THE AUTHORITY SINCE 1868

# THE
# WORLD
# ALMANAC
# & BOOK OF FACTS
# 1979

Published Annually by
NEWSPAPER ENTERPRISE ASSOCIATION, INC.
New York

# THE WORLD ALMANAC & BOOK OF FACTS 1979

**Publisher:** Jane D. Flatt
**Editor:** George E. Delury

**Managing Editor:** Vincent P. Bannan
**Associate Editors:** Hana Umlauf,
Barry Youngerman

**Assistant Editors:** Thomas J. McGuire,
Juliana N. Mace
**Senior Assistants:** Florence Byrnes,
June Foley Lindenman
**Assistant to the Editor:** Sally E. Armstrong

**Canadian Editor:** John Filion

Paperback cover design: Barbara Wilhelm

---

The editors acknowledge with thanks the many letters of helpful comment and criticism from users of THE WORLD ALMANAC, and invite further suggestions and observations. Because of the volume of mail directed to the editorial offices, it is not possible personally to reply to each letter writer. However, every communication is read by the editors and all comments and suggestions receive careful attention. Inquiries regarding contents should be sent to: The World Almanac, 200 Park Avenue, New York, NY 10017.

THE WORLD ALMANAC is published annually in November. Purchase orders should be sent to: Newspaper Enterprise Association, Inc., 1100 Central Trust Tower, Cincinnati, OH 45202

THE WORLD ALMANAC does not decide wagers.

The first edition of THE WORLD ALMANAC, a 120-page volume with 12 pages of advertising, was published by the New York World in 1868, 111 years ago. Annual publication was suspended in 1876. Joseph Pulitzer, publisher of the New York World, revived THE WORLD ALMANAC in 1886 with the goal of making it a "compendium of universal knowledge." It has been published annually since then. In 1931, it was acquired by the Scripps-Howard Newspapers; until 1951, it bore the imprint of the New York World-Telegram and thereafter, until 1967, that of the New York World-Telegram and Sun. It is now published in paper and clothbound editions by Newspaper Enterprise Association, Inc., a Scripps-Howard company.

---

**THE WORLD ALMANAC & BOOK OF FACTS 1979**
Copyright© Newspaper Enterprise Association, Inc. 1978
Library of Congress Catalog Card Number 4-3781
International Standard Serial Number (ISSN) 0084-1382
Newspaper Enterprise Association, Inc. (softcover) ISBN 0-911818-09-X
Newspaper Enterprise Association Inc. (hardcover) ISBN 0-911818-10-3
Doubleday and Co., Inc. ISBN 0-385-14667-1
Grosset & Dunlap, Inc. ISBN 0-448-16398-5
Microfilm Edition since 1868: Bell and Howell Co.
Printed in the United States of America

---

**NEWSPAPER ENTERPRISE ASSOCIATION, INC.**
200 Park Avenue, New York, NY 10017

# GENERAL INDEX

3

General Index

## Late News, Addenda, Changes

### Aerospace (pp. 141-147)

**Ocean Flights:** Three Americans accomplished the first transatlantic balloon crossing (Presque Isle, Me. to Miserey, Fr.) Aug. 11-17, 1978 (p. 143).

### Colleges and Universities (pp. 172-195)

Catholic Univ. of America president is now Dr. Edmund D. Pellegrino (p. 174).

Dominican College of Blauvelt presidency is now vacant (p. 175).

Franklin Univ. (Columbus, O.) president is now Dr. Frederick Bunte; enrollment is 4,189; faculty numbers 169 (p. 176).

LaGrange College president is now Dr. Charles L. Hagood·(p. 178).

Ohio Dominican president is now Sister Mary Andrew Matesich O.P. (p. 181).

Columbus Technical Inst. president is now Dr. Harold M. Nestor; enrollment is 6,500; faculty numbers 603 (p. 188).

Garden City Community Coll. president is now George

Chambers (p. 189).

### U.S. Population (pp. 205-263)

The April 1, 1970 population of Boone County, W. Va. was 25,118, *not* 2,118 (p. 260).

### National Defense (pp. 325-335)

Adm. Harry D. Train succeeded Adm. Isaac Kidd as Supreme Allied Commander Atlantic, North Atlantic Treaty Organization, Oct. 2, 1978 (p. 325).

A provision of the Defense Appropriation Authorization Act for fiscal year 1979 designates the Commandant of the Marine Corps as a member of the Joint Chiefs of Staff.

### Associations and Societies (pp. 336-349)

**Aluminum Association's** new address is 818 Connecticut Ave. NW, Washington, D.C. 20006 (p. 336).

**Television Bureau of Advertising:** correct address is 1345 Ave. of the Americas, New York, N.Y. 10019; membership is 350 (p. 348).

**American Television and Radio Artists:** membership is

35,000 (p. 348).

## 1978 Prizes and Awards (pp. 407-419)

**Nobel Prize in Chemistry:** Peter Mitchell, Britain, for his work in showing how plants and animals convert nutrition into energy; $165,000 (p. 407).

**Nobel Prize in Economics:** Herbert A Simon, U.S., for theories on economic decision-making; $165,000 (p. 409).

**Nobel Prize in Literature:** Isaac Bashevis Singer, Polish-born U.S. novelist and short-story writer in the Yiddish language; $165,000 (p. 408).

**Nobel Prize in Medicine or Physiology:** Daniel Nathans, Hamilton O. Smith, U.S., to share $165,000 award with Werner Arber, Switzerland, for genetic studies (p. 407).

**Nobel Prize in Physics:** Pyotr Kapitsa, U.S.S.R., for studies on supercold temperatures, $82,500; Arno Penzias and Robert Wilson, U.S., to share $82,500, for their discovery of residual "Big Bang" radiation (p. 407).

**Nobel Peace Prize:** Egyptian President Anwar Sadat and Israeli Prime Minister Menachem Begin to share $165,000 award for efforts to reach Arab-Israel peace (p. 408).

**Books, Allied Arts** (p. 414): **Academy of American Poets Fellowship** for distinguished poetic achievement, $10,000: Josephine Miles.

**Lamont Poetry Selection** by Acad. of American Poets: Ai, *Killing Floor.*

**Samuel Eliot Morison Award** for American History, by American Heritage Publishing Co.: David McCullough, *Path Between the Seas.*

**National Religious Book Awards** by Religious Book Review and Omni Publications: Sheldon Vanauken, *A Severe Mercy;* Peter Spier, *Noah's Ark.*

**Journalism Awards** (p. 415): **Associated Press Managing Eds. Public Service Award:** *Jackson* (Miss.) *Clarion-Ledger;* Northampton (Mass.) *Daily Hampshire Gazette.*

**National Assoc. of Bank Women Awards:** Bailey Morris, *Washington* (D.C.) *Star;* Mary Anne Hammond, New Eng. Merchants Natl. Bank *Beacon.*

**Howard W. Blakeslee Awards** of American Heart Assoc.: Gail Bronson, *Wall Street Journal;* Joann Rodgers, *Woman's Day.*

**Professional Football Writers of Amer. Awards:** Frank Luksa, *Dallas Times Herald;* Edwin Pope, *Miami Herald;* Gerald Eskenazi, *New York Times;* Marty Williams, *Dayton Daily News.*

**Penney-Missouri Magazine Awards,** by Missouri School of Journalism, $1000: Bil Gilbert, *Sports Illustrated;* Mark Dowie, *Mother Jones;* Berton Roueché, *New Yorker;* John McPhee, *New Yorker;* Frank Graham and Jack Star; John Davidson, *Texas Monthly* and Mavis Kennedy, *Washingtonian.*

**Broadcasting and Theater** (p. 416): **Robert F. Kennedy Awards:** Grand Prize: Bill Moyers, Tom Spain, Howard Stringer, Dan Lerner, CBS-TV, *CBS Reports: The Fire Next Door.*

**Emmy Awards,** by Academy of Television Arts and Sciences, for nighttime programs (a selection from among more than 40 award categories): a comedy series: All in the Family; drama series: The Rockford Files; limited series: Holocaust; comedy-variety series: The Muppet Show; classical performing arts show: Giselle; actor, limited series: Michael Moriarty, Holocaust; actress, limited series: Meryl Streep, Holocaust; supporting actress, limited series: Blanche Baker, Holocaust; actor, special: Fred Astaire, A Family Upside Down; actress, special: Joanne Woodward, See How She Runs; actor, comedy series: Carroll O'Connor, All in the Family; actress, comedy series: Jean Stapleton, All in the Family; supporting actor, comedy series: Rob Reiner, All in the Family; supporting actress, comedy series; Julie Kavner, Rhoda; actress, drama series: Sada Thompson, Family; actor, drama series: Edward Asner, Lou Grant; supporting actress, drama series: Nancy Merchand, Lou Grant; supporting actor, drama series: Robert Vaughn, Washington: Behind Closed Doors; actor, single performance in series: Barnard Hughes, Lou Grant; actress, sing. perf. in series: Rita Moreno, Rockford Files; supporting actor, sing. perf. in series: Ricardo Montalban, How the West Was Won.

Also, director, comedy series: Paul Bogart, All in the Family; director, drama series: Marvin J. Chomsky, Holocaust; director, comedy-variety series: Dave Powers, Carol Burnett Show; writers, comedy series: Bob Weiskopt, Bob Schiller, Barry Harman, Harve Brosten, All in the Family; writer, drama series: Gerald Green, Holocaust (p. 416).

**Miscellaneous Awards** (p. 417): **Kennedy Center/Rockefeller Foundation Piano Competition:** $10,000: Bradford Paul Gowen; $5,000: Donna Coleman; $3,000; Robert Weirich.

**Spingarn Award** by National Assoc. for the Advancement of Colored People: Andrew Young, 1977 (p. 419).

## Arts and Media (pp. 420-432)

Twenty-two year old Kylene J. Barker of Galax, Va. was chosen **Miss America** 1979 (p. 425).

## Volcanoes of the World (pp. 436-437)

The eruption of Vesuvio in 79 A.D. took place on Aug. 24, not Oct. 26.

## Bridges (pp. 450-452)

World's longest steel arch bridge is now the New River Gorge Bridge, New River Gorge, W.Va., longest span 1,700 feet (p. 451).

## Constitution (pp. 468-475)

Congress extended, Oct. 1978, the deadline for ratification of the Equal Rights Amendment to June 30, 1982 (p. 475).

Congress approved (Aug. 1978) and sent to the states a constitutional amendment that would give the District of Columbia full voting representation in Congress.

## Canada (pp. 497-512)

**British Columbia** total area is 366,255 sq. mi., *not* 255,285 sq. mi. (p. 499).

In Oct., 1978 by-elections, Liberals lost 5 Ontario seats to Conservatives, but retained a 7-seat majority in federal Parliament (p. 505).

## Nations of the World (pp. 513-607)

**Australia:** Northern Territory's self-government began Sept. 1978, with the opening of its Legislative Assembly; the Territory had rejected statehood status (p. 516).

**Belgium:** Social Christian Paul Vanden Boeynants agreed, Oct. 1978, to form a new government (p. 518).

**Brazil:** The electoral college chose Gen. Joao Baptista Figueiredo president, Oct. 1978, to take office Mar. 15, 1979 (p. 520).

**Chad:** Former rebel leader Hissen Habre was named president under a new national charter, Aug. 1978 (p. 523).

**Egypt:** Mustapha Khalil was installed as prime minister, Oct. 1978 (p. 532).

**Iceland:** Leftist leader Olafur Johannesson took over as prime minister, Sept. 1978, heading a 3-party coalition (p. 543).

**Kenya:** Daniel arap Moi was sworn in, Oct. 1978, to replace late President Kenyatta (p. 552).

**Panama:** President Aristides Royo assumed executive powers Oct. 1978, though Natl. Guard Cmmdr. Torrijos remained the leading political figure (p. 567).

**Portugal:** Political independent Carlos da Mota Pinto was asked, Oct. 1978, to form a new government (p. 570).

**Solomon Islands** was admitted as the 150th United Nations member, Sept. 1978 (p. 598).

**South Africa:** Pieter Botha was chosen prime minister, Sept. 1978; former Prime Minister John Vorster was sworn in as president in October (p. 577).

**Sweden:** Liberal leader Ola Ullsten became prime minister Oct. 1978 (p. 580).

**Switzerland:** The French-speaking northern Jura region voted for self-government, Sept. 1978; it will become the nation's 23rd canton, first since 1815 (p. 581).

**Tuvalu:** The island nation became completely independent of Great Britain Oct. 1978 (p. 591).

Three new judges were elected at the U.N. to the **World Court** Oct. 1978, to serve Feb. 1979-1988: Richard R. Baxter (U.S.), Roberto Ago (Italy), Abdullah Ali El-Erian (Egypt) (p. 599).

A bill was signed in 1978 increasing from $100 to $300 the amount of duty-free merchandise travelers may bring through **customs** into the U.S. A 10% duty now applies on purchases worth between $300 and $900. Still more liberal rules apply to travelers from Virgin Is., Guam, and American Samoa (p. 606).

# The World Almanac
### and Book of Facts for 1979

## The Top 10 News Stories of 1978

Middle East peace—at least between Israel and Egypt—became a real likelihood after a 12-day marathon **negotiation at Camp David**, Maryland, resulted in a "framework for peace" agreement between Israeli Prime Minister Begin and Egyptian President Anwar Sadat. Both leaders credited President Carter's firmness, patience, and persuasiveness with a major role in securing the promise of an Egyptian-Israeli peace treaty after 30 years of hostilities.

Elections of **two popes within two months** drew world attention to Vatican City and to the cardinals who might be called to the leadership of the Catholic Church. Pope Paul VI died August 6. His successor, the smiling John Paul I, elected August 26, died in his sleep September 28. The college of cardinals, on October 16, elected 58-year-old Karol Cardinal Wojtyla, a Pole, the first non-Italian Pope since 1523. Wojtyla chose the name John Paul II.

Loss of confidence in U.S. ability to stem **inflation** and massive trade deficits (caused by increasing oil imports) brought **the falling dollar** to record lows in world money markets. Worth 362 Japanese yen in 1968 and only 270 at the end of 1977, the dollar was worth less than 178 yen at the end of October, 1978. The flight from the dollar pushed the price of gold to a record $245 an ounce.

In a 5 to 4 decision in **the Bakke case**, the Supreme Court ruled that rigid quota systems were not permissable means to redress racial imbalances. While upholding affirmative action procedures in general, the Court held that the University of California Medical School's system, which had rejected Bakke, unfairly discriminated against qualified non-minority candidates.

Saddled with ever increasing property taxes, Californians voted 2 to 1 for **Proposition 13**, a measure which immediately cut property taxes 57% and set a limit on further increases. The "tax revolt" spread across the nation; similar proposals were made in several other states and in the U.S. Congress, as the public began to make clear its discontent with increasing government payrolls and waste.

Seldom had a **President's popularity** sunk so low as quickly as President Carter's. Charged with incompetence, indecisiveness, and confusion, Carter received an approval rating of only 39% in the August Gallup poll, the lowest for a new president since Harry Truman. However, after Carter's successful management of the Camp David negotiations, his popularity quickly rebounded to over 50%.

After months of bitter debate and with some minor changes and clarifications, the Senate, 68 to 32, voted approval of the **Panama Canal treaty** which will bring an end to the Canal Zone on September 1, 1979, and turn the canal over to full Panamanian control at the end of 1999.

Guilty verdicts were a matter of course in a series of **Soviet trials** of dissidents Anatoly Shcharansky and Alexander Ginzburg, an American businessman accused of currency violations, and two U.S. journalists and their newspapers accused of slandering the Soviet government. In each case Soviet courts blatantly violated Soviet law in refusing the defense various rights while accepting inaccurate and irrelevant evidence from the prosecution. U.S.-Soviet relations fell to their lowest level since detente began as the U.S. government cancelled the sale of a computer system to Tass and private U.S. organizations refused to attend meetings in the Soviet Union.

Aldo **Moro's kidnapping** and the shooting and maiming of other Italian government figures focused world attention on European terrorism. The kidnappers of the former Italian premier, the Red Brigades, demanded the release of other Brigades terrorists on trial in Turin. When the Italian government refused to negotiate with the kidnappers, Moro was "tried" and condemned by the terrorists, who left his lifeless body in a car in the center of Rome.

Reaffirming Congressional support for the **Equal Rights Amendment**, the House (233 to 189) and Senate (60 to 36) extended by 39 months, to June 30, 1982, the time available to the states for ratification of the constitutional amendment. The further progress of the amendment, which needs three more approvals by state legislatures to become law, was protected when Congress specifically refused to permit rescissions of ratifications already made.

Yet other stories vied for a ranking in the Top Ten, among them: the successful birth in England of the first baby to be conceived outside a mother's body, the long and bitter nationwide coal strike, the activities of Cuban troops in Africa, and the weeks-long strike that deprived New York City of its newspapers.

---

## Republicans Score Modest Midterm Gains

Republican efforts to hold on to major party status got a boost in Nov. 7, 1978, midterm election.

Modest but definite increases in the Republican presence in Congress and the state houses were achieved in an atmosphere of fiscal conservatism, as a majority of state electorates backed ballot proposals to curb state taxes or spending.

But Democrats in many states were able to defuse the issue by joining the tax-cut bandwagon.

In the most stricking example, California Governor (and presidential hopeful) Jerry Brown abandoned his opposition to Proposition 13 (a measure, approved in a June referendum, which cut real estate taxes severely). He then campaigned on a promise to work toward successful implementation in a new nationwide era of limited government, and rode that promise to a landslide 61% victory.

Incomplete returns showed voters backing major tax-spending curbs in 10 of the 18 states where such measures were on the ballot, but defeating them in 4 other states and giving 2 split decisions. Michigan voters showed commendable selectivity, supporting an amendment to limit state spending growth to the rise in personal income, but defeating a plan for a 43% property tax cut. In Maryland, 2 counties favored tax cuts, while wealthy Montgomery County voted one down.

Texas voters gave 4 to 1 backing to a package tying spending to economic growth, cutting farm and timber taxes, and raising exemptions for homesteads and the elderly. Property tax cuts were also approved in Nevada (by 3 to 1), Missouri (2 to 1), and Idaho, and similar cuts were leading in Alabama and Massachusetts.

Spending ceilings similar to the one approved in Michigan, which would keep the state government sector at a constant percentage of the economy, were approved in Hawaii and Arizona, and Illinois voters approved an advisory referendum on curbing expenditures. North Dakota voters approved a cut in income taxes.

Oregon voters resisted "Proposition 13 fever," by rejecting 2 property tax cut proposals, though each had been supported respectively by the Democratic and Republican gubernatorial candidates. Arkansas voters rejected sales tax exemptions for food and medicine, and Floridians turned down a package giving tax relief to business, the elderly, and the disabled.

A spending growth curb was rejected soundly in Colorado, where it had been opposed as insufficient by California's Proposition 13 author Howard Jarvis. Results in Nebraska and South Dakota were too close to call.

### Republican Gains in Congress

Democrats remained in firm control of both houses of Congress, but Republicans had a net gain of 3 Senate seats and 12 House seats.

Though they trailed behind the usual midterm gain of nonpresidential parties, Republicans may be in a better position to resist some of Pres. Carter's programs, by retiring such liberal stalwarts as Sens. Dick Clark of Iowa and Floyd Haskell of Colorado, both the target of national conservative opposition. Moderate and conservative Republicans also captured the seats of retiring liberal senators in Minnesota and South Dakota, dimming the prospects for such liberal priorities as national health care and the prospective Strategic Arms Limitation Treaty.

Nearly all incumbents in congressional leadership positions were re-elected. Only Republican Senate Deputy Minority Leader Robert Griffin was defeated. He had made the mistake of announcing he would not run and then changed his mind several months later.

Liberal Republican Sen. Charles Percy reversed a losing standing in the polls only after apologizing for past spending programs; after his re-election he told voters "your message has come through loud and clear".

Republicans increased their hold on governorships for the first time since 1969, picking up 6 new seats and giving them a stronger base for the 1980 presidential race.

The leading Republican presidential hopefuls running this year all won handily, including Gov. James Thompson of Illinois and Sen. Howard Baker of Tennessee, both garnering nearly 60% of the vote, and Ill. Rep. Philip Crane, the only declared candidate of either party.

The effect of Pres. Carter and his fluctuating popularity on the various races was difficult to gauge. In those states where he campaigned personally in recent weeks, Democrats won 12 gubernatorial or senatorial seats and lost 15, but many of his appearances had been for shaky candidates.

Analysts agreed that the recently-passed tax cut, and Carter's forceful announcement of anti-inflation and dollar-aid plans, helped defuse the Proposition 13 issue for fellow Democrats. His success at the Camp David Middle East peace talks removed any impulse the voters may have had to register dissent from his foreign policies by electing Republicans.

The voters' selective reaction to a host of other important ballot issues showed that no general move to the right had occurred. In the first statewide right-to-work referendum in 20 years, Missouri voters responded to organized labor's pleas and rejected a constitutional amendment that would have barred union shops, in which all employees must join unions.

Gay rights supporters scored their first electorial victories, as California voters rejected a provision (opposed by many conservative and liberal politicians) that would have required school boards to fire homosexuals or those "advocating" homosexuality. Seattle voters rejected a proposal to remove an existing gay rights ordinance. Dade County, Fla. once again rejected a gay rights provision, but by a lower margin than in the previous referendum. In Brooklyn, a contrite Cong. Frederick Richmond was reelected despite a homosexual scandal.

### Legalized Gambling

Legalized gambling proposals went down to defeat in 3 states. Casino gambling in Miami Beach was rejected by 72% of Florida voters, 60% of New Jerseyans opposed jai alai betting, and a majority in Virginia rejected pari-mutuel thoroughbred racing.

In environmental issues, proposals for a deposit on beverage containers in Nebraska and limiting public smoking in California lost. But Montana approved strict controls on nuclear power plants.

There were some bright spots for political feminists, but some disappointments as well.

Republican Nancy Kassebaum, daughter of former republican presidential candidate Alf Landon, became the first women to be elected to the Senate since Margaret Chase Smith last won in 1966. And Democratic Connecticut Governor Ella Grasso won a landslide re-election bid. But Senate candidate Jane Eskind was easily defeated by Republican celebrity Howard Baker.

Only 47 women were nominated for federal office by the major parties in 1978, a drop from the 1976 level. But the number of women Representatives will apparently remain at 16, despite the defeats of Reps. Helen Meyner of New Jersey and Martha Keys of Kansas, both from swing districts.

Nevada voters appeared to have defeated an advisory referendum asking if they wanted the state legislature to support the Equal Rights Amendment. In Florida, voters defeated a state equal rights amendment by a 60% margin.

Black representation in the House remained steady at 16, with incumbents re-elected by huge majorities in most cases, including Rep. Charles Diggs of Michigan, convicted of accepting payroll kickbacks from congressional staffers.

But the Senate lost its only black, as Republican Edward Brooke succumbed to the bad publicity of a divorce scandal and his admitted financial "mistatements" to Senate investigators. Mississippi civil rights activist Charles Evers lost his independent bid for a Senate seat, but picked up 25% of the vote.

### Sidelights

An unusually high number of incumbent Congressional candidates were running against their own record of proven or suspected misdeeds. The majority managed to win the forgiveness of their constituents.

Prominent among these were Diggs, Richmond, and colorful Pennsylvania Democrat Rep. Daniel Flood, who had been indicted for bribery, perjury, and conspiracy. Of 3 California Democratic representatives reprimanded by the House for their role in the "Koreagate" scandel, two were re-elected: Edward Roybal and Charles Wilson. John McFall was ousted.

Florida's Rep. J. Herbert Burke, who had been arrested for misbehaving outside a topless bar, was defeated. But former Ohio Rep. Wayne Hays, who had resigned after charges of sexual misconduct, won a place in the Ohio legislature.

Even before final reports were filed with the Federal Election Commission, preliminary figures showed that some 2,000 candidates for Senate and House seats had spent over $150 million to get their messages to the voters. In a reversal of pattern, Democratic candidates collected and spent more than Republicans.

Despite universal predictions of voter apathy and low turnout, early figures showed healthy vote totals in most parts of the country.

# The Ninety-Sixth Congress

## With 1978 Election Results

### The Senate

Terms are for 6 years and end Jan. 3 of the year preceding name. Annual salary $57,500. To be eligible for the U.S. Senate a person must be at least 30 years of age, a citizen of the United States for at least 9 years, and a resident of the state from which he is chosen. The Congress must meet annually on Jan. 3, unless it has, by law, appointed a different day.

**Senate officials** (95th Congress): President Pro Tempore James O. Eastland; Deputy President Pro Tempore Hubert H. Humphrey; Majority Leader Robert C. Byrd; Majority Whip Alan Cranston; Minority Leader Howard H. Baker Jr.; Minority Whip Ted Stevens.

Dem., 58; Rep., 41; Indep., 1; Total, 100. *Designates senior senator.
Preliminary and unofficial returns.

| Term ends | Senator (Party, home) | 1978 Election |
|---|---|---|
| **Alabama** | | |
| 1981 | Donald Steward* (D, Anniston) . . . . | 388,430 |
| | James D. Martin (R, Gadsden) . . . . | 311,214 |
| 1985 | Howell Heflin (D, Tuscumbia) . . . . . | Unopposed |
| **Alaska** | | |
| 1981 | Mike Gravel (D, Anchorage) | |
| 1985 | Ted Stevens* (R, Anchorage). . . . . | 68,994 |
| | Donald Hobbs (D, Anchorage) . . . . | 22,244 |
| **Arizona** | | |
| 1981 | Barry M. Goldwater* (R, Scottsdale) | |
| 1983 | Dennis DeConcini (D, Tucson) | |
| **Arkansas** | | |
| 1981 | Dale Bumpers* (D, Charleston) | |
| 1985 | David Pryor (D, Little Rock) . . . . . . | 400,017 |
| | Tom Kelly (R, Little Rock) . . . . . . . | 87,512 |
| **California** | | |
| 1981 | Alan Cranston* (D, Palm Springs) | |
| 1983 | S. I. (Sam) Hayakawa (R, Mill Valley) | |
| **Colorado** | | |
| 1981 | Gary Hart* (D, Denver) | |
| 1985 | William L. Armstrong (R, Aurora) . . . . . . | 480,652 |
| | Floyd K. Haskell (D, Littleton) . . . . . . . . | 330,222 |
| **Connecticut** | | |
| 1981 | Abraham A. Ribicoff* (D, Hartford) | |
| 1983 | Lowell P. Weicker Jr. (R, Greenwich) | |
| **Delaware** | | |
| 1983 | William V. Roth Jr.* (R, Wilmington) | |
| 1985 | Joseph R. Biden Jr. (D, Wilmington) . | 93,926 |
| | James H. Baxter (R, Georgetown) . . | 66,636 |
| **Florida** | | |
| 1981 | Richard Stone (D, Tallahassee) | |
| 1983 | Lawton Chiles* (D, Lakeland) | |
| **Georgia** | | |
| 1981 | Herman E. Talmadge* (D, Lovejoy) | |
| 1985 | Sam Nunn (D, Perry) . . . . . . . . . . | 546,657 |
| | John W. Stokes (R, Atlanta) . . . . . . | 107,832 |
| **Hawaii** | | |
| 1981 | Daniel K. Inouye* (D, Honolulu) | |
| 1983 | Spark M. Matsunaga (D, Honolulu) | |
| **Idaho** | | |
| 1981 | Frank Church* (D, Boise) | |
| 1985 | James A. McClure (R, Payette) . . . . | 193,340 |
| | Dwight Jensen (D, Boise) . . . . . . . | 89,360 |

| Term ends | Senator (Party, home) | 1978 Election |
|---|---|---|
| **Illinois** | | |
| 1981 | Adlai E. Stevenson 3d (D, Chicago) | |
| 1985 | Charles H. Percy* (R, Wilmette) . . . | 1,670,051 |
| | Alex Seith (D, Hinsdale) . . . . . . . . | 1,420,648 |
| **Indiana** | | |
| 1981 | Birch Bayh* (D, Indianapolis) | |
| 1983 | Richard G. Lugar (R, Indianapolis) | |
| **Iowa** | | |
| 1981 | C. Culver* (D, Cedar Rapids) | |
| 1985 | Robert W. Jepson (R, Davenport) . . | 420,416 |
| | Dick Clark (D, Des Moines) . . . . . . | 392,391 |
| **Kansas** | | |
| 1981 | Robert J. Dole* (R, Russell) | |
| 1985 | Nancy Landon Kassebaum (R, Wichita) . . . . . . . . . . . . . . . . . . . . . | 408,975 |
| | Bill Roy (D, Topeka) . . . . . . . . . . | 316,241 |
| **Kentucky** | | |
| 1981 | Wendell H. Ford (D, Owensboro) | |
| 1985 | Walter Huddleston* (D, Elizabethtown) . . . . . . . . . . . . . . . . . . . | 287,902 |
| | Louie Guenthner Jr. (R, Louisville) . . | 173,948 |
| **Louisiana** | | |
| 1981 | Russell B. Long* (D, Baton Rouge) | |
| 1985 | J. Bennett Johnston Jr. (D, Shreveport) . . . . . . . . . . . . . . . . . . . | Unopposed |
| **Maine** | | |
| 1983 | Edmund S. Muskie* (D, Waterville) | |
| 1985 | William S. Cohen (R, Bangor) . . . . . | 212,950 |
| | William D. Hathaway (D, Auburn) . . . | 128,128 |
| **Maryland** | | |
| 1981 | Charles C. Mathias* (R, Frederick) | |
| 1983 | Paul S. Sarbanes (D, Baltimore) | |
| **Massachusetts** | | |
| 1983 | Edward M. Kennedy* (D, Boston) | |
| 1985 | Paul E. Tsongas (D, Lowell) . . . . . . | 1,090,012 |
| | Edward W. Brooke (R, Boston) . . . . | 888,341 |
| **Michigan** | | |
| 1983 | Donald W. Riegle Jr.* (D, Flint) | |
| 1985 | Carl Levin (D, Detroit) . . . . . . . . . | 1,342,702 |
| | Robert P. Griffin (R, Traverse City) . . | 1,212,755 |
| **Minnesota** | | |
| 1983 | David Durenberger* (R, Minneapolis) | 952,529 |
| | Bob Short (D, Minneapolis) . . . . . . | 551,492 |
| 1985 | Rudolph E. Boschwitz (R, Wauzata) . | 889,681 |
| | Wendell Anderson (D, Rochester) . . | 648,220 |

| Term ends | Senator (Party, home) | 1978 Election |
|---|---|---|
| | **Mississippi** | |
| 1983 | John C. Stennis* (D, DeKalb) | |
| 1985 | Thad Cochran (R, Jackson) | 262,660 |
| | Maurice Danton (D, Columbia) | 185,080 |
| | James Charles Evers (Ind, Fayette) | 131,905 |
| | **Missouri** | |
| 1981 | Thomas F. Eagleton* (D, St. Louis) | |
| 1983 | John C. Danforth (R, Jefferson City) | |
| | **Montana** | |
| 1983 | John Melcher* (D, Forsyth) | |
| 1985 | Max Baucus (D, Missoula) | 136,081 |
| | Larry Williams (R, Kalispell) | 113,445 |
| | **Nebraska** | |
| 1983 | Edward Zorinsky* (D, Omaha) | |
| 1985 | James J. Exon (D, Lincoln) | 329,718 |
| | Donald Eugene Shasteen (R, Hastings) | 158,085 |
| | **Nevada** | |
| 1981 | Paul Laxalt (R, Carson City) | |
| 1983 | Howard W. Cannon* (D, Las Vegas) | |
| | **New Hampshire** | |
| 1981 | John A. Durkin* (D, Manchester) | |
| 1985 | Gordon J. Humphrey (R, Swapee) | 132,338 |
| | Thomas J. McIntyre (D, Laconia) | 127,930 |
| | **New Jersey** | |
| 1983 | Harrison A. Williams Jr.* (D, Bedminster) | |
| 1985 | Bill Bradley (D, Denville) | 1,063,211 |
| | Jeffrey Bell (R, Trenton) | 825,951 |
| | **New Mexico** | |
| 1983 | Harrison "Jack" Schmitt (R, Silver City) | |
| 1985 | Pete V. Domenici* (R, Albuquerque) | 181,932 |
| | Tony Anaya (D, Santa Fe) | 158,210 |
| | **New York** | |
| 1981 | Jacob K. Javits* (R,L, New York) | |
| 1983 | Daniel Patrick Moynihan (D, New York) | |
| | **North Carolina** | |
| 1981 | Robert Morgan (D, Lillington) | |
| 1985 | Jesse A. Helms* (R, Raleigh) | 617,194 |
| | John Randolph Ingram (D, Cary) | 513,152 |
| | **North Dakota** | |
| 1981 | Milton R. Young* (R, LaMoure) | |
| 1983 | Quentin N. Burdick (D, Fargo) | |
| | **Ohio** | |
| 1981 | John Glenn* (D, Columbia) | |
| 1983 | Howard M. Metzenbaum (D, Shaker Heights) | |
| | **Oklahoma** | |
| 1981 | Henry Bellmon* (R, Red Rock) | |
| 1985 | David Lyle Boren (D, Okla. City) | 490,494 |
| | Robert B. Kamm (R, Stillwater) | 246,856 |
| | **Oregon** | |
| 1981 | Robert W. Packwood (R, Lake Oswego) | |
| 1985 | Mark O. Hatfield* (R, Salem) | 549,603 |
| | Vern Cook (D, Gresham) | 340,945 |

| Term ends | Senator (Party, home) | 1978 Election |
|---|---|---|
| | **Pennsylvania** | |
| 1981 | Richard S. Schweiker* (R, Worcester) | |
| 1983 | H. John Heinz III (R, Pittsburgh) | |
| | **Rhode Island** | |
| 1983 | John H. Chafee (R, Warwick) | |
| 1985 | Claiborne Pell* (D, Newport) | 221,936 |
| | James G. Reynolds (R, Barrington) | 73,006 |
| | **South Carolina** | |
| 1981 | Ernest F. Hollings (D, Columbia) | |
| 1985 | Strom Thurmond* (R, Aiken) | 350,911 |
| | Charles D. Ravenel (D, Mt. Pleasant) | 279,290 |
| | **South Dakota** | |
| 1981 | George McGovern* (D, Mitchell) | |
| 1985 | Larry Pressler (R, Humboldt) | 171,563 |
| | Don Barnett (D, Rapid City) | 84,585 |
| | **Tennessee** | |
| 1983 | James R. Sasser (D, Nashville) | |
| 1985 | Howard H. Baker Jr.* (R, Huntsville) | 641,901 |
| | Jane Eskind (D, Nashville) | 465,706 |
| | **Texas** | |
| 1983 | Lloyd Bentsen (D, Houston) | |
| 1985 | John G. Tower* (R, Wichita Falls) | 1,144,246 |
| | Robert Krueger (D, New Braunfells) | 1,130,714 |
| | **Utah** | |
| 1981 | Jake Garn* (R, Salt Lake City) | |
| 1983 | Orrin G. Hatch (R, Salt Lake City) | |
| | **Vermont** | |
| 1981 | Patrick J. Leahy (D, Burlington) | |
| 1983 | Robert T. Stafford* (R, Rutland) | |
| | **Virginia** | |
| 1983 | Harry F. Byrd Jr.* (I, Winchester) | |
| 1985 | John William Warner (R, Middleburg) | 613,294 |
| | Andrew P. Miller (D, Richmond) | 608,782 |
| | **Washington** | |
| 1981 | Warren G. Magnuson* (D, Seattle) | |
| 1983 | Henry M. Jackson (D, Everett) | |
| | **West Virginia** | |
| 1983 | Robert C. Byrd* (D, Sophia) | |
| 1985 | Jennings Randolph (D, Charleston) | 248,333 |
| | Arch A. Moore Jr. (R, Glendale) | 243,795 |
| | **Wisconsin** | |
| 1981 | Gaylord A. Nelson (D, Madison) | |
| 1983 | William Proxmire* (D, Madison) | |
| | **Wyoming** | |
| 1983 | Malcolm Wallop* (R, Big Horn) | |
| 1985 | Alan Kooi Simpson (R, Cody) | 82,827 |
| | Raymond B. Whitaker (D, Casper) | 50,431 |

## The House of Representatives

Members' terms to Jan. 3, 1981. Annual salary $57,500; house speaker $75,000. To be eligible for membership, a person must be at least 25, a U.S. citizen for at least 7 years, and a resident of the state from which he is chosen.

**House Officials** (95th Congress): Speaker Thomas P. O'Neill; Majority Leader James Wright; Majority Whip John Brademas; Minority Leader John J. Rhodes; Minority Whip Robert H. Michel.

Democrats, 275, Republicans, 158. (Two races undecided at presstime—‡.) Total 435.

(Those marked * served in the 95th Congress.)

Bold face denotes the winner.

Preliminary and unofficial returns.

| Dist. | Representative (Party, Home) | 1978 Election |
|---|---|---|
| | **Alabama** | |
| 1. | **Jack Edwards*** (R, Mobile) | **70,264** |
| | L.W. Noonan (D, Mobile) | 39,776 |
| 2. | **William L. "Bill" Dickinson*** (R, Montgomery) | **58,346** |
| | Wendell Mitchell (D, Luverne) | 49,395 |
| 3. | **Bill Nichols*** (D, Sylacauga) | **Unopposed** |
| 4. | **Tom Bevill*** (D, Jasper) | **Unopposed** |
| 5. | **Ronnie G. Flippo*** (D, Florence) | **Unopposed** |
| 6. | **John H. Buchanan Jr.*** (R, Birmingham) | **59,154** |
| | Don Hawkins* (D, Birmingham) | 39,024 |
| 7. | **Richard C. Shelby** (D, Tuscaloosa) | **Unopposed** |
| | **Alaska At Large** | |
| | **Don Young*** (R, Anchorage) | **51,081** |
| | Patrick Rodey (D, Anchorage) | 41,487 |
| | **Arizona** | |
| 1. | **John J. Rhodes*** (R, Mesa) | **81,095** |
| | Ken Graves (D, Phoenix) | 33,169 |
| 2. | **Morris K. Udall*** (D, Tucson) | **67,832** |
| | Tom Richey (R, Sierra Vista) | 58,641 |
| 3. | **Bob Stump*** (D, Tolleson) | **Unopposed** |
| 4. | **Eldon Rudd*** (R, Scottsdale) | **90,733** |
| | Michael McCormick (D, Phoenix) | 48,630 |
| | **Arkansas** | |
| 1. | **Bill Alexander*** (D, Osceola) | **Unopposed** |
| 2. | **Edwin R. Bethune Jr.** (R, Searcy) | **65,238** |
| | Benton Douglas Brandon Jr. (D, Little Rock) | 61,423 |
| 3. | **John Paul Hammerschmidt*** (R, Harrison) | **129,625** |
| | William Curtis Mears (D, Hot Springs) | 35,539 |
| 4. | **Beryl Anthony Jr.** (D, El Dorado) | **Unopposed** |
| | **California** | |
| 1. | **Harold T. Johnson*** (D, Roseville) | **124,529** |
| | James E. Taylor (R, Auburn) | 85,196 |
| 2. | **Don H. Clausen*** (R, Crescent City) | **113,623** |
| | Norma Bork (D, Angwin) | 98,934 |
| 3. | **Robert T. Matsui** (D, Sacramento) | **104,488** |
| | Sandy Smoley (R, Sacramento) | 90,991 |
| 4. | **Vic Fazio** (D, Sacramento) | **87,405** |
| | Rex Hime (R, Sacramento) | 70,357 |
| 5. | **John L. Burton*** (D, San Francisco) | **105,110** |
| | Dolores Skore (R, San Rafael) | 52,075 |
| 6. | **Phillip Burton*** (D, San Francisco) | **81,140** |
| | Tom Spinosa (R, San Francisco) | 33,101 |
| 7. | **George Miller*** (D, Martinez) | **109,172** |
| | Paula Gordon (R, Walnut Creek) | 58,047 |
| 8. | **Ronald V. Dellums*** (D, Berkeley) | **94,433** |
| | Charles V. Hughes (R, Berkeley) | 70,090 |
| 9. | **Fortney H. Stark Jr.*** (D, Oakland) | **87,865** |
| | Robert S. Allen (R, Livermore) | 40,942 |
| 10. | **Don Edwards*** (D, San Jose) | **104,103** |
| | Rudy Hansen (R, San Jose) | 41,152 |
| 11. | **Leo J. Ryan*** (D, Belmont) | **92,135** |
| | Dave Welch (R, San Bruno) | 54,267 |
| 12. | **Paul N. McCloskey Jr.*** (R, Menlo Park) | **115,990** |
| | Kirsten Olsen (D, Palo Alto) | 34,190 |
| 13. | **Norman Y. Mineta*** (D, San Jose) | **99,899** |

| Dist. | Representative (Party, Home) | 1978 Election |
|---|---|---|
| | Dan O'Keefe (R, Cupertino) | 68,560 |
| 14. | **Norman D. Shumway** (R, Stockton) | **95,454** |
| | John J. McFall* (D, Manteca) | 76,113 |
| 15. | **Tony Coelho** (D, Merced) | **74,631** |
| | Chris Patterakis (R, Modesto) | 49,380 |
| 16. | **Leon E. Panetta*** (D, Carmel Valley) | **102,932** |
| | Eric Seastrand (R, Salinas) | 64,704 |
| 17. | **Charles Pashayan Jr.** (R, Fresno) | **80,642** |
| | John Krebs* (D, Fresno) | 67,246 |
| 18. | **William M. Thomas** (R, Bakersfield) | **84,437** |
| | Bob Sogge (D, Bakersfield) | 58,245 |
| 19. | **Robert J. Lagomarsino*** (R, Ventura) | **114,158** |
| | Jerry Zamos (D, Santa Barbara) | 48,385 |
| 20. | **Barry M. Goldwater Jr.*** (R, Burbank) | **127,918** |
| | Pat Lear (D, Encino) | 64,954 |
| 21. | **James C. Corman*** (D, Van Nuys) | **72,776** |
| | G. Walsh (R, Woodland Hills) | 43,745 |
| 22. | **Carlos J. Moorhead*** (R, Glendale) | **97,263** |
| | Robert S. Henry (D, Pasadena) | 53,536 |
| 23. | **Anthony C. Beilenson*** (D, Los Angeles) | **115,109** |
| | Joseph Barbara (R, Woodland Hills) | 60,046 |
| 24. | **Henry A. Waxman*** (D, Los Angeles) | **83,540** |
| | Howard G. Schaefer (R, Los Angeles) | 43,012 |
| 25. | **Edward R. Roybal*** (D, Los Angeles) | **45,188** |
| | Robert K. Watson (R, South Pasadena) | 21,681 |
| 26. | **John H. Rousselot*** (R, San Marino) | **Unopposed** |
| 27. | **Robert K. Dornan*** (R, Redondo Beach) | **24,091** |
| | Carey Peck (D, Santa Monica) | 21,765 |
| 28. | **Julian C. Dixon** (D, Los Angeles) | **Unopposed** |
| 29. | **Augustus F. Hawkins*** (D, Los Angeles) | **39,109** |
| | Uriah J. Fields (R, Los Angeles) | 7,969 |
| 30. | **George E. Danielson*** (D, Monterey Park) | **41,864** |
| | Henry Ares (R, Pico Rivera) | 16,773 |
| 31. | **Charles H. Wilson*** (D, Hawthorne) | **19,107** |
| | Don Grimshaw (R, Lawndale) | 10,131 |
| 32. | **Glenn M. Anderson*** (D, Harbor City) | **24,252** |
| | Sonya Mathison (R, San Pedro) | 8,630 |
| 33. | **Wayne Grisham** (R, La Mirada) | **40,122** |
| | Dennis S. Kazarian (D, Whittier) | 32,450 |
| 34. | **Dan Lungren** (R, Long Beach) | **43,969** |
| | Mark Hannaford* (D, Lakewood) | 35,202 |
| 35. | **Jim Lloyd*** (D, West Covina) | **45,102** |
| | David Dreier (R, Claremont) | 38,061 |
| 36. | **George E. Brown Jr.*** (D, Riverside) | **80,190** |
| | Dana Warren Carmody (R, Riverside) | 47,269 |
| 37. | **Jerry Lewis** (R, Highland) | **106,449** |
| | Dan Corcoran (D, Riverside) | 60,420 |
| 38. | **Jerry M. Patterson*** (D, Buena Park) | **74,426** |
| | Dan Goedeke (R, Santa Ana) | 52,437 |
| 39. | **William E. Dannemeyer** (R, Fullerton) | **110,513** |
| | William E. Farris (D, Orange) | 63,115 |
| 40. | **Robert E. Badham*** (R, Newport Beach) | **141,846** |
| | Jim McGuy (D, Newport Beach) | 75,074 |

| Dist. | Representative (Party, Home) | 1978 Election |
|---|---|---|
| 41. | **Bob Wilson\*** (R, San Diego) | **105,402** |
| | King Golden Jr (D, San Diego) | 76,113 |
| 42. | **Lionel Van Deerlin\*** (D, Chula Vista) | **83,572** |
| | Lawrence C. Mattera (R, San Diego) | 29,759 |
| 43. | **Clair W. Burgener\*** (R, La Jolla) | **164,417** |
| | Ruben B. Brooks (D, San Diego) | 75,277 |

### Colorado

| Dist. | Representative (Party, Home) | 1978 Election |
|---|---|---|
| 1. | **Pat Schroeder\*** (D, Denver) | **82,732** |
| | Gene Hutcheson (R, Denver) | 49,892 |
| 2. | **Tim Wirth\*** (D, Lakewood) | **98,887** |
| | Ed Scott (R, Lakewood) | 88,057 |
| 3. | **Ray Kogovsek** (D, Pueblo) | **70,566** |
| | Harold L. McCormick (R, Canon City) | 69,192 |
| 4. | **James P. (Jim) Johnson** (R, Fort Collins) | **103,181** |
| | Morgan Smith (D, Brighton) | 65,291 |
| 5. | **Ken Kramer** (R, Colorado Springs) | **91,935** |
| | Gerry Frank (D, Aurora) | 52,911 |

### Connecticut

| Dist. | Representative (Party, Home) | 1978 Election |
|---|---|---|
| 1. | **William R. Cotter\*** (D, Hartford) | **101,947** |
| | Ben F. Andrews Jr. (R, Hartford) | 67,228 |
| 2. | **Christopher J. Dodd\*** (D, Norwich) | **116,207** |
| | Thomas Hudson Connell (R, Vernon) | 51,406 |
| 3. | **Robert N. Giaimo\*** (D, North Haven) | **96,670** |
| | John G. Pucciano (R, Orange) | 66,730 |
| 4. | **Stewart B. McKinney\*** (R, Fairfield) | **81,905** |
| | Michael G. Morgan (D, Stamford) | 59,305 |
| 5. | **William R. Ratchford** (D, Danbury) | **95,472** |
| | George C. Guidera (R, Weston) | 86,714 |
| 6. | **Anthony Toby Moffett\*** (D, Unionville) | **119,025** |
| | Daniel F. Mackinnon (R, Suffield) | 66,551 |

### Delaware At Large

| | Representative (Party, Home) | 1978 Election |
|---|---|---|
| | **Thomas B. Evans Jr.\*** (R, Wilmington) | **91,787** |
| | Gary E. Hindes (D, Dover) | 64,819 |

### Florida

| Dist. | Representative (Party, Home) | 1978 Election |
|---|---|---|
| 1. | **Earl Dewitt Hutto** (D, Panama City) | **82,294** |
| | Warren Briggs (R, Pensacola) | 47,465 |
| 2. | **Don Fuqua\*** (D, Altha) | **108,058** |
| | Pete Brathwaite (R, Gainesville) | 24,158 |
| 3. | **Charles E. Bennett\*** (D, Jacksonville) | **Unopposed** |
| 4. | **Bill Chappell Jr.\*** (D, Ocala) | **109,918** |
| | Tom Boney (R, Keystone Heights) | 40,282 |
| 5. | **Richard Kelly\*** (R, New Port Richey) | **104,484** |
| | David Ryan Best (D, Orlando) | 100,035 |
| 6. | **C. W. Bill Young\*** (R, St. Petersburg) | **150,694** |
| | Jim Christison (D, Clearwater) | 40,654 |
| 7. | **Sam M. Gibbons\*** (D, Tampa) | **Unopposed** |
| 8. | **Andy Ireland\*** (D, Winter Haven) | **Unopposed** |
| 9. | **Bill Nelson** (D, Melbourne) | **81,486** |
| | Edward J. Gurney (R, Winter Park) | 53,219 |
| 10. | **L. A. (Skip) Bafalis\*** (R, Fort Meyers Beach) | **Unopposed** |
| 11. | **Dan Mica** (D, West Palm Beach) | **122,370** |
| | Bill James (R, Delray Beach) | 98,788 |
| 12. | **Edward J. Stack** (D, Hollywood) | **104,653** |
| | J. Herbert Burke\* (R, Hollywood) | 64,793 |
| 13. | **William Lehman\*** (D, N. Miami Beach) | **Unopposed** |
| 14. | **Claude Pepper\*** (D, Miami) | **63,167** |
| | Al Cardenas (R, Miami) | 37,310 |
| 15. | **Dante B. Fascell\*** (D, Miami) | **105,469** |
| | Herbert J. Hoodwin (R, Coral Gables) | 36,523 |

### Georgia

| Dist. | Representative (Party, Home) | 1978 Election |
|---|---|---|
| 1. | **Bo Ginn\*** (D, Millen) | **Unopposed** |
| 2. | **Dawson Mathis\*** (D, Albany) | **Unopposed** |
| 3. | **Jack Brinkley\*** (D, Columbus) | **Unopposed** |
| 4. | **Elliott H. Levitas\*** (D, Atlanta) | **60,184** |
| | Homer Cheung (R, Atlanta) | 14,206 |
| 5. | **Wyche Fowler Jr.\*** (D, Atlanta) | **52,739** |
| | Thomas P. Bowles Jr. (R, Atlanta) | 17,132 |
| 6. | **Newton Leroy Gingrich** (R, Carrollton) | **47,161** |
| | Virginia Shapard (D, Carrollton) | 39,434 |

| Dist. | Representative (Party, Home) | 1978 Election |
|---|---|---|
| 7. | **Larry P. McDonald\*** (D, Marietta) | **46,783** |
| | Earnest Norsworthy (R, Marietta) | 23,631 |
| 8. | **Billy Lee Evans\*** (D, Macon) | **Unopposed** |
| 9. | **Ed Jenkins\*** (D, Jasper) | **46,172** |
| | David G. Ashworth (R, Canton) | 13,743 |
| 10. | **Doug Barnard\*** (D, Augusta) | **Unopposed** |

### Hawaii

| Dist. | Representative (Party, Home) | 1978 Election |
|---|---|---|
| 1. | **Cecil (Cec) Heftel\*** (D, Honolulu) | **84,552** |
| | William D. Spillane (R, Honolulu) | 24,470 |
| 2. | **Daniel K. Akaka\*** (D, Honolulu) | **118,273** |
| | Charlie Isaak (R, Kailua) | 15,693 |

### Idaho

| Dist. | Representative (Party, Home) | 1978 Election |
|---|---|---|
| 1. | **Steven D. Symms\*** (R, Caldwell) | **86,438** |
| | Roy Truby (D, Boise) | 57,896 |
| 2. | **George Hansen\*** (R, Pocatello) | **79,983** |
| | Stan Kress (D, Firth) | 59,565 |

### Illinois

| Dist. | Representative (Party, Home) | 1978 Election |
|---|---|---|
| 1. | **Bennett M. Stewart** (D, Chicago) | **43,388** |
| | Rayner (R, Chicago) | 28,454 |
| 2. | **Morgan F. Murphy\*** (D, Chicago) | **67,897** |
| | James P. Wognum (R, Chicago) | 9,683 |
| 3. | **Martin A. Russo\*** (D, South Holland) | **92,930** |
| | Robert L. Dunne (R, Chicago) | 51,468 |
| 4. | **Edward J. Derwinski\*** (R, Flossmoor) | **90,567** |
| | Andrew Thomas (D, Flossmoor) | 45,476 |
| 5. | **John G. Fary\*** (D, Chicago) | **96,902** |
| | Joseph A. Barracca (R, Chicago) | 18,658 |
| 6. | **Henry J. Hyde\*** (R, Park Ridge) | **79,668** |
| | Jeanne P. Quinn (D, Oak Park) | 39,707 |
| 7. | **Cardiss Collins\*** (D, Chicago) | **61,815** |
| | James C. Holt (R, Chicago) | 9,590 |
| 8. | **Dan Rostenkowski\*** (D, Chicago) | **78,796** |
| | Carl C. LoDico (R, Chicago) | 13,262 |
| 9. | **Sidney R. Yates\*** (D, Chicago) | **83,690** |
| | John M. Collins (R, Chicago) | 27,586 |
| 10. | **John E. Porter** (R, Evanston) | **85,834** |
| | Abner J. Mikva\* (D, Evanston) | 84,790 |
| 11. | **Frank Annunzio\*** (D, Chicago) | **111,132** |
| | John Hoeger (R, Chicago) | 40,288 |
| 12. | **Philip M. Crane\*** (R, Mount Prospect) | **106,242** |
| | Gilbert Bogen (D, Highland Park) | 27,349 |
| 13. | **Robert M. McClory\*** (R, Lake Bluff) | **64,045** |
| | Frederick J. Steffen (D, Elgin) | 40,662 |
| 14. | **John N. Erlenborn\*** (R, Glen Ellyn) | **118,538** |
| | James A. Romanyak (D, Lisle) | 39,347 |
| 15. | **Tom Corcoran\*** (R, Ottawa) | **80,841** |
| | Tim L. Hall (D, Dwight) | 48,740 |
| 16. | **John B. Anderson\*** (R, Rockford) | **107,587** |
| | Ernest W. Dahlin (D, Rockford) | 55,631 |
| 17. | **George M. O'Brien\*** (R, Joliet) | **83,161** |
| | Clifford J. Sinclair (D, Joliet) | 37,923 |
| 18. | **Robert H. Michel\*** (R, Peoria) | **85,935** |
| | Virgil R. Grunkmeyer (D, Peoria) | 44,542 |
| 19. | **Tom Railsback\*** (R, Moline) | **Unopposed** |
| 20. | **Paul Findley\*** (R, Pittsfield) | **110,640** |
| | Victor Roberts (D, Springfield) | 48,145 |
| 21. | **Edward R. Madigan\*** (R, Lincoln) | **97,773** |
| | Ken Baughman (D, Monticello) | 27,132 |
| 22. | **Daniel B. Crane** (R, Danville) | **85,163** |
| | Terry L. Bruce (D, Olney) | 72,788 |
| 23. | **Melvin Price\*** (D, East St. Louis) | **74,065** |
| | Daniel J. Stack (R, Highland) | 25,022 |
| 24. | **Paul Simon\*** (D, Carbondale) | **108,124** |
| | John T. Anderson (R, Marion) | 56,571 |

### Indiana

| Dist. | Representative (Party, Home) | 1978 Election |
|---|---|---|
| 1. | **Adam Benjamin Jr.\*** (D, Hobart) | **72,367** |
| | Owen W. Crumpacker (R, Hammond) | 17,419 |
| 2. | **Floyd J. Fithian\*** (D, Lafayette) | **81,848** |
| | Jay Philip Oppenheim (R, Leesburg) | 52,834 |
| 3. | **John Brademas\*** (D, South Bend) | **63,610** |
| | Thomas L. Thorson (R, La Porte) | 49,372 |
| 4. | **Dan Quayle\*** (R, Fort Wayne) | **78,808** |
| | John D. Walda (D, Fort Wayne) | 42,773 |
| 5. | **Elwood H. Hillis\*** (R, Kokomo) | **92,495** |
| | Max Ervin Heiss (D, Anderson) | 44,919 |

| Dist. | Representative (Party, Home) | 1978 Election |
|-------|------------------------------|---------------|
| 6. | **David W. Evans\*** (D, Indianapolis) | **64,764** |
| | David G. Crane (R, Martinsville) | 59,380 |
| 7. | **John T. Myers\*** (R, Covington) | **84,875** |
| | Charlotte T. Zietlow (D, Bloomington) | 66,295 |
| 8. | **H. Joel Deckard\*** (R, Evansville) | **82,668** |
| | David L. Cornwell\* (D, Paoli) | 76,397 |
| 9. | **Lee H. Hamilton\*** (D, Columbus) | **101,967** |
| | Frank I. Hamilton Jr. (R, Greensburg) | 52,120 |
| 10. | **Philip R. Sharp\*** (D, Muncie) | **73,138** |
| | William Gould Frazier (R, Muncie) | 56,070 |
| 11. | **Andrew Jacobs Jr.\*** (D, Indianapolis) | **59,052** |
| | Charles E. Bosma (R, Beech Grove) | 44,486 |

### Iowa

| Dist. | Representative (Party, Home) | 1978 Election |
|-------|------------------------------|---------------|
| 1. | **Jim Leach\*** (R, Davenport) | **79,776** |
| | Richard E. Myers (D, Coralville) | 46,028 |
| 2. | **Thomas J. Tauke** (R, Dubuque) | **72,530** |
| | Michael T. Blouin\* (D, Dubuque) | 65,175 |
| 3. | **Charles E. Grassley\*** (R, New Hartford) | **104,549** |
| | John Knudson (D, Albion) | 34,774 |
| 4. | **Neal Smith\*** (D, Altoona) | **90,338** |
| | Charles E. Minor (R, Des Moines) | 47,399 |
| 5. | **Tom Harkin\*** (D, Ames) | **82,357** |
| | Julian B. Garret (R, Indianola) | 57,300 |
| 6. | **Berkley Bedell\*** (D, Spirit Lake) | **86,954** |
| | Willis Edgar Junder (R, Sioux City) | 44,580 |

### Kansas

| Dist. | Representative (Party, Home) | 1978 Election |
|-------|------------------------------|---------------|
| 1. | **Keith G. Sebelius\*** (R, Norton) | **Unopposed** |
| 2. | **James E. Jeffries** (R, Atchison) | **76,730** |
| | Martha Keys\* (D, Manhattan) | 70,796 |
| 3. | **Larry Winn Jr.\*** (R, Overland Park) | **Unopposed** |
| 4. | **Dan Glickman\*** (D, Wichita) | **109,499** |
| | James Paul Litsey (R, Wichita) | 43,486 |
| 5. | **Robert "Bob" Whittaker** (R, Augusta) | **85,331** |
| | Don Allegrucci (D, Pittsburg) | 62,731 |

### Kentucky

| Dist. | Representative (Party, Home) | 1978 Election |
|-------|------------------------------|---------------|
| 1. | **Carroll Hubbard Jr.\*** (D, Mayfield) | **Unopposed** |
| 2. | **William Natcher\*** (D, Bowling Green) | **Unopposed** |
| 3. | **Romano L. Mazzoli\*** (D, Louisville) | **35,911** |
| | Norbert Drummond Leveronne (R, Shively) | 17,051 |
| 4. | **M. Gene Snyder\*** (R, Brownsboro Farms) | **61,648** |
| | George Clarke Martin (D, Anchorage) | 31,913 |
| 5. | **Tim Lee Carter\*** (R, Tompkinsville) | **60,292** |
| | Jesse M. Ramey (D, Waynesburg) | 15,552 |
| 6. | **Larry J. Hopkins** (R, Lexington) | **52,550** |
| | Charles T. Easterly (D, Frankfort) | 48,083 |
| 7. | **Carl D. Perkins\*** (D, Hindman) | **51,896** |
| | Granville Thomas (R, London) | 16,076 |

### Louisiana

| Dist. | Representative (Party, Home) | 1978 Election |
|-------|------------------------------|---------------|
| 1. | **Bob Livingston\*** (R, New Orleans) | **Unopposed** |
| 2. | **Lindy (Mrs. Hale) Boggs\*** (D, New Orleans) | **Unopposed** |
| 3. | **David C. Treen\*** (R, Metairie) | **Unopposed** |
| 4. | Claude "Buddy" Leach ‡ (D, Leesville) | 65,570 |
| | James Hamilton Wilson (R, Vivian) | 65,322 |
| 5. | **Jerry Huckaby\*** (D, Ringgold) | **Unopposed** |
| 6. | **W. Henson Moore\*** (R, Baton Rouge) | **Unopposed** |
| 7. | **John Breaux\*** (D, Crowley) | **Unopposed** |
| 8. | **Gillis W. Long\*** (D, Alexandria) | **Unopposed** |

### Maine

| Dist. | Representative (Party, Home) | 1978 Election |
|-------|------------------------------|---------------|
| 1. | **David F. Emery\*** (R, Rockland) | **122,122** |
| | John Quinn (D, South Portland) | 70,151 |
| 2. | **Olympia J. Snowe** (R, Auburn) | **87,909** |
| | Markham L. Gartley (D, Greenville) | 71,194 |

### Maryland

| Dist. | Representative (Party, Home) | 1978 Election |
|-------|------------------------------|---------------|
| 1. | **Robert E. Bauman\*** (R, Easton) | **77,592** |
| | Joseph D. Quinn (D, Denton) | 44,913 |
| 2. | **Clarence D. Long\*** (D, Ruxton) | **93,896** |
| | Malcolm M. McKnight (R, Fork) | 48,752 |
| 3. | **Barbara A. Mikulski\*** (D, Baltimore) | **Unopposed** |
| 4. | **Marjorie S. Holt\*** (R, Severna Park) | **69,655** |
| | Sue F. Ward (D, Clinton) | 43,022 |

| Dist. | Representative (Party, Home) | 1978 Election |
|-------|------------------------------|---------------|
| 5. | **Gladys Noon Spellman\*** (D, Laurel) | **63,868** |
| | Saul J. Harris (R, Landover Hills) | 18,800 |
| 6. | **Beverly B. Byron** (D, Frederick) | **122,378** |
| | Melvin Perkins (R, Baltimore) | 14,286 |
| 7. | **Parren J. Mitchell\*** (D, Baltimore) | **Unopposed** |
| 8. | **Michael D. Barnes** (D, Kensington) | **79,644** |
| | Newton I. Steers Jr.\* (R, Bethesda) | 74,749 |

### Massachusetts

| Dist. | Representative (Party, Home) | 1978 Election |
|-------|------------------------------|---------------|
| 1. | **Silvio Conte\*** (R, Pittsfield) | **Unopposed** |
| 2. | **Edward P. Boland\*** (D, Springfield) | **98,861** |
| | Thomas P. Swank (R, West Brookfield) | 37,067 |
| 3. | **Joseph D. Early\*** (D, Worcester) | **117,581** |
| | Charles K. Macleod (R, Marlborough) | 38,505 |
| 4. | **Robert F. Drinan\*** (D, Chestnut Hill) | **Unopposed** |
| 5. | **James M. Shannon\*** (D, Lawrence) | **90,170** |
| | John J. Buckley (R, Belmont) | 48,671 |
| 6. | **Nicholas Mavroules** (D, Peabody) | **96,181** |
| | William E. Bronson (R, Manchester) | 83,446 |
| 7. | **Edward J. Markey\*** (D, Malden) | **Unopposed** |
| 8. | **Thomas P. O'Neill Jr.\*** (D, Cambridge) | **101,460** |
| | William A. Barnstead (R, Arlington) | 28,414 |
| 9. | **John J. Moakley\*** (D, Boston) | **Unopposed** |
| 10. | **Margaret Heckler\*** (R, Wellesley Hills) | **96,189** |
| | John J. Marino (D, Wellesley) | 62,212 |
| 11. | **Brian J. Donnelly** (D, Dorchester) | **Unopposed** |
| 12. | **Gerry E. Studds\*** (D, Cohasset) | **Unopposed** |

### Michigan

| Dist. | Representative (Party, Home) | 1978 Election |
|-------|------------------------------|---------------|
| 1. | **John Conyers\*** (D, Detroit) | **89,252** |
| | Robert S. Arnold (R, Detroit) | 6,900 |
| 2. | **Carl D. Pursell\*** (R, Plymouth) | **86,310** |
| | Earl Greene (D, Ann Arbor) | 43,289 |
| 3. | **Howard Wolpe** (D, Lansing) | **83,473** |
| | Garry Brown\* (R Schoolcraft) | 78,877 |
| 4. | **Dave Stockman\*** (R, St. Joseph) | **95,519** |
| | Morgan L. Hager Jr. (D, Benton Harbor) | 38,331 |
| 5. | **Harold S. Sawyer\*** (R, Rockford) | **91,507** |
| | Dale Robert Sprik (D, Grand Rapids) | 89,213 |
| 6. | **Bob Carr\*** (D, East Lansing) | **87,925** |
| | Michael H. Conlin (R, Jackson) | 65,634 |
| 7. | **Dale E. Kildee\*** (D, Flint) | **105,402** |
| | Gale M. Cronk (R, Fenton) | 29,958 |
| 8. | **Bob Traxler\*** (D, Bay City) | **103,170** |
| | Norman R. Hughes (R, Metamora) | 51,912 |
| 9. | **Guy Vander Jagt\*** (R, Luther) | **122,321** |
| | Howard M. LeRoux (D, North Muskegon) | 53,425 |
| 10. | **Donald Joseph Albosta** (D, St. Charles) | **91,268** |
| | Elford A. Cederberg\* (R, Midland) | 84,699 |
| 11. | **Robert W. Davis** (R, Gaylord) | **96,138** |
| | Keith McLeod (D, Marquette) | 79,091 |
| 12. | **David E. Bonior\*** (D, Mt. Clemens) | **80,965** |
| | Kirby Holmes (R, Utica) | 65,873 |
| 13. | **Charles C. Diggs Jr.\*** (D, Detroit) | **44,322** |
| | Dovie T. Pickett (R, Detroit) | 11,170 |
| 14. | **Lucien N. Nedzi\*** (D, Detroit) | **66,109** |
| | John Edward Getz (R, Grosse Pointe Farms) | 25,382 |
| 15. | **William D. Ford\*** (D, Taylor) | **69,372** |
| | Edgar Nieten (R, Romulus) | 16,297 |
| 16. | **John D. Dingell\*** (D, Trenton) | **79,927** |
| | Melvin E. Hever (R, Trenton) | 23,412 |
| 17. | **William M. Brodhead\*** (D, Detroit) | **Unopposed** |
| 18. | **James J. Blanchard\*** (D, Pleasant Ridge) | **81,586** |
| | Robert J. Salloum (R, Troy) | 21,058 |
| 19. | **William S. Broomfield\*** (R, Birmingham) | **101,466** |
| | Betty F. Collier (D, Drayton Plains) | 38,134 |

### Minnesota

| Dist. | Representative (Party, Home) | 1978 Election |
|-------|------------------------------|---------------|
| 1. | **Arlen Erdahl\*** (R, West St. Paul) | **109,831** |
| | Gerald Sikorski (D, Stillwater) | 80,148 |
| 2. | **Tom Hagedorn\*** (R, Truman) | **137,028** |
| | John F. Considine (D, Mankato) | 57,971 |

| Dist. | Representative (Party, Home) | 1978 Election |
|---|---|---|
| 3. | **Bill Frenzel*** (R, Golden Valley) | **125,396** |
| | Michael O. Freeman (D, Richfield) | 64,453 |
| 4. | **Bruce F. Vento*** (D, St. Paul) | **95,425** |
| | John Berg (R, St. Paul) | 68,989 |
| 5. | **Martin Olav Sabo** (D, Minneapolis) | **91,692** |
| | Mike Till, (R, Minneapolis) | 55,519 |
| 6. | **Richard Nolan*** (D, Waite Park) | **111,960** |
| | Russ Bjorhus (R, Litchfield) | 91,155 |
| 7. | **Arlan Stangeland*** (R, Barnesville) | **107,412** |
| | Gene Wenstrom (D, Elbow Lake). | 91,976 |
| 8. | **James L. Oberstar*** (D, Chisholm) | **Unopposed** |

### Mississippi

| Dist. | Representative (Party, Home) | 1978 Election |
|---|---|---|
| 1. | **Jamie L. Whitten*** (D, Charleston) | **57,344** |
| | Terrill K. Moffett (R, Oxford) | 25,575 |
| 2. | **David Bowen*** (D, Cleveland) | **57,645** |
| | M. Roland Byrd (R, Louisville) | 35,722 |
| 3. | **G. V. (Sonny) Montgomery*** (D, Meridian) | **95,660** |
| | Dorothy Eleanor Cleveland (R, Union) | 7,244 |
| 4. | **Jon Clifton Hinson** (R, Tylertown) | **67,915** |
| | John Hampton Stennis (D, Jackson) | 34,406 |
| 5. | **Trent Lott*** (R, Gulfport) | **Unopposed** |

### Missouri

| Dist. | Representative (Party, Home) | 1978 Election |
|---|---|---|
| 1. | **William (Bill) Clay*** (D, St. Louis) | **62,969** |
| | Bill White (R, Rock Hill) | 30,389 |
| 2. | **Robert A. Young*** (D, St. Ann) | **103,412** |
| | Bob Chase (R, St. Louis) | 79,973 |
| 3. | **Richard A. Gephardt*** (D, St. Louis) | **120,172** |
| | Lee Buchschacher (R, St. Louis) | 26,829 |
| 4. | **Ike Skelton** (D, Lexington) | **116,098** |
| | Bill Baker (R, Lee's Summit) | 43,742 |
| 5. | **Richard Bolling*** (D, Kansas City) | **81,483** |
| | Steven L. Walter (R, Kansas City) | 30,189 |
| 6. | **E. Thomas Coleman*** (R, Kansas City) | **95,721** |
| | Phil Snowden (D, Gladstone) | 75,163 |
| 7. | **Gene Taylor*** (R, Sarcoxie) | **104,443** |
| | Jim Thomas (D, Kimberling City) | 67,374 |
| 8. | **Richard H. Ichord*** (D, Houston) | **95,473** |
| | Donald D. Meyer (R, Labadie) | 62,467 |
| 9. | **Harold L. Volkmer*** (D, Hannibal) | **135,080** |
| | Jerry Dent (R, St. Peters) | 45,894 |
| 10. | **Bill D. Burlison*** (D, Cape Girardeau) | **98,910** |
| | James A. Weir (R, Cedar Hill) | 52,249 |

### Montana

| Dist. | Representative (Party, Home) | 1978 Election |
|---|---|---|
| 1. | **Pat Williams** (D, Helena) | **35,409** |
| | Jim Waltermire (R, Missoula) | 26,739 |
| 2. | **Ron Marlenee*** (R, Scobey) | **55,241** |
| | Thomas G. Monahan (D, Billings) | 45,311 |

### Nebraska

| Dist. | Representative (Party, Home) | 1978 Election |
|---|---|---|
| 1. | **Douglas K. Bereuter** (R, Utica) | **98,185** |
| | Hess Dyas (D, Lincoln) | 70,607 |
| 2. | **John J. Cavanaugh*** (D, Omaha) | **76,383** |
| | Harold J. Daub Jr. (R, Omaha) | 69,625 |
| 3. | **Virginia Smith*** (R, Chappell) | **138,432** |
| | Marilyn Fowler (D, Lexington) | 35,840 |

### Nevada

| Dist. | Representative (Party, Home) | 1978 Election |
|---|---|---|
| | **Jim Santini*** (D, Las Vegas) | **130,238** |
| | Bill O'Mara (R, Reno) | 43,836 |

### New Hampshire

| Dist. | Representative (Party, Home) | 1978 Election |
|---|---|---|
| 1. | **Norman E. D'Amours*** (D, Manchester) | **82,705** |
| | Daniel M. Hughes (R, Manchester) | 49,134 |
| 2. | **James C. Cleveland*** (R, New London) | **84,432** |
| | Edgar J. Helms (D, Concord) | 39,530 |

### New Jersey

| Dist. | Representative (Party, Home) | 1978 Election |
|---|---|---|
| 1. | **James J. Florio*** (D, Camden) | **105,353** |
| | Robert Mark-Deitch (R, Sicklerville) | 26,661 |
| 2. | **William J. Hughes*** (D, Ocean City) | **105,873** |
| | James H. Biggs (R, Island Heights) | 53,327 |
| 3. | **James J. Howard*** (D, Spring Lake Heights) | **80,226** |
| | Bruce G. Coe (R, Rumson) | 61,966 |
| 4. | **Frank Thompson Jr.*** (D, Trenton) | **68,714** |
| | Christopher H. Smith (R, Trenton) | 41,533 |
| 5. | **Millicent H. Fenwick*** (R, Bernardsville) | **102,186** |
| | John T. Fahy (D, Parsippany) | 39,023 |
| 6. | **Edwin B. Forsythe*** (R, Moorestown) | **87,919** |
| | W. Thomas McGann (D, Moorestown) | 55,888 |
| 7. | **Andrew Maguire*** (D, Ridgewood) | **78,358** |
| | Margaret S. Roukema (R, Ridgewood) | 69,543 |
| 8. | **Robert A. Roe*** (D, Patterson) | **69,498** |
| | Thomas Melani (R, Wayne) | 23,843 |
| 9. | **Harold C. Hollenbeck*** (R, East Rutherford) | **73,328** |
| | Nicholas S. Mastorelli (D, Secaucus) | 56,305 |
| 10. | **Peter W. Rodino Jr.*** (D, Newark) | **54,806** |
| | John L. Pelt (R, Newark) | 7,907 |
| 11. | **Joseph G. Minish*** (D, West Orange) | **84,836** |
| | Julius George Feld (R, South Orange) | 34,117 |
| 12. | **Matthew J. Rinaldo*** (R, Union) | **77,763** |
| | Richard McCormack (D, Kenilworth) | 29,776 |
| 13. | **James A. Courter** (R, Hackettstown) | **76,976** |
| | Helen S. Meyner* (D, Phillipsburg) | 72,081 |
| 14. | **Frank J. Guarini** (D, Jersey City) | **66,252** |
| | Henry J. Hill (R, Kearny) | 21,532 |
| 15. | **Edward J. Patten*** (D, Perth Amboy) | **55,905** |
| | Charles W. Wiley (R, Parlin) | 52,810 |

### New Mexico

| Dist. | Representative (Party, Home) | 1978 Election |
|---|---|---|
| 1. | **Manuel Lujan Jr.*** (R, Albuquerque) | **116,675** |
| | Robert M. Hawk (D, Albuquerque) | 70,083 |
| 2. | **Harold Runnels*** (D, Lovington) | **Unopposed** |

### New York

| Dist. | Representative (Party, Home) | 1978 Election |
|---|---|---|
| 1. | **William Carney** (R, C, Hauppauge) | **86,502** |
| | John Randolph (D, E. Patchogue) | 64,132 |
| 2. | **Thomas J. Downey*** (D, W. Islip) | **63,126** |
| | Harold J. Withers (R, C, North Babylon) | 52,159 |
| 3. | **Jerome A. Ambro*** (D, East Northport) | **70,035** |
| | Gregory W. Carman (R, C, Farmingdale) | 66,612 |
| 4. | **Norman F. Lent*** (R, C, East Rockaway) | **94,381** |
| | Everett A. Rosenblum (D, East Meadow) | 46,539 |
| 5. | **John W. Wydler*** (R, C, Garden City) | **84,692** |
| | John W. Matthews (D, L, South Hempstead) | 40,465 |
| 6. | **Lester Wolff*** (D, L, Great Neck) | **79,590** |
| | Stuart L. Ain (R, Roslyn Heights) | 43,748 |
| 7. | **Joseph P. Addabbo*** (D, L, Ozone Park) | **68,414** |
| | Mark Elliot Scott (C, Ozone Park) | 3,842 |
| 8. | **Benjamin S. Rosenthal*** (D, L, Flushing) | **73,202** |
| | Albert Lemishow (R, Flushing) | 15,196 |
| 9. | **Geraldine A. Ferraro** (D, Forest Hills) | **49,614** |
| | Alfred A. DelliBovi (R, C, Richmond Hill) | 40,588 |
| 10. | **Mario Biaggi*** (D, R, L, Bronx) | **75,091** |
| | Carmen Ricciardi (C, Queens) | 4,075 |
| 11. | **James H. Scheuer*** (D, L, Neponsit) | **57,529** |
| | Kenneth Harris (R, C, Belle Harbor) | 15,903 |
| 12. | **Shirley Chisholm*** (D, L, Brooklyn) | **24,020** |
| | Charles Gibbs (R, Brooklyn) | 3,425 |
| 13. | **Stephen J. Solarz*** (D, L, Brooklyn) | **66,954** |
| | Max Carasso (R, C, Brooklyn) | 15,725 |
| 14. | **Frederick W. Richmond*** (D, L, Brooklyn) | **29,706** |
| | Arthur Bramwell (R, Brooklyn) | 7,103 |
| 15. | **Leo C. Zefferetti*** (D, C, Brooklyn) | **46,818** |
| | Robert P. Whelan (R, Brooklyn) | 19,678 |
| 16. | **Elizabeth Holtzman*** (D, L, Brooklyn) | **58,703** |
| | Larry Penner (R, Brooklyn) | 9,808 |
| 17. | **John M. Murphy*** (D, Staten Island) | **52,342** |
| | John M. Peters (R, C, Staten Island) | 31,987 |
| 18. | **S. William Green*** (R, New York) | **58,274** |
| | Carter Burden (D, L, New York) | 51,902 |

| Dist. | Representative (Party, Home) | 1978 Election |
|---|---|---|
| 19. | **Charles B. Rangel*** (D, R, New York) | **55,545** |
| | E. Freeman Yearling (C, West Hempstead) | 1,584 |
| 20. | **Ted S. Weiss*** (D, L, New York) | **62,451** |
| | Harry Torczyner (R, New York) | 11,299 |
| 21. | **Robert Garcia*** (D, R, L, Bronx) | **23,473** |
| | Lawrence W. Lindsley Sr. (C, Bronx) | 492 |
| 22. | **Jonathan B. Bingham*** (D, L, Bronx) | **55,821** |
| | Anthony J. Geidel Jr. (R, C, Bronx) | 10,944 |
| 23. | **Peter A. Peyser** (D, Irvington) | **64,259** |
| | Angelo Martinelli (R, C, Yonkers) | 57,319 |
| 24. | **Richard L. Ottinger*** (D, Pleasantville) | **58,367** |
| | Michael R. Edelman (R, C, Yonkers) | 50,554 |
| 25. | **Hamilton Fish Jr.*** (R, Poughkeepsie) | **108,445** |
| | Gunars M. Ozols (D, Wappingers Fall) | 29,903 |
| 26. | **Benjamin A. Gilman*** (R, Middletown) | **85,212** |
| | Charles Emmet Holbrook (D, L, Congers) | 41,213 |
| 27. | **Matthew F. McHugh*** (D, Ithaca) | **81,492** |
| | Neil Tyler Wallace (R, C, Ithaca) | 65,932 |
| 28. | **Samuel S. Stratton*** (D, Amsterdam) | **126,703** |
| | Paul H. Tocker (R, C, Schenectady) | 32,616 |
| 29. | **Gerald B. H. Solomon** (R, C, Glenn Falls) | **96,625** |
| | Edward Pattison* (D, L, Troy) | 83,398 |
| 30. | **Robert C. McEwen*** (R, C, Ogdensburg) | **88,085** |
| | Norma Bartle (D, L, Oswego) | 57,220 |
| 31. | **Donald J. Mitchell*** (R, C, Herkimer) | **Unopposed** |
| 32. | **James M. Hanley*** (D, Syracuse) | **74,373** |
| | Peter Del Giorno (R, C, Syracuse) | 65,567 |
| 33. | **Gary A. Lee** (R, Ithaca) | **81,283** |
| | Roy A. Bernardi (D, Syracuse) | 57,835 |
| 34. | **Frank Horton*** (D, R, Rochester) | **119,878** |
| | Leo J. Kasperski (C, Fairport) | 17,757 |
| 35. | **Barber B. Conable*** (R, Rochester) | **94,322** |
| | Francis C. Repicci (D, Batavia) | 36,180 |
| 36. | **John J. La Falce*** (D, L, Tonawanda) | **97,876** |
| | Francina Joyce Cartonia (R, Williamsville) | 31,427 |
| 37. | **Henry J. Nowak*** (D, L, Buffalo) | **70,023** |
| | Charles Poth III (R, Buffalo) | 17,747 |
| 38. | **Jack Kemp*** (R, C, Buffalo) | **113,476** |
| | James A. Peck (L, West Seneca) | 6,192 |
| 39. | **Stanley N. Lundine*** (D, Jamestown) | **77,616** |
| | Crispin Maguire (R, C, Olean) | 54,644 |

### North Carolina

| Dist. | Representative (Party, Home) | 1978 Election |
|---|---|---|
| 1. | **Walter Jones*** (D, Farmville) | **66,916** |
| | James Milford Newcomb (R, Williamston) | 16,809 |
| 2. | **L. H. Fountain*** (D, Tarboro) | **62,019** |
| | Barry Lynn Gardner (R, Rocky Mount) | 16,370 |
| 3. | **Charles Whitely*** (D, Mt. Olive) | **54,049** |
| | Willard Jackson Blanchard (R, Salemburg) | 22,150 |
| 4. | **Ike Andrews*** (D, Siler City) | **Unopposed** |
| 5. | **Stephen L. Neal*** (D, Winston-Salem) | **68,787** |
| | Hamilton C. Horton (R, Winston-Salem) | 58,334 |
| 6. | **Richardson Preyer*** (D, Greensboro) | **58,138** |
| | George H. Bemus (R, Greensboro) | 26,876 |
| 7. | **Charles Rose*** (D, Fayetteville) | **53,779** |
| | Raymond Schrump (R, Fayetteville) | 23,140 |
| 8. | **W. G. (Bill) Hefner*** (D, Concord) | **62,467** |
| | Roger Lee Austin (R, Marshville) | 43,180 |
| 9. | **James G. Martin*** (R, Charlotte) | **66,207** |
| | Charles Kimball Maxwell (D, Charlotte) | 29,871 |
| 10. | **James T. Broyhill*** (R, Lenior) | **Unopposed** |
| 11. | **Lamar Gudger*** (D, Asheville) | **75,351** |
| | R. Curtis Ratcliff (R, Alexander) | 65,708 |

### North Dakota At Large

| | | 1978 Election |
|---|---|---|
| | **Mark Andrews*** (R, Mapleton) | **144,403** |
| | Bruce F. Hagen (D, Mandan) | 66,820 |

### Ohio

| Dist. | Representative (Party, Home) | 1978 Election |
|---|---|---|
| 1. | **Willis D. Gradison Jr.*** (R, Cincinnati) | **73,533** |
| | Timothy M. Burke (D, Cincinnati) | 38,597 |
| 2. | **Thomas A. Luken*** (D, Cincinnati) | **64,493** |
| | Stanley J. Aronoff (R, Cincinnati) | 58,694 |
| 3. | **Tony P. Hall** (D, Dayton) | **62,613** |
| | Dudley P. Kircher (R, Dayton) | 51,573 |
| 4. | **Tennyson Guyer*** (R, Findlay) | **85,359** |
| | John William Griffin (D, Miamisburg) | 39,040 |
| 5. | **Delbert Latta*** (R, Bowling Green) | **83,649** |
| | James Robert Sherck (D, Fremont) | 49,871 |
| 6. | **William H. Harsha*** (R, Portsmouth) | **85,409** |
| | Ted Strickland (D, Lucasville) | 46,198 |
| 7. | **Clarence J. Brown*** (R, Urbana) | **Unopposed** |
| 8. | **Thomas N. Kindness*** (R, Hamilton) | **81,130** |
| | Luella R. Schroeder (D, Fairfield) | 32,476 |
| 9. | **Thomas Ludlow Ashley*** (D, Maumee) | **72,373** |
| | John C. Hoyt (R, Toledo) | 34,202 |
| 10. | **Clarence E. Miller*** (R, Lancaster) | **99,263** |
| | James A. Plummer (D, Jackson) | 35,027 |
| 11. | **J. William Stanton*** (R, Painesville) | **88,957** |
| | Patrick James Donlin (D, Hubbard) | 37,008 |
| 12. | **Samuel L. Devine*** (R, Columbus) | **81,414** |
| | James L. Baumann (D, Columbus) | 62,098 |
| 13. | **Donald J. Pease*** (D, Oberlin) | **80,929** |
| | Mark W. Whitfield (R, Medina) | 43,336 |
| 14. | **John F. Seiberling*** (D, Akron) | **81,911** |
| | Walter J. Vogel (R, Akron) | 31,137 |
| 15. | **Chalmers P. Wylie*** (R, Columbus) | **91,166** |
| | Henry W. Eckhart (D, Columbus) | 37,064 |
| 16. | **Ralph S. Regula*** (R, Navarre) | **105,098** |
| | Owen S. Hand Jr. (D, Canton) | 29,628 |
| 17. | **John M. Ashbrook*** (R, Johnstown) | **81,828** |
| | Kenneth Robert Grier (D, Coshocton) | 40,358 |
| 18. | **Douglas Applegate*** (D, Steubenville) | **71,823** |
| | William J. Ress (R, New Philadelphia) | 48,884 |
| 19. | **Lyle Williams** (R, Niles) | **71,869** |
| | Charles J. Carney* (D, Youngstown) | 70,055 |
| 20. | **Mary Rose Oakar*** (D, Cleveland) | **Unopposed** |
| 21. | **Louis Stokes*** (D, Warrensville Heights) | **58,045** |
| | Bill Mack (R, Cleveland) | 9,589 |
| 22. | **Charles A. Vanik*** (D, Euclid) | **87,152** |
| | Richard W. Sander (R, Euclid) | 30,869 |
| 23. | **Ronald M. Mottl*** (D, Parma) | **99,690** |
| | Homer S. Taft (R, Bay Village) | 33,861 |

### Oklahoma

| Dist. | Representative (Party, Home) | 1978 Election |
|---|---|---|
| 1. | **James R. Jones*** (D, Tulsa) | **73,886** |
| | Paula Unruh (R, Tulsa) | 49,404 |
| 2. | **Michael Lynn Synar** (D, Muskogee) | **71,761** |
| | Gary Richardson (R, Muskogee) | 59,775 |
| 3. | **Wesley Wade Watkins*** (D, Ada) | **Unopposed** |
| 4. | **Tom Steed*** (D, Shawnee) | **63,894** |
| | Seward Eliot Robb (R, Norman) | 42,124 |
| 5. | **Mickey Edwards*** (R, Oklahoma City) | **69,138** |
| | Jesse Dennis Knipp (D, Oklahoma City) | 17,674 |
| 6. | **Glenn English*** (D, Cordell) | **103,510** |
| | Harold V. Hunter (R, Waukomis) | 36,446 |

### Oregon

| Dist. | Representative (Party, Home) | 1978 Election |
|---|---|---|
| 1. | **Les AuCoin** (D, Portland) | **157,916** |
| | Nick Bunick (R, Portland) | 94,366 |
| 2. | **Al Ullman*** (D, Baker) | **152,124** |
| | Terry H. Hicks (R, Dallas) | 67,604 |
| 3. | **Robert B. Duncan*** (D, Portland) | **Unopposed** |
| 4. | **James Weaver*** (D, Eugene) | **124,459** |
| | Jerry Lausmann (R, Medford) | 96,378 |

### Pennsylvania

| Dist. | Representative (Party, Home) | 1978 Election |
|---|---|---|
| 1. | **Michael Myers*** (D, Philadelphia) | **101,118** |
| | Samuel N. Fanelli (R, Philadelphia) | 37,621 |
| 2. | **William H. Gray III** (D, Philadelphia) | **127,838** |
| | Roland J. Atkins (R, Philadelphia) | 25,672 |

| Dist. Representative (Party, Home) | 1978 Election |
|---|---|
| 3. Raymond F. Lederer* (D, Philadelphia) | 84,185 |
| Raymond S. Kauffman (R, Philadelphia) | 33,379 |
| 4. Charles F. Dougherty (R, Philadelphia) | 108,640 |
| Joshua Eilberg* (D, Philadelphia) | 85,307 |
| 5. Richard T. Schulze* (R, West Chester) | 108,031 |
| Murray P. Zealor (D, Chester Springs) | 35,720 |
| 6. Gus Yatron* (D, Reading) | 106,198 |
| Stephen Mazur (R, Gilberton) | 37,490 |
| 7. Robert W. Edgar* (D, Broomall) | 79,657 |
| Eugene Daniel Kane (R, Drexel Hill) | 78,377 |
| 8. Peter H. Kostmayer* (D, New Hope) | 88,885 |
| G. Roger Bowers (R, Bensalem Twp.) | 56,481 |
| 9. Bud Shuster* (R, Everett) | 100,613 |
| Blaine Leroy Havice Jr. (D, Middleburg) | 33,766 |
| 10. Joseph M. McDade* (R, Clarks Summit) | 115,729 |
| Gene Basalyga (D, Blakely) | 35,920 |
| 11. Daniel J. Flood* (D, Wilkes-Barre) | 78,951 |
| Robert P. Hudock (R, Hazleton) | 69,327 |
| 12. John P. Murtha* (D, Johnstown) | 104,201 |
| Luther V. Elkin (R, Indiana) | 47,414 |
| 13. R. Lawrence Coughlin* (R, Norristown) | 109,426 |
| Alan Bendix Rubenstein (D, Gwynedd Valley) | 46,316 |
| 14. William S. Moorhead* (D, Pittsburgh) | 67,592 |
| Stan Thomas (R, Pittsburgh) | 49,900 |
| 15. Donald Lawrence Ritter (R, Coopersburg) | 65,796 |
| Fred B. Rooney* (D, Bethlehem) | 58,001 |
| 16. Robert S. Walker* (R, E. Petersburg) | 90,453 |
| Charles W. Boohar (D, Lancaster) | 27,023 |
| 17. Allen E. Ertel* (D, Montoursville) | 79,053 |
| Thomas Richard Rippon (R, Mifflinburg) | 53,382 |
| 18. Doug Walgren* (D, Pittsburgh) | 88,081 |
| Ted Jacob (R, Pittsburgh) | 65,160 |
| 19. William F. Goodling* (R, York) | 105,197 |
| Raj Kumar (D, Camp Hill) | 28,553 |
| 20. Joseph M. Gaydos* (D, McKeesport) | 97,427 |
| Kathleen M. Meyer (R, Pittsburgh) | 37,746 |
| 21. Donald A. Bailey (D, Greensburg) | 73,837 |
| Robert Miller (R, Greensburg) | 65,539 |
| 22. Austin J. Murphy* (D, Monongahela) | 99,589 |
| Marilyn Coyle Ecoff (R, Pittsburgh) | 39,561 |
| 23. William F. Clinger Jr. (R, Warren) | 73,072 |
| Joseph S. Ammerman* (D, Curwensville) | 61,607 |
| 24. Marc L. Marks* (R, Sharon) | 86,907 |
| Joseph P. Vigorito (D, Erie) | 48,687 |
| 25. Eugene V. Atkinson (D, Aliquippa) | 68,188 |
| Tim Shaffer (R, Prospect) | 62,029 |

### Rhode Island

| Dist. Representative (Party, Home) | 1978 Election |
|---|---|
| 1. Fernand St Germain* (D, Woonsocket) | 84,316 |
| Jerry Slocum (R, Newport) | 53,308 |
| 2. Edward P. Beard* (D, Cranston) | 83,180 |
| Claudine Camarada Schneider (R, Narragansett) | 75,625 |

### South Carolina

| Dist. Representative (Party, Home) | 1978 Election |
|---|---|
| 1. Mendel J. Davis* (D, Charleston) | 65,575 |
| C. C. Wannamaker (R, North Charleston) | 43,178 |
| 2. Floyd D. Spence* (R, Lexington) | 70,809 |
| Jack Solomon Bass (D, Columbia) | 52,696 |
| 3. Butler Derrick* (D, Edgefield) | 81,114 |
| Anthony Panuccio (R, Seneca) | 17,980 |
| 4. Carroll A. Campbell Jr. (R, Fountain Inn) | 51,488 |
| Max M. Heller (D, Greenville) | 45,357 |
| 5. Ken Holland* (D, Rock Hill) | Unopposed |

| Dist. Representative (Party, Home) | 1978 Election |
|---|---|
| 6. John W. Jenrette Jr.* (D, N. Myrtle Beach) | Unopposed |

### South Dakota

| Dist. Representative (Party, Home) | 1978 Election |
|---|---|
| 1. Leo K. Thorsness‡ (R, Sioux Falls) | 64,582 |
| Thomas A. Daschle (D, Aberdeen) | 64,543 |
| 2. James Abdnor* (R, Mitchell) | 68,714 |
| Robert Samuelson (D, Faith) | 54,441 |

### Tennessee

| Dist. Representative (Party, Home) | 1978 Election |
|---|---|
| 1. James Quillen* (R, Kingsport) | 92,716 |
| William Gordon Ball (D, Newport) | 53,853 |
| 2. John J. Duncan* (R, Knoxville) | 124,534 |
| Margaret Francis (D, Knoxville) | 55,069 |
| 3. Marilyn Lloyd* (D, Chattanooga) | 106,823 |
| Dan Rucker East (I, Chattanooga) | 13,335 |
| 4. Albert Gore Jr.* (D, Carthage) | Unopposed |
| 5. William Hill Boner (D, Nashville) | 68,433 |
| William Dean Goodwin (R, Nashville) | 47,288 |
| 6. Robin Beard* (R, Memphis) | 114,276 |
| C. Ronald Arline (D, Memphis) | 38,928 |
| 7. Ed Jones* (D, Yorkville) | 96,685 |
| Ross Earl Cook (R, Memphis) | 36,044 |
| 8. Harold E. Ford* (D, Memphis) | 80,522 |
| Duncan Ragsdale (R, Memphis) | 33,673 |

### Texas

| Dist. Representative (Party, Home) | 1978 Election |
|---|---|
| 1. Sam B. Hall* (D, Marshall) | 73,466 |
| Fred Hudson (R, Center) | 21,176 |
| 2. Charles Wilson* (D, Lufkin) | 65,391 |
| James H. Dillion (R, Woodville) | 28,611 |
| 3. James M. Collins* (R, Dallas) | Unopposed |
| 4. Ray Roberts* (D, McKinney) | 63,590 |
| Frank S. Glenn (R, Flint) | 38,201 |
| 5. Jim Mattox* (D, Dallas) | 35,435 |
| Thomas W. Pauken (R, Mesquite) | 34,558 |
| 6. William Philip Gramm (D, College Station) | 65,328 |
| Wes Mowery (R, Fort Worth) | 34,950 |
| 7. Bill Archer* (R, Houston) | 128,214 |
| Robert Laurence Hutchings (D, Houston) | 22,415 |
| 8. Robert Eckhardt* (D, Houston) | 39,429 |
| Nick Gearhart (R, Houston) | 24,673 |
| 9. Jack Brooks* (D, Beaumont) | 49,866 |
| Randy Evans (R, Lamarque) | 27,067 |
| 10. James J. Pickle* (D, Austin) | 94,512 |
| Emmett Leroy Hudspeth (R, Austin) | 29,295 |
| 11. Marvin Leath (D, Marlin) | 52,297 |
| Jack Burgess (R, Waco) | 49,312 |
| 12. Jim Wright* (D, Fort Worth) | 45,087 |
| Claude K. Brown (R, Bedford) | 21,045 |
| 13. Jack Hightower* (D, Vernon) | 74,647 |
| Clifford Alvin Jones (R, Perryton) | 24,780 |
| 14. Joe Wyatt Jr.* (D, Victoria) | 64,369 |
| Joy Yates (R, Corpus Christi) | 24,321 |
| 15. E. de la Garza* (D, Mission) | 53,816 |
| Robert Lendol McDonald (R, Pt. Isabel) | 27,444 |
| 16. Richard C. White* (D, Bethesda) | 53,090 |
| Michael Giere (R, El Paso) | 22,743 |
| 17. Charles W. Stenholm (D, Stamford) | 67,916 |
| Billy L. Fisher (R, Abilene) | 31,904 |
| 18. G. T. (Mickey) Leland (D, Houston) | 36,783 |
| Deborah Vee Vernier (SW, Houston) | 1,235 |
| 19. Kent Hance (D, Lubbock) | 54,580 |
| George Bush (R, Midland) | 47,992 |
| 20. Henry B. Gonzalez* (D, San Antonio) | Unopposed |
| 21. Thomas G. Loeffler (R, Hunt) | 82,418 |
| Nelson William Wolff (D, Leon Springs) | 63,231 |
| 22. Ronald E. Paul (R, Lake Jackson) | 54,626 |
| Bob Gammage* (D, Nassau Bay) | 53,441 |
| 23. Abraham Kazen Jr.* (D, Laredo) | Unopposed |
| 24. Martin Frost (D, Dallas) | 39,000 |
| Leo Berman (R, Arlington) | 32,972 |

### Utah

| Dist. Representative (Party, Home) | 1978 Election |
|---|---|
| 1. Gunn McKay* (D, Salt Lake City) | 93,749 |
| Jed J. Richardson (R, Provo) | 84,951 |

| Dist. | Representative (Party, Home) | 1978 Election |
|---|---|---|
| 2. | **Dan Marriott*** (R, Salt Lake City) | **121,251** |
| | Edwin Brown Firmage (D, Salt Lake City) | 68,839 |

### Vermont At Large

| | James M. Jeffords* (R, Rutland) | 90,775 |
|---|---|---|
| | Sarah Marie Dietz (D, Taftville) | 23,324 |

### Virginia

| 1. | **Paul S. Trible Jr.*** (R, Tappahannock) | **89,209** |
|---|---|---|
| | Lewis Burwell Puller (D, Hampton) | 34,578 |
| 2. | **G. William Whitehurst*** (R, Virginia Beach) | **Unopposed** |
| 3. | **David E. Satterfield*** (D, Richmond) | **Unopposed** |
| 4. | **Robert W. Daniel Jr.*** (R, Spring Grove) | **Unopposed** |
| 5. | **Dan Daniel*** (D, Danville) | **Unopposed** |
| 6. | **M. Caldwell Butler*** (R, Roanoke) | **Unopposed** |
| 7. | **J. Kenneth Robinson*** (R, Winchester) | **84,517** |
| | Lewis Perley Fickett Jr. (D, Fredericksburg) | 46,948 |
| 8. | **Herbert E. Harris II*** (D, Alexandria) | **56,168** |
| | John F. Herrity (R, Springfield) | 52,394 |
| 9. | **William C. Wampler*** (R, Bristol) | **76,822** |
| | Charles Champ Clark (D, Chilhowie) | 47,325 |
| 10. | **Joseph L. Fisher*** (D, Arlington) | **70,864** |
| | Frank R. Wolf (R, Vienna) | 61,963 |

### Washington

| 1. | **Joel Pritchard*** (R, Seattle) | **92,987** |
|---|---|---|
| | Janice Niemi (D, Seattle) | 49,852 |
| 2. | **Allan Byron Swift** (D, Bellingham) | **65,030** |
| | John Nance Garner (R, Everett) | 60,672 |
| 3. | **Don Bonker*** (D, Olympia) | **76,045** |
| | Richard H. Bennett Sr. (R, Issaquah) | 53,739 |
| 4. | **Mike McCormack*** (D, Richland) | **78,633** |
| | Susan Roylance (R, Kennewick) | 50,318 |
| 5. | **Thomas S. Foley*** (D, Spokane) | **68,578** |
| | Duane Alton (R, Spokane) | 60,278 |
| 6. | **Norman N. Dicks*** (D, Bremerton) | **63,996** |
| | James Edward Beaver (R, Tacoma) | 38,890 |
| 7. | **Michael Lowry** (D, Mercer Island) | **63,557** |
| | John E. Cunningham* (R, Seattle) | 54,984 |

| Dist. | Representative (Party, Home) | 1978 Election |
|---|---|---|
| | **West Virginia** | |
| 1. | **Robert H. Mollohan*** (D, Fairmont) | **76,155** |
| | Gene A. Haynes (R, Parkersburg) | 43,944 |
| 2. | **Harley O. Staggers*** (D, Keyser) | **69,621** |
| | Cleveland Keith Benedict (R, Lewisburg) | 56,182 |
| 3. | **John M. Slack*** (D, Charleston) | **74,373** |
| | David Michael Staton (R, South Charleston) | 51,317 |
| 4. | **Nick J. Rahall II*** (D, Beckley) | **Unopposed** |

### Wisconsin

| 1. | **Les Aspin*** (D, East Troy) | **76,852** |
|---|---|---|
| | William Watson Petrie III (R, Waterford) | 63,677 |
| 2. | **Robert W. Kastenmeier*** (D, Sun Prairie) | **98,072** |
| | James A. Wright (R, Baraboo) | 69,309 |
| 3. | **Alvin Baldus*** (D, Menomonie) | **94,165** |
| | Michael Steven Ellis (R, Elmwood) | 55,485 |
| 4. | **Clement J. Zablocki*** (D, Milwaukee) | **100,119** |
| | Elroy Charles Honadel (R, Oak Creek) | 51,443 |
| 5. | **Henry S. Reuss*** (D, Milwaukee) | **Unopposed** |
| 6. | **William A. Steiger*** (R, Oshkosh) | **112,969** |
| | Robert J. Steffes (D, Two Rivers) | 49,153 |
| 7. | **David R. Obey*** (D, Wausau) | **110,805** |
| | Vinton A. Vesta (R, Hayward) | 65,319 |
| 8. | **Toby Roth** (R, Appleton) | **101,858** |
| | Robert J. Cornell* (D, De Pere) | 73,951 |
| 9. | **F. James Sensenbrenner Jr.** (R, Shorewood) | **115,393** |
| | Matthew J. Flynn (D, Fox Point) | 73,768 |

### Wyoming At Large

| | **Richard Bruce Cheney** (R, Casper) | **76,010** |
|---|---|---|
| | William D. Bagley (D, Cheyenne) | 53,529 |

### Non-Voting Delegates

| District of Columbia | Walter E. Fauntroy* (D, D.C.) |
|---|---|
| Guam | Antonio Borja Won Pat* (D, Agana) |
| Virgin Islands | Melvin Evans (I, St. Croix) |
| Puerto Rico | Jaime Benitez* (Pop. D, Cayey) |

# The Races for Governor

In 1978, there were 36 Democrats, 13 Republicans and one independent serving as governors. As a result of the November 7 election, the roster became 32 Democrats and 18 Republicans.

| States | Democrats | Vote[1] | Republicans | Vote[1] |
|---|---|---|---|---|
| Alabama | Forrest James | 545,000 | Guy Hunt | 193,389 |
| Alaska | Chancy Croft | 18,712 | **Jay Hammond** | **37,245** |
| Arizona | **Bruce Babbitt*** | **382,519** | Evan Mechan | 241,008 |
| Arkansas | **William Clinton** | **336,630** | A. Lynn Lowe | 194,065 |
| California | **Edmund G. Brown*** | **3,826,266** | Evelle Younger | 2,485,706 |
| Colorado | **Richard D. Lamm*** | **483,506** | Ted Strickland | 317,029 |
| Connecticut | **Ella T. Grasso*** | **610,719** | Ronald Sarasin | 421,878 |
| Florida | **Robert Graham** | **1,377,261** | Jack Eckerd | 1,095,226 |
| Georgia | **George Busbee*** | **424,910** | Rodney Cook | 126,481 |
| Hawaii | **George R. Ariyoshi*** | **153,395** | John Leopold | 124,610 |
| Idaho | **John V. Evans*** | **168,032** | Allen Larsen | 113,460 |
| Illinois | Michael J. Bakalis | 1,234,435 | **James R. Thompson*** | **1,832,735** |
| Iowa | Jerome Fitzgerald | 342,595 | **Robert D. Ray*** | **489,271** |
| Kansas | **John Carlin** | **362,251** | Robert F. Bennet* | 345,972 |
| Maine | **Joseph Brennan** | **177,167** | Linwood Palmer | 126,133 |
| Maryland | **Harry Hughes** | **702,637** | J. Glenn Beale | 285,141 |
| Massachusetts | **Edward J. King*** | **1,026,125** | Francis W. Hatch | 923,733 |
| Michigan | William Fitzgerald | 1,135,526 | **William G. Milliken*** | **1,441,636** |
| Minnesota | Rudy Perpich* | 717,037 | **Albert Quie** | **824,080** |
| Nebraska | Gerald Whelan | 214,638 | **Charles Thone** | **272,309** |
| Nevada | Robert Rose | 75,213 | **Robert List** | **106,659** |

*(continued on page 49)*

## Political Divisions of the U.S. Senate and House of Representatives From 1855 (34th Cong.) to 1979-1981 (96th Cong.)

Source: Clerk of the House of Representatives

| Congress | Years | Senate | | | | | House of Representatives | | | | |
|---|---|---|---|---|---|---|---|---|---|---|---|
| | | Number of Senators | Democrats | Republicans | Other parties | Vacant | Number of Representatives | Democrats | Republicans | Other parties | Vacant |
| 34th.... | 1855-57 | 62 | 42 | 15 | 5 | | 234 | 83 | 108 | 43 | |
| 35th.... | 1857-59 | 64 | 39 | 20 | 5 | | 237 | 131 | 92 | 14 | |
| 36th.... | 1859-61 | 66 | 38 | 26 | 2 | | 237 | 101 | 113 | 23 | |
| 37th.... | 1861-63 | 50 | 11 | 31 | 7 | 1 | 178 | 42 | 106 | 28 | 2 |
| 38th.... | 1863-65 | 51 | 12 | 39 | | | 183 | 80 | 103 | | |
| 39th.... | 1865-67 | 52 | 10 | 42 | | | 191 | 46 | 145 | | |
| 40th.... | 1867-69 | 53 | 11 | 42 | | | 193 | 49 | 143 | | 1 |
| 41st.... | 1869-71 | 74 | 11 | 61 | | 2 | 243 | 73 | 170 | | |
| 42d.... | 1871-73 | 74 | 17 | 57 | | | 243 | 104 | 139 | | |
| 43d.... | 1873-75 | 74 | 19 | 54 | | 1 | 293 | 88 | 203 | | 2 |
| 44th.... | 1875-77 | 76 | 29 | 46 | | 1 | 293 | 181 | 107 | 3 | 2 |
| 45th.... | 1877-79 | 76 | 36 | 39 | 1 | | 293 | 156 | 137 | | |
| 46th.... | 1879-81 | 76 | 43 | 33 | | | 293 | 150 | 128 | 14 | 1 |
| 47th.... | 1881-83 | 76 | 37 | 37 | 2 | | 293 | 130 | 152 | 11 | |
| 48th.... | 1883-85 | 76 | 36 | 40 | | | 325 | 200 | 119 | 6 | |
| 49th.... | 1885-87 | 76 | 34 | 41 | | 1 | 325 | 182 | 140 | 2 | 1 |
| 50th.... | 1887-89 | 76 | 37 | 39 | | | 325 | 170 | 151 | 4 | |
| 51st.... | 1889-91 | 84 | 37 | 47 | | | 330 | 156 | 173 | 1 | |
| 52d.... | 1891-93 | 88 | 39 | 47 | 2 | | 333 | 231 | 88 | 14 | |
| 53d.... | 1893-95 | 88 | 44 | 38 | 3 | 3 | 356 | 220 | 126 | 10 | |
| 54th.... | 1895-97 | 88 | 39 | 44 | 5 | | 357 | 104 | 246 | 7 | |
| 55th.... | 1897-99 | 90 | 34 | 46 | 10 | | 357 | 134 | 206 | 16 | 1 |
| 56th.... | 1899-1901 | 90 | 26 | 53 | 11 | | 357 | 163 | 185 | 9 | |
| 57th.... | 1901-03 | 90 | 29 | 56 | 3 | 2 | 357 | 153 | 198 | 5 | 1 |
| 58th.... | 1903-05 | 90 | 32 | 58 | | | 386 | 178 | 207 | | 1 |
| 59th.... | 1905-07 | 90 | 32 | 58 | | | 386 | 136 | 250 | | |
| 60th.... | 1907-09 | 92 | 29 | 61 | | 2 | 386 | 164 | 222 | | |
| 61st.... | 1909-11 | 92 | 32 | 59 | | 1 | 391 | 172 | 219 | | |
| 62d.... | 1911-13 | 92 | 42 | 49 | | 1 | 391 | 228 | 162 | 1 | |
| 63d.... | 1913-15 | 96 | 51 | 44 | 1 | | 435 | 290 | 127 | 18 | |
| 64th.... | 1915-17 | 96 | 56 | 39 | 1 | | 435 | 231 | 193 | 8 | 3 |
| 65th.... | 1917-19 | 96 | 53 | 42 | 1 | | 435 | 210 | 216 | 9 | |
| 66th.... | 1919-21 | 96 | 47 | 48 | 1 | | 435 | 191 | 237 | 7 | |
| 67th.... | 1921-23 | 96 | 37 | 59 | | | 435 | 132 | 300 | 1 | 2 |
| 68th.... | 1923-25 | 96 | 43 | 51 | 2 | | 435 | 207 | 225 | 3 | |
| 69th.... | 1925-27 | 96 | 40 | 54 | 1 | 1 | 435 | 183 | 247 | 5 | |
| 70th.... | 1927-29 | 96 | 47 | 48 | 1 | | 435 | 195 | 237 | 3 | |
| 71st.... | 1929-31 | 96 | 39 | 56 | 1 | | 435 | 163 | 267 | 1 | 4 |
| 72d.... | 1931-33 | 96 | 47 | 48 | 1 | | 435 | 216 | 218 | 1 | |
| 73d.... | 1933-35 | 96 | 59 | 36 | 1 | | 435 | 313 | 117 | 5 | |
| 74th.... | 1935-37 | 96 | 69 | 25 | 2 | | 435 | 322 | 103 | 10 | |
| 75th.... | 1937-39 | 96 | 75 | 17 | 4 | | 435 | 333 | 89 | 13 | |
| 76th.... | 1939-41 | 96 | 69 | 23 | 4 | | 435 | 262 | 169 | 4 | |
| 77th.... | 1941-43 | 96 | 66 | 28 | 2 | | 435 | 267 | 162 | 6 | |
| 78th.... | 1943-45 | 96 | 57 | 38 | 1 | | 435 | 222 | 209 | 4 | |
| 79th.... | 1945-47 | 96 | 57 | 38 | 1 | | 435 | 243 | 190 | 2 | |
| 80th.... | 1947-49 | 96 | 45 | 51 | | | 435 | 188 | 246 | 1 | |
| 81st.... | 1949-51 | 96 | 54 | 42 | | | 435 | 263 | 171 | 1 | |
| 82d.... | 1951-53 | 96 | 48 | 47 | 1 | | 435 | 234 | 199 | 2 | |
| 83d.... | 1953-55 | 96 | 46 | 48 | 2 | | 435 | 213 | 221 | 1 | |
| 84th.... | 1955-57 | 96 | 48 | 47 | 1 | | 435 | 232 | 203 | | |
| 85th.... | 1957-59 | 96 | 49 | 47 | | | 435 | 234 | 201 | | |
| 86th.... | 1959-61 | 98 | 64 | 34 | | | 436 | 283 | 153 | | |
| 87th.... | 1961-63 | 100 | 64 | 36 | | | 437 | 262 | 175 | | |
| 88th.... | 1963-65 | 100 | 67 | 33 | | | 435 | 258 | 176 | | 1 |
| 89th.... | 1965-67 | 100 | 68 | 32 | | | 435 | 295 | 140 | | |
| 90th.... | 1967-69 | 100 | 64 | 36 | | | 435 | 248 | 187 | | |
| 91st.... | 1969-71 | 100 | 58 | 42 | | | 435 | 243 | 192 | | |
| 92d.... | 1971-73 | 100 | 54 | 44 | 2 | | 435 | 255 | 180 | | |
| 93d.... | 1973-75 | 100 | 56 | 42 | 2 | | 435 | 242 | 192 | 1 | |
| 94th.... | 1975-77 | 100 | 61 | 37 | 2 | | 435 | 291 | 144 | | |
| 95th.... | 1977-79 | 100 | 61 | 38 | 1 | | 435 | 292 | 143 | | |
| 96th.... | 1979-81 | 100 | 58 | 41 | 1 | | 435 | 275 | 158 | (2 undecided) | |

(1) Democrats organized House with help of other parties. (2) Democrats organized House due to Republican deaths. (3) Proclamation declaring Alaska a State issued Jan. 3, 1959. (4) Proclamation declaring Hawaii a State issued Aug. 21, 1959.

# Governors of States and Possessions

### Reflecting Nov. 7, 1978 election

| State | Capital | Governor | Party | Term years | Term expires | Annual salary |
|---|---|---|---|---|---|---|
| Alabama | Montgomery | Forrest "Fob" James | Dem. | 4 | Jan. 1983 | $28,955 |
| Alaska | Juneau | Jay Hammond | Rep. | 4 | Dec. 1982 | 52,992 |
| Arizona | Phoenix | Bruce E. Babbit | Dem. | 4 | Jan. 1983 | 50,000 |
| Arkansas | Little Rock | William Clinton | Dem. | 2 | Jan. 1981 | 35,000 |
| California | Sacramento | Edmund G. Brown Jr. | Dem. | 4 | Jan. 1983 | 49,100 |
| Colorado | Denver | Richard D. Lamm | Dem. | 4 | Jan. 1983 | 40,000 |
| Connecticut | Hartford | Ella T. Grasso | Dem. | 4 | Jan. 1983 | 42,000 |
| Delaware | Dover | Pierre S. du Pont | Rep. | 4 | Jan. 1981 | 35,000 |
| Florida | Tallahassee | Robert Graham | Dem. | 4 | Jan. 1983 | 50,000 |
| Georgia | Atlanta | George Busbee | Dem. | 4 | Jan. 1983 | 50,000 |
| Hawaii | Honolulu | George R. Ariyoshi | Dem. | 4 | Dec. 1982 | 50,000 |
| Idaho | Boise | John V. Evans | Dem. | 4 | Jan. 1983 | 40,000 |
| Illinois | Springfield | James R. Thompson | Rep. | 4 | Jan. 1983 | 50,000 |
| Indiana | Indianapolis | Otis R. Bowen | Rep. | 4 | Jan. 1981 | 36,000 |
| Iowa | Des Moines | Robert D. Ray | Rep. | 4 | Jan. 1983 | 55,000 |
| Kansas | Topeka | John Carlin | Dem. | 4 | Jan. 1983 | 45,000 |
| Kentucky | Frankfort | Julian Carroll | Dem. | 4 | Dec. 1979 | 35,000 |
| Louisiana | Baton Rouge | Edwin W. Edwards | Dem. | 4 | May 1980 | 50,000 |
| Maine | Augusta | Joseph E. Brennan | Dem. | 4 | Jan. 1983 | 35,000 |
| Maryland | Annapolis | Harold Hughes | Dem. | 4 | Jan. 1983 | 60,000 |
| Massachusetts | Boston | Edward J. King | Dem. | 4 | Jan. 1983 | 40,000 |
| Michigan | Lansing | William G. Milliken | Rep. | 4 | Jan. 1983 | 58,000 |
| Minnesota | St. Paul | Albert H. Quie | Rep. | 4 | Jan. 1983 | 58,000 |
| Mississippi | Jackson | Charles C. Finch | Dem. | 4 | Jan. 1980 | 43,000 |
| Missouri | Jefferson City | Joseph P. Teasdale | Dem. | 4 | Jan. 1981 | 37,500 |
| Montana | Helena | Thomas L. Judge | Dem. | 4 | Jan. 1981 | 35,000 |
| Nebraska | Lincoln | Charles Thone | Rep. | 4 | Jan. 1983 | 40,000 |
| Nevada | Carson City | Robert List | Rep. | 4 | Jan. 1983 | 50,000 |
| New Hampshire | Concord | Hugh Gallen | Dem. | 2 | Jan. 1981 | 42,000 |
| New Jersey | Trenton | Brendan T. Byrne | Dem. | 4 | Jan. 1982 | 65,000 |
| New Mexico | Sante Fe | Bruce King | Dem. | 4 | Jan. 1983 | 35,000 |
| New York | Albany | Hugh L. Carey | Dem. | 4 | Jan. 1983 | 85,000 |
| North Carolina | Raleigh | James B. Hunt Jr. | Dem. | 4 | Jan. 1981 | 47,700 |
| North Dakota | Bismarck | Arthur A. Link | Dem. | 4 | Jan. 1981 | 27,500 |
| Ohio | Columbus | James A. Rhodes | Rep | 4 | Jan. 1983 | 50,000 |
| Oklahoma | Oklahoma City | George Nigh | Dem. | 4 | Jan. 1983 | 42,500 |
| Oregon | Salem | Victor Atiyeh | Rep. | 4 | Jan. 1983 | 47,976 |
| Pennsylvania | Harrisburg | Richard Thornburgh | Rep | 4 | Jan. 1983 | 66,000 |
| Rhode Island | Providence | J. Joseph Garrahy | Dem. | 2 | Jan. 1981 | 42,500 |
| South Carolina | Columbia | Richard Riley | Dem. | 4 | Jan. 1983 | 39,000 |
| South Dakota | Pierre | William Janklow | Rep. | 4 | Jan. 1983 | 37,000 |
| Tennessee | Nashville | Lamar Alexander | Rep. | 4 | Jan. 1983 | 65,000 |
| Texas | Austin | William P. Clements | Rep. | 4 | Jan. 1983 | 71,400 |
| Utah | Salt Lake City | Scott M. Matheson | Dem. | 4 | Jan. 1981 | 40,000 |
| Vermont | Montpelier | Richard A. Snelling | Rep. | 2 | Jan. 1981 | 39,000 |
| Virginia | Richmond | John Dalton | Rep. | 4 | Jan. 1982 | 60,000 |
| Washington | Olympia | Dixy Lee Ray | Dem. | 4 | Jan. 1981 | 55,000 |
| West Virginia | Charleston | John D. Rockefeller 4th | Dem. | 4 | Jan. 1981 | 50,000 |
| Wisconsin | Madison | Lee Dreyfus | Rep. | 4 | Jan. 1983 | 44,920 |
| Wyoming | Cheyenne | Ed Herschler | Dem. | 4 | Jan. 1983 | 55,000 |

### Possessions

| | | | | | | |
|---|---|---|---|---|---|---|
| Guam | Agana | Ricardo J. Bordallo | Rep. | 4 | Jan. 1981 | 35,000 |
| Puerto Rico | San Juan | Carlos Romero Barcelo | N.P. | 4 | Jan. 1981 | 36,200 |
| Virgin Isls. | Charlotte Amalie | Juan Luis | Ind. | 4 | Jan. 1983 | 35,505 |

(continued from page 47)

| | | | | |
|---|---|---|---|---|
| New Hampshire | **Hugh Galen** | **133,124** | Meldrim Thomson* | 122,737 |
| New Mexico | **Bruce King*** | **173,189** | Joe Skeen | 169,229 |
| New York | **Hugh Carey*** | **2,410,988** | Perry Duryea | 2,136,939 |
| Ohio | Richard Celeste | 1,350,207 | **James A. Rhodes** | **1,397,809** |
| Oklahoma | **George Nigh** | **411,667** | Ron Shotts | 366,149 |
| Oregon | Robert Straub* | 408,686 | **Victor Atiyeh** | **496,714** |
| Pennsylvania | Peter Flaherty | 1,734,112 | **Richard Thornburg** | **1,954,952** |
| Rhode Island | **J. Joseph Garrahy*** | **191,204** | Lincoln Almond | 92,849 |
| South Carolina | **Richard Riley** | **381,871** | Edward L. Young | 235,017 |
| South Dakota | Roger McKellips | 112,869 | **William Janklow** | **147,561** |
| Tennessee | Jake Butcher | 523,928 | **Lamar Alexander** | **662,628** |
| Texas | John L. Hill | 1,164,367 | **William P. Clements** | **1,177,374** |
| Vermont | Edwin Granai | 42,230 | **Richard Snelling*** | **77,827** |
| Wisconsin | Martin Schreiber | 671,151 | **Lee Dreyfus** | **807,724** |
| Wyoming | **Ed Herschler** | **69,797** | John Ostlund | 67,556 |

(1) Preliminary unofficial returns. **Bold face type** denotes the winner. *Incumbent.

## Mayors and City Managers of Larger North American Cities

Reflecting Nov. 7, 1978 elections

*Asterisk before name denotes city manager. All others are mayors. For mayors, dates are those of expiration of term; for city managers, they are dates of appointment.

D, Democrat; R, Republican; N-P, Non-Partisan

| City | Name | Term |
|---|---|---|
| Abilene, Tex. | *Fred Sandlin | 1974, May |
| Akron, Oh. | John S. Ballard, R | 1979, Dec. |
| Alameda, Cal. | *John Goss | 1973, Dec. |
| Albany, Ga. | James H. Gray | 1980, Jan. |
| Albany, N.Y. | Erastus Corning 2d, D | 1979, Dec. |
| Albuquerque, N.M. | David Rusk, D | 1981, Dec. |
| Alexandria, La. | Carroll E. Lanier, D | 1981, Dec. |
| Alexandria, Va. | *Douglas Harman | 1976, Jan. |
| Alhambra, Cal. | *Donald L. Russell | 1976, July |
| Allen Park, Mich. | Frank J. Lada, D | 1979, Nov. |
| Allentown, Pa. | Frank Fischl Jr., R | 1982, Jan. |
| Alton, Ill. | Paul A. Lenz, N-P | 1981, Apr. |
| Altoona, Pa. | William C. Stouffer, R | 1980, Jan. |
| Amarillo, Tex. | Jerry Hodge, N-P | 1979, Apr. |
| Ames, Ia. | *Terry Sprenkel | 1976, Apr. |
| Anaheim, Cal. | *William O. Talley | 1976, July |
| Anchorage, Alas. | George M. Sullivan, R | 1981, Dec. |
| Anderson, Ind. | Robert Rock, D | 1979, Dec. |
| Anderson, S.C. | *Richard Burnette | 1976, Sept. |
| Ann Arbor, Mich. | *Sylvester Murray | 1973, Aug. |
| Appleton, Wis. | James P. Sutherland, N-P | 1980, Apr. |
| Arcadia, Cal. | *Lyle W. Alberg | 1978, Jan. |
| Arlington, Mass. | *Donald R. Marquis | 1966, Nov. |
| Arlington, Tex. | S.J. Stovall, N-P | 1979, Apr. |
| Arlington, Va. | *W.V. Ford | 1976, Feb. |
| Arlington Hts., Ill. | *L.A. Hanson | 1958, Nov. |
| Arvada, Col. | *Craig Kocian | 1977, Feb. |
| Asheville, N.C. | Roy Trantham, D | 1979, Nov. |
| Athens, Ga. | Upshaw Bentley, D | 1979, Nov. |
| Atlanta, Ga. | Maynard Jackson, N-P | 1981, Dec. |
| Atlantic City, N.J. | Joseph Lazarow, R | 1980, May |
| Auburn, N.Y. | *Bruce Clifford | 1966, Aug. |
| Augusta, Ga. | Lewis A. Newman, N-P | 1981, Nov. |
| Aurora, Col. | *Robert E. Brown | 1978, July |
| Aurora, Ill. | Jack Hill, N-P | 1981, Apr. |
| Austin, Tex. | *Dan H. Davidson | 1972, Aug. |
| Bakersfield, Cal. | *Harold E. Bergen | 1966, July |
| Baldwin Park, Cal. | *James Sexton | 1976, Mar. |
| Baltimore, Md. | William Schaefer, D | 1979, Dec. |
| Bangor, Me. | *John W. Flynn | 1977, Feb. |
| Baton Rouge, La. | W.W. Dumas, D | 1980, Dec. |
| Battle Creek, Mich. | *Gordon Jaeger | 1976, Mar. |
| Bay City, Mich. | *Carlton Laird | 1975, July |
| Baytown, Tex. | *Fritz Lanham | 1972, May |
| Beaumont, Tex. | *Ray A. Riley | 1978, Apr. |
| Belleville, Ill. | Charles E. Nichols, N-P | 1981, Apr. |
| Belleville, N.J. | Michael Marotti, D | 1979, May |
| Bellevue, Wash. | *William Parness | 1978, Sept. |
| Bellflower, Cal. | *John Jameson | 1978, July |
| Beloit, Wis. | *H. Herbert Holt | 1971, Mar. |
| Berkeley, Cal. | *Elijah B. Rogers | 1976, July |
| Bessemer, Ala. | Ed Porter, D | 1982, Oct. |
| Bethlehem, Pa. | Paul M. Marcincin, D | 1981, Dec. |
| Billings, Mont. | William Fox, D | 1979, May |
| Biloxi, Miss. | Jerry O'Keefe, D | 1981, July |
| Binghamton, N.Y. | Alfred J. Libous, R | 1981, Dec. |
| Birmingham, Ala. | David Vann, D | 1979, Nov. |
| Bismarck, N.D. | Eugene Leary, N-P | 1982, Apr. |
| Bloomfield, N.J. | John W. Kinder, R | 1980, Dec. |
| Bloomington, Ill. | *William Vail | 1976, Oct. |
| Bloomington, Ind. | Francis X. McCloskey, D | 1979, Dec. |
| Bloomington, Minn. | *John Pidgeon | 1967, Dec. |
| Boise, Ida. | Dick Eardley, N-P | 1981, Dec. |
| Bossier City, La. | Marvin E. Anding, D | 1981, June |
| Boston, Mass. | Kevin White, D | 1979, Dec. |
| Boulder, Col. | Ruth Carroll, N-P | 1979, Dec. |
| Bowie, Md. | *G.C. Moore | 1976, Apr. |
| Bowling Green, Ky. | *Charles W. Coates | 1977, Feb. |
| Bridgeport, Conn. | John Mandanici, D | 1979, Nov. |
| Bristol, Conn. | Michael Werner, R | 1979, Nov. |
| Brockton, Mass. | David L. Crosby, D | 1979, Dec. |
| Brookfield, Wis. | William Mitchell Jr., N-P | 1980, Apr. |
| Brookline, Mass. | Board of Selectmen | |
| Brooklyn Center, Minn. | *Gerald G. Splinter | 1977, Oct. |
| Brownsville, Tex. | Ruben Edelstein, N-P | 1979, Nov. |
| Bryan, Tex. | *vacant | |
| Buffalo, N.Y. | James D. Griffen, D | 1981, Dec. |
| Burbank, Cal. | D. Verner Gibson, R | 1979, Apr. |
| Burlington, Vt. | Gordon H. Paquette, D | 1979, Apr. |
| Calumet City, Ill. | Robert C. Stefaniak, D | 1981, Apr. |
| Cambridge, Mass. | *James L. Sullivan | 1974, Apr. |
| Camden, N.J. | Angelo Errichetti, D | 1981, July |
| Canton, Oh. | Stanley A. Cmich, R | 1979, Dec. |
| Cape Girardeau, Mo. | Paul Stehr, N-P | 1981, Apr. |
| Carson, Cal. | *E. Frederick Bien | 1968, May |
| Casper, Wyo. | *Kenneth Erickson | 1969, Oct. |
| Cedar Rapids, Ia. | Donald J. Canney, N-P | 1979, Dec. |
| Champaign, Ill. | *V. Eugene Miller | 1974, Sept. |
| Charleston, S.C. | Joseph P. Riley Jr., D | 1979, Dec. |
| Charleston, W. Va. | John G. Hutchinson, D | 1979, May |
| Charlotte, N.C. | *David A. Burkhalter | 1971, May |
| Charlottesville, Va. | *Cole Hendrix | 1971, Jan. |
| Chattanooga, Tenn. | Charles A. Rose, N-P | 1979, Apr. |
| Chesapeake, Va. | *John T. Maxwell | 1978, Sept. |
| Chester, Pa. | John Nacrelli, R | 1980, Jan. |
| Cheyenne, Wyo. | Donald Erickson, N-P | 1980, Dec. |
| Chicago, Ill. | Michael A. Bilandic, D | 1979, Apr. |
| Chicago Hts., Ill. | Charles Panici, R | 1979, May |
| Chicopee, Mass. | John Moylan, D | 1980, Jan. |
| Chula Vista, Cal. | Will T. Hyde | 1981, Apr. |
| Cicero, Ill. | Christy Berkos | 1980, Apr. |
| Cincinnati, Oh. | *William Donaldson | 1975, June |
| Clarksville, Tenn. | Ted Crozier, N-P | 1982, Dec. |
| Clearwater, Fla. | *Anthony Shoemaker | 1977, June |
| Cleveland, Oh. | Dennis J. Kucinich, D | 1979, Nov. |
| Cleveland Hgts., Oh. | *Richard Robinson | 1978, July |
| Clifton, N.J. | *William Holster | 1957, Jan. |
| Col. Spgs., Col. | *George H. Fellows | 1966, July |
| Columbia, Mo. | *vacant | |
| Columbia, S.C. | *Graydon V. Olive Jr. | 1970, Mar. |
| Columbus, Ga. | Harry Jackson, D | 1982, Dec. |
| Columbus, Oh. | Tom Moody, R | 1979, Dec. |
| Commerce, Cal. | *Robert Hinderliter | 1973, Aug. |
| Compton, Cal. | *Allen Parker | 1975, Dec. |
| Concord, Cal. | *Farrel A. Stewart | 1960, Apr. |
| Concord, N.H. | *vacant | |
| Coon Rapids, Minn. | *John K. Cottingham | 1969, July |
| Coral Gables, Fla. | *J. Martin Gainer | 1975, Jan. |
| Corpus Christi, Tex. | *R. Marvin Townsend | 1968, Jan. |
| Corvallis, Ore. | *C. Dean Smith | 1968, Jan. |
| Costa Mesa, Cal. | *Fred Sorsabal | 1970 |
| Council Bluffs, Ia. | *Michael G. Miller | 1978, Aug. |
| Covington, Ky. | George Wermeling, D | 1980, Jan. |
| Crystal, Minn. | *John Irving | 1964, Jan. |
| Culver City, Cal. | *Dale Jones | 1969, Aug. |
| Cuyahoga Falls, Oh. | Robert Quirk, D | 1981, Dec. |
| Dallas, Tex. | *George Schrader | 1972, Nov. |
| Daly City, Cal. | *David R. Rowe | 1969, Aug. |
| Danbury, Conn. | Donald Boughton, R | 1979, Nov. |
| Danville, Ill. | David S. Palmer, D | 1979, Apr. |
| Danville, Va. | *James W. Lord | 1971, Nov. |
| Dayton, Oh. | *James Alloway | 1974, Feb. |
| Daytona Bch., Fla. | *Howard D. Tipton | 1978, Oct. |
| Dearborn, Mich. | John O'Reilly, N-P | 1982, Jan. |
| Decatur, Ala. | Bill Dukes, D | 1980, Oct. |
| Decatur, Ill. | *Leslie T. Allen | 1972, Sept. |
| Denton, Tex. | Joe Mitchell, N-P | 1979, Apr. |
| Denver, Col. | William H. McNichols, N-P | 1979, July |
| Des Moines, Ia. | Richard E. Olson, N-P | 1979, Dec. |
| Des Plaines, Ill. | H.H. Volberding Sr., N-P | 1981, May |
| Detroit, Mich. | Coleman A. Young, N-P | 1981, Dec. |
| Dothan, Ala. | James W. Grant 3D, N-P | 1981, Oct. |
| Downers Grove, Ill. | *James R. Grisemer | 1972, Sept. |
| Dubuque, Ia. | *Gilbert D. Chavenelle | 1960, Dec. |
| Duluth, Minn. | Robert Beaudin, D | 1979, Dec. |
| Durham, N.C. | *Dean Hunter | 1978, Aug. |

| City | Name | Term | City | Name | Term |
|------|------|------|------|------|------|
| E. Chicago, Ind. | Robert A. Pastrick, D | 1979, Dec. | Hartford, Conn. | *John A. Sulik | 1978, Sept. |
| E. Cleveland, Oh. | *Edwin M. Robinson | 1976, Sept. | Harvey, Ill. | James A. Haines, R | 1979, Apr. |
| E. Detroit, Mich. | William Mihelich, N-P | 1977, Nov. | Hattiesburg, Miss. | A. L. Gerrard Jr., D | 1981, July |
| E. Hartford, Conn. | Richard H. Blackstone, D | 1979, Nov. | Haverhill, Mass. | George K. Katsaros, N-P | 1979, Dec. |
| E. Lansing, Mich. | *vacant | | Hawthorne, Cal. | *R. Kenneth Jue | 1977, Jan. |
| E. Orange, N.J. | Thomas H. Cooke, Jr., D | 1981, Dec. | Hayward, Cal. | *William Hanley | 1972, Feb. |
| E. Providence, R.I. | *Paul A. Flynn | 1972, Aug. | Hempstead, N.Y. | Dalton R. Miller, R | 1981, Apr. |
| E. St. Louis, Ill. | William Mason, D | 1979, May | Hialeah, Fla. | Dale Bennett, D | 1979, Nov. |
| Eau Claire, Wis. | *Stephen Atkins | 1978, Sept. | High Point, N.C. | *Cyrus L. Books | 1976, Aug. |
| Edina, Minn. | *Kenneth Rosland | 1977, Oct. | Highland Park, Ill. | Robert Buhai, N-P | 1979, Apr. |
| Edison, N.J. | Anthony Yelencsics, D | 1981, Dec. | Hoboken, N.J. | Steve Cappiello, N-P | 1981, July |
| El Cajon, Cal. | *Robert M. Applegate | 1968, Sept. | Holyoke, Mass. | Ernest Proulx, D | 1979, Dec. |
| El Monte, Cal. | *J. R. Castner | 1978, July | Hollywood, Fla. | *James Chandler | 1976, Nov. |
| El Paso, Tex. | Ray Salazar, D | 1979, Apr. | Honolulu, Ha. | Frank F. Fasi, D | 1981, Jan. |
| Elgin, Ill. | *Leo Wilson | 1972, Dec. | Hot Springs, Ark. | Tom Ellsworth, N-P | 1982, Dec. |
| Elizabeth, N.J. | Thomas G. Dunn, D | 1980, Dec. | Houston, Tex. | James McConn, N-P | 1980 Jan. |
| Elkhart, Ind. | Peter Sarantos, R | 1979, Dec. | Huntington, W. Va. | *Richard Barton | 1978, Feb. |
| Elmhurst, Ill. | *Robert T. Palmer | 1953, June | Huntington Beach, | | |
| Elmira, N.Y. | *Joseph E. Sartori | 1972, June | Cal. | *Floyd Belsito | 1976, June |
| Elyria, Oh. | Marguerite Bowman, R | 1979, Dec. | Huntsville, Ala. | Joe W. Davis, N-P | 1980, Oct. |
| Enfield, Conn. | *Robert F. Ledger Jr. | 1977, Mar. | Hutchinson, Kan. | *George Pyle | 1967, Sept. |
| Enid, Okla. | *Tom Sailors Jr. | 1969, Oct. | | | |
| Erie, Pa. | Louis J. Tullio, D | 1981, Dec. | | | |
| Escondido, Cal. | *Kenneth Lounsbery | 1976, Aug. | Independence, Mo. | *W. Robert Semple | 1978, June |
| Euclid, Oh. | Anthony Sustarsic, N-P | 1979, Nov. | Indianapolis, Ind. | William Hudnut, R | 1979, Dec. |
| Eugene, Ore. | *Charles T. Henry | 1975, July | Inglewood, Cal. | *Douglas W. Ayres | 1968, Apr. |
| Evanston, Ill. | *Edward A. Martin | 1971, Mar. | Inkster, Mich. | Terrel LeCesne, N-P | 1979, Nov. |
| Evansville, Ind. | Russell Lloyd, R | 1979, Dec. | Iowa City, Ia. | *Neal Berlin | 1975, Mar. |
| Everett, Mass. | George R. McCarthy, D | 1979, Dec. | Irving, Tex. | *Jack Huffman | 1973, Dec. |
| Everett, Wash. | Bill Moore, R | 1982, Jan. | Irvington, N.J. | Robert Miller, R | 1982, July |
| | | | Jackson, Mich. | *S.W. McAllister Jr. | 1974, Mar. |
| Fairborn, Oh. | *William Burns | 1977, Feb. | Jackson, Miss. | Dale Danks, D | 1981, July |
| Fairfield, Cal. | *B. Gale Wilson | 1956, Mar. | Jackson, Tenn. | Bob Conger, D | 1979, June |
| Fairfield, Conn. | John J. Sullivan, D | 1979, Nov. | Jacksonville, Fla. | Hans Tanzler Jr., D | 1979, July |
| Fair Lawn, N.J. | Louis Raffiani, D | 1980, Dec. | Jamestown, N.Y. | Steve Carlson, D | 1979, Dec. |
| Fall River, Mass. | Carlton Viveiros, D | 1980, Jan. | Janesville, Wis. | *Philip L. Deaton | 1976, Mar. |
| Fayetteville, Ark. | *Donald Grimes | 1972, Apr. | Jefferson City, Mo. | Robert Hyder, D | 1979, Apr. |
| Fayetteville, N.C. | *William G. Thomas 3d | 1976, Nov. | Jersey City, N.J. | Thomas F.X. Smith, D | 1981, July |
| Fitchburg, Mass. | David Gilmartin, D | 1980, Jan. | Johnson City, Tenn. | *William Ricker | 1971, Oct. |
| Flagstaff, Ariz. | *Kent McClain | 1973, Nov. | Johnstown, Pa. | Charles Tomlijanovic, D | 1982, Jan. |
| Flint, Mich. | *Nanette Lynn | 1978, July | Joliet, Ill. | *Robert H. Oldland | 1977, Aug. |
| Florissant, Mo. | James J. Eagan, D | 1979, Apr. | Joplin, Mo. | *James P. Berzina | 1977, Mar. |
| Fond du Lac, Wis. | *Myron J. Medin Jr. | 1967, Nov. | | | |
| Ft. Collins, Col. | *John Arnold | 1977, Oct. | | | |
| Ft. Lauderdale, Fla. | *Richard E. Anderson | 1975, July | Kalamazoo, Mich. | *Robert C. Bobb | 1976, Nov. |
| Ft. Lee, N.J. | Richard A. Nest | 1979, Dec. | Kansas City, Kan. | John Reardon, D | 1979, Apr. |
| Ft. Smith, Ark. | Jack Freeze, N-P | 1979, Dec. | Kansas City, Mo. | *Robert A. Kipp | 1974, Jan. |
| Ft. Wayne, Ind. | Robert Armstrong, R | 1979, Dec. | Kenosha, Wis. | Paul Saftig, N-P | 1980, Apr. |
| Ft. Worth, Tex. | *Robert Herchert | 1978, Aug. | Kettering, Oh. | *John W. Laney | 1976, Mar. |
| Fremont, Cal. | *Don Driggs | 1967, Jan. | Key West, Fla. | *Ronald J. Stack | 1974, June |
| Fresno, Cal. | *Gerald E. Newfarmer | 1978, July | Killeen, Tex. | *Mike Eastland | 1976, Apr. |
| Fullerton, Cal. | *Leslie R. White | 1976, July | Knoxville, Tenn. | Randell L. Tyree | 1979 Dec. |
| | | | Kokomo, Ind. | Arthur LaDow, R | 1979, Dec. |
| Gadsden, Ala. | Steve Means, D | 1982, Nov. | | | |
| Gainesville, Fla. | *B. Harold Farmer | 1968, Nov. | LaCrosse, Wis. | Patrick Zielke, N-P | 1979, Apr. |
| Galesburg, Ill. | *Thomas B. Herring | 1960, Nov. | La Habra, Cal. | *Lee Risner | 1970, Nov. |
| Galveston, Tex. | *Thomas Muehlenbeck | 1977, Aug. | La Mesa, Cal. | *Gayle T. Martin | 1975, June |
| Gardena, Cal. | *Craig McDowell | 1973, Dec. | La Mirada, Cal. | *Claude J. Klug | 1971, Aug. |
| Garden Grove, Cal. | *Richard R. Powers | 1972, Apr. | Lafayette, Ind. | James Riehle, D | 1979, Dec. |
| Garfield Hts., Oh. | Raymond Stachewicz, D | 1979, Dec. | Lafayette, La. | Kenneth Bowen, D | 1980, July |
| Garland, Tex. | *Fred Greene | 1977, Sept. | Lake Charles, La. | William E. Boyer, D | 1981, July |
| Gary, Ind. | Richard G. Hatcher, D | 1979, Dec. | Lakeland, Fla. | *Robert V. Youkey | 1960, Jan. |
| Gastonia, N.C. | *Gary Hicks | 1973, Dec. | Lakewood, Cal. | *Howard L. Chambers | 1976, Mar. |
| Glendale, Ariz. | *S.F. Van de Putte | 1960, Aug. | Lakewood, Col. | *Charles Anderson | 1978, Sept. |
| Glendale, Cal. | *J. Keithley | 1972, Sept. | Lakewood, Oh. | Anthony Sinagra, R | 1979, Dec. |
| Grand Forks, N.D. | Cyril P. O'Neill, D | 1980, Apr. | Lancaster, Pa. | Richard Scott, R | 1982, Jan. |
| Gr. Island, Neb. | *Dwight Johnson | 1978, Aug. | Lansing, Mich. | Gerald Graves, N-P | 1981, Dec. |
| Gr. Prairie, Tex. | *Clifford Johnson | 1962 Sept. | Laredo, Tex. | Aldo Tatangelo, N-P | 1982, Mar. |
| Gr. Rapids, Mich. | *Joseph G. Zainea | 1976, Oct. | Las Cruces, N.M. | *Kenneth E. Ohler | 1977, Aug. |
| Great Falls, Mont. | *Richard D. Thomas | 1973, May | Las Vegas, Nev. | *Russell Dorn | 1978, Jan. |
| Green Bay, Wis. | Michael Monfils, N-P | 1979, Apr. | Lawrence, Kan. | *Buford M. Watson Jr. | 1970, Jan. |
| Greensboro, N.C. | Jim Melvin, N-P | 1979, Dec. | Lawrence, Mass. | Lawrence LeFebre, N-P | 1979, Dec. |
| Greenville, S.C. | *John J. Dullea | 1971, Oct. | Lawton, Okla. | *Robert Metzinger | 1977, Jan. |
| Greenwich, Conn. | Ruth L. Sims, D | 1979, Dec. | Lexington, Ky. | James Amato, N-P | 1982, Jan. |
| Groton, Conn. | Donald Sweet, R | 1979, May | Lima, Oh. | Harry Moyer, N-P | 1981, Dec. |
| Gulfport, Miss. | Jack Barnett, D | 1981, July | Lincoln, Neb. | Helen Boosalis, D | 1979, May |
| | | | Linden, N.J. | John Gregorio, D | 1982, Dec. |
| Hackensack, N.J. | *Joseph J. Squillace | 1964, Oct. | Little Rock, Ark. | *Carleton E. McMullin | 1973, Nov. |
| Hagerstown, Md. | Varner L. Paddack, R | 1981, Apr. | Livermore, Cal. | *William H. Harness | 1957, Oct. |
| Hamden, Conn. | Lucien A. DiMeo, R | 1979, Nov. | Livonia, Mich. | Edward H. McNamara, | |
| Hamilton, Oh. | *Jack Kirsch | 1975, Dec. | | N-P | 1980, Jan. |
| Hammond, Ind. | Edward J. Raskosky, D | 1979, Dec. | Lombard, Ill. | *W. B. Browning | 1975, Sept. |
| Hampton, Va. | *C. E. Johnson | 1958, May | Long Beach, Cal. | John Dever | 1977, Jan. |
| Harlingen, Tex. | *W. T. Snyder Jr. | 1974, Dec. | Long Beach, N.Y. | *William McKenney | 1978, Jan. |
| Harrisburg, Pa. | Paul Doutrich, R | 1982, Jan. | Longview, Tex. | *Harry G. Mosley | 1952, July |

| City | Name | Term |
|---|---|---|
| Los Angeles, Cal. | Thomas Bradley, D | 1981, June |
| Louisville, Ky. | William Stansbury, D | 1980, Nov. |
| Lowell, Mass. | *William Taupier | 1975 Oct. |
| L. Merion, Pa. | *Thomas B. Fulweiler | 1968, Jan. |
| Lubbock, Tex. | *Larry Cunningham | 1975, Sept. |
| Lynchburg, Va. | *David B. Norman | 1970, Nov. |
| Lynn, Mass. | Antonio J. Marino N-P | 1980, Jan. |
| Lynwood, Cal. | *Edward J. Valliere | 1976, Nov. |
| | | |
| Macon, Ga. | Buckner Melton, D | 1979, Dec. |
| Madison, Wis. | Paul Soglin, N-P | 1979, Apr. |
| Madison Heights, Mich. | George Suarez, N-P | 1979, Dec. |
| Malden, Mass. | James Conway, D | 1980, Jan. |
| Manchester, Conn. | *Robert B. Weiss | 1966, Jan. |
| Manchester, N.H. | Charles Stanton, D | 1979, Dec. |
| Manitowoc, Wis. | Anthony V. Dufek, D | 1979, Apr. |
| Mansfield, Oh. | Richard A. Porter, R | 1979, Dec. |
| Marion, Ind. | Anthony Maidenberg, D | 1979, Dec. |
| McKeesport, Pa. | Thomas Fullard, R | 1980, Jan. |
| Medford, Mass. | *James Nicholson | 1970, Oct. |
| Melbourne, Fla. | *Samuel Halter | 1978, July |
| Memphis, Tenn. | Wyeth Chandler, N-P | 1979, Dec. |
| Mentor, Oh. | *Edward Podojil | 1977, Nov. |
| Meridian, Miss. | *Joel W. Forrester | 1959, July |
| Mesa, Ariz. | Wayne Pomeroy, N-P | 1980, June |
| Mesquite, Tex. | B. J. Smith, N-P | 1979, Apr. |
| Miami, Fla. | *Joseph Grassie | 1976 July |
| Miami Beach, Fla. | *Gavin O'Brien | 1978, July |
| Middletown, Oh. | *Dale F. Helsel | 1970, Oct. |
| Midland, Tex. | *James W. Brown | 1964, Nov. |
| Midwest City, Okla. | Irving P. Frank | 1978, Apr. |
| Milford, Conn. | Henry A. Povinelli, R | 1979, Nov. |
| Milwaukee, Wis. | Henry W. Maier, D | 1980, Apr. |
| Minneapolis, Minn. | Albert Hofstede, N-P | 1980, Jan. |
| Minnetonka, Minn. | *Carsten D. Leikvold | 1973, Dec. |
| Minot, N.D. | *R. A. Schempp | 1977, Nov. |
| Mobile, Ala. | Commission form of Govt.(a) | |
| Modesto, Cal. | *Garth Lipsky | 1974, Jan. |
| Moline, Ill. | Lawrence Lorenson, D | 1981, Apr. |
| Monroe, La. | W. Derwood Cann Jr., D | 1979, Apr. |
| Montclair, N.J. | Grant M. Gille, N-P | 1980, May |
| Montebello, Cal. | *Roy Pederson | 1969, Jan. |
| Monterey Park, Cal. | *Lloyd de Llamas | 1976, Sept. |
| Montgomery, Ala. | Jim Robinson, D | 1979, Nov. |
| Mt. Prospect, Ill. | *Terrance Burghard. | 1978, Oct. |
| Mt. Vernon, N.Y. | Thomas E. Sharpe, D | 1979, Dec. |
| Mountain View, Cal. | *Bruce Liedstrand | 1976, Aug. |
| Muncie, Ind. | Robert Cunningham, D | 1979, Dec. |
| Mundelein, Ill. | Colin McRae, N-P | 1981, Apr. |
| Muskegon, Mich. | *Paul F. Frederick | 1970, June |
| Muskogee, Okla. | *Paul McCauley | 1978, June |
| | | |
| Napa, Cal. | *William Bopf | 1977, Dec. |
| Nashua, N.H. | Morris Arel, D | 1979, Dec. |
| Nashville, Tenn. | Richard Fulton, D | 1979, Aug. |
| National City, Cal. | *Harry E. Gill. | 1977, Mar. |
| New Bedford, Mass. | John Markey, N-P | 1980, Jan. |
| New Britain, Conn. | William J. McNamara, D | 1979, Nov. |
| New Brunswick, N.J. | John Lynch Jr., D | 1982, Dec. |
| New Castle, Pa. | Francis J. Rogan, D | 1979, Dec. |
| New Haven, Conn. | Frank Logue, D | 1979, Dec. |
| New Kensington, Pa. | Verle N. Bevan, D | 1981, Dec. |
| New Orleans, La. | Ernest Morial, D | 1982, Apr. |
| New Rochelle, N.Y. | *C. Samuel Kissinger | 1975, Apr. |
| New York, N.Y. | Edward Koch, D | 1981, Dec. |
| Newark, N.J. | Kenneth Gibson, D | 1982, July |
| Newport, R.I. | *Paul Steinbrenner | 1976, May |
| Newport Beach, Cal. | *Robert L. Wynn. | 1971, Aug. |
| Newport News, Va. | *Frank Smiley | 1976, Oct. |
| Newton, Mass. | Theodore Mann, R | 1981, Dec. |
| Niagara Falls, N.Y. | *Donald J. O'Hara | 1976, May |
| Niles, Ill. | Nicholas B. Blase, D | 1981, Apr. |
| Norfolk, Va. | *Julian Hirst | 1975, Apr. |
| Norman, Okla. | *James D. Crosby | 1975, Oct. |
| No. Charleston, S.C. | John Bourne, R | 1982, June |
| North Chicago, Ill. | Leo F. Kukla, D | 1981, Apr. |
| No. Little Rock, Ark. | Eddie Powell, D | 1980, Dec. |
| Norwalk, Cal. | *William H. Kraus | 1972, May |
| Norwalk, Conn. | William A. Collins, D | 1979, Nov. |
| Norwich, Conn. | *Charles Whitty | 1973, June |
| Novato, Cal. | *Phillip J. Brown. | 1974, May |
| | | |
| Oak Lawn, Ill. | *Richard E. O'Neill | 1976, Sept. |
| Oak Park, Ill. | *Jack Gruber | 1976, May |
| Oak Park, Mich. | David Shepherd, D | 1979, Sept. |

| City | Name | Term |
|---|---|---|
| Oak Ridge, Tenn. | A. K. Bissell, N-P | 1979, June |
| Oakland, Cal. | *Cecil S. Riley | 1972, Sept. |
| Oceanside, Cal. | *Robert Bourcier | 1978, June |
| Odessa, Tex. | *Kerry R. Sweatt | 1978, Jan. |
| Ogden, Ut. | *L. D. Hunter. | 1977, Sept. |
| Oklahoma City, Okla. | *James Cook | 1976, Apr. |
| Omaha, Neb. | Al Veys, D | 1981, June |
| Ontario, Cal. | *Roger Hughbanks | 1975, July |
| Orange, Cal. | Robert Hoyt, N-P | 1980, Mar. |
| Orange, N.J. | Carmine Capone, R | 1980, July |
| Orlando, Fla. | Carl Langford, N-P | 1980, Oct. |
| Oshkosh, Wis. | *W. O. Frueh. | 1976, Aug. |
| Overland Park, Kan. | Ben Sykes, D | 1981, Apr. |
| Owensboro, Ky. | *Max Rhoads | 1959, Sept. |
| Oxnard, Cal. | *Paul E. Wolven | 1953, Feb. |
| | | |
| Pacifia, Cal. | *Albert St. Cyr. | 1978, July |
| Palm Springs, Cal. | *Don Blubaugh | 1973, Aug. |
| Palo Alto, Cal. | *George Sipel | 1972, Feb. |
| Parkersburg, W. Va. | Alvin K. Smith, D. | 1981, Dec. |
| Parma, Oh. | John Petruska, D | 1979, Dec. |
| Pasadena, Cal. | *Donald F. McIntyre. | 1973, June |
| Pasadena, Tex. | John Ray Harrison, D | 1981, May |
| Passaic, N.J. | Robert Hare, N-P | 1981, June |
| Paterson, N.J. | Lawrence Kramer, R | 1982, June |
| Pawtucket, R.I. | Dennis Lynch, D | 1980, Jan. |
| Pekin, Ill. | William L. Waldmeier, D | 1979, Apr. |
| Pensacola, Fla. | *Steve Garman | 1978, June |
| Peoria, Ill. | Richard E. Carver, R | 1981, May |
| Perth Amboy, N.J. | George J. Otlowski, N-P | 1980, June |
| Philadelphia, Pa. | Frank L. Rizzo, D | 1980, Jan. |
| Phoenix, Ariz. | *Marvin Andrews | 1976, Oct. |
| Pico Rivera, Cal. | *John Donlevy. | 1977, May |
| Pine Bluff, Ark. | Charles Moore, D | 1980, Dec. |
| Pittsburgh, Pa. | Richard S. Caliguiri, D | 1981, Dec. |
| Pittsfield, Mass. | Paul Brindle, D | 1979, Dec. |
| Plainfield, N.J. | Paul O'Keefe, R | 1982, Jan. |
| Pocatello, Ida. | *Charles W. Moss. | 1970, Sept. |
| Pomona, Cal. | *Ora E. Lampman. | 1978, Aug. |
| Pompano Bch., Fla. | *John Schoeberlein | 1975, May |
| Pontiac, Mich. | *vacant | |
| Port Arthur, Tex. | *George Dibrell | |
| Port Huron, Mich. | *Gerald R. Bouchard. | 1965, June |
| Portage, Mich. | *Donald Ziemke | 1974, Aug. |
| Portland, Me. | *A. J. Wilson Jr. | 1976, May |
| Portland, Ore. | Neil Goldschmidt, N-P | 1979, Dec. |
| Portsmouth, Oh. | *Barry Feldman | 1977, Jan. |
| Portsmouth, Va. | *Robert T. Williams | 1975, Apr. |
| Poughkeepsie, N.Y. | *William Cranston | 1974, June |
| Prichard, Ala. | A.J. Cooper Jr. | 1980, Oct. |
| Providence, R.I. | Vincent Cianci Jr., R. | 1983, Jan. |
| Provo, Ut. | Jim Ferguson, N-P | 1982, Jan. |
| Pueblo, Col. | *Fred E. Weisbroad | 1967, Feb. |
| | | |
| Quincy, Ill. | C. David Nuessen, R | 1981, Apr. |
| Quincy, Mass. | Arthur H. Tobin, D | 1980, Jan. |
| | | |
| Racine, Wis. | Stephen Olson, D | 1979, Apr. |
| Raleigh, N.C. | *Lawrence P. Zachery Jr. | 1973, Nov. |
| Rapid City, S.D. | Arthur La Croix, N-P | 1979, May |
| Reading, Pa. | Joseph Kuzminski, D | 1980, Jan. |
| Redlands, Cal. | *Chris Christiansen | 1978, Oct. |
| Redondo Beach, Cal. | *vacant | |
| Redwood City, Cal. | *James M. Fales Jr. | 1971, Aug. |
| Reno, Nev. | *Henry Etchemendy | 1978, May |
| Revere, Mass. | George V. Colella, D | 1979, Dec. |
| Richardson, Tex. | Raymond Noah, R | 1979, Apr. |
| Richfield, Minn. | *Wayne Burggraaff | 1968, Dec. |
| Richmond, Cal. | *Kenneth Smith | 1967, Sept. |
| Richmond, Ind. | Clifford Dickman, R | 1979, Dec. |
| Richmond, Va. | *William J. Leidinger | 1972, June |
| Riverside, Cal. | *William F. Cornett | 1976, Jan. |
| Roanoke, Va. | *Byron E. Haner. | 1973, Jan. |
| Rochester, Minn. | Alex Smekta, N-P | 1979, June |
| Rochester, N.Y. | *Elisha Freedman | 1974, Jan. |
| Rock Hill, S.C. | *Max Holland | 1965, Mar. |
| Rock Island, Ill. | *J. Neil Neilsen | 1977, Jan. |
| Rockford, Ill. | Robert McGaw, D | 1981, May |
| Rockville, Md. | *Larry N. Blick | 1972, Nov. |
| Rome, N.Y. | William A. Valentine, R | 1979, Dec. |
| Rosemead, Cal. | *Frank Tripepi | 1976, Feb. |
| Roseville, Mich. | *B. J. Nardelli | 1975, Nov. |
| Roseville, Minn. | *James Andre | 1974, May |
| Rosewell, N.M. | *Robert Owen | 1973, Oct. |
| Royal Oak, Mich. | *William Baldridge. | 1975, Sept. |

(a) Form of Government case being reviewed by U.S. Supreme Court.

| City | Name | Term | City | Name | Term |
|------|------|------|------|------|------|
| Sacramento, Cal. | *Walter Slipe | 1976, Apr. | Upland, Cal. | *S. Lee Travers | 1974, Oct. |
| Saginaw, Mich. | *Thomas Dalton | 1978, Sept. | Upper Arlington, Oh. | *H. W. Hyrne | 1968, May |
| St. Clair Shores, Mich. | *Donald J. Harm | 1962, Jan. | Urbana, Ill. | Jeffrey Markland, R. | 1981, Apr. |
| St. Cloud, Minn. | Al G. Loehr, N-P | 1980, Apr. | Utica, N.Y. | Stephen Pawlinga, D | 1979, Dec. |
| St. Joseph, Mo. | Gordon Weiser, R | 1982, Apr. | | | |
| St. Louis, Mo. | James F. Conway, D | 1981, Apr. | Vallejo, Cal. | *Ted McDonell | 1978, Sept. |
| St. Louis Pk., Minn. | *John Elwell | 1977, Oct. | Vancouver, Wash. | *Alan Harvey | 1969, May |
| St. Paul, Minn. | George Latimer, D | 1980, June | Ventura, Cal. | *Edward E. McCombs | 1970, Mar. |
| St. Petersburg, Fla. | *Raymond Harbaugh | 1970, Apr. | Victoria, Tex. | *John F. Lee | 1959, Sept. |
| Salem, Mass. | Jean Levesque, D | 1980, Jan. | Vineland, N.J. | Patrick R. Fiorilli, N-P | 1980, July |
| Salem, Ore. | *Robert S. Moore | 1968, Aug. | Virginia Beach, Va. | *George L. Hanbury | 1974, Nov. |
| Salina, Kan. | *Norris D. Olson | 1964, May | | | |
| Salinas, Cal. | *Robert Christofferson | 1972, Dec. | Waco, Tex. | *David F. Smith Jr. | 1970, Sept. |
| Salt Lake City, Ut. | Ted Wilson, D | 1979, Dec. | Walnut Creek, Cal. | *Thomas Dunne | 1972, Apr. |
| San Angelo, Tex. | Tom Parrett, D | 1979 May | Waltham, Mass. | Arthur J. Clark, D | 1980, Jan. |
| San Antonio, Tex. | *Thomas Huebner | 1977, Jan. | Warren, Mich. | Ted Bates, N-P | 1979, Nov. |
| San Bernardino, Cal. | *Marshall Julian | 1971, Nov. | Warwick, R.I. | Joseph Walsh, D | 1981, Jan. |
| San Buenaventura, Cal. | *Edward McCombs | 1970, Feb. | Wash. D.C. | Marion Barry, D | 1983, Jan. |
| San Diego, Cal. | *Hugh McKinley | 1975, Apr. | Waterbury, Conn. | Edward Bergin, D | 1979, Dec. |
| San Francisco, Cal. | George Moscone, D. | 1980, Jan. | Waterloo, Ia. | Leo Rooff, N-P | 1980, Jan. |
| San Jose, Cal. | *vacant | | Waukegan, Ill. | Bill Morris, D | 1981, May |
| San Leandro, Cal. | *Lee Riordan | 1976, Jan. | Waukesha, Wis. | Joseph Laporte, N-P | 1980, Apr. |
| San Mateo, Cal. | *Richard Delong | 1976, Sept. | Wausau, Wis. | John Kannenberg, N-P | 1980, Apr. |
| San Rafael, Cal. | *William J. Bielser | 1972, Dec. | Wauwatosa, Wis. | James A. Benz, N-P | 1980, Apr. |
| Sandusky, Oh. | *Frank Link | 1972, Jan. | West Allis, Wis. | Jack Barlich, N-P | 1980, Apr. |
| Santa Ana, Cal. | *Bruce C. Spragg | 1972, Sept. | W. Covina, Cal. | *Herman Fast | 1976, Aug. |
| Santa Barbara, Cal. | *Richard Thomas | 1977, Jan. | W. Hartford, Conn. | *William Brady | 1978, Jan. |
| Santa Cruz, Cal. | Lawrence Edler, N-P | 1979, Mar. | W. Haven, Conn. | Robert A. Johnson, D | 1979, Dec. |
| Santa Fe, N.M. | Arthur Trujillo, D | 1982, Mar. | W. New York, N.J. | Anthony DeFino, D | 1979, May |
| Santa Maria, Cal. | *Robert Grogan | 1963, Jan. | W. Palm Beach, Fla. | *Richard Simmons | 1968, Sept. |
| Santa Monica, Cal. | Donna O'Brien Swink, D | 1979, Apr. | Westland, Mich. | Thomas F. Taylor, N-P | 1981, Dec. |
| Santa Rosa, Cal. | *Kenneth R. Blackman | 1970, July | Westminster, Cal. | *Robert J. Huntley | 1967, July |
| Sarasota, Fla. | *Kenneth Thompson | 1950, Feb. | Weymouth, Mass. | Board of Selectmen | |
| Savannah, Ga. | *Arthur A. Mendonsa | 1971, Sept. | Wheaton, Ill. | Ralph Barger, R | 1979, Apr. |
| Schenectady, N.Y. | *Wayne V. Chapman | 1977, May | Wheeling, W. Va. | *Jack Maloney | 1977, Aug. |
| Scottsdale, Ariz. | William Jenkins, N-P | 1980, Apr. | White Plains, N.Y. | Alfred Del Vecchio, R | 1981, Dec. |
| Scranton, Pa. | Eugene Hickey, D | 1981, Dec. | Wichita, Kan. | *E. H. Denton | 1976, July |
| Seattle, Wash. | Charles Royer, D | 1982, Jan. | Wichita Falls, Tex. | *Gerald Fox | 1969, Feb. |
| Shaker Heights, Oh. | Walter C. Kelley, D | 1979, Dec. | Wilkes-Barre, Pa. | Walter Lisman, D | 1979, Dec. |
| Sheboygan, Wis. | Richard Suscha, R | 1981, Apr. | Williamsport, Pa. | Daniel Kirby, D | 1980, Jan. |
| Shreveport, La. | W. T. (Billy) Hanna Jr., D | 1982, Nov. | Wilmington, Del. | William T. McLaughlin, D | 1981, Jan. |
| Simi Valley, Cal. | *Richard Malcolm | 1974, May | Wilmington, N.C. | *Robert Cobb | 1977, Dec. |
| Sioux City, Ia. | *Gary F. Pokorny | 1974, Jan. | Winston-Salem, N.C. | *Orville W. Powell | 1972, Nov. |
| Sioux Falls, S.D. | Rick Knobe, R | 1979, May | Woonsocket, R.I. | Gerard Bouley, D | 1979, Nov. |
| Skokie, Ill. | *vacant | | Worcester, Mass. | *Francis J. McGrath | 1951, May |
| Somerville, Mass. | Thomas F. August, D | 1980, Jan. | Wyandotte, Mich. | William L. Cook, N-P | 1979, Apr. |
| South Bend, Ind. | Peter J. Nemeth, D | 1979, Dec. | Wyoming, Mich. | *James Sheeran | 1976, Nov. |
| So. Gate, Cal. | *Carl Zeise | 1966, Oct. | | | |
| So. S.F., Cal. | *C. W. Birkelo | 1978 | Yakima, Wash. | *Richard Zais Jr. | 1978, Nov. |
| Southfield, Mich. | *Peter Cristiano | 1968, July | Yonkers, N.Y. | *Pat Ravo | 1978, Jan. |
| Southgate, Mich. | *William Valusek | 1972, Feb. | York, Pa. | Elizabeth Marshall, D | 1982, Jan. |
| Spartanburg, S.C. | *W. H. Carstarphen | 1975, Mar. | Youngstown, Oh. | J. Philip Richley, D. | 1979, Dec. |
| Spokane, Wash. | *Terry Novak | 1978 July | | | |
| Springfield, Ill. | William C. Telford, R | 1979, Apr. | Zanesville, Oh. | *Frank Patrizio | 1975, Sept. |
| Springfield, Mass. | Theodore Dimauro, D | 1980, Jan. | | | |
| Springfield, Mo. | *Don G. Busch | 1971, Oct. | | | |

## Canadian Cities
(as of Oct. 15, 1978)

| City | Name | Term |
|------|------|------|
| Springfield, Oh. | *Thomas M. Bay | 1978, Sept. | | | |
| Stamford, Conn. | Louis A. Clapes, R | 1979, Nov. | Calgary, Alta. | Ross Alger | 1980, Oct. |
| Sterling Hts. Mich. | *Leonard Hendricks | 1976, Jan. | Charlottetown, P.E.I. | Francis Moran | 1980, Nov. |
| Stillwater, Okla. | Jon Patton, N-P | 1979, May | Edmonton, Alta. | C.J. Purves | 1980, Oct. |
| Stockton, Cal. | *Gerald Davenport | 1977, Jan. | Fredericton, N.B. | Elbridge C. Wilkins | 1980, May |
| Stratford, Conn. | *Michael Brown | 1978, May | Guelph, Ont. | Norman Jary | 1978, Nov. |
| Sunnyvale, Cal. | *Lee Ayres | 1977, Mar. | Halifax, N.S. | Edmund L. Morris | 1980, Oct. |
| Syracuse, N.Y. | Lee Alexander, D | 1981, Dec. | Hamilton, Ont. | Jack MacDonald | 1978, Nov. |
| | | | Hull, Que. | Gilles Rocheleau | 1979, Nov. |
| | | | Kingston, Ont. | Ken Keyes | 1978, Nov. |
| Tacoma, Wash. | *Erling O. Mork | 1975, June | Kitchener, Ont. | Morley Rosenberg | 1978, Nov. |
| Tallahassee, Fla. | *Daniel A. Kleman | 1974, Aug. | La Salle, Que. | Gerald Raymond | 1979, Nov. |
| Tampa, Fla. | William Poe, N-P. | 1979, Oct. | London, Ont. | Mrs. Jane Bigelow | 1978, Nov. |
| Taunton, Mass. | Joseph Amaral, D. | 1979, Dec. | Moncton, N.B. | G.D. Wheeler | 1980, June |
| Taylor, Mich. | Donald L. Zub, N-P | 1981, Nov. | Montreal, Que. | Jean Drapeau | 1978, Nov. |
| Teaneck, N.J. | *Werner H. Schmid | 1959, Mar. | Oshawa, Ont. | James Potticary | 1978, Nov. |
| Tempe, Ariz. | Harry E. Mitchell, D | 1980, July | Ottawa, Ont. | Lorry Greenberg | 1978, Nov. |
| Temple, Tex. | *Barney Knight | 1978, Dec. | Peterborough, Ont. | Cameron Wasson | 1978, Nov. |
| Terre Haute, Ind. | William Brighton, D | 1979, Dec. | Quebec, Que. | Jean Pelletier | 1979, Nov. |
| Thousand Oaks, Cal. | *Glenn Kendall | 1966 | Regina, Sask. | Henry H.P. Baker | 1979, Oct. |
| Titusville, Fla. | *Norman Hickey | 1974, June | Saint John, N.B. | Samuel Davis | 1980, May |
| Toledo, Oh. | *Walter Kane | 1977, Mar. | St. John's, Nfld. | Mrs. Dorothy Wyatt | 1981, Nov. |
| Topeka, Kan. | William McCormick, N-P | 1979, Apr. | Saskatoon, Sask. | C. Wright | 1979, Oct. |
| Torrance, Cal. | *Edward J. Ferraro | 1964, Mar. | Sault Ste. Marie, Ont. | Nicholas Trbovich | 1978, Nov. |
| Trenton, N.J. | Arthur Holland, D | 1982, June | Sherbrooke, Que. | Jacques O'Bready | 1978, Nov. |
| Troy, Mich. | Frank Gerstenecker, D | 1970, Feb. | Sudbury, Ont. | J. Gordon | 1978, Nov. |
| Troy, N.Y. | *J. Duncan Barrett | 1977, Aug. | Toronto, Ont. | Fred Beavis | 1978, Nov. |
| Tucson, Ariz. | Lewis Murphy, R | 1979, Dec. | Vancouver, B.C. | Jack Volrich | 1978, Nov. |
| Tulsa, Okla. | James M. Inhofe, R | 1980, May | Victoria, B.C. | Michael Young | 1979, Nov. |
| Tuscaloosa, Ala. | Ernest Collins, N-P | 1981, Oct. | Waterloo, Ont. | Mrs. M. Carroll | 1978, Nov. |
| Tyler, Tex. | *Ed Wagoner | 1977, June | Windsor, Ont. | Bert Weeks | 1978, Nov. |
| Univ. City, Mo. | *Victor Ellman | 1975, Dec. | Winnipeg, Man. | Robert Steen | 1980, Oct. |

# Laws Passed During 95th Congress, Second Session, 1978

Closing down its second session with a 34-hour marathon, the 95th Congress cleared a deluge of legislation, much of it major bills it had debated all year. The tax and energy bills, passed in barely readable penciled drafts, were cases in point.

In its final form, the $18.7-billion tax-cut bill which gave most of its benefits to persons earning $15,000 or more a year, rejected most of Pres. Jimmy Carter's tax reform proposals, including a controversial plan to end deductions for the "3-martini lunch." The bill did include an increase in personal exemptions from $750 to $1,000 and a $2.1 billion cut in capital gains taxes, 75% of which would benefit those making over $50,000 per year.

The energy bill, a gutted version of the president's 1977 proposals, contained $1 billion in tax credits to encourage energy conservation and a diluted form of Pres. Carter's proposed tax on the sale of gas-guzzling cars. The final bill lacked 2 of the president's biggest proposed energy-saving taxes on domestic crude oil and industrial use of oil and gas, but did incorporate the phased removal of federal price controls from new natural gas by 1985.

Bills passed and signed and other major actions during the second session included:

**Energy Research.** Authorized $6.08 billion for energy research in fiscal 1978 (signed Feb. 25). The bill did not provide $80 million for continued work on the Clinch River, Tenn., breeder reactor, a provision that provoked Pres. Carter to veto similar legislation in 1977.

**Supplemental Appropriations.** Provided $7.8 billion in fiscal 1978 supplemental appropriations, including funds for sewage treatment plant construction and Small Business Administration disaster loans (signed Mar. 7). The legislation also included an $80-million appropriation for the fast breeder reactor at Clinch River, Tenn. Ending a controversy that had delayed it for months, the bill rescinded $462 million appropriated in fiscal 1977 to build 2 B-1 bombers.

**Nuclear Technology.** Imposed new and stricter controls on export of nuclear technology and fuel, stipulating that the U.S. would end nuclear exports to any country that, in future, developed such weapons (signed Mar. 10).

**National Debt.** Extended temporary ceiling on the public debt, set at $752 billion, through July 31 (signed Mar. 27). If the temporary ceiling had expired on Mar. 31 as scheduled, the permanent ceiling of $400 billion, well below the current debt, would have come into effect. In further legislation, raised the permanent ceiling on the national debt to $798 billion, effective through Mar. 31, 1979 (signed Aug. 3).

## Retirement, Child Abuse

**Retirement Age.** Raised mandatory retirement age for most employees from age 65 to age 70 (signed Apr. 6).

**Child Abuse.** Extended the Child Abuse Prevention and Treatment Act of 1973 through Sept. 30, 1981, authorizing $112.5 million for prevention and treatment programs during those 4 years (signed Apr. 24). Expanded the definition of child abuse to include "sexual exploitation," expanding coverage to rape, prostitution, and incest as well as obscene or pornographic filming or depiction of children for commercial purposes.

**NYC Aid.** Gave New York City $1.65 billion in federal long-term loan guarantees, the cornerstone of a plan to restore the city's financial stability by fiscal 1983 (signed Aug. 8).

**Weapons.** House sustained, 206-191, a veto of a $37-billion weapons authorization bill (Sept. 7). Pres. Carter had vetoed the legislation chiefly because it had provided $2 billion for constructing a nuclear-powered aircraft.

**Foreign Military and Security Aid.** Authorized $2.8 billion in fiscal 1979 for military and security aid. In granting military aid, provided for a lifting of the arms embargo against Turkey and set conditions for ending economic sanctions against Rhodesia. Prohibited security aid to any nation that consistently violated human rights, except in cases certified as exceptional by the secretary of state (signed Sept. 26).

**Diplomatic Immunity.** Revised legal immunity granted by U.S. to foreign diplomats, repealing a 1790 law that had granted immunity to foreign diplomatic personnel from all criminal prosecutions and protection from civil damage suits. Such full immunity would be extended only to top-level diplomats and their families (signed Sept. 30).

**U.S. Customs.** Revised and simplified U.S. customs statutes, increasing duty-free allowance given to U.S. residents returning from abroad from $100 to $300 (signed Oct. 3).

**Public Works.** House sustained, 223-190, veto of $10.1 billion public works appropriation bill that Pres. Carter had attacked as inflationary and wasteful "pork barrel" legislation (Oct. 5). The bill contained several water projects to which Carter objected. In a stop-gap move, passed a $27-billion appropriations bill containing a compromise public works program and funds for other federal activities including public broadcasting and several drug abuse and health projects (signed Oct. 19).

**Civil Service.** Passed Civil Service Reform Act, revising federal procedures to make it easier to reward good workers and fire incompetent ones (signed Oct. 13).

**Veterans Benefits.** Provided a 7.3% cost-of-living increase for 2.2 million recipients of regular veteran's checks and 368,000 survivors of veterans; raised maximum federal home loan guarantee for veterans and the severely disabled (signed Oct. 18).

**Foreign Aid.** Authorized $9.1 billion in foreign aid as part of the administration's Middle East initiative, slating much of the aid for Egypt, Jordan and Israel. Also authorized Pres. Carter to give Syria up to $90 million in aid if he believed it would help the peace process. Aid also provided for Greece and Turkey toward efforts to arrange a Cyprus peace settlement (signed Oct. 18).

**ERA.** Extended by 39 months the deadline for states to ratify the Equal Rights Amendment.

## More Judgeships

**Judiciary.** Created 152 new federal judgeships, expanding the federal judiciary by one-quarter, in order to clear up the backlog of cases confronting the courts (signed Oct. 20).

**Intelligence Surveillance.** Required court approval before the government can conduct electronic surveillance in most foreign intelligence cases (signed Oct. 25).

**Airline Deregulation.** Passed Airline Deregulation bill, ending 40 years of federal control of the nation's airlines. Phased out government supervision of routes and fares through 1982 and authorized airlines to cut fares up to 50% without prior clearance (signed Oct. 24).

**Financial Disclosure.** Required public financial disclosure from the top 14,000 government officials, including the president, vice president, members of Congress, and the Supreme Court. This legislation, proposed by Pres. Carter in 1977, was the first time any across-the-board ethics standard had been applied to the 3 branches of government (signed Oct. 26).

**Full Employment.** Passed the Humphrey-Hawkins Bill requiring the president to set annual goals for employment, unemployment, production, and inflation for 5 years aimed at reducing the national jobless rate to 4% by 1983 and achieving zero inflation by 1988 (signed Oct. 27).

**Pregnancy Benefits.** Reversing a 1976 Supreme Court decision, required employers to give pregnant workers the same sick pay and long-term disability benefits they provide for other workers (signed Oct. 31).

**Endangered Species.** Extended by 18 months the Endangered Species Act, including a review procedure for exempting public works projects threatening endangered species. Provided special expedited review process for the Tellico Dam whose construction was stopped by the Supreme Court because it would cause the extinction of the snail darter (signing pending).

**Banking Reform.** Largely in reaction to the Bert Lance affair, limited the total amount of loans that can be made to a bank's officers, directors, and principal stockholders to 10% of the bank's capital. Also required that all such loans be publicly reported and barred bank officers from obtaining preferential loans from banks that have a correspondent relationship with their bank (signing pending).

# Major Decisions of the U.S. Supreme Court, 1977-78

Among notable actions in 1977-78, the Supreme Court:

Held unanimously that national banks could be sued in state courts in any county where they had a branch, thereby ruling that the law could not be interpreted as restricting suits to places where the national banks were chartered (Nov. 8, 1977).

In a 6-3 decision, ruled that police could require a motorist to get out of his car after he had been stopped for a minor traffic violation (Dec. 5, 1977).

Ruled unanimously that an employer could not deprive an employe who took maternity leave of her accumulated seniority. However, the court also held that employers were not legally bound to provide pregnancy or child-birth benefits (Dec. 6, 1977).

Held 5-4 that federal judges could force telephone companies to install electronic surveillance devices to help criminal investigations. In a second decision, 6-3, the court stated that federal judges were constitutionally empowered to authorize such surveillance (Dec. 7, 1977).

Ruled 7-2 that employers could require retirement before age 65 if such early retirement was a prerequisite of a company's long-standing pension plan (Dec. 12, 1977).

In a unanimous decision, ruled that the father of an illegitimate child had no right to veto the adoption of his child, even if a court had not found him to be unfit as a parent (Jan. 10, 1978).

Ruled, 5-3, that foreign governments could bring antitrust suits against U.S. corporations in U.S. courts. The court indicated that foreign governments, if they won such suits, could collect the usual triple damages (Jan. 11, 1978).

In a 5-2 ruling, affirmed a decision which upheld South Carolina's use of teacher tests that had disqualified 83% of black applicants but only 17.5% of white applicants (Jan. 16, 1978).

## Union Picketing Restricted

Decided, 6-3, that it was illegal for a construction union to picket a job site to enforce a so-called "prehiring agreement" with a contractor if the union was not the legal bargaining agent for the workers on the site (Jan. 17, 1978).

Held unanimously that an employer who won a job discrimination suit could not collect legal fees unless a judge ruled that the suit was "frivolous, unreasonable or groundless" (Jan. 23, 1978).

Declined to review, therefore let stand, an appellate court ruling which permitted companies to begin drilling for oil and gas on tracts off the New Jersey shore which they had leased from the federal government (Feb. 21, 1978).

Let stand, by refusing to review, a decision that the University of Missouri could not refuse to recognize Gay Lib, a student homosexual group, as an official campus organization (Feb. 21, 1978).

In an 8-0 decision, ruled that public school students suspended without a hearing could not collect more than $1 in damages unless they could prove that they had been harmed by their suspension (Mar. 21, 1978).

Ruled, 6-2, that the testimony of a key witness in a New York State gambling case was admissable in spite of the fact that the police had obtained the identity of the witness through an admittedly illegal search for evidence (Mar. 22, 1978).

Reversing a 5-year trend in backing the rights of aliens against state restriction, ruled that states could require U.S. citizenship as a prerequisite for joining their state police forces (Mar. 22, 1978).

Held, 6-2, that a judge could ignore the objections of a defendant and instruct a jury to disregard the fact that a defendant had refused to testify in his own behalf (Mar. 22, 1978).

Ruled, 7-0, that the federal courts could not act to circumvent government regulations on the building of nuclear power plants (Apr. 3, 1978).

Decided, 7-2, that television and radio networks did not have automatic access to the White House tape recordings of former Pres. Richard M. Nixon (Apr. 18, 1978).

Stayed an appeals court decision which would have allowed New Hampshire Gov. Meldrim Thomson Jr. to carry out a proclamation ordering all flags flown outside state office buildings lowered in observance of Good Friday (Mar. 24, 1978). Later, the Supreme Court refused to extend the stay and suggested the controversy be settled in the lower courts (Apr. 24, 1978).

Ruled, 6-2, that it was discriminatory under the Civil Rights Act of 1964 for an employer to charge women more than men to participate in a pension plan (Apr. 25, 1978).

## Corporations Can Spread Political Views

Decided, 5-4, that, under the provisions of the first amendment, corporations could not be barred from spending money to disseminate their views on political issues (Apr. 26, 1978).

Ruled, 6-3, that a municipal utility could not terminate service to a customer for non-payment of bills until it gave the customer a hearing (May 1, 1978).

In a 7-2 decision, held that federal agents must make only a "reasonable effort" to avoid intercepting private conversation when using court-ordered wiretaps in criminal investigations (May 15, 1978).

Held 8-1, that juries should not take children into consideration when applying "community standards" as a test for possibly obscene material (May 23, 1978).

Ruled, 7-2, that a judge in a criminal trial could be required to charge the jury that a defendant is presumed innocent. The judge in the case had only stated the prosecution must prove guilt beyond a reasonable doubt (May 30, 1978).

Decided, 5-3 that the news media were not entitled to special immunity from court-approved searches by police officers. On the broader issue, the court ruled that the police could obtain warrants to search the property of persons not suspected of any criminal wrongdoing (May 31, 1978).

Overturning a 1961 ruling, decided, 7-2, that municipalities were vulnerable to damage suits if their official policies deprived citizens of their civil rights (June 6, 1978).

Refused to issue a temporary stay of a lower court ruling permitting a neo-Nazi organization to hold a rally in Skokie, Ill. on June 25 (June 12, 1978).

Ruled, 8-0, to uphold a government regulation which prevented newspapers from acquiring radio or television stations in their communities (June 12, 1978).

## Double Jeopardy Reinterpreted

Handed down a series of decisions reinterpreting the constitutional prohibition against double jeopardy. Overturned, 5-4, a doctrine it had established in 1975 and 1977 which stated that in federal cases an indictment dismissed during a trial was to be considered a legal "acquittal,"even though the jury had not handed in a verdict. Ruled, 8-0, in 2 cases, that a defendant could not be subjected to a 2d trial if his conviction was reversed by an appeals court on the grounds that the evidence was not sufficient to justify a jury verdict of guilty (June 14, 1978).

Upheld, 6-3, a lower court ruling halting completion of a Tennessee Valley Authority dam because it was a threat to the habitat of the snail darter, a rare fish found only in a 17-mile stretch of the Little Tennessee River (June 15, 1978).

In 2 decisions, affirmed the right of unions to distribute their literature on company property. Ruled, 7-2, that an union could distribute material of a political nature at an employment site (June 22, 1978).

Affirmed, 5-4, a lower court decision ordering the University of California Medical School to admit Allan P. Bakke, who had claimed the school's minority-admissions plan had made him a victim of "reverse discrimination." Then, aligning 5-4, the court ruled that universities could consider race as one factor in choosing among applicants for admission (June 28, 1978).

Struck down, 7-1, the death penalty in Ohio and let stand rulings that death penalty laws in New York and Pennsylvania were unconstitutional because they did not make sufficient provision for consideration of mitigating circumstances (July 3, 1978).

# PERSONAL FINANCE

## Using the Consumer Price Index

Beginning in January 1978, the Bureau of Labor Statistics introduced a revised consumer price index for urban wage earners and clerical workers — about 40% of the population. The revised index (CPI-W) is based on a new, larger market basket of goods priced in 85 areas (29 more areas than for the old CPI). The new market basket includes TV and sound equipment and repairs, additional children's clothes, luggage, automotive body work, medical supplies such as crutches, and a variety of other goods and services which were not included in the old CPI.

In addition to the revised CPI, the Bureau also began to publish a completely new index for all urban dwellers, including the unemployed, the retired, and professional and managerial workers — about 80% of the U.S. population. This new urban index (CPI-U) takes into account the different ways price changes affect the purchasing habits of the poor and the moderately rich.

Both the CPI-W and the CPI-U use the same base year as the old CPI (1967=100) and were dovetailed into the old CPI. However, because of the many changes in sampling procedures, neither of the new indexes are strictly comparable with the old index.

### Which Index For You?

Which index should you use to calculate the impact of inflation on your life? If your income is near the poverty level, or if you are retired on a moderate income, you should probably use the new CPI-U. Otherwise, even if you are moderately rich, the CPI-W will probably be the best indicator for you.

The CPI (W and U) emerges each month as single numbers. At the end of the year an average is computed from the monthly figures. (Averaging does away with fluctuations caused by special situations that have nothing to do with inflation.)

For example, the average CPI for 1977 was 181.5. This means that the value of goods and services, which was set at 100% in 1967, cost 81.5% more in 1977.

Changes in prices and how they affect you can be calculated by comparing the CPI of one period against another. The 1977 CPI reading of 181.5 can be compared to the 1976 reading of 170.5. Dividing 181.5 by 170.5, the excess over 1 is the percentage increase for the year 1977; in this case, 6.45%.

Did your income increase by enough to keep up with this inflation? To make the comparison, dig out your old W-2 or income tax return forms, or find your old paycheck stubs. Both gross and takehome pay comparisons will be of interest to you, but take care to compare equals. Overtime pay should not be counted. Also, watch out for changes in deductions such as those for tax exemptions, credit union pay-

---

## Consumer Price Indexes, 1978

Source: Bureau of Labor Statistics, U.S. Labor Department

| (1967 = 100) | Dec. 1977 | January CPI-U | CPI-W | March CPI-U | CPI-W | May CPI-U | CPI-W |
|---|---|---|---|---|---|---|---|
| All Items | 186.1 | 187.2 | 187.1 | 189.8 | 189.7 | 193.3 | 193.3 |
| Food, beverages | 191.9 | 194.6 | 194.5 | 199.5 | 199.2 | 205.2 | 205.1 |
| Housing | 192.4 | 193.8 | 193.8 | 196.7 | 196.7 | 199.9 | 199.8 |
| Apparel, upkeep | 158.2 | 155.7 | 155.4 | 156.5 | 156.0 | 159.8 | 159.7 |
| Transportation | 178.8 | 179.0 | 179.1 | 179.9 | 180.0 | 183.2 | 183.4 |
| Medical care | 209.3 | 211.2 | 211.2 | 214.5 | 214.3 | 216.9 | 217.0 |
| Entertainment | 171.0 | 171.9 | 171.7 | 174.1 | 174.1 | 176.2 | 175.6 |
| Other goods, services | 177.8 | 178.5 | 178.4 | 179.3 | 179.6 | 180.4 | 180.6 |
| Services | 200.5 | 202.0 | 202.0 | 204.9 | 205.0 | 208.0 | 207.9 |
| Rent, for home | 157.9 | 158.8 | 158.8 | 160.5 | 160.5 | 162.7 | 162.6 |
| Household, less rent | 220.0 | 221.8 | 221.7 | 226.0 | 226.0 | 230.6 | 230.6 |
| Transportation | 192.9 | 193.7 | 194.0 | 194.9 | 195.2 | 195.5 | 195.7 |
| Medical care | 224.2 | 226.5 | 226.5 | 229.9 | 229.7 | 232.5 | 232.5 |
| Other services | 177.5 | 178.8 | 178.6 | 180.7 | 181.1 | 182.5 | 183.0 |
| All items less food | 183.1 | 183.8 | 183.8 | 185.9 | 185.8 | 189.0 | 188.8 |
| Commodities | 178.3 | 179.2 | 179.1 | 181.6 | 181.5 | 185.5 | 185.4 |
| Commodities less food | 168.4 | 168.6 | 168.5 | 170.0 | 169.9 | 173.0 | 172.8 |
| Nondurables | 182.9 | 183.9 | 183.8 | 186.8 | 186.6 | 190.7 | 190.7 |
| Energy | 211.3 | 211.8 | 211.7 | 214.3 | 214.1 | 217.7 | 217.5 |
| All items less energy | 184.4 | 184.4 | 185.5 | 185.6 | 188.1 | 191.7 | 191.7 |

---

## Average Consumer Price Indexes (CPI-W)

Source: Bureau of Labor Statistics, U.S. Labor Department

The Consumer Price Index (CPI-W) measures the average change in prices of goods and services purchased by urban wage earners and clerical workers. (1967 = 100)

| | 1971 Index | %+ | 1972 Index | %+ | 1973 Index | %+ | 1974 Index | %+ | 1975 Index | %+ | 1976 Index | %+ | 1977 Index | %+ |
|---|---|---|---|---|---|---|---|---|---|---|---|---|---|---|
| All items | 121.3 | 4.3 | 125.3 | 3.3 | 133.1 | 6.2 | 147.7 | 11.0 | 161.2 | 9.1 | 170.5 | 5.8 | 181.5 | 6.5 |
| Food, drink | 118.3 | 3.1 | 123.2 | 4.1 | 139.5 | 13.2 | 158.7 | 13.8 | 172.1 | 8.4 | 177.4 | 3.1 | 188.0 | 6.0 |
| Housing | 123.4 | 4.4 | 128.1 | 3.8 | 133.7 | 4.4 | 148.8 | 11.3 | 164.5 | 10.6 | 174.6 | 6.1 | 186.5 | 6.8 |
| Apparel, upkeep | 119.8 | 3.2 | 122.3 | 2.1 | 126.8 | 3.7 | 136.2 | 7.4 | 142.3 | 4.5 | 147.6 | 3.7 | 154.2 | 4.5 |
| Transportation | 118.6 | 5.2 | 119.9 | 1.1 | 123.8 | 3.3 | 137.7 | 11.2 | 150.6 | 9.4 | 165.5 | 9.9 | 177.2 | 7.1 |
| Medical care | 128.4 | 6.5 | 132.5 | 3.2 | 137.7 | 3.9 | 150.5 | 9.3 | 168.6 | 12.0 | 184.7 | 9.5 | 202.4 | 9.6 |
| Entertainment | 122.9 | 5.3 | 126.5 | 2.9 | 130.0 | 2.8 | 139.8 | 7.5 | 152.2 | 8.9 | 159.8 | 5.0 | 167.7 | 4.9 |
| Other | 122.4 | 4.8 | 127.5 | 4.2 | 132.5 | 3.9 | 142.0 | 7.2 | 153.9 | 8.4 | 162.7 | 5.7 | 172.2 | 5.8 |

nents, payroll bonds, and the like. These have nothing to do with inflation and should be added back to your take home pay.

### Measuring Your Paycheck

A. To compare year-to-year earnings in percent form, divide your 1977 earnings by those of 1976 and express the result as a percentage. For example, if you earned the gross wages of the average U.S. worker, your paychecks in 1976 showed about $176.29 per week as compared with $189.53 per week in 1977, an increase of 7.51%. Since prices rose by only 6.45% during 1977, the average worker made a slight gain in real gross income that year. You can do the same kind of calculation on your total 1976 and 1977 earnings by using your total annual income figures in place of weekly earnings figures.

B. Another way to handle the same figures takes a dollar form. For this calculation, assume your wage was $176.29 at the end of 1976. During 1977, prices increased by 6.45%. To match that price increase, your wages should have gone up to $187.66 ($176.29 times 1.0645) by the end of 1977.

While readings on a monthly basis may be misleading, you may want a rough idea of how much you are being affected by inflation right now. For example, if you had weekly earnings of $202.48 in May of 1978, compared to earnings of $189.53 in December, 1977, your income went up $6.83% (202.48 divided by 189.53 equals 1.06832 or 6.83%). The CPI-W went from 186.1 to 193.3 during the same period, a gain of 3.88%. This means the average worker made a apreciable gain on inflation in the first 5 months of 1978. You can make the same calculation for any month by using the latest CPI figures as they are issued by the Department of Labor and published in your local newspaper.

## Consumer Price Index by Cities

(1967 = 100, except Anchorage and Miami)

| City[1] | 1976 avg. | 1977 (2) | February, 1978 CPI-U | February, 1978 CPI-W | March, 1978 CPI-U | March, 1978 CPI-W | April, 1978 CPI-U | April, 1978 CPI-W | May, 1978 CPI-U | May, 1978 CPI-W |
|---|---|---|---|---|---|---|---|---|---|---|
| Anchorage, Alas. (10/67 = 100)[3] | — | — | — | — | 180.7 | 180.8 | — | — | 184.2 | 184.0 |
| Atlanta, Ga. | 169.2 | 184.5 | 186.1 | 186.5 | — | — | 188.5 | 188.9 | — | — |
| Baltimore, Md. | 173.9 | 190.7 | — | — | — | — | — | — | 198.0 | 198.4 |
| Boston, Mass. | 174.5 | 185.7(10) | — | — | 188.2 | 187.8 | — | — | 190.7 | 190.2 |
| Buffalo, N.Y. | 170.6 | 185.1(11) | 187.5 | 187.5 | — | — | 159.0 | 189.2 | — | — |
| Chicago, Ill.-Northwest Ind. | 165.1 | 180.0 | 184.2 | 183.8 | 186.3 | 185.6 | 187.3 | 186.6 | 189.0 | 188.2 |
| Cincinnati, Ohio-Ky.-Ind. | 170.1 | 186.7 | — | — | — | — | — | — | 197.5 | 197.6 |
| Cleveland, Ohio | 169.0 | 184.4(11) | 186.6 | 186.6 | — | — | 190.3 | 190.7 | — | — |
| Dallas-Ft. Worth, Tex. | 167.7 | 183.8(11) | 186.7 | 186.7 | — | — | 189.3 | 189.7 | — | — |
| Denver-Boulder, Col.[3] | — | — | — | — | 195.1 | 195.7 | — | — | 198.5 | 199.5 |
| Detroit, Mich. | 168.8 | 184.4 | 185.6 | 185.8 | 188.4 | 187.9 | 190.2 | 189.8 | 192.3 | 192.1 |
| Honolulu, Ha. | 162.8 | 174.9 | 178.0 | 177.5 | — | — | 181.4 | 181.3 | — | — |
| Houston, Tex. | 177.3 | 192.7(10) | — | — | — | — | — | — | — | — |
| Kansas City, Mo.-Kan. | 166.5 | 182.7 | 183.8 | 184.4 | — | — | 188.9 | 188.6 | — | — |
| Los Angeles-Long Beach, Anaheim, Cal. | 168.0 | 184.4 | 186.5 | 186.8 | 187.4 | 187.1 | 189.6 | 188.9 | 191.5 | 191.2 |
| Miami, Fla. (11/77 = 100)[3] | — | — | — | — | 102.2 | 102.3 | — | — | 102.8 | 103.3 |
| Milwaukee, Wis. | 167.1 | 186.6(11) | — | — | 186.3 | 186.5 | — | — | 188.7 | 189.5 |
| Minneapolis-St. Paul, Minn.-Wis. | 170.9 | 187.0(10) | — | — | — | — | — | — | — | — |
| New York, N.Y.-Northeast N.J. | 176.3 | 188.8 | 190.8 | 190.8 | 192.2 | 191.9 | 193.5 | 192.8 | 194.6 | 193.7 |
| Northeast Pa. (Scranton) | 170.9 | 182.8(11) | — | — | 187.0 | 187.2 | — | — | 190.0 | 190.8 |
| Philadelphia, Pa.-N.J. | 172.4 | 186.9 | 188.2 | 188.7 | 189.6 | 189.7 | 190.8 | 191.5 | 191.7 | 192.6 |
| Pittsburgh, Pa. | 168.3 | 183.5(10) | — | — | — | — | — | — | — | — |
| Portland, Ore.-Wash. | — | 183.8 | — | — | 191.7 | 191.9 | — | — | 195.3 | 196.1 |
| St. Louis, Mo.-Ill. | 165.1 | 180.6 | — | — | — | — | — | — | 189.5 | 187.9 |
| San Diego, Cal. | 170.7 | 186.6 | — | — | 191.4 | 191.2 | — | — | 195.5 | 195.4 |
| San Francisco-Oakland, Cal. | 168.0 | 187.3 | 189.2 | 189.5 | — | — | 192.8 | 192.4 | — | — |
| Seattle-Everett, Wash. | 164.5 | 182.5(11) | — | — | 187.2 | 186.8 | — | — | 193.5 | 192.5 |
| Washington, D.C.-Md.-Va. | 171.2 | 188.1(11) | — | — | 191.5 | 191.4 | — | — | 194.7 | 196.7 |

(1) The area listed includes the entire Standard Metropolitan Statistical Area, except New York and Chicago which include the Standard Consolidated Area. (2) Latest month in 1977: usually Dec., except (10) = Oct. and (11) = Nov. (3) Anchorage, Denver and Miami are new additions to the special CPI city indexes.

## Annual Average Purchasing Power of the Dollar

Source: Bureau of Labor Statistics, U.S. Labor Department

Obtained by dividing the index for 1967 (100.00) by the index for the given period and expressing the result in dollars and cents. Beginning 1961, wholesale prices include data for Alaska and Hawaii; beginning 1964, consumer prices include them.

| Year | As measured by— Wholesale prices | As measured by— Consumer prices | Year | Wholesale prices | Consumer prices | Year | Wholesale prices | Consumer prices |
|---|---|---|---|---|---|---|---|---|
| 1940 | $2.469 | $2.381 | 1967 | $1.000 | $1.000 | 1973 | $ .744 | $ .752 |
| 1950 | 1.222 | 1.387 | 1968 | .976 | .960 | 1974 | .625 | .677 |
| 1955 | 1.139 | 1.247 | 1969 | .939 | .911 | 1975 | .572 | .620 |
| 1960 | 1.054 | 1.127 | 1970 | .906 | .860 | 1976 | .546 | .587 |
| 1965 | 1.035 | 1.058 | 1971 | .878 | .824 | 1977 | .515 | .551 |
| 1966 | 1.002 | 1.029 | 1972 | .840 | .799 | 1978, May | .481 | .517 |

## Consumer Price Index (CPI-U) by Region and City Size

Source: Bureau of Labor Statistics, U.S. Labor Department

(City sizes: A=1.25 million or more; B=385,000 to 1.25 million; C=75,000 to 385,000; D=75,000 or less.)

| April, 1978 (Dec. 1977 = 100) | All items | Food and beverages | Housing | Apparel, upkeep | Transportation | Medical care | Entertainment | Other goods and services |
|---|---|---|---|---|---|---|---|---|
| **Northeast** | | | | | | | | |
| Size A | 102.3 | 105.0 | 101.9 | 100.7 | 100.5 | 102.7 | 103.3 | 100.6 |
| Size B | 102.7 | 104.9 | 102.3 | 100.0 | 102.1 | 102.8 | 102.7 | 101.7 |
| Size C | 103.2 | 105.5 | 103.2 | 100.4 | 102.4 | 103.1 | 101.8 | 101.2 |
| Size D | 102.2 | 105.1 | 102.2 | 97.4 | 101.0 | 102.6 | 103.5 | 100.5 |
| **North Central** | | | | | | | | |
| Size A | 103.4 | 105.8 | 104.3 | 99.2 | 101.1 | 103.0 | 102.3 | 100.8 |
| Size B | 103.1 | 104.9 | 103.6 | 102.4 | 101.0 | 104.2 | 101.2 | 101.7 |
| Size C | 102.8 | 105.7 | 103.2 | 98.2 | 101.3 | 102.7 | 102.4 | 100.0 |
| Size D | 103.1 | 106.1 | 103.1 | 97.9 | 101.0 | 105.7 | 103.8 | 101.5 |
| **South** | | | | | | | | |
| Size A | 102.7 | 105.1 | 102.8 | 101.6 | 101.4 | 102.1 | 101.7 | 100.7 |
| Size B | 103.2 | 105.3 | 103.6 | 100.8 | 101.1 | 103.7 | 103.4 | 100.9 |
| Size C | 103.4 | 105.9 | 104.3 | 99.5 | 101.1 | 102.5 | 102.1 | 101.8 |
| Size D | 102.7 | 106.2 | 102.0 | 100.6 | 101.4 | 104.3 | 103.6 | 102.1 |
| **West** | | | | | | | | |
| Size A | 103.0 | 105.9 | 103.0 | 100.2 | 101.3 | 103.1 | 102.8 | 102.2 |
| Size B | 103.5 | 106.3 | 103.5 | 100.1 | 102.5 | 102.4 | 102.5 | 101. |
| Size C | 102.9 | 106.9 | 102.6 | 99.2 | 101.6 | 103.3 | 101.3 | 101.7 |
| Size D | 102.6 | 105.8 | 101.7 | 100.4 | 101.6 | 103.8 | 105.2 | 102.5 |

The Northeast region includes cities from Boston to Pittsburgh; the North Central, cities from Cleveland to Grand Island, Neb. and from Minneapolis to St. Louis and Cincinnati; the South, cities from Baltimore to Dallas; the West, cities from Alamogordo, N. Mex., to Butte, Mont., Anchorage, and Honolulu.

## Annual Percent Change in Productivity and Related Data, 1967-77

Source: Bureau of Labor Statistics, U.S. Labor Department

| Item | 1967 | 1968 | 1969 | 1970 | 1971 | 1972 | 1973 | 1974 | 1975 | 1976 | 1977 |
|---|---|---|---|---|---|---|---|---|---|---|---|
| **Private business sector:** | | | | | | | | | | | |
| Output per hour of all persons | 2.3 | 3.3 | 0.3 | 0.7 | 3.2 | 2.9 | 1.9 | 2.7 | 1.8 | 4.2 | 2.6 |
| Real compensation per hour | 2.7 | 3.3 | 1.5 | 1.1 | 2.2 | 2.3 | 1.8 | -1.4 | 0.5 | 3.1 | 2.3 |
| Unit labor cost | 3.3 | 4.1 | 6.6 | 6.4 | 3.2 | 2.7 | 6.2 | 12.4 | 7.7 | 4.7 | 6.1 |
| Unit nonlabor payments | 2.1 | 3.6 | 1.0 | 1.3 | 6.9 | 5.4 | 5.0 | 4.3 | 16.1 | 5.1 | 3.1 |
| Implicit price deflator | 2.9 | 3.9 | 4.7 | 4.7 | 4.4 | 3.6 | 5.8 | 9.8 | 10.3 | 4.8 | 5.1 |
| **Nonfarm business sector:** | | | | | | | | | | | |
| Output per hour of all persons | 1.9 | 3.2 | -0.2 | 0.2 | 2.9 | 3.0 | 1.7 | 2.8 | 1.6 | 4.1 | 2.2 |
| Real compensation per hour | 2.9 | 3.0 | 1.0 | 0.7 | 2.2 | 2.4 | 1.4 | -1.4 | 0.5 | 2.8 | 2.2 |
| Unit labor cost | 3.8 | 3.9 | 6.6 | 6.5 | 3.5 | 2.7 | 6.0 | 12.6 | 7.9 | 4.4 | 6.4 |
| Unit nonlabor payments | 2.3 | 4.0 | 0.4 | 1.7 | 6.8 | 4.0 | 0.3 | 5.9 | 17.8 | 6.5 | 3.5 |
| Implicit price deflator | 3.3 | 4.0 | 4.5 | 4.9 | 4.5 | 3.1 | 4.1 | 10.5 | 10.9 | 5.1 | 5.4 |
| **Manufacturing:** | | | | | | | | | | | |
| Output per hour of all persons | 0.3 | 3.6 | 1.2 | -0.4 | 5.6 | 5.2 | 2.9 | -5.5 | 3.1 | 6.8 | 2.2 |
| Real compensation per hour | 2.2 | 2.7 | 1.1 | 0.8 | 2.2 | 2.2 | 1.0 | 1.1 | 1.9 | 2.6 | 2.2 |
| Unit labor cost | 4.8 | 3.3 | 5.2 | 7.2 | 1.0 | 0.4 | 4.3 | 16.1 | 7.8 | 1.7 | 6.5 |
| Unit nonlabor payments | -2.4 | 3.9 | -4.4 | -3.2 | 9.0 | 2.5 | -1.0 | 0.7 | 20.7 | 10.9 | NA |
| Implicit price deflator | 2.5 | 3.5 | 2.3 | 4.2 | 3.1 | 1.0 | 2.8 | 11.5 | 11.0 | 4.1 | NA |

## Average Weekly Earnings of Production Workers[1]

Source: Bureau of Labor Statistics, U.S. Labor Department

| | Private nonagricultural workers | | | | | | Manufacturing workers | | | | | |
|---|---|---|---|---|---|---|---|---|---|---|---|---|
| | Gross average weekly earnings | | Spendable average weekly earnings[12] | | | | Gross average weeky earnings | | Spendable average weekly earnings[2] | | | |
| | | | Worker with no dependents | | Worker with 3 dependents | | | | Worker with no dependents | | Worker with 3 dependents | |
| Year and month | Current dollars | 1967 dollars | Current dollars | 1967 dollars | Current dollars | 1967 dollars | Current dollars | 1967 dollars | Current dollars | 1967 dollars | Current dollars | 1967 dollars |
| 1971 | 127.28 | 104.93 | 103.78 | 85.56 | 112.41 | 92.67 | 142.44 | 117.43 | 114.97 | 94.78 | 124.24 | 102.42 |
| 1973 | 145.43 | 109.26 | 117.54 | 88.31 | 127.41 | 95.73 | 165.65 | 124.46 | 132.00 | 99.17 | 142.90 | 107.36 |
| 1974 | 154.45 | 104.57 | 124.14 | 84.05 | 134.37 | 90.97 | 176.00 | 119.16 | 139.80 | 94.52 | 150.94 | 102.19 |
| 1975 | 163.89 | 101.67 | 132.74 | 82.34 | 145.93 | 90.53 | 189.51 | 117.56 | 150.71 | 93.49 | 165.33 | 102.56 |
| 1976 | 176.29 | 103.40 | 143.90 | 84.40 | 156.50 | 91.79 | 207.60 | 121.76 | 166.55 | 97.68 | 180.03 | 105.59 |
| 1977 | 189.53 | 104.42 | 155.58 | 85.72 | 170.34 | 93.85 | 226.89 | 125.01 | 182.37 | 100.48 | 198.55 | 109.39 |
| 1978 Jan. | 193.25 | 103.29 | 157.87 | 84.38 | 172.83 | 92.37 | 231.86 | 123.92 | 185.40 | 99.09 | 201.82 | 107.87 |
| Feb. | 195.61 | 103.83 | 159.57 | 84.70 | 174.64 | 92.70 | 235.22 | 124.85 | 187.71 | 99.63 | 204.34 | 108.46 |
| Mar. | 198.89 | 104.84 | 161.93 | 85.36 | 177.11 | 93.36 | 240.78 | 126.93 | 191.55 | 100.98 | 208.50 | 109.91 |
| April. | 201.96 | 105.52 | 164.14 | 85.76 | 179.41 | 93.74 | 242.00 | 126.44 | 192.39 | 100.52 | 209.42 | 109.41 |
| May[p] | 202.48 | 104.75 | 164.51 | 85.11 | 179.80 | 93.02 | 242.41 | 125.11 | 192.81 | 99.75 | 209.88 | 108.58 |
| June[p] | 205.46 | NA | 166.66 | NA | 182.03 | NA | 246.04 | NA | 195.17 | NA | 212.45 | NA |

(1) Data relate to production workers in mining and manufacturing; to construction workers in contract construction; and to nonsupervisory workers in transportation and public utilities; wholesale and retail trade; finance, insurance, and real estate; and services. (2) Spendable average weekly earnings are based on gross average weekly earnings less the estimated amount of the worker's Federal, social security, and income taxes. (p)—preliminary.

# Federal Individual Income Tax

Source: Internal Revenue Service, U.S. Treasury Department.

## Who Must File

Every individual under 65 years of age who resided in the United States and had a gross income of $2,950 or more during the year must file a federal income tax return. Anyone 65 or older on the last day of the tax year is not required to file a return unless he had gross income of $3,700 or more during the year. A married couple both 65 or older, need not file unless their gross income is $6,300 or more.

A taxpayer with gross income of less than $2,950 (or less than $3,700 if 65 or older) should file a return to claim the refund of any taxes withheld, even if he is listed as a dependent by another taxpayer.

## Forms to Use

A taxpayer may, at his election, use form 1040 or Form 1040A. However, those taxpayers who choose to itemize deductions must use the longer form 1040.

## Deductions

A taxpayer may either itemize deductions or choose the standard deduction. For single taxpayers the standard deduction is $2,200. For married taxpayers filing a joint return it is $3,200. For married taxpayers filing separate returns the deduction is $1,600 each.

## Dates for Filing Returns

For individuals using the calendar year, Apr. 15 is final date (unless it falls on a Saturday, Sunday, or a legal holiday) for filing income tax returns and for payment of any tax due, and the first quarterly installment of the estimated tax. Other installments of estimated tax to be paid June 15, Sept. 15, and Jan. 15.

Apr. 15 is final date for filing declaration of estimated tax. Amended declarations may be filed June 15, Sept. 15, and Jan. 15.

Instead of paying the 4th installment a final income return may be filed by Jan. 31. Farmers may file a final return by Mar. 1 to satisfy estimated tax requirements.

## Joint Return

A husband and wife may make a return jointly, even if one has no income personally. Their tax will be twice the tax imposed if the income were cut in half and taxed at the married filing separate rate.

One provision stipulates that if one spouse dies, the survivor may compute his tax using joint return rates for the first two taxable years following, provided he or she was also entitled to file a joint return the year of the death, and furnishes over half the cost of maintaining in his household a home for a dependent child or stepchild. If the taxpayer remarries before the end of the taxable year these privileges are lost but he is permitted to file a joint return with his new spouse. An individual legally separated or divorced is not considered married.

## Estimated Tax

If total tax exceeds withheld tax by at least $100, declarations of estimated tax are required from (1) single individuals, heads of a household or surviving spouses, or a married person entitled to file a joint return whose spouse does not receive wages, who expects a gross income over $20,00; (2) married individuals with over $10,000 where both spouses receive wages; (3) married individuals with over $5,000 not entitled to file a joint return; and (4) individuals whose gross income can reasonably be expected to include more than $500 from sources other than wages subject to withholdings.

## Exemptions

Personal exemption is $750.

Every individual has an exemption of $750, to be deducted from gross income. A husband and a wife are each entitled to a $750 exemption. A taxpayer 65 or over on the last day of the year gets another exemption of $750. A person blind on the last day of the year gets another exemption of $750.

Exemption for dependents, over one-half of whose total support comes from the taxpayer and for whom the other dependency tests have been met, is $750. This applies to a child, stepchild, or adopted child as well as certain other relatives with less than $750 gross income; also to a child, stepchild, or adopted child of the taxpayer who is under 19 at the end of the year or was a full-time student during 5 months of the year even if he makes $750 or more. A dependent can be a non-relative if a member of the taxpayer's household and living there all year. There is a special $35 tax credit per dependent for 1978 or 2% of the first $9,000 of taxable income, whichever is greater.

In 1978, taxpayers can use $35 for age and $35 for blindness in computing general tax credit. However, most taxpayers will not have to compute this credit because it is incorporated into the tax tables.

Taxpayer gets the exemption for his child who is a student regardless of the student's age or earnings, provided the taxpayer provides over half of the student's total support. If the student gets a scholarship, this is not counted as support.

## Child and Disabled Dependent Care

To qualify, a taxpayer must be employed and provide over one-half the cost of maintaining a household for a dependent child under 15, a disabled dependent of any age, or a disabled spouse.

Taxpayers may be allowed a credit of an amount equal to 20% of employment related expenses.

For further information consult your local IRS office or the instructional material attached to your return form.

## Life Insurance

Life insurance paid to survivors is not taxed as income. Interest on life insurance left with the insurance company and paid to survivors at intervals is taxable when available. Surviving spouse has an exclusion of the prorata amount of principal payable at death plus up to $1,000 per year of interest earned when life insurance proceeds are payable in installments.

Regular payments under the Railroad Retirement Act, and those received as social security, are exempt.

## Dividends

The first $100 in dividends can be excluded from income. If husband and wife both receive $100 on their joint return they can exclude $200.

The exclusion does not apply to dividends from tax-exempt corporations, mutual savings banks, building and loan associations, and several others.

Dividends paid in stock or in stock rights are generally exempt from tax, except when paid in place of preferred stock dividends of the current or preceding year, or when the stockholder has an option to take stock or property or when the stock distribution is disproportionate.

## Deductible Medical Expenses

Expenses for medical care, not compensated for by insurance or other payment for taxpayer, spouse, and dependents, in excess of 3% of adjusted gross income are deductible. There is no limit to the maximum amount of medical expenses that can be deducted.

Medical care includes diagnosis, treatment and prevention of disease or for the purpose of affecting any structure or function of the body, and amounts paid for insurance to reimburse for hospitalization, surgical fees and other medical expenses.

Only medicine and drugs in excess of 1% of adjusted gross income may be included in medical expenses.

One-half the cost of medical care insurance premiums up to $150 can be deducted without regard to the 3% limitation. The other half plus any excess over $150 is included with other medical expenses subject to the 3% limit.

Medical expenses for a decedent paid by his estate within one year after his death may be treated as expenses of the decedent taxpayer.

Medical and hospital benefits provided by the employer may be exempt from individual income tax.

Disability income payments are excludable only if the payee is totally and permanently disabled and under age 65 at The end of the tax year. Up to $5,200 can be excluded but must be reduced by income above certain limits.

## Deductions for Contributions

Deductions up to 50% of taxpayers' adjusted gross income may be taken for contribution to most publicly supported charitable organizations, including churches or associations of churches, tax-exempt educational institutions, tax-exempt hospitals, and medical research organizations associated with a hospital. The deduction is generally limited to 20% for such organizations as private nonoperating foundations, and certain organizations that do not qualify for the 50% limitation.

Taxpayers also are permitted to carry over for five years certain contributions, generally to publicly supported organizations, which exceed the 50% allowable deduction the year the contribution was made.

Also permissible is the deduction as a charitable contribution of unreimbursed amounts up to $50 a school month spent to maintain an elementary or high school student, other than a dependent or relative, in taxpayer's home. There must be a written agreement between you and a qualified organization.

## Deductions for Interest Paid

Interest paid by the taxpayer is deductible.

If personal property is bought under a contract providing for payment by installments, and in which carrying charges are stated but interest is not ascertainable, then subject to limitation payments are held to include interest equal to 6% on average unpaid balance.

However, the amount charged to a customer's revolving charge account is solely for the privilege of deferring payment and is interest.

## Prizes and Awards

All prizes and awards must be reported in gross income, except when received without action by the recipient. To be exempt, awards must be received primarily in recognition of religious, charitable, scientific, educational, artistic, literary, or civic achievement. (Nobel and Pulitzer prizes exempt.)

## Deductions for Employees

An employee may take the standard deduction and deduct as well the following if in connection with his employment: transportation, except commuting; automobile expense, including gas, oil, and depreciation; however, meals and lodging are deductible as traveling expense only if the employee is away from home overnight.

An outside salesman—a salesman who works fulltime outside the office, using the latter only for incidentals—may deduct both the standard deduction and all his business expenses.

An employee who is reimbursed and is required to account to his employer for his business expenses will not be required to report either the reimbursement or the expenses on his tax return. Any allowance to the employee in excess of his expenses must be included in gross income. If he claims a deduction for an excess of expenses over reimbursement he will have to report the reimbursement and claim actual expenses.

An employee who is not required to account to his employer must report on his return the total amounts of reimbursements and expenses for travel, transportation, entertainment, etc., that he incurs under a reimbursement arrangement with his employer.

The expense of moving to a new place of employmen. may be deducted under certain circumstances regardless of whether the taxpayer is a new or continuing employee, or whether he pays his own expenses or is reimbursed by his employer. Reimbursement must be reported as income.

## Tax Credit for the Elderly

Subject to certain rules or exclusions, taxpayers 65 or older may claim a credit which varies according to filing status. Taxpayers should read IRS instructions carefully for full details.

The credit is limited to 15% of $2,500 for single taxpayers; 15% of $2,500 for married taxpayers filing a joint return when only one taxpayer is 65 or older; 15% of $3,750 for married taxpayers both 65 or older filing a joint return; and 15% of $1,875 for a married taxpayer filing a separate return.

## Net Capital Losses

An individual taxpayer may deduct capital losses up to $3,000 against his ordinary income. However, it takes $2 of net long-term capital loss to get $1 of offset against other income. He may carry the rest over to subsequent years at the same rate, no legal limit on the number of years.

## Income Averaging

Individuals with large fluctuations in their annual income may be able to take advantage of averaging provisions available to taxpayers whose income for a particular year exceeds 120% of their average income for the prior 4 years, if the excess is more than $3,000.

## Returns with Itemized Deductions for 1976

| Size of adjusted gross income | | Total deductions | | Standard deduction | | Itemized deductions | | |
|---|---|---|---|---|---|---|---|---|
| | | No. of returns | Amount (thousands) | No. of returns | Amount (thousands) | No. of returns | %² | Amount (thousands) |
| Total, all returns | | 84,016,427 | $246,915,533 | 58,118,746 | $113,697,501 | 25,897,681 | 30.8 | $133,218,032 |
| $1.00 to | $1,000 | 4,224,685 | 7,188,316 | 4,199,714 | 7,098,370 | 24,971 | 0.6 | 89,945 |
| 1,000 to | 2,000 | 5,246,344 | 8,979,536 | 5,182,670 | 8,840,553 | 63,674 | 1.2 | 138,983 |
| 2,000 to | 3,000 | 5,024,730 | 8,765,126 | 4,949,731 | 8,581,609 | 74,999 | 1.5 | 183,517 |
| 3,000 to | 4,000 | 4,507,324 | 8,080,527 | 4,340,817 | 7,585,454 | 166,507 | 3.7 | 495,072 |
| 4,000 to | 5,000 | 4,329,610 | 8,061,207 | 4,061,508 | 7,204,340 | 268,102 | 6.2 | 856,867 |
| 5,000 to | 6,000 | 4,643,143 | 8,995,540 | 4,239,678 | 7,642,759 | 403,465 | 8.7 | 1,352,782 |
| 6,000 to | 7,000 | 4,274,809 | 8,437,195 | 3,786,478 | 6,870,639 | 488,331 | 11.4 | 1,566,556 |
| 7,000 to | 8,000 | 3,933,453 | 8,075,607 | 3,356,922 | 6,146,474 | 576,531 | 14.7 | 1,929,133 |
| 8,000 to | 9,000 | 3,677,635 | 7,764,743 | 3,028,647 | 5,591,374 | 648,988 | 17.6 | 2,173,369 |
| 9,000 to | 10,000 | 3,361,705 | 7,555,525 | 2,562,826 | 4,785,589 | 798,879 | 23.8 | 2,769,937 |

| Size of adjusted gross income | | Total deductions | | Standard deduction | | Itemized deductions | | |
|---|---|---|---|---|---|---|---|---|
| | | No. of returns | Amount (thousands) | No. of returns | Amount (thousands) | No. of returns | %[2] | Amount (thousands) |
| 10,000 to | 11,000 | 3,211,078 | 7,472,170 | 2,308,634 | 4,440,726 | 902,444 | 28.1 | 3,071,444 |
| 11,000 to | 12,000 | 2,919,802 | 7,083,721 | 2,002,063 | 3,937,342 | 917,739 | 31.4 | 3,146,380 |
| 12,000 to | 13,000 | 2,919,380 | 7,583,273 | 1,846,772 | 3,786,178 | 1,072,608 | 36.7 | 3,797,095 |
| 13,000 to | 14,000 | 2,758,160 | 7,567,027 | 1,675,629 | 3,591,108 | 1,082,531 | 39.2 | 3,975,919 |
| 14,000 to | 15,000 | 2,725,375 | 8,005,730 | 1,568,832 | 3,620,811 | 1,156,543 | 42.4 | 4,384,919 |
| 15,000 to | 20,000 | 11,182,362 | 39,096,238 | 5,522,778 | 14,430,451 | 5,659,584 | 50.6 | 24,665,787 |
| 20,000 to | 25,000 | 6,662,024 | 27,804,857 | 2,237,830 | 6,153,564 | 4,424,194 | 66.4 | 21,651,293 |
| 25,000 to | 30,000 | 3,610,979 | 17,865,222 | 734,954 | 2,024,084 | 2,876,025 | 79.7 | 15,841,137 |
| 30,000 to | 50,000 | 3,632,248 | 23,732,900 | 453,165 | 1,244,577 | 3,179,083 | 87.5 | 22,488,322 |
| 50,000 to | 100,000 | 945,253 | 11,103,818 | 53,843 | 147,161 | 891,410 | 94.3 | 10,956,658 |
| 100,000 to | 200,000 | 184,284 | 4,282,101 | 4,728 | 12,930 | 179,556 | 97.4 | 4,269,171 |
| 200,000 to | 500,000 | 36,495 | 2,042,524 | 476 | 1,272 | 36,019 | 98.4 | 2,041,252 |
| 500,000 to | 1,000,000 | 4,179 | 656,638 | 37 | 99 | 4,142 | 99.1 | 656,539 |
| 1,000,000 or | more | 1,370 | 715,991 | 14 | 36 | 1,356 | 99.0 | 715,955 |

| Size of adjusted gross income | Medical and dental | | | Taxes paid | | | Contributions | | |
|---|---|---|---|---|---|---|---|---|---|
| | No. of returns | Amount (thousands) | Avg. | No. of returns | Amount (thousands) | Avg. | No. of returns | Amount (thousands) | Avg. |
| Total, all returns | 19,042,687 | $12,154,750 | $638 | 25,817,344 | $49,505,456 | $1,918 | 24,404,446 | $16,710,718 | $685 |
| $0 to $1,000 | 15,183 | 16,651 | 1,097 | 24,943 | 49,908 | 2,001 | 12,996 | 1,659 | 128 |
| (thousands) | | | | | | | | | |
| $1 to 2 | 25,969 | 25,950 | 999 | 51,184 | 35,172 | 687 | 34,670 | 15,821 | 456 |
| 2 to 3 | 44,245 | 52,433 | 1,185 | 71,735 | 43,302 | 604 | 48,705 | 15,347 | 315 |
| 3 to 4 | 145,914 | 150,107 | 1,029 | 162,574 | 123,131 | 757 | 126,480 | 50,099 | 396 |
| 4 to 5 | 235,304 | 259,376 | 1,102 | 258,623 | 204,213 | 790 | 218,738 | 100,848 | 461 |
| 5 to 6 | 344,257 | 497,597 | 1,445 | 384,474 | 298,257 | 776 | 327,084 | 140,003 | 428 |
| 6 to 7 | 423,667 | 365,286 | 862 | 488,008 | 447,847 | 918 | 444,748 | 174,326 | 392 |
| 7 to 8 | 513,862 | 601,353 | 1,170 | 574,801 | 500,041 | 870 | 521,741 | 236,530 | 453 |
| 8 to 9 | 548,800 | 497,420 | 906 | 645,962 | 583,446 | 903 | 566,737 | 222,688 | 393 |
| 9 to 10 | 659,968 | 591,489 | 896 | 797,225 | 763,414 | 958 | 737,354 | 325,254 | 441 |
| 10 to 11 | 743,270 | 599,976 | 807 | 899,490 | 903,647 | 1,005 | 819,266 | 336,386 | 411 |
| 11 to 12 | 733,746 | 480,511 | 655 | 917,739 | 969,426 | 1,056 | 830,717 | 330,268 | 398 |
| 12 to 13 | 844,766 | 542,917 | 643 | 1,069,843 | 1,171,002 | 1,095 | 988,226 | 410,223 | 415 |
| 13 to 14 | 836,275 | 509,135 | 609 | 1,080,855 | 1,278,051 | 1,182 | 1,002,584 | 422,520 | 421 |
| 14 to 15 | 862,148 | 501,728 | 582 | 1,153,974 | 1,459,932 | 1,265 | 1,086,759 | 457,126 | 421 |
| 15 to 20 | 4,103,978 | 2,403,817 | 586 | 5,651,019 | 8,493,920 | 1,503 | 5,358,373 | 2,527,823 | 472 |
| 20 to 25 | 3,093,283 | 1,505,446 | 487 | 4,420,449 | 8,260,288 | 1,869 | 4,272,512 | 2,317,353 | 542 |
| 25 to 30 | 1,982,652 | 875,447 | 442 | 2,876,017 | 6,506,305 | 2,262 | 2,812,981 | 1,816,828 | 646 |
| 30 to 50 | 2,200,315 | 1,151,161 | 523 | 3,177,482 | 9,691,802 | 3,050 | 3,108,527 | 2,919,476 | 939 |
| 50 to 100 | 564,867 | 395,254 | 700 | 890,141 | 4,791,401 | 5,383 | 869,255 | 1,751,487 | 2,015 |
| 100 to 200 | 97,569 | 93,521 | 959 | 179,361 | 1,789,111 | 9,975 | 175,383 | 905,762 | 5,164 |
| 200 to 500 | 19,615 | 33,589 | 1,712 | 35,950 | 752,088 | 20,920 | 35,197 | 611,713 | 17,379 |
| 500 to 1,000 | 2,326 | 3,796 | 1,632 | 4,139 | 207,956 | 50,243 | 4,070 | 255,397 | 62,751 |
| 1,000 or more | 708 | 790 | 1,116 | 1,356 | 181,797 | 134,069 | 1,343 | 365,782 | 272,362 |

| Size of adjusted gross income | Interest paid | | | Miscellaneous deductions | | | Total tax as % of taxable income |
|---|---|---|---|---|---|---|---|
| | No. of returns | Amount (thousands) | Avg. | No. of returns | Amount (thousands) | Avg. | |
| Total, all returns | 23,323,376 | $43,058,264 | $1,846 | 21,752,290 | $11,788,844 | $542 | 21.2 |
| $0 to $1,000 | 13,667 | 18,370 | 1,344 | 10,534 | 3,356 | 319 | [1] |
| (thousands) | | | | | | | |
| $1 to $2 | 27,355 | 47,076 | 1,721 | 31,974 | 14,964 | 468 | 10.5 |
| 2 to 3 | 32,153 | 48,667 | 1,514 | 34,773 | 23,768 | 684 | 6.5 |
| 3 to 4 | 110,424 | 143,674 | 1,301 | 100,552 | 28,062 | 279 | 11.2 |
| 4 to 5 | 180,187 | 234,507 | 1,301 | 164,885 | 57,923 | 351 | 13.0 |
| 5 to 6 | 272,954 | 356,464 | 1,306 | 286,909 | 60,461 | 211 | 13.4 |
| 6 to 7 | 398,875 | 470,660 | 1,180 | 373,539 | 108,439 | 290 | 13.3 |
| 7 to 8 | 438,865 | 463,275 | 1,056 | 450,757 | 127,933 | 284 | 14.0 |
| 8 to 9 | 531,438 | 633,819 | 1,193 | 503,025 | 235,996 | 469 | 14.7 |
| 9 to 10 | 679,479 | 861,660 | 1,268 | 617,015 | 228,120 | 370 | 15.2 |
| 10 to 11 | 778,456 | 967,709 | 1,243 | 742,899 | 263,726 | 355 | 15.4 |
| 11 to 12 | 824,958 | 1,076,540 | 1,305 | 760,416 | 289,634 | 381 | 15.8 |
| 12 to 13 | 979,184 | 1,338,491 | 1,367 | 898,229 | 334,462 | 372 | 16.0 |
| 13 to 14 | 988,220 | 1,434,315 | 1,451 | 917,875 | 331,899 | 362 | 16.5 |
| 14 to 15 | 1,058,618 | 1,562,383 | 1,476 | 1,000,532 | 403,751 | 404 | 16.7 |
| 15 to 20 | 5,358,686 | 9,057,522 | 1,690 | 4,951,719 | 2,182,706 | 441 | 17.6 |
| 20 to 25 | 4,186,317 | 7,686,374 | 1,836 | 3,827,839 | 1,881,831 | 492 | 19.2 |
| 25 to 30 | 2,674,349 | 5,286,978 | 1,977 | 2,506,251 | 1,355,580 | 541 | 20.9 |
| 30 to 50 | 2,868,029 | 6,786,034 | 2,366 | 2,659,459 | 1,939,850 | 729 | 24.4 |
| 50 to 100 | 743,358 | 2,939,192 | 3,954 | 725,440 | 1,079,324 | 1,488 | 33.6 |
| 100 to 200 | 145,272 | 1,014,905 | 6,986 | 150,762 | 465,872 | 3,090 | 43.9 |
| 200 to 500 | 28,219 | 416,685 | 14,766 | 31,899 | 227,177 | 7,122 | 53.6 |
| 500 to 1,000 | 3,236 | 115,147 | 35,583 | 3,772 | 74,243 | 19,683 | 62.2 |
| 1,000 or more | 1,077 | 97,819 | 90,825 | 1,245 | 69,767 | 56,038 | 67.9 |

(1) Estimate not shown because sample base is too small. (2) Percent of returns in each income category which are itemized.

## Individual Income Tax Returns for 1976

Source: Internal Revenue Service, U.S. Treasury Department

| Size of adjusted gross income | All returns | | | | Taxable returns | | |
|---|---|---|---|---|---|---|---|
| | Returns | | Adjusted gross income less deficit | | Returns | | Adjusted gross income less deficit |
| | Number | Percent of total | Amount ($000) | Average (dollars) | Number | Percent of total | Amount ($000) |
| Total. . . . . . . . . . . . . | 84,536,143 | 100.0 | 1,053,592,868 | 12,463 | 64,430,958 | 100.0 | 1,003,856,984 |
| No adjusted gross income . . . | 519,716 | 0.6 | −5,840,757 | −11,238 | 5,925 | (1) | −309,442 |
| $1 under $1,000. . . . . . . . | 4,224,685 | 5.0 | 2,410,282 | 571 | (1) | (1) | (1) |
| $1,000 under $2,000 . . . . . | 5,246,344 | 6.2 | 7,758,972 | 1,479 | 64,904 | 0.1 | 94,622 |
| $2,000 under $3,000 . . . . . | 5,024,730 | 5.9 | 12,556,851 | 2,499 | 1,110,995 | 1.7 | 3,109,186 |
| $3,000 under $4,000 . . . . . | 4,507,324 | 5.3 | 15,803,066 | 3,506 | 2,827,226 | 4.4 | 9,954,012 |
| $4,000 under $5,000 . . . . . | 4,329,610 | 5.1 | 19,530,138 | 4,511 | 2,795,997 | 4.3 | 12,622,172 |
| $5,000 under $6,000 . . . . . | 4,643,143 | 5.5 | 25,440,128 | 5,479 | 3,343,587 | 5.2 | 18,349,084 |
| $6,000 under $7,000 . . . . . | 4,274,809 | 5.1 | 27,745,893 | 6,491 | 3,523,040 | 5.5 | 22,914,834 |
| $7,000 under $8,000 . . . . . | 3,933,453 | 4.7 | 29,489,850 | 7,497 | 3,588,216 | 5.6 | 26,932,118 |
| $8,000 under $9,000 . . . . . | 3,677,635 | 4.4 | 31,234,812 | 8,493 | 3,483,073 | 5.4 | 29,580,751 |
| $9,000 under $10,000 . . . . | 3,361,705 | 4.0 | 31,883,099 | 9,484 | 3,251,700 | 5.0 | 30,840,713 |
| $10,000 under $11,000. . . . | 3,211,078 | 3.8 | 33,696,541 | 10,494 | 3,129,637 | 4.9 | 32,842,249 |
| $11,000 under $12,000. . . . | 2,919,802 | 3.5 | 33,561,479 | 11,494 | 2,872,639 | 4.5 | 33,016,670 |
| $12,000 under $13,000. . . . | 2,919,380 | 3.5 | 36,482,493 | 12,497 | 2,881,503 | 4.5 | 36,011,246 |
| $13,000 under $14,000. . . . | 2,758,160 | 3.3 | 37,210,802 | 13,491 | 2,726,172 | 4.2 | 36,780,713 |
| $14,000 under $15,000. . . . | 2,725,375 | 3.2 | 39,524,354 | 14,502 | 2,703,949 | 4.2 | 39,215,147 |
| $15,000 under $20,000. . . . | 11,182,362 | 13.2 | 193,943,679 | 17,344 | 11,113,620 | 17.2 | 192,764,008 |
| $20,000 under $25,000. . . . | 6,662,024 | 7.9 | 148,182,796 | 22,243 | 6,632,181 | 10.3 | 147,529,056 |
| $25,000 under $30,000. . . . | 3,610,979 | 4.3 | 98,282,796 | 27,218 | 3,594,334 | 5.6 | 97,820,248 |
| $30,000 under $50,000. . . . | 3,632,248 | 4.3 | 132,554,397 | 36,494 | 3,613,394 | 5.6 | 131,888,295 |
| $50,000 under $100,000. . . | 945,253 | 1.1 | 62,193,913 | 65,796 | 942,654 | 1.5 | 62,030,262 |
| $100,000 under $200,000 . . | 184,284 | 0.2 | 24,043,771 | 130,471 | 183,845 | 0.3 | 23,986,144 |
| $200,000 under $500,000 . . | 36,495 | (1) | 10,206,043 | 279,656 | 36,444 | 0.1 | 10,191,588 |
| $500,000 under $1,000,000 . . | 4,179 | (1) | 2,781,096 | 665,493 | 4,174 | (1) | 2,777,679 |
| $1,000,000 or more. . . . . . | 1,370 | (1) | 2,916,373 | 2,128,739 | 1,369 | (1) | 2,915,354 |

| Size of adjusted gross income | Taxable income | Income tax after credits | | Total income tax | | |
|---|---|---|---|---|---|---|
| | Amount ($000) | Number of returns | Amount ($000) | Amount ($000) | Percent of adjusted gross income | Average (dollars) |
| Total. . . . . . . . . . . . . . . . | 669,165,218 | 64,408,856 | 140,919,120 | 141,886,352 | 14.1 | 2,202 |
| No adjusted gross income. . . . . . | — | (1) | (1) | 30,429 | — | 5,136 |
| $1 under $1,000 . . . . . . . . . . | — | — | — | (1) | (1) | (1) |
| $1,000 under $2,000 . . . . . . . . | 42,809 | 64,751 | 3,871 | 4,500 | 4.8 | 69 |
| $2,000 under $3,000 . . . . . . . . | 508,118 | 1,110,767 | 32,996 | 33,264 | 1.1 | 30 |
| $3,000 under $4,000 . . . . . . . . | 2,930,776 | 2,827,201 | 327,622 | 328,081 | 3.3 | 116 |
| $4,000 under $5,000 . . . . . . . . | 5,196,102 | 2,795,873 | 676,219 | 677,163 | 5.4 | 242 |
| $5,000 under $6,000 . . . . . . . . | 8,743,170 | 3,343,250 | 1,173,913 | 1,174,773 | 6.4 | 351 |
| $6,000 under $7,000 . . . . . . . . | 11,652,372 | 3,522,418 | 1,545,751 | 1,546,578 | 6.7 | 439 |
| $7,000 under $8,000 . . . . . . . . | 14,354,492 | 3,587,920 | 2,010,273 | 2,011,413 | 7.5 | 561 |
| $8,000 under $9,000 . . . . . . . . | 16,729,602 | 3,482,812 | 2,462,538 | 2,462,864 | 8.3 | 707 |
| $9,000 under $10,000 . . . . . . . | 17,945,004 | 3,250,341 | 2,718,395 | 2,720,240 | 8.8 | 837 |
| $10,000 under $11,000 . . . . . . . | 19,711,815 | 3,127,751 | 3,037,026 | 3,038,868 | 9.3 | 971 |
| $11,000 under $12,000 . . . . . . . | 20,354,890 | 2,872,289 | 3,218,050 | 3,220,920 | 9.8 | 1,121 |
| $12,000 under $13,000 . . . . . . . | 22,498,657 | 2,881,191 | 3,598,797 | 3,599,380 | 10.0 | 1,249 |
| $13,000 under $14,000 . . . . . . . | 23,507,741 | 2,725,674 | 3,868,123 | 3,876,471 | 10.5 | 1,422 |
| $14,000 under $15,000 . . . . . . . | 25,288,492 | 2,702,594 | 4,221,209 | 4,222,280 | 10.8 | 1,562 |
| $15,000 under $20,000 . . . . . . . | 127,293,652 | 11,112,279 | 22,429,813 | 22,455,380 | 11.6 | 2,021 |
| $20,000 under $25,000 . . . . . . . | 102,845,093 | 6,631,352 | 19,753,961 | 19,772,110 | 13.4 | 2,981 |
| $25,000 under $30,000 . . . . . . . | 70,702,407 | 3,593,055 | 14,740,760 | 14,761,053 | 15.1 | 4,107 |
| $30,000 under $50,000 . . . . . . . | 98,850,779 | 3,611,457 | 24,011,812 | 24,116,669 | 18.3 | 6,674 |
| $50,000 under $100,000. . . . . . . | 48,365,600 | 941,009 | 16,032,130 | 16,238,674 | 26.2 | 17,227 |
| $100,000 under $200,000 . . . . . . | 19,249,964 | 183,138 | 8,274,933 | 8,457,343 | 35.3 | 46,003 |
| $200,000 under $500,000 . . . . . . | 8,078,165 | 36,231 | 4,162,163 | 4,326,924 | 42.5 | 118,728 |
| $500,000 under $1,000,000. . . . . . | 2,118,677 | 4,139 | 1,236,489 | 1,318,596 | 47.5 | 315,907 |
| $1,000,000 or more . . . . . . . . . | 2,196,841 | 1,353 | 1,382,191 | 1,491,311 | 51.2 | 1,089,343 |

(1) Less than 0.05 per cent.

# Social Security Programs

Source: Social Security Administration, U.S. Department of Health, Education, and Welfare

## Old-Age, Survivors, and Disability Insurance; Medicare; Supplemental Security Income

### Old-Age, Survivors, and Disability Insurance

Old-age, survivors, and disability insurance covers almost all jobs in which people work for wages or salaries, as well as most work of self-employed persons, whether in a city job, or in business, or on a farm.

Old-age, survivors, and disability insurance is paid for by a tax on earnings (for 1978 up to $17,700 and for 1979 up to $22,900; the taxable earnings base is now subject to adjustment when cost-of-living benefit increases have been made). The employed worker and his employer share the tax equally (cash tips count as covered wages if they amount to $20 or more from one place of employment. The worker reports them to his employer, who includes them in his social security tax reports, but only the worker pays contributions on the amount of the tips).

The employer deducts the tax each payday and sends it, with an equal amount as his own share, to the District Director of Internal Revenue. The collected taxes are deposited in the Federal Old-Age and Survivors Insurance Trust Fund and the Federal Disability Insurance Trust Fund; they can be used only to pay benefits, the cost of rehabilitation services, and administrative expenses.

### H.E.W. Reorganized

Under a March 1977 reorganization of the Department of Health, Education, and Welfare, the federal-state assistance program of aid to families with dependent children became the responsibility of the Social Security Administration. The reorganization placed the Medicare program under the newly created Health Care Financing Administration, which also now administers Medicaid, the federal-state medical assistance program. The Social Security Administration continues to provide services, such as those relating to contributions and premiums and maintenance of beneficiary records, for the Medicare program.

In Medicare, following the required annual review of hospital costs under the program, increases were made in the hospital insurance deductible amount (what the patient must pay for hospital services before reimbursement can begin) and in the cost-sharing for days above the number specified in the law.

The Commissioner of Social Security is James B. Cardwell. There are 632 district offices with 682 branch offices, and 30 teleservice centers where the public may obtain information about benefit rights.

### Benefit Increase, June 1978

Social Security checks delivered to beneficiaries in the first week of July 1978 reflected the fourth automatic cost-of-living increase in cash benefits under legislation enacted in 1972 and 1973. The 6.5-percent increase, which became effective in June, applied to benefits for all persons on the social security benefit rolls at the end of May.

Automatic increases are initiated whenever the Consumer Price Index (CPI) of the Bureau of Labor Statistics for the first calendar quarter of a year exceeds by at least 3 percent the CPI for the base quarter, which is either the first calendar quarter of the preceding year or the quarter in which an increase was legislated by Congress. In this case, the base quarter was the first quarter of 1977. The size of the benefit increase is determined by the actual percentage rise of the CPI during the quarters measured.

As a result of the general benefit-rate increase, the average monthly benefit for retired workers amounted to $287.86 for men (up $17.64) and $227.17 for women ($13.94 more). The average amount for disabled workers rose to $311.16 for men and $230.29 for women—increases of $19.16 and $14.16, respectively. The average benefit increase for entitled dependents ranged from $5.12 for children of disabled workers to $8.07 for wives and husbands of retired workers. Among survivors of decreased workers, average benefit increases were highest for nondisabled widows and widowers ($14.80) and lowest for disabled widows and widowers ($10.21).

Social security benefits are based on a worker's primary insurance amount (PIA), which is related by law to the average monthly earnings (AME) on which social security contributions have been paid. The full PIA is payable to a retired worker who becomes entitled to benefits at age 65 and to an entitled disabled worker at any age. Spouses and children of retired or disabled workers and survivors of deceased workers receive set proportions of the PIA subject to a family maximum amount. The PIA is calculated by applying varying percentages to succeeding parts of the AME. Whenever a cost-of-living benefit increase is implemented, these percentages are changed to reflect the percentage increase in benefits.

### Medicare

Under Medicare, protection against the costs of hospital care is provided for social security and railroad retirement beneficiaries aged 65 and over (beginning July 1966) and, effective July 1973, for persons entitled for 24 months to receive a social security disability benefit, certain persons with chronic kidney disease and their dependents, and, on a voluntary basis with payment of a special premium, persons aged 65 and over not otherwise eligible for hospital benefits; all those eligible for hospital benefits may enroll for medical benefits and pay a monthly premium and so may persons aged 65 and over who are not eligible for hospital benefits.

Persons eligible for both hospital and medical insurance or for medical insurance only may choose to have their covered services provided through a Health Maintenance Organization (a prepaid group health or other capitation plan that meets prescribed standards).

**Hospital insurance.**—In the 11th year of operation (July 1976-June 1977) about $58.7 billion was withdrawn from the hospital insurance trust fund for hospital and related benefits. About 25,316,000 persons were enrolled under the program as of July 1976—2,392,000 of them disabled beneficiaries under age 65.

The hospital insurance program pays the cost of covered services for hospital and posthospital care as follows:

- Up to 90 days of hospital care during a benefit period (spell of illness) starting the first day that care as a bed-patient is received in a hospital or skilled-nursing facility and ending when the individual has not been a bed-patient for 60 consecutive days. For the first 60 days, the hospital insurance pays for all but the first $144 of expenses; for the 61st day to 90th day, the program pays all but $36 a day for covered services. In addition, each person has a 60-day lifetime reserve that can be used after the 90 days of hospital care in a benefit period are exhausted, and all but $72 a day of expenses during the reserve days are paid. Once used, the reserve days are not replaced. (Payment for care in a mental hospital is limited to 190 days.)
- Up to 100 days' care in a skilled-nursing facility (skilled-nursing home) in each benefit period. Hospital insurance pays for all covered services for the first 20 days and all but $18 daily for the next 80 days. At least 3 days' hospital stay must precede these services, and the skilled-nursing facility must be entered within 14 days after leaving the hospital. (The 1972 law permits more than 14 days in certain circumstances.)
- Up to 100 visits by nurses or other health workers (not doctors) from a home health agency in the 365 days after release from a hospital or extended-care facility.

Money to pay these benefits comes from special contributions paid by workers, their employers, and the self-employed.

**Medical insurance.** Aged persons can receive benefits under this supplementary program only if they sign up for them and agree to a monthly premium ($8.20 to July 1979). The federal government pays the rest of the cost. In December of each year the Secretary of Health, Education, and Welfare announces the premium payable starting in July of the following year. The premiums are to be increased only when there is a general benefit increase in the year and it will rise no more than the percent by which the cash benefits have been increased since the last premium increase.

About 140 million bills were reimbursed under the medical insurance program from Jan. 1976 to July 1977 for a total of $7.5 billion. As of July 1976, 24,614,400 persons were enrolled — 2,168,500 of them disabled persons under age 65.

The medical insurance program pays 80% of the reasonable charges (after the first $60 in each calendar year) for the following services:

- Physicians' and surgeons' services, whether in the doctor's office, a clinic, or hospital or at home (but physician's charges for X-ray or clinical laboratory services for hospital bed-patients are paid in full and without meeting the deductible).
- Other medical and health services, such as diagnostic tests, surgical dressings and splints, and rental or purchase of medical equipment. Services of a physical therapist in independent practice, furnished in his office or the patient's home. A hospital or extended-care facility may provide covered outpatient physical therapy services under the medical insurance program to its patients who have exhausted their hospital insurance coverage.
- Physical therapy services furnished under the supervision of a practicing hospital, clinic, skilled nursing facility, or agency.
- Certain services by podiatrists.
- All outpatient services of a participating hospital (including diagnostic tests).
- Outpatient speech pathology services, under the same requirements as physical therapy.
- Services of licensed chiropractors who meet uniform standards, but only for treatment by means of manual manipulation of the spine and treatment of subluxation of the spine demonstrated by X-ray.
- Supplies related to colostomies are considered prosthetic devices and payable under the program.
- Home health services even without a hospital stay (up to 100 visits a year) are paid up to 100%.

To get medical insurance protection, persons approaching age 65 may enroll in the 7-month period that includes 3 months before the 65th birthday, the month of the birthday, and 3 months after the birthday, but if they wish coverage to begin in the month they reach 65 they must enroll in the 3 months **before** their birthday. Persons not enrolling within their first enrollment period may enroll later, during the first 3 months of each year but their premium is 10% higher for each 12-month period elapsed since they first could have enrolled.

The monthly premium is deducted from the cash benefit for persons receiving social security, railroad retirement, or civil service retirement benefits. Income from the medical premiums and the federal matching payments are put in a Supplementary Medical Insurance Trust Fund, from which benefits and administrative expenses are paid.

**Medicare card.** Persons qualifying for hospital insurance under social security receive a health insurance card similar to cards now used by Blue Cross and other health agencies. The card indicates whether the individual has taken out medical insurance protection. It is to be shown to the hospital, skilled nursing facility, home health agency, doctor, or whoever provides the covered services.

Payments are made only in the 50 states, Puerto Rico, the Virgin Islands, Guam, and American Samoa, except that hospital services may be provided in border areas immediately outside the U.S. if comparable services are not accessible in the U.S. for a beneficiary who becomes ill or is injured in the U.S.

### Amount of Work Required

To qualify for benefits for himself and his family, the worker must have been in covered employment long enough to become insured. Just how long depends on his date of birth (or if he dies or becomes disabled, the date of his death or disability).

A person is fully covered if he has one quarter of coverage for every year after 1950 (or year he reaches age 21) up to but not including the year in which he reaches age 62 or dies.

Certain provisions in the law permit special monthly payments under the social security program to persons aged 72 and over who are not eligible for regular social security benefits since they had little or no opportunity to earn social security work credits during their working lifetime.

To get disability benefits, the worker must also have credit for 5 out of 10 years before he becomes disabled. Persons disabled before age 31 can qualify with a briefer period of coverage.

### Work Years Required

The following table shows the number of work years required to be fully insured for old-age or survivors benefits, according to the year worker reaches retirement age or dies.

**Work credit for retirement benefits**

| If you reach 62 in | Years you need | If you reach 62 in | Years you need |
|---|---|---|---|
| 1974 | 6* | 1979 | 7 |
| 1975 | 6 | 1981 | 7½ |
| 1976 | 6¼ | 1983 | 8 |
| 1977 | 6½ | 1987 | 9 |
| 1978 | 6¾ | 1991 or later. | 10 |

*For 1974 a woman needs only 5¾ years.

**Deceased's work credit for survivor's benefits**

| Born after 1929, die at | Born before 1930, die before age 62 | Years needed |
|---|---|---|
| 28 or younger | | 1½ |
| 30 | | 2 |
| 32 | | 2½ |
| 34 | | 3 |
| 36 | | 3½ |
| 38 | | 4 |
| 40 | | 4½ |
| 42 | | 5 |
| 44 | 1973 | 5½ |
| 45 | 1974 | 5¾ |
| 46 | 1975 | 6 |
| 48 | 1977 | 6½ |
| 50 | 1979 | 7 |
| 52 | 1981 | 7½ |
| 54 | 1983 | 8 |
| 56 | 1985 | 8½ |
| 58 | 1987 | 9 |
| 60 | 1989 | 9½ |
| 62 or older | 1991 or later | 10 |

**Tax-rate schedule under old and new law**
[Percent of covered earnings]

| Year | Total Old law | Total New law | OASDI Old law | OASDI New law | HI Old law | HI New law |
|---|---|---|---|---|---|---|
| | Employees and employers, each | | | | | |
| 1977 | 5.85 | 5.85 | 4.95 | 4.95 | 0.90 | 0.90 |
| 1978 | 6.05 | 6.05 | 4.95 | 5.05 | 1.10 | 1.00 |
| 1979-80 | 6.05 | 6.13 | 4.95 | 5.08 | 1.10 | 1.05 |
| 1981 | 6.30 | 6.65 | 4.95 | 5.35 | 1.35 | 1.30 |
| 1982-84 | 6.30 | 6.70 | 4.95 | 5.40 | 1.35 | 1.30 |
| 1985 | 6.30 | 7.05 | 4.95 | 5.70 | 1.35 | 1.35 |
| 1986-89 | 6.45 | 7.15 | 4.95 | 5.70 | 1.50 | 1.45 |
| 1990-2010 | 6.45 | 7.65 | 4.95 | 6.20 | 1.50 | 1.45 |
| 2011 and after. | 7.45 | 7.65 | 5.95 | 6.20 | 1.50 | 1.45 |
| | Self-employed | | | | | |
| 1977 | 7.90 | 7.90 | 7.00 | 7.00 | 0.90 | 0.90 |
| 1978 | 8.10 | 8.10 | 7.00 | 7.10 | 1.10 | 1.00 |
| 1979-80 | 8.10 | 8.10 | 7.00 | 7.05 | 1.10 | 1.05 |
| 1981 | 8.35 | 9.30 | 7.00 | 8.00 | 1.35 | 1.30 |
| 1982-84 | 8.35 | 9.35 | 7.00 | 8.05 | 1.35 | 1.30 |
| 1985 | 8.35 | 9.90 | 7.00 | 8.55 | 1.35 | 1.35 |
| 1986-89 | 8.50 | 10.00 | 7.00 | 8.55 | 1.50 | 1.45 |
| 1990-2010 | 8.50 | 10.75 | 7.00 | 9.30 | 1.50 | 1.45 |
| 2011 and after. | 8.50 | 10.75 | 7.00 | 9..30 | 1.50 | 1.45 |

### What Aged Workers Get

When a person has enough work in covered employment and reaches retirement age (65 for full benefit, 62 for reduced benefit), he may retire and get monthly old-age benefits. If he continues to work and has earnings of more than $4,500 in 1979, $1 in benefits will be withheld for every $2 above $4,500. The amount that can be earned in a month without loss of any benefits is $270. The annual exempt amount and the monthly test are raised automatically or according to the rise in general earnings levels. The eligible worker who is 72 receives the full amount of benefit regardless of earnings.

A worker's benefit will be raised by 1% for each year after 1970 for which the worker between 65 and 72 did not receive benefits because of earnings from work. No increases are to be paid to the worker's dependents or survivors under this provision.

A special minimum benefit is payable to persons who worked 20 or more years under social security as an alternative to the regular minimum ($114.30 in June 1977) if a higher amount results. The highest minimum under this provision would be $230 a month in 1979 for a person with 30 or more years of coverage.

When a person receives old-age benefits, payments can also be made to certain of his dependents, including a wife 62 or over, dependent children under 18 or who became totally disabled before age 22 or who are full-time students not yet aged 22, a wife (regardless of age) if caring for an eligible child, and a dependent husband 62 or over.

The special benefit for persons aged 72 or over who do not meet the regular coverage requirements is $78.40 a month ($117.60 for a couple if both members are eligible). Like the monthly benefits, these payments are now subject to cost-of-living increases. The special payment is not made to persons on the public assistance or supplemental security income rolls.

Social Security benefits are not subject to income taxes.

A woman worker is eligible for a full old-age benefit at age 65, but she may retire at 62 and get 80% of her full benefit for the rest of her life; the nearer she is to 65 when she begins collecting her benefit, the larger it will be. (Benefits for men retiring before 65 are reduced at the same rate as benefits for women retiring before 65.)

A child can get benefits based on his mother's earnings on the same conditions as those entitling a child to benefits based on his father's earnings record.

| OASDI | June 1978 | May 1978 | June 1977 |
|---|---|---|---|
| **Monthly beneficiaries, total (in thousands) . . . . . . . . . . .** | **34,068** | **34,202** | **33,333** |
| Aged 65 and over, total . . . . . | 22,070 | 22,035 | 21,447 |
| Retired workers . . . . . . . . . | 16,055 | 16,025 | 15,549 |
| Survivors and dependents . . . | 5,870 | 5,864 | 5,725 |
| Special age-72 beneficiaries. . | 145 | 147 | 173 |
| Under age 65, total . . . . . . . . | 11,998 | 12,167 | 11,886 |
| Retired workers . . . . . . . . . | 1,869 | 1,896 | 1,831 |
| Disabled workers . . . . . . . . | 2,858 | 2,860 | 2,755 |
| Survivors and dependents . . . | 7,271 | 7,411 | 7,300 |
| **Total monthly benefits (in millions)¹ . . . . . . . . . . . .** | **$7,707** | **$7,245** | **$6,933** |

### Benefits for Worker's Spouse

The wife of a man who is getting social security retirement or disability payments may become entitled to wife's insurance benefits in a reduced amount when she reaches 62, or she may wait until she reaches 65 and get the entire amount of the wife's benefit, which is one-half of the husband's benefit. Benefits are also payable to the divorced wife of an insured worker if she was married to him for at least 20 years and he was contributing to or was ordered by a court to contribute to her support.

If a woman worker entitled to an old-age benefit has a dependent husband aged 65 or over, he may draw a benefit similar to a wife's benefit at 65 (or a reduced benefit at age 62).

### Benefits for Children of Retired or Disabled Workers

If a worker has children under 18 when he retires for age or disability they will get a benefit that is half his benefit, and so will his wife, even if she is under 62. Total benefits paid on a worker's earnings record are subject to a maximum and if the total paid to a family exceed that maximum, the individual dependents' benefits are adjusted downward.

(Total benefits paid to the family of a worker who retired in 1975 at age 65 with average monthly earnings of $1,175 can be no higher than $1,098.)

When his children reach 18, their benefits will stop, except that a child permanently and totally disabled before 22 may get a benefit as long as his disability meets the definition in the law. In addition, child's benefits are payable until the child reaches his 22nd birthday if he is attending school as a full-time student. Benefits may now be paid to a grandchild or step-grandchild of a worker or of his spouse, in special circumstances.

### What Disabled Workers Get

If a worker becomes so severely disabled that he is unable to work, he may be eligible to receive a monthly disability benefit that is the same amount he would receive as an old-age benefit if he were 65 at the start of his disability. When he reaches 65, his disability benefit becomes an old-age benefit.

Benefits like those provided for dependents of retired-worker beneficiaries may be paid to dependents of disabled beneficiaries.

### Survivor Benefits

If a worker should die while insured, one or more types of benefits would be payable to survivors.

1. A cash payment to cover burial expenses that amounts to 3 times the basic benefit but not more than $255, paid at the death of every insured worker.

2. A benefit for each child until the child reaches 18 (or up to age 22, if he is attending school). The monthly benefit of each child of a worker who has died is three-quarters of the amount the worker would have received if he had lived and drawn retirement benefits. A child with a permanent disability that began before age 22 may receive his benefit after that age.

3. A mother's benefit for the widow, if children under 18 are left in her care. Her benefit is 75% of the basic benefit and she draws it until the youngest child reaches 18. Payments stop then even if the child's benefit continues because he is attending school. They will start again when she is 62 (or 60), unless she marries. If she marries and the marriage is ended, she regains benefit rights. If she has a disabled child beneficiary aged 18 or over in her care, her benefits also continue.

Disabled widows and widowers qualify for benefits at age 50 at reduced rates that depend on age at entitlement. The widow or widower must have become totally disabled before or within 7 years after the spouse's death.

4. If there are no children entitled to receive benefits, the widow will receive a benefit that is 100% of the husband's basic amount, if it is first payable when she is 65. She may choose to get her benefit when she is 60; her benefit is then reduced by 19/40 of 1% for each month it is paid before she is 65. However, for widows aged 62 and over whose husbands claimed their benefits before 65, the benefit is the reduced amount he would be getting if he were alive but not less than 82 1/2% of his basic benefit. Dependent widowers aged 60 or over are entitled to survivor benefits on same basis as widows.

5. Dependent parents may be eligible for benefits, if they have been receiving at least half their support from the worker before his death, have reached age 62, and (except in certain circumstances) have not remarried since the worker's death. Each parent gets 75% of the basic benefit except that if only one parent survives the benefit is 82 1/2%.

The survivors of a woman worker receive benefits on the same basis as those of men workers. (Beginning March 1975, widowed father's benefits are payable on same basis as widowed mother's benefits).

### Maximum Benefits Payable

The illustrative table on page 66 shows a column heading for average monthly earnings of $1,475, but the benefit amounts shown in the column are not in general payable yet, since it will be some time before workers can have an average that high (years when the maximum creditable amount of earnings was lower than $17,700 — the 1978 maximum — must currently be included when the average is figured). Benefit amounts larger than those shown in the table will eventually be payable to persons who raise their average yearly earnings for social security purposes by earning, for a sufficient period, the highest creditable amount in years with the higher maximums specified in the law —$17,700 in 1978 and $22,900 in 1979 (higher amounts in the future whenever the base is raised under the automatic adjustment procedure).

#### Contribution and benefit base under old and new law

| Calendar year | Old law[1] | New law[2] |
|---|---|---|
| 1977 . . . . . . . . . | $16,500 | $16,500 |
| 1978 . . . . . . . . . | 17,700 | 17,700 |
| 1979 . . . . . . . . . | 18,900 | 22,900 |
| 1980 . . . . . . . . . | 20,400 | 25,900 |
| 1981 . . . . . . . . . | 21,900 | 29,700 |
| 1982 . . . . . . . . . | 23,400 | 31,800 |

(1) Estimated under automatic-adjustment provisions for 1979-82. (2) Stated in law for 1979-81. Estimated under automatic adjustment-provisions for 1982.

### Self-Employed

A self-employed person who has earnings of $400 or more in a year must report his earnings for income tax and social security tax purposes. If he is not a farmer he reports only net returns from his business. He need not add income from real estate, savings, dividends, loans, pensions or insurance policies if these are not part of his business.

A self-employed person who has net earnings of $400 or more in a year gets 4 quarters of coverage for that year. If his earnings are less than $400 in a year they do not count toward social security credits. The nonfarm self-employed person must make estimated payments of his social security taxes, on a quarterly basis, for taxable years after 1966, if combined estimated income tax and social security tax amount to at least $40.

The self-employed now have the option, comparable to that for farm workers, of reporting their earnings as ⅔ of their gross income from self-employment but not more than $1,600 a year. This option can be used only if actual net earnings from self-employment income is less than $1,600 and less than ⅔ of gross income and may be used only 5 times.

When a person has both taxable wages and earnings from self-employment, only as much of the self-employment income as will bring total earnings up to the current taxable maximum is subject to tax for social security purposes. A self-employed person pays the tax at a lower rate than the combined rate for an employee and his employer — about 1 ½ times what the employee alone pays.

### Farm Owners and Workers

Self-employed farmers whose gross annual earnings from farming are under $2,400 may report ⅔ of their gross earnings instead of net earnings for social security purposes. Cash or crop shares received from a tenant or share farmer count if the owner participated materially in production or management. The self-employed farmer pays contributions at the same rate as other self-employed, but he may make his tax returns annually.

**Farm workers.** Earnings from farm work count toward benefits (1) if the employer pays $150 or more in cash during the year; (2) if the employee works on 20 or more days for cash pay figured on a time basis. Under these rules a person gets credit for one calendar quarter for each $100 in cash pay in a year but no more than four quarters in any one year.

Foreign farm workers admitted to the United States on a temporary basis are not covered.

### Household Workers

Anyone working as maid, cook, laundress, nursemaid, baby-sitter, chauffeur, gardener and at other household tasks in the house of another, is covered by social security if he or she earns $50 or more in cash in three months from any one employer. Room and board do not count, but carfare counts if paid in cash. The job does not have to be regular or fulltime. The employee should get a card at the social security office and show it to the employer.

The employer deducts the amount of the social security tax from the worker's pay, adds an identical amount as his own tax and sends the total amount to the federal government, with the number of the employee's social security card.

### Supplemental Security Income

On Jan. 1, 1974, the supplemental security income program established by the 1972 Social Security Act amendments replaced the former federal grants to states for aid to the needy aged, blind, and disabled in the 50 states and the District of Columbia. The program provides both for federal payments based on uniform national standards and eligibil-

---

## Examples of OASDI Monthly Cash Benefits

(under the Social Security Act, effective June 1978)

| Beneficiary family | | Average monthly earnings of insured worker | | | | | | | | |
|---|---|---|---|---|---|---|---|---|---|---|
| | $76 or less | $200 | $400 | $550 | $750 | $900 | $1,100 | $1,275 | $1,475 | |
| Retired worker claiming benefits at age 65, or disabled worker: | | | | | | | | | | |
| Worker alone. . . . . . . . . . . . . . . . . . | $121.80 | $222.40 | $336.00 | $415.30 | $510.10 | $553.40 | $608.20 | $651.50 | $695.40 | |
| Worker with spouse claiming benefits at— | | | | | | | | | | |
| Age 65 or over . . . . . . . . . . . . . . | 182.70 | 333.60 | 504.00 | 623.00 | 765.20 | 830.10 | 912.30 | 977.30 | 1,043.10 | |
| Age 62 . . . . . . . . . . . . . . . . . | 167.50 | 305.80 | 462.00 | 571.10 | 701.50 | 761.00 | 836.30 | 895.90 | 956.20 | |
| Worker, spouse, and 1 child . . . . . . . . . . . | 182.70 | 333.60 | 612.70 | 751.60 | 892.70 | 968.30 | 1,064.00 | 1,140.00 | 1,216.90 | |
| Retired worker claiming benefits at age 62: | | | | | | | | | | |
| Worker alone. . . . . . . . . . . . . . . . . . | 97.50 | 178.00 | 268.80 | 332.30 | 408.10 | 442.80 | 486.60 | 521.20 | 556.40 | |
| Worker with spouse claiming benefits at— | | | | | | | | | | |
| Age 65 or over . . . . . . . . . . . . . . | 158.40 | 289.20 | 436.80 | 540.00 | 663.20 | 719.50 | 790.70 | 847.00 | 904.10 | |
| Age 62 . . . . . . . . . . . . . . . . . | 143.20 | 261.40 | 394.80 | 488.10 | 599.50 | 650.40 | 714.70 | 765.60 | 817.20 | |
| Widow or widower claiming benefits at— | | | | | | | | | | |
| Age 65 or over[1] . . . . . . . . . . . . . . | 121.80 | 222.40 | 336.00 | 415.30 | 510.10 | 553.40 | 608.20 | 651.50 | 695.40 | |
| Age 60 . . . . . . . . . . . . . . . . . | 87.10 | 159.10 | 240.30 | 297.00 | 364.80 | 395.70 | 434.90 | 465.90 | 497.30 | |
| Disabled widow or widower claiming benefits at age 50 . . . . . . . . . . . . . . . . . . | 61.00 | 111.30 | 168.10 | 207.80 | 255.20 | 276.80 | 304.20 | 325.90 | 347.80 | |
| 1 surviving child. . . . . . . . . . . . . . . . . | [2]121.80 | 166.80 | 252.00 | 311.50 | 382.60 | 415.10 | 456.20 | 488.70 | 521.60 | |
| Widow or widower aged 65 and over and 1 child. . | 182.70 | 333.60 | 588.00 | 726.80 | 892.70 | 968.30 | 1,064.00 | 1,140.00 | 1,216.90 | |
| Widowed mother or father and 1 child . . . . . . | 182.70 | 333.60 | 504.00 | 623.00 | 765.20 | 830.20 | 912.40 | 977.40 | 1,043.20 | |
| Widowed mother or father and 2 children . . . . . | 182.70 | 333.60 | 612.70 | 751.60 | 892.70 | 968.30 | 1,064.00 | 1,140.00 | 1,216.90 | |
| Maximum family benefits . . . . . . . . . . . . . | 182.70 | 333.60 | 612.70 | 751.60 | 892.70 | 968.30 | 1,064.00 | 1,140.00 | 1,216.90 | |

(1) Widow's or widower's benefit limited to amount spouse would have been receiving if still living but not less than 82½ percent of the PIA. (2) Sole survivors. NOTE: The higher monthly earnings shown in column headings on the right are not, in general, possible now, since earnings in some of the earlier years—when the maximum amount creditable was lower—must be included in the average. Therefore, the benefit amounts shown in these columns are not generally currently payable. (Effective June 1978, the highest average monthly earnings possible for a worker retiring at age 65 is $688).

ity requirements and for state supplementary payments varying from state to state. The Social Security Administration administers the federal payments financed from general funds of the Treasury—and the state supplements as well, if the state elects to have its supplementary program federally administered. The states may supplement the federal payment for all recipients and must supplement it for persons otherwise adversely affected by the transition from the former public assistance programs. In Aug. 1977, the number of persons receiving federal payments and federally administered state payments was 4,237,000, and the amount of these payments was $529,882,000. The average amount of combined federal payments and federally administered state payments was $125 for that month.

As a result of the 5.9 percent cost-of-living increase in social security benefits in June, 1977, the Federal SSI payment levels were raised in July, 1977, from $167.80 per month for an individual and $251.80 for a couple to $177.80 and $266.70 respectively.

### Public Assistance

In May 1977, 11.1 million persons received cash payments of $839.6 million under the federal-state program of aid to families with dependent children that averaged $234.03 per family and $75.56 per recipient. Under the child-support enforcement provisions of the Social Security Act, $34.3 million was collected and applied against assistance expenditures. In 42 states, 877,523 persons were receiving general assistance, financed entirely by state and local governments, that averaged $119.40. Emergency assistance was provided in 21 states for 41,348 families at an average payment of $165.70.

**Minimum and maximum monthly retired-worker benefits payable to individuals who retired at age 65, 1940—78**

| Year of attainment of age 65[1] | Minimum benefit | | Maximum benefit | | | |
|---|---|---|---|---|---|---|
| | Payment at the time of retirement | Payable effective June 1978 | Payable at the time of retirement | | Payable effective June 1978 | |
| | | | Men[2] | Women | Men[2] | Women |
| 1940 . . . | $10.00 | $121.80 | $41.20 | . . . | $235.60 | . . . |
| 1950 . . . | 10.00 | 121.80 | 45.20 | . . . | 251.80 | . . . |
| 1955 . . . | 30.00 | 121.80 | 98.50 | . . . | 278.10 | . . . |
| 1960 . . . | 33.00 | 121.80 | 119.00 | . . . | 314.90 | . . . |
| 1961 . . . | 33.00 | 121.80 | 120.00 | . . . | 317.30 | . . . |
| 1962 . . . | 40.00 | 121.80 | 121.00 | $123.00 | 320.20 | $325.60 |
| 1963 . . . | 40.00 | 121.80 | 122.00 | 125.00 | 322.90 | 330.50 |
| 1964 . . . | 40.00 | 121.80 | 123.00 | 127.00 | 325.60 | 336.00 |
| 1965 . . . | 44.00 | 121.80 | 131.70 | 135.90 | 325.60 | 336.00 |
| 1966 . . . | 44.00 | 121.80 | 132.70 | 135.90 | 328.00 | 336.00 |
| 1967 . . . | 44.00 | 121.80 | 135.90 | 140.00 | 336.00 | 346.00 |
| 1968 . . . | [3]55.00 | 121.80 | [3]156.00 | [3]161.60 | 341.10 | 353.20 |
| 1969 . . . | 55.00 | 121.80 | 160.50 | 167.30 | 351.10 | 365.90 |
| 1970 . . . | 64.00 | 121.80 | 189.80 | 196.40 | 360.80 | 373.50 |
| 1971 . . . | 70.40 | 121.80 | 213.10 | 220.40 | 368.30 | 380.70 |
| 1972 . . . | 70.40 | 121.80 | 216.10 | 224.70 | 373.50 | 388.20 |
| 1973 . . . | 84.50 | 121.80 | 266.10 | 276.40 | 383.10 | 398.00 |
| 1974 . . . | 84.50 | 121.80 | 274.60 | 284.90 | 395.30 | 410.20 |
| 1975 . . . | 93.80 | 121.80 | 316.30 | 333.70 | 410.20 | 432.70 |
| 1976 . . . | 101.40 | 121.80 | 364.00 | 378.80 | 436.90 | 454.70 |
| 1977 . . . | 107.90 | 121.80 | 412.70 | 422.40 | 465.60 | 476.50 |
| 1978 . . . | 114.30 | 121.80 | 459.80 | 459.80 | 489.70 | 489.70 |

(1) Assumes retirement at beginning of year. (2) Represents benefit for both men and women until 1962. (3) Effective for February 1968.

## Social Security Trust Funds

### Old-Age, Survivors, and Disability Insurance Trust Funds, 1937-1978

(thousands)

| Fiscal year: | Receipts | | | Expenditures | | | |
|---|---|---|---|---|---|---|---|
| | Net contrib. inc., transfers, and reimb. from gen'l rev. | Net interest received | Cash benefit payments and rehab. services | Transfers to R.R. ret. acct. | Administrative expenses | Total assets at end of period |
| 1937 . . . . . . . . . . . . | $ 265,000 | $ 2,262 | $ 27 | $. . . | $ 26,840 | $ 267,235 |
| 1940 . . . . . . . . . . . . | 550,000 | 42,489 | 15,805 | | 12,288 | 1,744,698 |
| 1945 . . . . . . . . . . . . | 1,309,919 | 123,854 | 239,834 | . . . | 26,950 | 6,613,381 |
| 1950 . . . . . . . . . . . . | 2,109,912 | 256,778 | 727,266 | . . . | 56,841 | 12,892,612 |
| 1955 . . . . . . . . . . . . | 5,087,154 | 438,029 | 4,333,147 | -9,551 | 103,202 | 21,141,001 |
| 1960 . . . . . . . . . . . . | 10,829,664 | 564,040 | 10,798,019 | 573,606 | 234,291 | 22,995,939 |
| 1965 . . . . . . . . . . . . | 17,032,456 | 648,372 | 16,618,084 | 459,253 | 379,145 | 22,187,184 |
| 1970 . . . . . . . . . . . . | 34,554,182 | 1,572,375 | 29,062,772 | 589,257 | 623,055 | 37,719,951 |
| 1975 . . . . . . . . . . . . | 63,872,883 | 2,803,838 | 62,547,281 | 1,010,299 | 1,100,693 | 48,138,321 |
| 1976 . . . . . . . . . . . . | 67,867,099 | 2,815,197 | 71,462,416 | 1,238,669 | 1,200,326 | 44,919,209 |
| 1976 (July-Sept.)[1] . . . . . . | 18,264,899 | 93,726 | 19,459,572 | | 304,448 | 43,513,811 |
| 1977 . . . . . . . . . . . . | 78,511,213 | 2,658,629 | 82,490,402 | 1,207,523 | 1,370,386 | 39,615,344 |
| 1978 (Oct. '77-June '78) . . | 63,942,088 | 2,281,419 | 66,943,866 | 1,618,461 | 1,087,214 | 36,189,332 |
| Cum. 1937-June '78 . . . . | 756,549,716 | 33,855,181 | 726,321,100 | 13,445,205 | 14,447,998 | 36,189,332 |

(1) Transitional quarter. Beginning Oct. 1976, federal fiscal year begins Oct. 1.

### Hospital Insurance Trust Fund, 1966-78

(thousands)

| Fiscal year: | Receipts | | | | Expenditures | | |
|---|---|---|---|---|---|---|---|
| | Net contribution income[1] | Transfers from general revenues[2] | Transfers from railroad retirement account[3] | Net interest[4] | Net hospital and related service benefits[5] | Administrative expenses[6] | Total assets |
| 1966 . . . . . . . . . . . . | $908,797 | . . . | . . . | $5,970 | . . . | $63,564 | $851,204 |
| 1967 . . . . . . . . . . . . | 2,688,684 | $337,850 | $16,200 | 45,903 | $2,507,773 | 88,848 | 1,343,221 |
| 1970 . . . . . . . . . . . . | 4,784,789 | 628,262 | 61,307 | 139,423 | 4,804,242 | 148,660 | 2,677,401 |
| 1972 . . . . . . . . . . . . | 5,225,891 | 551,351 | 63,782 | 190,105 | 6,109,139 | 166,370 | 2,858,725 |
| 1973 . . . . . . . . . . . . | 7,663,119 | 429,415 | 61,222 | 197,844 | 6,648,819 | 192,839 | 4,368,666 |
| 1974 . . . . . . . . . . . . | 10,606,551 | 498,780 | 96,163 | 408,273 | 7,785,596 | 258,066 | 7,934,772 |
| 1975 . . . . . . . . . . . . | 11,296,773 | 529,353 | 126,749 | 614,989 | 10,355,390 | 256,134 | 9,870,039 |
| 1976 . . . . . . . . . . . . | 12,039,194 | 658,430 | 130,904 | 715,744 | 12,270,382 | 308,215 | 10,835,714 |
| 1976 (July-Sept.)[7] . . . . . . | 3,367,940 | . . . | 135,863 | 11,951 | 3,315,251 | 88,408 | 10,947,810 |
| 1977 . . . . . . . . . . . . | 13,659,042 | 944,000 | . . . | 770,966 | 14,912,370 | 294,762 | 11,114,685 |
| 1978 (Oct. '77-June '78) . . | 12,126,235 | 830,938 | 196,506 | 788,361 | 13,005,320 | 237,391 | 11,814,015 |
| Cum. July '66-June '78 . . | 97,202,269 | 7,336,827 | 1,049,340 | 4,229,710 | 95,568,642 | 2,435,500 | 11,814,015 |

(1) Represents amounts appropriated (estimated tax collections with suitable subsequent adjustments), after deductions for refund of estimated amount of employee-tax overpayment. (2) Represents Federal Government transfers from general funds appropriations to meet costs of benefits for persons not insured for cash benefits under OASDHI or railroad retirement and for costs of benefits arising from military wage credits. (3) Represents receipts under the financial interchange with railroad retirement account with respect to

contributions for hospital insurance coverage of railroad workers. (4)Represents interest and profit on investments after transfers of interest on administrative expenses reimbursed to the OASI trust fund and on amounts transferred from railroad accounts. (5)Represents (1) payment vouchers on letters of credit issued to fiscal intermediaries under sec. 1816 and (2) direct payments to providers of services under sec. 1815 of the Social Security Act. (6)Subject to subsequent adjustment among all 4 social security trust funds, for allocated cost of each operation. (7)Transitional quarter. Beginning Oct. 1976, federal fiscal year begins Oct. 1.

## Supplementary Medical Insurance Trust Fund, 1967-78
### (thousands)

| Fiscal year: | Premium income[1] | Receipts Transfers from general revenues[2] | Net interest[3] | Net medical service benefits[4] | Adminis- trative expenses[5] | Total assets |
|---|---|---|---|---|---|---|
| 1967 | $646,682 | $623,000 | $14,052 | $664,261 | $133,682 | $485,791 |
| 1970 | 936,000 | 928,151 | 11,536 | 1,979,287 | 216,993 | 57,181 |
| 1973 | 1,462,607 | 1,430,451 | 45,049 | 2,391,232 | 245,861 | 745,722 |
| 1974 | 1,703,189 | 2,028,926 | 75,924 | 2,869,132 | 409,146 | 1,275,483 |
| 1975 | 1,886,962 | 2,329,590 | 105,539 | 3,765,397 | 404,458 | 1,424,413 |
| 1976 | 1,951,221 | 2,939,338 | 103,645 | 4,671,847 | 528,214 | 1,218,555 |
| 1976 (July-Sept.)[6] | 538,648 | 878,000 | 4,420 | 1,269,038 | 132,077 | 1,238,508 |
| 1977 | 2,192,903 | 5,052,944 | 136,710 | 5,866,922 | 474,717 | 2,279,426 |
| 1978 (Oct. '77-June '78) | 1,782,220 | 4,863,004 | 221,372 | 5,010,373 | 349,782 | 3,785,869 |
| Cum (July '67-June '78) | 17,259,888 | 25,302,266 | 808,651 | 35,816,539 | 3,768,599 | 3,785,869 |

(1) Represents voluntary premium payments from and in behalf of insured persons. (2) Represents Federal Government transfers from general funds appropriations to match aggregate premiums paid. (3) Represents interest and profit on investments after transfer of interest on administrative expenses reimbursed to the OASI trust fund (see footnote 5). (4) Represents payment vouchers on letters of credit issued to carriers under section 1842 of the Social Security Act. (5) Subject to subsequent adjustment among all 4 social security trust funds for allocated cost of each operation. (6) Transitional quarter. Beginning Oct. 1976, federal fiscal year begins Oct. 1.

---

# Employment and Training Services and Unemployment Insurance
### Source: Employment and Training Administration, U.S. Labor Department

## Employment Service

The Federal-State Employment Service consists of the U.S. Employment Service and affiliated state employment services with their network of about 2,500 local offices. During fiscal year 1977, these offices made a total of 5.9 million placements, of which 5.5 million were in nonagricultural and 400,000 agricultural industries. Overall, 4.1 million different individuals were placed in employment.

The employment service works to refer employable applicants to job openings that use their highest skills and helps the unemployed obtain services or training to make them employable. It also provides special attention to help older workers, youth, minorities, the poor, handicapped workers, migrants, seasonal farmworkers, and workers who lose their jobs because of foreign trade competition.

## Special Veterans Service

Veterans receive special services and absolute preference in placements at all employment service offices. During fiscal year 1977, these offices placed over 720,000 veterans in jobs, two-thirds of them veterans of the Vietnam era.

## Community Manpower System

The Comprehensive Employment and Training Act of 1973 sets up a community system to give people training and job-related services and place them in jobs. Under this system all states and cities, counties, and combinations of local units with populations of 100,000 or more receive federal grants to plan and run comprehensive employment and training programs in their localities.

Besides operating comprehensive programs, local governments plan and provide public service jobs for unemployed workers.

## National Activities

The federal role in the system is to provide support and technical assistance to local programs, insure proper use of federal money, and serve groups with special job disadvantages.

In addition to continuing programs for Indians and migrant and seasonal farmworkers, there are new and expanded efforts for youth. Programs authorized by the Youth Employment and Demonstration Projects Act of 1977 include the Young Adult Conservation Corps, which hires unemployed young people to work on public lands; Youth Incentive Entitlement Pilot Projects, providing part-time jobs and training to youth attending school; and Youth Community Conservation and Improvement Projects, which give unemployed youth paid work in community betterment.

The act also provides for Youth Employment and Training Programs to improve young people's job prospects. In addition, continuing programs are increasing opportunities for young people. Job Corps, which was training disadvantaged youth at 62 residential centers in mid-1978 plans to double the number of centers it operates so that it can serve 44,000 youth at any one time. The Summer Program for Economically Disadvantaged Youth supported over a million part-time jobs in 1978.

## Unemployment Insurance

Unlike old-age and survivors insurance, entirely a federal program, the unemployment insurance program is a Federal-State system which provides insured wage earners with partial replacement of wages lost during involuntary unemployment. The program protects most workers in industry. During calendar year 1978, an estimated 86.2 million jobs in commerce, industry, agriculture, and government, including the armed forces, are covered under the Federal-State system. In addition, an estimated 500,000 railroad workers are insured against unemployment by the Railroad Retirement Board.

Each state, as well as the District of Columbia and Puerto Rico, has its own law and operates its own program. The amount and duration of the weekly benefits are determined by state laws, based on prior wages and length of employment. States are required to extend the duration of benefits when unemployment rises to and remains above specified state or national levels; costs of extended benefits are shared by the state and federal governments.

Under the Federal Unemployment Tax Act, as amended in 1976, the tax rate is 3.4% on the first $6,000 paid to each employee of employers with one or more employees in 20 weeks of the year or a quarterly payroll of $1,500. A credit of up to 2.7% is allowed for taxes paid under state unemployment insurance laws that meet certain criteria, leaving the federal share at 0.7% of taxable wages.

## Social Security Requirement

The Social Security Act requires, as a condition of such grants, prompt payment of due benefits. The Federal Unemployment Tax Act provides safeguards for workers' right to benefits if they refuse jobs that fail to meet certain labor standards. Through the Unemployment Insurance Service of the Employment and Training Administration, the Secretary of Labor determines whether states qualify for grants and for tax offset credit for employers.

Benefits are financed solely by employer contributions, except in Alaska, Alabama, and New Jersey, where employees also contribute. Benefits are paid through the public employment offices, at which unemployed workers must register for work and to which they must report regularly for referral to a possible job during the time when they are drawing weekly benefit payments. During the 1977 calendar year, $8.4 billion in benefits was paid under state unemployment insurance programs to 7,985,000 beneficiaries, representing compensation for 137,667,200 weeks of unemployment. They received an average weekly payment of $78.77 for total unemployment for an average of 14.2 weeks.

### Federal Worker Benefits

Title 5, chapter 85 of the U.S. Code provided unemployment insurance protection during calendar year 1977 to about 2,878,300 federal civilian employees and about 2,133,400 members of the armed forces. Benefits for unemployed federal workers and ex-servicemen are financed through direct federal appropriations but are paid by the state agencies as agents of the federal government.

During calendar year 1977, a total of $275,371,600 was paid to 125,000 unemployed federal civilian workers for a total of 2,399,200 weeks of unemployment. The average weekly payment was $81.80 was paid for an average of 18.0 weeks. A total of $470,660,300 was paid to 234,100 unemployed ex-servicemen for 4,191,400 weeks of unemployment. The average weekly benefit was $84.13 and was paid for the average of 17.2 weeks.

## Employment Security

Selected unemployment insurance data by state
Calendar year 1977, state programs only

| | Insured claimants[1] (1,000) | Bene-ficiaries[2] (1,000) | Exhaustions[3] (1,000) | Initial claims[4] (1,000) | Benefits paid[5] (1,000) | Avg. weekly benefit for total unemployment | Funds available for benefits Dec. 31, 1977 (millions)[6] | Employers subject to state law Dec. 31, 1977 (1,000) |
|---|---|---|---|---|---|---|---|---|
| Alabama | 174 | 159 | 41 | 309 | 107,184 | 68.26 | 28 | 59 |
| Alaska | 52 | 50 | 15 | 88 | 85,406 | 86.69 | 75 | 9 |
| Arizona | 66 | 53 | 17 | 141 | 45,567 | 72.74 | 66 | 54 |
| Arkansas | 100 | 70 | 20 | 198 | 50,747 | 67.46 | 26 | 46 |
| California | 1,455 | 1,016 | 396 | 2,594 | 1,017,609 | 72.58 | 1,088 | 475 |
| Colorado | 78 | 71 | 29 | 165 | 65,321 | 87.25 | 57 | 60 |
| Connecticut | 185 | 166 | 53 | 365 | 193,150 | 83.20 | 27 | 72 |
| Delaware | 35 | 28 | 8 | 71 | 31,677 | 86.88 | 4 | 13 |
| District of Columbia | 37 | 31 | 14 | 45 | 55,435 | 105.09 | 7 | 17 |
| Florida | 251 | 194 | 101 | 468 | 166,466 | 63.34 | 111 | 170 |
| Georgia | 248 | 197 | 60 | 411 | 116,973 | 71.29 | 250 | 92 |
| Hawaii | 41 | 34 | 12 | 64 | 44,964 | 91.46 | 1 | 19 |
| Idaho | 38 | 32 | 9 | 83 | 24,054 | 77.37 | 62 | 21 |
| Illinois | 415 | 415 | 172 | 851 | 647,996 | 93.59 | −717 | 213 |
| Indiana | 226 | 153 | 44 | 422 | 97,864 | 70.05 | 261 | 85 |
| Iowa | 91 | 77 | 20 | 148 | 88,528 | 94.66 | 57 | 63 |
| Kansas | 63 | 49 | 17 | 94 | 55,715 | 78.82 | 155 | 50 |
| Kentucky | 156 | 124 | 32 | 293 | 90,282 | 71.30 | 146 | 59 |
| Lousiana | 152 | 113 | 42 | 225 | 143,764 | 85.22 | 125 | 67 |
| Maine | 71 | 69 | 22 | 195 | 51,607 | 69.50 | 3 | 23 |
| Maryland | 148 | 128 | 32 | 307 | 124,260 | 74.07 | 3 | 70 |
| Massachusetts | 294 | 238 | 96 | 533 | 281,242 | 79.78 | 106 | 112 |
| Michigan | 489 | 406 | 155 | 1,086 | 406,690 | 89.56 | 351 | 152 |
| Minnesota | 147 | 127 | 57 | 221 | 143,283 | 87.09 | 83 | 83 |
| Mississippi | 77 | 55 | 14 | 132 | 36,878 | 58.65 | 124 | 37 |
| Missouri | 218 | 167 | 55 | 476 | 134,511 | 74.05 | 121 | 91 |
| Montana | 38 | 28 | 9 | 69 | 26,412 | 75.88 | 7 | 20 |
| Nebraska | 41 | 32 | 9 | 69 | 23,695 | 72.19 | 53 | 34 |
| Nevada | 32 | 34 | 13 | 94 | 33,804 | 77.32 | 25 | 16 |
| New Hampshire | 42 | 31 | 2 | 59 | 16,563 | 67.19 | 41 | 21 |
| New Jersey | 479 | 371 | 179 | 746 | 516,702 | 83.16 | 69 | 154 |
| New Mexico | 30 | 21 | 7 | 64 | 21,063 | 58.08 | 38 | 25 |
| New York | 880 | 646 | 268 | 1,858 | 917,802 | 75.90 | −29 | 388 |
| North Carolina | 279 | 203 | 56 | 600 | 140,292 | 66.68 | 274 | 98 |
| North Dakota | 21 | 20 | 5 | 45 | 21,865 | 82.13 | 17 | 16 |
| Ohio | 415 | 316 | 78 | 871 | 367,777 | 91.77 | 221 | 181 |
| Oklahoma | 67 | 51 | 26 | 121 | 47,417 | 65.23 | 44 | 52 |
| Oregon | 130 | 102 | 28 | 308 | 96,480 | 74.66 | 91 | 58 |
| Pennsylvania | 755 | 672 | 145 | 1,614 | 803,592 | 92.34 | 24 | 195 |
| Puerto Rico | 126 | 126 | 92 | 255 | 90,185 | 46.11 | 11 | 44 |
| Rhode Island | 82 | 57 | 22 | 153 | 60,624 | 75.13 | −66 | 23 |
| South Carolina | 134 | 101 | 24 | 321 | 67,906 | 70.25 | 90 | 48 |
| South Dakota | 14 | 13 | 3 | 29 | 9,674 | 73.69 | 13 | 16 |
| Tennessee | 255 | 159 | 44 | 336 | 107,008 | 62.81 | 168 | 69 |
| Texas | 248 | 181 | 70 | 404 | 128,983 | 57.23 | 249 | 225 |
| Utah | 43 | 37 | 11 | 69 | 33,201 | 80.14 | 32 | 26 |
| Vermont | 24 | 20 | 5 | 45 | 20,780 | 73.00 | 8 | 12 |
| Virginia | 153 | 104 | 32 | 258 | 91,480 | 75.33 | 90 | 83 |
| Washington | 179 | 154 | 57 | 507 | 165,755 | 82.01 | −41 | 84 |
| West Virginia | 108 | 97 | 13 | 165 | 56,469 | 64.91 | 64 | 30 |
| Wisconsin | 247 | 178 | 116 | 424 | 177,127 | 87.90 | 231 | 92 |
| Wyoming | 13 | 7 | 12 | 45 | 7,330 | 78.66 | 45 | 13 |
| **Total** | **10,140** | **7,985** | **2,850** | **19,488** | **$8,357,160** | **$78.77** | **$4,387** | **4,233** |

(1) Claimants whose base-period earnings or whose employment — covered by the unemployment insurance program — was sufficient to make them eligible for unemployment insurance benefits as provided by state law. (2) Based on number of first payments. (3) Based on final payments. Some claimants shown, therefore, actually experienced their final week of compensable unemployment toward the end of the previous calendar year but received their final payments in the current calendar year. Similarly, some claimants who served their last week of compensable unemployment toward the end of the current calendar year did not receive their final payment in this calendar year and hence are not shown. A final week of compensable unemployment in a benefit year results in the exhaustion of benefit rights for the benefit year. Claimants who exhaust their benefit rights in one benefit year may be entitled to further benefits in the following benefit year. (4) Excludes intrastate transitional claims to reflect more nearly instances of new unemployment. Includes claims filed by interstate claimants in the Virgin Islands. (5) Adjusted for voided benefit checks and transfers under interstate combined wage plan. (6) Sum of balance in state clearing accounts, benefit payment accounts, and unemployment trust fund accounts maintained in the U.S. Treasury.

# Canadian Income Tax Rates

Source: Revenue Canada

## 1978 Rates of Federal Income Tax

| Taxable income $ | | Tax | |
|---|---|---|---|
| 761 or less | | 6% | |
| 761 | $ 46 | + 16% on next | $ 760 |
| 1,521 | 167 | + 17% on next | 1,521 |
| 3,042 | 426 | + 18% on next | 1,521 |
| 4,563 | 700 | + 19% on next | 3,042 |
| 7,605 | 1,278 | + 21% on next | 3,042 |
| 10,647 | 1,916 | + 23% on next | 3,042 |
| 13,689 | 2,616 | + 25% on next | 3,042 |
| 16,731 | 3,377 | + 28% on next | 4,563 |
| 21,294 | 4,654 | + 32% on next | 15,210 |
| 36,504 | 9,521 | + 36% on next | 22,815 |

| Taxable income | | Tax | |
|---|---|---|---|
| 59,319 | 17,735 | + 39% on next | 31,941 |
| 91,260 | 30,192 | + 43% on remainder | |

### 1978 Rates of Provincial Income Tax[1]

| | |
|---|---|
| Newfoundland | 58% |
| Prince Edward Island | 50% |
| Nova Scotia | 52.5% |
| New Brunswick | 55.5% |
| Ontario | 44% |
| Manitoba | 54%[2] |
| Saskatchewan | 58.5% |
| Alberta | 38.5% |
| British Columbia | 46% |

(1) Rates apply to basic federal tax payable. (2) A provincial surtax of 20% is added to basic provincial income tax in excess of $2,318.

---

# Canada: Taxable Returns by Income, 1975

Source: Revenue Canada Taxation Statistics

| Total income in dollars | Number | Per- cent | Total income (millions) | Per- cent | Taxed income (millions) | Federal tax (millions) | Per- cent |
|---|---|---|---|---|---|---|---|
| 0-1,500 | 9,268 | .11 | 6.6 | .01 | .8 | .2 | .00 |
| 1,500-2,000 | 3,816 | .15 | 6.7 | .01 | 1.4 | | .00 |
| 2,000-3,000 | 120,276 | 1.57 | 308.4 | .32 | 57.5 | .2 | .00 |
| 3,000-4,000 | 230,435 | 4.28 | 827.4 | 1.13 | 302.0 | 4.9 | .01 |
| 4,000-5,000 | 491,911 | 10.08 | 2,231.2 | 3.32 | 1,020.1 | 53.2 | .44 |
| 5,000-10,000 | 3,327,068 | 49.26 | 24,876.9 | 27.79 | 14,209.9 | 1,704.9 | 14.15 |
| 10,000-15,000 | 2,404,110 | 77.57 | 29,503.5 | 56.80 | 19,398.1 | 3,162.0 | 26.23 |
| 15,000-20,000 | 1,105,590 | 90.59 | 18,923.2 | 75.41 | 13,273.2 | 2,483.6 | 20.60 |
| 20,000-25,000 | 402,441 | 95.33 | 8,869.5 | 84.16 | 6,428.8 | 1,308.1 | 10.86 |
| 25,000-50,000 | 329,581 | 99.21 | 10,603.3 | 94.58 | 8,038.1 | 1,878.0 | 15.58 |
| 50,000-100,000 | 56,194 | 99.87 | 3,676.0 | 98.20 | 3,037.9 | 891.1 | 7.39 |
| 100,000-200,000 | 9,084 | 99.98 | 1,186.7 | 99.37 | 1,017.1 | 350.1 | 2.91 |
| 200,000 & over | 1,971 | 100.0 | 644.0 | 100.00 | 563.9 | 214.2 | 1.78 |

---

# Average Canadian Income and Taxes by Occupation, 1975

Source: Revenue Canada Taxation Statistics

| Occupation | Number[1] | Average income[2] | Average federal tax |
|---|---|---|---|
| Self-employed doctors and surgeons | 26,626 | $46,661 | $10,783 |
| Self-employed engineers and architects | 2,689 | 43,409 | 10,360 |
| Self-employed lawyers and notaries | 11,697 | 42,731 | 9,980 |
| Self-employed dentists | 5,851 | 40,871 | 9,318 |
| Self-employed accountants | 7,195 | 34,668 | 7,109 |
| Other self-employed professionals | 18,091 | 17,989 | 2,934 |
| Investors | 210,327 | 16,420 | 2,030 |
| Farmers | 162,223 | 16,149 | 1,989 |
| Property owners | 47,380 | 15,486 | 2,162 |
| Teachers and professors | 291,061 | 14,308 | 1,781 |
| Self-employed salesmen | 24,974 | 14,184 | 1,768 |

| Occupation | Number[1] | Average income[2] | Average federal tax |
|---|---|---|---|
| Armed forces employees | 71,956 | $13,435 | $1,609 |
| Federal government employees | 316,195 | 12,968 | 1,553 |
| Business proprietors | 280,612 | 12,875 | 1,555 |
| Provincial government employees | 409,907 | 12,629 | 1,497 |
| Municipal government employees | 367,542 | 12,360 | 1,390 |
| Business enterprise employees | 5,144,199 | 11,600 | 1,370 |
| Self-employed entertainers and artists | 6,657 | 10,743 | 1,117 |
| Employees of institutions | 544,107 | 9,898 | 995 |
| Pensioners | 150,569 | 9,762 | 626 |
| Unclassified employees | 134,477 | 8,426 | 755 |
| Fishermen | 15,293 | 8,027 | 645 |
| Unclassified | 242,117 | 5,903 | 310 |
| **Total** | **8,491,745** | **11,974** | **1,419** |

(1) Based on taxable income tax returns. (2) Average total income after business expense deductions but before personal deductions.

---

# Average Income in Selected Canadian Cities, 1975

Source: Revenue Canada Taxation Statistics

| City | Average income[1] | Rank | No. of tax returns |
|---|---|---|---|
| Oakville, Ont. | $11,714 | 1 | 37,430 |
| Burlington, Ont. | 11,527 | 2 | 54,276 |
| Sept-Isles, Que. | 11,191 | 3 | 14,715 |
| Brossard, Que. | 10,956 | 4 | 16,523 |
| Mississauga, Ont. | 10,838 | 5 | 124,377 |
| Prince George, B.C. | 10,634 | 6 | 32,259 |
| Bramalea, Ont. | 10,510 | 7 | 21,614 |
| Alberni, B.C. | 10,345 | 8 | 13,289 |
| Ottawa, Ont. | 10,287 | 9 | 289,897 |
| Sarnia, Ont. | 10,286 | 10 | 44,251 |
| Calgary, Alta. | 10,263 | 11 | 263,291 |
| Vancouver, B.C. | 10,233 | 12 | 614,111 |
| Edmonton, Alt. | 10,153 | 13 | 308,083 |
| Kamloops, B.C. | 10,135 | 14 | 30,076 |
| Langly, B.C. | 9,997 | 15 | 23,488 |
| Whitby, Ont. | 9,971 | 16 | 15,365 |
| Brampton, Ont. | 9,874 | 17 | 33,256 |
| Nanaimo, B.C. | 9,865 | 18 | 21,203 |
| Medicine Hat, Alta. | 9,756 | 19 | 18,114 |
| Regina, Sask. | 9,740 | 20 | 84,558 |
| Victoria, B.C. | 9,680 | 24 | 135,026 |
| Lethbridge, Alta. | 9,678 | 25 | 27,101 |
| Toronto, Ont. | 9,638 | 26 | 1,453,925 |
| Montreal, Ont. | 9,531 | 31 | 1,113,376 |
| Saskatoon, Sask. | 9,417 | 32 | 72,928 |
| Halifax, N.S. | 9,273 | 38 | 79,594 |
| Quebec, Que. | 9,262 | 39 | 210,348 |
| Windsor, Ont. | 9,238 | 40 | 141,698 |
| Hamilton, Ont. | 9,050 | 45 | 236,176 |
| St. John's Nfld. | 8,974 | 48 | 55,693 |
| Penticton, B.C. | 8,940 | 50 | 12,757 |
| Fredericton, N.B. | 8,860 | 56 | 28,837 |
| Kitchener, Ont. | 8,860 | 57 | 112,311 |
| Winnipeg, Man. | 8,324 | 77 | 354,390 |
| Charlottetown, P.E.I. | 8,013 | 88 | 14,023 |
| Cornwall, Ont. | 7,390 | 100 | 27,656 |

(1) Average total income after business expense deductions but before personal deductions.

## State Individual Income Taxes: Rates, Exemptions

Source: Tax Foundation, Inc. Data as of July 1, 1978
Footnotes at end of table.

| State | Taxable income | Percentage rates | Taxable income | Percentage rates | Personal exemp. Single | Married family head | Credit per depend. |
|---|---|---|---|---|---|---|---|
| Alabama[1] | First $1,000 | 1.5 | $3,001-$5,000 | 4.5 | $1,500 | $3,000 | $300 |
| | 1,001-3,000 | 3 | Over 5,000 | 5 | | | |
| Alaska | Rates range from 3% on first $2,000 to 14.5% over $400,000 | | | | Federal exemptions | | |
| Arizona[1 2 4] | First 1,000 | 2 | 3,001-4,000 | 5 | 1,000 | 2,000 | 600 |
| | 1,001-2,000 | 3 | 4,001-5,000 | 6 | | | |
| | 2,001-3,000 | 4 | 5,001-6,000 | 7 | Over 6,000 8 | | |
| Arkansas[3] | First 2,999 | 1 | 9,000-14,999 | 4.5 | 17.50 | 35 | 6 |
| | 3,000-5,999 | 2.5 | 15,000-24,999 | 6 | (tax credit) | | |
| | 6,000-8,999 | 3.5 | 25,000 and over | 7 | | | |
| California[1 2 4] | First 2,000 | 1 | 8,001-9,500 | 6 | (tax credit) | | |
| | 2,001-3,500 | 2 | 9,501-11,000 | 7 | 25 | 50 | 8 |
| | 3,501-5,000 | 3 | 11,001-12,500 | 8 | Heads of households have slightly lower | | |
| | 5,001-6,500 | 4 | 12,501-14,000 | 9 | tax rates. | | |
| | 6,501-8,000 | 5 | 14,001-15,500 | 10 | Over 15,500 11 | | |
| Colorado[1 4] | First 1,000 | 3 | 6,001-7,000 | 6 | 850 | 700 | 850 |
| | 1,001-2,000 | 3.5 | 7,001-8,000 | 6.5 | | | |
| | 2,001-3,000 | 4 | 8,001-9,000 | 7 | Surtax on intangible income over $5,000, | | |
| | 3,001-4,000 | 4.5 | 9,001-10,000 | 7.5 | 2%. A credit equal to 1/2 of 1% of net | | |
| | 4,001-5,000 | 5 | Over 10,000 | 8 | taxable income is allowed for income under | | |
| | 5,001-6,000 | 5.5 | | | $9,000. | | |
| Connecticut | 7% capital gains tax; tax on dividends earned if federal adjusted gross income is greater than or equal to $20,000; tax ranges from 1% on $20,000 through 9% on $100,000 and over. | | | | 100 | 200 | |
| Delaware[3] | First 1,000 | 1.6 | 8,001-20,000 | 8.8 | Exemptions apply only to adjusted gross | | |
| | 1,001-2,000 | 2.2 | 20,001-25,000 | 9.3 | incomes of more than $20,000 and net | | |
| | 2,001-3,000 | 3.3 | 25,001-30,000 | 9.9 | capital gains more than $100 (or $200 on | | |
| | 3,001-4,000 | 4.4 | 30,001-40,000 | 12.1 | joint returns). | | |
| | 4,001-5,000 | 5.5 | 40,001-50,000 | 13.2 | 600 | 1,200 | 600 |
| | 5,001-6,000 | 6.6 | 50,001-75,000 | 15.4 | | | |
| | 6,001-8,000 | 7.7 | 75,001-100,000 | 16.5 | Over 100,000 19.8 | | |
| Dist. of Col.[1 4] | First 1,000 | 2 | 5,001-10,000 | 7 | Federal exemptions | | |
| | 1,001-2,000 | 3 | 10,001-13,000 | 8 | | | |
| | 2,001-3,000 | 4 | 13,001-17,000 | 9 | | | |
| | 3,001-4,000 | 5 | 17,001-25,000 | 10 | | | |
| | 4,001-5,000 | 6 | Over 25,000 | 11 | | | |
| Georgia[3 5] | First 750 | 1 | 5,251-7,000 | 5 | 1,500 | 3,000 | 700 |
| | 751-2,250 | 2 | Over 7,000 | 6 | For married persons filing separately, | | |
| | 2,251-3,750 | 3 | | | rates range from 1% on the first $500 | | |
| | 3,751-5,250 | 4 | | | to 6% on $5,000 or more. For married couples filing jointly and heads of households, rates range from 1% on the first $1,000 to 6% on $10,000 or more. | | |
| Hawaii[1] | First 500 | 2.25 | 3,001-5,000 | 7.5 | 750 | 1,500 | 750 |
| | 501-1,000 | 3.25 | 5,001-10,000 | 8.5 | Special tax rates for heads of households. | | |
| | 1,001-1,500 | 4.5 | 10,001-14,000 | 9.5 | | | |
| | 1,501-2,000 | 5 | 14,001-20,000 | 10 | | | |
| | 2,001-3,000 | 6.5 | 20,001-30,000 | 10.5 | Over 30,000 11 | | |
| Idaho[2 3 4] | First 1,000 | 2 | 3,001-4,000 | 5.5 | Federal exemptions | | |
| | 1,001-2,000 | 4 | 4,001-5,000 | 6.5 | Each person (husband and wife filing jointly | | |
| | 2,001-3,000 | 4.5 | Over 5,000 | 7.5 | are deemed one person) filing return pays additional $10. | | |
| Illinois | Total net income | | 2.5 | | 1,000 | 2,000 | 1,000 |
| Indiana[4] | Adjusted gross | 2 | | | 1,000 | *2,000 | 500 |
| | *Lesser of $1,000 or adjusted gross income of each spouse, but not less than $500. | | | | | | |
| Iowa[3] | First 1,000 | 0.5 | 3,001-4,000 | 3.5 | (tax credit) 15 | 30 | 10 |
| | 1,001-2,000 | 1.25 | 4,001-7,000 | 5 | Net incomes $4,000 or less are not taxable. | | |
| | 2,001-3,000 | 2.75 | 7,001-9,000 | 6 | On up to 13% over $75,000 | | |
| Kansas[2 4] | First 2,000 | 2 | 5,001-7,000 | 5 | 750 | 1,500 | 750 |
| | 2,001-3,000 | 3.5 | 7,001-10,000 | 6.5 | 20,001-25,000 8.5 | | |
| | 3,001-5,000 | 4 | 10,001-20,000 | 7.5 | Over 25,000 9.5 | | |
| Kentucky[3] | First 3,000 | | 4,001-5,000 | 4 | | | |
| | 3,001-4,000 | 3 | 5,001-8,000 | 5 | (tax credit) | | |
| | | | Over 8,000 | 6 | 20 | 40 | 20 |

| State | Taxable income | Percentage rates | Taxable income | Percentage rates | Personal exemp. Single | Married family head | Credit per depend. |
|---|---|---|---|---|---|---|---|
| Louisiana . . . . | First 10,000<br>10,001-50,000 | 2<br>4 | Over 50,000 | 6 | 2,500 | 5,000 | 400 |

Credits are allowed new income which is taxed at 2%; additional $1,000 exemp. for blindness allowed for dependents.

| State | Taxable income | Percentage rates | Taxable income | Percentage rates | Single | Married family head | Credit per depend. |
|---|---|---|---|---|---|---|---|
| Maine : . . . . | First 2,000<br>2,001-4,000<br>4,001-6,000<br>6,001-8,000 | 1<br>2<br>3<br>6 | 8,001-10,000<br>10,001-15,000<br>15,001-25,000<br>Over 25,000 | 7<br>8<br>9.2<br>10 | 1,200 | 2,100 | 1,200 |
| Maryland . . . . | First 1,000<br>1,001-2,000 | 2<br>3 | 2,001-3,000<br>Over 3,000 | 4<br>5 | 800 | 1,600 | 800 |

An additional exemption of $800 is allowed for each dependent 65 or over.

| State | Taxable income | Percentage rates | | | Single | Married family head | Credit per depend. |
|---|---|---|---|---|---|---|---|
| Massachusetts | Earned and business income:<br>Interest, divs., capital gains on intangibles: | 5*<br><br>10* | | | 2,000 | 2,600-4,600 | 600 |

The exemptions shown are those allowed against business income, including salaries and wages. A specific exemption of $2,000 is allowed for each taxpayer. In addition, a dependency exemption of $600 is allowed for a dependent spouse who has income from all sources of less than $2,000. In the case of a joint return, the exemption is the smaller of (1) $4,600 or (2) $2,600 plus the income of the spouse having the smaller income.
*Plus 7.5% surtax.

| State | Taxable income | Percentage rates | Taxable income | Percentage rates | Single | Married family head | Credit per depend. |
|---|---|---|---|---|---|---|---|
| Michigan . . . . . | All taxable income | 4.6 | | | 1,500 | 3,000 | 1,500 |
| Minnesota . . . . | First 500<br>501-1,000<br>1,001-2,000<br>2,001-3,000<br>3,001-4,000<br>4,001-5,000 | 1.6<br>2.2<br>3.5<br>5.8<br>7.3<br>8.8 | 5,001- 7,000<br>7,001- 9,000<br>9,001-12,500<br>12,501-20,000<br>20,001-27,500<br>27,501-40,000<br>Over 40,000 | 10.2<br>11.5<br>12.8<br>14<br>15<br>16<br>17 | 40 | 80 | 40 |

An additional tax credit of $20 is allowed for each unmarried taxpayer aged 65 or older.

| State | Taxable income | Percentage rates | Taxable income | Percentage rates | Single | Married family head | Credit per depend. |
|---|---|---|---|---|---|---|---|
| Mississippi . . . | First 5,000 | 3 | Over 5,000 | 4 | 4,500 | 6,500 | 750 |
| Missouri . . . . . | First 1,000<br>1,001-2,000<br>2,001-3,000<br>3,001-4,000<br>4,001-5,000 | 1.5<br>2<br>2.5<br>3<br>3.5 | 5,001- 6,000<br>6,001- 7,000<br>7,001- 8,000<br>8,001-9,000<br>Over 9,000 | 4<br>4.5<br>5<br>5.5<br>6 | 1,200 | 2,400 | 400 |

An additional $800 exemption is allowed unmarried head of household.

| State | Taxable income | Percentage rates | Taxable income | Percentage rates | Single | Married family head | Credit per depend. |
|---|---|---|---|---|---|---|---|
| Montana . . . . . | First 1,000<br>1,001-2,000<br>2,001-4,000<br>4,001-6,000<br>6,001-8,000 | 2<br>3<br>4<br>5<br>6 | 8,001-10,000<br>10,001-14,000<br>14,001-20,000<br>20,001-35,000<br>Over 35,000 | 7<br>8<br>9<br>10<br>11 | 650 | 1,300 | 650 |

Additional surtax of 10% on tax liability.

**Nebraska**    Federal exemptions
The tax is imposed as a % of the taxpayer's Fed. income tax liability (not including surtax) before credits, with limited adjustments. For the year 1978 the rate was set at 16% by State Board of Equalization and Assessment.

**New Hampshire**    Interest and dividends (except interest on savings accounts).    5    4% commuter tax    $600 of each income is exempt; additional $600 exemptions are allowed to persons who are 65 or older, blind or handicapped and unable to work.

| State | Taxable income | Percentage rates | | | Single | Married family head | Credit per depend. |
|---|---|---|---|---|---|---|---|
| New Jersey . . . | First 20,000<br>Over 20,000 | 2<br>2.5 | | | 1,000 | 2,000 | 1,000 |

Additional credit of $1,000 allowed for the elderly, and disabled.

Commuter tax from 2.7% on net income under $1,000 to 15% on income over $25,000.

| State | Taxable income | Percentage rates | Taxable income | Percentage rates | | | |
|---|---|---|---|---|---|---|---|
| New Mexico . . . | First 2,000<br>2,001-3,000<br>3,001-4,000<br>4,001-5,000<br>5,001-6,000<br>6,001-7,000<br>7,001-8,000<br>8,001-10,000<br>10,000-12,000 | .8<br>.9<br>1.1<br>1.3<br>1.5<br>1.8<br>2.3<br>2.9<br>3.5 | 12,001-14,000<br>14,001-16,000<br>16,001-18,000<br>18,001-20,000<br>20,001-25,000<br>25,001-35,000<br>35,001-50,000<br>50,001-100,000<br>Over 100,000 | 4.2<br>4.9<br>5.6<br>6.3<br>7.0<br>7.5<br>8.0<br>8.5<br>9.0 | | | |

Federal exemptions

The income classes reported are for individuals. For joint returns and heads of households, a separate rate schedule is provided. A credit is allowed for state and local taxes for gross income of less than $8,000.

| State | Taxable income | Percentage rates | Taxable income | Percentage rates | Single | Married family head | Credit per depend. |
|---|---|---|---|---|---|---|---|
| New York . . . | First 1,000<br>1,001-3,000<br>3,001-5,000<br>5,001-7,000<br>7,001-9,000<br>9,001-11,000<br>11,001-13,000 | 2<br>3<br>4<br>5<br>6<br>7<br>8 | 13,001-15,000<br>15,001-17,000<br>17,001-19,000<br>19,001-21,000<br>21,001-23,000<br>Over 23,000 | 9<br>10<br>11<br>12<br>13<br>14 | 650 | 1,300 | 650 |

Income from unincorporated business is taxed at 5.5%. The following credit is allowed: $110 tax or less, full amount; $110 to $550 difference between $137.50 and 25% of amount of tax; $550 or more, no credit. Personal exemption increases to $700 per dependent in 1979, and $750 in 1980.

| State | Taxable income | Percentage rates | Taxable income | Per-centage rates | Personal exemp. Single | Married family head | Credit per depend. |
|---|---|---|---|---|---|---|---|
| North Carolina[3][4] | First 2,000<br>2,001-4,000<br>4,001-6,000 | 3<br>4<br>5 | 6,001-10,000<br>Over 10,000 | 6<br>7 | 1,000 | 2,000* | 600 |

*An additional exemption of $1,000 is allowed the spouse having the lower income; joint returns are not permitted.

| State | Taxable income | Percentage rates | Taxable income | Per-centage rates | Single | Married family head | Credit per depend. |
|---|---|---|---|---|---|---|---|
| North Dakota[3] | First 1,000<br>1,000-3,000<br>3,001-5,000<br>5,001-6,000 | 1<br>2<br>3<br>5 | 6,001-8,000<br>Over 8,000 | 7.5<br>10 | Federal exemptions<br>A credit of 25% of income tax liability is allowed up to a maximum of $100. | | |
| Ohio[4] . . . . . | First 5,000<br>5,001-10,000<br>10,001-15,000 | 0.5<br>1<br>2 | 15,001-20,000<br>20,001-40,000<br>over 40,000 | 2.5<br>3<br>3.5 | 650 | 1,300 | 650 |

Taxpayers age 65 or older are allowed a $25 credit, or if they have received a lump sum distribution from a pension, retirement or profit sharing plan during the tax year, they are allowed a credit equal to $25 times the taxpayer's expected remaining life. Credit may not exceed tax otherwise due. Credit is also allowed for an amount paid during the school year for elementary and secondary education or instruction or training of dependents who do not have a high school diploma.

| State | Taxable income | Percentage rates | Taxable income | Per-centage rates | Single | Married family head | Credit per depend. |
|---|---|---|---|---|---|---|---|
| Oklahoma[1][4] . . | First 1,000<br>1,001-2,500<br>2,501-3,750<br>3,751-5,000 | 0.5<br>1<br>2<br>3 | 5,001-6,250<br>6,251-7,500<br>Over 7,500 | 4<br>5<br>6 | 750 | 1,500 | 750 |

For joint returns and heads of households the rates shown apply to income classes twice as large.

Non-resident aliens are taxed at a flat rate of 6% of Oklahoma taxable income.

| State | Taxable income | Percentage rates | Taxable income | Per-centage rates | Single | Married family head | Credit per depend. |
|---|---|---|---|---|---|---|---|
| Oregon[1][4] . . . . | First 500<br>501-1,000<br>1,001-2,000<br>2,001-3,000 | 4<br>5<br>6<br>7 | 3,001-4,000<br>4,001-5,000<br>Over 5,000 | 8<br>9<br>10 | 750 | 1,500 | 750 |

A credit is provided in an amount and equal to 25% of the federal retirement income tax credit to the extent that such a credit is based on Oregon taxable income.

| State | Taxable income | Percentage rates | Taxable income | Per-centage rates | Single | Married family head | Credit per depend. |
|---|---|---|---|---|---|---|---|
| Pennsylvania . | 2.2% of specified classes of taxable income | | | | | | |
| Rhode Island . | 19% of modified federal income tax liability | | | | Federal Exemptions | | |
| South Carolina | First 2,000<br>2,001-4,000<br>4,001-6,000 | 2<br>3<br>4 | 6,001-8,000<br>8,001-10,000<br>Over 10,000 | 5<br>6<br>7 | 800 | 1,600 | 800 |
| Tennessee | Interest and dividends | 6 | | | Dividends from corporations, 75% of whose property is taxable in Tenn., are taxed at 4%. | | |
| Utah[1] . . . . . | First 750<br>751-1,500<br>1,501-2,250 | 2.25<br>3.25<br>4.25 | 2,251-3,000<br>3,001-3,750<br>3,751-4,500 | 5.25<br>6.25<br>7.25 | Over 4,500 | Federal exemptions<br>7.75 | |
| Vermont[3] . . . . | Federal exemptions. | | | | | | |

The tax is imposed at a rate of 25% of the fed. income tax liability of the taxpayer for the taxable year after certain credits (retirement income, investment, foreign tax, child and dependent care, and tax-free covenant bonds) but before any surtax on fed. liability, reduced by a % equal to the % of the taxpayer's adjusted gross income for the taxable year which is not Vermont income.

| State | Taxable income | Percentage rates | Taxable income | Per-centage rates | Single | Married family head | Credit per depend. |
|---|---|---|---|---|---|---|---|
| Virginia[3] . . . . | First 3,000<br>3,001-5,000 | 2<br>3 | 5,001-12,000<br>Over 12,000 | 5<br>5.75 | 600 | 1,200 | 600 |
| West Virginia[1][3] . | First 2,000<br>2,001-4,000<br>4,001-6,000<br>6,001-8,000<br>8,001-10,000<br>10,001-12,000<br>12,001-14,000<br>14,001-16,000<br>16,001-18,000<br>18,001-20,000<br>20,001-22,000<br>22,001-26,000 | 2.1<br>2.3<br>2.8<br>3.2<br>3.5<br>4<br>4.6<br>4.9<br>5.3<br>5.4<br>6<br>6.1 | 26,001-32,000<br>32,001-38,000<br>38,001-44,000<br>44,001-50,000<br>50,001-60,000<br>60,001-70,000<br>70,001-80,000<br>80,001-90,000<br>90,001-100,000<br>100,001-150,000<br>150,001-200,000<br>Over 200,000 | 6.5<br>6.8<br>7.2<br>7.5<br>7.9<br>8.2<br>8.6<br>8.8<br>9.1<br>9.3<br>9.5<br>9.6 | 600 | 1,200 | 600 |

For joint returns and a return of a surviving spouse, a separate rate schedule is provided.

| State | Taxable income | Percentage rates | Taxable income | Per-centage rates | Single | Married family head | Credit per depend. |
|---|---|---|---|---|---|---|---|
| Wisconsin[1][4] . . | First 1,000<br>1,001-2,000<br>2,001-3,000<br>3,001-4,000<br>4,001-5,000<br>5,001-6,000<br>6,001-7,000<br>7,001-8,000 | 3.1<br>3.4<br>3.6<br>4.8<br>5.4<br>5.9<br>6.5<br>7.6 | 8,001-9,000<br>9,001-10,000<br>10,001-11,000<br>11,001-12,000<br>12,001-13,000<br>13,001-14,000<br>Over 14,000 | 8.2<br>8.8<br>9.3<br>9.9<br>10.5<br>11.1<br>11.4 | (Tax Credit)<br>20 | 40 | 20 |

(1) A standard deduction and optional tax table are provided. In Louisiana, standard deduction is incorporated in tax tables.

(2) Community property state in which, in general, one-half of the community income is taxable to each spouse.

(3) A standard deduction is allowed.

(4) A limited general tax credit for taxpayers filing joint returns and a credit for home improvements is allowed in Ohio; a limited tax credit is allowed for sales taxes in Colorado, Massachusetts, Nebraska, and Vermont; for property taxes and city

income taxes in Michigan; for personal property taxes in Maryland and Wisconsin; for property taxes in D.C. if household income is less than $10,000, and in N.Y. if household income is less than $12,000; for installation of solar energy devices in Arizona, California, Kansas, New Mexico, North Carolina, and Oregon; for property taxes paid on pollution control property in Colorado; for installation of insulation in residences in Idaho; and for making an existing building accessible to the handicapped in Kansas.

(5) Tax credits are allowed: $15 for single person or married person filing separately if AGI is $3,000 or less. (For each dollar by which the federal AGI exceeds $3,000 the credit is reduced by $1 until no credit is allowed if federal AGI is $3,015 or more.) $30 for heads of households or married persons filing jointly with $6,000 or less AGI. (For each dollar by which federal AGI exceeds $6,000, credit is reduced by $1 until no credit is allowed if federal AGI is $6,030 or more.)

---

## State Retail Sales Taxes: Types and Rates

Source: Advisory Commission on Intergovernmental Relations

| State | Tangible personal property | Admissions | Selected service | | | Rates on other services and nonretail business |
|---|---|---|---|---|---|---|
| | | | Rest. meals | Transient lodging | Public utilities | |
| Alabama[2] | 4%[3] | 4% | 4% | 4% | ... | Gross rcpts of amus't operators, 4%, agric., mining and mfg. mach., 1.5% |
| Arizona[2] | 4 | 4 | 4 | 3 | 4 | Timbering, 1.5%; storage, apt., office rental, 3%. |
| Arkansas[2] | 3 | 3 | 3 | 3 | 3 | Printing, photographic services; rcpts. from coin-operated dev.; repair services incl. auto and elect., 3%. |
| California[2] | 4.75[5] | ... | 4.75 | ... | 14 | Renting, leasing, producing, fabricating, processing, pringting, 4.75% |
| Colorado[2] | 3 | ... | 3 | 3[10] | 3 | |
| Connecticut | 7 | ... | 7[7] | 7[10] | 7[13] | Storing for use or consumption of personal property items, 7%. |
| D. of C. | 5[3] | 5 | 6 | 6 | 5 | Duplicating, mailing, addressing and public stenographic services, 5%; sales of food for off-premise consumption, nonprescription medicines, 2%. |
| Florida | 4 | 4 | 4 | 4 | ... | Rental income of amus't mach., 4%. |
| Georgia | 3 | 3 | 3 | 3<br>3 | | Levies on amus's dev., 3%. |
| Hawaii[1] | 4 | 4 | 4 | 4 | ... | Sugar processors, pineapple farmers and selected businesses, 0.5%; insur. solicitors, 2% contractors, sales rep., professions, radio stations, 4%. |
| Idaho[6] | 3 | 3 | 3 | 3 | ... | Closed circuit TV boxing, wrestling, 5%. |
| Illinois[2] | 4 | ... | 4 | ... | ... | Property sold in connection with a sale of service, 4%, remodeling repairing and reconditioning of tangible personal property, 4%. |
| Indiana | 4 | ... | 4 | 4 | 4 | |
| Iowa | 3 | 3 | 3 | 3 | 3 | Laundry, dry cleaning, automobile and cold storage, photography, printing, repairs, barber and beauty parlor services, advt., dry cleaning equip. rentals and gross rcpts. from amus't dev., 3%. |
| Kansas[2] | 3 | 3 | 3 | 3 | 3 | Gross rcpts. from operation of coin-operated devices; commer. amus't, 3%. |
| Kentucky[2] | 5 | 5 | 5 | 5 | 5 | Storage, sewer services, photog. and photo fin., 5%; ticket sales to boxing or wrestling on closed circuit TV, 5% of gross rcpts; tax also applies to pay'ts for right to broadcast matches. |
| Louisiana[2] | 3 | 3 | 3 | 3 | ... | Food and prescpt'n. drugs, exempt. |
| Maine | 5 | ... | 5 | 5 | 5 | Proceeds from closed circuit TV, 5%. |
| Maryland[2] | 4[3] | 11 | 4[7] | 4 | 4 | Farm equip., 2%; mfg. equip., including that used in generation of electricity or in R.&S. sold to mfrs., 2%; watercraft, 3% |
| Mass. | 5 | ... | 7 | 5.7[9] | ... | |
| Michigan | 4 | ... | 4 | 4 | 4 | |
| Minnesota[2] | 4[3] | 4 | 4 | 4 | 4 | Food, medicines and clothing are exempt; coin-operated vending mach., 3% of gross sales. |
| Mississippi[1] | 5[3] | ... | 5 | 5 | 5 | Wholesaling, 0.125% (0.5% on sales of meat for human consumption; 5% on beer, alc. bevs., soft drinks and motor fuel); extracting or mining of minerals, specified miscellaneous bus. incl. bowling, pool halls, warehouses, laundry and dry cleaning, pest control services, specified repair services, 5%; cotton ginning, 15c per bale; sales of materials to railroads for use in track structures, 3%; tractors, indust. fuel and mfg. mach. sales over $500, 1%. |
| Missouri[2] | 3 | 3 | 3 | 3 | 3 | |
| Nebraska[2] | 2.5 | 2.5 | 2.5 | 2.5 | 2.5 | |

| State | Tangible personal property | Admissions | Selected service | | | Rates on other services and nonretail business |
|---|---|---|---|---|---|---|
| | | | Rest. meals | Trans-ient lodging | Public utilities | |
| Nevada[2] | 3[10] | ... | 3 | ... | | |
| New Jersey[2] | 5 | 5[11] | 5 | 5[9] | ... | |
| New Mexico[2] | 4[3] | 4 | 4 | 4 | 4 | |
| New York[2] | 4 | 4[11] | 4[7] | 4[9] | 4 | Safe deposit rentals, 4%. |
| North Carolina[2] | 3[3] | ... | 3 | 3 | ... | Farm and industrial machinery, 1% ($80 max.); airplanes, boats and locomotives, 2% ($120 max.); sales of horses and mules, 1%. |
| North Dakota | 4[3] | 4 | 4 | 4 | 4 | Severance of sand or gravel from the soil, 4%. |
| Ohio | 4 | ... | 4 | 4 | | |
| Oklahoma[2] | 2[3] | 2 | 2 | 2 | 2 | Advert. (exclusive of newspapers, periodicals, billboards), printing, auto storage, gross proceeds from amusement dev., 2%. |
| Pennsylvania[2] | 6 | ... | 6[7] | 6 | 6 | Cleaning, polishing, lubr. and insp. motor vehicles, rental income of coin-operated amuse. dev., 6%. |
| Rhode Island | 6 | ... | 6 | 6 | 6 | |
| South Carolina | 4 | ... | 4 | 4 | 4 | |
| South Dakota[2] | 4[3] | 4 | 4 | 3 | 3 | Farm mach. and agric. irrigation equip., 2%; gross rcpts. from professions (other than medical), 4%. |
| Tennessee | 4.5 | | 4.5 | 4.5 | 4.5 | Vending machines, 1.5% (except tobacco products, 2.5%); industrial, farm equipment and machinery, 1%. |
| Texas[2] | 4[3] | ... | 4 | ... | | |
| Utah | 4 | 4 | 4 | 4 | 4 | |
| Vermont | 3 | 3 | [12] | [12] | 3 | |
| Virginia[2] | 3[3] | ... | 3 | 3 | | |
| Washington[2] | 4.6 | 4.6 | 4.6 | 4.6 | ... | Rentals, auto, parking, other specified services, amusements, recreations, 4.5% (unless subject to county or city adm. taxes, when they remain taxable under the state business, occupation levy, 1%). |
| West Virginia | 3[3] | 3 | 3 | 3 | ... | All services except public util. and personal and professional services, 3%. |
| Wisconsin[2] | 4 | 4[11] | 4 | 4 | 4 | |
| Wyoming[2] | 3 | 3 | 3 | 3 | 3 | |

(1) All but a few states levy sales taxes of the single-stage retail type. Ha. and Miss. levy multiple-stage sales taxes. The N.M. and S.D. taxes have broad bases with respect to taxable services but they are not multiple-stage taxes. Wash. and W.Va. levy gross receipts taxes on all business, distinct from their sales taxes. Alaska also levies a gross receipts tax on businesses. The rates applicable to retailers, with exceptions, under these gross receipts taxes are as follows: Alaska 0.5% on gross receipts of $20,000-$100,000 and 0.25% on gross receipts in excess of $100,000; Wash., 0.44%, plus a 6% surtax; and W.Va., 0.55%. N.J. imposes a tax of 0.05% on retail stores with income in excess of $150,000, and an unincorporated business tax at the rate of 0.25% of 1% if gross receipts exceed $5,000.

(2) In addition to the State tax, sales taxes are also levied by certain cities and/or counties.

(3) Motor vehicles are taxed at the general sales tax rates with the following exceptions: Ala., 1.5%; Miss., 3%; and N.C., 2% ($120 maximum). Motor vehicles are exempt from the general sales and use taxes but are taxed under motor vehicle tax laws in Md., 4%; Minn., 4%; N.M., 2%; N.D. 4%; Okla., 2%; S.D. and W.Va., 3%; Tex., 4%; Va., 2%; and the D.C., 4%.

(4) Ariz. and Miss. also tax the transportation of oil and gas by pipeline. Ga., Mo., Okla., and Utah do not tax transportation of property. Miss. taxes taxicab transportation at the rate of 2%. Okla. does not tax fares of 15¢ or less on local transportation. Utah does not tax street railway fares.

(5) "Lease" excludes the use of tangible personal property for a period of less than one day for a charge of less than $10 when the privilege of using the property is restricted to use on the premises or at a business location of the grantor.

(6) A limited credit (or refund) in the form of a flat dollar amount per personal exemption is allowed against the personal income tax to compensate for (1) sales taxes paid on food in Col., D.C., and Neb.; and (2) all sales taxes paid in Ida., Mass., and Vt. Low-income taxpayers (adjusted gross income not over $6,000) are allowed a credit against D.C. tax liability ranging from $2 to $6 per personal exemption, depending on taxpayer's income bracket. A refund is allowed if credit exceeds tax liability.

(7) Restaurant meals below a specified price are exempt: Conn. and Md. less than $1; N.Y. less than $1 (when alcoholic beverages are sold, meals are taxable regardless of price); and Pa., 50¢ or less. In Mass., restaurant meals ($1 or more) which are taxed at 8% under the meals excise tax are exempt.

(8) Conn. exempts clothing for children under 10 years of age. Pa. and Wisc. exempt clothing with certain exceptions.

(9) In Col. and Conn., the first 30 consecutive days of rental or occupancy of rooms is taxable. Over 30 days is exempt. In Mass., transient lodging (in excess of $2 a day) is subject to a 5.7% (5% plus 14% surtax) room occupancy excise tax. In N.J. and N.Y., rooms which rent for $2 a day or less are exempt.

(10) Includes a statewide mandatory 1% county sales tax collected by the state and paid to the counties for support of local school districts.

(11) Md. taxes at 0.5% gross receipts derived from charges for rentals of sporting or recreational equipment, and admis-

sions, cover charges for tables, services or merchandise at any roof garden or cabaret. In N.J., admissions to a place of amusement are taxable if the charge is in excess of 75¢. N.Y. taxes admissions when the charge is over 10¢; exempt are participating sports (such as bowling and swimming), motion picture theaters, race tracks, boxing, wrestling, and live dramatic or musical performances. In Wis., sales of admissions to motion picture theaters costing 75¢ or less are exempt.

(12) Meals and rooms are exempt from sales tax, but are subject to a special excise tax of 5%.

(13) Gas, water, electricity, telephone and telegraph services provided to consumers through mains, lines or pipes are exempt. Gas and electric energy used for domestic heating are exempt. Interstate telephone calls are exempt, as are calls from coin-operated telephones.

(14) Beginning Jan. 1, 1975, a surcharge for efficiency is imposed at the rate of 1/10th mill ($0.0001) per kwh.

## State Estate Tax Rates and Exemptions

Source: Compiled by Tax Foundation from Commerce Clearing House data
As of Sept. 1, 1978. *See index for state inheritance tax rates and exemptions.*

| State (a) | Rates (on net estate after exemptions) (b) | Maximum rate applies above | Exemption |
|---|---|---|---|
| Alabama | Maximum federal credit (c, d) | $10,040,000 | $60,000 |
| Alaska | Maximum federal credit (c, d) | 10,040,000 | 60,000 |
| Arizona | 0.8% on first $50,000 to 16% (e) | 10,000,000 | 100,000 (f, g) |
| Arkansas | Maximum federal credit (c, d) | 10,040,000 | 60,000 (g) |
| Florida | Maximum federal credit (c, d) | 10,040,000 | 60,000 |
| Georgia | Maximum federal credit (c, d) | 10,040,000 | 60,000 |
| Massachusetts | 5% on first $50,000 to 16% | 4,000,000 | 30,000 (h) |
| Mississippi | 1% on first $60,000 to 16% | 10,000,000 | 60,000 (f, g) |
| New Mexico | Maximum federal credit (c, d) | 10,040,000 | 60,000 |
| New York | 2% on first $50,000 to 21% (e,i) | 10,100,000 | (f,g,i) |
| North Dakota | 4% on first $10,000 to 18% (e) | 80,000 | 60,000 (g) |
| Ohio | 2% on first $40,000 to 7% (e). | 500,000 | 5,000 (g, k) |
| Oklahoma | 1% on first $10,000 to 10% (e). | 10,000,000 | 60,000 (g,l,m) |
| South Carolina | 4% on first $40,000 to 6%. | 100,000 | 60,000 (g) |
| Utah | Maximum federal credit (c, d). | 10,400,000 | 60,000 (g) |
| Vermont | Maximum federal credit (e, n). | 10,040,000 | 60,000 (g) |

(a) Excludes states shown in table on page 77 which levy an estate tax, in addition to their inheritance taxes, to assure full absorption of the federal credit.

(b) The rates generally are in addition to graduated absolute amounts.

(c) Maximum federal credit allowed under the 1954 code for state estate taxes paid is expressed as a percentage of the taxable estate (after $60,000 exemption) in excess of $40,000, plus a graduated absolute amount.

(d) A tax on nonresident estates is imposed on the proportionate share of the net estate which the property located in the state bears to the entire estate wherever situated.

(e) An additional estate tax is imposed to assure full absorption of the federal credit.

(f) Insurance receives special treatment.

(g) Transfers to religious, charitable, educational, and municipal corporations are fully exempt. Limited in Mississippi to those located in U.S. or its possessions.

(h) Applies to net estates above $60,000.

(i) On net estate before exemption.

(j) The specific exemptions ($20,000 of the net estate transferred to spouse and $5,000 to lineal ancestors and descendants and certain other named relatives) are allowed in an amount equal to 2% of the first $50,000 and 3% of the next $100,000.

(k) Property is exempt to the extent transferred to surviving spouse not exceeding $30,000; for a child under 18, $7,000, and for each child 18 or over, $3,000.

(l) An estate valued at $100 or less is exempt.

(m) Exemption is a total aggregate of $60,000 for father, mother, child, and other named relatives.

(n) The tax is 30% of the federal estate tax liability. Taxes on estates of decedents dying after 12/31/76, but before 1/1/79, are reduced by the percentage that $120,000 is of the amount of the federal taxable estate; after 12/31/78, $240,000. The reduction shall not be more than 100%.

## City Income Tax in U.S. Cities over 50,000

Compiled by Tax Foundation from Commerce Clearing House data and other sources.

| City | Rates % 1978 | Rates % Orig. | Year began |
|---|---|---|---|
| **Cities with 500,000 or more inhabitants** | | | |
| Baltimore, Md. | (50% of state tax) | 1.0 | 1966 |
| Cleveland, Oh. | 1.0 | 0.5 | 1967 |
| Columbus, Oh. | 1.5 | 0.5 | 1947 |
| Detroit, Mich. | 2.0 | 1.0 | 1965 |
| Kansas City, Mo. | 1.0 | 0.5 | 1964 |
| New York, N.Y. | .4-2 | 0.4-2.0 | 1966 |
| Philadelphia, Pa. | 4.3125 | 1.5 | 1939 |
| Pittsburgh, Pa. | 1.0 | 1.0 | 1954 |
| St. Louis, Mo. | 1.0 | .25 | 1948 |
| **Cities with 100,000 to 499,999 inhabitants** | | | |
| Akron, Oh. | 1.5 | 1.0 | 1962 |
| Allentown, Pa. | 1.0 | 1.0 | 1958 |
| Birmingham, Ala. | 1.0 | 1.0 | 1970 |
| Canton, Oh. | 1.5 | 0.6 | 1954 |
| Cincinnati, Oh. | 2.0 | 1.0 | 1954 |
| Dayton, Oh. | 1.75 | 0.5 | 1949 |
| Erie, Pa. | 1.0 | 1.0 | 1948 |
| Flint, Mich. | 1.0 | 1.0 | 1965 |
| Grand Rapids, Mich. | 1.0 | 1.0 | 1967 |
| Lansing, Mich. | 1.0 | 1.0 | 1968 |
| Lexington, Ky. | 2.0 | 1.0 | 1952 |
| Louisville, Ky. | 2.0 | 1.0 | 1948 |
| Montgomery, Ala. | 1.0 | 1.0 | 1972 |
| Parma, Oh. | 1.0 | 0.5 | 1967 |
| Scranton, Pa. | 2.0 | 1.0 | 1948 |
| Toledo, Oh. | 1.5 | 1.0 | 1946 |
| Youngstown, Oh. | 1.5 | 0.3 | 1948 |
| **Cities with 50,000 to 99,999 inhabitants** | | | |
| Altoona, Pa. | 1.0 | 1.0 | 1948 |
| Bethlehem, Pa. | 1.0 | 1.0 | 1957 |
| Chester, Pa. | 1.0 | 1.0 | 1956 |
| Covington, Ky. | 2.5 | 1.0 | 1956 |
| Euclid, Oh. | 1.0 | 0.5 | 1967 |
| Gadsden, Ala. | 2.0 | 1.0 | 1956 |
| Hamilton, Oh. | 1.5 | 0.8 | 1960 |
| Harrisburg, Pa. | 1.0 | 1.0 | 1966 |
| Lakewood, Oh. | 1.0 | 1.0 | 1968 |
| Lancaster, Pa. | 0.5 | 0.5 | 1959 |
| Lima, Oh. | 1.0 | .75 | 1959 |
| Lorain, Oh. | 1.0 | 0.5 | 1967 |
| Pontiac, Mich. | 1.0 | 1.0 | 1968 |
| Reading, Pa. | 1.0 | 1.0 | 1969 |
| Saginaw, Mich. | 1.0 | 1.0 | 1965 |
| Springfield, Oh. | 2.0 | 1.0 | 1948 |
| Warren, Oh. | 1.0 | 0.5 | 1952 |
| Wilkes-Barre, Pa. | 1.0 | 1.0 | 1966 |
| Wilmington, Del. | 1.0 | 0.5 | 1970 |
| York, Pa. | 1.0 | 1.0 | 1965 |

## State Inheritance Tax Rates and Exemptions

Source: Compiled by Tax Foundation from Commerce Clearing House data.
As of Sept. 1, 1978

| State (a) | Rates (b) (per cent) Spouse, child, or parent | Brother or sister | Other than relative | Max. rate applies above ($1,000) | Exemptions (c) ($1,000) Spouse | Child or parent | Brother or sister | Other than relative |
|---|---|---|---|---|---|---|---|---|
| California | 3-14 | 6-20 | 10-24 | $400 | $60(d) | $5(e) | $2 | $0.3 |
| Colorado (f) | 3-9 | 4-11 | 11-20 | 500 | 75 | 25(e) | 3 | 0.5 (g) |
| Connecticut (i) | 2-8 | 4-10 | 8-14 | 1,000 | 50 | 10 | 3 | 0.5 |
| Delaware | 1-6 | 5-10 | 10-16 | 200 | 70 | 3 | 1 | None |
| District of Columbia | 1-8 | 5-23 | 5-23 | 1,000 | 5 | 5 | 1 | 1 |
| Hawaii | 2-7 | 3-8 | 3-10 | 200 | 100 | 50 | 5 | 5 |
| Idaho | 2-15 | 4-20 | 8-30 | 500 | 30(d) | 15(e) | 10 | 10 |
| Illinois | 2-14 | 2-14 | 10-30 | 500 | 20 | 20 | 10 | 0.1 |
| Indiana | 1-10 | 7-15 | 10-20 | 1,500(h) | 60 | 2(e) | 0.5 | 0.1 |
| Iowa | 1-8 | 5-10 | 10-15 | 150 | 80 | 10(e) | None | None |
| Kansas | 0.5-5 | 3-12.5 | 10-15 | 500 | 75 | 15 | 5 | 0.2 (g) |
| Kentucky | 2-10 | 4-16 | 6-16 | 500(j) | 20 | 5(e) | 1 | 0.5 |
| Louisiana | 2-3 | 5-7 | 5-10 | 25 | 5(d) | 5 | 1 | 0.5 |
| Maine | 5-10 | 8-14 | 14-18 | (h) | 50 | 25 | 1 | 1 |
| Maryland (k) | 1 | 10 | 10 | (l) | .15 (g) | .15 (g) | 0.15 (g) | 0.15 (g) |
| Massachusetts (m) | 1.8-11.8 | 5.5-19.3 | 8-19.3 | 1,000 | 30(n) | 15(n) | 5 (n) | 5 (n) |
| Michigan | 2-8 (o) | 2-8 (o) | 10-15 (o) | 750 | 30(e) | 5 | 5 | None . |
| Minnesota | 1.5-10 | 6-25 | 8-30 | 1,000 | 60 | 6(e) | 1.5 | 0.5 |
| Missouri | 1-6 | 3-18 | 5-30 | 400 | 20(p) | 5(e) | 0.5 | 0.1 (g) |
| Montana | 2-8 | 4-16 | 8-32 | 100 | 40 | 7(e) | 1.0 | None |
| Nebraska | 1 | 1 | 6-18 | 60 | 10 | 10 | 10 | 0.5 |
| New Hampshire | (q) | 15 | 15 | (l) | (q) | (q) | None | None |
| New Jersey | 1-16 | 11-16 | 15-16 | 3,200 | 15 | 15 | 0.5 (g) | 0.5 (g) |
| North Carolina | 1-12 | 4-16 | 8-17 | 3,000 | 10 | 2(e) | None | None |
| Oregon | 12 | 12 | 12 | 50(r) | 54(s) | None | None | None |
| Pennsylvania | 6 | 15 | 15 | (l) | None(t) | None(t) | None | None |
| Rhode Island | 2-9 | 3-10 | 8-15 | 1,000(u) | 10 | 10 | 5 | 1 |
| South Dakota (a) | (v) | 4-16 | 6-24 | 100 | 80(v) | 3(e) | 0.5 | 0.1 |
| Tennessee | 5.5-9.5 | 6.5-20 | 6.5-20 | 500 | 60 | 60 | 1 | .1 |
| Texas | 1-6 | 3-10 | 5-20 | 1,000 | 200(w) | 200(w) | 10 | 0.5 |
| Virginia | 1-5 | 2-10 | 5-15 | 1,000 | 5 | 5 | 2 | 1 |
| Washington | 1-10 | 3-20 | 10-25 | 500 | 5(d) | 5 | 1 | None |
| West Virginia | 3-13 | 4-18 | 10-30 | 1,000 | 30 | 10 | 10 | None |
| Wisconsin | 1.25-12.5 | 5-25 | 10-30(x) | 500 | 50 | 4 | 1 | 0.5 |
| Wyoming | 2 | 2 | 6 | (l) | 60 | 10 | 10 | None |

(a) In addition to an inheritance tax, all states listed also levy an estate tax, generally to assure full absorption of the federal credit. Exception is S.D.

(b) Rates generally apply to excess above graduated absolute amounts.

(c) Generally, transfers to governments or to solely charitable, educational, scientific, religious, literary, public, and other similar organizations in the U.S. are wholly exempt. Some states grant additional exemptions either for insurance, homestead, joint deposits, support allowance, disinherited minor children, orphaned, incompetent or blind children, and for previously or later taxed transfers. In many states, exemptions are deducted from the first bracket only.

(d) Community property state in which, in general, either all community property to the surviving spouse is exempt, or only one-half of the community property is taxable on the death of either spouse.

(e) Exemption for child (in thousands): $30 in Iowa; and $30 in S.D. Exemption for minor child is (in thousands): $12 in Cal.; $37.5 in Col.; $30 in Idaho; $5 in Ind.; $10 in Ky.; $30 in Minn.; $15 in Mon.; $5 in N.C. In Mo. the exemption for an insane, blind or otherwise incapacitated lineal descendant is (thousands) $15. In Mich. a widow receives $5,000 for every minor child to whom no property is transferred in addition to the normal exemption for a spouse.

(f) Col. imposes an additional tax of 10% upon the amount of tax computed at above rates.

(g) No exemption if share exceeds amount stated.

(h) Maximum rate for brother or sister and any other than relative in Indiana is $1 million. In Maine the maximum rate for any other than relative is $150 thousand.

(i) On estates an additional inheritance tax equal to 30% of the basic tax is imposed.

(j) Estates over $3 million are not subject to the inheritance tax but are subject to an estate tax equal to the amount of the federal credit.

(k) Where property of a decedent subject to administration in Md. is $5,000 or less, no inheritance taxes are due.

(l) Rate applies to entire share.

(m) Mass. imposes a 14% surtax in addition to the inheritance tax on all property or interests. This tax is suspended for estates of decedents dying on or after 1/1/76.

(n) No exemption if share exceeds amount stated except that the tax shall not reduce the share below the amount of the exemption. In addition there are certain exemptions for the spouse's home.

(o) There is no tax on the share of any beneficiary if the value of the share is less than $100. In addition each county collects an additional 0.5% of the tax collected.

(p) In addition, an exemption of ½ of the decedent's estate, or ⅓ if decedent is survived by lineal descendents.

(q) Spouses, minor children, parents, and minor adopted children in the decendent's line of succession are exempt.

(r) Net taxable estates are allowed an exemption of $50,000 if the decedent died in 1978, $70,000 if death occurs in 1979 or 1980, $100,000 if death occurs in 1981 or 1982, $200,000 if death occurs in 1983 or 1984 and $500,000 if death occurs in 1985 or 1986.

(s) Credit is allowed to surviving spouse, child or stepchild under 18 years or child who is incapable of self support. The credit is $54,000 in 1978, $51,000 in 1979 and 1980, $48,000 in 1981 and 1982, $36,000 in 1983 and 1984 and zero thereafter. Estates of descendants dying on or after 1/1/87 are not subject to inheritance tax.

(t) However, the $2,000 family exemption is specifically allowed as a deduction.

(u) Beneficiaries of estates worth more than $250,000 are liable for their share of the additional estate tax.

(v) The rates range from 3-6% for a spouse and child and from 3-12% for parents. Effective 7/1/79, exemption for spouse is $100,000.

(w) Increased to $250,00 from 1/1/82 through 8/31/85 and to $300,000 beginning 9/1/85. When more than one beneficiary (spouse, child or parent) receives property, and when the total exceeds the amount of the exemption, the exemption is divided proportionally.

(x) Maximum rate applies above $50,000.

# Federal Estate and Gift Tax

Source: Tax Foundation, Inc.

As a result of sweeping changes introduced by the Tax Reform Act of 1976, the federal government now taxes estates and gifts on an entirely different basis than previously applied. The major changes include the unification of estate and gift rates, the substitution of a unified credit for the previous estate and gift tax exemptions, and a new tax on generation-skipping.

## Estate Tax

Instead of the specific exemptions which were subtracted from the total estate (previously $60,000) or the lifetime gift total (previously $30,000), the new law provides for a unified credit against combined estate and gift taxes. For estates of decedents who die in 1977, the unified credit is $30,000; in 1978, $34,000; in 1979, $38,000; in 1980, $42,500; in 1981 and thereafter $47,000. The 1977 credit is in general equivalent to an exemption of $120,660; by 1981, to $175,625.

Estate taxes are computed by applying the unified rate schedule, shown below, to the total estate (minus allowable deductions) plus taxable gifts made after 1976. Gift taxes paid are subtracted from tax due, and credit also may be taken for state death taxes. The amount of the state tax credit is determined by the schedule shown in the table below or the actual state taxes paid, whichever is less. No state tax credit is available to an adjusted taxable estate (i.e., taxable estate minus $60,000) smaller than $40,000.

Deductions may be taken from the gross estate for funeral expenses, administration expenses, debts, charitable contributions, and, within limitations, bequests to the surviving spouse. A special deduction is allowed for estates passing to orphans, up to $5,000 per child multiplied by the number of years by which 21 exceeds the child's age. For instance, two orphaned children aged 7 and 9 would be entitled to a deduction of $130,000.

The marital deduction for small and medium-sized estates is increased to the larger of 50 percent of the adjusted gross estate or $250,000. A fractional interest rule eliminates the previous requirement for a consideration-furnished test. In general, each spouse's interest will be one-half, where property is jointly held with rights of survivorship and joint tenancy is created by a transfer subject to gift tax provisions.

The new law provides for real property passed on to family members for use in a closely held business, such as farming, to be valued on basis of such use, rather than fair market value on basis of highest and best use. In no case may this special valuation reduce the gross estate by more than $500,000.

Generation-skipping transfers which occur after April 30, 1976, in general are now subject to taxes substantially equivalent to those which would have been imposed had the property been transferred outright to each successive generation. However, an exclusion is provided for transfers to grandchildren up to $250,000 for each child of the decedent who serves as a conduit for the transfer (not for each grandchild).

A return must be filed for the estate of every U.S. citizen or resident whose gross estate exceeds $120,000 ($60,000 if the decedent dies before 1977; $36,000 for the estate of a nonresident who is not a citizen). The return is due nine months after death unless an extension is granted.

## Gift Tax

Any citizen or resident alien whose gifts to any one person exceed $3,000 within a calendar year will be liable for payment of a gift tax, at rates determined under the unified estate and gift tax schedule. Gift tax returns are filed on a quarterly basis and ordinarily are due a month and a half following any quarter in which a taxable gift was made (i.e., May 15, August 15, November 15, and February 15). After 1976, however, quarterly filing is not required until cumulative taxable gifts during the year exceed $25,000.

Gifts made by husband and wife to a third party may be considered as having been made one-half by each, provided both spouses consent to such division. For gifts between spouses, there is an unlimited deduction for the first $100,000 of lifetime gifts.

## Unified Rate Schedule for Estate and Gift Tax

| If the amount with respect to which the tentative tax to be computed is: | | | The tentative tax is: | | |
|---|---|---|---|---|---|
| Not over $10,000 | | | 18 percent of such amount. | | |
| Over $10,000 | but not over | $20,000. | $1,800, plus 20% | of the excess over | $10,000. |
| Over $20,000 | but not over | $40,000. | $3,800, plus 22% | of the excess over | $20,000. |
| Over $40,000 | but not over | $60,000. | $8,200, plus 24% | of the excess over | $40,000. |
| Over $60,000 | but not over | $80,000. | $13,000, plus 26% | of the excess over | $60,000. |
| Over $80,000 | but not over | $100,000. | $18,200, plus 28% | of the excess over | $80,000. |
| Over $100,000 | but not over | $150,000. | $23,800, plus 30% | of the excess over | $100,000. |
| Over $150,000 | but not over | $250,000. | $38,800, plus 32% | of the excess over | $150,000. |
| Over $250,000 | but not over | $500,000. | $70,800, plus 34% | of the excess over | $250,000. |
| Over $500,000 | but not over | $750,000. | $155,800, plus 37% | of the excess over | $500,000. |
| Over $750,000 | but not over | $1,000,000. | $248,300, plus 39% | of the excess over | $750,000. |
| Over $1,000,000 | but not over | $1,250,000. | $345,800, plus 41% | of the excess over | $1,000,000. |
| Over $1,250,000 | but not over | $1,500,000. | $448,300, plus 43% | of the excess over | $1,250,000. |
| Over $1,500,000 | but not over | $2,000,000. | $555,800, plus 45% | of the excess over | $1,500,000. |
| Over $2,000,000 | but not over | $2,500,000. | $780,800, plus 49% | of the excess over | $2,000,000. |
| Over $2,500,000 | but not over | $3,000,000. | $1,025,800, plus 53% | of the excess over | $2,500,000. |
| Over $3,000,000 | but not over | $3,500,000. | $1,290,800, plus 57% | of the excess over | $3,000,000. |
| Over $3,500,000 | but not over | $4,000,000. | $1,575,800, plus 61% | of the excess over | $3,500,000. |
| Over $4,000,000 | but not over | $4,500,000. | $1,880,800, plus 65% | of the excess over | $4,000,000. |
| Over $4,500,000 | but not over | $5,000,000. | $2,205,800, plus 69% | of the excess over | $4,500,000. |
| Over $5,000,000 | | | $2,550,800, plus 70% | of the excess over | $5,000,000. |

## State Death Tax Credit for Estate Tax

| Adjusted taxable estate from | to | Credit = + | % | Of excess over | Adjusted taxable estate from | to | Credit = + | % | Of excess over |
|---|---|---|---|---|---|---|---|---|---|
| $ 0 | $ 40,000 | 0 | 0 | $ 0 | 2,540,000 | 3,040,000 | 146,800 | 8.8 | 2,540,000 |
| 40,000 | 90,000 | 0 | .8 | 40,000 | 3,040,000 | 3,540,000 | 190,800 | 9.6 | 3,040,000 |
| 90,000 | 140,000 | 400 | 1.6 | 90,000 | 3,540,000 | 4,040,000 | 238,800 | 10.4 | 3,540,000 |
| 140,000 | 240,000 | 1,200 | 2.4 | 140,000 | 4,040,000 | 5,040,000 | 290,800 | 11.2 | 4,040,000 |
| 240,000 | 440,000 | 3,600 | 3.2 | 240,000 | 5,040,000 | 6,040,000 | 402,800 | 12 | 5,040,000 |
| 440,000 | 640,000 | 10,000 | 4 | 440,000 | 6,040,000 | 7,040,000 | 522,800 | 12.8 | 6,040,000 |
| 640,000 | 840,000 | 18,000 | 4.8 | 640,000 | 7,040,000 | 8,040,000 | 650,800 | 13.6 | 7,040,000 |
| 840,000 | 1,040,000 | 27,600 | 5.6 | 840,000 | 8,040,000 | 9,040,000 | 786,800 | 14.4 | 8,040,000 |
| 1,040,000 | 1,540,000 | 38,800 | 6.4 | 1,040,000 | 9,040,000 | 10,040,000 | 930,800 | 15.2 | 9,040,000 |
| 1,540,000 | 2,040,000 | 70,800 | 7.2 | 1,540,000 | 10,040,000 | | 1,082,800 | 16 | 10,040,000 |
| 2,040,000 | 2,540,000 | 106,800 | 8 | 2,040,000 | | | | | |

(1) The adjusted taxable estate equals the taxable estate minus $60,000.

## Savings by Individuals in the U.S.

Source: Federal Reserve System
(billions of dollars).

| | 1968 | 1970 | 1974 | 1975 | 1976 | 1977 | 1978[1] |
|---|---|---|---|---|---|---|---|
| Increase in financial assets. | 76.4 | 79.1 | 138.8 | 166.4 | 199.8 | 235.7 | 222.4 |
| Currency and demand deposits | 11.1 | 8.9 | 7.9 | 5.2 | 13.8 | 20.4 | 26.8 |
| Savings accounts | 31.1 | 43.6 | 57.2 | 84.8 | 108.1 | 108.3 | 106.6 |
| Securities. | 6.0 | −3.0 | 29.2 | 21.9 | 5.3 | 18.7 | 18.9 |
| U.S. Savings Bonds | 0.6 | 0.3 | 3.0 | 4.0 | 4.7 | 4.7 | 4.3 |
| Other U.S. Treasury sec. | 4.2 | −11.3 | 7.4 | 13.7 | −3.4 | −3.2 | −6.7 |
| U.S. Govt. agency securities | 1.4 | 4.6 | 4.1 | −3.2 | 3.5 | 3.9 | 3.2 |
| State & local obligations. | −0.5 | −0.9 | 8.2 | 6.1 | 5.1 | 8.8 | 8.5 |
| Corporation & foreign bonds | 4.2 | 9.5 | 4.7 | 8.0 | 2.1 | 1.1 | −2.1 |
| Commercial paper | 2.6 | −3.8 | 4.1 | −3.2 | −3.2 | 8.4 | 14.0 |
| Investment company shares | 5.9 | 2.8 | −0.7 | −0.1 | −1.0 | −1.0 | 0.4 |
| Other corporate stock | −12.4 | −4.3 | −1.5 | −3.6 | −2.4 | −4.1 | −2.7 |
| Private life insurance reserves | 4.6 | 5.1 | 6.4 | 5.3 | 6.7 | 7.9 | 7.8 |
| Private insured pension reserves | 2.9 | 3.3 | 6.2 | 10.3 | 15.3 | 14.9 | 16.0 |
| Private noninsured pension reserves | 6.5 | 7.1 | 10.9 | 12.8 | 12.8 | 21.0 | 16.2 |
| Government ins. & pension reserves | 6.1 | 8.9 | 12.6 | 15.0 | 18.1 | 19.8 | 0.5 |
| Miscellaneous financial assets | 8.0 | 5.3 | 8.5 | 11.0 | 19.7 | 24.6 | 29.6 |
| Gross investment in tangible assets. | 133.3 | 142.4 | 201.8 | 215.0 | 254.1 | 307.9 | 341.3 |
| Nonfarm homes | 24.7 | 24.5 | 42.9 | 43.0 | 57.5 | 76.3 | 90.3 |
| Noncorporate business construction & equipment. | 27.7 | 32.6 | 40.9 | 39.7 | 43.0 | 50.7 | 54.4 |
| Consumer durables | 80.0 | 84.9 | 122.0 | 132.6 | 156.6 | 178.4 | 198.0 |
| Inventories | 0.8 | 0.4 | −4.0 | −0.3 | −3.1 | 2.5 | −1.3 |
| Capital consumption allowances | 85.4 | 103.6 | 148.9 | 172.0 | 184.3 | 204.9 | 223.5 |
| Nonfarm homes | 10.5 | 12.8 | 19.8 | 22.2 | 24.4 | 28.3 | 31.7 |
| Noncorporate business plant and equipment. | 19.2 | 23.2 | 34.1 | 39.6 | 43.4 | 47.6 | 52.9 |
| Consumer durables | 55.7 | 67.5 | 95.0 | 110.2 | 116.6 | 128.9 | 138.8 |
| Net investment in tangible assets | 47.9 | 38.8 | 52.9 | 43.0 | 69.7 | 103.0 | 117.9 |
| Nonfarm homes | 14.3 | 11.7 | 23.1 | 20.9 | 33.2 | 48.0 | 58.5 |
| Noncorporate business construction and equipment | 8.6 | 9.4 | 6.8 | — | −0.4 | 3.1 | 1.4 |
| Consumer durables | 24.3 | 17.4 | 27.0 | 22.5 | 40.1 | 49.4 | 59.2 |
| Inventories | 0.8 | 0.4 | −4.0 | −0.3 | −3.1 | 2.5 | −1.3 |
| Increase in debt | 43.3 | 34.0 | 65.8 | 63.7 | 115.1 | 172.4 | 179.9 |
| Mortgage debt on nonfarm homes | 17.1 | 14.1 | 35.4 | 38.1 | 61.3 | 93.0 | 88.6 |
| Noncorporate business mortgage debt | 6.3 | 8.5 | 12.7 | 7.4 | 10.8 | 19.0 | 22.3 |
| Consumer credit | 10.0 | 5.9 | 10.2 | 9.4 | 23.6 | 35.0 | 51.6 |
| Security credit | 2.9 | −1.8 | −1.8 | 0.8 | 4.7 | 3.1 | 5.6 |
| Policy loans | 1.3 | 2.3 | 2.7 | 1.6 | 1.4 | 0.7 | 2.8 |
| Other debt | — | — | 6.6 | 6.5 | 13.4 | 20.6 | 8.9 |
| Individuals' saving. | 81.0 | 84.0 | 125.9 | 145.7 | 154.4 | 166.3 | 160.4 |
| Less Govt. ins. & pen. reserves | 6.1 | 8.9 | 12.6 | 15.0 | 18.1 | 19.8 | 0.5 |
| Net inv. in consumer durables | 24.3 | 17.4 | 27.0 | 22.5 | 40.1 | 49.4 | 59.2 |
| Capital gains dividends from invest. cos. | 2.5 | 0.9 | 0.5 | 0.2 | 0.5 | 0.6 | 0.9 |
| Net savings by farm corps. | — | −0.1 | −0.1 | 0.2 | — | — | 0.2 |
| Equals pers. saving, F/F basis | 48.2 | 56.9 | 86.0 | 108.0 | 96.3 | 97.0 | 100.3 |
| Personal saving, NIA basis. | 38.1 | 50.6 | 71.7 | 83.6 | 68.0 | 66.9 | 74.6 |
| Difference | 10.1 | 6.3 | 14.4 | 24.4 | 28.2 | 30.1 | 25.6 |

(1) 2d quarter, 1978, seasonally adjusted.

---

## Major Federal Tax Expenditures (Loopholes)

Source: Office of Management and Budget
(Estimates for fiscal year 1977)

Income tax provisions resulting in tax expenditures are defined as exceptions to the "normal structure" of individual and corporate income tax. They reduce tax liabilities for particular groups of taxpayers. The normal structure is nowhere defined in the tax code. Existing rates are accepted as "normal"; when the rate structure is changed, for whatever reason, the new rate structure becomes the new norm.

The following features of the tax system are defined as part of the normal tax structure and therefore **do not result in tax expenditures**: progressive rate schedules for individual income tax; personal exemptions and the minimum standard deduction; separate schedules for single and married persons, married persons filing separately, and heads of households; deduction of business expenses; exclusion of unrealized capital gains and losses; exclusion of gifts and bequests received; exclusion of the value of government services received in kind (e.g., food stamps); foreign tax credits; treatment of individuals and corporations as separate tax paying entities.

| Item | Amount (in millions) | |
|---|---|---|
| | Individual | Corporate |
| State and local tax deduction | $7,660 | — |
| Investment credit | 2,075 | $8,880 |
| Capital gains, lower tax on | 15,555 | 730 |
| Home mortgage interest deduction. | 4,490 | — |
| Employer pension contribution exclusion | 8,715 | — |
| Charitable contributions deduction | 5,250 | 670 |
| Home property tax deduction | 4,205 | — |
| Interest on State and local bonds exclusion | 1,905 | 3,470 |
| Corporate profits, lower tax on first $50,000 | — | 3,875 |
| Employer medical care and insurance payments exclusion | 5,560 | — |
| Social security retirement benefits exclusion | 3,790 | — |
| Percentage depletion allowance | 305 | 1,090 |
| Medical expense deduction | 2,230 | — |
| Unemployment insurance benefits exclusion | 1,500 | — |
| Interest on life insurance savings exclusion | 1,850 | — |
| Consumer credit interest deduction | 1,785 | — |
| Additional exemption for over 65 | 1,140 | — |
| Armed forces personnel benefits exclusion | 1,095 | — |
| Self-employed pension contributions exclusion | 1,390 | — |
| Expensing of research and development | 30 | 1,395 |
| Asset depreciation range | 100 | 1,955 |

# Directory of Federal Consumer and Information Offices

Source: Office of Consumer Affairs, U.S. Department of Health, Education, and Welfare

**Advertising:**
Director, Bureau of Consumer Protection, Federal Trade Commission, Washington, DC 20580; phone (202) 523-3727.

**Air travel-routes and service:**
Director, Office of Consumer Protection, Civil Aeronautics Board, Washington, DC 20423; phone (202) 673-5937.

**Air travel-safety:**
For general information contact the Community and Consumer Liaison Division, Federal Aviation Administration, APA-430, Washington, DC 20591; phone (202) 426-8058. For specific safety problems contact the above office marking correspondence APA-100; phone (202) 426-1960.

**Alcohol:**
Chief, Trade and Consumer Affairs Division, Bureau of Alcohol, Tobacco, and Firearms, Department of the Treasury, Washington, DC 20226; phone (202) 566-7581.

**Alcoholism, drug abuse, and mental illness:**
Office of Public Affairs, Alcohol, Drug Abuse and Mental Health Service, 5600 Fishers Lane, Rockville, MD 20857; phone (301) 443-3783.

**Antitrust:**
Bureau of Competition, Federal Trade Commission, Washington, DC 20580; phone (202) 523-3601.
Consumer Affairs Section, Antitrust Division, Justice Department, Washington, DC 20530; phone (202) 739-4173.

**Auto safety and highways:**
Director, Office of Public and Consumer Affairs, Transportation Department, Washington, DC 20590; phone (202) 426-4518.
National Highway Traffic Safety Administration; toll-free hotline **(800) 424-9393.** In Washington, DC call 426-0123.
Associate Administrator for Planning, Federal Highway Administration, Washington, DC 20590; phone (202) 426-0585.

**Banks:**
*Federal Credit Unions*
National Credit Union Administration, Washington, DC 20456; phone (202) 254-8760.
*Federally Insured Savings and Loans*
Consumer Division, Office of Community Investment, Federal Home Loan Bank Board, Washington, DC 20552; phone (202) 377-6237.
*Federal Reserve Banks*
Office of Saver and Consumer Affairs, Federal Reserve System, Washington, DC 20551; phone (202) 452-3000.
*National Banks*
Consumer Affairs, Office of the Comptroller of the Currency, Washington, DC 20219; phone (202) 447-1600.
*State Chartered Banks*
Office of Bank Customer Affairs, Federal Deposit Insurance Corporation, Washington, DC 20429; phone (202) 389-4427.

**Boating:**
Chief, Information and Administrative Staff, U.S. Coast Guard, Washington, DC 20590; phone (202) 426-1080.

**Bus Travel:**
Consumer Affairs Office, Interstate Commerce Commission, Washington, DC 20423; phone (202) 275-7252.

**Business:**
Office of the Ombudsman, Department of Commerce, Washington, DC 20230; phone (202) 377-3176.
Director, Women-in-Business and Consumer Affairs, Small Business Administration, 1441 L St. NW, Washington, DC 20416; phone (202) 653-6074.

**Child abuse:**
National Center on Child Abuse and Neglect, P.O. Box 1182, Washington DC 20013; phone (202) 755-0593.

**Childhood immunization:**
Office of the Assistant Secretary for Health, Office of Public Affairs, Washington, DC 20201; phone (202) 472-5663.

**Children and youth:**
Director of Public Affairs, Office of Human Development Services, Department of Health, Education, and Welfare, Washington, DC 20201; phone (202) 472-7257.

**Commodity trading:**
Consumer Hotline, Commodity Futures Trading Commission, 2033 K St. NW, Washington, DC 20581; toll-free hotline in California and states east of the Mississippi **(800) 424-9838;** states west of the Mississippi except California, **(800) 227-4428.** In Washington, D.C. call 254-8630.

**Consumer information:**
For a copy of the free *Consumer Information Catalog,* a listing of more than 200 selected Federal consumer publications on such topics as child care, automobiles, health, employment, housing, energy, etc., send a postcard to the Consumer Information Center, Pueblo, CO 81009.

**Copyrights:**
Copyright Office, Crystal Mall, 1921 Jefferson Davis Hwy., Arlington, VA 20559; phone (703) 557-8700.

**Credit:**
Director, Bureau of Consumer Protection, Federal Trade Commission, Washington, DC 20850; phone (202) 523-3727.

**Crime insurance:**
Federal Crime Insurance, Department of Housing and Urban Development, P.O. Box 41033, Washington, DC 20014; toll-free hotline **(800) 638-8780.** In Washington, D.C. call 652-2637.

**Customs:**
Public Information Division, U.S. Customs, Washington, DC 20229; phone (202) 566-8195.

**Discrimination:**
U.S. Commission on Civil Rights, 1121 Vermont Ave. Washington, DC 20425; phone (202) 254-6697.
Equal Employment Opportunity Commission, 2401 E. St. NW, Washington DC 20506; phone (202) 634-6930.
For complaints about discrimination in lending practices by financial and retail institutions based on race, color, religion, national origin, sex, marital status, age, or receipt of public assistance, contact the Housing and Credit Section, Civil Rights Division, Justice Department, Washington, DC 20530; phone (202) 739-4123. (Also see **Housing**)

**Drugs and cosmetics:**
Consumer Inquiry Section, Food and Drug Administration, 5600 Fishers Lane, Rockville, MD 20852; phone (301) 443-3170.

**Education grants and loans:**
Office of Public Affairs, Office of Education, Washington, DC 20202; phone (202) 245-7949. Toll-free hotline for Basic Education Opportunity Grants, **(800) 638-6700.** In Maryland, call **(800) 492-6602.**

**Elderly:**
Administration on Aging, Washington, DC 20201; phone (202) 245-2158.

**mployment and job training:**
Since nearly all employment and training programs are handled at the state or local levels, check your phone directory under your state government for the Employment Service or under your local government for the mayor's office. If you cannot reach these sources, you can obtain general information by writing to the Employment and Training Administration, Department of Labor, Washington, DC 20213; phone (202) 376-6905.

**nergy:**
Director, Office of Consumer Affairs, Department of Energy, Washington, DC 20585; phone (202) 252-5141.

**nergy efficiency:**
Information Office, National Bureau of Standards, Washington, DC 20234; phone (301) 921-3181.

**nvironment:**
Office of Public Awareness, Environmental Protection Agency, Washington, DC 20460; phone (202) 755-0700.

**ederal job information:**
Check for the Federal Job Information Center under the U.S. Government in your phone directory. If there is no listing, call toll-free directory assistance at **(800) 555-1212,** and ask for the number of the Federal Job Information Center in your state. In the Washington, D.C. metropolitan area contact the Civil Service Commission, 1900 E St. NW, Washington, DC 20415; phone (202) 737-9616.

**ederal regulations:**
For information on federal regulations and proposals, the Office of the Federal Register (OFR) is offering, among other services, recorded "Dial-a-Reg" phone messages. "Dial-a-Reg" gives advance information on significant documents to be published in the *Federal Register* the following work day. The service is currently available in three cities: Washington, D.C. telephone (202) 523-5022; Chicago telephone (312) 663-0884; and Los Angeles telephone (213) 688-6694.

**irearms:**
(See Alcohol)

**ish grading:**
National Marine Fisheries Service, Department of Commerce, Washington, DC 20235; phone (202) 634-7458.

**ish and wildlife:**
Fish and Wildlife Service, Office of Public Affairs, Washington, DC 20240; phone (202) 343-5634.

**lood insurance:**
National Flood Insurance, Department of Housing and Urban Development, Washington DC 20410; toll-free hotline **(800) 424-8872.** In Washington, D.C. call 755-9096.

**ood:**
Assistant Secretary for Food and Consumer Services, U.S. Department of Agriculture, Washington, DC 20250; phone (202) 447-4623.
Consumer Inquiry Section, Food and Drug Administration, 5600 Fishers Lane, Rockville, MD 20852; phone (301) 443-3170.

**raud:**
Director, Bureau of Consumer Protection, Federal Trade Commission, Washington, DC 20580; phone (202) 523-3727.

**landicapped:**
Director, Division of Public Information, Office of Human Development Services, Department of Health, Education, and Welfare, Washington, DC 20201; phone (202) 472-7257.

**lousing:**
Department of Housing and Urban Development, Division of Consumer Complaints, Washington, DC 20410; phone (202) 755-5353.
For complaints about housing discrimination call the housing discrimination hotline **(800) 424-8590.** In Washington, D.C. call 755-5490.

**Immigration and naturalization:**
Information Services, Immigration and Naturalization Service, 425 Eye St. NW, Washington, DC 20536; phone (202) 376-8449.

**Indian arts and crafts:**
Indian Arts and Crafts Board, Washington, DC 20240; phone (202) 343-2773.

**Job safety:**
Office of Information, Occupational Safety and Health Administration, Department of Labor, Washington, DC 20210; phone (202) 523-8151.

**Mail:**
*Fraud*
Check with your local postal inspector about problems relating to mail fraud and undelivered merchandise or contact the Chief Postal Inspector, U.S. Postal Inspection Service, Washington, DC 20260; phone (202) 245-5445.
*Service*
Check with your local postmaster or contact the Consumer Advocate, U.S. Postal Service, Room 5920, Washington, DC 20260; phone (202) 245-4514.

**Maps:**
Public Inquiries Office, Geological Survey, National Center, Reston, VA 22092; phone (703) 860-6167.

**Medicaid- Medicare:**
Health Care Financing Administration, Department of Health, Education, and Welfare, Washington, DC 20201; phone (202) 245-0312.

**Medical research:**
Division of Public Information, National Institutes of Health, 9000 Rockville Pike, Bethesda, MD 20014; phone (301) 496-5787.
Center for Disease Control, Attention, Public Inquiries, Atlanta, GA 30333; phone (404) 653-3311, ext. 3534.

**Mental illness:**
(See Alcoholism, drug abuse and mental illness)

**Metric information:**
(See Energy Efficiency, National Bureau of Standards)

**Moving:**
Interstate Commerce Commission; Washington, DC 20423; toll-free moving hotline **(800) 424-9312.** In Florida call **(800) 432-4537.** In Washington, D.C. call 275-7852.

**Parks and recreation areas:**
*National Forests*
Forest Service, U.S. Department of Agriculture, Washington, DC 20250; phone (202) 447-3760.
*National Parks and Historic Sites*
National Park Service, Washington, DC 20240; phone (202) 343-7394.
*Recreation Areas on Army Corps of Engineers Project Sites*
Recreation Resource Management Branch (CWO-R), Army Corps of Engineers, Washington, DC 20314; phone (202) 693-7177.
*Other Recreation Areas*
Office of Public Affairs, Department of the Interior, Washington, DC 20240; phone (202) 343-3171.

**Passports:**
For passport information check with your local post office or contact the Passport Office, Department of State, 1425 K St., NW, Washington, DC 20524; phone (202) 783-8200.

**Patents and trademarks:**
*Patents*
Commissioner, Patent Office, Department of Commerce, Washington, DC 20231; phone (703) 557-3080.
*Trademarks*
Commissioner, Trademark Office, Department of Commerce, Washington, DC 20231; phone (703) 557-3268.

**Pensions:**
Office of Communications, Pension Benefit Guaranty Corporation, 2020 K St. NW, Washington, DC 20006;

phone (202) 254-4817.

Labor Management Standards Administration, Department of Labor, Washington, DC 20210; phone (202) 523-8776.

**Physical fitness-sports:**

President's Council on Physical Fitness and Sports, 400 6th St. SW, Washington, DC 20201 phone (202) 755-8131.

**Product safety:**

Consumer Product Safety Commission, Consumer Services Branch, Washington, DC 20207; toll-free hotline **(800) 638-2666.** In Maryland call **(800) 492-2937.**

**Radio and television broadcasting interference:**

Consumer Assistance Office, Federal Communications Commission, Washington, DC 20554; phone (202) 632-7000.

**Runaway children:**

The National Runaway Hotline; toll-free **(800) 621-4000.** In Illinois call **(800) 972-6004.**

**Smoking:**

Office on Smoking and Health, 12420 Parklawn Dr., Room 158 Park Building, Rockville, MD 20852; phone (301) 443-1575.

**Social Security:**

Check your local phone directory under U.S. Government. If there is no listing check at your local post office for the schedule of visits by Social Security representatives, or write: Division of Public Inquiries, Social Security Administration, 6401 Security Blvd., Baltimore, MD 21235; phone (301) 594-7705.

**Solar heating:**

National Solar Heating and Cooling Information Center, P.O. Box 1607, Rockville, MD 20850; toll-free hotline is **(800) 523-2929.** In Pennsylvania, call **(800) 462-4983.**

**Stocks and Bonds:**

Consumer Liaison Office, Securities and Exchange Commission, Washington, DC 20549; phone (202) 523-5516.

**Taxes:**

The Internal Revenue Service (IRS) toll-free tax information number is listed in your tax package and is generally listed in your local telephone directory. If you cannot locate the number, call your information operator for the number for your area. If you wish to write, send the letter to your IRS District Director. Problem Resolution Program (PRP). Offices have been established in each district to solve unique problems and complaints which have not been satisfied through normal channels. Taxpayers may call the toll-free number and ask for the PRP Office.

**Train travel:**

AMTRAK (National Railroad Passenger Corp.) For consumer problems first try to contact a local AMTRAK consumer relations office listed in your phone directory. If there is not an office near you contact AMTRAK, Office of Consumer Relations, P.O. Box 2709, Washington, DC 20013; phone (202) 383-2121.

**Travel information:**

U.S. Travel Service, Department of Commerce, Washington, DC 20230; phone (202) 377-4553.

**Venereal disease:**

VD toll-free hotline **(800) 523-1885.** In Pennsylvania call **(800) 462-4966.**

**Veterans information:**

The Veterans Administration has toll-free numbers in all 50 states. Check your local phone directory, or call **(800) 555-1212** for toll-free directory assistance. For problems that can't be handled through local offices, write Veterans Administration, (271), 810 Vermont Ave. NW, Washington, DC 20420.

**Wages and Working conditions:**

Employment Standards Administration, Department of Labor, Washington, DC 20210; phone (202) 523-8743.

**Warranties:**

For a problem involving the failure of a seller to honor a warranty, contact the Division of Special Statutes, Federal Trade Commission, Washington, DC 20580; phone (202) 724-1100. Or you may contact the FTC regional office nearest you. They are listed in your telephone directory under U.S. Government.

## Canadian Consumer Associations

### Automobile Protection Association

The Automobile Protection Association (APA) is a nonprofit, independently-financed consumer group founded in 1969 to advise motorists on the quality of automotive products and services, to publicize and encourage legal action against what it considers dishonest or dangerous practices in the automobile industry, and to press federal and provincial governments for protective legislation. For a $10 annual fee members receive periodic APA bulletins as well as free legal consultation when needed. A list of recommended garages and automobile dealerships in the Montreal and Toronto areas is provided. Headquarters are at 292 St-Joseph West,

Montreal, Quebec H2V 2N7.

### Consumers' Association of Canada

The Consumers' Association of Canada (CAC) is a voluntary, non-profit organization founded in 1947 to represent consumer interests. It also provides members with information on consumer legislation and the results of its research and tests on consumer goods and services. The national office is at 200 First Avenue, Ottawa, Ontario K1S 2G6 branch offices are in each province and territory. CAC publishes bi-monthly, bilingual magazines, *Canadian Consumer* and *Le Consommateur Canadien* (circulation 140,000). Annual membership fee is $8.

## Consumer Installment Credit
Source: Federal Reserve System (amounts outstanding, millions of dollars)

| End of year or month | Total | By holder | | | | | By type | | | | |
| | | Commercial banks | Finance companies | Credit unions | Retailers and others | Automobile | Mobile homes | Home improvement | Revolving | All other |
|---|---|---|---|---|---|---|---|---|---|---|---|
| 1973 . . . . . | 146,434 | 71,871 | 35,404 | 19,609 | 19,550 | 50,065 | 11,698 | 6,950 | 9,092 | 68,629 |
| 1974 . . . . . | 157,454 | 75,846 | 36,087 | 21,895 | 23,626 | 52,871 | 14,618 | 8,522 | 11,078 | 70,364 |
| 1975 . . . . . | 164,955 | 78,667 | 35,994 | 25,666 | 24,628 | 55,879 | 14,423 | 9,405 | 12,311 | 72,937 |
| 1976 . . . . . | 185,489 | 89,511 | 38,639 | 30,546 | 26,793 | 66,116 | 14,572 | 10,990 | 14,392 | 79,418 |
| 1977 . . . . . | 216,572 | 105,291 | 44,015 | 37,036 | 30,231 | 79,352 | 15,014 | 12,952 | 17,986 | 91,269 |
| 1978, June . | 233,416 | 114,756 | 47,147 | 41,388 | 30,125 | 88,767 | 15,309 | 14,037 | 18,925 | 96,378 |

# Interest Laws and Consumer Finance Loan Rates

**Source:** Revised by Christian T. Jones, Editor Consumer Finance Law Bulletin, Chicago.

Most states have laws regulating interest rates. These laws fix a legal or conventional rate which applies when there is no contract for interest. They also fix a general maximum contract rate, but in many states there are so many exceptions that the general contract maximum actually applies only to exceptional cases.

**Legal rate of interest.** The legal or conventional rate of interest applies to money obligations when no interest rate is contracted for and also to judgments. The rate is usually 6% a year; 5% or 7% in some states.

**General maximum contract rates.** General interest laws in most states set the maximum rate between 8% and 12% per year. The general maximum is fixed by the state constitution rather than by statute at 10% per year in Arkansas, California, Tennessee, and Texas. Loans to corporations are frequently exempted or subject to a higher maximum. In recent years, it has also been common to provide special rates for home mortgage loans. Courts generally hold that installment sale charges are not interest, but installment sale charges are limited by laws in many states.

**Specific enabling acts.** In many states special statutes permit industrial loan companies and banks to charge interest and fees without regard to installment payments which yield 1.5% a month or more. Laws regulating charge accounts and

credit cards generally limit charges to 1.5% per month. Credit unions may generally charge 1% a month. Pawnbrokers' rates vary widely. Building and loan associations, and loans insured by the Federal Housing Administration, are also specially regulated.

**Consumer finance loan statutes.** Most consumer finance loan statutes are based on early models drafted by the Russell Sage Foundation (1916-42) to provide small loans to wage earners under license and other protective regulations. Since 1969, however, the model has frequently been the Uniform Consumer Credit Code which applies to credit sales and loans for consumer purposes up to $25,000. In general, licensed lenders may charge 2.5% or 3% a month for $300 or less and reduced rates for additional amounts up to $2,000 or more. A number of states permit add-on rates of 17% to 20% ($17 to $20 per $100) a year of the original principal for $300 and lower rates for additional amounts. An add-on of 17% ($17 per $100) per year yields about 2.5% per month when the loan is paid in equal monthly installments. In the table below unless otherwise stated, monthly and annual rates are based on reducing principal balances, annual add-on rates are based on the original principal for the full term, and two or more rates apply to different portions of balance or original principal.

## States with consumer finance loan laws and the rates of charge as of Oct. 1, 1978.

Maximum rate monthly unless otherwise stated.

**Ala.** . . Annual add-on: 15% to $500, 10% to $1,000, 8% to $2,000. Over $2,000, 8% add-on on entire balance. Higher rates for loans up to $300.

**Alas.** . . 3% to $500, 2% to $1,000, 1% to $5,000; or equivalent flat rate.

**Ariz.** . . 3% to $300, 2% to $600, 1.5% to $1,500, 1% to $2,500.

**Cal.** . . 2.5% to $225, 2% to $625, 1.5% to $1,650, 1% to $10,000 (1.5% min.).

**Colo.** . . 36% per annum to $300, 21% to $1,000, 15% to $25,000 (18% min.).

**Conn.** . Annual Add-on: 17% to $300, 11% to $5,000; 11% over $1,800 to $5,000 for certain secured loans.

**Del.** . . Annual Discount: 9% for 1st 36 mos., 6% for remaining months; plus 2% fee.

**Fla.** . . 30% per annum to $500, 24% to $1,000, 16% to $2,500.

**Ga.** . . 8% per annum discount for 18 months, add-on to 36½ months; 8% fee to $600, 4% on excess plus $2 per month; max. $3,000.

**Ha.** . . 3.5% to $100, 2.5% to $300.

**Ida.** . . 36% per year to $540, 21% to $1,800, 15% to $45,000 (18% min.).

**Ill.** . . 2.5% to $300, 2% to $600, 1.5% to $1,500; or equivalent flat rate.

**Ind.** . . 36% per year to $450, 21% to $1,500, 15% to $37,500 (18% min.).

**Ia.** . . 3% to $250, 2% to $400, 1.5% to $1,000; or equivalent flat rate.

**Kan.** . . 36% per year to $360, 21% to $1,200, 14.45% to $25,000 (18% min.).

**Ky.** . . 3% to $500, 2% to $1,200, 1.5% to $1,500.

**La.** . . 36% per annum to $800, 27% to $2,000, 21% to $3,500, 15% to $25,000 (18% min.).

**Me.** . . 30% per annum to $480, 21% to $1,600, 15% to $40,000 (18% min.).

**Md.** . . 2.75% to $300, 2% to $500, 1.25% to $1,200, 1.75% to $3,500; 1.5% to $5,000; 1.35% to $6,000.

**Mass.** . 18% per year plus $15 fee.

**Mich.** . . 2.5% to $400, 1.25% to $1,500.

**Minn.** . . 2.75% to $300, 1.5% to $600, 1.25% to $1,200 plus fee of $1 per $100.

**Miss.** . . 36% per annum to $600, 33% to $1,800, 24% to $4,500, 12% over $4,500.

**Mo.** . . 2.218% to $500, 10% per annum on any remainder.

**Mont.** . Annual add-on: 20% to $300, 16% to $500, 12% to

$1,000, 10% to $7,500. Special rate to $90.

**Neb.** . . 30% per annum to $300, 24% to $500, 18% to $1,000, 12% to $3,000.

**Nev.** . . 36% per annum to $300, 21% to $1,000, 15% to $10,000 (1.5% min.).

**N.H.** . . 2% to $600, 1.5% to $1,500; 1.5% on entire amount over $1,500 to $5,000.

**N.J.** . . 24% per annum to $500, 22% to $1,500, 18% to $2,500.

**N.M.** . . 3% to $150, 2.5% to $300, 1% to $2,500 (1.5% min.).

**N.Y.** . . 2.5% to $100, 2% to $300, 1.5% to $900, 1.25% to $2,500.

**N.C.** . . 3% to $300, 1.5% to $1,500.

**N.D.** . . 2.5% to $250, 2% to $500, 1.75% to $750, 1.5% to $1,000; 1.5% on entire amount over $1,000 to $3,500.

**Ohio** . . Annual add-on: 16% to $750, 11% to $1,500, 9% to $3,000; or equivalent simple interest rate.

**Okla.** . . 30% per annum to $300, 21% to $1,000, 15% to $25,000. (18% min.). Special rates to $100.

**Ore.** . . 3% to $300, 1.75% to $1,000, 1.25% to $5,000. Over $5,000, 1.5%.

**Pa.** . . . 9.5% per annum discount to 36 months, 6% for remaining time plus 2% fee; $5,000 max.

**P.R.** . . Annual Add-on: 20% to $300, 7% to $600.

**R.I.** . . 3% to $300, 2.5% for loans between $300 and $800; 2% for larger loans to $2,500.

**S.C.** . . 36% per annum to $300, 21% to $1,000, 15% to $25,000 (18% min.). Special rate to $150.

**S.D.** . . 2.5% to $300, 2% to $1,000, 1.5% to $1,500, 1% to $2,500; 1.5% on entire amount to $5,000. $2 minimum.

**Tenn.** . . 7.5% per annum discount plus fees; no size limit.

**Texas** . Annual add-on: 18% to $300, 8% to $2,500. Special rates to $100.

**Utah** . . 36% per year to $540, 21% to $1,800, 15% to $45,000 (18% min.).

**Vt.** . . . . Annual add-on of 14% to $1,500.

**Va.** . . . 2.5% to $500, 1.5% to $1,500; annual add-on of 17% to $500, 13% to %1,000, 11% to $1,500.

**Wash.** . 2.5% to $500, 1.75% to $1,000, 1% to $2,500.

**W.Va.** . 36% per year to $200, 24% to $600, 18% to $1,200.

**Wis.** . . Annual Discount: 9.5% on first $1,000, 8% to $3,000 up to 36 months; 18% per annum for larger loans.

**Wyo.** . . 36% per annum to $300, 21% to $1,000, 15% to $25,000 (18% min.).

# Business Directory

Source: World Almanac Questionnaire

Listed below are major U.S. corporations, and major foreign corporations with their U.S. headquarters, whose operation directly concern the American consumer. The address given is the mailing address of the company. At the end of each listing is a representative example of some of the company's subsidiaries or holdings. Names of parent companies, if applicable, appear in italics at the end of the listing.

Should you, as a dissatisfied consumer, wish to register a complaint beyond the local level, address your correspondence to the attention of the Consumer Complaint Office of the individual company. Be as specific as possible about the dealer's name and address, purchase date or date of service, price, name and serial number (if any) of the product, and places you may have sought relief, with dates. Include copies of receipts and guarantees and/or warranties. Don't forget your name and complete address and telephone number with area code.

**Company. . .Address. . .Chief executive officer. . .Business. . .Subsidiaries/Parent Co.**

**AMF Inc.. . .**777 Westchester Ave., White Plains, NY 10604. . .Rodney C. Gott. . .sports equipment, machinery, yachts. . .AMF Bowling Products; AMF Harley-Davidson.

**A-T-O Inc.. . .**4420 Sherwin Rd., Willoughby, OH 44094. . .Harry E. Figgie Jr.. . .fire-fighting equip., recreation prods.. . .Rawlings Sporting Goods; "Automatic" Sprinkler Corp.

**Addressograph Multigraph Corp.. . .**20600 Chagrin Blvd., Shaker Heights, OH 44122. . .Roy L. Ash. . .business equipment.

**Admiral Group. . .**1701 E. Woodfield Rd., Schaumberg, IL 60172. . .John J. Henry. . .major electronic machinery. . .Rockwell Intl.

**Alberto-Culver Co.. . .**2525 Armitage Ave., Melrose Park, IL 60160. . .Leonard H. Lavin. . .toiletries.

**Allegheny Airlines Inc.. . .**Washington National Airport, Wash., DC 20001. . .Edwin I. Colodny. . .transportation.

**Allegheny Ludlum Industries, Inc.. . .**2 Oliver Plaza, Pittsburgh, PA 15222. . .Robert J. Buckley. . .steel specialty metals & materials and consumer products.

**Ethan Allen, Inc.. . .**Ethan Allen Dr., Danbury, CT 06810. . .Nathan S. Ancell. . .furniture.

**Allied Chemical Corp.. . .**P.O. Box 4000R, Morristown, NJ 07960. . .John T. Connor. . .energy products and services.

**Allied Stores Corp.. . .**1141 Ave. of the Americas, N.Y., NY 10036. . .Thomas M. Macioce. . .dept. stores, shopping centers, discount stores. . .Bon Marche; Jordan Marsh.

**Allied Van Lines, Inc.. . .**P.O. Box 4403, Chicago, IL 60680. . .moving, storage.

**Allis Chalmers Corp.. . .**1205 S. 70th St., Milwaukee, WI 53201. . .David C. Scott. . .technology in solids, liquids, gases, agricultural equip., electrical prods., material handling equip., outdoor power equip.

**Aluminum Co. of America. . .**1501 Alcoa Bldg., Pittsburgh, PA 15219. . .W.H. Krome George. . .aluminum. . .Alcoa Building Products; Wear-Ever Aluminum.

**Amana Refrigeration, Inc.. . .**Amana, IA 52203. . .George C. Foerstner. . .major electrical appliances. . .Raytheon.

**Amerada Hess Corp.. . .**1185 Ave. of the Americas, N.Y., NY 10036. . .Leon Hess. . .crude oil, gas, petroleum prods.

**American Airlines. . .**633 3d Ave., N.Y., NY 10017. . .Albert V. Casey. . .air transportation. . .Flagship Intl.

**American Bakeries Co.. . .**10 Riverside Plaza, Chicago, IL 60606. . .G.P. Turci. . .wholesale bakery goods.

**American Brands, Inc.. . .**245 Park Ave., N.Y., NY 10017. . .Robert K. Heimann. . .industrial rubber prods., staples, locks, wholesaling & retailing businesses, distilled beverages. . .American Cigar; American Tobacco Co.; James B. Beam Distilling Co.; Duffy-Mott Co.; Andrew Jergens Co.; Sunshine Biscuits; Swingline.

**American Broadcasting Companies Inc.. . .**1330 Ave. of the Americas, N.Y., NY 10019. . .Leonard H. Goldenson. . .broadcasting, theater exhibition of motion pictures, recorded music, operation of scenic attractions.

**American Can Company. . .**American Lane, Greenwich, CT 06830. . .William F. May. . .diversified packaging.

**American Cigar.. . .**245 Park Ave., N.Y., NY 10017. . .Alvin Bernstein. . .cigars, smoking tobacco. . .American Brands, Inc.

**American Cyanamid Company. . .**Berdan Ave., Wayne, NJ 07470. . .J.G. Affleck. . .medical, agricultural prods., chemicals. . .Formica Corp.; Shulton.

**American Greetings Corp.. . .**10500 American Rd., Cleveland, OH 44144. . .Irving I. Stone. . .greeting cards.

**American Hoechst Corp.. . .**202-206 North, Somerville, NJ 08876. . .John G. Brookhuis. . .fibers, sunglasses, pharmaceuticals. . .Foster Grant Co./Hoechst AG.

**American Hoist & Derrick Co.. . .**63 S. Robert, St. Paul, MN 55107. . .Robert P. Fox. . .material handling equip.

**American Home Products Corp.. . .**685 3d Ave., N.Y., NY 10017. . .J.W. Culligan. . .household prods., housewares, drugs, food specialties.

**American Honda Motor Co., Inc.. . .**100 W. Almdra Blvd., Gardena, CA 90247. . .passenger vehicles.

**American Motors Corp.. . .**2777 Franklin Rd., Southfield, MI 48034. . .Roy D. Chapin. . .passenger vehicles, service parts. . .Jeep Corp.

**American Petrofina, Inc.. . .**8350 N. Central Exp., Dallas, TX 75206. . .R.I. Galland. . .petroleum, petrochemicals.

**American Standard, Inc.. . .**40 W. 40th St., N.Y., NY 10018. . .William A. Marquand. . .building, industrial prods., transportation, construction, and mining equipment.

**American Stores Co.. . .**One Rollins Pl., Wilmington, DE 19803. . .William R. Delley. . .retail food markets, dept. & drug stores, restaurants. . .Acme Markets.

**American Telephone & Telegraph Co.. . .**195 Broadway, N.Y., NY 10007. . .John D. deButts. . .communications. . .Western Electric.

**American Tobacco Co.. . .**245 Park Ave., N.Y., NY 10017. . .Robert K. Heimann. . .cigarettes. . .American Brands.

**Amstar Corp.. . .**1251 Ave. of Americas, N.Y., NY 10020. . .Robert T. Quittmeyer. . .sweeteners.

**Anaconda Co.. . .**1271 Ave. of the Americas, N.Y., NY 10020. . .John B. M. Place. . .copper, aluminum, uranium. . .Atlantic Richfield.

**Anchor Hocking Corp.. . .**109 N. Broad, Lancaster, OH 43130. . .George C. Barber. . .glass containers, metal and plastic closures.

**Anheuser-Busch, Inc.. . .**721 Pestalozzi St., St. Louis, MO 63118. . .August A. Busch III. . .brewer, mfg. baker's yeast and corn prods.. . .St. Louis National Baseball Club.

**Armour & Co.. . .**Greyhound Tower, Phoenix, AZ 85077. . .C.B. Cox. . .meat, poultry. . .Greyhound.

**Armstrong Cork Co.. . .**Liberty & Charlotte Sts., Lancaster, PA 17604. . .James H. Binns. . .home furnishings.

**Armstrong Rubber Co.. . .**500 Sargent Dr., New Haven, CT 06507. . .James A. Walsh. . .tires.

**Arrow Co.. . .**530 5th Ave., N.Y., NY 10036. . .John Currier. . .apparel. . .Cluett, Peabody.

**Arvin Industries, Inc.. . .**1531 13th St., Columbus, IN 47201. . .Eugene I. Anderson. . .auto parts, record players.

**Ashland Oil Co.. . .**1409 Winchester Ave., Ashland, KY 41101. . .Robert E. Yancey. . .petroleum prods.

**Associates Corp. of North America. . .**250 Carpenter Freeway, Dallas, TX 75222. . .Reese Overcash. . .financial services. . .Gulf & Western.

**Atlantic Richfield Co.. . .**515 Flower St., Los Angeles, CA 90071. . .Robert O. Anderson. . .petroleum. . .Anaconda.

**Avco Embassy Pictures Corp.. . .**6601 Romaine St., Los Angeles, CA 90038. . .William E. Chaikin. . .film distributor. . .Avco Corp.

**Avco Financial Services, Inc.. . .**620 Newport Center Dr., Newport Beach, CA 92660. . .H. Wallace Merryman. . .financial services, insurance. . .Avco Corp.

**Avis, Inc.. . .**900 Old Country Rd., Garden City, NY 11530. . .Colin M. Marshall. . .car rental. . .Norton Simon.

**Avery International Corp.. . .**415 Huntington Dr., San Marino, CA 91108. . .R. Stanton Avery. . .labels.

**Avon Products, Inc.. . .**9 West 57th St., N.Y., NY 10019. . .David W. Mitchell. . .cosmetics.

**BP North America Inc.. . .**620 5th Ave., N.Y., NY 10020. . .A. Manson. . .petroleum prods.

**Babcock & Wilcox Co.. . .**161 E. 42d St., N.Y., NY 10017. . .

.George G. Zipf. . .steam generating prods.

**Bali Co., Inc.. .** .7000 Hanes Mills Rd., Winston-Salem, NC 27105. . .Terry L. Johnson. . .bras, swimwear. . .*Hanes*.

**Ball Corp.. .** .345 S. High St., Muncie, IN 47302. . .J.W. Fisher. . .glass & metal containers.

**Bausch & Lomb**. . .One Lincoln First Square, Rochester, NY 14601. . .Jack D. Harby. . .ophthalmic, scientific instruments, optical prods.

**James B. Beam Distilling Co.. .** .500 N. Michigan Ave., Chicago, IL 60611. . .Everett Kovler. . .distilled beverages. . .*American Brands*.

**Beatrice Foods Co.. .** .120 La Salle St., Chicago, IL 60603. . .Wallace N. Rasmussen. . .foods. . .Buxton; Charmglow; Dannon; Royal Crown; Samsonite; Seven-Up; Louis Sherry; Stiffel.

**Beech Aircraft Corp.. .** .Wichita, KS 67201. . .Frank E. Hedrick. . .aircraft.

**Beech-Nut Corp.. .** .P.O. Box 127, Ft. Washington, PA 19034. . .Frank C. Nicholas. . .baby foods.

**Bell & Howell Co.. .** .7100 McCormick Rd., Lincolnwood, IL 60645.. . .Donald N. Frey. . .audio-visual instruments.

**Bendix Corp.. .** .The Bendix Center, Southfield, MI 48076. . .Wm. M. Agee. . .automotive, aerospace, electronics.

**Beneficial Personal Finance Co. Ltd.. .** .Beneficial Bldg., Wilmington, DE 19899. . .F.M.W. Caspersen. . .financial services. . .*Beneficial Corp*.

**Benrus Watch.. .** Rte. 7., Ridgefield, CT 06877. . .Victor K. Kiam II. . .watches. . .*Wells-Benrus*.

**Bethlehem Steel Corp.. .** .8th & Eaton Ave., Bethlehem, PA 18016. . .Lewis W. Foy. . .steel & steel prods.

**Betty Crocker.** .9200 Wayzata Blvd., Minneapolis, MN 55426. . .Donald L. Knutzen. . .dessert mixes. . .*General Mills*.

**Bic Pen Corp.. .** One Wiley St., Milford, CT 06460. . .Robert P. Adler. . .pens, lighters.

**Black & Decker Mfg. Co.. .** .701 E. Joppa Rd., Towson, MD 21204. . .Francis P. Lucier. . .power tools.

**H & R Block, Inc.. .** .4410 Main St., Kansas City, MO 64111. . .Henry W. Block. . .tax preparation.

**Blue Bell, Inc.. .** .335 Church Ct., Greensboro, NC 27401. . .L.K. Mann. . .clothing. . .*Wrangler*.

**Boeing Company.. .** .7755 E. Marginal Way So., Seattle, WA 98108. . .T.A. Wilson. . .aerospace.

**Boise Cascade Corp.. .** .P.O. Box 50, Boise, ID 83728. . .John B. Fery. . .timber, paper, wood prod.

**Borden, Inc.. .** .277 Park Ave., N.Y., NY 10017. . .Augustine R. Marusi. . .food, industrial and consumer prods.

**Borg-Warner Corp.. .** .200 S. Michigan Ave., Chicago, IL 60604. . .Robert O. Bass. . .air conditioning, transportation equip.

**Braniff Airways, Inc.. .** .7701 Lemmon Ave., Dallas, TX 75209. . .Russell Thayer. . .air carrier. . .*Braniff Intl*.

**Braun North America.. .** Prudential Tower Bldg., Boston, MA 02199. . .Richard S. Rohe. . .consumer prods.. . .*Gillette*.

**Brink's, Inc.. .** .One Crossroads of Commerce, Rolling Meadows, IL 60008. . .N.T. Camicia. . .armored car security. . .*Pittston*.

**Bristol-Myers Co.. .** .345 Park Ave., N.Y., NY 10022. . .Richard L. Gelb. . .toiletries, cosmetics, household prods., pharmaceuticals. . .Clairol; Drackett; Mead Johnson.

**Browning.. .** Rte. 1, Morgan, UT 84050. . .Harmon G. Williams. . .sports equip.. . .*Browning Arms*.

**Brown & Williamson Tobacco Corp.. .** .1600 West Hill St., Louisville, KY 40232. . .C.I. McCarty. . .cigarettes. . .Gimbel Brothers; Vita Food.

**Brunswick Corp.. .** .One Brunswick Plaza, Skokie, IL 60075. . .Jack F. Reichert. . .marine, medical, recreation prods.

**Bucilla Co.. .** .30-20 Thompson Rd., Long Island City, NY 11101. . .David L. Duensing. . .needlework crafts. . .*Greyhound*.

**Bucyrus-Erie Co.. .** .P.O. Box 56, S. Milwaukee, WI 53172. . .E.P. Berg. . .mining, construction equip.

**Bulova Watch Co., Inc.. .** .Bulova Park, Flushing, NY 11370. . .R. Mark Bourguin. . .watches, time pieces.

**Burlington Industries, Inc.. .** .1345 Ave. of the Americas, N.Y., NY. . .10019. . .Wm. A. Klopman. . .fabrics, hosiery, carpets, furniture. . .Lees Carpets.

**Burlington Northern Inc.. .** .176 E. 5th St., St. Paul, MN 55101. . .N.M. Lorentzen. . .transportation, natural resources.

**Buxton, Inc.. .** .265 Main St., Agawam, MA 01001. . .Wm. Henry Clay Jr.. . .leather goods. . .*Beatrice Foods*.

**CBS Inc.. .** .51 W. 52d St., N.Y., NY 10019. . .John D. Backe. . .broadcasting, recorded music, leisure prods.. . .CBS records; Columbia House.

**CNA Financial Corp.. .** .310 So. Michigan Ave., Chicago, IL

60604. . .Laurence A. Tisch. . .financial services.. . .*Loews Corp*.

**CPC International, Inc.. .** .International Plaza, Englewood Cliffs, NJ 07632. . .J.W. McKee Jr.. . .diversified food prods., polishes and dyes. . .Best Foods; Dutch Pantry; S.B. Thomas.

**Cadbury Schweppes USA Inc.. .** .1200 High Ridge Rd., Stamford, CT 06905. . .Robert E. Ix. . .chocolate bars, carbonated beverages, cocktail mixers. . .*Cadbury Schweppes Ltd*.

**Caloric Corp.. .** .Washington & Heffner Sts., Topton, PA 19562. . .Kenneth J. Haas. . .major appliances. . .*Raytheon Co*.

**Campbell Soup Co.. .** .Campbell Pl., Camden, NJ 08101. . .Harold A. Shaub. . .convenience foods. . .Godiva Chocolatier; Pepperidge Farm.

**Campbell Taggart, Inc.. .** .6211 Lemmon Ave., Dallas, TX 75209. . .C.B. Lane. . .bakeries, food prods.

**Canada Dry Corp.. .** .100 Park Ave., N.Y., NY 10017. . .Richard C. Beeson. . .soft drinks. . .*Norton Simon*.

**Cannon Mills Co.. .** .Kannapolis, NC 28081. . .Harold P. Hornaday. . .textiles.

**Capitol Records Inc.. .** .1750 N. Vine St., Los Angeles, CA 90028. . .V.B. Menon. . .records. . .*Capitol Industries*.

**Carborundum Co.. .** .P.O. Box 156, Niagara Falls, NY 14302. . .William H. Wendel. . .abrasives, air & water pollution control equip.

**Carnation Co.. .** .5045 Wilshire Blvd., Los Angeles, CA 90036. . .H.E. Olson. . .food prods.. . .*Contadina*.

**Carrier Corp.. .** .P.O. Box 4800, Syracuse, NY 13221. . .William J. Bailey. . .air conditioning, refrigerating, heating equip.. . .*Dempster Dumpster*.

**Carte Blanche Corp.. .** .3460 Wilshire Blvd., Los Angeles, CA 90010. . .P.K. Dunsire. . .travel, entertainment credit card. . .*Avco Corp*.

**Castle & Cooke, Inc.. .** .50 California St., San Francisco, CA 94111. . .D.J. Kirchhoff. . .food processing. . .*Dole*.

**Caterpillar Tractor Co.. .** .100 N.E. Adams St., Peoria, IL 61629. . .Lee L. Morgan. . .heavy duty earth-moving equip.

**Celanese Corp.. .** .1211 Ave. of the Americas, N.Y., NY 10036. . .John W. Brooks. . .chemicals, fibers, plastics.

**Certain Teed Corp.. .** .120 E. Lancaster Ave., Valley Forge, PA 19482. . .George J. Haufler. . .bldg. materials.

**Cessna Aircraft Co.. .** .P.O. Box 1521, Wichita, KS 67201. . .Malcolm S. Harned. . .aircraft.

**Champion Home Builders Co.. .** .5573 E. North St., Dryden, MI 48428. . .Joseph J. Morris. . .mobile homes.

**Champion Spark Plug Co.. .** .P.O. Box 910, Toledo, OH 43661. . .R.A. Stranahan Jr.. . .spark plugs.

**Chap Stick Co.. .** .1000 Robins Rd., Lynchburg, VA 24505. . .D.E. French. . .drugs, cosmetics, household prods.. . .*A.H. Robins*.

**Chemetron Corp.. .** .111 E. Wacker Dr., Chicago, IL 60601. . .John P. Gallagher. . .chemicals, gases, metals, healthcare prods.

**Chesebrough-Pond's Inc.. .** .33 Benedict Pl., Greenwich, CT 06830. . .Ralph E. Ward. . .cosmetics, toiletries, clothing, food prods.. . .Adolph's Ltd. Health-tex; Prince Matchabelli; Ragu.

**Chicago Pneumatic Tool Co.. .** .6 E. 44th St., N.Y., NY 10017. . .T.P. Latimer. . .compressors, pneumatic tools, automotive service tools.

**Chris Craft Industries, Inc.. .** .600 Madison Ave., N.Y., NY 10022. . .Herbert J. Siegel. . .boats.

**Chromalloy American Corp.. .** .641 Lexington Ave., N.Y., NY 10022. . .Joseph Friedman. . .agricultural equip., pharmaceuticals, textiles and apparel, marine and land transport.

**Chrysler Corp.. .** .P.O. Box 1919, Detroit, MI 48231. . .E.A. Cafiero. . .cars, trucks.

**Cities Service Co.. .** .P.O. Box 300, Tulsa, OK 74102. . .Robert V. Sellers. . .industrial chemicals, oil.

**Clorox Company.. .** .P.O. Box 24035, Oakland, CA 94623. . .Robert B. Shetterly. . .retail consumer prods.

**Club Mediterranée International Inc.. .** .40 W. 57th St., N.Y., NY 10019. . .Jacques Ganin. . .travel.

**Coats & Clark Inc.. .** .72 Cummings Point Rd., Stamford, CT 06902. . .R.G. Laidlaw. . .thread, yarn; slide fasteners.

**Coca-Cola Co.. .** .P.O. Drawer 1734, Atlanta, GA 30301. . .J. Paul Austin. . .syrups, concentrates for soft drinks, coffee, tea, & citrus prods.. . .Taylor Wine.

**Colgate-Palmolive Co.. .** .300 Park Ave., N.Y., NY 10022. . .David R. Foster. . .laundry, cleaning, personal, and health care prods., sports prods., foods. . .*Helena Rubenstein*.

**Collins & Aikman Corp.. .** .210 Madison Ave., N.Y., NY 10016. . .Donald F. McCullough. . .textiles.

**Columbia Pictures Industries, Inc.. .** .711 5th Ave., N.Y., NY 10022. . .Alan J. Herschfield. . .entertainment.

**Commonwealth Oil Refining Co., Inc.. .** .8626 Tesoro Dr., San

Antonio, TX 78217. . .Edward D. Dohery. . .petroleum, petrochemicals.

**Congoleum Industries. . .**195 Belgrove Dr., Kearny, NJ 07032. . .E.G. Nicholson. . .flooring. . .*Congoleum Corp.*

**Consolidated Foods Corp.. . .**135 S. La Salle, Chicago, IL 60603. . .John H. Bryan Jr.. . .foods, indentification prods., housewares, appliances, clothing. . .Electrolux; Fuller Brush; Gant; Popsicle; Sara Lee; Shasta; Tyco.

**Consolidated Rail Corp. (Conrail). . .**6 Penn Center Plaza, Phila., PA 19104: . .Edward G. Jordan. . .railroads.

**Continental Air Lines Inc.. . .**Los Angeles Intl. Airport, Los Angeles, CA 90009. . .Alexander Damm. . .airlines.

**Continental Group, Inc.. . .**633 3d Ave., N.Y., NY 10017. . .S. Bruce Smart Jr.. . .metals, machinery, plastic, paper prods.

**Continental Oil Co.. . .**High Ridge Park, Stamford, CT 06904. . .H.W. Blauvelt. . .oil, natural gas, plastics.

**Control Data Corp.. . .**P.O. Box 0, Minneapolis, MN 55440. . .Wm. C. Norris. . .computing, financial services.

**Converse. . .**55 Fordham Rd., Wilmington, MA 01887. . .J.P. O'Neil. . .athletic, recreational and leisure footwear. . .*Eltra.*

**Thomas Cook, Inc.. . .**380 Madison Ave., N.Y., NY 10017. . .David Lorretto. . .travel.

**Adolph Coors Co.. . .**East of Town, Golden, CO 80401. . .William K. Coors. . .brewery.

**Corning Glass Works. . .**Houghton Park, Corning, NY 14830. . .Amory Houghton Jr.. . .glass.

**Crane Co.. . .**300 Park Ave., N.Y. NY 10022. . .Dante C. Fabiani. . .fluid & pollution controls, steel, building prods.

**Crown Cork & Seal Co.. . .**9300 Ashton Rd., Phila., PA 19136. . .J.F. Connelly. . .cans, packaging machinery & equip.

**Crown Zellerbach Corp.. . .**One Bush St., San Francisco, CA 94119. . .C.R. Dahl. . .pulp, paper, packaging containers.

**Culligan International Co.. . .**One Culligan Pkwy., Northbrook, IL 60062. . .Donald L. Porth. . .water conditioning prods. and services.

**Dairylea Cooperative Inc.. . .**One Blue Hill Plaza, Pearl River, NY 10965. . .Richard E. Richmond. . .dairy prods.

**Dan River Inc.. . .**P.O. Box 6126, Greenville, SC 29606. . .Robert S. Small. . .textiles.

**Dante. . .**1290 Ave. of the Americas, N.Y., NY 10019. . .John L. Hannigan. . .men's fashion accessories. . .*Genesco.*

**Deere & Company.. . .**John Deere Rd., Moline, IL 61265. . .William A. Hewitt. . .farm, industrial, and outdoor power equip.

**Del Monte Corp.. . .**P.O. Box 3575, San Francisco, CA 94119. . .R.G. Landis. . .food prods.

**Delta Air Lines, Inc.. . .**Hartsfield Atlanta Intl. Airport, Atlanta, GA 30320. . .W.T. Beebe. . .air transportation.

**Diamond Shamrock Corp.. . .**1100 Superior Ave., Cleveland, OH 44114. . .W.H. Bricker. . .chemicals, oil and gas technology.

**Digital Equipment Corp.. . .**146 Main St., Maynard, MA 01754. . .Kenneth H. Olsen. . .computers.

**Walt Disney Productions.. . .**500 S. Buena Vista St., Burbank, CA 91521. . .E. Cardon Walker. . .motion pictures, amusement parks. . .Disneyland, Walt Disney World.

**Dr Pepper Co.. . .**5523 Mockingbird Lane, Dallas, TX 75222. . .W.W. Clements. . .soft drinks.

**Dow Chemical Co.. . .**2020 Dow Center, Midland, MI 48640. . .Z. Merszei. . .chemicals, pharmaceuticals, plastics, metals. . .Dow Corning.

**Duffy-Mott Co., Inc.. . .**370 Lexington Ave., N.Y., NY 10017. . .Raymond M. Anrig. . .fruit prods.. . .*American Brands.*

**Dunlop Tire & Rubber Corp.. . .**River Dr., Buffalo, NY 14240. . .tires.

**E.I. du Pont de Nemours & Co., Inc.. . .**1007 Market St., Wilmington, DE 19898. . .Edward R. Kane. . .chemicals, textile fibers, building material prods.

**Durkee Foods. . .**900 Union Commerce Bldg., Cleveland, OH 44115. . .R.E. Dorfmeyer. . .foods, food services. . .*SCM.*

**Dutch Boy Inc.. . .**500 Central Ave., Northfield, IL 60093. . .Peter R. Harvey. . .lighting prods., metal & plastic prods., paints and coatings.

**Eastern Air Lines Inc.. . .**Miami International Airport, Miami, FL 33148. . .Frank Borman. . .air transportation.

**Eastman Kodak Co.. . .**343 State, Rochester, NY 14650. . .Walter A. Fallon. . .photographic materials & equip.

**Electrolux. . .**2777 Summer St., Stamford, CT 06905. . .Charles A. McKee. . .household cleaning equip.. . .*Consolidated Foods.*

**Elizabeth Arden, Inc.. . .**691 5th Ave., N.Y., NY 10022. . .Richard D. Wood. . .*Eli Lilly.*

**Emerson Electric Co.. . .**8100 W. Florissant Ave., St. Louis, MO 63136. . .C.F. Knight. . .electronics.

**Emery Air Freight Corp.. . .**Old Danbury Rd., Wilton, CT 06897. . .John C. Emery Jr.. . .air freight forwarder.

**Ethyl Corp.. . .**330 S. 4th St., Richmond, VA 23219. . .Floyd D. Gottwald Jr.. . .petroleum and industrial chemicals, plastics.

**Ex-Cell-O Corp.. . .**2855 Coolidge, Troy, MI 48084. . .E. Paul Casey. . .industrial tools, abrasives.

**Exxon Corp.. . .**1251 Ave. of the Americas, N.Y., NY 10020. . .C.C. Garvin Jr.. . .chemical, oil, exploration prods.

**Fabergé, Inc.. . .**1345 Ave. of the Americas, N.Y., NY 10019. . .George Barrie. . .cosmetics, toiletries. . .Brut.

**Max Factor & Co.. . .**6922 Hollywood Blvd., Hollywood, CA 90028. . .Samuel Kalish. . .cosmetics. . .*Norton Simon.*

**Fairchild Camera and Instrument Corp.. . .**464 Ellis St., Mountain View, CA 94042. . .Wilfred J. Corrigan. . .electronic component systems.

**Fairmont Foods Co.. . .**P.O. Box 19683, Houston, TX 77024. . .E.W. Kelley. . .dairy foods.

**Farberware. . .**1500 Bassett Ave., Bronx, NY 10461. . .Fred R. Sullivan. . .electrical appliances, cookware. . .*Walter Kidde.*

**Fedders Corp.. . .**Woodbridge Ave., Edison, NJ 08817. . .Salvatore Giordano Jr.. . .air conditioners, home appliances. . .Norge.

**Federal Co.. . .**2900 Sterick Bldg., Memphis, TN 38103. . .L.K. McKee. . .food prods.

**Federated Department Stores, Inc.. . .**222 W. 7th St., Cincinnati, OH 45202. . .Harold Krensky. . .dept. stores. . .Bloomingdale's; Bullock's; Filene's; Lazarus; I. Magnin; Shillito's.

**Fiat Motors of North America, Inc.. . .**155 Chestnut Ridge Rd., Montvale, NJ 07645. . .Claudio Ferrari. . .automobiles.

**Fieldcrest Mills, Inc.. . .**Eden, NC 27288. . .William C. Battle. . .textiles. . .Karastan Rugs.

**Firestone Tire & Rubber Co.. . .**1200 Firestone Pkwy., Akron, OH 44317. . .Richard A. Riley. . .tires, rubber prods.

**Fleetwood Enterprises, Inc.. . .**3125 Myers St., Riverside, CA 92523. . .John C. Crean. . .mobile homes, travel trailers.

**Ford Motor Co.. . .**The American Rd., Dearborn, MI 48121. . .Henry Ford II. . .motor vehicles. . .Ford Tractor; Lincoln-Mercury.

**Formfit Rogers. . .**530 5th Ave., N.Y., NY 10036. . .Charles R. Carruth. . .lingerie, foundation garments. . .*Genesco.*

**Foster Grant Co., Inc.. . .**Rte. 202-206, Somerville North, NJ 08876. . .D. Markowitz. . .sunglasses. . .*American Hoechst.*

**Franklin Mint Corp.. . .**Franklin Center, PA 19091. . .Charles L. Andes. . .coins, medals, sculpture, crystal, and porcelain collectibles.

**R.T. French Co.. . .**One Mustard St., Rochester, NY 14609. . .E.I. Reveal. . .mustard, sauces.

**Frigidaire.. . .**300 Taylor St., Dayton, OH 45442. . .Emmett B. Lewis Jr.. . .major electrical appliances. . .*General Motors.*

**Fuller Brush Co.. . .**Westport Addition, P.O. Box 729, Great Bend, KS 67530. . .Nat Zivin. . .housewares, personal care prods.. . .*Consolidated Foods.*

**Gant Inc.. . .**40 Sargent Dr., New Haven, CT 06509. . .William R. Keegan. . .shirts.. . .*Consolidated Foods.*

**General Electric Co.. . .**3135 Easton Ave., Fairfield, CT 06431. . .R.H. Jones. . .electrical, electronic, atomic prods.

**General Foods Corp.. . .**250 North, White Plains, NY 10625. . .J.L. Ferguson. . .grocery prods., fast-food restaurants, seeds and gardening aids. . .W. Atlee Burpee; Burger Chef.

**General Host Corp.. . .**22 Gate House Rd., Stamford, CT 06902. . .Harris J. Ashton. . .foods, agricultural prods.. . .Van de Kamp's; Cudahy.

**General Mills, Inc.. . .**Box 1113, Minneapolis, MN 55440. . .H. Brewster Atwater. . .foods, toys, restaurants, apparel.. . .Betty Crocker; Gorton Group; Parker Brothers; Monet; Ship 'N Shore; The Talbots.

**General Motors Corp.. . .**Gen. Motors Bldg., Detroit, MI 48202. . .Thomas A. Murphy. . .motor vehicles, household appliances. . .AC Spark Plug; Buick; Cadillac; Chevrolet; Delco; Frigidaire; G.M. Acceptance Corp.

**General Telephone & Electronics Corp.. . .**One Stamford Forum, Stamford, CT 06904. . .Theodore F. Brophy. . .utilities. . .Sylvania Lighting.

**General Tire & Rubber Co.. . .**One General St., Akron, OH 44329. . .M.G. O'Neil. . .tires, rubber prods.

**Genesco, Inc.. . .**111 7th Ave. No., Nashville, TN 37203. . .John

L. Hannigan. . .apparel. . .Dante; Formfit Rogers; Hardy Amies; Johnston & Murphy Shoe Co., S.H. Kress; Plymouth Shops.

**Georgia-Pacific Corp.. . .**900 S.W. 5th Ave., Portland, OR 97204. . .T. Marshall Hahn Jr.. . .lumber, pulp, paper, chemicals.

**Gerber Products Co.. . .**445 State St., Fremont, MI 49412. . .John C. Suerth. . .baby foods, clothing, nursery accessories.

**Getty Oil Co.. . .**3810 Wilshire Blvd., Los Angeles, CA 90010. . .Harold E. Berg. . .petroleum prod.

**Gillette Co.. . .**Prudential Tower Bldg., Boston, MA 02199. . .Colman M. Mockler Jr.. . .razors, pens, leather goods, appliances. . .Braun No. Amer.; Paper Mate.

**Gimbel Brothers, Inc.. . .**1275 Broadway, N.Y., NY. . .C.I. McCarty. . .dept. store.. . *Brown & Williamson Tabacco Corp.*

**B.F. Goodrich Co.. . .**500 S. Main, Akron, OH 44318. . .O. Pendleton Thomas. . .rubber, chemical, plastic prods.

**Goodyear Tire & Rubber Co.. . .**1144 E. Market, Akron, OH 44316. . .Charles J. Pilliod Jr.. . .tires, rubber prods.. . .Kelly-Springfield.

**Gould Inc.. . .**10 Gould Center, Rolling Meadows, IL 60008. . .Daniel T. Carroll. . .electrical and industrial prods.

**W.R. Grace & Co.. . .**Grace Plaza, 1114 Ave. of the Americas, N.Y., NY 10036. . .J. Peter Grace. . .chemicals, natural resources, and consumer products and services.. . .Baker & Taylor Books; Channel; Herman's World of Sporting Goods; Hooton Chocolate.

**Great Atlantic & Pacific Tea Co.. . .**2 Paragon Dr., Montvale, NJ 07645. . .Jonathan L. Scott. . .retail food stores.

**Great Western United Corp.. . .**716 Metro Bank Bldg., Denver, CO 80202. . .W.H. Hunt. . .sugar refining, real estate, restaurants.. . .Shakey's.

**Green Giant Co.. . .**Hazeltine Gates, Chaska, MN 55318. . .Thomas H. Wyman.. . .restaurants, food processing.

**Greyhound Corp.. . .**111 W. Clarendon, Phoenix, AZ 85013. . .Gerald H. Trautman. . .meat and poultry packer, bus transportation, soap prods., food, financial services, pharmaceuticals. . .Armour; Bucilla; Carey Transportation.

**Gruen Industries, Inc.. . .**20 E. 46th St., N.Y., NY 10017. . .Charles F. Evans Jr.. . .watches, clocks.

**Grumman Corp.. . .**1111 Stewart, Bethpage, NY 11714. . .John C. Bierwirth. . .aerospace, marine prods., leisure-time vehicles, data services.

**Gulf Oil Corp.. . .**439 7th Ave., Pittsburgh, PA 15219. . .James E. Lee. . .oil, gas, chemicals, minerals.

**Gulf & Western Industries, Inc.. . .**One Gulf & Western Plaza, N.Y., NY 10023. . .David N. Judelson. . .diversified manufacturer. . .Her Majesty Industries; Consolidated Cigar; Schrafft Candy; Kayser-Roth; Associates Corp. of No. Amer.; Paramount Pictures; Simon & Schuster.

**Hamilton Beach.. . .**Scovill Sq., Waterbury, CT 06720. . .John J. Flaherty. . .electric housewares.. . *Scovill Manufacturing.*

**Hammond Organ Co.. . .**4200 W. Diversey, Chicago, IL 60639. . .Robert A. Pritzker. . .organs.. . *Marmon Group.*

**Hanes Corp.. . .**2000 W. 1st St., Winston-Salem, NC 27101. . .Robert E. Elberson. . .apparel, hosiery. . .Bali; L'eggs.

**Hardy Amies of London. . .**1290 Ave. of the Americas, N.Y., NY 10019. . .John L. Hannigan. . .menswear.. . *Genesco.*

**Hart Schaffner & Marx. . .**36 S. Franklin, Chicago, IL 60606. . .Jerome S. Gore. . .menswear, retail stores.

**Hartz Mountain Corp.. . .**700 S. 4th St., Harrison, NJ 07029. . .Leonard N. Stern. . .pet supplies.

**Havatampa Corp.. . .**P.O. Box 1909, Tampa, FL 33601. . .Doyle E. Carlton. . .cigars.

**Health-tex Inc.. . .**1411 Broadway, N.Y., NY 10018. . .Ralph E. Ward. . .children's apparel.. . *Chesebrough-Pond's.*

**H.J. Heinz Co.. . .**P.O. Box 57, Pittsburgh, PA 15230. . .Anthony J. F. O'Reilly. . .foods. . .Ore-Ida; Star-Kist.

**Helene Curtis Industries, Inc.. . .**4401 W. North Ave, Chicago, IL 60639. . .Walter Kaplan. . .toiletries and hair care.

**Henredon Furniture Industries, Inc.. . .**Henredon Rd., Hwy. 70, Morgantown, NC 28655. . .John Collett. . .furniture.

**Hershey Food Corp.. . .**19 E. Chocolate Ave., Hershey, PA 17033. . .Richard A. Zimmerman. . .confectionery, food prods. & services. . .H.B. Reese Candy.

**Hertz Corp.. . .**660 Madison Ave., N.Y., NY 10021. . .Frank A. Olson. . .car, truck renting and leasing. . .*RCA.*

**Heublein, Inc.. . .**Farmington, CT 06032. . .Hicks B. Waldron. . .alcoholic beverages, foods. . .Smirnoff.

**Hewlett-Packard Co.. . .**1501 Page Mill Rd., Palo Alto, CA 94304. . .John A. Young. . .electronics equip.

**Hilton Hotels Corp.. . .**9880 Wilshire Blvd., Beverly Hills, CA 90210. . .Barron Hilton. . .hotels.

**Hobart Corp.. . .**World Headquarters, Troy, OH 45374. . .David B. Meeker. . .food equip., appliances. . .Kitchenaid Home Appliances.

**Hoffman-La Roche Inc.. . .**340 Kingsland St., Nutley, NJ 07110. . .Robert B. Clark. . .pharmaceuticals, medical electronics.

**Holiday Inns Inc.. . .**3742 Lamar Ave., Memphis, TN 38118. . .L.M. Clymer. . .food and lodging, bus transportation, steamships.

**Honda Motor Co., Ltd.. . .**P.O. Box 50, Gardena, CA 90247. . .Kiyoshi Kawashima. . .motorcycles, cars, power prods.

**Honeywell, Inc.. . .**Honeywell Plaza, Minneapolis, MN 55408. . .E.W. Spencer. . .computers, automatic controls, instrumentation.

**H.P. Hood Inc.. . .**500 Rutherford Ave., Boston, MA 02129. . .John M. Fox. . .dairy and food prods.

**Hoover Ball & Bearing Co.. . .**P.O. Box 1003, Ann Arbor, MI 41806. . .J.F. Daly. . .aluminum, steel, plastic prods.

**Hoover Co.. . .**101 E. Maple St., No. Canton, OH 44720. . .Fred L. Tabacchi. . .electrical household appliances.

**Geo. A. Hormel & Co.. . .**501 16th Ave. N.E., Austin, MN 55912. . .I.J. Holton. . .meat packaging, pork and beef prods.

**Household Finance Corp., Consumer Div.. . .**W.E. Wehner. . .consumer finance.. . *Household Finance Corp.*

**Howard Johnson Co.. . .**One Howard Johnson Plaza, Boston, MA 02125. . .Howard B. Johnson. . .restaurants, motor lodges. . .Howard Johnson's Restaurants; Motor Lodge.

**Hunt-Wesson Foods, Inc.. . .**1645 W. Valencia Dr.. . .Fullerton, CA 92634. . .William K. Hood. . .food prods.. . *Norton Simon.*

**Ideal Toy Corp.. . .**184-10 Jamaica Ave., Hollis, NY 11423. . .Lionel A. Weintraub. . .toys.

**Ingredient Technology Corp. (**formerly, **Su Crest Corp.).**. . .120 Wall St., N.Y., NY 10005. . .Rudolph Eberstadt Jr.. . .sugar refining, related prods.

**Insilco Corp.. . .**1000 Research Pkwy., Meriden, CT 06450. . .Durand B. Blatz. . .diversified manufacturer. . .International Silver; Red Devil Paints and Chemicals; Rolodex.

**Interco Inc.. . .**P.O. Box 8777, St. Louis, MO 63102. . .John K. Riedy. . .apparel. . .Queen Casuals; Florsheim Shoe.

**International Business Machines Corp.. . .**Old Orchard Rd., Armonk, NY 10504. . .John R. Opel. . .information handling systems, equipment, services.

**International Harvester Co.. . .**401 N. Michigan Ave., Chicago, IL 60611. . .Brooks McCormick. . .agricultural, construction equipment.

**International Paper Co.. . .**220 E. 42d St., N.Y., NY 10017. . .J. Stanford Smith. . .paper, wood prods.

**International Silver Co.. . .**500 S. Broad St., Meriden, CT 06450. . .Durand B. Blatz. . .silver prods.. . *Insilco Corp.*

**International Telephone and Telegraph Corp.. . .**320 Park Ave., N.Y., NY 10022. . .H.S. Geneen. . .communication systems, multi-prods.. . .Sheraton Corp.

**Iroquois Brands, Ltd.. . .**41 W. Putnam Ave., Greenwich, CT 06830. . .Terence J. Fox. . .specialty foods, beverages. . .A-W Brands; Champale; Yoo-Hoo Chocolate Beverage.

**Jeep Corp.. . .**27777 Franklin Rd., Southfield, MI 48034. . .Gerald C. Meyers. . .vehicles. . *. American Motors.*

**Andrew Jergens Co.. . .**2535 Spring Grove Ave., Cincinnati, OH 45214. . .Kenneth C. Schuster. . .toiletries, cosmetics. . .*American Brands.*

**Johns-Manville Corp.. . .**P.O. Box 5108, Denver, CO 80217. . .J.A. McKinney. . .thermal insulations, pipe systems, building prods.

**Johnson & Johnson. . .**501 George St., New Brunswick, NJ 08903. . .D.R. Clare. . .surgical dressings, pharmaceuticals, health and baby prods.

**Johnson Outboards. . .**100 Sea Horse Dr., Waukegan, IL 60085. . .H.A. Jespersen. . .outboard motors.. . *Outboard Marine Corp.*

**Jonathan Logan, Inc.. . .**P.O. Box 122, Midtown Sta., N.Y., NY 10018. . .Richard J. Schwartz. . .apparel. . .Act III; Butte Knitting Mills; Etienne Aigner; Misty Harbor.

**Kaiser Aluminum & Chemical. . .**300 Lakeside Dr., Oakland, CA 94666. . .Cornell C. Maier. . .aluminum, chemicals, real estate.

**Kaiser Steel Corp.. . .**P.O. Box 58, Oakland, CA 94604. . .Mark

T. Anthony. . .iron, steel, and associated prods.

**Kane-Miller Corp.. . .**P.O. Box 7, Tarrytown, NY 10591. . .Stanley B. Kane. . .food processing. . .American Meat Packing.

**Keebler Co.. . .**One Hollow Tree Lane, Elmhurst, IL 60126. . .Arthur E. Larkin Jr.. . .cookies, crackers.

**Kellogg Co.. . .**235 Porter, Battle Creek, MI 49016. . .Joseph E. Lonning. . .food prods.. . .Mrs. Smith's Pie Co.; Salada Foods.

**Kentucky Fried Chicken-Retail Stores. . .**Box 92092, Los Angeles, CA 90009. . .Chet Rondinella. . .fast food restaurants. . .Collins Food Intl.

**Walter Kidde & Co., Inc.. . .**9 Brighton Rd., Clifton, NJ 07015. . .Fred R. Sullivan. . .safety, security prods., diversified consumer prods.. . .E.J. Burke Security; Farberware; Lucien Piccard.

**Kimberly-Clark Corp.. . .**N. Lake St., Neenah, WI 54956. . .Darwin E. Smith. . .paper and lumber prods.

**K mart Corp.. . .**3100 W. Big Beaver Rd., Troy, MI 48084. . .E.E. Wardlow. . .retail stores.

**Kraft, Inc.. . .**Kraft Ct., Glenview, IL 60025. . .William Beers. . .food prods.

**Kroger Co.. . .**1014 Vine St., Cincinnati, OH 45201. . .Lyle Everingham. . .supermarkets, drugstores, food prods.

**LTV Corp.. . .**P.O. Box 5003, Dallas, TX 75222. . .Paul Thayer. . .aerospace vehicles and equip.

**Land O'Lakes Inc.. . .**614 McKinley Pl., Minneapolis, MN 55413. . .Ralph Hofstad. . .agri-business, food prods.

**Lever Brothers Co.. . .**390 Park Ave., N.Y., NY 10022. . .Thomas S. Carroll. . .soaps, detergents, dentifrices, foods.

**Levi Strauss & Co.. . .**Embarcadero Center, San Francisco, CA 94106. . .Peter E. Haas. . .apparel.

**Levitz Furniture Corp.. . .**1317 NW 167th St., Miami, FL 33169. . .Robert M. Elliott. . .retail furniture stores.

**Libbey-Owens-Ford Co.. . .**811 Madison Ave., Toledo, OH 43695. . .R.G. Wingerter. . .glass and plastic prods.

**Libby, McNeil & Libby, Inc.. . .**200 S. Michigan Ave., Chicago, IL 60604. . .D.E. Guerrant. . .foods. . .Nestle.

**Liggett Group Inc.. . .**4100 Roxboro Rd., Durham, NC 27702. . .Raymond J. Mulligan. . .tobacco prods., spirits and wines, pet foods, home care prods., sporting goods. . .Austin, Nichols; L & M Tobacco; Pinkerton Tobacco; Allen Products (Alpo).

**Eli Lilly & Co.. . .**307 E. McCarty St., Indianapolis, IN 46206. . .Richard D. Wood. . .drugs, cosmetics. . .Elizabeth Arden.

**Thomas J. Lipton Inc.. . .**800 Sylvan Ave., Englewood Cliffs, NJ 07632. . .W.G. Barker. . .food prods.. . .Good Humor; Knox Gelatin.

**Litton Microwave Cooking Products. . .**1405 Xenium Lane N., Minneapolis, MN 55441. . .Charles B. Thornton. . .microwave ovens and prods.. . .Litton Industries.

**Lockheed Aircraft Corp.. . .**2555 N. Hollywood Way, Burbank, CA 91520. . .Lawrence O. Kitchen. . .aircraft.

**Loews Corp.. . .**666 5th Ave., N.Y., NY 10019. . .Laurence A. Tisch. . .tobacco prods., motion pictures, hotels. . .CNA Financial Corp.; Loew's Theatres; Lorillard Int'l. Sales.

**Longines-Wittnauer, Inc.. . .**145 Huguenot St., New Rochelle, NY 10810. . .R.E. Kirby. . .watches. . .Westinghouse Electric.

**Lorillard International Sales Corp.. . .**666 5th Ave., N.Y., NY 10019. . .Laurence A. Tisch. . .tobacco prods.. . .Loews Corp.

**M. Lowenstein & Sons, Inc.. . .**1430 Broadway, N.Y., NY 10018. . .L. Terrell Sovey Jr.. . .textiles. . .Wamsutta Fabrics.

**Lucky Stores, Inc.. . .**630 Clark Ave., Dublin, CA 94566. . .Wayne H. Fisher. . .supermarkets, restaurants, dept., fabric, and automotive stores.

**M C A Inc.. . .**100 Universal City Plaza, Universal City, CA 91608. . .Lew R. Wasserman. . .motion pictures; recreation services, record, music, book publishing; savings and loan operations. . .Columbia Savings & Loan; G.P. Putnam's Sons; Spencer Gifts; Universal City Studios.

**M E I Corp.. . .**733 Marquette Ave., Minneapolis, MN 55402. . .Donald E. Benson. . .soft drink bottler, distributor.

**Magic Chef Inc.. . .**740 King Edward Ave. S.E., Cleveland, TN 37311. . .S.B. Rymer Jr.. . .major electrical appliances, heating.

**Magnavox Consumer Electronics. . .**1700 Magnavox Way, Ft. Wayne, IN 48804. . .Alfred di Scipio. . .electrical, electronic components. . .North American Philips.

**Marmon Group, Inc.. . .**39 S. La Salle St., Chicago, IL 60603. . .Robert A. Pritzker. . .metal and copper prods., mining, CATV. . .Hammond Organ Co.

**Marriott Corp.. . .**5161 River Rd., Wash., DC 20016. . .J. Willard Marriott Jr.. . .food service, lodging and leisure time.

**Martin Marietta Corp.. . .**6801 Rockledge Dr., Bethesda, MD 20034. . .Thomas G. Pownall. . .diversified operations in construction, aerospace and defense, specialty chemicals.

**Masonite Corp.. . .**29 N. Wacker Dr., Chicago, IL 60606. . .Samuel S. Greeley. . .building materials.

**Massey-Ferguson Inc.. . .**1901 Bell Ave., Des Moines, IA 50315. . .J.E. Mitchell. . .farm machinery. . .Massey-Ferguson Ltd.

**Matsushita Electric Corp. of America. . .**One Panasonic Way, Secaucus, NJ 07094. . .A. Harada. . .electronic goods. . .Panasonic; Quasar Electronics.

**Mattel, Inc.. . .**5150 Rosecrans Ave., Hawthorne, CA 90250. . .Arthur S. Spear. . .toys, pet prods., entertainment. . .Ringling Bros.-Barnum & Bailey Circus.

**Maxell Corp. of America. . .**60 Oxford Dr., Moonachie, NJ 07074. . .Mr. Okada. . .recording tapes & batteries.

**Mayflower Corp.. . .**P.O. Box 107-B, Indianapolis, IN 46206. . .John Burnside Smith. . .movers.

**Maytag Co.. . .**403 W. 4th St. N., Newton, IA 50208. . .Daniel J. Krumm. . .appliances.

**Thom Mc An Shoe Co.. . .**67 Millbrook St., Worcester, MA 01606. . .Lawrence McGourty. . .retail shoe chain. . .Melville.

**McCall Pattern Co.. . .**230 Park Ave., N.Y., NY 10017. . .Earle K. Angstadt Jr.. . .patterns, craft books. . .Norton Simon.

**McDonald's Corp.. . .**McDonald's Plaza, Oak Brook, IL 60521. . .Edward H. Schmitt. . .fast food restaurants.

**McDonnell Douglas Corp.. . .**P.O. Box 516, St. Louis, MO 63166. . .Sanford N. McDonnell. . .aerospace.

**McGraw-Edison Co.. . .**333 W. River Rd., Elgin, IL 60120. . .E.J. Williams. . .electrical equip.. . .Speed Queen; Toastmaster.

**Mead Corp.. . .**Courthouse Plaza N.E., Dayton, OH 45463. . .Warren L. Batts. . .pulp, paper, school and office prods.. . .Stanley Furniture.

**Melville Corp.. . .**3000 Westchester Ave., Harrison, NY 10528. . .Francis C. Rooney Jr.. . .shoe stores, apparel, health and beauty aids. . .Foxmoor Casuals; Thom Mc An.

**Memorex Corp.. . .**San Tomas at Central Exp., Santa Clara, CA 95052. . .Robert C. Wilson. . .computer, communication prods.

**Mercedes-Benz of North America, Inc.. . .**One Mercedes Dr., P.O. Box 350, Montvale, NJ 07645. . .Karlfried Nordmann. . .cars, trucks, diesel engines.

**Merck & Co., Inc.. . .**Lincoln Ave., Rahway, NJ 07065. . .John J. Horan. . .pharmaceuticals. . .Calgon.

**Miles Laboratories, Inc.. . .**1127 Myrtle St., Elkhart, IN 46514. . .W.A. Compton. . .pharmaceuticals, chemicals, foods.

**Miller Brewing Co.. . .**4000 W. State St., Milwaukee, WI 53201. . .John A. Murphy. . .beer.

**Milton Bradley Co.. . .**1500 Main St., Springfield, MA 01115. . .James J. Shea Jr.. . .toys, educational products. . .Playskool.

**Mobil Corp.. . .**150 E. 42d St., N.Y., NY 10017. . .W.P. Tavoulareas.. . .petroleum, natural gas prods., diversified subs.. . .Container Corp. of America; Montgomery Ward.

**Mohasco Corp.. . .**57 Lyon St., Amsterdam, NY 12010. . .Herbert L. Shuttleworth 2d. . .home furnishings. . .Mohawk Carpet Mills.

**Monet Jewelers, Inc.. . .**16 E. 34th St., N.Y., NY 10016. . .Michael P. Chernow. . .jewelry. . .General Mills.

**Monsanto Company. . .**800 N. Lindbergh Blvd., St. Louis, MO 63166. . .John W. Hanley. . .chemicals, plastics, agricultural prods., man-made fibers, electronics.

**Montgomery Ward & Co.. . .**619 W. Chicago Ave., Chicago, IL 60610. . .Edward S. Donnell. . .retailing. . .Mobil.

**Morton-Norwich Products, Inc.. . .**110 N. Wacker Dr., Chicago, IL 60606. . .John W. Simmons. . .pharmaceuticals, household, food prods.. . .Morton Salt.

**Motorola, Inc.. . .**1303 E. Algonquin Rd., Schaumburg, IL 60196. . .Robert W. Galvin. . .electronics.

**NCR Corp.. . .**1700 S. Patterson Blvd., Dayton, OH 45479. . .Charles E. Exley Jr.. . .computers, electronic business equip.

**Nabisco, Inc.. . .**DeForest Ave., E. Hanover, NJ 07936. . .Robert M. Schaeberle. . .foods, pharmaceuticals, toys, furnishings.

**National Airlines, Inc.. . .**Miami Intl. Airport, Miami, FL 33159. . .L.B. Maytag. . .air transportation.

**National Broadcasting Co., Inc.. . .**30 Rockefeller Plaza, N.Y., NY 10021. . .Fred Silverman. . .broadcasting. . .RCA.

**National Car Rental System, Inc.. . .**5501 Green Valley Dr., Minneapolis, MN 55437. . .Gilbert R. Ellis. . .car rental. . .Household Finance.

**National Distillers & Chemical Corp.. . .**99 Park Ave., N.Y., NY 10016. . .Drummond C. Bell. . .wines and liquors, chemicals, textiles, metals. . .Almaden Vineyards.

**Nestlé Enterprises, Inc.. . .**100 Bloomingdale Rd., White Plains, NY 10605. . .D.E. Guerrant. . .foods. . .Libby, McNeill & Libby.

**Newhall Land and Farming Co.. . .**27050 Henry Mayo Rd., Valencia, CA 91355. . .James F. Dickason. . .real estate, gas exploration, recreation facilities.

**North American Philips Corp.. . .**100 E. 42d St., N.Y., NY 10017. . .Pieter C. Vink. . .electrical, electronic components. .Magnavox.

**Northrop Corp.. . .**1800 Century Park E., Los Angeles, CA 90067. . .Thomas V. Jones. . .aircraft, communications, electronics.

**Northwest Airlines, Inc.. . .**Minneapolis-St. Paul Intl. Airport, St. Paul, MN 55111. . .Donald W. Nyrop. . .air transportation.

**Northwest Industries, Inc.. . .**6300 Sears Tower, Chicago, IL 60606. . .Ben W. Heineman. . .tubular steel, chemicals, apparel. . .Fruit of the Loom.

**Norton Simon Inc.. . .**277 Park Ave., N.Y., NY 10017. . .David J. Mahoney. . .foods, cosmetics, apparel, soft drinks, distilled spirits, car rental. . .Avis; Canada Dry; Max Factor; Halston; Hunt-Wesson; McCall Pattern.

**Occidental Petroleum Corp.. . .**10889 Wilshire Blvd., Los Angeles, CA 90024. . .Armand Hammer. . .oil, gas, chemicals, coal.

**Olin Corp.. . .**120 Long Ridge Rd., Stamford, CT 06904. . .James F. Towey. . .chemicals, metals, paper, ammunition, sporting equip. . .Winchester Group.

**Olivetti Corp. of America. . .**500 Park Ave., N.Y., NY 10022. . .Guido Lorenzotti. . .office equipment, typewriters, computers, etc.

**Oneida Ltd.. . .**Sherrill Rd., Oneida, NY 13421. . .P.T. Noyes. . .silver, flatware, pewter.

**Oscar Mayer & Co., Inc.. . .**P.O. Box 7188, Madison, WI 53707. .P. Goff Beach. . .meat packing, food prods.. . .Claussen Pickle.

**Oster Corp.. . .**5055 N. Lydell Ave., Milwaukee, WI 53217. .W.J. Pfeif. . .small electric appliances. . .Sunbeam.

**Outboard Marine Corp.. . .**100 Sea Horse Dr., Waukegan, IL 60085. . .C.D. Strang. . .outboard motors, power equip.. . .Johnson Outboards.

**Owens-Corning Fiberglas Corp.. . .**Fiberglas Tower, Toledo, OH 43659. . .W.W. Boeschenstein. . .glass fiber materials.

**Owens-Illinois, Inc.. . .**P.O. Box 1035, Toledo, OH 43666. . .Edwin D. Dodd. . .glass and plastic containers, television bulbs.

**Pabst Brewing Co.. . .**917 W. Juneau Ave., Milwaukee, WI 53201. . .Frank C. DeGuire. . .brewery.

**Pan American World Airways. . .**200 Park Ave., Pan Am Bldg., N.Y., NY 10017. . .Wm. T. Seawell. . .air transportation.

**Panasonic Co.. . .**One Panasonic Way, Secaucus, NJ 07094. . .A. Harada. . .electronic goods. . .Matsushita Electric.

**Paper Mate. . .**Prudential Tower Bldg., Boston, MA 02199. . .William H. Holtsnider. . .pens. . .Gillette.

**Paramount Pictures Corp.. . .**One Gulf & Western Plaza, N.Y., NY 10023. . .David N. Judelson. . .motion pictures.. . .Gulf & Western.

**Parker Brothers. . .**190 Bridge St., Salem, MA 01970. . .Randolph P. Barton. . .games, toys. . .General Mills.

**Parker Pen Co.. . .**219 E. Court St., Janesville, WI 53545. . .George Parker. . .writing instruments, recreational equip., leisure clothing.

**Peavey Co.. . .**730 2d Ave. So., Minneapolis, MN 55402. . .Fredric H. Corrigan. . .foods, fabrics, crafts. . .Thunderbird Home Centers.

**Penn Dixie Industries, Inc.. . .**1345 Ave. of the Americas, N.Y., NY 10019. . .Jerome Castle. . .steel, cement.

**J.C. Penney Co., Inc.. . .**1301 Ave. of the Americas, N.Y., NY 10019. . .Donald V. Seibert. . .dept. stores, catalog sales, food, drugs, insurance.

**Pennwalt Corp.. . .**Pennwalt Bldg., 3 Pkwy., Phila., PA 19102. . .Wm. P. Drake. . .chemicals, health products.

**Pepperidge Farm Inc.. . .**P.O. Box 5500, Norwalk, CT 06856. . .R.G. McGovern. . .bakery prods.. . .Campbell Soup.

**PepsiCo, Inc.. . .**Anderson Hill Rd., Purchase, NY 10577. . .Andrall E. Pearson. . .soft drinks, snack foods, transportation, sporting goods.. . .Frito-Lay; Pepsi-Cola; PepsiCo Transportation; Wilson Sporting Goods.

**Pet Inc.. . .**Pet Plaza, 400 S. 4th St., St. Louis, MO 63166. . .Boyd F. Schenk. . .food prods., store equip.. . .Whitman's .

Chocolates, Stuckey's.

**Pfizer Inc.. . .**235 E. 42d St., N.Y., NY 10017. . .E.T. Pratt Jr.. . .pharmaceutical, hospital, agricultural, chemical prods.

**Philip Morris Inc.. . .**100 Park Ave., N.Y., NY 10017. . .Joseph F. Cullman 3d. . .cigarettes, beer, adhesives, chemicals, papers, greeting cards. . .Miller Brewing Co.; Mission Viejo.

**Pillsbury Co.. . .**608 2d Ave. So., Minneapolis, MN 55402.. . .Winston R. Wallin. . .food. . .Burger King.

**Pitney-Bowes, Inc.. . .**Walnut & Pacific, Stamford, CT 06904. . .Fred T. Allen. . .business systems, equip.

**Playtex, Intl.. . .**888 7th Ave., N.Y., NY 10019. . .Joel E. Smilow. . .personal prods.. . .Esmark.

**Polaroid Corp.. . .**549 Technology Sq., Cambridge, MA 02139. . .William J. McCune Jr.. . .photographic equip., supplies and optical goods.

**Potlatch Corp.. . .**P.O. Box 3591, San Francisco, CA 94119. . .Richard B. Madden. . .lumber, paper prods.

**Procter & Gamble Co.. . .**301 E. 6th St., Cincinnati, OH 45202. . .E.G. Harness. . .household, personal care, food prods.. . .Charmin; Folger Coffee.

**Pullman, Inc.. . .**200 S. Michigan Ave., Chicago, IL 60604. . .Samuel B. Casey Jr.. . .manufacture of transportation equip., engineering.

**Purex Corp.. . .**5101 Clark Ave., Lakewood, CA 90712. . .William R. Tincher. . .household cleaning prods., drugs, toiletries, foods, chemicals.

**Quaker Oats Co.. . .**Merchandise Mart Plaza, Chicago, IL 60654. . .Robert D. Stuart, Jr.. . .foods, pet foods, toys, chemicals, needlecraft kits, restaurants.

**Quaker State Oil Refining Corp.. . .**P.O. Box 989, Oil City, 16301. . .Q.E. Woods. . .petroleum prods., coal.

**Quasar Electronics Co.. . .**9401 W. Grand Ave., Franklin Park, IL 60131. . .R.T. Bloomberg. . .electrical prods.. . .Matsushita Electric.

**Questor Corp.. . .**1801 Spielbusch Ave., Toledo, OH 43691. . .P.M. Grieve. . .home environmental prods., auto parts, toys, sporting goods. . .Tinkertoy; Spalding.

**RCA Corp.. . .**Rockefeller Plaza, N.Y., NY 10020. . .Edgar H. Griffiths. . .electronics communications, diversified business.. . .Banquet Foods; Consumer Electronics; Hertz; NBC; Random House.

**Radio Shack. . .**2617 W. 7th St., Ft. Worth, TX 76107. . .Lewis F. Kornfeld. . .consumer electronics stores. . .Tandy Corp.

**Ralston Purina Co.. . .**835 S. 8th St., St. Louis, MO 63188. . .R. Hal Dean. . .feeds and grocery prods.

**Ramada Inns, Inc.. . .**3838 E. Van Buren, Phoenix, AZ 85008. . .M. William Isbell. . .hotel operation.

**Rath Packing Co.. . .**P.O. Box 330, Waterloo, IA 50704. . .Emmet A. McGuire. . .meat processing, food distribution.

**Raytheon Co.. . .**141 Spring St., Lexington, MA 02173. . .Thomas L. Phillips. . .diversified electronics. . .Amana Refrigeration; Caloric.

**Red Devil Paints & Chemicals. . .**30 Northwest St., Mt. Vernon, NY 10550. . .Durand B. Blatz. . .paints, wall coverings. . .Insilco.

**Revere Copper & Brass Inc.. . .**605 3d Ave., N.Y., NY 10016. . .William F. Collins. . .metal fabricators.

**Revlon, Inc.. . .**767 5th Ave., N.Y., NY 10022. . .Michael C. Bergerac. . .cosmetics, pharmaceuticals.

**Reynolds Metals Co.. . .**P.O. Box 27003, Richmond, VA 23261. . .David P. Reynolds. . .aluminum prods.

**R.J. Reynolds Industries, Inc.. . .**401 N. Main St., Winston-Salem, NC 27102. . .Colin Stokes. . .crude oil, petroleum, transportation, tobacco, food, and beverage prods.

**Richardson-Merrell Inc.. . .**10 Westport Rd., Wilton, CT 06897. . .J.S. Scott. . .pharmaceuticals. . .Vicks.

**Rival Manufacturing Co.. . .**36th St. & Bennington Ave., Kansas City, MO. . .I.H. Miller. . .small appliances.

**Robertshaw Controls Co.. . .**P.O. Box 26544, Richmond, VA 23261. . .Ralph S. Thomas. . .controls, control systems.

**A.H. Robins Co., Inc.. . .**1407 Cummings Dr., Richmond, VA 23220. . .W.L. Zimmer 3d. . .health care prods.. . .Chap Stick.

**Rockwell Intl.. . .**600 Grant St., Pittsburgh, PA 15219. . .Robert Anderson. . .aerospace, electronics, automotive, utility prods.. . .Admiral.

**Ronson Corp.. . .**One Ronson Rd., Bridgewater, NJ 08807. . .Louis V. Aronson 2d. . .cigarette lighters and accessories, personal care prods.

**Roper Corp.. . .**1905 W. Court St., Kankakee, IL 60901. . .C.M. Hoover. . .appliances, home and lawn prods.

**Royal Typewriter Co.. . .**2828 Beverly Blvd., Los Angeles, CA 90057. . .Charles B. Thornton. . .typewriters. . .*Litton Industries.*

**Rubbermaid Inc.. . .**1147 Akron Rd., Wooster, OH 44691. . .Donald E. Noble. . .rubber and plastic prods.

**Helena Rubenstein, Inc.. . .**300 Park Ave., N.Y., NY 10022. . .Peter H. Engel. . .cosmetics. . .*Colgate-Palmolive.*

**SCM Corp.. . .**299 Park Ave., N.Y., NY 10017. . .Paul H. Elicker. . .diversified manufacturer. . .Smith Corona; Durkee Foods.

**Safeway Stores, Inc.. . .**201 4th St., Oakland, CA 94660. . .W.S. Mitchell. . .retail food stores.

**St. Regis Paper Co.. . .**150 E. 42d St., N.Y., NY 10017. . .William R. Hazelton. . .pulp and paper machinery, building prods.

**Santa Fe Industries, Inc.. . .**224 S. Michigan Ave., Chicago, IL 60604. . .John S. Reed. . .transportation, real estate, construction, natural resources. . .Atchison, Topeka and Santa Fe Railway.

**Sara Lee, Kitchens of. . .**500 Waukegan Rd., Deerfield, IL 60015. . .Thomas F. Barnum. . .frozen bakery prods.. . .*Consolidated Foods.*

**Saxon Industries, Inc.. . .**1230 Ave. of the Americas. . .Stanley Lurie. . .paper and paper prods., photocopiers and supplies. . .Sphinx.

**Schering-Plough Corp.. . .**Galloping Hill Rd., Kenilworth, NJ 07033. . .W.H. Conzen. . .medicines, cosmetics, household prods.

**Schick, Inc.. . .**33 Riverside Ave., Westport, CT 06880. . .James W. Hart. . .personal care appliances.

**Jos. Schlitz Brewing Co.. . .**235 Galena St., Milwaukee, WI 53201. . .D.F. McKeithan. . .brewery.

**Scott Paper Co.. . .**Scott Plaza, Phila., PA 19113. . .Charles D. Dickey Jr.. . .paper prods.

**Scovill Manufacturing Co.. . .**Scovill Sq., Waterbury, CT 06720. . .M. Baldrige. . .automotive, housing prods., housewares, sewing notions. . .Hamilton Beach.

**Joseph E. Seagram & Sons, Inc.. . .**375 Park Ave., N.Y., NY 10022. . .Philip E. Beekman. . .distilled spirits & wine. . .*Seagram Co. Ltd.*

**G.D. Searle & Co.. . .**P.O. Box 1045, Skokie, IL 60076. . .Donald Rumsfeld. . .health care, pharmaceutical, diagnostic prods.. . .Vision Center, Hillman-Kohan Eyeglasses.

**Sears Roebuck & Co.. . .**Sears Tower, Chicago, IL 60684. . .Edward R. Telling. . .merchandising. . .Allstate Insurance.

**Seven-up Co.. . .**121 S. Meramec, St. Louis, MO 63105. . .William E. Winter. . .flavoring extracts, soft drinks.

**Shasta Beverages. . .**26901 Industrial Blvd., Hayward, CA 94545. . .Fred Schmid. . .soft drinks. . .*Consolidated Foods.*

**Shell Oil Co.. . .**P.O. Box 2463, Houston, TX 77001. . .John F. Bookout. . .oil, gas, chemicals.

**Sheller-Globe Corp.. . .**P.O. Box 962. . .Toledo, OH 43297. . .Chester Devenow. . .auto parts and accessories, vehicles.

**Sheraton Corp. of America. . .**470 Atlantic Ave., Boston, MA 02210. . .H.S. Geneen. . .hotels. . .*Intl. Telephone and Telegraph.*

**Sherwin-Williams Co.. . .**101 Prospect Ave. N.W., Cleveland, OH 44115. . .W.C. Fine. . .paints and related prods.

**Ship 'N Shore, Inc.. . .**Bridgewater Rd., Aston, PA 19014. . .Jon E. DeLuca. . .apparel. . .*General Mills.*

**Simmons Co.. . .**P.O. Box 49000, Atlanta, GA 30340. . .G.G. Simmons Jr.. . .bedding, furniture, caskets.

**Singer Co.. . .**30 Rockefeller Plaza, N.Y., NY 10020. . .Joseph B. Flavin. . .sewing prods., furniture, power tools.

**Skyline Corp.. . .**2520 By-Pass Rd., Elkhart, IN 46514. . .Arthur J. Decio. . .mobile and recreational vehicles.

**A.O. Smith. . .**3533 N. 27th. . .Milwaukee, WI 53216. . .L.B. Smith. . .water heating equip., electric motors.

**Smith Corona. . .**Locust Ave., New Canaan, CT 06840. . .P.J. Webbing. . .typewriters. . .*SCM Corp.*

**SmithKline Corp.. . .**1500 Spring Garden, Phila., PA 19101. . .Henry Wendt. . .pharmaceuticals, animal health prods., diagnostic instruments. . .Sea & Ski.

**Sony Corp. of America.. . .**9 W. 57th St., N.Y., NY 10019. . .Raymond Steiner. . .electronics.

**Southern Pacific Co.. . .**One Market Plaza, San Francisco, CA 94105. . .B.F. Biaggini. . .transportation, leasing.

**Spencer Foods, Inc.. . .**P.O. Box 1228, Spencer, IA 51301. . .Gerald L. Pearson. . .beef processing.

**Sperry and Hutchinson Co.. . .**S & H Bldg., 330 Madison Ave., N.Y., NY 10017. . .W.S. Beinecke. . .S & H stamps, carpeting,

furniture, banking, insurance.

**Sperry Rand Corp.. . .**1290 Ave. of the Americas, N.Y., NY 10019. . .J. Paul Lyet. . .electronic prods.. . .Sperry Remington Electric Shaver.

**Spiegel, Inc.. . .**1515 W. 22d St., Oak Brook, IL 60521. . .Henry A. Johnson. . .catalog merchandising. . .*Beneficial Corp.*

**Spring Mills, Inc.. . .**Executive Office Bldg., Ft. Mill, SC 29715. . .Peter G. Scotese. . .textiles, frozen foods.

**Squibb Corp.. . .**40 W. 57th St., N.Y., NY 10019. . .Richard M. Furlaud. . .drugs, confectionery, household prods.. . .Lanvin-Charles of the Ritz; Life Savers.

**A.E. Staley Manufacturing Co.. . .**2200 E. Eldorado, Decatur, IL 62525. . .Donald E. Nordlund. . .corn and soybean processing.

**Standard Brands Inc.. . .**625 Madison Ave., N.Y., NY 10022. . .F. Ross Johnson. . .foods, related prods.. . .Fleischmann Distilling; Julius Wile.

**Standard Oil Co. of California. . .**225 Bush, San Francisco, CA 94104. . .H.J. Haynes. . .petroleum.

**Standard Oil Co. (Indiana). . .**200 E. Randolph Dr., Chicago, IL 60601. . .George V. Myers. . .petroleum.

**Standard Oil Co. (Ohio). . .**Midland Bldg., Cleveland, OH 44115. . .Charles E. Spahr. . .petroleum, coal, uranium, chemicals, plastics.

**Stanley Home Products, Inc.. . .**333 Western Ave., Westfield, MA 01085. . .Homer G. Perkins. . .household and personal prods.

**Stanley Works. . .**195 Lake, New Britain, CT 06052. . .D.W. Davis. . .tools, hardware.

**Star-Kist Foods, Inc.. . .**582 Tuna St., Terminal Island, CA 90731. . .Anthony J.F. O'Reilly. . .canned fish. . .*H.J. Heinz.*

**Sterling Drug Inc.. . .**90 Park Ave., N.Y., NY 10016. . .W. Clarke Wescoe. . .pharmaceuticals. . .d-Con; Dorothy Gray.

**J.P. Stevens & Co., Inc.. . .**1185 Ave. of the Americas, N.Y., NY 10036. . .James D. Finley. . .fabrics, carpets, hosiery.

**Stokely-Van Camp, Inc.. . .**941 N. Meridian, Indianapolis, IN 46206. . .A.J. Stokley. . .canned fruits and vegetables.

**Studebaker-Worthington, Inc.. . .**One Dag Hammarskjold Plaza, N.Y., NY 10017. . .Derald H. Ruttenberg. . .cleaning, maintenance equip., lawn and garden tractors, automotive, construction prods.

**Sunbeam Appliance Co.. . .**2001 S. York Rd., Oak Brook, IL 60521. . .W.A. Crews. . .small electrical appliances. . .Sunbeam Corp.

**Sun Company, Inc.. . .**100 Matsonford Rd., Radnor, PA 19087. . .Theodore A. Burtis. . .petroleum.

**Sunshine Biscuits, Inc.. . .**245 Park Ave., N.Y., NY 10017. . .Edward J. Jennings Jr.. . .biscuits, crackers, snacks. . .*American Brands.*

**Swift & Co.. . .**115 W. Jackson, Chicago, IL 60604. . .William S. Watchman Jr.. . .food. . .*Esmark.*

**Swingline, Inc.. . .**32-00 Skillman Ave., Long Island City, NY 11101. . .Edward W. Whittemore. . .staplers, cutlery, fasteners. . .*American Brands.*

**Sylvania Lighting. . .**100 Endicott St., Danvers, MA 01923. . .Theodore F. Brophy. . .lighting prods.. . .*General Telephone & Electronics.*

**Talbots, Inc.. . .**175 Beal St., Hingham, MA 02402. . .Rudolph L. Talbot. . .apparel catalog sales.

**Talley Industries, Inc.. . .**P.O. Box 849, Mesa, AZ 85201. . .F.G. Talley. . .diversified manufacturing. . .Seth Thomas; Westclox.

**Tandy Corp.. . .**P.O. Box 17180, Fort Worth, TX 76102. . .C.D. Tandy. . .electronics. . .Radio Shack.

**Tappan Co.. . .**Tappan Park, Mansfield, OH 44901. . .D.C. Blasius. . .large kitchen appliances, heating & air conditioning equip.

**Teledyne, Inc.. . .**1901 Ave. of the Stars, Los Angeles, CA 90067. . .George Roberts. . .electronics, aerospace, geophysical prods.

**Texaco Inc.. . .**135 E. 42d St., N.Y., NY 10017. . .Maurice F. Granville. . .petrochemicals.

**Texas Instruments Inc.. . .**P.O. Box 225474, Dallas, TX 75265. . .J. Fred Bucy. . .electrical and electronic prods., digital watches.

**Textron Inc.. . .**40 Westminster St., Providence, RI 02903. . .Jospeh B. Collinson. . .aerospace, metal prods.. . .Gorham; Speidel; Talon.

**3M Co.. . .**3M Center, St. Paul, MN 55101. . .Raymond H. Herzog. . .automotive, building prods., chemicals, data processing.

**Trane Co.. . .**3600 Pammel Creek Rd., La Crosse, WI 54601. . .Thomas Hancock. . .air conditioning and heat transfer equip.

**Trans World Airlines Inc.. . .**605 3d Ave., N.Y., NY 10016. . .L.

Edwin Smart. . .air transportation.
**Tropicana Products, Inc.. . .**P.O. Box 338, Bradenton, FL
33506. . .A.T. Rossi. . .citrus processing.
**Tupperware. . .**N. Highway 441, Kissimmee, FL 32741. . .
.Thomas P. Mullaney. . .food containers, toys. . .*Dart Industries.*
**Twentieth Century-Fox Film Corp.. . .**P.O. Box 900, Beverly
Hills, CA 90213. . .Dennis C. Stanfill. . .motion pictures.

**United Air Lines, Inc.. . .**P.O. Box 66100, Chicago, IL 60666. .
.E.E. Carlson. . .air transportation. . .*UAL.*
**Union Carbide Corp.. . .**270 Park Ave., N.Y. NY 10017. . .William S. Sneath. . .agricultural, battery, carbon prods., chemicals, plastics.
**Union Pacific Corp.. . .**345 Park Ave., N.Y., NY 10022. . .F.E.
Barnett. . .transportation, natural resources, real estate.
**Uniroyal, Inc.. . .**Oxford Management & Research Center, Middlebury, CT 06749. . .Joseph P. Flannery. . .chemical, rubber,
plastic prods.
**United Brands Co.. . .**30 Rockefeller Plaza, N.Y., NY 10020. . .
.Seymour Milstein. . .foods, telecommunications, restaurants. .
.Chiquita; John Morrell.
**United Merchants and Manufacturers, Inc.. . .**1407 Broadway,
N.Y., NY 10018. . .Z.B. Lane Jr.. . .textiles, plastics, chemicals.
**United Parcel Service. . .**Greenwich Office Park #5, Greenwich, CT 06830. . .Harold Oberkotter. . .parcel delivery.
**United States Steel Corp.. . .**600 Grant St., Pittsburgh, PA
15230. . .David M. Roderick. . .steel, chemicals, transportation,
utilities.
**States Tobacco Co.. . .**100 W. Putnam Ave., Greenwich, CT 06830. . .L.F. Bantle. . .tobacco, pet foods, wines,
pens and pencils. . .Cadillac Pet Foods.
**United Technologies. . .**United Technologies Bldg., Hartford,
CT 06101. . .Harry J. Gray. . .high-technology prods.. . .Pratt &
Whitney Aircraft; Sikorsky Aircraft.
**Universal Leaf Tobacco Co., Inc.. . .**P.O. Box 25099, Richmond, VA 23260. . .Gordon L. Crenshaw. . .leaf tobacco.
**Upjohn Co.. . .**7000 Portage Rd., Kalamazoo, MI 49001. . .R.T.
Parfet Jr.. . .pharmaceuticals, chemicals.

**VF Corp.. . .**1047 N. Park Rd., Reading, PA 19610. . .M.O. Lee. .
.apparel. . .Vanity Fair; Kay Windsor.
**Volkswagen of America, Inc.. . .**7111 E. 11-Mile Rd., Warren,
MI 48092. . .James McLernon. . .passenger vehicles.
**Volvo, Inc.. . .**Volvo Dr., Rockleigh, NJ 07647. . .Bjorn Ahlstrom. .
.automobiles.

**Walgreen Co.. . .**200 Wilmot Rd., Deerfield, IL 60015. . .R.L.
Schmitt. . .drug, discount stores.
**Ward Foods, Inc.. . .**2 Penn Plaza, N.Y., NY 10001. . .Alvin L.
Erlich. . .foods.
**Warnaco Inc.. . .**350 Lafayette, Bridgeport, CT 06602. . .James
C. Walker. . .apparel. . .Hathaway. . .Rosanna; Puritan; White
Stag.
**Warner Communications. . .**75 Rockefeller Plaza, N.Y., NY
10019. . .Steven J. Ross. . .entertainment, communications. .
.Warner Books; Warner Bros.
**Warner-Lambert Co.. . .**201 Tabor Rd., Morris Plains, NJ

07950. . .E. Burke Giblin. . .health care prods., confectionery. .
.American Chicle; DuBarry; Good & Plenty.
**Wear-Ever Aluminum, Inc.. . .**1089 Eastern Ave., Chillicothe,
OH 45601. . .W.H. Krome George. . .aluminum. . .*Aluminum
Co. of America.*
**West Bend Co.. . .**400 W. Washington, West Bend, WI 53095. .
.Thomas P. Mullaney. . .cookware, electric housewares, humidifiers. . .*Dart Industries.*
**Western Airlines, Inc.. . .**6060 Avion Dr., Los Angeles, CA
90045. . .Arthur F. Kelly. . .air transportation.
**Western Union Telegraph Co.. . .**56 Marietta St., Atlanta, GA
30303. . .R.W. McFall. . .telecommunications. . .*Western Union
Corp.*
**Westinghouse Broadcasting Co., Inc.. . .**90 Park Ave., N.Y.,
NY 10016. . .R.E. Kirby. . .Radio, TV broadcasting, CATV. . .
.*Westinghouse Electric.*
**Westinghouse Electric Corp.. . .**Westinghouse Bldg., Gateway
Center, Pittsburgh, PA 15222. . .electricity transmission communications, watches. . .Longines-Wittnauer; Westinghouse
Broadcasting.
**West Point-Pepperell—Consumer Prods.. . .**1221 Ave. of the
Americas, N.Y., NY 10020. . .C.J. Kjorlien. . .towels, sheets,
blankets.
**Weyerhaeuser Co.. . .**Tacoma, WA 98401. . .George H. Weyerhaeuser. . .forest prods.
**Whirlpool Corp.. . .**Administrative Center, Benton Harbor, MI
49022. . .John H. Platts. . .major household appliances.
**White Consolidated Industries, Inc.. . .**11770 Berea Rd.,
Cleveland, OH 44111. . .R.H. Holdt. . .home prods.. . .Kelvinator; White Sewing Machine.
**White Motor Corp.. . .**35129 Curtis Blvd., Eastlake, OH 44094. .
.S.E. Knudsen. . .heavy duty trucks.
**Willamette Industries, Inc.. . .**1300 S.W. 5th Ave., Portland, OR
97201. . .Gene D. Knudson. . .lumber prods.
**Wilson Sporting Goods Co.. . .**2233 West St., River Grove, IL
60171. . .Gordon Hollywood. . .sports equip.. . .*PepsiCo.*
**Winn-Dixie Stores, Inc.. . .**5050 Edgewood Ct., Jacksonville, FL
32203. . .B.L. Thomas. . .retail grocery chain.
**Winnebago Industries, Inc.. . .**Junction 9 and 69, Forest City,
IA 50436. . .J. Harold Bragg. . .recreational vehicles.
**F.W. Woolworth Co.. . .**233 Broadway, N.Y., NY 10007. . .Edward F. Gibbons. . .retail general merchandise stores.
**Wm. Wrigley Jr. Co.. . .**410 N. Michigan Ave., Chicago, IL
60611. . .William Wrigley. . .chewing gum.

**Xerox Corp.. . .**High Ridge Park, Stamford, CT 06904. . .C. Peter McColough. . .copiers, duplicators, computer related
equip., textbook publishing.

**Yashica, Inc.—U.S.A.. . .**411 Sette Dr., Paramus, NJ 07652. .
.Mr. T. Kakutani. . .cameras, photographic supplies.
**Yoo-Hoo Chocolate Beverage Corp.. . .**600 Commercial Ave.,
Carlstadt, NJ 07072. . .Max A. Geller. . .soft drinks. . .*Iroquois
Brands.*

**Zale Corp.. . .**3000 Diamond Park, Dallas TX 75247. . .Donald
Zale. . .jewelry, footware, catalog sales, apparel, sporting
goods, furniture.
**Zenith Radio Corp.. . .**1000 Milwaukee Ave., Glenview, IL
60025. . .John J. Nevin. . .electronic home entertainment
prods.

---

## State & Local Government Receipts and Expenditures, 1973-1976

Source: Bureau of Economic Analysis, U.S. Commerce Department

(Estimated; in millions of dollars)

| | 1973 Current $ | 1967 $ | 1974 Current $ | 1967 $ | 1975 Current $ | 1967 $ | 1976 Current $ | 1967 $ |
|---|---|---|---|---|---|---|---|---|
| **Receipts** | 235,623 | 177,027 | 257,285 | 174,194 | 287,575 | 178,396 | 321,142 | 188,353 |
| Personal taxes | 36,137 | 27,150 | 39,206 | 26,544 | 43,375 | 26,908 | 49,551 | 29,062 |
| Corporate, business taxes | 104,688 | 78,654 | 113,349 | 76,743 | 121,790 | 75,552 | 135,990 | 79,760 |
| Social insurance payments | 12,085 | 29,080 | 13,904 | 9,414 | 15,904 | 9,866 | 18,137 | 10,638 |
| Grants-in-aid | 82,713 | 62,144 | 90,826 | 61,494 | 106,506 | 66,071 | 117,464 | 68,894 |
| **Expenditures** | 222,620 | 167,257 | 249,721 | 169,073 | 281,658 | 174,726 | 302,705 | 177,540 |
| Purchases of goods, services | 167,339 | 125,724 | 191,536 | 129,679 | 215,605 | 133,750 | 231,215 | 135,610 |
| Govt. workers' salaries | 97,139 | 72,982 | 106,458 | 72,077 | 119,226 | 73,962 | 129,237 | 75,799 |
| Transfer payments (pensions, welfare, etc.) | 20,324 | 15,270 | 20,532 | 13,901 | 23,768 | 14,744 | 25,933 | 15,210 |
| Net interest | −2,851 | −2,142 | −4,947 | −3,349 | −5,156 | −3,199 | −5,730 | −3,361 |
| Less temp. surpluses (− subsidies) | 1,803 | 1,355 | 1,975 | 1,337 | 2,209 | 1,370 | 2,909 | 1,706 |
| State grants to local govts. | 42,139 | 31,660 | 46,925 | 31,770 | 51,904 | 32,199 | 56,466 | 33,118 |
| **Surpluses** | 13,003 | 9,769 | 7,564 | 5,121 | 5,917 | 3,671 | 18,437 | 10,813 |

# ECONOMICS

## U.S. Budget Receipts and Outlays—1976-1978

**Source:** Treasury Department; Office of Management and Budget.
(1976 fiscal year ended June 30; 1977 and 1978 fiscal years ended Sept. 30)
(thousands of dollars)

| Classification | Fiscal 1976 | Transitional Quarter 1976 | Fiscal 1977 | Fiscal 1978 |
|---|---|---|---|---|
| **Net Receipts** | | | | |
| Individual income taxes | 131,602,555 | 38,800,969 | 156,725,183 | 182,000,000 |
| Corporation income taxes | 41,408,703 | 8,460,466 | 54,892,364 | 59,000,000 |
| Social insurance taxes and contributions: | | | | |
| Federal old-age and survivors insurance | 58,702,690 | 15,885,848 | 68,031,809 | NA |
| Federal disability insurance | 7,686,092 | 2,130,051 | 8,785,502 | NA |
| Federal hospital insurance | 11,995,098 | 3,458,803 | 13,484,042 | NA |
| Railroad retirement taxes | 1,525,144 | 328,310 | 1,908,494 | NA |
| **Total employment taxes and contributions** | **79,909,024** | **21,803,012** | **92,209,847** | **NA** |
| Other insurance and retirement: | | | | |
| Unemployment | 8,053,658 | 2,697,903 | 11,311,506 | NA |
| Federal supplementary medical insurance | 1,937,296 | 538,648 | 2,192,903 | NA |
| Federal employees retirement | 2,760,167 | 706,247 | 2,909,697 | NA |
| Civil service retirement and disability | 54,231 | 13,323 | 58,923 | NA |
| **Total social insurance taxes and contributions** | **92,714,377** | **25,759,134** | **108,682,876** | **123,600,000** |
| Excise taxes | 16,962,582 | 4,472,698 | 17,547,715 | 18,200,000 |
| Estate and gift taxes | 5,216,229 | 1,454,592 | 7,326,877 | 5,200,000 |
| Customs duties | 4,074,176 | 1,212,173 | 5,150,151 | 6,100,000 |
| Deposits of earnings-Federal Reserve Banks | 5,450,824 | 1,500,459 | 5,908,214 | NA |
| Petroleum import license fees | 1,890,326 | –49,812 | –12,617 | NA |
| All other miscellaneous receipts | 685,305 | 162,088 | 640,568 | NA |
| **Net Budget Receipts** | **300,005,077** | **81,772,766** | **6,536,165** | **401,200,** |
| **Net Outlays** | | | | |
| Legislative Branch | 779,052 | 224,882 | 976,492 | 1,000,000 |
| The Judiciary | 325,021 | 85,188 | 391,839 | 500,000 |
| Executive Office of the President: | | | | |
| The White House Office | 15,791 | 4,136 | 17,236 | NA |
| Office of Management and Budget | 23,591 | 5,373 | 26,536 | NA |
| **Total Executive Office** | **79,224** | **16,206** | **73,386** | **100,000** |
| Funds appropriated to the President: | | | | |
| Appalachian regional development | 319,283 | 73,539 | 248,868 | NA |
| Disaster relief | 291,137 | 71,321 | 294,016 | NA |
| Foreign assistance-security | 1,101,398 | 468,084 | 347,287 | NA |
| Foreign assistance-development-multilateral | 1,045,829 | 429,712 | 1,124,925 | NA |
| Foreign assistance-development-bilateral | 623,516 | 179,348 | 507,098 | NA |
| **Total funds appropriated to the President** | **3,524,692** | **1,221,437** | **2,497,204** | **5,200,000** |
| Agriculture Department: | | | | |
| Food stamp program | 5,774,500 | 1,366,642 | 5,398,795 | NA |
| Child Nutrition Program | 1,801,566 | 346,012 | 2,635,039 | NA |
| **Total Agriculture Department** | **12,796,311** | **3,849,622** | **16,737,730** | **21,600,000** |
| Commerce Department | 2,020,005 | 533,952 | 2,606,804 | 5,200,000 |
| Defense Department: | | | | |
| Military personnel | 25,063,518 | 6,358,317 | 25,714,935 | NA |
| Retired military personnel | 7,295,679 | 1,947,333 | 8,216,429 | NA |
| Operation and maintenance | 27,901,590 | 7,260,781 | 30,688,742 | NA |
| Procurement | 15,963,849 | 3,766,420 | 18,178,230 | NA |
| Research and development | 8,923,023 | 2,205,681 | 9,795,166 | NA |
| Military construction | 2,018,627 | 376,211 | 1,913,804 | NA |
| Family housing | 1,191,772 | 295,954 | 1,357,866 | NA |
| Civil defense | 79,835 | 17,621 | 92,728 | 2,500,000 |
| Corps of Engineers and civil functions | 2,124,252 | 582,545 | 2,279,998 | NA |
| **Total Defense Department** | **90,160,407** | **22,508,760** | **98,031,451** | **104,500,000** |
| Health, Education and Welfare Department: | | | | |
| National Institutes of Health | 2,349,289 | 471,704 | 2,253,040 | NA |
| Old-age and survivors benefits | 62,164,263 | 17,109,799 | 73,478,596 | NA |
| Public assistance (including health care and social services) | 16,675,438 | 4,399,141 | 19,777,109 | NA |
| Education Division | 6,903,749 | 1,751,003 | 7,783,479 | NA |
| **Total HEW** | **128,784,967** | **34,340,745** | **147,455,436** | **163,300,000** |
| Housing and Urban Development Department | 7,079,133 | 1,397,090 | 5,832,430 | 8,000,000 |
| Interior Department | 2,293,480 | 787,617 | 3,085,260 | 3,900,000 |
| Justice Department: | | | | |
| Federal Bureau of Investigation | 468,764 | 130,177 | 520,218 | NA |
| **Total Justice Department** | **2,241,574** | **550,633** | **2,349,726** | **2,500,000** |
| Labor Department: | | | | |
| Unemployment Trust Fund | 17,920,413 | 3,543,844 | 14,102,958 | NA |
| **Total Labor Department** | **25,742,379** | **5,905,346** | **22,374,056** | **22,900,000** |
| State Department | 1,061,820 | 316,144 | 1,131,820 | 1,300,000 |
| Transportation Department | 11,936,056 | 3,002,507 | 12,513,984 | 13,500,000 |
| Treasury Department: | | | | |
| Internal Revenue Service | 2,924,389 | 600,805 | 2,265,183 | NA |
| Interest on the public debt | 37,063,211 | 8,101,561 | 41,899,720 | NA |
| General revenue sharing | 6,242,926 | 1,587,642 | 6,760,092 | NA |
| **Total Treasury Department** | **44,335,468** | **9,699,089** | **49,560,182** | **56,300,000** |
| Energy Research and Development Agency | 3,759,025 | 1,051,211 | 5,020,477 | 6,600,000 |
| Environmental Protection Agency | 3,117,746 | 1,108,362 | 4,364,808 | 4,500,000 |

| Classification | Fiscal 1976 | Transitional Quarter 1976 | Fiscal 1977 | Fiscal 1978[1] |
|---|---|---|---|---|
| **Net Outlays (cont'd)** | | | | |
| General Services Administration | −92,142 | 3,202 | −31,100 | 100,000 |
| National Aeronautics and Space Administration | 3,669,502 | 953,026 | 3,943,817 | 4,000,000 |
| Veterans Administration | 18,414,835 | 3,957,459 | 18,019,353 | 18,800,000 |
| Independent agencies: | | | | |
| Action | 177,011 | 47,840 | 186,296 | NA |
| Arms Control and Disarmament Agency | 10,704 | 2,642 | 11,863 | NA |
| Board for International Broadcasting | 59,340 | 21,265 | 57,837 | NA |
| Civil Aeronautics Board | 90,939 | 22,193 | 102,707 | NA |
| Civil Service Commission | 8,320,440 | 2,352,986 | 9,260,119 | NA |
| Commission on Civil Rights | 7,863 | 1,873 | 9,476 | NA |
| Community Services Administration | 448,733 | 123,700 | 639,363 | NA |
| Consumer Product Safety Commission | 38,351 | 10,189 | 39,867 | NA |
| Corporation for Public Broadcasting | 70,000 | 26,000 | 103,000 | NA |
| District of Columbia | 464,738 | 173,110 | 315,717 | NA |
| Emergency Loan Guarantee Board | −5,570 | −3,872 | −5 014 | NA |
| Equal Employment Opportunity Commission | 56,143 | 16,204 | 71,729 | NA |
| Federal Communications Commission | 52,486 | 12,756 | 55,776 | NA |
| Federal Deposit Insurance Corporation | −478,330 | 133,280 | −851,645 | NA |
| Federal Energy Administration | 140,603 | −26,593 | 148,607 | NA |
| Federal Home Loan Bank Board | −78,853 | −178,167 | 1,913,355 | NA |
| Federal Maritime Commission | 7,784 | 1,892 | 8,449 | NA |
| Federal Mediation and Conciliation Service | 17,908 | 4,335 | 19,570 | NA |
| Federal Power Commission | 35,704 | 8,639 | 40,932 | NA |
| Federal Trade Commission | 43,729 | 11,117 | 51,703 | NA |
| Historical and Memorial Commissions | 12,788 | 5,839 | 7,850 | NA |
| Intergovernmental Agencies | 174,099 | 52,689 | 292,403 | NA |
| International Trade Commission | 9,715 | 2,472 | 10,806 | NA |
| Interstate Commerce Commission | 47,440 | 12,582 | 60,602 | NA |
| Legal Services Corporation | 84,634 | 51,769 | 125,004 | NA |
| National Credit Union Administration | −19,896 | 3,532 | −19,282 | NA |
| National Foundation on the Arts and Humanities | 151,860 | 43,895 | 192,753 | NA |
| National Labor Relations Board | 67,466 | 15,717 | 80,546 | NA |
| National Science Foundation | 731,905 | 206,475 | 752,035 | NA |
| Nuclear Regulatory Commission | 179,956 | 45,819 | 230,547 | NA |
| Postal Service | 1,719,650 | 937,742 | 2,267,449 | NA |
| Railroad Retirement Board | 3,482,102 | 936,792 | 3,858,848 | NA |
| Securities and Exchange Commission | 50,618 | 11,568 | 53,635 | NA |
| Selective Service System | 37,493 | 3,993 | 9,587 | NA |
| Small Business Administration | 436,164 | 78,144 | 699,974 | NA |
| Smithsonian Institution | 112,772 | 30,423 | 114,988 | NA |
| Temporary Study Commissions | 13,602 | 3,153 | 15,147 | NA |
| Tennessee Valley Authority | 930,318 | 232,130 | 1,099,559 | NA |
| U.S. Information Agency | 257,034 | 73,035 | 261,220 | NA |
| U.S. Railway Association | 329,020 | 3,150 | 735,500 | NA |
| Water Resources Council | 10,943 | 2,026 | 12,238 | NA |
| Other Independent agencies | 52,031 | 12,710 | 85,569 | NA |
| **Total independent agencies** | 18,285,947 | 5,527,046 | 20,014,438 | 24,600,000 |
| Undistributed offsetting receipts | −14,704,375 | −2,566,530 | −15,053,215 | −16,100,000 |
| **Net Budget Outlays** | 365,610,129 | 94,472,996 | 401,896,376 | 452,300,000 |
| Less net receipts | 300,005,077 | 81,772,766 | 356,861,331 | 401,200,000 |
| **Deficit** | −65,605,052 | −12,700,230 | −45,035,045 | −51,100,000 |

(1) Estimate. (NA) Not available.

# U.S. Net Receipts and Outlays

Source: Treasury Department; annual statements for year ending June 30[1] (thousands of dollars)

| Yearly average | Receipts | Expenditures | Yearly average | Receipts | Expenditures | Yearly average | Receipts | Expenditures |
|---|---|---|---|---|---|---|---|---|
| 1789-1800[1] | 5,717 | 5,776 | 1871-1875 | 336,830 | 287,460 | 1911-1915 | 710,227 | 720,252 |
| 1801-1810[2] | 13,056 | 9,086 | 1876-1880 | 288,124 | 255,598 | 1916-1920[6] | 3,483,652 | 8,065,333 |
| 1811-1820[2] | 21,032 | 23,943 | 1881-1885 | 366,961 | 257,691 | 1921-1925 | 4,306,673 | 3,578,989 |
| 1821-1830[2] | 21,928 | 16,162 | 1886-1890 | 375,448 | 279,134 | 1926-1930 | 4,069,138 | 3,182,807 |
| 1831-1840[2] | 30,461 | 24,495 | 1891-1895 | 352,891 | 363,599 | 1931-1935[4] | 2,770,973 | 5,214,874 |
| 1841-1850[2] | 28,545 | 34,097 | 1896-1900 | 434,877 | 457,451 | 1936-1940[4] | 4,960,614 | 10,192,367 |
| 1851-1860 | 60,237 | 60,163 | 1901-1905 | 559,481 | 535,559 | 1941-1945[4] | 25,951,137 | 66,037,928 |
| 1861-1865 | 160,907 | 683,785 | 1906-1910 | 628,507 | 639,178 | 1946-1950[5 7] | 39,047,243 | 42,334,534 |
| 1866-1870 | 447,301 | 377,642 | | | | | | |

| Fiscal year | Receipts | Expenditures | Fiscal year | Receipts | Expenditures | Fiscal year | Receipts | Expenditures |
|---|---|---|---|---|---|---|---|---|
| 1955 | 60,389,744 | 64,569,973 | 1965 | 93,071,797 | 96,506,904 | 1974 | 264,847,484 | 268,342,952 |
| 1960 | 77,763,460 | 76,539,413 | 1968[9] | 153,675,705 | 172,803,186 | 1975 | 281,037,466 | 324,641,586 |
| 1961 | 77,659,425 | 81,515,167 | 1970 | 193,843,791 | 194,968,258 | 1976 | 300,005,077 | 365,610,129 |
| 1962 | 81,409,092 | 87,786,767 | 1971 | 188,332,129 | 210,652,667 | 1976 Trans[3] | 81,772,766 | 94,472,996 |
| 1963 | 86,357,020 | 92,589,764 | 1972[8] | 215,262,639 | 238,285,907 | 1977[3] | 356,861,331 | 401,896,376 |
| 1964 | 89,458,664 | 97,684,375 | 1973 | 232,191,842 | 246,603,359 | 1978[10] | 401,200,000 | 452,300,000 |

(1) Average for period March 4, 1789, to Dec. 31, 1800. (2) Years ended Dec. 31, 1801 to 1842; average for 1841-1850 is for the period Jan. 1, 1841, to June 30, 1850. (3) Effective fiscal year 1977, fiscal year is reckoned Oct. 1-Sept. 30; transition quarter covers July 1, 1976-Sept. 30, 1976. (4) Expenditures for years 1932 through 1946 have been revised to include Government corps. (wholly owned) etc. (net). (5) Effective January 3, 1949, amounts refunded by the Government, principally for the overpayment of taxes, are being reported as deductions from total receipts rather than as expenditures. Also, effective July 1, 1948, payments to the Treasury, principally by wholly owned Government corporations for retirement of capital stock and for disposition of earnings, are excluded in reporting both budget receipts and expenditures. Neither of these changes affects the size of the budget surplus or deficit. Beginning 1931 figures in each case have been adjusted accordingly for comparative purposes. (6) Figures for 1918 through 1946 are revised to exclude statutory debt retirement (sinking fund, etc.). (7) Excludes $3 billion transferred to Foreign Economics Corporation Trust Fund, and includes $3 billion representing expenditures made from the FEC Trust Fund. (8) Effective fiscal year 1972 loan repayments and loan disbursements will be netted against expenditures and known as outlays. (9) From 1968, figures include trust funds (e.g. Social Security). (10) Estimate.

## Summary of U.S. Receipts by Source and Outlays by Function

Source: U.S. Treasury Department, and the Office of Management and Budget

(in millions)

| Net Receipts | Fiscal 1976 | 7/1-9/30 1976[1] | Fiscal 1977 | Fiscal 1978[2] |
|---|---|---|---|---|
| Individual income taxes | $130,794 | $38,715 | $156,725 | $178,828 |
| Corporation income taxes | 41,409 | 8,460 | 54,892 | 58,949 |
| Social insurance taxes and contributions: | | | | |
|   Employment taxes and contributions | 79,909 | 21,803 | 92,210 | 103,986 |
|   Unemployment insurance | 8,054 | 2,698 | 11,312 | 14,420 |
|   Contributions for other insurance and retirement | 4,752 | 1,259 | 5,167 | 5,716 |
| Excise taxes | 16,963 | 4,473 | 17,548 | 20,150 |
| Estate and gift taxes | 5,216 | 1,455 | 7,327 | 5,618 |
| Customs duties | 4,074 | 1,212 | 5,150 | 5,792 |
| Miscellaneous receipts | 8,026 | 1,612 | 6,531 | 6,928 |
| **Total** | **299,197** | **81,687** | **356,861** | **400,387** |
| **Net outlays** | | | | |
| National defense | 89,430 | 22,307 | 97,501 | 107,626 |
| International affairs | 5,567 | 2,180 | 4,831 | 6,747 |
| General science, space, and technology | 4,370 | 1,161 | 4,677 | 4,757 |
| Energy | 3,127 | 794 | 4,172 | 7,837 |
| Natural resources and environment | 8,124 | 2,532 | 10,000 | 12,125 |
| Agriculture | 2,502 | 584 | 5,526 | 9,106 |
| Commerce and housing credit | 3,795 | 1,391 | −31 | 3,515 |
| Transportation | 13,438 | 3,306 | 14,636 | 16,318 |
| Community and regional development | 4,709 | 1,340 | 6,283 | 9,694 |
| Education, training, employment and social services | 18,737 | 5,162 | 20,985 | 27,471 |
| Health | 33,448 | 8,720 | 38,785 | 44,261 |
| Income security | 126,598 | 32,710 | 137,004 | 147,640 |
| Veterans benefits and services | 18,432 | 3,962 | 18,038 | 18,916 |
| Administration of justice | 3,320 | 859 | 3,600 | 4,019 |
| General government | 2,927 | 878 | 3,357 | 4,119 |
| General purpose fiscal assistance | 7,235 | 2,092 | 9,499 | 9,860 |
| Interest | 34,589 | 7,246 | 38,092 | 43,841 |
| Undistributed offsetting receipts | −14,704 | −2,567 | −15,053 | −15,619 |
| **Total** | **365,643** | **94,657** | **401,902** | **462,234** |

(1) Transitional quarter; up to 1976, fiscal year ended June 30; beginning with 1977, fiscal year ends Sept. 30 of the year indicated.
(2) Estimate.

---

## U.S. Direct Investment Abroad, Countries and Industries

Source: Bureau of Economic Analysis, U.S. Commerce Department

(millions of dollars)

| | Direct investment position 1976 | Direct investment position 1977 | Equity and intercompany account outflows (inflows (−)) 1976 | Equity and intercompany account outflows (inflows (−)) 1977 | Reinvested earnings 1976 | Reinvested earnings 1977 | Interest, dividends, and earnings of unincorp. affiliates 1976 | Interest, dividends, and earnings of unincorp. affiliates 1977 | Income 1976 | Income 1977 |
|---|---|---|---|---|---|---|---|---|---|---|
| **Bulk all areas** | 136,396 | 148,782 | 3,918 | 4,904 | 7,696 | −385 | 11,303 | 12,540 | 18,999 | 19,851 |
| Petroleum | 28,408 | 30,887 | 1,316 | 1,613 | 738 | 266 | 4,385 | 4,478 | 5,123 | 5,481 |
| Manufacturing | 61,161 | 65,604 | 1,041 | 884 | 4,117 | −603 | 3,106 | 3,812 | 7,223 | 7,326 |
| Other | 46,827 | 52,291 | 1,561 | 2,406 | 2,841 | −47 | 3,812 | 4,250 | 6,653 | 7,044 |
| **Developed countries** | 100,398 | 108,047 | 2,880 | 2,546 | 6,133 | −1,054 | 5,327 | 6,810 | 11,461 | 11,889 |
| Canada | 33,932 | 35,398 | 115 | −409 | 2,451 | −535 | 1,385 | 1,425 | 3,837 | 3,341 |
| Petroleum | 7,181 | 7,722 | −27 | −30 | 724 | −88 | 282 | 355 | 1,006 | 992 |
| Manufacturing | 15,965 | 16,658 | 67 | −125 | 1,202 | −422 | 633 | 563 | 1,835 | 1,344 |
| Other | 10,786 | 11,018 | 74 | −255 | 525 | −26 | 471 | 506 | 996 | 1,006 |
| Europe | 55,139 | 60,591 | 2,408 | 2,733 | 3,084 | −364 | 3,085 | 4,406 | 6,169 | 7,125 |
| Petroleum | 12,726 | 13,926 | 1,347 | 1,279 | 33 | −106 | 547 | 895 | 580 | 822 |
| Manufacturing | 28,788 | 31,390 | 686 | 847 | 2,011 | −237 | 1,585 | 2,391 | 3,596 | 4,165 |
| Other | 13,625 | 15,274 | 376 | 607 | 1,040 | −21 | 954 | 1,120 | 1,993 | 2,139 |
| Other | 11,327 | 12,058 | 357 | 222 | 599 | −155 | 856 | 979 | 1,455 | 1,423 |
| Petroleum | 3,068 | 3,206 | 160 | 40 | 163 | −66 | 182 | 175 | 345 | 272 |
| Manufacturing | 5,013 | 5,317 | 24 | 130 | 256 | −79 | 281 | 332 | 536 | 509 |
| Other | 3,246 | 3,536 | 174 | 51 | 180 | −11 | 394 | 472 | 574 | 641 |
| **Developing countries** | 28,884 | 33,706 | 1,398 | 2,419 | 1,223 | 1,045 | 5,824 | 5,489 | 7,047 | 7,756 |
| Latin America | 23,934 | 27,739 | 439 | 2,090 | 1,323 | 219 | 2,157 | 2,371 | 3,479 | 3,913 |
| Petroleum | 2,932 | 3,378 | −599 | 196 | 227 | 29 | 222 | 333 | 449 | 589 |
| Manufacturing | 9,275 | 9,954 | 189 | 51 | 515 | 83 | 491 | 413 | 1,006 | 1,012 |
| Other | 11,727 | 14,407 | 849 | 1,843 | 580 | 107 | 1,444 | 1,625 | 2,024 | 2,313 |
| Other | 4,950 | 5,967 | 959 | 330 | −100 | 825 | 3,667 | 3,118 | 3,568 | 3,843 |
| Petroleum | −671 | −365 | 773 | 128 | −597 | 831 | 3,117 | 2,538 | 2,521 | 2,773 |
| Manufacturing | 2,120 | 2,285 | 76 | −19 | 132 | 52 | 117 | 112 | 250 | 296 |
| Other | 3,501 | 4,047 | 110 | 221 | 364 | −58 | 433 | 468 | 797 | 774 |
| **International and unallocated** | 7,114 | 7,029 | −360 | −62 | 340 | −376 | 152 | 241 | 492 | 205 |

## State Finances
### Revenues, Expenditures, Debts, Taxes, U.S. Aid, Military Contracts
Sources: Bureau of the Census, U.S. Treasury and Defense Departments

For fiscal 1977 (year ending June 30, 1976, except: New York, Mar. 31; Texas, Aug. 31, Alabama and Michigan, Sept. 30). Taxes are state income and sales (or gross receipts) taxes, and vehicle, etc., fees. *Military prime contracts.

| State | Revenues (thousands) | Expen- ditures (thousands) | Total debt (thousands) | Per cap. debt | Per cap. taxes | Per cap. U.S. aid | *Military contracts (thousands) |
|---|---|---|---|---|---|---|---|
| Alabama . . . . | $3,124,417 | $2,966,281 | $997,145 | $270.23 | $380.40 | $304 | $421,217 |
| Alaska . . . . . | 1,391,605 | 1,147,589 | 916,584 | 2,252.05 | 1,900.43 | 939 | 123,086 |
| Arizona. . . . . | 2,107,037 | 1,865,661 | 103,206 | 44.95 | 505.26 | 282 | 540,202 |
| Arkansas. . . . | 1,568,624 | 1,521,155 | 140,494 | 65.53 | 374.49 | 298 | 70,505 |
| California. . . . | 26,108,228 | 22,439,586 | 6,742,567 | 307.94 | 574.95 | 311 | 10,078,180 |
| Colorado. . . . | 2,394,258 | 2,151,503 | 197,266 | 75.32 | 411.33 | 273 | 379,169 |
| Connecticut . . | 2,857,967 | 2,656,060 | 3,173,424 | 1,021.05 | 468.83 | 288 | 1,974,323 |
| Delaware. . . . | 712,204 | 696,692 | 742,708 | 1,276.13 | 671.62 | 321 | 50,662 |
| Florida . . . . . | 5,707,077 | 5,391,507 | 2,003,353 | 237.03 | 387.46 | 235 | 1,060,877 |
| Georgia . . . . | 3,579,450 | 3,440,030 | 1,268,456 | 251.28 | 377.68 | 369 | 517,688 |
| Hawaii . . . . . | 1,456,564 | 1,502,093 | 1,486,277 | 1,660.64 | 766.15 | 447 | 223,805 |
| Idaho . . . . . . | 785,989 | 772,627 | 52,256 | 60.98 | 429.20 | 335 | 15,525 |
| Illinois . . . . . | 9,852,612 | 9,939,241 | 4,053,846 | 360.50 | 473.06 | 285 | 559,934 |
| Indiana . . . . . | 3,763,796 | 3,456,564 | 587,394 | 110.21 | 405.80 | 205 | 834,832 |
| Iowa . . . . . . | 2,542,726 | 2,552,312 | 123,951 | 43.05 | 448.94 | 248 | 280,750 |
| Kansas . . . . . | 1,766,107 | 1,718,799 | 402,809 | 173.18 | 416.60 | 236 | 363,265 |
| Kentucky. . . . | 2,980,435 | 2,848,694 | 2,040,599 | 590.11 | 451.24 | 294 | 221,461 |
| Louisiana. . . . | 3,685,114 | 3,646,738 | 1,769,239 | 451.22 | 438.32 | 315 | 390,651 |
| Maine. . . . . . | 1,024,998 | 981,474 | 564,071 | 519.88 | 431.76 | 380 | 323,276 |
| Maryland. . . . | 3,933,699 | 3,918,843 | 3,051,080 | 737.15 | 514.06 | 301 | 1,092,273 |
| Massachusetts | 5,669,948 | 5,520,145 | 5,167,658 | 893.75 | 507.48 | 360 | 2,395,491 |
| Michigan . . . . | 9,689,212 | 9,070,835 | 1,950,959 | 213.71 | 530.59 | 319 | 1,244,458 |
| Minnesota . . . | 4,385,035 | 4,157,681 | 1,236,667 | 311.11 | 625.30 | 308 | 656,230 |
| Mississippi . . . | 2,030,629 | 1,922,027 | 812,088 | 339.93 | 405.71 | 335 | 493,211 |
| Missouri . . . . | 3,099,660 | 2,790,077 | 440,415 | 91.73 | 332.87 | 238 | 2,361,070 |
| Montana . . . . | 850,823 | 783,421 | 101,392 | 133.24 | 410.51 | 457 | 173,731 |
| Nebraska . . . . | 1,119,368 | 1,042,162 | 59,297 | 37.99 | 392.64 | 236 | 79,915 |
| Nevada . . . . . | 762,457 | 632,780 | 54,603 | 86.26 | 519.86 | 325 | 27,875 |
| New Hampshire | 636,339 | 677,139 | 363,177 | 427.77 | 235.84 | 276 | 153,329 |
| New Jersey . . | 7,038,175 | 6,827,632 | 4,051,767 | 552.84 | 423.49 | 300 | 1,216,613 |
| New Mexico . . | 1,349,306 | 1,137,043 | 212,068 | 178.21 | 502.19 | 377 | 159,999 |
| New York . . . | 22,667,068 | 21,252,546 | 20,012,019 | 1,116.49 | 599.38 | 415 | 4,300,271 |
| North Carolina. | 4,574,592 | 4,357,782 | 807,475 | 146.15 | 431.63 | 274 | 373,506 |
| North Dakota . | 736,073 | 678,657 | 67,326 | 103.10 | 453.80 | 343 | 43,533 |
| Ohio . . . . . . | 8,975,675 | 8,168,648 | 3,205,246 | 299.53 | 333.69 | 235 | 1,164,100 |
| Oklahoma . . . | 2,283,116 | 2,138,132 | 937,252 | 333.42 | 405.19 | 278 | 292,796 |
| Oregon. . . . . | 2,638,018 | 2,272,393 | 2,431,243 | 1,023.25 | 409.57 | 352 | 77,945 |
| Pennsylvania . | 11,091,470 | 11,207,936 | 6,383,946 | 541.70 | 474.40 | 308 | 1,654,009 |
| Rhode Island . | 1,037,637 | 972,252 | 640,327 | 684.84 | 469.35 | 383 | 125,051 |
| South Carolina. | 2,414,949 | 2,334,336 | 1,311,389 | 455.98 | 412.93 | 279 | 175,418 |
| South Dakota . | 543,702 | 528,910 | 231,533 | 336.04 | 290.44 | 348 | 13,289 |
| Tennessee . . . | 2,933,213 | 2,854,020 | 1,203,163 | 279.87 | 355.79 | 277 | 709,718 |
| Texas. . . . . . | 8,847,332 | 7,829,437 | 2,124,976 | 165.63 | 370.23 | 225 | 2,778,375 |
| Utah . . . . . . | 1,237,698 | 1,177,333 | 145,536 | 114.78 | 418.99 | 306 | 226,754 |
| Vermont . . . . | 572,997 | 535,769 | 454,547 | 941.09 | 475.78 | 462 | 119,108 |
| Virginia . . . . . | 4,098,080 | 3,926,729 | 872,519 | 169.92 | 399.97 | 255 | 2,038,451 |
| Washington . . | 4,478,273 | 4,092,803 | 1,411,775 | 385.94 | 574.09 | 306 | 1,738,452 |
| West Virginia . | 1,875,742 | 1,832,035 | 1,334,820 | 718.03 | 485.97 | 339 | 91,795 |
| Wisconsin . . . | 4,931,994 | 4,455,535 | 1,684,708 | 362.22 | 587.68 | 321 | 416,394 |
| Wyoming. . . . | 563,376 | 448,313 | 73,279 | 180.49 | 574.72 | 458 | 19,429 |
| **Total or average. . .** | 204,474,864 | 191,237,957 | 90,199,895 | 418.29 | 486.76 | 305 | 45,539,537 |

## U.S. Customs and Internal Revenue Receipts
Source: Treasury Department
Gross. Not reduced by appropriations to Federal old-age and survivors insurance trust fund or refunds or receipts.

| Fiscal year | Customs | Internal Revenue | Fiscal year | Customs | Internal Revenue | Fiscal year | Customs | Internal Revenue |
|---|---|---|---|---|---|---|---|---|
| 1930 | $587,000,903 | $3,039,295,014 | 1955 | $606,396,634 | $66,288,691,586 | 1974 | $3,334,127,000 | $269,000,000,000 |
| 1935 | 343,353,034 | 3,277,690,028 | 1960 | 1,123,037,579 | 91,774,802,823 | 1975 | 3,675,532,000 | 293,800,000,000 |
| 1940 | 348,590,635 | 5,303,133,988 | 1965 | 1,477,548,820 | 114,428,991,753 | 1976 | 4,074,176,000 | 302,520,000,000 |
| 1945 | 354,775,542 | 43,902,001,929 | 1970 | 2,429,799,000 | 195,700,000,000 | T.Q.[1] | 1,212,173,000 | 75,463,000,000 |
| 1950 | 422,650,329 | 39,448,607,109 | 1973 | 3,175,268,000 | 237,800,000,000 | 1977 | 5,150,151,000 | 358,139,000,000 |

(1) Transitional quarter; July 1, 1976 through Sept. 30, 1976. Through 1976 the fiscal year ended June 30. From 1977 on, fiscal year ends Sept. 30.

## U.S. Business Indexes

Source: Federal Reserve System; F.W. Dodge Div., McGraw-Hill; U.S. Labor Department; U.S. Commerce Department

(1967 = 100, except as noted)

| | Industrial production | | | | | | | Industry | | Construction contracts | Nonagricultural employment Total[1] | Manufacturing | | | Prices[4] | |
|---|---|---|---|---|---|---|---|---|---|---|---|---|---|---|---|---|
| | | Market | | | | | | | | | | | | | | |
| | | | Products | | | | | | | | | | | | | |
| | | | | Final | | | | | | | | | | | | |
| Period | Total | Total | Total | Consumer goods | Equipment | Intermediate | Materials | Manufacturing | Capacity utilization in mfg. | | | Employment[2] | Payrolls | Total retail sales[3] | Consumer | Producer finished goods |
| 1963 | 76.5 | 76.4 | 75.5 | 81.3 | 67.5 | 79.9 | 76.7 | 75.8 | 83.5 | 86.1 | 86.1 | 87.7 | 76.0 | 79 | 91.8 | 93.8 |
| 1965 | 89.8 | 88.2 | 87.6 | 92.6 | 80.7 | 90.6 | 92.4 | 89.7 | 89.5 | 93.2 | 92.3 | 93.9 | 88.1 | 90 | 94.5 | 95.7 |
| 1970 | 107.8 | 106.9 | 105.3 | 109.0 | 100.1 | 112.9 | 109.2 | 106.4 | 79.2 | 123.1 | 107.7 | 98.0 | 114.1 | 119 | 116.3 | 110.3 |
| 1972 | 119.7 | 118.0 | 115.7 | 124.4 | 103.8 | 126.5 | 122.3 | 118.9 | 83.1 | 166.1 | 111.9 | 97.5 | 131.5 | 142 | 125.3 | 117.2 |
| 1974 | 129.3 | 127.3 | 125.1 | 128.9 | 120.0 | 135.3 | 132.4 | 129.4 | 84.2 | 173.9 | 119.1 | 102.1 | 157.1 | 171 | 147.7 | 147.5 |
| 1975 | 117.8 | 119.3 | 118.2 | 124.0 | 110.2 | 123.1 | 115.5 | 116.3 | 73.6 | 162.3 | 116.9 | 91.3 | 157.3 | 185 | 161.2 | 163.4 |
| 1976 | 129.8 | 129.3 | 127.3 | 136.8 | 114.3 | 137.2 | 130.6 | 129.5 | 80.1 | 190.2 | 120.6 | 95.2 | 177.1 | 204 | 170.5 | 170.3 |
| 1977 | 137.0 | 137.1 | 134.9 | 143.4 | 123.2 | 145.1 | 136.9 | 136.9 | 82.4 | 253.0 | 124.7 | 98.3 | 198.6 | 224 | 181.6 | 180.6 |
| 1978[5] | 145.3 | 144.3 | 141.6 | 147.3 | 133.8 | 154.8 | 146.9 | 145.6 | 84.1 | 286.0 | 130.6 | 102.1 | 224.2 | 246 | 196.7 | 195.9 |

(1) Employees only; excludes personnel in the Armed Forces. (2) Production workers only. (3) F.R. index based on Census Bureau figures. (4) Prices are not seasonally adjusted. Latest figure is final. (5) July 1978, except consumer prices which are June 1978.

## Producer Price Indexes

Source: Bureau of Labor Statistics, U.S. Labor Department

Producer Price Indexes measure average changes in prices received in primary markets of the U.S. by producers of commodities in all stages of processing.

| Commodity group (1967 = 100) | Annual Avg. 1977 | 1977 June | 1977 Dec. | 1978 Jan. | 1978 Apr. |
|---|---|---|---|---|---|
| All commodities | 194.2 | 194.5 | 198.2 | 199.9 | 206.4 |
| Farm products, processed foods, and feeds | 188.8 | 191.5 | 189.4 | 192.1 | 205.5 |
| Farm products | 192.5 | 192.8 | 188.3 | 192.2 | 213.6 |
| Processed foods and feeds | 186.1 | 190.1 | 189.3 | 191.3 | 200.2 |
| Industrial commodities | 195.1 | 194.7 | 200.0 | 201.5 | 206.0 |
| Textile products and apparel | 154.0 | 154.6 | 155.8 | 156.4 | 157.7 |
| Hides, skins, leathers, and related products | 179.5 | 179.4 | 181.5 | 186.1 | 192.2 |
| Fuels and related products and power | 302.2 | 304.3 | 312.0 | 312.8 | 317.3 |
| Chemicals and allied products | 192.7 | 193.9 | 194.1 | 194.0 | 197.0 |
| Rubber and plastic products | 167.5 | 167.5 | 170.0 | 169.9 | 172.7 |
| Lumber and wood products | 236.2 | 228.8 | 249.2 | 256.3 | 269.5 |
| Pulp, paper, and allied products | 186.4 | 187.3 | 187.6 | 188.2 | 191.6 |
| Metals and metal products | 209.0 | 207.7 | 213.3 | 215.2 | 223.8 |
| Machinery and equipment | 181.7 | 180.7 | 206.3 | 205.9 | 208.6 |
| Furniture and household durables | 151.4 | 151.5 | 154.2 | 155.6 | 158.3 |
| Nonmetallic mineral products | 200.4 | 200.6 | 206.6 | 212.7 | 218.0 |
| Transportation equipment (Dec. 1968 = 100) | 161.3 | 159.5 | 168.3 | 169.0 | 170.5 |
| Miscellaneous products | 164.4 | 163.5 | 169.7 | 171.5 | 181.2 |

## Indexes of Manufacturing, Industrial Countries

Source: Bureau of Labor Statistics, U.S. Labor Department (1967 = 100)

### Output per hour

| Country | 1960 | 1965 | 1970 | 1972 | 1973 | 1974 | 1975 | 1976 | 1977 |
|---|---|---|---|---|---|---|---|---|---|
| United States | 78.8 | 98.2 | 104.5 | 116.0 | 119.4 | 112.8 | 117.9 | 123.5 | 126.7 |
| 10 Foreign countries | 68.4 | 89.9 | 123.5 | 138.0 | 147.5 | 152.5 | 151.9 | 164.7 | N.A. |
| Canada | 75.1 | 93.6 | 114.7 | 128.1 | 133.4 | 135.6 | 133.4 | 137.8 | 143.3 |
| Japan | 52.6 | 79.1 | 146.5 | 161.0 | 179.0 | 180.3 | 172.4 | 194.8 | 206.6 |
| Belgium | 69.9 | 87.5 | 129.5 | 153.2 | 166.7 | 174.1 | 183.7 | 204.0 | N.A. |
| Denmark | 66.6 | 86.7 | 129.3 | 150.7 | 159.8 | 165.1 | 175.7 | 187.9 | 185.1 |
| France | 68.7 | 88.5 | 121.2 | 136.8 | 143.7 | 147.8 | 151.1 | 165.3 | 171.6 |
| W. Germany | 67.8 | 90.7 | 116.1 | 128.7 | 136.6 | 145.0 | 150.4 | 162.8 | 169.6 |
| Italy | 65.1 | 91.6 | 117.8 | 132.9 | 147.8 | 155.9 | 150.2 | 161.5 | 162.3 |
| Netherlands | 67.5 | 87.8 | 134.0 | 154.4 | 170.2 | 184.3 | 181.0 | 198.9 | N.A. |
| Sweden | 63.1 | 88.5 | 124.5 | 137.9 | 147.4 | 152.1 | 150.4 | 152.9 | 156.6 |
| United Kingdom | 76.8 | 92.4 | 108.6 | 121.2 | 126.3 | 127.6 | 124.4 | 128.7 | 126.6 |
| 8 European Countries | 69.2 | 90.9 | 118.8 | 133.8 | 141.9 | 147.9 | 149.0 | 160.4 | N.A. |
| Original EEC | 68.6 | 91.0 | 119.8 | 134.5 | 143.7 | 150.6 | 153.5 | 166.2 | N.A. |

### Unit labor costs in U.S. dollars

| Country | 1960 | 1965 | 1970 | 1972 | 1973 | 1974 | 1975 | 1976 | 1977 |
|---|---|---|---|---|---|---|---|---|---|
| United States | 97.7 | 92.6 | 116.5 | 118.1 | 123.2 | 143.1 | 152.4 | 158.4 | 168.3 |
| 10 Foreign countries | 82.6 | 97.2 | 112.5 | 143.7 | 173.3 | 197.3 | 238.2 | 228.9 | N.A. |
| Canada | 106.9 | 92.0 | 111.8 | 122.4 | 127.9 | 148.7 | 166.5 | 187.4 | 184.1 |
| Japan | 82.5 | 102.5 | 113.4 | 161.6 | 197.3 | 237.9 | 285.6 | 275.2 | 314.7 |
| Belgium | 74.9 | 94.3 | 101.4 | 128.6 | 153.6 | 180.2 | 222.9 | 212.8 | N.A. |
| Denmark | 74.7 | 91.8 | 104.4 | 117.3 | 147.6 | 170.2 | 201.8 | 198.9 | 220.2 |
| France | 81.7 | 98.3 | 98.9 | 120.0 | 147.9 | 158.7 | 206.4 | 195.0 | 205.6 |
| W. Germany | 76.5 | 94.4 | 125.7 | 164.3 | 211.7 | 236.3 | 270.0 | 258.1 | 293.4 |
| Italy | 76.5 | 97.1 | 119.2 | 152.2 | 172.5 | 183.1 | 246.2 | 213.2 | 244.6 |
| Netherlands | 65.4 | 91.8 | 108.7 | 139.2 | 174.0 | 194.0 | 246.2 | 240.1 | N.A. |
| Sweden | 80.5 | 93.3 | 105.1 | 132.8 | 148.5 | 165.2 | 216.7 | 241.3 | 258.5 |
| United Kingdom | 85.7 | 98.7 | 106.0 | 126.6 | 132.8 | 160.3 | 199.2 | 184.7 | 199.7 |
| 8 European countries | 79.1 | 96.0 | 113.6 | 143.0 | 174.1 | 194.3 | 236.2 | 224.2 | N.A. |
| Original EEC | 77.0 | 95.6 | 116.2 | 148.0 | 184.9 | 203.9 | 246.1 | 231.9 | N.A. |

## Gross National Product, National Income, and Personal Income

Source: Bureau of Economic Analysis, U.S. Commerce Department
includes Alaska and Hawaii beginning in 1960 (millions of dollars)

| | 1950 | 1960 | 1970 | 1975 | 1976 | 1977 |
|---|---|---|---|---|---|---|
| Gross national product . . . . . . . . . . . | 286,172 | 505,979 | 982,419 | 1,528,883 | 1,700,124 | 1,887,177 |
| Less: Capital consumption allowances. . . . . . | 23,853 | 47,712 | 90,827 | 161,954 | 177,801 | 195,191 |
| Equals: Net national product . . . . . . . . | 262,319 | 458,266 | 894,592 | 1,366,879 | 1,522,323 | 1,691,986 |
| Less: Indirect business tax and nontax liability . | 23,422 | 45,389 | 94,027 | 139,246 | 151,340 | 165,084 |
| Business transfer payments . . . . . . . . . | 778 | 1,974 | 3,983 | 7,599 | 8,277 | 9,631 |
| Statistical discrepancy . . . . . . . . . . . | 2,030 | −683 | −2,076 | 7,371 | 4,210 | 4,741 |
| Plus: Subsidies minus current surplus of government enterprises . . . . . . . . . . | 114 | 422 | 2,716 | 2,339 | 687 | 2,771 |
| Equals: National income . . . . . . . . . . . | 236,203 | 412,008 | 798,374 | 1,215,002 | 1,359,183 | 1,515,301 |
| Less: Corporate profits and inventory valuation adjustment . . . . . . . . . . | 2,272 | 9,760 | 37,549 | 95,902 | 127,003 | 144,171 |
| Contributions for social insurance . . . . . . . | 7,058 | 21,058 | 58,712 | 110,579 | 125,141 | 140,346 |
| Wage accruals less disbursement . . . . . . | 24 | 0 | 0 | 0 | 0 | 0 |
| Plus: Government transfer payment to persons. | 14,404 | 26,966 | 75,898 | 170,567 | 185,638 | 199,193 |
| Personal income interest. . . . . . . . . . . . | 8,929 | 23,284 | 64,284 | 115,529 | 126,291 | 141,161 |
| Dividends. . . . . . . . . . . . . . . | 8,803 | 12,890 | 22,884 | 31,885 | 37,898 | 43,651 |
| Business transfer payments . . . . . . . . . | 778 | 1,974 | 3,983 | 7,599 | 8,277 | 9,631 |
| Equals: Personal income . . . . . . . . . . . | 226,102 | 399,724 | 801,271 | 1,255,486 | 1,380,854 | 1,528,990 |

## National Income by Type of Income

| | (millions of dollars) | | | | | |
|---|---|---|---|---|---|---|
| | 1960 | 1965 | 1970 | 1975 | 1976 | 1977 |
| Compensation of employees. . . . . . . . . . | 294,932 | 396,543 | 609,150 | 931,079 | 1,036,775 | 1,153,444 |
| Wages and salaries. . . . . . . . . . . | 271,932 | 362,005 | 546,453 | 805,872 | 890,082 | 983,642 |
| Private . . . . . . . . . . . . . . | 222,782 | 292,145 | 430,481 | 630,431 | 702,453 | 782,859 |
| Government . . . . . . . . . . . . . | 49,150 | 69,860 | 115,972 | 175,441 | 187,629 | 200,783 |
| Supplements to wages, salary. . . . . . . . | 23,000 | 34,538 | 62,697 | 125,207 | 146,693 | 169,802 |
| Employer contrib. for social insurance . . | 11,780 | 16,698 | 30,680 | 60,079 | 69,674 | 79,376 |
| Other labor income . . . . . . . . . . . | 11,220 | 17,840 | 32,017 | 65,128 | 77,019 | 90,426 |
| Proprietors' income . . . . . . . . . . . . . . | 46,978 | 56,674 | 65,140 | 86,980 | 88,577 | 99,767 |
| Business and professional . . . . . . . . . . . | 35,558 | 44,106 | 51,208 | 63,509 | 70,170 | 79,530 |
| Inventory valuation adj. . . . . . . | 91 | -198 | -506 | -1,164 | -1,201 | -1,312 |
| Farm . . . . . . . . . . . . . . . . | 11,420 | 12,568 | 13,932 | 23,471 | 18,407 | 20,237 |
| Rental income of persons. . . . . . . . . . . . | 13,758 | 17,117 | 18,644 | 22,426 | 22,539 | 22,489 |
| Corp. prof., with inv. adjust. . . . . . . . . . . | 46,590 | 77,096 | 67,891 | 95,902 | 127,003 | 144,171 |
| Corp. profits before tax. . . . . . . . . . | 48,540 | 75,209 | 71,485 | 120,378 | 155,937 | 173,925 |
| Corp. profits tax liability . . . . . . . . | 22,696 | 30,876 | 34,477 | 49,811 | 64,258 | 71,825 |
| Corp. profits after tax . . . . . . . . . | 25,844 | 44,333 | 37,008 | 70,567 | 91,679 | 102,100 |
| Dividends . . . . . . . . . . . . | 12,890 | 19,120 | 22,884 | 31,885 | 37,898 | 43,651 |
| Undistributed profits . . . . . . . . | 12,954 | 25,213 | 14,124 | 38,682 | 53,781 | 58,449 |
| Inventory valuation adj. . . . . . . . . | 327 | -1,865 | -5,067 | -12,432 | -14,522 | -14,834 |
| Net interest . . . . . . . . . . . . . . . . | 9,760 | 18,529 | 37,549 | 78,615 | 84,289 | 95,430 |
| National income. . . . . . . . . . . . . . . . | 412,008 | 565,959 | 798,374 | 1,215,002 | 1,359,183 | 1,515,301 |

## Appropriations by the Federal Government

Source: U.S. Treasury Department (fiscal year)

| Year | Appropriations | Year | Appropriations | Year | Appropriations | Year | Appropriations |
|---|---|---|---|---|---|---|---|
| 1890 | $395,430,284.26 | 1940 | $13,349,202,681.73 | 1957 | $70,717,305,080.55 | 1969 | $203,049,351,090.91 |
| 1895 | 492,477,759.97 | 1944 | 118,411,173,965.24 | 1958 | 77,145,934,082.25 | 1970 | 222,200,021,901.52 |
| 1900 | 698,912,982.83 | 1945 | 73,067,712,071.39 | 1959 | 82,055,863,758.58 | 1971 | 247,623,820,964.75 |
| 1905 | 781,288,215.95 | 1950 | 52,867,672,466.21 | 1960 | 80,169,728,902.87 | 1972 | 247,638,104,722.57 |
| 1910 | 1,044,433,622.64 | 1951 | 67,966,083,088.46 | 1961 | 89,229,575,129.94 | 1973 | 275,554,945,383.88 |
| 1915 | 1,122,471,919.12 | 1952 | 127,788,153,262.97 | 1962 | 91,447,827,731.00 | 1974 | 311,728,034,150.99 |
| 1920 | 6,454,596,649.56 | 1953 | 94,916,821,231.67 | 1963 | 102,149,886,566.52 | 1975 | 374,124,469,875.62 |
| 1925 | 3,748,651,750.35 | 1954 | 74,744,844,304.88 | 1965 | 107,555,087,622.62 | 1976 | 403,740,395,600.61 |
| 1930 | 4,665,236,678.04 | 1955 | 54,761,172,461.58 | 1967 | 140,861,235,376.56 | T.Q.[1] | 111,767,892,878.83 |
| 1935 | 7,527,559,327.66 | 1956 | 63,857,731,203.86 | 1968 | 195,908,743,535.65 | 1977 | 466,559,809,964.06 |

(1) Transitional Quarter; July 1, 1976 through Sept. 30, 1976. Through 1976 the fiscal year ended June 30. From 1977 on, fiscal year ends Sept. 30.

## Public Debt of the U.S.

Source: U.S. Treasury Department

| Fiscal year | Gross debt | Per cap. | Fiscal year | Gross debt | Per cap. | Fiscal year | Gross debt | Per cap. |
|---|---|---|---|---|---|---|---|---|
| 1870 | $2,436,453,269 | $61.06 | 1930 | $16,185,309,831 | $131.51 | 1973 | $457,316,605,312 | $2,173.60 |
| 1880 | 2,090,908,872 | 41.60 | 1940 | 42,967,531,038 | 325.23 | 1974 | 474,234,815,732 | 2,238.07 |
| 1890 | 1,132,396,584 | 17.80 | 1950 | 256,087,352,351 | 1,688.30 | 1975 | 533,188,976,772 | 2,496.90 |
| 1900 | 1,263,416,913 | 16.60 | 1960 | 284,092,760,848 | 1,572.31 | 1976 | 620,432,971,265 | 2,883.83 |
| 1910 | 1,146,939,969 | 12.41 | 1965 | 313,818,898,984 | 1,612.70 | T.Q.[1] | 634,701,954,322 | 2,950.15 |
| 1920 | 24,299,321,467 | 228.23 | 1970 | 370,093,706,950 | 1,807.09 | 1977 | 698,839,928,356 | p3,223.18 |

(p) Preliminary. (1) Transitional Quarter; July 1, 1976 through Sept. 30, 1976. Through 1976 the fiscal year ended June 30. From 1977 on, fiscal year ends Sept. 30.

# National Income by Industry

Source: Bureau of Economic Analysis. U.S. Commerce Department
(millions of dollars)

| | 1960 | 1965 | 1970 | 1974 | 1975 | 1976 | 1977 |
|---|---|---|---|---|---|---|---|
| Agricul., forestry, fisheries | 17,468 | 20,366 | 24,455 | 42,199 | 42,827 | 40,519 | 44,594 |
| Farms | 16,452 | 18,805 | 22,191 | 38,692 | 39,379 | 36,155 | 39,814 |
| Agri. services, forestry, fisheries | 1,016 | 1,561 | 2,264 | 3,507 | 3,448 | 4,364 | 4,780 |
| Mining | 5,613 | 6,013 | 7,810 | 15,539 | 18,149 | 20,267 | 23,179 |
| Metal mining | 807 | 856 | 1,179 | 1,596 | 1,635 | 1,900 | 2,067 |
| Coal mining | 1,286 | 1,372 | 2,231 | 5,208 | 6,228 | 5,874 | 6,289 |
| Crude petroleum, natural gas | 2,606 | 2,670 | 3,099 | 6,661 | 8,075 | 10,232 | 12,483 |
| Nonmetallic min. & quar. | 914 | 1,115 | 1,301 | 2,074 | 2,211 | 2,261 | 2,340 |
| Contract construction | 20,972 | 29,840 | 43,821 | 62,233 | 61,795 | 67,701 | 77,232 |
| Manufacturing | 125,448 | 170,361 | 215,388 | 297,833 | 312,467 | 362,924 | 408,875 |
| Nondurable goods | 51,818 | 65,416 | 88,088 | 119,285 | 127,942 | 148,101 | 161,699 |
| Food, kindred products | 12,150 | 14,232 | 19,579 | 23,672 | 30,020 | 31,675 | 32,000 |
| Tobacco manufactures | 1,020 | 1,096 | 1,696 | 1,687 | 2,155 | 2,444 | 2,761 |
| Textile mill products | 4,484 | 5,872 | 7,525 | 9,915 | 8,754 | 10,502 | 11,778 |
| Apparel, other fabric prod. | 4,933 | 6,494 | 8,722 | 10,426 | 10,773 | 12,320 | 13,248 |
| Paper, allied products | 4,706 | 6,005 | 7,968 | 11,898 | 11,833 | 14,216 | 15,487 |
| Printing, pub., allied industry | 6,666 | 8,725 | 11,883 | 15,212 | 16,672 | 18,508 | 20,774 |
| Chemicals, allied products | 9,106 | 12,398 | 16,042 | 21,268 | 23,820 | 28,053 | 30,700 |
| Petroleum refining, related ind. | 4,396 | 4,811 | 6,632 | 13,977 | 12,893 | 17,342 | 19,384 |
| Rubber, misc. plastic products | 2,751 | 3,939 | 5,804 | 8,811 | 8,661 | 10,247 | 12,696 |
| Leather, leather products | 1,606 | 1,844 | 2,237 | 2,419 | 2,361 | 2,794 | 2,871 |
| Durable goods | 73,630 | 104,945 | 127,300 | 178,548 | 184,525 | 214,823 | 247,176 |
| Lumber, wood, except furn. | 3,362 | 4,534 | 5,537 | 10,596 | 8,936 | 11,469 | 13,363 |
| Furniture and fixtures | 2,098 | 2,904 | 3,715 | 4,792 | 4,588 | 5,293 | 6,044 |
| Stone, clay, glass products | 4,620 | 5,654 | 6,891 | 9,690 | 9,858 | 11,554 | 13,215 |
| Primary metal industries | 11,066 | 14,491 | 15,757 | 26,631 | 24,231 | 26,104 | 29,216 |
| Fabricated metal products | 8,124 | 11,475 | 14,812 | 22,815 | 24,300 | 27,887 | 30,946 |
| Machinery, except electrical | 11,919 | 18,239 | 24,353 | 33,455 | 36,801 | 40,890 | 46,989 |
| Electrical equip. and supplies | 10,496 | 14,855 | 20,132 | 25,762 | 26,646 | 29,916 | 34,778 |
| Transport equip. exc. autos. | 8,266 | 11,330 | 14,480 | 14,064 | 15,715 | 16,836 | 19,039 |
| Motor vehicles equipment | 8,399 | 14,455 | 12,086 | 17,712 | 19,045 | 28,403 | 34,775 |
| Instruments | 2,948 | 4,128 | 5,797 | 8,176 | 9,006 | 10,382 | 12,404 |
| Misc. manufacturing | 2,332 | 2,880 | 3,740 | 4,855 | 5,399 | 6,089 | 6,407 |
| Transportation | 18,141 | 23,069 | 30,308 | 44,248 | 44,455 | 51,567 | 58,383 |
| Railroad | 6,710 | 7,016 | 7,612 | 10,139 | 9,987 | 11,811 | 12,559 |
| Local suburban highway passenger | 1,619 | 1,897 | 2,308 | 2,763 | 2,933 | 3,231 | 3,470 |
| Motor freight trans., warehousing | 5,886 | 8,396 | 11,830 | 18,692 | 18,935 | 20,957 | 24,129 |
| Water transportation | 1,635 | 1,982 | 2,503 | 3,305 | 3,323 | 3,654 | 4,153 |
| Air transportation | 1,370 | 2,636 | 4,358 | 6,914 | 7,062 | 8,594 | 10,106 |
| Pipeline transportation | 350 | 390 | 528 | 641 | 820 | 1,002 | 1,246 |
| Transportation service | 571 | 752 | 1,169 | 1,794 | 1,935 | 2,318 | 2,720 |
| Communication | 8,228 | 11,497 | 17,600 | 24,516 | 27,066 | 31,431 | 34,955 |
| Telephone and telegraph | 7,293 | 10,255 | 15,887 | 22,167 | 24,358 | 27,927 | 31,059 |
| Radio broadcasting, television | 935 | 1,242 | 1,713 | 2,349 | 2,708 | 3,504 | 3,896 |
| Electric, gas, sanitary services | 8,923 | 11,442 | 14,864 | 18,442 | 24,302 | 27,232 | 29,540 |
| Wholesale and retail trade | 64,737 | 84,662 | 122,213 | 174,973 | 194,227 | 215,290 | 236,977 |
| Wholesale trade | 23,420 | 30,469 | 44,860 | 76,639 | 80,564 | 89,563 | 96,451 |
| Retail trade | 41,317 | 54,193 | 77,353 | 98,334 | 113,663 | 125,727 | 140,526 |
| Finance, ins. and real estate | 48,608 | 63,987 | 92,625 | 128,409 | 140,375 | 157,863 | 177,909 |
| Banking | 7,255 | 8,943 | 16,448 | 19,621 | 20,109 | 20,358 | 22,241 |
| Credit agencies, other than banks | −1,076 | −1,617 | −1,981 | −6,831 | −4,729 | −4,905 | −6,021 |
| Security, commodity brokers | 1,219 | 1,942 | 2,733 | 3,017 | 4,144 | 4,742 | 4,796 |
| Insurance carriers | 4,816 | 5,880 | 9,269 | 12,100 | 12,751 | 15,949 | 19,192 |
| Insurance agents, brokers, service | 2,070 | 2,957 | 4,223 | 5,852 | 6,704 | 8,146 | 9,319 |
| Real estate | 33,940 | 45,741 | 61,812 | 93,216 | 100,078 | 111,783 | 125,848 |
| Holding and other investment cos. | 384 | 141 | 121 | 1,434 | 1,318 | 1,790 | 2,531 |
| Services | 44,648 | 64,142 | 103,304 | 150,224 | 168,516 | 188,869 | 213,129 |
| Hotels, other lodging places | 2,114 | 2,964 | 4,659 | 6,193 | 6,952 | 7,977 | 8,897 |
| Personal services | 4,608 | 5,965 | 7,436 | 8,052 | 8,329 | 9,062 | 9,797 |
| Misc. business services | 5,091 | 8,399 | 14,051 | 22,030 | 23,928 | 27,618 | 31,654 |
| Automobile repair, serv., garages | 1,746 | 2,402 | 3,616 | 5,389 | 5,944 | 6,751 | 7,856 |
| Misc. repair services | 1,094 | 1,494 | 2,149 | 3,276 | 3,478 | 3,811 | 4,387 |
| Motion pictures | 891 | 1,201 | 1,581 | 1,745 | 1,842 | 2,414 | 2,872 |
| Amusement, recreation services | 1,662 | 2,201 | 3,321 | 4,622 | 5,268 | 5,906 | 6,552 |
| Medical, other health services | 10,636 | 15,790 | 29,472 | 46,250 | 54,075 | 61,109 | 69,425 |
| Legal services | 2,695 | 4,197 | 6,691 | 10,069 | 11,828 | 12,592 | 14,225 |
| Education services | 2,419 | 4,145 | 6,688 | 8,651 | 10,014 | 11,027 | 11,903 |
| Social Services | — | — | — | 14,212 | 5,003 | 5,698 | 6,792 |
| Nonprofit membership org. | 4,176 | 5,787 | 8,912 | | 11,016 | 11,822 | 12,830 |
| Misc. professional services | 3,719 | 5,629 | 9,673 | 13,548 | 15,030 | 16,587 | 18,795 |
| Private households | 3,797 | 3,968 | 5,055 | 5,587 | 5,809 | 6,495 | 7,144 |
| Government, government enterprises | 52,707 | 75,374 | 127,421 | 180,415 | 199,875 | 215,710 | 232,729 |
| Federal | 25,303 | 33,303 | 53,093 | 66,708 | 72,007 | 76,459 | 81,221 |
| General Government | 21,676 | 28,298 | 44,723 | 54,903 | 58,976 | 62,391 | 66,444 |
| Government enterprises | 3,627 | 5,005 | 8,370 | 11,805 | 13,031 | 14,068 | 14,777 |
| State & local. | 27,404 | 42,071 | 74,328 | 113,707 | 127,868 | 139,251 | 151,508 |
| General Government | 25,470 | 39,294 | 69,964 | 106,458 | 119,641 | 130,101 | 141,529 |
| Government enterprises | 1,934 | 2,777 | 4,364 | 7,249 | 8,227 | 9,150 | 9,979 |
| Domestic income | 415,493 | 560,753 | 799,809 | 1,139,031 | 1,234,054 | 1,379,373 | 1,537,502 |
| Rest of the world | 2,477 | 4,681 | 4,616 | 13,052 | 10,534 | 14,416 | 17,268 |
| All industries, total | 417,970 | 565,434 | 804,425 | 1,152,083 | 1,244,588 | 1,393,789 | 1,554,770 |

## U.S. Currency and Coin — June 30, 1978

Source: U.S. Treasury Department

### Amounts in Circulation and Outstanding

| Currency[1] | Amounts in circulation | Add amounts held by: United States Treasury | Add amounts held by: Federal Reserve Banks | Amounts outstanding |
|---|---|---|---|---|
| Federal Reserve Notes . . . . . . | $95,338,942,490 | $5,927,953 | $10,305,976,945 | $105,650,847,388 |
| United States Notes . . . . . . . . | 314,298,583 | 8,249,433 | . . . | 322,539,016 |
| Currency No Longer Issued . . . . | 279,407,977 | 271,669 | 36,996 | 279,716,462 |
| Total . . . . . . . . . . . . . . | 95,932,640,050 | 14,449,055 | 10,306,013,941 | 106,253,103,046 |
| Coin[2] | | | | |
| Dollars[3] . . . . . . . . . . . . . . . | 1,031,060,849 | 49,829,627 | 49,041,422 | [3]1,129,931,898 |
| Fractional Coin . . . . . . . . . . . | 9,324,197,909 | 272,747,350 | 235,805,741 | 9,832,751,000 |
| Total . . . . . . . . . . . . . . . | 10,355,258,758 | 322,576,977 | 284,847,163 | 10,962,682,898 |
| Total currency and coin. . . . . . . | 106,287,898,808 | 357,026,032 | 10,590,861,104 | 117,215,785,944 |

### Currency in Circulation by Denominations

| Denomination | Total currency in circulation | Federal Reserve Notes[4] | United States Notes | Currency no longer issued |
|---|---|---|---|---|
| 1 Dollar | $2,968,214,184 | $2,812,836,681 | $143,507 | $155,233,996 |
| 2 Dollars | 647,256,734 | 512,201,324 | 135,042,096 | 13,314 |
| 5 Dollars | 4,020,695,610 | 3,864,140,535 | 115,381,660 | 41,173,415 |
| 10 Dollars | 10,982,520,970 | 10,956,267,180 | 6,030 | 26,247,760 |
| 20 Dollars | 33,647,168,300 | 33,626,713,120 | 3,400 | 20,451,780 |
| 50 Dollars | 10,416,699,050 | 10,404,556,950 | . . . | 12,142,100 |
| 100 Dollars | 32,881,577,100 | 32,794,282,200 | 63,712,800 | 23,582,100 |
| 500 Dollars | 167,860,500 | 167,662,500 | . . . | 198,000 |
| 1,000 Dollars | 195,187,000 | 194,972,000 | . . . | 215,000 |
| 5,000 Dollars | 1,840,000 | 1,790,000 | . . . | 50,000 |
| 10,000 Dollars | 3,620,000 | 3,520,000 | . . . | 100,000 |
| Fractional parts | 487 | . . . | . . . | 487 |
| Partial notes[5] | 115 | . . . | 90 | 25 |
| Total currency | 95,932,640,050 | 95,338,942,490 | 314,289,583 | 279,407,977 |

### Comparative Totals of Money in Circulation — Selected Dates

| Date | Amounts (in millions) | Per capita[6] | Date | Amounts (in millions) | Per capita[6] | Date | Amounts (in millions) | Per capita[6] |
|---|---|---|---|---|---|---|---|---|
| June 30, 1978 | $106,287.9[7] | $486.42 | June 30, 1950 | 27,156.3 | 179.03 | June 30, 1920 | 5,467.6 | 51.36 |
| June 30, 1975 | 81,196.4 | 380.08 | June 30, 1945 | 26,746.4 | 191.14 | June 30, 1915 | 3,319.6 | 33.01 |
| June 30, 1970 | 54,351.0 | 265.39 | June 30, 1940 | 7,847.5 | 59.40 | June 30, 1910 | 3,148.7 | 34.07 |
| June 30, 1965 | 39,719.8 | 204.14 | June 30, 1935 | 5,567.1 | 43.75 | | | |
| June 30, 1960 | 32,064.6 | 177.47 | June 30, 1930 | $4,522.0 | $36.74 | | | |
| June 30, 1955 | $30,229.3 | $182.90 | June 30, 1925 | 4,815.2 | 41.56 | | | |

(1) Excludes gold certificates, 1934 Series — $1,277,800, at 6/30/74 which are issued only to Federal Reserve banks and do not appear in circulation. (2) Excludes coin sold to collectors at premium prices. (3) Includes $481,781,898 in standard silver dollars. (4) Issued on and after July 1, 1929. (5) Represents value of certain partial denominations not presented for redemption. (6) Based on Bureau of the Census estimates of population. (7) Highest amount to date.

The requirement for a gold reserve against U.S. notes was repealed by Public Law 90-269 approved Mar. 18, 1968. Silver certificates issued on and after July 1, 1929 became redeemable from the general fund on June 24, 1968. The amount of security after those dates has been reduced accordingly.

## U.S. Money in Circulation, by Denominations

Source: Fiscal Service, Bureau of Government Financial Operations, U.S. Treasury Department

Outside Treasury and Federal Reserve Banks. (millions of dollars)

| End of year | Total in circulation | Coin and small denomination | | | | | | Large denomination currency | | | | | | |
|---|---|---|---|---|---|---|---|---|---|---|---|---|---|---|
| | | Total | Coin | $1 | $2 | $5 | $10 | $20 | Total | $50 | $100 | $500 | $1,000 | $5,000 | $10,000 |
| 1950 | 27,741 | 19,305 | 1,554 | 1,113 | 64 | 2,049 | 5,998 | 8,529 | 8,438 | 2,422 | 5,043 | 368 | 588 | 4 | 12 |
| 1960 | 32,869 | 23,521 | 2,427 | 1,533 | 88 | 2,246 | 6,691 | 10,536 | 9,348 | 2,815 | 5,954 | 249 | 316 | 3 | 10 |
| 1970 | 57,093 | 39,639 | 6,281 | 2,310 | 136 | 3,161 | 9,170 | 18,581 | 17,454 | 4,896 | 12,084 | 215 | 252 | 3 | 4 |
| 1975 | 86,547 | 54,866 | 8,959 | 2,809 | 135 | 3,841 | 10,777 | 28,344 | 31,681 | 8,157 | 23,139 | 175 | 204 | 2 | 4 |
| 1976 | 93,716 | 57,644 | 9,483 | 2,858 | 637 | 3,905 | 10,775 | 29,986 | 36,072 | 9,026 | 26,668 | 172 | 200 | 2 | 4 |
| 1977 | 103,811 | 62,543 | 10,071 | 3,038 | 650 | 4,190 | 11,361 | 33,233 | 41,269 | 10,079 | 30,818 | 169 | 197 | 2 | 4 |

## Seigniorage on Coin and Silver Bullion

Source: Fiscal Service, U.S. Treasury Department

Seigniorage is the profit from coining money; it is the difference between the monetary value of coins and their cost, including the manufacturing expense.

| Fiscal year | Total | | Total |
|---|---|---|---|
| Jan. 1, 1935-June 30, 1965, cumulative | $2,525,927,763.84 | 1973 | $399,799,682.00 |
| 1968 | 383,141,339.00[1] | 1974 | 320,706,638.49 |
| 1969 | 250,170,276.34 | 1975 | 660,898,070.69 |
| 1970 | 274,217,884.01 | 1976 | 769,722,066.00 |
| 1971 | 399,652,811.18 | 1977 | 407,022,950.00 |
| 1972 | 580,586,683.00 | Cumulative Jan. 1, 1935-Sept. 30, 1977 | 8,457,384,530.69 |

(1) Revised to include seigniorage on clad coins.

# Bureau of the Mint

Source: Bureau of the Mint, U.S. Treasury Department

The first United States Mint was established in Philadelphia, Pa., then the nation's capital, by the Act of April 2, 1792, which provided for gold, silver, and copper coinage. Originally, supervision of the Mint was a function of the secretary of state, but it became (1799) an independent agency reporting directly to the president. When the Coinage Act of 1873 was passed, all mint and assay office activities were placed under a newly organized Bureau of the Mint in the Department of the Treasury.

The Bureau of the Mint manufactures all U.S. coins and distributes them through the Federal Reserve banks and branches. The Mint also maintains physical custody of the Treasury's monetary stocks of gold and silver, and refines and processes silver bullion. Functions performed by the Mint on a reimbursable basis include: the manufacture and sale of medals of a national character, the production and sale of numismatic coins and coin sets, and, as scheduling permits, the manufacture of foreign coins.

Amendments to the Coinage Act of 1965 (Public Law 19-607, Dec. 31, 1970) authorized the production of dollar coins and provided that the dollar and half dollar coins for general circulation be of the same nonsilver clad composition as the quarter dollars and dimes. The cladding is an alloy of 75 percent copper and 25 percent nickel, bonded to a core of pure copper. The coins were first minted in calendar year 1971. The legislation authorized the secretary of the treasury to mint and issue not more than 150 million one dollar pieces containing 40-percent silver for sale to the public at premium prices. The dollar coins which bore the likeness of President Eisenhower and a reverse design emblematic of the Apollo 11 moon landing were minted and issued from 1971 until early in 1975.

Public Law 93-127, Oct. 18, 1973, authorized the minting for issue after July 4, 1975, of dollar, half dollar, and quarter dollar coins with reverse designs emblematic of the Bicentennial and the obverse dates 1776-1976, for general issue; and the production of 45 million numismatic 40-percent silver coins of the same designs and denominations to be sold to the public at premium prices. Although the production of Bicentennial-design coins was terminated on Dec. 31, 1976, 40-percent silver coin sets continued to be packaged and sold after that date.

The composition of the five cent coin continues to be 75 percent copper, 25 percent nickel, while the one cent coins are 95 percent copper and 5 percent zinc.

Calendar year 1977 coinage production follows:

## Domestic Coinage Executed During Calendar Year 1977

| Denomination | Philadelphia | Denver | San Francisco | Total value | Total pieces |
|---|---|---|---|---|---|
| **Dollars — non-silver** | | | | | |
| 1977 | $12,596,000.00 | $32,983,006.00 | -0- | $45,579,006.00 | 45,579,006 |
| **Total dollars** | **$12,596,000.00** | **$32,983,006.00** | **-0-** | **$45,579,006.00** | **45,579,006** |
| **Subsidiary** | | | | | |
| Half dollars - 1977 | $21,799,000.00 | $15,724,553.00 | -0- | $37,523,553.00 | 75,047,106 |
| Quarters - 1977[1] | 117,139,000.00 | 64,131,244.50 | -0- | 181,270,244.50 | 725,080,978 |
| Dimes | 79,693,000.00 | 37,660,722.80 | -0- | 117,353,722.80 | 1,173,537,228 |
| **Total subsidiary** | **$218,631,000.00** | **$117,516,520.30** | **-0-** | **$336,147,520.30** | **1,973,665,312** |
| **Minor** | | | | | |
| Five-cent pieces | $29,268,800.00 | $14,865,673.60 | -0- | $44,134,473.60 | 882,689,472 |
| One-cent pieces[2] | 44,699,300.00 | 41,490,623.00 | -0- | 86,189,923.00 | 8,618,992,300 |
| **Total minor** | **$73,968,100.00** | **$56,356,296.60** | **-0-** | **$130,324,396.60** | **9,501,681,772** |
| **Total domestic coinage** | **$305,195,100.00** | **$206,855,822.90** | **-0-** | **$512,050,922.90** | **11,520,926,090** |

| Manufactured at San Francisco Assay Office | |
|---|---|
| 1977 Proof sets | 3,251,152 |
| Bicentennial 40% silver proof sets | 148,608 |
| Bicentennial 40% silver uncirc. sets | 70,794 |

(1) $1,838,000.00 manufactured at West Point Depository.
(2) $13,953,550.00 manufactured at West Point Depository.

| Coinage Executed for Foreign Governments | |
|---|---|
| Country | No. of pieces |
| Panama | 10,000,000 |
| Peru | 2,100,000 |
| Philippine | 1,088,000 |
| **Total** | **13,188,000** |

## Portraits on U.S. Treasury Bills, Bonds, Notes and Savings Bonds

| Denomination | Savings bonds | Treas. bills | Treas. bonds | Treas. notes |
|---|---|---|---|---|
| 25 | Washington | | | |
| 50 | Jefferson | | Jefferson | |
| 75 | Kennedy | | | |
| 100 | Cleveland | | Jackson | |
| 200 | F.D. Roosevelt | | | |
| 500 | Wilson | | Washington | |
| 1,000 | Lincoln | H. McCulloch | Lincoln | Lincoln |
| 5,000 | | J.G. Carlisle | Monroe | Monroe |
| 10,000 | T. Roosevelt | J. Sherman | Cleveland | Cleveland |
| 50,000 | | C. Glass | | |
| 100,000 | | A Gallatin | Grant | Grant |
| 1,000,000 | | O. Wolcott | T. Roosevelt | T. Roosevelt |
| 100,000,000 | | | | Madison |
| 500,000,000 | | | | McKinley |

## Large Denominations of U.S. Currency Discontinued

The largest denomination of United States currency now being issued is the $100 bill. Issuance of currency in denominations of $500, $1000, $5,000 and $10,000 has been discontinued because their use has declined sharply over the past two decades.

As large denomination bills reach the Federal Reserve Bank they are removed from circulation.

Because some of the discontinued currency is expected to be in the hands of holders for many years, the description of the various denominations below is continued:

## Portraits on U.S. Currency

| Amt. | Portrait | Embellishment on back | Amt. | Portrait | Embellishment on back |
|---|---|---|---|---|---|
| $ 1 | Washington | Great Seal of U.S. | $ 100 | Franklin | Independence Hall |
| 2 | Jefferson | Signers of Declaration | 500* | McKinley | Ornate denominational marking |
| 5 | Lincoln | Lincoln Memorial | 1,000* | Cleveland | Ornate denominational marking |
| 10 | Hamilton | U.S. Treasury | 5,000* | Madison | Ornate denominational marking |
| 20 | Jackson | White House | 10,000* | Chase | Ornate denominational marking |
| 50 | Grant | U.S. Capitol | 100,000* | Wilson | Ornate denominational marking |

*For use only in transactions between Federal Reserve System and Treasury Department.

# World Gold Production

Source: Bureau of Mines, U.S. Interior Department (in ounces)

| Year | Estimated world prod. | Africa | | | North and South America | | | | Colombia | Other | | | | |
|---|---|---|---|---|---|---|---|---|---|---|---|---|---|---|
| | | South Africa | Ghana | Zaire | United States | Canada | Mexico | Nicaragua | | Australia | India | Japan | Philippines | All other |
| 1970 | 47,522,342 | 32,164,107 | 707,900 | 180,590 | 1,743,322 | 2,408,574 | 198,241 | 115,173 | 201,519 | 619,922 | 104,200 | 225,189 | 602,715 | 8,220,890 |
| 1971 | 46,494,837 | 31,388,631 | 697,517 | 171,685 | 1,495,108 | 2,243,000 | 150,915 | 121,134 | 188,847 | 672,106 | 118,569 | 255,255 | 637,048 | 8,355,022 |
| 1972 | 44,843,374 | 29,245,273 | 724,051 | 140,724 | 1,449,943 | 2,078,567 | 146,061 | 112,340 | 188,137 | 754,866 | 105,776 | 243,027 | 606,730 | 9,047,879 |
| 1973 | 43,296,755 | 27,494,603 | 722,531 | 133,642 | 1,175,750 | 1,954,340 | 132,557 | 85,051 | 215,876 | 554,278 | 105,390 | 188,274 | 572,250 | 9,962,213 |
| 1974 | 39,941,080 | 24,388,203 | 566,617 | 130,603 | 1,126,886 | 1,698,392 | 134,454 | 82,639 | 265,195 | 522,127 | 101,114 | 139,727 | 536,338 | 10,248,785 |
| 1975 | 38,574,162 | 22,937,820 | 523,889 | 103,217 | 1,052,252 | 1,674,000 | 132,236 | 70,281 | 299,366 | 514,186 | 91,437 | 143,489 | 501,776 | 10,530,213 |
| 1976 | 39,882,557 | 22,935,988 | 532,473 | 102,882 | 1,048,037 | 1,685,983 | 162,811 | 75,855 | 297,861 | 497,693 | 100,696 | 137,669 | 501,197 | 11,803,412 |
| 1977[p] | NA | 22,000,000 | NA | NA | 1,100,347 | 1,680,600 | NA | NA | NA | 490,000 | NA | NA | NA | NA |

(p) preliminary (NA) not available.

# Gold Reserves of Central Banks and Governments

Source: IMF, *International Financial Statistics*
Millions of SDRs; valued at SDR 35 per ounce

| Year end | All countries[2] | Int'l Monetary Fund | United States | Canada | Japan | Belgium | France | Fed. Rep. of Germany | Italy | Netherlands | Switzerland | United Kingdom |
|---|---|---|---|---|---|---|---|---|---|---|---|---|
| 1963 | 39,845 | 2,312 | 15,596 | 817 | 289 | 1,371 | 3,175 | 3,844 | 2,343 | 1,601 | 2,820 | 2,484 |
| 1965 | 41,496 | 1,869 | 14,065 | 1,151 | 328 | 1,558 | 4,706 | 4,410 | 2,404 | 1,756 | 3,042 | 2,265 |
| 1967 | 39,362 | 2,682 | 12,065 | 1,015 | 338 | 1,480 | 5,234 | 4,228 | 2,400 | 1,711 | 3,089 | 1,291 |
| 1969 | 38,916 | 2,310 | 11,859 | 872 | 413 | 1,519 | 3,547 | 4,079 | 2,956 | 1,720 | 2,642 | 1,471 |
| 1970 | 36,996 | 4,339 | 11,972 | 791 | 532 | 1,470 | 3,532 | 3,980 | 2,887 | 1,787 | 2,731 | 1,349 |
| 1971 | 35,911 | 4,732 | 10,206 | 794 | 680 | 1,544 | 3,523 | 4,077 | 2,884 | 1,908 | 2,902 | 776 |
| 1973 | 35,608 | 5,370 | 9,659 | 768 | 739 | 1,476 | 3,532 | 4,116 | 2,887 | 1,902 | 2,912 | 734 |
| 1974 | 35,557 | 5,369 | 9,659 | 768 | 739 | 1,476 | 3,533 | 4,116 | 2,887 | 1,901 | 2,912 | 736 |
| 1975 | 35,518 | 5,370 | 9,615 | 768 | 739 | 1,476 | 3,533 | 4,116 | 2,887 | 1,901 | 2,912 | 736 |
| 1977 | 35,535 | 4,605 | 9,714 | 770 | 757 | 1,486 | 3,558 | 4,140 | 2,902 | 1,912 | 2,915 | 778 |

(1) Gold holdings are valued throughout at SDR 35 per ounce, equivalent to US $35 per ounce before December 1971, to US $38 per ounce from December 1971 through January 1973, to US $42.22 per ounce from February 1973 through June 1974 and to the US $ gold price as measured by the "basket" valuation of the SDR beginning with July 1974. (2) Excludes USSR, most other East European countries, and the People's Republic of China.

**Reserves not listed above, Dec. 31, 1977.** Algeria 193, Argentina 146, Australia 268, Austria 735, Republic of China (Taiwan) 84, Denmark 67, Egypt 85, Greece 131, India 257, Iran 132, Iraq 145, Kuwait 88, Lebanon 323, Libya 86, Mexico 61, Pakistan 57, Portugal 969, Saudi Arabia 108, South Africa 340, Spain 505, Sweden 208, Thailand 84, Turkey 127, Uruguay 125, Venezuela 394.

# U.S. and World Silver Production

Source: Bureau of Mines, U.S. Interior Department

Largest production of silver in the United States in 1915—74,961,075 fine ounces.

| Year (Cal.) | United States | | World | Year (Cal.) | United States | | World |
|---|---|---|---|---|---|---|---|
| | Fine ozs. | Value | Fine ozs. | | Fine ozs. | Value | Fine ozs. |
| 1930 . . . . | 50,748,127 | $19,538,000 | 248,708,426 | 1960. . . . | 36,000,000 | $33,305,858 | 241,300,000 |
| 1935 . . . . | 45,924,454 | 33,008,000 | 220,704,231 | 1965. . . . | 39,806,033 | 51,469,201 | 257,415,000 |
| 1940 . . . . | 69,585,734 | 49,483,000 | 275,387,000 | 1970. . . . | 45,006,000 | 79,697,000 | 310,891,000 |
| 1945 . . . . | 29,063,255 | 20,667,200 | 162,000,000 | 1975. . . . | 34,938,000 | 154,424,000 | 297,882,000 |
| 1950 . . . . | 43,308,739 | 38,291,545 | 203,300,000 | 1976. . . . | 34,328,000 | 149,328,000 | 304,899,000 |
| 1955 . . . . | 36,469,610 | 33,006,839 | 224,000,000 | 1977[p] . . . | 38,166,000 | 176,325,000 | NA |

(p) preliminary (NA) not available.

# 50 Stocks Most Widely Held by Insurance Cos., Mutual Funds, and Banks

Source: Vickers Associates, Inc.

Publicly-held issues throughout the U.S. in order of number of institutions, etc., which held shares, as of July 31, 1978.

| | | | | |
|---|---|---|---|---|
| Intl. Bus. Machines | Mobil Corp. | Caterpillar Tractor | Coca-Cola Co. | Intl. Tel. & Tel. |
| Amer. Tel. & Tel. | Dow Chemical | Union Carbide | Halliburton Co. | Johnson & Johnson |
| Exxon Corp. | Standard Oil, Ind. | General Tel. & El. | E.I. Du Pont | Pepsico Inc. |
| General Electric | Merck & Co. | Continental Oil | Texas Utilities | Goodyear Tire |
| General Motors | Citicorp | Gulf Oil | Pfizer, Inc. | Weyerhaeuser Co. |
| Eastman Kodak | Minn. Mng./Mfg. | Ford Motor | Tenneco, Inc. | Monsanto Co. |
| Texaco, Inc. | Amer. Home Products | Schlumberger, Ltd. | Intl. Paper | R.J. Reynolds Ind. |
| Xerox Corp. | Phillips Petroleum | Burroughs Corp. | Avon Products | Schering-Plough |
| Sears, Roebuck & Co. | Standard Oil of Cal. | Procter & Gamble | Warner-Lambert | J.C. Penney |
| Atlantic Richfield | K Mart | Philip Morris | Bristol-Myers | RCA Corp. |

# Corporations and Stocks

## Stock Exchanges Trade 7.03 Billion Shares in U.S. Firms

The Securities and Exchange Commission reported in 1978 that 7.03 billion shares of stock were traded on the New York, American, and other U.S. stock exchanges in 1977.

The N.Y. Stock Exchange listed 2,183 issues of 1,578 companies for a total of 26.9 billion shares, valued on July 31, 1978, at $864 billion. Average daily trading was 27,250,510 through July 31, 1978, compared to 21,361,580

in 1977.

The American Stock Exchange listed 1,200 issues of 1,151 companies, totaling 3.2 billion shares, valued July 31, 1978, at $37.6 billion. Average daily volume through July 31 was 2.7 million shares.

A 1975 count indicated that 25.3 million persons owned shares in American corporations. More recent counts are not available.

## N.Y. Stock Exchange Transactions and Seat Prices

Source: New York Stock Exchange

| Year | Yearly volumes Stock shares | Yearly volumes Bonds par values | Seat price High | Seat price Low | Year | Yearly volumes Stock shares | Yearly volumes Bonds par values | Seat price High | Seat price Low |
|---|---|---|---|---|---|---|---|---|---|
| 1900 | 138,981,000 | $579,293,000 | $47,500 | $37,500 | 1940 | 207,599,749 | 1,669,438,000 | 60,000 | 33,000 |
| 1905 | 260,569,000 | 1,026,254,000 | 85,000 | 72,000 | 1950 | 524,799,621 | 1,112,425,170 | 54,000 | 46,000 |
| 1910 | 163,705,000 | 634,863,000 | 94,000 | 65,000 | 1960 | 766,693,818 | 1,346,419,750 | 162,000 | 135,000 |
| 1915 | 172,497,000 | 961,700,000 | 74,000 | 38,000 | 1970 | 2,937,359,448 | 4,494,864,600 | 320,000 | 130,000 |
| 1920 | 227,636,000 | 3,868,422,000 | 115,000 | 85,000 | 1975 | 4,693,427,000 | 5,178,300,000 | 138,000 | 55,000 |
| 1925 | 459,717,623 | 3,427,042,210 | 150,000 | 99,000 | 1976 | *5,360,116,000 | 5,262,107,000 | 104,000 | 40,000 |
| 1929 | 1,124,800,410 | 2,996,398,000 | 625,000 | 550,000 | 1977 | 5,273,767,000 | 4,646,354,000 | 95,000 | 35,000 |
| 1930 | 810,632,546 | 2,720,301,800 | 480,000 | 205,000 | *Record high for trading in stocks. | | | | |
| 1935 | 381,635,752 | $3,339,458,000 | $140,000 | $65,000 | | | | | |

## American Stock Exchange Transactions and Seat Prices

Source: American Stock Exchange

| Year | Yearly volumes Stock shares | Yearly volumes Bonds par values | Seat price High | Seat price Low | Year | Yearly volumes Stock shares | Yearly volumes Bonds par values | Seat price High | Seat price Low |
|---|---|---|---|---|---|---|---|---|---|
| 1929 | 476,140,375 | $513,551,000 | $254,000 | $150,000 | 1960 | 286,039,982 | $32,670,000 | $60,000 | $51,000 |
| 1930 | 222,270,065 | 863,541,000 | 225,000 | 70,000 | 1965 | 534,221,999 | 146,927,000 | 80,000 | 55,000 |
| 1940 | 42,928,337 | 303,902,000 | 7,250 | 6,900 | 1970 | 843,116,260 | 641,270,000 | 180,000 | 70,000 |
| 1945 | 143,309,392 | 167,333,000 | 32,000 | 12,000 | 1975 | 457,610,360 | 259,128,000 | 72,000 | 34,000 |
| 1950 | 107,792,340 | 47,549,000 | 11,000 | 6,500 | 1977 | 653,128,700 | 284,696,000 | 52,000 | 21,000 |

## 50 U.S. Industrials with Largest Annual Sales and Income

Source: Reprinted by permission from The Fortune Directory; © 1978 Time Inc.

| Company | Sales (thousands) | Income (or loss) (thousands) | Company | Sales (thousands) | Income (or loss) (thousands) |
|---|---|---|---|---|---|
| General Motors Corp. | $54,961,300 | $3,337,500 | Westinghouse Electric Co. | $6,137,661 | $250,779 |
| Exxon Corp. | 54,126,219 | 2,422,964 | Occidental Petroleum Corp. | 6,006,019 | 217,912 |
| Ford Motor Co. | 37,841,500 | 1,672,800 | International Harvester Co. | 5,975,061 | 203,737 |
| Mobil Corp. | 32,125,828 | 1,004,670 | Eastman Kodak Co. | 5,966,986 | 643,448 |
| Texaco Inc. | 27,920,499 | 930,789 | RCA | 5,880,900 | 247,000 |
| Standard Oil of Cal. | 20,917,331 | 1,016,360 | Rockwell International | 5,858,700 | 144,100 |
| Intl. Business Machines Corp. | 18,133,184 | 2,719,414 | Caterpillar Tractor Co. | 5,848,900 | 445,100 |
| Gulf Oil Corp. | 17,840,000 | 752,000 | Union Oil of Cal. | 5,668,520 | 334,239 |
| General Electric Co. | 17,518,600 | 1,088,200 | United Technologies Corp. | 5,550,670 | 195,972 |
| Chrysler Corp. | 16,708,300 | 163,200 | Bethlehem Steel Corp. | 5,370,000 | (488,200) |
| Intl. Tel. & Tel. Corp. | 13,145,664 | 550,667 | Beatrice Foods Co. | 5,288,578 | 182,566 |
| Standard Oil Co. (Ind.) | 13,019,939 | 1,011,575 | Esmark Inc. | 5,280,160 | 66,970 |
| Atlantic Richfield Co. | 10,969,091 | 701,515 | Kraft Corp. | 5,238,807 | 154,115 |
| Shell Oil Co. | 10,112,062 | 735,094 | Xerox Corp. | 5,076,900 | 406,627 |
| U.S. Steel Corp. | 9,609,900 | 137,900 | General Foods Corp. | 4,909,737 | 177,338 |
| E.I. du Pont de Nemours. | 9,434,800 | 545,100 | R.J. Reynolds Industries | 4,816,022 | 423,516 |
| Continental Oil Co. | 8,700,317 | 380,626 | Ashland Oil Inc. | 4,785,578 | 164,265 |
| Western Electric | 8,134,604 | 490,076 | LTV Corp. | 4,703,296 | (38,706) |
| Tenneco Inc. | 7,440,300 | 426,900 | Monsanto Co. | 4,594,500 | 275,600 |
| Procter & Gamble Co. | 7,284,255 | 461,463 | Amerada Hess Corp. | 4,591,253 | 178,881 |
| Union Carbide Corp. | 7,036,100 | 385,100 | Firestone Tire & Rubber | 4,426,900 | 110,200 |
| Goodyear Tire & Rubber | 6,627,818 | 205,781 | Cities Service Co. | 4,388,200 | 210,200 |
| Sun Co. | 6,418,117 | 361,940 | Marathon Oil | 4,252,028 | 196,959 |
| Phillips Petroleum Co. | 6,284,185 | 516,902 | Boeing Co. | 4,018,800 | 180,300 |
| Dow Chemical Co. | 6,234,255 | 555,703 | Minn. Mining & Mfg. | 3,980,326 | 412,946 |

## 30 Largest Industrials Outside the U.S.

Source: Reprinted by permission from The Fortune Directory; © 1978 Time Inc.

| Company | Sales (thousands) | Income (or loss) (thousands) | Company | Sales (thousands) | Income (or loss) (thousands) |
|---|---|---|---|---|---|
| Royal Dutch/Shell Group, N-B | $39,680,211 | $2,338,691 | Nippon Steel, J | $8,910,800 | $95,192 |
| National Iranian Oil, Ir | 22,315,269 | 19,336,936 | DaimLer-Benz, G | 8,633,006 | 211,010 |
| British Petroleum, B | 20,940,927 | 530,797 | Peugeot-Citroën, F | 8,523,766 | 238,700 |
| Unilever, B-N | 15,965,116 | 456,789 | Nestlé, S | 8,392,275 | 346,633 |
| Philips' Gloeilampenfabrieken, N. | 12,702,569 | 258,255 | Thyssen, G | 8,325,059 | 65,744 |
| Française des Pétroles, F | 10,875,117 | 27,373 | Petrobrás, Br | 8,284,302 | 1,091,057 |
| Siemens, G | 10,640,951 | 272,971 | Hitachi, J | 8,222,247 | 255,340 |
| Volkswagenwerk, G | 10,409,715 | 179,759 | Imperial Chemical Ind., B | 8,139,127 | 394,476 |
| ENI, It | 10,367,524 | (249,391) | Mitsubishi Heavy Ind., J | 8,089,479 | 68,292 |
| Hoechst, G | 10,041,671 | 92,969 | Elf-Aquitaine, F | 7,754,775 | 358,974 |
| Renault, F | 10,018,305 | 4,070 | Nissan Motor, J | 7,677,346 | 293,019 |
| Petróleos de Venezuela, V | 9,628,101 | 1,818,179 | Matsushita Electric Ind., J | 6,887,743 | 283,996 |
| Toyota Motor, J | 9,601,206 | 453,377 | B.A.T. Industries, B | 6,615,941 | 357,987 |
| Bayer, G | 9,220,047 | 136,169 | St-Gobain-Pont-à-Mousson, F | 6,477,173 | 130,766 |
| BASF, G | 9,115,918 | 167,444 | Montedison, It | 6,183,520 | (514,686) |

National headquarters: B, Britain; Br, Brazil; F, France; G, West Germany; Ir, Iran; It, Italy; J, Japan; N, Netherlands; S, Switzerland; V, Venezuela.

## All Banks in U.S.—Number, Deposits

Source: Federal Reserve System

Comprises all national banks in the United States and all state commercial banks, trust companies, mutual stock savings banks, private and industrial banks, and special types of institutions that are treated as banks by the federal bank supervisory agencies.

| Year (As of June 30) | Total all banks | Number of banks — F.R.S. members — Total | Nat'l | State | Nonmembers Mutual savings | Other | Total all banks | Total deposits (millions of dollars) F.R.S. members Total | Nat'l | State | Nonmembers Mutual savings | Other |
|---|---|---|---|---|---|---|---|---|---|---|---|---|
| 1925 | 26,479 | 9,538 | 8,066 | 1,472 | 621 | 18,320 | 51,641 | 32,457 | 19,912 | 12,546 | 7,089 | 12,095 |
| 1930 | 23,855 | 8,315 | 7,247 | 1,068 | 604 | 14,936 | 59,828 | 38,069 | 23,235 | 14,834 | 9,117 | 12,642 |
| 1935 | 16,047 | 6,410 | 5,425 | 985 | 569 | 9,068 | 51,149 | 34,938 | 22,477 | 12,461 | 9,830 | 6,381 |
| 1940 | 14,955 | 6,398 | 5,164 | 1,234 | 551 | 8,008 | 70,770 | 51,729 | 33,014 | 18,715 | 10,631 | 8,410 |
| 1945 | 14,542 | 6,840 | 5,015 | 1,825 | 539 | 7,163 | 151,033 | 118,378 | 76,534 | 41,844 | 14,413 | 18,242 |
| 1950 | 14,674 | 6,885 | 4,971 | 1,914 | 527 | 7,262 | 163,770 | 122,707 | 82,430 | 40,277 | 19,927 | 21,137 |
| 1955 | 14,309 | 6,611 | 4,744 | 1,867 | 525 | 7,173 | 208,850 | 154,670 | 98,636 | 56,034 | 27,310 | 26,870 |
| 1960 | 14,006 | 6,217 | 4,542 | 1,675 | 513 | 7,276 | 249,163 | 179,519 | 116,178 | 63,341 | 35,316 | 34,328 |
| 1965 | 14,295 | 6,235 | 4,803 | 1,432 | 504 | 7,556 | 362,611 | 259,743 | 171,528 | 88,215 | 50,980 | 51,889 |
| 1970 | 14,167 | 5,803 | 4,637 | 1,166 | 496 | 7,868 | 502,658 | 346,229 | 254,261 | 91,967 | 69,285 | 87,145 |
| 1975, Dec. 31 | 15,108 | 5,787 | 4,741 | 1,046 | 475 | 8,846 | 897,101 | 590,999 | 447,590 | 143,409 | 110,569 | 195,533 |
| 1976, Dec. 31 | 15,145 | 5,758 | 4,735 | 1,023 | 473 | 8,914 | 961,980 | 618,859 | 469,378 | 149,481 | 123,654 | 219,467 |
| 1977, Dec. 31 | 15,174 | 5,668 | 4,654 | 1,014 | 467 | 9,039 | 1,074,426 | 683,611 | 520,167 | 163,443 | 134,916 | 255,898 |

## Bank Rates on Short-term Business Loans

Source: Federal Reserve System

Percent per annum. Short-term loans mature within one year.

| | | Ave. 35 cities | N.Y. C. | 7 Other N.E. | All size loans 8 No. Cent. | 7 S.E. | 8 S.W. | 4 West | Size of loan in $1,000 1-9 | 10-99 | 100 to 499 | 500 to 999 | 1,000 and over |
|---|---|---|---|---|---|---|---|---|---|---|---|---|---|
| 1967 | Aug. 1-15 | 5.95 | 5.66 | 6.29 | 5.92 | 5.92 | 6.01 | 6.02 | 6.58 | 6.46 | 6.16 | 5.89 | 5.72 |
| | Nov. 1-15 | 5.96 | 5.71 | 6.29 | 5.91 | 5.94 | 6.03 | 6.03 | 6.60 | 6.48 | 6.17 | 5.90 | 5.73 |
| 1970 | Aug. 1-15 | 8.50 | 8.24 | 8.89 | 8.47 | 8.49 | 8.53 | 8.54 | 9.15 | 9.07 | 8.75 | 8.46 | 8.25 |
| | Nov. 1-15 | 8.07 | 7.74 | 8.47 | 8.05 | 8.15 | 8.08 | 8.16 | 8.89 | 8.79 | 8.34 | 8.09 | 7.74 |
| 1974 | Feb. | 9.91 | 9.68 | 10.28 | 9.98 | 9.80 | 9.93 | 9.78 | 9.86 | 10.09 | 10.28 | 10.06 | 9.75 |
| | May | 11.15 | 11.08 | 11.65 | 11.09 | 10.88 | 10.82 | 11.19 | 10.50 | 11.06 | 11.41 | 11.32 | 11.06 |
| 1975 | Feb. | 9.94 | 9.61 | 10.31 | 9.87 | 10.24 | 10.01 | 9.99 | 10.94 | 10.73 | 10.25 | 9.93 | 9.73 |
| | May | 8.16 | 7.88 | 8.37 | 8.00 | 8.70 | 8.34 | 8.33 | 9.57 | 9.10 | 8.52 | 8.18 | 7.90 |
| 1976 | Aug. | 7.80 | 7.48 | 8.18 | 7.70 | 7.95 | 7.75 | 8.15 | 8.85 | 9.41 | 8.65 | 9.33 | 9.26 |
| | Nov. | 7.28 | 6.88 | 7.62 | 7.28 | 7.51 | 7.33 | 7.52 | 8.56 | 9.22 | 8.45 | 9.13 | 8.69 |

| | | Size of Loan in $1,000[1] | | | | | | |
|---|---|---|---|---|---|---|---|---|
| | | All sizes | 1-24 | 25-49 | 50-99 | 100-499 | 500-999 | 1,000 and over |
| 1977 | Feb. | 8.95 | 9.65 | 9.44 | 9.26 | 9.03 | 8.78 | 8.34 |
| | May | 9.01 | 9.82 | 9.63 | 9.37 | 9.04 | 8.90 | 8.53 |

(1) In Feb. 1977, The Quarterly Interest Rate Survey was replaced by the Survey of Terms of Bank Lending (STBL). The STBL is conducted in the middle month of each quarter at about 340 member and nonmember banks. The regional breakdown was discontinued at that time. The last previous revision began with the survey period of Feb. 1971. It incorporated a number of technical changes in coverage, sampling, and interest rate calculations.

# Federal Reserve System

The Federal Reserve System, central banking system of the U.S., was established Dec. 23, 1913, by an Act of Congress to give the country an elastic currency, to provide facilities for discounting commercial paper, and to improve supervision of banking. Today it is generally recognized that the primary function of the system is to foster a flow of credit and money that will facilitate orderly economic growth, a stable dollar, and a long-run balance in international payments.

The Federal Reserve System consists of the (1) Board of Governors of the Federal Reserve System; (2) Federal Open Market Committee; (3) 12 Fed. Reserve Banks and 25 branches; (4) member banks; (5) Fed. Advisory Council, and (6) the Consumer Advisory Council.

The 7 members of the Board of Governors in Washington are appointed by the President with the advice and consent of the Senate; G. William Miller is chairman. One of the Board's principal functions is in the area of monetary policy. The Board has authority to approve changes in discount rates, to change member bank reserve requirements within specified limits, to set margin requirements for certain kinds of stock transactions, and to set maximum interest rates payable on member banks' savings and time deposits. Another important duty of the Board relates to supervision of Federal Reserve Banks, state chartered member banks, and bank holding companies. Expenses of the Board of Governors are paid out of assessments upon the Reserve Banks. The Federal Reserve has also been given responsibility by the Congress for rule writing and enforcement of a number of consumer credit protection laws.

The Federal Open Market Committee is composed of the 7 members of the Board of Governors and 5 Federal Reserve Bank presidents elected annually. The Committee establishes System open market policy for the purchases and sales of securities and for operations in foreign currencies.

The Federal Advisory Council is composed of representatives of the banking industry from the 12 Federal Reserve Districts. The Council is required by law to meet with the Board at least 4 times yearly, to consult with and advise the Board on all matters within the Board's jurisdiction.

Congress established the Consumer Advisory Council in 1976. It consults with the Board at least 4 times a year on consumer-related matters. It had 23 members, broadly representative of consumer and creditor interests, at the end of 1977. Members are appointed for 3-year terms.

Rather than having one central bank in the political capital, as in central banking systems of most countries, the Federal Reserve System is divided into 12 districts, each with a Federal Reserve Bank—in Boston, New York, Philadelphia, Cleveland, Richmond, Atlanta, Chicago, St. Louis, Minneapolis, Kansas City, Dallas, and San Francisco. Reserve Banks are operated for public service. By statute, their stock is held entirely by member banks, which include all national banks and such state banks and trust companies as have been admitted to membership. Ownership of Reserve Bank stock is in the nature of an obligation incident to membership in the System and does not carry with it the attributes of control and financial interest ordinarily attached to stock ownership in corporations that are operated for profit. The amount of stock that member banks own is specified by law and dividends are limited to 6% per annum. In case of the liquidation of any Reserve Bank, its surplus would be paid entirely to the U.S. Each Reserve Bank has 9 directors, 6 of whom are chosen by member banks and 3 by the Board of Governors, including the chairman of the Reserve Bank board.

# Federal Deposit Insurance Corporation (FDIC)

The primary purpose of the Federal Deposit Insurance Corporation (FDIC) is to insure the deposits of all banks entitled to insurance benefits under the Federal Deposit Insurance Act. The major functions of the FDIC are to pay off depositors of insured banks closed without adequate provision having been made to pay depositors' claims, to act as receiver for all national banks placed in receivership and for state banks placed in receivership when appointed receiver by state authorities, and to prevent the continuance or development of unsafe and unsound banking practices. The FDIC's entire income consists of assessments on insured banks and income from investments; it receives no appropriations from Congress. It may borrow from the U.S. Treasury not to exceed $3 billion outstanding at any one time, but has made no such borrowings since it was organized in 1933. The FDIC surplus (Deposit Insurance Fund) as of Dec. 31, 1977 was 7.99 billion.

# Largest Bank in Each of 47 Foreign Countries

**Source:** 500 Largest Banks in the Free World, compiled by the American Banker, New York. (Copyright 1978) Based on deposits Dec. 31, 1977, or nearest fiscal year-end. For Canada, see Index.

(thousands)

| Country, bank | Deposits in U.S. $ | Country, bank | Deposits in U.S. $ |
|---|---|---|---|
| Argentina, Banco de la Nacion | $ 3,246,125 | Malaysia, Bank Bumiputra Malaysia Berhad | 1,305,913 |
| Austrailia, Commonwealth Bkng. Corp. | 12,852,485 | Mexico, Bancomer | 4,907,345 |
| Austria, Creditanstalt-Bankverein. | 9,466,967 | Netherlands, Coop. Centr. | |
| Belgium, Societe Generale de Banque. | 18,059,083 | Raiffeisen-Boerenleenbank | 25,760,115 |
| Brazil, Banco do Brasil | 26,482,165 | New Zealand, Bank of | 1,699,509 |
| Denmark, Danske Bank | 4,072,410 | Nigeria, Standard Bank Nigeria Ltd. | 1,929,138 |
| Egypt, National Bank of Egypt | 5,248,155 | Norway, Norske Creditbank. | 2,355,330 |
| Finland, Union Bank Ltd. | 3,178,656 | Pakistan, Habib Bank Ltd. | 1,678,464 |
| France, Banque Nationale de Paris | 51,721,528 | Peru, Banco de la Nacion | 1,805,365 |
| Germany, Deutsche Bank | 55,210,331 | Philippines, Philippine National Bank | 1,139,300 |
| Greece, National Bank of Greece | 7,335,387 | Portugal, Banco Portugues do Atlantico | 1,619,660 |
| Hong Kong, Hongkong & Shanghai | 12,924,693 | Saudi Arabia, National Commercial Bank | 3,990,148 |
| India, State Bank of India | 8,390,255 | Singapore, Oversea-Chinese Banking Corp. | 1,255,042 |
| Indonesia, Bank Bumi Daya | 2,087,447 | South Africa, Barclays Nat'l Bank Ltd. | 4,448,601 |
| Iran, Bank Melli Iran | 8,220,756 | Spain, Banco Central | 10,543,062 |
| Iraq, Rafidain Bank | 3,979,127 | Sweden, Post-Och Kreditbanken | 10,142,580 |
| Ireland, Bank of | 3,627,263 | Switzerland, Swiss Bank Corp. | 24,963,491 |
| Israel, Bank Leumile-Israel | 8,874,373 | Taiwan, Bank of | 5,092,368 |
| Italy, Banca Nazionale del Lavoro | 24,320,353 | Thailand, Bangkok Bank Ltd. | 2,273,042 |
| Japan, Dai-Ichi Kangyo Bank Ltd. | 33,544,751 | Turkey, Turkiye Is Bankasi | 3,212,934 |
| Jordan, Arab Bank, Ltd. | 2,644,547 | United Arab Emirates, Nat'l Bank of | |
| Korea, Bank of Seoul & Trust Co. | 2,154,984 | Abu Dhabi | 3,025,320 |
| Kuwait, National Bank of. | 2,074,427 | United Kingdom, Barclays Bank Ltd. | 37,109,464 |
| Libya, National Commercial Bank | 1,251,782 | Venezuela, Banco Nacional de Descuento | 1,544,460 |
| Luxembourg, Cie, Luxembourgeoise | 6,592,762 | | |

# 100 Largest U.S. Commercial Banks

Source: 300 Largest Commercial Banks in U.S., compiled by the American Banker, New York. (Copyright 1978) Based on deposits June 30, 1978.

| Rank | | Deposits | Rank | | Deposits |
|---|---|---|---|---|---|
| 1 | Bank of America NT&SA, San Francisco | $71,010,269,000 | 54 | Northwestern NB, Minneapolis | 1,916,465,000 |
| 2 | Citibank NA, New York | 60,889,533,000 | 55 | National Bank, Norfolk | 1,833,973,000 |
| 3 | Chase Manhattan Bank NA, New York | 43,497,466,000 | 56 | Riggs National Bank, Washington, D.C. | 1,830,957,000 |
| 4 | Manufacturers Hanover Trust Co., New York | 30,092,798,000 | 57 | Central National Bank, Cleveland | 1,744,763,000 |
| 5 | Morgan Guaranty Trust Co., New York | 25,765,063,000 | 58 | Banco Popular de Puerto Rico, San Juan | 1,743,562,407 |
| 6 | Chemical Bank, New York | 23,262,673,000 | 59 | Connecticut Bank & Trust Co., Hartford | 1,730,640,301 |
| 7 | Continental Illinois NB&T Co., Chicago | 18,353,150,000 | 60 | Industrial NB of Rhode Island, Providence | 1,717,596,000 |
| 8 | Bankers Trust Co., New York | 17,948,812,000 | 61 | First Union NB of North Carolina, Charlotte | 1,715,273,000 |
| 9 | First National Bank, Chicago | 16,714,313,000 | 62 | Lloyds Bank California, Los Angeles | 1,695,018,130 |
| 10 | Security Pacific Nat'l Bk, Los Angeles | 16,218,520,148 | 63 | First National Bank, Atlanta, Ga. | 1,668,457,000 |
| 11 | Wells Fargo Bank NA, San Francisco. | 13,712,536,000 | 64 | First National Bank, Minneapolis | 1,563,315,000 |
| 12 | Marine Midland Bank, Buffalo, N.Y. | 10,515,088,000 | 65 | American Fletcher NB&T Co., Indianapolis | 1,556,436,000 |
| 13 | Crocker National Bank, San Francisco | 10,485,558,000 | 66 | Trust Co. Bank, Atlanta, Ga. | 1,553,163,000 |
| 14 | United California Bank, Los Angeles | 9,786,687,000 | 67 | Hartford National Bank & Trust Co., Conn. | 1,514,423,000 |
| 15 | Irving Trust Co., New York | 8,679,207,078 | 68 | American National B&T Co., Chicago | 1,506,929,826 |
| 16 | Mellon Bank NA, Pittsburgh | 7,412,746,000 | 69 | Southeast First National Bank, Miami. | 1,475,550,000 |
| 17 | First National Bank, Boston | 7,374,310,000 | 70 | Citibank (New York State) NA, Rochester, N.Y. | 1,475,097,000 |
| 18 | National Bank of Detroit | 6,754,020,000 | 71 | First National Bank, St. Louis, Mo. | 1,462,107,000 |
| 19 | Bank of New York | 5,192,945,416 | 72 | Mercantile National Bank, Dallas | 1,428,046,063 |
| 20 | First Pennsylvania Bank NA, Philadelphia. | 4,945,179,000 | 73 | Bank of Hawaii, Honolulu | 1,424,408,092 |
| 21 | Seattle-First National Bank. | 4,807,294,000 | 74 | Shawmut Bank of Boston NA | 1,407,667,000 |
| 22 | Republic National Bank, Dallas | 4,590,337,000 | 75 | Provident National Bank, Philadelphia. | 1,407,518,000 |
| 23 | First National Bank, Dallas | 4,465,798,000 | 76 | American Security Bank NA, Washington, D.C. | 1,398,082,000 |
| 24 | Union Bank, Los Angeles | 4,216,153,000 | 77 | Michigan National Bank, Lansing | 1,383,063,000 |
| 25 | Harris Trust & Savings Bank, Chicago | 4,057,044,925 | 78 | Mercantile Trust Co. NA, St. Louis, Mo. | 1,382,556,065 |
| 26 | Valley National Bank, Phoenix, Ariz. | 3,429,251,469 | 79 | Indiana National Bank, Indianapolis | 1,372,976,419 |
| 27 | First City National Bank, Houston | 3,404,114,000 | 80 | Manuf. & Traders Trust Co., Buffalo, N.Y. | 1,358,384,247 |
| 28 | Philadelphia National Bank | 3,365,745,000 | 81 | Equitable Trust Co., Baltimore | 1,349,456,000 |
| 29 | Northern Trust Co., Chicago | 3,365,548,000 | 82 | Michigan National Bank, Detroit | 1,271,600,000 |
| 30 | North Carolina National Bank, Charlotte | 3,260,852,464 | 83 | First Security Bank of Utah NA, Ogden | 1,271,139,647 |
| 31 | Cleveland Trust Co. | 3,200,213,000 | 84 | First & Merchants NB, Richmond, Va. | 1,270,186,863 |
| 32 | Detroit Bank & Trust Co. | 3,193,068,000 | 85 | First National State Bank, Newark, N.J. | 1,262,508,000 |
| 33 | Wachovia B&T Co. NA, Winston-Salem, N.C. | 3,175,053,462 | 86 | American Bank & Trust Co., Reading, Pa. | 1,255,164,000 |
| 34 | Texas Commerce Bank NA, Houston. | 3,130,237,000 | 87 | New England Merchants NB, Boston | 1,254,068,308 |
| 35 | National Bank of No. America, New York | 3,028,918,000 | 88 | Ohio National Bank, Columbus | 1,250,374,807 |
| 36 | Rainier National Bank, Seattle | 3,016,240,144 | 89 | First National Bank, Baltimore | 1,244,617,000 |
| 37 | Girard Bank, Philadelphia | 2,993,154,000 | 90 | First National Bank, St. Paul, Minn. | 1,240,484,000 |
| 38 | First National Bank of Oregon, Portland | 2,985,503,000 | 91 | Arizona Bank, Phoenix | 1,232,657,522 |
| 39 | Manufacturers National Bank, Detroit. | 2,962,713,000 | 92 | Idaho First National Bank, Boise. | 1,216,043,152 |
| 40 | European American B&T Co., New York | 2,886,222,000 | 93 | Northwestern Bk., North Wilkesboro, N.C. | 1,214,734,000 |
| 41 | United States NB of Oregon, Portland | 2,834,655,000 | 94 | Whitney National Bank, New Orleans, La. | 1,212,133,356 |
| 42 | Citizens & Southern NB, Atlanta, Ga. | 2,818,027,000 | 95 | Sumitomo Bank of California, San Francisco | 1,203,180,439 |
| 43 | Pittsburgh National Bank | 2,730,993,181 | 96 | Industrial Valley B&T Co., Philadelphia | 1,200,207,000 |
| 44 | Fidelity Bank, Philadelphia | 2,396,048,000 | 97 | First National Bank, Louisville, Ky. | 1,189,528,373 |
| 45 | California First Bank of San Francisco | 2,355,046,000 | 98 | Continental Bank, Norristown, Pa. | 1,173,453,000 |
| 46 | Bank of Tokyo Trust Co., New York. | 2,354,347,646 | 99 | First Hawaiian Bank, Honolulu | 1,170,607,000 |
| 47 | Bank of California NA, San Francisco. | 2,265,088,000 | 100 | Bank of the Southwest NA, Houston | 1,156,750,000 |
| 48 | First National Bank, Phoenix, Ariz. | 2,251,295,000 | | | |
| 49 | Maryland National Bank, Baltimore | 2,208,077,000 | | | |
| 50 | Republic National Bank, New York | 2,207,012,379 | | | |
| 51 | Equibank NA, Pittsburgh | 2,025,904,000 | | | |
| 52 | First Wisconsin National Bank, Milwaukee | 2,016,443,000 | | | |
| 53 | National City Bank, Cleveland | 1,964,542,000 | | | |

---

## Bank Suspensions

Source: Federal Deposit Insurance Corp. Deposits in thousands of dollars. The figures represent banks which, during the periods shown, closed temporarily or permanently on account of financial difficulties; does not include banks whose deposit liabilities were assumed by other banks.

| Year | Susp. | Deposits | Year | Susp. | Deposits | Year | Susp. | Deposits | Year | Susp. | Deposits |
|---|---|---|---|---|---|---|---|---|---|---|---|
| 1929 | 659 | 230,643 | 1936 | 42 | 11,241 | 1959 | 3 | 2,593 | 1967 | 4 | 10,878 |
| 1930 | 1,352 | 853,363 | 1937 | 50 | 14,960 | 1960 | 1 | 6,930 | 1969 | 4 | 9,011 |
| 1931 | 2,294 | 1,690,669 | 1938 | 50 | 10,296 | 1961 | 5 | 8,936 | 1970 | 4 | 34,040 |
| 1932 | 1,456 | 715,626 | 1939 | 32 | 32,738 | 1963 | 2 | 23,444 | 1971 | 5 | 74,605 |
| 1933* | 4,004 | 3,598,975 | 1940 | 19 | 5,657 | 1964 | 7 | 23,438 | 1972 | 1 | 20,482 |
| 1934 | 9 | 1,968 | 1955(a) | 4 | 6,503 | 1965 | 3 | 42,889 | 1973 | 3 | 25,811 |
| 1935 | 24 | 9,091 | 1958 | 3 | 4,156 | 1966 | 1 | 774 | 1975 | 1 | 18,248 |
| | | | | | | | | | 1976 | 3 | 18,859 |

*Figures for 1933 comprise 628 banks with deposits of $360,413,000 suspended before or after the banking holiday (the holiday began March 6 and closed March 15) or placed in receivership during the holiday; 2,124 banks with deposits of $2,520,391,000 which were not licensed following the banking holiday and were placed in liquidation or receivership; and 1,252 banks with deposits of $718,171,000 which had not been licensed by June 20, 1933. (a) No suspensions in years 1945-1954, 1962, 1968, 1974, 1977.

## Civilian Employment of the Federal Government

Source: Workforce Analysis and Statistics Division, U.S. Civil Service Commission as of June 30, 1978

| Agency | All areas | United States | | | Outside United States | | |
|---|---|---|---|---|---|---|---|
| | | Total | Full-time | Part-time & intermittent | Total | Terri- tories | Foreign countries |
| Total, all agencies[1] | 2,929,100 | 2,801,188 | 2,564,282 | 236,906 | 127,912 | 35,486 | 92,426 |
| Percent distribution | 100 | 96 | 88 | 8 | 4 | 1 | 3 |
| Legislative branch | 41,474 | 41,388 | 40,341 | 1,047 | 86 | 16 | 70 |
| Congress | 19,909 | 19,909 | 19,908 | 1 | ... | ... | ... |
| Senate | 7,266 | 7,266 | 7,266 | ... | ... | ... | ... |
| House of Representatives | 12,632 | 12,632 | 12,632 | ... | ... | ... | ... |
| Comm. on Security and Coop. in Europe | 11 | 11 | 10 | 1 | ... | ... | ... |
| Architect of the Capitol | 2,313 | 2,313 | 2,037 | 276 | ... | ... | ... |
| General Accounting Office | 5,657 | 5,582 | 5,415 | 167 | 75 | 16 | 59 |
| Government Printing Office | 7,626 | 7,626 | 7,426 | 200 | ... | ... | ... |
| Library of Congress | 5,281 | 5,270 | 4,937 | 333 | 11 | ... | 11 |
| Tax Court | 203 | 203 | 200 | 3 | ... | ... | ... |
| Judicial branch | 13,079 | 12,919 | 12,198 | 721 | 160 | 160 | ... |
| United States Courts | 12,747 | 12,587 | 11,892 | 695 | 160 | 160 | ... |
| Supreme Court | 332 | 332 | 306 | 26 | ... | ... | ... |
| Executive branch | 2,874,547 | 2,746,881 | 2,511,743 | 235,138 | 127,666 | 35,310 | 92,356 |
| Executive Office of the President | 1,627 | 1,627 | 1,526 | 101 | ... | ... | ... |
| White House Office | 378 | 378 | 351 | 27 | ... | ... | ... |
| Office of the Vice President | 24 | 24 | 23 | 1 | ... | ... | ... |
| Office of Management and Budget | 593 | 593 | 580 | 13 | ... | ... | ... |
| Council of Economic Advisors | 33 | 33 | 32 | 1 | ... | ... | ... |
| Council on Environmental Quality | 66 | 66 | 57 | 9 | ... | ... | ... |
| Council on Wage and Price Stability | 49 | 49 | 42 | 7 | ... | ... | ... |
| Domestic Council | 54 | 54 | 51 | 3 | ... | ... | ... |
| Executive Mansions and Grounds | 87 | 87 | 87 | ... | ... | ... | ... |
| Office of Administration | 183 | 183 | 167 | 16 | ... | ... | ... |
| Office of Special Representatives Trade Negotiations | 53 | 53 | 47 | 6 | ... | ... | ... |
| Office of Science and Technology Policy | 38 | 38 | 26 | 12 | ... | ... | ... |
| National Security Council | 69 | 69 | 63 | 6 | ... | ... | ... |
| Executive departments | 1,777,195 | 1,676,097 | 1,596,819 | 79,278 | 101,098 | 15,119 | 85,979 |
| State[2] | 30,502 | 10,695 | 10,149 | 546 | 19,807 | ... | 19,807 |
| Treasury | 131,243 | 130,276 | 124,294 | 5,982 | 967 | 600 | 367 |
| Defense | 999,696 | 924,838 | 910,903 | 13,935 | 74,858 | 10,763 | 64,095 |
| Department of the Army | 365,193 | 328,603 | 322,781 | 5,822 | 36,590 | 3,945 | 32,645 |
| Department of the Navy | 317,048 | 295,467 | 291,150 | 4,317 | 21,581 | 4,900 | 16,681 |
| Department of the Air Force | 245,529 | 231,698 | 228,637 | 3,061 | 13,831 | 1,730 | 12,101 |
| Defense Logistics Agency | 48,733 | 48,340 | 48,010 | 330 | 393 | 55 | 338 |
| Other Defense Activities | 23,193 | 20,730 | 20,325 | 405 | 2,463 | 133 | 2,330 |
| Justice | 55,241 | 54,382 | 52,935 | 1,447 | 859 | 388 | 471 |
| Interior | 83,696 | 83,325 | 74,159 | 9,166 | 371 | 304 | 67 |
| Agriculture | 138,303 | 136,811 | 107,869 | 28,942 | 1,492 | 750 | 742 |
| Commerce | 41,580 | 40,776 | 35,144 | 5,632 | 804 | 626 | 178 |
| Labor | 21,895 | 21,798 | 20,784 | 1,014 | 97 | 60 | 37 |
| Health, Education, and Welfare | 161,050 | 160,233 | 149,913 | 10,320 | 817 | 770 | 47 |
| Housing and Urban Development | 17,928 | 17,757 | 17,170 | 587 | 171 | 171 | ... |
| Transportation | 76,037 | 75,191 | 74,019 | 1,172 | 846 | 686 | 160 |
| Department of Energy | 20,024 | 20,015 | 19,480 | 535 | 9 | 1 | 8 |
| Independent agencies | 1,095,725 | 1,069,157 | 913,398 | 155,759 | 26,568 | 20,191 | 6,377 |
| Action | 2,088 | 1,542 | 1,462 | 80 | 546 | 16 | 530 |
| Board of Governors, Fed. Res. System | 1,502 | 1,502 | 1,467 | 35 | ... | ... | ... |
| Canal Zone Government | 3,213 | ... | ... | ... | 3,213 | 3,213 | ... |
| Civil Service Commission | 8,900 | 8,879 | 7,132 | 1,747 | 21 | 21 | ... |
| Community Service Admin. | 1,111 | 1,111 | 1,091 | 20 | ... | ... | ... |
| Environmental Protection Agency | 13,100 | 13,089 | 11,689 | 1,400 | 11 | 11 | ... |
| Federal Communications Comm. | 2,209 | 2,202 | 2,199 | 3 | 7 | 7 | ... |
| Federal Trade Commission | 1,821 | 1,821 | 1,725 | 96 | ... | ... | ... |
| General Service Admin. | 38,629 | 38,527 | 37,118 | 1,409 | 102 | 89 | 13 |
| International Communications Agency | 8,569 | 3,411 | 3,356 | 55 | 5,158 | ... | 5,158 |
| Interstate Commerce Commission | 2,168 | 2,168 | 2,133 | 35 | ... | ... | ... |
| National Aeronautics and Space Admin. | 24,696 | 24,671 | 24,549 | 122 | 25 | 1 | 24 |
| National Labor Relations Board | 2,979 | 2,955 | 2,926 | 29 | 24 | 24 | ... |
| Nuclear Regulatory Comm. | 3,070 | 3,070 | 2,941 | 129 | ... | ... | ... |
| Panama Canal Company | 11,731 | 78 | 77 | 1 | 11,653 | 11,653 | ... |
| Securities and Exchange Comm. | 1,999 | 1,999 | 1,952 | 47 | ... | ... | ... |
| Selective Service System | 75 | 75 | 74 | 1 | ... | ... | ... |
| Small Business Admin. | 6,130 | 6,023 | 5,892 | 131 | 107 | 107 | ... |
| Tennessee Valley Authority | 45,417 | 45,412 | 44,952 | 460 | 5 | ... | 5 |
| U. S. Postal Service | 650,320 | 647,541 | 525,202 | 122,339 | 2,779 | 2,779 | ... |
| Veterans Administration | 239,760 | 237,331 | 211,484 | 25,847 | 2,429 | 2,166 | 263 |
| All other agencies | 26,238 | 25,750 | 23,977 | 1,773 | 488 | 104 | 384 |

(1) Excludes employees of Central Intelligence Agency, National Security Agency (not reported to the Civil Service Commission) and uncompensated employees. June 1978 total includes 40,898 employees exempted from personnel ceilings in the Youth Programs and Worker Trainee Opportunities Program. (2) Includes 6,071 employees in Agency for International Development (2,570 in the Washington, D.C. metropolitan area); employees in foreign countries include 437 paid from local currency trust funds established by foreign governments.

# U.S. Labor Force, Employment and Unemployment

Source: Bureau of Labor Statistics, U.S. Labor Department

(numbers in thousands; seasonally adjusted)

| | 1975[2] | 1976[2] | 1977[2] | 1978 Jan. | Feb. | Mar. | Apr. | May |
|---|---|---|---|---|---|---|---|---|
| **Labor force** | | | | | | | | |
| Total labor force (age 16 and over)[1] | 94,793 | 96,917 | 99,534 | 101,228 | 101,217 | 101,536 | 102,118 | 102,113 |
| Civilian labor force | 92,613 | 94,773 | 97,401 | 99,107 | 99,093 | 99,414 | 99,784 | 100,261 |
| Employed | 84,783 | 87,485 | 90,546 | 92,881 | 93,003 | 93,266 | 93,801 | 94,112 |
| Agriculture | 3,380 | 3,297 | 3,244 | 3,354 | 3,242 | 3,310 | 3,275 | 3,235 |
| Nonagricultural industries | 81,403 | 84,188 | 87,302 | 89,527 | 89,761 | 89,956 | 90,526 | 90,877 |
| Unemployed, total | 7,830 | 7,288 | 6,855 | 6,226 | 6,090 | 6,148 | 5,983 | 6,149 |
| Long term, 15 weeks and over | 2,483 | 2,339 | 1,911 | 1,688 | 1,568 | 1,463 | 1,384 | 1,358 |

**Unemployment rates** (unemployed in each group as percent of total group)

| | 1975[2] | 1976[2] | 1977[2] | Jan. | Feb. | Mar. | Apr. | May |
|---|---|---|---|---|---|---|---|---|
| Total, 16 years and over | 8.5 | 7.7 | 7.0 | 6.3 | 6.1 | 6.2 | 6.0 | 6.1 |
| Men, 20 years and over | 6.7 | 5.9 | 5.2 | 4.7 | 4.5 | 4.5 | 4.2 | 4.2 |
| Women, 20 years and over | 8.0 | 7.4 | 7.0 | 6.1 | 5.7 | 5.8 | 5.8 | 6.3 |
| Both sexes, 16 to 19 years | 19.9 | 19.0 | 17.7 | 16.0 | 17.4 | 17.3 | 16.9 | 16.5 |
| White, total | 7.8 | 7.0 | 6.2 | 5.5 | 5.3 | 5.3 | 5.2 | 5.2 |
| Men, 20 years and over | 6.2 | 5.4 | 4.6 | 4.0 | 3.9 | 4.0 | 3.6 | 3.6 |
| Women, 20 years and over | 7.5 | 6.8 | 6.2 | 5.5 | 5.0 | 4.9 | 5.1 | 5.4 |
| Both sexes, 16 to 19 years | 17.9 | 16.9 | 15.4 | 13.7 | 14.8 | 14.6 | 14.6 | 13.8 |
| Black and other, total | 13.9 | 13.1 | 13.1 | 12.7 | 11.8 | 12.4 | 11.8 | 12.3 |
| Men, 20 years and over | 11.7 | 10.6 | 10.0 | 9.8 | 8.6 | 8.5 | 8.8 | 8.8 |
| Women, 20 years and over | 11.5 | 11.3 | 11.7 | 10.8 | 10.1 | 11.4 | 10.5 | 10.9 |
| Both sexes, 16 to 19 years | 36.9 | 37.1 | 38.3 | 38.7 | 38.0 | 39.0 | 35.3 | 38.4 |
| Married men, spouse present | 5.1 | 4.2 | 3.6 | 2.9 | 2.9 | 3.0 | 2.8 | 2.9 |
| Married women, spouse present | 7.9 | 7.1 | 6.5 | 5.6 | 5.2 | 5.1 | 5.0 | 5.9 |
| Women who head families | 10.0 | 10.0 | 9.3 | 7.9 | 7.6 | 8.6 | 10.1 | 9.3 |
| Full-time workers | 8.1 | 7.3 | 6.5 | 5.8 | 5.7 | 5.6 | 5.4 | 5.6 |
| Part-time workers | 10.3 | 10.1 | 9.8 | 8.9 | 8.6 | 9.6 | 9.6 | 9.2 |
| Unemployed 15 weeks and over | 2.7 | 2.5 | 2.0 | 1.7 | 1.6 | 1.5 | 1.4 | 1.4 |
| White-collar workers | 4.7 | 4.6 | 4.3 | 3.6 | 3.5 | 3.4 | 3.5 | 3.6 |
| Clerical workers | 6.6 | 6.4 | 5.9 | 5.0 | 5.0 | 4.5 | 5.1 | 5.3 |
| Blue-collar workers | 11.7 | 9.4 | 8.1 | 7.1 | 7.1 | 7.1 | 6.5 | 6.6 |
| Nonfarm laborers | 15.6 | 13.7 | 12.0 | 11.0 | 11.5 | 11.9 | 10.0 | 8.7 |
| Service workers | 8.6 | 8.7 | 8.2 | 7.6 | 7.1 | 7.7 | 7.7 | 7.6 |
| Nonagricultural private wage and salary workers[2] | 9.2 | 7.9 | 7.0 | 6.2 | 6.1 | 6.0 | 5.9 | 5.9 |
| Construction | 18.1 | 15.6 | 12.7 | 11.7 | 11.5 | 11.3 | 9.5 | 9.2 |
| Manufacturing | 10.9 | 7.9 | 6.7 | 5.6 | 5.7 | 5.4 | 5.3 | 5.6 |
| Durable goods | 13.3 | 7.7 | 6.2 | 5.2 | 5.0 | 4.8 | 4.4 | 5.0 |
| Nondurable goods | 10.4 | 8.1 | 7.4 | 6.1 | 6.5 | 6.2 | 6.5 | 6.4 |
| Wholesale and retail trade | 8.7 | 8.6 | 8.0 | 7.1 | 7.1 | 7.3 | 7.2 | 6.8 |
| Finance and service industries | 6.6 | 6.5 | 6.0 | 5.3 | 5.1 | 5.1 | 5.2 | 5.3 |
| Government workers | 4.0 | 4.4 | 4.2 | 4.2 | 3.5 | 3.7 | 3.8 | 4.1 |

(1) Includes all military personnel. (2) Data for periods prior to January 1978 are not strictly comparable with current data because of recent expansion of the sample and revisions in estimation procedures.

## Employed Persons by Major Occupational Groups and Sex

**Annual averages 1976**

| Occupational group | Thousands of persons — Both sexes | Males | Females | Percent distribution — Both sexes | Males | Females |
|---|---|---|---|---|---|---|
| Total employed | 87,485 | 52,391 | 35,095 | 100.0 | 100.0 | 100.0 |
| White-collar workers | 43,700 | 21,551 | 22,148 | 49.9 | 41.1 | 63.1 |
| Professional and technical | 13,329 | 7,725 | 5,603 | 15.2 | 14.7 | 16.0 |
| Managers and administrators, except farm | 9,315 | 7,373 | 1,942 | 10.6 | 14.1 | 5.5 |
| Sales workers | 5,497 | 3,140 | 2,357 | 6.3 | 6.0 | 6.7 |
| Clinical workers | 15,558 | 3,314 | 12,245 | 17.8 | 6.3 | 34.9 |
| Blue-collar workers | 28,958 | 23,852 | 5,106 | 33.1 | 45.5 | 14.5 |
| Craft and kindred workers | 11,278 | 10,733 | 545 | 12.9 | 20.5 | 1.6 |
| Operatives, except transport. | 10,085 | 6,135 | 3,949 | 11.5 | 11.7 | 11.3 |
| Transport equipment operatives | 3,271 | 3,062 | 209 | 3.7 | 5.8 | .6 |
| Nonfarm laborers | 4,325 | 3,922 | 403 | 4.9 | 7.5 | 1.1 |
| Service workers | 12,005 | 4,622 | 7,384 | 13.7 | 8.8 | 21.0 |
| Private household workers | 1,125 | 30 | 1,095 | 1.3 | .1 | 3.1 |
| Other service workers | 10,880 | 4,592 | 6,289 | 12.4 | 8.8 | 17.9 |
| Farm workers | 2,822 | 2,365 | 458 | 3.2 | 4.5 | 1.3 |
| Farmers and farm managers | 1,514 | 1,423 | 90 | 1.7 | 2.7 | .3 |
| Farm laborers and supervisors | 1,309 | 942 | 367 | 1.5 | 1.8 | 1.0 |

## Employment and Unemployment in the U.S.

Civilian labor force, persons 16 years of age and over (in thousands)

| Year | Civilian labor force | Employed | Unemployed | Year | Civilian labor force | Employed | Unemployed |
|---|---|---|---|---|---|---|---|
| 1940 | 52,705 | 45,070 | 7,635 | 1972 | 86,542 | 81,702 | 4,840 |
| 1950 | 62,208 | 58,920 | 3,288 | 1973 | 88,714 | 84,409 | 4,304 |
| 1960 | 69,628 | 65,778 | 3,852 | 1974 | 91,011 | 85,936 | 5,076 |
| 1965 | 74,455 | 71,088 | 3,366 | 1975 | 92,613 | 84,783 | 7,830 |
| 1969 | 80,734 | 77,902 | 2,832 | 1976 | 94,773 | 87,485 | 7,288 |
| 1970 | 82,715 | 78,627 | 4,088 | 1977 | 97,401 | 90,546 | 6,855 |

## Per Capita Personal Income, by States and Regions

Source: Bureau of Economic Analysis, U.S. Commerce Department (Dollars)

| State and Region | 1970 | 1974 | 1975 | 1976 | 1977 |
|---|---|---|---|---|---|
| **United States** . . . . . . . | **3,893** | **5,428** | **5,861** | **6,403** | **7,019** |
| **New England** . . . . . . | **4,245** | **5,635** | **6,030** | **6,568** | **7,183** |
| Connecticut . . . . . . | 4,871 | 6,391 | 6,779 | 7,313 | 8,061 |
| Maine . . . . . . . . | 3,250 | 4,493 | 4,766 | 5,367 | 5,734 |
| Massachusetts . . . | 4,276 | 5,666 | 6,077 | 6,633 | 7,258 |
| New Hampshire . . . | 3,720 | 5,022 | 5,417 | 5,974 | 6,536 |
| Rhode Island . . . . | 3,878 | 5,287 | 5,709 | 6,187 | 6,775 |
| Vermont . . . . . . . | 3,447 | 4,580 | 4,924 | 5,414 | 5,823 |
| **Mideast** . . . . . . . | **4,384** | **5,928** | **6,380** | **6,878** | **7,499** |
| Delaware . . . . . . | 4,468 | 6,078 | 6,547 | 7,107 | 7,697 |
| District of Columbia . | 4,644 | 6,591 | 7,262 | 8,120 | 8,999 |
| Maryland . . . . . . | 4,267 | 5,951 | 6,403 | 6,995 | 7,572 |
| New Jersey . . . . . | 4,684 | 6,326 | 6,794 | 7,314 | 7,994 |
| New York . . . . . . | 4,605 | 6,076 | 6,519 | 6,929 | 7,537 |
| Pennsylvania . . . . | 3,879 | 5,402 | 5,841 | 6,402 | 7,011 |
| **Great Lakes** . . . . . . | **4,050** | **5,644** | **6,047** | **6,688** | **7,347** |
| Illinois . . . . . . . | 4,446 | 6,215 | 6,735 | 7,332 | 7,768 |
| Indiana . . . . . . . | 3,709 | 5,225 | 5,609 | 6,259 | 6,921 |
| Michigan . . . . . . | 4,041 | 5,670 | 5,991 | 6,765 | 7,619 |
| Ohio . . . . . . . . | 3,949 | 5,433 | 5,778 | 6,400 | 7,084 |
| Wisconsin . . . . . . | 3,712 | 5,182 | 5,616 | 6,136 | 6,890 |
| **Plains** . . . . . . . . . . | **3,657** | **5,267** | **5,719** | **6,110** | **6,830** |
| Iowa . . . . . . . . . | 3,643 | 5,327 | 5,894 | 6,172 | 6,878 |
| Kansas . . . . . . . | 3,725 | 5,505 | 5,958 | 6,507 | 7,134 |
| Minnesota . . . . . . | 3,819 | 5,422 | 5,779 | 6,237 | 7,129 |
| Missouri . . . . . . . | 3,654 | 5,007 | 5,476 | 5,968 | 6,654 |
| Nebraska . . . . . . | 3,657 | 5,196 | 5,882 | 6,112 | 6,720 |
| North Dakota . . . . | 3,077 | 5,879 | 5,888 | 5,773 | 6,190 |
| South Dakota . . . . | 3,108 | 4,753 | 5,009 | 5,097 | 5,957 |

| State and Region | 1970 | 1974 | 1975 | 1976 | 1977 |
|---|---|---|---|---|---|
| **Southeast** . . . . . . . . | **3,208** | **4,689** | **5,028** | **5,536** | **6,055** |
| Alabama. . . . . . . | 2,892 | 4,233 | 4,635 | 5,138 | 5,622 |
| Arkansas. . . . . . . | 2,791 | 4,271 | 4,510 | 4,923 | 5,540 |
| Florida . . . . . . . | 3,698 | 5,338 | 5,631 | 6,105 | 6,684 |
| Georgia . . . . . . . | 3,300 | 4,755 | 5,029 | 5,531 | 6,014 |
| Kentucky . . . . . . | 3,076 | 4,520 | 4,887 | 5,414 | 5,945 |
| Louisiana . . . . . . | 3,023 | 4,373 | 4,803 | 5,337 | 5,913 |
| Mississippi. . . . . . | 2,547 | 3,781 | 4,047 | 4,543 | 5,030 |
| North Carolina . . . | 3,200 | 4,624 | 4,940 | 5,478 | 5,935 |
| South Carolina . . . | 2,951 | 4,405 | 4,665 | 5,197 | 5,628 |
| Tennessee . . . . . | 3,079 | 4,506 | 4,804 | 5,305 | 5,785 |
| Virginia . . . . . . . | 3,677 | 5,337 | 5,772 | 6,314 | 6,865 |
| West Virginia . . . . | 3,038 | 4,425 | 4,962 | 5,476 | 5,986 |
| **Southwest** . . . . . . . . | **3,465** | **4,979** | **5,469** | **6,017** | **6,642** |
| Arizona . . . . . . . | 3,614 | 5,123 | 5,391 | 5,944 | 6,509 |
| New Mexico . . . . . | 3,045 | 4,328 | 4,843 | 5,298 | 5,857 |
| Oklahoma . . . . . . | 3,341 | 4,822 | 5,280 | 5,707 | 6,346 |
| Texas . . . . . . . . | 3,507 | 5,048 | 5,584 | 6,166 | 6,803 |
| **Rocky Mountain** . . . . | **3,540** | **5,153** | **5,571** | **6,074** | **6,618** |
| Colorado . . . . . . | 3,838 | 5,495 | 5,987 | 6,527 | 7,160 |
| Idaho . . . . . . . . | 3,243 | 5,028 | 5,179 | 5,678 | 5,980 |
| Montana . . . . . . | 3,395 | 4,976 | 5,388 | 5,669 | 6,125 |
| Utah . . . . . . . . | 3,169 | 4,462 | 4,900 | 5,422 | 5,923 |
| Wyoming . . . . . . | 3,672 | 5,653 | 6,123 | 6,764 | 7,562 |
| **Far West** . . . . . . . . | **4,310** | **5,910** | **6,474** | **7,104** | **7,788** |
| California . . . . . . | 4,423 | 6,015 | 6,575 | 7,219 | 7,911 |
| Nevada . . . . . . . | 4,583 | 6,063 | 6,625 | 7,198 | 7,988 |
| Oregon . . . . . . . | 3,677 | 5,312 | 5,769 | 6,368 | 7,007 |
| Washington . . . . . | 3,997 | 5,647 | 6,298 | 6,878 | 7,528 |
| Alaska . . . . . . . | 4,638 | 7,137 | 9,636 | 10,124 | 10,586 |
| Hawaii . . . . . . . | 4,599 | 6,134 | 6,708 | 7,183 | 7,677 |

---

## America's Richest People

Source: Dan Rottenberg in *Town and Country*, May, 1978.© 1978

Estimated worth. Family or individual (birth date). Source of wealth. Founder.

**$3 Billion to $5 Billion**

**du Ponts,** Wilmington, Del. Chemicals. Eleuthere Irenee (1771-1834), fndr.

**Mellons,** Pittsburgh, Pa. Mellon National Bank. Thomas (1813-1908), fndr.

**$2 Billion to $3 Billion**

**Gettys,** Los Angeles, Cal. Getty Oil. J. Paul (1892-1976), fndr.

**Daniel K. Ludwig** (b. 6/24/1897), N.Y., N.Y. Shipping, real estate.

**$1 Billion to $2 Billion**

**Rockefellers,** N.Y., N.Y. Standard Oil. John D. (1839-1937), fndr.

**$600 Million to $1 Billion**

**Fords,** Detroit, Mich. Ford Motor Co. Henry (1863-1947), fndr.

**Hunts,** Dallas, Tx. Oil. H.L. (1889-1974), fndr.

**Pews,** Philadelphia, Pa. Sun Oil. Joseph N. (1848-1912), fndr.

**Pritzkers,** Chicago, Ill. Hyatt Hotels, real estate, A.N. (b.1897), Jack (b. 1/6/1904), fndrs.

**$400 Million to $600 Million**

**Bechtels,** San Francisco, Cal. Engineering and construction mgmt. Stephen D. Sr. (b. 9/24/1900), Stephen D. Jr. (b. 1925), fndrs.

**Henry Crown** (b. 6/13/1896), Chicago, Ill. General Dynamics.

**Marvin Davis** (b. 1926), Colorado, Col. Oil.

**Michel Fribourg** (b. 1914), N.Y., N.Y. Continental Grain.

**William R. Hewlett** (b. 5/20/1913), Palo Alto, Cal. Hewlett-Packard.

**Klebergs,** Kingsville, Tx. King Ranch, real estate. Richard King (1824-1885), fndr.

**Charles Koch** (b. 11/1/1935), Witchita, Kan. Oil marketing.

**Ray Kroc** (b. 10/5/1902), Chicago, Ill. McDonald's.

**MacMillans,** Wayzata, Minn. Grain exporting. William Cargill (1844-1909), fndr.

**Samuel I. Newhouse** (b. 1895), N.Y., N.Y. Newspapers.

**David Packard** (b. 1913), Palo Alto, Cal. Hewlett-Packard.

**Phipps,** N.Y., N.Y. Carnegie Steel. Henry (1839-1930), fndr.

**Leonard Stern** (b. 3/28/38), N.Y., N.Y. Hartz Mountain pet foods, real estate.

**$300 Million to $400 Million**

**Walter Annenberg** (b. 1908), Philadelphia, Pa. and Palm Springs, Cal. Publishing: TV Guide, others.

**John T. Dorrance Jr.** (b. 2/7/1919), Philadelphia, Pa. Campbell Soup.

**Ernest Gallo** (b. 1909) and Julio Gallo (b. 1910), Modesto, Cal. Wine.

**J. Seward Johnson** (b. 1895), Princeton, N.J. Johnson & Johnson.

**Kennedys,** Hyannis, Mass. Real estate and investments. Joseph P. (1888-1969), fndr.

**Forrest E. Mars** (b. 1904), Washington, D.C. Candy.

**Milton J. Petrie** (b. 1906), N.Y., N.Y. Petri Stores, women's clothing.

**Pitcairns,** Philadelphia, Pa. Pittsburgh Plate Glass. John (1841-1916), fndr.

**Rosenwalds,** Philadelphia, Pa., N.Y., N.Y., New Orleans, La. Sears, Roebuck. Julius (1866-1932), fndr.

**DeWitt Wallace** (b. 11/12/1889), Chappaqua, N.Y. Reader's Digest.

## U.S. Balance of International Payments

Source: Bureau of Economic Analysis, U.S. Commerce Department
(millions of dollars)

| | 1955 | 1960 | 1965 | 1970 | 1974 | 1975 | 1976 | 1977 |
|---|---|---|---|---|---|---|---|---|
| **Exports of goods and services.** . . . . . | 19,948 | 28,861 | 41,090 | 65,659 | 146,086 | 155,655 | 171,274 | 183,214 |
| Merchandise, adjusted . . . . . . . . . . | 14,424 | 19,650 | 26,461 | 42,469 | 98,306 | 107,088 | 114,700 | 120,585 |
| Transfers under U.S. military agency sales contracts . . . . . . . . . . . . . . . . | 200 | 335 | 830 | 1,501 | 2,952 | 3,919 | 5,213 | 7,079 |
| Receipts of income on U.S. investments abroad . . . . . . . . . . . . . . . . . | 2,817 | 4,616 | 7,441 | 11,751 | 27,541 | 25,359 | 29,244 | 32,100 |
| Other services . . . . . . . . . . . . . . . | 2,507 | 4,261 | 6,359 | 9,938 | 17,287 | 19,289 | 22,124 | 23,451 |
| **Imports of goods and services.** . . . . . . | −17,795 | −23,729 | −32,801 | −60,005 | −137,182 | −132,595 | −161,913 | −193,727 |
| Merchandise, adjusted . . . . . . . . . . | −11,527 | −14,758 | −21,510 | −39,866 | −103,649 | −98,041 | −124,047 | −151,644 |
| Direct defense expenditures . . . . . . . | −2,901 | −3,087 | −2,952 | −4,855 | −5,032 | −4,795 | −4,901 | −5,745 |
| Payments of income on foreign investments in the U.S. . . . . . . . . . | −520 | −1,237 | −2,088 | −5,516 | −12,084 | −12,564 | −13,311 | −14,593 |
| Other services . . . . . . . . . . . . . . . | −2,847 | −4,646 | −6,252 | −9,771 | −16,417 | −17,194 | −19,655 | −21,746 |
| Unilateral transfers, net. . . . . . . . . . . | −2,498 | −2,308 | −2,854 | −3,294 | −7,186 | −4,615 | −5,022 | −4,708 |
| U.S. official reserve assets, net . . . . . . | 182 | 2,145 | 1,222 | 2,477 | −1,434 | −607 | −2,530 | −231 |
| U.S. Government assets, other than official reserve assets, net. . . . . . . . . . . . | −310 | −1,100 | −1,605 | −1,589 | 366 | −3,470 | −4,213 | −3,679 |
| U.S. private assets, net. . . . . . . . . . . | −1,255 | −5,144 | −5,335 | −10,228 | −33,643 | −35,368 | −43,865 | −30,740 |
| Foreign official assets in the U.S., net. . . . . ⎫ | | 1,473 | 132 | 6,907 | 10,981 | 6,907 | 18,073 | 37,124 |
| Other foreign assets in the U.S., net . . . . ⎬ | 1,357 | 821 | 607 | −550 | 23,696 | 8,643 | 18,897 | 13,746 |
| Allocations of special drawing rights . . . . ⎭ | — | — | — | 867 | — | — | — | — |
| Statistical discrepancy . . . . . . . . . . . | 371 | −1,019 | −457 | −244 | −1,684 | 5,449 | 9,300 | −998 |
| **Memoranda:** | | | | | | | | |
| Balance on merchandise trade . . . . . . | 2,897 | 4,892 | 4,951 | 2,603 | −5,343 | 9,047 | −9,353 | −31,059 |
| Balance on goods and services . . . . . . | 2,153 | 5,132 | 8,289 | 5,654 | 8,905 | 23,060 | 9,361 | −10,514 |
| Balance on goods, services, and remittances . . . . . . . . . . . . . . . . | 1,556 | 4,496 | 7,243 | 4,096 | 7,194 | 21,339 | 7,483 | −12,445 |
| Balance on current account. . . . . . . . | −345 | 2,824 | 5,435 | 2,360 | 1,719 | 18,445 | 4,339 | −15,221 |

Note.—Details may not add to totals because of rounding.

## Average Weekly Canadian Wages and Salaries, by Province

Source: Canadian Statistical Review, May 1978 (Canadian dollars)

| Year & month | Canada[1] | Nfld. | P.E.I. | N.S. | N.B. | Que. | Ont. | Man. | Sask. | Alta. | B.C. |
|---|---|---|---|---|---|---|---|---|---|---|---|
| 1970 . . . . . . | 126.82 | 117.70 | 83.82 | 104.21 | 104.01 | 122.38 | 131.52 | 115.88 | 114.87 | 128.15 | 137.97 |
| 1974 . . . . . . | 178.09 | 168.48 | 126.92 | 149.98 | 154.58 | 172.89 | 181.43 | 162.71 | 160.99 | 178.72 | 200.55 |
| 1975 . . . . . . | 203.34 | 196.50 | 149.84 | 172.40 | 182.40 | 199.22 | 204.86 | 186.01 | 188.31 | 207.39 | 229.97 |
| 1976 . . . . . . | 228.03 | 221.63 | 170.88 | 193.21 | 202.56 | 222.41 | 228.72 | 208.55 | 214.87 | 236.89 | 259.52 |
| 1977 . . . . . . | 249.95 | 242.43 | 187.73 | 212.09 | 223.34 | 244.77 | 249.46 | 228.28 | 235.61 | 261.96 | 284.13 |
| 1978 Jan. . . . | 255.55 | 247.38 | 194.44 | 219.83 | 230.76 | 252.82 | 252.57 | 231.63 | 242.28 | 270.03 | 291.54 |
| Feb. . . . . | 258.40 | 249.16 | 192.25 | 219.63 | 231.52 | 255.23 | 258.70 | 234.20 | 244.97 | 272.26 | 293.94 |

(1) Includes Yukon and Northwest Territories.

## Canadian Labor Force

Source: Statistics Canada; April, 1978, seasonally adjusted (thousands of workers)

| | Can. | Nfld. | P.E.I. | N.S. | N.B. | Que. | Ont. | Man. | Sask. | Alta. | B.C. |
|---|---|---|---|---|---|---|---|---|---|---|---|
| Labor force . . . . . . . . | 10,931 | 196 | 52 | 346 | 278 | 2,858 | 4,170 | 473 | 430 | 938 | 1,200 |
| Employed . . . . . . . . | 9,996 | 164 | 46 | 308 | 239 | 2,538 | 3,860 | 441 | 406 | 893 | 1,108 |
| Unemployed . . . . . . . | 935 | 32 | 6 | 38 | 39 | 320 | 310 | 32 | 24 | 45 | 92 |
| Percent Unemployed . . | 8.6 | 16.3 | 11.1 | 11.0 | 14.0 | 11.2 | 7.4 | 6.8 | 5.6 | 4.8 | 7.7 |

## Canadian Labor Force Characteristics

Source: Statistics Canada (thousands of workers)

| | Labor force | Total | Employed All workers[1] Agri-culture | Non-agri-culture | Paid workers Total | Non-agri-culture | Unem-ployed | Unem-ployed % |
|---|---|---|---|---|---|---|---|---|
| Year | | | | | | | | |
| 1950 . . . . . . | 5,163 | 4,976 | 1,018 | 3,958 | 3,522 | 3,411 | 186 | 3.6 |
| 1955 . . . . . . | 5,610 | 5,364 | 819 | 4,546 | 4,133 | 4,027 | 245 | 4.4 |
| 1960 . . . . . . | 6,411 | 5,965 | 683 | 5,282 | 4,843 | 4,732 | 446 | 7.0 |
| 1965 . . . . . . | 7,141 | 6,862 | 594 | 6,268 | 5,760 | 5,655 | 280 | 3.9 |
| 1970 . . . . . . | 8,374 | 7,879 | 511 | 7,368 | 6,839 | 6,740 | 495 | 5.9 |
| 1974 . . . . . . | 9,662 | 9,137 | 473 | 8,664 | 8,105 | 8,006 | 525 | 5.4 |
| 1975 . . . . . . | 10,060 | 9,363 | 486 | 8,877 | 8,448 | 8,310 | 697 | 6.9 |
| 1976 . . . . . . | 10,308 | 9,572 | 474 | 9,098 | 8,631 | 8,488 | 736 | 7.1 |
| 1977 . . . . . . | 10,616 | 9,754 | 468 | 9,287 | 8,776 | 8,631 | 862 | 8.1 |

(1) Including self-employed.

# Foreign Direct Investment in the U.S.

Source: Bureau of Economic Analysis, U.S. Commerce Department

(millions of dollars)

| Country | Position at yearend | | Equity and inter-company account inflows (outflows (-))[1] | | Reinvested earnings of incorporated affiliates[2] | | Income[3] | | Interest, dividends, and earnings of unincorporated affiliates[4] | |
|---|---|---|---|---|---|---|---|---|---|---|
| | 1976 | 1977 | 1976 | 1977 | 1976 | 1977 | 1976 | 1977 | 1976 | 1977 |
| Total. . . . . . . . . . . | 30,770 | 34,071 | 2,687 | 1,767 | 1,659 | 1,572 | 3,110 | 2,829 | 1,451 | 1,257 |
| By country: | | | | | | | | | | |
| Canada . . . . . . . . . . | 5,907 | 5,999 | 313 | 36 | 247 | 262 | 479 | 374 | 232 | 112 |
| Europe. . . . . . . . . . | 20,162 | 22,666 | 1,659 | 1,351 | 1,156 | 972 | 2,102 | 1,805 | 946 | 833 |
| Belgium and Luxembourg | (D) | 1,190 | (D) | (D) | (D) | 118 | (D) | 126 | 7 | 9 |
| France . . . . . . . . . . | 1,570 | 1,793 | 126 | 141 | 44 | 81 | 107 | 129 | 63 | 47 |
| Germany . . . . . . . . . | 2,097 | 2,494 | 594 | 299 | 94 | 75 | 136 | 148 | 42 | 72 |
| Italy . . . . . . . . . . . . | (D) | 281 | (D) | (D) | (D) | 13 | (D) | 22 | 13 | 10 |
| Netherlands . . . . . . . | 6,255 | 7,091 | 437 | 297 | 471 | 405 | 698 | 700 | 227 | 295 |
| Denmark and Ireland . . . . | 86 | 114 | −19 | 26 | 6 | 2 | 9 | 4 | 3 | 2 |
| United Kingdom . . . . . . | 5,802 | 6,337 | 402 | 316 | 331 | 220 | 731 | 459 | 401 | 239 |
| Sweden. . . . . . . . . . | 604 | 695 | 50 | 64 | 3 | 26 | 15 | 34 | 12 | 8 |
| Switzerland. . . . . . . . | 2,295 | 2,400 | 94 | 87 | 68 | 24 | 243 | 174 | 175 | 149 |
| Other . . . . . . . . . . . | 263 | 269 | −2 | −3 | 3 | 7 | 6 | 10 | 3 | 3 |
| Japan . . . . . . . . . . . | 1,178 | 1,741 | 544 | 370 | 43 | 203 | 94 | 248 | 51 | 45 |
| Australia, New Zealand, and South Africa . . . . . . . . . | 79 | 51 | 33 | −35 | 12 | 7 | 25 | 23 | 13 | 16 |
| Latin America . . . . . . . | 3,101 | 3,287 | 112 | 47 | 209 | 140 | 387 | 354 | 178 | 215 |
| Panama. . . . . . . . . . | 451 | 428 | 12 | −66 | 62 | 43 | 69 | 47 | 7 | 4 |
| Other Latin America. . . . | 141 | 121 | −31 | −14 | (*) | −6 | 38 | 2 | 38 | 8 |
| Other Western Hemisphere | 2,510 | 2,738 | 131 | 128 | 147 | 102 | 280 | 305 | 133 | 202 |
| Middle East . . . . . . . . | 201 | 194 | −17 | −1 | −1 | −5 | 7 | 2 | 8 | 8 |
| Israel . . . . . . . . . . . | 81 | 87 | (D) | 3 | 2 | 2 | 3 | 4 | 1 | 1 |
| Other . . . . . . . . . . . | 119 | 107 | (D) | −4 | −2 | −8 | 4 | −2 | 6 | 6 |
| Other Africa, Asia, and Pacific | 142 | 134 | 44 | −2 | −8 | −7 | 16 | 22 | 24 | 28 |
| Memorandum: OPEC[5] . . . . . | 163 | 157 | −5 | 1 | −1 | −7 | 5 | −1 | 6 | 6 |
| By Industry: | | | | | | | | | | |
| Petroleum . . . . . . . . . . . | 5,921 | 6,566 | 410 | 42 | 538 | 604 | 803 | 838 | 265 | 234 |
| Manufacturing. . . . . . . . | 12,620 | 13,706 | 625 | 747 | 609 | 377 | 949 | 843 | 340 | 467 |
| Trade . . . . . . . . . . . | 6,123 | 7,208 | 1,064 | 584 | 215 | 499 | 393 | 724 | 178 | 225 |
| Finance . . . . . . . . . . | 1,829 | 2,154 | 214 | 284 | 95 | 45 | 329 | 235 | 234 | 190 |
| Insurance . . . . . . . . . | 2,114 | 2,275 | 319 | 98 | 161 | 63 | 490 | 86 | 330 | 23 |
| Real estate . . . . . . . . | 799 | 779 | 52 | 29 | −28 | −49 | 11 | −14 | 39 | 35 |
| Other. . . . . . . . . . . . | 1,366 | 1,385 | 5 | −14 | 70 | 34 | 135 | 116 | 65 | 83 |

* Less than $500,000 (+). (D) Suppressed to avoid disclosure of data of individual companies. (1) Foreign parents' shares in net changes in capital stock and intercompany accounts with incorporated U.S. affiliates, and in equity in unincorporated U.S. affiliates. (2) Foreign parents' shares in the earnings of incorporated U.S. affiliates (net of U.S. income taxes), less their shares in the gross dividends of these affiliates. (3) Foreign parents' shares in the earnings of U.S. affiliates (net of U.S. income taxes), plus net interest paid on intercompany debt, less withholding taxes on dividends and interest. Also equals interest, dividends, and earnings of unincorporated affiliates plus reinvested earnings of incorporated affiliates. (4) Dividends and interest on intercompany debt credited to foreign parents by affiliates, less interest credited by foreign parents to affiliates, exclusive of withholding taxes; plus foreign parents' shares in the earnings of unincorporated U.S. affiliates. (5) Countries in the Organization of Petroleum Exporting Countries (OPEC) are: Algeria, Ecuador, Gabon, Indonesia, Iran, Iraq, Kuwait, Libya, Nigeria, Qatar, Saudi Arabia, Venezuela, and United Arab Emirates.

---

# Canadian Unemployment Insurance Commission

Source: Canadian Statistical Review, May 1978
(Canadian dollars)

| Year | Claims data | | | Benefits paid | | | | |
|---|---|---|---|---|---|---|---|---|
| | Benefi-ciaries[1][2] (000) | Claims received (000) | Weeks paid | Total paid[3] (thousands of dollars) | Regular | Sickness | Maternity | Retirement | Fishing |
| 1974 . . | 828 | 2,411 | 28,460 | 2,119,213 | 1,924,543 | 98,319 | 81,710 | 4,165 | 22,676 |
| 1975 . . | ... | 2,857 | 37,326 | 3,144,020 | 2,907,715 | 110,989 | 102,161 | 5,834 | 23,621 |
| 1976 . . | 701 | 2,675 | 36,189 | 3,342,246 | 3,019,686 | 129,802 | 139,624 | 18,048 | 28,881 |
| 1977 . . | 750 | 2,807 | 38,701 | 3,884,970 | 3,485,080 | 155,828 | 172,028 | 13,543 | 48,400 |

(1) Refer to the number of persons receiving $1.00 or more in unemployment insurance benefits during a specific week each month. (2) Annual figures are average of 12 months. (3) Includes adjustments for cancellation of warrants and collection of overpayments.

---

# Canadian Provincial Unemployment Rates

Source: Statistics Canada

| Year | Can. | Nfld. | P.E.I. | N.S. | N.B. | Que. | Ont. | Man. | Sask. | Alta. | B.C. |
|---|---|---|---|---|---|---|---|---|---|---|---|
| 1974 . . | 5.4 | 16.7 | ... | 6.7 | 9.2 | 7.3 | 4.1 | 3.1 | 2.8 | 2.7 | 6.0 |
| 1975 . . | 6.9 | 12.2 | ... | 7.8 | 9.9 | 8.1 | 6.3 | 4.5 | 2.9 | 4.1 | 8.5 |
| 1976 . . | 7.1 | 13.6 | 9.8 | 9.6 | 11.1 | 8.7 | 6.2 | 4.7 | 4.0 | 3.9 | 8.6 |
| 1977 . . | 8.1 | 15.9 | 10.0 | 10.7 | 13.4 | 10.3 | 7.0 | 5.9 | 4.5 | 4.4 | 8.5 |

## Total Value of Canadian Construction Work

Source: Statistics Canada (thousands of Canadian dollars)

| Province | 1976 New | 1976 Repair | 1976 Total | 1977 New | 1977 Repair | 1977 Total |
|---|---|---|---|---|---|---|
| Canada | 28,144,940 | 4,986,259 | 33,130,749 | 30,269,232 | 5,483,969 | 35,753,201 |
| Newfoundland | 636,284 | 96,744 | 733,028 | 491,872 | 101,434 | 593,306 |
| Prince Edward Island | 73,777 | 26,735 | 100,512 | 97,129 | 26,668 | 123,797 |
| Nova Scotia | 728,854 | 145,186 | 874,040 | 709,891 | 198,111 | 908,002 |
| New Brunswick | 766,657 | 126,322 | 892,979 | 754,441 | 129,238 | 883,679 |
| Quebec | 6,746,063 | 1,157,117 | 7,903,180 | 7,346,876 | 1,329,642 | 8,676,618 |
| Ontario | 8,370,048 | 1,695,906 | 10,065,954 | 8,618,843 | 1,856,666 | 10,475,509 |
| Manitoba | 1,054,355 | 233,260 | 1,287,615 | 1,153,742 | 232,232 | 1,385,974 |
| Saskatchewan | 1,197,348 | 224,242 | 1,421,590 | 1,322,750 | 234,634 | 1,557,384 |
| Alberta | 4,558,702 | 638,738 | 5,197,440 | 5,509,837 | 685,576 | 6,195,413 |
| British Columbia | 4,012,852 | 642,009 | 4,654,861 | 4,263,851 | 689,768 | 4,953,619 |

Includes residential, commerical, institutional, marine, road, highway and aerodrome, waterworks and sewage systems, and all other construction.

## Canadian Pulpwood, Wood Pulp, and Newsprint

Source: Canadian Statistical Review, May 1978 (thousands of tons)

| Year and month | Pulpwood production (thousand units[1]) | Wood pulp production[2] Total | Mechanical | Chemical | Wood pulp exports[3] | Newsprint production | Newsprint shipments Total | Domestic | Exports[4] |
|---|---|---|---|---|---|---|---|---|---|
| 1974 | 2,640 | 21,168 | 7,870 | 12,001 | 7,057 | 9,548 | 9,597 | 886 | 8,711 |
| 1975 | 16,444 | | | | 5,496 | 7,679 | 7,727 | 864 | 6,863 |
| 1976 | 15,093 | 17,590.2 | 6,843.4 | 10,687.2 | 6,742 | 8,915 | 8,712 | 885 | 7,827 |
| 1977 | 15,603 | 17,762.4 | 6,803.1 | 10,933.9 | 6,715 | 8,988 | 9,005 | 909 | 8,096 |

(1) 100 cu. ft. of solid wood; pulpwood produced for domestic use and excluding exports, but including receipts of purchased round-wood. (2) Total pulp production covers "screenings" which are already included in exports. "Screenings" are excluded throughout from mechanical and chemical pulp. (3) Customs exports. (4) Mill shipments destined for export.

## Telephones in North American Cities

Source: American Telephone and Telegraph Co., and Trans-Canada Telephone Systems (Jan. 1, 1976)

| City | Number | City | Number | City | Number | City | Number |
|---|---|---|---|---|---|---|---|
| Akron | 335,127 | Erie | 137,002 | Memphis | 574,196 | Royal Oaks, Mich. | 194,449 |
| Albany, N.Y. | 165,499 | Eugene-Spring | | Mexico City (area) | 1,526,373 | Sacramento | 486,309 |
| Albuquerque | 274,790 | field, Ore. | 135,232 | Miami | 980,834 | Saginaw, Mich. | 127,006 |
| Alexandria, Va. | 234,001 | Evansville | 123,872 | Milwaukee | 828,572 | St. Louis | 569,676 |
| Allentown, Pa. | 142,044 | Fayetteville | 126,714 | Minn.-St. Paul | 1,546,100 | St. Petersburg | 284,266 |
| Amarillo | 129,022 | Flint | 218,339 | Mobile | 217,449 | Salt Lake City | 457,747 |
| Anaheim, Cal. | 209,653 | Ft. Lauderdale | 368,603 | Modesto, Cal. | 109,753 | San Antonio | 399,796 |
| Anchorage | 115,242 | Fort Wayne | 167,466 | Monterey, Mex. | 192,907 | San Diego (area) | 989,465 |
| Ann Arbor, Mich. | 123,318 | Fort Worth | 336,027 | Montgomery | 144,811 | San Francisco | 794,464 |
| Atlanta, Ga. | 863,622 | Fremont City | 120,378 | Montreal, Que. | 1,238,156 | San Jose | 564,498 |
| Augusta, Ga. | 137,301 | Fresno | 241,449 | Mt. Vernon, N.Y. | 122,393 | San Mateo | 123,897 |
| Austin, Tex. | 296,905 | Gary | 121,767 | Nashville | 387,298 | Santa Ana | 409,708 |
| Bakersfield, Cal. | 160,316 | Grand Rapids | 291,266 | New Haven | 261,890 | Santa Barbara | 130,461 |
| Baltimore | 1,251,557 | Greensboro | 186,324 | New Orleans | 698,428 | Savannah | 140,112 |
| Baton Rouge | 266,974 | Greenville, S.C. | 166,978 | New York | 5,945,045 | Schenectady | 130,056 |
| Birmingham | 430,412 | Guadalajara, Mex. | 204,570 | Newark | 316,942 | Seattle | 605,917 |
| Boise | 115,023 | Halifax, N.S. | 141,503 | Newport Beach | 114,731 | Shreveport | 201,200 |
| Boston | 493,875 | Hamilton, Ont. | 214,815 | Newport News | 202,348 | Skokie, Ill. | 139,700 |
| Bridgeport | 176,307 | Harrisburg | 201,116 | Norfolk (Area) | 436,057 | South Bend | 135,139 |
| Buffalo | 428,459 | Hartford | 311,626 | Oak Lawn, Ill. | 115,732 | Southfield, Mich. | 109,628 |
| Calgary, Alta. | 421,584 | Hayward, Cal. | 137,235 | Oklahoma City | 575,581 | Spokane | 208,993 |
| Cambridge, Mass. | 110,145 | Hollywood, Fla. | 207,901 | Omaha | 422,300 | Springfield, Ill | 145,417 |
| Canton | 124,948 | Honolulu | 347,806 | Orange, Cal. | 108,766 | Springfield, Mass. | 150,654 |
| Cedar Rapids | 121,900 | Houston | 1,299,450 | Orlando | 236,015 | Springfield, Mo. | 119,519 |
| Champaign | 105,213 | Huntington Beach | 126,194 | Ottawa, Ont. | 424,807 | Stamford, Conn. | 110,543 |
| Charleston, S.C. | 195,224 | Huntsville, Ala. | 139,291 | Overland Pk., Kan. | 122,714 | Stockton, Cal. | 134,179 |
| Charleston, W. Va. | 169,461 | Indianapolis | 648,041 | Palo Alto | 150,895 | Sunnyvale, Cal. | 107,379 |
| Charlotte | 332,442 | Jackson, Miss. | 196,069 | Passaic | 138,300 | Syracuse | 257,866 |
| Chattanooga | 236,463 | Jacksonville | 409,591 | Paterson | 123,058 | Tacoma | 229,345 |
| Chicago | 2,540,611 | Jersey City | 178,204 | Pensacola | 141,476 | Tampa | 374,801 |
| Cincinnati | 727,700 | Kalamazoo | 148,278 | Peoria | 190,405 | Toledo | 302,513 |
| Clearwater | 188,532 | Kansas City, Kan. | 166,066 | Philadelphia | 1,675,541 | Topeka | 116,654 |
| Cleveland | 902,453 | Kansas City, Mo. | 337,326 | Phoenix | 872,105 | Toronto, Ont. (Metro). | 1,689,000 |
| Colorado Springs | 199,284 | Kitchener, Ont. | 123,737 | Pittsburgh | 802,937 | Tucson | 293,737 |
| Columbia, S.C. | 256,680 | Knoxville | 206,134 | Pomano | 179,761 | Tulsa | 382,944 |
| Columbus, Ga. | 133,569 | Lancaster, Pa. | 105,690 | Pompano Beach | 163,447 | Union City, N.J. | 124,431 |
| Columbus, Oh. | 467,362 | Lansing | 217,355 | Pontiac | 118,573 | Vancouver, B.C. | 424,736 |
| Corpus Christi | 140,836 | Las Vegas | 328,898 | Portland, Ore. | 472,249 | Victoria, B.C. | 153,908 |
| Covington | 117,526 | Lexington | 153,028 | Providence | 272,322 | Warren, Mich. | 300,385 |
| Dallas | 788,693 | Lincoln | 155,200 | Quebec City | 278,124 | Washington, D.C. | 1,020,944 |
| Davenport | 112,700 | Little Rock | 211,498 | Raleigh | 185,672 | West Palm Beach. | 269,214 |
| Dayton | 364,704 | Livonia, Mich. | 169,857 | Reading, Pa. | 157,210 | Wichita | 227,767 |
| Denver | 1,146,866 | London, Ont. | 183,186 | Regina, Sask. | 120,693 | Wilmington, Del. | 195,770 |
| Des Moines | 265,900 | Los Angeles | | Reno | 127,838 | Windsor, Ont. | 128,236 |
| Detroit | 1,492,384 | (Area) | 5,640,361 | Richmond, Va. | 369,880 | Winnipeg, Man. | 411,583 |
| Durham, N.C. | 106,987 | Louisville | 540,401 | Riverside, Cal. | 151,282 | Winston-Salem | 163,649 |
| East Orange, N.J. | 132,361 | Lubbock, Tex. | 153,782 | Roanoke, Va. | 125,397 | Winter Park | 122,981 |
| Edmonton, Alta. | 384,955 | Macon, Ga. | 113,011 | Rochester, N.Y. | 366,237 | Worchester | 138,924 |
| El Paso | 251,488 | Madison, Wis. | 191,035 | Rockford, Ill. | 180,768 | Youngstown | 186,222 |

# ENERGY

## Nuclear Power Reactors in U.S.

Source: U.S. Energy Research and Development Administration

| State | Site | Plant name | Capacity (kilowatts) | Utility | Commercial operation |
|---|---|---|---|---|---|
| Alabama | Decatur | Browns Ferry Unit 1 | 1,065,000 | Tennessee Valley Authority | 1974 |
| | Decatur | Browns Ferry Unit 2 | 1,065,000 | Tennessee Valley Authority | 1975 |
| | Decatur | Browns Ferry Unit 3 | 1,065,000 | Tennessee Valley Authority | 1977 |
| | Dothan | Joseph M. Farley Unit 1 | 829,000 | Alabama Power Co. | 1977 |
| | Dothan | Joseph M. Farley Unit 2 | 829,000 | Alabama Power Co. | 1979 |
| Arkansas | Russellville | Arkansas Unit 1 | 850,000 | Ark. Power & Light Co. | 1974 |
| | Russellville | Arkansas Unit 2 | 912,000 | Ark. Power & Light Co. | 1978 |
| California | Eureka | Humboldt Bay Unit 3 | 63,000 | Pacific Gas & Electric Co. | 1963 |
| | San Clemente | San Onofre Unit 1 | 430,000 | So. Calif. Ed. & San Diego Gas & El. Co. | 1968 |
| | Diablo Canyon | Diablo Canyon Unit 1 | 1,084,000 | Pacific Gas & Electric Co. | 1977 |
| | Diablo Canyon | Diablo Canyon Unit 2 | 1,106,000 | Pacific Gas & Electric Co. | 1978 |
| | Clay Station | Rancho Seco Station | 918,000 | Sacramento Munic. Utility District. | 1975 |
| Colorado | Platteville | Ft. St. Vrain Station | 330,000 | Public Service Co. of Colorado | 1977 |
| Connecticut | Haddam Neck | Haddam Neck | 575,000 | Conn. Yankee Atomic Power Co. | 1968 |
| | Waterford | Millstone Unit 1 | 652,000 | Northeast Nuclear Energy Co. | 1971 |
| | Waterford | Millstone Unit 2 | 828,000 | Northeast Nuclear Energy Co. | 1975 |
| Florida | Florida City | Turkey Point Unit 3 | 693,000 | Fla. Power & Light Co. | 1972 |
| | Florida City | Turkey Point Unit 4 | 693,000 | Fla. Power & Light Co. | 1973 |
| | Red Level | Crystal River Unit 3 | 825,000 | Florida Power Corp. | 1977 |
| | Ft. Pierce | St. Lucie Unit 1 | 810,000 | Fla. Power & Light Co. | 1976 |
| Georgia | Baxley | Edwin I. Hatch Unit 1 | 786,000 | Georgia Power Co. | 1975 |
| Illinois | Morris | Dresden Unit 1 | 200,000 | Commonwealth Edison Co. | 1960 |
| | Morris | Dresden Unit 2 | 794,000 | Commonwealth Edison Co. | 1970 |
| | Morris | Dresden Unit 3 | 794,000 | Commonwealth Edison Co. | 1971 |
| | Zion | Zion Unit 1 | 1,040,000 | Commonwealth Edison Co. | 197 |
| | Zion | Zion Unit 2 | 1,040,000 | Commonwealth Edison Co. | 197 |
| | Cordova | Quad-Cities Unit 1 | 789,000 | Comm. Ed. Co.-Ia.-Ill. Gas & Elec. Co. | 1972 |
| | Cordova | Quad-Cities Unit 2 | 789,000 | Comm. Ed. Co.-Ia.-Ill. Gas & Elec. Co. | 1972 |
| | Seneca | LaSalle County Unit 1 | 1,078,000 | Commonwealth Edison Co. | 1979 |
| Iowa | Palo | Duane Arnold Unit 1 | 538,000 | Iowa Electric Light and Power Co. | 1975 |
| Maine | Wiscasset | Maine Yankee | 790,000 | Me. Yankee Atomic Power Co. | 1972 |
| Maryland | Lusby | Calvert Cliffs Unit 1 | 845,000 | Baltimore Gas & Electric Co. | 1975 |
| | Lusby | Calvert Cliffs Unit 2 | 845,000 | Baltimore Gas & Electric Co. | 1977 |
| Massachusetts | Rowe | Yankee Station | 175,000 | Yankee Atomic Electric Co. | 1961 |
| | Plymouth | Pilgrim Unit 1 | 655,000 | Boston Edison Co. | 1972 |
| Michigan | Big Rock Point | Big Rock Point | 72,000 | Consumers Power Co. | 1965 |
| | South Haven | Palisades Station | 668,000 | Consumers Power Co. | 1971 |
| | Bridgman | Donald C. Cook Unit 1 | 1,054,000 | Ind. & Michigan Electric Co. | 1975 |
| | Bridgman | Donald C. Cook Unit 2 | 1,060,000 | Ind. & Michigan Electric Co. | 1978 |
| Minnesota | Monticello | Monticello | 545,000 | Northern States Power Co. | 1971 |
| | Red Wing | Prairie Island Unit 1 | 530,000 | Northern States Power Co. | 1973 |
| | Red Wing | Prairie Island Unit 2 | 530,000 | Northern States Power Co. | 1974 |
| Nebraska | Fort Calhoun | Ft. Calhoun Unit 1 | 457,000 | Omaha Public Power District | 1973 |
| | Brownville | Cooper Station | 778,000 | Neb. Pub. Power Dist.-Ia. Power & Light Co. | 1974 |
| New Jersey | Toms River | Oyster Creek Unit 1 | 650,000 | Jersey Central Power & Light Co. | 1969 |
| | Salem | Salem Unit 1 | 1,090,000 | Public Service Electric & Gas, N.J. | 1977 |
| | Salem | Salem Unit 2 | 1,115,000 | Public Service Electric & Gas, N.J. | 1979 |
| New York | Indian Point | Indian Point Unit 1 | 265,000 | Consolidated Edison Co. | 1962 |
| | Indian Point | Indian Point Unit 2 | 873,000 | Consolidated Edison Co. | 1973 |
| | Indian Point | Indian Point Unit 3 | 873,000 | Power Authority of State of N.Y. | 1976 |
| | Scriba | Nine Mile Point Unit 1 | 610,000 | Niagara Mohawk Power Co. | 1969 |
| | Ontario | R.E. Ginna Unit 1 | 490,000 | Rochester Gas & Electric Co. | 1970 |
| | Brookhaven | Shoreham Station | 819,000 | Long Island Lighting Co. | 1979 |
| | Scriba | James A. FitzPatrick | 821,000 | Power Authority of State of N.Y. | 1975 |
| North Carolina | Southport | Brunswick Steam Unit 1 | 821,000 | Carolina Power & Light Co. | 1977 |
| | Southport | Brunswick Steam Unit 2 | 821,000 | Carolina Power & Light Co. | 1975 |
| | Cowans Ford Dam. | Wm. B. McGuire Unit 1 | 1,180,000 | Duke Power Co. | 1979 |
| Ohio | Oak Harbor | Davis-Besse Unit 1 | 906,000 | Toledo Edison-Cleveland El. Illum. Co. | 1977 |
| | Moscow | Wm. H. Zimmer Unit 1 | 810,000 | Cincinnati Gas & Electric Co. | 1979 |
| Oregon | Prescott | Trojan Unit 1 | 1,130,000 | Portland Gen. Electric Co. | 1975 |
| Pennsylvania | Peach Bottom | Peach Bottom Unit 2 | 1,065,000 | Philadelphia Electric Co. | 1974 |
| | Peach Bottom | Peach Bottom Unit 3 | 1,065,000 | Philadelphia Electric Co. | 1974 |
| | Shippingport | Shippingport Station | 90,000 | U.S. Energy Research & Devel. Admin. | 1957 |
| | Shippingport | Beaver Valley Unit 1 | 852,000 | Duquesne Light Co.-Ohio Edison Co. | 1977 |
| | Middletown | Three Mile Island Unit 1 | 819,000 | Metropolitan Edison Co. | 1974 |
| | Middletown | Three Mile Island Unit 2 | 906,000 | Jersey Central Power & Light Co. | 1978 |
| South Carolina | Hartsville | H. B. Robinson Unit 2 | 712,000 | Carolina Power & Light Co. | 1971 |
| | Seneca | Oconee Unit 1 | 887,000 | Duke Power Co. | 1973 |
| | Seneca | Oconee Unit 2 | 887,000 | Duke Power Co. | 1974 |
| | Seneca | Oconee Unit 3 | 887,000 | Duke Power Co. | 1974 |
| Tennessee | Daisy | Sequoyah Unit 1 | 1,148,000 | Tennessee Valley Authority | 1978 |
| | Daisy | Sequoyah Unit 2 | 1,148,000 | Tennessee Valley Authority | 1979 |
| | Spring City | Watts Bar Unit 1 | 1,177,000 | Tennessee Valley Authority | 1979 |
| Vermont | Vernon | Vermont Yankee Station | 514,000 | Vt. Yankee Nuclear Power Corp. | 1972 |
| Virginia | Gravel Neck | Surry Unit 1 | 822,000 | Va. Electric & Power Co. | 1972 |
| | Gravel Neck | Surry Unit 2 | 822,000 | Va. Electric & Power Co. | 1973 |
| | Mineral | North Anna Unit 1 | 907,000 | Va. Electric & Power Co. | 1977 |
| | Mineral | North Anna Unit 2 | 907,000 | Va. Electric & Power Co. | 1977 |
| Washington | Richland | N-Reactor/WPPSS Steam. | 850,000 | U.S. Energy Research & Devel. Admin. | 1966 |
| Wisconsin | La Crosse | Genoa Station | 50,000 | Dairyland Power Cooperative | 1969 |
| | Two Creeks | Point Beach Unit 1 | 497,000 | Wis. Mich. Power Co. | 1970 |
| | Two Creeks | Point Beach Unit 2 | 497,000 | Wis. Mich. Power Co. | 1973 |
| | Carlton | Kewaunee Unit 1 | 535,000 | Wis. Public Service Corp. | 1974 |

Nuclear plant capacity (kilowatts): operable 47,606,000; being built 95,308,500; planned 87,914,000; Total 230,828,500.

## World Nuclear Power

Source: Energy Information Agency, U.S. Energy Department

| Country | Operational reactors | Capacity[1] | Generation[2] May 1978 | Country | Operational reactors | Capacity[1] | Generation[2] May 1978 |
|---|---|---|---|---|---|---|---|
| Argentina | 1 | 370,000 | 0.270 | Japan | 15 | 8,780,000 | 3.702 |
| Belgium | 3 | 1,740,000 | 1.287 | Netherlands | 2 | 520,000 | 0.380 |
| Canada | 8 | 4,790,000 | 2.469 | Pakistan | 1 | 140,000 | NA |
| Finland | 1 | 440,000 | 0.309 | Spain | 3 | 1,120,000 | 0.113 |
| France | 13 | 5,890,000 | 2.113 | Sweden | 6 | 3,850,000 | 1.543 |
| Germany, W. | 10 | 6,410,000 | 3.134 | Switzerland | 3 | 1,060,000 | 0.736 |
| Great Britain | 31 | 8,100,000 | 2.361 | Taiwan | 1 | 640,000 | 0.205 |
| India | 3 | 620,000 | 0.223 | U.S. | 67 | 50,470,000 | 21.262 |
| Italy | 3 | 630,000 | 0.370 | Total[2] | 171 | 95,570,000 | 40.477 |

(1) Kilowatts. (2) Billion kilowatt-hours. (3) Non-Communist countries. (NA) Not available.

---

## World Electricity Production

Source: UN Monthly Bulletin of Statistics, July 1978. (1977 production, in million kilowatt-hours.)

| | | | | | | | |
|---|---|---|---|---|---|---|---|
| U.S. | 2,209,404 | Italy | 166,572 | Sweden | 87,576 | Romania | 58,272 |
| USSR | 1,149,996 | China[1] | 121,000 | Australia | 82,464 | Mexico | 50,052 |
| Japan | 464,522 | Poland | 109,368 | South Africa | 80,196 | Yugoslvia | 48,636 |
| W. Germany | 335,316 | Spain | 93,708 | Norway | 72,492 | Belgium | 47,100 |
| Canada | 316,548 | E. Germany | 91,992 | Czechoslovakia | 66,300 | Switzerland | 44,124 |
| United Kingdom | 283,476 | India[2] | 90,840 | Netherlands | 58,296 | Austria | 37,680 |
| France | 210,348 | Brazil[3] | 88,380 | | | | |

(1) Estimate, 1975. (2) Excluding generation by industrial establishments. (3) 1976.

---

## World Production of Crude Petroleum

Source: Bureau of Mines, U.S. Interior Department
(thousands of 42-gallon barrels)

| Country | 1976 | 1977 | Percent of change | Country | 1976 | 1977 | Percent of change |
|---|---|---|---|---|---|---|---|
| **North America:** | | | | Turkey. . . . . | 25,254 | 19,428 | +4.5 |
| Canada . . . . . | 488,680 | 482,021 | −1.4 | United Arab | | | |
| Mexico[1] . . . . . | 327,285 | 358,090 | +9.4 | Emirates . . . . | 692,106 | 733,285 | +2.9 |
| United States[1] . | 2,971,686 | 2,985,360 | +0.3 | Total. . . . . . | 8,049,566 | 8,113,037 | 0.0 |
| Cuba (e). . . . . | 775 | 775 | 0.0 | **Africa:** | | | |
| Total. . . . . . | 3,788,426 | 3,825,471 | +0.9 | Algeria[1] . . . . . | 383,816 | 409,864 | +6.8 |
| **South America:** | | | | Angola. . . . . . | 33,217 | 70,810 | +92.6 |
| Argentina . . . | 145,561 | 157,248 | +8.0 | Congo . . . . . . | 14,274 | 12,045 | −15.6 |
| Barbados . . . . | 110 | 124 | +12.7 | Egypt . . . . . . | 120,180 | 150,925 | +25.6 |
| Bolivia . . . . . | 14,856 | 12,840 | −13.6 | Gabon. . . . . . | 82,042 | 81,144 | −1.1 |
| Brazil . . . . . . | 61,026 | 60,800 | −0.4 | Libya. . . . . . . | 704,011 | 759,200 | +7.8 |
| Chile. . . . . . . | 8,372 | 8,030 | −4.1 | Morocco. . . . . | 35 | 167 | +377.1 |
| Colombia . . . . | 53,376 | 50,735 | −5.0 | Nigeria . . . . . | 756,064 | 765,473 | +1.2 |
| Ecuador . . . . | 68,463 | 66,954 | −2.1 | Tunisia . . . . . | 28,600 | 34,675 | +21.2 |
| Peru . . . . . . | 27,936 | 33,276 | +19.1 | Zaire. . . . . . . | 9,075 | 8,255 | −9.0 |
| Trinidad . . . . . | 81,984 | 83,950 | +8.1 | Total. . . . . . | 2,131,315 | 2,292,558 | +7.4 |
| Venezuela . . . | 839,737 | 816,818 | −2.7 | **Asian area:** | | | |
| Total. . . . . . | 1,301,421 | 1,290,775 | −0.5 | Australia . . . . | 152,522 | 156,987 | +2.9 |
| **Western Europe:** | | | | Brunei . . . . . . | 75,030 | 76,650 | +3.0 |
| Austria. . . . . . | 13,466 | 12,462 | −7.5 | Burma. . . . . . | 8,183 | 10,400 | +27.1 |
| Denmark . . . . | 1,098 | 3,285 | +120.2 | India . . . . . . . | 64,632 | 75,787 | +17.3 |
| France. . . . . . | 7,710 | 7,557 | −2.0 | Indonesia . . . . | 550,319 | 615,123 | +11.8 |
| Germany, West. | 39,902 | 39,012 | −2.2 | Japan . . . . . . | 4,241 | 4,334 | +2.2 |
| Italy . . . . . . . | 7,553 | 7,889 | +4.5 | Malaysia . . . . | 60,547 | 66,984 | +10.6 |
| Netherlands. . . | 10,538 | 9,420 | −10.6 | New Zealand[1] . . | 3,776 | (e) 5,000 | +32.4 |
| Norway . . . . . | 101,900 | 101,887 | 0.0 | Pakistan. . . . . | 2,562 | 3,720 | +45.2 |
| Spain . . . . . . | 11,552 | 6,898 | −40.3 | Taiwan . . . . . | 1,555 | (e) 1,600 | +2.9 |
| United Kingdom | 89,006 | 271,653 | +205.2 | Thailand. . . . . | 57 | 103 | +80.7 |
| Yugoslavia . . . | 28,739 | 29,265 | +1.8 | Total. . . . . . | 921,068 | 1,016,688 | +10.2 |
| Total. . . . . . | 311,464 | 489,328 | +56.9 | **East Europe and China:** | | | |
| **Middle East:** | | | | Albania (e) . . . | 15,012 | 15,000 | −0.1 |
| Bahrain . . . . . | 21,228 | 21,236 | −0.2 | Bulgaria (e) . . . | 730 | 730 | 0.0 |
| Iran . . . . . . . | 2,168,237 | 2,080,051 | −4.1 | Czechoslovakia | (e)949 | 730 | −23.1 |
| Iraq . . . . . . . | 834,810 | 826,908 | −6.5 | Germany, East | | | |
| Israel . . . . . . | 268 | 256 | −4.5 | (e). . . . . . . | 2,500 | 2,500 | 0.0 |
| Kuwait . . . . . | 700,000 | 650,795 | −7.0 | Hungary . . . . . | 16,343 | 16,786 | +2.7 |
| Neutral Zone . . | 171,669 | 136,072 | −20.7 | China . . . . . . | 645,897 | 653,350 | +1.2 |
| Oman . . . . . . | 133,795 | 123,626 | −7.6 | Poland. . . . . . | 3,376 | 3,285 | −2.7 |
| Qatar . . . . . . | 178,120 | 162,285 | −10.7 | Romania . . . . | 109,559 | 109,186 | −0.3 |
| Saudi Arabia . . | 3,053,887 | 3,290,000 | +7.7 | USSR[1]. . . . . . | 3,822,000 | 3,991,050 | +4.4 |
| Syria . . . . . . | 69,685 | 74,095 | +6.3 | Total. . . . . . | 4,615,621 | 4,792,617 | +3.8 |
| | | | | Total World. . | 21,118,880 | 21,826,249 | +3.0 |

(e) Estimate. (1) Includes condensate.

## World Oil Supply and Demand Projections

Source: Central Intelligence Agency
(million barrels per day)

| | 1976 | 1977 | 1978 | 1979 | 1980 | 1985 |
|---|---|---|---|---|---|---|
| **Demand** (non-Communist) | **48.4** | **49.8-50.5** | **51.2-52.2** | **52.5-54.1** | **54.9-56.7** | **68.3-72.6** |
| United States | 16.7 | 17.8-18.3 | 18.2-19.0 | 18.4-19.7 | 19.3-20.7 | 22.2-25.6 |
| West Europe | 13.6 | 13.9-14.3 | 13.8-14.2 | 13.7-14.4 | 13.7-14.7 | 15.8-18.2 |
| Japan | 5.2 | 5.3-5.4 | 5.5-5.8 | 5.9-6.2 | 6.2-6.6 | 8.1-8.8 |
| Canada | 2.0 | 2.0-2.1 | 2.1-2.2 | 2.2-2.3 | 2.2-2.4 | 2.9-3.5 |
| Other developed[1] | 1.2 | 1.2 | 1.3 | 1.3 | 1.4 | 1.9 |
| Non-OPEC LDCs[2] | 6.7 | 7.1 | 7.5 | 7.8 | 8.5 | 12.0 |
| OPEC[3] countries | 2.1 | 2.3 | 2.5 | 2.8 | 3.0 | 4.0 |
| Other demand[4] | 0.9 | 0 | 0 | 0 | 0 | 0 |
| **Non-OPEC supply**[5] | **17.5** | **18.5** | **20.1** | **21.2** | **22.0** | **20.4-22.4** |
| United States | 9.7 | 9.6 | 10.2 | 10.2 | 10.0 | 10.0-11.0 |
| West Europe | 0.9 | 1.8 | 2.5 | 3.1 | 3.7 | 4.0-5.0 |
| Japan | 0 | 0 | 0 | 0 | 0 | 0.1 |
| Canada | 1.6 | 1.6 | 1.5 | 1.5 | 1.5 | 1.3-1.5 |
| Other developed[1] | 0.5 | 0.5 | 0.5 | 0.5 | 0.5 | 0.4 |
| Non-OPEC LDCs | 3.7 | 4.1 | 4.6 | 5.3 | 6.1 | 8.0-9.0 |
| Net Communist trade[6] | | | | | | |
| USSR-East Europe | 0.9 | 0.7 | 0.5 | 0.2 | — 0.3 | — 3.5 — 4.5 |
| China | 0.2 | 0.2 | 0.3 | 0.4 | 0.5 | 0 |
| **Required OPEC production**[7] | **30.9** | **31.3-32.0** | **31.1-32.1** | **31.3-32.9** | **32.9-34.7** | **46.7-51.2** |

(1) Australia, Israel, New Zealand, South Africa. (2) LDCs: less developed countries. (3) OPEC: Organization of Petroleum Exporting Countries. (4) Including stock changes and statistical discrepancy. (5) Including natural gas liquids. (6) Difference of Communist countries' exports and imports; minus sign indicates net Communist imports. (7) OPEC production capacity will reach 27.5-29.4 million barrels per day by 1985, exclusive of Saudi Arabia; Saudi projections are uncertain.

---

## U.S. Natural Gas Reserves

Source: American Gas Association

Estimates of proved reserves, which can be recovered under existing economic and operating conditions.

| Year | Natural gas (millions of cu. ft.) Discoveries, revisions and extensions | Change in underground storage[1] | Production[4] | Proved reserves at end of year | Natural gas liquids (1,000 42-gallon barrels) Discoveries, revisions and extensions | Production[4] | Proved reserves at end of year |
|---|---|---|---|---|---|---|---|
| 1946 | 17,632,864 | (2) | 4,915,774 | 159,703,813 | (2) | 129,262 | 3,163,219 |
| 1947 | 10,921,187 | (2) | 5,599,235 | 165,025,765 | 251,538 | 160,782 | 3,253,975 |
| 1948 | 13,823,090 | 51,202 | 5,975,001 | 172,925,056 | 470,557 | 183,749 | 3,540,783 |
| 1949 | 12,605,615 | 82,146 | 6,211,124 | 179,401,693 | 386,776 | 198,547 | 3,729,012 |
| 1950 | 11,985,361 | 52,935 | 6,855,244 | 184,584,745 | 766,062 | 227,411 | 4,267,663 |
| 1951 | 15,965,808 | 132,030 | 7,923,673 | 192,758,910 | 723,991 | 267,052 | 4,724,602 |
| 1952 | 14,267,606 | 197,766 | 8,592,716 | 198,631,566 | 556,838 | 284,789 | 4,996,651 |
| 1953 | 20,341,933 | 513,629[3] | 9,188,365 | 210,298,763 | 743,969 | 302,698 | 5,437,922 |
| 1954 | 9,547,074 | 90,408 | 9,375,314 | 210,560,931 | 107,350 | 300,815 | 5,244,457 |
| 1955 | 21,897,616 | 87,164 | 10,063,167 | 222,482,544 | 514,508 | 320,400 | 5,438,565 |
| 1956 | 24,716,115 | 133,241 | 10,848,685 | 236,483,215 | 809,820 | 346,053 | 5,902,332 |
| 1957 | 20,008,051 | 178,761 | 11,439,890 | 245,230,137 | 137,392 | 352,364 | 5,687,360 |
| 1958 | 18,896,724 | 57,582 | 11,422,651 | 252,761,792 | 858,206 | 341,548 | 6,204,018 |
| 1959 | 20,621,249 | 160,453 | 12,373,063 | 261,170,431 | 703,444 | 385,154 | 6,522,308 |
| 1960 | 13,893,978 | 281,273 | 13,019,356 | 262,326,326 | 725,130 | 431,379 | 6,816,059 |
| 1961 | 17,166,421 | 159,544 | 13,378,649 | 266,273,642 | 694,686 | 461,649 | 7,049,096 |
| 1962 | 19,483,958 | 159,231 | 13,637,973 | 272,278,858 | 732,549 | 470,128 | 7,311,517 |
| 1963 | 18,164,667 | 253,733 | 14,546,025 | 276,151,233 | 878,120 | 515,659 | 7,673,978 |
| 1964 | 20,252,139 | 195,110 | 15,347,028 | 281,251,454 | 608,744 | 536,090 | 7,746,632 |
| 1965 | 21,319,279 | 150,483 | 16,252,293 | 286,468,923 | 832,312 | 555,410 | 8,023,534 |
| 1966 | 20,220,432 | 134,523 | 17,491,073 | 289,332,805 | 894,116 | 588,684 | 8,328,966 |
| 1967 | 21,804,333 | 151,403 | 18,380,838 | 292,907,703 | 929,758 | 644,493 | 8,614,231 |
| 1968 | 14,697,008 | 118,568 | 19,373,427 | 287,349,852 | 685,659 | 701,782 | 8,598,108 |
| 1969 | 8,375,004 | 107,169 | 20,723,190 | 275,108,835 | 281,028 | 735,962 | 8,143,174 |
| 1970 | 37,196,359 | 402,018 | 21,960,804 | 290,746,408 | 307,579 | 747,812 | 7,702,941 |
| 1971 | 9,825,421 | 310,301 | 22,076,512 | 278,805,618 | 347,720 | 746,434 | 7,304,227 |
| 1972 | 9,634,563 | 156,563 | 22,511,898 | 266,084,846 | 238,273 | 755,941 | 6,786,559 |
| 1973 | 6,825,049 | (354,282) | 22,605,406 | 249,950,207 | 408,979 | 740,831 | 6,454,707 |
| 1974 | 8,679,184 | (178,424) | 21,318,470 | 237,132,497 | 619,841 | 724,099 | 6,350,449 |
| 1975 | 10,483,688 | 302,561 | 19,718,570 | 228,200,176 | 618,504 | 701,123 | 6,267,830 |
| 1976 | 7,555,468 | (187,550) | 19,542,020 | 216,026,074 | 834,766 | 700,629 | 6,401,967 |
| 1977 | 11,851,924 | 446,930 | 19,447,050 | 208,877,878 | 291,171 | 698,773 | 5,994,365 |

(1) Parentheses indicate decline. (2) Not estimated. (3) All native gas in storage reservoirs formerly classified as proved reserves is included in this figure. (4) Preliminary net production.

## U.S. Crude Petroleum Production by Chief States

Source: Bureau of Mines, U.S. Interior Department (thousands of 42-gallon barrels)

| Year | Ark. | Cal. | Ill. | Kan. | La. | Miss. | N.M. | N.D. | Okla. | Tex. | Wyo. |
|------|------|------|------|------|------|-------|------|------|-------|------|------|
| 1950 | 31,108 | 327,607 | 62,028 | 107,586 | 208,965 | 38,236 | 47,367 | .... | 164,599 | 829,874 | 61,631 |
| 1960 | 30,117 | 305,352 | 77,341 | 113,453 | 400,832 | 51,673 | 107,380 | 21,992 | 192,913 | 927,479 | 133,910 |
| 1965 | 25,930 | 316,428 | 63,708 | 104,733 | 594,853 | 56,183 | 119,166 | 26,350 | 203,441 | 1,000,749 | 138,314 |
| 1970 | 18,035 | 372,191 | 43,747 | 84,853 | 906,907 | 65,119 | 128,184 | 21,998 | 223,574 | 1,249,697 | 160,345 |
| 1972 | 18,519 | 347,022 | 34,874 | 73,744 | 891,827 | 61,100 | 110,525 | 20,624 | 207,633 | 1,301,685 | 140,011 |
| 1973 | 18,016 | 336,075 | 30,669 | 66,227 | 831,524 | 56,102 | 100,986 | 20,235 | 191,204 | 1,294,671 | 141,914 |
| 1974 | 16,527 | 323,003 | 27,553 | 61,691 | 737,324 | 50,779 | 98,695 | 19,697 | 177,785 | 1,262,126 | 139,997 |
| 1975 | 16,133 | 322,199 | 26,067 | 59,106 | 650,840 | 46,614 | 95,063 | 20,452 | 163,123 | 1,221,929 | 135,943 |
| 1976 | 18,097 | 326,021 | 26,272 | 58,714 | 606,501 | 46,072 | 92,130 | 21,725 | 161,426 | 1,189,523 | 134,149 |
| 1977[1] | 20,200 | 349,714 | 25,722 | 57,496 | 562,868 | 43,020 | 87,085 | 23,193 | 156,381 | 1,137,542 | 111,767 |

(1) Preliminary.

## U.S. Total Fuel Supply and Demand

Source: Bureau of Mines, U.S. Interior Department

(thousands of 42-gallon barrels)

| Year | Gasoline[1] Production | Total demand | Kerosene[2] Production | Total demand | Distillate fuel oil Production | Total demand | Residual fuel oil Production | Total demand |
|------|------------|--------------|------------|--------------|------------|--------------|------------|--------------|
| 1950[3] | 1,024,181 | 1,019,011 | 118,512 | 119,922 | 398,912 | 75,435 | 425,217 | 570,021 |
| 1960 | 1,522,497 | 1,525,126 | 136,842 | 133,188 | 667,050 | 695,165 | 332,147 | 577,934 |
| 1965 | 1,733,258 | 1,756,419 | 201,788 | 219,932 | 765,430 | 779,644 | 268,567 | 601,893 |
| 1970 | 2,135,838 | 2,165,598 | 313,544 | 358,146 | 897,097 | 928,109 | 257,510 | 824,073 |
| 1971 | 2,231,157 | 2,246,025 | 306,847 | 365,308 | 912,097 | 974,077 | 274,684 | 851,262 |
| 1972 | 2,352,310 | 2,384,734 | 313,554 | 379,984 | 963,625 | 1,067,321 | 292,519 | 937,707 |
| 1973 | 2,434,943 | 2,487,580 | 327,818 | 384,063 | 1,030,178 | 1,127,548 | 354,597 | 1,029,165 |
| 1974 | 2,371,004 | 2,436,681 | 290,780 | 346,706 | 974,025 | 1,076,771 | 390,491 | 968,185 |
| 1975 | 2,420,962 | 2,479,857 | 308,034 | 347,399 | 968,650 | 1,040,838 | 450,957 | 903,914 |
| 1976 | 2,549,627 | 2,597,305 | 323,114 | 350,565 | 1,070,209 | 1,146,695 | 503,953 | 1,025,148 |
| 1977[4] | 2,613,400 | 2,664,661 | 349,668 | 367,147 | 1,197,132 | 1,223,328 | 638,989 | 1,116,612 |

Demand usually exceeds the production; the difference is made up by dipping into stocks or by imports. (1) Includes special naphtha production. (2) Includes kerosene type jet fuel. (3) 1950 figures are on a 48-state basis. (4) Preliminary.

## U.S. Motor Fuel Supply and Demand

Source: Bureau of Mines, U.S. Interior Department

(thousands of 42-gallon barrels)

| Year | Supply[1] Production | Daily average | Demand Domestic | Export | Year | Supply[1] Production | Daily average | Demand Domestic | Export |
|------|------------|---------------|----------|--------|------|------------|---------------|----------|--------|
| 1945 | 793,431 | 2,174 | 696,333 | 88,059 | 1972 | 2,352,310 | 6,445 | 2,382,569 | 2,165 |
| 1950 | 1,024,481 | 2,806 | 994,290 | 24,721 | 1973 | 2,434,943 | 6,671 | 2,484,262 | 3,318 |
| 1955 | 1,373,950 | 3,764 | 1,329,788 | 34,521 | 1974 | 2,371,004 | 6,496 | 2,434,368 | 2,313 |
| 1960[2] | 1,522,497 | 4,171 | 1,511,670 | 13,456 | 1975 | 2,420,962 | 6,633 | 2,477,786 | 2,071 |
| 1965 | 1,733,258 | 4,749 | 1,750,028 | 6,391 | 1976 | 2,549,627 | 6,966 | 2,597,305 | 3,807 |
| 1970 | 2,135,838 | 5,852 | 2,162,642 | 2,956 | 1977[3] | 2,613,400 | 7,160 | 2,664,661 | 2,155 |
| 1971 | 2,231,157 | 6,113 | 2,242,921 | 3,104 | | | | | |

(1) Includes special naphtha. (2) Beginning with 1960 Alaska and Hawaii are included. (3) Preliminary.

## Coal and Coke Production in the U.S.

Source: Bureau of Mines, U.S. Interior Department

| Year | Penn. anthracite Production 1,000 net tons | Value $1,000 | Bituminous Production 1,000 net tons | Value $1,000 | Year | Penn. anthracite Production 1,000 net tons | Value $1,000 | Bituminous Production 1,000 net tons | Value $1,000 |
|------|------------|--------------|------------|--------------|------|------------|--------------|------------|--------------|
| 1945 | 54,934 | 323,944 | 577,617 | 1,768,204 | 1968 | 11,461 | 97,245 | 545,245 | 2,546,340 |
| 1950 | 44,077 | 392,398 | 516,311 | 2,500,374 | 1969 | 10,473 | 100,769 | 560,505 | 2,795,509 |
| 1955 | 26,205 | 206,097 | 464,633 | 2,092,383 | 1970 | 9,729 | 105,341 | 602,932 | 3,772,662 |
| 1960 | 18,817 | 147,116 | 415,512 | 1,950,421 | 1971 | 8,727 | 103,469 | 552,192 | 3,901,496 |
| 1962 | 16,894 | 134,094 | 422,149 | 1,891,555 | 1972 | 7,106 | 85,251 | 595,386 | 4,561,983 |
| 1963 | 18,267 | 153,503 | 458,928 | 2,013,390 | 1973 | 6,830 | 90,260 | 591,738 | 5,049,612 |
| 1964 | 17,184 | 148,648 | 486,998 | 2,165,582 | 1974 | 6,617 | 144,695 | 603,406 | 9,502,347 |
| 1965 | 14,866 | 122,021 | 512,088 | 2,276,022 | 1975 | 6,203 | 198,481 | 648,438 | 12,472,486 |
| 1966 | 12,941 | 100,663 | 533,881 | 2,421,293 | 1976 | 6,228 | 209,234 | 678,685 | 13,189,481 |
| 1967 | 12,256 | 96,160 | 552,026 | 2,555,377 | 1977 est. | 6,200 | 217,000 | 688,575 | 14,100,000 |

**Coke production** (1,000 net tons—value in $1,000)—(1968) 63,653, $1,157,359; (1969) 64,757, $1,355,260; (1970) 66,525, $1,849,160; (1971) 57,436, $1,745,693; (1972) 60,507, $2,012,486; (1973) 64,325, $2,442,151; (1974) 61,581, $4,510,150; (1975) 57,207, $4,835,654; (1976) 58,333, $5,021,616.

**Coke exports** (short tons)—(1968) 791,909; (1969) 1,629,000; (1970) 2,478,338; (1971) 1,508,639; (1972) 1,231,633; (1973) 1,394,980; (1974) 1,277,681; (1975) 1,272,906; (1976) 1,314,725; (1977) 1,240,577. **imports**—(1968) 94,085; (1969) 173,052; (1970) 152,879; (1971) 173,914; (1972) 185,023; (1973) 1,077,737; (1974) 3,540,326; (1975) 1,818,981; (1976) 1,311,472; (1977) 1,829,110.

**Anthracite exports** (net tons)—(1966) 766,025; (1967) 594,797; (1968) 518,159; (1969) 627,492; (1970) 789,499; (1971) 671,024; (1972) 743,451; (1973) 716,546; (1974) 735,173; (1975) 639,601; (1976) 615,167; (1977) 624,908.

## U.S. Petroleum and Natural Gas Production

Source: Bureau of Mines, U.S. Interior Department

| Year | Crude oil Production 1,000 bbls. | Value $1,000 | Natural gas liquids Production 1,000 bbls. | Value $1,000 | Total oil & N.G.L. 1,000 bbls. | Natural gas Marketed mil. cu. ft. | Value $1,000 |
|---|---|---|---|---|---|---|---|
| 1945 . . . . . | 1,713,655 | 2,094,250 | 112,004 | 187,564 | 1,828,539 | 3,944,021 | 191,006 |
| 1950 . . . . . | 1,973,574 | 4,963,380 | 181,961 | 419,605 | 2,155,693 | 6,282,060 | 408,521 |
| 1955 . . . . . | 2,484,428 | 6,870,380 | 281,371 | 619,006 | 2,766,325 | 9,405,351 | 978,357 |
| 1960 . . . . . | 2,574,933 | 7,420,181 | 340,157 | 808,385 | 2,915,365 | 12,771,038 | 1,789,970 |
| 1965 . . . . | 2,848,514 | 8,158,298 | 441,556 | 911,603 | 3,290,083 | 16,042,753 | 2,494,542 |
| 1970 . . . . | 3,517,450 | 11,173,726 | 605,916 | 1,275,112 | 4,123,366 | 21,920,642 | 3,745,680 |
| 1975 . . . . | 3,056,779 | 23,116,059 | 595,958 | 2,772,588 | 3,652,737 | 20,108,661 | 8,945,062 |
| 1976 . . . . | 2,976,180 | 24,229,540 | 587,045 | 3,284,089 | 3,563,225 | 19,952,438 | 11,571,776 |
| 1977[1] | 2,986,710 | 25,397,307 | 584,900 | 4,386,750 | 3,571,610 | 19,924,671 | 15,522,658 |

(1) Preliminary.

## Production of Electricity in the U.S. by Source

Source: Federal Power Commission

Amounts include both privately-owned and publicly-owned utilities.

| Calendar Year | Net production million kwh | Percentage produced by source Coal | Oil | Gas | Nuclear | Hydro | Other[1] | Fuel Consumption Coal 1,000 sht. tns. | Oil 1,000 bbls. | Gas million cu. ft. |
|---|---|---|---|---|---|---|---|---|---|---|
| 1971 | 1,612,593 | 44.3 | 13.6 | 23.2 | 2.4 | 16.5 | 0.05 | 327,887 | 396,468 | 3,975,971 |
| 1974 | 1,867,103 | 44.5 | 16.0 | 17.2 | 6.1 | 16.1 | 0.1 | 392,423 | 536,245 | 3,443,293 |
| 1975 | 1,917,638 | 44.5 | 15.1 | 15.6 | 9.0 | 15.6 | 0.2 | 406,029 | 506,128 | 3,157,584 |
| 1976 | 2,037,775 | 46.4 | 15.7 | 14.4 | 9.4 | 13.9 | 0.2 | 448,456 | 555,937 | 3,081,286 |
| 1977 | 2,124,580 | 46.4 | 16.8 | 14.4 | 11.8 | 10.4 | 0.2 | 477,229 | 623,742 | 3,191,948 |
| 1978[2] | 704,317 | 41.5 | 19.7 | 12.2 | 12.4 | 13.8 | 0.2 | 147,345 | 243,944 | 895,08 |

(1) Includes electricity produced from geothermal power, wood, and waste. (2) Four months.

## Fuel Economy in 1979 Autos; Comparative Miles per Gallon

Source: U.S. Environmental Protection Agency

The Environmental Protection Agency's fuel efficiency figures for 1979 model-year cars reflect a new, one-number system instead of the highway and city driving breakdowns of previous years. The single number is roughly equivalent to last year's city driving number. The EPA decided to use the single, lower figure because their tests showed that most people, in day-to-day driving situations, achieve fuel economy ratings closest to this number.

| Make, model | Cu. in. displcmt. | Cylinders | Trans.[1] | Mileage |
|---|---|---|---|---|
| AMC Concord . . . . . . | 121 | 4 | a | 20 |
| AMC Pacer . . . . . . . | 258 | 6 | a | 17 |
| AMC Spirit . . . . . . . | 121 | 4 | a | 20 |
| AMC Spirit . . . . . . . | 232 | 6 | m | 18 |
| AMC Spirit . . . . . . . | 258 | 6 | a | 17 |
| Audi Fox . . . . . . . | 97 | 4 | a | 20 |
| Audi 5000 . . . . . . . | 131 | 5 | a | 17 |
| Buick Century, Regal . . | 196 | 6 | a | 21 |
| Buick Century, Regal . . | 301 | 8 | a | 17 |
| Buick Electra . . . . . | 350 | 8 | a | 15 |
| Buick Opel . . . . . . . | 111 | 4 | a | 26 |
| Buick Riviera . . . . . | 350 | 8 | a | 16 |
| Buick Skylark . . . . . . | 231 | 6 | a | 19 |
| Cadillac Limo. . . . . . | 425 | 8 | a | 10 |
| Cadillac Seville . . . . . | 350 | 8 | a | 14 |
| Chevrolet . . . . . . . . | 250 | 6 | a | 16 |
| Chevrolet . . . . . . . . | 350 | 8 | a | 16 |
| Chevrolet Camaro . . . | 250 | 6 | a | 16 |
| Chevrolet Chevette . . . | 98 | 4 | a | 25 |
| Chevrolet Corvette . . . . | 350 | 8 | a | 16 |
| Chevrolet Malibu . . . . | 200 | 6 | a | 18 |
| Chevrolet Malibu . . . . . | 305 | 8 | a | 17 |
| Chevrolet Monte Carlo . | 231 | 6 | a | 19 |
| Chevrolet Monte Carlo . | 305 | 8 | a | 17 |
| Chevrolet Monza . . . . | 151 | 4 | a | 22 |
| Chevrolet Nova . . . . | 250 | 6 | a | 16 |
| Chevrolet Nova . . . . | 350 | 8 | a | 16 |
| Chrysler Cordoba . . . . | 318 | 8 | a | 16 |
| Chrysler LeBaron . . . . | 225 | 6 | a | 17 |
| Chrysler LeBaron . . . . | 360 | 8 | a | 14 |
| Chrysler Newport-N.Y. . | 225 | 6 | a | 17 |
| Chrysler Newport-N.Y. . | 318 | 8 | a | 16 |
| Chrysler Newport-N.Y. . | 360 | 8 | a | 14 |
| Datsun 2-Seater 280zx . | 168 | 6 | a | 16 |
| Datsun 210 . . . . . . . | 85 | 4 | a | 26 |
| Datsun 510 . . . . . . . | 119 | 4 | a | 24 |
| Dodge Aspen . . . . . . | 225 | 6 | a | 18 |
| Dodge Aspen . . . . . . . | 318 | 8 | a | 16 |

| Make, model | Cu. in. displcmt. | Cylinders | Trans.[1] | Mileage |
|---|---|---|---|---|
| Dodge Challenger . . . . | 98 | 4 | m | 26 |
| Dodge Colt . . . . . . . | 98 | 4 | m | 30 |
| Dodge Diplomat . . . . | 225 | 6 | a | 17 |
| Dodge Diplomat . . . . | 360 | 8 | a | 14 |
| Dodge Magnum . . . . . | 318 | 8 | a | 16 |
| Dodge Magnum . . . . . | 360 | 8 | a | 14 |
| Dodge St. Regis . . . . | 318 | 8 | a | 16 |
| Dodge St. Regis . . . . | 360 | 8 | a | 14 |
| Fiat 128 . . . . . . . . | 79 | 4 | m | 21 |
| Ford Fairmont . . . . . | 140 | 4 | a | 21 |
| Ford Fairmont . . . . . | 302 | 8 | a | 16 |
| Ford Fiesta . . . . . . | 98 | 4 | m | 28 |
| Ford Granada . . . . . | 250 | 6 | a | 17 |
| Ford Granada . . . . . | 302 | 8 | a | 16 |
| Ford LTD . . . . . . . | 351 | 8 | a | 14 |
| Ford LTD II . . . . . . | 302 | 8 | a | 14 |
| Ford Mustang . . . . . | 140 | 4 | a | 21 |
| Ford Mustang . . . . . | 171 | 6 | a | 18 |
| Ford Mustang . . . . . | 302 | 8 | a | 16 |
| Ford Pinto . . . . . . . | 140 | 4 | a | 21 |
| Ford Pinto . . . . . . . | 171 | 6 | a | 18 |
| Ford Thunderbird . . . . | 302 | 8 | a | 14 |
| Jaguar XJ . . . . . . . | 258 | 6 | a | 14 |
| Jaguar XJS . . . . . . . | 326 | 12 | a | 10 |
| Lincoln Contntl Mk V. . . | 400 | 8 | a | 12 |
| Mazda GLC. . . . . . . | 86 | 4 | a | 29 |
| Mazda rx7 . . . . . . . | 70 | 2 | a | 18 |
| Mercury Bobcat . . . . . | 140 | 4 | a | 21 |
| Mercury Bobcat . . . . . | 171 | 6 | a | 18 |
| Merc. Cougar. . . . . . | 302 | 8 | a | 14 |
| Merc. Cougar. . . . . . | 351 | 8 | a | 13 |
| Mercury Marquis . . . . | 302 | 8 | a | 15 |
| Mercury Marquis . . . . | 351 | 8 | a | 15 |
| Mercury Zephyr . . . . . | 140 | 4 | a | 20 |
| Mercury Zephyr . . . . . | 302 | 8 | a | 16 |
| Olds. Cutlass Sal. . . . . | 231 | 6 | a | 19 |
| Olds. Cutlass Sal. . . . . | 260 | 8 | a | 19 |
| Olds. Cutlass Sal. . . . . | 305 | 8 | a | 17 |

| Make, model | Cu. in. displcmt. | Cylinders | Trans.[1] | Mileage |
|---|---|---|---|---|
| Oldsmobile Delta 88. . . . | 231 | 6 | a | 18 |
| Oldsmobile Delta 88. . . | 301 | 8 | a | 17 |
| Oldsmobile Delta 88 Dsl | 350 | 8 | a | 21 |
| Oldsmobile 98 Dsl. . . . | 350 | 8 | a | 21 |
| Oldsmobile 98 . . . . . | 403 | 8 | a | 14 |
| Oldsmobile Omega . . . | 231 | 6 | a | 19 |
| Oldsmobile Omega . . . | 305 | 8 | a | 16 |
| Oldsmobile Starfire . . . | 151 | 4 | a | 22 |
| Plym. Arrow . . . . . . | 98 | 4 | m | 28 |
| Plymouth Horizon . . . . | 105 | 4 | m | 25 |
| Plymouth Lancer . . . . | 98 | 4 | m | 30 |
| Plym. Sapporo . . . . . | 98 | 4 | m | 26 |
| Plym. Sapporo . . . . . | 156 | 4 | a | 21 |
| Plym. Volare . . . . . . | 225 | 6 | a | 18 |
| Plym. Volare . . . . . . | 318 | 8 | a | 16 |
| Pontiac Cat.-Bonne . . . | 231 | 6 | a | 18 |
| Pontiac Cat.-Bonne . . . | 301 | 8 | a | 17 |
| Pontiac Firebird . . . . | 231 | 6 | a | 18 |
| Pontiac Firebird . . . . | 403 | 8 | a | 14 |
| Pontiac Grand Prix . . . | 231 | 6 | a | 19 |
| Pontiac Grand Prix . . . | 301 | 8 | a | 17 |
| Pontiac LeMans . . . . | 231 | 6 | a | 19 |
| Pontiac LeMans . . . . | 301 | 8 | a | 17 |
| Pontiac Phoenix . . . . | 231 | 6 | a | 19 |
| Pontiac Phoenix . . . . | 305 | 8 | a | 16 |
| Pontiac Sunbird . . . . | 151 | 4 | a | 22 |
| Porsche 930 . . . . . . | 201 | 6 | m | 12 |
| Renault LeCar . . . . . | 79 | 4 | m | 26 |
| Toyota Celica . . . . . | 134 | 4 | m | 18 |
| Toyota Corolla . . . . . | 71 | 4 | m | 31 |
| Toyota Corolla . . . . . | 97 | 4 | a | 23 |
| Toyota Corona . . . . . | 134 | 4 | a | 18 |
| Triumph Spitfire . . . . | 91 | 4 | m | 22 |
| Volswgn Beetle. . . . . | 97 | 4 | m | 20 |
| Volswgn Dasher . . . . | 97 | 4 | a | 20 |
| Volkswgn Diesl Rabt. . . . | 90 | 4 | m | 40 |
| Volswgn Rabbit . . . . . | 89 | 4 | a | 22 |
| Volswgn Scirocco . . . . | 97 | 4 | a | 24 |

(1) Type of transmission: a = automatic; m = manual.

## Measuring Energy

Source: House of Representatives Subcommittee on Energy

The following tables of equivalents contain those figures commonly used to compare different types of energy sources and their various measurements.

**Btu -** a British thermal unit — the amount of heat required to raise one pound of water one degree Fahrenheit. Equivalent to 1,055 joules or about 252 gram calories. A **therm** is usually 100,000 Btu but is sometimes used to refer to other units.

**Calorie -** the amount of heat required to raise one gram of water one degree Centigrade; abbreviated cal.; equivalent to about .003968 Btu. More common is the kilogram calorie, also called a **kilocalorie** and abbreviated Cal. or Kcal.; equivalent to about 3.97 Btu. (One Kcal is equivalent to one food calorie.)

### Btu Values of Energy Sources

(These are conventional or average values, not precise equivalents.)

**Coal** (per 2,000 lb. ton):
| | | |
|---|---|---|
| Anthracite | = | $25.4 \times 10^6$ Btu |
| Bituminous | = | $26.2 \times 10^6$ |
| Sub-bituminous | = | $19.0 \times 10^6$ |
| Lignite | = | $13.4 \times 10^6$ |

Average heating value of coal used to generate electricity in 1969 was $27.7 \times 10^6$ Btu.

**Natural gas** (per cubic foot):
| | | |
|---|---|---|
| Dry | = | 1,031 Btu |
| Wet | = | 1,103 |
| Liquid (avg.) | = | 4,100 |

**Electricity** — 1 kwh = 3,413 Btu

**Petroleum** (per barrel):
| | | |
|---|---|---|
| Crude oil | = | $5.60 \times 10^6$ Btu |
| Residual fuel oil | = | $6.29 \times 10^6$ |
| Distillate fuel oil | = | $5.83 \times 10^6$ |
| Gasoline (including av gas) | = | $5.25 \times 10^6$ |
| Jet fuel (kerosene) | = | $5.67 \times 10^6$ |
| Jet fuel (naphtha) | = | $5.36 \times 10^6$ |
| Kerosene | = | $5.67 \times 10^6$ |

**Nuclear** — gram of fissioned U-235 = $74 \times 10^6$ Btu

The Btu and calorie, being small amounts of energy, are usually expressed as follows when large numbers are involved.

| | |
|---|---|
| $1 \times 10^3$ Btu | = 1,000 |
| $1 \times 10^6$ | = 1,000,000 |

| | |
|---|---|
| $1 \times 10^9$ | = 1,000,000,000 |
| $1 \times 10^{12}$ | = 1 trillion |
| $1 \times 10^{15}$ | = 1 quadrillion |
| $1 \times 10^{18}$ | = 1 quintillion or 1 Q unit |
| One Q unit | = 38.46 billions tons of coal |
| | = 172.4 billion tons of oil |
| | = 968.9 trillion cubic ft. of natural gas |

### Other Conversion Factors

**Electricity** — 1 kwh.
| | |
|---|---|
| | = 0.88 lbs. of coal |
| | = 0.076 gallon of oil |
| | = 10.4 cu. ft. of natural gas |

**Natural gas** — 1 tcf
(trillion cubic feet)
| | |
|---|---|
| | = $39.3 \times 10^6$ tons of coal |
| | = $184 \times 10^6$ barrels of oil |

**Coal** — 1 mtce
(million tons of coal equivalent)
| | |
|---|---|
| | = $4.48 \times 10^6$ barrels of oil |
| | = 667,000 tons of oil |
| | = $25.19 \times 10^{12}$ cu. ft. of natural gas |

**Oil** — 1 million tons
($6.65 \times 10^6$ barrels)
| | |
|---|---|
| | = $4 \times 10^9$ kwh of electricity (when used to generate power) |
| | = $12 \times 10^9$ kwh unconverted |
| | = $1.5 \times 10^6$ tons of coal |
| | = $41.2 \times 10^6$ cu. ft. of natural gas |

### Approximate Conversion Factors for Oils

| To convert | Barrels to metric tons | Metric tons to barrels | Barrels/ days to tons/ year | Tons/year to barrels day |
|---|---|---|---|---|
| | | Multiply by — | | |
| Crude oil [1] | .136 | 7.33 | 49.8 | .0201 |
| Gasoline | .118 | 8.45 | 43.2 | .0232 |
| Kerosene | .128 | 7.80 | 46.8 | .0214 |
| Diesel fuel | .133 | 7.50 | 48.7 | .0205 |
| Fuel oil | .149 | 6.70 | 54.5 | .0184 |

(1) Based on world average gravity (excluding natural gas liquids).

## U.S. Crude Oil Reserves

Source: American Petroleum Institute

Estimates of proved reserves, which can be recovered under present economic relationships and known technology. Improved technology or higher world prices would increase estimates of reserves. Cumulative production for all years through Dec. 31, 1977 was 114,709,780 thousand barrels.

(thousands of 42-gallon barrels)

| Year | Discoveries, revisions, extensions | Production | Proved reserves at end of year | Change from previous year[1] | Year | Discoveries, revisions, extensions | Production | Proved reserves at end of year | Change from previous year[1] |
|---|---|---|---|---|---|---|---|---|---|
| 1946 | 2,658,062 | 1,726,348 | 20,873,560 | 931,714 | 1962 | 2,180,896 | 2,550,178 | 31,389,223 | (369,282) |
| 1947 | 2,464,570 | 1,850,445 | 21,487,685 | 614,125 | 1963 | 2,174,110 | 2,593,343 | 30,969,990 | (419,233) |
| 1948 | 3,795,207 | 2,002,448 | 23,280,444 | 1,792,759 | 1964 | 2,664,767 | 2,644,247 | 30,990,510 | 20,520 |
| 1949 | 3,187,845 | 1,818,800 | 24,649,489 | 1,369,045 | 1965 | 3,048,079 | 2,686,198 | 31,352,391 | 361,881 |
| 1950 | 2,562,685 | 1,943,776 | 25,268,398 | 618,909 | 1966 | 2,963,978 | 2,864,242 | 31,452,127 | 99,736 |
| 1951 | 4,413,954 | 2,214,321 | 27,468,031 | 2,199,633 | 1967 | 2,962,122 | 3,037,579 | 31,376,670 | (75,457) |
| 1952 | 2,749,288 | 2,256,765 | 27,960,554 | 492,523 | 1968 | 2,454,635 | 3,124,188 | 30,707,117 | (669,553) |
| 1953 | 3,296,130 | 2,311,856 | 28,944,828 | 984,274 | 1969 | 2,120,036 | 3,195,291 | 29,631,862 | (1,075,255) |
| 1954 | 2,873,037 | 2,257,119 | 29,560,746 | 615,918 | 1970 | 12,688,918 | 3,319,445 | 39,001,335 | 9,369,473 |
| 1955 | 2,870,724 | 2,419,300 | 30,012,170 | 451,424 | 1971 | 2,317,732 | 3,256,110 | 38,062,957 | (938,378) |
| 1956 | 2,974,336 | 2,551,857 | 30,434,649 | 422,479 | 1972 | 1,557,848 | 3,281,397 | 36,339,408 | (1,723,549) |
| 1957 | 2,424,800 | 2,559,044 | 30,300,405 | (134,244) | 1973 | 2,145,831 | 3,185,400 | 35,299,839 | (1,039,569) |
| 1958 | 2,608,242 | 2,372,730 | 30,535,917 | 235,512 | 1974 | 1,993,573 | 3,043,456 | 34,249,956 | (1,049,883) |
| 1959 | 3,666,745 | 2,483,315 | 31,719,347 | 1,183,430 | 1975 | 1,318,463 | 2,886,292 | 32,682,127 | (1,567,829) |
| 1960 | 2,365,328 | 2,471,464 | 31,613,211 | (106,136) | 1976 | 1,085,291 | 2,825,252 | 30,942,166 | (1,739,961) |
| 1961 | 2,657,567 | 2,512,273 | 31,758,505 | 145,294 | 1977 | 1,403,780 | 2,859,544 | 29,486,402 | (1,455,764) |

(1) Parentheses indicate decline.

## Industrial Minerals: Distribution, Resources, Reserves

**Source:** Organization for Economic Cooperation and Development

(Resource and reserve figures are based on average conservative estimates.)

| Minerals | Distribution of reserves, 1974 (% of world total) | Resources[1] 1975/76 (million metric tons) | Reserves[2] 1975/76 (million metric tons) | Ratio of reserves to 1975 demand in years[3] | Ratio of reserves to total demand 1974-2000[4] |
|---|---|---|---|---|---|
| Iron | USSR(31.1) Brazil(16.6) Canada(11.7) Australia(10.2) India(6.4) | 195,000 | 90,500 | 177 | 4.5 |
| Copper | U.S.(18.4) Chilie(18.4) USSR(7.9) Canada(6.8) Peru(6.5) Zambia(6.3) Zaire(5.6) | 1,500 | 408.2 | 62 | 1.3 |
| Lead | U.S.(35.6) Canada(11.5) USSR(10.9) Australia(10.9) Mexico(3.0) | 300 | 150.0 | 49 | 1.2 |
| Tin | China(23.6) Thailand(15.0) Malaysia(12.2) Bolivia(9.9) Indonesia(8.3) Brazil(6.0) | 37 | 10.2 | 44 | 1.3 |
| Zinc | Canada(22.8) U.S.(20.1) Australia(12.1) USSR(8.1) Ireland(5.4) | 245 | 135.0 | 41 | 1.1 |
| Aluminum | Australia(26.0) Guinea(26.0) Brazil(15.6) Jamaica(6.1) Greece(4.4) Cameroon(3.9) | 5,700 | 3,483 | over 200 | 4.0 |
| Titanium | Brazil(65.9) India(21.7) Australia(5.4) U.S.(3.5) Sierra Leone(1.7) Canada(1.6) | 1,234 | 340.1 | over 300 | 4.4 |
| Chromium | S. Africa(73.9) Rhodesia(19.7) USSR(2.9) Finland(1.2) India(0.5) Madagascar(0.4) Philippines(0.4) Turkey(0.4) Brazil(0.3) | 1,049 | 523.2 | over 200 | 5.7 |
| Cobalt | Zaire(27.7) New Caledonia(27.1) Zambia(14.2) Cuba(13.8) USSR(8.3) | 4.3 | 2.4 | 78 | 2.1 |
| Niobium | Brazil(75.8) Canada(7.6) USSR(6.3) Zaire(3.8) Uganda(2.9) Nigeria(2.7) | 14.6 | 10.0 | over 800 | over 10 |
| Manganese | S. Africa(45.0) USSR(37.5) Australia(8.0) Gabon(5.0) Brazil(2.2) | 3,265 | 1,814 | 197 | 4.9 |
| Molybdenum | U.S.(49.5) USSR(15.2) Canada(14.4) Chile(13.6) China(3.8) | 28.6 | 6.0 | 65 | 1.4 |
| Nickel | New Caledonia(43.7) Canada(16.1) USSR(9.6) Australia(9.2) Indonesia(8.4) Cuba(5.7) | 129.7 | 55.3 | 77 | 2.1 |
| Tantulum | Zaire(55.0) Nigeria(11.0) USSR(6.7) Thailand(6.7) Malaysia(5.4) Canada(4.8) Brazil(4.4) | 0.26 | 0.07 | 49 | 1.1 |
| Tungsten | China(53.6) Canada(12.1) USSR(8.9) N. Korea(6.4) U.S.(6.1) | 5.2 | 1.8 | 46 | 1.2 |
| Vanadium | USSR(74.7) S. Africa(18.7) Australia(1.4) Chilie(1.4) U.S.(1.1) | 56.2 | 9.7 | over 300 | 7.5 |
| Bismuth | Japan(25.6) Australia(19.5) U.S.(13.3) Mexico(6.2) Peru(5.1) | 0.13 | 0.06 | 22 | 0.5 |
| Mercury | Spain(40.6) USSR(10.1) Yugoslavia(10.1) China(10.1) U.S.(9.1) Italy(8.1) | 17,510 | 4,930 | 21 | 0.7 |
| Silver | USSR(26.7) U.S.(25.0) Mexico(13.3) Canada(11.7) Peru(10.0) Australia(3.3) | 0.70 | 0.19 | 16 | 0.4 |
| Platinum | S. Africa(71.3) USSR(26.7) Canada(1.8) U.S.(0.2) Colombia(0.2) | 0.026 | 0.009 | 110 | 3.1 |
| Asbestos | Canada(45.2) USSR(24.8) S. Africa(6.9) Australia(3.6) U.S.(3.0) | 249.4 | 145.1 | 35 | 0.9 |

(1) Seabed deposits not included; these are (in million metric tons): cobalt, 583; manganese, 36,425; nickel, 1,305; molybdenum, 78; vanadium, 107. Other minerals for which resource estimates are considerably increased if seabed deposits are included are titanium, aluminum, lead, copper, and to a smaller extent zinc, iron, and chromium. (2) Reserves are defined as that portion of the identified resources from which useable material can be economically and legally extracted at the time of determination. (3) Ie., iron will last 177 years if used at the 1975 rate. (4) Ie., there is 4.5 times more iron than total estimated demand between 1974 and 2000.

## U.S. Petroleum Imports by Source

**Source:** Department of Energy
(in thousands of barrels per day)

| Nation | 1973 | 1974 | 1975 | 1976 | 1977 |
|---|---|---|---|---|---|
| Algeria | 151.2 | 207.1 | 288.2 | 438.3 | 565.2 |
| Indonesia | 237.7 | 310.9 | 437.7 | 569.4 | 576.2 |
| Iran | 433.7 | 731.0 | 524.8 | 546.5 | 786.4 |
| Libya | 308.3 | 40.3 | 329.3 | 529.3 | 837.7 |
| Nigeria | 607.9 | 912.2 | 837.8 | 1,119.2 | 1,229.6 |
| Saudi Arabia | 740.3 | 675.2 | 891.6 | 1,365.8 | 1,523.8 |
| United Arab Emirates | 83.6 | 87.8 | 154.2 | 323.2 | 446.3 |
| Venezuela | 1,633.7 | 1,457.8 | 1,030.1 | 972.2 | 908.8 |
| Other OPEC[1] | 194.5 | 217.0 | 259.3 | 216.0 | 378.1 |
| **Total OPEC** | **4,390.9** | **4,669.3** | **4,753.0** | **6,079.9** | **7,252.2** |
| Arab OPEC Members | 1,377.4 | 1,106.4 | 1,790.1 | 2,773.0 | 3,636.5 |
| Bahamas | 170.8 | 159.3 | 152.0 | 116.5 | 168.0 |
| Canada | 1,312.9 | 1,067.6 | 845.2 | 599.3 | 502.8 |
| Neth'lands Antilles | 573.6 | 509.6 | 323.6 | 274.6 | 218.3 |
| Puerto Rico | 99.3 | 90.4 | 89.7 | 88.1 | 102.8 |
| Trinidad/Tobago | 250.6 | 241.2 | 240.9 | 272.6 | 286.0 |
| Virgin Islands | 329.2 | 391.7 | 406.5 | 422.3 | 468.7 |
| Mexico | 15.2 | 8.4 | 71.4 | 87.1 | 179.3 |
| Other non-OPEC | 523.5 | 384.2 | 306.1 | 373.5 | 657.1 |
| **Total non-OPEC** | **3,274.2** | **2,852.4** | **2,435.4** | **2,234.0** | **2,583.0** |
| **Total imports** (avg.) | **6,256.0** | **6,112.0** | **6,056.0** | **7,313.0** | **8,714.0** |

(1) Ecuador, Gabon, Iraq, Kuwait, Qatar. (2) Imports do not add to totals because OPEC figures include petroleum transshipped through, and usually refined in, other countries and counted again as imports from those countries.

## World's Largest Hydroelectric Generating Plants

Source: Bureau of Reclamation. U.S. Interior Department
UC—Under construction. Year—Initial operation.

| Name | Present megawatts | Ultimate megawatts | Year | Name | Present megawatts | Ultimate megawatts | Year |
|---|---|---|---|---|---|---|---|
| Itaipu, Brazil/Paraguay | —— | 12,870 | UC | Salto Grande, Argentina/ | | | |
| Grand Coulee, U.S.[1] | 4,163 | 10,080 | 1941 | Uruguay | —— | 1,890 | UC |
| Guri, Venezuela | 524 | 6,500 | 1967 | Dinorwic, Great Britain[1] | —— | 1,880 | UC |
| Sayanskaya, USSR | —— | 6,400 | UC | Ludington, U.S.[1] | 1,872 | 1,872 | 1973 |
| Krasnoyarsk, USSR | 6,096 | 6,096 | 1968 | St. Lawrence Power Dam, U.S./ | | | |
| La Grande 2, Canada | —— | 5,328 | UC | Canada | 1,824 | 1,824 | 1958 |
| Churchill Falls, Canada | 5,225 | 5,225 | 1971 | The Dalles, U.S. | 1,807 | 1,807 | 1957 |
| Bratsk, USSR | 4,100 | 4,600 | 1964 | Karakaya, Turkey | —— | 1,800 | UC |
| Sukhovo, USSR | —— | 4,500 | UC | Grand Maison, France | 1,200 | 1,800 | UC |
| Ust-Ipimsk, USSR | 720 | 4,320 | 1974 | Mica, Canada | —— | 1,740 | UC |
| Cabora Bassa, Mozambique | 2,000 | 4,000 | 1975 | Itaparica, Brazil | —— | 1,700 | UC |
| Tucurui, Brazil | —— | 3,960 | UC | Kemano, Canada | 813 | 1,670 | 1954 |
| Rogunsky, USSR | —— | 3,600 | UC | Blue Ridge, U.S.[1] | —— | 1,600 | UC |
| Paulo Afonso, Brazil | 1,524 | 3,409 | 1955 | Beauharnois, Canada | 1,021 | 1,574 | 1950 |
| Solteira, Brazil | 3,200 | 3,200 | 1973 | Kariba, Rhodesia/Zambia | 1,266 | 1,566 | 1959 |
| Inga I, Zaire | 360 | 2,820 | 1974 | San Carlos, Colombia | —— | 1,550 | UC |
| John Day, U.S. | 2,160 | 2,700 | 1968 | Raccoon Mountain, U.S.[1] | 1,530 | 1,530 | 1975 |
| Nurek, USSR | —— | 2,700 | UC | Tumut-3, Australia[1] | 1,500 | 1,500 | 1972 |
| Sao Simao, Brazil | —— | 2,680 | UC | Jupia, Brazil | 1,411 | 1,411 | 1966 |
| Volgograd-22nd Congress, | | | | McNary, U.S. | 980 | 1,406 | 1953 |
| USSR | 2,560 | 2,560 | 1958 | Cheboksary, USSR | 1,404 | 1,404 | 1972 |
| Chicoasen, Mexico | —— | 2,400 | UC | Marimbondo, Brazil | 1,400 | 1,400 | 1975 |
| Volga-V.I. Lenin, USSR | 2,300 | 2,300 | 1955 | Agua Vermelha, Brazil | —— | 1,380 | UC |
| Iron Gates I, Romania/Yugo- | | | | Saratov, USSR | 1,360 | 1,360 | 1967 |
| slavia | 2,300 | 2,300 | 1970 | Hoover, U.S. | 1,345 | 1,345 | 1936 |
| W.A.C. Bennett, Canada | 1,816 | 2,270 | 1969 | Wanapum, U.S. | 831 | 1,330 | 1964 |
| Foz Do Areia, Brazil | 2,250 | 2,250 | UC | Inguri, USSR | —— | 1,300 | UC |
| High Aswan (Sadd-el-Aali), | | | | Daniel Johnson, Canada | 650 | 1,292 | 1970 |
| Egypt | 2,100 | 2,100 | 1967 | Zeya, USSR | 300 | 1,290 | 1975 |
| Bath County, U.S.[1] | —— | 2,100 | UC | Takase, Japan[1] | —— | 1,280 | UC |
| Tarbela, Pakistan | 700 | 2,100 | 1977 | Priest Rapids, U.S. | 789 | 1,262 | 1959 |
| Itumbiara, Brazil | —— | 2,080 | UC | Castaic, U.S. | 1,060 | 1,250 | UC |
| Chief Joseph, U.S. | 1,024 | 2,069 | 1956 | Nizhne-Kanskaya, USSR | 624 | 1,248 | 1973 |
| Salto Santiago, Brazil | —— | 1,998 | UC | Malpaso, Mexico | 830 | 1,245 | 1968 |
| Robert Moses-Niagara, U.S. | 1,950 | 1,950 | 1961 | Keban, Turkey | 620 | 1,240 | 1974 |
| (1) Pumped storage installation. | | | | Liuchiahsia, China | —— | 1,225 | UC |

## Non-Federal Hydroelectric Plants in U.S.

Capacities of 150,000 Kilowatts or More as of Jan 1, 1978
Source: Federal Energy Regulatory Commission

Auxiliary and pumped storage units are not included in hydroelectric capacities.

| Plant | State | Owner | Kilowatts |
|---|---|---|---|
| Robert Moses, (Niagara) . . . | New York . . . . . . . . | Power Authority State of New York. . . . . . . | 1,950,000 |
| Rocky Reach . . . . . . . . . | Washington . . . . . . | Chelan County PUD[2] . . . . . . . . . . . | 1,213,100 |
| Robert Moses, (Massena) . . | New York . . . . . . . | Power Authority State of New York. . . . . . . | 912,000 |
| Wanapum . . . . . . . . . . | Washington . . . . . . | Grant County PUD No. 2. . . . . . . . . . | 831,250 |
| Priest Rapids. . . . . . . . | Washington . . . . . . | Grant County PUD No. 2. . . . . . . . . . | 788,500 |
| Wells . . . . . . . . . . . | Washington . . . . . | Douglas County PUD No. 1 . . . . . . . . . | 774,250 |
| Boundary . . . . . . . . . | Washington . . . . . | Seattle Department of Lighting . . . . . . . | 551,000 |
| Conowingo . . . . . . . . | Maryland. . . . . . . | Susquehanna Pow. Co., Phila. Elec. Pow. Co... | 474,480 |
| Hells Canyon . . . . . . . | Oregon. . . . . . . . | Idaho Power Company. . . . . . . . . . . | 391,500 |
| Brownlee . . . . . . . . . | Idaho . . . . . . . . | Idaho Power Company . . . . . . . . . . . | 360,400 |
| Ross . . . . . . . . . . . | Washington . . . . . | Seattle Department of Lighting Company . . . . | 360,000 |
| Edward G. Hyatt. . . . . . | California. . . . . . . | California Department of Water Resources . . . | 351,000 |
| Cowans Ford . . . . . . . | North Carolina. . . . | Duke Power Company . . . . . . . . . . . | 350,000 |
| Smith Mt. . . . . . . . . | Virginia . . . . . . . | Appalachian Power Company. . . . . . . . | 300,200 |
| Mossyrock . . . . . . . . | Washington . . . . . | City of Tacoma . . . . . . . . . . . . . | 300,000 |
| New Colgate . . . . . . . | California. . . . . . | Yuba County Water Agency . . . . . . . . | 284,400 |
| Noxon Rapids . . . . . . | Montana . . . . . . | The Washington Water Power Company . . . | 282,880 |
| Round Butte . . . . . . . | Oregon. . . . . . . | Portland General Electric Company . . . . . | 247,050 |
| Safe Harbor . . . . . . . | Pennsylvania . . . . | Safe Harbor Water Power Corporation. . . . | 226,500 |
| Walter Bouldin[1] . . . . . | Alabama . . . . . . | Alabama Power Company . . . . . . . . . | 225,000 |
| Rock Island . . . . . . . | Washington . . . . | Chelan County PUD No. 1. . . . . . . . . | 212,100 |
| Swift No. 1 . . . . . . . | Washington . . . . | Pacific Power and Light Company . . . . . | 204,000 |
| Cabinet Gorge . . . . . . | Idaho . . . . . . . | The Washington Water Power Company. . . . | 200,000 |
| Saluda . . . . . . . . . | South Carolina . . . | South Carolina Electric and Gas Company . . . | 197,500 |
| Oxbow . . . . . . . . . | Oregon. . . . . . . | Idaho Power Company . . . . . . . . . . | 190,000 |
| White Rock. . . . . . . . | California. . . . . . | Sacramento Municipal Utility District . . . . | 190,000 |
| Caribou No. 1 & 2 . . . . | California. . . . . . | Pacific Gas and Electric Company . . . . . | 184,800 |
| Gaston . . . . . . . . . | North Carolina . . . | Virginia Electric and Power Company . . . . | 177,920 |
| Lay Dam . . . . . . . . | Alabama . . . . . . | Alabama Power Company . . . . . . . . . | 117,000 |
| Osage . . . . . . . . . | Missouri . . . . . . | Union Electric Company of Missouri . . . . . | 172,000 |
| Kerr . . . . . . . . . . | Montana . . . . . . | The Montana Power Company . . . . . . . | 168,000 |
| Lewis Smith . . . . . . . | Alabama . . . . . . | Alabama Power Company . . . . . . . . . | 157,500 |
| Keowee . . . . . . . . . | South Carolina . . . | Duke Power Company . . . . . . . . . . | 157,500 |
| James B. Black . . . . . . | California. . . . . . | Pacific Gas and Electric Company . . . . . | 154,800 |
| Martin Dam. . . . . . . . | Alabama . . . . . . | Alabama Power Company . . . . . . . . . | 154,200 |

(1) Units out of service Feb. 1975 in dam failure. (2) Public utility district.

# MANUFACTURES AND MINERALS

## General Statistics for Major Industry Groups

Source: Bureau of the Census

The estimates for 1976 in the following table are based upon reports from a representative sample of about 70,000 manufacturing establishments.

| Industry | All employees | | Production workers | | | Value added by mfr. |
|---|---|---|---|---|---|---|
| | Number (1,000) | Payroll (millions) | Number (1,000) | Manhours (millions) | Wages (millions) | |
| Food & kindred products | 1,535.9 | 17,289.0 | 1,066.5 | 2,103.2 | 10,806.1 | 52,759.7 |
| Tobacco mfg. | 64.8 | 704.0 | 54.8 | 102.6 | 543.5 | 4,127.8 |
| Textile mill prods. | 875.8 | 7,368.4 | 765.2 | 1,518.5 | 5,769.4 | 14,495.1 |
| Apparel and other textile prods. | 1,270.6 | 8,562.6 | 1,109.2 | 2,003.7 | 6,459.7 | 16,859.9 |
| Lumber & wood prods. | 628.7 | 6,142.9 | 543.2 | 1,039.6 | 4,816.6 | 13,453.6 |
| Furniture & fixtures | 425.6 | 3,772.4 | 352.0 | 664.8 | 2,690.4 | 7,370.3 |
| Paper & allied prods. | 614.8 | 8,046.5 | 477.5 | 967.7 | 5,692.1 | 20,603.7 |
| Printing & publishing | 1,085.8 | 12,680.0 | 629.3 | 1,163.1 | 6,737.2 | 27,647.3 |
| Chemicals & allied prods. | 851.2 | 12,365.2 | 520.1 | 1,032.1 | 6,518.4 | 51,407.5 |
| Petroleum & coal prods. | 144.5 | 2,436.8 | 100.2 | 205.6 | 1,577.7 | 13,168.9 |
| Rubber & plastic prods. | 627.4 | 6,741.7 | 489.0 | 938.4 | 4,517.9 | 15,950.3 |
| Leather & leather prods. | 247.1 | 1,805.0 | 216.0 | 391.1 | 1,378.7 | 3,558.6 |
| Stone, clay & glass prods. | 599.0 | 7,085.8 | 474.0 | 938.9 | 5,144.8 | 16,772.9 |
| Primary metal industries | 1,106.0 | 16,974.7 | 875.0 | 1,712.8 | 12,639.4 | 34,181.9 |
| Fabricated metal prods. | 1,471.4 | 18,382.3 | 1,122.9 | 2,216.7 | 12,595.7 | 39,145.0 |
| Machinery, except electric | 1,959.8 | 26,479.6 | 1,332.1 | 2,633.4 | 15,831.0 | 57,357.0 |
| Electric, electronic equip. | 1,578.5 | 19,253.1 | 1,080.3 | 2,086.6 | 10,891.1 | 41,746.4 |
| Transportation equip. | 1,667.6 | 26,441.6 | 1,205.6 | 2,419.3 | 17,296.0 | 55,657.3 |
| Instruments & related prods. | 518.0 | 6,598.2 | 321.7 | 624.1 | 3,213.5 | 16,386.2 |
| Misc. mfg. industries | 410.0 | 3,868.0 | 317.4 | 592.1 | 2,446.4 | 8,821.9 |
| Administrative & auxiliary[1] | 1,070.5 | 20,390.9 | — | — | — | |
| **All industries total** | **18,753.0** | **233,388.7** | **13,052.0** | **25,354.2** | **137,565.4** | **511,471.1** |

(1) In addition to the employment and payroll for operating manufacturing establishments, manufacturing concerns reported separately for central administrative offices or auxiliary units (e.g., research laboratories, storage warehouses, power plants, garages, repair shops, etc.) which serve the manufacturing establishments of a company rather than the public.

## Manufacturing Production Worker Statistics

Source: Bureau of Labor Statistics, U.S. Labor Department (p — preliminary)

| Year | All employees | Production workers | Payroll index 1967 = 100 | Avg. weekly earnings | Avg. hourly earnings | Avg. hrs. per wk. |
|---|---|---|---|---|---|---|
| 1955 | 16,882,000 | 13,288,000 | 61.1 | $75.70 | $1.86 | 40.7 |
| 1960 | 16,796,000 | 12,586,000 | 68.9 | 89.72 | 2.26 | 39.7 |
| 1965 | 18,062,000 | 13,434,000 | 88.1 | 107.53 | 2.61 | 41.2 |
| 1970 | 19,349,000 | 14,020,000 | 114.1 | 133.73 | 3.36 | 39.8 |
| 1973 | 20,068,000 | 14,760,000 | 149.2 | 166.06 | 4.08 | 40.7 |
| 1974 | 20,046,000 | 14,613,000 | 157.1 | 176.40 | 4.41 | 40.0 |
| 1975 | 18,347,000 | 13,070,000 | 151.0 | 189.51 | 4.81 | 39.4 |
| 1976 | 18,956,000 | 13,625,000 | 172.4 | 207.60 | 5.19 | 40.0 |
| 1977 | 19,554,000 | 14,066,000 | NA | 226.89 | 5.63 | 40.3 |
| 1978, Jan. | 19,749,000 | 14,197,000 | NA | 231.86 | 5.93 | 39.1 |
| Feb. | 19,790,000 | 14,228,000 | NA | 235.22 | 5.94 | 39.6 |
| Mar. | 19,924,000 | 14,341,000 | NA | 240.78 | 5.96 | 40.4 |
| Apr. | 20,040,000 | 14,432,000 | NA | 242.00 | 5.99 | 40.4 |
| May[p] | 20,164,000 | 14,539,000 | NA | 242.61 | 6.02 | 40.3 |
| June[p] | 20,407,000 | 14,713,000 | NA | 246.04 | 6.06 | 40.6 |

## Personal Consumption Expenditures for the U.S.

Source: Bureau of Economic Analysis, U.S. Commerce Department (millions of dollars)

| Product | 1950 | 1955 | 1960 | 1965 | 1970 | 1975 | 1976 | 1977 |
|---|---|---|---|---|---|---|---|---|
| Food and tobacco | 58,120 | 72,236 | 87,979 | 106,966 | 147,140 | 224,319 | 241,982 | 261,763 |
| Clothing accessories and jewelry | 23,709 | 27,982 | 32,219 | 40,304 | 55,619 | 81,971 | 88,678 | 95,561 |
| Personal care | 2,438 | 3,162 | 5,242 | 7,617 | 10,920 | 14,228 | 15,164 | 16,736 |
| Housing | 21,286 | 34,339 | 48,117 | 65,469 | 93,986 | 150,151 | 166,355 | 184,592 |
| Household operation | 29,086 | 36,890 | 46,126 | 61,322 | 87,793 | 142,672 | 158,672 | 176,878 |
| Medical care | 9,104 | 13,206 | 20,002 | 30,053 | 49,853 | 89,155 | 104,385 | 117,977 |
| Personal business | 6,556 | 9,524 | 14,233 | 18,049 | 31,336 | 51,558 | 55,847 | 60,449 |
| Transportation | 25,415 | 34,583 | 42,391 | 58,205 | 78,032 | 125,493 | 150,404 | 192,104 |
| Recreation | 11,147 | 14,979 | 17,855 | 25,907 | 40,999 | 66,527 | 73,037 | 81,200 |
| Private educ. and research | 1,685 | 2,677 | 3,746 | 5,684 | 9,874 | 15,459 | 17,057 | 18,800 |
| Religious and welfare activities | 2,340 | 3,323 | 4,872 | 6,055 | 8,539 | 12,979 | 14,188 | 15,384 |
| Foreign travel and other—net | 655 | 1,619 | 2,121 | 2,858 | 4,705 | 4,965 | 4,475 | 5,063 |
| **Total personal consumption expenditures** | **191,966** | **253,665** | **324,903** | **430,154** | **618,796** | **979,070** | **1,090,244** | **1,206,507** |

## General Manufacturing Statistics for States

Source: Bureau of the Census, U.S. Commerce Department

| 1976 States | All employees | | Production workers | | | Value added by mfr. (millions) | Value of shipments (millions) | Capital expend. (millions) |
|---|---|---|---|---|---|---|---|---|
| | Number (1,000) | Payroll (millions) | Number (1,000) | Man-hrs. (millions) | Wages (millions) | | | |
| U.S. total . . . . . . . | 18,753.0 | 233,388.7 | 13,052.0 | 25,354.2 | 137,565.4 | 511,471.1 | 1,185,695.3 | 40,552.8 |
| Alabama. . . . . . . . | 330.3 | 3,357.7 | 265.1 | 511.7 | 2,388.2 | 7,716.1 | 17,988.1 | 1,151.9 |
| Alaska . . . . . . . . | 7.9 | 120.6 | 6.2 | 11.5 | 90.1 | 503.6 | 991.8 | 170.6 |
| Arizona . . . . . . . . | 99.0 | 1,237.1 | 62.5 | 120.1 | 651.7 | 2,882.4 | 6,232.9 | 183.2 |
| Arkansas . . . . . . . | 188.3 | 1,849.5 | 152.8 | 295.3 | 1,201.2 | 4,278.0 | 10,604.8 | 472.7 |
| California . . . . . . . | 1,600.1 | 21,214.7 | 1,041.3 | 2,021.8 | 11,202.3 | 46,297.4 | 102,041.0 | 2,867.1 |
| Colorado . . . . . . . | 142.9 | 1,870.8 | 92.2 | 180.4 | 1,015.5 | 3,989.8 | 9,535.5 | 385.2 |
| Connecticut . . . . . . | 405.4 | 5,315.0 | 249.2 | 492.3 | 2,635.7 | 10,095.8 | 18,397.4 | 479.9 |
| Delaware . . . . . . . | 66.0 | 1,063.6 | 32.2 | 62.1 | 383.3 | 1,580.7 | 5,042.7 | 159.7 |
| Dist. of Columbia . . . | 17.9 | 277.8 | 8.6 | 13.9 | 121.8 | 553.2 | 932.0 | 20.0 |
| Florida . . . . . . . . | 331.4 | 3,516.4 | 225.9 | 432.9 | 1,959.9 | 8,280.0 | 18,091.3 | 867.0 |
| Georgia . . . . . . . . | 468.9 | 4,506.1 | 362.4 | 708.3 | 2,950.1 | 11,092.6 | 28,391.4 | 852.9 |
| Hawaii . . . . . . . . | 24.2 | 266.4 | 17.1 | 30.8 | 153.9 | 700.3 | 1,854.8 | 55.6 |
| Idaho . . . . . . . . . | 52.5 | 613.6 | 38.9 | 75.1 | 396.3 | 1,525.0 | 3,448.1 | 159.9 |
| Illinois . . . . . . . . | 1,255.8 | 16,831.3 | 825.4 | 1,595.2 | 9,557.1 | 36,084.5 | 82,351.3 | 2,335.2 |
| Indiana . . . . . . . . | 677.0 | 9,159.2 | 498.3 | 969.0 | 6,107.7 | 19,982.8 | 45,180.9 | 1,475.1 |
| Iowa . . . . . . . . . | 231.1 | 2,994.8 | 164.0 | 312.8 | 1,910.3 | 7,798.6 | 20,772.3 | 709.5 |
| Kansas . . . . . . . . | 167.5 | 1,950.0 | 121.2 | 239.8 | 1,257.6 | 4,859.2 | 14,657.5 | 328.3 |
| Kentucky . . . . . . . | 277.0 | 3,058.1 | 209.9 | 397.3 | 2,039.4 | 8,645.3 | 20,268.5 | 521.6 |
| Louisiana . . . . . . . | 189.8 | 2,395.2 | 140.1 | 287.8 | 1,576.0 | 8,423.4 | 25,225.2 | 1,560.8 |
| Maine . . . . . . . . | 99.0 | 930.1 | 81.0 | 153.7 | 676.4 | 2,041.4 | 4,422.8 | 507.4 |
| Maryland . . . . . . . | 242.8 | 3,126.2 | 164.4 | 316.6 | 1,810.2 | 6,681.6 | 14,762.2 | 421.0 |
| Massachusetts . . . . | 590.9 | 6,942.9 | 387.5 | 743.8 | 3,660.8 | 14,420.6 | 26,918.4 | 781.6 |
| Michigan . . . . . . . | 1,049.9 | 17,107.2 | 740.8 | 1,503.2 | 10,792.9 | 32,389.8 | 80,326.7 | 2,636.1 |
| Minnesota . . . . . . | 305.5 | 3,892.8 | 212.2 | 380.9 | 2,127.5 | 8,473.0 | 20,439.5 | 494.9 |
| Mississippi . . . . . . | 209.5 | 1,817.0 | 170.0 | 331.3 | 1,306.5 | 4,393.1 | 10,867.6 | 336.9 |
| Missouri . . . . . . . | 424.4 | 5,059.8 | 290.0 | 553.7 | 2,961.3 | 11,121.0 | 27,468.8 | 597.5 |
| Montana . . . . . . . | 21.7 | 269.8 | 16.9 | 34.0 | 202.7 | 771.1 | 2,524.9 | 85.6 |
| Nebraska . . . . . . . | 87.8 | 986.6 | 63.1 | 125.0 | 634.5 | 2,692.1 | 8,773.3 | 167.5 |
| Nevada . . . . . . . . | 13.6 | 144.4 | 7.7 | 14.4 | 86.9 | 354.2 | 724.8 | 53.0 |
| New Hampshire . . . | 87.8 | 883.2 | 65.7 | 124.6 | 540.4 | 1,832.4 | 3,495.4 | 137.6 |
| New Jersey . . . . . . | 735.7 | 9,703.8 | 458.4 | 906.5 | 4,851.1 | 20,287.5 | 45,711.3 | 1,216.3 |
| New Mexico . . . . . . | 30.2 | 273.0 | 23.1 | 42.1 | 175.3 | 635.2 | 1,534.0 | 119.5 |
| New York . . . . . . . | 1,455.3 | 18,786.8 | 906.9 | 1,740.5 | 9,243.1 | 38,849.3 | 76,067.1 | 2,303.7 |
| North Carolina . . . . | 738.9 | 6,655.2 | 591.8 | 1,141.9 | 4,504.7 | 15,822.1 | 35,818.9 | 1,294.6 |
| North Dakota . . . . . | 14.2 | 139.4 | 8.8 | 16.4 | 78.7 | 387.0 | 1,236.2 | 54.9 |
| Ohio . . . . . . . . . | 1,283.0 | 17,855.4 | 888.7 | 1,752.7 | 11,235.4 | 37,724.5 | 83,715.9 | 2,265.5 |
| Oklahoma . . . . . . . | 150.1 | 1,743.0 | 100.1 | 194.8 | 953.1 | 3,607.7 | 10,126.0 | 410.6 |
| Oregon . . . . . . . . | 187.8 | 2,371.4 | 145.2 | 272.5 | 1,674.7 | 5,392.2 | 12,229.2 | 378.2 |
| Pennsylvania . . . . . | 1,310.2 | 16,491.7 | 915.7 | 1,749.6 | 9,873.8 | 32,221.6 | 71,918.5 | 2,000.5 |
| Rhode Island . . . . . | 115.1 | 1,150.0 | 88.9 | 166.0 | 719.8 | 2,294.8 | 4,532.7 | 143.4 |
| South Carolina . . . . | 371.3 | 3,406.2 | 299.2 | 591.6 | 2,382.5 | 7,163.9 | 16,610.1 | 868.0 |
| South Dakota . . . . . | 21.8 | 216.5 | 16.3 | 31.9 | 149.8 | 493.9 | 1,608.5 | 48.8 |
| Tennessee . . . . . . | 478.7 | 4,686.3 | 359.8 | 694.4 | 3,039.9 | 10,723.6 | 24,755.5 | 781.3 |
| Texas . . . . . . . . | 824.6 | 9,852.0 | 560.3 | 1,113.6 | 5,661.1 | 27,600.0 | 77,120.1 | 4,768.1 |
| Utah . . . . . . . . . | 71.2 | 779.4 | 47.9 | 89.3 | 463.5 | 1,708.7 | 4,640.6 | 141.9 |
| Vermont . . . . . . . | 41.1 | 449.8 | 28.9 | 55.0 | 247.6 | 952.3 | 2,056.2 | 95.6 |
| Virginia . . . . . . . . | 377.3 | 3,851.0 | 288.9 | 560.7 | 2,547.7 | 9,367.7 | 20,470.5 | 907.4 |
| Washington . . . . . . | 244.1 | 3,594.4 | 163.3 | 307.3 | 2,086.8 | 7,296.9 | 18,842.8 | 662.2 |
| West Virginia . . . . . | 120.0 | 1,520.8 | 89.0 | 168.6 | 1,023.9 | 3,557.7 | 7,937.6 | 288.8 |
| Wisconsin . . . . . . . | 519.9 | 6,611.4 | 370.8 | 717.4 | 4,223.6 | 14,905.5 | 35,427.3 | 913.1 |
| Wyoming . . . . . . . | 7.0 | 82.9 | 4.9 | 10.0 | 54.9 | 279.0 | 833.2 | 30.5 |

## Employees in Non-Agricultural Establishments

Source: Bureau of Labor Statistics, U.S. Labor Department (p-preliminary)

(thousands)

### Annual Average by Industry Division

| Year | Total | Mining | Contr./ construc- tion | Manu- factur- ing | Trans. and public utilities | Whole., retail trade | Finance, insur., real estate | Service, miscel- laneous | Govern- ment |
|---|---|---|---|---|---|---|---|---|---|
| 1955 . . . . | 50,675 | 792 | 2,802 | 16,882 | 4,141 | 10,535 | 2,335 | 6,274 | 6,914 |
| 1960 . . . . | 54,234 | 712 | 2,885 | 16,796 | 4,004 | 11,391 | 2,669 | 7,423 | 8,353 |
| 1965 . . . . | 60,815 | 632 | 3,186 | 18,062 | 4,036 | 12,716 | 3,023 | 9,087 | 10,074 |
| 1970 . . . . | 70,920 | 623 | 3,536 | 19,369 | 4,504 | 15,040 | 3,687 | 11,621 | 12,561 |
| 1973 . . . . | 76,896 | 644 | 4,015 | 20,068 | 4,644 | 16,674 | 4,091 | 13,021 | 13,739 |
| 1974 . . . . | 78,413 | 694 | 3,957 | 20,046 | 4,696 | 17,017 | 4,208 | 13,617 | 14,177 |
| 1975 . . . . | 77,051 | 745 | 3,512 | 18,347 | 4,498 | 17,000 | 4,223 | 14,006 | 14,720 |
| 1976 . . . . | 79,443 | 783 | 3,594 | 18,956 | 4,509 | 17,694 | 4,316 | 14,644 | 14,948 |
| 1977 . . . . | 82,142 | 831 | 3,844 | 19,554 | 4,589 | 18,292 | 4,508 | 15,333 | 15,190 |

## Profits of Manufacturing Corporations by Industry Groups

Source: Federal Trade Commission

| Industry Group | Before Income Taxes | | | Profits After Taxes | | |
|---|---|---|---|---|---|---|
| | | Pct. of sales | | | Pct. of sales | |
| (Amounts estimated in millions of dollars) | 1977 | 1977 | 1976 | 1977 | 1977 | 1976 |
| **Durable goods** . . . . . . . . . . . . . . . . . . . . . . . . | **57,939** | **8.8** | **8.6** | **34,841** | **5.3** | **5.2** |
| Transportation equipment . . . . . . . . . . . . . . | 13,781 | 8.5 | 8.1 | 8,122 | 5.0 | 4.8 |
| Motor vehicles and equipment[1] . . . . . . . . . . | 10,241 | 9.2 | 9.2 | 6,133 | 5.5 | 5.6 |
| Electrical and electronic equipment . . . . . . . | 9,510 | 9.4 | 8.0 | 5,383 | 5.3 | 4.5 |
| Machinery, except electrical. . . . . . . . . . . . | 14,788 | 12.4 | 11.7 | 9,131 | 7.6 | 7.3 |
| Fabricated metal products. . . . . . . . . . . . . | 5,899 | 8.2 | 8.3 | 3,458 | 4.8 | 4.8 |
| Primary iron and steel . . . . . . . . . . . . . . | 1,058 | 1.9 | 5.7 | 864 | 1.5 | 4.1 |
| Primary nonferrous metal . . . . . . . . . . . . | 1,257 | 4.8 | 5.3 | 873 | 3.4 | 3.8 |
| Stone, clay, and glass products. . . . . . . . . | 2,775 | 8.6 | 8.1 | 1,686 | 5.2 | 5.0 |
| Instruments and related products. . . . . . . . | 4,564 | 15.0 | 13.5 | 2,725 | 9.0 | 7.9 |
| Other durable goods. . . . . . . . . . . . . . . | 4,308 | 7.3 | 6.9 | 2,594 | 4.4 | 4.2 |
| **Nondurable goods.** . . . . . . . . . . . . . . . . . . | **57,170** | **8.3** | **8.8** | **35,526** | **5.2** | **5.5** |
| Food and kindred products . . . . . . . . . . . | 9,247 | 5.1 | 5.7 | 5,575 | 3.1 | 3.4 |
| Tobacco manufactures . . . . . . . . . . . . . | 2,270 | 13.7 | 15.3 | 1,239 | 7.5 | 8.5 |
| Textile mill products . . . . . . . . . . . . . . | 1,577 | 4.6 | 4.5 | 828 | 2.4 | 2.4 |
| Paper and allied products . . . . . . . . . . . | 3,632 | 7.9 | 9.3 | 2,367 | 5.2 | 5.8 |
| Printing and publishing . . . . . . . . . . . . | 4,809 | 10.3 | 9.4 | 2,663 | 5.7 | 5.1 |
| Chemicals and allied products . . . . . . . . . | 13,063 | 11.6 | 12.2 | 8,060 | 7.2 | 7.5 |
| Petroleum and coal products . . . . . . . . . . | 17,790 | 10.4 | 12.0 | 12,179 | 7.1 | 8.3 |
| Rubber and miscellaneous plastic products . . . | 2,287 | 6.8 | 6.6 | 1,322 | 3.9 | 3.8 |
| Other nondurable products . . . . . . . . . . . | 2,497 | 5.5 | 5.2 | 1,295 | 2.9 | 2.8 |
| **All Manufacturing Corps** . . . . . . . . . . . . . . . . . . . | **115,111** | **8.6** | **8.7** | **70,366** | **5.2** | **5.4** |

(1) Included in major industry above.

---

## Annual Rates of Profit on Stockholders' Equity

Source: Federal Trade Commission

(Each rate is the arithmetic mean of 4 quarterly rates, each on an annual basis.)

| By industry after taxes: by percent | 1950 | 1960 | 1965 | 1970[1] | 1974[2] | 1975 | 1976 | 1977 |
|---|---|---|---|---|---|---|---|---|
| All manufacturing corporations, except newspapers | 15.4 | 9.2 | 13.0 | 9.3 | 14.9 | 11.6 | 13.9 | 14.2 |
| **Durable goods industries.** . . . . . . . . . . . | 16.8 | 8.6 | 13.8 | 8.3 | 12.6 | 10.3 | 13.7 | 14.5 |
| Metals and metal fabricating industries . . . . | 16.9 | 8.6 | 14.2 | * | * | * | * | * |
| Transportation equipment . . . . . . . . | 21.5 | 11.7 | 18.5 | 6.3 | 8.0 | 7.5 | 16.0 | 17.4 |
| Motor vehicles and equipment. . . . . . | 25.2 | 13.5 | 19.5 | 6.1 | 6.9 | 6.2 | 17.1 | 18.7 |
| Aircraft and parts . . . . . . . . . . . . | * | 7.4 | 15.1 | 6.8 | 10.6 | 11.0 | 12.8 | 15.0 |
| Electrical machinery, equipment and supplies. . | 20.8 | 9.5 | 13.5 | 9.1 | 11.1 | 9.0 | 12.8 | 15.2 |
| Machinery, except electrical. . . . . . . . . | 14.0 | 7.6 | 14.1 | 9.9 | 13.2 | 13.7 | 15.4 | 16.7 |
| Metalworking machinery and equipment . . . . | * | 5.3 | 14.4 | 8.3 | * | * | * | * |
| Other fabricated metal products . . . . . . . | 15.9 | 5.6 | 13.2 | 8.6 | 16.6 | 13.2 | 15.3 | 15.7 |
| Primary metal industries . . . . . . . . . . | 14.5 | 7.2 | 10.6 | 7.0 | 16.4 | 8.6 | 8.5 | 4.7 |
| Blast furnaces, steel works and foundries . . | 14.3 | 7.2 | 9.8 | 4.3 | 16.8 | 10.9 | 9.0 | 3.6 |
| Nonferrous metals . . . . . . . . . . . . | 15.0 | 7.1 | 11.9 | 10.7 | 15.8 | 5.0 | 7.4 | 7.0 |
| **Other durable goods industries** . . . . . . . . . | 16.3 | 8.6 | 12.2 | * | * | * | * | * |
| Lumber and wood products, except furniture . . . | 17.4 | 3.6 | 10.0 | 5.9 | * | * | * | * |
| Furniture and fixtures . . . . . . . . . . . . | 15.1 | 6.5 | 13.3 | 7.9 | * | * | * | * |
| Stone, clay and glass products . . . . . . . . | 17.6 | 9.9 | 10.2 | 6.9 | 10.6 | 8.3 | 11.9 | 13.3 |
| Instruments and related products . . . . . . . | 16.7 | 11.6 | 17.5 | 14.2 | 16.1 | 13.5 | 14.7 | 16.9 |
| Miscellaneous manufacturing and ordnance . . . | 12.2 | 9.2 | 10.7 | 10.0 | * | * | * | * |
| **Nondurable goods industries** . . . . . . . . . . | 14.0 | 9.8 | 12.2 | 10.3 | 17.2 | 12.9 | 14.2 | 13.9 |
| Chemicals: petroleum, rubber, and plastics . . . . | 15.4 | 10.8 | 13.0 | * | * | * | * | * |
| Chemicals and allied products . . . . . . . . | 17.8 | 12.2 | 15.2 | 11.5 | 18.2 | 15.2 | 15.5 | 15.1 |
| Basic chemicals and related products . . . . . | * | 11.1 | 14.3 | 8.5 | 17.4 | 13.3 | 14.2 | 13.5 |
| Drugs. . . . . . . . . . . . . . . . . . . . | * | 16.8 | 20.3 | 17.6 | 18.8 | 17.8 | 18.0 | 18.2 |
| Petroleum refining and related industries. . . . | 13.8 | 10.1 | 11.8 | 11.0 | 21.0 | 12.5 | 14.1 | 13.6 |
| Petroleum refining . . . . . . . . . . . . | * | 10.1 | 11.8 | 11.0 | * | * | * | * |
| Rubber and miscellaneous plastics products . . . | 16.7 | 9.1 | 11.7 | 7.1 | 14.4 | 8.0 | 10.8 | 12.1 |
| **Other nondurable goods industries** . . . . . . . . | 12.8 | 8.5 | 11.1 | * | * | * | * | * |
| Food and kindred products . . . . . . . . . . | 12.3 | 8.7 | 10.7 | 10.8 | 14.0 | 14.4 | 14.9 | 13.3 |
| Dairy products . . . . . . . . . . . . . . | * | * | 10.6 | 10.2 | * | * | * | * |
| Bakery products . . . . . . . . . . . . . | * | * | 9.3 | 8.8 | * | * | * | * |
| Alcoholic beverages . . . . . . . . . . . | * | 7.1 | 9.3 | 10.5 | * | * | * | * |
| Tobacco manufactures . . . . . . . . . . . | 11.5 | 13.4 | 13.5 | 15.7 | 15.6 | 15.9 | 15.9 | 17.5 |
| Textile mill products . . . . . . . . . . . . | 12.6 | 5.8 | 10.8 | 5.1 | 8.2 | 4.2 | 8.0 | 8.6 |
| Apparel and other fabricated textile products . . . | 10.1 | 7.7 | 12.6 | 11.9 | * | * | * | * |
| Paper and allied products . . . . . . . . . . | 16.1 | 8.5 | 9.4 | 7.0 | 17.8 | 12.6 | 13.8 | 12.4 |
| Printing and publishing, except newspapers . . . | 11.5 | 10.6 | 14.1 | 11.2 | 13.2 | 12.8 | 15.1 | 17.4 |
| Leather and leather products . . . . . . . . . | 10.9 | 6.3 | 11.6 | 9.4 | * | * | * | * |

*—Not available. (1) Includes newspapers for the first time. (2) Profits for 1974 include equity in earnings (net of taxes) of nonconsolidated subsidiaries. In prior years this component was included in adjustment to earned surplus.

## Retail Store Sales

Source: Bureau of the Census, U.S. Commerce Department (millions of dollars)

| Kind of business | 1976 | 1977 | Kind of business | 1976 | 1977 |
|---|---|---|---|---|---|
| All retail stores . . . . . . . . . . | 642,507 | 708,344 | Apparel group. . . . . . . . . . . . | 33,188 | 33,527 |
| **Durable goods stores** . . . | **210,530** | **238,815** | Men's and boys' wear stores. . | 6,683 | 6,694 |
| Automotive group. . . . . . . . . | 125,685 | 143,682 | Women's apparel, accessory | | |
| Motor vehicle, other | | | stores . . . . . . . . . . . . . | 12,702 | 12,814 |
| automotive dealers . . . . . . | 115,596 | 131,418 | Shoe stores . . . . . . . . . . . | 5,575 | 5,766 |
| Tire, battery, accessory | | | Food group . . . . . . . . . . . . | 145,939 | 156,313 |
| dealers. . . . . . . . . . . . . | 10,089 | 12,264 | Grocery stores. . . . . . . . . . | 136,100 | 145,900 |
| Furniture and appliance group . . | 31,368 | 34,499 | General merchandise group | | |
| Furniture, home furnishings | | | with stores. . . . . . . . . . | 79,258 | 89,231 |
| stores . . . . . . . . . . . . . | 18,665 | 20,843 | Department stores, excl. | | |
| Household appliance, radio | | | mail order . . . . . . . . . . . | 62,900 | 71,583 |
| TV stores . . . . . . . . . . | 9,784 | 10,654 | Mail order (catalog sales). . . . | 6,099 | 6,751 |
| Lumber, building, hardware | | | Variety stores . . . . . . . . . | 7,598 | 7,958 |
| group. . . . . . . . . . . . . . | 32,226 | 37,958 | Eating and drinking places. . . . | 58,008 | 63,825 |
| Lumber, building materials | | | Gasoline service stations . . . . | 51,265 | 56,538 |
| dealers. . . . . . . . . . . . . | 22,206 | 26,706 | Drug and proprietary stores. . . . | 20,716 | 22,380 |
| Hardware stores. . . . . . . . . | 5,659 | 6,431 | Liquor stores . . . . . . . . . . | 12,734 | 13,084 |
| **Nondurable goods stores. . . .** | **431,977** | **469,529** | | | |

Total retail stores sales (millions of dollars) — (1955) 183,851; (1956) 189,729; (1957) 200,002; (1958) 200,353; (1959) 215,413; (1960) 219,529; (1961) 218,992; (1962) 235,563; (1963) 246,666; (1964) 261,870; (1965) 284,128; (1966) 303,956; (1967) 292,956; (1968) 325,109; (1969) 348,492; (1970) 371,082; (1971) 410,024; (1972) 449,069; (1973) 502,453; (1974) 534,511; (1975) 584,423.

## Cotton, Wool, Silk, and Man-Made Fibers Production

Source: Economics, Statistics, and Cooperatives Service, U.S. Agriculture Department

Cotton and wool from reports of the Agriculture Department; silk, rayon, and non-cellulosic man-made fibers from Textile Organon, a publication of the Textile Economics Bureau, Inc.

| Year | Cotton[1] U.S. (million bales) | Cotton[1] World | Wool[2] U.S. (million pounds) | Wool[2] World | Silk World (mil. lbs.) | Rayon & acetate U.S. (million pounds) | Rayon & acetate World | Man-made fibers[1] Non-cellulosic[4] U.S.[4] (million pounds) | Man-made fibers[1] Non-cellulosic[4] World |
|---|---|---|---|---|---|---|---|---|---|
| 1940 . . . . . . . | 12.6 | 31.2 | 434.0 | 4,180 | 130 | 471.2 | 2,485.3 | 4.6 | 4.6 |
| 1950 . . . . . . . | 10.0 | 30.6 | 249.3 | 4,000 | 42 | 1,259.4 | 3,552.8 | 145.9 | 177.4 |
| 1960 . . ? . . . . | 14.2 | 46.2 | 298.9 | 5,615 | 68 | 1,028.5 | 5,749.1 | 854.2 | 1,779.1 |
| 1965 . . . . . . . | 15.0 | 55.0 | 224.8 | 5,836 | 72 | 1,527.0 | 7,359.4 | 2,062.4 | 4,928.9 |
| 1967 . . . . . . . | 7.4 | 49.7 | 211.4 | 6,040 | 75 | 1,388.1 | 7,297.4 | 2,662.1 | 6,013.0 |
| 1968 . . . . . . . | 10.9 | 54.7 | 197.9 | 6,295 | 82 | 1,594.3 | 7,779.0 | 3,632.1 | 7,906.0 |
| 1969 . . . . . . . | 10.0 | 53.2 | 182.8 | 6,261 | 86 | 1,576.2 | 7,835.0 | 4,029.3 | 9,211.0 |
| 1970 . . . . . . . | 10.2 | 53.6 | 176.8 | 6,163 | 90 | 1,373.2 | 7,564.0 | 4,053.5 | 10,363.0 |
| 1971 . . . . . . . | 10.5 | 59.8 | 172.2 | 6,033 | 90 | 1,390.9 | 7,590.0 | 4,761.0 | 12,352.0 |
| 1972 . . . . . . . | 13.7 | 62.9 | 168.6 | 5,631 | 93 | 1,394.3 | 7,838.0 | 5,927.0 | 14,043.0 |
| 1973 . . . . . . . | 13.0 | 63.2 | 153.2 | 5,508 | 97 | 1,357.0 | 8,071.0 | 6,997.4 | 16,820.0 |
| 1974 . . . . . . . | 11.5 | 64.3 | 138.7 | 5,728 | 99 | 1,198.8 | 7,803.0 | 6,906.5 | 16,486.0 |
| 1975 . . . . . . . | 8.3 | 54.3 | 123.4 | 5,732 | 106 | 749.0 | 6,536.0 | 6,432.2 | 16,233.0 |
| 1976 . . . . . . . | 10.6 | 57.5 | 113.9 | 5,580 | 108 | 848.1 | 6,980.0 | 7,293.7 | 18,760.0 |
| 1977 . . . . . . . | 14.4 | 63.7 | 112.0 | 5,527 | 108 | 887.7 | 7,175.0 | 6,691.3 | 19,938.8 |

(1) Year beginning Aug. 1. (2) Grease basis. (3) Includes filament yarn and staple and tow fiber. (4) Includes textile glass fiber. (5) 480-pound net weight bales, U.S. beginning 1960 and world beginning 1965. (6) 1966 to date, excludes Olefin.

## Work Stoppages (Strikes) in the U.S.

Source: Bureau of Labor Statistics, U.S. Labor Department

| | Number stoppages | Workers involved (thousands) | Man days idle (thousands) | | Number stoppages | Workers involved (thousands) | Man days idle (thousands) |
|---|---|---|---|---|---|---|---|
| Average 1935-1939 | 2,862 | 1,130 | 16,900 | 1962. . . . . . . . . . | 3,614 | 1,230 | 18,600 |
| War Period | | | | 1963. . . . . . . . . . | 3,362 | 941 | 16,100 |
| Dec. 8, 1941-Aug. | | | | 1964. . . . . . . . . . | 3,655 | 1,640 | 22,900 |
| 14, 1945 . . . . . . . | 14,371 | 6,744 | 36,300 | 1965. . . . . . . . . . | 3,963 | 1,550 | 23,300 |
| Year . . . . . . . . . . | | | | 1966. . . . . . . . . . | 4,405 | 1,960 | 25,400 |
| 1947. . . . . . . . . . | 3,693 | 2,170 | 34,600 | 1967. . . . . . . . . . | 4,595 | 2,870 | 42,100 |
| 1948. . . . . . . . . . | 3,419 | 1,960 | 34,100 | 1968. . . . . . . . . . | 5,045 | 2,649 | 49,018 |
| 1949. . . . . . . . . . | 3,606 | 3,030 | 50,500 | 1969. . . . . . . . . . | 5,700 | 2,481 | 42,869 |
| 1950. . . . . . . . . . | 4,843 | 2,410 | 38,800 | 1970. . . . . . . . . . | 5,716 | 3,305 | 66,414 |
| 1951. . . . . . . . . . | 4,737 | 2,220 | 22,900 | 1971. . . . . . . . . . | 5,138 | 3,280 | 47,589 |
| 1952. . . . . . . . . . | 5,117 | 3,540 | 59,100 | 1972. . . . . . . . . . | 5,010 | 1,714 | 27,066 |
| 1953. . . . . . . . . . | 5,091 | 2,400 | 28,300 | 1973. . . . . . . . . . | 5,353 | 2,251 | 27,948 |
| 1954. . . . . . . . . . | 3,468 | 1,530 | 22,600 | 1974. . . . . . . . . . | 6,074 | 2,778 | 47,991 |
| 1955. . . . . . . . . . | 4,320 | 2,650 | 28,200 | 1975. . . . . . . . . . | 5,031 | 1,746 | 31,237 |
| 1956. . . . . . . . . . | 3,825 | 1,900 | 33,100 | 1976. . . . . . . . . . | 5,648 | 2,420 | 37,859 |
| 1957. . . . . . . . . . | 3,673 | 1,390 | 16,500 | 1977p . . . . . . . . . | 5,600 | 2,300 | 36,000 |
| 1958. . . . . . . . . . | 3,694 | 2,060 | 23,900 | 1978p January. . . . . | 271 | 87 | 4,689 |
| 1959. . . . . . . . . . | 3,708 | 1,880 | 69,000 | February. . . . | 267 | 70 | 4,221 |
| 1960. . . . . . . . . . | 3,333 | 1,320 | 19,100 | March . . . . . | 349 | 126 | 4,290 |
| 1961. . . . . . . . . . | 3,367 | 1,450 | 16,300 | (p) Preliminary | | | |

## Occupational Earnings in Selected Metropolitan Areas

**Source:** Bureau of Labor Statistics, U.S. Labor Department

(Average earnings[1] for selected occupations studied in 6 broad industry divisions: manufacturing, transportation, communication, and other public utilities; wholesale trade; retail trade; finance, insurance, and real estate; and selected services, March-May 1977)

| Occupations | Birmingham, Ala. | Detroit, Mich. | Norfolk-Virginia Beach-Portsmouth, Va.-N.C. | St. Louis, Mo.-Ill. | San Jose, Calif. | Toledo, Ohio-Mich. | Worcester, Mass. |
|---|---|---|---|---|---|---|---|
| **Office workers** | | | **Average weekly earnings, straight-time** | | | | |
| Accounting clerks[2] | $194.50 | $233.50 | $172.00 | $207.00 | $188.50 | $208.50 | $193.50 |
| Computer operators[2] | 204.50 | 303.00 | — | 252.00 | 264.00 | 230.00 | 218.00 |
| Computer programmers, business[2] | 301.00 | 377.50 | — | 300.00 | 377.50 | 277.00 | 328.00 |
| Computer systems analysts, business[2] | 366.50 | 438.00 | 344.00 | 390.50 | 445.00 | 371.50 | 363.00 |
| Drafters[2] | 302.00 | 416.50 | — | 315.00 | 299.00 | 313.50 | 272.00 |
| File clerks[2] | 149.00 | 197.00 | — | 160.50 | — | — | — |
| Keypunch operators[2] | 149.50 | 198.00 | 138.00 | 184.50 | 200.00 | 198.50 | 164.50 |
| Messengers | 131.00 | 148.50 | — | 133.00 | 163.00 | 135.50 | 123.50 |
| Registered industrial nurses | 227.00 | 311.00 | — | 258.00 | 278.00 | 260.50 | 236.00 |
| Secretaries | 183.50 | 257.50 | 172.50 | 194.00 | 217.50 | 211.50 | 189.00 |
| Stenographers, general | 164.50 | 191.00 | 154.50 | 170.00 | 189.00 | 192.00 | 164.00 |
| Typists[2] | 145.50 | 197.00 | 162.50 | 172.00 | 197.50 | 162.00 | 158.00 |
| **Maintenance, custodial, and material movement workers** | | | **Average hourly earnings, straight-time** | | | | |
| Carpenters | $6.44 | $8.34 | $— | $7.11 | $7.68 | $7.12 | $5.93 |
| Electricians | 6.89 | 8.60 | 6.92 | 7.64 | 8.19 | 7.77 | 6.49 |
| Stationary engineers | 7.03 | 8.24 | — | 7.28 | 7.59 | 7.12 | 6.17 |
| Trades helpers | 5.56 | 6.69 | 4.38 | 6.11 | 6.10 | 6.33 | 4.21 |
| Machinists | 6.85 | 8.12 | 5.92 | 7.54 | 7.97 | 7.35 | 6.69 |
| Mechanics (motor vehicles) | 5.90 | 8.10 | 5.83 | 7.12 | 8.45 | 7.82 | 6.58 |
| Painters | 5.95 | 8.33 | — | 7.20 | 7.83 | 7.21 | — |
| Guards and watchmen | 2.74 | 4.89 | 3.36 | 3.21 | 3.90 | 3.37 | 3.56 |
| Janitors, porters and cleaners | 2.74 | 4.95 | 3.03 | 3.80 | 4.62 | 4.61 | 3.70 |
| Material handling laborers | 3.66 | 6.41 | 3.75 | 5.71 | 5.41 | 6.10 | 5.05 |
| Shipping packers | 4.12 | 6.08 | — | 5.19 | 4.51 | 5.85 | 4.42 |
| Shipping clerks | 4.99 | 7.07 | 4.26 | 5.51 | — | 5.93 | 4.56 |
| Truckdrivers, local | 4.63 | 7.14 | 4.36 | 7.09 | 7.74 | 7.20 | 6.06 |

(1) Weekly earnings relate to regular straight-time salaries that are paid for standard workweeks. Hourly earnings exclude premium pay for overtime, weekends, holidays, or late shifts. (2) More than one skill level surveyed. Earnings are for the highest level surveyed.

## Employment Status of Civilian Labor Force

**Source:** Bureau of Labor Statistics, U.S. Labor Department

(thousands)

| Employment status | Annual average 1976 | 1977 | 1977 Oct. | Nov. | Dec. | 1978 Jan. | Feb. | Mar. | Apr. |
|---|---|---|---|---|---|---|---|---|---|
| Total noninstitutional population | 156,048 | 158,559 | 159,334 | 159,522 | 159,736 | 159,937 | 160,128 | 160,313 | 160,504 |
| Total labor force | 96,917 | 99,534 | 100,205 | 101,009 | 101,048 | 101,228 | 101,217 | 101,536 | 102,118 |
| Civilian noninstitutional population | 153,904 | 156,426 | 157,201 | 157,389 | 157,608 | 157,816 | 158,004 | 158,190 | 158,386 |
| Civilian labor force | 94,773 | 97,401 | 98,071 | 98,877 | 98,919 | 99,107 | 99,093 | 99,414 | 99,784 |
| Employed | 87,485 | 90,546 | 91,383 | 92,214 | 92,609 | 92,881 | 93,003 | 93,266 | 93,801 |
| Agriculture | 3,297 | 3,244 | 3,243 | 3,357 | 3,323 | 3,354 | 3,242 | 3,310 | 3,275 |
| Nonagricultural industries | 84,188 | 87,302 | 88,140 | 88,857 | 89,286 | 89,527 | 89,761 | 89,956 | 90,526 |
| Unemployed | 7,288 | 6,855 | 6,688 | 6,663 | 6,310 | 6,226 | 6,090 | 6,148 | 5,983 |
| Unemployment rate | 7.7 | 7.0 | 6.8 | 6.7 | 6.4 | 6.3 | 6.1 | 6.2 | 6.0 |
| Not in labor force | 59,130 | 59,025 | 59,130 | 58,512 | 58,689 | 58,709 | 58,911 | 58,776 | 58,602 |
| **Men, 20 years and over** | | | | | | | | | |
| Civilian noninstitutional population | 64,561 | 65,796 | 66,161 | 66,257 | 66,364 | 66,467 | 66,556 | 66,645 | 66,740 |
| Civilian labor force | 51,527 | 52,464 | 52,739 | 52,971 | 53,122 | 53,153 | 53,142 | 53,242 | 53,263 |
| Employed | 48,486 | 49,737 | 50,118 | 50,459 | 50,688 | 50,673 | 50,759 | 50,833 | 51,038 |
| Agriculture | 2,359 | 2,308 | 2,326 | 2,330 | 2,346 | 2,394 | 2,283 | 2,289 | 2,295 |
| Nonagricultural industries | 46,128 | 47,429 | 47,792 | 48,129 | 48,342 | 48,279 | 48,476 | 48,544 | 48,743 |
| Unemployed | 3,041 | 2,727 | 2,621 | 2,512 | 2,434 | 2,480 | 2,383 | 2,409 | 2,225 |
| Unemployment rate | 5.9 | 5.2 | 5.0 | 4.7 | 4.6 | 4.7 | 4.5 | 4.5 | 4.2 |
| Not in labor force | 13,034 | 13,332 | 13,422 | 13,286 | 13,242 | 13,314 | 13,414 | 13,403 | 13,477 |
| **Women, 20 years and over** | | | | | | | | | |
| Civilian noninstitutional population | 72,917 | 74,160 | 74,561 | 74,669 | 74,783 | 74,892 | 74,996 | 75,093 | 75,198 |
| Civilian labor force | 34,276 | 35,685 | 35,984 | 36,451 | 36,418 | 36,595 | 36,654 | 36,849 | 37,117 |
| Employed | 31,730 | 33,199 | 33,537 | 33,923 | 34,009 | 34,348 | 34,569 | 34,722 | 34,948 |
| Agriculture | 511 | 537 | 525 | 589 | 543 | 517 | 604 | 628 | 623 |
| Nonagricultural industries | 31,218 | 32,662 | 33,012 | 33,334 | 33,466 | 33,831 | 33,965 | 34,094 | 34,325 |
| Unemployed | 2,546 | 2,486 | 2,447 | 2,528 | 2,409 | 2,247 | 2,085 | 2,127 | 2,169 |
| Unemployment rate | 7.4 | 7.0 | 6.8 | 6.9 | 6.6 | 6.1 | 5.7 | 5.8 | 5.8 |
| Not in labor force | 38,641 | 38,474 | 38,577 | 38,218 | 38,365 | 38,297 | 38,342 | 38,244 | 38,081 |

# Labor Union Membership

**Source:** U.S. Labor Department

AFL-CIO unions with a membership of 25,000 or over (Aug., 1978)

| Union | Members | Union | Members |
|---|---|---|---|
| Actors and Artists of America, Associated | 85,000 | Retail Clerks International Association | 646,000 |
| Air Line Pilots Association | 44,000 | Retail, Wholesale and Department Store Union | 131,000 |
| Aluminum Workers International Union | 26,000 | Roofers, Damp & Waterproof Workers Association, United Slate, Tile & Composition | 27,000 |
| Bakery and Confectionery Workers International Union of America | 115,000 | Rubber, Cork, Linoleum & Plastic Workers of America, United | 159,000 |
| Barbers, Hairdressers and Cosmetologists' International Union of America, the Journeymen | 34,000 | Seafarers International Union of North America | 94,000 |
| Boilermakers, Iron Ship Builders, Blacksmiths, Forgers and Helpers, International Brotherhood of | 130,000 | Service Employees International Union, AFL-CIO | 505,000 |
| Bricklayers, Masons, and Plasterers International Union of America | 112,000 | Sheet Metal Workers International Association | 120,000 |
| | | Stage Employes & Moving Picture Machine Operators of the United States & Canada, International Alliance of Theatrical | 50,000 |
| Carpenters and Joiners of America, United Brotherhood of | 675,000 | State, County & Municipal Employees, American Federation of | 685,000 |
| Cement, Lime and Gypsum Workers International Union, United | 26,000 | Steelworkers of America, United | 954,000 |
| Chemical Workers Union, International | 51,000 | Teachers, American Federation of | 420,000 |
| Clothing and Textile Workers Union, Amalgamated | 301,000 | Textile Workers of America, United | 31,000 |
| Communications Workers of America | 478,000 | Transit Union, Amalgamated | 89,000 |
| | | Transport Workers Union of America | 93,000 |
| Dolls, Toys, Playthings, Novelties and Allied Products of the United States and Canada, AFL-CIO, International Union of | 33,000 | Transportation Union, United | 122,000 |
| | | Typographical Union, International | 61,000 |
| Electrical, Radio and Machine Workers International Union of | 238,000 | Upholsterers' International Union of North America | 46,000 |
| Electrical Workers, International Brotherhood of | 814,000 | Utility Workers Union of America | 52,000 |
| Engineers, International Union of Operating | 300,000 | Woodworkers of America, International | 53,000 |
| Fire Fighters, International Association of | 148,000 | | |
| Firemen and Oilers, International Brotherhood of | 38,000 | | |
| Furniture Workers of America, United | 26,000 | | |

## Independent Unions

### (Feb., 1978)

| Union | Members | Union | Members |
|---|---|---|---|
| Garment Workers of America, United | 32,000 | Automobile, Aerospace and Agricultural Implement Workers of America, International Union, United | 1,544,859 |
| Garment Workers Union, International Ladies' | 350,000 | Distributive Workers of America | 50,000 |
| Glass and Ceramic Workers of North America, United | 26,000 | Education Association, National | 1,470,212 |
| Glass Bottle Blowers' Association of the United States and Canada | 75,000 | Electrical, Radio, and Machine Workers of America, United | 163,000 |
| Glass Workers Union, American Flint | 31,000 | Federal Employees, National Federation of | 100,000 |
| Government Employees, American Federation of | 254,000 | Government Employees, National Assn. of | 96,817 |
| Grain Millers, American Federation of | 35,000 | Locomotive Engineers, Brotherhood of | 39,245 |
| Graphic Arts International Union | 83,000 | Longshoremen's and Warehousemen's Union International | 55,000 |
| Hotel and Restaurant Employees' and Bartenders' International Union | 398,000 | Mine Workers of America, United | 220,000 |
| | | Nurses' Association, American | 196,499 |
| Industrial Workers of America, International Union, Allied | 84,000 | Plant Guard Workers of America; Intl. Union, United | 34,000 |
| Iron Workers, International Association of Bridge and Structural | 160,000 | Police, Fraternal Order of | 147,000 |
| | | Postal Supervisors, National Assn. of | 35,000 |
| Laborers' International Union of North America | 475,000 | Rural Letter Carrier's Assn., National | 49,135 |
| Leather Goods, Plastics and Novelty Workers Union, International | 30,000 | Teamsters, Chauffeurs, Warehousemen and Helpers of America, Int'l Brotherhood of | 1,973,272 |
| Letter Carriers, National Association of | 151,000 | Telecommunications International Union | 65,000 |
| Longshoremen's Association, International | 62,000 | Treasury Employees Union, National | 50,000 |
| | | University Professors, American Assn. of | 72,265 |
| Machinists and Aerospace Workers, International Association of | 653,000 | | |
| Maintenance of Way Employees, Brotherhood of | 73,000 | | |
| Maritime Union of America, National | 30,000 | | |
| Meat Cutters and Butcher Workmen of North America, Amalgamated | 442,000 | ## Canadian Unions | |
| Molders and Allied Workers Union, International | 50,000 | ### Independent Unions (1977) | |
| Musicians, American Federation of | 187,000 | | |
| Newspaper Guild, The | 26,000 | Civil Service Assn. of Ontario, The | 57,000 |
| | | Teachers' Federation, Quebec | 85,000 |
| Office and Professional Employees International Union | 77,000 | Teachers' Federation, Ontario Secondary School | 37,050 |
| Oil, Chemical and Atomic Workers Internaional Union | 145,000 | ### CNTU Unions (1977) | |
| Painters & Allied Trades of the United States and Canada, International Brotherhood of | 160,000 | Public Service Employees Inc., Federation of | 24,000 |
| Paper Workers International Union, United | 261,000 | Social Affairs Federation | 65,000 |
| Plasterers' & Cement Masons' International Association of the United States and Canada, Operative | 50,000 | ### CLC Unions (1977) | |
| Plumbing and Pipe Fitting Industry of the United States & Canada, United Association of Journeymen & Apprentices of the | 228,000 | Automobile, Aerospace and Agricultural Implement Workers of America, International Union, United | 119,020 |
| Postal Workers Union, American | 254,000 | Food and Allied Workers, Canadian | 59,208 |
| Printing and Graphics Communications Union, International | 99,000 | Paperworkers Union, Canadian | 54,741 |
| | | Postal Workers, Canadian Union of | 22,528 |
| Railway, Airline and Steamship Clerks, Freight Handlers, Express & Station Employes, Brotherhood of | 107,000 | Provincial Govt. Employees, National Union of | 96,752 |
| | | Public Employees, Canadian Union of | 236,136 |
| Railway Carmen of the United States & Canada, Brotherhood | 51,000 | Public Service Alliance of Canada | 148,835 |
| | | Railway, Transport and General Workers, Canadian Brotherhood of | 33,000 |
| | | Steelworkers of America, United | 175,227 |

# U.S. Mineral Production

Source: Bureau of Mines. U.S. Interior Department

Production as measured by mine shipments, sales, or marketable production (including consumption by producers)

| Mineral fuels | | 1976 Quantity | 1976 Value (thousands) | 1977p Quantity | 1977p Value (thousands) |
|---|---|---|---|---|---|
| Asphalt and related bitumens (native): | | | | | |
| Bituminous limestone & sandstone & gilsonite | short tons | 2,011,500 | $17,647 | 1,920,000 | $18,040 |
| Carbon dioxide, natural(e) | thousand cubic feet | 1,356,834 | 298 | 1,355,000 | 338 |
| Coal: Bituminous and lignite[1] | thousand short tons | 678,685 | 13,189,481 | 685,000 | 14,400,000 |
| Pennsylvania anthracite | thousand short tons | 6,228 | 209,234 | 6,200 | 217,000 |
| Helium: Crude | million cubic feet | 585 | 7,020 | 492 | 5,904 |
| Grade A | million cubic feet | 754 | 18,928 | 874 | 22,339 |
| Natural gas | million cubic feet | 19,952,438 | 11,571,776 | 19,924,671 | 15,522,658 |
| Natural gas liquids: Gasoline products | thousand 42-gal. bbls. | 149,679 | 985,442 | 149,660 | 1,167,315 |
| LP gases | thousand 42-gal. bbls. | 437,366 | 2,298,647 | 435,240 | 3,219,435 |
| Peat | thousand short tons | 947 | 17,096 | 974 | 20,413 |
| Petroleum (crude) | thousand 42-gal. bbls. | 2,976,180 | 24,229,540 | 2,986,710 | 25,397,307 |
| **Total mineral fuels** | | XX | **52,545,000** | XX | **59,991,000** |
| **Non metals (except fuels)** | | | | | |
| Abrasive stones[2] | short tons | 2,696 | 1,404 | W | W |
| Asbestos | short tons | 114,842 | 23,693 | 105,400 | 26,040 |
| Barite | thousand short tons | 1,234 | 28,689 | 1,549 | 36,139 |
| Boron minerals | thousand short tons | 1,246 | 184,852 | 1,436 | 235,899 |
| Bromine | thousand pounds | 439,538 | 107,653 | W | W |
| Calcium chloride | short tons | 648,929 | 32,889 | 761,780 | 38,705 |
| Cement: Portland | thousand short tons | 69,163 | 2,330,402 | 73,957 | 2,663,520 |
| Masonry | thousand short tons | 3,267 | 139,564 | 3,669 | 166,704 |
| Natural and slag | thousand short tons | NA | NA | NA | NA |
| Clays | thousand short tons | 52,390 | 528,745 | 56,251 | 563,527 |
| Diatomite | short tons | W | W | 637,000 | 66,08. |
| Feldspar | short tons | 739,684 | 17,531 | 765,000 | 18,832 |
| Fluorspar | short tons | 188,270 | 17,927 | 179,591 | 16,872 |
| Garnet (abrasive) | short tons | 24,565 | 2,740 | W | W |
| Gem stones (e) | | NA | 8,907 | NA | 6,849 |
| Gypsum | thousand short tons | 11,980 | 59,888 | 13,851 | 76,181 |
| Lime | thousand short tons | 20,229 | 609,010 | 19,660 | 690,446 |
| Magnesium compounds from sea water and brine (except for metals) | short tons, MgO equivalent | W | W | W | W |
| Mica: Scrap | thousand short tons | 127 | 5,686 | 164 | 8,133 |
| Sheet | pounds | 5,000 | 3 | NA | NA |
| Perlite | short tons | 553,000 | 9,397 | 602,000 | 10,765 |
| Phosphate rock | thousand short tons | 49,241 | 949,365 | 49,221 | 770,060 |
| Potassium salts | thousand short tons K₂O equivalent | 2,500 | 202,635 | 2,540 | 210,082 |
| Pumice | thousand short tons | 4,134 | 10,500 | 4,109 | 12,507 |
| Pyrites | thousand long tons | 750 | 8,213 | W | W |
| Salt | thousand short tons | 44,191 | 430,959 | 42,934 | 440,450 |
| Sand and gravel | thousand short tons | 885,156 | 1,774,030 | 898,188 | 1,861,243 |
| Sodium carbonate (natural) | thousand short tons | 5,216 | 259,253 | 6,138 | 336,722 |
| Sodium sulfate (natural) | thousand short tons | 663 | 32,655 | 647 | 29,402 |
| Stone[3] | thousand short tons | 901,660 | 2,221,000 | 915,566 | 2,305,370 |
| Sulfur: Frasch process mines | thousand long tons | 5,860 | 299,999 | 6,200 | 302,558 |
| Talc, soapstone, and pyrophillite | short tons | 1,092,433 | 9,902 | 1,054,224 | 14,413 |
| Tripoli | short tons | 124,281 | 776 | W | W |
| Vermiculite | short tons | 304 | 14,032 | 349 | 18,126 |

Value of items that cannot be disclosed: Aplite, brucite, emery, graphite, iodine, kyanite, lithium minerals, magnesite, greensand marl, olivine, staurolite, wollastonite, and values of nonmetal items indicated by symbol W:

| | | | | | |
|---|---|---|---|---|---|
| | | XX | 224,473 | XX | 293,850 |
| **Total nonmetals** | | XX | **10,547,000** | XX | **11,219,000** |
| **Metals** | | | | | |
| Antimony ore concentrate, antimony content | short tons | 283 | 600 | 770 | W |
| Bauxite | thousand long tons, dried equivalent | 1,958 | 26,645 | 2,000 | 27,500 |
| Beryllium concentrate | short tons, gross weight | W | W | W | W |
| Copper (recoverable content of ores, etc.) | short tons | 1,605,586 | 2,234,975 | 1,503,966 | 2,009,297 |
| Gold (recoverable content of ores, etc.) | troy ounces | 1,048,037 | 131,340 | 1,100,347 | 163,192 |
| Iron ore (excluding iron sinter) | thousand long tons, gr. wgt. | 76,697 | 1,860,102 | 53,696 | 1,365,033 |
| Lead (recoverable content of ores, etc.) | short tons | 609,546 | 281,610 | 592,491 | 363,789 |
| Manganese ore (35% or more Mn) | short tons, gross wgt. | — | — | — | — |
| Manganiferous ore (5 to 35% Mn) | short tons, gross wgt. | 256,633 | 2,260 | W | W |
| Mercury | 76-pound flasks | 23,133 | 2,806 | 32,000 | 4,640 |
| Molybdenum (content of concentrate) | thousand pounds | 114,527 | 33,494 | 122,750 | 451,900 |
| Nickel (content of ore and concentrate) | short tons | 16,469 | W | 17,958 | W |
| Rare-earth metal concentrates | short tons | W | W | W | W |
| Silver (recoverable content of ores, etc.) | thousand troy ozs. | 34,328 | 149,328 | 38,166 | 176,325 |
| Titanium concentrate, ilmenite | short tons, gross weight | 617,896 | 27,578 | W | W |
| Tungsten ore and concentrate | thousand pounds | 5,869 | 37,266 | 7,000 | 67,700 |
| Uranium (recoverable content U₃O₈) | thousand pounds | 25,146 | 404,830 | 28,000 | 560,000 |
| Vanadium (recoverable in ore and concentrate) | short tons | 7,376 | 81,279 | 6,200 | 67,227 |
| Zinc (recoverable content of ores, etc.) | short tons | 484,513 | 358,541 | 449,620 | 309,338 |
| Value of items that cannot be disclosed: symbol W | | XX | 153,452 | XX | 188,578 |
| **Total metals** | | XX | **6,086,000** | XX | **5,755,000** |
| **Grand total mineral production** | | XX | **69,178,000** | XX | **76,965,000** |

(e) Estimate. (NA) Not available. (W) Withheld to avoid disclosing individual company confidential data: included with "Value of items that cannot be disclosed." (XX) Not applicable. (p) Preliminary.
(1) Includes a small quantity of anthracite mined in states other than Pennsylvania.
(2) Grindstones, pulpstones, grinding pebbles, sharpening stones, and tube mill liners.
(3) Excludes abrasive stone, bituminous limestone, bituminous sandstone, and soapstone, all included elsewhere.

## U.S. Mineral Production—Leading States

Source: Bureau of Mines, U.S. Interior Department

| State | 1976 Value (thousands) | Percent of U.S. total | Principal minerals, in order of value |
|---|---|---|---|
| Texas | $18,143,204 | 26.23 | Petroleum, natural gas, natural gas liquids, cement. |
| Louisiana | 8,652,107 | 12.51 | Petroleum, natural gas, natural gas liquids, sulfur. |
| West Virginia | 3,498,001 | 5.06 | Coal, natural gas, petroleum, natural gas liquids. |
| California | 3,483,373 | 5.04 | Petroleum, cement, natural gas, sand and gravel. |
| Pennsylvania | 3,041,186 | 4.40 | Coal, cement, stone, lime. |
| Kentucky | 3,114,589 | 4.50 | Coal, petroleum, stone, natural gas. |
| Oklahoma | 2,789,974 | 4.03 | Petroleum, natural gas, natural gas liquids, coal. |
| New Mexico | 2,510,127 | 3.63 | Petroleum, natural gas, copper, natural gas liquids. |
| Wyoming | 1,851,599 | 2.68 | Petroleum, sodium compounds, coal, natural gas. |
| Arizona | 1,726,621 | 2.50 | Copper, molybdenum, sand and gravel, cement. |

### Value of U.S. Mineral Production

(millons of dollars)

Production as measured by mine shipments sales or marketable production.

| Year[1] | Fuels | Nonme-tallic | Metals | Total[2] | Year[1] | Fuels | Nonme-tallic | Metals | Total[2] |
|---|---|---|---|---|---|---|---|---|---|
| 1930 | 2,500 | 973 | 501 | 3,980 | 1972 | 22,061 | 6,482 | 3,642 | 32,185 |
| 1940 | 2,662 | 784 | 752 | 4,198 | 1973 | 25,012 | 7,413 | 4,362 | 36,787 |
| 1950 | 8,689 | 1,882 | 1,351 | 11,862 | 1974 | 40,937 | 8,639 | 5,501 | 55,077 |
| 1960 | 12,142 | 3,868 | 2,022 | 18,032 | 1975 | 47,559 | 9,516 | 5,191 | 62,266 |
| 1965 | 14,047 | 4,933 | 2,544 | 21,524 | 1976 | 52,545 | 10,547 | 6,086 | 69,178 |
| 1969 | 17,965 | 5,624 | 3,333 | 26,921 | 1977[P] | 59,991 | 11,219 | 5,755 | 76,965 |
| 1970 | 20,152 | 5,712 | 3,928 | 29,792 | | | | | |
| 1971 | 21,247 | 6,058 | 3,406 | 30,711 | | | | | |

(1) Excludes Alaska and Hawaii, 1930-53. (2) Data may not add to total because of rounding figures. (P) Preliminary.

---

## U.S. Pig Iron and Steel Output

Source: American Iron and Steel Institute (net tons)

| Year | Total pig iron | Pig iron and ferro-alloys | Raw steel | Year | Total pig iron | Pig iron and ferro-alloys | Raw steel |
|---|---|---|---|---|---|---|---|
| 1940 | 46,071,666 | 47,398,529 | 66,982,686 | 1973 | 100,837,000 | 103,089,000 | 150,799,000 |
| 1945 | 53,223,169 | 54,919,029 | 79,701,648 | 1974 | 95,909,000 | 98,332,000 | 145,720,000 |
| 1950 | 64,586,907 | 66,400,311 | 96,836,075 | 1975 | 101,208,000 | 103,345,000 | 116,642,000 |
| 1955 | 76,857,417 | 79,263,865 | 117,036,085 | 1976 | 86,870,000 | 88,780,000 | 128,000,000 |
| 1960 | 66,480,648 | 68,566,384 | 99,281,601 | 1977 | 81,328,000 | 83,111,000 | 125,333,000 |
| 1965 | 88,184,901 | 90,918,040 | 131,461,601 | | | | |
| 1970 | 91,435,000 | 93,851,000 | 131,514,000 | | | | |

Steel figures include only that portion of the capacity and production of steel for castings used by foundries which were operated by companies producing steel ingots.

### Raw Steel Production

(thousands of net tons)

| State | 1975 | 1976 | 1977 | State | 1975 | 1976 | 1977 |
|---|---|---|---|---|---|---|---|
| New York | 3,401 | 4,799 | 3,958 | Illinois | 9,552 | 11,030 | 10,872 |
| Pennsylvania | 25,761 | 26,696 | 25,737 | Michigan | 9,093 | 10,382 | 10,051 |
| R.I., Conn., N.J., Del., Md. | 5,094 | 5,870 | 5,306 | Minn., Mo., Okla., Texas | 5,399 | 5,079 | 6,753 |
| Va., W.Va., Ga., Fla., N.C., S.C., | 4,795 | 5,403 | 5,484 | Ariz., Colo., Utah, Wash., Ore., Ha. | 4,380 | 4,431 | 4,758 |
| Kentucky | 2,081 | 2,206 | 2,289 | California | 3,351 | 3,398 | 3,224 |
| Ala., Tenn., Miss., Ark. | 4,308 | 4,109 | 3,963 | Total | 116,642 | 128,000 | 125,333 |
| Ohio | 19,620 | 22,419 | 21,466 | | | | |
| Indiana | 19,807 | 22,178 | 21,472 | | | | |

---

## U.S. Copper, Lead, and Zinc Production

Source: Bureau of Mines, U.S. Interior Department

| Year | Copper Mil. lbs. | Copper $1,000 | Lead[1] Short tons | Lead[1] $1,000 | Zinc Short tons | Zinc Mil. dol. | Year | Copper Mil. lbs. | Copper $1,000 | Lead[1] Short tons | Lead[1] $1,000 | Zinc Short tons | Zinc Mil. dol. |
|---|---|---|---|---|---|---|---|---|---|---|---|---|---|
| 1950 | 1,823 | 379,122 | 418,809 | 113,078 | 591,454 | 167 | 1974 | 3,194 | 2,468,964 | 668,870 | 298,742 | 499,872 | 359 |
| 1960 | 2,286 | 733,708 | 228,899 | 53,562 | 334,101 | 87 | 1975 | 2,827 | 1,814,763 | 621,464 | 267,230 | 469,355 | 366 |
| 1965 | 2,703 | 957,028 | 301,147 | 93,959 | 611,153 | 178 | 1976 | 3,211 | 2,234,975 | 609,546 | 281,610 | 484,513 | 359 |
| 1970 | 3,439 | 1,984,484 | 571,767 | 178,609 | 534,136 | 164 | 1977 | 3,008 | 2,009,297 | 592,491 | 363,789 | 449,620 | 309 |
| 1973 | 3,436 | 2,044,346 | 603,024 | 196,465 | 478,850 | 198 | | | | | | | |

(1) Production from domestic ores.

# TRADE AND TRANSPORTATION

## Notable Steamships and Motorships

Source: Lloyd's Register of Shipping as of Aug. 25, 1978

Gross tonnage is a measurement of enclosed space (1 gross ton = 100 cu. ft.) Deadweight tonnage is the weight (long tons) of cargo, fuel, etc., which a vessel is designed to carry safely.

### Oil Tankers

| Name, registry | Dwght. ton. | Lgth. ft. | Bdth. ft. |
|---|---|---|---|
| Pierre Guillaumat, Fr. | 555,031 | 1359 | 206 |
| Bellamya, Fr. | 553,662 | 1359 | 206 |
| Batillus, Fr. | 550,000 | 1358 | 206 |
| Esso Atlantic, Liber. | 516,893 | 1333 | 233 |
| Esso Pacific, Liber. | 516,423 | 1333 | 233 |
| Nissei Maru, Jap. | 484,337 | 1243 | 203 |
| Globtik London, Br. | 483,939 | 1243 | 203 |
| Globtik Tokyo, Br. | 483,664 | 1243 | 203 |
| Esso Mediterranean, Liber. | 446,500 | 1241 | 223 |
| Berge Empress, Nor. | 423,700 | 1252 | 223 |
| Hilda Knudsen, Nor. | 423,639 | 1240 | 226 |
| Esso Deutschland, W. Ger. | 421,678 | 1240 | 226 |
| Al Rekkah, Kuw. | 414,366 | 1200 | 229 |
| Berge Emperor, Nor. | 414,000 | 1285 | 223 |
| Jinko Maru, Jap. | 413,549 | 1200 | 229 |
| Chevron So. America, Liber. | 413,159 | 1200 | 229 |
| Aiko Maru, Jap. | 413,012 | 1200 | 229 |
| Chevron No. America, Liber. | 412,612 | 1200 | 229 |
| Golar Patricia, Liber. | 409,500 | 1236 | 226 |
| Coraggio, It. | 409,500 | 1240 | 226 |
| Esso Japan, Liber. | 406,640 | 1187 | 229 |
| David Packard, Liber. | 406,592 | 1200 | 229 |
| Esso Tokyo, Liber. | 406,258 | 1187 | 229 |
| Bonn, W. Ger. | 392,607 | 1214 | 209 |
| Shat-Al Arab, Iraq | 392,543 | 1221 | 209 |
| Wahran, Alger. | 392,372 | 1221 | 210 |
| Esso Madrid, Liber. | 388,119 | 1225 | 210 |
| Esso Caribbean, Liber. | 388,916 | 1241 | 223 |
| Berlin, Liber. | 386,612 | 1213 | 210 |
| Brazilian Hope, Liber. | 386,600 | 1213 | 210 |
| Bremen, Liber. | 386,600 | 1213 | 210 |
| Jarmada, Nor. | 380,000 | 1225 | 210 |
| Esso Le Havre, Pan. | 380,000 | 1225 | 210 |
| Titus, Nor. | 380,000 | 1225 | 209 |
| Brazilian Pride, Liber. | 372,280 | 1193 | 208 |
| Brazilian Splendour, Liber. | 372,201 | 1193 | 208 |
| Nisseki Maru, Jap. | 366,813 | 1138 | 179 |
| Al Andalus, Kuw. | 362,946 | 1188 | 175 |
| La Santa Maria, Sp. | 362,942 | 1189 | 175 |
| Adria Maru, Jap. | 183,572 | 1023 | 156 |
| Arafura Maru, Jap. | 180,626 | 1023 | 156 |
| Larina, Liber. | 175,934 | 984 | 157 |
| Romantic, Liber. | 174,107 | 995 | 151 |
| Rhetoric, Liber. | 173,668 | 995 | 151 |
| Kimizuru Maru, Jap. | 172,182 | 948 | 157 |
| Oder Maru, Jap. | 171,500 | 984 | 157 |
| Cedros, Liber. | 170,418 | 995 | 142 |
| Cetra Centaurus, Fr. | 170,414 | 981 | 143 |
| Cetra Vela, Fr. | 169,317 | 967 | 155 |
| Champagne, Fr. | 169,300 | 967 | 155 |
| Garden Green, Liber. | 169,147 | 967 | 155 |
| English Bridge, Br. | 169,080 | 965 | 145 |
| Sir John Hunter, Br. | 169,080 | 965 | 145 |
| Sir Alexander Glen, Br. | 169,080 | 965 | 144 |

### World's Largest Passenger Ships

| Name, registry | Dwght. ton. | Lgth. ft. | Bdth. ft. |
|---|---|---|---|
| Queen Elizabeth 2, Br. | 66,852 | 963 | 105 |
| France, Fr. | 66,348 | 1035 | 110 |
| Canberra, Br. | 44,807 | 818 | 102 |
| Oriana, Br. | 41,910 | 804 | 97 |
| United States, Br. | 38,216 | 990 | 101 |
| Rotterdam, Neth. Antil. | 37,783 | 748 | 94 |
| Leonardo Da Vinci, It. | 33,340 | 767 | 92 |
| Eugenio C., It. | 30,567 | 713 | 96 |
| Festivale, Pan. | 30,213 | 760 | 90 |

### Container, Liquefied Gas, Misc. Ships

| Name, registry | Dwght. ton. | Lgth. ft. | Bdth. ft. |
|---|---|---|---|
| Hoegh Gandria, Nor. | 95,683 | 943 | 142 |
| Golar Freeze, Liber. | 85,158 | 943 | 142 |
| Gimi, Liber. | 84,855 | 963 | 136 |
| Hilli, Liber. | 84,855 | 961 | 136 |
| LNG Aquarius, U.S. | 83,102 | 936 | 143 |
| Larbi Ben M'Hidi, Alger. | 80,328 | 924 | 136 |
| Mostefa Ben-Boulaid, Alger. | 82,243 | 914 | 134 |
| Ben Franklin, Liber. | 80,071 | 894 | 134 |
| LNG Challenger, Br. | 76,496 | 857 | 131 |
| Norman Lady, Br. | 76,416 | 818 | 131 |
| Gastor, Pan. | 68,247 | 902 | 138 |
| El Paso Paul Kayser, Liber. | 66,808 | 920 | 136 |
| El Paso Consolidated, Liber. | 66,808 | 920 | 136 |
| El Paso Sonatrach, Liber. | 66,807 | 920 | 136 |
| Palace Tokyo, Jap. | 64,378 | 807 | 131 |
| Cardigan Bay, Br. | 58,899 | 950 | 106 |
| Kowloon Bay, Br. | 58,889 | 950 | 106 |
| Liverpool Bay, Br. | 58,889 | 950 | 106 |
| Tokyo Bay, Br. | 58,889 | 950 | 106 |
| Osaka Bay, Br. | 58,889 | 950 | 106 |
| Nedlloyd Delft, Neth. | 58,716 | 941 | 106 |
| Nedlloyd Dejima, Neth. | 58,716 | 941 | 106 |
| City of Edinburgh, Br. | 58,440 | 950 | 106 |
| Benavon, Br. | 58,440 | 950 | 106 |
| Benalder, Br. | 58,440 | 950 | 106 |
| Hamburg Express, W. Ger. | 58,088 | 943 | 105 |
| Tokio Express, W. Ger. | 58,082 | 943 | 105 |
| Bremen Express, W. Ger. | 57,535 | 941 | 106 |
| Hongkong Express, W. Ger. | 57,525 | 941 | 106 |
| Kasuga Maru, Jap. | 57,500 | 948 | 105 |
| Korrigan, Fr. | 57,249 | 946 | 105 |
| Esso Fuji, Pan. | 55,896 | 807 | 131 |
| Geomitra, Br. | 53,128 | 849 | 114 |
| Genota, Br. | 53,128 | 849 | 113 |
| Toyama, Nor. | 52,196 | 902 | 106 |
| Elbe Maru, Jap. | 51,623 | 882 | 105 |
| Kitano Maru, Jap. | 51,159 | 856 | 105 |
| Kurama Maru, Jap. | 51,139 | 856 | 105 |
| Kamakura Maru, Jap. | 51,139 | 856 | 105 |
| Rhine Maru, Jap. | 51,085 | 856 | 105 |
| Nihon, Swed. | 50,805 | 902 | 105 |
| Selandia, Den. | 49,890 | 900 | 106 |
| Jutlandia, Den. | 49,890 | 900 | 106 |
| Gouldia | 48,662 | 843 | 114 |
| Gari, Br. | 48,662 | 842 | 114 |
| Gastrana, Br. | 48,662 | 842 | 114 |
| Gadila, Br. | 48,662 | 842 | 114 |
| Gadinia, Br. | 48,662 | 842 | 114 |
| Yusho Maru, Jap. | 47,783 | 744 | 114 |
| Hoegh Swallow, Nor. | 45,755 | 752 | 105 |

### Bulk, Ore, Bulk Oil, & Ore Oil Carriers

| Name, registry | Dwght. ton. | Lgth. ft. | Bdth. ft. |
|---|---|---|---|
| Svealand, Swed. | 282,450 | 1109 | 179 |
| Docecanyon, Liber. | 271,235 | 1113 | 180 |
| Licorne Pacifique, Fr. | 271,000 | 1111 | 176 |
| Jose Bonifacio, Braz. | 270,358 | 1106 | 179 |
| Tarfala, Swed. | 265,000 | 1099 | 170 |
| Mary F. Koch, Liber. | 265,000 | 1099 | 170 |
| Torne, Swed. | 265,000 | 1099 | 170 |
| Usa Maru, Jap. | 264,523 | 1105 | 179 |
| Nordic Conqueror, Liber. | 264,485 | 1101 | 176 |
| Lauderdale, Br. | 260,424 | 1101 | 176 |
| Licorne Atlantique, Fr. | 258,268 | 1101 | 176 |
| Seiko Maru, Jap. | 248,300 | 1069 | 170 |
| La Loma, Br. | 245,288 | 1069 | 170 |
| Hoegh Hood, Nor. | 244,677 | 1069 | 170 |
| Hoegh Hill, Nor. | 241,447 | 1069 | 170 |
| Konkar Dinos, Gr. | 231,045 | 1075 | 160 |
| Berger Vanga, Liber. | 227,561 | 1030 | 164 |
| Berge Adria, Nor. | 227,561 | 1030 | 164 |
| Andros Antares, Liber. | 227,480 | 1061 | 158 |
| San Giusto, It. | 227,408 | 1091 | 149 |
| World Recovery, Liber. | 227,406 | 1075 | 161 |
| Ambrosiana, It. | 227,400 | 1091 | 149 |
| Berge Brioni, Nor. | 227,187 | 1030 | 165 |
| Konkar Theodoros, Liber. | 225,000 | 1091 | 164 |
| Andros Atlas, Gr. | 224,074 | 1061 | 158 |
| Andros Aries, Gr. | 223,808 | 1061 | 158 |
| Sysla, Nor. | 223,500 | 1096 | 149 |
| Alva Bay, Br. | 222,331 | 1091 | 149 |
| Alva Sea, Br. | 221,457 | 1090 | 149 |
| Tartar, Nor. | 215,621 | 1075 | 164 |
| Jarl Malmros, Swed. | 215,500 | 1075 | 164 |
| Tantalus, Br. | 214,592 | 1075 | 164 |
| Atsuta Maru, Jap. | 214,017 | 1075 | 164 |
| Tsurumi Maru, Jap. | 213,842 | 1075 | 164 |
| Sensho Maru, Jap. | 191,018 | 983 | 154 |

| Name, registry | Gross ton. | Lgth. ft. | Bdth. ft. | Name, registry | Gross ton. | Lgth. ft. | Bdth. ft. |
|---|---|---|---|---|---|---|---|
| Sun River, Jap. | 45,647 | 734 | 106 | Pioneer Louise, Liber. | 40,300 | 698 | 120 |
| Polar Alaska Liber. | 44,088 | 798 | 111 | World Concord, Liber. | 39,500 | 734 | 106 |
| Arctic Tokyo, Liber. | 44,088 | 798 | 111 | World Creation, Liber. | 39,411 | 734 | 106 |
| Act 7, Br. | 43,992 | 815 | 106 | Verrazano Bridge, Jap. | 39,153 | 867 | 105 |
| Australian Venture, Austral. | 43,878 | 815 | 106 | Seven Seas Bridge, Jap. | 39,152 | 867 | 105 |
| Gas Gemini, Liber. | 42,252 | 748 | 120 | Tokuho Maru, Jap. | 39,117 | 705 | 105 |
| Remuera Bay, Br. | 42,007 | 824 | 105 | Izumisan Maru, Jap. | 38,872 | 705 | 105 |
| Kanayama Maru, Jap. | 41,939 | 734 | 113 | World Vigour, Liber. | 38,859 | 734 | 106 |
| Sea-Land Exchange, U.S. | 41,555 | 946 | 105 | New York Maru, Jap. | 38,825 | 862 | 105 |
| Sea-Land Commerce, U.S. | 41,127 | 946 | 105 | Kiso Maru, Jap. | 38,540 | 857 | 105 |
| Sea-Land Trade, U.S. | 41,127 | 946 | 105 | Svendborg Maersk, Den. | 38,540 | 856 | 105 |
| Sea-Land Market, U.S. | 41,127 | 946 | 105 | | | | |
| Sea-Land Resource, U.S. | 41,127 | 946 | 105 | **Nuclear Powered Merchant Ships** | | | |
| Sea-Land Finance, U.S. | 41,127 | 946 | 105 | Arktika, USSR | 18,172 | 485 | 98 |
| Sea-Land Galloway, U.S. | 41,127 | 946 | 105 | Sibir, USSR | 18,171 | 485 | 98 |
| Sea-Land Mclean, U.S. | 41,127 | 946 | 105 | Otto Hahn, W. Ger. | 16,871 | 564 | 76 |
| Bridgestone Maru V, Jap. | 40,934 | 690 | 106 | Savannah, U.S. | 15,585 | 595 | 78 |
| Nyhammer, Nor. | 40,396 | 757 | 105 | Lenin, USSR | 14,067 | 439 | 90 |
| | | | | Mutsu, Jap. | 8,214 | 428 | 62 |

## U.S. Exports and Imports of Leading Commodities

Source: Office of International Economic Research, U.S. Commerce Department (millions of dollars)

| Commodity | Exports 1975 | Exports 1976 | Exports 1977 | Imports 1975 | Imports 1976 | Imports 1977 |
|---|---|---|---|---|---|---|
| **Total** | $107,592 | $114,992 | $120,163 | $96,116 | $120,687 | $146,817 |
| **Food and live animals** | 15,484 | 15,710 | 14,103 | 8,503 | 10,267 | 12,490 |
| Meat | 528 | 798 | 797 | 1,141 | 1,447 | 1,273 |
| Dairy products and eggs | 134 | 128 | 182 | ... | ... | ... |
| Cheese | ... | ... | ... | 165 | 207 | 215 |
| Fish | 268 | 332 | 476 | 1,356 | 1,855 | 2,056 |
| Grains and preparations | 11,642 | 10,911 | 8,755 | 180 | 150 | 150 |
| Wheat and wheat flour | 5,292 | 4,041 | 2,882 | ... | ... | ... |
| Rice | 858 | 629 | 730 | ... | ... | ... |
| Corn | 4,448 | 5,223 | 4,139 | ... | ... | ... |
| Fruit and nuts | 871 | 976 | 1,080 | 637 | 760 | 959 |
| Vegetables | 406 | 559 | 518 | 355 | 426 | 592 |
| Sugar | ... | ... | ... | 1,865 | 1,154 | 1,079 |
| Coffee, green | ... | ... | ... | 1,561 | 2,632 | 3,861 |
| **Beverage and tobaccos** | 1,308 | 1,524 | 1,847 | 1,420 | 1,624 | 1,663 |
| Alcoholic beverages | ... | ... | ... | 1,033 | 1,174 | 1,282 |
| Tobacco, unmanufactured | 852 | 922 | 1,094 | 343 | 392 | 319 |
| **Crude materials, inedible, other than fuels** | 9,784 | 10,891 | 12,815 | 5,566 | 7,014 | 7,944 |
| Synthetic rubber | 261 | 329 | 327 | ... | ... | ... |
| Ores and metal scrap | 1,355 | 1,285 | 1,197 | 1,978 | 2,251 | 2,234 |
| Coal | 3,259 | 2,910 | 2,655 | ... | ... | ... |
| Petroleum and products | 908 | 998 | 1,276 | 24,814 | 31,993 | 42,136 |
| **Animal and vegetable oils and fats** | 944 | 978 | 1,341 | 554 | 464 | 538 |
| **Chemicals** | 8,691 | 9,959 | 10,827 | 3,696 | 4,772 | 5,432 |
| Medicinal and pharmaceutical | 866 | 997 | 1,081 | 235 | 269 | 318 |
| **Machinery and transport equipment** | 45,668 | 49,501 | 51,037 | 23,457 | 29,824 | 35,494 |
| Automotive engines and parts | 763 | 943 | 990 | 1,040 | 1,384 | 1,607 |
| Agricultural machinery | 704 | 707 | 716 | 474 | 496 | 504 |
| Tractors and parts | 752 | 928 | 868 | 430 | 456 | 564 |
| Metalworking machinery | 922 | 953 | 730 | 361 | 362 | 434 |
| Textile and leather machinery | 486 | 457 | 423 | 518 | 636 | 638 |
| Other nonelectrical machinery | 160 | 208 | 555 | 1,157 | 1,299 | 1,540 |
| Electrical apparatus | 7,582 | 9,278 | 10,285 | 4,911 | 7,424 | 8,432 |
| **Transport equipment** | 16,452 | 17,388 | 17,611 | 11,487 | 14,378 | 17,557 |
| New motor vehicles | 5,127 | 5,390 | 5,719 | 7,124 | 8,928 | 10,626 |
| Aircraft, parts and accessories | 6,136 | 6,104 | 5,866 | 519 | 434 | 601 |
| **Other manufactured goods** | 16,592 | 17,781 | 18,590 | 23,927 | 30,180 | 36,278 |
| Rubber manufactures | 544 | 491 | 588 | ... | ... | ... |
| Paper and manufactures | 1,447 | 1,624 | 1,517 | 1,673 | 2,103 | 2,392 |
| Gem diamonds | 237 | 306 | 336 | 730 | 1,018 | 1,453 |
| Manufactures of metals n.e.c. | 1,891 | 2,089 | 2,339 | 8,945 | 9,899 | 12,246 |
| Iron and steel-mill products | 2,382 | 1,833 | 1,608 | 4,037 | 3,809 | 5,281 |
| Nonferrous base metals | 1,090 | 1,089 | 1,058 | 2,063 | 2,941 | 3,369 |
| Textiles other than clothing | 1,625 | 1,971 | 1,959 | 1,219 | 1,635 | 1,772 |
| Clothing | 382 | 488 | 586 | 2,562 | 3,634 | 4,154 |
| **Other transactions** | 3,162 | 2,749 | 3,224 | 2,518 | 25,538 | 2,692 |

## U.S. Merchandise Exports and Imports, by Continent

Source: Office of International Economic Research, U.S. Commerce Department (millions of dollars)

| Year | Exports Western Hemis. | Exports Europe | Exports Asia & Oceania | Exports Africa | General imports Western Hemis. | General imports Europe | General imports Asia & Oceania | General imports Africa |
|---|---|---|---|---|---|---|---|---|
| 1965 | 9,932 | 9,397 | 7,129 | 1,071 | 9,257 | 6,292 | 4,999 | 867 |
| 1970 | 15,611 | 14,817 | 11,294 | 1,502 | 16,928 | 11,395 | 10,515 | 1,090 |
| 1972 | 19,690 | 16,180 | 12,387 | 1,500 | 21,930 | 15,744 | 16,279 | 1,578 |
| 1973 | 25,033 | 23,160 | 20,388 | 2,081 | 27,322 | 19,812 | 19,745 | 2,557 |
| 1974 | 35,746 | 30,070 | 28,937 | 3,204 | 40,332 | 24,410 | 28,943 | 6,551 |
| 1975 | 38,843 | 32,732 | 31,246 | 4,266 | 37,773 | 21,465 | 28,590 | 8,277 |
| 1976 | 41,074 | 35,900 | 33,229 | 4,396 | 43,356 | 23,645 | 41,131 | 12,522 |
| 1977 | 43,687 | 36,296 | 35,288 | 4,563 | 50,309 | 28,331 | 51,312 | 16,854 |

# U.S. Foreign Trade with Leading Countries

Source: Office of International Economic Research, U.S. Commerce Department

(millions of dollars)

| Exports from the U.S. to the following areas and countries and imports into the U.S. from those areas and countries: | Exports | | | Imports | | |
|---|---|---|---|---|---|---|
| | 1975 | 1976 | 1977 | 1975 | 1976 | 1977 |
| Total | $107,592 | $114,992 | $120,163 | $96,116 | $120,678 | $146,81 |
| Western Hemisphere | 38,843 | 41,074 | 43,687 | 37,773 | 43,356 | 50,30 |
| Canada | 21,744 | 24,106 | 25,749 | 21,729 | 26,237 | 29,35 |
| 19 American Republics | 15,655 | 15,487 | 16,346 | 11,835 | 13,228 | 16,33 |
| Central American Common Market | 968 | 1,153 | 1,478 | 819 | 1,208 | 1,52 |
| Latin American Free Trade Ass'n | ... | ... | ... | ... | | |
| Dominican Republic | 453 | 432 | 424 | 634 | 523 | 63 |
| Panama | 317 | 358 | 346 | 194 | 142 | 15 |
| Bahamas | 208 | 199 | 224 | 880 | 670 | 1,05 |
| Jamaica | 381 | 301 | 293 | 308 | 312 | 34 |
| Netherlands Antilles | 228 | 248 | 304 | 1,558 | 1,174 | 1,28 |
| Trinidad and Tobago | 256 | 309 | 306 | 1,170 | 1,500 | 1,65 |
| Europe | 32,732 | 35,900 | 36,296 | 21,465 | 23,645 | 28,33 |
| OECD countries (excludes depend. and Yugo.) | 29,575 | 32,047 | 33,338 | 20,473 | 22,398 | 27,07 |
| Western Europe | 29,945 | 32,396 | 33,752 | 20,737 | 22,783 | 27,41 |
| European Economic Community | 22,865 | 25,409 | 26,476 | 16,611 | 17,844 | 22,08 |
| Belgium and Luxembourg | 2,417 | 2,993 | 3,117 | 1,190 | 1,119 | 1,44 |
| Denmark | 445 | 444 | 532 | 461 | 560 | 58 |
| France | 3,031 | 3,446 | 3,503 | 2,137 | 2,509 | 3,03 |
| Germany, Federal Republic of | 5,194 | 5,731 | 5,982 | 5,382 | 5,592 | 7,21 |
| Ireland | 190 | 280 | 378 | 176 | 201 | 23 |
| Italy | 2,867 | 3,071 | 2,788 | 2,397 | 2,530 | 3,03 |
| Netherlands | 4,194 | 4,643 | 4,796 | 1,083 | 1,080 | 1,44 |
| United Kingdom | 4,527 | 4,801 | 5,380 | 3,784 | 4,254 | 5,06 |
| European Free Trade Association | ... | | ... | | | |
| Austria | 181 | 197 | 245 | 238 | 237 | 28 |
| Finland | 261 | 243 | 195 | 148 | 189 | 27 |
| Iceland | 32 | 35 | 36 | 85 | 124 | 15 |
| Norway | 510 | 500 | 541 | 403 | 651 | 75 |
| Portugal | 427 | 400 | 551 | 157 | 128 | 14 |
| Sweden | 925 | 1,029 | 1,099 | 877 | 918 | 99 |
| Switzerland | 1,153 | 1,173 | 1,359 | 867 | 1,025 | 1,08 |
| Greece | 450 | 591 | 539 | 111 | 146 | 17 |
| Spain | 2,164 | 2,020 | 1,875 | 831 | 914 | 97 |
| Turkey | 608 | 451 | 424 | 145 | 222 | 14 |
| Yugoslavia | 328 | 298 | 357 | 260 | 385 | 33 |
| Eastern Europe | 2,787 | 3,504 | 2,544 | 728 | 856 | 91 |
| Asia | 28,906 | 30,539 | 32,411 | 27,082 | 39,460 | 49,59 |
| Near East | 8,946 | 10,044 | 11,020 | 5,431 | 9,104 | 12,98 |
| Egypt | 683 | 810 | 982 | 28 | 93 | 17 |
| Iran | 3,244 | 2,772 | 2,731 | 1,400 | 1,480 | 2,78 |
| Iraq | 310 | 382 | 211 | 19 | 110 | 38 |
| Israel | 1,551 | 1,409 | 1,447 | 313 | 423 | 57 |
| Jordan | 195 | 234 | 302 | 1 | 1 | |
| Kuwait | 366 | 472 | 548 | 111 | 38 | 21 |
| Lebanon | 369 | 49 | 124 | 33 | 5 | 4 |
| Saudi Arabia | 1,502 | 2,774 | 3,575 | 2,625 | 5,213 | 6,35 |
| Japan | 9,563 | 10,145 | 10,522 | 11,268 | 15,504 | 18,62 |
| East and South Asia | 10,093 | 10,214 | 10,697 | 10,224 | 14,649 | 17,78 |
| China, Republic of (Taiwan) | 1,659 | 1,635 | 1,798 | 1,938 | 2,989 | 3,68 |
| Hong Kong | 808 | 1,117 | 1,292 | 1,575 | 2,413 | 2,91 |
| India | 1,290 | 1,136 | 779 | 548 | 708 | 78 |
| Indonesia | 810 | 1,035 | 763 | 2,221 | 3,004 | 3,49 |
| Korea, Republic of | 1,762 | 2,015 | 2,371 | 1,416 | 2,404 | 2,89 |
| Malaysia | 393 | 536 | 561 | 766 | 940 | 1,32 |
| Pakistan | 372 | 394 | 293 | 49 | 70 | 5 |
| Philippines | 832 | 818 | 876 | 754 | 883 | 1,10 |
| Singapore | 994 | 965 | 1,172 | 532 | 695 | 87 |
| Thailand | 357 | 347 | 510 | 217 | 275 | 35 |
| Vietnam | 213 | 1 | ... | 6 | 1 | |
| Oceania | 2,340 | 2,690 | 2,877 | 1,508 | 1,671 | 1,72 |
| Australia | 1,815 | 2,185 | 2,356 | 1,147 | 1,211 | 1,18 |
| New Zealand and Samoa | 414 | 417 | 405 | 246 | 330 | 35 |
| Africa | 4,266 | 4,396 | 4,563 | 8,277 | 12,552 | 16,85 |
| North Africa excluding Egypt | 1,339 | 1,342 | 1,477 | 2,489 | 4,645 | 7,00 |
| Algeria | 632 | 487 | 527 | 1,359 | 2,209 | 3,06 |
| Ethiopia | 70 | 78 | 58 | 49 | 94 | 9 |
| Libya | 232 | 277 | 314 | 1,046 | 2,243 | 3,79 |
| Morocco | 200 | 297 | 372 | 10 | 17 | 2 |
| Tunisia | 90 | 82 | 111 | 26 | 56 | 1 |
| Western and equatorial Africa | 1,170 | 1,418 | 1,676 | 4,457 | 6,090 | 7,51 |
| Angola | 53 | 35 | 38 | 426 | 264 | 31 |
| Ghana | 100 | 133 | 146 | 150 | 155 | 21 |
| Ivory Coast | 78 | 64 | 89 | 160 | 248 | 31 |
| Liberia | 90 | 85 | 91 | 97 | 99 | 10 |
| Nigeria | 536 | 770 | 958 | 3,282 | 4,938 | 6,09 |
| Central and southern Africa | 1,762 | 1,641 | 1,413 | 1,323 | 1,818 | 2,33 |
| Kenya | 49 | 43 | 77 | 36 | 60 | 9 |
| South Africa | 1,302 | 1,348 | 1,054 | 841 | 925 | 1,26 |
| Zaire | 188 | 99 | 114 | 67 | 193 | 17 |

## Merchant Fleets of the World

Source: Maritime Administration, U.S. Dept. of Commerce

Oceangoing steam and motor ships of 1,000 gross tons and over as of June 30, 1977, excludes ships operating exclusively on the Great Lakes and inland waterways and special types such as channel ships, icebreakers, cable ships, etc., and merchant ships owned by any military force. Tonnage is in thousands. Gross tonnage is a volume measurement; each cargo gross ton represents 100 cubic ft. of enclosed space. Deadweight tonnage is the carrying capacity of a ship in long tons (2,240 lbs.).

| Country of registry | Total no. | Gross tons | Dwt. tons | Bulk carriers No. | Bulk carriers Dwt. | Freighters No. | Freighters Dwt. | Tankers No. | Tankers Dwt. |
|---|---|---|---|---|---|---|---|---|---|
| Total-All Countries . . . . | 23,902 | 369,606 | 626,715 | 4,752 | 171,559 | 13,040 | 107,060 | 5,414 | 345,200 |
| United States¹ . . . . . . | 846 | 13,010 | 19,113 | 18 | 529 | 495 | 6,961 | 271 | 11,219 |
| Privately owned. . . . | 577 | 10,829 | 16,520 | 18 | 529 | 296 | 4,907 | 257 | 11,034 |
| Government owned | 269 | 2,181 | 2,593 | — | — | 199 | 2,054 | 14 | 185 |
| Algeria . . . . . . . . | 52 | 927 | 1,498 | 6 | 95 | 28 | 167 | 18 | 1,236 |
| Argentina. . . . . . . . | 162 | 1,414 | 1,994 | 15 | 298 | 92 | 857 | 48 | 811 |
| Australia . . . . . . . . | 86 | 1,284 | 1,939 | 33 | 1,099 | 38 | 392 | 15 | 448 |
| Bangladesh . . . . . . | 17 | 92 | 132 | — | — | 15 | 128 | 2 | 4 |
| Belgium. .` . . . . . . . | 80 | 1,511 | 2,458 | 25 | 1,250 | 39 | 491 | 15 | 702 |
| Brazil. . . . . . . . . . | 272 | 3,236 | 5,255 | 38 | 1,593 | 169 | 1,371 | 59 | 2,280 |
| British Colonies . . . . . | 97 | 2,084 | 3,521 | 35 | 1,323 | 30 | 177 | 30 | 2,015 |
| *Bulgaria . . . . . . . . | 110 | 850 | 1,218 | 28 | 373 | 59 | 377 | 19 | 456 |
| Canada. . . . . . . . . . | 73 | 402 | 553 | 14 | 208 | 22 | 89 | 27 | 244 |
| Chile . . . . . . . . . | 42 | 385 | 591 | 6 | 139 | 30 | 308 | 5 | 142 |
| China (Taiwan) . . . . | 149 | 1,437 | 2,219 | 32 | 820 | 95 | 724 | 14 | 617 |
| *China (People's Rep.) . . | 381 | 3,423 | 5,100 | 44 | 933 | 249 | 2,511 | 64 | 1,582 |
| Colombia . . . . . . . . | 37 | 253 | 317 | 1 | 2 | 35 | 286 | 1 | 29 |
| *Cuba . . . . . . . . . | 73 | 519 | 717 | 5 | 49 | 58 | 576 | 8 | 82 |
| Cyprus . . . . . . . . | 533 | 2,824 | 4,120 | 40 | 467 | 450 | 2,993 | 37 | 626 |
| *Czechoslovakia . . . . . | 13 | 144 | 214 | 5 | 160 | 8 | 54 | — | — |
| Denmark . . . . . . . . | 374 | 5,133 | 8,514 | 45 | 1,232 | 249 | 1,945 | 72 | 5,321 |
| Ecuador . . . . . . . . | 19 | 164 | 247 | — | — | 8 | 67 | 11 | 180 |
| Egypt. . . . . . . . . | 66 | 333 | 467 | — | — | 48 | 230 | 11 | 197 |
| Finland . . . . . . . . | 195 | 2,115 | 3,407 | 31 | 680 | 105 | 569 | 52 | 2,148 |
| France . . . . . . . . | 461 | 11,774 | 20,660 | 60 | 2,820 | 239 | 2,303 | 156 | 15,511 |
| Gabon . . . . . . . . | 5 | 106 | 183 | 1 | 15 | 3 | 28 | 1 | 140 |
| Germany (West). . . . . | 652 | 9,207 | 15,124 | 80 | 4,121 | 478 | 4,086 | 89 | 6,903 |
| *Germany (East) . . . . . | 161 | 1,295 | 1,847 | 18 | 369 | 128 | 949 | 11 | 503 |
| Ghana . . . . . . . . | 19 | 127 | 166 | — | — | 19 | 166 | — | — |
| Greece . . . . . . . . | 1,969 | 24,844 | 41,617 | 577 | 15,944 | 1,005 | 9,596 | 331 | 15,842 |
| India . . . . . . . . . | 343 | 5,257 | 8,502 | 94 | 4,033 | 205 | 2,363 | 33 | 2,038 |
| Indonesia. . . . . . . . | 189 | 757 | 991 | 10 | 110 | 129 | 665 | 21 | 126 |
| Iran . . . . . . . . . | 48 | 621 | 1,022 | — | — | 41 | 474 | 7 | 548 |
| Iraq . . . . . . . . . | 31 | 825 | 1,518 | — | — | 14 | 119 | 17 | 1,399 |
| Ireland . . . . . . . . | 21 | 192 | 293 | 10 | 269 | 8 | 17 | 3 | 7 |
| Israel . . . . . . . . . | 46 | 415 | 546 | 9 | 277 | 37 | 269 | — | — |
| Italy . . . . . . . . . | 627 | 10,882 | 17,805 | 156 | 7,091 | 193 | 1,403 | 228 | 9,101 |
| Ivory Coast. . . . . . . | 14 | 106 | 139 | — | — | 14 | 139 | — | — |
| Japan. . . . . . . . . | 2,097 | 39,856 | 67,837 | 599 | 24,206 | 924 | 7,571 | 546 | 35,997 |
| Korea (South) . . . . . | 197 | 1,605 | 2,697 | 34 | 490 | 128 | 772 | 35 | 1,435 |
| Kuwait . . . . . . . . | 65 | 1,860 | 3,256 | 1 | 9 | 52 | 935 | 12 | 2,312 |
| Lebanon . . . . . . . | 50 | 162 | 204 | 3 | 5 | 45 | 186 | — | — |
| Liberia . . . . . . . . | 2,722 | 80,709 | 154,292 | 1,042 | 42,629 | 639 | 6,661 | 1,025 | 104,878 |
| Libya . . . . . . . . . | 20 | 788 | 1,482 | — | — | 8 | 37 | 12 | 1,445 |
| Malaysia . . . . . . . | 36 | 455 | 681 | 12 | 447 | 18 | 138 | 4 | 91 |
| Maldives . . . . . . . | 40 | 117 | 153 | 1 | 5 | 39 | 148 | — | — |
| Mexico . . . . . . . . | 49 | 509 | 770 | 3 | 61 | 16 | 139 | 29 | 567 |
| Morocco . . . . . . . | 31 | 126 | 192 | 2 | 50 | 25 | 102 | 4 | 40 |
| Netherlands . . . . . . | 472 | 5,252 | 8,285 | 37 | 1,004 | 350 | 2,546 | 78 | 4,685 |
| New Zealand . . . . . . | 28 | 170 | 201 | 10 | 35 | 16 | 115 | 2 | 51 |
| Nigeria . . . . . . . . | 24 | 297 | 492 | 1 | 16 | 22 | 206 | 1 | 270 |
| Norway. . . . . . . . . | 1,003 | 29,190 | 51,946 | 326 | 18,122 | 304 | 2,509 | 342 | 31,240 |
| Pakistan . . . . . . . . | 50 | 445 | 589 | 2 | 31 | 40 | 473 | 1 | 27 |
| Panama . . . . . . . . | 1,699 | 16,136 | 26,385 | 270 | 6,029 | 1,157 | 8,446 | 231 | 11,692 |
| Peru . . . . . . . . . | 42 | 391 | 593 | 10 | 255 | 27 | 261 | 5 | 77 |
| Philippines . . . . . . | 158 | 946 | 1,420 | 10 | 238 | 97 | 594 | 29 | 548 |
| Poland . . . . . . . . | 303 | 3,044 | 4,578 | 79 | 1,885 | 205 | 1,660 | 15 | 1,015 |
| Portugal . . . . . . . ▲ | 99 | 1,182 | 1,897 | 5 | 124 | 64 | 493 | 24 | 1,246 |
| Qatar . . . . . . . . . | 1 | 72 | 138 | — | — | — | — | 1 | 138 |
| *Romania . . . . . . . . | 121 | 1,078 | 1,627 | 28 | 699 | 84 | 487 | 7 | 433 |
| Saudi Arabia . . . . . . | 35 | 595 | 1,051 | — | — | 21 | 97 | 11 | 947 |
| Singapore . . . . . . . | 485 | 5,898 | 10,012 | 52 | 1,858 | 318 | 2,423 | 95 | 5,634 |
| Somalia . . . . . . . . | 221 | 1,569 | 2,294 | 24 | 504 | 182 | 1,572 | 13 | 210 |
| South Africa . . . . . . | 52 | 440 | 567 | 4 | 88 | 44 | 402 | 3 | 61 |
| Spain . . . . . . . . . | 481 | 6,281 | 10,919 | 64 | 1,980 | 262 | 1,172 | 126 | 7,664 |
| Sweden . . . . . . . . | 335 | 8,208 | 14,204 | 92 | 4,936 | 146 | 1,347 | 91 | 7,905 |
| Switzerland . . . . . . | 27 | 262 | 392 | 6 | 200 | 19 | 186 | 2 | 6 |
| Thailand . . . . . . . . | 31 | 177 | 281 | 1 | 2 | 19 | 126 | 11 | 153 |
| Tunisia . . . . . . . . | 18 | 93 | 142 | 3 | 36 | 11 | 42 | 4 | 64 |
| Turkey . . . . . . . . | 128 | 1,068 | 1,595 | 14 | 478 | 71 | 496 | 28 | 589 |
| United Arab Emirates . . | 10 | 114 | 204 | — | — | 9 | 69 | 1 | 135 |
| United Kingdom . . . . . | 1,526 | 33,358 | 56,012 | 355 | 15,387 | 723 | 7,161 | 426 | 33,310 |
| Uruguay . . . . . . . . | 15 | 132 | 203 | — | — | 9 | 53 | 6 | 150 |
| *U.S.S.R.² . . . . . . . . | 2,439 | 15,360 | 19,754 | 163 | 2,042 | 1,717 | 10,670 | 468 | 6,809 |
| Venezuela . . . . . . . | 49 | 487 | 685 | 3 | 16 | 30 | 255 | 15 | 405 |
| *Vietnam . . . . . . . . | 20 | 84 | 125 | 1 | 3 | 16 | 79 | 3 | 43 |
| Yugoslavia . . . . . . . | 245 | 2,159 | 3,209 | 45 | 1,252 | 175 | 1,551 | 15 | 349 |
| Zaire . . . . . . . . . | 11 | 106 | 152 | — | — | 9 | 128 | — | — |

*Source material limited. (1) Excludes 95 non-merchant type ships which are currently in the National Defense Reserve Fleet. (2) Includes U.S. government-owned ships transferred to USSR under lend-lease agreements, 31 of which are still under that registry.

## Shortest Navigable Distances Between Ports

Source: Distances Between Ports, 1965. Defense Mapping Agency Hydrographic Center
Distances shown are in nautical miles (1,852 meters or about 6,076.115 feet) To get statute miles, multiply by 1.15.

| TO | FROM | New York | Montreal | Colon[1] |
|---|---|---|---|---|
| Algiers, Algeria | | 3,617 | 3,600 | 4,745 |
| Amsterdam, Netherlands | | 3,438 | 3,162 | 4,825 |
| Baltimore, Md. | | 417 | 1,769 | 1,901 |
| Barcelona, Spain | | 3,714 | 3,697 | 4,842 |
| Boston, Mass. | | 386 | 1,308 | 2,157 |
| Buenos Aires, Argentina | | 5,817 | 6,455 | 5,472 |
| Cape Town, S. Africa[2] | | 6,786 | 7,118 | 6,494 |
| Cherbourg, France | | 3,154 | 2,878 | 4,541 |
| Cobh, Ireland | | 2,901 | 2,603 | 4,308 |
| Copenhagen, Denmark | | 3,846 | 3,570 | 5,233 |
| Dakar, Senegal | | 3,335 | 3,566 | 3,694 |
| Galveston, Tex. | | 1,882 | 3,165 | 1,492 |
| Gibraltar[3] | | 3,204 | 3,187 | 4,332 |
| Glasgow, Scotland | | 3,086 | 2,691 | 4,508 |
| Halifax, N.S. | | 600 | 895 | 2,295 |
| Hamburg, W. Germany | | 3,674 | 3,398 | 5,061 |
| Hamilton, Bermuda | | 697 | 1,572 | 1,659 |
| Havana, Cuba | | 1,186 | 2,473 | 998 |
| Helsinki, Finland | | 4,309 | 4,033 | 5,696 |
| Istanbul, Turkey | | 5,001 | 4,984 | 6,129 |
| Kingston, Jamaica | | 1,474 | 2,690 | 551 |
| Lagos, Nigeria | | 4,883 | 5,130 | 5,049 |
| Lisbon, Portugal | | 2,972 | 2,943 | 4,152 |
| Marseille, France | | 3,891 | 3,874 | 5,019 |
| Montreal, Quebec | | 1,460 | | 3,126 |
| Naples, Italy | | 4,181 | 4,164 | 5,309 |
| Nassau, Bahamas | | 962 | 2,274 | 1,166 |
| New Orleans, La. | | 1,708 | 2,991 | 1,389 |
| New York, N.Y. | | | 1,460 | 1,974 |
| Norfolk, Va. | | 294 | 1,700 | 1,779 |
| Oslo, Norway | | 3,827 | 3,165 | 5,053 |
| Piraeus, Greece | | 4,688 | 4,671 | 5,816 |
| Port Said, Egypt | | 5,123 | 5,106 | 6,251 |
| Rio de Janeiro, Brazil | | 4,770 | 5,354 | 4,367 |
| St. John's, Nfld. | | 1,093 | 1,043 | 2,695 |
| San Juan, Puerto Rico | | 1,399 | 2,445 | 993 |
| Southampton, England | | 3,189 | 2,913 | 4,576 |

| TO | FROM | San. Fran. | Vancouver | Panama |
|---|---|---|---|---|
| Acapulco, Mexico | | 1,833 | 2,613 | 1,426 |
| Anchorage, Alas. | | 1,872 | 1,444 | 5,093 |
| Bombay, India | | 9,794 | 9,578 | 12,962 |
| Calcutta, India | | 8,991 | 8,728 | 12,154 |
| Colon, Panama[1] | | 3,298 | 4,076 | 44 |
| Jakarta, Indonesia | | 7,641 | 7,360 | 10,637 |
| Haiphong, Vietnam | | 6,496 | 6,231 | 9,673 |
| Hong Kong | | 6,044 | 5,777 | 9,195 |
| Honolulu, Hawaii | | 2,091 | 2,423 | 4,685 |
| Los Angeles, Cal. | | 371 | 1,161 | 2,913 |
| Manila, Philippines | | 6,221 | 5,976 | 9,347 |
| Melbourne, Australia | | 6,970 | 7,343 | 7,928 |
| Pusan, S. Korea | | 4,914 | 4,623 | 8,074 |
| Saigon, Vietnam | | 6,878 | 6,664 | 10,017 |
| San Francisco, Cal. | | | 812 | 3,245 |
| Seattle, Wash. | | 807 | 126 | 4,020 |
| Shanghai, China | | 5,396 | 5,110 | 8,566 |
| Singapore | | 7,353 | 7,078 | 10,505 |
| Suva, Fiji | | 4,749 | 5,183 | 6,325 |
| Valparaiso, Chile | | 5,140 | 5,915 | 2,616 |
| Vancouver, B.C. | | 812 | | 4,032 |
| Vladivostok, USSR | | 4,563 | 4,378 | 7,741 |
| Yokohama, Japan | | 4,536 | 4,262 | 7,682 |

| TO | FROM | Port Said | Cape Town[2] | Singapore |
|---|---|---|---|---|
| Bombay, India | | 3,049 | 4,616 | 2,441 |
| Calcutta, India | | 4,695 | 5,638 | 1,649 |
| Dar es Salaam, Tanzania | | 3,238 | 2,365 | 4,042 |
| Jakarta, Indonesia | | 5,293 | 5,276 | 525 |
| Hong Kong | | 6,462 | 7,006 | 1,454 |
| Kuwait | | 3,360 | 5,176 | 3,833 |
| Manila, Philippines | | 6,348 | 6,777 | 1,330 |
| Melbourne, Australia | | 7,842 | 5,963 | 3,844 |
| Saigon, Vietnam | | 5,667 | 6,263 | 649 |
| Singapore | | 5,018 | 5,614 | |
| Yokohama, Japan | | 7,907 | 8,503 | 2,889 |

(1) Colon on the Atlantic is 44 nautical miles from Panama (port) on the Pacific. (2) Cape Town is 35 nautical miles northwest of the Cape of Good Hope. (3) Gibraltar (port) is 24 nautical miles east of the Strait of Gibraltar.

## Notable Ocean Passages by Ships

| Time | From | To | Naut. mi. | Date | Ship |
|---|---|---|---|---|---|
| **Sailing Vessels** | | | | | |
| 16d . . . . . | Liverpool. . . . | New York . . . . | 3,150 | Nov. 1846 | Yorkshire |
| 76d 6h . . . . | San Francisco . | Boston . . . . . . | ... | 1853 | Northern Light |
| 12d 6h . . . . | Boston Light. . . | Light Rock . . . . | ... | 1854 | James Baines |
| 89d . . . . . | New York . . . . | San Francisco . . | 15,091 | 1854 | Flying Cloud |
| 89d 20h. . . . | New York . . . . | San Francisco . . | 13,700 | 1860 | Andrew Jackson |
| 63d 18h 15m. | Liverpool. . . . . | Melbourne . . . . | ... | 1868-69 | Thermopylae |
| 13d 1h 25m . | New York . . . . | Liverpool . . . . . | 3,150 | ... | Red Jacket |
| 36d . . . . . | 50 S. Lat. . . . . | Golden Gate . . . | ... | ... | Starr King |
| 12d 12h. . . . | Equator . . . . . | San Francisco . . | ... | ... | Golden Fleece |
| 12d 4h 1m . . | Sandy Hook. . . | England. . . . . . | 3,013 | 1905 | Atlantic |
| **Atlantic Crossings by Power Vessels** | | | | | |
| 29d 4h . . . . | Savannah . . . . | Liverpool . . . . . | ... | May 22, 1819 | Savannah (Amer.) (a) |
| 15d . . . . . | Bristol . . . . . | New York . . . . . | ... | Apr. 1838 | Great Western (Br.) |
| 14d 8h . . . . | Liverpool. . . . | New York . . . . . | 3,150 | July 1840 | Britannia (Br.) (b) |
| 9d 13h . . . . | Liverpool. . . . | New York . . . . . | 3,054 | Aug. 1852 | Baltic (Amer.) |
| 5d 15h 20m . | Southampton . . | New York . . . . . | 3,189 | 1898 | Kaiser Wilhelm Der Grosse (Ger.) |
| 5d 7h 38m . . | Sandy Hook. . . | Plymouth . . . . . | 3,082 | Sept. 1900 | Deutschland (Ger.) |
| 4d 11h 42m . | Queenstown . . . | New York. . . . . | 2,780 | 1909 | Lusitania (Br.) |
| 5d 6h 21m . . | New York . . . . | Cherbourg . . . . | 3,227 | Oct. 1924 | Leviathan (Amer.) |
| 4d 17h 42m . | Cherbourg. . . . | Ambrose Lt. . . . | 3,164 | July 1929 | Bremen (Ger.)* |
| 4d 14h 30m . | New York . . . . | Plymouth . . . . . | 3,082 | July 1929 | Bremen (Ger.) |
| 4d 16h 48m . | Cherbourg. . . . | New York . . . . . | 3,149 | July 1933 | Europa (Ger.) |
| 4d 13h 58m . | Gibraltar . . . . . | Ambrose Lt. . . . | 3,181 | Aug. 1933 | Rex (Ital.) |
| 4d 14h 27m . | Cherbourg. . . . | Ambrose Lt. . . . | 3,092 | Nov. 1934 | Bremen (Ger.) |
| 3d 23h 02m . | Bishop's Rock. . | Ambrose Lt. . . . | 2,906 | July-Aug. 1937 | Normandie (Fr.) |
| 3d 22h 07m . | New York . . . . | Southampton . . . | 2,936 | Aug. 1937 | Normandie (Fr.) |
| 3d 20h 42m . | Ambrose Lt.. . . | Bishop's Rock . . | 3,120 | Aug. 10-14, 1938 | Queen Mary (Br.) |
| 3d 21h 48m . | Bishop's Rock. . | Ambrose Lt. . . . | 3,120 | Aug. 3-8, 1948 | Queen Mary (Br.) |
| 3d 10h 40m . | Ambrose Lt.. . . | Bishop's Rock . . | 2,942 | July 3-7, 1952 | United States (U.S.)* (e) |
| 3d 11h 24m . | Bishop's Rock. . | Ambrose Lt. . . . | 2,912 | Aug. 20, 1973 | Sea-Land Exchange (U.S.) (k) |
| **Other Ocean Passages** | | | | | |
| 3d 00h 36m . | San Pedro. . . . | Honolulu . . . . . | 2,226 | June 1928 | U.S.S. Lexington |
| 86d . . . . . | Halifax. . . . . . | Vancouver . . . . | 7,295 | July-Sept. 1944 | St. Roch (Can.) (c) |
| 3d 2h 30m . . | San Francisco . | Oahu, Hawaii. . . | 2,091 | July 16-19, 1945 | U.S.S. Indianapolis (d) |
| 4d 8h 51m . . | Gibraltar . . . . . | Newport News . . | 3,360 | Nov. 26, 1945 | U.S.S. Lake Champlain |
| 7d 18h 36m . | Japan . . . . . . | San Francisco . . | 5,000 | July-Aug. 4, 1950 | U.S.S. Boxer |

| Time | From | To | Naut. mi. | Date | Ship |
|---|---|---|---|---|---|
| 7d 13h .... | Yokosuka .... | Alameda .... | 5,000 | June 1-9, 1951 | U.S.S. Philippine Sea |
| 8d 11h .... | Nantucket .... | Portland, Eng. . . | 3,161 | Feb. 25-Mar. 4, '58 | U.S.S. Skate (f) |
| 7d 5h ..... | Lizard Head. . . | Nantucket, Mass. | ... | Mar. 23-29, 1958 | U.S.S. Skate (f) |
| 45d ...... | Pearl Harbor. . . | Iceland (via N. | | | |
| | | Pole) ...... | ... | July 23-Aug. 7, '58 | U.S.S. Nautilus (g) |
| 84d ...... | New London. . . | Rehoboth, Del. . . | 41,500 | Feb. 16-May 10, '60 | U.S.S. Triton (h) |
| 5d ...... | Baffin Bay .... | NW Passage, Pac | 850 | Aug. 15-20, 1960 | U.S.S. Seadragon (i) |
| 12d 16h 22m. | New York .... | Cape Town .. | 6,786 | Oct. 30-Nov. 11, '62 | African Comet* |
| 5d 6h ..... | Kobe....... | Race Rock, B.C.. | 4,126 | Aug. 24, 1973 | Sea-Land Trade (U.S.) |

*Maiden voyage. (a) The Savannah, a fully rigged sailing vessel with steam auxiliary (over 300 tons, 98.5 ft. long, beam 25.8 ft., depth 12.9 ft.) was launched in the East River in 1818. It was the first ship to use steam in crossing any ocean. It was supplied with engines and detachable iron paddle wheels. On its famous voyage it used steam 105 hours. (b) First Cunard liner. (c) First ship to complete NW Passage in one season. (d) Carried Hiroshima atomic bomb in World War II. (e) Set world speed record; average speed eastbound on maiden voyage 35.59 knots (about 41 m.p.h.). (f) First atomic submarine to cross Atlantic both ways submerged. (g) World's first atomic submarine also first to make undersea voyage under polar ice cap, 1,830 mi. from Point Barrow, Alaska, to Atlantic Ocean, Aug. 1-4, 1958, reaching North Pole Aug. 3. Second undersea transit of the North Pole made by submarine USS Skate Aug. 11, 1958, during trip from New London, Conn., and return. (h) World's largest submarine. Nuclear-powered Triton was submerged during nearly all its voyage around the globe. It duplicated the route of Ferdinand Magellan's circuit (1519-1522) 30,708 mi., starting from St. Paul Rocks off the NE coast of Brazil, Feb. 24-Apr. 25, 1960, then sailed to Cadiz, Spain, before returning home. (i) First underwater transit of Northwest Passage. (k) Fastest freighter crossing of Atlantic.

## Value of U.S. Exports, Imports, and Merchandise Balance

Source: Office of International Economic Research, U.S. Commerce Department (millions of dollars)

| Year | Principal Census trade totals | | | | | Other Census totals | | |
|---|---|---|---|---|---|---|---|---|
| | U.S. exports and reexports excluding military grant-aid | U.S. general imports f.a.s. transaction values[1] | U.S. merchandise balance f.a.s.[1] | U.S. general imports c.i.f. | U.S. balance exports f.a.s. imports c.i.f. | Military grant-aid shipments | Exports of domestic merchandise | Re-exports |
| 1950 | 9,997 | 8,954 | 1,043 | — | — | 282 | 10,146 | 133 |
| 1955 | 14,298 | 11,566 | 2,732 | — | — | 1,256 | 15,426 | 128 |
| 1960 | 19,659 | 15,073 | 4,586 | — | — | 949 | 20,408 | 201 |
| 1965 | 26,742 | 21,427 | 5,315 | — | — | 773 | 27,178 | 343 |
| 1970[2] | 42,664 | 40,114 | 2,550 | 42,591 | 73 | 565 | 42,594 | 634 |
| 1975 | 107,589 | 96,573 | 11,017 | 103,846 | 3,744 | 461 | 106,561 | 1,489 |
| 1977 | 121,144 | [3]147,696 | −26,552 | [3]157,574 | −36,430 | 62 | 119,005 | 2,201 |

Note: Export values include both commercially-financed shipments and shipments under government-financed programs such as AID and PL-480. (1) Prior to 1974, imports are customs values, i.e. generally at prices in principal foreign markets. (2) Beginning 1970, includes nonmonetary gold valued as follows in millions of dollars in 1970-77 respectively: Exports - 4, 24, 28, 50, 89, 459, 348, and 1,043; imports - 162, 221, 358, 356, 397, 457, 331, and 674. (3) 1977 imports are based on the date of importation, other years on the date of entry. This change in timing increased 1977 imports by $205 million.

## U.S. Foreign Trade, by Economic Classes

| Economic class | 1965 | 1970 | 1973 | 1974 | 1975 | 1976 | 1977 |
|---|---|---|---|---|---|---|---|
| Exports, total . . . . . . . . . . . . | 29,128 | 45,114 | 70,246 | 97,144 | 106,102 | 113,318 | 117,966 |
| Excluding military grant-aid . . . . . . | ... | ... | 69,730 | 96,545 | 105,641 | 113,133 | 117,899 |
| Crude foods . . . . . . . . . . . . . . | 2,587 | 2,748 | 8,805 | 10,390 | 11,804 | 11,420 | 9,438 |
| Manufactured foods . . . . . . . . . . | 1,590 | 1,921 | 3,522 | 4,195 | 4,221 | 4,764 | 5,356 |
| Crude materials . . . . . . . . . . . . | 2,887 | 4,492 | 7,828 | 11,170 | 10,883 | 11,805 | 13,976 |
| Agricultural . . . . . . . . . . . . . | 1,942 | 2,524 | 5,290 | 6,981 | 5,747 | 6,765 | 8,804 |
| Semimanufactures . . . . . . . . . . . | 4,114 | 6,866 | 9,246 | 14,193 | 12,815 | 13,969 | 14,107 |
| Finished manufactures . . . . . . . . . | 16,008 | 26,563 | 40,845 | 57,196 | 66,379 | 71,365 | 75,084 |
| Excluding military grant-aid . . . . . | ... | ... | 40,330 | 56,597 | 65,918 | 71,175 | 75,022 |
| Imports, total[1] . . . . . . . . . . . | 22,293 | 40,748 | 69,476 | 100,997 | 96,902 | 121,795 | 147,848 |
| Crude foods . . . . . . . . . . . . . . | 2,008 | 2,579 | 3,562 | 3,721 | 3,642 | 5,225 | 7,065 |
| Manufactured foods . . . . . . . . . . | 1,877 | 3,519 | 5,517 | 6,810 | 5,953 | 6,277 | 6,755 |
| Crude materials . . . . . . . . . . . . | 3,709 | 4,126 | 7,831 | 20,000 | 23,570 | 32,080 | 40,822 |
| Agricultural . . . . . . . . . . . . . | 864 | 797 | 1,091 | 1,349 | 1,280 | 1,620 | 1,732 |
| Semimanufactures . . . . . . . . . . . | 4,964 | 7,263 | 13,129 | 22,077 | 17,326 | 20,495 | 24,182 |
| Finished manufactures . . . . . . . . . | 8,871 | 22,464 | 39,437 | 48,390 | 46,411 | 57,716 | 69,025 |

(1) Customs values are shown for imports.

## Total Exports and Exports Financed by Foreign Aid

| | 1965 | 1970 | 1973 | 1974 | 1975 | 1976 | 1977 |
|---|---|---|---|---|---|---|---|
| Exports, total . . . . . . . . . . . . | 27,530 | 43,224 | 71,339 | 98,507 | 107,592 | 114,992 | 120,163 |
| Agricultural commodities . . . . . . . . | 6,306 | 7,349 | 17,861 | 22,260 | 22,097 | 23,281 | 24,234 |
| Nonagricultural commodities . . . . . . | 20,445 | 35,310 | 52,962 | 75,648 | 85,094 | 91,522 | 95,867 |
| Manufactured goods (domestic) . . . . | 17,439 | 29,343 | 44,731 | 63,523 | 70,950 | 77,241 | 80,453 |
| Military grant—aid . . . . . . . . . . | 779 | 565 | 516 | 599 | 461 | 190 | 62 |
| Export financed under P.L.-480 . . . | 1,323 | 1,021 | 755 | 760 | 1,181 | 1,078 | 1,074 |
| Sales for foreign currency . . . . . . | 899 | 276 | 4 | — | — | — | — |
| Donations, including disaster relief . . . | 253 | 255 | 209 | 272 | 257 | 307 | 368 |
| Barter for strategic goods . . . . . . . | 19 | — | — | — | — | — | — |
| Long-term dollar credit sales . . . . . | 152 | 490 | 542 | 488 | 924 | 771 | 706 |

## Value of Principal Agricultural Exports

| Commodity | Avg. 1961-65 | Avg. 1966-70 | 1965 | 1970 | 1974 | 1975 | 1976 | 1977 |
|---|---|---|---|---|---|---|---|---|
| Wheat and wheat products . . . . . | 1,268 | 1,197 | 1,214 | 1,144 | 4,678 | 5,292 | 4,086 | 2,932 |
| Feed grains . . . . . . . . . . . . . | 841 | 1,082 | 1,162 | 1,099 | 4,727 | 5,492 | 5,979 | 4,862 |
| Rice . . . . . . . . . . . . . . . . . | 178 | 311 | 244 | 314 | 853 | 858 | 629 | 698 |
| Fodders and feeds . . . . . . . . . . | 179 | 386 | 278 | 496 | 1,287 | 987 | 449 | 592 |
| Oilseeds and products . . . . . . . . | 774 | 1,182 | 1,029 | 1,642 | 4,865 | NA | 5,070 | 6,630 |
| Cotton, raw . . . . . . . . . . . . . | 639 | 408 | 495 | 377 | 1,353 | 991 | 1,049 | 1,529 |

# Commerce at Principal North American Ports
## Handling 1,000,000 tons or more per year
Source: Corps of Engineers, Department of the Army; Statistics Canada

U.S. data 1976; Canadian data 1977 (short tons)

### Major Ports

| | |
|---|---|
| Port of New York, N.Y. & N.J. | 179,586,763 |
| New Orleans, La. | 155,990,247 |
| Houston, Tex. | 89,897,598 |
| Baton Rouge, La. | 66,702,534 |
| Baltimore Hbr. and channels, Md. | 52,437,192 |
| Philadelphia Hbr., Pa. | 50,603,564 |
| Norfolk Hbr., Va. | 50,055,402 |
| Beaumont, Tex. | 43,939,073 |
| Tampa Hbr., Fla. | 39,904,415 |
| Vancouver, B.C. | 39,031,196 |
| Corpus Christi, Tex. | 38,558,753 |
| Mobile Hbr., Ala. | 35,379,310 |
| Sept-Isles, Que. | 35,031,196 |
| Long Beach, Cal. | 31,457,099 |
| Los Angeles Hbr., Cal. | 30,931,489 |
| Port Arthur, Tex. | 30,687,203 |
| Marcus Hook, Pa. and vicinity | 28,680,539 |
| Texas City, Tex. | 28,516,499 |
| Paulsboro N.J. and vicinity | 26,213,298 |
| Boston, Mass. | 26,172,442 |
| Portland Hbr., Me. | 25,373,621 |
| Port Cartier, Que. | 23,978,093 |
| Port of metropolitan St. Louis | 23,954,882 |
| Pascagoula Hbr., Miss. | 23,927,049 |
| Thunder Bay, Ont. | 21,934,763 |
| Portland, Ore. | 21,492,513 |
| Lake Charles, La. | 20,221,283 |
| Richmond Hbr., Ca. | 20,165,240 |
| Montreal, Que. | 18,044,084 |
| Seattle Hbr., Wash. | 16,777,890 |
| Huntington, W. Va. | 15,930,959 |
| Quebec, Que. | 15,078,262 |
| Jacksonville Hbr., Fla. | 14,397,951 |
| Hamilton, Ont. | 13,352,976 |
| Port of Newport News, Va. | 13,344,253 |
| New Castle, Del. and vicinity | 12,693,084 |
| Halifax, N.S. | 12,082,772 |
| Memphis, Tenn. | 12,046,218 |
| Port Everglades Hbr., Fla. | 12,020,700 |
| St. John, N.B. | 11,146,197 |
| New Haven Hbr., Conn. | 11,069,899 |
| Clairton-Elizabeth, Pa. | 10,627,014 |
| Cincinnati, Oh. | 10,581,359 |
| Port of Albany, N.Y. | 10,146,459 |

### Other U.S. Ports

| | |
|---|---|
| Tacoma Hbr., Wash. | 10,227,464 |
| Freeport Hbr., Tex. | 9,710,609 |
| Charleston Hbr., S.C. | 9,664,865 |
| Longview, Wash. | 9,223,526 |
| El Segundo, Wash. | 8,750,145 |
| Camden-Gloucester, N.J. | 8,715,042 |
| Port of Wilmington, N.C. | 7,950,333 |
| Anacortes Hbr., Wash. | 7,491,649 |
| Galveston, Tex. | 7,302,900 |
| Coos Bay, Ore. | 7,116,085 |
| Oakland Hbr., Cal. | 6,634,278 |

| | |
|---|---|
| St. Paul, Minn. | 5,977,5 |
| Aliquippa-Rochester, Pa. | 5,965,3 |
| Harbor Island, Tex. | 5,195,8 |
| Fall River Hbr., Mass. | 4,739,0 |
| Mount Vernon, Ind. | 4,550,5 |
| Port Jefferson, N.Y. | 4,409,2 |
| Matagorda Ship Channel, Port Lavaca, Tex. | 4,256,3 |
| Astoria, Ore. | 4,167,9 |
| Everett Hbr., Wash. | 4,143,0 |
| Miami Hbr., Fla. | 3,708,7 |
| New London Hbr., Conn. | 3,342,2 |
| Bridgeport Hbr., Conn. | 3,265,1 |
| Nashville, Tenn. | 3,246,7 |
| Port Angeles Hbr., Wash. | 3,241,4 |
| Victoria, Tex. | 3,238,5 |
| Portsmouth Hbr., N.M. | 3,143,3 |
| Grays.Hbr. and Chehalis River, Wash. | 3,142,6 |
| Minneapolis, Minn. | 3,086,5 |
| Canaveral Hbr., Fla. | 3,078,7 |
| Helena, Ark. | 3,051,0 |
| Vancouver, Wash. | 3,039,6 |
| Vicksburg, Miss. | 3,001,3 |
| Greenville, Miss. | 2,739,0 |
| Wilmington Hbr., Del. | 2,653,2 |
| Brownsville, Tex. | 2,584,9 |
| Pensacola Hbr., Fla. | 2,548,4 |
| Morehead City Hbr., N.C. | 2,503,6 |
| San Diego Hbr., Cal. | 2,184,6 |
| Charlotte Hbr., Fla. | 2,057,0 |
| San Francisco Hbr., Cal. | 1,956,4 |
| Kansas City, Mo. | 1,827,9 |
| Chattanooga, Tenn. | 1,804,4 |
| Humboldt Hbr. and Bay, Cal. | 1,775,5 |
| Bellingham Bay and Hbr., Wash. | 1,760,5 |
| Brunswick Hbr., Ga. | 1,685,8 |
| Georgetown Hbr., S.C. | 1,666,4 |
| Salem Hbr., Mass. | 1,651,0 |
| Washington Hbr., D.C. | 1,538,1 |
| Port of Richmond, Va. | 1,537,2 |
| Port of Hopewell, Va. | 1,491,2 |
| Hempstead Hbr., N.Y. | 1,488,3 |
| Ventura Hbr., Cal. | 1,487,9 |
| Stockton, Cal. | 1,469,9 |
| San Luis Obispo Hbr., Cal. | 1,457,1 |
| Weedon Island, Fla. | 1,385,2 |
| Searsport Hbr., Me | 1,313,4 |
| Moss Landing Hbr., Cal. | 1,306,9 |
| Port Townsend Hbr., Wash. | 1,223,5 |
| Panama City Hbr., Fla. | 1,208,6 |
| Palm Beach Hbr., Fla. | 1,026,0 |

### Alaska, Hawaii, Puerto Rico

| | |
|---|---|
| San Juan Hbr., P.R. | 9,321,3 |
| Honolulu Hbr., Ha. | 7,189,5 |
| Barbers Point, Oahu, Ha. | 6,593,4 |
| Anchorage, Alas. | 2,932,4 |
| Ketchikan Hbr., Alas. | 1,559,0 |
| Kahului Hbr., Maui, Ha. | 1,276,4 |

## Commerce at Great Lakes Ports

| | | | |
|---|---|---|---|
| Port of Chicago, Ill. | 40,574,524 | Sandusky Hbr., Oh. | 5,370,0 |
| Duluth-Superior Hbr., Minn. & Wis. | 32,654,531 | Milwaukee Hbr., Wis. | 3,546,7 |
| Port of Detroit, Mich. | 26,407,938 | Port Dolomite, Mich. | 3,457,4 |
| Toledo Hbr., Oh. | 25,001,674 | Port Inland, Mich. | 3,361,5 |
| Indiana Hbr., Ind. | 19,490,752 | St. Clair, Mich. | 3,355,1 |
| Cleveland Hbr., Oh. | 18,167,579 | Huron Hbr., Oh. | 2,855,7 |
| Conneaut Hbr., Oh. | 16,464,534 | Alpena Hbr., Mich. | 2,835,4 |
| Port of Buffalo, N.Y. | 12,267,468 | Fairport Hbr., Oh. | 2,677,0 |
| Taconite Hbr., Minn. | 12,189,112 | Drummond Island, Mich. | 2,511,3 |
| Escanaba, Mich. | 11,934,366 | Green Bay Hbr., Wis. | 2,340,5 |
| Ashtabula Hbr., Oh. | 11,700,411 | Ludington Hbr., Mich. | 2,338,7 |
| Calcite, Mich. | 11,313,470 | Muskegon Hbr., Mich. | 2,270,8 |
| Silver Bay, Minn. | 11,025,905 | Buffington Hbr., Ind. | 2,181,3 |
| Gary Hbr., Ind. | 9,921,693 | Erie Hbr., Pa. | 1,157,6 |
| Stoneport, Mich. | 9,766,015 | Port Washington Hbr., Wis. | 1,066,0 |
| Lorain Hbr., Oh. | 7,439,113 | Oswego Hbr., N.Y. | 1,014,1 |
| Presque Isle Hbr., Mich. | 6,840,553 | | |

---

## Automotive Exports from U.S.
Source: Bureau of Economic Analysis, U.S. Commerce Department (in millions)

| | Total value | | | | Total value | | | | Total value | |
|---|---|---|---|---|---|---|---|---|---|---|
| | Vehicles | Automotive | | | Vehicles | Automotive* | | | Vehicles | Automotiv* |
| 1940 | $147 | $259 | | 1965 | $739 | $1,929 | | 1974 | $3,728 | $8,162 |
| 1950 | 406 | 746 | | 1969 | 1,575 | 3,888 | | 1975 | 5,084 | 10,077 |
| 1955 | 747 | 1,276 | | 1970 | 1,416 | 3,652 | | 1976 | 5,335 | 11,243 |
| 1960 | 634 | 1,266 | | 1973 | 2,713 | 6,343 | | 1977 | 5,669 | 12,132 |

*Includes new and used passenger cars and trucks, trailers, parts for assembly, and garage equipment.

## Important Waterways and Canals

**The St. Lawrence & Great Lakes Waterway,** the largest inland navigation system on the continent, extends from the Atlantic Ocean to Duluth at the western end of Lake Superior, a distance of 2,342 miles. With the deepening of channels and locks to 27 ft., ocean carriers are able to penetrate to ports in the Canadian interior and the American midwest.

The major canals are those of the St. Lawrence Great Lakes waterway — the 3 new canals of the St. Lawrence Seaway, with their 7 locks, providing navigation for vessels of 26-foot draught from Montreal to Lake Ontario; the Welland Ship Canal by-passing the Niagara River between Lake Ontario and Lake Erie with its 8 locks, and the Sault Ste. Marie Canal and lock between Lake Huron and Lake Superior. These 16 locks overcome a drop of 580 ft. from the head of the lakes to Montreal. From Montreal to Lake Ontario the former bottleneck of narrow, shallow canals and of slow passage through 22 locks has been overcome, giving faster and safer movement for larger vessels. The new locks and linking channels now accommodate all but the largest ocean-going vessels and the upper St. Lawrence and Great Lakes are open to 80% of the world's saltwater fleet.

Subsidiary Canadian canals or branches include the St. Peters Canal between Bras d'Or Lakes and the Atlantic Ocean in Nova Scotia; the St. Ours and Chambly Canals on the Richelieu River, Quebec; the Ste. Anne and Carillon Canals on the Ottawa River; the Rideau Canal between the Ottawa River and Lake Ontario, the Trent and Murrary Canals between Lake Ontario and Georgian Bay in Ontario and the St. Andrew's Canal on the Red River. The commercial value of these canals is not great but they are maintained to control water levels and permit the passage of small vessels and pleasure craft. The Canso Canal, completed 1957, permits shipping to pass through the causeway connecting Cape Breton Island with the Nova Scotia mainland.

The 1977 navigation season began on April 4 and ended when the last commercial vessel cleared the St. Lawrence Seaway system on December 26. This marked the latest closing in the 19-year history of the waterway.

Cargo tonnage on the Montreal - Lake Ontario Section of the Seaway was over 63 million tons during 1977 — the second best tonnage year. Bulk cargo, totaling 56.5 million tons, was principally responsible for the overall increase. General cargo in 1977 rose 50% and accounted for 6.8 million tons.

**Addresses:** St. Lawrence Seaway Development Corporation (U.S.), P.O. Box 520, Massena, N.Y., David W. Oberlin, Administrator, and St. Lawrence Seaway Authority (Canada), Ottawa, Ont., Mr. Paul D. Normandeau, president.

**The Welland Canal** overcomes the 326-ft. drop of Niagara Falls and the rapids of the Niagara River. It has 8 locks, each 859 ft. long, 80 ft. wide and 30 ft. deep. Regulations permit ships of 730-ft. length and 75-ft. beam to transit.

### Panama Canal

The Panama Canal is a lock and lake canal, crossing the Isthmus of Panama from the Caribbean Sea in a southeasterly direction to the Bay of Panama of the Pacific Ocean. It is 50 mi. long from deep water to deep water, at least 500 ft. wide at the bottom of excavated channels, 110 ft. wide in lock chambers, which have a usable length of 1,000 ft. Depth varies, but is not less than 40 ft. Time in transit is about 8 hours.

Gatun Dam blocks the Chagres River near its Atlantic mouth, creating Gatun Lake, 23 3/4 mi. long, 85 ft. above sea level, about 45 ft. deep. Ships ascend to the lake by locks and then pass through Gaillard (formerly Culebra) Cut, 8 mi. long.

Cargo tonnage on the Panama Canal in fiscal 1977 amounted to 123.1 million compared with 117.4 million tons in 1976. Transit of oceangoing ships in fiscal 1977 totaled 11,997 compared with 12,280 in fiscal 1976. Toll collections in fiscal 1977 were $164.6 million, $135.0 million in 1976.

Improvements have included the widening of the 8-mile long channel through Gaillard Cut from 300 to 500 ft., costing $60 million; illumination of Gaillard Cut and installation of new towing locomotives at the locks costing $8 million.

**Thatcher Ferry Bridge,** opened 1962, spans Panama Canal 201 ft. above the water level near Balboa. It is a steel-arch bridge, about one mi. long, with 3 spans and 4 lanes. It cost $20 million authorized by the U.S. Congress in 1956.

## Fastest Scheduled Train Runs in U.S. and Canada

Source: Donald M. Steffee; figures are based on 1978 timetables

### Electric Traction-Passenger-(80 mph and over)

| Railroad | Train | From | To | Dis. | Time | Speed |
|---|---|---|---|---|---|---|
| Amtrak | Metroliners(6) | Baltimore | Wilmington | 68.4 | 44 | 93.3 |
| Amtrak | Metroliner | Baltimore | Wilmington | 68.4 | 45 | 91.2 |
| Amtrak | Metroliners(5) | Baltimore | Wilmington | 68.4 | 46 | 89.2 |
| Amtrak | Metroliner | Metro Park | Trenton | 33.9 | 24 | 84.7 |
| Amtrak | Metroliners(8) | Wilmington | Baltimore | 68.4 | 50 | 82.1 |
| Amtrak | Metroliner | Baltimore | Philadelphia | 94.0 | 69 | 81.9 |
| Amtrak | Metroliners(4) | Wilmington | Baltimore | 68.4 | 51 | 80.5 |

### Diesel Traction—Passenger—(80 mph and over)

| Railroad | Train | From | To | Dis. | Time | Speed |
|---|---|---|---|---|---|---|
| Canadian National | Turbotrain | Kingston | Guildwood | 145.1 | 102 | 85.4 |
| Canadian National | Turbotrains(2) | Kingston | Dorval | 165.8 | 120 | 82.9 |
| Canadian National | Turbotrains(2) | Dorval | Kingston | 165.8 | 121 | 82.2 |
| Canadian National | Turbotrain | Guildwood | Kingston | 145.1 | 106 | 82.1 |
| Amtrak | Southwest Limited | Garden City | Lamar | 99.9 | 73 | 82.1 |
| Canadian National | Turbotrain | Kingston | Guildwood | 145.1 | 107 | 81.4 |
| Amtrak | Southwest Limited | Dodge City | Hutchinson | 120.1 | 90 | 80.1 |

### Diesel Traction—Freight—(62 mph and over)

| Railroad | Train | From | To | Dis. | Time | Speed |
|---|---|---|---|---|---|---|
| Union Pacific | BASV | North Platte | Cheyenne | 225.4 | 205 | 66.0 |
| Union Pacific | Super Van | North Platte | Cheyenne | 225.4 | 215 | 62.9 |
| Santa Fe | Six trains | Gallup | Winslow | 125.8 | 120 | 62.9 |
| Santa Fe | No. 991 | Winslow | Gallup | 125.8 | 120 | 62.9 |
| Santa Fe | No. 199 | Kingman | Seligman | 88.1 | 85 | 62.2 |

### Fastest Scheduled Passenger Train Runs in Japan and European Countries

| Country | Train | From | To | Dis. | Time | Speed |
|---|---|---|---|---|---|---|
| Japan | Hikari Train | Nagoya | Shizouka | 108.2 | 59 | 110.0 |
| Great Britain | High Speed Trains(6) | Swindon | Reading | 41.3 | 24 | 103.2 |
| France | Etendard | St. Pierre des Corps | Poitiers | 62.7 | 37 | 101.5 |
| West Germany | Nymphenburg | Dortmund | Bielefeld | 61.0 | 41 | 89.3 |
| Italy | Two Trains | Rome | Naples | 130.3 | 95 | 82.3 |
| | Two trains | Naples | Rome | 130.3 | 95 | 82.3 |
| Sweden | No. 121 | Hallsberg | Skovde | 70.8 | 56 | 75.9 |
| | No. 130 | Skovde | Hallsberg | 70.8 | 56 | 75.9 |

## Automobile Factory Sales

Source: Motor Vehicle Manufacturers Association, Detroit, Mich.—wholesale values

| Year | Passenger Cars Number | Value | Motor Trucks, Buses Number | Value | Total Number | Value |
|---|---|---|---|---|---|---|
| 1900 | 4,192 | $4,899,433 | ... | ... | 4,190 | $4,899,443 |
| 1910 | 181,000 | 215,340,000 | 6,000 | 9,660,000 | 187,000 | 225,000,000 |
| 1920 | 1,905,560 | 1,809,170,963 | 321,789 | 423,249,410 | 2,227,349 | 2,232,420,37_ |
| 1930 | 2,787,456 | 1,644,083,152 | 575,364 | 390,752,061 | 3,362,820 | 2,034,853,213 |
| 1940 | 3,717,385 | 2,370,654,083 | 754,901 | 567,820,414 | 4,472,286 | 2,938,474,497 |
| 1950 | 6,665,863 | 8,468,137,000 | 1,337,193 | 1,707,748,000 | 8,003,056 | 10,175,885,000 |
| 1960 | 6,674,796 | 12,164,234,000 | 1,194,475 | 2,350,680,000 | 7,869,271 | 14,514,914,000 |
| 1965 | 9,305,561 | 18,380,036,000 | 1,751,805 | 3,733,664,000 | 11,057,366 | 22,113,700,00_ |
| 1970 | 6,546,817 | 14,630,217,000 | 1,692,440 | 4,819,752,000 | 8,239,257 | 19,449,969,00_ |
| 1975 | 6,712,852 | 23,400,000,000 | 2,272,160 | 9,900,000,000 | 8,985,012 | 33,300,000,000 |
| 1977 | 9,198,956 | NA | 3,440,335 | NA | 12,639,291 | NA |

After July 1, 1964 all tactical vehicles are excluded. Federal excise taxes are excluded in all years.

## Passenger Car Production, U.S. Plants

Source: Motor Vehicle Manufacturers Association of the U.S., Inc.

| | 1976 | 1977 | 1978 7 mos. | | 1976 | 1977 | 1978 7 mos. |
|---|---|---|---|---|---|---|---|
| **American Motors Corp.** | | | | Mark V | 60,296 | 84,593 | 40,896 |
| Spirit (Gremlin) | 39,419 | 27,054 | 8,964 | Versailles | — | 20,867 | 5,617 |
| Concord (Hornet) | 63,722 | 67,535 | 57,675 | **Total Lincoln-Merc.** | **559,745** | **794,494** | **475,930** |
| AMX | — | 1,952 | 824 | **Total Ford Motor** | **2,053,799** | **2,555,867** | **1,543,869** |
| Pacer | 74,030 | 40,034 | 9,358 | **General Motors Corp.** | | | |
| Matador | 36,747 | 20,419 | 4,803 | Chevrolet | 370,934 | 590,113 | 304,324 |
| **Total American** | **213,918** | **156,994** | **81,624** | Corvette | 47,431 | 46,357 | 29,447 |
| **Chrysler Corp.** | | | | Monte Carlo | 364,233 | 356,065 | 205,317 |
| Horizon | — | 6,282 | 100,490 | Malibu (Chevelle) | 319,812 | 271,939 | 225,317 |
| Voyager (Valiant) | 50,664 | 12,927 | 7,717 | Camaro | 201,653 | 229,637 | 181,185 |
| Volare | 435,625 | 327,429 | 137,522 | Nova | 391,309 | 363,181 | 194,683 |
| Fury | 114,265 | 114,603 | 49,176 | Monza (Vega) | 157,348 | 79,134 | 102,115 |
| Gran Fury | 57,466 | 30,822 | — | Chevette | 154,381 | 192,431 | 184,539 |
| **Total Plymouth** | **658,020** | **492,063** | **294,905** | Acadian | — | — | 8,595 |
| Chrysler | 127,466 | 130,128 | 45,001 | **Total Chevrolet** | **2,012,412** | **2,133,403** | **1,435,522** |
| Imperial (Le Baron) | — | 116,936 | 87,810 | Pontiac | 151,695 | 221,870 | 116,415 |
| **Total Chry-Plym.** | **785,486** | **739,127** | **427,716** | Grand Prix | 271,276 | 268,990 | 131,558 |
| Omni | — | 5,888 | 75,723 | Le Mans | 89,713 | 72,058 | 73,710 |
| Sportsman (Dart) | 77,906 | 47,706 | 23,989 | Firebird | 125,018 | 169,856 | 119,936 |
| Aspen | 342,509 | 259,540 | 103,087 | Phoenix (Ventura) | 86,750 | 87,565 | 41,667 |
| Monaco (Coronet) | 77,656 | 77,164 | 28,246 | Astre | 43,103 | 20,019 | — |
| Royal Monaco | — | 30,739 | — | Sunbird | 17,076 | 35,599 | 52,995 |
| Diplomat (Dodge) | 49,845 | 76,195 | 43,018 | **Total Pontiac** | **784,631** | **875,957** | **536,281** |
| **Total Dodge** | **547,916** | **497,232** | **274,063** | Oldsmobile | 304,071 | 403,373 | 248,776 |
| **Total Chrysler Corp.** | **1,333,402** | **1,236,359** | **701,779** | Toronado | 24,781 | 33,057 | 13,427 |
| **Ford Motor Co.** | | | | Cutlass | 560,055 | 580,866 | 250,114 |
| Ford | 248,550 | 275,668 | 132,193 | Omega | 67,127 | 55,844 | 31,531 |
| LTD II (Torino) | 198,307 | 232,839 | 108,068 | Starfire | 8,391 | 6,701 | 10,197 |
| Thunderbird (Elite) | 212,938 | 365,986 | 222,020 | **Total Oldsmobile** | **964,425** | **1,079,841** | **554,045** |
| Club Wagon | 34,982 | 46,589 | 23,533 | Buick | 309,099 | 384,835 | 183,497 |
| Granada | 415,390 | 357,076 | 155,933 | Riviera | 22,940 | 23,573 | 10,336 |
| Maverick | 92,378 | 48,792 | — | Century (Regal) | 345,201 | 284,167 | 227,641 |
| Fairmont | — | 111,713 | 197,370 | Skylark (Apollo) | 128,599 | 102,272 | 76,032 |
| Pinto | 108,140 | 152,195 | 108,108 | Skyhawk | 11,830 | 6,355 | 16,416 |
| Mustang | 183,369 | 170,315 | 120,714 | **Total Buick** | **817,669** | **801,202** | **513,922** |
| **Total Ford** | **1,494,054** | **1,761,373** | **1,067,939** | Cadillac | 233,575 | 267,581 | 147,094 |
| Mercury | 91,509 | 170,478 | 90,501 | Eldorado | 39,995 | 52,483 | 26,840 |
| Cougar (Montego) | 139,049 | 164,437 | 31,371 | Seville | 39,275 | 49,190 | 36,881 |
| XR-7 | — | 47,536 | 116,117 | **Total Cadillac** | **312,845** | **369,254** | **210,815** |
| Monarch | 133,734 | 119,601 | 57,125 | **Total Gen. Mts.** | **4,891,982** | **5,259,657** | **3,250,585** |
| Comet | 31,510 | 12,237 | — | Checker Motors | 4,792 | 4,777 | 2,621 |
| Zephyr | — | 27,931 | 57,731 | Volkswagen | — | — | 4,586 |
| Bobcat | 39,063 | 40,835 | 20,470 | **Total Passenger Cars** | **8,497,893** | **9,213,654** | **5,585,064** |
| Capri | — | — | 528 | | | | |
| Lincoln | 64,584 | 105,979 | 55,574 | | | | |

## Minimum Legal Age for Purchase of Alcoholic Beverages

In the U.S. and Canada

| | Years | | Years | | Years | | Years |
|---|---|---|---|---|---|---|---|
| Alabama | 19 | Indiana | 21 | New Brunswick | 19 | Quebec | 18 |
| Alaska | 19 | Iowa | 18 | Newfoundland | 19 | Rhode Island | 18 |
| Alberta | 18 | Kansas (a) | 18 | New Hampshire | 18 | Saskatchewan | 18 |
| Arizona | 19 | Kentucky | 21 | New Jersey | 18 | South Carolina (d) | 21 |
| Arkansas | 21 | Louisiana | 18 | New Mexico | 21 | South Dakota (a) | 21 |
| British Columbia | 19 | Maine | 20 | New York | 18 | Tennessee | 18 |
| California | 21 | Manitoba | 18 | North Carolina (b) | 21 | Texas | 18 |
| Colorado (c) | 21 | Maryland (b) | 21 | North Dakota | 21 | Utah | 21 |
| Connecticut | 18 | Massachusetts | 18 | Northwest Territories | 19 | Vermont | 18 |
| Delaware | 20 | Michigan | 18 | Nova Scotia | 19 | Virginia (f) | 18 |
| Dist. of Col. (b) | 21 | Minnesota | 19 | Ohio (a) | 21 | Washington | 21 |
| Florida | 18 | Mississippi (e) | 18 | Oklahoma (a) | 21 | West Virginia | 18 |
| Georgia | 18 | Missouri | 21 | Oregon | 21 | Wisconsin | 18 |
| Hawaii | 18 | Montana | 18 | Ontario | 18 | Wyoming | 19 |
| Idaho | 19 | Nebraska | 19 | Pennsylvania | 21 | Yukon Territory | 19 |
| Illinois (c) | 21 | Nevada | 21 | Prince Edward Island | 18 | | |

(a) 3.2 Beer 18. (b) Light wine, beer 18. (c) Wine, beer 19. (d) Wine, beer 18. (e) Beer not over 4% by wgt. and wine 18. (f) Beer 18.

## Highway Mileage Between Selected Canadian and U.S. Cities

| | CALGARY | EDMONTON | HALIFAX | LONDON | MONCTON | MONTREAL | OTTAWA | QUEBEC | REGINA | ST. JOHN | SAULT STE. MARIE | THUNDER BAY | TORONTO | VANCOUVER | WINNIPEG |
|---|---|---|---|---|---|---|---|---|---|---|---|---|---|---|---|
| BANGOR, ME. | 2592 | 2595 | 450 | 762 | 287 | 310 | 436 | 241 | 2115 | 188 | 936 | 1331 | 651 | 3250 | 1760 |
| BOSTON, MASS. | 2620 | 2639 | 683 | 675 | 520 | 333 | 458 | 390 | 2142 | 421 | 958 | 1403 | 564 | 3168 | 1812 |
| BUFFALO, N.Y. | 2106 | 2125 | 1141 | 142 | 978 | 383 | 350 | 533 | 1628 | 879 | 532 | 977 | 102 | 2878 | 1377 |
| BUTTE, MONT. | 378 | 561 | 2950 | 1859 | 2787 | 2309 | 2033 | 2470 | 629 | 2739 | 1533 | 1303 | 1972 | 764 | 875 |
| CALGARY, ALTA. | | 183 | 3073 | 2246 | 2910 | 2282 | 2202 | 2432 | 478 | 2862 | 1601 | 1271 | 2142 | 659 | 832 |
| DETROIT, MICH. | 1915 | 1934 | 1336 | 122 | 1204 | 576 | 475 | 738 | 1437 | 1156 | 246 | 691 | 235 | 2505 | 1149 |
| DULUTH, MINN. | 1240 | 1243 | 1842 | 777 | 1679 | 1051 | 925 | 1199 | 763 | 1631 | 425 | 195 | 865 | 1898 | 408 |
| EDMONTON, ALTA. | 183 | | 3076 | 2249 | 2913 | 2285 | 2205 | 2435 | 497 | 2865 | 1632 | 1274 | 2145 | 842 | 835 |
| FARGO, N.D. | 989 | 1172 | 2092 | 1048 | 1929 | 1502 | 1175 | 1764 | 511 | 1881 | 675 | 445 | 1161 | 1654 | 233 |
| HALIFAX, N.S. | 3073 | 3076 | | 1243 | 163 | 791 | | 657 | 2596 | 262 | 1417 | 1812 | 1132 | 3731 | 2241 |
| LONDON, ONT. | 2246 | 2249 | 1243 | | 1080 | 452 | 359 | 602 | 1769 | 1032 | 403 | 985 | 111 | 2904 | 1414 |
| MONCTON, N.B. | 2910 | 2913 | 163 | 1080 | | 628 | 754 | 494 | 2433 | 99 | 1254 | 1649 | 969 | 3568 | 2078 |
| MONTREAL, QUE. | 2282 | 2285 | 791 | 452 | 628 | | 126 | 150 | 1805 | 580 | 626 | 1021 | 341 | 2940 | 1450 |
| OTTAWA, ONT. | 2202 | 2205 | 917 | 359 | 754 | 126 | | 274 | 1725 | 706 | 500 | 941 | 248 | 2860 | 1370 |
| QUEBEC, QUE. | 2432 | 2435 | 657 | 602 | 494 | 150 | 274 | | 1955 | 446 | 774 | 1171 | 491 | 3090 | 1600 |
| REGINA, SASK. | 478 | 497 | 2596 | 1769 | 2433 | 1805 | 1725 | 1955 | | 2385 | 1146 | 794 | 1665 | 1136 | 355 |
| ST. JOHN, N.B. | 2862 | 2865 | 262 | | 99 | 580 | 706 | 446 | 2385 | | 1206 | 1601 | 921 | 3520 | 2030 |
| SAULT STE. MARIE | 1601 | 1632 | 1417 | 403 | 1254 | 626 | 500 | 774 | 1146 | 1206 | | 445 | 440 | 2201 | 797 |
| SEATTLE, WASH. | 762 | 945 | 3494 | 2489 | 3331 | 2693 | 2577 | 2934 | 1092 | 3283 | 2077 | 1883 | 2600 | 146 | 1444 |
| THUNDER BAY, ONT. | 1271 | 1274 | 1812 | 985 | 1649 | 1021 | 941 | 1171 | 794 | 1601 | 445 | | 881 | 1929 | 439 |
| TORONTO, ONT. | 2142 | 2145 | 1132 | 111 | 969 | 341 | 248 | 491 | 1665 | 921 | 440 | 881 | | 2800 | 1310 |
| VANCOUVER, B.C. | 659 | 842 | 3731 | 2904 | 3568 | 2940 | 2860 | 3090 | 1136 | 3520 | 2201 | 1929 | 2800 | | 1490 |
| WINNIPEG, MAN. | 832 | 835 | 2241 | 1414 | 2078 | 1450 | 1370 | 1600 | 355 | 2030 | 797 | 439 | 1310 | 1490 | |

## Car, Truck, and Bus Drivers in the U.S.

Source: Federal Highway Administration, estimated total licenses in force during 1977.

| State | No. of drivers | State | No. of drivers | State | No. of drivers | State | No. of drivers |
|---|---|---|---|---|---|---|---|
| Alabama | 2,122,679 | Illinois | 6,741,192 | Montana | 515,643 | Rhode Island | 600,213 |
| Alaska | 225,781 | Indiana | 3,474,158 | Nebraska | 1,025,244 | South Carolina | 1,741,432 |
| Arizona | 1,419,363 | Iowa | 1,984,650 | Nevada | 478,818 | South Dakota | 470,531 |
| Arkansas | 1,402,035 | Kansas | 1,768,749 | New Hampshire | 584,143 | Tennessee | 2,597,025 |
| California | 14,579,000 | Kentucky | 1,993,756 | New Jersey | 4,294,084 | Texas | 8,192,443 |
| Colorado | 1,878,330 | Louisiana | 2,223,033 | New Mexico | 774,436 | Utah | 771,066 |
| Connecticut | 1,912,713 | Maine | 667,681 | New York | 8,970,091 | Vermont | 331,679 |
| Delaware | 383,749 | Maryland | 2,529,740 | North Carolina | 3,490,420 | Virginia | 3,277,231 |
| Dist. of Col. | 349,685 | Massachusetts | 3,652,145 | North Dakota | 394,940 | Washington | 2,339,215 |
| Florida | 6,572,489 | Michigan | 6,150,000 | Ohio | 8,505,035 | West Virginia | 1,367,093 |
| Georgia | 3,163,940 | Minnesota | 2,598,123 | Oklahoma | 1,874,891 | Wisconsin | 2,840,543 |
| Hawaii | 534,028 | Mississippi | 1,572,875 | Oregon | 1,754,349 | Wyoming | 309,275 |
| Idaho | 595,292 | Missouri | 3,100,117 | Pennsylvania | 7,025,750 | Total | 138,120,893 |

## Trucking: Employees, Payroll, Registration, Taxes

Source: American Trucking Assns.

| 1976 | Trucks registered | Employment in trucking | Wages and salaries ($1,000) | Payments of federal and state highway users taxes ($1,000) | 1976 | Trucks registered | Employment in trucking | Wages and salaries ($1,000) | Payments of federal and state highway users taxes ($1,000) |
|---|---|---|---|---|---|---|---|---|---|
| Ala. | 595,957 | 163,100 | 1,688,900 | 170,015 | Mon. | 237,713 | 50,900 | 507,014 | 56,568 |
| Alas. | 86,763 | 15,300 | 283,953 | 24,695 | Neb. | 369,403 | 92,000 | 909,052 | 90,761 |
| Ariz. | 390,381 | 115,500 | 1,300,530 | 124,243 | Nev. | 123,702 | 42,400 | 495,359 | 38,393 |
| Ark. | 429,549 | 135,000 | 1,228,600 | 112,481 | N.H. | 75,183 | 28,500 | 284,886 | 24,011 |
| Cal. | 2,690,495 | 1,190,000 | 15,483,090 | 909,120 | N.J. | 354,087 | 212,400 | 2,678,576 | 163,118 |
| Col. | 491,638 | 146,500 | 1,659,406 | 106,951 | N.M. | 275,655 | 56,600 | 598,148 | 72,534 |
| Conn. | 142,456 | 127,200 | 1,555,274 | 50,612 | N.Y. | 824,203 | 408,300 | 5,385,068 | 269,306 |
| Del. | 60,210 | 29,900 | 366,843 | 24,095 | N.C. | 812,676 | 313,600 | 3,014,636 | 245,295 |
| Dist. of Col. | 12,926 | 10,900 | 165,636 | 7,761 | N.D. | 219,612 | 37,300 | 358,303 | 39,192 |
| Fla. | 922,327 | 283,000 | 3,028,666 | 263,290 | Oh. | 907,277 | 334,100 | 4,077,356 | 339,149 |
| Ga. | 700,246 | 216,500 | 2,279,312 | 165,306 | Okla. | 683,197 | 168,000 | 1,745,352 | 148,781 |
| Ha. | 66,578 | 21,200 | 240,450 | 15,569 | Ore. | 332,410 | 120,700 | 1,379,601 | 107,151 |
| Ida. | 240,210 | 49,500 | 495,594 | 60,247 | Pa. | 1,114,504 | 452,800 | 5,334,436 | 376,727 |
| Il. | 1,094,482 | 341,000 | 4,364,118 | 372,088 | R.I. | 68,419 | 35,800 | 369,205 | 19,318 |
| Ind. | 763,985 | 321,000 | 3,769,182 | 255,709 | S.C. | 342,809 | 145,000 | 1,376,485 | 93,332 |
| Ia. | 560,484 | 165,100 | 1,737,182 | 155,873 | S.D. | 187,081 | 38,000 | 339,948 | 41,264 |
| Kan. | 568,193 | 149,200 | 1,527,808 | 120,601 | Tenn. | 617,286 | 143,300 | 1,441,311 | 178,072 |
| Ky. | 596,768 | 154,100 | 1,624,522 | 180,412 | Tex. | 2,248,660 | 683,000 | 7,357,959 | 653,041 |
| La. | 620,692 | 167,800 | 1,797,306 | 148,700 | Ut. | 262,066 | 60,000 | 634,620 | 55,456 |
| Me. | 132,181 | 55,400 | 517,824 | 40,920 | Vt. | 56,397 | 18,700 | 185,616 | 22,526 |
| Md. | 342,206 | 123,200 | 1,441,809 | 125,319 | Va. | 506,267 | 181,400 | 1,956,943 | 207,534 |
| Mass. | 299,873 | 167,700 | 1,913,121 | 90,632 | Wash. | 668,046 | 194,800 | 2,390,585 | 186,361 |
| Mich. | 921,917 | 317,600 | 4,331,428 | 307,258 | W. Va. | 224,560 | 88,200 | 999,129 | 83,852 |
| Minn. | 659,071 | 191,500 | 2,127,373 | 172,757 | Wis. | 412,499 | 156,900 | 1,761,673 | 130,832 |
| Miss. | 387,627 | 106,400 | 959,089 | 105,559 | Wy. | 138,890 | 25,300 | 280,526 | 47,128 |
| Mo. | 684,595 | 241,400 | 2,703,197 | 179,498 | U.S. Total | 26,524,412 | 9,093,000 | 104,451,913 | 7,979,413 |

# Highway Mileage Between Selected Cities

**Cities In The East**

| | ALBANY, N.Y. | ATLANTA, GA. | BALTIMORE, MD. | BANGOR, ME. | BIRMINGHAM, ALA. | BOSTON, MASS. | BUFFALO, N.Y. | CHARLESTON, W. VA. | CHICAGO, ILL. | CINCINNATI, OHIO | CLEVELAND, OHIO | DETROIT, MICH. | INDIANAPOLIS, IND. | JACKSON, MISS. | JACKSON-VILLE... |
|---|---|---|---|---|---|---|---|---|---|---|---|---|---|---|---|
| ALBANY | | 988 | 321 | 366 | 1091 | 170 | 283 | 712 | 807 | 707 | 466 | 536 | 766 | 1379 | 111 |
| ATLANTA | 988 | | 671 | 1315 | 155 | 1070 | 876 | 519 | 707 | 467 | 692 | 726 | 539 | 400 | 31 |
| BALTIMORE | 321 | 671 | | 632 | 800 | 400 | 366 | 391 | 690 | 497 | 348 | 510 | 565 | 998 | 79 |
| BANGOR | 366 | 1315 | 632 | | 1407 | 233 | 652 | 1018 | 1174 | 1094 | 827 | 892 | 1136 | 1635 | 142 |
| BIRMINGHAM | 1091 | 155 | 800 | 1407 | | 1210 | 932 | 589 | 661 | 499 | 742 | 743 | 492 | 243 | 42 |
| BOSTON | 170 | 1070 | 400 | 233 | 1210 | | 458 | 781 | 974 | 861 | 640 | 707 | 931 | 1446 | 120 |
| BUFFALO | 283 | 876 | 366 | 652 | 932 | 458 | | 439 | 520 | 428 | 186 | 249 | 486 | 1115 | 108 |
| CHARLESTON | 712 | 519 | 391 | 1018 | 589 | 781 | 439 | | 483 | 202 | 268 | 357 | 301 | 786 | 67 |
| CHICAGO | 807 | 707 | 690 | 1174 | 661 | 974 | 520 | 483 | | 294 | 345 | 269 | 188 | 747 | 101 |
| CINCINNATI | 707 | 467 | 497 | 1094 | 499 | 861 | 428 | 202 | 294 | | 244 | 251 | 104 | 678 | 78 |
| CLEVELAND | 466 | 692 | 348 | 827 | 742 | 640 | 186 | 268 | 345 | 244 | | 168 | 300 | 924 | 97 |
| DETROIT | 536 | 726 | 510 | 892 | 743 | 707 | 249 | 357 | 269 | 251 | 168 | | 277 | 931 | 103 |
| INDIANAPOLIS | 766 | 539 | 565 | 1136 | 492 | 931 | 486 | 301 | 188 | 104 | 300 | 277 | | 631 | 85 |
| JACKSON | 1379 | 400 | 998 | 1635 | 243 | 1446 | 1115 | 786 | 747 | 678 | 924 | 931 | 631 | | 59 |
| JACKSONVILLE | 1117 | 315 | 794 | 1426 | 427 | 1201 | 1080 | 671 | 1017 | 783 | 971 | 1039 | 852 | 597 | |
| LOUISVILLE | 827 | 428 | 602 | 1198 | 362 | 964 | 537 | 266 | 304 | 108 | 351 | 363 | 114 | 573 | 76 |
| MEMPHIS | 1217 | 366 | 951 | 1594 | 247 | 1340 | 924 | 615 | 548 | 487 | 737 | 726 | 444 | 210 | 67 |
| MIAMI | 1468 | 665 | 1143 | 1773 | 765 | 1539 | 1431 | 1043 | 1377 | 1133 | 1322 | 1387 | 1197 | 920 | 34 |
| NASHVILLE | 1090 | 251 | 732 | 736 | 201 | 1126 | 717 | 409 | 452 | 289 | 532 | 544 | 293 | 375 | 57 |
| NEW ORLEANS | 1476 | 517 | 1153 | 1747 | 359 | 1556 | 1248 | 936 | 929 | 820 | 1060 | 1077 | 839 | 182 | 56 |
| NEW YORK | 147 | 863 | 192 | 450 | 988 | 211 | 367 | 566 | 828 | 635 | 486 | 626 | 716 | 1232 | 97 |
| NORFOLK | 560 | 592 | 249 | 881 | 753 | 543 | 561 | 397 | 874 | 600 | 531 | 699 | 698 | 996 | 66 |
| PHILADELPHIA | 233 | 771 | 99 | 541 | 897 | 303 | 360 | 481 | 758 | 571 | 425 | 578 | 639 | 1153 | 88 |
| PITTSBURGH | 457 | 737 | 230 | 819 | 763 | 576 | 220 | 233 | 459 | 278 | 127 | 287 | 355 | 972 | 89 |
| PORTLAND, ME. | 275 | 1185 | 513 | 128 | 1325 | 106 | 574 | 895 | 1089 | 967 | 752 | 817 | 1037 | 1552 | 129 |
| RICHMOND | 472 | 545 | 144 | 773 | 697 | 543 | 473 | 309 | 786 | 512 | 443 | 611 | 620 | 944 | 64 |
| ST. LOUIS | 1016 | 513 | 804 | 1379 | 503 | 1188 | 723 | 538 | 291 | 338 | 540 | 513 | 239 | 505 | 88 |
| TAMPA | 1331 | 464 | 986 | 1620 | 552 | 1383 | 1263 | 884 | 1187 | 948 | 1166 | 1201 | 1005 | 678 | 19 |
| TRENTON | 223 | 783 | 128 | 520 | 915 | 289 | 358 | 513 | 780 | 590 | 435 | 594 | 660 | 1163 | 92 |
| WASHINGTON | 367 | 640 | 39 | 673 | 767 | 440 | 372 | 335 | 687 | 497 | 362 | 516 | 567 | 1000 | 75 |

| | LOUISVILLE, KY. | MEMPHIS, TENN. | MIAMI, FLA. | NASHVILLE, TENN. | NEW OR-LEANS, LA. | NEW YORK, N.Y. | NORFOLK, VA. | PHILADEL-PHIA, PA. | PITTSBURGH, PA. | PORTLAND, ME. | RICHMOND, VA. | ST. LOUIS, MO. | TAMPA, FLA. | TRENTON, N.J. | WASHING-... |
|---|---|---|---|---|---|---|---|---|---|---|---|---|---|---|---|
| ALBANY | 827 | 1217 | 1468 | 1090 | 1476 | 147 | 560 | 233 | 457 | 275 | 472 | 1016 | 1331 | 223 | 36 |
| ATLANTA | 428 | 366 | 665 | 251 | 517 | 863 | 592 | 771 | 737 | 1185 | 545 | 553 | 464 | 783 | 64 |
| BALTIMORE | 602 | 951 | 1143 | 732 | 1153 | 192 | 249 | 99 | 230 | 513 | 144 | 804 | 986 | 128 | 3 |
| BANGOR | 1198 | 1594 | 1773 | 736 | 1747 | 450 | 881 | 541 | 819 | 128 | 773 | 1379 | 1620 | 520 | 67 |
| BIRMINGHAM | 362 | 247 | 765 | 201 | 359 | 988 | 753 | 897 | 763 | 1325 | 697 | 503 | 552 | 915 | 76 |
| BOSTON | 964 | 1340 | 1539 | 1126 | 1556 | 211 | 543 | 303 | 576 | 106 | 543 | 1188 | 1383 | 289 | 44 |
| BUFFALO | 537 | 924 | 1431 | 717 | 1248 | 367 | 561 | 360 | 220 | 574 | 473 | 723 | 1263 | 358 | 37 |
| CHARLESTON | 266 | 615 | 1043 | 409 | 936 | 566 | 397 | 481 | 233 | 895 | 309 | 538 | 884 | 513 | 35 |
| CHICAGO | 304 | 548 | 1377 | 452 | 929 | 828 | 874 | 758 | 459 | 1089 | 786 | 291 | 1187 | 780 | 68 |
| CINCINNATI | 108 | 487 | 1133 | 289 | 820 | 635 | 600 | 571 | 278 | 967 | 512 | 338 | 948 | 590 | 49 |
| CLEVELAND | 351 | 737 | 1322 | 532 | 1060 | 486 | 531 | 425 | 127 | 752 | 443 | 540 | 1166 | 435 | 36 |
| DETROIT | 363 | 726 | 1387 | 544 | 1077 | 626 | 699 | 578 | 287 | 817 | 611 | 513 | 1201 | 594 | 51 |
| INDIANAPOLIS | 114 | 444 | 1197 | 293 | 839 | 716 | 698 | 639 | 355 | 1037 | 620 | 239 | 1005 | 660 | 56 |
| JACKSON | 573 | 210 | 920 | 375 | 182 | 1232 | 996 | 1153 | 972 | 1552 | 944 | 505 | 678 | 1163 | 100 |
| JACKSONVILLE | 766 | 672 | 345 | 577 | 568 | 979 | 661 | 889 | 893 | 1293 | 646 | 881 | 194 | 921 | 75 |
| LOUISVILLE | | 365 | 1078 | 180 | 719 | 759 | 693 | 682 | 398 | 1070 | 575 | 267 | 865 | 705 | 60 |
| MEMPHIS | 365 | | 1017 | 220 | 399 | 1142 | 958 | 1057 | 786 | 1446 | 845 | 294 | 782 | 1064 | 91 |
| MIAMI | 1078 | 1017 | | 916 | 878 | 1327 | 1013 | 1230 | 1237 | 1649 | 994 | 1222 | 248 | 1276 | 110 |
| NASHVILLE | 180 | 220 | 916 | | 536 | 929 | 713 | 838 | 568 | 1232 | 625 | 295 | 908 | 853 | 69 |
| NEW ORLEANS | 719 | 399 | 878 | 536 | | 1353 | 1101 | 1239 | 1113 | 1655 | 1057 | 699 | 644 | 1270 | 115 |
| NEW YORK | 759 | 1142 | 1327 | 929 | 1353 | | 441 | 91 | 363 | 317 | 330 | 961 | 1176 | 70 | 22 |
| NORFOLK | 693 | 958 | 1013 | 713 | 1101 | 441 | | 348 | 400 | 649 | 88 | 930 | 859 | 359 | 19 |
| PHILADELPHIA | 682 | 1057 | 1230 | 838 | 1239 | 91 | 348 | | 294 | 409 | 240 | 881 | 1083 | 32 | 13 |
| PITTSBURGH | 398 | 786 | 1237 | 568 | 1113 | 363 | 400 | 294 | | 682 | 312 | 599 | 1045 | 205 | 22 |
| PORTLAND, ME. | 1070 | 1446 | 1649 | 1232 | 1655 | 317 | 649 | 409 | 682 | | 649 | 1294 | 1488 | 395 | 54 |
| RICHMOND | 575 | 845 | 994 | 625 | 1057 | 330 | 88 | 240 | 312 | 649 | | 842 | 842 | 277 | 10 |
| ST. LOUIS | 267 | 294 | 1222 | 295 | 699 | 961 | 930 | 881 | 599 | 1294 | 842 | | 1030 | 897 | 80 |
| TAMPA | 865 | 782 | 248 | 908 | 644 | 1176 | 859 | 1083 | 1045 | 1488 | 842 | 1030 | | 1109 | 94 |
| TRENTON | 705 | 1064 | 1276 | 853 | 1270 | 70 | 359 | 32 | 205 | 395 | 277 | 897 | 1109 | | 16 |
| WASHINGTON | 605 | 917 | 1105 | 697 | 1150 | 226 | 195 | 136 | 229 | 549 | 107 | 804 | 947 | 169 | |

## *Directions for Use of Mileage Charts

To measure mileage between the east and west charts there are 5 key cities: Chicago, Jackson (Miss.), Memphis, New Orleans and St. Louis.

Plot your course between the city listed nearest your home town and whichever of the 5 key cities you desire to pass through to the city of your destination. Add the mileage shown and this will give you the approximate total mileage.

For example: The mileage between Cheyenne and Philadelphia through St. Louis: Philadelphia to St. Louis - 881 miles, St. Louis to Cheyenne - 910; the total is 1,791 miles. (continued

(continued)

# Highway Mileage Between Selected Cities

**Cities In The West**

| | ALBUQUERQUE, N.M. | BOISE, IDA. | CHEYENNE, WY. | CHICAGO, ILL | DALLAS, TEX. | DENVER, COL | DES MOINES, IA. | FARGO, N.D. | HELENA, MON. | HOUSTON, TEX. | JACKSON, MISS. | KANSAS CITY, MO. | LITTLE ROCK, ARK. | LOS ANGELES, CAL. | MEMPHIS, TENN. |
|---|---|---|---|---|---|---|---|---|---|---|---|---|---|---|---|
| ALBUQUERQUE | | 980 | 545 | 1285 | 650 | 432 | 1032 | 1310 | 1111 | 844 | 1062 | 791 | 901 | 805 | 1032 |
| BOISE | 980 | | 766 | 1726 | 1637 | 867 | 1397 | 1228 | 494 | 1825 | 2063 | 1446 | 1833 | 887 | 1913 |
| CHEYENNE | 545 | 766 | | 967 | 880 | 101 | 632 | 823 | 700 | 1143 | 1282 | 657 | 1053 | 1182 | 1127 |
| CHICAGO | 1285 | 1726 | 967 | | 936 | 1018 | 330 | 657 | 1478 | 1092 | 747 | 505 | 652 | 2106 | 548 |
| DALLAS | 650 | 1637 | 880 | 936 | | 784 | 704 | 1110 | 1571 | 245 | 411 | 498 | 330 | 1410 | 468 |
| DENVER | 432 | 867 | 101 | 1018 | 784 | | 674 | 901 | 792 | 1028 | 1219 | 613 | 962 | 1162 | 1058 |
| DES MOINES | 1032 | 1397 | 632 | 330 | 704 | 674 | | 491 | 1162 | 948 | 828 | 207 | 581 | 1788 | 608 |
| FARGO, N.D. | 1310 | 1228 | 823 | 657 | 1110 | 901 | 491 | | 822 | 1364 | 1271 | 636 | 1054 | 1935 | 1061 |
| HELENA | 1111 | 494 | 700 | 1478 | 1571 | 792 | 1162 | 822 | | 1813 | 1922 | 1261 | 1666 | 1234 | 1720 |
| HOUSTON | 844 | 1825 | 1143 | 1092 | 245 | 1028 | 948 | 1364 | 1813 | | 433 | 744 | 439 | 1554 | 572 |
| JACKSON | 1062 | 2063 | 1282 | 747 | 411 | 1219 | 828 | 1271 | 1922 | 433 | | 613 | 257 | 1864 | 210 |
| KANSAS CITY | 791 | 1446 | 657 | 505 | 498 | 613 | 207 | 636 | 1261 | 744 | 613 | | 409 | 1620 | 467 |
| LITTLE ROCK | 901 | 1833 | 1053 | 652 | 330 | 962 | 581 | 1045 | 1666 | 439 | 257 | 409 | | 1698 | 139 |
| LOS ANGELES | 805 | 887 | 1182 | 2106 | 1410 | 1162 | 1788 | 1935 | 1234 | 1554 | 1864 | 1620 | 1698 | | 1823 |
| MEMPHIS | 1032 | 1913 | 1127 | 548 | 468 | 1058 | 627 | 1061 | 1720 | 572 | 210 | 467 | 139 | 1823 | |
| MILWAUKEE | 1390 | 1763 | 1019 | 87 | 1063 | 1039 | 358 | 573 | 1392 | 1163 | 826 | 564 | 727 | 2145 | 632 |
| MINNEAPOLIS | 1223 | 1446 | 821 | 418 | 964 | 845 | 254 | 239 | 1056 | 1211 | 1062 | 461 | 833 | 1996 | 852 |
| NEW ORLEANS | 1145 | 2140 | 1376 | 929 | 500 | 1284 | 1028 | 1479 | 2070 | 358 | 182 | 846 | 434 | 1916 | 399 |
| OKLAHOMA CITY | 545 | 1489 | 702 | 826 | 212 | 616 | 566 | 900 | 1392 | 458 | 587 | 357 | 350 | 1353 | 482 |
| OMAHA | 892 | 1267 | 491 | 465 | 672 | 537 | 139 | 436 | 1056 | 917 | 882 | 208 | 623 | 1698 | 671 |
| PHOENIX | 449 | 1020 | 924 | 1753 | 1021 | 826 | 1449 | 1726 | 1147 | 1158 | 1456 | 1238 | 1337 | 389 | 1470 |
| PORTLAND, ORE. | 1461 | 435 | 1211 | 2131 | 2057 | 1285 | 1819 | 1590 | 657 | 2282 | 2506 | 1901 | 2284 | 994 | 2367 |
| RENO | 1036 | 427 | 995 | 1970 | 1695 | 1040 | 1638 | 1639 | 905 | 1888 | 2104 | 1665 | 2030 | 476 | 2083 |
| ST. LOUIS | 1057 | 1701 | 910 | 291 | 651 | 863 | 349 | 812 | 1498 | 801 | 505 | 254 | 357 | 1862 | 294 |
| SALT LAKE CITY | 612 | 363 | 457 | 1443 | 1262 | 512 | 1089 | 1215 | 500 | 1453 | 1685 | 1118 | 1444 | 730 | 1570 |
| SAN FRANCISCO | 1132 | 654 | 1209 | 2183 | 1773 | 1267 | 1851 | 1873 | 1134 | 1955 | 2203 | 1893 | 2032 | 403 | 2162 |
| SEATTLE | 1511 | 529 | 1279 | 2031 | 2136 | 1377 | 1766 | 1505 | 611 | 2354 | 2601 | 1904 | 2273 | 1177 | 2362 |
| SIOUX FALLS | 1082 | 1295 | 654 | 525 | 844 | 655 | 282 | 230 | 960 | 1110 | 1013 | 390 | 799 | 1817 | 858 |
| TUCSON | 454 | 1191 | 999 | 1739 | 951 | 845 | 1462 | 1746 | 1270 | 1070 | 1362 | 1255 | 1278 | 512 | 1417 |
| WICHITA | 620 | 1663 | 590 | 711 | 386 | 512 | 403 | 731 | 1241 | 629 | 733 | 202 | 472 | 1384 | 549 |

| | MILWAUKEE, WIS. | MINNEAPOLIS, MINN. | NEW ORLEANS, LA. | OKLAHOMA CITY, OKLA. | OMAHA, NEB. | PHOENIX, ARIZ. | PORTLAND, ORE. | RENO, NEV. | ST. LOUIS, MO. | SALT LAKE CITY, UTAH | SAN FRANCISCO, CAL. | SEATTLE, WASH. | SIOUX FALLS, S.D. | TUCSON, ARIZ. | WICHITA, KAN. |
|---|---|---|---|---|---|---|---|---|---|---|---|---|---|---|---|
| ALBUQUERQUE | 1390 | 1223 | 1145 | 545 | 892 | 449 | 1461 | 1036 | 1057 | 612 | 1132 | 1511 | 1082 | 454 | 620 |
| BOISE | 1763 | 1446 | 2140 | 1489 | 1267 | 1020 | 435 | 427 | 1701 | 363 | 654 | 525 | 1295 | 1191 | 1663 |
| CHEYENNE | 1019 | 821 | 1376 | 702 | 491 | 924 | 1211 | 995 | 910 | 457 | 1209 | 1279 | 654 | 999 | 590 |
| CHICAGO | 87 | 418 | 929 | 826 | 465 | 1753 | 2131 | 1970 | 291 | 1443 | 2183 | 2031 | 525 | 1739 | 711 |
| DALLAS | 1063 | 964 | 500 | 212 | 672 | 1021 | 2057 | 1695 | 651 | 1262 | 1773 | 2136 | 844 | 951 | 386 |
| DENVER | 1039 | 845 | 1284 | 616 | 537 | 826 | 1285 | 1040 | 863 | 512 | 1267 | 1377 | 655 | 845 | 512 |
| DES MOINES | 358 | 254 | 1028 | 566 | 139 | 1449 | 1819 | 1638 | 349 | 1089 | 1851 | 1766 | 282 | 1462 | 403 |
| FARGO, N.D. | 573 | 239 | 1479 | 900 | 436 | 1726 | 1590 | 1639 | 812 | 1215 | 1873 | 1505 | 230 | 1746 | 731 |
| HELENA | 1392 | 1056 | 2070 | 1392 | 1056 | 1147 | 657 | 905 | 1498 | 500 | 1134 | 611 | 960 | 1270 | 1241 |
| HOUSTON | 1163 | 1211 | 358 | 458 | 917 | 1158 | 2282 | 1888 | 801 | 1453 | 1955 | 2354 | 1110 | 1070 | 629 |
| JACKSON | 826 | 1062 | 182 | 587 | 882 | 1456 | 2506 | 2104 | 505 | 1685 | 2203 | 2601 | 1013 | 1362 | 733 |
| KANSAS CITY | 564 | 461 | 846 | 357 | 208 | 1238 | 1901 | 1665 | 254 | 1118 | 1893 | 1904 | 390 | 1255 | 202 |
| LITTLE ROCK | 727 | 833 | 434 | 350 | 623 | 1337 | 2284 | | 357 | 1444 | 2032 | 2273 | 799 | 1278 | 472 |
| LOS ANGELES | 2145 | 1996 | 1916 | 1353 | 1698 | 389 | 994 | 476 | 1862 | 730 | 403 | 1177 | 1817 | 512 | 1384 |
| MEMPHIS | 632 | 852 | 399 | 482 | 671 | 1470 | 2367 | 2083 | 294 | 1570 | 2162 | 2362 | 858 | 1417 | 549 |
| MILWAUKEE | | 334 | 1034 | 905 | 501 | 1833 | 2069 | 2003 | 371 | 1502 | 2203 | 2045 | 507 | 1819 | 792 |
| MINNEAPOLIS | 334 | | 1251 | 818 | 364 | 1671 | 1721 | 1797 | 553 | 1246 | 2001 | 1673 | 221 | 1677 | 650 |
| NEW ORLEANS | 1034 | 1251 | | 684 | 1065 | 1527 | 2591 | 2199 | 699 | 1773 | 2278 | 2645 | 1265 | 1436 | 840 |
| OKLAHOMA CITY | 905 | 818 | 684 | | 477 | 989 | 1926 | 1529 | 523 | 1112 | 1692 | 1975 | 644 | 941 | 168 |
| OMAHA | 501 | 364 | 1065 | 477 | | 1325 | 1700 | 1500 | 453 | 955 | 1720 | 1657 | 187 | 1341 | 309 |
| PHOENIX | 1833 | 1671 | 1527 | 989 | 1325 | | 1273 | 762 | 1492 | 688 | 794 | 1510 | 1481 | 123 | 1040 |
| PORTLAND, ORE. | 2069 | 1721 | 2591 | 1926 | 1700 | 1273 | | 566 | 2113 | 807 | 669 | 173 | 1580 | 1396 | 1854 |
| RENO | 2003 | 1797 | 2199 | 1529 | 1500 | 762 | 566 | | 1906 | 531 | 227 | 760 | 1472 | 912 | 1542 |
| ST. LOUIS | 371 | 553 | 699 | 523 | 453 | 1492 | 2113 | 1879 | | 1381 | 2133 | 2102 | 632 | 1457 | 460 |
| SALT LAKE CITY | 1502 | 1246 | 1773 | 1112 | 953 | 688 | 807 | 531 | 1381 | | 755 | 869 | 941 | 820 | 1020 |
| SAN FRANCISCO | 2203 | 2001 | 2278 | 1692 | 1720 | 794 | 669 | 227 | 2133 | 755 | | 858 | 1696 | 921 | 1730 |
| SEATTLE | 2045 | 1673 | 2645 | 1975 | 1657 | 1510 | 173 | 760 | 2102 | 869 | 858 | | 1526 | 1666 | 1842 |
| SIOUX FALLS | 507 | 221 | 1265 | 644 | 187 | 1481 | 1580 | 1472 | 632 | 941 | 1696 | 1526 | | 1536 | 493 |
| TUCSON | 1819 | 1677 | 1436 | 941 | 1341 | 123 | 1396 | 912 | 1457 | 820 | 921 | 1666 | 1536 | | 1074 |
| WICHITA | 792 | 650 | 840 | 168 | 309 | 1040 | 1854 | 1542 | 460 | 1020 | 1730 | 1842 | 493 | 1074 | |

## Motor Vehicle Registrations, Taxes, Motor Fuel, Drivers' Ages

Source: Federal Highway Adm.

| State, 1977 | Driver's age Jan. 1, 1978 (1) Regular | Driver's age Jan. 1, 1978 (2) Juvenile | Registered autos, buses & trucks number | State gas tax per gal. cents | Motor fuel adjusted net total tax receipts $1,000 | Motor fuel consumption Highway 1,000 gallons | Motor fuel consumption Non-highway 1000 gallons | Motor fuel consumption Total 1000 gallons |
|---|---|---|---|---|---|---|---|---|
| Alabama | 16 | | 2,673,549 | 7 | 179,014 | 2,295,126 | 47,796 | 2,342,92 |
| Alaska | 16 | | 257,401 | 8 | 18,018 | 217,458 | 47,521 | 264,97 |
| Arizona | 16 | | 1,554,128 | 8 | 118,734 | 1,457,406 | 48,549 | 1,505,95 |
| Arkansas | 16 | | 1,422,805 | 8.5 | 120,420 | 1,437,884 | 23,879 | 1,461,76 |
| California | 16/18 | 14 | 14,957,812 | 7 | 815,264 | 11,991,826 | 276,378 | 12,268,20 |
| Colorado | 21 | 16 | 2,162,875 | 7 | 103,859 | 1,529,194 | 62,377 | 1,591,57 |
| Connecticut | 16/18 | | 2,089,639 | 11 | 162,548 | 1,472,772 | 27,796 | 1,500,56 |
| Delaware | 16/18 | | 373,905 | 9 | 32,878 | 328,904 | 5,593 | 334,49 |
| Dist. of Col. | 18 | 16 | 260,509 | 10 | 22,659 | 237,678 | 3,378 | 241,05 |
| Florida | 16/18 | | 6,095,739 | 8 | 391,032 | 4,846,201 | 131,635 | 4,977,83 |
| Georgia | 16 | | 3,496,270 | 8 | 251,597 | 3,318,079 | 52,131 | 3,370,21 |
| Hawaii | 15 | | 521,159 | 7.5 | 27,566 | 320,527 | 13,081 | 333,60 |
| Idaho | 16 | 14 | 717,568 | 9.5 | 52,187 | 548,656 | 40,906 | 589,56 |
| Illinois | 16/18 | | 6,860,900 | 7.5 | 408,301 | 5,634,782 | 233,832 | 5,868,61 |
| Indiana | 16/18 | | 3,585,961 | 8 | 260,317 | 3,258,729 | 75,993 | 3,334,72 |
| Iowa | 16/18 | 14 | 2,221,923 | 7 | 130,315 | 1,846,490 | 171,543 | 2,018,03 |
| Kansas | 16 | 14 | 1,926,400 | 8 | 114,543 | 1,446,996 | 123,353 | 1,570,34 |
| Kentucky | 16 | | 2,449,708 | 9 | 186,731 | 2,030,585 | 30,976 | 2,061,56 |
| Louisiana | 15/17 | 15 | 2,421,528 | 8 | 179,560 | 2,225,608 | 52,917 | 2,278,52 |
| Maine | 15/17 | 15 | 718,886 | 9 | 54,588 | 614,194 | 11,215 | 625,40 |
| Maryland | 16/18 | | 2,587,110 | 9 | 191,898 | 2,099,437 | 23,082 | 2,122,51 |
| Massachusetts | 17/18 | 16½ | 3,519,589 | 8.5 | 215,899 | 2,528,085 | 31,513 | 3,559,59 |
| Michigan | 16/18 | 14 | 5,986,053 | 9 | 424,156 | 5,047,682 | 176,045 | 5,223,72 |
| Minnesota | 16/18 | 15 | 2,813,270 | 9 | 200,639 | 2,222,231 | 161,462 | 2,383,69 |
| Mississippi | 15 | | 1,493,966 | 9 | 136,223 | 1,437,048 | 27,154 | 1,464,20 |
| Missouri | 16 | | 3,052,607 | 7 | 208,571 | 3,021,031 | 131,115 | 3,152,14 |
| Montana | 15/16 | | 671,879 | 7.75 | 45,812 | 520,998 | 42,667 | 563,66 |
| Nebraska | 16 | 14 | 1,257,644 | 8.5 | 85,467 | 977,333 | 85,288 | 1,062,62 |
| Nevada | 16 | 14 | 548,809 | 6 | 30,733 | '495,339 | '15,542 | '510,88 |
| New Hampshire | 16/18 | 16 | 593,363 | 9 | 42,503 | 453,370 | 6,489 | 459,85 |
| New Jersey | 17 | 16 | 4,407,247 | 8 | 299,287 | 3,548,505 | 55,526 | 3,604,03 |
| New Mexico | 15/16 | | 907,002 | 7 | 63,464 | 884,026 | 15,549 | 899,57 |
| New York | 17/18 | 16 | 7,730,045 | 8 | 501,750 | 6,121,273 | 303,556 | 6,424,82 |
| North Carolina | 16/18 | | 4,079,313 | 9 | 305,809 | 3,334,011 | 72,907 | 3,406,91 |
| North Dakota | 16 | 14 | 580,411 | 7 | 31,025 | 412,033 | 91,194 | 503,22 |
| Ohio | 16/18 | 14 | 7,504,260 | 7 | 401,196 | 5,887,931 | 134,025 | 6,021,95 |
| Oklahoma | 16 | | 2,296,385 | 6.5 | 126,974 | 1,968,726 | 50,119 | 2,018,84 |
| Oregon | 16 | 14 | 1,776,331 | 7 | 93,077 | 1,526,673 | 49,632 | 1,576,30 |
| Pennsylvania | 17/18 | 16 | 8,101,725 | 9 | 512,071 | 5,672,574 | 125,324 | 5,797,89 |
| Rhode Island | 16/18 | | 605,385 | 10 | 41,550 | 402,487 | 13,204 | 415,69 |
| South Carolina | 16 | 15 | 1,857,555 | 8 | 155,722 | 1,765,400 | 33,484 | 1,798,88 |
| South Dakota | 16 | 14 | 560,673 | 8 | 36,882 | 467,976 | 68,618 | 536,59 |
| Tennessee | 16 | | 2,996,117 | 7 | 222,505 | 2,748,407 | 43,666 | 2,792,07 |
| Texas | 16/18 | 15 | 9,489,010 | 5 | 456,334 | 9,068,288 | 178,074 | 9,246,36 |
| Utah | 16 | | 908,420 | 7 | 53,883 | 765,451 | 27,805 | 793,25 |
| Vermont | 18 | 16 | 320,426 | 9 | 23,331 | 288,589 | 6,151 | 294,74 |
| Virginia | 16/18 | | 3,256,746 | 9 | 271,246 | 2,976,964 | 52,553 | 3,029,51 |
| Washington | 16/18 | | 2,894,790 | 9 | 206,274 | 2,064,266 | 56,698 | 2,120,96 |
| West Virginia | 18 | 16 | 1,136,379 | 8.5 | 84,610 | 973,597 | 10,702 | 984,29 |
| Wisconsin | 16/18 | 14 | 2,667,102 | 7 | 174,963 | 2,490,300 | 106,107 | 2,596,40 |
| Wyoming | 16 | 14 | 375,956 | 8 | 33,190 | 397,763 | 47,473 | 445,23 |
| **Total** | | | 143,744,233 | | 9,307,175 | 119,626,889 | 3,723,573 | 123,350,46 |

(1) Unrestricted operation of private passenger car. When 2 ages are shown, license is issued at lower age upon completion of approved driver education course. (2) Juvenile license issued for use between home and school in Iowa, Kan., Me., Mich., Neb., Nev. N.H., N.D., Oreg.; restricted to daylight or curfew hours in Idaho, Ill., La., Mass., Minn., N.Y., Pa., S.C., S.D., Tenn., Wis.; hardship cases in Ohio, Texas, Wyo.; for agricultural pursuits in Mich., Wyo., S.C.

## Auto Registrations, Taxes, Motor Fuel, Drivers' Ages in Canada

Source: Statistics Canada

| Province | Driver's Age Minimum (1976) | Driver's Age Minor (1976) | Registered[1] road motor vehicles (1976)[4] | Province gas tax per gal. (1976)[4] | Motor fuel[2] net tax collect's (C $1,000) (1976) | Fuel consumption on roads and highways 1976[3] Gasoline 1,000 gallons | Fuel consumption on roads and highways 1976[3] Diesel 1,000 gallons | Fuel consumption on roads and highways 1976[3] Liquified petroleum 1,000 gallons |
|---|---|---|---|---|---|---|---|---|
| Newfoundland | 17 | — | 178,110 | 27 | 37,708 | 121,634 | 18,440 | 106 |
| P.E.I. | 16 | — | 57,551 | 21 | 8,320 | 37,217 | 1,887 | — |
| Nova Scotia | 16 | — | 362,526 | 21 | 57,565 | 244,013 | 19,855 | 175 |
| New Brunswick | 18 | 16 | 300,506 | 20 | 49,475 | 212,916 | 23,391 | 74 |
| Quebec | 18 | 16 | 2,907,670 | 19 | 424,317 | 1,811,081 | 295,770 | 847 |
| Ontario | 16 | — | 4,102,344 | 19 | 587,093 | 2,634,600 | 315,832 | 1,038 |
| Manitoba | 16 | — | 568,534 | 18 | 65,610 | 298,136 | 39,885 | 717 |
| Saskatchewan | 16 | — | 653,408 | 15 | 59,018 | 309,929 | 44,217 | 522 |
| Alberta | 16 | 14 | 1,168,377 | 10 | 90,585 | 696,777 | 99,488 | 2,714 |
| British Columbia | 18 | 16 | 1,457,570 | 17 | 177,244 | 750,945 | 95,681 | 952 |
| Yukon and N.W.T. | 16 | — | 29,713 | 14 | 6,846 | 18,025 | 14,510 | — |
| **Total** | | | 11,786,309 | | 1,563,782 | 7,135,281 | 967,957 | 7,144 |

(1) Registrations include: passenger automobiles (including taxis and for-hire cars) 9,016,258; trucks and truck tractors 2,266,383; buses 50,437; motorcycles 341,297; registered mopeds 54,483; and other road vehicles (ambulances, fire trucks, etc.) 57,451. (2) Includes some taxes on other fuels (i.e., not highway). (3) Net sales of gasoline, diesel fuel and liquified petroleum gas at road-use tax rates. (4) Fiscal year April 1, 1976 to March 31, 1977.

## Memorable Manned Space Flights

Sources: National Aeronautics and Space Administration and The World Almanac.

| rew, date | Mission name | Orbits[1] | Duration | Remarks |
|---|---|---|---|---|
| uri A. Gagarin (4/12/61) . . . . . . . . | Vostok 1 | 1 | 1h 48m. . . . . . | First manned orbital flight. |
| an B. Shepard Jr. (5/5/61) . . . . . . . . . | Mercury-Redstone 3 | (2) | 15m 22s . . | First American in space. |
| rgil I. Grissom (7/21/61) . . . . . . . | Mercury-Redstone 4 | (2) | 15m 37s . . | Spacecraft sank. Grissom rescued. |
| erman S. Titov (8/6-7/61). . . . . . . | Vostok 2 | 16 | 25h 18m. . . . . . | First space flight of more than 24 hrs. |
| hn H. Glenn Jr. (2/20/62) . . . . . . . | Mercury-Atlas 6 | 3 | 4h 55m 23s . . | First American in orbit. |
| Scott Carpenter (5/24/62) . . . . . . . | Mercury-Atlas 7 | 3 | 4h 56m 05s . . | Manual retrofire error caused 250 mi. landing overshoot. |
| drian G. Nikolayev (8/11-15/62) . . . . . . | Vostok 3 | 64 | 94h 22m. . . . . . | Vostok 3 and 4 made first group flight. |
| avel R. Popovich (8/12-15/62) . . . . . . | Vostok 4 | 48 | 70h 57m. . . . . . | On first orbit it came within 3 miles of Vostok 3. |
| alter M. Schirra, Jr. (10/3/62) . . . . . . | Mercury-Atlas 8 | 6 | 9h 13m 11s . . | Closest splashdown to target to date (4.5 mi.). |
| Gordon Cooper (5/15-16/63) . . . . . . | Mercury-Atlas 9 | 22 | 34h 19m 49s . . | First U.S. evaluation of effects on man of one day in space. |
| alery F. Bykovsky (6/14-6/19/63) . . . . | Vostok 5 | 81 | 119h 06m. . . . . . | Vostok 5 and 6 made 2d group flight. |
| alentina V. Tereshkova (6/16-19/63) . . . . . . | Vostok 6 | 48 | 70h 50m. . . . . . | First woman in space. |
| adimir M. Komarov, onstantin P. Feoktistov, oris B. Yegorov (10/12/64) . . . . . . . | Voskhod 1 | 16 | 24h 17m. . . . . . | First 3-man orbital flight: first without space suits. |
| vel I. Belyayev, eksei A. Leonov (3/18/65) . . . . . . . . | Voskhod 2 | 17 | 26h 02m. . . . . . | Leonov made first "space walk" (10 min.) |
| rgil I. Grissom, John ', Young (3/23/65). . . . | Gemini-Titan 3 | 3 | 4h 53m 00s . . | First manned spacecraft to change its orbital path. |
| mes A. McDivitt, dward H. White 2d, (6/3-7/65). . . . . . . . | Gemini-Titan 4 | 62 | 97h 56m 11s . . | White was first American to "walk in space" (20 min.). |
| Gordon Cooper Jr., arles Conrad Jr. (8/21-29/65) . . . . . . | Gemini-Titan 5 | 120 | 190h 55m 14s . . | First use of fuel cells for electric power; evaluated guidance and navigation system. |
| ank Borman, James A. ovell Jr. (12/4-18/65) . . | Gemini-Titan 7 | 206 | 330h 35m 31s . . | Longest duration Gemini flight |
| alter M. Schirra Jr., homas P. Stafford (12/15-16/65) . . . . . | Gemini-Titan 6-A | 16 | 25h 51m 24s . . | Completed world's first space rendezvous with Gemini 7. |
| eil A. Armstrong, avid R. Scott (3/16-17/66) . . . . . . | Gemini-Titan 8 | 6.5 | 10h 41m 26s . . | First docking of one space vehicle with another; mission aborted, control malfunction. |
| hn W. Young, chael Collins (7/18-21/66) . . . . . . | Gemini-Titan 10 | 43 | 70h 46m 39s . . | First use of Agena target vehicle's propulsion systems; rendezvoused with Gemini 8. |
| arles Conrad Jr., chard F. Gordon Jr. (9/12-15/66) . . . . . . | Gemini-Titan 11 | 44 | 71h 17m 08s . . | Docked, made 2 revolutions of earth tethered; set Gemini altitude record (739.2 mi.). |
| mes A. Lovell Jr., Edwin Aldrin Jr. (11/11-15/66) | Gemini-Titan 12 | 59 | 94h 34m 31s . . | Final Gemini mission; record 5½ hrs. of extravehicular activity. |
| adimir M. Komarov (4/23/67) . . . . . . . . | Soyuz 1 | 17 | 26h 40m. . . . . . | Crashed after re-entry killing Komarov. |
| alter M. Schirra Jr., onn F. Eisele, Walter Cunningham (10/11-22/68) . . . . . | Apollo-Saturn 7 | 163 | 260h 09m 03s . . | First manned flight of Apollo spacecraft command-service module only. |
| eorgi T. Beregovoi (10/26-30/68) . . . . . | Soyuz 3 | 64 | 94h 51m. . . . . . | Made rendezvous with unmanned Soyuz 2. |
| ank Borman, James A. ovell Jr., William A. Anders (12/21-27/68) . | Apollo-Saturn 8 | 10[9] | 147h 00m 42s . . . . | First flight to moon (command-service module only); views of lunar surface televised to earth. |
| adimir A. Shatalov (1/14-17/69) . . . . . . | Soyuz 4 | 45 | 71h 14m. . . . . . | Docked with Soyuz 5. |
| ris V. Volyanov, eksei S. Yeliseyev, vgeny V. Khrunov (1/15-18/69) . . . . . . | Soyuz 5 | 46 | 72h 46m. . . . . . | Docked with Soyuz 4; Yeliseyev and Khrunov transferred to Soyuz 4. |
| mes A. McDivitt, David R. cott, Russell L. hweickart (3/3-13/69) . | Apollo-Saturn 9 | 151 | 241h 00m 54s . . | First manned flight of lunar module. |

*(continued)*

| Crew, date | Mission name | Orbits[1] | Duration | Remarks |
|---|---|---|---|---|
| Thomas P. Stafford, Eugene A. Cernan, John W. Young (5/18-26/69). . . . | Apollo-Saturn 10 | 31[4] | 192h 03m 23s . . | First lunar module orbit of moon. |
| Neil A. Armstrong, Edwin E. Aldrin Jr., Michael Collins (7/16-24/69) . . . . . . | Apollo-Saturn 11 | 30[3] | 195h 18m 35s . . | First lunar landing made by Armstrong and Aldrin; collected 48.5 lbs. of soil, rock samples; lunar stay time 21 h, 36m, 21 s. |
| Georgi S. Shonin, Valery N. Kubasov (10/11-16/69) | Soyuz 6 | 79 | 118h 42m. . . . . | First welding of metals in space. Space lab construction tests made; Soyuz 6, 7 and 8 — first time 3 spacecraft 7 crew orbited earth at once. |
| Anatoly V. Filipchenko, Vladislav N. Volkov, Viktor V. Gorbatko (10/12-17/69) . . . . . | Soyuz 7 | 79 | 118h 41m. . . . . | |
| Vladimir A. Shatalov, Aleksei S. Yeliseyev (10/13-18/69) . . . . . | Soyuz 8 | 79 | 118h 41m. . . . . | Orbiting space laboratory construction tests were made. |
| Charles Conrad Jr., Richard F. Gordon, Alan L. Bean (11/14-24/69) . . . . . | Apollo-Saturn 12 | 45[3] | 244h 36m 25s . . | Conrad and Bean made 2d moon landing; collected 74.7 lbs. of samples, lunar stay time 31 h, 31 m. |
| James A. Lovell Jr., Fred W. Haise Jr., John L. Swigart Jr. (4/11-17/70) | Apollo-Saturn 13 | . . . | 142h 54m 41s . . | Aborted after service module oxygen tank ruptured; crew returned safely using lunar module oxygen and power. |
| Alan B. Shepard Jr., Stuart A. Roosa, Edgar D. Mitchell (1/31-2/9/71). . . . . | Apollo-Saturn 14 | 34[3] | 216h 01m 57s . . | Shepard and Mitchell made 3d moon landing, collected 96 lbs. of lunar samples; lunar stay 33 h, 31 m. |
| Vladimir A. Shatalov, Aleksei S. Yeliseyev, Nikolai Rukavishnikov (4/22-24/71) . . . . . . | Soyuz 10 | 32 | 47h 46m. . . . | Docked with prototype Salyut orbiting space station for 5½ hrs, then mission was aborted. |
| Georgi T. Dobrovolsky, Vladislav N. Volkov, Viktor I. Patsayev (6/6-30/71) . . . . . . . | Soyuz 11 | 360 | 569h 40m. . . . . | Docked with Salyut space station; and orbited in Salyut for 23 days; crew died during re-entry from loss of pressurization. |
| David R. Scott, Alfred M. Worden, James B. Irwin (7/26-8/7/71). . . . . . | Apollo-Saturn 15 | 74[3] | 295h 11m 53s . . | Scott and Irwin made 4th moon landing; first lunar rover use; first deep space walk; 170 lbs. of samples; 66 h, 55 m. stay. |
| Charles M. Duke Jr., Thomas K. Mattingly, John W. Young (4/16-27/72) . . . . . . | Apollo-Saturn 16 | 64[3] | 265h 51m 05s . . | Young and Duke made 5th moon landing; collected 213 lbs. of lunar samples; lunar stay line 71 h, 2 m. |
| Eugene A. Cernan, Ronald E. Evans, Harrison H. Schmitt (12/7-19/72) . . . . . . | Apollo-Saturn 17 | 75[3] | 301h 51m 59s . . | Cernan and Schmitt made 6th manned lunar landing; collected 243 lbs. of samples; record lunar stay of 75 h. |
| Charles Conrad Jr., Joseph P. Kerwin, Paul J. Weitz (5/25-6/22/73). . . . . | Skylab 2 | . . . | 672h 49m 49s . . | First American manned orbiting space station; made long-flights tests, crew repaired damage caused during boost. |
| Alan L. Bean, Jack R. Lousma, Owen K. Garriott (7/28-9/25/73). . . . . | Skylab 3 | . . . | 1,427h 09m 04s . . | Crew systems and operational tests, exceeded pre-mission plans for scientific activities; space walk total 13h, 44 m. |
| Gerald P. Carr, Edward G. Gibson, William Pogue (11/16/73-2/8/74). . . | Skylab 4 | . . . | 2,017h 16m 30s . . | Final Skylab mission; record space walk of 7 h, 1 m., record space walks total for a mission 22 h, 21 m. |
| Alexi Leonov, Valeri Kubason (7/15-7/21/75) . | Soyuz 19 | 96 | 143h 31m | |
| Vance Brand, Thomas P. Stafford, Donald K. Slayton (7/15-7/24/75). . . . . | Apollo 18 | 136 | 217h 30m. . . . . . | U.S.-USSR joint flight. Crews linked-up in space, conducted experiments, shared meals, and held a joint news conference. |
| Boris Yolynov, Vitaly Zhobovov (7/26-8/24/76) | Soyuz 21 | . . . | 50 days . . | Conducted experiments aboard Salyut 5. |
| Viktor Gorbatko, Yuri Glazkov (2/7-2/25/77) . . | Soyuz 24 | . . . | 18 days . . | Docked with Salyut 5. |
| Georgi Grechko, Yuri Romanenko (12/10/77-3/16/78) . . | Soyuz 26 | . . . | 96 days . . | Docked with Salyut 6. Conducted scientific experiments. Set new space endurance record. |
| Vladimir Dzhanibekov, Oleg Markarov (1/10-1/16/78) . . . . . . . | Soyuz 27 | . . . | 6 days . . | Joined Soyuz 26 crew on Salyut 6. |

(1) The Americans measure orbital flights in revolutions while the Soviets use "orbits." (2) suborbital. (3) Moon orbits in command module. (4) Moon orbits.
Fire aboard spacecraft Apollo I on the ground at Cape Kennedy, Fla. killed Virgil I. Grissom, Edward H. White and Roger B. Chaffee on Jan. 27, 1967. There were the only U.S. astronauts killed in space tests.

## Notable Ocean and Intercontinental Flights

(Certified by the Federation Aeronautique Internationale as of Jan., 1978)

| | From | To | Miles | Time | Date |
|---|---|---|---|---|---|
| | | **Dirigible Balloons** | | | |
| ritish R-34(1)..... | East Fortune, Scot...... | Mineola, N.Y..... | ..... | 108 hrs. | July 2-6, 1919 |
| | Mineola, N.Y...... | Pulham, Eng...... | ..... | 75 hrs. | July 9-13, 1919 |
| mundsen-Ellsworth-Nobile expedition... | Spitsbergen........ | Teller, Alas...... | ..... | 80 hrs. | May 11-14, 1926 |
| raf Zeppelin..... | Friedrichshafen.... | Lakehurst, N.J..... | 6,630 | 4d 15h 46m | Oct. 11-15, 1928 |
| ndenburg Zeppelin.. | Germany........ | Lakehurst, N.J..... | ..... | 51h 17m | June 30-July 2, 1936 |
| | Lakehurst, N.J..... | Frankfort, Ger..... | ..... | 42h 53m | Aug. 9-11, 1936 |
| SN ZPG-2 Blimp... | S. Weymouth, Mass..... | Africa | | | |
| | Africa......... | Key West, Fla...... | 7,000 | 275h | Mar. 4-16, 1957 |
| | | **Airplanes** | | | |
| SN NC-4....... | Rockaway, N.Y..... | Lisbon, Port..... | ..... | ....... | May 8-27, 1919 |
| hn Alcock-A.W. Brown (2).... | St. John's, Nfld..... | Clifden, Ireland.... | 1,960 | 16h 12m | June 14-15, 1919 |
| ichard E. Byrd (3).. | Spitsbergen....... | North Pole...... | 1,545 | 15h 30m | May 9, 1926 |
| harles Lindbergh (4).. | Mineola, N.Y..... | Paris........ | 3,610 | 33h 29m 30s | May 20-21, 1927 |
| Levin-. | Roosevelt Field | | | | |
| C. Chamberlin (5)... | Mineola, N.Y..... | Isleben, Germany.... | 3,911 | 42h 31m | June 4-6, 1927 |
| aron G. von Huene-feld, crew (6).... | Dublin......... | Greenly Isl., Lab..... | ..... | 37 hrs. | Apr. 12-13, 1928 |
| r Hubert Wilkins (9).. | Point Barrow, Alaska... | Spitsbergen....... | ..... | ....... | Apr. 16, 1928 |
| r Chas. Kingsford-Smith, crew (7)... | Oakland, Cal...... | Brisbane, Aust...... | ..... | ....... | May 31-June 8, 1928 |
| melia Earhart Put-nam, W. Stultz, L. Gordon...... | Trepassy, Nfld..... | Burry Port, Wales... | ..... | 20h 40m | June 17-18, 1928 |
| ichard E. Byrd (8).. | Bay of Wales..... | South Pole...... | ..... | ....... | Nov. 28-29, 1929 |
| . Coste-M. Bellonte.. | Paris........ | Valley Stream, N.Y... | 4,100 | 37h 18m 30s | Sept. 1-2, 1930 |
| iley Post-Harold Gatty...... | Harbor Grace, Nfld.... | England....... | 2,200 | 16h 17m | June 23-24, 1931 |
| yde Pangborn-Hugh Herndon Jr. (10)... | Tokyo......... | Wenatchee, Wash.... | 4,458 | 41h 34m | Oct. 3-5, 1931 |
| melia Earhart Putnam (11)... | Harbor Grace, Nfld.... | Ireland....... | 2,026 | 14h 56m | May 20-21, 1932 |
| mes A. Mollison (12). | Portmarnock, Ire..... | Pennfield, N.B..... | ..... | ....... | Aug. 18, 1932 |
| hina Clipper (Pan Am. Airways) (13).. | San Francisco..... | Manila, P.I...... | ..... | ....... | Nov. 22-28, 1935 |
| | Manila, P.I...... | San Francisco..... | ..... | ....... | Dec. 1-6, 1935 |
| romoff, Yumasheff, Danilin (USSR).... | Moscow, USSR..... | San Jacinto, Cal.... | 6,262 | 62h 02m | July 12-14, 1937 |
| ouglas C. Corrigan.. | New York....... | Dublin, Ire...... | ..... | 28h 13m | July 17-18, 1938 |
| 29 (C.J. Miller).... | Honolulu....... | Washington, D.C.... | 4,640 | 17h 21m | Sept. 1, 1945 |
| -54 (Maj. G.E. Cain) | Tokyo........ | Washington, D.C.... | ..... | 31h 24m | Sept. 3, 1945 |
| ol. David C. Schilling, USAF (14)..... | England....... | Limestone, Me..... | 3,300 | 10h 01m | Sept. 22, 1950 |
| has. F. Blair Jr..... | New York....... | London........ | 3,500 | 7h 48m | Jan 31, 1951 |
| has. F. Blair Jr. (15). | Bardufoss, Norway... | Fairbanks, Alas.... | 3,300 | 10h 29m | May 29, 1951 |
| has. F. Blair Jr..... | Fairbanks, Alaska... | New York...... | 3,450 | 9h 31m | May 30, 1950 |
| anberra Bomber.... | England....... | Australia...... | ..... | 20h 20m | Mar. 16, 1952 |
| wo U.S. S-55 Heli-copters (16)..... | Westover AFB, Mass.... | Prestwick, Scotland... | 3,410 | 42h 30m | July 15-31, 1952 |
| anberra Bomber (17). | Aldergrove, N.Ire.... | Gander, Nfld...... | 2,073 | 4h 34m | Aug. 26, 1952 |
| | Gander, Nfld....... | Aldergrove, N.Ire.... | 2,073 | 3h 25m | Aug. 26, 1952 |
| ritish Comet..... | London-Tokyo..... | Tokyo-London..... | 20,400 | 74h 52m | Apr. 3-7, 1953 |
| ritish Comet..... | London........ | Rio de Janeiro.... | 6,000 | 12h 30m | Sept. 13-14, 1953 |
| anberra Bomber.... | New York....... | Paris........ | ..... | 22h 23m | Nov. 7, 1954 |
| lax Conrad (solo).. | London (round trip)... | New York...... | 6,920 | 14h 21m 45.4s | Aug. 23, 1955 |
| apt. William F. Judd. | New York....... | Paris........ | ..... | 24h 11m | Jan. 29-30, 1956 |
| hree USAF F-100Cs. | London........ | Los Angeles..... | 6,710 | 14h 5m | May 13, 1957 |
| irit of St. Louis II (USAF F-100F jet). | McGuire AFB, N.J.... | Le Bourget, Paris... | ..... | 6h 38m | May 21, 1957 |
| SAF KC-135..... | Tokyo........ | Lajes AFB, Azores... | 10,230 | 18h 48m | Apr. 7-8, 1958 |
| lax Conrad (solo)... | New York....... | Palermo, Sicily.... | 4,440 | 32h 55m | June 22-23, 1958 |
| SAF KC-135..... | Yokota AB, Japan.... | Washington, D.C.... | 7,100 | 12h 28m | Sept. 12, 1958 |
| lax Conrad (solo)... | Chicago........ | Rome........ | 5,000 | 34h 3m | Mar. 5-6, 1959 |
| lax Conrad (solo)... | Casablanca, Mor..... | Los Angeles..... | 7,700 | 58h 36m | June 2-4, 1959 |
| SSR TU-114 (18).. | Moscow........ | New York...... | 5,092 | 11h 6m | June 28, 1959 |
| eing 707 airliner... | San Francisco..... | Sydney, Australia... | 7,630 | 16h 10m | July 2, 1959 |
| eing 707-320..... | New York....... | Moscow....... | c.5,090 | 8h 54m | July 23, 1959 |
| lax Conrad (solo)... | Casablanca, Mor..... | El Paso, Tex...... | 6,911 | 56h 26m | Nov. 22-26, 1959 |
| ol. J.B. Swindal.... | Washington, D.C.... | Moscow....... | 5,004 | 8h 39m 02.2s | May 19, 1963 |
| Irs. Jerrie Mock (19).. | Columbus, Oh..... | Columbus, Oh..... | 23,206 | 29d 11h 59m | Mar. 19-Apr. 18, 1964 |
| an Merriam (20).... | Oakland, Cal...... | Oakland, Cal...... | 27,750 | 56d | Mar. 17-May 12, 1964 |
| oncorde GB...... | London........ | Washington, D.C.... | 3,662 | 3h 34m 48s | May 29, 1976 |
| eing 747 (21)..... | San Francisco..... | San Francisco..... | 26,382 | 54h 7m 12s | Oct. 28-31, 1977 |

**Notable first flights:** (1) Atlantic aerial round trip. (2) Non-stop transatlantic flight. (3) Polar flight. (4) Solo transatlantic flight in the yan monoplane the "Spirit of St. Louis." (5) Transatlantic passenger flight. (6) East-West transatlantic crossing. (7) U.S. to Australia ght. (8) South Pole flight. (9) Trans-Arctic flight. (10) Non-stop Pacific flight. (11) Woman's transoceanic solo flight. (12) Westbound ansatlantic solo flight. (13) Pacific airmail and U.S. to Philippines crossing. (14) Non-stop jet transatlantic flight. (15) Solo across North le. (16) Transatlantic helicopter flight. (17) Transatlantic round trip on same day. (18) Non-stop between Moscow and New York. (19) rst woman pilot to circle globe; First woman to fly both North Atlantic and Pacific. (20) Followed route Amelia Earhart partly com-eted in 1937. (21) Speed record around the world over both the earth's poles.

# International Aeronautical Records

Source: The National Aeronautic Association, 806 15th St. NW, Washington, DC 20005, representative in the United States of the Federation Aeronautique Internationale, certifying agency for world aviation and space records. The International Aeronautical Federation was formed in 1905 by representatives from Belgium, France, Germany, Great Britain, Spain, Italy, Switzerland, and the United States with headquarters in Paris. Regulations for the control of official records were signed Oct. 14, 1905. World records are defined as maximum performance, regardless of class or type of aircraft used. Records to Apr., 1978.

## World Air Records—Maximum Performance in Any Class

**Speed over a straight course** — 3,529.56 kph. (2,193.16 mi.) — Capt. Elden W. Joersz, USAF, Lockheed SR-71; Beale AFB, Cal., July 28, 1976.

**Speed over a closed circuit** — 3,367,221 kph. (2,092,294 mph) — Maj. Adolphus H. Bledsoe Jr., USAF, Lockheed SR-71; Beale AFB, Cal., July 27, 1976.

**Distance in a straight line** — 20,168.78 kms (12,532.28 mi.) — Maj. Clyde P. Evely, USAF, Boeing B52-P; Kadena, Okinawa, to Madrid, Spain, Jan. 11, 1962.

**Distance over a closed circuit** — 18,245.5 kms (11,336.92 mi.) — Capt. William Stevenson, USAF, Boeing B52-H; Seymour-Johnson, N.C., June 6-7, 1962.

**Altitude** — 37,650 meters (123,523.58 feet) — Alexander Fedotov, USSR, E-266M; Podmoskovnoye, USSR, Aug. 31, 1977.

**Altitude in horizontal flight** — 25,929,031 meters (85,068,997 ft.) — Capt. Robert C. Helt, USAF, Lockheed SR-71; Beale AFB, Cal., July 28, 1976.

## Manned Space Craft

**Duration** — 84 days 1 hr. 15 min. 30.8 sec. — Gerald P. Carr, Edward G. Gibson, William R. Pogue, U.S.; Skylab 3; Nov. 16, 1973-Feb. 8, 1974.

**Altitude** — 377,668.9 kms (234,672.5 mi) — Frank Borman, James A. Lovell Jr., William Anders, Apollo 8; Dec. 21-27, 1968.

**Greatest mass lifted** — 127,980 kgs. (282,197 lbs) — Frank Borman, James S. Lovell Jr., William Anders, Apollo 8; Dec. 21-27, 1968.

**Distance** — 55,474,039 kms. (34,469,970 mi.) — Gerald P. Carr, Edward G. Gibson, William R. Pogue, U.S.; Skylab 3; Nov. 16, 1973-Feb. 8, 1974.

## World "Class" Records

All other records, international in scope, are termed World "Class" records and are divided into classes: airships, free balloons, airplanes, seaplanes, amphibians, gliders, and rotorplanes. Airplanes (Class C) are sub-divided into four groups: Group I — piston engine aircraft, Group II — turboprop aircraft, Group III — jet aircraft, Group IV — rocket powered aircraft. A partial listing of world records follows:

## Airplanes (Class C, Group I—piston engine)

**Distance, closed circuit** — 14,441.26 kms (8,974 mi.) — James R. Bede, U.S., BD-2, Columbus, Oh. to Kansas City course, Nov. 7-8, 1969.

**Distance in a straight line. Airline (international)** — 18,081.99 kms. (11,235.6 miles) — Cmdr. Thomas D. Davies, USN; Cmdr. Eugene P. Rankin, USN; Cmdr. Walter S. Reid, USN, and Lt. Cmdr. Ray A. Tabeling, USN; Lockheed P2V-1; from Pearce Field, Perth, Australia, to Port Columbus, Oh., Sept. 29-Oct. 1, 1946.

**Maximum speed over 3-kilometer measured course (international)** — 776,449 kph. (482.462 mph) — Darryl Greenamyer; Grumman F8F Bearcat; Edwards AFB, Cal., Aug. 16, 1969.

**Speed for 100 kilometers (62,137 miles) without payload (international)** — 755.668 kph. (469.549 mph.) — Jacqueline Cochran, U.S.; North American P-51; Coachella Valley, Cal., Dec. 10, 1947.

**Speed for 1,000 kilometers (621,369 miles) without payload** — 693.78 kph. (431.09 mph.) — Jacqueline Cochran, U.S.; North American P-51; Santa Rosasummit, Cal. — Flagstaff, Ariz. course, May 24, 1948.

**Speed for 5,000 kilometers (3,106.849 miles) without payload** — 544.59 kph. (338.39 mph.) — Capt. James Bauer, USAF, Boeing B-29; Dayton, Oh., June 28, 1946.

**Speed around the world** — 327.73 kph (203.64 mph) — D.N. Dalton, Australia; Beechcraft Duke; Brisbane, Aust., July 20-25, 1975. Time: 5 days, 2 hours; 19 min., 57 sec.

## Light Airplanes—(Class C-1.d)

**Distance in a straight line** — 12,341.26 kms. (7,668.48 miles) — Max Conrad, U.S.; Piper Comanche; Casablanca, Morocco to Los Angeles, June 2-4, 1959.

**Speed for 100 kilometers** — (62,137 miles) in a closed circuit — 519.480 kph. (322.780 mph.) — Miss R. M. Sharpe, Great Britain; Vickers Supermarine Spitfire 5-B; Wolverhampton, June 17, 1950.

## Helicopters (Class E-1)

**Distance in a straight line** — 3,561.55 kms. (2,213.04 miles) — Robert G. Ferry, U.S.; Hughes YOH-6A helicopter; Culver City, Cal., to Daytona Beach, Fla., Apr. 6-7, 1966.

**Speed over 3-km. course** — 348.971 kph. (216.839 mph.) — Byron Graham, U.S.; Sikorsky S-67 helicopter; Windsor Locks, Conn., Dec. 14, 1970.

## Gliders (Class D—single place)

**Distance, straight line** — 1,460.8 kms. (907.7 miles) — Hans Werner Grosse, West Germany; ASK12 sailplane; Luebeck to Biarritz, Apr. 25, 1972.

**Altitude above sea level** — 14,102 meters (46,267 feet) — Paul F. Bikle, U.S.; Sailplane Schweizer SCG 123E; Mojave, Lancaster, Ca., Feb. 25, 1961.

## Airplanes (Class C, Group II—Turboprop)

**Distance in a straight line** — 14,052.95 kms. (8,732.09 miles) — Lt. Col. Edgar L. Allison Jr., USAF, Lockheed HC-130 Hercules aircraft; Taiwan to Scott AFB, Ill.; Feb. 20, 1972.

**Speed over a 15-25 km. course** — Cmdr. D.H. Lilienthal, USN, Lockheed P3C Orion aircraft; 806.10 kph. (501.44 mph); Jan. 27, 1971.

**Altitude** — 15,549 meters (51,014 ft.) — Donald R. Wilson, U.S.; LTV L450F aircraft; Greenville, Tex., Mar. 27, 1972.

**Speed for 1,000 kilometers (621.369 miles) without payload** — 871.38 kph. (541.449 mph.) — Ivan Soukhomline, USSR; TU-114 swept wing monoplane, Sternberg, USSR; Mar. 24, 1960.

**Speed for 5,000 kilometers (3,106.849 miles) without payload** — 877.212 kph. (545.072 mph.) — Ivan Soukhomline, USSR; TU-114 swept wing monoplane, Sternberg, USSR; Apr. 9, 1960.

## Airplanes (Class C-1, Group III—Jet-powered)

**Distance in a straight line** — 20,168.78 kms. (12,532.28 mi.) — Maj. Clyde P. Evely, USAF, Boeing B52-H, Kadena, Okinawa, to Madrid, Spain, Jan. 10-11, 1962.

**Distance in a closed circuit** — 18,245.05 kms. (11,336.92 miles) — Capt. William Stevenson, USAF, Boeing B52H, Seymour-Johnson, N.C., June 6-7, 1962.

**Altitude** — 36,650 meters (123,523.58 ft.) — Alexander Fedotov, USSR; E-266 airplane; Podmoskovnoye, USSR, Aug. 31, 1977.

**Speed over a 3-kilometer course** — 1,452.777 kph. (902.769 mph) — Lt. Hunt Hardisty, USN; McDonnell F4H Phantom, White Sands, N.M., Aug. 29, 1961.

**Speed for 100 kilometers in a closed circuit** — 2,605 kph. (1,618.7 mph.) — Alexander Fedotov, USSR; E-266 airplane, Apr. 8, 1973.

**Speed for 500 kilometers in a closed circuit** — 2,981.5 kph. (1,852.61 mph.) — Mikhail Komarov, USSR; E-266 airplane, Oct. 5, 1967.

**Speed for 1,000 kilometers in a closed circuit** — 3,367.221 kph (2,192.294 mph) — Maj. Adolphus H. Bledsoe Jr., USAF Lockheed R-71; Beale, AFB, Cal., July 27, 1976.

**Speed for 2,000 kilometers in closed circuit** — 1,708.817 kph. (1,061.808 mph.) — Maj. H. J. Deutschendorf Jr., USA Convair B-58 Hustler Bomber; Edwards AFB, Cal., Jan. 12, 1961.

## Free Balloons (Tenth category, over 4,000 cubic meters)

**Altitude** — 34,668 meters (113,739.9 feet) — Cmdr. Malcolm D. Ross, USNR; Lee Lewis Memorial Winzen Research Balloon; Gulf of Mexico, May 4, 1961.

## FAI Course Records

**Los Angeles to New York** — 1,954.79 kph (1,214.65 mph) — Capt. Robert G. Sowers, USAF; Convair B58 Hustler; elapsed time: 2 hrs. 58.71 sec., Mar. 5, 1962.

**New York to Los Angeles** — 1,741 kph (1,081.80 mph) — Capt. Robert G. Sowers, USAF; Convair B58 Hustler; elapsed time: 2 hrs. 15 min. 50.08 sec., Mar. 5, 1962.

**New York to Paris** — 1,753.068 kph (1,089.36 mph) — Maj. W. R. Payne, U.S.; Convair B58 Hustler; elapsed time: 3 hrs 19 min. 44 sec., May 26, 1961.

**London to New York** — 945,423 kph (587.457 mph) — Maj. Burl D. Dayenport, USAF; Boeing KC-135; June 27, 1958; elapsed time: 5 hrs. 53 min. 12.77 sec.

**Baltimore to Moscow, USSR** — 906.64 kph (563.36 mph) — Col. James B. Swindal, USAF; Boeing VC-137 (707); elapsed time: 8 hrs. 33 min. 45.4 sec., May 19, 1963.

**Belfast to Gander, Newfoundland** — 774.25 kph (481.099 mph) — Wing Commander R. P. Beamont, Great Britain; Canberra bomber, Aug. 31, 1951; elapsed time: 4 hrs. 18 min. 24.4 sec.

**New York to London** — 2,908.026 kph (1,806.964 mph) — Maj. James V. Sullivan, USAF; Lockheed SR-71; elapsed time 1 hr. 54 min. 56.4 sec., Sept. 1, 1974.

**London to Los Angeles** — 2,310.353 kph (1,435.587 mph) — Capt. Harold B. Adams, USAF; Lockheed SR-71; elapsed time: 3 hrs. 47 min. 39 sec., Sept. 13, 1974.

---

## Aviation Hall of Fame

The Aviation Hall of Fame at Dayton, Oh., is dedicated to honoring aviation's outstanding pioneers.

Allen, William M.
Arnold, Henry "Hap"
Balchen, Bernt
Baldwin, Thomas S.
Beachey, Lincoln
Beech, Walter H.
Bell, Alexander Graham
Bell, Lawrence D.
Boeing, William E.
Byrd, Richard E.
Cessna, Clyde V.
Chamberlin, Clarence D.
Chanute, Octave
Chennault, Claire L.
Cunningham, Alfred A.
Curtiss, Glenn H.
deSeversky, Alexander P.
Doolittle, James H.
Douglas, Donald W.
Eaker, Ira C.

Earhart, (Putnam), Amelia
Ellyson, Theodore G.
Ely, Eugene B.
Fleet, Reuben H.
Foulois, Benjamin D.
Gabreski, Franciss
Glenn Jr., John H.
Goddard, George W.
Goddard, Robert H.
Gross, Robert E.
Grumman, Leroy R.
Guggenheim, Harry F.
Hegenberger, Albert F.
Hughes, Howard R.
Johnson, Clarence L.
Kenney, George C.
Kindelberger, James H.
Knabenshue, A. Roy
Lahm, Frank P.
Langley, Samuel P.

Lear, William P. Sr.
LeMay, Curtis E.
LeVier, Anthony W.
Lindbergh, Charles A.
Link, Edwin A.
Loening, Grover C.
Luke Jr., Frank
Macready, John A.
Martin, Glenn A.
McDonnell, James S.
Mitchell, William "Billy"
Montgomery, John J.
Moss, Sanford A.
Northrop, John K.
Odlum, Jacqueline Cochran
Patterson, William A.
Post, Wiley H.
Read, Albert C.
Reeve, Robert C.
Richardson, Holden C.

Rickenbacker, Edward V.
Rodgers, Calbraith P.
Rogers, "Will"
Ryan, T. Claude
Selfridge, Thomas E.
Shepard Jr., Alan B.
Sikorsky, Igor I.
Smith, C.R.
Spaatz, Carl A.
Sperry Sr., Elmer A.
Taylor, Charles E.
Towers, John H.
Trippe, Juan T.
Turner, Roscoe
Twining, Nathan F.
Wade, Leigh
Walden, Henry W.
Wright, Orville
Wright, Wilbur
Yeager, Charles E.

---

## The Busiest Airports, 1977

### (Total take-offs and landings)

### United States
Source: U.S. Transportation Department

| | |
|---|---|
| Chicago O'Hare International | 741,272 |
| Santa Ana | 639,624 |
| Van Nuys | 592,863 |
| Long Beach | 573,858 |
| Atlanta International | 516,558 |
| Los Angeles International | 500,976 |
| San Jose, Cal. | 487,005 |
| Denver Stapleton | 466,206 |
| Oakland International | 457,469 |
| Opa Locka (Miami, Fla.) | 450,288 |
| Phoenix Sky Harbor | 429,703 |
| Seattle Boeing | 424,030 |

### Canada
Source: Aviation Statistics Centre, Statistics Canada

| | |
|---|---|
| St. Hubert, Que. | 282,222 |
| Pitt Meadows, B.C. | 258,494 |
| Toronto International, Ont. | 243,173 |
| Buttonville, Ont. | 240,063 |
| Vancouver International, B.C. | 235,825 |
| St. Andrews, Man. | 231,714 |
| Hamilton City, Ont. | 225,295 |
| Edmonton Municipal, Alta. | 213,060 |
| Calgary International, Alta. | 208,170 |
| Ottawa International, Ont. | 201,758 |
| Springbank, Alta. | 201,608 |
| Langley, B.C. | 194,846 |

## Notable Trips Around the World

(Certified by Federation Aeronautique Internationale as of Jan., 1978)

Fast circuits of the earth have been a subject of wide interest since Jules Verne, French novelist, described an imaginary trip by Phileas Fogg in Around the World in 80 Days, assertedly occurring Oct. 2 to Dec. 20, 1872.

| | Terminal | Miles | Time | Date |
|---|---|---|---|---|
| Nellie Bly | New York, N.Y. | | 72d 06h 11m | 1889 |
| George Francis Train | New York, N.Y. | | 67d 12h 03m | 1890 |
| Charles Fitzmorris | Chicago | | 60d 13h 29m | 1901 |
| J. W. Willis Sayre | Seattle | | 54d 09h 42m | 1903 |
| Col. Burnlay-Campbell | | | 40d 19h 30m | 1907 |
| Andre Jaeger-Schmidt | | | 39d 19h 42m 38s | 1911 |
| John Henry Mears | | | 35d 21h 36m | 1913 |
| Two U.S. Army airplanes | Seattle (57 hops, 21 countries) | 26,103 | 35d 01h 11m | 1924 |
| Edward S. Evans and Linton Wells (New York World) (1) | New York | 18,400 | 28d 14h 36m 05s | June 16-July 14, 1926 |
| John H. Mears and Capt. C.B.D. Collyer | New York | | 23d 15h 21m 03s | June 29-July 22, 1928 |
| Graf Zeppelin | Friedrichshafen, Ger. via Tokyo, Los Angeles, Lakehurst, N.J. | 21,700 | 20d 04h | Aug. 14-Sept. 4, 1929 |
| Wiley Post and Harold Gatty (Monoplane Winnie Mae) | Roosevelt Field, N.Y. via Arctic Circle | 15,474 | 8d 15h 51m | June 23-July 1, 1931 |
| Wiley Post (Monoplane Winnie Mae) (2) | Floyd Bennett Field, N.Y. via Arctic Circle | 15,596 | 115h 36m 30s | July 15-22, 1933 |
| H. R. Ekins (Scripps-Howard Newspapers in race) (Zeppelin Hindenburg to Germany air planes from Frankfurt) | Lakehurst, N.J., via Frankfurt, Germany | 25,654 | 18d 11h 14m 33s | Sept. 30-Oct. 19, 1936 |
| Howard Hughes and 4 assistants | New York, Paris, Moscow, Siberia, Fairbanks | 14,824 | 3d 19h 08m 10s | July 10-13, 1938 |
| Mrs. Clara Adams (Pan American Clipper) | Port Washington, N.Y., return Newark, N.J. | | 16d 19h 04m | June 28-July 15, 1939 |
| Globester, U.S. Air Transport Command | Washington, D.C. | 23,279 | 149h 44m | Sept. 28-Oct. 4, 1945 |
| Capt. William P. Odom (A-26 Reynolds Bombshell) | New York, via Paris, Cairo, Tokyo, Alaska | 20,000 | 78h 55m 12s | Apr. 12-16, 1947 |
| America, Pan American 4-engine Lockheed Constellation (3) | New York | 22,219 | 101h 32m | June 17-30, 1947 |
| Col. Edward Eagan | New York | 20,559 | 147h 15m | Dec. 13, 1948 |
| USAF B-50 Lucky Lady II (Capt. James Gallagher) (4) | Fort Worth, Texas | 23,452 | 94h 01m | Feb. 26-Mar. 2, 1949 |
| Jean-Marie Audibert | Paris | | 4d 19h 38m | Dec. 11-15, 1952 |
| Pamela Martin | Midway Airport, Chicago | | 90h 59m | Dec. 5-8, 1953 |
| Three USAF B-52 Stratofortresses (5) | Merced, Cal., via Nfld., Morocco, Saudi Arabia, India, Ceylon, P.I., Guam | 24,325 | 45h 19m | Jan. 15-18, 1957 |
| Joseph Cavoli | Cleveland, Oh. | | 89h 13m 37s | Jan. 31-Feb. 4, 1958 |
| Peter Gluckmann (solo) | San Francisco | 22,800 | 29d | Aug. 22-Sept. 20, 1959 |
| Milton Reynolds | San Francisco | | 51h 45m 22s | Jan. 12-14, 1960 |
| Sue Snyder | Chicago | 21,219 | 62h 59m | June 22-24, 1960 |
| Max Conrad (solo) | Miami, Fla. | 25,946 | 8d 18h 35m 57s | Feb. 28-Mar. 8, 1961 |
| Sam Miller & Louis Fodor | New York | | 46h 28m | Aug. 3-4, 1963 |
| Henry G. Beaird | Wichita, Kan. | 22,992 | 65h 38m 49s | May 23-26, 1966 |
| Robert & Joan Wallick | Manila, Philippines | 23,129 | 5d 6h 17m 10s | June 2-7, 1966 |
| Arthur Godfrey, Richard Merrill Fred Austin, Karl Keller | New York | 23,333 | 86h 9m 01s | June 4-7, 1966 |
| Trevor K. Brougham | Darwin, Australia | 24,800 | 5d 05h 57m | Aug. 5-10, 1972 |
| Walter H. Mullikin, Albert Frink, Lyman Watt, Frank Cassaniti, Edward Shields | New York | 23,137 | 1d 22h 50s | May 1-3,1976 |
| Arnold Palmer | Denver, Col. | 22,985 | 57h 25m 42s | May 17-19, 1976 |

(1) Mileage by train and auto, 4,110; by plane, 6,300; by steamship, 8,000. (2) First to fly solo around northern circumference of the world, also first to fly twice around the world. (3) Inception of regular commercial global air service. (4) First non-stop round-the-world flight, refueled 4 times in flight. (5) First non-stop global flight by jet planes; refueled in flight by KC-97 aerial tankers; average speed approx. 525 mph.

---

## U.S. Scheduled Airline Traffic

Source: Air Transport Association of America (thousands)

| | 1975 | 1976 | 1977 |
|---|---|---|---|
| **Passenger traffic** | | | |
| Revenue passengers enplaned | 205,062 | 223,318 | 240,326 |
| Revenue passenger miles | 162,810,160 | 178,988,026 | 193,218,837 |
| Available seat miles | 303,006,243 | 322,821,649 | 345,566,005 |
| **Cargo traffic** (ton miles) | 5,892,606 | 6,210,435 | 6,573,871 |
| Freight | 4,766,119 | 5,074,193 | 5,385,130 |
| Express | 29,190 | 22,003 | 41,417 |
| U.S. Mail | 1,097,297 | 1,114,239 | 1,147,324 |
| **Overall traffic and service** | | | |
| Nonscheduled traffic—total ton miles | 1,348,205 | 1,588,220 | 1,674,174 |
| Total revenue ton miles—all services | 23,533,743 | 25,709,152 | 27,582,944 |
| Total available ton miles—all services | 49,288,695 | 51,708,842 | 54,789,420 |

## Air Line Distances Between Selected Cities of the World

Source: Defense Mapping Agency Aerospace Center (statute miles)
Point-to-point measurements are usually from City Hall

| | Bangkok | Berlin | Cairo | Cape-town | Caracas | Chicago | Hong Kong | Hono-lulu | Lima | London |
|---|---|---|---|---|---|---|---|---|---|---|
| Bangkok | .... | 5,352 | 4,523 | 6,300 | 10,555 | 8,570 | 1,077 | 6,609 | 12,244 | 5,944 |
| Berlin | 5,352 | .... | 1,797 | 5,961 | 5,238 | 4,414 | 5,443 | 7,320 | 6,896 | 583 |
| Cairo | 4,523 | 1,797 | .... | 4,480 | 6,342 | 6,141 | 5,066 | 8,848 | 7,726 | 2,185 |
| Capetown | 6,300 | 5,961 | 4,480 | .... | 6,366 | 8,491 | 7,376 | 11,535 | 6,072 | 5,989 |
| Caracas | 10,555 | 5,238 | 6,342 | 6,366 | .... | 2,495 | 10,165 | 6,021 | 1,707 | 4,655 |
| Chicago | 8,570 | 4,414 | 6,141 | 8,491 | 2,495 | .... | 7,797 | 4,256 | 3,775 | 3,958 |
| Hong Kong | 1,077 | 5,443 | 5,066 | 7,376 | 10,165 | 7,797 | .... | 5,556 | 11,418 | 5,990 |
| Honolulu | 6,609 | 7,320 | 8,848 | 11,535 | 6,021 | 4,256 | 5,556 | .... | 5,947 | 7,240 |
| London | 5,944 | 583 | 2,185 | 5,989 | 4,655 | 3,958 | 5,990 | 7,240 | 6,316 | .... |
| Madrid | 6,337 | 1,165 | 2,087 | 5,308 | 4,346 | 4,189 | 6,558 | 7,872 | 5,907 | 785 |
| Melbourne | 4,568 | 9,918 | 8,675 | 6,425 | 9,717 | 9,673 | 4,595 | 5,505 | 8,059 | 10,500 |
| Mexico City | 9,793 | 6,056 | 7,700 | 8,519 | 2,234 | 1,690 | 8,788 | 3,789 | 2,639 | 5,558 |
| Montreal | 8,338 | 3,740 | 5,427 | 7,922 | 2,438 | 745 | 7,736 | 4,918 | 3,970 | 3,254 |
| Moscow | 4,389 | 1,006 | 1,803 | 6,279 | 6,177 | 4,987 | 4,437 | 7,047 | 7,862 | 1,564 |
| New Delhi | 1,813 | 3,598 | 2,758 | 5,769 | 8,833 | 7,486 | 2,339 | 7,412 | 10,432 | 4,181 |
| New York | 8,669 | 3,979 | 5,619 | 7,803 | 2,120 | 714 | 8,060 | 4,969 | 3,639 | 3,469 |
| Paris | 5,877 | 548 | 1,998 | 5,786 | 4,732 | 4,143 | 5,990 | 7,449 | 6,370 | 214 |
| Peking | 2,046 | 4,584 | 4,698 | 8,044 | 8,950 | 6,604 | 1,217 | 5,077 | 10,349 | 5,074 |
| Rio de Janeiro | 9,994 | 6,209 | 6,143 | 3,781 | 2,804 | 5,282 | 11,009 | 8,288 | 2,342 | 5,750 |
| Rome | 5,494 | 737 | 1,326 | 5,231 | 5,195 | 4,824 | 5,774 | 8,040 | 6,750 | 895 |
| San Francisco | 7,931 | 5,672 | 7,466 | 10,248 | 3,902 | 1,859 | 6,905 | 2,398 | 4,518 | 5,367 |
| Singapore | 883 | 6,164 | 5,137 | 6,008 | 11,402 | 9,372 | 1,605 | 6,726 | 11,689 | 6,747 |
| Stockholm | 5,089 | 528 | 2,096 | 6,423 | 5,471 | 4,331 | 5,063 | 6,875 | 7,166 | 942 |
| Tokyo | 2,865 | 5,557 | 5,958 | 9,154 | 8,808 | 6,314 | 1,791 | 3,859 | 9,631 | 5,959 |
| Warsaw | 5,033 | 322 | 1,619 | 5,935 | 5,559 | 4,679 | 5,147 | 7,366 | 7,215 | 905 |
| Washington, D.C. | 8,807 | 4,181 | 5,822 | 7,895 | 2,047 | 596 | 8,155 | 4,838 | 3,509 | 3,674 |

| | Madrid | Mel-bourne | Mexico City | Mon-treal | Mos-cow | Nai-robi | New Delhi | New York | Paris | Peking |
|---|---|---|---|---|---|---|---|---|---|---|
| Bangkok | 6,337 | 4,568 | 9,793 | 8,338 | 4,389 | 4,483 | 1,813 | 8,669 | 5,877 | 2,046 |
| Berlin | 1,165 | 9,918 | 6,056 | 3,740 | 1,006 | 3,949 | 3,598 | 3,979 | 548 | 4,584 |
| Cairo | 2,087 | 8,675 | 7,700 | 5,427 | 1,803 | 2,186 | 2,758 | 5,619 | 1,998 | 4,698 |
| Capetown | 5,308 | 6,425 | 8,519 | 7,922 | 6,279 | 2,542 | 5,769 | 7,803 | 5,786 | 8,044 |
| Caracas | 4,346 | 9,717 | 2,234 | 2,438 | 6,177 | 7,178 | 8,833 | 2,120 | 4,732 | 8,950 |
| Chicago | 4,189 | 9,673 | 1,690 | 745 | 4,987 | 8,011 | 7,486 | 714 | 4,143 | 6,604 |
| Hong Kong | 6,558 | 4,595 | 8,788 | 7,736 | 4,437 | 5,449 | 2,339 | 8,060 | 5,990 | 1,217 |
| Honolulu | 7,872 | 5,505 | 3,789 | 4,918 | 7,047 | 10,741 | 7,412 | 4,969 | 7,449 | 5,077 |
| London | 785 | 10,500 | 5,558 | 3,254 | 1,564 | 4,231 | 4,181 | 3,469 | 214 | 5,074 |
| Madrid | .... | 10,758 | 5,643 | 3,448 | 2,147 | 3,841 | 4,530 | 3,593 | 655 | 5,745 |
| Melbourne | 10,758 | .... | 8,426 | 10,395 | 8,950 | 7,153 | 6,329 | 10,359 | 10,430 | 5,643 |
| Mexico City | 5,643 | 8,426 | .... | 2,317 | 6,676 | 9,219 | 9,120 | 2,090 | 5,725 | 7,753 |
| Montreal | 3,448 | 10,395 | 2,317 | .... | 4,401 | 7,267 | 7,012 | 331 | 3,432 | 6,519 |
| Moscow | 2,147 | 8,950 | 6,676 | 4,401 | .... | 3,930 | 2,698 | 4,683 | 1,554 | 3,607 |
| New Delhi | 4,530 | 6,329 | 9,120 | 7,012 | 2,698 | 3,374 | .... | 7,318 | 4,102 | 2,353 |
| New York | 3,593 | 10,359 | 2,090 | 331 | 4,683 | 7,364 | 7,318 | .... | 3,636 | 6,844 |
| Paris | 655 | 10,430 | 5,725 | 3,432 | 1,554 | 4,022 | 4,102 | 3,636 | .... | 5,120 |
| Peking | 5,745 | 5,643 | 7,753 | 6,519 | 3,607 | 5,727 | 2,353 | 6,844 | 5,120 | .... |
| Rio de Janeiro | 5,045 | 8,226 | 4,764 | 5,078 | 7,170 | 5,560 | 8,753 | 4,801 | 5,684 | 10,768 |
| Rome | 851 | 9,929 | 6,377 | 4,104 | 1,483 | 3,339 | 3,684 | 4,293 | 690 | 5,063 |
| San Francisco | 5,803 | 7,856 | 1,887 | 2,543 | 5,885 | 9,597 | 7,691 | 2,572 | 5,577 | 5,918 |
| Singapore | 7,080 | 3,759 | 10,327 | 9,203 | 5,228 | 4,638 | 2,571 | 9,534 | 6,673 | 2,771 |
| Stockholm | 1,653 | 9,630 | 6,012 | 3,714 | 716 | 4,281 | 3,414 | 3,986 | 1,003 | 4,133 |
| Tokyo | 6,706 | 5,062 | 7,035 | 6,471 | 4,660 | 6,999 | 3,638 | 6,757 | 6,053 | 1,307 |
| Warsaw | 1,427 | 9,598 | 6,337 | 4,022 | 721 | 3,801 | 3,277 | 4,270 | 852 | 4,325 |
| Washington, D.C. | 3,792 | 10,180 | 1,885 | 489 | 4,876 | 7,551 | 7,500 | 205 | 3,840 | 6,942 |

| | Rio de Janiero | Rome | San Fran-cisco | Singa-pore | Stock-holm | Teheran | Tokyo | Vienna | Warsaw | Wash., D.C. |
|---|---|---|---|---|---|---|---|---|---|---|
| Bangkok | 9,994 | 5,494 | 7,931 | 883 | 5,089 | 3,391 | 2,865 | 5,252 | 5,033 | 8,807 |
| Berlin | 6,209 | 737 | 5,672 | 6,164 | 528 | 2,185 | 5,557 | 326 | 322 | 4,181 |
| Cairo | 6,143 | 1,326 | 7,466 | 5,137 | 2,096 | 1,234 | 5,958 | 1,481 | 1,619 | 5,822 |
| Capetown | 3,781 | 5,231 | 10,248 | 6,008 | 6,423 | 5,241 | 9,154 | 5,656 | 5,935 | 7,895 |
| Caracas | 2,804 | 5,195 | 3,902 | 11,402 | 5,471 | 7,320 | 8,808 | 5,372 | 5,559 | 2,047 |
| Chicago | 5,282 | 4,824 | 1,859 | 9,372 | 4,331 | 6,502 | 6,314 | 4,698 | 4,679 | 596 |
| Hong Kong | 11,009 | 5,774 | 6,905 | 1,605 | 5,063 | 3,843 | 1,791 | 5,431 | 5,147 | 8,155 |
| Honolulu | 8,288 | 8,040 | 2,398 | 6,726 | 6,875 | 8,070 | 3,859 | 7,632 | 7,366 | 4,838 |
| London | 5,750 | 895 | 5,367 | 6,747 | 942 | 2,743 | 5,959 | 771 | 905 | 3,674 |
| Madrid | 5,045 | 851 | 5,803 | 7,080 | 1,653 | 2,978 | 6,706 | 1,128 | 1,427 | 3,792 |
| Melbourne | 8,226 | 9,929 | 7,856 | 3,759 | 9,630 | 7,826 | 5,062 | 9,790 | 9,598 | 10,180 |
| Mexico City | 4,764 | 6,377 | 1,887 | 10,327 | 6,012 | 8,184 | 7,035 | 6,320 | 6,337 | 1,885 |
| Montreal | 5,078 | 4,104 | 2,543 | 9,203 | 3,714 | 5,880 | 6,471 | 4,009 | 4,022 | 489 |
| Moscow | 7,170 | 1,483 | 5,885 | 5,228 | 716 | 1,532 | 4,660 | 1,043 | 721 | 4,876 |
| New Delhi | 8,753 | 3,684 | 7,691 | 2,571 | 3,414 | 1,583 | 3,638 | 3,465 | 3,277 | 7,500 |
| New York | 4,801 | 4,293 | 2,572 | 9,534 | 3,986 | 6,141 | 6,757 | 4,234 | 4,270 | 205 |
| Paris | 5,684 | 690 | 5,577 | 6,673 | 1,003 | 2,625 | 6,053 | 645 | 852 | 3,840 |
| Peking | 10,768 | 5,063 | 5,918 | 2,771 | 4,133 | 3,490 | 1,307 | 4,648 | 4,325 | 6,942 |
| Rio de Janeiro | • .... | 5,707 | 6,613 | 9,785 | 6,683 | 7,374 | 11,532 | 6,127 | 6,455 | 4,779 |
| Rome | 5,707 | .... | 6,259 | 6,229 | 1,245 | 2,127 | 6,142 | 477 | 820 | 4,497 |
| San Francisco | 6,613 | 6,259 | .... | 8,448 | 5,399 | 7,362 | 5,150 | 5,994 | 5,854 | 2,441 |
| Singapore | 9,785 | 6,229 | 8,448 | .... | 5,936 | 4,103 | 3,300 | 6,035 | 5,843 | 9,662 |
| Stockholm | 6,683 | 1,245 | 5,399 | 5,936 | .... | 2,173 | 5,053 | 780 | 494 | 4,183 |
| Tokyo | 11,532 | 6,142 | 5,150 | 3,300 | 5,053 | 4,775 | .... | 5,689 | 5,347 | 6,791 |
| Warsaw | 6,455 | 820 | 5,854 | 5,843 | 494 | 1,879 | 5,689 | 347 | .... | 4,472 |
| Washington, D.C. | 4,779 | 4,497 | 2,441 | 9,662 | 4,183 | 6,341 | 6,791 | 4,438 | 4,472 | .... |

# AGRICULTURE
## World and Regional Food Production, 1972 to 1977
Source: UN Food and Agriculture Organization

(1961-65 = 100)

| Region | 1972 | 1973 | 1974 | 1975 | 1976 | 1977 | Change 1976 to 1977 | Annual rate of change 1961-70 % | Annual rate of change 1970-77 % |
|---|---|---|---|---|---|---|---|---|---|
| Developing market economies[2] | 125 | 129 | 132 | 140 | 145 | 148 | + 2 | 2.9 | 2.8 |
| Latin America | 128 | 132 | 139 | 144 | 154 | 156 | + 1 | 3.5 | 3.3 |
| Far East | 122 | 133 | 131 | 143 | 143 | 143 | + 4 | 2.7 | 2.8 |
| Near East | 137 | 130 | 141 | 151 | 158 | 158 | — | 3.0 | 4.0 |
| Africa | 117 | 113 | 120 | 123 | 127 | 127 | — | 2.6 | 1.3 |
| Asian centrally planned economies | 125 | 130 | 134 | 138 | 140 | 142 | + 1 | 2.8 | 2.3 |
| Total, developing countries | 125 | 130 | 133 | 139 | 143 | 146 | + 3 | 2.9 | 2.6 |
| Developed market economies[2] | 122 | 125 | 129 | 133 | 135 | 137 | + 2 | 2.5 | 2.4 |
| Western Europe | 119 | 123 | 129 | 128 | 126 | 128 | + 1 | 2.3 | 1.4 |
| North America | 122 | 124 | 126 | 135 | 141 | 144 | + 2 | 2.4 | 3.2 |
| Oceania | 126 | 139 | 132 | 141 | 150 | 143 | − 4 | 3.4 | 2.8 |
| Eastern Europe and the USSR | 122 | 141 | 136 | 130 | 140 | 140 | — | 3.2 | 1.9 |
| Total, developed countries | 122 | 129 | 131 | 132 | 136 | 138 | + 1 | 2.7 | 2.3 |
| World | 123 | 129 | 131 | 135 | 139 | 14 | + 1 | 2.8 | 2.4 |

Note: Food production covers crops and livestock only. (1) Preliminary. (2) Including countries in other regions not specified.

## Food Production Per Capita in Developing Regions, 1972-77
Source: UN Food and Agriculture Organization

(1961-65 = 100)

| Region | 1972 | 1973 | 1974 | 1975 | 1976 | 1977[1] | Change 1975 to 1976 % | Annual rate of change 1961-70 % | Annual rate of change 1970-76 % |
|---|---|---|---|---|---|---|---|---|---|
| Developing market economies[2] | 99 | 100 | 100 | 103 | 104 | 103 | − 1 | 0.3 | + 0.2 |
| Latin America | 101 | 101 | 103 | 104 | 109 | 107 | − 2 | 0.5 | + 0.5 |
| Far East | 98 | 104 | 99 | 106 | 103 | 105 | + 2 | 0.2 | + 0.2 |
| Near East | 108 | 100 | 105 | 109 | 111 | 108 | − 3 | 0.4 | + 1.1 |
| Africa | 94 | 88 | 91 | 91 | 91 | 89 | − 3 | 0.1 | − 1.4 |
| Total developing countries | 102 | 104 | 104 | 107 | 107 | 106 | − 1 | 0.6 | + 0.3 |

(1) Preliminary. (2) Including countries in other regions not specified.

## Food Intake Below Critical Minimum Limit in Developing Regions
Source: UN Food and Agriculture Organization

(Estimated)

The critical minimum limit for food intake is 1.2 times the Basal Metabolic Rate (BMR).

| Region | Total Population (millions) 1969-71 | Total Population (millions) 1972-74 | Percentage below 1.2 BMR 1969-71 | Percentage below 1.2 BMR 1972-74 | Total number below 1.2 BMR (millions) 1969-71 | Total number below 1.2 BMR (millions) 1972-74 |
|---|---|---|---|---|---|---|
| Africa | 278 | 301 | 25 | 28 | 70 | 83 |
| Far East | 968 | 1,042 | 25 | 29 | 256 | 297 |
| Latin America | 279 | 302 | 16 | 15 | 44 | 46 |
| Near East | 167 | 182 | 18 | 16 | 31 | 29 |
| MSA[1] | 954 | 1,027 | 27 | 30 | 255 | 307 |
| Other developing market economies | 738 | 800 | 20 | 18 | 146 | 148 |
| Total developing market economies | 1,692 | 1,827 | 24 | 25 | 401 | 455 |

(1) Countries most severely affected by food shortages.

## World Daily Dietary Energy Supply in Relation to Requirements
Source: UN Food and Agriculture Organization

| Region | Dietary energy[3] 1961-63 | 1964-66 | 1969-71 | 1972-74 | Supply as percent of requirement 1961-63 | 1964-66 | 1969-71 | 1972-74 |
|---|---|---|---|---|---|---|---|---|
| Developing market economies[1] | 2,110 | 2,130 | 2,190 | 2,180 | 92 | 93 | 96 | 95 |
| MSA[2] countries | 2,040 | 2,030 | 2,080 | 2,030 | 91 | 90 | 92 | 90 |
| Others | 2,210 | 2,250 | 2,330 | 2,360 | 95 | 96 | 100 | 101 |
| Africa | 2,070 | 2,100 | 2,150 | 2,110 | 89 | 90 | 92 | 91 |
| Far East | 2,010 | 2,000 | 2,070 | 2,040 | 91 | 90 | 94 | 92 |
| Latin America | 2,400 | 2,470 | 2,530 | 2,540 | 101 | 104 | 106 | 107 |
| Near East | 2,290 | 2,340 | 2,410 | 2,440 | 93 | 95 | 98 | 100 |
| Asian centrally planned economies | 1,960 | 2,110 | 2,200 | 2,290 | 83 | 90 | 94 | 97 |
| Total developing countries | 2,060 | 2,120 | 2,200 | 2,210 | 89 | 92 | 95 | 96 |
| Developed market economies | 3,130 | 3,170 | 3,280 | 3,340 | 123 | 124 | 129 | 131 |
| Western Europe | 3,200 | 3,230 | 3,330 | 3,390 | 125 | 126 | 130 | 132 |
| North America | 3,320 | 3,360 | 3,500 | 3,530 | 126 | 127 | 133 | 134 |
| Oceania | 3,300 | 3,320 | 3,320 | 3,370 | 124 | 125 | 125 | 127 |
| Eastern Europe and the U.S.S.R. | 3,240 | 3,270 | 3,420 | 3,460 | 126 | 127 | 133 | 135 |
| Total developed countries | 3,170 | 3,200 | 3,330 | 3,380 | 124 | 125 | 132 | 132 |
| World | 2,410 | 2,460 | 2,540 | 2,550 | 101 | 103 | 106 | 107 |

(1) Including countries in other regions not specified. (2) Most severely affected by food shortages. (3) Kilocalories per capita.

## Agricultural Products — U.S. and World Production and Exports

Source: Foreign Agricultural Service, U.S. Agriculture Department

| 1977[1] Commodity | Unit | Production U.S. | World | %U.S. | Exports[2] U.S. | World | %U.S. |
|---|---|---|---|---|---|---|---|
| Wheat | Mil Mt | 55 | 382 | 14.4 | 30.3 | 74.2 | 40.8 |
| Oats | Mil Mt | 11 | 52 | 20.9 | .1 | 1.1 | 13.4 |
| Corn | Mil Mt | 162 | 344 | 47.0 | 45.5 | 64.2 | 70.8 |
| Barley | Mil Mt | 9 | 164 | 5.6 | 1.2 | 14.5 | 8.2 |
| Soybeans | Mil Mt | 35[3] | 61[3] | 57.5 | 16.2[4] | 19.6[4] | 82.7 |
| Rice[5] | Mil Mt | 5 | 363 | 1.2 | 2.2[4] | 8.4[4][6] | 26.5 |
| Lard[4] | 1,000 Mt | 464 | N/A | [7] | 82.6 | N/A | [7] |
| Tallow and Grease[4] | 1,000 Mt | 2,735 | N/A | [7] | 1,299 | N/A | [7] |
| Tobacco, unmfd[4][8] | 1,000 Mt | 869 | 5,541 | 15.6 | 240.0 | 1,269.0 | 22.8 |
| Edible veg. oils[9] | Mil Mt | 7.1[3] | 30.8[3] | 23.0 | 4.5[4][10] | 11.8[4][10][11] | 38.1 |
| Cotton[12] | Mil Bales | 14.4 | 63.7 | 22.6 | 5.6 | 19.5 | 28.7 |

(1) Crop 77-78 as follows: Wheat, oats and barley, beginning July 1; corn Oct 1; rice and cotton, August 1; (2) Trade figures for wheat, oats, corn and barley are preliminary; (3) Year beginning September 1, 1976; (4) Calendar year 1977; (5) Production listed on rough basis; trade listed on milled basis; (6) Aggregate of differing local marketing years; (7) Percentage not available; (8) Production figures listed as farm weight; trade figures listed as dry weight; (9) Includes palm oil; (10) Includes oil equivalent of exported oilseeds; (11) Exports from producing countries; (12) Bales of 480 lbs. net weight; all figures preliminary;

## Grain, Hay, Potato, Cotton, Soybean, Tobacco Production

Source: Statistical Reporting Service U S Agriculture Department

| 1977 State | Barley 1,000 bushels | Corn, grain 1,000 bushels | Cotton lint 1,000 bales | All hay 1,000 tons | Oats 1,000 bushels | Potatoes 1,000 cwt | Soybeans 1,000 bushels | Tobacco 1,000 pounds | All wheat 1,000 bushels |
|---|---|---|---|---|---|---|---|---|---|
| Alabama | — | 10,875 | 280 | 1,008 | 1,025 | 2,010 | 33,600 | 1,102 | 2,520 |
| Alaska | — | — | — | — | — | — | — | — | — |
| Arizona | 4,180 | 3,000 | 1,110 | 1,461 | — | 1,755 | — | — | 10,080 |
| Arkansas | — | 2,279 | 1,050 | 1,404 | 3,500 | — | 101,200 | — | 25,740 |
| California | 53,200 | 28,652 | 2,880 | 7,729 | 5,304 | 21,840 | — | — | 43,700 |
| Colorado | 13,570 | 80,620 | — | 2,793 | 1,426 | 11,284 | — | — | 57,100 |
| Connecticut | — | — | — | 161 | — | 466 | — | 6,054 | — |
| Delaware | 840 | 10,360 | — | 47 | — | 1,113 | 5,175 | — | 1,054 |
| Florida | — | 10,465 | 5 | 452 | 540 | 6,207 | 7,848 | 25,238 | 377 |
| Georgia | 259 | 24,000 | 80 | 752 | 2,750 | — | 21,800 | 134,875 | 3,300 |
| Hawaii | — | — | — | — | — | — | — | — | — |
| Idaho | 39,950 | 2,408 | — | 4,459 | 2,565 | 88,200 | — | — | 50,730 |
| Illinois | 378 | 1,152,900 | — | 3,708 | 20,740 | 460 | 327,450 | — | 68,370 |
| Indiana | 320 | 633,420 | — | 2,384 | 7,950 | 1,496 | 139,320 | 19,000 | 55,800 |
| Iowa | — | 1,091,200 | — | 7,225 | 81,125 | 473 | 245,820 | — | 3,145 |
| Kansas | 2,340 | 161,280 | — | 5,294 | 9,450 | — | 27,720 | — | 344,850 |
| Kentucky | 1,150 | 126,900 | 0.7 | 3,093 | 315 | — | 40,120 | 470,456 | 10,138 |
| Louisiana | — | 3,380 | 660 | 715 | 378 | 173 | 62,980 | 135 | 918 |
| Maine | — | — | — | 340 | 1,500 | 28,320 | — | — | — |
| Maryland | 3,570 | 43,200 | — | 530 | 1,166 | 240 | 8,320 | 29,900 | 4,366 |
| Massachusetts | — | — | — | 233 | — | 888 | — | 1,919 | — |
| Michigan | 988 | 191,250 | — | 2,855 | 18,700 | 10,243 | 20,880 | — | 33,000 |
| Minnesota | 52,530 | 600,000 | — | 8,136 | 161,840 | 15,023 | 133,350 | — | 131,894 |
| Mississippi | — | 5,760 | 1,650 | 1,172 | 585 | 117 | 74,825 | — | 3,570 |
| Missouri | 296 | 205,200 | 235 | 5,700 | 7,250 | — | 144,000 | 5,750 | 60,450 |
| Montana | 55,480 | 748 | — | 3,907 | 5,600 | 2,016 | — | — | 130,920 |
| Nebraska | 1,530 | 628,650 | — | 7,464 | 38,860 | 1,695 | 40,120 | — | 103,250 |
| Nevada | 1,235 | — | 1.7 | 879 | 220 | 5,250 | — | — | 1,560 |
| New Hampshire | — | — | — | 185 | — | 71 | — | — | — |
| New Jersey | 816 | 6,650 | — | 306 | 387 | 2,147 | 4,071 | — | 1,302 |
| New Mexico | 1,326 | 10,260 | 151 | 1,124 | — | 551 | — | — | 9,137 |
| New York | 440 | 51,200 | — | 4,639 | 15,370 | 12,082 | 299 | — | 6,825 |
| North Carolina | 2,200 | 86,190 | 52 | 521 | 3,150 | 2,711 | 29,040 | 741,710 | 6,000 |
| North Dakota | 98,670 | 16,116 | — | 3,229 | 60,000 | 20,800 | 3,800 | — | 229,907 |
| Ohio | 561 | 380,100 | — | 3,558 | 24,780 | 3,086 | 116,610 | 24,910 | 72,380 |
| Oklahoma | 4,200 | 7,790 | 440 | 3,520 | 5,980 | — | 6,050 | — | 175,500 |
| Oregon | 8,930 | 1,140 | — | 2,437 | 5,200 | 25,774 | — | — | 45,320 |
| Pennsylvania | 6,250 | 106,720 | — | 3,889 | 18,550 | 6,375 | 1,943 | 23,530 | 8,910 |
| Rhode Island | — | — | — | 15 | — | 943 | — | — | — |
| South Carolina | 840 | 22,320 | 110 | 396 | 2,530 | — | 26,000 | 138,380 | 2,755 |
| South Dakota | 26,880 | 126,850 | — | 6,292 | 132,300 | 1,062 | 9,150 | — | 71,964 |
| Tennessee | 507 | 47,450 | 255 | 1,820 | 1,075 | 405 | 50,600 | 143,590 | 10,080 |
| Texas | 3,400 | 148,500 | 5,527 | 4,676 | 24,000 | 3,339 | 19,760 | — | 117,500 |
| Utah | 6,210 | 1,157 | — | 1,842 | 550 | 1,296 | — | — | 4,716 |
| Vermont | — | — | — | 721 | — | 235 | — | — | — |
| Virginia | 4,048 | 30,800 | 0.3 | 1,083 | 1,496 | 3,463 | 7,955 | 141,038 | 6,355 |
| Washington | 9,450 | 5,088 | — | 2,432 | 1,505 | 48,685 | — | — | 101,305 |
| West Virginia | 378 | 3,996 | — | 830 | 492 | 154 | — | 3,060 | 310 |
| Wisconsin | 1,566 | 286,000 | — | 12,002 | 76,050 | 18,038 | 6,528 | 23,540 | 3,075 |
| Wyoming | 7,315 | 2,550 | — | 1,639 | 1,710 | 1,474 | — | — | 5,620 |
| **Total U.S.** | **415,803** | **6,357,424** | **14,496** | **131,057** | **747,914** | **352,010** | **1,716,334** | **1,934,187** | **2,025,793** |

(1) Equiv. to 480 lbs.

## Production of Chief U.S. Crops

Source: Statistical Reporting Service, U.S. Agriculture Department

| Year | Corn grain 1,000 bushels | Oats 1,000 bushels | Barley 1,000 bushels | Sorghums for grain 1,000 bushels | All wheat 1,000 bushels | Rye 1,000 bushels | Flax-seed 1,000 bushels | Cotton lint 1,000 bales | Cotton seed 1,000 tons |
|---|---|---|---|---|---|---|---|---|---|
| 1970 | 4,152,243 | 915,236 | 416,091 | 683,179 | 1,351,558 | 36,840 | 29,416 | 10,192 | 4,068 |
| 1972 | 5,579,832 | 690,616 | 421,719 | 801,350 | 1,546,209 | 28,256 | 13,883 | 13,704 | 5,393 |
| 1973 | 5,670,712 | 659,136 | 417,434 | 923,224 | 1,710,787 | 24,677 | 16,408 | 12,974 | 5,016 |
| 1974 | 4,701,402 | 600,655 | 298,669 | 622,711 | 1,781,918 | 17,506 | 14,083 | 11,540 | 4,510 |
| 1975 | 5,828,961 | 642,042 | 374,386 | 753,046 | 2,122,459 | 15,958 | 15,553 | 8,302 | 3,211 |
| 1976 | 6,266,359 | 546,315 | 372,461 | 719,817 | 2,142,362 | 14,951 | 7,820 | 10,581 | 4,149 |
| 1977 | 6,357,424 | 747,914 | 415,803 | 790,647 | 2,025,793 | 16,998 | 16,105 | 14,496 | 5,531 |

| Year | Tobacco 1,000 lbs. | All hay 1,000 tons | Beans dry edible 1,000 cwt. | Peas dry edible 1,000 cwt. | Peanuts 1,000 lbs. | Soy-beans 1,000 bushels | Pota-toes 1,000 cwt. | Sweet pota-toes 1,000 cwt. |
|---|---|---|---|---|---|---|---|---|
| 1970 | 1,906,453 | 126,969 | 17,399 | 3,315 | 2,983,121 | 1,127,100 | 325,716 | 13,164 |
| 1972 | 1,749,085 | 128,565 | 17,983 | 2,103 | 3,274,761 | 1,270,608 | 296,359 | 12,170 |
| 1973 | 1,742,105 | 134,217 | 16,274 | 1,665 | 3,473,837 | 1,547,543 | 300,013 | 12,156 |
| 1974 | 1,989,728 | 126,384 | 20,330 | 3,228 | 3,667,604 | 1,216,287 | 342,395 | 13,339 |
| 1975 | 2,181,775 | 132,210 | 17,442 | 2,731 | 3,857,122 | 1,547,383 | 322,254 | 13,225 |
| 1976 | 2,135,829 | 120,006 | 17,786 | 2,150 | 3,750,890 | 1,287,560 | 357,674 | 13,432 |
| 1977 | 1,934,187 | 131,057 | 16,288 | 1,023 | 3,681,312 | 1,716,334 | 352,010 | 12,516 |

| Year | Five seed crops* 1,000 lbs. | Sugar and seed 1,000 tons | Sugar beets 1,000 tons | Pecans 1,000 tons | Al-monds 1,000 tons | Wal-nuts 1,000 tons | Fil-berts 1,000 tons | Oranges and tan-gerines** 1,000 boxes | Grape-fruit** 1,000 boxes |
|---|---|---|---|---|---|---|---|---|---|
| 1970 | 251,934 | 23,996 | 26,378 | 77.6 | 124.0 | 111.8 | 9.3 | 189,970 | 53,910 |
| 1972 | 170,396 | 28,332 | 28,410 | 91.6 | 125.0 | 116.8 | 10.2 | 196,480 | 64,250 |
| 1973 | 175,147 | 25,827 | 24,499 | 137.9 | 134.0 | 175.0 | 12.3 | 229,790 | 65,640 |
| 1974 | 179,918 | 25,140 | 22,123 | 68.7 | 189.0 | 156.5 | 6.7 | 221,050 | 65,500 |
| 1975 | 161,609 | 28,344 | 29,704 | 124.2 | 160.0 | 199.3 | 12.1 | 243,060 | 61,610 |
| 1976 | 143,006 | 28,120 | 29,386 | 51.6 | 233.0 | 183.7 | 7.2 | 248,140 | 70,080 |
| 1977 | 147,123 | 27,656 | 25,115 | 124.8 | 255.0 | 195.6 | 11.6 | 250,020 | 74,500 |

*Five seed crops include alfalfa, red clover, ladino clover, lespedeza, and timothy. **Crop year ending in year cited.

---

## Production of Principal Field Crops in Canada

Source: Statistics Canada

| 1977 | Wheats 1,000 bushels | Oats 1,000 bushels | Barley 1,000 bushels | Ryes 1,000 bushels | Flaxseed 1,000 bushels |
|---|---|---|---|---|---|
| Canada | 722,036 | 279,011 | 528,906 | 15,499 | 24,000 |
| Prince Edward Island | 564 | 2,240 | 1,358 | — | — |
| Nova Scotia | 171 | 660 | 186 | — | — |
| New Brunswick | 265 | 1,345 | 199 | — | — |
| Quebec | 2,736 | 21,242 | 1,985 | 248 | — |
| Ontario | 30,900 | 21,424 | 15,478 | 1,271 | — |
| Manitoba | 101,000 | 58,000 | 94,000 | 2,750 | 12,600 |
| Saskatchewan | 467,000 | 80,000 | 165,000 | 6,000 | 9,500 |
| Alberta | 117,000 | 90,000 | 243,000 | 5,000 | 1,900 |
| British Columbia | 2,400 | 4,100 | 7,700 | 180 | — |

| | Mixed grains 1,000 bushels | Corn grains 1,000 bushels | Soybeans 1,000 bushels | Rapeseed 1,000 bushels | Potatoes 1,000 c.w.t. |
|---|---|---|---|---|---|
| Canada | 78,737 | 169,394 | 19,000 | 78,300 | 54,841 |
| Prince Edward Island | 4,267 | — | — | — | 11,913 |
| Nova Scotia | 243 | — | — | — | 623 |
| New Brunswick | 180 | — | — | — | 11,093 |
| Quebec | 4,475 | 13,644 | — | — | 8,032 |
| Ontario | 44,122 | 154,200 | 19,000 | — | 10,760 |
| Manitoba | 8,000 | 1,550 | — | 11,400 | 5,500 |
| Saskatchewan | 4,200 | — | — | 34,500 | 420 |
| Alberta | 13,000 | — | — | 31,000 | 3,700 |
| British Columbia | 250 | — | — | 1,400 | 2,800 |

| | Mustard seed 1,000 pounds | Sunflower seed 1,000 pounds | Tame hay 1,000 tons | Fodder corn 1,000 tons | Sugar beets 1,000 tons |
|---|---|---|---|---|---|
| Canada | 175,000 | 175,000 | 27,266 | 16,665 | 1,111 |
| Prince Edward Island | — | — | 268 | 91 | — |
| Nova Scotia | — | — | 360 | 128 | — |
| New Brunswick | — | — | 349 | 65 | — |
| Quebec | — | — | 4,957 | 3,836 | 75 |
| Ontario | — | — | 7,432 | 11,765 | — |
| Manitoba | 36,000 | 175,000 | 2,600 | 350 | 440 |
| Saskatchewan | 105,000 | — | 3,000 | — | — |
| Alberta | 34,000 | — | 6,400 | — | 596 |
| British Columbia | — | — | 1,900 | 430 | — |

(1) Excluding Newfoundland.

## U.S. Farms by State—Number, Acreage, and Value

Source: U S Bureau of the Census

| State 1974 | Farms (Number) | Average size of farm (acres) | Value of land and buildings (per acre) | Farms 2000 acres or more | Farms 10-49 acres | Land in farms (acres) |
|---|---|---|---|---|---|---|
| Alabama | 56,678 | 209 | $ 364 | 643 | 15,475 | 11,852,946 |
| Alaska | 291 | 5,612 | 42 | 37 | 40 | 1,633,070 |
| Arizona | 5,803 | 6,539 | 111 | 877 | 1,253 | 37,944,191 |
| Arkansas | 50,959 | 287 | 419 | 787 | 8,537 | 14,641,677 |
| California | 67,674 | 493 | 653 | 2,813 | 24,162 | 33,385,619 |
| Colorado | 25,501 | 1,408 | 188 | 4,061 | 2,800 | 35,902,165 |
| Connecticut | 3,421 | 129 | 1,525 | 6 | 888 | 440,056 |
| Delaware | 3,400 | 185 | 971 | 17 | 783 | 630,605 |
| Florida | 32,466 | 407 | 685 | 1,006 | 10,940 | 13,199,365 |
| Georgia | 54,911 | 253 | 474 | 723 | 11,118 | 13,878,294 |
| Hawaii | 3,020 | 702 | 485 | 70 | 812 | 2,118,976 |
| Idaho | 23,680 | 603 | 339 | 1,246 | 4,251 | 14,274,258 |
| Illinois | 111,049 | 262 | 846 | 229 | 13,420 | 29,094,794 |
| Indiana | 87,915 | 191 | 720 | 125 | 17,325 | 16,785,208 |
| Iowa | 126,104 | 262 | 719 | 150 | 9,841 | 33,044,768 |
| Kansas | 79,188 | 605 | 296 | 3,819 | 5,127 | 47,945,722 |
| Kentucky | 102,053 | 141 | 427 | 159 | 20,945 | 14,431,713 |
| Louisiana | 33,240 | 275 | 512 | 594 | 9,233 | 9,133,275 |
| Maine | 6,436 | 237 | 341 | 28 | 728 | 1,523,696 |
| Maryland | 15,163 | 174 | 1,060 | 57 | 3,399 | 2,634,395 |
| Massachusetts | 4,497 | 134 | 961 | 9 | 1,185 | 601,734 |
| Michigan | 64,094 | 169 | 553 | 62 | 12,233 | 10,832,234 |
| Minnesota | 98,537 | 280 | 429 | 443 | 6,846 | 27,605,228 |
| Mississippi | 53,620 | 267 | 379 | 938 | 10,351 | 14,300,498 |
| Missouri | 115,711 | 258 | 396 | 509 | 13,919 | 29,801,127 |
| Montana | 23,324 | 2,665 | 112 | 7,411 | 1,550 | 62,158,351 |
| Nebraska | 67,597 | 683 | 282 | 3,719 | 3,384 | 46,172,012 |
| Nevada | 2,076 | 5,209 | 85 | 342 | 317 | 10,813,610 |
| New Hampshire | 2,412 | 210 | 564 | 5 | 360 | 506,464 |
| New Jersey | 7,409 | 130 | 1,807 | 18 | 2,215 | 961,395 |
| New Mexico | 11,282 | 4,170 | 78 | 2,610 | 1,694 | 47,046,388 |
| New York | 43,682 | 215 | 510 | 67 | 5,093 | 9,410,706 |
| North Carolina | 91,280 | 123 | 590 | 237 | 30,195 | 11,243,933 |
| North Dakota | 42,710 | 992 | 195 | 3,789 | 773 | 42,387,424 |
| Ohio | 92,158 | 170 | 706 | 76 | 16,163 | 15,668,238 |
| Oklahoma | 69,719 | 475 | 302 | 2,191 | 6,001 | 33,082,848 |
| Oregon | 26,753 | 682 | 250 | 1,731 | 8,292 | 18,241,445 |
| Pennsylvania | 53,171 | 154 | 734 | 45 | 8,368 | 8,186,378 |
| Rhode Island | 597 | 102 | 1,500 | 2 | 177 | 61,068 |
| South Carolina | 29,275 | 211 | 467 | 312 | 7,677 | 6,177,024 |
| South Dakota | 42,825 | 1,074 | 145 | 4,444 | 1,549 | 45,977,776 |
| Tennessee | 93,659 | 140 | 467 | 233 | 24,759 | 13,103,224 |
| Texas | 174,068 | 771 | 243 | 10,038 | 20,951 | 134,185,289 |
| Utah | 12,184 | 871 | 188 | 822 | 2,948 | 10,610,050 |
| Vermont | 5,906 | 282 | 462 | 14 | 402 | 1,667,561 |
| Virginia | 52,699 | 184 | 558 | 264 | 11,521 | 9,678,307 |
| Washington | 29,410 | 567 | 350 | 1,657 | 8,739 | 16,661,902 |
| West Virginia | 16,909 | 207 | 300 | 60 | 2,160 | 3,496,606 |
| Wisconsin | 89,479 | 197 | 434 | 118 | 8,176 | 17,624,826 |
| Wyoming | 8,018 | 4,274 | 80 | 2,607 | 403 | 34,271,918 |
| **Total** | **2,314,013** | **440** | **336** | **62,225** | **379,543** | **1,017,030,357** |

## Livestock on Farms in the U.S.

Source: Statistical Reporting Service: U.S. Agriculture Department (thousands)

| Year (On Jan. 1) | All cattle | Milk cows | All sheep | Hogs | Horses* and mules | Year (On Jan. 1) | All cattle | Milk cows | All sheep | Hogs |
|---|---|---|---|---|---|---|---|---|---|---|
| 1890 | 60,014 | 15,000 | 44,518 | 48,130 | 18,054 | 1965 | 109,000 | ²15,380 | 25,127 | 57,030 |
| 1900 | 59,739 | 16,544 | 48,105 | 51,055 | 21,004 | 1968 | 109,371 | 13,115 | 22,223 | ²58,818 |
| 1910 | 58,993 | 19,450 | 50,239 | 48,072 | 24,211 | 1969 | 110,015 | 12,550 | 21,350 | ²60,829 |
| 1920 | 70,400 | 21,455 | 40,743 | 60,159 | 25,742 | 1970 | 112,369 | 12,091 | 20,423 | ²57,046 |
| 1925 | 63,373 | 22,575 | 38,543 | 55,770 | 22,569 | 1971 | 114,578 | 11,909 | 19,731 | ²67,285 |
| 1930 | 61,003 | 23,032 | 51,565 | 55,705 | 19,124 | 1972 | 117,862 | 11,776 | 18,739 | ²62,412 |
| 1935 | 68,846 | 26,082 | 51,808 | 39,066 | 16,683 | 1973 | 121,539 | 11,622 | 17,641 | ²59,017 |
| 1940 | 68,039 | 24,940 | 52,107 | 61,165 | 14,478 | 1974 | 127,788 | 11,297 | 16,310 | ²60,614 |
| 1945 | 85,573 | 27,770 | 46,520 | 59,373 | 11,950 | 1975¹ | 132,028 | 11,220 | 14,515 | ²54,693 |
| 1950 | 77,963 | 23,853 | 29,826 | 58,937 | 7,781 | 1976 | 127,980 | 11,087 | 13,311 | ²49,267 |
| 1955 | 96,592 | 23,462 | 31,582 | 50,474 | 4,309 | 1977 | 122,810 | 11,035 | 12,766 | ²54,934 |
| 1960 | 96,236 | 19,527 | 33,170 | 59,026 | 3,089 | 1978 | 116,265 | 10,930 | 12,387 | ²57,587 |

*Discontinued in 1960. (1) Total estimated value on farms as of Jan. 1, 1978, was as follows (avg. value per head in parentheses): cattle and calves $27,028,660,000 ($232.00); sheep and lambs $638,509,000 ($51.50); hogs $3,635,352,000 ($63.10); (2) New series, milk cows and heifers that have calved, beginning 1965. (3) As of Dec. 1 of preceeding year.

## Harvested Acreage of Principal U.S. Crops

Source: Statistical Reporting Service: U.S. Agriculture Department (thousands of acres)

| State | 1975 | 1976 | 1977 | State | 1975 | 1976 | 1977 |
|---|---|---|---|---|---|---|---|
| Alabama | 3,426 | 3,524 | 3,499 | Nebraska | 17,659 | 17,758 | 18,111 |
| Arizona | 1,045 | 1,266 | 1,182 | Nevada | 513 | 528 | 490 |
| Arkansas | 7,838 | 7,930 | 8,230 | New Hampshire | 113 | 116 | 113 |
| California | 6,392 | 6,475 | 6,131 | New Jersey | 442 | 509 | 53 |
| Colorado | 5,904 | 5,830 | 5,837 | New Mexico | 1,310 | 1,031 | 1,313 |
| Connecticut | 148 | 146 | 141 | New York | 4,181 | 4,241 | 4,22 |
| Delaware | 521 | 510 | 511 | North Carolina | 4,783 | 4,757 | 4,68 |
| Florida | 1,340 | 1,436 | 1,358 | North Dakota | 19,589 | 20,684 | 19,78 |
| Georgia | 4,713 | 4,794 | 3,770 | Ohio | 10,456 | 10,698 | 10,83 |
| Hawaii | 112 | 107 | 106 | Oklahoma | 10,004 | 9,705 | 10,32 |
| Idaho | 4,293 | 4,410 | 4,235 | Oregon | 2,654 | 2,744 | 2,61 |
| Illinois | 22,958 | 23,030 | 23,361 | Pennsylvania | 4,356 | 4,334 | 4,38 |
| Indiana | 12,135 | 12,476 | 12,634 | Rhode Island | 17 | 17 | 16 |
| Iowa | 24,334 | 24,316 | 24,320 | South Carolina | 2,682 | 2,661 | 2,675 |
| Kansas | 21,608 | 21,465 | 22,477 | South Dakota | 15,261 | 12,886 | 14,970 |
| Kentucky | 4,564 | 4,774 | 5,071 | Tennessee | 4,553 | 4,721 | 5,047 |
| Louisiana | 3,725 | 4,265 | 4,563 | Texas | 23,093 | 21,539 | 23,267 |
| Maine | 409 | 402 | 404 | Utah | 1,157 | 1,116 | 1,009 |
| Maryland | 1,541 | 1,563 | 1,533 | Vermont | 547 | 548 | 543 |
| Massachusetts | 162 | 164 | 160 | Virginia | 2,812 | 2,797 | 2,783 |
| Michigan | 6,412 | 6,490 | 6,500 | Washington | 4,770 | 4,907 | 4,657 |
| Minnesota | 20,323 | 21,256 | 21,738 | West Virginia | 747 | 735 | 714 |
| Mississippi | 5,450 | 5,985 | 6,198 | Wisconsin | 9,181 | 9,263 | 9,37 |
| Missouri | 13,162 | 13,600 | 14,063 | Wyoming | 1,876 | 1,904 | |
| Montana | 8,931 | 9,104 | 9,111 | **Total U.S.** | **324,202** | **325,517** | **331,33** |

Crop acreages included are corn, sorghum, oats, barley, wheat, rice, rye, soybeans, flaxseed, peanuts, sunflower seed (1975-77), popcorn, cotton, all hay, dry edible beans, dry edible peas, potatoes, sweet potatoes, tobacco, sugarcane and sugar beets.

## Harvested Acreage of Principal Canadian Crops

Source: Statistics Canada (thousands of acres)

| Province | 1974 | 1975 | 1976 | 1977 | Province | 1974 | 1975 | 1976 | 1977 |
|---|---|---|---|---|---|---|---|---|---|
| Prince Edward Island | 339 | 350 | 373 | 372 | Manitoba | 8,778 | 9,006 | 9,353 | 9,47 |
| Nova Scotia | 186 | 205 | 227 | 230 | Saskatchewan | 25,359 | 25,392 | 25,851 | 26,02 |
| New Brunswick | 291 | 296 | 308 | 306 | Alberta | 16,717 | 17,646 | 18,115 | 17,49 |
| Quebec | 3,941 | 3,991 | 4,041 | 3,902 | British Columbia | 1,026 | 1,042 | 1,078 | 1,12 |
| Ontario | 7,611 | 7,664 | 8,214 | 8,173 | **Total** | **64,247** | **65,592** | **67,559** | **67,09** |

Crops included are winter wheat, spring wheat, oats, barley, fall rye, spring rye, flaxseed, mixed grains, corn for grain, buckwheat, peas, dry beans, soybeans, rapeseed, potatoes, mustard seed, sunflower seed, tame hay, fodder corn, field roots and sugar beets.

## Wool Production

Source: Statistical Reporting Service: U.S. Agriculture Department

| | Sheep shorn (1,000) | Shorn wool (1,000 lbs.) | Value ($1,000) | Price per lb. (cents) | Pulled wool (1,000 lbs.) | Total wool (1,000 lbs |
|---|---|---|---|---|---|---|
| 1970 | 19,163 | 161,587 | 57,162 | 35.4 | 15.200 | 176.787 |
| 1971 | 19,036 | 160,156 | 31,416 | 19.6 | 12.000 | 172.156 |
| 1972 | 18,770 | 158,506 | 55,496 | 35.0 | 9.700 | 168.206 |
| 1973 | 17,425 | 143,738 | 118,839 | 82.7 | 8.000 | 151.738 |
| 1974 | 15,956 | 131,382 | 77,788 | 59.2 | 5.700 | 137.082 |
| 1975 | 14,403 | 119,535 | 53,505 | 44.7 | 5.300 | 124.835 |
| 1976 | 13,669 | 110,817 | 73,148 | 65.7 | 4.000 | 114.817 |
| 1977 | 13,191 | 106,927 | 77,010 | 72.0 | 1.700 | 108.627 |

## Egg Production in the U.S.

Source: Statistical Reporting Service: U.S. Agriculture Department (millions of eggs)

| State | 1975 | 1976 | 1977 | State | 1975 | 1976 | 1977 | State | 1975 | 1976 | 1977 | State | 1975 | 1976 | 197 |
|---|---|---|---|---|---|---|---|---|---|---|---|---|---|---|---|
| Ala. | 2,951 | 2,919 | 3,183 | Ind. | 3,156 | 3,091 | 3,004 | Neb. | 782 | 737 | 739 | S.C. | 1,384 | 1,282 | 1,24 |
| Alas. | 5.0 | 6.0 | 6.2 | Ia. | 2,058 | 2,040 | 2,004 | Nev. | 4.3 | 5.2 | 3.1 | S.D. | 698 | 620 | 57 |
| Ariz. | 159 | 143 | 140 | Kan. | 599 | 564 | 530 | N.H. | 260 | 237 | 210 | Tenn. | 1,002 | 974 | 99 |
| Ark. | 3,594 | 3,752 | 3,812 | Ky. | 518 | 541 | 556 | N.J. | 620 | 548 | 446 | Tex. | 2,360 | 2,357 | 2,3 |
| Cal. | 8,467 | 8,635 | 8,345 | La. | 658 | 671 | 598 | N.M. | 234 | 270 | 288 | Ut. | 321 | 283 | 3 |
| Col. | 480 | 505 | 508 | Me. | 1,708 | 1,791 | 1,849 | N.Y. | 1,984 | 1,903 | 1,825 | Vt. | 115 | 114 | 1 |
| Conn. | 702 | 803 | 863 | Md. | 331 | 327 | 308 | N.C. | 2,802 | 2,756 | 2,968 | Va. | 767 | 800 | 8 |
| Del. | 115 | 129 | 128 | Mass. | 402 | 343 | 354 | N.D. | 132 | 120 | 99 | Wash. | 1,082 | 1,058 | 1,08 |
| Fla. | 2,779 | 2,846 | 2,998 | Mich. | 1,467 | 1,520 | 1,530 | Oh. | 2,109 | 1,994 | 1,934 | W.Va | 256 | 230 | 1 |
| Ga. | 5,284 | 5,591 | 5,535 | Minn. | 2,209 | 2,238 | 2,120 | Okla. | 430 | 458 | 487 | Wis. | 1,194 | 1,094 | 9 |
| Ha. | 209 | 218 | 218 | Miss. | 1,707 | 1,719 | 1,775 | Ore. | 519 | 532 | 525 | Wy. | 26.6 | 26.4 | 2 |
| Ida. | 184 | 192 | 192 | Mo. | 1,241 | 1,193 | 1,168 | Pa. | 2,800 | 2,701 | 2,943 | **Total** | | | |
| Ill. | 1,507 | 1,398 | 1,389 | Mon. | 199 | 185 | 175 | R.I. | 59.2 | 51.5 | 50.7 | **U.S.** | **64,626** | **64,511** | **64,5** |

Note: The egg and chicken production year runs from Dec. 1 of the previous year through Nov. 1.

## Egg Production in Canada

Source: Statistics Canada
(thousand dozens)

| Province | 1975 | 1976 | 1977 | Province | 1975 | 1976 | 1977 |
|---|---|---|---|---|---|---|---|
| ewfoundland | 6,740 | 6,810 | 7,135 | Manitoba | 50,531 | 49,286 | 50,270 |
| ince Edward Island | 2,373 | 2,496 | 2,625 | Saskatchewan | 20,880 | 18,629 | 19,522 |
| va Scotia | 17,756 | 16,744 | 17,531 | Alberta | 42,875 | 39,168 | 40,403 |
| ew Brunswick | 9,019 | 8,758 | 9,141 | British Columbia | 54,535 | 56,505 | 58,402 |
| uebec | 74,036 | 79,667 | 75,200 | Total | 462,547 | 454,466 | 458,678 |
| ntario | 183,802 | 176,403 | 178,449 | | | | |

Gross farm value of eggs (1974) $289,981,000; (1975) $282,469,000; (1976) $308,342,000; (1977) $313,398,000. Average price of eggs d for consumption (1974) $.59; (1975) $.57; (1976) $.64; (1977) $.65. Number and value of chicken and fowl (1974) 242,355,000 - 38,103,000; (1975) 226,342,000 - $311,007,000; (1976) 251,734,000 - $353,404,000; (1977) 259,556,000 - $365,480,000. Gross farm income from eggs, chicken and fowl (1974) $627,994,000; (1975) $593,476,000; (1976) $661,746,000; (1977) $678,878,000.

## Grain Receipts at U.S. Grain Centers

Source: Chicago Board of Trade (thousands bushels)

| 1977 | Wheat | Corn | Oats | Rye | Barley | Soybeans | Total |
|---|---|---|---|---|---|---|---|
| hicago | 14,105 | 91,350 | 172 | — | 11 | 26,596 | 132,234 |
| uluth | 152,361 | 6,148 | 10,850 | 1,050 | 55,061 | — | 225,470 |
| nid | 71,771 | — | — | — | — | — | 71,771 |
| utchinson | 65,784 | 18 | — | — | 3 | 3 | 65,808 |
| ansas City | 78,936 | 51,831 | 730 | — | 6 | 9,251 | 140,754 |
| ilwaukee | 527 | 25,635 | 156 | — | 17,121 | 1,606 | 45,045 |
| inneapolis | 124,201 | 77,339 | 39,001 | 2,729 | 33,518 | 32,817 | 309,604 |
| maha | 19,555 | 42,695 | 1,997 | 15 | 35 | 5,368 | 69,665 |
| eoria | 130 | 16,891 | 23 | 15 | — | 99 | 17,158 |
| oux City | 1,270 | 1,246 | 6,288 | 2 | 10 | 292 | 9,108 |
| t. Joseph | 3,470 | 7,192 | 3,078 | — | — | 2,402 | 16,142 |
| t. Louis | 29,776 | 15,988 | 125 | — | — | 19,353 | 65,242 |
| oledo | — | — | — | — | — | — | — |
| ichita | 45,321 | 762 | — | — | 219 | 6,258 | 52,560 |
| **Total** | **607,207** | **337,094** | **62,420** | **3,811** | **105,984** | **104,045** | **1,220,561** |

## Grain Storage Capacity at Principal Grain Centers in U.S.

Source: Chicago Board of Trade
(bushels)

| ties | Capacity | Cities | Capacity |
|---|---|---|---|
| lantic Coast | 35,500,000 | Texas High Plains | 76,800,000 |
| eat Lakes | | Enid | 66,100,000 |
| Toledo | 38,300,000 | Gulf Points | |
| Buffalo | 16,700,000 | South Mississippi | 41,600,000 |
| Chicago | 53,600,000 | North Texas Gulf | 28,200,000 |
| Milwaukee | 9,100,000 | South Texas Gulf | 14,000,000 |
| Duluth | 76,200,000 | Plains | |
| ver Points | | Wichita | 55,400,000 |
| Minneapolis | 111,100,000 | Topeka | 61,600,000 |
| Peoria | 6,600,000 | Salina | 26,300,000 |
| St. Louis | 25,500,000 | Hutchinson | 42,000,000 |
| Sioux City | 11,600,000 | Hastings-Grand Island | 24,100,000 |
| Omaha-Council Bluffs | 35,300,000 | Lincoln | 39,600,000 |
| Atchison | 24,500,000 | Pacific N.W. | |
| St. Joseph | 20,600,000 | Puget Sound | 9,500,000 |
| Kansas City | 72,400,000 | Portland | 24,900,000 |
| outhwest | | California Ports | 14,300,000 |
| Forth Worth | 57,600,000 | | |

**Atlantic Coast** — Albany, N.Y., Philadelphia, Pa., Baltimore, Md., Norfolk, Va., North Charleston, S.C. **Gulf Points** — ew Orleans, Baton Rouge, Ama. Belle Chase, La., Mobile, Ala., Pascagoula, Miss. **North Texas Gulf** — Houston, Galves-n, Beaumont, Port Arthur, Texas. **South Texas Gulf** — Corpus Christi, Brownsville, Texas. **Pacific N.W.** — Seattle, Ta-ma, Wash., Portland, Oreg., Columbia River **Calif. Ports** — San Francisco, Stockton, Sacramento, Los Angeles. **Texas igh Plains** — Amarillo, Lubbock, Hereford, Plainview, Texas.

## U.S. Meat and Lard Production and Consumption

Source: Economics, Statistics, and Cooperatives Service; U.S. Agriculture Department (million lbs.)

| | Beef | | Veal | | Lamb and mutton | | Pork (exclud. lard) | | All meats | | Lard | |
|---|---|---|---|---|---|---|---|---|---|---|---|---|
| ear | Pro-duc-tion | Con-sump-tion | Pro-duc-tion | Con-sump-tion | Pro-duc-tion | Con-sump-tion | Pro-duc-tion | Con-sump-tion | Pro-duc-tion | Con-sump-tion | Pro-duc-tion | Con-sump-tion |
| 940 | 7,175 | 7,257 | 981 | 981 | 876 | 873 | 10,044 | 9,701 | 19,076 | 18,812 | 2,288 | 1,901 |
| 950 | 9,534 | 9,529 | 1,230 | 1,206 | 597 | 596 | 10,714 | 10,390 | 22,075 | 21,721 | 2,631 | 1,891 |
| 960 | 14,753 | 15,147 | 1,109 | 1,093 | 768 | 852 | 13,905 | 13,838 | 30,535 | 30,930 | 2,562 | 1,358 |
| 965 | 18,727 | 19,060 | 1,020 | 992 | 651 | 716 | 12,781 | 12,870 | 33,179 | 33,638 | 2,045 | 1,225 |
| 970 | 21,685 | 22,926 | 588 | 581 | 551 | 657 | 14,699 | 14,661 | 37,523 | 38,825 | 1,913 | 939 |
| 975 | 23,976 | 25,398 | 873 | 876 | 410 | 430 | 11,779 | 11,852 | 37,038 | 38,556 | 1,012 | 632 |
| 977 | 25,279 | 27,038 | 834 | 836 | 351 | 371 | 13,247 | 13,200 | 39,711 | 41,445 | 1,037 | 502 |

## Net Income per Farm by States

Source: Economics, Statistics, and Cooperatives Service, U.S. Agriculture Department (dollars)

| State | 1969 | 1970 | 1971 | 1972 | 1973 | 1974 | 1975 | 1976 |
|---|---|---|---|---|---|---|---|---|
| Alabama | 2,941 | 2,744 | 3,185 | 4,232 | 6,732 | 4,886 | 5,209 | 5,952 |
| Alaska | 2,797 | 4,306 | 3,368 | 3,690 | 4,561 | 3,942 | 8,917 | 10,207 |
| Arizona | 23,578 | 18,295 | 23,114 | 25,480 | 40,104 | 65,828 | 41,076 | 63,855 |
| Arkansas | 3,734 | 4,570 | 4,327 | 5,609 | 11,798 | 12,402 | 10,416 | 7,627 |
| California | 16,735 | 15,520 | 17,685 | 23,384 | 38,940 | 44,093 | 38,781 | 39,362 |
| Colorado | 6,714 | 7,946 | 8,930 | 10,629 | 16,476 | 15,916 | 14,460 | 8,992 |
| Connecticut | 8,300 | 9,728 | 9,296 | 8,675 | 12,420 | 11,906 | 9,730 | 9,692 |
| Delaware | 12,480 | 6,974 | 8,361 | 11,954 | 28,550 | 21,619 | 24,874 | 23,81? |
| Florida | 12,531 | 10,824 | 14,878 | 19,266 | 25,197 | 23,579 | 27,612 | 27,61? |
| Georgia | 4,596 | 4,310 | 5,240 | 5,637 | 10,240 | 8,390 | 7,361 | 7,65? |
| Hawaii | 10,018 | 11,017 | 14,342 | 17,164 | 16,317 | 80,944 | 32,696 | 13,64? |
| Idaho | 6,972 | 7,269 | 7,029 | 9,752 | 16,584 | 21,615 | 10,859 | 8,04? |
| Illinois | 6,275 | 4,788 | 5,931 | 6,366 | 13,131 | 11,490 | 17,691 | 10,63? |
| Indiana | 4,927 | 3,262 | 5,342 | 4,257 | 11,225 | 5,976 | 9,551 | 8,97? |
| Iowa | 7,581 | 7,434 | 5,990 | 9,085 | 19,068 | 10,497 | 11,998 | 6,64? |
| Kansas | 4,477 | 6,208 | 7,198 | 10,546 | 16,962 | 10,955 | 7,984 | 6,48? |
| Kentucky | 3,046 | 2,843 | 2,938 | 3,811 | 4,461 | 5,150 | 4,041 | 4,43? |
| Louisiana | 3,405 | 4,242 | 5,010 | 5,825 | 10,724 | 12,131 | 7,022 | 6,82? |
| Maine | 5,663 | 6,093 | 5,664 | 6,081 | 18,166 | 23,478 | 8,220 | 19,10? |
| Maryland | 6,082 | 5,667 | 4,421 | 6,621 | 11,523 | 7,729 | 9,083 | 9,55? |
| Massachusetts | 6,273 | 6,438 | 6,054 | 6,215 | 7,890 | 7,182 | 7,116 | 8,68? |
| Michigan | 3,438 | 3,261 | 2,952 | 4,466 | 6,262 | 7,022 | 6,001 | 4,62? |
| Minnesota | 5,358 | 6,772 | 6,145 | 7,798 | 19,173 | 13,151 | 9,186 | 5,33? |
| Mississippi | 3,179 | 3,557 | 3,988 | 4,889 | 7,307 | 5,214 | 3,435 | 4,84? |
| Missouri | 2,626 | 2,955 | 3,138 | 4,345 | 7,865 | 4,005 | 4,438 | 2,30? |
| Montana | 7,457 | 9,168 | 7,521 | 13,835 | 22,829 | 14,829 | 14,540 | 10,45? |
| Nebraska | 7,182 | 6,442 | 6,913 | 10,096 | 17,798 | 8,169 | 14,707 | 6,85? |
| Nevada | 11,893 | 11,483 | 12,409 | 17,563 | 27,070 | 13,285 | 11,294 | 9,92? |
| New Hampshire | 4,882 | 4,924 | 5,260 | 6,901 | 9,209 | 6,416 | 6,968 | 8,14? |
| New Jersey | 7,610 | 6,671 | 6,178 | 5,451 | 10,592 | 11,402 | 6,580 | 7,68? |
| New Mexico | 7,015 | 9,158 | 9,226 | 10,403 | 16,247 | 10,900 | 14,787 | 11,77? |
| New York | 6,052 | 5,794 | 5,588 | 4,915 | 7,043 | 5,880 | 4,302 | 5,11? |
| North Carolina | 3,729 | 3,813 | 3,744 | 4,926 | 8,297 | 7,838 | 7,916 | 9,37? |
| North Dakota | 6,935 | 5,440 | 8,196 | 13,943 | 35,692 | 24,840 | 17,455 | 8,621 |
| Ohio | 3,163 | 3,224 | 3,080 | 3,823 | 5,355 | 6,216 | 6,536 | 5,99? |
| Oklahoma | 2,579 | 3,291 | 3,022 | 4,013 | 8,320 | 4,339 | 3,473 | 2,29? |
| Oregon | 4,549 | 4,080 | 3,878 | 5,751 | 10,628 | 12,648 | 8,478 | 7,00? |
| Pennsylvania | 4,065 | 4,187 | 3,695 | 4,036 | 6,034 | 5,553 | 4,392 | 4,97? |
| Rhode Island | 6,547 | 8,837 | 7,851 | 7,866 | 5,676 | 8,453 | 12,075 | 12,54? |
| South Carolina | 2,777 | 2,769 | 3,105 | 3,750 | 5,668 | 6,593 | 4,506 | 3,90? |
| South Dakota | 6,513 | 6,941 | 7,722 | 11,641 | 23,151 | 12,964 | 10,498 | 4,96? |
| Tennessee | 1,745 | 1,781 | 1,748 | 2,261 | 3,464 | 2,195 | 1,605 | 2,89? |
| Texas | 3,289 | 4,249 | 3,457 | 4,795 | 10,211 | 4,339 | 4,296 | 4,54? |
| Utah | 3,965 | 4,353 | 4,700 | 6,145 | 10,634 | 6,421 | 4,429 | 5,40? |
| Vermont | 6,078 | 6,792 | 7,065 | 8,658 | 9,241 | 7,044 | 7,683 | 11,17? |
| Virginia | 2,161 | 2,266 | 1,960 | 2,952 | 4,831 | 3,888 | 3,371 | 2,78? |
| Washington | 7,577 | 5,611 | 7,199 | 10,763 | 19,203 | 20,264 | 19,345 | 12,29? |
| West Virginia | 791 | 641 | 625 | 956 | 1,484 | 1,076 | 519 | 30? |
| Wisconsin | 5,129 | 5,273 | 5,938 | 6,403 | 8,637 | 6,910 | 7,428 | 6,69? |
| Wyoming | 5,095 | 5,895 | 6,401 | 11,675 | 14,788 | 6,751 | 2,495 | 24? |
| Total U.S. | 4,766 | 4,790 | 5,030 | 6,504 | 11,727 | 9,232 | 8,637 | 7,203 |

## Farm Income—Cash Receipts from Marketings

Source: Economics, Statistics, and Cooperatives Service: U.S. Agriculture Department

($1,000)

| 1976 State | Crops | Live- stock | Gov't pay'ts | Total |
|---|---|---|---|---|
| Alabama | 624,722 | 993,226 | 13,115 | 1,631,063 |
| Alaska | 5,216 | 4,126 | 151 | 9,493 |
| Arizona | 699,005 | 541,115 | 4,936 | 1,245,056 |
| Arkansas | 1,237,025 | 1,059,002 | 9,097 | 2,305,124 |
| California | 6,148,682 | 2,953,178 | 12,983 | 9,114,843 |
| Colorado | 530,591 | 1,446,017 | 22,780 | 1,999,388 |
| Connecticut | 93,678 | 137,281 | 443 | 231,402 |
| Delaware | 98,757 | 182,805 | 290 | 281,852 |
| Florida | 1,840,106 | 692,680 | 5,440 | 2,538,226 |
| Georgia | 1,103,337 | 1,165,684 | 9,783 | 2,278,804 |
| Hawaii | 260,847 | 62,410 | 391 | 323,648 |
| Idaho | 793,330 | 455,090 | 9,277 | 1,257,697 |
| Illinois | 4,243,954 | 1,866,939 | 9,700 | 6,120,593 |
| Indiana | 1,995,998 | 1,334,757 | 6,016 | 3,336,771 |
| Iowa | 2,967,826 | 4,041,870 | 26,767 | 7,036,463 |
| Kansas | 1,614,397 | 1,917,163 | 50,824 | 3,582,384 |
| Kentucky | 896,536 | 729,592 | 6,591 | 1,632,719 |
| Louisiana | 868,417 | 405,489 | 7,453 | 1,281,359 |
| Maine | 174,987 | 268,081 | 2,083 | 445,151 |
| Maryland | 255,071 | 428,292 | 1,514 | 684,877 |
| Massachusetts | 100,560 | 114,163 | 599 | 215,322 |
| Michigan | 884,776 | 815,799 | 7,300 | 1,707,875 |
| Minnesota | 1,720,943 | 2,181,606 | 59,085 | 3,961,634 |
| Mississippi | 989,588 | 682,220 | 28,557 | 1,700,365 |
| Missouri | 1,053,027 | 1,577,728 | 30,874 | 2,661,629 |
| Montana | 543,594 | 453,381 | 10,497 | 1,007,472 |
| Nebraska | 1,690,740 | 2,176,886 | 36,614 | 3,904,240 |
| Nevada | 42,288 | 107,484 | 1,323 | 151,095 |
| New Hampshire | 21,610 | 57,688 | 689 | 79,987 |
| New Jersey | 224,717 | 109,603 | 833 | 335,153 |
| New Mexico | 193,923 | 518,402 | 15,502 | 727,827 |
| New York | 474,757 | 1,223,614 | 5,979 | 1,704,350 |
| North Carolina | 1,748,541 | 1,073,071 | 7,784 | 2,829,396 |
| North Dakota | 1,171,511 | 484,362 | 22,744 | 1,678,617 |
| Ohio | 1,617,874 | 1,163,911 | 7,297 | 2,789,082 |
| Oklahoma | 663,084 | 1,248,848 | 27,679 | 1,939,611 |
| Oregon | 666,702 | 355,774 | 5,277 | 1,027,753 |
| Pennsylvania | 500,069 | 1,300,409 | 5,774 | 1,806,252 |
| Rhode Island | 15,082 | 12,956 | 87 | 28,125 |
| South Carolina | 553,932 | 285,482 | 5,285 | 844,699 |
| South Dakota | 372,451 | 1,417,116 | 88,068 | 1,877,635 |
| Tennessee | 635,168 | 675,368 | 11,392 | 1,321,928 |
| Texas | 3,109,198 | 3,189,219 | 111,735 | 6,410,152 |
| Utah | 97,121 | 262,186 | 5,611 | 364,918 |
| Vermont | 18,492 | 244,825 | 1,187 | 264,504 |
| Virginia | 482,101 | 554,976 | 7,225 | 1,044,302 |
| Washington | 1,231,157 | 523,110 | 5,007 | 1,759,274 |
| West Virginia | 37,190 | 103,442 | 2,591 | 143,223 |
| Wisconsin | 541,755 | 2,486,884 | 14,282 | 3,042,921 |
| Wyoming | 82,781 | 303,320 | 7,113 | 393,214 |
| Total U.S. | 47,937,214 | 46,388,630 | 733,624 | 95,059,468 |

## Average Prices Received by U.S. Farmers

Source: Statistical Reporting Service; U.S. Agriculture Department

The figures represent dollars per 100 lbs. for hogs, beef cattle, veal calves, sheep, lamb, and milk (wholesale), dollars per head for milk cows; cents per lb. for milk fat (in cream), chickens, broilers, turkeys, and wool; cents for eggs per dozen.

Weighted calendar year prices for livestock and livestock products other than wool. 1943 through 1963, wool prices are weighted on marketing year basis. The marketing year has been changed (1964) from a calendar year to a Dec.-Nov. basis for hogs, chickens, broilers and eggs.

| Year | Hogs | Cattle (beef) | Calves (veal) | Sheep | Lambs | Cows (milk) | Milk (wholesale) | Milk fat (in cream) | Chickens (excl. broilers) | Broilers | Turkeys | Eggs | Wool |
|---|---|---|---|---|---|---|---|---|---|---|---|---|---|
| 1930 | 8.84 | 7.71 | 9.68 | 4.74 | 7.76 | 74.20 | 2.21 | 34.5 | ... | ... | 20.2 | 23.7 | 19.5 |
| 1940 | 5.39 | 7.56 | 8.83 | 3.95 | 8.10 | 61.00 | 1.82 | 28.0 | 13.0 | 17.3 | 15.2 | 18.0 | 28.4 |
| 1950 | 18.00 | 23.30 | 26.30 | 11.60 | 25.10 | 198.00 | 3.89 | 62.0 | 22.0 | 27.4 | 32.9 | 36.3 | 62.1 |
| 1960 | 15.30 | 20.40 | 22.90 | 5.61 | 17.90 | 223.00 | 4.21 | 60.5 | 12.2 | 16.9 | 25.4 | 36.1 | 42.0 |
| 1965 | 19.60 | 19.90 | 22.00 | 6.34 | 22.80 | 212.00 | 4.23 | 61.1 | 8.9 | 15.0 | 22.2 | 33.7 | 47.1 |
| 1970 | 22.70 | 27.10 | 34.50 | 7.51 | 26.40 | 332.00 | 5.71 | 70.0 | 9.1 | 13.6 | 22.6 | 39.1 | 35.5 |
| 1972 | 25.10 | 33.50 | 44.70 | 7.28 | 29.10 | 397.00 | 6.07 | 67.5 | 8.9 | 14.1 | 22.2 | 30.9 | 35.0 |
| 1973 | 38.40 | 42.80 | 56.60 | 12.70 | 35.10 | 496.00 | 7.14 | 67.2 | 15.1 | 24.0 | 38.2 | 52.5 | 82.7 |
| 1974 | 34.20 | 35.60 | 35.20 | 11.30 | 37.00 | 500.00 | 8.33 | 63.5 | 9.7 | 21.5 | 28.0 | 53.3 | 59.1 |
| 1975 | 46.10 | 32.30 | 27.20 | 11.20 | 42.10 | 412.00 | 8.75 | 71.0 | 9.9 | 26.3 | 34.8 | 52.5 | 44.7 |
| 1976 | 43.30 | 33.70 | 34.10 | 13.20 | 46.90 | 477.00 | 9.66 | 83.4 | 13.0 | 23.6 | 31.7 | 58.4 | 65.7 |
| 1977 | 39.40 | 34.40 | 36.90 | 13.40 | 51.30 | 504.00 | 9.72 | 91.4 | 12.1 | 23.6 | 35.5 | 55.7 | 72.0 |

The figures represent cents per lb. for cotton, apples, and peanuts; dollars per bushel for oats, wheat, corn, barley, and soybeans; dollars per 100 lbs. for rice, sorghum, and potatoes; dollars per ton for cottonseed and baled hay.

Weighted crop year prices. Crop years are as follows: apples, June-May; wheat, oats, barley, hay and potatoes, July-June; cotton, rice, peanuts and cottonseed, August-July; soybeans, September-August; and corn and sorghum grain, October-September.

| Crop Year | Corn | Wheat | Upland Cotton[1] | Oats | Barley | Rice | Soybeans | Sorghum | Peanuts | Cottonseed | Hay | Potatoes | Apples |
|---|---|---|---|---|---|---|---|---|---|---|---|---|---|
| 1930 | .663 | .550 | 9.46 | 0.31 | .420 | 1.74 | 1.34 | 1.02 | 3.46 | 22.00 | 11.00 | 1.47 | ... |
| 1940 | .674 | .601 | 9.83 | 0.30 | .393 | 1.80 | .892 | .873 | 3.33 | 21.70 | 9.78 | .850 | ... |
| 1950 | 2.00 | 1.52 | 39.90 | 0.79 | 1.19 | 5.09 | 2.47 | 1.88 | 10.9 | 86.60 | 21.10 | 1.50 | ... |
| 1960 | 1.74 | .997 | 30.08 | 0.60 | .838 | 4.55 | 2.13 | 1.49 | 10.0 | 42.50 | 21.70 | 2.00 | 4.79 |
| 1965 | 1.35 | 1.16 | 29.26 | 0.62 | 1.02 | 4.93 | 2.54 | 1.76 | 11.4 | 46.70 | 23.20 | 2.53 | 4.32 |
| 1970 | 1.33 | 1.33 | 22.81 | 0.62 | .973 | 5.17 | 2.85 | 2.04 | 12.8 | 56.50 | 26.10 | 1.21 | 6.97 |
| 1972 | 1.57 | 1.76 | 27.20 | 72.5 | 1.21 | 6.73 | 4.37 | 2.45 | 14.5 | 49.50 | 31.30 | 3.01 | 8.92 |
| 1973 | 2.55 | 3.95 | 44.40 | 1.18 | 2.14 | 13.80 | 5.68 | 3.82 | 16.2 | 100.00 | 41.60 | 4.89 | 10.70 |
| 1974 | 3.02 | 4.09 | 42.70 | 1.53 | 2.81 | 11.20 | 6.64 | 4.95 | 17.9 | 136.0 | 50.90 | 4.01 | 11.10 |
| 1975 | 2.54 | 3.56 | 51.10 | 1.46 | 2.42 | 8.35 | 4.92 | 4.23 | 19.6 | 97.00 | 52.20 | 4.48 | 8.80 |
| 1976 | 2.15 | 2.73 | 63.80 | 1.56 | 2.25 | 7.02 | 6.81 | 3.63 | 20.0 | 103.00 | 60.30 | 3.59 | 8.80 |
| 1977 | 2.03 | 2.31 | 51.40 | 1.14 | 1.80 | 9.43 | 5.79 | 3.09 | 21.0 | 71.00 | 54.00 | 3.64 | 11.30 |

(1) Beginning 1964, 480 lb. net weight bales.

## Index Numbers of Prices Received by Farmers

Source: Statistical Reporting Service; U.S. Agriculture Department (index 1910-14 = 100 per cent)

| Year | All farm products | All crops | Livestock[1] | Food grains | Feed grains and Hay | Cotton | Tobacco | Oil-bearing crops | Fruit | Commercial vegetables | Potatoes Sweetpot[2] | Meat animals | Dairy products | Poultry and eggs | | Ratio of prices received to prices paid by farmers |
|---|---|---|---|---|---|---|---|---|---|---|---|---|---|---|---|---|
| | | | | | | | | | | | | | | | Year | ratio |
| 1910 | 104 | 105 | 102 | 109 | 96 | 118 | 84 | 120 | 100 | ... | 83 | 101 | 100 | 104 | 1967 | 100 |
| 1920 | 211 | 235 | 190 | 249 | 202 | 262 | 233 | 208 | 188 | 294 | 171 | 202 | 222 | 99 | 1968 | 99 |
| 1930 | 125 | 115 | 134 | 93 | 106 | 104 | 140 | 111 | 149 | 128 | 162 | 133 | 142 | 128 | 1969 | 100 |
| 1940 | 100 | 90 | 109 | 84 | 85 | 83 | 134 | 103 | 81 | 122 | 89 | 108 | 120 | 98 | 1970 | 98 |
| 1950 | 258 | 233 | 280 | 224 | 193 | 282 | 402 | 276 | 194 | 211 | 166 | 340 | 249 | 186 | 1971 | 96 |
| 1960 | 239 | 222 | 253 | 203 | 152 | 254 | 500 | 214 | 244 | 230 | 203 | 296 | 259 | 160 | 1972 | 101 |
| 1965 | 245 | 230 | 260 | 163 | 174 | 245 | 513 | 265 | 240 | 262 | 293 | 315 | 260 | 144 | 1973 | 124 |
| 1970 | 274 | 225 | 325 | 162 | 179 | 183 | 604 | 265 | 217 | 292 | 218 | 405 | 350 | 147 | 1974 | 117 |
| 1975 | 463 | 452 | 474 | 426 | 400 | 348 | 899 | 529 | 313 | 458 | 400 | 567 | 537 | 235 | 1975 | 103 |
| 1976 | 464 | 443 | 485 | 355 | 387 | 504 | 906 | 551 | 294 | 456 | 375 | 569 | 591 | 233 | 1976 | 97 |
| 1977 | 456 | 431 | 481 | 275 | 316 | 509 | 972 | 652 | 358 | 496 | 363 | 564 | 594 | 228 | 1977 | 90 |

(1) Livestock and livestock products. (2) For fresh market and processing beginning 1952. (3) Including dry edible beans.

## Farm Employment—Annual Averages

Source: Statistical Reporting Service; U.S. Agriculture Department (Index 1910-14 = 100 per cent)

| Year | Total Aver. no. (1,000) | Total Index % | Family Aver. no. (1,000) | Family Index % | Hired Aver. no. (1,000) | Hired Index % | Year | Total Aver. no. (1,000) | Total Index % | Family Aver. no. (1,000) | Family Index % | Hired Aver. no. (1,000) | Hired Index % |
|---|---|---|---|---|---|---|---|---|---|---|---|---|---|
| 1920 | 13,432 | 99 | 10,041 | 99 | 3,391 | 100 | 1960 | 7,057 | 52 | 5,172 | 52 | 1,885 | 55 |
| 1930 | 12,497 | 92 | 9,307 | 92 | 3,190 | 94 | 1970 | 4,523 | 34 | 3,348 | 33 | 1,175 | 35 |
| 1940 | 10,979 | 82 | 8,300 | 81 | 2,679 | 79 | 1976 | 4,374 | 32 | 2,997 | 29 | 1,377 | 41 |
| 1950 | 9,926 | 75 | 7,597 | 73 | 2,329 | 69 | 1977 | 4,152 | 31 | 2,856 | 28 | 1,295 | 38 |

## Canadian Farm Cash Receipts

Source: Statistics Canada
(millions of Canadian Dollars)
Cash receipts from farming operations excluding supplementary payments. Excludes Newfoundland

### Crops

| Year and Quarter | Total cash receipts | Total crops | Wheat | Barley | C.W.B. Advance[1] payments | Deferred grain receipts | Other grains[2] | Pota- toes | Fruits | Vege- tables | Flori- culture and nursery | Tobacco | Other[3] crops |
|---|---|---|---|---|---|---|---|---|---|---|---|---|---|
| 1973 | 6,861.31 | 2,704.64 | 1,201.25 | 330.28 | 6.47 | −305.24 | 579.56 | 159.97 | 140.85 | 161.49 | 92.34 | 142.81 | 194.86 |
| 1974 | 8,868.86 | 4,168.59 | 2,054.53 | 564.64 | 11.42 | −320.57 | 796.23 | 211.48 | 140.23 | 191.68 | 117.76 | 207.68 | 193.52 |
| 1975 | 9,998.19 | 4,802.12 | 2,525.62 | 615.18 | −13.90 | −69.63 | 655.30 | 164.81 | 130.50 | 242.59 | 143.37 | 198.19 | 210.11 |
| 1976 | 10,038.54 | 4,621.64 | 2,056.13 | 506.19 | 58.44 | 149.18 | 650.02 | 213.17 | 136.28 | 244.54 | 170.26 | 236.90 | 200.54 |
| 1977 | 10,171.95 | 4,429.00 | 1,797.43 | 436.53 | 5.67 | 112.24 | 866.09 | 203.50 | 159.01 | 243.62 | 191.71 | 182.63 | 230.56 |

### Livestock and Products

| Year and Quarter | Total | Cattle | Hogs | Dairy products | Poultry | Eggs | Other products[4] | Total forest & maple products | Provincial income stabilization plan | Dairy Supple- mentary payments | Deficiency[5] payments |
|---|---|---|---|---|---|---|---|---|---|---|---|
| 1973 | 3,920.54 | 1,479.51 | 825.49 | 849.46 | 437.94 | 243.79 | 84.35 | 44.61 | — | 131.02 | 60.50 |
| 1974 | 4,384.42 | 1,680.58 | 778.09 | 1,095.90 | 472.15 | 269.10 | 88.60 | 43.17 | 15.58 | 221.06 | 36.04 |
| 1975 | 4,817.95 | 1,817.98 | 886.47 | 1,343.29 | 419.35 | 260.17 | 90.69 | 45.97 | 49.79 | 259.77 | 22.60 |
| 1976 | 4,996.28 | 1,963.34 | 840.17 | 1,331.31 | 479.55 | 282.51 | 99.40 | 53.66 | 83.32 | 258.87 | 24.79 |
| 1977 | 5,245.81 | 2,088.89 | 844.11 | 1,422.64 | 495.83 | 281.17 | 113.17 | 62.01 | 117.02 | 269.45 | 48.69 |

(1) Represents participation payments made by the Canadian Wheat Board direct to producers on crops delivered in previous years. (2) Includes oats, rye, flaxseed, rapeseed, soybeans, and corn. (3) Includes sugar beets, clover and grass seed, hay, clover, mustard seed, sunflower seed, hops, dry beans and dry peas and miscellaneous products. (4) Including sheep and lambs. (5) Made under the authority of the Agricultural Stabilization Act.

## Canadian Farm Cash Receipts by Province

Source: Statistics Canada
(thousands of Canadian dollars)

| Province | 1973 | 1974 | 1975 | 1976 | 1977 |
|---|---|---|---|---|---|
| Prince Edward Island | 73,304 | 84,693 | 83,427 | 104,950 | 88,599 |
| Nova Scotia | 96,499 | 103,537 | 116,236 | 123,025 | 128,158 |
| New Brunswick | 95,822 | 103,233 | 100,043 | 113,205 | 109,579 |
| Quebec | 980,080 | 1,149,617 | 1,342,037 | 1,363,213 | 1,430,953 |
| Ontario | 1,992,585 | 2,486,908 | 2,649,785 | 2,827,347 | 2,875,224 |
| Manitoba | 619,429 | 825,371 | 935,004 | 894,545 | 910,598 |
| Saskatchewan | 1,467,146 | 2,039,831 | 2,468,789 | 2,285,293 | 2,130,918 |
| Alberta | 1,201,211 | 1,686,475 | 1,876,103 | 1,849,739 | 1,994,519 |
| British Columbia | 335,230 | 389,199 | 426,765 | 477,225 | 503,400 |
| **Total** | **6,861,306** | **8,868,864** | **9,998,189** | **10,038,542** | **10,171,948** |

## Canadian Production of Sawn Lumber

Source: Canadian Statistical Review (May, 1978)
(million feet, board measure)

| Year | Canada[1] | N.S. | N.B. | Que. | Ont. | Sask. | Alta. | B.C. |
|---|---|---|---|---|---|---|---|---|
| 1974... | 13,499 | 188 | 342 | 2,210 | 1,260 | 139 | 618 | 8,755 |
| 1975... | 11,283 | 162 | 256 | 1,930 | 948 | 127 | 391 | 7,469 |
| 1976... | 15,431 | 159 | 321 | 2,364 | 1,175 | 156 | 511 | 10,745 |
| 1977... | 17,582 | 194 | 308 | 2,700 | 1,412 | 217 | 620 | 12,038 |

(1) Excludes Newfoundland, P.E.I., Manitoba, the Yukon, and the Northwest Territories which, together, account for less than 1% of the total.

## Average Farm Wages

Source: Economics, Statistics, and Cooperatives Service, U.S. Agriculture Department

(dollars per hour)

| Method of pay: | 1975 | 1976 | 1977 | | 1975 | 1976 | 1977 |
|---|---|---|---|---|---|---|---|
| All hired farm workers | 2.43 | 2.66 | 2.87 | Machine operators | 2.50 | 2.72 | 2.92 |
| Paid by piece-rate | 2.96 | 3.14 | 3.48 | Maintenance and bookkeeping | 3.15 | 3.45 | (5) |
| Paid by other than piece-rate | 2.38 | 2.61 | 2.82 | Supervisors | 4.00 | 4.39 | 4.63 |
| Paid by hour only[1] | 2.39 | 2.60 | 2.84 | Other agricultural workers | 2.76 | 3.11[5] | 3.37 |
| Paid cash wages only[2] | 2.60 | 2.81 | 3.06 | | | | |
| Paid by hour cash wages only[3] | 2.45 | 2.65 | 2.90 | Indexes[4] | | | |
| Type of work performed: | | | | (1910-14=100) | 1,612 | 1,764 | |
| Field and livestock workers | 2.26 | 2.47 | 2.65 | (1967=100) | 190 | 208 | |
| Packinghouse workers | 2.52 | 2.80 | 2.97 | | | | |

(1) May include perquisites such as room and board, includes only those paid by the hour. (2) Does not include perquisites, includes all methods of pay. (3) Does not include perquisites, includes only those paid by the hour. (4) Indexes are based on all hired farm workers and are adjusted for seasonal variation. (5) Maintainance and bookkeeping included with other workers in 1976 and 1977.

## Government Payments by Programs, by States

Source: Economics, Statistics, and Cooperatives Service: U.S. Agriculture Department ($1,000)

| 1976 State | Conservation[1] | Sugar Act | Feed Grain Program | Wheat Program | Cotton | Cropland Adjustment | Great Plains Conservation | Misc. Program[2] | Total |
|---|---|---|---|---|---|---|---|---|---|
| Alabama | 5,734 | — | 332 | 6 | 5,598 | 948 | — | 596 | 13,115 |
| Alaska | 124 | — | — | — | — | — | — | 27 | 151 |
| Arizona | 2,024 | — | 15 | 37 | 1,663 | 95 | — | 1,102 | 4,936 |
| Arkansas | 3,515 | — | 12 | — | 4,958 | 99 | — | 513 | 9,097 |
| California | 4,586 | 640 | 1,810 | 1,736 | 15 | 2 | — | 4,194 | 12,983 |
| Colorado | 3,633 | — | 3,226 | 11,153 | — | 445 | 1,648 | 2,675 | 22,780 |
| Connecticut | 371 | — | — | — | — | 24 | — | 48 | 443 |
| Delaware | 263 | — | 7 | — | — | 17 | — | 3 | 290 |
| Florida | 4,497 | — | 129 | — | 102 | 471 | — | 241 | 5,440 |
| Georgia | 5,292 | — | 565 | 9 | 1,894 | 1,113 | — | 910 | 9,783 |
| Hawaii | 389 | — | — | — | — | — | — | 2 | 391 |
| Idaho | 5,105 | — | 364 | 1,566 | — | 12 | — | 2,230 | 9,277 |
| Illinois | 6,087 | — | 2,377 | 438 | — | 432 | — | 366 | 9,700 |
| Indiana | 4,324 | — | 453 | 558 | — | 433 | — | 248 | 6,016 |
| Iowa | 7,974 | — | 17,423 | 88 | — | 520 | — | 762 | 26,767 |
| Kansas | 6,883 | — | 9,712 | 31,729 | — | 499 | 1,526 | 475 | 50,824 |
| Kentucky | 5,053 | — | 450 | 145 | 70 | 637 | — | 236 | 6,591 |
| Louisiana | 3,754 | (3) | 17 | 3 | 3,298 | 31 | — | 353 | 7,453 |
| Maine | 1,954 | — | — | — | — | 26 | — | 103 | 2,083 |
| Maryland | 1,320 | — | 25 | 2 | — | 35 | — | 132 | 1,514 |
| Massachusetts | 443 | — | — | — | — | 27 | — | 129 | 599 |
| Michigan | 4,890 | — | 1,013 | 143 | — | 833 | — | 421 | 7,300 |
| Minnesota | 6,172 | — | 45,388 | 871 | — | 909 | — | 5,745 | 59,085 |
| Mississippi | 4,991 | — | 58 | 1 | 22,492 | 352 | — | 663 | 28,557 |
| Missouri | 7,949 | — | 14,327 | 2,515 | 4,218 | 1,055 | — | 810 | 30,874 |
| Montana | 5,689 | — | 212 | 1,522 | — | 87 | 810 | 2,177 | 10,497 |
| Nebraska | 5,374 | (2) | 16,878 | 11,592 | — | 817 | 1,242 | 713 | 36,614 |
| Nevada | 842 | — | 1 | 55 | — | 1 | — | 425 | 1,323 |
| New Hampshire | 587 | — | — | — | — | 1 | — | 101 | 689 |
| New Jersey | 715 | — | 4 | — | — | 68 | — | 46 | 833 |
| New Mexico | 2,019 | — | 2,818 | 5,104 | 1,824 | 1,400 | 641 | 1,696 | 15,502 |
| New York | 5,008 | — | 269 | 39 | — | 401 | — | 262 | 5,979 |
| North Carolina | 4,740 | — | 824 | 218 | 505 | 597 | — | 900 | 7,784 |
| North Dakota | 4,835 | (1) | 5,616 | 9,313 | — | 397 | 763 | 1,821 | 22,744 |
| Ohio | 4,901 | — | 200 | 859 | — | 480 | — | 857 | 7,297 |
| Oklahoma | 5,793 | — | 2,014 | 14,573 | 3,047 | 384 | 1,586 | 282 | 27,679 |
| Oregon | 3,156 | — | 74 | 1,077 | — | 5 | — | 965 | 5,277 |
| Pennsylvania | 4,875 | — | 126 | 108 | — | 343 | — | 322 | 5,774 |
| Rhode Island | 77 | — | — | — | — | — | — | 10 | 87 |
| South Carolina | 2,470 | — | 240 | 76 | 1,192 | 850 | — | 457 | 5,285 |
| South Dakota | 3,757 | — | 50,908 | 22,956 | — | 608 | 938 | 8,901 | 88,068 |
| Tennessee | 4,230 | — | 234 | 28 | 6,142 | 574 | — | 184 | 11,392 |
| Texas | 17,735 | — | 10,482 | 15,262 | 51,266 | 2,663 | 3,824 | 10,503 | 111,735 |
| Utah | 1,712 | — | 437 | 951 | — | 33 | — | 2,478 | 5,611 |
| Vermont | 1,051 | — | 1 | — | — | 5 | — | 130 | 1,187 |
| Virginia | 5,727 | — | 258 | 94 | 5 | 176 | — | 965 | 7,225 |
| Washington | 3,842 | — | 23 | 276 | — | 11 | — | 855 | 5,007 |
| West Virginia | 2,168 | — | 3 | 1 | — | 18 | — | 401 | 2,591 |
| Wisconsin | 4,516 | — | 6,179 | 9 | — | 1,002 | — | 2,576 | 14,282 |
| Wyoming | 1,819 | — | 41 | 257 | — | 24 | 597 | 4,375 | 7,113 |
| United States | 194,965 | 634 | 195,545 | 135,370 | 108,289 | 19,860 | 13,575 | 65,386 | 733,624 |

(1) Includes amounts paid under Appalachian Region, Agricultural and Emergency Conservation Programs. (2) Includes Rice Disaster Program, National Wool Act Program, Milk Indemnity Program, Beekeepers Indemnity Program, Hay and Cattle Transportation Payments, Forestry Incentive Program, Water Bank Program and other miscellaneous programs.

## U.S. Farm Marketing, Supply, Related Service Cooperatives

Source: Economics, Statistics, and Cooperatives Service, U.S. Agriculture Department

Marketing season 1975-76[1]; a marketing season includes the period during which the farm products of a specified year are moved into the channels of trade. Marketing seasons overlap.

| State | Number of cooperatives | Memberships | Net business[2] | State | Number of cooperatives | Memberships | Net business[2] |
|---|---|---|---|---|---|---|---|
| Alabama | 98 | 101,698 | 511,844 | Maryland | 37 | 59,765 | 382,148 |
| Alaska | 1 | 15 | 11,465 | Massachusetts | 17 | 10,965 | 158,365 |
| Arizona | 18 | 89,639 | 283,087 | Michigan | 141 | 137,946 | 1,068,202 |
| Arkansas[2] | 121 | 106,820 | 812,619 | Minnesota | 1,048 | 597,557 | 2,909,767 |
| California[2] | 277 | 85,285 | 3,922,342 | Mississippi | 133 | 118,593 | 501,342 |
| Colorado | 81 | 48,615 | 482,873 | Missouri | 146 | 239,717 | 1,005,871 |
| Connecticut | 8 | 5,065 | 108,881 | Montana | 226 | 73,752 | 316,226 |
| Delaware | 7 | 17,165 | 57,209 | Nebraska | 336 | 246,065 | 1,374,912 |
| Florida | 86 | 60,050 | 948,633 | Nevada | 3 | 305 | 14,737 |
| Georgia | 94 | 154,488 | 843,525 | New Hampshire | 7 | 6,202 | 57,472 |
| Hawaii | 18 | 2,183 | 24,285 | New Jersey | 33 | 16,221 | 177,308 |
| Idaho | 60 | 39,498 | 266,033 | New Mexico | 23 | 6,832 | 74,211 |
| Illinois | 279 | 308,519 | 2,661,155 | New York | 247 | 140,718 | 1,472,131 |
| Indiana | 106 | 365,135 | 1,311,114 | North Carolina | 38 | 132,289 | 449,994 |
| Iowa | 447 | 326,981 | 2,989,547 | North Dakota | 664 | 201,387 | 1,216,593 |
| Kansas | 261 | 204,716 | 1,675,209 | Ohio | 199 | 213,547 | 1,500,457 |
| Kentucky | 82 | 232,389 | 360,735 | Oklahoma | 151 | 132,462 | 736,039 |
| Louisiana | 100 | 18,519 | 360,726 | Oregon | 66 | 54,655 | 663,847 |
| Maine | 10 | 7,025 | 95,834 | Pennsylvania | 98 | 76,805 | 957,108 |

*(continued)*

| State | Number of cooperatives | Member-ships | Net business[2] | State | Number of cooperatives | Member-ships | Net business[2] |
|---|---|---|---|---|---|---|---|
| Rhode Island | 1 | 865 | 15,157 | Virginia | 114 | 190,125 | 511,570 |
| South Carolina | 21 | 63,957 | 170,252 | Washington | 138 | 76,669 | 1,169,168 |
| South Dakota | 314 | 168,723 | 647,111 | West Virginia | 67 | 67,506 | 86,012 |
| Tennessee | 103 | 157,245 | 388,774 | Wisconsin | 494 | 372,891 | 2,103,583 |
| Texas | 440 | 133,073 | 1,675,285 | Wyoming | 29 | 8,673 | 65,746 |
| Utah | 39 | 19,919 | 288,124 | Foreign | — | 275 | 56,517 |
| Vermont | 8 | 6,879 | 163,172 | **Total** | **7,535** | **5,906,379** | **40,104,317** |

(1) Preliminary. (2) The volume of a Hawaiian sugar co-op based in California is included in the dollar volume of California.

---

## Farm-Real Estate Debt Outstanding by Lender Groups

Source: Economics, Statistics, and Cooperatives Service, U.S. Agriculture Department

| | Total farm-real estate debt[1] $1,000 | Federal land banks[1] $1,000 | Amounts held by principal lender groups | | | |
|---|---|---|---|---|---|---|
| | | | Farmers Home Administration[2] $1,000 | Life insurance companies[3] $1,000 | All commercial banks $1,000 | Other[4] $1,000 |
| 1951 | 6,112,286 | 991,439 | 256,724 | 1,352,635 | 985,954 | 2,525,534 |
| 1952 | 6,662,327 | 1,026,906 | 290,529 | 1,541,874 | 1,017,360 | 2,785,658 |
| 1953 | 7,240,937 | 1,095,257 | 330,087 | 1,716,022 | 1,069,398 | 3,030,173 |
| 1954 | 7,930,931 | 1,187,046 | 352,199 | 1,892,773 | 1,091,949 | 3,215,964 |
| 1955 | 8,245,278 | 1,279,787 | 378,108 | 2,051,784 | 1,161,308 | 3,374,291 |
| 1956 | 9,012,016 | 1,480,204 | 412,670 | 2,271,784 | 1,275,429 | 3,571,929 |
| 1957 | 9,821,525 | 1,722,381 | 462,942 | 2,476,543 | 1,298,113 | 3,861,546 |
| 1958 | 10,382,475 | 1,897,187 | 540,762 | 2,578,958 | 1,315,530 | 4,050,038 |
| 1959 | 11,091,390 | 2,065,372 | 608,101 | 2,661,229 | 1,407,548 | 4,349,140 |
| 1960 | 12,082,409 | 2,335,124 | 676,224 | 2,819,542 | 1,523,051 | 4,728,468 |
| 1961 | 12,820,304 | 2,539,044 | 722,870 | 2,974,609 | 1,591,762 | 4,992,019 |
| 1962 | 13,899,105 | 2,803,103 | 948,346 | 3,161,757 | 1,640,790 | 5,345,109 |
| 1963 | 15,167,821 | 3,024,013 | 1,057,923 | 3,391,183 | 1,870,216 | 5,824,486 |
| 1964 | 16,803,505 | 3,281,797 | 1,171,373 | 3,780,537 | 2,136,571 | 6,433,227 |
| 1965 | 18,894,240 | 3,686,755 | 1,284,913 | 4,287,671 | 2,416,634 | 7,218,267 |
| 1966 | 21,186,886 | 4,240,227 | 1,497,313 | 4,801,677 | 2,607,404 | 8,040,265 |
| 1967 | 23,077,186 | 4,914,522 | 1,663,067 | 5,213,587 | 2,770,010 | 8,516,000 |
| 1968 | 25,142,401 | 5,563,204 | 1,844,046 | 5,539,600 | 3,060,551 | 9,135,000 |
| 1969 | 27,397,370 | 6,081,229 | 2,054,382 | 5,763,500 | 3,333,259 | 10,165,000 |
| 1970 | 29,182,766 | 6,671,222 | 2,279,620 | 5,733,900 | 3,545,024 | 10,953,000 |
| 1971 | 30,346,083 | 7,145,363 | 2,440,043 | 5,610,300 | 3,772,377 | 11,378,000 |
| 1972 | 32,207,666 | 6,879,753 | 2,618,131 | 5,564,300 | 4,218,482 | 11,927,000 |
| 1973 | 35,757,754 | 9,050,067 | 2,835,202 | 5,643,300 | 4,792,185 | 13,437,000 |
| 1974 | 41,252,870 | 10,901,352 | 3,013,440 | 5,964,800 | 5,458,278 | 15,915,000 |
| 1975 | 46,288,419 | 13,402,441 | 3,214,657 | 6,297,400 | 5,966,282 | 17,407,639 |
| 1976 | 51,068,946 | 15,949,720 | 3,368,747 | 6,726,000 | 6,296,286 | 18,728,193 |
| 1977[5] | 56,056,182 | 18,454,578 | 3,655,146 | 7,270,084 | 6,781,410 | 19,894,964 |

(1) Includes data for joint stock land banks and Federal Farm Mortgage Corporations. (2) Includes loans made directly by FmHA for farm ownership, soil and water loans to individuals, recreation loans to individuals, Indian tribe land acquisition, grazing associations, and irrigation drainage and soil conservation associations. Also includes loans for rural housing on farm tracts and labor housing. (3) Taken from Life Insurance Institute Tally sheet. (4) Estimated by ERS, USDA 1965-73 revised June, 1974. (5) Preliminary.

---

## Civilian Consumption of Major Food Commodities per Person

Source: Economics, Statistics, and Cooperatives Service, U.S. Agriculture Department

| Commodity[1] | 1960 | 1970 | 1977[2] | Commodity[1] | 1960 | 1970 | 1977[2] |
|---|---|---|---|---|---|---|---|
| **Meats** | 134.1 | 151.4 | 154.8 | Processed: | | | |
| Beef | 64.3 | 84.1 | 93.2 | Canned fruit | 22.6 | 23.3 | 19.9 |
| Veal | 5.2 | 2.4 | 3.2 | Canned juice | 13.0 | 14.6 | 15.6 |
| Lamb and mutton | 4.3 | 2.9 | 1.5 | Frozen (including juices) | 9.1 | 9.8 | 11.9 |
| Pork | 60.3 | 62.0 | 56.9 | Chilled citrus juices | 2.1 | 4.7 | 6.0 |
| **Fish** (edible weight) | 10.3 | 11.8 | 12.8 | Dried | 3.1 | 2.7 | 2.7 |
| **Poultry products:** | | | | **Vegetables:** | | | |
| Eggs | 42.4 | 39.5 | 34.5 | Fresh[3] | 96.0 | 91.0 | 93.2 |
| Chicken (ready-to-cook) | 27.8 | 40.5 | 44.9 | Canned (excluding potatoes and sweet potatoes) | 43.4 | 51.2 | 53.3 |
| Turkey (ready-to-cook) | 6.2 | 8.0 | 9.2 | Frozen (excluding potatoes) | 7.0 | 9.6 | 10.3 |
| **Dairy products:** | | | | Potatoes[4] | 105.0 | 115.3 | 120.6 |
| Cheese | 8.3 | 11.5 | 16.3 | Sweet potatoes[4] | 6.5 | 5.2 | 4.9 |
| Condensed and evaporated milk | 13.7 | 7.1 | 3.3 | **Grains:** | | | |
| Fluid milk and cream (product weight) | 321.0 | 296.0 | 289.4 | Wheat flour[5] | 118 | 110 | 108 |
| Ice cream (product weight) | 18.3 | 17.7 | 17.7 | Rice | 6.1 | 6.7 | 8.0 |
| **Fats and Oils**—Total fat content | 45.3 | 53.0 | 54.4 | **Other:** | | | |
| Butter (actual weight) | 7.5 | 5.3 | 4.4 | Coffee | 11.6 | 10.5 | 6.9 |
| Margarine (actual weight) | 9.4 | 11.0 | 11.6 | Tea | .6 | .7 | .9 |
| Lard | 7.6 | 4.7 | 3.4 | Cocoa | 2.9 | 3.1 | 2.7 |
| Shortening | 12.6 | 17.3 | 17.6 | Peanuts (shelled) | 4.9 | 5.9 | 6.4 |
| Other edible fats and oils | 11.5 | 18.2 | 21.6 | Dry edible beans | 7.3 | 5.9 | 6.0 |
| **Fruits:** | | | | Melons | 23.2 | 21.2 | 21.3 |
| Fresh | 90.0 | 79.1 | 80.3 | Sugar (refined) | 97.4 | 101.8 | 93.2 |
| Citrus | 32.5 | 27.9 | 24.4 | | | | |
| Noncitrus | 57.5 | 51.2 | 55.9 | | | | |

(1) Quantity in pounds, retail weight unless otherwise shown. Data on calendar year basis except for dried fruits, fresh citrus fruits, peanuts, and rice which are on a crop-year basis. (2) Preliminary. (3) Commercial production for sale as fresh produce. (4) Including fresh equivalent of processed. (5) White, whole wheat, and semolina flour including use in bakery products.

## Federal Food Program Costs

Source: Food and Nutrition Service, U.S. Agriculture Department (millions of dollars)

| Calendar year | Food stamps Total value | Bonus[1] | WIC[2] | Food distribution[3] Needy persons[4] | Schools | Institu- tions | Child nutrition School lunch | School bkfst. | Child care | Supp. food | Special milk | Total costs |
|---|---|---|---|---|---|---|---|---|---|---|---|---|
| 1971 | 3,105 | 1,699[1] | — | 331 | 296 | 26 | 647 | 22 | 14 | 20 | 92 | 3,147 |
| 1975 | 8,325 | 5,073[1] | 119 | 37 | 364 | 15 | 1,385 | 99 | 57 | 65 | 133 | 7,347 |
| 1976p | 8,613 | 5,262[1] | 177 | 41 | 407 | 16 | 1,543 | 113 | 94 | 140 | 150 | 7,943 |
| 1977p | 8,272 | 5,014 | 289 | 50 | 503 | 19 | 1,700 | 154 | 117 | 122 | 151 | 8,119 |
| 1978, 1st qtr. p | 2,137 | 1,348 | 92 | 13 | 194 | 5 | 537 | 54 | 37 | — | 41 | 2,321 |
| 2d qtr. p | 2,058 | 1,285 | 101 | 10 | 105 | 9 | 483 | 48 | 37 | 18 | 36 | 2,132 |

(1) Includes Food Certificate Program. (2) Special Supplemental Food Program for Women, Infants, and Children. (3) Cost of food delivered to state distribution centers. (4) Represents cost of the Needy Family Program, Supplemental Food Program, and the Nutrition Program for the Elderly.

## Food Stamps—Costs and Benefits

| Fiscal year | Average persons participating per month | Value per year Total purchase | Bonus | Avg. bonus per participant per month Current $ | 1967 $ |
|---|---|---|---|---|---|
| 1962 | 142,817 | $ 35,202,266 | $ 13,152,695 | 7.67 | 8.47 |
| 1965 | 424,652 | 85,471,989 | 32,505,096 | 6.38 | 6.75 |
| 1970 | 4,340,030 | 1,089,960,761 | 549,663,811 | 10.55 | 9.07 |
| 1974 | 12,861,526 | 4,727,450,579 | 2,718,296,427 | 17.61 | 11.87 |
| 1975 | 17,064,196 | 7,265,641,706 | 4,385,501,248 | 21.41 | 13.62 |
| 1976 | 18,548,715 | 8,700,208,987 | 5,326,505,192 | 23.93 | — |
| 1977p | 17,057,598 | 8,339,804,533 | 5,057,723,608 | 24.71 | — |
| 1978p | 16,135,015 | 8,284,629,025 | 5,152,634,946 | 26.61 | — |

(p) preliminary. The Food Stamp Program enables low-income families to buy more food of greater variety to improve their diets. If a household meets eligibility requirements it receives food stamps based on its net income and the number of people in the household. Major reform measures will go into effect after Jan. 1, 1979, to lower the net income eligibility standards to the official poverty level ($6,500 for a family of four for fiscal year 1978); change the allowable deductions; eliminate the food stamp purchase requirement; streamline administration; and reduce the potential for fraud or abuse. County and city welfare departments administer the program locally.

---

## Giant Trees of the U.S.

Source: The American Forestry Association

There are approximately 1,180 different species of trees native to the continental U.S., including a few imports that have become naturalized to the extent of reproducing themselves in the wild state.

The oldest living trees in the world are reputed to be the bristlecone pines, the majority of which are found growing on the arid crags of California's White Mts. Some of them are estimated to be more than 4,600 years old. The largest known bristlecone pine is the "Patriarch," believed to be 1,500 years old. The oldest known redwoods are about 3,500 years old.

Recognition as the National Champion of each species is determined by total mass of each tree, based on this formula: the circumference in inches as measured at a point 4 1/2 feet above the ground plus the total height of the tree, plus 1/4 of the average crown spread in feet. In case of a tie the Champion is determined on the basis of circumference. It is not possible, due to lack of space, to list all the 661 trees registered with the American Forestry Assn.

(Figure in parentheses is year of most recent measurement)

| Species | Height (Ft.) | Location |
|---|---|---|
| Acacia, Koa (1969) | 140 | Kau, Ha. |
| Ailanthus, Tree-of-Heaven (1972) | 60 | Long Island, N.Y. |
| Alder, European (1974) | 68 | Princeton, Ill. |
| Apple, Southern Crab (1976) | 46 | Williamsburg, Va. |
| Ash, Blue (1970) | 86 | Danville, Ky. |
| Aspen, Bigtooth (1972) | 93 | Walker, N.Y. |
| Bald Cypress, Common (1977) | 138 | Windsor, N.C. |
| Basswood, American (1971) | 115 | Grand Traverse Co. Mich. |
| Bayberry, Pacific (1972) | 38 | Siuslaw Natl. Forest, Ore. |
| Beech, American (1976) | 161 | Three Oaks, Mich. |
| Birch, River (1974) | 95 | Cumberland For., Va. |
| Blackbead, Catclaw (1976) | 88 | Sarasota, Fla. |
| Blackhaw, Rusty (1961) | 25 | nr. Washington, Ark. |
| Bladdernut, American (1972) | 36 | nr. Utica, Mich. |
| Boxelder (1976) | 110 | Lenawee Co., Mich. |
| Buckeye, Painted (1972) | 144 | Union County, Ga. |
| Buckthorn, Cascara (1977) | 37 | Seaside, Ore. |
| Buckwheat tree (1967) | 30 | nr. Crooked Creek, Fla. |
| Buffaloberry, Silver (1975) | 22 | Malheur Co., Ore. |
| Bumelia, Gum (1977) | 80 | Robertson Co., Tex. |
| Butternut (1973) | 102 | Portland, Ore. |
| Buttonbush, Common (1977) | 23 | nr. High Springs, Fla. |
| Button-Mangrove (1974) | 52 | Palm Beach, Fla. |
| Cajeput (1975) | 66 | Sarasota, Fla. |
| Camphor-tree (1977) | 72 | Hardee Co., Fla. |

| Species | Height (Ft.) | Location |
|---|---|---|
| Casuarina, Horsetail (1968) | 89 | Olowalo, Maui, Ha. |
| Catalpa, Northern (1972) | 94 | Lansing, Mich. |
| Cedar, Port-Orford (1972) | 219 | Siskiyou Natl. Forest, Ore. |
| Cercocarpus, Birchleaf (1972) | 34 | Central Point, Ore. |
| Cherry, Black (1972) | 114 | Lawrence, Mich. |
| Chestnut, American (1975) | 66 | Sherwood, Ore. |
| Chinaberry (1967) | 75 | Koahe, So. Kuona, Ha. |
| Chinkapin, Golden (1954) | 127 | nr. Annapolis, Cal. |
| Chokecherry, Common (1972) | 66 | Ada, Mich. |
| Coconut (1968) | 94 | Hilo, Ha. |
| Coffeetree, Kentucky (1976) | 110 | Van Buren Co., Mich. |
| Cottonwood, Black (1969) | 147 | Unionvalle, Ore. |
| Cypress, Monterey (1975) | 97 | Brookings, Ore. |
| Dahoon (1975) | 72 | Osceola For., Fla. |
| Desert Willow (1976) | 56 | Gila Co., Ariz. |
| Devil's-walkingstick (1976) | 51 | San Felasco Hammock, Fla. |
| Devilwood (1972) | 37 | Mayo, Fla. |
| Dogwood, Pacific (1975) | 50 | nr. Clatskanie, Ore. |
| Douglas Fir (1972) | 221 | Olympic Natl. Pk., Wash. |
| Doveplum (1965) | 45 | Miami, Fla. |
| Elder, Blackbead (1972) | 42 | nr. Prescott, Ore. |
| Elm, American (1974) | 92 | White Creek, N.Y. |
| False-Mastic (1975) | 70 | Lignumvitae Key, Fla. |
| Fig, Florida Strangler (1973) | 80 | Old Cutler Hammock, Fla. |
| Fir, Noble (1972) | 278 | Gifford Pinchot Natl. Forest, Wash. |

(continued)

| (continued) Species | Height (Ft.) | Location | Species | Height (Ft.) | Location |
|---|---|---|---|---|---|
| Franklinia (1973) | 38 | McLean, Va. | Peppertree (1973) | 47 | San Juan Capistrano, Cal. |
| Grapefruit (1972) | 38 | Ellenton, Fla. | Pinckneya (1972) | 21 | nr. Mt. Pleasant, Fla. |
| Gumbo-limbo (1973) | 50 | Homestead, Fla. | Pine, Ponderosa (1974) | 223 | Plumas, Cal. |
| Hackberry, Common (1972) | 118 | Allegany Co., Md. | Plum, American (1972) | 35 | Oakland Co., Mich. |
| Hawthorn (1967) | 50 | Glenview, Ill. | Poison Sumac (1972) | 20 | Robin's Island, N.Y. |
| Hemlock, Western (1972) | 164 | Olympic Natl. Pk., Wash. | Pondcypress (1972) | 135 | nr. Newton, Ga. |
| Hercules-club (1961) | 38 | Little Rock, Ark. | Poplar, Balsam (1976) | 128 | Champion, Mich. |
| Hickory, Pignut (1972) | 125 | nr. Brunswick, Ga. | Possumhaw (1976) | 30 | Congaree Swamp, S.C. |
| Holly, Tawnyberry (1973) | 55 | Homestead, Fla. | Redbay (1972) | 58 | Randolph Co., Ga. |
| Honeylocust, Thornless (1976) | 130 | Washtenaw Co., Mich. | Redwood, Coast (1972) | 362 | Humboldt Redwoods State Park, Cal. |
| Hophornbeam, Eastern (1976) | 73 | Traverse Co., Mich. | Royalpalm, Florida (1973) | 80 | Homestead, Fla. |
| Hoptree, Common (1972) | 31 | Ada, Mich. | Sassafras (1972) | 100 | Owensboro, Ky. |
| Hornbeam, American (1975) | 65 | Milton, N.Y. | Seagrape (1972) | 57 | Miami, Fla. |
| Joshua-tree (1967) | 32 | San Bernardino Natl. Forest, Cal. | Sequoia, Giant (1975) | 275 | Sequoia Natl. Pk., Cal. |
| Juniper, Western (1954) | 87 | Stanislaus Natl. Forest, Cal. | Serviceberry, Downy (1975) | 50 | New Philadelphia, Oh. |
| | | | Silk-oak (1972) | 78 | nr. La Belle, Fla. |
| Larch, Western (1972) | 177 | nr. Kootenai Natl. Forest, Mont. | Silktree (1971) | 41 | Gilmer, Tex. |
| | | | Silverbell, Two-wing (1971) | 55 | Tallahassee, Fla. |
| Laurelcherry, Carolina (1972) | 44 | Dellwood, Fla. | Smoketree, American (1974) | 47 | Lewiston, Ida. |
| Lebbek (1968) | 65 | Lahaina, Maui, Ha. | Soapberry, Western (1972) | 67 | Newton County, Tex. |
| Loblolly-Bay (1972) | 84 | Ocala Natl. Forest, Fla. | Sourwood (1972) | 118 | nr. Robbinsville, N.C. |
| Locust, Black (1974) | 96 | Dansville, N.Y. | Sparkleberry Tree (1977) | 30 | Pensacola, Fla. |
| Lysiloma, Bahama (1973) | 79 | Homestead, Fla. | Spruce, Sitka (1973) | 216 | Seaside, Ore. |
| Madrone, Pacific (1974) | 79 | Humboldt Co., Cal. | Sugarberry (1976) | 78 | Society Hill, S.C. |
| Magnolia, Cucumber tree (1974) | 92 | Bel Air, Md. | Sumac, Shining (1974) | 55 | Grenada Co., Miss. |
| Mangrove, Red (1975) | 75 | Everglades Natl. Pk., Fla. | Sweetleaf, Common (1972) | 55 | Tallahassee, Fla. |
| Maple, Red (1972) | 125 | nr. Armada, Mich. | Sycamore, Cal. (1945) | 116 | nr. Santa Barbara, Cal. |
| Mesquite, Velvet (1972) | 55 | Coronado Natl. Forest, Ariz. | Tamarack (1972) | 95 | Jay, Me. |
| Mountain-Ash, Showy (1972) | 58 | nr. Gould City, Mich. | Tamarisk, Five-Stamen (1972) | 37 | Albuquerque, N.M. |
| Mountain-Laurel (1972) | 20 | Chattahoochee Natl. Forest, Ga. | Tanoak (1969) | 100 | Kneeland, Cal. |
| | | | Tesota (1972) | 31 | nr. Quartzsite, Ariz. |
| Mulberry, White (1976) | 82 | Battle Creek, Mich. | Torreya, Cal. (1945) | 141 | nr. Mendocino, Cal. |
| Oak, California white (1973) | 120 | nr. Gridley, Cal. | Trifoliate-Orange (1968) | 26 | Harrisburg, Pa. |
| Oleander, Common (1963) | 22 | Phoenix, Ariz. | Tupelo, Black (1969) | 117 | Harrison Co., Tex. |
| Osage-Orange (1972) | 51 | Charlotte Co., Va. | (1969) | 139 | nr. Houston, Tex. |
| Palmetto, Cabbage (1972) | 90 | Highlands Hammock State Pk., Fla. | Wahoo, Eastern (1974) | 20 | Warrensburg, Mo. |
| | | | Walnut, Cal. (1973) | 116 | Santa Rosa, Cal. |
| Paloverde, Blue (1976) | 53 | Riverside Co., Cal. | Willow, Crack (1972) | 112 | nr. Utica, Mich. |
| Paulownia, Royal (1969) | 105 | Philadelphia, Pa. | Winterberry, Common (1971) | 40 | Wildwood, Fla. |
| Pawpaw, Blue (1972) | 41 | nr. Smith Mills, Ky. | Witch Hazel, Common (1976) | 43 | Muskegon, Mich. |
| Pear (1976) | 57 | Clawson, Mich. | Yaupon (1972) | 45 | nr. Devers, Tex. |
| Pecan (1972) | 124 | Mer Rouge, La. | Yellow-Poplar (1972) | 124 | Bedford, Va. |
| | | | Yellowwood (1967) | 58 | Morrisville, Pa. |
| | | | Yew, Pacific (1969) | 60 | nr. Mineral, Wash. |
| | | | Yucca, Aloe (1972) | 15 | Lakeland, Fla. |

---

# Giant Trees of Canada

**Source:** Native Trees of Canada by R.C. Hosie; Canadian Forestry Service, Dept. of Fisheries & Forestry

There are nearly 140 species of trees native to Canada on which information is easily available. A "native" tree is defined as a single-stemmed perennial woody plant growing to a height of more than 10 feet, and which is indigenous to Canada. Most of the "giant" trees in Canada are to be found in the forest regions. These regions reflect differences caused by terrain, soil, and climate. The 9 forest regions are: The Grassland, Boreal, Great Lakes-St. Lawrence, Columbia, Deciduous, Coast, Subalpine, Acadian, and Montane.

It is difficult to obtain precise records of single trees of outstanding heights. Given below are several common species of trees native to Canada showing the usual or normal height of the species. But many exceptions have been noted. For example, the Douglas Fir, whose average range in height is given at 150 to 200 ft. with diameters of up to 9 ft., occasionally may attain heights above 300 ft. and diameters of 15 ft. or more. The Sitka Spruce is also known to have reached heights of at least 280 ft., and the Western White Pine is recorded as having attained 200 ft.

| Species | Height (ft.) | Forest region | Species | Height (ft.) | Forest region |
|---|---|---|---|---|---|
| Alpine Fir | 65-100 | Subalpine; N. W. Boreal | Sitka Spruce | 125-175 | Coast |
| Amabilis Fir | 80-125 | Coast & coastal parts of Subalpine | Sugar Maple | 80-90 | Gt. Lakes-St. Lawrence |
| | | | Sycamore | Up to 150 | Deciduous |
| Balsam Poplar | 60-80 | Boreal, Great Lakes-St. Lawrence & Acadian | Western Hemlock | 120-160 | Coast & Columbia |
| Black Cottonwood | 80-125 | Throughout B.C. and western Alberta | Western Larch | 100-180 | Southern part of Columbia & Montane, B.C. |
| Black Maple | 80-90 | Ontario to Montreal Is. | Western Red Cedar | 150-200 | Coast & Columbia |
| Douglas Fir | 150-200 | Coast | Western White Pine | 90-110 | S. Coast & Columbia |
| Eastern Cottonwood | 75-100 | Gt. Lakes-St. Lawrence | White Birch | Med.-80 | Throughout Canada |
| Eastern White Pine | 100-175 | Through east Canada | White Elm | 60-80 | G. Lakes-St. Lawrence & Acadian |
| Engelmann Spruce | 100-120 | Southern Subalpine | | | |
| Grand Fir | 100-125 | S. Coast & Columbia | White Oak | Med.-100 | Southern Ontario |
| Mockernut Hickory | 75-90 | Deciduous | White Spruce | 80-120 | Boreal |
| Silver Maple | 80-90 | S.E. parts of G. Lakes-St. Lawrence | Yellow Cypress | 60-80 | Coast & in coastal parts of Subalpine |

# Food and Nutrition

Food contains proteins, carbohydrates, fats, water, vitamins and minerals. Nutrition is the way your body takes in and uses these ingredients to maintain proper functioning. If you aren't eating foods that your body needs, you suffer from poor nutrition and, sooner or later, your health will deteriorate.

## Protein

Proteins are composed of amino acids and are indispensable in the diet. They build, maintain, and repair the body. Best sources: eggs, milk, soybeans, nuts, fish, meat, poultry. No one of these foods will supply all the necessary proteins.

## Fats

Fats provide energy by furnishing calories to the body, and by carrying vitamins A, D, E, and K. They are the most concentrated source of energy in the diet. Best sources: butter, margarine, salad oils, nuts, cream, eggs, most cheeses, lard, meat.

## Carbohydrates

Carbohydrates provide energy for body function and activity by supplying immediate calories. The 3 forms of carbohydrates are sugars, starches, and cellulose. Best sources: wheats and cereals, legumes, nuts, potatoes (with skin), fruits, honey.

## Water

Water dissolves and transports other nutrients throughout the body aiding the process of digestion, absorption, circulation, and excretion. It also helps regulate body temperature. We get water from all foods.

## Vitamins

Vitamin A—promotes good eyesight and helps keep the skin and mucous membranes resistant to infection. Best sources: liver, carrots, sweet potatoes, kale, collard greens, turnips, whole milk.

Vitamin B1 (thiamine)—essential to the nervous system, heart, liver. Best Sources: meat, fish, poultry, wheat germ, brewers' yeast, brown rice, whole grain cereals.

Vitamin B2 (riboflavin)—an aid to healthy eyes. Best sources: liver, almonds, wheat germ, mushrooms, turnip greens, whole milk, milk products.

Vitamin B6 (pyridoxine)—important in the regulation of the central nervous system. Best sources: whole grains, meats, nuts, brewers' yeast.

Vitamin B12 (cobalamin)—necessary for the formation of red blood cells. Best sources: meat, fish, eggs, soybeans.

Niacin—maintains the health of skin, tongue, and digestive system. Best sources: poultry, peanuts, fish, organ meats, milk and milk products, eggs.

Other B vitamins are—biotin, choline, folic acid (folacin), inositol, PABA (para-aminobenzoic acid), and pantothenic acid.

Vitamin C (ascorbic acid)—maintains collagen, a protein necessary for the formation of skin, ligaments, and bones. It helps heal wounds and mend fractures, and aids in resisting some types of virus and bacterial infections. Best sources: citrus fruits and juices, turnips, broccoli, Brussels sprouts, potatoes and sweet potatoes, tomatoes, cabbage.

Vitamin D—important for bone development. Best sources: sunlight, fortified milk and milk products, fish, egg yolks, organ meats.

Vitamin E (tocopherol)—helps protect red blood cells. May aid the circulatory system and counteract the aging process. Best sources: wheat germ, whole grains, eggs, peanuts, organ meats, margarine, vegetable oils, green leafy vegetables.

Vitamin K—necessary for formation of prothrombin, which helps blood to clot. Best sources: green leafy vegetables, tomatoes, egg yolks, oats, wheat, rye.

## Minerals

Calcium—the most abundant mineral in the body, works with phosphorus in building and maintaining bones and teeth. Best sources: whole sesame seeds, cheese, milk and milk products, and blackstrap molasses.

Phosphorus—the 2nd most abundant mineral, performs more functions than any other mineral, and plays a part in nearly every chemical reaction in the body. Best source: wheat germ, brewers' yeast, powdered skim milk.

Iron—the 2d most essential trace element in the body, it is necessary for the formation of myoglobin, which transports oxygen to muscle tissue, and hemoglobin, which transports oxygen in the blood. Best sources: organ meats, molasses, beans, green leafy vegetables, and shellfish.

Other minerals—chromium, cobalt, copper, fluorine, iodine, magnesium, manganese, molybdenum, potassium, selenium, sodium, sulfur, and zinc.

---

## Recommended Daily Dietary Allowances

Source: Food and Nutrition Board, National Research Council

The allowances are amounts of nutrients recommended as adequate for maintenance of good nutrition in healthy persons in the U.S. Diets should be based on a variety of common foods in order to provide other nutrients for which human requirements have been less well defined.

| | Years From-up to | Weight (kg) | (lbs.) | Hgt. (in.) | Calories | Protein (grams) | Calcium (mg.) | Iron (mg.) | Vit A (I.U.) | Thiamin (mg.) | Riboflavin (mg.) | Niacin (mg.) | Ascorbic acid (mg.) |
|---|---|---|---|---|---|---|---|---|---|---|---|---|---|
| Infants . . . . . | 0.0-0.5 | 6 | 14 | 24 | kg × 117 | kg × 2.2 | 360 | 10 | 1,400 | 0.3 | 0.4 | 5 | 35 |
| | 0.5-1.0 | 9 | 20 | 28 | kg × 108 | kg × 2.0 | 540 | 15 | 2,000 | 0.5 | 0.6 | 8 | 35 |
| Children . . . . | 1-3 | 13 | 28 | 34 | 1,300 | 23 | 800 | 15 | 2,000 | 0.7 | 0.8 | 9 | 40 |
| | 4-6 | 20 | 44 | 44 | 1,800 | 30 | 800 | 10 | 2,500 | 0.9 | 1.1 | 12 | 40 |
| | 7-10 | 30 | 66 | 54 | 2,400 | 36 | 800 | 10 | 3,300 | 1.2 | 1.2 | 16 | 40 |
| Males . . . . . . | 11-14 | 44 | 97 | 63 | 2,800 | 44 | 1,200 | 18 | 5,000 | 1.4 | 1.5 | 18 | 45 |
| | 15-18 | 61 | 134 | 69 | 3,000 | 54 | 1,200 | 18 | 5,000 | 1.5 | 1.8 | 20 | 45 |
| | 19-22 | 67 | 147 | 69 | 3,000 | 54 | 800 | 10 | 5,000 | 1.5 | 1.8 | 20 | 45 |
| | 23-50 | 70 | 154 | 69 | 2,700 | 56 | 800 | 10 | 5,000 | 1.4 | 1.6 | 18 | 45 |
| | 51 + | 70 | 154 | 69 | 2,400 | 56 | 800 | 10 | 5,000 | 1.2 | 1.5 | 16 | 45 |
| Females . . . . | 11-14 | 44 | 97 | 62 | 2,400 | 44 | 1,200 | 18 | 4,000 | 1.2 | 1.3 | 16 | 45 |
| | 15-18 | 54 | 119 | 65 | 2,100 | 48 | 1,200 | 18 | 4,000 | 1.1 | 1.4 | 14 | 45 |
| | 19-22 | 58 | 128 | 65 | 2,100 | 46 | 800 | 18 | 4,000 | 1.1 | 1.4 | 14 | 45 |
| | 23-50 | 58 | 128 | 65 | 2,000 | 46 | 800 | 18 | 4,000 | 1.0 | 1.2 | 13 | 45 |
| | 51 + | 58 | 128 | 65 | 1,800 | 46 | 800 | 18 | 4,000 | 1.0 | 1.1 | 12 | 45 |
| Pregnant . . | . . . | . . . | . . . | . . . | +300 | +30 | 1,200 | 18 | 5,000 | +0.3 | +0.3 | +2 | 60 |
| Lactating . . | . . . | . . . | . . . | . . . | +500 | +20 | 1,200 | 18 | 6,000 | +0.3 | +0.5 | +4 | 80 |

## Nutritive Value of Food (Calories, Proteins, etc.)

Source: Home and Garden Bulletin No. 72 (revised April 1977), U.S. Agriculture Department
Available for $1.05 from Supt. of Documents, U. S. Government Printing Office, Washington, DC 20402

| Food | Measure | Food Energy (calories) | Protein (grams) | Fat (grams) | Saturated fats (grams) | Carbohydrate (grams) | Calcium (milligrams) | Iron (milligrams) | Vitamin A (I.U.) | Thiamin (milligrams) | Riboflavin (milligrams) | Niacin (milligrams) | Ascorbic acid (milligrams) |
|---|---|---|---|---|---|---|---|---|---|---|---|---|---|
| **Dairy products** | | | | | | | | | | | | | |
| Cheese, cheddar. | 1 oz. | 115 | 7 | 9 | 6.1 | T | 204 | .2 | 300 | .01 | .11 | T | 0 |
| Cheese, cottage, small curd. | 1 cup | 220 | 26 | 9 | 6.0 | 6 | 126 | .3 | 340 | .04 | .34 | .3 | 0 |
| Cheese, cream. | 1 oz. | 100 | 2 | 10 | 6.2 | 1 | 23 | .3 | 400 | T | .06 | T | 0 |
| Cheese, Swiss. | 1 oz. | 105 | 8 | 8 | 5.0 | 1 | 272 | T | 240 | .01 | .10 | T | 0 |
| Cheese, pasteurized process spread, American. | 1 oz. | 82 | 5 | 6 | 3.8 | 2 | 159 | .1 | 220 | .01 | .12 | T | 0 |
| Half-and-Half. | 1 tbsp. | 20 | T | 2 | 1.1 | 1 | 16 | T | 70 | .01 | .02 | T | T |
| Cream, sour. | 1 tbsp. | 25 | T | 3 | 1.6 | 1 | 14 | T | 90 | T | .02 | T | T |
| Milk, whole. | 1 cup | 150 | 8 | 8 | 5.1 | 11 | 291 | .1 | 310 | .09 | .40 | .2 | 2 |
| Milk, nonfat (skim). | 1 cup | 85 | 8 | T | .3 | 12 | 302 | .1 | 500 | .09 | .37 | .2 | 2 |
| Buttermilk. | 1 cup | 100 | 8 | 2 | 1.3 | 12 | 285 | .1 | 80 | .08 | .38 | .1 | 2 |
| Milkshake, chocolate | 10.6 oz. | 355 | 9 | 8 | 5.0 | 63 | 396 | .9 | 260 | .14 | .67 | .4 | 0 |
| Ice Cream, hardened. | 1 cup | 270 | 5 | 14 | 8.9 | 32 | 176 | .1 | 540 | .05 | .33 | .1 | 1 |
| Sherbet. | 1 cup | 270 | 2 | 4 | 2.4 | 59 | 103 | .3 | 190 | .03 | .09 | .1 | 4 |
| Yogurt, fruit-flavored. | 8 oz. | 230 | 10 | 3 | 1.8 | 42 | 343 | .2 | 120 | .08 | .40 | .2 | 1 |
| **Eggs** | | | | | | | | | | | | | |
| Fried in butter. | 1 | 85 | 5 | 6 | 2.4 | 1 | 26 | .9 | 290 | .03 | .13 | T | 0 |
| Hard-cooked. | 1 | 80 | 6 | 6 | 1.7 | 1 | 28 | 1.0 | 260 | .04 | .14 | T | 0 |
| Scrambled in butter. | 1 | 95 | 6 | 7 | 2.8 | 1 | 47 | .9 | 310 | .04 | .16 | T | 0 |
| **Fats & oils** | | | | | | | | | | | | | |
| Butter. | 1 tbsp. | 100 | T | 12 | 7.2 | T | 3 | T | 430 | T | T | T | 0 |
| Margarine. | 1 tbsp. | 100 | T | 12 | 2.1 | T | 3 | T | 470 | T | T | T | 0 |
| Salad dressing, blue cheese. | 1 tbsp. | 75 | 1 | 8 | 1.6 | 1 | 12 | T | 30 | T | .02 | T | T |
| Salad dressing, French. | 1 tbsp. | 65 | T | 6 | 1.1 | 3 | 2 | .1 | - | - | - | - | - |
| Salad dressing, Italian. | 1 tbsp. | 85 | T | 9 | 1.6 | 1 | 2 | T | - | T | T | T | - |
| Mayonnaise. | 1 tbsp. | 100 | T | 11 | 2.0 | T | 3 | .1 | 40 | T | .01 | T | - |
| **Meat, poultry, fish** | | | | | | | | | | | | | |
| Bluefish, baked with butter or margarine. | 3 oz. | 135 | 22 | 4 | - | 0 | 25 | 0.6 | 40 | .09 | .08 | 1.6 | - |
| Clams, raw, meat only. | 3 oz. | 65 | 11 | 1 | - | 2 | 59 | 5.2 | 90 | .08 | .15 | 1.1 | 8 |
| Crabmeat, white or king, canned. | 1 cup | 135 | 24 | 3 | .6 | 1 | 61 | 1.1 | - | .11 | .11 | 2.6 | - |
| Fish sticks, breaded, cooked, frozen. | 1 oz. | 50 | 5 | 3 | - | 2 | 3 | .1 | 0 | .01 | .02 | .5 | - |
| Salmon, pink, canned. | 3 oz. | 120 | 17 | 5 | .9 | 0 | 167 | .7 | 60 | .03 | .16 | 6.8 | - |
| Sardines, Atlantic, canned in oil. | 3 oz. | 175 | 20 | 9 | 3.0 | 0 | 372 | 2.5 | 190 | .02 | .17 | 4.6 | - |
| Shrimp, French fried. | 3 oz. | 190 | 17 | 9 | 2.3 | 9 | 61 | 1.7 | - | .03 | .07 | 2.3 | - |
| Tuna, canned in oil. | 3 oz. | 170 | 24 | 7 | 1.7 | 0 | 7 | 1.6 | 70 | .04 | .10 | 10.1 | - |
| Bacon, broiled or fried crisp. | 2 slices | 85 | .4 | 8 | 2.5 | 1 | 2 | .5 | 0 | .08 | .05 | .8 | - |
| Ground beef, broiled, 10% fat. | 3 oz. | 185 | 23 | 10 | 4.0 | 0 | 10 | 3.0 | 20 | .08 | .20 | 5.1 | - |
| Roast beef, relatively lean. | 3 oz. | 165 | 25 | 7 | 2.8 | 0 | 11 | 3.2 | 10 | .06 | .19 | 4.5 | - |
| Beef steak, lean and fat. | 3 oz. | 330 | 20 | 27 | 11.3 | 0 | 9 | 2.5 | 50 | .05 | .15 | 4.0 | - |
| Beef & vegetable stew. | 1 cup | 220 | 16 | 11 | 4.9 | 15 | 29 | 2.9 | 2,400 | .15 | .17 | 4.7 | 17 |
| Lamb, chop, lean and fat. | 3.1 oz. | 360 | 18 | 32 | 14.8 | 0 | 8 | 1.0 | - | .11 | .19 | 4.1 | - |
| Ham, light cure, lean and fat. | 3 oz. | 245 | 18 | 19 | 6.8 | 0 | 8 | 2.2 | 0 | .40 | .15 | 3.1 | - |
| Pork, chop, lean and fat. | 2.7 oz. | 305 | 19 | 25 | 8.9 | 0 | 9 | 2.7 | 0 | .75 | .22 | 4.5 | - |
| Bologna. | 1 slice | 85 | 3 | 8 | 3.0 | T | 2 | .5 | - | .05 | .06 | .7 | - |
| Frankfurter, cooked. | 1 | 170 | 7 | 15 | 5.6 | 1 | 3 | .8 | - | .08 | .11 | 1.4 | - |
| Sausage, pork link, cooked. | 1 link | 60 | 2 | 6 | 2.1 | T | 1 | .3 | 0 | .10 | .04 | .5 | - |
| Veal, cutlet, braised or boiled. | 3 oz. | 185 | 23 | 9 | 4.0 | 0 | 9 | 2.7 | - | .06 | .21 | 4.6 | - |
| Chicken, drumstick, fried, bones removed | 1.3 oz. | 90 | 12 | 4 | 1.1 | T | 6 | .9 | 50 | .03 | .15 | 2.7 | - |
| Chicken, half broiler, broiled, bones removed | 6.2 oz. | 240 | 42 | 7 | 2.2 | 0 | 16 | 3.0 | 160 | .09 | .34 | 15.5 | - |
| Chicken a la king. | 1 cup | 470 | 27 | 34 | 12.7 | 12 | 127 | 2.5 | 1,130 | .10 | .42 | 5.4 | 12 |
| Chicken potpie, baked, 1/3 of 9 in. diam. pie. | 1 piece | 545 | 23 | 31 | 11.3 | 42 | 70 | 3.0 | 3,090 | .34 | .31 | 5.5 | 5 |
| **Fruits & products** | | | | | | | | | | | | | |
| Apple, raw, 2-3/4 in. diam. | 1 | 80 | T | 1 | - | 20 | 10 | .4 | 120 | .04 | .03 | .1 | 6 |
| Applejuice. | 1 cup | 120 | T | T | - | 30 | 15 | 1.5 | - | .02 | .05 | .2 | 2 |
| Applesauce, canned, sweetened. | 1 cup | 230 | 1 | T | - | 61 | 10 | 1.3 | 100 | .05 | .03 | .1 | 3 |
| Banana, raw. | 1 | 100 | 1 | T | - | 26 | 10 | .8 | 230 | .06 | .07 | .8 | 12 |
| Cherries, sweet, raw. | 10 | 45 | 1 | T | - | 12 | 15 | .3 | 70 | .03 | .04 | .3 | 7 |
| Fruit cocktail, canned, in heavy syrup | 1 cup | 195 | 1 | T | - | 50 | 23 | 1.0 | 360 | .05 | .03 | 1.0 | 5 |
| Grapefruit, raw, medium, white. | 1/2 | 45 | 1 | T | - | 12 | 19 | .5 | 10 | .05 | .02 | .2 | 44 |
| Grapes, Thompson seedless. | 10 | 35 | T | T | - | 9 | 6 | .2 | 50 | .03 | .02 | .2 | 2 |
| Lemonade, frozen, diluted. | 1 cup | 105 | T | T | - | 28 | 2 | .1 | 10 | .01 | .02 | .2 | 17 |
| Cantaloupe, 5-in. diam. | 1/2 | 80 | 2 | T | - | 20 | 38 | 1.1 | 9,240 | .11 | .08 | 1.6 | 90 |
| Orange, 2-5/8 in. diam. | 1 | 65 | 1 | T | - | 16 | 54 | .5 | 260 | .13 | .05 | .5 | 66 |
| Orange juice, frozen, diluted. | 1 cup | 120 | 2 | T | - | 29 | 25 | .2 | 540 | .23 | .03 | .9 | 120 |
| Peach, raw, 2-1/2 in. diam. | 1 | 40 | 1 | T | - | 10 | 9 | .5 | 1,330 | .02 | .05 | 1.0 | 7 |
| Peaches, canned in syrup. | 1 cup | 200 | 1 | T | - | 51 | 10 | .8 | 1,100 | .03 | .05 | 1.5 | 8 |
| Pear, raw, Bartlett, 2-1/2 in. diam. | 1 | 100 | 1 | 1 | - | 25 | 13 | .5 | 30 | .03 | .07 | .2 | 7 |
| Pineapple, heavy syrup pack, crushed, chunks. | 1 cup | 190 | 1 | T | - | 49 | 28 | .8 | 130 | .20 | .05 | .5 | 18 |
| Raisins, seedless. | 1 cup | 420 | 4 | T | - | 112 | 90 | 5.1 | 30 | .16 | .12 | .7 | 1 |
| Strawberries, whole. | 1 cup | 55 | 1 | 1 | - | 13 | 31 | 1.5 | 90 | .04 | .10 | .9 | 88 |
| Watermelon, 4 by 8 in. wedge. | 1 wedge | 110 | 2 | 1 | - | 27 | 30 | 2.1 | 2,510 | .13 | .13 | .9 | 30 |
| **Grain products** | | | | | | | | | | | | | |
| Bagel, egg. | 1 | 165 | 6 | 2 | .5 | 28 | 9 | 1.2 | 30 | .14 | .10 | 1.2 | 0 |
| Biscuit, 2 in. diam., from home recipe. | 1 | 105 | 2 | 5 | 1.2 | 13 | 34 | .4 | T | .08 | .08 | .7 | T |
| Bread, raisin. | 1 slice | 65 | 2 | 1 | .2 | 13 | 18 | .6 | T | .09 | .06 | .6 | T |
| Bread, white, enriched, soft-crumb. | 1 slice | 70 | 2 | 1 | .2 | 13 | 21 | .6 | T | .10 | .06 | .8 | T |
| Bread, whole wheat, soft-crumb. | 1 slice | 65 | 3 | 1 | .1 | 14 | 24 | .8 | T | .09 | .03 | .8 | T |
| Oatmeal or rolled oats. | 1 cup | 130 | 5 | 2 | .4 | 23 | 22 | 1.4 | 0 | .19 | .05 | .2 | 0 |
| Bran flakes (40% bran), added sugar, salt, iron, vitamins | 1 cup | 105 | 4 | 1 | - | 28 | 19 | 12.4 | 1,650 | .41 | .49 | 4.1 | 12 |
| Corn flakes, added sugar, salt, iron, vitamins. | 1 cup | 95 | 2 | T | - | 21 | T | 0.6 | 1,180 | .29 | .35 | 2.9 | 9 |
| Rice, puffed, added iron, thiamin, niacin. | 1 cup | 60 | 1 | T | - | 13 | 3 | .3 | 0 | .07 | .01 | .7 | 0 |

(continued)

*(continued)*

| Food | Measure | Food Energy (calories) | Protein (grams) | Fat (grams) | Saturated fats (grams) | Carbohydrate (grams) | Calcium (milligrams) | Iron (milligrams) | Vitamin A (I.U.) | Thiamin (milligrams) | Riboflavin (milligrams) | Niacin (milligrams) | Ascorbic acid (milligrams) |
|---|---|---|---|---|---|---|---|---|---|---|---|---|---|
| Wheat, shredded, plain, 1 biscuit or 1/2 cup | 1 serving | 90 | 2 | 1 | - | 20 | 11 | .9 | 0 | .06 | .03 | 1.1 | 0 |
| Cake, angel food, 1/12 of cake | 1 | 135 | 3 | T | - | 32 | 50 | .2 | 0 | .03 | .08 | .3 | 0 |
| Coffeecake, 1/6 cake | 1 | 230 | 5 | 7 | 2.0 | 38 | 44 | 1.2 | 120 | .14 | .15 | 1.3 | T |
| Cupcake, 2-1/2 in. diam., with chocolate icing | 1 | 130 | 2 | 5 | 2.0 | 21 | 47 | .4 | 60 | .05 | .06 | .4 | T |
| Cake, devil's food with chocolate icing, 1/16 of 2 layer cake | 1 | 235 | 3 | 8 | 3.1 | 40 | 41 | 1.0 | 100 | .07 | .10 | .6 | T |
| Boston cream pie with custard filling, 1/12 of cake | 1 | 210 | 3 | 6 | 1.9 | 34 | 46 | .7 | 140 | .09 | .11 | .8 | T |
| Fruitcake, dark, 1/30 of loaf | 1 | 55 | 1 | 2 | .5 | 9 | 11 | .4 | 20 | .02 | .02 | .2 | T |
| Cake, pound, 1/17 of loaf | 1 | 160 | 2 | 10 | 2.5 | 16 | 6 | .5 | 80 | .05 | .06 | .4 | 0 |
| Brownies, with nuts, from commercial recipe | 1 | 85 | 1 | 4 | .9 | 13 | 9 | .4 | 20 | .03 | .02 | .2 | T |
| Cookies, chocolate chip, from home recipe | 4 | 205 | 2 | 12 | 3.5 | 24 | 14 | .8 | 40 | .06 | .06 | .5 | T |
| Vanilla wafers | 10 | 185 | 2 | 6 | - | 30 | 16 | .6 | 50 | .10 | .09 | .8 | 0 |
| Crackers, graham | 2 | 55 | 1 | 1 | .3 | 10 | 6 | .5 | 0 | .02 | .08 | .5 | 0 |
| Crackers, saltines | 4 | 50 | 1 | 1 | .3 | 8 | 2 | .5 | 0 | .05 | .05 | .4 | 0 |
| Danish pastry, round piece | 1 | 275 | 5 | 15 | 4.7 | 30 | 33 | 1.2 | 200 | .18 | .19 | 1.7 | T |
| Doughnut, cake type | 1 | 100 | 1 | 5 | 1.2 | 13 | 10 | .4 | 20 | .05 | .05 | .4 | T |
| Macaroni and cheese, from home recipe | 1 cup | 430 | 17 | 22 | 9.8 | 40 | 362 | 1.8 | 860 | .20 | .40 | 1.8 | T |
| Muffin, corn | 1 | 125 | 3 | 4 | 1.2 | 19 | 42 | .7 | 120 | .10 | .10 | .7 | T |
| Noodles, enriched, cooked | 1 cup | 200 | 7 | 2 | - | 37 | 16 | 1.4 | 110 | .22 | .13 | 1.9 | 0 |
| Pancake, plain, from home recipe | 1 | 60 | 2 | 2 | .5 | 9 | 27 | .4 | 30 | .06 | .07 | .5 | T |
| Pie, apple, 1/7 of pie | 1 | 345 | 3 | 15 | 3.9 | 51 | 11 | .9 | 40 | .15 | .11 | 1.3 | 2 |
| Pie, banana cream, 1/7 of pie | 1 | 285 | 6 | 12 | 3.8 | 40 | 86 | 1.0 | 330 | .11 | .22 | 1.0 | 1 |
| Pie, cherry, 1/7 of pie | 1 | 350 | 4 | 15 | 4.0 | 52 | 19 | .9 | 590 | .16 | .12 | 1.4 | T |
| Pie, lemon meringue, 1/7 of pie | 1 | 305 | 4 | 12 | 3.7 | 45 | 17 | 1.0 | 200 | .09 | .12 | .7 | 4 |
| Pie, pecan, 1/7 of pie | 1 | 495 | 6 | 27 | 4.0 | 61 | 55 | 3.7 | 190 | .26 | .14 | 1.0 | T |
| Pie, pumpkin, 1/7 of pie | 1 | 275 | 5 | 15 | 5.4 | 32 | 66 | 1.0 | 3,210 | .11 | .18 | 1.0 | T |
| Pizza, cheese, 1/8 of 12 in. diam. pie | 1 | 145 | 6 | 4 | 1.7 | 22 | 86 | 1.1 | 230 | .16 | .18 | 1.6 | 4 |
| Popcorn, popped, plain | 1 cup | 25 | 1 | T | - | 5 | 1 | .2 | - | - | .01 | .1 | 0 |
| Pretzels, stick | 10 | 10 | T | T | - | 2 | 1 | T | 0 | .01 | .01 | .1 | 0 |
| Rice, white, enriched, instant, cooked | 1 cup | 180 | 4 | T | T | 40 | 5 | 1.3 | 0 | .21 | ** | 1.7 | 0 |
| Rolls, enriched, brown & serve | 1 | 85 | 2 | 2 | .4 | 14 | 20 | .5 | T | .10 | .06 | .9 | T |
| Rolls, frankfurter & hamburger | 1 | 120 | 3 | 2 | .5 | 21 | 30 | .8 | T | .16 | .10 | 1.3 | T |
| Spaghetti with meat balls & tomato sauce, from home recipe | 1 cup | 330 | 19 | 12 | 3.3 | 39 | 124 | 3.7 | 1,590 | .25 | .30 | 4.0 | 22 |
| **Legumes, nuts, seeds** | | | | | | | | | | | | | |
| Beans, Great Northern, cooked | 1 cup | 210 | 14 | 1 | - | 38 | 90 | 4.9 | 0 | .25 | .13 | 1.3 | 0 |
| Peanuts, roasted in oil, salted | 1 cup | 840 | 37 | 72 | 13.7 | 27 | 107 | 3.0 | - | .46 | .19 | 24.8 | 0 |
| Peanut butter | 1 tbsp. | 95 | 4 | 8 | 1.5 | 3 | 9 | .3 | - | .02 | .02 | 2.4 | 0 |
| **Sugars & sweets** | | | | | | | | | | | | | |
| Candy, caramels | 1 oz. | 115 | 1 | 3 | 1.6 | 22 | 42 | .4 | T | .01 | .05 | .1 | T |
| Candy, milk chocolate | 1 oz. | 145 | 2 | 9 | 5.5 | 16 | 65 | .3 | 80 | .02 | .10 | .1 | T |
| Fudge, chocolate | 1 oz. | 115 | 1 | 3 | 1.3 | 21 | 22 | .3 | T | .01 | .03 | .1 | T |
| Candy, hard | 1 oz. | 110 | 0 | T | - | 28 | 6 | .5 | 0 | 0 | 0 | 0 | 0 |
| Honey | 1 tbsp. | 65 | T | 0 | 0 | 17 | 1 | .1 | 0 | T | .01 | .1 | T |
| Jams & Preserves | 1 tbsp. | 55 | T | T | - | 14 | 4 | .2 | T | T | .01 | T | T |
| **Vegetables** | | | | | | | | | | | | | |
| Asparagus, canned, spears | 4 spears | 15 | 2 | T | - | 3 | 15 | 1.5 | 640 | .05 | .08 | .6 | 12 |
| Beans, lima, thick-seeded | 1 cup | 170 | 10 | 1 | - | 32 | 34 | 2.9 | 390 | .12 | .09 | 1.7 | 29 |
| Beans, green, from frozen, cuts | 1 cup | 35 | 2 | T | - | 8 | 54 | .9 | 780 | .09 | .12 | .5 | 7 |
| Beets, canned, diced or sliced | 1 cup | 65 | 2 | T | - | 15 | 32 | 1.2 | 30 | .02 | .05 | .2 | 5 |
| Broccoli, cooked | 1 stalk | 45 | 6 | 1 | - | 8 | 158 | 1.4 | 4,500 | .16 | .36 | 1.4 | 162 |
| Cabbage, raw, coarsely shredded or sliced | 1 cup | 15 | 1 | T | - | 4 | 34 | .3 | 90 | .04 | .04 | .02 | 33 |
| Carrots, raw, 7-1/2 by 1-1/8 in. | 1 | 30 | 1 | T | - | 7 | 27 | .5 | 7,930 | .04 | .04 | .4 | 6 |
| Cauliflower, raw | 1 cup | 31 | 3 | T | - | 6 | 29 | 1.3 | 70 | .13 | .12 | .8 | 90 |
| Celery, raw | 1 stalk | 5 | T | T | - | 2 | 16 | .1 | 110 | .01 | .01 | .1 | 4 |
| Corn, sweet, cooked | 1 ear | 70 | 2 | 1 | - | 16 | 2 | .5 | 310 | .09 | .08 | 1.1 | 7 |
| Corn, cream style | 1 cup | 210 | 5 | 2 | - | 51 | 8 | 1.5 | 840 | .08 | .13 | 2.6 | 13 |
| Cucumber, with peel | 6-8 slices | 5 | T | T | - | 1 | 7 | .3 | 70 | .01 | .01 | .1 | 3 |
| Lettuce, iceberg, chopped | 1 cup | 5 | T | T | - | 2 | 11 | .3 | 180 | .03 | .03 | .2 | 3 |
| Mushrooms, raw | 1 cup | 20 | 2 | T | - | 3 | 4 | .6 | T | .07 | .32 | 2.9 | 2 |
| Peas, frozen, cooked | 1 cup | 110 | 8 | T | - | 19 | 30 | 3.0 | 960 | .43 | .14 | 2.7 | 21 |
| Potatoes, baked, peeled | 1 | 145 | 4 | T | - | 33 | 14 | 1.1 | T | .15 | .07 | 2.7 | 31 |
| Potatoes, mashed, milk added | 1 cup | 135 | 4 | 2 | .7 | 27 | 50 | .8 | 40 | .17 | .11 | 2.1 | 21 |
| Potato chips | 10 | 115 | 1 | 8 | 2.1 | 10 | 8 | .4 | T | .04 | .01 | 1.0 | 3 |
| Potato salad | 1 cup | 250 | 7 | 7 | 2.0 | 41 | 80 | 1.5 | 350 | .20 | .18 | 2.8 | 28 |
| Sauerkraut, canned | 1 cup | 40 | 2 | T | - | 9 | 85 | 1.2 | 120 | .07 | .09 | .5 | 33 |
| Spinach, chopped, from frozen | 1 cup | 45 | 6 | 1 | - | 8 | 232 | 4.3 | 16,200 | .14 | .31 | .8 | 39 |
| Squash, summer, cooked | 1 cup | 30 | 2 | T | - | 7 | 53 | .8 | 820 | .11 | .17 | 1.7 | 21 |
| Sweet potatoes, baked in skin, peeled | 1 | 160 | 2 | 1 | - | 37 | 46 | 1.0 | 9,230 | .10 | .08 | .8 | 25 |
| Tomatoes, raw | 1 | 25 | 1 | T | - | 6 | 16 | .6 | 1,110 | .07 | .05 | .9 | 28 |
| Tomato catsup | 1 tbsp. | 15 | T | T | - | 4 | 3 | .1 | 210 | .01 | .01 | .2 | 2 |
| Tomato juice | 1 cup | 45 | 2 | T | - | 10 | 17 | 2.2 | 1,940 | .12 | .07 | 1.9 | 39 |
| **Miscellaneous** | | | | | | | | | | | | | |
| Beer | 12 fl. oz. | 150 | 1 | 0 | 0 | 14 | 18 | T | - | - | .11 | 2.2 | - |
| Gin, rum, vodka, whisky, 86 proof | 1-1/2 fl. oz. | 105 | - | 0 | 0 | T | - | - | - | - | - | - | - |
| Wine, table | 3-1/2 fl. oz. | 85 | T | 0 | 0 | 4 | 9 | .4 | - | T | .01 | .1 | - |
| Cola-type beverage | 12 fl. oz. | 145 | 0 | 0 | 0 | 37 | - | - | 0 | 0 | 0 | 0 | 0 |
| Ginger ale | 12 fl. oz. | 115 | 0 | 0 | 0 | 29 | - | - | 0 | 0 | 0 | 0 | 0 |
| Gelatin dessert | 1 cup | 140 | 4 | 0 | 0 | 34 | - | - | - | - | - | - | - |
| Mustard, prepared | 1 tsp. | 5 | T | T | - | T | 4 | .1 | - | - | - | - | - |
| Olives, pickled, green | 4 medium | 15 | T | 2 | .2 | T | 8 | .2 | 40 | - | - | - | - |
| Pickles, dill, whole | 1 | 5 | T | T | - | 1 | 17 | .7 | 70 | T | .01 | T | 4 |
| Popsicle, 3 fl. oz. | 1 | 70 | 0 | 0 | 0 | 18 | 0 | T | 0 | 0 | 0 | 0 | 0 |
| Soup, cream of chicken, prepared with milk | 1 cup | 180 | 7 | 10 | 4.2 | 15 | 172 | .5 | 610 | .05 | .27 | .7 | 2 |
| Soup, cream of mushroom, prepared with milk | 1 cup | 215 | 7 | 14 | 5.4 | 16 | 191 | .5 | 250 | .05 | .34 | .7 | 1 |
| Soup, tomato, prepared with water | 1 cup | 90 | 2 | 3 | .5 | 16 | 15 | .7 | 1,000 | .05 | .05 | 1.2 | 12 |

T — Indicates trace * — Varies by brand

# ENVIRONMENT

## Estimated Total Pollution Control Expenditures

Source: Council on Environmental Quality (billions of 1976 dollars). Does not include research, conservation, and enhancement programs.

| Pollutant/source | 1976 | | | 1985 | | | Cumulative 1976-85 | | |
|---|---|---|---|---|---|---|---|---|---|
| | O&M[1] | Capital costs[2] | Total annual costs[3] | O&M[1] | Capital costs[2] | Total annual costs[3] | O&M[1] | Capital costs[2] | Total costs[3] |
| Air pollution | | | | | | | | | |
| Public | 0.1 | 0.1 | 0.2 | 0.6 | 0.2 | 0.8 | 4.3 | 1.9 | 6.2 |
| Private | | | | | | | | | |
| Mobile | 3.4 | 2.0 | 5.4 | 0.8 | 7.5 | 8.3 | 18.4 | 53.8 | 72.2 |
| Industrial | 1.9 | 2.2 | 4.1 | 4.3 | 5.1 | 9.4 | 30.5 | 36.6 | 67.1 |
| Utilities | 1.2 | 1.2 | 2.4 | 4.0 | 4.0 | 8.0 | 24.9 | 24.9 | 49.8 |
| **Subtotal** | **6.6** | **5.5** | **12.1** | **9.7** | **16.8** | **26.5** | **78.1** | **117.2** | **195.3** |
| Water pollution | | | | | | | | | |
| Public | 2.6 | 7.7 | 10.3 | 6.4 | 15.3 | 21.7 | 44.3 | 120.4 | 164.7 |
| Private | | | | | | | | | |
| Industrial | 1.9 | 1.6 | 3.5 | 7.5 | 5.9 | 13.4 | 45.2 | 36.5 | 81.7 |
| Utilities | .8 | .5 | 1.3 | 1.5 | .9 | 2.4 | 11.8 | 7.1 | 18.9 |
| **Subtotal** | **5.3** | **9.8** | **15.1** | **15.4** | **22.1** | **37.5** | **101.3** | **164.0** | **265.3** |
| Radiation | | | | | | | | | |
| Nuclear powerplant | (4) | (4) | (4) | (4) | (4) | 0.1 | 0.1 | 0.3 | 0.4 |
| Solid wastes | | | | | | | | | |
| Public | 2.0 | 0.3 | 2.3 | 2.2 | 0.8 | 3.0 | 21.2 | 4.9 | 26.1 |
| Private | 3.8 | 0.9 | 4.7 | 5.0 | 1.3 | 6.3 | 47.0 | 9.9 | 56.9 |
| **Subtotal** | **5.8** | **1.2** | **7.0** | **7.2** | **2.1** | **9.3** | **68.2** | **14.8** | **83.0** |
| Land reclamation | | | | | | | | | |
| Surface mining | 0.1 | NA | 0.1 | 0.7 | NA | 0.7 | 5.4 | NA | 5.4 |
| Toxic substances | NA | NA | NA | 0.2 | NA | 0.2 | 1.1 | NA | 1.1 |
| Noise | NA | NA | NA | 0.4 | NA | 0.4 | 1.8 | 2.0 | 3.8 |
| **Total** | **17.8** | **16.5** | **34.3** | **33.6** | **41.4** | **75.1** | **256.0** | **298.3** | **554.3** |

(1) Operating and maintenance costs. (2) Interest and depreciation. (3) O&M plus capital costs. (4) Less than 0.05. (5) Incremental and total costs are assumed to be the same. (NA) Not available.

---

## Investment for Pollution Control by U.S. Industries

Source: Bureau of Economic Analysis, U.S. Commerce Department
(millions of dollars)

| | 1977 Pollution abatement | | | | | 1978[1] Pollution abatement | | | | |
|---|---|---|---|---|---|---|---|---|---|---|
| | Air | Water | Solid waste | Total | Percent of investment[2] | Air | Water | Solid waste | Total | Percent of investment[2] |
| **All industries[3]** | 3,693 | 2,785 | 461 | 6,939 | 5.06 | 3,651 | 2,912 | 591 | 7,154 | 4.74 |
| **Manufacturing** | 2,032 | 1,993 | 258 | 4,282 | 7.02 | 1,930 | 1,898 | 331 | 4,159 | 6.18 |
| Durable goods | 941 | 636 | 91 | 1,668 | 5.90 | 953 | 674 | 107 | 1,734 | 5.49 |
| Primary metals | 607 | 295 | 26 | 927 | 15.73 | 578 | 282 | 28 | 888 | 14.41 |
| Blast furnaces, steel works | 282 | 182 | 5 | 470 | 16.70 | 330 | 192 | 12 | 534 | 19.45 |
| Nonferrous metals | 262 | 103 | 19 | 383 | 17.05 | 196 | 81 | 14 | 291 | 11.63 |
| Electrical machinery | 30 | 65 | 15 | 111 | 3.37 | 40 | 72 | 16 | 128 | 3.44 |
| Machinery, except electrical | 51 | 49 | 5 | 104 | 1.78 | 48 | 65 | 10 | 123 | 1.82 |
| Transportation equipment | 58 | 74 | 31 | 163 | 3.09 | 88 | 113 | 36 | 236 | 3.96 |
| Motor vehicles | 49 | 63 | 30 | 142 | 3.53 | 76 | 102 | 31 | 209 | 4.66 |
| Aircraft | 9 | 11 | 1 | 21 | 2.09 | 11 | 11 | 4 | 26 | 2.10 |
| Stone, clay, and glass | 107 | 39 | 4 | 149 | 7.31 | 114 | 48 | 8 | 170 | 7.30 |
| Other durables | 88 | 116 | 10 | 213 | 3.61 | 86 | 93 | 9 | 189 | 2.85 |
| Nondurable goods | 1,091 | 1,357 | 167 | 2,615 | 7.98 | 977 | 1,224 | 224 | 2,425 | 6.78 |
| Food including beverage | 71 | 96 | 8 | 176 | 4.24 | 78 | 114 | 22 | 214 | 4.66 |
| Textiles | 11 | 23 | 1 | 35 | 3.75 | 11 | 20 | 7 | 37 | 3.53 |
| Paper | 188 | 256 | 23 | 468 | 13.78 | 132 | 192 | 26 | 349 | 9.59 |
| Chemicals | 249 | 414 | 38 | 701 | 10.16 | 256 | 376 | 51 | 682 | 9.24 |
| Petroleum | 531 | 546 | 90 | 1,167 | 8.23 | 458 | 500 | 116 | 1,074 | 7.00 |
| Rubber | 31 | 12 | 4 | 47 | 3.26 | 30 | 16 | 1 | 48 | 2.96 |
| Other nondurables | 9 | 9 | 2 | 21 | 1.20 | 12 | 7 | 2 | 21 | 0.97 |
| **Nonmanufacturing** | 1,661 | 792 | 204 | 2,657 | 3.50 | 1,721 | 1,014 | 260 | 2,995 | 3.59 |
| Mining | 38 | 32 | 27 | 97 | 2.18 | 59 | 54 | 47 | 161 | 3.06 |
| Railroad | 4 | 23 | 2 | 28 | 0.97 | 1 | 44 | 1 | 46 | 1.38 |
| Air transportation | 12 | 1 | 1 | 14 | 0.83 | 14 | 4 | 1 | 19 | 0.88 |
| Other transportation | 11 | 10 | 2 | 23 | 0.95 | 4 | 12 | 1 | 17 | 0.90 |
| Public utilities | 1,525 | 654 | 121 | 2,300 | 8.80 | 1,571 | 833 | 151 | 2,556 | 8.73 |
| Electric | 1,514 | 636 | 121 | 2,271 | 10.44 | 1,557 | 807 | 151 | 2,515 | 10.37 |
| Gas and other | 11 | 18 | 1 | 30 | 0.68 | 14 | 26 | (5) | 40 | 0.80 |
| Communication, commercial and other[4] | 73 | 72 | 51 | 195 | 0.51 | 72 | 67 | 59 | 198 | 0.48 |

(1) Planned (2) Pollution control as a percent of total plant and equipment investment. (3) Excludes agricultural business; real estate operators; medical, legal, educational, and cultural services; and nonprofit organizations. (4) Includes trade, service, construction, finance, and insurance. (5) Less than $500,000.

# Environmental Quality Index

**Source:** National Wildlife Federation.
Adapted from the Feb.-Mar., 1978 issue of *National Wildlife* magazine.

In 1969, the National Wildlife Federation began to record an index of environmental quality which measures progress or decline in 7 environmental areas. The index represents the judgment of environmental protection experts and advocates influenced by very high standards of environmental quality.

**Wildlife:** The year was marked by the worst weather in a century and a Congress that hindered at least as much as it helped. The gains: Congress gave $169.3 million to the U.S. Fish & Wildlife Service; a new U.S. law required reclamation of strip-mined land; laws governing endangered species and water quality halted questionable projects in Tennessee, Maine and North Dakota; the Bureau of Land Management reduced livestock overgrazing and restricted fences. But a fierce winter and a dry spring brought heavy losses among birds and fish; wildlife lost water rights to developers and drainers. And Congress spent $10.3 billion on public works projects.

**Air:** Some 4,000 deaths and 4 million sick days were caused last year by auto emissions alone, but Congress allowed car makers a fourth cleanup delay—until 1982—and permitted violations of healthful sulfur dioxide levels. Also, Congress gave power plants until 1982 to comply with cleanup deadlines, despite a study revealing that as many as 21,000 people east of the Mississippi die prematurely each year because of power plant pollution. EPA successes: the requirement that heavily polluted areas permit new industries only if additional pollution is offset by reductions elsewhere, and the ban on fluorocarbons in aerosol products.

**Minerals:** In a watershed year for energy and minerals, the U.S. seemed ready to move toward a national energy program; energy efficiency generated corporate concern; federal funding for research in solar and geothermal energy was increased; companies tested new techniques to use waste products as fuel; homeowners insulated; the Alaska pipeline opened. However, mineral imports rose again; domestic oil and natural gas discoveries stayed low; and the Interstate Commerce Commission kept freight rates for scrap iron 2 to 3 times higher than for virgin materials.

**Water:** The good news—the U.S. got its first national drinking water standard; the bad—evidence of toxic contamination increased. Most industrial polluters met their cleanup deadline; at least 50 rivers were improved dramatically; and industrial waste dumped at sea declined. Less encouraging: only 4,150 of 12,500 cities met the deadline for installing secondary treatment facilities, and the largest source of water pollution—urban and agricultural runoff —remained uncontrolled.

**Forests:** The housing construction resurgence meant that a timber famine predicted for 2020 could come sooner. Conservationists worked toward new harvesting methods and new products using wood wastes; new computerized techniques and better coordination in forest fire fighting; biodegradable chemicals and viruses for use against gypsy and tussock moths. Also, tax breaks and other incentives to increase yields of the small private woodlots that make up more than half the U.S. woodlands were in the works. And the new Forest Service national advisory group earmarked $27 million for habitat improvement, and began to determine which of 60 million undeveloped acres could be included in the Wilderness Preservation System.

**Soil:** The loss of soil to erosion continued to be the main problem, but there were a couple of checks: Crop surpluses may encourage farmers to take land out of production, and rising fuel costs encourages them to use soil-saving minimum tillage programs. The second problem remained runoff from farmland, carrying toxic chemicals into most waterways, and the third, the loss of farmland to urban development—in the U.S., an average of 1 million acres per year. A positive development: 42 states now have laws designed to save soil.

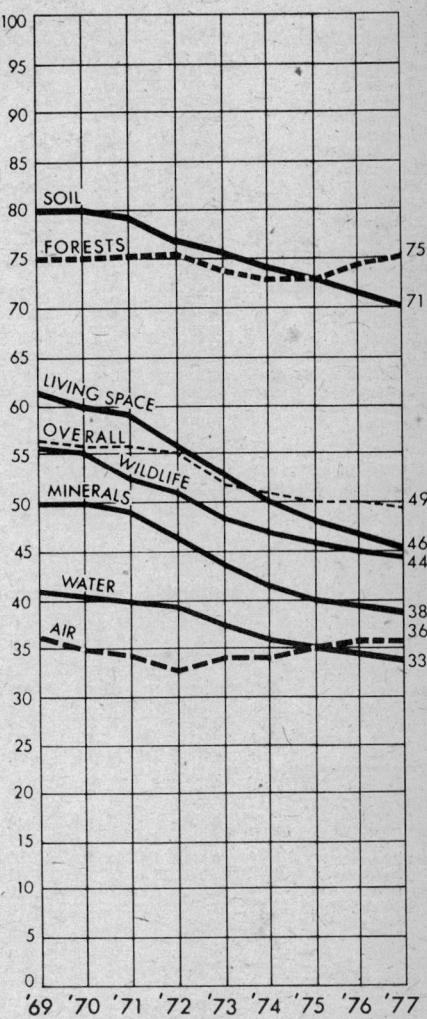

**Living space:** On the plus side, the Land and Water Conservation Fund Act was amended to provide 50% more funds for purchasing parks, wildlife and recreation areas; in California, the town of Petaluma reported that its first 5-year growth management program was a success; in Maryland, Montgomery County's high court upheld limits on growth; in New York, the Suffolk County Farmlands Preservation Program saved more than 200 Long Island acres; EPA geared up to implement the Resource Conservation and Recovery Act of 1976. Disappointments: further degradation of cities and more construction in flood plains; continued overdevelopment in coastal areas:

## U.S. Forest Land by State and Region

Source: Forest Service, U.S. Agriculture Department, 1970.

| State or region | Land area (1,000 acres) | Area forested | Percent forested | State or region | Land area (1,000 acres) | Area forested | Percent forested |
|---|---|---|---|---|---|---|---|
| Connecticut | 3,116 | 2,186 | 70 | Arkansas | 33,324 | 18,277 | 55 |
| Maine | 19,797 | 17,748 | 90 | Florida | 35,179 | 17,932 | 51 |
| Massachusetts | 5,013 | 3,520 | 70 | Georgia | 37,295 | 25,545 | 69 |
| New Hampshire | 5,781 | 5,131 | 89 | Louisiana | 28,867 | 15,380 | 53 |
| Rhode Island | 671 | 433 | 65 | Mississippi | 30,290 | 16,913 | 56 |
| Vermont | 5,935 | 4,391 | 74 | North Carolina | 31,367 | 20,613 | 66 |
| **New England** | **40,314** | **33,410** | **83** | Oklahoma | 44,149 | 9,340 | 21 |
| Delaware | 1,268 | 391 | 31 | South Carolina | 19,366 | 12,493 | 65 |
| Maryland | 6,369 | 2,960 | 47 | Tennessee | 26,474 | 13,136 | 50 |
| New Jersey | 4,820 | 2,463 | 51 | Texas | 168,300 | 24,091 | 14 |
| New York | 30,636 | 17,377 | 57 | Virginia | 25,496 | 16,389 | 64 |
| Pennsylvania | 28,816 | 17,832 | 62 | **South** | **512,791** | **211,884** | **41** |
| West Virginia | 15,413 | 12,172 | 79 | Alaska | 365,481 | 119,051 | 33 |
| **Mid Atlantic** | **87,324** | **53,196** | **61** | California | 100,091 | 42,408 | 42 |
| Michigan | 36,492 | 19,273 | 53 | Hawaii | 4,106 | 1,974 | 48 |
| Minnesota | 50,745 | 18,984 | 37 | Oregon | 61,574 | 30,404 | 49 |
| North Dakota | 44,339 | 421 | 1 | Washington | 42,665 | 23,098 | 54 |
| South Dakota (east) | 41,727 | 334 | 1 | **Pacific Coast** | **573,917** | **216,935** | **38** |
| Wisconsin | 34,858 | 14,945 | 43 | Arizona | 72,688 | 18,583 | 26 |
| **Lake States** | **208,162** | **53,959** | **26** | Colorado | 66,485 | 22,534 | 34 |
| Illinois | 35,761 | 3,789 | 11 | Idaho | 52,933 | 21,591 | 41 |
| Indiana | 23,161 | 3,908 | 17 | Montana | 93,248 | 22,777 | 24 |
| Iowa | 35,867 | 2,455 | 7 | Nevada | 70,264 | 7,660 | 11 |
| Kansas | 52,515 | 1,344 | 3 | New Mexico | 77,766 | 18,313 | 24 |
| Kentucky | 25,504 | 11,968 | 47 | South Dakota (west) | 6,878 | 1,399 | 20 |
| Missouri | 44,189 | 14,919 | 34 | Utah | 52,697 | 15,288 | 29 |
| Nebraska | 48,974 | 1,045 | 2 | Wyoming | 62,342 | 10,085 | 16 |
| Ohio | 26,251 | 6,498 | 25 | **Rocky Mountain** | **555,315** | **138,234** | **25** |
| **Central** | **292,225** | **45,928** | **16** | | | | |
| Alabama | 32,678 | 21,770 | 67 | **Total U.S.** | **2,270,050** | **¹753,549** | **33** |

(1) Of this total, 499,697,000 acres are of commercial quality (136 million acres are government owned); 17,246,000 acres are productive but reserved; 2,281,000 acres are deferred for possible reserve status; and 233,891,000 acres are unproductive or awaiting survey.

## Major U.S. and Canadian Public Zoological Parks

Source: Ronald T. Reuther, Past President, American Association of Zoological Parks and Aquariums. Figures are for 1978; budget, metro population, and attendance are in millions. (e) estimate

| Zoo | Budget | Metro pop. | Atten-dance | Acres | Species | Major Attractions |
|---|---|---|---|---|---|---|
| San Diego | $14.3 | 1.6 | 3.3 | 128 | 813 | Bus tours, primates, walk-through bird cages. |
| Bronx (N.Y.C.) | 12.0 | 17.3 | 2.2 | 252 | 640 | World of Darkness, World of Birds, Wild Asia. |
| Brookfield (Chicago) | 8.2 | 7.8 | 1.4 | 200 | 630 | Porpoise show, tropical world, baboon island. |
| Toronto | 7.9 | 2.8 | 1.0 | 710 | 390 | Zoogeographic biodomes, monorail. |
| National (Washington, D.C.) | 7.0 | 3.1 | 3.0 e | 165 | 452 | Giant pandas, flight cage, lions & tigers. |
| San Diego (Wild Animal Park) | 6.4 | 1.6 | 1.1 | 1800 | 225 | 5 1/2 mile monorail, Nairobi Village, bird show. |
| Detroit | 4.7 | 4.5 | 1.1 | 122 | 487 | Penguinarium, great ape house. |
| Milwaukee | 4.1 | 1.4 | 1.3 | 180 | 504 | Zoogeographic design, bird house, aquarium. |
| Philadelphia | 4.0 | 5.3 | 1.1 | 42 | 494 | Reptiles, African plains, great apes, monorail. |
| St. Louis | 3.6 | 2.3 | 2.0 e | 83 | 641 | Cat country, aquatic house. |
| Los Angeles | 3.1 + | 8.9 | 1.5 | 113 | 536 | Zoogeographic design, hoof animals, birds. |
| Cincinnati | 2.3 | 1.5 | 0.7 | 62 | 629 | Walk-through cat exhibit, great apes, aquarium. |
| Calgary | 1.8 | 0.5 | 0.7 | 204 | 307 | Children's zoo, aquatic house, dinosaurs. |
| Buffalo | 1.8 | 1.4 | 0.4 | 23.5 | 318 | Children's zoo, giraffe house. |
| Cleveland | 1.7 | 2.4 | 0.5 | 125 | 302 | Children's farm, pachyderm building, hoofed animals. |
| Oklahoma City | 1.6 | 0.8 | 0.5 | 150 | 439 | Hoofed animals, carnivores, birds of prey. |
| Baltimore | 1.5 | 2.1 | 0.4 | 142 | 313 | Pachyderm bldg., children's zoo. |
| Lincoln Park (Chicago) | 1.5 + | 7.8 | 4.0 e | 35 | 537 | Small mammal house, great ape house, sea lions. |
| Arizona-Sonora Desert Museum (Tucson) | 1.5 | 0.5 | 0.5 | 186 | 192 | Plants, animals, desert geology. |
| Denver | 1.5 | 1.3 | 0.9 | 76 | 398 | Walk-through bird house, primates, hoofed animals, cats. |
| Pittsburgh | 1.4 | 2.1 | 0.5 | 65 | 374 | Underground zoo, aquazoo, children's zoo. |
| San Antonio | 1.4 | 0.9 | 0.9 | 50 | 711 | Hoofed animals, great apes. |
| San Francisco | 1.4 + | 4.8 | 0.9 | 124 | 299 | Great apes, monkey island, bears. |
| Dallas | 1.3 | 2.7 | 0.6 | 50 | 761 | Birds and reptiles, hoofed animals, primates, pachyderms. |
| Houston | 1.3 + | 2.4 | 2.0 e | 43 | 528 | Small mammals, reptiles, great apes, bird house. |
| Phoenix | 1.3 | 1.4 | 0.7 | 125 | 295 | Safari train, Arizona wildlife, children's zoo. |
| Columbus | 1.2 | 1.1 | 0.4 | 92 | 778 | Reptiles, great apes. |

# Mammals: Orders and Major Families

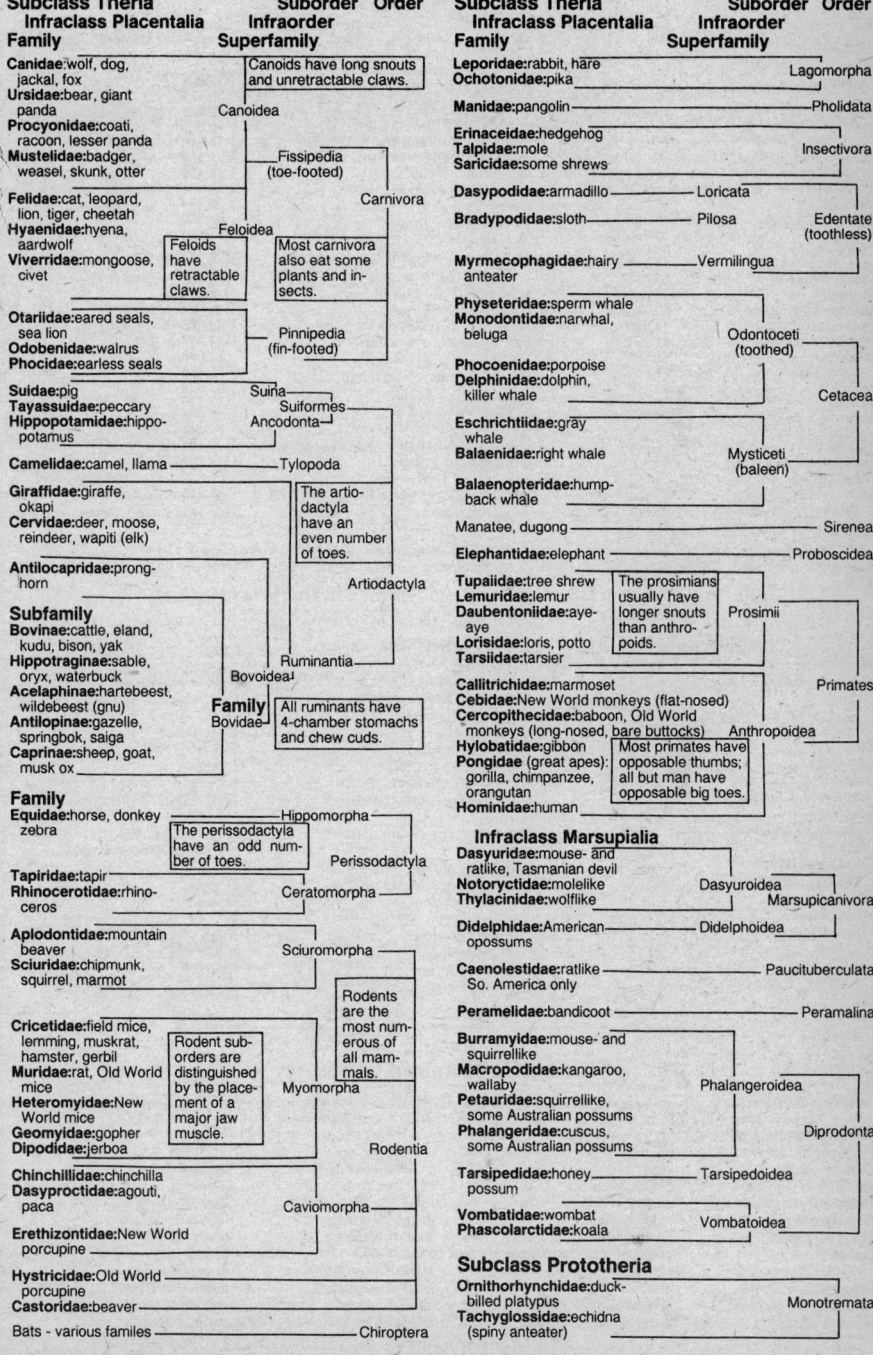

**Subclass Theria**
**Infraclass Placentalia**
Family | Suborder Order Infraorder Superfamily

**Canidae:**wolf, dog, jackal, fox
**Ursidae:**bear, giant panda
**Procyonidae:**coati, racoon, lesser panda
**Mustelidae:**badger, weasel, skunk, otter

Canoids have long snouts and unretractable claws.

Canoidea

Fissipedia (toe-footed)

**Felidae:**cat, leopard, lion, tiger, cheetah
**Hyaenidae:**hyena, aardwolf
**Viverridae:**mongoose, civet

Feloidea

Feloids have retractable claws.

Most carnivora also eat some plants and insects.

Carnivora

**Otariidae:**eared seals, sea lion
**Odobenidae:**walrus
**Phocidae:**earless seals

Pinnipedia (fin-footed)

**Suidae:**pig
**Tayassuidae:**peccary
**Hippopotamidae:**hippopotamus

Suina
Suiformes
Ancodonta

**Camelidae:**camel, llama — Tylopoda

**Giraffidae:**giraffe, okapi
**Cervidae:**deer, moose, reindeer, wapiti (elk)

The artiodactyla have an even number of toes.

**Antilocapridae:**pronghorn

Artiodactyla

## Subfamily
**Bovinae:**cattle, eland, kudu, bison, yak
**Hippotraginae:**sable, oryx, waterbuck
**Acelaphinae:**hartebeest, wildebeest (gnu)
**Antilopinae:**gazelle, springbok, saiga
**Caprinae:**sheep, goat, musk ox

Ruminantia

Bovoidea

## Family
**Bovidae**

All ruminants have 4-chamber stomachs and chew cuds.

## Family
**Equidae:**horse, donkey, zebra

Hippomorpha

The perissodactyla have an odd number of toes.

Perissodactyla

**Tapiridae:**tapir
**Rhinocerotidae:**rhinoceros

Ceratomorpha

**Aplodontidae:**mountain beaver
**Sciuridae:**chipmunk, squirrel, marmot

Sciuromorpha

Rodents are the most numerous of all mammals.

**Cricetidae:**field mice, lemming, muskrat, hamster, gerbil
**Muridae:**rat, Old World mice
**Heteromyidae:**New World mice
**Geomyidae:**gopher
**Dipodidae:**jerboa

Rodent suborders are distinguished by the placement of a major jaw muscle.

Myomorpha

Rodentia

**Chinchillidae:**chinchilla
**Dasyproctidae:**agouti, paca

Caviomorpha

**Erethizontidae:**New World porcupine

**Hystricidae:**Old World porcupine
**Castoridae:**beaver

Bats - various families — Chiroptera

---

**Subclass Theria**
**Infraclass Placentalia**
Family | Suborder Order Infraorder Superfamily

**Leporidae:**rabbit, hare
**Ochotonidae:**pika

Lagomorpha

**Manidae:**pangolin — Pholidata

**Erinaceidae:**hedgehog
**Talpidae:**mole
**Saricidae:**some shrews

Insectivora

**Dasypodidae:**armadillo — Loricata

**Bradypodidae:**sloth — Pilosa

Edentate (toothless)

**Myrmecophagidae:**hairy anteater — Vermilingua

**Physeteridae:**sperm whale
**Monodontidae:**narwhal, beluga

Odontoceti (toothed)

**Phocoenidae:**porpoise
**Delphinidae:**dolphin, killer whale

Cetacea

**Eschrichtiidae:**gray whale
**Balaenidae:**right whale

Mysticeti (baleen)

**Balaenopteridae:**humpback whale

Manatee, dugong — Sirenea

**Elephantidae:**elephant — Proboscidea

**Tupaiidae:**tree shrew
**Lemuridae:**lemur
**Daubentoniidae:**aye-aye
**Lorisidae:**loris, potto
**Tarsiidae:**tarsier

The prosimians usually have longer snouts than anthropoids.

Prosimii

**Callitrichidae:**marmoset
**Cebidae:**New World monkeys (flat-nosed)
**Cercopithecidae:**baboon, Old World monkeys (long-nosed, bare buttocks)
**Hylobatidae:**gibbon
**Pongidae** (great apes): gorilla, chimpanzee, orangutan
**Hominidae:**human

Anthropoidea

Most primates have opposable thumbs; all but man have opposable big toes.

Primates

### Infraclass Marsupialia
**Dasyuridae:**mouse- and ratlike, Tasmanian devil
**Notoryctidae:**molelike
**Thylacinidae:**wolflike

Dasyuroidea

Marsupicanivora

**Didelphidae:**American opossums — Didelphoidea

**Caenolestidae:**ratlike So. America only — Paucituberculata

**Peramelidae:**bandicoot — Peramalina

**Burramyidae:**mouse- and squirrellike
**Macropodidae:**kangaroo, wallaby
**Petauridae:**squirrellike, some Australian possums
**Phalangeridae:**cuscus, some Australian possums

Phalangeroidea

Diprodonta

**Tarsipedidae:**honey possum — Tarsipedoidea

**Vombatidae:**wombat
**Phascolarctidae:**koala

Vombatoidea

### Subclass Prototheria
**Ornithorhynchidae:**duck-billed platypus
**Tachyglossidae:**echidna (spiny anteater)

Monotremata

## Some Endangered Species in North America

Source: U.S. Fish and Wildlife Service, U.S. Interior Department

| Common name | Scientific name | Range |
|---|---|---|
| **Mammals** | | |
| Wood bison | Bison bison athabascae | Canada (Alberta) |
| Black-footed ferret | Mustela nigripes | U.S., Canada |
| Northern kit fox | Vulpus velox hebes | Canada |
| West Indian (Florida) manatee | Trichechus manatus | Caribbean (So. Amer.) |
| Sonoran pronghorn | Antilocapra americana sonoriensis | U.S. (Ariz.), Mexico |
| Hawaiian monk seal | Monachus schauinslandi | U.S. (Hawaii) |
| Eastern timber wolf | Canis lupus lycaon | U.S. (Minn., Mich.) |
| Northern Rocky Mountain wolf | Canis lupus irremotus | U.S. (Wy., Mont.) |
| Red wolf | Canis rufus | U.S. (Tex., La.) |
| Eastern cougar | Felis concolor cougar | U.S. |
| **Birds** | | |
| Bald eagle | Haliaeetus leucocephalus | U.S. (most states) |
| Masked bobwhite (quail) | Colinus virginianus ridgwayi | U.S. (Ariz., N.M.) Mexico |
| California condor | Gymnogyps californianus | U.S. (Cal.) |
| Whooping crane | Grus americana | U.S., Canada |
| Eskimo curlew | Numenius borealis | Canada to Argentina |
| American peregrine falcon | Falco peregrinus anatum | Canada to Mexico |
| Arctic peregrine falcon | Falco peregrinus tundrius | Canada to Mexico |
| Aleutian Canada goose | Branta canadensis leucopareia | U.S., Japan |
| Brown pelican | Pelecanus occidentalis | U.S. to South America |
| Attwater's greater prairie chicken | Tympanuchus cupido attwateri | U.S. (Tex.) |
| Bachman's warbler (wood) | Vermivora bachmanii | U.S., Cuba |
| Kirtland's warbler (wood) | Dendroica Kirtlandii | U.S., Bahamas |
| Ivory-billed woodpecker | Campephilus principalis | U.S., Cuba |
| **Reptiles** | | |
| American alligator | Alligator mississippiensis | U.S. (Southeast) |
| American crocodile | Crocodylus acutus | U.S. (Fla.) to So. Amer. |

## Some Other Endangered Species in the World

Source: U.S. Fish and Wildlife Service, U.S. Interior Department

| Common name | Scientific name | Range |
|---|---|---|
| **Mammals** | | |
| Asian wild ass | Equus hemionus | Iran to Mongolia |
| Dugong | Dugong dugon | East Africa to Okinawa |
| Slender-horned (Rhim) gazelle | Gazella leptoceros | North Africa |
| Gorilla | Gorilla gorilla | Central and West Africa |
| Orangutan | Pongo pygmaeus | Indonesia, Malaysia, Brunei |
| Great Indian rhinoceros | Rhinoceros unicornus | India, Nepal |
| Javan rhinoceros | Rhinoceros sondaicus | Indonesia, Burma, Thailand |
| Sumatran rhinoceros | Didermocerus sumatrensis | Bangladesh to Vietnam to Indonesia |
| Northern white rhinoceros | Ceratotherium simum cottoni | Sudan, Zaire, Uganda, Central African Empire |
| Blue whale | Balaenoptera musculus | Oceanic |
| Humpback whale | Megaptera novaeangliae | Oceanic |
| Sperm whale | Physeter catodon | Oceanic |
| **Birds** | | |
| Great Indian bustard | Choriotis nigriceps | India, Pakistan |
| Japanese crane | Grus japonensis | Japan, China, Korea, USSR |
| Chinese egret | Egretta eulophotes | China, Korea |
| Japanese crested ibis | Nipponia nippon | Japan, China, Korea, USSR |

## A Collection of Animal Collectives

The English language boasts an abundance of names to describe groups of things, particularly pairs or aggregations of animals. Some of these words have fallen into comparative disuse, but many of them are still in service, helping to enrich the vocabularies of those who like their language to be precise, who tire of hearing a group referred to as "a bunch of," or who enjoy the sound of words that aren't overworked.

| | | | |
|---|---|---|---|
| **band** of gorillas | **clowder** of cats | **exaltation** of larks | **husk** of hares |
| **bed** of clams, oysters | **clutch** of chicks | **flight** of birds | **kindle** or **kendle** of kittens |
| **bevy** of quail, swans | **clutter** of cats | **flock** of sheep, geese | **knot** of toads |
| **brace** of ducks | **colony** of ants | **gaggle** of geese | **leap** of leopards |
| **brood** of chicks | **congregation** of plovers | **gam** of whales | **leash** of greyhounds, foxes |
| **cast** of hawks | **covey** of quail, partridge | **gang** of elks | **litter** of pigs |
| **cete** of badgers | **cry** of hounds | **grist** of bees | **mob** of kangaroos |
| **charm** of goldfinches | **down** of hares | **herd** of elephants | **murder** of crows |
| **chattering** of choughs | **drift** of swine | **hive** of bees | **muster** of peacocks |
| **cloud** of gnats | **drove** of cattle, sheep | **horde** of gnats | **mute** of hounds |

| | | |
|---|---|---|
| **nest** of vipers | **school** of fish | **sounder** of boars, swine |
| **nest, nide** of pheasants | **sedge** or **siege** of cranes | **span** of mules |
| **pack** of hounds, wolves | **shoal** of fish, pilchards | **spring** of teals |
| **pair** of horses | **skein** of geese | **swarm** of bees |
| **pod** of whales, seals | **skulk** of foxes | **team** of ducks, horses |
| **pride** of lions | **sleuth** of bears | **tribe** or **trip** of goats |

| |
|---|
| **troop** of kangaroos, monkeys |
| **volery** of birds |
| **watch** of nightingales |
| **wing** of plovers |
| **yoke** of oxen |

## Young of Animals Have Special Names

The young of many animals, birds and fish have come to be called by special names. A young eel, for example, is an elver. Many young animals, of course, are often referred to simply as infants, babies, younglets, or younglings.

**bunny:** rabbit.
**calf:** cattle, elephant, antelope, rhino, hippo, whale, etc.
**cheeper:** grouse, partridge, quail.
**chick, chicken:** fowl.
**cockerel:** rooster.
**codling, sprag:** codfish.
**colt:** horse (male).
**cub:** lion, bear, shark, fox, etc.
**cygnet:** swan.
**duckling:** duck.
**eaglet:** eagle.
**elver:** eel.
**eyas:** hawk, others.
**fawn:** deer.

**filly:** horse (female).
**fingerling:** fish generally.
**flapper:** wild fowl.
**fledgling:** birds generally.
**foal:** horse, zebra, others.
**fry:** fish generally.
**gosling:** goose.
**heifer:** cow.
**joey:** kangaroo, others.
**kid:** goat.
**kit:** fox, beaver, rabbit, cat.
**kitten, kitty, catling:** cats, other fur-bearers.
**lamb, lambkin, cosset, hog:** sheep.
**leveret:** hare.

**nestling:** birds generally.
**owlet:** owl.
**parr, smolt, grilse:** salmon.
**piglet, shoat, farrow, suckling:** pig.
**polliwog, tadpole:** frog.
**poult:** turkey.
**pullet:** hen.
**pup:** dog, seal, sea lion, fox.
**puss, pussy:** cat.
**spike, blinker, tinker:** mackerel.
**squab:** pigeon.
**squeaker:** pigeon, others.
**whelp:** dog, tiger, beasts of prey.
**yearling:** cattle, sheep, horse, etc.

## Speeds of Animals

Source: Natural History magazine, March 1974.
Copyright © The American Museum of Natural History, 1974.

| Animal | Mph | Animal | Mph | Animal | Mph |
|---|---|---|---|---|---|
| Cheetah | 70 | Mongolian wild ass | 40 | Human | 27.89 |
| Pronghorn antelope | 61 | Greyhound | 39.35 | Elephant | 25 |
| Wildebeest | 50 | Whippet | 35.50 | Black mamba snake | 20 |
| Lion | 50 | Rabbit (domestic) | 35 | Six-lined race runner | 18 |
| Thomson's gazelle | 50 | Mule deer | 35 | Wild turkey | 15 |
| Quarterhorse | 47.5 | Jackal | 35 | Squirrel | 12 |
| Elk | 45 | Reindeer | 32 | Pig (domestic) | 11 |
| Cape hunting dog | 45 | Giraffe | 32 | Chicken | 9 |
| Coyote | 43 | White-tailed deer | 30 | Spider (Tegenaria atrica) | 1.17 |
| Gray fox | 42 | Wart hog | 30 | Giant tortoise | 0.17 |
| Hyena | 40 | Grizzly bear | 30 | Three-toed sloth | 0.15 |
| Zebra | 40 | Cat (domestic) | 30 | Garden snail | 0.03 |

Most of these measurements are for maximum speeds over approximate quarter-mile distances. Exceptions are the lion and elephant, whose speeds were clocked in the act of charging; the whippet, which was timed over a 200-yard course; the cheetah over a 100-yard distance; man for a 15-yard segment of a 100-yard run (of 13.6 seconds); and the black mamba, six-lined race runner, spider, giant tortoise, three-toed sloth, and garden snail, which were measured over various small distances.

## Gestation, Longevity, and Incubation of Animals

Longevity figures were supplied by Ronald T. Reuther, of the Zoological Society of Philadelphia. They refer to animals in captivity; the potential life span of animals is rarely attained in nature. Maximum longevity figures are from the Biology Data Book, 1972. Figures on gestation and incubation are averages based on estimates by leading authorities.

| Animal | | Gestation (day) | Average longevity (years) | Maximun longevity (yrs., mos.) | Animal | Gestation (day) | Average longevity (years) | Maximum longevity (yrs., mos.) |
|---|---|---|---|---|---|---|---|---|
| Ass | | 365 | 12 | 35-10 | Leopard | 98 | 12 | 19-4 |
| Baboon | | 187 | 20 | 35-7 | Lion | 100 | 15 | 25-1 |
| Bear: | Black | 219 | 18 | 36-10 | Monkey (rhesus) | 164 | 15 | — |
| | Grizzly | 225 | 25 | — | Moose | 240 | 12 | — |
| | Polar | 240 | 20 | 34-8 | Mouse (meadow) | 21 | 3 | — |
| Beaver | | 122 | 5 | 20-6 | Mouse (dom. white) | 19 | 3 | 3-6 |
| Buffalo (American) | | 278 | 15 | — | Opossum (American) | 14-17 | 1 | — |
| Bactrian camel | | 406 | 12 | 29-5 | Pig (domestic) | 112 | 10 | 27 |
| Cat (domestic) | | 63 | 12 | 28 | Puma | 90 | 12 | 19 |
| Chimpanzee | | 231 | 20 | 44-6 | Rabbit (domestic) | 37 | 5 | 13 |
| Chipmunk | | 31 | 6 | 8 | Rhinocerous (black) | 450 | 15 | — |
| Cow | | 284 | 15 | 30 | Rhinocerous (white) | — | 20 | — |
| Deer (white-tailed) | | 201 | 8 | 17-6 | Sea lion (California) | 350 | 12 | 28 |
| Dog (domestic) | | 61 | 12 | 20 | Sheep (domestic) | 154 | 12 | 20 |
| Elephant (African) | | — | 35 | 60 | Squirrel (gray) | 44 | 10 | — |
| Elephant (Asian) | | 645 | 40 | 70 | Tiger | 105 | 16 | 26-3 |
| Elk | | 250 | 15 | 26-6 | Wolf (maned) | 63 | 5 | — |
| Fox (red) | | 52 | 7 | 14 | Zebra (Grant's) | 365 | 15 | — |
| Giraffe | | 425 | 10 | 33-7 | | | | |
| Goat (domestic) | | 151 | 8 | 18 | **Incubation time** (days) | | | |
| Gorilla | | 257 | 20 | 39-4 | Chicken . . . . . . . . . . . . . . . . . . . . . . . . . 21 | | | |
| Guinea pig | | 68 | 4 | 7-6 | Duck. . . . . . . . . . . . . . . . . . . . . . . . . . . . 30 | | | |
| Hippopotamus | | 238 | 25 | — | Goose . . . . . . . . . . . . . . . . . . . . . . . . . . . 30 | | | |
| Horse | | 330 | 20 | 46 | Pigeon. . . . . . . . . . . . . . . . . . . . . . . . . . . 18 | | | |
| Kangaroo | | 42 | 7 | — | Turkey. . . . . . . . . . . . . . . . . . . . . . . . . . . 26 | | | |

# Major Venomous Animals

## Snakes

**Coral snake** - several species, 2 to 4 ft. long, in Americas south of Canada; bite is nearly painless; very slow onset of paralysis, difficulty breathing; mortality high without anti-venin.

**Rattlesnake** - variety of species, 2 to 8 ft. long, throughout W. Hemisphere. Rapid onset of symptoms of severe pain, swelling; mortality low, but amputation of affected limb is sometimes necessary; anti-venin. Probably high mortality for Mojave rattler.

**Cottonmouth water moccasin** - less than 6 ft. long, wetlands of Southern U.S. from Virginia to Texas. Rapid onset of symptoms of severe pain, swelling; mortality low, but tissue destruction, caused by the venom's effect on the blood, can be extensive; anti-venin.

**Copperhead** - less than 4 ft. long, from New England to Texas; pain and swelling; very seldom fatal.

**Fer-de-lance** - up to 7 ft. long, Martinique only; venom attacks nerves and blood; probably high mortality.

**Bushmaster** - up to 9 ft. long, jungles of C. and S. America; few bites recorded; probably low mortality.

**Yellow-beard** - up to 7 ft. long, from tropical Mexico to Brazil; severe tissue damage common; low mortality; anti-venin.

**Asian pit vipers** - variety of species from 2 to 5 ft. long throughout Asia; reactions and mortality vary but most bites cause tissue damage and mortality is generally low.

**Sharp-nosed pit viper** - up to 5 ft. long, in eastern China and Indo-China; the most toxic of Asian pit vipers; very rapid onset of swelling and tissue damage, internal bleeding; moderate mortality; anti-venin.

**Boomslang** - under 6 ft. long, in African savannahs; rapid onset of nausea and dizziness, often followed by slight recovery and then sudden death from internal hemorrhaging; bites rare, mortality high; anti-venin.

**European vipers** - various species from 1 to 3 ft. long; bleeding and tissue damage; mortality low; anti-venins.

**Puff adder** - up to 5 ft. long, fat; south of the Sahara and throughout the Middle East; rapid large swelling, great pain, dizziness; moderate mortality often from internal bleeding; anti-venin.

**Gaboon viper** - over 6 ft. long, fat; 2-inch fangs; south of the Sahara; massive tissue damage, internal bleeding; mortality rate not clear.

**Saw-scaled or carpet viper** - up to 2 ft. long, in dry areas from India to Africa; severe bleeding, fever; high mortality, venom 3 times more toxic than common cobra's; anti-venin.

**Desert horned viper** - several varieties of varying sizes, in dry areas of Africa and western Asia; swelling and tissue damage; low mortality; anti-venin.

**Russel's viper or tic-palonga** - over 5 ft. long, throughout Asia; internal bleeding; mortality rate not clear; bite reports common; anti-venin.

**Black mamba** - up to 14 ft. long, fast-moving; S. and C. Africa; rapid onset of dizziness, difficulty breathing, erratic heart-beat; mortality high, nears 100% without anti-venin.

**Kraits** - various species in S. Asia; rapid onset of sleepiness; numbness; kraits are among the most lethal snakes in the world with up to 50% mortality even with anti-venin treatment.

**Common or Asian cobra** - 4 to 8 ft. long, throughout S. Asia; considerable tissue damage, sometimes paralysis; mortality probably not more than 10%; anti-venin. Egyptian cobra is similar in toxicity.

**King cobra** - up to 16 ft. long, large hood; throughout S. Asia; rapid swelling, dizziness, loss of consciousness, difficulty breathing, erratic heart-beat; mortality varies sharply with amount of venom involved, most bites involve non-fatal amounts; anti-venin.

**Yellow or Cape cobra** - 7 ft. long, in Southern Africa; most toxic venom of any cobra; rapid onset of swelling, breathing and cardiac difficulties; mortality high without treatment; anti-venin.

**Ringhala and spitting cobras** - 5 ft. and 7 ft. long; southern Africa; squirt venom through holes in front of fangs as a defense; venom is severely irritating and can cause blindness.

**Australian brown snakes** - several types, varying sizes; very slow onset of symptoms of cardiac or respiratory distress; moderate mortality; anti-venin.

**Tiger snake** - 2 to 6 ft. long, S. Australia; pain, numbness, mental disturbances with rapid onset of paralysis; may be the most deadly of all land snakes though anti-venin is quite effective.

**Death adder** - less than 3 ft. long, Australia; rapid onset of faintness, cardiac and respiratory distress; at least 50% mortality without anti-venin.

**Taipan** - up to 11 ft. long, in Australia and New Guinea; rapid paralysis with severe breathing difficulty; mortality nears 100% without anti-venin.

**Sea snakes** - many varieties of varying sizes; throughout Pacific and Indian oceans except NE Pacific; almost painless bite, variety of muscle pain, paralysis; mortality rate about 15%, many bites are not envenomed; some anti-venins.

*Notes:* Not all snake bites by venomous snakes are actually envenomed; for a variety of reasons, the snake may be temporarily lacking in venom or fail to inject it. Any animal bite, however, carries the danger of tetanus and no bite by a venomous snake should go untreated. Anti-venins are not certain cures; they are only an aid in the treatment of bites. Mortality rates above are for envenomed bites; low mortality, up to 5% result in death; moderate, up to 15%; high, over 15%. Even in cases in which the victim recovers fully, prolonged hospitalization and extensive, continuous medical procedures are usually required.

## Lizards

**Gila monster** - up to 30 inches long with heavy body and tail, in high desert in southwest U.S. and N. Mexico; immediate severe pain followed by vomiting, thirst, difficulty swallowing, weakness approaching paralysis; mortality very low with medical treatment, otherwise high; anti-venin.

**Mexican beaded lizard** - similar to Gila monster, Mexican west-coast; reaction and mortality rate similar to Gila monster; anti-venin.

## Insects

**Ants, bees, wasps, hornets, etc.** All are of the order *Hymenoptera* (winged) with global distribution. Usual reaction is piercing pain in area of sting. Never directly fatal, except in cases of massive multiple stings. Many people suffer allergic reactions - swelling, rashes, partial paralysis —and a few may die within minutes from severe sensitivity to the venom (anaphylactic shock).

## Spiders, scorpions

**Black widow** - small, round-bodied with hour-glass marking; the widow and its relatives are found around the world in tropical and temperate zones; slow to rapid onset of sharp pain spreading from the bite to the rest of the body, weakness, clammy skin, muscular rigidity, breathing difficulty and, in small children, convulsions; low mortality.

**Brown recluse or fiddleback** - small, oblong body; native to Midwest and South U.S. but can be found anywhere in U.S. today; slow onset of pain and severe ulceration at place of bite; in severe cases fever, nausea, and stomach cramps; ulceration may last months; very low mortality.

*Atrax* **spiders** - several varieties, often large, found in Australia; slow onset of breathing and circulation difficulties; low mortality.

**Tarantulas** - large, hairy spiders found around the world; contrary to popular belief, American tarantulas, and probably all others, are **harmless**, though their bite may cause some pain and swelling.

**Scorpions** - crab-like body with stinger in tail, various sizes, many varieties throughout tropical and subtropical areas; various symptoms may include severe pain spreading from the wound, numbness, severe emotional agitation, cramps; severe reactions include vomiting, diarrhea, respiratory failure; moderate, perhaps high, mortality, particularly in children; anti-venins.

## Sea Life

**Sea wasps** - jellyfish, with tentacles up to 30 ft. long, in the South Pacific; very rapid onset of circulatory problems; high mortality largely because of the speed of toxic reaction; anti-venin.

**Portuguese man-of-war** - jellyfish-like, with tentacles up to 70 ft. long, in most warm water areas; immediate severe pain; not fatal, though shock may cause death in a rare case.

**Octopi** - global distribution, usually in warm waters; all varieties produce venom (inserted into a wound made with the mouth), but only a few can cause death; rapid onset of paralysis with breathing difficulty.

**Stingrays** - several varieties of differing sizes, found in tropical and temperate seas and some fresh water; drives a venom-

ous spine in the tail into the victim; severe pain, rapid onset of nausea, vomiting, breathing difficulties; wound area may ulcerate, gangrene may appear; seldom fatal.

**Stonefish** - brownish, slimy fish which lies motionless as a rock on bottom in relatively shallow water, throughout S. Pacific and Indian oceans; spines on back and around tail carry venom; extraordinary pain, rapid paralysis; low mortality, especially when medical care and anti-venin are available.

**Cone-shells** - molluscs in small, beautiful shells in shallow waters of the S. Pacific and Indian oceans; shoot barbs into victims; paralysis; low mortality.

---

## American Kennel Club Registrations

| | 1977 | 1976 | | 1977 | 1976 |
|---|---|---|---|---|---|
| 1—Poodles | 112,300 | 126,799 | 68—American Staffordshire Terriers | 904 | 732 |
| 2—Doberman Pinschers | 79,254 | 73,615 | 69—Rhodesian Ridgeback | 872 | 846 |
| 3—German Shepherd Dogs | 67,072 | 74,723 | 70—Australian Terriers | 847 | 939 |
| 4—Cocker Spaniels | 52,955 | 46,862 | 71—Bullmastiffs | 821 | 676 |
| 5—Irish Setters | 43,367 | 54,917 | 72—Welsh Terriers | 782 | 888 |
| 6—Labrador Retrievers | 41,275 | 39,929 | 73—Standard Schnauzers | 772 | 785 |
| 7—Beagles | 40,850 | 44,156 | 74—Salukis | 743 | 737 |
| 8—Dachshunds | 35,087 | 38,927 | 75—Soft-Coated Wheaten Terriers | 650 | 539 |
| 9—Miniature Schnauzers | 35,072 | 36,816 | 76—Kerry Blue Terriers | 621 | 661 |
| 10—Golden Retrievers | 30,263 | 27,612 | 77—Papillons | 547 | 490 |
| 11—Shetland Sheepdogs | 24,464 | 23,950 | 78—Belgian Sheepdogs | 534 | 552 |
| 12—Collies | 23,386 | 25,161 | 79—Giant Schnauzers | 499 | 565 |
| 13—Lhasa Apsos | 22,354 | 21,145 | 80—Pulik | 480 | 609 |
| 14—Yorkshire Terriers | 21,573 | 20,392 | 81—Italian Greyhounds | 478 | 506 |
| 15—Siberian Huskies | 20,196 | 20,598 | 82—Bearded Collies | 446 | 998 |
| 16—Pekingese | 19,891 | 20,400 | 83—Pointers | 429 | 439 |
| 17—Brittany Spaniels | 19,267 | 20,222 | 84—Manchester Terriers | 406 | 536 |
| 18—English Springer Spaniels | 18,579 | 16,842 | 85—Belgian Tervuren | 397 | 430 |
| 19—Great Danes | 17,892 | 19,869 | 86—Irish Terriers | 385 | 273 |
| 20—Pomeranians | 15,943 | 15,241 | 87—Bedlington Terriers | 380 | 370 |
| 21—Chihuahuas | 15,841 | 16,478 | 88—Japanese Chin | 368 | 356 |
| 22—Old English Sheepdogs | 14,403 | 15,364 | 89—Welsh Corgis (Cardigan) | 364 | 356 |
| 23—Basset Hounds | 14,368 | 14,997 | 90—Black and Tan Coonhounds | 326 | 357 |
| 24—Shih Tzu | 14,189 | 12,562 | 91—Bernese Mountain Dogs | 324 | 292 |
| 25—St. Bernards | 13,186 | 17,537 | 92—American Water Spaniels | 323 | 302 |
| 26—German Shorthaired Pointers | 13,093 | 14,269 | 93—Norwich Terriers | 295 | 278 |
| 27—Boxers | 12,951 | 13,057 | 94—Tibetan Terriers | 275 | 242 |
| 28—Boston Terriers | 10,753 | 10,806 | 95—Staffordshire Bull Terriers | 256 | 291 |
| 29—Samoyeds | 9,640 | 10,147 | 96—Briards | 254 | 216 |
| 30—Afghan Hounds | 9,416 | 10,045 | 97—Dandie Dinmont Terriers | 226 | 235 |
| 31—Alaskan Malamutes | 8,371 | 8,324 | 98—Skye Terriers | 216 | 226 |
| 32—Chow Chows | 7,649 | 6,211 | 99—French Bulldogs | 195 | 208 |
| 33—Norwegian Elkhounds | 7,280 | 8,037 | 100—Greyhounds | 188 | 148 |
| 34—Scottish Terriers | 7,073 | 7,202 | 101—Brussels Griffons | 178 | 219 |
| 35—Airedale Terriers | 6,745 | 6,835 | 102—Lakeland Terriers | 176 | 171 |
| 36—Dalmatians | 6,694 | 7,241 | 103—Kuvaszok | 170 | 158 |
| 37—Bulldogs | 6,549 | 6,554 | 104—Flat-Coated Retrievers | 156 | 132 |
| 38—Cairn Terriers | 6,359 | 6,432 | 105—Sealyham Terriers | 154 | 98 |
| 39—West Highland White Terriers | 6,332 | 6,072 | 106—Irish Water Spaniels | 142 | 89 |
| 40—Maltese | 6,197 | 6,183 | 107—Welsh Springer Spaniels | 137 | 108 |
| 41—Pugs | 6,066 | 6,660 | 108—Scottish Deerhounds | 124 | 158 |
| 42—Keeshonden | 6,040 | 5,871 | 109—Wirehaired Pointing Griffons | 117 | 137 |
| 43—Weimaraners | 5,519 | 6,243 | 110—Border Terriers | 110 | 104 |
| 44—Fox Terriers | 4,254 | 4,673 | 111—Komondorok | 99 | 99 |
| 45—Chesapeake Bay Retrievers | 2,906 | 2,650 | 112—Foxhounds (American) | 84 | 69 |
| 46—Silky Terriers | 2,728 | 2,829 | 113—Affenpinschers | 77 | 63 |
| 47—Welsh Corgis (Pembroke) | 2,179 | 2,061 | 114—Clumber Spaniels | 61 | 55 |
| 48—Newfoundlands | 2,096 | 2,113 | 115—English Toy Spaniels | 58 | 46 |
| 49—Rottweilers | 1,878 | 1,406 | 116—Otter Hounds | 49 | 52 |
| 50—Vizslas | 1,877 | 1,867 | 117—Curly-Coated Retrievers | 45 | 15 |
| 51—Basenjis | 1,702 | 1,674 | 118—Belgian Malinois | 36 | 34 |
| 52—Bichons Frises | 1,619 | 1,512 | 119—Field Spaniels | 31 | 42 |
| 53—English Setters | 1,579 | 1,756 | 120—Harriers | 15 | 25 |
| 54—Bloodhounds | 1,578 | 1,446 | 121—Sussex Spaniels | 7 | 14 |
| 55—Borzois | 1,535 | 1,658 | 122—Foxhounds (English) | 4 | 9 |
| 56—Irish Wolfhounds | 1,383 | 1,409 | | | |
| 57—Great Pyrenees | 1,364 | 1,529 | | 1,013,650 | 1,048,648 |
| 58—Akitas | 1,332 | 1,213 | | | |
| 59—Gordon Setters | 1,329 | 1,383 | | | |
| 60—Miniature Pinschers | 1,316 | 1,126 | | | |
| 61—Schipperkes | 1,272 | 1,260 | | | |
| 62—Bouviers Des Flandres | 1,204 | 1,053 | | | |
| 63—Whippets | 1,146 | 1,050 | | | |
| 64—Bull Terriers | 1,057 | 929 | | | |
| 65—English Cocker Spaniels | 1,024 | 942 | | | |
| 66—German Wirehaired Pointers | 969 | 1,021 | | | |
| 67—Mastiffs | 936 | 810 | | | |

### Registrations By Groups

| | 1977 | 1976 |
|---|---|---|
| Sporting | 235,450 | 237,849 |
| Hound | 116,750 | 125,800 |
| Working | 307,000 | 318,300 |
| Terrier | 73,300 | 75,300 |
| Toy | 105,450 | 103,550 |
| Non-Sporting | 175,700 | 187,849 |

# EDUCATION

## American Colleges and Universities

### Student and Faculty Figures for Spring Term, 1978

**Source:** World Almanac questionnaires and U.S. Office of Education

(For Canadian Colleges and Universities, see Index)

All coeducational unless followed by (M) for men only, or (W) for women only. Even though marked (M) or (W) some ar̄ coeducational at graduate level and in evening and summer divisions. Asterisk (*) denotes landgrant college.

Governing official is president unless otherwise designated. Year is that of founding. The word college is part of the nam̄ unless another designation is given.

Affiliation: C-county; D-religious denomination; Di-district; F-federal; Mu-municipal; P-private; S-state; T-territorial govt̄ Each institution listed has an enrollment of at least 200 students of college grade. Number of teachers is the total numbē of individuals on teaching staff. Enrollment and faculty in italics includes all branches and campuses.

(A) Designates colleges that have not provided up-to-date information.

(See Index for typical tuition fees)

### Senior Colleges

| Name, address | Year | Governing official and affiliation | | Stu-dents | Teach-ers |
|---|---|---|---|---|---|
| Abilene Christian, Abilene, TX 79601 | 1906 | John C. Stevens | P | *5,003* | *16̄* |
| Adams, State, Alamosa, CO 81102 | 1921 | Milton Byrd | S | 2,400 | 10̄ |
| Adelphi Univ., Garden City, NY 11530 | 1896 | Timothy Costello | P | 10,500 | 36̄ |
| Adrian, Adrian, MI 49221 | 1859 | John H. Dawson | P,D | 912 | 78 |
| Agnes Scott, Decatur, GA 30030 | 1889 | Marvin Perry Jr | P | 566 | 67 |
| Akron, Univ. of, Akron, OH 44325 | 1870 | Dominic J. Guzzetta | S | 23,931 | 63̄ |
| Alabama A&M Univ., Normal, AL 35762 | 1875 | Richard D. Morrison | S | 4,613 | 24̄ |
| Alabama State Univ., Montgomery, AL 36101 | 1874 | Levi Watkins | S | 4,754 | 24̄ |
| Alabama, Univ. of, University, AL 35486 | 1831 | David Mathews | S | 16,920 | 68̄ |
| at Birmingham, Birmingham, AL 35294 | 1966 | S.R. Hill Jr | S | 13,000 | 1,198 |
| at Huntsville, Huntsville, AL 35807 | 1950 | Benjamin B. Graves | S | *4,000* | *19̄* |
| Alaska, Univ. of*, Fairbanks, AK 99701 | 1917 | Robert W. Hiatt | S | *18,254* | *42̄* |
| Albany Coll. of Pharmacy, Albany, NY 12208 | 1881 | Dean Walter Singer | P | 600 | 25 |
| Albany State, Albany, GA 31705 | 1903 | Charles Hays | S | 2,011 | 119 |
| Albertus Magnus (W), New Haven, CT 06511 | 1925 | Sr. Francis Heffernan | D | *540* | *3̄* |
| Albion, Albion, MI 49224 | 1835 | Bernard Tagg Lomas | P | 1,748 | 106 |
| Albright, Reading, PA 19604 | 1856 | Dr. Morley Mays | D | 1,425 | 82 |
| Albuquerque, Univ. of, Albuquerque, NM 87140 | 1920 | Laurence Smith | D | *2,662* | *9̄* |
| Alcorn State Univ., Lorman, MS 39096 | 1871 | Walter Washington | S | 2,776 | 136 |
| Alderson-Broaddus, Philippi, WV 26416 | 1871 | Richard E. Shearer | P,D | 971 | 66 |
| Alfred Univ., Alfred, NY 14802 | 1836 | M. Richard Rose | P | 2,000 | 16̄ |
| Allegheny, Meadville, PA 16335 | 1815 | Lawrence L. Pelletier | P | 1,798 | 127 |
| Alliance, Cambridge Springs, PA 16403 | 1912 | Arthur Auten | P | 203 | 23 |
| Alma, Alma, MI 48801 | 1886 | Robert D. Swanson | D | 1,135 | 72 |
| Alvernia, Reading, PA 19607 | 1958 | Sister Mary Victorine | P | 830 | 53 |
| Alverno (W), Milwaukee, WI 53215 | 1936 | Sister Joel Read | D | 857 | 104 |
| American Cons. of Music, Chicago, IL 60603 | 1886 | Leo Heim | P | 2,500 | 160 |
| American International, Springfield, MA 01075 | 1885 | Harry J. Courniotes | P | 2,200 | 90 |
| American Univ., Washington DC 20016 | 1893 | Joseph J. Sisco | D | 12,583 | 360 |
| Amherst, Amherst, MA 01002 | 1821 | John William Ward | P | 1,487 | 150 |
| Anderson, Anderson, IN 46011 | 1917 | Robert H. Reardon | P,D | 1,919 | 151 |
| Andrews Univ., Berrien Springs, MI 49104 | 1874 | Joseph Smoot | D | *2,837* | *19̄* |
| Angelo State Univ., San Angelo, TX 76901 | 1928 | Lloyd Vincent | S | 4,660 | 19̄ |
| Anna Maria, Paxton, MA 01612 | 1946 | B. Madore, Act | P | 1,193 | 99 |
| Annhurst, Woodstock, CT 06281 | 1941 | Paul Buchanan | D | 347 | 35 |
| Antioch, Yellow Spgs., OH 45387 | 1852 | Dr. Wm. Birenbaum | P | 8,379 | 26̄ |
| Appalachian Bible Inst., Bradley, WV 25818 | 1950 | Lester E. Pipkin | P | 222 | 1̄ |
| Appalachian State Univ., Boone, NC 28608 | 1899 | Herbert W. Wey, Chan | S | 10,208 | 540 |
| Aquinas, Grand Rapids, MI 49506 | 1922 | Norbert J. Hruby | P | 1,800 | 119 |
| Arizona, State Univ., Tempe, AZ 85281 | 1885 | John W. Schwada | S | 35,278 | 1,660 |
| Arizona, Univ. of*, Tucson, AZ 85721 | 1885 | John Paul Schaefer | S | 31,754 | 1,579 |
| Arkansas, Batesville, AR 72501 | 1872 | Dan C. West | D,P | 515 | 43 |
| Arkansas Tech, Russellville, AR 72801 | 1909 | Kenneth Kersh | S | 2,390 | 125 |
| Arkansas State Univ., State Univ., AR 72467 | 1909 | Carl Whillock | S | *8,116* | *34̄* |
| Arkansas, State Coll. of, Conway, AR 72032 | 1907 | Jefferson Farris | S | 5,280 | 212 |
| Arkansas, Univ. of*, Fayetteville, AR 72701 | 1871 | Charles Bishop | S | *30,652* | *1,57̄* |
| at Little Rock, Little Rock, AR 72204 | 1927 | G. Robert Ross, Chan. | S | 10,000 | 450 |
| at Pine Bluff, Pine Bluff, AR 71601 | 1873 | Herman Smith Jr., Chan. | S | 2,972 | 166 |
| Armstrong, Berkeley, CA 94704 | 1918 | John E. Armstrong | P | 615 | 23 |
| Armstrong State, Savannah, GA 31406 | 1935 | Henry L. Ashmore | S | 3,200 | 170 |
| Art Center Coll. of Design, Pasadena, CA 91103 | 1930 | Donald R. Kubly | P | 1,425 | 181 |
| Art Inst. of Chicago, Chicago, IL 60603 | 1869 | Donald Irving, Dir. | P | 1,688 | 70 |
| Asbury, Wilmore, KY 40390 | 1890 | Dennis F. Kinlaw | P | 1,257 | 93 |
| Ashland, Ashland, OH 44805 | 1878 | Dr. Arthur Schultz | P | 2,127 | 106 |
| Assumption, Worcester, MA 01609 | 1904 | Rev. Wm. Dufault, Act. | D | 1,836 | 70 |
| Athenaeum of Ohio, Cincinnati, OH 45212 | 1829 | Rev. J.R. Favret. | Mu | *300* | *14̄* |
| Athens State, Athens AL 35611 | 1822 | Sidney Sandridge | S | 1,475 | 40 |
| Atlanta College of Art, Atlanta, GA 30309 | 1928 | William Voos | P | 700 | 22 |
| Atlantic Christian, Wilson, NC 27893 | 1902 | Harold C. Doster | D | 1,658 | 117 |
| Atlantic Union, So. Lancaster, MA 01561 | 1882 | R. Dale McCune | D | 798 | 74 |
| Auburn Univ.*, Auburn, AL 36830 | 1856 | Harry Philpott | S | *22,000* | *1,20̄* |
| Augsburg, Minneapolis, MN 55454 | 1869 | Oscar A. Anderson | D,P | 1,751 | 79 |
| Augusta, Augusta, GA 30904 | 1925 | George A. Christenberry | S | 3,574 | 14̄ |
| Augustana, Rock Island, IL 61201 | 1860 | J. Thomas Tredway | D | 2,041 | 11̄ |
| Augustana, Sioux Falls, SD 57102 | 1860 | Charles L. Balcer | P | 2,228 | 140 |
| Aurora, Aurora, IL 60507 | 1893 | Lloyd Richardson | P | 840 | 87 |
| Austin, Sherman, TX 75090 | 1849 | John D. Moseley | P | 1,198 | 88 |
| Austin Peay State Univ., Clarksville, TN 37040 | 1927 | Robert O. Riggs | S | 4,872 | 180 |
| Averett, Danville, VA 24541 | 1859 | Conwell A. Anderson | P,D | 982 | 61 |

172

| ame, address | Year | Governing official and affiliation | | Stu-dents | Teach-ers |
|---|---|---|---|---|---|
| vila, Kansas City, MO 64145 | 1916 | Sister Olive Dallavis | D | 1,961 | 59 |
| zusa Pacific, Azusa CA 91702 | 1899 | Paul Sago | D,P | 2,113 | 84 |
| abson, Babson Park, MA 02157 | 1919 | Ralph Sorenson | P | 2,812 | 79 |
| aker Univ., Baldwin City, KS 66006 | 1858 | Jerald C. Walker | P | 955 | 58 |
| aldwin-Wallace, Berea, OH 44017 | 1845 | A.B. Bonds Jr. | P | 3,058 | 113 |
| all State Univ., Muncie, IN 47306 | 1918 | John J. Pruis | S | 16,977 | 948 |
| altimore, Univ. of, Baltimore, MD 21201 | 1925 | H. Mebane Turner | P | 5,474 | 115 |
| aptist Bible College of Pa., Clarks Summit, PA 18411 | 1932 | Ernest Pickering | D | 933 | 43 |
| aptist Coll. at Charleston, Charleston, SC 29411 | 1960 | John Hamrick | D | 2,310 | 77 |
| arat (W), Lake Forest, IL 60045 | 1858 | Judith Cagney | P | 805 | 39 |
| arber-Scotia, Concord, NC 28025 | 1867 | Mable McLean | P,D | 451 | 22 |
| ard, Annandale-on-Hudson, NY 12504 | 1860 | Leon Botstein | P | 701 | 64 |
| arnard (W), New York, NY 10027 | 1889 | Jacquelyn Mattfeld | P | 2,053 | 134 |
| arrington, Barrington, RI 02806 | 1900 | Harold Fickett, Jr. | P | 561 | 35 |
| arry, Miami, FL 33161 | 1940 | Sister M. Trinita Flood | P,D | 1,636 | 117 |
| ates, Lewiston, ME 04240 | 1864 | Thomas H. Reynolds | P | 1,322 | 105 |
| aylor Univ., Waco, TX 76706 | 1845 | Abner V. McCall | D | 9,474 | 385 |
| eaver, Glenside, PA 19038 | 1853 | Edward D. Gates | P | 1,859 | 57 |
| elhaven, Jackson, MS 39202 | 1883 | Howard J. Cleland | D | 611 | 44 |
| ellarmine, Louisville, KY 40205 | 1950 | Eugene Petrick | D | 1,782 | 57 |
| ellevue, Bellevue, NE 68005 | 1966 | Richard Winchell | P | 1,909 | 23 |
| elmont, Nashville, TN 37203 | 1951 | Herbert C. Gabhart | D | 1,267 | 106 |
| elmont Abbey, Belmont, NC 28012 | 1876 | Rev. Neil W. Tobin | P | 668 | 56 |
| eloit, Beloit, WI 53511 | 1846 | Martha Peterson | P | 1,194 | 91 |
| emidji State, Bemidji, MN 56601 | 1919 | Robert Decker | S | 4,384 | 225 |
| enedict, Columbia, SC 29204 | 1870 | Henry Ponder | P | 1,982 | 113 |
| enedictine, Atchison KS 66002 | 1971 | Rev. Gerard Senecal | D,P | 979 | 85 |
| enjamin Franklin Univ., Washington, DC 20036 | 1925 | Mrs. Clephane Kennedy | P | 1,000 | 34 |
| ennett (W), Greensboro, NC 27420 | 1873 | Isaac H. Miller | P | 618 | 59 |
| ennington, Bennington, VT 05201 | 1935 | Joseph Iseman, Act. | D | 597 | 82 |
| entley, Waltham, MA 02154 | 1917 | Gregory Adamian | P | 4,871 | 224 |
| erea, Berea, KY 40404 | 1855 | W.D. Weatherford. | P | 1,500 | 145 |
| erry, Mount Berry, GA 30149 | 1902 | John R. Bertrand | P | 1,671 | 77 |
| ethany, Lindsborg, KS 67456 | 1881 | Arvin Hahn | P | 784 | 61 |
| ethany, Bethany, WV 26032 | 1840 | William Tucker | P,D | 1,029 | 82 |
| ethany Bible, Santa Cruz, CA 95066 | 1919 | C. Morse Ward | D,P | 576 | 30 |
| ethany Nazarene, Bethany, OK 73008 | 1899 | John Knight | P,D | 1,272 | 75 |
| ethel, North Newton, KS 67117 | 1887 | Harold Schultz | D | 638 | 44 |
| ethel, McKenzie, TN 38201 | 1842 | William L. Odom | P,D | 304 | 34 |
| ethel, St. Paul, MN 55112 | 1871 | Carl Lundquist. | P | 1,680 | 115 |
| iola, La Mirada, CA 90639 | 1908 | O.P. Bronson | D | 1,464 | 85 |
| ethune-Cookman, Daytona Beach, FL 32015 | 1904 | J. Richard Chase | P | 2,282 | 130 |
| irmingham Southern, Birmingham, AL 35204 | 1856 | Neal R. Berte | Mu | 1,006 | 70 |
| iscayne, Miami, FL 33054 | 1962 | Rev. John McDonnell. | D | 14,974 | 83 |
| ishop, Dallas, TX 75241 | 1881 | Milton K. Curry Jr. | P | 1,733 | 91 |
| lack Hills State, Spearfish, SD 57783 | 1883 | M. Fitzgerald, Act. | S | 2,366 | 115 |
| lackburn, Carlinville, IL 62626 | 1837 | John Alberti | D | 643 | 55 |
| loomfield, Bloomfield, NJ 07003 | 1868 | Merle F. Allshouse | P | 1,800 | 90 |
| loomsburg State, Bloomsburg, PA 17815 | 1839 | James McCormick | S | 6,400 | 298 |
| lue Mountain (W), Blue Mountain, MS 38610 | 1873 | E. Harold Fisher. | D | 330 | 25 |
| luefield, Bluefield, VA 24605 | 1922 | Dr. Chas. Tyer. | P | 372 | 19 |
| luefield State, Bluefield, WV 24701 | 1895 | Wm. H. Brothers, Act. | P | 2,401 | 72 |
| luffton, Bluffton, OH 45817 | 1899 | Benjamin Sprunger | P | 690 | 58 |
| ob Jones Univ., Greenville, SC 29614 | 1927 | Bob Jones, III | D | 5,040 | 338 |
| oca Raton, Boca Raton, FL 33431 | 1963 | Thomas Carlin. | D | 510 | 34 |
| oise State, Boise, ID 83725 | 1932 | Dr. John Keiser | S | 10,419 | 411 |
| oston, Chestnut Hill, MA 02167 | 1863 | Rev. J. Donald Monan | S | 13,968 | 541 |
| oston State, Boston, MA 02115 | 1852 | Kermit C. Merrissey | S | 5,805 | 295 |
| oston Conserv. of Music, Boston, MA 02215 | 1867 | George Brambilla | P | 509 | 33 |
| oston Univ., Boston, MA 02215 | 1869 | John Silber | P | 22,671 | 1,880 |
| owdoin, Brunswick, ME 04011 | 1794 | Willard Enteman | P | 1,340 | 91 |
| owie State*, Bowie, MD 20715 | 1865 | Samuel L. Meyers | S | 1,817 | 157 |
| owling Green State Univ., Bowling Green, OH 43403 | 1910 | Hollis A. Moore Jr. | S | 17,042 | 716 |
| radford, Bradford, MA 01830 | 1803 | Jack L. Armstrong | P | 347 | 42 |
| radley Univ., Peoria, IL 61625. | 1897 | Martin G. Abegg | P | 5,000 | 259 |
| randeis Univ., Waltham, MA 02154 | 1948 | Marver Bernstein | P | 2,943 | 410 |
| renau, Gainesville, GA 30501 | 1878 | James T. Rogers | P | 795 | 40 |
| rescia, Owensboro, KY 42301 | 1950 | Sister Geo. Ann Cecil. | P | 876 | 51 |
| riar Cliff, Sioux City, IA 51104. | 1930 | Chas. Bensman | D | 1,000 | 54 |
| ridgeport Engineering Inst., Bridgeport, CT 06606 | 1924 | William J. Owens | P | 414 | 80 |
| ridgeport, Univ. of, Bridgeport, CT 06602 | 1927 | Leland Miles | P | 7,700 | 250 |
| ridgewater, Bridgewater, VA 22812 | 1880 | Dr. Wayne F. Geisert | P | 829 | 51 |
| ridgewater State, Bridgewater, MA 02324 | 1840 | Adrian Rondileau | S | 7,550 | 280 |
| righam Young Univ., Provo, UT 84602 | 1875 | Dallin U. Oaks. | P,D | 26,470 | 1,259 |
| rooks Inst. of Santa Barbara, Santa Barbara, CA | 1945 | Raymond Lisle, Dean. | P | 1,036 | 55 |
| rooklyn Law School, Brooklyn, NY 11201 | 1901 | Ernest Brooks II. | P | 780 | 42 |
| rown Univ., Providence, RI 02912 | 1764 | Howard R. Swearer | P | 6,737 | 460 |
| ryan, Dayton, TN 37321. | 1930 | Theodore Mercer | P | 511 | 32 |
| ryant, Smithfield RI 02917. | 1863 | William O'Hara | P | 3,931 | 115 |
| ryn Mawr (W), Bryn Mawr, PA 19010 | 1885 | Harris L. Wofford Jr. | P | 1,601 | 188 |
| ucknell Univ., Lewisburg, PA 17837 | 1846 | George O'Brien | P | 3,200 | 261 |
| uena Vista, Storm Lake, IA 50588 | 1891 | Keith G. Briscoe. | D,P | 1,094 | 70 |
| utler Univ., Indianapolis, IN 46208 | 1855 | John G. Johnson | P | 4,025 | 150 |
| abrini, Radnor, PA 19087 | 1957 | Sr. Mary Sullivan | D,P | 570 | 30 |
| aldwell, Caldwell, NJ 07006 | 1939 | Sr. M. Anne John O'Laughlin | D,P | 850 | 73 |
| alifornia Baptist, Riverside, CA 92504 | 1950 | James R. Staples | P | 822 | 51 |
| al. Coll. of Arts and Crafts, Oakland, CA 94618 | 1907 | Harry Xavier Ford | P | 1,150 | 110 |
| al. College of Podiatric Med., San Francisco, CA 94120 | 1914 | Richard Allen | P | 380 | 48 |
| al. Inst. of the Arts, Valencia, CA 91355 | 1961 | Robert Fitzpatrick | P | 621 | 92 |
| al. Inst. of Tech., Pasadena, CA 91125 | 1920 | Robert Christy, Act. | P | 1,541 | 738 |
| al. Lutheran, Thousand Oaks, CA 91360 | 1959 | Dr. Mark Mathews | P | 1,638 | 68 |
| al. Maritime Academy, Vallejo, CA 94590 | 1929 | R. Adm. Joseph Rizza | S | 468 | 27 |
| al. Polytechnic State Univ., San Luis Obispo, CA 93407 | 1901 | Robert Kennedy. | S | 15,158 | 800 |
| al. State, Bakersfield, CA 93309 | 1970 | Jacob Frankel | S | 3,035 | 194 |
| al. State, California, PA 15419 | 1874 | John Watkins | S | 4,937 | 331 |

| Name, address | Year | Governing official and affiliation | | Students | Teachers |
|---|---|---|---|---|---|
| Cal. State, Dominguez Hills, CA 90747 | 1960 | Donald Gerth | S | 6,000 | 316 |
| Cal. State, Rohnert Park, CA 94928 | 1960 | P. Diamandopoulos | S | 6,024 | 42 |
| Cal. State, San Bernardino, CA 92407 | 1962 | John Pfau | S | 4,200 | 18 |
| Cal. State, Turlock, CA 95380 | 1957 | Walter Olson | S | 3,525 | 16 |
| Cal. State Polytechnic Univ., Pomona, CA 91768 | 1938 | Hugh La Bounty Jr. | S | 14,100 | 49 |
| Cal. State Univ., Northridge, CA 91330 | 1958 | James W. Cleary | S | 27,360 | 90 |
| Cal. State Univ., Chico, CA 95929 | 1887 | Stanford Cazier | S | 12,791 | 65 |
| Cal. State Univ., Fresno, CA 93740 | 1911 | Norman Baxter | S | 14,951 | 944 |
| Cal. State Univ., Fullerton, CA 92634 | 1959 | L. Donald Shields | S | 21,572 | 1,18 |
| Cal. State Univ., Hayward, CA 94542 | 1957 | Ellis McCune | S | 12,800 | 75 |
| Cal. State Univ., Long Beach, CA 90840 | 1949 | Stephen Horn | S | 31,157 | 1,60 |
| Cal. State Univ., Los Angeles, CA 90032 | 1947 | J.A. Greenlee | S | 25,600 | 1,46 |
| Cal. State Univ., Sacramento, CA 95819 | 1947 | James Bond | S | 20,415 | 1,11 |
| Cal. State Univ., San Francisco, CA 94132 | 1899 | Paul F. Romberg | S | 23,409 | 1,50 |
| Cal., Univ. of*, Berkeley, CA 94720 | 1868 | David S. Saxon | S | 128,478 | 7,00 |
| Berkeley Campus, Berkeley, CA 94720 | 1873 | Albert H. Bowker, Chan. | S | 30,001 | 2,42 |
| Davis Campus, Davis, CA 95616 | 1905 | James Meyer, Chan. | S | 17,197 | 1,26 |
| Irvine Campus, Irvine, CA 92717 | 1965 | D.G. Aldrich, Chan. | S | 9,682 | 718 |
| Los Angeles Campus, Los Angeles, CA 90024 | 1919 | Charles Young, Chan. | S | 32,131 | 2,26 |
| Riverside Campus, Riverside, CA 92502 | 1907 | Ivan Hinderaker, Chan. | S | 5,058 | 766 |
| San Diego Campus, La Jolla, CA 92093 | 1912 | William D. McElroy, Chan. | S | 8,875 | 944 |
| San Francisco Campus, San Francisco, CA 94122 | 1873 | F. A. Sooy, Chan. | S | 3,295 | 1,41 |
| Santa Barbara Campus, Santa Barbara, CA 93106 | 1898 | Vernon Cheadle, Chan. | S | 14,584 | 947 |
| Santa Cruz Campus, Santa Cruz, CA 95064 | 1965 | R.L. Sinsheimer, Chan. | S | 6,097 | 346 |
| Calumet, Whiting, IN 46394 | 1951 | Rev. James McCabe | D,P | 1,736 | 51 |
| Calvin, Grand Rapids, MI 49506 | 1876 | Anthony Dickema | P,D | 4,088 | 200 |
| Cameron, Lawton, OK 73505 | 1908 | Don Owen | S | 5,538 | 234 |
| Campbell, Bules Creek, NC 27506 | 1887 | Norman A. Wiggins | D,P | 2,450 | 14 |
| Campbellsville, Campbellsville, KY 42718 | 1906 | William R. Davenport | P,D | 686 | 50 |
| Canisius, Buffalo, NY 14208 | 1870 | Rev. James Demske | P | 3,052 | 162 |
| Capital Univ., Columbus, OH 43209 | 1850 | Thomas H. Langevin | D | 2,619 | 163 |
| Capitol Inst. of Tech., Kensington, MD 20795 | 1927 | G.W. Trexler | P | 401 | 11 |
| Cardinal Stritch, Milwaukee, WI 53217 | 1937 | Sister M. Kliebhan | D | 1,100 | 118 |
| Carleton, Northfield, MN 55057 | 1866 | Robert Edwards | P | 1,661 | 135 |
| Carlow (W), Pittsburgh, PA 15213 | 1929 | Sister Jane Scully | D,P | 901 | 96 |
| Carnegie-Mellon, Univ., Pittsburgh, PA 15213 | 1900 | Richard M. Cyert | P | 4,768 | 430 |
| Carroll, Helena, MT 59601 | 1909 | Francis Kevins | D,P | 1,433 | 11 |
| Carroll, Waukesha, WI 53186 | 1846 | Robert V. Cramer | P | 1,225 | 103 |
| Carson-Newman, Jefferson City, TN 37760 | 1851 | John A. Fincher | P,D | 1,540 | 110 |
| Carthage, Kenosha, WI 53140 | 1847 | Erno Dahl | D | 1,604 | 103 |
| Case Western Reserve Univ., Cleveland OH 44106 | 1826 | L.A. Toepfer | P | 8,108 | 1,258 |
| Castleton State, Castleton, VT 05735 | 1867 | Donald Wilson | S | 2,088 | 85 |
| Catawba, NC 28144 | 1851 | M.L. Shotzberger | P,D | 918 | 72 |
| Cathedral (M), Douglaston, NY 11362 | 1914 | Rev. Thomas Gradilone | D | 200 | 33 |
| Catholic Univ. of America, Washington, DC 20064 | 1887 | Clarence C. Walton | D | 7,237 | 398 |
| Cath. Univ. of Puerto Rico, Ponce, PR 00731 | 1948 | F.J. Carreras | D,P | 10,026 | 426 |
| Cedar Crest (W), Allentown, PA 18104 | 1867 | Pauline Tompkins | D | 745 | 82 |
| Cedarville, Cedarville, OH 45314 | 1887 | James Jeremiah | D,P | 1,250 | 68 |
| Centenary (W), Hackettstown, NJ 07840 | 1867 | Charles Dick | P | 511 | 44 |
| Centenary Coll. of La, Shreveport, LA 71104 | 1825 | Dr. Donald Webb | D,P | 934 | 62 |
| Central Bible, Springfield, MO 65802 | 1922 | Rev. Philip Crouch | D,P | 1,147 | 51 |
| Central, Pella, IA 50219 | 1853 | Kenneth J. Weller | P | 1,352 | 9 |
| Central Connecticut State, New Britain, CT 06050 | 1849 | F. Don James | S | 12,757 | 655 |
| Central Methodist, Fayette, MO 65248 | 1854 | Dr. Joe Howell | D | 567 | 55 |
| Central Mich. Univ., Mt. Pleasant, MI 48859 | 1892 | Harold Abel | S | 16,004 | 75 |
| Central Missouri St. Univ., Warrensburg, MO 64093 | 1871 | Warren C. Lovinger | S | 10,145 | 41 |
| Central New England, Worcester, MA 01608 | 1905 | Edward Mattar III | P | 1,150 | 35 |
| Central State Univ., Edmond, OK 73034 | 1890 | Bill Lillard | S | 11,382 | 432 |
| Central State Univ., Wilberforce, OH 45384 | 1887 | Lionel H. Newsom | S | 2,280 | 113 |
| Central Washington State, Ellensburg, WA 98926 | 1890 | James E. Brooks | S | 7,666 | 330 |
| Central Wesleyan, Central, SC 29630 | 1906 | Claude Rickman | D | 347 | 29 |
| Centre Coll. of Ky. Danville, KY 40422 | 1819 | Thos. Spragens | P | 799 | 77 |
| Chadron State, Chadron, NE 69337 | 1911 | Edwin Nelson | S | 2,132 | 90 |
| Chaminade Univ. of Honolulu, Honolulu, HI 96816 | 1955 | Rev D. Schuyler | D | 2,348 | 18 |
| Chapman, Orange, CA 92666 | 1861 | D. Chamberlin, Act. | D | 3,551 | 180 |
| Charleston, Coll. of, Charleston, SC 29401 | 1770 | Theodore Stern | S | 4,562 | 215 |
| Chatham (W), Pittsburgh, PA 15232 | 1869 | Dr. A Arthuis | P | 590 | 50 |
| Chestnut Hill (W), Philadelphia, PA 19118 | 1924 | Sister Mary Xavier | P,D | 857 | 83 |
| Cheyney State, Cheyney, PA 19319 | 1837 | Wade Wilson | S | 2,801 | 220 |
| Chicago Academy of Fine Arts, Chicago, IL 60601 | 1902 | Richard Hamper | P | 257 | 30 |
| Chicago Coll. of Osteopathic, Chicago, IL 60615 | 1900 | Thaddeus Kawalek | P | 383 | 188 |
| Chicago State Univ., Chicago, IL 60628 | 1867 | Benjamin Alexander | P | 7,007 | 294 |
| Chicago Technical, Chicago, IL 60616 | 1904 | Leslie Morey | P | 451 | 16 |
| Chicago, Univ. of, Chicago, IL 60637 | 1891 | Mrs. Hanna Gray | P | 9,425 | 1,039 |
| Christian Brothers, Memphis, TN 38104 | 1871 | Bro. Bernard LoCoco | D | 940 | 7 |
| Christopher Newport, Newport News, Va 23606 | 1960 | James Windsor | S | 3,717 | 156 |
| Cincinnati, Univ. of, Cincinnati, OH 45221 | 1819 | Henry Winkler | S | 38,239 | 1,69 |
| Citadel, The Military (M), Charleston, SC 29409 | 1842 | Lt. Gen. George Seignious | S | 3,205 | 192 |
| Claflin, Orangeburg, SC 29115 | 1869 | Hubert V. Manning | D | 895 | 56 |
| Claremont Men's, Claremont, CA 91711 | 1946 | Jack Lee Stark | P | 800 | 78 |
| Clarion State, Clarion, PA 16214 | 1867 | Clayton Sommers | S | 4,695 | 254 |
| Clark, Atlanta, GA 30314 | 1869 | Elias Blake Jr. | D | 1,764 | 12 |
| Clark Univ., Worcester, MA 01610 | 1887 | Mortimer Appley | P | 2,777 | 205 |
| Clarke (W), Dubuque, IA 52001 | 1843 | Meneve Dunham | P | 676 | 55 |
| Clarkson Coll. of Tech. Potsdam, NY 13676 | 1896 | Robert A. Plane | P | 3,235 | 202 |
| Cleary, Ypsilanti, MI 48197 | 1883 | James Perry | P | 1,200 | 42 |
| Clemson Univ.*, Clemson, SC 29631 | 1889 | Robert C. Edwards | S | 10,787 | 608 |
| Cleveland Inst. of Art, Cleveland, OH 44106 | 1882 | Joseph McCullough | P | 782 | 82 |
| Cleveland Inst. of Music, Cleveland, OH 44106 | 1920 | Grant Johannesen | P | 246 | 30 |
| Cleveland State Univ., Cleveland, OH 44115 | 1964 | Walter Waetjen | S | 16,467 | 70 |
| Coe, Cedar Rapids, IA 52402 | 1851 | Leo Nussbaum | P,D | 1,070 | 81 |
| Coker, Hartsville, SC 29550 | 1908 | C.H. Womble | P | 409 | 36 |
| Colby, Waterville, ME 04901 | 1813 | Robert E. L. Strider II | P | 1,593 | 135 |
| Colby-Sawyer, New London, NH 03257 | 1837 | Louis Vaccaro | P | 720 | 71 |
| Colgate Univ., Hamilton, NY 13346 | 1819 | Thomas Bartlett | P | 2,485 | 214 |
| Colorado, Colo. Spgs., CO 80903 | 1874 | Lloyd E. Worner | P | 1,850 | 130 |
| Colorado Sch. of Mines, Golden, CO 80401 | 1874 | Guy McBride Jr. | S | 2,204 | 133 |

| ame, address | Year | Governing official and affiliation | Stu-dents | Teach-ers |
|---|---|---|---|---|
| olorado State Univ.*, Fort Collins, CO 80523 | 1879 | A.R. Chamberlain | S | 17,426 | 952 |
| olorado, Univ. of (A), Boulder, CO 80302 | 1876 | R.C. Rautenstraus | S | 30,428 | 2,729 |
| Colorado Springs, Colorado Springs, CO 80907 | 1965 | Donald Schwartz, Chan. | S | 4,309 | 150 |
| olorado Women's (W), Denver, CO 80220 | 1888 | Sherry Manning | P | 425 | 39 |
| olumbia (W), Columbia, SC 29203 | 1854 | Ralph Mirse | P,D | 876 | 78 |
| olumbia Bible, Columbia, SC 29203 | 1851 | W. Merle Hill | P | 2,218 | 74 |
| olumbia Union, Takoma Park, MD 20012 | 1923 | J. Robertson McQuilkin | P | 980 | 40 |
| olumbia Union, Takoma Park, MD 20012 | 1904 | Colin Standish * | D | 914 | 69 |
| olumbia Univ., New York, NY 10027 | 1754 | William McGill | P | 16,853 | 1,440 |
| Teachers College, New York, NY 10027 | 1887 | L.A. Cremin | P | 5,922 | 403 |
| olumbus, Columbus, GA 31907 | 1958 | Thomas Y. Whitley | S | 4,961 | 208 |
| olumbus Coll. of Art & Design, Columbus, OH 43215 | 1870 | Joseph Canzani, Dean | P | 593 | 54 |
| oncord, Athens, WV 24712 | 1872 | Meredith Freeman | S | 1,730 | 90 |
| oncordia, Bronxville, NY 10708 | 1881 | Ralph Schultz | D | 415 | 45 |
| oncordia, Moorhead, MN 56560 | 1891 | Paul Dovre | D | 2,647 | 148 |
| oncordia, St. Paul, MN 55104 | 1893 | Gerhardt Hyatt | D | 600 | 50 |
| oncordia Teachers, River Forest, IL 60305 | 1864 | Paul A. Zimmerman | D | 1,206 | 103 |
| oncordia Teachers, Seward, NE 68434 | 1894 | M.J. Stelmachowicz | P | 1,039 | 107 |
| onnecticut, New London, CT 06320 | 1911 | Oakes Ames | P | 1,942 | 144 |
| onnecticut, Univ. of, Storrs, CT 06268 | 1881 | Glenn Ferguson | S | 22,186 | 1,407 |
| onverse (W), Spartanburg, SC 29301 | 1889 | Robert T. Coleman, Jr. | P | 1,800 | 67 |
| ooper Union, New York, NY 10003 | 1859 | John White | P | 915 | 51 |
| oppin State, Baltimore, MD 21216 | 1900 | Calvin Burnett | S | 3,105 | 143 |
| ornell, Mt. Vernon, IA 52314 | 1853 | Philip Secor | P | 900 | 79 |
| ornell Univ.*, Ithaca, NY 14853 | 1865 | Frank Rhodes | S | 16,721 | 1,559 |
| ovenant, Lookout Mt., TN 37350 | 1955 | Martin Essenburg | D | 553 | 31 |
| reighton Univ., Omaha, NE 68178 | 1878 | Rev. Joseph Labaj | D,P | 4,757 | 812 |
| ulver-Stockton, Canton, MO 63435 | 1853 | Orville Wake, Act. | P | 462 | 40 |
| umberland, Williamsburg, KY 40769 | 1889 | J.M. Boswell | D,P | 1,850 | 100 |
| urry, Milton, MA 02186 | 1879 | John S. Hafer | P | 912 | 53 |
| aemen, Amherst, NY 14226 | 1947 | R.S. Marshall | P | 1,100 | 89 |
| akota State, Madison, SD 57042 | 1881 | Richard Bowen | S | 900 | 70 |
| akota Wesleyan Univ., Mitchell, SD 57301 | 1885 | Donald E. Messer | D | 562 | 32 |
| allas Baptist, Dallas, TX 75211 | 1963 | W.E. Thorn | D,P | 981 | 57 |
| allas, Univ. of, Irving, TX 75061 | 1956 | Bryan F. Smith, Chan. | P | 1,911 | 127 |
| ana, Blair, NE 68008 | 1884 | Robert Glass, Act. | D | 473 | 34 |
| artmouth, Hanover, NH 03755 | 1769 | John George Kemeny | P,D | 2,172 | 120 |
| avid Lipscomb, Nashville, TN 37203 | 1891 | Williard Collins | P | 2,154 | 112 |
| avidson, Davidson, NC 28036 | 1837 | Samuel R. Spencer Jr. | P,D | 1,356 | 95 |
| avis & Elkins, Elkins, WV 26241 | 1904 | Gordon Hermanson | P,D | 938 | 82 |
| ayton, Univ. of, Dayton, OH 45469 | 1850 | Rev. R.A. Roesch | D,P | 9,611 | 338 |
| elaware State*, Dover, DE 19901 | 1850 | M. Ludwig | P,D | 800 | 63 |
| elaware, Univ. of*, Newark, DE 19711 | 1890 | Luna I. Mishoe | S | 2,128 | 120 |
| el. Valley Coll. of S&A, Doylestown, PA 18901 | 1833 | E.A. Trabant | P | 18,900 | 811 |
| elta State Univ., Cleveland, MS 38733 | 1896 | Joshua Feldstein | S | 1,339 | 78 |
| enison Univ., Granville, OH 43023 | 1924 | Kent Wyatt | S | 3,240 | 175 |
| enver, Univ. of, Denver, CO 80210 | 1831 | Robert C. Good | P | 2,091 | 156 |
| ePaul Univ., Chicago, IL 60604 | 1864 | Maurice B. Mitchell | P | 7,835 | 457 |
| ePauw Univ., Greencastle, IN 46135 | 1898 | Rev. J.R. Cortelyou | D | 11,300 | 565 |
| | 1837 | Richard Rosser | P,D | 2,384 | 145 |
| etroit Coll. of Business, Dearborn, MI 48126 | 1962 | Robert Sneden | P | 2,065 | 101 |
| etroit Coll. of Law, Detroit, MI 48201 | 1891 | G. Cameron Buchanan | P | 948 | 20 |
| etroit Inst. of Tech., Detroit, MI 48201 | 1877 | H. Thompson | P | 1,400 | 145 |
| etroit, Univ. of, Detroit, MI 48221 | 1877 | Rev. M. Carron | P | 7,633 | 543 |
| eVry Inst. of Tech., Dallas, TX 75285 | 1969 | Douglas Kerr | P | 752 | 42 |
| eVry Inst. of Tech., Chicago, IL 60618 | 1931 | Samuel Edmonds | P | 2,907 | 100 |
| eVry Inst. of Tech., Phoenix, AZ 85016 | 1967 | F. Roger Hess | P | 2,220 | 89 |
| ickinson (A), Carlisle, PA 17013 | 1773 | Samuel Banks | P | 1,660 | 120 |
| ickinson School of Law, Carlisle, PA 17013 | 1834 | Dale F. Shughart | P | 445 | 32 |
| ickinson State, Dickinson, ND 58601 | 1918 | R.C. Gillund | S,P | 1,100 | 70 |
| illard Univ., New Orleans, LA 70122 | 1869 | Samuel Cook | D,P | 1,141 | 89 |
| istrict of Columbia, Univ. of, Washington, DC 20009 | 1851 | Wendell Russell | Mu | 1,310 | 132 |
| oane, Crete, NE 68333 | 1872 | Philip C. Heckman | P | 625 | 43 |
| . Martin Luther, New Ulm, MN 56073 | 1884 | Rev. Conrad Frey | D | 739 | 70 |
| ominican Coll. of Blauvelt, Blauvelt, NY 10913 | 1952 | Sister Natalie Casey | P | 1,135 | 78 |
| ominican Coll. of San Rafael, San Rafael, CA 94901 | 1890 | Sister M. Samuel Conlan | D,P | 722 | 112 |
| ordt, Sioux Center, IA 51250 | 1955 | B.J. Haan | P | 990 | 50 |
| owling, Oakdale, NY 11769 | 1959 | V.P. Meskill | P | 2,224 | 219 |
| rake Univ., Des Moines, IA 50311 | 1881 | Wilbur C. Miller | P | 6,458 | 277 |
| rew Univ., Madison, NJ 07940 | 1866 | Paul Hardin | P | 2,112 | 173 |
| rexel Univ., Philadelphia, PA 19104 | 1891 | William W. Hagerty | P | 10,183 | 310 |
| rury, Springfield, MO 65802 | 1873 | William Everheart | P | 2,214 | 156 |
| ubuque, Univ. of, Dubuque, IA 52001 | 1852 | Walter F. Peterson | P,D | 788 | 59 |
| uke Univ., Durham, NC 27706 | 1838 | Terry Sanford | P,D | 9,970 | 1,253 |
| uquesne Univ., Pittsburgh, PA 15219 | 1878 | Rev. J. McAnulty | P | 7,457 | 462 |
| yke, Cleveland, OH 44114 | 1848 | John Corfias | P | 1,640 | 28 |
| Youville, Buffalo, NY 14201 | 1908 | Sister Mary C. Barton | P,D | 1,400 | 90 |
| arlham, Richmond, IN 47374 | 1847 | Franklin Wallin | D,P | 1,082 | 118 |
| ast Carolina Univ., Greenville, NC 27834 | 1907 | L.W. Jenkins, Chan. | S | 13,899 | 700 |
| ast Central Univ., Ada, OK 74820 | 1909 | Stanley Wagner | S | 3,800 | 149 |
| ast Stroudsburg State, E. Stroudsburg, PA 18301 | 1891 | Darrell Holmes | S | 4,023 | 228 |
| ast Tennessee State Univ., Johnson City, TN 37601 | 1911 | Delos Culp | S | 10,288 | 426 |
| ast Texas Baptist, Marshall, TX 75670 | 1912 | Jerry Dawson | D,P | 799 | 37 |
| ast Texas State Univ., Commerce, TX 75428 | 1889 | F.H. McDowell | S | 9,827 | 425 |
| astern, St. Davids, PA 19087 | 1952 | Daniel E. Weiss | D | 693 | 37 |
| astern Conn. State, Willimantic, CT 06226 | 1889 | Charles Richard Webb | S | 2,342 | 210 |
| astern Illinois Univ., Charleston, IL 61920 | 1895 | Daniel Marvin | S | 9,923 | 505 |
| astern Kentucky Univ., Richmond, KY 40475 | 1906 | Julius Powell | S | 13,510 | 569 |
| astern Maine Voc. Tech Inst., Bangor, ME 04401 | 1965 | Francis Sprague | S | 1,550 | 45 |
| astern Mennonite, Harrisonburg, VA 22801 | 1917 | Myron S. Augsburger | P,D | 1,007 | 68 |
| astern Michigan Univ., Ypsilanti, MI 48197 | 1849 | James Brickley | S | 18,931 | 752 |
| astern Montana, Billings, MT 59101 | 1927 | J. Van de Wetering | S | 3,453 | 166 |
| astern Nazarene, Wollaston, MA 02170 | 1918 | Donald Irwin | P | 817 | 60 |
| astern New Mexico Univ., Portales, NM 88130 | 1934 | Warren Armstrong | S | 4,266 | 250 |
| astern Oregon State, LaGrande, OR 97850 | 1929 | Rodney A. Briggs | S | 1,471 | 105 |

| Name, address | Year | Governing official and affiliation | | Students | Teachers |
|---|---|---|---|---|---|
| Eastern Washington State, Cheney, WA 99004 | 1890 | H.G. Frederickson | S | 7,000 | 35 |
| Eckerd, St. Petersburg, FL 33733 | 1958 | Billy D. Wireman | D | 863 | 6 |
| Edgecliff, Cincinnati, OH 45206 | 1935 | Sr. M. Molitor | D | 971 | 6 |
| Edgewood, Madison, WI 53711 | 1927 | Sister Cecilia Carey | P,D | 624 | 6 |
| Edinboro State, Edinboro, PA 16444 | 1857 | Chester T. McNerney | S | 6,755 | 4. |
| Elizabeth City State Univ., Eliz. City, NC 27909 | 1891 | Marion Thorpe, Chan. | S | 1,629 | 11 |
| Elizabethtown, Elizabethtown, PA 17022 | 1899 | Morely J. Mays | P | 1,633 | 14 |
| Elmhurst, Elmhurst, IL 60126 | 1871 | Ivan Frick | P,D | 2,653 | 17 |
| Elmira, Elmira, NY 14901 | 1855 | Leonard Grant | P | 3,139 | 24 |
| Elon, Elon College, NC 27244 | 1889 | J.F. Young | P | 2,175 | 9 |
| Embry Riddle Aero. Univ., Daytona Beach, FL 32014 | 1926 | Jack R. Hunt | P | 2,250 | 18 |
| Emerson, Boston, MA 02116 | 1880 | Gus Turbeville | P | 1,434 | 9 |
| Emmanuel (W), Boston, MA 02115 | 1919 | Sister Mary McCarthy | D,P | 1,390 | 10 |
| Emory & Henry, Emory, VA 24327 | 1836 | Thomas F. Chilcote | P | 794 | 6 |
| Emory Univ., Atlanta, GA 30322 | 1836 | S.S. Atwood | D,P | 7,334 | 9 |
| Emporia Kansas State, Emporia, KS 66801 | 1857 | John Visser | S | 6,007 | 33 |
| Erskine, Due West, SC 29639 | 1839 | M.S. Bell | D | 771 | 6 |
| Eureka, Eureka, IL 61530 | 1855 | Daniel Gilbert | P | 410 | 3 |
| Evangel, Springville, MO 65802 | 1955 | Robert Spence | P | 1,291 | 6 |
| Evansville, Univ. of, Evansville, IN 47702 | 1854 | Wallace B. Graves | D | 4,904 | 2. |
| Evergreen State, Olympia, WA 98505 | 1967 | Daniel Evans | S | 2,600 | 13 |
| Fairfield Univ., Fairfield, CT 06430 | 1942 | Rev. Thomas Fitzgerald | P | 4,791 | 17 |
| Fairleigh Dickinson Univ., Rutherford, NJ 07070 | 1942 | Jerome Pollack | P | 12,134 | 55 |
| Fairmont State, Fairmont, WV 26554 | 1867 | Eston K. Feaster | S | 5,072 | 18 |
| Faith Baptist Bible, Ankeny, IA 50021 | 1921 | David Nettleton | P | 600 | 2 |
| Fayetteville St. Univ., Fayetteville, NC 28301 | 1877 | Charles Lyons Jr. | S | 2,136 | 7 |
| Felician, Lodi, NJ 07644 | 1942 | Sr. Mary Lawniczak | P,D | 822 | 3 |
| Ferris State, Big Rapids, MI 49507 | 1884 | Robert Ewigleben | S | 9,934 | 53 |
| Ferrum, Ferrum, VA 24088 | 1913 | Joseph T. Hart | D,P | 1,344 | 7 |
| Findlay, Findlay, OH 45840 | 1882 | Glen R. Rasmusson | P,D | 931 | 7 |
| Fisk Univ., Nashville, TN 37203 | 1867 | Walter Leonard | P | 1,281 | 7 |
| Fitchburg State, Fitchburg, MA 01420 | 1894 | Vincent J. Mars | S | 6,626 | 28 |
| Flagler, St. Augustine, FL 32084 | 1968 | William L. Proctor | P | 680 | 3 |
| Florida Atlantic Univ., Boca Raton, FL 33431 | 1961 | G.L. Creech | S | 7,000 | 35 |
| Florida A.&M. Univ.*, Tallahassee, FL 32307 | 1887 | Benjamin Luther Perry Jr. | S | 5,725 | 38 |
| Florida Inst. of Tech., Melbourne, FL 32901 | 1958 | Jerome P. Keuper | P | 4,287 | 3. |
| Florida Memorial, Miami, FL 33054 | 1879 | Willie Robinson | P | 940 | 4 |
| Florida Southern, Lakeland, FL 33802 | 1885 | Robert Davis | P | 1,581 | 8 |
| Florida State Univ., Tallahassee, FL 32306 | 1857 | Bernard Sliger | S | 21,356 | 1,1. |
| Florida Tech. Univ., Orlando, FL 32816 | 1963 | Trevor Colbourn | S | 10,605 | 39 |
| Florida Univ. of*, Gainesville, FL 32611 | 1853 | Robert Marston | S | 29,952 | 2,96 |
| Fontbonne, St. Louis, MO 63105 | 1917 | Sister Jane Hassett | P,D | 901 | 7 |
| Fordham Univ., Bronx, NY 10458 | 1841 | Rev. James C. Finley | P | 15,027 | 46 |
| Ft. Hays State, Hays, KS 67601 | 1902 | G. Tomanek | S | 4,690 | 18 |
| Ft. Lauderdale, Ft. Lauderdale, FL 33301 | 1956 | Lyle E. Anderson | P | 661 | 4 |
| Fort Lewis, Durango, CO 81301 | 1911 | Rexer Berndt | S | 2,800 | 16 |
| Fort Valley State*, Fort Valley, GA 31030 | 1895 | Cleveland W. Pettigrew | S | 1,800 | 15 |
| Fort Wayne Bible, Fort Wayne, IN 46807 | 1904 | Timothy Warner | D,P | 607 | 4 |
| Fort Wright, Spokane, WA 99204 | 1907 | Sr. Katherine Gray | P | 343 | 3 |
| Framingham State, Framingham, MA 01701 | 1839 | D. Justin McCarthy | S | 4,748 | 24 |
| Francis Marion, Florence, SC 29501 | 1970 | Walter D. Smith | S | 2,720 | 11 |
| Franklin, Franklin, IN 46131 | 1834 | Edwin A. Penn | P,D | 685 | 6 |
| Franklin, Univ., Columbus, OH 43215 | 1902 | Joseph Frasch | P | 3,875 | 13 |
| Franklin and Marshall, Lancaster, PA 17604 | 1787 | Keith Spalding | P | 1,974 | 12 |
| Franklin Pierce, Rindge, NH 03461 | 1962 | Walter Peterson | P | 1,102 | 5 |
| Freed-Hardeman, Henderson, TN 38340 | 1869 | E. Claude Gardner | D | 1,413 | 7 |
| Free Will Baptist Bible, Nashville, TN 37205 | 1942 | L.C. Johnson | D,P | 550 | 2 |
| Fresno Pacific, Fresno, CA 93702 | 1944 | Edmund Janzen | Mu | 719 | 4 |
| Friends, Univ., Wichita, KS 67213 | 1898 | Harold C. Cope | D,P | 858 | 6 |
| Frostburg State, Frostburg, MD 21532 | 1898 | Nelson Guild | S | 3,186 | 20 |
| Furman Univ., Greenville, SC 29613 | 1826 | John Johns | P | 2,721 | 18 |
| Gallaudet, Washington, DC 20002 | 1864 | Edward C. Merrill Jr. | P | 943 | 12 |
| Gannon, Erie, PA 16501 | 1944 | Rev. Msgr. W.J. Nash | P | 3,644 | 21 |
| Gardner-Webb, Boiling Springs, NC 28017 | 1905 | C. Williams | D,P | 1,242 | 7 |
| General Motors Inst., Flint, MI 48502 | 1919 | W. Cottingham | P | 2,175 | 15 |
| Geneva, Beaver Falls, PA 15010 | 1848 | Edwin C. Clarke | D | 1,395 | 9 |
| George Fox, Newberg, OR 97132 | 1891 | David Le Shana | D | 630 | 4 |
| George Mason Univ., Fairfax, VA 22030 | 1956 | Robert Krug, Act. | S | 8,771 | 3 |
| Geo. Peabody Coll. for Teachers, Nashville, TN 37203 | 1875 | John Dunworth | P | 2,000 | 15 |
| Geo. Washington Univ., Washington, DC 20052 | 1821 | Lloyd H. Elliott | P | 11,544 | 99 |
| George Williams, Downers Grove, IL 60515 | 1890 | Richard E. Hamlin | P | 1,895 | 7 |
| Georgetown, Georgetown, KY 40324 | 1829 | Robert L. Mills | D | 1,010 | 6 |
| Georgetown Univ. (A), Washington, DC 20057 | 1789 | Rev. Timothy Healy | P | 11,043 | 1,01 |
| Georgia, Milledgeville, GA 31061 | 1889 | J. Whitney Bunting | S | 3,510 | 9 |
| Georgia Inst. Of Tech.*, Atlanta, GA 30332 | 1885 | Joseph M. Pettit | S | 10,741 | 75 |
| Georgia Southern, Statesboro, GA 30458 | 1906 | Pope A. Duncan | S | 6,114 | 30 |
| Georgia Southwestern, Americus, GA 31709 | 1908 | William B. King | S | 2,409 | 12 |
| Georgia State Univ., Atlanta, GA 30303 | 1913 | Noah N. Langdale Jr. | S | 20,686 | 80 |
| Georgia, Univ. of*, Athens, GA 30602 | 1785 | Fred C. Davison | S | 21,665 | 1,69 |
| Georgian Court, Lakewood, NJ 08701 | 1908 | Sister Maria Cordis | P,D | 950 | 8 |
| Gettysburg, Gettysburg, PA 17325 | 1832 | Chas. Glassick | P | 1,900 | 13 |
| Glassboro State, Glassboro, NJ 08028 | 1923 | Mark Chamberlain | S | 10,331 | 40 |
| Glenville State, Glenville, WV 26351 | 1872 | Wm. Simmons | S | 1,406 | 7 |
| Goddard, Plainfield, VT 05667 | 1938 | John Hall, Act. | P | 980 | 7 |
| Golden Gate Univ., San Francisco, CA 94105 | 1901 | Otto Butz | P | 9,431 | 4 |
| Gonzaga Univ., Spokane, WA 99258 | 1887 | Bernard Coughlin | P | 3,200 | 17 |
| Gordon, Wenham, MA 01984 | 1889 | Richard Gross | P | 980 | 7 |
| Goshen, Goshen, IN 46526 | 1894 | J. Lawrence Burkholder | D,P | 1,214 | 5 |
| Goucher (W), Towson, MD 21204 | 1885 | Rhoda Dorsey | S | 882 | 9 |
| Governors State Univ., Park Forest South, IL 60466 | 1969 | L. Malamuth II | S | 3,600 | 15 |
| Grace Coll. of the Bible, Omaha, NE 68108 | 1943 | Robert Benton | P | 500 | 3 |
| Graceland, Lamoni, IA 50140 | 1895 | Franklin Hough, Act. | P,D | 1,234 | 8 |
| Grambling State Univ., Grambling, LA 71245 | 1901 | Ralph W.E. Jones | S | 3,749 | 20 |
| Grand Canyon, Phoenix, AZ 85061 | 1949 | William R. Hintze | D,P | 1,137 | 6 |
| Grand Valley State, Allendale, MI 49401 | 1960 | Arend Lubbers | S | 7,540 | 28 |

| me, address | Year | Governing official and affiliation | | Stu-dents | Teach-ers |
|---|---|---|---|---|---|
| and View, Des Moines, IA 50316 | 1896 | Karl F. Langrock | D,P | 1,063 | 66 |
| eat Falls, Coll. of, Great Falls, MT 59405 | 1932 | Msgr. A.M. Brown | P,D | 1,223 | 89 |
| een Mountain, Poultney, VT 05764 | 1834 | James Pollock | P | 383 | 29 |
| eenville, Greenville, IL 62246 | 1892 | O.R. Herron | D,P | 856 | 66 |
| nnell, Grinnell, IA 50112 | 1846 | A. Richard Turner | P | 1,158 | 102 |
| ove City, Grove City, PA 16127 | 1876 | Charles S. MacKenzie | P | 2,241 | 100 |
| ilford, Greensboro, NC 27410 | 1837 | Grimsley T. Hobbs | D | 1,649 | 100 |
| stavus Adolphus, St. Peter, MN 56082 | 1862 | Edward Lindell | D,P | 2,200 | 145 |
| vynedd-Mercy, Gwynedd Valley, PA 19437 | 1948 | Sister Isabelle Keiss | D,P | 1,092 | 113 |
| hnemann Medical, Philadelphia, PA 19102 | 1848 | William Likoff | P | 794 | 327 |
| milton, Clinton, NY 13323 | 1812 | J.M. Carovano | P | 1,600 | 130 |
| mline Univ., St. Paul, MN 55104 | 1854 | Jerry E. Hudson | P | 1,816 | 148 |
| mpden-Sydney (M), Hampden-Sydney, VA 23943 | 1776 | Josiah Bunting III | D,P | 736 | 56 |
| mpton Institute, Hampton, VA 23668 | 1868 | Carl M. Hill, Act | P | 2,618 | 248 |
| nover, Hanover, IN 47243 | 1827 | John E. Horner | D,P | 901 | 71 |
| rdin-Simmons Univ., Abilene, TX 79601 | 1891 | Elwin L. Skiles | D | 1,641 | 117 |
| rding, Searcy, AR 72143 | 1924 | Clinton L. Ganus Jr. | D | 2,987 | 157 |
| rris Teachers, St. Louis, MO 63103 | 1857 | Richard Stumpe | MU | 1,300 | 65 |
| rtford, Univ. of, W. Hartford, CT 06117 | 1877 | S. Trachtenberg | P | 9,420 | 410 |
| rtwick, Oneonta, NY 13820 | 1928 | Earl Deubler Jr., Act. | P | 1,550 | 120 |
| rvard Univ.*, Cambridge, MA 02138 | 1636 | Derek Curtis Bok | P | 20,498 | 3,860 |
| rvey Mudd, Claremont, CA 91711 | 1955 | D. Kenneth Baker | P | 481 | 52 |
| stings, Hastings, NE 68901 | 1882 | Clyde B. Matters | P | 720 | 54 |
| verford, Haverford, PA 19401 | 1833 | Stephen Cary, Act. | P | 894 | 72 |
| waii, Univ. of, Honolulu, HI 96822 | 1907 | Fujio Matsuda | S | 47,214 | 2,302 |
| ald Engineering, San Francisco, CA 94109 | 1863 | James Dietz | P | 1,000 | 70 |
| idelberg, Tiffin, OH 44883 | 1850 | Leslie H. Fishel Jr. | P,D | 1,018 | 107 |
| nderson State Univ., Arkadelphia, AR 71923 | 1890 | Martin Garrison | P | 3,333 | 175 |
| ndrix, Conway, AR 72032 | 1884 | Roy Schilling, Jr. | D | 1,058 | 54 |
| gh Point, High Point, NC 27262 | 1924 | Wendell M. Patton | D | 1,132 | 60 |
| lsdale, Hillsdale, MI 49242 | 1844 | George C. Roche III. | P | 1,029 | 70 |
| ram, Hiram, OH 44234 | 1850 | Elmer Jagow | P,D | 1,156 | 110 |
| bart & William Smith, Geneva, NY 14456 | 1822 | Allan A. Kuusisto | P | 1,700 | 132 |
| fstra Univ., Hempstead, NY 11550 | 1935 | James Shuart | P | 9,420 | 604 |
| llins (W), Hollins Coll., VA 24020 | 1842 | Carroll Brewster | P | 990 | 91 |
| ly Cross, Coll. of the, Worcester, MA 01610 | 1843 | Rev. John Brooks | D | 2,565 | 195 |
| ly Family, Philadelphia, PA 19114 | 1954 | Sister Mary Lillian | D,P | 1,102 | 84 |
| ly Names, Oakland, CA 94619 | 1868 | Sister M. Irene Woodward | P | 619 | 43 |
| od, Frederick, MD 21701 | 1893 | Martha Church | P,D | 1,506 | 117 |
| pe, Holland, MI 49423 | 1866 | Gordon Van Wylen | P | 2,330 | 140 |
| ughton, Houghton, NY 14744 | 1883 | D.R. Chamberlain | P,D | 1,220 | 84 |
| uston, Univ. of, Houston, TX 77004 | 1927 | William Hinton | D | 1,850 | 85 |
| Downtown College, Houston, TX 77002 | 1974 | Philip G. Hoffman | P | 40,000 | 1,200 |
| ward Payne, Brownwood, TX 76801 | 1889 | J. Don Boney, Chan. | S | 4,517 | 179 |
| ward Univ., Washington, DC 20059 | 1867 | Roger L. Brooks | P | 1,422 | 90 |
| mboldt State Univ., Arcata, CA 95521 | 1913 | James E. Cheek | P | 9,815 | 1,908 |
| ntingdon, Montgomery, AL 36106 | 1854 | Alistair McCrone | S | 7,442 | 425 |
| ntington, Huntington, IN 46750 | 1897 | Allen Jackson | D,P | 651 | 52 |
| ron, Huron, SD 57350 | 1883 | E. DeWitt Baker | P | 530 | 30 |
| sson, Bangor, ME 04401 | 1898 | Wendell Jahnke | P | 315 | 26 |
| ston-Tillotson, Austin, TX 78702 | 1876 | Delmont Merrill | P | 1,100 | 42 |
| | | John T. King | D | 850 | 49 |
| aho, Coll. of, Caldwell, ID 83605 | 1891 | William Cassell | P | 893 | 46 |
| aho State Univ., Pocatello, ID 83209 | 1901 | Myron Coulter | S | 9,843 | 499 |
| aho, Univ. of*, Moscow, ID 83843 | 1889 | Richard D. Gibb | S | 8,168 | 400 |
| nois, Jacksonville, IL 62650 | 1829 | Donald Mundinger | P | 684 | 45 |
| nois Benedictine, Lisle, IL 60532 | 1887 | Richard Becker | P,D | 1,405 | 87 |
| nois Coll. of Optometry, Chicago, IL 60616 | 1872 | Alfred Rosenbloom | P | 574 | 65 |
| nois Coll. of Pod. Med., Chicago, IL 60610 | 1912 | P.R. Brachman | P | 596 | 90 |
| nois Inst. of Technology, Chicago, IL 60616 | 1892 | Thomas L. Martin Jr. | P | 6,806 | 757 |
| nois State Univ., Normal, IL 61761 | 1857 | Gene Budig | S | 17,986 | 949 |
| nois, Univ. of*, Urbana, IL 61801 | 1867 | John E. Corbally | S | 64,531 | 7,558 |
| Chicago Circle*, Chicago, IL 60680 | 1965 | Donald Riddle, Chan. | S | 20,252 | 975 |
| Medical Center*, Chicago, IL 60680 | 1896 | Joseph Begando, Chan. | S | 4,538 | 3,801 |
| Urbana-Champaign*, Urbana, IL 61801 | 1867 | Jack W. Peltason, Chan. | S | 33,552 | 2,261 |
| nois Wesleyan Univ., Bloomington, IL 61701 | 1850 | Robert Eckley | P,D | 1,682 | 124 |
| maculata, Immaculata, PA 19345 | 1920 | Sister Mary Antione | P,D | 1,038 | 137 |
| maculate Heart, Los Angeles, CA 90027 | 1916 | Nancy Heer | P | 701 | 40 |
| arnate Word, San Antonio, TX 78209 | 1881 | Sr. Margaret Slattery | D | 1,450 | 84 |
| diana Central Univ., Indianapolis, IN 46227 | 1902 | Gene Sease | P,D | 3,316 | 138 |
| diana State Univ., Terre Haute, IN 47809 | 1865 | Richard Landini | S | 14,462 | 782 |
| diana Univ., Bloomington, IN 47401 | 1820 | John W. Ryan | S | 77,948 | 3,223 |
| diana Univ. of Pa. Indiana, PA 15701 | 1875 | Robert C. Wilburn | S | 11,420 | 610 |
| ter Amer. Univ. of P.R. San Juan, PR 00936 | 1962 | A. Leslie Leonard | P | 1,809 | 140 |
| ona, New Rochelle, NY 10801 | 1912 | Ramon A. Cruz | P | 28,516 | 508 |
| wa State Univ.*, Ames, IA 50011 | 1940 | John Driscoll | P,D | 4,926 | 256 |
| wa, Univ. of, Iowa City, IA 52242 | 1858 | W. Robert Parks | S | 22,803 | 1,800 |
| wa Wesleyan, Mt. Pleasant, IA 52641 | 1847 | Willard L. Boyd | S | 21,271 | 1,193 |
| aca, Ithaca, NY 14850 | 1842 | Louis Haselmayer | P,D | 678 | 70 |
| | 1892 | James J. Whalen | P | 4,476 | 276 |
| ckson State Univ., Jackson, MS 39217 | 1877 | John A. Peoples Jr. | S | 7,928 | 882 |
| cksonville State Univ., Jacksonville, AL 36265 | 1883 | Ernest Stone | S | 7,500 | 300 |
| cksonville Univ., Jacksonville, FL 32211 | 1934 | Robert H. Spiro | P | 2,014 | 135 |
| mes Madison Univ., Harrisonburg, VA 22801 | 1908 | Ronald Carrier | S | 7,659 | 380 |
| mestown, Jamestown, ND 58401 | 1883 | J.N. Anderson | P,D | 543 | 52 |
| rvis Christian, Hawkins, TX 75765 | 1912 | E.W. Rand | P | 548 | 48 |
| rsey City State, Jersey City, NJ 07305 | 1927 | William Maxwell | S | 7,500 | 309 |
| nn Brown Univ., Siloam Springs, AR 72761 | 1919 | John E. Brown Jr. | P | 671 | 48 |
| nn Carroll Univ., Cleveland, OH 44118 | 1886 | Rev. Henry Birkenhauer | D | 3,637 | 172 |
| nn F. Kennedy Univ., Orinda, CA 94563 | 1964 | Robert Fisher | P | 650 | 85 |
| nn Marshall Law School, Chicago, IL 60604 | 1899 | Louis Bird | P | 1,500 | 80 |
| nn Wesley, Owosso, MI 48867 | 1909 | H.C. Roost | P | 520 | 45 |

*Oldest college in the United States

| Name, address | Year | Governing official and affiliation | | Students | Teachers |
|---|---|---|---|---|---|
| Johns Hopkins Univ., Baltimore, MD 21218 | 1876 | Steven Muller | P | 10,000 | 7 |
| Johnson C. Smith Univ., Charlotte, NC 28216 | 1867 | Wilbert Greenfield | P,D | 1,635 | |
| Johnson State, Johnston, VT 05656 | 1866 | E. Elmendorf | S | 1,253 | 10 |
| Johnson & Wales, Providence, RI 02903 | 1914 | Morris J. Gaebe | P | 5,500 | 10 |
| Jones, Jacksonville, FL 32211 | 1918 | Delores C. Jones | P | 432 | 1 |
| at Orlando, Orlando, FL 32803 | 1953 | Jack Jones | P | 1,565 | |
| Judson, Marion, AL 36756 | 1838 | N. McCrummen | D | 450 | |
| Juilliard School, The, New York, NY 10023 | 1905 | Peter Mennin | P | 1,000 | 20 |
| Juniata, Huntingdon, PA 16652 | 1876 | Frederick M. Binder | P | 1,130 | 7 |
| Kalamazoo, Kalamazoo, MI 49007 | 1833 | George N. Rainsford | D | 1,501 | 8 |
| Kan. City Art Inst., Kansas City, MO 64111 | 1885 | John W. Lottes | P | 722 | 5 |
| Kan. City Coll. of Osteop. Med., Kansas City, MO 64124 | 1916 | Rudolph Bremen | P | 578 | 1 |
| Kansas Newman, Wichita, KS 67213 | 1933 | Rev. Roman S. Galiardi | D,P | 598 | 5 |
| Kansas State Univ.*, Manhattan, KS 66506 | 1863 | Duane Acker | P | 18,220 | 97 |
| Kansas, Univ. of, Lawrence, KS 66045 | 1865 | Archie R. Dykes, Chan. | S | 24,372 | 1,2 |
| Kansas Wesleyan, Salina, KS 67401 | 1886 | Daniel Bratton | D | 427 | |
| Kean Coll. of New Jersey, Union, NJ 07083 | 1855 | Nathan Weiss | P | 12,450 | 3 |
| Kearney State, Kearney, NE 68847 | 1905 | Brendan McDonald | S | 5,814 | 23 |
| Keene State, Keene, NH 03431 | 1909 | Leo Redfern | S | 2,998 | 14 |
| Kendall, Evanston, IL 60201 | 1934 | Andrew Cothran | P | 325 | 2 |
| Kent State Univ., Kent, OH 44240 | 1910 | Brage Golding | S | 28,024 | 1,1 |
| Kentucky State Univ.*, Frankfort, KY 40601 | 1886 | W.A. Butts | S | 2,389 | 22 |
| Kentucky, Univ. of*, Lexington, KY 40506 | 1878 | Otis A. Singletary | S | 21,282 | 1,40 |
| Kentucky Wesleyan (A), Owensboro, KY 42301 | 1858 | William James | P | 708 | 7 |
| Kenyon, Gambier, OH 43022 | 1824 | Philip Jordan Jr. | P | 1,384 | 12 |
| Keuka (W), Keuka Park, NY 14478 | 1890 | William Boyle, Jr. | P | 600 | 5 |
| King, Bristol, TN 37620 | 1867 | Powell A. Fraser | D | 301 | 4 |
| King's, Briarcliff Manor, NY 10510 | 1938 | Robert A. Cook | P | 792 | 6 |
| King's, Wilkes-Barre, PA 18711 | 1946 | Rev. Charles Sherrer | D | 2,088 | 10 |
| Kirksville Coll. of Osteop. Med., Kirksville, MO 63501 | 1892 | H.C. Moore | P | 491 | 8 |
| Knox, Galesburg, IL 61401 | 1837 | E. Inman Fox | P | 1,021 | 9 |
| Knoxville, Knoxville, TN 37921 | 1875 | Rutherford Adkins | P | 735 | 6 |
| Kutztown State, Kutztown, PA 19530 | 1866 | Lawrence M. Stratton | S | 5,187 | 29 |
| Ladycliff, Highland Falls, NY 10928 | 1933 | Rev. Francis J. Breidenbach | P | 500 | 3 |
| Lafayette, Easton, PA 18042 | 1826 | K.R. Bergethon | P,D | 2,147 | 16 |
| LaGrange, LaGrange, GA 30240 | 1831 | Waights Henry Jr. | D | 800 | 5 |
| Lake Erie (W), Painesville, OH 44077 | 1856 | Paul Newland, Act. | P | 498 | 8 |
| Lake Forest, Lake Forest, IL 60045 | 1857 | Eugene Hotchkiss | P,D | 1,072 | 4 |
| Lakeland, Sheboygan, WI 53081 | 1864 | Ralph Mirse | D | 576 | 4 |
| Lake Superior State, Sault Ste. Marie, MI 49783 | 1946 | Kenneth Shouldice | S | 2,457 | 13 |
| Lamar Univ., Beaumont, TX 77710 | 1923 | John E. Gray | S | 12,723 | 4 |
| Lander, Greenwood, SC 29646 | 1872 | Larry Jackson | P | 1,578 | 9 |
| Lane, Jackson, TN 38301 | 1882 | Herman Stone Jr. | D,P | 551 | 5 |
| Langston Univ.*, Langston, OK 73050 | 1897 | Thos. English | S | 1,201 | 6 |
| LaRoche, Pittsburgh, PA 15237 | 1963 | Mary Coultas | P | 1,009 | 9 |
| La Salle, Philadelphia, PA 19141 | 1863 | Bro. Patrick Ellis | D,P | 5,600 | 37 |
| La Verne, La Verne, CA 91750 | 1891 | Armen Sarafian | P | 2,737 | 25 |
| Lawrence Inst. of Tech., Southfield, MI 48075 | 1932 | W.H. Buell | P | 4,584 | 20 |
| Lawrence Univ., Appleton, WI 54911 | 1847 | Thomas S. Smith | P | 1,300 | 14 |
| Lebanon Valley, Annville, PA 17003 | 1866 | Frederick Sample | P | 1,100 | 11 |
| Lee, Cleveland, TN 37311 | 1918 | Charles Conn | D,P | 1,197 | 5 |
| Lehigh Univ., Bethlehem, PA 18015 | 1865 | W. Deming Lewis | P | 6,261 | 60 |
| Le Moyne, Syracuse, NY 13214 | 1946 | W. O'Halloran | P,D | 1,767 | 14 |
| Le Moyne-Owen, Memphis, TN 38126 | 1870 | Walter Walker | P | 1,040 | 6 |
| Lenoir-Rhyne, Hickory, NC 28601 | 1891 | Albert Anderson | D,P | 1,139 | 9 |
| Lesley (W), Cambridge, MA 02138 | 1909 | Don A. Orton | P | 1,311 | 10 |
| Lewis Univ., Lockport, IL 60441 | 1930 | Bro. Vincent Neil, Act. | P,D | 4,222 | 2 |
| Lewis & Clark, Portland, OR 97219 | 1867 | John R. Howard | P | 2,976 | 20 |
| Limestone, Gaffney, SC 29340 | 1845 | Jack Jones Early | P | 835 | 6 |
| Lincoln Christian, Lincoln, IL 62656 | 1944 | Robert Phillips | P,D | 646 | 3 |
| Lincoln Memorial Univ., Harrogate, TN 37752 | 1897 | Frank W. Welch | P | 917 | 10 |
| Lincoln Univ., Jefferson City, MO 65101 | 1866 | James Frank | S | 2,400 | 16 |
| Lincoln Univ., Lincoln Univ., PA 19352 | 1854 | Herman Branson | S | 1,103 | 10 |
| Lincoln Univ., San Francisco, CA 94118 | 1919 | T. Kong Lee, Chan. | P | 867 | 5 |
| Lindenwood, St. Charles, MO 63301 | 1827 | William Spencer | P | 1,727 | 8 |
| Linfield, McMinnville, OR 97128 | 1849 | Charles Walker | P | 1,000 | 8 |
| Livingston Univ., Livingston, AL 35470 | 1835 | Asa Green | S | 1,348 | 6 |
| Livingstone, Salisbury, NC 28144 | 1879 | F. George Shipman | D | 909 | 5 |
| Lock Haven State, Lock Haven, PA 17745 | 1870 | Francis Hamblin | S | 2,125 | 19 |
| Loma Linda Univ., Loma Linda, CA 92350 | 1905 | V. Norskov Olsen | D | 5,033 | 1,50 |
| Lone Mountain, San Francisco, CA 94118 | 1898 | Sister Gertrude Patch | P | 900 | 6 |
| Long Island Univ., Brooklyn, NY 11201 | 1926 | Edward Clark | P | 7,004 | 24 |
| C.W. Post, Greenvale, NY 11548 | 1954 | Edward Cook | P | 10,803 | 33 |
| Longwood, Farmville, VA 23901 | 1839 | Henry I. Willett, Jr. | P | 2,320 | 15 |
| Loras, Dubuque, IA 52001 | 1839 | P. Di Pasquale Jr. | P | 1,529 | 9 |
| Los Angeles Baptist, Newhall, CA 91322 | 1927 | John Dunkin | D,P | 375 | 2 |
| Louisiana, Pineville, LA 71360 | 1906 | Robert Lynn | P | 1,170 | 5 |
| Louisiana St. Univ.*, Baton Rouge, LA 70803 | 1860 | Martin Woodin | S | 47,150 | 4,74 |
| Baton Rouge Campus, Baton Rouge, LA 70803 | 1860 | Paul Murrill, Chan. | S | 23,886 | 1,23 |
| Law Center, Baton Rouge, LA 70803 | 1906 | Winston Day, Act. Dean | S | 994 | 3 |
| Medical Center, New Orleans, LA 70112 | 1931 | Allen Copping, Chan. | S | 2,239 | 1,96 |
| New Orleans Campus, New Orleans, LA 70122 | 1956 | Homer L. Hitt, Chan. | S | 14,161 | 46 |
| Shreveport Campus, Shreveport, LA 71105 | 1967 | Donald Shipp, Chan. | S | 3,111 | 13 |
| Louisiana Tech. Univ., Ruston, LA 71272 | 1894 | F.J. Taylor | S | 9,017 | 33 |
| Louisville, Univ. of, Louisville, KY 40208 | 1798 | James G. Miller | S | 16,300 | 1,27 |
| Lowell, Univ. of, Lowell, MA 01854 | 1894 | John B. Duff | S | 12,550 | 41 |
| Loyola, Baltimore, MD 21210 | 1852 | Rev. J.A. Sellinger | D,P | 4,529 | 23 |
| Loyola Univ., Chicago, IL 60611 | 1870 | Rev. R.C. Baumhart | D | 14,917 | 1,14 |
| Loyola Univ., New Orleans, LA 70118 | 1912 | Rev. James Carter | D | 4,500 | 25 |
| Loyola Marymount Univ., Los Angeles, CA 90045 | 1911 | Rev. D.P. Merrifield | D | 5,303 | 33 |
| Lubbock Christian, Lubbock, TX 79407 | 1957 | H.M. Pruitt | D | 1,069 | 6 |
| Luther, Decorah, IA 52101 | 1861 | Elwin D. Farwell | P | 1,849 | 14 |
| Lycoming, Williamsport, PA 17701 | 1812 | F. Blumer | D | 1,229 | 7 |
| Lynchburg, Lynchburg, VA 24504 | 1903 | Carey Brewer | P | 2,158 | 12 |
| Lyndon State, Lyndonville, VT 05851 | 1911 | Janet Murphy | S | 963 | 5 |

| ame, address | Year | Governing official and affiliation | | Students | Teachers |
|---|---|---|---|---|---|
| acalester, St. Paul, MN 55105 | 1874 | John B. Davis Jr. | P,D | 1,676 | 120 |
| acMurray, Jacksonville, IL 62650 | 1846 | John Wittich | P,D | 730 | 67 |
| adonna, Livonia, MI 48150 | 1947 | Sr. Mary VandeVeyver | P,D | 2,208 | 111 |
| aine Maritime Academy, Castine, ME 04421 | 1941 | E.A. Rodgers, Supt. | S | 640 | 45 |
| aine System, Univ. of*, Bangor, ME 04401 | 1865 | P. McCarthy, Chan. | S | 26,750 | 1,136 |
| at Augusta, Augusta, ME 04330 | 1965 | K. Allen, Act. | S | 2,966 | 232 |
| at Farmington, Farmington, ME 04938 | 1864 | Einar Olsen | S | 1,898 | 95 |
| at Ft. Kent, Ft. Kent, ME 04743 | 1878 | Richard J. Spath | S | 598 | 28 |
| at Machias, Machias, ME 04654 | 1909 | Arthur Buswell | S | 743 | 56 |
| at Orono*, Orono, ME 04473 | 1865 | Howard Neville | S | 10,688 | 656 |
| at Portland-Gorham, Portland, ME 04103 | 1878 | N.E. Miller | S | 7,602 | 544 |
| at Presque Isle, Presque Isle, ME 04769 | 1903 | P. McCarthy, Chan. | S | 1,269 | 69 |
| alone, Canton, OH 44709 | 1892 | Lon D. Randall | D | 896 | 69 |
| anchester, N. Manchester, IN 46962 | 1889 | Alfred B. Helman | D | 1,171 | 91 |
| anhattan, Riverdale, NY 10471 | 1853 | Brother J.S. Sullivan | P | 4,310 | 325 |
| anhattan Sch. of Music, New York, NY 10027 | 1917 | John O. Crosby | P | 750 | 185 |
| anhattanville, Purchase, NY 10577 | 1841 | Barbara K. Debs | P | 2,296 | 151 |
| ankato State Univ., Mankato, MN 56001 | 1867 | Douglas Moore | S | 12,827 | 565 |
| ansfield State, Mansfield, PA 16933 | 1857 | Lawrence Park | S | 2,900 | 260 |
| arian, Indianapolis, IN 46222 | 1851 | Louis C. Gatto | S,P | 808 | 84 |
| arian Coll. of Fond du Lac, Fond du Lac, WI 54935 | 1936 | James Hanlon | P,D | 514 | 45 |
| arietta, Marietta, OH 45750 | 1835 | Sherrill Cleland | P | 1,647 | 115 |
| arion, Marion, IN 46952 | 1920 | Robert Luckey | D | 870 | 70 |
| arist, Poughkeepsie, NY 12601 | 1946 | Linus Richard Foy | D | 1,881 | 118 |
| arquette Univ., Milwaukee, WI 53233 | 1881 | Rev. J.P. Raynor | P | 13,210 | 807 |
| ars Hill, Mars Hill, NC 28754 | 1856 | Fred Blake Bentley | D | 1,756 | 120 |
| arshall Univ., Huntington, WV 25701 | 1837 | Robert B. Hayes | S | 11,221 | 395 |
| ary Baldwin, Staunton, VA 24401 | 1842 | Virginia Lester | D,P | 671 | 60 |
| ary Hardin Baylor, Belton, TX 76513 | 1845 | Bobby E. Parker | P | 1,117 | 165 |
| ary Washington, Fredericksburg, VA 22401 | 1908 | Prince B. Woodard | S | 2,292 | 138 |
| arycrest, Davenport, IA 52804 | 1939 | Ron Van Ryswyk | P | 1,084 | 98 |
| arygrove, Detroit, MI 48221 | 1910 | Raymond Fleck | D | 1,700 | 164 |
| aryland Inst. of Art, Baltimore, MD 21217 | 1826 | T.E. Klitzke, Act. | P | 1,923 | 110 |
| aryland, Univ. of*, College Park, MD 20742 | 1807 | John S. Toll | S | 77,000 | 6,010 |
| 　Eastern Shore, Princess Anne, MD 21853 | 1882 | William P. Hytche, Chan. | S | 1,014 | 88 |
| arylhurst, Marylhurst, OR 97036 | 1893 | Sr. V.A. Baxter | D | 1,828 | 74 |
| arymount, Salina, KS 67401 | 1922 | Sr. Mary Buser | D,P | 832 | 70 |
| arymount (W)., Tarrytown, NY 10591 | 1907 | Robert Christin | P | 922 | 115 |
| arymount Coll. of Va., Arlington, VA 22207 | 1950 | Sr. M. Majella Berg | P | 734 | 89 |
| arymount Manhattan, New York, NY 10021 | 1936 | Colette Mahoney | P | 1,851 | 150 |
| aryville, Maryville, TN 37801 | 1819 | Wayne Anderson | D,P | 580 | 50 |
| aryville, St. Louis, MO 63141 | 1872 | C. Pritchard, Act. | P,D | 1,072 | 92 |
| arywood, Scranton, PA 18509 | 1915 | Sister M. Coleman Noe | P | 2,956 | 211 |
| assachusetts Coll. Of Art, Boston, MA 02215 | 1873 | John Nolan | S | 1,736 | 120 |
| ass. Coll. of Pharmacy, Boston, MA 02115 | 1823 | Raymond A. Gosselin | P | 1,300 | 120 |
| ass. Institute of Tech.*, Cambridge, MA 02139 | 1861 | Jerome Wiesner | P | 7,972 | 972 |
| ass. Maritime Academy, Buzzards Bay, MA 02532 | 1891 | Lee Harrington | S | 850 | 44 |
| assachusetts, Univ. of*, Boston, MA 02108 | 1863 | Robert C. Wood | S | 29,045 | 1,892 |
| 　Boston Campus, Boston, MA 02125 | 1964 | Carlo L. Golino, Chan. | S | 6,600 | 500 |
| ayville State, Mayville, ND 58257 | 1889 | James Schobel | S | 824 | 55 |
| cKendree, Lebanon, IL 62254 | 1828 | Julian Murphy | D | 749 | 54 |
| cMurry, Abilene, TX 79605 | 1923 | Tom K. Kim | D,P | 1,218 | 73 |
| cNeese State Univ., Lake Charles, LA 70609 | 1939 | Thomas S. Leary | S | 5,525 | 260 |
| cPherson, McPherson, KS 67460 | 1887 | Paul Hoffman | P,D | 515 | 36 |
| edaille, Buffalo, NY 14214 | 1875 | C.R. MacRoy, Act. | P | 582 | 20 |
| edical Coll. of Ga., Augusta, GA 30902 | 1828 | William Moretz | S | 2,224 | 440 |
| edical Coll. of Pa., Philadelphia, PA 19129 | 1850 | Robert J. Slater | P | 836 | 423 |
| edical Univ. of S.C., Charleston, SC 29401 | 1824 | William McCord | S | 2,020 | 630 |
| ed. & Dentistry of NJ, Newark, NJ 07103 | 1956 | S.S. Bergen Jr. | S | 1,542 | 549 |
| eharry Medical, Nashville, TN 37208 | 1876 | Lloyd C. Elam | P | 790 | 240 |
| emphis State Univ., Memphis, TN 38152 | 1912 | Billy Jones | S | 22,000 | 724 |
| enlo, Menlo Park, CA 94025 | 1927 | Richard O'Brien | P | 890 | 80 |
| ercer Univ., Macon, GA 31207 | 1833 | Rufus C. Harris | P,D | 3,622 | 150 |
| ercy, Dobbs Ferry, NY 10522 | 1950 | Donald Grunewald | S | 5,675 | 340 |
| ercy Coll. of Detroit, Detroit, MI 48219 | 1941 | Sister Agnes Mary Mansour | D | 1,936 | 120 |
| ercyhurst, Erie, PA 16501 | 1926 | Marion Shane | P | 1,426 | 104 |
| eredith (W) Raleigh, NC 27611 | 1891 | John Edgar Weems | D,P | 1,544 | 114 |
| errimack, No. Andover, MA 01845 | 1947 | Rev. John A. Coughlan | S | 1,875 | 118 |
| esa, Grand Junction, CO 81501 | 1925 | John Tomlinson | P | 2,716 | 163 |
| essiah, Grantham, PA 17027 | 1909 | D. Ray Hostetter | P | 966 | 86 |
| ethodist, Fayetteville, NC 28301 | 1956 | Richard Pearce | P | 803 | 50 |
| etropolitan State, Denver, CO 80204 | 1965 | James D. Palmer | S | 12,921 | 602 |
| iami Univ., Oxford, OH 45056 | 1809 | Phillip R. Shriver | S | 17,534 | 827 |
| iami, Univ. of, Coral Gables, FL 33124 | 1926 | Henry K. Stanford | P | 16,877 | 1,290 |
| ichigan State Univ., East Lansing, MI 48824 | 1855 | Clifton R. Wharton Jr. | S | 43,459 | 2,687 |
| ichigan Tech Univ., Houghton, MI 49931 | 1885 | Raymond L. Smith | S | 6,387 | 342 |
| ichigan, Univ. of, Ann Arbor, MI 48104 | 1817 | Robben W. Fleming | S | 44,372 | 5,362 |
| id-America Nazarene, Olathe, KS 66061 | 1968 | R. Curtis Smith | D | 1,033 | 60 |
| iddle Tenn. State Univ., Murfreesboro, TN 37132 | 1911 | M.G. Scarlett | S | 10,400 | 457 |
| iddlebury, Middlebury, VT 05753 | 1800 | Olin Robinson | P | 1,917 | 155 |
| idland Lutheran, Fremont, NE 68025 | 1883 | L. Dale Lund | D,P | 852 | 78 |
| idwestern State Univ., Wichita Falls, TX 76308 | 1922 | John Barker | S | 4,600 | 157 |
| iles, Birmingham, AL 35208 | 1905 | W. Clyde Williams | D | 1,245 | 89 |
| illersville State, Millersville, PA 17551 | 1854 | William Duncan | S | 6,292 | 329 |
| illigan, Milligan Coll., TN 37682 | 1866 | Jess W. Johnson | P | 695 | 60 |
| illikin Univ., Decatur, IL 62522 | 1901 | J. Roger Miller. | P,D | 1,520 | 122 |
| ills (W), Oakland, CA 94613 | 1852 | Barbara White. | P | 957 | 109 |
| illsaps, Jackson, MS 39210 | 1890 | Edward Collins | D | 955 | 77 |
| ilton, Milton, WI 53563 | 1867 | Joseph Kipper | P | 500 | 46 |
| ilwaukee Sch. of Eng., Milwaukee, WI 53201 | 1903 | Karl O. Werwath | P | 1,311 | 73 |
| pls. Coll. of Art & Design, Minneapolis, MN 55404 | 1886 | J. Hausman | P | 960 | 78 |
| innesota, Univ. of* Minneapolis, MN 55455 | 1851 | C.P. Magrath | S | 82,401 | 5,601 |
| 　Duluth Campus*, Duluth, MN 55812 | 1947 | Robt. Heller(Prov.) | S | 6,561 | 466 |
| 　Morris Campus*, Morris, MN 56267 | 1960 | John Imholte (Prov.) | S | 1,740 | 104 |
| inot State, Minot, ND 58701 | 1913 | Gordon Olson | S | 2,026 | 136 |
| isericordia, Dallas, PA 18612 | 1924 | Sister Ann Gallagher | D | 933 | 100 |
| ississippi, Clinton, MS 39058 | 1826 | Lewis Nobles | D,P | 3,088 | 150 |

| Name, address | Year | Governing official and affiliation | | Students | Teachers |
|---|---|---|---|---|---|
| Mississippi Industrial, Holly Springs, MS 38635 | 1905 | E.E. Rankin | D,P | 400 | 2 |
| Miss. Univ. for Women (W), Columbus, MS 39701 | 1884 | James Strobel | S | 2,862 | 1 |
| Mississippi State Univ.*, Miss. State, MS 39762 | 1878 | James McComas | S | 11,829 | 6 |
| Mississippi, Univ. of, University, MS 38677 | 1848 | P.L. Fortune Jr., Chan. | S | 8,989 | 5 |
| Mississippi Valley State Univ., Itta Bena, MS 38941 | 1950 | E.A. Boykins | S | 3,228 | 1 |
| Missouri Baptist, St. Louis, MO 63141 | 1968 | R. Sutherland | D,P | 525 | 3 |
| Missouri Inst. of Tech., Kansas City, MO 64108 | 1931 | C.R. LeValley | P | 624 | 2 |
| Missouri Southern State, Joplin, MO 64801 | 1966 | Leon Billingsly | S | 3,659 | 1 |
| Missouri, Univ. of*, Columbia, MO 65201 | 1839 | James Olson | S | 50,283 | 2,7 |
| at Columbia*, Columbia, MO 65211 | 1839 | Barbara Uehling, Chan. | S | 23,474 | 3,9 |
| at Kansas City*, Kansas City, MO 64110 | 1933 | George Russell, Chan. | S | 10,554 | 1,0 |
| at Rolla*, Rolla, MO 65401 | 1870 | James Pogue, Chan. | S | 4,881 | 8 |
| at St. Louis*, St. Louis, MO 63121 | 1963 | A. Grobman, Chan. | S | 11,374 | 7 |
| Missouri Valley, Marshall, MO 65340 | 1889 | Donald Zimeke | P | 513 | |
| Missouri Western State, St. Joseph, MO 64507 | 1915 | Marvin Looney | P | 3,769 | 1 |
| Mobile, Mobile, AL 36613 | 1961 | William K. Weaver Jr. | P | 1,250 | |
| Molloy, Rockville Ctre, NY 11570 | 1955 | Sister Janet Fitzgerald | D | 1,374 | |
| Monmouth, Monmouth, IL 61462 | 1853 | DeBow Freed | P | 700 | |
| Monmouth, W. Long Branch, NJ 07764 | 1933 | Richard Stonesifer | P | 3,936 | 20 |
| Montana Coll. of Mineral Science & Tech., Butte, MT 59701 | 1893 | Fred W. DeMoney | S | 1,008 | |
| Montana State Univ., Bozeman, MT 59717 | 1893 | Wm. Tietz Jr. | S | 9,803 | 57 |
| Montana, Univ. of, Missoula, MT 59812 | 1893 | Richard Bowers | S | 8,381 | 49 |
| Montclair State, Upper Montclair, NJ 07043 | 1908 | David W.D. Dickson | S | 14,780 | 49 |
| Monterey Inst. of Foreign Studies, Monterey, CA 93940 | 1955 | Jack Kolbert | P | 460 | |
| Montevallo, Univ. of, Montevallo, AL 35115 | 1896 | James Vickrey | S | 3,004 | 1 |
| Moody Bible Institute, Chicago, IL 60610 | 1883 | George Sweeting | P,D | 3,159 | 1 |
| Moore Coll. of Art (W), Philadelphia, PA 19103 | 1844 | H.J. Burgart | P | 700 | |
| Moorehead State, Moorehead, MN 56560 | 1887 | Roland Dille | S | 4,821 | 34 |
| Moravian, Bethlehem, PA 18018 | 1807 | Herman E. Collier Jr. | D,P | 1,524 | 13 |
| Morehead State Univ., Morehead, KY 40351 | 1923 | Morris Norfleet | S | 7,318 | 34 |
| Morehouse (M), Atlanta, GA 30314 | 1867 | Hugh Gloster | P | 1,405 | 10 |
| Morgan State, Baltimore, MD 21239 | 1867 | A. Billingsley | S | 6,361 | 28 |
| Morningside, Sioux City, IA 51106 | 1893 | Thomas S. Thompson | D,P | 1,559 | 8 |
| Morris Brown, Atlanta, GA 30314 | 1881 | Robert Threatt | P,D | 1,503 | 8 |
| Morris Harvey, Charleston, WV 25304 | 1888 | Thomas Voss | P | 2,156 | 8 |
| Mt. Holyoke (W), S. Hadley, MA 01075 | 1837 | Elizabeth Kennan | P | 1,850 | 1 |
| Mt. Marty, Yankton, SD 57078 | 1936 | William Tucker | P | 571 | 5 |
| Mt. Mary (W), Milwaukee, WI 53222 | 1913 | Sister Mary Nora Barber | P,D | 1,125 | 1 |
| Mt. Mercy, Cedar Rapids, IA 52402 | 1928 | Sister Mary Hennessey | P,D | 900 | 8 |
| Mt. St. Joseph (W), Mt. St. Joseph, OH 45051 | 1920 | Robert Wolverton | P,D | 894 | 10 |
| Mt. St. Mary, Newburgh, NY 12550 | 1959 | Sr. Ann Sakac | P,D | 973 | 8 |
| Mt. St. Mary's, Los Angeles, CA 90049 | 1925 | Sr. Magdalen Coughlin | D,P | 1,066 | |
| Mt. St. Mary's, Emmitsburg, MD 21727 | 1808 | Robt. Wickenheiser | P | 1,318 | 6 |
| Mt. St. Vincent, Coll. of, Riverdale, NY 10471 | 1847 | Sister Doris Smith | P | 1,106 | |
| Mt. Union, Alliance, OH 44601 | 1846 | Ronald Weber | P | 1,149 | |
| Mt. Vernon, Washington, DC 20007 | 1875 | Peter Pelham | P | 450 | |
| Mt. Vernon Nazarene, Mount Vernon, OH 43050 | 1964 | L. Guy Nees | D | 879 | |
| Muhlenberg, Allentown, PA 18104 | 1848 | John H. Morey | P,D | 1,825 | 11 |
| Multnomah Sch. of the Bible, Portland, OR 97220 | 1936 | Willard M. Aldrich | P | 746 | 4 |
| Mundelein, Chicago, IL 60660 | 1930 | Sr. Susan Rink | P | 1,425 | 16 |
| Murray State Univ., Murray, KY 42071 | 1922 | C. Curris | S | 7,355 | 35 |
| Muskingum, New Concord, OH 43762 | 1837 | Russell Hutchinson, Act. | P | 969 | |
| Nasson, Springvale, ME 04083 | 1912 | William Cole | P | 500 | 4 |
| National Coll. of Business, Rapid City, SD 57709 | 1941 | John Hauer | P | 1,128 | 4 |
| National Coll. of Chiropractic, Lombard, IL 60148 | 1906 | Joseph Janse | P | 860 | 4 |
| National Coll. of Education, Evanston, IL 60201 | 1886 | Calvin Gross | P | 3,610 | 1 |
| Nazareth Coll., Nazareth, MI 49074 | 1924 | John S. Lore | P | 541 | 6 |
| Nazareth Coll. of Rochester, Rochester, NY 14610 | 1924 | Robert Kidera | P | 2,658 | 7 |
| Nebraska Univ. of*, Lincoln, NE 68583 | 1869 | R. Roskens | S | 39,185 | 1,70 |
| at Omaha, Omaha, NE 68101 | 1908 | D. Weber, Ed. Dr. | S | 15,000 | 5 |
| Nebraska Wesleyan Univ., Lincoln, NE 68504 | 1887 | John White Jr. | D | 1,108 | 8 |
| Nevada Univ. of*, Reno, NV 89557 | 1864 | Joseph Crowley | S | 9,181 | 39 |
| at Las Vegas, Las Vegas, NV 89154 | 1957 | Brock Dixon | S | 8,929 | 31 |
| New England, Henniker, NH 03242 | 1946 | J.K. Cummiskey | P | 1,327 | |
| New England Cons. of Music, Boston, MA 02115 | 1867 | J.S. Ballinger | P | 628 | |
| New Hampshire, Manchester, NH 03104 | 1932 | Edward Shapiro | P | 3,295 | |
| New Hampshire, Univ. of*, Durham, NH 03824 | 1866 | Eugene Mills | S | 11,220 | |
| New Haven, Univ. of*, New Haven, CT 06516 | 1920 | Phillip Kaplan | P | 6,889 | 1 |
| New Jersey Inst. of Tech., Newark, NJ 07102 | 1881 | Paul H. Newell Jr. | S | 5,665 | 24 |
| New Mexico Highlands Univ., Las Vegas, NM 87701 | 1893 | John Aragon | S | 2,000 | 1 |
| N. Mexico Inst. of Min. & Tech., Socorro, NM 87801 | 1889 | Kenneth Ford | S | 891 | 7 |
| New Mexico State Univ.*, Las Cruces, NM 88003 | 1888 | Gerald W. Thomas | S | 11,423 | 6 |
| New Mexico, Univ. of*, Albuquerque, NM 87131 | 1889 | William Davis | S | 21,625 | 7 |
| New Orleans, Univ. of, New Orleans, LA 70122 | 1958 | Homer Hitt, Chan. | S | 14,260 | 6 |
| New Rochelle, Coll. of (W), New Rochelle, NY 10801 | 1904 | Sister Dorothy Ann Kelly | P | 2,979 | 2 |
| New School for Soc. Research, New York, NY 10011 | 1919 | John R. Everett | P | 25,000 | 1,05 |
| New York City, Univ. of, New York, NY 10021 | 1847 | Robert J. Kibbee, Chan. | Mu | 269,929 | 15,1 |
| Bernard M. Baruch, New York, NY 10010 | 1919 | Joel Segall | Mu | 13,239 | 45 |
| Brooklyn, Brooklyn, NY 11210 | 1930 | John W. Kneller | Mu | 19,402 | 89 |
| City, New York, NY 10031 | 1847 | Robert E. Marshak | Mu | 15,247 | 72 |
| Medgar Evers, Brooklyn, NY 11225 | 1969 | Richard D. Trent | Mu | 3,028 | 1 |
| Hunter, New York, NY 10021 | 1870 | Jacqueline G. Wexler | Mu | 17,816 | 1,32 |
| John Jay Coll. of Criminal Just., New York, NY 10019 | 1965 | Gerald Lynch | Mu | 6,719 | 2 |
| Herbert H. Lehman, Bronx, NY 10468 | 1931 | Leonard Lief | Mu | 9,971 | 51 |
| Queens, Flushing, NY 11367 | 1937 | Saul B. Cohen | Mu | 20,507 | 1,33 |
| Staten Island, Staten Island, NY 10301 | 1976 | Edmond Volpe | Mu | 10,908 | 42 |
| York, Jamaica, NY 11451 | 1966 | Milton G. Bassin | Mu | 4,315 | 2 |
| N.Y. Inst. of Technology, Old Westbury, NY 11568 | 1957 | Alexander Schure | P | 11,050 | 18 |
| New York Law School, New York, NY 10013 | 1891 | F. Shapiro, Dean | P | 1,308 | 11 |
| New York, State Univ. of, Albany, NY 12210 | 1948 | C.R. Wharton Jr., Chan. | S | 343,946 | 14,13 |
| State Univ., Albany, NY 12222 | 1844 | V.J. O'Leary, Act. | S | 14,679 | 72 |
| " " Buffalo, NY 14214 | 1846 | Robert Ketter | S | 21,111 | 93 |
| " " Binghamton, NY 13901 | 1946 | Clifford D. Clark | S | 9,916 | 48 |
| " " Stony Brook, NY 11790 | 1957 | John Toll | S | 15,006 | 63 |
| State Univ. Colleges, Brockport, NY 14420 | 1867 | Albert W. Brown | S | 10,033 | 5 |
| " " Buffalo, NY 14222 | 1867 | Elbert K. Fretwell | S | 11,260 | 57 |
| " " Cortland, NY 13045 | 1866 | Richard Jones | S | 5,615 | 3 |

| ame, address | Year | Governing official and affiliation | | Stu-dents | Teach-ers |
|---|---|---|---|---|---|
| "   "   Fredonia, NY 14063 | 1867 | Dallas K. Beal | S | 4,977 | 258 |
| "   "   Geneseo, NY 14454 | 1867 | Robert Macvittie | S | 5,153 | 303 |
| "   "   New Paltz, NY 12561 | 1885 | Peter Vukasin, Act. | S | 7,543 | 362 |
| "   "   Oneonta, NY 13820 | 1887 | Clifford Craven | S | 6,427 | 347 |
| "   "   Oswego, NY 13126 | 1861 | Virginia Radley | S | 8,272 | 401 |
| "   "   Old Westbury, NY 11568 | 1965 | John Maguire | S | 2,252 | 79 |
| "   "   "   Plattsburgh, NY 12901 | 1889 | Joseph C. Burke | S | 6,067 | 296 |
| "   "   "   Potsdam, NY 13676 | 1867 | Thomas Barrington | S | 4,964 | 263 |
| "   "   "   Purchase, NY, 10577 | 1965 | Michael Hammond | S | 2,546 | 107 |
| "   "   "   Utica, NY 13502 | 1966 | William Kunsela | S | 2,840 | 41 |
| "   "   Empire State, Saratoga Spgs., NY 12866 | 1971 | James Hall | S | 3,110 | 94 |
| Buffalo Health Sciences Ctr., Buffalo, NY 14214 | 1846 | F.C. Pannill, V.P. | S | 2,966 | 354 |
| College of Ceramics, Alfred, NY 14802 | 1900 | W.G. Lawrence, Dean | S | 625 | 40 |
| Env'm't'l. Sci. & Forestry, Syracuse, NY 13210 | 1911 | Edward Palmer | S | 2,147 | 107 |
| Downstate Medical Center, Brooklyn, NY 11203 | 1858 | Calvin H. Plimpton | S | 1,447 | 454 |
| Health Sciences Center, Stony Brook, NY 11790 | 1957 | James H. Oaks, V.P. | S | 1,355 | 175 |
| Maritime (M), Bronx, NY 10465 | 1874 | Sheldon Kinney | S | 1,085 | 74 |
| Upstate Medical Center, Syracuse, NY 13210 | 1834 | Richard P. Schmidt | S | 866 | 274 |
| ew York Univ., New York, NY 10003 | 1831 | John Sawhill | P | 40,199 | 5,160 |
| ewberry, Newberry, SC 29108 | 1856 | Glenn Whitesides | P | 835 | 50 |
| ewcomb Coll. of Tulane Univ., New Orleans, LA 70118 | 1886 | F. Lawrence, Act. Dean | P | 1,540 | 137 |
| iagara Univ., Niagara Univ., NY 14109 | 1856 | V. Rev. G. Mahoney | D | 4,460 | 246 |
| icholls State Univ., Thibodaux, LA 70301 | 1948 | Vernon Galliano | S | 6,410 | 262 |
| ichols, Dudley, MA 01570 | 1815 | Lowell Smith | P | 703 | 35 |
| orfolk State, Norfolk, VA 23540 | 1935 | Lyman Brooks | S | 6,260 | 405 |
| orth Adams State, North Adams, MA 01247 | 1894 | James Amsler | S | 2,181 | 117 |
| orth Alabama, Univ., Florence, AL 35630 | 1872 | Robt. Guillot | S | 5,000 | 200 |
| orth Carolina Central U., Durham, NC 27707 | 1910 | A. Whiting, Chan. | S | 4,855 | 228 |
| orth Carolina, Univ. of, Chapel Hill, NC 27514 | 1972 | William Friday | S | 104,786 | 6,325 |
| A&T State Univ., Greensboro, NC 27411. | 1891 | Lewis Dowdy, Chan. | S | 5,515 | 316 |
| at Asheville, Asheville, NC 28804 | 1927 | William Highsmith | S | 1,618 | 85 |
| at Chapel Hill, Chapel Hill, NC 27514 | 1776 | N.F. Taylor | S | 20,293 | 1,730 |
| at Charlotte, Charlotte, NC 28223 | 1946 | D.W. Colvard, Chan. | S | 8,504 | 380 |
| at Greensboro, Greensboro, NC 27412 | 1891 | J.S. Ferguson, Chan. | S | 9,964 | 521 |
| at Wilmington, Wilmington, NC 28401 | 1947 | Wm. H. Wagoner, Chan. | S | 3,561 | 190 |
| J.C. School of the Arts, Winston-Salem, NC 27107 | 1965 | R. Suderburg, Chan. | S | 600 | 80 |
| J.C. State Univ. at Raleigh, NC 27650 | 1862 | Joab Thomas | S | 17,730 | 1,053 |
| orth Carolina Wesleyan, Rocky Mount, NC 27801 | 1956 | S. Bruce Petteway | D | 624 | 30 |
| orth Central Bible, Minneapolis, MN 55404 | 1930 | E.M. Clark | P | 595 | 12 |
| orth Central, Naperville, IL 60540 | 1861 | Gael D. Swing | P | 1,086 | 74 |
| orth Dakota State Univ., Fargo, ND 58102 | 1890 | L.D. Loftsgard | S | 6,600 | 475 |
| orth Dakota, Univ. of*, Grand Forks, ND 58202 | 1883 | Thomas Clifford | P | 8,858 | 640 |
| orth Florida, Univ. of, Jacksonville, FL 32216 | 1965 | Thos. Carpenter | S | 4,302 | 140 |
| orth Georgia, Dahlonega, GA 30533. | 1873 | John H. Owen | S | 1,753 | 100 |
| orth Park, Chicago, IL 60625 | 1891 | Lloyd Ahlem | D | 1,313 | 109 |
| orth Texas State Univ., Denton, TX 76203 | 1890 | C.C. Nolen | S | 15,990 | 638 |
| ortheast Louisiana Univ., Monroe, LA 71209 | 1931 | Dwight Vines | S | 9,098 | 359 |
| ortheast Missouri St., Univ., Kirksville, MO 63501 | 1867 | Charles T. McClain | S | 5,248 | 254 |
| ortheastern Illinois Univ., Chicago, IL 60625 | 1961 | Ronald Williams | S | 10,148 | 341 |
| ortheastern Okla. State, Tahlequah, OK 74464 | 1909 | Robert Collier | S | 5,469 | 226 |
| ortheastern Univ., Boston, MA 02115 | 1898 | Kenneth Ryder | P | 38,587 | 727 |
| orthern Arizona Univ., Flagstaff, AZ 86011 | 1899 | J. Lawrence Walkup | S | 11,502 | 572 |
| orthern Colorado, Univ. of, Greeley, CO 80639 | 1890 | Richard R. Bond | S | 11,048 | 620 |
| orthern Illinois Univ., DeKalb, Il 60115 | 1899 | Wm. Monat, Act. | S | 24,737 | 1,046 |
| orthern Iowa, Univ. of, Cedar Falls, IA 50613 | 1876 | John Kamerick | S | 12,054 | 595 |
| orthern Kentucky Univ., Highland Hts., KY 41076 | 1968 | A.D. Albright | S | 7,000 | 325 |
| orthern Michigan Univ., Marquette, MI 49855 | 1899 | John X. Jamrich | S | 8,977 | 341 |
| orthern Montana, Havre, MT 59501 | 1929 | H.W. Gardner, Act. | S | 1,020 | 72 |
| orthern State, Aberdeen, SD 57401 | 1901 | Joseph McFadden | S | 2,425 | 114 |
| orthland, Ashland, WI 54806 | 1892 | Malcolm McLean | D | 700 | 46 |
| orthrop Univ., Inglewood, CA 90306 | 1942 | B.J. Shell | P | 1,827 | 137 |
| orthwest Bible, Minot, ND 58701 | 1934 | Laud Vaught | D,P | 217 | 12 |
| orthwest Christian, Eugene, OR 97401 | 1895 | Barton A. Dowdy | P | 371 | 15 |
| orthwest Col. of the Assemblies of God, Kirkland, WA 98033 | 1934 | D.V. Hurst | D | 689 | 30 |
| orthwest Missouri State, Univ., Maryville, MO 64468 | 1905 | B.D. Owens | S | 4,103 | 250 |
| orthwest Nazarene, Nampa, ID 83651. | 1913 | Kenneth Pearsall | D,P | 1,249 | 65 |
| orthwestern, Orange City, IA 51041 | 1882 | H. Rowenhorst | P | 760 | 46 |
| orthwestern State Univ., Nathicohes, LA 71457 | 1884 | René Bienvenu | S | 6,358 | 283 |
| orthwestern Okla. St. Univ., Alva, OK 73717 | 1897 | Joe Struckle | S | 1,920 | 71 |
| orthwestern Univ., Evanston, IL 60201 | 1851 | Robert Henry Strotz | P | 15,323 | 1,292 |
| orwich, Univ., Northfield, VT 05663 | 1819 | Loring Hart | P | 1,686 | 120 |
| orthwood Inst., Midland, MI 48640 | 1959 | T.J. Brown, Chan. | P | 2,000 | 75 |
| otre Dame, Coll of, Belmont CA 94002 | 1851 | Sr. Catharine Cunningham. | P,D | 771 | 36 |
| otre Dame, Manchester, NH 03104 | 1950 | Sr. Jeannette Vezeau | P,D | 500 | 37 |
| otre Dame (W), Cleveland, OH 44121. | 1922 | Sister Mary Marthe | D,P | 618 | 61 |
| otre Dame Coll. of OH, S.Euclid, OH 44121 | 1922 | Sr. Mary Marthe. | D,P | 541 | 36 |
| otre Dame of Maryland, Baltimore, MD 21210 | 1873 | Sister Kathleen Feeley | P | 750 | 57 |
| otre Dame, Univ. of, Notre Dame, IN 46556 | 1842 | Rev. T.M. Hesburgh | D,P | 8,498 | 756 |
| ova Univ., Ft. Lauderdale, FL 33314 | 1964 | Abraham Fischler | P | 8,143 | 393 |
| yack, Nyack, NY 10960 | 1882 | Thomas Bailey | D,P | 691 | 40 |
| Oakland City, Oakland City, IN 47660. | 1885 | J.W. Murray | D,P | 450 | 29 |
| Oakland Univ., Rochester, MI 48063 | 1957 | Donald D. O'Dowd | S | 10,457 | 488 |
| Oakwood, Huntsville, AL 35806 | 1896 | C.B. Rock | D | 1,300 | 64 |
| Oberlin, Oberlin, OH 44074 | 1833 | E. Danenberg | P | 2,700 | 226 |
| Occidental, Los Angeles, CA 90041 | 1887 | Richard C. Gilman | P | 1,650 | 120 |
| Oglethorpe Univ. Atlanta, GA 30319. | 1835 | Manning Pattillo Jr. | P | 864 | 32 |
| Ohio Dominican, Columbus, OH 43219 | 1911 | Sister M. Suzanne Uhrhane | D | 910 | 71 |
| Ohio Coll. of Podiatric Med., Cleveland, OH 44106 | 1916 | Abe Rubin | P | 536 | 20 |
| Ohio Inst. of Technology, Columbus, OH 43209 | 1952 | Richard A. Czerniak | P | 2,978 | 102 |
| Ohio Northern Univ., Ada, OH 45810 | 1871 | R.B. Loeschner | D,P | 2,527 | 158 |
| Ohio State Univ.*, Columbus, OH 43210 | 1870 | Harold L. Enarson | S | 54,579 | 3,533 |
| Ohio Univ., Athens, OH 45701 | 1804 | Charles J. Ping | S | 12,205 | 685 |
| Ohio Wesleyan Univ., Delaware, OH 43015 | 1842 | Thomas Wenzlau | D,P | 2,240 | 160 |
| Oklahoma Baptist Univ., Shawnee, OK 74801 | 1910 | E. Eugene Hall | P | 1,549 | 120 |
| Oklahoma Christian, Oklahoma City, OK 73111 | 1950 | J. Johnson | P,D | 1,493 | 50 |
| Oklahoma City Univ., Oklahoma City, OK 73106 | 1904 | Dolphus Whitten Jr. | D | 2,741 | 104 |

| Name, address | Year | Governing official and affiliation | | Students | Teachers |
|---|---|---|---|---|---|
| Okla. Coll. of Liberal Arts, Chickasha, OK 73018 | 1908 | Roy Troutt | S | 1,200 | 5 |
| Oklahoma Panhandle St. Univ., Goodwell, OK 73939 | 1909 | Thomas L. Palmer | S | 1,115 | 7 |
| Oklahoma State Univ.*, Stillwater, OK 74074 | 1890 | Lawrence Boger | S | 27,232 | 1,10 |
| Oklahoma Univ. of, Norman, OK 73019 | 1890 | Paul F. Sharp | S | 24,910 | 1,33 |
| Old Dominion Univ., Norfolk, VA 23508 | 1930 | A.B. Rollins Jr. | S | 14,188 | 59 |
| Olivet, Olivet, MI 49076 | 1844 | Donald A. Morris | P | 709 | 4 |
| Olivet Nazarene, Kankakee, IL 60901 | 1907 | Leslie Parrott | P | 1,853 | 8 |
| Oral Roberts Univ., Tulsa, OK 74171 | 1963 | Granville Oral Roberts | P | 3,800 | 300 |
| Orangeburg-Calhoun Tech, Orangeburg, SC 29115 | 1968 | M. Rudy Groomes | S | 1,400 | 5 |
| Oregon College of Educ., Monmouth, OR 97361 | 1882 | G. Leinwand | S | 3,228 | 20 |
| Oregon Inst. of Tech., Klamath Falls, OR 97601 | 1947 | Kenneth Light | S | 2,236 | 15 |
| Oregon State Univ.*, Corvallis, OR 97331 | 1868 | R. MacVicar | S | 16,511 | 1,30 |
| Oregon, Univ. of, Eugene, OR 97403 | 1876 | William Boyd | S | 16,701 | 2,15 |
| Osteopathic Med. & Sur., Coll. of, Des Moines, IA 50312 | 1898 | J.L. Azneer | P | 523 | 5 |
| Otis Art Inst., Los Angeles, CA 90057 | 1918 | Peter Clothier, Act. Dir. | C | 460 | 11 |
| Ottawa Univ., Ottawa, KS 66067 | 1865 | Milton Froyd, Act. | P | 1,000 | 5 |
| Otterbein, Westerville, OH 43081 | 1847 | Thomas Jefferson Kerr. | D,P | 1,447 | 7 |
| Ouachita Baptist Univ., Arkadelphia, AR 71923 | 1886 | Daniel R. Grant | P | 1,574 | 10 |
| Our Lady of Angels, Aston, PA 19014 | 1965 | Sr. Marie Cunningham | D | 646 | 3 |
| Our Lady of Elms, Col. of (W), Chicopee, MA 01013 | 1928 | Edward D'Alessio | D | 440 | 6 |
| Our Lady of the Lake, Univ., San Antonio, TX 78285 | 1911 | Sr. Eliz. Sueltenfuss | P | 1,659 | 9 |
| Ozarks, Coll. of the, Clarksville, AR 72830 | 1834 | Robert Qualls | D,P | 604 | 3 |
| Ozarks, School of the, Pt. Lookout, MO 65726 | 1906 | M. Graham Clark | P | 1,138 | 7 |
| | | | | | |
| Pace Univ., New York, NY 10038 | 1906 | Edward J. Mortola | P | 14,575 | 78 |
| Pacific Christian, Fullerton, CA 92631 | 1928 | Medford Jones | D,P | 859 | 1 |
| Pacific Lutheran Univ., Tacoma, WA 98447 | 1890 | William Rieke | P,D | 3,228 | 19 |
| Pacific States Univ., Los Angeles, CA 90006 | 1928 | Steven Kase | | 650 | 5 |
| Pacific Union, Angwin, CA 94508 | 1882 | J.W. Cassel, Jr. | D,P | 2,100 | 12 |
| Pacific Univ. Forest Grove, OR 97116 | 1849 | James Miller | P,D | 1,055 | 7 |
| Pacific, Univ. of the, Stockton, CA 95211 | 1851 | Stanley McCaffrey | P | 5,800 | 40 |
| Paine, Augusta, GA 30901 | 1882 | J.S. Scott Jr. | D | 752 | 5 |
| Palm Beach Atlantic, W., Palm Beach, FL 33041 | 1968 | George Borders | P,D | 551 | 3 |
| | | | | | |
| Pan American Univ., Edinburg, TX 78539 | 1927 | Ralph Schilling | S | 7,183 | 32 |
| Park, Parkville, MO 64152 | 1875 | Harold Condit | D | 2,150 | 4 |
| Parsons School of Design, New York, NY 10011 | 1896 | John R. Everett | P | 3,000 | 250 |
| Paul Quinn, Waco, TX 76704 | 1872 | R.D. Manning | D,P | 494 | 3 |
| Peabody Cons. of Music, Baltimore, MD 21202 | 1857 | Richard F. Goldman | P | 505 | 9 |
| Pembroke St. Univ., Pembroke, NC 28372 | 1887 | English E. Jones | S | 1,874 | 11 |
| Penn Col. of Optometry, Philadelphia, PA 19141 | 1919 | Norman F. Wallis | P | 545 | 9 |
| Penn. Coll. of Podiatric Med., Phila., PA 19107 | 1963 | James Bates | P | 456 | 13 |
| Penn. State Univ.*, University Park, PA 16802 | 1855 | John W. Oswald | S | 60,180 | 2,61 |
| Pennsylvania Univ. of Philadelphia, PA 19104 | 1755 | Martin Meyerson | P | 21,667 | 3,19 |
| Pepperdine Univ., Malibu, CA 90265 | 1937 | William S. Banowsky | D,P | 8,185 | 36 |
| Peru State, Peru, NE 68421 | 1865 | Larry Tangeman | S | 765 | 4 |
| Pfeiffer, Misenheimer, NC 28109 | 1885 | Douglas Reid Sasser | P | 929 | 5 |
| Phila. College of Art, Philadelphia, PA 19102 | 1876 | Thomas Schutte | P | 2,120 | 7 |
| Phila. Coll. of Bible, Philadelphia, PA 19103 | 1913 | D.B. MacCorkle | P,D | 1,534 | 6 |
| Phila. Coll. of Osteopathic Med., Philadelphia, PA 19131 | 1898 | Thomas Rowland Jr. | P | 813 | 9 |
| Phila. Coll. of Pharm. & Science, Philadelphia, PA 19104 | 1821 | John Bergen | P | 1,156 | 6 |
| Phila. Coll. of Textiles & Science, Philadelphia, PA 19144 | 1884 | D.B. Partridge | P | 2,235 | 16 |
| Philander Smith, Little Rock, AR 72203 | 1868 | Walter Hazzard | D | 701 | 5 |
| Phillips Univ., Enid, OK 73701 | 1907 | Samuel Curl | P | 1,439 | 7 |
| Piedmont, Demorest, GA 30535 | 1897 | James E. Walker | P | 489 | 3 |
| Piedmont Bible, Winston-Salem, NC 27101 | 1945 | Donald Drake | D | 447 | 1 |
| Pikeville, Pikeville, KY 41501 | 1889 | Jackson Hall | D,P | 650 | 5 |
| | | | | | |
| Pine Manor (W), Chestnut Hill, MA 02167 | 1911 | Rosemary Ashby | P | 489 | 2 |
| Pittsburgh State U., Pittsburg, KS 66762 | 1903 | James Appleberry | S | 5,182 | 245 |
| Pittsburgh, Univ. of, Pittsburgh, PA 15260 | 1787 | Wesley W. Posvar | S | 35,188 | 4,31 |
| Pitzer, Claremont, CA 91711 | 1963 | Robert Atwell | S | 750 | 6 |
| Plymouth State, Plymouth, NH 03264 | 1870 | Kasper Marking | S | 3,298 | 134 |
| Point Park, Pittsburgh, PA 15222 | 1960 | John Hopkins | P | 1,936 | 8 |
| Polytechnic Institute, Brooklyn, NY 11201 | 1854 | George Bugliarello | P | 4,362 | 21 |
| Pomona, Claremont, CA 91711 | 1887 | David Alexander | P | 1,311 | 130 |
| Portland State Univ., Portland, OR 97207 | 1946 | Joseph Blumel | P | 14,016 | 732 |
| Portland, Univ. of, Portland, OR 97203 | 1901 | Rev. P.E. Waldschmidt | P | 2,540 | 105 |
| Prairie View A & M Univ., Prairie View, TX 77445 | 1886 | Alvin Thomas | S | 5,080 | 278 |
| Pratt Institute Brooklyn, NY 11205 | 1887 | Richardson Pratt Jr. | P | 4,400 | 450 |
| Presbyterian, Clinton, SC 29325 | 1880 | Marc C. Weersing | D | 837 | 4 |
| Princeton Univ., Princeton, NJ 08540 | 1746 | William G. Bowen | P | 5,967 | 74 |
| Principia, Elsah, IL 62028 | 1898 | David K. Andrews | P | 876 | 7 |
| Providence, Providence, RI 02918 | 1917 | Rev. T.R. Peterson | P | 5,123 | 207 |
| Puerto Rico, Univ. of*, San Juan, PR 00936 | 1903 | A. Carrion | S | 50,225 | 2,64 |
| Puget Sound, Univ. of, Tacoma, WA 98416 | 1888 | Philip M. Phibbs | P | 5,375 | 264 |
| Purdue Univ.*, W. Lafayette, IN 47907 | 1869 | Arthur G. Hansen | S | 40,997 | 2,37 |
| | | | | | |
| Queens (W), Charlotte, NC 28274 | 1857 | Billy Wireman | P | 591 | 37 |
| Quincy, Quincy, IL 62301 | 1860 | Rev. G. Brinkman | D,P | 1,646 | 74 |
| Quinnipiac, Hamden, CT 06518 | 1929 | Harry Bennett, Act. | P | 3,400 | 175 |
| | | | | | |
| Radcliffe (W), Cambridge, MA 02138 | 1879 | Matina Souretia Horner | P | 2,070 | (a) |
| Radford, Radford, VA 24141 | 1910 | Donald N. Dedmon | S | 5,623 | 275 |
| Ramapo, Coll. of N.J., Mahwah, NJ 07430 | 1969 | George T. Potter | S | 4,080 | 160 |
| Randolph-Macon, Ashland, VA 23005 | 1830 | Luther W. White III | P,D | 931 | 72 |
| Randolph-Macon Woman's (W), Lynchburg, VA 24503 | 1891 | Robert Spivey | P | 788 | 65 |
| Redlands, Univ. of, Redlands, CA 92373 | 1907 | Eugene Dawson | P | 2,367 | 12 |
| Reed, Portland, OR 97202 | 1911 | Paul Bragdon | P | 1,162 | 176 |
| Regis, Denver, CO 80121 | 1877 | Rev. David M. Clarke | D,P | 990 | 8 |
| Regis (W), Weston, MA 02193 | 1927 | Sister Therese Higgins | P | 1,052 | 56 |
| Rensselaer Poly. Inst., Troy, NY 12181 | 1824 | George M. Low | P | 5,700 | 344 |
| Rhode Island, Providence, RI 02908 | 1854 | David E. Sweet | P | 9,600 | 366 |
| R.I. School of Design, Providence, RI 02903 | 1877 | Ms. Lee Hall | P | 1,458 | 88 |
| Rhode Island, Univ. of, Kingston, RI 02881 | 1888 | Frank Newman | S | 16,527 | 84 |
| Rice Univ., Houston, TX 77001 | 1891 | Norman Hackerman | P | 3,650 | 350 |

(a) Radcliffe students are taught by the Harvard faculty.

| Name, address | Year | Governing official and affiliation | Stu- dents | Teach- ers |
|---|---|---|---|---|
| Richmond, Univ. of, Richmond, VA 23173. | 1830 | E. Bruce Heilman | P | 4,655 | 193 |
| Ricker, Houlton, ME 04730 | 1848 | W. Abbott | P | 709 | 55 |
| Rider, Lawrenceville, NJ 08648 | 1865 | Frank N. Elliott | P | 5,680 | 300 |
| Rio Grande, Rio Grande, OH 45674 | 1876 | Paul Hayes | P | 1,083 | 45 |
| Ripon, Ripon, WI 54971 | 1851 | Bernard S. Adams | P | 949 | 65 |
| Rivier Nashua, NH 03060 | 1933 | Sister Doris Benoit | P | 1,516 | 41 |
| Roanoke, Salem, VA 24153 | 1842 | Norman Fintel | D | 1,280 | 65 |
| Robert Morris, Coraopolis, PA 15108 | 1921 | Charles Sewall | P | 3,771 | 83 |
| Roberta Wesleyan, Rochester, NY 14624 | 1866 | Paul I. Adams | D,P | 640 | 50 |
| Rochester Inst. of Tech., Rochester, NY 14623 | 1829 | Paul A. Miller | P | 12,514 | 544 |
| Rochester, Univ. of, Rochester, NY 14627 | 1850 | Robert Sproull | P | 8,005 | 1,259 |
| Rockford, Rockford, IL 61101 | 1847 | John Spence, Act. | P | 1,150 | 104 |
| Rockhurst, Kansas City, MO 64110 | 1910 | Rev. Robert Weiss | D | 3,481 | 77 |
| Rocky Mountain, Billings, MT 59102 | 1847 | B. Alton | D,P | 515 | 35 |
| Roger Williams, Bristol, RI 02809 | 1948 | Wm. Rizzini, Act. | P | 3,300 | 76 |
| Rollins, Winter Park, FL 32789 | 1885 | Thaddeus Seymour | P | 3,732 | 93 |
| Roosevelt Univ., Chicago, IL 60605 | 1945 | Rolf A. Weil | P | 7,024 | 260 |
| Rosary, River Forest, IL 60305 | 1901 | Sister Candida Lund | P | 855 | 67 |
| Rosary Hill, Buffalo, NY 14226 | 1948 | Robert S. Marshall | P | 1,200 | 115 |
| Rose-Hulman Inst. of Tech., (M) Terre Haute, IN 47803 | 1874 | S.F. Hulbert | P | 1,150 | 70 |
| Rosemont, Rosemont, PA 19010 | 1921 | Sister Ann Marie Durst | D | 610 | 84 |
| Russell Sage, Troy, NY 12180 | 1916 | William Kahl | P | 4,837 | 153 |
| Rust, Holly Spgs., MS 38635 | 1866 | W.A. McMillan | D,P | 670 | 33 |
| Rutgers Univ.*, New Brunswick, NJ 08903 | 1766 | Edward J. Bloustein | S | 49,045 | 2,536 |
| Sacred Heart, Coll. of the, Santurce, PR 00914 | 1935 | Pedro Gonzalez Ramos | D | 5,051 | 81 |
| Sacred Heart Univ., Bridgeport, CT 06606 | 1963 | Robert Kidera | P | 2,481 | 139 |
| Saginaw Valley State, Univ. Center, MI 48710 | 1964 | Jack Ryder | S | 3,116 | 91 |
| St. Ambrose, Davenport, IA 52803 | 1882 | William Bakrow | D,P | 1,657 | 65 |
| St. Andrews Presbyterian, Laurinburg, NC 28352 | 1962 | A.P. Perkinson Jr. | D | 568 | 55 |
| St. Anslem's, Manchester, NH 03102 | 1889 | Rev. B.P. Donnelly | D,P | 1,884 | 142 |
| St. Augustine's, Raleigh, NC 27611 | 1867 | Prezell R. Robinson. | P | 1,775 | 73 |
| St. Benedict, Coll. of (W), St. Joseph, MN 56374 | 1913 | Beverly Miller | D,P | 1,993 | 85 |
| St. Bernard, St. Bernard, AL 35138 | 1891 | Robert Kaffer | D | 450 | 52 |
| St. Bonaventure Univ., St. Bonaventure, NY 14778 | 1858 | V. Rev. M. Doyle | D | 2,680 | 110 |
| St. Catherine, Coll. of (W), St. Paul, MN 55105 | 1905 | Sister Alberta Huber | D | 2,100 | 150 |
| St. Cloud State Univ., St. Cloud, MN 56301 | 1869 | Charles J. Graham | S | 11,312 | 461 |
| St. Edward's Univ., Austin, TX 78704 | 1896 | Stephen Walsh | P | 2,073 | 124 |
| St. Elizabeth, Coll. of (W), Convent Station, NJ 07961 | 1899 | Sister Eliz. Ann Maloney | D,P | 681 | 83 |
| St. Francis, Fort Wayne, IN 46808 | 1890 | Sister M. Jo Ellen Scheetz. | D | 1,329 | 75 |
| St. Francis, Brooklyn, NY 11201 | 1884 | Donald Sullivan | P | 3,972 | 187 |
| St. Francis, Loretto, PA 15940 | 1847 | Rev. Christian Oravec | D | 1,502 | 64 |
| St. Francis, Coll. of, Joliet, IL 60435 | 1930 | John Orr | P | 2,927 | 135 |
| St. John Fisher, Rochester, NY 14618 | 1948 | Rev. C.J. Lavery | P,D | 1,827 | 112 |
| St. John's, Annapolis, MD 21404 | 1696 | Richard D. Weigle. | P | 651 | |
| St. John's Univ., Collegeville, MN 56321 | 1857 | V. Rev. Michael Blecker | D | 1,894 | |
| St. John's Univ., Jamaica, NY 11439 | 1870 | V. Rev. Joseph T. Cahill | P,D | 16,700 | 489 |
| St. Joseph, West Hartford, CT 06117 | 1932 | Sr. Mary O'Connor | D,P | 1,138 | 62 |
| St. Joseph's, Rensselaer, IN 47978 | 1889 | Rev. Charles Banet | D | 1,032 | 55 |
| St. Joseph's, Brooklyn, NY 11205 | 1916 | Sr. G.A. O'Connor | D | 1,124 | 53 |
| St. Joseph's, North Windham, ME 04062 | 1912 | Bernard Currier | D | 866 | 60 |
| St. Joseph's, Philadelphia, PA 19131 | 1851 | Rev. Donald MacLean | D | 5,395 | 125 |
| St. Lawrence Univ., Canton, NY 13617 | 1856 | Frank Peter Piskor | P | 2,200 | 160 |
| St. Leo, St. Leo, FL 33574 | 1889 | Thomas Southard. | P,D | 1,003 | 69 |
| St. Louis Coll. of Pharmacy, St. Louis, MO 63110 | 1864 | Charles C. Rabe | P | 686 | 35 |
| St. Louis Univ., St. Louis, MO 63103. | 1818 | Rev. Edw. Drummond | P | 10,393 | 1,812 |
| Park, Cahokia, IL 62206 | 1927 | Leon Z. Seltzer (Dean) | P | 796 | 44 |
| St. Martin's, Olympia, WA 98503 | 1895 | Fr. John C. Scott | D,P | 739 | 35 |
| St. Mary, Coll. of, Omaha, NE 68124 | 1923 | Sister Mary A. Costello. | P,D | 454 | 48 |
| St. Mary (W), Leavenworth, KS 66048 | 1923 | Sr. Mary J. McGilley | D | 782 | 43 |
| St. Mary of the Plains Coll., Dodge City, KS 67801 | 1952 | Michael McCarthy | D,P | 567 | 58 |
| St. Mary-of-the Woods (W), St. Mary-of-the-Woods, IN 47876 | 1840 | Sister Jeanne Knoerle | D,P | 645 | 41 |
| St. Mary's, Notre Dame, IN 46556 | 1844 | John Duggan | D,P | 1,781 | 246 |
| St. Mary's, Winona, MN 55987 | 1913 | Peter Clifford | D,P | 1,197 | 64 |
| St. Mary's Coll. of Cal., Moraga, CA 94575. | 1863 | Bro. Mel Anderson | P | 1,845 | 61 |
| St. Mary's Coll. of Maryland, St. Mary's City, MD 20686 | 1839 | J. Renwick Jackson Jr.. | S | 1,172 | 67 |
| St. Mary's Dominican (W), New Orleans, LA 70118 | 1860 | Sr. Mary Gerald Shea | D,P | 875 | 32 |
| St. Mary's Univ., San Antonio, TX 78284 | 1852 | Rev. James Young | D | 3,072 | 150 |
| St. Michael's, Winooski, VT 05404 | 1904 | Edward L. Henry | P,D | 2,200 | 105 |
| St. Norbert, DePere, WI 54115 | 1898 | Neil Webb | D | 1,531 | 85 |
| St. Olaf, Northfield, MN 55057 | 1874 | Sidney A. Rand | D,P | 2,974 | 245 |
| St. Paul Bible, Bible College, MN 55375 | 1916 | Francis W. Grubbs | P | 562 | 24 |
| St. Paul's, Lawrenceville, VA 23868 | 1888 | James Alvin Russell Jr. | P | 627 | 43 |
| St. Peter's, Jersey City, NJ 07306 | 1872 | V. Rev. V.R. Yanitelli | D | 4,458 | 132 |
| St. Rose, Coll. of, Albany, NY 12203 | 1920 | Thomas Manion | P | 2,083 | 167 |
| St. Scholastica, Coll. of, Duluth, MN 55811 | 1912 | Bruce Stender | P | 1,174 | 81 |
| St. Teresa, Coll. of (W), Winona, MN 55987 | 1907 | Sister Joyce Rowland | D | 1,036 | 92 |
| St. Thomas Aquinas, Sparkill, NY 10976 | 1952 | D. McNelis | P | 1,065 | 50 |
| St. Thomas, Coll. of, St. Paul, MN 55105 | 1885 | Msgr. Terrence Murphy | D | 4,140 | 136 |
| St. Thomas, Univ. of, Houston, TX 77006 | 1947 | Rev. Patrick Braden | P | 1,769 | 100 |
| St. Vincent (M), Latrobe, PA 15650 | 1846 | Rev. Cecil Diethrich. | P | 900 | 89 |
| St. Xavier, Chicago, IL 60655. | 1847 | Sr. M. Chekouras | D | 1,450 | 141 |
| Salem (W), Winston-Salem, NC 27108 | 1772 | M. Cuninggim | P,D | 625 | 70 |
| Salem, Salem, WV 26426 | 1888 | Dallas Bailey Jr.. | P | 1,394 | 78 |
| Salem State, Salem, MA 01970 | 1854 | Edward Penson | S | 7,490 | 270 |
| Salisbury State, Salisbury, MD 21801 | 1925 | Norman Crawford Jr.. | S | 4,299 | 167 |
| Salve Regina, Newport, RI 02840 | 1934 | Sister Lucille McKillop | D | 1,605 | 120 |
| Sam Houston State Univ., Huntsville, TX 77341 | 1879 | E.T. Bowers | S | 10,694 | 403 |
| Samford Univ., Birmingham, AL 35209 | 1841 | Leslie S. Wright | D,P | 4,121 | 195 |
| San Diego, Univ. Of, San Diego, CA 92110 | 1949 | Author E. Hughes | P,D | 3,399 | 139 |
| San Diego State Univ., San Diego, CA 92182 | 1897 | Thomas Day | S | 29,971 | 1,260 |
| San Francisco Art Inst., San Francisco, CA 94133. | 1871 | Stephen Goldstine | P | 845 | 62 |
| San Francisco, Univ. of, San Francisco, CA 94117 | 1855 | Rev. J. LoSchiavo. | P | 6,392 | 247 |
| Sangamon State Univ., Springfield, IL 62708 | 1969 | Robert Spencer | S | 3,792 | 185 |
| San Jose State Univ., San Jose, CA 95192 | 1857 | John H. Bunzel | S | 26,358 | 910 |
| Santa Clara, Univ. of, Santa Clara, CA 95053 | 1851 | William Rewak | D,P | 7,295 | 238 |

| Name, address | Year | Governing official and affiliation | | Students | Teachers |
|---|---|---|---|---|---|
| Sante Fe, Coll. of, Sante Fe, NM 87501 | 1947 | Bro. Cyprian Luke | P | 1,280 | 61 |
| Sarah Lawrence, Bronxville, NY 10708 | 1926 | Charles DeCarlo | P | 863 | 149 |
| Savannah State, Savannah, GA 31404 | 1890 | Clyde Hall, Act. | S | 2,334 | 143 |
| Scranton, Univ. of, Scranton, PA 18510 | 1888 | Rev. William Byron | D | 4,460 | 145 |
| Scripps (W), Claremont, CA 91711 | 1926 | John Chandler | P | 597 | 64 |
| Seattle Pacific Univ., Seattle, WA 98119 | 1891 | David L. McKenna | D,P | 2,276 | 187 |
| Seattle Univ., Seattle, WA 98122 | 1891 | Rev. William Sullivan | D | 3,646 | 174 |
| Selma Univ., Selma, AL 36701 | 1878 | M.C. Cleveland Jr. | D,P | 620 | 28 |
| Seton Hall Univ., S. Orange, NJ 07079 | 1856 | Robert T. Conley | D | 9,131 | 340 |
| Seton Hill (W), Greensburg, PA 15601 | 1883 | Eileen Farrell | D | 862 | 51 |
| Shaw Coll. at Detroit, Detroit, MI 48202 | 1936 | Romallus Murphy | P | 1,037 | 57 |
| Shaw Univ., Raleigh, NC 27611 | 1865 | John Fleming, Act. | P | 1,335 | 68 |
| Shenandoah Coll. of Music, Winchester, VA 22601 | 1875 | Robert P. Parker | D | 742 | 91 |
| Shepherd, Shepherdstown, WV 25443 | 1871 | James Butcher | S | 2,826 | 109 |
| Shippensburg State, Shippensburg, PA 17257 | 1871 | Gilmore B. Seavers | S | 6,041 | 276 |
| Shorter, Rome, GA 30161 | 1873 | Randall H. Minor | D,P | 796 | 48 |
| Siena, Loundonville, NY 12211 | 1937 | Rev. Hugh F. Hines | P | 2,750 | 112 |
| Siena Heights, Adrian, MI 49221 | 1919 | Louis Vaccaro | P | 1,017 | 54 |
| Simmons (W), Boston, MA 02115 | 1899 | William J. Holmes | P | 2,644 | 200 |
| Simpson, Indianola, IA 50125 | 1860 | Richard Lancaster | P | 835 | 77 |
| Simpson, San Francisco, CA 94134 | 1921 | Mark W. Lee | D,P | 280 | 24 |
| Sioux Falls, Sioux Falls, SD 57101 | 1884 | Owen Halleen | D,P | 681 | 42 |
| Skidmore, Saratoga Spgs., NY 12866 | 1903 | Joseph C. Palamountian Jr. | P | 2,050 | 164 |
| Slippery Rock State, Slippery Rock, PA 16057 | 1889 | James Roberts, Act. | S | 5,754 | 327 |
| Smith (W), Northampton, MA 01060 | 1875 | Jill Kerr Conway | P | 2,518 | 240 |
| South Univ. of the, Sewanee, TN 37375 | 1857 | James J. Bennett | D,P | 1,112 | 108 |
| South Alabama, Univ. of, Mobile, AL 36688 | 1963 | Frederick Whiddon | S | 6,935 | 367 |
| South Carolina St.*, Orangeburg, SC 29117 | 1896 | M.M. Nance Jr. | S | 3,897 | 240 |
| South Carolina, Univ. of*, Columbia, SC 29208 | 1801 | William Patterson | S | 22,285 | 1,453 |
| S.D. Sch. of Mines & Tech., Rapid City, SD 57701 | 1885 | Richard Schleusener | S | 1,812 | 112 |
| South Dakota State Univ.*, Brookings, SD 57007 | 1881 | Sherwood Berg | S | 6,500 | 301 |
| South Dakota, Univ. of, Vermillion, SD 57069 | 1862 | Charles D. Lein | S | 6,500 | 350 |
| South Florida, Univ. of, Tampa, FL 33620 | 1956 | John Lott Brown | S | 22,812 | 1,042 |
| South Texas Coll. of Law, Houston, TX 77002 | 1923 | G.R. Walker | P | 1,013 | 47 |
| Southeast Missouri St. Univ., Cape Girardeau, MO 63701 | 1873 | Robert Leestamar | S | 8,584 | 377 |
| Southeastern Bible, Lakeland, FL 33801 | 1935 | Cyril Homer | D,P | 1,189 | 39 |
| Southeastern Louisiana Univ., Hammond, LA 70402 | 1925 | Clea E. Parker | S | 6,754 | 240 |
| Southeastern Mass. Univ., N. Dartmouth, MA 02747 | 1895 | Donald E. Walker | S | 7,314 | 333 |
| Southeastern Okla. St. Univ., Durant, OK 74701 | 1909 | Leon Hibbs | S | 4,417 | 139 |
| Southeastern Univ., Washington, DC 20024 | 1879 | Barkev Kibarian | S | 1,125 | 120 |
| Southern Arkansas Univ., Magnolia, AR 71753 | 1909 | Harold Brinson | S | 2,213 | 157 |
| Southern Benedictine, St. Bernard, AL 35138 | 1892 | Robert Kaffer | D | 427 | 27 |
| Southern California, Costa Mesa, CA 92626 | 1920 | Wayne Kraiss | D | 660 | 32 |
| Southern Cal., Univ. of, Los Angeles, CA 90007 | 1880 | John R. Hubbard | P | 27,879 | 1,679 |
| Southern Coll. of Optometry, Memphis, TN 38104 | 1932 | Spurgeon B. Eure | P | 587 | 50 |
| Southern Colorado, Univ. of, Pueblo, CO 81001 | 1933 | Richard Pesqueira | S | 6,000 | 285 |
| Southern Conn. State, New Haven, CT 06515 | 1893 | Manson Van B. Jennings | S | 7,000 | 443 |
| Southern Illinois Univ., Edwardsville, IL 62026 | 1965 | Kenneth Shaw | S | 12,060 | 610 |
| Southern Illinois Univ., Carbondale, IL 62901 | 1869 | Warren Brandt | S | 22,537 | 1,143 |
| Southern Methodist Univ., Dallas, TX 75275 | 1911 | J. Zumberge | D,P | 8,677 | 523 |
| Southern Missionary, Collegedale, TN 37315 | 1892 | Frank Knittel | P | 1,682 | 120 |
| Southern Miss. Univ. of, Hattiesburg, MS 39401 | 1910 | Aubrey Lucas | S | 11,830 | 590 |
| Southern Oregon State, Ashland, OR 97520 | 1925 | James K. Sours | S | 4,500 | 215 |
| Southern State, Magnolia, AR 71753 | 1909 | Harold T. Brinson | S | 2,325 | 200 |
| Southern Tech. Inst., Marietta, GA 30060 | 1948 | Joseph Pettit | S | 1,938 | 90 |
| Southern Univ., Baton Rouge, LA 70813 | 1880 | Jesse Stone Jr. | S | 9,022 | 476 |
| Southern Utah State, Cedar City, UT 84720 | 1897 | R.C. Braithwaite | S | 1,912 | 120 |
| Southwest Baptist, Bolivar, MO 65613 | 1878 | James L. Sells | P,D | 1,328 | 89 |
| Southwest St. Univ., Marshall, MN 56258 | 1967 | Jon Wefald | S | 1,719 | 106 |
| Southwest Mo. St. Univ., Springfield, MO 65802 | 1905 | Duane Meyer | S | 12,306 | 514 |
| Southwest Texas St. Univ., San Marcos, TX 78666 | 1899 | Lee Smith | S | 14,034 | 674 |
| Southwestern, Winfield, KS 67156 | 1885 | Donald Ruthenberg | D,P | 695 | 48 |
| Southwestern La., Univ. of, Lafayette, LA 70504 | 1898 | Ray Authement | S | 14,102 | 575 |
| Southwestern at Memphis, Memphis, TN 38112 | 1848 | James Daughdrill Jr. | D | 973 | 86 |
| Southwestern Okla. St. Univ., Weatherford, OK 73096 | 1901 | Leonard Campbell | S | 5,403 | 205 |
| Southwestern Union, Keene, TX 76059 | 1893 | Donald McAdams | D | 754 | 49 |
| Southwestern Univ., Georgetown, TX 78626 | 1840 | L. Durwood Fleming | D,P | 963 | 72 |
| Spalding, Louisville, KY 40203 | 1920 | Sister Eileen Egan | D,P | 1,005 | 59 |
| Spelman (W), Atlanta, GA 30314 | 1881 | Donald Stewart | P | 1,283 | 95 |
| Spring Arbor, Spring Arbor, MI 49283 | 1873 | E.A. Voller | D,P | 782 | 49 |
| Spring Garden, Philadelphia, PA 19118 | 1851 | Daniel DeLucca | P | 1,424 | 56 |
| Spring Hill, Mobile, AL 36608 | 1830 | Rev. Paul S. Tipton | D | 1,046 | 49 |
| Springfield, Springfield, MA 01109 | 1885 | Wilbert Locklin | P | 2,600 | 150 |
| Stanford Univ., Stanford, CA 94305 | 1885 | Richard W. Lyman | P | 11,710 | 1,755 |
| Stephen F. Austin State Univ., Nacogdoches, TX 75962 | 1923 | Wm. Johnson | S | 10,756 | 441 |
| Stephens (W), Columbia, MO 65243 | 1833 | Arland Christ-Janer | P | 1,645 | 142 |
| Sterling, Sterling, KS 67579 | 1887 | C. Schoenherr | P,D | 509 | 36 |
| Stetson Univ., De Land, FL 32720 | 1883 | Pope A. Duncan | D,P | 2,839 | 130 |
| Steubenville Coll. of, Steubenville, OH 43952 | 1947 | Rev. M. Scanlon | P | 860 | 45 |
| Stevens Inst. of Tech., Hoboken, NJ 07030 | 1870 | Kenneth C. Rogers | P | 2,050 | 130 |
| Stillman, Tuscaloosa, AL 35401 | 1876 | Harold N. Stinson | P | 700 | 35 |
| Stockton State, Pomona, NJ 08240 | 1969 | Richard Bjork | S | 4,668 | 169 |
| Stonehill, N. Easton, MA 02356 | 1948 | Rev. Bartley Macphaidin | D,P | 2,000 | 110 |
| Strayer, Washington, DC 20005 | 1898 | Murray Donoho III | P | 1,700 | 35 |
| Suffolk Univ., Boston, MA 02114 | 1906 | Thomas Fulham | P | 6,373 | 122 |
| Sul Ross State Univ., Alpine, TX 79830 | 1917 | C.R. Richardson | S | 2,257 | 76 |
| Susquehanna Univ., Selinsgrove, PA 17870 | 1858 | Gustave W. Weber | P | 1,700 | 115 |
| Swarthmore, Swarthmore, PA 19081 | 1864 | Theodore Friend | P | 1,260 | 137 |
| Sweet Briar, Sweet Briar, VA 24595 | 1901 | Harold B. Whiteman Jr. | P | 682 | 71 |
| Syracuse Univ., Syracuse, NY 13210 | 1870 | M.A. Eggers | P | 15,000 | 900 |
| Tabor, Hillsboro, KS 67063 | 1908 | Roy Just | P | 510 | 28 |
| Talladega, Talladega, AL 35160 | 1867 | Joseph Gayles | P | 586 | 41 |
| Tampa, Tampa, FL 33609 | 1890 | Jack H. Jones | P | 1,274 | 70 |
| Tampa, Univ. of, Tampa, FL 33606 | 1931 | Richard Cheshire | P | 2,360 | 83 |
| Tarkio, Tarkio, MO 64491 | 1883 | Frank Bretz | P | 635 | 31 |
| Tarleton State Univ., Stephenville, TX 76402 | 1899 | Wm. Trogdon | S | 3,317 | 174 |

| Name, address | Year | Governing official and affiliation | | Stu-dents | Teach-ers |
|---|---|---|---|---|---|
| Taylor Univ., Upland, IN 46989 | 1846 | Robert Baptista | P | 1,525 | 83 |
| Temple Univ., Philadelphia, PA 19122 | 1884 | Marvin Wachman | S | 36,339 | 1,713 |
| Tennessee State Univ.*, Nashville, TN 37203 | 1912 | F. Humphries | S | 5,244 | 368 |
| Tennessee System, Univ. of*, Knoxville, TN 37916 | 1794 | Edward Boling | S | 50,467 | 3,493 |
| Ctr. for Health Sci.*, Memphis, TN 38103 | 1911 | T. Farmer, Chan. | S | 2,552 | 752 |
| at Chattanooga*, Chattanooga, TN 37401 | 1886 | James Drinnon Jr., Chan. | S | 5,951 | 245 |
| at Knoxville*, Knoxville, TN 37916 | 1794 | Jack Reese, Chan. | S | 29,771 | 1,741 |
| at Martin*, Martin, TN 38238 | 1927 | Larry T. McGehee, Chan. | S | 5,002 | 240 |
| at Nashville*, Nashville, TN 37203 | 1971 | Charles Smith, Act. Chan. | S | 5,100 | 160 |
| Tennessee Tech. Univ., Cookeville, TN 38501 | 1915 | Arliss Roaden | S | 7,120 | 339 |
| Tennessee Temple, Chattanooga, TN 37404 | 1946 | Lee Roberson, Chan. | P,D | 3,770 | 145 |
| Tennessee Wesleyan, Athens, TN 37303 | 1857 | George Naff Jr. | D | 445 | 32 |
| Texas, Tyler, TX 75701 | 1894 | Allen C. Hancock | P | 592 | 37 |
| Texas A & I Univ., Kingsville, TX 78363 | 1925 | Duane Leach | S | 6,388 | 293 |
| Texas A & M Univ.*, College Station, TX 77843 | 1876 | Jack K. Williams | S | 28,000 | 2,000 |
| Prairie View A. & M. Univ., Prairie View, TX 77445 | 1876 | Alvin Thomas | S | 5,007 | 716 |
| Tarleton State Univ., Stephenville, TX 76402 | 1899 | William O. Trogdon | S | 2,983 | 150 |
| Texas Christian Univ., Fort Worth, TX 76129 | 1873 | J.M. Moudy, Chan. | P,D | 6,200 | 380 |
| Texas Eastern Univ., Tyler, TX 75701 | 1971 | James Stewart Jr. | S | 1,834 | 77 |
| Texas Lutheran, Seguin, TX 78155 | 1891 | Chas. Oestreich | P | 1,074 | 59 |
| Texas Southern Univ., Houston, TX 77004 | 1947 | Granville Sawyer | S | 9,147 | 453 |
| Texas System, Univ. of, Austin, TX 78701 | 1881 | Charles A. LeMaistre | S | 96,145 | 5,971 |
| at Arlington, Arlington, TX 76019 | 1895 | Wendell Nedderman | S | 17,201 | 750 |
| at Austin, Austin, TX 78712 | 1881 | L. Rogers | S | 41,660 | 2,254 |
| at Dallas, Dallas, TX 75080 | 1969 | Bryce Jordan | S | 5,333 | 276 |
| at El Paso, El Paso, TX 79968 | 1913 | Arleigh Templeton | S | 15,836 | 509 |
| Health Science Center, Dallas, TX 75235 | 1943 | Charles Sprague | S | 1,312 | 375 |
| at Houston, Houston, TX 77025 | 1905 | Truman Blocker Jr., Act. | S | 2,162 | 557 |
| at San Antonio, San Antonio, TX 78284 | 1959 | Frank Harrison | S | 1,749 | 501 |
| Medical Branch, Galveston, TX 77550 | 1881 | William Levin | S | 1,468 | 418 |
| at Permian Basin, Odessa, TX 79762 | 1969 | V.R. Cardozier | S | 1,575 | 70 |
| at San Antonio, San Antonio, TX 78285 | 1969 | James Wagener, Act. | S | 1,849 | 261 |
| Texas Tech. Univ., Lubbock, TX 79409 | 1923 | M. Cecil Mackey Jr. | S | 22,358 | 984 |
| Texas Wesleyan, Fort Worth, TX 76105 | 1891 | Jon Fleming | D | 1,642 | 68 |
| Texas Woman's Univ., Denton, TX 76204 | 1901 | Mary B. Huey | S | 9,023 | 585 |
| Thiel, Greenville, PA 16125 | 1866 | Louis Almen | D | 1,050 | 61 |
| Thomas, Waterville, ME 04901 | 1894 | John L. Thomas Jr. | P | 1,000 | 40 |
| Thomas Jefferson Univ., Philadelphia, PA 19107 | 1824 | Geo. Norwood Jr., Act. | P | 1,700 | 1,400 |
| Thomas More, Ft. Mitchell, KY 41017 | 1921 | Richard A. DeGraff | P | 1,296 | 50 |
| Tiffin Univ., Tiffin, OH 44883 | 1918 | Richard Pfeiffer | P | 475 | 11 |
| Tift (W), Forsyth, GA 31029 | 1847 | Robert W. Jackson | P,D | 500 | 36 |
| Toccoa Falls, Toccoa Falls, GA 30577 | 1907 | Alvin Moser, Admin. Officer | P | 425 | 28 |
| Toledo, Univ. of, Toledo, OH 43606 | 1872 | Glen R. Driscoll | S | 17,500 | 650 |
| Tougaloo, Tougaloo, MS 39174 | 1869 | George A. Owens | P | 830 | 52 |
| Towson State Univ., Baltimore, MD 21204 | 1865 | James L. Fisher | S | 14,591 | 692 |
| Transylvania Univ., Lexington, KY 40508 | 1780 | William Kelly | P | 722 | 59 |
| Trenton State, Trenton, NJ 08625 | 1855 | C.B. Brower | S | 11,000 | 388 |
| Trevecca Nazarene, Nashville, TN 37210 | 1901 | Mark Moore | P | 1,008 | 45 |
| Trinity, Hartford, CT 06106 | 1823 | Theodore Lockwood | P | 2,000 | 135 |
| Trinity, Deerfield, IL 60015 | 1897 | Harry Evans | P | 950 | 36 |
| Trinity, Burlington, VT 05401 | 1925 | Catherine McNamee | D | 450 | 32 |
| Trinity, Washington, DC 20017 | 1897 | Sr. Roseanne Fleming | D | 900 | 109 |
| Trinity Univ., San Antonio, TX 78284 | 1869 | Bruce Thomas | P,D | 3,570 | 211 |
| Tri-State Univ., Angola, IN 46703 | 1894 | Carl Elliott | P | 1,377 | 81 |
| Troy State Univ. System, Troy, AL 36081 | 1887 | Ralph W. Adams | S | 11,294 | 250 |
| Tufts Univ., Medford, MA 02155 | 1852 | Jean Mayer | P | 6,800 | 904 |
| Tulane Univ., New Orleans, LA 70118 | 1834 | Sheldon Hackney | P | 9,221 | 660 |
| Tulsa, Univ. of, Tulsa, OK 74104 | 1894 | J. Paschal Twyman | P | 6,362 | 315 |
| Tusculum, Greenville, TN 37743 | 1794 | Thomas Voss | P | 434 | 28 |
| Tuskegee Institute, Tuskegee Inst., AL 36088 | 1881 | Luther H. Foster | P | 3,616 | 325 |
| Union, Barbourville, KY 40906 | 1879 | Mahlon A. Miller | D,P | 1,113 | 46 |
| Union, Lincoln, NE 68506 | 1891 | Myrl O. Manley | D | 923 | 53 |
| Union, Schenectady, NY 12308 | 1795 | Vacant | P | 3,180 | 167 |
| Union Univ., Jackson, TN 38301 | 1825 | Robert E. Craig | D,P | 1,046 | 58 |
| U.S. Air Force Academy, Col. Springs, CO 80840 | 1955 | Lt. Gen. J. Allen, Supt. | F | 4,000 | 550 |
| U.S. Coast Guard Acad., New London, CT 06320 | 1876 | R. Adm. Malcolm Clark, Supt. | F | 916 | 120 |
| U.S. International Univ., San Diego, CA 92131 | 1952 | William Rust | P | 2,500 | 132 |
| U.S. Merch. Marine Acad., Kings Point, NY 11024 | 1943 | Rear Adm. A. Engel, Supt. | F | 1,068 | 81 |
| U.S. Military Academy, West Point, NY 10996 | 1802 | Lt. Gen. A. Goodpaster, | F | 4,400 | 595 |
| U.S. Naval Academy, Annapolis, MD 21402 | 1845 | Kinnaird McKee, Supt. | F | 4,300 | 540 |
| Upper Iowa Univ., Fayette, IA 52142 | 1857 | Aldrich Paul | P | 509 | 41 |
| Upsala, E. Orange, NJ 07019 | 1893 | W. Weller Jr., Chan. | P | 1,701 | 129 |
| Urbana, Urbana, OH 43078 | 1850 | Roland Patzer | P,D | 465 | 34 |
| Ursinus, Collegeville, PA 19426 | 1869 | Richard Richter | P | 1,706 | 80 |
| Ursuline, Cleveland, OH 44124 | 1871 | Sister M. Kenan Dulzer | D,P | 815 | 87 |
| Utah State Univ.*, Logan, UT 84322 | 1888 | Glen L. Taggert | S | 9,436 | 463 |
| Utah, Univ. of, Salt Lake City, UT 84112 | 1850 | David P. Gardner | S | 21,880 | 1,050 |
| Valdosta State, Valdosta, GA 31601 | 1906 | S. Walter Martin | S | 5,128 | 252 |
| Valley City State, Valley City, ND 58072 | 1890 | Ted De Vries | S | 1,000 | 52 |
| Valparaiso Univ., Valparaiso, IN 46383 | 1859 | Albert Huegli | P | 3,537 | 343 |
| Vanderbilt Univ., Nashville, TN 37240 | 1873 | Alexander Heard, Chan. | P | 6,933 | 1,687 |
| Vassar, Poughkeepsie, NY 12601 | 1861 | Virginia Smith | P | 2,250 | 225 |
| Vermont, Univ. of*, Burlington, VT 05401 | 1791 | Lattie Coor | S | 10,702 | 709 |
| Villa Maria (W), Erie, PA 16415 | 1925 | Sr. M. Lawrence Antoun | P | 508 | 72 |
| Villanova Univ., Villanova, PA 19085 | 1842 | Rev. John M. Driscoll | D,P | 9,619 | 572 |
| Virgin Island, Coll. of the, St. Thomas, VI 00801 | 1962 | L.C. Wanlass | T | 2,119 | 120 |
| Virginia Commonwealth Univ., Richmond, VA 23284 | 1838 | Edmund Ackell | S | 18,366 | 1,262 |
| Virginia Intermont, Bristol, VA 24201 | 1894 | Floyd Turner | P | 811 | 52 |
| Virginia Military Inst. (M), Lexington, VA 24450 | 1839 | Lt. Gen. R. Irby | S | 1,349 | 132 |
| Virginia Poly. Inst. & State Univ.*, Blacksburg, VA 24061 | 1872 | William Lavery | S | 19,648 | 1,505 |
| Virginia State*, Petersburg, VA 23803 | 1882 | Thomas Law. | S | 5,379 | 229 |
| Virginia Union Univ., Richmond, VA 23220 | 1865 | Allix B. James | P,D | 1,423 | 80 |
| Virginia, Univ. of, Charlottesville, VA 22903 | 1819 | F. Hereford Jr. | S | 15,900 | 1,279 |
| Virginia Wesleyan, Norfolk, VA 23502 | 1961 | Lambuth M. Clarke | P,D | 737 | 38 |
| Viterbo, La Crosse, WI 54601 | 1890 | Rev. J. Thomas Finucan | P,D | 941 | 90 |
| Voorhees, Denmark, SC 29042 | 1897 | Lester Brown | D,P | 1,018 | 49 |

| Name, address | Year | Governing official and affiliation | | Students | Teachers |
|---|---|---|---|---|---|
| Wabash (M), Crawfordsville, IN 47933 | 1832 | Lewis S. Salter | P | 860 | 66 |
| Wagner, Staten Island NY 10301 | 1883 | John Satterfield | P | 2,442 | 105 |
| Wake Forest Univ., Winston-Salem, NC 27109. | 1834 | James R. Scales | D | 4,516 | 781 |
| Walla Walla, College Place, WA 99324 | 1892 | N.C. Sorensen | P | 1,947 | 130 |
| Walsh Coll. of Accounting, Troy, MI 48084 | 1922 | Jeffrey Barry | P | 1,172 | 72 |
| Warner Pacific, Portland, OR 97215. | 1937 | E.J. Gilliam | D,P | 649 | 38 |
| Warren Wilson, Swannanoa, NC 28778. | 1894 | Reuben H. Holden | P,D | 505 | 59 |
| Wartburg, Waverly, IA 50677. | 1852 | W. Jellema. | P,D | 1,197 | 79 |
| Washburn Univ. of Topeka, Topeka, KS 66621 | 1865 | John W. Henderson | Mu | 5,488 | 317 |
| Washington, Chestertown, MD 21620 | 1782 | Joseph McLain | P | 780 | 66 |
| Washington and Jefferson, Washington, PA 15301 | 1787 | Howard J. Burnett | P | 1,265 | 124 |
| Washington and Lee Univ., Lexington, VA 24450 | 1749 | Robert Huntley | P | 1,703 | 147 |
| Washington State Univ., Pullman, WA 99164. | 1890 | Glenn Terrell | S | 15,933 | 1,031 |
| Washington Tech. Inst., Washington, DC 20008 | 1966 | C.L. Dennard | S | 4,142 | 194 |
| Washington Univ., St. Louis, MO 63130. | 1853 | W.H. Danforth, Chan. | P | 11,265 | 2,141 |
| Washington, Univ. of*, Seattle, WA 98195 | 1861 | John R. Hogness | S | 37,120 | 2,118 |
| Way Coll. of Emporia, The, Emporia, KS 66801 | 1882 | V.P. Wierwille | D | 476 | 64 |
| Wayland Baptist, Plainview, TX 79072. | 1908 | Roy C. McClung | P | 1,162 | 52 |
| Wayne State, Wayne, NE 68787. | 1910 | Lyle Seymour | S | 2,579 | 90 |
| Wayne State Univ., Detroit, MI 48202 | 1868 | Thomas N. Bonner | S | 34,818 | 1,600 |
| Waynesburg, Waynesburg, PA 15370. | 1849 | Joseph Marsh | D,P | 802 | 61 |
| Weber State, Ogden, UT 84408 | 1889 | Joseph Bishop. | S | 8,741 | 455 |
| Webster, St. Louis, MO 63119 | 1915 | Leigh Gerdine | P | 3,998 | 325 |
| Wellesley (W), Wellesley, MA 02181 | 1875 | Barbara W. Newell | P | 2,093 | 261 |
| Wells (W), Aurora, NY 13026. | 1868 | Frances Farenthold. | P | 513 | 69 |
| Wesleyan (W), Macon, GA 31201 | 1836 | W. Earl Strickland. | D | 570 | 53 |
| Wesleyan Univ., Middletown, CT 06457 | 1831 | Colin G. Campbell | P | 2,500 | 250 |
| West Chester State, West Chester, PA 19380 | 1871 | Charles Mayo | S | 9,152 | 519 |
| West Coast Univ., Los Angeles, CA 90020 | 1909 | Victor Elconin | P | 1,240 | 200 |
| West Florida, Univ. of, Pensacola, FL 32504 | 1963 | James Robinson | S | 5,108 | 215 |
| West Georgia, Carrollton, GA 30117 | 1933 | Maurice Townsend | S | 5,366 | 269 |
| West Liberty State, West Liberty, WV 26074 | 1837 | James L. Chapman. | S | 2,452 | 147 |
| West Texas State Univ., Canyon, TX 79016 | 1909 | Lloyd Watkins | S | 6,558 | 348 |
| W. Va. Inst. of Tech., Montgomery, WV 25136 | 1895 | Leonard C. Nelson | S | 3,312 | 199 |
| West Virginia State, Institute, WV 25112 | 1891 | Harold M. McNeill. | S | 3,519 | 186 |
| West Virginia Univ.*, Morgantown, WV 26505 | 1867 | Gene Budig | S | 20,964 | 1,175 |
| W. Virginia Wesleyan, Buckhannon, WV 26201 | 1890 | R.E. Sleeth | D | 1,805 | 132 |
| Western Baptist Bible, Salem, OR 97302. | 1946 | W.T. Younger | D,P | 438 | 38 |
| Western Carolina Univ., Cullonhee, NC 28723 | 1889 | H.F. Robinson, Chan. | S | 6,380 | 307 |
| Western Conn. State, Danbury, CT 06810 | 1903 | Robert Bersi | S | 4,981 | 251 |
| Western Illinois Univ., Macomb, IL 61455 | 1899 | L. Malpass | S | 14,744 | 773 |
| Western Kentucky Univ., Bowling Green, Ky 42101 | 1906 | Dero Downing | S | 13,386 | 626 |
| Western Maryland, Westminster, MD 21157 | 1867 | Ralph C. John | P | 2,147 | 146 |
| Western Mich. Univ., Kalamazoo, MI 49008 | 1903 | John T. Bernhard | S | 21,033 | 888 |
| Western Montana, Dillon, MT 59725. | 1893 | George Bandy | S | 823 | 43 |
| Western New England, Springfield, MA 01119 | 1919 | Richard Gottier | P | 4,989 | 266 |
| Western New Mexico Univ, Silver City, NM 88061 | 1893 | John Snedeker | S | 1,916 | 60 |
| Western State Col. of Colo., Gunnison, CO 81230 | 1901 | John Mellon | S | 3,350 | 130 |
| Western Washington St., Bellingham, WA 98225 | 1899 | Paul Olscamp | S | 8,697 | 439 |
| Westfield State, Westfield, MA 01085. | 1839 | Robert L. Randolph. | S | 4,239 | 184 |
| Westmar, Le Mars, IA 51031 | 1890 | Ben F. Wade | D | 642 | 50 |
| Westminster, Fulton, MO 65251 | 1851 | J.H. Saunders | P | 700 | 60 |
| Westminster, New Wilmington, PA 16142. | 1852 | Earland I. Carlson. | P | 1,850 | 113 |
| Westminster, Salt Lake City, UT 84105. | 1875 | Helmut Hofmann | P | 1,476 | 58 |
| Westminster Choir, Princeton, NJ 08540 | 1926 | Ray E. Robinson | P | 460 | 57 |
| Westmont, Santa Barbara, CA 93108 | 1940 | David Winter. | P,D | 979 | 55 |
| Wheaton, Wheaton, IL 60187. | 1860 | Hudson T. Armerding. | P | 2,135 | 180 |
| Wheaton (W), Norton, MA 02766 | 1834 | Alice F. Emerson | P | 1,100 | 115 |
| Wheeling, Wheeling, WV 26003 | 1954 | Rev. Charles Currie | D | 1,041 | 77 |
| Wheelock, Boston, MA 02215 | 1889 | Gordon L. Marshall | P | 907 | 95 |
| White Plains, Coll. of, White Plains, NY 10603 | 1923 | Edward Mortola | P | 800 | 55 |
| Whitman, Walla Walla, WA 99362 | 1859 | Robert Skotheim | P | 1,112 | 88 |
| Whittier, Whittier, CA 90608 | 1901 | W.R. Newsom | P | 1,785 | 126 |
| Whitworth, Spokane, WA 99251 | 1890 | Edward B. Lindaman | P | 1,868 | 152 |
| Wichita State Univ., Wichita, KS 67208 | 1895 | Clark Ahlberg | S | 14,842 | 852 |
| Widener, Chester, PA 19013 | 1821 | Clarence R. Moll | P | 3,341 | 236 |
| Wilberforce Univ., Wilberforce, OH 45384 | 1856 | Charles Taylor | D,P | 1,107 | 62 |
| Wiley, Marshall, TX 75670 | 1873 | Robert Hayes Sr. | D | 544 | 41 |
| Wilkes, Wilkes-Barre, PA 18703 | 1933 | Robert Capin | P | 2,767 | 158 |
| Willamette Univ., Salem, OR 97301 | 1842 | Robert Lisensky. | P | 1,753 | 148 |
| William Carey, Hattiesburg, MS 39401 | 1906 | J. Ralph Noonkester | D | 2,042 | 90 |
| William Jewell, Liberty, MO 64068. | 1849 | Thomas Field | P,D | 1,619 | 133 |
| Wm. and Mary, Coll. of, Williamsburg, VA 23185 | 1693 | Thomas A. Graves Jr. | S | 6,011 | 464 |
| Wm. Mitchell Coll. of Law, St. Paul, MN 55105. | 1900 | Ronald Hachey | P | 1,050 | 100 |
| Wm. Paterson, Wayne, NJ 07470 | 1855 | William McKeefery | S | 12,999 | 443 |
| William Penn, Oskaloosa, IA 52577 | 1873 | Duane Moon. | P | 650 | 40 |
| William Woods (W), Fulton, MO 65251 | 1870 | Randall B. Cutlip | P | 1,086 | 100 |
| Williams, Williamstown, MA 01267. | 1793 | John W. Chandler. | P | 1,863 | 160 |
| Wilmington, Wilmington, OH 45177 | 1870 | Robert E. Lucas. | D | 1,022 | 102 |
| Wilson (W), Chambersburg, PA 17201 | 1869 | Margaret Waggoner | P,D | 285 | 50 |
| Wingate, Wingate, NC 28174. | 1896 | Thomas Corts | P | 1,478 | 69 |
| Winona State Univ., Winona, MN 55987. | 1858 | Robt. Hanson | S | 4,626 | 164 |
| Winston-Salem St. Univ., Winston-Salem, NC 27102 | 1892 | Kenneth Williams, Chan. | S | 1,987 | 149 |
| Winthrop, Rock Hill, SC 29733. | 1886 | Charles Vail | S | 4,267 | 206 |
| Wisconsin, Univ. of*, Madison, WI 53706 | 1971 | Edwin Young | S | 143,440 | 6,615 |
| Eau Claire, Eau Claire, WI 54701 | 1916 | Leonard Haas, Chas. | S | 9,974 | 501 |
| Green Bay, Green Bay, WI 54302. | 1969 | Edward W. Weidner, Chan. | S | 3,641 | 160 |
| La Crosse, La Crosse, WI 54601 | 1909 | Kenneth Lindner, Chan. | S | 7,756 | 333 |
| Madison, Madison, WI 53706 | 1849 | Irving Shain | S | 39,022 | 2,500 |
| Milwaukee, Milwaukee, WI 53201. | 1885 | Werner Baum, Chan. | S | 24,686 | 846 |
| Oshkosh, Oshkosh, WI 54901 | 1871 | Robert Birnbaum, Chan. | S | 10,225 | 587 |
| Parkside, Kenosha, WI 53140 | 1969 | Alan Guskin, Chan. | S | 4,984 | 167 |
| Platteville, Platteville, WI 53818 | 1866 | Warren Carrier, Chan. | S | 4,352 | 311 |
| River Falls, River Falls, WI 54022 | 1874 | George Field, Chan. | S | 4,873 | 238 |
| Stevens Point, Stevens Point, WI 54481 | 1894 | Lee S. Dreyfus, Chan. | S | 8,522 | 435 |
| Stout, Menomonie, WI 54751 | 1893 | Robert Swanson, Chan. | S | 6,066 | 293 |
| Superior, Superior, WI 54880 | 1896 | Karl W. Meyer, Chan.. | S | 2,450 | 155 |

| address | Year | Governing official and affiliation | | Stu-dents | Teach-ers |
|---|---|---|---|---|---|
| Whitewater, Whitewater, WI 53190 | 1868 | James Connor, Chan. | S | 9,388 | 418 |
| Wittenberg Univ., Springfield, OH 45501 | 1845 | W.A. Kinnison | P,D | 4,355 | 156 |
| Wofford, Spartanburg, SC 29301 | 1854 | J.M. Lesesne Jr. | P,D | 1,000 | 100 |
| Woodbury, Los Angeles, CA 90017 | 1884 | Bethel Johnson | P | 1,600 | 75 |
| Wooster, Coll. of, Wooster, OH 44691 | 1866 | Henry Copeland | P | 1,896 | 141 |
| Worcester Polytechnic Inst., Worcester, MA 01609 | 1865 | George W. Hazzard | P | 2,750 | 190 |
| Worcester State, Worcester, MA 01602 | 1874 | Joseph Orze | S | 5,811 | 197 |
| Wright State Univ., Dayton, OH 45431 | 1964 | R.J. Kegerreis | S | 14,362 | 657 |
| Wyoming, Univ. of*, Laramie, WY 82071 | 1886 | William Carlson | S | 8,900 | 850 |
| Xavier Univ. of La., New Orleans, LA 70125 | 1925 | Norman C. Francis | D | 1,700 | 158 |
| Xavier Univ., Cincinnati, OH 45207 | 1831 | Rev. Robert Mulligan | P | 6,493 | 175 |
| Yale Univ., New Haven, CT 06520. | 1701 | A.B. Giamatti | P | 9,526 | 1,580 |
| Yankton, Yankton, SD 57078. | 1881 | Orlan Mitchell | P | 244 | 30 |
| Yeshiva Univ., New York, NY 10033. | 1886 | Norman Lamm | P | 6,677 | 1,260 |
| York College of Pa., York, PA 17405 | 1941 | R.V. Iosue | P | 3,100 | 85 |
| Youngstown State Univ., Youngstown, OH 44503 | 1908 | John J. Coffelt. | S | 13,917 | 760 |

## Community and Junior Colleges

Enrollment and faculty figures in italics includes all branches and campuses

| address | Year | Governing official and affiliation | | Stu-dents | Teach-ers |
|---|---|---|---|---|---|
| Abraham Baldwin Agric., Tifton, GA 31794 | 1908 | Stanley Anderson. | S | 2,431 | 111 |
| Adirondacks Community, Glens Falls, NY 12801 | 1960 | Charles R. Eisenhart | S | 2,037 | 65 |
| Aeronautics, Academy of, Flushing, NY 11371 | 1932 | Walter M. Hartung | P | 1,500 | 55 |
| Aims Comm., Greeley, CO 80631 | 1968 | Richard Laughlin | C | 4,000 | 200 |
| Air Force, Comm. Coll. of the, Lackland AFB, TX 78236 | 1972 | Col. Lyle Kaapke | F | 79,608 | 8,855 |
| Alabama Christian, Montgomery, AL 36069 | 1942 | E.R. Brannan | D,P | 1,352 | 105 |
| Alameda, Coll. of, Alameda, CA 94501 | 1970 | Jeanette Poore | C,S | 7,337 | 241 |
| Albany Junior, Albany, GA 31707 | 1966 | B.R. Tilley | S | 2,148 | 100 |
| Albany, Junior Coll. of, Albany, NY 12208 | 1957 | William Kahl | P | 1,045 | 42 |
| Albemarle, Coll. of, Elizabeth City, NC 27909 | 1960 | J.P. Chesson Jr. | S | 1,100 | 58 |
| Alexander City State Jr., Alexander City, AL 35010 | 1965 | W. Byron Causey | S | 1,500 | 47 |
| Allen Co. Comm. Jr., Iola, KS 66749 | 1923 | Bill R. Spencer | C | 747 | 52 |
| Allan Hancock, Santa Maria, CA 93454. | 1920 | Gary Edelbrock | S | 12,728 | 122 |
| Allegany Community, Cumberland, MD 21502 | 1961 | W. Ardell Haines | C,S | 1,813 | 124 |
| Allegheny Co., Comm. Coll. of, Pittsburgh, PA 15222 | 1965 | John B. Hirt | C | 38,480 | 1,510 |
| Alpena Community, Alpena, MI 49707 | 1952 | Herbert N. Stoutenberg | S | 1,850 | 110 |
| Alvin Comm., Alvin, TX 77511 | 1948 | A.R. Allbright | S | 2,603 | 79 |
| Amarillo, Amarillo, TX 79178 | 1929 | Charles Lutz Jr. | Mu | 4,069 | 197 |
| American Academy of Art, Chicago, IL 60604 | 1923 | I. Shapiro. | P | 864 | 26 |
| American River, Sacramento, CA 95841 | 1955 | Kenneth Boettcher | Di | 22,767 | 363 |
| Anderson, Anderson, SC 29621 | 1911 | Ray P. Rust | D | 994 | 46 |
| Andrew, Cuthbert, GA 31740. | 1854 | Walter Murphy | D | 373 | 20 |
| Angelina, Lufkin, TX 75901 | 1968 | Jack W. Hudgins | S | 1,475 | 88 |
| Anne Arundel Comm., Arnold, MD 21012. | 1961 | Justus D. Sundermann. | C,S | 5,668 | 265 |
| Anoke-Ramsey Comm., Coon Rapids, MN 55433 | 1965 | Neil Christenson | S | 2,747 | 72 |
| Anson Tech. Inst., Ansonville, NC 28007 | 1962 | H.B. Monroe. | S | 504 | 18 |
| Antelope Valey, Lancaster, CA 93534 | 1929 | Clinton Stine | S | 4,665 | 200 |
| Aquinas Junior, Milton, MA 02186 | 1956 | Sr. Mary Morgan | D,P | 394 | 25 |
| Aquinas Junior, Nashville, TN 37205 | 1961 | Sister Robert Ann Britton | D,P | 350 | 12 |
| Arapahoe Community, Littleton, CO 80120. | 1966 | Joseph K. Bailey | S | 5,100 | 300 |
| Arizona Western, Yuma, AZ 85364 | 1963 | Marvin Knudson | S | 3,900 | 421 |
| Art Academy of Cincinnati, Cincinnati, OH 45202 | 1887 | Roger Williams, Dir. | P | 171 | 9 |
| Asheville Buncombe Tech. Inst., Asheville, NC 28801 | 1959 | Harvey Haynes | S | 1,686 | 135 |
| Ashland Community, Ashland, KY 41101 | 1957 | Robert Goodpaster | S | 1,253 | 62 |
| Atlantic Comm., Mays Landing, NJ 08330 | 1964 | L.R. Winchell Jr. | C,S | 2,307 | 123 |
| Austin Comm., Austin, MN 55912 | 1940 | Arlan Burmeister | S | 800 | 50 |
| Bacone, Muskogee, OK 74401. | 1880 | Dean Chavers | P | 478 | 39 |
| Bakersfield, Bakersfield, CA 93305 | 1913 | John J. Collins | S | 13,083 | 452 |
| Baltimore, Com. Col. of, Baltimore, MD 21215 | 1947 | Harry Bard. | Mu | 11,700 | 350 |
| Barstow, Barstow, CA 92311. | 1959 | J.W. Edwin Spear. | S | 1,900 | 33 |
| Barton County Comm., Great Bend, KS 67530. | 1965 | Jimmie Downing. | C | 1,902 | 109 |
| Bay de Noe Comm., Escanaba, MI 49829 | 1962 | Edwin E. Wuehle | C | 1,121 | 85 |
| Bay Path Junior, Longmeadow, MA 01106 | 1897 | Randle Elliott | P | 607 | 34 |
| Beal, Bangor, ME 04401 | 1891 | David Tibbetts | P | 468 | 15 |
| Beaufort Co. Tech. Inst., Washington, NC 27889. | 1967 | James P. Blanton | S,C | 1,025 | 36 |
| Beaver Co., Com. Col. of, Monaca, PA 15061 | 1966 | Richard Adams | S | 2,000 | 60 |
| Becker Junior, Worcester, MA 01609 | 1784 | Lloyd H. Van Buskirk | P | 1,300 | 60 |
| Beckley, Beckley, WV 25801. | 1933 | John Saunders | P | 1,257 | 16 |
| Bee County, Beeville, TX 78102 | 1965 | Grady C. Hogue. | S | 2,219 | 125 |
| Belleville Area, Belleville, IL 62221 | 1946 | William Keel | S | 7,156 | 141 |
| Bellevue Community, Bellevue, WA 98008 | 1966 | Thos. O'Connell. | S | 8,764 | 114 |
| Belmont Technical, St. Clairsville, OH 43950 | 1969 | Paul Tien. | S | 1,200 | 40 |
| Bennett, Millbrook, NY 12545 | 1891 | J. William Nystrom | P | 249 | 35 |
| Bergen Community, Paramus, NJ 07652 | 1965 | Sidney Silverman | C,S | 9,743 | 513 |
| Berkeley School, The, Little Falls, NJ 07424 | 1931 | Larry Luing | S | 400 | 14 |
| Berkshire Community, Pittsfield, MA 01201. | 1960 | Jonathan M. Daube. | S | 3,500 | 80 |
| Big Bend Community, Moses Lake, WA 98837. | 1962 | Peter DeVries . | S | 2,000 | 45 |
| Biscayne Southern, Charlotte, NC 28232. | 1972 | Charles Palmer | P | 425 | 32 |
| Bismarck Junior, Bismarck, ND 58501 | 1939 | Kermit Lidstrom. | Mu | 2,179 | 91 |
| Black Hawk, Moline, IL 61265. | 1946 | Richard J. Puffer | S,Di | 7,545 | 153 |
| Blackhawk Technical Inst., Janesville, WI 53545. | 1968 | O.L. Johnson (Dir.) | Di | 1,693 | 97 |
| Bladen Tech. Inst., Dublin, NC 28332 | 1967 | Geo. Resseguie . | S | 400 | 20 |
| Blinn, Brenham, TX 77833 | 1883 | James H. Atkinson | C,S | 2334 | 113 |
| Bliss, Columbus, OH 43214 | 1899 | Gerald J. Wickham | P | 500 | 24 |
| Bluefield, Bluefield, VA 24605 | 1922 | Charles L. Tyer | D | 634 | 33 |
| Blue Mountain Comm., Pendleton, OR 97801 | 1962 | Ronald L. Daniels | C,S, | 1,820 | 91 |
| Blue Ridge Comm., Weyers Cave, VA 24486 | 1965 | James A. Armstrong | S | 1,500 | 42 |
| Boca Raton, Coll. of, Boca Raton, FL 33431 | 1963 | Donald Ross. | P | 456 | 36 |
| Brainerd Comm., Brainerd, MN 56401. | 1938 | Curtis Murton Jr. | S | 600 | 55 |
| Brandywine, Wilmington, DE 19803 | 1966 | C.R. Moll. | D | 1,375 | 45 |

| Name, address | Year | Governing official and affiliation | | Stu-dents | Teach-ers |
|---|---|---|---|---|---|
| Brazosport, Lake Jackson, TX 77566 | 1968 | W.A. Bass | Di | 4,282 | 7 |
| Brevard, Brevard, NC 28712 | 1853 | J.C. Martinson Jr. | D,P | 602 | 4 |
| Brevard Comm., Coca, FL 32922 | 1960 | Maxwell King | S | 8,816 | 30 |
| Brewton Parker, Mt. Vernon, GA 30445 | 1904 | J. Theodore Phillips | D | 1,052 | 4 |
| Bristol Community, Fall River, MA 02720 | 1965 | Jack Hudnall | S | 5,810 | 9 |
| Brookdale Comm., Lincroft, NJ 07738 | 1967 | Donald H. Smith | C | 9,011 | 13 |
| Broome Community, Binghamton, NY 13902 | 1946 | Peter Blomerley | S | 4,686 | 14 |
| Broward Community, Ft. Lauderdale, FL 33301 | 1960 | Hugh Adams | S | 16,000 | 27 |
| Brunswick Junior, Brunswick, GA 31520 | 1961 | John W. Teel | S | 1,068 | 5 |
| Bucks County Comm., Newtown, PA 18940 | 1965 | Charles Rollins | C,S | 7,609 | 34 |
| Butler County Comm., Butler, PA 16001 | 1966 | Thomas Ten Hoeve Jr. | C | 2,012 | 12 |
| Butler County Comm. Jr., El Dorado, KS 67042 | 1927 | Carl Heinrich | C | 1,760 | 6 |
| Butte Community, Oroville, CA 95965 | 1967 | Albert Schlueter | S | 7,716 | 35 |
| Cabrillo Comm. Coll., Aptos, CA 95003 | 1959 | John C. Petersen | S | 10,209 | 18 |
| Caldwell Comm. Coll. & Tech. Inst., Lenoir, NC 28645 | 1964 | H. Edwin Beam | C,S | 1,300 | 12 |
| Camden County, Blackwood, NJ 08012 | 1967 | Otto R. Mauke | C | 6,660 | 34 |
| Canada, Redwood City, CA 94061 | 1968 | J.W. Wenrich | C | 8,300 | 35 |
| Canyons, Coll. of the, Valencia, CA 91355 | 1968 | Robert Rockwell | C | 3,439 | 10 |
| Cape Cod Comm., W. Barnstable, MA 02668 | 1960 | James F. Hall | S | 4,685 | 22 |
| Cape Fear Tech. Inst., Wilmington, NC 28401 | 1964 | M.J. McLeod | S | 3,902 | 40 |
| Carl-Albert Junior, Poteau, OK 74953 | 1934 | Joe E. White | S | 1,375 | 4 |
| Carl Sandburg, Galesburg, IL 61401 | 1966 | Eltis Henson | S | 2,400 | 19 |
| Carteret Tech. Inst., Morehead City, NC 28557 | 1964 | Donald Bryant | S | 913 | 6 |
| Casper, Casper, WY 82601 | 1945 | Tilghman Aley | S | 3,584 | 188 |
| Catawba Valley Tech. Inst., Hickory, NC 28601 | 1958 | Robert E. Paap | S | 2,228 | 120 |
| Catonsville Comm., Baltimore, MD 21228 | 1957 | Robert Barringer | C,S | 8,881 | 41 |
| Cayuga Co. Comm., Auburn, NY 13021 | 1953 | John Anthony | S | 2,829 | 84 |
| Cazenovia (W), Cazenovia, NY 13035 | 1824 | Stephen Schneeweiss | P | 350 | 38 |
| Cecil Community, North East, MD 21901 | 1968 | William O'Connor | C,S | 1,472 | 90 |
| Central Arizona, Coolidge, AZ 85228 | 1969 | Don Pence | C | 4,200 | 57 |
| Central Carolina Tech. Inst., Sanford, NC 27330 | 1962 | James F. Hockaday | S | 1,870 | 72 |
| Central, McPherson, KS 67460 | 1884 | Bruce L. Kline | P | 212 | 23 |
| Central Florida Comm., Ocala, FL 32670 | 1957 | Henry E. Goodlett | S | 2,357 | 189 |
| Central Oregon Comm., Bend, OR 97701 | 1949 | Frederick Boyle | S | 2,500 | 80 |
| Central Piedmont Comm., Charlotte, NC 28204 | 1963 | Richard H. Hagemeyer | S | 18,947 | 692 |
| Central Nebr. Tech. Comm., Grand Island, NE 68801 | 1966 | Chester Guasman | C | 16,072 | 13 |
| Central Texas, Killeen, TX 76541 | 1967 | L.M. Morton Jr. | S | 5,000 | 12 |
| Central Virginia Comm., Lynchburg, VA 24502 | 1966 | Donald Puyear | S | 3,003 | 121 |
| Central Wyoming, Riverton, WY 82501 | 1966 | William Day | C,S | 2,210 | 33 |
| Central YMCA Comm., Chicago, IL 60606 | 1960 | Donald A. Canar | P | 3,885 | 370 |
| Centralia, Centralia, WA 98531 | 1925 | Nels W. Hanson | S | 4,182 | 200 |
| Cerritos Community, Norwalk, CA 90650 | 1955 | Wilford Michael | S | 22,063 | 720 |
| Cerro Coso Comm., Ridgecrest, CA 93555 | 1973 | Richard Meyers | S | 4,527 | 68 |
| Chabot, Hayward, CA 94545 | 1961 | Reed L. Buffington | Di | 19,348 | 900 |
| Chaffey, Alta Loma, CA 91701 | 1883 | K.C. Hinrichsen | S | 11,644 | 461 |
| Champlain, Burlington, VT 05402 | 1878 | C. Bader Brouilette | P | 1,174 | 63 |
| Charles Co. Comm., La Plata, MD 20646 | 1958 | J.N. Carsey | S | 2,146 | 115 |
| Charles S. Mott Comm., Flint, MI 48503 | 1923 | Charles Pappas | C | 9,710 | 436 |
| Chattanooga St. Tech. Comm., Chattanooga, TN 37406 | 1973 | Charles W. Branch | S | 5,000 | 76 |
| Chemeketa Comm., Salem, OR 97303 | 1969 | Arthur A. Binnie | C | 29,000 | 196 |
| Chesapeake, Wye Mills, MD 21679 | 1965 | Robert Schleiger | C | 1,815 | 31 |
| Chicago, City Colleges of, Chicago, IL 60601 | 1911 | Oscar Shabat, Chan. | Mu | 106,774 | 1,400 |
|   Daley, Chicago, IL 60652 | 1960 | Virginia R. Keehan | S | 4,689 | 150 |
|   Kennedy-King, Chicago, IL 60621 | 1935 | Ewen Akin | S | 9,484 | 300 |
|   Loop, Chicago, IL 60601 | 1962 | David H. Heller | S | 8,106 | 250 |
|   Malcolm X., Chicago, IL 60612 | 1911 | James C. Griggs | S | 5,600 | 175 |
|   Olive-Harvey, Chicago, IL 60628 | 1957 | Eugene T. Speller | S | 5,147 | 175 |
|   Truman, Chicago, IL 60640 | 1956 | Wallace B. Appelson | S | 5,397 | 175 |
|   Wright, Chicago, IL 60634 | 1934 | Ernest Clements | S | 6,880 | 250 |
| Chipola Junior, Marianna, FL 32446 | 1947 | Raymond M. Deming | S | 999 | 47 |
| Chowan, Murfreesboro, NC 27855 | 1848 | Bruce E. Whitaker | D | 987 | 54 |
| Cisco Junior, Cisco, TX 76437 | 1941 | Norman Wallace | S | 1,625 | 69 |
| Citrus, Azusa, CA 91702 | 1915 | Robert Haugh | S | 10,049 | 174 |
| Clackamas Comm., Oregon City, OR 97045 | 1966 | John Hakanson | S | 9,000 | 745 |
| Claremore Junior, Claremore, OK 74017 | 1971 | Richard Mosier | S | 2,000 | 80 |
| Clarendon, Clarendon, TX 79226 | 1926 | Kenneth D. Vaughan | S | 432 | 21 |
| Clark, Vancouver, WA 98663 | 1933 | Richard A. Jones | S | 4,256 | 129 |
| Clark Co. Comm., N. Las Vegas, NV 89030 | 1971 | Chas. Donnelly | S | 5,800 | 60 |
| Clark Tech., Springfield, OH 45501 | 1962 | Richard Brinkman | S | 2,010 | 110 |
| Clatsop Community, Astoria, OR 97103 | 1962 | Philip Bainer | S | 6,545 | 148 |
| Clayton Junior, Morrow, GA 30260 | 1965 | Harry S. Downs | S | 3,139 | 86 |
| Cleveland Co. Tech. Inst., Shelby, NC 28150 | 1965 | James Petty | S | 1,810 | 130 |
| Cleveland State Comm., Cleveland, TN 37311 | 1967 | D.F. Adkisson | S | 3,600 | 94 |
| Clinton Community, Clinton, IA 52732 | 1946 | Dean F. Travis | S | 804 | 5 |
| Clinton Community, Plattsburgh, NY 12901 | 1966 | Albert B. Light | S | 1,400 | 31 |
| Cloud County Comm., Concordia, KS 66901 | 1965 | James P. Ihrig | C | 1,275 | 91 |
| Coahoma Junior, Clarksdale, MS 38614 | 1949 | James Earl Miller | S | 1,302 | 66 |
| Coastal Carolina Comm., Jacksonville, NC 28540 | 1964 | James Henderson Jr. | S | 2,500 | 250 |
| Cochise Comm., Douglas, AZ 85607 | 1962 | John R. Edwards Jr. | S | 4,173 | 284 |
| Coffeyville Comm. Jr., Coffeyville, KS 67337 | 1923 | Russell Graham | S | 744 | 49 |
| Colby Comm., Colby, KS 67701 | 1964 | James Tangeman | S | 1,996 | 81 |
| Colorado Mountain, Glenwood Spgs., CO 81601 | 1967 | Elbie L. Gann | C | 5,238 | 24 |
| Colorado Northwestern Comm., Rangely, CO 81648 | 1962 | James H. Bos | Di | 3,680 | 121 |
| Columbia Greene Comm., Hudson, NY 12534 | 1966 | Edward J. Owen | S | 1,218 | 37 |
| Columbia Junior, Columbia, CA 95310 | 1968 | Harvey Rhodes | S | 3,000 | 150 |
| Columbia State Comm., Columbia, TN 38401 | 1966 | Harold S. Pryor | S | 2,156 | 91 |
| Columbus Tech. Inst., Columbus, OH 43215 | 1963 | Clarence Schauer | S | 4,966 | 264 |
| Compton Comm., Compton, CA 90221 | 1927 | Abel B. Sykes Jr. | S | 6,832 | 268 |
| Concordia, Milwaukee, WI 53208 | 1881 | Wilbert Rosin | D | 476 | 43 |
| Connors State, Warner, OK 74469 | 1908 | Melvin Self | S | 1,800 | 64 |
| Cooke County, Gainesville, TX 76240 | 1924 | Alton Laird | S | 1,718 | 116 |
| Copiah-Lincoln Junior, Wesson, MS 39191 | 1928 | Billy Thames | S | 1,365 | 9 |
| Corning Community, Corning, NY 14830 | 1956 | Donald H. Hangen | S | 3,171 | 112 |
| Cottey (W), Nevada, MO 64772 | 1884 | Evelyn Milam | P | 355 | 34 |
| Cowley County Comm., Arkansas City, KS 67005 | 1922 | Owen Nelson | C | 1,419 | 41 |
| Crafton Hills, Yucaipa, CA 92399 | 1972 | Wm. Moore | S | 3,416 | 167 |

| Name, address | Year | Governing official and affiliation | | Stu-dents | Teach-ers |
|---|---|---|---|---|---|
| ...raven Comm., New Bern, NC 28560 | 1965 | Thurman E. Brock | S | 1,293 | 65 |
| ...owder, Neosho, MO 64850 | 1963 | Dell Reed | S | 1,100 | 40 |
| ...uesta, San Luis Obispo, CA 93406 | 1963 | Frank Martinez | C | 6,811 | 84 |
| ...umberland County, Vineland, NJ 08360 | 1963 | Philip Phelan | C | 1,750 | 65 |
| ...urry, Milton, MA 02186 | 1879 | John S. Hafer | P | 1,027 | 54 |
| ...uyahoga, Community, Cleveland, OH 44115 | 1962 | Nolen Ellison, Chan. | C | 27,474 | 468 |
| ...uyamaca, El Cajon, CA 92020 | 1977 | Wallace F. Cohen | Di | 2,700 | 45 |
| ...ypress, Cypress, CA 90630 | 1966 | Jack A. Scott | Di | 12,000 | 200 |
| ...abney S. Lancaster, Comm., Clifton Forge, VA 24422 | 1967 | John F. Backels | S | 900 | 47 |
| ...allas Co. Comm. Col. System, Dallas, TX 75202 | 1965 | Bill J. Priest | C | 32,790 | 2,412 |
| ...alton, Jr., Dalton, GA 30720 | 1967 | Derrell Roberts | S | 1,600 | 75 |
| ...anville Junior, Danville, IL 61832 | 1946 | William Langas | S | 3,350 | 99 |
| ...avenport Coll. of Business, Grand Rapids, MI 49502 | 1866 | Robert W. Sneden | P | 1,311 | 46 |
| ...avidson County Comm., Lexington, NC 27292 | 1959 | Grady Love | S | 2,597 | 198 |
| ...avis Jr. Coll. of Business, Toledo, OH 43604 | 1858 | Ruth L. Davis | P | 1,197 | 41 |
| ...awson Comm., Glendive, MT 59330 | 1940 | James Hoffman | C | 730 | 43 |
| ...aytona Beach Comm., Daytona Beach, FL 32015 | 1958 | Charles Polk | S | 7,500 | 145 |
| ...ean Junior, Franklin, MA 02038 | 1865 | Richard Crockford | P | 1,606 | 51 |
| ...eAnza, Cupertino, CA 95014 | 1967 | A. Robert DeHart | C | 21,000 | 755 |
| ...eKalb Community, Clarkston, GA 30021 | 1964 | W.W. Scott | C,S | 18,000 | 271 |
| ...elgado, New Orleans, LA 70119 | 1921 | Marvin E. Thames | S | 10,725 | 280 |
| ...el Mar, Corpus Christi, TX 78404 | 1935 | Jean Richardson | Di | 10,624 | 248 |
| ...elaware County Comm., Media, PA 19063 | 1967 | Douglas Libby Jr. | C | 4,800 | 250 |
| ...elaware Tech. Comm., Dover, DE 19901 | 1966 | P.K. Weatherly | S | 3,500 | 600 |
| ...elta, University Ctr., MI 48710 | 1957 | Donald Carlyon | C | 8,150 | 385 |
| ...enver, Comm. Coll. of, Denver, CO 80203 | 1968 | G.O. Smith, Act. | S | 15,739 | 766 |
| ...es Moines Area Comm., Ankeny, IA 50021 | 1966 | Paul Lowery | S | 10,037 | 235 |
| ...esert, Coll. of the, Palm Desert, CA 92260 | 1958 | F.D. Stout | S | 11,352 | 303 |
| ...iablo Valley, Pleasant Hill, CA 94523 | 1949 | William P. Niland | Di | 17,040 | 552 |
| ...istrict One Tech. Inst., Eau Claire, WI 54701 | 1912 | Norbert Wurtzel, Dir. | S | 2,147 | 120 |
| ...ixie, St. George, UT 84770 | 1911 | Wm. Kerr | S | 1,343 | 75 |
| ...odge City Community, Dodge City, KS 67801 | 1935 | Charles M. Barnes | C | 1,200 | 73 |
| ...onnelly, Kansas City, KS 66102 | 1949 | Rev. Raymond Davern | D | 844 | 42 |
| ...undalk Community, Baltimore, MD 21222 | 1969 | John E. Ravekes | C | 2,200 | 65 |
| ...u Page, Coll. of, Glen Ellyn, IL 60137 | 1965 | Rodney Berg | S | 16,000 | 264 |
| ...urham Tech. Inst., Durham, NC 27703 | 1965 | John Crumpton Jr. | S,C | 2,000 | 130 |
| ...utchess Community, Poughkeepsie, NY 12601 | 1957 | John J. Connolly | S | 5,975 | 132 |
| ...yersburg State Comm., Dyersburg, TN 38024 | 1969 | Edward Eller | S | 1,191 | 70 |
| ...ast Central Junior, Decatur, MS 39327 | 1928 | Charles V. Wright | S | 1,129 | 54 |
| ...ast Central Junior, Union, MO 63084 | 1968 | Donald D. Shook | Di | 1,400 | 45 |
| ...ast Los Angeles, Los Angeles, CA 90022 | 1945 | A. Rodriguez | Di | 18,000 | 700 |
| ...ast Mississippi Jr., Scooba, MS 39358 | 1927 | C. Cheatham | S | 1,311 | 49 |
| ...astern Arizona, Thatcher, AZ 85552 | 1888 | W.M. McGrath | S,C | 3,826 | 239 |
| ...astern Iowa Comm., Davenport, IA 52806 | 1966 | James Loper, Act. Supt. | S,Di | 2,864 | 158 |
| ...astern Maine Voc. Tech., Bangor, ME 04401 | 1965 | Francis Sprague, Dir. | S | 2,280 | 100 |
| ...astern Oklahoma State, Wilburton, OK 74578 | 1907 | James Miller | S | 1,785 | 89 |
| ...astern Utah, Coll. Of, Price, UT 84501 | 1937 | Dean McDonald | S | 1,885 | 75 |
| ...astern Wyoming, Torrington, WY 82240 | 1948 | Charles Rogers | Di | 1,500 | 120 |
| ...astfield, Mesquite, TX 75149 | 1970 | Byron McClenney | C | 11,800 | 402 |
| ...dgecombe Tech. Inst., Tarboro, NC 27886 | 1968 | Charles McIntyre | C,S | 1,000 | 60 |
| ...dison Community, Ft. Myers, FL 33901 | 1962 | David G. Robinson | S | 3,400 | 121 |
| ...dmonds Community, Lynnwood, WA 98036 | 1965 | James Warren | S | 4,600 | 185 |
| ...dward Williams, Hackensack, NJ 07601 | 1964 | Jerome Pollack | P | 398 | 9 |
| ...l Camino, Torrance, CA 90506 | 1947 | Stuart E. Marsee | Di | 28,454 | 620 |
| ...l Centro, Dallas, TX 75202 | 1966 | Ruby H. Herd | C | 7,733 | 193 |
| ...l Paso Community, El Paso, TX 79904 | 1971 | Ray Salazan | C | 9,800 | 347 |
| ...l Reno Jr., El Reno, OK 73036 | 1938 | Bill S. Cole | S | 801 | 57 |
| ...lgin Community, Elgin, IL 60120 | 1949 | Mark L. Hopkins | S | 5,500 | 340 |
| ...lizabeth Seton, Yonkers, NY 10701 | 1960 | Sr. Mary Ellen Brosnan | P | 989 | 81 |
| ...lizabethtown Comm., Elizabethtown, KY 42701 | 1964 | James Owen, Dir. | S | 1,440 | 65 |
| ...llsworth Comm., Iowa Falls, IA 50126 | 1890 | G.P. Warford (Dean) | S | 724 | 54 |
| ...mmanuel, Franklin Spgs., GA 30639 | 1919 | C.Y. Melton | P,D | 415 | 26 |
| ...ndicott Junior (W), Beverly, MA 01915 | 1939 | Eleanor Tupper | P | 841 | 64 |
| ...rie Community, Buffalo, NY 14221 | 1946 | Oscar Smuckler, Act. | S | 10,296 | 325 |
| ...ssex Community, Baltimore, MD 21237 | 1957 | Vernon Wanty | C | 9,467 | 413 |
| ...ssex County, Newark, NJ 07102 | 1968 | J. Harry Smith | C | 6,749 | 257 |
| ...verett Comm., Everett, WA 98201 | 1941 | Nina Haynes, Act. | S | 7,900 | 150 |
| ...ashion Inst. of Tech., New York, NY 10001 | 1944 | Marvin J. Feldman | S | 8,444 | 164 |
| ...aulkner State Jr., Bay Minette, AL 36507 | 1963 | L. Sibert | S | 2,347 | 78 |
| ...ayetteville Tech. Inst., Fayetteville, NC 28303 | 1961 | Howard Boudreau | S | 4,709 | 213 |
| ...eather River, Quincy, CA 95971 | 1968 | Dale P. Wren | S | 1,837 | 53 |
| ...ergus Falls Comm., Fergus Falls, MN 56537 | 1960 | W.A. Waage | S | 631 | 29 |
| ...inger Lakes, Comm. Coll. of, Canandaigua, NY 14424 | 1965 | Charles Meder | S | 2,330 | 65 |
| ...isher Junior, Boston, MA 02116 | 1903 | Scott Fisher | P | 2,115 | 97 |
| ...lathead Valley Comm., Kalispell, MT 59901 | 1967 | R.C. Mattson, Act. | S,C | 1,407 | 100 |
| ...lorida Jr., Jacksonville, FL 32202 | 1966 | Benjamin R. Wygal | S | 75,158 | 1,580 |
| ...lorida Keys Comm., Key West, FL 33040 | 1965 | John S. Smith | S | 1,348 | 50 |
| ...lorissant Valley Comm. (A), St. Louis, MO 63135 | 1962 | Raymond J. Stith | Di | 6,869 | 350 |
| ...loyd Junior, Rome, GA 30161 | 1970 | David McCorkle | S | 1,445 | 55 |
| ...oothill, Los Altos Hills, CA 94022 | 1958 | James Fitzgerald | S | 15,550 | 650 |
| ...orest Park Comm., St. Louis, MO 63110 | 1962 | Ralph H. Lee | Di | 8,704 | 367 |
| ...orsyth Tech. Inst., Winston-Salem, NC 27103 | 1960 | Harley Affeldt | S | 2,174 | 127 |
| ...t. Steilacoom Comm., Tacoma, WA 98498 | 1967 | Marion O. Oppelt | S | 10,050 | 424 |
| ...ox Valley Tech. Inst., Appleton, WI 54913 | 1967 | William Sirek, Dir. | S | 33,000 | 255 |
| ...ranklin Inst., Boston, MA 02116 | 1908 | Michael Mazzola | P | 1,028 | 34 |
| ...resno City, Fresno, CA 93741 | 1910 | Clyde McCully | Di | 17,902 | 232 |
| ...ullerton, Fullerton, CA 92634 | 1913 | Philip W. Borst | S | 19,430 | 350 |
| ...ulton-Montgomery Comm., Johnstown, NY 12095 | 1963 | Hadley S. DePuy | S | 1,565 | 57 |
| ...adsden State Junior, Gadsden, AL 35903 | 1963 | A.D. Naylor * | S | 3,677 | 126 |
| ...ainesville Junior, Gainesville, GA 30501 | 1964 | Hugh Mills Jr. | S | 1,550 | 60 |
| ...alveston, Galveston, TX 77550 | 1967 | Melvin M. Plexco | S | 2,203 | 80 |
| ...arden City Comm., Jr., Garden City, KS 67846 | 1919 | Raymond Wamsley | C,S | 1,464 | 64 |
| ...aston, Dallas, NC 28034 | 1963 | Joseph L Mills | S | 3,000 | 91 |

| Name, address | Year | Governing official and affiliation | | Stu-dents | Teach-er |
|---|---|---|---|---|---|
| Gateway Tech. Inst., Kenosha, WI 53140 | 1911 | Keith Stoehr, Dir. | Di | 12,188 | 22 |
| Gavilan, Gilroy, CA 95020 | 1919 | Rudy Melone | S | 2,500 | 14 |
| Genesee Community, Batavia, NY 14020 | 1966 | Stuart Steiner | S | 2,093 | 8 |
| George C. Wallace St. Comm., Dothan, AL 36301 | 1965 | Phillip J. Hamm | S | 2,239 | 9 |
| Germanna Comm., Locust Grove, VA 22508 | 1970 | Arnold E. Wirtala | S | 1,050 | 4 |
| Glen Oaks Comm., Centreville, MI 49032 | 1965 | Justus Sundermann | S | 900 | 6 |
| Glendale Comm., Glendale, CA 91208 | 1927 | John Grande | S | 7,752 | 36 |
| Gloucester County, Sewell, NJ 08080 | 1966 | William Apetz | C | 2,500 | 11 |
| Gogebic Community, Ironwood, MI 49938 | 1932 | R. Ernest Dear | S | 1,200 | 5 |
| Golden West, Huntgtn. Bch., CA 92647 | 1965 | R. Dudley Boyce | S | 23,063 | 55 |
| Goldey Beacom, Wilmington, DE 19808 | 1886 | William Ott | P | 1,450 | 12 |
| Gordon Junior, Barnesville, GA 30204 | 1852 | Jerry M. Williamson | P | 1,104 | 5 |
| Grahm Junior, Boston, MA 02215 | 1950 | Arthur Griffin | P | 831 | 7 |
| Grand Rapids Junior, Grand Rapids, MI 49502 | 1914 | Richard Calkins | Mu | 7,301 | 23 |
| Grand View, Des Moines, IA 50316 | 1896 | K.F. Langrock | P | 858 | 4 |
| Grays Harbor, Aberdeen, WA 98520 | 1930 | Joseph Malik | S | 2,959 | 23 |
| Grayson County Junior, Denison, TX 75020 | 1964 | Truman Wester | S,C | 4,900 | 5 |
| Greater Hartford Comm., Hartford, CT 06105 | 1967 | Arthur C. Banks Jr. | S | 3,100 | 5 |
| Green River Comm., Auburn, WA 98002 | 1965 | Melvin Lindbloom | S | 6,500 | 29 |
| Greenfield Comm., Greenfield, MA 01301 | 1962 | Lewis Turner | S | 2,000 | 10 |
| Greenville Tech., Greenville, SC 29606 | 1962 | Thomas Barton Jr. | S | 10,000 | 13 |
| Grossmont, El Cajon, CA 92020 | 1961 | Erv. F. Metzgar | Di | 15,761 | 27 |
| Guilford Tech. Inst., Jamestown, NC 27282 | 1958 | Woodrow Sugg | C | 3,300 | 24 |
| Gulf Coast Comm., Panama City, FL 32401 | 1957 | Lawrence Tyree | S | 3,000 | 20 |
| Hagerstown Junior, Hagerstown, MD 21740 | 1946 | Atlee Kepler | C | 2,116 | 6 |
| Halifax Co. Tech. Inst., Weldon, NC 27890 | 1967 | Phillip W. Taylor | S,C | 840 | 9 |
| Harcum Junior, Bryn Mawr, PA 19010 | 1915 | Michael A. Duzy | P | 750 | 6 |
| Harrisburg Area Comm., Harrisburg, PA 17110 | 1964 | James Odon Jr. | Di,S | 4,823 | 11 |
| Hartford Community, Bel Air, MD 21014 | 1957 | A.C. O'Connell | S | 2,630 | 8 |
| Hartford State Tech., Hartford, CT 06106 | 1946 | L. Barrell | S | 1,419 | 8 |
| Hartnell, Salinas, CA 93901 | 1920 | Gibb R. Madsen | S | 7,309 | 27 |
| Haskell Indian Junior, Lawrence, KS 66044 | 1884 | Wallace Galluzzi | F | 1,086 | 8 |
| Hawkeye Inst. of Tech., Waterloo, IA 50704 | 1966 | John Hawse | S | 21,642 | 44 |
| Haywood Tech. Inst., Clyde, NC 28721 | 1965 | J.H. Nanney | S | 1,600 | 16 |
| Hazard Community, Hazard, KY 41701 | 1968 | J. Marvin Jolly, Dir. | S | 292 | 2 |
| Henderson Community, Henderson, KY 42420 | 1960 | Marshall Arnold, Dir. | S | 803 | 5 |
| Henderson County, Athens, TX 75751 | 1946 | T.M. Harvey | S | 1,786 | 9 |
| Henry Ford Comm., Dearborn, MI 48128 | 1938 | Stuart M. Bundy | Mu | 14,856 | 60 |
| Herkimer Co. Comm., Herkimer, NY 13350 | 1966 | Robert McLaughlin | S | 1,747 | 6 |
| Hesston, Hesston, KS 67062 | 1909 | Laban Peachey | D | 650 | 7 |
| Hibbing Comm., Hibbing, MN 55746 | 1916 | Jennis Bapst | S | 575 | 4 |
| Highland Comm., Freeport, IL 61032 | 1961 | Howard Sims | S | 1,814 | 10 |
| Highland Comm., Highland, KS 66035 | 1858 | Jack D. Nutt | S | 996 | 3 |
| Highline Comm., Midway, WA 98031 | 1961 | Shirley Gordon | S | 7,095 | 35 |
| Hilbert, Hamburg, NY 14075 | 1957 | Sr. E. Paczesny | P | 658 | 2 |
| Hill Junior, Hillsboro, TX 76645 | 1962 | Oran Bailey | S | 700 | 5 |
| Hillsborough Comm., Tampa, FL 33622 | 1968 | F. Scaglione | C | 11,045 | 26 |
| Hinds Junior, Raymond, MS 39154 | 1917 | Robert Mayo | C,S | 8,516 | 33 |
| Hiwassee, Madisonville, TN 37354 | 1849 | Horace N. Barker | D | 650 | 13 |
| Hocking Technical, Nelsonville, OH 45764 | 1968 | John J. Light | S | 2,100 | 12 |
| Holding Tech. Inst., Raleigh, NC 27603 | 1963 | R. LeMay Jr. | S | 1,362 | 8 |
| Holmes Junior, Goodman, MS 39079 | 1925 | Frank Branch | S | 1,338 | 6 |
| Holyoke Community, Holyoke, MA 01040 | 1946 | David Bartley | S | 4,996 | 28 |
| Honolulu Comm., Honolulu, HI 96817 | 1920 | C. Yoshioka | S | 6,544 | 49 |
| Hopkinsville Comm., Hopkinsville, KY 42240 | 1965 | Thomas Riley | S | 1,345 | 6 |
| Horry-Georgetown Tech., Conway, SC 29526 | 1965 | W.F. Anderson | S | 3,300 | 6 |
| Housatonic Comm., Bridgeport, CT 06608 | 1966 | V. Darnowski | S | 2,724 | 10 |
| Houston Comm. Coll., Houston, TX 77007 | 1971 | J.B. Whiteley | S | 26,000 | 1,37 |
| Howard Community, Columbia, MD 21044 | 1970 | Alfred Smith Jr. | C | 1,450 | 6 |
| Howard Coll. at Big Spring, Big Spring, TX 79720 | 1945 | Charles Hays | S | 1,056 | 4 |
| Hudson Valley Comm., Troy, NY 12180 | 1953 | J. Fitzgibbons | S | 6,932 | 24 |
| Humphreys, Stockton, CA 95207 | 1896 | John Humphreys | P | 299 | 2 |
| Hutchinson Comm. Jr., Hutchinson, KS 67501 | 1928 | A.H. Elland | S | 2,416 | 17 |
| Illinois Central, E. Peoria, IL 61635 | 1967 | Leon Perley | Di | 11,972 | 18 |
| Illinois Eastern Comm., Olney, IL 62450 | 1968 | James Spencer, Chan. | C | 5,262 | 8 |
| Illinois Valley Comm., Oglesby, IL 61348 | 1924 | Alfred Wisgoski | S | 3,100 | 14 |
| Imperial Valley, Imperial, CA 92251 | 1922 | Terrell Spencer | S | 4,565 | 21 |
| Independence Comm. Jr., Independence, KS 67301 | 1925 | Neil Edds | C | 937 | 7 |
| Indian Hills Comm., Ottumwa, IA 52501 | 1966 | Lyle A. Hellyer | C | 1,095 | 9 |
| Indian Hills Comm., Centerville, IA 52544 | 1930 | Lyle Hellyer | S | 1,228 | 9 |
| Indian River Comm., Ft. Pierce, FL 33450 | 1959 | Herman Heise | S | 4,300 | 8 |
| Indian Valley, Novato, CA 94947 | 1971 | Ernest H. Berg | C | 3,064 | 14 |
| Indiana Vocational Tech., Indianapolis, IN 46206 | 1963 | Glenn W. Sample | S | 12,042 | 91 |
| Inver Hills Comm., Inver Grove Hts., MN 55075 | 1970 | Curtis Johnson | S | 3,000 | 16 |
| Iowa Central Comm., Ft. Dodge, IA 50501 | 1966 | Edwin Barbour | S | 2,520 | 14 |
| Iowa Lakes Comm., Estherville, IA 51334 | 1967 | Richard Blacker, Supt. | S,C | 1,372 | 6 |
| Iowa Western Comm., Council Bluff, IA 51501 | 1966 | Robert Looft | S | 1,782 | 11 |
| Isothermal Comm., Spindle, NC 28160 | 1966 | Fred J. Eason | S | 1,046 | 4 |
| Itasca Comm., Grand Rapids, MN 55744 | 1922 | Leo Keskinen, Act. | S | 570 | 3 |
| Itawamba Junior, Fulton, MS 38843 | 1948 | W.O. Benjamin | S | 2,450 | 10 |
| Jackson Comm., Jackson, MI 49201 | 1928 | Harold Sheffer | C | 11,988 | 10 |
| Jackson State Comm., Jackson, TN 38301 | 1967 | W.L. Nelms | S | 2,275 | 6 |
| Jamestown Community, Jamestown, NY 14701 | 1950 | C.W Ingle, Act. | S | 3,397 | 10 |
| Jeff Davis State Jr., Brewton, AL 36426 | 1965 | W.P. Patterson | S | 900 | 4 |
| Jefferson, Hillsboro, MO 63050 | 1963 | B.R. Henry | Di | 5,200 | 20 |
| Jefferson Community, Louisville, KY 40201 | 1968 | Ronald Horvath, Dir. | S | 6,086 | 30 |
| Jefferson Community, Watertown, NY 13601 | 1961 | John Henderson | C | 1,466 | 5 |
| Jefferson State Jr., Birmingham, AL 35215 | 1965 | George Layton | S | 8,118 | 20 |
| John A. Logan, Carterville, IL 62918 | 1967 | Robert Tarvin | S | 4,183 | 7 |
| John C. Calhoun St. Comm., Decatur, AL 35602 | 1965 | J.R. Chasteen | S | 4,223 | 12 |
| John Tyler Comm., Chester, VA 23831 | 1967 | James Walpole | S | 909 | 8 |
| Johnson County Comm., Overland Park, KS 66210 | 1968 | John E. Cleek | C,S | 5,544 | 11 |
| Joliet Junior, Joliet, IL 60436 | 1901 | H.D. McAninch | S | 9,000 | 40 |
| Jones County Junior, Ellisville, MS 39437 | 1911 | Thos. Terrell Tisdale | S,Di | 2,002 | 11 |

| ame, address | Year | Governing official and affiliation | | Stu-dents | Teach-ers |
|---|---|---|---|---|---|
| alamazoo Valley Comm., Kalamazoo, MI 49009 | 1966 | Dale B. Lake. | Di | 6,157 | 92 |
| ankakee Comm., Kankakee, IL 60901 | 1966 | L.H. Horton Jr. | S | 3,526 | 99 |
| an. City Kan. Comm., Kansas City, KS 66112 | 1923 | A.L. Davies | C | 2,934 | 92 |
| apiolani Comm., Honolulu, HI 96814 | 1965 | J.S. Tsunoda, Prov. | S | 4,500 | 95 |
| askaskia, Centralia, IL 62801 | 1965 | Paul Blowers | S | 1,600 | 54 |
| atharine Gibbs School, New York, NY 10017 | 1917 | Miss Edith Foster | P | 1,000 | 25 |
| auai Community, Lihue, HI 96766 | 1965 | Edward White, Provost. | S | 1,256 | 75 |
| ellogg Community, Battle Crrek, MI 49016 | 1956 | Richard F. Whitmore | S | 6,635 | 232 |
| endall, Evanston, IL 60204 | 1934 | Andrew Cothran | D | 400 | 25 |
| ennesaw Junior, Marietta, GA 30061 | 1963 | Horace W. Sturgis | S | 3,211 | 94 |
| ettering Coll. of Med. Arts, Kettering, OH 45429 | 1967 | Winton Beaven, Dean | D | 412 | 40 |
| eystone Junior, La Plume, PA 18440 | 1868 | John B. Hibbard. | P | 850 | 52 |
| igore, Kilgore, TX 75662 | 1935 | Stewart McLaurin. | S,Di | 3,716 | 135 |
| irg's, Charlotte, NC 28204 | 1901 | Richard Poyner | P | 450 | 11 |
| irtland Comm., Roscommon, MI 48653 | 1966 | Raymond D. Homer | F | 1,100 | 26 |
| irkwood Comm., Cedar Rapids, IA 52406 | 1966 | Selby Ballantyne (Supt.) | S | 4,128 | 266 |
| ishwaukee, Malta, IL 60150 | 1968 | W. Lamar Fly | S | 3,300 | 75 |
| abette Comm. Jr., Parsons, KS 67357 | 1923 | James J. Altendorf | C,S | 736 | 52 |
| ackawanna Jr., Scranton, PA 18503 | 1894 | S. J. Budash. | P | 1,798 | 201 |
| ake City Comm., Lake City, FL 32055 | 1947 | Herbert E. Phillips. | S | 2,996 | 139 |
| ake County, Coll. of, Grayslake, IL 60030 | 1968 | Richard Erzen | S | 8,401 | 405 |
| ake Land, Hattoon, IL 61938 | 1966 | Robert D. Webb. | Di | 3,980 | 347 |
| akeland, Mentor, OH 44060 | 1966 | Wayne Rodehorst. | C | 6,342 | 280 |
| ake Michigan, Benton Harbor, MI 49022 | 1946 | James Lehman | S | 3,104 | 207 |
| ake Region Jr., Devils Lake, ND 58301 | 1941 | Merril Berg. | S | 1,132 | 57 |
| ake Sumter Comm., Leesburg, FL 32748 | 1962 | Paul P. Williams | Di | 2,135 | 115 |
| akeshore Tech Inst., Cleveland, WI 53015 | 1912 | Frederick Nierode. | Mu | 3,958 | 115 |
| akewood Comm., White Bear L., MN 55110 | 1967 | N. Christenson, Act. | S | 2,474 | 93 |
| amar Community, Lamar, CO 81052 | 1937 | Carl Westbrook | S | 501 | 43 |
| ane Com nunity, Eugene, OR 97405 | 1965 | Eldon G. Schafer | C | 13,685 | 361 |
| ansing Community, Lansing, MI 48914 | 1957 | Philip Gannon | S | 15,901 | 816 |
| aramie County Comm., Cheyenne, Wy 82001 | 1968 | Harlan L. Heglar | S,C | 3,205 | 205 |
| aredo Junior, Laredo, TX 78040 | 1946 | D. Arechiga | Mu | 3,206 | 135 |
| asell Junior (W), Newton, MA 02166 | 1851 | Arthur Griffin. | P | 631 | 76 |
| assen Comm., Susanville, CA 96130 | 1925 | Robert Theiler. | Di | 3,100 | 215 |
| atter-Day Saints Bus., Salt Lake City, UT 84111 | 1886 | R.F. Kirkham | P | 800 | 25 |
| ee, Baytown, TX 77520 | 1934 | Jim Sturgeon | Di | 5,009 | 169 |
| ees-McRae, Banner Elk, NC 28604 | 1900 | H.C. Evans Jr. | D | 750 | 45 |
| ehigh County Comm., Schnecksville, PA 18078 | 1966 | John G. Berrier | C | 2,452 | 102 |
| eicester Jr., Leicester, MA 01524. | 1784 | L. Van Burkirk | P | 209 | 26 |
| enoir Comm., Kinston, NC 28501 | 1960 | Jesse L. McDaniel | S | 1,972 | 111 |
| ewis and Clark Comm., Godfrey, IL 62035 | 1971 | Wilbur R.L. Trimpe | S | 4,153 | 184 |
| exington Technical Inst., Lexington, KY 40506 | 1965 | William Price. | S | 1,600 | 85 |
| ima Technical, Lima, OH 45804 | 1971 | James S. Biddle. | S | 1,050 | 47 |
| incoln Land Comm., Springfield, IL 62708 | 1967 | Robert L. Poorman | S,C | 5,972 | 255 |
| incoln, Lincoln, IL 62656 | 1865 | Dale Brummet. | D | 487 | 48 |
| incoln Trail, Robinson, IL 62454. | 1969 | Joseph Piland | S | 2,000 | 103 |
| inn Benton Comm., Albany, OR 97321 | 1967 | Raymond J. Needham | S | 6,333 | 552 |
| ong Beach City, Long Beach, CA 90808. | 1927 | Frank Pearce | Mu | 31,065 | 1,187 |
| ongview Community, Lee's Summit, MO 64063 | 1969 | William D. Hatley | Di | 5,138 | 229 |
| orain County Comm., Elyria, OH 44035 | 1964 | Omar Olson | C,S | 5,298 | 239 |
| os Angeles City, Los Angeles, CA 90029 | 1929 | J.L. Heinselman, Act. | C,S | 19,727 | 650 |
| os Angeles Harbor, Wilmington, CA 90744 | 1949 | Eugene A. Pimentel. | S | 12,258 | 425 |
| os Angeles Pierce, Woodland Hills, CA 91364 | 1947 | Edward Liston | S | 23,500 | 750 |
| os Angeles Southwest, Los Angeles, CA 90047 | 1967 | Franklin Turner | S | 6,250 | 225 |
| .A. Trade Technical, Los Angeles, CA 90015 | 1949 | Fred Brinkman | Mu | 18,528 | 945 |
| os Angeles Valley, Van Nuys, CA 91401 | 1949 | Alice Thurston. | S | 21,523 | 640 |
| ouisburg, Louisburg, NC 27549 | 1787 | J. Allen Norris Jr. | D | 576 | 39 |
| ouisiana State Univ. | | | | | |
| at Alexandria, Alexandria, LA 71301 | 1960 | R. Cleveland, Chan. | S | 1,647 | 83 |
| at Eunice, Eunice, LA 70735 | 1967 | Anthony Mumphrey, Chan. | S | 1,112 | 44 |
| ower Columbia, Longview, WA 98632 | 1934 | David Story | S | 2,685 | 84 |
| urleen B. Wallace St. Jr., Andalusia, AL 36420 | 1969 | W.H. McWhorter | S | 1,072 | 50 |
| uzerne County Comm., Nanticoke, PA 18634. | 1966 | Byron Rinehimer | C | 1,800 | 120 |
| lacomb County Comm., Warren, MI 48093 | 1963 | R.F. Roelofs | S | 24,000 | 865 |
| lacCormac Junior, Chicago, IL 60604 | 1904 | Gordon Borchardt. | P | 400 | 21 |
| lacon Junior, Macon, GA 31206 | 1968 | William Wright. | S | 2,506 | 82 |
| ladison Area Technical, Madison, WI 53703. | 1912 | Norman P. Mitby, Dir.. | Di | 7,383 | 220 |
| ladison Business, Madison, WI 53703 | 1856 | Stuart E. Sears | D | 296 | 17 |
| laine, Univ of | | | | | |
| at Augusta, ME 04330 | 1965 | K.W. Allen, Act. | S | 3,160 | 232 |
| lainland, Coll. of the, Texas City, TX 77590 | 1967 | Fred Taylor | Di | 2,080 | 239 |
| lalcolm X, Chicago, IL 60612 | 1911 | Samuel Huffman | Mu | 6,830 | 215 |
| lanatee Junior, Bradenton, FL 33507 | 1957 | W. Wetzler. | S | 4,161 | 198 |
| lanchester Comm., Manchester, CT 06040 | 1963 | Ronald Denison | S | 5,000 | 110 |
| laple Woods Comm., Kansas City, MO 64156 | 1969 | John M. Gazda | Mu | 1,972 | 39 |
| laria, Albany, NY 12208 | 1958 | Sr. L. Fitzgerald | P | 488 | 48 |
| laria Regina, Syracuse, NY 13208 | 1961 | Sr. Mary Rosalie | P | 421 | 34 |
| laricopa Tech. Comm., Phoenix, AZ 85004 | 1968 | N. Bruemmer, Dean | C | 5,196 | 366 |
| larin, Coll. of, Kentfield, CA 94904 | 1926 | I.P. Diamond. | S | 7,390 | 225 |
| larion Institute, Marion, AL 36756. | 1842 | Maj. Gen. Barfield. | P | 370 | 35 |
| larshalltown Comm., Marshalltown, IA 50158. | 1927 | Paul Kegel. | S | 1,034 | 65 |
| lartin, Pulaski, TN 38478. | 1870 | Bill Starnes | D | 300 | 24 |
| lartin Tech. Inst. Williamston, NC 27892 | 1968 | Joseph B. Carter | S,C | 1,250 | 65 |
| lass. Bay Comm., Watertown, MA 02181 | 1961 | John McKenzie | S | 4,096 | 248 |
| lassasoit Comm., Brockton, MA 02402 | 1966 | John Musselman | S | 5,900 | 300 |
| lattatuck Comm., Waterbury, CT 06708 | 1967 | Charles B. Kinney. | S | 3,088 | 120 |
| laui Community, Kahului, HI 96732. | 1965 | Sanae Moikeha, Provost | S | 1,615 | 82 |
| lcCook, McCook, NE 69001. | 1926 | Elmer Kuntz | S | 646 | 46 |
| lcDowell Tech. Inst., Marion, NC 28752 | 1964 | John Price | S | 514 | 36 |
| lcHenry County, Crystal Lake, IL 60014. | 1967 | James Davis. | Di | 4,100 | 130 |
| lcLennan Comm., Waco, TX 76708 | 1965 | Wilbur Ball. | S | 3,535 | 176 |
| ledgar Evers, Brooklyn, NY 11225 | 1968 | Richard D. Trent | Mu | 3,500 | 180 |
| leramec Community, St. Louis, MO 63122 | 1962 | Glynn E. Clark. | Di | 7,070 | 378 |
| lerced, Merced, CA 95340 | 1962 | Lowell Barker | S | 7,706 | 300 |

| Name, address | Year | Governing official and affiliation | | Stu-dents | Teach-ers |
|---|---|---|---|---|---|
| Mercer County Comm., Trenton, NJ 08690 | 1966 | John P. Hanley | D | 7,274 | 15 |
| Mercy, Dobbs Ferry, NY 10522 | 1950 | Donald Grunewald | P | 4,300 | 27 |
| Meridian Jr., Meridian, MS 39301 | 1937 | William F. Scaggs | Mu | 2,857 | 22 |
| Merritt, Oakland, CA 94619 | 1964 | Donald Godbold | Di | 10,500 | 350 |
| Mesabi Comm., Virginia, MN 55792 | 1918 | Gilbert Staupe | S | 850 | 3 |
| Metropolitan Comm., Minneapolis, MN 55403 | 1967 | Rafael Cortada | S | 4,000 | 16 |
| Metropolitan Comm., Kansas City, MO 64111 | 1916 | Ervin Harlacher, Chan. | S | 15,329 | 27 |
| Miami-Dade Comm., Miami, FL 33176 | 1960 | Peter Masiko Jr. | S | 40,296 | 88 |
| Miami-Jacobs Jr. Coll. of Bus., Dayton, OH 45401 | 1860 | Charles P. Harbottle | P | 1,003 | 5 |
| Michael J. Owens Tech., Perrysburg, OH 43551 | 1967 | Jacob H. See | S | 2,991 | 6 |
| Mid Michigan Comm., Harrison, MI 48625 | 1965 | Eugene W. Gillaspy | S | 2,000 | 8 |
| Mid-Plains Comm., No. Platte, NE 69101 | 1967 | Kenneth L. Aten | C | 1,748 | 6 |
| Mid-State Tech. Inst., Wis. Rapids, WI 54494 | 1967 | Earl F. Jaeger | Di,S | 6,000 | 25 |
| Middle Georgia, Cochran, GA 31014 | 1884 | Louis C. Alderman Jr. | S | 1,695 | 10 |
| Middlesex Comm., Middletown, CT 06457 | 1966 | Philip Wheaton | S | 2,166 | 4 |
| Middlesex County, Edison, NJ 08817 | 1966 | Robert Harris | C | 14,600 | 25 |
| Midland, Midland, TX 79701 | 1972 | Al G. Langford | S | 1,600 | 10 |
| Midlands Tech., Columbia, SC 29250 | 1974 | Robert Grigsby Jr. | S,C | 8,500 | 25 |
| Miles Comm., Miles City, MT 59301 | 1939 | Vernon R. Kailey | Di | 850 | 49 |
| Milwaukee Area Tech., Milwaukee, WI 53203 | 1911 | William Ramsey | Di | 77,600 | 2,33 |
| Mineral Area, Flat River, MO 63601 | 1922 | Richard Caster | Di | 917 | 5 |
| Mira Costa, Oceanside, CA 92054 | 1934 | John MacDonald | S | 5,400 | 19 |
| Mississippi Delta Jr., Moorhead, MS 38761 | 1926 | J.T. Hall | S,C | 1,441 | 9 |
| Mississippi Gulf Coast Jr., Perkinston, MS 39573 | 1925 | J.J. Hayden Jr. | S | 8,365 | 32 |
| Mitchell, New London, CT 06320 | 1938 | Robert C. Weller | P | 732 | 4 |
| Mitchell Comm., Statesville, NC 28677 | 1852 | Charles Poindexter | S | 1,581 | 6 |
| Moberly Area Junior, Moberly, MO 65270 | 1927 | Andrew Komar Jr. | S | 765 | 6 |
| Modesto Junior, Modesto, CA 95350 | 1921 | Kenneth Griffin | S | 17,058 | 56 |
| Mohawk Valley Comm., Utica, NY 13501 | 1946 | G.H. Robertson | S | 7,143 | 14 |
| Mohegan Comm., Norwich, Ct 06360 | 1970 | Robert N. Rue | S | 1,841 | 9 |
| Monroe Community, Rochester, NY 14623 | 1961 | Moses Koch | S | 10,029 | 28 |
| Monroe County Comm., Monroe, MI 48161 | 1964 | Ronald Campbell | C,S | 2,100 | 5 |
| Montcalm Comm., Sidney, MI 48885 | 1965 | C.J. Bedore | C | 1,050 | 27 |
| Monterey Peninsula, Monterey, CA 93940 | 1947 | George J. Faul | S | 8,000 | 42 |
| Montgomery Comm., Rockville, MD 20850 | 1946 | William Strasser | C | 13,984 | 69 |
| Montgomery Co. Comm., Blue Bell, PA 19422 | 1964 | Leroy Brendlinger | C | 5,813 | 31 |
| Montreat-Anderson, Montreat, NC 28757 | 1916 | Silas M. Vaughn | P | 449 | 2 |
| Moorpark, Moorpark, CA 93021 | 1967 | W. Ray Hearon | C | 9,397 | 45 |
| Morame Valley Comm., Palos Hills, IL 60465 | 1968 | James Koeller | S | 10,516 | 379 |
| Morgan Comm., Ft. Morgan, CO 80701 | 1970 | Robert W. Johnson | S | 1,000 | 1 |
| Morris, County Coll. of, Dover, NJ 07801 | 1965 | Sherman H. Masten | C | 8,717 | 35 |
| Morristown, (A) Morristown, TN 37814 | 1881 | Raymond White | D | 233 | 1 |
| Morse Sch. of Bus. Inc., Hartford, CT 06103 | 1860 | Michael Taub | P | 350 | 3 |
| Motlow State Comm., Tullahoma, TN 37388 | 1969 | Harry D. Wagner | S | 1,140 | 4 |
| Mt. Aloysius Junior, Cresson, PA 16630 | 1939 | J.P. Gallagher | P | 489 | 3 |
| Mt. Hood Comm., Gresham, OR 97030 | 1965 | R.S. Nicholson | Di | 10,000 | 40 |
| Mt. Ida Junior, Newton Centre, MA 02159 | 1899 | B.E. Carlson | P | 710 | 4 |
| Mt. Olive, Mt. Olive, NC 28365 | 1951 | Williams B. Raper | D,P | 377 | 33 |
| Mt. San Antonio, Walnut, CA 91789 | 1946 | Eldon Pearce | Di | 23,815 | 75 |
| Mt. San Jacinto, San Jacinto, CA 92383 | 1963 | Milo P. Johnson | S | 2,500 | 47 |
| Mt. Wachusett Comm., Gardner, MA 01440 | 1963 | Arthur F. Haley | S | 2,969 | 17 |
| Mountain View, Dallas, TX 75211 | 1970 | David Sims | S | 6,500 | 25 |
| Murray State, Tishomingo, OK 73460 | 1908 | Clyde Kindell | S | 1,357 | 49 |
| Muskegon Business, Muskegon, MI 49442 | 1885 | Robert Jewell | P | 750 | 55 |
| Muskegon Comm., Muskegon, MI 49442 | 1926 | J.G. Thompson | C | 4,762 | 200 |
| Napa, Napa, CA 94558 | 1962 | George Clark | C | 8,000 | 388 |
| Nash Tech. Inst., Rocky Mount, NC 27801 | 1968 | Jack D. Ballard | S | 813 | 35 |
| Nassau Community, Garden City, NY 11530 | 1959 | George Chambers | C | 17,595 | 474 |
| Navarro, Corsicana, TX 75110 | 1946 | Kenneth Walker | C | 2,018 | 11 |
| Nebraska Western, Scottsbluff, NE 69361 | 1928 | Alex Easton | Mu | 761 | 5 |
| Neosho County Comm. Jr., Chanute, KS 66720 | 1936 | J.C. Sanders | C | 622 | 48 |
| New Hampshire Tech. Inst., Concord, NH 03301 | 1965 | D. Larrabee Sr. | S | 2,200 | 16 |
| New Hampshire Voc. Tech., Manchester, NY 03102 | 1945 | R.E. Mandeville, Dir. | S | 700 | 57 |
| New Mexico Junior, Hobbs, NM 88240 | 1965 | Jodie Smith | S | 1,154 | 58 |
| New Mexico Military Inst. (M), Roswell, NM 88201 | 1891 | Robert Kemble | S | 940 | 56 |
| New River Community, Dublin, VA 24084 | 1966 | H.R. Edwards | S | 2,325 | 135 |
| New York City, Univ. of, New York, NY 10021 | 1847 | Robert Kibbee | C | 269,929 | 15,116 |
| Bronx Comm., Bronx, NY 10453 | 1957 | Roscoe C. Brown Jr. | Mu | 13,905 | 593 |
| Hostos Comm., Bronx, NY 10451 | 1968 | Candido DeLeon | C | 2,871 | 202 |
| Kingsborough Comm., Brooklyn, NY 11235 | 1963 | Leon M. Goldstein | Mu | 9,052 | 262 |
| LaGuardia Comm., Long Is. City, NY 11101 | 1968 | Joseph Shenker | Mu | 6,120 | 315 |
| Manhattan Comm., New York, NY 10019 | 1964 | Joshua Smith | Mu | 9,200 | 32 |
| New York City Comm., Brooklyn, NY 11201 | 1946 | Peter Caffey, Act. | Mu | 13,378 | 46 |
| Queensborough Comm., Bayside, NY 11364 | 1958 | Kurt R. Schmeller | C | 10,387 | 42 |
| New York, State Univ. of | | | | | |
| Agric. & Tech. Inst., Alfred, NY 14802 | 1908 | David H. Huntington | S | 4,138 | 221 |
| " " " Canton, NY 13617 | 1906 | Earl MacArthur | S | 2,614 | 122 |
| " " " Cobleskill, NY 12043 | 1911 | Walton A. Brown | S | 2,683 | 145 |
| " " " Delhi, NY 13753 | 1913 | Francis Hennessy | S | 2,825 | 125 |
| " " " Farmingdale, NY 11735 | 1912 | F.A. Cipriani | S | 13,049 | 314 |
| " " " Morrisville, NY 13408 | 1908 | Royson N. Whipple | S | 2,997 | 144 |
| Niagara County Comm., Sanborn, NY 14132 | 1962 | Jack C. Watson | S | 3,835 | 123 |
| Normandale Comm., Bloomington, MN 55431 | 1968 | Dale Lorenz | S | 4,500 | 19 |
| North Central Michigan, Petoskey, MI 49770 | 1958 | A.D. Shankland | S,C | 1,569 | 66 |
| North Central Tech. Inst., Wausau, WI 54401 | 1912 | L.B. Hoyt, Dir. | C | 2,502 | 44 |
| North County Comm., Saranac Lake, NY 12983 | 1967 | P.J. Cayan | S | 1,376 | 48 |
| N. Dak. St. Sch. of Science, Wahpeton, ND 58075 | 1903 | Clair I. Blikre | S | 3,176 | 168 |
| North Florida Junior, Madison, FL 32340 | 1958 | Stephen McMahon | S | 1,034 | 55 |
| North Greenville, Tigerville, SC 29688 | 1892 | George Silver | D,P | 632 | 38 |
| North Harris County, Houston, TX 77037 | 1972 | W.W. Thorne | S | 1,500 | 75 |
| North Hennepin Comm., Brooklyn Pk., MN 55445 | 1966 | John F. Helling | S | 3,372 | 143 |
| North Idaho, Coeur d'Alene, ID 83814 | 1933 | Barry Schuler | Di | 2,337 | 117 |
| North Iowa Area Comm., Mason City, IA 50401 | 1918 | David Randall Pierce | S | 2,014 | 90 |
| North Shore Community, Beverly, MA 01915 | 1965 | George Traicoff | S | 6,392 | 358 |
| Northampton Co. Area Comm., Bethlehem, PA 18017 | 1966 | Richard Richardson Jr. | C | 3,900 | 209 |
| Northeast Alabama State Jr., Rainsville, AL 35986 | 1965 | E.R. Knox | S | 2,978 | 14 |

| ame, address | Year | Governing official and affiliation | | Stu-dents | Teach-ers |
|---|---|---|---|---|---|
| ortheast Miss. Junior, Booneville, MS 38829 | 1948 | Harold T. White | S | 1,556 | 95 |
| ortheast Neb. Tech. Comm., Norfolk, NE 68701 | 1973 | Robert P. Cox | S | 1,166 | 91 |
| ortheast Wisc. Tech. Inst., Green Bay, WI 54303 | 1916 | K.W. Hanbenschild, Dir. | Di | 3,050 | 650 |
| ortheastern Junior, Sterling, CO 80751 | 1941 | Ervin S. French | C | 1,977 | 110 |
| ortheastern Okla. A&M, Miami, OK 74354 | 1919 | D.D. Creech | S | 2,561 | 129 |
| orthern Essex Comm., Haverhill, MA 01830 | 1960 | J.R. Dimitry | S | 5,857 | 347 |
| orthern Oklahoma, Tonkawa, OK 74653 | 1901 | Edwin Vineyard | S | 2,023 | 67 |
| orthern Virginia Comm., Annandale, VA 22003 | 1965 | Richard Ernst | S | 26,557 | 1,477 |
| orthland Comm., Thief R. Falls, MN 56701 | 1965 | Alex Easton | S | 650 | 27 |
| orthwest Community, Powell, WY 82435 | 1965 | Sinclair Orendorff | S | 1,409 | 88 |
| orthwest Miss. Junior, Senotobia, MS 38668 | 1927 | Henry B. Koon | S | 2,743 | 130 |
| orthwestern Conn. Comm., Winsted, CT 06098 | 1965 | Regina Duffy | S | 1,901 | 58 |
| orthwestern Michigan, Traverse City, MI 49684 | 1951 | William J. Yankee | S | 2,605 | 97 |
| orwalk Community, Norwalk, CT 06854 | 1961 | E.I.L. Baker | S | 2,887 | 92 |
| orwalk State Tech., Norwalk, CT 06854 | 1961 | P.A. Marino | S | 2,000 | 65 |
| akland Comm., Bloomfield Hills, MI 48013 | 1964 | Derek Nunney, Act. | C | 18,825 | 290 |
| cean County, Toms River, NJ 08753 | 1969 | William Koehnline | S | 11,694 | 751 |
| dessa, Odessa, TX 79760 | 1964 | Andrews S. Moreland | C | 4,634 | 230 |
| hlone, Fremont, CA 94538 | 1946 | Philip Speegle | S | 3,650 | 125 |
| kaloosa-Walton Jr., Niceville, FL 32578 | 1966 | W.B. Richter | Di | 7,860 | 350 |
| klahoma Sch. of Business, Acctg., | 1963 | J.E. McCracken | S | 2,866 | 155 |
| Law & Finance, Tulsa, OK 74103 | 1919 | H. Everett Pope Jr. | P | 489 | 28 |
| lney Central, Olney, IL 62450 | 1963 | Paul Thompson | S | 1,576 | 63 |
| lympic, Bremerton, WA 98310 | 1946 | Henry Milander | S | 7,500 | 350 |
| nondaga Comm., Syracuse, NY 13215 | 1961 | A. Paloumpis | S | 6,024 | 181 |
| rangeburg-Calhoun Tech., Orangeburg, SC 29115 | 1966 | M. Rudy Groomes | C,S | 3,269 | 58 |
| range Coast, Costa Mesa, CA 92626 | 1948 | Robert Moore | C | 25,529 | 898 |
| range County Comm., Middletown, NY 10940 | 1950 | Robert T. Novak | S | 4,988 | 138 |
| scar Rose Junior, Midwest City, OK 73110 | 1970 | Joe Leone | S | 8,493 | 300 |
| tero Junior, La Junta, CO 81050 | 1941 | William L. McDivitt | S | 885 | 43 |
| ttumwa Heights, Ottumwa, IA 52501 | 1925 | Sr. Bernadine Pieper | P | 310 | 27 |
| aducah Comm., Paducah, KY 42201 | 1932 | Donald J. Clemens, Dir. | S | 1,307 | 50 |
| alm Beach Junior, Lake Worth, FL 33461 | 1933 | Harold C. Manor | S | 10,586 | 172 |
| alomar Comm., San Marcos, CA 92069 | 1946 | Frederick R. Huber | S | 15,515 | 600 |
| alo Verde, Blythe, CA 92225 | 1947 | George W. Pennell | S | 750 | 20 |
| anola Junior, Carthage, TX 75633 | 1947 | Arthur Johnson | S | 850 | 39 |
| aris Junior, Paris, TX 75460 | 1924 | Louis B. Williams | Di | 2,430 | 107 |
| arkersburg Comm., Parkersburg, WV 26101 | 1971 | Jerry Jones | S | 3,672 | 88 |
| arkland, Champaign, IL 61820 | 1966 | William M. Staerkel | Di,S | 6,967 | 318 |
| asadena City, Pasadena, CA 91106 | 1924 | E.H. Floyd | S | 20,700 | 712 |
| asco-Hernando Comm., Dade City, FL 33525 | 1972 | Milton O. Jones | S | 1,700 | 174 |
| assaic Co. Comm., Paterson, NJ 07505 | 1968 | Gustavo Mellander | C | 1,236 | 94 |
| atrick Henry State Jr., Monroeville, AL 36460 | 1965 | Cecil Murphy | S | 1,013 | 57 |
| aul D. Camp Comm., Franklin, VA 23851 | 1968 | Perry Adams | S | 1,253 | 54 |
| aul Smith's Coll. of Arts & Sci., Paul Smiths, NY 12970 | 1937 | T.N. Stainback. | P | 1,246 | 81 |
| earl River Junior, Poplarville, MS 39470 | 1921 | S. David Frazier. | S | 531 | 34 |
| eirce Junior, Philadelphia, PA 19102 | 1865 | M.R. White | S | 2,500 | 106 |
| eninsula, Port Angeles, WA 98362 | 1961 | Thomas M. Peirce III | P | 1,407 | 71 |
| enn Valley Comm., Kansas City, MO 64112 | 1915 | Paul G. Cornaby | S | 2,463 | 120 |
| ensacola Jr., Pensacola, FL 32504 | 1948 | Thomas M. Law | S | 6,219 | 237 |
| eralta Comm., Oakland, CA 94610 | 1964 | T. Felton Harrison. | Di | 14,635 | 470 |
| hiladelphia, Comm., Coll. of, Philadelphia, PA 19107 | 1965 | Thos. Fryer Jr. | Di | 34,559 | 1,108 |
| | | Allen T. Bonnell | C | 12,592 | 383 |
| hillips County Comm., Helena, AR 72342 | 1965 | John Easley | S | 4,724 | 100 |
| hoenix, Phoenix, AZ 85013 | 1920 | William Berry | C | 13,051 | 562 |
| iedmont Tech., Greenwood, SC 29646 | 1966 | Lex Walters | S | 3,300 | 300 |
| iedmont Tech. Inst., Roxboro, NC 27573 | 1970 | Edward W. Cox | S | 877 | 59 |
| iedmont Virginia Comm., Charlottesville, VA 22901 | 1972 | James Walpole | S | 2,028 | 107 |
| ikes Peak Comm., Colorado Springs, CO 80906 | 1968 | Donald McInnis | S | 5,200 | 105 |
| ima Comm., Tucson, AZ 85709 | 1970 | Irwin Spector | S | 19,996 | 998 |
| ne Manor Junior (W), Chestnut Hill, MA 02167 | 1911 | Rosemary Ashby | P | 377 | 47 |
| tt Tech. Inst., Greenville, NC 27834 | 1961 | W.E. Fulford Jr. | S,C | 1,626 | 90 |
| olk Comm., Winter Haven, FL 33880 | 1964 | Frederick T. Lenfestey | S | 5,428 | 185 |
| orterville, Porterville, CA 93257 | 1927 | O.H. Shires | S | 3,686 | 143 |
| ortland Comm., Portland, OR 97219 | 1961 | Amo De Bernardis | Di | 32,966 | 321 |
| ost Junior, Waterbury, CT 06708 | 1890 | Harold Harlow | P | 1,320 | 63 |
| otomac State, Keyser, WV 26726 | 1901 | A.G. Slonaker, Dean | S | 1,005 | 57 |
| rairie State, Chicago Hts., IL 60411 | 1958 | Richard Creal | S | 5,800 | 93 |
| ratt Community, Pratt, KS 67124 | 1938 | Norman Myers | C | 1,638 | 74 |
| resentation, Aberdeen, SD 57401 | 1951 | Sr. Lynn Marie Welbig | D,P | 396 | 46 |
| rince George's Comm., Largo, MD 20870 | 1958 | Robert Bickford | C | 11,830 | 569 |
| uerto Rico Jr., Rio Piedras, PR 00928 | 1949 | Federico J. Modesto | P | 5,691 | 218 |
| uincy Jr., Quincy, MA 02169 | 1958 | Edward Pierce. | Mu | 4,201 | 150 |
| uinebaug Valley Comm., Danielson, CT 06239 | 1971 | Robert E. Miller | S | 569 | 9 |
| uinsigamond Comm., Worcester, MA 01606 | 1963 | Paul Preus | S | 5,107 | 309 |
| andolph Tech. Inst., Asheboro, NC 27203 | 1962 | M.H. Branson | S | 1,400 | 40 |
| anger Junior, Ranger, TX 76470 | 1926 | Jack Elsom | S | 850 | 50 |
| eading Area Comm., Reading, PA 19603 | 1971 | Lewis Ogle | S | 887 | 74 |
| edwoods, Coll. of the, Eureka, CA 95501 | 1964 | Donald Weichert | S | 8,000 | 120 |
| eedley, Reedley, CA 93654 | 1926 | R.A. Cattant | S | 3,401 | 157 |
| einhardt, Waleska, GA 30183 | 1893 | Allen O. Jernigan | D | 797 | 44 |
| end Lake, Ina, IL 62846 | 1967 | H.J. Haberaecker, Act. | S | 2,475 | 59 |
| hode Island Jr., Warwick, RI 02886 | 1964 | William F. Flanagan | S | 8,500 | 474 |
| ichard J. Daley, Chicago, IL 60652 | 1960 | Virginia Keehan | C | 7,766 | 185 |
| ichland, Dallas, TX 75243 | 1972 | E. Biggerstaff Jr. | C | 11,200 | 428 |
| ichland Comm., Decatur, IL 62523 | 1971 | Murray Deutsch | Di | 3,422 | 88 |
| ichmond Tech. Inst., Hamlet, NC 28345 | 1964 | Joseph Nanney | S | 1,122 | 78 |
| icks, Rexburg, ID 83440 | 1888 | Henry B. Eyring | D | 5,740 | 234 |
| o Hondo, Comm., Whittier, CA 90608 | 1960 | L.A. Grandy | C,S | 13,656 | 555 |
| verside City, Riverside, CA 92506 | 1916 | Foster Davidoff | S | 14,064 | 469 |
| obeson Tech. Inst., Lumberton, NC 28358 | 1965 | R. Craig Allen | S | 1,145 | 45 |

| Name, address | Year | Governing official and affiliation | | Students | Teacher |
|---|---|---|---|---|---|
| Rochester Comm., Rochester, MN 55901 | 1915 | Charles Hill | S | 2,950 | 14 |
| Rocklnd Comm., Suffern, NY 10901 | 1957 | Seymour Eskow | S | 7,943 | 15 |
| Rock Valley, Rockford, IL 61101 | 1964 | Karl Jacobs | Di | 8,540 | 12 |
| Rockingham Comm., Wentworth, NC 27375 | 1966 | Gerald B. James | S,C | 3,086 | 12 |
| Rogue Comm., Grants Pass. OR 97526 | 1970 | Henry O. Pete | S | 1,490 | 6 |
| Sacramento City, Sacramento, CA 95822 | 1916 | M.J. Fujimoto | S | 15,572 | 45 |
| Saddleback, Mission Viejo, CA 92675 | 1967 | R.A. Lombardi | S | 13,773 | 68 |
| St. Clair County Comm., Pt. Huron, MI 48060 | 1923 | Richard L. Norris | C | 3,316 | 17 |
| St. John's, Winfield KS 67156 | 1893 | Rev. M.J. Stelmachowicz | D | 285 | 3 |
| St. John's River Comm., Palatka, FL 32077 | 1958 | Robert L. McLendon Jr. | S | 1,500 | 5 |
| St. Louis Community, St. Louis, MO 63110 | 1962 | Richard Greenfield, Chan. | Di | 25,147 | 62 |
| at Florissant Valley, St. Louis, MO 63135 | 1962 | Raymond Smith | Di | 8,460 | 47 |
| at Forest Park, St. Louis, MO 63110 | 1963 | Philip Carlock, Act. | C | 7,912 | 20 |
| at Meramec, St. Louis, MO 63122 | 1962 | Glynn Clark | Di | 9,040 | 43 |
| St. Mary's Jr., Minneapolis, MN 55454 | 1964 | Sr. Anne Joachim Moore | D,P | 821 | 10 |
| St. Mary's (W), Raleigh, NC 27611 | 1842 | John T. Rice | D | 510 | 4 |
| St. Petersburg Junior, St. Petersburg, FL 33733 | 1927 | Michael Bennett | S | 13,018 | 29 |
| Salem Community, Penns Grove, NJ 08069 | 1972 | Herbert C. Donaghay | C | 923 | 5 |
| Sampson Tech. Inst., Clinton, NC 28328 | 1965 | Bruce Howell | S | 745 | 8 |
| San Antonio, San Antonio, TX 78284 | 1925 | Jerome Weynand | S | 21,402 | 1,19 |
| San Bernardino Valley, San Bernardino, CA 92403 | 1926 | Arthur Jensen | S | 15,585 | 49 |
| San Diego City, San Diego, CA 92101 | 1914 | Allen Repashy | S | 5,250 | 14 |
| San Diego, Mesa, San Diego, CA 92111 | 1963 | Ellis Benson | C,Mu | 9,214 | 34 |
| San Francisco, City Coll. of, San Francisco, CA 94112 | 1935 | K.S. Washington | C,Mu | 24,498 | 98 |
| San Jacinto, Pasadena, TX 77505 | 1961 | Thomas M. Spencer | S | 11,448 | 48 |
| San Joaquin Delta Comm., Stockton, CA 95207 | 1935 | Dale Parnell | S,Di | 20,710 | 54 |
| San Jose City, San Jose, CA 95128 | 1921 | Theodore Murguia | C | 14,713 | 75 |
| San Luis Obispo Co. Comm., San Luis Obispo, CA 93406 | 1965 | Merlin Eisenbise | C | 5,504 | 20 |
| San Mateo, Coll. of, San Mateo, CA 94402. | 1922 | David H. Mertes | C | 17,000 | 60 |
| Sandhills Comm., Southern Pines, NC 28387 | 1963 | Raymond A. Stone | S | 1,592 | 8 |
| Santa Ana, Santa Ana, CA 92706 | 1915 | John E. Johnson | S | 23,288 | 78 |
| Santa Barbara City, Santa Barbara, CA 93109 | 1908 | Glenn Gooder | Di,S | 8,613 | 24 |
| Santa Fe Community, Gainesville, FL 32602 | 1965 | Alan Robertson | S | 6,056 | 32 |
| Santa Monica, Santa Monica, CA 90405 | 1929 | Richard Moore | Mu | 18,419 | 20 |
| Santa Rosa Junior, Santa Rosa, CA 95401. | 1918 | Roy Mikalson | C | 15,861 | 56 |
| Sauk Valley, Dixon, IL 61021 | 1965 | George Cole. | S | 3,261 | 15 |
| Schenectady Co. Comm., Schenectady, NY 12305 | 1967 | Robert Larsson | S | 2,745 | 4 |
| Schoolcraft, Livonia, MI 48151 | 1964 | C. Nelson Grote. | S | 6,816 | 91 |
| Schreiner, Kerrville, TX 78028 | 1923 | Sam Junkin | D,P | 477 | 3 |
| Scottsdale Comm., Scottsdale, AZ 85251 | 1970 | Ray Cattan, Exec. Dean | C | 5,100 | 20 |
| S.D. Bishop State Jr., Mobile, AL 36603 | 1965 | Sanford Bishop | S | 1,650 | 7 |
| Seattle Central Comm., Seattle, WA 98122 | 1966 | Robert Terry. | S | 8,129 | 33 |
| Selma Univ., Selma, AL 36701 | 1878 | M.C. Cleveland Jr. | D,P | 620 | 2 |
| Seminole Comm., Sanford, FL 32771 | 1965 | E.S. Weldon | S | 5,509 | 30 |
| Sequoias, Coll. of the, Visalia, CA 93277 | 1925 | Ivan Crookshanks | Di | 6,592 | 33 |
| Seward County Comm., Liberal, KS 67901. | 1967 | Wade Kirk | C,S | 1,059 | 4 |
| Shasta, Redding, CA 96001 | 1950 | Dale Miller | C | 12,800 | 48 |
| Shelby State Comm., Memphis, TN 38104 | 1972 | Jess Parrish | S | 4,326 | 23 |
| Sheldon Jackson, Sitka, AK 99835 | 1878 | H.H. Holloway | D | 297 | 28 |
| Sheridan, Sheridan, WY 82801. | 1948 | Gordon Ward | S | 720 | 5 |
| Shoreline Comm., Seattle, WA 98133 | 1964 | Richard S. White | S | 8,000 | 32 |
| Sierra, Rocklin, CA 95677 | 1914 | G.C. Angove. | C | 8,328 | 35 |
| Sinclair Comm., Dayton, OH 45402 | 1887 | David Ponitz | C | 12,634 | 55 |
| Siskiyous, Coll. of the Weed, CA 96094. | 1957 | Eugene Schumacher | Di | 3,500 | 16 |
| Skagit Valley, Mt. Vernon, WA 98273 | 1926 | Norwood Cole. | S | 15,662 | 37 |
| Skyline, San Bruno, CA 94066 | 1969 | J.C. Petersen | C | 7,842 | 28 |
| Snead State Jr., Boaz, AL 35957 | 1935 | Virgil McCain Jr.. | S | 1,635 | 13 |
| Snow, Ephraim, UT 84627 | 1888 | J.M. Higbee | S | 1,103 | 49 |
| Solano Comm., Suisun City, CA 94585 | 1945 | William Wilson. | S | 9,285 | 334 |
| Somerset Comm., Somerset, KY 42501 | 1965 | Roscoe Kelley. | S | 800 | 45 |
| Somerset County, Somerville, NJ 08876 | 1968 | Joseph Fink | C,S | 3,700 | 190 |
| South Florida Jr., Avon Park, FL 33825 | 1965 | William Stallard | S | 1,400 | 39 |
| South Georgia, Douglas, GA 31533 | 1906 | Denton Coker | S | 1,263 | 78 |
| South Oklahoma City, Oklahoma City, OK 73159 | 1972 | Dale L. Gibson | S | 5,458 | 144 |
| South Plains, Levelland, TX 79336. | 1957 | Marvin L. Baker | Di | 2,538 | 17 |
| Southeast Comm., Fairbury, NE 68352 | 1941 | Daniel Gerber, Dir. | C,S | 852 | 3 |
| Southeastern Comm., Burlington, IA 52655. | 1966 | C.W. Callison, Supt. | S | 1,782 | 13 |
| Southeastern Comm., Keokuk, IA 52632 | 1953 | C.W. Callison | S | 414 | 30 |
| Southeastern Comm., Whiteville, NC 28472 | 1965 | W.R. McCarter | S | 1,666 | 105 |
| Southeastern Illinois, Harrisburg, IL 62946 | 1960 | Harry Abell | S | 1,850 | 66 |
| Southern Baptist, Walnut Ridge, AR 72476. | 1941 | D.J. Nicholas | P | 694 | 44 |
| Southern Idaho, Coll. of, Twin Falls, ID 83301 | 1965 | James L. Taylor. | S | 3,190 | 83 |
| Southern Ohio, Cincinnati, OH 45202 | 1927 | H.W. Nagel | P | 1,600 | 66 |
| Southern Seminary Jr., Buena Vista, VA 24416 | 1867 | J.T. Kanipe Jr.. | P | 293 | 29 |
| Southern Union State Jr., Wadley, AL 36276. | 1922 | Ray Jones | S | 1,710 | 58 |
| Southwest Mississippi Jr., Summit, MS 39666 | 1929 | Horace Holmes | S | 1,105 | 59 |
| Southwest Texas Junior, Uvalde, TX 78801 | 1946 | Wayne Matthews | S | 2,129 | 140 |
| Southwest Virginia Comm., Richlands, VA 24641 | 1968 | Charles King. | S | 2,013 | 49 |
| Southwestern, Chula Vista, CA 92010 | 1961 | C.S. DeVore | S | 11,761 | 400 |
| Southwestern, Okla. City, OK 73127 | 1966 | Hugh Morgan | S | 1,500 | 75 |
| Southwestern Comm., Creston, IA 50801. | 1966 | John A. Smith | S | 550 | 41 |
| Southwestern Michigan, Dowagiac, MI 49047 | 1964 | R.M. Owens | Di | 2,400 | 140 |
| Southwestern Oregon Comm., Coos Bay, OR 97420 | 1961 | Jack E. Brookins | S | 3,429 | 200 |
| Spartanburg Methodist, Spartanburg, SC 29301. | 1911 | James S. Barrett | D | 1,008 | 66 |
| Spartanburg Tech, Spartanburg, SC 29303 | 1963 | Joe D. Gault | S | 3,097 | 217 |
| Spokane Comm., Spokane, WA 99202 | 1963 | Lloyd Stannard | S | 3,600 | 33 |
| Spokane Falls Comm., Spokane, WA 99204 | 1970 | Gerald Saling | S | 3,904 | 131 |
| Spoon River, Canton, IL 61520. | 1959 | Hearl C. Bishop | S | 1,476 | 40 |
| Springfield Tech. Comm., Springfield, MA 01105 | 1967 | Robert Geitz | S | 5,794 | 200 |
| Springfield Coll. in Illinois, Springfield, IL 62702 | 1929 | Sr. Mary Ann Luth | D | 541 | 43 |
| State Fair Comm., Sedalia, MO 65301 | 1966 | Fred E. Davis | Di | 1,545 | 97 |
| State Tech Inst., Memphis, TN 38134 | 1967 | Charles Whitehead | S | 5,803 | 147 |
| Staten Island Comm., Staten Island, NY 10301 | 1955 | Edmund Volpe. | Mu | 12,325 | 540 |
| Sue Bennett, London, KY 40741 | 1897 | Earl F. Hays | D | 287 | 16 |
| Suffolk County Comm., Selden, NY 11784 | 1959 | Albert M. Ammerman. | S | 19,601 | 454 |
| Sullivan County Comm., Loch Sheldrake, NY 12759 | 1962 | Richard F. Grego | S | 1,740 | 71 |
| Sumter Area Tech, Sumter, SC 29150 | 1963 | L.E. Terrell Jr., Act. | S | 2,000 | 110 |

| Name, address | Year | Governing official and affiliation | | Students | Teachers |
|---|---|---|---|---|---|
| Suomi, Hancock, MI 49930 | 1896 | Ralph J. Jalkanen | P,D | 371 | 30 |
| Surry Community, Dobson, NC 27017 | 1964 | Swanson Richards | S | 1,358 | 73 |
| Tacoma Comm., Tacoma, WA 98465 | 1965 | L.P. Stevens | S | 6,015 | 327 |
| Taft, Taft, CA 93268 | 1922 | Wendell Reeder | Di | 1,056 | 46 |
| Tallahassee Comm., Tallahassee, FL 32304 | 1965 | Fred W. Turner | S | 2,900 | 114 |
| Tarrant County Junior, Ft. Worth, TX 76102 | 1965 | Joe B. Rushing | C | 19,554 | 402 |
| Tech. Inst. of Alamance, Burlington, NC 27215 | 1958 | William Taylor | S | 9,783 | 2,207 |
| Temple Junior, Temple, TX 76501 | 1926 | Marvin Felder | S | 1,914 | 101 |
| Texarkana, Texarkana, TX 75501 | 1927 | Carl M. Nelson | S | 2,946 | 128 |
| Texas Southmost, Brownsville, TX 78520 | 1926 | A.L. Oliveira | Mu | 4,600 | 125 |
| Thames Valley State Tech., Norwich, CT 06360 | 1963 | Donald Welter | S | 1,680 | 33 |
| Thomas Nelson Comm., Hampton, VA 23670 | 1968 | Gerald O. Cannon | S | 4,662 | 194 |
| Thornton Comm., So. Holland, IL 60473 | 1927 | Nathan A. Ivey | Di | 10,964 | 131 |
| Three Rivers Comm., Poplar Bluff, MO 63901 | 1966 | J.L. Bottenfield | S | 1,562 | 50 |
| Tidewater Comm., Portsmouth, VA 23703 | 1968 | George Pass | S | 11,250 | 216 |
| Tomkins-Courtland Comm., Groton, NY 13053 | 1967 | Hushang Bahar | S | 2,793 | 48 |
| Treasure Valley Comm., Ontario, OR 97914 | 1962 | Emery Skinner | Di | 1,441 | 52 |
| Tri-County Tech., Pendleton, SC 29670 | 1962 | Don Garrison | S | 2,304 | 362 |
| Trident Tech., Charleston, SC 29411 | 1964 | Richard Waldroup Jr. | S | 7,356 | 241 |
| Trinidad State Junior, Trinidad, CO 81082 | 1925 | Thomas Sullivan | S | 1,400 | 143 |
| Triton, River Grove, IL 60171 | 1964 | Brent Knight | Mu | 23,675 | 1,183 |
| Truett McConnell, Cleveland, GA 30528 | 1946 | Ronald Weitman | D | 730 | 48 |
| Tunxis Community, Farmington, CT 06032 | 1970 | Benjamin G. Davis | S | 2,557 | 134 |
| Tyler Junior, Tyler, TX 75701 | 1926 | Harry E. Jenkins | S | 10,284 | 238 |
| Ulster County Comm., Stone Ridge, NY 12484 | 1961 | Robert T. Brown | S | 2,681 | 87 |
| Umpqua Comm., Roseburg, OR 97470 | 1964 | I.S. Hakanson | Di | 8,100 | 140 |
| Union, Cranford, NJ 07016 | 1933 | Saul Orkin | P | 4,735 | 100 |
| Union County Tech. Inst., Scotch Plains, NJ 07076 | 1960 | Harvey Charles | C | 4,188 | 300 |
| Utica Junior, Utica, MS 39175 | 1903 | J. Louis Stokes | S | 1,085 | 71 |
| Valencia Comm., Orlando, FL 32802 | 1967 | James F. Gollattscheck | S | 5,101 | 145 |
| Ventura, Ventura, CA 93003 | 1927 | Richard A. Glenn | S | 13,739 | 481 |
| Vermillion Comm., Ely, MN 55731 | 1922 | Ralph R. Doty | S | 385 | 25 |
| Vermont, Comm. Coll. of, Montpelier, VT 05602 | 1970 | Peter Smith | S | 2,000 | 455 |
| Vermont Technical, Randolph Center, VT 05061 | 1962 | Ned Herrin Jr. | S | 630 | 50 |
| Victor Valley, Victorville, CA 92392 | 1961 | B.W. Wadsworth | Di | 3,200 | 156 |
| Victoria, Victoria, TX 77901 | 1925 | Roland E. Bing | C | 2,400 | 60 |
| Villa Julie, Stevenson, MD 21153 | 1952 | Sister Mary S. Manuszak | P | 610 | 69 |
| Vincennes Univ., Vincennes, IN 47591 | 1801 | Isaac K. Beckes | S | 3,343 | 186 |
| Virginia Highlands Comm., Abingdon, VA 24210 | 1969 | Emma Schulken | S | 1,333 | 66 |
| Virginia Western Comm., Roanoke, VA 24015 | 1966 | Harold H. Hopper | S | 4,408 | 140 |
| Wabash Valley, Mt. Carmel, IL 62863 | 1960 | John Gwaltney | S | 2,800 | 94 |
| Wake Tech. Inst., Raleigh, NC 27603 | 1963 | Robert LeMay Jr. | S | 1,422 | 98 |
| Waldorf, Forest City, IA 50436 | 1903 | Paul Mork | P | 492 | 33 |
| Walker, Jasper, AL 35501 | 1938 | David J. Rowland | S | 674 | 40 |
| Walla Walla Comm, Walla Walla, WA 99362 | 1967 | Eldon Dietrich | S | 3,602 | 95 |
| Walters State Comm., Morristown, TN 37814 | 1970 | Jack E. Campbell | S | 2,669 | 75 |
| Washington State Comm., Spokane, WA 92207 | 1963 | Max M. Synder | S | 18,978 | 326 |
| Washtenaw Comm., Ann Arbor, MI 48106 | 1965 | Gunder Myran | C | 6,800 | 359 |
| Waterbury State Tech., Waterbury, CT 06708 | 1964 | Kenneth Fogg | S | 1,234 | 76 |
| Waubonsee Comm., Sugar Grove, IL 60554 | 1966 | F.D. Etheredge | C | 5,334 | 245 |
| Waukesha Co. Tech. Inst., Pewaukee, WI 53072 | 1923 | R. Anderson | S,Di | 30,000 | 812 |
| Wayne Community, Goldsboro, NC 27530 | 1957 | Clyde Erwin Jr. | S | 2,000 | 120 |
| Wayne County Comm., Detroit, MI 48201 | 1967 | Reginald Wilson | S | 16,177 | 735 |
| Weatherford Jr., Weatherford, TX 76086 | 1869 | E.W. Mince | C | 1,453 | 74 |
| Wenatchee Valley, Wenatchee, WA 98801 | 1939 | William Steward | S | 3,689 | 168 |
| Wentworth Institute, Boston, MA 02115 | 1904 | Edward I. Kirkpatrick | P | 1,900 | 191 |
| Wesley, Dover, DE 19901 | 1873 | R.J. Cooke | D | 1,053 | 56 |
| West Hills, Coalinga, CA 93210 | 1932 | Robert A. Annand | S | 2,000 | 150 |
| West Los Angeles, Culver City, CA 90230 | 1968 | H. Zeitlin | Di | 7,483 | 244 |
| West Shore Comm., Scottville, MI 49454 | 1967 | John Eaton | S | 2,745 | 86 |
| West Valley, Saratoga, CA 95070 | 1963 | James P. Hardy | S | 23,000 | 750 |
| West Virginia North, Comm., Wheeling, WV 26003 | 1972 | Daniel B. Crowder | S | 5,103 | 153 |
| Westark Comm., Ft. Smith, AR 72901 | 1928 | James Kraps | S | 3,339 | 129 |
| Westbrook (W), Portland, ME 04103 | 1831 | James F. Dickinson | P | 796 | 70 |
| Westchester Comm., Valhalla, NY 10595 | 1946 | Joseph N. Hankin | S | 8,017 | 181 |
| Western Iowa Tech., Sioux City, IA 51102 | 1966 | Robert Kiser | S | 1,324 | 82 |
| Western Okla. State, Altus, OK 73521 | 1926 | W.C. Burris | S | 1,612 | 43 |
| Western Piedmont Comm., Morganton, NC 28655 | 1964 | Gordon Blank | S | 1,560 | 55 |
| Western Texas, Snyder, TX 79549 | 1969 | Robert Clinton | C,S | 1,182 | 80 |
| Western Wisc. Tech. Inst., LaCrosse, WI 54601 | 1912 | Charles Richardson, Dir. | C,Mu | 3,584 | 175 |
| Wharton County Junior, Wharton, TX 77488 | 1946 | Theodore Nicksick Jr. | C | 2,022 | 92 |
| Wilkes Community, Wilkesboro, NC 28697 | 1964 | Howard Thompson | S | 2,225 | 101 |
| William Rainey Harper, Palatine, IL 60067 | 1965 | Robert E. Lahti | S | 19,575 | 933 |
| Williamsport Area Comm., Williamsport, PA 17701 | 1965 | William Fedderson | S,C | 3,065 | 210 |
| Willmar Comm., Willmar, MN 56201 | 1962 | John Torgelson | S | 788 | 27 |
| Wilson Co. Tech. Inst., Wilson, NC 27893 | 1958 | Ernest B. Parry | C,S | 1,231 | 43 |
| Wingate, Wingate, NC 28174 | 1896 | Thomas Corts | D | 1,323 | 72 |
| Wisconsin Center, Univ. of | | | | | |
|   at Barron, Rice Lake, WI 54868 | 1966 | John Meggers, Dean | S | 466 | 28 |
|   at Manitowoc, Manitowoc, WI 54220 | 1933 | C. Natunewicz, Dean | S | 309 | 12 |
|   at Marathon, Wausau, WI 54401 | 1947 | W.R. Peters, Dean | S | 840 | 35 |
|   at Marshfield/Wood, Marshfield, WI 54449 | 1964 | Norbert Koopman, Dean | S | 500 | 22 |
|   at Richland, Richland Ctr., WI 53581 | 1967 | Marjorie Wallace, Dean | S | 326 | 9 |
|   at Rock County, Janesville, WI 53545 | 1966 | T. Walterman, Dean | S | 622 | 27 |
|   at Sheboygan, Sheboygan, WI 53081 | 1933 | K.M. Bailey, Dean | S | 631 | 24 |
|   at Washington, West Bend, WI 53095 | 1968 | R.O. Thompson, Dean | S | 590 | 22 |
| Worthington Comm., Worthington, MN 56187 | 1936 | Leon Flancher | S | 762 | 47 |
| Yakima Valley, Yakima, WA 98907 | 1928 | William Russell | S | 6,600 | 122 |
| Yavapai Prescott, AZ 86301 | 1967 | Joseph Russo | S | 4,570 | 138 |
| York, York, NE 68467 | 1890 | Dale Larsen | D,P | 345 | 23 |
| York Technical, Rock Hill, SC 29730 | 1962 | Baxter Hood | S | 2,034 | 57 |
| Young Harris, Young Harris, GA 30582 | 1886 | Ray Farley | D | 499 | 25 |
| Yuba Comm., Marysville, CA 95901 | 1927 | Daniel G. Walker | C,S | 7,047 | 223 |

# Canadian Colleges and Universities

**Source:** Statistics Canada, World Almanac Questionnaire

All coeducational unless followed by (M) for men only. Governing official is president unless otherwise designated. Eac institution listed has an enrollment of at least 200 students of college grade. Number of teachers is the total number of indi viduals on teaching staff. Enrollment and faculty in italics include all branches and campuses.

| Name | Location | Year | Governing official | Students[1] | Teacher |
|------|----------|------|--------------------|-------------|---------|
| Acadia Univ. | Wolfville, N.S. | 1838 | A.M. Sinclair. | 2,700 | 22 |
| Alberta, Univ. of | Edmonton, Alta. | 1906 | Harry E. Gunning | 19,491 | 1,57 |
| Bishop's Univ. | Lennoxville, Que. | 1843 | Christopher Nicholl | 928 | 8 |
| Brandon Univ. | Brandon, Man. | 1899 | H.J. Perkins. | 1,227 | 16 |
| British Columbia, Univ. of | Vancouver, B.C. | 1908 | Douglas T. Kenny | 24,258 | 1,81 |
| Brock Univ. | St. Catharines, Ont. | 1964 | A.J. Earp. | 2,491 | 22 |
| Calgary, Univ. of | Calgary, Alta. | 1945 | W.A. Cochrane | 10,691 | 93 |
| Carleton Univ. | Ottawa, Ont. | 1942 | Michael Oliver. | 8,763 | 88 |
| Concordia Univ. (2) | Montreal, Que. | 1974 | John O'Brien, Rector | 10,094 | 60 |
| Dalhousie Univ. | Halifax, N.S. | 1818 | Henry D. Hicks | 7,216 | 69 |
| Guelph, Univ. of | Guelph, Ont. | 1964 | Donald F. Forster | 10,367 | 85 |
| King's Coll., Univ. of | Halifax, N.S. | 1789 | John F. Godfrey. | 350 | 1 |
| Lakehead Univ. | Thunder Bay, Ont. | 1965 | G.A. Horrower | 2,885 | 25 |
| Laurentian Univ. | Sudbury, Ont. | 1960 | Henry B.M. Best | 2,881 | 40 |
| Laval Universite | Quebec, Que. | 1852 | Jean-Guy Paquet, Rector | 16,675 | 1,38 |
| Lethbridge, Univ. of | Lethbridge, Alta. | 1967 | W.E. Beckel | 1,500 | 15 |
| Manitoba, Univ. of | Winnipeg, Man. | 1877 | Ralph Campbell | 20,334 | 1,39 |
| McGill Univ. | Montreal, Que. | 1821 | Robert E. Bell, Prin. | 15,723 | 1,32 |
| McMaster Univ. | Hamilton, Ont. | 1887 | A.N. Bourns | 10,200 | 90 |
| Mem. Univ. of Newfoundland (2) | St. John's, Nfld. | 1925 | M.O. Morgan | 6,635 | 77 |
| Moncton, Univ. de | Moncton, N.B. | 1963 | Jean Cadieux, Rector | 3,000 | 26 |
| Montreal, Universite de | Montreal, Que. | 1920 | Paul Lacoste, Rector | 22,863 | 1,80 |
| Mount Allison Univ. | Sackville, N.B. | 1840 | W.S.H. Crawford | 1,475 | 13 |
| Mount St. Vincent Univ. | Halifax, N.S. | 1925 | Margaret Fulton. | 1,540 | 15 |
| New Brunswick, Univ. of. | Fredericton, N.B. | 1785 | John M. Anderson | 5,923 | 55 |
| Nova Scotia Coll. of Arts & Design. | Halifax, N.S. | 1887 | Garry Neill Kennedy | 468 | 3 |
| Nova Scotia Technical. | Halifax, N.S. | 1907 | Clair Callghan. | 588 | 7 |
| Ontario Inst. for Studies in Education | Toronto, Ont. | 1965 | Clifford C. Pitt. | 2,573 | 16 |
| Ottawa, Univ. of (2) | Ottawa, Ont. | 1848 | Roger Guindon | 10,541 | 93 |
| Prince Edward Island, Univ. of | Charlottetown, P.E.I. | 1969 | Peter Meincke. | 1,463 | 11 |
| Quebec, Universite du (2) | Ste-Foy, Que. | 1969 | Robert Depres. | 11,086 | 1,18 |
| Queen's Univ. | Kingston, Ont. | 1841 | R.L. Watts | 10,287 | 87 |
| Regina, Univ. of. | Regina, Sask. | 1974 | Lloyd I. Barber | 3,718 | 38 |
| Royal Military Coll. of Can. (M) | Kingston, Ont. | 1876 | J.R. Dacey. | 570 | 14 |
| Ryerson Polytechnical Inst. | Toronto, Ont. | 1948 | Walter G. Pitman | 11,000 | 57 |
| Sainte-Anne, Universite | Church Point, N.S. | 1890 | Charles J. Gaudet, Recteur | 318 | 3 |
| Saint Paul University | Ottawa, Ont. | 1866 | Rev. Henri Goudreault | 404 | 4 |
| St. Francis Xavier Univ. | Antigonish, N.S. | 1853 | Rev. G.A. MacKinnon | 2,403 | 16 |
| St. Mary's Univ. | Halifax, N.S. | 1802 | D. Owen Carrigan | 2,475 | 16 |
| Saskatchewan, Univ. of | Saskatoon, Sask. | 1907 | R.W. Begg | 10,437 | 97 |
| Sherbrooke, Univ. of. | Sherbrooke, Que. | 1954 | Yves Martin | 6,340 | 65 |
| Simon Fraser Univ. | Burnaby, B.C. | 1965 | Pauline Jewett | 8,994 | 42 |
| Toronto, Univ. of | Toronto, Ont. | 1827 | James M. Ham | 31,408 | 2,79 |
| Trent Univ. | Peterborough, Ont. | 1963 | T.E.W. Nind | 2,376 | 18 |
| Victoria, Univ. of | Victoria, B.C. | 1963 | Howard E. Petch | 5,202 | 48 |
| Waterloo, Univ. of | Waterloo, Ont. | 1957 | B.C. Mathews | 18,739 | 73 |
| Western Ontario, Univ. of | London, Ont. | 1878 | George E. Connell | 17,520 | 1,33 |
| Wilfrid Laurier Univ. | Waterloo, Ont. | 1973 | N.H. Tayler | 3,268 | 20 |
| Windsor, Univ. of (2) | Windsor, Ont. | 1857 | John Francis Leddy | 7,404 | 50 |
| Winnipeg, Univ. of | Winnipeg, Man. | 1871 | Henry E. Duckeorth | 2,756 | 18 |
| York Univ. | Downsview, Ont. | 1959 | H. Ian Macdonald | 23,654 | 1,85 |

(1) Total full-time enrollment including undergraduates and graduates for the academic year 1977-78. (2) Enrollment and staff figures apply to 1976-77 academic year.

---

# Typical Tuition Fees at Canadian Colleges and Universities

**Source:** World Almanac Questionnaire, Statistics Canada

Undergraduate tuition fees at universities and colleges with enrollment of 5,000 full day-time students or more. Fee is fo 1978-79 academic year. Figures followed by (a) apply to 1977-78.

| Institution | Tuition | Institution | Tuition |
|-------------|---------|-------------|---------|
| Alberta, University of | $550-$825 | Ottawa, University of | $697-917(a |
| British Columbia, University of | 573-960 | Queen's University of Kingston | 700-825(a |
| Calgary, University of | 275-550(1) | Quebec, Universite du | 250(2)(a |
| Carleton University, Ottawa | 920-980 | Ryerson Polytechnical Institute | 528 |
| Concordia University | 450-540(a) | Saskatchewan, University of | 625-90 |
| Dalhousie University. | 765-885 | Sherbrooke, University of. | 465-65 |
| Guelph, University of | 338-403(1) | Simon Fraser University | 786(3 |
| Laval Universite. | 252-342(3) | Toronto, University of | 575-1,575(a |
| Manitoba, University of | 450-800 | Victoria, University of | 54 |
| Montreal, Universite de | 270-320(3) | Waterloo, University of | 780-82 |
| Memorial University of Newfoundland | 300(1) | Western Ontario, University of | 689-87 |
| McGill University. | 570-719 | Windsor, University of | 745-826(a |
| McMaster University | 680-750 | York University. | 750-76 |
| New Brunswick, University of | 740 | | |

(1) Per semester. (2) Per session. (3) Per trimester.

# Tuition Fees at Selected U.S. Colleges and Universities

**Source: World Almanac Questionnaire**

The College Entrance Examination Board has estimated that the average cost in a private college in the fall of 1978 was $5,110, a 6% increase over the previous year. The cost at a public college averaged $3,054.

Fees for tuition charged per year by colleges and universities for courses, use of libraries, laboratories and other facilities are a major part of student expenses. Tuition varies considerably, depending on the type of institution, its control and location. The lowest tuition fees are those of state-controlled or other public-controlled institutions for residents of their state, city, etc. Students from other states or areas have to pay more. In the following list, such state or other public institutions are shown with two figures. The lower one is the tuition fee for residents, the higher one the tuition fee for students from other states or areas.

*(Tuition does not include room, board, or other expenses.)*

| School | Tuition | School | Tuition | School | Tuition |
|---|---|---|---|---|---|
| Adams State | $ 447-1,787 | Dana | 2,300 | Notre Dame, Univ. of | 3,480 |
| Agnes Scott | 2,900 | Dayton, Univ. of | 2,200 | Oberlin | 3,975 |
| Akron, Univ. of | 840-1,800 | Delaware, Univ. of | 1,000-2,170 | Occidental | 4,400 |
| Alabama State | 495-825 | Delta State Univ. | 554-1,304 | Ohio Univ. | 990-2,265 |
| Alabama, Univ. of | 688-1,413 | Detroit College of Law | 2,400 | Oklahoma State Univ. | 500-1,500 |
| Albion | 3,432 | Eastern New Mexico Univ. | 526-1,334 | Old Dominion Univ. | 744-1,344 |
| Albright | 3,050 | Evergreen State | 618-1,983 | Oral Roberts Univ. | 1,900 |
| Allegheny | 3,600 | Fairleigh Dickinson Univ. | 2,912 | Paine | 2,650 |
| Alma | 3,348 | Florida State Univ. | 705-1,740 | Paul Quinn | 1,500 |
| Amherst | 4,550 | Fordham Univ. | 3,100 | Pennsylvania State Univ. | 1,452-2,832 |
| Appalachian State Univ. | 604-2,324 | Framingham State | 500-1,250 | Peru State | 510-900 |
| Arizona, Univ. of | 450-1,640 | Georgetown | 2,200-2,300 | Pfeiffer | 1,870 |
| Arkansas, Univ. of | 460-1,090 | George Washington Univ. | 2,800 | Quinnipiac | 2,950 |
| Auburn | 600-1,200 | Georgia State Univ. | 570-1,695 | Radcliffe | 4,450 |
| Augusta | 496-1,210 | Goucher | 3,320 | Redlands, Univ. of | 4,100 |
| Austin | 2,950 | Green Mountain | 3,400 | Reed | 4,230 |
| Austin Peay State Univ. | 477-1,413 | Hastings | 2,400 | Rhode Island | 548-1,706 |
| Avila | 2,200 | Hope | 3,055 | Richmond, Univ. of | 4,555 |
| Baker | 2,020 | Idaho, College of | 2,950 | Rutgers, Univ. | 760-1,520 |
| Baldwin-Wallace | 3,132 | Indiana State Univ. | 821-1,689 | St. Bonaventure Univ. | 1,450 |
| Ball State | 840-1,800 | Iowa State Univ. | 735-1,701 | St. Louis Univ. | 3,000 |
| Baltimore, Univ. of | 700-1,600 | Ithaca | 3,860 | St. Olaf | 3,325 |
| Baylor | 1,760 | Jacksonville State Univ. | 500 | St. Paul Bible | 1,200 |
| Beaver | 3,600 | Jersey City State | 704-1,408 | Selma Univ. | 1,074 |
| Blue Mountain | 1,080 | John Brown Univ. | 2,920 | Southern Methodist Univ. | 3,534 |
| Bob Jones | 1,161 | John Carroll Univ. | 2,600 | Southern Miss., Univ. of | 660-1,460 |
| Boston | 3,645 | Juilliard School | 3,000 | Tabor | 2,300 |
| Bowdoin | 4,600 | Kentucky, Univ. of | 768-1,838 | Tampa, Univ. of | 2,895 |
| Brandeis Univ. | 4,635 | Knoxville | 1,626-2,922 | Temple Univ. | 1,450-2,650 |
| Bridgeport, Univ. of | 3,360 | Kutztown State | 950-1,780 | Tennessee, Univ. of | 495-1,395 |
| Brown | 5,050 | Lock Haven State | 475-890 | Tiffin Univ. | 1,700 |
| Bryan | 1,870 | Lowell, Univ. of | 475-1,150 | Trenton State | 700-1,400 |
| Cabrini | 2,530 | Lubbock, Christian | 1,856 | Utah, Univ. of | 589-1,474 |
| Cal. Lutheran | 2,600 | Marquette Univ. | 3,100 | Ursinus | 3,300 |
| Canisius | 2,650 | Memphis State Univ. | 442-1,378 | Vassar | 4,025 |
| Carleton | 5,277 | Montclair State | 704-1,408 | Vermont, Univ. of | 1,300-3,735 |
| Carnegie-Mellon | 4,000 | Montana State Univ. | 550-1,500 | Virginia State | 790-1,250 |
| Case Western Reserve Univ. | 3,900 | Muskingum | 3,600 | Washington, Univ. of | 880-2,394 |
| Central New England | 1,890 | Nazareth | 2,800 | West Virginia Inst. of Tech. | 1,768-2,669 |
| Chicago State Univ. | 590-1,610 | Nebr. Wesleyan Univ. | 2,500 | Worcester State | 500-1,250 |
| Clemson Univ. | 830-1,780 | New England | 3,550 | Wyoming, Univ. of | 430-1,720 |
| Colorado, Univ. of | 380-1,510 | New Mexico, Univ. of | 576-1,716 | Yale Univ. | 5,150 |
| Dakota Wesleyan Univ. | 1,865 | New Orleans, Univ. of | 424-1,254 | Yankton | 2,340 |

---

# Federal Funds for Education, 1978

**Source: National Center for Health Statistics, U.S. Health, Education, and Welfare Department**

Includes grants, loans, and directly administered services. Estimated. (thousands of dollars)

| Type of support, level, and program | | | |
|---|---|---|---|
| **Elementary-secondary education** | **$5,578,721** | Vocational-technical education | $3,501,000 |
| School asst.—federally affected areas | 496,000 | Veterans' education | 605,600 |
| Educationally deprived/Economic | | General continuing education | 189,874 |
| Opportunity Programs | 3,351,007 | Training, federal, state, and local personnel | 81,651 |
| Supporting services | 363,448 | **Grants, total** | **17,959,262** |
| Teacher corps | 18,522 | **Loans, total** | **486,763** |
| Vocational education | 389,979 | Student loan program, Nat. Def. Ed. Act | 382,000 |
| Dependents' schools abroad | 321,533 | College facilities loans | 104,763 |
| Public lands revenue for schools | 198,089 | **Total grants and loans** | **18,446,025** |
| Assistance in special areas | 118,825 | **Other federal funds, total** | **6,616,954** |
| Veterans' education | 84,200 | Applied research and development | 2,336,000 |
| Emergency school asst. | 200,277 | School lunch and milk programs | 2,171,590 |
| Other | 36,841 | Training of federal personnel | 1,172,389 |
| **Higher education** | **8,002,416** | U.S. academies | 333,348 |
| Basic research | 1,483,000 | Professional training, military | 839,041 |
| Research facilities | 326,000 | **Library services** | **307,471** |
| Training grants, | | Grants to public libraries | 52,614 |
| fellowships, and traineeships | 834,052 | National library services | 254,857 |
| Facilities and equipment | 157,316 | **International education** | **97,404** |
| Other institutional support | 472,543 | Educational exchange program | 36,744 |
| Other student assistance | 4,729,505 | AID projects | 53,934 |
| **Vocational-tech. and continuing ed.** | **4,378,125** | ACTION (including Peace Corps) | 4,744 |
| | | | *(Continued)* |

(Continued)

| | | | |
|---|---|---|---|
| Other international educ. and training . . | 1,982 | Educational television facilities . . . . . | 120,081 |
| **Other . . . . . . . . . . . . . . . . . . . . .** | **532,100** | Education in federal correctional inst. . . | 14,871 |
| Agricultural extension service . . . . . . | 240,273 | Other education and training . . . . . . . | 156,875 |

## Fall Enrollment and Teachers in Full-time Day Schools
### Public Elementary and Secondary Day Schools, Fall 1977
Source: National Center for Education Statistics, U.S. Health, Education and Welfare Dept.

| | Local admin. units | Teachers[1] | Pupils enrolled Elementary | Secondary | High school graduates |
|---|---|---|---|---|---|
| **United States . . . . . . . . . . . . . . . . .** | **16,200** | **2,188,000** | **24,775,000** | **18,973,000** | **2,840,000** |
| Alabama . . . . . . . . . . . . . . | 127 | NA | NA | NA | NA |
| Alaska . . . . . . . . . . . . . . . | 51 | 4,915 | 50,398 | 39,946 | 4,526 |
| Arizona . . . . . . . . . . . . . . | 234 | 24,189 | 358,889 | 154,928 | 27,223 |
| Arkansas . . . . . . . . . . . . . | 385 | 22,463 | 240,447 | 218,331 | 27,628 |
| California . . . . . . . . . . . . . | 1,044 | 207,000 | 2,540,582 | 1,748,588 | 266,143 |
| Colorado . . . . . . . . . . . . . | 203 | 28,994 | 287,613 | 274,194 | 36,647 |
| Connecticut . . . . . . . . . . . | 165 | NA | NA | NA | NA |
| Delaware . . . . . . . . . . . . . | 26 | 6,029 | 57,967 | 60,033 | 8,164 |
| District of Columbia . . . . . . . | 1 | 6,022 | 65,616 | 54,259 | 5,335 |
| Florida . . . . . . . . . . . . . . | 67 | 70,598 | 776,714 | 758,856 | 88,137 |
| Georgia . . . . . . . . . . . . . . | 188 | NA | NA | NA | NA |
| Hawaii . . . . . . . . . . . . . . | 1 | 7,891 | 90,299 | 82,057 | 11,637 |
| Idaho . . . . . . . . . . . . . . . | 115 | 9,561 | 105,591 | 95,842 | 13,029 |
| Illinois . . . . . . . . . . . . . . | 1,030 | 107,000 | 1,451,352 | 733,603 | 142,040 |
| Indiana . . . . . . . . . . . . . . | 305 | 52,649 | 585,346 | 558,376 | 76,406 |
| Iowa . . . . . . . . . . . . . . . | 449 | 33,331 | 306,345 | 282,415 | 43,720 |
| Kansas . . . . . . . . . . . . . . | 307 | 25,613 | 266,232 | 179,893 | 33,216 |
| Kentucky . . . . . . . . . . . . . | 181 | 32,860 | 441,632 | 255,368 | 41,755 |
| Louisiana . . . . . . . . . . . . . | 66 | 40,794 | 577,452 | 261,548 | 48,219 |
| Maine . . . . . . . . . . . . . . . | 281 | 13,425 | 166,704 | 79,064 | NA |
| Maryland . . . . . . . . . . . . . | 24 | 42,637 | 421,448 | 415,464 | 55,503 |
| Massachusetts . . . . . . . . . . | 409 | 66,224 | 603,204 | 561,330 | 75,386 |
| Michigan . . . . . . . . . . . . . | 581 | 87,452 | 1,065,004 | 971,072 | 135,162 |
| Minnesota . . . . . . . . . . . . | 440 | 44,574 | 405,051 | 435,401 | 68,166 |
| Mississippi . . . . . . . . . . . . | 152 | 24,831 | 277,132 | 224,893 | 27,639 |
| Missouri . . . . . . . . . . . . . | 558 | 49,618 | 614,938 | 316,294 | 64,471 |
| Montana . . . . . . . . . . . . . | 595 | NA | NA | NA | NA |
| Nebraska . . . . . . . . . . . . . | 1,138 | 17,859 | 159,126 | 145,205 | 23,110 |
| Nevada . . . . . . . . . . . . . . | 17 | 6,055 | 72,651 | 70,793 | 8,011 |
| New Hampshire . . . . . . . . . | 168 | 9,600 | 119,413 | 55,205 | 11,477 |
| New Jersey . . . . . . . . . . . . | 610 | 78,701 | 890,092 | 531,256 | 97,494 |
| New Mexico . . . . . . . . . . . | 88 | 13,832 | 142,872 | 139,024 | 17,988 |
| New York . . . . . . . . . . . . . | 744 | 164,270 | 1,598,667 | 1,630,881 | 215,100 |
| North Carolina . . . . . . . . . . | 145 | NA | 816,645 | 365,186 | 71,146 |
| North Dakota . . . . . . . . . . . | 341 | 7,389 | 53,105 | 66,980 | 10,839 |
| Ohio . . . . . . . . . . . . . . . | 616 | 105,286 | 1,283,428 | 898,551 | 156,220 |
| Oklahoma . . . . . . . . . . . . . | 623 | 31,177 | 320,427 | 274,041 | 38,577 |
| Oregon . . . . . . . . . . . . . . | 333 | 24,312 | 274,570 | 198,709 | 30,258 |
| Pennsylvania . . . . . . . . . . . | 505 | 113,100 | 1,054,040 | 1,074,833 | 160,600 |
| Rhode Island . . . . . . . . . . . | 40 | 9,112 | 93,579 | 73,050 | 10,796 |
| South Carolina . . . . . . . . . . | 92 | 29,666 | 373,796 | 246,927 | 37,780 |
| South Dakota . . . . . . . . . . . | 195 | 8,072 | 93,987 | 49,643 | 11,293 |
| Tennessee . . . . . . . . . . . . | 148 | 40,029 | 541,869 | 336,555 | 49,290 |
| Texas . . . . . . . . . . . . . . . | 1,113 | 147,544 | 1,516,676 | 1,326,166 | 163,574 |
| Utah . . . . . . . . . . . . . . . | 40 | 12,933 | 173,486 | 143,846 | 19,801 |
| Vermont . . . . . . . . . . . . . | 274 | 6,170 | 61,557 | 41,377 | 6,699 |
| Virginia . . . . . . . . . . . . . . | 141 | 60,082 | 640,927 | 441,257 | 66,738 |
| Washington . . . . . . . . . . . . | 302 | 33,691 | 395,237 | 381,226 | 50,876 |
| West Virginia . . . . . . . . . . . | 55 | 20,674 | 234,174 | 167,195 | 24,719 |
| Wisconsin . . . . . . . . . . . . . | 436 | 52,940 | 505,518 | 412,345 | 72,367 |
| Wyoming . . . . . . . . . . . . . | 51 | 5,025 | 48,805 | 43,516 | 5,861 |
| **Outlying Areas:** | | | | | |
| American Samoa . . . . . . . . . | 1 | 488 | 7,022 | 2,269 | 411 |
| Canal Zone . . . . . . . . . . . . | 1 | 370 | 5,104 | 3,688 | 638 |
| Guam . . . . . . . . . . . . . . . | 1 | NA | NA | NA | NA |
| Puerto Rico . . . . . . . . . . . . | 1 | NA | NA | NA | NA |
| Virgin Islands . . . . . . . . . . . | 1 | 1,421 | 15,894 | 9,677 | 791 |

(1) Full and part-time teachers. (NA) Not available.

## National Spelling Bee Champions

The National Spelling Bee, conducted by Scripps-Howard Newspapers and other newspapers since 1939, was instituted by the Louisville (Ky.) Courier-Journal in 1925. Children under 16 years of age sponsored by participating newspapers are eligible to compete for the cash prizes and prize trips.

In the 1978 spelldown, the runner-up missed "crescive" (which means increasing, or capable of growth). The winner spelled it correctly, and also the final word, "deification".

**Recent winners are:**
**1978** — 1. Peg McCarthy, 13, Topeka (Topeka Capital-Times). 2. Lyn Sue Kahng, 12, San Diego (San Diego Union Union). 3. Julie Won, 13, Mechanicsburg (Harrisburg Patriot and Evening News).
**1977** — 1. John Paola, 14, Pittsburgh (Pittsburgh Press). 2. Joan O'Leary, 13, Yonkers, N.Y. (N.Y. Daily News). 3. Joseph Fumic, 13, Cleveland (Cleveland Press).

# Public School Attendance, Teachers, Expenditures

Source: National Center for Education Statistics, U.S. Health, Education and Welfare Department

| School year | Pop. 5 to 17 yrs. | Pupils — Enrolled | Pupils — Av. daily attend. | Teachers[1] — Male | Teachers[1] — Female | Teachers[1] — Total | Salary[2] | Total expend. |
|---|---|---|---|---|---|---|---|---|
| 900 . . . . | 21,404,322 | 15,503,110 | 10,632,772 | 126,588 | 296,474 | 423,062 | $325 | $214,964,618 |
| 910 . . . . | 24,239,948 | 17,813,852 | 12,827,307 | 110,481 | 412,729 | 523,210 | 485 | 426,250,434 |
| 920 . . . . | 27,728,788 | 21,578,316 | 16,150,035 | 95,654 | 583,648 | 679,302 | 871 | 1,036,151,209 |
| 930 . . . | 31,571,322 | 25,678,015 | 21,264,886 | 141,771 | 712,492 | 854,263 | 1,420 | 2,316,790,384 |
| 940 . . . . | 29,805,259 | 25,433,542 | 22,042,151 | 194,725 | 680,752 | 875,477 | 1,441 | 2,344,048,927 |
| 950 . . . . | 30,788,000 | 25,111,427 | 22,283,845 | 194,968 | 718,703 | 913,671 | 3,010 | 5,837,643,000 |
| 960 . . . . | 43,881,000 | 36,086,771 | 32,477,440 | 392,700 | 962,300 | 1,355,000 | 5,174 | 15,613,255,000 |
| 968 (Fall) . | 52,288,000 | 44,961,662 | 41,157,000 | 617,805 | 1,324,980 | 1,942,785 | 8,200 | 35,511,170,000 |
| 970 (Fall). | 52,435,000 | 45,909,088 | 42,495,346 | 649,250 | 1,411,865 | 2,061,115 | 9,570 | 44,423,865,000 |
| 971 (Fall). | 52,133,000 | 46,081,000 | 42,544,000 | 668,000 | 1,395,000 | 2,063,000 | 10,100 | 48,513,986,000 |
| 972 (Fall). | 51,637,000 | 45,744,000 | 42,408,000 | 702,000 | 1,400,000 | 2,102,000 | 10,608 | 51,905,025,000 |
| 974 . . . . | 51,485,000 | 46,441,189 | 41,438,054 | 722,868 | 1,432,580 | 2,155,448 | 11,185 | 56,970,355,000 |
| 975 (Fall) p | 50,364,000 | 44,838,490 | 41,373,473 | 748,000 | 1,455,000 | 2,203,000 | 13,967 | 67,102,569,000 |
| 976 (Fall) p | ......... | 44,335,000 | 40,834,949 | 663,209 | 1,288,732 | 2,193,000 | 13,397 | 74,801,266,000 |

1) Prior to 1954 includes other nonsupervisory instructional staff (librarians and guidance and psychological personnel). (2) Average annual salary per member of instructional staff, including supervisors and principals. (p) preliminary.

---

# Cost per Pupil by State

Source: National Center for Education Statistics, U. S. Health, Education and Welfare Department
Expenditures per pupil in average daily attendance in public elementary and secondary day schools, 1975-76.

| State | Total | Current | Capital outlay | Interest on school debt |
|---|---|---|---|---|
| United States . . | $1,699 | $1,509 | $143 | $46 |
| Alabama . . . . . . . | 1,195 | 1,130 | 57 | 8 |
| Alaska . . . . . . . . | 3,710 | 3,009 | 566 | 135 |
| Arizona . . . . . . . | 1,753 | 1,420 | 301 | 32 |
| Arkansas . . . . . . | 1,161 | 1,007 | 125 | 29 |
| California . . . . . . | 1,721 | 1,510 | 186 | 25 |
| Colorado . . . . . . | 1,605 | 1,456 | 84 | 64 |
| Connecticut . . . . | 1,687 | 1,598 | 23 | 66 |
| Delaware . . . . . . | 1,871 | 1,693 | 103 | 75 |
| District of Columbia | 2,125 | 2,002 | 123 | ... |
| Florida . . . . . . . . | 1,576 | 1,369 | 170 | 37 |
| Georgia . . . . . . . | 1,323 | 1,162 | 140 | 22 |
| Hawaii . . . . . . . . | 1,817 | 1,616 | 196 | 5 |
| Idaho . . . . . . . . | 1,368 | 1,125 | 211 | 32 |
| Illinois . . . . . . . . | 1,848 | 1,581 | 198 | 69 |
| Indiana . . . . . . . | 1,446 | 1,248 | 146 | 51 |
| Iowa . . . . . . . . | 1,653 | 1,505 | 114 | 33 |
| Kansas . . . . . . . | 1,538 | 1,412 | 100 | 27 |
| Kentucky . . . . . . | 1,122 | 1,021 | 59 | 42 |
| Louisiana . . . . . . | 1,391 | 1,258 | 98 | 35 |
| Maine . . . . . . . . | 1,406 | 1,221 | 150 | 36 |
| Maryland . . . . . . | 2,054 | 1,743 | 264 | 47 |
| Massachusetts . . | 2,059 | 1,890 | 116 | 53 |
| Michigan . . . . . . | 1,902 | 1,683 | 151 | 68 |
| Minnesota . . . . . | 1,911 | 1,651 | 198 | 61 |
| Mississippi . . . . . | 1,072 | 999 | 55 | 18 |
| Missouri . . . . . . . | 1,389 | 1,250 | 108 | 31 |
| Montana . . . . . . . | 1,745 | 1,586 | 136 | 23 |
| Nebraska . . . . . . | 1,477 | 1,413 | 30 | 34 |

| State | Total | Current | Capital outlay | Interest on school debt |
|---|---|---|---|---|
| Nevada . . . . . . . | $1,617 | $1,354 | $180 | $82 |
| New Hampshire . . | 1,493 | 1,289 | 158 | 46 |
| New Jersey . . . . . | 2,122 | 1,951 | 106 | 64 |
| New Mexico . . . . | 1,509 | 1,284 | 204 | 21 |
| New York . . . . . . | 2,580 | 2,419 | 81 | 80 |
| North Carolina . . . | 1,394 | 1,221 | 160 | 12 |
| North Dakota . . . . | 1,408 | 1,261 | 124 | 23 |
| Ohio . . . . . . . . | 1,481 | 1,303 | 144 | 33 |
| Oklahoma . . . . . . | 1,278 | 1,152 | 111 | 15 |
| Oregon . . . . . . . | 1,995 | 1,786 | 172 | 36 |
| Pennsylvania . . . . | 1,914 | 1,682 | 146 | 85 |
| Rhode Island . . . . | 1,722 | 1,613 | 11 | 99 |
| South Carolina . . . | 1,278 | 1,112 | 135 | 30 |
| South Dakota . . . . | 1,445 | 1,310 | 116 | -19 |
| Tennessee . . . . . . | 1,214 | 1,045 | 156 | 13 |
| Texas . . . . . . . . | 1,487 | 1,274 | 152 | 61 |
| Utah . . . . . . . . | 1,471 | 1,172 | 267 | 32 |
| Vermont . . . . . . . | 1,504 | 1,384 | 74 | 45 |
| Virginia . . . . . . . | 1,488 | 1,310 | 128 | 50 |
| Washington . . . . . | 1,684 | 1,546 | 105 | 32 |
| West Virginia . . . . | 1,382 | 1,225 | 139 | 18 |
| Wisconsin . . . . . . | 1,792 | 1,598 | 148 | 46 |
| Wyoming . . . . . . | 2,142 | 1,670 | 411 | 61 |
| **Outlying areas** | | | | |
| American Samoa . . | 897 | 897 | ... | ... |
| Canal Zone . . . . . | 1,396 | 1,329 | 67 | ... |
| Guam . . . . . . . . | 1,834 | 1,560 | 274 | ... |
| Puerto Rico . . . . . | 636 | 632 | 5 | ... |
| Virgin Islands . . . . | 1,651 | 1,513 | 138 | ... |

---

# Canadian Fall Enrollment, Teachers, Expenditures in Day Schools

## Full-time Public Elementary and Secondary Day Schools — 1976-1977

Source: Statistics Canada

| | Enrollment — Elementary Kdgn.- Gr. 8 | Enrollment — Secondary Gr. 9 and up | Enrollment — Total | Teachers — Elementary Kdgn.- Gr. 8 | Teachers — Secondary Gr. 9 and up | Teachers — Total | School board expenditure per pupil[4] 1976 (calendar year) (e) |
|---|---|---|---|---|---|---|---|
| Canada . . . . . | 3,660,224 | 1,621,429 | 5,281,653 | 122,970[2] | 72,260[2] | 267,465 | $1,654 |
| Nfld. . . . . | 120,174 | 37,512 | 157,686 | 5,698 | 1,996 | 7,694 | 1,245 |
| P.E.I. . . . . | 20,024 | 7,879 | 27,903 | 918 | 515 | 1,433 | 1,437 |
| N.S. . . . . | 144,388 | 56,891 | 201,279 | 7,046 | 3,477 | 10,523 | 1,424 |
| N.B. . . . . | 112,083 | 51,234 | 163,317 | 4,886 | 2,796 | 7,682 | 1,245 |
| Que. . . . . | 945,910 | 372,440 | 1,318,350 | (1) | (1) | 72,235[3] | 1,642 |
| Ont. . . . . | 1,331,403 | 641,737 | 1,973,140 | 60,052 | 36,809 | 96,861 | 1,758 |
| Man. . . . . | 156,818 | 68,880 | 225,698 | 7,234 | 4,194 | 11,428 | 1,592 |
| Sask. . . . . | 153,082 | 66,109 | 219,191 | 7,065 | 3,624 | 10,689 | 1,457 |
| Alta. . . . . | 299,302 | 141,768 | 441,070 | 14,416 | 7,206 | 21,622 | 1,634 |
| B.C. . . . . | 362,572 | 173,665 | 536,237 | 14,917 | 11,436 | 26,353 | 1,751 |
| Yuk. . . . . | 3,616 | 1,250 | 4,866 | 208 | 62 | 270 | 2,281 |
| N.W.T. . . . . | 10,852 | 2,064 | 12,916 | 530 | 145 | 675 | 2,568 |

e) Estimate. (1) Data not available. (2) Excludes Quebec. (3) Source: Advance Statistics of Education, 1977-78. (4) Includes provincial expenditures made on behalf of school boards.

## Public Libraries in Selected North American Cities

Source: World Almanac questionnaire

First figure in parentheses denotes number of branches-2d figure indicates number of bookmobiles. (*) indicates county library syste (†) indicates state library system; (A) designates library has not provided up-to-date information.

| City | No. bound volumes | Circulation | Cost of operation | City | No. bound volumes | Circulation | Cost of operatio |
|---|---|---|---|---|---|---|---|
| Akron, Oh.* (17-3) | 868,590 | 2,022,444 | $ 3,146,183 | Newark, N.J. (10-1) | 1,250,000 | 1,810,000 | $3,350,0 |
| Albuquerque, N.M. (8-1) | 350,000 | 1,350,000 | 1,746,462 | New Haven, Conn. (8-0) | 526,736 | 466,874 | 1,085,4 |
| Anaheim, Cal. (3-1) | 300,000 | 1,012,243 | 2,500,000 | New Orleans, La. (11-2) | 751,295 | 1,305,513 | 2,610,6 |
| Atlanta, Ga. (27-7) | 1,083,672 | 2,106,812 | 5,000,000 | New York City | 4,768,931 | None | 17,855,0 |
| Austin, Tex. (13-5) | 567,523 | 2,446,825 | 3,446,180 | N.Y.C. branches (83-4) | 3,527,968 | 9,259,666 | 23,559,0 |
| Baltimore, Md. (33-2) | 2,220,767 | 2,359,695 | 9,482,464 | Brooklyn* (57-0) | 3,648,282 | 6,398,092 | 14,145,1 |
| Baton Rouge, La.* (8-0) | 334,135 | 880,556 | 1,203,589 | Queens* (56-0) | 3,376,863 | 6,046,116 | 18,558,9 |
| Birmingham, Ala.* (16-2) | 807,660 | 2,020,474 | 2,500,000 | Norfolk, Va. (11-2) | 601,539 | 1,154,146 | 2,090,6 |
| Boston, Mass. (28-1) | 4,070,851 | 2,278,226 | 8,876,474 | Oakland, Cal. (19-4) | 750,000 | 1,728,680 | 3,369,5 |
| Buffalo, N.Y.* (55-4) | 3,072,063 | 4,646,907 | 9,600,000 | Okla. City, Okla.* (12)A | 600,000 | 1,540,842 | 2,031,0 |
| Calgary, Alta. (12-4) | 681,759 | 2,900,624 | 4,722,145 | Omaha, Neb. (9-1) | 522,352 | 1,700,855 | 1,941,6 |
| Charlotte, N.C.* (15-0) | 655,231 | 1,701,784 | 2,149,176 | Ottawa, Ont. (7-2) | 593,639 | 2,168,049 | 4,523,0 |
| Chicago, Ill. (87-0) | 6,813,340 | 6,924,142 | 38,083,065 | Philadelphia, Pa. (46-2) | 3,040,254 | 5,613,971 | 17,324,0 |
| Cincinnati, Oh.* (37-3) | 3,188,959 | 5,438,253 | 7,800,000 | Phoenix, Ariz. (9)A | 998,012 | 2,997,859 | 3,809,2 |
| Cleveland, Oh. (34-2) | 2,797,450 | 2,730,706 | 13,011,999 | Pittsburgh, Pa. (20-5) | 2,049,828 | 3,070,460 | 7,410,1 |
| Columbus, Oh.* (22-3) | 1,153,096 | 2,923,764 | 6,300,918 | Portland, Ore.* (16-3) | 1,107,579 | 2,807,697 | 4,185,0 |
| Corpus Christi, Tex. (4-2) | 284,541 | 660,852 | 896,338 | Quebec, P.Q. (6-0) | 140,000 | 300,000 | 500,0 |
| Dallas, Tex. (17-3) | 1,727,800 | 3,822,643 | 6,383,221 | Regina, Sask. (4-3) | 300,000 | 1,177,829 | 2,648,3 |
| Dayton, Oh.* (19-1) | 1,302,269 | 4,132,154 | 4,100,000 | Richmond, Va. (6-2) | 565,810 | 1,018,773 | 1,362,8 |
| Denver, Col. (21-2) | 1,600,000 | 3,000,000 | 7,000,000 | Rochester, N.Y. (11-2) | 885,214 | 1,539,385 | 4,255,9 |
| Des Moines, Ia. (5-3) | 410,000 | 1,224,725 | 1,500,000 | Sacramento, Cal. (26-3) | 983,256 | 3,984,128 | 6,304,5 |
| Detroit, Mich. (26-4) | 2,405,694 | 2,044,876 | 12,500,000 | St. Catharines, Ont. (3-0) | 219,810 | 892,660 | 1,323,8 |
| Edmonton, Alta. (10-3) | 715,000 | 3,300,000 | 6,400,000 | St. Louis, Mo. (21-0) | 1,364,000 | 1,823,000 | 4,311,0 |
| El Paso, Tex. (7-4) | 391,651 | 925,478 | 1,301,745 | St. Paul, Minn. (10-1) | 746,371 | 1,996,297 | 2,409,9 |
| Ft. Worth, Tex. (7-4) | 736,305 | 2,048,058 | 2,234,501 | St. Petersburg, Fla. (3-3) | 388,279 | 1,210,483 | 1,086,2 |
| Hamilton, Ont. (10-2) | 750,000 | 1,736,279 | 4,202,268 | San Antonio, Tex. (9-5) | 954,825 | 2,297,850 | 2,331,6 |
| Honolulu, Ha.† (19-P) | 1,761,892 | 4,597,248 | 5,010,699 | San Diego, Cal. (28-1) | 1,462,510 | 4,203,170 | 4,859,8 |
| Houston, Tex. (30 -) | 1,874,092 | 5,149,175 | 9,800,000 | San Francisco, Cal. (26-1) | 1,615,044 | 2,691,636 | 7,567,8 |
| Indianapolis, Ind.* (21-4) | 1,285,152 | 3,625,727 | 5,880,384 | San Jose, Cal. (16-1) | 750,000 | 2,999,827 | 5,664,0 |
| Jacksonville, Fla. (10-3) | 1,022,735 | 2,017,035 | 2,427,924 | Saskatoon, Sask. (5-3) | 320,674 | 1,159,442 | 1,935,0 |
| Jersey City, N.J. (10-2) | 685,900 | 467,075 | 2,027,062 | Seattle, Wash. (22-4) | 1,493,712 | 4,391,104 | 6,426,3 |
| Kansas City, Mo. (13-0) | 1,186,484 | 871,955 | 2,874,856 | Syracuse, N.Y.* (8-1) | 419,042 | 928,976 | 2,390,9 |
| Kitchener, Ont. (2-4) | 389,182 | 1,089,494 | 1,614,680 | Tampa, Fla.* (14-1) | 600,000 | 1,981,000 | 3,765,0 |
| London, Ont. (10-2) | 509,505 | 1,717,093 | 3,516,464 | Toledo, Oh.* (17-4) | 1,255,038 | 2,774,373 | 3,857,1 |
| Long Beach, Cal. (11-1) | 706,763 | 2,024,243 | 5,155,721 | Toronto, Ont. (24-1) | 1,066,755 | 4,851,142 | 9,866,7 |
| Los Angeles, Cal.* (93-8) | 4,267,126 | 11,502,891 | 22,499,240 | Tucson, Ariz. (13-2) | 704,181 | 2,472,978 | 3,753,2 |
| Louisville, Ky.* (23-4) | 979,000 | 1,546,960 | 3,600,000 | Tulsa, Okla.* (20-2) | 713,768 | 1,638,132 | 2,641,8 |
| Memphis, Tenn.* (20-4) | 1,448,281 | 2,615,332 | 4,820,607 | Vancouver, B.C. (16-1) | 805,000 | 4,182,800 | 6,600,0 |
| Miami, Fla.* (19-7) | 1,275,637 | 2,659,312 | 10,004,000 | Washington, D.C.* (27-4) | 1,930,341 | 1,538,235 | 9,167,4 |
| Milwaukee, Wis. (12-3) | 2,366,716 | 3,388,905 | 7,900,000 | Wichita, Kan. (9-0) | 378,072 | 1,166,792 | 1,067,2 |
| Minneapolis, Minn. (15-1) | 1,454,462 | 2,515,399 | 5,712,672 | Windsor, Ont. (8-0) | 420,554 | 983,959 | 2,889,4 |
| Mobile, Ala. (5-1) | 368,442 | 791,953 | 1,301,665 | Winnipeg, Man. (10-2) | 604,385 | 1,692,954 | 2,639,5 |
| Montreal, P.Q. (16-1) | 1,203,373 | 2,293,461 | 3,061,300 | Yonkers, N.Y. (5-2) | 346,396 | 790,900 | 2,131,1 |
| Nashville, Tenn.* (15-3) | 502,106 | 1,512,362 | 2,966,240 | | | | |

## Major U.S. Academic Libraries

Source: World Almanac questionnaire

(A) designates library has not provided up-to-date information.

| Institution | No. bound volumes | Microfilm units | Enroll- ment | Staff Prof. | Staff Total | Annual acquis tion expense |
|---|---|---|---|---|---|---|
| Harvard Univ. | 9,547,576 | 1,501,444 | 16,075 | 220 | 845 | $3,272,03 |
| Yale Univ. | 6,884,604 | 992,994 | 9,526 | 179 | 621 | 2,513,91 |
| Univ. of Illinois, Urbana-Champaign | 5,575,617 | 1,343,465 | 35,552 | 142 | 453 | 2,558,01 |
| Univ. of California, Berkeley | 5,000,000 | 1,084,450 | 30,000 | 170 | 559 | 2,535,39 |
| Univ. of Michigan, Ann Arbor | 4,917,381 | 1,301,936 | 35,954 | 139 | 533 | 2,426,32 |
| Columbia Univ. (A) | 4,623,344 | 1,386,267 | 15,978 | 142 | 539 | NA |
| Stanford Univ. | 4,363,593 | 1,630,598 | 12,765 | 135 | 487 | 2,882,49 |
| Indiana Univ. | 4,220,987 | 1,271,750 | 68,112 | 165 | 614 | 2,742,46 |
| Cornell Univ. | 3,980,000 | 1,650,000 | 16,377 | 113 | 416 | 2,300,00 |
| Univ. of California, Los Angeles | 3,908,053 | 1,513,356 | 30,000 | 152 | 535 | 2,241,34 |
| Univ. of Chicago | 3,886,130 | 572,833 | 7,645 | 74 | 309 | 1,596,05 |
| Univ. of Texas, Austin (A) | 3,878,535 | 1,359,212 | 43,998 | 119 | 464 | NA |
| Duke Univ. | 3,869,558 | 273,712 | 9,129 | 90 | 194 | 1,561,39 |
| Michigan State Univ. | 3,450,000 | 1,000,000 | 44,211 | 74 | 173 | 1,365,25 |
| Univ. of Minnesota, Twin Cities | 3,363,576 | 941,976 | 44,743 | 132 | 446 | 1,729,74 |
| Univ. of Wisconsin, Madison | 3,238,152 | 1,339,646 | 39,000 | 112 | 429 | 1,339,64 |
| Univ. of Washington | 3,236,944 | 2,397,288 | 36,656 | 115 | 467 | 2,178,84 |
| Ohio State Univ. | 3,126,131 | 1,375,962 | 47,486 | 87 | 389 | 1,803,34 |
| New York Univ. | 3,033,734 | 1,126,567 | 15,579 | 64 | 291 | 1,539,37 |
| Princeton Univ. | 3,000,000 | 1,095,090 | 5,967 | 100 | 350 | 1,612,96 |
| Univ. of Pennsylvania (A) | 2,713,905 | 1,027,044 | 14,739 | 92 | 317 | NA |
| Northwestern Univ. (A) | 2,536,611 | 617,150 | 12,769 | 98 | 330 | NA |
| Univ. of North Carolina, Chapel Hill | 2,274,173 | 1,198,980 | 21,296 | 83 | 251 | 1,791,72 |
| Univ. of Pittsburgh | 2,174,868 | 938,931 | 22,354 | 141 | 348 | 1,632,09 |
| Univ. of Virginia | 2,143,226 | 643,925 | 15,499 | 76 | 261 | 1,848,31 |
| Johns Hopkins Univ. | 2,101,525 | 993,789 | 6,448 | 56 | 220 | 1,174,14 |
| Univ. of Iowa | 2,055,581 | 1,085,581 | 22,766 | 73 | 181 | 2,085,67 |
| Rutgers Univ. (A) | 1,927,021 | 1,079,289 | 37,440 | 99 | 314 | NA |
| Univ. of Missouri, Columbia | 1,882,394 | 1,778,760 | 23,474 | 55 | 161 | 1,230,0 |

## 105 Years of Public Schools

Source: National Center for Education Statistics, U.S. Health, Education and Welfare Department

| Pupils and teachers (thousands) | 1869-70 | 1899-1900 | 1909-10 | 1919-20 | 1929-30 | 1939-40 | 1949-50 | 1959-60 | 1969-70 | 1973-74 |
|---|---|---|---|---|---|---|---|---|---|---|
| Total U.S. population | 39,818 | 75,995 | 90,492 | 104,512 | 121,770 | 130,880 | 148,665 | 179,323 | 203,212 | 209,843 |
| Population 5-17 years of age | 12,055 | 21,573 | 24,009 | 27,556 | 31,417 | 30,150 | 30,168 | 43,881 | 52,490 | 51,485 |
| Percent aged 5-17 years | 30.3 | 28.4 | 26.5 | 26.4 | 25.8 | 23.0 | 20.3 | 24.5 | 25.8 | 24.5 |
| **Enrollment (thousands)** | | | | | | | | | | |
| Elementary and secondary | 6,872 | 15,503 | 17,814 | 21,578 | 25,678 | 25,434 | 25,111 | 36,087 | 45,619 | 45,409 |
| Percent pop. 5-17 enrolled | 57.0 | 71.9 | 74.2 | 78.3 | 81.7 | 84.4 | 83.2 | 82.2 | 86.9 | 88.2 |
| Percent in high schools | 1.2 | 3.3 | 5.1 | 10.2 | 17.1 | 26.0 | 22.7 | 23.5 | 28.5 | 31.0 |
| High school graduates | .... | 62 | 111 | 231 | 592 | 1,143 | 1,063 | 1,627 | 2,589 | 2,762 |
| Average school term (in days) | 132.2 | 144.3 | 157.5 | 161.9 | 172.7 | 175.0 | 177.9 | 178.0 | 178.9 | 178.7 |
| Total instructional staff | .... | .... | .... | 678 | 880 | 912 | 962 | 1,464 | 2,253 | 2,425 |
| Teachers, librarians: Men | 78 | 127 | 110 | 93 | 140 | 195 | 195 | 402 | 691 | 766 |
| Women | 123 | 296 | 413 | 565 | 703 | 681 | 719 | 985 | 1,440 | 1,521 |
| Percent men | 38.7 | 29.9 | 21.1 | 14.1 | 16.6 | 22.2 | 21.3 | 29.0 | 33.4 | 33.5 |
| **Receipts & expenditures (millions)** | | | | | | | | | | |
| Total receipts | .... | $219 | $433 | $970 | $2,088 | $2,260 | $5,437 | $14,746 | $40,267 | $58,231 |
| Total expenditures | $63 | 214 | 426 | 1,036 | 2,316 | 2,344 | 5,837 | 15,613[1] | 40,683 | 56,970 |
| Current elem. and secondary | .... | 179 | 356 | 861 | 1,843 | 1,941 | 4,687 | 12,329 | 34,218 | 50,025 |
| Capital outlay | .... | 35 | 69 | 153 | 370 | 257 | 1,014 | 2,661 | 4,659 | 4,979 |
| Interest on school debt | .... | .... | .... | 18 | 92 | 130 | 100 | 489 | 1,171 | 1,514 |
| Other | .... | .... | .... | 3 | 9 | 13 | 35 | 132 | 636 | 453 |
| **Salaries and pupil cost** | | | | | (Data in unadjusted dollars) | | | | | |
| Average annual teacher salary[2] | $189 | $325 | $485 | $2,130 | $3,869 | $3,894 | $5,928 | $8,213 | $10,917 | $11,185 |
| Expenditure per capita total pop. | 1.59 | 2.83 | 4.71 | 24.24 | 51.85 | 48.40 | 77.34 | 138.21 | 247.23 | 271.49 |
| Current expenditure per pupil ADA[3] | .... | 16.67 | 27.85 | 130.41 | 236.25 | 238.05 | 411.29 | 595.50 | 1,007.65 | 1,207.21 |

(1) Because of a modification of the scope, "current expenditures for elementary and secondary schools" data for 1959-60 and later years are not entirely comparable with data for prior years. (2) Includes supervisors, principals, teachers and other non-supervisory instructional staff. (3) "ADA" means average daily attendance in elementary and secondary day schools.

## Family Income, 1969-76, in Constant 1976 Dollars

Source: U.S. Bureau of the Census

| All Races | 1976 | 1975 | 1974 | 1973 | 1972 | 1971 | 1970 | 1969 |
|---|---|---|---|---|---|---|---|---|
| Number (000) | 56,710 | 56,245 | 55,698 | 55,053 | 54,373 | 53,296 | 52,227 | 51,586 |
| Percent | 100.0 | 100.0 | 100.0 | 100.0 | 100.0 | 100.0 | 100.0 | 100.0 |
| Under $3,000 | 3.9 | 4.2 | 4.1 | 3.9 | 4.2 | 4.6 | 4.8 | 4.5 |
| $3,000 to $4,999 | 6.4 | 6.8 | 5.9 | 5.9 | 6.1 | 6.4 | 6.2 | 6.0 |
| $5,000 to $6,999 | 7.8 | 7.8 | 7.3 | 7.2 | 7.1 | 7.4 | 7.1 | 7.0 |
| $7,000 to $9,999 | 11.8 | 12.2 | 11.7 | 11.2 | 11.5 | 12.1 | 11.9 | 11.4 |
| $10,000 to $11,999 | 8.1 | 8.3 | 8.4 | 7.9 | 8.0 | 8.8 | 8.7 | 8.9 |
| $12,000 to $14,999 | 12.2 | 12.6 | 13.1 | 12.4 | 13.1 | 13.8 | 14.0 | 14.0 |
| $15,000 to $24,999 | 32.0 | 31.6 | 31.6 | 33.8 | 32.7 | 32.0 | 32.3 | 32.9 |
| $25,000 and over | 17.8 | 16.4 | 17.9 | 17.8 | 17.2 | 14.9 | 15.0 | 15.4 |
| Median income (76 dollars) | 14,958 | 14,510 | 14,894 | 15,437 | 15,126 | 14,457 | 14,465 | 14,648 |
| Median income (current dollars) | 14,958 | 13,719 | 12,902 | 12,051 | 11,116 | 10,285 | 9,867 | 9,433 |
| **White** | | | | | | | | |
| Number (000) | 50,083 | 49,873 | 49,440 | 48,919 | 48,477 | 47,641 | 46,535 | 46,022 |
| Percent | 100.0 | 100.0 | 100.0 | 100.0 | 100.0 | 100.0 | 100.0 | 100.0 |
| Under $3,000 | 3.1 | 3.4 | 3.3 | 3.1 | 3.4 | 3.8 | 4.0 | 3.7 |
| $3,000 to $4,999 | 5.3 | 5.9 | 5.0 | 5.0 | 5.2 | 5.5 | 5.5 | 5.4 |
| $5,000 to $6,999 | 7.3 | 7.3 | 6.8 | 6.5 | 6.5 | 6.8 | 6.6 | 6.4 |
| $7,000 to $9,999 | 11.4 | 11.9 | 11.2 | 10.6 | 11.0 | 11.6 | 11.3 | 10.8 |
| $10,000 to $11,999 | 8.1 | 8.3 | 8.3 | 7.8 | 8.0 | 8.7 | 8.7 | 8.7 |
| $12,000 to $14,999 | 12.3 | 12.9 | 13.4 | 12.6 | 13.4 | 14.2 | 14.3 | 14.3 |
| $15,000 to $24,999 | 33.4 | 32.8 | 32.9 | 35.4 | 34.1 | 33.5 | 33.7 | 34.4 |
| $25,000 and over | 19.1 | 17.5 | 19.1 | 19.0 | 18.4 | 15.9 | 16.0 | 16.4 |
| Median income (76 dollars) | 15,537 | 15,091 | 15,478 | 16,134 | 15,715 | 15,001 | 15,006 | 15,208 |
| Median income (current dollars) | 15,537 | 14,268 | 13,408 | 12,595 | 11,549 | 10,672 | 10,236 | 9,794 |
| **Black** | | | | | | | | |
| Number (000) | 5,804 | 5,586 | 5,491 | 5,440 | 5,265 | 5,157 | 4,928 | 4,774 |
| Percent | 100.0 | 100.0 | 100.0 | 100.0 | 100.0 | 100.0 | 100.0 | 100.0 |
| Under $3,000 | 10.1 | 11.3 | 11.3 | 11.2 | 11.4 | 11.2 | 12.2 | 11.6 |
| $3,000 to $4,999 | 16.0 | 15.1 | 14.3 | 13.6 | 14.2 | 14.3 | 13.3 | 12.4 |
| $5,000 to $6,999 | 12.4 | 12.1 | 11.9 | 13.0 | 12.5 | 12.9 | 11.5 | 12.8 |
| $7,000 to $9,999 | 14.9 | 15.0 | 16.2 | 16.1 | 15.5 | 16.5 | 17.3 | 17.3 |
| $10,000 to $11,999 | 7.6 | 9.4 | 8.8 | 8.5 | 8.2 | 9.9 | 9.3 | 10.2 |
| $12,000 to $14,999 | 11.3 | 10.8 | 10.6 | 10.9 | 11.2 | 11.0 | 11.2 | 11.9 |
| $15,000 to $24,999 | 20.8 | 20.2 | 20.7 | 20.4 | 20.4 | 19.3 | 19.7 | 18.7 |
| $25,000 and over | 6.8 | 6.1 | 6.2 | 6.3 | 6.7 | 4.9 | 5.4 | 5.1 |
| Median income (76 dollars) | 9,242 | 9,285 | 9,242 | 9,312 | 9,340 | 9,052 | 9,205 | 9,315 |
| Median income (current dollars) | 9,242 | 8,779 | 8,006 | 7,269 | 6,864 | 6,440 | 6,279 | 5,999 |

Median income means that one half of American families had more income than that shown, and one half had less. Income figures here refer to gross income before taxes. The figures show that while incomes of white families have improved slightly in the last 8 years, the incomes of black families have declined slightly. The disparity is particularly marked in 1972-1973, when white family median income in constant dollars exceeded 1969 income by nearly $1,000, while black family income in 1972 barely exceeded 1969 income and fell even lower in 1973. Recovery from the recession which followed 1973 has nearly restored white income to 1972 levels, while black family income has not recovered nearly so well. The figures also tend to suggest, however, that all families have experienced slight increases in income since 1968, particularly those in the top and bottom income groups.

## Educational Attainment by Age, Race, and Sex

Source: U.S. Bureau of the Census (Number of persons in thousands)

| 1977 Age, race and sex | Total Pop. | Elementary | | | High School | | | | College | | | | |
|---|---|---|---|---|---|---|---|---|---|---|---|---|---|
| | | None | 1-7 | 8 | 1 | 2 | 3 | 4 | 1 | 2 | 3 | 4 | 5 or more |
| **White** | | | | | | | | | | | | | |
| Total, 14 years old and over | 144,795 | 884 | 11,152 | 14,129 | 9,239 | 10,474 | 8,268 | 50,805 | 8,099 | 9,064 | 3,628 | 11,598 | 7,45 |
| 14-17 | 14,057 | 37 | 1,819 | 3,595 | 3,591 | 3,115 | 1,705 | 176 | 6 | 13 | — | — | — |
| 18-19 | 6,977 | 16 | 79 | 162 | 263 | 511 | 1,430 | 3,643 | 774 | 77 | 15 | 8 | |
| 20-24 | 16,544 | 48 | 231 | 285 | 498 | 705 | 696 | 7,276 | 1,885 | 2,038 | 1,141 | 1,448 | 29 |
| 25-44 | 48,367 | 178 | 1,631 | 1,563 | 1,659 | 1,811 | 1,788 | 19,862 | 3,326 | 3,816 | 1,483 | 6,263 | 4,45 |
| 45-64 | 38,829 | 239 | 3,382 | 4,032 | 2,002 | 2,507 | 1,964 | 15,319 | 1,552 | 2,265 | 678 | 2,833 | 2,05 |
| 65 and over | 20,020 | 365 | 4,014 | 4,491 | 1,228 | 1,291 | 687 | 4,530 | 556 | 852 | 311 | 1,462 | 65 |
| **Male, 14 years old and over** | 69,555 | 441 | 5,574 | 6,935 | 4,387 | 4,842 | 3,930 | 21,854 | 3,951 | 4,600 | 1,868 | 6,232 | 4,94 |
| 14-17 | 7,154 | 28 | 1,027 | 1,854 | 1,812 | 1,580 | 786 | 60 | 1 | 8 | — | — | — |
| 18-19 | 3,423 | 10 | 40 | 75 | 128 | 277 | 777 | 1,721 | 357 | 26 | 7 | 5 | |
| 20-24 | 8,196 | 26 | 106 | 142 | 252 | 340 | 369 | 3,452 | 964 | 1,033 | 626 | 717 | 16 |
| 25 and over | 50,782 | 378 | 4,401 | 4,864 | 2,195 | 2,644 | 1,999 | 16,621 | 2,629 | 3,533 | 1,235 | 5,510 | 4,77 |
| 25-29 | 7,568 | 32 | 151 | 114 | 195 | 237 | 206 | 2,704 | 657 | 775 | 340 | 1,336 | 82 |
| 30-34 | 6,443 | 26 | 167 | 189 | 205 | 272 | 202 | 2,199 | 463 | 563 | 237 | 960 | 96 |
| 35-39 | 5,123 | 34 | 228 | 231 | 188 | 273 | 188 | 1,897 | 278 | 405 | 123 | 607 | 67 |
| 40-44 | 4,773 | 20 | 280 | 287 | 207 | 251 | 169 | 1,787 | 265 | 301 | 102 | 538 | 56 |
| 45-54 | 10,048 | 49 | 821 | 896 | 503 | 611 | 570 | 3,448 | 426 | 661 | 180 | 1,028 | 85 |
| 55-64 | 8,589 | 60 | 949 | 1,195 | 426 | 552 | 387 | 2,916 | 335 | 503 | 137 | 579 | 55 |
| 65-74 | 5,518 | 74 | 1,071 | 1,161 | 332 | 324 | 207 | 1,282 | 160 | 243 | 83 | 319 | 26 |
| 75 and over | 2,720 | 84 | 735 | 791 | 138 | 124 | 70 | 388 | 44 | 82 | 33 | 144 | 6 |
| **Female, 14 years old and over** | 75,239 | 443 | 5,578 | 7,194 | 4,852 | 5,632 | 4,338 | 28,951 | 4,147 | 4,463 | 1,760 | 5,365 | 2,51 |
| 14-17 | 6,903 | 9 | 794 | 1,741 | 1,779 | 1,536 | 919 | 116 | 5 | 5 | — | — | — |
| 18-19 | 3,554 | 6 | 39 | 87 | 135 | 233 | 653 | 1,922 | 417 | 52 | 8 | 3 | |
| 20-24 | 8,348 | 22 | 125 | 143 | 246 | 364 | 326 | 3,823 | 921 | 1,005 | 515 | 730 | 12 |
| 25 and over | 56,434 | 405 | 4,622 | 5,223 | 2,693 | 3,499 | 2,439 | 23,089 | 2,805 | 3,401 | 1,237 | 4,632 | 2,38 |
| 25-29 | 7,623 | 21 | 139 | 140 | 207 | 312 | 251 | 3,327 | 635 | 675 | 231 | 1,199 | 48 |
| 30-34 | 6,538 | 9 | 203 | 179 | 217 | 360 | 231 | 2,968 | 441 | 482 | 180 | 780 | 48 |
| 35-39 | 5,368 | 8 | 207 | 201 | 242 | 357 | 277 | 2,554 | 316 | 316 | 155 | 467 | 26 |
| 40-44 | 4,931 | 29 | 255 | 222 | 198 | 282 | 264 | 2,426 | 271 | 300 | 115 | 376 | 19 |
| 45-54 | 10,638 | 56 | 702 | 741 | 512 | 701 | 570 | 4,990 | 447 | 631 | 205 | 709 | 37 |
| 55-64 | 9,554 | 75 | 909 | 1,200 | 561 | 642 | 437 | 3,964 | 343 | 470 | 156 | 518 | 27 |
| 65-74 | 7,238 | 72 | 1,156 | 1,388 | 461 | 540 | 276 | 2,021 | 250 | 331 | 144 | 384 | 21 |
| 75 and over | 4,544 | 136 | 1,051 | 1,152 | 296 | 304 | 133 | 839 | 103 | 196 | 50 | 198 | 8 |
| **Black** | | | | | | | | | | | | | |
| Total, 14 years old and over | 17,398 | 236 | 2,976 | 1,747 | 1,564 | 1,740 | 1,583 | 4,725 | 839 | 724 | 282 | 645 | 33 |
| 14-17 | 2,322 | 3 | 401 | 657 | 568 | 461 | 212 | 17 | 2 | 2 | — | — | |
| 18-19 | 1,057 | 5 | 22 | 24 | 69 | 150 | 323 | 367 | 94 | 1 | 1 | | |
| 20-24 | 2,322 | 11 | 42 | 63 | 106 | 150 | 201 | 1,014 | 256 | 232 | 107 | 123 | 1 |
| 25-44 | 5,801 | 27 | 375 | 218 | 378 | 559 | 512 | 2,335 | 373 | 357 | 118 | 385 | 22 |
| 45-64 | 3,986 | 78 | 1,151 | 529 | 319 | 357 | 299 | 830 | 87 | 107 | 45 | 100 | 8 |
| 65 and over | 1,853 | 112 | 986 | 258 | 125 | 63 | 36 | 161 | 26 | 23 | 10 | 37 | 1 |
| **Male, 14 years old and over** | 7,914 | 152 | 1,490 | 794 | 755 | 726 | 635 | 2,068 | 383 | 356 | 138 | 259 | 16 |
| 14-17 | 1,158 | 1 | 233 | 321 | 289 | 213 | 92 | 5 | 2 | 2 | — | — | |
| 18-19 | 494 | 3 | 9 | 16 | 49 | 83 | 154 | 145 | 33 | 1 | 1 | | |
| 20-24 | 1,058 | 8 | 30 | 27 | 48 | 66 | 76 | 484 | 106 | 113 | 47 | 45 | |
| 25 and over | 5,205 | 139 | 1,219 | 430 | 368 | 363 | 313 | 1,434 | 242 | 240 | 90 | 214 | 15 |
| 25-29 | 854 | 1 | 30 | 24 | 39 | 44 | 54 | 369 | 83 | 68 | 33 | 75 | 3 |
| 30-34 | 665 | 2 | 43 | 9 | 37 | 53 | 59 | 278 | 46 | 50 | 15 | 47 | 2 |
| 35-39 | 548 | 2 | 54 | 29 | 47 | 58 | 36 | 204 | 27 | 24 | 13 | 31 | 2 |
| 40-44 | 530 | 11 | 65 | 36 | 53 | 46 | 43 | 175 | 22 | 31 | 6 | 18 | 2 |
| 45-54 | 1,044 | 37 | 273 | 131 | 109 | 94 | 73 | 207 | 40 | 36 | 12 | 16 | 1 |
| 55-64 | 787 | 23 | 321 | 108 | 46 | 50 | 37 | 134 | 10 | 18 | 9 | 10 | 2 |
| 65-74 | 539 | 35 | 297 | 68 | 29 | 13 | 13 | 46 | 10 | 9 | 1 | 10 | |
| 75 and over | 237 | 28 | 137 | 23 | 7 | 6 | — | 21 | 3 | 4 | — | 6 | |
| **Female, 14 years old and over** | 9,484 | 84 | 1,486 | 952 | 809 | 1,014 | 948 | 2,658 | 456 | 368 | 144 | 386 | 17 |
| 14-17 | 1,164 | 2 | 167 | 337 | 279 | 248 | 119 | 12 | — | — | — | — | |
| 18-19 | 563 | 2 | 13 | 7 | 20 | 67 | 170 | 223 | 61 | — | — | — | |
| 20-24 | 1,265 | 3 | 12 | 36 | 58 | 83 | 126 | 531 | 150 | 119 | 61 | 78 | |
| 25 and over | 6,493 | 77 | 1,293 | 573 | 453 | 615 | 534 | 1,892 | 245 | 249 | 84 | 308 | 17 |
| 25-29 | 1,044 | 3 | 45 | 23 | 54 | 87 | 79 | 454 | 74 | 75 | 19 | 90 | 4 |
| 30-34 | 836 | 3 | 22 | 13 | 59 | 101 | 93 | 346 | 55 | 50 | 18 | 49 | 2 |
| 35-39 | 718 | 3 | 39 | 25 | 50 | 89 | 76 | 279 | 42 | 35 | 6 | 44 | 2 |
| 40-44 | 665 | 3 | 80 | 56 | 39 | 81 | 72 | 230 | 24 | 24 | 9 | 30 | 1 |
| 45-54 | 1,211 | 4 | 228 | 143 | 91 | 132 | 135 | 317 | 19 | 32 | 16 | 57 | 3 |
| 55-64 | 941 | 13 | 328 | 146 | 70 | 82 | 54 | 172 | 17 | 22 | 8 | 17 | 1 |
| 65-74 | 695 | 23 | 321 | 112 | 73 | 38 | 23 | 71 | 3 | 8 | 8 | 8 | |
| 75 and over | 381 | 25 | 228 | 55 | 15 | 5 | 2 | 22 | 10 | 3 | — | 13 | |

## Median Income by Sex, Age, Education, Occupation, and Race

**Source:** U.S. Bureau of the Census

(B-base less than 75,000; — represents zero or rounds to zero; . . .-not applicable. Median income means that half the working population made more than that and half made less.)

| | All persons 1976 No. (000) | 1976 Median income ($) | 1975 Median income ($) | % Change 77$ | % Change 76$ | Year-round full-time workers 1976 No. (000) | 1976 Median income ($) | 1975 Median income ($) | % Change 77$ | % Change 76$ |
|---|---|---|---|---|---|---|---|---|---|---|
| **All Males . . . . . . . . . . . . .** | **72,775** | **9,426** | **8,853** | **6.5** | **0.7** | **38,197** | **13,859** | **12,934** | **7.2** | **1.3** |
| **Race** | | | | | | | | | | |
| White . . . . . . . . . . . . . | 64,946 | 9,937 | 9,300 | 6.8 | 1.0 | 34,681 | 14,272 | 13,233 | 7.9 | 2.0 |
| Black . . . . . . . . . . . . . | 6,651 | 5,983 | 5,560 | 7.6 | 1.7 | 2,953 | 10,222 | 9,848 | 3.8 | −1.9 |
| Hispanic . . . . . . . . . . . | 3,099 | 7,050 | 6,777 | 4.0 | −1.6 | 1,548 | 10,422 | 9,588 | 8.7 | 2.8 |
| **Age** | | | | | | | | | | |
| 14-19 . . . . . . . . . . . . | 7,401 | 1,032 | 974 | 6.0 | 0.2 | 566 | 5,617 | 5,657 | −0.7 | −6.1 |
| 20-24 . . . . . . . . . . . . | 8,966 | 5,841 | 5,484 | 6.5 | 0.7 | 3,491 | 8,949 | 8,521 | 5.0 | −0.7 |
| 25-34 . . . . . . . . . . . . | 15,678 | 11,717 | 10,922 | 7.3 | 1.4 | 10,745 | 13,240 | 12,585 | 5.2 | −0.5 |
| 35-44 . . . . . . . . . . . . | 11,117 | 14,326 | 13,120 | 9.2 | 3.2 | 8,502 | 15,693 | 14,652 | 7.1 | 1.3 |
| 45-54 . . . . . . . . . . . . | 11,147 | 14,094 | 13,007 | 8.4 | 2.4 | 8,310 | 15,889 | 14,751 | 7.7 | 1.8 |
| 55-64 . . . . . . . . . . . . | 9,369 | 11,523 | 10,556 | 9.2 | 3.2 | 5,771 | 14,718 | 13,305 | 10.6 | 4.6 |
| 65 & over . . . . . . . . . . | 9,098 | 5,293 | 4,959 | 6.7 | 0.9 | 812 | 11,668 | 11,425 | 2.1 | −3.4 |
| **Occupation of longest job** | | | | | | | | | | |
| **White collar . . . . . . . . .** | **23,465** | **13,751** | **12,902** | **6.6** | **0.8** | **17,836** | **15,852** | **14,902** | **6.4** | **0.6** |
| Professional, technical . . | 8,170 | 15,272 | 14,167 | 7.8 | 1.9 | 6,272 | 16,939 | 15,796 | 7.2 | 1.4 |
| Managers . . . . . . . . . . | 7,933 | 15,584 | 14,759 | 5.6 | −0.2 | 6,769 | 16,674 | 15,787 | 5.6 | −0.1 |
| Sales . . . . . . . . . . . | 3,671 | 10,446 | 10,248 | 1.9 | −3.6 | 2,311 | 14,586 | 13,840 | 5.4 | −0.4 |
| Clerical . . . . . . . . . . | 3,691 | 10,343 | 10,031 | 3.1 | −2.5 | 2,484 | 12,843 | 12,096 | 6.2 | 0.4 |
| **Blue collar . . . . . . . . . .** | **28,035** | **9,482** | **8,812** | **7.6** | **1.7** | **16,011** | **12,469** | **11,616** | **7.3** | **1.5** |
| Craftsmen . . . . . . . . . | 11,897 | 11,836 | 10,759 | 10.0 | 4.0 | 7,953 | 13,638 | 12,588 | 8.3 | 2.4 |
| Operatives . . . . . . . . . | 10,806 | 9,102 | 8,577 | 6.1 | 0.3 | 6,313 | 11,688 | 11,006 | 6.2 | 0.4 |
| Laborers . . . . . . . . . . | 5,332 | 3,940 | 3,991 | −1.3 | −6.7 | 1,745 | 10,104 | 9,057 | 11.6 | 5.5 |
| **Service . . . . . . . . . . . .** | **5,988** | **4,931** | **4,503** | **9.5** | **3.5** | **2,734** | **10,030** | **9,488** | **5.7** | **−0.1** |
| Private household . . . . | 76 | 574 | 515 | 11.5 | 5.4 | 3 | (B) | — | . . . | . . . |
| Other . . . . . . . . . . . | 5,912 | 5,042 | 4,580 | 10.1 | 4.1 | 2,731 | 10,036 | 9,488 | 5.8 | — |
| **Farm . . . . . . . . . . . . . . .** | **2,962** | **2,626** | **2,469** | **6.4** | **0.6** | **1,603** | **6,003** | **5,935** | **1.1** | **−4.4** |
| **Education** (workers age 25 or over) | | | | | | | | | | |
| Elementary . . . . . . . . . | 11,484 | 5,819 | 5,473 | 6.3 | 0.5 | 3,985 | 10,173 | 9,628 | 5.7 | −0.1 |
| High School: 1-3 years . . | 7,839 | 9,536 | 8,825 | 8.1 | 2.2 | 4,249 | 12,301 | 11,412 | 7.8 | 1.9 |
| 4 years . . . . . | 18,178 | 12,393 | 11,799 | 5.0 | −0.7 | 12,198 | 14,295 | 13,283 | 7.6 | 1.7 |
| College: 1-3 years . . . . . | 8,040 | 13,347 | 12,859 | 3.8 | −1.9 | 5,532 | 15,514 | 14,985 | 3.5 | −2.1 |
| 4 years . . . . . | 5,849 | 16,466 | 15,469 | 6.4 | 0.6 | 4,441 | 18,236 | 17,009 | 7.2 | 1.4 |
| 5 or more years | 5,019 | 18,456 | 17,484 | 5.6 | −0.2 | 3,735 | 20,597 | 19,531 | 5.5 | −0.3 |
| **All females . . . . . . . . . . .** | **63,170** | **3,576** | **3,385** | **5.6** | **−0.1** | **18,116** | **8,312** | **7,719** | **7.7** | **1.8** |
| **Race** | | | | | | | | | | |
| White . . . . . . . . . . . . . | 55,026 | 3,606 | 3,420 | 5.4 | −0.3 | 15,669 | 8,376 | 7,737 | 8.3 | 2.4 |
| Black . . . . . . . . . . . . . | 7,188 | 3,398 | 3,107 | 9.4 | 3.4 | 2,138 | 7,831 | 7,392 | 5.9 | 0.2 |
| Hispanic . . . . . . . . . . . | 2,568 | 3,359 | 3,202 | 4.9 | −0.8 | 695 | 7,129 | 6,577 | 8.4 | 2.5 |
| **Age** | | | | | | | | | | |
| 14-19 . . . . . . . . . . . . | 6,720 | 897 | 867 | 3.5 | −2.2 | 383 | 5,205 | 4,568 | 13.9 | 7.7 |
| 20-24 . . . . . . . . . . . . | 8,103 | 3,839 | 3,526 | 8.9 | 2.9 | 2,691 | 6,966 | 6,598 | 5.6 | −0.2 |
| 25-34 . . . . . . . . . . . . | 11,943 | 5,372 | 5,052 | 6.3 | 0.5 | 4,845 | 8,939 | 8,401 | 6.4 | 0.6 |
| 35-44 . . . . . . . . . . . . | 8,568 | 5,158 | 4,705 | 9.6 | 3.6 | 3,541 | 8,734 | 8,084 | 8.0 | 2.1 |
| 45-54 . . . . . . . . . . . . | 8,388 | 5,331 | 5,066 | 5.2 | −0.5 | 3,794 | 8,546 | 7,980 | 7.1 | 1.3 |
| 55-64 . . . . . . . . . . . . | 7,659 | 4,054 | 3,900 | 3.9 | −1.7 | 2,525 | 8,451 | 7,785 | 8.6 | 2.6 |
| 65 & over . . . . . . . . . . | 11,788 | 2,816 | 2,642 | 6.6 | 0.8 | 337 | 8,591 | 7,250 | 18.5 | 12.0 |
| **Occupation of longest job** | | | | | | | | | | |
| **White collar . . . . . . . . .** | **26,660** | **5,811** | **5,382** | **8.0** | **2.1** | **12,877** | **8,853** | **8,288** | **6.8** | **1.0** |
| Professional, technical . . | 6,673 | 8,362 | 7,862 | 6.4 | 0.6 | 3,476 | 11,072 | 10,506 | 5.4 | −0.4 |
| Managers . . . . . . . . . . | 2,309 | 7,511 | 6,860 | 9.5 | 3.5 | 1,466 | 9,804 | 9,125 | 7.4 | 1.6 |
| Sales . . . . . . . . . . . | 3,048 | 2,285 | 1,984 | 15.2 | 8.9 | 734 | 6,272 | 5,460 | 14.9 | 8.6 |
| Clerical . . . . . . . . . . | 14,630 | 5,683 | 5,322 | 6.8 | 1.0 | 7,201 | 8,128 | 7,562 | 7.5 | 1.6 |
| **Blue collar . . . . . . . . . .** | **6,502** | **4,618** | **4,157** | **11.1** | **5.0** | **2,718** | **6,808** | **6,368** | **6.9** | **1.1** |
| Craftsmen . . . . . . . . . | 696 | 5,323 | 4,847 | 9.8 | 3.8 | 347 | 7,765 | 7,268 | 6.8 | 1.0 |
| Operatives . . . . . . . . . | 5,280 | 4,689 | 4,177 | 12.3 | 6.1 | 2,231 | 6,649 | 6,251 | 6.4 | 0.6 |
| Laborers . . . . . . . . . . | 525 | 2,791 | 2,645 | 5.5 | −0.2 | 140 | 7,613 | 6,937 | 9.7 | 3.8 |
| **Service . . . . . . . . . . . .** | **10,788** | **1,854** | **1,646** | **12.6** | **6.5** | **2,409** | **5,674** | **5,204** | **9.0** | **3.1** |
| Private household . . . . . | 1,936 | 699 | 712 | −1.8 | −7.2 | 149 | 2,570 | 2,413 | 6.5 | 0.7 |
| Other . . . . . . . . . . . | 8,851 | 2,327 | 2,164 | 7.5 | 1.7 | 2,261 | 5,840 | 5,414 | 7.9 | 2.0 |
| **Education** (workers age 25 or over) | | | | | | | | | | |
| Elementary . . . . . . . . . | 9,762 | 2,595 | 2,396 | 8.3 | 2.4 | 1,200 | 5,993 | 5,460 | 9.8 | 3.8 |
| High School: 1-3 years . . . . | 7,603 | 3,423 | 3,308 | 3.5 | −2.2 | 1,837 | 6,800 | 6,355 | 7.0 | 1.2 |
| 4 years . . . . . | 18,297 | 4,925 | 4,549 | 8.3 | 2.4 | 6,864 | 8,377 | 7,777 | 7.7 | 1.8 |
| College: 1-3 years . . . . . . | 6,242 | 5,502 | 5,403 | 1.8 | −3.7 | 2,277 | 9,475 | 9,126 | 3.8 | −1.8 |
| 4 years . . . . . | 4,099 | 7,643 | 7,459 | 2.5 | −3.1 | 1,708 | 11,010 | 10,264 | 7.3 | 1.4 |
| 5 or more years | 2,344 | 10,499 | 10,345 | 1.5 | −4.0 | 1,156 | 13,569 | 12,879 | 5.4 | −0.4 |

# The Principal Languages of the World

Source: Sidney S. Culbert, Assoc. Professor of Psychology, University of Washington

Total number of speakers of languages spoken by at least one million persons (midyear 1978)

| Language | Millions |
|---|---|
| Achinese (Indonesia) | 2 |
| Afrikaans (S. Africa) | 7 |
| Albanian | 3 |
| Amharic (Ethiopia) | 9 |
| Arabic | 138 |
| Armenian | 4 |
| Assamese[1] (India) | 13 |
| Aymara (Bolivia; Peru) | 1 |
| Azerbaijani (USSR; Iran) | 8 |
| Bahasa (see Malay-Indonesian) | |
| Balinese | 3 |
| Baluchi (Pakistan; Iran) | 3 |
| Batak (Indonesia) | 2 |
| Bemba (S. Central Africa) | 2 |
| Bengali[1] (Bangladesh; India) | 136 |
| Berber[2] (N. Africa) | |
| Bhili (India) | 4 |
| Bihari (India) | 22 |
| Bikol (Philippines) | 2 |
| Bisaya (see Cebuano, Panay-Hiliagynon, and Samar-Leyte) | |
| Bugi (Indonesia) | 2 |
| Bulgarian | 9 |
| Burmese | 24 |
| Byelorussian (mainly USSR) | 9 |
| Cambodian (Cambodia, Asia) | 7 |
| Canarese (see Kannada) | |
| Cantonese (China) | 49 |
| Catalan (Spain; France; Andorra) | 6 |
| Cebuano (Philippines) | 9 |
| Chinese[3] | |
| Chuang[7] (China) | 9 |
| Chuvash (USSR) | 2 |
| Czech | 11 11 |
| Danish | 5 |
| Dayak (Borneo) | 1 |
| Dutch (see Netherlandish) | |
| Edo (W. Africa) | 1 |
| Efik | 2 |
| English | 374 |
| Esperanto | 1 |
| Estonian | 1 |
| Ewe (W. Africa) | 3 |
| Fang-Bulu (W. Africa) | 1 |
| Finnish | 5 |
| Flemish (see Netherlandish) | |
| French | 98 |
| Fula (W. Africa) | 9 |
| Galician (Spain) | 3 |
| Galla (see Oromo) | |
| Ganda (or Luganda)(E. Africa) | 3 |
| Georgian (USSR) | 4 |
| German | 120 |
| Gilaki (Iran) | 2 |
| Gondi (India) | 2 |
| Greek | 10 |
| Guarani (mainly Paraguay) | 3 |
| Gujarati[1] (India) | 32 |
| Hakka (China) | 22 |
| Hausa (W. and Central Africa) | 20 |
| Hebrew | 3 |
| Hindi[1,4] | 224 |
| Hindustani[4] | |
| Hungarian (or Magyar) | 13 |
| Ibibio (see Efik) | |
| Ibo (or Igbo)(W. Africa) | 11 |
| Ijaw (W. Africa) | 1 |
| Ilocano (Philippines) | 4 |

| Language | Millions |
|---|---|
| Iloko (see Ilocano) | |
| Indonesian (see Malay-Indonesian) | |
| Italian | 61 |
| Japanese | 114 |
| Javanese | 46 |
| Kamba (E. Africa) | 1 |
| Kanarese (see Kannada) | |
| Kannada[1] (India) | 30 |
| Kanuri (W. and Central Africa) | 3 |
| Kashmiri[1] | 3 |
| Kazakh (USSR) | 6 |
| Khalkha (Mongolia) | 2 |
| Kikongo (see Kongo) | |
| Kikuyu (or Gekoyo)(Kenya) | 3 |
| Kimbundu (see Mbundu-Kimbundu) | |
| Kirghiz (USSR) | 2 |
| Kituba (Congo River) | 3 |
| Kongo (Congo River) | 2 |
| Konkani (India) | 2 |
| Korean | 56 |
| Kurdish (S.W. of Caspian Sea) | 7 |
| Kurukh (or Oraon)(India) | 1 |
| Lao[5] (Laos, Asia) | 3 |
| Latvian (or Lettish) | 2 |
| Lingala (see Ngala) | |
| Lithuanian | 3 |
| Luba-Lulua (Zaire) | 3 |
| Luganda (see Ganda) | |
| Luhya (or Luhia)(Kenya) | 1 |
| Luo (Kenya) | 2 |
| Luri (Iran) | 2 |
| Macedonian (Yugoslavia) | 2 |
| Madurese (Indonesia) | 8 |
| Makua (S.E. Africa) | 3 |
| Malagasy (Madagascar) | 8 |
| Malay-Indonesian | 103 |
| Malayalam[1] (India) | 28 |
| Malinke-Bambara-Dyula (Africa) | 6 |
| Mandarin (China) | 680 |
| Marathi[1] (India) | 53 |
| Mazandarani (Iran) | 2 |
| Mbundu (Umbundu group)(S.Angola) | 3 |
| Mbundu (Kimbundu group)(Angola) | 2 |
| Mende (Sierra Leone) | 1 |
| Meo (see Miao) | |
| Miao (and Meo)(S.E.Asia) | 3 |
| Min (China) | 40 |
| Minankabau (Indonesia) | 4 |
| Moldavian (inc. with Romanian) | |
| Mongolian (see Khalkha) | |
| Mordvin (USSR) | 1 |
| Moré (see Mossi) | |
| Mossi (or Moré)(W. Africa) | 3 |
| Ndongo (see Mbundu-Kimbundu) | |
| Nepali (Nepal; India) | 10 |
| Netherlandish (Dutch and Flemish) | 20 |
| Ngala (or Lingala)(Africa) | 2 |
| Norwegian | 5 |
| Nyamwezi-Sukuma (S.E. Africa) | 2 |
| Nyanja (S.E. Africa) | 3 |
| Oraon (see Kurukh) | |
| Oriya[1] (India) | 25 |
| Oromo (Ethiopia) | 7 |
| Panay-Hiliagynon (Philippines) | 4 |
| Panjabi (see Punjabi) | |
| Pashto (see Pushtu) | |
| Pedi (see Sotho, Northern) | |

| Language | Million |
|---|---|
| Persian | |
| Polish | |
| Portuguese | 13 |
| Provencal (Southern France) | |
| Punjabi[1] (India; Pakistan) | 6 |
| Pushtu (mainly Afghanistan) | |
| Quechua (S. America) | |
| Rajasthani (India) | |
| Romanian | |
| Ruanda (S. Central Africa) | |
| Rundi (S. Central Africa) | |
| Russian (Great Russian only) | 2 |
| Samar-Leyte (Philippines) | |
| Sango (Central Africa) | |
| Santali (India) | |
| Sepedi (see Sotho, Northern) | |
| Serbo-Croatian (Yugoslavia) | 1 |
| Shan (Burma) | |
| Shona (S.E. Africa) | |
| Siamese (see Thai) | |
| Sindhi[1] (India; Pakistan) | |
| Sinhalese (Sri Lanka) | 1 |
| Slovak | |
| Slovene (Yugoslavia) | |
| Somali (E. Africa) | |
| Sotho, Northern (S. Africa) | |
| Sotho, Southern (S. Africa) | |
| Spanish | 23 |
| Sundanese (Indonesia) | |
| Swahili (E. Africa) | |
| Swedish | |
| Tagalog (Philippines) | |
| Tajiki (USSR) | |
| Tamil[1] (India; Sri Lanka) | 5 |
| Tatar (or Kazan-Turkic)(USSR) | |
| Telugu[1] (India) | 5 |
| Thai[5] | |
| Thonga (S.E. Africa) | |
| Tibetan | |
| Tigrinya (Ethiopia) | |
| Tiv (E. Central Nigeria) | |
| Tswana (S. Africa) | |
| Tulu (India) | |
| Turkish | |
| Turkoman (USSR) | |
| Twi-Fante (or Akan)(W.Africa) | |
| Uighur (Sinkiang, China) | |
| Ukrainian (mainly USSR) | 4 |
| Umbundu (see Mbundu) | |
| Urdu[1] (Pakistan; India) | 6 |
| Uzbek (USSR) | 1 |
| Vietnamese | 4 |
| Visayan (see Cebuano, Panay-Hiliagynon, and Samar-Leyte) | |
| White Russian (see Byelorussian) | |
| Wolof (W. Africa) | |
| Wu (China) | |
| Xhosa (S. Africa) | |
| Yi (China) | |
| Yiddish[6] | |
| Yoruba (W. Africa) | 1 |
| Zhuang[7] (China)(see Chuang) | |
| Zulu (S. Africa) | |

(1) One of the fifteen languages of the Constitution of India. (2) Here considered a group of dialects. (3) See Mandarin, Cantonese, Wu, Min and Hakka. The "national language" (Guoyu) or "common speech" (Putonghua) is a standardized form of Mandarin as spoken in the area of Peking. (4) Hindi and Urdu are essentially the same language, Hindustani. As the official language of India it is written in the Devanagari script and called Hindi. As the official language of Pakistan it is written in a modified Arabic script and called Urdu. (5) Thai includes Central, Southwestern, Northern and Northeastern Thai. The distinction between Northeastern Thai and Lao is political rather than linguistic. (6) Yiddish is usually considered a variant of German, though it has its own standard grammar, dictionaries, a highly developed literature, and is written in Hebrew characters. (7) A group of Thai-like dialects.

# UNITED STATES POPULATION

## Changing Population Patterns

By Manuel D. Plotkin
Director, U.S. Bureau of the Census

Population trends that emerged after the 1970 census continued to hold true during 1977. The population of the U.S. was estimated to be 217.7 million as 1978 began, an increase of 1.7 million, or 0.79 percent during 1977. The Census Bureau estimates the population gain was the result of 3.3 million births, 1.9 million deaths, and net immigration of about 305,000.

There are several measures of the Nation's birth rate; all rose slightly in 1977. The crude rate was 15.3 births per 1,000 of population, up from the 1976 rate of 14.7. The total fertility rate, viewed by demographers as more indicative of the actual trend of births, went from 1,768 in 1976 to 1,815 per 1,000 women in 1977. This implies that an estimated 1.8 children would be born to each woman in her lifetime if the 1977 birth rate were to continue. For the population to exactly replace itself, each woman would have to bear 2.1 children. That figure—2.1 children—is what women under 35 years of age reported in 1977 they expected to have, on the average, during their lives.

### Childbearing Postponed

An increasing proportion of young married women are postponing motherhood. Among women aged 20 to 24 who had ever married, the proportion who were childless in 1977 was 43 percent, up from 36 percent in 1970. For the 25- to 29-year age group, the proportion had risen from 16 to 24 percent. Postponement in childbearing has an important consequence in expanding the number of social, educational, and occupational goals a young woman can pursue.

The declining birth rate has resulted in declines in kindergarten and elementary school enrollments. On the other hand, between 1970 and 1977, high school enrollment climbed by 7 percent and college enrollment grew by a large 38 percent. Most of the increase this decade has occurred among students 25 to 34 years old, and among women. For example, while there was a 15 percent increase in male enrollment for the 22- to 24-year age group, for females the increase was 69 percent. Total enrollment in schools and colleges was 61.3 million in the fall of 1977, about the same level as in 1976. The number of college graduates in the U.S. increased from 13.4 million to 20.6 million from 1970 to 1977.

### Marriages Postponed

Other social trends continue to shape America's lifestyle as the 1980s approach. As more young adults postpone marriage, the proportion of women in their early twenties who had never married increased from 36 to 45 percent during the 1970-77 period. Also, the divorce rate continues to rise. There were 84 divorced persons for every 1,000 persons in an intact marriage in 1977, compared with 47 per 1,000 in 1970. At the beginning of the decade, there were approximately three marriages for each divorce in the U.S.; in 1977 there were 2,176,000 marriages and 1,097,000 divorces. The Census Bureau estimates that some 38 percent of first marriages of women now in their late twenties may eventually end in divorce.

Families headed by a woman with no husband present represent a growing proportion of all families. There were more than one-third again as many of these families in 1977 as in 1970. Another large increase this decade has been in the number of unrelated couples of opposite sexes living together—an 83 percent increase to just under one million couples. Along with the reduced birth rate, these changes in household composition led to a decline in the average household size from 3.14 persons in 1970 to only 2.86 in 1977.

### "Baby Boom" Impact

The very large number of children born in the post World War Two "baby boom" continues to have a impact on the population. The 25- to 34-year age group has grown 32 percent since 1970. At the same time, the elderly—those 65 and over—have increased 18 percent. The declining birth rate has caused a drop of 6.4 million in the number of children under 14 since the start of the decade. These factors have combined to raise the median age of the population from 27.9 in 1970 to 29.4 in 1977.

Nonmetropolitan areas grew at a faster rate in 1977 than the metropolitan areas of the Nation—continuing the historic reversal which began about 1970. Metropolitan areas have grown 0.8 percent since 1970 (7 million persons), while nonmetropolitan areas grew 1.2 percent (4 million persons). While the growth rates have reversed, far more people live in the Nation's metropolitan areas—157.5 million, compared to 57 million for nonmetropolitan areas.

While the white population in central cities of metropolitan areas declined by 8 percent during the 7 years since 1970, the black population there increased 6 percent. In the suburbs of metropolitan areas, the black population has increased at a rate of 4.2 percent a year since 1970, while the white population increased by 1.3 percent last year.

The "sunbelt" states of California, Florida and Texas have received about 40 percent of the population growth of 13 million in the U.S. since 1970. The rate of population increase between 1970 and 1977 was fastest in Alaska, Nevada, Arizona, Florida, Wyoming, Idaho and Utah, in that order.

In 1977, the total labor force, including the Armed Forces, passed the 100 million mark for the first time. About 97.4 million persons were in the civilian labor force, nearly 15 million more than in 1970, and 28 million more than 1960. Women constituted 41 percent of the civilian labor force in 1977, and accounted for 57 percent of the increase between 1970 and 1977.

During this period, the proportion of working wives rose from 40 percent to 46 percent. Female householders maintaining a family with no husband present increased from 5.7 million in 1970 to 7.9 million in 1977.

### Family Income Up

Median family income, in constant dollars, was 3 percent higher in 1976 than in 1975. It was $14,960 in 1976, about $500 higher than that for 1970 in 1976 constant dollars. White families had a median income of $15,540 in 1976; the sum was $9,240 for black families and $10,260 for Spanish origin families during 1976.

About 12 percent of the population—25 million persons—lived in poverty in 1976. In 1969, about the same proportion lived below the poverty level, compared with 22 percent, or 39 million in 1959.

In 1976, as in earlier years, relatively large proportions of poor persons were black, persons of Spanish origin, children under 18 years old, the elderly, and persons in families of female householders with no husband present. The latter category had the largest proportion of poor.

Other significant population characteristics in 1977 include the following:

• Women made marked gains in employment in professional and related services, with 867,000 more women working in this field in 1977 than in 1975.

• Among persons moving to metropolitan areas, twice as many moved to the suburbs as moved to the central cities between 1975 and 1977. The Northeast and North Central regions of the country had net outmigration during this period, while the South and West had net inmigration.

• The death rate of Americans edged downward to a historic low of 8.8 per 1,000 in 1977, compared with 8.9 in both 1976 and 1975.

• In 1977, both the black and Spanish origin populations has rather large proportions of young persons, mainly because their birth rates were above the national average.

• Although the fertility rate increased in 1977, young women continued to delay childbearing longer than a few years ago; about 43 percent of the ever-married women 20 to 24 years old in 1977, compared with 36 percent in 1970 and 24 percent in 1960, had borne no children.

## Population of the U.S., 1960-1970

| Region, division, and state | 1970 Census | 1960 Census | Pct. + or − | 1970 Urban | 1970 Rural | Pct. Urban | Rank 1970 | Rank 1960 |
|---|---|---|---|---|---|---|---|---|
| United States. . . . . . . . . . | 203,235,298 | 179,323,175 | 13.3 | 149,324,930 | 53,886,996 | 73.5 | . . . | . . . |
| **Regions:** | | | | | | | | |
| Northeast . . . . . . . . . . . | 48,999,999 | 44,677,819 | 9.7 | 39,449,818 | 9,590,885 | 80.4 | . . . | . . . |
| North Central . . . . . . . . . | 56,577,067 | 51,619,139 | 9.6 | 40,480,760 | 16,090,903 | 71.6 | . . . | . . . |
| South. . . . . . . . . . . . . | 62,798,347 | 54,973,113 | 14.2 | 40,539,961 | 22,255,406 | 64.6 | . . . | . . . |
| West . . . . . . . . . . . . . | 34,809,359 | 28,053,104 | 24.1 | 28,854,391 | 5,949,802 | 82.9 | . . . | . . . |
| **New England . . . . . . . . .** | 11,847,186 | 10,509,367 | 12.7 | 9,043,517 | 2,798,146 | 76.4 | . . . | . . . |
| Maine. . . . . . . . . . . . . | 993,663 | 969,265 | 2.5 | 504,157 | 487,891 | 50.8 | 38 | 36 |
| New Hampshire. . . . . . . . | 737,681 | 606,921 | 21.5 | 416,040 | 321,641 | 56.4 | 42 | 45 |
| Vermont. . . . . . . . . . . | 444,732 | 389,881 | 14.1 | 142,889 | 301,441 | 32.2 | 49 | 47 |
| Massachusetts . . . . . . . . | 5,689,170 | 5,148,578 | 10.5 | 4,810,449 | 878,721 | 84.6 | 10 | 9 |
| Rhode Island . . . . . . . . | 949,723 | 859,488 | 10.5 | 824,930 | 121,795 | 87.1 | 39 | 39 |
| Connecticut . . . . . . . . | 3,032,217 | 2,535,234 | 19.6 | 2,345,052 | 686,657 | 77.4 | 24 | 25 |
| **Middle Atlantic . . . . . . . .** | 37,152,813 | 34,168,452 | 8.7 | 30,406,301 | 6,792,739 | 81.7 | . . . | . . . |
| New York . . . . . . . . . . | 18,241,266 | 16,782,304 | 8.4 | 15,602,486 | 2,634,481 | 85.6 | 2 | 1 |
| New Jersey . . . . . . . . . | 7,168,164 | 6,066,782 | 18.2 | 6,373,405 | 794,759 | 88.9 | 8 | 8 |
| Pennsylvania . . . . . . . . | 11,793,909 | 11,319,366 | 4.2 | 8,430,410 | 3,363,499 | 71.5 | 3 | 3 |
| **East North Central. . . . . .** | 40,252,678 | 36,225,024 | 11.1 | 30,091,847 | 10,160,629 | 74.8 | . . . | . . . |
| Ohio . . . . . . . . . . . . | 10,652,017 | 9,706,397 | 9.7 | 8,025,775 | 2,625,242 | 75.3 | 6 | 5 |
| Indiana . . . . . . . . . . | 5,913,669 | 4,662,498 | 11.4 | 3,372,060 | 1,821,609 | 64.9 | 11 | 11 |
| Illinois. . . . . . . . . . . | 11,113,976 | 10,081,158 | 10.2 | 9,229,821 | 1,884,155 | 83.0 | 5 | 4 |
| Michigan . . . . . . . . . . | 8,875,083 | 7,823,194 | 13.4 | 6,553,773 | 2,321,310 | 73.8 | 7 | 7 |
| Wisconsin . . . . . . . . . | 4,417,933 | 3,951,777 | 11.8 | 2,910,418 | 1,507,313 | 65.9 | 16 | 15 |
| **West North Central . . . . .** | 16,324,389 | 15,394,115 | 6.0 | 10,388,913 | 5,930,274 | 63.7 | . . . | . . . |
| Minnesota . . . . . . . . . | 3,805,069 | 3,413,864 | 11.5 | 2,527,308 | 1,277,663 | 66.4 | 19 | 18 |
| Iowa . . . . . . . . . . . . | 2,825,041 | 2,757,537 | 2.4 | 1,616,405 | 1,207,971 | 57.2 | 25 | 24 |
| Missouri . . . . . . . . . . | 4,677,399 | 4,319,813 | 8.3 | 3,277,662 | 1,398,839 | 70.1 | 13 | 13 |
| North Dakota . . . . . . . . | 617,761 | 632,446 | -2.3 | 273,442 | 344,319 | 44.3 | 46 | 44 |
| South Dakota . . . . . . . . | 666,257 | 680,514 | -2.1 | 296,628 | 368,879 | 44.6 | 45 | 40 |
| Nebraska . . . . . . . . . . | 1,483,791 | 1,411,330 | 5.1 | 912,598 | 570,895 | 61.5 | 35 | 34 |
| Kansas . . . . . . . . . . | 2,249,071 | 2,178,611 | 3.2 | 1,484,870 | 761,708 | 66.1 | 28 | 28 |
| **South Atlantic . . . . . . . .** | 30,671,337 | 25,971,732 | 18.1 | 19,523,920 | 11,147,417 | 63.7 | . . . | . . . |
| Delaware . . . . . . . . . . | 548,104 | 446,292 | 22.8 | 395,569 | 152,535 | 72.2 | 47 | 46 |
| Maryland . . . . . . . . . . | 3,922,399 | 3,100,689 | 26.5 | 3,003,935 | 918,464 | 76.6 | 18 | 21 |
| District of Columbia. . . . . | 756,510 | 763,956 | -1.0 | 756,510 | . . . | 100.0 | 41 | . . . |
| Virginia . . . . . . . . . . | 4,648,494 | 3,966,949 | 17.2 | 2,934,841 | 1,713,653 | 63.1 | 14 | 14 |
| West Virginia . . . . . . . . | 1,744,237 | 1,860,421 | -6.2 | 679,491 | 1,064,746 | 39.0 | 34 | 30 |
| North Carolina. . . . . . . . | 5,082,059 | 4,556,155 | 11.5 | 2,285,168 | 2,796,891 | 45.0 | 12 | 12 |
| South Carolina . . . . . . . | 2,590,516 | 2,382,594 | 8.7 | 1,232,195 | 1,358,321 | 47.6 | 26 | 26 |
| Georgia . . . . . . . . . . | 4,589,575 | 3,943,116 | 16.4 | 2,768,074 | 1,821,501 | 60.3 | 15 | 16 |
| Florida . . . . . . . . . . | 6,789,443 | 4,951,560 | 37.1 | 5,468,137 | 1,321,306 | 80.5 | 9 | 10 |
| **East South Central. . . . . .** | 12,804,552 | 12,050,126 | 6.3 | 6,987,943 | 5,815,527 | 54.6 | . . . | . . . |
| Kentucky . . . . . . . . . . | 3,219,311 | 3,038,156 | 6.0 | 1,684,053 | 1,534,653 | 52.3 | 23 | 22 |
| Tennessee. . . . . . . . . . | 3,924,164 | 3,567,089 | 10.0 | 2,305,307 | 1,618,380 | 58.7 | 17 | 17 |
| Alabama . . . . . . . . . . | 3,444,165 | 3,266,740 | 5.4 | 2,011,941 | 1,432,224 | 58.4 | 21 | 19 |
| Mississippi . . . . . . . . . | 2,216,912 | 2,178,141 | 1.8 | 986,642 | 1,230,270 | 44.5 | 29 | 29 |
| **West South Central . . . . .** | 19,322,458 | 16,951,255 | 14.0 | 14,028,098 | 5,292,462 | 72.6 | . . . | . . . |
| Arkansas . . . . . . . . . . | 1,923,295 | 1,786,272 | 7.7 | 960,865 | 962,430 | 50.0 | 32 | 31 |
| Louisiana . . . . . . . . . . | 3,643,180 | 3,257,022 | 11.9 | 2,406,150 | 1,235,156 | 66.1 | 20 | 20 |
| Oklahoma . . . . . . . . . . | 2,559,253 | 2,328,284 | 9.9 | 1,740,137 | 819,092 | 68.0 | 27 | 27 |
| Texas. . . . . . . . . . . . | 11,196,730 | 9,579,677 | 16.9 | 8,920,946 | 2,275,784 | 79.7 | 4 | 6 |
| **Mountain . . . . . . . . . . .** | 8,283,585 | 6,855,060 | 20.8 | 6,054,979 | 2,226,583 | 73.1 | . . . | . . . |
| Montana . . . . . . . . . . | 694,409 | 674,767 | 2.9 | 370,676 | 323,733 | 53.4 | 44 | 41 |
| Idaho . . . . . . . . . . . | 713,008 | 667,191 | 6.9 | 385,434 | 327,133 | 54.1 | 43 | 42 |
| Wyoming. . . . . . . . . . | 332,416 | 330,066 | 0.7 | 201,111 | 131,305 | 60.5 | 50 | 48 |
| Colorado. . . . . . . . . . | 2,207,259 | 1,753,947 | 25.8 | 1,733,311 | 473,948 | 78.5 | 30 | 33 |
| New Mexico . . . . . . . . . | 1,016,000 | 951,023 | 6.8 | 708,775 | 307,225 | 69.8 | 37 | 37 |
| Arizona. . . . . . . . . . . | 1,772,482 | 1,302,161 | 36.1 | 1,408,864 | 362,036 | 79.6 | 33 | 35 |
| Utah . . . . . . . . . . . . | 1,059,273 | 890,627 | 18.9 | 851,472 | 207,801 | 80.4 | 36 | 38 |
| Nevada. . . . . . . . . . . | 488,738 | 285,278 | 71.3 | 395,336 | 93,402 | 80.9 | 48 | 49 |
| **Pacific . . . . . . . . . . . .** | 26,525,774 | 21,198,044 | 25.1 | 22,799,412 | 3,723,219 | 86.0 | . . . | . . . |
| Washington . . . . . . . . . | 3,409,169 | 2,853,214 | 19.5 | 2,476,468 | 932,701 | 72.6 | 22 | 23 |
| Oregon. . . . . . . . . . . | 2,091,385 | 1,768,687 | 18.2 | 1,402,704 | 688,681 | 67.1 | 31 | 32 |
| California. . . . . . . . . . | 19,953,134 | 15,717,204 | 27.0 | 18,136,045 | 1,817,089 | 90.9 | 1 | 2 |
| Alaska. . . . . . . . . . . | 302,173 | 226,167 | 33.6 | 145,512 | 154,870 | 48.4 | 51 | 50 |
| Hawaii . . . . . . . . . . . | 769,913 | 632,772 | 21.7 | 638,683 | 129,878 | 83.1 | 40 | 43 |

Urban and rural figures do not equal total 1970 population because of errors discovered by Census Bureau after tabulation.

## U.S. Area and Population: 1790 to 1970

Source: U.S. Bureau of the Census

Area figures represent area on indicated date including in some cases considerable areas not then organized or settled, and not covered by the census. Area figures have been adjusted to bring them into agreement with remeasurements made in 1940. *Changes in land and water area between 1960 and 1970 due to construction of dams and reservoirs. Also total area of Texas reduced approximately one square mile in the Chamizal agreement between U.S. and Mexico.

| Census date | Area (square miles) | | | Population | | | |
|---|---|---|---|---|---|---|---|
| | Gross | Land | Water | Number | Per sq. mile of land | Increase over preceding census Number | % |
| 1790 (Aug. 2) . . . . . . . . . | 888,811 | 864,746 | 24,065 | 3,929,214 | 4.5 | (X) | (X) |
| 1800 (Aug. 4) . . . . . . . . . | 888,811 | 864,746 | 24,065 | 5,308,483 | 6.1 | 1,379,269 | 35.1 |
| 1810 (Aug. 6) . . . . . . . . . | 1,716,003 | 1,681,828 | 34,175 | 7,239,881 | 4.3 | 1,931,398 | 36.4 |
| 1820 (Aug. 7) . . . . . . . . . | 1,788,006 | 1,749,462 | 38,544 | 9,638,453 | 5.5 | 2,398,572 | 33.1 |
| 1830 (June 1) . . . . . . . . . | 1,788,006 | 1,749,462 | 38,544 | 12,866,020 | 7.4 | 3,227,567 | 33.5 |
| 1840 (June 1) . . . . . . . . . | 1,788,006 | 1,749,462 | 38,544 | 17,069,453 | 9.8 | 4,203,433 | 32.7 |
| 1850 (June 1) . . . . . . . . . | 2,992,747 | 2,940,042 | 52,705 | 23,191,876 | 7.9 | 6,122,423 | 35.9 |
| 1860 (June 1) . . . . . . . . . | 3,022,387 | 2,969,640 | 52,747 | 31,443,321 | 10.6 | 8,251,445 | 35.6 |
| 1870 (June 1) . . . . . . . . . | 3,022,387 | 2,969,640 | 52,747 | '39,818,449 | '13.4 | 8,375,128 | 26.6 |
| 1880 (June 1) . . . . . . . . . | 3,022,387 | 2,969,640 | 52,747 | 50,155,783 | 16.9 | 10,337,334 | 26.0 |
| 1890 (June 1) . . . . . . . . . | 3,022,387 | 2,969,640 | 52,747 | 62,947,714 | 21.2 | 12,791,931 | 25.5 |
| 1900 (June 1) . . . . . . . . . | 3,022,387 | 2,969,834 | 52,553 | 75,994,575 | 25.6 | 13,046,861 | 20.7 |
| 1910 (Apr. 15) . . . . . . . . | 3,022,387 | 2,969,565 | 52,822 | 91,972,266 | 31.0 | 15,977,691 | 21.0 |
| 1920 (Jan. 1) . . . . . . . . . | 3,022,387 | 2,969,451 | 52,936 | 105,710,620 | 35.6 | 13,738,354 | 14.9 |
| 1930 (Apr. 1) . . . . . . . . . | 3,022,387 | 2,977,128 | *45,259 | 122,775,046 | 41.2 | 17,064,426 | 16.1 |
| 1940 (Apr. 1) . . . . . . . . . | 3,022,387 | 2,977,128 | 45,259 | 131,669,275 | 44.2 | 8,894,229 | 7.2 |
| 1950 (Apr. 1)² . . . . . . . . | 3,615,211 | 3,552,206 | 63,005 | 151,325,798 | 42.6 | 19,161,229 | 14.5 |
| 1960 (Apr. 1)² . . . . . . . . | 3,615,123 | 3,540,911 | 74,212 | 179,323,175 | 50.5 | 27,997,377 | 18.5 |
| 1970* (Apr. 1)² . . . . . . . . | 3,615,122 | 3,536,855 | 78,267 | 203,211,926 | 57.5 | 23,888,751 | 13.3 |

(X) Not applicable. (1) Revised to include adjustments for underenumeration in Southern States; unrevised number is 38,558,371. (2) Includes Alaska and Hawaii.

## Population, Urban and Rural, by Race: 1960 and 1970

Source: U.S. Bureau of the Census

An urbanized area comprises at least one city of 50,000 inhabitants (central city) plus contiguous, closely settled areas (urban fringe). (thousands)

| Year and area | 1960 | | | 1970 | | |
|---|---|---|---|---|---|---|
| | Total | White | Negro and other | Total | White | Negro and other |
| Population, total. . . . . . . . . . . . . . . . . . | 179,323 | 158,832 | 20,491 | 203,212 | 177,749 | 25,463 |
| Urban. . . . . . . . . . . . . . . . . . . . . . . . . . . . . | 125,269 | 110,428 | 14,840 | 149,325 | 128,773 | 20,552 |
| Inside urbanized areas. . . . . . . . . . . . . | 95,848 | 83,770 | 12,070 | 118,447 | 100,952 | 17,495 |
| Central cities . . . . . . . . . . . . . . . . . . | 57,976 | 47,627 | 10,348 | 63,922 | 49,547 | 14,375 |
| Urban fringe . . . . . . . . . . . . . . . . . . | 37,873 | 36,143 | 1,731 | 54,525 | 51,405 | 3,120 |
| Outside urbanized areas. . . . . . . . . . . . | 29,420 | 26,658 | 2,762 | 30,878 | 27,822 | 3,057 |
| Rural. . . . . . . . . . . . . . . . . . . . . . . . . . . . . . | 54,054 | 48,403 | 5,651 | 53,887 | 48,976 | 4,911 |

## Congressional Apportionment

| | 1970 | 1960 | | 1970 | 1960 | | 1970 | 1960 | | 1970 | 1960 | | 1970 | 1960 |
|---|---|---|---|---|---|---|---|---|---|---|---|---|---|---|
| Ala.. . | 7 | 8 | Ida.. . | 2 | 2 | Minn.. . | 8 | 8 | N. D.. . | 1 | 2 | Vt.. . . | 1 | 1 |
| Alas.. | 1 | 1 | Ill.. . . | 24 | 24 | Miss.. . | 5 | 5 | Oh.. . . | 23 | 24 | Va.. . . | 10 | 10 |
| Ariz.. | 4 | 3 | Ind.. . | 11 | 11 | Mo.. . . | 10 | 10 | Okla.. . | 6 | 6 | Wash.. | 7 | 7 |
| Ark.. . | 4 | 4 | Ia.. . . | 6 | 7 | Mon.. . | 2 | 2 | Ore.. . | 4 | 4 | W. Va.. | 4 | 5 |
| Cal.. . | 43 | 38 | Kan.. . | 5 | 5 | Neb.. . | 3 | 3 | Pa.. . . | 25 | 27 | Wis.. . | 9 | 10 |
| Col.. . | 5 | 4 | Ky.. . . | 7 | 7 | Nev.. . | 1 | 1 | R. I.. . | 2 | 2 | Wy.. . | 1 | 1 |
| Conn.. | 6 | 6 | La.. . . | 8 | 8 | N. H.. . | 2 | 2 | S. C.. . | 6 | 6 | | | |
| Del.. . | 1 | 1 | Me.. . . | 2 | 2 | N. J.. . | 15 | 15 | S. D.. . | 2 | 2 | Totals. | 435 | 435 |
| Fla.. . | 15 | 12 | Md.. . | 8 | 8 | N. M.. . | 2 | 2 | Tenn.. . | 8 | 9 | | | |
| Ga.. . | 10 | 10 | Mass.. | 12 | 12 | N. Y.. . | 39 | 41 | Tex.. . | 24 | 23 | | | |
| Ha.. . | 2 | 2 | Mich.. | 19 | 19 | N. C.. . | 11 | 11 | Ut.. . . | 2 | 2 | | | |

The chief reason the Constitution provided for a census of the population every 10 years was to give a basis for apportionment of representatives among the states. This apportionment largely determines the number of electoral votes allotted to each state.

The number of representatives of each state in Congress is determined by the state's population, but each state is entitled to one representative regardless of population. A Congressional apportionment has been made after each decennial census except that of 1920.

Under provisions of a law that became effective Nov. 15, 1941, apportionment of representatives is made by the method of equal proportions. In the application of this method, the apportionment is made so that the average population per representative has the least possible variation between one state and any other. The first House of Representatives, in 1790, had 65 members, or one representative for each 30,000 of the estimated population, as provided by the Constitution. As the population grew, the number of representatives was increased but the total membership has been fixed at 435 since 1912.

## U.S. Population by Officia

(Members of the Armed Forces overseas (

| State | 1790 | 1800 | 1810 | 1820 | 1830 | 1840 | 1850 | 1860 | 1870 | 188 |
|---|---|---|---|---|---|---|---|---|---|---|
| Ala. | | 1,250 | 9,046 | 127,901 | 309,527 | 590,756 | 771,623 | 964,201 | 996,992 | 1,262,50 |
| Alas. | | | | | | | | | | |
| Ariz. | | | | | | | | | 9,658 | 40,44 |
| Ark. | | | 1,062 | 14,273 | 30,388 | 97,574 | 209,897 | 435,450 | 484,471 | 802,52 |
| Cal. | | | | | | | 92,597 | 379,994 | 560,247 | 864,69 |
| Col. | | | | | | | | 34,277 | 39,864 | 194,32 |
| Conn. | 237,946 | 251,002 | 261,942 | 275,248 | 297,675 | 309,978 | 370,792 | 460,147 | 537,454 | 622,70 |
| Del. | 59,096 | 64,273 | 72,674 | 72,749 | 76,748 | 78,085 | 91,532 | 112,216 | 125,015 | 146,60 |
| D.C. | | 14,023 | 24,023 | 33,039 | 39,834 | 43,712 | 51,687 | 75,080 | 131,700 | 177,62 |
| Fla. | | | | | 34,730 | 54,477 | 87,445 | 140,424 | 187,748 | 269,49 |
| Ga. | 82,548 | 162,686 | 252,433 | 340,989 | 516,823 | 691,392 | 906,185 | 1,057,286 | 1,184,109 | 1,542,18 |
| Ha. | | | | | | | | | | |
| Ida. | | | | | | | | | 14,999 | 32,61 |
| Ill. | | | 12,282 | 55,211 | 157,445 | 476,183 | 851,470 | 1,711,951 | 2,539,891 | 3,077,87 |
| Ind. | | 5,641 | 24,520 | 147,178 | 343,031 | 685,866 | 988,416 | 1,350,428 | 1,680,637 | 1,978,30 |
| Ia. | | | | | | 43,112 | 192,214 | 674,913 | 1,194,020 | 1,624,61 |
| Kan. | | | | | | | | 107,206 | 364,399 | 996,09 |
| Ky. | 73,677 | 220,995 | 406,511 | 564,317 | 687,917 | 779,828 | 982,405 | 1,155,684 | 1,321,011 | 1,648,69 |
| La. | | | 76,556 | 153,407 | 215,739 | 352,411 | 517,762 | 708,002 | 726,915 | 939,94 |
| Me. | 96,540 | 151,719 | 228,705 | 298,335 | 399,455 | 501,793 | 583,169 | 628,279 | 626,915 | 648,93 |
| Md. | 319,728 | 341,548 | 380,546 | 407,350 | 447,040 | 470,019 | 583,034 | 687,049 | 780,894 | 934,94 |
| Mass. | 378,787 | 422,845 | 472,040 | 523,287 | 610,408 | 737,699 | 994,514 | 1,231,066 | 1,457,351 | 1,783,08 |
| Mich. | | | 4,762 | 8,896 | 31,639 | 212,267 | 397,654 | 749,113 | 1,184,059 | 1,636,93 |
| Minn. | | | | | | | 6,077 | 172,023 | 439,706 | 780,77 |
| Miss. | | 8,850 | 40,352 | 75,448 | 136,621 | 375,651 | 606,526 | 791,305 | 827,922 | 1,131,59 |
| Mo. | | | 19,783 | 66,586 | 140,455 | 383,702 | 682,044 | 1,182,012 | 1,721,295 | 2,168,38 |
| Mon. | | | | | | | | | 20,595 | 39,15 |
| Neb. | | | | | | | | 28,841 | 122,993 | 452,40 |
| Nev. | | | | | | | | 6,857 | 42,491 | 62,26 |
| N.H. | 141,885 | 183,858 | 214,460 | 244,161 | 269,328 | 284,574 | 317,976 | 326,073 | 318,300 | 346,99 |
| N.J. | 184,139 | 211,149 | 245,562 | 277,575 | 320,823 | 373,306 | 489,555 | 672,035 | 906,096 | 1,131,11 |
| N.M. | | | | | | | 61,547 | 93,516 | 91,874 | 119,56 |
| N.Y. | 340,120 | 589,051 | 959,049 | 1,372,812 | 1,918,608 | 2,428,921 | 3,097,394 | 3,880,735 | 4,382,759 | 5,082,87 |
| N.C. | 393,751 | 478,103 | 555,500 | 638,829 | 737,987 | 753,419 | 869,039 | 992,622 | 1,071,361 | 1,399,75 |
| N.D. | | | | | | | | | *2,405 | 36,90 |
| Oh. | | 45,365 | 230,760 | 581,434 | 937,903 | 1,519,467 | 1,980,329 | 2,339,511 | 2,665,260 | 3,198,06 |
| Okla. | | | | | | | | | | |
| Ore. | | | | | | | 13,294 | 52,465 | 90,923 | 174,76 |
| Pa. | 434,373 | 602,365 | 810,091 | 1,049,458 | 1,348,233 | 1,724,033 | 2,311,786 | 2,906,215 | 3,521,951 | 4,282,89 |
| R.I. | 68,825 | 69,122 | 76,931 | 83,059 | 97,199 | 108,830 | 147,545 | 174,620 | 217,353 | 276,53 |
| S.C. | 249,073 | 345,591 | 415,115 | 502,741 | 581,185 | 594,398 | 668,507 | 703,708 | 705,606 | 995,57 |
| S.D. | | | | | | | | *4,837 | *11,776 | 98,26 |
| Tenn. | 35,691 | 105,602 | 261,727 | 422,823 | 681,904 | 829,210 | 1,002,717 | 1,109,801 | 1,258,520 | 1,542,35 |
| Tex. | | | | | | | 212,592 | 604,215 | 818,579 | 1,591,74 |
| Ut. | | | | | | | 11,380 | 40,273 | 86,786 | 143,96 |
| Vt. | 85,425 | 154,465 | 217,895 | 235,981 | 280,652 | 291,948 | 314,120 | 315,098 | 330,551 | 332,28 |
| Va. | 821,287 | 880,200 | 974,600 | 1,065,366 | 1,211,405 | 1,239,797 | 1,421,661 | 1,596,318 | 1,225,163 | 1,512,56 |
| Wash. | | | | | | | | 1,201 | 11,594 | 23,955 | 75,11 |
| W. Va. | | | | | | | | | 442,014 | 618,45 |
| Wis. | | | | | | 30,945 | 305,391 | 775,881 | 1,054,670 | 1,315,49 |
| Wy. | | | | | | | | | 9,118 | 20,78 |
| U.S. | 3,929,214 | 5,308,483 | 7,239,881 | 9,638,453 | 12,866,020 | 17,069,453 | 23,191,876 | 31,443,321 | 38,558,371 | 50,155,78 |

*1860 figure is for Dakota Territory; 1870 figures are for parts of Dakota Territory. (1) U.S. total includes persons (5,318 in 1830 and 6,100 in 1840) on public ships in the service of the United States not credited to any region, division, or state.

## Density of Population by States

(Per square mile, land area only)

| State | 1920 | 1960 | 1970 | State | 1920 | 1960 | 1970 | State | 1920 | 1960 | 1970 |
|---|---|---|---|---|---|---|---|---|---|---|---|
| Ala. | 45.8 | 64.2 | 67.9 | Ky. | 60.1 | 76.2 | 81.2 | N. D. | 9.2 | 9.1 | 8.9 |
| Alas.* | 0.1 | 0.4 | 0.5 | La. | 39.6 | 72.2 | 81.0 | Oh. | 141.4 | 236.6 | 260.0 |
| Ariz. | 2.9 | 11.5 | 15.6 | Me. | 25.7 | 31.3 | 32.1 | Okla. | 29.2 | 33.8 | 37.2 |
| Ark. | 33.4 | 34.2 | 37.0 | Md. | 145.8 | 313.5 | 396.6 | Ore. | 8.2 | 18.4 | 21.7 |
| Cal. | 22.0 | 100.4 | 127.6 | Mass. | 479.2 | 657.3 | 727.0 | Pa. | 194.5 | 251.4 | 262.3 |
| Col. | 9.1 | 16.9 | 21.3 | Mich. | 63.8 | 137.6 | 156.2 | R. I. | 566.4 | 819.3 | 905.5 |
| Conn. | 286.4 | 520.6 | 623.7 | Minn. | 29.5 | 43.0 | 48.0 | S. C. | 55.2 | 78.7 | 85.7 |
| Del. | 113.5 | 225.2 | 276.5 | Miss. | 38.6 | 46.0 | 46.9 | S. D. | 8.3 | 9.0 | 8.8 |
| D. C. | 7,292.9 | 12,523.9 | 12,401.8 | Mo. | 49.5 | 62.6 | 67.8 | Tenn. | 56.1 | 86.2 | 94.9 |
| Fla. | 17.7 | 91.5 | 125.5 | Mon. | 3.8 | 4.6 | 4.8 | Tex. | 17.8 | 36.4 | 42.7 |
| Ga. | 49.3 | 67.8 | 79.0 | Neb. | 16.9 | 18.4 | 19.4 | Ut. | 5.5 | 10.8 | 12.9 |
| Ha.* | 39.9 | 98.5 | 119.8 | Nev. | .7 | 2.6 | 4.4 | Vt. | 38.6 | 42.0 | 47.9 |
| Ida. | 5.2 | 8.1 | 8.6 | N. H. | 49.1 | 67.2 | 81.7 | Va. | 57.4 | 99.5 | 116.9 |
| Ill. | 115.7 | 180.4 | 199.4 | N. J. | 420.0 | 805.5 | 953.1 | Wash. | 20.3 | 42.8 | 51.2 |
| Ind. | 81.3 | 128.8 | 143.9 | N. M. | 2.9 | 7.8 | 8.4 | W. Va. | 60.9 | 77.2 | 72.5 |
| Ia. | 43.2 | 49.2 | 50.5 | N. Y. | 217.9 | 350.6 | 381.3 | Wis. | 47.6 | 72.6 | 81.1 |
| Kan. | 21.6 | 26.6 | 27.5 | N. C. | 52.5 | 93.2 | 104.1 | Wy. | 2.0 | 3.4 | 3.4 |
| | | | | | | | | U.S. | *29.9 | 50.6 | 57.5 |

*For purposes of comparison, Alaska and Hawaii included in above tabulation for 1920, even though not states then.

# Census from 1790 to 1970

other U.S. nationals overseas are not included.)

| State | 1890 | 1900 | 1910 | 1920 | 1930 | 1940 | 1950 | 1960 | 1970 |
|---|---|---|---|---|---|---|---|---|---|
| Ala. | 1,513,401 | 1,828,697 | 2,138,093 | 2,348,174 | 2,646,248 | 2,832,961 | 3,061,743 | 3,266,740 | 3,444,164 |
| Alas. | ........ | ........ | ........ | ........ | ........ | ........ | ........ | 226,167 | 302,173 |
| Ariz. | 88,243 | 122,931 | 204,354 | 334,162 | 435,573 | 499,261 | 749,587 | 1,302,161 | 1,772,482 |
| Ark. | 1,128,211 | 1,311,564 | 1,574,449 | 1,752,204 | 1,854,482 | 1,949,387 | 1,909,511 | 1,786,272 | 1,923,295 |
| Cal. | 1,213,398 | 1,485,053 | 2,377,549 | 3,426,861 | 5,677,251 | 6,907,387 | 10,586,223 | 15,717,204 | 19,953,134 |
| Col. | 413,249 | 539,700 | 799,024 | 939,629 | 1,035,791 | 1,123,296 | 1,325,089 | 1,753,947 | 2,207,259 |
| Conn. | 746,258 | 908,420 | 1,114,756 | 1,380,631 | 1,606,903 | 1,709,242 | 2,007,280 | 2,535,234 | 3,032,217 |
| Del. | 168,493 | 184,735 | 202,322 | 223,003 | 238,380 | 266,505 | 318,085 | 446,292 | 548,104 |
| D.C. | 230,392 | 278,718 | 331,069 | 437,571 | 486,869 | 663,091 | 802,178 | 763,956 | 756,510 |
| Fla. | 391,422 | 528,542 | 752,619 | 968,470 | 1,468,211 | 1,897,414 | 2,771,305 | 4,951,560 | 6,789,443 |
| Ga. | 1,837,353 | 2,216,331 | 2,609,121 | 2,895,832 | 2,908,506 | 3,123,723 | 3,444,578 | 3,943,116 | 4,589,575 |
| Ha. | ........ | ........ | ........ | ........ | ........ | ........ | ........ | 632,772 | 769,913 |
| Ida. | 88,548 | 161,772 | 325,594 | 431,866 | 445,032 | 524,873 | 588,637 | 667,191 | 713,008 |
| Ill. | 3,826,352 | 4,821,550 | 5,638,591 | 6,485,280 | 7,630,654 | 7,897,241 | 8,712,176 | 10,081,158 | 11,113,976 |
| Ind. | 2,192,404 | 2,516,462 | 2,700,876 | 2,930,390 | 3,238,503 | 3,427,796 | 3,934,224 | 4,662,498 | 5,193,669 |
| Ia. | 1,912,297 | 2,231,853 | 2,224,771 | 2,404,021 | 2,470,939 | 2,538,268 | 2,621,073 | 2,757,537 | 2,825,041 |
| Kan. | 1,428,108 | 1,470,495 | 1,690,949 | 1,769,257 | 1,880,999 | 1,801,028 | 1,905,299 | 2,178,611 | 2,249,071 |
| Ky. | 1,858,635 | 2,147,174 | 2,289,905 | 2,416,630 | 2,614,589 | 2,845,627 | 2,944,806 | 3,038,156 | 3,219,311 |
| La. | 1,118,588 | 1,381,625 | 1,656,388 | 1,798,509 | 2,101,593 | 2,363,880 | 2,683,516 | 3,257,022 | 3,643,180 |
| Me. | 661,086 | 694,466 | 742,371 | 768,014 | 797,423 | 847,226 | 913,774 | 969,265 | 993,663 |
| Md. | 1,042,390 | 1,188,044 | 1,295,346 | 1,449,661 | 1,631,526 | 1,821,244 | 2,343,001 | 3,100,689 | 3,922,399 |
| Mass. | 2,238,947 | 2,805,346 | 3,366,416 | 3,852,356 | 4,249,614 | 4,316,721 | 4,690,514 | 5,148,578 | 5,689,170 |
| Mich. | 2,093,890 | 2,420,982 | 2,810,173 | 3,668,412 | 4,842,325 | 5,256,106 | 6,371,766 | 7,823,194 | 8,875,083 |
| Minn. | 1,310,283 | 1,751,394 | 2,075,708 | 2,387,125 | 2,563,953 | 2,792,300 | 2,982,483 | 3,413,864 | 3,805,069 |
| Miss. | 1,289,600 | 1,551,270 | 1,797,114 | 1,790,618 | 2,009,821 | 2,183,796 | 2,178,914 | 2,178,141 | 2,216,912 |
| Mo. | 2,679,185 | 3,106,665 | 3,293,335 | 3,404,055 | 3,629,367 | 3,784,664 | 3,954,653 | 4,319,813 | 4,677,399 |
| Mon. | 142,924 | 243,329 | 376,053 | 548,889 | 537,606 | 559,456 | 591,024 | 674,767 | 694,409 |
| Neb. | 1,062,656 | 1,066,300 | 1,192,214 | 1,296,372 | 1,377,963 | 1,315,834 | 1,325,510 | 1,411,330 | 1,483,791 |
| Nev. | 47,355 | 42,335 | 81,875 | 77,407 | 91,058 | 110,247 | 160,083 | 285,278 | 488,738 |
| N.H. | 376,530 | 411,588 | 430,572 | 443,083 | 465,293 | 491,524 | 533,242 | 606,921 | 737,681 |
| N.J. | 1,444,933 | 1,883,669 | 2,537,167 | 3,155,900 | 4,041,334 | 4,160,165 | 4,835,329 | 6,066,782 | 7,168,164 |
| N.M. | 160,282 | 195,310 | 327,301 | 360,350 | 423,317 | 531,818 | 681,187 | 951,023 | 1,016,000 |
| N.Y. | 6,003,174 | 7,268,894 | 9,113,614 | 10,385,227 | 12,588,066 | 13,479,142 | 14,830,192 | 16,782,304 | 18,241,266 |
| N.C. | 1,617,949 | 1,893,810 | 2,206,287 | 2,559,123 | 3,170,276 | 3,571,623 | 4,061,929 | 4,556,155 | 5,082,059 |
| N.D. | 190,983 | 319,146 | 577,056 | 646,872 | 680,845 | 641,935 | 619,636 | 632,446 | 617,761 |
| Oh. | 3,672,329 | 4,157,545 | 4,767,121 | 5,759,394 | 6,646,697 | 6,907,612 | 7,946,627 | 9,706,397 | 10,652,017 |
| Okla. | 258,657 | 790,391 | 1,657,155 | 2,028,283 | 2,396,040 | 2,336,434 | 2,233,351 | 2,328,284 | 2,559,253 |
| Ore. | 317,704 | 413,536 | 672,765 | 783,389 | 953,786 | 1,089,684 | 1,521,341 | 1,768,687 | 2,091,385 |
| Pa. | 5,258,113 | 6,302,115 | 7,665,111 | 8,720,017 | 9,631,350 | 9,900,180 | 10,498,012 | 11,319,366 | 11,793,909 |
| R.I. | 345,506 | 428,556 | 542,610 | 604,397 | 687,497 | 713,346 | 791,896 | 859,488 | 949,723 |
| S.C. | 1,151,149 | 1,340,316 | 1,515,400 | 1,683,724 | 1,738,765 | 1,899,804 | 2,117,027 | 2,382,594 | 2,509,516 |
| S.D. | 348,600 | 401,570 | 583,888 | 636,547 | 692,849 | 642,961 | 652,740 | 680,514 | 666,257 |
| Tenn. | 1,767,518 | 2,020,616 | 2,184,789 | 2,337,885 | 2,616,556 | 2,915,841 | 3,291,718 | 3,567,089 | 3,924,164 |
| Tex. | 2,235,527 | 3,048,710 | 3,896,542 | 4,663,228 | 5,824,715 | 6,414,824 | 7,711,194 | 9,579,677 | 11,196,730 |
| Ut. | 210,779 | 276,749 | 373,351 | 449,396 | 507,847 | 550,310 | 688,862 | 890,627 | 1,059,273 |
| Vt. | 332,422 | 343,641 | 355,956 | 352,428 | 359,611 | 359,231 | 377,747 | 389,881 | 444,732 |
| Va. | 1,655,980 | 1,854,184 | 2,061,612 | 2,309,187 | 2,421,851 | 2,677,773 | 3,318,680 | 3,966,949 | 4,648,494 |
| Wash. | 357,232 | 518,103 | 1,141,990 | 1,356,621 | 1,563,396 | 1,736,191 | 2,378,962 | 2,853,214 | 3,409,169 |
| W. Va. | 762,794 | 958,800 | 1,221,119 | 1,463,701 | 1,729,205 | 1,901,974 | 2,005,553 | 1,860,421 | 1,744,237 |
| Wis. | 1,693,330 | 2,069,042 | 2,333,860 | 2,632,067 | 2,939,006 | 3,137,587 | 3,434,575 | 3,951,777 | 4,417,933 |
| Wy. | 62,555 | 92,531 | 145,965 | 194,402 | 225,565 | 250,742 | 290,529 | 330,066 | 332,416 |
| U.S. | 62,947,714 | 75,994,575 | 91,972,266 | 105,710,620 | 122,775,046 | 131,669,275 | 150,697,361 | 179,323,175 | 203,235,298 |

## U.S. Center of Population, 1790-1970

**Center of Population** is that point which may be considered as center of population gravity of the U.S. or that point upon which the U.S. would balance if it were a rigid plane without weight and the population distributed thereon with each individual being assumed to have equal weight and to exert an influence on a central point proportional to his distance from that point.

| Year | N. Lat. | | W.Long. | | Approximate location |
|---|---|---|---|---|---|
| 1790 | 39 16 | 30 | 76 11 | 12 | 23 miles east of Baltimore, Md. |
| 1800 | 39 16 | 6 | 76 56 | 30 | 18 miles west of Baltimore, Md. |
| 1810 | 39 11 | 30 | 77 37 | 12 | 40 miles northwest by west of Washington, D.C. (in Va.) |
| 1820 | 39 5 | 42 | 78 33 | 0 | 16 miles east of Moorefield, W. Va.[1] |
| 1830 | 38 57 | 54 | 79 16 | 54 | 19 miles west-southwest of Moorefield, W. Va.[1] |
| 1840 | 39 2 | 0 | 80 18 | 0 | 16 miles south of Clarksburg, W. Va.[1] |
| 1850 | 38 59 | 0 | 81 19 | 0 | 23 miles southeast of Parkersburg, W. Va.[1] |
| 1860 | 39 0 | 24 | 82 48 | 48 | 20 miles south by east of Chillicothe, Oh. |
| 1870 | 39 12 | 0 | 83 35 | 42 | 48 miles east by north of Cincinnati, Oh. |
| 1880 | 39 4 | 8 | 84 39 | 40 | 8 miles west by south of Cincinnati, Oh. (in Ky.) |
| 1890 | 39 11 | 56 | 85 32 | 53 | 20 miles east of Columbus, Ind. |
| 1900 | 39 9 | 36 | 85 48 | 54 | 6 miles southeast of Columbus, Ind. |
| 1910 | 39 10 | 12 | 86 32 | 20 | In the city of Bloomington, Ind. |
| 1920 | 39 10 | 21 | 86 43 | 15 | 8 miles south-southeast of Spencer, Owen County, Ind. |
| 1930 | 39 3 | 45 | 87 8 | 6 | 3 miles northeast of Linton, Greene County, Ind. |
| 1940 | 38 56 | 54 | 87 22 | 35 | 2 miles southeast by east of Carlisle, Haddon township, Sullivan County, Ind. |
| 1950 (Inc. Alaska & Hawaii) | 38 48 | 15 | 88 22 | 8 | 3 miles northeast of Louisville, Clay County, Ill. |
| 1960 | 38 35 | 58 | 89 12 | 35 | 6 1/2 miles northwest of Centralia, Ill. |
| 1970 | 38 27 | 47 | 89 42 | 22 | 5 miles east southeast of Mascoutah, St. Clair County, Ill. |

(1) West Virginia was set off from Virginia Dec. 31, 1862, and admitted as a state June 20, 1863.

# Rankings of U.S. Standard Metropolitan Statistical Areas

**Source:** U.S. Bureau of the Census

Metropolitan areas are ranked by 1976 provisional population size based on new SMSA definitions and compared with a ranking of areas as defined in the 1970 census. Included are 264 of the 281 Standard Metropolitan Statistical Areas (SMSAs) as defined through December 1977 by the Office of Federal Statistical Policy and Standards, excluding 4 areas in Puerto Rico not covered in the report.

Asterisk (*) indicates 13 New England County Metropolitan Areas comprised of 26 New England SMSAs.

| SMSA | 1974 (P) Rank | Pop. | 1970 Rank | Pop. |
|---|---|---|---|---|
| New York, N.Y.-N.J. | 1 | 9,526,700 | 1 | 9,973,716 |
| Chicago, Ill. | 2 | 7,006,400 | 3 | 6,977,267 |
| Los Angeles-Long Beach, Cal. | 3 | 7,004,400 | 2 | 7,041,980 |
| Philadelphia, Pa.-N.J. | 4 | 4,822,400 | 4 | 4,824,110 |
| Detroit, Mich. | 5 | 4,389,900 | 5 | 4,435,051 |
| Boston-Lowell-Brockton Lawrence-Haverhill, Mass.-N.H.* | 6 | 3,905,600 | 6 | 3,848,593 |
| San Francisco-Oakland, Cal. | 7 | 3,158,900 | 7 | 3,109,247 |
| Washington, D.C.-Md.-Va. | 8 | 3,035,700 | 8 | 2,910,111 |
| Nassau-Suffolk, N.Y.[1] | 9 | 2,675,300 | 9 | 2,555,868 |
| Dallas-Ft. Worth, Tex.[3] | 10 | 2,585,300 | 12 | 2,377,623 |
| Houston, Tex. | 11 | 2,392,100 | 16 | 1,999,316 |
| St. Louis, Mo.-Ill. | 12 | 2,386,300 | 10 | 2,410,884 |
| Pittsburgh, Pa. | 13 | 2,306,300 | 11 | 2,401,362 |
| Baltimore, Md. | 14 | 2,152,400 | 13 | 2,071,016 |
| Minneapolis-St.Paul, Minn.-Wis. | 15 | 2,033,400 | 17 | 1,965,391 |
| Newark, N.J. | 16 | 1,988,300 | 15 | 2,057,468 |
| Cleveland, Oh. | 17 | 1,960,200 | 14 | 2,063,729 |
| Atlanta, Ga. | 18 | 1,802,700 | 18 | 1,595,517 |
| Anaheim-Santa Ana-Garden Grove, Cal. | 19 | 1,755,600 | 20 | 1,421,233 |
| San Diego, Cal. | 20 | 1,623,400 | 23 | 1,357,854 |
| Miami, Fla. | 21 | 1,466,800 | 26 | 1,267,792 |
| Denver-Boulder, Col.[1] | 22 | 1,442,500 | 27 | 1,239,545 |
| Seattle-Everett, Wash. | 23 | 1,421,700 | 19 | 1,424,605 |
| Milwaukee, Wis. | 24 | 1,407,300 | 21 | 1,403,884 |
| Tampa-St. Petersburg, Fla. | 25 | 1,370,400 | 30 | 1,088,549 |
| Cincinnati, Oh.-Ky.-Ind. | 26 | 1,362,200 | 22 | 1,387,287 |
| Buffalo, N.Y. | 27 | 1,320,900 | 24 | 1,349,211 |
| Kansas City, Mo.-Kan. | 28 | 1,278,100 | 25 | 1,273,926 |
| Riverside-San Bernardino-Ontario, Cal. | 29 | 1,255,500 | 28 | 1,139,149 |
| Phoenix, Ariz. | 30 | 1,243,200 | 36 | 971,228 |
| San Jose, Cal. | 31 | 1,198,900 | 31 | 1,065,313 |
| Indianapolis, Ind. | 32 | 1,139,700 | 29 | 1,111,352 |
| New Orleans, La. | 33 | 1,109,400 | 32 | 1,046,470 |
| Portland, Oreg.-Wash. | 34 | 1,108,800 | 35 | 1,007,130 |
| Columbus, Oh. | 35 | 1,072,100 | 34 | 1,017,847 |
| Hartford-New Britain-Bristol, Conn.* | 36 | 1,060,400 | 33 | 1,035,195 |
| San Antonio, Tex. | 37 | 987,200 | 38 | 888,179 |
| Rochester, N.Y. | 38 | 972,300 | 37 | 961,516 |
| Sacramento, Cal. | 39 | 903,200 | 43 | 803,793 |
| Louisville, Ky.-Ind. | 40 | 884,200 | 39 | 867,330 |
| Memphis, Tenn.-Ark.-Miss. | 41 | 874,800 | 42 | 834,103 |
| Fort Lauderdale-Hollywood, Fla. | 42 | 850,800 | 61 | 620,100 |
| Providence-Warwick-Pawtucket, R.I.* | 43 | 846,300 | 40 | 855,495 |
| Dayton, Oh. | 44 | 835,700 | 41 | 852,531 |
| Birmingham, Ala. | 45 | 803,200 | 46 | 767,230 |
| Bridgeport-Stamford-Norwalk-Danbury, Conn.* | 46 | 801,500 | 44 | 792,814 |
| Salt Lake City-Ogden, Ut.[3] | 47 | 797,400 | 51 | 705,458 |
| Albany-Schenectady-Troy, N.Y. | 48 | 793,300 | 45 | 777,977 |
| Toledo, Ohio-Mich. | 49 | 783,900 | 47 | 762,658 |
| Norfolk-Virginia Beach-Portsmouth, Va.-N.C. | 50 | 771,700 | 49 | 732,600 |
| Greensboro-Winston-Salem-High Point, N.C. | 51 | 769,200 | 50 | 724,129 |
| New Haven-West Haven-Waterbury, Meriden, Conn.* | 52 | 763,000 | 48 | 744,948 |
| Nashville-Davidson, Tenn. | 53 | 761,000 | 52 | 699,271 |
| Oklahoma City, Okla. | 54 | 760,400 | 53 | 699,092 |
| Honolulu, Ha. | 55 | 718,400 | 58 | 630,528 |
| Jacksonville, Fla. | 56 | 700,700 | 60 | 621,827 |
| Akron, Oh. | 57 | 667,000 | 54 | 679,239 |
| Syracuse, N.Y. | 58 | 651,400 | 56 | 636,596 |
| Worcester-Fitchburg-Leominster, Mass.* | 59 | 648,200 | 55 | 637,037 |
| Gary-Hammond-East Chicago, Ind. | 60 | 644,000 | 57 | 633,367 |

| SMSA | 1974 (P) Rank | Pop. | 1970 Rank | Pop. |
|---|---|---|---|---|
| Northeast Pennsylvania | 61 | 635,000 | 59 | 621,882 |
| Allentown-Bethlehem-Easton, Pa.-N.J. | 62 | 622,700 | 63 | 594,382 |
| Springfield-Chicopee-Holyoke, Mass.* | 63 | 595,800 | 65 | 583,031 |
| Tulsa, Okla. | 64 | 595,600 | 67 | 549,154 |
| Charlotte-Gastonia, N.C.[3] | 65 | 594,700 | 66 | 557,785 |
| New Brunswick-Perth Amboy-Sayreville, N.J.[1] | 66 | 592,700 | 64 | 583,813 |
| Richmond, Va. | 67 | 592,200 | 68 | 547,542 |
| Orlando, Fla. | 68 | 586,700 | 77 | 453,270 |
| Omaha, Neb.-Ia. | 69 | 581,400 | 69 | 542,646 |
| Jersey City, N.J. | 70 | 572,900 | 62 | 607,839 |
| Grand Rapids, Mich. | 71 | 568,100 | 70 | 539,225 |
| Youngstown-Warren, Oh. | 72 | 534,900 | 71 | 537,124 |
| Greenville-Spartanburg, S.C. | 73 | 529,200 | 74 | 473,454 |
| Wilmington, Del-N.J.-Md. | 74 | 519,100 | 73 | 499,493 |
| Flint, Mich. | 75 | 514,700 | 72 | 508,664 |
| Long Branch-Asbury Park, N.J.[1] | 76 | 492,800 | 75 | 461,849 |
| Raleigh-Durham, N.C.[3] | 77 | 480,000 | 80 | 419,254 |
| West Palm Beach-Boca Raton, Fla. | 78 | 470,200 | 97 | 348,993 |
| New Bedford-Fall River, Mass.* | 79 | 464,100 | 78 | 444,301 |
| Fresno, Cal. | 80 | 462,500 | 81 | 413,329 |
| Austin, Tex. | 81 | 461,200 | 94 | 360,463 |
| Tucson, Ariz. | 82 | 453,900 | 96 | 351,667 |
| Oxnard-Simi Valley-Ventura, Cal. | 83 | 452,500 | 87 | 378,497 |
| Paterson-Clifton-Passaic, N.J. | 84 | 449,000 | 76 | 460,782 |
| Lansing-East Lansing, Mich. | 85 | 447,400 | 79 | 424,271 |
| Knoxville, Tenn. | 86 | 439,600 | 84 | 409,409 |
| Harrisburg, Pa. | 87 | 428,600 | 83 | 410,505 |
| El Paso, Tex. | 88 | 425,200 | 95 | 359,291 |
| Tacoma, Wash. | 89 | 420,500 | 82 | 412,344 |
| Baton Rouge, La. | 90 | 420,200 | 89 | 375,628 |
| Mobile, Ala. | 91 | 416,600 | 88 | 376,690 |
| Canton, Oh. | 92 | 402,300 | 85 | 393,789 |
| Johnson City-Kingsport-Bristol, Tenn.-Va.[1] | 93 | 400,800 | 90 | 373,591 |
| Wichita, Kan. | 94 | 391,900 | 86 | 389,352 |
| Chattanooga, Tenn.-Ga. | 95 | 391,100 | 91 | 370,857 |
| Albuquerque, N.M. | 96 | 388,200 | 103 | 333,266 |
| Charleston-North Charleston, S.C. | 97 | 377,300 | 101 | 336,036 |
| Davenport-Rock Island-Moline, Ia.-Ill. | 98 | 373,000 | 92 | 362,638 |
| Columbia, S.C. | 99 | 372,700 | 108 | 322,880 |
| Fort Wayne, Ind. | 100 | 370,300 | 93 | 361,984 |
| Little Rock-North Little Rock, Ark. | 101 | 362,600 | 107 | 323,296 |
| Peoria, Ill. | 102 | 359,200 | 99 | 341,979 |
| Newport News-Hampton, Va. | 103 | 355,500 | 104 | 333,140 |
| Beaumont-Port Arthur-Orange, Tex. | 104 | 355,500 | 98 | 347,568 |
| Bakersfield, Cal. | 105 | 354,300 | 105 | 330,234 |
| Shreveport, La. | 106 | 352,600 | 102 | 333,826 |
| York, Pa. | 107 | 351,500 | 106 | 329,540 |
| Lancaster, Pa. | 108 | 345,200 | 109 | 320,079 |
| Las Vegas, Nev. | 109 | 343,400 | 124 | 273,288 |
| Des Moines, Ia. | 110 | 333,000 | 110 | 313,562 |
| Utica-Rome, N.Y. | 111 | 332,100 | 100 | 340,477 |
| Trenton, N.J. | 112 | 318,700 | 111 | 304,116 |
| Spokane, Wash. | 113 | 310,700 | 116 | 287,487 |
| Binghamton, N.Y.-Pa. | 114 | 307,300 | 112 | 302,672 |
| Madison, Wis. | 115 | 306,900 | 115 | 290,272 |
| Reading, Pa. | 116 | 305,900 | 113 | 296,382 |
| Stockton, Cal. | 117 | 301,800 | 114 | 291,073 |
| Corpus Christi, Tex. | 118 | 298,400 | 119 | 284,832 |
| Jackson, Miss. | 119 | 291,500 | 131 | 258,906 |
| Huntington-Ashland, W.Va.-Ky.-Oh. | 120 | 290,800 | 117 | 286,935 |

| SMSA | 1974 (P) Rank | Pop. | 1970 Rank | Pop. |
|---|---|---|---|---|
| Lexington-Fayette, Ky. | 121 | 290,500 | 126 | 266,701 |
| Huntsville, Ala. | 122 | 288,200 | 120 | 282,450 |
| Evansville, Ind.-Ky. | 123 | 286,800 | 118 | 284,959 |
| Appleton-Oshkosh, Wis. | 124 | 286,700 | 122 | 276,948 |
| Santa Barbara-Santa Maria-Lompoc, Cal. | 125 | 286,300 | 128 | 264,324 |
| Colorado Springs, Col. | 126 | 285,700 | 138 | 239,288 |
| Vallejo-Fairfield-Napa, Cal. | 127 | 284,300 | 135 | 251,129 |
| Augusta, Ga.-S.C. | 128 | 284,000 | 123 | 275,787 |
| Lakeland-Winter Haven, Fla.[1] | 129 | 278,300 | 143 | 228,515 |
| Pensacola, Fla. | 130 | 277,300 | 137 | 243,075 |
| South Bend, Ind. | 131 | 276,400 | 121 | 280,031 |
| Erie, Pa. | 132 | 275,000 | 129 | 263,654 |
| Salinas-Seaside-Monterey, Cal. | 133 | 271,500 | 136 | 247,450 |
| Rockford, Ill. | 134 | 270,400 | 125 | 272,063 |
| Johnstown, Pa. | 135 | 268,300 | 130 | 262,822 |
| Lorain-Elyria, Oh. | 136 | 266,400 | 134 | 256,843 |
| Duluth-Superior, Minn.-Wis. | 137 | 264,400 | 127 | 265,350 |
| Kalamazoo-Portage, Mich. | 138 | 264,100 | 132 | 257,723 |
| Charleston, W.Va. | 139 | 254,600 | 133 | 257,140 |
| Santa Rosa, Cal. | 140 | 253,300 | 155 | 204,885 |
| Montgomery, Ala. | 141 | 253,000 | 146 | 225,911 |
| Ann Arbor, Mich. | 142 | 248,100 | 140 | 234,103 |
| Hamilton-Middletown, Oh. | 143 | 246,000 | 145 | 226,207 |
| Manchester-Nashua, N.H.* | 144 | 245,100 | 147 | 223,941 |
| Eugene-Springfield, Ore. | 145 | 244,600 | 151 | 215,401 |
| New London-Norwich, Conn.* | 146 | 244,000 | 141 | 230,654 |
| Macon, Ga. | 147 | 239,600 | 144 | 226,782 |
| Poughkeepsie, N.Y.[1] | 148 | 235,100 | 148 | 222,295 |
| Modesto, Cal. | 149 | 230,900 | 157 | 194,506 |
| McAllen-Pharr-Edenburg, Tex. | 150 | 230,300 | 161 | 181,535 |
| Portland, Me.* | 151 | 230,300 | 150 | 215,980 |
| Fayetteville, N.C. | 152 | 229,500 | 152 | 212,042 |
| Columbus, Ga.-Ala. | 153 | 229,300 | 139 | 238,584 |
| Melbourne-Titusville-Cocoa, Fla.[1] | 154 | 228,100 | 142 | 230,006 |
| Saginaw, Mich. | 155 | 226,100 | 149 | 219,743 |
| Salem, Ore. | 156 | 213,500 | 159 | 186,658 |
| Roanoke, Va. | 157 | 212,500 | 156 | 203,153 |
| Lima, Oh. | 158 | 211,700 | 153 | 210,074 |
| Daytona Beach, Fla.[1] | 159 | 210,500 | 171 | 169,487 |
| Savannah, Ga. | 160 | 210,600 | 154 | 207,987 |
| Killeen-Temple, Tex.[1] | 161 | 204,600 | 180 | 159,794 |
| Lubbock, Tex. | 162 | 199,600 | 164 | 179,295 |
| Atlantic City, N.J. | 163 | 189,100 | 167 | 175,043 |
| Springfield, Mo. | 164 | 186,400 | 172 | 168,053 |
| Galveston-Texas City, Tex. | 165 | 186,300 | 170 | 169,812 |
| Springfield, Ill. | 166 | 184,300 | 168 | 171,020 |
| Springfield, Oh. | 167 | 183,400 | 158 | 187,606 |
| Lincoln, Neb. | 168 | 182,900 | 173 | 167,972 |
| Battle Creek, Mich. | 169 | 182,300 | 163 | 180,129 |
| Wheeling, W. Va.-Oh. | 170 | 181,300 | 160 | 181,954 |
| Fort Smith, Ark.-Okla. | 171 | 181,200 | 178 | 160,421 |
| Topeka, Kan. | 172 | 180,700 | 162 | 180,619 |
| Brownsville-Harlingen-San Benito, Tex. | 173 | 179,500 | 189 | 140,368 |
| Muskegon-Norton Shores-Muskegon Heights, Mich. | 174 | 178,300 | 165 | 175,410 |
| Racine, Wis. | 175 | 175,700 | 169 | 170,838 |
| Green Bay, Wis. | 176 | 173,300 | 181 | 158,244 |
| Biloxi-Gulfport, Miss. | 177 | 172,700 | 179 | 160,070 |
| Terre Haute, Ind. | 178 | 171,300 | 166 | 175,143 |
| Provo-Orem, Ut. | 179 | 170,300 | 191 | 137,776 |
| Asheville, N.C. | 180 | 168,300 | 177 | 161,059 |
| Anchorage, Alas. | 181 | 167,500 | 202 | 126,385 |
| Cedar Rapids, Ia. | 182 | 166,900 | 176 | 163,213 |
| Champaign-Urbana-Rantoul, Ill. | 183 | 165,500 | 175 | 163,281 |
| Steubenville-Weirton, Oh.-W. Va. | 184 | 164,200 | 174 | 166,385 |
| Santa Cruz, Cal.[1] | 185 | 162,900 | 204 | 123,790 |
| Sarasota, Fla.[1] | 186 | 161,400 | 209 | 120,413 |
| Fort Myers, Fla.[1] | 187 | 160,900 | 228 | 105,216 |
| Yakima, Wash.[1] | 188 | 159,500 | 186 | 145,212 |
| Waco, Tex. | 189 | 155,400 | 184 | 147,553 |
| St. Cloud, Minn.[1] | 190 | 155,200 | 194 | 134,585 |
| Amarillo, Tex. | 191 | 154,300 | 187 | 144,396 |
| Lake Charles, La. | 192 | 153,100 | 185 | 145,415 |
| Parkersburg-Marietta, W. Va.-Oh.[2] | 193 | 152,400 | 183 | 148,132 |
| Fayetteville-Springdale, Ark.[1] | 194 | 149,600 | 201 | 127,846 |
| Reno, Nev. | 195 | 149,100 | 207 | 121,068 |
| Pittsfield, Mass.* | 196 | 148,000 | 182 | 149,402 |
| Jackson, Mich. | 197 | 147,000 | 188 | 143,274 |
| Lynchburg, Va. | 198 | 146,700 | 193 | 134,744 |
| Clarksville-Hopkinsville, Tenn.-Ky.[1] | 199 | 142,200 | 211 | 118,945 |
| Boise City, Ida. | 200 | 139,700 | 222 | 112,230 |
| Anderson, Ind. | 201 | 138,300 | 190 | 138,451 |
| Alexandria, La.[2] | 202 | 137,800 | 196 | 131,749 |
| Tallahassee, Fla. | 203 | 137,200 | 225 | 109,355 |
| Waterloo-Cedar Falls, Ia. | 204 | 135,600 | 195 | 132,916 |
| Altoona, Pa. | 205 | 133,800 | 192 | 135,356 |
| Vineland-Millville-Bridgeton, N.J. | 206 | 133,600 | 206 | 121,374 |
| Abilene, Tex. | 207 | 131,500 | 205 | 122,164 |
| Mansfield, Oh. | 208 | 130,000 | 197 | 129,997 |
| Wilmington, N.C. | 209 | 129,600 | 227 | 107,219 |
| Wichita Falls, Tex. | 210 | 129,200 | 200 | 128,642 |
| Fargo-Moorhead, N.D.-Minn. | 211 | 128,600 | 210 | 120,261 |
| Monroe, La. | 212 | 128,600 | 218 | 115,387 |
| Muncie, Ind. | 213 | 128,400 | 198 | 129,219 |
| Longview, Tex. | 214 | 127,900 | 208 | 120,770 |
| Gainesville, Fla. | 215 | 127,000 | 229 | 104,764 |
| Lafayette, La. | 216 | 127,000 | 223 | 111,643 |
| Petersburg-Colonial Heights-Hopewell, Va.[1] | 217 | 126,500 | 199 | 128,809 |
| Decatur, Ill. | 218 | 126,400 | 203 | 125,010 |
| Bradenton, Fla.[1] | 219 | 125,700 | 236 | 97,115 |
| Tuscaloosa, Ala. | 220 | 125,100 | 217 | 116,029 |
| Pueblo, Col. | 221 | 124,500 | 212 | 118,238 |
| Kenosha, Wis. | 222 | 124,300 | 213 | 117,917 |
| Florence, Ala.[1] | 223 | 123,800 | 214 | 117,743 |
| Eau Claire, Wis.[1] | 224 | 123,500 | 219 | 114,936 |
| Fort Collins, Col.[1] | 225 | 120,700 | 247 | 89,900 |
| Sioux City, Ia.-Neb. | 226 | 119,800 | 216 | 116,189 |
| Bay City, Mich. | 227 | 119,300 | 215 | 117,339 |
| Bloomington-Normal, Ill. | 228 | 118,700 | 230 | 104,389 |
| Texarkana, Tex.-Ark. | 229 | 117,800 | 220 | 113,488 |
| Williamsport, Pa.[1] | 230 | 115,300 | 221 | 113,296 |
| Anniston, Ala.[1] | 231 | 113,600 | 231 | 103,092 |
| Lafayette-West Lafayette, Ind. | 232 | 113,200 | 224 | 109,378 |
| Richland-Kennewick, Wash.[1] | 233 | 112,800 | 243 | 93,356 |
| Lawton, Okla. | 234 | 109,200 | 226 | 108,144 |
| Greely, Col.[1] | 235 | 108,900 | 248 | 89,297 |
| Tyler, Tex. | 236 | 108,900 | 237 | 97,096 |
| Pascagoula-Moss Point, Miss.[1] | 237 | 108,300 | 249 | 87,975 |
| Kokomo, Ind.[1] | 238 | 103,200 | 233 | 99,848 |
| Albany, Ga.[1] | 239 | 101,700 | 238 | 96,683 |
| Odessa, Tex. | 240 | 100,900 | 244 | 92,660 |
| Sioux Falls, S.D. | 241 | 100,700 | 241 | 95,209 |
| Grand Fork, N.D.-Minn.[1] | 242 | 100,000 | 240 | 95,537 |
| Billings, Mon. | 243 | 99,600 | 250 | 87,367 |
| St. Joseph, Mo. | 244 | 99,400 | 234 | 98,828 |
| Elmira, N.Y.[1] | 245 | 99,400 | 232 | 101,537 |
| Burlington, N.C.[1] | 246 | 99,000 | 239 | 96,502 |
| Kankakee, Ill.[1] | 247 | 96,200 | 235 | 97,250 |
| Gadsden, Ala. | 248 | 96,200 | 242 | 94,144 |
| Dubuque, Ia. | 249 | 95,600 | 246 | 90,609 |
| Lewiston-Auburn, Me.* | 250 | 94,100 | 245 | 91,279 |
| Bloomington, Ind. | 251 | 90,300 | 252 | 85,221 |
| Panama City, Fla.[1] | 252 | 90,100 | 259 | 75,283 |
| Rochester, Minn.[1] | 253 | 89,900 | 253 | 84,104 |
| La Crosse, Wis.[1] | 254 | 87,800 | 257 | 80,468 |
| Columbia, Mo.[1] | 255 | 85,700 | 256 | 80,935 |
| Pine Bluff, Ark. | 256 | 83,900 | 251 | 85,329 |
| Great Falls, Mon. | 257 | 83,600 | 255 | 81,804 |
| Laredo, Tex. | 258 | 82,700 | 260 | 72,859 |
| Sherman-Denison, Tex. | 259 | 81,900 | 254 | 83,225 |
| Owensboro, Ky.[1] | 260 | 81,000 | 258 | 79,486 |
| San Angelo, Tex. | 261 | 77,200 | 261 | 71,047 |
| Bryan-College Station, Tex. | 262 | 73,000 | 263 | 57,978 |
| Midland, Tex. | 263 | 71,400 | 262 | 65,433 |
| Lawrence, Kan.[1] | 264 | 64,534 | 264 | 57,932 |

(1) New SMSA established since 1970 census.
(2) New SMSA established in Nov. 1971, and area definition changed in Apr. 1973.
(3) Merger of 2 existing SMSAs since 1970 census; rank and population given for 1970 refer to the merger of the 2 SMSAs.

## How the Cities Grew

Source: U.S. Bureau of the Census

(cities over 100,000 ranked by 1975 population estimates)

| Rank | City | 1975 | 1970 | 1960 | 1950 | 1900 | 1850 | 1790 |
|---|---|---|---|---|---|---|---|---|
| 1 | New York, N.Y. | 7,481,613 | 7,895,563 | 7,781,984 | 7,891,957 | 3,437,202 | [1]696,115 | [1]49,401 |
| | Bronx | 1,355,482 | 1,471,701 | 1,424,815 | 1,451,277 | 200,507 | 8,032 | 1,781 |
| | Brooklyn | 2,408,234 | 2,602,012 | 2,627,319 | 2,738,175 | 1,166,582 | 138,882 | 4,495 |
| | Manhattan | 1,429,033 | 1,539,233 | 1,698,281 | 1,960,101 | 1,850,093 | 515,547 | 33,131 |
| | Queens | 1,963,705 | 1,987,174 | 1,809,578 | 1,550,849 | 152,999 | 18,593 | 6,159 |
| | Staten Island | 325,159 | 295,443 | 221,991 | 191,555 | 67,021 | 15,061 | 3,835 |
| 2 | Chicago, Ill. | 3,099,391 | 3,369,357 | 3,550,404 | 3,620,962 | 1,698,575 | 29,963 | ... |
| 3 | Los Angeles, Cal. | 2,727,399 | 2,811,801 | 2,479,015 | 1,970,358 | 102,479 | 1,610 | ... |
| 4 | Philadelphia, Pa. | 1,815,808 | 1,949,996 | 2,002,512 | 2,071,605 | 1,293,697 | 121,376 | 28,522 |
| 5 | Houston, Tex. | 1,397,562 | 1,282,443 | 938,219 | 596,163 | 44,633 | 2,396 | ... |
| 6 | Detroit, Mich. | 1,335,085 | 1,514,063 | 1,670,144 | 1,849,568 | 285,704 | 21,019 | ... |
| 7 | Baltimore, Md. | 851,698 | 905,787 | 939,024 | 949,708 | 508,957 | 169,054 | 13,603 |
| 8 | Dallas, Tex. | 822,745 | 844,621 | 679,684 | 434,462 | 42,638 | ... | ... |
| 9 | San Diego, Cal. | 774,489 | 697,471 | 573,224 | 334,387 | 17,700 | ... | ... |
| 10 | San Antonio, Tex. | 773,248 | 708,582 | 587,718 | 408,442 | 53,321 | 3,488 | ... |
| 11 | Indianapolis, Ind. | 725,077 | 740,000 | 476,258 | 427,173 | 169,164 | 8,091 | ... |
| 12 | Washington, D.C. | 711,518 | 756,668 | 763,956 | 802,178 | 278,718 | 40,001 | ... |
| 13 | Honolulu, Ha. | 705,381 | 630,528 | 294,194 | 248,034 | 39,306 | ... | ... |
| 14 | Milwaukee, Wis. | 665,796 | 717,372 | 741,324 | 637,392 | 285,315 | 20,061 | ... |
| 15 | Phoenix, Ariz. | 664,721 | 589,016 | 439,170 | 106,818 | 5,544 | ... | ... |
| 16 | San Francisco, Cal. | 664,520 | 715,674 | 740,316 | 775,357 | 342,782 | [2]34,776 | ... |
| 17 | Memphis, Tenn. | 661,319 | 657,007 | 497,524 | 396,000 | 102,320 | 8,841 | ... |
| 18 | Cleveland, Oh. | 638,793 | 750,879 | 876,050 | 914,808 | 381,768 | 17,034 | ... |
| 19 | Boston, Mass. | 636,725 | 641,071 | 697,197 | 801,444 | 560,892 | 136,881 | 18,320 |
| 20 | Jacksonville, Fla. | 562,283 | 528,865 | 201,030 | 204,517 | 28,429 | 1,045 | ... |
| 21 | New Orleans, La. | 559,770 | 593,471 | 627,525 | 570,445 | 287,104 | 116,375 | ... |
| 22 | San Jose, Cal. | 555,707 | 461,212 | 204,196 | 95,280 | 21,500 | ... | ... |
| 23 | Columbus, Oh. | 535,610 | 540,025 | 471,316 | 375,901 | 125,560 | 17,832 | ... |
| 24 | St. Louis, Mo. | 524,964 | 622,236 | 750,026 | 856,796 | 575,238 | 77,860 | ... |
| 25 | Denver, Col. | 488,434 | 514,678 | 493,887 | 415,786 | 133,859 | ... | ... |
| 26 | Seattle, Wash. | 487,091 | 530,831 | 557,087 | 467,591 | 80,671 | ... | ... |
| 27 | Kansas City, Mo. | 472,529 | 507,330 | 475,539 | 456,622 | 163,752 | ... | ... |
| 28 | Pittsburgh, Pa. | 458,651 | 520,089 | 604,332 | 676,806 | 321,616 | 46,601 | ... |
| 29 | Nashville-Davidson, Tenn.[3] | 446,941 | 447,877 | 170,874 | 174,307 | 80,865 | 10,165 | ... |
| 30 | Atlanta, Ga. | 436,057 | 495,039 | 487,455 | 331,314 | 89,872 | 2,572 | ... |
| 31 | Cincinnati, Oh. | 412,564 | 453,514 | 502,550 | 503,998 | 325,902 | 115,435 | ... |
| 32 | Buffalo, N.Y. | 407,160 | 462,768 | 532,759 | 580,132 | 352,387 | 42,261 | ... |
| 33 | El Paso, Tex. | 385,691 | 322,261 | 276,687 | 130,435 | 15,906 | ... | ... |
| 34 | Minneapolis, Minn. | 378,112 | 434,400 | 482,872 | 521,718 | 202,718 | ... | ... |
| 35 | Omaha, Neb. | 371,455 | 358,452 | 301,598 | 251,117 | 102,555 | ... | ... |
| 36 | Toledo, Oh. | 367,650 | 383,062 | 318,003 | 303,616 | 131,822 | 3,829 | ... |
| 37 | Oklahoma City, Okla. | 365,916 | 368,164 | 324,253 | 243,504 | 10,037 | ... | ... |
| 38 | Miami, Fla. | 365,082 | 334,859 | 291,688 | 249,276 | 1,681 | ... | ... |
| 39 | Fort Worth, Tex. | 358,364 | 393,455 | 356,263 | 278,778 | 26,688 | ... | ... |
| 40 | Portland, Ore. | 356,732 | 382,352 | 372,676 | 373,628 | 90,426 | ... | ... |
| 41 | Newark, N.J. | 339,568 | 381,930 | 405,220 | 438,776 | 246,070 | 38,894 | ... |
| 42 | Louisville, Ky. | 335,954 | 361,706 | 390,639 | 369,129 | 204,731 | 43,194 | 200 |
| 43 | Long Beach, Cal. | 335,602 | 361,427 | 344,168 | 250,767 | 2,252 | ... | ... |
| 44 | Tulsa, Okla. | 331,726 | 330,350 | 261,685 | 182,740 | 1,390 | ... | ... |
| 45 | Oakland, Cal. | 330,651 | 361,561 | 367,548 | 384,575 | 66,960 | ... | ... |
| 46 | Tucson, Ariz. | 303,137 | 267,464 | 212,892 | 45,454 | 7,531 | ... | ... |
| 47 | Austin, Tex. | 301,147 | 255,869 | 186,545 | 132,459 | 22,258 | 629 | ... |
| 48 | Baton Rouge, La. | 293,286 | 271,064 | 152,419 | 125,629 | 11,269 | 3,905 | ... |
| 49 | Norfolk, Va. | 286,694 | 307,951 | 304,869 | 213,513 | 46,624 | 14,326 | 2,959 |
| 50 | Charlotte, N.C. | 281,417 | 274,640 | 201,564 | 134,042 | 18,091 | 1,065 | ... |
| 51 | Birmingham, Ala. | 280,799 | 310,904 | 340,887 | 326,037 | 38,415 | ... | ... |
| 52 | Tampa, Fla. | 280,340 | 277,714 | 274,970 | 124,681 | 15,839 | ... | ... |
| 53 | St. Paul, Minn. | 279,535 | 309,866 | 313,411 | 311,349 | 163,065 | 1,112 | ... |
| 54 | Albuquerque, N.M. | 279,401 | 243,751 | 201,189 | 96,815 | 6,238 | ... | ... |
| 55 | Rochester, N.Y. | 267,173 | 295,011 | 318,611 | 332,488 | 162,608 | 36,403 | ... |
| 56 | Wichita, Kan. | 264,901 | 276,554 | 254,698 | 168,279 | 24,671 | ... | ... |
| 57 | Sacramento, Cal. | 260,822 | 257,105 | 191,667 | 137,572 | 29,282 | 6,820 | ... |
| 58 | Akron, Oh. | 251,747 | 275,425 | 290,351 | 274,605 | 42,728 | 3,266 | ... |
| 59 | Jersey City, N.J. | 243,756 | 260,350 | 276,101 | 299,017 | 206,433 | 6,856 | ... |
| 60 | St. Petersburg, Fla. | 234,389 | 216,159 | 181,298 | 96,738 | 1,575 | ... | ... |
| 61 | Richmond, Va. | 232,652 | 249,431 | 219,958 | 230,310 | 85,050 | 27,570 | 3,761 |
| 62 | Corpus Christi, Tex. | 214,838 | 204,525 | 167,690 | 108,287 | 4,703 | ... | ... |
| 63 | Virginia Beach, Va. | 213,954 | 172,106 | 8,091 | 5,390 | ... | ... | ... |
| 64 | Dayton, Oh. | 205,986 | 244,564 | 262,332 | 243,872 | 85,333 | 10,977 | ... |
| 65 | Mobile, Ala. | 196,441 | 190,026 | 194,856 | 129,009 | 38,469 | 20,515 | ... |
| 66 | Des Moines, Ia. | 194,168 | 201,404 | 208,982 | 177,965 | 62,139 | ... | ... |
| 67 | Anaheim, Cal. | 193,616 | 166,408 | 104,184 | 14,566 | 1,456 | ... | ... |
| 68 | Yonkers, N.Y. | 192,509 | 204,297 | 190,634 | 152,798 | 47,931 | ... | ... |
| 69 | Grand Rapids, Mich. | 187,946 | 197,649 | 177,313 | 176,515 | 87,565 | 2,686 | ... |
| 70 | Lexington-Fayette, Ky.[5] | 186,048 | 174,323 | 62,810 | 55,534 | 26,369 | 8,159 | 834 |
| 71 | Shreveport, La. | 185,711 | 182,064 | 164,372 | 127,206 | 16,013 | 1,728 | ... |
| 72 | Jackson, Miss. | 185,415 | 180,814 | 144,422 | 98,271 | 7,816 | 1,881 | ... |
| 73 | Fort Wayne, Ind. | 185,200 | 184,853 | 161,776 | 133,607 | 45,115 | 4,282 | ... |
| 74 | Knoxville, Tenn. | 183,383 | 174,587 | 111,827 | 124,769 | 32,637 | 2,076 | ... |
| 75 | Syracuse, N.Y. | 182,543 | 197,297 | 216,038 | 220,583 | 103,374 | 22,271 | ... |
| 76 | Colorado Springs, Col. | 180,472 | 141,207 | 70,194 | 45,472 | 21,038 | ... | ... |
| 77 | Santa Ana, Cal. | 177,304 | 155,710 | 100,350 | 45,533 | 4,933 | ... | ... |
| 78 | Fresno, Cal. | 176,528 | 167,427 | 133,929 | 91,699 | 12,470 | ... | ... |
| 79 | Flint, Mich. | 174,218 | 193,317 | 196,940 | 163,143 | 13,103 | ... | ... |

| Rank | City | 1975 | 1970 | 1960 | 1950 | 1900 | 1850 | 1790 |
|------|------|------|------|------|------|------|------|------|
| 80 | Spokane, Wash. | 173,698 | 170,516 | 181,608 | 161,721 | 36,848 | ... | ... |
| 81 | Warren, Mich. | 172,755 | 179,260 | 89,246 | 727 | 350 | ... | ... |
| 82 | Worcester, Mass. | 171,566 | 176,572 | 186,587 | 203,486 | 118,421 | 17,049 | 2,095 |
| 83 | Springfield, Mass. | 170,790 | 163,905 | 174,463 | 162,399 | 62,059 | 11,766 | 1,574 |
| 84 | Salt Lake City, Ut. | 169,917 | 175,885 | 189,454 | 182,121 | 53,531 | ... | ... |
| 85 | Madison, Wis. | 168,196 | 171,809 | 126,706 | 96,056 | 19,164 | 1,525 | ... |
| 86 | Kansas City, Kan. | 168,149 | 178,885 | 121,901 | 129,553 | 51,418 | ... | ... |
| 87 | Providence, R.I. | 167,724 | 179,116 | 207,493 | 248,674 | 175,597 | 41,513 | 6,380 |
| 88 | Gary, Ind. | 167,546 | 188,398 | 178,320 | 133,911 | ... | ... | ... |
| 89 | Lubbock, Tex. | 163,525 | 149,101 | 128,691 | 71,747 | ... | ... | ... |
| 90 | Lincoln, Neb. | 163,112 | 152,639 | 128,521 | 98,884 | 40,159 | ... | ... |
| 91 | Chattanooga, Tenn. | 162,842 | 167,838 | 130,009 | 131,041 | 30,154 | ... | ... |
| 92 | Anchorage, Alas. | 161,018 | 126,385 | 44,237 | 11,254 | ... | ... | ... |
| 93 | Columbus, Ga. | 160,103 | 167,377 | 116,779 | 79,611 | 17,614 | 5,942 | ... |
| 94 | Greensboro, N.C. | 155,848 | 147,948 | 119,574 | 74,389 | 10,035 | ... | ... |
| 95 | Montgomery, Ala. | 153,343 | 140,102 | 134,393 | 106,525 | 30,346 | 8,728 | ... |
| 96 | Fort Lauderdale, Fla. | 152,959 | 139,590 | 83,648 | 36,328 | ... | ... | ... |
| 97 | Paterson, N.J. | 152,568 | 144,824 | 143,663 | 139,336 | 105,171 | 11,334 | ... |
| 98 | Tacoma, Wash. | 151,267 | 154,407 | 147,979 | 143,673 | 37,714 | ... | ... |
| 99 | Riverside, Cal. | 150,612 | 140,089 | 84,332 | 46,764 | 7,973 | ... | ... |
| 100 | Huntington Beach, Cal. | 149,706 | 115,960 | 11,492 | 5,237 | ... | ... | ... |
| 101 | Las Vegas, Nev. | 146,030 | 125,787 | 64,405 | 24,624 | ... | ... | ... |
| 102 | Rockford, Ill. | 145,459 | 147,370 | 126,706 | 92,927 | 31,051 | ... | ... |
| 103 | Bridgeport, Conn. | 142,960 | 156,542 | 156,748 | 158,809 | 70,996 | 6,080 | ... |
| 104 | Little Rock, Ark. | 141,143 | 132,483 | 107,813 | 102,213 | 38,307 | 2,167 | ... |
| 105 | Winston-Salem, N.C.[4] | 141,018 | 133,683 | 111,135 | 87,811 | 13,650 | ... | ... |
| 106 | Torrance, Cal. | 139,776 | 134,968 | 100,991 | 22,241 | ... | ... | ... |
| 107 | Newport News, Va. | 138,760 | 138,177 | 113,662 | 42,358 | 19,635 | ... | ... |
| 108 | Amarillo, Tex. | 138,743 | 127,010 | 137,969 | 74,246 | 1,442 | ... | ... |
| 109 | Hartford, Conn. | 138,152 | 158,017 | 162,178 | 177,397 | 72,850 | 13,555 | 2,683 |
| 110 | Huntsville, Ala. | 136,419 | 139,282 | 72,365 | 16,437 | 8,068 | 2,863 | ... |
| 111 | Raleigh, N.C. | 134,231 | 122,830 | 93,931 | 65,679 | 13,643 | 4,518 | ... |
| 112 | Evansville, Ind. | 133,566 | 138,764 | 141,543 | 128,635 | 59,007 | 3,235 | ... |
| 113 | Glendale, Cal. | 132,360 | 132,664 | 119,442 | 95,702 | ... | ... | ... |
| 114 | Youngstown, Oh. | 132,203 | 140,909 | 166,689 | 168,330 | 44,885 | ... | ... |
| 115 | Springfield, Mo. | 131,557 | 120,096 | 95,865 | 66,731 | 23,267 | 415 | ... |
| 116 | Erie, Pa. | 127,895 | 129,265 | 138,440 | 130,803 | 52,733 | 5,858 | ... |
| 117 | New Haven, Conn. | 126,845 | 137,707 | 152,048 | 164,443 | 108,027 | 20,345 | 4,487 |
| 118 | Lansing, Mich. | 126,805 | 131,403 | 107,807 | 92,129 | 16,485 | ... | ... |
| 119 | Peoria, Ill. | 125,983 | 126,963 | 103,162 | 111,856 | 56,100 | 5,095 | ... |
| 120 | Hampton, Va. | 125,013 | 120,779 | 89,258 | 5,966 | 2,764 | ... | ... |
| 121 | Macon, Ga. | 121,157 | 122,423 | 69,764 | 70,252 | 23,272 | 5,720 | ... |
| 122 | Lakewood, Col. | 120,350 | 92,743 | ... | ... | ... | ... | ... |
| 123 | Topeka, Kan. | 119,203 | 125,011 | 119,484 | 76,791 | 33,608 | ... | ... |
| 124 | Hollywood, Fla. | 119,002 | 106,873 | 35,237 | 14,351 | ... | ... | ... |
| 125 | Garden Grove, Cal. | 118,454 | 121,155 | 84,238 | ... | ... | ... | ... |
| 126 | Aurora, Col. | 118,060 | 76,477 | 48,548 | 11,421 | 202 | ... | ... |
| 127 | Fremont, Cal. | 117,862 | 100,869 | 43,790 | ... | ... | ... | ... |
| 128 | Hialeah, Fla. | 117,682 | 102,452 | 66,972 | 19,676 | ... | ... | ... |
| 129 | Stockton, Cal. | 117,600 | 109,963 | 86,321 | 70,853 | 17,506 | ... | ... |
| 130 | South Bend, Ind. | 117,478 | 127,328 | 132,445 | 115,911 | 35,999 | 1,652 | ... |
| 131 | Livonia, Mich. | 114,881 | 110,109 | 66,702 | 17,534 | ... | ... | ... |
| 132 | Beaumont, Tex. | 113,696 | 117,548 | 119,175 | 94,014 | 9,427 | ... | ... |
| 133 | Orlando, Fla. | 113,179 | 100,081 | 88,135 | 52,367 | 2,481 | ... | ... |
| 134 | Independence, Mo. | 112,615 | 112,766 | 62,328 | 36,963 | 6,974 | ... | ... |
| 135 | Columbia, S.C. | 111,616 | 113,542 | 97,433 | 86,914 | 21,103 | 6,060 | ... |
| 136 | Garland, Tex. | 111,322 | 81,437 | 38,501 | 10,571 | 819 | ... | ... |
| 137 | Arlington, Tex. | 110,543 | 90,229 | 44,775 | 7,692 | 1,079 | ... | ... |
| 138 | Berkeley, Cal. | 110,465 | 114,091 | 111,268 | 113,805 | 13,214 | ... | ... |
| 139 | Savannah, Ga. | 110,348 | 118,349 | 149,245 | 119,638 | 54,244 | 15,312 | ... |
| 140 | Albany, N.Y. | 110,311 | 115,781 | 129,726 | 134,995 | 94,151 | 50,763 | 3,498 |
| 141 | Cedar Rapids, Ia. | 108,998 | 110,642 | 92,035 | 72,296 | 25,656 | ... | ... |
| 142 | Portsmouth, Va. | 108,674 | 110,963 | 114,773 | 80,039 | 17,427 | 8,626 | ... |
| 143 | Pasadena, Cal. | 108,220 | 112,951 | 116,407 | 104,577 | 3,117 | ... | ... |
| 144 | Waterbury, Conn. | 107,065 | 108,033 | 107,130 | 104,477 | 45,859 | ... | ... |
| 145 | Allentown, Pa. | 106,624 | 109,871 | 108,347 | 106,756 | 35,416 | 3,779 | ... |
| 146 | Pueblo, Col. | 105,312 | 99,978 | 91,181 | 63,685 | 28,157 | ... | ... |
| 147 | Alexandria, Va. | 105,220 | 110,927 | 91,023 | 61,787 | 14,528 | 8,734 | 2,748 |
| 148 | Stamford, Conn. | 105,151 | 108,798 | 92,713 | 74,293 | 15,997 | ... | ... |
| 149 | Hammond, Ind. | 104,892 | 107,983 | 111,698 | 87,594 | 12,376 | ... | ... |
| 150 | Chesapeake, Va. | 104,459 | 89,580 | 73,637 | 110,371 | ... | ... | ... |
| 151 | Elizabeth, N.J. | 104,405 | 112,654 | 107,698 | 112,817 | 52,130 | 5,583 | ... |
| 152 | Irving, Tex. | 103,703 | 98,961 | 45,985 | 2,621 | ... | ... | ... |
| 153 | Ann Arbor, Mich. | 103,542 | 100,035 | 67,340 | 48,251 | 14,509 | ... | ... |
| 154 | Sunnyvale, Cal. | 102,462 | 95,976 | 52,898 | 9,829 | ... | ... | ... |
| 155 | Cambridge, Mass. | 102,420 | 100,361 | 107,761 | 120,740 | 91,886 | 15,215 | 2,115 |
| 156 | San Bernardino, Cal. | 102,076 | 109,203 | 91,992 | 63,058 | 6,150 | ... | ... |
| 157 | Canton, Oh. | 101,852 | 110,053 | 113,631 | 118,912 | 30,667 | 2,603 | ... |
| 158 | Trenton, N.J. | 101,365 | 104,786 | 114,167 | 128,009 | 73,307 | 6,461 | ... |
| 159 | Durham, N.C. | 101,224 | 95,438 | 78,302 | 71,311 | 6,679 | ... | ... |
| 160 | Roanoke, Va. | 100,585 | 105,637 | 97,110 | 91,921 | 21,495 | 8,477 | ... |

(1) Population shown for years prior to 1900 is for New York and its boroughs as constituted under the act of consolidation in 1898. (2) Population shown is for 1862 as given in State census for that year; 1850 returns for San Francisco were destroyed by fire. (3) Figure for 1970 is for the Metropolitan Government of Nashville and Davidson County (consolidated 1963); figures for previous years are for Nashville city. (4) Winston city and Salem town consolidated as Winston-Salem city between 1910 and 1920. Figure for 1900 represents combined population of Winston and Salem. (5) Lexington city and Fayette county governments consolidated in 1974. Figure for 1970 is for combined populations; figures for previous years are for Lexington city.

# Population by Age — States: 1976

Source: U.S. Bureau of the Census (thousands)

| State | Total | Under 5 years | 5-13 years | 14-17 years | 18-20 years | 21-44 years | 45-64 years | 65 yr. and over |
|---|---|---|---|---|---|---|---|---|
| **United States** | **214,659** | **15,339** | **32,955** | **16,896** | **12,641** | **70,194** | **43,700** | **22,934** |
| **New England** | **12,221** | **753** | **1,870** | **951** | **718** | **3,949** | **2,579** | **1,400** |
| Maine | 1,070 | 76 | 168 | 86 | 62 | 330 | 219 | 128 |
| New Hampshire | 822 | 57 | 130 | 65 | 46 | 272 | 160 | 91 |
| Vermont | 476 | 34 | 77 | 38 | 30 | 157 | 87 | 53 |
| Massachusetts | 5,809 | 347 | 877 | 450 | 352 | 1,881 | 1,220 | 682 |
| Rhode Island | 927 | 57 | 139 | 70 | 53 | 286 | 205 | 116 |
| Connecticut | 3,117 | 183 | 478 | 243 | 174 | 1,023 | 688· | 330 |
| **Middle Atlantic** | **37,282** | **2,355** | **5,570** | **2,824** | **2,019** | **11,865** | **8,390** | **4,259** |
| New York | 18,084 | 1,146 | 2,705 | 1,351 | 975 | 5,856 | 3,982 | 2,068 |
| New Jersey | 7,336 | 464 | 1,127 | 570 | 384 | 2,337 | 1,668 | 787 |
| Pennsylvania | 11,862 | 745 | 1,738 | 903 | 660 | 3,672 | 2,740 | 1,404 |
| **East North Central** | **40,934** | **2,964** | **6,478** | **3,307** | **2,450** | **13,353** | **8,226** | **4,157** |
| Ohio | 10,690 | 770 | 1,674 | 849 | 644 | 3,483 | 2,182 | 1,089 |
| Indiana | 5,302 | 399 | 846 | 425 | 317 | 1,733 | 1,042 | 540 |
| Illinois | 11,229 | 814 | 1,737 | 891 | 646 | 3,652 | 2,318 | 1,171 |
| Michigan | 9,104 | 670 | 1,491 | 751 | 564 | 3,015 | 1,780 | 834 |
| Wisconsin | 4,609 | 311 | 732 | 390 | 279 | 1,470 | 904 | 523 |
| **West North Central** | **16,805** | **1,166** | **2,550** | **1,374** | **1,011** | **5,327** | **3,310** | **2,066** |
| Minnesota | 3,965 | 271 | 633 | 337 | 243 | 1,297 | 738 | 445 |
| Iowa | 2,870 | 194 | 441 | 238 | 163 | 886 | 581 | 367 |
| Missouri | 4,778 | 331 | 704 | 375 | 282 | 1,521 | 957 | 608 |
| North Dakota | 643 | 48 | 99 | 58 | 41 | 195 | 127 | 75 |
| South Dakota | 686 | 52 | 105 | 59 | 44 | 200 | 139 | 86 |
| Nebraska | 1,553 | 112 | 233 | 127 | 94 | 489 | 302 | 196 |
| Kansas | 2,310 | 158 | 334 | 180 | 144 | 738 | 466 | 289 |
| **South Atlantic** | **33,989** | **2,449** | **5,138** | **2,615** | **2,030** | **11,214** | **6,837** | **3,707** |
| Delaware | 582 | 41 | 92 | 47 | 38 | 198 | 115 | 51 |
| Maryland | 4,144 | 267 | 660 | 334 | 253 | 1,439 | 841 | 350 |
| District of Columbia | 702 | 47 | 98 | 47 | 46 | 254 | 137 | 72 |
| Virginia | 5,032 | 351 | 769 | 397 | 326 | 1,749 | 1,000 | 441 |
| West Virginia | 1,821 | 136 | 270 | 137 | 96 | 561 | 405 | 214 |
| North Carolina | 5,469 | 412 | 846 | 421 | 338 | 1,860 | 1,079 | 513 |
| South Carolina | 2,848 | 235 | 464 | 233 | 184 | 964 | 530 | 240 |
| Georgia | 4,970 | 405 | 810 | 392 | 303 | 1,702 | 915 | 443 |
| Florida | 8,421 | 555 | 1,129 | 606 | 446 | 2,487 | 1,815 | 1,383 |
| **East South Central** | **13,661** | **1,070** | **2,153** | **1,097** | **800** | **4,400** | **2,670** | **1,473** |
| Kentucky | 3,428 | 264 | 532 | 272 | 203 | 1,110 | 674 | 373 |
| Tennessee | 4,214 | 310 | 639 | 324 | 238 | 1,401 | 849 | 453 |
| Alabama | 3,665 | 285 | 581 | 298 | 216 | 1,173 | 724 | 388 |
| Mississippi | 2,354 | 211 | 401 | 202 | 142 | 715 | 423 | 259 |
| **West South Central** | **21,204** | **1,729** | **3,365** | **1,700** | **1,273** | **6,940** | **4,032** | **2,164** |
| Arkansas | 2,109 | 164 | 321 | 166 | 114 | 646 | 421 | 277 |
| Louisiana | 3,841 | 320 | 658 | 332 | 236 | 1,235 | 706 | 355 |
| Oklahoma | 2,766 | 207 | 400 | 210 | 162 | 889 | 558 | 339 |
| Texas | 12,488 | 1,038 | 1,986 | 992 | 762 | 4,170 | 2,347 | 1,193 |
| **Mountain** | **9,833** | **845** | **1,565** | **824** | **620** | **3,252** | **1,846** | **880** |
| Montana | 753 | 57 | 116 | 67 | 45 | 237 | 154 | 77 |
| Idaho | 831 | 74 | 132 | 71 | 50 | 260 | 161 | 81 |
| Wyoming | 390 | 32 | 60 | 32 | 24 | 127 | 81 | 34 |
| Colorado | 2,583 | 197 | 392 | 209 | 170 | 925 | 473 | 218 |
| New Mexico | 1,168 | 102 | 198 | 107 | 76 | 377 | 213 | 94 |
| Arizona | 2,270 | 198 | 356 | 187 | 134 | 724 | 436 | 235 |
| Utah | 1,228 | 139 | 213 | 103 | 86 | 394 | 199 | 94 |
| Nevada | 610 | 46 | 96 | 49 | 35 | 208 | 129 | 47 |
| **Pacific** | **28,730** | **2,007** | **4,267** | **2,204** | **1,721** | **9,893** | **5,809** | **2,830** |
| Washington | 3,612 | 245 | 549 | 286 | 218 | 1,235 | 706 | 374 |
| Oregon | 2,329 | 163 | 338 | 179 | 131 | 770 | 481 | 266 |
| California | 21,520 | 1,488 | 3,170 | 1,634 | 1,279 | 7,430 | 4,397 | 2,121 |
| Alaska | 382 | 37 | 71 | 34 | 30 | 147 | 54 | 9 |
| Hawaii | 887 | 74 | 139 | 70 | 62 | 310 | 171 | 60 |

## Immigration by Country of Last Residence 1820-1976

Source: U.S. Immigration and Naturalization Service (thousands)

| Country | 1820-1975, total | 1951-1960, total | 1961-1970, total | 1972 | 1973 | 1974 | 1975 | 1976[1] | Percent 1820-1975 | Percent 1961-1970 | Percent 1971-1976[1] |
|---|---|---|---|---|---|---|---|---|---|---|---|
| **All countries** | 47,099 | 2,515.5 | 3,321.7 | 384.7 | 400.1 | 394.9 | 386.2 | 502.3 | 100.0 | 100.0 | 100.0 |
| **Europe** | 35,961 | 1,325.6 | 1,123.4 | 86.3 | 91.2 | 80.4 | 72.8 | 91.6 | 76.4 | 33.8 | 21.1 |
| Austria[2] | } 4,312 | } 67.1 | 20.6 | 2.3 | 1.6 | .7 | .5 | .6 } | } 9.2 | } .6 | .3 |
| Hungary | | } 36.6 | 5.4 | .5 | 1.0 | .9 | .6 | .7 } | | } .2 | .2 |
| Belgium | 201 | 18.6 | 9.2 | .5 | .4 | .4 | .4 | .7 | .4 | .3 | .1 |
| Czechoslovakia | 136 | .9 | 3.3 | 1.2 | .9 | .4 | .3 | .4 | .3 | .1 | .2 |
| Denmark | 363 | 11.0 | 9.2 | .5 | .4 | .5 | .3 | .5 | .8 | .3 | .1 |
| Finland | 33 | 4.9 | 4.2 | .3 | .3 | .2 | .2 | .2 | .1 | .1 | .1 |
| France | 742 | 51.1 | 45.2 | 2.9 | 2.6 | 2.2 | 1.8 | 2.6 | 1.6 | 1.4 | .6 |
| Germany[2] | 6,954 | 477.8 | 190.8 | 7.8 | 7.6 | 7.2 | 5.9 | 8.6 | 14.8 | 5.7 | 1.9 |
| Great Britain[3] | 4,852 | 195.5 | 210.0 | 11.5 | 11.9 | 11.7 | 12.2 | 16.0 | 10.3 | 6.3 | 3.1 |
| Greece | 629 | 47.6 | 86.0 | 10.5 | 10.3 | 10.6 | 9.8 | 10.8 | 1.3 | 2.6 | 2.7 |
| Ireland[4] | 4,720 | 57.3 | 37.5 | 1.4 | 1.6 | 1.3 | 1.1 | 1.3 | 10.0 | 1.1 | .3 |
| Italy | 5,270 | 185.5 | 214.1 | 22.4 | 22.3 | 15.0 | 11.0 | 10.0 | 11.2 | 6.4 | 4.2 |
| Netherlands | 356 | 52.3 | 30.6 | 1.0 | 1.0 | 1.0 | .8 | 1.2 | .8 | .9 | .3 |
| Norway[2] | 855 | 22.9 | 15.5 | .4 | .4 | .4 | .4 | .4 | 1.8 | .5 | .1 |
| Poland[2] | 503 | 10.0 | 53.5 | 3.8 | 4.1 | 3.5 | 3.5 | 4.0 | 1.1 | 1.6 | .9 |
| Portugal | 411 | 19.6 | 76.1 | 9.5 | 10.0 | 10.7 | 11.3 | 13.7 | .9 | 2.3 | 2.7 |
| Spain | 246 | 7.9 | 44.7 | 4.3 | 5.5 | 4.7 | 2.6 | 3.4 | .5 | 1.3 | 1.0 |
| Sweden | 1,270 | 21.7 | 17.1 | .7 | .6 | .6 | .5 | .8 | 2.7 | .5 | .2 |
| Switzerland | 346 | 17.7 | 18.5 | 1.0 | .7 | .7 | .7 | 1.0 | .7 | .6 | .2 |
| U.S.S.R.[2,5] | 3,354 | .6 | 2.3 | .4 | .9 | .9 | 4.7 | 9.2 | 7.1 | .1 | .7 |
| Yugoslavia | 106 | 8.2 | 20.4 | 2.8 | 5.2 | 5.0 | 2.9 | 2.9 | .2 | .6 | .9 |
| Other Europe | 300 | 10.8 | 9.2 | .9 | 1.9 | 1.9 | 1.4 | 2.8 | .6 | .3 | .4 |
| **Asia** | 2,275 | 153.3 | 427.8 | 116.0 | 120.0 | 127.0 | 129.2 | 184.4 | 4.8 | 12.9 | 31.7 |
| China[6] | 488 | 9.7 | 34.8 | 8.5 | 9.2 | 10.0 | 9.2 | 12.9 | 1.0 | 1.0 | 2.4 |
| Hong Kong | [7]143 | 15.5 | 75.0 | 10.9 | 10.3 | 10.7 | 12.5 | 16.9 | .3 | 2.3 | 2.8 |
| India | 107 | 2.0 | 27.2 | 15.6 | 12.0 | 11.7 | 14.3 | 20.2 | .2 | .8 | 3.7 |
| Iran | [7]26 | 3.4 | 10.3 | 2.9 | 2.9 | 2.5 | 2.2 | 3.7 | .1 | .3 | .7 |
| Israel | [7]70 | 25.5 | 29.6 | 3.0 | 2.9 | 2.9 | 3.5 | 6.4 | .1 | .9 | .9 |
| Japan | 391 | 46.3 | 40.0 | 5.0 | 6.1 | 5.4 | 4.8 | 6.0 | .8 | 1.2 | 1.3 |
| Jordan | [7]29 | 5.8 | 11.7 | 2.4 | 2.1 | 2.5 | 2.3 | 3.1 | .1 | .3 | .6 |
| Korea | [7]150 | 6.2 | 34.5 | 18.1 | 22.3 | 27.5 | 28.1 | 37.5 | .3 | 1.0 | 6.0 |
| Lebanon | [7]35 | 4.5 | 15.2 | 3.0 | 2.6 | 3.0 | 4.0 | 6.8 | .1 | .5 | .9 |
| Philippines | [8]268 | 19.3 | 98.4 | 28.7 | 30.2 | 32.5 | 31.3 | 46.4 | .6 | 3.0 | 8.1 |
| Turkey | 382 | 3.5 | 10.1 | 1.5 | 1.4 | 1.4 | 1.1 | 1.3 | .8 | .3 | .3 |
| Other Asia | 184 | 11.7 | 40.9 | 16.3 | 18.0 | 16.9 | 15.8 | 23.3 | .4 | 1.2 | 4.0 |
| **America** | 8,348 | 996.9 | 1,716.4 | 173.2 | 179.6 | 178.8 | 174.7 | 213.5 | 17.7 | 51.7 | 44.7 |
| Argentina | [9]83 | 19.5 | 49.7 | 2.5 | 2.9 | 2.9 | 2.8 | 3.3 | .2 | 1.5 | .7 |
| Brazil | [9]52 | 13.8 | 29.3 | 1.8 | 1.8 | 1.6 | 1.4 | 1.7 | .1 | .9 | .4 |
| Canada | 4,048 | 378.0 | 413.3 | 18.6 | 14.8 | 12.3 | 11.2 | 14.9 | 8.6 | 12.4 | 3.9 |
| Columbia | [9]119 | 18.0 | 72.0 | 5.2 | 5.3 | 5.9 | 6.4 | 7.1 | .3 | 2.2 | 1.5 |
| Cuba | [10]395 | 78.9 | 208.5 | 19.9 | 22.5 | 17.4 | 25.6 | 35.0 | .8 | 6.3 | 5.8 |
| Dominican Rep. | [9]170 | 9.9 | 93.3 | 10.8 | 14.0 | 15.7 | 14.1 | 15.0 | .4 | 2.8 | 3.4 |
| Ecuador | [9]70 | 9.8 | 36.8 | 4.4 | 4.2 | 4.8 | 4.7 | 5.6 | .1 | 1.1 | 1.2 |
| El Salvador | [9]31 | 5.9 | 15.0 | 2.0 | 2.0 | 2.3 | 2.4 | 3.1 | .1 | .4 | .5 |
| Guatemala | [9]30 | 4.7 | 15.9 | 1.7 | 1.8 | 1.6 | 1.9 | 2.6 | .1 | .5 | .5 |
| Haiti | [9]65 | 4.4 | 34.5 | 5.5 | 4.6 | 3.8 | 5.0 | 6.5 | .1 | 1.0 | 1.3 |
| Honduras | [9]28 | 6.0 | 15.7 | 1.0 | 1.4 | 1.4 | 1.4 | 1.6 | .1 | .5 | .3 |
| Mexico | 1,912 | 299.8 | 453.9 | 64.2 | 70.4 | 71.9 | 62.6 | 74.5 | 4.1 | 13.7 | 16.2 |
| Panama | [9]39 | 11.7 | 19.4 | 1.6 | 1.7 | 1.7 | 1.7 | 2.3 | .1 | .6 | .4 |
| Peru | [9]35 | 7.4 | 19.1 | 1.5 | 1.8 | 2.0 | 2.3 | 3.3 | .1 | .6 | .5 |
| West Indies | 637 | 29.8 | 133.9 | 24.2 | 21.6 | 24.4 | 22.3 | 24.6 | 1.4 | 4.0 | 5.8 |
| Other America | 633 | 99.2 | 106.2 | 8.3 | 8.7 | 9.3 | 9.0 | 12.4 | 1.3 | 3.2 | 2.3 |
| **Africa** | 104 | 14.1 | 29.0 | 5.5 | 5.5 | 5.2 | 5.9 | 7.7 | .2 | .9 | 1.5 |
| **Australia and New Zealand** | 111 | 11.5 | 19.6 | 2.6 | 2.5 | 2.0 | 1.8 | 2.7 | .2 | .6 | .6 |
| All other countries | 300 | 14.0 | 5.7 | 1.2 | 1.3 | 1.4 | 1.8 | 2.4 | .6 | .2 | .4 |

(1) For 1976, 15 months, ending Sept. 30. (2) 1938-1945, Austria included with Germany; 1899-1919, Poland included with Austria-Hungary, Germany, and U.S.S.R. (3) Beginning 1952, includes data for United Kingdom not specified, formerly included with "Other Europe." (4) Comprises Eire and Northern Ireland. (5) Europe and Asia. (6) Beginning 1957, includes Taiwan. (7) Prior to 1951, included with "Other Asia." (8) Prior to 1951, Philippines included with "All other countries." (9) Prior to 1951, included with "Other America." (10) Prior to 1951, included with "West Indies."

## Poverty by Family Status, Sex, and Race

Source: U.S. Bureau of the Census
(In 1976, according to poverty level defined in table below. Thousands)

| | 1976 No. | 1976 %* | 1975 No. | 1975 %* | 1974r No. | 1974r %* | 1973 No. | 1973 %* |
|---|---|---|---|---|---|---|---|---|
| **Total poor** | **24,975** | **11.8** | **25,877** | **12.3** | **23,370** | **11.2** | **22,973** | **11.1** |
| In families | 19,632 | 10.3 | 20,789 | 10.9 | 18,817 | 9.9 | 18,299 | 9.7 |
| Head | 5,311 | 9.4 | 5,450 | 9.7 | 4,922 | 8.8 | 4,828 | 8.8 |
| Related children | 10,081 | 15.8 | 10,882 | 16.8 | 9,967 | 15.1 | 9,453 | 14.2 |
| Other relatives | 4,240 | 6.0 | 4,457 | 6.4 | 3,928 | 5.7 | 4,018 | 5.9 |
| Unrelated individuals | 5,344 | 24.9 | 5,088 | 25.1 | 4,553 | 24.1 | 4,674 | 25.6 |
| **In male-head families** | **10,603** | **6.4** | **11,943** | **7.1** | **10,355** | **6.2** | **10,121** | **6.0** |
| Head | 2,768 | 5.6 | 3,020 | 6.2 | 2,598 | 5.4 | 2,635 | 5.5 |
| Related children | 4,497 | 8.5 | 5,284 | 9.8 | 4,605 | 8.3 | 4,282 | 7.6 |
| Other relatives | 3,337 | 5.2 | 3,638 | 5.7 | 3,151 | 5.0 | 3,204 | 5.1 |
| Unrelated male individuals | 1,787 | 19.7 | 1,667 | 19.9 | 1,547 | 19.5 | 1,495 | 19.8 |
| **In female-head families** | **9,029** | **37.3** | **8,846** | **37.5** | **8,462** | **36.5** | **8,178** | **37.5** |
| Head | 2,543 | 33.0 | 2,430 | 32.5 | 2,324 | 32.1 | 2,193 | 32.2 |
| Related children | 5,583 | 52.0 | 5,597 | 52.7 | 5,361 | 51.5 | 5,171 | 52.1 |
| Other relatives | 903 | 15.7 | 819 | 15.0 | 777 | 14.1 | 814 | 16.0 |
| Unrelated female individuals | 3,557 | 28.7 | 3,422 | 28.9 | 3,007 | 27.3 | 3,179 | 29.7 |
| **Total white poor** | **16,713** | **9.1** | **17,770** | **9.7** | **15,736** | **8.6** | **15,142** | **8.4** |
| In families | 12,500 | 7.5 | 13,799 | 8.3 | 12,181 | 7.3 | 11,412 | 6.9 |
| Head | 3,560 | 7.1 | 3,838 | 7.7 | 3,352 | 6.8 | 3,219 | 6.6 |
| Female | 1,379 | 25.2 | 1,394 | 25.9 | 1,289 | 24.8 | 1,190 | 24.5 |
| Related children | 6,034 | 11.3 | 6,748 | 12.5 | 6,079 | 11.0 | 5,462 | 9.7 |
| Other relatives | 2,906 | 4.7 | 3,213 | 5.2 | 2,750 | 4.5 | 2,731 | 4.5 |
| Unrelated individuals | 4,213 | 22.7 | 3,972 | 22.7 | 3,555 | 21.8 | 3,730 | 23.7 |
| **Total black poor** | **7,595** | **31.1** | **7,545** | **31.3** | **7,182** | **30.3** | **7,388** | **31.4** |
| In families | 6,576 | 30.1 | 6,533 | 30.1 | 6,255 | 29.3 | 6,560 | 30.8 |
| Head | 1,617 | 27.9 | 1,513 | 27.1 | 1,479 | 26.9 | 1,527 | 28.1 |
| Female | 1,122 | 52.2 | 1,004 | 50.1 | 1,010 | 52.2 | 974 | 52.7 |
| Related children | 3,758 | 40.4 | 3,884 | 41.4 | 3,713 | 39.6 | 3,822 | 40.6 |
| Other relatives | 1,201 | 17.8 | 1,136 | 16.9 | 1,063 | 16.4 | 1,211 | 18.7 |
| Unrelated individuals | 1,019 | 39.8 | 1,011 | 42.1 | 927 | 39.3 | 828 | 37.9 |

r-revised. *Percent of total population in that general category who fell below poverty level. For example, of all black female heads of households in 1974, 52.2 per cent were poor.

## Estimated Poverty Level, 1977, by Family Size and Sex of Head

| Number of family members | Total | Non-Farm Total | Non-Farm Male | Non-Farm Female | Farm Total | Farm Male | Farm Female |
|---|---|---|---|---|---|---|---|
| 1 member | $3,060 | $3,070 | $3,210 | $2,970 | $2,600 | $2,700 | $2,500 |
| Under 65 yrs. | 3,140 | 3,150 | 3,270 | 3,020 | 2,710 | 2,780 | 2,570 |
| 65 yrs. and over | 2,900 | 2,910 | 2,940 | 2,900 | 2,470 | 2,500 | 2,460 |
| 2 members | 3,930 | 3,950 | 3,960 | 3,900 | 3,330 | 3,340 | 3,230 |
| Head under 65 yrs. | 4,050 | 4,070 | 4,090 | 3,970 | 3,480 | 3,480 | 3,360 |
| Head 65 yrs. and over | 3,640 | 3,670 | 3,670 | 3,650 | 3,120 | 3,120 | 3,110 |
| 3 members | 4,810 | 4,830 | 4,860 | 4,700 | 4,110 | 4,110 | 3,970 |
| 4 members | 6,160 | 6,190 | 6,190 | 6,160 | 5,270 | 5,270 | 5,150 |
| 5 members | 7,280 | 7,320 | 7,330 | 7,240 | 6,250 | 6,250 | 6,220 |
| 6 members | 8,200 | 8,260 | 8,270 | 8,210 | 7,010 | 7,010 | 7,030 |
| 7 members or more | 10,120 | 10,210 | 10,240 | 9,980 | 8,590 | 8,590 | 8,970 |

## Poverty Level, 1976

| Numbers of family members | Total | Non-Farm Total | Non-Farm Male | Non-Farm Female | Farm Total | Farm Male | Farm Female |
|---|---|---|---|---|---|---|---|
| 1 member | $2,877 | $2,884 | $3,016 | $2,788 | $2,438 | $2,532 | $2,348 |
| Under 65 yrs. | 2,954 | 2,959 | 3,069 | 2,840 | 2,542 | 2,608 | 2,413 |
| 65 years and over | 2,720 | 2,730 | 2,758 | 2,722 | 2,322 | 2,344 | 2,313 |
| 2 members | 3,688 | 3,711 | 3,721 | 3,660 | 3,128 | 3,133 | 3,033 |
| Head under 65 yrs. | 3,806 | 3,826 | 3,846 | 3,733 | 3,267 | 3,271 | 3,159 |
| Head 65 yrs. and over | 3,417 | 3,445 | 3,447 | 3,428 | 2,928 | 2,928 | 2,922 |
| 3 members | 4,515 | 4,540 | 4,565 | 4,414 | 3,858 | 3,864 | 3,734 |
| 4 members | 5,786 | 5,815 | 5,818 | 5,790 | 4,950 | 4,953 | 4,840 |
| 5 members | 6,838 | 6,876 | 6,884 | 6,799 | 5,870 | 5,871 | 5,847 |
| 6 members | 7,706 | 7,760 | 7,766 | 7,709 | 6,585 | 6,584 | 6,607 |
| 7 members or more | 9,505 | 9,588 | 9,622 | 9,375 | 8,072 | 8,068 | 8,428 |

## Income Distribution by Population Fifths

Source: U.S. Bureau of the Census

| Families, 1976 | Top income of each fifth Lowest | Top income of each fifth Second | Top income of each fifth Third | Top income of each fifth Fourth | Average Top 5% | Percent distribution of total income Lowest fifth | Percent distribution of total income Second fifth | Percent distribution of total income Third fifth | Percent distribution of total income Fourth fifth | Percent distribution of total income Highest fifth | Percent distribution of total income Top 5% |
|---|---|---|---|---|---|---|---|---|---|---|---|
| Total | $7,441 | $12,400 | $17,300 | $23,923 | $37,047 | 5.4 | 11.8 | 17.6 | 24.1 | 41.1 | 15.6 |
| White | 8,073 | 13,036 | 17,930 | 24,500 | 38,018 | 5.8 | 12.1 | 17.7 | 23.9 | 40.6 | 15.4 |
| Black and other | 4,320 | 7,529 | 12,275 | 18,271 | 28,441 | 4.6 | 9.9 | 16.5 | 25.3 | 43.7 | 15.6 |
| Black | 4,160 | 7,164 | 11,670 | 17,400 | 27,000 | 4.8 | 10.0 | 16.4 | 25.5 | 43.5 | 15.3 |

## Aid to Families with Dependent Children

Source: Office of Research and Statistics, Social Security Administration

| December, 1977 State | No. of families | Number of recipients Total[1] | Children | Payments to recipients Total amount | Average per- family | recipient | % change from Dec., 1976 No. of recip. | Amount |
|---|---|---|---|---|---|---|---|---|
| Alabama | 56,770 | 170,810 | 124,866 | $6,346,401 | $111.79 | $37.15 | 2.4 | 5.2 |
| Alaska | 4,753 | 12,485 | 8,988 | 1,390,600 | 292.57 | 111.38 | 18.5 | 21.2 |
| Arizona | 17,939 | 53,599 | 39,954 | 2,518,712 | 140.40 | 46.99 | -9.1 | -7.1 |
| Arkansas | 29,832 | 90,626 | 67,162 | 4,166,333 | 139.66 | 45.97 | -4.1 | .8 |
| California | 481,076 | 1,433,732 | 974,376 | 148,934,936 | 309.59 | 103.88 | * | 10.9 |
| Colorado | 30,922 | 87,961 | 61,738 | 6,376,050 | 206.20 | 72.49 | -4.4 | -4.9 |
| Connecticut | 44,650 | 135,796 | 95,997 | 13,822,987 | 309.59 | 101.79 | .8 | 16.9 |
| Delaware | 10,856 | 31,536 | 22,434 | 2,233,252 | 205.72 | 70.82 | 3.6 | 6.4 |
| Dist. of Columbia | 31,884 | 95,249 | 67,126 | 7,620,655 | 239.01 | 80.01 | 1.2 | 4.6 |
| Florida | 84,679 | 246,306 | 181,202 | 12,124,585 | 143.18 | 49.23 | 2.1 | 14.3 |
| Georgia | 81,457 | 225,573 | 167,404 | 8,377,743 | 102.85 | 37.14 | -11.6 | -2.1 |
| Guam | 1,348 | 4,952 | 3,695 | 263,520 | 195.49 | 53.21 | 19.2 | 23.7 |
| Hawaii | 18,196 | 58,368 | 39,369 | 6,709,095 | 368.71 | 114.94 | 5.7 | 10.0 |
| Idaho | 6,878 | 19,706 | 13,590 | 1,715,232 | 249.38 | 87.04 | 1.0 | 2.2 |
| Illinois | 221,871 | 733,639 | 522,621 | 57,635,359 | 259.77 | 78.56 | -5.5 | -7.2 |
| Indiana | 52,748 | 157,160 | 113,476 | 9,462,900 | 179.40 | 60.21 | -6.3 | * |
| Iowa | 32,095 | 94,477 | 63,536 | 8,354,517 | 260.31 | 88.43 | -1.3 | 7.9 |
| Kansas | 27,231 | 72,252 | 52,092 | 6,081,243 | 223.32 | 84.17 | -4.1 | -2.8 |
| Kentucky | 61,185 | 172,906 | 123,143 | 10,075,611 | 164.67 | 58.27 | -17.1 | -13.5 |
| Louisiana | 64,007 | 210,610 | 157,435 | 7,793,256 | 121.76 | 37.00 | -5.6 | -1.7 |
| Maine | 19,918 | 59,937 | 40,961 | 4,071,503 | 204.41 | 67.93 | -.2 | 7.8 |
| Maryland | 72,487 | 208,817 | 145,683 | 13,083,637 | 180.50 | 62.66 | -2.3 | 2.8 |
| Massachusetts | 123,101 | 367,813 | 249,010 | 37,025,468 | 300.77 | 100.66 | -.8 | -.8 |
| Michigan | 198,943 | 622,563 | 432,002 | 61,683,026 | 310.05 | 99.08 | -4.7 | 2.4 |
| Minnesota | 47,182 | 131,888 | 90,618 | 12,809,704 | 271.50 | 97.13 | .5 | 4.1 |
| Mississippi | 52,233 | 168,204 | 127,857 | 2,438,141 | 46.68 | 14.50 | -4.4 | -3.7 |
| Missouri | 73,103 | 217,143 | 155,433 | 12,552,896 | 171.72 | 57.81 | -20.3 | 2.0 |
| Montana | 6,376 | 17,828 | 12,646 | 1,167,843 | 183.16 | 65.51 | -.4 | 5.4 |
| Nebraska | 12,004 | 35,276 | 25,014 | 3,010,105 | 250.76 | 85.33 | 2.4 | 31.1 |
| Nevada | 3,906 | 10,850 | 7,748 | 653,729 | 167.37 | 60.25 | -15.4 | -7.0 |
| New Hampshire | 7,815 | 22,624 | 15,439 | 1,645,646 | 210.58 | 72.74 | -10.1 | 3.4 |
| New Jersey(e) | 143,595 | 464,316 | 324,907 | 38,997,571 | 271.58 | 83.99 | 3.7 | 7.7 |
| New Mexico | 16,687 | 51,872 | 36,906 | 2,512,364 | 150.56 | 48.43 | -7.3 | 1.4 |
| New York(e) | 364,775 | 1,172,832 | 808,510 | 133,599,474 | 366.25 | 113.91 | -5.6 | -7.1 |
| North Carolina | 72,861 | 197,804 | 144,092 | 11,408,692 | 156.58 | 57.68 | -1.3 | 6.0 |
| North Dakota | 4,806 | 13,634 | 9,618 | 1,159,187 | 241.20 | 85.02 | -.9 | .5 |
| Ohio(e) | 176,318 | 524,116 | 360,941 | 35,236,518 | 199.85 | 67.23 | -8.3 | -3.5 |
| Oklahoma | 28,580 | 87,716 | 65,007 | 5,879,075 | 205.71 | 67.02 | -1.8 | .8 |
| Oregon | 44,127 | 122,541 | 81,239 | 11,816,148 | 267.78 | 96.43 | .4 | 8.8 |
| Pennsylvania | 207,073 | 644,519 | 437,747 | 58,259,061 | 281.35 | 90.39 | -.5 | 2.0 |
| Puerto Rico[2] | 43,470 | 183,182 | 132,033 | 2,148,195 | 49.42 | 11.73 | -6.5 | 5.9 |
| Rhode Island | 17,097 | 51,535 | 35,854 | 5,314,584 | 310.85 | 103.13 | -2.2 | 18.4 |
| South Carolina | 49,121 | 142,238 | 103,029 | 4,142,386 | 84.33 | 29.12 | 2.7 | 5.9 |
| South Dakota | 7,594 | 22,169 | 16,190 | 1,324,434 | 174.41 | 59.74 | -8.7 | -16.0 |
| Tennessee | 59,926 | 167,852 | 122,505 | 6,211,683 | 103.66 | 37.01 | -17.3 | -13.7 |
| Texas | 97,736 | 307,015 | 228,578 | 10,190,927 | 104.27 | 33.19 | -4.4 | -.8 |
| Utah | 13,078 | 38,027 | 27,721 | 3,259,459 | 249.23 | 85.71 | 3.8 | 8.6 |
| Vermont | 6,297 | 19,312 | 12,838 | 1,625,164 | 258.09 | 84.15 | -15.1 | -9.1 |
| Virgin Islands[2] | 1,148 | 3,701 | 2,996 | 148,057 | 128.97 | 40.00 | -1.0 | .8 |
| Virginia | 58,795 | 166,301 | 118,766 | 10,991,257 | 186.94 | 66.09 | -4.5 | -2.2 |
| Washington | 49,715 | 143,005 | 92,985 | 13,231,166 | 266.14 | 92.52 | .2 | 8.3 |
| West Virginia | 21,667 | 63,040 | 45,363 | 4,278,112 | 197.45 | 67.86 | -2.6 | 15.1 |
| Wisconsin | 68,644 | 196,850 | 136,952 | 20,678,695 | 301.25 | 105.05 | -1.9 | 6.1 |
| Wyoming | 2,378 | 6,258 | 4,553 | 455,241 | 191.44 | 72.75 | -4.6 | -2.5 |
| **Total** | **3,532,933** | **10,760,521** | **7,551,936** | **$855,012,135** | **$242.01** | **$79.46** | **-3.8** | **1.6** |

(e) Estimated. (1) Includes as recipients the children and one or both parents or one caretaker relative other than a parent in families in which the requirements of such adults were considered in determining the amount of assistance. (2) Incomplete. Data for foster care not reported by Puerto Rico and the Virgin Islands. * Change of less than 0.05%.

## Welfare Recipients and Payments, 1955-1977

| Category | | 1955, Dec. | 1960, Dec. | 1965, Dec. | 1970, Dec. | 1975, Dec. (b) | 1976, Dec. | 1977, Dec. |
|---|---|---|---|---|---|---|---|---|
| Old age: | Recipients | 2,538,000 | 2,305,000 | 2,087,000 | 2,082,000 | 2,333,685 | 2,175,442 | 2,050,921 |
| | Total amt. | $127,003,000 | $135,759,000 | $131,674,000 | $161,642,000 | $217,002,000 | $209,553,000 | $198,166,000 |
| | Avg. amt. | $50.05 | $58.90 | $63.10 | $77.65 | $92.99 | $96.33 | $96.62 |
| | (a)Avg. real $ | 62.41 | 66.38 | 66.75 | 66.78 | 57.65 | 56.50 | 53.23 |
| AFDC: | Recipients | 2,192,000 | 3,073,000 | 4,396,000 | 9,659,000 | 11,389,000 | 11,215,463 | 10,760,521 |
| | Total amt. | $51,472,000 | $87,051,000 | $144,355,000 | $485,877,000 | $824,648,000 | $844,786,586 | $855,012,135 |
| | Avg. amt. | $23.50 | $28.35 | $32.85 | $50.30 | $72.40 | $75.32 | $79.46 |
| | (a)Avg. real $ | 29.30 | 31.95 | 34.76 | 43.26 | 44.89 | 44.18 | 43.78 |
| Blind: | Recipients | 104,000 | 107,000 | 85,100 | 81,000 | 75,315 | 77,223 | 77,362 |
| | Total amt. | $5,803,000 | $7,215,000 | $6,922,000 | $8,446,000 | $11,220,000 | $11,991,000 | $12,316,000 |
| | Avg. amt. | $55.55 | $67.45 | $81.35 | $104.35 | $148.97 | $155.28 | $159.20 |
| | (a)Avg. real $ | 69.27 | 76.02 | 86.07 | 89.74 | 92.36 | 91.07 | 87.72 |
| Disabled: | Recipients | 241,000 | 369,000 | 557,000 | 935,000 | 1,950,625 | 2,033,487 | 2,109,409 |
| | Total amt. | $11,750,000 | $20,711,000 | $37,035,000 | $91,325,000 | $279,073,000 | $299,723,000 | $317,176,000 |
| | Avg. amt. | $48.75 | $56.15 | $66.50 | $97.65 | $143.07 | $147.39 | $150.36 |
| | (a)Avg. real $ | 60.79 | 63.28 | 70.36 | 83.98 | 88.70 | 86.45 | 82.85 |

(a) Dollar amounts adjusted to represent actual purchasing power in terms of average value of dollar during 1967. (b) Administration of the public assistance programs of Old-age Assistance, Aid to the Blind, and Aid to the Disabled was transferred to the Social Security Administration by Public Law 92-603 effective 1/1/74.

## Jewish Population by Countries and Cities

Source: American Jewish Year Book 1978.

| | |
|---|---|
| Europe (including Asiatic USSR and Turkey) | 4,158,870 |
| America, North, Central, and South | 6,693,005 |
| Asia | 3,154,860 |
| Africa | 177,790 |
| Australia and New Zealand | 75,000 |
| **Total** | **14,259,525** |

### Europe

| | |
|---|---|
| Albania | 300 |
| Austria | 12,000 |
| Belgium | 41,000 |
| Bulgaria | 7,000 |
| Czechoslovakia | 12,000 |
| Denmark | 7,500 |
| Finland | 1,320 |
| France | 650,000 |
| Germany | 33,000 |
| Gibraltar | 650 |
| Great Britain | 410,000 |
| Greece | 6,000 |
| Hungary | 80,000 |
| Ireland | 4,400 |
| Italy | 38,500 |
| Luxembourg | 1,000 |
| Malta | 50 |
| Netherlands | 30,000 |
| Norway | 950 |
| Poland | 6,000 |
| Portugal | 600 |
| Romania | 60,000 |
| Spain | 9,000 |
| Sweden | 16,000 |
| Switzerland | 21,000 |
| Turkey | 27,000 |
| USSR | 2,678,000 |
| Yugoslavia | 6,000 |

### North America

| | |
|---|---|
| Canada | 305,000 |
| Mexico | 37,500 |
| United States | 5,775,935 |

### Central America and West Indies

| | |
|---|---|
| Barbados | 70 |
| Costa Rica | 2,500 |
| Cuba | 1,500 |
| Curaçao | 700 |
| Dominican Republic | 200 |
| El Salvador | 350 |
| Guatemala | 2,000 |
| Haiti | 150 |
| Honduras | 200 |
| Jamaica | 500 |
| Nicaragua | 200 |
| Panama | 2,000 |
| Trinidad | 300 |

### South America

| | |
|---|---|
| Argentina | 300,000 |
| Bolivia | 2,000 |
| Brazil | 150,000 |
| Chile | 27,000 |
| Colombia | 12,000 |
| Ecuador | 1,000 |
| Paraguay | 1,200 |
| Peru | 5,200 |
| Surinam | 500 |
| Uruguay | 50,000 |
| Venezuela | 15,000 |

### Asia

| | |
|---|---|
| Afghanistan | 200 |
| Burma | 200 |
| China | 30 |
| Cyprus | 30 |
| Hong Kong | 200 |
| India | 8,000 |
| Indonesia | 100 |
| Iran | 80,000 |
| Iraq | 350 |
| Israel | 3,059,000 |
| Japan | 400 |
| Lebanon | 400 |
| Pakistan | 250 |
| Philippines | 200 |
| Singapore | 500 |
| Syria | 4,500 |
| Yemen | 500 |

### Australia and New Zealand

| | |
|---|---|
| Australia | 70,000 |
| New Zealand | 5,000 |

### Africa

| | |
|---|---|
| Algeria | 1,000 |
| Egypt | 400 |
| Ethiopia | 28,000 |
| Kenya | 400 |
| Libya | 40 |
| Morocco | 18,000 |
| Rep. of South Africa | 118,000 |
| Rhodesia | 3,800 |
| Tunisia | 7,000 |
| Zaire | 750 |
| Zambia | 400 |

### World Cities

| City | Pop. | City | Pop. |
|---|---|---|---|
| Adelaide | 1,600 | Manchester (greater) | 35,000 |
| Amsterdam | 20,000 | Marseilles | 65,000 |
| Antwerp | 13,000 | Melbourne | 34,000 |
| Athens | 2,800 | Mexico, D. F. | 32,500 |
| Auckland | 1,500 | Milan | 9,000 |
| Basel | 2,300 | Montevideo | 48,000 |
| Belgrade | 1,500 | Montreal | 115,000 |
| Berlin (both sectors) | 6,000 | Moscow | 285,000 |
| Bogota | 5,500 | Nice | 20,000 |
| Bombay (and district) | 6,970 | Ottawa | 7,500 |
| Bordeaux | 6,400 | Paris | 300,000 |
| Brisbane | 1,500 | Perth | 3,200 |
| Brussels | 24,500 | Porto Alegre | 12,000 |
| Bucharest | 40,000 | Prague | 3,000 |
| Budapest | 65,000 | Rabat | 2,500 |
| Cape Town | 25,650 | Recife | 3,000 |
| Copenhagen | 7,000 | Rio de Janeiro | 55,000 |
| Durban | 5,990 | Rome | 10,000 |
| Geneva | 3,250 | Salisbury | 2,000 |
| Glasgow | 13,000 | San-Jose | 2,500 |
| Goteborg | 4,000 | Sao Paulo | 75,000 |
| Guatemala City | 1,500 | Sofia | 4,000 |
| Haifa | 210,000 | Stockholm | 8,000 |
| Istanbul | 23,000 | Strasbourg | 12,000 |
| Izmir | 2,500 | Sydney | 28,500 |
| Jerusalem | 266,000 | Tel Aviv-Jaffa | 394,000 |
| Johannesburg | 57,500 | Toronto | 115,000 |
| Kiev | 170,000 | Toulouse | 18,000 |
| Leeds | 18,000 | Vancouver | 12,000 |
| Leningrad | 165,000 | Valparaiso | 4,000 |
| Lima | 5,000 | Vienna | 9,000 |
| Liverpool | 6,500 | Wellington | 1,500 |
| London (greater) | 280,000 | Warsaw | 5,000 |
| Lyons | 20,000 | Winnipeg | 20,000 |
| Madrid | 3,000 | Zurich | 6,150 |
| Malmo | 4,000 | | |

### U.S. Cities and Counties

| Place | Pop. | Place | Pop. |
|---|---|---|---|
| Alameda and Contra Costa Co., Cal. | 28,000 | Detroit, Mich. | 80,000 |
| Albany, NY | 13,500 | Essex Co., NJ | 95,000 |
| Alexandria, Va. | 16,000 | Fort Lauderdale, Fla. | 40,000 |
| Atlanta, Ga. | 21,000 | Framingham, Mass. | 16,000 |
| Atlantic City, NJ | 11,800 | Hartford (inc. New Britain). | 23,500 |
| Baltimore, Md. | 92,000 | Hollywood, Fla. | 30,000 |
| Bergen Co., NJ | 100,000 | Houston, Tex. | 26,000 |
| Boston (inc. Brockton) | 170,000 | Indianapolis, Ind. | 11,000 |
| Bridgeport, Conn. | 14,500 | Kansas City, Mo. | 22,000 |
| Buffalo, NY | 22,000 | Las Vegas, Nev. | 11,000 |
| Camden, NJ | 26,000 | Long Beach, Cal. | 16,000 |
| Chicago Metro Area | 253,000 | Los Angeles Metro | 455,000 |
| Cincinnati, Oh. | 30,000 | Lynn, Mass. | 19,000 |
| Cleveland, Oh. | 80,000 | Miami, Fla. | 225,000 |
| Columbus, Oh. | 13,000 | Milwaukee, Wis. | 23,900 |
| Dallas, Tex. | 20,000 | Minneapolis, Minn. | 22,090 |
| Denver, Col. | 30,000 | Montgomery Co., Md. | 53,335 |
| Monmouth Co., NJ | 25,000 | Pittsburgh, Pa. | 51,000 |
| Morris Co., NJ | 15,000 | Prince George's Co., Md. | 16,000 |
| New Haven, Conn. | 20,000 | Raritan Valley, NJ | 18,000 |
| New Orleans, La. | 10,600 | Richmond, Va. | 10,000 |
| New York, (greater) | 1,998,000 | Rochester, NY | 21,500 |
| New York City | 1,228,000 | Rockland Co., NY | 25,000 |
| Manhattan | 171,000 | San Diego, Cal. | 21,000 |
| Brooklyn | 514,000 | San Francisco, Cal. | 75,000 |
| Bronx | 143,000 | San Jose, Cal. | 13,000 |
| Queens | 379,000 | Seattle, Wash. | 13,000 |
| Staten Island | 21,000 | Springfield, Mass. | 11,000 |
| Nassau-Suffolk | 605,000 | Stamford, Conn. | 10,800 |
| Westchester | 165,000 | St. Louis, Mo. | 60,000 |
| Ocean Co., NJ | 12,000 | Syracuse, NY | 11,000 |
| Orange Co., Cal. | 35,000 | Union Co., NJ | 39,000 |
| Palm Beach Co., Fla. | 35,000 | Washington, DC (greater) | 120,000 |
| Philadelphia Metro. | 350,000 | Worcester, Mass. | 10,000 |
| Phoenix, Ariz. | 25,000 | | |

## Black Population by States

Source: U.S. Bureau of the Census (estimated July 1, 1975)

| State | Pop. | State | Pop. | State | Pop. | State | Pop. |
|---|---|---|---|---|---|---|---|
| Ala. | 919,900 | Ill. | 1,534,300 | Mon.[1] | 1,995 | R.I. | 27,600 |
| Alas.[1] | 8,911 | Ind. | 388,600 | Neb. | 46,300 | S.C. | 867,000 |
| Ariz. | 67,400 | Ia. | 40,300 | Nev. | 35,600 | S.D.[1] | 1,627 |
| Ark. | 356,100 | Kan. | 107,700 | N.H.[1] | 2,505 | Tenn. | 651,200 |
| Cal. | 1,601,100 | Ky. | 244,300 | N.J. | 870,500 | Tex. | 1,529,600 |
| Col. | 86,800 | La. | 1,134,000 | N.M.[1] | 19,555 | Ut.[1] | 6,617 |
| Conn. | 187,900 | Me.[1] | 2,800 | N.Y. | 2,382,200 | Vt.[1] | 761 |
| Del. | 85,300 | Md. | 828,500 | N.C. | 1,193,300 | Va. | 930,800 |
| D.C. | 511,400 | Mass. | 211,200 | N.D.[1] | 2,494 | Wash. | 80,400 |
| Fla. | 1,179,000 | Mich. | 1,080,300 | Oh. | 1,033,600 | W.Va. | 64,400 |
| Ga. | 1,288,100 | Minn. | 39,900 | Okla. | 191,400 | Wis. | 143,500 |
| Ha.[1] | 7,573 | Miss. | 840,500 | Ore. | 30,700 | Wy.[1] | 2,568 |
| Ida.[1] | 2,130 | Mo. | 507,300 | Pa. | 1,049,200 | Total | 24,426,736 |

(1) 1970 census figures.

# U.S. Places of 5,000 or More Population—With ZIP and Area Codes

**Source:** U.S. Bureau of the Census; U.S. Postal Service; N.Y. Telephone Co.

The listings below show the official urban population of the United States. "Urban population" is defined as all persons living in (a) places of 5,000 inhabitants or more, incorporated as cities, villages, boroughs (except Alaska), and towns (except in New England, New York, New Jersey, Pennsylvania and Wisconsin), but excluding those persons living in the rural portions of extended cities; (b) unincorporated places of 5,000 inhabitants or more; and (c) other territory, incorporated or unincorporated, included in urbanized areas.

The non-urban portion of an extended city contains one or more areas, each at least 5 square miles in extent and with a population density of less than 100 persons per square mile. The area or areas constitute at least 25 percent of the legal city's land area of a total of 25 square miles or more.

In New England, New York, New Jersey, Pennsylvania, and Wisconsin, minor civil divisions called "towns" often include rural areas and one or more urban areas. Only the urban areas of these "towns" are included here, except in the case of New England where entire town populations, which may include some rural population, are shown in italics. Boroughs in Alaska may contain one or more urban areas which are included here.

(u) means place is unincorporated.

Where special censuses were taken after April 1, 1970, the year appears after the name of the place.

*The ZIP Code of each place appears before the name of that place, if it is obtainable. Area Code appears in parentheses after the name of the state or, if a state has more than one number, after the name of the place.*

*CAUTION—Where an asterisk (\*) appears before the ZIP Code, ask your local postmaster for the correct ZIP Code for a specific address within the place listed.*

| ZIP code | Place | 1970 | 1960 |
|---|---|---|---|
| | **Alabama (205)** | | |
| 35950 | Albertville | 9,963 | 8,250 |
| 35010 | Alexander City | 12,358 | 13,140 |
| 36420 | Andalusia | 10,092 | 10,263 |
| 36201 | Anniston | 31,533 | 33,657 |
| | Anniston Northwest(u) | 6,609 | |
| 35611 | Athens | 14,360 | 9,330 |
| 36502 | Atmore | 8,293 | 8,173 |
| 35954 | Attalla | 7,510 | 8,257 |
| 36830 | Auburn | 22,767 | 16,261 |
| 36507 | Bay Minette | 6,727 | 5,197 |
| 35020 | Bessemer | 33,428 | 33,052 |
| *35203 | Birmingham | 300,910 | 340,887 |
| 35226 | Bluff Park(u) | 12,431 | |
| 35957 | Boaz | 5,635 | 4,654 |
| 36426 | Brewton | 6,747 | 6,309 |
| 35215 | Center Point(u) | 15,675 | |
| 36611 | Chickasaw | 8,447 | 10,002 |
| 35045 | Clanton | 5,868 | 5,683 |
| 35055 | Cullman | 12,601 | 10,883 |
| 36322 | Daleville | 5,182 | 693 |
| 35601 | Decatur | 38,044 | 29,217 |
| 36732 | Demopolis | 7,651 | 7,377 |
| 36301 | Dothan | 36,733 | 31,440 |
| 36330 | Enterprise | 15,591 | 11,410 |
| 36027 | Eufaula | 9,102 | 8,357 |
| 35064 | Fairfield 1975 | 12,976 | 15,816 |
| 36532 | Fairhope | 5,720 | 4,858 |
| 35630 | Florence | 34,031 | 31,649 |
| 35214 | Forestdale(u) | 6,091 | |
| 36201 | Fort McClellan(u) | 5,334 | |
| 35967 | Fort Payne | 8,435 | 7,029 |
| 36360 | Fort Rucker(u) | 14,242 | |
| 35068 | Fultondale | 5,163 | 2,001 |
| *35901 | Gadsden | 53,928 | 58,088 |
| 35071 | Gardendale | 6,537 | 4,712 |
| 36037 | Greenville | 8,033 | 6,894 |
| 35976 | Guntersville | 6,491 | 6,592 |
| 35640 | Hartselle | 7,355 | 5,000 |
| 35209 | Homewood | 21,137 | 20,289 |
| 35020 | Hueytown 1976 | 12,127 | 5,997 |
| *35804 | Huntsville | 139,282 | 72,365 |
| 35210 | Irondale 1975 | 5,200 | 3,501 |
| 36545 | Jackson | 5,957 | 4,959 |
| 36265 | Jacksonville | 7,715 | 5,678 |
| 35501 | Jasper | 10,798 | 10,799 |
| 36863 | Lanett | 6,908 | 7,674 |
| 35094 | Leeds | 6,991 | 6,162 |
| 35228 | Midfield | 6,340 | 3,556 |
| *36601 | Mobile | 190,026 | 194,856 |
| *36104 | Montgomery | 133,386 | 134,393 |
| 35223 | Mountain Brook | 19,509 | 12,680 |
| 35660 | Muscle Shoals | 6,907 | 4,084 |
| 35476 | Northport | 9,435 | 5,245 |
| 36801 | Opelika | 19,027 | 15,678 |
| 36467 | Opp | 6,493 | 5,535 |
| 36360 | Ozark | 13,555 | 9,534 |
| 35125 | Pell City | 5,602 | 4,165 |
| 36867 | Phenix City | 25,281 | 27,630 |
| 36272 | Piedmont | 5,063 | 4,794 |
| 35127 | Pleasant Grove 1977 | 5,774 | 3,097 |
| 36067 | Prattville | 13,116 | 6,616 |
| 36610 | Prichard | 41,578 | 47,371 |
| 35901 | Rainbow City 1977 | 5,268 | |
| 36274 | Roanoke | 5,251 | 5,288 |
| 35653 | Russellville | 7,814 | 6,628 |
| 36571 | Saraland | 7,840 | 4,595 |
| 35768 | Scottsboro 1976 | 12,917 | 6,449 |
| 36701 | Selma | 27,379 | 28,385 |

| ZIP code | Place | 1970 | 1960 |
|---|---|---|---|
| 35660 | Sheffield | 13,115 | 13,491 |
| 35150 | Sylacauga | 12,255 | 12,857 |
| 35160 | Talladega | 17,662 | 17,742 |
| 35217 | Tarrant City | 6,835 | 7,810 |
| 36081 | Troy | 11,482 | 10,234 |
| 35401 | Tuscaloosa | 65,773 | 63,370 |
| 35674 | Tuscumbia | 8,828 | 8,994 |
| 36083 | Tuskegee | 11,028 | 7,240 |
| 35216 | Vestavia Hills 1975 | 14,199 | 4,029 |
| 36201 | West End-Cobb(u) | 5,515 | 5,485 |
| | **Alaska (907)** | | |
| *99502 | Anchorage | 48,081 | 44,237 |
| 99702 | Eielson(u) | 6,149 | |
| 99506 | Elmendorf(u) | 6,018 | |
| 99701 | Fairbanks | 14,771 | 13,311 |
| 99505 | Fort Richardson(u) | 10,751 | |
| 99703 | Fort Wainwright(u) | 9,097 | |
| 99801 | Juneau | 6,050 | 6,797 |
| 99901 | Ketchikan | 6,994 | 6,483 |
| 99503 | Spenard(u) | 18,089 | 9,074 |
| | **Arizona (602)** | | |
| 85321 | Ajo(u) | 5,881 | 7,049 |
| 85323 | Avondale 1975 | 6,526 | 6,151 |
| 85603 | Bisbee | 8,328 | 9,914 |
| 85222 | Casa Grande 1975 | 13,598 | 8,311 |
| 85224 | Chandler 1975 | 20,034 | 9,531 |
| 85533 | Clifton | 5,087 | 4,191 |
| 85228 | Coolidge 1975 | 6,711 | 4,990 |
| 85607 | Douglas 1975 | 12,422 | 11,925 |
| 85231 | Eloy 1975 | 6,493 | 4,899 |
| 86001 | Flagstaff 1975 | 31,370 | 18,214 |
| 85613 | Fort Huachuca(u) | 6,659 | |
| *85301 | Glendale 1975 | 67,298 | 15,893 |
| 85501 | Globe 1975 | 6,396 | 6,217 |
| 86025 | Holbrook 1975 | 5,093 | 3,438 |
| 86401 | Kingman 1975 | 7,397 | 4,525 |
| 85301 | Luke(u) | 5,047 | |
| *85201 | Mesa 1975 | 100,763 | 33,772 |
| 85621 | Nogales 1975 | 8,946 | 7,286 |
| 86040 | Page(u) 1975 | 5,892 | 2,960 |
| 85253 | Paradise Valley 1975 | 9,121 | |
| 85345 | Peoria 1975 | 7,758 | 2,593 |
| *85026 | Phoenix 1975 | 669,005 | 439,170 |
| 86301 | Prescott 1975 | 16,888 | 12,861 |
| 85546 | Safford 1975 | 5,947 | 4,648 |
| *85251 | Scottsdale 1975 | 78,065 | 10,026 |
| 85635 | Sierra Vista 1975 | 20,121 | 3,121 |
| 85713 | South Tucson 1975 | 6,218 | 7,004 |
| 85351 | Sun City(u) | 13,670 | |
| *85282 | Tempe 1975 | 93,882 | 24,897 |
| *85726 | Tucson 1975 | 298,683 | 212,892 |
| 85364 | West Yuma(u) | 5,552 | 2,781 |
| 86047 | Winslow 1975 | 7,663 | 8,862 |
| 85364 | Yuma 1975 | 30,081 | 23,974 |
| | **Arkansas (501)** | | |
| 71923 | Arkadelphia 1975 | 10,227 | 8,069 |
| 72501 | Batesville 1974 | 7,085 | 6,207 |
| 72015 | Benton 1975 | 16,724 | 10,399 |
| 72712 | Bentonville 1975 | 6,707 | 3,649 |
| *72315 | Blytheville | 24,752 | 20,797 |
| 72021 | Brinkley | 5,275 | 4,636 |
| 71701 | Camden | 15,147 | 15,828 |

| ZIP code | Place | 1970 | 1960 |
|---|---|---|---|
| 72032 | Conway 1973 | 16,772 | 9,791 |
| 71635 | Crossett 1975 | 6,295 | 5,370 |
| 71639 | Dumas 1974 | 5,290 | 3,540 |
| 71730 | El Dorado | 25,283 | 25,292 |
| 72701 | Fayetteville 1976 | 34,036 | 20,274 |
| 72335 | Forrest City | 12,521 | 10,544 |
| 72901 | Fort Smith 1977 | 68,006 | 52,991 |
| 72601 | Harrison 1975 | 8,867 | 6,580 |
| 72342 | Helena 1971 | 10,201 | 11,500 |
| 71801 | Hope | 8,830 | 8,399 |
| 71901 | Hot Springs | 35,631 | 28,337 |
| 72076 | Jacksonville 1975 | 24,391 | 14,488 |
| 72401 | Jonesboro 1974 | 28,962 | 21,418 |
| *72201 | Little Rock 1974 | 139,703 | 107,813 |
| 71753 | Magnolia 1973 | 11,527 | 10,651 |
| 72104 | Malvern 1974 | 9,848 | 9,566 |
| 72360 | Marianna | 6,196 | 5,134 |
| 71654 | McGehee 1977 | 5,413 | ..... |
| 71655 | Monticello 1972 | 7,034 | 4,412 |
| 72110 | Morrilton | 6,814 | 5,997 |
| 72653 | Mountain Home 1976 | 6,415 | 2,105 |
| 72112 | Newport 1976 | 7,854 | 7,007 |
| *72114 | North Little Rock 1976 | 62,040 | 58,032 |
| 72370 | Osceola 1975 | 8,371 | 6,189 |
| 72450 | Paragould | 10,639 | 9,947 |
| 72455 | Pocahantas 1974 | 5,448 | 3,665 |
| 71601 | Pine Bluff | 57,389 | 44,037 |
| 72756 | Rogers 1976 | 14,982 | 5,700 |
| 72801 | Russellville 1975 | 13,909 | 8,921 |
| 72143 | Searcy 1973 | 10,867 | 7,272 |
| 72116 | Sherwood 1976 | 6,744 | 1,222 |
| 72761 | Siloam Springs 1975 | 6,433 | 3,953 |
| 72204 | Southwest Little Rock(u) | 13,231 | ..... |
| 72764 | Springdale 1977 | 20,875 | 10,076 |
| 72160 | Stuttgart | 10,477 | 9,661 |
| 75501 | Texarkana 1976 | 21,192 | 19,788 |
| 72472 | Trumann 1974 | 6,402 | 4,511 |
| 72956 | Van Buren 1975 | 9,452 | 6,787 |
| 71671 | Warren | 6,433 | 6,752 |
| 72390 | West Helena 1973 | 10,838 | 8,385 |
| 72301 | West Memphis 1973 | 28,236 | 19,374 |
| 72396 | Wynne 1974 | 7,292 | 4,922 |

## California

| ZIP code | Place | | 1970 | 1960 |
|---|---|---|---|---|
| 94501 | Alameda | (415) | 70,968 | 63,855 |
| 94507 | Alamo-Danville(u) | (415) | 14,059 | ..... |
| 94706 | Albany | (415) | 14,674 | 14,804 |
| *91802 | Alhambra | (213) | 62,125 | 54,807 |
| 90249 | Alondra Park(u) | (213) | 12,193 | ..... |
| 91001 | Altadena(u) | (213) | 42,415 | 40,568 |
| 95116 | Alum Rock(u) | (408) | 18,355 | 18,942 |
| *92803 | Anaheim | (714) | 166,408 | 104,184 |
| 96007 | Anderson | (916) | 5,492 | 4,492 |
| 94509 | Antioch | (415) | 28,060 | 17,305 |
| 92307 | Apple Valley(u) | (714) | 6,702 | ..... |
| 95003 | Aptos(u) | (408) | 8,704 | ..... |
| 91006 | Arcadia | (213) | 45,138 | 41,005 |
| 95521 | Arcata | (707) | 8,985 | 5,235 |
| 95825 | Arden-Arcade(u) | (916) | 82,492 | 73,352 |
| 93420 | Arroyo Grande | (805) | 7,454 | 3,291 |
| 90701 | Artesia | (213) | 14,757 | 9,993 |
| 93203 | Arvin 1975 | (805) | 6,014 | ..... |
| 94577 | Ashland(u) | (415) | 14,810 | ..... |
| 93422 | Atascadero(u) | (805) | 10,290 | 5,983 |
| 94025 | Atherton | (415) | 8,085 | 7,717 |
| 95301 | Atwater | (209) | 11,640 | 7,318 |
| 95603 | Auburn | (916) | 6,570 | 5,586 |
| 92505 | August School Area(u) | (209) | 6,735 | ..... |
| 91746 | Avocado Heights(u) | (213) | 9,810 | ..... |
| 91702 | Azusa | (213) | 25,217 | 20,497 |
| *93302 | Bakersfield | (805) | 69,515 | 56,848 |
| 91706 | Baldwin Park | (213) | 47,285 | 33,951 |
| 92220 | Banning | (714) | 12,034 | 10,250 |
| 92311 | Barstow 1975 | (714) | 16,812 | 11,644 |
| 95903 | Beale East(u) | (916) | 7,029 | ..... |
| 92223 | Beaumont | (714) | 5,484 | 4,288 |
| 90201 | Bell | (213) | 21,836 | 19,450 |
| 90706 | Bellflower | (213) | 51,454 | 45,909 |
| 90201 | Bell Gardens | (213) | 29,308 | ..... |
| 94002 | Belmont | (415) | 23,538 | 15,996 |
| 94510 | Benicia | (415) | 7,349 | 6,070 |
| *94704 | Berkeley | (415) | 116,716 | 111,268 |
| *90213 | Beverly Hills | (213) | 33,416 | 30,817 |
| 92314 | Big Bear(u) | (714) | 5,268 | 1,562 |
| 92316 | Bloomington(u) | (714) | 11,957 | ..... |
| 92225 | Blythe | (714) | 7,047 | 6,023 |
| 92227 | Brawley 1974 | (714) | 13,940 | 12,703 |
| 92621 | Brea | (714) | 18,447 | 8,487 |
| 95605 | Broderick-Bryte(u) | (916) | 12,782 | ..... |
| *90620 | Buena Park | (714) | 63,646 | 46,401 |
| *91505 | Burbank | (213) | 88,871 | 90,155 |
| 94010 | Burlingame | (415) | 27,320 | 24,036 |
| 92231 | Calexico 1974 | (714) | 12,829 | 7,992 |
| 93725 | Calwa | (714) | 5,191 | ..... |
| 93010 | Camarillo | (213) | 19,219 | ..... |
| 93010 | Camarillo Heights(u) | (213) | 5,892 | 1,704 |
| 95124 | Cambrian Park(u) | (408) | 5,316 | ..... |
| 95008 | Campbell | (408) | 24,770 | 11,863 |
| 95010 | Capitola | (408) | 5,080 | 2,021 |
| 92007 | Cardiff-by-the-Sea(u) | (714) | 5,724 | 3,149 |
| 92008 | Carlsbad | (714) | 14,944 | 9,253 |
| 95608 | Carmichael(u) | (916) | 37,625 | 20,455 |
| 93013 | Carpinteria | (805) | 6,982 | ..... |
| 90744 | Carson | (213) | 71,150 | ..... |
| 94546 | Castro Valley(u) | (415) | 44,760 | 37,120 |
| 95307 | Ceres | (805) | 6,029 | 4,406 |
| 90701 | Cerritos | (213) | 15,856 | 3,508 |
| 94541 | Cherryland(u) | (415) | 9,969 | ..... |
| 95926 | Chico | (916) | 19,580 | 14,757 |
| 95926 | Chico North(u) | (916) | 6,856 | ..... |
| 93555 | China Lake(u) | (805) | 11,105 | ..... |
| 91710 | Chino 1975 | (714) | 27,490 | 10,305 |
| *92010 | Chula Vista | (714) | 67,901 | 42,034 |
| 95610 | Citrus Heights(u) | (714) | 21,760 | ..... |
| 91711 | Claremont | (714) | 23,464 | 12,633 |
| 93612 | Clovis | (209) | 13,856 | 5,546 |
| 92236 | Coachella | (714) | 8,353 | 4,854 |
| 93210 | Coalinga | (408) | 6,161 | 5,965 |
| 92324 | Colton 1975 | (714) | 18,686 | 18,666 |
| 90022 | Commerce | (213) | 10,536 | 9,555 |
| 90220 | Compton | (213) | 78,547 | 71,812 |
| *94520 | Concord | (415) | 85,164 | 36,000 |
| 93212 | Corcoran | (209) | 5,249 | 4,976 |
| 91720 | Corona | (714) | 27,519 | 13,336 |
| 92118 | Coronado | (714) | 20,020 | 18,039 |
| 94925 | Corte Madera | (415) | 8,464 | 5,962 |
| *92626 | Costa Mesa | (714) | 72,660 | 37,550 |
| *91722 | Covina | (213) | 30,395 | 20,124 |
| 91730 | Cucamonga(u) | (714) | 5,796 | ..... |
| 90201 | Cudahy | (213) | 16,998 | ..... |
| 90230 | Culver City | (213) | 34,451 | 32,163 |
| 95014 | Cupertino | (408) | 18,216 | 3,664 |
| 90630 | Cypress | (714) | 31,569 | 1,753 |
| *94017 | Daly City | (415) | 66,922 | 44,791 |
| 95616 | Davis | (916) | 23,488 | 8,910 |
| 90250 | Del Aire(u) | (213) | 11,930 | ..... |
| 93215 | Delano | (805) | 14,559 | 11,913 |
| 91765 | Diamond Bar(u) | (714) | 10,576 | ..... |
| 93618 | Dinuba | (805) | 7,917 | 6,103 |
| 90810 | Dominguez(u) | (213) | 5,980 | ..... |
| *90241 | Downey | (213) | 88,445 | 82,505 |
| 91010 | Duarte | (213) | 14,981 | 13,962 |
| 94566 | Dublin(u) | (415) | 13,641 | ..... |
| 90220 | East Compton(u) | (213) | 5,853 | ..... |
| 90638 | East La Mirada(u) | (213) | 12,339 | ..... |
| 90022 | East Los Angeles(u) | (213) | 105,033 | 104,270 |
| 94303 | East Palo Alto (u) | (415) | 18,099 | ..... |
| 93523 | Edwards(u) | (805) | 10,331 | ..... |
| *92020 | El Cajon | (714) | 52,273 | 37,618 |
| 92243 | El Centro 1977 | (714) | 22,660 | 16,811 |
| 94530 | El Cerrito | (415) | 25,190 | 25,437 |
| 93017 | El Encanto Heights(u) | (213) | 6,225 | ..... |
| *91734 | El Monte | (213) | 68,892 | 13,163 |
| 93446 | El Paso de Robles | (213) | 7,168 | 6,677 |
| 93030 | El Rio(u) | (805) | 6,173 | 6,966 |
| 90245 | El Segundo | (213) | 15,620 | 14,219 |
| 92630 | El Toro(u) | (714) | 8,654 | ..... |
| 92709 | El Toro Station(u) | (714) | 6,970 | ..... |
| 92024 | Encinitas(u) | (714) | 5,375 | 2,786 |
| 96001 | Enterprise(u) | (916) | 11,486 | 4,946 |
| *92025 | Escondido | (714) | 36,792 | 16,377 |
| 92501 | Eureka | (707) | 24,337 | 28,137 |
| 94930 | Fairfax | (415) | 7,661 | 5,813 |
| 94533 | Fairfield | (707) | 44,146 | 14,968 |
| 95628 | Fair Oaks(u) | (916) | 11,256 | ..... |
| 92028 | Fallbrook(u) | (714) | 6,945 | 4,814 |
| 93015 | Fillmore | (805) | 6,285 | 4,808 |
| 90001 | Florence-Graham(u) | (213) | 42,895 | 38,164 |
| 95828 | Florin(u) | (916) | 9,646 | ..... |
| 95630 | Folsom | (916) | 5,810 | 3,925 |
| 92335 | Fontana 1975 | (714) | 23,629 | 14,659 |
| 94404 | Foster City(u) | (415) | 9,522 | ..... |
| 92708 | Fountain Valley | (714) | 31,886 | 2,068 |
| 95019 | Freedom(u) | (408) | 5,563 | 4,206 |
| *94536 | Fremont | (415) | 100,869 | 43,790 |
| *93706 | Fresno | (209) | 165,972 | 133,929 |
| 92631 | Fullerton | (714) | 85,987 | 56,180 |
| *90247 | Gardena | (213) | 41,021 | 35,943 |
| 95205 | Garden Acres(u) | (213) | 7,870 | ..... |
| *92640 | Garden Grove | (714) | 120,967 | 84,238 |
| 92392 | George(u) | (714) | 7,404 | ..... |
| 95020 | Gilroy | (408) | 12,665 | 7,348 |
| 92509 | Glen Avon(u) | (714) | 5,759 | 3,416 |
| *91209 | Glendale | (213) | 132,664 | 119,442 |
| 91740 | Glendora | (213) | 31,380 | 20,752 |
| 92324 | Grand Terrace(u) | (714) | 5,901 | ..... |
| 95945 | Grass Valley | (916) | 5,149 | 4,876 |
| 92041 | Grossmont-Mt. Helix(u) | (714) | 8,723 | ..... |
| 93433 | Grover City | (805) | 5,939 | 5,210 |
| 91745 | Hacienda Heights(u) | (213) | 35,969 | ..... |
| 93230 | Hanford | (408) | 15,179 | 10,133 |
| 90716 | Hawaiian Gardens(u) | (213) | 9,052 | ..... |
| 90250 | Hawthorne | (213) | 53,304 | 33,035 |
| *94544 | Hayward | (415) | 93,058 | 72,700 |
| 95448 | Healdsburg | (707) | 5,438 | 4,816 |
| 92343 | Hemet | (714) | 12,252 | 5,416 |

| ZIP code | Place | | 1970 | 1960 | ZIP code | Place | | 1970 | 1960 |
|---|---|---|---|---|---|---|---|---|---|
| 92343 | Hemet East(u) | (714) | 8,598 | 1,936 | 93454 | Orcutt(u) | (805) | 8,500 | 1,414 |
| 90254 | Hermosa Beach | (213) | 17,412 | 16,115 | 94563 | Orinda Village(u) | (415) | 6,790 | 5,568 |
| 92346 | Highland(u) | (714) | 12,669 | ..... | 95965 | Oroville | (916) | 7,536 | 6,115 |
| 94010 | Hillsborough | (415) | 8,753 | 7,554 | 92010 | Otay-Castle Park(u) | (714) | 15,445 | ..... |
| 95023 | Hollister | (408) | 7,663 | 6,071 | *93030 | Oxnard | (805) | 71,225 | 40,265 |
| 91720 | Home Gardens(u) | (714) | 5,116 | 1,541 | 94044 | Pacifica | (415) | 36,020 | 20,995 |
| *92647 | Huntingdon Beach | (714) | 115,960 | 11,492 | 93950 | Pacific Grove | (408) | 13,505 | 12,121 |
| 90255 | Huntington Park 1976 | (213) | 37,851 | 29,920 | 93550 | Palmdale | (805) | 8,511 | ..... |
| 92032 | Imperial Beach | (714) | 20,244 | 17,773 | 92260 | Palm Desert(u) | (714) | 6,171 | 1,295 |
| 92201 | Indio | (714) | 14,459 | 9,745 | 92262 | Palm Springs | (714) | 20,936 | 13,468 |
| *90306 | Inglewood | (213) | 89,985 | 63,390 | 94302 | Palo Alto | (415) | 55,835 | 52,287 |
| 93017 | Isla Vista(u) | (408) | 13,441 | ..... | 90274 | Palos Verdes Estates | (213) | 13,631 | 9,564 |
| 94707 | Kensington(u) | (415) | 5,823 | ..... | 90274 | Palos Verdes Peninsula(u) | (213) | 38,918 | ..... |
| 91011 | La Canada-Flintridge(u) | (213) | 20,652 | 18,338 | 95569 | Paradise(u) | (916) | 14,539 | 8,268 |
| 91214 | La Crescenta-Montrose(u) | (213) | 19,620 | ..... | 90723 | Paramount | (213) | 34,734 | 27,249 |
| 90045 | Ladera Heights(u) | (213) | 6,535 | ..... | 95823 | Parkway-Sacramento So.(u) | (916) | 28,574 | ..... |
| 94549 | Lafayette | (415) | 20,484 | 7,114 | *91109 | Pasadena | (213) | 112,951 | 116,407 |
| *92651 | Laguna Beach | (714) | 14,550 | 9,288 | 92055 | Pendleton North(u) | (714) | 11,803 | ..... |
| 92653 | Laguna Hills(u) | (805) | 13,676 | ..... | 92055 | Pendleton South(u) | (714) | 13,692 | ..... |
| 90631 | La Habra | (213) | 41,350 | 25,136 | 94952 | Petaluma | (707) | 24,870 | 14,035 |
| 92040 | Lakeside(u) | (714) | 11,991 | ..... | 90660 | Pico Rivera | (213) | 54,170 | 49,150 |
| *90714 | Lakewood | (213) | 83,025 | 67,126 | 94611 | Piedmont | (415) | 10,917 | 11,117 |
| 90638 | La Mirada | (714) | 30,808 | 22,444 | 94564 | Pinole | (415) | 13,266 | 6,064 |
| 93241 | Lamont(u) | (805) | 7,007 | 6,177 | 94565 | Pittsburg | (415) | 20,651 | 19,062 |
| 93534 | Lancaster(u) | (805) | 32,728 | 26,012 | 92670 | Placentia | (714) | 21,948 | 5,861 |
| 90624 | La Palma | (714) | 9,687 | 622 | 95667 | Placerville | (916) | 5,416 | 4,439 |
| *91747 | La Puente | (213) | 31,092 | 24,723 | 94523 | Pleasant Hill | (415) | 24,610 | 23,844 |
| 94939 | Larkspur | (415) | 10,487 | 5,710 | 94566 | Pleasanton | (415) | 18,328 | 4,203 |
| 91750 | La Verne | (213) | 12,965 | 6,516 | *91766 | Pomona | (213) | 87,384 | 67,157 |
| 90260 | Lawndale | (213) | 24,825 | 21,740 | 93257 | Porterville | (209) | 12,602 | 7,991 |
| 92045 | Lemon Grove(u) | (714) | 19,690 | 19,348 | 93257 | Porterville West(u) | (209) | 6,200 | ..... |
| 93245 | Lemoore Station(u) | (408) | 9,210 | ..... | 93041 | Port Hueneme | (805) | 14,295 | 11,067 |
| 90304 | Lennox(u) | (213) | 16,121 | 31,224 | 92064 | Poway(u) | (714) | 9,422 | 1,921 |
| 95207 | Lincoln Village(u) | (916) | 6,112 | ..... | 95670 | Rancho Cordova(u) | (916) | 30,451 | 7,429 |
| 95901 | Linda(u) | (916) | 7,731 | 6,129 | 95014 | Rancho Rinconada(u) | (408) | 5,149 | ..... |
| 93247 | Lindsay | (209) | 5,206 | 5,397 | 96080 | Red Bluff | (916) | 7,676 | 7,202 |
| 95062 | Live Oak(u) (Santa Cruz) | (408) | 6,443 | 3,518 | 96001 | Redding | (916) | 16,659 | 12,773 |
| 94550 | Livermore | (415) | 37,703 | 16,058 | 92373 | Redlands 1975 | (714) | 36,566 | 26,829 |
| 95240 | Lodi 1975 | (209) | 32,065 | 22,229 | *90277 | Redondo Beach | (213) | 57,451 | 46,986 |
| 92354 | Loma Linda 1975 | (714) | 7,651 | ..... | 94064 | Redwood City | (415) | 55,686 | 46,290 |
| 90717 | Lomita | (213) | 19,784 | ..... | 93654 | Reedley | (209) | 8,131 | 5,850 |
| 93436 | Lompoc | (805) | 25,284 | 14,415 | 92376 | Rialto 1975 | (714) | 31,069 | 18,567 |
| *90801 | Long Beach | (213) | 358,879 | 344,168 | *94802 | Richmond | (415) | 79,043 | 71,854 |
| 90720 | Los Alamitos | (714) | 11,346 | 4,312 | 93555 | Ridgecrest | (805) | 7,629 | ..... |
| 94022 | Los Altos | (415) | 24,726 | 19,696 | 95673 | Rio Linda(u) | (916) | 7,524 | 2,189 |
| 94022 | Los Altos Hills | (415) | 6,865 | 3,412 | 92502 | Riverside | (714) | 140,089 | 84,332 |
| *90052 | Los Angeles | (213) | 2,809,813 | 2,479,015 | 94572 | Rodeo(u) | (415) | 5,356 | ..... |
| 93635 | Los Banos | (209) | 9,188 | 5,272 | 94928 | Rohnert Park | (707) | 6,133 | ..... |
| 95030 | Los Gatos | (408) | 23,735 | 9,036 | 90274 | Rolling Hills Estates | (213) | 6,735 | 3,941 |
| 90262 | Lynwood | (213) | 43,354 | 31,614 | 95401 | Roseland(u) | (707) | 5,105 | 4,510 |
| 93637 | Madera | (209) | 16,044 | 14,430 | 91770 | Rosemead | (213) | 40,972 | 15,476 |
| 90266 | Manhattan Beach | (213) | 35,352 | 33,934 | 95678 | Roseville | (916) | 18,221 | 13,421 |
| 95336 | Manteca 1975 | (209) | 17,488 | 8,242 | 90720 | Rossmoor(u) | (714) | 12,922 | ..... |
| 93933 | Marina(u) | (408) | 8,343 | 3,310 | 91745 | Rowland Heights(u) | (213) | 16,881 | ..... |
| 94553 | Martinez | (415) | 16,506 | 9,604 | 92509 | Rubidoux(u) | (714) | 13,969 | ..... |
| 95901 | Marysville | (916) | 9,353 | 9,553 | *95813 | Sacramento | (916) | 257,105 | 191,660 |
| 95655 | Mather(u) | (916) | 7,027 | ..... | 93901 | Salinas | (408) | 58,896 | 28,957 |
| 90270 | Maywood | (213) | 16,996 | 14,588 | 94960 | San Anselmo | (415) | 13,031 | 11,584 |
| 95023 | Meiners Oaks-Mira Monte(u) | (805) | 7,025 | ..... | *94403 | San Bernardino 1975 | (714) | 102,303 | 91,922 |
| 94025 | Menlo Park | (415) | 26,826 | 26,957 | 94066 | San Bruno | (415) | 36,254 | 29,063 |
| 95340 | Merced | (209) | 22,670 | 20,068 | | San Buenaventura (*See Ventura*) | (805) | | |
| 94030 | Millbrae | (415) | 20,792 | 15,873 | 94070 | San Carlos | (415) | 26,053 | 21,370 |
| 94941 | Mill Valley | (415) | 12,942 | 10,411 | 92672 | San Clemente | (714) | 17,063 | 8,527 |
| 95035 | Milpitas | (408) | 27,149 | 6,572 | *92109 | San Diego | (714) | 697,027 | 573,224 |
| 91752 | Mira Loma(u) | (714) | 8,482 | 3,982 | 91773 | San Dimas | (213) | 15,692 | ..... |
| 92675 | Mission Viejo(u) | (714) | 11,933 | ..... | *91340 | San Fernando | (213) | 16,571 | 16,093 |
| *95350 | Modesto | (209) | 61,712 | 36,585 | *94101 | San Francisco | (415) | 715,674 | 740,316 |
| 91016 | Monrovia | (213) | 30,562 | 27,079 | 91776 | San Gabriel | (213) | 29,336 | 22,561 |
| 91763 | Montclair 1975 | (714) | 21,072 | 13,546 | 93657 | Sanger | (209) | 10,088 | 8,072 |
| 90640 | Montebello | (213) | 42,807 | 32,097 | *95101 | San Jose | (408) | 445,779 | 204,196 |
| 93940 | Monterey | (408) | 26,302 | 22,618 | 94577 | San Leandro | (415) | 68,698 | 65,962 |
| 91754 | Monterey Park | (213) | 49,166 | 37,821 | 94580 | San Lorenzo(u) | (415) | 24,633 | 23,773 |
| 94556 | Moraga(u) | (415) | 14,205 | ..... | 93401 | San Luis Obispo | (805) | 28,036 | 20,437 |
| 95037 | Morgan Hill | (408) | 6,485 | 3,151 | 91108 | San Marino | (213) | 14,177 | 13,658 |
| 93442 | Morro Bay | (805) | 7,109 | ..... | 94402 | San Mateo | (415) | 78,991 | 69,870 |
| *94042 | Mountain View | (415) | 54,304 | 30,889 | 94806 | San Pablo | (415) | 21,461 | 19,687 |
| 92405 | Muscoy(u) | (714) | 7,091 | ..... | *94901 | San Rafael | (415) | 38,977 | 20,460 |
| 94558 | Napa | (707) | 35,978 | 22,170 | *92711 | Santa Ana | (714) | 155,762 | 100,350 |
| 92050 | National City | (714) | 43,184 | 32,771 | *93102 | Santa Barbara | (805) | 70,215 | 58,768 |
| 94560 | Newark | (415) | 27,153 | 9,884 | *95050 | Santa Clara | (408) | 87,717 | 58,880 |
| 91321 | Newhall(u) | (213) | 9,651 | 4,705 | 95060 | Santa Cruz | (408) | 32,076 | 25,596 |
| *92660 | Newport Beach | (714) | 49,422 | 26,564 | 90670 | Santa Fe Springs | (213) | 14,750 | 16,342 |
| 91760 | Norco | (714) | 14,511 | ..... | 93454 | Santa Maria | (805) | 32,749 | 20,027 |
| 94025 | North Fair Oaks(u) | (415) | 9,740 | ..... | 93454 | Santa Maria South(u) | (805) | 7,129 | ..... |
| 95660 | North Highlands(u) | (916) | 31,854 | 21,271 | *90406 | Santa Monica | (213) | 88,289 | 83,249 |
| 92135 | North Island(u) | (714) | 6,892 | ..... | 93060 | Santa Paula | (805) | 18,001 | 13,279 |
| 90650 | Norwalk | (213) | 91,827 | 88,739 | 95402 | Santa Rosa | (707) | 50,006 | 31,027 |
| 94947 | Novato | (415) | 31,006 | 17,881 | 92071 | Santee(u) | (714) | 21,107 | ..... |
| 95361 | Oakdale | (209) | 6,594 | 4,980 | 95070 | Saratoga | (408) | 27,110 | 14,861 |
| *94615 | Oakland | (415) | 361,561 | 367,548 | 94965 | Sausalito | (415) | 6,158 | 5,331 |
| 92054 | Oceanside | (714) | 40,494 | 24,971 | 90740 | Seal Beach | (213) | 24,441 | 6,994 |
| 93308 | Oildale(u) | (805) | 20,879 | ..... | 93955 | Seaside | (408) | 35,935 | 19,353 |
| 93023 | Ojai | (805) | 5,591 | 4,495 | 93662 | Selma | (209) | 7,459 | 6,934 |
| 95961 | Olivehurst(u) | (916) | 8,100 | 4,835 | 93263 | Shafter | (805) | 5,327 | 4,576 |
| *91761 | Ontario 1975 | (714) | 63,186 | 46,617 | 91024 | Sierra Madre | (213) | 12,140 | 9,732 |
| 95060 | Opal Cliffs(u) | (408) | 5,425 | 3,825 | 90806 | Signal Hill | (213) | 5,588 | 4,627 |
| *92667 | Orange | (714) | 77,365 | 26,444 | *93065 | Simi Valley | (805) | 59,832 | ..... |
| 95662 | Orangevale(u) | (916) | 16,493 | ..... | 92075 | Solana Beach(u) | (714) | 5,023 | ..... |
| | | | | | 95073 | Soquel(u) | (408) | 5,795 | ..... |

| ZIP code | Place | 1970 | 1960 |
|---|---|---|---|
| 91733 | South El Monte . . . . . . (213) | 13,443 | 4,850 |
| 90280 | South Gate . . . . . . . . . (213) | 56,909 | 53,831 |
| 95705 | South Lake Tahoe . . . . (916) | 12,921 | ..... |
| 95350 | South Modesto(u) . . . . . (209) | 7,889 | 5,465 |
| 91030 | South Pasadena . . . . . . (213) | 22,979 | 19,706 |
| 94080 | South San Francisco . . . (415) | 46,646 | 39,418 |
| 91770 | South San Gabriel(u) . . . (213) | 5,051 | ..... |
| 95144 | South San Jose Hills(u) . (213) | 12,386 | ..... |
| 90605 | South Whittier(u) . . . . . (213) | 46,641 | ..... |
| 95991 | South Yuba(u) . . . . . . . (916) | 5,352 | 3,200 |
| *92077 | Spring Valley(u) . . . . . . (714) | 29,742 | ..... |
| 94305 | Stanford(u) . . . . . . . . . (415) | 8,691 | ..... |
| 90680 | Stanton . . . . . . . . . . . (714) | 18,186 | 11,163 |
| *95204 | Stockton 1975 . . . . . . . (209) | 117,986 | 86,321 |
| 92381 | Sun City(u) . . . . . . . . . (714) | 5,519 | ..... |
| 92388 | Sun City(u) . . . . . . . . . (714) | 5,519 | ..... |
| *94086 | Sunnymead(u) . . . . . . . (714) | 6,708 | 3,404 |
| 96130 | Sunnyvale . . . . . . . . . (408) | 95,408 | 52,898 |
| 91780 | Susanville . . . . . . . . . (916) | 6,608 | 5,598 |
| 91360 | Temple City . . . . . . . . (213) | 31,034 | ..... |
| 94920 | Thousand Oaks . . . . . . (805) | 35,873 | ..... |
| *90510 | Tiburon . . . . . . . . . . . (415) | 6,209 | ..... |
| 95396 | Torrance . . . . . . . . . . (213) | 134,968 | 100,991 |
| 93274 | Tracy 1975 . . . . . . . . . (209) | 16,055 | 11,289 |
| 95380 | Tulare . . . . . . . . . . . . (209) | 16,235 | 13,824 |
| 92680 | Turlock . . . . . . . . . . . (209) | 13,992 | 9,116 |
| 92705 | Tustin . . . . . . . . . . . . (714) | 21,180 | 2,006 |
| 92277 | Tustin-Foothills(u) . . . . (714) | 26,598 | ..... |
| 92278 | Twentynine Palms(u) . . . (714) | 5,667 | ..... |
| 95482 | Twentynine Palms Base(u) (714) | 5,647 | ..... |
| 94587 | Ukiah . . . . . . . . . . . . (707) | 10,095 | 9,900 |
| 91786 | Union City . . . . . . . . . (415) | 14,724 | 6,618 |
| 95688 | Upland 1975 . . . . . . . . (714) | 37,253 | 15,918 |
| 91744 | Vacaville . . . . . . . . . . (707) | 21,690 | 10,898 |
| 94590 | Valinda(u) . . . . . . . . . (213) | 18,837 | ..... |
| 93437 | Vallejo . . . . . . . . . . . (707) | 71,710 | 60,877 |
| *93001 | Vandenburg(u) . . . . . . . (805) | 13,193 | ..... |
| 92392 | Ventura . . . . . . . . . . . (805) | 57,964 | 29,114 |
| 90043 | Victorville 1975 . . . . . . (714) | 12,344 | ..... |
| 93277 | View Park-Windsor Hills(u) (213) | 12,268 | ..... |
| 92083 | Visalia . . . . . . . . . . . (209) | 27,268 | 15,791 |
| 91789 | Vista . . . . . . . . . . . . (714) | 24,688 | ..... |
| *94596 | Walnut . . . . . . . . . . . (213) | 5,992 | 934 |
| 94596 | Walnut Creek . . . . . . . (415) | 39,844 | 9,903 |
| 90255 | Walnut Creek West(u) . . (415) | 8,330 | ..... |
| 93280 | Walnut Park(u) . . . . . . (213) | 8,925 | ..... |
| 95076 | Wasco . . . . . . . . . . . (805) | 8,269 | 6,841 |
| 90044 | Watsonville . . . . . . . . (408) | 14,569 | 13,293 |
| 90502 | West Athens(u) . . . . . . (213) | 13,311 | ..... |
| 90247 | West Carson(u) . . . . . . (213) | 15,918 | ..... |
| *91793 | West Compton(u) . . . . . (213) | 5,605 | ..... |
| 90069 | West Covina . . . . . . . . (213) | 68,034 | 50,645 |
| 92683 | West Hollywood(u) . . . . (213) | 34,622 | 28,870 |
| 95351 | Westminster . . . . . . . . (714) | 59,874 | 25,750 |
| 90047 | West Modesto(u) . . . . . (209) | 6,135 | 1,897 |
| 94565 | Westmont(u) . . . . . . . . (213) | 29,310 | ..... |
| 91746 | West Pittsburg(u) . . . . . (415) | 5,969 | 5,188 |
| 95991 | West Puente Valley(u) . . (213) | 20,733 | ..... |
| *90606 | West Sacramento(u) . . . (916) | 12,002 | ..... |
| *90605 | West Whittier-Los Nietos(u) (213) | 20,845 | ..... |
| 90222 | Whittier . . . . . . . . . . . (213) | 72,863 | 33,663 |
| 95695 | Willowbrook(u) . . . . . . (213) | 32,328 | ..... |
| 92686 | Woodland . . . . . . . . . (916) | 20,677 | 13,524 |
| 96097 | Yorba Linda . . . . . . . . (714) | 11,856 | ..... |
| 95991 | Yreka City . . . . . . . . . (916) | 5,394 | 4,759 |
| 92399 | Yuba City . . . . . . . . . (916) | 13,986 | 11,507 |
| | Yucaipa(u) . . . . . . . . . (714) | 19,284 | ..... |

## Colorado (303)

| | | | |
|---|---|---|---|
| 81101 | Alamosa . . . . . . . . . . | 6,985 | 6,205 |
| 80401 | Applewood(u) . . . . . . . | 8,214 | ..... |
| *80001 | Arvada . . . . . . . . . . . | 49,083 | 19,242 |
| 80010 | Aurora . . . . . . . . . . . | 74,974 | 48,548 |
| *80302 | Boulder . . . . . . . . . . . | 66,870 | 37,718 |
| 80601 | Brighton . . . . . . . . . . | 8,309 | 7,055 |
| 80020 | Broomfield . . . . . . . . . | 7,261 | ..... |
| 81212 | Canon City . . . . . . . . | 9,206 | 8,973 |
| *80901 | Colorado Springs . . . . . | 135,060 | 70,194 |
| 80022 | Commerce City . . . . . . | 17,407 | 8,970 |
| 81321 | Cortez . . . . . . . . . . . | 6,032 | 6,764 |
| 81625 | Craig 1977 . . . . . . . . . | 6,677 | ..... |
| *80202 | Denver . . . . . . . . . . . | 514,678 | 493,887 |
| 80022 | Derby(u) . . . . . . . . . . | 10,206 | 10,124 |
| 81301 | Durango . . . . . . . . . . | 10,333 | 10,530 |
| 80110 | Englewood . . . . . . . . . | 33,695 | 33,398 |
| 80913 | Fort Carson(u) . . . . . . | 19,399 | ..... |
| 80521 | Fort Collins . . . . . . . . | 43,337 | 25,027 |
| 80701 | Fort Morgan . . . . . . . . | 7,594 | 7,379 |
| 80401 | Golden . . . . . . . . . . . | 9,817 | 7,118 |
| 81501 | Grand Junction . . . . . . | 20,170 | 18,694 |
| 80631 | Greeley . . . . . . . . . . . | 38,902 | 26,314 |
| 81050 | La Junta . . . . . . . . . . | 7,938 | 8,026 |
| 80215 | Lakewood . . . . . . . . . | 92,743 | ..... |
| 81052 | Lamar . . . . . . . . . . . | 7,797 | 7,369 |
| 80120 | Littleton . . . . . . . . . . | 26,466 | 13,670 |
| 80120 | Littleton Southeast(u) . . | 22,899 | ..... |
| 80501 | Longmont . . . . . . . . . | 23,209 | 11,489 |
| 80537 | Loveland . . . . . . . . . . | 16,220 | 9,734 |

| ZIP code | Place | 1970 | 1960 |
|---|---|---|---|
| 81401 | Montrose . . . . . . . . . . | 6,496 | 5,044 |
| 80233 | North Glenn . . . . . . . . | 27,937 | ..... |
| 81501 | Orchard Mesa(u) . . . . . | 5,824 | 4,956 |
| *81003 | Pueblo . . . . . . . . . . . | 97,453 | 91,181 |
| 80911 | Security-Widefield(u) . . . | 15,297 | 9,017 |
| 80221 | Sherrelwood(u) . . . . . . | 18,868 | ..... |
| 80751 | Sterling . . . . . . . . . . . | 10,636 | 10,751 |
| 80906 | Stratton Meadows(u) . . . | 6,223 | ..... |
| 80229 | Thornton . . . . . . . . . . | 13,326 | 11,353 |
| 81082 | Trinidad . . . . . . . . . . | 9,901 | 10,691 |
| 80229 | Welby(u) . . . . . . . . . . | 6,875 | ..... |
| 80030 | Westminster . . . . . . . . | 19,432 | 13,850 |
| 80221 | Westminster East(u) . . . | 7,576 | ..... |
| 80033 | Wheat Ridge . . . . . . . . | 29,778 | ..... |

## Connecticut (203)

*See Note on Page 219*

| | | | |
|---|---|---|---|
| 06401 | Ansonia . . . . . . . . . . | 21,160 | 19,819 |
| 06001 | Avon . . . . . . . . . . . . | 8,352 | 5,273 |
| 06037 | Berlin . . . . . . . . . . . . | 14,149 | 11,250 |
| 06801 | Bethel . . . . . . . . . . . | 10,945 | 8,200 |
| 06002 | Bloomfield . . . . . . . . . | 18,301 | 13,613 |
| 06405 | Branford . . . . . . . . . . | 20,444 | 16,610 |
| *06602 | Bridgeport . . . . . . . . . | 156,542 | 156,748 |
| 06010 | Bristol . . . . . . . . . . . | 55,487 | 45,499 |
| 06804 | Brookfield . . . . . . . . . | 9,688 | 3,405 |
| 06019 | Canton . . . . . . . . . . . | 6,868 | 4,783 |
| 06410 | Cheshire . . . . . . . . . . | 19,051 | 13,383 |
| 06413 | Clinton . . . . . . . . . . . | 10,267 | 4,166 |
| 06413 | Clinton Center(u) . . . . . | 5,957 | 2,693 |
| 06415 | Colchester . . . . . . . . . | 6,603 | 4,648 |
| 06340 | Conning Towers-Nautilus Park(u) . | 9,791 | 3,457 |
| 06238 | Coventry . . . . . . . . . . | 8,140 | 6,356 |
| 06416 | Cromwell . . . . . . . . . . | 7,400 | 6,780 |
| 06810 | Danbury . . . . . . . . . . | 50,781 | 22,928 |
| 06820 | Darien . . . . . . . . . . . | 20,411 | 18,437 |
| 06418 | Derby . . . . . . . . . . . | 12,599 | 12,132 |
| 06424 | East Hampton . . . . . . . | 7,078 | 5,403 |
| 06108 | East Hartford . . . . . . . | 57,583 | 43,977 |
| 06512 | East Haven . . . . . . . . | 25,120 | 21,388 |
| 06333 | East Lyme . . . . . . . . . | 11,399 | 6,782 |
| 06016 | East Windsor . . . . . . . | 8,513 | 7,500 |
| 06029 | Ellington . . . . . . . . . . | 7,707 | 5,580 |
| 06082 | Enfield . . . . . . . . . . . | 46,189 | 31,464 |
| 06430 | Fairfield . . . . . . . . . . | 56,487 | 46,183 |
| 06032 | Farmington . . . . . . . . | 14,390 | 10,813 |
| 06033 | Glastonbury . . . . . . . . | 20,651 | 14,497 |
| 06035 | Granby . . . . . . . . . . . | 6,150 | 4,968 |
| 06830 | Greenwich . . . . . . . . . | 59,755 | 53,793 |
| 06351 | Griswold . . . . . . . . . . | 7,763 | 6,472 |
| 06340 | Groton . . . . . . . . . . . | 38,244 | 29,937 |
| 06340 | Groton Borough . . . . . . | 8,933 | 10,111 |
| 06437 | Guilford . . . . . . . . . . | 12,033 | 7,913 |
| 06514 | Hamden . . . . . . . . . . | 49,357 | 41,056 |
| *06101 | Hartford . . . . . . . . . . | 158,017 | 162,178 |
| 06239 | Killingly . . . . . . . . . . | 13,573 | 11,298 |
| 06339 | Ledyard . . . . . . . . . . | 14,837 | 5,395 |
| 06759 | Litchfield . . . . . . . . . . | 7,399 | 6,264 |
| 06443 | Madison . . . . . . . . . . | 9,768 | 4,567 |
| 06040 | Manchester . . . . . . . . | 47,994 | 42,102 |
| 06250 | Mansfield . . . . . . . . . | 19,994 | 14,638 |
| 06450 | Meriden . . . . . . . . . . | 55,959 | 51,850 |
| 06762 | Middlebury . . . . . . . . . | 5,542 | 4,785 |
| 06457 | Middletown . . . . . . . . | 36,924 | 33,250 |
| 06460 | Milford . . . . . . . . . . . | 50,858 | 41,662 |
| 06468 | Monroe . . . . . . . . . . . | 12,047 | 6,402 |
| 06353 | Montville . . . . . . . . . . | 15,662 | 7,759 |
| 06770 | Naugatuck . . . . . . . . . | 23,034 | 19,511 |
| *06050 | New Britain . . . . . . . . | 83,441 | 82,201 |
| 06840 | New Canaan . . . . . . . . | 17,455 | 13,466 |
| 06810 | New Fairfield . . . . . . . . | 6,991 | 3,355 |
| *06510 | New Haven . . . . . . . . | 137,707 | 152,048 |
| 06111 | Newington . . . . . . . . . | 26,037 | 17,664 |
| 06320 | New London . . . . . . . . | 31,630 | 34,182 |
| 06776 | New Milford . . . . . . . . | 14,601 | 8,318 |
| 06470 | Newtown . . . . . . . . . . | 16,942 | 11,373 |
| 06471 | North Branford . . . . . . | 10,778 | 6,771 |
| 06473 | North Haven . . . . . . . . | 22,194 | 15,935 |
| 06856 | Norwalk . . . . . . . . . . | 79,113 | 67,775 |
| 06360 | Norwich . . . . . . . . . . | 41,739 | 38,506 |
| 06475 | Old Saybrook . . . . . . . | 8,468 | 5,274 |
| 06477 | Orange . . . . . . . . . . . | 13,524 | 8,547 |
| 02891 | Pawcatuck(u) . . . . . . . | 5,255 | 4,389 |
| 06374 | Plainfield . . . . . . . . . . | 11,957 | 8,884 |
| 06062 | Plainville . . . . . . . . . . | 16,733 | 13,149 |
| 06782 | Plymouth . . . . . . . . . . | 10,321 | 8,981 |
| 06480 | Portland . . . . . . . . . . | 8,812 | 7,496 |
| 06712 | Prospect . . . . . . . . . . | 6,543 | 4,367 |
| 06260 | Putnam . . . . . . . . . . . | 6,918 | 6,952 |
| | Putnam . . . . . . . . . . . | 8,598 | 8,412 |
| 06875 | Redding . . . . . . . . . . | 5,590 | 3,359 |
| 06877 | Ridgefield . . . . . . . . . | 18,188 | 8,165 |
| | Ridgefield Center(u) . . . | 5,878 | 2,954 |
| 06067 | Rocky Hill . . . . . . . . . | 11,103 | 7,404 |
| 06483 | Seymour . . . . . . . . . . | 12,776 | 10,100 |
| 06484 | Shelton . . . . . . . . . . . | 27,165 | 18,190 |
| 06070 | Simsbury . . . . . . . . . . | 17,475 | 10,138 |

| ZIP code | Place | 1970 | 1960 |
|---|---|---|---|
| 06071 | Somers. | 6,893 | 3,702 |
| 06488 | Southbury | 7,852 | 5,918 |
| 06489 | Southington | 30,946 | 22,797 |
| 06074 | South Windsor. | 15,553 | 9,460 |
| 06075 | Stafford | 8,680 | 7,476 |
| *06904 | Stamford. | 108,798 | 92,713 |
| 06378 | Stonington | 15,940 | 13,969 |
| 06268 | Storrs(u) | 10,691 | 6,054 |
| 06497 | Stratford | 49,775 | 45,012 |
| 06078 | Suffield. | 8,634 | 6,779 |
| 06787 | Thomaston. | 6,233 | 5,850 |
| 06277 | Thompson. | 7,580 | 6,217 |
| 06084 | Tolland. | 7,857 | 2,950 |
| 06790 | Torrington. | 31,952 | 30,045 |
| 06611 | Trumbull. | 31,394 | 20,379 |
| 06060 | Vernon | 27,237 | 16,961 |
| 06492 | Wallingford. | 35,714 | 29,920 |
| *06701 | Waterbury. | 108,033 | 107,130 |
| 06385 | Waterford. | 17,227 | 15,391 |
| 06795 | Watertown. | 18,610 | 14,837 |
| 06107 | West Hartford. | 68,031 | 62,382 |
| 06516 | West Haven. | 52,851 | 43,002 |
| 06880 | Weston. | 7,417 | 4,039 |
| 06880 | Westport. | 27,414 | 20,955 |
| 06109 | Wethersfield. | 26,662 | 20,561 |
| 06226 | Willimantic. | 14,402 | 13,881 |
| 06897 | Wilton. | 13,572 | 8,026 |
| 06094 | Winchester. | 11,106 | 10,496 |
| 06280 | Windham. | 19,626 | 16,973 |
| 06095 | Windsor. | 22,502 | 19,467 |
| 06096 | Windsor Locks. | 15,080 | 11,411 |
| 06098 | Winsted. | 8,954 | 8,136 |
| 06716 | Wolcott. | 12,495 | 8,889 |
| 06525 | Woodbridge. | 7,673 | 5,182 |
| 06798 | Woodbury. | 5,869 | 3,910 |

### Delaware (302)

| ZIP code | Place | 1970 | 1960 |
|---|---|---|---|
| 19711 | Brookside Park(u) | 7,856 | ...... |
| 19703 | Claymont(u) | 6,584 | ...... |
| 19901 | Dover. | 17,488 | 7,250 |
| 19901 | Dover Base(u) | 8,106 | ...... |
| 19805 | Elsmere. | 8,415 | 7,319 |
| 19963 | Milford | 5,314 | 5,795 |
| 19711 | Newark. | 21,298 | 11,404 |
| 19973 | Seaford | 5,537 | 4,430 |
| *19899 | Wilmington. | 80,386 | 95,827 |
| 19720 | Wilmington Manor —Chelsea—Leedom | 10,134 | ...... |

### District of Columbia (202)

| ZIP code | Place | 1970 | 1960 |
|---|---|---|---|
| *20013 | Washington | 756,510 | 763,956 |
|  | Northeast. | 184,439 | 197,536 |
|  | Northwest. | 347,337 | 374,165 |
|  | Southeast. | 194,365 | 173,988 |
|  | Southwest. | 30,369 | 18,267 |

### Florida

| ZIP code | Place | 1970 | 1960 |
|---|---|---|---|
| 33821 | Arcadia. | (813) | 5,658 | 5,889 |
| 33823 | Auburndale | (813) | 5,386 | 5,595 |
| 33825 | Avon Park | (813) | 6,712 | 6,073 |
| 32807 | Azalea Park(u) | (305) | 7,367 | ...... |
| 33830 | Bartow | (813) | 12,891 | 12,849 |
| 33505 | Bayshore Gardens(u). | (813) | 9,255 | 2,297 |
| 33430 | Belle Glade | (305) | 15,949 | 11,273 |
| 33432 | Boca Raton | (305) | 28,506 | 6,961 |
| 33435 | Boynton Beach | (305) | 18,115 | 10,467 |
| *33506 | Bradenton | (813) | 21,040 | 19,380 |
| 33511 | Brandon(u). | (813) | 12,749 | 1,665 |
| 33314 | Broadview Park-RockHill(u) | (305) | 6,049 | ...... |
| 33311 | Browardale(u) | (305) | 17,444 | ...... |
| 33142 | Browns Village(u) | (305) | 23,442 | ...... |
| 33054 | Bunche Park(u) | (305) | 5,773 | ...... |
| 33904 | Cape Coral(u) | (813) | 10,193 | ...... |
| 33055 | Carol City(u). | (305) | 27,361 | 21,749 |
| 33023 | Carver Ranch Estates(u). | (305) | 5,515 | ...... |
| 32707 | Casselberry. | (305) | 9,438 | 2,463 |
| 33505 | Cedar Hammock-Bradenton South(u) | (813) | 10,820 | ...... |
| 32324 | Chattahoochee | (904) | 7,944 | 9,699 |
| *33515 | Clearwater. | (813) | 52,074 | 34,653 |
| 32922 | Cocoa | (305) | 16,110 | 12,294 |
| 32931 | Cocoa Beach | (305) | 9,952 | 3,475 |
| 32922 | Cocoa West(u) | (305) | 5,779 | 3,975 |
| 33064 | Collier Manor-Cresthaven(u) | (305) | 7,202 | ...... |
| 32809 | Conway(u) | (305) | 8,642 | ...... |
| 33134 | Coral Gables | (305) | 42,494 | 34,793 |
| 32536 | Crestview | (904) | 7,952 | 7,467 |
| 33157 | Cutler Ridge(u) | (305) | 17,441 | 7,005 |
| 33004 | Dania | (305) | 9,013 | 7,065 |
| 33314 | Davie | (305) | 5,859 | ...... |
| *32015 | Daytona Beach | (904) | 45,327 | 37,395 |
| 33441 | Deerfield Beach. | (305) | 16,662 | 9,573 |
| 32720 | De Land | (904) | 11,641 | 10,775 |
| 33444 | Delray Beach | (305) | 19,915 | 12,230 |
| 33528 | Dunedin | (813) | 17,639 | 8,444 |
| 33610 | East Lake-Orient Park(u) | (813) | 5,711 | ...... |
| 33940 | East Naples (u) | (813) | 6,152 | ...... |
| 32542 | Eglin(u). | (904) | 7,769 | ...... |
| 33614 | Egypt Lake(u) | (813) | 7,556 | ...... |
| 33533 | Englewood(u) | (813) | 5,108 | 2,877 |
| 32726 | Eustis. | (904) | 6,722 | 6,189 |
| 32034 | Fernandina Beach | (904) | 6,955 | 7,276 |
| 33030 | Florida City | (305) | 5,133 | 4,114 |
| *33310 | Fort Lauderdale. | (305) | 139,590 | 82,648 |
| *33902 | Fort Myers. | (813) | 27,351 | 22,523 |
| 33901 | Fort Myers Southwest(u). | (813) | 5,086 | ...... |
| 33450 | Fort Pierce. | (305) | 29,721 | 25,256 |
| 32548 | Fort Walton Beach | (904) | 19,994 | 12,147 |
| *32601 | Gainesville. | (904) | 64,510 | 29,701 |
| 32960 | Gifford(u). | (305) | 5,772 | 3,509 |
| 33170 | Goulds(u) | (305) | 6,690 | 5,121 |
| 33581 | Gulf Gate Estates(u) | (813) | 5,874 | ...... |
| 33737 | Gulfport | (813) | 9,976 | 9,730 |
| 33844 | Haines City | (813) | 8,956 | 9,135 |
| 33009 | Hallandale | (305) | 23,849 | 10,483 |
| *33010 | Hialeah. | (305) | 102,452 | 66,972 |
| 32805 | Holden Heights(u). | (305) | 6,206 | ...... |
| 32017 | Holly Hill | (904) | 8,191 | 4,182 |
| *33022 | Hollywood | (305) | 106,873 | 35,237 |
| 33030 | Homestead | (305) | 13,674 | 9,152 |
| 33030 | Homestead Base(u) | (305) | 8,257 | ...... |
| 32937 | Indian Harbour Beach | (305) | 5,371 | ...... |
| *32201 | Jacksonville | (305) | 528,865 | 201,030 |
| 33156 | Kendall(u) | (305) | 35,497 | ...... |
| 33040 | Key West | (305) | 29,312 | 33,956 |
| 32741 | Kissimmee | (305) | 7,119 | 6,845 |
| 33618 | Lake Carroll(u) | (813) | 5,577 | ...... |
| 32055 | Lake City. | (813) | 10,575 | 9,465 |
| 32208 | Lake Forest(u) | (305) | 5,216 | ...... |
| 33803 | Lake Holloway(u) | (305) | 6,227 | 3,172 |
| *33802 | Lakeland. | (813) | 41,552 | 41,350 |
| 33612 | Lake Magdalene(u). | (813) | 9,266 | ...... |
| 33403 | Lake Park | (305) | 6,993 | 3,589 |
| 33853 | Lake Wales | (813) | 8,240 | 8,346 |
| 33460 | Lake Worth | (305) | 23,714 | 20,758 |
| 33460 | Lantana | (305) | 7,126 | 5,021 |
| 33540 | Largo. | (813) | 22,031 | 5,302 |
| 33313 | Lauderdale Lakes. | (813) | 10,577 | ...... |
| 33313 | Lauderhill | (305) | 8,465 | 132 |
| 32748 | Leesburg. | (305) | 11,869 | 11,172 |
| 33614 | Leto(u) | (904) | 8,458 | ...... |
| 33064 | Lighthouse Point | (813) | 9,071 | 2,453 |
| 32060 | Live Oak. | (305) | 6,830 | 6,544 |
| 32810 | Lockhart(u) | (904) | 5,809 | ...... |
| 32751 | Maitland | (305) | 7,157 | 3,570 |
| 33063 | Margate. | (305) | 8,867 | 2,646 |
| 32446 | Marianna. | (305) | 6,741 | 7,152 |
| *32901 | Melbourne. | (904) | 40,236 | 11,982 |
| 33314 | Melrose Park (u) | (305) | 6,111 | ...... |
| 32952 | Merritt Island(u) | (305) | 29,233 | 3,554 |
| *33152 | Miami. | (305) | 334,859 | 291,688 |
| 33139 | Miami Beach. | (305) | 87,072 | 63,145 |
| 33153 | Miami Shores | (305) | 9,425 | 8,865 |
| 33166 | Miami Springs | (305) | 13,279 | 11,229 |
| 32570 | Milton. | (904) | 5,360 | 4,108 |
| 32754 | Mims(u) | (305) | 8,309 | 1,307 |
| 33023 | Miramar | (305) | 23,997 | 5,485 |
| 32506 | Myrtle Grove(u) | (904) | 16,186 | ...... |
| 33940 | Naples | (813) | 12,042 | 4,655 |
| 33552 | New Port Richey 1973 | (813) | 7,137 | 3,520 |
| 32069 | New Smyrna Beach | (904) | 10,580 | 8,781 |
| 33308 | North Andrews Terrace(u) | (305) | 7,082 | ...... |
| 33903 | North Fort Myers(u) | (813) | 8,798 | ...... |
| 33314 | North Lauderdale 1974. | (305) | 9,285 | ...... |
| 33161 | North Miami | (305) | 34,767 | 28,708 |
| 33160 | North Miami Beach | (305) | 30,544 | 21,405 |
| 33408 | North Palm Beach | (305) | 9,035 | 2,684 |
| 33169 | Norwood(u) | (305) | 14,973 | ...... |
| 33308 | Oakland Park | (813) | 16,261 | 5,331 |
| 32670 | Ocala. | (904) | 22,583 | 13,598 |
| 32548 | Ocean City(u) | (904) | 5,267 | ...... |
| 33054 | Opa-Locka 1976 | (305) | 13,129 | 9,810 |
| 32073 | Orange Park. | (904) | 7,619 | 2,624 |
| *32802 | Orlando | (305) | 99,006 | 88,135 |
| 32074 | Ormond Beach | (904) | 14,063 | 8,658 |
| 32074 | Ormond By-The-Sea(u) | (904) | 6,002 | 3,476 |
| 33476 | Pahokee | (305) | 5,663 | 4,709 |
| 32077 | Palatka | (904) | 9,444 | 11,028 |
| 32905 | Palm Bay | (305) | 7,176 | 2,808 |
| 33480 | Palm Beach | (305) | 9,086 | 6,055 |
| 33403 | Palm Beach Gardens | (305) | 6,102 | 1 |
| 33561 | Palmetto. | (813) | 7,422 | 5,556 |
| 33619 | Palm River-Clair Mel(u) | (813) | 8,536 | ...... |
| 32401 | Panama City. | (904) | 32,096 | 33,275 |
| 33023 | Pembroke Pines. | (305) | 15,496 | 1,429 |
| *32502 | Pensacola | (904) | 59,507 | 56,752 |
| 33157 | Perrine(u) | (305) | 10,257 | 6,424 |
| 32347 | Perry | (904) | 7,701 | 8,080 |
| 32808 | Pine Hills(u) | (305) | 13,882 | ...... |
| 33565 | Pinellas Park | (813) | 22,287 | 10,848 |
| 33566 | Plant City | (813) | 15,451 | 15,711 |
| 33314 | Plantation | (813) | 23,523 | 4,772 |
| *33060 | Pompano Beach | (305) | 38,587 | 15,992 |

| ZIP code | Place | | 1970 | 1960 |
|---|---|---|---|---|
| 33064 | Pompano Beach Highlands(u) | (305) | 5,014 | ..... |
| 33950 | Port Charlotte(u) | (813) | 10,769 | 3,197 |
| 32351 | Quincy | (904) | 8,334 | 8,874 |
| 33156 | Richmond Heights(u) | (305) | 6,663 | 4,311 |
| 33312 | Riverland Village– | | | |
| | Lauderdale Isles(u) | (305) | 5,512 | ..... |
| 33404 | Riviera Beach | (305) | 21,401 | 13,046 |
| 32955 | Rockledge | (305) | 10,523 | 3,481 |
| 32084 | St. Augustine | (904) | 12,352 | 14,734 |
| 32769 | St. Cloud | (305) | 5,041 | 4,353 |
| *33730 | St. Petersburg 1976 | (813) | 236,413 | 181,298 |
| 33706 | St. Petersburg Beach | (813) | 8,024 | 6,268 |
| 32771 | Sanford | (904) | 17,393 | 19,175 |
| *33578 | Sarasota | (813) | 40,237 | 34,083 |
| 33579 | Sarasota Southeast(u) | (813) | 6,885 | ..... |
| 32937 | Satelite Beach | (305) | 6,558 | 825 |
| 33870 | Sebring | (813) | 7,223 | 6,939 |
| 33143 | South Miami | (305) | 11,780 | 9,846 |
| 33157 | South Miami Heights(u) | (305) | 10,395 | ..... |
| 32937 | South Patrick Shores(u) | (305) | 10,313 | ..... |
| 32401 | Springfield | (904) | 5,949 | 4,628 |
| 33304 | Sunrise 1972 | (305) | 11,693 | ..... |
| 33614 | Sweetwater Creek(u) | (813) | 19,453 | ..... |
| *32303 | Tallahassee | (904) | 72,624 | 48,174 |
| 33313 | Tamarac 1975 | | 22,614 | ..... |
| *33602 | Tampa | (813) | 277,753 | 274,970 |
| 33589 | Tarpon Springs | (813) | 7,118 | 6,768 |
| 33617 | Temple Terrace | (813) | 7,347 | 3,812 |
| 33905 | Tice(u) | (813) | 7,254 | 4,377 |
| 32780 | Titusville | (305) | 30,515 | 6,410 |
| 33740 | Treasure Island | (813) | 6,120 | 3,506 |
| 33620 | University (Hillsborough)(u) | (813) | 10,039 | ..... |
| 32580 | Valparaiso | (904) | 6,504 | 5,975 |
| 33595 | Venice | (813) | 6,648 | 3,444 |
| 32960 | Vero Beach | (305) | 11,908 | 8,849 |
| 32960 | Vero Beach South(u) | (305) | 7,330 | ..... |
| 32507 | Warrington(u) | (904) | 15,848 | 16,752 |
| 33505 | West Bradenton(u) | (813) | 6,162 | ..... |
| 32446 | West End(u) | (904) | 5,289 | 3,124 |
| 33144 | West Miami | (305) | 5,494 | 5,296 |
| *33401 | West Palm Beach | (305) | 57,375 | 56,208 |
| 32505 | West Pensacola(u) | (904) | 20,924 | ..... |
| 33880 | West Winter Haven(u) | (813) | 7,716 | 5,050 |
| 33165 | Westwood Lakes(u) | (305) | 12,811 | 22,517 |
| 33305 | Wilton Manors | (813) | 10,948 | 8,257 |
| 32787 | Winter Garden, 1976 | (305) | 6,238 | 5,513 |
| 33880 | Winter Haven | (813) | 16,136 | 16,277 |
| 32789 | Winter Park | (305) | 21,895 | 17,162 |

## Georgia

| | | | | |
|---|---|---|---|---|
| *31701 | Albany | (912) | 72,623 | 55,890 |
| 31709 | Americus | (912) | 16,091 | 13,472 |
| 30601 | Athens | (404) | 44,342 | 31,355 |
| *30304 | Atlanta | (404) | 497,421 | 487,455 |
| *30901 | Augusta | (404) | 59,864 | 70,626 |
| 31717 | Bainbridge | (912) | 10,887 | 12,714 |
| 31723 | Blakely | (912) | 5,267 | 3,580 |
| 31520 | Brunswick | (912) | 19,585 | 21,703 |
| 31728 | Cairo | (912) | 8,061 | 7,427 |
| 30117 | Carrollton | (404) | 13,520 | 10,973 |
| 30120 | Cartersville | (404) | 10,138 | 8,668 |
| 30125 | Cedartown | (404) | 9,253 | 9,340 |
| 30341 | Chamblee | (404) | 9,127 | 6,635 |
| 31014 | Cochran | (912) | 5,161 | 4,714 |
| 30337 | College Park | (404) | 18,203 | 23,469 |
| *31902 | Columbus | (404) | 155,028 | 116,779 |
| 31015 | Cordele | (912) | 10,733 | 10,609 |
| 30209 | Covington | (404) | 10,267 | 8,167 |
| 30720 | Dalton | (404) | 18,872 | 17,868 |
| 31742 | Dawson | (912) | 5,383 | 5,062 |
| *30030 | Decatur | (404) | 21,943 | 22,026 |
| 31520 | Dock Junction(u) | (912) | 6,009 | 5,417 |
| 30340 | Doraville | (404) | 9,157 | 4,437 |
| 31533 | Douglas | (912) | 10,195 | 8,736 |
| 30134 | Douglasville | (404) | 5,472 | 4,462 |
| 31021 | Dublin | (912) | 15,143 | 13,814 |
| 31023 | Eastman | (912) | 5,416 | 5,118 |
| 30344 | East Point | (404) | 39,315 | 35,633 |
| 30635 | Elberton | (404) | 6,438 | 7,107 |
| 31750 | Fitzgerald | (912) | 8,187 | 8,781 |
| 30050 | Forest Park | (404) | 19,994 | 14,201 |
| 31905 | Fort Benning(u) | (404) | 27,495 | ..... |
| 30905 | Fort Gordon(u) | (404) | 15,589 | ..... |
| 30741 | Fort Oglethorpe 1974 | (404) | 5,083 | 2,251 |
| 31030 | Fort Valley | (912) | 9,251 | 8,310 |
| 30501 | Gainesville | (404) | 15,459 | 16,523 |
| 31408 | Garden City | (404) | 5,790 | 5,451 |
| 30223 | Griffin | (404) | 22,734 | 21,735 |
| 30354 | Hapeville | (404) | 9,567 | 10,082 |
| 31545 | Jesup | (912) | 9,091 | 7,304 |
| 30728 | La Fayette | (404) | 6,044 | 5,588 |
| 30240 | La Grange | (404) | 23,301 | 23,632 |
| 30245 | Lawrenceville | (404) | 5,115 | 3,804 |
| *31201 | Macon | (912) | 122,423 | 69,764 |
| 30060 | Marietta | (404) | 27,216 | 25,565 |
| 31034 | Midway-Hardwick(u) | (404) | 14,047 | 16,909 |
| 31061 | Milledgeville | (404) | 11,601 | 11,117 |
| 30655 | Monroe | (404) | 8,071 | 6,826 |

| ZIP code | Place | | 1970 | 19 |
|---|---|---|---|---|
| 31768 | Moultrie | (912) | 14,400 | 15,7 |
| 30263 | Newnan | (404) | 11,205 | 12,1 |
| 31069 | Perry | (912) | 7,771 | 6,0 |
| 30161 | Rome | (404) | 30,759 | 32,2 |
| 30075 | Roswell | (404) | 5,430 | 2,9 |
| 31522 | St. Simons(u) | (912) | 5,346 | 3,1 |
| 31082 | Sandersville | (404) | 5,546 | 5,4 |
| *31401 | Savannah | (912) | 118,349 | 149,2 |
| 30080 | Smyrna | (404) | 19,157 | 10,1 |
| 30458 | Statesboro | (912) | 14,616 | 8,3 |
| 30747 | Summerville | (404) | 5,043 | 4,7 |
| 30401 | Swainsboro | (912) | 7,325 | 5,9 |
| 30286 | Thomaston | (404) | 10,024 | 9,3 |
| 31792 | Thomasville | (912) | 18,155 | 18,2 |
| 30824 | Thomson | (404) | 6,503 | 4,5. |
| 31794 | Tifton | (912) | 12,179 | 9,9 |
| 30577 | Toccoa | (404) | 6,971 | 7,3 |
| 31601 | Valdosta | (912) | 32,303 | 30,6 |
| 30474 | Vidalia | (912) | 9,507 | 7,5 |
| 31093 | Warner Robins | (912) | 33,491 | 18,6 |
| 31501 | Waycross | (912) | 18,996 | 20,9 |
| 30830 | Waynesboro | (912) | 5,530 | 5,3 |
| 30680 | Winder | (404) | 6,605 | 5,5. |
| 31406 | Windsor Forest(u) | (912) | 7,288 | |

## Hawaii (808)

| | | | |
|---|---|---|---|
| 96701 | Aiea | 12,560 | 11,8 |
| 96706 | Ewa Beach | 7,765 | 4,6 |
| 96701 | Halawa Heights | 5,809 | |
| 96824 | Hickam Housing | 7,352 | |
| 96720 | Hilo | 26,353 | 25,9 |
| *96813 | Honolulu | 324,871 | 294,1 |
| 96732 | Kahului | 8,280 | 4,2 |
| 96734 | Kailua | 33,783 | 25,6 |
| 96744 | Kaneohe | 29,903 | 14,4 |
| 96734 | Maunawili | 5,303 | |
| 96734 | Mokapu | 7,860 | |
| 96792 | Nanakuli | 6,506 | 2,7 |
| 96782 | Pacific Palisades | 7,846 | |
| 96782 | Pearl City | 19,552 | |
| 96786 | Schofield Barracks | 13,516 | |
| 96786 | Wahiawa | 17,598 | 15,5 |
| 96793 | Wailuku | 7,979 | 6,9 |
| 96797 | Waipahu | 24,150 | |

## Idaho (208)

| | | | |
|---|---|---|---|
| 83221 | Blackfoot | 8,716 | 7,3 |
| *83708 | Boise City | 74,990 | 34,4 |
| 83318 | Burley 1976 | 8,773 | 7,5 |
| 83605 | Caldwell | 14,219 | 12,2 |
| 83814 | Coeur D'Alene 1975 | 17,994 | 14,2 |
| 83401 | Idaho Falls 1975 | 37,126 | 33,1 |
| 83338 | Jerome 1974 | 5,625 | 4,7 |
| 83501 | Lewiston | 26,068 | 12,6 |
| 83843 | Moscow | 14,146 | 11,1 |
| 83647 | Mountain Home 1974 | 6,755 | 5,9 |
| 83648 | Mountain Home Base(u) | 6,038 | |
| 83651 | Nampa | 20,768 | 18,8 |
| 83661 | Payette 1976 | 5,235 | 4,4 |
| 83201 | Pocatello 1975 | 42,565 | 28,5 |
| 83440 | Rexburg 1973 | 9,761 | 4,7 |
| 83301 | Twin Falls | 21,914 | 20,1 |

## Illinois

| | | | | |
|---|---|---|---|---|
| 60101 | Addison 1976 | (312) | 28,019 | 6,74 |
| 60658 | Alsip 1974 | (312) | 15,694 | 3,77 |
| 62002 | Alton 1975 | (618) | 35,741 | 43,04 |
| *60004 | Arlington Heights 1976 | (312) | 71,012 | 27,8 |
| *60507 | Aurora | (312) | 74,182 | 63,71 |
| 60010 | Barrington 1976 | (312) | 9,410 | 5,43 |
| 60607 | Bartonville 1976 | (309) | 6,145 | 7,25 |
| 60510 | Batavia 1974 | (312) | 10,816 | 7,49 |
| 62618 | Beardstown | (217) | 6,222 | 6,29 |
| *62220 | Belleville | (618) | 41,699 | 37,26 |
| 60104 | Bellwood 1971 | (312) | 21,473 | 20,72 |
| 61008 | Belvidere | (815) | 14,061 | 11,24 |
| 60106 | Bensenville 1976 | (312) | 13,876 | 9,14 |
| 62812 | Benton | (618) | 6,833 | 7,02 |
| 60162 | Berkeley | (312) | 6,152 | 5,79 |
| 60402 | Berwyn | (312) | 52,502 | 54,22 |
| 62010 | Bethalto 1976 | (618) | 8,373 | 3,23 |
| 60108 | Bloomingdale 1975 | (312) | 8,788 | 1,26 |
| 61701 | Bloomington 1975 | (309) | 41,409 | 36,27 |
| 60406 | Blue Island 1975 | (312) | 21,190 | 19,61 |
| 60439 | Bolingbrook 1976 | (217) | 31,143 | |
| 60914 | Bourbonnais 1976 | (815) | 10,620 | 3,33 |
| 60915 | Bradley 1972 | (815) | 10,631 | 8,08 |
| 60455 | Bridgeview 1972 | (312) | 13,495 | 7,33 |
| 60153 | Broadview 1971 | (312) | 9,470 | 8,58 |
| 60513 | Brookfield | (312) | 20,284 | 20,42 |
| 60090 | Buffalo Grove 1974 | (312) | 18,390 | 1,49 |
| 60459 | Burbank 1976 | (312) | 29,448 | |
| 62206 | Cahokia | (815) | 20,649 | 15,82 |
| 62914 | Cairo | (618) | 6,277 | 9,34 |

| ZIP code | Place | 1970 | 1960 | ZIP code | Place | 1970 | 1960 |
|---|---|---|---|---|---|---|---|
| 60409 | Calumet City 1976 (312) | 38,761 | 25,000 | 61301 | La Salle (312) | 10,736 | 11,897 |
| 60643 | Calumet Park (312) | 10,069 | 8,448 | 62439 | Lawrenceville (618) | 5,863 | 5,492 |
| 61520 | Canton (309) | 14,217 | 13,588 | 60439 | Lemont 1976 (312) | 5,197 | 3,397 |
| 62901 | Carbondale (815) | 22,816 | 14,670 | 61048 | Libertyville 1976. (312) | 14,730 | 8,560 |
| 62626 | Carlinville (217) | 5,675 | 5,440 | 62656 | Lincoln (217) | 17,582 | 16,890 |
| 62821 | Carmi (618) | 6,033 | 6,152 | 60645 | Lincolnwood (312) | 12,529 | 11,744 |
| 60187 | Carol Stream 1975 (312) | 8,537 | 836 | 60532 | Lisle 1976 (312) | 5,329 | 4,219 |
| 60110 | Carpentersville 1975 (312) | 24,869 | 17,424 | 62056 | Litchfield (217) | 7,190 | 7,330 |
| 62801 | Centralia (815) | 15,217 | 13,904 | 60441 | Lockport (815) | 9,985 | 7,560 |
| 62206 | Centreville (618) | 11,378 | 12,769 | 60148 | Lombard 1974 (312) | 36,839 | 22,561 |
| 61820 | Champaign (217) | 56,532 | 49,583 | 61111 | Loves Park 1975 (815) | 12,198 | 9,086 |
| 61920 | Charleston 1975 (217) | 18,162 | 10,505 | 60534 | Lyons (312) | 11,124 | 9,936 |
| 62233 | Chester (618) | 5,310 | 4,460 | 60050 | McHenry 1976 (815) | 8,459 | 3,336 |
| *60607 | Chicago (312) | 3,366,957 | 3,550,404 | 61455 | Macomb 1975 (309) | 23,495 | 12,135 |
| 60411 | Chicago Heights (312) | 40,900 | 34,331 | 62060 | Madison (618) | 7,042 | 6,861 |
| 60415 | Chicago Ridge 1974 (312) | 12,576 | 5,748 | 62959 | Marion 1975 (618) | 13,176 | 11,274 |
| 61523 | Chillicothe 1976. (309) | 5,982 | 3,054 | 60426 | Markham (312) | 15,987 | 11,704 |
| 60650 | Cicero (312) | 67,058 | 69,130 | 62258 | Mascoutah (618) | 5,045 | 3,625 |
| 60514 | Clarendon Hills (312) | 6,750 | 5,885 | 60443 | Matteson 1974 (312) | 6,086 | 3,225 |
| 61727 | Clinton 1977 (217) | 7,604 | 7,355 | 61938 | Mattoon 1972 (217) | 19,270 | 19,088 |
| 62234 | Collinsville 1977 (618) | 18,909 | 14,217 | 60153 | Maywood (312) | 29,019 | 27,330 |
| 60477 | Country Club Hills 1975 (312) | 12,239 | 3,421 | *60160 | Melrose Park (312) | 22,716 | 22,291 |
| 60525 | Countryside 1973 (312) | 5,434 | ...... | 61342 | Mendota (815) | 6,902 | 6,154 |
| 60435 | Crest Hill 1973 (815) | 8,322 | 5,887 | 62960 | Metropolis (618) | 6,940 | 7,339 |
| 60445 | Crestwood 1973 (312) | 7,557 | 1,213 | 60445 | Midlothian 1974 (312) | 14,241 | 6,605 |
| 61611 | Creve Coeur 1975 (309) | 6,594 | 6,684 | 61264 | Milan 1975. (309) | 6,036 | 3,065 |
| 60014 | Crystal Lake 1975 (815) | 16,797 | 8,314 | 61265 | Moline (309) | 46,237 | 42,705 |
| 61832 | Danville (717) | 42,570 | 41,856 | 61462 | Monmouth (309) | 11,022 | 10,372 |
| 60559 | Darien 1973 (312) | 9,770 | ...... | 60450 | Morris 1977 (815) | 8,563 | 7,935 |
| *62521 | Decatur (217) | 90,397 | 78,004 | 61550 | Morton 1975. (309) | 13,243 | 5,325 |
| 60015 | Deerfield 1972 (312) | 18,867 | 11,786 | 60053 | Morton Grove (312) | 26,369 | 20,533 |
| 60115 | De Kalb (815) | 32,949 | 18,486 | 62863 | Mount Carmel (618) | 8,096 | 8,594 |
| *60016 | Des Plaines 1973 (312) | 55,594 | 34,886 | 60056 | Mount Prospect 1975 (312) | 48,975 | 18,906 |
| 61021 | Dixon (815) | 18,147 | 19,565 | 62864 | Mount Vernon 1977. (618) | 16,861 | 15,566 |
| 60419 | Dolton 1974 (312) | 26,321 | 18,746 | 60060 | Mundelein 1976 (312) | 17,315 | 10,526 |
| 60515 | Downers Grove 1975. (312) | 38,776 | 21,154 | 62966 | Murphysboro 1976 (618) | 9,629 | 8,673 |
| 62832 | Du Quoin (618) | 6,691 | 6,558 | 60540 | Naperville 1977 (312) | 35,062 | 12,933 |
| 62024 | East Alton (618) | 7,309 | 7,630 | 60648 | Niles 1971 (312) | 32,432 | 20,393 |
| 60411 | East Chicago Heights 1973 (312) | 6,405 | 3,270 | 61761 | Normal 1975 (309) | 32,091 | 13,357 |
| 61244 | East Moline (309) | 20,832 | 16,732 | 60656 | Norridge 1971 (312) | 18,043 | 14,087 |
| 61611 | East Peoria 1977 (309) | 21,710 | 12,310 | 60542 | North Aurora 1974 (312) | 5,344 | 2,088 |
| *62201 | East St. Louis (618) | 69,996 | 81,712 | 60062 | Northbrook 1977 (312) | 30,067 | 11,635 |
| 62025 | Edwardsville 1977 (618) | 11,982 | 9,996 | 60064 | North Chicago (312) | 47,275 | 22,938 |
| 62401 | Effingham 1976 (217) | 10,772 | 8,172 | 60093 | Northfield (312) | 5,010 | 4,005 |
| 60120 | Elgin 1976 (312) | 61,116 | 49,447 | 60164 | Northlake (312) | 14,212 | 12,318 |
| 60007 | Elk Grove Village 1974. (312) | 25,303 | 6,608 | 61111 | North Park(u) (815) | 15,679 | ...... |
| 60126 | Elmhurst (312) | 48,887 | 36,991 | 60546 | North Riverside 1971 (312) | 7,849 | 7,989 |
| 60635 | Elmwood Park (309) | 26,160 | 23,866 | 60521 | Oak Brook 1975 (312) | 5,251 | 324 |
| *60204 | Evanston (312) | 80,113 | 79,283 | 60452 | Oak Forest 1975 (312) | 22,220 | 3,724 |
| 60642 | Evergreen Park 1971. (312) | 25,981 | 24,178 | *60454 | Oak Lawn 1974. (312) | 62,245 | 27,471 |
| 62837 | Fairfield (312) | 5,897 | 6,362 | *60301 | Oak Park (312) | 62,511 | 61,093 |
| 62208 | Fairview Heights (618) | 8,625 | ...... | 62269 | O'Fallon 1973 (618) | 10,045 | 4,018 |
| 62839 | Flora (618) | 5,283 | 5,331 | 62450 | Olney (618) | 8,974 | 8,780 |
| 60422 | Flossmoor 1975. (312) | 8,310 | 4,624 | 60462 | Orland Park 1975. (312) | 13,137 | 2,592 |
| 60130 | Forest Park (312) | 15,472 | 14,452 | 61350 | Ottawa (815) | 18,716 | 19,408 |
| 60131 | Franklin Park (312) | 20,348 | 18,322 | 60067 | Palatine 1976 (312) | 31,447 | 11,504 |
| 61032 | Freeport (815) | 27,736 | 26,628 | 60463 | Palos Heights 1977 (312) | 10,725 | 3,775 |
| 60030 | Gages Lake-Wildwood(u) (312) | 5,337 | ...... | 60465 | Palos Hills 1972. (312) | 9,778 | 3,766 |
| 61401 | Galesburg 1971 (309) | 34,501 | 37,243 | 62557 | Pana (217) | 6,326 | 6,432 |
| 61254 | Geneseo 1977 (815) | 6,154 | 5,169 | 61944 | Paris (217) | 9,971 | 9,823 |
| 60134 | Geneva 1974 (312) | 9,140 | 7,646 | 60466 | Park Forest (312) | 30,638 | 29,993 |
| 60022 | Glencoe (312) | 10,675 | 10,472 | 60466 | Park Forest South 1976 (312) | 5,832 | ...... |
| 60137 | Glendale Heights 1977 (312) | 18,364 | 173 | 60068 | Park Ridge (312) | 42,614 | 32,659 |
| 60137 | Glen Ellyn 1977 (312) | 24,785 | 15,972 | 61554 | Pekin 1974. (309) | 32,315 | 28,146 |
| 60025 | Glenview 1975 (312) | 30,551 | 18,132 | *61601 | Peoria (309) | 126,963 | 103,162 |
| 60425 | Glenwood 1975 (312) | 10,409 | 882 | 61614 | Peoria Heights 1975 (309) | 8,239 | 7,064 |
| 62040 | Granite City (618) | 40,685 | 40,073 | 61354 | Peru (815) | 11,772 | 10,460 |
| 60030 | Grayslake 1974. (312) | 5,062 | 3,762 | 61764 | Pontiac (815) | 10,595 | 8,435 |
| 60103 | Hanover Park 1972. (312) | 19,609 | 451 | 60469 | Posen (312) | 5,498 | 4,517 |
| 62946 | Harrisburg (618) | 9,535 | 9,171 | 61356 | Princeton 1976 (815) | 7,025 | 6,250 |
| 60033 | Harvard 1976 (312) | 5,156 | 4,248 | 60070 | Prospect Heights(u) (312) | 13,333 | ...... |
| 60426 | Harvey (312) | 34,636 | 29,071 | 62301 | Quincy (217) | 45,288 | 43,793 |
| 60656 | Harwood Heights 1971. (312) | 8,837 | 5,688 | 60656 | Rantoul (217) | 25,562 | 22,116 |
| 60429 | Hazel Crest 1974. (312) | 13,229 | 6,205 | 60471 | Richton Park 1976 (312) | 8,016 | 933 |
| 62948 | Herrin (618) | 9,623 | 9,474 | 60627 | Riverdale (312) | 15,806 | 12,008 |
| 60457 | Hickory Hills 1974. (312) | 13,951 | 2,707 | 60305 | River Forest (312) | 13,402 | 12,695 |
| 62249 | Highland (618) | 5,981 | 4,943 | 60171 | River Grove (312) | 11,465 | 8,464 |
| 60035 | Highland Park (312) | 32,263 | 25,532 | 60546 | Riverside (312) | 10,432 | 9,750 |
| 60162 | Hillside 1971. (312) | 9,466 | 7,794 | 60472 | Robbins (312) | 9,641 | 7,511 |
| 60521 | Hinsdale 1977. (312) | 16,844 | 12,859 | 62454 | Robinson (217) | 7,178 | 7,226 |
| 60172 | Hoffman Estates 1974 (312) | 31,549 | 8,296 | 61068 | Rochelle 1974. (815) | 8,850 | 7,008 |
| 60456 | Hometown (312) | 6,729 | 7,479 | 61071 | Rock Falls (815) | 10,287 | 10,261 |
| 60430 | Homewood 1976 (312) | 19,679 | 13,371 | *61125 | Rockford (815) | 147,370 | 126,706 |
| 60942 | Hoopeston (217) | 6,461 | 6,606 | 61201 | Rock Island (309) | 50,166 | 51,863 |
| 60143 | Itasca 1975 (312) | 6,148 | 3,564 | 60008 | Rolling Meadows 1974 (312) | 19,785 | 10,879 |
| 62650 | Jacksonville (217) | 20,553 | 21,690 | 60441 | Romeoville 1971. (815) | 15,336 | 3,574 |
| 62052 | Jerseyville 1976. (217) | 7,432 | 7,420 | 60172 | Roselle 1976 (312) | 10,213 | 3,581 |
| *60431 | Joliet 1975. (815) | 74,140 | 66,780 | 60073 | Round Lake Beach 1974. (312) | 10,525 | 5,011 |
| 60458 | Justice (312) | 9,473 | 2,803 | 60174 | St. Charles 1974. (815) | 15,144 | 9,269 |
| 60901 | Kankakee (815) | 30,944 | 27,666 | 62881 | Salem 1977 (618) | 7,183 | 6,165 |
| 61109 | Ken Rock(u) (815) | 5,945 | ...... | 60548 | Sandwich (815) | 5,056 | 3,842 |
| 61443 | Kewanee (815) | 15,762 | 16,324 | 60411 | Sauk Village 1974 (312) | 9,956 | 4,687 |
| 60525 | La Grange (312) | 17,814 | 15,285 | 60172 | Schaumburg 1976 (312) | 43,580 | 986 |
| 60525 | La Grange Highlands(u) (312) | 6,842 | ...... | 60176 | Schiller Park (312) | 12,712 | 5,687 |
| 60525 | La Grange Park (312) | 15,459 | 13,793 | 62225 | Scott(u) (618) | 7,871 | ...... |
| 60044 | Lake Bluff (312) | 5,008 | 3,494 | 61282 | Silvis (815) | 5,907 | 3,973 |
| 60045 | Lake Forest 1977 (312) | 15,243 | 10,687 | 60076 | Skokie 1971. (312) | 68,911 | 59,364 |
| 60047 | Lake Zurich 1975 (312) | 6,789 | 3,458 | 60473 | South Holland 1972 (312) | 25,220 | 10,412 |
| 60438 | Lansing 1973 (312) | 28,232 | 18,098 | 60459 | South Stickney(u) (see Burbank) (312) | | |

| ZIP code | Place | | 1970 | 1960 |
|---|---|---|---|---|
| *62703 | Springfield | (217) | 91,753 | 83,271 |
| 61362 | Spring Valley | (815) | 5,605 | 5,371 |
| 60475 | Steger 1973 | (312) | 9,285 | 6,432 |
| 61081 | Sterling | (815) | 16,113 | 15,688 |
| 60402 | Stickney | (312) | 6,601 | 6,239 |
| 60103 | Streamwood | (312) | 18,176 | 4,821 |
| 61364 | Streator | (312) | 15,600 | 16,868 |
| 60501 | Summit | (312) | 11,569 | 10,374 |
| 62221 | Swansea 1975 | (618) | 5,473 | 3,018 |
| 60178 | Sycamore | (815) | 7,843 | 6,961 |
| 62568 | Taylorville | (217) | 10,927 | 8,801 |
| 60477 | Tinley Park 1977 | (312) | 23,207 | 6,392 |
| 61801 | Urbana | (217) | 32,800 | 27,294 |
| 62471 | Vandalia | (618) | 5,160 | 5,537 |
| 60181 | Villa Park 1971 | (312) | 25,546 | 20,391 |
| 61571 | Washington 1977 | (309) | 10,045 | 5,919 |
| 62204 | Washington Park | (618) | 9,524 | 6,601 |
| 60970 | Watseka | (217) | 5,294 | 5,219 |
| 60084 | Wauconda 1974 | (312) | 5,662 | 3,227 |
| 60085 | Waukegan 1975 | (312) | 65,133 | 55,719 |
| 60153 | Westchester | (312) | 20,033 | 18,092 |
| 60185 | West Chicago 1975 | (312) | 12,689 | 6,854 |
| 61120 | West End(u) | (815) | 7,554 | ..... |
| 60558 | Western Springs 1974 | (312) | 13,728 | 10,838 |
| 62896 | West Frankfort | (618) | 8,854 | 9,027 |
| 60559 | Westmont 1977 | (312) | 13,823 | 5,997 |
| 61604 | West Peoria(u) | (309) | 6,873 | ..... |
| 60187 | Wheaton 1976 | (312) | 39,360 | 24,312 |
| 60090 | Wheeling 1974 | (312) | 18,106 | 7,169 |
| 60091 | Wilmette | (312) | 32,134 | 28,268 |
| 60093 | Winnetka | (312) | 13,998 | 13,368 |
| 60191 | Wood Dale 1973 | (312) | 10,494 | 3,071 |
| 60515 | Woodridge 1974 | (312) | 16,827 | 542 |
| 62095 | Wood River | (618) | 13,186 | 11,694 |
| 60098 | Woodstock | (815) | 10,226 | 8,897 |
| 60482 | Worth 1971 | (312) | 12,153 | 8,196 |
| 60099 | Zion 1975 | (312) | 17,511 | 11,941 |

## Indiana

| ZIP code | Place | | 1970 | 1960 |
|---|---|---|---|---|
| 46001 | Alexandria | (317) | 5,600 | 5,582 |
| *46011 | Anderson | (317) | 70,787 | 49,061 |
| 46703 | Angola | (219) | 5,117 | 4,746 |
| 46706 | Auburn | (219) | 7,388 | 6,350 |
| 47421 | Bedford | (812) | 13,087 | 13,024 |
| 46107 | Beech Grove 1973 | (317) | 14,651 | 10,973 |
| 46408 | Black Oak(u) | (219) | 9,624 | ..... |
| 47401 | Bloomington | (812) | 43,262 | 31,357 |
| 46714 | Bluffton | (219) | 8,297 | 6,238 |
| 47601 | Boonville | (812) | 5,736 | 4,801 |
| 47834 | Brazil | (317) | 8,163 | 8,853 |
| 46112 | Brownsburg | (317) | 5,751 | 4,478 |
| 46032 | Carmel 1976 | (317) | 15,181 | 1,442 |
| 46303 | Cedar Lake 1976 | (812) | 7,764 | ..... |
| 47111 | Charlestown | (812) | 5,933 | 5,726 |
| 46304 | Chesterton | (219) | 6,177 | 4,335 |
| 47130 | Clarksville 1974 | (812) | 14,117 | 8,088 |
| 47842 | Clinton | (317) | 5,340 | 5,843 |
| 46725 | Columbia City 1977 | (219) | 5,022 | ..... |
| 47201 | Columbus | (812) | 26,457 | 20,778 |
| 47331 | Connersville | (317) | 17,604 | 17,698 |
| 47933 | Crawfordsville | (317) | 13,842 | 14,231 |
| 46307 | Crown Point 1973 | (219) | 13,420 | 8,443 |
| 46733 | Decatur | (219) | 8,445 | 8,327 |
| 46312 | East Chicago | (219) | 46,982 | 57,669 |
| 46405 | East Gary | (219) | 9,858 | 9,309 |
| 46514 | Elkhart | (219) | 43,152 | 40,274 |
| 46036 | Elwood | (317) | 11,196 | 11,793 |
| *47708 | Evansville | (812) | 138,764 | 141,543 |
| *46802 | Fort Wayne | (219) | 178,021 | 161,776 |
| 46041 | Frankfort | (317) | 14,956 | 15,302 |
| 46131 | Franklin | (317) | 11,477 | 9,453 |
| *46401 | Gary | (219) | 175,415 | 178,320 |
| 46933 | Gas City | (317) | 5,742 | 4,469 |
| 46526 | Goshen 1976 | (219) | 18,709 | 13,718 |
| 46135 | Greencastle | (317) | 8,852 | 8,506 |
| 46140 | Greenfield 1973 | (317) | 10,808 | 9,049 |
| 47240 | Greensburg | (317) | 9,766 | 9,523 |
| 46142 | Greenwood 1975 | (317) | 16,097 | 7,169 |
| 46319 | Griffith 1974 | (219) | 17,681 | 9,483 |
| *46320 | Hammond | (219) | 107,885 | 111,698 |
| 47348 | Hartford City | (317) | 8,207 | 8,053 |
| 46322 | Highland | (219) | 24,947 | 16,284 |
| 46342 | Hobart 1977 | (219) | 22,268 | 16,680 |
| 46750 | Huntington | (219) | 16,217 | 16,185 |
| *46206 | Indianapolis | (317) | 746,302 | 476,258 |
| 47546 | Jasper | (812) | 8,641 | 6,737 |
| 47130 | Jeffersonville | (817) | 20,008 | 19,522 |
| 46755 | Kendallville | (219) | 6,838 | 6,765 |
| 46901 | Kokomo | (317) | 44,042 | 47,197 |
| *47901 | Lafayette | (317) | 44,955 | 42,330 |
| 46350 | La Porte | (219) | 22,140 | 21,157 |
| 46226 | Lawrence | (317) | 16,917 | 10,103 |
| 46052 | Lebanon | (317) | 9,766 | 9,523 |
| 47441 | Linton | (812) | 5,450 | 5,736 |
| 46947 | Logansport | (219) | 19,255 | 21,106 |
| 46356 | Lowell 1975 | (219) | 5,305 | 2,270 |
| 47250 | Madison | (812) | 13,081 | 10,488 |

| ZIP code | Place | | 1970 | 196 |
|---|---|---|---|---|
| 46952 | Marion | (317) | 39,607 | 37,85 |
| 46151 | Martinsville | (812) | 9,723 | 7,52 |
| 46410 | Merrillville 1973 | (219) | 25,978 | ... |
| 46360 | Michigan City | (219) | 39,369 | 36,65 |
| 46544 | Mishawaka 1977 | (219) | 39,002 | 33,36 |
| 46158 | Mooresville | (317) | 5,800 | 3,85 |
| 47620 | Mount Vernon 1974 | (812) | 7,092 | 5,97 |
| *47302 | Muncie | (317) | 69,082 | 68,60 |
| 46321 | Munster 1977 | (219) | 20,164 | 10,31 |
| 46150 | New Albany | (812) | 38,402 | 37,81 |
| 47362 | New Castle | (317) | 21,215 | 20,34 |
| 46774 | New Haven | (317) | 5,728 | 3,39 |
| 46060 | Noblesville | (317) | 10,189 | 7,66 |
| 46962 | North Manchester | (219) | 5,791 | 4,37 |
| 46970 | Peru | (317) | 14,139 | 14,45 |
| 46168 | Plainfield 1977 | (317) | 8,650 | 5,46 |
| 46563 | Plymouth | (219) | 7,661 | 7,55 |
| 46368 | Portage 1973 | (219) | 20,624 | 11,82 |
| 47371 | Portland | (317) | 7,115 | 6,99 |
| 47670 | Princeton | (618) | 7,431 | 7,90 |
| 47374 | Richmond | (317) | 43,999 | 44,14 |
| 46173 | Rushville | (317) | 6,686 | 7,26 |
| 47167 | Salem 1975 | (618) | 5,323 | 4,54 |
| 47274 | Seymour | (618) | 13,352 | 11,62 |
| 46176 | Shelbyville | (317) | 15,094 | 14,31 |
| *46624 | South Bend | (219) | 125,580 | 132,44 |
| 46224 | Speedway | (317) | 14,649 | 9,62 |
| 47586 | Tell City 1974 | (812) | 8,515 | 6,60 |
| *47808 | Terre Haute | (812) | 70,335 | 72,50 |
| 46072 | Tipton | (317) | 5,313 | 5,60 |
| 46383 | Valparaiso 1974 | (219) | 20,544 | 15,22 |
| 47591 | Vincennes | (219) | 19,867 | 18,04 |
| 46992 | Wabash | (219) | 13,379 | 12,62 |
| 46580 | Warsaw 1974 | (219) | 9,679 | 7,23 |
| 47501 | Washington | (618) | 11,358 | 10,84 |
| 46408 | West Glen Park(u) | (219) | 5,940 | ... |
| 47906 | West Lafayette 1975 | (317) | 20,372 | 12,68 |
| 46394 | Whiting | (219) | 7,152 | 8,13 |
| 47394 | Winchester | (317) | 5,493 | 5,74 |

## Iowa

| ZIP code | Place | | 1970 | 196 |
|---|---|---|---|---|
| 50511 | Algona | (515) | 6,032 | 5,70 |
| 50010 | Ames 1975 | (515) | 43,561 | 27,00 |
| 50021 | Ankeny 1975 | (515) | 13,212 | 2,96 |
| 50022 | Atlantic 1976 | (712) | 7,324 | 6,89 |
| 52722 | Bettendorf 1975 | (319) | 24,290 | 11,53 |
| 50036 | Boone | (712) | 12,468 | 12,46 |
| 52601 | Burlington | (319) | 32,366 | 32,43 |
| 51401 | Carroll 1976 | (717) | 9,218 | 7,68 |
| *50613 | Cedar Falls 1974 | (319) | 33,154 | 21,19 |
| *52401 | Cedar Rapids 1975 | (319) | 108,987 | 92,03 |
| 52544 | Centerville | (515) | 6,531 | 6,62 |
| 50049 | Chariton | (515) | 5,009 | 5,04 |
| 50616 | Charles City 1974 | (515) | 9,119 | 9,96 |
| 51012 | Cherokee | (317) | 7,272 | 7,72 |
| 51632 | Clarinda 1972 | (712) | 5,312 | 5,90 |
| 50428 | Clear Lake City 1973 | (515) | 6,876 | 6,15 |
| 52732 | Clinton | (319) | 34,719 | 33,58 |
| 52240 | Coralville | (319) | 6,130 | 2,35 |
| 51501 | Council Bluffs | (712) | 60,348 | 55,64 |
| 50801 | Creston | (712) | 8,234 | 7,66 |
| *52802 | Davenport 1975 | (319) | 99,836 | 88,98 |
| 52101 | Decorah | (319) | 7,458 | 6,43 |
| 51442 | Denison | (319) | 6,218 | 4,93 |
| *50318 | Des Moines | (515) | 201,404 | 208,98 |
| 52001 | Dubuque 1975 | (319) | 61,728 | 56,60 |
| 51334 | Estherville | (712) | 8,108 | 7,92 |
| 50707 | Evansdale | (319) | 5,038 | 5,73 |
| 52556 | Fairfield | (515) | 8,715 | 8,05 |
| 50501 | Fort Dodge | (515) | 31,263 | 28,39 |
| 52627 | Fort Madison | (319) | 13,996 | 15,247 |
| 51534 | Glenwood 1977 | (712) | 5,002 | ... |
| 50112 | Grinnell | (515) | 8,685 | 7,367 |
| 51537 | Harlan 1976 | (712) | 5,251 | 4,35 |
| 50644 | Independence | (319) | 5,910 | 5,49 |
| 50125 | Indianola 1975 | (515) | 9,611 | 7,06 |
| 52240 | Iowa City 1974 | (319) | 47,744 | 33,443 |
| 50126 | Iowa Falls | (515) | 6,454 | 5,56 |
| 52632 | Keokuk | (319) | 14,631 | 16,31 |
| 50138 | Knoxville | (515) | 7,755 | 7,817 |
| 51031 | Le Mars | (712) | 6,767 | 6,767 |
| 52060 | Maquoketa | (319) | 5,677 | 5,909 |
| 52302 | Marion 1976 | (319) | 18,190 | 10,882 |
| 50158 | Marshalltown 1975 | (515) | 26,506 | 22,521 |
| 50401 | Mason City | (515) | 30,379 | 30,642 |
| 52641 | Mount Pleasant | (319) | 7,007 | 7,33 |
| 52761 | Muscatine | (319) | 22,405 | 20,997 |
| 50208 | Newton | (515) | 15,619 | 15,381 |
| 52070 | Oelwein | (319) | 7,735 | 8,282 |
| 52577 | Oskaloosa | (315) | 11,224 | 11,053 |
| 52501 | Ottumwa | (515) | 29,610 | 33,871 |
| 50219 | Pella | (515) | 6,668 | 5,198 |
| 50220 | Perry | (515) | 6,906 | 6,442 |
| 51566 | Red Oak | (717) | 6,210 | 6,421 |
| 51601 | Shenandoah 1976 | (712) | 6,242 | 6,567 |
| *51101 | Sioux City | (712) | 85,925 | 89,159 |
| 51301 | Spencer | (712) | 10,278 | 8,864 |

| ZIP code | Place | | 1970 | 1960 |
|---|---|---|---|---|
| 50588 | Storm Lake 1975 | (712) | 8,589 | 7,728 |
| 50322 | Urbandale 1975 | (515) | 16,410 | 5,821 |
| 52353 | Washington | (319) | 6,317 | 6,037 |
| *50701 | Waterloo 1975 | (319) | 73,064 | 71,755 |
| 50677 | Waverly 1975 | (515) | 7,351 | 6,357 |
| 50595 | Webster City | (515) | 8,488 | 8,520 |
| 50265 | West Des Moines 1975 | (515) | 20,712 | 11,949 |
| 50311 | Windsor Heights | (515) | 6,303 | 4,715 |

## Kansas

| ZIP code | Place | | 1970 | 1960 |
|---|---|---|---|---|
| 67410 | Abilene | (913) | 6,661 | 6,746 |
| 67005 | Arkansas City | (316) | 13,216 | 14,262 |
| 66002 | Atchison | (913) | 12,565 | 12,529 |
| 67010 | Augusta | (316) | 5,977 | 6,434 |
| 66720 | Chanute | (316) | 10,341 | 10,849 |
| 67337 | Coffeyville | (316) | 15,116 | 17,382 |
| 66901 | Concordia | (913) | 7,221 | 7,022 |
| 67037 | Derby | (316) | 7,947 | 6,458 |
| 67801 | Dodge City | (316) | 14,127 | 13,520 |
| 67042 | El Dorado | (316) | 12,308 | 12,523 |
| 66801 | Emporia | (316) | 23,327 | 18,190 |
| 66205 | Fairway | (913) | 5,133 | 5,398 |
| 66027 | Fort Leavenworth(u) | (913) | 8,060 | ..... |
| 66701 | Fort Scott | (913) | 8,967 | 9,410 |
| 67846 | Garden City | (316) | 14,790 | 11,811 |
| 67735 | Goodland | (316) | 5,510 | 4,459 |
| 67530 | Great Bend | (316) | 16,123 | 16,670 |
| 67601 | Hays | (913) | 15,396 | 11,947 |
| 67060 | Haysville | (316) | 6,483 | 5,836 |
| 67501 | Hutchinson | (316) | 36,885 | 37,574 |
| 67301 | Independence | (316) | 10,347 | 11,222 |
| 66749 | Iola | (316) | 6,493 | 6,885 |
| 66441 | Junction City | (913) | 19,018 | 18,700 |
| *66110 | Kansas City | (913) | 168,213 | 121,901 |
| 66044 | Lawrence | (913) | 45,698 | 32,858 |
| 66048 | Leavenworth | (913) | 25,147 | 22,052 |
| 66206 | Leawood | (913) | 10,349 | 7,466 |
| 66215 | Lenexa | (913) | 5,242 | 2,487 |
| 67901 | Liberal | (316) | 13,789 | 13,813 |
| 67460 | McPherson | (316) | 10,851 | 9,996 |
| 66502 | Manhattan | (913) | 27,575 | 22,993 |
| 66203 | Merriam | (913) | 10,851 | 5,084 |
| 66222 | Mission | (316) | 8,376 | 4,626 |
| 67114 | Newton | (316) | 15,439 | 14,877 |
| 66442 | North Fort Riley(u) | (913) | 12,469 | ..... |
| 66061 | Olathe | (316) | 17,917 | 10,987 |
| 66067 | Ottawa | (913) | 11,036 | 10,673 |
| 66204 | Overland Park | (913) | 79,034 | ..... |
| 67357 | Parsons | (316) | 13,015 | 13,929 |
| 66762 | Pittsburg | (316) | 20,171 | 18,678 |
| 66208 | Prairie Village | (913) | 28,138 | 25,356 |
| 67124 | Pratt | (316) | 6,736 | 8,156 |
| 66203 | Roeland Park | (913) | 9,974 | 8,949 |
| 67665 | Russell | (913) | 5,371 | 6,113 |
| 67401 | Salina | (913) | 37,714 | 43,202 |
| *66203 | Shawnee | (913) | 20,482 | 9,072 |
| *66603 | Topeka | (913) | 125,011 | 119,484 |
| 67152 | Wellington | (316) | 8,072 | 8,809 |
| *67202 | Wichita | (316) | 276,554 | 254,698 |
| 67156 | Winfield | (316) | 11,405 | 11,117 |

## Kentucky

| ZIP code | Place | | 1970 | 1960 |
|---|---|---|---|---|
| 41101 | Ashland | (606) | 29,245 | 31,283 |
| 40004 | Bardstown | (502) | 5,816 | 4,798 |
| 41073 | Bellevue | (606) | 8,847 | 9,336 |
| 40403 | Berea | (606) | 6,956 | 4,302 |
| 42101 | Bowling Green | (502) | 36,705 | 28,338 |
| 40218 | Buechel(u) | (502) | 5,359 | ..... |
| 42718 | Campbellsville | (502) | 7,598 | 6,966 |
| 42330 | Central City | (502) | 5,450 | 3,694 |
| 40701 | Corbin | (606) | 7,317 | 7,119 |
| *41011 | Covington | (606) | 52,535 | 60,376 |
| 41031 | Cynthiana | (606) | 6,356 | 5,641 |
| 40422 | Danville | (606) | 11,542 | 9,010 |
| 41074 | Dayton | (606) | 8,751 | 9,050 |
| 42701 | Elizabethtown | (502) | 11,748 | 9,641 |
| 41018 | Elsmere | (606) | 5,161 | 4,607 |
| 41018 | Erlanger | (606) | 12,676 | 7,072 |
| 41139 | Flatwoods | (606) | 7,380 | 3,741 |
| 41042 | Florence | (606) | 11,661 | 5,837 |
| 42223 | Fort Campbell North(u) | (502) | 13,616 | ..... |
| 40121 | Fort Knox(u) | (502) | 37,608 | ..... |
| 41017 | Fort Mitchell | (606) | 6,982 | 525 |
| 41075 | Fort Thomas | (606) | 16,338 | 14,896 |
| 40601 | Frankfort | (502) | 21,902 | 18,365 |
| 42134 | Franklin | (502) | 6,553 | 5,319 |
| 40324 | Georgetown | (606) | 8,629 | 6,986 |
| 42141 | Glasgow | (502) | 11,301 | 10,069 |
| 40330 | Harrodsburg | (502) | 6,741 | 6,061 |
| 41701 | Hazard | (606) | 5,459 | 5,958 |
| 42420 | Henderson | (502) | 22,976 | 16,892 |
| 42240 | Hopkinsville | (502) | 21,250 | 19,465 |
| 40299 | Jeffersontown | (502) | 9,701 | 3,431 |
| 40033 | Lebanon | (502) | 5,528 | 4,813 |
| *40511 | Lexington | (606) | 108,137 | 62,810 |
| *40201 | Louisville | (502) | 361,706 | 390,639 |
| 41016 | Ludlow | (606) | 5,815 | 6,233 |
| 42431 | Madisonville | (502) | 15,332 | 13,110 |
| 42066 | Mayfield | (502) | 10,724 | 10,762 |
| 41056 | Maysville | (606) | 7,411 | 8,484 |
| 40965 | Middlesborough | (606) | 11,878 | 12,607 |
| 40351 | Morehead | (606) | 7,191 | 4,170 |
| 40353 | Mount Sterling | (606) | 5,083 | 5,370 |
| 42071 | Murray | (502) | 13,537 | 9,303 |
| *41071 | Newport | (606) | 25,998 | 30,070 |
| 40356 | Nicholasville | (606) | 5,829 | 4,275 |
| 40219 | Okolona(u) | (502) | 17,643 | ..... |
| 42301 | Owensboro | (502) | 50,329 | 42,471 |
| 42001 | Paducah | (502) | 31,627 | 34,479 |
| 40361 | Paris | (606) | 7,823 | 7,791 |
| 41501 | Pikeville | (606) | 5,205 | 4,754 |
| 40258 | Pleasure Ridge Park(u) | (502) | 28,566 | 10,612 |
| 42445 | Princeton | (502) | 6,292 | 5,618 |
| 40160 | Radcliff | (502) | 7,881 | 3,384 |
| 40475 | Richmond | (606) | 16,861 | 12,168 |
| 42276 | Russellville | (502) | 6,456 | 5,861 |
| 40207 | St. Matthews | (502) | 13,152 | 8,738 |
| 40216 | Shively | (502) | 19,139 | 15,155 |
| 42501 | Somerset | (606) | 10,436 | 7,112 |
| 40272 | Valley Station(u) | (502) | 24,471 | 10,533 |
| 40383 | Versailles | (606) | 5,679 | 4,060 |
| 40391 | Winchester | (606) | 13,402 | 10,187 |

## Louisiana

| ZIP code | Place | | 1970 | 1960 |
|---|---|---|---|---|
| 70510 | Abbeville | (318) | 10,996 | 10,414 |
| 71301 | Alexandria | (318) | 41,557 | 40,279 |
| 70714 | Baker | (504) | 8,281 | 4,823 |
| 71220 | Bastrop | (318) | 14,713 | 15,193 |
| *70821 | Baton Rouge | (504) | 165,963 | 152,419 |
| 70360 | Bayou Cane(u) | (504) | 9,077 | 3,173 |
| 70380 | Bayou Vista(u) | (504) | 5,121 | ..... |
| 70427 | Bogalusa | (318) | 18,412 | 21,423 |
| 71010 | Bossier City | (318) | 41,595 | 32,776 |
| 71322 | Bunkie | (318) | 5,395 | 5,188 |
| 71101 | Cooper Road(u) | | 9,034 | ..... |
| 70433 | Covington | (504) | 7,170 | 6,754 |
| 70526 | Crowley | (318) | 16,104 | 15,617 |
| 70726 | Denham Springs | (504) | 6,752 | 5,991 |
| 70634 | De Ridder | (318) | 8,030 | 7,188 |
| 70346 | Donaldsonville | (504) | 7,367 | 6,082 |
| 70535 | Eunice | (318) | 11,390 | 11,326 |
| 71334 | Ferriday | (318) | 5,239 | 4,563 |
| 70538 | Franklin | (504) | 9,325 | 8,673 |
| 70053 | Gretna | (504) | 24,875 | 21,967 |
| 70401 | Hammond | (504) | 12,487 | 10,563 |
| 70123 | Harahan | (504) | 13,037 | 9,275 |
| 70058 | Harvey(u) | (504) | 6,347 | ..... |
| 70360 | Houma 1975 | (504) | 30,562 | 22,561 |
| 70544 | Jeanerette | (504) | 6,322 | 5,568 |
| 70121 | Jefferson Heights(u) | (504) | 16,489 | 19,353 |
| 70546 | Jenning | (318) | 11,783 | 11,887 |
| 71251 | Jonesboro | (318) | 5,072 | 3,848 |
| 70548 | Kaplan | (318) | 5,540 | 5,267 |
| 70062 | Kenner | (504) | 29,858 | 17,037 |
| 70501 | Lafayette | (318) | 68,908 | 40,400 |
| 70501 | Lafayette Southwest | (318) | 5,396 | 6,682 |
| 70601 | Lake Charles | (318) | 77,998 | 63,392 |
| 71254 | Lake Providence | (318) | 6,183 | 5,781 |
| 70068 | Laplace(u) | (504) | 5,953 | 3,541 |
| 71446 | Leesville | (318) | 8,928 | 4,689 |
| 70123 | Little Farms(u) | (504) | 15,713 | ..... |
| 71052 | Mansfield | (318) | 6,432 | 5,839 |
| 70072 | Marrero(u) | (504) | 29,015 | ..... |
| *70004 | Metairie(u) | (504) | 136,477 | ..... |
| 71055 | Minden | (318) | 13,996 | 12,785 |
| 71201 | Monroe | (318) | 56,374 | 52,219 |
| 70380 | Morgan City | (504) | 16,586 | 13,540 |
| 71457 | Natchitoches | (318) | 15,974 | 13,924 |
| 70560 | New Iberia | (318) | 30,147 | 29,062 |
| *70113 | New Orleans | (504) | 593,471 | 627,525 |
| 71459 | North Fort Polk(u) | (318) | 7,955 | ..... |
| 71463 | Oakdale | (318) | 7,301 | 6,618 |
| 70570 | Opelousas | (318) | 20,387 | 17,417 |
| 71360 | Pineville | (318) | 8,951 | 8,636 |
| 70764 | Plaquemine | (504) | 7,739 | 7,689 |
| 70767 | Port Allen | (504) | 5,728 | 5,026 |
| 70578 | Rayne | (318) | 9,510 | 8,634 |
| 70084 | Reserve(u) | (504) | 6,381 | 5,297 |
| 71270 | Ruston | (318) | 17,365 | 13,991 |
| 70582 | St. Martinville | (318) | 7,153 | 6,468 |
| 70807 | Scotlandville(u) | (504) | 22,557 | ..... |
| *71102 | Shreveport | (318) | 182,064 | 164,372 |
| 70458 | Slidell | (504) | 16,101 | 6,356 |
| 71459 | South Fort Polk(u) | (318) | 15,600 | ..... |
| 71075 | Springhill | (318) | 6,496 | 6,437 |
| 70663 | Sulphur | (318) | 14,959 | 11,429 |
| 71282 | Tallulah | (318) | 9,643 | 9,413 |
| 71285 | Terry(u) | (504) | 13,382 | ..... |
| 70301 | Thibodaux | (504) | 15,028 | 13,403 |
| 71373 | Vidalia | (318) | 5,538 | 4,313 |
| 70586 | Ville Platte | (318) | 9,692 | 7,512 |
| 71291 | West Monroe | (318) | 14,868 | 15,215 |
| 70094 | Westwego | (504) | 11,402 | 9,815 |

| ZIP code | Place | 1970 | 1960 |
|---|---|---|---|
| 71483 | Winnfield . . . . . . . . . . . (318) | 7,142 | 7,022 |
| 71295 | Winnsboro . . . . . . . . . . (318) | 5,349 | 4,437 |

## Maine (207)
*See Note on Page 219*

| ZIP code | Place | 1970 | 1960 |
|---|---|---|---|
| 04210 | Auburn . . . . . . . . . . | 24,151 | 24,449 |
| 04330 | Augusta . . . . . . . . . | 21,945 | 21,680 |
| 04401 | Bangor 1975. . . . . . | 32,205 | 38,912 |
| 04530 | Bath . . . . . . . . . | 9,679 | 10,717 |
| 04915 | Belfast . . . . . . . . | 5,957 | 6,140 |
| 04005 | Biddeford. . . . . . | 19,983 | 19,255 |
| 04412 | Brewer . . . . . . | 9,300 | 9,009 |
| 04011 | Brunswick Center(u) | 10,867 | 9,444 |
| ..... | Brunswick. . . . | 16,195 | 15,797 |
| 04107 | Cape Elizabeth . | 7,873 | 5,505 |
| 04736 | Caribou. . . . . | 10,419 | 12,464 |
| ..... | Fairfield. . . . | 5,684 | 5,829 |
| 04105 | Falmouth. . . . | 6,291 | 5,976 |
| ..... | Farmington. . . | 5,657 | 5,001 |
| 04345 | Gardiner . . . | 6,685 | 6,897 |
| ..... | Gorham . . . | 7,839 | 5,767 |
| 04730 | Houlton Center(u). | 6,760 | 5,976 |
| ..... | Houlton. . . . | 8,111 | 8,289 |
| ..... | Kennebunk. . | 5,646 | 551 |
| 03904 | Kittery Center(u) | 7,363 | 8,051 |
| ..... | Kittery . . . | 11,028 | 10,689 |
| 04240 | Lewiston . . | 41,779 | 40,804 |
| 04750 | Limestone . . | 10,360 | 13,102 |
| 04250 | Lisbon . . . | 6,544 | 5,042 |
| 04750 | Loring(u) . . | 7,881 | ..... |
| ..... | Madawaska . | 5,585 | 5,507 |
| 04462 | Millinocket Center(u) | 7,558 | 7,318 |
| ..... | Millinocket . | 7,742 | 7,453 |
| 04064 | Old Orchard Beach Ctr.(u). | 5,273 | 4,431 |
| ..... | Old Orchard Beach. | 5,404 | 4,580 |
| 04468 | Old Town . . | 9,057 | 8,626 |
| 04473 | Orono Center(u) | 9,146 | 3,234 |
| ..... | Orono . . . | 9,989 | 8,341 |
| *04101 | Portland . . | 65,116 | 72,566 |
| 04769 | Presque Isle . | 11,452 | 12,886 |
| 04841 | Rockland . . | 8,505 | 8,769 |
| 04276 | Rumford Compact(u) | 6,198 | 7,233 |
| ..... | Rumford . . | 9,363 | 10,005 |
| 04072 | Saco . . . | 11,678 | 10,515 |
| 04073 | Sanford Center(u) | 10,457 | 10,936 |
| ..... | Sanford. . . | 15,812 | 14,962 |
| 04074 | Scarborough. | 7,845 | 6,418 |
| 04976 | Skowhegan Center(u) | 6,571 | 6,667 |
| ..... | Skowhegan . | 7,601 | 7,661 |
| 04106 | South Portland | 23,267 | 22,788 |
| ..... | Topsham. . . | 5,022 | 3,818 |
| 04901 | Waterville . | 18,192 | 19,001 |
| 04092 | Westbrook. . | 14,444 | 13,820 |
| 04082 | Windham. . | 6,593 | 4,498 |
| 04901 | Winslow Center(u) | 5,389 | 3,640 |
| ..... | Winslow . . | 7,299 | 5,891 |
| 03909 | York . . . | 5,690 | 4,663 |

## Maryland (301)

| ZIP code | Place | 1970 | 1960 |
|---|---|---|---|
| 21001 | Aberdeen . . . | 12,375 | 9,679 |
| 21005 | Aberdeen Proving Ground(u) | 7,403 | ..... |
| 20331 | Andrews(u) . . | 6,418 | ..... |
| *21401 | Annapolis . . | 30,095 | 23,385 |
| 21227 | Arbutus(u) . . | 22,745 | 22,402 |
| 20853 | Aspen Hill(u) . | 16,823 | ..... |
| 20783 | Avenel-Hilandale(u) | 19,520 | ..... |
| 21905 | Bainbridge Center(u) | 5,257 | ..... |
| *21233 | Baltimore. . | 905,759 | 939,024 |
| 21014 | Bel Air . . . | 6,307 | 4,300 |
| 20705 | Beltsville(u) . | 8,912 | ..... |
| 20014 | Bethesda(u) . | 71,621 | 56,527 |
| 20021 | Birchwood City(u) | 13,514 | ..... |
| 20710 | Bladensburg. . | 7,488 | 3,103 |
| 20715 | Bowie. . . | 35,028 | 1,072 |
| 21225 | Brooklyn(u) . | 13,896 | ..... |
| 20705 | Calverton(u) . | 6,543 | ..... |
| 21613 | Cambridge . | 11,595 | 12,239 |
| 20031 | Camp Springs(u) | 22,776 | ..... |
| 20027 | Carmody Hills-Pepper Mill(u) | 6,335 | ..... |
| 21228 | Catonsville(u) | 54,812 | 37,372 |
| 20027 | Chapel Oaks-Cedar Heights(u) | 6,049 | ..... |
| 20785 | Cheverly(u) . | 6,808 | 5,223 |
| 20015 | Chevy Chase(u) | 16,424 | ..... |
| 20783 | Chillum(u) . | 35,656 | ..... |
| 20904 | Colesville(u) . | 9,455 | ..... |
| 20740 | College Park. | 26,156 | 18,482 |
| 21043 | Columbia(u) . | 8,815 | ..... |
| 20027 | Coral Hills(u) | 9,058 | ..... |
| 21502 | Cumberland . | 29,724 | 33,415 |
| 21222 | Defense Heights(u) | 6,775 | ..... |
| 20028 | District Heights | 7,659 | 7,524 |
| 21222 | Dundalk(u) . | 85,377 | 82,428 |
| 21601 | Easton . . . | 6,809 | 6,337 |
| 21219 | Edgemere(u). | 10,352 | 11,775 |
| 21040 | Edgewood(u) . | 8,551 | 1,670 |

| ZIP code | Place | 1970 | 19.. |
|---|---|---|---|
| 21921 | Elkton. . . | 5,362 | 5,9.. |
| *21043 | Ellicott(u) . | 9,435 | ..... |
| 21221 | Essex(u) . . | 38,193 | 35,2.. |
| 21061 | Ferndale(u) . | 9,929 | ..... |
| 20028 | Forestville(u) . | 16,188 | ..... |
| 20755 | Fort Meade(u) . | 16,699 | ..... |
| 21701 | Frederick. . | 23,641 | 21,74.. |
| 21532 | Frostburg. . | 7,327 | 6,72.. |
| 20760 | Gaithersburg. | 8,344 | 3,8.. |
| 21061 | Glen Burnie(u) | 38,608 | ..... |
| 20801 | Good Luck(u) | 10,584 | ..... |
| 20770 | Greenbelt . | 18,199 | 7,4.. |
| 21740 | Hagerstown . | 35,862 | 36,6.. |
| 21740 | Halfway(u) . | 6,106 | 4,25.. |
| 20852 | Halpine(u) . | 6,118 | ..... |
| 21078 | Havre De Grace. | 9,791 | 8,5.. |
| 20031 | Hillcrest Heights. | 24,037 | 15,2.. |
| *20780 | Hyattsville . | 14,998 | 15,16.. |
| 21085 | Joppatowne(u) | 9,092 | ..... |
| 20904 | Kemp Mill(u) | 10,037 | ..... |
| 20785 | Kentland(u) . | 9,649 | ..... |
| 20785 | Landover(u) . | 5,597 | ..... |
| 20787 | Langley Park(u) | 11,564 | 11,5.. |
| 20801 | Lanham-Seabrook(u) | 13,244 | ..... |
| 21227 | Lansdowne-Baltimore Highlands(u) | 17,770 | 13,1.. |
| 20810 | Laurel . . | 10,525 | 8,50.. |
| 20653 | Lexington Pk.-Patuxent R.(u) | 9,136 | ..... |
| 21090 | Linthicum(u) . | 9,775 | ..... |
| 21093 | Lutherville-Timonium(u) | 24,055 | 12,20.. |
| 20810 | Maryland City(u) | 7,102 | ..... |
| 21220 | Middle River(u) | 19,935 | 10,82.. |
| 20852 | Montrose(u) . | 5,902 | ..... |
| 20822 | Mount Rainier. | 8,180 | 9,85.. |
| 20784 | New Carrollton(u) | 14,870 | 3,3.. |
| 20854 | North Potomac(u) | 12,784 | ..... |
| 20012 | North Takoma Park(u) | 7,373 | ..... |
| 21113 | Odenton(u) . | 5,989 | 1,9.. |
| 21206 | Overlea(u) . | 13,124 | 10,79.. |
| 21117 | Owings Mills(u) | 7,360 | 3,8.. |
| 20021 | Oxon Hill(u) . | 11,974 | ..... |
| 20785 | Palmer Park(u) | 8,172 | ..... |
| 21234 | Parkville(u) . | 33,589 | 27,23.. |
| 21128 | Perry Hall(u) . | 5,446 | ..... |
| 21208 | Pikesville(u) . | 25,395 | 18,73.. |
| 20016 | Potomac Valley(u) | 5,122 | ..... |
| 21227 | Pumphrey(u) . | 6,426 | ..... |
| 21133 | Randallstown(u) | 33,683 | ..... |
| 20853 | Randolph(u) . | 13,215 | ..... |
| 21136 | Reisterstown(u) | 12,568 | 4,2.. |
| 20840 | Riverdale. . | 5,724 | 4,38.. |
| 20840 | Riverdale Hgts.-E. Pines(u) | 8,941 | ..... |
| 21122 | Riviera Beach(u) | 7,464 | 4,9.. |
| *20850 | Rockville . | 41,821 | 26,09.. |
| 21237 | Rosedale(u) . | 19,417 | ..... |
| 21801 | Salisbury. . | 15,252 | 16,30.. |
| 20027 | Seat Pleasant | 7,217 | 5,36.. |
| 21146 | Severna Park(u) | 16,358 | 3,72.. |
| *20907 | Silver Spring(u) | 77,411 | 66,34.. |
| 21061 | South Gate(u) | 9,356 | ..... |
| 20795 | South Kensington(u) | 10,289 | ..... |
| 20810 | South Laurel(u) | 13,345 | ..... |
| 20023 | Suitland-Silver Hills(u) | 30,355 | 10,30.. |
| 20012 | Takoma Park. | 18,507 | 16,79.. |
| 21204 | Towson(u) . | 77,768 | 19,09.. |
| 20601 | Waldorf(u) . | 7,368 | 1,04.. |
| 20028 | Walker Mill(u) | 7,103 | ..... |
| 21157 | Westminster. | 7,207 | 6,12.. |
| 20902 | Wheaton(u) . | 66,280 | 54,63.. |
| 20903 | White Oak(u) . | 19,769 | ..... |
| 21207 | Woodlawn-Woodmoor(u) | 28,821 | ..... |

## Massachusetts
*See Note on Page 219*

| ZIP code | Place | 1970 | 19.. |
|---|---|---|---|
| 02351 | Abington . . . . . (617) | 12,334 | 10,60.. |
| 01720 | Acton. . . . . (617) | 14,770 | 7,23.. |
| 02743 | Acushnet. . . . (617) | 7,767 | 5,75.. |
| 01220 | Adams Center(u) . . (413) | 11,256 | 11,94.. |
| ..... | Adams. . . . . (413) | 11,772 | 12,39.. |
| 01001 | Agawam . . . . (413) | 21,717 | 15,71.. |
| 01913 | Amesbury Center(u) . (617) | 10,088 | 9,62.. |
| ..... | Amesbury . . . (617) | 11,388 | 10,78.. |
| 01002 | Amherst Center . . (413) | 17,926 | 10,30.. |
| ..... | Amherst . . . . (413) | 26,331 | 13,71.. |
| 01810 | Andover . . . . (617) | 23,695 | 17,13.. |
| 02174 | Arlington . . . . (617) | 53,534 | 49,95.. |
| 01721 | Ashland . . . . (617) | 8,882 | 7,77.. |
| 01331 | Athol Center(u) . . (413) | 9,723 | 10,16.. |
| ..... | Athol. . . . . (413) | 11,185 | 11,63.. |
| 02703 | Attleboro . . . . (617) | 32,907 | 27,11.. |
| 01501 | Auburn . . . . (617) | 15,347 | 14,04.. |
| 02322 | Avon . . . . . (617) | 5,295 | 4,30.. |
| *01432 | Ayer . . . . . (617) | 7,393 | 14,92.. |
| 02630 | Barnstable. . . . (617) | 19,842 | 13,46.. |
| 01730 | Bedford . . . . (617) | 13,513 | 10,96.. |
| 01007 | Belchertown. . . (413) | 5,936 | 5,18.. |
| 02019 | Bellingham . . . (617) | 13,967 | 6,77.. |
| 02178 | Belmont . . . . (617) | 28,285 | 28,71.. |

| ZIP code | Place | | 1970 | 1960 |
|---|---|---|---|---|
| 01915 | Beverly | (617) | 38,348 | 36,108 |
| 01821 | Billerica | (617) | 31,648 | 17,867 |
| 01504 | Blackstone | (617) | 6,566 | 5,130 |
| *02109 | Boston | (617) | 641,071 | 697,197 |
| 02532 | Bourne | (617) | 12,636 | 14,011 |
| 02184 | Braintree | (617) | 35,050 | 31,069 |
| 02324 | Bridgewater | (617) | 11,829 | 10,276 |
| *02403 | Brockton | (617) | 89,040 | 72,813 |
| 02146 | Brookline | (617) | 58,886 | 54,044 |
| 01803 | Burlington | (617) | 21,980 | 12,852 |
| *02138 | Cambridge | (617) | 100,361 | 107,716 |
| 02021 | Canton | (617) | 17,100 | 12,771 |
| 01824 | Chelmsford | (617) | 31,432 | 15,130 |
| 02150 | Chelsea | (413) | 30,625 | 33,749 |
| *01021 | Chicopee | (617) | 66,676 | 61,553 |
| 01510 | Clinton | (617) | 13,383 | 12,848 |
| 02025 | Cohasset | (617) | 6,954 | 5,840 |
| 01742 | Concord | (617) | 16,148 | 12,517 |
| 01226 | Dalton | (413) | 7,505 | 6,436 |
| 01923 | Danvers | (617) | 26,151 | 21,926 |
| 02714 | Dartmouth | (617) | 18,800 | 14,607 |
| 02026 | Dedham | (617) | 25,938 | 23,869 |
| 02638 | Dennis | (617) | 6,454 | 3,727 |
| 01826 | Dracut | (617) | 18,214 | 13,674 |
| 01570 | Dudley | (617) | 8,087 | 6,510 |
| 02332 | Duxbury | (617) | 7,636 | 4,727 |
| 02333 | East Bridgewater | (617) | 8,347 | 6,139 |
| 01027 | Easthampton | (413) | 13,012 | 12,326 |
| 01028 | East Longmeadow | (413) | 13,029 | 10,294 |
| 02334 | Easton | (617) | 12,157 | 9,078 |
| 01249 | Everett | (617) | 42,485 | 43,544 |
| 02719 | Fairhaven | (617) | 16,332 | 14,339 |
| *02722 | Fall River | (617) | 96,898 | 99,942 |
| *02540 | Falmouth Center(u) | (617) | 5,806 | 3,308 |
| ..... | Falmouth | (617) | 15,942 | 13,037 |
| 01420 | Fitchburg | (617) | 43,343 | 43,021 |
| 01433 | Fort Devens(u) | (413) | 12,019 | ..... |
| 02035 | Foxborough | (617) | 14,218 | 10,136 |
| 01701 | Framingham | (617) | 64,048 | 44,526 |
| 02038 | Franklin Center(u) | (617) | 8,863 | 6,391 |
| ..... | Franklin | (617) | 17,830 | 10,530 |
| 01440 | Gardner | (617) | 19,748 | 19,038 |
| 01833 | Georgetown | (617) | 5,290 | 3,755 |
| 01930 | Gloucester | (617) | 27,941 | 25,789 |
| 01519 | Grafton | (413) | 11,659 | 10,627 |
| 01033 | Granby | (413) | 5,473 | 4,221 |
| 01230 | Great Barrington | (413) | 7,537 | 6,624 |
| 01301 | Greenfield Center(u) | (413) | 14,642 | 14,389 |
| ..... | Greenfield | (617) | 18,116 | 17,690 |
| 01450 | Groton | (617) | 5,109 | 3,904 |
| 01834 | Groveland | (617) | 5,382 | 3,297 |
| 01936 | Hamilton | (617) | 6,373 | 5,488 |
| 02339 | Hanover | (617) | 10,107 | 5,923 |
| 02341 | Hanson | (617) | 7,148 | 4,370 |
| 01451 | Harvard | (617) | 12,494 | 2,563 |
| 02645 | Harwich | (617) | 5,892 | 3,747 |
| 01830 | Haverhill | (617) | 46,120 | 46,346 |
| 02043 | Hingham | (617) | 18,845 | 15,378 |
| 02343 | Holbrook | (617) | 11,775 | 10,104 |
| 01520 | Holden | (617) | 12,564 | 10,117 |
| 01746 | Holliston | (413) | 12,069 | 6,222 |
| 01040 | Holyoke | (617) | 50,112 | 52,689 |
| 01748 | Hopkinton | (617) | 5,981 | 4,932 |
| 01749 | Hudson Center(u) | (617) | 14,283 | 7,987 |
| ..... | Hudson | (617) | 16,084 | 9,666 |
| 02045 | Hull | (617) | 9,961 | 7,055 |
| 02601 | Hyannis(u) | (617) | 6,847 | 5,139 |
| 01938 | Ipswich(u) | (617) | 5,022 | 4,617 |
| ..... | Ipswich | (617) | 10,750 | 8,544 |
| 02364 | Kingston | (617) | 5,999 | 4,302 |
| 01523 | Lancaster | (413) | 6,095 | 3,958 |
| *01842 | Lawrence | (617) | 66,915 | 70,933 |
| 01238 | Lee | (617) | 6,426 | 5,271 |
| 01524 | Leicester | (617) | 9,140 | 8,177 |
| 01240 | Lenox | (617) | 5,804 | 4,253 |
| 01453 | Leominster | (617) | 32,939 | 27,929 |
| 01273 | Lexington | (617) | 31,886 | 27,691 |
| 01773 | Lincoln | (413) | 7,567 | 5,613 |
| 01460 | Littleton | (617) | 6,380 | 5,109 |
| 01106 | Longmeadow | (413) | 15,630 | 10,565 |
| *01853 | Lowell | (617) | 94,239 | 92,107 |
| 01056 | Ludlow | (617) | 17,580 | 13,805 |
| 01462 | Lunenburg | (617) | 7,419 | 6,334 |
| *01901 | Lynn | (617) | 90,294 | 94,478 |
| 01940 | Lynnfield | (617) | 10,826 | 8,398 |
| 02148 | Malden | (617) | 56,127 | 57,676 |
| 01944 | Manchester | (617) | 5,151 | 3,932 |
| 02048 | Mansfield | (617) | 9,939 | 7,773 |
| 01945 | Marblehead | (617) | 21,295 | 18,521 |
| 01752 | Marlborough | (617) | 27,936 | 18,819 |
| 02050 | Marshfield | (617) | 15,223 | 6,748 |
| 01754 | Maynard | (617) | 9,710 | 7,695 |
| 02052 | Medfield | (617) | 9,821 | 6,021 |
| 02155 | Medford | (617) | 64,397 | 64,971 |
| 02053 | Medway | (617) | 7,938 | 5,168 |
| 02176 | Melrose | (617) | 33,180 | 29,619 |
| 01844 | Methuen | (617) | 35,456 | -28,114 |
| 02346 | Middleborough Center(u) | (617) | 6,259 | 6,003 |
| ..... | Middleborough | (617) | 13,607 | 11,065 |
| 01757 | Milford Center(u) | (617) | 13,740 | 13,722 |
| ..... | Milford | (617) | 19,352 | 15,749 |
| 01527 | Millbury | (617) | 11,987 | 9,623 |
| 02054 | Millis | (617) | 5,686 | 4,374 |
| 02186 | Milton | (617) | 27,190 | 26,375 |
| 01057 | Monson | (413) | 7,355 | 6,712 |
| 01351 | Montague | (413) | 8,451 | 7,836 |
| 01760 | Natick | (617) | 31,057 | 28,831 |
| 02192 | Needham | (617) | 29,748 | 25,793 |
| *02741 | New Bedford | (617) | 101,777 | 102,477 |
| 01950 | Newburyport | (617) | 15,807 | 14,004 |
| 02158 | Newton | (617) | 91,066 | 92,384 |
| 01247 | North Adams | (413) | 19,195 | 19,905 |
| 01060 | Northampton | (617) | 29,664 | 30,058 |
| 01845 | North Andover | (617) | 16,284 | 10,908 |
| *02760 | North Attleborough | (617) | 18,665 | 14,777 |
| 01532 | Northborough | (617) | 9,218 | 6,687 |
| 01534 | Northbridge | (617) | 11,795 | 10,800 |
| 01864 | North Reading | (617) | 11,264 | 8,331 |
| 02060 | North Scituate(u) | (617) | 5,507 | 3,421 |
| 02766 | Norton | (617) | 9,487 | 6,818 |
| 02061 | Norwell | (617) | 7,796 | 5,207 |
| 02062 | Norwood | (617) | 30,815 | 24,898 |
| 01364 | Orange | (413) | 6,104 | 6,154 |
| 01253 | Otis(u) | (413) | 5,596 | ..... |
| 01540 | Oxford Center(u) | (617) | 6,109 | 6,985 |
| ..... | Oxford | (617) | 10,345 | 9,282 |
| 01069 | Palmer | (413) | 11,680 | 10,358 |
| 01960 | Peabody | (617) | 48,080 | 32,202 |
| 02359 | Pembroke | (617) | 11,193 | 4,919 |
| 01463 | Pepperell | (617) | 5,887 | 4,336 |
| 01866 | Pinehurst | (617) | 5,681 | 1,991 |
| 01201 | Pittsfield | (413) | 57,020 | 57,879 |
| *02360 | Plymouth Center(u) | (617) | 6,940 | 6,488 |
| ..... | Plymouth | (617) | 18,606 | 14,445 |
| 02169 | Quincy | (617) | 87,966 | 87,409 |
| 02368 | Randolph | (617) | 27,035 | 18,900 |
| 02767 | Raynham | (617) | 6,705 | 4,150 |
| 01867 | Reading | (617) | 22,539 | 19,259 |
| 02769 | Rehoboth | (617) | 6,512 | 4,953 |
| 02151 | Revere | (617) | 43,159 | 40,080 |
| 02370 | Rockland | (617) | 15,674 | 13,119 |
| 01966 | Rockport | (617) | 5,636 | 4,616 |
| 01970 | Salem | (617) | 40,556 | 39,211 |
| 02563 | Sandwich | (617) | 5,239 | 2,082 |
| 01906 | Saugus | (617) | 25,110 | 20,666 |
| 02066 | Scituate | (617) | 16,973 | 11,214 |
| 02771 | Seekonk | (617) | 11,116 | 8,399 |
| 02067 | Sharon | (617) | 12,367 | 10,070 |
| 01545 | Shrewsbury | (617) | 19,196 | 16,622 |
| 02725 | Somerset | (617) | 18,088 | 12,196 |
| 02143 | Somerville | (617) | 88,779 | 94,697 |
| 01772 | Southborough | (617) | 5,798 | 3,996 |
| 01550 | Southbridge Center(u) | (617) | 14,261 | 15,889 |
| ..... | Southbridge | (617) | 17,057 | 16,523 |
| 01075 | South Hadley | (413) | 17,033 | 14,956 |
| 01077 | Southwick | (413) | 6,330 | 5,139 |
| 02664 | South Yarmouth(u) | (617) | 5,380 | 2,029 |
| 01562 | Spencer Center | (617) | 5,895 | 5,593 |
| ..... | Spencer | (617) | 8,779 | 7,838 |
| *01101 | Springfield | (413) | 163,905 | 174,463 |
| 02180 | Stoneham | (617) | 20,725 | 17,821 |
| 02072 | Stoughton | (617) | 23,459 | 16,328 |
| 01776 | Sudbury | (617) | 13,506 | 7,447 |
| 01907 | Swampscott | (617) | 13,578 | 13,294 |
| 02777 | Swansea | (617) | 12,640 | 9,916 |
| 02780 | Taunton | (617) | 43,756 | 41,132 |
| 01468 | Templeton | (617) | 5,863 | 5,371 |
| 01876 | Tewksbury | (617) | 22,755 | 15,902 |
| 01983 | Topsfield | (413) | 5,225 | 3,351 |
| 01376 | Turners Falls(u) | (617) | 5,168 | 4,917 |
| 01569 | Uxbridge | (617) | 8,253 | 7,789 |
| 01880 | Wakefield | (617) | 25,402 | 24,295 |
| 02081 | Walpole | (617) | 18,149 | 14,068 |
| 02154 | Waltham | (413) | 61,582 | 55,413 |
| 01082 | Ware Center(u) | (413) | 6,509 | 6,650 |
| ..... | Ware | (617) | 8,187 | 7,517 |
| 02571 | Wareham | (617) | 11,492 | 9,461 |
| 02172 | Watertown | (617) | 39,307 | 39,092 |
| 01778 | Wayland | (617) | 13,461 | 10,444 |
| 01570 | Webster Center(u) | (617) | 12,432 | 12,072 |
| ..... | Webster | (617) | 14,917 | 13,680 |
| 02181 | Wellesley | (617) | 28,051 | 26,071 |
| 01581 | Westborough | (617) | 12,594 | 9,599 |
| 01583 | West Boylston | (617) | 6,369 | 5,526 |
| 02379 | West Bridgewater | (617) | 7,152 | 5,061 |
| 01085 | Westfield | (413) | 31,433 | 26,302 |
| 01886 | Westford | (617) | 10,368 | 6,261 |
| 02193 | Weston | (617) | 10,870 | 8,261 |
| 02790 | Westport | (612) | 9,791 | 6,641 |
| 01089 | West Springfield | (413) | 28,461 | 24,924 |
| 02090 | Westwood | (617) | 12,750 | 10,354 |
| 02188 | Weymouth | (617) | 54,610 | 48,177 |
| 01588 | Whitinsville(u) | (617) | 5,210 | 5,102 |
| 02382 | Whitman | (617) | 13,059 | 10,485 |
| 01095 | Wilbraham | (413) | 11,984 | 7,387 |
| 01267 | Williamstown | (413) | 8,454 | 7,322 |
| 01887 | Wilmington | (413) | 17,102 | 12,475 |
| 01475 | Winchendon | (617) | 6,635 | 6,237 |

| ZIP code | Place | | 1970 | 1960 |
|---|---|---|---|---|
| 01890 | Winchester | (617) | 22,269 | 19,376 |
| 02152 | Winthrop | (617) | 20,335 | 20,303 |
| 01801 | Woburn | (617) | 37,406 | 31,214 |
| *01613 | Worcester | (617) | 176,572 | 186,587 |
| 02093 | Wrentham | (617) | 7,315 | 6,685 |
| 02675 | Yarmouth | (617) | 12,033 | 5,504 |

## Michigan

| ZIP code | Place | | 1970 | 1960 |
|---|---|---|---|---|
| 49221 | Adrian | (313) | 20,382 | 20,347 |
| 49224 | Albion | (517) | 12,112 | 12,749 |
| 48101 | Allen Park | (313) | 40,747 | 37,494 |
| 48801 | Alma | (517) | 9,611 | 8,978 |
| 49707 | Alpena | (313) | 13,805 | 14,682 |
| *48106 | Ann Arbor | (313) | 99,797 | 67,340 |
| *49016 | Battle Creek | (616) | 38,931 | 44,169 |
| 48706 | Bay City | (517) | 49,449 | 53,604 |
| 48809 | Belding | (616) | 5,121 | 4,887 |
| 49022 | Benton Central(u) | (616) | 8,067 | ..... |
| 49022 | Benton Harbor | (616) | 16,481 | 19,136 |
| 48072 | Berkley | (313) | 21,879 | 23,275 |
| 48009 | Beverly Hills | (313) | 13,598 | 8,633 |
| 49307 | Big Rapids | (616) | 11,995 | 8,686 |
| *48012 | Birmingham | (313) | 26,170 | 25,525 |
| 49601 | Cadillac | (616) | 9,990 | 10,112 |
| 48724 | Carrollton(u) | (517) | 7,300 | ..... |
| 48015 | Center Line | (313) | 10,379 | 10,164 |
| 48813 | Charlotte | (517) | 8,244 | 7,657 |
| 49721 | Cheboygan | (616) | 5,553 | 5,859 |
| 48017 | Clawson | (313) | 17,617 | 14,795 |
| 49036 | Coldwater | (517) | 9,155 | 8,880 |
| 49041 | Comstock(u) | (616) | 5,003 | ..... |
| 49321 | Comstock Park(u) | (616) | 5,766 | ..... |
| 49508 | Cutlerville(u) | (616) | 6,267 | ..... |
| 48423 | Davison 1976 | (313) | 6,193 | 3,761 |
| *48120 | Dearborn | (313) | 104,199 | 112,007 |
| 48127 | Dearborn Heights | (313) | 80,069 | ..... |
| *48233 | Detroit | (313) | 1,513,601 | 1,670,144 |
| 49047 | Dowagiac | (313) | 6,583 | 7,208 |
| 48020 | Drayton Plains(u) | (616) | 16,462 | ..... |
| 48021 | East Detroit | (313) | 45,920 | 45,756 |
| 49506 | East Grand Rapids | (616) | 12,565 | 10,924 |
| 48823 | East Lansing | (616) | 47,540 | 30,198 |
| 49001 | Eastwood(u) | (517) | 9,682 | ..... |
| 48229 | Ecorse | (616) | 17,515 | 17,328 |
| 49829 | Escanaba | (313) | 15,368 | 15,391 |
| 48024 | Farmington | (906) | 10,329 | 6,881 |
| 48430 | Fenton | (313) | 8,284 | 6,142 |
| 48220 | Ferndale | (313) | 30,850 | 31,347 |
| 48134 | Flat Rock | (313) | 5,643 | 4,696 |
| *48502 | Flint | (313) | 193,317 | 196,940 |
| 48433 | Flushing 1976 | (313) | 8,313 | 3,761 |
| 48026 | Fraser 1977 | (313) | 13,986 | 7,027 |
| 48135 | Garden City | (313) | 41,864 | 38,017 |
| 49837 | Gladstone | (313) | 5,237 | 5,267 |
| 48439 | Grand Blanc | (406) | 5,132 | 1,565 |
| 49417 | Grand Haven | (313) | 11,844 | 11,066 |
| 48837 | Grand Ledge | (616) | 6,032 | 5,165 |
| *49501 | Grand Rapids | (517) | 197,649 | 177,313 |
| 49418 | Grandville | (616) | 10,764 | 7,975 |
| 48838 | Greenville | (616) | 7,493 | 7,440 |
| 48138 | Grosse Ile(u) | (616) | 8,306 | ..... |
| 48236 | Grosse Pointe | (313) | 6,637 | 6,631 |
| 48236 | Grosse Pointe Farms | (313) | 11,701 | 12,172 |
| 48236 | Grosse Pointe Park | (313) | 15,641 | 15,457 |
| 48236 | Grosse Pointe Woods | (313) | 21,878 | 18,580 |
| 48212 | Hamtramck | (313) | 27,245 | 34,137 |
| 48236 | Harper Woods | (313) | 20,186 | 19,995 |
| 49058 | Hastings | (616) | 6,501 | 6,375 |
| 48030 | Hazel Park | (313) | 23,784 | 25,631 |
| 48203 | Highland Park | (313) | 35,444 | 38,063 |
| 49242 | Hillsdale | (517) | 7,728 | 7,629 |
| 49423 | Holland | (616) | 26,479 | 24,777 |
| 48842 | Holt(u) | (517) | 6,980 | 4,818 |
| 49931 | Houghton | (906) | 6,067 | 3,393 |
| 48843 | Howell | (517) | 5,224 | 4,861 |
| 48070 | Huntington Woods | (313) | 8,536 | 8,746 |
| 48141 | Inkster | (313) | 38,595 | 39,097 |
| 48846 | Ionia | (517) | 6,361 | 6,754 |
| 49801 | Iron Mountain | (906) | 8,702 | 9,299 |
| 49938 | Ironwood | (906) | 8,711 | 10,265 |
| 49849 | Ishpeming | (906) | 8,245 | 8,857 |
| *49201 | Jackson | (517) | 45,484 | 50,720 |
| 49428 | Jenison(u) | (616) | 11,266 | ..... |
| *49001 | Kalamazoo | (616) | 85,555 | 82,089 |
| 49508 | Kentwood 1976 | (616) | 25,731 | ..... |
| 49788 | Kincheloe(u) | (906) | 6,331 | ..... |
| 49801 | Kingsford | (906) | 5,276 | 5,084 |
| 49843 | K.I. Sawyer(u) | (906) | 8,224 | ..... |
| 49015 | Lakeview(u) | (517) | 11,391 | 10,384 |
| 48144 | Lambertville(u) | (313) | 5,711 | 1,168 |
| *48924 | Lansing | (517) | 131,403 | 107,807 |
| 48446 | Lapeer | (313) | 6,314 | 6,160 |
| 48503 | Lapeer Heights(u) | (313) | 7,130 | ..... |
| 48146 | Lincoln Park | (313) | 52,984 | 53,933 |
| *48150 | Livonia | (313) | 110,109 | 66,702 |
| 48071 | Madison Heights | (313) | 38,599 | 33,343 |

| ZIP code | Place | | 1970 | 196_ |
|---|---|---|---|---|
| 49660 | Manistee | (616) | 7,723 | 8,32 |
| 49855 | Marquette | (906) | 21,967 | 19,82 |
| 49068 | Marshall | (517) | 7,253 | 6,73 |
| 48040 | Marysville | (313) | 5,610 | 4,06 |
| 48854 | Mason | (517) | 5,468 | 4,52 |
| 48122 | Melvindale | (313) | 13,862 | 13,08 |
| 49858 | Menominee | (906) | 10,748 | 11,28 |
| 48640 | Midland | (517) | 35,176 | 27,77 |
| 48161 | Monroe | (313) | 23,894 | 22,96 |
| 48043 | Mount Clemens | (313) | 20,476 | 21,01 |
| 48858 | Mount Pleasant | (517) | 20,524 | 14,87 |
| *49440 | Muskegon | (616) | 44,631 | 46,48 |
| 49444 | Muskegon Heights | (616) | 17,304 | 19,55 |
| 49866 | Negaunee | (906) | 5,248 | 6,12 |
| 49120 | Niles | (616) | 12,988 | 13,84 |
| 48167 | Northville | (313) | 5,400 | 3,96 |
| 49441 | Norton Shores | (616) | 22,271 | ..... |
| 48050 | Novi | (313) | 9,668 | 6,39 |
| 48237 | Oak Park | (313) | 36,762 | 36,63 |
| 48864 | Okemos(u) | (517) | 7,770 | ..... |
| 48867 | Owosso | (517) | 17,179 | 17,00 |
| 49770 | Petroskey | (616) | 6,342 | 6,13 |
| 48170 | Plymouth | (313) | 11,758 | 8,76 |
| *48053 | Pontiac | (313) | 85,279 | 82,23 |
| 49081 | Portage 1977 | (616) | 36,533 | ..... |
| 48060 | Port Huron | (313) | 35,794 | 36,08 |
| 48024 | Quakertown North(u) | ..... | 7,101 | ..... |
| 48218 | River Rouge | (313) | 15,947 | 18,14 |
| 48192 | Riverview | (313) | 11,342 | 7,23 |
| 48063 | Rochester | (313) | 7,054 | 5,43 |
| 48066 | Roseville | (313) | 60,529 | 50,19 |
| *48068 | Royal Oak | (313) | 88,238 | 80,61 |
| *48065 | Saginaw | (517) | 91,849 | 98,26 |
| *48083 | St. Clair Shores | (313) | 88,093 | 76,65 |
| 48879 | St. Johns | (517) | 6,672 | 5,62 |
| 49085 | St. Joseph | (616) | 11,042 | 11,75 |
| 48176 | Saline 1974 | (517) | 6,050 | 2,33 |
| 49783 | Sault Ste. Marie | (906) | 15,136 | 18,72 |
| 48075 | Southfield | (313) | 69,285 | 31,50 |
| 48198 | Southgate | (313) | 33,909 | 29,40 |
| 49090 | South Haven | (313) | 6,471 | 6,14 |
| *48078 | Sterling Heights 1976 | (313) | 92,904 | ..... |
| 49091 | Sturgis | (616) | 9,295 | 8,91 |
| 48180 | Taylor 1976 | (313) | 77,490 | ..... |
| 49286 | Tecumseh | (517) | 7,120 | 7,04 |
| 49093 | Three Rivers | (616) | 7,355 | 7,09 |
| 49684 | Traverse City | (616) | 18,048 | 18,43 |
| 48183 | Trenton | (313) | 24,127 | 18,43 |
| 48084 | Troy | (313) | 39,419 | 19,40 |
| 49464 | Walker 1976 | (616) | 13,349 | ..... |
| *48089 | Warren | (313) | 179,260 | 89,24 |
| 48184 | Wayne | (313) | 21,054 | 16,03 |
| 48185 | Westland | (313) | 86,749 | ..... |
| 49007 | Westwood(u) | (616) | 9,143 | ..... |
| 48753 | Wurtsmith(u) | (517) | 6,932 | ..... |
| *48192 | Wyandotte | (313) | 41,061 | 43,51 |
| 49509 | Wyoming | (616) | 56,560 | 45,82 |
| 48197 | Ypsilanti | (313) | 29,538 | 20,957 |

## Minnesota

| ZIP code | Place | | 1970 | 1960 |
|---|---|---|---|---|
| 56007 | Albert Lea | (507) | 19,418 | 17,108 |
| 56308 | Alexandria | (612) | 6,973 | 6,713 |
| 55303 | Anoka | (612) | 13,295 | 10,562 |
| 55068 | Apple Valley 1975 | (612) | 15,315 | ..... |
| 55112 | Arden Hills | (612) | 5,149 | 3,930 |
| 55912 | Austin | (507) | 25,074 | 27,908 |
| 56601 | Bemidji | (218) | 11,490 | 9,958 |
| 55433 | Blaine | (612) | 20,625 | 7,570 |
| 55420 | Bloomington 1975 | (612) | 79,119 | 50,498 |
| 56401 | Brainerd | (612) | 11,667 | 12,898 |
| 55429 | Brooklyn Center | (612) | 35,173 | 24,356 |
| 55429 | Brooklyn Park 1972 | (612) | 29,945 | 10,197 |
| 55337 | Burnsville | (612) | 19,940 | ..... |
| 55316 | Champlin 1972 | (612) | 6,298 | 1,271 |
| 55317 | Chanhassen 1971 | (612) | 5,054 | 244 |
| 55318 | Chaska 1972 | (612) | 5,398 | 2,501 |
| 55719 | Chisholm 1975 | (218) | 6,085 | 7,144 |
| 55720 | Cloquet | (218) | 8,699 | 9,013 |
| 55421 | Columbia Heights | (612) | 23,837 | 17,533 |
| 55433 | Coon Rapids | (612) | 30,505 | 14,931 |
| 55016 | Cottage Grove | (218) | 13,419 | ..... |
| 56716 | Crookston | (612) | 8,312 | 8,546 |
| 55428 | Crystal | (612) | 30,925 | 24,283 |
| 56501 | Detroit Lakes | (612) | 5,797 | 5,633 |
| *55806 | Duluth | (218) | 100,578 | 106,884 |
| 55121 | Eagan 1977 | (612) | 19,276 | ..... |
| 56721 | East Grand Forks 1975 | (612) | 8,397 | 6,998 |
| 55343 | Eden Prairie 1975 | (612) | 9,109 | ..... |
| 55424 | Edina | (612) | 44,046 | 28,501 |
| 56031 | Fairmont | (507) | 10,751 | 9,745 |
| 55113 | Falcon Heights | (612) | 5,641 | 5,927 |
| 55021 | Faribault | (507) | 16,595 | 16,926 |
| 56537 | Fergus Falls | (218) | 12,443 | 13,733 |
| 55421 | Fridley | (612) | 29,233 | 15,173 |
| 55427 | Golden Valley | (612) | 24,246 | 14,559 |
| 55744 | Grand Rapids | (218) | 7,247 | 7,265 |
| 55033 | Hastings | (612) | 12,195 | 8,965 |

| ZIP code | Place | | 1970 | 1960 |
|---|---|---|---|---|
| 55746 | Hibbing 1976 | (218) | 16,126 | 17,731 |
| 55343 | Hopkins | (612) | 13,428 | 11,370 |
| 55350 | Hutchinson | (612) | 8,031 | 6,207 |
| 56649 | International Falls | (218) | 6,439 | 6,778 |
| 55075 | Inver Grove Heights | (612) | 12,148 | ..... |
| 55044 | Lakeville | (612) | 7,556 | 924 |
| 55355 | Litchfield | (612) | 5,262 | 5,078 |
| 55110 | Little Canada 1974 | (612) | 5,977 | 3,512 |
| 56345 | Little Falls | (612) | 7,467 | 7,551 |
| 56001 | Mankato | (507) | 30,895 | 23,797 |
| 55369 | Maple Grove 1975 | (612) | 10,039 | 2,213 |
| 55109 | Maplewood | (612) | 25,222 | 18,519 |
| 56258 | Marshall 1977 | (507) | 10,194 | 6,681 |
| 55118 | Mendota Heights | (612) | 6,165 | 5,028 |
| *55401 | Minneapolis | (612) | 434,400 | 482,872 |
| 55343 | Minnetonka | (612) | 35,737 | 25,037 |
| 56265 | Montevideo | (612) | 5,661 | 5,693 |
| 56560 | Moorhead | (218) | 29,687 | 22,934 |
| 56267 | Morris | (612) | 5,366 | 4,199 |
| 55364 | Mound | (612) | 7,572 | 5,440 |
| 55112 | Mounds View | (612) | 10,641 | 6,146 |
| 55112 | New Brighton | (612) | 19,507 | 6,448 |
| 54428 | New Hope | (612) | 23,180 | 3,552 |
| 56073 | New Ulm | (507) | 13,051 | 11,114 |
| 55057 | Northfield | (507) | 10,235 | 8,707 |
| 56001 | North Mankato 1975 | (507) | 8,071 | 5,927 |
| 55109 | North St. Paul | (612) | 11,950 | 8,520 |
| 55119 | Oakdale | (612) | 7,304 | ..... |
| 55391 | Orono | (612) | 6,787 | 5,643 |
| 55060 | Owatonna | (507) | 15,341 | 13,409 |
| 56164 | Pipestone | (507) | 5,328 | 5,324 |
| 55427 | Plymouth | (612) | 18,077 | 9,576 |
| 55066 | Red Wing | (507) | 10,441 | 10,528 |
| 55423 | Richfield | (612) | 47,231 | 42,523 |
| 55422 | Robbinsdale | (612) | 16,845 | 16,381 |
| 55901 | Rochester | (507) | 53,766 | 40,663 |
| 55113 | Roseville | (612) | 34,438 | 23,997 |
| 55418 | St. Anthony | (612) | 9,239 | 5,084 |
| 56301 | St. Cloud 1975 | (612) | 40,715 | 33,815 |
| 55426 | St. Louis Park | (612) | 48,922 | 43,310 |
| *55101 | St. Paul | (612) | 309,714 | 313,411 |
| 55071 | St. Paul Park | (612) | 5,587 | 3,267 |
| 56082 | St. Peter | (507) | 8,339 | 8,484 |
| 56379 | Sauk Rapids | (612) | 5,051 | 4,038 |
| 55379 | Shakopee | (612) | 6,876 | 5,201 |
| 55112 | Shoreview | (612) | 10,995 | 7,157 |
| 55075 | South St. Paul | (612) | 25,016 | 22,032 |
| 55432 | Spring Lake Park | (612) | 6,417 | 3,260 |
| 55082 | Stillwater | (612) | 10,191 | 8,310 |
| 56701 | Thief River Falls 1975 | (218) | 8,929 | 7,151 |
| 55792 | Virginia | (218) | 12,450 | 14,034 |
| 56093 | Waseca 1975 | (507) | 7,804 | 5,898 |
| 55118 | West St. Paul | (612) | 18,799 | 13,101 |
| 55110 | White Bear Lake | (612) | 23,313 | 12,849 |
| 56201 | Willmar | (612) | 12,869 | 10,417 |
| 55987 | Winona | (507) | 26,438 | 24,895 |
| 55119 | Woodbury | (612) | 6,184 | ..... |
| 56187 | Worthington | (507) | 9,916 | 9,015 |

## Mississippi (601)

| ZIP code | Place | 1970 | 1960 |
|---|---|---|---|
| 39730 | Aberdeen | 6,507 | 6,450 |
| 38821 | Amory | 7,236 | 6,474 |
| 39520 | Bay St. Louis | 6,752 | 5,073 |
| *39530 | Biloxi 1975 | 46,497 | 44,053 |
| 38829 | Booneville | 5,895 | 3,480 |
| 39601 | Brookhaven | 10,700 | 9,885 |
| 39046 | Canton | 10,503 | 9,707 |
| 38614 | Clarksdale | 21,673 | 21,105 |
| 38732 | Cleveland 1975 | 14,043 | 10,172 |
| 39056 | Clinton 1976 | 12,100 | 3,438 |
| 39429 | Columbia | 7,587 | 7,117 |
| 39701 | Columbus | 25,795 | 24,771 |
| 38834 | Corinth | 11,581 | 11,453 |
| 39532 | D'Iberville(u) | 7,288 | 3,005 |
| 38701 | Greenville | 39,648 | 41,502 |
| 38930 | Greenwood | 22,400 | 20,436 |
| 38901 | Grenada | 9,944 | 7,914 |
| 39501 | Gulfport | 40,791 | 30,204 |
| 39401 | Hattiesburg | 38,277 | 34,989 |
| 38635 | Holly Springs | 5,728 | 5,621 |
| 38751 | Indianola | 8,947 | 6,714 |
| *39205 | Jackson | 153,968 | 144,422 |
| 39090 | Kosciusko | 7,266 | 6,800 |
| 39440 | Laurel | 24,145 | 27,889 |
| 38756 | Leland | 6,000 | 6,295 |
| 39560 | Long Beach 1975 | 7,113 | 4,770 |
| 39339 | Louisville | 6,626 | 5,066 |
| 39648 | McComb | 11,969 | 12,020 |
| 39301 | Meridian 1974 | 46,087 | 49,374 |
| 39563 | Moss Point | 19,321 | 6,631 |
| 39120 | Natchez | 19,704 | 23,791 |
| 38652 | New Albany | 6,426 | 5,151 |
| 39564 | Ocean Springs | 9,580 | 5,025 |
| 38655 | Oxford City | 13,846 | 5,283 |
| 39567 | Pascagoula | 27,264 | 17,155 |
| 39208 | Pearl(u) | 9,623 | 5,081 |
| 39465 | Petal(u) | 6,986 | 4,007 |
| 39350 | Philadelphia | 6,274 | 5,017 |
| 39466 | Picayune | 10,467 | 7,834 |
| 38671 | Southaven(u) | 8,931 | ..... |
| 39759 | Starkville | 11,369 | 9,041 |
| 38801 | Tupelo | 20,471 | 17,221 |
| 39180 | Vicksburg | 25,478 | 29,143 |
| 39501 | West Gulfport(u) | 6,996 | 3,323 |
| 39773 | West Point | 8,714 | 8,550 |
| 38967 | Winona | 5,521 | 4,282 |
| 39194 | Yazoo City | 11,688 | 11,236 |

## Missouri

| ZIP code | Place | | 1970 | 1960 |
|---|---|---|---|---|
| 63123 | Affton(u) | (314) | 24,264 | ..... |
| 65605 | Aurora | (417) | 5,359 | 4,683 |
| 63011 | Ballwin | (314) | 10,656 | 5,710 |
| 63137 | Bellefontaine Neighbors | (314) | 14,084 | 13,650 |
| 63133 | Bel-Ridge | (314) | 5,346 | 4,395 |
| 64012 | Belton | (816) | 12,179 | 4,897 |
| 63134 | Berkeley | (314) | 19,743 | 18,676 |
| 64015 | Blue Springs | (816) | 6,779 | 2,555 |
| 65233 | Boonville | (816) | 7,514 | 7,090 |
| 63114 | Breckenridge Hills | (314) | 7,011 | 6,299 |
| 63144 | Brentwood | (314) | 11,248 | 12,250 |
| 63044 | Bridgeton | (314) | 19,992 | 7,820 |
| 64628 | Brookfield | (816) | 5,491 | 5,694 |
| 63701 | Cape Girardeau | (314) | 31,282 | 24,947 |
| 64836 | Carthage | (417) | 11,035 | 11,264 |
| 63830 | Caruthersville | (314) | 7,350 | 8,643 |
| 63834 | Charleston | (314) | 5,131 | 5,911 |
| 64601 | Chillicothe | (816) | 9,519 | 9,236 |
| 63105 | Clayton | (314) | 16,100 | 15,245 |
| 64735 | Clinton | (816) | 7,504 | 6,925 |
| 65201 | Columbia | (314) | 58,812 | 36,650 |
| 63128 | Concord(u) | (314) | 21,217 | ..... |
| 63126 | Crestwood | (314) | 15,123 | 11,106 |
| 63141 | Creve Coeur 1976 | (314) | 10,660 | 5,122 |
| 63136 | Dellwood | (314) | 7,137 | 4,720 |
| 63020 | De Soto | (314) | 5,984 | 5,804 |
| 63131 | Des Peres 1975 | (314) | 7,130 | 4,362 |
| 63841 | Dexter | (314) | 6,024 | 5,519 |
| 64024 | Excelsior Springs | (816) | 9,411 | 6,473 |
| 63640 | Farmington | (314) | 6,590 | 5,618 |
| 63135 | Ferguson | (314) | 28,759 | 22,149 |
| 63028 | Festus | (314) | 7,530 | 7,021 |
| *63033 | Florissant | (314) | 65,908 | 38,166 |
| 65473 | Fort Leonard Wood(u) | (314) | 33,799 | ..... |
| 65251 | Fulton | (314) | 12,248 | 11,131 |
| 64118 | Gladstone | (816) | 23,422 | 14,502 |
| 63122 | Glendale | (314) | 6,981 | 7,048 |
| 64030 | Grandview | (816) | 17,456 | 6,027 |
| 63401 | Hannibal | (314) | 18,698 | 20,028 |
| 64701 | Harrisonville | (816) | 5,052 | 3,510 |
| *63042 | Hazelwood | (314) | 14,082 | 6,045 |
| *64051 | Independence | (816) | 111,630 | 62,328 |
| 63755 | Jackson | (314) | 5,896 | 4,875 |
| 65101 | Jefferson City | (314) | 32,407 | 28,228 |
| 63136 | Jennings | (314) | 19,379 | 19,965 |
| 64801 | Joplin | (417) | 39,256 | 38,958 |
| *64108 | Kansas City | (816) | 507,330 | 475,539 |
| 63857 | Kennett | (314) | 10,090 | 9,098 |
| 63140 | Kinloch | (314) | 5,629 | 6,501 |
| 63501 | Kirksville | (816) | 15,560 | 13,123 |
| 63122 | Kirkwood | (314) | 31,679 | 29,421 |
| 63124 | Ladue | (314) | 10,359 | 9,466 |
| 65536 | Lebanon | (417) | 8,616 | 8,220 |
| 64063 | Lee's Summit | (816) | 16,230 | 8,267 |
| 63125 | Lemay(u) | (314) | 40,516 | ..... |
| 64067 | Lexington | (816) | 5,388 | 4,845 |
| 64068 | Liberty | (816) | 13,704 | 8,909 |
| 63552 | Macon | (816) | 5,301 | 4,547 |
| 63863 | Malden | (816) | 5,374 | 5,007 |
| 63011 | Manchester | (314) | 5,031 | 2,021 |
| 63143 | Maplewood | (314) | 12,785 | 12,552 |
| 65340 | Marshall | (816) | 12,051 | 9,572 |
| 63043 | Maryland Heights(u) | (314) | 8,805 | ..... |
| 64468 | Maryville | (816) | 9,970 | 7,807 |
| 65265 | Mexico | (314) | 11,807 | 12,889 |
| 65270 | Moberly | (816) | 12,988 | 13,170 |
| 65708 | Monett | (417) | 5,937 | 5,359 |
| 64850 | Neosho | (417) | 7,517 | 7,452 |
| 64772 | Nevada | (417) | 9,736 | 8,416 |
| 63121 | Normandy | (314) | 6,236 | 4,452 |
| 64116 | North Kansas City 1974 | (816) | 5,046 | 5,657 |
| 63366 | O'Fallon | (314) | 7,018 | 3,770 |
| 63124 | Olivette | (314) | 9,156 | 8,257 |
| 63114 | Overland | (314) | 24,819 | 22,763 |
| 63133 | Pagedale | (314) | 5,044 | 5,106 |
| 63775 | Perryville | (314) | 5,149 | 5,117 |
| 63120 | Pine Lawn | (314) | 5,745 | 5,943 |
| 63901 | Poplar Bluff | (816) | 16,653 | 15,926 |
| 64133 | Raytown | (314) | 33,306 | 17,083 |
| 63117 | Richmond Heights | (314) | 13,802 | 15,622 |
| 63124 | Rock Hill | (314) | 6,815 | 6,523 |
| 65401 | Rolla | (314) | 13,571 | 11,132 |
| 63074 | St. Ann | (314) | 18,215 | 12,155 |
| 63301 | St. Charles | (314) | 31,834 | 21,189 |
| 63114 | St. John | (314) | 8,960 | 7,342 |

| ZIP code | Place | | 1970 | 1960 |
|---|---|---|---|---|
| *64501 | St. Joseph | (816) | 72,691 | 79,673 |
| *63155 | St. Louis | (314) | 622,236 | 750,026 |
| 63126 | Sappington(u) | (314) | 10,603 | ..... |
| 65301 | Sedalia | (816) | 22,847 | 23,874 |
| 63119 | Shrewsbury | (314) | 5,896 | 4,730 |
| 63801 | Sikeston | (314) | 14,699 | 13,765 |
| 63138 | Spanish Lake(u) | (314) | 15,647 | ..... |
| *65801 | Springfield | (417) | 120,096 | 95,865 |
| 63080 | Sullivan | (314) | 5,111 | 4,098 |
| 64683 | Trenton | (816) | 6,063 | 6,262 |
| 63084 | Union | (314) | 5,183 | 3,937 |
| 63130 | University City | (314) | 47,527 | 51,249 |
| 64093 | Warrensburg | (816) | 13,125 | 9,689 |
| 63090 | Washington | (314) | 8,499 | 7,961 |
| 64870 | Webb City | (417) | 6,923 | 6,740 |
| 63119 | Webster Groves | (314) | 27,457 | 28,990 |
| 63112 | Wellston | (314) | 7,050 | 7,979 |
| 65775 | West Plains | (417) | 6,893 | 5,836 |
| 65301 | Whiteman | (816) | 5,040 | ..... |
| 63134 | Woodson Terrace | (314) | 5,880 | 6,048 |

## Montana (406)

| ZIP code | Place | 1970 | 1960 |
|---|---|---|---|
| 59711 | Anaconda | 9,771 | 12,054 |
| *59101 | Billings | 61,581 | 52,851 |
| 59715 | Bozeman | 18,670 | 13,361 |
| 59701 | Butte | 23,368 | 27,877 |
| 59701 | Floral Park(u) | 5,113 | 4,079 |
| 59330 | Glendive 1977 | 5,892 | 7,058 |
| *59401 | Great Falls | 60,091 | 55,244 |
| 59501 | Havre | 10,558 | 10,740 |
| 59601 | Helena | 22,730 | 20,227 |
| 59901 | Kalispell | 10,526 | 10,151 |
| 59457 | Lewistown | 6,437 | 7,408 |
| 59047 | Livingston | 6,883 | 8,229 |
| 59402 | Malmstrom(u) | 8,374 | ..... |
| 59301 | Miles City 1976 | 9,622 | 9,665 |
| 59801 | Missoula | 29,497 | 27,090 |
| 59801 | Missoula West(u) | 9,148 | ..... |
| 59701 | Silver Bow Park(u) | 5,524 | 4,798 |

## Nebraska

| ZIP code | Place | | 1970 | 1960 |
|---|---|---|---|---|
| 69301 | Alliance 1977 | (308) | 7,987 | 7,845 |
| 68310 | Beatrice | (402) | 12,389 | 12,132 |
| 68005 | Bellevue 1974 | (402) | 21,145 | 8,831 |
| 68008 | Blair | (402) | 6,106 | 4,931 |
| 69337 | Chadron | (308) | 5,921 | 5,079 |
| 68601 | Columbus | (402) | 15,471 | 12,476 |
| 68352 | Fairbury | (402) | 5,265 | 5,572 |
| 68355 | Falls City | (402) | 5,444 | 5,598 |
| 68025 | Fremont | (402) | 22,962 | 19,698 |
| 69341 | Gering 1976 | (308) | 6,680 | 4,585 |
| 68801 | Grand Island | (308) | 31,269 | 25,742 |
| 68901 | Hastings | (402) | 23,580 | 21,412 |
| 68949 | Holdrege | (308) | 5,635 | 5,226 |
| 68847 | Kearney 1976 | (308) | 19,350 | 14,210 |
| 68128 | La Vista 1974 | (402) | 7,640 | 1,004 |
| 68850 | Lexington | (402) | 5,654 | 5,572 |
| *68501 | Lincoln | (402) | 149,518 | 128,521 |
| 69001 | McCook | (308) | 8,285 | 8,301 |
| 68137 | Millard | (402) | 7,460 | 1,014 |
| 68410 | Nebraska City | (402) | 7,441 | 7,252 |
| 68701 | Norfolk | (402) | 16,607 | 13,640 |
| 69101 | North Platte | (308) | 19,447 | 17,184 |
| 68113 | Offutt East(u) | (402) | 5,195 | ..... |
| 68113 | Offutt West(u) | (402) | 8,445 | ..... |
| *68108 | Omaha | (402) | 346,929 | 301,598 |
| 68046 | Papillion 1974 | (402) | 6,493 | 2,235 |
| 68048 | Plattsmouth | (402) | 6,371 | 6,244 |
| 69361 | Scottsbluff | (308) | 14,507 | 13,377 |
| 68434 | Seward | (402) | 5,294 | 4,208 |
| 69162 | Sidney 1976 | (308) | 6,092 | 8,004 |
| 68776 | South Sioux City 1976 | (402) | 6,504 | 7,200 |
| 68787 | Wayne | (402) | 5,379 | 4,217 |
| 68467 | York | (402) | 6,778 | 6,173 |

## Nevada (702)

| ZIP code | Place | 1970 | 1960 |
|---|---|---|---|
| 89005 | Boulder City | 5,223 | 4,059 |
| 89701 | Carson City | 15,468 | 5,163 |
| 89112 | East Las Vegas(u) | 6,501 | ..... |
| 89801 | Elko | 7,621 | 6,298 |
| 89015 | Henderson | 16,395 | 12,525 |
| *89114 | Las Vegas | 125,787 | 64,405 |
| 89110 | Nellis(u) | 6,449 | ..... |
| 89030 | North Las Vegas | 36,216 | 18,422 |
| 89109 | Paradise(u) | 24,477 | ..... |
| *89501 | Reno | 72,863 | 51,470 |
| 89431 | Sparks | 24,187 | 16,618 |
| 89110 | Sunrise Manor(u) | 10,886 | ..... |
| 89109 | Vegas Creek(u) | 8,970 | ..... |
| 89101 | Winchester(u) | 13,981 | ..... |

## New Hampshire (603)

*See note on page 219*

| ZIP code | Place | 1970 | 1960 |
|---|---|---|---|
| 03102 | *Bedford* | 5,859 | 3,636 |
| 03570 | Berlin | 15,256 | 17,821 |

| ZIP code | Place | 1970 | 1960 |
|---|---|---|---|
| 03743 | Claremont | 14,221 | 13,563 |
| 03301 | Concord | 30,022 | 28,991 |
| 03038 | Derry Compact(u) | 6,090 | 4,468 |
| 03038 | *Derry* | 11,712 | 6,987 |
| 03820 | Dover | 20,850 | 19,131 |
| 03824 | Durham Compact(u) | 7,221 | 4,688 |
| | *Durham* | 8,869 | 5,504 |
| 03833 | Exeter Compact(u) | 6,439 | 5,896 |
| | *Exeter* | 8,892 | 7,243 |
| 03235 | Franklin | 7,292 | 6,742 |
| 03045 | Goffstown | 9,284 | 7,230 |
| 03842 | Hampton Compact(u) | 5,407 | 3,281 |
| | *Hampton* | 8,011 | 5,379 |
| 03755 | Hanover Compact(u) | 6,147 | 5,649 |
| | *Hanover* | 8,494 | 7,329 |
| 03106 | Hookset | 5,564 | 3,713 |
| 03051 | Hudson | 10,638 | 5,876 |
| 03431 | Keene | 20,467 | 17,562 |
| 03246 | Laconia | 14,888 | 15,288 |
| 03766 | Lebanon | 9,725 | 9,299 |
| 03516 | *Littleton* | 5,290 | 5,003 |
| 03053 | *Londonderry* | 5,346 | 2,457 |
| *03101 | Manchester | 87,754 | 88,282 |
| 03054 | *Merrimack* | 8,595 | 2,989 |
| 03055 | *Milford* | 6,622 | 4,863 |
| 03060 | Nashua | 55,820 | 39,096 |
| 03773 | *Newport* | 5,899 | 5,458 |
| 03076 | *Pelham* | 5,408 | 2,605 |
| 03801 | Portsmouth | 25,717 | 26,900 |
| 03867 | Rochester | 17,938 | 15,927 |
| 03079 | *Salem* | 20,142 | 9,210 |
| 03874 | *Seabrook 1974* | 5,128 | 2,209 |
| 03878 | Somersworth | 9,026 | 8,529 |

## New Jersey

| ZIP code | Place | | 1970 | 1960 |
|---|---|---|---|---|
| 08201 | Absecon | (609) | 6,094 | 4,320 |
| 07401 | Allendale | (201) | 6,240 | 4,092 |
| 07712 | Asbury Park | (201) | 16,533 | 17,366 |
| *08401 | Atlantic City | (609) | 47,859 | 59,544 |
| 07716 | Atlantic Highlands | (201) | 5,102 | 4,119 |
| 08106 | Audubon | (609) | 10,802 | 10,440 |
| 08007 | Barrington | (609) | 8,409 | 7,943 |
| 07002 | Bayonne | (201) | 72,743 | 74,215 |
| 07109 | Belleville | (201) | 37,629 | 35,005 |
| 08030 | Bellmawr | (609) | 15,618 | 11,853 |
| 07719 | Belmar | (201) | 5,782 | 5,190 |
| 07621 | Bergenfield | (201) | 29,000 | 27,203 |
| 07922 | Berkeley Hts. Twp. | (201) | 13,078 | 8,721 |
| 07924 | Bernardsville | (201) | 6,652 | 5,515 |
| 07003 | Bloomfield | (201) | 52,029 | 51,867 |
| 07403 | Bloomingdale | (201) | 7,797 | 5,293 |
| 07603 | Bogota | (201) | 8,960 | 7,965 |
| 07005 | Boonton | (201) | 9,261 | 7,981 |
| 08805 | Bound Brook | (201) | 10,450 | 10,263 |
| 08723 | Brick Twp. | (201) | 35,057 | 16,299 |
| 08302 | Bridgeton | (609) | 20,435 | 20,966 |
| 08203 | Brigantine | (609) | 6,741 | 4,201 |
| 08015 | Browns Mills(u) | (609) | 7,144 | ..... |
| 08016 | Burlington | (609) | 11,991 | 12,687 |
| 07405 | Butler | (201) | 7,051 | 5,414 |
| *07006 | Caldwell | (201) | 8,677 | 6,942 |
| *08101 | Camden | (609) | 102,551 | 117,159 |
| 08701 | Candlewood(u) | (201) | 5,629 | ..... |
| 07072 | Carlstadt | (201) | 6,724 | 6,042 |
| 07008 | Carteret | (201) | 23,137 | 20,502 |
| 07009 | Cedar Grove Twp. | (201) | 15,582 | 14,603 |
| 07928 | Chatham | (201) | 9,566 | 9,517 |
| *08002 | Cherry Hill Twp. | (201) | 64,395 | 31,522 |
| 08077 | Cinnaminson Twp. | | 16,962 | 8,302 |
| 07066 | Clark Twp. | (201) | 18,829 | 12,195 |
| 08312 | Clayton | (609) | 5,193 | 4,711 |
| 07010 | Cliffside Park | (201) | 18,891 | 17,642 |
| 07721 | Cliffwood-Cliffwood Beach(u) | (201) | 7,056 | ..... |
| *07015 | Clifton | (201) | 82,437 | 82,084 |
| 07624 | Closter | (201) | 8,604 | 7,767 |
| 08108 | Collingswood | (609) | 17,422 | 17,370 |
| 07016 | Cranford Twp. | (201) | 27,391 | 26,424 |
| 07626 | Cresskill | (201) | 8,298 | 7,290 |
| 08075 | Delran Twp. | (609) | 10,065 | 5,327 |
| 07627 | Demarest | (201) | 5,133 | 4,231 |
| 07834 | Denville Twp. | (201) | 14,045 | 10,632 |
| 08096 | Deptford Twp. | (609) | 24,232 | 17,878 |
| 07801 | Dover | (201) | 15,039 | 13,034 |
| 07628 | Dumont | (201) | 20,155 | 18,882 |
| 08812 | Dunellen | (201) | 7,072 | 6,840 |
| 08816 | East Brunswick Twp. | (201) | 34,166 | 19,965 |
| *07019 | East Orange | (201) | 75,471 | 77,259 |
| 07407 | East Paterson | (201) | 20,511 | 19,344 |
| 07073 | East Rutherford | (201) | 8,536 | 7,769 |
| 08520 | East Windsor Twp. 1974 | (609) | 19,788 | 2,298 |
| 07724 | Eatontown | (201) | 14,619 | 10,334 |
| 08817 | Edison Twp. | (201) | 67,120 | 44,799 |
| *07207 | Elizabeth | (201) | 112,654 | 107,698 |
| 07630 | Emerson | (201) | 8,428 | 6,849 |
| *07631 | Englewood | (201) | 24,985 | 26,057 |
| 07632 | Englewood Cliffs | (201) | 5,938 | 2,913 |
| 08053 | Evesham Twp. | (609) | 13,477 | 4,543 |

| ZIP code | Place | | 1970 | 1960 |
|---|---|---|---|---|
| 08618 | Ewing Twp. | (609) | 32,831 | 26,628 |
| 07006 | Fairfield | (201) | 6,884 | ..... |
| 07701 | Fair Haven | (201) | 6,142 | 5,858 |
| 07410 | Fair Lawn | (201) | 37,975 | 36,421 |
| 07022 | Fairview | (201) | 10,698 | 9,399 |
| 07023 | Fanwood | (201) | 8,920 | 7,963 |
| 08518 | Florence-Roebling(u) | (609) | 7,551 | ..... |
| 07932 | Florham Park | (201) | 8,094 | 7,222 |
| 08640 | Fort Dix(u) | (609) | 26,290 | ..... |
| 07024 | Fort Lee | (201) | 30,631 | 21,815 |
| 07417 | Franklin Lakes | (201) | 7,550 | 3,316 |
| 07728 | Freehold | (201) | 10,545 | 9,140 |
| 07026 | Garfield | (201) | 30,797 | 29,253 |
| 07027 | Garwood | (201) | 5,260 | 5,426 |
| 08028 | Glassboro | (609) | 12,938 | 10,253 |
| 07028 | Glen Ridge | (201) | 8,518 | 8,322 |
| 07452 | Glen Rock | (201) | 13,011 | 12,896 |
| 08030 | Gloucester City | (609) | 14,707 | 15,511 |
| 07093 | Guttenberg | (201) | 5,754 | 5,118 |
| *07602 | Hackensack | (201) | 36,008 | 30,521 |
| 07840 | Hackettstown | (201) | 9,472 | 5,276 |
| 08108 | Haddon Twp. | (201) | 18,192 | 17,099 |
| 08033 | Haddonfield | (609) | 13,118 | 13,201 |
| 08035 | Haddon Heights | (609) | 9,365 | 9,260 |
| 07508 | Haledon | (201) | 6,767 | 6,161 |
| 08037 | Hammonton | (609) | 11,464 | 9,854 |
| 07981 | Hanover Twp. | (201) | 10,700 | 9,329 |
| 07029 | Harrison | (201) | 11,811 | 11,743 |
| 07604 | Hasbrouck Heights | (201) | 13,651 | 13,046 |
| 07506 | Hawthorne | (201) | 19,173 | 17,735 |
| 07730 | Hazlet Twp. | (201) | 22,239 | 15,334 |
| 08904 | Highland Park | (201) | 14,385 | 11,049 |
| 08520 | Hightstown | (609) | 5,431 | 4,317 |
| 07642 | Hillsdale | (201) | 11,768 | 8,734 |
| 07205 | Hillside Twp. | (201) | 21,636 | 22,304 |
| 07030 | Hoboken | (201) | 45,380 | 48,441 |
| 07843 | Hopatcong | (201) | 9,052 | 3,391 |
| 08560 | Hopewell Twp. (Mercer) | (609) | 10,030 | 7,818 |
| 07111 | Irvington | (201) | 59,743 | 59,379 |
| 08527 | Jackson Twp. | (609) | 18,276 | 5,939 |
| *07303 | Jersey City | (201) | 260,350 | 276,101 |
| 07734 | Keansburg | (201) | 9,720 | 6,854 |
| 07032 | Kearny | (201) | 37,585 | 37,472 |
| 08824 | Kendall Park(u) | (201) | 7,412 | ..... |
| 07033 | Kenilworth | (201) | 9,165 | 8,379 |
| 07735 | Keyport | (201) | 7,205 | 6,440 |
| 07405 | Kinnelon | (201) | 7,600 | 4,331 |
| 07034 | Lake Hiawatha(u) | (201) | 11,389 | ..... |
| 07871 | Lake Mohawk(u) | (201) | 6,262 | 4,647 |
| 07054 | Lake Parsippany(u) | (201) | 7,488 | ..... |
| 08701 | Lakewood(u) | (201) | 17,874 | 13,004 |
| 08879 | Laurence Harbor(u) | (201) | 6,715 | ..... |
| 07605 | Leonia | (201) | 8,847 | 8,384 |
| 07035 | Lincoln Park | (201) | 9,034 | 6,048 |
| 07036 | Linden | (201) | 41,409 | 39,931 |
| 08021 | Lindenwold 1973 | (609) | 16,265 | 7,335 |
| 08221 | Linwood | (609) | 6,159 | 3,847 |
| 07424 | Little Falls Twp. | (201) | 11,727 | 9,730 |
| 07643 | Little Ferry | (201) | 9,064 | 6,176 |
| 07739 | Little Silver | (201) | 6,010 | 5,202 |
| 07039 | Livingston Twp. | (201) | 30,127 | 23,124 |
| 07644 | Lodi | (201) | 25,163 | 23,502 |
| 07740 | Long Branch | (201) | 31,774 | 26,228 |
| 07071 | Lyndhurst Twp. | (201) | 22,729 | 21,867 |
| 07940 | Madison | (201) | 16,710 | 15,122 |
| 08049 | Magnolia | (609) | 5,893 | 4,199 |
| 07430 | Mahwah Twp. | (201) | 10,800 | 7,376 |
| 08835 | Manville | (201) | 13,029 | 10,995 |
| 08052 | Maple Shade Twp. | (609) | 16,464 | 12,947 |
| 07040 | Maplewood Twp. | (201) | 24,932 | 23,977 |
| 08402 | Margate City | (609) | 10,576 | 9,474 |
| 07746 | Marlboro Twp. | (201) | 12,273 | 8,038 |
| 08053 | Marlton(u) | (609) | 10,180 | ..... |
| 07747 | Matawan | (201) | 9,136 | 5,097 |
| 07607 | Maywood | (201) | 11,087 | 11,460 |
| 08641 | McGuire(u) | (609) | 10,933 | ..... |
| 08619 | Mercerville-Hamilton Sq.(u) | (609) | 24,465 | ..... |
| 08840 | Metuchen | (201) | 16,031 | 14,041 |
| 08846 | Middlesex | (201) | 15,038 | 10,520 |
| 07748 | Middletown Twp. | (201) | 54,623 | 39,675 |
| 07432 | Midland Park | (201) | 8,159 | 7,543 |
| 07041 | Millburn Twp. | (201) | 21,089 | 18,799 |
| 08850 | Milltown | (201) | 6,470 | 5,435 |
| 08332 | Millville | (609) | 21,366 | 19,096 |
| 07434 | Monroe Twp. (Gloucester) | (201) | 14,071 | 9,396 |
| *07042 | Montclair | (201) | 44,043 | 43,129 |
| 07645 | Montvale | (201) | 7,327 | 3,699 |
| 07045 | Montville Twp. | (201) | 11,846 | 6,772 |
| 08057 | Moorestown-Lenola(u) | (609) | 14,179 | ..... |
| 07950 | Morris Plains | (201) | 5,540 | 4,703 |
| 07960 | Morristown | (201) | 17,662 | 17,712 |
| 07092 | Mountainside | (201) | 7,520 | 6,325 |
| 08059 | Mount Ephraim | (609) | 5,625 | 5,447 |
| 08060 | Mount Holly Twp. | (609) | 12,713 | 13,271 |
| 08753 | Neptune Twp. | (609) | 27,863 | 21,487 |
| 08753 | Neptune City | (609) | 5,502 | 4,916 |
| *07102 | Newark | (201) | 381,930 | 405,220 |
| *08901 | New Brunswick | (201) | 41,885 | 40,139 |
| 08511 | New Hanover | (201) | 27,410 | 28,528 |

| ZIP code | Place | | 1970 | 1960 |
|---|---|---|---|---|
| 07646 | New Milford | (201) | 19,149 | 18,810 |
| 07974 | New Providence | (201) | 13,796 | 10,243 |
| 07724 | New Shrewsbury | (201) | 8,395 | 7,313 |
| 07860 | Newton | (201) | 7,297 | 6,563 |
| 07032 | North Arlington | (201) | 18,096 | 17,477 |
| 07047 | North Bergen Twp. | (201) | 47,751 | 42,387 |
| 08902 | North Brunswick Twp. | (201) | 16,691 | 10,099 |
| 07006 | North Caldwell | (201) | 6,733 | 4,163 |
| 08225 | Northfield | (609) | 8,875 | 5,849 |
| 07508 | North Haledon | (201) | 7,614 | 6,026 |
| 07060 | North Plainfield | (201) | 21,796 | 16,993 |
| 07647 | Northvale | (201) | 5,177 | 2,892 |
| 07110 | Nutley | (201) | 31,913 | 29,513 |
| 07755 | Oakhurst(u) | (201) | 5,558 | 4,374 |
| 07436 | Oakland | (201) | 14,420 | 9,446 |
| 08226 | Ocean City | (609) | 10,575 | 7,618 |
| 07757 | Oceanport | (201) | 7,503 | 4,937 |
| 08857 | Old Bridge(u) | (201) | 25,176 | ..... |
| 07649 | Oradell | (201) | 8,903 | 7,487 |
| *07050 | Orange | (201) | 32,566 | 35,789 |
| 07650 | Palisades Park | (201) | 13,351 | 11,943 |
| 08065 | Palmyra | (609) | 6,969 | 7,036 |
| 07652 | Paramus | (201) | 28,381 | 23,238 |
| 07656 | Park Ridge | (201) | 8,709 | 6,389 |
| *07055 | Passaic | (201) | 55,124 | 53,963 |
| *07510 | Paterson | (201) | 144,824 | 143,663 |
| 08066 | Paulsboro | (609) | 8,084 | 8,121 |
| 08110 | Pennsauken Twp. | (609) | 36,394 | 33,771 |
| 08069 | Penns Grove | (609) | 5,727 | 6,176 |
| 08070 | Pennsville Center(u) | (609) | 11,014 | ..... |
| 07440 | Pequannock Twp. | (201) | 14,350 | 10,553 |
| *08861 | Perth Amboy | (201) | 38,798 | 38,007 |
| 08865 | Phillipsburg | (201) | 17,849 | 18,502 |
| 08021 | Pine Hill | (609) | 5,132 | 3,939 |
| 08854 | Piscataway Twp. | (201) | 36,418 | 19,890 |
| 08071 | Pitman | (609) | 10,257 | 8,644 |
| *07061 | Plainfield | (201) | 46,862 | 45,330 |
| 08232 | Pleasantville | (609) | 13,778 | 15,172 |
| 08742 | Point Pleasant | (201) | 15,968 | 10,182 |
| 07442 | Pompton Lakes | (201) | 11,397 | 9,445 |
| 08540 | Princeton | (609) | 12,331 | 11,890 |
| 08540 | Princeton North(u) | (609) | 5,488 | 4,506 |
| 07508 | Prospect Park | (201) | 5,176 | 5,201 |
| *07065 | Rahway | (201) | 29,114 | 27,699 |
| 08057 | Ramblewood(u) | (609) | 5,556 | ..... |
| 07446 | Ramsey | (201) | 12,571 | 9,527 |
| 07970 | Randolph Twp. | (201) | 13,296 | 7,295 |
| 08869 | Raritan | (201) | 6,691 | 6,137 |
| 07701 | Red Bank | (201) | 12,847 | 12,482 |
| 07657 | Ridgefield | (201) | 11,308 | 10,788 |
| 07660 | Ridgefield Park | (201) | 13,990 | 12,701 |
| *07451 | Ridgewood | (201) | 27,547 | 25,391 |
| 07456 | Ringwood | (201) | 10,393 | 4,182 |
| 07661 | River Edge | (201) | 12,850 | 13,264 |
| 08075 | Riverside Twp. | (609) | 8,591 | 8,474 |
| 07662 | Rochell Park Twp. | (201) | 6,380 | 6,119 |
| 07866 | Rockaway | (201) | 6,383 | 5,413 |
| 07203 | Roselle | (201) | 22,585 | 21,032 |
| 07204 | Roselle Park | (201) | 14,227 | 12,546 |
| 07760 | Rumson | (201) | 7,421 | 6,405 |
| 08078 | Runnemede | (201) | 10,475 | 8,396 |
| *07070 | Rutherford | (201) | 20,802 | 20,473 |
| 07662 | Saddle Brook Twp. | (201) | 15,975 | 13,834 |
| 08079 | Salem | (609) | 7,648 | 8,941 |
| 08872 | Sayreville | (201) | 32,508 | 22,553 |
| 07076 | Scotch Plains Twp. | (201) | 22,279 | 18,491 |
| 07094 | Secaucus | (201) | 13,228 | 12,154 |
| 08083 | Somerdale | (609) | 6,510 | 4,839 |
| 08244 | Somers Point | (609) | 7,919 | 4,504 |
| 08876 | Somerville | (201) | 13,652 | 12,458 |
| 08879 | South Amboy | (201) | 9,338 | 8,422 |
| 07079 | South Orange | (201) | 16,971 | 16,175 |
| 07080 | South Plainfield | (201) | 21,142 | 17,879 |
| 08882 | South River | (201) | 15,428 | 13,397 |
| 07871 | Sparta Twp. | (201) | 10,819 | 6,717 |
| 08884 | Spotswood | (201) | 7,891 | 5,788 |
| 07081 | Springfield Twp. | (201) | 15,740 | 14,467 |
| 08084 | Stratford | (609) | 9,801 | 4,308 |
| 07747 | Strathmore | (201) | 7,874 | ..... |
| 07901 | Summit | (201) | 23,620 | 23,677 |
| 07666 | Teaneck Twp. | (201) | 42,355 | 42,085 |
| 07670 | Tenafly | (201) | 14,827 | 14,264 |
| 08753 | Toms River | (201) | 7,303 | 6,062 |
| 07512 | Totowa | (201) | 11,580 | 10,897 |
| *08608 | Trenton | (609) | 104,786 | 114,167 |
| 07083 | Union Twp. | (201) | 53,077 | 51,499 |
| 07735 | Union Beach | (201) | 6,472 | 5,862 |
| 07087 | Union City | (201) | 57,305 | 52,180 |
| 07458 | Upper Saddle River | (201) | 7,949 | 3,570 |
| 08406 | Ventnor City | (609) | 10,385 | 8,688 |
| 07044 | Verona | (201) | 15,067 | 13,782 |
| 08360 | Vineland | (609) | 47,399 | 37,685 |
| 07463 | Waldwick | (201) | 12,313 | 10,495 |
| 07057 | Wallington | (201) | 10,284 | 9,261 |
| 07465 | Wanaque | (201) | 8,636 | 7,126 |
| 07882 | Washington | (201) | 5,943 | 5,723 |
| 07675 | Washington Twp. (Bergen) | (201) | 10,577 | 6,654 |
| 07470 | Wayne Twp. | (201) | 49,141 | 29,353 |
| 07087 | Weehawken Twp. | (201) | 13,383 | 13,504 |

| ZIP code | Place | | 1970 | 1960 |
|---|---|---|---|---|
| 07006 | West Caldwell | (201) | 11,913 | 8,314 |
| *07091 | Westfield | (201) | 33,720 | 31,447 |
| 07764 | West Long Branch | (201) | 6,845 | 5,337 |
| 07480 | West Milford Twp. | (201) | 17,304 | 8,157 |
| 07093 | West New York | (201) | 40,627 | 35,547 |
| 07052 | West Orange | (201) | 43,715 | 39,895 |
| 07424 | West Paterson | (201) | 11,692 | 7,602 |
| 08093 | Westville | (201) | 5,170 | 4,951 |
| 07675 | Westwood | (201) | 11,105 | 9,046 |
| 07885 | Wharton | (201) | 5,535 | 5,006 |
| 08610 | White Horse-Yardville(u) | (201) | 18,680 | ..... |
| 07886 | White Meadow Lake(u) | (201) | 8,499 | ..... |
| 08046 | Willingboro Twp. 1973 | (609) | 44,607 | 11,861 |
| 08095 | Winslow Twp. | (609) | 11,202 | 9,142 |
| 07095 | Woodbridge Twp. | (201) | 98,944 | 78,846 |
| 08096 | Woodbury | (609) | 12,408 | 12,453 |
| 07675 | Woodcliff Lake | (201) | 5,506 | 2,742 |
| 07075 | Wood-Ridge | (201) | 8,311 | 7,964 |
| 07481 | Wyckoff Twp. | (201) | 16,039 | 11,205 |

## New Mexico (505)

| ZIP code | Place | | 1970 | 1960 |
|---|---|---|---|---|
| 88310 | Alamogordo | | 23,035 | 21,723 |
| *87101 | Albuquerque | | 243,751 | 201,189 |
| 88210 | Artesia | | 10,315 | 12,000 |
| 88101 | Cannon(u) | | 5,461 | ..... |
| 88220 | Carlsbad | | 21,297 | 25,541 |
| 88101 | Clovis | | 28,495 | 23,713 |
| 88030 | Deming | | 8,343 | 6,764 |
| 87401 | Farmington | | 21,979 | 23,786 |
| 87301 | Gallup | | 14,596 | 14,089 |
| 87020 | Grants | | 8,768 | 10,274 |
| 88240 | Hobbs | | 26,025 | 26,275 |
| 88330 | Holloman(u) | | 8,001 | ..... |
| 88001 | Las Cruces | | 37,857 | 29,367 |
| 87701 | Las Vegas (city) | | 7,528 | 7,790 |
| 87701 | Las Vegas (town) | | 6,307 | 6,028 |
| 87544 | Los Alamos(u) | | 11,310 | 12,584 |
| 88260 | Lovington | | 8,915 | 9,660 |
| 87107 | North Valley(u) | | 10,366 | ..... |
| 88130 | Portales | | 10,554 | 9,695 |
| 87740 | Raton | | 6,962 | 8,146 |
| 88201 | Roswell | | 33,908 | 39,593 |
| 87115 | Sandia(u) | | 6,867 | ..... |
| 87501 | Santa Fe | | 41,167 | 33,394 |
| 88061 | Silver City | | 8,557 | 6,972 |
| 87801 | Socorro | | 5,849 | 5,271 |
| 87105 | South Valley(u) | | 29,389 | ..... |
| 88401 | Tucumcari | | 7,189 | 8,143 |

## New York

| ZIP code | Place | | 1970 | 1960 |
|---|---|---|---|---|
| *12207 | Albany | (518) | 115,781 | 129,726 |
| 11507 | Albertson(u) | (516) | 6,825 | ..... |
| 14411 | Albion | (716) | 5,122 | 5,182 |
| 11701 | Amityville | (516) | 9,794 | 8,318 |
| 12010 | Amsterdam | (518) | 25,524 | 28,772 |
| 12603 | Arlington(u) | (914) | 11,203 | 8,317 |
| 13021 | Auburn | (315) | 34,599 | 35,249 |
| *11702 | Babylon | (516) | 12,897 | 11,062 |
| 11510 | Baldwin(u) | (516) | 34,525 | 30,204 |
| 13027 | Baldwinsville | (315) | 6,298 | 5,985 |
| 14020 | Batavia | (716) | 17,338 | 18,210 |
| 14810 | Bath | (607) | 6,053 | 6,166 |
| 11705 | Bayport(u) | (516) | 8,232 | ..... |
| 11706 | Bay Shore(u) | (516) | 11,119 | ..... |
| 11709 | Bayville | (516) | 6,147 | 3,962 |
| 12508 | Beacon | (914) | 13,255 | 13,922 |
| 11710 | Bellmore(u) | (516) | 18,431 | 12,784 |
| 11714 | Bethpage(u) | (516) | 18,555 | ..... |
| *13902 | Binghamton | (607) | 64,123 | 75,941 |
| 10913 | Blauvelt(u) | (914) | 5,426 | ..... |
| 11716 | Bohemia(u) | (516) | 8,926 | ..... |
| 11717 | Brentwood(u) | (516) | 28,327 | 15,387 |
| 10510 | Briarcliff Manor | (914) | 6,521 | 5,105 |
| 14420 | Brockport | (716) | 7,878 | 5,256 |
| 10708 | Bronxville | (914) | 6,674 | 6,744 |
| *14240 | Buffalo | (716) | 462,768 | 532,759 |
| 14424 | Canadaigua 1971 | (315) | 10,753 | 9,370 |
| 13032 | Canastota | (315) | 5,033 | 4,896 |
| 13617 | Canton | (315) | 6,398 | 5,046 |
| 11514 | Carle Place(u) | (516) | 6,326 | ..... |
| 12414 | Catskill | (518) | 5,317 | 5,825 |
| 11516 | Cedarhurst | (516) | 6,941 | 6,954 |
| 11720 | Centereach(u) | (516) | 9,427 | 8,524 |
| 11722 | Central Islip(u) | (516) | 36,391 | ..... |
| 12065 | Clifton Knolls(u) | (518) | 5,771 | ..... |
| 12047 | Cohoes | (518) | 18,653 | 20,129 |
| 11724 | Cold Spring Harbor | (914) | 5,450 | 1,705 |
| 12205 | Colonie | (518) | 8,701 | 6,992 |
| 11725 | Commack(u) | (516) | 24,138 | 9,613 |
| 10920 | Congers(u) | (914) | 5,928 | ..... |
| 11726 | Copiague(u) | (516) | 19,632 | 14,081 |
| 14830 | Corning | (607) | 15,792 | 17,085 |
| 13045 | Cortland | (607) | 19,621 | 19,181 |
| 10520 | Croton-on-Hudson | (914) | 7,523 | 6,812 |
| 14437 | Dansville | (716) | 5,436 | 5,460 |
| 11729 | Deer Park(u) | (516) | 32,274 | 16,726 |

| ZIP code | Place | | 1970 | 1960 |
|---|---|---|---|---|
| 14043 | Depew | (716) | 22,158 | 13,586 |
| 13214 | DeWitt(u) | (315) | 10,032 | ..... |
| 11746 | Dix Hills(u) | (516) | 10,050 | ..... |
| 10522 | Dobbs Ferry | (914) | 10,353 | 9,264 |
| 14048 | Dunkirk | (716) | 16,855 | 18,205 |
| 14052 | East Aurora | (716) | 7,033 | 6,791 |
| 10709 | Eastchester(u) | (914) | 23,750 | ..... |
| 12302 | East Glenville(u) | (518) | 5,898 | ..... |
| 11746 | East Half Hollow Hills(u) | (516) | 9,691 | ..... |
| 11576 | East Hills | (516) | 8,624 | 7,184 |
| 11730 | East Islip(u) | (516) | 6,861 | ..... |
| 11758 | East Massapequa(u) | (516) | 15,926 | 14,779 |
| 11554 | East Meadow(u) | (516) | 46,290 | 46,036 |
| 11743 | East Neck(u) | (516) | 5,221 | 3,789 |
| 11731 | East Northport(u) | (516) | 12,392 | 8,387 |
| 11772 | East Patchogue(u) | (516) | 8,092 | ..... |
| 14445 | East Rochester | (716) | 8,347 | 8,155 |
| 11518 | East Rockaway | (516) | 11,795 | 10,721 |
| 13902 | East Vestal(u) | (607) | 10,472 | ..... |
| *14901 | Elmira | (607) | 39,945 | 46,517 |
| 11003 | Elmont(u) | (516) | 29,363 | 30,138 |
| 11731 | Elwood(u) | (516) | 15,031 | ..... |
| 13760 | Endicott | (607) | 16,556 | 18,775 |
| 13760 | Endwell(u) | (607) | 15,999 | ..... |
| 13219 | Fairmount(u) | (315) | 15,317 | ..... |
| 14450 | Fairport | (716) | 6,474 | 5,507 |
| 12601 | Fairview(u) | (914) | 8,517 | 8,626 |
| 11735 | Farmingdale | (516) | 9,297 | 6,128 |
| *11001 | Floral Park | (516) | 18,466 | 17,499 |
| 11010 | Franklin Square(u) | (516) | 32,156 | 32,483 |
| 14063 | Fredonia | (716) | 10,326 | 8,477 |
| 11520 | Freeport | (516) | 40,374 | 34,419 |
| 13069 | Fulton | (315) | 14,003 | 14,261 |
| 11530 | Garden City | (516) | 25,373 | 23,948 |
| 11040 | Garden City Park(u) | (516) | 7,488 | ..... |
| 14454 | Geneseo | (716) | 5,714 | 3,284 |
| 14456 | Geneva | (315) | 16,793 | 17,286 |
| 11542 | Glen Cove | (516) | 25,770 | 23,817 |
| 12801 | Glens Falls | (518) | 17,222 | 18,580 |
| 12078 | Gloversville | (518) | 19,677 | 21,741 |
| *11022 | Great Neck | (516) | 10,798 | 10,171 |
| 11020 | Great Neck Plaza | (516) | 6,043 | 4,948 |
| 11740 | Greenlawn(u) | (516) | 8,493 | 5,422 |
| 11746 | Half Hollow Hills(u) | (516) | 12,081 | ..... |
| 14075 | Hamburg | (716) | 10,215 | 9,145 |
| 10528 | Harrison Town | (914) | 21,544 | 19,201 |
| 10530 | Hartsdale(u) | (914) | 12,226 | ..... |
| 10706 | Hastings-on-Hudson | (914) | 9,479 | 8,979 |
| 11787 | Hauppauge(u) | (516) | 13,957 | ..... |
| 10927 | Haverstraw | (914) | 8,198 | 5,771 |
| *11551 | Hempstead | (516) | 39,411 | 34,641 |
| 13350 | Herkimer | (315) | 8,960 | 9,396 |
| 11040 | Herricks(u) | (516) | 9,112 | ..... |
| 11557 | Hewlett(u) | (516) | 6,796 | ..... |
| *11802 | Hicksville(u) | (516) | 49,820 | 50,405 |
| 10977 | Hillcrest(u) | (914) | 5,357 | ..... |
| 11741 | Holbrook-Holtsville(u) | (516) | 12,103 | ..... |
| 14843 | Hornell | (607) | 12,144 | 13,907 |
| 14845 | Horseheads Village | (607) | 7,989 | 7,207 |
| 12534 | Hudson | (518) | 8,940 | 11,075 |
| 12839 | Hudson Falls | (518) | 7,917 | 7,752 |
| 11743 | Huntington(u) | (516) | 12,601 | 11,255 |
| 11746 | Huntington Station(u) | (516) | 28,817 | 23,438 |
| 13357 | Ilion | (315) | 9,808 | 10,199 |
| 11696 | Inwood(u) | (516) | 8,433 | 10,362 |
| 10533 | Irvington | (914) | 5,878 | 5,494 |
| 11558 | Island Park | (516) | 5,396 | 3,846 |
| 11751 | Islip | (516) | 7,692 | ..... |
| 14850 | Ithaca | (607) | 26,226 | 28,799 |
| 14701 | Jamestown | (716) | 39,795 | 41,818 |
| 10535 | Jefferson Valley-Yorktown(u) | (914) | 9,008 | ..... |
| 11753 | Jericho(u) | (516) | 14,010 | 10,795 |
| 13790 | Johnson City | (607) | 18,025 | 19,118 |
| 12095 | Johnstown | (518) | 10,045 | 10,390 |
| 14217 | Kenmore | (716) | 20,980 | 21,261 |
| 11754 | Kings Park(u) | (516) | 5,555 | 4,949 |
| 11024 | Kings Point | (516) | 5,614 | 5,410 |
| 12401 | Kingston | (914) | 25,544 | 29,260 |
| 14218 | Lackawanna | (716) | 28,657 | 29,564 |
| 11755 | Lake Grove 1975 | (516) | 9,359 | ..... |
| 14086 | Lancaster | (716) | 13,365 | 12,254 |
| 10538 | Larchmont | (914) | 7,203 | 6,789 |
| 12110 | Latham(u) | (914) | 9,661 | ..... |
| 11559 | Lawrence | (516) | 6,566 | 5,907 |
| 14482 | Le Roy | (716) | 5,118 | 4,662 |
| 11756 | Levittown(u) | (516) | 65,440 | 65,276 |
| 11757 | Lindenhurst | (516) | 28,359 | 20,905 |
| 13365 | Little Falls | (315) | 7,629 | 8,935 |
| 14094 | Lockport | (716) | 25,399 | 26,443 |
| 11791 | Locust Grove(u) | (516) | 11,626 | 11,558 |
| 11561 | Long Beach(u) | (516) | 33,127 | 26,473 |
| 12211 | Loudonville(u) | (518) | 9,299 | ..... |
| 11563 | Lynbrook | (516) | 23,151 | 19,881 |
| 10541 | Mahopac(u) | (914) | 5,265 | 1,337 |
| 12953 | Malone | (518) | 8,048 | 8,737 |
| 11565 | Malverne | (516) | 10,036 | 9,968 |
| 10543 | Mamaroneck | (914) | 18,909 | 17,673 |
| 11030 | Manhasset(u) | (516) | 8,541 | ..... |
| 11050 | Manorhaven | (516) | 5,488 | 3,566 |

| ZIP code | Place | | 1970 | 1960 |
|---|---|---|---|---|
| 1758 | Massapequa(u) | (516) | 26,821 | 32,900 |
| 1762 | Massapequa Park | (516) | 22,112 | 19,904 |
| 3662 | Massena | (315) | 14,042 | 15,478 |
| 3211 | Mattydale(u) | (315) | 8,292 | ..... |
| 2118 | Mechanicville | (518) | 6,247 | 6,831 |
| 4103 | Medina | (716) | 6,415 | 6,681 |
| 1746 | Melville(u) | (516) | 6,641 | ..... |
| 1566 | Merrick(u) | (516) | 25,904 | 18,789 |
| 0940 | Middletown | (914) | 22,607 | 23,475 |
| 1501 | Mineola | (516) | 21,744 | 20,519 |
| 0952 | Monsey(u) | (914) | 8,797 | ..... |
| 2701 | Monticello | (914) | 5,991 | 5,222 |
| 0549 | Mt. Kisco | (914) | 8,172 | 6,805 |
| 0551 | Mount Vernon | (914) | 72,788 | 76,010 |
| 0954 | Nanuet(u) | (914) | 10,447 | ..... |
| 1767 | Nesconset(u) | (516) | 10,048 | 1,964 |
| 4513 | Newark 1975 | (315) | 10,717 | 12,868 |
| 2550 | Newburgh | (914) | 26,219 | 30,979 |
| 1590 | New Cassel(u) | (516) | 8,721 | ..... |
| 0956 | New City(u) | (914) | 27,344 | ..... |
| 1040 | New Hyde Park | (516) | 10,116 | 10,808 |
| 2561 | New Paltz | (914) | 6,058 | 3,041 |
| 0802 | New Rochelle | (914) | 75,385 | 76,812 |
| 2550 | New Windsor | (914) | 8,803 | 4,041 |
| 0001 | New York | (212) | 7,895,563 | 7,781,984 |
| 0451 | Bronx | (212) | 1,471,701 | 1,424,815 |
| 1201 | Brooklyn | (212) | 2,602,102 | 2,627,319 |
| 0001 | Manhattan | (212) | 1,539,233 | 1,696,281 |
| *(Q) | Queens | (212) | 1,987,174 | 1,809,578 |

*) There are 4 P.O.s for Queens: 11101 for L.I. City; 11690 Far Rockaway; 11351 Flushing; and 11431 Jamaica.

| ZIP code | Place | | 1970 | 1960 |
|---|---|---|---|---|
| 10314 | Staten Island | (212) | 295,443 | 221,991 |
| 14302 | Niagara Falls | (716) | 85,615 | 102,394 |
| 13745 | Nimmonsburg-Chenango Br.(u) | (607) | 5,059 | ..... |
| 12309 | Niskayuna(u) | (518) | 6,186 | ..... |
| 11701 | North Amityville(u) | (516) | 11,936 | ..... |
| 11703 | North Babylon(u) | (716) | 39,526 | ..... |
| 11710 | North Bellmore(u) | (516) | 22,893 | 19,639 |
| 11713 | North Bellport(u) | (516) | 5,903 | ..... |
| 11752 | North Great River(u) | (516) | 12,080 | ..... |
| 11757 | North Lindenhurst(u) | (516) | 11,117 | ..... |
| 11758 | North Massapequa(u) | (516) | 23,123 | ..... |
| 11566 | North Merrick(u) | (516) | 13,650 | 12,976 |
| 11040 | North New Hyde Park(u) | (516) | 18,154 | 17,929 |
| 11772 | North Patchogue(u) | (516) | 5,232 | ..... |
| 10803 | North Pelham(u) | (914) | 5,184 | 5,326 |
| 11768 | Northport | (516) | 7,494 | 5,972 |
| 13212 | North Syracuse | (315) | 8,687 | 7,412 |
| 10591 | North Tarrytown | (914) | 8,334 | 8,818 |
| 14120 | North Tonawanda | (716) | 36,012 | 34,757 |
| 11580 | North Valley Stream(u) | (516) | 14,881 | 17,239 |
| 11793 | North Wantagh(u) | (516) | 15,053 | ..... |
| 13815 | Norwich | (607) | 8,843 | 9,175 |
| 10960 | Nyack | (914) | 6,659 | 6,062 |
| 11769 | Oakdale(u) | (516) | 7,334 | ..... |
| 11572 | Oceanside(u) | (516) | 35,372 | 30,448 |
| 13669 | Ogdensburg | (315) | 14,554 | 16,122 |
| 11804 | Old Bethpage(u) | (516) | 7,084 | ..... |
| 14760 | Olean | (716) | 19,169 | 21,868 |
| 13421 | Oneida | (315) | 11,658 | 11,677 |
| 13820 | Oneonta | (602) | 16,030 | 13,412 |
| 10562 | Ossining | (914) | 21,659 | 18,662 |
| 13126 | Oswego | (315) | 20,913 | 22,155 |
| 11771 | Oyster Bay(u) | (516) | 6,822 | ..... |
| 11772 | Patchogue 1975 | (516) | 11,283 | 8,838 |
| 10965 | Pearl River(u) | (914) | 17,146 | ..... |
| 10566 | Peekskill | (914) | 19,283 | 18,737 |
| 10803 | Pelham Manor | (914) | 6,673 | 6,114 |
| 14527 | Penn Yan | (315) | 5,293 | 5,770 |
| 11714 | Plainedge(u) | (516) | 10,759 | 21,973 |
| 11803 | Plainview(u) | (516) | 31,695 | 27,710 |
| 12901 | Plattsburg | (518) | 18,715 | 20,172 |
| 12903 | Plattsburgh Base(u) | (518) | 7,078 | ..... |
| 10570 | Pleasantville | (914) | 7,110 | 5,877 |
| 10573 | Port Chester | (914) | 25,803 | 24,960 |
| 11777 | Port Jefferson 1975 | (516) | 5,800 | ..... |
| 11776 | Port Jefferson Station(u) | (516) | 7,403 | 1,041 |
| 12771 | Port Jervis | (914) | 8,852 | 9,268 |
| 11050 | Port Washington(u) | (516) | 15,923 | 15,657 |
| 13676 | Potsdam | (315) | 10,303 | 7,765 |
| *12601 | Poughkeepsie | (914) | 32,029 | 38,330 |
| 12144 | Rensselaer | (518) | 10,136 | 10,506 |
| 11901 | Riverhead(u) | (516) | 7,585 | 5,830 |
| *14603 | Rochester | (716) | 296,233 | 318,611 |
| 11570 | Rockville Centre | (516) | 27,444 | 26,355 |
| 12205 | Roessleville(u) | (518) | 5,476 | ..... |
| 13440 | Rome | (315) | 50,148 | 51,646 |
| 11779 | Ronkonkoma(u) | (516) | 7,484 | 4,220 |
| 11575 | Roosevelt(u) | (516) | 15,008 | 12,883 |
| 11577 | Roslyn Heights(u) | (516) | 7,242 | ..... |
| 12303 | Rotterdam(u) | (518) | 25,214 | 16,871 |
| 10580 | Rye | (914) | 15,869 | 14,225 |
| 11780 | St. James(u) | (516) | 10,500 | 3,524 |
| 14779 | Salamanca | (716) | 7,877 | 8,480 |
| 11754 | San Remo(u) | (516) | 8,302 | 3,160 |
| 12983 | Saranac Lake | (518) | 6,086 | 6,421 |
| 12866 | Saratoga Springs | (518) | 18,845 | 16,630 |

| ZIP code | Place | | 1970 | 1960 |
|---|---|---|---|---|
| 11782 | Sayville(u) | (516) | 11,680 | ..... |
| 10583 | Scarsdale | (914) | 19,229 | 17,968 |
| *12301 | Schenectady | (518) | 77,958 | 81,682 |
| 12302 | Scotia | (518) | 7,370 | 7,625 |
| 11579 | Sea Cliff | (516) | 5,890 | 5,669 |
| 11783 | Seaford(u) | (516) | 17,379 | 14,718 |
| 11784 | Selden(u) | (516) | 11,613 | 1,604 |
| 13148 | Seneca Falls | (315) | 7,794 | 7,439 |
| 11733 | Setauket-South Setauket(u) | (516) | 6,857 | ..... |
| 11967 | Shirley(u) | (516) | 6,280 | ..... |
| 14225 | Sloan | (716) | 5,216 | 5,803 |
| 13209 | Solvay | (315) | 8,280 | 8,732 |
| 11735 | South Farmingdale(u) | (516) | 20,464 | 16,318 |
| 11741 | South Holbrook(u) | (516) | 6,700 | ..... |
| 11746 | South Huntington(u) | (516) | 9,115 | 7,084 |
| 14904 | Southport(u) | (607) | 8,685 | 6,698 |
| 11790 | South Stony Brook(u) | (516) | 15,329 | ..... |
| 11581 | South Valley Stream(u) | (516) | 6,595 | ..... |
| 11590 | South Westbury(u) | (516) | 10,978 | 11,977 |
| 10977 | Spring Valley | (914) | 18,112 | 6,538 |
| 11790 | Stony Brook(u) | (516) | 6,391 | 3,548 |
| 10980 | Stony Point(u) | (914) | 8,270 | 3,330 |
| 10901 | Suffern | (914) | 8,273 | 5,094 |
| 11791 | Syosset(u) | (516) | 10,084 | ..... |
| *13201 | Syracuse | (315) | 197,297 | 216,038 |
| 10983 | Tappan(u) | (914) | 7,424 | ..... |
| 10591 | Tarrytown | (914) | 11,115 | 11,109 |
| 10594 | Thornwood(u) | (914) | 6,874 | ..... |
| 14150 | Tonawanda | (716) | 21,898 | 21,561 |
| *12180 | Troy | (518) | 62,918 | 67,492 |
| 10707 | Tuckahoe | (914) | 6,236 | 6,423 |
| 11553 | Uniondale(u) | (516) | 22,077 | 20,041 |
| *13503 | Utica | (315) | 91,340 | 100,410 |
| 10989 | Valley Cottage(u) | (914) | 6,007 | ..... |
| *11580 | Valley Stream | (516) | 40,413 | 38,629 |
| 11731 | Vernon Valley(u) | (516) | 7,925 | 5,998 |
| 13850 | Vestal-Twin Orchards(u) | (607) | 8,303 | ..... |
| 10901 | Viola(u) | (914) | 5,136 | ..... |
| 12586 | Walden | (914) | 5,277 | 4,851 |
| 11793 | Wantagh(u) | (516) | 21,873 | 34,172 |
| 12590 | Wappingers Falls | (914) | 5,607 | 4,447 |
| 13165 | Waterloo | (315) | 5,418 | 5,098 |
| 13601 | Watertown | (315) | 30,787 | 33,306 |
| 12189 | Watervliet | (518) | 12,404 | 13,917 |
| 14892 | Waverly | (607) | 5,261 | 5,950 |
| 14580 | Webster | (716) | 5,037 | 3,060 |
| 14895 | Wellsville | (716) | 5,815 | 5,967 |
| 11758 | West Amityville(u) | (516) | 6,424 | ..... |
| 11704 | West Babylon(u) | (516) | 12,893 | ..... |
| 11590 | Westbury | (516) | 15,362 | 14,757 |
| 14905 | West Elmira(u) | (607) | 5,901 | 5,763 |
| 10993 | West Haverstraw | (914) | 8,558 | 5,020 |
| 11552 | West Hempstead(u) | (516) | 20,375 | ..... |
| 11795 | West Islip(u) | (516) | 17,374 | ..... |
| 12203 | Westmere(u) | (518) | 6,364 | ..... |
| 10994 | West Nyack(u) | (914) | 5,510 | ..... |
| 11796 | West Sayville(u) | (516) | 7,386 | ..... |
| 13219 | Westvale(u) | (315) | 7,253 | ..... |
| *10602 | White Plains | (914) | 50,346 | 50,485 |
| 14221 | Williamsville | (716) | 6,835 | 6,316 |
| 11596 | Williston Park | (516) | 9,154 | 8,255 |
| 11598 | Woodmere(u) | (516) | 19,831 | 14,011 |
| 11798 | Wyandanch(u) | (516) | 15,716 | ..... |
| 11980 | Yaphank(u) | (516) | 5,460 | ..... |
| *10701 | Yonkers | (914) | 204,297 | 190,634 |
| 10598 | Yorktown Heights(u) | (914) | 6,805 | 2,478 |

## North Carolina

| ZIP code | Place | | 1970 | 1960 |
|---|---|---|---|---|
| 27910 | Ahoskie | (919) | 5,105 | 4,583 |
| 28001 | Albemarle | (704) | 11,126 | 12,261 |
| 27203 | Asheboro | (919) | 10,797 | 9,449 |
| *28801 | Asheville | (704) | 57,681 | 60,192 |
| 28012 | Belmont | (704) | 5,054 | 5,007 |
| 28607 | Boone | (919) | 8,754 | 3,686 |
| 28712 | Brevard | (704) | 5,243 | 4,857 |
| 27215 | Burlington | (919) | 35,930 | 33,199 |
| 28542 | Camp Le Jeune Central(u) | (919) | 34,549 | ..... |
| 28716 | Canton | (704) | 5,158 | 5,068 |
| 27510 | Carrboro | (919) | 5,058 | 1,997 |
| 27511 | Cary 1975 | (919) | 14,671 | 3,356 |
| 27514 | Chapel Hill | (919) | 25,537 | 12,573 |
| *28202 | Charlotte | (704) | 241,178 | 201,564 |
| 28533 | Cherry Point(u) | (919) | 12,029 | ..... |
| 28021 | Cherryville | (704) | 5,258 | 3,607 |
| 28328 | Clinton | (919) | 7,157 | 7,461 |
| 28025 | Concord | (704) | 18,464 | 17,799 |
| 28334 | Dunn | (919) | 8,302 | 7,566 |
| *27700 | Durham | (919) | 95,438 | 78,302 |
| 27288 | Eden | (919) | 15,871 | ..... |
| 27909 | Elizabeth City | (919) | 14,069 | 14,062 |
| *28302 | Fayetteville | (919) | 53,510 | 47,106 |
| 28043 | Forest City | (704) | 7,179 | 6,556 |
| 28307 | Fort Bragg(u) | (919) | 46,995 | ..... |
| 28052 | Gastonia | (704) | 47,142 | 37,276 |
| 27530 | Goldsboro | (919) | 26,810 | 28,873 |
| 27253 | Graham | (919) | 8,172 | 7,723 |
| *27420 | Greensboro | (919) | 144,076 | 119,574 |
| 27834 | Greenville | (919) | 29,063 | 22,860 |

| ZIP code | Place | | 1970 | 1960 |
|---|---|---|---|---|
| 28532 | Havelock | (919) | 5,263 | 2,433 |
| 27536 | Henderson | (919) | 13,896 | 12,740 |
| 28739 | Hendersonville | (704) | 6,443 | 5,911 |
| 28601 | Hickory | (704) | 20,569 | 19,328 |
| *27260 | High Point | (919) | 63,259 | 62,063 |
| 28540 | Jacksonville | (919) | 16,289 | 13,491 |
| 28081 | Kannapolis(u) | (704) | 36,293 | 34,647 |
| 28086 | Kings Mountain | (704) | 8,465 | 8,008 |
| 28501 | Kinston | (919) | 23,020 | 24,819 |
| 28352 | Laurinburg | (919) | 8,859 | 8,242 |
| 28645 | Lenoir | (704) | 14,705 | 10,257 |
| 27292 | Lexington | (704) | 17,205 | 16,093 |
| 28092 | Lincolnton | (704) | 5,293 | 5,699 |
| 28358 | Lumberton | (919) | 16,961 | 15,305 |
| 28110 | Monroe | (704) | 11,282 | 10,882 |
| 28115 | Mooresville | (704) | 8,808 | 6,918 |
| 28557 | Morehead City | (919) | 5,233 | 5,583 |
| 28655 | Morganton | (704) | 13,625 | 9,186 |
| 27030 | Mount Airy | (919) | 7,325 | 7,055 |
| 28120 | Mount Holly | (704) | 5,107 | 4,037 |
| 28560 | New Bern | (919) | 14,660 | 15,717 |
| 28540 | New River Gieger(u) | (919) | 8,699 | ..... |
| 28658 | Newton | (704) | 7,857 | 6,658 |
| 28012 | North Belmont(u) | (704) | 10,672 | 8,328 |
| 27565 | Oxford | (919) | 7,178 | 6,978 |
| *27611 | Raleigh | (919) | 123,793 | 93,931 |
| 27320 | Reidsville | (919) | 13,636 | 14,267 |
| 27870 | Roanoke Rapids | (919) | 13,508 | 13,320 |
| 28379 | Rockingham | (919) | 5,852 | 5,512 |
| 27801 | Rocky Mount | (919) | 34,284 | 32,147 |
| 27573 | Roxboro | (919) | 5,370 | 5,147 |
| 28144 | Salisbury | (704) | 22,515 | 21,297 |
| 27330 | Sanford | (919) | 11,716 | 12,253 |
| 27530 | Seymour-Johnson(u) | (919) | 8,172 | ..... |
| 28150 | Shelby | (704) | 16,328 | 17,698 |
| 27577 | Smithfield | (919) | 6,677 | 6,117 |
| 28387 | Southern Pines | (919) | 5,937 | 5,198 |
| 28677 | Statesville | (704) | 20,007 | 19,844 |
| 27886 | Tarboro | (919) | 9,425 | 8,411 |
| 27360 | Thomasville | (704) | 15,230 | 15,190 |
| 27889 | Washington | (919) | 8,961 | 9,939 |
| 28786 | Waynesville | (704) | 6,488 | 6,159 |
| 28025 | West Concord(u) | (704) | 5,347 | 5,510 |
| 27892 | Williamston | (919) | 6,570 | 6,924 |
| 28401 | Wilmington | (919) | 46,169 | 44,013 |
| 27893 | Wilson | (919) | 29,347 | 28,753 |
| *27102 | Winston-Salem | (919) | 133,683 | 111,135 |

### North Dakota (701)

| ZIP code | Place | 1970 | 1960 |
|---|---|---|---|
| 58501 | Bismark 1975 | 38,123 | 27,670 |
| 58301 | Devils Lake 1974 | 7,354 | 6,299 |
| 58601 | Dickinson 1975 | 12,496 | 9,971 |
| 58102 | Fargo | 53,965 | 46,662 |
| 58237 | Grafton 1973 | 5,931 | 5,885 |
| 58201 | Grand Forks(u) 1976 | 42,581 | 34,451 |
| 58201 | Grand Forks Base(u) | 10,474 | ..... |
| 58401 | Jamestown 1971 | 15,078 | 15,163 |
| 58554 | Mandan 1973 | 11,400 | 10,525 |
| 58701 | Minot 1975 | 32,823 | 30,604 |
| 58701 | Minot Base(u) | 12,077 | ..... |
| 58072 | Valley City | 7,843 | 7,809 |
| 58075 | Wahpeton 1975 | 8,257 | 5,876 |
| 58078 | West Fargo 1976 | 7,919 | 3,328 |
| 58801 | Williston | 11,280 | 11,866 |

### Ohio

| ZIP code | Place | | 1970 | 1960 |
|---|---|---|---|---|
| 45810 | Ada | (419) | 5,309 | 3,918 |
| *44309 | Akron | (216) | 275,425 | 290,351 |
| 44601 | Alliance | (216) | 26,547 | 28,362 |
| 44001 | Amherst | (419) | 9,902 | 6,750 |
| 44805 | Ashland | (419) | 19,872 | 17,419 |
| 44004 | Ashtabula | (216) | 24,313 | 24,559 |
| 45701 | Athens | (614) | 24,168 | 16,470 |
| 44202 | Aurora | (216) | 6,549 | 4,049 |
| 44515 | Austintown(u) | (216) | 29,393 | ..... |
| 44011 | Avon | (216) | 7,214 | 6,002 |
| 45404 | Avondale(u) | (513) | 5,240 | ..... |
| 44012 | Avon Lake | (216) | 12,261 | 9,403 |
| 44203 | Barberton | (216) | 33,052 | 33,805 |
| 44140 | Bay Village | (216) | 18,163 | 14,489 |
| 44122 | Beachwood | (216) | 9,631 | 6,089 |
| 44146 | Bedford | (216) | 17,552 | 15,223 |
| 44146 | Bedford Heights | (216) | 13,063 | 5,275 |
| 43906 | Bellaire | (614) | 9,655 | 11,502 |
| 43311 | Bellefontaine | (513) | 11,255 | 11,424 |
| 44811 | Bellevue | (216) | 8,604 | 8,286 |
| 45714 | Belpre | (614) | 7,189 | 5,418 |
| 44017 | Berea | (216) | 22,465 | 16,592 |
| 43209 | Bexley | (614) | 14,888 | 14,319 |
| 43004 | Blacklick Estates(u) | (614) | 8,351 | ..... |
| 45242 | Blue Ash | (513) | 8,324 | 8,341 |
| 44512 | Boardman(u) | (216) | 30,852 | ..... |
| 43402 | Bowling Green | (419) | 21,760 | 13,574 |
| 44141 | Brecksville | (216) | 9,137 | 5,435 |
| 45211 | Bridgetown(u) | (513) | 13,352 | ..... |
| 44141 | Broadview Heights | (216) | 11,463 | 6,209 |

| ZIP code | Place | | 1970 | 196_ |
|---|---|---|---|---|
| 44144 | Brooklyn | (216) | 13,142 | 10,733 |
| 44142 | Brook Park | (216) | 30,774 | 12,856 |
| 44212 | Brunswick | (216) | 15,852 | 11,725 |
| 43506 | Bryan | (419) | 7,008 | 7,361 |
| 44820 | Bucyrus | (419) | 13,111 | 12,276 |
| 43725 | Cambridge | (614) | 13,656 | 14,562 |
| 44405 | Campbell | (216) | 12,577 | 13,406 |
| *44711 | Canton | (216) | 110,053 | 113,631 |
| 45822 | Celina | (419) | 8,072 | 7,659 |
| 45459 | Centerville | (513) | 10,333 | 3,490 |
| 45211 | Cheviot | (513) | 11,135 | 10,701 |
| 45601 | Chillicothe | (614) | 24,842 | 24,957 |
| 44505 | Churchill(u) | (216) | 7,457 | ..... |
| *45234 | Cincinnati | (513) | 451,455 | 502,550 |
| 43113 | Circleville | (614) | 11,687 | 11,059 |
| *44101 | Cleveland | (216) | 750,879 | 876,050 |
| 44118 | Cleveland Heights | (216) | 60,767 | 61,813 |
| 43410 | Clyde | (419) | 5,503 | 4,826 |
| *43216 | Columbus | (614) | 540,025 | 471,316 |
| 44030 | Conneaut | (219) | 14,552 | 10,557 |
| 43812 | Coshocton | (614) | 13,747 | 13,106 |
| 45238 | Covedale(u) | (513) | 6,639 | ..... |
| 44827 | Crestline | (419) | 5,947 | 5,521 |
| 45341 | Crystal Lakes(u) | (513) | 5,851 | 1,569 |
| *44222 | Cuyahoga Falls | (219) | 49,678 | 47,322 |
| *45401 | Dayton | (513) | 242,917 | 262,332 |
| 45236 | Deer Park | (513) | 7,415 | 8,423 |
| 43512 | Defiance | (419) | 16,281 | 14,553 |
| 43015 | Delaware | (614) | 15,008 | 13,282 |
| 45833 | Delphos | (419) | 7,608 | 6,961 |
| 44622 | Dover | (614) | 11,516 | 11,300 |
| 44112 | East Cleveland | (216) | 39,600 | 37,991 |
| 44094 | Eastlake | (216) | 19,690 | 12,467 |
| 43920 | East Liverpool(u) | (216) | 20,020 | 22,306 |
| 43920 | East Liverpool North | (216) | 6,223 | ..... |
| 44413 | East Palestine | (216) | 5,604 | 5,232 |
| 43520 | Eaton | (513) | 6,020 | 5,034 |
| *44035 | Elyria | (216) | 53,427 | 43,782 |
| 45322 | Englewood | (513) | 7,885 | 1,515 |
| 44117 | Euclid | (216) | 71,552 | 62,998 |
| 45324 | Fairborn | (513) | 32,267 | 19,453 |
| 45014 | Fairfield | (614) | 14,680 | 9,734 |
| 44313 | Fairlawn | (216) | 6,102 | ..... |
| 44126 | Fairview Park | (216) | 21,681 | 14,624 |
| 45840 | Findlay | (419) | 35,800 | 30,344 |
| 45405 | Forest Park | (513) | 15,139 | ..... |
| 45426 | Fort McKinley(u) | (513) | 11,536 | ..... |
| 44830 | Fostoria | (419) | 16,037 | 15,732 |
| 45005 | Franklin | (513) | 10,075 | 7,917 |
| 43420 | Fremont | (419) | 18,490 | 18,767 |
| 43230 | Gahanna | (614) | 12,400 | 2,717 |
| 44833 | Galion | (419) | 13,123 | 12,650 |
| 45631 | Gallipolis | (614) | 7,490 | 8,775 |
| 44125 | Garfield Heights | (216) | 41,417 | 38,455 |
| 44041 | Geneva | (216) | 6,449 | 5,677 |
| 44420 | Girard | (216) | 14,119 | 12,997 |
| 45237 | Golf Manor | (513) | 5,170 | 4,648 |
| 43212 | Grandview Heights | (614) | 8,460 | 8,270 |
| 45218 | Greenhills | (513) | 6,092 | 5,407 |
| 45331 | Greenville | (513) | 12,380 | 10,585 |
| 43123 | Grove City | (614) | 13,911 | 8,107 |
| *45012 | Hamilton | (513) | 67,865 | 72,354 |
| 43055 | Heath | (614) | 6,768 | 2,426 |
| 44143 | Highland Heights | (216) | 5,926 | 2,929 |
| 43026 | Hilliard | (614) | 8,369 | 5,633 |
| 45133 | Hillsboro | (513) | 5,584 | 5,474 |
| 44425 | Hubbard | (216) | 8,583 | 7,137 |
| 45424 | Huber Heights(u) | (513) | 18,943 | ..... |
| 44839 | Huron | (216) | 6,896 | 5,197 |
| 44131 | Independence | (216) | 7,034 | 6,868 |
| 45243 | Indian Hill | (513) | 5,651 | 4,526 |
| 45638 | Ironton | (614) | 15,030 | 15,745 |
| 45640 | Jackson | (614) | 6,843 | 6,980 |
| 44240 | Kent | (216) | 28,183 | 17,836 |
| 43326 | Kenton | (419) | 8,315 | 8,747 |
| 45236 | Kenwood(u) | (513) | 15,789 | ..... |
| 45429 | Kettering | (513) | 71,864 | 54,462 |
| 44094 | Kirtland | (216) | 5,530 | ..... |
| 44432 | Knollwood(u) | (513) | 5,353 | ..... |
| 44107 | Lakewood | (216) | 70,173 | 66,154 |
| 43130 | Lancaster | (614) | 32,911 | 29,916 |
| 45036 | Lebanon | (513) | 7,934 | 5,993 |
| *45802 | Lima | (419) | 53,734 | 51,037 |
| 45215 | Lincoln Heights | (513) | 6,099 | 7,798 |
| 43228 | Lincoln Village(u) | (513) | 11,215 | ..... |
| 45215 | Lockland | (513) | 5,288 | 5,292 |
| 43138 | Logan | (614) | 6,269 | 6,417 |
| 43140 | London | (614) | 6,481 | 6,379 |
| *44052 | Lorain | (216) | 78,185 | 68,932 |
| 44641 | Louisville | (216) | 6,298 | 5,116 |
| 45140 | Loveland | (513) | 7,144 | 5,008 |
| 44124 | Lyndhurst | (213) | 19,749 | 16,805 |
| 44056 | Macedonia | (213) | 6,375 | ..... |
| 45243 | Madeira | (513) | 6,713 | 6,744 |
| 44124 | Madison North(u) | (216) | 6,882 | ..... |
| *44901 | Mansfield | (419) | 55,047 | 47,325 |
| 44137 | Maple Heights | (216) | 34,093 | 31,667 |
| 45750 | Marietta | (614) | 16,861 | 16,847 |
| 43302 | Marion | (419) | 38,646 | 37,079 |

| ZIP code | Place | | 1970 | 1960 |
|---|---|---|---|---|
| 43935 | Martins Ferry | (614) | 10,757 | 11,919 |
| 43040 | Marysville | (513) | 5,744 | 4,952 |
| 45040 | Mason | (513) | 5,677 | 4,952 |
| 44646 | Massillon | (216) | 32,539 | 31,236 |
| 43537 | Maumee | (419) | 15,937 | 12,063 |
| 44124 | Mayfield Heights | (216) | 22,139 | 13,478 |
| 44256 | Medina | (216) | 10,913 | 8,235 |
| 44060 | Mentor | (216) | 36,912 | 4,354 |
| 44060 | Mentor-on-the-Lake | (216) | 6,517 | 3,290 |
| 45342 | Miamisburg | (513) | 14,797 | 9,893 |
| 44017 | Middleburg Heights | (216) | 12,367 | 7,282 |
| 45042 | Middletown | (513) | 48,767 | 42,115 |
| 43938 | Mingo Junction | (614) | 5,278 | 4,987 |
| 45242 | Montgomery | (513) | 5,683 | 3,075 |
| 45231 | Mount Healthy | (513) | 7,446 | 6,553 |
| 45050 | Mount Vernon | (614) | 13,373 | 13,284 |
| 43545 | Napoleon | (419) | 7,791 | 6,739 |
| 43055 | Newark | (614) | 41,836 | 41,790 |
| 45344 | New Carlisle | (513) | 6,112 | 4,107 |
| 44663 | New Philadelphia | (614) | 15,184 | 14,241 |
| 44444 | Newton Falls | (216) | 5,378 | 5,038 |
| 44446 | Niles | (216) | 21,581 | 19,545 |
| 44720 | North Canton | (216) | 15,228 | 7,727* |
| 45239 | North College Hill | (513) | 12,363 | 12,035 |
| 45070 | North Olmsted | (216) | 34,861 | 16,290 |
| 45414 | Northridge(u) | (513) | 10,084 | |
| 44039 | North Ridgeville | (216) | 13,152 | 8,057 |
| 44133 | North Royalton | (216) | 12,807 | 9,290 |
| 44203 | Norton | (216) | 12,308 | |
| 44857 | Norwalk | (419) | 13,386 | 12,900 |
| 45212 | Norwood | (513) | 30,420 | 34,580 |
| 44819 | Oakwood City | (513) | 10,095 | 10,493 |
| 44074 | Oberlin | (614) | 8,761 | 8,198 |
| 43616 | Oregon | (419) | 16,563 | 13,319 |
| 44667 | Orrville | (216) | 7,408 | 6,511 |
| 45431 | Overlook-Page Manor(u) | (513) | 19,719 | |
| 45056 | Oxford | (513) | 15,868 | 7,828 |
| 44077 | Painesville | (216) | 16,536 | 16,116 |
| 44077 | Painesville Southwest(u) | (216) | 5,461 | |
| 44129 | Parma | (216) | 100,216 | 82,845 |
| 44130 | Parma Heights | (216) | 27,192 | 18,100 |
| 44124 | Pepper Pike | (216) | 5,382 | 3,217 |
| 43551 | Perrysburg | (419) | 7,693 | 5,519 |
| 45356 | Piqua | (513) | 20,741 | 19,219 |
| 43452 | Port Clinton | (419) | 7,202 | 6,870 |
| 45662 | Portsmouth | (614) | 27,633 | 33,637 |
| 44266 | Ravenna | (216) | 11,780 | 10,918 |
| 45215 | Reading | (513) | 14,617 | 12,832 |
| 43068 | Reynoldsburg | (614) | 13,921 | 7,793 |
| 44143 | Richmond Heights | (213) | 9,220 | 5,068 |
| 43217 | Rickenbacker Base(u) | (614) | 5,623 | |
| 44270 | Rittman | (216) | 6,308 | 5,410 |
| 44116 | Rocky River | (216) | 22,958 | 18,097 |
| 43460 | Rossford | (419) | 5,302 | 4,406 |
| 45217 | St. Bernard | (513) | 6,080 | 6,778 |
| 45885 | St. Marys | (419) | 7,699 | 7,737 |
| 44460 | Salem | (216) | 14,186 | 13,854 |
| 44870 | Sandusky | (419) | 32,674 | 31,989 |
| 44870 | Sandusky South(u) | (419) | 8,501 | 4,724 |
| 44131 | Seven Hills | (216) | 12,700 | 5,708 |
| 43947 | Shadyside | (614) | 5,070 | 5,028 |
| 44120 | Shaker Heights | (216) | 36,306 | 36,460 |
| 45241 | Sharonville | (513) | 11,393 | 3,890 |
| 44054 | Sheffield Lake | (216) | 8,734 | 6,884 |
| 44875 | Shelby | (419) | 9,847 | 9,106 |
| 45415 | Shiloh(u) | (419) | 11,368 | |
| 45365 | Sidney | (513) | 16,332 | 14,663 |
| 45236 | Silverton | (513) | 6,588 | 6,682 |
| 44139 | Solon | (216) | 11,519 | 6,333 |
| 44121 | South Euclid | (216) | 29,579 | 27,569 |
| 45246 | Springdale | (513) | 8,127 | 3,556 |
| 45501 | Springfield | (513) | 81,941 | 82,723 |
| 43952 | Steubenville | (614) | 30,771 | 32,495 |
| 44224 | Stow | (216) | 19,847 | 12,194 |
| 44240 | Streetsboro | (216) | 7,966 | |
| 44136 | Strongsville | (216) | 15,182 | 8,504 |
| 44471 | Struthers | (216) | 15,343 | 15,631 |
| 43560 | Sylvania | (419) | 12,031 | 5,187 |
| 44278 | Tallmadge | (216) | 15,274 | 10,246 |
| 44883 | Tiffin | (419) | 21,596 | 21,478 |
| 45371 | Tipp City | (513) | 5,090 | 4,267 |
| 43601 | Toledo | (419) | 383,105 | 318,003 |
| 43964 | Toronto | (614) | 7,705 | 7,780 |
| 45067 | Trenton | (513) | 5,278 | 3,064 |
| 45426 | Trotwood | (513) | 6,997 | 4,992 |
| 45373 | Troy | (513) | 17,186 | 13,685 |
| 44087 | Twinsburg | (216) | 6,432 | 4,098 |
| 44683 | Uhrichsville | (614) | 5,731 | 6,201 |
| 44118 | University Heights | (216) | 17,055 | 16,641 |
| 43221 | Upper Arlington | (614) | 38,727 | 28,486 |
| 43351 | Upper Sandusky | (419) | 5,645 | 4,941 |
| 43078 | Urbana | (513) | 11,237 | 10,461 |
| 45377 | Vandalia | (513) | 10,796 | 6,342 |
| 45891 | Van Wert | (419) | 11,320 | 11,323 |
| 44089 | Vermilion | (216) | 9,872 | 4,785 |
| 44281 | Wadsworth | (216) | 13,142 | 10,635 |
| 45895 | Wapakoneta | (513) | 7,324 | 6,756 |
| *44481 | Warren | (216) | 63,494 | 59,648 |
| 44122 | Warrensville Heights | (216) | 18,925 | 10,609 |
| 43160 | Washington | (513) | 12,495 | 12,388 |
| 45692 | Wellston | (614) | 5,410 | 5,728 |
| 43968 | Wellsville | (419) | 5,891 | 7,117 |
| 45449 | West Carrollton | (513) | 10,748 | 4,749 |
| 43081 | Westerville | (614) | 12,530 | 7,011 |
| 44145 | Westlake | (216) | 15,689 | 12,906 |
| 43213 | Whitehall | (614) | 25,263 | 20,818 |
| 44092 | Wickliffe | (216) | 21,354 | 15,760 |
| 44890 | Willard | (419) | 5,510 | 5,457 |
| 44094 | Willoughby | (614) | 18,634 | 15,058 |
| 44094 | Willoughby Hills | (614) | 5,247 | 4,241 |
| 44094 | Willowick | (614) | 21,237 | 18,749 |
| 45177 | Wilmington | (513) | 10,051 | 8,915 |
| 44691 | Wooster | (216) | 18,703 | 17,046 |
| 43085 | Worthington | (614) | 15,326 | 9,239 |
| 45433 | Wright-Patterson(u) | (513) | 10,151 | |
| 45215 | Wyoming | (513) | 9,089 | |
| 45385 | Xenia | (513) | 25,373 | 20,445 |
| *44501 | Youngstown | (216) | 140,909 | 166,689 |
| 43701 | Zanesville | (614) | 33,045 | 39,077 |

## Oklahoma

| ZIP code | Place | | 1970 | 1960 |
|---|---|---|---|---|
| 74820 | Ada | (405) | 14,859 | 14,347 |
| 73521 | Altus | (405) | 23,302 | 21,225 |
| 73717 | Alva | (405) | 7,440 | 6,258 |
| 73005 | Anadarko | (405) | 6,682 | 6,299 |
| 73401 | Ardmore | (918) | 20,881 | 20,184 |
| 74003 | Bartlesville | (918) | 29,683 | 27,893 |
| 73008 | Bethany | (405) | 22,694 | 12,342 |
| 74631 | Blackwell | (405) | 8,645 | 9,588 |
| 74012 | Broken Arrow | (918) | 11,787 | 5,928 |
| 73018 | Chickasha | (405) | 14,194 | 14,866 |
| 74017 | Claremore | (918) | 9,084 | 6,639 |
| 73601 | Clinton | (405) | 8,513 | 9,617 |
| 74023 | Cushing | (405) | 7,529 | 8,619 |
| 73115 | Del City | (405) | 27,133 | 12,934 |
| 73533 | Duncan | (405) | 19,718 | 20,009 |
| 74701 | Durant | (405) | 11,118 | 10,467 |
| 73034 | Edmond | (405) | 16,633 | 8,577 |
| 73644 | Elk City | (405) | 7,323 | 8,196 |
| 73036 | El Reno | (405) | 14,510 | 11,015 |
| 73701 | Enid | (405) | 44,986 | 38,859 |
| 73503 | Fort Sill(u) | (405) | 21,217 | |
| 73542 | Frederick | (405) | 6,132 | 5,879 |
| 73044 | Guthrie | (405) | 9,575 | 9,502 |
| 73942 | Guymon | (918) | 7,674 | 5,760 |
| 74437 | Henryetta | (918) | 6,430 | 6,551 |
| 74848 | Holdenville | (405) | 5,181 | 5,712 |
| 74743 | Hugo | (405) | 6,585 | 6,287 |
| 74745 | Idabel | (405) | 5,946 | 4,967 |
| 73501 | Lawton | (918) | 74,470 | 61,697 |
| 74501 | McAlester | (918) | 18,802 | 17,419 |
| 74354 | Miami | (405) | 13,880 | 12,869 |
| 73110 | Midwest City | (405) | 48,212 | 36,058 |
| 73060 | Moore | (918) | 18,761 | 1,783 |
| 74401 | Muskogee | (918) | 37,331 | 38,059 |
| 73064 | Mustang, 1976 | (405) | 5,725 | 198 |
| 73069 | Norman | (405) | 52,117 | 33,412 |
| *73125 | Oklahoma City | (918) | 368,377 | 324,253 |
| 74447 | Okmulgee | (918) | 15,180 | 15,951 |
| 73075 | Pauls Valley | (405) | 5,769 | 6,856 |
| 73077 | Perry | (405) | 5,341 | 5,210 |
| 74601 | Ponca City | (405) | 25,940 | 24,411 |
| 74953 | Poteau | (918) | 5,500 | 4,428 |
| 74361 | Pryor | (918) | 7,057 | 6,476 |
| 74063 | Sand Springs | (918) | 10,565 | 7,754 |
| 74066 | Sapulpa | (918) | 15,159 | 14,282 |
| 74868 | Seminole | (918) | 7,878 | 11,464 |
| 74801 | Shawnee | (405) | 25,075 | 24,326 |
| 74074 | Stillwater | (405) | 31,126 | 23,965 |
| 73086 | Sulphur | (405) | 5,158 | 4,737 |
| 74464 | Tahlequah | (918) | 9,254 | 5,840 |
| 73120 | The Village | (405) | 13,695 | 12,118 |
| *74101 | Tulsa | (918) | 330,350 | 261,685 |
| 74301 | Vinita | (918) | 5,847 | 6,027 |
| 73132 | Warr Acres | (405) | 9,887 | 7,135 |
| 73096 | Weatherford | (405) | 7,959 | 4,499 |
| 74884 | Wewoka | (918) | 5,284 | 5,954 |
| 73801 | Woodward | (405) | 9,412 | 7,747 |
| 73099 | Yukon 1975 | (405) | 12,980 | 3,076 |

## Oregon (503)

| ZIP code | Place | 1970 | 1960 |
|---|---|---|---|
| 97321 | Albany | 18,181 | 12,926 |
| 97601 | Altamont(u) | 15,746 | 10,811 |
| 97520 | Ashland | 12,342 | 9,119 |
| 97103 | Astoria | 10,244 | 11,239 |
| 97814 | Baker | 9,354 | 9,986 |
| 97005 | Beaverton | 18,577 | 5,937 |
| 97701 | Bend | 13,710 | 11,936 |
| 97420 | Coos Bay | 13,466 | 7,084 |
| 97330 | Corvallis | 35,056 | 20,669 |
| 97424 | Cottage Grove | 6,004 | 3,895 |
| 97338 | Dallas | 6,361 | 5,072 |
| *97401 | Eugene | 79,028 | 50,977 |
| 97116 | Forest Grove | 8,275 | 5,628 |
| 97301 | Four Corners(u) | 5,823 | 4,743 |

| ZIP code | Place | 1970 | 1960 |
|---|---|---|---|
| 97027 | Gladstone | 6,254 | 3,854 |
| 97526 | Grants Pass | 12,455 | 10,118 |
| 97030 | Gresham | 10,030 | 3,944 |
| 97303 | Hayesville(u) | 5,518 | 4,568 |
| 97123 | Hillsboro | 14,675 | 8,232 |
| 97303 | Keizer(u) | 11,405 | 5,288 |
| 97601 | Klamath Falls | 15,775 | 16,949 |
| 97850 | La Grande | 9,645 | 9,014 |
| 97034 | Lake Oswego | 14,615 | 8,906 |
| 97355 | Lebanon | 6,636 | 5,858 |
| 97128 | McMinnville | 10,125 | 7,656 |
| 97501 | Medford | 28,454 | 24,425 |
| 97222 | Milwaukie | 16,444 | 9,099 |
| 97361 | Monmouth | 5,237 | 2,229 |
| 97132 | Newberg | 6,507 | 4,204 |
| 97365 | Newport | 5,188 | 5,344 |
| 97459 | North Bend | 8,553 | 7,512 |
| 97914 | Ontario | 6,523 | 5,101 |
| 97045 | Oregon City | 9,176 | 7,996 |
| 97801 | Pendleton | 13,197 | 14,434 |
| *97208 | Portland | 379,967 | 372,676 |
| 97470 | Roseburg | 14,461 | 11,467 |
| 97051 | St. Helens | 6,212 | 5,022 |
| *97301 | Salem | 68,480 | 49,142 |
| 97477 | Springfield | 26,874 | 19,616 |
| 97058 | The Dalles | 10,423 | 10,493 |
| 97223 | Tigard | 5,302 | ..... |
| 97068 | West Linn | 7,091 | 3,933 |
| 97071 | Woodburn | 7,495 | 3,120 |

## Pennsylvania

| ZIP code | Place | | 1970 | 1960 |
|---|---|---|---|---|
| 19001 | Abington(u) | (215) | 8,594 | ..... |
| 19018 | Aldan | (215) | 5,001 | 4,324 |
| 15001 | Aliquippa | (412) | 22,277 | 26,369 |
| *18101 | Allentown | (215) | 109,527 | 108,347 |
| *16603 | Altoona | (814) | 63,115 | 69,407 |
| 19002 | Ambler | (215) | 7,800 | 6,765 |
| 15003 | Ambridge | (412) | 11,324 | 13,865 |
| 18403 | Archbald | (717) | 6,118 | 5,642 |
| 19003 | Ardmore(u) | (215) | 5,131 | ..... |
| 15068 | Arnold | (412) | 8,174 | 9,437 |
| 15202 | Avalon | (412) | 7,010 | 6,859 |
| 15005 | Baden | (412) | 5,536 | 6,109 |
| 19004 | Bala-Cynwyd(u) | (215) | 6,483 | ..... |
| 15234 | Baldwin | (412) | 26,729 | 24,489 |
| 18013 | Bangor | (215) | 5,425 | 5,766 |
| 15009 | Beaver | (412) | 6,100 | 6,160 |
| 15010 | Beaver Falls | (412) | 14,375 | 16,240 |
| 16823 | Bellefonte | (814) | 6,828 | 6,088 |
| 15202 | Bellevue | (412) | 11,586 | 11,412 |
| 18603 | Berwick | (717) | 12,274 | 13,353 |
| 15102 | Bethel Park | (412) | 34,791 | 23,650 |
| *18016 | Bethlehem | (215) | 72,686 | 75,408 |
| 18447 | Blakely | (717) | 6,391 | 6,374 |
| 17815 | Bloomsburg | (717) | 11,652 | 10,655 |
| 15104 | Braddock | (412) | 8,795 | 12,337 |
| 16701 | Bradford | (814) | 12,672 | 15,061 |
| 19406 | Brandywine Village(u) | (215) | 11,411 | ..... |
| 15227 | Brentwood | (412) | 13,732 | 13,706 |
| 19405 | Bridgeport | (215) | 5,630 | 5,306 |
| 15017 | Bridgeville | (412) | 6,717 | 7,112 |
| 19007 | Bristol | (215) | 12,085 | 12,364 |
| 19015 | Brookhaven 1973 | (215) | 7,262 | 5,280 |
| 19010 | Bryn Mawr(u) | (215) | 5,815 | ..... |
| 16001 | Butler | (412) | 18,691 | 20,975 |
| 15419 | California | (412) | 6,635 | 5,978 |
| 17011 | Camp Hill | (717) | 9,931 | 8,559 |
| 15317 | Canonsburg | (814) | 11,439 | 11,877 |
| 18407 | Carbondale | (717) | 12,808 | 13,595 |
| 17013 | Carlisle | (717) | 18,079 | 16,623 |
| 15106 | Carnegie | (412) | 10,864 | 11,887 |
| 15108 | Carnot-Moon(u) | (412) | 13,093 | ..... |
| 15234 | Castle Shannon | (412) | 11,899 | 11,836 |
| 18032 | Catasauqua | (215) | 5,702 | 5,062 |
| 19095 | Cedarbrook-Melrose Park(u) | (215) | 9,980 | ..... |
| 19428 | Cedar Heights(u) | (215) | 6,326 | ..... |
| 17201 | Chambersburg | (717) | 17,315 | 17,670 |
| 15022 | Charleroi | (412) | 6,723 | 8,148 |
| 19380 | Chatwood(u). | (215) | 7,168 | 3,621 |
| *19003 | Chester | (215) | 56,331 | 63,658 |
| 15025 | Clairton | (412) | 15,051 | 18,389 |
| 16214 | Clarion | (814) | 6,095 | 4,958 |
| 18411 | Clarks Summit | (712) | 5,376 | 3,693 |
| 16830 | Clearfield | (814) | 8,176 | 9,270 |
| 19018 | Clifton Heights | (215) | 8,348 | 8,005 |
| 19320 | Coatesville | (215) | 12,331 | 12,971 |
| 19023 | Collingdale | (215) | 10,605 | 10,268 |
| 17512 | Columbia | (717) | 11,237 | 12,075 |
| 15425 | Connellsville | (412) | 11,643 | 12,814 |
| 19428 | Conshohocken | (215) | 10,195 | 10,259 |
| 15108 | Coraopolis | (412) | 8,435 | 9,643 |
| 16407 | Corry | (814) | 7,435 | 7,744 |
| 15205 | Crafton | (412) | 8,233 | 8,418 |
| 17821 | Danville | (717) | 6,176 | 6,889 |
| 19023 | Darby | (215) | 13,729 | 14,059 |
| 18519 | Dickson City | (717) | 7,698 | 7,738 |
| 15033 | Donora | (412) | 8,825 | 11,131 |

| ZIP code | Place | | 1970 | 1960 |
|---|---|---|---|---|
| 15216 | Dormont | (412) | 12,856 | 13,098 |
| 19335 | Downingtown 1977 | (215) | 7,655 | 5,598 |
| 18901 | Doylestown | (215) | 8,270 | 5,917 |
| 15801 | Du Bois | (814) | 10,112 | 10,667 |
| 18512 | Dunmore | (717) | 17,300 | 18,917 |
| 15110 | Duquesne | (412) | 11,410 | 15,019 |
| 18642 | Duryea | (717) | 5,264 | 5,626 |
| 18042 | Easton | (215) | 29,450 | 31,955 |
| 18301 | East Stroudsburg | (717) | 7,894 | 7,674 |
| 15005 | Economy 1976 | (412) | 8,379 | 5,925 |
| 15218 | Edgewood | (412) | 5,138 | 5,124 |
| 18704 | Edwardsville | (717) | 5,633 | 5,711 |
| 17022 | Elizabethtown | (717) | 8,072 | 6,780 |
| 16117 | Ellwood City | (412) | 10,857 | 12,413 |
| 18049 | Emmaus | (214) | 11,511 | 10,262 |
| 17522 | Ephrata | (717) | 9,662 | 7,688 |
| *16501 | Erie | (814) | 129,231 | 138,440 |
| 15223 | Etna | (412) | 5,819 | 5,519 |
| 16121 | Farrell | (814) | 11,022 | 13,793 |
| 19031 | Flourtown(u) | (215) | 9,149 | ..... |
| 19032 | Folcroft | (215) | 9,810 | 7,013 |
| 15221 | Forest Hills | (412) | 9,561 | 8,796 |
| 18704 | Forty Fort | (717) | 6,114 | 6,431 |
| 19015 | Fountain Hill | (215) | 5,384 | 5,428 |
| 17931 | Frackville | (215) | 5,445 | 5,654 |
| 16323 | Franklin | (814) | 8,629 | 9,586 |
| 15143 | Franklin Park | (412) | 5,310 | ..... |
| 18052 | Fullerton(u) | (215) | 7,908 | ..... |
| 19004 | General Wayne(u) | (215) | 5,368 | ..... |
| 17325 | Gettysburg. | (717) | 7,275 | 7,960 |
| 15045 | Glassport | (412) | 7,450 | 8,418 |
| 19036 | Glenolden | (215) | 8,697 | 7,249 |
| 19038 | Glenside(u) | (215) | 17,353 | ..... |
| 15601 | Greensburg | (412) | 17,077 | 17,383 |
| 15220 | Green Tree | (412) | 6,441 | 5,226 |
| 16125 | Greenville | (412) | 8,704 | 8,765 |
| 16127 | Grove City | (814) | 8,312 | 8,368 |
| 17331 | Hanover | (717) | 15,623 | 15,538 |
| *17105 | Harrisburg | (717) | 68,061 | 79,697 |
| 19040 | Hatboro | (215) | 8,880 | 7,315 |
| 19044 | Hatboro West(u) | (215) | 13,542 | ..... |
| 18201 | Hazleton | (717) | 30,426 | 32,056 |
| 18055 | Hellertown | (215) | 6,615 | 6,716 |
| 17033 | Hershey(u) | (717) | 7,047 | 6,851 |
| 18042 | Highland Park (Northampton)(u) | (717) | 5,500 | ..... |
| 16648 | Hollidaysburg | (814) | 6,262 | 6,475 |
| 16001 | Homeacre-Lyndora(u) | (412) | 8,415 | ..... |
| 15120 | Homestead | (412) | 6,309 | 7,502 |
| 18431 | Honesdale | (717) | 5,224 | 5,569 |
| 16652 | Huntingdon | (717) | 6,987 | 7,234 |
| 15701 | Indiana | (412) | 16,100 | 13,005 |
| 15644 | Jeannette | (412) | 15,209 | 16,565 |
| 15344 | Jefferson | (412) | 8,512 | 8,280 |
| 19401 | Jefferson-Trooper(u) | (215) | 13,022 | ..... |
| 19046 | Jenkintown | (215) | 5,990 | 5,017 |
| 17740 | Jersey Shore | (717) | 5,322 | 5,613 |
| 18229 | Jim Thorpe. | (717) | 5,456 | 5,945 |
| *15901 | Johnstown | (814) | 42,476 | 53,949 |
| 16735 | Kane | (814) | 5,001 | 5,380 |
| 18704 | Kingston | (717) | 18,325 | 20,261 |
| 16201 | Kittanning | (814) | 6,231 | 6,793 |
| 19444 | Lafayette Hills-Plymouth Meeting(u) | (215) | 8,275 | ..... |
| *17604 | Lancaster | (717) | 57,690 | 61,055 |
| 19446 | Lansdale | (215) | 18,451 | 12,612 |
| 19050 | Lansdowne | (215) | 14,090 | 12,601 |
| 18232 | Lansford | (717) | 5,168 | 5,958 |
| 15650 | Latrobe | (412) | 11,749 | 11,932 |
| 17042 | Lebanon | (717) | 28,572 | 30,045 |
| 18235 | Lehighton | (215) | 6,095 | 6,318 |
| 17837 | Lewisburg | (717) | 6,376 | 5,523 |
| 17044 | Lewistown | (717) | 11,098 | 12,640 |
| 17543 | Lititz | (717) | 7,072 | 5,987 |
| 17745 | Lock Haven | (717) | 11,427 | 11,748 |
| 15068 | Lower Burrell | (814) | 13,654 | 11,952 |
| *15134 | McKeesport | (412) | 37,977 | 45,489 |
| 15136 | McKees Rocks | (412) | 11,901 | 13,185 |
| 17948 | Mahanoy City | (215) | 7,257 | 8,536 |
| 17545 | Manheim | (717) | 5,434 | 4,790 |
| 16335 | Meadville | (814) | 16,573 | 16,671 |
| 17055 | Mechanicsburg | (717) | 9,385 | 8,123 |
| *19063 | Media | (215) | 6,444 | 5,803 |
| 19066 | Merion(u) | (215) | 5,686 | ..... |
| 17057 | Middletown | (717) | 9,080 | 11,182 |
| 15059 | Midland | (412) | 5,271 | 6,425 |
| 17551 | Millersville | (717) | 6,396 | 3,824 |
| 15209 | Millvale | (412) | 5,815 | 6,624 |
| 17847 | Milton | (717) | 7,723 | 7,972 |
| 17954 | Minersville | (215) | 6,012 | 6,606 |
| 15061 | Monaca | (412) | 7,486 | 8,394 |
| 15062 | Monessen | (412) | 15,216 | 18,424 |
| 15063 | Monongahela | (412) | 7,113 | 8,388 |
| 15146 | Monroeville | (412) | 29,011 | 22,446 |
| 17754 | Montoursville | (717) | 5,985 | 5,211 |
| 19067 | Morrisville | (215) | 11,309 | 7,790 |
| 17851 | Mount Carmel | (717) | 9,317 | 10,760 |
| 17552 | Mount Joy | (717) | 5,041 | 3,292 |
| 15210 | Mount Oliver | (412) | 5,487 | 5,960 |

| ZIP code | Place | | 1970 | 1960 |
|---|---|---|---|---|
| 15666 | Mount Pleasant | (412) | 5,895 | 6,107 |
| 15120 | Munhall | (412) | 16,574 | 17,312 |
| 18634 | Nanticoke | (717) | 14,632 | 15,601 |
| 19072 | Narbeth | (215) | 5,151 | 5,109 |
| 18064 | Nazareth | (215) | 5,815 | 6,209 |
| 15066 | New Brighton | (412) | 7,637 | 8,397 |
| *16101 | New Castle | (412) | 38,559 | 44,790 |
| 17070 | New Cumberland | (717) | 9,803 | 9,257 |
| 15068 | New Kensington | (412) | 20,312 | 23,485 |
| *19401 | Norristown | (215) | 38,169 | 38,925 |
| 18067 | Northampton | (215) | 8,389 | 8,866 |
| 19003 | North Ardmore(u) | (215) | 5,856 | |
| 15104 | North Braddock | (412) | 10,838 | 13,204 |
| 19038 | North Hills-Ardsley(u) | (215) | 13,096 | |
| 19074 | Norwood | (215) | 7,229 | 6,729 |
| 19126 | Oak Lane(u) | (215) | 6,192 | |
| 15139 | Oakmont | (412) | 7,550 | 7,504 |
| 19117 | Ogontz(u) | (215) | 5,463 | 2,254 |
| 16301 | Oil City | (814) | 15,033 | 17,692 |
| 18518 | Old Forge | (717) | 9,522 | 8,928 |
| 18447 | Olyphant | (717) | 5,422 | 5,864 |
| 19075 | Oreland(u) | (215) | 9,261 | |
| 18071 | Palmerton | (717) | 5,620 | 5,942 |
| 17078 | Palmyra | (717) | 7,615 | 6,999 |
| 19301 | Paoli(u) | (215) | 5,835 | |
| 17331 | Parkville(u) | (717) | 5,120 | 4,516 |
| 19004 | Pencoyd | (215) | 6,650 | |
| 19401 | Penn Sq.-Plymouth Valley(u) | (215) | 20,238 | |
| 19151 | Penn Wynne(u) | (215) | 6,038 | |
| 18944 | Perkasie | (215) | 5,451 | 4,650 |
| *19104 | Philadelphia | (215) | 1,949,996 | 2,002,512 |
| 19460 | Phoenixville | (215) | 14,823 | 13,797 |
| *15219 | Pittsburgh | (412) | 520,117 | 604,332 |
| *18640 | Pittston | (717) | 11,113 | 12,407 |
| 18705 | Plains(u) | (717) | 6,606 | |
| 15236 | Pleasant Hills | (412) | 10,409 | 8,573 |
| 15239 | Plum | (412) | 21,932 | 10,241 |
| 18651 | Plymouth | (717) | 9,536 | 10,401 |
| 15133 | Port Vue | (412) | 5,862 | 6,635 |
| 19464 | Pottstown | (215) | 25,355 | 26,144 |
| 17901 | Pottsville | (717) | 19,715 | 21,659 |
| 19076 | Prospect Park | (215) | 7,250 | 6,596 |
| 15767 | Punxsutawney | (814) | 7,792 | 8,805 |
| 18951 | Quakertown | (215) | 7,276 | 6,305 |
| *19603 | Reading | (215) | 87,643 | 98,177 |
| 17356 | Red Lion | (717) | 5,645 | 5,594 |
| 15853 | Ridgway | (814) | 6,022 | 6,387 |
| 19078 | Ridley Park | (215) | 9,025 | 7,387 |
| 19001 | Roslyn(u) | (215) | 18,380 | |
| 19046 | Rydal(u) | (215) | 5,083 | |
| 15857 | St. Marys | (814) | 7,470 | 8,065 |
| 18840 | Sayre | (717) | 7,473 | 7,917 |
| 17972 | Schuylkill Haven | (215) | 6,125 | 6,470 |
| 15683 | Scottdale | (814) | 5,818 | 6,244 |
| *18503 | Scranton | (717) | 102,696 | 111,443 |
| 17870 | Selinsgrove | (717) | 5,116 | 3,948 |
| 15143 | Sewickley | (412) | 5,660 | 6,157 |
| 17872 | Shamokin | (717) | 11,719 | 13,674 |
| 16146 | Sharon | (412) | 22,653 | 25,267 |
| 19079 | Sharon Hill | (215) | 7,464 | 7,123 |
| 15215 | Sharpsburg | (412) | 5,453 | 6,096 |
| 16150 | Sharpsville | (814) | 6,126 | 6,061 |
| 17976 | Shenandoah | (215) | 8,287 | 11,073 |
| 19607 | Shillington | (215) | 6,249 | 5,639 |
| 17257 | Shippensburg | (717) | 6,536 | 6,138 |
| 15501 | Somerset | (814) | 6,269 | 6,347 |
| 18964 | Souderton | (215) | 6,366 | 5,381 |
| 17701 | South Williamsport | (717) | 7,153 | 6,972 |
| 15144 | Springdale | (412) | 5,202 | 5,602 |
| 16801 | State College | (814) | 33,778 | 22,409 |
| 17113 | Steelton | (717) | 8,556 | 11,266 |
| 18360 | Stroudsburg | (717) | 5,451 | 6,070 |
| 16323 | Sugar Creek | (814) | 5,944 | |
| 17801 | Sunbury | (717) | 13,025 | 13,687 |
| 19081 | Swarthmore | (215) | 6,156 | 5,753 |
| 15218 | Swissvale | (412) | 13,819 | 15,089 |
| 18704 | Swoyersville | (717) | 6,786 | 6,751 |
| 18252 | Tamaqua | (215) | 9,246 | 10,173 |
| 15084 | Tarentum | (412) | 7,379 | 8,232 |
| 18517 | Taylor | (717) | 6,977 | 6,148 |
| 16354 | Titusville | (814) | 7,331 | 8,356 |
| 15145 | Turtle Creek | (412) | 8,308 | 10,607 |
| 16686 | Tyrone | (814) | 7,072 | 7,792 |
| 15401 | Uniontown | (814) | 16,282 | 17,942 |
| 15690 | Vandergrift | (412) | 7,889 | 8,742 |
| 16365 | Warren | (814) | 12,998 | 14,505 |
| 15301 | Washington | (412) | 19,827 | 23,545 |
| 17268 | Waynesboro | (717) | 10,011 | 10,427 |
| 15370 | Waynesburg | (412) | 5,152 | 5,188 |
| 19380 | West Chester | (215) | 19,301 | 15,705 |
| 18201 | West Hazleton | (717) | 6,059 | 6,278 |
| 15122 | West Mifflin | (412) | 28,070 | 27,289 |
| 15905 | Westmont | (814) | 6,673 | 6,573 |
| 18643 | West Pittston | (717) | 7,074 | 6,998 |
| 15229 | West View | (412) | 8,312 | 8,079 |
| 17404 | West York | (717) | 5,314 | 5,526 |
| 18052 | Whitehall | (412) | 16,551 | 16,075 |
| 15131 | White Oak | (412) | 9,304 | 9,047 |
| *18701 | Wilkes-Barre | (717) | 58,856 | 63,551 |
| 15221 | Wilkinsburg | (412) | 26,780 | 30,066 |
| 17701 | Williamsport | (717) | 37,918 | 41,967 |
| 19090 | Willow Grove(u) | (215) | 16,494 | |
| 15025 | Wilson | (215) | 8,406 | 8,465 |
| 15963 | Windber | (814) | 6,332 | 6,994 |
| 19610 | Wyomissing | (215) | 7,136 | 5,044 |
| 19050 | Yeadon | (215) | 12,136 | 11,610 |
| *17405 | York | (717) | 50,335 | 54,504 |

## Rhode Island (401)

*See Note on Page 219*

| ZIP code | Place | 1970 | 1960 |
|---|---|---|---|
| 02806 | Barrington | 17,554 | 13,826 |
| 02809 | Bristol | 17,860 | 14,570 |
| 02830 | Burrillville | 10,087 | 9,119 |
| 02863 | Central Falls | 18,716 | 19,858 |
| 02816 | Coventry | 22,947 | 15,432 |
| 02910 | Cranston | 74,287 | 66,766 |
| 02864 | Cumberland | 26,605 | 18,792 |
| 02818 | East Greenwich | 9,577 | 6,100 |
| 02914 | East Providence | 48,207 | 41,955 |
| 02814 | Glocester | 5,160 | 3,397 |
| 02833 | Hopkinton | 5,392 | 4,174 |
| 02919 | Johnston | 22,037 | 17,160 |
| 02881 | Kingston(u) | 5,601 | 2,616 |
| 02865 | Lincoln | 16,182 | 13,551 |
| 02840 | Middletown | 29,290 | 12,675 |
| 02882 | Narragansett | 7,138 | 3,444 |
| 02840 | Newport | 34,562 | 47,049 |
| 02843 | Newport East(u) | 10,285 | 2,643 |
| 02852 | North Kingstown | 29,793 | 18,977 |
| 02908 | North Providence | 24,337 | 18,220 |
| 02876 | North Smithfield | 9,349 | 7,632 |
| *02860 | Pawtucket | 76,984 | 81,001 |
| 02871 | Portsmouth | 12,521 | 8,251 |
| *02904 | Providence | 179,116 | 207,498 |
| 02857 | Scituate | 7,489 | 5,210 |
| 02917 | Smithfield | 13,468 | 9,442 |
| 02879 | South Kingstown | 16,913 | 11,942 |
| 02878 | Tiverton | 12,559 | 9,461 |
| *02880 | Wakefield-Peacedale(u) | 6,331 | 5,569 |
| 02885 | Warren | 10,523 | 8,750 |
| 02887 | Warwick | 83,694 | 68,504 |
| 02891 | Westerly Center(u) | 13,654 | 9,698 |
| 02891 | Westerly | 17,248 | 14,267 |
| 02893 | West Warwick | 24,323 | 21,414 |
| 02895 | Woonsocket | 46,820 | 47,080 |

## South Carolina (803)

| ZIP code | Place | 1970 | 1960 |
|---|---|---|---|
| 29620 | Abbeville | 5,515 | 5,436 |
| 29801 | Aiken | 13,436 | 11,243 |
| 29621 | Anderson | 27,556 | 41,316 |
| 29407 | Avondale-Moorland(u) | 5,236 | |
| 29902 | Beaufort | 9,434 | 6,298 |
| 29627 | Belton | 5,257 | 5,106 |
| 29512 | Bennettsville | 7,468 | 6,963 |
| 29611 | Berea | 7,186 | |
| 29020 | Camden | 8,532 | 6,842 |
| 29033 | Cayce | 9,967 | 8,517 |
| *29401 | Charleston | 66,945 | 65,925 |
| 29404 | Charleston Base(u) | 6,238 | |
| 29408 | Charleston Yard(u) | 13,565 | |
| 29631 | Cheraw | 5,627 | 5,171 |
| 29706 | Chester | 7,045 | 6,906 |
| 29631 | Clemson | 5,578 | 1,587 |
| 29325 | Clinton | 8,138 | 7,937 |
| *29201 | Columbia | 113,542 | 97,433 |
| 29526 | Conway | 8,151 | 8,563 |
| 29532 | Darlington | 6,990 | 6,710 |
| 29536 | Dillon | 6,391 | 6,173 |
| 29640 | Easley | 11,175 | 8,283 |
| 29501 | Florence | 25,997 | 24,722 |
| 29206 | Forest Acres | 6,808 | 3,842 |
| 29340 | Gaffney | 13,253 | 10,435 |
| 29605 | Gantt(u) | 11,386 | |
| 29440 | Georgetown | 10,449 | 12,261 |
| *29602 | Greenville 1976 | 57,849 | 66,188 |
| 29646 | Greenwood | 21,069 | 16,644 |
| 29651 | Greer | 10,642 | 8,967 |
| 29410 | Hanahan(u) 1974 | 11,518 | |
| 29550 | Hartsville | 8,017 | 6,392 |
| 29560 | Lake City | 6,247 | 6,059 |
| 29720 | Lancaster | 9,186 | 7,999 |
| 29360 | Laurens | 10,298 | 9,598 |
| 29571 | Marion | 7,435 | 7,174 |
| 29662 | Mauldin 1973 | 5,480 | 1,462 |
| 29464 | Mount Pleasant | 6,879 | 5,116 |
| 29574 | Mullins | 6,006 | 6,299 |
| 29577 | Myrtle Beach | 9,035 | 7,834 |
| 29108 | Newberry | 9,218 | 8,208 |
| 29841 | North Augusta | 12,883 | 10,348 |
| 29115 | Orangeburg | 13,252 | 13,852 |
| 29905 | Parris Island(u) | 8,868 | |
| 29730 | Rock Hill | 33,846 | 29,404 |
| 29407 | St. Andrews(u) | 9,202 | |
| 29678 | Seneca | 6,382 | 5,227 |

| ZIP code | Place | 1970 | 1960 |
|---|---|---|---|
| 29150 | Shannontown(u) | 7,491 | 7,064 |
| 29152 | Shaw(u) | 5,819 | ..... |
| 29681 | Simpsonville 1974 | 6,209 | 2,282 |
| *29301 | Spartanburg | 44,546 | 44,352 |
| 29150 | Sumter | 24,555 | 23,062 |
| 29687 | Taylors(u) | 6,831 | 1,071 |
| 29379 | Union | 10,775 | 10,191 |
| 29607 | Wade-Hampton(u) | 17,152 | ..... |
| 29488 | Walterboro | 6,257 | 5,417 |
| 29169 | West Columbia | 7,838 | 6,410 |
| 29745 | York | 5,081 | 4,758 |

## South Dakota (605)

| ZIP code | Place | 1970 | 1960 |
|---|---|---|---|
| 57401 | Aberdeen | 26,476 | 23,073 |
| 57006 | Brookings | 13,717 | 10,558 |
| 57706 | Ellsworth(u) | 6,207 | ..... |
| 57350 | Huron | 14,299 | 14,180 |
| 57754 | Lead | 5,420 | 6,211 |
| 57042 | Madison | 6,315 | 5,420 |
| 57301 | Mitchell | 13,425 | 12,555 |
| 57501 | Pierre | 9,699 | 10,088 |
| 57701 | Rapid City | 43,836 | 42,399 |
| *57101 | Sioux Falls | 72,488 | 65,466 |
| 57785 | Sturgis 1974 | 5,162 | 4,639 |
| 57069 | Vermillion | 9,128 | 6,102 |
| 57201 | Watertown | 13,388 | 14,077 |
| 57078 | Yankton | 11,919 | 9,279 |

## Tennessee

| ZIP code | Place | | 1970 | 1960 |
|---|---|---|---|---|
| 37701 | Alcoa | (615) | 7,739 | 6,395 |
| 37303 | Athens | (615) | 11,790 | 12,103 |
| 38008 | Bolivar | (901) | 6,674 | 3,338 |
| 37620 | Bristol | (615) | 20,064 | 17,582 |
| 38012 | Brownsville | (901) | 7,011 | 5,424 |
| *37401 | Chattanooga | (615) | 119,923 | 130,009 |
| 37040 | Clarksville 1975 | (615) | 52,621 | 22,021 |
| 37311 | Cleveland | (615) | 20,651 | 16,196 |
| 38401 | Columbia | (615) | 21,471 | 17,624 |
| 38501 | Cookeville 1975 | (615) | 17,070 | 7,805 |
| 38019 | Covington | (901) | 5,801 | 5,298 |
| 38555 | Crossville | (615) | 5,381 | 4,668 |
| 37055 | Dickson | (615) | 5,665 | 5,028 |
| 38024 | Dyersburg | (901) | 14,523 | 12,499 |
| 37801 | Eagleton Village(u) | (615) | 5,345 | 5,068 |
| 37412 | East Ridge | (615) | 21,799 | 19,570 |
| 37643 | Elizabethton | (615) | 12,269 | 10,896 |
| 37334 | Fayetteville | (615) | 7,030 | 6,804 |
| 42223 | Fort Campbell South(u) | (615) | 9,279 | ..... |
| 37064 | Franklin 1974 | (615) | 11,298 | 6,977 |
| 37066 | Gallatin 1976 | (615) | 14,374 | 7,901 |
| 37075 | Greater Hendersonville(u) | (615) | 11,996 | ..... |
| 37743 | Greeneville | (615) | 13,722 | 11,759 |
| 37748 | Harriman | (615) | 8,734 | 5,931 |
| 37343 | Hixson(u) | (615) | 6,188 | ..... |
| 38343 | Humboldt | (901) | 10,066 | 8,482 |
| 38301 | Jackson 1977 | (901) | 41,145 | 34,376 |
| 37760 | Jefferson City | (615) | 5,124 | 4,550 |
| 37601 | Johnson City | (615) | 33,770 | 31,187 |
| *37662 | Kingsport | (615) | 31,938 | 26,314 |
| 37665 | Kingsport North(u) | (615) | 13,118 | ..... |
| *37901 | Knoxville | (615) | 174,587 | 111,827 |
| 37766 | La Follette | (615) | 6,902 | 6,204 |
| 37416 | Lake Hills-Murray Hills(u) | (615) | 7,806 | ..... |
| 38464 | Lawrenceburg | (615) | 8,889 | 8,042 |
| 37087 | Lebanon | (615) | 12,492 | 10,512 |
| 37771 | Lenoir City | (615) | 5,324 | 4,979 |
| 37091 | Lewisburg | (615) | 7,207 | 6,338 |
| 38351 | Lexington | (901) | 5,024 | 3,943 |
| 37110 | Mc Minnville | (615) | 10,662 | 9,013 |
| 37355 | Manchester | (615) | 6,208 | 3,930 |
| 38237 | Martin | (901) | 7,781 | 4,750 |
| 37801 | Maryville | (615) | 13,808 | 10,348 |
| *38101 | Memphis | (901) | 623,530 | 497,524 |
| 38358 | Milan | (901) | 7,313 | 5,208 |
| 38053 | Millington | (901) | 21,177 | 6,059 |
| 37814 | Morristown | (615) | 20,318 | 21,267 |
| 37130 | Murfreesboro | (615) | 26,360 | 18,991 |
| *37202 | Nashville-Davidson | (615) | **447,877 | 170,874 |
| 37821 | Newport | (615) | 7,328 | 6,448 |
| 37830 | Oak Ridge | (901) | 28,319 | 27,169 |
| 38242 | Paris | (615) | 9,892 | 9,325 |
| 38478 | Pulaski | (615) | 6,989 | 6,616 |
| 37415 | Red Bank | (615) | 12,715 | 10,777 |
| 37854 | Rockwood | (901) | 5,259 | 5,345 |
| 38372 | Savannah | (615) | 5,576 | 4,315 |
| 37160 | Shelbyville | (615) | 12,262 | 10,466 |
| 37167 | Smyrna | (615) | 5,698 | 3,612 |
| 37379 | Soddy-Daisy | (615) | 7,569 | ..... |
| 37311 | South Cleveland(u) | (615) | 5,070 | 1,512 |
| 38583 | Sparta 1975 | (615) | 5,038 | 4,510 |
| 37172 | Springfield | (615) | 9,720 | 9,221 |
| 37388 | Tullahoma | (615) | 15,311 | 12,242 |
| 38261 | Union City | (901) | 11,925 | 8,837 |
| 37398 | Winchester | (615) | 5,256 | 4,760 |

**Comprises the Metropolitan Government of Nashville and Davidson County.

| ZIP code | Place | | 1970 | 1960 |
|---|---|---|---|---|

## Texas

| ZIP code | Place | | 1970 | 1960 |
|---|---|---|---|---|
| *79604 | Abilene | (915) | 89,653 | 90,368 |
| 78209 | Alamo Heights | (512) | 6,933 | 7,552 |
| 78332 | Alice | (512) | 20,121 | 20,861 |
| 79830 | Alpine | (915) | 5,971 | 4,740 |
| 77511 | Alvin | (713) | 10,671 | 5,643 |
| *79105 | Amarillo | (806) | 127,010 | 137,969 |
| 79714 | Andrews | (915) | 8,625 | 11,135 |
| 77515 | Angleton | (713) | 9,770 | 7,312 |
| 78336 | Aransas Pass | (512) | 5,813 | 6,956 |
| *76010 | Arlington | (817) | 90,032 | 44,775 |
| 75751 | Athens | (214) | 9,582 | 7,086 |
| 75551 | Atlanta | (214) | 5,007 | 4,076 |
| *78710 | Austin | (512) | 251,808 | 186,545 |
| 75149 | Balch Springs | (214) | 10,464 | 6,821 |
| 77414 | Bay City | (713) | 13,445 | 11,656 |
| 77520 | Baytown | (713) | 43,980 | 28,159 |
| *77704 | Beaumont | (713) | 117,548 | 119,175 |
| 76021 | Bedford | (814) | 10,049 | 2,706 |
| 78102 | Beeville | (512) | 13,506 | 13,811 |
| 77401 | Bellaire | (713) | 19,009 | 19,872 |
| 76704 | Bellmead | (817) | 7,698 | 5,127 |
| 76513 | Belton | (817) | 8,696 | 8,163 |
| 76126 | Benbrook | (817) | 8,169 | 3,254 |
| 79720 | Big Spring | (915) | 28,735 | 31,230 |
| 75418 | Bonham | (214) | 7,698 | 7,357 |
| 79007 | Borger | (806) | 14,195 | 20,911 |
| 76230 | Bowie | (817) | 5,185 | 4,566 |
| 76825 | Brady | (915) | 5,557 | 5,338 |
| 76024 | Breckenridge | (817) | 5,944 | 6,273 |
| 77833 | Brenham | (713) | 8,922 | 7,740 |
| 77611 | Bridge City(u) | (713) | 8,164 | 4,677 |
| 79316 | Brownfield | (806) | 9,647 | 10,286 |
| 78520 | Brownsville | (512) | 52,522 | 48,040 |
| 76801 | Brownwood | (915) | 17,368 | 16,974 |
| 77801 | Bryan | (713) | 33,719 | 27,542 |
| 76354 | Burkburnett | (817) | 9,230 | 7,621 |
| 76028 | Burleson | (817) | 7,713 | 2,345 |
| 76520 | Cameron | (713) | 5,546 | 5,640 |
| 79015 | Canyon | (806) | 8,333 | 5,864 |
| 78834 | Carrizo Springs | (512) | 5,374 | 5,699 |
| 75006 | Carrollton | (214) | 13,855 | 4,242 |
| 75633 | Carthage | (214) | 5,392 | 5,262 |
| 78213 | Castle Hills | (512) | 5,311 | 2,622 |
| 79201 | Childress | (817) | 5,408 | 6,399 |
| 76031 | Cleburne | (817) | 16,015 | 15,381 |
| 77327 | Cleveland | (713) | 5,627 | 5,838 |
| 77531 | Clute City | (713) | 6,023 | 4,501 |
| 76834 | Coleman | (915) | 5,608 | 6,371 |
| 77840 | College Station | (713) | 17,676 | 11,396 |
| 79512 | Colorado City | (915) | 5,227 | 6,457 |
| 75428 | Commerce | (214) | 9,534 | 5,789 |
| 77301 | Conroe | (713) | 11,969 | 9,192 |
| 76522 | Copperas Cove | (817) | 10,818 | 4,567 |
| *78408 | Corpus Christi | (512) | 204,525 | 167,690 |
| 75110 | Corsicana | (214) | 19,972 | 20,344 |
| 75835 | Crockett | (713) | 6,616 | 5,356 |
| 78839 | Crystal City | (512) | 8,104 | 9,101 |
| 77954 | Cuero | (516) | 6,956 | 7,338 |
| 79022 | Dalhart | (806) | 5,705 | 5,160 |
| *75260 | Dallas | (214) | 844,401 | 679,684 |
| 77536 | Deer Park | (713) | 12,773 | 4,865 |
| 78840 | Del Rio | (512) | 21,330 | 18,612 |
| 75020 | Denison | (214) | 24,923 | 22,748 |
| 76201 | Denton | (214) | 39,874 | 26,844 |
| 75115 | De Soto | (214) | 6,617 | 1,969 |
| 77539 | Dickinson(u) | (713) | 10,776 | 4,715 |
| 78537 | Donna | (517) | 7,365 | 7,522 |
| 79029 | Dumas | (806) | 9,771 | 8,477 |
| 75116 | Duncanville | (214) | 14,105 | 3,774 |
| 78852 | Eagle Pass | (512) | 15,364 | 12,094 |
| 78539 | Edinburg | (512) | 17,163 | 18,706 |
| 77957 | Edna | (713) | 5,332 | 5,038 |
| 77437 | El Campo | (713) | 9,332 | 7,700 |
| *79910 | El Paso | (915) | 322,261 | 276,687 |
| 75119 | Ennis | (214) | 11,046 | 9,347 |
| 76039 | Euless | (817) | 19,316 | 4,263 |
| 78355 | Falfurrias | (512) | 6,355 | 6,515 |
| 75234 | Farmers Branch | (714) | 27,492 | 13,441 |
| 76119 | Forest Hill | (817) | 8,236 | 3,221 |
| 79906 | Fort Bliss(u) | (915) | 13,288 | ..... |
| 76544 | Fort Hood(u) | (817) | 32,597 | ..... |
| 78234 | Fort Sam Houston(u) | (512) | 10,553 | ..... |
| 79735 | Fort Stockton | (915) | 8,283 | 6,373 |
| *76101 | Fort Worth | (817) | 393,476 | 356,268 |
| 78624 | Fredericksburg | (512) | 5,326 | 4,629 |
| 77541 | Freeport | (713) | 11,997 | 11,619 |
| 77546 | Friendswood | (713) | 5,675 | ..... |
| 76240 | Gainesville | (214) | 13,830 | 13,083 |
| 77547 | Galena Park | (713) | 10,479 | 10,852 |
| 77550 | Galveston | (713) | 61,809 | 67,175 |
| *75040 | Garland | (214) | 81,437 | 38,501 |
| 78626 | Georgetown | (512) | 6,395 | 5,218 |
| 75647 | Gladewater | (214) | 5,574 | 5,742 |
| 78629 | Gonzales | (512) | 5,854 | 5,829 |
| 76046 | Graham | (817) | 7,477 | 8,505 |
| 75050 | Grand Prairie | (214) | 50,904 | 30,386 |
| 76051 | Grapevine | (817) | 7,023 | 2,821 |

| ZIP code | Place | | 1970 | 1960 |
|---|---|---|---|---|
| 5401 | Greenville | (214) | 22,043 | 19,087 |
| 7619 | Groves | (713) | 18,067 | 17,304 |
| 6117 | Haltom City | (817) | 28,127 | 23,133 |
| 6550 | Harlingen | (512) | 33,503 | 41,207 |
| 5652 | Henderson | (214) | 10,187 | 9,666 |
| 9045 | Hereford | (806) | 13,414 | 7,652 |
| 5205 | Highland Park | (214) | 10,133 | 10,411 |
| 6645 | Hillsboro | (214) | 7,224 | 7,402 |
| 7563 | Hitchcock | (713) | 5,565 | 5,216 |
| 3861 | Hondo | (512) | 5,487 | 4,992 |
| 7013 | Houston | (713) | 1,232,802 | 938,219 |
| 7340 | Huntsville | (713) | 17,610 | 11,999 |
| 6053 | Hurst | (817) | 27,215 | 10,165 |
| 6367 | Iowa Park | (817) | 5,796 | 3,295 |
| 5061 | Irving | (214) | 97,260 | 45,985 |
| 7029 | Jacinto City | (713) | 9,563 | 9,547 |
| 5766 | Jacksonville | (214) | 9,734 | 9,590 |
| 5951 | Jasper | (713) | 6,251 | 4,889 |
| 9745 | Kermit | (915) | 7,884 | 10,465 |
| 8028 | Kerrville | (512) | 12,672 | 8,901 |
| 5662 | Kilgore | (214) | 9,495 | 10,092 |
| 8541 | Killeen | (817) | 35,507 | 23,377 |
| 8363 | Kingsville | (512) | 28,915 | 25,297 |
| 8236 | Lackland(u) | (512) | 19,141 | ...... |
| 7566 | Lake Jackson | (713) | 13,376 | 9,651 |
| 7568 | La Marque | (713) | 16,131 | 13,969 |
| 9631 | Lamesa | (915) | 11,559 | 12,438 |
| 6550 | Lampasas | (817) | 5,922 | 5,061 |
| 5146 | Lancaster | (214) | 10,522 | 7,501 |
| 7571 | La Porte | (713) | 7,149 | 4,512 |
| 6040 | Laredo | (512) | 69,024 | 60,678 |
| 7573 | League City | (713) | 10,818 | ...... |
| 9336 | Levelland | (806) | 11,445 | 10,153 |
| 5067 | Lewisville | (817) | 9,264 | 3,956 |
| 7575 | Liberty | (713) | 5,591 | 6,127 |
| 9339 | Littlefield | (806) | 6,738 | 7,236 |
| 8644 | Lockhart | (512) | 6,489 | 6,084 |
| 5601 | Longview 1975 | (214) | 51,953 | 40,050 |
| 9408 | Lubbock | (806) | 149,101 | 128,691 |
| 5901 | Lufkin | (713) | 23,049 | 17,641 |
| 8501 | McAllen | (713) | 37,636 | 32,728 |
| 5069 | McKinney | (512) | 15,193 | 13,763 |
| 6661 | Marlin | (214) | 6,351 | 6,918 |
| 5670 | Marshall | (214) | 22,937 | 23,846 |
| 8368 | Mathis | (512) | 5,351 | 6,075 |
| 8570 | Mercedes | (512) | 9,355 | 10,943 |
| 5149 | Mesquite | (214) | 55,131 | 27,526 |
| 8650 | Mexia | (214) | 5,943 | 6,121 |
| 9701 | Midland | (915) | 59,463 | 62,625 |
| 6067 | Mineral Wells | (817) | 18,411 | 11,053 |
| 8572 | Mission | (512) | 13,043 | 14,081 |
| 9756 | Monahans | (915) | 8,333 | 8,567 |
| 5455 | Mount Pleasant | (214) | 9,459 | 8,027 |
| 5961 | Nacogdoches | (713) | 22,544 | 12,674 |
| 7868 | Navasota | (214) | 5,111 | 4,937 |
| 7630 | Nederland | (713) | 16,810 | 12,036 |
| 8130 | New Braunfels | (512) | 17,859 | 15,631 |
| 6118 | North Richland Hills | (817) | 16,514 | 8,662 |
| 9760 | Odessa | (915) | 78,380 | 80,338 |
| 7630 | Orange | (713) | 24,457 | 25,605 |
| 5801 | Palestine | (214) | 14,525 | 13,974 |
| 9065 | Pampa | (806) | 21,726 | 24,664 |
| 5460 | Paris | (214) | 23,441 | 20,977 |
| 7501 | Pasadena | (713) | 89,277 | 58,737 |
| 7581 | Pearland | (713) | 6,444 | 1,497 |
| 8061 | Pearsall 1976 | (512) | 6,495 | 4,957 |
| 9772 | Pecos | (915) | 12,682 | 12,728 |
| 9070 | Perryton | (806) | 7,810 | 7,903 |
| 8577 | Pharr | (512) | 15,829 | 14,106 |
| 9072 | Plainview | (806) | 19,096 | 18,735 |
| 5074 | Plano | (214) | 17,872 | 3,695 |
| 8064 | Pleasanton | (512) | 5,407 | 3,467 |
| 7640 | Port Arthur | (713) | 57,371 | 66,676 |
| 8374 | Portland | (512) | 7,302 | 2,538 |
| 7979 | Port Lavaca | (512) | 10,491 | 8,864 |
| 7651 | Port Neches | (713) | 10,894 | 8,696 |
| 5475 | Randolph(u) | (512) | 5,329 | ...... |
| 8580 | Raymondville | (512) | 7,987 | 9,385 |
| 5080 | Richardson | (214) | 48,582 | 16,810 |
| 6118 | Richland Hills | (817) | 8,865 | 7,804 |
| 7469 | Richmond | (713) | 5,777 | 3,868 |
| 8582 | Rio Grande City(u) | (512) | 5,676 | 5,835 |
| 7019 | River Oaks | (817) | 8,193 | 8,444 |
| 8380 | Robstown | (512) | 11,217 | 10,266 |
| 7471 | Rosenberg | (713) | 12,098 | 9,698 |
| 6901 | San Angelo | (915) | 63,884 | 58,815 |
| 8284 | San Antonio | (512) | 654,153 | 587,718 |
| 8586 | San Benito | (512) | 15,176 | 16,422 |
| 8589 | San Juan | (512) | 5,070 | 4,371 |
| 8666 | San Marcos | (512) | 18,860 | 12,713 |
| 8155 | Seguin | (512) | 15,934 | 14,299 |
| 9360 | Seminole | (915) | 5,007 | 5,737 |
| 5090 | Sherman | (214) | 29,061 | 24,988 |
| 7656 | Silsbee | (713) | 7,271 | 6,277 |
| 8387 | Sinton | (512) | 5,563 | 6,008 |
| 9364 | Slaton | (806) | 6,583 | 6,568 |
| 9549 | Snyder | (915) | 11,171 | 13,850 |
| 7587 | South Houston | (713) | 11,527 | 7,523 |
| 6401 | Stephenville | (817) | 9,277 | 7,359 |

| ZIP code | Place | | 1970 | 1960 |
|---|---|---|---|---|
| 75482 | Sulphur Springs | (214) | 10,642 | 9,160 |
| 79556 | Sweetwater | (915) | 12,020 | 13,914 |
| 76574 | Taylor | (817) | 9,616 | 9,434 |
| 76501 | Temple | (817) | 33,431 | 30,419 |
| 75160 | Terrell | (214) | 14,182 | 13,803 |
| 78209 | Terrell Hills | (512) | 5,225 | 5,572 |
| 75501 | Texarkana | (214) | 30,497 | 30,218 |
| 77590 | Texas City | (713) | 38,908 | 32,065 |
| 79088 | Tulia | (806) | 5,294 | 4,410 |
| 75701 | Tyler | (214) | 57,770 | 51,230 |
| 78148 | Universal City | (512) | 7,613 | ...... |
| 77608 | University Park | (214) | 23,498 | 23,202 |
| 78801 | Uvalde | (512) | 10,764 | 10,293 |
| 76384 | Vernon | (817) | 11,454 | 12,141 |
| 77901 | Victoria | (512) | 41,349 | 33,047 |
| 77662 | Vidor | (713) | 9,738 | ...... |
| *76701 | Waco | (817) | 95,326 | 97,808 |
| 75165 | Waxahachie | (214) | 13,452 | 12,749 |
| 76086 | Weatherford | (817) | 11,750 | 9,759 |
| 78596 | Weslaco | (512) | 15,313 | 15,649 |
| 77005 | West University Place | (713) | 13,317 | 14,628 |
| 77488 | Wharton | (713) | 7,881 | 5,734 |
| 76108 | White Settlement | (817) | 13,449 | 11,513 |
| *76307 | Wichita Falls | (817) | 96,265 | 101,724 |
| 77995 | Yoakum | (512) | 5,755 | 5,761 |

## Utah (801)

| ZIP code | Place | 1970 | 1960 |
|---|---|---|---|
| 84003 | American Fork | 7,713 | 6,373 |
| 84010 | Bountiful | 27,751 | 17,039 |
| 84302 | Brigham City | 14,007 | 11,728 |
| 84720 | Cedar City | 8,946 | 7,543 |
| 84015 | Clearfield | 13,316 | 8,833 |
| 84121 | Cottonwood(u) | 8,431 | ...... |
| 84109 | East Millcreek(u) | 26,579 | ...... |
| 84119 | Granger-Hunter(u) | 9,029 | ...... |
| 84106 | Granite Park(u) | 9,573 | ...... |
| 84117 | Holladay(u) | 23,014 | ...... |
| 84037 | Kaysville | 6,192 | 3,608 |
| 84118 | Kearns(u) | 17,247 | 17,172 |
| 84041 | Layton | 13,603 | 9,027 |
| 84321 | Logan | 22,333 | 18,731 |
| 84044 | Magna(u) | 5,509 | 6,442 |
| 84047 | Midvale | 7,840 | 5,802 |
| 84117 | Mount Olympus(u) | 5,909 | ...... |
| 84107 | Murray | 21,206 | 16,806 |
| 84404 | North Ogden | 5,257 | 2,621 |
| *84401 | Ogden | 69,478 | 70,197 |
| 84057 | Orem | 25,729 | 18,394 |
| 84062 | Pleasant Grove | 5,327 | 4,772 |
| 84501 | Price | 6,218 | 6,802 |
| 84601 | Provo | 53,131 | 36,047 |
| 84067 | Roy | 14,356 | 9,239 |
| 84770 | St. George | 7,097 | 5,130 |
| *84101 | Salt Lake City | 175,885 | 189,454 |
| 84070 | Sandy City | 6,438 | 3,322 |
| 84403 | South Ogden | 9,991 | 7,405 |
| 84115 | South Salt Lake | 7,810 | 9,520 |
| 84660 | Spanish Fork | 7,284 | 6,472 |
| 84663 | Springville | 8,790 | 7,913 |
| 84015 | Sunset | 6,268 | 4,235 |
| 84074 | Tooele | 12,539 | 9,133 |
| 84403 | Washington Terrace | 7,241 | 6,441 |
| 74070 | White City(u) | 6,402 | ...... |

## Vermont (802)

*See Note on Page 219*

| ZIP code | Place | 1970 | 1960 |
|---|---|---|---|
| 05641 | Barre | 10,209 | 10,387 |
| ...... | Barre | 6,509 | 4,580 |
| 05201 | Bennington | 14,586 | 13,002 |
| ...... | Bennington | 7,950 | 8,023 |
| 05301 | Brattleboro Center(u) | 9,055 | 9,315 |
| ...... | Brattleboro | 12,239 | 11,734 |
| 05401 | Burlington | 38,633 | 35,531 |
| 05446 | Colchester | 8,776 | 4,718 |
| 05451 | Essex | 10,951 | 7,090 |
| 05452 | Essex Junction | 6,511 | 5,340 |
| 05047 | Hartford | 6,355 | |
| 05753 | Middlebury | 6,532 | 5,305 |
| 05602 | Montpelier | 8,609 | 8,782 |
| 05101 | Rockingham | 5,501 | 5,704 |
| 05701 | Rutland | 19,293 | 18,325 |
| 05478 | St. Albans | 8,082 | 8,806 |
| 05819 | St. Johnsbury | 8,409 | 8,869 |
| 05401 | South Burlington | 10,032 | 6,903 |
| 05156 | Springfield Center(u) | 5,632 | 6,600 |
| ...... | Springfield | 10,063 | 9,934 |
| 05401 | Williston Road Section(u) | 5,376 | 3,259 |
| 05404 | Winooski | 7,309 | 7,420 |

## Virginia

| ZIP code | Place | | 1970 | 1960 |
|---|---|---|---|---|
| *22313 | Alexandria | (703) | 110,927 | 91,023 |
| 22003 | Annandale(u) | (703) | 27,405 | ...... |
| *22210 | Arlington(u) | (703) | 174,284 | 163,401 |
| 22041 | Bailey's Crossroads(u) | (703) | 7,295 | ...... |

| ZIP code | Place | | 1970 | 1960 |
|---|---|---|---|---|
| 24523 | Bedford | (804) | 6,011 | 5,921 |
| 22307 | Belleview(u) | (703) | 8,299 | ..... |
| 24060 | Blacksburg | (703) | 9,384 | 7,070 |
| 24605 | Bluefield | (703) | 5,286 | 4,235 |
| 23235 | Bon Air(u) | (804) | 10,771 | ..... |
| 24201 | Bristol | (703) | 14,857 | 17,144 |
| 24416 | Buena Vista | (703) | 6,425 | 6,300 |
| *22906 | Charlottesville | (804) | 38,880 | 29,427 |
| *23320 | Chesapeake | (804) | 89,580 | ..... |
| 23831 | Chester(u) | (804) | 5,556 | 1,290 |
| 24073 | Christiansburg | (703) | 7,857 | 3,653 |
| 24422 | Clifton Forge | (703) | 5,501 | 5,268 |
| 24078 | Collinsville(u) | (703) | 6,015 | 3,586 |
| 23834 | Colonial Heights | (804) | 15,097 | 9,587 |
| 24426 | Covington | (703) | 10,060 | 11,062 |
| 22701 | Culpeper | (703) | 6,056 | 2,412 |
| 22191 | Dale City(u) | (703) | 13,857 | ..... |
| 24541 | Danville | (804) | 46,391 | 46,577 |
| 23847 | Emporia | (804) | 5,300 | 5,535 |
| 22030 | Fairfax | (703) | 21,970 | 13,585 |
| *22046 | Falls Church | (703) | 10,772 | 10,192 |
| 22060 | Fort Belvoir(u) | (703) | 14,591 | ..... |
| 22308 | Fort Hunt(u) | (703) | 10,415 | ..... |
| 23801 | Fort Lee(u) | (804) | 12,435 | ..... |
| 23851 | Franklin | (804) | 6,880 | 7,264 |
| 22401 | Fredericksburg | (703) | 14,450 | 13,639 |
| 22630 | Front Royal | (703) | 8,211 | 7,949 |
| 24333 | Galax | (703) | 6,278 | 5,254 |
| 22306 | Groveton(u) | (703) | 11,761 | ..... |
| *23360 | Hampton | (804) | 120,779 | 89,258 |
| 22801 | Harrisonburg | (703) | 14,605 | 11,916 |
| 23075 | Highland Springs(u) | (804) | 7,345 | ..... |
| 23860 | Hopewell | (804) | 23,471 | 17,895 |
| 22303 | Huntington(u) | (703) | 5,559 | ..... |
| 22042 | Jefferson(u) | (804) | 25,432 | ..... |
| 22041 | Lake Barcroft(u) | (703) | 11,605 | ..... |
| 23228 | Lakeside(u) | (804) | 11,137 | ..... |
| 24450 | Lexington | (703) | 7,597 | 7,537 |
| 22312 | Lincolnia(u) | (703) | 10,761 | ..... |
| 22030 | Long Branch(u) | (703) | 21,634 | ..... |
| *24505 | Lynchburg | (804) | 54,083 | 54,790 |
| 22110 | Manassas | (703) | 9,164 | 3,555 |
| 22110 | Manassas Park | (703) | 6,844 | 5,342 |
| 22030 | Mantua(u) | (703) | 6,911 | ..... |
| 24354 | Marion | (703) | 8,158 | 8,385 |
| 24112 | Martinsville | (804) | 19,653 | 18,798 |
| 22101 | McLean(u) | (703) | 17,698 | ..... |
| 23111 | Mechanicsville(u) | (804) | 5,189 | ..... |
| *23607 | Newport News | (804) | 138,177 | 113,662 |
| *23501 | Norfolk | (804) | 307,951 | 304,869 |
| 22151 | North Springfield(u) | (703) | 8,631 | ..... |
| 23803 | Petersburg | (804) | 36,103 | 36,750 |
| 23662 | Poquoson | (804) | 5,441 | 4,278 |
| *23705 | Portsmouth | (804) | 110,963 | 114,773 |
| 24301 | Pulaski | (703) | 10,279 | 10,469 |
| 22134 | Quantico Station(u) | (703) | 6,213 | ..... |
| 24141 | Radford | (703) | 11,596 | 9,371 |
| 22070 | Reston(u) | (703) | 5,723 | ..... |
| *23232 | Richmond | (804) | 249,431 | 219,958 |
| *24001 | Roanoke | (703) | 92,115 | 97,110 |
| 22310 | Rose Hill(u) | (703) | 14,492 | ..... |
| 24153 | Salem | (703) | 21,982 | 16,058 |
| 22044 | Seven Corners(u) | (703) | 5,590 | ..... |
| 24592 | South Boston | (804) | 6,889 | 5,974 |
| *22150 | Springfield | (703) | 11,613 | 10,783 |
| 24401 | Staunton | (703) | 24,504 | 22,232 |
| 22170 | Sterling Park(u) | (703) | 8,321 | ..... |
| 23434 | Suffolk 1977 | (804) | 46,574 | 12,609 |
| 22180 | Vienna | (703) | 17,146 | 11,440 |
| 24179 | Vinton | (703) | 6,347 | 3,432 |
| *23458 | Virginia Beach | (804) | 172,106 | 8,091 |
| 22980 | Waynesboro | (703) | 16,707 | 15,694 |
| 22152 | West Springfield(u) | (703) | 14,143 | ..... |
| 23185 | Williamsburg | (804) | 9,069 | 6,832 |
| 22601 | Winchester | (703) | 14,643 | 15,110 |
| 22191 | Woodbridge-Marumsco(u) | (703) | 25,412 | ..... |
| 24382 | Wytheville | (703) | 6,069 | 5,634 |

## Washington

| ZIP code | Place | | 1970 | 1960 |
|---|---|---|---|---|
| 98520 | Aberdeen | (206) | 18,489 | 18,741 |
| 98221 | Anacortes | (206) | 7,701 | 8,414 |
| 98002 | Auburn | (206) | 21,653 | 11,933 |
| *98009 | Bellevue | (206) | 61,196 | 12,809 |
| 98225 | Bellingham | (206) | 39,375 | 34,688 |
| 98011 | Bothell | (206) | 5,420 | 2,237 |
| 98310 | Bremerton | (206) | 35,307 | 28,922 |
| 98607 | Camas | (206) | 5,790 | 5,666 |
| 98531 | Centralia | (206) | 10,054 | 8,586 |
| 98532 | Chehalis | (206) | 5,727 | 5,199 |
| 99004 | Cheney | (509) | 6,358 | 3,173 |
| 99403 | Clarkston | (509) | 6,312 | 6,209 |
| 99213 | Dishman(u) | (509) | 9,079 | ..... |
| 98020 | Edmonds | (206) | 23,998 | 8,016 |
| 98926 | Ellensburg | (509) | 13,568 | 8,625 |
| 98823 | Ephrata | (509) | 5,255 | 6,548 |
| *98201 | Everett | (206) | 53,622 | 40,304 |
| 99011 | Fairchild(u) | (509) | 6,754 | ..... |
| 98466 | Fircrest | (206) | 5,651 | 3,565 |

| ZIP code | Place | | 1970 | 1 |
|---|---|---|---|---|
| 98433 | Fort Lewis(u) | (206) | 38,054 | |
| 98550 | Hoquiam | (206) | 10,466 | 10, |
| 98626 | Kelso | (206) | 10,296 | 8, |
| 99336 | Kennewick | (509) | 15,212 | 14, |
| 98031 | Kent | (206) | 16,596 | 9,0 |
| 98033 | Kirkland | (206) | 14,970 | 6,0 |
| 98503 | Lacey | (206) | 9,696 | |
| 98499 | Lakes District(u) | (206) | 48,195 | |
| 98632 | Longview | (206) | 28,373 | 23,3 |
| 98036 | Lynwood | (206) | 16,919 | 7, |
| 98438 | McChord(u) | (206) | 6,515 | |
| 98040 | Mercer Island | (206) | 19,047 | |
| 98837 | Moses Lake | (509) | 10,310 | 11,2 |
| 98273 | Mount Vernon | (206) | 8,804 | 7,1 |
| 98277 | Oak Harbor | (206) | 9,167 | 3,0 |
| *98501 | Olympia | (206) | 23,296 | 18,2 |
| 99214 | Opportunity(u) | (509) | 16,604 | 12,4 |
| 98444 | Parkland(u) | (206) | 21,012 | |
| 99301 | Pasco | (509) | 13,920 | 14,5 |
| 98362 | Port Angeles | (206) | 16,367 | 12,6 |
| 98368 | Port Townsend | (206) | 5,241 | 5,0 |
| 99163 | Pullman | (509) | 20,509 | 12,9 |
| 98052 | Redmond | (206) | 11,020 | 1,4 |
| 98055 | Renton | (206) | 25,878 | 18,4 |
| 99352 | Richland | (509) | 26,290 | 23,5 |
| *98109 | Seattle | (206) | 530,831 | 557,0 |
| 98584 | Shelton | (206) | 6,515 | 5,0 |
| 98290 | Snohomish | (206) | 5,174 | 3,8 |
| 98387 | Spanaway(u) | (206) | 5,768 | |
| *99210 | Spokane | (509) | 170,516 | 181,6 |
| 98944 | Sunnyside | (509) | 6,751 | 6,2 |
| *98402 | Tacoma | (509) | 154,407 | 147,9 |
| 98948 | Toppenish | (509) | 5,744 | 5,6 |
| 99268 | Town and Country(u) | (509) | 6,484 | |
| 98502 | Turnwater | (206) | 5,373 | 3,0 |
| 98406 | University Place(u) | (206) | 13,230 | |
| *98660 | Vancouver | (206) | 41,859 | 32,4 |
| 99362 | Walla Walla | (509) | 23,619 | 24,5 |
| 98801 | Wenatchee | (206) | 16,912 | 16,7 |
| *98901 | Yakima | (509) | 45,588 | 43,2 |

## West Virginia (304)

| ZIP code | Place | 1970 | 1 |
|---|---|---|---|
| 25801 | Beckley | 19,884 | 18,6 |
| 24701 | Bluefield | 15,921 | 19,2 |
| 26201 | Buckhannon | 7,261 | 6,3 |
| *25301 | Charleston | 71,505 | 85,7 |
| 26301 | Clarksburg | 24,864 | 28,1 |
| 25064 | Dunbar | 9,151 | 11,0 |
| 26241 | Elkins | 8,287 | 8,3 |
| 26554 | Fairmont | 26,093 | 27,4 |
| 26354 | Grafton | 6,433 | 5,7 |
| *25701 | Huntington | 74,315 | 83,6 |
| 26726 | Keyser | 6,586 | 6,1 |
| 25401 | Martinsburg | 14,626 | 15,1 |
| 26505 | Morgantown | 29,431 | 22,4 |
| 26041 | Moundsville | 13,560 | 15,1 |
| 26155 | New Martinsville | 6,528 | 5,6 |
| 25143 | Nitro | 8,019 | 6,8 |
| 26105 | Parkersburg | 44,208 | 44,7 |
| 25550 | Point Pleasant | 6,122 | 5,7 |
| 25177 | St. Albans | 14,356 | 15,1 |
| 25303 | South Charleston | 16,333 | 19,1 |
| 26101 | Vienna | 11,549 | 9,3 |
| 26062 | Weirton | 27,131 | 28,2 |
| 26452 | Weston | 7,323 | 8,7 |
| 26505 | Westover | 5,086 | 4,1 |
| 26003 | Wheeling | 48,188 | 53,4 |
| 25661 | Williamson | 5,831 | 6,7 |

## Wisconsin

| ZIP code | Place | | 1970 | 1 |
|---|---|---|---|---|
| 54301 | Allouez(u) 1976 | (414) | 15,159 | |
| 54409 | Antigo | (715) | 9,005 | 9,6 |
| 54911 | Appleton | (414) | 56,377 | 48,4 |
| 54806 | Ashland | (715) | 9,615 | 10,1 |
| 54304 | Ashwaubenor(u) | (414) | 9,323 | |
| 53913 | Baraboo | (608) | 7,931 | 7,6 |
| 53916 | Beaver Dam | (414) | 14,265 | 13,1 |
| 53511 | Beloit 1974 | (608) | 35,957 | 32,8 |
| 54923 | Berlin | (414) | 5,338 | 4,8 |
| 53005 | Brookfield 1974 | (414) | 33,371 | 19,8 |
| 53209 | Brown Deer | (414) | 12,582 | 11,2 |
| 53105 | Burlington | (414) | 7,479 | 5,8 |
| 53012 | Cedarburg | (414) | 7,697 | 5,2 |
| 54729 | Chippewa Falls | (715) | 12,351 | 11,7 |
| 53110 | Cudahy | (414) | 22,078 | 17,9 |
| 53115 | Delavan | (414) | 5,526 | 4,8 |
| 54115 | De Pere 1976 | (414) | 14,626 | 10,0 |
| 54701 | Eau Claire | (715) | 44,619 | 37,9 |
| 53122 | Elm Grove | (414) | 7,201 | 4,9 |
| 54935 | Fond Du Lac | (414) | 35,515 | 32,7 |
| 53538 | Fort Atkinson | (414) | 9,164 | 7,9 |
| 53217 | Fox Point | (414) | 7,939 | 7,3 |
| 53132 | Franklin | (414) | 12,247 | 10,0 |
| 53022 | Germantown 1974 | (414) | 8,219 | 62 |

| ZIP code | Place | | 1970 | 1960 |
|---|---|---|---|---|
| 53209 | Glendale | (414) | 13,426 | 9,537 |
| 53024 | Grafton 1973 | (414) | 7,169 | 3,748 |
| *54305 | Green Bay 1976 | (414) | 88,304 | 62,888 |
| 53220 | Greenfield | (414) | 24,424 | 17,636 |
| 53130 | Hales Corners | (414) | 7,771 | 5,549 |
| 53027 | Hartford | (414) | 6,499 | 5,627 |
| 54016 | Hudson 1973 | (715) | 5,322 | 4,325 |
| 53545 | Janesville | (608) | 46,426 | 35,164 |
| 53549 | Jefferson | (414) | 5,429 | 4,548 |
| 54130 | Kaukauna | (414) | 11,308 | 10,096 |
| 53140 | Kenosha | (414) | 78,805 | 67,899 |
| 54136 | Kimberly | (414) | 6,131 | 5,322 |
| 54601 | La Crosse 1976 | (608) | 48,864 | 47,575 |
| 54140 | Little Chute | (414) | 5,522 | 5,099 |
| *53701 | Madison 1974 | (608) | 168,671 | 126,706 |
| 53701 | Madison town 1975 | (608) | 5,995 | 4,925 |
| 54220 | Manitowoc | (414) | 33,430 | 32,275 |
| 54143 | Marinette 1976 | (715) | 12,157 | 13,329 |
| 54449 | Marshfield | (715) | 15,619 | 14,153 |
| 54952 | Menasha | (414) | 14,836 | 14,647 |
| 53051 | Menomonee Falls | (414) | 31,697 | 18,276 |
| 54751 | Menomonie | (715) | 11,275 | 8,624 |
| 53092 | Mequon | (414) | 12,150 | 8,543 |
| 54452 | Merrill | (715) | 9,502 | 9,451 |
| 53562 | Middleton | (608) | 8,286 | 4,410 |
| *53203 | Milwaukee 1975 | (414) | 669,022 | 741,324 |
| 53716 | Monona | (608) | 10,420 | 8,178 |
| 53566 | Monroe | (608) | 8,654 | 8,050 |
| 53150 | Muskego | (414) | 11,573 | ..... |
| 54956 | Neenah | (414) | 22,902 | 18,057 |
| 53151 | New Berlin | (414) | 26,910 | 15,788 |
| 54961 | New London | (414) | 5,801 | 5,288 |
| 53154 | Oak Creek 1976 | (414) | 15,510 | 9,372 |
| 53066 | Oconomowoc | (414) | 8,741 | 6,682 |
| 54901 | Oshkosh | (414) | 53,082 | 45,110 |
| 53511 | Perry Go Place(u) | (608) | 5,912 | 4,475 |
| 53818 | Platteville | (608) | 9,599 | 6,957 |
| 53073 | Plymouth | (414) | 5,810 | 5,128 |
| 53901 | Portage | (608) | 7,821 | 7,822 |
| 53074 | Port Washington | (414) | 8,752 | 5,984 |
| 53821 | Prairie Du Chien | (608) | 5,540 | 5,649 |
| *53401 | Racine | (414) | 95,162 | 89,144 |
| 54501 | Rhinelander | (715) | 8,218 | 8,790 |

| ZIP code | Place | | 1970 | 1960 |
|---|---|---|---|---|
| 54868 | Rice Lake | (715) | 7,278 | 7,303 |
| 53581 | Richland Center | (608) | 5,086 | 4,746 |
| 54971 | Ripon | (414) | 7,053 | 6,163 |
| 54022 | River Falls | (715) | 7,238 | 4,857 |
| 53207 | St. Francis 1974 | (414) | 9,951 | 10,065 |
| 54166 | Shawano | (715) | 6,488 | 6,103 |
| 53081 | Sheboygan | (414) | 48,484 | 45,747 |
| 53211 | Shorewood | (414) | 15,576 | 15,990 |
| 53172 | South Milwaukee | (414) | 23,297 | 20,307 |
| 54656 | Sparta | (608) | 6,258 | 6,080 |
| 54481 | Stevens Point | (715) | 23,479 | 17,837 |
| 53589 | Stoughton | (608) | 6,096 | 5,555 |
| 54235 | Sturgeon Bay 1976 | (414) | 7,764 | 7,353 |
| 53590 | Sun Prairie | (608) | 9,935 | 4,008 |
| 54880 | Superior | (715) | 32,237 | 33,563 |
| 54660 | Tomah | (608) | 5,647 | 5,321 |
| 54241 | Two Rivers 1974 | (414) | 13,243 | 12,393 |
| 53094 | Watertown | (414) | 15,683 | 13,943 |
| 53186 | Waukesha | (414) | 39,695 | 30,004 |
| 53963 | Waupun | (414) | 7,946 | 7,935 |
| 54401 | Wausau | (715) | 32,806 | 31,943 |
| 54401 | Wausau West(u) | (715) | 6,399 | 4,105 |
| 53213 | Wauwatosa | (414) | 58,676 | 56,923 |
| 53214 | West Allis | (414) | 71,649 | 68,157 |
| 53095 | West Bend | (414) | 16,555 | 9,969 |
| 53217 | Whitefish Bay | (414) | 17,402 | 18,390 |
| 53190 | Whitewater 1977 | (414) | 10,942 | 6,380 |
| 54494 | Wisconsin Rapids 1975 | (715) | 18,134 | 15,042 |

## Wyoming (307)

| ZIP code | Place | 1970 | 1960 |
|---|---|---|---|
| 82601 | Casper | 39,361 | 38,930 |
| 82001 | Cheyenne | 40,914 | 43,505 |
| 82414 | Cody | 5,161 | 4,838 |
| 81716 | Gillette | 7,194 | 3,580 |
| 82520 | Lander | 7,125 | 4,182 |
| 82070 | Laramie | 23,143 | 17,520 |
| 82301 | Rawlins | 7,855 | 8,968 |
| 82501 | Riverton | 7,995 | 6,845 |
| 82901 | Rock Springs | 11,657 | 10,371 |
| 82801 | Sheridan | 10,856 | 11,651 |
| 82401 | Worland | 5,055 | 5,806 |

# 1970 Census and Areas of Counties and States

Source: U.S. Bureau of the Census
With names of county seats or court houses

## Alabama

(67 counties, 50,708 sq. mi. land; pop., 3,444,165)

| County | Pop. Apr. 1 1970 | County seat or court house | Land area sq. mi. |
|---|---|---|---|
| Autauga | 24,460 | Prattville | 599 |
| Baldwin | 59,382 | Bay Minette | 1,578 |
| Barbour | 22,543 | Clayton | 891 |
| Bibb | 13,812 | Centreville | 625 |
| Blount | 26,853 | Oneonta | 639 |
| Bullock | 11,824 | Union Springs | 615 |
| Butler | 22,007 | Greenville | 773 |
| Calhoun | 103,092 | Anniston | 611 |
| Chambers | 36,356 | Lafayette | 597 |
| Cherokee | 15,606 | Centre | 556 |
| Chilton | 25,180 | Clanton | 699 |
| Choctaw | 16,589 | Butler | 911 |
| Clarke | 26,724 | Grove Hill | 1,232 |
| Clay | 12,636 | Ashland | 603 |
| Cleburne | 10,996 | Heflin | 574 |
| Coffee | 34,872 | Elba | 677 |
| Colbert | 49,632 | Tuscumbia | 596 |
| Conecuh | 15,645 | Evergreen | 850 |
| Coosa | 10,662 | Rockford | 650 |
| Covington | 34,079 | Andalusia | 984 |
| Crenshaw | 13,188 | Luverne | 611 |
| Cullman | 52,445 | Cullman | 730 |
| Dale | 52,938 | Ozark | 559 |
| Dallas | 55,296 | Selma | 976 |
| De Kalb | 41,981 | Fort Payne | 778 |
| Elmore | 33,661 | Wetumpka | 624 |
| Escambia | 34,912 | Brewton | 962 |
| Etowah | 94,144 | Gadsden | 555 |
| Fayette | 16,252 | Fayette | 627 |
| Franklin | 23,933 | Russellville | 644 |
| Geneva | 21,924 | Geneva | 577 |
| Greene | 10,650 | Eutaw | 627 |
| Hale | 15,888 | Greensboro | 662 |
| Henry | 13,254 | Abbeville | 554 |
| Houston | 56,574 | Dothan | 575 |
| Jackson | 39,202 | Scottsboro | 1,079 |
| Jefferson | 644,991 | Birmingham | 1,115 |
| Lamar | 14,335 | Vernon | 605 |
| Lauderdale | 68,111 | Florence | 662 |
| Lawrence | 27,281 | Moulton | 685 |
| Lee | 61,268 | Opelika | 612 |
| Limestone | 41,699 | Athens | 546 |
| Lowndes | 12,897 | Hayneville | 715 |
| Macon | 24,841 | Tuskegee | 616 |
| Madison | 186,540 | Huntsville | 803 |
| Marengo | 23,819 | Linden | 978 |
| Marion | 23,788 | Hamilton | 743 |
| Marshall | 54,211 | Guntersville | 571 |
| Mobile | 317,308 | Mobile | 1,240 |
| Monroe | 20,883 | Monroeville | 1,032 |
| Montgomery | 167,790 | Montgomery | 790 |
| Morgan | 77,306 | Decatur | 570 |
| Perry | 15,388 | Marion | 734 |
| Pickens | 20,326 | Carrollton | 887 |
| Pike | 25,038 | Troy | 673 |
| Randolph | 18,331 | Wedowee | 581 |
| Russell | 45,394 | Phenix City | 627 |
| St. Clair | 27,956 | Ashville & Pell City | 640 |
| Shelby | 38,037 | Columbiana | 798 |
| Sumter | 16,974 | Livingston | 915 |
| Talladega | 65,280 | Talladega | 750 |
| Tallapoosa | 33,840 | Dadeville | 704 |
| Tuscaloosa | 116,029 | Tuscaloosa | 1,333 |
| Walker | 56,246 | Jasper | 805 |
| Washington | 16,241 | Chatom | 1,066 |
| Wilcox | 16,303 | Camden | 899 |
| Winston | 16,654 | Double Springs | 615 |

## Alaska

(29 divisions, 566,432 sq. mi. land; pop., 302,173)

| Census division | Pop. Apr. 1, 1970 | Land area sq. mi. |
|---|---|---|
| Aleutian Islands | 8,057 | 14,583 |
| Anchorage | 126,385 | 927 |
| Angoon | 503 | 2,825 |
| Barrow | 2,663 | 57,587 |

| Census division | Pop. Apr. 1 1970 | Land area sq. mi. |
|---|---|---|
| Bethel | 7,767 | 19,642 |
| Bristol Bay Borough | 1,147 | 531 |
| Bristol Bay | 3,485 | 36,565 |
| Cordova-McCarthy | 1,857 | 15,481 |
| Fairbanks | 45,864 | 7,074 |
| Haines | 1,504 | 2,128 |
| Juneau | 13,556 | 1,286 |
| Kenai-Cook Inlet | 14,250 | 12,474 |
| Ketchikan | 10,041 | 1,345 |
| Kobuk | 4,434 | 42,978 |
| Kodiak | 9,409 | 5,375 |
| Kuskokwim | 2,306 | 56,562 |
| Matanuska-Susitna | 6,509 | 25,730 |
| Nome | 5,749 | 24,968 |
| Outer Ketchikan | 1,676 | 3,762 |
| Prince of Wales | 2,106 | 3,485 |
| Seward | 2,336 | 3,727 |
| Sitka | 6,106 | 2,296 |
| Skagway-Yakutat | 2,157 | 8,646 |
| Southeast Fairbanks | 4,179 | 17,713 |
| Upper Yukon | 1,684 | 84,142 |
| Valdez-Chitina-Whittier | 3,098 | 18,619 |
| Wade Hampton | 3,917 | 16,770 |
| Wrangell-Petersburg | 4,913 | 6,178 |
| Yukon-Koyukuk | 4,758 | 73,053 |

## Arizona

*(14 counties, 113,417 sq. mi. land; pop. 1,772,482)*

| County | Pop. Apr. 1 1970 | County seat or court house | Land area sq. mi. |
|---|---|---|---|
| Apache | 32,304 | Saint Johns | 11,171 |
| Cochise | 61,918 | Bisbee | 6,256 |
| Coconino | 48,326 | Flagstaff | 18,540 |
| Gila | 29,255 | Globe | 4,748 |
| Graham | 16,578 | Safford | 4,618 |
| Greenlee | 10,330 | Clifton | 1,879 |
| Maricopa | 968,487 | Phoenix | 9,155 |
| Mohave 1974. | 35,714 | Kingman | 13,217 |
| Navajo | 47,559 | Holbrook | 9,910 |
| Pima 1975 | 449,544 | Tucson | 9,240 |
| Pinal | 68,579 | Florence | 5,364 |
| Santa Cruz | 13,966 | Nogales | 1,246 |
| Yavapai | 37,005 | Prescott | 8,091 |
| Yuma | 60,827 | Yuma | 9,983 |

## Arkansas

*(75 counties, 51,945 sq. mi. land; pop. 1,923,295)*

| County | Pop. Apr. 1 1970 | County seat or court house | Land area sq. mi. |
|---|---|---|---|
| Arkansas | 23,347 | DeWitt & Stuttgart | 1,015 |
| Ashley | 24,976 | Hamburg | 928 |
| Baxter | 15,319 | Mountain Home | 551 |
| Benton | 50,476 | Bentonville | 851 |
| Boone | 19,073 | Harrison | 586 |
| Bradley | 12,778 | Warren | 651 |
| Calhoun | 5,573 | Hampton | 629 |
| Carroll | 12,301 | Berryville and Eureka Spring | 626 |
| Chicot | 18,164 | Lake Village | 643 |
| Clark | 21,537 | Arkadelphia | 878 |
| Clay | 18,771 | Corning; Piggott | 639 |
| Cleburne | 10,349 | Heber Springs | 554 |
| Cleveland | 6,605 | Rison | 601 |
| Columbia | 25,952 | Magnolia | 768 |
| Conway | 16,805 | Morrilton | 561 |
| Craighead | 52,068 | Jonesboro and Lake City | 716 |
| Crawford | 25,677 | Van Buren | 596 |
| Crittenden | 48,106 | Marion | 608 |
| Cross | 19,783 | Wynne | 625 |
| Dallas | 10,022 | Fordyce | 672 |
| Desha | 18,761 | Arkansas City | 736 |
| Drew | 15,157 | Monticello | 832 |
| Faulkner | 31,578 | Conway | 641 |
| Franklin | 11,301 | Charleston and Ozark | 613 |
| Fulton | 7,699 | Salem | 608 |
| Garland | 54,131 | Hot Spgs. Nat'l Pk. | 658 |
| Grant | 9,711 | Sheridan | 631 |
| Greene | 24,765 | Paragould | 579 |
| Hempstead | 19,308 | Hope | 726 |
| Hot Spring | 21,963 | Malvern | 621 |
| Howard | 11,412 | Nashville | 569 |
| Independence | 22,723 | Batesville | 752 |
| Izard | 7,381 | Melbourne | 574 |
| Jackson | 20,452 | Newport | 629 |
| Jefferson | 85,329 | Pine Bluff | 873 |
| Johnson | 13,630 | Clarksville | 673 |
| Lafayette | 10,018 | Lewisville | 523 |
| Lawrence | 16,320 | Walnut Ridge | 590 |

| County | Pop. Apr. 1 1970 | County seat or court house | Land area sq. mi. |
|---|---|---|---|
| Lee | 18,884 | Marianna | 608 |
| Lincoln | 12,913 | Star City | 563 |
| Little River | 11,194 | Ashdown | 486 |
| Logan | 16,789 | Booneville & Paris | 718 |
| Lonoke | 26,249 | Lonoke | 796 |
| Madison | 9,453 | Huntsville | 832 |
| Marion | 7,000 | Yellville | 584 |
| Miller | 33,385 | Texarkana | 623 |
| Mississippi | 62,060 | Blytheville and Osceola | 904 |
| Monroe | 15,657 | Clarendon | 607 |
| Montgomery | 5,821 | Mount Ida | 775 |
| Nevada | 10,111 | Prescott | 616 |
| Newton | 5,844 | Jasper | 822 |
| Ouachita | 30,896 | Camden | 736 |
| Perry | 5,634 | Perryville | 551 |
| Phillips | 40,046 | Helena | 686 |
| Pike | 8,711 | Murfreesboro | 600 |
| Poinsett | 26,843 | Harrisburg | 760 |
| Polk | 13,297 | Mena | 859 |
| Pope | 28,607 | Russellville | 812 |
| Prairie | 10,249 | Des Arc and De Valls Bluff | 661 |
| Pulaski | 287,189 | Little Rock | 765 |
| Randolph | 12,645 | Pocahontas | 647 |
| St. Francis | 30,799 | Forest City | 635 |
| Saline | 36,107 | Benton | 724 |
| Scott | 8,207 | Waldron | 898 |
| Searcy | 7,731 | Marshall | 664 |
| Sebastian | 79,237 | Fort Smith; Greenwood | 527 |
| Sevier | 11,272 | De Queen | 522 |
| Sharp | 8,233 | Ash Flat | 581 |
| Stone | 6,838 | Mountain View | 608 |
| Union | 45,428 | El Dorado | 1,050 |
| Van Buren | 8,275 | Clinton | 699 |
| Washington | 77,370 | Fayetteville | 958 |
| White | 39,253 | Searcy | 1,041 |
| Woodruff | 11,566 | Augusta | 591 |
| Yell | 14,208 | Danville and Dardanelle | 929 |

## California

*(58 counties, 156,361 sq. mi. land; pop. 19,953,134)*

| County | Pop. Apr. 1 1970 | County seat or court house | Land area sq. mi. |
|---|---|---|---|
| Alameda | 1,073,184 | Oakland | 733 |
| Alpine | 484 | Markleeville | 727 |
| Amador | 11,821 | Jackson | 583 |
| Butte | 101,969 | Oroville | 1,645 |
| Calaveras | 13,585 | San Andreas | 1,024 |
| Colusa | 12,430 | Colusa | 1,152 |
| Contra Costa | 555,805 | Martinez | 735 |
| Del Norte | 14,580 | Crescent City | 1,007 |
| El Dorado | 43,833 | Placerville | 1,715 |
| Fresno | 413,329 | Fresno | 5,966 |
| Glenn | 17,521 | Willows | 1,314 |
| Humboldt | 99,692 | Eureka | 3,586 |
| Imperial | 74,492 | El Centro | 4,241 |
| Inyo | 15,571 | Independence | 10,130 |
| Kern | 329,281 | Bakersfield | 8,152 |
| Kings | 66,717 | Hanford | 1,396 |
| Lake | 19,548 | Lakeport | 1,261 |
| Lassen | 16,796 | Susanville | 4,561 |
| Los Angeles | 7,040,697 | Los Angeles | 4,069 |
| Madera | 41,519 | Madera | 2,145 |
| Marin | 206,758 | San Rafael | 520 |
| Mariposa | 6,015 | Mariposa | 1,453 |
| Mendocino | 51,101 | Ukiah | 3,511 |
| Merced | 104,629 | Merced | 1,958 |
| Modoc | 7,469 | Alturas | 4,097 |
| Mono | 4,016 | Bridgeport | 3,027 |
| Monterey | 247,450 | Salinas | 3,324 |
| Napa | 79,140 | Napa | 787 |
| Nevada | 26,346 | Nevada City | 973 |
| Orange | 1,420,676 | Santa Ana | 782 |
| Placer | 77,632 | Auburn | 1,431 |
| Plumas | 11,707 | Quincy | 2,566 |
| Riverside | 459,074 | Riverside | 7,176 |
| Sacramento | 634,190 | Sacramento | 975 |
| San Benito | 18,226 | Hollister | 1,396 |
| San Bernardino 1975 | 696,064 | San Bernardino | 20,117 |
| San Diego | 1,357,854 | San Diego | 4,261 |
| San Francisco | 715,674 | San Francisco | 45 |
| San Joaquin 1975 | 299,831 | Stockton | 1,412 |
| San Luis Obispo | 105,690 | San Luis Obispo | 3,183 |
| San Mateo | 556,605 | Redwood City | 447 |
| Santa Barbara | 264,324 | Santa Barbara | 2,737 |
| Santa Clara | 1,066,174 | San Jose | 1,300 |
| Santa Cruz | 123,790 | Santa Cruz | 440 |
| Shasta | 77,640 | Redding | 3,788 |
| Sierra | 2,365 | Downieville | 958 |
| Siskiyou | 33,225 | Yreka | 6,262 |
| Solano | 171,989 | Fairfield | 823 |
| Sonoma | 204,885 | Santa Rosa | 1,604 |
| Stanislaus | 194,506 | Modesto | 1,511 |

| County | Pop. Apr. 1 1970 | County seat or court house | Land area sq. mi. |
|---|---|---|---|
| Sutter | 41,935 | Yuba City | 603 |
| Tehama | 29,517 | Red Bluff | 2,982 |
| Trinity | 7,615 | Weaverville | 3,173 |
| Tulare | 188,322 | Visalia | 4,812 |
| Tuolumne | 22,169 | Sonora | 2,252 |
| Ventura | 378,497 | Ventura | 1,863 |
| Yolo | 91,788 | Woodland | 1,028 |
| Yuba | 44,736 | Marysville | 639 |

## Colorado

*(63 counties, 103,766 sq. mi. land; pop. 2,207,259)*

| County | Pop. Apr. 1 1970 | County seat or court house | Land area sq. mi. |
|---|---|---|---|
| Adams | 185,789 | Brighton | 1,237 |
| Alamosa | 11,422 | Alamosa | 719 |
| Arapahoe | 162,142 | Littleton | 797 |
| Archuleta 1977 | 3,594 | Pagosa Springs | 1,364 |
| Baca | 5,674 | Springfield | 2,563 |
| Bent | 6,493 | Las Animas | 1,519 |
| Boulder | 131,889 | Boulder | 748 |
| Chaffee | 10,162 | Salida | 1,038 |
| Cheyenne | 2,396 | Cheyenne Wells | 1,772 |
| Clear Creek | 4,819 | Georgetown | 394 |
| Conejos | 7,846 | Conejos | 1,268 |
| Costilla | 3,091 | San Luis | 1,213 |
| Crowley | 3,086 | Ordway | 802 |
| Custer | 1,120 | Westcliffe | 737 |
| Delta 1977 | 18,949 | Delta | 1,154 |
| Denver | 514,678 | Denver | 95 |
| Dolores | 1,641 | Dove Creek | 1,026 |
| Douglas | 8,407 | Castle Rock | 843 |
| Eagle | 7,498 | Eagle | 1,681 |
| Elbert | 3,903 | Kiowa | 1,864 |
| El Paso | 235,972 | Colorado Springs | 2,157 |
| Fremont | 21,942 | Canon City | 1,561 |
| Garfield 1977 | 18,800 | Glenwood Springs | 2,996 |
| Gilpin | 1,272 | Central City | 148 |
| Grand | 4,107 | Hot Sulphur Springs | 1,854 |
| Gunnison | 7,578 | Gunnison | 3,220 |
| Hinsdale | 202 | Lake City | 1,054 |
| Huerfano | 6,590 | Walsenburg | 1,574 |
| Jackson | 1,811 | Walden | 1,622 |
| Jefferson | 235,300 | Golden | 783 |
| Kiowa | 2,029 | Eads | 1,767 |
| Kit Carson | 7,530 | Burlington | 2,171 |
| Lake | 8,282 | Leadville | 379 |
| La Plata | 19,199 | Durango | 1,683 |
| Larimer | 89,900 | Fort Collins | 2,611 |
| Las Animas | 15,744 | Trinidad | 4,794 |
| Lincoln | 4,836 | Hugo | 2,593 |
| Logan | 18,852 | Sterling | 1,822 |
| Mesa 1977 | 66,848 | Grand Junction | 3,301 |
| Mineral | 786 | Creede | 921 |
| Moffat 1977 | 10,303 | Craig | 4,743 |
| Montezuma | 12,952 | Cortez | 2,094 |
| Montrose | 18,366 | Montrose | 2,238 |
| Morgan | 20,105 | Fort Morgan | 1,278 |
| Otero | 23,523 | LaJunta | 1,254 |
| Ouray | 1,546 | Ouray | 540 |
| Park | 2,185 | Fairplay | 2,162 |
| Phillips | 4,131 | Holyoke | 680 |
| Pitkin | 6,185 | Aspen | 973 |
| Prowers | 13,258 | Lamar | 1,621 |
| Pueblo | 118,238 | Pueblo | 2,405 |
| Rio Blanco 1977 | 5,100 | Meeker | 3,263 |
| Rio Grande | 10,494 | Del Norte | 915 |
| Routt 1977 | 10,516 | Steamboat Springs | 2,330 |
| Saguache | 3,827 | Saguache | 3,144 |
| San Juan | 831 | Silverton | 391 |
| San Miguel | 1,949 | Telluride | 1,283 |
| Sedgwick | 3,405 | Julesburg | 544 |
| Summit | 2,665 | Breckenridge | 604 |
| Teller | 3,316 | Cripple Creek | 553 |
| Washington | 5,550 | Akron | 2,526 |
| Weld | 89,297 | Greeley | 4,002 |
| Yuma | 8,544 | Wray | 2,379 |

## Connecticut

*(8 counties, 4,862 sq. mi. land; opo. 3,032,217)*

| County | Pop. Apr. 1 1970 | County seat or court house | Land area sq. mi. |
|---|---|---|---|
| Fairfield | 792,814 | Bridgeport | 626 |
| Hartford | 816,737 | Hartford | 739 |
| Litchfield | 144,091 | Litchfield | 925 |
| Middlesex | 115,018 | Middletown | 372 |
| New Haven | 744,948 | New Haven | 604 |
| New London | 230,654 | Norwich | 667 |
| Tolland | 103,440 | Rockville | 416 |
| Windham | 84,515 | Putnam | 514 |

## Delaware

*(3 counties, 1,982 sq. mi. land; pop. 548,104)*

| County | Pop. Apr. 1 1970 | County seat or court house | Land area sq. mi. |
|---|---|---|---|
| Kent | 81,892 | Dover | 594 |
| New Castle | 385,856 | Wilmington | 438 |
| Sussex | 80,356 | Georgetown | 950 |

## District of Columbia

*(61 sq. mi. land; pop. 756,510)*

## Florida

*(67 counties, 54,090 sq. mi. land; pop. 6,789,443)*

| County | Pop. Apr. 1 1970 | County seat or court house | Land area sq. mi. |
|---|---|---|---|
| Alachua | 104,764 | Gainesville | 916 |
| Baker | 9,242 | Macclenny | 585 |
| Bay | 75,283 | Panama City | 747 |
| Bradford | 14,625 | Starke | 294 |
| Brevard | 230,006 | Titusville | 1,011 |
| Broward | 620,100 | Fort Lauderdale | 1,219 |
| Calhoun | 7,624 | Blountstown | 561 |
| Charlotte | 27,559 | Punta Gorda | 703 |
| Citrus | 19,196 | Inverness | 560 |
| Clay | 32,059 | Green Cove Spgs. | 593 |
| Collier | 38,040 | Naples | 2,006 |
| Columbia | 25,250 | Lake City | 784 |
| Dade | 1,267,792 | Miami | 2,042 |
| De Soto | 13,060 | Arcadia | 648 |
| Dixie | 5,480 | Cross City | 692 |
| Duval | 528,865 | Jacksonville | 766 |
| Escambia | 205,334 | Pensacola | 665 |
| Flagler | 4,454 | Bunnell | 487 |
| Franklin | 7,065 | Apalachicola | 536 |
| Gadsden | 39,184 | Quincy | 512 |
| Gilchrist | 3,551 | Trenton | 346 |
| Glades | 3,669 | Moore Haven | 753 |
| Gulf | 10,096 | Port St. Joe | 565 |
| Hamilton | 7,787 | Jasper | 514 |
| Hardee | 14,889 | Wauchula | 629 |
| Hendry | 11,859 | La Belle | 1,187 |
| Hernando | 17,004 | Brooksville | 484 |
| Highlands | 29,507 | Sebring | 997 |
| Hillsborough | 490,265 | Tampa | 1,038 |
| Holmes | 10,720 | Bonifay | 482 |
| Indian River | 35,992 | Vero Beach | 506 |
| Jackson | 34,434 | Marianna | 935 |
| Jefferson | 8,778 | Monticello | 605 |
| Lafayette | 2,892 | Mayo | 549 |
| Lake | 69,305 | Tavares | 961 |
| Lee | 105,216 | Fort Myers | 785 |
| Leon | 103,047 | Tallahassee | 670 |
| Levy | 12,756 | Bronson | 1,083 |
| Liberty | 3,379 | Bristol | 839 |
| Madison | 13,481 | Madison | 703 |
| Manatee | 97,115 | Bradenton | 739 |
| Marion | 69,030 | Ocala | 1,600 |
| Martin | 28,035 | Stuart | 556 |
| Monroe | 52,586 | Key West | 1,034 |
| Nassau | 20,626 | Fernandina Beach | 650 |
| Okaloosa | 88,187 | Crestview | 944 |
| Okeechobee | 11,233 | Okeechobee | 777 |
| Orange | 344,311 | Orlando | 910 |
| Osceola | 25,267 | Kissimmee | 1,313 |
| Palm Beach | 348,993 | West Palm Beach | 2,023 |
| Pasco 1973 | 108,865 | Dade City | 742 |
| Pinellas | 522,329 | Clearwater | 265 |
| Polk | 228,026 | Bartow | 1,858 |
| Putnam | 36,424 | Palatka | 779 |
| St. Johns | 31,035 | Saint Augustine | 605 |
| St. Lucie | 50,836 | Fort Pierce | 584 |
| Santa Rosa | 37,741 | Milton | 1,032 |
| Sarasota | 120,413 | Sarasota | 587 |
| Seminole | 83,692 | Sanford | 305 |
| Sumter | 14,839 | Bushnell | 555 |
| Suwannee | 15,559 | Live Oak | 686 |
| Taylor | 13,641 | Perry | 1,051 |
| Union | 8,112 | Lake Butler | 241 |
| Volusia | 169,487 | De Land | 1,062 |
| Wakulla 1974 | 8,546 | Crawfordville | 601 |
| Walton | 16,087 | De Funiak Springs | 1,053 |
| Washington | 11,453 | Chipley | 585 |

## Georgia

*(159 counties, 58,073 sq. mi. land; pop. 4,589,575)*

| County | Pop. Apr. 1 1970 | County seat or court house | Land area sq. mi. |
|---|---|---|---|
| Appling | 12,726 | Baxley | 513 |
| Atkinson | 5,879 | Pearson | 318 |
| Bacon | 8,233 | Alma | 293 |
| Baker | 3,875 | Newton | 355 |
| Baldwin | 34,240 | Milledgeville | 255 |
| Banks | 6,833 | Homer | 231 |
| Barrow | 16,859 | Winder | 171 |
| Bartow | 32,911 | Cartersville | 461 |
| Ben Hill | 13,171 | Fitzgerald | 255 |
| Berrien | 11,556 | Nashville | 468 |

| County | Pop. Apr. 1 1970 | County seat or court house | Land area sq. mi. | County | Pop. Apr. 1 1970 | County seat or court house | Land area sq. mi. |
|---|---|---|---|---|---|---|---|
| Bibb | 143,418 | Macon | 254 | Oconee | 7,915 | Watkinsville | 186 |
| Bleckley | 10,291 | Cochran | 219 | Oglethorpe | 7,598 | Lexington | 435 |
| Brantley | 5,940 | Nahunta | 447 | Paulding | 17,520 | Dallas | 318 |
| Brooks | 13,743 | Quitman | 491 | Peach | 15,990 | Fort Valley | 151 |
| Bryan | 6,539 | Pembroke | 443 | Pickens | 9,620 | Jasper | 225 |
| Bulloch | 31,585 | Statesboro | 685 | Pierce | 9,281 | Blackshear | 342 |
| Burke | 18,255 | Waynesboro | 831 | Pike | 7,316 | Zebulon | 230 |
| Butts | 10,560 | Jackson | 185 | Polk | 29,656 | Cedartown | 312 |
| Calhoun | 6,606 | Morgan | 289 | Pulaski | 8,066 | Hawkinsville | 253 |
| Camden | 11,334 | Woodbine | 653 | Putnam | 9,394 | Eatonton | 339 |
| Candler | 6,412 | Metter | 250 | Quitman | 2,180 | Georgetown | 156 |
| Carroll | 45,404 | Carrollton | 495 | Rabun | 8,327 | Clayton | 368 |
| Catoosa | 28,271 | Ringgold | 167 | Randolph | 8,734 | Cuthbert | 436 |
| Charlton | 5,680 | Folkston | 796 | Richmond | 162,437 | Augusta | 323 |
| Chatham | 187,816 | Savannah | 445 | Rockdale | 18,152 | Conyers | 128 |
| Chattahoochee | 25,813 | Cusseta | 253 | Schley | 3,097 | Ellaville | 162 |
| Chattooga | 20,541 | Summerville | 317 | Screven | 12,591 | Sylvania | 651 |
| Cherokee | 31,059 | Canton | 415 | Seminole | 7,059 | Donalsonville | 246 |
| Clarke | 65,177 | Athens | 116 | Spalding | 39,514 | Griffin | 201 |
| Clay | 3,636 | Fort Gaines | 200 | Stephens | 20,331 | Toccoa | 173 |
| Clayton | 98,126 | Jonesboro | 149 | Stewart | 6,511 | Lumpkin | 452 |
| Clinch | 6,405 | Homerville | 797 | Sumter | 26,931 | Americus | 488 |
| Cobb | 196,793 | Marietta | 343 | Talbot | 6,625 | Talbotton | 390 |
| Coffee | 22,828 | Douglas | 612 | Taliaferro | 2,423 | Crawfordville | 195 |
| Colquitt | 32,298 | Moultrie | 563 | Tattnall | 16,557 | Reidsville | 490 |
| Columbia | 22,327 | Appling | 290 | Taylor | 7,865 | Butler | 403 |
| Cook | 12,129 | Adel | 233 | Telfair | 11,394 | McRae | 440 |
| Coweta | 32,310 | Newnan | 442 | Terrell | 11,416 | Dawson | 329 |
| Crawford | 5,748 | Knoxville | 315 | Thomas | 34,562 | Thomasville | 541 |
| Crisp | 18,087 | Cordele | 292 | Tift | 27,288 | Tifton | 266 |
| Dade | 9,910 | Trenton | 168 | Toombs | 19,151 | Lyons | 368 |
| Dawson | 3,639 | Dawsonville | 211 | Towns | 4,565 | Hiawassee | 166 |
| Decatur | 22,310 | Bainbridge | 575 | Treutlen | 5,647 | Soperton | 194 |
| De Kalb | 415,387 | Decatur | 269 | Troup | 44,466 | La Grange | 415 |
| Dodge | 15,658 | Eastman | 498 | Turner | 8,790 | Ashburn | 293 |
| Dooly | 10,404 | Vienna | 395 | Twiggs | 8,222 | Jeffersonville | 364 |
| Dougherty | 89,639 | Albany | 324 | Union | 6,811 | Blairsville | 309 |
| Douglas | 28,659 | Douglasville | 202 | Upson | 23,505 | Thomaston | 334 |
| Early | 12,682 | Blakely | 524 | Walker | 50,691 | La Fayette | 445 |
| Echols | 1,924 | Statenville | 425 | Walton | 23,404 | Monroe | 330 |
| Effingham | 13,632 | Springfield | 480 | Ware | 33,525 | Waycross | 912 |
| Elbert | 17,262 | Elberton | 358 | Warren | 6,669 | Warrenton | 284 |
| Emanuel | 18,357 | Swainsboro | 686 | Washington | 17,480 | Sandersville | 674 |
| Evans | 7,290 | Claxton | 186 | Wayne | 17,858 | Jesup | 645 |
| Fannin | 13,357 | Blue Ridge | 394 | Webster | 2,362 | Preston | 195 |
| Fayette | 11,364 | Fayetteville | 199 | Wheeler | 4,596 | Alamo | 306 |
| Floyd | 73,742 | Rome | 514 | White | 7,742 | Cleveland | 243 |
| Forsyth | 16,928 | Cumming | 219 | Whitfield | 55,108 | Dalton | 281 |
| Franklin | 12,784 | Carnesville | 263 | Wilcox | 6,998 | Abbeville | 383 |
| Fulton | 607,592 | Atlanta | 530 | Wilkes | 18,184 | Washington | 468 |
| Gilmer | 8,956 | Ellijay | 439 | Wilkinson | 9,393 | Irwinton | 458 |
| Glascock | 2,280 | Gibson | 143 | Worth | 14,770 | Sylvester | 579 |
| Glynn | 50,528 | Brunswick | 412 | | | | |
| Gordon | 23,570 | Calhoun | 358 | | | | |
| Grady | 17,826 | Cairo | 466 | | | | |
| Greene | 10,212 | Greensboro | 403 | | | | |
| Gwinnett | 72,349 | Lawrenceville | 437 | | | | |
| Habersham | 20,691 | Clarkesville | 282 | | | | |
| Hall | 59,405 | Gainesville | 378 | | | | |
| Hancock | 9,019 | Sparta | 478 | | | | |
| Haralson | 15,927 | Buchanan | 285 | | | | |
| Harris | 11,520 | Hamilton | 465 | | | | |

## Hawaii

(4 counties, 6,425 sq. mi. land; pop. 769,913)

| County | Pop. Apr. 1 1970 | County seat or court house | Land area sq. mi. |
|---|---|---|---|
| Hawaii | 63,468 | Hilo | 4,037 |
| Honolulu | 630,528 | Honolulu | 596 |
| Kauai | 29,761 | Lihue | 619 |
| Maui* | 46,156 | Wailuku | 1,173 |

*Includes population of Kalawao County (279) shown separately in 1960 but included with Maui County in 1970.

## Idaho

(44 counties, 82,677 sq. mi. land; pop. 713,008)

| County | Pop. Apr. 1 1970 | County seat or court house | Land area sq. mi. |
|---|---|---|---|
| Hart | 15,814 | Hartwell | 231 | Ada | 112,230 | Boise | 1,043 |
| Heard | 5,354 | Franklin | 297 | Adams | 2,877 | Council | 1,371 |
| Henry | 23,724 | McDonough | 331 | Bannock | 52,200 | Pocatello | 1,122 |
| Houston | 62,924 | Perry | 380 | Bear Lake | 5,801 | Paris | 984 |
| Irwin | 8,036 | Ocilla | 372 | Benewah | 6,230 | Saint Maries | 788 |
| Jackson | 21,093 | Jefferson | 346 | Bingham | 29,167 | Blackfoot | 2,084 |
| Jasper | 5,760 | Monticello | 373 | Blaine 1977 | 8,748 | Hailey | 2,647 |
| Jeff Davis | 9,425 | Hazlehurst | 331 | Boise | 1,763 | Idaho City | 1,910 |
| Jefferson | 17,174 | Louisville | 530 | Bonner | 15,560 | Sandpoint | 1,733 |
| Jenkins | 8,332 | Millen | 351 | Bonneville 1975 | 58,499 | Idaho Falls | 1,836 |
| Johnson | 7,727 | Wrightsville | 313 | Boundary | 5,484 | Bonners Ferry | 1,275 |
| Jones | 12,218 | Gray | 402 | Butte | 2,925 | Arco | 2,239 |
| Lamar | 10,688 | Barnesville | 181 | Camas | 728 | Fairfield | 1,054 |
| Lanier | 5,031 | Lakeland | 177 | Canyon | 61,288 | Caldwell | 578 |
| Laurens | 32,738 | Dublin | 810 | Caribou | 6,534 | Soda Springs | 1,746 |
| Lee | 7,044 | Leesburg | 355 | Cassia | 17,017 | Burley | 2,544 |
| Liberty | 17,569 | Hinesville | 514 | Clark | 741 | Dubois | 1,751 |
| Lincoln | 5,895 | Lincolnton | 193 | Clearwater | 10,871 | Orofino | 2,521 |
| Long | 3,746 | Ludowici | 402 | Custer | 2,967 | Challis | 4,929 |
| Lowndes | 55,112 | Valdosta | 508 | Elmore | 17,479 | Mountain Home | 3,048 |
| Lumpkin | 8,728 | Dahlonega | 292 | Franklin | 7,373 | Preston | 664 |
| McDuffie | 15,276 | Thomson | 253 | Fremont | 8,710 | Saint Anthony | 1,864 |
| McIntosh | 7,371 | Darien | 426 | Gem | 9,387 | Emmett | 555 |
| Macon | 12,933 | Oglethorpe | 403 | Gooding | 8,645 | Gooding | 720 |
| Madison | 13,517 | Danielsville | 281 | Idaho | 12,891 | Grangeville | 8,516 |
| Marion | 5,099 | Buena Vista | 365 | Jefferson | 11,740 | Rigby | 1,096 |
| Meriwether | 19,461 | Greenville | 499 | Jerome | 10,253 | Jerome | 595 |
| Miller | 6,424 | Colquitt | 287 | | | | |
| Mitchell | 18,956 | Camilla | 510 | | | | |
| Monroe | 10,991 | Forsyth | 398 | | | | |
| Montgomery | 6,099 | Mount Vernon | 237 | | | | |
| Morgan | 9,904 | Madison | 356 | | | | |
| Murray | 12,986 | Chatsworth | 342 | | | | |
| Muscogee | 167,377 | Columbus | 220 | | | | |
| Newton | 26,282 | Covington | 271 | | | | |

| County | Pop. Apr. 1 1970 | County seat or court house | Land area sq. mi. |
|---|---|---|---|
| Kootenai | 35,332 | Coeur d'Alene | 1,249 |
| Latah | 24,898 | Moscow | 1,090 |
| Lemhi | 5,566 | Salmon | 4,580 |
| Lewis | 3,867 | Nezperce | 476 |
| Lincoln | 3,057 | Shoshone | 1,203 |
| Madison | 13,452 | Rexberg | 473 |
| Minidoka | 15,731 | Rupert | 750 |
| Nez Perce | 30,376 | Lewiston | 844 |
| Oneida | 2,864 | Malad City | 1,191 |
| Owyhee | 6,422 | Murphy | 7,641 |
| Payette 1975 | 14,390 | Payette | 402 |
| Power | 4,864 | American Falls | 1,413 |
| Shoshone 1976 | 18,938 | Wallace | 2,609 |
| Teton | 2,351 | Driggs | 457 |
| Twin Falls | 41,807 | Twin Falls | 1,947 |
| Valley | 3,609 | Cascade | 3,676 |
| Washington 1976 | 8,485 | Weiser | 1,462 |

## Illinois

*(102 counties, 55,748 sq. mi. land; pop. 11,113,976)*

| County | Pop. Apr. 1 1970 | County seat or court house | Land area sq. mi. |
|---|---|---|---|
| Adams | 70,861 | Quincy | 862 |
| Alexander | 12,015 | Cairo | 229 |
| Bond | 14,012 | Greenville | 378 |
| Boone | 25,440 | Belvidere | 283 |
| Brown | 5,586 | Mount Sterling | 306 |
| Bureau | 38,541 | Princeton | 866 |
| Calhoun | 5,675 | Hardin | 247 |
| Carroll | 19,276 | Mount Carroll | 456 |
| Cass | 14,219 | Virginia | 371 |
| Champaign | 163,281 | Urbana | 1,000 |
| Christian | 35,948 | Taylorville | 709 |
| Clark | 16,216 | Marshall | 505 |
| Clay | 14,735 | Louisville | 464 |
| Clinton | 28,315 | Carlyle | 434 |
| Coles | 47,815 | Charleston | 506 |
| Cook | 5,493,766 | Chicago | 954 |
| Crawford | 19,824 | Robinson | 443 |
| Cumberland | 9,772 | Toledo | 347 |
| De Kalb | 71,654 | Sycamore | 636 |
| De Witt | 16,975 | Clinton | 399 |
| Douglas | 18,997 | Tuscola | 420 |
| Du Page | 490,822 | Wheaton | 331 |
| Edgar | 21,591 | Paris | 628 |
| Edwards | 7,090 | Albion | 225 |
| Effingham | 24,608 | Effingham | 481 |
| Fayette | 20,752 | Vandalia | 703 |
| Ford | 16,382 | Paxton | 488 |
| Franklin | 38,329 | Benton | 434 |
| Fulton | 41,900 | Lewistown | 877 |
| Gallatin | 7,418 | Shawneetown | 328 |
| Greene | 17,014 | Carrollton | 543 |
| Grundy | 26,535 | Morris | 432 |
| Hamilton | 8,665 | McLeansboro | 435 |
| Hancock | 23,664 | Carthage | 797 |
| Hardin | 4,914 | Elizabethtown | 183 |
| Henderson | 8,451 | Oquawka | 376 |
| Henry | 53,217 | Cambridge | 826 |
| Iroquois | 33,532 | Watseka | 1,122 |
| Jackson | 55,008 | Murphysboro | 605 |
| Jasper | 10,741 | Newton | 495 |
| Jefferson | 31,848 | Mount Vernon | 573 |
| Jersey | 18,492 | Jerseyville | 376 |
| Jo Daviess | 21,766 | Galena | 606 |
| Johnson | 7,550 | Vienna | 345 |
| Kane | 251,005 | Geneva | 520 |
| Kankakee | 97,250 | Kankakee | 678 |
| Kendall | 26,374 | Yorkville | 320 |
| Knox | 60,939 | Galesburg | 728 |
| Lake | 382,638 | Waukegan | 457 |
| La Salle | 111,409 | Ottawa | 1,150 |
| Lawrence | 17,522 | Lawrenceville | 374 |
| Lee | 37,947 | Dixon | 728 |
| Livingston | 40,690 | Pontiac | 1,043 |
| Logan | 33,538 | Lincoln | 622 |
| McDonough | 36,653 | Macomb | 582 |
| McHenry | 111,555 | Woodstock | 610 |
| McLean | 104,389 | Bloomington | 1,173 |
| Macon | 125,010 | Decatur | 578 |
| Macoupin | 44,557 | Carlinville | 872 |
| Madison | 250,911 | Edwardsville | 733 |
| Marion | 38,986 | Salem | 579 |
| Marshall | 13,302 | Lacon | 391 |
| Mason | 16,180 | Havana | 541 |
| Massac | 13,889 | Metropolis | 245 |
| Menard | 9,685 | Petersburg | 312 |
| Mercer | 17,294 | Aledo | 556 |
| Monroe | 18,831 | Waterloo | 382 |
| Montgomery | 30,260 | Hillsboro | 705 |
| Morgan | 36,174 | Jacksonville | 561 |
| Moultrie | 13,263 | Sullivan | 326 |
| Ogle | 42,867 | Oregon | 758 |
| Peoria | 195,318 | Peoria | 623 |
| Perry | 19,757 | Pinckneyville | 439 |
| Piatt | 15,509 | Monticello | 437 |
| Pike | 19,185 | Pittsfield | 828 |

| County | Pop. Apr. 1 1970 | County seat or court house | Land area sq. mi. |
|---|---|---|---|
| Pope | 3,857 | Golconda | 381 |
| Pulaski | 8,741 | Mound City | 204 |
| Putnam | 5,007 | Hennepin | 160 |
| Randolph | 31,379 | Chester | 594 |
| Richland | 16,829 | Olney | 364 |
| Rock Island | 166,734 | Rock Island | 424 |
| St. Clair | 285,199 | Belleville | 673 |
| Saline | 25,721 | Harrisburg | 383 |
| Sangamon | 161,335 | Springfield | 879 |
| Schuyler | 8,135 | Rushville | 434 |
| Scott | 6,096 | Winchester | 251 |
| Shelby | 22,589 | Shelbyville | 752 |
| Stark | 7,510 | Toulon | 291 |
| Stephenson | 48,861 | Freeport | 568 |
| Tazewell | 118,649 | Pekin | 652 |
| Union | 16,071 | Jonesboro | 416 |
| Vermilion | 97,047 | Danville | 899 |
| Wabash | 12,841 | Mt. Carmel | 222 |
| Warren | 21,595 | Monmouth | 541 |
| Washington | 13,780 | Nashville | 564 |
| Wayne | 17,004 | Fairfield | 715 |
| White | 17,312 | Carmi | 502 |
| Whiteside | 62,877 | Morrison | 687 |
| Will | 247,825 | Joliet | 847 |
| Williamson | 49,021 | Marion | 429 |
| Winnebago | 246,623 | Rockford | 519 |
| Woodford | 28,012 | Eureka | 528 |

## Indiana

*(92 counties, 36,097 sq. mi. land; pop. 5,193,669)*

| County | Pop. Apr. 1 1970 | County seat or court house | Land area sq. mi. |
|---|---|---|---|
| Adams | 26,871 | Decatur | 345 |
| Allen | 280,455 | Fort Wayne | 671 |
| Bartholomew | 57,022 | Columbus | 402 |
| Benton | 11,262 | Fowler | 409 |
| Blackford | 15,888 | Hartford City | 167 |
| Boone | 30,870 | Lebanon | 427 |
| Brown | 9,057 | Nashville | 319 |
| Carroll | 17,734 | Delphi | 374 |
| Cass | 40,456 | Logansport | 415 |
| Clark | 75,876 | Jeffersonville | 384 |
| Clay | 23,933 | Brazil | 364 |
| Clinton | 30,547 | Frankfort | 407 |
| Crawford | 8,033 | English | 312 |
| Daviess | 26,602 | Washington | 430 |
| Dearborn | 29,430 | Lawrenceburg | 306 |
| Decatur | 22,738 | Greensburg | 370 |
| DeKalb | 30,837 | Auburn | 366 |
| Delaware | 129,219 | Muncie | 396 |
| Dubois | 30,934 | Jasper | 433 |
| Elkhart | 126,529 | Goshen | 468 |
| Fayette | 26,216 | Connersville | 215 |
| Floyd | 55,622 | New Albany | 149 |
| Fountain | 18,257 | Covington | 397 |
| Franklin | 16,943 | Brookville | 394 |
| Fulton | 16,984 | Rochester | 368 |
| Gibson | 30,444 | Princeton | 498 |
| Grant | 83,955 | Marion | 421 |
| Greene | 26,894 | Bloomfield | 549 |
| Hamilton | 54,532 | Noblesville | 401 |
| Hancock | 35,096 | Greenfield | 305 |
| Harrison | 20,423 | Corydon | 479 |
| Hendricks | 53,974 | Danville | 417 |
| Henry | 52,603 | New Castle | 400 |
| Howard | 83,198 | Kokomo | 293 |
| Huntington | 34,970 | Huntington | 369 |
| Jackson | 33,187 | Brownstown | 520 |
| Jasper | 20,429 | Rensselaer | 562 |
| Jay | 23,575 | Portland | 386 |
| Jefferson | 27,006 | Madison | 366 |
| Jennings | 19,454 | Vernon | 377 |
| Johnson | 61,138 | Franklin | 315 |
| Knox | 41,546 | Vincennes | 516 |
| Kosciusko | 48,127 | Warsaw | 540 |
| Lagrange | 20,890 | Lagrange | 381 |
| Lake | 546,253 | Crown Point | 513 |
| La Porte | 105,342 | La Porte | 607 |
| Lawrence | 38,038 | Bedford | 459 |
| Madison | 138,522 | Anderson | 453 |
| Marion | 793,769 | Indianapolis | 392 |
| Marshall | 34,986 | Plymouth | 443 |
| Martin | 10,969 | Shoals | 345 |
| Miami | 39,246 | Peru | 377 |
| Monroe | 85,221 | Bloomington | 386 |
| Montgomery | 33,930 | Crawfordsville | 507 |
| Morgan | 44,176 | Martinsville | 406 |
| Newton | 11,606 | Kentland | 413 |
| Noble | 31,382 | Albion | 412 |
| Ohio | 4,289 | Rising Sun | 87 |
| Orange | 16,968 | Paoli | 405 |
| Owen | 12,163 | Spencer | 390 |
| Parke | 14,670 | Rockville | 445 |
| Perry | 19,075 | Cannelton | 384 |
| Pike | 12,281 | Petersburg | 335 |
| Porter | 87,114 | Valparaiso | 425 |
| Posey | 21,740 | Mount Vernon | 412 |

| County | Pop. Apr. 1 1970 | County seat or court house | Land area sq. mi. | County | Pop. Apr. 1 1970 | County seat or court house | Land area sq. mi. |
|---|---|---|---|---|---|---|---|
| Pulaski | 12,534 | Winamac | 433 | Marshall | 41,076 | Marshalltown | 574 |
| Putnam | 26,932 | Greencastle | 490 | Mills | 11,832 | Glenwood | 447 |
| Randolph | 28,915 | Winchester | 457 | Mitchell | 13,108 | Osage | 467 |
| Ripley | 21,138 | Versailles | 442 | Monona | 12,069 | Onawa | 699 |
| Rush | 20,352 | Rushville | 409 | Monroe | 9,357 | Albia | 435 |
| St. Joseph | 245,045 | South Bend | 466 | Montgomery | 12,781 | Red Oak | 422 |
| Scott | 17,144 | Scottsburg | 193 | Muscatine | 37,181 | Muscatine | 443 |
| Shelby | 37,797 | Shelbyville | 409 | O'Brien | 17,522 | Primghar | 575 |
| Spencer | 17,134 | Rockport | 396 | Osceola | 8,555 | Sibley | 398 |
| Starke | 19,280 | Knox | 310 | Page | 18,537 | Clarinda | 535 |
| Steuben | 20,159 | Angola | 309 | Palo Alto | 13,289 | Emmetsburg | 561 |
| Sullivan | 19,889 | Sullivan | 457 | Plymouth | 24,322 | Le Mars | 863 |
| Switzerland | 6,306 | Vevay | 221 | Pocahontas | 12,793 | Pocahontas | 581 |
| Tippecanoe | 109,378 | Lafayette | 500 | Polk | 286,130 | Des Moines | 578 |
| Tipton | 16,650 | Tipton | 261 | Pottawattamie | 86,991 | Council Bluffs | 963 |
| Union | 6,582 | Liberty | 168 | Poweshiek | 18,803 | Montezuma | 589 |
| Vanderburgh | 168,772 | Evansville | 241 | Ringgold | 6,373 | Mount Ayr | 538 |
| Vermillion | 16,793 | Newport | 263 | Sac | 15,573 | Sac City | 578 |
| Vigo | 114,528 | Terre Haute | 415 | Scott | 142,687 | Davenport | 454 |
| Wabash | 35,553 | Wabash | 398 | Shelby | 15,528 | Harlan | 587 |
| Warren | 8,705 | Williamsport | 368 | Sioux | 27,996 | Orange City | 766 |
| Warrick | 27,972 | Boonville | 391 | Story | 62,783 | Nevada | 568 |
| Washington | 19,278 | Salem | 516 | Tama | 20,147 | Toledo | 720 |
| Wayne | 79,109 | Richmond | 405 | Taylor | 8,790 | Bedford | 528 |
| Wells | 23,821 | Bluffton | 368 | Union | 13,557 | Creston | 425 |
| White | 20,995 | Monticello | 497 | Van Buren | 8,643 | Keosauqua | 487 |
| Whitely | 23,395 | Columbia City | 337 | Wapello | 42,149 | Ottumwa | 437 |
| | | | | Warren | 27,432 | Indianola | 558 |
| | | | | Washington | 18,967 | Washington | 568 |
| | | | | Wayne | 8,405 | Corydon | 532 |
| | | | | Webster | 48,391 | Fort Dodge | 718 |
| | | | | Winnebago | 12,990 | Forest City | 401 |
| | | | | Winneshiek | 21,758 | Decorah | 688 |
| | | | | Woodbury | 103,052 | Sioux City | 871 |
| | | | | Worth | 8,984 | Northwood | 400 |
| | | | | Wright | 17,294 | Clarion | 577 |

## Iowa

*(99 counties; 55,941 sq. mi. land; pop. 2,825,041)*

| County | Pop. Apr. 1 1970 | County seat or court house | Land area sq. mi. |
|---|---|---|---|
| Adair | 9,487 | Greenfield | 569 |
| Adams | 6,322 | Corning | 426 |
| Allamakee | 14,968 | Waukon | 636 |
| Appanoose | 15,007 | Centerville | 523 |
| Audubon | 9,595 | Audubon | 448 |
| Benton | 22,885 | Vinton | 718 |
| Black Hawk | 132,916 | Waterloo | 568 |
| Boone | 26,470 | Boone | 573 |
| Bremer | 22,737 | Waverly | 439 |
| Buchanan | 21,762 | Independence | 568 |
| Buena Vista | 20,693 | Storm Lake | 572 |
| Butler | 16,953 | Allison | 582 |
| Calhoun | 14,292 | Rockwell City | 571 |
| Carroll | 22,912 | Carroll | 574 |
| Cass | 17,007 | Atlantic | 559 |
| Cedar | 17,655 | Tipton | 585 |
| Cerro Gordo | 49,223 | Mason City | 575 |
| Cherokee | 17,269 | Cherokee | 573 |
| Chickasaw | 14,969 | New Hampton | 505 |
| Clarke | 7,581 | Oscea | 429 |
| Clay | 18,464 | Spencer | 580 |
| Clayton | 20,606 | Elkader | 779 |
| Clinton | 56,749 | Clinton | 693 |
| Crawford | 19,116 | Denison | 716 |
| Dallas | 26,085 | Adel | 597 |
| Davis | 8,207 | Bloomfield | 509 |
| Decatur | 9,737 | Leon | 530 |
| Delaware | 18,770 | Manchester | 572 |
| Des Moines | 46,982 | Burlington | 408 |
| Dickinson | 12,565 | Spirit Lake | 380 |
| Dubuque | 90,609 | Dubuque | 612 |
| Emmet | 14,009 | Estherville | 394 |
| Fayette | 26,898 | West Union | 728 |
| Floyd | 19,860 | Charles City | 503 |
| Franklin | 13,255 | Hampton | 586 |
| Fremont | 9,282 | Sidney | 524 |
| Greene | 12,716 | Jefferson | 569 |
| Grundy | 14,119 | Grundy Center | 501 |
| Guthrie | 12,243 | Guthrie Center | 596 |
| Hamilton | 18,383 | Webster City | 577 |
| Hancock | 13,506 | Garner | 570 |
| Hardin | 22,248 | Eldora | 574 |
| Harrison | 16,240 | Logan | 696 |
| Henry | 18,114 | Mount Pleasant | 440 |
| Howard | 11,442 | Cresco | 471 |
| Humboldt | 12,519 | Dakota City | 435 |
| Ida | 9,283 | Ida Grove | 431 |
| Iowa | 15,419 | Marengo | 584 |
| Jackson | 20,839 | Maquoketa | 644 |
| Jasper | 35,425 | Newton | 731 |
| Jefferson | 15,774 | Fairfield | 436 |
| Johnson 1974 | 75,025 | Iowa City | 619 |
| Jones | 19,868 | Anamosa | 585 |
| Keokuk | 13,943 | Sigourney | 579 |
| Kossuth | 22,937 | Algona | 979 |
| Lee | 42,996 | Fort Madison and Keokuk | 527 |
| Linn | 163,213 | Cedar Rapids | 717 |
| Louisa | 10,682 | Wapello | 403 |
| Lucas | 10,163 | Chariton | 434 |
| Lyon | 13,340 | Rock Rapids | 588 |
| Madison | 11,558 | Winterset | 564 |
| Mahaska | 22,177 | Oskaloosa | 572 |
| Marion | 26,352 | Knoxville | 498 |

## Kansas

*(105 counties, 81,787 sq. mi. land; pop. 2,249,071)*

| County | Pop. Apr. 1 1970 | County seat or court house | Land area sq. mi. |
|---|---|---|---|
| Allen | 15,043 | Iola | 505 |
| Anderson | 8,501 | Garnett | 577 |
| Atchison | 19,165 | Atchison | 427 |
| Barber | 7,016 | Medicine Lodge | 1,146 |
| Barton | 30,663 | Great Bend | 894 |
| Bourbon | 15,215 | Fort Scott | 639 |
| Brown | 11,685 | Hiawatha | 577 |
| Butler | 38,658 | El Dorado | 1,442 |
| Chase | 3,408 | Cottonwood Falls | 774 |
| Chautauqua | 4,642 | Sedan | 647 |
| Cherokee | 21,549 | Columbus | 586 |
| Cheyenne | 4,256 | Saint Francis | 1,027 |
| Clark | 2,896 | Ashland | 983 |
| Clay | 9,890 | Clay Center | 635 |
| Cloud | 13,466 | Concordia | 711 |
| Coffey | 7,397 | Burlington | 617 |
| Comanche | 2,702 | Coldwater | 800 |
| Cowley | 35,012 | Winfield | 1,136 |
| Crawford | 37,850 | Girard | 598 |
| Decatur | 4,988 | Oberlin | 899 |
| Dickinson | 19,993 | Abilene | 855 |
| Doniphan | 9,107 | Troy | 388 |
| Douglas | 57,932 | Lawrence | 471 |
| Edwards | 4,581 | Kinsley | 617 |
| Elk | 3,858 | Howard | 647 |
| Ellis | 24,730 | Hays | 900 |
| Ellsworth | 6,146 | Ellsworth | 717 |
| Finney | 19,029 | Garden City | 1,301 |
| Ford | 22,587 | Dodge City | 1,091 |
| Franklin | 20,007 | Ottawa | 577 |
| Geary | 28,111 | Junction City | 374 |
| Gove | 2,940 | Gove | 1,070 |
| Graham | 4,751 | Hill City | 891 |
| Grant | 5,961 | Ulysses | 571 |
| Gray | 4,516 | Cimarron | 872 |
| Greeley | 1,819 | Tribune | 783 |
| Greenwood | 9,141 | Eureka | 1,133 |
| Hamilton | 2,747 | Syracuse | 992 |
| Harper | 7,871 | Anthony | 801 |
| Harvey | 27,236 | Newton | 540 |
| Haskell | 3,672 | Sublette | 580 |
| Hodgerman | 2,662 | Jetmore | 860 |
| Jackson | 10,342 | Holton | 656 |
| Jefferson | 11,945 | Oskaloosa | 510 |
| Jewell | 6,099 | Mankato | 910 |
| Johnson | 220,073 | Olathe | 476 |
| Kearny | 3,047 | Lakin | 855 |
| Kingman | 8,886 | Kingman | 864 |
| Kiowa | 4,088 | Greensburg | 720 |
| Labette | 25,775 | Oswego | 654 |
| Lane | 2,707 | Dighton | 720 |
| Leavenworth | 53,340 | Leavenworth | 466 |
| Lincoln | 4,582 | Lincoln | 725 |
| Linn | 7,770 | Mound City | 606 |
| Logan | 3,814 | Oakley | 1,073 |

| County | Pop. Apr. 1 1970 | County seat or court house | Land area sq. mi. | County | Pop. Apr. 1 1970 | County seat or court house | Land area sq. mi. |
|---|---|---|---|---|---|---|---|
| Lyon | 32,071 | Emporia | 841 | Green | 10,350 | Greensburg | 282 |
| McPherson | 24,778 | McPherson | 896 | Greenup | 33,192 | Greenup | 351 |
| Marion | 13,935 | Marion | 945 | Hancock | 7,080 | Hawesville | 187 |
| Marshall | 13,139 | Marysville | 883 | Hardin | 78,421 | Elizabeth | 616 |
| Meade | 4,912 | Meade | 979 | Harlan | 37,370 | Harlan | 469 |
| Miami | 19,254 | Paola | 592 | Harrison | 14,158 | Cynthiana | 308 |
| Mitchell | 8,010 | Beloit | 714 | Hart | 13,980 | Munfordville | 420 |
| Montgomery | 39,949 | Independence | 628 | Henderson | 36,031 | Henderson | 433 |
| Morris | 6,432 | Council Grove | 697 | Henry | 10,910 | New Castle | 289 |
| Morton | 3,576 | Elkhart | 728 | Hickman | 6,264 | Clinton | 246 |
| Nemaha | 11,825 | Seneca | 708 | Hopkins | 38,167 | Madisonville | 553 |
| Neosho | 18,812 | Erie | 587 | Jackson | 10,005 | McKee | 337 |
| Ness | 4,791 | Ness City | 1,081 | Jefferson | 695,055 | Louisville | 375 |
| Norton | 7,279 | Norton | 872 | Jessamine | 17,430 | Nicholasville | 177 |
| Osage | 13,352 | Lyndon | 707 | Johnson | 17,539 | Paintsville | 264 |
| Osborne | 6,416 | Osborne | 886 | Kenton | 129,440 | Independence | 165 |
| Ottawa | 6,183 | Minneapolis | 723 | Knott | 14,698 | Hindman | 356 |
| Pawnee | 8,484 | Larned | 755 | Knox | 23,689 | Barbourville | 373 |
| Phillips | 7,888 | Phillipsburg | 897 | Larue | 10,672 | Hodgenville | 260 |
| Pottawatomie | 11,755 | Westmoreland | 820 | Laurel | 27,386 | London | 446 |
| Pratt | 10,056 | Pratt | 729 | Lawrence | 10,726 | Louisa | 425 |
| Rawlins | 4,393 | Atwood | 1,078 | Lee | 6,587 | Beattyville | 210 |
| Reno | 60,765 | Hutchinson | 1,260 | Leslie | 11,623 | Hyden | 409 |
| Republic | 8,498 | Belleville | 718 | Letcher | 23,165 | Whitesburg | 339 |
| Rice | 12,320 | Lyons | 725 | Lewis | 12,355 | Vanceburg | 486 |
| Riley | 56,788 | Manhattan | 597 | Lincoln | 16,663 | Stanford | 340 |
| Rooks | 7,628 | Stockton | 886 | Livingston | 7,596 | Smithland | 311 |
| Rush | 5,117 | LaCrosse | 724 | Logan | 21,793 | Russellville | 563 |
| Russell | 9,428 | Russell | 867 | Lyon | 5,562 | Eddyville | 216 |
| Saline | 46,592 | Salina | 720 | McCracken | 58,281 | Paducah | 250 |
| Scott | 5,606 | Scott City | 724 | McCreary | 12,548 | Whitley City | 418 |
| Sedgwick | 350,694 | Wichita | 1,007 | McLean | 9,062 | Calhoun | 257 |
| Seward | 16,062 | Liberal | 646 | Madison | 42,730 | Richmond | 446 |
| Shawnee | 155,322 | Topeka | 548 | Magoffin | 10,443 | Salyersville | 303 |
| Sheridan | 3,859 | Hoxie | 893 | Marion | 16,714 | Lebanon | 343 |
| Sherman | 7,792 | Goodland | 1,055 | Marshall | 20,381 | Benton | 303 |
| Smith | 6,757 | Smith Center | 893 | Martin | 9,377 | Inez | 231 |
| Stafford | 5,943 | Saint John | 795 | Mason | 17,273 | Maysville | 238 |
| Stanton | 2,287 | Johnson | 676 | Meade | 18,796 | Brandenburg | 305 |
| Stevens | 4,198 | Hugoton | 731 | Menifee | 4,050 | Frenchburg | 210 |
| Sumner | 23,553 | Wellington | 1,186 | Mercer | 15,960 | Harrodsburg | 256 |
| Thomas | 7,501 | Colby | 1,070 | Metcalfe | 8,177 | Edmonton | 296 |
| Trego | 4,436 | Wakeeney | 901 | Monroe | 11,642 | Tompkinsville | 334 |
| Wabaunsee | 6,397 | Alma | 792 | Montgomery | 15,364 | Mount Sterling | 204 |
| Wallace | 2,215 | Sharon Springs | 911 | Morgan | 10,019 | West Liberty | 369 |
| Washington | 9,249 | Washington | 891 | Muhlenberg | 27,537 | Greenville | 481 |
| Wichita | 3,274 | Leoti | 724 | Nelson | 23,477 | Bardstown | 437 |
| Wilson | 11,317 | Fredonia | 574 | Nicholas | 6,508 | Carlisle | 204 |
| Woodson | 4,789 | Yates Center | 497 | Ohio | 18,790 | Hartford | 596 |
| Wyandotte | 186,845 | Kansas City | 152 | Oldham | 14,687 | La Grange | 184 |
|  |  |  |  | Owen | 7,470 | Owenton | 351 |
|  |  |  |  | Owsley | 5,023 | Booneville | 197 |
|  |  |  |  | Pendleton | 9,949 | Falmouth | 279 |
|  |  |  |  | Perry | 26,259 | Hazard | 341 |
|  |  |  |  | Pike | 61,059 | Pikeville | 782 |
|  |  |  |  | Powell | 7,704 | Stanton | 173 |
|  |  |  |  | Pulaski | 35,234 | Somerset | 653 |
|  |  |  |  | Robertson | 2,163 | Mount Olivet | 101 |
|  |  |  |  | Rockcastle | 12,305 | Mount Vernon | 311 |
|  |  |  |  | Rowan | 17,010 | Morehead | 290 |
|  |  |  |  | Russell | 10,542 | Jamestown | 238 |
|  |  |  |  | Scott | 17,948 | Georgetown | 284 |
|  |  |  |  | Shelby | 18,999 | Shelbyville | 383 |
|  |  |  |  | Simpson | 13,054 | Franklin | 239 |
|  |  |  |  | Spencer | 5,488 | Taylorsville | 193 |
|  |  |  |  | Taylor | 17,138 | Campbellsville | 277 |
|  |  |  |  | Todd | 10,823 | Elkton | 376 |
|  |  |  |  | Trigg | 8,620 | Cadiz | 408 |
|  |  |  |  | Trimble | 5,349 | Bedford | 146 |
|  |  |  |  | Union | 15,882 | Morganfield | 340 |
|  |  |  |  | Warren | 57,884 | Bowling Green | 546 |
|  |  |  |  | Washington | 10,728 | Springfield | 307 |
|  |  |  |  | Wayne | 14,268 | Monticello | 440 |
|  |  |  |  | Webster | 13,282 | Dixon | 339 |
|  |  |  |  | Whitley | 24,145 | Williamsburg | 459 |
|  |  |  |  | Wolfe | 5,669 | Campton | 227 |
|  |  |  |  | Woodford | 14,434 | Versailles | 193 |

## Kentucky

*(120 counties, 39,650 sq. mi. land; pop. 3,219,311)*

| County | Pop. Apr. 1 1970 | County seat or court house | Land area sq. mi. |
|---|---|---|---|
| Adair | 13,037 | Columbia | 370 |
| Allen | 12,598 | Scottsville | 351 |
| Anderson | 9,358 | Lawrenceburg | 206 |
| Ballard | 8,276 | Wickliffe | 259 |
| Barren | 28,677 | Glasgow | 468 |
| Bath | 9,235 | Owingsville | 287 |
| Bell | 31,121 | Pineville | 370 |
| Boone | 32,812 | Burlington | 249 |
| Bourbon | 18,476 | Paris | 300 |
| Boyd | 52,376 | Catlettsburg | 159 |
| Boyle | 21,861 | Danville | 183 |
| Bracken | 7,227 | Brooksville | 204 |
| Breathitt | 14,221 | Jackson | 494 |
| Breckinridge | 14,789 | Hardinsburg | 554 |
| Bullitt | 26,090 | Shepherdsville | 300 |
| Butler | 9,723 | Morgantown | 443 |
| Caldwell | 13,179 | Princeton | 357 |
| Calloway | 27,692 | Murray | 384 |
| Campbell | 88,704 | Alexandria | 149 |
| Carlisle | 5,354 | Bardwell | 195 |
| Carroll | 8,523 | Carrollton | 130 |
| Carter | 19,850 | Grayson | 397 |
| Casey | 12,930 | Liberty | 435 |
| Christian | 56,224 | Hopkinsville | 725 |
| Clark | 24,090 | Winchester | 259 |
| Clay | 18,481 | Manchester | 474 |
| Clinton | 8,174 | Albany | 190 |
| Crittenden | 8,493 | Marion | 365 |
| Cumberland | 6,850 | Burkesville | 310 |
| Daviess | 79,486 | Owensboro | 462 |
| Edmonson | 8,751 | Brownsville | 298 |
| Elliott | 5,933 | Sandy Hook | 240 |
| Estill | 12,752 | Irvine | 260 |
| Fayette | 174,323 | Lexington | 280 |
| Fleming | 11,366 | Flemingsburg | 350 |
| Floyd | 35,889 | Prestonsburg | 399 |
| Franklin | 34,481 | Frankfort | 211 |
| Fulton | 10,183 | Hickman | 203 |
| Gallatin | 4,134 | Warsaw | 100 |
| Garrard | 9,457 | Lancaster | 236 |
| Grant | 9,999 | Williamstown | 249 |
| Graves | 30,939 | Mayfield | 60 |
| Grayson | 16,445 | Leitchfield | 496 |

## Louisiana

*(64 parishes, 44,930 sq. mi. land; pop. 3,643,180)*

| Parish | Pop. Apr. 1 1970 | Parish seat or court house | Land area sq. mi. |
|---|---|---|---|
| Acadia | 52,109 | Crowley | 663 |
| Allen | 20,794 | Oberlin | 774 |
| Ascension | 37,086 | Donaldsville | 301 |
| Assumption | 19,654 | Napoleonville | 356 |
| Avoyelles | 37,751 | Marksville | 832 |
| Beauregard | 22,888 | De Ridder | 1,181 |
| Bienville | 16,024 | Arcadia | 832 |
| Bossier | 63,703 | Benton | 849 |
| Caddo | 230,184 | Shreveport | 899 |
| Calcasieu | 145,415 | Lake Charles | 1,105 |
| Caldwell | 9,354 | Columbia | 551 |
| Cameron | 8,149 | Cameron | 1,441 |
| Catahoula | 11,769 | Harrisonburg | 742 |

| Parish | Pop. Apr. 1 1970 | Parish seat or court house | Land area sq. mi. |
|---|---|---|---|
| Claiborne | 17,024 | Homer | 763 |
| Concordia | 22,578 | Vidalia | 718 |
| De Soto | 22,764 | Mansfield | 894 |
| East Baton Rouge | 285,167 | Baton Rouge | 459 |
| East Carroll | 12,884 | Lake Providence | 436 |
| East Feliciana | 17,657 | Clinton | 454 |
| Evangeline | 31,932 | Ville Platte | 669 |
| Franklin | 23,946 | Winnsboro | 648 |
| Grant | 13,671 | Colfax | 670 |
| Iberia | 57,397 | New Iberia | 589 |
| Iberville | 30,746 | Plaquemine | 627 |
| Jackson | 15,963 | Jonesboro | 582 |
| Jefferson | 338,229 | Gretna | 369 |
| Jefferson Davis | 29,554 | Jennings | 658 |
| Lafayette | 111,643 | Lafayette | 283 |
| Lafourche | 68,941 | Thibodaux | 1,141 |
| La Salle | 13,295 | Jena | 643 |
| Lincoln | 33,880 | Ruston | 469 |
| Livingston | 36,511 | Livingston | 654 |
| Madison | 15,065 | Tallulah | 661 |
| Morehouse | 32,463 | Bastrop | 804 |
| Natchitoches | 35,219 | Natchitoches | 1,292 |
| Orleans | 593,471 | New Orleans | 197 |
| Ouachita | 115,387 | Monroe | 638 |
| Plaquemines | 25,225 | Pointe a la Hacke | 1,030 |
| Pointe Coupee | 22,002 | New Roads | 563 |
| Rapides | 118,078 | Alexandria | 1,318 |
| Red River | 9,226 | Coushatta | 406 |
| Richland | 21,774 | Rayville | 576 |
| Sabine | 18,638 | Many | 873 |
| St. Bernard | 51,185 | Chalmette | 514 |
| St. Charles | 29,550 | Hahnville | 294 |
| St. Helena | 9,937 | Greensburg | 420 |
| St. James | 19,733 | Convent | 253 |
| St. John The Baptist | 23,813 | Edgard | 227 |
| St. Landry | 80,364 | Opelousas | 932 |
| St. Martin | 32,453 | Saint Martinville | 736 |
| St. Mary | 60,752 | Franklin | 624 |
| St. Tammany | 63,585 | Covington | 887 |
| Tangipahoa | 65,875 | Amite | 808 |
| Tensas | 9,732 | Saint Joseph | 626 |
| Terrebonne | 76,049 | Houma | 1,368 |
| Union | 18,447 | Farmerville | 885 |
| Vermilion | 43,071 | Abbeville | 1,205 |
| Vernon | 53,794 | Leesville | 1,351 |
| Washington | 41,987 | Franklinton | 665 |
| Webster | 39,939 | Minden | 615 |
| West Baton Rouge | 16,684 | Port Allen | 203 |
| West Carroll | 13,028 | Oak Grove | 356 |
| West Feliciana | 11,376 | Saint Francisville | 405 |
| Winn | 16,369 | Winnfield | 950 |

## Maine

*(16 counties, 30,920 sq. mi. land; pop. 993,663)*

| County | Pop. Apr. 1 1970 | County seat or court house | Land area sq. mi. |
|---|---|---|---|
| Androscoggin | 91,279 | Auburn | 474 |
| Aroostook | 94,078 | Houlton | 6,821 |
| Cumberland | 192,528 | Portland | 879 |
| Franklin | 22,444 | Farmington | 1,709 |
| Hancock | 34,590 | Ellsworth | 1,536 |
| Kennebec | 95,306 | Augusta | 872 |
| Knox | 29,013 | Rockland | 369 |
| Lincoln | 20,537 | Wiscasset | 454 |
| Oxford | 43,457 | South Paris | 2,080 |
| Penobscot | 125,393 | Bangor | 3,390 |
| Piscataquis | 16,285 | Dover-Foxcroft | 3,892 |
| Sagadahoc | 23,452 | Bath | 257 |
| Somerset | 40,597 | Skowhegan | 3,894 |
| Waldo | 23,328 | Belfast | 737 |
| Washington | 29,859 | Machias | 2,554 |
| York | 111,576 | Alfred | 1,001 |

## Maryland

*(23 cos., 1 ind. city, 9,891 sq. mi. land; pop. 3,922,399)*

| Allegany | 84,044 | Cumberland | 428 |
|---|---|---|---|
| Anne Arundel | 298,042 | Annapolis | 423 |
| Baltimore | 620,409 | Towson | 598 |
| Calvert | 20,682 | Prince Frederick | 217 |
| Caroline | 19,781 | Denton | 321 |
| Carroll | 69,006 | Westminster | 456 |
| Cecil | 53,291 | Elkton | 362 |
| Charles | 47,678 | La Plata | 459 |
| Dorchester | 29,405 | Cambridge | 594 |
| Frederick | 84,927 | Frederick | 665 |
| Garrett | 21,476 | Oakland | 659 |
| Harford | 115,378 | Bel Air | 453 |
| Howard | 62,394 | Ellicott City | 251 |
| Kent | 16,146 | Chestertown | 281 |
| Montgomery | 522,809 | Rockville | 495 |
| Prince Georges | 661,082 | Upper Marlboro | 485 |

| County | Pop. Apr. 1 1970 | County seat or court house | Land area sq. mi. |
|---|---|---|---|
| Queen Annes | 18,422 | Centreville | 375 |
| St. Marys | 47,388 | Leonardtown | 373 |
| Somerset | 18,924 | Princess Anne | 339 |
| Talbot | 23,682 | Easton | 261 |
| Washington | 103,829 | Hagerstown | 459 |
| Wicomico | 54,236 | Salisbury | 381 |
| Worcester | 24,442 | Snow Hill | 479 |
| Independent City | | | |
| Baltimore | 905,787 | ... | 78 |

## Massachusetts

*(14 counties, 7,826 sq. mi. land; pop. 5,689,170)*

| Barnstable | 96,656 | Barnstable | 393 |
|---|---|---|---|
| Berkshire | 149,402 | Pittsfield | 941 |
| Bristol | 444,301 | Taunton | 554 |
| Dukes | 6,117 | Edgartown | 104 |
| Essex | 637,887 | Salem | 494 |
| Franklin | 59,210 | Greenfield | 708 |
| Hampden | 459,050 | Springfield | 619 |
| Hampshire | 123,981 | Northampton | 529 |
| Middlesex | 1,397,465 | Cambridge | 825 |
| Nantucket | 3,774 | Nantucket | 46 |
| Norfolk | 604,854 | Dedham | 394 |
| Plymouth | 333,314 | Plymouth | 654 |
| Suffolk | 735,190 | Boston | 56 |
| Worcester | 637,037 | Worcester | 1,509 |

## Michigan

*(83 counties; 56,817 sq. mi. land; pop. 8,875,083)*

| Alcona | 7,113 | Harrisville | 678 |
|---|---|---|---|
| Alger | 8,568 | Munising | 905 |
| Allegan | 66,575 | Allegan | 826 |
| Alpena | 30,708 | Alpena | 565 |
| Antrim | 12,612 | Bellaire | 476 |
| Arenac | 11,149 | Standish | 367 |
| Baraga | 7,789 | L'Anse | 901 |
| Barry | 38,166 | Hastings | 554 |
| Bay | 117,339 | Bay City | 447 |
| Benzie | 8,593 | Beulah | 316 |
| Berrien | 163,940 | Saint Joseph | 580 |
| Branch | 37,906 | Coldwater | 506 |
| Calhoun | 141,963 | Marshall | 709 |
| Cass | 43,312 | Cassopolis | 491 |
| Charlevoix | 16,541 | Charlevoix | 414 |
| Cheboygan | 16,573 | Cheboygan | 721 |
| Chippewa | 32,412 | Sault Sainte Marie | 1,590 |
| Clare | 16,695 | Harrison | 571 |
| Clinton | 48,492 | Saint Johns | 572 |
| Crawford | 6,482 | Grayling | 561 |
| Delta | 35,924 | Escanaba | 1,177 |
| Dickinson | 23,753 | Iron Mountain | 757 |
| Eaton | 68,892 | Charlotte | 571 |
| Emmet | 18,331 | Petoskey | 461 |
| Genesee | 445,589 | Flint | 642 |
| Gladwin | 13,471 | Gladwin | 503 |
| Gogebic | 20,676 | Bessemer | 1,107 |
| Grand Traverse | 39,175 | Traverse City | 462 |
| Gratiot | 39,246 | Ithaca | 566 |
| Hillsdale | 37,171 | Hillsdale | 600 |
| Houghton | 34,652 | Houghton | 1,017 |
| Huron | 34,083 | Bad Axe | 819 |
| Ingham | 261,039 | Mason | 559 |
| Ionia | 45,848 | Ionia | 575 |
| Iosco | 24,905 | Iawas City | 544 |
| Iron | 13,813 | Crystal Falls | 1,171 |
| Isabella | 44,594 | Mount Pleasant | 572 |
| Jackson | 143,274 | Jackson | 698 |
| Kalamazoo | 201,550 | Kalamazoo | 562 |
| Kalkaska | 5,272 | Kalkaska | 566 |
| Kent | 411,044 | Grand Rapids | 857 |
| Keweenaw | 2,264 | Eagle River | 538 |
| Lake | 5,661 | Baldwin | 571 |
| Lapeer | 52,361 | Lapeer | 658 |
| Leelanau | 10,872 | Leland | 345 |
| Lenawee | 81,951 | Adrian | 753 |
| Livingston | 58,967 | Howell | 572 |
| Luce | 6,789 | Newberry | 902 |
| Mackinac | 9,660 | Saint Ignace | 1,014 |
| Macomb | 625,309 | Mount Clemens | 480 |
| Manistee | 20,393 | Manistee | 553 |
| Marquette | 64,686 | Marquette | 1,828 |
| Mason | 22,612 | Ludington | 499 |
| Mecosta | 27,992 | Big Rapids | 560 |
| Menominee | 24,587 | Menominee | 1,038 |
| Midland | 63,769 | Midland | 520 |
| Missaukee | 7,126 | Lake City | 565 |
| Monroe | 119,172 | Monroe | 557 |
| Montcalm | 39,660 | Stanton | 712 |
| Montmorency | 5,247 | Atlanta | 555 |
| Muskegon | 157,426 | Muskegon | 501 |
| Newaygo | 27,992 | White Cloud | 849 |
| Oakland | 907,871 | Pontiac | 867 |
| Oceana | 17,984 | Hart | 536 |
| Ogemaw | 11,903 | West Branch | 571 |

| County | Pop. Apr. 1 1970 | County seat or court house | Land area sq. mi. |
|---|---|---|---|
| Ontonagon | 10,548 | Ontonagon | 1,316 |
| Osceola | 14,838 | Reed City | 581 |
| Oscoda 1977 | 6,305 | Mio | 563 |
| Otsego | 10,422 | Gaylord | 527 |
| Ottawa | 128,181 | Grand Haven | 563 |
| Presque Isle | 12,836 | Rogers City | 648 |
| Roscommon | 9,892 | Roscommon | 521 |
| Saginaw | 219,743 | Saginaw | 814 |
| St. Clair | 120,175 | Port Huron | 734 |
| St. Joseph | 47,392 | Centreville | 506 |
| Sanilac | 35,181 | Sandusky | 961 |
| Schoolcraft | 8,226 | Manistique | 1,181 |
| Shiawassee | 63,075 | Corunna | 540 |
| Tuscola | 48,603 | Caro | 815 |
| Van Buren | 56,173 | Paw Paw | 603 |
| Washtenaw | 234,103 | Ann Arbor | 711 |
| Wayne | 2,670,368 | Detroit | 605 |
| Wexford | 19,717 | Cadillac | 559 |

## Minnesota

(87 counties; 79,289 sq. mi. land; pop., 3,805,069)

| County | Pop. Apr. 1 1970 | County seat or court house | Land area sq. mi. |
|---|---|---|---|
| Aitkin | 11,403 | Aitkin | 1,828 |
| Anoka | 154,401 | Anoka | 424 |
| Becker | 24,372 | Detroit Lakes | 1,297 |
| Beltrami | 26,373 | Bemidji | 2,507 |
| Benton | 20,841 | Foley | 402 |
| Big Stone | 7,941 | Ortonville | 490 |
| Blue Earth | 52,322 | Mankato | 737 |
| Brown | 28,887 | New Ulm | 610 |
| Carlton | 28,072 | Carlton | 862 |
| Carver | 28,331 | Chaska | 359 |
| Cass | 17,323 | Walker | 1,998 |
| Chippewa | 15,109 | Montevideo | 582 |
| Chisago | 17,492 | Center City | 419 |
| Clay | 46,608 | Moorhead | 1,045 |
| Clearwater | 8,013 | Bagley | 1,000 |
| Cook | 3,423 | Grand Marais | 1,346 |
| Cottonwood | 14,887 | Windom | 636 |
| Crow Wing | 34,826 | Brainerd | 995 |
| Dakota | 139,808 | Hastings | 576 |
| Dodge | 13,037 | Mantorville | 435 |
| Douglas | 22,910 | Alexandria | 647 |
| Faribault | 20,896 | Blue Earth | 711 |
| Fillmore | 21,916 | Preston | 859 |
| Freeborn | 38,064 | Albert Lea | 701 |
| Goodhue | 34,804 | Red Wing | 753 |
| Grant | 7,462 | Elbow Lake | 546 |
| Hennepin | 960,080 | Minneapolis | 567 |
| Houston | 17,556 | Caledonia | 565 |
| Hubbard | 10,583 | Park Rapids | 932 |
| Isanti | 16,560 | Cambridge | 438 |
| Itasca | 35,530 | Grand Rapids | 2,633 |
| Jackson | 14,352 | Jackson | 696 |
| Kanabec | 9,775 | Mora | 524 |
| Kandiyohi | 30,548 | Willmar | 783 |
| Kittson | 6,853 | Hallock | 1,123 |
| Koochiching | 17,131 | International Falls | 3,127 |
| Lac Qui Parle | 11,164 | Madison | 768 |
| Lake | 13,351 | Two Harbors | 2,062 |
| Lake of the Woods 1974 | 4,196 | Baudette | 1,311 |
| Le Sueur | 21,332 | Le Center | 440 |
| Lincoln | 8,143 | Ivanhoe | 531 |
| Lyon | 24,273 | Marshall | 709 |
| McLeod | 27,662 | Glencoe | 488 |
| Mahnomen | 5,638 | Mahnomen | 563 |
| Marshall | 13,060 | Warren | 1,789 |
| Martin | 24,316 | Fairmont | 703 |
| Meeker | 18,387 | Litchfield | 619 |
| Mille Lacs | 15,703 | Milaca | 571 |
| Morrison | 26,949 | Little Falls | 1,127 |
| Mower | 43,783 | Austin | 703 |
| Murray | 12,508 | Slayton | 703 |
| Nicollet | 24,518 | Saint Peter | 432 |
| Nobles | 23,208 | Worthington | 712 |
| Norman | 10,008 | Ada | 885 |
| Olmstead | 84,104 | Rochester | 654 |
| Otter Tail | 46,097 | Fergus Falls | 1,962 |
| Pennington 1975 | 14,589 | Thief River Falls | 622 |
| Pine | 16,821 | Pine City | 1,414 |
| Pipestone | 12,791 | Pipestone | 464 |
| Polk | 34,435 | Crookston | 2,013 |
| Pope | 11,107 | Glenwood | 669 |
| Ramsey | 476,350 | Saint Paul | 155 |
| Red Lake | 5,388 | Red Lake Falls | 432 |
| Redwood | 20,024 | Redwood Falls | 874 |
| Renville | 21,139 | Olivia | 979 |
| Rice | 41,582 | Faribault | 496 |
| Rock | 11,346 | Luverne | 485 |
| Roseau | 11,569 | Roseau | 1,676 |
| St. Louis | 220,693 | Duluth | 6,092 |
| Scott | 32,423 | Shakopee | 353 |
| Sherburne | 18,344 | Elk River | 431 |
| Sibley | 15,845 | Gaylord | 583 |
| Stearns | 95,400 | Saint Cloud | 1,342 |
| Steele | 26,931 | Owatonna | 425 |

| County | Pop. Apr. 1 1970 | County seat or court house | Land area sq. mi. |
|---|---|---|---|
| Stevens | 11,218 | Morris | 558 |
| Swift | 13,177 | Benson | 739 |
| Todd | 22,114 | Long Prairie | 942 |
| Traverse | 6,254 | Wheaton | 568 |
| Wabasha | 17,224 | Wabasha | 522 |
| Wadena | 12,412 | Wadena | 536 |
| Waseca | 16,663 | Waseca | 415 |
| Washington | 82,948 | Stillwater | 386 |
| Watonwan | 13,298 | Saint James | 433 |
| Wilkin | 9,389 | Breckenridge | 752 |
| Winona | 44,409 | Winona | 620 |
| Wright | 38,933 | Buffalo | 674 |
| Yellow Medicine | 14,523 | Granite Falls | 753 |

## Mississippi

(82 counties, 47,296 sq. mi. land; pop. 2,216,912)

| County | Pop. Apr. 1 1970 | County seat or court house | Land area sq. mi. |
|---|---|---|---|
| Adams | 37,293 | Natchez | 449 |
| Alcorn | 27,179 | Corinth | 405 |
| Amite | 13,763 | Liberty | 729 |
| Attala | 19,570 | Kosciusko | 724 |
| Benton | 7,505 | Ashland | 412 |
| Bolivar | 49,409 | Cleveland & Rosedale | 923 |
| Calhoun | 14,623 | Pittsboro | 575 |
| Carroll | 9,397 | Carrollton & Vaiden | 637 |
| Chickasaw | 16,805 | Houston & Okolona | 506 |
| Choctaw | 8,440 | Ackerman | 417 |
| Claiborne | 10,086 | Port Gibson | 489 |
| Clarke | 15,049 | Quitman | 697 |
| Clay | 18,840 | West Point | 414 |
| Coahoma | 40,447 | Clarksdale | 569 |
| Copiah | 24,764 | Hazlehurst | 780 |
| Covington | 14,002 | Collins | 416 |
| De Soto | 35,885 | Hernando | 476 |
| Forrest | 57,849 | Hattiesburg | 468 |
| Franklin | 8,011 | Meadville | 568 |
| George | 12,459 | Lucedale | 481 |
| Greene | 8,545 | Leakesville | 728 |
| Grenada | 19,854 | Grenada | 431 |
| Hancock 1977 | 19,360 | Bay Saint Louis | 482 |
| Harrison | 134,582 | Gulfport | 585 |
| Hinds | 214,973 | Jackson & Raymond | 876 |
| Holmes | 23,120 | Lexington | 769 |
| Humphreys | 14,601 | Belzoni | 421 |
| Issaquena | 2,737 | Mayersville | 414 |
| Itawamba | 16,847 | Fulton | 541 |
| Jackson | 87,975 | Pascagoula | 736 |
| Jasper | 15,994 | Bat Springs & Paulding | 683 |
| Jefferson | 9,295 | Fayette | 521 |
| Jefferson Davis | 12,936 | Prentiss | 414 |
| Jones | 56,357 | Ellisville & Laurel | 702 |
| Kemper | 10,233 | De Kalb | 757 |
| Lafayette | 24,181 | Oxford | 668 |
| Lamar | 15,209 | Purvis | 500 |
| Lauderdale | 67,087 | Meridian | 708 |
| Lawrence | 11,137 | Monticello | 433 |
| Leake | 17,075 | Carthage | 586 |
| Lee | 46,148 | Tupelo | 455 |
| Leflore | 42,111 | Greenwood | 592 |
| Lincoln | 26,198 | Brookhaven | 586 |
| Lowndes | 49,700 | Columbus | 508 |
| Madison | 29,737 | Canton | 727 |
| Marion | 22,871 | Columbia | 550 |
| Marshall | 24,027 | Holly Springs | 710 |
| Monroe | 34,043 | Aberdeen | 769 |
| Montgomery | 12,918 | Winona | 403 |
| Neshoba | 20,802 | Philadelphia | 568 |
| Newton | 18,983 | Decatur | 580 |
| Noxubee | 14,288 | Macon | 695 |
| Oktibbeha | 28,752 | Starkville | 454 |
| Panola | 26,829 | Batesville & Sardis | 693 |
| Pearl River | 27,802 | Poplarville | 828 |
| Perry | 9,065 | New Augusta | 653 |
| Pike | 31,813 | Magnolia | 409 |
| Pontotoc | 17,363 | Pontotoc | 501 |
| Prentiss | 20,133 | Booneville | 418 |
| Quitman | 15,888 | Marks | 412 |
| Rankin | 43,933 | Brandon | 775 |
| Scott | 21,369 | Forest | 615 |
| Sharkey | 9,937 | Rolling Fork | 436 |
| Simpson | 19,947 | Mendenhall | 587 |
| Smith | 13,561 | Raleigh | 642 |
| Stone | 8,101 | Wiggins | 448 |
| Sunflower | 37,047 | Indianola | 694 |
| Tallahatchie | 19,338 | Charleston & Sumner | 644 |
| Tate | 18,544 | Senatobia | 405 |
| Tippah | 15,852 | Ripley | 464 |
| Tishomingo | 14,940 | Iuka | 443 |
| Tunica | 11,854 | Tunica | 458 |
| Union | 19,096 | New Albany | 422 |
| Walthall | 12,500 | Tylertown | 403 |

| County | Pop. Apr. 1 1970 | County seat or court house | Land area sq. mi. |
|---|---|---|---|
| Warren | 44,981 | Vicksburg | 581 |
| Washington | 70,581 | Greenville | 734 |
| Wayne | 16,650 | Waynesboro | 827 |
| Webster | 10,047 | Walthall | 416 |
| Wilkinson | 11,099 | Woodville | 674 |
| Winston | 18,406 | Louisville | 606 |
| Yalobusha | 11,915 | Coffeeville & Water Valley | 488 |
| Yazoo | 27,314 | Yazoo City | 938 |

## Missouri

*(114 cos., 1 ind. city, 68,995 sq. mi. land; pop. 4,677,399)*

| County | Pop. Apr. 1 1970 | County seat or court house | Land area sq. mi. |
|---|---|---|---|
| Adair | 22,472 | Kirksville | 572 |
| Andrew | 11,913 | Savannah | 436 |
| Atchison | 9,240 | Rockport | 549 |
| Audrain | 25,362 | Mexico | 692 |
| Barry | 19,597 | Cassville | 783 |
| Barton | 10,431 | Lamar | 594 |
| Bates | 15,468 | Butler | 841 |
| Benton | 9,695 | Warsaw | 735 |
| Bollinger | 8,820 | Marble Hill | 621 |
| Boone | 80,935 | Columbia | 685 |
| Buchanan | 86,915 | Saint Joseph | 404 |
| Butler | 33,529 | Poplar Bluff | 715 |
| Caldwell | 8,351 | Kingston | 430 |
| Callaway | 25,991 | Fulton | 835 |
| Camden | 13,315 | Camdenton | 640 |
| Cape Girardeau | 49,350 | Jackson | 574 |
| Carroll | 12,565 | Carrollton | 697 |
| Carter | 3,878 | Van Buren | 506 |
| Cass | 39,448 | Harrisonville | 698 |
| Cedar | 9,424 | Stockton | 496 |
| Chariton | 11,084 | Keytesville | 754 |
| Christian | 15,124 | Ozark | 567 |
| Clark | 8,260 | Kahoka | 506 |
| Clay | 123,702 | Liberty | 412 |
| Clinton | 12,462 | Plattsburg | 420 |
| Cole | 46,228 | Jefferson City | 384 |
| Cooper | 14,732 | Boonville | 566 |
| Crawford | 14,828 | Steelville | 760 |
| Dade | 6,850 | Greenfield | 504 |
| Dallas | 10,054 | Buffalo | 537 |
| Daviess | 8,420 | Gallatin | 563 |
| De Kalb | 7,305 | Maysville | 423 |
| Dent | 11,457 | Salem | 756 |
| Douglas | 9,268 | Ava | 809 |
| Dunklin | 33,742 | Kennett | 543 |
| Franklin | 55,127 | Union | 934 |
| Gasconade | 11,878 | Hermann | 519 |
| Gentry | 8,060 | Albany | 488 |
| Greene | 152,929 | Springfield | 677 |
| Grundy | 11,819 | Trenton | 435 |
| Harrison | 10,257 | Bethany | 720 |
| Henry | 18,451 | Clinton | 734 |
| Hickory | 4,481 | Hermitage | 377 |
| Holt | 6,654 | Oregon | 458 |
| Howard | 10,561 | Fayette | 472 |
| Howell | 23,521 | West Plains | 920 |
| Iron | 9,529 | Ironton | 554 |
| Jackson | 654,178 | Independence | 603 |
| Jasper | 79,852 | Carthage | 642 |
| Jefferson | 105,248 | Hillsboro | 668 |
| Johnson | 34,172 | Warrensburg | 826 |
| Knox | 5,692 | Edina | 512 |
| Laclede | 19,944 | Lebanon | 770 |
| Lafayette | 26,626 | Lexington | 632 |
| Lawrence | 24,585 | Mount Vernon | 619 |
| Lewis | 10,993 | Monticello | 508 |
| Lincoln | 18,041 | Troy | 625 |
| Linn | 15,125 | Linneus | 622 |
| Livingston | 15,368 | Chillicothe | 530 |
| McDonald | 12,357 | Pineville | 540 |
| Macon | 15,432 | Macon | 798 |
| Madison | 8,641 | Fredericktown | 496 |
| Maries | 6,851 | Vienna | 525 |
| Marion | 28,121 | Palmyra | 438 |
| Mercer | 4,910 | Princeton | 455 |
| Miller | 15,026 | Tuscumbia | 600 |
| Mississippi | 16,647 | Charleston | 415 |
| Moniteau | 10,742 | California | 419 |
| Monroe | 9,542 | Paris | 669 |
| Montgomery | 11,000 | Montgomery City | 534 |
| Morgan | 10,083 | Versailles | 592 |
| New Madrid | 23,420 | New Madrid | 679 |
| Newton | 32,981 | Neosho | 629 |
| Nodaway | 22,467 | Maryville | 877 |
| Oregon | 9,180 | Alton | 784 |
| Osage | 10,994 | Linn | 608 |
| Ozark | 6,226 | Gainesville | 732 |
| Pemiscot | 26,373 | Caruthersville | 493 |
| Perry | 14,393 | Perryville | 471 |
| Pettis | 34,137 | Sedalia | 679 |
| Phelps | 29,567 | Rolla | 677 |
| Pike | 16,928 | Bowling Green | 681 |
| Platte | 32,081 | Platte City | 427 |
| Polk | 15,415 | Bolivar | 637 |
| Pulaski | 53,967 | Waynesville | 551 |
| Putnam | 5,916 | Unionville | 518 |
| Ralls | 7,764 | New London | 478 |
| Randolph | 22,434 | Huntsville | 473 |
| Ray | 17,599 | Richmond | 573 |
| Reynolds | 6,106 | Centerville | 817 |
| Ripley | 9,803 | Doniphan | 639 |
| St. Charles | 92,954 | St. Charles | 551 |
| St. Clair | 7,667 | Osceola | 697 |
| St. Francis | 36,875 | Farmington | 457 |
| St. Louis | 951,671 | Clayton | 499 |
| Ste. Genevieve | 12,867 | Ste. Genevieve | 499 |
| Saline | 24,837 | Marshall | 757 |
| Schuyler | 4,665 | Lancaster | 306 |
| Scotland | 5,499 | Memphis | 441 |
| Scott | 33,250 | Benton | 421 |
| Shannon | 7,196 | Eminence | 999 |
| Shelby | 7,906 | Shelbyville | 501 |
| Stoddard | 25,771 | Bloomfield | 823 |
| Stone | 9,921 | Galena | 449 |
| Sullivan | 7,572 | Milan | 654 |
| Taney | 13,023 | Forsyth | 615 |
| Texas | 18,320 | Houston | 1,183 |
| Vernon | 19,065 | Nevada | 838 |
| Warren | 9,699 | Warrenton | 426 |
| Washington | 15,086 | Potosi | 760 |
| Wayne | 8,546 | Greenville | 766 |
| Webster | 15,562 | Marshfield | 590 |
| Worth | 3,359 | Grant City | 267 |
| Wright | 13,667 | Hartville | 684 |
| **Independent City** | | | |
| St. Louis | 623,236 | ..... | 61 |

## Montana

*(57 counties, 145,587 sq. mi. land; pop. 694,409)*

| County | Pop. Apr. 1 1970 | County seat or court house | Land area sq. mi. |
|---|---|---|---|
| Beaverhead | 8,187 | Dillon | 5,551 |
| Big Horn 1976 | 10,618 | Hardin | 5,023 |
| Blaine | 6,727 | Chinook | 4,275 |
| Broadwater | 2,526 | Townsend | 1,193 |
| Carbon | 7,080 | Red Lodge | 2,066 |
| Carter | 1,956 | Ekalaka | 3,313 |
| Cascade | 81,804 | Great Falls | 2,661 |
| Chouteau | 6,473 | Fort Benton | 3,927 |
| Custer 1976 | 12,979 | Miles City | 3,756 |
| Daniels | 3,083 | Scobey | 1,443 |
| Dawson 1977 | 11,387 | Glendive | 2,370 |
| Deer Lodge | 15,652 | Anaconda | 740 |
| Fallon | 4,050 | Baker | 1,633 |
| Fergus | 12,611 | Lewistown | 4,242 |
| Flathead | 39,460 | Kalispell | 5,137 |
| Gallatin | 32,505 | Bozeman | 2,517 |
| Garfield | 1,796 | Jordan | 4,455 |
| Glacier | 10,783 | Cut Bank | 2,964 |
| Golden Valley | 931 | Ryegate | 1,176 |
| Granite | 2,737 | Philipsburg | 1,733 |
| Hill | 17,358 | Havre | 2,927 |
| Jefferson | 5,238 | Boulder | 1,652 |
| Judith Basin | 2,667 | Stanford | 1,880 |
| Lake | 14,445 | Polson | 1,494 |
| Lewis & Clark | 33,281 | Helena | 3,476 |
| Liberty | 2,359 | Chester | 1,439 |
| Lincoln | 18,063 | Libby | 3,714 |
| McCone | 2,875 | Circle | 2,607 |
| Madison | 5,014 | Virginia City | 3,528 |
| Meagher | 2,122 | White Sulphur Springs | 2,354 |
| Mineral | 2,958 | Superior | 1,222 |
| Missoula | 58,263 | Missoula | 2,612 |
| Musselshell | 3,734 | Roundup | 1,887 |
| Park | 11,197 | Livingston | 2,626 |
| Petroleum | 675 | Winnett | 1,655 |
| Phillips | 5,386 | Malta | 5,213 |
| Pondera | 6,611 | Conrad | 1,645 |
| Powder River | 2,862 | Broadus | 3,288 |
| Powell | 6,660 | Deer Lodge | 2,336 |
| Prairie | 1,752 | Terry | 1,730 |
| Ravalli | 14,409 | Hamilton | 2,382 |
| Richland | 9,837 | Sidney | 2,079 |
| Roosevelt | 10,365 | Wolf Point | 2,385 |
| Rosebud, 1976 | 9,578 | Forsyth | 5,037 |
| Sanders | 7,093 | Thompson Falls | 2,778 |
| Sheridan | 5,779 | Plentywood | 1,694 |
| Silver Bow | 41,981 | Butte | 715 |
| Stillwater | 4,632 | Columbus | 1,794 |
| Sweet Grass | 2,980 | Big Timber | 1,840 |
| Teton | 6,116 | Choteau | 2,294 |
| Toole | 5,839 | Shelby | 1,950 |
| Treasure | 1,069 | Hysham | 985 |
| Valley | 11,471 | Glasgow | 4,974 |
| Wheatland | 2,529 | Harlowton | 1,420 |
| Wibaux | 1,465 | Wibaux | 890 |
| Yellowstone | 87,367 | Billings | 2,642 |
| Yellowstone Nat. Park | 64 | ..... | 269 |

| County | Pop. Apr. 1 1970 | County seat or court house | Land area sq. mi. |
|---|---|---|---|

## Nebraska

*(93 counties, 76,483 sq. mi. land; pop. 1,483,791)*

| County | Pop. Apr. 1 1970 | County seat or court house | Land area sq. mi. |
|---|---|---|---|
| Adams | 30,533 | Hastings | 562 |
| Antelope | 9,047 | Neligh | 853 |
| Arthur | 606 | Arthur | 704 |
| Banner | 1,034 | Harrisburg | 738 |
| Blaine | 847 | Brewster | 710 |
| Boone | 8,190 | Albion | 683 |
| Box Butte | 10,094 | Alliance | 1,065 |
| Boyd | 3,752 | Butte | 538 |
| Brown | 4,021 | Ainsworth | 1,216 |
| Buffalo | 31,222 | Kearney | 949 |
| Burt | 9,247 | Tekamah | 483 |
| Butler | 9,461 | David City | 582 |
| Cass | 18,076 | Plattsmouth | 555 |
| Cedar | 12,192 | Hartington | 742 |
| Chase | 4,129 | Imperial | 890 |
| Cherry | 6,846 | Valentine | 5,966 |
| Cheyenne | 10,778 | Sidney | 1,186 |
| Clay | 8,266 | Clay Center | 570 |
| Colfax | 9,498 | Schuyler | 406 |
| Cuming | 12,034 | West Point | 571 |
| Custer | 14,092 | Broken Bow | 2,558 |
| Dakota 1976 | 15,683 | Dakota City | 255 |
| Dawes | 9,761 | Chadron | 1,386 |
| Dawson | 19,771 | Lexington | 975 |
| Deuel | 2,717 | Chappell | 436 |
| Dixon | 7,453 | Ponca | 475 |
| Dodge | 34,782 | Fremont | 528 |
| Douglas | 389,455 | Omaha | 335 |
| Dundy | 2,926 | Benkelman | 921 |
| Fillmore | 8,137 | Geneva | 577 |
| Franklin | 4,566 | Franklin | 578 |
| Frontier | 3,982 | Stockville | 962 |
| Furnas | 6,897 | Beaver City | 722 |
| Gage | 25,731 | Beatrice | 858 |
| Garden | 2,929 | Oshkosh | 1,678 |
| Garfield | 2,411 | Burwell | 569 |
| Gosper | 2,178 | Elwood | 464 |
| Grant | 1,019 | Hyannis | 764 |
| Greeley | 4,000 | Greeley | 570 |
| Hall | 42,851 | Grand Island | 537 |
| Hamilton | 8,867 | Aurora | 537 |
| Harlan | 4,357 | Alma | 556 |
| Hayes | 1,530 | Hayes Center | 711 |
| Hitchcock | 4,051 | Trenton | 712 |
| Holt | 12,933 | O'Neil | 2,405 |
| Hooker | 939 | Mullen | 722 |
| Howard | 6,807 | Saint Paul | 564 |
| Jefferson | 10,436 | Fairbury | 577 |
| Johnson | 5,743 | Tecumseh | 377 |
| Kearney | 6,707 | Minden | 512 |
| Keith | 8,487 | Ogallala | 1,032 |
| Keya Paha | 1,340 | Springview | 768 |
| Kimball | 6,009 | Kimball | 953 |
| Knox | 11,723 | Center | 1,107 |
| Lancaster | 167,972 | Lincoln | 845 |
| Lincoln | 29,538 | North Platte | 2,522 |
| Logan | 991 | Stapleton | 570 |
| Loup | 854 | Taylor | 574 |
| McPherson | 623 | Tryon | 856 |
| Madison | 27,402 | Madison | 572 |
| Merrick | 8,751 | Central City | 480 |
| Morrill | 5,813 | Bridgeport | 1,402 |
| Nance | 5,142 | Fullerton | 439 |
| Nemaha | 8,976 | Auburn | 400 |
| Nuckolls | 7,404 | Nelson | 579 |
| Otoe | 15,576 | Nebraska City | 619 |
| Pawnee | 4,473 | Pawnee City | 433 |
| Perkins | 3,423 | Grant | 885 |
| Phelps | 9,553 | Holdrege | 544 |
| Pierce | 8,493 | Pierce | 573 |
| Platte | 26,544 | Columbus | 667 |
| Polk | 6,468 | Osceola | 432 |
| Red Willow | 12,191 | McCook | 686 |
| Richardson | 12,277 | Falls City | 550 |
| Rock | 2,231 | Bassett | 1,009 |
| Saline | 12,809 | Wilber | 575 |
| Sarpy 1974 | 73,479 | Papillion | 239 |
| Saunders | 17,108 | Wahoo | 759 |
| Scotts Bluff | 36,432 | Gering | 726 |
| Seward | 14,460 | Seward | 571 |
| Sheridan | 7,285 | Rushville | 2,462 |
| Sherman | 4,725 | Loup City | 567 |
| Sioux | 2,034 | Harrison | 2,063 |
| Stanton | 5,758 | Stanton | 431 |
| Thayer | 7,779 | Hebron | 577 |
| Thomas | 954 | Thedford | 716 |
| Thurston | 6,942 | Pender | 388 |
| Valley | 5,783 | Ord | 569 |
| Washington | 13,310 | Blair | 386 |
| Wayne | 10,400 | Wayne | 443 |
| Webster | 5,396 | Red Cloud | 575 |
| Wheeler | 1,051 | Bartlett | 576 |
| York | 13,685 | York | 577 |

## Nevada

*(16 cos., 1 ind. city, 109,889 sq. mi. land; pop. 488,738)*

| County | Pop. Apr. 1 1970 | County seat or court house | Land area sq. mi. |
|---|---|---|---|
| Churchill | 10,513 | Fallon | 4,883 |
| Clark | 273,288 | Las Vegas | 7,874 |
| Douglas | 6,882 | Minden | 703 |
| Elko | 13,958 | Elko | 17,162 |
| Esmeralda | 629 | Goldfield | 3,570 |
| Eureka | 948 | Eureka | 4,182 |
| Humboldt | 6,375 | Winnemucca | 9,702 |
| Lander | 2,666 | Austin | 5,621 |
| Lincoln | 2,557 | Pioche | 10,649 |
| Lyon | 8,221 | Yerington | 2,030 |
| Mineral | 7,051 | Hawthorne | 3,765 |
| Nye | 5,599 | Tonopah | 18,064 |
| Pershing | 2,670 | Lovelock | 6,001 |
| Storey | 695 | Virginia City | 262 |
| Washoe | 121,068 | Reno | 6,366 |
| White Pine | 10,150 | Ely | 8,904 |
| Independent City | | | |
| Carson City | 15,468 | Carson City | 150 |

## New Hampshire

*(10 counties, 9,027 sq. mi. land; pop. 737,681)*

| County | Pop. Apr. 1 1970 | County seat or court house | Land area sq. mi. |
|---|---|---|---|
| Belknap | 32,367 | Laconia | 400 |
| Carroll | 18,548 | Ossipee | 938 |
| Cheshire | 52,364 | Keene | 715 |
| Coos | 34,291 | Lancaster | 1,820 |
| Grafton | 54,914 | Woodsville | 1,732 |
| Hillsborough | 223,941 | Nashua | 887 |
| Merrimack | 80,925 | Concord | 930 |
| Rockingham | 138,951 | Exeter | 691 |
| Strafford | 70,431 | Dover | 376 |
| Sullivan | 30,949 | Newport | 539 |

## New Jersey

*(21 counties, 7,521 sq. mi. land; pop. 7,168,164)*

| County | Pop. Apr. 1 1970 | County seat or court house | Land area sq. mi. |
|---|---|---|---|
| Atlantic | 175,043 | Mays Landing | 569 |
| Bergen | 897,148 | Hackensack | 234 |
| Burlington | 323,132 | Mount Holly | 819 |
| Camden | 456,291 | Camden | 221 |
| Cape May | 59,554 | Cape May Court House | 267 |
| Cumberland | 121,374 | Bridgeton | 500 |
| Essex | 932,526 | Newark | 130 |
| Gloucester | 172,681 | Woodbury | 329 |
| Hudson | 607,839 | Jersey City | 47 |
| Hunterdon | 69,718 | Flemington | 423 |
| Mercer | 304,116 | Trenton | 228 |
| Middlesex | 583,813 | New Brunswick | 312 |
| Monmouth | 461,849 | Freehold | 476 |
| Morris | 383,454 | Morristown | 468 |
| Ocean | 208,470 | Toms River | 642 |
| Passaic | 460,782 | Paterson | 192 |
| Salem | 60,346 | Salem | 365 |
| Somerset | 198,372 | Somerville | 307 |
| Sussex | 77,528 | Newton | 527 |
| Union | 543,116 | Elizabeth | 103 |
| Warren | 73,960 | Belvidere | 362 |

## New Mexico

*(32 counties, 121,412 sq. mi. land; pop. 1,016,000)*

| County | Pop. Apr. 1 1970 | County seat or court house | Land area sq. mi. |
|---|---|---|---|
| Bernalillo | 315,774 | Albuquerque | 1,169 |
| Catron | 2,198 | Reserve | 6,897 |
| Chaves | 43,335 | Roswell | 6,084 |
| Colfax | 12,170 | Raton | 3,764 |
| Curry | 39,517 | Clovis | 1,403 |
| De Baca | 2,547 | Fort Sumner | 2,356 |
| Dona Ana | 69,773 | Las Cruces | 3,804 |
| Eddy | 41,119 | Carlsbad | 4,167 |
| Grant | 22,030 | Silver City | 3,970 |
| Guadalupe | 4,969 | Santa Rosa | 2,998 |
| Harding | 1,348 | Mosquero | 2,134 |
| Hidalgo | 4,734 | Lordsburg | 3,447 |
| Lea | 49,554 | Lovington | 4,393 |
| Lincoln | 7,560 | Carrizozo | 4,858 |
| Los Alamos | 15,198 | Los Alamos | 108 |
| Luna | 11,706 | Deming | 2,957 |
| McKinley | 43,208 | Gallup | 5,454 |
| Mora | 4,673 | Mora | 1,940 |
| Otero | 41,097 | Alamogordo | 6,638 |
| Quay | 10,903 | Tucumcari | 2,875 |
| Rio Arriba | 25,170 | Tierra Amarilla | 5,843 |
| Roosevelt | 16,479 | Portales | 2,454 |
| Sandoval | 17,492 | Bernalillo | 3,714 |
| San Juan | 52,517 | Aztec | 5,500 |
| San Miguel | 21,951 | Las Vegas | 4,741 |
| Santa Fe | 54,774 | Santa Fe | 1,902 |
| Sierra | 7,189 | Truth or Consequences | 4,166 |
| Socorro | 9,763 | Socorro | 6,603 |
| Taos | 17,516 | Taos | 2,256 |

| County | Pop. Apr. 1 1970 | County seat or court house | Land area sq. mi. |
|---|---|---|---|
| Torrance | 5,290 | Estancia | 3,346 |
| Union | 4,925 | Clayton | 3,816 |
| Valencia | 40,576 | Los Lunas | 5,656 |

## New York

(62 counties, 47,831 sq. mi. land; pop., 18,241,266)

| County | Pop. Apr. 1 1970 | County seat or court house | Land area sq. mi. |
|---|---|---|---|
| Albany | 286,742 | Albany | 526 |
| Allegany | 46,458 | Belmon | 1,047 |
| Bronx | 1,471,701 | Bronx | 41 |
| Broome | 221,815 | Binghamton | 714 |
| Cattaraugus | 81,666 | Little Valley | 1,318 |
| Cayuga | 77,439 | Auburn | 698 |
| Chautauqua | 147,305 | Mayville | 1,081 |
| Chemung | 101,537 | Elmira | 415 |
| Chenango | 46,368 | Norwich | 903 |
| Clinton | 72,934 | Plattsburgh | 1,059 |
| Columbia | 51,519 | Hudson | 645 |
| Cortland | 45,894 | Cortland | 502 |
| Delaware | 44,718 | Delhi | 1,443 |
| Dutchess | 222,295 | Poughkeepsie | 813 |
| Erie | 1,113,491 | Buffalo | 1,058 |
| Essex | 34,631 | Elizabethtown | 1,823 |
| Franklin | 43,931 | Malone | 1,674 |
| Fulton | 52,637 | Johnstown | 498 |
| Genesee | 58,722 | Batavia | 501 |
| Greene | 33,136 | Catskill | 653 |
| Hamilton | 4,714 | Lake Pleasant | 1,735 |
| Herkimer | 67,633 | Herkimer | 1,435 |
| Jefferson | 88,508 | Watertown | 1,294 |
| Kings | 2,602,012 | Brooklyn | 70 |
| Lewis | 23,644 | Lowville | 1,291 |
| Livingston | 54,041 | Geneseo | 638 |
| Madison | 62,864 | Wampsville | 661 |
| Monroe | 711,917 | Rochester | 675 |
| Montgomery | 55,883 | Fonda | 408 |
| Nassau | 1,428,838 | Mineola | 289 |
| New York | 1,539,233 | New York | 23 |
| Niagara | 235,720 | Lockport | 532 |
| Oneida | 273,037 | Utica | 1,223 |
| Onondaga | 472,835 | Syracuse | 794 |
| Ontario | 78,849 | Canandaigua | 651 |
| Orange | 221,657 | Goshen | 833 |
| Orleans | 37,305 | Albion | 396 |
| Oswego | 100,897 | Oswego | 964 |
| Otsego | 56,181 | Cooperstown | 1,013 |
| Putnam, 1975 | 68,765 | Carmel | 231 |
| Queens | 1,987,174 | Jamaica | 108 |
| Rensselaer | 152,510 | Troy | 665 |
| Richmond | 295,443 | Saint George | 58 |
| Rockland | 229,903 | New City | 176 |
| St. Lawrence | 112,309 | Canton | 2,768 |
| Saratoga | 121,764 | Ballston Spa | 818 |
| Schenectady | 161,078 | Schenectady | 207 |
| Schoharie | 24,750 | Schoharie | 624 |
| Schuyler | 16,737 | Watkins Glen | 330 |
| Seneca | 35,083 | Ovid & Waterloo | 330 |
| Steuben | 99,546 | Bath | 1,410 |
| Suffolk | 1,127,030 | Riverhead | 929 |
| Sullivan | 52,580 | Monticello | 980 |
| Tioga | 46,513 | Owego | 524 |
| Tompkins | 77,064 | Ithaca | 482 |
| Ulster | 141,241 | Kingston | 1,141 |
| Warren | 49,402 | Lake George | 887 |
| Washington | 52,725 | Hudson Falls | 836 |
| Wayne, 1975 | 82,194 | Lyons | 606 |
| Westchester | 894,406 | White Plains | 443 |
| Wyoming | 37,688 | Warsaw | 598 |
| Yates | 19,831 | Penn Yan | 343 |

## North Carolina

(100 counties, 48,798 sq. mi. land; pop., 5,082,059)

| County | Pop. Apr. 1 1970 | County seat or court house | Land area sq. mi. |
|---|---|---|---|
| Alamance | 96,362 | Graham | 428 |
| Alexander | 19,466 | Taylorsville | 259 |
| Alleghany | 8,134 | Sparta | 225 |
| Anson | 23,488 | Wadesboro | 533 |
| Ashe | 19,571 | Jefferson | 426 |
| Avery | 12,655 | Newland | 245 |
| Beaufort | 35,980 | Washington | 826 |
| Bertie | 20,528 | Windsor | 698 |
| Bladen | 26,477 | Elizabethtown | 883 |
| Brunswick | 24,223 | Southport | 856 |
| Buncombe | 145,056 | Asheville | 657 |
| Burke | 60,364 | Morganton | 511 |
| Cabarrus | 74,629 | Concord | 363 |
| Caldwell | 56,699 | Lenoir | 469 |
| Camden | 5,453 | Camden | 239 |
| Carteret | 31,603 | Beaufort | 536 |
| Caswell | 19,055 | Yanceyville | 428 |
| Catawba | 90,873 | Newton | 394 |
| Chatham | 29,554 | Pittsboro | 709 |
| Cherokee | 16,330 | Murphy | 452 |
| Chowan | 10,764 | Edenton | 173 |
| Clay | 5,180 | Hayesville | 209 |
| Cleveland | 72,556 | Shelby | 468 |
| Columbus | 46,937 | Whiteville | 945 |
| Craven | 62,554 | New Bern | 699 |
| Cumberland | 212,042 | Fayetteville | 654 |
| Currituck | 6,976 | Currituck | 246 |
| Dare | 6,995 | Manteo | 391 |
| Davidson | 95,627 | Lexington | 549 |
| Davie | 18,855 | Mocksville | 265 |
| Duplin | 38,015 | Kenansville | 815 |
| Durham | 132,681 | Durham | 295 |
| Edgecombe | 52,341 | Tarboro | 510 |
| Forsyth | 215,118 | Winston-Salem | 419 |
| Franklin | 26,820 | Louisburg | 491 |
| Gaston | 148,415 | Gastonia | 356 |
| Gates | 8,524 | Gatesville | 337 |
| Graham | 6,562 | Robbinsville | 292 |
| Granville | 32,762 | Oxford | 537 |
| Greene | 14,967 | Snow Hill | 267 |
| Guilford | 288,645 | Greensboro | 655 |
| Halifax | 53,884 | Halifax | 734 |
| Harnett | 49,667 | Lillington | 603 |
| Haywood | 41,710 | Waynesville | 551 |
| Henderson | 42,804 | Hendersonville | 378 |
| Hertford | 23,529 | Winton | 353 |
| Hoke | 16,436 | Raeford | 389 |
| Hyde | 5,571 | Swanquarter | 613 |
| Iredell | 72,197 | Statesville | 572 |
| Jackson | 21,593 | Sylva | 491 |
| Johnston | 61,737 | Smithfield | 797 |
| Jones | 9,779 | Trenton | 467 |
| Lee | 30,467 | Sanford | 256 |
| Lenoir | 55,204 | Kinston | 400 |
| Lincoln | 32,682 | Lincolnton | 297 |
| McDowell | 30,648 | Marion | 436 |
| Macon | 15,788 | Franklin | 513 |
| Madison | 16,003 | Marshall | 450 |
| Martin | 24,730 | Williamston | 455 |
| Mecklenburg | 354,656 | Charlotte | 530 |
| Mitchell | 13,447 | Bakersville | 215 |
| Montgomery | 19,267 | Troy | 488 |
| Moore | 39,048 | Carthage | 704 |
| Nash | 59,122 | Nashville | 544 |
| New Hanover | 82,996 | Wilmington | 185 |
| Northampton | 24,009 | Jackson | 536 |
| Onslow | 103,126 | Jacksonville | 765 |
| Orange | 57,707 | Hillsboro | 400 |
| Pamlico | 9,467 | Bayboro | 338 |
| Pasquotank | 26,824 | Elizabeth City | 228 |
| Pender | 18,149 | Burgaw | 871 |
| Perquimans | 8,351 | Hertford | 246 |
| Person | 25,914 | Roxboro | 401 |
| Pitt | 73,900 | Greenville | 655 |
| Polk | 11,735 | Columbus | 239 |
| Randolph | 76,358 | Asheboro | 798 |
| Richmond | 39,889 | Rockingham | 475 |
| Robeson | 84,842 | Lumberton | 949 |
| Rockingham | 72,402 | Wentworth | 569 |
| Rowan | 90,035 | Salisbury | 523 |
| Rutherford | 47,337 | Rutherfordton | 563 |
| Sampson | 44,954 | Clinton | 945 |
| Scotland | 26,929 | Laurinburg | 319 |
| Stanly | 42,822 | Albemarle | 398 |
| Stokes | 23,782 | Danbury | 457 |
| Surry | 51,415 | Dobson | 536 |
| Swain | 8,835 | Bryson City | 524 |
| Transylvania | 19,713 | Brevard | 382 |
| Tyrrell | 3,806 | Columbia | 390 |
| Union | 54,714 | Monroe | 639 |
| Vance | 32,691 | Henderson | 249 |
| Wake | 229,006 | Raleigh | 858 |
| Warren | 15,810 | Warrenton | 424 |
| Washington | 14,038 | Plymouth | 343 |
| Watauga | 23,404 | Boone | 317 |
| Wayne | 85,408 | Goldsboro | 557 |
| Wilkes | 49,524 | Wilkesboro | 757 |
| Wilson | 57,486 | Wilson | 375 |
| Yadkin | 24,599 | Yadkinville | 336 |
| Yancey | 12,629 | Burnsville | 312 |

## North Dakota

(53 counties, 69,273 sq. mi. land; pop., 617,761)

| County | Pop. Apr. 1 1970 | County seat or court house | Land area sq. mi. |
|---|---|---|---|
| Adams | 3,832 | Hettinger | 989 |
| Barnes | 14,669 | Valley City | 1,479 |
| Benson | 8,245 | Minnewaukan | 1,403 |
| Billings | 1,198 | Medora | 1,139 |
| Bottineau | 9,496 | Bottineau | 1,677 |
| Bowman | 3,901 | Bowman | 1,170 |
| Burke | 4,739 | Bowbells | 1,119 |
| Burleigh, 1975 | 46,079 | Bismarck | 1,625 |
| Cass | 73,653 | Fargo | 1,749 |
| Cavalier 1973 | 10,971 | Langdon | 1,512 |
| Dickey | 6,976 | Ellendale | 1,143 |
| Divide | 4,564 | Crosby | 1,300 |

| County | Pop. Apr. 1 1970 | County seat or court house | Land area sq. mi. |
|---|---|---|---|
| Dunn | 4,895 | Manning | 1,992 |
| Eddy | 4,103 | New Rockford | 635 |
| Emmons | 7,200 | Linton | 1,503 |
| Foster | 4,832 | Carrington | 645 |
| Golden Valley | 2,611 | Beach | 1,014 |
| Grand Forks | 61,102 | Grand Forks | 1,438 |
| Grant | 5,009 | Carson | 1,666 |
| Griggs | 4,184 | Cooperstown | 710 |
| Hettinger | 5,075 | Mott | 1,134 |
| Kidder | 4,362 | Steele | 1,358 |
| La Moure | 7,117 | La Moure | 1,136 |
| Logan | 4,245 | Napoleon | 1,001 |
| McHenry | 8,977 | Towner | 1,879 |
| McIntosh | 5,545 | Ashley | 992 |
| McKenzie | 6,127 | Watford City | 2,735 |
| McLean | 11,251 | Washburn | 2,065 |
| Mercer | 6,175 | Stanton | 1,042 |
| Morton | 20,310 | Mandan | 1,920 |
| Mountrail | 8,437 | Stanley | 1,819 |
| Nelson | 5,807 | Lakota | 995 |
| Oliver | 2,322 | Center | 721 |
| Pembina | 10,728 | Cavalier | 1,124 |
| Pierce | 6,323 | Rugby | 1,038 |
| Ramsey | 12,915 | Devils Lake | 1,248 |
| Ransom | 7,102 | Lisbon | 861 |
| Renville | 3,828 | Mohall | 886 |
| Richland | 18,089 | Wahpeton | 1,449 |
| Rolette | 11,549 | Rolla | 913 |
| Sargent | 5,937 | Forman | 853 |
| Sheridan | 3,232 | McClusky | 989 |
| Sioux | 3,632 | Fort Yates | 1,103 |
| Slope | 1,484 | Amidon | 1,225 |
| Stark | 19,613 | Dickinson | 1,316 |
| Steele | 3,749 | Finley | 710 |
| Stutsman | 23,550 | Jamestown | 2,264 |
| Towner | 4,645 | Cando | 1,043 |
| Traill | 9,571 | Hillsboro | 861 |
| Walsh | 16,251 | Grafton | 1,286 |
| Ward | 58,560 | Minot | 2,044 |
| Wells | 7,847 | Fessenden | 1,299 |
| Williams | 19,301 | Williston | 2,064 |

## Ohio

*(88 counties, 40,975 sq. mi. land; pop., 10,652,017)*

| County | Pop. Apr. 1 1970 | County seat or court house | Land area sq. mi. |
|---|---|---|---|
| Adams | 18,957 | West Union | 587 |
| Allen | 111,144 | Lima | 410 |
| Ashland | 43,303 | Ashland | 424 |
| Ashtabula | 98,237 | Jefferson | 700 |
| Athens | 55,747 | Athens | 504 |
| Auglaize | 38,602 | Wapakoneta | 400 |
| Belmont | 80,917 | Saint Clairsville | 534 |
| Brown | 26,635 | Georgetown | 490 |
| Butler | 226,207 | Hamilton | 471 |
| Carroll | 21,579 | Carrollton | 390 |
| Champaign | 30,491 | Urbana | 432 |
| Clark | 157,115 | Springfield | 402 |
| Clermont | 95,887 | Batavia | 458 |
| Clinton | 31,464 | Wilmington | 410 |
| Columbiana | 108,310 | Lisbon | 534 |
| Coshocton | 33,486 | Coshocton | 562 |
| Crawford | 50,364 | Bucyrus | 404 |
| Cuyahoga | 1,720,835 | Cleveland | 456 |
| Darke | 49,141 | Greenville | 605 |
| Defiance | 36,949 | Defiance | 412 |
| Delaware | 42,908 | Delaware | 450 |
| Erie | 75,909 | Sandusky | 264 |
| Fairfield | 73,301 | Lancaster | 505 |
| Fayette | 25,461 | Washington C. H. | 404 |
| Franklin | 833,249 | Columbus | 538 |
| Fulton | 33,071 | Wauseon | 407 |
| Gallia | 25,239 | Gallipolis | 471 |
| Geauga | 62,977 | Chardon | 407 |
| Greene | 125,057 | Xenia | 415 |
| Guernsey | 37,665 | Cambridge | 528 |
| Hamilton | 923,205 | Cincinnati | 414 |
| Hancock | 61,217 | Findlay | 532 |
| Hardin | 30,813 | Kenton | 467 |
| Harrison | 17,013 | Cadiz | 401 |
| Henry | 27,058 | Napoleon | 416 |
| Highland | 28,996 | Hillsboro | 549 |
| Hocking | 20,322 | Logan | 421 |
| Holmes | 23,024 | Millersburg | 424 |
| Huron | 49,587 | Norwalk | 497 |
| Jackson | 27,174 | Jackson | 419 |
| Jefferson | 96,193 | Steubenville | 411 |
| Knox | 41,795 | Mount Vernon | 531 |
| Lake | 197,200 | Painesville | 231 |
| Lawrence | 56,868 | Ironton | 456 |
| Licking | 107,799 | Newark | 686 |
| Logan | 35,072 | Bellefontaine | 460 |
| Lorain | 256,843 | Elyria | 495 |
| Lucas | 483,594 | Toledo | 343 |
| Madison | 23,318 | London | 463 |
| Mahoning | 304,545 | Youngstown | 415 |
| Marion | 64,724 | Marion | 405 |
| Medina | 82,717 | Medina | 425 |
| Meigs | 19,799 | Pomeroy | 436 |
| Mercer | 35,558 | Celina | 444 |
| Miami | 84,342 | Troy | 407 |
| Monroe | 15,739 | Woodsfield | 456 |
| Montgomery | 608,413 | Dayton | 459 |
| Morgan | 12,375 | McConnelsville | 420 |
| Morrow | 21,348 | Mount Gilead | 403 |
| Muskingum | 77,826 | Zanesville | 651 |
| Noble | 10,428 | Caldwell | 398 |
| Ottawa | 37,099 | Port Clinton | 261 |
| Paulding | 19,329 | Paulding | 417 |
| Perry | 27,434 | New Lexington | 410 |
| Pickaway | 40,071 | Circleville | 504 |
| Pike | 19,114 | Waverly | 443 |
| Portage | 125,868 | Ravenna | 495 |
| Preble | 34,719 | Eaton | 427 |
| Putnam | 31,134 | Ottawa | 486 |
| Richland | 129,997 | Mansfield | 496 |
| Ross | 61,211 | Chillicothe | 687 |
| Sandusky | 60,983 | Fremont | 409 |
| Scioto | 76,951 | Portsmouth | 608 |
| Seneca | 60,696 | Tiffin | 551 |
| Shelby | 37,748 | Sidney | 408 |
| Stark | 372,210 | Canton | 576 |
| Summit | 553,371 | Akron | 408 |
| Trumbull | 232,579 | Warren | 608 |
| Tuscarawas | 77,211 | New Philadelphia | 569 |
| Union | 23,786 | Marysville | 434 |
| Van Wert | 29,194 | Van Wert | 409 |
| Vinton | 9,420 | McArthur | 411 |
| Warren | 85,505 | Lebanon | 408 |
| Washington | 57,160 | Marietta | 641 |
| Wayne | 87,123 | Wooster | 561 |
| Williams | 33,669 | Bryan | 421 |
| Wood | 89,722 | Bowling Green | 619 |
| Wyandot | 21,826 | Upper Sandusky | 406 |

## Oklahoma

*(77 counties, 68,782 sq. mi. land; pop., 2,559,253)*

| County | Pop. Apr. 1 1970 | County seat or court house | Land area sq. mi. |
|---|---|---|---|
| Adair | 15,141 | Stillwell | 570 |
| Alfalfa | 7,224 | Cherokee | 868 |
| Atoka | 10,972 | Atoka | 991 |
| Beaver | 6,282 | Beaver | 1,790 |
| Beckham | 15,754 | Sayre | 907 |
| Blaine | 11,794 | Watonga | 917 |
| Bryan | 25,552 | Durant | 889 |
| Caddo | 28,931 | Anadarko | 1,272 |
| Canadian | 32,245 | El Reno | 897 |
| Carter | 37,349 | Ardmore | 830 |
| Cherokee | 23,174 | Tahlequah | 756 |
| Choctaw | 15,141 | Hugo | 778 |
| Cimarron | 4,145 | Boise City | 1,843 |
| Cleveland | 81,839 | Norman | 527 |
| Coal | 5,525 | Coalgate | 526 |
| Comanche | 108,144 | Lawton | 1,084 |
| Cotton | 6,832 | Walters | 651 |
| Craig | 14,722 | Vinita | 764 |
| Creek | 45,532 | Sapulpa | 936 |
| Custer | 22,665 | Arapaho | 980 |
| Delaware | 17,767 | Jay | 707 |
| Dewey | 5,656 | Taloga | 1,018 |
| Ellis | 5,129 | Arnett | 1,242 |
| Garfield | 56,343 | Enid | 1,054 |
| Garvin | 24,874 | Pauls Valley | 814 |
| Grady | 29,354 | Chickasha | 1,096 |
| Grant | 7,117 | Medford | 1,007 |
| Greer | 7,979 | Mangum | 633 |
| Harmon | 5,136 | Hollis | 545 |
| Harper | 5,151 | Buffalo | 1,041 |
| Haskell | 9,578 | Stigler | 602 |
| Hughes | 13,228 | Holdenville | 807 |
| Jackson | 30,902 | Altus | 810 |
| Jefferson | 7,125 | Waurika | 780 |
| Johnston | 7,870 | Tishomingo | 638 |
| Kay | 48,791 | Newkirk | 950 |
| Kingfisher | 12,857 | Kingfisher | 904 |
| Kiowa | 12,532 | Hobart | 1,027 |
| Latimer | 8,601 | Wilburton | 737 |
| Le Flore | 32,137 | Poteau | 1,560 |
| Lincoln | 19,482 | Chandler | 973 |
| Logan | 19,645 | Guthrie | 751 |
| Love | 5,637 | Marietta | 513 |
| McClain | 14,157 | Purcell | 573 |
| McCurtain | 28,642 | Idabel | 1,800 |
| McIntosh | 12,472 | Eufaula | 608 |
| Major | 7,529 | Fairview | 963 |
| Marshall | 7,682 | Madill | 366 |
| Mayes | 23,302 | Pryor | 648 |
| Murray | 10,669 | Sulphur | 423 |
| Muskogee | 59,542 | Muskogee | 818 |
| Noble | 10,043 | Perry | 743 |
| Nowata | 9,773 | Nowata | 537 |
| Okfuskee | 10,683 | Okemah | 637 |
| Oklahoma | 527,717 | Oklahoma City | 700 |

| County | Pop. Apr. 1 1970 | County seat or court house | Land area sq. mi. |
|---|---|---|---|
| Okmulgee | 35,358 | Okmulgee | 700 |
| Osage | 29,750 | Pawhuska | 2,272 |
| Ottawa | 29,800 | Miami | 464 |
| Pawnee | 11,338 | Pawnee | 61 |
| Payne | 50,654 | Stillwater | 694 |
| Pittsburg | 37,521 | McAlester | 1,241 |
| Pontotoc | 27,867 | Ada | 714 |
| Pottawatomie | 43,134 | Shawnee | 794 |
| Pushmataha | 9,385 | Antlers | 1,420 |
| Roger Mills | 4,452 | Cheyenne | 1,140 |
| Rogers | 28,425 | Claremore | 685 |
| Seminole | 25,144 | Wewoka | 630 |
| Sequoyah | 23,370 | Sallisaw | 696 |
| Stephens | 35,902 | Duncan | 891 |
| Texas | 16,352 | Guymon | 2,062 |
| Tillman | 12,901 | Frederick | 901 |
| Tulsa | 399,982 | Tulsa | 573 |
| Wagoner | 22,163 | Wagoner | 563 |
| Washington | 42,302 | Bartlesville | 424 |
| Washita | 12,141 | Cordell | 1,009 |
| Woods | 11,920 | Alva | 1,298 |
| Woodward | 15,537 | Woodward | 1,251 |

## Oregon

*(36 counties, 96,184 sq. mi. land; pop., 2,091,385)*

| County | Pop. Apr. 1 1970 | County seat or court house | Land area sq. mi. |
|---|---|---|---|
| Baker | 14,919 | Baker | 3,068 |
| Benton | 53,776 | Corvallis | 668 |
| Clackamas | 166,088 | Oregon City | 1,884 |
| Clatsop | 28,473 | Astoria | 805 |
| Columbia | 28,790 | Saint Helens | 639 |
| Coos | 56,515 | Coquille | 1,604 |
| Crook | 9,985 | Prineville | 2,975 |
| Curry | 13,006 | Gold Beach | 1,627 |
| Deschutes | 30,442 | Bend | 3,031 |
| Douglas | 71,743 | Roseburg | 5,063 |
| Gilliam | 2,342 | Condon | 1,208 |
| Grant | 6,996 | Canyon City | 4,530 |
| Harney | 7,215 | Burns | 10,166 |
| Hood River | 13,187 | Hood River | 523 |
| Jackson | 94,533 | Medford | 2,812 |
| Jefferson | 8,548 | Madras | 1,793 |
| Josephine | 35,746 | Grants Pass | 1,625 |
| Klamath | 50,021 | Klamath Falls | 5,970 |
| Lake | 6,343 | Lakeview | 8,231 |
| Lane | 215,401 | Eugene | 4,552 |
| Lincoln | 25,755 | Newport | 986 |
| Linn | 71,914 | Albany | 2,283 |
| Malheur | 23,169 | Vale | 9,858 |
| Marion | 151,309 | Salem | 1,166 |
| Morrow | 4,465 | Heppner | 2,060 |
| Multnomah | 554,668 | Portland | 423 |
| Polk | 35,349 | Dallas | 736 |
| Sherman | 2,139 | Moro | 830 |
| Tillamook | 18,034 | Tillamook | 1,115 |
| Umatilla | 44,923 | Pendleton | 3,227 |
| Union | 19,377 | La Grande | 2,032 |
| Wallowa | 6,247 | Enterprise | 3,178 |
| Wasco | 20,133 | The Dalles | 2,381 |
| Washington | 157,920 | Hillsboro | 716 |
| Wheeler | 1,849 | Fossil | 1,707 |
| Yamhill | 40,213 | McMinnville | 711 |

## Pennsylvania

*(67 counties, 44,966 sq. mi. land; pop., 11,793,909)*

| County | Pop. Apr. 1 1970 | County seat or court house | Land area sq. mi. |
|---|---|---|---|
| Adams | 56,937 | Gettysburg | 526 |
| Allegheny | 1,605,133 | Pittsburgh | 728 |
| Armstrong | 75,590 | Kittanning | 652 |
| Beaver | 208,418 | Beaver | 440 |
| Bedford (1973) | 43,278 | Bedford | 1,018 |
| Berks | 296,382 | Reading | 862 |
| Blair | 135,356 | Hollidaysburg | 530 |
| Bradford | 57,962 | Towanda | 1,148 |
| Bucks | 416,728 | Doylestown | 614 |
| Butler | 127,941 | Butler | 794 |
| Cambria | 186,785 | Ebensburg | 692 |
| Cameron | 7,096 | Emporium | 401 |
| Carbon | 50,573 | Jim Thorpe | 404 |
| Centre | 99,267 | Bellefonte | 1,115 |
| Chester | 277,746 | West Chester | 761 |
| Clarion | 38,414 | Clarion | 597 |
| Clearfield | 74,619 | Clearfield | 1,139 |
| Clinton | 37,721 | Lock Haven | 899 |
| Columbia | 55,114 | Bloomsburg | 484 |
| Crawford | 81,342 | Meadville | 1,012 |
| Cumberland | 158,177 | Carlisle | 555 |
| Dauphin | 223,713 | Harrisburg | 518 |
| Delaware | 601,715 | Media | 184 |
| Elk | 37,770 | Ridgeway | 807 |
| Erie | 263,654 | Erie | 813 |
| Fayette | 154,667 | Uniontown | 802 |
| Forest | 4,926 | Tionesta | 419 |
| Franklin | 100,833 | Chambersburg | 754 |
| Fulton | 10,776 | McConnellsburg | 435 |

| County | Pop. Apr. 1 1970 | County seat or court house | Land area sq. mi. |
|---|---|---|---|
| Greene | 36,090 | Waynesburg | 578 |
| Huntingdon | 39,108 | Huntingdon | 895 |
| Indiana | 79,451 | Indiana | 825 |
| Jefferson | 43,695 | Brookville | 652 |
| Juniata | 16,712 | Mifflintown | 386 |
| Lackawanna | 234,107 | Scranton | 454 |
| Lancaster | 320,079 | Lancaster | 946 |
| Lawrence | 107,374 | New Castle | 367 |
| Lebanon | 99,665 | Lebanon | 363 |
| Lehigh | 255,304 | Allentown | 348 |
| Luzerne | 342,329 | Wilkes-Barre | 886 |
| Lycoming | 113,296 | Williamsport | 1,216 |
| McKean | 51,915 | Smethport | 992 |
| Mercer | 127,225 | Mercer | 670 |
| Mifflin | 45,268 | Lewistown | 431 |
| Monroe | 45,422 | Stroudsburg | 611 |
| Montgomery | 623,956 | Norristown | 496 |
| Montour | 16,508 | Danville | 130 |
| Northampton | 214,545 | Easton | 376 |
| Northumberland | 99,190 | Sunbury | 453 |
| Perry | 28,615 | New Bloomfield | 551 |
| Philadelphia | 1,949,996 | Philadelphia | 129 |
| Pike | 11,818 | Milford | 542 |
| Potter | 16,395 | Coudersport | 1,092 |
| Schuylkill | 160,089 | Pottsville | 784 |
| Snyder | 29,269 | Middleburg | 327 |
| Somerset | 76,037 | Somerset | 1,078 |
| Sullivan | 5,961 | Laporte | 478 |
| Susquehanna | 34,344 | Montrose | 833 |
| Tioga | 39,691 | Wellsboro | 1,146 |
| Union | 28,603 | Lewisburg | 318 |
| Venango | 62,353 | Franklin | 678 |
| Warren | 47,682 | Warren | 905 |
| Washington | 210,876 | Washington | 857 |
| Wayne | 29,581 | Honesdale | 741 |
| Westmoreland | 376,935 | Greensburg | 1,024 |
| Wyoming | 19,082 | Tunkhannock | 398 |
| York | 272,603 | York | 909 |

## Rhode Island

*(5 counties, 1,049 sq. mi. land; pop., 949,723)*

| County | Pop. Apr. 1 1970 | County seat or court house | Land area sq. mi. |
|---|---|---|---|
| Bristol | 45,937 | Bristol | 25 |
| Kent | 142,382 | East Greenwich | 173 |
| Newport | 94,228 | Newport | 115 |
| Providence | 581,470 | Providence | 416 |
| Washington | 85,706 | West Kingston | 321 |

## South Carolina

*(46 counties, 30,225 sq. mi. land; pop., 2,590,516)*

| County | Pop. Apr. 1 1970 | County seat or court house | Land area sq. mi. |
|---|---|---|---|
| Abbeville | 21,112 | Abbeville | 506 |
| Aiken | 91,023 | Aiken | 1,087 |
| Allendale | 9,783 | Allendale | 418 |
| Anderson | 105,474 | Anderson | 749 |
| Bamberg | 15,950 | Bamberg | 395 |
| Barnwell | 17,176 | Barnwell | 553 |
| Beaufort | 51,136 | Beaufort | 579 |
| Berkeley | 56,199 | Moncks Corner | 1,110 |
| Calhoun | 10,780 | Saint Matthews | 377 |
| Charleston | 247,650 | Charleston | 939 |
| Cherokee | 36,791 | Gaffney | 394 |
| Chester | 29,811 | Chester | 584 |
| Chesterfield | 33,667 | Chesterfield | 790 |
| Clarendon | 25,604 | Manning | 599 |
| Colleton | 27,622 | Walterboro | 1,049 |
| Darlington | 53,442 | Darlington | 543 |
| Dillon | 28,838 | Dillon | 407 |
| Dorchester | 32,276 | Saint George | 569 |
| Edgefield | 15,692 | Edgefield | 482 |
| Fairfield | 19,999 | Winnsboro | 696 |
| Florence | 89,636 | Florence | 805 |
| Georgetown | 33,500 | Georgetown | 812 |
| Greenville | 240,774 | Greenville | 792 |
| Greenwood | 49,686 | Greenwood | 446 |
| Hampton | 15,878 | Hampton | 562 |
| Horry | 69,992 | Conway | 1,154 |
| Jasper | 11,885 | Ridgeland | 652 |
| Kershaw | 34,727 | Camden | 781 |
| Lancaster | 43,328 | Lancaster | 502 |
| Laurens | 49,713 | Laurens | 711 |
| Lee | 18,323 | Bishopville | 409 |
| Lexington | 89,012 | Lexington | 717 |
| McCormick | 7,955 | McCormick | 360 |
| Marion | 30,270 | Marion | 491 |
| Marlboro | 27,151 | Bennettsville | 483 |
| Newberry | 29,273 | Newberry | 635 |
| Oconee | 40,728 | Walhalla | 654 |
| Orangeburg | 69,789 | Orangeburg | 1,106 |
| Pickens | 58,956 | Pickens | 492 |
| Richland | 233,868 | Columbia | 748 |
| Saluda | 14,528 | Saluda | 458 |
| Spartanburg | 173,724 | Spartanburg | 831 |
| Sumter | 79,425 | Sumter | 672 |
| Union | 29,230 | Union | 514 |

| County | Pop. Apr. 1 1970 | County seat or court house | Land area sq. mi. |
|---|---|---|---|
| Williamsburg | 34,243 | Kingstree | 935 |
| York | 85,216 | York | 684 |

## South Dakota

*(67 counties, 75,955 sq. mi. land; pop., 666,257)*

| County | Pop. Apr. 1 1970 | County seat or court house | Land area sq. mi. |
|---|---|---|---|
| Aurora | 4,183 | Plankinton | 709 |
| Beadle | 20,877 | Huron | 1,259 |
| Bennett | 3,088 | Martin | 1,181 |
| Bon Homme | 8,577 | Tyndall | 560 |
| Brookings | 22,158 | Brookings | 800 |
| Brown | 36,920 | Aberdeen | 1,674 |
| Brule | 5,870 | Chamberlain | 818 |
| Buffalo | 1,739 | Gannvalley | 482 |
| Butte | 7,825 | Belle Fourche | 2,250 |
| Campbell | 2,866 | Mound City | 732 |
| Charles Mix | 9,994 | Lake Andes | 1,097 |
| Clark | 5,515 | Clark | 964 |
| Clay | 12,923 | Vermillion | 405 |
| Codington | 19,140 | Watertown | 687 |
| Corson | 4,994 | McIntosh | 2,470 |
| Custer | 4,698 | Custer | 1,557 |
| Davison | 17,319 | Mitchell | 432 |
| Day | 8,713 | Webster | 1,036 |
| Deuel | 5,686 | Clear Lake | 639 |
| Dewey | 5,170 | Timber Lake | 2,351 |
| Douglas | 4,569 | Armour | 435 |
| Edmunds | 5,548 | Ipswich | 1,154 |
| Fall River | 7,505 | Hot Springs | 1,743 |
| Faulk | 3,893 | Faulkton | 996 |
| Grant | 9,005 | Milbank | 681 |
| Gregory | 6,710 | Burke | 997 |
| Haakon | 2,802 | Philip | 1,816 |
| Hamlin | 5,520 | Hayti | 511 |
| Hand | 5,883 | Miller | 1,432 |
| Hanson | 3,781 | Alexandria | 430 |
| Harding | 1,855 | Buffalo | 2,682 |
| Hughes | 11,632 | Pierre | 748 |
| Hutchinson | 10,379 | Olivet | 815 |
| Hyde | 2,515 | Highmore | 863 |
| Jackson | 1,531 | Kadoka | 808 |
| Jerauld | 3,310 | Wessington Spgs | 527 |
| Jones | 1,882 | Murdo | 973 |
| Kingsbury | 7,657 | De Smet | 818 |
| Lake | 11,456 | Madison | 567 |
| Lawrence | 17,453 | Deadwood | 800 |
| Lincoln | 11,761 | Canton | 576 |
| Lyman | 4,060 | Kennebec | 1,683 |
| McCook | 7,246 | Salem | 575 |
| McPherson | 5,022 | Leola | 1,147 |
| Marshall | 5,965 | Britton | 848 |
| Meade | 17,020 | Sturgis | 3,465 |
| Mellette | 2,420 | White River | 1,306 |
| Miner | 4,454 | Howard | 570 |
| Minnehaha | 95,209 | Sioux Falls | 813 |
| Moody | 7,622 | Flandreau | 523 |
| Pennington | 59,349 | Rapid City | 2,779 |
| Perkins | 4,769 | Bison | 2,860 |
| Potter | 4,449 | Gettysburg | 869 |
| Roberts | 11,678 | Sisseton | 1,108 |
| Sanborn | 3,697 | Woonsocket | 570 |
| Shannon | 8,198 | (Attached to Fall River) | 2,100 |
| Spink | 10,595 | Redfield | 1,505 |
| Stanley | 2,457 | Fort Pierre | 1,414 |
| Sully | 2,362 | Onida | 1,004 |
| Todd | 6,606 | (Attached to Tripp) | 1,388 |
| Tripp | 8,171 | Winner | 1,620 |
| Turner | 9,872 | Parker | 612 |
| Union | 9,643 | Elk Point | 452 |
| Walworth | 7,842 | Selby | 718 |
| Washabaugh | 1,389 | (Attached to Jackson) | 1,061 |
| Yankton | 19,039 | Yankton | 519 |
| Zeibach | 2,221 | Dupree | 1,981 |

## Tennessee

*(95 counties, 41,328 sq. mi. land; pop., 3,924,164)*

| County | Pop. Apr. 1 1970 | County seat or court house | Land area sq. mi. |
|---|---|---|---|
| Anderson | 60,300 | Clinton | 335 |
| Bedford | 25,039 | Shelbyville | 482 |
| Benton | 12,126 | Camden | 392 |
| Bledsoe | 7,643 | Pikeville | 404 |
| Blount | 63,744 | Maryville | 575 |
| Bradley | 50,686 | Cleveland | 334 |
| Campbell | 26,045 | Jacksboro | 451 |
| Cannon | 8,467 | Woodbury | 271 |
| Carroll | 25,741 | Huntingdon | 596 |
| Carter | 42,259 | Elizabethton | 348 |
| Cheatham | 13,199 | Ashland City | 305 |
| Chester | 9,927 | Henderson | 285 |
| Claiborne | 19,420 | Tazewell | 444 |
| Clay | 6,624 | Celina | 233 |
| Cocke | 25,283 | Newport | 424 |
| Coffee | 32,572 | Manchester | 434 |

| County | Pop. Apr. 1 1970 | County seat or court house | Land area sq. mi. |
|---|---|---|---|
| Crockett | 14,402 | Alamo | 269 |
| Cumberland | 20,733 | Crossville | 678 |
| Davidson | 447,877 | Nashville | 508 |
| Decatur | 9,457 | Decaturville | 337 |
| De Kalb | 11,151 | Smithville | 278 |
| Dickson | 21,977 | Charlotte | 485 |
| Dyer | 30,427 | Dyersburg | 529 |
| Fayette | 22,692 | Somerville | 704 |
| Fentress | 12,593 | Jamestown | 498 |
| Franklin | 27,289 | Winchester | 553 |
| Gibson | 47,871 | Trenton | 607 |
| Giles | 22,138 | Pulaski | 619 |
| Grainger | 13,948 | Rutledge | 282 |
| Greene | 47,630 | Greeneville | 613 |
| Grundy | 10,631 | Altamont | 358 |
| Hamblen | 38,696 | Morristown | 155 |
| Hamilton | 255,077 | Chattanooga | 550 |
| Hancock | 6,719 | Sneedville | 230 |
| Hardeman | 22,435 | Bolivar | 656 |
| Hardin | 18,212 | Savannah | 587 |
| Hawkins | 33,757 | Rogersville | 480 |
| Haywood | 19,596 | Brownsville | 519 |
| Henderson | 17,360 | Lexington | 515 |
| Henry | 23,749 | Paris | 567 |
| Hickman | 12,096 | Centerville | 610 |
| Houston | 5,853 | Erin | 201 |
| Humphreys | 13,560 | Waverly | 530 |
| Jackson | 8,141 | Gainesboro | 323 |
| Jefferson | 24,940 | Dandridge | 274 |
| Johnson | 11,569 | Mountain City | 293 |
| Knox | 276,293 | Knoxville | 508 |
| Lake | 8,074 | Tiptonville | 167 |
| Lauderdale | 20,271 | Ripley | 477 |
| Lawrence | 29,097 | Lawrenceburg | 634 |
| Lewis | 6,761 | Hohenwald | 285 |
| Lincoln | 24,318 | Fayetteville | 580 |
| Loudon | 24,266 | Loudon | 237 |
| McMinn | 35,462 | Athens | 432 |
| McNairy | 18,369 | Selmer | 569 |
| Macon | 12,315 | Lafayette | 304 |
| Madison | 65,774 | Jackson | 560 |
| Marion | 20,577 | Jasper | 506 |
| Marshall | 17,319 | Lewisburg | 377 |
| Maury | 44,028 | Columbia | 614 |
| Meigs | 5,219 | Decatur | 191 |
| Monroe | 23,475 | Madisonville | 660 |
| Montgomery | 62,721 | Clarksville | 539 |
| Moore | 3,568 | Lynchburg | 124 |
| Morgan | 13,619 | Wartburg | 539 |
| Obion | 30,247 | Union City | 556 |
| Overton | 14,866 | Livingston | 441 |
| Perry | 5,238 | Linden | 411 |
| Pickett | 3,774 | Byrdstown | 158 |
| Polk | 11,669 | Benton | 434 |
| Putnam | 35,487 | Cookeville | 405 |
| Rhea | 17,202 | Dayton | 312 |
| Roane | 38,881 | Kingston | 350 |
| Robertson | 29,102 | Springfield | 476 |
| Rutherford | 59,428 | Murfreesboro | 612 |
| Scott | 14,762 | Huntsville | 544 |
| Sequatchie | 6,331 | Dunlap | 273 |
| Sevier | 28,241 | Sevierville | 597 |
| Shelby | 722,111 | Memphis | 755 |
| Smith | 12,509 | Carthage | 323 |
| Stewart | 7,319 | Dover | 470 |
| Sullivan | 127,329 | Blountville | 413 |
| Sumner | 56,266 | Gallatin | 534 |
| Tipton | 28,001 | Covington | 459 |
| Trousdale | 5,155 | Hartsville | 114 |
| Unicoi | 15,254 | Erwin | 185 |
| Union | 9,072 | Maynardville | 212 |
| Van Buren | 3,758 | Spencer | 254 |
| Warren | 26,972 | McMinnville | 439 |
| Washington | 73,924 | Jonesboro | 323 |
| Wayne | 12,365 | Waynesboro | 739 |
| Weakley | 28,827 | Dresden | 576 |
| White | 16,329 | Sparta | 382 |
| Williamson | 34,423 | Franklin | 593 |
| Wilson | 36,999 | Lebanon | 567 |

## Texas

*(254 counties, 262,134 sq. mi. land; pop., 11,196,730)*

| County | Pop. Apr. 1 1970 | County seat or court house | Land area sq. mi. |
|---|---|---|---|
| Anderson | 27,789 | Palestine | 1,072 |
| Andrews | 10,372 | Andrews | 1,504 |
| Angelina | 49,349 | Lufkin | 738 |
| Aransas | 8,902 | Rockport | 275 |
| Archer | 5,759 | Archer City | 913 |
| Armstrong | 1,895 | Claude | 907 |
| Atascosa | 18,696 | Jourdanton | 1,206 |
| Austin | 13,381 | Bellville | 663 |
| Bailey | 8,487 | Muleshoe | 835 |
| Bandera | 4,747 | Bandera | 763 |
| Bastrop | 17,297 | Bastrop | 890 |
| Baylor | 5,221 | Seymour | 845 |
| Bee | 22,737 | Beeville | 842 |

| County | Pop. Apr. 1 1970 | County seat or court house | Land area sq. mi | County | Pop. Apr. 1 1970 | County seat or court house | Land area sq. mi |
|---|---|---|---|---|---|---|---|
| Bell | 124,483 | Belton | 1,047 | Hood | 6,368 | Granbury | 426 |
| Bexar | 830,460 | San Antonio | 1,246 | Hopkins | 20,710 | Sulphur Springs | 793 |
| Blanco | 3,567 | Johnson City | 719 | Houston | 17,855 | Crockett | 1,237 |
| Borden | 888 | Gail | 907 | Howard | 37,796 | Big Spring | 911 |
| Bosque | 10,966 | Meridian | 990 | Hudspeth | 2,392 | Sierra Blanca | 4,554 |
| Bowie | 67,813 | Boston | 891 | Hunt | 47,948 | Greenville | 826 |
| Brazoria | 108,312 | Angleton | 1,423 | Hutchinson | 24,443 | Stinnett | 875 |
| Brazos | 57,978 | Bryan | 586 | Irion | 1,070 | Mertzon | 1,073 |
| Breaster | 7,780 | Alpine | 6,204 | Jack | 6,711 | Jacksboro | 945 |
| Briscoe | 2,794 | Silverton | 874 | Jackson | 12,975 | Edna | 850 |
| Brooks | 8,005 | Falfurrias | 904 | Jasper | 24,692 | Jasper | 907 |
| Brown | 25,877 | Brownwood | 938 | Jeff Davis | 1,527 | Fort Davis | 2,259 |
| Burleson | 9,999 | Caldwell | 670 | Jefferson | 246,402 | Beaumont | 951 |
| Burnet | 11,420 | Burnet | 996 | Jim Hogg | 4,654 | Hebbronville | 1,143 |
| Caldwell | 21,178 | Lockhart | 544 | Jim Wells | 33,032 | Alice | 845 |
| Calhoun | 17,831 | Port Lavaca | 527 | Johnson | 45,769 | Cleburne | 740 |
| Callahan | 8,205 | Baird | 856 | Jones | 16,106 | Anson | 956 |
| Cameron | 140,368 | Brownsville | 896 | Karnes | 13,462 | Karnes City | 758 |
| Camp | 8,005 | Pittsburg | 192 | Kaufman | 32,392 | Kaufman | 815 |
| Carson | 6,358 | Panhandle | 900 | Kendall | 6,964 | Boerne | 670 |
| Cass | 24,133 | Linden | 941 | Kenedy | 678 | Sarita | 1,394 |
| Castro | 10,394 | Dimmitt | 880 | Kent | 1,434 | Jayton | 880 |
| Chambers | 12,187 | Anahuac | 616 | Kerr | 19,454 | Kerrville | 1,101 |
| Cherokee | 32,008 | Rusk | 1,049 | Kimble | 3,904 | Junction | 1,274 |
| Childress | 6,605 | Childress | 699 | King | 464 | Guthrie | 944 |
| Clay | 8,079 | Henrietta | 1,102 | Kinney | 2,006 | Brackettville | 1,393 |
| Cochran | 5,326 | Morton | 783 | Kleberg | 33,166 | Kingsville | 851 |
| Coke | 3,087 | Robert Lee | 911 | Knox | 5,972 | Benjamin | 851 |
| Coleman | 10,288 | Coleman | 1,280 | Lamar | 36,062 | Paris | 984 |
| Collin | 66,920 | McKinney | 836 | Lamb | 17,770 | Littlefield | 1,022 |
| Collingsworth | 4,755 | Wellington | 894 | Lampasas | 9,323 | Lampasas | 726 |
| Colorado | 17,638 | Columbus | 949 | La Salle | 5,014 | Cotulla | 1,500 |
| Comal | 24,165 | New Braunfels | 567 | Lavaca | 17,903 | Hallettsville | 975 |
| Comanche | 11,898 | Comanche | 944 | Lee | 8,048 | Giddings | 637 |
| Concho | 2,937 | Paint Rock | 1,004 | Leon | 8,738 | Centerville | 1,102 |
| Cooke | 23,471 | Gainesville | 985 | Liberty | 33,014 | Liberty | 1,180 |
| Coryell | 35,311 | Gatesville | 1,043 | Limestone | 18,100 | Groesbeck | 931 |
| Cottle | 3,204 | Paducah | 900 | Lipscomb | 3,486 | Lipscomb | 934 |
| Crane | 4,172 | Crane | 795 | Live Oak | 6,697 | George West | 1,055 |
| Crockett 1977 | 4,177 | Ozona | 2,794 | Llano | 6,979 | Llano | 941 |
| Crosby | 9,085 | Crosbyton | 911 | Loving | 164 | Mentone | 648 |
| Culberson | 3,429 | Van Horn | 3,851 | Lubbock | 179,295 | Lubbock | 893 |
| Dallam | 6,012 | Dalhart | 1,494 | Lynn | 9,107 | Tahoka | 915 |
| Dallas | 1,327,695 | Dallas | 859 | McCulloch | 8,571 | Brady | 1,066 |
| Dawson | 16,604 | Lamesa | 902 | McLennan | 147,553 | Waco | 1,000 |
| Deaf Smith | 18,999 | Hereford | 1,510 | McMullen | 1,095 | Tilden | 1,159 |
| Delta | 4,927 | Cooper | 276 | Madison | 7,693 | Madisonville | 480 |
| Denton | 75,633 | Denton | 911 | Marion | 8,517 | Jefferson | 380 |
| Dewitt | 18,660 | Cuero | 910 | Martin | 4,774 | Staton | 911 |
| Dickens | 3,737 | Dickens | 931 | Mason | 3,356 | Mason | 935 |
| Dimmit | 9,039 | Carrizo Springs | 1,344 | Matagorda | 27,913 | Bay City | 1,157 |
| Donley | 3,641 | Clarendon | 905 | Maverick | 18,093 | Eagle Pass | 1,289 |
| Duval | 11,722 | San Diego | 1,814 | Medina | 20,249 | Hondo | 1,352 |
| Eastland | 18,092 | Eastland | 952 | Menard | 2,646 | Menard | 914 |
| Ector | 91,805 | Odessa | 907 | Midland | 65,433 | Midland | 939 |
| Edwards | 2,107 | Rocksprings | 2,076 | Milam | 20,028 | Cameron | 1,028 |
| Ellis | 46,638 | Waxahachie | 940 | Mills | 4,212 | Goldthwaite | 734 |
| El Paso | 359,291 | El Paso | 1,057 | Mitchell | 9,073 | Colorado City | 920 |
| Erath | 18,141 | Stephenville | 1,085 | Montague | 15,326 | Montague | 932 |
| Falls | 17,300 | Marlin | 764 | Montgomery | 49,479 | Conroe | 1,090 |
| Fannin | 22,705 | Bonham | 905 | Moore | 14,060 | Dumas | 909 |
| Fayette | 17,650 | La Grange | 934 | Morris | 12,310 | Daingerfield | 260 |
| Fisher | 6,344 | Roby | 904 | Motley | 2,178 | Matador | 980 |
| Floyd | 11,044 | Floydada | 993 | Nacogdoches | 36,362 | Nacogdoches | 902 |
| Foard | 2,211 | Crowell | 676 | Navarro | 31,150 | Corsicana | 1,070 |
| Fort Bend | 52,314 | Richmond | 869 | Newton | 11,657 | Newton | 949 |
| Franklin | 5,291 | Mount Vernon | 293 | Nolan | 16,220 | Sweetwater | 922 |
| Freestone | 11,116 | Fairfield | 865 | Nueces | 237,544 | Corpus Christi | 841 |
| Frio 1976 | 12,702 | Pearsall | 1,116 | Ochiltree | 9,704 | Perryton | 907 |
| Gaines | 11,593 | Seminole | 1,489 | Oldham | 2,258 | Vega | 1,478 |
| Galveston | 169,812 | Galveston | 399 | Orange | 71,170 | Orange | 359 |
| Garza | 5,289 | Post | 914 | Palo Pinto | 28,962 | Palo Pinto | 948 |
| Gillespie | 10,553 | Fredericksburg | 1,055 | Panola | 15,894 | Carthage | 869 |
| Glasscock | 1,155 | Garden City | 863 | Parker | 33,888 | Weatherford | 903 |
| Goliad | 4,869 | Goliad | 871 | Parmer | 10,509 | Farwell | 859 |
| Gonzales | 16,375 | Gonzales | 1,056 | Pecos | 13,748 | Fort Stockton | 4,740 |
| Gray | 26,949 | Pampa | 934 | Polk | 14,457 | Livingston | 1,100 |
| Grayson | 83,225 | Sherman | 940 | Potter | 90,511 | Amarillo | 909 |
| Gregg | 75,929 | Longview | 282 | Presidio | 4,842 | Marfa | 3,892 |
| Grimes | 11,855 | Anderson | 801 | Rains | 3,752 | Emory | 210 |
| Guadalupe | 33,554 | Seguin | 714 | Randall | 53,885 | Canyon | 914 |
| Hale | 34,137 | Plainview | 979 | Reagan | 3,239 | Big Lake | 1,132 |
| Hall | 6,015 | Memphis | 885 | Real | 2,013 | Leakey | 622 |
| Hamilton | 7,198 | Hamilton | 844 | Red River | 14,298 | Clarksville | 1,033 |
| Hansford | 6,351 | Spearman | 907 | Reeves | 16,526 | Pecos | 2,608 |
| Hardeman | 6,795 | Quanah | 687 | Refugio | 9,494 | Refugio | 774 |
| Hardin | 29,996 | Kountze | 897 | Roberts | 967 | Miami | 899 |
| Harris | 1,741,912 | Houston | 1,723 | Robertson | 14,389 | Franklin | 877 |
| Harrison | 44,841 | Marshall | 894 | Rockwall | 7,046 | Rockwall | 147 |
| Hartley | 2,782 | Channing | 1,488 | Runnels | 12,108 | Ballinger | 1,058 |
| Haskell | 8,512 | Haskell | 877 | Rusk | 34,102 | Henderson | 939 |
| Hays | 27,642 | San Marcos | 650 | Sabine | 7,187 | Hemphill | 456 |
| Hemphill | 3,084 | Canadian | 904 | San Augustine | 7,858 | San Augustine | 473 |
| Henderson | 26,466 | Athens | 943 | San Jacinto | 6,702 | Coldspring | 624 |
| Hidalgo | 181,535 | Edinburg | 1,543 | San Patricio | 47,288 | Sinton | 685 |
| Hill | 22,596 | Hillsboro | 1,010 | San Saba | 5,540 | San Saba | 1,120 |
| Hockley | 20,396 | Levelland | 908 | Schleicher | 2,277 | Eldorado | 1,331 |

| County | Pop. Apr. 1 1970 | County seat or court house | Land area sq. mi. |
|---|---|---|---|
| Scurry | 15,760 | Snyder | 904 |
| Shackelford | 3,323 | Albany | 887 |
| Shelby | 19,672 | Center | 778 |
| Sherman | 3,657 | Stratford | 916 |
| Smith | 97,096 | Tyler | 934 |
| Somervell | 2,793 | Glen Rose | 197 |
| Starr | 17,707 | Rio Grande City | 1,211 |
| Stephens | 8,414 | Breckenridge | 899 |
| Sterling | 1,056 | Sterling City | 914 |
| Stonewall | 2,397 | Aspermont | 926 |
| Sutton 1977 | 4,736 | Sonora | 1,493 |
| Swisher | 10,373 | Tulia | 896 |
| Tarrant | 716,317 | Fort Worth | 861 |
| Taylor | 97,853 | Abilene | 912 |
| Terrell | 1,940 | Sanderson | 2,391 |
| Terry | 14,118 | Brownfield | 899 |
| Throckmorton | 2,205 | Throckmorton | 920 |
| Titus | 16,702 | Mount Pleasant | 418 |
| Tom Green | 71,047 | San Angelo | 1,500 |
| Travis | 295,516 | Austin | 1,012 |
| Trinity | 7,628 | Groveton | 707 |
| Tyler | 12,417 | Woodville | 919 |
| Upshur | 20,976 | Gilmer | 584 |
| Upton | 4,697 | Rankin | 1,312 |
| Uvalde | 17,348 | Uvalde | 1,588 |
| Val Verde | 27,471 | Del Rio | 3,241 |
| Van Zandt | 22,155 | Canton | 845 |
| Victoria | 53,766 | Victoria | 892 |
| Walker | 27,680 | Huntsville | 790 |
| Waller | 14,285 | Hempstead | 509 |
| Ward | 13,019 | Monahans | 827 |
| Washington | 18,842 | Brenham | 594 |
| Webb | 72,859 | Laredo | 3,306 |
| Wharton | 36,729 | Wharton | 1,076 |
| Wheeler | 6,434 | Wheeler | 914 |
| Wichita | 120,563 | Wichita Falls | 611 |
| Wilbarger | 15,355 | Vernon | 952 |
| Willacy | 15,570 | Raymondville | 591 |
| Williamson | 37,305 | Georgetown | 1,104 |
| Wilson | 13,041 | Floresville | 802 |
| Winkler | 9,640 | Kermit | 887 |
| Wise | 19,687 | Decatur | 922 |
| Wood | 18,589 | Quitman | 721 |
| Yoakum | 7,344 | Plains | 830 |
| Young | 15,400 | Graham | 888 |
| Zapata | 4,352 | Zapata | 957 |
| Zavala | 11,370 | Crystal City | 1,291 |

## Utah

*(29 counties, 82,096 sq. mi. land; pop. 1,059,273)*

| County | Pop. Apr. 1 1970 | County seat or court house | Land area sq. mi. |
|---|---|---|---|
| Beaver | 3,800 | Beaver | 2,584 |
| Box Elder | 28,129 | Brigham City | 5,603 |
| Cache | 42,331 | Logan | 1,174 |
| Carbon | 15,647 | Price | 1,476 |
| Daggett | 666 | Manila | 682 |
| Davis | 99,028 | Farmington | 297 |
| Duchesne | 7,299 | Duchesne | 3,255 |
| Emery | 5,137 | Castle Dale | 4,439 |
| Garfield | 3,157 | Panguitch | 5,158 |
| Grand | 6,688 | Moab | 3,682 |
| Iron | 12,177 | Parowan | 3,300 |
| Juab | 4,574 | Nephi | 3,412 |
| Kane | 2,421 | Kanab | 3,904 |
| Millard | 6,988 | Fillmore | 6,793 |
| Morgan | 3,983 | Morgan | 603 |
| Piute | 1,164 | Junction | 754 |
| Rich | 1,615 | Randolph | 1,023 |
| Salt Lake | 458,607 | Salt Lake City | 764 |
| San Juan | 9,606 | Monticello | 7,707 |
| Sanpete | 10,976 | Manti | 1,597 |
| Sevier | 10,103 | Richfield | 1,929 |
| Summit | 5,879 | Coalville | 1,849 |
| Tooele | 21,545 | Tooele | 6,923 |
| Uintah | 12,684 | Vernal | 4,487 |
| Utah | 137,776 | Provo | 2,014 |
| Wasatch | 5,863 | Heber City | 1,191 |
| Washington | 13,669 | Saint George | 2,427 |
| Wayne | 1,483 | Loa | 2,486 |
| Weber | 126,278 | Ogden | 581 |

## Vermont

*(14 counties, 9,267 sq. mi. land; pop. 444,732)*

| County | Pop. Apr. 1 1970 | County seat or court house | Land area sq. mi. |
|---|---|---|---|
| Addison | 24,266 | Middlebury | 784 |
| Bennington | 29,282 | Bennington | 672 |
| Caledonia | 22,789 | Saint Johnsbury | 612 |
| Chittenden | 99,131 | Burlington | 533 |
| Essex | 5,416 | Guildhall | 663 |
| Franklin | 31,282 | Saint Albans | 637 |
| Grand Isle | 3,574 | North Hero | 83 |
| Lamoille | 13,309 | Hyde Park | 474 |
| Orange | 17,676 | Chelsea | 690 |
| Orleans | 20,153 | Newport | 715 |
| Rutland | 52,637 | Rutland | 927 |
| Washington | 47,659 | Montpelier | 707 |
| Windham | 33,476 | Newfane | 784 |
| Windsor | 44,082 | Woodstock | 962 |

## Virginia

*(96 cos., 38 ind. cities, 39,780 sq. mi. land; pop. 4,648,494)*

| County | Pop. Apr. 1 1970 | County seat or court house | Land area sq. mi. |
|---|---|---|---|
| Accomack | 29,004 | Accomac | 476 |
| Albemarle | 37,780 | Charlottesville | 740 |
| Alleghany | 12,461 | Covington | 444 |
| Amelia | 7,592 | Amelia, C.H. | 366 |
| Amherst | 26,072 | Amherst | 470 |
| Appomattox | 9,784 | Appomattox | 345 |
| Arlington | 174,284 | Arlington | 26 |
| Augusta | 44,220 | Staunton | 986 |
| Bath | 5,192 | Warm Springs | 540 |
| Bedford | 26,728 | Bedford | 727 |
| Bland | 5,423 | Bland | 369 |
| Botetourt | 18,193 | Fincastle | 548 |
| Brunswick | 16,172 | Lawrenceville | 579 |
| Buchanan | 32,071 | Grundy | 508 |
| Buckingham | 10,597 | Buckingham | 582 |
| Campbell | 43,319 | Rustburg | 529 |
| Caroline | 13,925 | Bowling Green | 545 |
| Carroll | 23,092 | Hillsville | 494 |
| Charles City | 6,158 | Charles City | 181 |
| Charlotte | 12,366 | Charlotte Courthouse | 470 |
| Chesterfield | 77,045 | Chesterfield | 442 |
| Clarke | 8,102 | Berryville | 174 |
| Craig | 3,524 | New Castle | 336 |
| Culpeper | 18,218 | Culpeper | 389 |
| Cumberland | 6,179 | Cumberland | 291 |
| Dickenson | 16,077 | Clintwood | 332 |
| Dinwiddie | 25,046 | Dinwiddie | 507 |
| Essex | 7,099 | Tappahannock | 250 |
| Fairfax | 455,032 | Fairfax | 399 |
| Fauquier | 26,375 | Warrenton | 660 |
| Floyd | 9,775 | Floyd | 383 |
| Fluvanna | 7,621 | Palmyra | 288 |
| Franklin | 28,163 | Rocky Mount | 716 |
| Frederick | 28,893 | Winchester | 405 |
| Giles | 16,741 | Pearisburg | 363 |
| Gloucester | 14,059 | Gloucester | 228 |
| Goochland 1976 | 11,221 | Goochland | 289 |
| Grayson | 15,439 | Independence | 452 |
| Greene | 5,248 | Stanardsville | 153 |
| Greensville | 9,604 | Emporia | 299 |
| Halifax | 30,076 | Halifax | 796 |
| Hanover | 37,479 | Hanover | 465 |
| Henrico | 154,364 | Richmond | 229 |
| Henry | 50,901 | Martinsville | 381 |
| Highland | 2,529 | Monterey | 416 |
| Isle of Wight | 18,285 | Isle of Wight | 317 |
| James City | 17,853 | Williamsburg | 152 |
| King and Queen | 5,491 | King and Queen | 318 |
| King George | 8,039 | King George | 176 |
| King William | 7,497 | King William | 278 |
| Lancaster | 9,126 | Lancaster | 137 |
| Lee | 20,321 | Jonesville | 438 |
| Loudoun | 37,150 | Leesburg | 517 |
| Louisa | 14,004 | Louisa | 517 |
| Lunenburg | 11,687 | Lunenburg | 442 |
| Madison | 8,638 | Madison | 327 |
| Mathews | 7,168 | Mathews | 89 |
| Mecklenburg | 29,426 | Boydton | 612 |
| Middlesex | 6,295 | Saluda | 130 |
| Montgomery | 47,157 | Christiansburg | 394 |
| *Nansemond | 35,166 | Suffolk | 408 |
| Nelson | 11,702 | Lovingston | 471 |
| New Kent | 5,300 | New Kent | 210 |
| Northampton | 14,442 | Eastville | 220 |
| Northumberland | 9,239 | Heathsville | 190 |
| Nottoway | 14,260 | Nottoway | 308 |
| Orange | 13,792 | Orange | 355 |
| Page | 16,581 | Luray | 316 |
| Patrick | 15,282 | Stuart | 464 |
| Pittsylvania | 58,789 | Chatham | 1,001 |
| Powhatan | 7,696 | Powhatan | 269 |
| Prince Edward | 14,379 | Farmville | 357 |
| Prince George | 29,092 | Prince George | 276 |
| Prince William | 111,102 | Manassas | 347 |
| Pulaski | 29,564 | Pulaski | 328 |
| Rappahannock | 5,199 | Washington | 267 |
| Richmond | 6,504 | Warsaw | 190 |
| Roanoke | 67,339 | Salem | 262 |
| Rockbridge | 16,637 | Lexington | 601 |
| Rockingham | 47,890 | Harrisonburg | 865 |
| Russell | 24,533 | Lebanon | 483 |
| Scott | 24,376 | Gate City | 539 |
| Shenandoah | 22,852 | Woodstock | 507 |
| Smyth | 31,349 | Marion | 435 |
| Southampton | 18,582 | Courtland | 602 |
| Spotsylvania | 16,424 | Spotsylvania | 409 |
| Stafford | 24,587 | Stafford | 270 |
| Surry | 5,882 | Surry | 277 |
| Sussex | 11,464 | Sussex | 494 |
| Tazewell | 39,816 | Tazewell | 522 |

| County | Pop. Apr. 1 1970 | County seat or court house | Land area sq. mi. |
|---|---|---|---|
| Warren | 15,301 | Front Royal | 219 |
| Washington | 40,835 | Abingdon | 574 |
| Westmoreland | 12,142 | Montross | 229 |
| Wise | 35,947 | Wise | 412 |
| Wythe | 22,139 | Wytheville | 460 |
| York | 33,203 | Yorktown | 129 |

*1/1/74 merged with ind. city of Suffolk.

**Independent cities**

| County | Pop. Apr. 1 1970 | County seat or court house | Land area sq. mi. |
|---|---|---|---|
| Alexandria | 110,927 | | 15 |
| Bedford | 6,011 | | 7 |
| Bristol | 14,857 | | 4 |
| Buena Vista | 6,425 | | 3 |
| Charlottesville | 38,880 | | 10 |
| Chesapeake | 89,580 | | 341 |
| Clifton Forge | 5,501 | | 4 |
| Colonial Heights | 15,097 | | 8 |
| Covington | 10,060 | | 4 |
| Danville | 46,391 | | 17 |
| Emporia | 5,300 | | 2 |
| Fairfax | 21,970 | | 6 |
| Falls Church | 10,772 | | 2 |
| Franklin | 6,880 | | 4 |
| Fredericksburg | 14,450 | | 6 |
| Galax | 6,278 | | 7 |
| Hampton | 120,779 | | 55 |
| Harrisonburg | 14,605 | | 6 |
| Hopewell | 23,471 | | 9 |
| Lexington | 7,597 | | 3 |
| Lynchburg | 54,083 | | 25 |
| Martinsville | 19,653 | | 11 |
| Newport News | 138,177 | | 69 |
| Norfolk | 307,951 | | 53 |
| Norton | 4,172 | | 4 |
| Petersburg | 36,103 | | 8 |
| Portsmouth | 110,963 | | 29 |
| Radford | 11,596 | | 5 |
| Richmond | 249,431 | | 60 |
| Roanoke | 92,115 | | 27 |
| Salem | 21,982 | | 14 |
| South Boston | 6,889 | | 5 |
| Staunton | 24,504 | | 9 |
| Suffolk | 9,858 | | 2 |
| Virginia Beach | 172,106 | | 259 |
| Waynesboro | 16,707 | | 7 |
| Williamsburg | 9,069 | | 5 |
| Winchester | 14,643 | | 3 |

## Washington

*(39 counties, 66,570 sq. mi. land; pop., 3,409,169)*

| County | Pop. Apr. 1 1970 | County seat or court house | Land area sq. mi. |
|---|---|---|---|
| Adams | 12,014 | Ritzville | 1,894 |
| Asotin | 13,799 | Asotin | 633 |
| Benton | 67,540 | Prosser | 1,722 |
| Chelan | 41,103 | Wenatchee | 2,918 |
| Clallam | 34,770 | Port Angeles | 1,753 |
| Clark | 128,454 | Vancouver | 627 |
| Columbia | 4,439 | Dayton | 853 |
| Cowlitz | 68,616 | Kelso | 1,144 |
| Douglas | 16,787 | Waterville | 1,831 |
| Ferry | 3,655 | Republic | 2,202 |
| Franklin | 25,816 | Pasco | 1,253 |
| Garfield | 2,911 | Pomeroy | 709 |
| Grant | 41,881 | Ephrata | 2,675 |
| Grays Harbor | 59,553 | Montesano | 1,910 |
| Island | 27,011 | Coupeville | 212 |
| Jefferson | 10,661 | Port Townsend | 1,805 |
| King | 1,159,375 | Seattle | 2,128 |
| Kitsap | 101,732 | Port Orchard | 393 |
| Kittitas | 25,039 | Ellensburg | 2,317 |
| Klickitat | 12,138 | Goldendale | 1,908 |
| Lewis | 45,467 | Chehalis | 2,423 |
| Lincoln | 9,572 | Davenport | 2,306 |
| Mason | 20,918 | Shelton | 962 |
| Okanogan | 25,867 | Okanogan | 5,301 |
| Pacific | 15,796 | South Bend | 908 |
| Pend Oreille | 6,025 | Newport | 1,402 |
| Pierce | 411,027 | Tacoma | 1,676 |
| San Juan | 3,856 | Friday Harbor | 179 |
| Skagit | 52,381 | Mount Vernon | 1,735 |
| Skamania | 5,845 | Stevenson | 1,672 |
| Snohomish | 265,236 | Everett | 2,098 |
| Spokane | 287,487 | Spokane | 1,758 |
| Stevens | 17,405 | Colville | 2,481 |
| Thurston | 76,894 | Olympia | 714 |
| Wahkiakum | 3,592 | Cathlamet | 261 |
| Walla Walla | 42,176 | Walla Walla | 1,262 |
| Whatcom | 81,950 | Bellingham | 2,126 |
| Whitman | 37,900 | Colfax | 2,153 |
| Yakima | 144,971 | Yakima | 4,268 |

## West Virginia

*(55 counties, 24,070 sq. mi. land; pop., 1,744,237)*

| County | Pop. Apr. 1 1970 | County seat or court house | Land area sq. mi. |
|---|---|---|---|
| Barbour | 14,030 | Philippi | 341 |
| Berkeley | 36,356 | Martinsburg | 316 |
| Boone | 2,118 | Madison | 501 |
| Braxton | 12,666 | Sutton | 511 |
| Brooke | 29,685 | Wellsburg | 88 |
| Cabell | 106,918 | Huntington | 279 |
| Calhoun | 7,046 | Grantsville | 281 |
| Clay | 9,330 | Clay | 343 |
| Doddridge | 6,389 | West Union | 319 |
| Fayette | 49,332 | Fayetteville | 663 |
| Gilmer | 7,782 | Glenville | 339 |
| Grant | 8,607 | Petersburg | 478 |
| Greenbrier | 32,090 | Lewisburg | 1,026 |
| Hampshire | 11,710 | Romney | 639 |
| Hancock | 39,749 | New Cumberland | 83 |
| Hardy | 8,855 | Moorefield | 585 |
| Harrison | 73,028 | Clarksburg | 418 |
| Jackson | 20,903 | Ripley | 461 |
| Jefferson | 21,280 | Charles Town | 211 |
| Kanawha | 229,515 | Charleston | 907 |
| Lewis | 17,847 | Weston | 392 |
| Lincoln | 18,912 | Hamlin | 438 |
| Logan | 46,269 | Logan | 456 |
| McDowell | 50,666 | Welch | 533 |
| Marion | 61,356 | Fairmont | 311 |
| Marshall | 37,598 | Moundsville | 304 |
| Mason | 24,306 | Point Pleasant | 433 |
| Mercer | 63,206 | Princeton | 417 |
| Mineral | 23,109 | Keyser | 330 |
| Mingo | 32,780 | Williamson | 423 |
| Monongalia | 63,714 | Morgantown | 365 |
| Monroe | 11,272 | Union | 473 |
| Morgan | 8,547 | Berkeley Springs | 233 |
| Nicholas | 22,552 | Summersville | 642 |
| Ohio | 64,197 | Wheeling | 106 |
| Pendleton | 7,031 | Franklin | 695 |
| Pleasants | 7,274 | St. Marys | 129 |
| Pocahontas | 8,870 | Marlinton | 943 |
| Preston | 25,455 | Kingwood | 645 |
| Putnam | 27,625 | Winfield | 348 |
| Raleigh | 70,080 | Beckley | 605 |
| Randolph | 24,596 | Elkins | 1,036 |
| Ritchie | 10,145 | Harrisville | 452 |
| Roane | 14,111 | Spencer | 486 |
| Summers | 13,213 | Hinton | 350 |
| Taylor | 13,878 | Grafton | 174 |
| Tucker | 7,447 | Parsons | 421 |
| Tyler | 9,929 | Middlebourne | 256 |
| Upshur | 19,092 | Buckhannon | 352 |
| Wayne | 37,581 | Wayne | 513 |
| Webster | 9,809 | Webster Springs | 551 |
| Wetzel | 20,314 | New Martinsville | 363 |
| Wirt | 4,154 | Elizabeth | 235 |
| Wood | 86,818 | Parkersburg | 368 |
| Wyoming | 30,095 | Pineville | 504 |

## Wisconsin

*(72 counties, 54,464 sq. mi. land; pop., 4,417,933)*

| County | Pop. Apr. 1 1970 | County seat or court house | Land area sq. mi. |
|---|---|---|---|
| Adams | 9,234 | Friendship | 646 |
| Ashland | 16,743 | Ashland | 1,038 |
| Barron | 33,955 | Barron | 864 |
| Bayfield | 11,683 | Washburn | 1,460 |
| Brown | 158,244 | Green Bay | 524 |
| Buffalo | 13,743 | Alma | 711 |
| Burnett | 9,276 | Grantsburg | 840 |
| Calumet | 27,604 | Chilton | 322 |
| Chippewa | 47,717 | Chippewa Falls | 1,018 |
| Clark | 30,361 | Neillsville | 1,221 |
| Columbia | 40,150 | Portage | 776 |
| Crawford | 15,252 | Prairie du Chien | 568 |
| Dane | 290,272 | Madison | 1,198 |
| Dodge | 69,004 | Juneau | 889 |
| Door | 20,106 | Sturgeon Bay | 492 |
| Douglas | 44,657 | Superior | 1,305 |
| Dunn | 29,154 | Menomonie | 853 |
| Eau Claire, 1975 | 72,237 | Eau Claire | 647 |
| Florence | 3,298 | Florence | 487 |
| Fond Du Lac | 84,567 | Fond du Lac | 725 |
| Forest (1973) | 8,265 | Crandon | 1,007 |
| Grant | 48,398 | Lancaster | 1,147 |
| Green | 26,714 | Monroe | 585 |
| Green Lake | 16,878 | Green Lake | 354 |
| Iowa | 19,306 | Dodgeville | 762 |
| Iron | 6,533 | Hurley | 747 |
| Jackson | 15,325 | Black River Falls | 999 |
| Jefferson | 60,060 | Jefferson | 564 |
| Juneau | 18,455 | Mauston | 774 |
| Kenosha | 117,917 | Kenosha | 272 |
| Kewaunee | 18,961 | Kewaunee | 330 |
| La Crosse | 80,468 | La Crosse | 451 |
| Lafayette | 17,456 | Darlington | 643 |
| Langlade | 19,220 | Antigo | 856 |
| Lincoln | 23,499 | Merrill | 892 |
| Manitowoc | 82,294 | Manitowoc | 590 |
| Marathon | 97,457 | Wausau | 1,586 |
| Marinette | 35,810 | Marinette | 1,378 |

| County | Pop. Apr. 1 1970 | County seat or court house | Land area sq. mi. | County | Pop. Apr. 1 1970 | County seat or court house | Land area sq. mi. |
|---|---|---|---|---|---|---|---|
| Marquette | 8,865 | Montello | 455 | Waushara | 14,795 | Wautoma | 627 |
| Menominee | 2,607 | Keshena | 360 | Winnebago | 129,946 | Oshkosh | 448 |
| Milwaukee | 1,054,249 | Milwaukee | 237 | Wood | 65,362 | Wisconsin Rapids | 807 |
| Monroe | 31,610 | Sparta | 915 | | | | |
| Oconto | 25,553 | Oconto | 1,001 | | | | |
| Oneida | 24,427 | Rhinelander | 1,112 | | | | |
| Outaramie | 119,398 | Appleton | 634 | | | | |

## Wyoming

*(23 counties, 97,203 sq. mi. land; pop., 332,416)*

| County | Pop. Apr. 1 1970 | County seat or court house | Land area sq. mi. | County | Pop. Apr. 1 1970 | County seat or court house | Land area sq. mi. |
|---|---|---|---|---|---|---|---|
| Ozaukee | 54,461 | Port Washington | 236 | Albany | 26,431 | Laramie | 4,248 |
| Pepin | 7,319 | Durand | 235 | Big Horn | 10,202 | Basin | 3,157 |
| Pierce | 26,652 | Ellsworth | 590 | Campbell | 12,957 | Gillette | 4,756 |
| Polk | 26,666 | Balsam Lake | 931 | Carbon | 13,354 | Rawlins | 7,905 |
| Portage | 47,541 | Stevens Point | 806 | Converse | 5,938 | Douglas | 4,281 |
| Price | 14,520 | Phillips | 1,260 | Crook | 4,535 | Sundance | 2,882 |
| Racine | 170,838 | Racine | 337 | Fremont | 28,352 | Lander | 9,106 |
| Richland | 17,079 | Richland Center | 583 | Goshen | 10,885 | Torrington | 2,228 |
| Rock | 131,970 | Janesville | 721 | Hot Springs | 4,952 | Thermopolis | 2,022 |
| Rusk | 14,238 | Ladysmith | 906 | Johnson | 5,587 | Buffalo | 4,175 |
| St. Croix | 34,354 | Hudson | 734 | Laramie | 56,360 | Cheyenne | 2,703 |
| Sauk | 39,057 | Baraboo | 841 | Lincoln | 8,640 | Kemmerer | 4,085 |
| Sawyer | 9,670 | Hayward | 1,259 | Natrona | 51,264 | Casper | 5,342 |
| Shawano | 32,650 | Shawano | 919 | Niobrara | 2,924 | Lusk | 2,614 |
| Sheboygan | 96,660 | Sheboygan | 505 | Park | 17,752 | Cody | 6,959 |
| Taylor | 16,958 | Medford | 975 | Platte | 6,486 | Wheatland | 2,086 |
| Trempealeau | 23,344 | Whitehall | 735 | Sheridan | 17,852 | Sheridan | 2,532 |
| Vernon | 24,557 | Viroqua | 802 | Sublette | 3,755 | Pinedale | 4,851 |
| Vilas | 10,958 | Eagle River | 867 | Sweetwater | 18,391 | Green River | 10,429 |
| Walworth | 63,444 | Elkhorn | 557 | Teton | 4,823 | Jackson | 4,000 |
| Washburn | 10,601 | Shell Lake | 817 | Uinta | 7,100 | Evanston | 2,086 |
| Washington | 63,839 | West Bend | 429 | Washakie | 7,569 | Worland | 2,262 |
| Waukesha | 231,338 | Waukesha | 554 | Weston | 6,307 | Newcastle | 2,407 |
| Waupaca | 37,780 | Waupaca | 751 | | | | |

# 1970 Population of Outlying Areas

Source: U.S. Bureau of the Census

## Puerto Rico

| ZIP code | Municipios | Pop. April 1 | Land area sq. mile | ZIP code | Municipios | Pop. April 1 | Land area sq. mile | ZIP code | Municipios | Pop. April 1 | Land area sq. mile |
|---|---|---|---|---|---|---|---|---|---|---|---|
| 00601 | Adjuntas | 18,691 | 66 | 00653 | Guanica | 14,889 | 37 | 00720 | Orocovis | 20,201 | 63 |
| 00602 | Aguada | 25,658 | 30 | 00654 | Guayama | 36,249 | 65 | 00723 | Patillas | 17,828 | 48 |
| 00603 | Aguadilla | 51,355 | 36 | 00656 | Guayanilla | 18,144 | 42 | 00724 | Penuelas | 15,973 | 44 |
| 00607 | Aguas Buenas | 18,600 | 30 | 00657 | Guaynabo | 67,042 | 27 | 00731 | Ponce | 158,981 | 116 |
| 00609 | Aibonito | 20,044 | 31 | 00658 | Gurabo | 18,289 | 28 | 00742 | Quebradillas | 15,582 | 23 |
| 00610 | Anasco | 19,416 | 40 | 00659 | Hatillo | 21,913 | 42 | 00743 | Rincon | 9,094 | 14 |
| 00612 | Arecibo | 73,468 | 127 | 00660 | Hormigueros | 10,827 | 11 | 00745 | Rio Grande | 22,032 | 61 |
| 00615 | Arroyo | 13,033 | 15 | 00661 | Humacao | 36,023 | 45 | 00747 | Sabana Grande | 16,343 | 37 |
| 00617 | Barceloneta | 20,792 | 34 | 00662 | Isabela | 30,430 | 56 | 00751 | Salinas | 21,837 | 69 |
| 00618 | Barranquitas | 20,118 | 33 | 00664 | Jayuya | 13,588 | 39 | 00753 | San German | 27,990 | 54 |
| 00619 | Bayamon | 156,192 | 44 | 00665 | Juana Diaz | 36,270 | 61 | *00936- | | | |
| 00623 | Cabo Rojo | 26,060 | 72 | 00666 | Juncos | 21,814 | 26 | | San Juan | 463,242 | 47 |
| 00625 | Caguas | 95,661 | 58 | 00667 | Lajas | 16,545 | 60 | 00754 | San Lorenzo | 27,755 | 53 |
| 00627 | Camuy | 19,922 | 46 | 00669 | Lares | 25,263 | 62 | 00755 | San Sebastian | 30,157 | 71 |
| 00630 | Carolina | 107,643 | 48 | 00670 | Las Marias | 7,841 | 44 | 00757 | Santa Isabel | 16,056 | 34 |
| 00632 | Catano | 26,459 | 5 | 00671 | Las Piedras | 18,112 | 33 | 00758 | Toa Alta | 18,964 | 27 |
| 00633 | Cayey | 38,432 | 50 | 00672 | Loiza | 39,062 | 53 | 00759 | Toa Baja | 46,384 | 24 |
| 00635 | Ceiba | 18,312 | 27 | 00673 | Luquillo | 10,390 | 26 | 00760 | Tujillo Alto | 30,669 | 21 |
| 00638 | Ciales | 15,595 | 66 | 00701 | Manati | 30,559 | 46 | 00761 | Utuado | 35,494 | 115 |
| 00639 | Cidra | 23,892 | 36 | 00706 | Maricao | 5,991 | 37 | 00762 | Vega Alta | 22,810 | 28 |
| 00640 | Coamo | 26,468 | 77 | 00707 | Maunabo | 10,792 | 21 | 00763 | Vega Baja | 35,327 | 47 |
| 00642 | Comerio | 18,819 | 28 | 00708 | Mayaguez | 85,857 | 77 | 00765 | Vieques | 7,767 | 52 |
| 00643 | Corozal | 24,545 | 42 | 00716 | Moca | 22,361 | 51 | 00766 | Villalba | 18,733 - | 37 |
| 00645 | Culebra | 732 | 10 | 00717 | Morovis | 19,059 | 39 | 00767 | Yabucoa | 30,165 | 55 |
| 00646 | Dorado | 17,388 | 23 | 00718 | Naguabo | 17,996 | 52 | 00768 | Yauco | 35,103 | 68 |
| 00648 | Faiardo | 23,032 | 31 | 00719 | Naranjito | 19,913 | 28 | | Total | 2,712,033 | 3,421 |

| ZIP code | Area | Pop. April 1 | Land area sq. mile | ZIP code | Area | Pop. April 1 | Land area sq. mile | ZIP code | Area | Pop. April 1 | Land area sq. mile |
|---|---|---|---|---|---|---|---|---|---|---|---|
| | **American Samoa** | | | | Asan | 2,629 | 6 | | **Virgin Islands** | | |
| 96920 | American Samoa | 27,159 | 76 | | Barrigada | 6,356 | 9 | | St. Croix | 31,779 | 80 |
| | | | | | Chalan-Pago-Ordot | 2,931 | 6 | 00830 | St. John | 1,729 | 20 |
| | | | | | Dededo | 10,780 | 30 | 00801 | St. Thomas | 28,960 | 32 |
| | **Canal Zone** | | | | Inarajan | 1,897 | 19 | 00801 | Charlotte Amalie | 12,220 | |
| | Canal Zone | 44,198 | 362 | | Mangilao | 3,228 | 10 | 00820 | Christiansted | 3,020 | |
| | Balboa | 32,552 | 222 | | Merizo | 1,529 | 6 | 00840 | Frederiksted | 1,531 | |
| | Cristobal | 11,646 | 140 | | Mongmong-Too-Maite | | | | Total | 62,468 | 132 |
| | | | | | | 6,057 | 2 | | | | |
| | | | | | Piti | 1,284 | 7 | | **Trust Territory of Pacific Islands** | | |
| | **Guam** | | | | Santa Rita | 8,109 | 17 | | Mariana district | 9,640 | 184 |
| 96910 | Guam | 84,996 | 209 | | Sinajana | 3,506 | 1 | | Marshall district | 22,888 | 70 |
| | Agana | 2,119 | 1 | | Talofofo | 1,935 | 17 | | Palau district | 11,210 | 192 |
| | Agana Hts. | 3,156 | 1 | | Tamuning | 10,218 | 6 | | Ponape district | 18,536 | 176 |
| | Agat | 4,308 | 10 | | Umatac | 813 | 6 | | Truk district | 21,041 | 49 |
| | | | | | Yigo | 11,542 | 35 | | Yap district | 7,625 | 46 |
| | | | | | Yona | 2,599 | 20 | | Total | 90,940 | 717 |

# Women 1978: Demonstrations, Boycotts, Lawsuits

## By Hana Umlauf

On a hot, muggy Sunday in the summer of 1978, nearly 100,000 women, men, and children marched dozens of blocks to gather on the Washington, D.C., mall to demonstrate their support for an extension of the 7-year deadline for ratification of the Equal Rights Amendment. The day, July 9, had been chosen because it was the first anniversary of the death of Alice Paul, a monumental leader in the movement for women's suffrage in the first decades of this century. Despite the heat and discomfort of the day, the gathering had none of the belligerence of many of the city's anti-war demonstrations, but rather resembled a family reunion.

The intent of the march was to show the depth and variety of support for the ERA and to launch a renewed nationwide campaign for ratification of the amendment. Pres. Jimmy Carter, calling the ERA the "bedrock" for strengthening and broadening opportunities for women and minorities, sent a statement of support for the extension of the ratification deadline.

### Committee Supports Extension

The hopes of the demonstrators were at least partially fulfilled just 9 days later when, following an often impassioned debate, the House Judiciary Committee voted, 19-15, to send to the full House a resolution in favor of extending the ratification deadline by 3 years and 3 months. The committee also rejected a proposal to allow states to rescind approval of the amendment. ERA supporters greeted the committee action optimistically as a solid indication that the resolution would be passed in the House. Rep. Don Edwards (D, Cal.) explained, "This is a very conservative committee and getting through here is the tough battle." Nevertheless, the resolution still must be approved by the House Rules Committee as well as the Senate where a filibuster is a possibility. The extension may also face a court fight by opponents because the Judiciary Committee decided that a simple majority vote rather than the two-thirds majority required to launch the amendment in 1972 would be sufficient to approve the extension.

The heated day-long debate that preceded the vote centered on the fine points of the extension, such as the time limit, the need for an amendment, and the right of states to withdraw their ratification. Rep. Barbara Jordan (D, Tex.), who asked "Who can limit the time during which I can attempt to protect and guarantee my personhood in the community of humankind?", exemplified one side of the debate. On the other side, Rep. Charles E. Wiggins (R, Cal.) argued that he found it "a repugnant idea that an issue could run for 14 years."

Passage of the extension is crucial for supporters of the ERA. The current deadline is Mar. 22, 1979, and the ERA is still 3 short of the 38 states needed for ratification. Supporters had been dealt a serious blow in June when Illinois, which had been made the centerpiece of the proponents' campaign to regain lost momentum, twice rejected the proposed ERA.

### ERA Convention Boycott Working

The record for ERA ratification has been disappointing — no state has ratified the amendment since 1977 — despite the apparent success of the convention boycott of states that have not ratified the ERA. NOW, the prime mover behind the boycott, estimated in April that the boycott had cost the 15 states involved $100 million. Two states, Missouri and Nevada, have filed suits against NOW, charging the organization with violation of federal anti-trust laws. Estimates indicate that Chicago has lost as many as 92,250 conventioneers and $18.4 million as a result of the boycott. The estimated loss for Atlanta stands at $16 million, St. Louis at $10 million, Las Vegas at $8 million, and New Orleans at $10 to $12 million. NOW attributes its success in part to the support of more than 120 organizations, including the United Automobile Workers, National Education Association, Common Cause, and American Association of University Women.

The pro-ERA boycott has come under fire for several reasons. Some state officials feel the boycott is counterproductive because it penalizes an entire state for the deeds of a small number of officials. STOP ERA head Phyllis Schlafly feels the boycott has no political effect but rather is a "deliberate malicious campaign against people like waiters and maids in hotels and restaurants and taxicab drivers who don't have anything to do with ratification." Others feel that the campaign injures women more than men because they constitute the majority of workers in the convention industry.

Despite the difficulties facing the ERA, its supporters are determined to keep fighting. Although the general consensus is that defeat of the ERA would be a public relations disaster, there is no talk of quitting. Betty Friedan believes the stakes are simply too high: "If it is blocked, I honestly feel that not only will there be further erosion, but laws can be outright repealed. Without the ERA you have to keep inventing the wheel all over again, fighting piece by piece against the erosion of everything we've won instead of getting on to the next set of issues we need to deal with, for men as well as for women."

### Piece-by-Piece Fight Shows Gains

Friedan's piece-by-piece battle did show some important gains over the past year. In a major victory, a Louisiana federal district court held that equal employment requirements set as preconditions for government contracts were valid and enforceable and that the regulations implementing them were constitutional under the due process clause. The court also ruled that the government could refuse to contract with firms that do not adopt seniority systems that intend to provide affirmative action relief to females. The rulings were important, said Assistant Secretary for Employment Standards Donald Elisburg, because they confirmed that the government could set the terms and conditions of its contracts, including Equal Employment Opportunity requirements, without a hearing, and "we can require changes in seniority systems where women or minorities are underrepresented in better paying, high opportunity jobs."

In December 1977, the Supreme Court held that women who took maternity leaves could not be deprived of their seniority when they returned. However, the court affirmed its 1976 ruling that an employer was not required to allow a worker to use accumulated sick-leave credit to remain on the payroll when she left temporarily for childbirth. Not all women's rights advocates were encouraged by the court's action because of the conflicting nature of the 2 decisions. Susan Deller Ross, clinical director of the American Civil Liberties Union women's rights project, concluded "Discrimination against pregnant workers is sometimes illegal and sometimes is not, the court said. The decision showed the importance of a new federal law to make all discrimination against pregnant workers illegal." Justice John Paul Stevens agreed, writing a separate opinion to point out the conflict. Stevens observed that "although some discrimination against pregnancy...is permissable, discrimination against pregnant or formerly pregnant employes is not."

## Equal Opportunity on Federal Construction Sites

Responding to lobbying by women's organizations since 1971, the Labor Department issued regulations, effective May 8, 1978, for equal employment opportunity for women on all federal or federally-assisted construction work. The regulations established nationwide goals and timetables for a 3-year period for all contractors and subcontractors holding government or government-assisted contracts in excess of $10,000. Along with special affirmative action steps to hire and promote minorities and women, contractors are now required to ensure and maintain a working environment free of harassment, intimidation, and coercion. Contractors are also required to direct recruitment to minority, female, and community organizations as well as schools and other institutions with female and minority members.

In April, the Supreme Court ruled that employers who required women to contribute a greater percentage of their salaries to pension plans than men were in violation of Title VII of the 1964 Civil Rights Act. Employers had defended the pension plans by arguing that women, on the average, lived longer than men and were, consequently, likely to receive about 15% more in benefits after retirement. The court pointed out, however, that there was no assurance that any individual female employee would live as long or longer than the average male employee. As a result, some women received smaller pay checks than men while they were working, but would receive no compensating advantage when they retired.

## NYC Recognizes Wife-Beating as Crime

In another major step forward, the New York City Police Department, reversing a long-standing practice, agreed in an out-of-court settlement to arrest wife beaters. The settlement was made in a 1,000-word consent agreement signed for the police department by New York City's corporation counsel and by lawyers for 71 women. The suit in which the settlement was made, was brought by the women in 1976. They had accused the police and administrative arm of the city's family court of unlawfully denying them assistance after they had reported beatings.

Lawyers for the women described the suit as the first comprehensive challenge in the U.S. to official treatment of wives beaten by their husbands and hailed it as a precedent with far-reaching repercussions. Laurie Woods, a lawyer for the women, called it "the first official recognition by any law enforcement agency in New York that wife assault is serious and pervasive," and noted that battered women are now "officially entitled to the same police protection as victims of other crimes."

Progress in winning rights for women was also evident in various branches of the armed forces.

In July, Federal District Court Judge John J. Sirica rejected a federal statute that barred Navy women from sea duty on other than transport and hospital ships. The statute, Sirica found, also limited the range of duties and assignments available to some 25,000 Navy women on shore because some shore billets were open only to people who have served aboard ships from which women were barred. Although Sirica's ruling only applied to Navy women, it was presumed that it would lead to lawsuits by women seeking to broaden opportunities for combat-related service in other branches of the armed forces. Kathleen Willert Peratis, director of the American Civil Liberties Union's Women's Rights Project hailed the ruling as "a fabulous decision," commenting, "It strikes down one of the last legal barriers to job training and advancement for women."

In another decision, the Air Force, breaking with the policy of the other services, decided to allow women enrolled in the Air Force Academy to remain in school if they became pregnant. However, pregnant students who married would still have to leave the academy. The decision was based on the consideration of marriage as a "permanent condition", while pregnancy was viewed as a "temporary disability". The decision, it was said privately, stemmed from the opinion that dismissal due to pregnancy was a violation of a woman's constitutional rights.

# America's 25 Most Influential Women in 1978

The following women, listed alphabetically, were chosen by The World Almanac co-sponsoring newspapers.

**Bella Abzug,** former Democratic Congresswoman from New York, is currently co-chair of the National Advisory Committee on Women.

**Erma Bombeck,** nationally-syndicated columnist, is the best-selling author of *The Grass is Always Greener Over the Septic Tank* and other books.

**Helen Gurley Brown,** editor of *Cosmopolitan* since 1965, was an advertising copywriter when she wrote the best-seller, *Sex and the Single Girl.*

**Anita Bryant,** entertainer, author, is the leader of Save Our Children.

**Rosalynn Carter,** first lady, is the honorary chairman of the President's Commission on Mental Health.

**Jane Fonda,** actress, political activist, won excellent reviews in 1978 for her performance in *Coming Home.*

**Betty Ford,** former first lady, made headlines in 1978 when she sought medical attention for a drug-dependency problem.

**Betty Friedan,** author of *The Feminine Mystique,* was a founding member of the National Organization for Women and the National Women's Political Caucus.

**Katharine Graham,** publisher of *The Washington Post,* also controls the parent company which owns *Newsweek* and radio and television stations.

**Patricia Roberts Harris,** secretary of HUD, was the first black woman to reach cabinet rank as well as ambassadorial rank, having served as ambassador to Luxemburg during Pres. Johnson's term.

**Barbara Jordan,** Democratic Congresswoman from Texas, serves on the House Judiciary Committee.

**Coretta Scott King,** civil rights leader, has become increasingly prominent since the assassination of her husband, Rev. Martin Luther King Jr.

**Juanita Kreps,** secretary of commerce, was formerly vice president of Duke University where she began her teaching career in economics in 1955.

**Maggie Kuhn,** retired social worker, in 1970 at age 64 organized the Gray Panthers, a network of highly vocal older people dedicated to improving conditions for senior citizens.

**Ann Landers,** nationally-syndicated columnist, dispenses personal advice to readers all over the world.

**Virginia Johnson Masters,** sex researcher, is the co-author of *Human Sexual Response* and *Human Sexual Inadequacy.*

**Margaret Mead,** anthropologist, has studied 7 cultures, written 17 books, and is a major intellectual force.

**Mary Tyler Moore,** television actress, is one of the heads of Mary Tyler Moore Productions.

**Jacqueline Kennedy Onassis,** former first lady, is currently an editor at Doubleday and Co.

**Sylvia Porter,** financial and consumer columnist since 1939, today appears in more than 340 newspapers.

**Phyllis Schlafly,** author, politician, housewife, is the chief spokesman for STOP-ERA force and publishes the monthly *Phyllis Schlafly Report.*

**Gloria Steinem,** feminist, an articulate spokeswoman for the rights of women and blacks, helped found *Ms* and the National Women's Political Caucus.

**Helen Thomas,** White House Correspondent for United Press International, joined UPI as a wire service reporter in 1943.

**Abigail Van Buren,** personal advice columnist, has written "Dear Abby" since 1956 and now appears in newspapers all over the world.

**Barbara Walters,** currently broadcast journalist at ABC-TV, was the first woman to anchor an evening news program.

## Presidential Election Statistics
### Popular and Electoral Vote, 1972 and 1976

| States | 1972 Electoral Vote Nixon | 1972 Electoral Vote McGovern | 1972 Republican Nixon | 1972 Democrat McGovern | 1976 Electoral Vote Carter | 1976 Electoral Vote Ford | 1976 Democrat Carter | 1976 Republican Ford | 1976 Indep. McCarthy | 1976 Libert. MacBride |
|---|---|---|---|---|---|---|---|---|---|---|
| Ala. . . . | 9 | | 728,701 | 256,923 | 9 | | 659,170 | 504,070 | | 1,481 |
| Alas. . . | 3 | | 55,349 | 32,967 | | 3 | 44,058 | 71,555 | | 6,785 |
| Ariz. . . | 6 | | 402,812 | 198,540 | | 6 | 295,602 | 418,642 | 19,229 | 7,647 |
| Ark. . . . | 6 | | 445,751 | 198,899 | 6 | | 498,604 | 267,903 | 639 | |
| Cal. . . . | 45 | | 4,602,096 | 3,475,847 | | 45 | 3,742,284 | 3,882,244 | | 56,388 |
| Col. . . . | 7 | | 597,189 | 329,980 | | 7 | 460,353 | 584,367 | 26,107 | 5,330 |
| Conn. . . . | 8 | | 810,763 | 555,498 | | 8 | 647,895 | 719,261 | | |
| Del. . . . | 3 | | 140,357 | 92,283 | 3 | | 122,596 | 109,831 | 2,437 | |
| D.C. . . . | | 3 | 35,226 | 127,627 | 3 | | 137,818 | 27,873 | | 274 |
| Fla. . . . | 17 | | 1,857,759 | 718,117 | 17 | | 1,636,000 | 1,469,531 | 23,643 | |
| Ga. . . . | 12 | | 881,496 | 289,529 | 12 | | 979,409 | 483,743 | | |
| Ha. . . . | 4 | | 168,865 | 101,409 | 4 | | 147,375 | 140,003 | | 3,923 |
| Ida. . . . | 4 | | 199,384 | 80,826 | | 4 | 126,549 | 204,151 | | 3,558 |
| Ill. . . . . | 26 | | 2,788,179 | 1,913,472 | | 26 | 2,271,295 | 2,364,269 | 55,939 | 8,057 |
| Ind. . . . | 13 | | 1,405,154 | 708,568 | | 13 | 1,014,714 | 1,185,958 | | |
| Ia. . . . | 8 | | 706,207 | 496,206 | | 8 | 619,931 | 632,863 | 20,051 | 1,452 |
| Kan. . . . | 7 | | 619,812 | 270,287 | | 7 | 430,421 | 502,752 | 13,185 | 3,242 |
| Ky. . . . | 9 | | 676,446 | 371,159 | 9 | | 615,717 | 531,852 | 6,837 | 814 |
| La. . . . | 10 | | 686,852 | 298,142 | 10 | | 661,365 | 587,446 | 6,588 | 3,325 |
| Me. . . . | 4 | | 256,458 | 160,584 | | 4 | 232,279 | 236,320 | 10,874 | |
| Md. . . . | 10 | | 829,305 | 505,781 | 10 | | 759,612 | 672,661 | | |
| Mass. . . | | 14 | 1,112,078 | 1,332,540 | 14 | | 1,429,475 | 1,030,276 | 65,637 | 135 |
| Mich. . . | 21 | | 1,961,721 | 1,459,435 | | 21 | 1,696,714 | 1,893,742 | 47,905 | 5,406 |
| Minn. . . | 10 | | 898,269 | 802,346 | 10 | | 1,070,440 | 819,395 | 35,490 | 3,529 |
| Miss. . . | 7 | | 505,125 | 126,782 | 7 | | 381,309 | 366,846 | 4,074 | 2,609 |
| Mo. . . . | 12 | | 1,154,058 | 698,531 | 12 | | 999,163 | 928,808 | 24,329 | |
| Mon. . . . | 4 | | 183,976 | 120,197 | | 4 | 149,259 | 173,703 | | |
| Neb. . . . | 5 | | 406,298 | 169,991 | | 5 | 233,287 | 359,219 | 9,383 | 1,476 |
| Nev. . . . | 3 | | 115,750 | 66,016 | | 3 | 92,479 | 101,273 | | 1,519 |
| N.H.. . . | 4 | | 213,724 | 116,435 | | 4 | 147,645 | 185,935 | 4,095 | 936 |
| N.J. . . . | 17 | | 1,845,502 | 1,102,211 | | 17 | 1,444,653 | 1,509,688 | 32,717 | 9,449 |
| N.M. . . . | 4 | | 235,606 | 141,084 | | 4 | 201,148 | 211,419 | | 1,110 |
| N.Y. . . . | 41 | | 4,192,778 | 2,951,084 | 41 | | 3,389,558 | 3,100,791 | | 12,197 |
| N.C. . . . | 13 | | 1,054,889 | 438,705 | 13 | | 927,365 | 741,960 | | 2,219 |
| N.D.. . . | 3 | | 174,109 | 100,384 | | 3 | 136,078 | 153,470 | 2,952 | 256 |
| Oh. . . . | 25 | | 2,441,827 | 1,558,889 | 25 | | 2,011,621 | 2,000,505 | 58,258 | 8,961 |
| Okla. . . | 8 | | 759,025 | 247,147 | | 8 | 532,442 | 545,708 | 14,101 | |
| Ore. . . . | 6 | | 486,686 | 392,760 | | 6 | 490,407 | 492,120 | 40,207 | |
| Pa. . . . | 27 | | 2,714,521 | 1,796,951 | 27 | | 2,328,677 | 2,205,604 | 50,584 | |
| R.I. . . . | 4 | | 220,383 | 194,645 | 4 | | 227,636 | 181,249 | | 715 |
| S.C. . . . | 8 | | 477,044 | 186,824 | 8 | | 450,807 | 346,149 | | |
| S.D. . . . | 4 | | 166,476 | 139,945 | | 4 | 147,068 | 151,505 | | 1,619 |
| Tenn. . . | 10 | | 813,147 | 357,293 | 10 | | 825,879 | 633,969 | 5,004 | 1,375 |
| Tex. . . . | 26 | | 2,298,896 | 1,154,289 | 26 | | 2,082,319 | 1,953,300 | 20,118 | |
| Ut. . . . | 4 | | 323,643 | 126,284 | | 4 | 182,110 | 337,908 | 3,907 | 2,438 |
| Vt. . . . . | 3 | | 117,149 | 68,174 | | 3 | 78,789 | 100,387 | 4,001 | |
| Va. . . . | 11* | | 988,493 | 438,887 | | 12 | 813,896 | 836,554 | | 4,648 |
| Wash. . . | 9 | | 837,135 | 568,334 | | 8** | 717,323 | 777,732 | 36,986 | 5,042 |
| W.Va. . . | 6 | | 484,964 | 277,435 | 6 | | 435,864 | 314,726 | | |
| Wis. . . . | 11 | | 989,430 | 810,174 | 11 | | 1,040,232 | 1,004,987 | 34,943 | 3,814 |
| Wyo. . . | 3 | | 100,464 | 44,358 | | 3 | 62,239 | 92,717 | 624 | 89 |
| **TOTAL .** | **520** | **17** | **47,165,234** | **28,168,110** | **297** | **240** | **40,825,839** | **39,147,770** | **680,390** | **171,627** |

*One elector in Virginia for John Hospers and Theodora Nathan. **One elector in Washington for Reagan.

## Presidential Election Returns by Counties

Compiled from official returns by The World Almanac.

### Alabama

| County | 1972 McGovern (D) | Nixon (R) | 1976 Carter (D) | Ford (R) |
|---|---|---|---|---|
| utauga | 1,593 | 5,367 | 4,640 | 4,512 |
| aldwin | 2,923 | 15,104 | 9,191 | 13,256 |
| arbour | 1,846 | 4,985 | 4,730 | 3,758 |
| bb | 837 | 3,332 | 2,850 | 1,591 |
| lount | 1,582 | 6,486 | 6,645 | 4,233 |
| ullock | 2,321 | 2,178 | 3,536 | 1,482 |
| utler | 1,401 | 4,685 | 4,271 | 2,909 |
| alhoun | 5,832 | 20,364 | 20,466 | 11,763 |
| hambers | 2,076 | 8,716 | 6,164 | 5,488 |
| herokee | 1,182 | 3,179 | 4,668 | 1,492 |
| hilton | 1,356 | 7,349 | 5,550 | 4,725 |
| hoctaw | 1,934 | 3,055 | 3,911 | 3,033 |
| larke | 2,031 | 5,256 | 4,737 | 4,126 |
| lay | 507 | 3,948 | 2,946 | 1,883 |
| lebume | 581 | 3,420 | 2,490 | 1,436 |
| offee | 2,160 | 9,076 | 7,844 | 4,683 |
| olbert | 4,811 | 11,215 | 11,996 | 4,471 |
| onecuh | 1,042 | 3,214 | 3,086 | 1,812 |
| oosa | 773 | 2,672 | 2,533 | 1,196 |
| ovington | 1,547 | 9,278 | 7,081 | 4,977 |
| renshaw | 1,085 | 3,129 | 3,372 | 1,801 |
| ullman | 3,571 | 14,390 | 12,961 | 6,899 |
| ale | 1,594 | 8,346 | 6,346 | 4,996 |
| allas | 5,427 | 8,644 | 8,866 | 7,144 |
| eKalb | 3,759 | 9,434 | 9,759 | 6,597 |
| more | 1,891 | 8,461 | 6,646 | 6,551 |
| scambia | 1,598 | 8,883 | 5,957 | 4,934 |
| owah | 7,372 | 20,851 | 25,020 | 10,333 |
| ayette | 836 | 4,240 | 4,076 | 2,165 |
| ranklin | 1,840 | 5,877 | 6,279 | 3,345 |
| eneva | 1,049 | 5,851 | 5,983 | 2,663 |
| reene | 3,235 | 1,404 | 2,900 | 903 |
| ale | 1,779 | 2,859 | 3,236 | 2,034 |
| enry | 853 | 3,414 | 3,144 | 2,052 |
| ouston | 2,358 | 12,622 | 8,787 | 10,672 |
| ackson | 2,985 | 6,202 | 10,989 | 3,913 |
| efferson | 57,288 | 135,095 | 99,531 | 113,590 |
| amar | 766 | 3,283 | 3,860 | 1,739 |
| auderdale | 5,112 | 14,410 | 15,549 | 7,226 |
| awrence | 1,416 | 4,433 | 6,810 | 1,415 |
| ee | 3,622 | 11,571 | 8,427 | 9,884 |
| mestone | 2,079 | 6,188 | 8,803 | 2,997 |
| owndes | 2,559 | 1,990 | 3,732 | 1,621 |
| acon | 3,636 | 1,931 | 5,915 | 1,387 |
| adison | 13,108 | 38,899 | 35,497 | 20,959 |
| arengo | 2,645 | 5,156 | 4,731 | 3,841 |
| arion | 986 | 5,927 | 6,244 | 3,036 |
| arshall | 3,894 | 12,090 | 13,696 | 6,006 |
| obile | 20,694 | 62,639 | 50,264 | 53,835 |
| onroe | 1,636 | 5,155 | 3,669 | 3,476 |
| ontgomery | 12,723 | 35,353 | 24,641 | 29,360 |
| organ | 5,004 | 18,100 | 16,547 | 9,058 |
| erry | 2,718 | 2,800 | 4,486 | 2,164 |
| ckens | 1,933 | 4,071 | 3,776 | 2,969 |
| ke | 1,624 | 5,690 | 5,387 | 4,363 |
| andolph | 1,330 | 4,427 | 3,539 | 2,286 |
| ussell | 2,644 | 6,034 | 8,077 | 4,150 |
| . Clair | 1,859 | 6,952 | 5,653 | 4,877 |
| helby | 1,538 | 9,390 | 7,197 | 9,035 |
| umter | 2,737 | 2,686 | 3,457 | 2,191 |
| alladega | 4,567 | 12,763 | 10,577 | 6,425 |
| allapoosa | 2,113 | 8,535 | 7,614 | 5,237 |
| uscaloosa | 8,272 | 21,172 | 20,275 | 16,021 |
| alker | 3,724 | 14,581 | 16,232 | 7,389 |
| ashington | 1,096 | 3,282 | 3,471 | 2,171 |
| ilcox | 3,254 | 2,641 | 3,723 | 1,824 |
| inston | 779 | 4,971 | 4,134 | 3,710 |
| **Totals** | **256,923** | **728,701** | **659,170** | **504,070** |

### Alabama Vote Since 1932

932 (Pres.), Roosevelt, Dem., 207,910; Hoover, Rep., 34,675; Foster, Com., 406; Thomas, Soc. 2,030; Upshaw, Proh., 13.

936 (Pres.), Roosevelt, Dem., 238,195; Landon, Rep., 35,358; Colvin, Proh., 719; Browder, Com., 679; Lemke, Union, 549; Thomas, Soc., 242.

940 (Pres.), Roosevelt, Dem., 250,726; Willkie, Rep., 42,174; Babson, Proh., 698; Browder, Com., 509; Thomas, Soc., 100.

944 (Pres.), Roosevelt, Dem., 198,918; Dewey, Rep., 44,540; Watson, Proh., 1,095; Thomas, Soc., 190.

948 (Pres.), Thurmond, States' Rights, 171,443; Dewey, Rep., 40,930; Wallace, Prog., 1,522; Watson, Proh., 1,085.

952 (Pres.), Eisenhower, Rep., 149,231; Stevenson, Dem.,

275,075; Hamblen, Proh., 1,814.

1956 (Pres.), Stevenson, Dem., 290,844; Eisenhower, Rep. 195,694; Independent electors, 20,323.

1960 (Pres.), Kennedy, Dem., 324,050; Nixon, Rep., 237,981; Faubus, States' Rights, 4,367; Decker, Proh., 2,106; King, Afro-Americans, 1,485; scattering, 236.

1964 (Pres.), Dem. 209,848 (electors unpledged); Goldwater, Rep., 479,085; scattering, 105.

1968 (Pres.), Nixon, Rep., 146,923; Humphrey, Dem., 196,579; Wallace, 3d party, 691,425; Munn, Proh., 4,022.

1972 (Pres.), Nixon, Rep., 728,701; McGovern, Dem., 219,108 plus 37,815 Natl. Demo. Party of Alabama; Schmitz, Conservative, 11,918; Munn., Proh., 8,551.

1976 (Pres.), Carter, Dem., 659,170; Ford, Rep., 504,070; Maddox, Am. Ind., 9,198; Bubar, Proh., 6,669; Hall, Comm., 1,954; MacBride, Libertarian, 1,481.

### Alaska

| County | 1972 McGovern (D) | Nixon (R) | 1976 Carter (D) | Ford (R) |
|---|---|---|---|---|
| No. 1 | 1,526 | 2,529 | 1,983 | 2,994 |
| No. 2 | 967 | 1,386 | 1,022 | 1,423 |
| No. 3 | 1,393 | 1,549 | 1,152 | 1,710 |
| No. 4 | 2,968 | 4,277 | 3,214 | 5,252 |
| No. 5 | 903 | 1,689 | 1,307 | 2,071 |
| No. 6 | 849 | 2,384 | 1,486 | 2,882 |
| No. 7 | 2,854 | 4,527 | 2,935 | 4,105 |
| No. 8 | 2,454 | 5,275 | 3,368 | 5,412 |
| No. 9 | 2,501 | 6,759 | 1,726 | 2,561 |
| No. 10 | 2,854 | 6,882 | 2,839 | 6,837 |
| No. 11 | 1,337 | 2,686 | 3,568 | 6,588 |
| No. 12 | 727 | 1,117 | 2,700 | 6,381 |
| No. 13 | 178 | 293 | 2,099 | 4,057 |
| No. 14 | 843 | 1,042 | 856 | 1,380 |
| No. 15 | 1,235 | 919 | 538 | 746 |
| No. 16 | 1,004 | 902 | 876 | 1,063 |
| No. 17 | 5,535 | 7,672 | 1,149 | 1,074 |
| No. 18 | 640 | 1,202 | 804 | 942 |
| No. 19 | 1,155 | 1,114 | 1,415 | 1,893 |
| No. 20 | ... | ... | 6,706 | 10,306 |
| No. 21 | ... | ... | 1,229 | 749 |
| No. 22 | ... | ... | 1,086 | 1,129 |
| **Totals** | **32,967** | **55,349** | **44,058** | **71,555** |

### Alaska Vote Since 1960

1960 (Pres.), Kennedy, Dem., 29,809; Nixon, Rep. 30,953.

1964 (Pres.), Johnson, Dem., 44,329; Goldwater, Rep., 22,930.

1968 (Pres.), Nixon, Rep., 37,600; Humphrey, Dem., 35,411; Wallace, 3d party, 10,024.

1972 (Pres.), Nixon, Rep., 55,349; McGovern, Dem., 32,967; Schmitz, American, 6,906.

1976 (Pres.), Carter, Dem., 44,058; Ford, Rep., 71,555; MacBride, Libertarian, 6,785.

### Arizona

| County | 1972 McGovern (D) | Nixon (R) | 1976 Carter (D) | Ford (R) |
|---|---|---|---|---|
| Apache | 3,145 | 3,394 | 6,583 | 3,447 |
| Cochise | 6,023 | 11,706 | 9,281 | 9,921 |
| Coconino | 6,250 | 10,611 | 9,450 | 11,036 |
| Gila | 4,295 | 5,673 | 6,440 | 5,136 |
| Graham | 1,863 | 3,575 | 3,050 | 3,659 |
| Greenlee | 2,013 | 1,758 | 2,601 | 1,532 |
| Maricopa | 95,135 | 244,593 | 144,613 | 258,262 |
| Mohave | 2,588 | 6,755 | 6,504 | 7,601 |
| Navajo | 4,003 | 6,999 | 7,323 | 6,796 |
| Pima | 56,223 | 73,154 | 71,214 | 77,264 |
| Pinal | 6,404 | 10,584 | 10,595 | 9,354 |
| Santa Cruz | 1,866 | 2,137 | 2,265 | 2,312 |
| Yavapai | 3,977 | 12,277 | 7,685 | 12,998 |
| Yuma | 4,755 | 9,596 | 7,998 | 9,324 |
| **Totals** | **198,540** | **402,812** | **295,602** | **418,642** |

### Arizona Vote Since 1932

1932 (Pres.), Roosevelt, Dem., 79,264; Hoover, Rep., 36,104; Thomas, Soc., 2030; Foster. Com., 406.

1936 (Pres.), Roosevelt, Dem., 86,722; Landon, Rep., 33,433; Lemke, Union, 3,307; Colvin, Proh., 384; Thomas, Soc., 317.

1940 (Pres.), Roosevelt, Dem., 95,267; Willkie, Rep., 54,030; Babson, Proh., 742.

1944 (Pres.), Roosevelt, Dem., 80,826; Dewey, Rep., 56,287; Watson, Proh., 421.

1948 (Pres.), Truman, Dem., 95,251; Dewey, Rep., 77,597; Wallace, Prog., 3,310; Watson, Proh., 786; Teichert, Soc. Lab., 121.

1952 (Pres.), Eisenhower, Rep., 152,042; Stevenson, Dem., 108,528.

1956 (Pres.), Eisenhower, Rep., 176,990; Stevenson, Dem., 112,880; Andrews, Ind. 303.

1960 (Pres.), Kennedy, Dem., 176,781; Nixon, Rep., 221,241; Haas, Soc. Lab., 469.

1964 (Pres.), Johnson, Dem., 237,753; Goldwater, Rep., 242,535; Haas, Soc. Labor, 482.

1968 (Pres.), Nixon, Rep., 266,721; Humphrey, Dem., 170,514; Wallace, 3d party, 46,573; McCarthy, New Party, 2,751; Halstead, Soc. Worker, 85; Cleaver, Peace and Freedom, 217; Bloman, Soc. Labor, 75.

1972 (Pres.), Nixon, Rep., 402,812; McGovern, Dem., 198,540; Schmitz, American, 21,208; Soc. Worker, 30,945. (Due to ballot peculiarities in 3 counties (particularly Pima), thousands of voters cast ballots for the Socialist Workers Party *and* one of the major candidates. Court ordered both votes counted as official.

1976 (Pres.), Carter, Dem., 295,602; Ford, Rep., 418,642; McCarthy, Ind., 19,229; MacBride, Libertarian, 7,647; Camejo, Soc. Workers, 928; Anderson, American, 564; Maddox, Am. Ind., 85.

## Arkansas

| County | 1972 McGovern (D) | 1972 Nixon (R) | 1976 Carter (D) | 1976 Ford (R) |
|---|---|---|---|---|
| Arkansas | 1,849 | 5,225 | 5,640 | 2,480 |
| Ashley | 1,680 | 5,506 | 5,253 | 3,092 |
| Baxter | 2,677 | 6,754 | 5,766 | 5,885 |
| Benton | 4,083 | 14,621 | 11,289 | 12,670 |
| Boone | 1,862 | 5,484 | 5,388 | 3,959 |
| Bradley | 1,368 | 3,218 | 3,567 | 1,134 |
| Calhoun | 707 | 1,298 | 2,014 | 495 |
| Carroll | 1,401 | 3,565 | 3,791 | 2,804 |
| Chicot | 1,469 | 2,858 | 3,868 | 1,621 |
| Clark | 2,741 | 4,173 | 6,641 | 1,816 |
| Clay | 1,933 | 4,381 | 5,664 | 1,893 |
| Cleburne | 1,400 | 2,870 | 5,726 | 1,992 |
| Cleveland | 734 | 1,837 | 2,320 | 646 |
| Columbia | 2,193 | 5,801 | 4,708 | 4,287 |
| Conway | 3,009 | 4,187 | 6,443 | 2,177 |
| Craighead | 5,843 | 11,312 | 13,840 | 6,213 |
| Crawford | 1,520 | 6,974 | 5,946 | 4,764 |
| Crittenden | 3,246 | 7,971 | 8,249 | 5,202 |
| Cross | 1,221 | 3,743 | 4,198 | 1,909 |
| Dallas | 1,402 | 2,152 | 3,266 | 1,012 |
| Desha | 1,665 | 3,385 | 4,228 | 1,372 |
| Drew | 1,168 | 3,334 | 3,750 | 1,730 |
| Faulkner | 4,604 | 6,746 | 11,423 | 3,904 |
| Franklin | 1,252 | 3,678 | 3,703 | 1,973 |
| Fulton | 960 | 2,030 | 2,670 | 1,038 |
| Garland | 5,207 | 15,602 | 15,707 | 10,394 |
| Grant | 1,147 | 2,414 | 3,797 | 1,047 |
| Greene | 2,263 | 6,128 | 7,495 | 2,690 |
| Hempstead | 2,047 | 4,963 | 5,397 | 2,859 |
| Hot Spring | 2,872 | 5,378 | 7,809 | 2,187 |
| Howard | 1,069 | 2,682 | 3,207 | 1,575 |
| Independence | 2,630 | 5,076 | 7,116 | 2,878 |
| Izard | 1,108 | 2,001 | 3,328 | 1,394 |
| Jackson | 2,092 | 4,196 | 6,456 | 1,783 |
| Jefferson | 10,346 | 16,888 | 21,001 | 8,034 |
| Johnson | 2,045 | 4,107 | 5,044 | 2,173 |
| Lafayette | 952 | 2,460 | 2,342 | 1,467 |
| Lawrence | 1,751 | 3,981 | 5,167 | 1,708 |
| Lee | 1,907 | 3,540 | 3,463 | 1,574 |
| Lincoln | 1,115 | 2,318 | 3,045 | 699 |
| Little River | 1,091 | 2,550 | 3,142 | 1,431 |
| Logan | 1,956 | 4,964 | 5,313 | 2,909 |
| Lonoke | 2,504 | 5,298 | 7,761 | 2,522 |
| Madison | 1,889 | 3,372 | 2,926 | 2,502 |
| Marion | 1,108 | 2,331 | 2,979 | 2,045 |
| Miller | 2,855 | 8,355 | 6,821 | 4,737 |
| Mississippi | 3,544 | 10,931 | 10,292 | 6,009 |
| Monroe | 1,578 | 2,897 | 3,556 | 1,285 |
| Montgomery | 688 | 1,555 | 2,420 | 924 |
| Nevada | 1,179 | 2,513 | 3,101 | 1,163 |
| Newton | 831 | 1,924 | 1,840 | 1,641 |
| Ouachita | 3,931 | 6,620 | 8,946 | 2,753 |
| Perry | 810 | 1,445 | 2,310 | 8 |
| Phillips | 4,283 | 6,235 | 7,774 | 3,3 |
| Pike | 798 | 2,316 | 2,822 | 1,2 |
| Poinsett | 1,908 | 7,010 | 6,835 | 2,7 |
| Polk | 1,120 | 3,609 | 3,505 | 2,4 |
| Pope | 3,302 | 6,917 | 8,355 | 4,3 |
| Prairie | 873 | 2,186 | 2,836 | 8 |
| Pulaski | 33,611 | 57,576 | 63,541 | 37,6 |
| Randolph | 1,525 | 2,578 | 4,551 | 1,5 |
| St. Francis | 2,674 | 5,692 | 6,851 | 3,6 |
| Saline | 4,503 | 7,972 | 12,008 | 4,1 |
| Scott | 771 | 2,424 | 2,880 | 1,4 |
| Searcy | 853 | 3,163 | 2,067 | 1,7 |
| Sebastian | 5,770 | 25,219 | 15,698 | 17,6 |
| Sevier | 1,048 | 2,526 | 3,391 | 1,4 |
| Sharp | 1,154 | 2,677 | 3,532 | 2,1 |
| Stone | 958 | 1,989 | 2,718 | 1,0 |
| Union | 3,531 | 11,925 | 8,257 | 7,9 |
| Van Buren | 1,594 | 2,622 | 4,004 | 1,6 |
| Washington | 7,108 | 17,523 | 15,610 | 14,1 |
| White | 4,161 | 8,701 | 11,412 | 4,7 |
| Woodruff | 1,183 | 1,989 | 3,040 | 8 |
| Yell | 1,669 | 3,310 | 5,785 | 1,9 |
| **Totals** | **198,899** | **445,751** | **498,604** | **267,9** |

## Arkansas Vote Since 1932

1932 (Pres.), Roosevelt, Dem., 189,602; Hoover, Rep, 28,467; Thomas, Soc., 1,269; Harvey, Ind., 1,049; Foste Com., 175.

1936 (Pres.), Roosevelt, Dem. 146,765; Landon, Rep, 32,039; Thomas, Soc., 446; Browder, Com., 164; Lemk Union, 4.

1940 (Pres.), Roosevelt, Dem., 158,622; Willkie, Rep, 42,121; Babson, Proh., 793; Thomas, Soc., 305.

1944 (Pres.), Roosevelt, Dem., 148,965; Dewey, Rep 63,551; Thomas, Soc. 438.

1948 (Pres.), Truman, Dem., 149,659; Dewey, Rep., 50,95 Thurmond, States' Rights, 40,068; Thomas, Soc., 1,03 Wallace, Prog., 751; Watson, Proh., 1.

1952 (Pres.), Eisenhower, Rep., 177,155; Stevenson, Dem 226,330; Hamblen, Proh., 886; MacArthur, Christian N tionalist, 458; Haas, Soc. Lab. 1.

1956 (Pres.), Stevenson, Dem., 213,277; Eisenhower, Rep 186,287; Andrews, Ind., 7,008.

1960 (Pres.), Kennedy, Dem., 215,049; Nixon, Rep 184,508; National States' Rights, 28,952.

1964 (Pres.), Johnson, Dem., 314,197; Goldwater, Rep 243,264; Kasper, Nat'l. States Rights, 2,965.

1968 (Pres.), Nixon, Rep., 189,062; Humphrey, Dem 184,901; Wallace, 3d party, 235,627.

1972 (Pres.), Nixon, Rep., 445,751; McGovern, Dem 198,899; Schmitz, Amer. Party, 3,016.

1976 (Pres.), Carter, Dem., 498,604; Ford, Rep., 267,90 McCarthy, Ind., 639; Anderson, American, 389.

## California

| County | 1972 McGovern (D) | 1972 Nixon (R) | 1976 Carter (D) | 1976 Ford (R) |
|---|---|---|---|---|
| Alameda | 259,254 | 201,862 | 235,988 | 155,28 |
| Alpine | 195 | 366 | 189 | 25 |
| Amador | 2,705 | 3,533 | 4,037 | 3,69 |
| Butte | 18,401 | 28,819 | 24,203 | 28,40 |
| Calaveras | 2,268 | 4,119 | 3,607 | 3,69 |
| Colusa | 1,810 | 2,715 | 2,340 | 2,73 |
| Contra Costa | 111,718 | 139,044 | 123,742 | 126,59 |
| Del Norte | 2,156 | 2,927 | 2,789 | 2,48 |
| El Dorado | 8,654 | 11,330 | 12,763 | 12,47 |
| Fresno | 72,682 | 79,051 | 74,958 | 72,53 |
| Glenn | 2,681 | 4,569 | 3,501 | 4,09 |
| Humboldt | 21,132 | 22,345 | 23,500 | 18,03 |
| Imperial | 7,982 | 14,178 | 10,244 | 10,61 |
| Inyo | 2,006 | 4,873 | 2,635 | 3,90 |
| Kern | 41,327 | 71,686 | 50,567 | 58,02 |
| Kings | 7,274 | 10,509 | 8,061 | 8,26 |
| Lake | 4,715 | 6,477 | 6,374 | 5,46 |
| Lassen | 3,134 | 3,618 | 3,801 | 3,00 |
| Los Angeles | 1,189,977 | 1,549,717 | 1,221,893 | 1,174,92 |
| Madera | 6,580 | 7,835 | 7,625 | 6,84 |
| Marin | 47,414 | 54,123 | 43,590 | 53,42 |
| Mariposa | 1,487 | 2,122 | 2,093 | 2,01 |
| Mendocino | 9,435 | 11,128 | 10,653 | 9,78 |
| Merced | 13,914 | 17,737 | 16,637 | 14,84 |
| Modoc | 1,271 | 2,085 | 1,733 | 1,91 |
| Mono | 828 | 1,872 | 1,025 | 1,60 |
| Monterey | 32,545 | 47,004 | 36,849 | 40,89 |
| Napa | 14,529 | 23,403 | 18,048 | 20,83 |
| Nevada | 5,693 | 8,004 | 7,926 | 8,17 |

| | 1972 (D) | (R) | 1976 (D) | (R) |
|---|---|---|---|---|
| Orange | 176,847 | 448,291 | 232,246 | 408,632 |
| Placer | 16,911 | 18,597 | 21,026 | 18,154 |
| Plumas | 3,057 | 2,952 | 3,429 | 2,884 |
| Riverside | 71,591 | 108,120 | 96,228 | 97,774 |
| Sacramento | 137,287 | 141,218 | 144,203 | 123,110 |
| San Benito | 2,582 | 3,961 | 3,122 | 3,398 |
| San Bernardino | 85,986 | 144,689 | 109,636 | 113,265 |
| San Diego | 206,455 | 371,627 | 263,654 | 353,302 |
| San Francisco | 170,882 | 127,461 | 133,733 | 103,561 |
| San Joaquin | 44,062 | 61,646 | 48,733 | 50,277 |
| San Luis Obispo | 20,779 | 28,566 | 24,926 | 27,785 |
| San Mateo | 109,745 | 135,377 | 102,896 | 117,338 |
| Santa Barbara | 50,609 | 67,075 | 55,018 | 60,922 |
| Santa Clara | 208,506 | 237,334 | 208,023 | 219,188 |
| Santa Cruz | 32,336 | 34,799 | 37,772 | 31,872 |
| Shasta | 17,214 | 16,618 | 19,200 | 17,273 |
| Sierra | 658 | 629 | 841 | 680 |
| Siskiyou | 6,434 | 7,563 | 7,060 | 7,070 |
| Solano | 24,766 | 31,314 | 33,682 | 26,136 |
| Sonoma | 43,746 | 57,697 | 50,353 | 50,555 |
| Stanislaus | 35,005 | 39,521 | 38,448 | 32,937 |
| Sutter | 5,409 | 10,224 | 6,966 | 8,745 |
| Tehama | 5,175 | 6,054 | 6,990 | 6,110 |
| Trinity | 1,621 | 1,868 | 2,172 | 1,989 |
| Tulare | 21,775 | 36,048 | 25,551 | 31,864 |
| Tuolumne | 4,596 | 5,894 | 6,492 | 6,104 |
| Ventura | 49,307 | 95,310 | 68,529 | 82,670 |
| Yolo | 23,694 | 17,969 | 23,533 | 18,376 |
| Yuba | 4,435 | 6,623 | 6,451 | 5,496 |
| **Totals** | **3,475,847** | **4,602,096** | **3,742,284** | **3,882,244** |

## Colorado

| County | 1972 McGovern (D) | Nixon (R) | 1976 Carter (D) | Ford (R) |
|---|---|---|---|---|
| Adams | 24,170 | 40,372 | 40,551 | 35,392 |
| Alamosa | 1,540 | 2,916 | 2,052 | 2,599 |
| Arapahoe | 18,631 | 52,283 | 33,685 | 63,154 |
| Archuleta | 300 | 606 | 632 | 768 |
| Baca | 527 | 1,645 | 1,164 | 1,303 |
| Bent | 787 | 1,525 | 1,268 | 1,156 |
| Boulder | 29,494 | 40,766 | 33,284 | 42,830 |
| Chaffee | 1,354 | 2,859 | 2,064 | 2,925 |
| Cheyenne | 400 | 815 | 625 | 610 |
| Clear Creek | 815 | 1,557 | 1,069 | 1,477 |
| Conejos | 1,140 | 1,658 | 1,698 | 1,426 |
| Costilla | 744 | 602 | 1,033 | 392 |
| Crowley | 414 | 1,094 | 667 | 834 |
| Custer | 154 | 495 | 259 | 491 |
| Delta | 1,903 | 4,890 | 3,232 | 4,980 |
| Denver | 98,062 | 121,995 | 112,229 | 105,960 |
| Dolores | 166 | 498 | 374 | 343 |
| Douglas | 1,048 | 3,625 | 2,459 | 5,078 |
| Eagle | 1,306 | 1,920 | 1,502 | 2,963 |
| Elbert | 451 | 1,416 | 1,068 | 1,279 |
| El Paso | 21,234 | 53,892 | 32,911 | 50,929 |
| Fremont | 2,813 | 6,701 | 4,886 | 5,647 |
| Garfield | 2,088 | 4,452 | 2,852 | 4,699 |
| Gilpin | 362 | 516 | 563 | 451 |
| Grand | 685 | 1,721 | 910 | 1,703 |
| Gunnison | 1,187 | 2,231 | 1,250 | 2,568 |
| Hinsdale | 44 | 172 | 83 | 189 |
| Huerfano | 1,341 | 1,620 | 1,932 | 1,182 |
| Jackson | 178 | 623 | 279 | 455 |
| Jefferson | 31,555 | 80,082 | 52,782 | 87,080 |
| Kiowa | 372 | 849 | 529 | 598 |
| Kit Carson | 824 | 2,316 | 1,647 | 1,888 |
| Lake | 1,263 | 1,556 | 1,549 | 1,57. |
| La Plata | 2,830 | 5,691 | 3,843 | 6,228 |
| Larimer | 13,731 | 27,462 | 19,005 | 32,169 |
| Las Animas | 3,222 | 3,659 | 4,459 | 2,615 |
| Lincoln | 685 | 1,678 | 1,059 | 1,276 |
| Logan | 2,426 | 5,352 | 3,543 | 4,256 |
| Mesa | 6,358 | 15,527 | 8,807 | 17,924 |
| Mineral | 96 | 247 | 167 | 235 |
| Moffat | 591 | 1,928 | 1,451 | 2,099 |
| Montezuma | 1,223 | 3,391 | 1,993 | 3,002 |
| Montrose | 1,870 | 4,571 | 3,164 | 4,838 |
| Morgan | 2,081 | 5,365 | 3,798 | 4,603 |
| Otero | 2,929 | 6,016 | 4,118 | 4,597 |
| Ouray | 186 | 669 | 333 | 645 |
| Park | 386 | 1,001 | 741 | 1,034 |
| Philips | 687 | 1,480 | 1,173 | 1,142 |
| Pitkin | 2,531 | 2,064 | 2,194 | 2,955 |
| Prowers | 1,860 | 3,272 | 2,861 | 2,578 |
| Pueblo | 19,620 | 25,607 | 25,841 | 18,518 |
| Rio Blanco | 414 | 1,586 | 627 | 1,439 |
| Rio Grande | 1,029 | 2,787 | 1,475 | 2,627 |
| Routt | 1,613 | 2,629 | 2,130 | 2,822 |
| Saguache | 578 | 1,062 | 1,059 | 1,094 |
| San Juan | 140 | 238 | 167 | 221 |
| San Miguel | 426 | 583 | 674 | 622 |
| Sedgwick | 588 | 4,129 | 773 | 902 |
| Summit | 707 | 1,082 | 1,087 | 1,826 |
| Teller | 535 | 1,440 | 986 | 1,410 |
| Washington | 643 | 1,837 | 1,211 | 1,440 |
| Weld | 11,690 | 24,695 | 16,501 | 21,976 |
| Yuma | 1,066 | 2,873 | 2,025 | 2,350 |
| **Total** | **329,980** | **597,189** | **460,353** | **584,367** |

## California Vote Since 1932

1932 (Pres.), Roosevelt, Dem., 1,324,157; Hoover, Rep., 847,902; Thomas, Soc., 63,299; Upshaw, Proh., 20,637; Harvey, Liberty, 9,827; Foster, Com., 1,023.

1936 (Pres.), Roosevelt, Dem., 1,766,836; Landon, Rep., 836,431; Colvin, Proh., 12,917; Thomas, Soc., 11,325; Browder, Com., 10,877.

1940 (Pres.), Roosevelt, Dem., 1,877,618; Willkie, Rep., 1,351,419; Thomas, Prog., 16,506; Browder, Com., 13,586; Babson, Proh., 9,400.

1944 (Pres.), Roosevelt, Dem., 1,988,564; Dewey, Rep., 1,512,965; Watson, Proh., 14,770; Thomas, Soc., 3,923; Teichert, Soc. Lab., 327.

1948 (Pres.), Truman, Dem., 1,913,134; Dewey, Rep., 1,895,269; Wallace, Prog., 190,381; Watson, Proh., 16,926; Thomas, Soc., 3,459; Thurmond, States' Rights, 1,228; Teichert, Soc. Lab., 195; Dobbs, Soc. Wkr., 133.

1952 (Pres.), Eisenhower, Rep., 2,897,310; Stevenson, Dem., 2,197,548; Hallinan, Prog., 24,106; Hamblen, Proh., 15,653; MacArthur, (Tenny Ticket), 3,326; (Kellems Ticket) 178; Haas, Soc. Lab., 273; Hoopes, Soc., 206; Scattered, 3,249.

1956 (Pres.), Eisenhower, Rep., 3,027,668; Stevenson, Dem., 2,420,136; Holtwick, Proh., 11,119; Andrews, Constitution, 6,087; Haas, Soc. Lab., 300; Hoopes, Soc., 123; Dobbs, Soc. Workers, 96; Smith, Christian Nat'l., 8.

1960 (Pres.), Kennedy, Dem., 3,224,099; Nixon, Rep., 3,259,722; Decker, Proh., 21,706; Haas, Soc. Lab., 1,051.

1964 (Pres.), Johnson, Dem., 4,171,877; Goldwater, Rep., 2,879,108; Hass, Soc. Labor, 489; DeBerry, Soc. Worker, 378; Munn, Proh., 305; Hensley, Universal, 19.

1968 (Pres.), Nixon, Rep., 3,467,664; Humphrey, Dem., 3,244,318; Wallace, 3d party, 487,270; Peace and Freedom party, 27,707; McCarthy, Alternative, 20,721; Gregory, write-in, 3,230; Mitchell, Communist, 260; Munn, Prohibition, 59; Blomen, Socialist, 341; Soeters, Defense, 17.

1972 (Pres.), Nixon, Rep., 4,602,096; McGovern, Dem., 3,475,847; Schmitz, Amer., 232,554; Spock, Peace and Freedom, 55,167; Hall, Communist, 373; Hospers, Libertarian, 980; Munn, Prohibition, 53; Fisher, Soc. Labor, 197; Jenness, Soc. Workers, 574; Green, Universal, 21.

1976 (Pres.), Carter, Dem., 3,742,284; Ford, Rep., 3,882,244; MacBride, Libertarian, 56,388; Maddox, Am. Ind., 51,098; Wright, People's, 41,731; Camejo, Soc. Workers, 17,259; Hall, Comm., 12,766; write-in, McCarthy, 58,412; other write-in, 4,935.

## Colorado Vote Since 1932

1932 (Pres.), Roosevelt, Dem., 250,877; Hoover, Rep., 189,617; Thomas, Soc., 14,018; Upshaw, Proh., 1,928

1936 (Pres.), Roosevelt, Dem., 295,081; Landon, Rep., 18,267; Lemke, Union, 9,962; Thomas, Soc., 1,593; Browder, Com., 497; Aiken, Soc. Labor, 336.

1940 (Pres.), Roosevelt, Dem., 265,554; Willkie, Rep., 279,576; Thomas, Soc., 1,899; Babson, Proh., 1,597; Browder, Com., 378.

1944 (Pres.), Roosevelt, Dem., 234,331; Dewey, Rep., 268,731; Thomas, Soc., 1,977.

1948 (Pres.), Truman, Dem., 267,288; Dewey, Rep., 239,714; Wallace, Prog., 6,115; Thomas, Soc., 1,678; Dobbs, Soc. Workers, 228; Teichert, Soc. Lab., 214.

1952 (Pres.), Eisenhower, Rep., 379,782; Stevenson, Dem., 245,504; MacArthur, Constitution, 2,181; Hallinan, Prog., 1,919; Hoopes, Soc., 365; Haas, Soc. Lab., 352.

1956 (Pres.), Eisenhower, Rep., 394,479; Stevenson, Dem.,

263,997; Haas, Soc. Lab., 3,308; Andrews, Ind., 759; Hoopes, Soc., 531.

1960 (Pres.), Kennedy, Dem., 330,629; Nixon, Rep., 402,242; Haas, Soc. Lab., 2,803; Dobbs, Soc. Workers, 572.

1964 (Pres.), Johnson, Dem., 476,024; Goldwater, Rep., 296,767; Haas, Soc. Labor, 302; DeBerry, Soc. Worker, 2,537; Munn, Proh., 1,356.

1968 (Pres.), Nixon, Rep., 409,345; Humphrey, Dem., 335,174; Wallace, 3d party, 60,813; Blomen, Soc., 3,016; Gregory, New-party, 1,393; Munn, Proh., 275; Halstead, Soc. Work., 235.

1972 (Pres.), Nixon, Rep., 597,189; McGovern, Dem., 329,980; Fisher, Soc. Labor, 4,361; Hospers, Libertarian, 1,111; Hall, Com., 432; Jenness, Soc. Wrks., 555; Munn, Proh., 467; Schmitz, American, 17,269; Spock, Peoples, 2,403.

1976 (Pres.), Carter, Dem., 460,353; Ford, Rep., 584,367; McCarthy, Ind., 26,107; MacBride, Libertarian, 5,330.

## Connecticut

| | 1972 | | 1976 | |
| | McGovern | Nixon | Carter | Ford |
| County | (D) | (R) | (D) | (R) |
|---|---|---|---|---|
| Fairfield | 125,128 | 233,188 | 148,353 | 209,458 |
| Hartford | 174,837 | 194,095 | 191,257 | 175,064 |
| Litchfield | 27,929 | 43,478 | 32,419 | 40,705 |
| Middlesex | 23,573 | 33,249 | 29,097 | 31,115 |
| New Haven | 135,132 | 200,818 | 157,402 | 174,342 |
| New London | 32,935 | 58,516 | 45,908 | 47,231 |
| Tolland | 19,505 | 25,798 | 23,079 | 23,703 |
| Windham | 16,459 | 21,621 | 20,380 | 17,643 |
| **Totals** | **555,498** | **810,763** | **647,895** | **719,261** |

### Connecticut Vote Since 1932

1932 (Pres.), Roosevelt, Dem., 281,632; Hoover, Rep., 288,420; Thomas, Soc., 22,767.

1936 (Pres.), Roosevelt, Dem., 382,129; Landon, Rep., 278,685; Lemke, Union, 21,805; Thomas, Soc., 5,683; Browder, Com., 1,193.

1940 (Pres.), Roosevelt, Dem., 417,621; Willkie, Rep., 361,021; Browder, Com., 1,091; Aiken, Soc. Lab., 971; Willkie, Union, 798.

1944 (Pres.), Roosevelt, Dem., 435,146; Dewey, Rep., 390,527; Thomas, Soc., 5,097; Teichert, Soc. Lab., 1,220.

1948 (Pres.), Truman, Dem., 423,297; Dewey, Rep., 437,754; Wallace, Prog., 13,713; Thomas, Soc., 6,964; Teichert, Soc. Lab., 1,184; Dobbs, Soc. Workers, 606.

1952 (Pres.), Eisenhower, Rep., 611,012; Stevenson, Dem., 481,649; Hoopes, Soc., 2,244; Hallinan, Peoples, 1,466; Haas, Soc. Lab., 535; write-in, 5.

1956 (Pres.), Eisenhower, Rep., 711,837; Stevenson, Dem., 405,079; scattered, 205.

1960 (Pres.), Kennedy, Dem., 657,055; Nixon, Rep., 565,813.

1964 (Pres.), Johnson, Dem., 826,269; Goldwater, Rep., 390,996; scattered, 1,313.

1968 (Pres.), Nixon, Rep., 556,721; Humphrey, Dem., 621,561; Wallace, 3d party, 76,650; scattered, 1,300.

1972 (Pres.), Nixon, Rep., 810,763; McGovern, Dem., 555,498; Schmitz, Amer. Party, 17,239; scattered, 777.

1976 (Pres.), Carter, Dem., 647,895; Ford, Rep., 719,261; Maddox, George Wallace Party, 7,101; LaRouche, U.S. Labor, 1,789.

## Delaware

| | 1972 | | 1976 | |
| | McGovern | Nixon | Carter | Ford |
| County | (D) | (R) | (D) | (R) |
|---|---|---|---|---|
| Kent | 10,463 | 17,712 | 16,523 | 12,604 |
| New Castle | 70,190 | 100,681 | 87,521 | 80,074 |
| Sussex | 11,630 | 21,964 | 18,552 | 17,153 |
| **Totals** | **92,283** | **140,357** | **122,596** | **109,831** |

### Delaware Vote Since 1932

1932 (Pres.), Hoover, Rep., 57,074; Roosevelt, Dem., 54,319; Thomas, Soc., 1,376; Foster, Com., 133.

1936 (Pres.), Roosevelt, Dem., 69,702; Landon, Rep. 54,014 Lemke, Union, 442; Thomas, Soc., 179; Browder, Com. 52.

1940 (Pres.), Roosevelt, Dem., 74,559; Willkie, Rep., 61,440 Babson, Proh., 220; Thomas, Soc., 115.

1944 (Pres.), Roosevelt, Dem., 68,166; Dewey, Rep., 56,747 Watson, Proh., 294; Thomas, Soc., 154.

1948 (Pres.), Truman, Dem., 67,813; Dewey, Rep., 69,688 Wallace, Prog., 1,050; Watson, Proh., 343; Thomas, Soc. 250; Teichert, Soc. Lab., 29.

1952 (Pres.), Eisenhower, Rep., 90,059; Stevenson, Dem 83,315; Haas, Soc. Lab., 242; Hamblen, Proh., 234; Halli nan, Prog., 155; Hoopes, Soc., 20.

1956 (Pres.), Eisenhower, Rep. 98,057; Stevenson, Dem 79,421; Oltwick, Proh., 400; Haas, Soc. Lab., 110.

1960 (Pres.), Kennedy, Dem., 99,590; Nixon, Rep., 96,373 Faubus, States' Rights, 354; Decker, Proh., 284; Haas Soc. Lab., 82.

1964 (Pres.), Johnson, Dem., 122,704; Goldwater, Rep 78,078; Haas, Soc. Lab., 113; Munn, Proh., 425.

1968 (Pres.), Nixon, Rep., 96,714; Humphrey, Dem., 89,194 Wallace, 3d party, 28,459.

1972 (Pres.), Nixon, Rep., 140,357; McGovern, Dem. 92,283; Schmitz, Amer. Party, 2,638; Munn, Proh., 238.

1976 (Pres.), Carter, Dem., 122,596; Ford, Rep., 109,831 McCarthy, non-partisan, 2,437; Anderson, American 645; LaRouche, U.S. Labor, 136; Bubar, Proh., 103; Le vin, Soc. Labor, 86.

## District of Columbia

| | 1972 | | 1976 | |
| | McGovern | Nixon | Carter | Ford |
| County | (D) | (R) | (D) | (R) |
|---|---|---|---|---|
| **Totals** | **127,627** | **35,226** | **137,818** | **27,87** |

### District of Columbia Vote Since 1964

1964 (Pres.), Johnson, Dem., 169,796; Goldwater, Rep. 28,801.

1968 (Pres.), Nixon, Rep., 31,012; Humphrey, Dem. 139,566.

1972 (Pres.), Nixon, Rep., 35,226; McGovern, Dem. 127,627; Reed, Soc. Worker, 316; Hall, Comm. 252.

1976 (Pres.), Carter, Dem., 137,818; Ford, Rep., 27,873 Camejo, Soc. Workers, 545; MacBride, Libertarian, 274 Hall, Comm., 219; LaRouche, U.S. Labor 157.

## Florida

| | 1972 | | 1976 | |
| | McGovern | Nixon | Carter | Ford |
| County | (D) | (R) | (D) | (R) |
|---|---|---|---|---|
| Alachua | 17,245 | 22,536 | 27,895 | 15,546 |
| Baker | 379 | 1,943 | 2,985 | 1,058 |
| Bay | 3,914 | 20,245 | 14,858 | 14,208 |
| Bradford | 1,217 | 3,652 | 3,868 | 1,680 |
| Brevard | 16,854 | 62,773 | 46,421 | 44,470 |
| Broward | 74,127 | 196,528 | 176,491 | 161,411 |
| Calhoun | 461 | 2,069 | 2,487 | 1,153 |
| Charlotte | 3,874 | 12,888 | 10,300 | 12,703 |
| Citrus | 2,607 | 8,848 | 9,438 | 7,973 |
| Clay | 1,748 | 10,467 | 8,410 | 8,468 |
| Collier | 3,201 | 13,501 | 8,764 | 14,643 |
| Columbia | 1,664 | 6,723 | 6,683 | 3,947 |
| Dade | 177,693 | 256,529 | 303,047 | 211,148 |
| De Soto | 852 | 2,958 | 2,715 | 2,000 |
| Dixie | 367 | 1,628 | 2,169 | 558 |
| Duval | 46,530 | 122,154 | 105,912 | 74,997 |
| Escambia | 14,078 | 56,071 | 38,279 | 41,471 |
| Flagler | 493 | 1,409 | 2,086 | 1,262 |
| Franklin | 490 | 2,277 | 1,859 | 1,054 |
| Gadsden | 3,829 | 5,995 | 6,798 | 3,535 |
| Gilchrist | 247 | 1,306 | 1,807 | 522 |
| Glades | 253 | 1,019 | 1,311 | 624 |
| Gulf | 713 | 2,628 | 2,641 | 1,584 |
| Hamilton | 626 | 1,741 | 2,053 | 794 |
| Hardee | 647 | 3,563 | 2,670 | 2,189 |
| Hendry | 739 | 2,763 | 2,337 | 1,843 |
| Hernando | 2,110 | 6,296 | 7,717 | 5,793 |
| Highlands | 2,458 | 9,645 | 7,318 | 8,317 |
| Hillsborough | 45,305 | 106,956 | 94,589 | 78,504 |
| Holmes | 309 | 3,819 | 3,256 | 1,850 |
| Indian River | 3,316 | 11,741 | 8,512 | 9,818 |
| Jackson | 2,220 | 8,904 | 7,687 | 4,795 |
| Jefferson | 1,049 | 2,108 | 2,310 | 1,361 |

| | 1972 (D) | (R) | 1976 (D) | (R) |
|---|---|---|---|---|
| Lafayette | 173 | 1,060 | 1,126 | 523 |
| Lake | 4,803 | 23,079 | 14,369 | 19,976 |
| Lee | 9,404 | 36,738 | 30,567 | 38,038 |
| Leon | 15,555 | 27,479 | 28,729 | 23,739 |
| Levy | 862 | 3,273 | 4,025 | 1,965 |
| Liberty | 222 | 1,199 | 1,137 | 620 |
| Madison | 1,187 | 3,236 | 3,218 | 1,761 |
| Manatee | 8,058 | 32,664 | 24,342 | 29,300 |
| Marion | 5,397 | 19,505 | 16,963 | 16,163 |
| Martin | 2,946 | 11,296 | 8,785 | 11,682 |
| Monroe | 4,469 | 11,688 | 11,079 | 8,232 |
| Nassau | 1,293 | 5,078 | 5,896 | 3,136 |
| Okaloosa | 2,843 | 23,303 | 14,210 | 18,598 |
| Okeechobee | 621 | 2,581 | 3,184 | 1,598 |
| Orange | 23,840 | 94,516 | 58,442 | 70,451 |
| Osceola | 1,875 | 9,320 | 6,893 | 7,062 |
| Palm Beach | 40,825 | 108,670 | 96,705 | 98,236 |
| Pasco | 11,330 | 29,249 | 33,710 | 28,306 |
| Pinellas | 77,197 | 179,541 | 141,879 | 150,003 |
| Polk | 16,419 | 60,748 | 47,286 | 44,238 |
| Putnam | 2,901 | 8,741 | 9,597 | 5,040 |
| St. Johns | 2,549 | 8,919 | 7,412 | 6,660 |
| St. Lucie | 4,593 | 14,258 | 12,386 | 11,502 |
| Santa Rosa | 1,491 | 12,669 | 8,020 | 9,122 |
| Sarasota | 12,235 | 48,939 | 26,293 | 44,157 |
| Seminole | 6,503 | 27,658 | 19,609 | 26,655 |
| Sumter | 1,107 | 3,695 | 4,721 | 2,212 |
| Suwannee | 1,027 | 4,435 | 4,718 | 2,405 |
| Taylor | 754 | 4,109 | 3,370 | 1,983 |
| Union | 253 | 1,314 | 1,480 | 544 |
| Volusia | 21,637 | 52,656 | 49,161 | 37,523 |
| Wakulla | 539 | 2,466 | 2,353 | 1,580 |
| Walton | 988 | 6,217 | 5,196 | 2,927 |
| Washington | 606 | 3,777 | 3,566 | 2,313 |
| **Totals** | **718,117** | **1,857,759** | **1,636,000** | **1,469,531** |

## Florida Vote Since 1932

1932 (Pres.), Roosevelt, Dem., 206,307; Hoover, Rep., 69,170; Thomas, Soc., 775.

1936 (Pres.), Roosevelt, Dem., 249,117; Landon, Rep., 78,248; Thomas, Soc., 775.

1940 (Pres.), Roosevelt, Dem., 359,334; Willkie, Rep., 126,158.

1944 (Pres.), Roosevelt, Dem., 339,377; Dewey, Rep., 143,215.

1948 (Pres.), Truman, Dem., 281,988; Dewey, Rep., 194,280; Thurmond, States' Rights, 89,755; Wallace, Prog., 11,620.

1952 (Pres.), Eisenhower, Rep., 544,036; Stevenson, Dem., 444,950; scattered, 351.

1956 (Pres.), Eisenhower, Rep., 643,849; Stevenson, Dem., 480,371.

1960 (Pres.), Kennedy, Dem., 748,700; Nixon, Rep., 795,476.

1964 (Pres.), Johnson, Dem., 948,540; Goldwater, Rep., 905,941.

1968 (Pres.), Nixon, Rep., 886,804; Humphrey, Dem., 676,794; Wallace, 3d party, 624,207.

1972 (Pres.), Nixon, Rep., 1,857,759; McGovern, Dem., 718,117; scattered, 7,407.

1976 (Pres.), Carter, Dem., 1,636,000; Ford, Rep., 1,469,531; McCarthy, Ind., 23,643; Anderson, Amer., 21,325.

## Georgia

| | 1972 McGovern (D) | Nixon (R) | 1976 Carter (D) | Ford (R) |
|---|---|---|---|---|
| **County** | | | | |
| Appling | 512 | 2,755 | 3,585 | 961 |
| Atkinson | 309 | 924 | 1,560 | 347 |
| Bacon | 192 | 1,771 | 2,395 | 594 |
| Baker | 345 | 965 | 1,162 | 305 |
| Baldwin | 1,435 | 4,826 | 4,674 | 3,612 |
| Banks | 356 | 1,336 | 2,387 | 330 |
| Barrow | 867 | 3,423 | 4,756 | 1,364 |
| Bartow | 1,590 | 4,836 | 8,166 | 1,876 |
| Ben Hill | 703 | 2,104 | 2,449 | 814 |
| Berrien | 371 | 2,285 | 3,394 | 555 |
| Bibb | 10,201 | 27,402 | 31,902 | 12,819 |
| Bleckley | 377 | 2,308 | 2,605 | 972 |
| Brantley | 338 | 1,587 | 2,294 | 358 |
| Brooks | 643 | 2,430 | 2,653 | 1,102 |
| Bryan | 263 | 1,409 | 2,045 | 761 |
| Bulloch | 1,524 | 5,683 | 5,199 | 3,156 |
| Burke | 1,058 | 2,846 | 3,014 | 1,565 |
| Butts | 727 | 1,968 | 2,898 | 819 |
| Calhoun | 495 | 892 | 1,394 | 436 |
| Camden | 753 | 2,380 | 2,962 | 995 |
| Candler | 238 | 1,427 | 1,388 | 646 |

| | 1972 | | 1976 | |
|---|---|---|---|---|
| Carroll | 2,158 | 8,296 | 10,050 | 3,640 |
| Catoosa | 894 | 6,008 | 6,020 | 3,799 |
| Charlton | 310 | 1,244 | 1,750 | 452 |
| Chatham | 15,566 | 38,079 | 32,075 | 24,160 |
| Chattahoochee | 121 | 345 | 506 | 178 |
| Chattooga | 923 | 3,188 | 4,686 | 1,087 |
| Cherokee | 1,159 | 5,509 | 6,539 | 2,609 |
| Clarke | 6,090 | 11,465 | 11,342 | 6,610 |
| Clay | 283 | 632 | 947 | 295 |
| Clayton | 3,740 | 23,681 | 21,432 | 12,905 |
| Clinch | 239 | 1,127 | 1,414 | 383 |
| Cobb | 7,688 | 43,977 | 45,002 | 34,324 |
| Coffee | 607 | 3,934 | 4,601 | 1,417 |
| Colquitt | 930 | 6,900 | 6,928 | 2,181 |
| Columbia | 946 | 4,839 | 4,674 | 3,423 |
| Cook | 525 | 2,135 | 2,882 | 670 |
| Coweta | 1,560 | 5,751 | 6,195 | 3,044 |
| Crawford | 512 | 1,167 | 1,842 | 378 |
| Crisp | 682 | 3,623 | 3,747 | 1,328 |
| Dade | 148 | 2,110 | 2,263 | 1,388 |
| Dawson | 230 | 828 | 1,384 | 370 |
| Decatur | 1,196 | 4,292 | 3,736 | 2,500 |
| DeKalb | 30,671 | 104,750 | 86,872 | 67,160 |
| Dodge | 884 | 4,346 | 5,267 | 848 |
| Dooly | 590 | 1,904 | 2,441 | 655 |
| Dougherty | 3,625 | 12,878 | 11,461 | 9,337 |
| Douglas | 982 | 6,610 | 7,805 | 3,959 |
| Early | 513 | 2,396 | 2,405 | 1,157 |
| Echols | 68 | 404 | 585 | 111 |
| Effingham | 497 | 3,175 | 2,906 | 1,654 |
| Elbert | 884 | 2,875 | 4,730 | 961 |
| Emanuel | 916 | 3,684 | 4,603 | 1,493 |
| Evans | 375 | 1,666 | 1,631 | 746 |
| Fannin | 949 | 3,873 | 3,402 | 2,646 |
| Fayette | 450 | 3,401 | 3,718 | 2,837 |
| Floyd | 3,372 | 15,485 | 15,151 | 7,713 |
| Forsyth | 549 | 2,968 | 4,693 | 1,443 |
| Franklin | 435 | 2,022 | 4,192 | 687 |
| Fulton | 74,329 | 96,256 | 129,849 | 61,552 |
| Gilmer | 768 | 2,729 | 2,499 | 1,261 |
| Glascock | 41 | 578 | 704 | 371 |
| Glynn | 3,002 | 9,443 | 9,459 | 5,403 |
| Gordon | 870 | 4,344 | 6,052 | 1,698 |
| Grady | 874 | 3,732 | 3,758 | 1,209 |
| Greene | 919 | 1,679 | 2,534 | 652 |
| Gwinnett | 2,986 | 18,181 | 20,838 | 13,912 |
| Habersham | 172 | 971 | 5,120 | 1,315 |
| Hall | 2,440 | 10,686 | 12,804 | 5,093 |
| Hancock | 1,502 | 1,595 | 2,117 | 651 |
| Haralson | 767 | 3,460 | 4,550 | 1,301 |
| Harris | 701 | 2,617 | 2,861 | 1,544 |
| Hart | 784 | 2,308 | 4,605 | 860 |
| Heard | 276 | 1,239 | 1,593 | 433 |
| Henry | 1,460 | 5,155 | 5,717 | 2,622 |
| Houston | 2,556 | 13,576 | 13,164 | 5,404 |
| Irwin | 335 | 1,851 | 2,012 | 561 |
| Jackson | 1,055 | 4,124 | 5,931 | 1,239 |
| Jasper | 463 | 1,289 | 1,852 | 689 |
| Jeff Davis | 302 | 1,857 | 2,405 | 622 |
| Jefferson | 1,184 | 2,777 | 3,115 | 1,309 |
| Jenkins | 484 | 1,769 | 1,820 | 563 |
| Johnson | 417 | 2,201 | 2,210 | 698 |
| Jones | 861 | 2,483 | 3,471 | 1,317 |
| Lamar | 666 | 1,844 | 2,785 | 847 |
| Lanier | 193 | 850 | 1,269 | 207 |
| Laurens | 2,130 | 7,350 | 8,617 | 3,281 |
| Lee | 390 | 1,441 | 1,727 | 1,110 |
| Liberty | 1,217 | 2,337 | 3,328 | 979 |
| Lincoln | 340 | 1,246 | 1,583 | 576 |
| Long | 236 | 764 | 1,243 | 222 |
| Lowndes | 2,015 | 7,812 | 8,830 | 4,512 |
| Lumpkin | 385 | 1,477 | 2,301 | 547 |
| Macon | 837 | 2,005 | 3,013 | 638 |
| Madison | 572 | 2,600 | 3,367 | 1,115 |
| Marion | 164 | 850 | 1,314 | 291 |
| McDuffie | 996 | 2,990 | 3,024 | 1,694 |
| McIntosh | 893 | 1,367 | 1,978 | 535 |
| Meriwether | 1,213 | 3,420 | 4,330 | 1,450 |
| Miller | 118 | 1,269 | 1,536 | 476 |
| Mitchell | 1,120 | 2,400 | 4,495 | 1,572 |
| Monroe | 789 | 2,181 | 2,962 | 1,078 |
| Montgomery | 337 | 1,370 | 1,610 | 626 |
| Morgan | 668 | 2,007 | 2,274 | 904 |
| Murray | 644 | 2,643 | 3,511 | 889 |
| Muscogee | 18,234 | 28,449 | 24,092 | 13,496 |
| Newton | 1,380 | 4,647 | 6,294 | 2,137 |
| Oconee | 464 | 2,029 | 2,228 | 1,184 |
| Oglethorpe | 326 | 1,712 | 1,854 | 811 |
| Paulding | 1,004 | 2,814 | 5,420 | 1,432 |
| Peach | 2,413 | 3,747 | 3,989 | 1,163 |
| Pickens | 520 | 2,101 | 2,571 | 973 |
| Pierce | 269 | 1,982 | 2,628 | 544 |
| Pike | 423 | 1,432 | 1,903 | 776 |
| Polk | 1,317 | 4,929 | 6,115 | 1,944 |
| Pulaski | 444 | 1,966 | 2,318 | 485 |
| Putnam | 604 | 1,963 | 2,040 | 835 |
| Quitman | 140 | 502 | 677 | 313 |
| Rabun | 366 | 1,477 | 2,398 | 591 |
| Randolph | 798 | 1,603 | 2,186 | 747 |
| Richmond | 9,219 | 24,362 | 24,042 | 17,893 |
| Rockdale | 791 | 3,560 | 4,640 | 2,974 |

| County | 1972 (D) | (R) | 1974 (D) | (R) |
|---|---|---|---|---|
| Schley | 162 | 694 | 783 | 268 |
| Screven | 575 | 2,402 | 2,168 | 1,176 |
| Seminole | 376 | 1,851 | 2,074 | 681 |
| Spalding | 1,702 | 7,183 | 7,593 | 3,739 |
| Stephens | 871 | 3,773 | 5,560 | 1,340 |
| Stewart | 353 | 1,020 | 1,632 | 433 |
| Sumter | 1,268 | 4,533 | 5,328 | 2,053 |
| Talbot | 508 | 990 | 1,634 | 459 |
| Taliaferro | 372 | 585 | 748 | 236 |
| Tattnall | 492 | 2,892 | 3,556 | 1,326 |
| Taylor | 514 | 1,590 | 1,962 | 504 |
| Telfair | 687 | 2,245 | 3,534 | 637 |
| Terrell | 686 | 2,057 | 2,348 | 1,168 |
| Thomas | 2,171 | 6,668 | 6,147 | 3,263 |
| Tift | 816 | 4,591 | 5,185 | 2,162 |
| Toombs | 675 | 4,080 | 4,047 | 2,126 |
| Towns | 404 | 1,573 | 1,786 | 1,175 |
| Treutlen | 210 | 1,346 | 1,567 | 465 |
| Troup | 2,056 | 8,350 | 7,699 | 4,422 |
| Turner | 437 | 2,120 | 2,265 | 416 |
| Twiggs | 1,113 | 1,363 | 2,515 | 513 |
| Union | 742 | 2,317 | 2,795 | 1,154 |
| Upson | 896 | 4,892 | 4,219 | 2,897 |
| Walker | 1,574 | 8,728 | 8,007 | 4,807 |
| Walton | 1,140 | 3,994 | 5,402 | 1,687 |
| Ware | 1,724 | 6,578 | 7,719 | 2,661 |
| Warren | 475 | 1,175 | 1,335 | 720 |
| Washington | 1,246 | 3,901 | 3,865 | 1,657 |
| Wayne | 733 | 3,677 | 4,489 | 1,499 |
| Webster | 108 | 483 | 622 | 165 |
| Wheeler | 294 | 1,093 | 1,378 | 344 |
| White | 343 | 1,537 | 2,125 | 625 |
| Whitfield | 1,955 | 8,591 | 10,475 | 4,498 |
| Wilcox | 315 | 1,863 | 2,153 | 346 |
| Wilkes | 646 | 2,195 | 2,461 | 1,067 |
| Wilkinson | 751 | 2,196 | 2,652 | 837 |
| Worth | 542 | 2,942 | 2,790 | 1,156 |
| **Totals** | 289,529 | 881,496 | 979,409 | 483,743 |

## Georgia Vote Since 1932

1932 (Pres.), Roosevelt, Dem., 234,118; Hoover, Rep., 19,863; Upshaw, Proh., 1,125; Thomas, Soc., 461; Foster, Com., 23.

1936 (Pres.), Roosevelt, Dem., 255,364; Landon, Rep., 36,942; Colvin, Proh., 660; Lemke, Union, 141; Thomas, Soc., 68.

1940 (Pres.), Roosevelt, Dem., 265,194; Willkie, Rep., 23,934; Ind. Dem., 22,428; total, 46,362; Babson, Proh., 983.

1944 (Pres.), Roosevelt, Dem., 268,187; Dewey, Rep., 56,506; Watson, Proh., 36.

1948 (Pres.), Truman, Dem., 254,646; Dewey, Rep., 76,691; Thurmond, States' Rights, 85,055; Wallace, Prog., 1,636; Watson, Proh., 732.

1952 (Pres.), Eisenhower, Rep., 198,979; Stevenson, Dem., 456,823; Liberty Party, 1.

1956 (Pres.), Stevenson, Dem., 444,388; Eisenhower, Rep., 222,778; Andrews, Ind., write-in, 1,754.

1960 (Pres.), Kennedy, Dem., 458,638; Nixon, Rep., 274,472; write-in, 239.

1964 (Pres.), Johnson, Dem., 522,557; Goldwater, Rep., 616,600.

1968 (Pres.), Nixon, Rep., 380,111; Humphrey, Dem., 334,440; Wallace, 3d party, 535,550; write-in, 162.

1972 (Pres.), Nixon, Rep., 881,496; McGovern, Dem., 289,529; Schmitz, Amer. Party, 2,288; scattered.

1976 (Pres.), Carter, Dem., 979,409; Ford, Rep., 483,743; write-in, 4,306.

## Hawaii

| County | 1972 McGovern (D) | Nixon (R) | 1976 Carter (D) | Ford (R) |
|---|---|---|---|---|
| Hawaii | 11,652 | 16,832 | 15,960 | 15,366 |
| Honolulu | 76,957 | 132,844 | 111,389 | 108,041 |
| Kauai | 5,401 | 7,571 | 8,105 | 6,278 |
| Maui | 7,339 | 11,618 | 11,921 | 10,318 |
| **Totals** | 101,409 | 168,865 | 147,375 | 140,003 |

## Hawaii Vote Since 1960

1960 (Pres.), Kennedy, Dem., 92,410; Nixon, Rep., 92,295.

1964 (Pres.), Johnson, Dem., 163,249; Goldwater, Rep., 44,022.

1968 (Pres.), Nixon, Rep., 91,425; Humphrey, Dem.,

---

141,324; Wallace, 3d party, 3,469.

1972 (Pres.), Nixon, Rep., 168,865; McGovern, Dem., 101,409.

1976 (Pres.), Carter, Dem., 147,375; Ford, Rep., 140,003; MacBride, Libertarian, 3,923.

## Idaho

| County | 1972 McGovern (D) | Nixon (R) | 1976 Carter (D) | Ford (R) |
|---|---|---|---|---|
| Ada | 12,687 | 36,665 | 21,125 | 41,135 |
| Adams | 293 | 963 | 639 | 809 |
| Bannock | 7,840 | 12,856 | 10,261 | 13,172 |
| Bear Lake | 716 | 2,213 | 960 | 2,094 |
| Benewah | 1,062 | 1,494 | 1,549 | 1,458 |
| Bingham | 2,476 | 6,886 | 4,347 | 7,327 |
| Blaine | 1,240 | 2,113 | 1,604 | 2,178 |
| Boise | 256 | 676 | 433 | 684 |
| Bonner | 2,599 | 4,405 | 4,065 | 4,549 |
| Bonneville | 4,199 | 13,134 | 7,230 | 15,793 |
| Boundary | 860 | 1,587 | 1,217 | 1,456 |
| Butte | 387 | 788 | 663 | 751 |
| Camas | 95 | 344 | 160 | 288 |
| Canyon | 5,630 | 18,383 | 9,460 | 17,263 |
| Caribou | 614 | 2,069 | 1,110 | 2,253 |
| Cassia | 1,080 | 4,576 | 1,881 | 4,575 |
| Clark | 64 | 339 | 169 | 334 |
| Clearwater | 1,412 | 1,590 | 1,752 | 1,469 |
| Custer | 274 | 989 | 516 | 850 |
| Elmore | 1,153 | 3,078 | 2,164 | 2,808 |
| Franklin | 611 | 2,787 | 1,157 | 2,720 |
| Freemont | 819 | 2,621 | 1,445 | 2,581 |
| Gem | 1,069 | 2,717 | 1,978 | 2,401 |
| Gooding | 1,030 | 3,124 | 1,923 | 2,909 |
| Idaho | 1,622 | 3,235 | 2,323 | 3,185 |
| Jefferson | 715 | 2,983 | 1,745 | 3,599 |
| Jerome | 888 | 3,661 | 1,800 | 3,188 |
| Kootenai | 5,162 | 9,958 | 7,225 | 10,493 |
| Latah | 4,548 | 6,043 | 5,314 | 6,846 |
| Lemhi | 526 | 1,812 | 1,159 | 1,685 |
| Lewis | 635 | 961 | 898 | 824 |
| Lincoln | 313 | 1,120 | 615 | 909 |
| Madison | 710 | 3,606 | 1,320 | 4,190 |
| Minidoka | 1,423 | 4,097 | 2,441 | 3,600 |
| Nez Perce | 5,081 | 6,232 | 6,324 | 6,151 |
| Oneida | 402 | 1,204 | 637 | 1,065 |
| Owyhee | 463 | 1,630 | 1,054 | 1,519 |
| Payette | 1,113 | 3,577 | 2,195 | 3,115 |
| Power | 625 | 1,405 | 1,286 | 1,374 |
| Shoshone | 3,020 | 3,868 | 3,216 | 3,570 |
| Teton | 298 | 862 | 514 | 904 |
| Twin Falls | 3,344 | 13,075 | 6,085 | 12,659 |
| Valley | 537 | 1,324 | 897 | 1,374 |
| Washington | 935 | 2,264 | 1,693 | 2,044 |
| **Totals** | 80,826 | 199,384 | 126,549 | 204,151 |

## Idaho Vote Since 1932

1932 (Pres.), Roosevelt, Dem., 109,479; Hoover, Rep., 71,312; Harvey, Lib., 4,712; Thomas, Soc., 526; Foster, Com., 491.

1936 (Pres.), Roosevelt, Dem., 125,683; Landon, Rep., 66,256; Lemke, Union, 7,684.

1940 (Pres.), Roosevelt, Dem., 127,842; Willkie, Rep., 106,553; Thomas, Soc., 497; Browder, Com., 276.

1944 (Pres.), Roosevelt, Dem., 107,399; Dewey, Rep., 100,137; Watson, Proh., 503; Thomas, Soc., 282.

1948 (Pres.), Truman, Dem., 107,370; Dewey, Rep., 101,514; Wallace, Prog., 4,972; Watson, Proh., 628; Thomas, Soc., 332.

1952 (Pres.), Eisenhower, Rep., 180,707; Stevenson Dem., 95,081; Hallinan, Prog., 443; write-in, 23.

1956 (Pres.), Eisenhower, Rep., 166,979; Stevenson, Dem., 105,868; Andrews, Ind., 126; write-in, 16.

1960 (Pres.), Kennedy, Dem., 138,853; Nixon, Rep., 161,597.

1964 (Pres.), Johnson, Dem., 148,920; Goldwater, Rep., 143,557.

1968 (Pres.), Nixon, Rep., 165,369; Humphrey, Dem., 89,273; Wallace, 3d party, 36,541.

1972 (Pres.), Nixon, Rep., 199,384; McGovern, Dem., 80,826; Schmitz, American, 28,869; Spock, Peoples, 903.

1976 (Pres.), Carter, Dem., 126,549; Ford, Rep., 204,151; Maddox, Amer., 5,935; MacBride, Libertarian, 3,558; LaRouche, U.S. Labor, 739.

## Illinois

| County | 1972 McGovern (D) | Nixon (R) | 1976 Carter (D) | Ford (R) |
|---|---|---|---|---|
| Adams | 9,055 | 20,731 | 11,926 | 18,189 |
| Alexander | 2,482 | 3,669 | 3,246 | 2,349 |

| County | 1972 (D) | (R) | 1976 (D) | (R) |
|---|---|---|---|---|
| Bond | 2,704 | 4,475 | 3,682 | 3,716 |
| Boone | 3,131 | 7,003 | 4,458 | 6,470 |
| Brown | 1,203 | 1,780 | 1,533 | 1,519 |
| Bureau | 6,133 | 12,786 | 7,566 | 10,854 |
| Calhoun | 1,299 | 1,705 | 1,549 | 1,364 |
| Carroll | 2,571 | 6,041 | 3,372 | 5,059 |
| Cass | 2,803 | 4,414 | 3,589 | 3,524 |
| Champaign | 24,743 | 33,700 | 26,858 | 34,546 |
| Christian | 7,556 | 10,072 | 9,306 | 7,445 |
| Clark | 2,965 | 5,706 | 4,071 | 4,506 |
| Clay | 2,844 | 5,283 | 3,837 | 3,860 |
| Clinton | 4,756 | 7,931 | 6,275 | 7,245 |
| Coles | 7,988 | 13,681 | 8,639 | 11,021 |
| Cook | 1,063,268 | 1,234,307 | 1,180,814 | 987,498 |
| Crawford | 3,477 | 6,568 | 5,007 | 5,522 |
| Cumberland | 2,083 | 3,257 | 2,752 | 2,518 |
| DeKalb | 12,375 | 18,910 | 11,535 | 18,193 |
| DeWitt | 2,672 | 5,025 | 3,477 | 4,137 |
| Douglas | 2,656 | 5,840 | 3,826 | 4,635 |
| DuPage | 57,043 | 172,341 | 72,137 | 175,055 |
| Edgar | 3,889 | 7,195 | 5,058 | 5,842 |
| Edwards | 1,055 | 3,017 | 1,648 | 2,379 |
| Effingham | 4,431 | 8,752 | 5,952 | 7,194 |
| Fayette | 4,192 | 6,574 | 5,128 | 5,059 |
| Ford | 1,934 | 5,656 | 2,690 | 4,801 |
| Franklin | 8,545 | 10,121 | 12,818 | 7,420 |
| Fulton | 7,529 | 12,328 | 9,314 | 9,588 |
| Gallatin | 1,844 | 2,148 | 2,611 | 1,499 |
| Greene | 2,824 | 4,673 | 4,057 | 3,706 |
| Grundy | 3,584 | 8,725 | 5,534 | 7,581 |
| Hamilton | 2,006 | 3,282 | 3,036 | 2,433 |
| Hancock | 3,592 | 7,519 | 4,730 | 6,043 |
| Hardin | 1,140 | 1,915 | 1,602 | 1,393 |
| Henderson | 1,744 | 2,689 | 2,152 | 2,210 |
| Henry | 8,368 | 14,796 | 9,822 | 12,849 |
| Iroquois | 3,723 | 11,995 | 5,167 | 10,129 |
| Jackson | 13,146 | 12,393 | 12,940 | 10,152 |
| Jasper | 2,114 | 3,461 | 2,772 | 2,794 |
| Jefferson | 6,396 | 9,448 | 8,989 | 7,422 |
| Jersey | 3,317 | 5,164 | 4,625 | 4,273 |
| JoDaviess | 3,318 | 5,763 | 3,979 | 5,478 |
| Johnson | 1,293 | 2,826 | 2,182 | 2,417 |
| Kane | 27,525 | 64,546 | 34,057 | 59,275 |
| Kankakee | 13,434 | 26,866 | 18,394 | 23,003 |
| Kendall | 2,525 | 9,373 | 4,202 | 9,011 |
| Knox | 9,333 | 17,315 | 11,525 | 14,123 |
| Lake | 47,416 | 92,052 | 57,741 | 92,231 |
| LaSalle | 21,405 | 31,190 | 23,105 | 25,114 |
| Lawrence | 2,818 | 5,347 | 4,044 | 4,345 |
| Lee | 4,788 | 10,636 | 6,076 | 8,674 |
| Livingston | 5,110 | 13,217 | 5,174 | 10,097 |
| Logan | 4,395 | 10,277 | 5,686 | 8,623 |
| Macon | 20,296 | 29,596 | 28,243 | 24,893 |
| Macoupin | 9,662 | 13,583 | 11,910 | 10,242 |
| Madison | 43,289 | 55,385 | 56,457 | 44,183 |
| Marion | 6,968 | 10,755 | 9,834 | 8,729 |
| Marshall | 2,141 | 4,452 | 2,570 | 4,017 |
| Mason | 2,901 | 4,897 | 3,947 | 3,847 |
| Massac | 1,831 | 4,313 | 3,666 | 3,226 |
| McDonough | 5,143 | 10,573 | 5,464 | 9,683 |
| McHenry | 12,090 | 36,114 | 16,799 | 37,115 |
| McLean | 14,824 | 31,060 | 16,601 | 28,493 |
| Menard | 1,587 | 3,657 | 2,301 | 3,137 |
| Mercer | 3,477 | 5,452 | 4,090 | 4,816 |
| Monroe | 2,958 | 6,479 | 3,984 | 5,602 |
| Montgomery | 6,858 | 9,025 | 8,322 | 7,379 |
| Morgan | 5,674 | 11,103 | 7,403 | 8,885 |
| Moultrie | 2,350 | 3,143 | 3,332 | 2,803 |
| Ogle | 4,743 | 13,512 | 6,463 | 11,073 |
| Peoria | 27,264 | 50,324 | 34,606 | 46,526 |
| Perry | 4,084 | 6,968 | 5,976 | 5,286 |
| Piatt | 2,394 | 5,057 | 3,509 | 4,442 |
| Pike | 3,883 | 5,940 | 5,006 | 4,975 |
| Pope | 773 | 1,440 | 1,070 | 1,187 |
| Pulaski | 1,683 | 2,485 | 2,489 | 1,836 |
| Putnam | 1,112 | 1,665 | 1,344 | 1,572 |
| Randolph | 6,440 | 9,761 | 8,693 | 8,190 |
| Richland | 2,553 | 5,558 | 3,485 | 4,434 |
| Rock Island | 32,529 | 37,548 | 35,994 | 34,007 |
| St. Clair | 46,636 | 50,519 | 59,177 | 40,333 |
| Saline | 5,226 | 7,660 | 7,472 | 5,970 |
| Sangamon | 25,720 | 50,458 | 38,017 | 43,309 |
| Schuyler | 1,534 | 2,994 | 2,014 | 2,635 |
| Scott | 1,145 | 2,228 | 1,424 | 1,789 |
| Shelby | 4,389 | 7,217 | 61,172 | 5,234 |
| Stark | 993 | 2,529 | 1,146 | 2,191 |
| Stephenson | 6,404 | 13,584 | 7,192 | 11,678 |
| Tazewell | 15,576 | 31,937 | 22,821 | 28,951 |
| Union | 3,428 | 5,034 | 5,003 | 3,531 |
| Vermilion | 14,413 | 24,863 | 18,438 | 19,751 |
| Wabash | 1,985 | 4,310 | 2,781 | 3,388 |
| Warren | 2,969 | 7,021 | 3,808 | 5,822 |
| Washington | 2,327 | 5,179 | 3,222 | 4,485 |
| Wayne | 2,763 | 6,400 | 4,303 | 5,211 |
| White | 3,678 | 6,052 | 5,306 | 4,600 |
| Whiteside | 7,909 | 17,305 | 11,255 | 14,308 |
| Will | 33,633 | 65,155 | 51,103 | 61,784 |
| Williamson | 9,202 | 14,101 | 13,600 | 10,703 |
| Winnebago | 35,937 | 57,682 | 42,399 | 52,736 |
| Woodford | 3,558 | 9,622 | 4819 | 8,899 |
| **Totals** | **1,913,472** | **2,788,179** | **2,271,295** | **2,364,269** |

## Illinois Vote Since 1932

1932 (Pres.), Roosevelt, Dem., 1,882,304; Hoover, Rep., 1,432,756; Thomas, Soc., 67,258; Foster, Com., 15,582; Upshaw, Proh., 6,388; Reynolds, Soc. Lab., 3,638.

1936 (Pres.), Roosevelt, Dem., 2,282,999; Landon, Rep., 1,570,393; Lemke, Union, 89,439; Thomas, Soc., 7,530; Colvin, Proh., 3,439; Aiken, Soc. Lab., 1,921.

1940 (Pres.), Roosevelt, Dem., 2,149,934; Willkie, Rep., 2,047,240; Thomas, Soc., 10,914; Babson, Proh., 9,190.

1944 (Pres.), Roosevelt, Dem., 2,079,479; Dewey, Rep., 1,939,314; Teichert, Soc. Lab., 9,677; Watson, Proh., 7,411; Thomas, Soc., 180.

1948 (Pres.), Truman, Dem., 1,994,715; Dewey, Rep., 1,961,103; Watson, Proh., 11,959; Thomas, Soc., 11,522; Teichert, Soc. Lab., 3,118.

1952 (Pres.), Eisenhower, Rep., 2,457,327; Stevenson, Dem., 2,013,920; Haas, Soc. Lab., 9,363; write-in, 448.

1956 (Pres.), Eisenhower, Rep., 2,623,327; Stevenson, Dem., 1,775,682; Haas, Soc. Lab., 8,342; write-in, 56.

1960 (Pres.), Kennedy, Dem., 2,377,846; Nixon, Rep., 2,368,988; Haas, Soc. Lab., 10,560; write-in, 15.

1964 (Pres.), Johnson, Dem., 2,796,833; Goldwater, Rep., 1,905,946; write-in, 62.

1968 (Pres.), Nixon, Rep., 2,174,774; Humphrey, Dem., 2,039,814; Wallace, 3d party, 390,958; Blomen, Soc. Labor, 13,878; write-in, 325.

1972 (Pres.), Nixon, Rep., 2,788,179; McGovern, Dem., 1,913,472; Fisher, Soc. Labor, 12,344; Schmitz, Amer., 2,471; Hall, Communist, 4,541; others, 2,229.

1976 (Pres.), Carter, Dem., 2,271,295; Ford, Rep., 2,364,269; McCarthy, Ind., 55,939; Hall, Comm., 9,250; MacBride, Libertarian, 8,057; Camejo, Soc. Workers, 3,615; Blomen, Soc. Labor, 2,422; LaRouche, U.S. Labor, 2,018; write-in, 1,968.

## Indiana

| County | 1972 McGovern (D) | Nixon (R) | 1976 Carter (D) | Ford (R) |
|---|---|---|---|---|
| Adams | 3,971 | 7,549 | 4,908 | 6,280 |
| Allen | 38,621 | 76,924 | 44,744 | 71,321 |
| Bartholomew | 6,974 | 17,365 | 11,203 | 14,771 |
| Benton | 1,566 | 3,703 | 2,071 | 3,093 |
| Blackford | 2,311 | 3,876 | 3,174 | 2,886 |
| Boone | 3,235 | 9,874 | 5,686 | 9,214 |
| Brown | 1,443 | 2,737 | 2,381 | 2,466 |
| Carroll | 2,214 | 5,885 | 3,606 | 4,797 |
| Cass | 5,317 | 12,681 | 7,610 | 10,342 |
| Clark | 10,838 | 16,111 | 16,670 | 12,732 |
| Clay | 3,742 | 7,146 | 5,433 | 5,674 |
| Clinton | 4,283 | 9,849 | 6,682 | 8,199 |
| Crawford | 1,801 | 2,623 | 2,721 | 2,181 |
| Daviess | 3,538 | 8,490 | 4,952 | 6,829 |
| Dearborn | 4,137 | 7,689 | 6,348 | 6,176 |
| Decatur | 2,994 | 6,761 | 4,365 | 5,555 |
| Dekalb | 4,354 | 8,834 | 6,151 | 7,860 |
| Delaware | 17,936 | 32,468 | 25,151 | 26,417 |
| Dubois | 6,365 | 6,637 | 7,385 | 6,383 |
| Elkhart | 12,659 | 31,009 | 17,581 | 27,291 |
| Fayette | 3,519 | 7,273 | 5,519 | 5,704 |
| Floyd | 9,243 | 13,198 | 12,744 | 11,259 |
| Fountain | 2,977 | 5,979 | 4,089 | 4,903 |
| Franklin | 2,131 | 4,324 | 3,234 | 3,557 |
| Fulton | 2,150 | 6,170 | 3,488 | 5,083 |
| Gibson | 5,633 | 9,115 | 8,430 | 7,105 |
| Grant | 7,912 | 20,969 | 13,468 | 16,847 |
| Greene | 4,450 | 8,453 | 7,263 | 6,442 |
| Hamilton | 4,151 | 20,247 | 7,857 | 21,828 |
| Hancock | 3,069 | 11,019 | 6,191 | 10,072 |
| Harrison | 3,927 | 5,910 | 5,685 | 4,911 |
| Hendricks | 4,384 | 17,699 | 9,066 | 16,725 |
| Henry | 5,610 | 14,538 | 10,137 | 11,620 |
| Howard | 8,083 | 23,089 | 14,815 | 19,571 |
| Huntington | 4,908 | 10,858 | 6,515 | 9,182 |
| Jackson | 4,984 | 9,546 | 7,610 | 7,615 |
| Jasper | 1,920 | 6,369 | 3,286 | 5,398 |
| Jay | 3,349 | 6,090 | 4,124 | 4,606 |
| Jefferson | 4,267 | 6,722 | 6,139 | 5,573 |
| Jennings | 2,903 | 5,156 | 4,430 | 4,505 |

| | 1972 (D) | 1972 (R) | 1976 (D) | 1976 (R) |
|---|---|---|---|---|
| Johnson | 5,067 | 17,537 | 10,075 | 16,414 |
| Knox | 6,089 | 11,940 | 9,612 | 9,100 |
| Kosciusko | 4,233 | 16,216 | 7,328 | 14,505 |
| LaGrange | 1,658 | 4,152 | 2,835 | 3,876 |
| Lake | 88,510 | 115,480 | 120,700 | 90,119 |
| LaPorte | 13,222 | 26,243 | 18,217 | 21,989 |
| Lawrence | 4,278 | 10,936 | 7,908 | 9,278 |
| Madison | 20,921 | 39,036 | 29,811 | 32,437 |
| Marion | 102,166 | 206,065 | 145,274 | 177,767 |
| Marshall | 4,349 | 11,908 | 6,424 | 9,707 |
| Martin | 2,021 | 3,470 | 2,827 | 2,702 |
| Miami | 3,889 | 9,477 | 6,257 | 8,263 |
| Monroe | 15,241 | 19,953 | 16,609 | 18,938 |
| Montgomery | 3,431 | 10,997 | 5,320 | 9,509 |
| Morgan | 3,390 | 11,980 | 7,181 | 10,983 |
| Newton | 252 | 3,771 | 2,236 | 3,204 |
| Noble | 4,250 | 7,916 | 5,875 | 6,885 |
| Ohio | 922 | 1,368 | 1,300 | 1,027 |
| Orange | 2,932 | 5,715 | 4,031 | 4,399 |
| Owen | 1,708 | 3,896 | 3,103 | 2,896 |
| Parke | 2,207 | 5,014 | 3,158 | 3,929 |
| Perry | 4,277 | 5,204 | 5,620 | 4,088 |
| Pike | 2,648 | 4,252 | 3,938 | 3,138 |
| Porter | 8,943 | 26,877 | 16,468 | 25,489 |
| Posey | 3,586 | 6,771 | 5,298 | 5,136 |
| Pulaski | 1,863 | 4,243 | 2,813 | 3,586 |
| Putnam | 3,339 | 7,879 | 5,116 | 6,063 |
| Randolph | 3,409 | 8,754 | 5,330 | 6,891 |
| Ripley | 3,601 | 6,594 | 4,792 | 5,293 |
| Rush | 1,764 | 5,965 | 3,052 | 4,723 |
| St. Joseph | 41,629 | 64,808 | 49,156 | 50,358 |
| Scott | 2,785 | 3,564 | 4,229 | 2,657 |
| Shelby | 4,028 | 10,794 | 7,098 | 8,918 |
| Spencer | 3,867 | 5,518 | 4,796 | 4,166 |
| Starke | 2,994 | 5,520 | 4,753 | 4,354 |
| Steuben | 2,401 | 5,636 | 3,323 | 5,079 |
| Sullivan | 3,624 | 5,338 | 5,198 | 3,747 |
| Switzerland | 1,612 | 1,872 | 2,150 | 1,329 |
| Tippecanoe | 14,598 | 31,565 | 17,850 | 29,186 |
| Tipton | 2,095 | 5,674 | 3,428 | 4,776 |
| Union | 765 | 2,043 | 1,160 | 1,631 |
| Vanderburgh | 22,163 | 47,806 | 34,911 | 37,975 |
| Vermillion | 3,515 | 4,764 | 4,791 | 3,674 |
| Vigo | 18,898 | 29,730 | 24,684 | 23,555 |
| Wabash | 4,601 | 10,011 | 5,704 | 8,534 |
| Warren | 1,164 | 2,746 | 1,906 | 2,377 |
| Warrick | 4,296 | 8,520 | 7,804 | 7,200 |
| Washington | 3,086 | 4,758 | 4,409 | 3,794 |
| Wayne | 7,655 | 21,610 | 12,306 | 16,697 |
| Wells | 3,244 | 6,425 | 4,250 | 5,596 |
| White | 2,675 | 7,419 | 3,963 | 6,287 |
| Whitley | 3,838 | 7,489 | 5,445 | 6,761 |
| **Totals** | **708,568** | **1,405,154** | **1,014,714** | **1,185,958** |

## Indiana Vote Since 1932

1932 (Pres.), Roosevelt, Dem., 862,054; Hoover, Rep., 677,184; Thomas, Soc., 21,388; Upshaw, Proh., 10,399; Foster, Com., 2,187; Reynolds, Soc. Lab., 2,070.

1936 (Pres.), Roosevelt, Dem., 943,974; Landon, Rep., 691,570; Lemke, Union, 19,407; Thomas, Soc., 3,856; Browder, Com., 1,090.

1940 (Pres.), Roosevelt, Dem., 874,063; Willkie, Rep., 899,466; Babson, Proh., 6,437; Thomas, Soc., 2,075; Aiken, Soc. Lab., 706.

1944 (Pres.), Roosevelt, Dem., 781,403; Dewey, Rep., 875,891; Watson, Proh., 12,574; Thomas, Soc., 2,223.

1948 (Pres.), Truman, Dem., 807,833; Dewey, Rep., 821,079; Watson, Proh., 14,711; Wallace, Prog., 9,649; Thomas, Soc., 2,179; Teichert, Soc. Lab., 763.

1952 (Pres.), Eisenhower, Rep., 1,136,259; Stevenson, Dem., 801,530; Hamblen, Proh., 15,335; Hallinan, Prog., 1,222; Haas, Soc. Lab., 979.

1956 (Pres.), Eisenhower, Rep., 1,182,811; Stevenson, Dem., 783,908; Holtwick, Proh., 6,554; Haas, 1,334.

1960 (Pres.), Kennedy, Dem., 952,358; Nixon, Rep., 1,175,120; Decker, Proh., 6,746; Haas, Soc. Lab., 1,136.

1964 (Pres.), Johnson, Dem., 1,170,848; Goldwater, Rep., 911,118; Munn, Proh., 8,266; Haas, Soc. Lab., 1,374.

1968 (Pres.), Nixon, Rep., 1,067,885; Humphrey, Dem., 806,659; Wallace, 3d party, 243,108; Munn, Prohibition, 4,616; Halstead, Soc. Worker, 1,293; Gregory, 36.

1972 (Pres.), Nixon, Rep., 1,405,154; McGovern, Dem., 708,568; Reed, Soc. Worker, 5,575; Fisher, Soc. Labor, 1,688; Spock, Peace & Freedom, 4,544.

1976 (Pres.), Carter, Dem., 1,014,714; Ford, Rep., 1,185,958; Anderson, American, 14,048; Camejo, Soc. Worker, 5,695; LaRouche, U.S. Labor, 1,947.

# Iowa

| | 1972 McGovern (D) | 1972 Nixon (R) | 1976 Carter (D) | 1976 For (R) |
|---|---|---|---|---|
| County | | | | |
| Adair | 1,642 | 3,041 | 2,294 | 2,32 |
| Adams | 1,161 | 1,814 | 1,507 | 1,38 |
| Allamakee | 2,271 | 4,150 | 2,568 | 3,64 |
| Appanoose | 2,283 | 4,321 | 3,424 | 3,03 |
| Audubon | 1,533 | 2,515 | 2,104 | 1,97 |
| Benton | 4,282 | 5,273 | 5,514 | 5,01 |
| Black Hawk | 21,721 | 30,929 | 29,508 | 30,99 |
| Boone | 5,057 | 6,271 | 6,595 | 5,41 |
| Bremer | 3,122 | 6,333 | 4,203 | 6,25 |
| Buchanan | 3,609 | 5,277 | 4,258 | 4,79 |
| Buena Vista | 3,460 | 5,685 | 4,227 | 5,12 |
| Butler | 1,682 | 4,615 | 2,503 | 4,20 |
| Calhoun | 2,446 | 3,821 | 3,001 | 3,21 |
| Carroll | 4,608 | 4,415 | 5,333 | 4,09 |
| Cass | 1,923 | 5,234 | 2,866 | 4,58 |
| Cedar | 2,465 | 4,452 | 3,354 | 4,30 |
| Cerro Gordo | 9,460 | 11,856 | 11,189 | 10,60 |
| Cherokee | 2,780 | 4,726 | 3,358 | 3,99 |
| Chickasaw | 3,134 | 3,836 | 3,503 | 3,43 |
| Clarke | 1,590 | 2,241 | 2,333 | 1,73 |
| Clay | 2,887 | 4,564 | 3,776 | 4,54 |
| Clayton | 3,366 | 5,447 | 3,804 | 4,82 |
| Clinton | 9,895 | 12,768 | 11,746 | 12,40 |
| Crawford | 3,018 | 4,493 | 3,903 | 3,87 |
| Dallas | 5,085 | 6,143 | 6,722 | 5,82 |
| Davis | 1,806 | 2,287 | 2,426 | 1,63 |
| Decatur | 1,880 | 2,638 | 2,698 | 1,93 |
| Delaware | 2,944 | 4,848 | 3,168 | 4,16 |
| Des Moines | 8,869 | 10,216 | 11,268 | 9,02 |
| Dickinson | 2,373 | 3,739 | 3,074 | |
| Dubuque | 18,417 | 17,272 | 20,548 | 17,45 |
| Emmet | 1,970 | 3,436 | 2,720 | 2,87 |
| Fayette | 4,413 | 7,263 | 5,220 | 6,61 |
| Floyd | 3,338 | 4,726 | 4,646 | 4,36 |
| Franklin | 1,986 | 3,643 | 2,682 | 3,05 |
| Fremont | 1,210 | 2,642 | 1,964 | 2,16 |
| Greene | 2,152 | 3,371 | 3,094 | 2,81 |
| Grundy | 1,844 | 4,706 | 2,410 | 4,17 |
| Guthrie | 2,258 | 3,655 | 2,873 | 2,64 |
| Hamilton | 2,913 | 4,803 | 3,953 | 3,93 |
| Hancock | 2,349 | 3,706 | 2,975 | 3,12 |
| Hardin | 3,516 | 5,969 | 4,479 | 4,68 |
| Harrison | 2,369 | 4,721 | 3,228 | 3,48 |
| Henry | 2,721 | 5,066 | 3,882 | 3,84 |
| Howard | 2,439 | 2,980 | 2,917 | 2,61 |
| Humboldt | 2,062 | 3,622 | 2,677 | 3,07 |
| Ida | 1,490 | 2,819 | 1,868 | 2,59 |
| Iowa | 2,578 | 4,202 | 3,367 | 3,92 |
| Jackson | 3,704 | 4,975 | 4,467 | 4,22 |
| Jasper | 7,007 | 9,133 | 8,783 | 7,72 |
| Jefferson | 2,362 | 4,628 | 3,377 | 3,74 |
| Johnson | 20,922 | 14,823 | 20,208 | 16,09 |
| Jones | 3,468 | 4,962 | 4,245 | 4,46 |
| Keokuk | 2,619 | 3,831 | 3,482 | 2,92 |
| Kossuth | 4,393 | 5,841 | 5,190 | 4,65 |
| Lee | 7,510 | 9,748 | 9,017 | 8,19 |
| Linn | 31,370 | 36,503 | 38,252 | 36,51 |
| Louisa | 1,707 | 2,806 | 2,089 | 2,28 |
| Lucas | 1,759 | 2,851 | 733 | 2,07 |
| Lyon | 1,407 | 3,788 | 1,870 | 3,55 |
| Madison | 2,234 | 3,480 | 3,109 | 2,68 |
| Mahaska | 3,382 | 6,374 | 4,838 | 5,26 |
| Marion | 4,643 | 6,583 | 6,226 | 5,42 |
| Marshall | 6,618 | 10,798 | 8,695 | 9,56 |
| Mills | 1,060 | 3,531 | 1,908 | 2,72 |
| Mitchell | 2,449 | 3,395 | 2,906 | 2,88 |
| Monona | 2,189 | 3,237 | 2,661 | 2,63 |
| Monroe | 1,736 | 2,357 | 2,360 | 1,58 |
| Montgomery | 1,559 | 4,391 | 2,229 | 3,67 |
| Muscatine | 4,917 | 8,436 | 6,567 | 7,69 |
| O'Brien | 2,224 | 5,159 | 2,732 | 4,64 |
| Osceola | 1,317 | 2,262 | 1,309 | 1,95 |
| Page | 1,790 | 6,200 | 2,865 | 5,34 |
| Palo Alto | 2,845 | 3,141 | 3,182 | 2,62 |
| Plymouth | 4,033 | 6,339 | 4,284 | 5,59 |
| Pocahontas | 2,241 | 3,138 | 3,055 | 2,70 |
| Polk | 59,169 | 70,245 | 71,917 | 62,31 |
| Pottawattamie | 8,074 | 19,722 | 14,754 | 17,26 |
| Poweshiek | 3,718 | 4,785 | 4,360 | 4,19 |
| Ringgold | 1,003 | 2,264 | 1,739 | 1,54 |
| Sac | 2,452 | 4,017 | 2,996 | 3,34 |
| Scott | 23,810 | 34,135 | 29,771 | 35,02 |
| Shelby | 2,259 | 4,052 | 2,851 | 3,30 |
| Sioux | 2,867 | 10,721 | 3,322 | 9,44 |
| Story | 13,972 | 16,617 | 15,717 | 18,39 |
| Tama | 3,693 | 5,058 | 4,580 | 4,37 |
| Taylor | 1,247 | 3,042 | 1,947 | 2,05 |
| Union | 2,112 | 3,734 | 2,955 | 2,87 |
| Van Buren | 1,268 | 2,272 | 1,807 | 1,80 |
| Wapello | 8,348 | 9,301 | 10,249 | 6,78 |
| Warren | 5,143 | 7,332 | 7,653 | 6,09 |
| Washington | 2,784 | 5,187 | 3,448 | 4,21 |
| Wayne | 1,574 | 2,681 | 2,145 | 1,78 |
| Webster | 8,358 | 11,133 | 10,543 | 9,06 |
| Winnebago | 2,324 | 4,300 | 2,950 | 3,31 |
| Winneshiek | 4,401 | 5,877 | 4,158 | 4,76 |

| | 1972 | | 1976 | |
| | (D) | (R) | (D) | (R) |
|---|---|---|---|---|
| Woodbury | 16,974 | 23,757 | 19,664 | 22,853 |
| Worth | 2,034 | 2,564 | 2,399 | 1,964 |
| Wright | 2,780 | 4,278 | 3,637 | 3,544 |
| **Total** | **496,206** | **706,207** | **619,931** | **632,863** |

## Iowa Vote Since 1932

1932 (Pres.), Roosevelt, Dem., 598,019; Hoover, Rep., 414,433; Thomas, Soc., 20,467; Upshaw, Proh., 2,111; Coxey, Farm-Lab., 1,094; Foster, Com., 559.

1936 (Pres.), Roosevelt, Dem., 621,756; Landon, Rep., 487,977; Lemke, Union, 29,687; Thomas, Soc., 1,373; Colvin, Proh., 1,182; Browder, Comm., 506; Aiken, Soc. Lab., 252.

1940 (Pres.), Roosevelt, Dem., 578,800; Willkie, Rep., 632,370; Babson, Proh., 2,284; Browder, Com., 1,524; Aiken, Soc. Lab., 452.

1944 (Pres.), Roosevelt, Dem., 499,876; Dewey, Rep., 547,267; Watson, Proh., 3,752; Thomas, Soc., 1,511; Teichert, Soc. Lab., 193.

1948 (Pres.), Truman, Dem., 522,380; Dewey, Rep., 494,018; Wallace, Prog., 12,125; Teichert, Soc. Lab., 4,274; Watson, Proh., 3,382; Thomas, Soc., 1,829; Dobbs, Soc. Workers, 26.

1952 (Pres.), Eisenhower, Rep., 808,906; Stevenson, Dem., 451,513; Hallinan, Prog., 5,085; Hamblen, Proh., 2,882; Hoopes, Soc., 219; Haas, Soc. Lab., 139; scattering 29.

1956 (Pres.), Eisenhower, Rep., 729,187; Stevenson, Dem., 501,858; Andrews (A.C.P. of Iowa), 3,202; Hoopes, Soc., 192; Haas, Soc. Lab., 125.

1960 (Pres.), Kennedy, Dem., 550,565; Nixon, Rep., 722,381; Haas, Soc. Lab., 230; Write-in, 634.

1964 (Pres.), Johnson, Dem., 733,030; Goldwater, Rep., 449,148; Haas, S. L., 182; DeBerry, S. W., 159; Munn, P., 1,902.

1968 (Pres.), Nixon, Rep., 619,106; Humphrey, Dem., 476,699; Wallace, 3d party, 66,422; Munn, Proh., 362; Halstead, Soc. Worker, 3,377; Cleaver, Peace and Freedom, 1,332; Blomen, S. L., 241.

1972 (Pres.), Nixon, Rep., 706,207; McGovern, Dem., 496,206; Schmitz, American, 22,056; Jenness, Soc. Worker, 488; Fisher, Soc. Labor, 195; Hall, Communist, 272; Green, Universal, 199; scattered, 321.

1976 (Pres.), Carter, Dem., 619,931; Ford, Rep., 632,863; McCarthy, Ind., 20,051; Anderson, American, 3,040; MacBride, Libertarian, 1,452.

## Kansas

| | 1972 | | 1976 | |
| | McGovern | Nixon | Carter | Ford |
| County | (D) | (R) | (D) | (R) |
|---|---|---|---|---|
| Allen | 1,610 | 3,938 | 2,746 | 3,269 |
| Anderson | 1,035 | 2,718 | 1,886 | 1,872 |
| Atchison | 2,404 | 5,471 | 4,108 | 4,030 |
| Barber | 727 | 2,308 | 1,494 | 1,568 |
| Barton | 3,481 | 8,479 | 5,497 | 7,311 |
| Bourbon | 1,912 | 4,776 | 3,237 | 3,589 |
| Brown | 1,038 | 4,314 | 1,745 | 3,407 |
| Butler | 4,669 | 11,045 | 8,540 | 8,390 |
| Chase | 315 | 1,184 | 643 | 922 |
| Chautauqua | 378 | 1,546 | 866 | 1,159 |
| Cherokee | 2,806 | 6,019 | 5,154 | 3,957 |
| Cheyenne | 399 | 1,440 | 758 | 1,008 |
| Clark | 311 | 1,142 | 680 | 761 |
| Clay | 887 | 3,562 | 1,610 | 3,085 |
| Cloud | 1,806 | 3,832 | 2,976 | 2,954 |
| Coffey | 782 | 2,667 | 1,549 | 2,145 |
| Comanche | 281 | 1,052 | 630 | 719 |
| Cowley | 3,592 | 10,332 | 7,095 | 7,513 |
| Crawford | 6,683 | 9,652 | 9,021 | 7,225 |
| Decatur | 616 | 1,707 | 1,011 | 1,232 |
| Dickinson | 1,957 | 6,515 | 3,672 | 4,759 |
| Doniphan | 690 | 2,856 | 1,428 | 2,469 |
| Douglas | 11,646 | 15,316 | 11,922 | 14,277 |
| Edwards | 757 | 1,534 | 1,304 | 1,001 |
| Elk | 428 | 1,522 | 865 | 1,087 |
| Ellis | 4,113 | 5,463 | 6,280 | 4,719 |
| Ellsworth | 1,028 | 2,087 | 1,573 | 1,618 |
| Finney | 2,062 | 4,335 | 3,813 | 3,711 |
| Ford | 2,804 | 6,232 | 4,934 | 4,679 |
| Franklin | 2,056 | 6,011 | 3,607 | 4,760 |
| Geary | 1,708 | 4,299 | 2,843 | 3,230 |
| Gove | 466 | 1,226 | 848 | 860 |
| Graham | 488 | 1,440 | 936 | 1,112 |
| Grant | 476 | 1,469 | 1,151 | 1,226 |

| | 1972 | | 1976 | |
| | McGovern | Nixon | Carter | Ford |
| | (D) | (R) | (D) | (R) |
|---|---|---|---|---|
| Gray | 511 | 1,235 | 1,111 | 837 |
| Greeley | 212 | 639 | 479 | 389 |
| Greenwood | 951 | 3,157 | 1,737 | 2,319 |
| Hamilton | 394 | 941 | 746 | 560 |
| Harper | 729 | 2,628 | 1,681 | 1,777 |
| Harvey | 3,555 | 8,287 | 6,003 | 6,624 |
| Haskell | 383 | 1,036 | 676 | 761 |
| Hodgeman | 331 | 853 | 697 | 576 |
| Jackson | 1,191 | 3,363 | 2,129 | 2,725 |
| Jefferson | 1,237 | 3,679 | 2,470 | 3,225 |
| Jewell | 716 | 2,242 | 1,111 | 1,592 |
| Johnson | 24,324 | 76,161 | 35,605 | 75,798 |
| Kearny | 325 | 876 | 658 | 674 |
| Kingman | 1,107 | 2,756 | 2,142 | 1,839 |
| Kiowa | 406 | 1,559 | 764 | 1,180 |
| Labette | 3,210 | 6,399 | 5,294 | 4,640 |
| Lane | 294 | 943 | 646 | 651 |
| Leavenworth | 4,727 | 10,762 | 8,022 | 8,407 |
| Lincoln | 476 | 1,649 | 985 | 1,225 |
| Linn | 876 | 2,593 | 1,681 | 1,873 |
| Logan | 428 | 1,164 | 694 | 957 |
| Lyon | 3,720 | 9,157 | 5,634 | 7,062 |
| Marion | 1,478 | 4,373 | 2,483 | 3,519 |
| Marshall | 1,823 | 4,127 | 3,004 | 3,226 |
| McPherson | 2,858 | 7,457 | 5,366 | 6,187 |
| Meade | 526 | 1,712 | 983 | 1,109 |
| Miami | 2,140 | 5,234 | 4,000 | 3,999 |
| Mitchell | 1,030 | 2,830 | 1,700 | 2,095 |
| Montgomery | 3,685 | 11,717 | 7,157 | 8,864 |
| Morris | 704 | 2,471 | 1,337 | 1,698 |
| Morton | 363 | 1,165 | 735 | 738 |
| Nemaha | 1,777 | 3,422 | 2,586 | 2,759 |
| Neosho | 2,559 | 5,034 | 3,842 | 4,038 |
| Ness | 652 | 1,539 | 1,106 | 1,016 |
| Norton | 778 | 2,688 | 1,337 | 2,201 |
| Osage | 1,522 | 4,073 | 2,755 | 2,945 |
| Osborne | 724 | 2,182 | 1,190 | 1,574 |
| Ottawa | 705 | 2,065 | 1,393 | 1,629 |
| Pawnee | 1,110 | 2,370 | 1,959 | 1,692 |
| Phillips | 827 | 2,919 | 1,264 | 2,317 |
| Pottawatomie | 1,298 | 3,947 | 2,316 | 3,483 |
| Pratt | 1,214 | 3,253 | 2,307 | 2,427 |
| Rawlins | 560 | 1,553 | 903 | 1,148 |
| Reno | 8,183 | 15,714 | 14,620 | 11,212 |
| Republic | 1,059 | 2,421 | 1,617 | 2,294 |
| Rice | 1,825 | 3,843 | 3,056 | 2,584 |
| Riley | 5,333 | 11,120 | 6,540 | 9,518 |
| Rooks | 904 | 2,457 | 1,412 | 1,664 |
| Rush | 806 | 1,629 | 1,359 | 1,170 |
| Russell | 1,011 | 3,168 | 1,453 | 3,165 |
| Saline | 5,406 | 12,592 | 8,476 | 11,218 |
| Scott | 449 | 1,547 | 919 | 1,195 |
| Sedgwick | 39,220 | 83,949 | 63,989 | 69,828 |
| Seward | 989 | 3,866 | 1,907 | 3,604 |
| Shawnee | 20,383 | 43,727 | 28,578 | 37,101 |
| Sheridan | 552 | 1,134 | 793 | 838 |
| Sherman | 785 | 2,225 | 1,573 | 1,671 |
| Smith | 818 | 2,600 | 1,333 | 2,009 |
| Stafford | 844 | 2,200 | 1,659 | 1,430 |
| Stanton | 259 | 754 | 489 | 510 |
| Stevens | 408 | 1,392 | 901 | 1,262 |
| Summer | 2,685 | 6,941 | 5,385 | 4,645 |
| Thomas | 943 | 2,300 | 1,802 | 2,246 |
| Trego | 621 | 1,369 | 1,003 | 1,025 |
| Wabaunsee | 622 | 2,461 | 1,354 | 1,921 |
| Wallace | 214 | 782 | 486 | 600 |
| Washington | 996 | 3,301 | 1,564 | 2,543 |
| Wichita | 288 | 794 | 614 | 593 |
| Wilson | 1,043 | 3,568 | 2,047 | 2,682 |
| Woodson | 550 | 1,592 | 904 | 1,104 |
| Wyandotte | 28,206 | 34,157 | 37,478 | 23,141 |
| **Totals** | **270,287** | **619,812** | **430,421** | **502,752** |

## Kansas Vote Since 1932

1932 (Pres.), Roosevelt, Dem., 424,204; Hoover, Rep., 349,498; Thomas, Soc., 18,276.

1936 (Pres.), Roosevelt, Dem., 464,520; Landon, Rep., 397,727; Thomas, Soc., 2,766; Lemke, Union, 494.

1940 (Pres.), Roosevelt, Dem., 364,725; Willkie, Rep., 489,169; Babson, Proh., 4,056; Thomas, Soc., 2,347.

1944 (Pres.), Roosevelt, Dem., 287,458; Dewey, Rep., 442,096; Watson, Proh., 2,609; Thomas, Soc., 1,613.

1948 (Pres.), Truman, Dem., 351,902; Dewey, Rep., 423,039; Watson, Proh., 6,468; Wallace, Prog., 4,603; Thomas, Soc., 2,807.

1952 (Pres.), Eisenhower, Rep., 616,302; Stevenson, Dem., 273,296; Hamblen, Proh., 6,038; Hoopes, Soc., 530.

1956 (Pres.), Eisenhower, Rep., 566,878; Stevenson, Dem., 296,317; Holtwick, Proh., 3,048.

1960 (Pres.), Kennedy, Dem., 363,213; Nixon, Rep., 561,474; Decker, Proh., 4,138.

1964 (Pres.), Johnson, Dem., 464,028; Goldwater, Rep., 386,579; Munn, Proh., 5,393; Haas, Soc. Labor, 1,901.

1968 (Pres.), Nixon, Rep., 478,674; Humphrey, Dem., 302,996; Wallace, 3d, 88,921; Munn, Proh., 2,192.
1972 (Pres.), Nixon, Rep., 619,812; McGovern, Dem., 270,287; Schmitz, Cons., 21,808; Munn, Proh., 4,188.
1976 (Pres.), Carter, Dem., 430,421; Ford, Rep., 502,752; McCarthy, Ind., 13,185; Anderson, Amer., 4,724; MacBride, Libertarian, 3,242; Maddox, Cons., 2,118.

## Kentucky

| | 1972 | | 1976 | |
| | McGovern | Nixon | Carter | Ford |
| County | (D) | (R) | (D) | (R) |
|---|---|---|---|---|
| Adair | 1,610 | 3,859 | 2,366 | 3,201 |
| Allen | 1,259 | 3,025 | 2,231 | 2,508 |
| Anderson | 1,302 | 2,298 | 2,388 | 1,682 |
| Ballard | 1,411 | 1,542 | 2,794 | 649 |
| Barren | 3,384 | 6,070 | 5,878 | 3,797 |
| Bath | 1,347 | 1,919 | 2,113 | 938 |
| Bell | 3,219 | 6,518 | 5,284 | 5,035 |
| Boone | 2,595 | 7,355 | 5,602 | 5,602 |
| Bourbon | 1,860 | 3,180 | 3,504 | 2,260 |
| Boyd | 6,434 | 12,812 | 11,150 | 9,106 |
| Boyle | 2,395 | 4,317 | 4,095 | 3,511 |
| Bracken | 873 | 1,628 | 1,577 | 879 |
| Breathitt | 2,677 | 1,346 | 3,544 | 1,014 |
| Breckinridge | 1,921 | 3,574 | 3,347 | 2,698 |
| Bullitt | 2,827 | 4,517 | 5,623 | 3,639 |
| Butler | 835 | 2,941 | 1,588 | 2,363 |
| Caldwell | 1,345 | 2,952 | 3,016 | 1,808 |
| Calloway | 3,468 | 5,167 | 8,141 | 3,171 |
| Campbell | 8,585 | 20,025 | 12,423 | 15,798 |
| Carlisle | 872 | 1,169 | 1,985 | 435 |
| Carroll | 1,306 | 1,228 | 2,251 | 815 |
| Carter | 2,591 | 4,082 | 3,915 | 3,185 |
| Casey | 913 | 3,727 | 1,602 | 3,379 |
| Christian | 4,063 | 7,414 | 7,845 | 4,964 |
| Clark | 2,020 | 4,506 | 4,575 | 3,114 |
| Clay | 1,709 | 4,046 | 1,674 | 3,652 |
| Clinton | 659 | 2,632 | 987 | 2,354 |
| Crittenden | 859 | 2,248 | 1,715 | 1,596 |
| Cumberland | 686 | 2,294 | 853 | 1,653 |
| Daviess | 8,168 | 17,234 | 14,114 | 12,826 |
| Edmonson | 722 | 2,327 | 1,418 | 1,976 |
| Elliott | 1,499 | 782 | 1,987 | 455 |
| Estill | 1,322 | 3,054 | 2,034 | 2,250 |
| Fayette | 19,828 | 42,362 | 28,012 | 35,170 |
| Fleming | 1,455 | 2,484 | 2,317 | 1,647 |
| Floyd | 7,544 | 6,099 | 10,151 | 3,108 |
| Franklin | 5,601 | 7,781 | 10,475 | 5,536 |
| Fulton | 1,024 | 1,807 | 2,370 | 1,060 |
| Gallatin | 612 | 719 | 1,164 | 436 |
| Garrard | 1,441 | 3,143 | 1,887 | 2,045 |
| Grant | 1,054 | 2,086 | 2,336 | 1,212 |
| Graves | 3,701 | 6,098 | 8,982 | 3,195 |
| Grayson | 1,839 | 4,155 | 3,064 | 3,658 |
| Green | 1,209 | 2,755 | 2,085 | 2,397 |
| Greenup | 4,491 | 6,828 | 6,880 | 5,062 |
| Hancock | 791 | 1,583 | 1,562 | 1,124 |
| Hardin | 4,060 | 8,740 | 7,977 | 6,965 |
| Harlan | 4,349 | 6,527 | 7,300 | 4,624 |
| Harrison | 1,780 | 2,732 | 3,582 | 1,911 |
| Hart | 2,307 | 3,582 | 3,189 | 2,013 |
| Henderson | 3,889 | 6,231 | 7,916 | 4,053 |
| Henry | 1,688 | 1,919 | 2,985 | 1,192 |
| Hickman | 976 | 1,430 | 2,035 | 585 |
| Hopkins | 3,129 | 7,133 | 7,749 | 5,115 |
| Jackson | 436 | 5,303 | 680 | 2,766 |
| Jefferson | 88,143 | 142,436 | 122,731 | 130,262 |
| Jessamine | 1,269 | 3,819 | 2,795 | 3,081 |
| Johnson | 1,840 | 4,607 | 3,683 | 4,891 |
| Kenton | 12,672 | 28,076 | 18,833 | 22,087 |
| Knott | 2,774 | 1,479 | 4,762 | 962 |
| Knox | 1,805 | 5,017 | 3,642 | 4,931 |
| Larue | 1,483 | 2,449 | 2,207 | 1,409 |
| Laurel | 2,274 | 7,276 | 3,813 | 6,186 |
| Lawrence | 1,529 | 2,392 | 2,402 | 1,838 |
| Lee | 744 | 1,629 | 1,091 | 1,449 |
| Leslie | 913 | 3,299 | 1,478 | 3,770 |
| Letcher | 2,908 | 4,213 | 4,590 | 3,122 |
| Lewis | 1,200 | 3,124 | 1,929 | 2,383 |
| Lincoln | 1,882 | 3,623 | 3,198 | 2,694 |
| Livingston | 1,065 | 1,673 | 2,497 | 878 |
| Logan | 2,459 | 3,573 | 4,850 | 2,430 |
| Lyon | 687 | 1,030 | 1,606 | 585 |
| McCracken | 7,576 | 11,260 | 14,956 | 6,997 |
| McCreary | 684 | 3,203 | 1,827 | 3,272 |
| McLean | 1,191 | 2,298 | 2,346 | 1,212 |
| Madison | 4,328 | 8,659 | 7,299 | 6,581 |
| Magoffin | 2,024 | 2,243 | 2,451 | 1,793 |
| Marion | 2,351 | 2,370 | 3,520 | 1,723 |
| Marshall | 2,806 | 4,290 | 6,906 | 2,578 |
| Martin | 661 | 2,495 | 1,267 | 2,120 |
| Mason | 2,459 | 3,529 | 3,397 | 2,529 |
| Meade | 1,541 | 2,492 | 3,030 | 1,755 |
| Menifee | 732 | 596 | 1,041 | 304 |
| Mercer | 1,707 | 3,575 | 3,411 | 2,45 |
| Metcalfe | 1,308 | 1,896 | 1,877 | 1,35 |
| Monroe | 768 | 3,770 | 1,412 | 3,35 |
| Montgomery | 1,657 | 2,868 | 3,141 | 2,03 |
| Morgan | 1,815 | 1,535 | 2,897 | 97 |
| Muhlenberg | 3,246 | 5,596 | 7,058 | 4,29 |
| Nelson | 2,828 | 3,495 | 4,454 | 2,80 |
| Nicholas | 804 | 1,076 | 1,582 | 73 |
| Ohio | 906 | 2,392 | 3,508 | 3,76 |
| Oldham | 1,311 | 3,041 | 2,819 | 3,69 |
| Owen | 1,161 | 1,456 | 2,332 | 67 |
| Owsley | 251 | 1,328 | 305 | 1,05 |
| Pendleton | 909 | 1,966 | 2,147 | 1,23 |
| Perry | 3,601 | 5,373 | 5,633 | 4,43 |
| Pike | 9,513 | 12,535 | 14,320 | 9,17 |
| Powell | 1,230 | 1,766 | 1,859 | 1,14 |
| Pulaski | 3,080 | 10,602 | 5,752 | 9,22 |
| Robertson | 421 | 456 | 546 | 27 |
| Rockcastle | 968 | 3,437 | 1,408 | 2,58 |
| Rowen | 2,169 | 3,245 | 3,541 | 2,24 |
| Russell | 1,169 | 3,992 | 1,803 | 2,88 |
| Scott | 1,642 | 3,255 | 3,118 | 2,40 |
| Shelby | 2,074 | 3,893 | 3,841 | 2,91 |
| Simpson | 1,325 | 2,285 | 2,782 | 1,48 |
| Spencer | 481 | 1,120 | 1,209 | 74 |
| Taylor | 1,859 | 4,035 | 3,456 | 3,33 |
| Todd | 1,222 | 1,964 | 2,436 | 1,09 |
| Trigg | 1,514 | 1,767 | 2,727 | 99 |
| Trimble | 757 | 935 | 1,568 | 51 |
| Union | 1,855 | 2,701 | 3,540 | 1,71 |
| Warren | 5,934 | 12,481 | 9,657 | 9,43 |
| Washington | 1,552 | 2,378 | 2,376 | 1,76 |
| Wayne | 1,853 | 3,514 | 2,537 | 3,24 |
| Webster | 1,712 | 2,396 | 3,523 | 1,40 |
| Whitley | 2,199 | 6,788 | 4,212 | 6,10 |
| Wolfe | 957 | 936 | 1,777 | 65 |
| Woodford | 1,268 | 3,363 | 2,689 | 2,64 |
| **Totals** | 371,159 | 676,446 | 615,717 | 531,852 |

### Kentucky Vote Since 1932

1932 (Pres.), Roosevelt, Dem., 580,574; Hoover, Rep., 394,716; Upshaw, Proh., 2,252; Thomas, Soc., 3,853; Reynolds, Soc. Lab., 1,396; Foster, Com., 272.

1936 (Pres.), Roosevelt, Dem., 541,944; Landon, Rep., 369,702; Lemke, Union, 12,501; Colvin, Proh., 929; Thomas, S., 627; Aiken, S. L., 294; Browder, Com., 204.

1940 (Pres.), Roosevelt, Dem., 557,222; Willkie, Rep., 410,384; Babson, Proh., 1,443; Thomas, Soc., 1,014.

1944 (Pres.), Roosevelt, Dem., 472,589; Dewey, Rep., 392,448; Watson, Proh., 2,023; Thomas, Soc., 535; Teichert, Soc. Lab., 326.

1948 (Pres.), Truman, Dem., 466,756; Dewey, Rep., 341,210; Thurmond, States' Rights, 10,411; Wallace Prog., 1,567; Thomas, Soc., 1,284; Watson, Proh., 1,245; Teichert, Soc. Lab., 185.

1952 (Pres.), Eisenhower, Rep., 495,029; Stevenson, Dem., 495,729; Hamblen, Proh., 1,161; Haas, Soc. Lab., 893; Hallinan, Proh., 336.

1956 (Pres.), Eisenhower, Rep., 572,192; Stevenson, Dem., 476,453; Byrd, States' Rights, 2,657; Holtwick, Proh., 2,145; Haas, Soc. Lab., 358.

1960 (Pres.), Kennedy, Dem., 521,855; Nixon, Rep., 602,607.

1964 (Pres.), Johnson, Dem., 669,659; Goldwater, Rep., 372,977; John Kasper, Nat'l. States Rights, 3,469.

1968 (Pres.), Nixon, Rep., 462,411; Humphrey, Dem., 397,547; Wallace, 3d p., 193,098; Halstead, S. W., 2,843.

1972 (Pres.), Nixon, Rep., 676,446; McGovern, Dem., 371,159; Schmitz, Amer., 17,627; Jenness, Soc. Worker, 685; Hall, Comm., 464; Spock, Peoples, 1,118.

1976 (Pres.), Carter, Dem., 615,717; Ford, Rep., 531,852; Anderson, American, 8,308; McCarthy, Ind., 6,837; Maddox, Amer. Independent, 2,328.

## Louisiana

| | 1972 | | 1976 | |
| | McGovern | Nixon | Carter | Ford |
| Parish | (D) | (R) | (D) | (R) |
|---|---|---|---|---|
| Acadia | 4,406 | 9,698 | 10,814 | 6,29 |
| Allen | 2,029 | 3,581 | 5,373 | 2,08 |
| Ascension | 3,324 | 5,187 | 9,100 | 4,43 |
| Assumption | 2,065 | 3,751 | 4,401 | 3,11 |
| Avoyelles | 3,395 | 6,225 | 8,104 | 4,57 |

| County | 1972 (D) | 1972 (R) | 1976 (D) | 1976 (R) |
|---|---|---|---|---|
| Beauregard | 1,728 | 4,955 | 5,322 | 3,196 |
| Bienville | 1,890 | 3,384 | 3,402 | 2,499 |
| Bossier | 2,914 | 12,856 | 8,062 | 12,132 |
| Caddo | 15,649 | 47,215 | 30,593 | 42,627 |
| Calcasieu | 15,330 | 24,778 | 33,980 | 17,485 |
| Caldwell | 508 | 2,306 | 1,830 | 1,890 |
| Cameron | 739 | 1,391 | 2,432 | 819 |
| Catahoula | 823 | 2,683 | 2,547 | 2,086 |
| Claiborne | 1,551 | 3,432 | 2,891 | 3,216 |
| Concordia | 2,142 | 4,521 | 3,892 | 3,849 |
| DeSoto | 2,596 | 4,017 | 4,630 | 3,601 |
| . Baton Rouge | 23,617 | 52,648 | 49,956 | 51,655 |
| East Carroll | 1,661 | 1,736 | 2,367 | 1,681 |
| East Feliciana | 1,603 | 1,992 | 3,485 | 1,668 |
| Evangeline | 2,919 | 5,523 | 7,578 | 3,715 |
| Franklin | 1,272 | 4,967 | 3,824 | 3,947 |
| Grant | 859 | 3,626 | 3,670 | 2,280 |
| Iberia | 5,143 | 11,812 | 9,984 | 10,392 |
| Iberville | 3,650 | 3,972 | 7,254 | 3,822 |
| Jackson | 1,477 | 4,152 | 3,605 | 3,310 |
| Jefferson | 20,981 | 75,348 | 53,257 | 71,787 |
| Jefferson Davis | 2,551 | 5,903 | 6,376 | 3,603 |
| Lafayette | 8,740 | 22,939 | 19,918 | 22,805 |
| Lafourche | 5,713 | 13,936 | 14,131 | 11,434 |
| LaSalle | 651 | 3,858 | 2,961 | 3,161 |
| Lincoln | 2,589 | 6,736 | 4,971 | 6,828 |
| Livingston | 1,898 | 7,481 | 9,875 | 5,555 |
| Madison | 2,249 | 2,420 | 4,933 | 2,096 |
| Morehouse | 2,355 | 5,770 | 4,017 | 5,418 |
| Natchitoches | 3,180 | 6,994 | 6,692 | 5,248 |
| Orleans | 60,790 | 88,075 | 93,130 | 70,925 |
| Ouachita | 6,920 | 24,860 | 15,738 | 24,082 |
| Plaquemines | 990 | 6,595 | 2,614 | 6,052 |
| Pointe Coupee | 3,133 | 3,192 | 5,147 | 2,567 |
| Rapides | 8,422 | 22,036 | 20,851 | 17,766 |
| Red River | 957 | 2,245 | 1,906 | 1,728 |
| Richland | 1,335 | 4,304 | 3,495 | 3,630 |
| Sabine | 1,332 | 4,935 | 4,555 | 3,531 |
| St. Bernard | 3,189 | 15,198 | 12,969 | 12,707 |
| St. Charles | 2,788 | 5,469 | 6,872 | 4,270 |
| St. Helena | 943 | 1,446 | 2,622 | 1,046 |
| St. James | 2,633 | 3,112 | 4,531 | 2,751 |
| St. John | 2,815 | 3,525 | 5,700 | 3,597 |
| St. Landry | 7,421 | 12,510 | 15,631 | 9,956 |
| St. Martin | 3,202 | 6,337 | 7,992 | 4,112 |
| St. Mary | 4,435 | 11,117 | 9,401 | 8,919 |
| St. Tammany | 3,949 | 15,438 | 14,691 | 15,822 |
| Tangipahoa | 5,227 | 11,607 | 14,432 | 9,242 |
| Tensas | 1,568 | 1,729 | 2,081 | 1,553 |
| Terrebonne | 4,415 | 13,753 | 10,627 | 12,895 |
| Union | 1,465 | 4,322 | 3,600 | 4,139 |
| Vermilion | 3,876 | 8,909 | 11,246 | 6,133 |
| Vernon | 1,345 | 6,225 | 6,202 | 3,970 |
| Washington | 2,947 | 8,162 | 10,000 | 5,677 |
| Webster | 2,859 | 8,829 | 7,286 | 7,550 |
| W. Baton Rouge | 1,849 | 2,626 | 3,809 | 1,913 |
| West Carroll | 571 | 2,997 | 2,595 | 2,407 |
| West Feliciana | 1,079 | 1,001 | 1,890 | 990 |
| Winn | 1,490 | 4,235 | 3,543 | 3,209 |
| **Totals** | **298,142** | **686,852** | **661,365** | **587,446** |

## Louisiana Vote Since 1932

1932 (Pres.), Roosevelt, Dem., 249,418; Hoover, Rep., 18,863.

1936 (Pres.), Roosevelt, Dem., 292,894; Landon, Rep., 36,791.

1940 (Pres.), Roosevelt, Dem., 319,751; Willkie, Rep., 52,446.

1944 (Pres.), Roosevelt, Dem., 281,564; Dewey, Rep., 67,750.

1948 (Pres.), Thurmond, States' Rights, 204,290; Truman, Dem., 136,344; Dewey, Rep., 72,657; Wallace, Prog., 3,035.

1952 (Pres.), Eisenhower, Rep., 306,925; Stevenson, Dem., 345,027.

1956 (Pres.), Eisenhower, Rep., 329,047; Stevenson, Dem., 243,977; Andrews, States' Rights, 44,520.

1960 (Pres.), Kennedy, Dem., 407,339; Nixon, Rep., 230,890; States' Rights (unpledged) 169,572.

1964 (Pres.), Johnson, Dem., 387,068; Goldwater, Rep., 509,225.

1968 (Pres.), Nixon, Rep., 257,535; Humphrey, Dem., 309,615; Wallace, 3d party, 530,300.

1972 (Pres.), Nixon, Rep., 686,852; McGovern, Dem., 298,142; Schmitz, American, 52,099; Jenness, Soc. Worker, 14,398.

1976 (Pres.), Carter, Dem., 661,365; Ford, Rep., 587,446; Maddox, American, 10,058; Hall, Comm., 7,417; McCarthy, Ind., 6,588; MacBride, Libertarian, 3,325.

# Maine

| County | 1972 McGovern (D) | 1972 Nixon (R) | 1976 Carter (D) | 1976 Ford (R) |
|---|---|---|---|---|
| Androscoggin | 19,509 | 19,406 | 26,484 | 16,330 |
| Aroostook | 11,474 | 19,051 | 15,484 | 15,550 |
| Cumberland | 33,326 | 51,268 | 47,007 | 48,959 |
| Franklin | 2,988 | 5,958 | 5,140 | 5,799 |
| Hancock | 4,191 | 11,889 | 6,725 | 12,064 |
| Kennebec | 16,379 | 24,617 | 23,473 | 22,534 |
| Knox | 3,601 | 8,478 | 5,922 | 8,315 |
| Lincoln | 2,903 | 7,580 | 4,818 | 7,554 |
| Oxford | 6,661 | 12,114 | 10,340 | 10,551 |
| Penobscot | 18,552 | 30,186 | 24,672 | 29,016 |
| Piscataquis | 2,518 | 4,617 | 3,727 | 4,084 |
| Sagadahoc | 3,414 | 6,463 | 5,529 | 5,988 |
| Somerset | 5,921 | 10,079 | 9,465 | 8,868 |
| Waldo | 2,941 | 6,480 | 4,853 | 6,289 |
| Washington | 3,742 | 7,820 | 6,644 | 7,039 |
| York | 22,464 | 30,152 | 31,996 | 27,380 |
| **Totals** | **160,584** | **256,458** | **232,279** | **236,320** |

## Maine Vote Since 1932

1932 (Pres.), Roosevelt, Dem., 128,907; Hoover, Rep., 166,631; Thomas, Soc., 2,439; Reynolds, Soc. Lab., 255; Foster, Com., 162.

1936 (Pres.), Landon, Rep., 168,823; Roosevelt, Dem., 126,333; Lemke, Union, 7,581; Thomas, Soc., 783; Colvin, Proh., 334; Browder, Com., 257; Aiken, Soc. Lab., 129.

1940 (Pres.), Roosevelt, Dem., 156,478; Willkie, Rep., 165,951; Browder, Com., 411.

1944 (Pres.), Roosevelt, Dem., 140,631; Dewey, Rep., 155,434; Teichert, Soc. Lab., 335.

1948 (Pres.), Truman, Dem., 111,916; Dewey, Rep., 150,234; Wallace, Prog., 1,884; Thomas, Soc., 547; Teichert, Soc. Lab., 206.

1952 (Pres.), Eisenhower, Rep., 232,353; Stevenson, Dem., 118,806; Hallinan, Prog., 332; Haas, Soc. Lab., 156; Hoopes, Soc., 138; scattered, 1.

1956 (Pres.), Eisenhower, Rep., 249,238; Stevenson, Dem., 102,468.

1960 (Pres.), Kennedy, Dem., 181,159; Nixon, Rep., 240,608.

1964 (Pres.), Johnson, Dem., 262,264; Goldwater, Rep., 118,701.

1968 (Pres.), Nixon, Rep., 169,254; Humphrey, Dem., 217,312; Wallace, 3d party, 6,370.

1972 (Pres.), Nixon, Rep., 256,458; McGovern, Dem., 160,584; scattered, 229.

1976 (Pres.), Carter, Dem., 232,279; Ford, Rep., 236,320; McCarthy, Ind., 10,874; Bubar, Proh., 3,495.

# Maryland

| County | 1972 McGovern (D) | 1972 Nixon (R) | 1976 Carter (D) | 1976 Ford (R) |
|---|---|---|---|---|
| Allegany | 10,808 | 20,687 | 15,967 | 15,435 |
| Anne Arundel | 26,082 | 71,707 | 54,351 | 61,353 |
| Baltimore | 70,309 | 175,897 | 118,505 | 143,293 |
| Calvert | 2,232 | 4,024 | 4,626 | 3,439 |
| Caroline | 1,567 | 4,325 | 3,017 | 3,114 |
| Carroll | 4,408 | 16,847 | 9,940 | 15,661 |
| Cecil | 4,113 | 10,759 | 8,950 | 7,833 |
| Charles | 4,502 | 9,665 | 9,525 | 7,792 |
| Dorchester | 2,136 | 6,859 | 4,528 | 4,768 |
| Frederick | 8,235 | 19,907 | 14,542 | 17,941 |
| Garrett | 1,510 | 5,480 | 3,332 | 4,640 |
| Harford | 8,737 | 25,141 | 19,890 | 24,309 |
| Howard | 10,668 | 19,265 | 20,533 | 21,200 |
| Kent | 2,168 | 4,036 | 3,211 | 2,821 |
| Montgomery | 100,228 | 133,090 | 131,098 | 122,674 |
| Prince George's | 79,914 | 116,166 | 111,743 | 81,027 |
| Queen Anne's | 1,712 | 4,380 | 3,457 | 3,479 |
| St. Mary's | 3,571 | 7,689 | 7,227 | 5,640 |
| Somerset | 2,036 | 4,342 | 3,472 | 3,254 |
| Talbot | 2,181 | 6,620 | 3,715 | 5,848 |
| Washington | 10,039 | 24,234 | 15,902 | 20,194 |
| Wicomico | 5,510 | 13,115 | 9,412 | 10,537 |
| Worcester | 1,792 | 5,584 | 4,076 | 4,647 |
| BALTIMORE CITY | 141,323 | 119,486 | 178,593 | 81,762 |
| **Totals** | **505,781** | **829,305** | **759,612** | **672,661** |

## Maryland Vote Since 1932

1932 (Pres.), Roosevelt, Dem., 314,314; Hoover, Rep.,

184,184; Thomas, Soc., 10,489; Reynolds, Soc. Lab., 1,036; Foster, Com., 1,031.

1936 (Pres.), Roosevelt, Dem., 389,612; Landon, Rep., 231,435; Thomas, Soc., 1,629; Aiken, Soc. Lab., 1,305; Browder, Com., 915.

1940 (Pres.), Roosevelt, Dem., 384,546; Willkie, Rep., 269,534; Thomas, Soc., 4,093; Browder, Com., 1,274; Aiken, Soc. Lab., 657.

1944 (Pres.), Roosevelt, Dem., 315,490; Dewey, Rep., 292,949.

1948 (Pres.), Truman, Dem., 286,521; Dewey, Rep., 294,814; Wallace, Prog., 9,983; Thomas, Soc., 2,941; Thurmond, States' Rights, 2,476; Wright, write-in, 2,294.

1952 (Pres.), Eisenhower, Rep., 499,424; Stevenson, Dem., 395,337; Hallinan, Prog., 7,313.

1956 (Pres.), Eisenhower, Rep., 559,738; Stevenson, Dem., 372,613.

1960 (Pres.), Kennedy, Dem., 565,800; Nixon, Rep., 489,538.

1964 (Pres.), Johnson, Dem., 730,912; Goldwater, Rep., 385,495; write-in, 50.

1968 (Pres.), Nixon, Rep., 517,995; Humphrey, Dem., 538,310; Wallace, 3d party, 178,734.

1972 (Pres.), Nixon, Rep., 829,305; McGovern, Dem., 505,781; Schmitz, American Party, 18,726.

1976 (Pres.), Carter, Dem., 759,612; Ford, Rep., 672,661.

## Massachusetts

| County | 1972 McGovern (D) | Nixon (R) | 1976 Carter (D) | Ford (R) |
|---|---|---|---|---|
| Barnstable | 22,636 | 36,340 | 31,268 | 39,295 |
| Berkshire | 35,391 | 30,380 | 39,337 | 27,462 |
| Bristol | 103,163 | 84,390 | 116,318 | 69,957 |
| Dukes | 2,001 | 2,312 | 2,513 | 2,365 |
| Essex | 157,324 | 138,040 | 165,710 | 125,538 |
| Franklin | 11,968 | 16,088 | 14,985 | 14,837 |
| Hampden | 94,945 | 86,164 | 110,028 | 70,008 |
| Hampshire | 28,572 | 24,529 | 34,947 | 22,219 |
| Middlesex | 345,343 | 269,064 | 359,919 | 260,044 |
| Nantucket | 952 | 1,418 | 1,115 | 1,399 |
| Norfolk | 150,232 | 134,459 | 155,342 | 136,628 |
| Plymouth | 69,124 | 76,062 | 83,663 | 74,684 |
| Suffolk | 166,250 | 85,272 | 142,010 | 80,623 |
| Worcester | 144,139 | 127,560 | 172,320 | 105,217 |
| **Totals** | **1,332,540** | **1,112,078** | **1,429,475** | **1,030,276** |

## Massachusetts Vote Since 1932

1932 (Pres.), Roosevelt, Dem., 800,148; Hoover, Rep., 736,959; Thomas, Soc., 34,305; Foster, Com., 4,821; Reynolds, Soc. Lab., 2,668; Upshaw, Proh., 1,142.

1936 (Pres.), Roosevelt, Dem., 942,716; Landon, Rep., 768,613; Lemke, Union, 118,639; Thomas, Soc., 5,111; Browder, Com., 2,930; Aiken, Soc. Lab., 1,305; Colvin, Proh., 1,032.

1940 (Pres.), Roosevelt, Dem., 1,076,522; Willkie, Rep., 939,700; Thomas, Soc., 4,091; Browder, Com., 3,806; Aiken, Soc. Lab., 1,492; Babson, Proh., 1,370.

1944 (Pres.), Roosevelt, Dem., 1,035,296; Dewey, Rep., 921,350; Teichert, Soc. Lab., 2,780; Watson, Proh., 973.

1948 (Pres.), Truman, Dem., 1,151,788; Dewey, Rep., 909,370; Wallace, Prog., 38,157; Teichert, Soc. Lab., 5,535; Watson, Proh., 1,663.

1952 (Pres.), Eisenhower, Rep., 1,292,325; Stevenson, Dem., 1,083,525; Hallinan, Prog., 4,636; Haas, Soc. Lab., 1,957; Hamblen, Proh., 886; scattered, 69; blanks, 41,150.

1956 (Pres.), Eisenhower, Rep., 1,393,197; Stevenson, Dem., 948,190; Haas, Soc. Lab., 5,573; Holtwick, Proh., 1,205; others, 341.

1960 (Pres.), Kennedy, Dem., 1,487,174; Nixon, Rep., 976,750; Haas, Soc. Lab., 3,892; Decker, Proh., 1,633; others, 31; blank and void, 26,024.

1964 (Pres.), Johnson, Dem., 1,786,422; Goldwater, Rep., 549,727; Haas, Soc. Lab., 4,755; Munn, Proh., 3,735; scattered, 159; blank, 48,104.

1968 (Pres.), Nixon, Rep., 766,844; Humphrey, Dem., 1,469,218; Wallace, 3d party, 87,088; Blomen, Soc. Labor, 6,180; Munn, Prohibition, 2,369; scattered, 53; blanks, 25,394.

1972 (Pres.), Nixon, Rep., 1,112,078; McGovern, Dem., 1,332,540; Soc. Worker, 10,600; Fisher, Soc. Labor, 129; Schmitz, American, 2,877; Spock, Peoples, 101; Hall, Communist, 46; Hospers, Libertarian, 43; scattered, 342.

1976 (Pres.), Carter, Dem., 1,429,475; Ford, Rep., 1,030,276; McCarthy, Ind., 65,637; Camejo, Soc. Workers, 8,138; Anderson, American, 7,555; La Rouche, U.S. Labor, 4,922.

## Michigan

| County | 1972 McGovern (D) | Nixon (R) | 1976 Carter (D) | Ford (R) |
|---|---|---|---|---|
| Alcona | 1,195 | 2,434 | 2,038 | 2,32 |
| Alger | 1,803 | 2,035 | 2,379 | 1,72 |
| Allegan | 7,883 | 18,407 | 9,794 | 19,33 |
| Alpena | 5,104 | 6,513 | 6,310 | 6,38 |
| Antrim | 2,000 | 4,068 | 3,032 | 4,36 |
| Arenac | 1,829 | 2,588 | 2,695 | 2,68 |
| Baraga | 1,517 | 1,905 | 1,778 | 1,78 |
| Barry | 5,484 | 10,393 | 6,967 | 11,17 |
| Bay | 21,712 | 23,094 | 25,958 | 23,17 |
| Benzie | 1,310 | 2,686 | 1,891 | 3,08 |
| Berrien | 18,597 | 43,047 | 25,163 | 40,83 |
| Branch | 4,887 | 8,388 | 6,301 | 8,25 |
| Calhoun | 22,154 | 32,531 | 25,229 | 30,39 |
| Cass | 4,982 | 10,398 | 7,843 | 9,89 |
| Charlevoix | 2,831 | 4,522 | 3,953 | 5,14 |
| Cheboygan | 2,985 | 4,529 | 3,880 | 4,89 |
| Chippewa | 4,744 | 7,028 | 6,022 | 7,02 |
| Clare | 2,434 | 4,402 | 4,153 | 4,87 |
| Clinton | 5,770 | 13,438 | 7,549 | 13,47 |
| Crawford | 1,143 | 1,953 | 1,889 | 2,35 |
| Delta | 8,003 | 7,647 | 9,027 | 7,80 |
| Dickinson | 5,339 | 5,989 | 6,134 | 5,92 |
| Eaton | 8,986 | 20,413 | 12,083 | 22,12 |
| Emmet | 3,081 | 4,288 | 4,013 | 5,91 |
| Genesee | 73,896 | 85,747 | 88,967 | 80,00 |
| Gladwin | 2,016 | 3,484 | 3,719 | 3,79 |
| Gogebic | 4,984 | 5,631 | 6,341 | 3,95 |
| Grand Traverse | 5,810 | 11,421 | 7,263 | 13,50 |
| Gratiot | 4,370 | 9,904 | 5,429 | 9,52 |
| Hillsdale | 3,942 | 9,261 | 5,427 | 9,30 |
| Houghton | 6,402 | 9,053 | 7,352 | 8,04 |
| Huron | 4,456 | 9,832 | 5,721 | 9,29 |
| Ingham | 53,458 | 63,376 | 47,890 | 66,72 |
| Ionia | 6,240 | 10,898 | 6,820 | 11,73 |
| Iosco | 3,065 | 5,750 | 4,875 | 5,50 |
| Iron | 3,512 | 3,630 | 4,401 | 3,22 |
| Isabella | 7,446 | 9,682 | 7,281 | 10,57 |
| Jackson | 19,350 | 34,220 | 24,726 | 32,87 |
| Kalamazoo | 33,324 | 50,405 | 33,411 | 51,46 |
| Kalkaska | 924 | 1,855 | 1,957 | 2,28 |
| Kent | 67,587 | 104,041 | 59,000 | 126,80 |
| Keweenaw | 456 | 715 | 658 | 60 |
| Lake | 1,548 | 1,532 | 2,179 | 1,59 |
| Lapeer | 5,531 | 11,615 | 9,503 | 12,34 |
| Leelanau | 1,855 | 3,809 | 2,437 | 4,24 |
| Lenawee | 11,018 | 19,125 | 14,610 | 18,39 |
| Livingston | 7,634 | 16,856 | 12,415 | 19,43 |
| Luce | 862 | 1,579 | 1,099 | 1,37 |
| Mackinac | 1,937 | 3,096 | 2,463 | 3,10 |
| Macomb | 82,346 | 147,777 | 121,176 | 132,49 |
| Manistee | 3,625 | 5,070 | 4,479 | 5,53 |
| Marquette | 11,555 | 13,249 | 12,837 | 12,98 |
| Mason | 3,697 | 6,811 | 4,541 | 6,81 |
| Mecosta | 3,799 | 7,158 | 4,725 | 7,28 |
| Menominee | 4,657 | 6,060 | 5,596 | 5,63 |
| Midland | 9,504 | 16,473 | 11,959 | 17,63 |
| Missaukee | 924 | 2,647 | 1,688 | 2,94 |
| Monroe | 17,726 | 23,263 | 23,290 | 20,67 |
| Montcalm | 5,402 | 9,591 | 6,684 | 10,43 |
| Montmorency | 914 | 1,798 | 1,684 | 1,88 |
| Muskegon | 22,804 | 36,428 | 27,013 | 35,54 |
| Newaygo | 3,978 | 8,254 | 5,622 | 8,25 |
| Oakland | 129,400 | 241,613 | 164,266 | 244,27 |
| Oceana | 2,525 | 4,992 | 3,427 | 5,23 |
| Ogemaw | 2,056 | 3,367 | 3,545 | 3,21 |
| Ontonagon | 2,140 | 3,040 | 3,104 | 2,46 |
| Osceola | 1,706 | 4,441 | 2,603 | 4,46 |
| Oscoda | 678 | 1,561 | 1,108 | 1,54 |
| Otsego | 1,912 | 2,854 | 2,724 | 3,15 |
| Ottawa | 15,119 | 42,169 | 16,381 | 49,19 |
| Presque Isle | 2,440 | 3,372 | 3,334 | 3,54 |
| Roscommon | 2,187 | 4,136 | 3,691 | 4,60 |
| Saginaw | 29,424 | 47,920 | 36,280 | 46,76 |
| St. Clair | 15,712 | 23,471 | 22,734 | 26,31 |
| St. Joseph | 5,119 | 18,438 | 7,306 | 11,78 |
| Sanilac | 3,780 | 11,031 | 6,042 | 10,59 |
| Schoolcraft | 1,759 | 2,310 | 2,158 | 1,93 |
| Shiawassee | 3,932 | 15,489 | 12,202 | 15,11 |
| Tuscola | 5,449 | 12,198 | 7,932 | 12,05 |
| Van Buren | 7,159 | 13,903 | 10,366 | 13,61 |
| Washtenaw | 55,350 | 50,535 | 50,917 | 56,80 |

| | 1972 | | 1976 | |
|---|---|---|---|---|
| | (D) | (R) | (D) | (R) |
| yne...... | 514,913 | 435,877 | 548,767 | 348,588 |
| xford...... | 3,048 | 5,221 | 4,519 | 5,670 |
| **Totals......** | **1,459,435** | **1,961,721** | **1,696,714** | **1,893,742** |

## Michigan Vote Since 1932

32 (Pres.), Roosevelt, Dem., 871,700; Hoover, Rep., 739,894; Thomas, Soc., 39,025; Foster, Com., 9,318; Upshaw, Proh., 2,893; Reynolds, Soc. Lab., 1,041; Harvey, Lib., 217.

36 (Pres.), Roosevelt, Dem., 1,016,794; Landon, Rep., 699,733; Lemke, Union, 75,795; Thomas, Soc., 8,208; Browder, Com., 3,384; Aiken, Soc. Lab., 600; Colvin, Proh., 579.

40 (Pres.), Roosevelt, Dem., 1,032,991; Willkie, Rep., 1,039,917; Thomas, Soc., 7,593; Browder, Com., 2,834; Babson, Proh., 1,795; Aiken, Soc. Lab., 795.

44 (Pres.), Roosevelt, Dem., 1,106,899; Dewey, Rep., 1,084,423; Watson, Proh., 6,503; Thomas, Soc., 4,598; Smith, America First, 1,530; Teichert, Soc. Lab., 1,264.

48 (Pres.), Truman, Dem., 1,003,448; Dewey, Rep., 1,038,595; Wallace, Prog., 46,515; Watson, Proh., 13,052; Thomas, Soc., 6,063; Teichert, Soc. Lab., 1,263; Dobbs, Soc. Workers, 672.

52 (Pres.), Eisenhower, Rep., 1,551,529; Stevenson, Dem., 1,230,657; Hamblen, Proh., 10,331; Hallinan, Prog., 3,922; Haas, Soc. Lab., 1,495; Dobbs, Soc. Workers, 655; scattered, 3.

56 (Pres.), Eisenhower, Rep., 1,713,647; Stevenson, Dem., 1,359,898; Holtwick, Proh., 6,923.

60 (Pres.), Kennedy, Dem., 1,687,269; Nixon, Rep., 1,620,428; Dobbs, Soc. Workers, 4,347; Decker, Proh., 2,029; Daly, Tax Cut, 1,767; Haas, Soc. Lab., 1,718; Ind. American, 539.

64 (Pres.), Johnson, Dem., 2,136,615; Goldwater, Rep., 1,060,152; DeBerry, Soc. Workers, 3,817; Haas, Soc. Lab., 1,704; Proh. (no candidate listed), 699; scattering, 145.

68 (Pres.), Nixon, Rep., 1,370,665; Humphrey, Dem., 1,593,082; Wallace, 3d party, 331,968; Halstead, Soc. Worker, 4,099; Blomen, Soc. Labor, 1,762; Cleaver, New Politics, 4,585; Munn, Prohib., 60; scattering, 29.

72 (Pres.), Nixon, Rep., 1,961,721; McGovern, Dem., 1,459,435; Schmitz, Amer., 63,321; Fisher, Soc. Labor, 2,437; Jenness, Soc. Worker, 1,603; Hall, Communist, 1,210.

76 (Pres.), Carter, Dem., 1,696,714; Ford, Rep., 1,893,742; McCarthy, Ind., 47,905; MacBride, Libertarian, 5,406; Wright, People's, 3,504; Camejo, Soc. Workers, 1,804; LaRouche, U.S. Labor, 1,366; Levin, Soc. Labor, 1,148; scattering, 2,160.

## Minnesota

| | 1972 | | 1976 | |
|---|---|---|---|---|
| | McGovern | Nixon | Carter | Ford |
| County | (D) | (R) | (D) | (R) |
| in........ | 2,687 | 3,241 | 4,308 | 2,476 |
| ka........ | 28,031 | 29,546 | 48,173 | 27,863 |
| ker........ | 4,695 | 6,033 | 6,597 | 5,611 |
| rami........ | 5,194 | 5,947 | 7,540 | 5,214 |
| ton........ | 4,282 | 4,652 | 6,235 | 4,099 |
| Stone........ | 2,185 | 1,748 | 2,581 | 1,332 |
| e Earth........ | 10,638 | 12,702 | 12,930 | 11,998 |
| wn........ | 4,347 | 7,791 | 5,792 | 7,479 |
| ton........ | 7,116 | 5,445 | 9,247 | 4,371 |
| ver........ | 4,852 | 8,546 | 7,574 | 8,199 |
| s........ | 3,347 | 4,906 | 5,424 | 4,443 |
| ppewa........ | 3,630 | 3,787 | 4,648 | 3,254 |
| sago........ | 4,174 | 4,718 | 6,625 | 3,874 |
| y........ | 9,076 | 11,089 | 10,876 | 10,317 |
| arwater........ | 1,751 | 1,819 | 2,437 | 1,374 |
| k........ | 742 | 1,047 | 1,018 | 1,034 |
| onwood........ | 2,802 | 4,396 | 3,813 | 3,906 |
| w Wing........ | 7,328 | 8,774 | 10,653 | 8,072 |
| ota........ | 28,479 | 34,967 | 44,253 | 37,542 |
| ge........ | 1,921 | 3,863 | 3,009 | 3,446 |
| glas........ | 5,501 | 6,678 | 7,097 | 5,910 |
| bault........ | 3,519 | 6,503 | 5,049 | 5,577 |
| nore........ | 3,155 | 7,107 | 4,758 | 5,984 |
| ebom........ | 7,163 | 9,747 | 9,470 | 8,220 |

| | 1972 | | 1976 | |
|---|---|---|---|---|
| | McGovern (D) | Nixon (R) | Carter (D) | Ford (R) |
| Goodhue........ | 6,147 | 11,107 | 8,926 | 9,967 |
| Grant........ | 2,085 | 1,899 | 2,624 | 1,635 |
| Hennepin........ | 205,943 | 228,951 | 257,380 | 211,892 |
| Houston........ | 2,467 | 5,186 | 3,861 | 4,853 |
| Hubbard........ | 2,136 | 3,294 | 3,196 | 2,985 |
| Isanti........ | 3,660 | 3,715 | 6,013 | 3,159 |
| Itasca........ | 8,683 | 7,558 | 12,979 | 6,646 |
| Jackson........ | 3,304 | 3,599 | 4,311 | 2,870 |
| Kanabec........ | 1,979 | 2,395 | 3,188 | 1,943 |
| Kandiyohi........ | 7,241 | 6,624 | 9,992 | 6,664 |
| Kittson........ | 1,584 | 1,832 | 2,008 | 1,555 |
| Koochiching........ | 3,396 | 3,681 | 4,846 | 2,893 |
| LacQuiParle........ | 2,845 | 2,773 | 3,647 | 2,292 |
| Lake........ | 3,640 | 2,575 | 3,973 | 2,313 |
| Lake O'Woods.... | 672 | 877 | 1,105 | 757 |
| Le Sueur........ | 4,725 | 5,388 | 6,556 | 4,565 |
| Lincoln........ | 2,148 | 1,881 | 2,594 | 1,599 |
| Lyon........ | 5,614 | 5,820 | 7,122 | 5,036 |
| McLeod........ | 4,538 | 7,820 | 6,249 | 6,519 |
| Mahnomen........ | 1,397 | 1,246 | 1,590 | 905 |
| Marshall........ | 2,790 | 3,264 | 3,744 | 2,605 |
| Martin........ | 3,816 | 7,569 | 5,672 | 6,484 |
| Meeker........ | 3,601 | 5,097 | 5,295 | 4,097 |
| Millie Lacs........ | 3,221 | 4,291 | 5,172 | 3,212 |
| Morrison........ | 5,993 | 5,714 | 8,176 | 4,590 |
| Mower........ | 10,286 | 9,929 | 12,837 | 8,163 |
| Murray........ | 2,893 | 2,959 | 3,685 | 2,605 |
| Nicollet........ | 4,680 | 6,230 | 5,777 | 6,071 |
| Nobles........ | 5,464 | 4,951 | 6,034 | 4,503 |
| Norman........ | 2,444 | 2,536 | 2,946 | 1,983 |
| Olmsted........ | 9,817 | 23,806 | 14,676 | 24,030 |
| Otter Tail........ | 7,881 | 13,519 | 11,881 | 12,113 |
| Pennington........ | 2,892 | 3,548 | 3,787 | 3,023 |
| Pine........ | 3,794 | 3,881 | 5,442 | 3,057 |
| Pipestone........ | 2,758 | 3,543 | 3,272 | 3,018 |
| Polk........ | 7,366 | 8,139 | 9,078 | 6,522 |
| Pope........ | 2,910 | 2,610 | 3,746 | 2,251 |
| Ramsey........ | 108,392 | 95,716 | 133,682 | 86,480 |
| Red Lake........ | 1,409 | 1,052 | 1,748 | 737 |
| Redwood........ | 3,177 | 5,776 | 4,525 | 4,926 |
| Renville........ | 4,499 | 5,329 | 5,762 | 4,482 |
| Rice........ | 6,065 | 9,195 | 10,590 | 8,311 |
| Rock........ | 2,089 | 3,470 | 2,769 | 2,892 |
| Roseau........ | 2,396 | 2,844 | 3,215 | 2,382 |
| St. Louis........ | 61,103 | 41,435 | 75,040 | 35,331 |
| Scott........ | 6,745 | 7,310 | 9,912 | 7,154 |
| Sherburne........ | 4,070 | 4,332 | 6,678 | 4,361 |
| Sibley........ | 2,433 | 4,543 | 3,752 | 3,871 |
| Stearns........ | 19,315 | 18,951 | 25,027 | 19,574 |
| Steele........ | 4,010 | 7,678 | 6,263 | 7,053 |
| Stevens........ | 2,870 | 2,830 | 3,171 | 2,484 |
| Swift........ | 3,823 | 2,673 | 4,428 | 2,190 |
| Todd........ | 4,270 | 5,387 | 6,530 | 4,278 |
| Traverse........ | 1,744 | 1,276 | 2,020 | 1,130 |
| Wabasha........ | 3,017 | 5,158 | 4,286 | 4,484 |
| Wadena........ | 2,430 | 3,408 | 3,164 | 3,048 |
| Waseca........ | 2,767 | 5,064 | 4,002 | 4,582 |
| Washington........ | 16,102 | 19,142 | 26,454 | 20,716 |
| Watonwan........ | 2,229 | 3,960 | 3,177 | 3,351 |
| Wilkin........ | 1,739 | 2,292 | 2,103 | 1,882 |
| Winona........ | 8,080 | 10,910 | 10,939 | 10,436 |
| Wright........ | 8,695 | 9,996 | 13,379 | 9,314 |
| Yellow Med........ | 3,462 | 3,683 | 4,337 | 2,946 |
| **Totals......** | **802,346** | **898,269** | **1,070,440** | **819,395** |

## Minnesota Vote Since 1932

1932 (Pres.), Roosevelt, Dem., 600,806; Hoover, Rep., 363,959; Thomas, Soc., 25,476; Foster, Com., 6,101; Coxey, Farm.-Lab., 5,731; Reynolds, Ind., 770.

1936 (Pres.), Roosevelt, Dem., 698,811; Landon, Rep., 350,461; Lemke, Union, 74,296; Thomas, Soc., 2,872; Browder, Com., 2,574; Aiken, Soc., 961.

1940 (Pres.), Roosevelt, Dem., 644,196; Willkie, Rep., 596,274; Thomas, Soc., 5,454; Browder, Com., 2,711; Aiken, Ind., 2,553.

1944 (Pres.), Roosevelt, Dem., 589,864; Dewey, Rep., 527,416; Thomas, Soc., 5,073; Teichert, Ind. Gov't., 3,176.

1948 (Pres.), Truman, Dem., 692,966; Dewey, Rep., 483,617; Wallace, Prog., 27,866; Thomas, Soc., 4,646; Teichert, Soc. Lab., 2,525; Dobbs, Soc. Workers, 606.

1952 (Pres.), Eisenhower, Rep., 763,211; Stevenson, Dem., 608,458; Hallinan, Prog., 2,666; Haas, Soc. Lab., 2,383; Hamblen, Proh., 2,147; Dobbs, Soc. Workers, 618.

1956 (Pres.), Eisenhower, Rep., 719,302; Stevenson, Dem., 617,525; Haas, Soc. Lab. (Ind. Gov.), 2,080; Dobbs, Soc. Workers, 1,098.

1960 (Pres.), Kennedy, Dem., 779,993; Nixon, Rep., 757,915; Dobbs, Soc. Workers, 3,077; Industrial Gov., 962.

1964 (Pres.), Johnson, Dem., 991,117; Goldwater, Rep.,

559,624; DeBerry, Soc. Workers, 1,177; Haas, Industrial Gov., 2,544.

1968 (Pres.), Nixon, Rep., 658,643; Humphrey, Dem., 857,738; Wallace, 3d party, 68,931; scattered, 2,443; Halstead, Soc. Worker, 808; Blomen, Ind. Gov't., 285; Mitchell, Communist, 415; Cleaver, Peace, 935; McCarthy, write-in, 585; scattered, 170.

1972 (Pres.), Nixon, Rep., 898,269; McGovern, Dem., 802,346; Schmitz, American, 31,407; Spock, Peoples, 2,805; Fisher, Soc. Labor, 4,261; Jenness, Soc. Worker, 940; Hall, Communist, 662; scattered, 962.

1976 (Pres.), Carter, Dem., 1,070,440; Ford, Rep., 819,395; McCarthy, Ind., 35,490; Anderson, American, 13,592; Camejo, Soc. Workers, 4,149; MacBride, Libertarian, 3,529; Hall, Comm., 1,092.

## Mississippi

| | 1972 | | 1976 | |
|---|---|---|---|---|
| County | McGovern (D) | Nixon (R) | Carter (D) | Ford (R) |
| Adams | 3,697 | 8,500 | 6,619 | 6,431 |
| Alcorn | 982 | 5,732 | 6,995 | 3,430 |
| Amite | 1,185 | 2,846 | 2,574 | 2,256 |
| Attala | 1,103 | 4,738 | 4,068 | 3,146 |
| Benton | 701 | 1,483 | 2,375 | 790 |
| Bolivar | 3,616 | 7,397 | 7,561 | 5,136 |
| Calhoun | 245 | 3,023 | 2,724 | 1,892 |
| Carroll | 580 | 1,777 | 1,566 | 1,561 |
| Chickasaw | 579 | 3,753 | 2,891 | 2,581 |
| Choctaw | 326 | 2,301 | 1,520 | 1,562 |
| Claiborne | 2,076 | 1,521 | 2,657 | 1,078 |
| Clarke | 954 | 4,561 | 2,816 | 2,935 |
| Clay | 1,410 | 4,035 | 3,514 | 3,017 |
| Coahoma | 3,708 | 6,602 | 6,412 | 4,269 |
| Copiah | 1,803 | 5,498 | 4,267 | 4,108 |
| Covington | 642 | 3,842 | 2,862 | 2,591 |
| DeSoto | 1,557 | 7,917 | 7,756 | 6,240 |
| Forrest | 2,933 | 14,418 | 7,914 | 10,770 |
| Franklin | 561 | 2,361 | 1,578 | 1,719 |
| George | 270 | 3,979 | 3,072 | 1,957 |
| Greene | 513 | 2,884 | 2,127 | 1,538 |
| Grenada | 1,471 | 4,800 | 3,263 | 3,569 |
| Hancock | 745 | 5,133 | 3,855 | 3,765 |
| Harrison | 4,761 | 28,962 | 16,569 | 19,207 |
| Hinds | 12,679 | 49,877 | 28,748 | 45,803 |
| Holmes | 3,459 | 3,158 | 4,616 | 2,438 |
| Humphreys | 892 | 2,334 | 2,172 | 1,445 |
| Issaquena | 395 | 701 | 567 | 325 |
| Itawamba | 509 | 4,419 | 4,480 | 2,153 |
| Jackson | 2,534 | 22,204 | 12,533 | 17,177 |
| Jasper | 935 | 3,597 | 3,109 | 2,356 |
| Jefferson | 1,457 | 1,131 | 2,562 | 782 |
| Jefferson Davis | 1,005 | 2,830 | 2,747 | 1,868 |
| Jones | 2,790 | 16,489 | 10,139 | 11,098 |
| Kemper | 837 | 2,748 | 2,436 | 1,680 |
| Lafayette | 1,545 | 5,391 | 4,375 | 3,735 |
| Lamar | 493 | 5,022 | 3,109 | 4,056 |
| Lauderdale | 3,453 | 18,337 | 9,813 | 14,273 |
| Lawrence | 709 | 3,394 | 2,242 | 2,109 |
| Leake | 1,053 | 4,217 | 3,415 | 2,952 |
| Lee | 1,632 | 10,730 | 8,504 | 7,366 |
| Leflore | 2,038 | 6,779 | 6,135 | 5,872 |
| Lincoln | 1,070 | 7,593 | 4,043 | 6,084 |
| Lowndes | 2,398 | 10,098 | 6,181 | 8,003 |
| Madison | 3,464 | 5,047 | 6,240 | 4,838 |
| Marion | 1,693 | 6,805 | 5,283 | 5,300 |
| Marshall | 1,875 | 3,326 | 6,769 | 2,242 |
| Monroe | 1,279 | 7,273 | 6,097 | 4,737 |
| Montgomery | 925 | 3,210 | 2,410 | 2,278 |
| Neshoba | 812 | 6,815 | 3,891 | 3,859 |
| Newton | 597 | 5,585 | 2,741 | 3,813 |
| Noxubee | 1,052 | 2,239 | 2,121 | 1,860 |
| Oktibbeha | 1,880 | 6,160 | 4,339 | 5,194 |
| Panola | 2,091 | 5,284 | 5,517 | 3,341 |
| Pearl River | 901 | 7,487 | 5,024 | 4,332 |
| Perry | 446 | 2,689 | 1,965 | 1,527 |
| Pike | 2,332 | 6,542 | 5,749 | 5,659 |
| Pontotoc | 488 | 4,476 | 4,066 | 2,245 |
| Prentiss | 398 | 4,607 | 4,431 | 2,362 |
| Quitman | 790 | 2,524 | 2,621 | 1,287 |
| Rankin | 1,913 | 12,187 | 6,937 | 11,507 |
| Scott | 1,213 | 5,244 | 3,643 | 3,649 |
| Sharkey | 655 | 1,426 | 1,283 | 1,024 |
| Simpson | 871 | 5,669 | 3,600 | 4,291 |
| Smith | 329 | 4,419 | 2,434 | 3,147 |
| Stone | 293 | 2,467 | 1,648 | 1,575 |
| Sunflower | 1,874 | 5,389 | 4,322 | 3,456 |
| Tallahatchie | 835 | 3,442 | 2,991 | 2,146 |
| Tate | 1,151 | 3,966 | 3,747 | 2,497 |
| Tippah | 569 | 3,937 | 4,260 | 1,887 |
| Tishomingo | 443 | 4,177 | 3,734 | 1,969 |
| Tunica | 858 | 1,446 | 1,695 | 951 |
| Union | 658 | 5,477 | 5,021 | 2,507 |
| Walthall | 747 | 3,110 | 2,650 | 2,110 |
| Warren | 3,480 | 10,420 | 6,299 | 8 |
| Washington | 4,623 | 9,634 | 9,650 | 7, |
| Wayne | 975 | 4,648 | 3,306 | 3, |
| Webster | 403 | 3,624 | 2,218 | 1. |
| Wilkinson | 1,409 | 1,608 | 2,514 | 1. |
| Winston | 1,354 | 5,155 | 3,956 | 3, |
| Yalobusha | 797 | 2,944 | 2,603 | 1, |
| Yazoo | 2,008 | 5,555 | 4,053 | 4, |
| **Totals** | **126,782** | **505,125** | **381,309** | **366,** |

### Mississippi Vote Since 1932

1932 (Pres.), Roosevelt, Dem., 140,168; Hoover, Re 5,180; Thomas, Soc., 686.

1936 (Pres.), Roosevelt, Dem., 157,318; Landon, Re Howard faction, 2,760; Rowlands faction, 1,675 to 4,435; Thomas, Soc., 329.

1940 (Pres.), Roosevelt, Dem., 168,252; Willkie, Ind. Re 4,550; Rep., 2,814; total, 7,364; Thomas, Soc., 103.

1944 (Pres.), Roosevelt, Dem., 158,515; Dewey, Rep., 3,7 Reg. Dem., 9,964; Ind. Rep., 7,859.

1948 (Pres.), Thurmond, States' Rights, 167,538; Trum Dem., 19,384; Dewey, Rep., 5,043; Wallace, Prog., 225.

1952 (Pres.), Eisenhower, Ind. vote pledged to Rep. can date, 112,966; Stevenson, Dem., 172,566.

1956 (Pres.), Stevenson, Dem., 144,498; Eisenhower, Re 56,372; Black and Tan Grand Old Party, 4,313; to 60,685; Byrd, Independent, 42,966.

1960 (Pres.), Democratic unpledged electors, 116,2 Kennedy, Dem., 108,362; Nixon, Rep., 73,561. Mississ pi's victorious slate of 8 unpledged Democratic elect cast their votes for Sen. Harry F. Byrd (D-Va.).

1964 (Pres.), Johnson, Dem., 52,618; Goldwater, Re 356,528.

1968 (Pres.), Nixon, Rep., 88,516; Humphrey, De 150,644; Wallace, 3d party, 415,349.

1972 (Pres.), Nixon, Rep., 505,125; McGovern, De 126,782; Schmitz, American, 11,598; Jenness, S Worker, 2,458.

1976 (Pres.), Carter, Dem., 381,309; Ford, Rep., 366,8 Anderson, American, 6,678; McCarthy, Ind., 4,074; Ma dox, Ind., 4,049; Camejo, Soc. Workers, 2,805; MacBri Libertarian, 2,609.

## Missouri

| | 1972 | | 1976 | |
|---|---|---|---|---|
| County | McGovern (D) | Nixon (R) | Carter (D) | Fo (I |
| Adair | 2,286 | 6,157 | 3,684 | 5,2 |
| Andrew | 1,686 | 4,180 | 3,042 | 3,1 |
| Atchison | 1,509 | 2,927 | 1,126 | 1,9 |
| Audrain | 3,706 | 7,197 | 5,600 | 5,3 |
| Barry | 3,167 | 7,295 | 5,046 | 5,0 |
| Barton | 1,140 | 4,026 | 2,326 | 2,7 |
| Bates | 3,020 | 5,314 | 4,288 | 3,3 |
| Benton | 1,423 | 3,537 | 2,684 | 2,7 |
| Bollinger | 1,818 | 3,069 | 2,740 | 2,1 |
| Boone | 13,666 | 17,488 | 17,674 | 16,3 |
| Buchanan | 11,395 | 21,850 | 17,427 | 16,4 |
| Butler | 3,466 | 9,198 | 6,759 | 5,6 |
| Caldwell | 1,231 | 3,167 | 2,113 | 2,0 |
| Callaway | 3,036 | 6,313 | 4,843 | 5,1 |
| Camden | 1,761 | 4,996 | 3,975 | 4,4 |
| Cape Girardeau | 6,280 | 15,693 | 10,440 | 12,6 |
| Carroll | 1,927 | 4,100 | 3,114 | 2,9 |
| Carter | 565 | 1,257 | 1,154 | 8 |
| Cass | 3,731 | 9,242 | 9,008 | 7,1 |
| Cedar | 1,152 | 3,520 | 2,192 | 2,7 |
| Chariton | 1,999 | 2,812 | 3,055 | 2,1 |
| Christian | 1,945 | 6,305 | 3,830 | 4,5 |
| Clark | 1,403 | 2,499 | 1,679 | 1,5 |
| Clay | 14,538 | 33,017 | 26,609 | 24,9 |
| Clinton | 1,944 | 3,924 | 3,424 | 2,8 |
| Cole | 4,754 | 16,685 | 7,949 | 14,3 |
| Cooper | 2,332 | 5,172 | 3,087 | 3,6 |
| Crawford | 2,248 | 4,595 | 3,565 | 3,2 |
| Dade | 747 | 2,624 | 1,681 | 2,0 |
| Dallas | 1,085 | 3,120 | 2,453 | 2,4 |
| Daviess | 1,430 | 2,840 | 2,250 | 1,9 |
| DeKalb | 1,339 | 2,766 | 2,023 | 1,7 |
| Dent | 1,710 | 3,024 | 2,931 | 2,4 |
| Douglas | 1,209 | 3,773 | 1,981 | 2,6 |
| Dunklin | 2,776 | 5,926 | 7,107 | 3,9 |
| Franklin | 7,464 | 13,785 | 11,695 | 12,2 |
| Gasconade | 1,226 | 4,944 | 1,702 | 3,9 |
| Gentry | 1,642 | 2,984 | 2,249 | 1,7 |
| Greene | 20,155 | 48,348 | 33,824 | 37,6 |
| Grundy | 1,428 | 3,969 | 2,597 | 2,6 |

|  | 1972 | | 1976 | |
|---|---|---|---|---|
|  | (D) | (R) | (D) | (R) |
| arrison | 1,383 | 3,574 | 2,304 | 2,478 |
| nry | 3,125 | 5,802 | 5,282 | 4,168 |
| ckory | 622 | 1,851 | 1,398 | 1,403 |
| lt | 1,011 | 2,578 | 1,529 | 1,777 |
| ward | 2,041 | 2,613 | 2,769 | 1,690 |
| well | 2,795 | 7,253 | 5,265 | 4,692 |
| n | 1,346 | 2,203 | 2,646 | 1,765 |
| ckson | 92,830 | 129,989 | 130,120 | 101,401 |
| sper | 7,652 | 22,482 | 14,910 | 17,086 |
| fferson | 13,787 | 21,947 | 25,159 | 18,261 |
| hnson | 3,044 | 7,228 | 5,551 | 5,513 |
| ox | 1,031 | 1,986 | 1,319 | 1,216 |
| clede | 2,186 | 6,152 | 4,381 | 4,067 |
| fayette | 4,063 | 9,187 | 6,410 | 6,823 |
| wrence | 3,130 | 8,445 | 5,315 | 5,784 |
| wis | 1,695 | 2,738 | 2,486 | 1,983 |
| coln | 2,784 | 5,127 | 4,473 | 3,581 |
| n | 3,073 | 4,595 | 4,092 | 3,114 |
| vingston | 2,662 | 5,253 | 3,819 | 3,010 |
| Donald | 1,787 | 4,339 | 3,111 | 2,949 |
| acon | 2,844 | 4,538 | 4,296 | 3,360 |
| adison | 1,451 | 2,837 | 2,229 | 1,739 |
| aries | 1,219 | 2,082 | 1,796 | 1,485 |
| arion | 4,171 | 7,197 | 6,124 | 5,501 |
| ercer | 607 | 1,592 | 1,177 | 1,025 |
| ller | 1,598 | 5,682 | 2,739 | 4,095 |
| ssissippi | 1,470 | 2,727 | 3,366 | 1,733 |
| oniteau | 1,395 | 3,963 | 2,462 | 3,077 |
| nroe | 2,299 | 2,141 | 3,039 | 1,585 |
| ntgomery | 1,691 | 3,707 | 2,535 | 2,665 |
| organ | 1,685 | 4,021 | 2,738 | 2,831 |
| w Madrid | 3,500 | 4,735 | 5,319 | 2,798 |
| wton | 4,291 | 10,701 | 7,045 | 7,142 |
| daway | 3,322 | 5,942 | 4,875 | 4,558 |
| egon | 1,352 | 2,118 | 2,564 | 1,122 |
| sage | 1,485 | 4,266 | 2,015 | 3,224 |
| ark | 625 | 2,119 | 1,341 | 1,754 |
| miscot | 2,017 | 4,897 | 4,681 | 2,541 |
| rry | 1,953 | 4,736 | 2,801 | 4,086 |
| ttis | 5,016 | 10,065 | 7,887 | 7,344 |
| elps | 3,567 | 7,598 | 6,261 | 6,153 |
| ke | 2,659 | 4,452 | 3,770 | 3,355 |
| atte | 4,183 | 8,764 | 8,651 | 8,103 |
| lk | 2,245 | 5,409 | 3,663 | 3,893 |
| laski | 1,903 | 4,243 | 4,370 | 2,865 |
| tnam | 571 | 2,112 | 1,097 | 1,444 |
| alls | 1,371 | 1,827 | 2,318 | 1,334 |
| andolph | 3,814 | 5,195 | 5,839 | 3,594 |
| y | 2,844 | 4,205 | 5,535 | 2,853 |
| eynolds | 1,031 | 1,541 | 2,143 | 879 |
| pley | 1,361 | 2,810 | 2,577 | 1,640 |
| Charles | 11,034 | 25,677 | 22,063 | 26,105 |
| Clair | 1,410 | 2,847 | 2,271 | 1,808 |
| Francois | 4,658 | 8,812 | 8,852 | 7,002 |
| e. Genevieve | 2,247 | 2,900 | 3,091 | 2,241 |
| Louis | 160,801 | 264,147 | 196,915 | 246,988 |
| aline | 3,460 | 6,641 | 5,890 | 4,883 |
| huyler | 991 | 1,495 | 1,417 | 1,193 |
| otland | 1,269 | 1,918 | 1,449 | 1,286 |
| ott | 3,646 | 7,316 | 8,075 | 5,473 |
| annon | 1,134 | 1,623 | 1,960 | 989 |
| elby | 1,569 | 2,057 | 2,227 | 1,453 |
| oddard | 2,636 | 6,282 | 6,097 | 3,989 |
| one | 1,094 | 4,180 | 2,358 | 3,457 |
| llivan | 1,588 | 2,611 | 2,313 | 2,141 |
| ney | 1,435 | 4,982 | 3,626 | 4,696 |
| xas | 2,737 | 5,104 | 4,638 | 3,338 |
| rnon | 3,057 | 4,892 | 4,921 | 3,715 |
| arren | 1,225 | 3,530 | 2,164 | 3,214 |
| ashington | 2,229 | 3,818 | 3,543 | 2,526 |
| ayne | 1,746 | 3,091 | 2,987 | 1,963 |
| ebster | 2,343 | 5,095 | 3,759 | 3,510 |
| orth | 727 | 1,170 | 969 | 771 |
| right | 1,368 | 4,350 | 2,781 | 3,397 |
| T. LOUIS CITY | 119,817 | 72,402 | 118,703 | 58,367 |
| rite-in Vote | 1,384 | 206 | 1,576 | 1,365 |
| **Totals** | **698,531** | **1,154,058** | **999,163** | **928,808** |

## Missouri Vote Since 1932

'32 (Pres.), Roosevelt, Dem., 1,025,406; Hoover, Rep., 564,713; Thomas, Soc., 16,374; Upshaw, Proh., 2,429; Foster, Com., 568; Reynolds, Soc. Lab., 404.

'36 (Pres.), Roosevelt, Dem., 1,111,403; Landon, Rep., 697,891; Lemke, Union, 14,630; Thomas, Soc., 3,454; Colvin, Proh., 908; Browder, Com., 417; Aiken, Soc. Lab., 292.

'40 (Pres.), Roosevelt, Dem., 958,476; Willkie, Rep., 871,009; Thomas, Soc., 2,226; Babson, Proh., 1,809; Aiken, Soc. Lab., 209.

'44 (Pres.), Roosevelt, Dem., 807,357; Dewey, Rep., 761,175; Thomas, Soc., 1,750; Watson, Proh., 1,175; Teichert, Soc. Lab., 221.

'48 (Pres.), Truman, Dem., 917,315; Dewey, Rep., 655,039; Wallace, Prog., 3,998; Thomas, Soc., 2,222.

1952 (Pres.), Eisenhower, Rep., 959,429; Stevenson, Dem., 929,830; Hallinan, Prog., 987; Hamblen, Proh., 885; MacArthur, Christian Nationalist, 302; America First, 233; Hoopes, Soc., 227; Haas, Soc. Lab., 169.

1956 (Pres.), Stevenson, Dem., 918,273; Eisenhower, Rep., 914,299.

1960 (Pres.), Kennedy, Dem., 972,201; Nixon, Rep., 962,221.

1964 (Pres.), Johnson, Dem., 1,164,344; Goldwater, Rep., 653,535.

1968 (Pres.), Nixon, Rep., 811,932; Humphrey, Dem., 791,444; Wallace, 3d party, 206,126.

1972 (Pres.), Nixon, Rep., 1,154,058; McGovern, Dem., 698,531.

1976 (Pres.), Carter, Dem., 999,163; Ford, Rep., 928,808; McCarthy, Ind., 24,329.

# Montana

|  | 1972 | | 1976 | |
|---|---|---|---|---|
|  | McGovern | Nixon | Carter | Ford |
| County | (D) | (R) | (D) | (R) |
| Beaverhead | 775 | 2,460 | 1,013 | 2,461 |
| Big Horn | 1,552 | 2,148 | 1,962 | 1,615 |
| Blaine | 1,151 | 1,513 | 1,356 | 1,349 |
| Broadwater | 411 | 916 | 557 | 820 |
| Carbon | 1,292 | 2,378 | 1,853 | 2,121 |
| Carter | 218 | 726 | 344 | 558 |
| Cascade | 12,899 | 16,159 | 14,678 | 15,289 |
| Chouteau | 1,149 | 2,027 | 1,568 | 1,814 |
| Custer | 1,875 | 3,486 | 2,425 | 3,120 |
| Daniels | 570 | 973 | 797 | 816 |
| Dawson | 1,685 | 3,207 | 2,201 | 2,639 |
| Deer Lodge | 3,979 | 2,373 | 3,859 | 2,197 |
| Fallon | 531 | 1,034 | 847 | 934 |
| Fergus | 1,652 | 4,082 | 2,470 | 3,556 |
| Flathead | 5,412 | 10,417 | 7,827 | 10,494 |
| Gallatin | 5,096 | 10,663 | 6,215 | 11,062 |
| Garfield | 173 | 695 | 273 | 625 |
| Glacier | 1,469 | 2,143 | 1,755 | 1,892 |
| Golden Valley | 170 | 359 | 255 | 302 |
| Granite | 422 | 804 | 509 | 746 |
| Hill | 3,061 | 3,759 | 3,878 | 3,274 |
| Jefferson | 904 | 1,281 | 1,210 | 1,387 |
| Judith Basin | 557 | 961 | 772 | 809 |
| Lake | 2,260 | 4,172 | 3,253 | 3,809 |
| Lewis & Clark | 6,081 | 10,719 | 8,118 | 10,155 |
| Liberty | 365 | 808 | 506 | 638 |
| Lincoln | 2,402 | 3,276 | 3,146 | 3,017 |
| Madison | 669 | 1,780 | 870 | 1,688 |
| McCone | 562 | 854 | 749 | 730 |
| Meagher | 230 | 674 | 364 | 565 |
| Mineral | 659 | 706 | 819 | 679 |
| Missoula | 13,784 | 15,557 | 15,099 | 16,350 |
| Musselshell | 689 | 1,202 | 922 | 1,117 |
| Park | 1,923 | 3,771 | 2,364 | 3,281 |
| Petroleum | 87 | 232 | 110 | 211 |
| Phillips | 828 | 1,659 | 1,117 | 1,347 |
| Pondera | 1,215 | 1,890 | 1,413 | 1,666 |
| Powder River | 267 | 844 | 429 | 683 |
| Powell | 1,050 | 1,720 | 1,302 | 1,610 |
| Prairie | 303 | 685 | 415 | 597 |
| Ravalli | 2,480 | 4,611 | 3,504 | 4,894 |
| Richland | 1,438 | 2,645 | 1,961 | 2,189 |
| Roosevelt | 1,464 | 2,304 | 2,061 | 1,822 |
| Rosebud | 777 | 1,486 | 1,413 | 1,538 |
| Sanders | 1,197 | 1,779 | 1,725 | 1,738 |
| Sheridan | 1,197 | 1,500 | 1,560 | 1,114 |
| Silver Bow | 11,704 | 7,967 | 11,377 | 7,506 |
| Stillwater | 716 | 1,698 | 1,143 | 1,446 |
| Sweet Grass | 350 | 1,260 | 502 | 1,135 |
| Teton | 1,121 | 1,991 | 1,506 | 1,730 |
| Toole | 897 | 1,679 | 1,080 | 1,469 |
| Treasure | 176 | 377 | 239 | 315 |
| Valley | 1,973 | 3,210 | 2,352 | 2,520 |
| Wheatland | 445 | 761 | 535 | 755 |
| Wibaux | 283 | 390 | 352 | 308 |
| Yellowstone | 13,602 | 25,205 | 18,329 | 25,201 |
| **Totals** | **120,197** | **183,976** | **149,259** | **173,703** |

## Montana Vote Since 1932

1932 (Pres.), Roosevelt, Dem., 127,286; Hoover, Rep., 78,078; Thomas, Soc., 7,891; Foster, Com., 1,775; Harvey, Lib., 1,449.

1936 (Pres.), Roosevelt, Dem., 159,690; Landon, Rep., 63,598; Lemke, Union, 5,549; Thomas, Soc., 1,066; Browder, Com., 385; Colvin, Proh., 224.

1940 (Pres.), Roosevelt, Dem., 145,698; Willkie, Rep., 99,579; Thomas, Soc., 1,443; Babson, Proh., 664; Browder, Com., 489.

1944 (Pres.), Roosevelt, Dem., 112,556; Dewey, Rep., 93,163; Thomas, Soc., 1,296; Watson, Proh., 340.

1948 (Pres.), Truman, Dem., 119,071; Dewey, Rep., 96,770; Wallace, Prog., 7,313; Thomas, Soc., 695; Watson, Proh., 429.

1952 (Pres.), Eisenhower, Rep., 157,394; Stevenson, Dem., 106,213; Hallinan, Prog., 723; Hamblen, Proh., 548; Hoopes, Soc., 159.

1956 (Pres.), Eisenhower, Rep., 154,933; Stevenson, Dem., 116,238.

1960 (Pres.), Kennedy, Dem., 134,891; Nixon, Rep., 141,841; Decker, Proh., 456; Dobbs, Soc. Workers, 391.

1964 (Pres.), Johnson, Dem., 164,246; Goldwater, Rep., 113,032; Kasper, Nat'l States Rights, 519; Munn, Proh., 499; DeBerry, Soc. Worker, 332.

1968 (Pres.), Nixon, Rep., 138,835; Humphrey, Dem., 114,117; Wallace, 3d party, 20,015; Halstead, Soc. Worker, 457; Munn, Prohibition 510; Caton, New Reform, 470.

1972 (Pres.), Nixon, Rep., 183,976; McGovern, Dem., 120,197; Schmitz, American, 13,430.

1976 (Pres.), Carter, Dem., 149,259; Ford, Rep., 173,703; Anderson, American, 5,772.

## Nebraska

| County | 1972 McGovern (D) | Nixon (R) | 1976 Carter (D) | Ford (R) |
|---|---|---|---|---|
| Adams | 3,359 | 8,841 | 4,949 | 7,612 |
| Antelope | 851 | 3,228 | 1,325 | 2,488 |
| Arthur | 45 | 236 | 64 | 193 |
| Banner | 96 | 404 | 210 | 281 |
| Blaine | 56 | 343 | 133 | 281 |
| Boone | 883 | 2,406 | 1,329 | 2,035 |
| Box Butte | 960 | 3,431 | 1,516 | 2,956 |
| Boyd | 506 | 1,419 | 792 | 1,004 |
| Brown | 330 | 1,462 | 557 | 1,239 |
| Buffalo | 2,988 | 8,587 | 4,296 | 8,083 |
| Burt | 900 | 2,937 | 1,373 | 2,507 |
| Butler | 1,812 | 2,301 | 2,336 | 1,808 |
| Cass | 1,805 | 4,503 | 3,202 | 3,800 |
| Cedar | 1,807 | 2,995 | 2,225 | 2,415 |
| Chase | 307 | 1,318 | 724 | 1,146 |
| Cherry | 463 | 2,610 | 906 | 2,197 |
| Cheyenne | 950 | 3,120 | 1,663 | 2,285 |
| Clay | 861 | 2,542 | 1,369 | 2,254 |
| Colfax | 1,107 | 2,799 | 1,666 | 2,363 |
| Cuming | 1,019 | 3,810 | 1,367 | 3,298 |
| Custer | 1,147 | 4,836 | 1,985 | 3,935 |
| Dakota | 1,748 | 2,879 | 2,290 | 2,629 |
| Dawes | 711 | 2,987 | 1,278 | 2,435 |
| Dawson | 1,424 | 6,211 | 2,393 | 5,411 |
| Deuel | 224 | 1,001 | 398 | 775 |
| Dixon | 941 | 2,299 | 1,286 | 1,981 |
| Dodge | 3,826 | 9,837 | 5,276 | 8,972 |
| Douglas | 48,201 | 101,579 | 61,692 | 92,980 |
| Dundy | 221 | 1,003 | 457 | 774 |
| Fillmore | 1,270 | 2,511 | 1,483 | 2,098 |
| Franklin | 599 | 1,510 | 941 | 1,170 |
| Frontier | 324 | 1,315 | 588 | 994 |
| Furnas | 676 | 2,282 | 1,126 | 1,844 |
| Gage | 3,588 | 6,298 | 4,506 | 5,199 |
| Garden | 204 | 1,161 | 445 | 928 |
| Garfield | 209 | 903 | 343 | 726 |
| Gosper | 242 | 829 | 332 | 654 |
| Grant | 69 | 376 | 116 | 313 |
| Greeley | 760 | 1,005 | 877 | 787 |
| Hall | 4,218 | 10,987 | 6,077 | 10,931 |
| Hamilton | 907 | 2,960 | 1,337 | 2,737 |
| Harlan | 539 | 1,549 | 879 | 1,325 |
| Hayes | 123 | 486 | 267 | 411 |
| Hitchcock | 364 | 1,339 | 786 | 898 |
| Holt | 1,053 | 4,147 | 1,751 | 3,389 |
| Hooker | 52 | 394 | 98 | 326 |
| Howard | 945 | 1,691 | 1,316 | 1,362 |
| Jefferson | 1,476 | 3,008 | 2,067 | 2,628 |
| Johnson | 917 | 1,637 | 1,115 | 1,298 |
| Kearney | 759 | 2,203 | 1,218 | 1,827 |
| Keith | 665 | 2,513 | 1,139 | 2,485 |
| Keya Paha | 146 | 563 | 245 | 405 |
| Kimball | 437 | 1,650 | 696 | 1,257 |
| Knox | 1,289 | 3,318 | 1,922 | 2,610 |
| Lancaster | 25,924 | 42,573 | 28,193 | 38,937 |
| Lincoln | 3,220 | 7,502 | 5,352 | 7,074 |
| Logan | 73 | 320 | 195 | 283 |
| Loup | 58 | 345 | 140 | 299 |
| McPherson | 42 | 247 | 104 | 221 |
| Madison | 2,224 | 8,580 | 3,433 | 7,844 |
| Merrick | 887 | 2,418 | 1,360 | 2,229 |
| Morrill | 520 | 1,740 | 971 | 1,351 |
| Nance | 641 | 1,413 | 936 | 1,119 |
| Nemaha | 909 | 2,600 | 1,404 | 2,092 |
| Nuckolls | 999 | 2,089 | 1,424 | 1,752 |
| Otoe | 1,718 | 4,815 | 2,436 | 3,715 |
| Pawnee | 524 | 1,299 | 845 | 990 |
| Perkins | 354 | 1,165 | 622 | 981 |
| Phelps | 735 | 3,356 | 1,166 | 3,2 |
| Pierce | 653 | 2,451 | 1,004 | 2,1 |
| Platte | 2,855 | 7,871 | 3,681 | 7,2 |
| Polk | 827 | 2,050 | 1,190 | 1,7 |
| Red Willow | 931 | 3,701 | 1,722 | 2,9 |
| Richardson | 1,508 | 3,662 | 2,415 | 3,1 |
| Rock | 138 | 937 | 255 | 7 |
| Saline | 2,654 | 2,828 | 3,205 | 2,3 |
| Sarpy | 3,904 | 11,514 | 7,384 | 11,9 |
| Saunders | 2,501 | 4,282 | 3,504 | 3,8 |
| Scotts Bluff | 2,764 | 8,649 | 4,297 | 6,8 |
| Seward | 2,087 | 3,707 | 2,609 | 3,2 |
| Sheridan | 481 | 2,386 | 810 | 2,0 |
| Sherman | 811 | 1,099 | 1,078 | 9 |
| Sioux | 129 | 639 | 329 | 5 |
| Stanton | 478 | 1,662 | 763 | 1,4 |
| Thayer | 978 | 2,274 | 1,315 | 1,9 |
| Thomas | 73 | 397 | 103 | 3 |
| Thurston | 840 | 1,565 | 1,020 | 1,2 |
| Valley | 771 | 2,011 | 1,042 | 1,5 |
| Washington | 1,401 | 4,290 | 2,233 | 3,7 |
| Wayne | 902 | 2,659 | 1,089 | 2,5 |
| Webster | 696 | 1,631 | 1,130 | 1,2 |
| Wheeler | 84 | 361 | 146 | 2 |
| York | 1,318 | 4,651 | 1,655 | 4,2 |
| **Totals** | 169,991 | 406,298 | 233,287 | 359,2 |

### Nebraska Vote Since 1932

1932 (Pres.), Roosevelt, Dem., 359,082; Hoover, Rep 201,177; Thomas, Soc., 9,876.

1936 (Pres.), Roosevelt, Dem., 347,454; Landon, Rep 248,731; Lemke, Union, 12,847.

1940 (Pres.), Roosevelt, Dem., 263,677; Willkie, Rep 352,201.

1944 (Pres.), Roosevelt, Dem., 233,246; Dewey, Re 329,880.

1948 (Pres.), Truman, Dem., 224,165; Dewey, Rep 264,774.

1952 (Pres.), Eisenhower, Rep., 421,603; Stevenson Dem 188,057.

1956 (Pres.), Eisenhower, Rep., 378,108; Stevenson, Dem 199,029.

1960 (Pres.), Kennedy, Dem., 232,542; Nixon, Rep 380,553.

1964 (Pres.), Johnson, Dem., 307,307; Goldwater, Rep 276,847.

1968 (Pres.), Nixon, Rep., 321,163; Humphrey, Dem 170,784; Wallace, 3d party, 44,904.

1972 (Pres.), Nixon, Rep., 406,298; McGovern, Dem 169,991; scattered 817.

1976 (Pres.), Carter, Dem., 233,287; Ford, Rep., 359,21 McCarthy, Ind., 9,383; Maddox, Amer. Ind., 3,378; Ma Bride, Libertarian, 1,476.

## Nevada

| County | 1972 McGovern (D) | Nixon (R) | 1976 Carter (D) | Ford (R) |
|---|---|---|---|---|
| Churchill | 1,038 | 2,970 | 1,800 | 2,3 |
| Clark | 36,807 | 53,101 | 51,178 | 48,2 |
| Douglas | 983 | 2,898 | 1,934 | 3,0 |
| Elko | 1,467 | 3,886 | 1,955 | 3,2 |
| Esmeralda | 127 | 273 | 214 | 18 |
| Eureka | 139 | 371 | 163 | 2 |
| Humboldt | 713 | 1,659 | 1,074 | 1,3 |
| Lander | 468 | 798 | 518 | 5 |
| Lincoln | 382 | 841 | 642 | 7 |
| Lyon | 959 | 2,813 | 1,866 | 2,0 |
| Mineral | 768 | 2,111 | 1,361 | 1,1 |
| Nye | 802 | 1,287 | 1,261 | 1,0 |
| Pershing | 365 | 853 | 633 | 6 |
| Storey | 226 | 508 | 310 | 2 |
| Washoe | 17,106 | 33,539 | 21,687 | 29,2 |
| White Pine | 1,546 | 2,446 | 2,009 | 1,5 |
| CARSON CITY | 2,120 | 5,396 | 3,874 | 5,2 |
| **Totals** | 66,016 | 115,750 | 92,479 | 101,2 |

### Nevada Vote Since 1932

1932 (Pres.), Roosevelt, Dem., 28,756; Hoover, Rep 12,674.

1936 (Pres.), Roosevelt, Dem., 31,925; Landon, Rep 11,923.

1940 (Pres.), Roosevelt, Dem., 31,945; Willkie, Rep., 21,22

1944 (Pres.), Roosevelt, Dem., 29,623; Dewey, Rep., 24,61

1948 (Pres.), Truman, Dem., 31,291; Dewey, Rep., 29,35 Wallace, Prog., 1,469.

'52 (Pres.), Eisenhower, Rep., 50,502; Stevenson, Dem., 31,688.

'56 (Pres.), Eisenhower, Rep., 56,049; Stevenson, Dem., 40,640.

'60 (Pres.), Kennedy, Dem., 54,880; Nixon, Rep., 52,387.

'64 (Pres.), Johnson, Dem., 79,339; Goldwater, Rep., 56,094.

'68 (Pres.), Nixon, Rep., 73,188; Humphrey, Dem., 60,598; Wallace, 3d party, 20,432.

'72 (Pres.), Nixon, Rep., 115,750; McGovern, Dem. 66,016.

'76 (Pres.), Carter Dem., 92,479; Ford, Rep., 101,273; MacBride, Libertarian, 1,519; Maddox, Amer. Inc., 1,497; scattered 5,108.

## New Hampshire

| | 1972 | | 1976 | |
| | McGovern | Nixon | Carter | Ford |
| County | (D) | (R) | (D) | (R) |
|--------|------|------|------|------|
| Belknap | 4,610 | 11,536 | 6,143 | 9,876 |
| Carroll | 2,395 | 8,525 | 3,374 | 8,561 |
| Cheshire | 9,157 | 13,390 | 10,388 | 12,554 |
| Coos | 5,829 | 9,468 | 7,385 | 7,094 |
| Grafton | 8,388 | 16,605 | 8,996 | 14,430 |
| Hillsborough | 34,739 | 65,274 | 45,554 | 53,581 |
| Merrimack | 11,737 | 25,354 | 14,865 | 21,853 |
| Rockingham | 21,998 | 38,825 | 30,051 | 36,738 |
| Strafford | 12,028 | 16,846 | 14,566 | 14,569 |
| Sullivan | 5,554 | 7,901 | 6,323 | 6,679 |
| **Totals** | **116,435** | **213,724** | **147,645** | **185,935** |

### New Hampshire Vote Since 1932

'32 (Pres.), Roosevelt, Dem., 100,680; Hoover, Rep., 103,629; Thomas, Soc., 947; Foster, Com., 264.

'36 (Pres.), Roosevelt, Dem., 108,640; Landon, Rep., 104,642; Lemke, Union, 4,819; Browder, Com., 193.

'40 (Pres.), Roosevelt, Dem., 125,292; Willkie, Rep., 110,127.

'44 (Pres.), Roosevelt, Dem., 119,663; Dewey, Rep., 109,916; Thomas, Soc., 46.

'48 (Pres.), Truman, Dem., 107,995; Dewey, Rep., 121,299; Wallace, Prog., 1,970; Thomas, Soc., 86; Teichert, Soc. Lab., 83; Thurmond, States' Rights, 7.

'52 (Pres.), Eisenhower, Rep., 166,287; Stevenson, Dem., 106,663.

'56 (Pres.), Eisenhower, Rep., 176,519; Stevenson, Dem., 90,364; Andrews, Const., 111.

'60 (Pres.), Kennedy, Dem., 137,772; Nixon, Rep., 157,989.

'64 (Pres.), Johnson, Dem., 182,065; Goldwater, Rep., 104,029.

'68 (Pres.), Nixon, Rep., 154,903; Humphrey, Dem., 130,589; Wallace, 3d party, 11,173; New Party, 421; Halstead, Soc. Worker, 104.

'72 (Pres.), Nixon, Rep., 213,724; McGovern, Dem., 116,435; Schmitz, American, 3,386; Jenness, Soc. Worker, 368; scattered, 142.

'76 (Pres.), Carter, Dem., 147,645; Ford, Rep., 185,935; McCarthy, Ind., 4,095; MacBride, Libertarian, 936; Reagan, write-in, 388; La Rouche, U.S. Labor, 186; Camejo, Soc. Workers, 161; Levin, Soc. Labor, 66; scattered, 215.

## New Jersey

| | 1972 | | 1976 | |
| | McGovern | Nixon | Carter | Ford |
| County | (D) | (R) | (D) | (R) |
|--------|------|------|------|------|
| Atlantic | 28,203 | 45,667 | 41,965 | 36,733 |
| Bergen | 147,155 | 285,458 | 180,738 | 237,331 |
| Burlington | 41,520 | 70,805 | 63,309 | 60,960 |
| Camden | 75,202 | 111,935 | 108,854 | 82,801 |
| Cape May | 8,729 | 22,621 | 16,489 | 19,498 |
| Cumberland | 18,692 | 26,409 | 29,165 | 20,535 |
| Essex | 161,270 | 170,036 | 174,434 | 133,911 |
| Gloucester | 25,509 | 44,806 | 38,726 | 34,888 |
| Hudson | 89,977 | 136,895 | 116,241 | 92,636 |
| Hunterdon | 9,031 | 21,282 | 12,592 | 19,616 |
| Mercer | 62,180 | 69,303 | 69,621 | 58,453 |
| Middlesex | 88,397 | 149,033 | 122,859 | 113,539 |
| Monmouth | 63,176 | 124,830 | 88,956 | 110,104 |
| Morris | 50,937 | 113,469 | 63,749 | 105,921 |
| Ocean | 27,710 | 77,979 | 56,413 | 77,875 |

| | McGovern | Nixon | Carter | Ford |
|--------|------|------|------|------|
| Passaic | 63,302 | 108,511 | 76,194 | 85,102 |
| Salem | 8,609 | 16,371 | 12,826 | 11,639 |
| Somerset | 26,537 | 56,524 | 36,258 | 51,260 |
| Sussex | 8,585 | 25,977 | 14,759 | 23,613 |
| Union | 90,482 | 148,290 | 106,267 | 118,019 |
| Warren | 10,008 | 19,301 | 14,238 | 15,254 |
| **Totals** | **1,102,211** | **1,845,502** | **1,444,653** | **1,509,688** |

### New Jersey Vote Since 1932

1932 (Pres.), Roosevelt, Dem., 806,630; Hoover, Rep., 775,684; Thomas, Soc., 42,998; Foster, Com., 2,915; Reynolds, Soc. Lab., 1,062; Upshaw, Proh., 774.

1936 (Pres.), Roosevelt, Dem., 1,083,549; Landon, Rep., 719,421; Lemke, Union, 9,405; Thomas, Soc., 3,895; Browder, Com., 1,590; Colvin, Proh., 916; Aiken, Soc. Lab., 346.

1940 (Pres.), Roosevelt, Dem., 1,016,404; Willkie, Rep., 944,876; Browder, Com., 8,814; Thomas, Soc., 2,823; Babson, Proh., 851; Aiken, Soc. Lab., 446.

1944 (Pres.) Roosevelt, Dem., 987,874; Dewey, Rep., 961,335; Teichert, Soc. Lab., 6,939; Watson, Nat'l Proh., 4,255; Thomas, Soc., 3,385.

1948 (Pres.), Truman, Dem., 895,455; Dewey, Rep., 981,124; Wallace, Prog., 42,683; Watson, Proh., 10,593; Thomas, Soc., 10,521; Dobbs, Soc. Workers, 5,825; Teichert, Soc. Lab., 3,354.

1952 (Pres.), Eisenhower, Rep., 1,373,613; Stevenson, Dem., 1,015,902; Hoopes, Soc., 8,593; Haas, Soc. Lab., 5,815; Hallinan, Prog., 5,589; Krajewski, Poor Man's, 4,203; Dobbs, Soc. Workers, 3,850; Hamblen, Proh., 989.

1956 (Pres.), Eisenhower, Rep., 1,606,942; Stevenson Dem., 850,337; Holtwick, Proh., 9,147; Haas, Soc. Lab., 6,736; Andrews, Conservative, 5,317; Dobbs, Soc. Workers, 4,004; Krajewski, American Third Party, 1,829.

1960 (Pres.), Kennedy, Dem., 1,385,415; Nixon, Rep., 1,363,324; Dobbs, Soc. Workers, 11,402; Lee, Conservative, 8,708; Haas, Soc. Lab., 4,262.

1964 (Pres.), Johnson, Dem., 1,867,671; Goldwater, Rep., 963,843; DeBerry, Soc. Workers, 8,181; Haas, Soc. Labor, 7,075.

1968 (Pres.), Nixon, Rep., 1,325,467; Humphrey, Dem., 1,264,206; Wallace, 3d party, 262,187; Halstead, Soc. Worker, 8,667; Gregory, Peace Freedom, 8,084; Blomen, Soc. Labor, 6,784.

1972 (Pres.), Nixon, Rep., 1,845,502; McGovern, Dem., 1,102,211; Schmitz, American, 34,378; Spock, Peoples, 5,355; Fisher, Soc. Labor, 4,544; Jenness, Soc. Worker, 2,233; Mahalchik, Amer. First, 1,743; Hall Communist, 1,263.

1976 (Pres.), Carter, Dem., 1,444,653; Ford, Rep., 1,509,688; McCarthy, Ind., 32,717; MacBride, Libertarian, 9,449; Maddox, American, 7,716; Levin, Soc. Labor, 3,686; Hall, Comm., 1,662; LaRouche, U.S. Labor, 1,650; Camejo, Soc. Workers, 1,184; Wright, People's, 1,044; Bubar, Proh., 554; Zeidler, Socialist, 469.

## New Mexico

| | 1972 | | 1976 | |
| | McGovern | Nixon | Carter | Ford |
| County | (D) | (R) | (D) | (R) |
|--------|------|------|------|------|
| Bernalillo | 48,753 | 79,993 | 63,949 | 76,614 |
| Catron | 271 | 829 | 517 | 602 |
| Chaves | 4,296 | 11,493 | 7,119 | 10,631 |
| Colfax | 1,855 | 2,663 | 2,653 | 2,259 |
| Curry | 2,416 | 8,392 | 5,004 | 6,232 |
| De Baca | 270 | 752 | 597 | 556 |
| Dona Ana | 9,416 | 14,562 | 12,036 | 13,888 |
| Eddy | 5,040 | 9,921 | 9,073 | 7,698 |
| Grant | 4,081 | 4,431 | 5,176 | 4,095 |
| Guadalupe | 1,202 | 1,297 | 1,379 | 1,047 |
| Harding | 220 | 522 | 285 | 387 |
| Hidalgo | 562 | 1,051 | 938 | 891 |
| Lea | 3,429 | 12,478 | 6,533 | 8,773 |
| Lincoln | 696 | 2,528 | 1,415 | 2,320 |
| Los Alamos | 2,435 | 5,039 | 2,890 | 5,383 |
| Luna | 1,560 | 2,958 | 2,872 | 2,966 |
| McKinley | 5,124 | 5,366 | 6,856 | 4,617 |
| Mora | 1,135 | 1,165 | 1,438 | 904 |
| Otero | 2,981 | 7,033 | 5,333 | 5,914 |
| Quay | 1,161 | 3,224 | 2,095 | 2,059 |
| Rio Arriba | 5,642 | 4,351 | 7,125 | 3,213 |
| Roosevelt | 1,612 | 4,727 | 3,111 | 3,269 |
| Sandoval | 3,293 | 3,507 | 5,072 | 4,110 |
| San Juan | 4,296 | 30,788 | 8,615 | 10,852 |

| | 1972 | | 1976 | |
|---|---|---|---|---|
| | (D) | (R) | (D) | (R) |
| San Miguel | 4,663 | 4,434 | 5,204 | 3,162 |
| Santa Fe. | 10,761 | 12,211 | 14,127 | 11,576 |
| Sierra | 934 | 2,074 | 1,564 | 1,665 |
| Socorro | 1,994 | 2,658 | 2,606 | 2,265 |
| Taos | 3,472 | 3,617 | 4,414 | 3,012 |
| Torrance | 908 | 1,758 | 1,526 | 1,462 |
| Union. | 496 | 1,545 | -975 | 1,146 |
| Valencia | 6,110 | 8,239 | 8,566 | 7,851 |
| **Totals** | **141,084** | **235,606** | **201,148** | **211,419** |

## New Mexico Vote Since 1932

1932 (Pres.), Roosevelt, Dem., 95,089; Hoover, Rep., 54,217; Thomas, Soc., 11,776; Harvey, Lib., 389; Foster, Com., 135.

1936 (Pres.), Roosevelt, Dem., 105,838; Landon, Rep., 61,710; Lemke, Union, 942; Thomas, Soc., 343; Browder, Com., 43.

1940 (Pres.), Roosevelt, Dem., 103,699; Willkie, Rep., 79,315.

1944 (Pres.), Roosevelt, Dem., 81,389; Dewey, Rep., 70,688; Watson, Proh., 148.

1948 (Pres.), Truman, Dem., 105,464; Dewey, Rep., 80,303; Wallace, Prog., 1,037; Watson, Proh., 127; Thomas, Soc., 83; Teichert, Soc. Lab., 49.

1952 (Pres.), Eisenhower, Rep., 132,170; Stevenson, Dem., 105,661; Hamblen, Proh., 297; Hallinan, Ind. Prog., 225; MacArthur, Christian National, 220; Haas, Soc. Lab., 35.

1956 (Pres.), Eisenhower, Rep., 146,788; Stevenson, Dem., 106,098; Holtwick, Proh., 607; Andrews, Ind., 364; Haas, Soc. Lab., 69.

1960 (Pres.), Kennedy, Dem., 156,027; Nixon, Rep., 153,733; Decker, Proh., 777; Haas, Soc. Lab., 570.

1964 (Pres.), Johnson, Dem., 194,017; Goldwater, Rep., 131,838; Haas, Soc. Labor, 1,217; Munn, Proh., 543.

1968 (Pres.), Nixon, Rep., 169,692; Humphrey, Dem., 130,081; Wallace, 3d party, 25,737; Chavez, 1,519; Halstead, Soc. Worker, 252.

1972 (Pres.), Nixon, Rep., 235,606; McGovern, Dem., 141,084; Schmitz, Amer., 8,767; Jenness, Soc. Worker, 474.

1976 (Pres.), Carter, Dem., 201,148; Ford, Rep., 211,419; Camejo, Soc. Worker, 2,462; MacBride, Libertarian, 1,110; Zeidler, Soc., 240; Bubar, Proh., 211.

## New York

| | 1972 | | 1976 | |
|---|---|---|---|---|
| | McGovern | Nixon | Carter | Ford |
| County | (D-L*) | (R-C**) | (D-L) | (R-C) |
| Albany | 67,297 | 81,848 | 71,616 | 69,592 |
| Allegany | 4,812 | 13,426 | 6,134 | 11,769 |
| Broome | 37,154 | 55,736 | 39,827 | 50,340 |
| Cattaraugus | 10,909 | 21,906 | 13,768 | 19,469 |
| Cayuga | 11,907 | 22,774 | 13,348 | 19,775 |
| Chatauqua | 26,253 | 37,158 | 27,447 | 33,730 |
| Chemung | 12,650 | 26,200 | 17,207 | 20,640 |
| Chenango | 5,695 | 13,770 | 7,356 | 12,384 |
| Clinton | 9,703 | 17,048 | 11,555 | 15,433 |
| Columbia | 7,558 | 17,995 | 10,514 | 15,871 |
| Cortland | 5,234 | 12,885 | 6,947 | 11,222 |
| Delaware | 5,243 | 15,136 | 7,254 | 12,443 |
| Dutchess | 27,872 | 68,864 | 37,531 | 51,312 |
| Erie | 218,105 | 256,462 | 229,397 | 220,310 |
| Essex | 4,955 | 11,763 | 6,556 | 10,194 |
| Franklin | 5,266 | 10,959 | 7,248 | 8,846 |
| Fulton | 7,303 | 15,200 | 9,323 | 12,161 |
| Genesee | 8,631 | 17,107 | 10,803 | 14,567 |
| Greene | 5,260 | 14,213 | 7,740 | 11,370 |
| Hamilton | 731 | 2,597 | 1,052 | 2,306 |
| Herkimer | 9,487 | 20,194 | 12,875 | 15,362 |
| Jefferson | 11,629 | 23,123 | 13,503 | 20,401 |
| Lewis | 2,987 | 6,591 | 3,764 | 5,840 |
| Livingston | 7,031 | 15,886 | 9,629 | 14,044 |
| Madison | 6,241 | 18,392 | 8,822 | 15,674 |
| Monroe | 120,031 | 196,579 | 134,739 | 167,303 |
| Montgomery | 9,460 | 16,640 | 11,271 | 13,281 |
| Niagara | 38,991 | 54,777 | 43,667 | 46,101 |
| Oneida | 33,642 | 78,549 | 47,779 | 57,655 |
| Onondaga | 61,895 | 140,039 | 76,097 | 115,474 |
| Ontario | 11,012 | 23,828 | 14,044 | 21,118 |
| Orange | 25,778 | 63,556 | 40,362 | 49,685 |
| Orleans | 4,371 | 10,938 | 5,927 | 8,994 |
| Oswego | 11,317 | 29,109 | 16,332 | 23,949 |
| Otsego | 7,898 | 17,364 | 9,787 | 14,796 |
| Putnam | 7,747 | 21,673 | 11,963 | 18,523 |

| | 1972 | | 1976 | |
|---|---|---|---|---|
| | (D) | (R) | (D) | (R) |
| Rensselaer | 24,019 | 48,864 | 28,979 | 40 |
| Rockland | 35,771 | 64,753 | 48,673 | 52 |
| St. Lawrence | 15,286 | 26,145 | 17,503 | 22 |
| Saratoga | 17,899 | 40,582 | 23,768 | 38 |
| Schenectady | 29,619 | 47,529 | 31,838 | 40 |
| Schoharie | 3,730 | 8,644 | 5,250 | 7 |
| Schuyler | 1,937 | 4,945 | 2,885 | 4 |
| Seneca | 4,441 | 9,368 | 5,745 | 7 |
| Steuben | 9,462 | 28,708 | 14,685 | 23 |
| Sullivan | 9,847 | 17,035 | 14,189 | 13 |
| Tioga | 5,470 | 13,396 | 6,969 | 11 |
| Tompkins | 12,344 | 17,605 | 12,808 | 15 |
| Ulster | 21,371 | 46,883 | 30,190 | 35 |
| Warren. | 5,760 | 16,649 | 7,264 | 14 |
| Washington | 5,677 | 16,136 | 7,262 | 13 |
| Wayne | 8,203 | 23,379 | 12,061 | 19, |
| Wyoming | 4,365 | 11,184 | 5,737 | 9 |
| Yates | 1,958 | 6,639 | 2,903 | 5 |
| **Outside** | | | | |
| **N.Y. Metro Area** | 1,068,404 | 1,914,829 | 1,281,893 | 1,607 |
| | | | | |
| Nassau | 252,831 | 438,723 | 302,869 | 329 |
| Suffolk | 132,441 | 316,452 | 208,263 | 248 |
| Westchester | 154,412 | 262,901 | 173,153 | 208 |
| **N.Y. Suburban** | 539,684 | 1,018,076 | 684,285 | 786, |
| | | | | |
| Bronx | 243,345 | 196,754 | 238,786 | 96 |
| Kings | 387,768 | 373,903 | 419,382 | 190 |
| New York | 354,326 | 178,515 | 337,438 | 117 |
| Queens | 328,316 | 426,015 | 379,907 | 244 |
| Richmond | 29,241 | 84,686 | 47,867 | 56 |
| **N.Y City** | 1,342,996 | 1,259,873 | 1,423,380 | 706 |
| **N.Y. Metro Area** | 1,882,680 | 2,277,949 | 2,107,665 | 1,493 |
| **D/R Total** | 2,767,956 | 3,824,642 | 3,244,165 | 2,825, |
| **2d Party** | | | | |
| **(Lib/Con)** | 83,128 | 368,136 | 145,393 | 274, |
| | | | | |
| **Totals** | **2,951,084** | **4,192,778** | **3,389,558** | **3,100** |

*Democratic and Liberal  **Republican and Conservative

## New York Vote Since 1932

1932 (Pres.), Roosevelt, Dem., 2,534,959; Hoover, Re 1,937,963; Thomas, Soc., 177,397; Foster, Com., 27,9 Reynolds, Soc. Lab., 10,339.

1936 (Pres.), Roosevelt, Dem., 3,018,298; American La 274,924; total 3,293,222; Landon, Rep., 2,180,6 Thomas, Soc., 86,879; Browder, Com., 35,609.

1940 (Pres.), Roosevelt, Dem., 2,834,500; American La 417,418; total, 3,251,918; Willkie, Rep., 3,027,4 Thomas, Soc., 18,950; Babson, Proh., 3,250.

1944 (Pres.), Roosevelt, Dem., 2,478,598; American La 496,405; Liberal, 329,325; total, 3,304,238; Dewey, Re 2,987,647; Teichert, Ind. Gov't., 14,352; Thomas, S 10,553.

1948 (Pres.), Truman, Dem., 2,557,642; Liberal, 222,5 total, 2,780,204; Dewey, Rep., 2,841,163; Wallace, Am Lab., 509,559; Thomas, Soc., 40,879; Teichert, I Gov't., 2,729; Dobbs, Soc. Workers, 2,675.

1952 (Pres.), Eisenhower, Rep., 3,952,815; Stevenson, De 2,687,890, Liberal, 416,711; total, 3,104,601; Hallin American Lab., 64,211; Hoopes, Soc., 2,664; Dobbs, S Workers, 2,212; Haas,Ind. Gov't., 1,560; scattering, 1 blank and void, 87,813.

1956 (Pres.), Eisenhower, Rep., 4,340,340; Stevenson, De 2,458,212; Liberal, 292,557; total, 2,750,769; write votes for Andrews, 1,027; Werdel, 492; Haas, 1 Hoopes, 82; others, 476.

1960 (Pres.), Kennedy, Dem., 3,423,909; Liberal, 406,1 total, 3,830,085; Nixon, Rep., 3,446,419; Dobbs, S Workers, 14,319; scattering, 256; blank and void, 88,89

1964 (Pres.), Johnson, Dem., 4,913,156; Goldwater, Re 2,243,559; Haas, Soc. Labor, 6,085; DeBerry, Soc. Wo ers, 3,215; scattering, 188; blank and void, 151,383.

1968 (Pres.), Nixon, Rep., 3,007,932; Humphrey, De 3,378,470; Wallace, 3d party, 358,864; Blomen, Soc. bor, 8,432; Halstead, Soc. Worker, 11,851; Gregory, Fr dom and Peace, 24,517; blank, void, and scatteri 171,624.

1972 (Pres.), Nixon, Rep., 3,824,642; Conservative, 368,1 McGovern, Dem., 2,767,956; Liberal, 183,128; Reed, S Worker, 7,797; Fisher, Soc. Labor, 4,530; Hall, Comn nist, 5,641; blank, void, or scattered, 161,641.

1976 (Pres.), Carter, Dem., 3,389,558; Ford, Re 3,100,791; MacBride, Libertarian, 12,197; Hall, Comn 10,270; Camejo, Soc. Worker, 6,996; LaRouche, U.S. L bor, 5,413; blank, void, or scattered, 143,037.

## North Carolina

| County | 1972 McGovern (D) | Nixon (R) | 1976 Carter (D) | Ford (R) |
|---|---|---|---|---|
| ance | 6,833 | 22,046 | 17,371 | 12,680 |
| ander | 2,468 | 5,865 | 5,287 | 4,661 |
| hany | 1,304 | 2,158 | 2,550 | 1,532 |
| on | 2,188 | 3,551 | 4,796 | 1,608 |
| . | 3,313 | 5,784 | 5,193 | 4,937 |
| y | 627 | 3,510 | 1,869 | 3,085 |
| fort | 2,901 | 6,915 | 5,728 | 4,677 |
| e | 1,819 | 2,874 | 4,117 | 1,332 |
| en | 2,201 | 4,205 | 6,009 | 1,546 |
| swick | 2,500 | 6,153 | 7,377 | 3,636 |
| ombe | 12,626 | 32,091 | 26,633 | 22,461 |
| e | 6,197 | 14,447 | 14,254 | 10,070 |
| arrus | 5,336 | 18,384 | 12,049 | 12,455 |
| well | 4,886 | 12,976 | 11,894 | 9,872 |
| den | 556 | 909 | 1,231 | 562 |
| eret | 2,805 | 8,463 | 7,080 | 5,786 |
| well | 1,922 | 2,983 | 3,707 | 1,761 |
| wba | 7,744 | 24,106 | 16,862 | 18,696 |
| ham | 3,624 | 6,175 | 6,397 | 4,279 |
| okee | 2,411 | 4,113 | 3,571 | 3,210 |
| wan | 936 | 1,906 | 1,862 | 1,019 |
| . | 797 | 1,545 | 1,569 | 1,428 |
| eland | 4,994 | 13,726 | 14,406 | 8,106 |
| mbus | 3,305 | 8,468 | 11,148 | 3,184 |
| en | 2,384 | 9,372 | 7,553 | 5,881 |
| berland | 9,853 | 24,376 | 24,297 | 14,226 |
| tuck | 718 | 1,578 | 1,999 | 954 |
| . | 634 | 1,986 | 2,191 | 1,680 |
| dson | 7,691 | 24,875 | 17,859 | 18,813 |
| e | 1,578 | 5,613 | 3,635 | 4,772 |
| lin | 2,857 | 7,153 | 7,696 | 3,912 |
| am | 15,566 | 25,576 | 22,425 | 18,945 |
| ombe | 4,635 | 8,244 | 8,001 | 4,850 |
| yth | 20,928 | 46,415 | 39,561 | 38,886 |
| klin | 2,341 | 5,431 | 5,405 | 2,630 |
| on | 8,462 | 27,956 | 22,878 | 19,727 |
| . | 1,177 | 1,264 | 2,291 | 722 |
| am | 1,057 | 1,699 | 1,791 | 1,621 |
| ville | 2,918 | 6,037 | 5,244 | 2,955 |
| ne | 847 | 2,788 | 2,740 | 1,356 |
| ord | 25,800 | 61,381 | 46,826 | 45,441 |
| ax | 4,241 | 8,908 | 7,892 | 5,257 |
| nett | 3,347 | 10,259 | 8,992 | 5,935 |
| wood | 4,515 | 8,903 | 10,692 | 5,885 |
| derson | 2,701 | 12,134 | 8,155 | 10,830 |
| ford | 1,928 | 2,794 | 3,986 | 1,517 |
| e | 1,466 | 1,927 | 3,186 | 920 |
| e | 403 | 1,112 | 1,084 | 623 |
| ell | 5,088 | 16,736 | 13,295 | 11,573 |
| son | 3,169 | 4,709 | 5,223 | 3,536 |
| nston | 3,488 | 14,272 | 10,301 | 8,511 |
| es | 1,093 | 1,650 | 2,016 | 948 |
| . | 2,024 | 5,836 | 5,104 | 3,691 |
| oir | 3,672 | 11,065 | 7,650 | 7,715 |
| oln | 5,100 | 8,597 | 9,462 | 6,682 |
| on | 1,749 | 4,134 | 4,406 | 3,673 |
| ison | 2,039 | 3,273 | 3,433 | 2,446 |
| tin | 1,840 | 4,188 | 4,518 | 1,931 |
| owell | 2,348 | 6,570 | 6,246 | 4,450 |
| klenburg | 33,730 | 77,546 | 63,198 | 61,715 |
| hell | 800 | 4,240 | 2,031 | 3,728 |
| tgomery | 2,175 | 4,417 | 4,308 | 2,872 |
| re | 3,627 | 9,406 | 7,373 | 7,577 |
| n | 4,503 | 12,679 | 8,937 | 8,477 |
| Hanover | 5,984 | 19,060 | 14,504 | 13,687 |
| hamptom | 3,233 | 2,997 | 5,118 | 1,238 |
| ow | 2,424 | 10,343 | 7,954 | 5,953 |
| nge | 12,634 | 11,632 | 15,755 | 9,302 |
| lico | 919 | 1,847 | 2,113 | 1,068 |
| . | 2,115 | 3,906 | 4,302 | 2,651 |
| quotank | 1,415 | 3,327 | 4,422 | 2,063 |
| der | 723 | 1,299 | 1,666 | 909 |
| umans | 2,246 | 5,941 | 3,977 | 3,038 |
| on | 5,858 | 14,406 | 11,636 | 9,532 |
| . | 1,416 | 3,121 | 3,155 | 2,605 |
| dolph | 5,346 | 18,724 | 12,714 | 14,337 |
| mond | 3,508 | 5,692 | 8,793 | 2,848 |
| eson | 7,391 | 11,362 | 20,695 | 4,907 |
| ngham | 5,530 | 14,519 | 13,413 | 9,362 |
| an | 6,834 | 20,735 | 15,363 | 14,644 |
| erford | 4,140 | 9,506 | 10,361 | 6,718 |
| pson | 4,888 | 9,684 | 8,869 | 6,968 |
| tland | 1,938 | 3,485 | 4,430 | 1,932 |
| ly | 5,218 | 12,459 | 9,262 | 8,845 |
| es | 3,254 | 7,118 | 6,647 | 6,029 |
| y | 4,706 | 10,497 | 10,024 | 7,403 |
| in | 1,101 | 2,052 | 2,141 | 1,608 |
| sylvania | 2,321 | 5,860 | 4,636 | 4,089 |
| ell | 459 | 676 | 900 | 403 |
| . | 3,886 | 10,264 | 10,578 | 6,184 |
| ce | 3,117 | 6,491 | 5,620 | 3,813 |
| e | 22,807 | 56,808 | 44,005 | 44,291 |
| ren | 1,698 | 2,603 | 3,185 | 1,427 |
| hington | 1,546 | 2,559 | 2,840 | 1,486 |
| auga | 3,451 | 6,017 | 5,358 | 5,400 |
| Wayne | 5,234 | 14,352 | 9,265 | 9,607 |
| Wilkes | 4,634 | 13,105 | 10,176 | 11,768 |
| Wilson | 4,166 | 12,060 | 8,209 | 6,795 |
| Yadkin | 1,592 | 6,824 | 4,497 | 5,916 |
| Yancey | 2,278 | 3,106 | 3,932 | 2,688 |
| **Totals** | **438,705** | **1,054,889** | **927,365** | **741,960** |

### North Carolina Vote Since 1932

1932 (Pres.), Roosevelt, Dem., 497,566; Hoover, Rep., 208,344; Thomas, Soc., 5,591.

1936 (Pres.), Roosevelt, Dem., 616,141; Landon, Rep., 223,283; Thomas, Soc., 21; Browder, Com., 11; Lemke, Union 2.

1940 (Pres.), Roosevelt, Dem., 609,015; Willkie, Rep., 213,633.

1944 (Pres.), Roosevelt, Dem., 527,399; Dewey, Rep., 263,155.

1948 (Pres.), Truman, Dem., 459,070; Dewey, Rep., 258,572; Thurmond, States' Rights, 69,652; Wallace, Prog., 3,915.

1952 (Pres.), Eisenhower, Rep., 558,107; Stevenson, Dem., 652,803.

1956 (Pres.), Eisenhower, Rep., 575,062; Stevenson, Dem., 590,530.

1960 (Pres.), Kennedy, Dem., 713,136; Nixon, Rep., 655,420.

1964 (Pres.), Johnson, Dem., 800,139; Goldwater Rep., 624,844.

1968 (Pres.), Nixon, Rep., 627,192; Humphrey, Dem., 464,113; Wallace, 3d party, 496,188.

1972 (Pres.), Nixon, Rep., 1,054,889; McGovern, Dem., 438,705; Schmitz, American, 25,018.

1976 (Pres.), Dem., 927,365; Ford, Rep., 741,960; Anderson, American, 5,607; MacBride, Libertarian, 2,219; LaRouche, U.S. Labor, 755.

## North Dakota

| County | 1972 McGovern (D) | Nixon (R) | 1976 Carter (D) | Ford (R) |
|---|---|---|---|---|
| Adams | 665 | 1,177 | 959 | 940 |
| Barnes | 2,804 | 4,518 | 3,321 | 4,011 |
| Benson | 1,635 | 2,050 | 1,973 | 1,689 |
| Billings | 192 | 509 | 285 | 351 |
| Bottineau | 1,369 | 3,263 | 1,987 | 2,638 |
| Bowman | 643 | 1,111 | 911 | 1,033 |
| Burke | 651 | 1,446 | 899 | 1,087 |
| Burleigh | 5,841 | 13,909 | 9,188 | 13,680 |
| Cass | 14,073 | 21,770 | 17,879 | 22,583 |
| Cavalier | 1,867 | 2,898 | 2,178 | 2,046 |
| Dickey | 1,266 | 2,277 | 1,612 | 2,027 |
| Divide | 774 | 1,230 | 1,057 | 881 |
| Dunn | 644 | 1,438 | 1,051 | 1,041 |
| Eddy | 911 | 1,022 | 1,123 | 890 |
| Emmons | 1,115 | 2,194 | 1,459 | 1,370 |
| Foster | 861 | 1,352 | 1,147 | 1,120 |
| Golden Valley | 362 | 774 | 479 | 663 |
| Grand Forks | 9,416 | 13,361 | 11,545 | 13,820 |
| Grant | 596 | 1,569 | 952 | 1,205 |
| Griggs | 901 | 1,312 | 1,122 | 1,086 |
| Hettinger | 726 | 1,511 | 1,095 | 1,135 |
| Kidder | 557 | 1,315 | 936 | 954 |
| La Moure | 1,399 | 2,110 | 1,718 | 1,735 |
| Logan | 554 | 1,408 | 809 | 944 |
| McHenry | 1,554 | 2,765 | 1,994 | 2,043 |
| McIntosh | 521 | 2,440 | 912 | 1,785 |
| McKenzie | 937 | 1,913 | 1,335 | 1,595 |
| McLean | 1,703 | 3,575 | 2,815 | 2,729 |
| Mercer | 784 | 2,567 | 1,298 | 1,982 |
| Morton | 3,312 | 5,494 | 5,241 | 4,921 |
| Mountrail | 1,391 | 2,038 | 2,189 | 1,430 |
| Nelson | 1,358 | 1,625 | 1,610 | 1,336 |
| Oliver | 293 | 669 | 529 | 575 |
| Pembina | 1,801 | 3,317 | 2,274 | 2,810 |
| Pierce | 973 | 1,970 | 1,434 | 1,396 |
| Ramsey | 2,384 | 3,954 | 3,096 | 3,293 |
| Ransom | 1,355 | 2,056 | 1,715 | 1,696 |
| Renville | 702 | 1,121 | 1,008 | 812 |
| Richland | 3,367 | 5,194 | 4,592 | 4,991 |
| Rolette | 1,803 | 1,713 | 2,531 | 1,094 |
| Sargent | 1,331 | 1,616 | 1,644 | 1,344 |
| Sheridan | 334 | 1,460 | 569 | 935 |
| Sioux | 557 | 561 | 697 | 354 |
| Slope | 249 | 413 | 347 | 355 |
| Stark | 2,636 | 5,115 | 4,076 | 4,374 |

| | 1972 | | 1976 | |
|---|---|---|---|---|
| | (D) | (R) | (D) | (R) |
| Steele | 892 | 1,063 | 1,066 | 835 |
| Stutsman | 3,589 | 6,269 | 4,883 | 5,653 |
| Towner | 944 | 1,349 | 1,216 | 993 |
| Traill | 1,892 | 3,118 | 2,352 | 2,800 |
| Walsh | 2,908 | 3,991 | 3,555 | 3,518 |
| Ward | 6,706 | 13,900 | 9,484 | 12,751 |
| Wells | 1,297 | 2,519 | 1,742 | 1,941 |
| Williams | 2,989 | 4,800 | 4,189 | 4,230 |
| Totals | 100,384 | 174,109 | 136,078 | 153,470 |

## North Dakota Vote Since 1932

1932 (Pres.), Roosevelt, Dem., 178,350; Hoover, Rep., 71,772; Harvey, Lib., 1,817; Thomas, Soc., 3,521; Foster, Com., 830.

1936 (Pres.), Roosevelt, Dem., 163,148; Landon, Rep., 72,751; Lemke, Union, 36,708; Thomas, Soc., 552; Browder, Com., 360; Colvin, Proh., 197.

1940 (Pres.), Roosevelt, Dem., 124,036; Willkie, Rep., 154,590; Thomas, Soc., 1,279; Knuttson, Com., 545; Babson, Proh., 325.

1944 (Pres.), Roosevelt, Dem., 100,144; Dewey, Rep., 118,535; Thomas, Soc., 943, Watson, Proh., 549.

1948 (Pres.), Truman, Dem., 95,812; Dewey, Rep., 115,139; Wallace, Prog., 8,391; Thomas, Soc., 1,000, Thurmond, States' Rights, 374.

1952 (Pres.), Eisenhower, Rep., 191,712; Stevenson, Dem., 76,694; MacArthur, Christian Nationalist, 1,075; Hallinan, Prog., 344; Hamblen, Proh., 302.

1956 (Pres.), Eisenhower, Rep., 156,766; Stevenson, Dem., 96,742; Andrews, American, 483.

1960 (Pres.), Kennedy, Dem., 123,963; Nixon, Rep., 154,310; Dobbs, Soc. Workers, 158.

1964 (Pres.), Johnson, Dem., 149,784; Goldwater, Rep., 108,207; DeBerry, Soc. Worker, 224; Munn, Proh., 174.

1968 (Pres.), Nixon, Rep., 138,669; Humphrey, Dem., 94,769; Wallace, 3d party, 14,244; Halstead, Soc. Worker, 128; Munn, Prohibition, 38; Troxell, Ind., 34.

1972 (Pres.), Nixon, Rep., 174,109; McGovern, Dem., 100,384; Jenness, Soc, Worker, 288; Hall, Communist, 87 Schmitz, American, 5,646.

1976 (Pres.), Carter, Dem., 136,078; Ford, Rep., 153,470; Anderson, American, 3,698; McCarthy, Ind., 2,952; Maddox, Amer. Ind., 269; MacBride, Libertarian, 256; scattering, 371.

## Ohio

| County | 1972 McGovern (D) | Nixon (R) | 1976 Carter (D) | Ford (R) |
|---|---|---|---|---|
| Adams | 2,709 | 4,980 | 4,450 | 4,197 |
| Allen | 10,184 | 26,966 | 14,627 | 23,721 |
| Ashland | 4,302 | 12,470 | 7,205 | 9,761 |
| Ashtabula | 15,052 | 22,762 | 20,883 | 16,885 |
| Athens | 9,977 | 9,735 | 9,896 | 8,387 |
| Auglaize | 4,617 | 11,900 | 5,840 | 9,772 |
| Belmont | 14,800 | 17,628 | 21,162 | 13,550 |
| Brown | 3,770 | 6,772 | 5,432 | 4,549 |
| Butler | 21,194 | 50,380 | 35,123 | 49,625 |
| Carroll | 2,755 | 5,984 | 5,006 | 5,091 |
| Champaign | 3,626 | 8,756 | 4,748 | 6,526 |
| Clark | 19,725 | 34,447 | 26,135 | 26,745 |
| Clermont | 8,276 | 22,936 | 14,850 | 19,616 |
| Clinton | 2,709 | 8,140 | 4,959 | 6,597 |
| Columbiana | 15,683 | 27,308 | 23,096 | 22,318 |
| Coshocton | 3,790 | 8,082 | 5,827 | 6,361 |
| Crawford | 5,518 | 14,632 | 7,553 | 10,801 |
| Cuyahoga | 317,670 | 329,493 | 349,186 | 255,594 |
| Darke | 6,534 | 13,862 | 9,901 | 11,580 |
| Defiance | 4,377 | 8,914 | 5,850 | 7,526 |
| Delaware | 4,452 | 12,950 | 7,058 | 12,285 |
| Erie | 10,889 | 16,714 | 13,843 | 14,742 |
| Fairfield | 7,746 | 21,909 | 13,361 | 19,098 |
| Fayette | 2,344 | 6,970 | 4,477 | 5,719 |
| Franklin | 117,562 | 219,771 | 141,624 | 189,645 |
| Fulton | 3,615 | 8,387 | 4,850 | 7,891 |
| Gallia | 2,341 | 6,506 | 4,971 | 5,198 |
| Geauga | 7,329 | 15,624 | 10,449 | 15,004 |
| Greene | 12,736 | 25,349 | 20,245 | 22,598 |
| Guernsey | 4,757 | 9,648 | 7,573 | 7,746 |
| Hamilton | 119,054 | 239,212 | 135,605 | 211,267 |
| Hancock | 6,084 | 18,111 | 8,548 | 15,983 |
| Hardin | 3,535 | 8,713 | 4,650 | 6,076 |
| Harrison | 2,388 | 4,554 | 4,070 | 3,509 |
| Henry | 3,145 | 8,099 | 4,592 | 7,656 |
| Highland | 3,464 | 8,524 | 6,327 | |
| Hocking | 2,874 | 5,407 | 5,126 | |
| Holmes | 1,507 | 3,752 | 2,242 | |
| Huron | 5,491 | 10,942 | 7,742 | |
| Jackson | 3,410 | 7,351 | 6,699 | |
| Jefferson | 16,198 | 21,531 | 22,318 | 1. |
| Knox | 5,370 | 10,705 | 7,361 | |
| Lake | 27,523 | 42,488 | 40,734 | 3( |
| Lawrence | 7,112 | 15,125 | 12,072 | 1( |
| Licking | 12,460 | 28,070 | 19,247 | 2: |
| Logan | 3,786 | 10,938 | 5,949 | |
| Lorain | 36,634 | 51,102 | 52,387 | 3: |
| Lucas | 90,142 | 88,401 | 103,658 | 7: |
| Madison | 2,484 | 8,372 | 4,885 | |
| Mahoning | 62,428 | 64,144 | 75,837 | 4: |
| Marion | 7,970 | 17,197 | 10,962 | 1: |
| Medina | 10,643 | 21,010 | 16,251 | 1: |
| Meigs | 2,335 | 5,961 | 5,262 | |
| Mercer | 5,798 | 8,587 | 6,724 | |
| Miami | 9,121 | 21,226 | 13,074 | 1: |
| Monroe | 2,483 | 3,721 | 4,296 | |
| Montgomery | 82,231 | 120,998 | 106,468 | 10( |
| Morgan | 1,554 | 3,679 | 2,727 | |
| Morrow | 2,527 | 6,886 | 4,870 | |
| Muskingum | 10,313 | 19,897 | 14,178 | 1: |
| Noble | 1,449 | 3,274 | 2,612 | |
| Ottawa | 6,465 | 9,772 | 9,646 | |
| Paulding | 2,283 | 4,553 | 3,229 | |
| Perry | 3,728 | 6,716 | 6,268 | |
| Pickaway | 2,978 | 9,661 | 5,907 | |
| Pike | 3,531 | 5,037 | 5,734 | |
| Portage | 20,769 | 23,294 | 24,417 | 1: |
| Preble | 3,472 | 8,993 | 5,850 | |
| Putnam | 3,729 | 8,185 | 5,035 | |
| Richland | 13,468 | 31,117 | 23,065 | 2: |
| Ross | 5,879 | 15,573 | 10,743 | 1: |
| Sandusky | 8,308 | 15,489 | 11,202 | 1: |
| Scioto | 11,008 | 19,998 | 18,019 | 1: |
| Seneca | 8,180 | 13,939 | 10,074 | 1: |
| Shelby | 4,721 | 9,089 | 6,414 | |
| Stark | 51,565 | 92,110 | 70,012 | 7: |
| Summit | 108,534 | 112,419 | 123,711 | 8( |
| Trumbull | 35,278 | 47,680 | 53,828 | 3( |
| Tuscarawas | 12,255 | 18,413 | 16,880 | 1 |
| Union | 2,447 | 8,389 | 4,377 | |
| Van Wert | 3,644 | 9,545 | 5,689 | |
| Vinton | 1,537 | 2,725 | 2,629 | |
| Warren | 6,941 | 20,210 | 13,349 | 1( |
| Washington | 5,814 | 14,023 | 8,914 | 1 |
| Wayne | 9,260 | 20,368 | 13,087 | 1( |
| Williams | 4,278 | 9,083 | 4,920 | |
| Wood | 13,494 | 21,080 | 16,926 | 1! |
| Wyandot | 2,771 | 6,414 | 4,043 | |
| Totals | 1,558,889 | 2,441,827 | 2,011,621 | 2,00( |

## Ohio Vote Since 1932

1932 (Pres.), Roosevelt, Dem., 1,301,695; Hoover, R 1,227,679; Thomas, Soc., 64,094; Upshaw, Proh., 7 Foster, Com., 7,221; Reynolds, Soc. Lab., 1,968.

1936 (Pres.), Roosevelt, Dem., 1,747,122; Landon, R 1,127,709; Lemke, Union, 132,212; Browder, Com., 5, Thomas, Soc., 117; Aiken, Soc. Lab., 14.

1940 (Pres.), Roosevelt, Dem., 1,733,139; Willkie, R 1,586,773.

1944 (Pres.), Roosevelt, Dem., 1,570,763; Dewey, R 1,582,293.

1948 (Pres.), Truman, Dem., 1,452,791; Dewey, R 1,445,684; Wallace, Prog., 37,596.

1952 (Pres.), Eisenhower, Rep., 2,100,391; Stevenson, D 1,600,367.

1956 (Pres.), Eisenhower, Rep., 2,262,610; Stevenson, D 1,439,655.

1960 (Pres.), Kennedy, Dem., 1,944,248; Nixon, R 2,217,611.

1964 (Pres.), Johnson, Dem., 2,498,331; Goldwater, R 1,470,865.

1968 (Pres.), Nixon, Rep., 1,791,014; Humphrey, D 1,700,586; Wallace, 3d party, 467,495; Gregory, Munn, Prohibition, 19; Blomen, Soc. Labor, 120; stead, Soc. Worker, 69; Mitchell Communist, 23.

1972 (Pres.), Nixon, Rep., 2,441,827; McGovern, D 1,558,889; Fisher, Soc. Labor, 7,107; Hall, Commu 6,437; Schmitz, American, 80,067; Wallace, Ind., 460.

1976 (Pres.), Carter, Dem., 2,011,621; Ford, R 2,000,505; McCarthy, Ind., 58,258; Maddox, Amer. I 15,529; MacBride, Libertarian, 8,961; Hall, Con 7,817; Camejo, Soc. Workers, 4,717; LaRouche, U.S. bor, 4,335; scattered, 130.

## Oklahoma

| County | 1972 McGovern (D) | Nixon (R) | 1976 Carter (D) | Ford (R) |
|---|---|---|---|---|
| ir......... | 1,601 | 4,720 | 3,183 | 3,013 |
| lfa | 641 | 3,208 | 1,725 | 2,113 |
| ka | 993 | 2,905 | 3,276 | 1,098 |
| ver | 522 | 2,562 | 1,213 | 1,801 |
| kham | 1,608 | 4,472 | 4,530 | 2,351 |
| ne | 963 | 3,958 | 2,297 | 2,682 |
| an | 3,144 | 5,397 | 7,410 | 2,848 |
| do | 2,921 | 7,683 | 7,382 | 3,854 |
| adian | 2,751 | 11,400 | 7,288 | 9,766 |
| ter | 4,577 | 9,368 | 8,319 | 6,668 |
| rokee | 2,899 | 7,080 | 6,006 | 4,443 |
| octaw | 1,798 | 3,399 | 4,269 | 1,821 |
| arron | 323 | 1,350 | 962 | 872 |
| veland | 11,126 | 25,777 | 20,054 | 22,098 |
| al | 680 | 1,461 | 1,774 | 769 |
| nanche | 4,559 | 19,759 | 12,910 | 13,163 |
| on | 798 | 2,050 | 1,911 | 1,127 |
| g | 1,642 | 4,163 | 3,577 | 2,540 |
| ek | 3,705 | 12,396 | 8,964 | 8,458 |
| ter | 2,298 | 7,267 | 4,597 | 4,847 |
| aware | 2,135 | 5,476 | 4,924 | 3,642 |
| vey | 626 | 2,106 | 1,540 | 1,230 |
| | 473 | 2,059 | 1,256 | 1,429 |
| field | 4,557 | 19,348 | 8,969 | 14,202 |
| vin | 2,685 | 7,245 | 6,797 | 3,905 |
| dy | 3,440 | 7,762 | 7,155 | 4,686 |
| nt | 805 | 2,829 | 1,853 | 1,685 |
| er | 1,004 | 2,154 | 2,113 | 1,164 |
| mon | 568 | 1,319 | 1,371 | 666 |
| per | 385 | 1,976 | 978 | 1,303 |
| kell | 1,408 | 2,815 | 3,388 | 1,401 |
| hes | 1,787 | 3,497 | 4,185 | 1,715 |
| kson | 2,054 | 5,519 | 4,914 | 3,189 |
| erson | 969 | 1,709 | 2,303 | 956 |
| nston | 983 | 2,205 | 2,765 | 1,127 |
| | 4,246 | 17,244 | 9,371 | 12,441 |
| gfisher | 912 | 4,861 | 2,372 | 3,443 |
| va | 1,495 | 3,711 | 3,403 | 1,971 |
| mer | 1,239 | 2,520 | 2,661 | 1,312 |
| Flore | 3,433 | 7,932 | 8,033 | 4,907 |
| coln | 1,919 | 6,512 | 4,988 | 4,429 |
| an | 2,760 | 6,543 | 4,594 | 4,382 |
| e | 671 | 1,407 | 1,923 | 846 |
| Clain | 1,350 | 4,241 | 4,048 | 2,444 |
| Curtain | 2,568 | 6,441 | 7,560 | 3,423 |
| ntosh | 1,686 | 3,216 | 4,145 | 1,822 |
| or | 512 | 3,203 | 1,357 | 2,282 |
| shall | 1,113 | 2,273 | 2,939 | 1,358 |
| yes | 2,656 | 7,535 | 6,298 | 5,040 |
| ray | 1,294 | 2,983 | 2,932 | 1,563 |
| skogee | 7,380 | 15,161 | 14,678 | 10,287 |
| le | 999 | 4,085 | 2,278 | 2,634 |
| vata | 1,096 | 3,293 | 2,195 | 2,077 |
| uskee | 1,328 | 2,862 | 2,663 | 1,630 |
| ahoma | 46,986 | 156,437 | 87,185 | 119,120 |
| nulgee | 4,494 | 8,706 | 8,499 | 5,333 |
| ge | 2,968 | 9,288 | 6,832 | 6,398 |
| awa | 3,657 | 8,348 | 7,446 | 4,985 |
| nee | 1,135 | 4,280 | 3,031 | 3,111 |
| ne | 5,644 | 17,019 | 9,987 | 13,481 |
| sburg | 4,748 | 9,989 | 10,743 | 4,807 |
| totoc | 3,160 | 8,762 | 7,466 | 4,895 |
| awatomie | 4,822 | 13,308 | 11,255 | 9,090 |
| nmatcha | 1,016 | 2,456 | 2,987 | 1,360 |
| er Mills | 420 | 1,696 | 1,346 | 873 |
| ers | 2,607 | 9,697 | 7,368 | 7,318 |
| ninole | 2,746 | 6,879 | 5,874 | 4,237 |
| quoyah | 2,519 | 6,842 | 5,873 | 3,938 |
| phens | 3,623 | 10,309 | 9,795 | 7,099 |
| as | 924 | 5,726 | 2,591 | 3,919 |
| nan | 1,256 | 3,331 | 2,852 | 1,802 |
| sa | 32,779 | 125,278 | 65,298 | 108,653 |
| goner | 2,257 | 6,569 | 5,879 | 5,071 |
| shington | 3,658 | 16,347 | 6,898 | 14,560 |
| shita | 1,305 | 3,578 | 3,304 | 2,165 |
| ods | 1,234 | 4,413 | 2,530 | 2,788 |
| dward | 1,104 | 5,350 | 2,807 | 3,782 |
| otals | 247,147 | 759,025 | 532,442 | 545,708 |

### Oklahoma Vote Since 1932

32 (Pres.), Roosevelt, Dem., 515,468; Hoover, Rep., 88,165.

36 (Pres.), Roosevelt, Dem., 501,069; Landon, Rep., 245,122; Thomas, Soc., 2,221; Colvin, Proh., 1,328.

40 (Pres.), Roosevelt, Dem., 474,313; Willkie, Rep., 348,872; Babson, Proh., 3,027.

44 (Pres.), Roosevelt, Dem., 401,549; Dewey, Rep., 319,424; Watson, Proh., 1,663.

8 (Pres.), Truman, Dem., 452,782; Dewey, Rep., 268,817.

1952 (Pres.), Eisenhower, Rep., 518,045; Stevenson, Dem., 430,939.

1956 (Pres.), Eisenhower, Rep., 473,769; Stevenson, Dem., 385,581.

1960 (Pres.), Kennedy, Dem., 370,111; Nixon, Rep., 533,039.

1964 (Pres.), Johnson, Dem., 519,834; Goldwater, Rep., 412,665.

1968 (Pres.), Nixon, Rep., 449,697; Humphrey, Dem., 301,658; Wallace, 3d party, 191,731.

1972 (Pres.), Nixon, Rep. 759,025; McGovern, Dem., 247,147; Schmitz, American, 23,728.

1976 (Pres.), Carter, Dem., 532,442; Ford, Rep., 545,708; McCarthy, Ind., 14,101.

## Oregon

| County | 1972 McGovern (D) | Nixon (R) | 1976 Carter (D) | Ford (R) |
|---|---|---|---|---|
| Baker | 2,047 | 3,441 | 3,306 | 3,340 |
| Benton | 10,842 | 14,906 | 11,887 | 15,555 |
| Clackamas | 32,540 | 41,767 | 42,504 | 47,671 |
| Clatsop | 6,017 | 5,998 | 6,690 | 6,178 |
| Columbia | 5,997 | 5,348 | 8,005 | 5,226 |
| Coos | 11,778 | 10,370 | 14,168 | 9,481 |
| Crook | 1,743 | 2,167 | 2,536 | 2,093 |
| Curry | 2,108 | 2,832 | 3,227 | 2,962 |
| Deschutes | 6,319 | 7,747 | 9,480 | 9,054 |
| Douglas | 9,009 | 15,881 | 14,965 | 16,500 |
| Gilliam | 335 | 665 | 508 | 612 |
| Grant | 932 | 1,781 | 1,393 | 1,640 |
| Harney | 1,004 | 1,693 | 1,567 | 1,652 |
| Hood River | 2,330 | 3,152 | 3,114 | 3,210 |
| Jackson | 14,529 | 24,003 | 23,384 | 24,237 |
| Jefferson | 1,229 | 1,816 | 1,769 | 1,810 |
| Josephine | 5,090 | 9,911 | 9,061 | 10,726 |
| Klamath | 5,719 | 11,169 | 9,659 | 11,649 |
| Lake | 777 | 1,619 | 1,381 | 1,575 |
| Lane | 46,177 | 47,739 | 56,479 | 46,245 |
| Lincoln | 5,117 | 6,112 | 6,685 | 5,755 |
| Linn | 11,178 | 15,079 | 15,776 | 14,128 |
| Malheur | 1,870 | 5,908 | 3,507 | 5,682 |
| Marion | 23,908 | 36,441 | 33,781 | 35,497 |
| Morrow | 718 | 1,059 | 1,162 | 1,091 |
| Multnomah | 125,470 | 118,219 | 129,060 | 112,400 |
| Polk | 5,908 | 8,985 | 8,141 | 8,528 |
| Sherman | 330 | 677 | 491 | 567 |
| Tillamook | 3,544 | 4,120 | 4,456 | 4,033 |
| Umatilla | 6,090 | 10,470 | 7,985 | 9,345 |
| Union | 3,272 | 5,073 | 4,280 | 5,111 |
| Wallowa | 899 | 1,909 | 1,310 | 1,693 |
| Wasco | 3,749 | 4,537 | 4,560 | 4,258 |
| Washington | 27,890 | 43,958 | 34,847 | 52,376 |
| Wheeler | 267 | 474 | 402 | 355 |
| Yamhill | 6,008 | 9,660 | 8,881 | 9,885 |
| Totals | 392,760 | 486,686 | 490,407 | 492,120 |

### Oregon Vote Since 1932

1932 (Pres.), Roosevelt, Dem., 213,871; Hoover, Rep., 136,019; Thomas, Soc., 15,450; Reynolds, Soc. Lab., 1,730; Foster, Com., 1,681.

1936 (Pres.), Roosevelt, Dem., 266,733; Landon, Rep., 122,706; Lemke, Union, 21,831; Thomas, Soc., 2,143; Aiken, Soc. Lab., 500; Browder, Com., 104; Colvin, Proh., 4.

1940 (Pres.), Roosevelt, Dem., 258,415; Willkie, Rep., 219,555; Aiken, Soc. Lab., 2,487; Thomas, Soc., 398; Browder, Com., 191; Babson, Proh., 154.

1944 (Pres.), Roosevelt, Dem., 248,635; Dewey, Rep., 225,365; Thomas, Soc., 3,785; Watson, Proh., 2,362.

1948 (Pres.), Truman, Dem., 243,147; Dewey, Rep., 260,904; Wallace, Prog., 14,978; Thomas, Soc., 5,051.

1952 (Pres.), Eisenhower, Rep., 420,815; Stevenson, Dem., 270,579; Hallinan, Ind., 3,665.

1956 (Pres.), Eisenhower, Rep., 406,393; Stevenson, Dem., 329,204.

1960 (Pres.), Kennedy, Dem., 367,402; Nixon, Rep., 408,060.

1964 (Pres.), Johnson, Dem., 501,017; Goldwater, Rep., 282,779; write-in, 2,509.

1968 (Pres.), Nixon, Rep., 408,433; Humphrey, Dem., 358,866; Wallace, 3d party, 49,683; write-in, McCarthy, 1,496; N. Rockefeller, 69; others, 1,075.

1972 (Pres.), Nixon, Rep., 486,686; McGovern, Dem., 392,760; Schmitz, Amer., 46,211; write-in, 2,289.

1976 (Pres.), Carter, Dem., 490,407; Ford, Rep., 492,120; McCarthy, Ind., 40,207; write-in, 7,142.

## Pennsylvania

| | 1972 | | 1976 | |
|---|---|---|---|---|
| | McGov-ern | Nixon | Carter | Ford |
| County | (D) | (R) | (D) | (R) |
| Adams | 5,529 | 13,593 | 8,771 | 12,133 |
| Allegheny | 282,496 | 371,737 | 328,343 | 303,127 |
| Armstrong | 10,490 | 17,557 | 15,179 | 13,378 |
| Beaver | 31,570 | 43,637 | 46,117 | 33,593 |
| Bedford | 3,836 | 11,243 | 6,652 | 9,355 |
| Berks | 36,563 | 66,172 | 50,994 | 54,452 |
| Blair | 10,023 | 33,126 | 18,397 | 28,290 |
| Bradford | 5,204 | 15,050 | 7,913 | 12,851 |
| Bucks | 56,784 | 99,684 | 79,838 | 85,628 |
| Butler | 14,695 | 29,665 | 22,611 | 26,366 |
| Cambria | 27,950 | 43,825 | 38,797 | 32,469 |
| Cameron | 828 | 1,935 | 1,319 | 1,616 |
| Carbon | 7,774 | 11,639 | 10,791 | 8,883 |
| Centre | 13,194 | 20,683 | 17,867 | 21,177 |
| Chester | 31,118 | 72,726 | 42,712 | 67,686 |
| Clarion | 4,509 | 10,073 | 6,585 | 8,360 |
| Clearfield | 9,246 | 16,780 | 13,714 | 13,626 |
| Clinton | 4,772 | 8,205 | 6,532 | 5,858 |
| Columbia | 7,222 | 14,187 | 12,051 | 11,508 |
| Crawford | 9,371 | 18,393 | 14,712 | 15,301 |
| Cumberland | 14,562 | 42,099 | 23,008 | 39,950 |
| Dauphin | 22,587 | 54,307 | 34,342 | 46,819 |
| Delaware | 94,144 | 175,414 | 117,252 | 148,679 |
| Elk | 4,710 | 7,900 | 6,713 | 6,159 |
| Erie | 42,022 | 61,542 | 55,385 | 49,641 |
| Fayette | 22,475 | 27,288 | 32,232 | 20,021 |
| Forest | 509 | 1,374 | 1,017 | 1,135 |
| Franklin | 9,456 | 24,093 | 14,643 | 20,009 |
| Fulton | 1,192 | 2,515 | 1,737 | 2,219 |
| Greene | 5,562 | 7,890 | 8,769 | 5,293 |
| Huntingdon | 3,394 | 9,606 | 5,410 | 7,843 |
| Indiana | 10,833 | 18,122 | 14,650 | 15,786 |
| Jefferson | 5,024 | 11,631 | 7,456 | 9,437 |
| Juniata | 2,156 | 4,412 | 3,105 | 3,991 |
| Lackawanna | 45,465 | 58,838 | 57,685 | 43,354 |
| Lancaster | 24,223 | 81,036 | 35,533 | 72,106 |
| Lawrence | 17,595 | 23,712 | 23,337 | 18,546 |
| Lebanon | 6,683 | 25,008 | 11,785 | 20,880 |
| Lehigh | 33,325 | 58,023 | 46,620 | 46,895 |
| Luzerne | 51,128 | 81,358 | 74,655 | 60,058 |
| Lycoming | 11,999 | 28,913 | 18,635 | 22,648 |
| McKean | 4,513 | 11,958 | 6,424 | 10,305 |
| Mercer | 18,087 | 27,961 | 25,041 | 22,469 |
| Mifflin | 3,667 | 9,989 | 6,210 | 7,698 |
| Monroe | 5,619 | 12,701 | 9,544 | 10,228 |
| Montgomery | 91,959 | 173,662 | 112,644 | 155,480 |
| Montour | 1,755 | 4,386 | 2,727 | 3,259 |
| Northampton | 32,335 | 41,822 | 42,514 | 32,926 |
| Northumberland | 13,885 | 25,912 | 18,939 | 19,283 |
| Perry | 2,731 | 8,082 | 4,605 | 7,454 |
| Philadelphia | 431,736 | 344,096 | 494,579 | 239,000 |
| Pike | 1,385 | 4,568 | 2,775 | 4,241 |
| Potter | 1,710 | 4,422 | 2,983 | 3,828 |
| Schuylkill | 26,077 | 44,071 | 33,905 | 31,944 |
| Snyder | 1,834 | 7,308 | 3,097 | 6,557 |
| Somerset | 8,743 | 19,739 | 13,452 | 15,960 |
| Sullivan | 885 | 1,886 | 1,347 | 1,584 |
| Susquehanna | 4,154 | 9,476 | 6,075 | 8,331 |
| Tioga | 3,733 | 10,028 | 5,795 | 8,417 |
| Union | 2,278 | 6,905 | 3,405 | 6,309 |
| Venango | 6,302 | 13,991 | 8,653 | 12,270 |
| Warren | 4,877 | 10,018 | 7,412 | 8,508 |
| Washington | 34,781 | 42,587 | 49,317 | 32,827 |
| Wayne | 2,733 | 8,948 | 4,244 | 7,811 |
| Westmoreland | 59,322 | 75,085 | 74,217 | 59,172 |
| Wyoming | 2,112 | 6,423 | 3,628 | 5,705 |
| York | 27,520 | 63,606 | 41,281 | 56,912 |
| Totals | 1,796,951 | 2,714,521 | 2,328,677 | 2,205,604 |

### Pennsylvania Vote Since 1932

1932 (Pres.), Roosevelt, Dem., 1,295,948; Hoover, Rep., 1,453,540; Thomas, Soc., 91,119; Upshaw, Proh., 11,319; Foster, Com., 5,658; Cox, Jobless, 725; Reynolds, Indust., 659.

1936 (Pres.), Roosevelt, Dem., 2,353,788; Landon, Rep., 1,690,300; Lemke, Royal Oak, 67,467; Thomas, Soc., 14,375; Colvin, Proh., 6,691; Browder, Com., 4,060; Aiken, Ind., Lab., 1,424.

1940 (Pres.), Roosevelt, Dem., 2,171,035; Willkie, Rep., 1,889,848; Thomas, Soc., 10,967; Browder, Com., 4,519; Aiken, Ind. Gov., 1,518.

1944 (Pres.), Roosevelt, Dem., 1,940,479; Dewey, Rep., 1,835,054; Thomas, Soc., 11,721; Watson, Proh., 5,750; Teichert, Ind. Gov., 1,789.

1948 (Pres.), Truman, Dem., 1,752,426; Dewey, Rep., 1,902,197; Wallace, Prog., 55,161; Thomas, Soc., 11,325;

Watson, Proh., 10,338; Dobbs, Militant Workers, 2, Teichert, Ind. Gov., 1,461.

1952 (Pres.), Eisenhower, Rep., 2,415,789; Stevenson, D 2,146,269; Hamblen, Proh., 8,771; Hallinan, Prog., 4, Hoopes, Soc., 2,684; Dobbs, Militant Workers, 1, Haas, Ind. Gov., 1,347; scattered, 155.

1956 (Pres.), Eisenhower, Rep., 2,585,252; Stevenson, D 1,981,769; Haas, Soc. Lab., 7,447; Dobbs, Militant W ers, 2,035.

1960 (Pres.), Kennedy, Dem., 2,556,282; Nixon, F 2,439,956; Haas, Soc. Lab., 7,185; Dobbs, Soc. Worl 2,678; scattering, 440.

1964 (Pres.), Johnson, Dem., 3,130,954; Goldwater, R 1,673,657; DeBerry, Soc. Worker, 10,456; Haas, Soc. bor, 5,092; scattering, 2,531.

1968 (Pres.), Nixon, Rep., 2,090,017; Humphrey, D 2,259,405; Wallace, 3d party, 378,582; Blomen, Soc. bor, 4,977; Halstead, Soc. Worker, 4,862; Gregory, 7, others, 2,264.

1972 (Pres.), Nixon, Rep., 2,714,521; McGovern, D 1,796,951; Schmitz, American, 70,593; Jenness, Worker, 4,639; Hall, Communist, 2,686; others, 2,715.

1976 (Pres.), Carter, Dem., 2,328,677; Ford, R 2,205,604; McCarthy, Ind., 50,584; Maddox, Cons tion, 25,344; Camejo, Soc. Workers, 3,009; LaRou U.S. Labor, 2,744; Hall, Comm., 1,891; others, 2,934.

## Rhode Island

| | 1972 | | 1976 | |
|---|---|---|---|---|
| | McGov-ern | Nixon | Carter | F |
| County | (D) | (R) | (D) | |
| Bristol | 9,928 | 12,009 | 11,228 | 1( |
| Kent | 29,004 | 40,534 | 35,855 | 34 |
| Newport | 12,844 | 19,142 | 17,768 | 15 |
| Providence | 129,232 | 129,418 | 144,805 | 103 |
| Washington | 13,637 | 19,280 | 17,980 | 17 |
| Totals | 194,645 | 220,383 | 227,636 | 181 |

### Rhode Island Vote Since 1932

1932 (Pres.), Roosevelt, Dem., 146,604; Hoover, R 115,266; Thomas, Soc., 3,138; Foster, Com., 546; R nolds, Soc. Lab., 433; Upshaw, Proh., 183.

1936 (Pres.), Roosevelt, Dem., 165,238; Landon, R 125,031; Lemke, Union, 19,569; Aiken, Soc. Lab., ! Browder, Com., 411.

1940 (Pres.), Roosevelt, Dem., 182,182; Willkie, R 138,653; Browder, Com., 239; Babson, Proh., 74.

1944 (Pres.), Roosevelt, Dem., 175,356; Dewey, R 123,487; Watson, Proh., 433.

1948 (Pres.), Truman, Dem., 188,736; Dewey, R 135,787; Wallace, Prog., 2,619; Thomas, Soc., 429; chert, Soc. Lab., 131.

1952 (Pres.), Eisenhower, Rep., 210,935; Stevenson, De 203,293; Hallinan, Prog., 187; Haas, Soc. Lab., 83.

1956 (Pres.), Eisenhower, Rep., 225,819; Stevenson, De 161,790.

1960 (Pres.), Kennedy, Dem., 258,032; Nixon, R 147,502.

1964 (Pres.), Johnson, Dem., 315,463; Goldwater, R 74,615.

1968 (Pres.), Nixon, Rep., 122,359; Humphrey, De 246,518; Wallace, 3d party, 15,678; Halstead, S Worker, 383.

1972 (Pres.), Nixon, Rep., 220,383; McGovern, De 194,645; Jenness, Soc. Worker, 729.

1976 (Pres.), Carter, Dem., 227,636; Ford, Rep., 181,2 MacBride, Libertarian, 715; Camejo, Soc. Workers, 4 Hall, Comm., 334; Levin, Soc. Labor, 188.

## South Carolina

| | 1972 | | 1976 | |
|---|---|---|---|---|
| | McGov-ern | Nixon | Carter | F |
| County | (D) | (R) | (D) | |
| Abbeville | 1,347 | 3,265 | 4,700 | 1, |
| Aiken | 5,745 | 21,117 | 14,927 | 16, |
| Allendale | 1,383 | 1,740 | 2,634 | 1,! |
| Anderson | 5,241 | 17,514 | 19,002 | 9, |
| Bamberg | 1,680 | 2,537 | 3,330 | 9. |

| | 1972 (D) | 1972 (R) | 1976 (D) | 1976 (R) |
|---|---|---|---|---|
| Barnwell | 1,560 | 3,955 | 4,083 | 2,569 |
| Beaufort | 3,237 | 5,929 | 6,049 | 5,935 |
| Berkeley | 4,497 | 9,345 | 9,741 | 6,981 |
| Calhoun | 1,148 | 1,867 | 2,055 | 1,382 |
| Charleston | 16,856 | 39,832 | 34,328 | 34,010 |
| Cherokee | 2,107 | 7,570 | 7,765 | 3,931 |
| Chester | 2,352 | 4,724 | 5,200 | 2,982 |
| Chesterfield | 2,938 | 5,230 | 7,687 | 2,537 |
| Clarendon | 3,276 | 3,958 | 5,489 | 3,040 |
| Colleton | 2,376 | 5,738 | 5,134 | 3,324 |
| Darlington | 4,414 | 11,756 | 10,165 | 6,678 |
| Dillon | 1,604 | 4,364 | 5,089 | 2,527 |
| Dorchester | 3,606 | 8,095 | 8,046 | 6,695 |
| Edgefield | 1,326 | 2,812 | 3,216 | 1,878 |
| Fairfield | 2,491 | 2,608 | 4,155 | 1,817 |
| Florence | 7,451 | 18,107 | 16,294 | 13,539 |
| Georgetown | 4,446 | 6,114 | 7,169 | 4,068 |
| Greenville | 10,163 | 46,360 | 35,923 | 39,099 |
| Greenwood | 3,400 | 9,370 | 9,976 | 5,974 |
| Hampton | 2,086 | 2,891 | 3,923 | 1,773 |
| Horry | 4,437 | 15,324 | 15,720 | 9,339 |
| Jasper | 1,203 | 1,650 | 2,903 | 1,221 |
| Kershaw | 2,531 | 8,035 | 6,211 | 6,126 |
| Lancaster | 2,461 | 9,016 | 8,324 | 4,997 |
| Laurens | 2,650 | 8,141 | 7,440 | 5,300 |
| Lee | 1,996 | 3,076 | 3,869 | 2,357 |
| Lexington | 4,069 | 25,327 | 14,339 | 21,442 |
| Marion | 844 | 1,302 | 5,927 | 3,076 |
| Marlboro | 2,535 | 4,719 | 5,409 | 1,961 |
| McCormick | 2,999 | 3,838 | 1,774 | 640 |
| Newberry | 2,035 | 7,325 | 5,034 | 4,931 |
| Oconee | 1,739 | 6,825 | 8,447 | 3,805 |
| Orangeburg | 7,652 | 11,711 | 13,652 | 8,794 |
| Pickens | 2,255 | 11,776 | 8,505 | 8,029 |
| Richland | 20,875 | 38,500 | 36,855 | 32,727 |
| Saluda | 1,022 | 3,095 | 2,715 | 2,085 |
| Spartanburg | 9,723 | 31,187 | 27,925 | 20,456 |
| Sumter | 5,795 | 10,892 | 10,471 | 9,332 |
| Union | 2,676 | 8,337 | 6,363 | 3,463 |
| Williamsburg | 5,213 | 5,729 | 8,745 | 5,275 |
| York | 6,374 | 14,441 | 14,099 | 9,843 |
| **Totals** | **186,824** | **477,044** | **450,807** | **346,149** |

## South Carolina Vote Since 1932

1932 (Pres.), Roosevelt, Dem., 102,347; Hoover, Rep., 1,978; Thomas, Soc., 82.

1936 (Pres.), Roosevelt, Dem., 113,791; Landon, Rep., Tolbert faction 953, Hambright faction 693, total, 1,646.

1940 (Pres.), Roosevelt, Dem., 95,470; Willkie, Rep., 1,727.

1944 (Pres.), Roosevelt, Dem., 90,601; Dewey, Rep., 4,547; Southern Democrats, 7,799; Watson, Proh., 365; Rep. Tolbert faction, 63.

1948 (Pres.), Thurmond, States' Rights, 102,607; Truman, Dem., 34,423; Dewey, Rep., 5,386; Wallace, Prog., 154; Thomas, Soc., 1.

1952 (Pres.), Eisenhower ran on two tickets. Under State law vote cast for two Eisenhower slates of electors could not be combined. Eisenhower, Ind., 158,289; Rep., 9,793; total, 168,082; Stevenson, Dem., 173,004; Hamblen, Proh., 1.

1956 (Pres.), Stevenson, Dem., 136,372; Byrd, Ind., 88,509; Eisenhower, Rep., 75,700; Andrews, Ind., 2.

1960 (Pres.), Kennedy, Dem., 198,129; Nixon, Rep., 188,558; write-in, 1.

1964 (Pres.), Johnson, Dem., 215,700; Goldwater, Rep., 309,048; write-ins: Nixon, 1, Wallace, 5; Powell, 1; Thurmond, 1.

1968 (Pres.), Nixon, Rep., 254,062; Humphrey, Dem., 197,486; Wallace, 3d party, 215,430.

1972 (Pres.), Nixon, Rep., 477,044; McGovern, Dem., 184,559, United Citizens, 2,265; Schmitz, American, 10,075; write-in, 17.

1976 (Pres.), Carter, Dem., 450,807; Ford, Rep., 346,149; Anderson, American, 2,996; Maddox, Amer. Ind., 1,950; write-in, 681.

## South Dakota

| County | 1972 McGovern (D) | 1972 Nixon (R) | 1976 Carter (D) | 1976 Ford (R) |
|---|---|---|---|---|
| Aurora | 1,257 | 1,075 | 1,269 | 831 |
| Beadle | 4,297 | 5,922 | 4,846 | 4,758 |
| Bennett | 476 | 808 | 481 | 610 |
| Bon Homme | 2,368 | 2,116 | 2,154 | 1,897 |
| Brookings | 4,701 | 5,182 | 4,685 | 5,278 |

| | 1972 (D) | 1972 (R) | 1976 (D) | 1976 (R) |
|---|---|---|---|---|
| Brown | 8,216 | 8,134 | 8,888 | 7,609 |
| Brule | 1,665 | 1,421 | 1,534 | 1,175 |
| Buffalo | 275 | 221 | 240 | 194 |
| Butte | 1,085 | 2,452 | 1,366 | 2,055 |
| Campbell | 361 | 1,169 | 489 | 897 |
| Chas. Mix | 2,691 | 2,020 | 2,593 | 1,779 |
| Clark | 1,336 | 1,617 | 1,376 | 1,449 |
| Clay | 2,821 | 2,518 | 2,593 | 2,647 |
| Codington | 4,601 | 4,936 | 4,680 | 4,504 |
| Corson | 689 | 975 | 967 | 846 |
| Custer | 798 | 1,476 | 995 | 1,373 |
| Davison | 4,710 | 3,796 | 4,510 | 3,688 |
| Day | 2,719 | 1,971 | 2,610 | 1,617 |
| Deuel | 1,370 | 1,357 | 1,465 | 1,177 |
| Dewey | 699 | 1,008 | 706 | 820 |
| Douglas | 887 | 1,434 | 975 | 1,315 |
| Edmunds | 1,646 | 1,567 | 1,629 | 1,294 |
| Fall River | 1,107 | 2,374 | 1,537 | 2,046 |
| Faulk | 986 | 1,004 | 1,063 | 868 |
| Grant | 2,231 | 2,247 | 2,398 | 2,051 |
| Gregory | 1,555 | 1,670 | 1,658 | 1,475 |
| Haakon | 366 | 1,021 | 477 | 812 |
| Hamlin | 1,276 | 1,693 | 1,402 | 1,452 |
| Hand | 1,307 | 1,806 | 1,477 | 1,510 |
| Hanson | 1,022 | 876 | 1,005 | 693 |
| Harding | 253 | 637 | 459 | 470 |
| Hughes | 2,037 | 4,231 | 2,506 | 3,997 |
| Hutchinson | 2,248 | 3,092 | 2,062 | 2,822 |
| Hyde | 533 | 789 | 572 | 687 |
| Jackson | 261 | 581 | 313 | 532 |
| Jerauld | 829 | 988 | 845 | 821 |
| Jones | 346 | 642 | 374 | 515 |
| Kingsbury | 1,632 | 2,320 | 1,762 | 1,844 |
| Lake | 2,886 | 2,919 | 2,930 | 2,530 |
| Lawrence | 2,533 | 4,795 | 3,102 | 4,206 |
| Lincoln | 2,617 | 3,201 | 2,957 | 3,105 |
| Lyman | 744 | 1,166 | 831 | 892 |
| Marshall | 1,646 | 1,500 | 1,721 | 1,233 |
| McCook | 1,993 | 1,963 | 1,822 | 1,744 |
| McPherson | 579 | 1,950 | 693 | 1,662 |
| Meade | 1,633 | 3,146 | 2,478 | 3,096 |
| Mellette | 433 | 637 | 429 | 508 |
| Miner | 1,337 | 1,059 | 1,289 | 839 |
| Minnehaha | 22,386 | 22,447 | 22,068 | 23,286 |
| Moody | 1,895 | 1,648 | 1,942 | 1,475 |
| Pennington | 8,592 | 13,654 | 10,058 | 13,352 |
| Perkins | 900 | 1,691 | 1,262 | 1,298 |
| Potter | 858 | 1,389 | 908 | 1,136 |
| Roberts | 2,976 | 2,187 | 2,890 | 1,915 |
| Sanborn | 1,074 | 1,064 | 1,025 | 881 |
| Shannon | 1,246 | 356 | 756 | 901 |
| Spink | 2,321 | 2,547 | 2,650 | 2,003 |
| Stanley | 492 | 779 | 548 | 637 |
| Sully | 414 | 773 | 505 | 630 |
| Todd | 907 | 806 | 826 | 583 |
| Tripp | 1,538 | 2,592 | 1,822 | 1,980 |
| Turner | 1,993 | 3,007 | 1,906 | 2,694 |
| Union | 2,554 | 2,271 | 2,540 | 2,297 |
| Walworth | 1,287 | 2,416 | 1,516 | 2,187 |
| Washabaugh | 211 | 245 | 276 | 229 |
| Yankton | 3,835 | 4,366 | 3,987 | 4,029 |
| Ziebach | 378 | 486 | 370 | 369 |
| **Totals** | **139,945** | **166,476** | **147,068** | **151,505** |

## South Dakota Vote Since 1932

1932 (Pres.), Roosevelt, Dem., 183,515; Hoover, Rep., 99,212; Harvey, Lib., 3,333; Thomas, Soc., 1,551; Upshaw, Proh., 463; Foster, Com., 364.

1936 (Pres.), Roosevelt, Dem., 160,137; Landon, Rep., 125,977; Lemke, Union, 10,338.

1940 (Pres.), Roosevelt, Dem., 131,862; Willkie, Rep., 177,065.

1944 (Pres.), Roosevelt, Dem., 96,711; Dewey, Rep., 135,365.

1948 (Pres.), Truman, Dem., 117,653; Dewey, Rep., 129,651; Wallace, Prog., 2,801.

1952 (Pres.), Eisenhower, Rep., 203,857; Stevenson, Dem., 90,426.

1956 (Pres.), Eisenhower, Rep., 171,569; Stevenson, Dem., 122,288.

1960 (Pres.), Kennedy, Dem., 128,070; Nixon, Rep., 178,417.

1964 (Pres.), Johnson, Dem., 163,010; Goldwater, Rep., 130,108.

1968 (Pres.), Nixon, Rep., 149,841; Humphrey, Dem., 118,023; Wallace, 3d party, 13,400.

1972 (Pres.), Nixon, Rep., 166,476; McGovern, Dem., 139,945; Jenness, Soc. Worker, 994.

1976 (Pres.), Carter, Dem., 147,068; Ford, Rep., 151,505; MacBride, Libertarian, 1,619; Hall, Comm., 318; Camejo, Soc. Workers, 168.

## Tennessee

| County | 1972 McGovern (D) | Nixon (R) | 1976 Carter (D) | Ford (R) |
|---|---|---|---|---|
| Anderson | 6,713 | 13,865 | 13,455 | 10,494 |
| Bedford | 2,565 | 4,262 | 7,228 | 3,023 |
| Benton | 1,479 | 2,614 | 4,088 | 1,678 |
| Bledsoe | 899 | 1,952 | 1,757 | 1,620 |
| Blount | 5,303 | 16,078 | 12,096 | 13,851 |
| Bradley | 2,804 | 10,440 | 8,776 | 9,136 |
| Campbell | 1,629 | 4,909 | 5,206 | 4,277 |
| Cannon | 911 | 1,615 | 2,463 | 908 |
| Carroll | 2,290 | 5,784 | 5,581 | 4,031 |
| Carter | 2,191 | 11,102 | 7,443 | 8,934 |
| Cheatham | 1,321 | 2,235 | 4,225 | 1,376 |
| Chester | 961 | 2,787 | 2,532 | 1,949 |
| Claiborne | 1,230 | 3,632 | 3,461 | 3,227 |
| Clay | 648 | 982 | 1,671 | 982 |
| Cocke | 805 | 5,268 | 3,141 | 5,004 |
| Coffee | 2,973 | 6,416 | 8,017 | 3,848 |
| Crockett | 735 | 2,642 | 2,963 | 1,694 |
| Cumberland | 1,482 | 4,593 | 4,543 | 4,119 |
| Davidson | 48,869 | 82,636 | 99,007 | 60,662 |
| Decatur | 1,187 | 2,368 | 2,432 | 1,637 |
| De Kalb | 1,243 | 2,014 | 3,222 | 1,443 |
| Dickson | 2,619 | 3,645 | 6,551 | 2,285 |
| Dyer | 1,600 | 6,066 | 5,937 | 4,391 |
| Fayette | 2,067 | 3,264 | 3,853 | 2,133 |
| Fentress | 665 | 2,154 | 1,953 | 1,767 |
| Franklin | 2,896 | 4,136 | 6,788 | 2,619 |
| Gibson | 3,625 | 9,900 | 10,356 | 5,563 |
| Giles | 1,875 | 2,914 | 5,225 | 1,952 |
| Grainger | 828 | 2,842 | 2,018 | 2,805 |
| Greene | 2,764 | 9,772 | 7,070 | 8,664 |
| Grundy | 1,005 | 1,364 | 2,850 | 850 |
| Hamblen | 2,563 | 8,879 | 7,504 | 6,989 |
| Hamilton | 20,657 | 58,469 | 45,348 | 47,969 |
| Hancock | 393 | 1,813 | 764 | 1,309 |
| Hardeman | 1,550 | 3,494 | 3,934 | 2,254 |
| Hardin | 1,202 | 4,401 | 3,438 | 3,362 |
| Hawkins | 2,608 | 7,791 | 5,931 | 6,407 |
| Haywood | 1,966 | 3,123 | 3,681 | 1,952 |
| Henderson | 1,313 | 5,122 | 3,366 | 4,152 |
| Henry | 2,694 | 4,613 | 7,162 | 2,585 |
| Hickman | 1,393 | 1,943 | 3,590 | 1,154 |
| Houston | 870 | 800 | 1,990 | 407 |
| Humphreys | 1,973 | 2,263 | 4,021 | 1,338 |
| Jackson | 1,085 | 956 | 2,959 | 591 |
| Jefferson | 1,357 | 5,925 | 3,995 | 5,459 |
| Johnson | 450 | 3,362 | 1,464 | 2,986 |
| Knox | 24,076 | 64,747 | 53,034 | 56,013 |
| Lake | 536 | 1,147 | 1,933 | 591 |
| Lauderdale | 1,771 | 3,597 | 4,747 | 2,105 |
| Lawrence | 2,824 | 6,438 | 7,140 | 4,967 |
| Lewis | 1,138 | 1,056 | 2,391 | 617 |
| Lincoln | 1,867 | 3,266 | 5,732 | 1,724 |
| Loudon | 1,604 | 5,357 | 4,683 | 4,458 |
| McMinn | 2,838 | 7,423 | 7,020 | 6,638 |
| McNairy | 1,610 | 4,774 | 4,293 | 3,388 |
| Macon | 653 | 2,295 | 1,951 | 2,063 |
| Madison | 5,203 | 15,481 | 12,989 | 11,364 |
| Marion | 1,929 | 3,711 | 4,615 | 2,965 |
| Marshall | 1,526 | 2,593 | 4,457 | 1,674 |
| Maury | 3,262 | 7,371 | 8,747 | 5,327 |
| Meigs | 539 | 1,052 | 1,254 | 975 |
| Monroe | 2,870 | 5,657 | 5,368 | 5,335 |
| Montgomery | 5,691 | 7,839 | 12,310 | 5,923 |
| Moore | 356 | 608 | 1,101 | 331 |
| Morgan | 1,084 | 2,531 | 2,953 | 1,949 |
| Obion | 2,243 | 5,800 | 7,204 | 2,986 |
| Overton | 1,573 | 1,947 | 3,897 | 1,115 |
| Perry | 937 | 900 | 1,660 | 520 |
| Pickett | 357 | 957 | 948 | 986 |
| Polk | 1,431 | 2,285 | 3,284 | 1,835 |
| Putnam | 3,738 | 6,038 | 8,485 | 4,079 |
| Rhea | 1,312 | 3,842 | 3,735 | 3,449 |
| Roane | 3,433 | 8,742 | 9,216 | 7,121 |
| Robertson | 2,985 | 4,175 | 7,547 | 2,505 |
| Rutherford | 5,811 | 11,256 | 14,854 | 7,921 |
| Scott | 679 | 2,775 | 2,260 | 2,432 |
| Sequatchie | 629 | 1,298 | 1,733 | 1,065 |
| Sevier | 1,128 | 8,273 | 3,993 | 7,608 |
| Shelby | 81,089 | 161,922 | 147,893 | 128,646 |
| Smith | 1,260 | 1,812 | 3,753 | 1,332 |
| Stewart | 1,098 | 790 | 2,442 | 510 |
| Sullivan | 10,007 | 27,593 | 23,353 | 22,087 |
| Sumner | 4,596 | 10,020 | 13,848 | 7,946 |
| Tipton | 1,853 | 5,542 | 5,667 | 3,329 |
| Trousdale | 539 | 663 | 1,385 | 332 |
| Unicoi | 822 | 3,877 | 2,526 | 3,211 |
| Union | 570 | 1,927 | 1,631 | 1,801 |
| Van Buren | 364 | 629 | 1,085 | 346 |
| Warren | 2,118 | 3,565 | 6,666 | 2,364 |
| Washington | 5,284 | 17,343 | 13,951 | 14,770 |
| Wayne | 673 | 2,898 | 1,891 | 2,597 |
| Weakley | 2,027 | 5,836 | 6,605 | 2,875 |
| White | 1,392 | 2,252 | 3,874 | 1,382 |
| Williamson | 2,616 | 7,556 | 8,183 | 7,880 |
| Wilson | 3,906 | 6,486 | 10,537 | 4,696 |
| **Totals** | **357,293** | **813,147** | **825,879** | **633,969** |

## Tennessee Vote Since 1932

1932 (Pres.), Roosevelt, Dem., 259,817; Hoover, Rep., 126,806; Upshaw, Proh., 1,995; Thomas, Soc., 1,786; Foster, Com., 234.

1936 (Pres.), Roosevelt, Dem., 327,083; Landon, Rep., 146,516; Thomas, Soc., 685; Colvin, Proh., 632; Browder, Com., 319; Lemke, Union, 296.

1940 (Pres.), Roosevelt, Dem., 351,601; Willkie, Rep., 169,153; Babson, Proh., 1,606; Thomas, Soc., 463.

1944 (Pres.), Roosevelt, Dem., 308,707; Dewey, Rep., 200,311; Watson, Proh., 882; Thomas, Soc., 892.

1948 (Pres.), Truman, Dem., 270,402; Dewey, Rep., 202,914; Thurmond, States' Rights, 73,815; Wallace, Prog., 1,864; Thomas, Soc., 1,288.

1952 (Pres.), Eisenhower, Rep., 446,147; Stevenson, Dem., 443,710; Hamblen, Proh., 1,432; Hallinan, Prog., 885; MacArthur, Christian Nationalist, 379.

1956 (Pres.), Eisenhower, Rep., 462,288; Stevenson, Dem., 456,507; Andrews, Ind., 19,820; Holtwick, Proh., 789.

1960 (Pres.), Kennedy, Dem., 481,453; Nixon, Rep., 556,577; Faubus, States' Rights, 11,304; Decker, Proh., 2,458.

1964 (Pres.), Johnson, Dem. 635,047; Goldwater, Rep., 508,965; write-in, 34.

1968 (Pres.), Nixon, Rep., 472,592; Humphrey, Dem., 351,233; Wallace, 3d party, 424,792.

1972 (Pres.), Nixon, Rep., 813,147; McGovern, Dem., 357,293; Schmitz, American, 30,373; write-in, 369.

1976 (Pres.), Carter, Dem., 825,879; Ford, Rep., 633,969; Anderson, American, 5,769; McCarthy, Ind., 5,004; Maddox, Am. Ind., 2,303; MacBride, Libertarian, 1,375; Hall, Comm., 547; LaRouche, U.S. Labor, 512; Bubar, Proh., 442; Miller, Ind., 316; write-in, 230.

## Texas

| County | 1972 McGovern (D) | Nixon (R) | 1976 Carter (D) | Ford (R) |
|---|---|---|---|---|
| Anderson | 2,233 | 5,826 | 5,499 | 4,17 |
| Andrews | 677 | 2,615 | 1,777 | 2,12 |
| Angelina | 4,970 | 11,453 | 9,750 | 7,22 |
| Aransas | 844 | 2,037 | 2,136 | 1,98 |
| Archer | 632 | 1,494 | 1,577 | 96 |
| Armstrong | 177 | 768 | 513 | 50 |
| Atascosa | 1,804 | 3,400 | 4,565 | 2,41 |
| Austin | 1,043 | 3,084 | 2,313 | 2,68 |
| Bailey | 465 | 1,837 | 1,356 | 1,25 |
| Bandera | 434 | 1,796 | 1,183 | 1,55 |
| Bastrop | 1,906 | 3,097 | 4,788 | 2,38 |
| Baylor | 598 | 1,190 | 1,335 | 78 |
| Bee | 2,067 | 3,779 | 3,690 | 2,95 |
| Bell | 6,848 | 17,525 | 17,499 | 15,12 |
| Bexar | 91,662 | 137,572 | 146,581 | 121,17 |
| Blanco | 460 | 1,215 | 923 | 1,01 |
| Borden | 96 | 330 | 234 | 15 |
| Bosque | 1,014 | 2,947 | 2,954 | 1,91 |
| Bowie | 5,227 | 14,722 | 12,445 | 9,59 |
| Brazoria | 11,350 | 21,045 | 21,711 | 19,47 |
| Brazos | 5,692 | 14,243 | 10,628 | 15,68 |
| Brewster | 904 | 1,524 | 1,227 | 1,36 |
| Briscoe | 349 | 642 | 823 | 28 |
| Brooks | 1,657 | 1,117 | 2,782 | 64 |
| Brown | 2,171 | 5,990 | 5,577 | 4,48 |
| Burleson | 1,361 | 1,762 | 2,924 | 1,14 |
| Burnet | 1,227 | 3,438 | 3,818 | 2,77 |
| Caldwell | 1,974 | 3,171 | 3,647 | 2,23 |
| Calhoun | 1,936 | 3,614 | 3,642 | 2,37 |
| Callahan | 665 | 2,223 | 2,241 | 1,58 |
| Cameron | 13,340 | 20,816 | 25,310 | 16,44 |
| Camp | 1,041 | 1,599 | 2,146 | 1,13 |
| Carson | 561 | 1,868 | 1,542 | 1,26 |
| Cass | 1,981 | 5,303 | 5,134 | 3,71 |
| Castro | 751 | 1,685 | 2,033 | 1,00 |
| Chambers | 1,206 | 2,390 | 2,927 | 1,83 |
| Cherokee | 2,467 | 5,743 | 6,509 | 3,92 |
| Childress | 729 | 1,716 | 1,578 | 1,04 |
| Clay | 1,023 | 1,893 | 2,568 | 1,20 |
| Cochran | 415 | 1,106 | 1,031 | 70 |
| Coke | 358 | 751 | 844 | 51 |
| Coleman | 721 | 2,386 | 2,264 | 1,66 |
| Collin | 4,783 | 17,667 | 14,039 | 21,60 |
| Collingsworth | 501 | 1,250 | 1,169 | 62 |
| Colorado | 1,502 | 3,495 | 3,028 | 2,99 |
| Comal | 1,823 | 6,761 | 4,068 | 6,37 |
| Comanche | 1,176 | 2,608 | 3,414 | 1,29 |
| Concho | 350 | 709 | 715 | 47 |
| Cooke | 1,702 | 6,317 | 4,483 | 4,80 |
| Coryell | 1,235 | 5,077 | 4,710 | 4,14 |

| County | 1972 (D) | 1972 (R) | 1976 (D) | 1976 (R) |
|---|---|---|---|---|
| Cottle | 571 | 564 | 1,047 | 311 |
| Crane | 349 | 1,123 | 664 | 963 |
| Crockett | 329 | 851 | 804 | 802 |
| Crosby | 1,021 | 1,503 | 2,176 | 897 |
| Culberson | 238 | 555 | 407 | 373 |
| Dallam | 327 | 1,271 | 1,029 | 936 |
| Dallas | 129,662 | 305,112 | 196,303 | 263,081 |
| Dawson | 846 | 3,247 | 2,162 | 2,474 |
| Deaf Smith | 1,240 | 3,690 | 2,613 | 2,776 |
| Delta | 581 | 957 | 1,563 | 421 |
| Denton | 9,720 | 19,138 | 18,887 | 20,440 |
| DeWitt | 1,357 | 3,755 | 2,540 | 2,754 |
| Dickens | 534 | 708 | 1,222 | 343 |
| Dimmit | 1,078 | 1,172 | 1,721 | 890 |
| Donley | 350 | 1,229 | 1,095 | 704 |
| Duval | 3,729 | 623 | 4,267 | 661 |
| Eastland | 1,630 | 4,106 | 4,320 | 2,340 |
| Ector | 5,449 | 21,386 | 10,802 | 18,973 |
| Edwards | 109 | 520 | 258 | 412 |
| Ellis | 3,839 | 8,779 | 9,991 | 6,996 |
| El Paso | 32,435 | 49,981 | 45,477 | 42,697 |
| Erath | 1,648 | 4,777 | 4,821 | 2,925 |
| Falls | 1,825 | 3,017 | 4,227 | 2,261 |
| Fannin | 2,295 | 3,826 | 5,845 | 2,102 |
| Fayette | 1,400 | 3,882 | 3,428 | 3,030 |
| Fisher | 933 | 1,207 | 1,993 | 573 |
| Floyd | 841 | 2,181 | 1,991 | 1,402 |
| Foard | 312 | 369 | 706 | 240 |
| Fort Bend | 4,541 | 10,475 | 11,264 | 17,354 |
| Franklin | 546 | 1,059 | 1,636 | 758 |
| Freestone | 1,283 | 2,459 | 2,679 | 1,674 |
| Frio | 1,588 | 1,904 | 2,598 | 1,280 |
| Gaines | 669 | 1,923 | 1,880 | 1,643 |
| Galveston | 22,565 | 30,936 | 37,873 | 25,251 |
| Garza | 446 | 1,153 | 957 | 751 |
| Gillespie | 526 | 3,490 | 1,260 | 3,541 |
| Glasscock | 75 | 288 | 190 | 218 |
| Goliad | 464 | 1,018 | 875 | 846 |
| Gonzales | 1,164 | 2,707 | 3,219 | 1,789 |
| Gray | 1,367 | 7,968 | 3,872 | 6,010 |
| Grayson | 6,952 | 16,769 | 17,015 | 11,981 |
| Gregg | 5,325 | 19,927 | 9,827 | 17,582 |
| Grimes | 1,116 | 2,243 | 2,656 | 1,473 |
| Guadalupe | 3,404 | 8,287 | 6,054 | 6,766 |
| Hale | 2,135 | 7,051 | 5,580 | 5,390 |
| Hall | 607 | 1,303 | 1,633 | 671 |
| Hamilton | 685 | 1,931 | 1,981 | 1,176 |
| Hansford | 202 | 1,947 | 983 | 1,401 |
| Hardeman | 614 | 1,357 | 1,403 | 805 |
| Hardin | 2,952 | 5,190 | 6,558 | 4,046 |
| Harris | 215,916 | 365,672 | 321,897 | 357,336 |
| Harrison | 4,333 | 9,600 | 7,796 | 7,787 |
| Hartley | 206 | 946 | 774 | 811 |
| Haskell | 950 | 1,744 | 2,512 | 838 |
| Hays | 4,068 | 5,406 | 7,005 | 5,714 |
| Hemphill | 214 | 942 | 707 | 858 |
| Henderson | 2,741 | 6,263 | 8,245 | 4,659 |
| Hidalgo | 18,366 | 22,920 | 35,021 | 19,199 |
| Hill | 1,882 | 4,481 | 5,927 | 2,680 |
| Hockley | 1,625 | 4,084 | 3,949 | 3,137 |
| Hood | 949 | 1,743 | 3,181 | 1,857 |
| Hopkins | 1,710 | 3,903 | 4,992 | 2,556 |
| Houston | 1,844 | 3,317 | 3,179 | 2,229 |
| Howard | 2,714 | 7,343 | 6,984 | 4,899 |
| Hudspeth | 250 | 467 | 479 | 395 |
| Hunt | 3,655 | 9,535 | 8,543 | 6,676 |
| Hutchinson | 1,405 | 7,411 | 3,691 | 6,137 |
| Irion | 111 | 363 | 297 | 302 |
| Jack | 775 | 1,719 | 1,814 | 1,049 |
| Jackson | 1,163 | 2,743 | 2,524 | 1,884 |
| Jasper | 2,746 | 4,575 | 5,422 | 3,167 |
| Jeff Davis | 202 | 382 | 309 | 288 |
| Jefferson | 29,909 | 45,819 | 47,581 | 32,451 |
| Jim Hogg | 848 | 765 | 1,645 | 429 |
| Jim Wells | 4,404 | 5,283 | 7,961 | 3,547 |
| Johnson | 3,968 | 10,042 | 10,864 | 7,194 |
| Jones | 1,050 | 3,202 | 3,318 | 2,072 |
| Karnes | 1,780 | 2,639 | 2,996 | 1,675 |
| Kaufman | 2,795 | 5,100 | 6,302 | 3,867 |
| Kendall | 484 | 2,681 | 1,190 | 2,543 |
| Kenedy | 88 | 124 | 139 | 65 |
| Kent | 223 | 465 | 474 | 171 |
| Kerr | 1,511 | 6,039 | 3,767 | 6,021 |
| Kimble | 266 | 971 | 759 | 846 |
| King | 75 | 143 | 100 | 96 |
| Kinney | 234 | 425 | 516 | 318 |
| Kleberg | 4,481 | 5,312 | 5,803 | 3,771 |
| Knox | 638 | 1,148 | 1,498 | 551 |
| Lamar | 2,865 | 7,736 | 8,601 | 4,443 |
| Lamb | 1,350 | 3,981 | 3,374 | 2,413 |
| Lampasas | 688 | 2,251 | 2,376 | 1,563 |
| LaSalle | 567 | 1,073 | 1,294 | 677 |
| Lavaca | 1,429 | 3,288 | 3,458 | 2,466 |
| Lee | 920 | 1,877 | 1,937 | 1,348 |
| Leon | 863 | 1,699 | 2,085 | 1,161 |
| Liberty | 3,311 | 6,111 | 7,086 | 4,552 |
| Limestone | 1,452 | 2,949 | 3,825 | 2,045 |
| Lipscomb | 156 | 1,226 | 644 | 911 |
| Live Oak | 610 | 1,745 | 1,656 | 1,287 |
| Llano | 766 | 2,164 | 2,361 | 1,947 |
| Loving | 7 | 55 | 35 | 47 |
| Lubbock | 15,353 | 43,564 | 24,797 | 38,478 |
| Lynn | 697 | 1,766 | 1,575 | 1,166 |
| Madison | 561 | 1,540 | 1,885 | 1,062 |
| Marion | 1,106 | 1,680 | 1,860 | 1,291 |
| Martin | 287 | 935 | 907 | 698 |
| Mason | 369 | 1,096 | 814 | 805 |
| Matagorda | 2,473 | 5,003 | 4,971 | 3,679 |
| Maverick | 1,710 | 1,477 | 2,840 | 924 |
| McCulloch | 753 | 1,769 | 1,888 | 1,300 |
| McLennan | 15,947 | 33,377 | 30,091 | 25,370 |
| McMullen | 88 | 304 | 194 | 217 |
| Medina | 1,507 | 4,059 | 3,681 | 3,252 |
| Menard | 273 | 644 | 543 | 441 |
| Midland | 4,388 | 18,905 | 7,725 | 19,178 |
| Milam | 2,159 | 3,554 | 4,871 | 2,404 |
| Mills | 388 | 1,089 | 1,012 | 684 |
| Mitchell | 699 | 1,790 | 1,730 | 1,058 |
| Montague | 1,286 | 3,463 | 4,087 | 2,182 |
| Montgomery | 4,358 | 15,067 | 13,718 | 15,739 |
| Moore | 863 | 3,620 | 2,767 | 2,759 |
| Morris | 1,162 | 2,699 | 3,071 | 1,843 |
| Motley | 230 | 657 | 522 | 428 |
| Nacogdoches | 3,656 | 8,757 | 6,697 | 7,315 |
| Navarro | 3,246 | 6,039 | 6,995 | 4,012 |
| Newton | 1,636 | 1,946 | 3,468 | 1,011 |
| Nolan | 1,338 | 3,634 | 3,094 | 2,431 |
| Nueces | 33,277 | 41,682 | 52,755 | 32,797 |
| Ochiltree | 298 | 2,861 | 1,084 | 2,471 |
| Oldham | 173 | 666 | 554 | 354 |
| Orange | 7,172 | 13,234 | 15,177 | 9,147 |
| Palo Pinto | 2,181 | 5,058 | 5,170 | 2,684 |
| Panola | 1,511 | 4,324 | 3,731 | 3,218 |
| Parker | 3,184 | 7,152 | 8,186 | 4,692 |
| Parmer | 495 | 2,304 | 1,914 | 1,487 |
| Pecos | 847 | 2,419 | 1,971 | 2,234 |
| Polk | 1,760 | 3,048 | 4,384 | 2,529 |
| Potter | 6,264 | 18,891 | 11,917 | 13,819 |
| Presidio | 674 | 785 | 1,232 | 687 |
| Rains | 532 | 865 | 1,339 | 510 |
| Randall | 3,470 | 18,557 | 9,074 | 17,115 |
| Reagan | 244 | 703 | 563 | 666 |
| Real | 150 | 483 | 510 | 448 |
| Red River | 1,361 | 3,112 | 3,670 | 1,652 |
| Reeves | 1,510 | 2,427 | 2,613 | 1,711 |
| Refugio | 1,060 | 1,937 | 2,218 | 1,537 |
| Roberts | 71 | 467 | 202 | 350 |
| Robertson | 1,976 | 1,977 | 3,741 | 1,244 |
| Rockwall | 610 | 1,890 | 1,828 | 2,087 |
| Runnels | 739 | 2,752 | 2,068 | 2,203 |
| Rusk | 2,867 | 8,179 | 6,063 | 6,800 |
| Sabine | 936 | 1,333 | 2,391 | 904 |
| San Augustine | 753 | 1,508 | 1,817 | 1,047 |
| San Jacinto | 1,020 | 1,296 | 2,406 | 1,094 |
| San Patricio | 5,097 | 7,179 | 9,469 | 5,853 |
| San Saba | 567 | 1,106 | 1,408 | 582 |
| Schleicher | 250 | 630 | 468 | 516 |
| Scurry | 1,223 | 3,777 | 2,639 | 2,797 |
| Shackelford | 331 | 909 | 764 | 748 |
| Shelby | 1,792 | 4,292 | 4,680 | 2,695 |
| Sherman | 169 | 996 | 718 | 679 |
| Smith | 8,041 | 23,671 | 16,856 | 22,238 |
| Somervell | 284 | 703 | 1,054 | 332 |
| Starr | 3,320 | 2,389 | 4,646 | 664 |
| Stephens | 678 | 2,259 | 1,796 | 1,621 |
| Sterling | 94 | 286 | 174 | 202 |
| Stonewall | 394 | 662 | 812 | 252 |
| Sutton | 245 | 705 | 768 | 831 |
| Swisher | 1,300 | 1,790 | 2,811 | 753 |
| Tarrant | 69,187 | 151,586 | 122,287 | 124,433 |
| Taylor | 6,024 | 22,417 | 14,453 | 19,822 |
| Terrell | 124 | 467 | 321 | 317 |
| Terry | 1,099 | 3,057 | 2,859 | 2,113 |
| Throckmorton | 348 | 568 | 658 | 356 |
| Titus | 1,703 | 3,671 | 4,205 | 2,603 |
| Tom Green | 6,082 | 15,784 | 11,064 | 12,316 |
| Travis | 54,147 | 70,561 | 78,585 | 71,031 |
| Trinity | 826 | 1,467 | 2,100 | 1,042 |
| Tyler | 1,321 | 2,955 | 3,322 | 1,965 |
| Upshur | 1,879 | 4,736 | 4,902 | 3,272 |
| Upton | 256 | 1,186 | 686 | 869 |
| Uvalde | 1,438 | 3,883 | 2,299 | 3,103 |
| Val Verde | 2,049 | 4,052 | 4,603 | 3,476 |
| Van Zandt | 1,939 | 4,839 | 6,449 | 3,385 |
| Victoria | 4,226 | 11,246 | 7,326 | 9,594 |
| Walker | 2,940 | 5,082 | 5,105 | 4,974 |
| Waller | 1,538 | 2,263 | 2,828 | 1,992 |
| Ward | 1,049 | 2,687 | 2,046 | 2,123 |
| Washington | 1,323 | 3,862 | 2,635 | 3,820 |
| Webb | 8,435 | 6,011 | 10,362 | 4,222 |
| Wharton | 3,481 | 6,271 | 5,914 | 4,682 |
| Wheeler | 502 | 1,766 | 1,598 | 1,273 |
| Wichita | 10,948 | 25,197 | 22,017 | 19,024 |
| Wilbarger | 1,139 | 3,183 | 3,280 | 2,145 |
| Willacy | 1,384 | 2,317 | 2,984 | 1,542 |
| Williamson | 3,806 | 6,998 | 9,355 | 7,481 |
| Wilson | 2,072 | 2,953 | 3,973 | 1,926 |
| Winkler | 602 | 2,467 | 1,382 | 1,842 |
| Wise | 1,741 | 4,230 | 5,133 | 2,856 |
| Wood | 1,842 | 4,746 | 4,107 | 3,076 |

| | 1972 | | 1976 | |
|---|---|---|---|---|
| | (D) | (R) | (D) | (R) |
| Yoakum | 457 | 1,952 | 1,181 | 1,477 |
| Young | 1,486 | 3,353 | 3,473 | 2,652 |
| Zapata | 768 | 695 | 1,216 | 462 |
| Zavala | 1,122 | 1,288 | 1,822 | 735 |
| | | | | |
| Totals | 1,154,289 | 2,298,896 | 2,082,319 | 1,953,300 |

## Texas Vote Since 1932

1932 (Pres.), Roosevelt, Dem., 760,348; Hoover, Rep., 97,959; Thomas, Soc., 4,450; Harvey, Lib., 324; Foster, Com., 207; Jackson Party, 104.

1936 (Pres.), Roosevelt, Dem., 734,485; Landon, Rep., 103,874; Lemke, Union, 3,281; Thomas, Soc., 1,075; Colvin, Proh., 514; Browder, Com., 253.

1940 (Pres.), Roosevelt, Dem., 840,151; Willkie, Rep., 199,152; Babson, Proh., 925; Thomas, Soc., 728; Browder, Com., 212.

1944 (Pres.), Roosevelt, Dem., 821,605; Dewey, Rep., 191,425; Texas Regulars, 135,439; Watson, Proh., 1,017; Thomas, Soc., 594; America First, 250.

1948 (Pres.), Truman, Dem., 750,700; Dewey, Rep., 282,240; Thurmond, States' Rights, 106,909; Wallace, Prog., 3,764; Watson, Proh., 2,758; Thomas, Soc., 874.

1952 (Pres.), Eisenhower, Rep., 1,102,878; Stevenson, Dem., 969,228; Hamblen, Proh., 1,983; MacArthur, Christian Nationalist, 833; MacArthur, Constitution, 730; Hallinan, Prog., 294.

1956 (Pres.), Eisenhower, Rep., 1,080,619; Stevenson, Dem., 859,958; Andrews, Ind., 14,591.

1960 (Pres.), Kennedy, Dem., 1,167,932; Nixon, Rep., 1,121,699; Sullivan, Constitution, 18,169; Decker, Proh., 3,870; write-in, 15.

1964 (Pres.), Johnson, Dem., 1,663,185; Goldwater, Rep., 958,566; Lightburn, Constitution, 5,060.

1968 (Pres.), Nixon, Rep., 1,227,844; Humphrey, Dem., 1,266,804; Wallace, 3d party, 584,269; write-in, 489.

1972 (Pres.), Nixon, Rep., 2,298,896; McGovern, Dem., 1,154,289; Schmitz, American, 6,039; Jenness, Soc. Worker, 8,664; others, 3,393.

1976 (Pres.), Carter, Dem., 2,082,319; Ford, Rep., 1,953,300; McCarthy, Ind., 20,118; Anderson, American, 11,442; Camejo, Soc. Workers, 1,723; write-in, 2,982.

## Utah

| | 1972 | | 1976 | |
|---|---|---|---|---|
| | McGov- | Nixon | Carter | Ford |
| | ern | | | |
| County | (D) | (R) | (D) | (R) |
| Beaver | 682 | 1,332 | 963 | 1,088 |
| Box Elder | 2,134 | 9,880 | 3,353 | 9,319 |
| Cache | 4,018 | 16,538 | 5,430 | 16,636 |
| Carbon | 3,335 | 3,956 | 5,157 | 3,360 |
| Daggett | 50 | 204 | 131 | 217 |
| Davis | 7,954 | 29,706 | 14,084 | 31,216 |
| Duchesne | 629 | 2,183 | 1,110 | 2,619 |
| Emery | 769 | 1,666 | 1,771 | 1,717 |
| Garfield | 242 | 1,290 | 539 | 1,163 |
| Grand | 560 | 1,837 | 931 | 1,781 |
| Iron | 1,098 | 5,085 | 1,700 | 4,757 |
| Juab | 691 | 1,629 | 1,091 | 1,290 |
| Kane | 218 | 1,146 | 330 | 1,094 |
| Millard | 777 | 2,689 | 1,224 | 2,484 |
| Morgan | 363 | 1,456 | 701 | 1,356 |
| Piute | 102 | 475 | 265 | 377 |
| Rich | 120 | 604 | 248 | 541 |
| Salt Lake | 64,489 | 132,066 | 86,659 | 144,100 |
| San Juan | 677 | 1,893 | 1,182 | 1,856 |
| Sanpete | 1,220 | 3,995 | 1,925 | 3,683 |
| Sevier | 820 | 3,700 | 1,564 | 3,686 |
| Summit | 836 | 2,209 | 1,282 | 2,316 |
| Tooele | 2,621 | 5,641 | 4,371 | 4,657 |
| Unitah | 716 | 4,712 | 1,342 | 4,017 |
| Utah | 10,828 | 42,179 | 18,327 | 49,328 |
| Wasatch | 693 | 2,046 | 1,092 | 1,940 |
| Washington | 956 | 5,176 | 1,893 | 5,944 |
| Wayne | 183 | 597 | 334 | 555 |
| Weber | 14,503 | 37,753 | 23,111 | 34,811 |
| | | | | |
| Totals | 126,284 | 323,643 | 182,110 | 337,908 |

## Utah Vote Since 1932

1932 (Pres.), Roosevelt, Dem., 116,750; Hoover, Rep., 84,795; Thomas, Soc., 4,087; Foster, Com., 947.

1936 (Pres.), Roosevelt, Dem., 150,246; Landon, Rep., 64,555; Lemke, Union, 1,121; Thomas, Soc., 432;

Browder, Com., 280; Colvin, Proh., 43.

1940 (Pres.), Roosevelt, Dem., 154,277; Willkie, Rep., 93,151; Thomas, Soc., 200; Browder, Com., 191.

1944 (Pres.), Roosevelt, Dem., 150,088; Dewey, Rep., 97,891; Thomas, Soc., 340.

1948 (Pres.), Truman, Dem., 149,151; Dewey, Rep., 124,402; Wallace, Prog., 2,679; Dobbs, Soc. Workers, 73.

1952 (Pres.), Eisenhower, Rep., 194,190; Stevenson, Dem., 135,364.

1956 (Pres.), Eisenhower, Rep., 215,631; Stevenson, Dem., 118,364.

1960 (Pres.), Kennedy, Dem., 169,248; Nixon, Rep., 205,361; Dobbs, Soc. Workers, 100.

1964 (Pres.), Johnson, Dem., 219,628; Goldwater, Rep., 181,785.

1968 (Pres.), Nixon, Rep., 238,728; Humphrey, Dem., 156,665; Wallace, 3d party, 26,906; Halstead, Soc. Worker, 89; Peace and Freedom, 180.

1972 (Pres.), Nixon, Rep., 323,643; McGovern, Dem., 126,284; Schmitz, American, 28,549.

1976 (Pres.), Carter, Dem., 182,110; Ford, Rep., 337,908; Anderson, American, 13,304; McCarthy, Ind., 3,907; MacBride, Libertarian, 2,438; Maddox, Am. Ind., 1,162; Camejo, Soc. Workers, 268; Hall, Comm., 121.

## Vermont

| | 1972 | | 1976 | |
|---|---|---|---|---|
| | McGov- | Nixon | Carter | Ford |
| | ern | | | |
| County | (D) | (R) | (D) | (R) |
| Addison | 3,262 | 6,467 | 4,164 | 5,726 |
| Bennington | 4,804 | 7,542 | 5,443 | 6,712 |
| Caledonia | 3,094 | 6,762 | 3,511 | 5,488 |
| Chittenden | 16,163 | 23,063 | 17,992 | 22,013 |
| Essex | 655 | 1,441 | 1,002 | 1,161 |
| Franklin | 3,898 | 8,109 | 5,610 | 6,190 |
| Grand Isle | 743 | 1,259 | 866 | 1,004 |
| Lamoille | 1,659 | 4,164 | 2,016 | 3,535 |
| Orange | 2,332 | 5,389 | 3,171 | 4,768 |
| Orleans | 2,793 | 4,906 | 3,561 | 4,075 |
| Rutland | 8,261 | 14,143 | 7,613 | 9,867 |
| Washington | 7,596 | 12,421 | 8,764 | 10,919 |
| Windham | 5,925 | 9,062 | 6,794 | 7,928 |
| Windsor | 6,989 | 12,421 | 8,282 | 11,001 |
| | | | | |
| Totals | 68,174 | 117,149 | 78,789 | 100,387 |

## Vermont Vote Since 1932

1932 (Pres.), Roosevelt, Dem., 56,266; Hoover, Rep., 78,984; Thomas, Soc., 1,533; Foster, Com., 195.

1936 (Pres.), Landon, Rep., 81,023; Roosevelt, Dem., 62,124; Browder, Com., 405.

1940 (Pres.), Roosevelt, Dem., 64,269; Willkie, Rep., 78,371; Browder, Com., 411.

1944 (Pres.), Roosevelt, Dem., 53,820; Dewey, Rep., 71,527.

1948 (Pres.), Truman, Dem., 45,557; Dewey, Rep., 75,926; Wallace, Prog., 1,279; Thomas, Soc., 585.

1952 (Pres.), Eisenhower, Rep., 109,717; Stevenson, Dem., 43,355; Hallinan, Prog., 282; Hoopes, Soc., 185.

1956 (Pres.), Eisenhower, Rep., 110,390; Stevenson, Dem., 42,549; scattered, 39.

1960 (Pres.), Kennedy, Dem., 69,186; Nixon, Rep., 98,131.

1964 (Pres.), Johnson, Dem., 107,674; Goldwater, Rep., 54,868.

1968 (Pres.), Nixon, Rep., 85,142; Humphrey, Dem., 70,255; Wallace, 3d party, 5,104; Halstead, Soc. Worker, 295; Gregory, New Party, 579.

1972 (Pres.), Nixon, Rep., 117,149; McGovern, Dem., 68,174; Spock, Liberty Union, 1,010; Jenness, Soc. Worker, 296; scattered, 318.

1976 (Pres.), Carter, Dem., 77,798; Carter, Ind. Vermonter, 991; Ford, Rep., 100,387; McCarthy, Ind., 4,001; Camejo, Soc. Workers, 430; LaRouche, U.S. Labor, 196; scattered, 99.

## Virginia

| | 1972 | | 1976 | |
|---|---|---|---|---|
| | McGov- | Nixon | Carter | Ford |
| | ern | | | |
| County | (D) | (R) | (D) | (R) |
| Accomack | 2,406 | 6,496 | 4,807 | 4,494 |
| Albemarle | 4,303 | 8,447 | 7,310 | 9,084 |
| Alleghany | 1,069 | 2,584 | 2,462 | 1,756 |

| | 1972 (D) | (R) | 1976 (D) | (R) |
|---|---|---|---|---|
| Amelia | 778 | 1,606 | 1,715 | 1,634 |
| Amherst | 1,512 | 4,909 | 3,675 | 3,956 |
| Appomattox | 684 | 2,788 | 1,702 | 1,964 |
| Arlington | 25,877 | 39,406 | 32,536 | 30,972 |
| Augusta | 1,766 | 9,106 | 5,626 | 8,452 |
| Bath | 462 | 1,127 | 1,029 | 888 |
| Bedford | 1,501 | 5,286 | 4,766 | 4,189 |
| Bland | 527 | 1,352 | 961 | 1,047 |
| Botetourt | 1,519 | 3,806 | 4,021 | 3,343 |
| Brunswick | 2,130 | 3,072 | 3,071 | 2,387 |
| Buchanan | 3,566 | 4,801 | 5,791 | 3,850 |
| Buckingham | 1,186 | 2,107 | 2,179 | 1,487 |
| Campbell | 2,055 | 11,676 | 4,354 | 7,442 |
| Caroline | 1,814 | 2,086 | 3,064 | 1,648 |
| Carroll | 1,583 | 5,247 | 4,010 | 4,820 |
| Charles City | 1,177 | 535 | 1,455 | 439 |
| Charlotte | 1,182 | 2,501 | 2,312 | 2,023 |
| Chesterfield | 3,823 | 24,934 | 14,126 | 27,812 |
| Clarke | 715 | 1,816 | 1,276 | 1,440 |
| Craig | 425 | 774 | 1,103 | 546 |
| Culpeper | 1,316 | 3,707 | 2,892 | 3,659 |
| Cumberland | 969 | 1,371 | 1,302 | 1,284 |
| Dickenson | 2,711 | 3,633 | 4,583 | 3,471 |
| Dinwiddie | 1,901 | 3,314 | 3,873 | 2,413 |
| Essex | 808 | 1,482 | 1,306 | 1,380 |
| Fairfax | 54,844 | 112,135 | 92,037 | 110,424 |
| Fauquier | 2,039 | 4,654 | 4,002 | 4,715 |
| Floyd | 708 | 2,444 | 1,728 | 2,071 |
| Fluvanna | 637 | 1,438 | 1,415 | 1,296 |
| Franklin | 2,273 | 4,674 | 6,439 | 3,532 |
| Frederick | 1,604 | 5,367 | 3,389 | 5,162 |
| Giles | 1,869 | 3,671 | 3,779 | 2,731 |
| Gloucester | 1,292 | 3,642 | 3,156 | 3,025 |
| Goochland | 1,254 | 2,127 | 2,259 | 2,104 |
| Grayson | 1,603 | 3,565 | 3,146 | 3,021 |
| Greene | 318 | 1,208 | 895 | 1,095 |
| Greensville | 1,197 | 1,608 | 2,413 | 1,137 |
| Halifax | 2,384 | 5,469 | 4,352 | 4,045 |
| Hanover | 2,200 | 11,095 | 6,069 | 11,559 |
| Henrico | 8,420 | 52,536 | 21,729 | 45,405 |
| Henry | 4,042 | 7,556 | 9,680 | 5,612 |
| Highland | 206 | 774 | 493 | 629 |
| Isle of Wight | 2,305 | 3,555 | 4,145 | 2,718 |
| James City | 1,992 | 3,372 | 3,000 | 3,186 |
| King George | 658 | 1,675 | 1,513 | 1,383 |
| King and Queen | 708 | 1,033 | 1,111 | 778 |
| King William | 797 | 1,839 | 1,501 | 1,597 |
| Lancaster | 1,009 | 2,683 | 1,581 | 2,381 |
| Lee | 2,825 | 4,957 | 5,415 | 4,679 |
| Loudoun | 3,941 | 9,417 | 7,995 | 9,192 |
| Louisa | 1,338 | 2,545 | 2,857 | 2,151 |
| Lunenburg | 1,044 | 2,464 | 1,739 | 1,816 |
| Madison | 639 | 1,864 | 1,466 | 1,710 |
| Mathews | 730 | 2,164 | 1,309 | 1,908 |
| Mecklenburg | 2,804 | 6,381 | 4,076 | 4,423 |
| Middlesex | 724 | 1,697 | 1,312 | 1,608 |
| Montgomery | 3,692 | 9,348 | 7,539 | 7,971 |
| Nelson | 954 | 2,145 | 2,426 | 1,516 |
| New Kent | 633 | 1,370 | 1,338 | 1,259 |
| Northampton | 1,246 | 2,587 | 2,459 | 2,043 |
| Northumberland | 884 | 2,332 | 1,814 | 2,167 |
| Nottoway | 1,308 | 2,979 | 2,558 | 2,486 |
| Orange | 1,032 | 2,758 | 2,309 | 2,549 |
| Page | 1,585 | 4,326 | 3,401 | 3,780 |
| Patrick | 942 | 2,951 | 2,740 | 2,349 |
| Pittsylvania | 4,429 | 12,108 | 7,929 | 9,173 |
| Powhatan | 810 | 1,751 | 1,528 | 2,010 |
| Prince Edward | 1,585 | 3,199 | 2,448 | 2,734 |
| Prince George | 1,084 | 2,405 | 2,630 | 2,254 |
| Prince William | 7,266 | 20,149 | 15,215 | 15,446 |
| Pulaski | 2,311 | 6,281 | 5,546 | 4,764 |
| Rappahannock | 471 | 1,055 | 1,071 | 881 |
| Richmond | 435 | 1,565 | 864 | 1,391 |
| Roanoke | 5,318 | 19,920 | 13,120 | 13,587 |
| Rockbridge | 956 | 3,009 | 2,525 | 2,157 |
| Rockingham | 2,026 | 10,025 | 5,349 | 9,768 |
| Russell | 3,367 | 5,010 | 6,014 | 4,287 |
| Scott | 2,474 | 5,125 | 4,496 | 4,313 |
| Shenandoah | 1,422 | 7,128 | 3,364 | 6,296 |
| Smyth | 2,280 | 6,409 | 5,246 | 5,032 |
| Southampton | 1,498 | 3,225 | 3,399 | 2,366 |
| Spotsylvania | 1,775 | 3,577 | 4,210 | 3,210 |
| Stafford | 1,901 | 5,222 | 4,900 | 4,451 |
| Surry | 988 | 1,067 | 1,829 | 929 |
| Sussex | 1,645 | 2,120 | 2,497 | 1,360 |
| Tazewell | 3,181 | 7,233 | 7,565 | 5,565 |
| Warren | 1,508 | 3,718 | 3,221 | 2,985 |
| Washington | 3,028 | 8,805 | 6,547 | 6,865 |
| Westmoreland | 1,113 | 2,331 | 2,355 | 1,909 |
| Wise | 4,402 | 6,739 | 7,134 | 5,691 |
| Wythe | 1,431 | 4,553 | 3,578 | 4,231 |
| York | 2,302 | 7,745 | 4,736 | 5,603 |
| **Total** | **251,451** | **621,848** | **489,208** | **540,351** |
| **CITIES** | | | | |
| Alexandria | 15,409 | 20,235 | 19,858 | 16,880 |
| Bedford | 529 | 1,407 | 1,122 | 1,043 |
| Bristol | 1,157 | 2,665 | 3,343 | 2,943 |
| Buena Vista | 373 | 990 | 993 | 771 |
| Charlottesville | 5,240 | 7,935 | 6,846 | 6,673 |

| | 1972 (D) | (R) | 1976 (D) | (R) |
|---|---|---|---|---|
| Chesapeake | 7,289 | 17,722 | 17,651 | 12,851 |
| Clifton Forge | 575 | 1,127 | 993 | 770 |
| Colonial Heights | 541 | 5,304 | 2,409 | 4,291 |
| Covington | 948 | 1,910 | 1,820 | 1,173 |
| Danville | 4,148 | 12,463 | 6,425 | 10,235 |
| Emporia | 565 | 1,340 | 899 | 1,055 |
| Fairfax | 2,274 | 5,063 | 3,464 | 4,174 |
| Falls Church | 1,895 | 2,967 | 2,202 | 2,323 |
| Franklin | 738 | 1,416 | 1,116 | 1,127 |
| Fredericksburg | 1,702 | 3,211 | 2,550 | 2,527 |
| Galax | 524 | 1,497 | 1,218 | 1,128 |
| Hampton | 10,648 | 21,897 | 19,202 | 15,021 |
| Harrisonburg | 992 | 3,626 | 1,803 | 3,376 |
| Hopewell | 1,485 | 5,229 | 3,691 | 3,764 |
| Lexington | 695 | 1,345 | 945 | 1,027 |
| Lynchburg | 4,208 | 13,259 | 8,227 | 14,564 |
| Manassas | N.A. | N.A. | 1,646 | 1,992 |
| Manassas Park | N.A. | N.A. | 709 | 444 |
| Martinsville | 2,292 | 3,879 | 3,491 | 3,147 |
| Newport News | 12,233 | 27,169 | 23,058 | 20,914 |
| Norfolk | 25,737 | 38,385 | 39,295 | 28,099 |
| Norton | 463 | 823 | 811 | 577 |
| Petersburg | 5,156 | 6,710 | 7,852 | 5,041 |
| Poquoson | N.A. | N.A. | 1,140 | 1,461 |
| Portsmouth | 13,124 | 20,090 | 22,837 | 12,872 |
| Radford | 1,121 | 2,577 | 2,240 | 1,844 |
| Richmond | 33,055 | 46,244 | 44,687 | 37,176 |
| Roanoke | 9,498 | 18,541 | 20,696 | 14,738 |
| Salem | 1,744 | 5,649 | 4,404 | 4,196 |
| South Boston | 709 | 1,865 | 1,001 | 1,389 |
| Staunton | 1,416 | 5,531 | 2,951 | 4,681 |
| Suffolk | 4,827 | 7,502 | 9,246 | 6,066 |
| Virginia Beach | 10,373 | 38,074 | 25,824 | 34,593 |
| Waynesboro | 1,061 | 4,163 | 2,209 | 3,528 |
| Williamsburg | 1,274 | 1,786 | 1,468 | 1,654 |
| Winchester | 1,418 | 4,647 | 2,346 | 4,075 |
| **Total** | **187,436** | **366,645** | **324,688** | **296,203** |
| **Aggregate** | **438,887** | **988,493** | **813,896** | **836,554** |

## Virginia Vote Since 1932

1932 (Pres.), Roosevelt, Dem., 203,979; Hoover, Rep., 89,637; Thomas, Soc., 2,382; Upshaw, Proh., 1,843; Foster, Com., 86; Cox, Ind. 15.

1936 (Pres.), Roosevelt, Dem., 234,980; Landon, Rep., 98,366; Colvin, Proh., 594; Thomas, Soc., 313; Lemke, Union, 233; Browder, Com., 98.

1940 (Pres.), Roosevelt, Dem., 235,961; Willkie, Rep., 109,363; Babson, Proh., 882; Thomas, Soc., 282; Browder, Com., 71; Aiken, Soc. Lab., 48.

1944 (Pres.), Roosevelt, Dem., 242,276; Dewey, Rep., 145,243; Watson, Proh., 459; Thomas, Soc., 417; Teichert, Soc. Lab., 90.

1948 (Pres.), Truman, Dem., 200,786; Dewey, Rep., 172,070; Thurmond, States' Rights, 43,393; Wallace, Prog., 2,047; Thomas, Soc., 726; Teichert, Soc. Lab., 234.

1952 (Pres.), Eisenhower, Rep., 349,037; Stevenson, Dem., 268,677; Haas, Soc. Lab., 1,160; Hoopes, Social Dem., 504; Hallinan, Prog., 311.

1956 (Pres.), Eisenhower, Rep., 386,459; Stevenson, Dem., 267,760; Andrews, States' Rights, 42,964; Hoopes, Soc. Dem., 444; Haas, Soc. Lab., 351.

1960 (Pres.), Kennedy, Dem., 362,327; Nixon, Rep., 404,521; Coiner, Conservative, 4,204; Haas, Soc. Lab., 397.

1964 (Pres.), Johnson, Dem., 558,038; Goldwater, Rep., 481,334; Haas, Soc. Lab., 2,895.

1968 (Pres.), Nixon, Rep., 590,319; Humphrey, Dem., 442,387; Wallace, 3d party, *320,272; Blomen, Soc. Labor, 4,671; Munn, Prohibition, 601; Gregory, Peace and Freedom, 1,680.

*10,561 votes for Wallace were omitted in the count.

1972 (Pres.), Nixon, Rep., 988,493; McGovern, Dem., 438,887; Schmitz, American, 19,721; Fisher, Soc. Labor, 9,918.

1976 (Pres.), Carter, Dem., 813,896; Ford, Rep., 836,554; Camejo, Soc. Workers, 17,802; Anderson, American, 16,686; LaRouche, U.S. Labor, 7,508; MacBride, Libertarian, 4,648.

## Washington

| | 1972 McGovern (D) | Nixon (R) | 1976 Carter (D) | Ford (R) |
|---|---|---|---|---|
| County | | | | |
| Adams | 1,110 | 3,083 | 1,790 | 2,795 |
| Asotin | 2,559 | 2,912 | 2,898 | 2,752 |
| Benton | 9,824 | 18,517 | 11,306 | 22,135 |
| Chelan | 5,889 | 10,470 | 7,623 | 10,492 |

| | 1972 | | 1976 | |
| | (D) | (R) | (D) | (R) |
|---|---|---|---|---|
| Clallam | 5,620 | 9,372 | 8,268 | 9,132 |
| Clark | 27,179 | 28,775 | 31,080 | 27,938 |
| Columbia | 533 | 1,445 | 829 | 1,153 |
| Cowlitz | 12,682 | 14,431 | 14,958 | 12,531 |
| Douglas | 2,420 | 4,512 | 3,809 | 4,547 |
| Ferry | 560 | 815 | 814 | 776 |
| Franklin | 3,867 | 5,972 | 4,369 | 5,671 |
| Garfield | 481 | 1,004 | 616 | 892 |
| Grant | 5,487 | 9,370 | 7,777 | 9,192 |
| Grays Harbor | 11,786 | 10,839 | 13,478 | 9,464 |
| Island | 3,149 | 7,495 | 5,859 | 7,804 |
| Jefferson | 2,096 | 2,770 | 2,913 | 2,794 |
| King | 212,509 | 298,707 | 248,743 | 279,382 |
| Kitsap | 17,011 | 25,831 | 25,701 | 23,124 |
| Kittitas | 4,299 | 5,464 | 4,858 | 4,765 |
| Klickitat | 2,293 | 3,061 | 2,890 | 2,573 |
| Lewis | 6,946 | 12,071 | 9,026 | 10,933 |
| Lincoln | 1,453 | 3,647 | 1,978 | 2,925 |
| Mason | 3,907 | 4,873 | 6,060 | 4,758 |
| Okanogan | 3,835 | 5,796 | 5,543 | 5,455 |
| Pacific | 3,585 | 3,349 | 4,278 | 2,781 |
| Pend Oreille | 1,071 | 1,746 | 1,533 | 1,516 |
| Pierce | 56,933 | 84,265 | 78,238 | 74,668 |
| San Juan | 906 | 1,786 | 1,467 | 1,998 |
| Skagit | 9,233 | 14,212 | 12,718 | 13,060 |
| Skamania | 1,153 | 1,288 | 1,436 | 1,102 |
| Snohomish | 39,471 | 60,032 | 55,623 | 55,375 |
| Spokane | 44,337 | 74,320 | 55,660 | 68,290 |
| Stevens | 2,390 | 4,839 | 3,824 | 4,719 |
| Thurston | 14,596 | 22,297 | 21,247 | 21,000 |
| Wahkiakum | 796 | 818 | 942 | 704 |
| Walla Walla | 5,364 | 12,579 | 7,012 | 10,883 |
| Whatcom | 15,027 | 22,585 | 19,739 | 20,007 |
| Whitman | 6,248 | 9,548 | 6,197 | 8,168 |
| Yakima | 19,729 | 32,240 | 24,223 | 29,478 |
| **Totals** | **568,334** | **837,135** | **717,323** | **777,732** |

## Washington Vote Since 1932

1932 (Pres.), Roosevelt, Dem., 353,260; Hoover, Rep., 208,645; Harvey, Lib., 30,308; Thomas, Soc., 17,080; Foster, Com., 2,972; Upshaw, Proh., 1,540; Reynolds, Soc. Lab., 1,009.

1936 (Pres.), Roosevelt, Dem., 459,579; Landon, Rep., 206,892; Lemke, Union, 17,463; Thomas, Soc., 3,496; Browder, Com., 1,907; Pellsy, Christian, 1,598; Colvin, Proh., 1,041; Aiken, Soc. Lab., 362.

1940 (Pres.), Roosevelt, Dem., 462,145; Willkie, Rep., 322,123; Thomas, Soc., 4,586; Browder, Com., 2,626; Babson, Proh., 1,686; Aiken, Soc. Lab., 667.

1944 (Pres.), Roosevelt, Dem., 486,774; Dewey, Rep., 361,689; Thomas, Soc., 3,824; Watson, Proh., 2,396; Teichert, Soc. Lab., 1,645.

1948 (Pres.), Truman, Dem., 476,165; Dewey, Rep., 386,315; Wallace, Prog., 31,692; Watson, Proh., 6,117; Thomas, Soc., 3,534; Teichert, Soc. Lab., 1,133; Dobbs, Soc. Workers, 103.

1952 (Pres.), Eisenhower, Rep., 599,107; Stevenson, Dem., 492,845; MacArthur, Christian Nationalist, 7,290; Hallinan, Prog., 2,460; Haas, Soc. Lab., 633; Hoopes, Soc., 254; Dobbs, Soc. Workers, 119.

1956 (Pres.), Eisenhower, Rep., 620,430; Stevenson, Dem., 523,002; Haas, Soc. Lab., 7,457.

1960 (Pres.), Kennedy, Dem., 599,298; Nixon, Rep., 629,273; Haas, Soc. Lab., 10,895; Curtis, Constitution, 1,401; Dobbs, Soc. Workers, 705.

1964 (Pres.), Johnson, Dem., 779,699; Goldwater, Rep., 470,366; Haas, Soc. Labor, 7,772; DeBerry, Freedom Soc., 537.

1968 (Pres.), Nixon, Rep., 588,510; Humphrey, Dem., 616,037; Wallace, 3d party, 96,990; Blomen, Soc. Labor, 488; Cleaver, Peace and Freedom, 1,609; Halstead, Soc. Worker, 270; Mitchell, Free Ballot, 377.

1972 (Pres.), Nixon, Rep., 837,135; McGovern, Dem., 568,334; Schmitz, American, 58,906; Spock, Ind., 2,644; Fisher, Soc. Labor, 1,102; Jenness, Soc. Worker, 623; Hall, Communist, 566; Hospers, Libertarian, 1,537.

1976 (Pres.), Carter, Dem., 717,323; Ford, Rep., 777,732; McCarthy, Ind., 36,986; Maddox, Amer. Ind., 8,585; Anderson, American, 5,046; MacBride, Libertarian, 5,042; Wright, People's, 1,124; Camejo, Soc. Workers, 905; LaRouche, U.S. Labor, 903; Hall, Comm., 817; Levin, Soc. Labor, 713; Zeidler, Socialist, 358.

## West Virginia

| | 1972 | | 1976 | |
| | McGovern | Nixon | Carter | Ford |
| County | (D) | (R) | (D) | (R) |
|---|---|---|---|---|
| Barbour | 2,258 | 4,432 | 3,647 | 3,235 |
| Berkeley | 4,523 | 10,954 | 8,216 | 8,935 |
| Boone | 5,342 | 5,985 | 8,528 | 3,072 |
| Braxton | 2,771 | 3,155 | 4,012 | 1,913 |
| Brooke | 5,226 | 7,544 | 8,197 | 4,792 |
| Cabell | 14,312 | 29,582 | 20,811 | 19,644 |
| Calhoun | 1,528 | 1,992 | 2,173 | 1,283 |
| Clay | 1,830 | 2,168 | 2,662 | 1,282 |
| Doddridge | 645 | 2,284 | 1,245 | 1,804 |
| Fayette | 9,966 | 11,876 | 15,496 | 5,459 |
| Gilmer | 1,359 | 2,056 | 2,245 | 1,371 |
| Grant | 614 | 3,556 | 1,323 | 2,976 |
| Greenbrier | 4,423 | 8,827 | 8,291 | 5,862 |
| Hampshire | 1,637 | 3,084 | 3,104 | 2,097 |
| Hancock | 6,727 | 10,634 | 10,627 | 6,771 |
| Hardy | 1,510 | 2,690 | 2,993 | 1,858 |
| Harrison | 12,910 | 22,196 | 21,467 | 15,172 |
| Jackson | 3,007 | 7,226 | 5,334 | 5,360 |
| Jefferson | 2,782 | 4,822 | 5,166 | 3,864 |
| Kanawha | 38,032 | 65,021 | 53,602 | 42,213 |
| Lewis | 2,062 | 5,778 | 3,960 | 3,736 |
| Lincoln | 3,876 | 4,673 | 5,260 | 2,997 |
| Logan | 10,045 | 9,533 | 13,122 | 4,021 |
| Marion | 11,864 | 16,095 | 17,800 | 10,391 |
| Marshall | 6,378 | 10,966 | 8,641 | 6,705 |
| Mason | 4,008 | 7,129 | 6,769 | 5,205 |
| McDowell | 7,826 | 17,846 | 10,557 | 4,107 |
| Mercer | 3,276 | 7,157 | 14,761 | 10,791 |
| Mineral | 5,585 | 7,484 | 5,898 | 5,130 |
| Mingo | 10,721 | 16,758 | 8,655 | 3,010 |
| Monongalia | 2,114 | 3,716 | 16,163 | 11,827 |
| Monroe | 1,118 | 3,014 | 3,297 | 2,750 |
| Morgan | 6,811 | 8,942 | 1,929 | 2,369 |
| Nicholas | 3,628 | 5,907 | 6,235 | 3,462 |
| Ohio | 10,491 | 18,435 | 11,817 | 12,476 |
| Pendleton | 1,248 | 2,207 | 2,104 | 1,554 |
| Pleasants | 1,207 | 2,025 | 1,699 | 1,608 |
| Pocahontas | 1,635 | 2,391 | 2,330 | 1,740 |
| Preston | 2,977 | 7,807 | 5,595 | 5,719 |
| Putnam | 4,771 | 8,265 | 8,226 | 6,334 |
| Raleigh | 10,586 | 19,150 | 19,768 | 10,637 |
| Randolph | 3,809 | 6,923 | 7,265 | 4,822 |
| Ritchie | 990 | 3,635 | 1,941 | 2,874 |
| Roane | 2,386 | 4,253 | 3,519 | 3,216 |
| Summers | 2,518 | 3,895 | 3,943 | 2,254 |
| Taylor | 2,085 | 4,385 | 3,905 | 2,891 |
| Tucker | 1,457 | 2,163 | 2,323 | 1,396 |
| Tyler | 1,125 | 3,362 | 1,817 | 2,514 |
| Upshur | 1,795 | 6,449 | 3,513 | 4,789 |
| Wayne | 6,251 | 9,775 | 9,958 | 6,009 |
| Webster | 2,069 | 2,114 | 2,931 | 971 |
| Wetzel | 3,276 | 6,046 | 5,042 | 3,793 |
| Wirt | 691 | 1,442 | 1,182 | 1,031 |
| Wood | 10,886 | 27,315 | 17,025 | 18,348 |
| Wyoming | 4,468 | 7,926 | 7,775 | 4,286 |
| **Totals** | **277,435** | **484,964** | **435,864** | **314,726** |

## West Virginia Vote Since 1932

1932 (Pres.), Roosevelt, Dem., 405,124; Hoover, Rep., 330,731; Thomas, Soc., 5,133; Upshaw, Proh., 2,342; Foster, Com., 444.

1936 (Pres.), Roosevelt, Dem., 502,582; Landon, Rep., 325,358; Colvin, Prog., 1,173; Thomas, Soc., 832.

1940 (Pres.), Roosevelt, Dem., 495,662; Willkie, Rep., 372,414.

1944 (Pres.), Roosevelt, Dem., 392,777; Dewey, Rep., 322,819.

1948 (Pres.), Truman, Dem., 429,188; Dewey, Rep., 316,251; Wallace, Prog., 3,311.

1952 (Pres.), Eisenhower, Rep., 419,970; Stevenson, Dem., 453,578.

1956 (Pres.), Eisenhower, Rep., 449,297; Stevenson, Dem., 381,534.

1960 (Pres.), Kennedy, Dem., 441,786; Nixon, Rep., 395,995.

1964 (Pres.), Johnson, Dem., 538,087; Goldwater, Rep., 253,953.

1968 (Pres.), Nixon, Rep., 307,555; Humphrey, Dem., 374,091; Wallace, 3d party, 72,560.

1972 (Pres.), Nixon, Rep., 484,964; McGovern, Dem., 277,435.

1976 (Pres.), Carter, Dem., 435,864; Ford, Rep., 314,726.

## Wisconsin

| County | 1972 McGovern (D) | 1972 Nixon (R) | 1976 Carter (D) | 1976 Ford (R) |
|---|---|---|---|---|
| Adams | 1,833 | 2,200 | 3,089 | 2,377 |
| Ashland | 3,771 | 3,478 | 4,688 | 3,045 |
| Barron | 5,376 | 8,418 | 8,678 | 7,393 |
| Bayfield | 2,736 | 3,045 | 3,885 | 2,624 |
| Brown | 26,511 | 37,101 | 33,572 | 36,571 |
| Buffalo | 2,461 | 3,079 | 3,448 | 2,844 |
| Burnett | 2,389 | 2,972 | 3,720 | 2,573 |
| Calumet | 4,804 | 6,446 | 6,241 | 6,589 |
| Chippewa | 8,210 | 8,451 | 11,538 | 8,137 |
| Clark | 4,617 | 7,138 | 7,238 | 6,095 |
| Columbia | 7,083 | 10,122 | 9,457 | 10,075 |
| Crawford | 2,487 | 3,705 | 3,629 | 3,393 |
| Dane | 79,567 | 56,020 | 82,321 | 63,466 |
| Dodge | 9,898 | 17,068 | 13,643 | 17,335 |
| Door | 3,430 | 6,503 | 4,553 | 6,557 |
| Douglas | 11,054 | 8,419 | 13,478 | 6,999 |
| Dunn | 5,681 | 6,660 | 7,862 | 6,751 |
| Eau Claire | 14,300 | 15,883 | 18,263 | 16,388 |
| Florence | 757 | 971 | 965 | 922 |
| Fond duLac | N.A. | N.A. | 16,571 | 22,226 |
| Forest | 1,678 | 1,856 | 2,574 | 1,604 |
| Grant | 6,915 | 11,873 | 9,639 | 12,016 |
| Green | 3,634 | 7,422 | 5,632 | 7,085 |
| Green Lake | 2,174 | 5,046 | 3,411 | 5,020 |
| Iowa | 3,131 | 4,387 | 4,252 | 4,195 |
| Iron | 1,648 | 1,723 | 2,399 | 1,340 |
| Jackson | 2,445 | 3,937 | 3,735 | 3,406 |
| Jefferson | 9,303 | 14,621 | 12,577 | 15,528 |
| Juneau | 2,943 | 4,833 | 4,512 | 4,242 |
| Kenosha | 19,441 | 24,041 | 27,585 | 22,349 |
| Kewaunee | 3,360 | 4,802 | 4,607 | 4,447 |
| La Crosse | 12,152 | 21,992 | 16,674 | 24,188 |
| La Fayette | 2,804 | 4,898 | 3,839 | 4,131 |
| Langlade | 3,011 | 4,368 | 4,134 | 4,630 |
| Lincoln | 4,175 | 6,206 | 5,800 | 5,672 |
| Manitowoc | 16,489 | 16,599 | 19,819 | 16,039 |
| Marathon | 18,500 | 21,454 | 24,934 | 21,898 |
| Marinette | 5,900 | 8,740 | 8,482 | 8,591 |
| Marquette | 1,537 | 2,682 | 2,516 | 2,607 |
| Menominee | 608 | 355 | 766 | 324 |
| Milwaukee | 210,802 | 191,874 | 249,739 | 192,008 |
| Monroe | 3,640 | 7,625 | 6,465 | 7,242 |
| Oconto | 4,041 | 6,511 | 6,541 | 6,232 |
| Oneida | 4,262 | 6,811 | 7,216 | 7,347 |
| Outagamie | 17,477 | 27,533 | 23,079 | 28,363 |
| Ozaukee | 8,503 | 15,759 | 11,271 | 19,817 |
| Pepin | 1,409 | 1,458 | 1,955 | 1,312 |
| Pierce | 5,611 | 5,899 | 8,035 | 5,676 |
| Polk | 5,738 | 6,567 | 8,489 | 6,159 |
| Portage | 13,564 | 9,346 | 15,912 | 9,520 |
| Price | 2,831 | 3,694 | 4,028 | 3,204 |
| Racine | 27,778 | 38,490 | 36,740 | 37,088 |
| Richland | 2,492 | 5,062 | 3,634 | 4,466 |
| Rock | 21,033 | 30,361 | 28,048 | 28,325 |
| Rusk | 3,075 | 3,007 | 4,050 | 2,724 |
| St. Croix | 7,488 | 8,553 | 10,601 | 7,685 |
| Sauk | 6,980 | 10,285 | 9,204 | 9,577 |
| Sawyer | 1,765 | 3,081 | 3,055 | 2,720 |
| Shawano | 3,940 | 8,807 | 6,751 | 8,505 |
| Sheboygan | 21,114 | 21,500 | 24,226 | 22,332 |
| Taylor | 2,934 | 4,125 | 4,101 | 3,591 |
| Trempealeau | 4,232 | 5,723 | 6,218 | 5,341 |
| Vernon | 3,407 | 6,836 | 5,534 | 6,132 |
| Vilas | 1,907 | 4,422 | 3,209 | 4,929 |
| Walworth | 8,598 | 17,823 | 12,418 | 18,091 |
| Washburn | 2,336 | 3,220 | 3,503 | 2,787 |
| Washington | 10,434 | 15,338 | 14,422 | 18,798 |
| Waukesha | 34,573 | 59,399 | 47,487 | 70,418 |
| Waupaca | 4,418 | 11,040 | 6,857 | 10,849 |
| Waushara | 2,094 | 4,466 | 3,485 | 4,449 |
| Winnebago | 20,450 | 29,488 | 24,485 | 32,149 |
| Wood | 10,415 | 14,806 | 14,728 | 15,479 |
| **Totals** | **810,174** | **989,430** | **1,040,232** | **1,004,987** |

### Wisconsin Vote Since 1932

1932 (Pres.), Roosevelt, Dem., 707,410; Hoover, Rep., 347,741; Thomas, Soc., 53,379; Foster, Com., 3,112; Upshaw Proh., 2,672; Reynolds, Soc., Lab., 494.

1936 (Pres.), Roosevelt, Dem., 802,984; Landon, Rep., 380,828; Lemke, Union, 60,297; Thomas, Soc., 10,626; Browder, Com., 2,197; Colvin, Proh., 1,071; Aiken, Soc. Lab., 557.

1940 (Pres.), Roosevelt, Dem., 704,821; Willkie, Rep., 679,260; Thomas, Soc., 15,071; Browder, Com., 2,394; Babson, Proh., 2,148; Aiken, Soc. Lab., 1,882.

1944 (Pres.), Roosevelt, Dem., 650,413; Dewey, Rep., 674,532; Thomas, Soc., 13,205; Teichert, Soc. Lab., 1,002.

1948 (Pres.), Truman, Dem., 647,310; Dewey, Rep., 590,959; Wallace, Prog., 25,282; Thomas, Soc., 12,547; Teichert, Soc. Lab., 399; Dobbs, Soc. Work., 303.

1952 (Pres.), Eisenhower, Rep., 979,744; Stevenson, Dem., 622,175; Hallinan, Ind., 2,174; Dobbs, Ind., 1,350; Hoopes, Ind., 1,157; Haas, Ind., 770.

1956 (Pres.), Eisenhower, Rep., 954,844; Stevenson, Dem., 586,768; Andrews, Ind., 6,918; Hoopes, Soc., 754; Haas, Soc. Lab., 710; Dobbs, Soc. Workers, 564.

1960 (Pres.), Kennedy, Dem., 830,805; Nixon, Rep., 895,175; Dobbs, Soc. Workers, 1,792; Haas, Soc. Lab., 1,310.

1964 (Pres.), Johnson, Dem., 1,050,424; Goldwater, Rep., 638,495; DeBerry, Soc. Worker, 1,692; Haas, Soc. Lab., 1,204.

1968 (Pres.), Nixon, Rep., 809,997; Humphrey, Dem., 748,804; Wallace, 3d party, 127,835; Blomen, Soc. Labor, 1,338; Halstead, Soc. Worker, 1,222; scattered, 2,342.

1972 (Pres.) Nixon, Rep., 989,430; McGovern, Dem., 810,174; Schmitz, American, 47,525; Spock, Ind., 2,701; Fisher, Soc. Labor, 998; Hall, Communist, 663; Reed, Ind., 506; scattered, 893.

1976 (Pres.), Carter, Dem., 1,040,232; Ford, Rep., 1,004,987; McCarthy, Ind., 34,943; Maddox, Amer. Ind., 8,552; Zeidler, Socialist, 4,298; MacBride, Liber., 3,814; Camejo, Soc. Work., 1,691; Wright, People's, 943; Hall, Comm., 749; LaRouche, U.S. Lab., 738; Levin, Soc. Lab., 389; Scattered, 2,839.

## Wyoming

| County | 1972 McGovern (D) | 1972 Nixon (R) | 1976 Carter (D) | 1976 Ford (R) |
|---|---|---|---|---|
| Albany | 4,873 | 7,021 | 4,663 | 6,734 |
| Big Horn | 1,049 | 3,244 | 1,618 | 3,117 |
| Campbell | 783 | 2,953 | 1,620 | 3,306 |
| Carbon | 2,292 | 4,037 | 3,010 | 3,556 |
| Converse | 682 | 2,312 | 1,150 | 2,188 |
| Crook | 339 | 1,760 | 653 | 1,438 |
| Fremont | 3,248 | 7,359 | 4,423 | 6,584 |
| Goshen | 1,515 | 3,629 | 2,262 | 2,764 |
| Hot Springs | 689 | 1,678 | 958 | 1,413 |
| Johnson | 436 | 2,203 | 797 | 2,042 |
| Laramie | 7,791 | 15,010 | 12,040 | 14,061 |
| Lincoln | 969 | 2,459 | 1,555 | 2,464 |
| Natrona | 6,514 | 15,649 | 8,640 | 13,761 |
| Niobrara | 289 | 1,245 | 427 | 1,042 |
| Park | 1,950 | 5,890 | 2,656 | 5,878 |
| Platte | 925 | 2,200 | 1,593 | 1,844 |
| Sheridan | 2,874 | 6,432 | 3,206 | 5,382 |
| Sublette | 304 | 1,348 | 528 | 1,284 |
| Sweetwater | 3,713 | 5,175 | 5,575 | 4,937 |
| Teton | 810 | 2,182 | 1,204 | 2,667 |
| Uinta | 968 | 2,011 | 1,559 | 2,124 |
| Washakie | 825 | 2,604 | 1,168 | 2,361 |
| Weston | 520 | 2,063 | 934 | 1,770 |
| **Totals** | **44,358** | **100,464** | **62,239** | **92,717** |

### Wyoming Vote Since 1932

1932 (Pres.), Roosevelt, Dem., 54,370; Hoover, Rep., 39,583; Thomas, Soc., 2,829; Foster, Com., 180.

1936 (Pres.), Roosevelt, Dem., 62,624; Landon, Rep., 38,739; Lemke, Union, 1,653; Thomas, Soc., 200; Browder, Com., 91; Colvin, Proh., 75.

1940 (Pres.), Roosevelt, Dem., 59,287; Willkie, Rep., 52,633; Babson, Proh., 172; Thomas, Soc., 148.

1944 (Pres.), Roosevelt, Dem., 49,419; Dewey, Rep., 51,921.

1948 (Pres.), Truman, Dem., 52,354; Dewey, Rep., 47,947; Wallace, Prog., 931; Thomas, Soc., 137; Teichert, Soc. Lab., 56.

1952 (Pres.), Eisenhower, Rep., 81,047; Stevenson, Dem., 47,934; Hamblen, Proh., 194; Hoopes, Soc., 40; Haas, Soc. Lab., 36.

1956 (Pres.), Eisenhower, Rep., 74,573; Stevenson, Dem., 49,554.

1960 (Pres.), Kennedy, Dem., 63,331; Nixon, Rep., 77,451.

1964 (Pres.), Johnson, Dem., 80,718; Goldwater, Rep., 61,998.

1968 (Pres.), Nixon, Rep., 70,927; Humphrey, Dem., 45,173; Wallace, 3d party, 11,105.

1972 (Pres.), Nixon, Rep., 100,464; McGovern, Dem., 44,358; Schmitz, American, 748.

1976 (Pres.), Carter, Dem., 62,239; Ford, Rep., 92,717; McCarthy, Ind., 624; Reagan, Ind., 307; Anderson, Amer., 290; MacBride, Libertarian, 89; Brown, Ind., 47; Maddox, Amer. Ind., 30.

## Major Parties' Popular and Electoral Vote for President

(F) Federalist; (D) Democrat; (R) Republican; (DR) Democrat Republican; (NR) National Republican;
(W) Whig; (P) People's; (PR) Progressive; (SR) States' Rights; (LR) Liberal Republican; Asterisk (*)—See notes.

| Year | President elected | Popular | Elec. | Losing candidate | Popular | Elec. |
|------|-------------------|---------|-------|------------------|---------|-------|
| 1789 | George Washington (F) | Unknown | 69 | No opposition | | |
| 1792 | George Washington (F) | Unknown | 132 | No opposition | | |
| 1796 | John Adams (F). | Unknown | 71 | Thomas Jefferson (DR) | Unknown | 68 |
| 1800* | Thomas Jefferson (DR) | Unknown | 73 | Aaron Burr (DR) | Unknown | 73 |
| 1804 | Thomas Jefferson (DR) | Unknown | 162 | Charles Pinckney (F) | Unknown | 14 |
| 1808 | James Madison (DR). | Unknown | 122 | Charles Pinckney (F) | Unknown | 47 |
| 1812 | James Madison (DR). | Unknown | 128 | DeWitt Clinton (F) | Unknown | 89 |
| 1816 | James Monroe (DR) | Unknown | 183 | Rufus King (F) | Unknown | 34 |
| 1820 | James Monroe (DR) | Unknown | 231 | John Quincy Adams (DR) | Unknown | 1 |
| 1824* | John Quincy Adams (NR) | 105,321 | 84 | Andrew Jackson (D) | 155,872 | 99 |
| | | | | Henry Clay (DR) | 46,587 | 37 |
| | | | | William H. Crawford (DR) | 44,282 | 41 |
| 1828 | Andrew Jackson (D) | 647,231 | 178 | John Quincy Adams (NR) | 509,097 | 83 |
| 1832 | Andrew Jackson (D) | 687,502 | 219 | Henry Clay (DR) | 530,189 | 49 |
| 1836 | Martin Van Buren (D) | 762,678 | 170 | William H. Harrison (W) | 548,007 | 73 |
| 1840 | William H. Harrison (W) | 1,275,017 | 234 | Martin Van Buren (D) | 1,128,702 | 60 |
| 1844 | James K. Polk (D) | 1,337,243 | 170 | Henry Clay (W). | 1,299,068 | 105 |
| 1848 | Zachary Taylor (W). | 1,360,101 | 163 | Lewis Cass (D) | 1,220,544 | 127 |
| 1852 | Franklin Pierce (D) | 1,601,474 | 254 | Winfield Scott (W) | 1,386,578 | 42 |
| 1856 | James C. Buchanan (D) | 1,927,995 | 174 | John C. Fremont (R) | 1,391,555 | 114 |
| 1860 | Abraham Lincoln (R) | 1,866,352 | 180 | Stephen A. Douglas (D) | 1,375,157 | 12 |
| | | | | John C. Breckinridge (D) | 845,763 | 72 |
| | | | | John Bell (Const. Union) | 589,581 | 39 |
| 1864 | Abraham Lincoln (R) | 2,216,067 | 212 | George McClellan (D) | 1,808,725 | 21 |
| 1868 | Ulysses S. Grant (R) | 3,015,071 | 214 | Horatio Seymour (D). | 2,709,615 | 80 |
| 1872* | Ulysses S. Grant (R) | 3,597,070 | 286 | Horace Greeley (D-LR) | 2,834,079 | . . . |
| 1876* | Rutherford B. Hayes (R). | 4,033,950 | 185 | Samuel J. Tilden (D) | 4,284,757 | 184 |
| 1880 | James A. Garfield (R) | 4,449,053 | 214 | Winfield S. Hancock (D) | 4,442,030 | 155 |
| 1884 | Grover Cleveland (D) | 4,911,017 | 219 | James G. Blaine (R) | 4,848,334 | 182 |
| 1888* | Benjamin Harrison (R) | 5,444,337 | 233 | Grover Cleveland (D) | 5,540,050 | 168 |
| 1892 | Grover Cleveland (D) | 5,554,414 | 277 | Benjamin Harrison (R) | 5,190,802 | 145 |
| | | | | James Weaver (P) | 1,027,329 | 22 |
| 1896 | William McKinley (R) | 7,035,638 | 271 | William J. Bryan (D-P) | 6,467,946 | 176 |
| 1900 | William McKinley (R) | 7,219,530 | 292 | William J. Bryan (D) | 6,358,071 | 155 |
| 1904 | Theodore Roosevelt (R) | 7,628,834 | 336 | Alton B. Parker (D) | 5,084,491 | 140 |
| 1908 | William H. Taft (R) | 7,679,006 | 321 | William J. Bryan (D) | 6,409,106 | 162 |
| 1912 | Woodrow Wilson (D) | 6,286,214 | 435 | Theodore Roosevelt (PR) | 4,216,020 | 88 |
| | | | | William H. Taft (R) | 3,483,922 | 8 |
| 1916 | Woodrow Wilson (D) | 9,129,606 | 277 | Charles E. Hughes (R). | 8,538,221 | 254 |
| 1920 | Warren G. Harding (R) | 16,152,200 | 404 | James M. Cox (D) | 9,147,353 | 127 |
| 1924 | Calvin Coolidge (R). | 15,725,016 | 382 | John W. Davis (D) | 8,385,586 | 136 |
| | | | | Robert M. LaFollette (PR) | 4,822,856 | 13 |
| 1928 | Herbert Hoover (R). | 21,392,190 | 444 | Alfred E. Smith (D) | 15,016,443 | 87 |
| 1932 | Franklin D. Roosevelt (D) | 22,821,857 | 472 | Herbert Hoover (R) | 15,761,841 | 59 |
| | | | | Norman Thomas (Socialist) | 884,781 | . . . |
| 1936 | Franklin D. Roosevelt (D) | 27,751,597 | 523 | Alfred Landon (R) | 16,679,583 | 8 |
| 1940 | Franklin D. Roosevelt (D) | 27,243,466 | 449 | Wendell Willkie (R). | 22,304,755 | 82 |
| 1944 | Franklin D. Roosevelt (D) | 25,602,505 | 432 | Thomas E. Dewey (R) | 22,006,278 | 99 |
| 1948 | Harry S. Truman (D) | 24,105,812 | 303 | Thomas E. Dewey (R) | 21,970,065 | 189 |
| | | | | J. Strom Thurmond (SR) | 1,169,021 | 39 |
| | | | | Henry A. Wallace (PR) | 1,157,172 | . . . |
| 1952 | Dwight D. Eisenhower (R) | 33,936,252 | 442 | Adlai E. Stevenson (D) | 27,314,992 | 89 |
| 1956* | Dwight D. Eisenhower (R) | 35,585,316 | 457 | Adlai E. Stevenson (D) | 26,031,322 | 73 |
| 1960* | John F. Kennedy (D) | 34,227,096 | 303 | Richard M. Nixon (R). | 34,108,546 | 219 |
| 1964 | Lyndon B. Johnson (D) | 43,126,506 | 486 | Barry M. Goldwater (R) | 27,176,799 | 52 |
| 1968 | Richard M. Nixon (R) | 31,785,480 | 301 | Hubert H. Humphrey (D) | 31,275,166 | 191 |
| | | | | George C. Wallace (3d party) | 9,906,473 | 46 |
| 1972* | Richard M. Nixon (R) | 47,165,234 | 520 | George S. McGovern (D) | 28,168,110 | 17 |
| 1976* | Jimmy Carter (D) | 40,825,839 | 297 | Gerald R. Ford (R) | 39,147,770 | 240 |

1800—Elected by House of Representatives because of tied electoral vote.
1824—Elected by House of Representatives. No candidate polled a majority.
1872—Greeley died Nov. 29, 1872. His electoral votes were split among 4 individuals.
1876—Fla., La., Ore., and S. C. election returns were disputed. Congress in joint session (Mar. 2, 1877) declared Hayes and Wheeler elected President and Vice-President.
1888—Cleveland had more votes than Harrison but the 233 electoral votes cast for Harrison against the 168 for Cleveland elected Harrison president.
1956—Democrats elected 74 electors but one from Alabama refused to vote for Stevenson.
1960—Sen. Harry F. Byrd (D-Va.) received 15 electoral votes.
1972—John Hospers of Cal. and Theodora Nathan of Ore. received one vote from an elector of Virginia.
1976—Ronald Reagan of Cal. received one vote from an elector of Washington.

## Electoral Votes for President, 1960-76

The Constitution, Article 2, Section 1 (consult index), provides for the appointment of electors, the counting of the electoral ballots and the procedure in the event of a tie. (*see Electoral College.*)

| State | 1960 R | 1960 D | 1964 R | 1964 D | 1968 R | 1968 D | 1968 3d | 1972 R | 1972 D | 1976 R | 1976 D |
|---|---|---|---|---|---|---|---|---|---|---|---|
| Ala. | | 5 | 10 | | | | 10 | 9 | | | 9 |
| Alas. | 3 | | | 3 | 3 | | | 3 | | 3 | |
| Ariz. | 4 | | 5 | | 5 | | | 6 | | 6 | |
| Ark. | | 8 | | 6 | | | 6 | 6 | | | 6 |
| Cal. | 32 | | | 40 | 40 | | | 45 | | 45 | |
| Col. | 6 | | | 6 | 6 | | | 7 | | 7 | |
| Conn. | | 8 | | 8 | | 8 | | | 8 | | 8 |
| Del. | | 3 | | 3 | 3 | | | 3 | | | 3 |
| D.C. | | | | 3 | | 3 | | | 3 | | 3 |
| Fla. | 10 | | 14 | | 14 | | | 17 | | | 17 |
| Ga. | | 12 | 12 | | | | 12 | 12 | | | 12 |
| Ha. | | 3 | | 4 | | 4 | | 4 | | | 4 |
| Ida. | 4 | | 4 | | 4 | | | 4 | | 4 | |
| Ill. | | 27 | | 26 | 26 | | | 26 | | 26 | |
| Ind. | 13 | | | 13 | 13 | | | 13 | | 13 | |
| Ia. | 10 | | | 9 | 9 | | | 8 | | 8 | |
| Kan. | 8 | | | 7 | 7 | | | 7 | | 7 | |
| Ky. | 10 | | | 9 | 9 | | | 9 | | | 9 |
| La. | | 10 | 10 | | | | 10 | 10 | | | 10 |
| Me. | 5 | | | 4 | | 4 | | 4 | | 4 | |
| Md. | | 9 | | 10 | | 10 | | | 10 | | 10 |
| Mass. | | 16 | | 14 | | 14 | | | 14 | | 14 |
| Mich. | | 20 | | 21 | | 21 | | 21 | | 21 | |
| Minn. | | 11 | | 10 | | 10 | | | 10 | | 10 |
| Miss. | | (¹) | 7 | | | | 7 | 7 | | | 7 |
| Mo. | | 13 | | 12 | | 12 | | 12 | | | 12 |
| Mon. | 4 | | | 4 | 4 | | | 4 | | 4 | |
| Neb. | 6 | | | 5 | 5 | | | 5 | | 5 | |
| Nev. | | 3 | | 3 | 3 | | | 3 | | 3 | |
| N.H. | 4 | | | 4 | 4 | | | 4 | | 4 | |
| N.J. | 16 | | | 17 | 17 | | | 17 | | 17 | |
| N.M. | | 4 | | 4 | 4 | | | 4 | | 4 | |
| N.Y. | | 45 | | 43 | | 43 | | 41 | | | 41 |
| N.C. | | 14 | | 13 | 12 | | (³) | 13 | | | 13 |
| N.D. | 4 | | | 4 | 4 | | | 3 | | 3 | |
| Oh. | 25 | | | 26 | 26 | | | 25 | | | 25 |
| Okla. | 7 | | 8 | | 8 | | | 8 | | 8 | |
| Ore. | 6 | | | 6 | 6 | | | 6 | | 6 | |
| Pa. | | 32 | | 29 | | 29 | | 27 | | | 27 |
| R.I. | | 4 | | 4 | | 4 | | | 4 | | 4 |
| S.C. | | 8 | 8 | | 8 | | | 8 | | | 8 |
| S.D. | 4 | | | 4 | 4 | | | 4 | | 4 | |
| Tenn. | 11 | | | 11 | 11 | | | 10 | | | 10 |
| Tex. | | 24 | | 25 | | 25 | | 26 | | | 26 |
| Ut. | 4 | | | 4 | 4 | | | 4 | | 4 | |
| Vt. | 3 | | | 3 | 3 | | | 3 | | 3 | |
| Va. | 12 | | | 12 | 12 | | | *11 | | 12 | |
| Wash. | 9 | | | 9 | | 9 | | 9 | | *8 | |
| W.Va. | | 8 | | 7 | | 7 | | 6 | | | 6 |
| Wis. | 12 | | | 12 | 12 | | | 11 | | | 11 |
| Wy. | 3 | | | 3 | 3 | | | 3 | | 3 | |
| **Totals** | 219 | 303 | 52 | 486 | 301 | 191 | 46 | 520 | 17 | 240 | 297 |
| **Plurality** | | '84 | | 434 | 110 | | | *503 | | | 57 |

(1) In 1960 Sen. Harry F. Byrd (D-Va.) got 15 electoral votes including those of 8 unpledged Miss. Dem. electors, 6 unpledged Ala. Dem., and one Okla. Rep. (2) First Presidential election. (3) In 1968 in N. C. one Rep. elector cast his ballot for Wallace. (4) In 1972 one Rep. elector in Va. cast his ballot for John Hospers. (5) In 1976 one Rep. elector in Wash. cast his ballot for Reagan.

---

## Voter Turnout in Presidential Elections

**Source:** League of Women Voters

National average of voting age population voting: 1960—63%; 1964—62%; 1968—60%; 1972—55.4%; 1976—56.5%. The sharp drop in 1972 reflects the expansion of eligibility with the enfranchisement of 18 to 21 year olds.

| State | 1976 Registered voters voting | 1976 Voting age population voting | 1972 Voting age population voting | State | 1976 Registered voters voting | 1976 Voting age population voting | 1972 Voting age population voting | State | 1976 Registered voters voting | 1976 Voting age population voting | 1972 Voting age population voting |
|---|---|---|---|---|---|---|---|---|---|---|---|
| Ala. | 63% | 47% | 44% | Ky. | 68 | 49 | 48 | N.D. | * | 71 | 70 |
| Alas. | 59 | 53 | 48 | La. | 69 | 50 | 45 | Oh. | 89 | 56 | 57 |
| Ariz. | 78 | 49 | 52 | Me. | n/a | 66 | 63 | Okla. | n/a | 57 | 57 |
| Ark. | 71 | 48 | 49 | Md. | 74 | 50 | 50 | Ore. | 78 | 62 | 62 |
| Cal. | 79 | 51 | 60 | Mass. | 82 | 62 | 62 | Pa. | 80 | 55 | 56 |
| Col. | 81 | 61 | 61 | Mich. | 72 | 59 | 59 | R.I. | 77 | 63 | 62 |
| Conn. | 84 | 64 | 66 | Minn. | 77 | 73 | 68 | S.C. | 72 | 52 | 40 |
| Del. | 78 | 58 | 64 | Miss. | 70 | 50 | 46 | S.D. | 71 | 64 | 71 |
| D.C. | 59 | 31 | 32 | Mo. | 82 | 58 | 57 | Tenn. | 69 | 50 | 44 |
| Fla. | 77 | 50 | 51 | Mon. | 75 | 66 | 69 | Tex. | 64 | 48 | 45 |
| Ga. | 64 | 43 | 38 | Neb. | 74 | 58 | 56 | Ut. | 78 | 70 | 70 |
| Ha. | 85 | 52 | 51 | Nev. | 82 | 49 | 52 | Vt. | 73 | 64 | 61 |
| Ida. | 68 | 63 | 65 | N.H. | 71 | 59 | 64 | Va. | 81 | 49 | 46 |
| Ill. | 76 | 61 | 63 | N.J. | 79 | 58 | 60 | Wash. | 77 | 62 | 62 |
| Ind. | 76 | 61 | 61 | N.M. | 81 | 55 | 61 | W.Va. | 69 | 59 | 65 |
| Ia. | n/a | 64 | 64 | N.Y. | 78 | 52 | 56 | Wis. | n/a | 65 | 63 |
| Kan. | 86 | 59 | 59 | N.C. | 66 | 44 | 44 | Wy. | 82 | 60 | 65 |

*No statewide registration. n/a—not available.

---

## Party Nominees for President and Vice President

Asterisk (*) denotes winning ticket

| | Democratic | | Republican | |
|---|---|---|---|---|
| Year | President | Vice President | President | Vice President |
| 1916 | Woodrow Wilson* | Thomas R. Marshall | Charles E. Hughes | Charles W. Fairbanks |
| 1920 | James M. Cox | Franklin D. Roosevelt | Warren G. Harding* | Calvin Coolidge |
| 1924 | John W. Davis | Charles W. Bryan | Calvin Coolidge* | Charles G. Dawes |
| 1928 | Alfred E. Smith | Joseph T. Robinson | Herbert Hoover* | Charles Curtis |
| 1932 | Franklin D. Roosevelt* | John N. Garner | Herbert Hoover | Charles Curtis |
| 1936 | Franklin D. Roosevelt* | John N. Garner | Alfred M. Landon | Frank Knox |
| 1940 | Franklin D. Roosevelt* | Henry A. Wallace | Wendell L. Willkie | Charles McNary |
| 1944 | Franklin D. Roosevelt* | Harry S. Truman | Thomas E. Dewey | John W. Bricker |
| 1948 | Harry S. Truman* | Alben W. Barkley | Thomas E. Dewey | Earl Warren |
| 1952 | Adlai E. Stevenson | John J. Sparkman | Dwight D. Eisenhower* | Richard M. Nixon |
| 1956 | Adlai E. Stevenson | Estes Kefauver | Dwight D. Eisenhower* | Richard M. Nixon |
| 1960 | John F. Kennedy* | Lyndon B. Johnson | Richard M. Nixon | Henry Cabot Lodge |
| 1964 | Lyndon B. Johnson* | Hubert H. Humphrey | Barry M. Goldwater | William E. Miller |
| 1968 | Hubert H. Humphrey | Edmund S. Muskie | Richard M. Nixon* | Spiro T. Agnew |
| 1972 | George S. McGovern | R. Sargent Shriver Jr. | Richard M. Nixon* | Spiro T. Agnew |
| 1976 | Jimmy Carter* | Walter F. Mondale | Gerald R. Ford | Robert J. Dole |

# Presidents of the U.S.

| No. | Name | Politics | Born | in | Inaug. | at age | Died | at age |
|---|---|---|---|---|---|---|---|---|
| 1 | George Washington | Fed. | 1732, Feb. 22 | Va. | 1789 | 57 | 1799, Dec. 14 | 67 |
| 2 | John Adams | Fed. | 1735, Oct. 30 | Mass. | 1797 | 61 | 1826, July 4 | 90 |
| 3 | Thomas Jefferson | Dem.-Rep. | 1743, Apr. 13 | Va. | 1801 | 57 | 1826, July 4 | 83 |
| 4 | James Madison | Dem.-Rep. | 1751, Mar. 16 | Va. | 1809 | 57 | 1836, June 28 | 85 |
| 5 | James Monroe | Dem.-Rep. | 1753, Apr. 28 | Va. | 1817 | 58 | 1831, July 4 | 73 |
| 6 | John Quincy Adams | Dem.-Rep. | 1767, July 11 | Mass. | 1825 | 57 | 1848, Feb. 23 | 80 |
| 7 | Andrew Jackson | Dem. | 1767, Mar. 15 | S.C. | 1829 | 61 | 1845, June 8 | 78 |
| 8 | Martin Van Buren | Dem. | 1782, Dec. 5 | N.Y. | 1837 | 54 | 1862, July 24 | 79 |
| 9 | William Henry Harrison | Whig | 1773, Feb. 9 | Va. | 1841 | 68 | 1841, Apr. 4 | 68 |
| 10 | John Tyler | Whig | 1790, Mar. 29 | Va. | 1841 | 51 | 1862, Jan. 18 | 71 |
| 11 | James Knox Polk | Dem. | 1795, Nov. 2 | N.C. | 1845 | 49 | 1849, June 15 | 53 |
| 12 | Zachary Taylor | Whig | 1784, Nov. 24 | Va. | 1849 | 64 | 1850, July 9 | 65 |
| 13 | Millard Fillmore | Whig | 1800, Jan. 7 | N.Y. | 1850 | 50 | 1874, Mar. 8 | 74 |
| 14 | Franklin Pierce | Dem. | 1804, Nov. 23 | N.H. | 1853 | 48 | 1869, Oct. 8 | 64 |
| 15 | James Buchanan | Dem. | 1791, Apr. 23 | Pa. | 1857 | 65 | 1868, June 1 | 77 |
| 16 | Abraham Lincoln | Rep. | 1809, Feb. 12 | Ky. | 1861 | 52 | 1865, Apr. 15 | 56 |
| 17 | Andrew Johnson | (1) | 1808, Dec. 29 | N.C. | 1865 | 56 | 1875, July 31 | 66 |
| 18 | Ulysses Simpson Grant | Rep. | 1822, Apr. 27 | Oh. | 1869 | 46 | 1885, July 23 | 63 |
| 19 | Rutherford Birchard Hayes | Rep. | 1822, Oct. 4 | Oh. | 1877 | 54 | 1893, Jan. 17 | 70 |
| 20 | James Abram Garfield | Rep. | 1831, Nov. 19 | Oh. | 1881 | 49 | 1881, Sept. 19 | 49 |
| 21 | Chester Alan Arthur | Rep. | 1829, Oct. 5 | Vt. | 1881 | 50 | 1886, Nov. 18 | 57 |
| 22 | Grover Cleveland | Dem. | 1837, Mar. 18 | N.J. | 1885 | 47 | 1908, June 24 | 71 |
| 23 | Benjamin Harrison | Rep. | 1833, Aug. 20 | Oh. | 1889 | 55 | 1901, Mar. 13 | 67 |
| 24 | Grover Cleveland | Dem. | 1837, Mar. 18 | N.J. | 1893 | 55 | 1908, June 24 | 71 |
| 25 | William McKinley | Rep. | 1843, Jan. 29 | Oh. | 1897 | 54 | 1901, Sept. 14 | 58 |
| 26 | Theodore Roosevelt | Rep. | 1858, Oct. 27 | N.Y. | 1901 | 42 | 1919, Jan. 6 | 60 |
| 27 | William Howard Taft | Rep. | 1857, Sept. 15 | Oh. | 1909 | 51 | 1930, Mar. 8 | 72 |
| 28 | Woodrow Wilson | Dem. | 1856, Dec. 28 | Va. | 1913 | 56 | 1924, Feb. 3 | 67 |
| 29 | Warren Gamaliel Harding | Rep. | 1865, Nov. 2 | Oh. | 1921 | 55 | 1923, Aug. 2 | 57 |
| 30 | Calvin Coolidge | Rep. | 1872, July 4 | Vt. | 1923 | 51 | 1933, Jan. 5 | 60 |
| 31 | Herbert Clark Hoover | Rep. | 1874, Aug. 10 | Ia. | 1929 | 54 | 1964, Oct. 20 | 90 |
| 32 | Franklin Delano Roosevelt | Dem. | 1882, Jan. 30 | N.Y. | 1933 | 51 | 1945, Apr. 12 | 63 |
| 33 | Harry S. Truman | Dem. | 1884, May 8 | Mo. | 1945 | 60 | 1972, Dec. 26 | 88 |
| 34 | Dwight David Eisenhower | Rep. | 1890, Oct. 14 | Tex. | 1953 | 62 | 1969, Mar. 28 | 78 |
| 35 | John Fitzgerald Kennedy | Dem. | 1917, May 29 | Mass. | 1961 | 43 | 1963, Nov. 22 | 46 |
| 36 | Lyndon Baines Johnson | Dem. | 1908, Aug. 22 | Tex. | 1963 | 55 | 1973, Jan. 22 | 6✗ |
| 37 | Richard Milhous Nixon (2) | Rep. | 1913, Jan. 9 | Cal. | 1969 | 56 | | |
| 38 | Gerald Rudolph Ford | Rep. | 1913, July 14 | Neb. | 1974 | 61 | | |
| 39 | Jimmy (James Earl) Carter | Dem. | 1924, Oct. 1 | Ga. | 1977 | 52 | | |

(1) Andrew Johnson — a Democrat, nominated vice president by Republicans and elected with Lincoln on National Union ticket. (2) Resigned Aug. 9, 1974.

# Presidents, Vice Presidents, Congresses

| President | Service | Vice President | Congress |
|---|---|---|---|
| 1 George Washington | Apr. 30, 1789—Mar. 3, 1797 | 1 John Adams | 1, 2, 3, 4 |
| 2 John Adams | Mar. 4, 1797—Mar. 3, 1801 | 2 Thomas Jefferson | 5, 6 |
| 3 Thomas Jefferson | Mar. 4, 1801—Mar. 3, 1805 | 3 Aaron Burr | 7, 8 |
| " | Mar. 4, 1805—Mar. 3, 1809 | 4 George Clinton | 9, 10 |
| 4 James Madison | Mar. 4, 1809—Mar. 3, 1813 | "(1) | 11, 12 |
| " | Mar. 4, 1813—Mar. 3, 1817 | 5 Elbridge Gerry (2) | 13, 14 |
| 5 James Monroe | Mar. 4, 1817—Mar. 3, 1825 | 6 Daniel D. Tompkins | 15, 16, 17, 18 |
| 6 John Quincy Adams | Mar. 4, 1825—Mar. 3, 1829 | 7 John C. Calhoun | 19, 20 |
| 7 Andrew Jackson | Mar. 4, 1829—Mar. 3, 1833 | "(3) | 21, 22 |
| " | Mar. 4, 1833—Mar. 3, 1837 | 8 Martin Van Buren | 23, 24 |
| 8 Martin Van Buren | Mar. 4, 1837—Mar. 3, 1841 | 9 Richard M. Johnson | 25, 26 |
| 9 William Henry Harrison (4) | Mar. 4, 1841—Apr. 4, 1841 | 10 John Tyler | 27 |
| 10 John Tyler | Apr. 6, 1841—Mar. 3, 1845 | | 27, 28 |
| 11 James K. Polk | Mar. 4, 1845—Mar. 3, 1849 | 11 George M. Dallas | 29, 30 |
| 12 Zachary Taylor (4) | Mar. 5, 1849—July 9, 1850 | 12 Millard Fillmore | 31 |
| 13 Millard Fillmore | July 10, 1850—Mar. 3, 1853 | | 31, 32 |
| 14 Franklin Pierce | Mar. 4, 1853—Mar. 3, 1857 | 13 William R. King (5) | 33, 34 |
| 15 James Buchanan | Mar. 4, 1857—Mar. 3, 1861 | 14 John C. Breckinridge | 35, 36 |
| 16 Abraham Lincoln | Mar. 4, 1861—Mar. 3, 1865 | 15 Hannibal Hamlin | 37, 38 |
| "(4) | Mar. 4, 1865—Apr. 15, 1865 | 16 Andrew Johnson | 39 |
| 17 Andrew Johnson | Apr. 15, 1865—Mar. 3, 1869 | | 39, 40 |
| 18 Ulysses S. Grant | Mar. 4, 1869—Mar. 3, 1873 | 17 Schuyler Colfax | 41, 42 |
| " | Mar. 4, 1873—Mar. 3, 1877 | 18 Henry Wilson (6) | 43, 44 |
| 19 Rutherford B. Hayes | Mar. 4, 1877—Mar. 3, 1881 | 19 William A. Wheeler | 45, 46 |
| 20 James A. Garfield (4) | Mar. 4, 1881—Sept. 19, 1881 | 20 Chester A. Arthur | 47 |
| 21 Chester A. Arthur | Sept. 20, 1881—Mar. 3, 1885 | | 47, 48 |
| 22 Grover Cleveland (7) | Mar. 4, 1885—Mar. 3, 1889 | 21 Thomas A. Hendricks (8) | 49, 50 |
| 23 Benjamin Harrison | Mar. 4, 1889—Mar. 3, 1893 | 22 Levi P. Morton | 51, 52 |
| 24 Grover Cleveland (7) | Mar. 4, 1893—Mar. 3, 1897 | 23 Adlai E. Stevenson | 53, 54 |
| 25 William McKinley | Mar. 4, 1897—Mar. 3, 1901 | 24 Garret A. Hobart (9) | 55, 56 |
| "(4) | Mar. 4, 1901—Sept. 14, 1901 | 25 Theodore Roosevelt | 57 |
| 26 Theodore Roosevelt | Sept. 14, 1901—Mar. 3, 1905 | | 57, 58 |
| " | Mar. 4, 1905—Mar. 3, 1909 | 26 Charles W. Fairbanks | 59, 60 |

| | President | Service | | Vice President | Congress |
|---|---|---|---|---|---|
| 27 | William H. Taft | Mar. 4, 1909—Mar. 3, 1913 | 27 | James S. Sherman (10) | 61, 62 |
| 28 | Woodrow Wilson | Mar. 4, 1913—Mar. 3, 1921 | 28 | Thomas R. Marshall | 63, 64, 65, 66 |
| 29 | Warren G. Harding (4) | Mar. 4, 1921—Aug. 2, 1923 | 29 | Calvin Coolidge | 67 |
| 30 | Calvin Coolidge | Aug. 3, 1923—Mar. 3, 1925 | | | 68 |
| | " | Mar. 4, 1925—Mar. 3, 1929 | 30 | Charles G. Dawes | 69, 70 |
| 31 | Herbert C. Hoover | Mar. 4, 1929—Mar. 3, 1933 | 31 | Charles Curtis | 71, 72 |
| 32 | Franklin D. Roosevelt (16) | Mar. 4, 1933—Jan. 20, 1941 | 32 | John N. Garner | 73, 74, 75, 76 |
| | " | Jan. 20, 1941—Jan. 20, 1945 | 33 | Henry A. Wallace | 77, 78 |
| | "(4) | Jan. 20, 1945—Apr. 12, 1945 | 34 | Harry S. Truman | 79 |
| 33 | Harry S. Truman | Apr. 12, 1945—Jan. 20, 1949 | | | 79, 80 |
| | " | Jan. 20, 1949—Jan. 20, 1953 | 35 | Alben W. Barkley | 81, 82 |
| 34 | Dwight D. Eisenhower | Jan. 20, 1953—Jan. 20, 1961 | 36 | Richard M. Nixon | 83, 84, 85, 86 |
| 35 | John F. Kennedy (4) | Jan. 20, 1961—Nov. 22, 1963 | 37 | Lyndon B. Johnson | 87, 88 |
| 36 | Lyndon B. Johnson | Nov. 22, 1963—Jan. 20, 1965 | | | 88 |
| | " | Jan. 20, 1965—Jan. 20, 1969 | 38 | Hubert H. Humphrey | 89, 90 |
| 37 | Richard M. Nixon | Jan. 20, 1969—Jan. 20, 1973 | 39 | Spiro T. Agnew (11) | 91, 92, 93 |
| | "(12) | Jan. 20, 1973—Aug. 9, 1974 | 40 | Gerald R. Ford (13) | 93 |
| 38 | Gerald R. Ford (14) | Aug. 9, 1974—Jan. 20, 1977 | 41 | Nelson A. Rockefeller (15) | 93, 94 |
| 39 | Jimmy (James Earl) Carter | Jan. 20, 1977— | 42 | Walter F. Mondale | 95 |

(1) Died Apr. 20, 1812. (2) Died Nov. 23, 1814. (3) Resigned Dec. 28, 1832, to become U.S. Senator. (4) Died in office. (5) Died Apr. 18, 1853. (6) Died Nov. 22, 1875. (7) Terms not consecutive. (8) Died Nov. 25, 1885. (9) Died Nov. 21, 1899. (10) Died Oct. 30, 1912. (11) Resigned Oct. 10, 1973. (12) Resigned Aug. 9, 1974. (13) First non-elected vice president, chosen under 25th Amendment procedure. (14) First non-elected president. (15) 2d non-elected vice president, sworn in Dec. 19, 1974. (16) First president to be inaugurated under 20th Amendment, Jan. 20, 1937.

# Vice Presidents of the U.S.

The numerals given vice presidents do not coincide with those given presidents, because some presidents had none and some had more than one.

| | Name | Birthplace | Year | Residence | Inaug. | Politics | Place of death | Year | Age |
|---|---|---|---|---|---|---|---|---|---|
| 1 | John Adams | Quincy, Mass. | 1735 | Mass. | 1789 | Fed. | Quincy, Mass. | 1826 | 90 |
| 2 | Thomas Jefferson | Shadwell, Va. | 1743 | Va. | 1797 | Rep. | Monticello, Va. | 1826 | 83 |
| 3 | Aaron Burr | Newark, N.J. | 1756 | N.Y. | 1801 | Rep. | Staten Island, N.Y. | 1836 | 80 |
| 4 | George Clinton | Ulster Co., N.Y. | 1739 | N.Y. | 1805 | Rep. | Washington, D.C. | 1812 | 73 |
| 5 | Elbridge Gerry | Marblehead, Mass. | 1744 | Mass. | 1813 | Rep. | Washington, D.C. | 1814 | 70 |
| 6 | Daniel D. Tompkins | Scarsdale, N.Y. | 1774 | N.Y. | 1817 | Rep. | Staten Island, N.Y. | 1825 | 51 |
| 7 | John C. Calhoun (1) | Abbeville, S.C. | 1782 | S.C. | 1825 | Rep. | Washington, D.C. | 1850 | 68 |
| 8 | Martin Van Buren | Kinderhook, N.Y. | 1782 | N.Y. | 1833 | Dem. | Kinderhook, N.Y. | 1862 | 79 |
| 9 | Richard M. Johnson | Louisville, Ky. | 1780 | Ky. | 1837 | Dem. | Frankfort, Ky. | 1850 | 70 |
| 10 | John Tyler | Greenway, Va. | 1790 | Va. | 1841 | Whig. | Richmond, Va. | 1862 | 71 |
| 11 | George M. Dallas | Philadelphia, Pa. | 1792 | Pa. | 1845 | Dem. | Philadelphia, Pa. | 1864 | 72 |
| 12 | Millard Fillmore | Summerhill, N.Y. | 1800 | N.Y. | 1849 | Whig. | Buffalo, N.Y. | 1874 | 74 |
| 13 | William R. King | Sampson Co., N.C. | 1786 | Ala. | 1853 | Dem. | Dallas Co., Ala. | 1853 | 67 |
| 14 | John C. Breckinridge | Lexington, Ky. | 1821 | Ky. | 1857 | Dem. | Lexington, Ky. | 1875 | 54 |
| 15 | Hannibal Hamlin | Paris, Me. | 1809 | Me. | 1861 | Rep. | Bangor, Me. | 1891 | 81 |
| 16 | Andrew Johnson | Raleigh, N.C. | 1808 | Tenn. | 1865 | (2) | Carter Co., Tenn. | 1875 | 66 |
| 17 | Schuyler Colfax | New York City, N.Y. | 1823 | Ind. | 1869 | Rep. | Makato, Minn. | 1885 | 62 |
| 18 | Henry Wilson | Farmington, N.H. | 1812 | Mass. | 1873 | Rep. | Washington, D.C. | 1875 | 63 |
| 19 | William A. Wheeler | Malone, N.Y. | 1819 | N.Y. | 1877 | Rep. | Malone, N.Y. | 1887 | 68 |
| 20 | Chester A. Arthur | Fairfield, Vt. | 1830 | N.Y. | 1881 | Rep. | New York City, N.Y. | 1886 | 56 |
| 21 | Thomas A. Hendricks | Muskingum Co., Oh. | 1819 | Ind. | 1885 | Dem. | Indianapolis, Ind. | 1885 | 66 |
| 22 | Levi P. Morton | Shoreham, Vt. | 1824 | N.Y. | 1889 | Rep. | Rhinebeck, N.Y. | 1920 | 96 |
| 23 | Adlai E. Stevenson (3) | Christian Co., Ky. | 1835 | Ill. | 1893 | Dem. | Chicago, Ill. | 1914 | 78 |
| 24 | Garret A. Hobart | Long Branch, N.J. | 1844 | N.J. | 1897 | Rep. | Paterson, N.J. | 1899 | 55 |
| 25 | Theodore Roosevelt | New York City, N.Y. | 1858 | N.Y. | 1901 | Rep. | Oyster Bay, N.Y. | 1919 | 60 |
| 26 | Charles W. Fairbanks | Unionville Centre, Oh. | 1852 | Ind. | 1905 | Rep. | Indianapolis, Ind. | 1918 | 66 |
| 27 | James S. Sherman | Utica, N.Y. | 1855 | N.Y. | 1909 | Rep. | Utica, N.Y. | 1912 | 57 |
| 28 | Thomas R. Marshall | N. Manchester, Ind. | 1854 | Ind. | 1913 | Dem. | Washington, D.C. | 1925 | 71 |
| 29 | Calvin Coolidge | Plymouth, Vt. | 1872 | Mass. | 1921 | Rep. | Northampton, Mass. | 1933 | 60 |
| 30 | Charles G. Dawes | Marietta, Oh. | 1865 | Ill. | 1925 | Rep. | Evanston, Ill. | 1951 | 85 |
| 31 | Charles Curtis | Topeka, Kan. | 1860 | Kan. | 1929 | Rep. | Washington, D.C. | 1936 | 76 |
| 32 | John Nance Garner | Red River Co., Tex. | 1868 | Tex. | 1933 | Dem. | Uvalde, Tex. | 1967 | 98 |
| 33 | Henry Agard Wallace | Adair County, Ia. | 1888 | Iowa | 1941 | Dem. | Danbury, Conn. | 1965 | 77 |
| 34 | Harry S. Truman | Lamar, Mo. | 1884 | Mo. | 1945 | Dem. | Kansas City, Mo. | 1972 | 88 |
| 35 | Alben W. Barkley | Graves County, Ky. | 1877 | Ky. | 1949 | Dem. | Lexington, Va. | 1956 | 78 |
| 36 | Richard M. Nixon | Yorba Linda, Cal. | 1913 | Cal. | 1953 | Rep. | | | |
| 37 | Lyndon B. Johnson | Johnson City, Tex. | 1908 | Tex. | 1961 | Dem. | San Antonio, Tex. | 1973 | 64 |
| 38 | Hubert H. Humphrey | Wallace, S.D. | 1911 | Minn. | 1965 | Dem. | Waverly, Minn. | 1978 | 66 |
| 39 | Spiro T. Agnew | Baltimore, Md. | 1918 | Md. | 1969 | Rep. | | | |
| 40 | Gerald R. Ford | Omaha, Neb. | 1913 | Mich. | 1973 | Rep. | | | |
| 41 | Nelson A. Rockefeller | Bar Harbor, Me. | 1908 | N.Y. | 1974 | Rep. | | | |
| 42 | Walter F. Mondale | Ceylon, Minn. | 1928 | Minn. | 1977 | Dem. | | | |

(1) John C. Calhoun resigned Dec. 28, 1832, having been elected to the Senate to fill a vacancy. (2) Andrew Johnson — a Democrat nominated by Republicans and elected with Lincoln on the National Union Ticket. (3) Adlai E. Stevenson, 23d vice president, was grandfather of Democratic candidate for president, 1952 and 1956.

## The Continental Congress: Meetings, Presidents

| Meeting places | Dates of meetings | Congress presidents | Date elected |
|---|---|---|---|
| Philadelphia | Sept. 5 to Oct. 26, 1774 | Peyton Randolph, Va. (1) | Sept. 5, 1774 |
| " | " | Henry Middleton, S.C. | Oct. 22, 1774 |
| Philadelphia | May 10, 1775 to Dec. 12, 1776 | Peyton Randolph, Va. | May 10, 1775 |
| " | " | John Hancock, Mass. | May 24, 1775 |
| Baltimore | Dec. 20, 1776 to Mar. 4, 1777 | " | " |
| Philadelphia | Mar. 5 to Sept. 18, 1777 | | |
| Lancaster, Pa. | Sept. 27, 1777 (one day) | | |
| York, Pa. | Sept. 30, 1777 to June 27, 1778 | Henry Laurens, S.C. | Nov. 1, 1777(4) |
| Philadelphia | July 2, 1778 to June 21, 1783 | John Jay, N.Y. | Dec. 10, 1778 |
| " | " | Samuel Huntington, Conn. | Sept. 28, 1779 |
| " | " | Thomas McKean, Del. | July 10, 1781 |
| " | " | John Hanson, Md. (2) | Nov. 5, 1781 |
| " | " | Elias Boudinot, N.J. | Nov. 4, 1782 |
| Princeton, N.J. | June 30 to Nov. 4, 1783 | Thomas Mifflin, Pa. | Nov. 3, 1783 |
| Annapolis, Md. | Nov. 26, 1783 to June 3, 1784 | | |
| Trenton, N.J. | Nov. 1 to Dec. 24, 1784 | Richard Henry Lee, Va. | Nov. 30, 1784 |
| New York City | Jan. 11 to Nov. 4, 1785 | | |
| " | Nov. 7, 1785 to Nov. 3, 1786 | John Hancock, Mass. (3) | Nov. 23, 1785 |
| " | " | Nathaniel Gorman, Mass. | June 6, 1786 |
| " | Nov. 6, 1786 to Oct. 30, 1787 | Arthur St. Clair, Pa. | Feb. 2, 1787 |
| " | Nov. 5, 1787 to Oct. 21, 1788 | Cyrus Griffin, Va. | Jan. 22, 1788 |
| " | Nov. 3, 1788 to Mar. 2, 1789 | " | " |

(1) Resigned Oct. 22, 1774. (2) Titled "President of the United States in Congress Assembled," John Hanson is considered by some to be the first U.S. President as he was the first to serve under the Articles of Confederation. He was, however, little more than presiding officer of the Congress, which retained full executive power. He could be considered the head of government, but not head of state. (3) Resigned May 29, 1786, without serving, because of illness. (4) Articles of Confederation agreed upon, Nov. 15, 1777; last ratification from Maryland, Mar. 1, 1781.

## Cabinets of the U. S.

### Secretaries of State

The Department of Foreign Affairs was created by act of Congress July 27, 1789, and the name changed to Department of State on Sept. 15.

| President | Secretary | Home | Apptd. |
|---|---|---|---|
| Washington | Thomas Jefferson | Va. | 1789 |
| " | Edmund Randolph | " | 1794 |
| " | Timothy Pickering | Pa. | 1795 |
| Adams, J. | " | " | 1795 |
| " | John Marshall | Va. | 1800 |
| Jefferson | James Madison | " | 1801 |
| Madison | Robert Smith | Md. | 1809 |
| " | James Monroe | Va. | 1811 |
| Monroe | John Quincy Adams | Mass. | 1817 |
| Adams, J.Q. | Henry Clay | Ky. | 1825 |
| Jackson | Martin Van Buren | N.Y. | 1829 |
| " | Edward Livingston | La. | 1831 |
| " | Louis McLane | Del. | 1833 |
| " | John Forsyth | Ga. | 1834 |
| Van Buren | " | " | 1837 |
| Harrison, W.H. | Daniel Webster | Mass. | 1841 |
| Tyler | " | " | 1841 |
| " | Abel P. Upshur | Va. | 1843 |
| " | John C. Calhoun | S.C. | 1844 |
| Polk | " | " | 1845 |
| " | James Buchanan | Pa. | 1845 |
| Taylor | " | " | 1849 |
| " | John M. Clayton | Del. | 1849 |
| Fillmore | " | " | 1850 |
| " | Daniel Webster | Mass. | 1850 |
| " | Edward Everett | " | 1852 |
| Pierce | William L. Marcy | N.Y. | 1853 |
| Buchanan | " | " | 1857 |
| " | Lewis Cass | Mich. | 1857 |
| " | Jeremiah S. Black | Pa. | 1860 |
| Lincoln | " | " | 1861 |
| " | William H. Seward | N.Y. | 1861 |
| Johnson, A. | " | " | 1865 |
| Grant | Elihu B. Washburne | Ill. | 1869 |
| " | Hamilton Fish | N.Y. | 1869 |
| Hayes | " | " | 1877 |
| " | William M. Evarts | " | 1877 |
| Garfield | " | " | 1881 |
| " | James G. Blaine | Me. | 1881 |
| Arthur | " | " | 1881 |
| " | F.T. Frelinghuysen | N.J. | 1881 |
| Cleveland | " | " | 1885 |
| " | Thomas F. Bayard | Del. | 1885 |
| Harrison, B. | " | " | 1889 |
| " | James G. Blaine | Me. | 1889 |
| " | John W. Foster | Ind. | 1892 |
| Cleveland | Walter Q. Gresham | Ill. | 1893 |
| " | Richard Olney | Mass. | 1895 |
| McKinley | " | " | 1897 |
| " | John Sherman | Oh. | 1897 |
| " | William R. Day | " | 1898 |
| " | John Hay | D.C. | 1898 |
| Roosevelt, T. | " | " | 1901 |
| " | Elihu Root | N.Y. | 1905 |
| " | Robert Bacon | " | 1909 |
| Taft | " | " | 1909 |
| " | Philander C. Knox | Pa. | 1909 |
| Wilson | " | " | 1913 |
| " | William J. Bryan | Neb. | 1913 |
| " | Robert Lansing | N.Y. | 1915 |
| " | Bainbridge Colby | " | 1920 |
| Harding | Charles E. Hughes | " | 1921 |
| Coolidge | " | " | 1923 |
| " | Frank B. Kellogg | Minn. | 1925 |
| Hoover | " | " | 1929 |
| " | Henry L. Stimson | N.Y. | 1929 |
| Roosevelt, F.D. | Cordell Hull | Tenn. | 1933 |
| " | E.R. Stettinius Jr. | Va. | 1944 |
| Truman | " | " | 1945 |
| " | James F. Byrnes | S.C. | 1945 |
| " | George C. Marshall | Pa. | 1947 |
| " | Dean G. Acheson | Conn. | 1949 |
| Eisenhower | John Foster Dulles | N.Y. | 1953 |
| " | Christian A. Herter | Mass. | 1959 |
| Kennedy | Dean Rusk | N.Y. | 1961 |
| Johnson, L.B. | " | " | 1963 |
| Nixon | William P. Rogers | N.Y. | 1969 |
| " | Henry A. Kissinger | D.C. | 1973 |
| Ford | " | " | 1974 |
| Carter | Cyrus R. Vance | N.Y. | 1977 |

## Secretaries of the Treasury

The Treasury Department was organized by act of Congress Sept. 2, 1789.

| President | Secretary | Home | Apptd. | President | Secretary | Home | Apptd. |
|---|---|---|---|---|---|---|---|
| Washington | Alexander Hamilton | N.Y. | 1789 | Hayes | John Sherman | Oh. | 1877 |
| " | Oliver Wolcott | Conn. | 1795 | Garfield | William Windom | Minn. | 1881 |
| Adams, J. | " | " | 1797 | Arthur | Charles J. Folger | N.Y. | 1881 |
| " | Samuel Dexter | Mass. | 1801 | " | Walter Q. Gresham | Ind. | 1884 |
| Jefferson | " | " | 1801 | " | Hugh McCulloch | " | 1884 |
| " | Albert Gallatin | Pa. | 1801 | Cleveland | Daniel Manning | N.Y. | 1885 |
| Madison | " | Pa. | 1809 | Cleveland | Charles S. Fairchild | " | 1887 |
| " | George W. Campbell | Tenn. | 1814 | Harrison, B. | William Windom | Minn. | 1889 |
| " | Alexander J. Dallas | Pa. | 1814 | " | Charles Foster | Oh. | 1891 |
| " | William H. Crawford | Ga. | 1816 | Cleveland | John G. Carlisle | Ky. | 1893 |
| Monroe | " | " | 1817 | McKinley | Lyman J. Gage | Ill. | 1897 |
| Adams, J.Q. | Richard Rush | Pa. | 1825 | Roosevelt, T. | " | " | 1901 |
| Jackson | Samuel D. Ingham | Pa. | 1829 | " | Leslie M. Shaw | Ia. | 1902 |
| " | Louis McLane | Del. | 1831 | " | George B. Cortelyou | N.Y. | 1907 |
| " | William J. Duane | Pa. | 1833 | Taft | Franklin MacVeagh | Ill. | 1909 |
| " | Roger B. Taney | Md. | 1833 | Wilson | William G. McAdoo | N.Y. | 1913 |
| " | Levi Woodbury | N.H. | 1834 | " | Carter Glass | Va. | 1918 |
| Van Buren | " | " | 1837 | " | David F. Houston | Mo. | 1920 |
| Harrison, W.H. | Thomas Ewing | Oh. | 1841 | Harding | Andrew W. Mellon | Pa. | 1921 |
| Tyler | " | " | 1841 | Coolidge | " | " | 1923 |
| " | Walter Forward | Pa. | 1841 | Hoover | " | " | 1929 |
| " | John C. Spencer | N.Y. | 1843 | " | Ogden L. Mills | N.Y. | 1932 |
| " | George M. Bibb | Ky. | 1844 | Roosevelt, F.D. | William H. Woodin | " | 1933 |
| Polk | Robert J. Walker | Miss. | 1845 | " | Henry Morenthau, Jr. | " | 1934 |
| Taylor | William M. Meredith | Pa. | 1849 | Truman | Fred M. Vinson | Ky. | 1945 |
| Fillmore | Thomas Corwin | Oh. | 1850 | " | John W. Snyder | Mo. | 1946 |
| Pierce | James Guthrie | Ky. | 1853 | Eisenhower | George M. Humphrey | Oh. | 1953 |
| Buchanan | Howell Cobb | Ga. | 1857 | " | Robert B. Anderson | Conn. | 1957 |
| " | Phillip F. Thomas | Md. | 1860 | Kennedy | C. Douglas Dillon | N.J. | 1961 |
| " | John A. Dix | N.Y. | 1861 | Johnson, L.B. | " | " | 1963 |
| Lincoln | Salmon P. Chase | Oh. | 1861 | " | Henry H. Fowler | Va. | 1965 |
| " | William P. Fessenden | Me. | 1864 | " | Joseph W. Barr | Ind. | 1968 |
| " | Hugh McCulloch | Ind. | 1865 | Nixon | David M. Kennedy | Ill. | 1969 |
| Johnson, A. | " | " | 1865 | " | John B. Connally | Tex. | 1970 |
| Grant | George S. Boutwell | Mass. | 1869 | " | George P. Shultz | Ill. | 1972 |
| " | William A. Richardson | Mass. | 1873 | " | William E. Simon | N.J. | 1974 |
| " | Benjamin H. Bristow | Ky. | 1874 | Ford | " | " | 1974 |
| " | Lot M. Morrill | Me. | 1876 | Carter | W. Michael Blumenthal | Mich. | 1977 |

## Secretaries of Defense

The Department of Defense, originally designated the National Military Establishment, was created Sept. 18, 1947. It is headed by the secretary of defense, who is a member of the president's cabinet.

The departments of the army, of the navy, and of the air force function within the Department of Defense, and their respective secretaries are no longer members of the president's cabinet.

| President | Secretary | Home | Apptd. | President | Secretary | Home | Apptd. |
|---|---|---|---|---|---|---|---|
| Truman | James V. Forrestal | N.Y. | 1947 | Johnson, L.B. | Robert S. McNamara | Mich. | 1963 |
| " | Louis A. Johnson | W.Va. | 1949 | " | Clark M. Clifford | Md. | 1968 |
| " | George C. Marshall | Pa. | 1950 | Nixon | Melvin R. Laird | Wis. | 1969 |
| " | Robert A. Lovett | N.Y. | 1951 | " | Elliot L. Richardson | Mass. | 1973 |
| Eisenhower | Charles E. Wilson | Mich. | 1953 | " | James R. Schlesinger | Va. | 1973 |
| " | Neil H. McElroy | Oh. | 1957 | Ford | " | " | 1974 |
| " | Thomas S. Gates Jr. | Pa. | 1959 | " | Donald H. Rumsfeld | Ill. | 1975 |
| Kennedy | Robert S. McNamara | Mich. | 1961 | Carter | Harold Brown | Cal. | 1977 |

## Secretaries of the Armed Services

### Not members of the president's Cabinet

The Department of Defense; created Sept. 18, 1947, consolidated the navy, army, air force into a single department.

| Secretary of the Air Force | Appointed |
|---|---|
| W. Stuart Symington | Sept. 18, 1947 |
| Thomas K. Finletter | Apr. 24, 1950 |
| Harold E. Talbot | Feb. 4, 1953 |
| Donald A. Quarles | Aug. 12, 1955 |
| James H. Douglas | Mar. 26, 1957 |
| Dudley C. Sharpe | Dec. 10, 1959 |
| Eugene M. Zuckert | Jan. 23, 1961 |
| Dr. Harold Brown | July 10, 1965 |
| Robert C. Seamans Jr. | Jan. 20, 1969 |
| John L. McLucas | July 19, 1973 |
| Thomas C. Reed | Jan. 2, 1976 |
| John C. Stetson | Apr. 6, 1977 |

| Secretary of the Army | Appointed |
|---|---|
| Kenneth C. Royall | Sept. 18, 1947 |
| Gordon Gray* | June 20, 1949 |
| Frank Pace Jr. | Apr. 12, 1950 |
| Earl D. Johnson (acting) | Jan. 20, 1953 |
| Robert T. Stevens | Feb. 4, 1953 |
| Wilber M. Brucker | July 21, 1955 |

| | |
|---|---|
| Elvis J. Stahr Jr. | Jan. 23, 1961 |
| Cyrus R. Vance | May 21, 1962 |
| Stephen Ailes | Jan. 20, 1964 |
| Stanley R. Resor | June 17, 1965 |
| Robert F. Froehlke | June 15, 1971 |
| Howard H. Callaway | May 2, 1973 |
| Norman R. Augustine (acting) | July 3, 1975 |
| Martin R. Hoffman | Aug. 5, 1975 |
| Clifford L. Alexander Jr. | Jan. 19, 1977 |

*In addition, Gordon Gray was acting secretary of the army from Apr. 28, 1949, and under secretary from May 25, 1949, until June 20, 1949.

| Secretary of the Navy | Appointed |
|---|---|
| John L. Sullivan | Sept. 18, 1947 |
| Francis P. Matthews | May 25, 1949 |
| Dan A. Kimball | July 31, 1951 |
| Robert B. Anderson | Feb. 4, 1953 |
| Charles S. Thomas | May 3, 1954 |
| Thomas S. Gates Jr. | Apr. 1, 1957 |
| William B. Franke | June 1, 1958 |

**Secretary of the Navy** (cont.)

| | | |
|---|---|---|
| John B. Connally Jr. | Jan. 23, 1961 | |
| Fred Korth | Dec. 11, 1961 | |
| Paul H. Nitze | Oct. 14, 1963 | |
| John T. McNaughton | June 6, 1967 | |
| Paul R. Ignatius | Aug. 4, 1967 | |
| John H. Chafee | Jan. 20, 1969 | |
| John W. Warner | Apr. 7, 1972 | |
| J. William Middendorf 2d | June 10, 1974 | |
| W. Graham Claytor Jr. | Jan. 19, 1977 | |

## Secretaries of War

The War (and Navy) Department was created by act of Congress Aug. 7, 1789, and Gen. Henry Knox was commissioned secretary of war under that act Sept. 12, 1789.

| President | Secretary | Home | Apptd. | President | Secretary | Home | Apptd. |
|---|---|---|---|---|---|---|---|
| Washington | Henry Knox | Mass. | 1789 | Grant | John A. Rawlins | Ill. | 1869 |
| " | Timothy Pickering | Pa. | 1795 | " | William T. Sherman | Oh. | 1869 |
| " | James McHenry | Md. | 1796 | " | William W. Belknap | Ia. | 1869 |
| Adams, J. | " | " | 1797 | " | Alphonso Taft | Oh. | 1876 |
| " | Samuel Dexter | Mass. | 1800 | Grant | James D. Cameron | Pa. | 1876 |
| Jefferson | Henry Dearborn | " | 1801 | Hayes | George W. McCrary | Ia. | 1877 |
| Madison | William Eustis | Mass. | 1809 | " | Alexander Ramsey | Minn. | 1879 |
| " | John Armstrong | N.Y. | 1813 | Garfield | Robert T. Lincoln | Ill. | 1881 |
| Madison | James Monroe | Va. | 1814 | Arthur | " | " | 1881 |
| " | William H. Crawford | Ga. | 1815 | Cleveland | William C. Endicott | Mass. | 1885 |
| Monroe | John C. Calhoun | S.C. | 1817 | Harrison, B. | Redfield Proctor | Vt. | 1890 |
| Adams, J.Q. | James Barbour | Va. | 1825 | " | Stephen B. Elkins | W.Va. | 1891 |
| " | Peter B. Porter | N.Y. | 1828 | Cleveland | Daniel S. Lamont | N.Y. | 1893 |
| Jackson | John H. Eaton | Tenn. | 1829 | McKinley | Russel A. Alger | Mich. | 1897 |
| " | Lewis Cass | Oh. | 1831 | " | Eihu Root | N.Y. | 1899 |
| " | Benjamin F. Butler | N.Y. | 1837 | Roosevelt, T. | " | " | 1901 |
| Van Buren | Joel R. Poinsett | S.C. | 1837 | " | William H. Taft | Oh. | 1904 |
| Harrison, W.H. | John Bell | Tenn. | 1841 | " | Luke E. Wright | Tenn. | 1908 |
| Tyler | " | " | 1841 | Taft | Jacob M. Dickinson | " | 1909 |
| Tyler | John C. Spencer | N.Y. | 1841 | " | Henry L. Stimson | N.Y. | 1911 |
| " | James M. Porter | Pa. | 1843 | Wilson | Lindley M. Garrison | N.J. | 1913 |
| " | William Wilkins | " | 1844 | " | Newton D. Baker | Oh. | 1916 |
| Polk | William L. Marcy | N.Y. | 1845 | Harding | John W. Weeks | Mass. | 1921 |
| Taylor | George W. Crawford | Ga. | 1849 | Coolidge | " | " | 1923 |
| Fillmore | Charles M. Conrad | La. | 1850 | " | Dwight F. Davis | Mo. | 1925 |
| Pierce | Jefferson Davis | Miss. | 1853 | Hoover | James W. Good | Ill. | 1929 |
| Buchanan | John B. Floyd | Va. | 1857 | Hoover | Patrick J. Hurley | Okla. | 1929 |
| " | Joseph Holt | Ky. | 1861 | Roosevelt, F.D. | George H. Dem | Ut. | 1933 |
| Lincoln | Simon Cameron | Pa. | 1861 | " | Harry H. Woodring | Kan. | 1937 |
| " | Edwin M. Stanton | Pa. | 1862 | Roosevelt, F.D. | Henry L. Stimson | N.Y. | 1940 |
| Johnson, A. | " | " | 1865 | Truman | Robert P. Patterson | N.Y. | 1945 |
| " | John M. Schofield | Ill. | 1868 | " | *Kenneth C. Royall | N.C. | 1947 |

## Secretaries of the Navy

The Navy Department was created by act of Congress Apr. 30, 1798.

| President | Secretary | Home | Apptd. | President | Secretary | Home | Apptd. |
|---|---|---|---|---|---|---|---|
| Adams, J. | Benjamin Stoddert | Md. | 1798 | Lincoln | Gideon Welles | Conn. | 1861 |
| Jefferson | " | " | 1801 | Johnson, A. | " | " | 1865 |
| " | Robert Smith | " | 1801 | Grant | Adolph E. Borie | Pa. | 1869 |
| Madison | Paul Hamilton | S.C. | 1809 | " | George M. Robeson | N.J. | 1869 |
| " | William Jones | Pa. | 1813 | Hayes | Richard W. Thompson | Ind. | 1877 |
| " | Benjamin Williams Crowninshield | Mass. | 1814 | " | Nathan Goff Jr. | W.Va. | 1881 |
| Monroe | " | " | 1817 | Garfield | William H. Hunt | La. | 1881 |
| " | Smith Thompson | N.Y. | 1818 | Arthur | William E. Chandler | N.H. | 1882 |
| " | Samuel L. Southard | N.J. | 1823 | Cleveland | William C. Whitney | N.Y. | 1885 |
| Adams, J.Q. | " | " | 1825 | Harrison, B. | Benjamin F. Tracy | N.Y. | 1889 |
| Jackson | John Branch | N.C. | 1829 | Cleveland | Hilary A. Herbert | Ala. | 1893 |
| " | Levi Woodbury | N.H. | 1831 | McKinley | John D. Long | Mass. | 1897 |
| " | Mahlon Dickerson | N.J. | 1834 | Roosevelt T. | " | " | 1901 |
| Van Buren | " | " | 1837 | " | William H. Moody | " | 1920 |
| " | James K. Paulding | N.Y. | 1838 | " | Paul Morton | Ill. | 1904 |
| Harrison, W.H. | George E. Badger | N.C. | 1841 | " | Charles J. Bonaparte | Md. | 1905 |
| Tyler | " | " | 1841 | " | Victor H. Metcalf | Cal. | 1906 |
| " | Abel P. Upshur | Va. | 1841 | " | Truman H. Newberry | Mich. | 1908 |
| " | David Henshaw | Mass. | 1843 | Taft | George von L. Meyer | Mass. | 1909 |
| " | Thomas W. Gilmer | Va. | 1844 | Wilson | Josephus Daniels | N.C. | 1913 |
| " | John Y. Mason | " | 1844 | Harding | Edwin Denby | Mich. | 1921 |
| Polk | George Bancroft | Mass. | 1845 | Coolidge | " | " | 1923 |
| " | John Y. Mason | Va. | 1846 | " | Curtis D. Wilbur | Cal. | 1924 |
| Taylor | William B. Preston | " | 1849 | Hoover | Charles Francis Adams | Mass. | 1929 |
| Fillmore | William A. Graham | N.C. | 1850 | Roosevelt, F.D. | Claude A. Swanson | Va. | 1933 |
| " | John P. Kennedy | Md. | 1852 | " | Charles Edison | N.J. | 1940 |
| Pierce | James C. Dobbin | N.C. | 1853 | " | Frank Knox | Ill. | 1940 |
| Buchanan | Isaac Toucey | Conn. | 1857 | " | *James V. Forrestal | N.Y. | 1944 |
| | | | | Truman | " | " | 1945 |

*Last members of Cabinet. The War Department became the Department of the Army and the Navy Department became branches of the Department of Defense, created Sept. 18, 1947.

## Attorneys General

The office of attorney general was organized by act of Congress Sept. 24, 1789. The Department of Justice was created June 22, 1870.

| President | Attorney General | Home | Apptd. | President | Attorney General | Home | Apptd. |
|---|---|---|---|---|---|---|---|
| Washington | Edmund Randolph | Va. | 1789 | Garfield | Wayne MacVeagh | Pa. | 1881 |
| " | William Bradford | Pa. | 1794 | Arthur | Benjamin H. Brewster | " | 1881 |
| " | Charles Lee | Va. | 1795 | Cleveland | Augustus Garland | Ark. | 1885 |
| Adams, J. | " | " | 1797 | Harrison, B. | William H. H. Miller | Ind. | 1889 |
| Jefferson | Levi Lincoln | Mass. | 1801 | Cleveland | Richard Olney | Mass. | 1893 |
| " | John Breckenridge | Ky. | 1805 | " | Judson Harmon | Oh. | 1895 |
| Jefferson | Caesar A. Rodney | Del. | 1807 | McKinley | Joseph McKenna | Cal. | 1897 |
| Madison | " | " | 1809 | " | John W. Griggs | N.J. | 1898 |
| " | William Pinkney | Md. | 1811 | " | Philander C. Knox | Pa. | 1901 |
| " | Richard Rush | Pa. | 1814 | Roosevelt, T. | " | " | 1901 |
| Monroe | " | " | 1817 | " | William H. Moody | Mass. | 1904 |
| " | William Wirt | Va. | 1817 | " | Charles J. Bonaparte | Md. | 1906 |
| Adams, J.Q. | " | " | 1825 | Taft | George W. Wickersham | N.Y. | 1909 |
| Jackson | John McP. Berrien | Ga. | 1829 | Wilson | J.C. McReynolds | Tenn. | 1913 |
| " | Roger B. Taney | Md. | 1831 | " | Thomas W. Gregory | Tex. | 1914 |
| " | Benjamin F. Butler | N.Y. | 1833 | " | A. Mitchell Palmer | Pa. | 1919 |
| Van Buren | " | " | 1837 | Harding | Harry M. Daugherty | Oh. | 1921 |
| " | Felix Grundy | Tenn. | 1838 | Coolidge | " | " | 1923 |
| " | Henry D. Gilpin | Pa. | 1840 | " | Harlan F. Stone | N.Y. | 1924 |
| Harrison, W.H. | John J. Crittenden | Ky. | 1841 | " | John G. Sargent | Vt. | 1925 |
| Tyler | " | " | 1841 | Hoover | William D. Mitchell | Minn. | 1929 |
| " | Hugh S. Legare | S.C. | 1841 | Roosevelt, F.D. | Homer S. Cummings | Conn. | 1933 |
| " | John Nelson | Md. | 1843 | " | Frank Murphy | Mich. | 1939 |
| Polk | John Y. Mason | Va. | 1845 | " | Robert H. Jackson | N.Y. | 1940 |
| " | Nathan Clifford | Me. | 1846 | " | Francis Biddle | Pa. | 1941 |
| " | Isaac Toucey | Conn. | 1848 | Truman | Tom C. Clark | Tex. | 1945 |
| Taylor | Reverdy Johnson | Md. | 1849 | " | J. Howard McGrath | R.I. | 1949 |
| Fillmore | John J. Crittenden | Ky. | 1850 | " | J.P. McGranery | Pa. | 1952 |
| Pierce | Caleb Cushing | Mass. | 1853 | Eisenhower | H. Brownell Jr. | N.Y. | 1953 |
| Buchanan | Jeremiah S. Black | Pa. | 1857 | " | William P. Rogers | Md. | 1957 |
| " | Edwin M. Stanton | Pa. | 1860 | Kennedy | Robert F. Kennedy | Mass. | 1961 |
| Lincoln | Edward Bates | Mo. | 1861 | Johnson, L.B. | " | " | 1963 |
| " | James Speed | Ky. | 1864 | " | N. de B. Katzenbach | Ill. | 1965 |
| Johnson, A. | " | " | 1865 | " | Ramsey Clark | Tex. | 1967 |
| " | Henry Stanbery | Oh. | 1866 | Nixon | John N. Mitchell | N.Y. | 1969 |
| " | William M. Evarts | N.Y. | 1868 | " | Richard G. Kleindienst | Ariz. | 1972 |
| Grant | Ebenezer R. Hoar | Mass. | 1869 | " | Elliot L. Richardson | Mass. | 1973 |
| " | Amos T. Akerman | Ga. | 1870 | " | William B. Saxbe | Oh. | 1974 |
| " | George H. William | Ore. | 1871 | Ford | " | " | 1974 |
| " | Edwards Pierrepont | N.Y. | 1875 | " | Edward H. Levi | Ill. | 1975 |
| " | Alphonso Taft | Oh. | 1876 | Carter | Griffin B. Bell | Ga. | 1977 |
| Hayes | Charles Devens | Mass. | 1877 | | | | |

## Secretaries of the Interior

The Department of Interior was created by act of Congress Mar. 3, 1849

| President | Secretary | Home | Apptd. | President | Secretary | Home | Apptd. |
|---|---|---|---|---|---|---|---|
| Taylor | Thomas Ewing | Oh. | 1849 | " | James R. Garfield | Oh. | 1907 |
| Fillmore | Thomas M. T. McKennan | Pa. | 1850 | Taft | Richard A. Ballinger | Wash. | 1909 |
| Fillmore | Alex H. H. Stuart | Va. | 1850 | " | Walter L. Fisher | Ill. | 1911 |
| Pierce | Robert McClelland | Mich. | 1853 | Wilson | Franklin K. Lane | Cal. | 1913 |
| Buchanan | Jacob Thompson | Miss. | 1857 | " | John B. Payne | Ill. | 1920 |
| Lincoln | Caleb B. Smith | Ind. | 1861 | Harding | Albert B. Fall | N.M. | 1921 |
| " | John P. Usher | " | 1863 | " | Hubert Work | Col. | 1923 |
| Johnson, A. | " | " | 1865 | Coolidge | " | " | 1923 |
| " | James Harlan | Ia. | 1865 | " | Roy O. West | Ill. | 1929 |
| " | Orville H. Browning | Ill. | 1866 | Hoover | Ray Lyman Wilbur | Cal. | 1929 |
| Grant | Jacob D. Cox | Oh. | 1869 | Roosevelt, F.D. | Harold L. Ickes | Ill. | 1933 |
| " | Columbus Delano | " | 1870 | Truman | " | " | 1945 |
| " | Zachariah Chandler | Mich. | 1875 | " | Julius A. Krug | Wis. | 1946 |
| Hayes | Carl Schurz | Mo. | 1877 | " | Oscar L. Chapman | Col. | 1950 |
| Garfield | Sam J. Kirkwood | Ia. | 1881 | Eisenhower | Douglas McKay | Ore. | 1953 |
| Arthur | Henry M. Teller | Col. | 1882 | " | Fred A Seaton | Neb. | 1956 |
| Cleveland | Lucius Q.C. Lamar | Miss. | 1885 | Kennedy | Stewart L. Udall | Ariz. | 1961 |
| " | William F. Vilas | Wis. | 1888 | Johnson, L.B. | " | " | 1963 |
| Harrison, B. | John W. Noble | Mo. | 1889 | Nixon | Walter J. Hickel | Alas. | 1969 |
| Cleveland | Hoke Smith | Ga. | 1893 | " | Rogers C.B. Morton | Md. | 1971 |
| " | David R. Francis | Mo. | 1896 | Ford | " | " | 1974 |
| McKinley | Cornelius N. Bliss | N.Y. | 1897 | " | Thomas S. Kleppe | N.D. | 1975 |
| " | Ethan A. Hitchcock | Mo. | 1898 | Carter | Cecil D. Andrus | Ida. | 1977 |
| Roosevelt, T. | " | " | 1901 | | | | |

## Secretaries of Agriculture

The Department of Agriculture was created by act of Congress May 15, 1862. On Feb. 8, 1889, its commissioner was renamed secretary of agriculture and became a member of the cabinet.

| President | Secretary | Home | Apptd. | President | Secretary | Home | Apptd. |
|---|---|---|---|---|---|---|---|
| Cleveland | Norman J. Colman | Mo. | 1889 | McKinley | James Wilson | Ia. | 1897 |
| Harrison, B. | Jeremiah M. Rusk | Wis. | 1889 | Roosevelt, T. | " | " | 1901 |
| Cleveland | J. Sterling Morton | Neb. | 1893 | Taft | " | " | 1909 |

| President | Secretary | Home | Apptd. | President | Secretary | Home | App |
|---|---|---|---|---|---|---|---|
| Wilson | David F. Houston | Mo. | 1913 | " | Charles F. Brannan | Col. | 19 |
| " | Edward T. Meredith | Ia. | 1920 | Eisenhower | Ezra Taft Benson | Ut. | 19 |
| Harding | Henry C. Wallace | Ia. | 1921 | Kennedy | Orville L. Freeman | Minn. | 19 |
| Coolidge | " | " | 1923 | Johnson, L.B. | " | " | 19 |
| " | Howard M. Gore | W.Va. | 1924 | Nixon | Clifford M. Hardin | Ind. | 19 |
| " | W.M. Jardine | Kan. | 1925 | " | Earl L. Butz | Ind. | 19 |
| Hoover | Arthur M. Hyde | Mo. | 1929 | Ford | " | " | 19 |
| Roosevelt, F.D. | Henry A. Wallace | Ia. | 1933 | " | John A. Knebel | Va. | 19 |
| " | Claude R. Wickard | Ind. | 1940 | Carter | Bob Bergland | Minn. | 19 |
| Truman | Clinton P. Anderson | N.M. | 1945 | | | | |

## Secretaries of Commerce and Labor

The Department of Commerce and Labor, created by Congress Feb. 14, 1903, was divided by Congress Mar. 4, 1913, in separate departments of Commerce and Labor. The secretary of each was made a cabinet member.

### Secretaries of Commerce and Labor

| President | Secretary | Home | Apptd. |
|---|---|---|---|
| Roosevelt, T. | Geo. B. Cortelyou | N.Y. | 1903 |
| " | Victor H. Metcalf | Cal. | 1904 |
| " | Oscar S. Straus | N.Y. | 1906 |
| Taft | Charles Nagel | Mo. | 1909 |

### Secretaries of Labor

| President | Secretary | Home | Apptd. |
|---|---|---|---|
| Wilson | William B. Wilson | Pa. | 1913 |
| Harding | James J. Davis | Pa. | 1921 |
| Coolidge | " | " | 1923 |
| Hoover | " | " | 1929 |
| " | William N. Doak | Va. | 1930 |
| Roosevelt, F.D. | Frances Perkins | N.Y. | 1933 |
| Truman | L.B. Schwellenbach | Wash. | 1945 |
| " | Maurice J. Tobin | Mass. | 1949 |
| Eisenhower | Martin P. Durkin | Ill. | 1953 |
| " | James P. Mitchell | N.J. | 1953 |
| Kennedy | Arthur J. Goldberg | Ill. | 1961 |
| " | W. Willard Wirtz | Ill. | 1962 |
| Johnson, L.B. | W. Willard Wirtz | Ill. | 1963 |
| Nixon | George P. Shultz | Ill. | 1969 |
| " | James D. Hodgson | Cal. | 1970 |
| " | Peter J. Brennan | N.Y. | 1973 |
| Ford | " | " | 1974 |
| " | John T. Dunlop | Cal. | 1975 |
| " | W.J. Usery Jr. | Ga. | 1976 |
| Carter | F. Ray Marshall | Tex. | 1977 |

### Secretaries of Commerce

| President | Secretary | Home | App |
|---|---|---|---|
| Wilson | William C. Redfield | N.Y. | 19 |
| " | Josh. W. Alexander | Mo. | 19 |
| Harding | Herbert C. Hoover | Cal. | 19 |
| Coolidge | " | " | 19 |
| " | William F. Whiting | Mass. | 19 |
| Hoover | Robert P. Lamont | Ill. | 19 |
| " | Roy D. Chapin | Mich. | 19 |
| Roosevelt, F.D. | Daniel C. Roper | S.C. | 19 |
| " | Harry L. Hopkins | N.Y. | 19 |
| " | Jesse Jones | Tex. | 19 |
| " | Henry A. Wallace | Ia. | 19 |
| Truman | " | " | 19 |
| Truman | W. Averell Harriman | N.Y. | 19 |
| " | Charles Sawyer | Oh. | 19 |
| Eisenhower | Sinclair Weeks | Mass. | 19 |
| " | Lewis L. Strauss | N.Y. | 19 |
| " | Frederick H. Mueller | Mich. | 19 |
| Kennedy | Luther H. Hodges | N.C. | 19 |
| Johnson, L.B. | John T. Connor | N.J. | 19 |
| " | Alex B. Trowbridge | N.J. | 19 |
| " | C.R. Smith | N.Y. | 19 |
| Nixon | Maurice H. Stans | Minn. | 19 |
| " | Peter G. Peterson | Ill. | 19 |
| " | Frederick B. Dent | S.C. | 19 |
| Ford | " | " | 19 |
| " | Rogers C.B. Morton | Md. | 19 |
| " | Elliot L. Richardson | Mass. | 19 |
| Carter | Juanita M. Kreps | N.C. | 19 |

## Secretaries of Health, Education, and Welfare

The Department of Health, Education, and Welfare was created by act of Congress Apr. 11, 1953.

| President | Secretary | Home | Apptd. | President | Secretary | Home | App |
|---|---|---|---|---|---|---|---|
| Eisenhower | Oveta Culp Hobby | Tex. | 1953 | Johnson, L.B. | Wilbur J. Cohen | Mich. | 196 |
| " | Marion B. Folsom | N.Y. | 1955 | Nixon | Robert H. Finch | Cal. | 196 |
| " | Arthur S. Flemming | Oh. | 1958 | " | Elliot L. Richardson | Mass. | 197 |
| Kennedy | Abraham A. Ribicoff | Conn. | 1961 | " | Casper W. Weinberger | Cal. | 197 |
| " | Anthony J. Celebrezze | Oh. | 1962 | Ford | " | " | 197 |
| Johnson, L.B. | " | " | 1963 | " | Forrest D. Mathews | Ala. | 197 |
| " | John W. Gardner | N.Y. | 1965 | Carter | Joseph A. Califano, Jr. | D.C. | 197 |

## Secretaries of Housing and Urban Development

The Department of Housing and Urban Development was created by act of Congress Sept. 9, 1965.

| President | Secretary | Home | Apptd. | President | Secretary | Home | App |
|---|---|---|---|---|---|---|---|
| Johnson, L.B. | Robert C. Weaver | Wash. | 1966 | Ford | " | " | 197 |
| " | Robert C. Wood | Mass. | 1968 | " | Carla Anderson Hills | Cal. | 197 |
| Nixon | George W. Romney | Mich. | 1969 | Carter | Patricia Roberts Harris | D.C. | 197 |
| " | James T. Lynn | Oh. | 1973 | | | | |

## Secretaries of Transportation

The Department of Transportation was created by act of Congress Oct. 15, 1966.

| President | Secretary | Home | Apptd. | President | Secretary | Home | App |
|---|---|---|---|---|---|---|---|
| Johnson, L.B. | Alan S. Boyd | Fla. | 1966 | Ford | Claude S. Brinegar | Cal. | 197 |
| Nixon | John A. Volpe | Mass. | 1969 | " | William T. Coleman Jr. | Pa. | 197 |
| " | Claude S. Brinegar | Cal. | 1973 | Carter | Brock Adams | Wash. | 197 |

## Secretary of Energy

The Department of Energy was created by federal law Aug. 4, 1977.

| President | Secretary | Home | Apptd. |
|---|---|---|---|
| Carter | James R. Schlesinger | Va. | 1977 |

## Postmasters General

Congress established the Post Office Department as a branch of the Treasury Sept. 22, 1789. The postmaster general was made a member of the Cabinet Mar. 9, 1829. The Postal Reorganization Act of 1970 replaced the department with the U.S. Postal Service, an independent federal agency. Its head, the postmaster general, is not a member of the Cabinet.

| President | Postmaster General | Home | Apptd. | President | Postmaster General | Home | Apptd. |
|---|---|---|---|---|---|---|---|
| Washington | Samuel Osgood | Mass. | 1789 | Arthur | Timothy O. Howe | Wis. | 1881 |
| " | Timothy Pickering | Pa. | 1791 | " | Walter Q. Gresham | Ind. | 1883 |
| " | Joseph Habersham | Ga. | 1795 | " | Frank Hatton | Iowa | 1884 |
| Adams, J. | " | " | 1797 | Cleveland | William F. Vilas | Wis. | 1885 |
| Jefferson | " | " | 1801 | " | Don M. Dickinson | Mich. | 1888 |
| " | Gideon Granger | Conn. | 1801 | Harrison, B. | John Wanamaker | Pa. | 1889 |
| Madison | " | " | 1809 | Cleveland | Wilson S. Bissell | N.Y. | 1893 |
| " | Return J. Meigs Jr. | Ohio | 1814 | " | William L. Wilson | W.Va. | 1895 |
| Monroe | " | " | 1817 | McKinley | James A. Gary | Md. | 1897 |
| " | John McLean | " | 1823 | " | Charles E. Smith | Pa. | 1898 |
| Adams, J.Q. | " | " | 1825 | Roosevelt, T. | " | " | 1901 |
| Jackson | William T. Barry | Ky. | 1829 | " | Henry C. Payne | Wis. | 1902 |
| " | Amos Kendall | " | 1835 | " | Robert J. Wynne | Pa. | 1904 |
| Van Buren | " | " | 1837 | " | George B. Cortelyou | N.Y. | 1905 |
| " | John M. Niles | Conn. | 1840 | " | George von L. Meyer | Mass. | 1907 |
| Harrison, W.H. | Francis Granger | N.Y. | 1841 | Taft | Frank H. Hitchcock | " | 1909 |
| Tyler | " | N.Y. | 1841 | Wilson | Albert S. Burleson | Tex. | 1913 |
| " | Charles A. Wickliffe | Ky. | 1841 | Harding | Will H. Hays | Ind. | 1921 |
| Polk | Cave Johnson | Tenn. | 1845 | " | Hubert Work | Colo. | 1922 |
| Taylor | Jacob Collamer | Vt. | 1849 | " | Harry S. New | Ind. | 1923 |
| Fillmore | Nathan K. Hall | N.Y. | 1850 | Coolidge | " | " | 1923 |
| " | Samuel D. Hubbard | Conn. | 1852 | Hoover | Walter F. Brown | Ohio | 1929 |
| " | James Campbell | Pa. | 1853 | Roosevelt, F.D. | James A. Farley | N.Y. | 1933 |
| Buchanan | Aaron V. Brown | Tenn. | 1857 | " | Frank C. Walter | Pa. | 1940 |
| " | Joseph Holt | Ky. | 1859 | Truman | Robert E. Hannegan | Mo. | 1945 |
| " | Horatio King | Me. | 1861 | " | Jesse M. Donaldson | Mo. | 1947 |
| Lincoln | Montgomery Blair | D.C. | 1861 | Eisenhower | A.E. Summerfield | Mich. | 1953 |
| " | William Dennison | Ohio | 1864 | Kennedy | J. Edward Day | Calif. | 1961 |
| Johnson, A. | " | " | 1865 | " | John A. Gronouski | Wis. | 1963 |
| " | Alex W. Randall | Wis. | 1866 | Johnson, L.B. | " | " | 1963 |
| Grant | John A.J. Creswell | Md. | 1869 | " | Lawrence F. O'Brien | Mass. | 1965 |
| " | James W. Marshall | Va. | 1874 | " | W. Marvin Watson | Texas | 1968 |
| " | Marshall Jewell | Conn. | 1874 | Nixon | Winton M. Blount | Ala. | 1969 |
| " | James N. Tyner | Ind. | 1876 | (Appointed) (1). | Elmer T. Klassen | Md. | 1971 |
| Hayes | David McK. Key | Tenn. | 1877 | " | Benjamin F. Bailar | D.C. | 1975 |
| Hayes | Horace Maynard | Tenn. | 1880 | " | William F. Bolger | Conn. | 1978 |
| Garfield | Thomas L. James | N.Y. | 1881 | (1) Appointed by Postal Service Board of Governors. | | | |

## Law on Succession to the Presidency

If by reason of death, resignation, removal from office, inability, or failure to qualify there is neither a president nor vice president to discharge the powers and duties of the office of president, then the speaker of the House of Representatives shall upon his resignation as speaker and as representative, act as president. The same rule shall apply in the case of the death, resignation, removal from office, or inability of an individual acting as president.

If at the time when a speaker is to begin the discharge of the powers and duties of the office of president there is no speaker, or the speaker fails to qualify as acting president, then the president pro tempore of the Senate, upon his resignation as president pro tempore and as senator, shall act as president.

An individual acting as president shall continue to act until the expiration of the then current presidential term, except that (1) if his discharge of the powers and duties of the office is founded in whole or in part in the failure of both the president-elect and the vice president-elect to qualify, then he shall act only until a president or vice president qualifies, and (2) if his discharge of the powers and duties of the office is founded in whole or in part on the inability of the president or vice president, then he shall act only until the removal of the disability of one of such individuals.

If, by reason of death, resignation, removal from office, or failure to qualify, there is no president pro tempore to act as president, then the officer of the United States who is highest on the following list, and who is not under disability to discharge the powers and duties of president, shall act as president; the secretaries of state, treasury, defense, attorney general; secretaries of interior, agriculture, commerce, labor; health, education and welfare; housing and urban development; transportation.

*(Legislation approved July 18, 1947; amended Sept. 9, 1965, and Oct. 15, 1966. See also Constitutional Amendment XXV.)*

## Burial Places of the Presidents

| | | | | | |
|---|---|---|---|---|---|
| Washington | Mt. Vernon, Va. | Fillmore | Buffalo, N.Y. | T. Roosevelt | Oyster Bay, N.Y. |
| J. Adams | Quincy, Mass. | Pierce | Concord, N.H. | Taft | Arlington Nat'l. Cem'y. |
| Jefferson | Charlottesville, Va. | Buchanan | Lancaster, Pa. | Wilson | Washington Cathedral |
| Madison | Montpelier Station, Va. | Lincoln | Springfield, Ill. | Harding | Marion, Oh. |
| Monroe | Richmond, Va. | A. Johnson | Greeneville Tenn. | Coolidge | Plymouth, Vt. |
| J.Q. Adams | Quincy, Mass. | Grant | New York City | Hoover | West Branch, Ia. |
| Jackson | Nashville, Tenn. | Hayes | Fremont, Oh. | F.D. Roosevelt | Hyde Park, N.Y. |
| Van Buren | Kinderhook, N.Y. | Garfield | Cleveland, Oh. | Truman | Independence, Mo. |
| W.H. Harrison | North Bend, Oh. | Arthur | Albany, N.Y. | Eisenhower | Abilene, Kan. |
| Tyler | Richmond, Va. | Cleveland | Princeton, N.J. | Kennedy | Arlington Nat'l. Cem'y. |
| Polk | Nashville, Tenn. | B. Harrison | Indianapolis, Ind. | L.B. Johnson | Stonewall, Tex. |
| Taylor | Louisville, Ky. | McKinley | Canton, Oh. | | |

# BIOGRAPHIES OF U.S. PRESIDENTS

## George Washington

George Washington, first president, was born Feb. 22, 1732 (Feb. 11, 1731. old style), the son of Augustine Washington and Mary Ball, at Wakefield on Pope's Creek, Westmoreland Co., Va. His early childhood was spent on the Ferry farm, near Fredericksburg. His father died when George was 11. He studied mathematics and surveying and when 16 went to live with his half brother Lawrence, who built and named Mount Vernon. George surveyed the lands of William Fairfax in the Shenandoah Valley, keeping a diary. He accompanied Lawrence to Barbados, West Indies, contracted small pox, and was deeply scarred. Lawrence died in 1752 and George acquired his property by inheritance. He valued land and when he died owned 70,000 acres in Virginia and 40,000 acres in what is now West Virginia.

Washington's military service began in 1753 when Gov. Dinwiddie of Virginia sent him on missions deep into Ohio country. He clashed with the French and had to surrender Fort Necessity July 3, 1754. He was an aide to Braddock and at his side when the army was ambushed and defeated on a march to Ft. Duquesne, July 9, 1755. He helped take Fort Duquesne from the French in 1758.

After his marriage to Martha Dandridge Custis, a widow, in 1759, Washington managed his family estate at Mount Vernon. Although not at first for independence, he opposed British exactions and took charge of the Virginia troops before war broke out. He was made commander-in-chief by the Continental Congress June 15, 1775.

The successful issue of a war filled with hardships was due to his leadership. He was resourceful, a stern disciplinarian, and the one strong, dependable force for unity. He favored a federal government and became chairman of the Constitutional Convention of 1787. He helped get the Constitution ratified and was unanimously elected president by the electoral college and inaugurated, Apr. 30, 1789, on the balcony of New York's Federal Hall.

He was reelected 1792, but refused to consider a 3d term and retired to Mount Vernon. He suffered acute laryngitis after a ride in snow and rain around his estate, was bled profusely, and died Dec. 14, 1799.

## John Adams

John Adams, 2d president, Federalist, was born in Braintree (Quincy), Mass., Oct. 30, 1735 (Oct. 19, o. s.), the son of John Adams, a farmer, and Susanna Boylston. He was a great-grandson of Henry Adams who came from England in 1636. He was graduated from Harvard, 1755, taught school, studied law. In 1765 he argued against taxation without representation before the royal governor. In 1770 he defended the British soldiers who fired on civilians in the "Boston Massacre." He was a delegate to the first Continental Congress, and signed the Declaration of Independence. He was a commissioner to France, 1778, with Benjamin Franklin and Arthur Lee; won recognition of the U.S. by The Hague, 1782; was first American minister to England, 1785-1788, and was elected vice president, 1788 and 1792.

In 1796 Adams was chosen president by the electors. Intense antagonism to America by France cause agitation for war, led by Alexander Hamilton. Adams, breaking with Hamilton, opposed war.

To fight alien influence and muzzle criticism Adams supported the Alien and Sedition laws of 1798, which led to his defeat for reelection. He died July 4, 1826, on the same day as Jefferson (the 50th anniversary of the Declaration of Independence).

## Thomas Jefferson

Thomas Jefferson, 3d president, was born Apr. 13, 1743 (Apr. 2, o. s.), at Shadwell, Va., the son of Peter Jefferson, a civil engineer of Welsh descent who raised tobacco, and Jane Randolph. His father died when he was 14, leaving him 2,750 acres and his slaves. Jefferson attended the College of William and Mary, 1760-1762, read classics in Greek and Latin and played the violin. In 1769 he was elected to the House of Burgesses. In 1770 he began building Monticello near Charlottesville. He was a member of the Virginia Committee of Correspondence and the Continental Congress. Named a member of the committee to draw up a Declaration of Independence, he wrote the basic draft. He was a member of the Virginia House of Delegates, 1776-79, elected governor to succeed Patrick Henry, 1779, reelected 1780, resigned June 1781, amid charges of ineffectual military preparation. During his term he wrote the statute on religious freedom. In the Continental Congress, 1783, he drew up an ordinance for the Northwest Territory, forbidding slavery after 1800; its terms were put into the Ordinance 1787. He was sent to Paris with Benjamin Franklin and John Adams to negotiate commercial treaties, 1784; made minister to France, 1785.

Washington appointed him secretary of state, 1789. Jefferson's strong faith in the consent of the governed, as opposed to executive control favored by Hamilton, secretary of the treasury, often led to conflict: Dec. 31, 1793, he resigned. He was the Republican candidate for president in 1796; beaten by John Adams, he became vice president. In 1800, Jefferson and Aaron Burr received equal electoral college vote for president. The House of Representatives elected Jefferson. Major events of his administration were the Louisiana Purchase, 1803, and the Lewis and Clark Expedition. He established the Univ. of Virginia and designed its buildings. He died July 4, 1826, on the same day as John Adams.

## James Madison

James Madison, 4th president, Republican, was born Mar. 16, 1751 (Mar. 5, 1750, o. s.) at Port Conway, King George Co., Va., eldest son of James Madison and Eleanor Rose Conway. Madison was graduated from Princeton 1771; studied theology, 1772; sat in the Virginia Constitutional Convention, 1776. He was a member of the Continental Congress. He was chief recorder at the Constitution Convention in 1787, and supported ratification in the Federalist Papers, written with Alexander Hamilton and John Jay. He was elected to the House of Representatives in 1789 helped frame the Bill of Rights and fought the Alien and Sedition Acts. He became Jefferson's secretary of state, 1801.

Elected president in 1808, Madison was a "strict constructionist," opposed to the free interpretation of the Constitution by the Federalists. He was reelected in 1812 by the votes of the agrarian South and recently admitted western states. Caught between British and French maritime restrictions, the U.S. drifted into war, declared June 18, 1812. The war ended in a stalemate. He retired in 1817 to his estate at Montpelier. There he edited his famous papers on the Constitutional Convention. He became rector of the Univ. of Virginia, 1826. He died June 28, 1836.

## James Monroe

James Monroe, 5th president, Republican, was born Apr. 28, 1758, in Westmoreland Co., Va., the son of Spence Monroe and Eliza Jones, who were of Scottish and Welsh descent, respectively. He attended the College of William and Mary, fought in the 3d Virginia Regiment at White Plains, Brandywine, Monmouth, and was wounded at Trenton. He studied law with Thomas Jefferson, 1780, was a member of the Virginia House of Delegates and of Congress, 1783-86. He opposed ratification of the Constitution because it lacked a bill of rights; was U.S. senator, 1790; minister to France, 1794-96; governor of Virginia, 1799-1802, and 1811. Jefferson sent him to France as minister, 1803. He helped R. Livingston negotiate the Louisiana Purchase, 1803. He ran against Madison for president in 1808. He was elected to the Virginia Assembly, 1810-1811; was secretary of state under Madison, 1811-1817.

In 1816 Monroe was elected president; in 1820 reelected

th all but one electoral college vote. Monroe's administraon became the "Era of Good Feeling." He obtained Flor-
a from Spain; settled boundaries with Canada, and elimi-
ed border forts. He supported the anti-slavery position
at led to the Missouri Compromise. His most significant
ntribution was the "Monroe Doctrine," which became a
rnerstone of U.S. foreign policy. Monroe retired to Oak
ll, Va. Financial problems forced him to sell his property.
e moved to New York City to live with a daughter. He
d there July 4, 1831.

## John Quincy Adams

John Quincy Adams, 6th president, independent Federal-
, was born July 11, 1767, at Braintree (Quincy), Mass., the
n of John and Abigail Adams. His father was the 2d presi-
nt. He was educated in Paris, Leyden, and Harvard, grad-
ting in 1787. He served as American minister in various
uropean capitals, and helped draft the War of 1812 peace
eaty. He was U.S. Senator, 1803-08. President Monroe
ade him secretary of state, 1817, and he negotiated the ces-
on of the Floridas from Spain, supported exclusion of slav-
y in the Missouri Compromise, and helped formulate the
onroe Doctrine. In 1824 he was elected president by the
ouse after he failed to win an electoral college majority.
is expansion of executive powers was strongly opposed
d he was beaten in 1828 by Jackson. In 1831 he entered
ongress and served 17 years with distinction. He opposed
avery, the annexation of Texas, and the Mexican War. He
lped establish the Smithsonian Institution. He had a
roke in the House and died in the Speaker's Room, Feb.
, 1848.

## Andrew Jackson

Andrew Jackson, 7th president, was a Jeffersonian-
epublican, later a Democrat. He was born in the Waxhaws
strict, New Lancaster Co., S.C., Mar. 15, 1767, the post-
umous son of Andrew Jackson and Elizabeth Hutchinson,
ho were Irish immigrants. At 13, he joined the militia in
e Revolution and was captured.

He read law in Salisbury, N.C., moved to Nashville,
enn., speculated in land, married, and practiced law. In
796 he helped draft the constitution of Tennessee and for a
ar occupied its one seat in Congress. He was in the Senate
1797, and again in 1823. He defeated the Creek Indians at
orseshoe Bend, Ala., 1814. With 6,000 backwoods fighters
e defeated Packenham's 12,000 British troops at the Chal-
ette, outside New Orleans, Jan. 8, 1815. In 1818 he briefly
vaded Spanish Florida to quell Seminoles and outlaws
ho harassed frontier settlements. In 1824 he ran for presient against John Quincy Adams and had the most popular
d electoral votes but not a majority; the election was de-
ded by the House, which chose Adams. In 1828 he de-
ated Adams, carrying the West and South. He was a noisy
ebater and a duelist and introduced rotation in office called
e "spoils system." Suspicious of privilege, he ruined the
ank of the United States by depositing federal funds with
ate banks. Though "Let the people rule" was his slogan,
e at times supported strict constructionist policies against
e expansionist West. He killed the Congressional caucus
r nominating presidential candidates and substituted the
ational convention, 1832. When South Carolina refused to
ollect imports under his protective tariff he ordered army
d naval forces to Charleston. Jackson recognized the
epublic of Texas, 1836. He died at the Hermitage, June 8,
845.

## Martin Van Buren

Martin Van Buren, 8th president, Democrat, was born
ec. 5, 1782, at Kinderhook, N.Y., the son of Abraham
an Buren, a Dutch farmer, and Mary Hoes. He was surro-
ate of Columbia County, N.Y., state senator and attorney
eneral. He was U.S. senator 1821, reelected, 1827, elected
overnor of New York, 1828. He helped swing eastern sup-
ort to Jackson in 1828 and was his secretary of state
829-31. In 1832 he was elected vice president. He was a

consummate politician, known as "the little magician," and
influenced Jackson's policies. In 1836 he defeated William
Henry Harrison for president and took office as the Panic of
1837 initiated a 5-year nationwide depression. He inaugurated the independent treasury system. His refusal to spend
land revenues led to his defeat by Harrison in 1840. He lost
the Democratic nomination of 1844 to Polk. In 1848 he ran
for president on the Free Soil ticket and lost. He died July
24, 1862, at Kinderhook.

## William Henry Harrison

William Henry Harrison, 9th president, Whig, who served
only 31 days, was born in Berkeley, Charles City Co., Va.,
Feb. 9, 1773, the 3d son of Benjamin Harrison, signer of the
Declaration of Independence. He attended Hampden Sydney College. He was secretary of the Northwest Territory,
1798; its delegate in Congress, 1799; first governor of Indi-
ana Territory, 1800; and superintendent of Indian affairs.
With 900 men he routed Tecumseh's Indians at Tippecanoe,
Nov. 7, 1811. A major general, he defeated British and
Indians at Battle of the Thames, Oct. 5, 1813. He served in
Congress, 1816-19; Senate, 1825-28. In 1840, when 68, he
was elected president with a "log cabin and hard cider" slogan. He caught pneumonia during the inauguration and died
Apr. 4, 1841.

## John Tyler

John Tyler, 10th president, independent Whig, was born
Mar. 29, 1790, in Greenway, Charles City Co., Va., son of
John Tyler and Mary Armistead. His father was governor of
Virginia, 1808-11. Tyler was graduated from William and
Mary, 1807; member of the House of Delegates, 1811; in
congress, 1816-21; in Virginia legislature, 1823-25; governor
of Virginia, 1825-26; U.S. senator, 1827-36. In 1840 he was
elected vice president and, on Harrison's death, succeeded
him. He favored pre-emption, allowing settlers to get government land; rejected a national bank bill and thus alienated most Whig supporters; refused to honor the spoils system. He signed the resolution annexing Texas, Mar. 1, 1845.
He accepted renomination, 1844, but withdrew before election. In 1861, he chaired an unsuccessful Washington conference called to avert civil war. After its failure he supported secession, sat in the provisional Confederate
Congress, became a member of the Confederate House, but
died, Jan. 18, 1862, before it met.

## James Knox Polk

James Knox Polk, 11th president, Democrat, was born in
Mecklenburg Co., N.C., Nov. 2, 1795, the son of Samuel
Polk, farmer and surveyor of Scotch-Irish descent, and Jane
Knox. He graduated from the Univ. of North Carolina,
1818; member of the Tennessee state legislature, 1823-25.
He served in Congress 1825-39 and as speaker 1835-39. He
was governor of Tennessee 1839-41, but was defeated 1841
and 1843. In 1844, when both Clay and Van Buren announced opposition to annexing Texas, the Democrats made
Polk the first dark horse nominee because he demanded control of all Oregon and annexation of Texas. Polk reestablished the independent treasury system originated by
Van Buren. His expansionist policy was opposed by Clay,
Webster, Calhoun; he sent troops under Zachary Taylor to
the Mexican border and, when Mexicans attacked, declared
war existed. The Mexican war ended with the annexation of
California and much of the Southwest as part of America's
"manifest destiny." He compromised on the Oregon boundary ("54-40 or fight!") by accepting the 49th parallel and
giving Vancouver to the British. Polk died in Nashville, June
15, 1849.

## Zachary Taylor

Zachary Taylor, 12th president, Whig, who served only
16 months, was born Nov. 24, 1784, in Orange Co., Va., the
son of Richard Taylor, later collector of the port of Louisville, Ky., and Sarah Strother. Taylor was commissioned
first lieutenant, 1808; fought in the War of 1812; the Black

Hawk War, 1832; and the second Seminole War, 1837. He was called Old Rough and Ready. He settled on a plantation near Baton Rouge, La. In 1845 Polk sent him with an army to the Rio Grande. When the Mexicans attacked him, Polk declared war. Taylor was successful at Palo Alto and Resaca de la Palma, 1846; occupied Monterey. Polk made him major general but sent many of his troops to Gen. Winfield Scott. Outnumbered 4-1, he defeated Santa Anna at Buena Vista, 1847. A national hero, he received the Whig nomination in 1848, and was elected president. He resumed the spoils system and though once a slave-holder worked to have California admitted as a free state. He died in office July 9, 1850.

## Millard Fillmore

Millard Fillmore, 13th president, Whig, was born Jan. 7, 1800, in Cayuga Co., N.Y., the son of Nathaniel Fillmore and Phoebe Miller. He taught school and studied law; admitted to the bar, 1823. He was a member of the state assembly, 1829-32; in Congress, 1833-35 and again 1837-43. He opposed the entrance of Texas as slave territory and voted for a protective tariff. In 1844 he was defeated for governor of New York. In 1848 he was elected vice president and succeeded as president July 10, 1850, after Taylor's death. Fillmore favored the Compromise of 1850 and signed the Fugitive Slave Law. His policies pleased neither expansionists nor slave-holders and he was not renominated in 1852. In 1856 he was nominated by the American (Know-Nothing) party and accepted by the Whigs, but defeated by Buchanan. He died in Buffalo, Mar. 8, 1874.

## Franklin Pierce

Franklin Pierce, 14th president, Democrat, was born in Hillsboro, N. H., Nov. 23, 1804, the son of Benjamin Pierce, veteran of the Revolution and governor of New Hampshire, 1827. He graduated from Bowdoin, 1824. A lawyer, he served in the state legislature 1829-33; in Congress, supporting Jackson, 1833-37; U.S. senator, 1837-42. He enlisted in the Mexican War, became brigadier general under Gen. Winfield Scott. In 1852 Pierce was nominated on the 49th ballot over Lewis Cass, Stephen A. Douglas, and James Buchanan, and defeated Gen. Scott, Whig. Though against slavery, Pierce was influenced by Southern pro-slavery men. He ignored the Ostend Manifesto that the U.S. either buy or take Cuba. He approved the Kansas-Nebraska Act, leaving slavery to popular vote ("squatter sovereignty"), 1854. He signed a reciprocity treaty with Canada and approved the Gadsden Purchase from Mexico, 1853. Denied renomination by the Democrats, he spent most of his remaining years in Concord, N.H., where he died Oct. 8, 1869.

## James Buchanan

James Buchanan, 15th president, Federalist, later Democrat, was born of Scottish descent near Mercersburg, Pa., Apr. 23, 1791. He graduated Dickinson, 1809; was a volunteer in the War of 1812; member, Pennsylvania legislature, 1814-16; Congress, 1820-31; Jackson's minister to Russia, 1831-33; U.S. senator 1834-45. As Polk's secretary of state, 1845-49, he ended the Oregon dispute with Britain, supported the Mexican War and annexation of Texas. As minister to Britain, 1853, he signed the Ostend Manifesto. Nominated by Democrats, he was elected, 1856, over John C. Fremont (Republican) and Millard Fillmore (American Know-Nothing and Whig tickets). On slavery he favored popular sovereignty and choice by state constitutions; he accepted the pro-slavery Dred Scott decision as binding. He denied the right of states to secede. A strict constructionist, he desired to keep peace and found no authority for using force. He died at Wheatland, near Lancaster, Pa., June 1, 1868.

## Abraham Lincoln

Abraham Lincoln, 16th president, Republican, was born Feb. 12, 1809, in a log cabin on a farm then in Hardin Co.,

Ky., now in Larue. He was the son of Thomas Lincoln, carpenter, and Nancy Hanks.

The Lincolns moved to Spencer Co., Ind., near Gentryville, when Abe was 7. Nancy died 1818, and his father married Mrs. Sarah Bush Johnston, 1819; she had a favorable influence on Abe. In 1830 the family moved to Macon C Ill. Lincoln lost election to the Illinois General Assembly 1832, but later won 4 times, beginning in 1834. He enlisted in the militia for the Black Hawk War, 1832. In New Sale he ran a store, surveyed land, and was postmaster.

In 1837 Lincoln was admitted to the bar and became partner in a Springfield, Ill., law office. He was elected Congress, 1847-49. He opposed the Mexican War. He supported Zachary Taylor, 1848. He opposed the Kansas Nebraska Act and extension of slavery, 1854. He failed, his bid for the Senate, 1855. He supported John C. Fremont 1856.

In 1858 Lincoln had Republican support in the Illinois legislature for the Senate but was defeated by Stephen Douglas, Dem., who had sponsored the Kansas-Nebraska Act.

Lincoln was nominated for president by the Republic party on an anti-slavery platform, 1860. He ran against Douglas, a northern Democrat; John C. Breckinridge southern pro-slavery Democrat; John Bell, Constitution Union party. When he won the election, South Carolina ceded from the Union Dec. 20, 1860, followed in 1861 by Southern states.

The Civil War erupted when Fort Sumter was attacked Apr. 12, 1861. On Sept. 22, 1862, 5 days after the battle Antietam, he announced that slaves in territory then in bellion would be free Jan. 1, 1863, date of the Emancipation Proclamation. His speeches, including his Gettysburg a Inaugural addresses, are remembered for their eloquence.

Lincoln was reelected, 1864, over Gen. George B. McClellan, Democrat. Lee surrendered Apr. 9, 1865. On Apr. Lincoln was shot by actor John Wilkes Booth in Ford Theatre, Washington. He died the next day.

## Andrew Johnson

Andrew Johnson, 17th president, Democrat, was born Raleigh, N.C., Dec. 29, 1808, the son of Jacob Johnson porter at an inn and church sexton, and Mary McDonough He was apprenticed to a tailor but ran away and eventual settled in Greenville, Tenn. He became an alderman, 182 mayor, 1830; state representative and senator, 1835-41 member of Congress, 1843-53; governor of Tennessee 1853-57; U.S. senator, 1857-62. He supported John Breckinridge against Lincoln in 1860. He had held slave but opposed secession and tried to prevent his home sta Tennessee, from seceding. In Mar. 1862, Lincoln appointed him military governor of occupied Tennessee. In 1864 was nominated for vice president with Lincoln on the N tional Union ticket to win Democratic support. He su ceeded Lincoln as president April 15, 1865. In a controversy with Congress over the president's power over the South, proclaimed, May 26, 1865, an amnesty to all Confederate except certain leaders if they would ratify the 13th Amendment abolishing slavery. States doing so added anti-Neg provisions that enraged Congress, which restored milita control over the South. When Johnson removed Edwin Stanton, secretary of war, without notifying the Senate, th repudiating the Tenure of Office Act, the House impeach him for this and other reasons. He was tried by the Sena and acquitted by only one vote, May 26, 1868. He return to the Senate in 1875. Johnson died July 31, 1875.

## Ulysses Simpson Grant

Ulysses S. Grant, 18th president, Republican, was born Point Pleasant, Oh., Apr. 27, 1822, son of Jesse R. Grant, tanner, and Hannah Simpson. The next year the fami moved to Georgetown, Oh. Grant was named Hiram Ulysses, but on entering West Point, 1839, his name was entered as Ulysses Simpson and he adopted it. he was graduated 1843; served under Gens. Taylor and Scott in the Mexica War; resigned, 1854; worked in St. Louis until 1860, th went to Galena, Ill. With the start of the Civil War, he w

amed colonel of the 21st Illinois Vols., 1861, then brigadier
general; took Forts Henry and Donelson; fought at Shiloh,
took Vicksburg. After his victory at Chattanooga, Lincoln
placed him in command of the Union Armies. He accepted
Lee's surrender at Appomattox, Apr., 1865. President John-
on appointed Grant secretary of war when he suspended
Stanton, but Grant was not confirmed. He was nominated
or president by the Republicans and elected over Horatio
Seymour, Democrat. The 15th Amendment, amnesty bill,
and civil service reform were events of his administration.
The Liberal Republicans and Democrats opposed him with
Horace Greeley, 1872, but he was reelected. An attempt by
the Stalwarts (Old Guard) to nominate him in 1880 failed.
In 1884 the collapse of Grant & Ward, investment house,
left him penniless. He wrote his personal memoirs while ill
with cancer and completed them 4 days before his death at
Mt. McGregor, N.Y., July 23, 1885. The book realized over
450,000.

### Rutherford Birchard Hayes

Rutherford B. Hayes, 19th president, Republican, was
born in Delaware, Oh., Oct. 4, 1822, the posthumous son of
Rutherford Hayes, a farmer, and Sophia Birchard. He was
raised by his uncle Sardis Birchard. He graduated from
Kenyon College, 1842, and Harvard Law School, 1845. He
practiced law in Lower Sandusky, Oh., now Fremont; was
city solicitor of Cincinnati, 1858-61. In the Civil War, he
was major of the 23d Ohio Vols., was wounded several
times, and rose to the rank of brevet major general, 1864.
He served in Congress 1864-67, supporting Reconstruction
and Johnson's impeachment. He was elected governor of
Ohio, 1867 and 1869; beaten in the race for Congress, 1872;
reelected governor, 1875. In 1876 he was nominated for
president and believed he had lost the election to Samuel J.
Tilden, Democrat. But a few Southern states submitted 2
different sets of electoral votes and the result was in dispute.
An electoral commission, appointed by Congress, 8 Republicans and 7 Democrats, awarded all disputed votes to
Hayes allowing him to become president by one electoral
vote. Hayes, keeping a promise to southerners, withdrew
troops from areas still occupied in the South, ending the era
of Reconstruction. He proceeded to reform the civil service,
alienating political spoilsmen. He advocated repeal of the
Tenure of Office Act. He supported sound money and specie
payments. Hayes died in Fremont, Oh., Jan. 17, 1893.

### James Abram Garfield

James A. Garfield, 20th president, Republican, was born
Nov. 19, 1831, in Orange, Cuyahoga Co., Oh., the son of
Abram Garfield and Eliza Ballou. His father died in 1833.
He worked as a canal bargeman, farmer, and carpenter; attended Western Reserve Eclectic, later Hiram College, and
was graduated from Williams in 1856. He taught at Hiram,
and later became principal. He was in the Ohio senate in
1859. Anti-slavery and anti-secession, he volunteered for the
war, became colonel of the 42d Ohio Infantry and brigadier
in 1862. He fought at Shiloh, was chief of staff for Rosecrans and was made major general for gallantry at Chickamauga. He entered Congress as a radical Republican in
1863; supported specie payment as against paper money
(greenbacks). On the electoral commission in 1876 he voted
for Hayes against Tilden on strict party lines. He was sena-
tor-elect in 1880 when he became the Republican nominee
for president. He was chosen as a compromise over Gen.
Grant, James G. Blaine, and John Sherman. This alienated
the Grant following but Garfield was elected. On July 2,
1881, Garfield was shot by mentally disturbed office-seeker,
Charles J. Guiteau, while entering a railroad station in
Washington. He died Sept. 19, 1881, at Elberon, N.J.

### Chester Alan Arthur

Chester A. Arthur, 21st president, Republican, was born
at Fairfield, Vt., Oct. 5, 1829, the son of the Rev. William
Arthur, from County Antrim, Ireland, and Malvina Stone.
He graduated Union College, 1848, taught school at Pownall, Vt., studied law in New York. In 1853 he argued in a
fugitive slave case that slaves transported through N.Y.
State were thereby freed; in 1885 he obtained a ruling that
Negroes were to be treated the same as whites on street cars.
He was made collector of the Port of New York, 1871. President Hayes, reforming the civil service, forced Arthur to
resign, 1879. This made the New York machine stalwarts
enemies of Hayes. Arthur and the stalwarts tried to nominate Grant for a 3d term in 1880. When Garfield was nominated, Arthur received 2d place in the interests of harmony.
When Garfield died, Arthur became president. He supported civil service reform and the tariff of 1883. He was
defeated for renomination by James G. Blaine. He died in
New York City Nov. 18, 1886.

### Grover Cleveland

*(According to a ruling of the State Dept., Grover Cleveland
is both the 22d and the 24th president, because his 2 terms
were not consecutive. By individuals, he is only the 22d.)*

Grover Cleveland, 22d and 24th president, Democrat, was
born in Caldwell, N.J. Mar. 18, 1837, the son of Richard F.
Cleveland, a Presbyterian minister, and Ann Neale. He was
named Steven Grover, but dropped the Stephen. He clerked
in Clinton and Buffalo, N.Y., taught at the N.Y. City Institution for the Blind; was admitted to the bar in Buffalo,
1859; became assistant district attorney, 1863; sheriff, 1871;
mayor, 1881; governor of New York, 1882. He was an independent, honest administrator who hated corruption. He
was nominated for president over Tammany Hall opposition, 1884, and defeated Republican James G. Blaine. He
enlarged the civil service, vetoed many pension raids on the
Treasury. In 1888 he was defeated by Benjamin Harrison,
although his popular vote was larger. Reelected over Harrison in 1892, he faced a money crisis brought about by lowering of the gold reserve, circulation of paper and exorbitant
silver purchases under the Sherman Act; obtained a repeal
of the latter and a reduced tariff. A severe depression and
labor troubles racked his administration but he refused to
interfere in business matters and rejected Jacob Coxey's demand for unemployment relief. He broke the Pullman strike,
1894. In 1896, the Democrats repudiated his administration
and chose silverite William Jennings Bryan as their candidate. Cleveland died in Princeton, N.J., June 24, 1908.

### Benjamin Harrison

Benjamin Harrison, 23d president, Republican, was born
at North Bend, Oh., Aug. 20, 1833. His great-grandfather,
Benjamin Harrison, was a signer of the Declaration of Independence; his grandfather, William Henry Harrison, was 9th
President; his father, John Scott Harrison, was a member of
Congress. His mother was Elizabeth F. Irwin. He attended
school on his father's farm; graduated from Miami Univ. at
Oxford, Oh., 1852; admitted to the bar, 1853, and practiced
in Indianapolis. In the Civil War, he rose to the rank of brevet brigadier general, fought at Kenesaw Mountain, Peachtree Creek, Nashville, and in the Atlanta campaign. He
failed to be elected governor of Indiana, 1876; but became
senator, 1881, and worked for the G. A. R. pensions vetoed
by Cleveland. In 1888 he defeated Cleveland for president
despite having fewer popular votes. He expanded the pension list; signed the McKinley high tariff bill and the Sherman Silver Purchase Act. During his administration, 6 states
were admitted to the union. He was defeated for reelection,
1892. He represented Venezuela in a boundary arbitration
with Great Britain in Paris, 1899. He died at Indianapolis,
Mar. 13, 1901.

### William McKinley

William McKinley, 25th president, Republican, was born
in Niles, Oh., Jan. 29, 1843, the son of William McKinley,
an ironmaker, and Nancy Allison. McKinley attended
school in Poland, Oh., and Allegheny College, Meadville,
Pa., and enlisted for the Civil War at 18 in the 23d Ohio, in
which Rutherford B. Hayes was a major. He rose to captain
and in 1865 was made brevet major. He studied law in the
Albany, N.Y., law school; opened an office in Canton, Oh.,

in 1867, and campaigned for Grant and Hayes. He served in the House of Representatives, 1877-83, 1885-91, and led the fight for passage of the McKinley Tarriff, 1890. Defeated for reelection on the issue in 1890, he was governor of Ohio, 1892-96. He had support for president in the convention that nominated Benjamin Harrison in 1892. In 1896 he was elected president on a protective tariff, sound money (gold standard) platform over William Jennings Bryan, Democratic proponent of free silver. McKinley was reluctant to intervene in Cuba but the loss of the battleship Maine at Havana crystallized opinion. He demanded Spain's withdrawal from Cuba; Spain made some concessions but Congress announced state of war as of Apr. 21. He was reelected in the 1900 campaign, defeating Bryan's anti-imperialist arguments with the promise of a "full dinner pail". McKinley was respected for his conciliatory nature, but conservative on business issues. On Sept. 6, 1901, while welcoming citizens at the Pan-American Exposition, Buffalo, N.Y., he was shot by Leon Czolgosz, an anarchist. He died Sept. 14.

## Theodore Roosevelt

Theodore Roosevelt, 26th president, Republican, was born in N.Y. City, Oct. 27, 1858, the son of Theodore Roosevelt, collector of the port, and Martha Bulloch. He was a 5th cousin of Franklin D. Roosevelt and an uncle of Mrs. Eleanor Roosevelt. Roosevelt graduated from Harvard, 1880; attended Columbia Law School briefly; sat in the N.Y. State Assembly, 1882-84; ranched in North Dakota, 1884-86; failed election as mayor of N.Y. City, 1886; member of U.S. Civil Service Commission, 1889; president, N.Y. Police Board, 1895, supporting the merit system; assistant secretary of the Navy under McKinley, 1897-98. In the war with Spain, he organized the 1st U.S. Volunteer Cavalry (Rough Riders) as lieutenant colonel; led the charge up Kettle Hill at San Juan. Elected New York governor, 1898-1900, he fought the spoils system and achieved taxation of corporation franchises. Nominated for vice president, 1900, he became nation's youngest president when McKinley died. As president he fought corruption of politics by big business; dissolved Northern Securities Co. and others for violating, anti-trust laws; intervened in coal strike on behalf of the public, 1902; obtained Elkins Law forbidding rebates to favored corporations, 1903; Hepburn Law regulating railroad rates, 1906; Pure Food and Drugs Act, 1906, Reclamation Act and employers' liability laws. He organized conservation, mediated the peace between Japan and Russia, 1905; won the Nobel Peace Prize. He was the first to use the Hague Court of International Arbitration. By recognizing the new Republic of Panama he made Panama Canal possible. He was reelected in 1904.

In 1908 he obtained the nomination of William H. Taft, who was elected. Feeling that Taft had abandoned his policies, Roosevelt unsuccessfully sought the nomination in 1912. He bolted the party and ran on the Progressive "Bull Moose", ticket against Taft and Woodrow Wilson, splitting the Republicans and insuring Wilson's election. He was shot during the campaign but recovered. In 1916 he supported Charles E. Hughes, Republican. A strong friend of Britain, he fought American isolation in World War I. He wrote some 40 books on many topics; his *Winning of the West* is best known. He died Jan. 6, 1919, at Sagamore Hill, Oyster Bay, N.Y.

## William Howard Taft

William Howard Taft, 27th president, Republican, was born in Cincinnati, Oh., Sept. 15, 1857, the son of Alphonso Taft and Louisa Maria Torrey. His father was secretary of war and attorney general in Grant's cabinet; minister to Austria and Russia under Arthur. Taft was graduated from Yale, 1878; Cincinnati Law School, 1880; became law reporter for Cincinnati newspapers; was assistant prosecuting attorney, 1881-83; assistant county solicitor, 1885; judge, superior court, 1887; U.S. solicitor-general, 1890; federal circuit judge, 1892. In 1900 he became head of the U.S. Philippines Commission and was first civil governor of the Philippines, 1901-04; secretary of war, 1904; provisional governor of Cuba, 1906. He was groomed for president by Roosevelt

and elected over Bryan, 1908. His administration dissolved Standard Oil and tobacco trusts; instituted Dept. of Labor; drafted direct election of senators and income tax amendments. His tariff and conservation policies angered progressives; though renominated he was opposed by Roosevelt; the result was Democrat Woodrow Wilson's election. Taft with some reservations, supported the League of Nations. He was professor of constitutional law, Yale, 1913-21; chief justice of the U.S., 1921-30; illness forced him to resign. He died in Washington, Mar. 8, 1930.

## Woodrow Wilson

Woodrow Wilson, 28th president, Democrat, was born at Staunton, Va., Dec. 28, 1856, as Thomas Woodrow Wilson, son of a Presbyterian minister, the Rev. Joseph Ruggles Wilson and Janet (Jessie) Woodrow. In his youth Wilson lived in Augusta, Ga., Columbia, S.C., and Wilmington. N.C. He attended Davidson College, 1873-74; was graduated from Princeton, A.B., 1879; A.M., 1882; read law at the Univ. of Virginia, 1881; practiced law, Atlanta, 1882-83; Ph.D., Johns Hopkins, 1886. He taught at Bryn Mawr, 1885-88; at Wesleyan, 1888-90; was professor of jurisprudence and political economy at Princeton, 1890-1910; president of Princeton, 1902-1910; governor of New Jersey, 1911-13. In 1912 he was nominated for president with the aid of William Jennings Bryan, who sought to block James "Champ" Clark and Tammany Hall. Wilson won the election because the Republican vote for Taft was split by the Progressives under Roosevelt.

Wilson protected American interests in revolutionary Mexico and fought for American rights on the high seas. His sharp warnings to Germany led to the resignation of his secretary of state, Bryan, a pacifist. In 1916 he was reelected by a slim margin with the slogan, "He kept us out of war." Wilson's attempts to mediate in the war failed. After 4 American ships had been sunk by the Germans, he secured a declaration of war against Germany on Apr. 6, 1917.

Wilson proposed peace Jan. 8, 1918, on the basis of his "Fourteen Points," a state paper with worldwide influence. His doctrine of self-determination continues to play a major role in territorial disputes. The Germans accepted his terms and an armistice, Nov. 11.

Wilson went to Paris to help negotiate the peace treaty, the crux of which he considered the League of Nations. The Senate demanded reservations that would not make the U.S. subordinate to the votes of other nations in case of war. Wilson refused to consider any reservations and toured the country to get support. He suffered a stroke, Oct., 1919. An invalid for months, he clung to his executive powers while his wife and doctor sought to shield him from affairs which would tire him.

He was awarded the 1919 Nobel Peace Prize, but the treaty embodying the League of Nations was rejected by the Senate, 1920. He died Feb. 3, 1924.

## Warren Gamaliel Harding

Warren Gamaliel Harding, 29th president, Republican, was born near Corsica, now Blooming Grove, Oh., Nov. 2, 1865, the son of Dr. George Tyron Harding, a physician, and Phoebe Elizabeth Dickerson. He attended Ohio Central College. He was state senator, 1900-04; lieutenant governor, 1904-06; defeated for governor, 1910; chosen U.S. senator, 1915. He supported Taft, opposed federal control of food and fuel; voted for anti-strike legislation, woman's suffrage, and the Volstead prohibition enforcement act over President Wilson's veto; and opposed the League of Nations. In 1920 he was nominated for president and defeated James M. Cox in the election. The Republicans capitalized on war weariness and fear that Wilson's League of Nations would curtail U.S. sovereignty. Harding stressed a return to "normalcy"; worked for tariff revision and repeal of excess profits law and high income taxes. Two Harding appointees, Albert B. Fall (interior) and Harry Daugherty (attorney general), became involved in the Teapot Dome scandal that embittered Harding's last days. He called the International Conference on Limitation of Armaments, 1921-22. Returning from a

to Alaska he became ill and died in San Francisco, Aug.
23.

## Calvin Coolidge

alvin Coolidge, 30th president, Republican, was born in
nouth, Vt., July 4, 1872, the son of John Calvin Coo-
e, a storekeeper, and Victoria J. Moor, and named John
in Coolidge. Coolidge graduated from Amherst in 1895.
entered Republican state politics and served as mayor of
thampton, Mass., state senator, lieutenant governor,
in 1919, governor. In Sept., 1919, Coolidge attained
onal prominence by calling out the state guard in the
on police strike. He declared: "There is no right to
e against the public safety by anybody, anywhere, any-
." This brought his name before the Republican conven-
of 1920, where he was nominated for vice president. He
eeded to the presidency on Harding's death. He oped the League of Nations; approved the World Court;
ed the soldiers' bonus bill, which was passed over his
. In 1924 he was reelected by a huge majority. He reed the national debt by $2 billion in 3 years. He twice
ed the McNary-Haugen farm bill, which would have
ided relief to financially hard-pressed farmers. With Re-
licans eager to renominated him he announced, Aug. 2,
7: "I do not choose to run for president in 1928." He
in Northampton, Jan. 5, 1933.

## Herbert Hoover

erbert C. Hoover, 31st president, Republican, was born
West Branch, Ia., Aug. 10, 1874, son of Jesse Clark
over, a blacksmith, and Hulda Randall Minthorn.
over grew up in Indian Territory (now Oklahoma) and
gon; won his A.B. in engineering at Stanford, 1891. He
ked briefly with U.S. Geological Survey and western
es; then was a mining engineer in Australia, Asia, Eu-
e, Africa, America. While chief engineer, imperial mines,
na, he directed food relief for victims of Boxer Rebellion,
0. He directed American Relief Committee, London,
4-15; U.S. Comm. for Relief in Belgium, 1915-1919; was
. Food Administrator, 1917-1919; American Relief Ad-
istrator, 1918-1923, feeding children in defeated nations;
ssian Relief, 1918-1923. He was secy. of commerce,
1-28. He was elected president over Alfred E. Smith,
8. In 1929 the stock market crashed and the economy
apsed. During the depression, Hoover opposed federal
to the unemployed. He was defeated in the 1932 election
Franklin D. Roosevelt. President Truman made him co-
inator of European Food Program, 1947, chairman of
Commission for Reorganization of the Executive
nch, 1947-49. He founded the Hoover Institution on
r, Revolution, and Peace at Stanford Univ. He died in
. City, Oct. 20, 1964.

## Franklin Delano Roosevelt

ranklin D. Roosevelt, 32d president, Democrat, was
n near Hyde Park, N.Y., Jan. 30, 1882, the son of James
osevelt and Sara Delano. He graduated Harvard, 1904;
ended Columbia Law School; was admitted to the bar.
went to the N.Y. Senate, 1910 and 1913. In 1913 Presi-
t Wilson made him assistant secretary of the navy.
Roosevelt ran for vice president, 1920, with James Cox
d was defeated. From 1920 to 1928 he was a N.Y. lawyer
d vice president of Fidelity & Deposit Co. In Aug., 1921,
ao paralyzed his legs. He learned to walk with leg braces
d a cane.
Roosevelt was elected governor of New York, 1928 and
80. In 1932, W. G. McAdoo, pledged to John N. Garner,
ew his votes to Roosevelt, who was nominated. The de-
ssion and the promise to repeal prohibition insured his
ction. He asked emergency powers, proclaimed the New
al, and put into effect a vast number of administrative
nges. Foremost was the use of public funds for relief and
olic works, resulting in deficit financing. He greatly ex-
ded the controls of the central government over busi-
ss, and by an excess profits tax and progressive income
es produced a redistribution of earnings on an unprece-

dented scale. The Wagner Act gave labor many advantages
in organizing and collective bargaining. He was the last
president inaugurated on Mar. 4 (1933) and the first inaugurated on Jan. 20 (1937).

Roosevelt was the first president to use radio for "fireside
chats." When the Supreme Court nullified some New Deal
laws, he sought power to "pack" the court with additional
justices, but Congress refused to give him the authority. He
was the first president to break the "no 3d term" tradition
(1940) and was elected to a 4th term, 1944, despite failing
health. He was openly hostile to fascist governments before
World War II and launched a lend-lease program on behalf
of the Allies. He wrote the principles of fair dealing into the
Atlantic Charter, Aug. 14, 1941 (with Winston Churchill),
and urged the Four Freedoms (freedom of speech, of worship, from want, from fear) Jan. 6, 1941. When Japan attacked Pearl Harbor, Dec. 7, 1941, the U.S. entered the war.
He conferred with allied heads of state at Casablanca, Jan.,
1943; Quebec, Aug., 1943; Teheran, Nov.-Dec., 1943; Cairo,
Dec., 1943; Yalta, Feb., 1945. He died at Warm Springs,
Ga., Apr. 12, 1945.

## Harry S. Truman

Harry S. Truman, 33d president, Democrat, was born at
Lamar, Mo., May 8, 1884, the son of John Anderson Truman and Martha Ellen Young. A family disagreement on
whether his middle name was Shippe or Solomon, after
names of 2 grandfathers, resulted in his using only the middle initial S. He attended public schools in Independence,
Mo., worked for the Kansas City Star, 1901, and as railroad
timekeeper, and helper in Kansas City banks up to 1905. He
ran his family's farm, 1906-17. He was commissioned a first
lieutenant and took part in the Vosges, Meuse-Argonne, and
St. Mihiel actions in World War I. After the war he ran a
haberdashery, became judge of Jackson Co. Court, 1922-24;
attended Kansas City School of Law, 1923-25.

Truman was elected U.S. senator in 1934; reelected 1940.
In 1944 with Roosevelt's backing he was nominated for vice
president and elected. On Roosevelt's death Truman became
president. In 1948 he was elected president although polls
had predicted his defeat.

Truman authorized the first uses of the atomic bomb (Hi-
roshima and Nagasaki, Aug. 6 and 9, 1945), bringing World
War II to a rapid end. He was responsible for creating
NATO, the Marshall Plan, and what came to be called the
Truman Doctrine (to aid nations such as Greece and Tur-
key, threatened by Russian or other communist takeover).
He broke a Russian blockade of West Berlin with a massive
airlift, 1948-49. When communist North Korea invaded
South Korea, June, 1950, he won UN approval for a "police
action" and sent in forces under Gen. Douglas MacArthur.
When MacArthur sought to pursue North Koreans into
China, Truman removed him from command.

On the domestic front, Truman was responsible for higher
minimum-wage, increased social-security, and aid-for-
housing laws. Truman died Dec. 26, 1972, in Independence,
Mo.

## Dwight David Eisenhower

Dwight D. Eisenhower, 34th president, Republican, was
born Oct. 14, 1890, at Denison, Tex., the son of David Jacob Eisenhower and Ida Elizabeth Stover. The next year, the
family moved to Abilene, Kan. He graduated from West
Point, 1915. He was a lieutenant colonel at Camp Colt, Gettysburg, Pa., 1918. He was on the American military mission to the Philippines, 1935-39 and during 4 of those years
on the staff of Gen. Douglas MacArthur. He was made
commander of Allied forces landing in North Africa, 1942,
full general, 1943. He became supreme Allied commander in
Europe, 1943, and as such led the Normandy invasion June
6, 1944. He was given the rank of general of the army Dec.
20, 1944, made permanent in 1946. On May 7, 1945, he received the surrender of the Germans at Rheims. He returned
to the U.S. to serve as chief of staff, 1945-1948. In 1948, Eisenhower published Crusade in Europe, his war memoirs,
which quickly became a best seller. From 1948 to 1953, he

was president of Columbia Univ., but took leave of absence in 1950, to command NATO forces.

Eisenhower resigned from the army and was nominated for president by the Republicans, 1952. He defeated Adlai E. Stevenson in the election. He was renominated and again defeated Stevenson, 1956. He called himself a moderate, favored "free market system" vs. government price and wage controls; kept goverment out of labor disputes; reorganized defense establishment; promoted missile programs. With support of John Foster Dulles, his secretary of state, he continued foreign aid; sped end of Korean fighting; endorsed Taiwan and SE Asia defense treaties; backed UN in condemning Anglo-French raid on Egypt; advocated "open skies" policy of mutual inspection to USSR. He sent U.S. troops to Little Rock, Ark., Sept., 1957, during the segregation crisis and ordered Marines into Lebanon July-Aug., 1958.

During his retirement at his farm near Gettysburg, Pa., Eisenhower took up the role of elder statesman, counseling his 3 successors in the White House. He died Mar. 28, 1969, in Washington.

## John Fitzgerald Kennedy

John F. Kennedy, 35th president, Democrat, was born May 29, 1917, in Brookline, Mass., the son of Joseph P. Kennedy, financier, who later became ambassador to Great Britain, and Rose Fitzgerald. He entered Harvard, attended the London School of Economics briefly in 1935, received a B.S., from Harvard, 1940. He served in the Navy, 1941-1945, commanded a PT boat in the Solomons and won the Navy and Marine Corps Medal. He wrote *Profiles in Courage*, which won a Pulitzer prize. He served as representative in Congress, 1947-1953; was elected to the Senate in 1952, reelected 1958. He nearly won the vice presidential nomination in 1956.

In 1960, Kennedy won the Democratic nomination for president and defeated Richard M. Nixon, Republican. He was the first Roman Catholic president.

Kennedy's most important act was his successful demand Oct. 22, 1962, that the Soviet Union dismantle its missile bases in Cuba. He established a quarantine of arms shipments to Cuba and continued surveillance by air. He defied Soviet attempts to force the Allies out of Berlin. He made the steel industry rescind a price rise. He backed civil rights, a mental health program, arbitration of railroad disputes, and expanded medical care for the aged. Astronaut flights and satellite orbiting were greatly developed during his administration.

On Nov. 22, 1963, Kennedy was assassinated in Dallas, Tex.

## Lyndon Baines Johnson

Lyndon B. Johnson, 36th president, Democrat, was born near Stonewall, Tex., Aug. 27, 1908, son of Sam Ealy Johnson and Rebekah Baines. His family moved to Johnson City in 1913. He received a B.S. degree at Southwest Texas State Teachers College, 1930, attended Georgetown Univ. Law School, Washington, 1935. He taught public speaking in Houston High School, 1930-32; served as secretary to Rep. R. M. Kleberg, 1932-35. In 1937 Johnson won a contest to fill the vacancy caused by the death of a representative and in 1938 was elected to the full term, after which he returned for 4 terms. He was elected U.S. senator in 1948 and reelected in 1954. He became Democratic whip, 1951, and leader, 1953. Johnson was Texas' favorite son for the Democratic presidential nomination in 1956 and had strong support in the 1960 convention, where the nominee, John F. Kennedy, asked him to run for vice president. His campaigning helped overcome religious bias against Kennedy in the South.

Johnson became president on the death of Kennedy. Johnson worked hard for welfare legislation, signed civil rights, anti-proverty, and tax reduction laws, and averted strikes on railroads. He was elected to a full term, 1964. The war in Vietnam overshadowed other developments, 1965-68.

In face of increasing division in the nation and his own party over his handling of the war, Johnson announced he would not seek another term, Mar. 31, 1968.

Retiring to his ranch near Johnson City, Tex., John wrote his memoirs and oversaw the construction of the L don Baines Johnson Library on the campus of the Univ Texas in Austin. He died Jan. 22, 1973.

## Richard Milhous Nixon

Richard M. Nixon, 37th president, Republican, was only president to resign without completing an elected te He was born in Yorba Linda, Cal., Jan. 9, 1913, the sol Francis Anthony Nixon and Hannah Milhous. In 1922, family moved to Whittier, Cal. Nixon graduated from W tier College, 1934; Duke Univ. Law School, 1937. A practicing law in Whittier and serving briefly in the Offic Price Administration in 1942, he entered the navy, servin the South Pacific, and was discharged as a lieuten commander.

Nixon was elected to the House of Representatives 1946 and 1948. He achieved prominence as the House American Activities Committee member who forced showdown that resulted in the Alger Hiss perjury con tion. In 1950 Nixon moved to the Senate.

He was elected vice president in the Eisenhower landsli of 1952 and 1956. With Eisenhower's endorsement, Ni won the Republican nomination in 1960. He was defea by Democrat John F. Kennedy, returned to Cal. and defeated in his race for governor, 1962.

In 1968, he won the presidential nomination and went to defeat Democrat Hubert H. Humphrey.

Nixon became the first U.S. president to visit China Russia (1972). He and his foreign affairs advisor, Henry Kissinger, achieved a detente with China and a partial s tegic arms limitation agreement with the Soviet Union.

In 1971, faced with trade and balance of payments defi and inflation, Nixon announced wage and price controls devaluation of the dollar. Nixon appointed 4 new Supre Court justices, including the chief justice, thus altering court's balance in favor of a more conservative view.

Reelected 1972, Nixon secured a cease-fire agreement Vietnam and completed the withdrawal of U.S. troo Early in 1973, Nixon ended most wage and price contr and announced a further devaluation of the dollar.

Nixon's 2d term was cut short by a series of scandals ginning with the burglary of Democratic party natio headquarters in the Watergate office complex on June 1972. From the beginning, Nixon denied any White Ho involvement in the Watergate break-in. On July 16, 197: White House aide, under questioning by a Senate comr tee, revealed that most of Nixon's office conversations phone calls had been recorded. Nixon claimed execu privilege to keep the tapes secret and the courts and C gress sought the tapes for criminal proceedings against mer White House aides and for a House inquiry into po ble impeachment.

On Oct. 10, 1973, Nixon fired the Watergate special pr ecutor and the attorney general resigned in protest. public outcry which followed caused Nixon to appoin new special prosecutor and to turn over to the courts a nu ber of subpoenaed tape recordings. Public reaction a brought the initiation of a formal inquiry into impeachme

On July 24, 1974, the Supreme Court ruled that Nixo claim of executive privilege must fall before the special pr ecutor's subpoenas of tapes relevant to criminal trial p ceedings. That same day, the House Judiciary Commi opened debate on impeachment. On July 30, the commi recommended House adoption of 3 articles of impeach charging Nixon with obstruction of justice, abuse of pow and contempt of Congress.

On Aug. 5, Nixon released transcripts of conversati held 6 days after the Watergate break-in showing that Nix had known of, approved, and directed Watergate cover activities. Nixon resigned from office Aug. 9 and retired San Clemente, Cal.

## Gerald Rudolph Ford

Gerald R. Ford, 38th president, Republican, was b July 14, 1913, in Omaha, Neb., son of Leslie King and I

ay Gardner, and was named Leslie Jr. When he was 2,
parents were divorced and his mother moved with the
to Grand Rapids, Mich. There she met and married Ge-
R. Ford, who formally adopted the boy and gave him
own name.

He graduated from the Univ. of Michigan, 1935 and was
st valuable player on the 1934 football team. He turned
wn a professional football bid, went to Yale Law School
graduated, 1941.

He began practicing law in Grand Rapids, but in 1942
ed the navy and served in the Pacific, leaving the service
946 as a lieutenant commander.

Back in Grand Rapids, he resumed his law practice. He
ered congress in 1948 and continued to win elections,
nding 25 years in the House, 8 of them as Republican
der.

As congressman and GOP leader, he was consistently
servative, opposing much social welfare legislation but
ing support to final passage of civil rights bills.

On Oct. 12, 1973, after Vice President Spiro T. Agnew
gned, Ford was nominated by President Nixon to replace
n. It was the first use of the procedures set out in the 25th
nendment.

When Nixon resigned Aug. 9, 1974, Ford became presi-
nt, the first to serve without being chosen in a national
ction. On Sept. 8 he pardoned Nixon for any federal
mes he might have committed as president. Ford vetoed
bills in his first 21 months in office, including aid bills for
using, schools, health, day care, and farms; strip mining
bs, jobs creation, and tax cuts extension, saying most
uld prove too costly. He sought to solve the energy crises
urging an end to oil and natural gas price controls. He

visited China. In 1976, he was defeated in the election by
Democrat Jimmy Carter.

### Jimmy (James Earl) Carter

Jimmy (James Earl) Carter, 39th president, Democrat,
was the first president from the Deep South since before the
Civil War. He was born Oct. 1, 1924, at Plains, Ga., where
his parents, James and Lillian Gordy Carter, had a farm and
several businesses.

After studying at Georgia Tech, he entered the Naval
Academy at Annapolis. On graduating, he entered the
Navy's nuclear submarine program as an aide to Adm. Hy-
man Rickover, and also studied nuclear physics at Union
College, Schenectady.

His father died in 1953 and Carter left the Navy to take
over the family businesses — peanut-raising, warehousing,
and cotton-ginning. He became a Baptist Church deacon, a
Sunday school teacher, and public school board member,
was elected to the Georgia state senate, was defeated for
governor, 1966, but elected in 1970.

Carter won the Democratic nomination and defeated
President Gerald R. Ford in the election of 1976.

As president, Carter launched a campaign on behalf of
worldwide human rights, calling in his inaugural address,
for people in all nations to join the U.S. in an effort to
achieve human freedom and dignity.

By 1978, there were complaints from some segments that
he had failed to carry out the hopes and promises of his
campaign.

---

## Wives and Children of the Presidents

Listed in order of presidential administrations.

| me | State | Born | Married | Died | Sons | Daughters |
|---|---|---|---|---|---|---|
| rtha Dandridge Custis Washington | Va. | 1732 | 1759 | 1802 | ... | ... |
| gail Smith Adams | Mass. | 1744 | 1764 | 1818 | 3 | 2 |
| rtha Wayles Skelton Jefferson | Va. | 1748 | 1772 | 1782 | 1 | 5 |
| rothea "Dolley" Payne Todd Madison | N.C. | 1768 | 1794 | 1849 | ... | ... |
| zabeth Kortright Monroe | N.Y. | 1768 | 1786 | 1830 | ... | (1) |
| uise Catherine Johnson Adams | Md. (2) | 1775 | 1797 | 1852 | 3 | 1 |
| chel Donelson Robards Jackson | Va. | 1767 | 1791 | 1828 | ... | ... |
| nnah Hoes Van Buren | N.Y. | 1783 | 1807 | 1819 | 4 | ... |
| na Symmes Harrison | N.J. | 1775 | 1795 | 1864 | 6 | 4 |
| titia Christian Tyler | Va. | 1790 | 1813 | 1842 | 3 | 4 |
| ia Gardiner Tyler | N.Y. | 1820 | 1844 | 1889 | 5 | 2 |
| rah Childress Polk | Tenn. | 1803 | 1824 | 1891 | ... | ... |
| rgaret Smith Taylor | Md. | 1788 | 1810 | 1852 | 1 | 5 |
| igail Powers Fillmore | N.Y. | 1798 | 1826 | 1853 | 1 | 1 |
| roline Carmichael McIntosh Fillmore | N.J. | 1813 | 1858 | 1881 | ... | ... |
| ne Means Appleton Pierce | N.H. | 1806 | 1834 | 1863 | 3 | ... |
| ry Todd Lincoln | Ky. | 1818 | 1842 | 1882 | 4 | ... |
| za McCardle Johnson | Tenn. | 1810 | 1827 | 1876 | 3 | 2 |
| lia Dent Grant | Mo. | 1826 | 1848 | 1902 | 3 | 1 |
| cy Ware Webb Hayes | Oh. | 1831 | 1852 | 1889 | 7 | 1 |
| cretia Rudolph Garfield | Oh. | 1832 | 1858 | 1918 | 4 | 1 |
| en Lewis Herndon Arthur | Va. | 1837 | 1859 | 1880 | 2 | 1 |
| ances Folsom Cleveland | N.Y. | 1864 | 1886 | 1947 | 2 | 3 |
| roline Lavinia Scott Harrison | Oh. | 1832 | 1853 | 1892 | 1 | 1 |
| ary Scott Lord Dimmick Harrison | Pa. | 1858 | 1896 | 1948 | ... | 1 |
| a Saxton McKinley | Oh. | 1847 | 1871 | 1907 | ... | 2 |
| ice Hathaway Lee Roosevelt | Mass. | 1861 | 1880 | 1884 | ... | 1 |
| ith Kermit Carow Roosevelt | Conn. | 1861 | 1886 | 1948 | 4 | 1 |
| len Herron Taft | Oh. | 1861 | 1886 | 1943 | 2 | 1 |
| en Louise Axson Wilson | Ga. | 1860 | 1885 | 1914 | ... | 3 |
| ith Bolling Galt Wilson | Va. | 1872 | 1915 | 1961 | ... | ... |
| orence Kling De Wolfe Harding | Oh. | 1860 | 1891 | 1924 | ... | ... |
| ace Anna Goodhue Coolidge | Vt. | 1879 | 1905 | 1957 | 2 | ... |
| u Henry Hoover | Ia. | 1875 | 1899 | 1944 | 2 | ... |
| ne Eleanor Roosevelt Roosevelt | N.Y. | 1884 | 1905 | 1962 | 4 | (1) | 1 |
| ss Wallace Truman | Mo. | 1885 | 1919 | ... | ... | 1 |
| amie Geneva Doud Eisenhower | Ia. | 1896 | 1916 | ... | 1 | (1) | ... |
| cqueline Lee Bouvier Kennedy | N.Y. | 1929 | 1953 | ... | 1 | (1) | 1 |
| audia "Lady Bird" Alta Taylor Johnson | Tex. | 1912 | 1934 | ... | ... | 2 |
| elma Catherine Patricia Ryan Nixon | Nev. | 1912 | 1940 | ... | ... | 2 |
| zabeth Bloomer Warren Ford | Ill. | 1918 | 1948 | ... | 3 | 1 |
| osalynn Smith Carter | Ga. | 1927 | 1946 | ... | 3 | 1 |

mes Buchanan, 15th president, was unmarried. (1) plus one infant, deceased. (2) Born London, father a Md. citizen.

## Presidents Pro Tempore of the Senate

Until 1890, presidents "pro tem" were named "for the occasion only." Beginning with that year, they have served "u⊐ the Senate otherwise ordered." Sen. John J. Ingalls, chosen under the old rule in 1887, was again elected, under the new ru in 1890. Party designations are D, Democrat; R, Republican.

| Name | Party | State | Elected | Name | Party | State | Elect⊐ |
|------|-------|-------|---------|------|-------|-------|--------|
| John J. Ingalls | R | Kan. | Apr. 3, 1890 | George H. Moses | R | N.H. | Mar. 6, 19 |
| Charles F. Manderson | R | Neb. | Mar. 2, 1891 | Key Pittman | D | Nev. | Mar. 9, 19 |
| Isham G. Harris | D | Tenn. | Mar. 22, 1893 | William H. King | D | Ut. | Nov. 19, 19 |
| Matt W. Ransom | D | N.C. | Jan. 7, 1895 | Pat Harrison | D | Miss. | Jan. 6, 19 |
| Isham G. Harris | D | Tenn. | Jan. 10, 1895 | Carter Glass | D | Va. | July 10, 19 |
| William P. Frye | R | Me. | Feb. 7, 1896 | Kenneth McKellar | D | Tenn. | Jan. 6, 19 |
| Charles Curtis | R | Kan. | Dec. 4, 1911 | Arthur H. Vandenberg | R | Mich. | Jan. 4, 19 |
| Augustus O. Bacon | D | Ga. | Jan. 15, 1912 | Kenneth McKellar | D | Tenn. | Jan. 3, 19 |
| Jacob H. Gallinger | R | N.H. | Feb. 12, 1912 | Styles Bridges | R | N.H. | Jan. 3, 19 |
| Henry Cabot Lodge | R | Mass. | Mar. 25, 1912 | Walter F. George | D | Ga. | Jan. 5, 19 |
| Frank B. Brandegee | R | Conn. | May 25, 1912 | Carl Hayden | D | Ariz. | Jan. 3, 19 |
| James P. Clarke | D | Ark. | Mar. 23, 1915 | Richard B. Russell | D | Ga. | Jan. 3, 19 |
| Willard Saulsbury | D | Del. | Dec. 14, 1916 | Allen J. Ellender | D | La. | Jan. 22, 19 |
| Albert B. Cummins | R | Ia. | May 19, 1919 | James O. Eastland | D | Miss. | July 28, 19 |

## Speakers of the House of Representatives

Party designations: A, American; D, Democratic; DR, Democratic Republican; F, Federalist;
R, Republican; W, Whig. *Served only one day.

| Name | Party | State | Tenure | Name | Party | State | Tenure |
|------|-------|-------|--------|------|-------|-------|--------|
| Frederick Muhlenberg | F | Pa. | 1789-1791 | Schuyler Colfax | R | Ind. | 1863-18 |
| Jonathan Trumbull | F | Conn. | 1791-1793 | *Theodore M. Pomeroy | R | N.Y. | 1869-18 |
| Frederick Muhlenberg | F | Pa. | 1793-1795 | James G. Blaine | R | Me. | 1869-18 |
| Jonathan Dayton | F | N.J. | 1795-1799 | Michael C. Kerr | D | Ind. | 1875-18 |
| Theodore Sedgwick | F | Mass. | 1799-1801 | Samuel J. Randall | D | Pa. | 1876-18 |
| Nathaniel Macon | DR | N.C. | 1801-1807 | Joseph W. Keifer | R | Oh. | 1881-18 |
| Joseph B. Varnum | DR | Mass. | 1807-1811 | John G. Carlisle | D | Ky. | 1883-18 |
| Henry Clay | DR | Ky. | 1811-1814 | Thomas B. Reed | R | Me. | 1889-18 |
| Langdon Cheves | DR | S.C. | 1814-1815 | Charles F. Crisp | D | Ga. | 1891-18 |
| Henry Clay | DR | Ky. | 1815-1820 | Thomas B. Reed | R | Me. | 1895-18 |
| John W. Taylor | DR | N.Y. | 1820-1821 | David B. Henderson | R | Ia. | 1899-19 |
| Philip P. Barbour | DR | Va. | 1821-1823 | Joseph G. Cannon | R | Ill. | 1903-19 |
| Henry Clay | DR | Ky. | 1823-1825 | Champ Clark | D | Mo. | 1911-19 |
| John W. Taylor | D | N.Y. | 1825-1827 | Frederick H. Gillett | R | Mass. | 1919-19 |
| Andrew Stevenson | D | Va. | 1827-1834 | Nicholas Longworth | R | Oh. | 1925-19 |
| John Bell | D | Tenn. | 1834-1835 | John N. Garner | D | Tex. | 1931-19 |
| James K. Polk | D | Tenn. | 1835-1839 | Henry T. Rainey | D | Ill. | 1933-19 |
| Robert M. T. Hunter | D | Va. | 1839-1841 | Joseph W. Byrns | D | Tenn. | 1935-19 |
| John White | W | Ky. | 1841-1843 | William B. Bankhead | D | Ala. | 1936-19 |
| John W. Jones | D | Va. | 1843-1845 | Sam Rayburn | D | Tex. | 1940-19 |
| John W. Davis | D | Ind. | 1845-1847 | Joseph W. Martin Jr. | R | Mass. | 1947-19 |
| Robert C. Winthrop | W | Mass. | 1847-1849 | Sam Rayburn | D | Tex. | 1949-19 |
| Howell Cobb | D | Ga. | 1849-1851 | Joseph W. Martin Jr. | R | Mass. | 1953-19 |
| Linn Boyd | D | Ky. | 1851-1855 | Sam Rayburn | D | Tex. | 1955-19 |
| Nathaniel P. Banks | A | Mass. | 1856-1857 | John W. McCormack | D | Mass. | 1962-19 |
| James L. Orr | D | S.C. | 1857-1859 | Carl Albert | D | Okla. | 1971-19 |
| William Pennington | R | N.J. | 1860-1861 | Thomas P. O'Neill Jr. | D | Mass. | 1977- |
| Galusha A. Grow | R | Pa. | 1861-1863 | | | | |

## National Political Parties

As of June, 1978

### Republican Party

**National Headquarters**—310 First St., SE, Washington, DC 20003.

**Chairman**—Bill Brock.

**Co-Chairman**—Mary Crisp.

**Vice Chairmen**—Ray C. Bliss, Ranny Riecker, Mary H. Boatwright, Clarke Reed, Bernard M. Shanley, Paula F. Hawkins, David B. Kennedy, Jo Anne Gray.

**Secretary**—June Gibbs.

**Treasurer**—William T. McManus.

**General Counsel**—William C. Cramer.

**Finance Chairman**—Ted H. Welch.

### Democratic Party

**National Headquarters**—1625 Massachusetts Ave., NW, Washi⊐ ton, DC 20036.

**Chairman**—John White.

**Vice Chairpersons**—Coleman Young, Carmela G. Lacayo.

**Secretary**—Dorothy V. Bush.

**Treasurer**—Evan S. Dobelle.

**Finance Chairman**—Charles Manatt.

## Other Major Political Organizations

### American Party

(PO Box 990, Pigeon Forge, TN 37863)

**Chairman**—Thomas J. Anderson.

### Americans For Democratic Action

(1411 K St. NW, Washington, DC 20005)

**President**—George McGovern.

**National Director**—Leon Shull.

**Chairperson Exec. Comm.**—Cushing Dolbeare.

### Comm. on Political Education, AFL-CIO

(AFL-CIO Building, 815 16th St., Wash., DC 20006)

**Chairman**—George Meany.

**Secretary-Treasurer**—Lane Kirkland.

National Director—Alexander E. Barkan.

## Conservative Party of the State of N.Y.
(468 Park Ave. So., New York, NY 10016)
Chairman—J. Daniel Mahoney.
Executive Director—Serphin R. Maltese.
Secretary—Barbara A. Keating.
Treasurer—James E. O'Doherty.

## Liberal Party of New York State
(1560 Broadway, New York, NY 10036)
Chairman—Donald S. Harrington.
First Vice Chairman—David Dubinsky.
Secretary—Ben Davidson.
Treasurer—Bernice Benedick.
Executive Director—James F. Notaro.
Assistant Executive Director—Patrick W. Giagnacova.

## Libertarian Party
(1516 P St. NW, Washington, DC 20005)
Chairman—David P. Bergland.
Vice-Chairwoman—Mary Louise Hanson.
Secretary—Sylvia Sanders.
Treasurer—Paul S. Allen.

National Director—Chris Hocker.

## National States' Rights Party
(P.O. Box 1211, Marietta, GA 30061)
Chairman—J.B. Stoner.
Secretary—Edward R. Fields.
Treasurer—Peter Xavier.

## Prohibition National Committee
(P.O. Box 2635, Denver, CO 80201)
National Chairman—Charles Wesley Ewing.
Executive Secretary—Earl F. Dodge.
National Secretary—Roger C. Storms.

## Socialist Labor Party
In Minnesota: Industrial Gov't. Party
(914 Industrial Ave., Palo Alto, CA 94303)
National Secretary—Nathan Karp.

## Socialist Workers Party
(14 Charles Lane, New York, NY 10014)
National Secretary—Jack Barnes.
Organization Secretary—Barry Sheppard.

## America's Third Parties

Since 1860, there have been only 4 presidential elections in which all third parties together polled more than 10% of the vote: the Populists (James Baird Weaver) in 1892, the National Progressives (Theodore Roosevelt) in 1912, the La Follette Progressives in 1924, and George Wallace's American Party in 1968. In 1948, the combined third parties (Henry Wallace's Progressives, Strom Thurmond's States' Rights party or Dixiecrats, Prohibition, Socialists, and others) received only 5.75% of the vote. In most elections since 1860, fewer than one vote in 20 has been cast for a third party. The only successful third party in American history was the Republican Party in the election of Abraham Lincoln in 1860.

### Major Third Parties

| Party | Presidential nominee | Election | Issues | Strength in |
|---|---|---|---|---|
| Anti-Masonic | William Wirt | 1832 | Against secret societies and oaths | Pa., Vt. |
| Free Soil | Martin Van Buren | 1848 | Anti-slavery | New York, Ohio |
| American (Know Nothing) | Millard Fillmore | 1856 | Anti-immigrant | Northeast, South |
| Greenback | Peter Cooper | 1876 | For "cheap money," | |
| Greenback | James B. Weaver | 1880 | labor rights | National |
| Prohibition | (numerous) | 1872 | Anti-liquor | National |
| Populist | James B. Weaver | 1892 | for "cheap money," end of national banks | South, West |
| Socialist | Eugene V. Debs | 1900-20 | For public ownership | National |
| Socialist | Norman Thomas | 1928-48 | Liberal reforms | National |
| Progressive (Bull Moose) | Theodore Roosevelt | 1912 | Against high tariffs | Midwest, West |
| Union | William Lemke | 1936 | Anti "New Deal" | National |
| Progressive | Robert M. LaFollette | 1924 | Farmer & labor rights | Midwest, West |
| States' Rights | Strom Thurmond | 1948 | For segregation | South |
| Progressive | Henry Wallace | 1948 | Anti-cold war | New York, California |
| American | George Wallace | 1968 | For states' rights | South |
| American | John G. Schmitz | 1972 | For "law and order" | California, Ohio |

## The Electoral College

The president and the vice president of the United States are the only elective federal officials not elected by direct vote of the people. They are elected by the members of the Electoral College, an institution that has survived since the founding of the nation despite repeated attempts in Congress to alter or abolish it. In the elections of 1824, 1876 and 1888 the presidential candidate receiving the largest popular vote failed to win a majority of the electoral votes.

On presidential election day, the first Tuesday after the first Monday in November of every 4th year, each state chooses as many electors as it has senators and representatives in Congress. In 1964, for the first time, as provided by the 23d Amendment to the Constitution, the District of Columbia voted for 3 electors. Thus, with 100 senators and 435 representatives, there are 538 members of the Electoral College, with a majority of 270 electoral votes needed to elect the president and vice president.

Political parties customarily nominate their lists of electors at their respective state conventions. An elector cannot be a member of Congress or any person holding federal office.

Some states print the names of the candidates for president and vice president at the top of the November ballot while others list only the names of the electors. In either case, the electors of the party receiving the highest vote are elected. The electors meet on the first Monday after the 2d Wednesday in December in their respective state capitals or in some other place prescribed by state legislatures. By long-established custom they vote for their party nominees, although the Constitution does not require them to do so. All of the state's electoral votes are then awarded to the winners. The only Constitutional requirement is that at least one of the persons each elector votes for shall not be an inhabitant of that elector's home state.

Certified and sealed lists of the votes of the electors in each state are mailed to the president of the U.S. Senate. He opens them in the presence of the members of the Senate and House of Representatives in a joint session held on Jan. 6 (the next day if that falls on a Sunday), and the electoral votes of all the states are then counted. If no candidate for president has a majority, the House of Representatives chooses a president from among the 3 highest candidates, with all representatives from each state combining to cast one vote for that state. If no candidate for vice president has a majority, the Senate chooses from the top 2, with the senators voting as individuals.

In 1977, Pres. Carter urged elimination of the electoral college system and substitution of a plurality of the national popular vote.

# UNITED STATES GOVERNMENT
## The Carter Administration
As of Aug. 1, 1978

Terms of office of the president and vice president, from Jan. 20, 1977 to Jan. 20, 1981. No person may be elected president of the United States for more than two 4-year terms.

**President** — Jimmy (James Earl) Carter of Georgia. Receives salary of $200,000 a year taxable, and in addition an expense allowance, also taxable, of $50,000 to assist in defraying expenses resulting from his official duties. Also there may be expended not exceeding $100,000, nontaxable, a year for travel expenses and official entertainment. Congress has provided lifetime pensions of $60,000 a year, free mailing privileges, free office space, and up to $90,000 a year for office help for ex-Presidents and $20,000 annually for their widows.

**Vice President** — Walter F. Mondale of Minnesota, salary $75,000 a year and $10,000 for expenses, all of which is taxable.

For succession to presidency, see Succession in Index.

### The Cabinet
(Salaries $66,000 each)

**Secretary of State** — Cyrus R. Vance, N.Y.
**Secretary of Treasury** — W. Michael Blumenthal, Mich.
**Secretary of Defense** — Harold S. Brown, Cal.
**Attorney General** — Griffin B. Bell, Ga.
**Secretary of Interior** — Cecil D. Andrus, Ida.
**Secretary of Agriculture** — Bob Bergland, Minn.
**Secretary of Commerce** — Juanita M. Kreps, N.C.
**Secretary of Labor** — F. Ray Marshall, Tex.
**Secretary of Health, Education, and Welfare** — Joseph A. Califano Jr., Wash., D.C.
**Secretary of Housing and Urban Development** — Patricia Roberts Harris, Wash., D.C.
**Secretary of Transportation** — Brock Adams, Wash.
**Secretary of Energy** — James R. Schlesinger, Va.

### The White House Staff
1600 Pennsylvania Ave. NW 20500

**Assistant to the President** — Hamilton Jordan.
**Press Secretary to the President** — Jody Powell.
**Counsel to the President** — Robert Lipshutz.
**Personal Assistant to the President** — Susan Clough.
**Press Secretary to the First Lady** — Mary Finch Hoyt.
**Physician to the President.** — R. Adm. William M. Lukash, USN.
**Chief Usher** — Rex W. Scouten.

### Executive Agencies

**National Security Council — Assistant to the President for Natl. Security Affairs** — Zbigniew Brzezinski.
**Council of Economic Advisers** — Charles Schultze.
**Council on Environmental Quality** — Charles Warren, chmn.
**Central Intelligence Agency** — Adm. Stansfield Turner, dir.
**Office of Management and Budget** — James McIntyre, dir.
**Special Representative for Trade Negotiations** — Robert Strauss.

### Department of State
2201 C St. NW 20520

**Secretary of State** — Cyrus R. Vance.
**Deputy Secretary** — Warren Christopher.
**Under Sec. for Political Affairs** — David D. Newsom.
**Under Sec. for Security Assistance, Science and Technology** — Lucy Wilson Benson.
**Under Sec. for Economic Affairs** — Richard N. Cooper.
**Deputy Under Secretary** — Ben H. Read (for management).
**Ambassadors at Large** — Alfred L. Atherton Jr., Arthur J. Goldberg, Elliot L. Richardson, Gerard C. Smith.
**Counselor** — Matthew Nimetz.
**Legal Advisor** — Herbert J. Hansell.
**Assistant Secretaries for:**
 **Administration** — John M. Thomas.
 **African Affairs** — Richard M. Moose Jr.

**Conngressional Relations** — Douglas J. Bennett Jr.
**Economic Affairs** — Julius L. Katz.
**European Affairs** — George S. Vest.
**East Asian & Pacific Affairs** — Richard Holbrooke.
**Inter-American Affairs** — Viron P. Vaky.
**International Organization Affairs** — Charles William Maynes.
**Near-Eastern & S. Asian Affairs** — Harold H. Saunders
**Public Affairs** — Hodding Carter 3d.
**Bureau of Counsular Affairs** — Barbara M. Watson, asst. secretary.
**Chief of Protocol** — Kit Dobelle.
**Dir. General, Foreign Service** — Harry G. Barnes.
**Dir. of Intelligence & Research** — William G. Bowdler.
**Bureau of Oceans and Internatl. Environmental and Scientific Affairs** — Asst. Sec. (vacant).
**Dir. of Politico-Military Affairs** — Leslie H. Gelb.
**Insp. Gen. Foreign Service** — Theodore L. Eliot Jr.
**Foreign Service Inst.** — George S. Springsteen, dir.
**Agency for International Development** — John J. Gilligan, admin.
**ACTION** — Sam Brown.
**U.S. Rep. to the UN and Rep. in the Security Council** — Andrew Young, amb.

### Treasury Department
1500 Pennsylvania Ave. NW 20220

**Secretary of the Treasury** — W. Michael Blumenthal.
**Deputy Sec. of the Treasury** — Robert Carswell.
**Under Sec. for Monetary Affairs** — Anthony M. Solomon.
**Under Sec.** — Bette Anderson.
**General Counsel** — Robert H. Mundheim.
**Assistant Secretaries:** — Roger C. Altman, C. Fred Bergsten, Daniel H. Brill, William J. Beckham Jr., Richard J. Davis, Gene E. Godley, Joseph Laitin.
**Bureaus:**
 **Alcohol, Tobacco, and Firearms** — Rex D. Davis. dir.
 **Comptroller of the Currency** — John G. Heimann.
 **Customs** — Robert E. Chasen, comm.
 **Engraving & Printing** — Seymour Berry, dir.
 **Government Financial Operations** — D. A. Pagliai, comm.
 **Internal Revenue Service** — Jerome Kurtz, comm.
 **Mint** — Stella B. Hackel, dir.
 **Public Debt** — H. J. Hintgen, comm.
 **Treasurer of the U.S.** — Azie Morton.
 **U.S. Secret Service** — H. Stuart Knight, dir.

### Department of Defense
The Pentagon 20301

**Secretary of Defense** — Harold S. Brown.
**Deputy Sec.** — Charles W. Duncan Jr.
**Research and Engineering** — William J. Perry.
**Asst. Secretaries of Defense:**
 **Comptroller** — Fred P. Wacker.
 **Communications, Command, Control & Intelligence** — Gerald P. Dineen.
 **Health Affairs** — Vacant
 **International Security Affairs** — David E. McGiffert
 **Legislative Affairs** — Jack L. Stempler.
 **Manpower, Reserve Affairs & Logistics** — John P. White.
 **Program Analysis & Evaluation** — Russell Murray 2d.
 **Public Affairs** — Thomas B. Ross.
**General Counsel** — Dianne Siemer.
**Joint Chiefs of Staff, chairman** — Gen. David C. Jones, USAF.
**NATO Affairs** — Robert W. Komer.

## Department of the Army
The Pentagon 20310

Secretary of the Army — Clifford L. Alexander Jr.
Under Secretary — Walter B. LaBerge.
Assistant Secretaries for:
  Finance Management — Hadlai A. Hull.
  Civil Works — vacant.
  Installations, Logistics and Financial Management — Alan J. Gibbs.
  Research, Development and Acquisition — Percy A. Pierre.
  Manpower & Reserve Affairs — Robert L. Nelson.
Chief of Public Affairs — Brig. Gen. Robert B. Solomon.
Chief of Staff — Gen. Bernard C. Rogers.
General Counsel — Jill Wine-Volner.
Comptroller of the Army — Lt. Gen. Richard L. West.
Surgeon General — Lt. Gen. Charles C. Pixley.
Adjutant General — Brig. Gen. James C. Pennington.
Inspector General — Lt. Gen. Richard D. Trefry.
Judge Advocate General — Maj. Gen. Wilton B. Persons Jr.
Deputy Chiefs of Staff:
  Logistics — Lt. Gen. Eivind H. Johansen.
  Operations & Plans — Lt. Gen. Edward C. Meyer.
  Research, Development, Acquisition — Lt. Gen. Donald R. Keith.
  Personnel — Lt. Gen. DeWitt C. Smith Jr.
Ass't. Chief of Staff, Intellingence — Maj. Gen. Edmund R. Thompson.
Chief of Engineers — Lt. Gen. John W. Morris.
Chief, Nat. Guard Bureau — Maj. Gen. LaVern E. Weber.
Chief, Army Reserve — Maj. Gen. Henry Mohr.
Commanders:
  U.S. Army Material Development and Readiness Command — Gen. John R. Guthrie.
  U.S. Army Forces Command — Gen. Robert W. Shoemaker.
  U.S. Army Training and Doctrine Command — Gen. Donn A. Starry.
  First U.S. Army — Lt. Gen. Jeffrey G. Smith.
  Fifth U.S. Army — Lt. Gen. William B. Caldwell 3d.
  Sixth U.S. Army — Lt. Gen. Eugene P. Forrester.
  Military Dist. of Washington — Maj. Gen. Kenneth E. Dohleman.
  XVIII Airborne Corps, Ft. Bragg, N.C. — Lt. Gen. Volney Warner.
  III Corps and Ft. Hood, Tex. — Lt. Gen. Marvin D. Fuller.

## Department of the Navy
The Pentagon 20350

Secretary of the Navy — W. Graham Claytor Jr.
Under Secretary — R. James Woolsey.
Assistant Secretaries for:
  Financial Management — George A. Peapples.
  Installations & Logistics — vacant.
  Manpower, Reserve Affairs, & Logistics — Edward Hidalgo.
  Research, Engineering, & Systems — Dr. David E. Mann.
Judge Advocate General — R. Adm. W. O. Miller.
Chief of Naval Operations — Adm. Thomas B. Hayward.
Chief of Naval Materiel — Adm. F. H. Michaelis.
Chief of Information — R. Adm. David M. Cooney.
Bureau Chiefs:
  Medicine & Surgery — V. Adm. W. P. Arentzen.
  Naval Personnel — V. Adm. Robert B. Baldwin.
Military Sealift Command — R. Adm. J. D. Johnson Jr.
U.S. Marine Corps: (zip code: 20380)
  Commandant — Gen. Louis H. Wilson.
  Asst. Commandant — Gen. Robert H. Barrow.
  Chief of Staff — Lt. Gen. Lawrence F. Snowden.
Commandants, Naval Districts:
  4th, Philadelphia — R. Adm. Frederick F. Palmer.
  5th, Norfolk — R. Adm. William H. Ellis.
  6th, Charleston — R. Adm. Roy F. Hoffman.

8th, New Orleans — V. Adm. P. N. Charbonnet Jr.
9th, Great Lakes — R. Adm. Thomas W. McNamara.
11th, San Diego — R. Adm. J. E. Langille 3d.
13th, Seattle — R. Adm. Henry D. Arnold.
14th, Pearl Harbor — R. Adm. R. B. Wentworth Jr.
Naval District, Wash., D.C. — R. Adm. Ralph H. Carnahan.

## Department of the Air Force
The Pentagon 20330

Secretary of the Air Force — John C. Stetson.
Under Secretary — Hans Mark.
Assistant Secretaries for:
  Financial Management — John A. Hewitt Jr.
  Research, Development & Logistics — John J. Martin.
  Manpower, Reserve Affairs & Installations — Antonia Handler Chayes.
General Counsel — Peter B. Hamilton.
Director of Information — Brig. Gen. H. J. Dalton Jr.
Director of Space Systems — Brig. Gen. W. L. Shields Jr.
Chief of Staff — Gen. Lew Allen Jr.
Vice Chief of Staff — Gen. James A. Hill.
Chief, National Guard Bureau — Maj. Gen. John T. Guice, USA.
Chief of Air Force Reserves — Maj. Gen. William Lyon.
Surgeon General — Lt. Gen. Paul W. Myers.
Judge Advocate — Maj. Gen. Walter D. Reed.
Inspector General — Lt. Gen. John T. Flynn.
Deputy Chiefs of Staff:
  Systems and Logistics — Lt. Gen. John R. Kelley Jr.
  Programs and Resources — Lt. Gen. Abbott C. Greenleaf.
  Personnel — Lt. Gen. Bennie L. Davis.
  Research and Development — Lt. Gen. Thomas P. Stafford.
  Plans and Operations — Lt. Gen. Andrew B. Anderson.
Major Air Commands:
  NORAD/ADCOM — Gen. James E. Hill.
  AF Logistics Command — Gen. F. Michael Rogers.
  AF Systems Command — Gen. Alton D. Slay.
  Air Training Command — Lt. Gen. John W. Roberts.
  Air University — Lt. Gen. Raymond B. Furlong.
  Military Airlift Command — Gen. William J. Moore Jr.
  Strategic Air Command — Gen. Richard D. H. Ellis.
  Tactical Air Command — Lt. Gen. Wilbur L. Creech.
  Alaskan Air Command — Lt. Gen. Winfield W. Scott Jr.
  Pacific Air Forces — Lt. Gen. James D. Hughes.
  USAF Europe — Gen. William J. Evans.
  USAF Security Service — Brig. Gen. Kenneth D. Burns.
  AF Communications Service — Maj. Gen. Robert E. Sadler.
  USAF Acct. and Finance Center — Maj. Gen. Lucius Theus.

## Department of Justice
Constitution Ave. & 10th St. NW 20530

Attorney General — Griffin B. Bell.
Deputy Attorney General — Benjamin R. Civiletti.
Solicitor General — Wade H. McCree.
Assistant Attorneys General:
  Antitrust Division — John H. Shenefield.
  Civil Division — Barbara Allen Babcock.
  Civil Rights Division — Drew S. Days.
  Criminial Division — Philip H. Heymann.
  Drug Enforcement Admin. — Peter B. Bensinger.
  Land & Natural Resources Division — James W. Moorman.
  Legal Counsel — John M. Harmon.
  Office of Legislative Affairs — Patricia M. Wald.
  Office of Management & Finance — Kevin D. Rooney.
  Public Information — Terrence B. Adamson.
  Tax Division — M. Carr Ferguson.
Fed. Bureau of Investigation — William H. Webster.
Board of Immigration Appeals — David L. Milhollan, chairman.
Bureau of Prisons — Norman A. Carlson.

Community Relations Ser. — Gilbert G. Pompa.
Immigration and Naturalization Service — Leonel J. Castillo, commissioner.
Law Enforcement Assistance Admin. — James M. H. Gregg (acting).
Pardon Attorney — John R. Stanish.
U.S. Parole Commission — Cecil C. McCall.

## Department of the Interior
### C St. between 18th & 19th Sts. NW 20240
Secretary of the Interior — Cecil D. Andrus.
Under Secretary — James A. Joseph.
Assistant Secretaries for:
  Fish, Wildlife and Parks — Robert Herbst.
  Energy & Minerals — Joan M. Davenport.
  Land and Water Resources — Guy Richard Martin.
  Policy, Budget, and Administration — vacant.
  Indian Affairs — Forrest J. Gerard.
Bureau of Land Management — Frank Gregg, dir.
Bureau of Mines — vacant.
Bureau of Reclamation — Keith Higginson, comm.
Fish & Wildlife Service — Lynn Greenwalt.
Geological Survey — H. W. Menard Jr., dir.
National Park Service — William J. Whalen.
Public Affairs — D. Chris Carlson.
Office of Water Research and Technology — Gary D. Cobb, dir.
Solicitor — Leo Krulitz.

## Department of Agriculture
### 14th & Independence Ave. SW 20250
Secretary of Agriculture — Bob Bergland.
Deputy Secretary — vacant.
Administration — Joan S. Wallace.
Conservation, Research, & Education — M. Rupert Cutler.
Internat. Affairs & Commodity Programs — Dale E. Hathaway.
Food & Consumer Service — Carol Tucker Foreman.
Marketing Services — P. R. Smith.
Rural Development — Alex P. Mercure.
Economics, Policy Analysis and Budget — Howard W. Hjort, dir.
Governmental & Public Affairs — James C. Webster, dir.
Agricultural Marketing Service — Barbara L. Schlei, admin.
Agric. Stabilization & Converv. Service — Ray Fitzgerald, admin.
Animal & Plant Health Inspection Ser. — F. J. Mulhern.
Economics, Statistics, and Cooperatives Service — Kenneth R. Farrell, admin.
Energy — Weldon Barton, dir.
Farmers Home Admin. — Gordon Cavanaugh, admin.
Fed. Crop Insurance Corp. — James Deal, mgr.
Federal Grain Inspection Service — Leland E. Bartlett.
Food & Nutrition Serv. — Lewis B. Straus, admin.
Food Safety and Quality Service — Robert Angelotti.
Foreign Agric. Service — Thomas R. Hughes, admin.
Forest Service — John R. McGuire, chief.
General Counsel — Sara Weddington.
Inspector General — Thomas McBride.
International Development Staff — William A. Faught, dir.
Rural Electrific. Admin. — David Hamil, admin.
Science & Education Admin. — Anson R. Bertrand, dir.
Soil Conservation Service — Ronello M. Davis, admin.

## Department of Commerce
### 14th St. between Constitution & E St. NW 20230
Secretary of Commerce — Juanita M. Kreps.
Under Secretary — Sidney Harman.
General Counsel — C. L. Haslam.
Maritime Affairs — Robert J. Blackwell.
Science & Technology — Jordan J. Baruch.
Administration — Elsa A. Porter.
Bureau of the Census — Manuel D. Plotkin.
Bureau of Economic Analysis — George Jaszi.
Bureau of Export Development — W. D. Moran.

Bureau of East-West Trade — Alan A. Reich.
Bureau of Domestic Business Development — Robert E. Shephard.
Industry & Trade Admin. — Frank A. Weil.
Chief Economist — Courtenay M. Slater.
Natl. Oceanic & Atmospheric Admin. — Richard A. Frank, admin.
Natl. Technical Info. Service — William T. Knox, director.
Economic Develop. Admin. — Robert T. Hall.
Natl. Bureau of Standards — Ernest Ambler.
Office of Minority Business Enterprise — Randolph T. Blackwell, dir.
Office of Product Standards — Howard I. Forman.
Natl. Telecomm & Information Admin. — John M. Richardson, dir.
Tourism — Fabian Chavez Jr.

## Department of Labor
### 200 Constitution Ave. NW 20210
Secretary of Labor — F. Ray Marshall.
Under Secretary — Robert Brown.
Executive Assistant-Counselor — Paul Jensen.
Assistant Secretaries for:
  Administration and Management — Alfred M. Zuck.
  Employment Standards — Donald Elisberg.
  Employment and Training — Ernest Green.
  Occupational Safety & Health — Eula Bingham.
  Policy, Evaluation and Research — Arnold H. Packer.
Solicitor of Labor — Carin A. Clauss.
Bureau of Labor Statistics — Julius Shiskin.
Dep. Under Secy. for Internatl. Affairs — Howard D. Samuel.
Office of Information, Publications & Reports — John W. Leslie.

## Department of Health, Education, and Welfare
### 330 Independence Ave. SW 20201
Secretary of HEW — Joseph A. Califano Jr.
Under Secretary — Hale Champion.
Assistant Secretaries for:
  Management and Budget — Leonard Schaeffer.
  Public Affairs — Eileen Shanahan.
  Health — Dr. Julius B. Richmond, Surgeon General.
  Planning and Evaluation — Henry Aaron.
  Education — Dr. Mary Berry.
  Human Development Services — Arabella Martinez.
  Legislation — Richard Warden.
  Personnel Administration — Thomas McFee.
General Counsel — Peter Libassi.
Office for Civil Rights — David S. Tatel.
Office of Consumer Affairs — Lee Richardson (act.)
Health Care Financing Admin. — Robert A. Derzon.
Social Security Admin. — Don Wortman (act.)

## Department of Housing and Urban Development
### 451 7th St. SW 20410
Secretary of Housing & Urban Development — Patricia Roberts Harris.
Under Secretary — Jay Janis.
Assistant Secretaries for:
  Administration — William A. Medina.
  Community Planning & Development — Robert C. Embry.
  Fair Housing and Equal Opportunity — Chester C. McGuire.
  Federal Housing Commissioner — Lawrence B. Simons.
  Legislation and Intergovernmental Relations — Harry K. Schwartz.
  Neighborhoods, Voluntary Assns. & Consumer Protection — Geno Baroni.
  Policy Development & Research — Donna E. Shalala.
President, Govt. Natl. Mortgage Assn. — John Dalton.
Public Affairs — Bill Wise.
International Affairs — Tila M. deHancock.
Labor Relations — Elizabeth Raymond.
General Counsel — Ruth T. Prokop.
Federal Insurance Administrator — Gloria M. Jimenez.

Fed. Diaster Assistance Admin. — William H. Wilcox.
New Community Development Admin. — William J. White.
Inspector General — Carl Dempsey (act.).

## Department of Transportation

### 400 7th St. SW 20590

Secretary of Transportation — Brock Adams.
Deputy Secretary — Alan A. Butchman.
Assistant Secretaries — Edward W. Scott Jr., Chester C. Davenport, Mortimer L. Downey, Terrence L. Bracy.
General Counsel — Linda H. Kamm.
National Highway Traffic Safety Admin. — Joan Claybrook.
U. S. Coast Guard Commandant — John B. Hayes.
Federal Aviation Admin. — Langhorne M. Bond.
Federal Highway Admin. — Karl S. Bowers (act.).
Federal Railroad Admin. — John M. Sullivan.

Urban Mass Transportation Admin. — Dr. Richard S. Page.
St. Lawrence Seaway Development Corp. — David W. Oberlin, admin.
Research & Special Programs Admin. — John J. Fearnsides (act.).

## Department of Energy

### Independence Ave. & 10th St. SW 20003

Secretary of Energy — James R. Schlesinger.
Deputy Secy. — John F. O'Leary.
Federal Energy Regulatory Comm. — Charles B. Curtis, chmn.
Off. of Hearings & Appeals — Melvin Goldstein, dir.
Inspector General — Joseph Seltzer (act.).
Off. of Economic Opportunity — Marion A. Bowden, dir.
Economic Regulatory Admin. — David J. Bardin.
Energy Research — John M. Deutch, dir.
International Affairs — Harry E. Bergold.

---

## State Officials, Salaries, Party Membership

Compiled from data supplied by state officials, mid-1978

### Alabama

Governor — George C. Wallace, D., $28,955.
Lt. Gov. — Jere Beasley, D., $50 per legislative day, plus annual salary of $300 per month.
Sec. of State — Mrs. Agnes Baggett, D., $22,959.
Atty. Gen. — Bill Baxley, D., $33,500.
Treasurer — Mrs. Annie Laurie Gunter, D., $22,959.
Legislature: meets annually the first Tuesday in Feb. except in 4th year (2d Tuesday in Jan.), at Montgomery. Members receive $50 per day during legislative sessions, limited to 30 days, plus annual salary of $300 per month.
Senate — Dem., 35; Rep., 0. Total, 5.
House — Dem., 103; Rep., 2. Total, 105.

### Alaska

Governor — Jay S. Hammond, R., $52,992.
Lt. Gov. — Lowell Thomas Jr., R., $47,304.
Atty. General — Avrum M. Gross, D., $47,304.
Legislature: meets annually in January at Juneau, for as long as may be necessary. First session in odd years. Members receive $11,750 per year plus $50 per diem while out of town, $35 if from Juneau, while in session. Also, $4,000 for stenographic services and other expenses.
Senate — Dem., 12; Rep., 8. Total, 20.
House — Dem., 25; Rep., 15. Total, 40.

### Arizona

Governor — Bruce Babbitt, D., $50,000.
Sec. of State — Rose Mofford, D., $28,000.
Atty. Gen. — John LaSota, R., $45,000.
Treasurer — Bart Fleming, R., $30,000.
Legislature: meets annually in January at Phoenix. Each member receives an annual salary of $6,000.
Senate — Dem., 16; Rep., 14. Total, 30.
House — Dem., 22; Rep., 38. Total, 60.

### Arkansas

Governor — David Pryor, D., $35,000.
Lt. Gov. — Joe Purcell, D., $14,000.
Sec. of State — Winston Bryant, D., $22,500.
Atty. Gen. — Bill Clinton, D., $26,500.
Treasurer — Mrs. Nancy J. Hall, D., $22,500.
General Assembly: meets odd years in January at Little Rock. Members receive $7,500 per year, $45 a day while in regular session, plus 13c a mile travel expense.
Senate — Dem., 34; Rep., 1. Total, 35.
House — Dem., 97; Rep., 3. Total, 100.

### California

(salaries effective Jan., 1979)
Governor — Edmund G. Brown Jr., D., $49,100.
Lt. Gov. — Mervyn M. Dymally, D., $42,500.
Sec. of State — March Fong Eu, D., $42,500.
Controller — Kenneth Cory, D., $42,500.
Atty. Gen. — Evelle J. Younger, R., $47,500.
Treasurer — Jesse M. Unruh, D., $42,500.
Legislature: meets at Sacramento; regular sessions commence on the first Monday in Dec. of every even-numbered year; each session lasts 2 years. Members receive $25,555 per year plus mileage and $40 per diem.
Senate — Dem., 26; Rep., 14. Total, 40.

Assembly — Dem., 57; Rep., 23. Total, 80.

### Colorado

Governor — Dick Lamm, D., $40,000.
Lt. Gov. — George Brown, D., $25,000.
Secy. of State — Mary Estill Buchanan, R., $25,000.
Atty. Gen. — J.D. MacFarlane, D., $32,500.
Treasurer — Roy Romer, D., $25,000.
General Assembly: meets annually in January at Denver. Members receive $7,600 annually, plus $35 per day for non-session meetings up to a maximum of $1,050 in any calendar year.
Senate — Dem., 17; Rep., 18. Total, 35.
House — Dem., 30; Rep., 35. Total, 65.

### Connecticut

(salaries, except governor, effective Mar., 1979)
Governor — Ella T. Grasso. D., $42,000.
Lt. Gov. — Robert K. Killian, D., $25,000.
Sec. of State — Gloria Schaffer, D., $25,000.
Treasurer — Henry E. Parker, D., $25,000.
Comptroller — J. Edward Caldwell, D., $25,000.
Atty. Gen. — Carl R. Ajello, D., $38,500.
General Assembly: meets annually odd years in January and even years in February at Hartford. Salary $15,000 per 2-year term plus $2,000 per 2-year term for expenses, plus 12c per mile travel allowance.
Senate — Dem., 22; Rep., 14. Total, 36.
House — Dem., 91; Rep., 60. Total, 151.

### Delaware

Governor — Pierre S. duPont 4th, R., $35,000.
Lt. Gov. — James D. McGinnis, D., $12,000.
Sec. of State — Glenn C. Kenton, R., $19,900.
Atty. Gen. — Richard R. Wier Jr., D., $30,000.
Treasurer — Thomas R. Carper, D., $18,000.
General Assembly: meets annually at Dover from the 2d Tuesday in January to midnight June 30. Members receive $9,000 base salary.
Senate — Dem., 13; Rep., 8. Total, 21.
House — Dem., 26; Rep., 15. Total, 41.

### Florida

Governor — Reubin Askew, D., $50,000.
Lt. Gov. — J.H. Williams, D., $36,000.
Sec. of State — Bruce A Smathers, D., $40,000.
Comptroller — Gerald Lewis, D., $40,000.
Atty. Gen. — Robert L. Shevin, D., $40,000.
Treasurer — Bill Gunter, D., $40,000.
Legislature: meets annually in April at Tallahassee. Members receive $12,000 per year plus expense allowance while on official business.
Senate — Dem., 30; Rep., 9; Ind., 1. Total, 40.
House — Dem., 92; Rep., 28. Total, 120.

### Georgia

Governor — George Busbee, D., $50,000.
Lt. Gov. — Zell Miller, D., $25,000.
Sec. of State — Ben W. Fortson Jr., D., $38,400.
Comptroller General — Johnnie L. Caldwell, D., $38,400.
Atty. Gen. — Arthur K. Bolton, D., $46,000.

**General Assembly:** meets annually at Atlanta. Members receive $7,200 per year. During session $36 per day for expenses.
**Senate** — Dem., 52; Rep., 4. Total, 56.
**House** — Dem., 155; Rep., 24, Ind., 1. Total, 180.

### Hawaii
**Governor** — George R. Ariyoshi, D., $50,000.
**Lt. Gov.** — Nelson K. Doi, D., $45,000.
**Dir., Budg. & Finance** — Eileen Anderson, D., $42,500.
**Atty. Gen.** — Ronald Amemiya, D., $42,500.
**Comptroller** — Hideo Murakami, D., $42,500.
**Legislature:** meets annually in January at Honolulu. Members receive $12,000 per year plus expenses.
**Senate** — Dem., 18. Rep., 7. Total, 25.
**House** — Dem., 41. Rep., 10. Total, 51.

### Idaho
(salaries effective Jan., 1979)
**Governor** — John V. Evans, D., $40,000.
**Lt. Gov.** — William J. Murphy, D., $12,000.
**Sec. of State** — Pete T. Cenarrusa, R., $28,000.
**Treasurer** — Marjorie Ruth Moon, D., $28,000.
**Atty. Gen.** — Wayne L. Kidwell, R., $35,000.
**Legislature:** meets on the Monday after the first day in January at Boise. Members receive $3,000 per year, plus $25 per day when authorized, plus travel allowances.
**Senate** — Dem., 15; Rep., 20. Total, 35.
**House** — Dem., 22; Rep., 48. Total, 70.

### Illinois
**Governor** — James R. Thompson, R., $50,000.
**Lt. Gov.** — Dave Oneal, R., $37,500.
**Sec. of State** — Alan J. Dixon, D., $42,500.
**Comptroller** — Michael J. Bakalis, D., $40,000.
**Atty. Gen.** — William J Scott, R., $42,500.
**Treasurer** — Donald R. Smith, R., $40,000.
**General Assembly:** meets each year in January at Springfield. Members receive $20,000 per annum.
**Senate** — Dem., 34; Rep., 25. Total, 59.
**House** — Dem., 93; Rep., 83; Ind., 1. Total, 177.

### Indiana
**Governor** — Otis R. Bowen, R., $36,000 ($48,000 in 1980) plus discretionary expenses.
**Lt. Gov.** — Robert Orr, R., $23,500 ($34,000 in 1980), also $6,000 per year as president of Senate.
**Sec. of State** — Larry Conrad, D., $34,000.
**Atty. Gen.** — Theodore L. Sendak, R., $34,000.
**Treasurer** — Jack L. New, D., $34,000.
**General Assembly:** meets annually in January. Members receive $8,000 per year after Nov. 1978, plus $44 per day while in session, $12.50 per day while not in session.
**Senate** — Dem., 28; Rep., 22. Total, 50.
**House** — Dem., 48, Rep., 52. Total, 100.

### Iowa
**Governor** — Robert D. Ray, R., $55,000 plus $5,000 expenses.
**Lt. Gov.** — Arthur A. Neu, R., $18,000 plus personal expenses and travel allowances at same rate as for a senator.
**Sec. of State** — Melvin D. Synhorst, R., $30,000.
**Atty. Gen.** — Richard C. Turner, R., $40,000.
**Treasurer** — Maurice E. Baringer, R., $30,000.
**General Assembly:** meets annually in January at Des Moines. Members receive $12,000 annually plus maximum expense allowance of $30 per day for first 120 days of first session, and first 100 days of 2d session; mileage expenses at 15c a mile.
**Senate** — Dem., 26; Rep., 24. Total, 50.
**House** — Dem., 59; Rep., 41. Total, 100.

### Kansas
(salaries effective 1979)
**Governor** — Robert F. Bennett, R., $45,000.
**Lt. Gov.** — Shelby Smith, R., $13,500 plus expenses.
**Sec. of State** — Mrs. Elwill M. Shanahan, R., $27,000.
**Atty. Gen.** — Curt Schneider, D., $40,000.
**Treasurer** — Joan Finney, D., $27,000.
**Legislature:** meets annually in January at Topeka. Members receive $35 a day plus $44 a day expenses while in session, plus $400 per month while not in session.
**Senate** — Dem., 19; Rep., 21. Total, 40.
**House** — Dem., 65; Rep., 60. Total, 125.

### Kentucky
**Governor** — Julian Carroll, D., $35,000.
**Lt. Gov.** — Thelma Stovall, D., $31,272.
**Sec. of State** — Drexel Davis, D., $31,272.

**Atty. Gen.** — Robert Stephens, D., $31,272.
**Treasurer** — Francis Mills, D., $31,272.
**General Assembly:** meets even years in January at Frankfort. Members receive $50 per day during session and $75 per day and $750 per month for expenses.
**Senate** — Dem., 30; Rep., 8. Total, 38.
**House** — Dem., 78; Rep., 22. Total, 100.

### Louisiana
**Governor** — Edwin W. Edwards, D., $50,000.
**Lt. Gov.** — James E. Fitzmorris Jr., D., $40,000.
**Sec. of State** — Paul Hardy, D., $35,000.
**Atty. Gen.** — William J. Guste Jr., D., $35,000.
**Treasurer** — Mary Evelyn Parker, D., $35,000.
**Legislature:** meets annually for 60 legislative days commencing on 3d Monday in April. Members receive $50 per day and mileage at 16c a mile for 8 round trips, plus $1,000 per month expense allowance.
**Senate** — Dem., 39; Rep., 0. Total, 39.
**House** — Dem., 102; Rep., 3. Total, 105.

### Maine
**Governor** — James B. Longley, I., $35,000.
**Sec. of State** — Markham L. Gartley, D., $20,000.
**Atty. Gen.** — Joseph E. Brennan, D., $25,500.
**Treasurer** — Leighton Cooney, D., $15,000.
**Legislature:** meets biennially in January at Augusta. Members receive $4,500 for regular sessions, $2,500 for special session plus expenses; presiding officers receive 50% more.
**Senate** — Dem., 12; Rep., 21. Total, 33.
**House** — Dem., 87; Rep., 63; (one vacancy). Total, 151.

### Maryland
**Governor** — Marvin Mandel, D. (suspended), $60,000 (in 1979).
**Lt. Gov.** — Blair Lee 3d, D. (acting Governor), $44,856.
**Comptroller** — Louis L. Goldstein, D., $44,856.
**Atty. Gen.** — Francis B. Burch, D., $44,856.
**Treasurer** — William S. James, D., $44,856.
**General Assembly:** meets 90 days annually on the 3d Wednesday in January at Annapolis. Members receive $16,000 per year.
**Senate** — Dem., 39; Rep., 8. Total, 47.
**House** — Dem., 126; Rep., 15. Total, 141.

### Massachusetts
**Governor** — Michael S. Dukakis, D., $40,000.
**Lt. Gov.** — Thomas P. O'Neill 3d, D., $30,000.
**Sec. of the Commonwealth** — Paul Guzzi, D., $30,000.
**Atty. Gen.** — Francis X. Belloti, D., $37,500.
**Treasurer** — Robert Q. Crane, D., $30,000.
**General Court (Legislature):** meets each January in Boston. Salaries $16,072 per annum.
**Senate** — Dem., 33; Rep., 7. Total, 40.
**House** — Dem., 192; Rep., 43; Ind., 3; (2 vacancies). Total, 240.

### Michigan
**Governor** — William G. Milliken, R., $58,000.
**Lt. Gov.** — James J. Damman, R., $40,000.
**Sec. of State** — Richard H. Austin, D., $45,000.
**Atty. Gen.** — Frank J. Kelley, D., $45,000.
**Treasurer** — Allison Green, Non-Part., $41,800.
**Legislature:** meets annually in January at Lansing. Members receive $24,000 per year, plus $4,600 expense allowance.
**Senate** — Dem., 24; Rep., 14. Total, 38.
**House** — Dem., 68; Rep., 42. Total, 110.

### Minnesota
**Governor** — Rudy Perpich, DFL, $58,000.
**Lt. Gov.** — Alec G. Olson, DFL, $36,000.
**Sec. of State** — Joan Anderson Growe, DFL, $30,000.
**Atty. Gen.** — Warren Spannaus, DFL., $49,000.
**Treasurer** — Jim Lord, DFL., $30,000.
**Legislature:** meets for a total of 120 days within every 2 years at St. Paul. Members receive $16,500 per year beginning in 1979, plus expense allowance during session.
**Senate** — DFL., 48; IR, 19. Total, 67.
**House** — DFL., 100; IR, 34. Total, 134.
(DFL means Democratic-Farmer-Labor. IR means Independent Republican.)

### Mississippi
**Governor** — Cliff Finch, D., $43,000 ($53,000 in 1980).
**Lt. Gov.** — Evelyn Gandy, D., $15,000 per regular legislative session, plus expense allowance.
**Sec. of State** — Heber Ladner, D., $34,000.
**Atty. Gen.** — A.L. Summer, D., $41,000.
**Treasurer** — Edwin Lloyd Pittman, D., $34,000.

**Legislature:** meets annually in January at Jackson. Members receive $8,100 per regular session plus travel allowance, and $210 per month while not in session.
Senate — Dem., 50; Rep., 2. Total, 52.
House — Dem., 119; Rep., 2; Ind., 1. Total, 122.

## Missouri
Governor — Joseph P. Teasdale, D., $37,500.
Lt. Gov. — William C. Phelps, R., $16,000.
Sec. of State — James C. Kirkpatrick, D., $25,000.
Atty. Gen. — John Ashcroft, R., $25,000.
Treasurer — James I. Spainhower, D., $20,000.
**General Assembly:** meets in Jefferson City annually, first Wednesday after first Monday in January; adjournment in odd-numbered years by June 30, in even-numbered years by May 15. Members receive $15,000 annually beginning in 1979.
Senate — Dem., 22; Rep., 12. Total, 34.
House — Dem., 112; Rep., 51. Total, 163.

## Montana
Governor — Thomas L. Judge, D., $35,000.
Lt. Gov. — Ted Schwinden, D., $25,000.
Sec. of State — Frank Murray, D., $22,500.
Atty. Gen. — Mike Greely, D., $32,500.
**Legislative Assembly:** meets biennially in January at Helena. Members receive $33.22 per legislative day plus $40 per day for expenses while in session.
Senate — Dem., 25; Rep., 25. Total, 50.
House — Dem., 57; Rep., 43. Total, 100.

## Nebraska
(salaries, except governor, effective 1979)
Governor — J. James Exon, D., $40,000.
Lt. Gov. — Gerald T. Whelan, D., $32,000.
Sec. of State — Allen J. Beermann, R., $32,000.
Atty. Gen. — Paul Douglas, R., $39,000.
Treasurer — Frank Marsh, R., $32,000.
**Legislature:** meets annually in January at Lincoln. Members receive salary of $4,800 annually plus travelling expenses for one round trip to and from session.
Unicameral body composed of 49 members who are elected on a nonpartisan ballot and are classed as senators.

## Nevada
(salaries effective 1979)
Governor — Mike O'Callaghan, D., $50,000.
Lt. Gov. — Robert Rose, D., $8,000 plus $60 per day when acting as governor and president of the Senate during legislative sessions.
Sec. of State — William D. Swackhamer, D., $32,500.
Comptroller — Wilson McGowen, R., $31,500.
Atty. Gen. — Robert List, R., $40,000.
Treasurer — Michael Mirabelli, D., $31,500.
**Legislature:** meets odd years in January at Carson City. Members receive $80 per day for 60 days (20 days for special sessions), plus per diem of $40 per day for entire length of session. Travel allowance of 10c per mile.
Senate — Dem., 17; Rep., 3. Total, 20.
Assembly — Dem., 35; Rep., 5. Total, 40.

## New Hampshire
Governor — Meldrim Thomson, Jr., R., $42,000.
Sec. of State — William M. Gardner, D., $29,500.
Atty. Gen. — Thomas D. Rath, $36,500.
Comptroller — Arthur H. Fowler.
Treasurer — Robert W. Flanders, R., $29,500.
**General Court (Legislature):** meets odd years in January at Concord. Members receive $200; presiding officers $250.
Senate — Dem., 12; Rep., 12. Total, 24.
House — Rep., 219; Dem., 176; (5 vacancies). Total, 400.

## New Jersey
Governor — Brendan Byrne, D., $65,000.
Sec. of State — Donald Lan, $49,000.
Atty. Gen. — John J. Degnan, $49,000.
Treasurer — Clifford Goldman, $49,000.
**Legislature:** meets annually in January at Trenton. Members receive $10,000 per year, except president of Senate and speaker of Assembly who receive 1/3 more.
Senate — Dem., 27; Rep., 13. Total, 40.
Assembly — Dem., 54; Rep. 26. Total, 80.

## New Mexico
Governor — Jerry Apodaca, D., $35,000.
Lt. Gov. — Robert E. Ferguson, D., $15,000, $75 per day when presiding over Senate. Acting governor, $75 per day.
Sec. of State — Ernestine D. Evans, D., $30,000.

Atty. Gen. — Toney Anaya, D., $35,000.
Treasurer — Edward Murphy, D., $30,000.
**Legislature:** meets in January at Sante Fe; odd years for 60 days, even years for 30 days. Members receive $24 per day while in session.
Senate — Dem., 33; Rep., 9. Total, 42.
House — Dem., 48; Rep., 22. Total, 70.

## New York
Governor — Hugh L. Carey, D., $85,000.
Lt. Gov. — Mary Anne Krupsak, D., $60,000.
Sec. of State — Mario M. Cuomo, D., $47,800.
Comptroller — Arthur Levitt, D., $60,000.
Atty. Gen. — Louis J. Lefkowitz R., $60,000.
**Legislature:** meets annually in January at Albany. Members receive $23,500 per year.
Senate — Dem., 24; Rep., 36. Total, 60.
Assembly — Dem., 88; Rep., 61; 1 Lib. Total, 150.

## North Carolina
Governor — James B. Hunt, D., $47,700 plus $10,000 per year expenses.
Lt. Gov. — James C. Green, D., $39,500 per year, plus $20 per day not to exceed 120 days per regular session; $10,000 per year expense allowance.
Sec. of State — Thad Eure, D., $39,500.
Atty. Gen. — Rufus L. Edmisten, D., $44,500.
Treasurer — Harlan E. Boyles, D., $39,500.
**General Assembly:** meets odd years in January at Raleigh. Members receive $6,000 annual salary and $1,800 annual expense allowance, plus $44 per diem subsistence and travel allowance while in session.
Senate — Dem., 47; Rep., 3. Total, 50.
House — Dem., 114; Rep., 6. Total, 120.

## North Dakota
Governor — Arthur A. Link, D., $27,500.
Lt. Gov. — Wayne Sanstead, D., $5,000.
Sec. of State — Ben Meier, R., $22,500.
Atty. Gen. — Allen I. Olson, R., $25,000.
Treasurer — Walter Christensen, $22,500.
**Legislative Assembly:** meets odd years in January at Bismarck. Members receive $65 per day during session and $150 per month when not in session.
Senate — Dem., 18; Rep., 32. Total, 50.
House — Dem., 50; Rep., 50. Total, 100.

## Ohio
Governor — James A. Rhodes, R., $50,000.
Lt. Gov. — Richard F. Celeste, D., $30,000.
Sec. of State — Ted W. Brown, R., $38,000.
Atty. Gen. — William J. Brown, D., $38,000.
Treasurer — Gertrude W. Donahey, D., $38,000.
**General Assembly:** meets at Columbus on first Monday in January in odd-numbered years; no later than Mar. 15 of following year for 2d session. Members receive $17,500 per annum.
Senate — Dem., 21; Rep., 12. Total, 33.
House — Dem., 62; Rep., 37. Total, 99.

## Oklahoma
Governor — David L. Boren, D., $42,500.
Lt. Gov. — George Nigh, D., $24,000.
Sec. of State — Jerome W. Byrd, D., $18,500.
Atty. Gen. — Larry Derryberry, D., $27,500.
Treasurer — Leo Winters, D., $22,000.
**Legislature:** meets each year in January at Oklahoma City. Members receive $12,948.
Senate — Dem., 39; Rep., 9. Total, 48.
House — Dem., 79; Rep., 22. Total, 101.

## Oregon
Governor — Robert W. Straub, D., $47,976, plus $1,000 monthly expenses.
Sec. of State — Norma Paulus, R., $39,492.
Atty. Gen. — James A. Redden, R., $39,492.
Treasurer — Clay Meyers, R., $39,492.
**Legislative Assembly:** meets odd years in January at Salem. Members receive $600 monthly and $44 expenses per day while in session; $175 per month while not in session.
Senate — Dem., 24; Rep., 6. Total, 30.
House — Dem., 36; Rep., 24. Total, 60.

## Pennsylvania
Governor — Milton J. Shapp, D., $66,000.
Lt. Gov. — Ernest P. Kline, D., $49,500.
Sec. of the Commonwealth — Barton A. Fields, D., $38,500.

**Atty. Gen.** — Gerald Gornish, D. (act.), $44,000.
**Treasurer** — Robert E. Casey, D., $42,500.
**General Assembly** — meets annually in January at Harrisburg. Members receive $18,720 per year plus $7,500 for expenses.
**Senate** — Dem., 30; Rep., 20. Total, 50.
**House** — Dem., 116; Rep., 84; (3 vacancies). Total, 203.

### Rhode Island

**Governor** — J. Joseph Garrahy, D., $42,500.
**Lt. Gov.** — Thomas R. DiLuglio, D., $25,500.
**Sec. of State** — Robert F. Burns, D., $25,500.
**Atty. Gen.** — Julius C. Michaelson, D., $31,875.
**Treasurer** — Anthony J. Solomon, D., $25,500.
**General Assembly:** meets annually in January at Providence. Members receive $5 per day for 60 days, and travel allowance of 8c per mile.
**Senate** — Dem., 45; Rep., 5. Total, 50.
**House** — Dem., 83; Rep., 17. Total, 100.

### South Carolina

**Governor** — James B. Edwards, R., $39,000.
**Lt. Gov.** — W. Brantley Harvey Jr., D., $16,250.
**Sec. of State** — O. Frank Thornton, D., $34,000.
**Comptroller Gen.** — Earle E. Morris Jr., D., $34,000.
**Atty. Gen.** — Daniel R. McLeod, D., $34,000.
**Treasurer** — G.L. Patterson Jr., D., $34,000.
**General Assembly:** meets annually in January at Columbia. Members receive $7,000 per year and expense allowance of $25 per day, plus travel and postage allowance.
**Senate** — Dem., 43; Rep., 3. Total, 46.
**House** — Dem. 111; Rep., 13. Total, 124.

### South Dakota

**Governor** — Harvey Wollman, D., $37,000.
**Lt. Gov.** — vacant, $5,000 per 30-day legislative session, $8,000 for 45-day session, plus $40 per legislative day.
**Sec. of State** — Lorna B. Herseth, D., $24,000.
**Treasurer** — David Volk, R., $24,000.
**Atty. Gen.** — William J. Janklow, R., $31,500.
**Legislature:** meets annually in January at Pierre. Members receive $3,600 for 45-day session in odd-numbered years, and $2,400 for 30-day session in even-numbered years, plus $50 per legislative day.
**Senate** — Dem., 11; Rep., 24. Total, 35.
**House** — Dem., 22; Rep., 48. Total, 70.

### Tennessee

**Governor** — Ray Blanton, D., $65,000 (in 1979).
**Lt. Gov.** — John S. Wilder, D., $8,308.
**Sec. of State** — Gentry Crowell, D., $43,680.
**Comptroller** — William Snodgrass, D., $48,360.
**Atty. Gen.** — Brooks McLemore, D., $50,388.
**General Assembly:** meets annually in January at Nashville. Members receive $8,308 yearly plus $66.47 expenses for each day in session, plus mileage and expense allowances.
**Senate** — Dem., 23; Rep., 9; Ind., 1. Total, 33.
**House** — Dem., 66; Rep., 32; Ind., 1. Total, 99.

### Texas

**Governor** — Dolph Briscoe, D., $71,400.
**Lt. Gov.** — Bill Hobby, D., $10,000, plus living quarters. Governor's salary when acting as governor.
**Sec. of State** — Steve Oaks, D., $42,700.
**Comptroller** — Bob Bullock, D., $45,200.
**Atty. Gen.** — John L. Hill, D., $45,200.
**Treasurer** — Warren G. Harding, D., $45,200.
**Legislature:** meets odd years in January at Austin. Members receive annual salary not exceeding $7,200, per diem while in session, and travel allowance.
**Senate** — Dem., 28; Rep., 3. Total, 31.
**House** — Dem., 132; Rep., 18. Total, 150.

### Utah

**Governor** — Scott M. Matheson, D., $40,000.
**Sec. of State/Lt. Gov.** — David S. Monson, R., $26,500.
**Atty. Gen.** — Robert B. Hansen, R., $30,000.
**Treasurer** — Linn C. Baker, D., $26,500.
**Legislature:** convenes for 60 days on 2d Monday in January in odd-numbered years; for 20 days in even-numbered years; members receive $25 per day, $15 daily expenses, and mileage.
**Senate** — Dem., 17; Rep., 12. Total, 29.
**House** — Dem., 35; Rep., 40. Total, 75.

### Vermont

**Governor** — Richard A. Snelling, R., $39,000.
**Lt. Gov.** — T. Garry Buckley, R., $16,700.

**Sec. of State** — James A. Guest, D., $21,200.
**Atty. Gen.** — M. Jerome Diamond, D., $21,200.
**Treasurer** — Emory H. Hebard, R., $21,200.
**General Assembly:** meets odd years in January at Montpelier. Members receive $200 weekly while in session, with a limit of 6,750 for a regular session and $40 per day for special session, plus specified expenses.
**Senate** — Dem., 9; Rep., 21. Total, 30.
**House** — Dem., 68; Rep., 70; R/D, 4; D/R, 3; I/D, 1; D/I, 3; I, 1. Total, 150.

### Virginia

**Governor** — John N. Dalton, R., $60,000.
**Lt. Gov.** — Charles S. Robb, D., $16,000.
**Atty. Gen.** — J. Marshall Coleman, R., $45,000.
**Sec. of the Commonwealth** — Frederick T. Gray Jr., R., $21,400.
**Treasurer** — Robert C. Watts Jr., R., $37,900.
**General Assembly:** meets every year in January at Richmond. Members receive $5,475 annually plus expense and mileage allowances.
**Senate** — Dem., 35; Rep., 5. Total, 40.
**House** — Dem., 76; Rep., 21; Ind., 3. Total, 100.

### Washington

**Governor** — Dixy Lee Ray, R., $55,000.
**Lt. Gov.** — John A. Cherberg, D., $30,000.
**Sec. of State** — Bruce K. Chapman, R., $27,000.
**Atty. Gen.** — Slade Gorton, R., $41,200.
**Treasurer** — Robert S. O'Brien, D., $32,500.
**Legislature:** meets odd years in January at Olympia. Members receive $9,800 (1979) annually, plus $40 per day while in session for subsistence and lodging.
**Senate** — Dem., 30; Rep., 19. Total, 49.
**House** — Dem., 62; Rep., 36. Total, 98.

### West Virginia

**Governor** — John D. Rockefeller 4th, D., $50,000.
**Sec. of State** — A. James Manchin, D., $30,000.
**Atty. Gen.** — Chauncey Browning Jr., D., $35,000.
**Treasurer** — Larry Bailey, D., $35,000.
**Comm. of Agric.** — Gus R. Douglas, D., $32,500.
**Legislature:** meets annually in January at Charleston. Members receive compensation fixed by citizens' commission.
**Senate** — Dem., 28; Rep., 6. Total, 34.
**House** — Dem., 91; Rep., 9. Total, 100.

### Wisconsin

**Governor** — (acting) Martin J. Schreiber, D., $49,920.
**Lt. Gov.** — vacant, $28,668.
**Sec. of State** — Douglas La Follette, D., $13,500.
**Treasurer** — Charles P. Smith, D., $22,140.
**Atty. Gen.** — Bronson C. LaFollette, D., $36,450.
**Legislature:** meets in January at Madison. Members receive $17,843 annually plus $30 per day expenses.
**Senate** — Dem., 22; Rep., 11. Total, 33.
**Assembly** — Dem., 66; Rep., 32; (1 vacancy). Total, 99.

### Wyoming

**Governor** — Ed Herschler, D., $55,000.
**Sec. of State** — Thyra Thomson, R., $37,500.
**Atty. Gen.** — vacant.
**Treasurer** — Edwin J. Wirtzenburger, R., $37,500.
**Legislature:** meets odd years in January, even years in February, at Cheyenne. Members receive $30 per day while in session, plus $36 per day for expenses.
**Senate** — Dem., 12; Rep., 18. Total, 30.
**House** — Dem., 27; Rep. 34; Ind. 1. Total, 62.

### Puerto Rico

**Governor** — Carlos Romero-Barcelo, $36,200.
**Secretaries** (all at $26,200):
   **Agric.** — Heriberto J. Martinez Torres.
   **Commerce** — Juan H. Cintron.
   **Educ.** — Carlos Chardon.
   **Health** — Dr. Jaime Rivera Dueno.
   **Justice** — Miguel Gimenez Munoz.
   **Labor** — Carlos S. Quirós.
   **Public Works** — Manuel A. Pietrantoni
   **Social Services** — Dr. Jenaro Collazo.
   **State** — Reinaldo Paniagua.
   **Treasury** — Julio Cesar Perez.
All officials belong to the New Progressive party.
**Legislative Assembly:** composed of a Senate of 27 members and a House of Representatives of 51 members. Meets annually, in January at San Juan. Members receive $15,000 plus expenses and travel allowances.

# Judiciary of the U.S.

Data as of July, 1978

## Justices of the United States Supreme Court

The Supreme Court comprises the chief justice of the United States and 8 associate justices, all appointed by the president with advice and consent of the Senate. Salaries: chief justice $75,000 annually, associate justice $72,500.

| Name; apptd from Chief Justices in italics | Service Term | Yrs. | Born | Died |
|---|---|---|---|---|
| John Jay, N. Y. | 1789-1795 | 5 | 1745 | 1829 |
| John Rutledge, S. C. | 1789-1791 | 1 | 1739 | 1800 |
| William Cushing, Mass. | 1789-1810 | 20 | 1732 | 1810 |
| James Wilson, Pa. | 1789-1798 | 8 | 1742 | 1798 |
| John Blair, Va. | 1789-1796 | 6 | 1732 | 1800 |
| James Iredell, N. C. | 1790-1799 | 9 | 1751 | 1799 |
| Thomas Johnson, Md. | 1791-1793 | 1 | 1732 | 1819 |
| William Paterson, N. J. | 1793-1806 | 13 | 1745 | 1806 |
| John Rutledge, S.C. | 1795(a) | | 1739 | 1800 |
| Samuel Chase, Md. | 1796-1811 | 15 | 1741 | 1811 |
| Oliver Ellsworth, Conn. | 1796-1800 | 4 | 1745 | 1807 |
| Bushrod Washington, Va. | 1798-1829 | 31 | 1762 | 1829 |
| Alfred Moore, N. C. | 1799-1804 | 4 | 1755 | 1810 |
| John Marshall, Va. | 1801-1835 | 34 | 1755 | 1835 |
| William Johnson, S. C. | 1804-1834 | 30 | 1771 | 1834 |
| Henry B. Livingston, N. Y. | 1806-1823 | 16 | 1757 | 1823 |
| Thomas Todd, Ky. | 1807-1826 | 18 | 1765 | 1826 |
| Joseph Story, Mass. | 1811-1845 | 33 | 1779 | 1845 |
| Gabriel Duval, Md. | 1811-1835 | 22 | 1752 | 1844 |
| Smith Thompson, N. Y. | 1823-1843 | 20 | 1768 | 1843 |
| Robert Trimble, Ky. | 1826-1828 | 2 | 1777 | 1828 |
| John McLean, Oh. | 1829-1861 | 32 | 1785 | 1861 |
| Henry Baldwin, Pa. | 1830-1844 | 14 | 1780 | 1844 |
| James M. Wayne, Ga. | 1835-1867 | 32 | 1790 | 1867 |
| Roger B. Taney, Md. | 1836-1864 | 28 | 1777 | 1864 |
| Philip P. Barbour, Va. | 1836-1841 | 4 | 1783 | 1841 |
| John Catron, Tenn. | 1837-1865 | 28 | 1786 | 1865 |
| John McKinley, Ala. | 1837-1852 | 15 | 1780 | 1852 |
| Peter V. Daniel, Va. | 1841-1860 | 19 | 1784 | 1860 |
| Samuel Nelson, N. Y. | 1845-1872 | 27 | 1792 | 1873 |
| Levi Woodbury, N. H. | 1845-1851 | 5 | 1789 | 1851 |
| Robert C. Grier, Pa. | 1846-1870 | 23 | 1794 | 1870 |
| Benjamin R. Curtis, Mass. | 1851-1857 | 6 | 1809 | 1874 |
| John A. Campbell, Ala. | 1853-1861 | 8 | 1811 | 1889 |
| Nathan Clifford, Me. | 1858-1881 | 23 | 1803 | 1881 |
| Noah H. Swayne, Oh. | 1862-1881 | 18 | 1804 | 1884 |
| Samuel F. Miller, Ia. | 1862-1890 | 28 | 1816 | 1890 |
| David Davis, Ill. | 1862-1877 | 14 | 1815 | 1886 |
| Stephen J. Field, Cal. | 1863-1897 | 34 | 1816 | 1899 |
| Salmon P. Chase, Oh. | 1864-1873 | 8 | 1808 | 1873 |
| William Strong, Pa. | 1870-1880 | 10 | 1808 | 1895 |
| Joseph P. Bradley, N. J. | 1870-1892 | 21 | 1813 | 1892 |
| Ward Hunt, N. Y. | 1872-1882 | 9 | 1810 | 1886 |
| Morrison R. Waite, Oh. | 1874-1888 | 14 | 1816 | 1888 |
| John M. Harlan, Ky. | 1877-1911 | 34 | 1833 | 1911 |
| William B. Woods, Ga. | 1880-1887 | 6 | 1824 | 1887 |
| Stanley Matthews, Oh. | 1881-1889 | 7 | 1824 | 1889 |
| Horace Gray, Mass. | 1881-1902 | 20 | 1828 | 1902 |
| Samuel Blatchford, N. Y. | 1882-1893 | 11 | 1820 | 1893 |
| Lucius Q. C. Lamar, Miss. | 1888-1893 | 5 | 1825 | 1893 |
| Melville W. Fuller, Ill. | 1888-1910 | 21 | 1833 | 1910 |
| David J. Brewer, Kan. | 1889-1910 | 20 | 1837 | 1910 |
| Henry B. Brown, Mich. | 1890-1906 | 15 | 1836 | 1913 |
| George Shiras Jr., Pa. | 1892-1903 | 10 | 1832 | 1924 |
| Howell E. Jackson, Tenn. | 1893-1895 | 2 | 1832 | 1895 |
| Edward D. White, La. | 1894-1910 | 16 | 1845 | 1921 |
| Rufus W. Peckman, N. Y. | 1895-1909 | 13 | 1838 | 1909 |
| Joseph McKenna, Cal. | 1898-1925 | 26 | 1843 | 1926 |
| Oliver W. Holmes, Mass. | 1902-1932 | 29 | 1841 | 1935 |
| William R. Day, Oh. | 1903-1922 | 19 | 1849 | 1923 |
| William H. Moody, Mass. | 1906-1910 | 3 | 1853 | 1917 |
| Horace H. Lurton, Tenn. | 1909-1914 | 4 | 1844 | 1914 |
| Charles E. Hughes, N. Y. | 1910-1916 | 5 | 1862 | 1948 |
| Willis Van Devanter, Wy. | 1910-1937 | 26 | 1859 | 1941 |
| Joseph R. Lamar, Ga. | 1910-1916 | 5 | 1857 | 1916 |
| Edward D. White, La. | 1910-1921 | 10 | 1845 | 1921 |
| Mahlon Pitney, N. J. | 1912-1922 | 10 | 1858 | 1924 |
| James C. McReynolds, Tenn. | 1914-1941 | 26 | 1862 | 1946 |
| Louis D. Brandeis, Mass. | 1916-1939 | 22 | 1856 | 1941 |
| John H. Clarke, Oh. | 1916-1922 | 5 | 1857 | 1945 |
| William H. Taft, Conn. | 1921-1930 | 8 | 1857 | 1930 |
| George Sutherland, Ut. | 1922-1938 | 15 | 1862 | 1942 |
| Pierce Butler, Minn. | 1922-1939 | 16 | 1866 | 1939 |
| Edward T. Sanford, Tenn. | 1923-1930 | 7 | 1865 | 1930 |
| Harlan F. Stone, N. Y. | 1925-1941 | 16 | 1872 | 1946 |
| Charles E. Hughes, N. Y. | 1930-1941 | 11 | 1862 | 1948 |
| Owen J. Roberts, Pa. | 1930-1945 | 15 | 1875 | 1955 |
| Benjamin N. Cardozo, N.Y. | 1932-1938 | 6 | 1870 | 1938 |
| Hugo L. Black, Ala. | 1937-1971 | 34 | 1886 | 1971 |
| Stanley F. Reed, Ky. | 1938-1957 | 19 | 1884 | |
| Felix Frankfurter, Mass. | 1939-1962 | 23 | 1882 | 1965 |
| William O. Douglas, Conn. | 1939-1975 | 36 | 1898 | |
| Frank Murphy, Mich. | 1940-1949 | 9 | 1890 | 1949 |
| Harlan F. Stone, N. Y. | 1941-1946 | 5 | 1872 | 1946 |
| James F. Byrnes, S. C. | 1941-1942 | 1 | 1879 | 1972 |
| Robert H. Jackson, N. Y. | 1941-1954 | 12 | 1892 | 1954 |
| Wiley B. Rutledge, Ia. | 1943-1949 | 6 | 1894 | 1949 |
| Harold H. Burton, Oh. | 1945-1958 | 13 | 1888 | 1964 |
| Fred M. Vinson, Ky. | 1946-1953 | 7 | 1890 | 1953 |
| Tom C. Clark, Tex. | 1949-1967 | 18 | 1899 | 1977 |
| Sherman Minton, Ind. | 1949-1956 | 7 | 1890 | 1965 |
| Earl Warren, Cal. | 1953-1969 | 16 | 1891 | 1974 |
| John Marshall Harlan, N. Y. | 1955-1971 | 16 | 1899 | 1971 |
| William J. Brennan Jr., N. J. | 1956 | | 1906 | |
| Charles E. Whittaker, Mo. | 1957-1962 | 5 | 1901 | 1973 |
| Potter Stewart, Oh. | 1958 | | 1915 | |
| Byron R. White, Col. | 1962 | | 1917 | |
| Arthur J. Goldberg, Ill. | 1962-1965 | 3 | 1908 | |
| Abe Fortas, Tenn. | 1965-1969 | 4 | 1910 | |
| Thurgood Marshall, N.Y. | 1967 | | 1908 | |
| Warren E. Burger, Va. | 1969 | | 1907 | |
| Harry A. Blackmun, Minn. | 1970 | | 1908 | |
| Lewis F. Powell Jr., Va. | 1971 | | 1907 | |
| William H. Rehnquist, Ariz. | 1971 | | 1924 | |
| John Paul Stevens, Ill. | 1975 | | 1920 | |

(a) Rejected Dec. 15, 1795.

## U.S. Court of Customs and Patent Appeals

Washington, DC 20439 (Salaries, $57,500)
**Chief Judge** — Howard T. Markey.
**Associate Judges** — Giles S. Rich, Phillip B. Baldwin, Donald E. Lane, Jack R. Miller.

## U.S. Customs Court

New York, NY 10007 (Salaries, $54,500)
**Chief Judge** — Edward D. Re.
**Judges** — Paul P. Rao, Morgan Ford, Scovel Richardson, Frederick Landis, James L. Watson, Herbert N. Maletz, Bernard Newman, Nils A. Boe.

## U.S. Court of Claims

Washington, DC 20005 (Salaries, $57,500)
**Chief Judge** — Daniel M. Friedman.
**Associate Judges** — Oscar H. Davis, Shiro Kashiwa, Robert L. Kunzig, Marion T. Bennett, Philip Nichols Jr.

## U.S. Tax Court

Washington DC 20217 (Salaries, $54,500)
**Chief Judge** — C. Moxley Featherston.

**Judges** — Arnold Raum, Irene F. Scott, William M. Fay, William M. Drennen, Theodore Tannenwald Jr., Charles R. Simpson, Leo H. Irwin, Samuel B. Sterrett, William Quealy, William A. Goffe, Cynthia H. Hall, Darrell D. Wiles, Richard C. Wilbur, Herbert L. Chabot.

# U.S. Courts of Appeals

(Salaries, $57,500. CJ means Chief Judge)

**District of Columbia** — David L. Bazelon, CJ; J. Skelly Wright, Carl McGowan, Edward Allen Tamm, Harold Leventhal, Spottswood W. Robinson III, Roger Robb, George E. MacKinnon, Malcolm Richard Wilkey; Clerk's Office, Washington, DC 20001.

**First Circuit** (Me., Mass., N.H., R.I., Puerto Rico) — Frank M. Coffin, CJ; Levin H. Campbell, Hugh H. Bownes; Clerk's Office, Boston, MA 02109.

**Second Circuit** (Conn., N.Y., Vt.) — Irving R. Kaufman, CJ; Wilfred Feinberg, Walter R. Mansfield, William H. Mulligan, James L. Oakes, William H. Timbers, Murray I. Gurfein, Ellsworth Van Graafeiland, Thomas J. Meskill; Clerk's Office, New York, NY 10007.

**Third Circuit** (Del., N.J., Pa., Virgin Is.) — Collins J. Seitz, CJ; Ruggero J. Aldisert, Arlin M. Adams, John J. Gibbons, Max Rosenn, James Hunter 3d, Joseph F. Weis Jr., Leonard I. Garth, A. Leon Higginbotham Jr.; Clerk's Office, Philadelphia, PA 19106.

**Fourth Circuit** (Md., N.C., S.C., Va., W.Va.) — Clement F. Haynsworth Jr., CJ; Harrison L. Winter, Kenneth K. Hall, John D. Butzner Jr., Donald Stuart Russell, H. Emory Widener Jr.; Clerk's Office, Richmond, VA 23219.

**Fifth Circuit** (Ala., Fla., Ga., La., Miss., Tex., Canal Zone) — John R. Brown, CJ; Homer Thornberry, James P. Coleman, Irving L. Goldberg, Robert A. Ainsworth Jr., John C. Godbold, Lewis R. Morgan, Charles Clark, Thomas G. Gee, Paul H. Roney, Gerald B. Tjoflat, James C. Hill, Peter T. Fay, Alvin B. Rubin; Clerk's Office, New Orleans, LA 70130.

**Sixth Circuit** (Ky., Mich., Ohio, Tenn.) — Harry Phillips, CJ; Paul C. Weick, George Clifton Edwards Jr., Anthony J. Celebrezze, John W. Peck, Albert J. Engel, Pierce Lively, Gilbert S. Merritt, Damon J. Keith; Clerk's Office, Cincinnati, OH 45202.

**Seventh Circuit** (Ill., Ind., Wis.) — Thomas E. Fairchild, CJ; Luther M. Swygert, Walter J. Cummings, Wilbur F. Pell Jr., Robert A. Sprecher, Philip W. Tone, Harlington Wood Jr., William J. Bauer; Clerk's Office, Chicago, IL 60604.

**Eighth Circuit** (Ark., Ia., Minn., Mo., Neb., N.D., S.D.) — Floyd R. Gibson, CJ; Donald P. Lay, Gerald W. Heaney, Myron H. Bright, Donald R. Ross, Roy L. Stephenson, William H. Webster, J. Smith Henley; Clerk's Office, St. Louis, MO 63101.

**Ninth Circuit** (Ariz., Cal., Ida., Mont., Nev., Ore., Wash., Alaska, Ha., Guam) — James R. Browning, CJ; Walter Ely, Shirley M. Hufstedler, Eugene A. Wright, Ozell M. Trask, Joseph T. Sneed, Herbert Y. C. Choy, J. Clifford Wallace, Alfred T. Goodwin, Anthony M. Kennedy, J. Blaine Anderson, Procter Hug Jr., Thomas Tang; Clerk's Office, San Francisco, CA 94101.

**Tenth Circuit** (Col., Kan., N.M., Okla., Ut., Wy.) — Oliver Seth, CJ; William J. Holloway Jr., Robert H. McWilliams, James E. Barrett, William E. Doyle, Monroe G. McKay; Clerk's Office, Denver, CO 80202.

**Temporary Emergency Court of Appeals** — Edward Allen Tamm, CJ; Clerk's Office, Washington, DC 20001.

# U.S. District Courts

(Salaries, $54,500. CJ means Chief Judge)

**Alabama — Northern:** Frank H. McFadden, CJ; Sam C. Pointer Jr., James Hughes Hancock, J. Foy Guin Jr.; Clerk's Office, Birmingham 35203. **Middle:** Frank M. Johnson Jr., CJ; Robert E. Varner; Clerk's Office, Montgomery 36101. **Southern:** Virgil Pittman, CJ; William Brevard Hand; Clerk's Office, Mobile 36602.

**Alaska** — James A. Von der Heydt, CJ; James M. Fitzgerald; Clerk's Office, Anchorage 99510.

**Arizona** — Walter Early Craig, CJ; C. A. Muecke, William P. Copple, William C. Frey, Mary Ann Richey; Clerk's Office, Phoenix 85025.

**Arkansas — Eastern:** Garnett Thomas Eisele, CJ; Terry L. Shell, Elsijane Trimble Roy; Clerk's Office, Little Rock 72203. **Western:** Paul X. Williams, CJ; Terry L. Shell; Clerk's Office, Fort Smith 72901.

**California — Northern:** Robert F. Peckham, CJ; Lloyd H. Burke, Stanley A. Weigel, Robert H. Schnacke, Samuel Conti, Spencer M. Williams, Charles B. Renfrew; William H. Orrick Jr., William H. Schwarzer, William A. Ingram, Cecil F. Poole; Clerk's Office, San Francisco 94102. **Eastern:** Thomas J. MacBride, CJ; M. D. Crocker, Philip C. Wilkins; Clerk's Office, San Francisco 94102. **Central:** Albert Lee Stephens Jr., CJ; Francis C. Whelan, Irving Hill, A. Andrew Hauk, William P. Gray, Warren J. Ferguson, Manuel L. Real, Harry Pregerson, David W. Williams, Robert J.

Kelleher, Wm. Matthew Byrne Jr., Lawrence T. Lydick, Malcolm M. Lucas, Robert Firth, Robert M. Takasugi, Laughlin E. Waters; Clerk's Office, Los Angeles 90012. **Southern:** Edward J. Schwartz, CJ; Howard B. Turrentine, Gordon Thompson Jr., Leland C. Nielsen, William B. Enright; Clerk's Office, San Diego 92189.

**Colorado** — Fred M. Winner, CJ; Sherman G. Finesilver, Richard P. Matsch; Clerk's Office, Denver 80294.

**Connecticut** — T. Emmet Clarie, CJ; T. F. Gilroy Daly, Jon O. Newman; Clerk's Office, New Haven 06505.

**Delaware** — James L. Latchum, CJ; Walter K. Stapleton, Murray M. Schwartz; Clerk's Office, Wilmington 19801.

**District of Columbia** — William B. Bryant, CJ; George L. Hart Jr., Oliver Gasch, John Lewis Smith Jr., Aubrey E. Robinson Jr., Joseph C. Waddy, Gerhard A. Gesell, John H. Pratt, June L. Green, Barrington D. Parker, Charles R. Richey, Thomas A. Flannery, Louis F. Oberdorfer; Clerk's Office, Washington, DC 20001.

**Florida — Northern:** Winston E. Arnow, CJ; William H. Stafford Jr.; Clerk's Office, Tallahassee 32302. **Middle:** George C. Young, CJ; Ben Krentzman, Howell W. Melton, William Terrell Hodges, John A. Reed Jr.; Clerk's Office, Jacksonville 32201. **Southern:** C. Clyde Atkins, CJ; Joe Eaton, James Lawrence King, Norman C. Roettger Jr.; Sidney M. Aronovitz, William H. Hoeveler; Clerk's Office, Miami 33101.

**Georgia — Northern:** Albert J. Henderson Jr., CJ; William C. O'Kelley, Charles A. Moye Jr., Richard C. Freeman, Newell Edenfield, Harold L. Murphy; Clerk's Office, Atlanta 30303. **Middle:** J. Robert Elliott, CJ; Wilbur D. Owens Jr.; Clerk's Office, Macon 31202. **Southern:** Anthony A. Alaimo, CJ; Alexander A. Lawrence; Clerk's Office, Savannah 31402.

**Hawaii** — Samuel P. King, CJ; Dick Yin Wong; Clerk's Office, Honolulu 96801.

**Idaho** — Ray McNichols, CJ; Marion J. Callister; Clerk's Office, Boise 83724.

**Illinois — Northern:** James B. Parsons, CJ; Hubert L. Will, Bernard M. Decker, Frank J. McGarr, Thomas R. McMillen, Prentice H. Marshall, Joel M. Flaum, Alfred Y. Kirkland, John F. Grady, George N. Leighton, John Powers Crowley, Nicholaus J. Bue, Stanley J. Roszkowski; Clerk's Office, Chicago 60604. **Eastern:** Henry S. Wise, CJ; James L. Foreman; Clerk's Office, Danville 61832. **Southern:** Robert D. Morgan, CJ; J. Waldo Ackerman; Clerk's Office, Peoria 61601.

**Indiana — Northern:** Jesse E. Eschbach, CJ; Allen Sharp, Phil M. McNagny Jr.; Clerk's Office, Hammond 46325. **Southern:** William E. Steckler, CJ; Cale J. Holder, S. Hugh Dillin, James E. Noland; Clerk's Office, Indianapolis 46204.

**Iowa — Northern:** Edward J. McManus, CJ; Clerk's Office, Cedar Rapids 52407. **Southern:** William C. Hanson, CJ; Clerk's Office, Des Moines 50309.

**Kansas** — Frank G. Theis, CJ; Earl E. O'Connor, Richard Dean Rodgers, Wesley E. Brown; Clerk's Office, Wichita 67201.

**Kentucky — Eastern:** Bernard T. Moynahan Jr., CJ; Howard David Hermansdorfer, Eugene E. Siler Jr.; Clerk's Office, Lexington 40501. **Western:** Charles M. Allen, CJ; Eugene E. Siler Jr., Edward H. Johnstone, Thomas A. Ballantine; Clerk's Office, Louisville 40202.

**Louisiana — Eastern:** Frederick J. R. Heebe, CJ; Edward J. Boyle Sr., Lansing L. Mitchell, Fred J. Cassibry, R. Blake West, Jack M. Gordon, Morey L. Sear, Charles Schwartz Jr.; Clerk's Office, New Orleans 70130. **Middle:** E. Gordon West; Clerk's Office, Baton Rouge 70801. **Western:** Nauman S. Scott, CJ; Tom Stagg, W. Eugene Davis, Earl Ernest Veron; Clerk's Office, Shreveport 71161.

**Maine** — Edward Thaxter Gignoux; Clerk's Office, Portland 04101.

**Maryland** — Edward S. Northrop, CJ; Frank A. Kaufman, Alexander Harvey 2d, James R. Miller Jr., Joseph H. Young, Herbert F. Murray, C. Stanley Blair; Clerk's Office, Baltimore 21202.

**Massachusetts** — Andrew A. Caffrey, CJ; W. Arthur Garrity Jr., Frank H. Freedman, Joseph L. Tauro, Walter Jay Skinner; Clerk's Office, Boston 02109.

**Michigan — Eastern:** Cornelia G. Kennedy, CJ; Lawrence Gubow, John Feikens, Philip Pratt, Robert E. DeMascio, Charles W. Joiner, James Harvey, James P. Churchill, Ralph B. Guy Jr.; Clerk's Office, Detroit 48226. **Western:** Noel P. Fox, CJ; Wendell A. Miles; Clerk's Office, Grand Rapids 49503.

**Minnesota** — Edward J. Devitt, CJ; Miles W. Lord, Donald D. Alsop, Harry H. MacLaughlin; Clerk's Office, St. Paul 55101.

**Mississippi — Northern:** William C. Keady, CJ; Orma R. Smith; Clerk's Office, Oxford 38655. **Southern:** Dan M. Russell Jr., CJ; William Harold Cox, Walter L. Nixon Jr.; Clerk's Office, Jackson 39205.

**Missouri — Eastern:** James H. Meridith, CJ; William R. Collinson, H. Kenneth Wangelin, John F. Nangle, Edward D. Filippine; Clerk's Office, St. Louis 63101. **Western:** John W. Oliver, CJ; William R. Collinson, Elmo B. Hunter, H. Kenneth Wangelin, Russell G. Clark; Clerk's Office, Kansas City 64106.

**Montana — Russell E. Smith, CJ; James F. Battin; Clerk's Office Great Falls 59807.**

**Nebraska — Warren K. Urbom, CJ; Robert V. Denney, Albert G. Schatz; Clerk's Office, Omaha 68101.**

**Nevada — Roger D. Foley, CJ; Bruce R. Thompson; Clerk's Office, Las Vegas 89101.**

**New Hampshire — vacant; Clerk's Office, Concord 03301.**

**New Jersey — Lawrence A. Whipple, CJ; George H. Barlow, Clarkson S. Fisher, Frederick B. Lacey, Vincent P. Biunno, Herbert J. Stern, H. Curtis Meanor, John F. Gerry, Stanley S. Brotman; Clerk's Office, Trenton 08605.**

**New Mexico — H. Vearle Payne, CJ; Howard C. Bratton, Edwin L. Mechem; Clerk's Office, Albuquerque 87103.**

**New York — Northern:** James T. Foley, CJ; Howard G. Munson; Clerk's Office, Albany 12201. **Eastern:** Jacob Mishler, CJ; Jack B. Weinstein, Mark A. Costantino, Edward R. Neaher, Thomas C. Platt Jr., Henry Bramwell, George C. Pratt, Charles P. Sifton, Eugene H. Nickerson; Clerk's Office, Brooklyn 11201. **Southern:** David N. Edelstein, CJ; Edward Weinfeld, Lloyd F. MacMahon, Charles H. Tenney, Marvin E. Frankel, Constance Baker Motley, Milton Pollack, Morris E. Lasker, Lawrence W. Pierce, Lee P. Gagliardi, Charles L. Brieant, Whitman Knapp, Charles E. Stewart Jr., Thomas P. Griesa, Robert L. Carter, Robert J. Ward, Kevin Thomas Duffy, William C. Conner, Richard Owen, Henry F. Werker, Gerard L. Goettel, Charles S. Haight Jr., Vincent L. Broderick; Clerk's Office, N. Y. City 10007. **Western:** John T. Curtin, CJ; Harold P. Burke, John T. Elfvin; Clerk's Office, Buffalo 14202.

**North Carolina — Eastern:** John D. Larkins Jr., CJ; Franklin T. Dupree Jr.; Clerk's Office, Raleigh 27611. **Middle:** Eugene A. Gordon, CJ; Hiram H. Ward; Clerk's Office, Greensboro 27402. **Western:** Woodrow Wilson Jones, CJ; James B. McMillan; Clerk's Office, Asheville 28802.

**North Dakota — Paul Benson, CJ; Bruce M. Van Sickle; Clerk's Office, Bismarck 58501.**

**Ohio — Northern:** Frank J. Battisti, CJ; Don J. Young, William K. Thomas, Thomas D. Lambros, Robert B. Krupansky, Nicholas J. Walinski, Leroy J. Contie Jr., John M. Manos; Clerk's Office, Cleveland 44114. **Southern:** David S. Porter, CJ; Joseph P. Kinneary, Timothy S. Hogan, Carl B. Rubin, Robert M. Duncan; Clerk's Office, Columbus 43215.

**Oklahoma — Northern:** Allen E. Barroa, CJ; Frederick A. Daugherty, H. Dale Cook; Clerk's Office, Tulsa 74103. **Eastern:** Joseph W. Morris, CJ; Frederick A. Daugherty, H. Dale Cook; Clerk's Office, Muskogee 74401. **Western:** Frederick A. Daugherty, CJ; Luther B. Eubanks, H. Dale Cook, Ralph G. Thompson; Clerk's Office, Oklahoma City 73102.

**Oregon — Otto R. Skopil Jr., CJ; Robert C. Belloni, James M. Burns; Clerk's Office, Portland 97207.**

**Pennsylvania — Eastern:** Joseph S. Lord 3d, CJ; Alfred L. Luongo, John P. Fullam, Charles R. Weiner, E. Mac Troutman, John B. Hannum, Daniel H. Huyett 3d, Donald W. VanArtsdalen, J. William Ditter Jr., Edward R. Becker, Raymond J. Broderick,

Clarence C. Newcomer, Clifford Scott Green, Louis Charles Bechtle, Herbert A. Fogel, Joseph L. McGlynn Jr., Edward N. Cahn; Clerk's Office, Philadelphia 19106. **Middle:** William J. Nealon Jr., CJ; Dixon Herman, Malcolm Muir; Clerk's Office, Scranton 18501. **Western:** Gerald J. Weber, CJ; William W. Knox, Hubert I. Teitelbaum, Barron P. McCune, Daniel J. Snyder Jr., Maurice B. Cohill Jr.; Clerk's Office, Pittsburgh 15230.

**Rhode Island — Raymond J. Pettine, CJ; Francis J. Boyle; Clerk's Office, Providence 02901.**

**South Carolina — J. Robert Martin Jr., CJ; Robert W. Hemphill, Charles E. Simons Jr., Solomon Blatt Jr., Robert F. Chapman; Clerk's Office, Columbia 29202.**

**South Dakota — Fred J. Nichol, CJ; Andrew A. Bogue; Clerk's Office, Sioux Falls 57102.**

**Tennessee — Eastern:** Frank W. Wilson, CJ; Robert L. Taylor, C. G. Neese; Clerk's Office, Knoxville 37901. **Middle:** L. Clure Morton, CJ; Clerk's Office, Nashville 37203. **Western:** Bailey Brown, CJ; Robert M. McRae Jr., Harry W. Wellford; Clerk's Office, Memphis 38103.

**Texas — Northern:** Halbert O. Woodward, CJ; William M. Taylor Jr., Eldon B. Mahon, Robert M. Hill, Robert W. Porter, Patrick E. Higginbotham; Clerk's Office, Dallas 75242. **Southern:** Reynaldo G. Garza, CJ; John V. Singleton Jr., Woodrow B. Seals, Carl O. Bue Jr., Owen D. Cox, Robert O'Conor Jr., Ross N. Sterling, Finis E. Cowan; Clerk's Office, Houston 77208. **Eastern:** Joe J. Fisher, CJ; William Wayne Justice, William M. Steger; Clerk's Office, Beaumont 77704. **Western:** Adrian A. Spears, CJ; Dorwin W. Suttle, Jack Roberts, William S. Sessions, John H. Wood Jr.; Clerk's Office, San Antonio 78206.

**Utah — Aldon J. Anderson; Clerk's Office, Salt Lake City 84101.**

**Vermont — James S. Holden, CJ; Albert W. Coffrin; Clerk's Office, Burlington 05401.**

**Virginia — Eastern:** Richard B. Kellam, CJ; Robert R. Merhige Jr., John A. MacKenzie, Albert V. Bryan Jr., D. Dortch Warriner, J. Calvitt Clarke; Clerk's Office, Norfolk 23501. **Western:** James C. Turk, CJ; Glen M. Williams; Clerk's Office, Roanoke 24006.

**Washington — Eastern:** Marshall A. Neill, CJ; Clerk's Office, Spokane 99210. **Western:** Walter T. McGovern; Morell E. Sharp, Donald S. Voorhees; Clerk's Office, Seattle 98104.

**West Virginia — Northern:** Robert Earl Maxwell, CJ; Charles H. Haden 2d; Clerk's Office, Elkins 26241. **Southern:** Dennis Raymond Knapp, CJ; John T. Copenhaver Jr., Charles H. Haden 2d; Clerk's Office, Charleston 25329.

**Wisconsin — Eastern:** John W. Reynolds, CJ; Myron L. Gordon, Robert W. Warren; Clerk's Office, Milwaukee 53202. **Western:** James E. Doyle; Clerk's Office, Madison 53701.

**Wyoming — Clarence A. Brimmer; Clerk's office, Cheyenne 82001.**

## U.S. Territorial District Courts

**Canal Zone — Clerk's Office, Balboa Heights.**

**Guam — Cristobal C. Duenas; Clerk's Office, P.O. Box DC, Agana 96910.**

**Puerto Rico — Jose V. Toledo, CJ; Hernan G. Pesquera, Juan R. Torruella; Clerk's Office, San Juan 00904.**

**Virgin Islands — Almeric L. Christian, CJ; Warren H. Young; Clerk's Office, Charlotte Amalie, St. Thomas 00801.**

---

## The Federal Judicial System

The Federal judicial system begins with the District Court. There are 94 of these courts, at least one in each state, in Washington, D.C., and in certain territories. Called courts of general jurisdiction, they have power to determine the facts and pass judgment in criminal cases involving violations of federal law and in civil cases where the amount of the suit is $10,000 or more and the contending parties reside in different states. Other types of cases handled by District Courts include suits in admiralty (maritime matters involving navigational waters), bankruptcy, patents, trademarks, and copyrights.

Equal to the District Courts are special courts which handle only certain issues: the U.S. Customs Court, the Tax Court, and the Court of Claims, which hears suits against the U.S. government.

These trial courts are responsible for finding the facts in a case and for applying the law to the facts found.

The District Courts and special courts are trial courts. Above them are several levels of appellate courts. The U.S. Courts of Appeals, often called circuit courts, sit in 10 judicial circuits and

Washington, D.C. They hear appeals from the District Courts and the Tax Court, and will review decisions of federal administrative agencies if it appears that such decisions may be unreasonable or arbitrary. The U.S. Court of Customs and Patent Appeals hears appeals from the Customs Court.

Appellate courts, theoretically, do not review the trial court's findings of fact. The job of the appellate court is to decide whether the trial judge applied the law properly. If an appellate court decides that there was error in the application of the law, it can simply reverse the lower court's decision and end the case there. But it can also send the case back to the lower court for retrial or for other proceedings that may be appropriate.

Ultimately, all decisions of these courts can be reviewed by the U.S. Supreme Court, which is also the first court of appeal from the U.S. Court of Claims. Besides reviewing federal court decisions, the Supreme Court is empowered to hear suits between the states and to review state supreme court decisions if an issue of federal law or the Constitution is involved.

# U.S. Government Independent Agencies

Source: General Services Administration
Address: Washington, DC. Location and ZIP codes of agencies in parentheses, as of July, 1978.

**ACTION** — Sam Brown, dir. (806 Connecticut Ave., NW, 20525).

**Administrative Conference of the United States** — Robert A. Anthony, chmn. (2120 L St., NW, 20037).

**American Battle Monuments Commission** — Mark W. Clark, chmn. (Forrestal Bldg., 20314).

**Appalachian Regional Commission** — Robert W. Scott, Federal co-chmn.; Gov. James B. Hunt Jr., states co-chmn. (1666 Connecticut Ave. NW, 20235).

**Arms Control & Disarmament Agency** — Paul C. Warnke, dir. (Department of State Bldg. 20451).

**Central Intelligence Agency** — Adm. Stansfield Turner, dir. (Wash., DC 20505).

**Civil Aeronautics Board** — Alfred E. Kahn, chmn. (1825 Connecticut Ave. NW, 20428).

**Civil Service Commission** — Alan K. Campbell, chmn. (1900 E. St. NW, 20415).

**Commission on Civil Rights** — Arthur S. Flemming, chmn. (1121 Vermont Ave. NW, 20425).

**Commission of Fine Arts** — J. Carter Brown, chmn. (708 Jackson Pl. NW, 20006).

**Commodity Futures Trading Commission** — William T. Bagley, chmn. (2033 K St. NW, 20581).

**Community Services Administration** — Graciela Olivarez, dir. (1200 19th St. NW, 20506).

**Consumer Product Safety Commission** — S John Byington, chmn. (1111 18th St. NW, 20036).

**Environmental Protection Agency** — Douglas M. Castle, adm. (401 M St., SW, 20460).

**Equal Employment Opportunity Commission** — Eleanor Holmes Norton, chmn. (2401 E St., NW, 20506).

**Export-Import Bank of the United States** — John L. Moore Jr., pres. and chmn. (811 Vermont Ave. NW, 20571).

**Farm Credit Administration** — Galen B. Brubaker, chmn. (490 L'Enfant Plaza East SW, 20578).

**Federal Communications Commission** — Charles D. Ferris, chmn. (1919 M St. NW, 20554).

**Federal Deposit Insurance Corporation** — George A. LeMaistre, chmn. (550 17th St. NW, 20429).

**Federal Election Commission** — Thomas E. Harris, chmn. (1325 K St. NW, 20463).

**Federal Home Loan Bank Board** — Robert H. McKinney, chmn. (320 First St. NW, 20552).

**Federal Maritime Commission** — Richard J. Daschbach, chmn. (1100 L St. NW, 20573).

**Federal Mediation and Conciliation Service** — Wayne L. Horvitz, dir. (2100 K St. NW, 20427).

**Federal Reserve System** — Chairman, board of governors: G. William Miller. (20th St. & Constitution Ave. NW, 20551).

**Federal Trade Commission** — Commissioners: Michael Pertschuk, chmn., Paul Rand Dixon, Elizabeth Hanford Dole, David A. Clanton, vacancy (Pennsylvania Ave. at 6th St. NW, 20580).

**Foreign Claims Settlement Comm. of the U.S.** — Chairman: vacancy. (1111 20th St., NW, 20579).

**General Accounting Office** — Comptroller general of the U.S.; Elmer B. Staats. (441 G St. NW, 20548).

**General Services Administration** — Joel W. (Jay) Solomon, adm. (18th & F Sts. NW, 20405).

**Government Printing Office** — Public printer: John J. Boyle (North Capitol and H Sts. NW, 20401).

**Indian Claims Commission** — Jerome K. Kuykendall, chmn. (1730 K St. NW, 20006).

**Inter-American Foundation** — Chairman: vacancy. (1515 Wilson Blvd., Rosslyn, VA 22209).

**International Communication Agency** — John E. Reinhardt, Dir. (1750 Pennsylvania Ave. NW, 20547).

**Interstate Commerce Commission** — A. Daniel O'Neal, chmn. (12th St. and Constitution Ave. NW, 20423).

**Library of Congress** — Daniel J. Boorstin, Librarian (10 First St. SE, 20540).

**National Academy of Sciences — National Academy of Engineering — National Research Council — Institute of Medicine** — Presidents: Philip Handler (NAS), Courtland D. Perkins (NA of Eng.), David A. Hamburg, M.D. (Inst. of Med.) (2101 Constitution Ave. NW 20418).

**National Aeronautics and Space Administration** — Robert A. Frosch, admin. (400 Maryland Ave., SW 20546).

**National Credit Union Administration** — Lawrence Connell, adm. (2025 M. St. NW, 20456).

**National Foundation on the Arts and Humanities** — Livingston L. Biddle Jr. chmn. (arts). Joseph D. Duffey chmn. (arts: 2401 E St. NW, 20506; humanities: 806 15th St. NW, 20506).

**National Labor Relations Board** — John H. Fanning chmn. (1717 Pennsylvania Ave. NW, 20570).

**National Mediation Board** — George S. Ives, chmn (1425 K St. NW, 20572).

**National Science Foundation** — Norman Hackerman chmn. (1800 G St. NW, 20550).

**National Transportation Safety Board** — James B King, chmn. (800 Independence Ave. SW, 20594).

**Nuclear Regulatory Commission** — Joseph M. Hendrie, chmn. (1717 H St. NW, 20555).

**Occupational Safety and Health Review Commission** — Timothy F. Cleary, chmn. (1825 K St. NW, 20006).

**Overseas Private Investment Corporation** — Rutherford M. Poats, acting pres. (1129 20th St. NW, 20527).

**Pennsylvania Avenue Development Corporation** — Elwood R. Quesada, chmn. (425 13th St. NW, 20004).

**Pension Benefit Guaranty Corporation** — Matthew M. Lind, exec. dir. (2020 K St. NW, 20006).

**Postal Rate Commission** — Clyde S. DuPont, chmn. (2000 L St. NW, 20268).

**Railroad Retirement Board** — William P. Adams, chmn. (Rm. 444, 425 13th St. NW, 20004), Main Office (844 Rush St., Chicago, IL 60611).

**Renegotiation Board** — Goodwin Chase, chmn. (2000 M St. NW, 20446).

**Securities and Exchange Commission** — Commissioners: Harold M. Williams, chmn.; Irving M. Pollack, Philip Loomis Jr., John R. Evans, Roberta S. Karmel. (500 N. Capitol St., 20549).

**Selective Service System** — Robert E. Shuck, acting dir. (600 E St. NW, 20435).

**Small Business Administration** — A. Vernon Weaver, admin. (1441 L St. NW, 20416).

**Smithsonian Institution** — S. Dillon Ripley, secy. (1000 Jefferson Dr. SW, 20560).

**Tennessee Valley Authority** — Chairman, board of directors: S. David Freeman. (400 Commerce Ave., Knoxville, TN 37902 and Woodward Bldg. 15th and H Sts. NW, Washington, D.C. 20444).

**United States International Trade Commission** — Daniel Minchew, chmn. (701 E St. NW, 20436).

**United States Postal Service** — William F. Bolger, postmaster general (475 L'Enfant Plaza West SW, 20260).

**Veterans Administration** — Max Cleland, adm. (810 Vermont Ave. NW, 20420).

# NATIONAL DEFENSE

Data as of Aug., 1978

**Chairman, Joint Chiefs of Staff**
David C. Jones (USAF)

he Joint Chiefs of Staff consists of the Chairman of the Joint Chiefs of Staff; the Chief of Staff, U.S. Army; the Chief of val Operations; and the Chief of Staff, U.S. Air Force. The Marine Corps commandant attends meetings regularly, and sits coequal of the other members when matters directly concerning the Marine Corps are being considered.

## Army

**Date of Rank**

**General of the Army**

| | | |
|---|---|---|
| dley, Omar N. | Sept. | 20, 1950 |

**Chief of Staff—Bernard W. Rogers**

**Generals**

| | | |
|---|---|---|
| nchard, George S. | Jul. | 1, 1975 |
| thrie, John R. | May | 1, 1977 |
| g Jr., Alexander M. | Mar. | 18, 1974 |
| nnessey, John J. | Nov. | 8, 1974 |
| owlton, William A. | Jun. | 1, 1976 |
| esen, Frederick J. | Oct. | 1, 1976 |
| gers, Bernard W. | Nov. | 7, 1974 |
| rry, Donn A. | Jul. | 1, 1977 |
| sey Jr., John W. | Nov. | 1, 1976 |

## Air Force

**Chief of Staff—Lew Allen Jr.**

**Generals**

| | | |
|---|---|---|
| en, James R. | Aug. | 1, 1977 |
| en Jr., Lew | Aug. | 1, 1977 |
| ech, Wilbur L. | May | 1, 1978 |
| s, Richard H. | Sept. | 30, 1973 |
| ns, William J. | Aug. | 30, 1975 |
| l, James A. | July | 10, 1978 |
| l, James E. | Dec. | 21, 1977 |
| yser, Robert E. | Sept. | 1, 1975 |
| es, David C. | Sept. | 1, 1971 |
| ore Jr., William G. | Apr. | 1, 1977 |
| aly, John W. | Aug. | 1, 1978 |

| | | |
|---|---|---|
| Poe, Bryce, II | Feb. | 2, 1978 |
| Roberts, John W. | Mar. | 15, 1977 |
| Slay, Alton D. | Apr. | 1, 1978 |

## Navy

**Chief of Naval Operations**
Admiral Thomas B. Hayward (aviation)

**Admirals**

| | | |
|---|---|---|
| Davis, Donald C. | May | 9, 1978 |
| Hayward, Thomas B. (aviation) | Aug. | 12, 1976 |
| Kidd, Isaac C. | Dec. | 1, 1971 |
| Long, Robert L.J. | July | 5, 1977 |
| Michaelis, Frederick H. (aviation) | Apr. | 19, 1975 |
| Rickover, Hyman G. (retired) | Nov. | 16, 1973 |
| Shear, Harold E. | May | 24, 1974 |
| Weisner, Maurice F. (aviation) | Sept. | 1, 1972 |

## Marine Corps

**Corps Commandant, with rank of General**

| | | |
|---|---|---|
| Louis H. Wilson | July | 1, 1975 |

**Asst. Commandant with rank of General**

| | | |
|---|---|---|
| Robert H. Barrow | July | 1, 1978 |

## Coast Guard

**Commandant, with rank of Admiral**

| | | |
|---|---|---|
| John B. Hayes. | May | 31, 1978 |

**Vice Commandant, with rank of Vice Admiral**

| | | |
|---|---|---|
| Robert Scarborough | June | 30, 1978 |

## United States Unified and Specified Commands

antic Command—Admiral Isaac C. Kidd, USN

rth American Air Defense Command—General James E. Hill, USAF

S. European Command—General Alexander Haig Jr., USA

cific Command—Admiral Maurice Weisner, USN

S. Southern Command—General Dennis P. McAuliffe, USA

Strategic Air Command—General Richard H. Ellis, USAF

U.S. Readiness Command—General John J. Hennessey, USA

Military Air Lift Command—General William G. Moore Jr., USAF

## North Atlantic Treaty Organization International Commands

pr. Allied Commander, Europe (SACEUR)—Gen. Alexander Haig Jr., USA

puty SACEUR—Gen. Sir Harry Tuzo (UK), Gen. Gerd Schmuckle (Germany)

in-C Allied Forces, Northern Europe—Gen. Peter Whitely (UK)

in-C Allied Forces, Central Europe—Gen. F.J. Schulze, (Germany)

in-C Allied Forces, Southern Europe—Adm. Harold E.

Shear, USN

Supr. Allied Commander Atlantic (SACLANT)—Adm. Isaac Kidd, USN

Deputy SACLANT—Adm. David A. Loram (UK)

Commander Strike Force South—V. Adm. James D. Watkins, USN

Allied Commander in Chief, Channel—Adm. Sir Edward Ashmore (UK)

## Principal U.S. Military Training Centers

### Army

| Name, P.O. address | Zip | Nearest city | Name, P.O. address | Zip | Nearest city |
|---|---|---|---|---|---|
| erdeen Proving Ground, MD | 21005 | Aberdeen | Fort Eustis, VA | 23604 | Newport News |
| arlisle Barracks, PA | 17013 | Carlisle | | | |
| rt Belvoir, VA | 22060 | Alexandria | Fort Gordon, GA | 30905 | Augusta |
| rt Benning, GA | 31905 | Columbus | Fort Wadsworth, NY | 10305 | Staten Island |
| rt Bliss, TX | 79916 | El Paso | Fort Benjamin Harrison, IN | 46216 | Indianapolis |
| rt Bragg, NC | 28307 | Fayetteville | Fort Sam Houston, TX | 78234 | San Antonio |
| rt Devens, MA | 01433 | Ayer | Fort Huachuca, AZ | 85613 | Sierra Vista |
| rt Dix, NJ | 08640 | Trenton | Fort Jackson, SC | 29207 | Columbia |

| Name, P.O. address | Zip | Nearest city | Name, P.O. address | Zip | Nearest city |
|---|---|---|---|---|---|
| Fort Knox, KY | 40121 | Louisville | Fort Sill, OK | 73503 | Lawton |
| Fort Leavenworth, KS | 66027 | Leavenworth | Fort Leonard Wood, MO | 65473 | Rolla |
| Fort Lee, VA | 23801 | Petersburg | Redstone Arsenal, AL | 35809 | Huntsville |
| Fort McClellan, AL | 36205 | Anniston | Rock Island Arsenal, IL | 61202 | Rock Island |
| Fort Monmouth, NJ | 07703 | Red Bank | The Judge Advocate | | Charlottes- |
| Fort Rucker, AL | 36362 | Dothan | General School, VA | 22901 | ville |

## Navy

| | | | | | |
|---|---|---|---|---|---|
| Great Lakes, IL | 60088 | Waukegan | Orlando, FL | 32813 | Orlando |
| San Diego, CA | 92133 | San Diego | | | |

## Marine Corps

| Name | Zip | Nearest city | Name | Zip | Nearest city |
|---|---|---|---|---|---|
| MCB Camp Lejeune, NC | 28542 | Jacksonville | MCAS (Helo) New River, NC | 28540 | Jacksonville |
| MCB Camp Pendleton, CA | 92055 | Oceanside | MCAS Iwakuni, Japan | FPO Seattle 98764 | Iwakuni |
| MCB Camp Butler, Okinawa | FPO Seattle 98773 | Futenma, Okinawa | MCAS Kaneohe Bay, | | |
| MCB Twentynine Palms, CA | 92278 | Palm Springs | Oahu, HI | FPO San Francisco 96615 | Kailua |
| MCDEC Quantico, VA | 22134 | Quantico | MCAS (Helo) Futenma, | | |
| MCRD Parris Island, SC | 29905 | Beaufort | Okinawa | FPO Seattle 98764 | Futenma |
| MCRD San Diego, CA | 92140 | San Diego | | | |
| MCAS Cherry Point, NC | 28533 | Cherry Point | MCAS Beaufort, SC | 29902 | Beaufort |
| MCAS El Toro (Santa Ana), CA | 92709 | Santa Ana | MCAS Yuma, AZ | 85364 | Yuma |
| MCAS (Helo) Santa Ana, CA | 92709 | Santa Ana | | | |

MCB = Marine Corps Base. MCDEC = Marine Corps Development & Education Command. MCAS = Marine Corps Air Station. Helo = Helicopter.

## Air Force

| Name | Zip | Nearest city | Name | Zip | Nearest city |
|---|---|---|---|---|---|
| Chanute AFB, IL | 61863 | Rantoul | Maxwell AFB, AL | 36112 | Montgomery |
| Columbus AFB, MS | 39701 | Columbus | Moody AFB, GA | 31601 | Valdosta |
| Craig AFB, AL | 36701 | Selma | Nellis AFB, NV | 89191 | Las Vegas |
| Fairchild AFB, MS | 99011 | Spokane | Randolph AFB, TX | 78148 | San Antonio |
| Keesler AFB, MS | 39534 | Biloxi | Reese AFB, TX | 79401 | Lubbock |
| Lackland AFB, TX | 78236 | San Antonio | Sheppard AFB, TX | 76311 | Wichita Falls |
| Laughlin AFB, TX | 78840 | Del Rio | Vance AFB, OK | 73701 | Enid |
| Lowry AFB, CO | 80230 | Denver | Webb AFB, TX | 79720 | Big Spring |
| Mather AFB, CA | 95655 | Sacramento | Williams AFB, AZ | 85224 | Chandler |

## Personal Salutes and Honors

The United States national salute, 21 guns, is also the salute to a national flag. The independence of the United States commemorated by the salute to the union — one gun for each state — fired at noon on July 4 at all military posts prov with suitable artillery.

A-21-gun salute on arrival and departure, with 4 ruffles and flourishes, is rendered to the President of the United States an ex-President and to a President-elect. The national anthem or *Hail to the Chief*, as appropriate, is played for the Presic and the national anthem for the others. A 21-gun salute on arrival and departure with 4 ruffles and flourishes, also is dered to the sovereign or chief of state of a foreign country or a member of a reigning royal family; the national anthem o or her country is played. The music is considered an inseparable part of the salute and will immediately follow the ruffles flourishes without pause.

| Rank | Salute—guns Arrive—Leave | | Ruffles, flour- ishes | Music |
|---|---|---|---|---|
| Vice President of United States | 19 | | 4 | Hail Columbia |
| Speaker of the House | 19 | | 4 | March |
| American or foreign ambassador | 19 | | 4 | Nat. anthem of officia |
| Premier or prime minister | 19 | | 4 | Nat. anthem of officia |
| Secretary of Defense, Army, Navy or Air Force | 19 | 19 | 4 | March |
| Other Cabinet members, Senate President pro tempore, Governor, or Chief Justice of U.S. | 19 | | 4 | March |
| Chairman, Joint Chiefs of Staff | 19 | 19 | 4 | |
| Army Chief of Staff, Chief of Naval Operations, Air Force Chief of Staff, Marine Commandant | 19 | 19 | 4 | General's or Admiral's March |
| General of the Army, General of the Air Force, Fleet Admiral | 19 | 19 | 4 | |
| Generals, Admirals | 17 | 17 | 4 | |
| Assistant Secretaries of Defense, Army, Navy or Air Force | 17 | 17 | 4 | March |
| Chairman of a Committee of Congress | 17 | | 4 | March |

**Other salutes** (on arrival only) include 15 guns for American envoys or ministers and foreign envoys or ministers acc ited to the United States; 15 guns for a lieutenant general or vice admiral; 13 guns for a major general or rear admiral (u half); 13 guns for American ministers resident and ministers resident accredited to the U.S.; 11 guns for a brigadier gener rear admiral (lower half); 11 guns for American charges d'affaires and like officials accredited to U.S.; and 11 guns for suls general accredited to U.S.

## Military Units, U.S. Army and Air Force

**Army units. Squad.** In infantry usually ten men under a staff sergeant. **Platoon.** In infantry 4 squads under a lieuten **Company.** Headquarters section and 4 platoons under a captain. (Company in the artillery is a battery; in the caval troop.) **Battalion.** Hdqts. and 4 or more companies under a lieutenant colonel. (Battalion size unit in the cavalry is a sq ron.) **Brigade.** Hdqts. and 3 or more battalions under a colonel. **Division.** Hdqts. and 3 brigades with artillery, combat port, and combat service support units under a major general. **Army Corps.** Two or more divisions with corps troops un

itenant general. **Field Army.** Hdqts. and two or more corps with field Army troops under a general.
**Air Force Units. Flight.** Small components of a squadron organized for special purpose such as medical evacuation flights.
**uadron.** The basic organized unit of the Air Force, used by operational as well as support forces but not limited by num-
s of personnel assigned; two to three tactical squadrons are assigned to a tactical wing. **Group.** Terminology used for spe-
 tactical forces and for many support elements. They do not necessarily have subordinate units assigned. **Wing.** Used for
tical and support forces. A tactical wing usually has two to three operational squadrons assigned. **Division.** An organiza-
al component of operational numbered Air Forces consisting of two to three wings, also used to designate numerous sup-
t and research components. **Air Force.** An intermediate echelon of command directly under the headquarters of a large
rational command, usually with four to seven subordinate divisions. **Major command.** A major subdivision of the Air
rce that is assigned a major segment of the USAF mission, usually two or four subordinate Air Force elements.

## U.S. Army Insignia and Chevrons

Source: Department of the Army

| Grade | Insignia |
|---|---|
| **neral of the Armies** | |

eneral John J. Pershing, the only person to have held
s rank, was authorized to prescribe his own insignia, but
er wore in excess of four stars. The rank originally was
ablished by Congress for George Washington in 1799,
1 he was promoted to the rank by joint resolution of Con-
ss, approved by Pres. Ford Oct. 19, 1976.

| Grade | Insignia |
|---|---|
| **neral of Army** | Five silver stars fastened together in a circle and the coat of arms of the United States in gold color metal with shield and crest enameled. |
| **neral** | Four silver stars |
| **utenant General** | Three silver stars |
| **ajor General** | Two silver stars |
| **igadier General** | One silver star |
| **lonel** | Silver eagle |
| **utenant Colonel** | Silver oak leaf |
| **ajor** | Gold oak leaf |
| **ptain** | Two silver bars |
| **st Lieutenant** | One silver bar |
| **cond Lieutenant** | One gold bar |

**Warrant officers**

Grade Four—Silver bar with 4 enamel black bands.
Grade Three—Silver bar with 3 enamel black bands.
Grade Two—Silver bar with 2 enamel black bands.
Grade One—Silver bar with 1 enamel black band.

**Non-commissioned Officers**

**Sergeant Major of the Army (E-9).** Same as Command Sergeant Major (below). Also wears distinctive red and white shield on lapel.

**Command Sergeant Major (E-9).** Three chevrons above three arcs with a 5-pointed star with a wreath around the star between the chevrons and arcs.

**Sergeant Major (E-9).** Three chevrons above three arcs with a five-pointed star between the chevrons and arcs.

**First Sergeant (E-8).** Three chevrons above three arcs with a lozenge between the chevrons and arcs.

**Master Sergeant (E-8).** Three chevrons above three arcs.

**Platoon Sergeant or Sergeant First Class (E-7).** Three chevrons above two acrs.

**Staff Sergeant (E-6).** Three chevrons above one arc.

**Sergeant (E-5).** Three chevrons.

**Corporal (E-4).** Two chevrons.

**Specialists**

**Specialist Seven (E-7).** Three arcs above the eagle device.

**Specialist Six (E-6).** Two arcs above the eagle device.

**Specialist Five (E-5).** One arc above the eagle device.

**Specialist Four (E-4).** Eagle device only.

**Other enlisted**

**Private First Class (E-3).** One chevron above one arc.

**Private (E-2).** One chevron.

**Private (E-1).** None.

## U.S. Army

Source: Department of the Army

### Army Military Personnel on Active Duty[1]

| June 30[2] | Total strength | Commissioned officers Total | Male | Female[3] | Warrant officers Male[4] | Female | Enlisted personnel Total | Male | Female |
|---|---|---|---|---|---|---|---|---|---|
| 40 | 267,767 | 17,563 | 16,624 | 939 | 763 | — | 249,441 | 249,441 | |
| 42 | 3,074,184 | 203,137 | 190,662 | 12,475 | 3,285 | — | 2,867,762 | 2,867,762 | |
| 43 | 6,993,102 | 557,657 | 521,435 | 36,222 | 21,919 | 0 | 6,413,526 | 6,358,200 | 55,325 |
| 44 | 7,992,868 | 740,077 | 692,351 | 47,726 | 36,893 | 10 | 7,215,888 | 7,144,601 | 71,287 |
| 45 | 8,266,373 | 835,403 | 772,511 | 62,892 | 56,216 | 44 | 7,374,710 | 7,283,930 | 90,780 |
| 46 | 1,889,690 | 257,300 | 240,643 | 16,657 | 9,826 | 18 | 1,622,546 | 1,605,847 | 16,699 |
| 50 | 591,487 | 67,784 | 63,375 | 4,409 | 4,760 | 22 | 518,921 | 512,370 | 6,551 |
| 55 | 1,107,606 | 111,347 | 106,173 | 5,174 | 10,552 | 48 | 985,659 | 977,943 | 7,716 |
| 60 | 871,348 | 91,056 | 86,832 | 4,224 | 10,141 | 39 | 770,112 | 761,833 | 8,279 |
| 65 | 967,049 | 101,812 | 98,029 | 3,783 | 10,285 | 23 | 854,929 | 846,409 | 8,520 |
| 66 | 1,197,468 | 106,468 | 102,347 | 4,121 | 11,296 | 22 | 1,079,682 | 1,070,503 | 9,179 |
| 67 | 1,440,120 | 127,393 | 122,685 | 4,708 | 16,090 | 34 | 1,296,603 | 1,286,862 | 9,741 |
| 68 | 1,567,900 | 145,988 | 140,919 | 5,069 | 20,158 | 27 | 1,401,727 | 1,391,016 | 10,711 |
| 69 | 1,509,637 | 148,836 | 143,699 | 5,137 | 23,734 | 20 | 1,337,047 | 1,316,326 | 10,721 |
| 70 | 1,319,735 | 143,704 | 138,469 | 5,235 | 23,005 | 13 | 1,153,013 | 1,141,537 | 11,476 |
| 71 | 1,120,822 | 130,261 | 125,240 | 5,021 | 18,670 | 19 | 971,872 | 960,047 | 11,825 |
| 72 | 807,985 | 105,364 | 100,961 | 4,403 | 15,907 | 19 | 686,695 | 674,346 | 12,349 |
| 73 | 798,177 | 101,194 | 96,936 | 4,258 | 14,990 | 21 | 681,972 | 665,515 | 16,457 |
| 74 | 780,464 | 91,873 | 87,504 | 4,369 | 14,106 | 19 | 674,466 | 648,138 | 26,328 |
| 75 | 781,316 | 89,756 | 85,184 | 4,572 | 13,214 | 22 | 678,324 | 640,621 | 37,703 |
| 76 (Apr. 30) | 766,979 | 85,515 | 80,588 | 4,927 | 12,748 | 30 | 668,686 | 625,792 | 42,894 |
| 77 (Mar. 31) | 774,664 | 84,984 | 79,599 | 5,385 | 13,005 | 36 | 676,639 | 631,410 | 45,229 |
| 78 (May 31) | 772,202 | 96,553 | 90,749 | 5,804 | 13,160 | 57 | 662,432 | 614,961 | 47,471 |

(1) Represents strength of the active Army, including Philippine Scouts, retired Regular Army personnel on extended active duty, and
tional Guard and Reserve personnel on extended active duty; excludes U.S. Military Academy cadets, contract surgeons, and National
ard and Reserve personnel not on extended active duty.
(2) Data for 1940 to 1947 include personnel in the Army Air Forces and its predecessors (Air Service and Air Corps).
(3) Includes: women doctors, dentists, and Medical Service Corps officers for 1946 and subsequent years, women in the Army Nurse
rps for all years, and the Women's Army Corps and Women's Medical Specialists Corps (dieticians, physical therapists, and occupa-
nal specialists) for 1943 and subsequent years.
(4) Act of Congress approved April 27, 1926, directed the appointment as warrant officers of field clerks still in active service. Includes
ght officers as follows: 1943, 5,700; 1944, 13,615; 1945, 31,117; 1946, 2,580.

## U.S. Navy Insignia
**Source:** Department of the Navy

### Navy
Stripes and corps device are of gold embroidery.

**Stripes**

Fleet Admiral . . . . . 1 two inch with 4 one-half inch.
Admiral . . . . . . . . 1 two inch with 3 one-half inch.
Vice Admiral. . . . . . 1 two inch with 2 one-half inch.
Rear Admiral . . . . . 1 two inch with 1 one-half inch.
Commodore
(War time only) . . . 1 two inch.
Captain. . . . . . . . 4 one-half inch.
Commander . . . . . . 3 one-half inch.
Lieut. Commander . . 2 one-half inch, with 1 one-quarter
inch between.
Lieutenant . . . . . . 2 one-half inch.
Lieutenant (j.g.) . . . . 1 one-half inch with one-quarter
inch above.
Ensign . . . . . . . . 1 one-half inch.
Warrant Officers—One 1/2″ (1/2″ for Warrant officer W-1)
broken with 1/2″ intervals of blue as follows:
Chief Warrant Officer W-4—1 break
Chief Warrant Officer W-3—2 breaks, 2″ apart

Chief Warrant Officer W-2—3 breaks, 2″ apart
The breaks are symmetrically centered on outer face of
sleeve.
Enlisted personnel (non-Commissioned petty officers).
rating badge worn on the upper left arm, consisting
spread eagle, appropriate number of chevrons, and
tered specialty mark.

### Marine Corps
Marine Corps and Army officer insignia are similar.
rine Crops and Army enlisted insignia, although basic
similar, differ in color, design, and fewer Marine Corps
divisions. The Marine Corps' distinctive cap and collar o
ment is a combination of the American eagle, globe, and
chor.

### Coast Guard
Coast Guard insignia follow Navy custom, with cer
minor changes such as the officer cap insignia. The C
Guard shield is worn on both sleeves of officers and on
right sleeve of all enlisted men.

## U.S. Naval Budget Appropriations

| Fiscal year | Total amount | Shipbuilding conversion and modernization | Aircraft and missile procurement | Military construction | All othe expenditu |
|---|---|---|---|---|---|
| 1940 . . . . . . . . | $885,769 | $328,819,394 | $24,011,998 | $72,503,151 | $460,435. |
| 1945 . . . . . . . . | 29,380,421,832 | 7,228,192,871 | 3,541,009,589 | 1,576,096,922 | 17,035,122. |
| 1950 . . . . . . . . | 4,065,484,778 | 281,328,056 | 452,723,233 | 86,054,932 | 3,245,378. |
| 1960 . . . . . . . . | 11,848,690,002 | 1,380,031,231 | 2,027,098,025 | 284,928,383 | 8,228,632. |
| 1970 . . . . . . . . | 2,501,628,282 | 2,065,660,211 | 3,183,464,921 | 333,271,852 | 16,919,231 |
| 1973. . . . . . . . | 25,425,000,000 | 2,962,000,000 | 3,673,000,000 | 486,000,000 | 18,122,000. |
| 1975. . . . . . . . | 27,934,000,000 | 3,111,000,000 | 3,516,000,000 | 578,000,000 | 20,730,000. |
| 1977. . . . . . . . | 36,538,000,000 | 5,700,000,000 | 4,934,000,000 | 690,000,000 | 25,214,000. |
| 1978 (plan) . . . . . | 39,735,000,000 | 5,903,000,000 | 5,846,000,000 | 531,000,000 | 27,555,000. |

## U.S. Navy Personnel on Active Duty

| June 30 | Officers[1] | Nurses | Enlisted[2] | Off. Cand. | Total |
|---|---|---|---|---|---|
| 1940 . . . . . . . . | 13,162 | 442 | 144,824 | 2,569 | 160,9 |
| 1945 . . . . . . . . | 320,293 | 11,086 | 2,988,207 | 61,231 | 3,380,8 |
| 1950 . . . . . . . . | 42,687 | 1,964 | 331,860 | 5,037 | 381,5 |
| 1960 . . . . . . . . | 67,456 | 2,103 | 544,040 | 4,385 | 617,9 |
| 1970 . . . . . . . . | 78,488 | 2,273 | 605,899 | 6,000 | 692,6 |
| 1975 . . . . . . . . | 65,900 | — | 483,500 | — | 549,4 |
| 1977 . . . . . . . . | 63,300 | — | 466,600 | — | 529,9 |
| 1978 . . . . . . . . | 62,300 | — | 462,300 | — | 524,6 |

(1) Nurses are included after 1973. (2) Officer candidates are included after 1973.

## Marine Corps Personnel On Active Duty

| Yr. | Officers | Enl. | Total | Yr. | Officers | Enl. | Total | Yr. | Officers | Enl. | Tot |
|---|---|---|---|---|---|---|---|---|---|---|---|
| 1955 . . | 18,417 | 186,753 | 205,170 | 1965 . . . | 17,258 | 172,955 | 190,213 | 1975. . | 18,100 | 174,100 | 192, |
| 1960 . . | 16,203 | 154,408 | 170,621 | 1970 . . . | 24,941 | 234,796 | 259,737 | 1978. . . | 18,600 | 171,800 | 190, |

## The Medal of Honor

The Medal of Honor is the highest military award for bravery that can be given to any individual in the United States. The first Army Medals were awarded on March 25, 1863, and the first Navy Medals went to sailors and Marines on April 3, 1863.

The Medal of Honor, established by Joint Resolution of Congress, 12 July 1862 (amended by Act of 9 July 1918 and Act of 25 July 1963) is awarded in the name of Congress to a person who, while a member of the Armed Forces, distinguishes himself conspicuously by gallantry and intrepidity at the risk of his life above and beyond the call of duty while engaged in an action against any enemy of the United States; while engaged in military operations involving conflict with an opposing foreign force; or while serving with friendly foreign forces engaged in an armed conflict against an opposing armed force in which the United States is not a belligerent party. The deed performed must be been one of

personal bravery or self-sacrifice so conspicuous as to cle
distinguish the individual above his comrades and must h
involved risk of life. Incontestable proof of the performa
of service is exacted and each recommendation for aware
this decoration is considered on the standard of extraor
nary merit.

Prior to World War I, the 2,625 Army Medal of Ho
awards up to that time were reviewed to determine wh
past awards met new stringent criteria. The Army remo
911 names from the list, most of them former members
volunteer infantry group during the Civil War who had t
induced to extend their enlistments when they were pr
ised the Medal.

Since that review Medals of Honor have been awarde
the following numbers:

World War I . . . . . . 124   Korean War . . . . . .
World War II . . . . . . 431   Vietnam (to date) . . . .

## U.S. Air Force

Source: Department of the Air Force

e Army Air forces were started Aug. 1, 1907, as the Aeronau- Division of the Signal Corps, U.S. Army. The division con- of one officer and two enlisted men, and it was more than a before it carried out its first mission in an airplane of its own. the U.S. entered World War I (April 6, 1917), the Aviation ce, as it was called then, had 55 planes and 65 officers, only 35 om were fliers. On the day the Japanese struck at Pearl Har- Dec. 7, 1941), the Army Air Forces, as they had been re-

named 6 months previously, has 10,329 planes, of which only 2,846 were suited for combat service. But when the Army's air arm reached its peak during World War II (in July, 1944), it had 79,908 of all types of aircraft and (in May 1945) 43,248 combat aircraft and (in March, 1944) 2,411,294 officers and enlisted men. The Air Force was established under the Armed Services Unification Act of July 26, 1947.

### USAF Personnel at Home and Overseas — Officers and Enlisted Men

| June 30 | Continental U.S. | Overseas | Total | June 30 | Continental U.S. | Overseas | Total |
|---|---|---|---|---|---|---|---|
| | 40,229 | 10,936 | 51,165 | 1965 | 635,430 | 189,232 | 824,662 |
| | 1,153,373 | 1,128,886 | 2,282,259 | 1970 | 531,386 | 255,819 | 787,205 |
| | 317,816 | 93,461 | 411,277 | 1973 | 515,439 | 171,399 | 686,838 |
| | 689,635 | 270,311 | 959,946 | 1975 | 457,484 | 150,853 | 608,337 |
| | 651,674 | 268,161 | 919,835 | 1977 | 451,724 | 129,232 | 580,956 |
| | 607,383 | 207,369 | 814,752 | 1978 | 439,762 | 130,454 | 570,216 |

Since 1957 continental U.S. includes Air Force Academy Cadets as follows: (1957) 504; (1960) 1,949; (1963) 2,660; (1964) 3; (1965) 2,907; (1966) 3,152; (1967) 3,361; (1968) 3,652; (1969) 3,941; (1970) 4,144; (1971) 2,997; (1972) 2,885; (1973) 4,356; 4) 4,412; (1975) 4,414; (1976) 4,415; (1977) 4,680; (1978) 4,524.
Since 1960 Overseas includes Alaska and Hawaii. All figures include Mobilized Personnel.

### USAF Military Personnel

| June 30 | Officers & airmen | Male commissioned officers USAF (Reg.) & RA | USAFR & ORC | ANG & NG | AFUS & AUS | Total warrant officers |
|---|---|---|---|---|---|---|
| | 959,946 | 23,463 | 105,587 | 984 | 2 | 3,961 |
| | 814,752 | 49,584 | 72,115 | 248 | 3 | 4,069 |
| | 824,662 | 62,076 | 62,537 | 280 | 54 | 2,532 |
| | 787,205 | 63,678 | 65,852 | 168 | 105 | 639 |
| | 603,317 | 57,854 | 42,131 | 128 | 28 | 39 |
| | 580,956 | 56,657 | 41,557 | 139 | 21 | 9 |
| | 570,216 | 56,838 | 39,598 | 148 | 18 | 2 |

) Selected reserves only.

### Female Commissioned Officers, and Enlisted Personnel

| June 30 | Female commissioned officers Total | WAF | Nurses | WMSC | Female WO | Enlisted personnel Total | Male | Female |
|---|---|---|---|---|---|---|---|---|
| | 3,858 | 679 | 3,020 | 159 | 5 | 685,063 | 679,412 | 5,651 |
| | 4,099 | 708 | 3,185 | 206 | 1 | 690,177 | 685,436 | 4,741 |
| | 4,667 | 1,072 | 3,407 | 188 | 0 | 657,402 | 648,415 | 8,987 |
| | 4,981 | 1,542 | 3,236 | 203 | 0 | 503,176 | 477,944 | 25,232 |
| | 5,264 | 1,849 | 3,085 | 330 | 0 | 482,573 | 447,961 | 34,612 |
| | 5,762 | 2,269 | 3,112 | 381 | 0 | 478,139 | 437,253 | 40,886 |

## Veteran Population

Source: Veterans Administration

| | June 1978 |
|---|---|
| rans in civil life, end of month — Total | 29,948,000 |
| Veterans — Total | 26,482,000 |
| ietnam Era — Total (a) | 8,680,000 |
|   And service in Korean Conflict | 538,000 |
|   No service in Korean Conflict | 8,142,000 |
| orean Conflict — Total (includes line 4) | 5,906,000 |
|   And service in WW II | 1,209,000 |
|   No service in WW II | 4,697,000 |
| orld War II (includes line 7) | 12,957,000 |
| orld War I | 686,000 |
| panish-American War | 319 |
| rice between Korean Conflict (January 31, 1955) | |
| nd Vietnam (August 5, 1964) only (b) | 3,070,000 |

a) Service after Aug. 4, 1964; (b) excludes men who served on active duty for training only.

### Pension Cases and Compensation Payments

| scal ear | Living veteran cases No. | Deceased veteran cases No. | Total cases No. | Total disbursement Dollars | Fiscal year | Living veteran cases No. | Deceased veteran cases No. | Total cases No. | Total disbursement Dollars |
|---|---|---|---|---|---|---|---|---|---|
| ) | 415,654 | 122,290 | 537,944 | 106,093,850 | 1965 | 3,204,275 | 1,277,009 | 4,481,284 | 3,901,598,010 |
| ) | 752,520 | 241,019 | 993,529 | 138,462,130 | 1970 | 3,127,338 | 1,487,176 | 4,614,514 | 5,113,649,490 |
| ) | 602,622 | 318,461 | 921,083 | 159,974,056 | 1971 | 3,222,394 | 1,584,167 | 4,806,561 | 5,726,485,000 |
| ) | 419,627 | 349,916 | 769,543 | 316,418,029 | 1972 | 3,268,826 | 1,641,370 | 4,910,196 | 6,045,214,000 |
| ) | 542,610 | 298,223 | 840,833 | 418,432,808 | 1973 | 3,256,746 | 1,654,287 | 4,911,033 | 6,426,647,000 |
| ) | 610,122 | 239,176 | 849,298 | 429,138,465 | 1974 | 3,241,263 | 1,627,482 | 4,868,745 | 6,615,599,000 |
| ) | 2,368,238 | 658,123 | 3,026,361 | 2,009,462,298 | 1975 | 3,226,701 | 1,628,146 | 4,854,847 | 7,600,000,000 |
| ) | 2,668,786 | 808,303 | 3,477,089 | 2,634,292,537 | 1976 | 3,235,778 | 1,630,830 | 4,866,608 | 8,074,488,000 |
| ) | 3,008,935 | 950,802 | 3,959,737 | 3,314,761,383 | 1977 | 3,272,821 | 1,628,488 | 4,901,309 | 8,874,720,000 |

## Monthly Pay Scale

F

### Commissioned Officers

| Pay grade | Army rank | Navy rank | Under 2 | Over 2 | Over 3 | Over 4 | Over 6 | Ove 8 |
|---|---|---|---|---|---|---|---|---|
| | Rank or pay grade | | | Cumulative years of service | | | | |
| O-10[1] | General* | Admiral | $3,126.30 | $3,236.40 | $3,236.40 | $3,236.40 | $3,336.40 | $3,36 |
| O-9 | Lieutenant General | Vice Admiral | 2,770.80 | 2,843.70 | 2,904.00 | 2,904.00 | 2,904.00 | 2,97 |
| O-8 | Major General | Rear Admiral (up. half) | 2,509.50 | 2,584.80 | 2,646.30 | 2,646.30 | 2,646.30 | 2,84 |
| O-7 | Brigadier General | Rear Admiral (low half) | 2,085.30 | 2,227.20 | 2,227.20 | 2,227.20 | 2,326.80 | 2,32 |
| O-6 | Colonel | Captain | 1,545.60 | 1,698.60 | 1,809.00 | 1,809.00 | 1,809.00 | 1,80 |
| O-5 | Lieutenant Colonel | Commander | 1,236.30 | 1,452.00 | 1,551.90 | 1,551.90 | 1,551.90 | 1,55 |
| O-4 | Major | Lieutenant Comdr. | 1,042.20 | 1,268.40 | 1,353.60 | 1,353.60 | 1,378.20 | 1,43 |
| O-3 | Captain | Lieutenant | 968.40 | 1,082.70 | 1,157.10 | 1,280.40 | 1,341.60 | 1,39 |
| O-2 | First Lieutenant | Lieutenant (J.G.) | 844.20 | 922.20 | 1,107.90 | 1,145.10 | 1,168.80 | 1,16 |
| O-1 | Second Lieutenant | Ensign | 732.90 | 762.90 | 922.20 | 922.20 | 922.20 | 92 |
| *Commissioned officers with over 4 years service as enlisted members* | | | | | | | | |
| O-3 | Captain | Lieutenant | 0.00 | 0.00 | 0.00 | 0.00 | 0.00 | |
| O-2 | First Lieutenant | Lieutenant (J.G.) | 0.00 | 0.00 | 0.00 | 0.00 | 0.00 | 1,20 |
| O-1[1] | Second Lieutenant | Ensign | 0.00 | 0.00 | 0.00 | 0.00 | 984.90 | 1,02 |

### Warrant Officers

| W-4 | Chief Warrant | Comm. Warrant | 986.40 | 1,058.40 | 1,058.40 | 1,082.70 | 1,131.90 | 1,18 |
|---|---|---|---|---|---|---|---|---|
| W-3 | Chief Warrant | Comm. Warrant | 897.00 | 972.90 | 972.90 | 984.90 | 996.60 | 1,06 |
| W-2 | Chief Warrant | Comm. Warrant | 785.40 | 849.30 | 849.30 | 874.20 | 922.20 | 97 |
| W-1 | Warrant Officer | Warrant Officer | 654.30 | 750.30 | 750.30 | 812.70 | 849.30 | 88 |

### Enlisted Personnel[2]

| E-9[3] | Sergeant Major** | Master C.P.O. | 0.00 | 0.00 | 0.00 | 0.00 | 0.00 | |
|---|---|---|---|---|---|---|---|---|
| E-8[3] | Master Sergeant. | Senior C.P.O. | 0.00 | 0.00 | 0.00 | 0.00 | 0.00 | 94 |
| E-7 | Sgt. 1st Class | Chief Petty Officer | 656.70 | 708.60 | 735.00 | 760.50 | 786.90 | 81 |
| E-6 | Staff Sergeant | Petty Officer 1st Class | 567.00 | 618.30 | 644.10 | 671.10 | 696.00 | 72 |
| E-5 | Sergeant | Petty Officer 2nd Cl. | 498.00 | 541.80 | 568.20 | 592.80 | 631.50 | 65 |
| E-4 | Corporal | Petty Officer 3rd Cl. | 478.50 | 505.20 | 534.90 | 576.60 | 599.40 | 59 |
| E-3 | Private 1st Class | Seaman | 460.20 | 485.40 | 504.90 | 525.00 | 525.00 | 52 |
| E-2 | Private | Seaman Apprentice. | 443.10 | 443.10 | 443.10 | 443.10 | 443.10 | 44 |
| E-1 | Private | Seaman Recruit. | 397.50 | 397.50 | 397.50 | 397.50 | 397.50 | 39 |

**The pay scale also applies to:** Coast Guard and Marine Corps, National Oceanic and Atmospheric Administration, Public Health vice, National Guard, and the Organized Reserves.

*Basic pay is limited to $3,958.20 by Level V of the Executive Schedule. Four star General or Admiral—personal money allowanc $2,200 per annum, or $4,000 if Chief of Staff of the Army, Chief of Staff of the Air Force, Chief of Naval Operations, Commandant o Marine Corps, or Commandant of the Coast Guard. Three star General or Admiral—personal money allowance of $500 per annum.

**A new title of Chief Master Sergeant created in 1965 rates E-9 classification.

(1) While serving as Chairman of Joint Chiefs of Staff, Chief of Staff of the Army, Chief of Naval Operations, Chief of Staff of the Forces, or Commandant of the Marine Corps, basic pay for this grade is $4,848.00 regardless of years of service, limited by Exec Schedule to $3,958.20

(2) Air Force enlisted personnel pay grades, E-9, Chief Master Sergeant; E-8, Sr. Master Sergeant; E-7, Master Sergeant; E-6, Tech Sergeant; E-5, Staff Sergeant; E-4, Sergeant; E-3, Airman 1st Class; E-2, Airman; E-1, Basic Airman.

Marine Corps enlisted ranks are as follows: E-9, Sergeant Major and Master Gunnery Sergeant; E-8, First Sergeant and Master Serge E-7, Gunnery Sergeant; E-6, Staff Sergeant; E-5, Sergeant; E-4, Corporal; E-3, Lance Corporal; E-2, Private, First Class Marine; E-1, vate.

Marine Corps and Air Force officer ranks are same as Army.

(3) While serving as Sergeant Major of the Army, Master Chief Petty Officer of the Navy, Chief Master Sergeant of the Air Forc Sergeant Major of the Marine Corps, basic pay for this grade is $1,754.40 regardless of years of service.

## American Military Actions, 1900-1973

1900—Occupation of Puerto Rico (ceded to U.S., 1899).

1900—500 Marines, 1,500 Army troops help relieve Peking in Boxer Rebellion.

1900-1902—Occupation of Cuba.

1900-1902—Guerrilla war in Philippines.

1903—Sailors and Marines from U.S.S. Nashville stop Colombian Army at Panama.

1904—Brief intervention in Dominican Republic.

1906-1909—Intervention in Cuba.

1909—Brief intervention in Honduras.

1910, 1912-1913—Intervention in Nicaragua.

1911—Intervention (to collect customs) in Honduras, Nicaragua, Dominican Republic.

1912-1917—Intervention in Cuba.

1914—Intervention in Dominican Republic.

1914—April 21 to Nov. 23. Marines in Vera Cruz.

1914—Navy and Marines enter Haiti, stay until 1934.

1916—Gen. John J. Pershing and 10,000 into Northern Mexico to stop raids by Pancho Villa, Mar. 15-Nov. 24.

1916-1924—Marines in Dominican Republic.

1917—Apr. 6 to Nov. 11, 1918. War with Germany,

Austria-Hungary.

1918-1920—Expeditions into North Russia, Siberia.

1918-1923—Occupation of Germany.

1922-1924—Marines in Nicaragua.

1926-1933—Marines in Nicaragua.

1927—1,000 Marines in China.

1941-1945—War with Japan, Germany, Italy and allies.

1950-1953—U.S. and other UN countries aid the Repu of Korea to repel North Korean invaders; U.S. Navy tects Taiwan.

1956—U.S. Fleet evacuates U.S. nationals during Suez sis.

1957—U.S. Fleet to Near East during Jordan crisis.

1958—Navy, Marines and Army units support Lebanon

1960—Navy patrol in Caribbean to protect Guatemala Nicaragua.

1961—Army units to Vietnam.

1962—Units of Navy on Cuban quarantine duty. Marin Thailand.

1962-1965—U.S. Military Assistance Command, Vietr units of Army, Navy, Air Force, Marine Corps, C

# Uniformed Services
1978

## Commissioned Officers

| | | Cumulative years of service | | | | | | Basic allowances for quarters | |
|---|---|---|---|---|---|---|---|---|---|
| Over 10 | Over 12 | Over 14 | Over 16 | Over 18 | Over 20 | Over 22 | Over 26 | Without dependents | With dependents |
| 3,360.30 | 3,618.00 | 3,618.00 | 3,876.60 | 3,876.60 | 4,136.10* | 4,136.10* | 4,393.80* | $339.30 | $424.20 |
| 2,978.10 | 3,101.40 | 3,101.40 | 3,360.30 | 3,360.30 | 3,618.00 | 3,618.00 | 3,876.60 | 339.30 | 424.20 |
| 2,843.70 | 2,978.10 | 2,978.10 | 3,101.40 | 3,236.40 | 3,360.30 | 3,495.00 | 3,495.00 | 339.30 | 424.20 |
| | | | | | | | | | |
| 2,462.10 | 2,462.10 | 2,584.80 | 2,843.70 | 3,039.00 | 3,039.00 | 3,039.00 | 3,039.00 | 339.30 | 424.20 |
| 1,809.00 | 1,809.00 | 1,870.50 | 2,166.90 | 2,277.60 | 2,326.80 | 2,462.10 | 2,670.00 | 304.50 | 371.40 |
| 1,599.30 | 1,684.80 | 1,797.30 | 1,932.30 | 2,043.30 | 2,104.80 | 2,178.60 | 2,178.60 | 280.80 | 338.10 |
| 1,537.50 | 1,624.20 | 1,698.60 | 1,772.40 | 1,821.90 | 1,821.90 | 1,821.90 | 1,821.90 | 249.90 | 301.80 |
| 1,464.60 | 1,537.50 | 1,575.30 | 1,575.30 | 1,575.30 | 1,575.30 | 1,575.30 | 1,575.30 | 219.90 | 271.20 |
| 1,168.80 | 1,168.80 | 1,168.80 | 1,168.80 | 1,168.80 | 1,168.80 | 1,168.80 | 1,168.80 | 190.80 | 241.50 |
| 922.20 | 922.20 | 922.20 | 922.20 | 922.20 | 922.20 | 922.20 | 922.20 | 148.80 | 193.80 |
| | | | | | | | | | |
| 1,464.60 | 1,537.50 | 1,599.30 | 1,599.30 | 1,599.30 | 1,599.30 | 1,599.30 | 1,599.30 | 219.90 | 271.20 |
| 1,268.40 | 1,317.30 | 1,353.60 | 1,353.60 | 1,353.60 | 1,353.60 | 1,353.60 | 1,353.60 | 190.80 | 241.50 |
| 1,058.40 | 1,095.30 | 1,145.10 | 1,145.10 | 1,145.10 | 1,145.10 | 1,145.10 | 1,145.10 | 148.80 | 193.80 |

## Warrant Officers

| Over 10 | Over 12 | Over 14 | Over 16 | Over 18 | Over 20 | Over 22 | Over 26 | Without dependents | With dependents |
|---|---|---|---|---|---|---|---|---|---|
| 1,231.20 | 1,317.30 | 1,378.20 | 1,427.10 | 1,464.60 | 1,512.90 | 1,563.30 | 1,684.80 | 240.90 | 290.70 |
| 1,131.90 | 1,168.80 | 1,206.00 | 1,242.00 | 1,280.40 | 1,329.90 | 1,378.20 | 1,427.10 | 214.80 | 264.60 |
| 1,009.50 | 1,046.40 | 1,082.70 | 1,120.50 | 1,157.10 | 1,193.70 | 1,242.00 | 1,242.00 | 186.90 | 237.30 |
| 922.20 | 960.30 | 996.60 | 1,033.50 | 1,069.50 | 1,107.90 | 1,107.90 | 1,107.90 | 168.60 | 218.40 |

## Enlisted Personnel

| Over 10 | Over 12 | Over 14 | Over 16 | Over 18 | Over 20 | Over 22 | Over 26 | Without dependents | With dependents |
|---|---|---|---|---|---|---|---|---|---|
| 1,120.80 | 1,146.30 | 1,172.40 | 1,199.40 | 1,225.80 | 1,249.80 | 1,315.80 | 1,443.30 | 181.80 | 255.60 |
| 966.60 | 992.40 | 1,018.50 | 1,044.90 | 1,069.20 | 1,069.20 | 1,159.80 | 1,289.40 | 167.40 | 236.40 |
| 837.30 | 863.70 | 902.70 | 928.20 | 954.30 | 966.60 | 1,031.70 | 1,159.80 | 142.50 | 219.90 |
| 748.20 | 786.90 | 811.50 | 837.30 | 850.20 | 850.20 | 850.20 | 850.20 | 129.30 | 202.20 |
| 683.70 | 708.60 | 721.80 | 721.80 | 721.80 | 721.80 | 721.80 | 721.80 | 124.20 | 185.70 |
| 599.40 | 599.40 | 599.40 | 599.40 | 599.40 | 599.40 | 599.40 | 599.40 | 109.80 | 163.50 |
| 525.00 | 525.00 | 525.00 | 525.00 | 525.00 | 525.00 | 525.00 | 525.00 | 98.10 | 142.50 |
| 443.10 | 443.10 | 443.10 | 443.10 | 443.10 | 443.10 | 443.10 | 443.10 | 86.70 | 142.50 |
| 397.50 | 397.50 | 397.50 | 397.50 | 397.50 | 397.50 | 397.50 | 397.50 | 81.90 | 142.50 |

*Limited under existing law to $3,958.20

### Basic Allowances for Subsistence

his allowance, the quarters allowance, and any other allowance are not subject to income tax.

cers — Subsistence (food) is paid to all officers regardless of rank . . . . . . . . . . . . . . . . . . . . . . . . . . . . . $55.61 per month
sted members:   When on leave or authorized to mess separately . . . . . . . . . . . . . . . . . . . . . . . . . . . . $2.84 per day
When rations in kind are not available . . . . . . . . . . . . . . . . . . . . . . . . . . . . . . . . . . . . . . . . $3.20 per day
When assigned to duty under emergency conditions where
no government messing facilities are available . . . . . . . . . . . . . . . . . . . . $ 4.25 per day (maximum rate)

### Family Separation Allowance

nder certain conditions of family separation of more than 30 days, a member in Pay Grades E-4 (with over 4 years' service) and above
be allowed $30 a month in addition to any other allowances to which he is entitled. When separated from family and required to main-
a home for his family and one for himself, the member is entitled to an additional monthly basic allowance for quarters at the "without
ndents" rate for his grade.

---

uard.
5—Navy, Marines, Army units to Dominican Republic.
5—American commanders in Vietnam authorized to
end U.S. Armed Force into combat.
9—President Nixon announces, June 8, first phase of
ithdrawal of U.S. troops from Vietnam.

1970—Army units participate in Cambodian sanctuary operations, Apr. 29-June 30.
1973—Last U.S. troops leave Vietnam, U.S. Military Assistance Command deactivated, March 29.
1973—End of all U.S. bombing operations over Indochina, Aug. 15.

---

## The Federal Service Academies

, Military Academy, West Point, N.Y. Founded 1802. Awards B.S. degree and Army commission for a 5-year ervice obligation. For admissions information, write Admissions Office, USMA, West Point, NY 10996.

, Naval Academy, Annapolis, Md. Founded 1845. Awards B.S. degree and Navy or Marine Corps commis-on for a 5-year service obligation. For admissions inforation, write Dean of Admissions, Naval Academy, Annapolis, MD 21402.

, Air Force Academy, Colorado Springs, Colo. Founded 954. Awards B.S. degree and Air Force commission for a -year service obligation. For admissions information, write Registrar, U.S. Air Force Academy, CO 80840.

U.S. Coast Guard Academy, New London, Conn. Founded 1876. Awards B.S. degree and Coast Guard commission for a 5-year service obligation. For admissions information, write Admissions Office, Coast Guard Academy, New London, CT 06320.

U.S. Merchant Marine Academy, Kings Point, N.Y. Founded 1943. Awards B.S. degree, a license as a deck or engineer officer, and a U.S. Naval Reserve commission. Service obligations vary according to options taken by the graduating ensign. For admissions information, write Admission Office, U.S. Merchant Marine Academy, Kings Point, NY 11024.

## Strategic Nuclear Armaments: U.S. and USSR

Source: International Institute for Strategic Services, London

### United States

| Land-based missiles[1] | | Range[2] (statute miles) | Estimated warhead yield[3] | Deployed (July 1977) |
|---|---|---|---|---|
| ICBM | Titan 2 | 7,000 | 5-10 MT | 54 |
| | Minuteman 2 | 7,000 | 1-2 MT | 450 |
| | Minuteman 3 | 7,500 | 3x170 KT | 550 |

| Sea-based missiles | | | | |
|---|---|---|---|---|
| SLBM (nuclear subs) | Polaris A3 | 2,880 | 3x200 KT | 160 |
| | Poseidon C3 | 2,880 | 10x50 KT | 496 |

| | | Range[8] (statute miles) | Weapons load (lb) | Deployed (July 1976) |
|---|---|---|---|---|
| Aircraft[7] | | | | |
| Long-range | B-52D | 11,500 | 60,000 | 373[8] |
| | B-52G-H | 12,500 | 70,000 | |
| Medium range | FB-111A | 3,800 | 37,500 | 68 |
| Strike aircraft; land-based | F-105D | 2,100 | 16,500 | (350)[9] |
| | F-4C-J | 2,300 | 16,000 | |
| | F-111A/E | 3,800 | 25,000 | |
| | A-7D | 3,400 | 15,000 | |
| Strike aircraft; carrier-based | A-4 | 2,055 | 10,000 | (200)[9] |
| | A-6A | 3,225 | 18,000 | |
| | A-7A/B/E | 3,400 | 15,000 | |
| | F-4 | 2,000 | 16,000 | |

### Soviet Union

| Land-based missiles[1] | | Range[2] (statute miles) | Estimated warhead yield[3] | Deplo (Ju 197 |
|---|---|---|---|---|
| ICBM | SS-7 Saddler | 6,900 | 5 MT | {10 |
| | SS-8 Sasin | 6,900 | 5 MT | |
| | SS-9 Scarp | 7,500 | 18-25 MT[4] | 23 |
| | SS-11 Sego | 6,500 | 1-2 MT[5] | 84 |
| | SS-13 Savage | 5,000 | 1 MT | 6 |
| | SS-17 | 6,500 | 4x KT | 6 |
| | SS-18 | 7,500 | 15-25 MT[6] | 5 |
| | SS-19 | 6,500 | 6x KT | 14 |

| Sea-based missiles | | | | |
|---|---|---|---|---|
| SLBM (nuclear subs) | SS-N-6-Sawfly | 1,750 | MT | 54 |
| | SS-N-8 | 4,800 | MT | 28 |

| | | Range[8] (statute miles) | Weapons load (lb) | Deplo (Ju 197 |
|---|---|---|---|---|
| Aircraft[7] | | | | |
| | Tu-95 Bear | 8,000 | 40,000 | 1C |
| | Mya-4 Bison | 6,000 | 20,000 | 3 |
| | Tu-16 Badger | 4,000 | 20,000 | 74 |
| | Backfire B | 5,500 | 20,000 | 6 |
| | Il-28 Beagle | 2,500 | 4,850 | |
| | Su-7 Fitter A | 900 | 4,500 | |
| | Tu-22 Blinder | 1,400 | 12,000 | |
| | MiG-21 Fishbed J/K/L | 1,150 | 2,000 | (1,000 |
| | MiG-27 Flogger D | 1,800 | 2,800 | |
| | Su-17/20 Fitter C | 1,100 | 5,000 | |
| | Su-19A Fencer | 1,800 | 8,000 | |

(1) ICBM = intercontinental ballistic missile. IRBM = intermediate-range ballistic missile. MRBM = medium-range missile. SLBM submarine-launched ballistic missile. SLCM = sub-launched cruise missile. (2) Operation range depends upon the payload car use of maximum payload may reduce missile range by up to 25%. (3) MT = megaton range = 1,000,000 tons of TNT equivaler over; KT = kiloton range = 1,000 tons of TNT equivalent or more, but less than 1 MT. (4) Some SS-9 missiles carry 3 warhead 4-5 MT each. (5) Some SS-11 missiles may carry 3xKT warheads. (6) Some SS-18 may carry 8xMT warheads. (7) All aircraft li are dual-capable and many, especially in the categories of strike aircraft, would be more likely to carry conventional than nuc weapons. (8) Theoretical maximum range, with internal fuel only, at optimum altitude and speed. Ranges for strike aircraft assum weapons load. Especially in the case of strike aircraft, therefore, range falls sharply for flights at lower altitude, at higher speed with full weapons load. (9) Figures in parentheses are estimates of Europe-based systems only.

---

## Women in the Armed Forces

Expansion of military women's programs began in the Department of Defense in fiscal year 1973. The planned end strength for fiscal year 1983 is approximately 199,000 which is 11.1% of the planned strength of the active forces.

Although women are prohibited by law and directives based on law from serving in combat positions, policy changes in the department have resulted in making possible the assignment of women to almost all other career fields. Career progression for women is now comparable to that for male personnel. Women are routinely assigned to overseas locations formerly closed to female personnel. Test programs have been initiated to place women in pilot training and in command of activities and units which have missions other than administration of women.

Admission of women to the service academies began in the fall of 1976 and will further the goal of increased numbers of women officers. The academies will provide single track education, allowing only for minor variations in the cadet program based on physiological differences between men and women.

**Women's Army Corps** — MG Gen. M.E. Clarke, WAC Director, Dept. of Army, Washington, DC 20310; 5,789 officers, 47,374 enlisted women; wide variety of assignments, world-wide; subsidizes some college training.

**Army Nurse Corps** — Brig. Gen. N.N. Parks, Chief, Army Nurse Corps, Office of the Surgeon General, Dept. of Army, Washington, DC 20310; 2,653 female officers; nursing and supervision assignments, world-wide; subsidizes

some training; corps includes men.

**Navy** — Fully integrated, no director for women. For formation: Commander, Naval Recruiting, Dept. of Na Washington, DC 22230; 3,809 officers, 19,275 women; v ety of assignments, world-wide.

**Navy Nurse Corps** — Rear Adm. Maxine Condor, Di tor, Navy Nurse Corps, Bureau of Medicine and Surge Dept. of Navy, Washington, DC 20372; 2,306 female cers; nursing and supervision assignments at U.S. and eign bases, and shipboard; subsidizes some training; co includes men.

**Air Force** — Fully integrated, no director for women. information: USAF Recruiting Service, Randolph Air Fo Base, TX 78148; 5,557 officers, 38,944 enlisted women; v ety of assignments, world-wide.

**Air Force Nurse Corps** — Brig. Gen. Clare M. Garre Chief, Air Force Nurse Corps, Office of the Surgeon G eral, USAF, Washington, DC 20314; 3,099 female offic nursing and supervision assignments; world-wide; subsid training; corps includes men.

**Women Marines** — Brig. Gen. Margaret A. Brewer, rector of Information, Headquarters, Marine Corps, Wa ington, DC 20380; 429 officers, 4,140 enlisted women.

**Coast Guard Women** — Fully integrated, no comman U.S. Coast Guard, Washington, DC 20590; 70 officers, enlisted women.

## Casualties in Principal Wars of the U.S.

on Revolutionary War casualties is from **The Toll of Independence**, Howard H. Peckham, ed., U. of Chicago Press,

prior to World War I are based on incomplete records in many cases. Casualty data are confined to dead and
·d personnel and therefore exclude personnel captured or missing in action who were subsequently returned to military
Dash (—) indicates information is not available.

| Wars | Branch of service | Number serving | Casualties | | | |
|---|---|---|---|---|---|---|
| | | | Battle deaths | Other deaths | Wounds not mortal[a] | Total |
| ·tionary War | Total | — | 6,824 | 18,500 | 8,445 | 33,769 |
| 5-1783 | Army | 184,000 | 5,992 | — | 7,988 | 13,980 |
| | Navy & | to | — | — | — | — |
| | Marines | 250,000 | 832 | — | 457 | 1,289 |
| · 1812 | Total | ·286,730 | 2,260 | — | 4,505 | 6,765 |
| 2-1815 | Army | — | 1,950 | — | 4,000 | 5,950 |
| | Navy | — | 265 | — | 439 | 704 |
| | Marines | — | 45 | — | 66 | 111 |
| an War | Total | ·78,718 | 1,733 | 11,550 | 4,152 | 17,435 |
| 6-1848 | Army | — | 1,721 | 11,500 | 4,102 | 17,373 |
| | Navy | — | 1 | — | 3 | 4 |
| | Marines | — | 11 | — | 47 | 58 |
| ·ar | Total | ·2,213,363 | 140,414 | 224,097 | 281,881 | 646,392 |
| on forces only) | Army | 2,128,948 | 138,154 | 221,374 | 280,040 | 639,568 |
| 1-1865 | Navy | — | 2,112 | 2,411 | 1,710 | 6,233 |
| | Marines | 84,415 | 148 | 312 | 131 | 591 |
| federate forces | Total | — | 74,524 | 59,297 | — | 133,821 |
| mate)¹ | Army | 600,000 | — | — | — | — |
| 3-1866 | Navy | to | — | — | — | — |
| | Marines | 1,500,000 | — | — | — | — |
| ·h-American | Total | 306,760 | 385 | 2,061 | 1,662 | 4,108 |
| | Army⁴ | 280,564 | 369 | 2,061 | 1,594 | 4,024 |
| 3 | Navy | 22,875 | 10 | 0 | 47 | 57 |
| | Marines | 3,321 | 6 | 0 | 21 | 27 |
| War I | Total | 4,743,826 | 53,513 | 63,195 | 204,002 | 320,710 |
| 16, 1917- | Army⁵ | 4,057,101 | 50,510 | 55,868 | 193,663 | 300,041 |
| ·11, 1918 | Navy | 599,051 | 431 | 6,856 | 819 | 8,106 |
| | Marines | 78,839 | 2,461 | 390 | 9,520 | 12,371 |
| | Coast Gd. | 8,835 | 111 | 81 | — | 192 |
| War II | Total | 16,353,659 | 292,131 | 115,185 | 670,846 | 1,078,162 |
| ·7, 1941- | Army⁶ | 11,260,000 | 234,874 | 83,400 | 565,861 | 884,135 |
| ·. 31, 1946² | Navy⁷ | 4,183,466 | 36,950 | 25,664 | 37,778 | 100,392 |
| | Marines · | 669,100 | 19,733 | 4,778 | 67,207 | 91,718 |
| | Coast Gd. | 241,093 | 574 | 1,343 | — | 1,917 |
| ·n War | Total | 5,764,143 | 33,629 | 20,617 | 103,284 | 157,530 |
| ·e 25, 1950- | Army | 2,834,000 | 27,704 | 9,429 | 77,596 | 114,729 |
| 27, 1953³ | Navy | 1,177,000 | 458 | 4,043 | 1,576 | 6,077 |
| | Marines | 424,000 | 4,267 | 1,261 | 23,744 | 29,272 |
| | Air Force | 1,285,000 | 1,200 | 5,884 | 368 | 7,452 |
| | Coast Gd. | 44,143 | — | — | — | — |
| ·m (preliminary)¹⁰ | Total | 8,744,000 | 46,616 | 10,386 | 153,329 | 210,291 |
| ·. 4, 1964- | Army | 4,368,000 | 30,717 | 7,194 | 96,811 | 134,711 |
| 27, 1973 | Navy | 1,842,000 | 1,535 | 909 | 4,180 | 6,618 |
| | Marines | 794,000 | 12,025 | 1,680 | 51,399 | 66,103 |
| | Air Force | 1,740,000 | 1,339 | 603 | 939 | 2,859 |

·uthoritative statistics for the Confederate Forces are not available. An estimated 26,000-31,000 Confederate per-
·died in Union prisons.
·ata are for the period Dec. 1, 1941 through Dec. 31, 1946 when hostilities were officially terminated by Presiden-
·oclamation, but few battle deaths or wounds not mortal were incurred after the Japanese acceptance of Allied
·terms on Aug. 14, 1945. Numbers serving from Dec. 1, 1941-Aug. 31, 1945 were: Total—14,903,213; Ar-
·0,420,000; Navy—3,883,520; and Marine Corps—599,693.
·entative final data based upon information available as of Sept. 30, 1954, at which time 24 persons were still car-
·s missing in action.
·umber serving covers the period April 21-Aug. 13, 1898, while dead and wounded data are for the period May
·31, 1898. Active hostilities ceased on Aug. 13, 1898, but ratifications of the treaty of peace were not exchanged
·en the United States and Spain until April 11, 1899.
·ncludes Air Service Battle deaths and wounds not mortal include casualties suffered by American forces in North-
·ssia to Aug. 25, 1919 and in Siberia to April 1, 1920. Other deaths covered the period April 1, 1917-Dec. 31, 1918.
·ncludes Army Air Forces.
·attle deaths and wounds not mortal include casualties incurred in Oct. 1941 due to hostile action.
·Marine Corps data for World War II, the Spanish-American War and prior wars represent the number of individuals
·led, whereas all other data in this column represent the total number (incidence) of wounds.
·s reported by the Commissioner of Pensions in his Annual Report for Fiscal Year 1903.
·Number serving covers the period Aug. 4 1964-Jan. 27, 1973 (date of ceasefire). Number of casualties incurred in
·ction with the conflict in Vietnam from Jan. 1, 1961-Sept. 30, 1977. Includes casualties incurred in Mayaguez Inci-
·Wounds not mortal exclude 150,375 persons not requiring hospital care.

## American Military Cemeteries and Memorials on Foreign Soil

Administered by the American Battle Monuments Commission, Washington, DC 20314
(Numbers of graves and numbers of commemorated missing in parentheses)
All of the cemeteries are closed to further interments.

### World War I Cemeteries

Aisne-Marne, Belleau (Aisne) France (2,288-1,060)
Brookwood (Surrey) England (468-563)
Flanders Field, Waregem, Belgium (368-43)
Meuse-Argonne, Romagne (Meuse), France (14,246-954)
Oise-Aisne, Seringes (Aisne), near Fere-en-Tardenois (Aisne), France (6,012-241)
St. Mihiel, Thiaucourt (M. et M.), France (4,153-284)
Somme, Bony (Aisne), France (1,844-284)
Suresnes (Seine), France (1,541-974). In this cemetery rest also 24 of our unknown dead of World War II. The World War I chapel was, by the addition of two loggias, converted into a shrine to commemorate our dead of both wars. Senior representatives of the American and French governments assemble here on ceremonial occasions to pay homage to our military dead of these wars.

### World War I Monuments

Audenarde, Belgium.
Bellicourt (Aisne), France.
Brest (Finistere), France.
Cantigny (Somme), France.
Chateau-Thierry (Aisne), Fr.
Gibraltar.
Remmel, Ypres, Belgium.
Montfaucon (Meuse), France.
Montsec (Meuse), France.
Sommepy (Marne), France.
Tours (Indre et Loire), France.

### World War II Cemetery Memorials

Ardennes, Neupre (Neuville-en-Condroz), Belgium (5,319)
Brittany, St. James (Manche), France (4,410-498)
Cambridge, Cambridge, England (3,811-5,125)
Epinal, Epinal (Vosges), France (5,255-424)
Florence, Florence (Tuscany), Italy (4,402-1,409)
Henri-Chapelle, Henri-Chapelle, Belgium (7,989-450)
Lorraine, St. Avold (Moselle), France (10,489-444)
Luxembourg, Hamm, Luxembourg (5,076-370)
Manila, Manila, Rep. of the Philippines (17,206-36,279)
Netherlands, Margraten, Holland (8,301-1,722)
Normandy, St. Laurent (Calvados), Fr. (9,386-1,557)
North Africa, Carthage, Tunisia (2,841-3,724)
Rhone, Draguignan (Var), France (861-293)
Sicily-Rome, Nettuno, Italy (7,862-3,094)

### World War II Memorials

To commemorate those who met their deaths American coastal waters of the Atlantic and Pacific the commission has erected a memorial in Battery NYC, on which are inscribed 4,596 names, and at the dio of San Francisco, Cal., which carries 412 names.
Honolulu Cemetery a memorial was erected which the names of 18,093 missing of World War II and missing resulting from the Korean operations.
The commission also maintains a cemetery in Mexi where the remains of 750 Americans who gave their the Mexican War (1846-1848) are buried.

---

## World War II Merchant Marine Casualties

Source: U.S. Coast Guard

Died from direct causes while serving on American flag ships, 845; died in prisoner-of-war camps, 37; listed as m 4,780.

There were 572 released prisoners of war, and one prisoner unaccounted for. Another 500 men died while serving eign flag ships under U.S. control.

The number of U.S. flag ships lost was 605 of 6,000,000 deadweight tons.

---

## Debts Owed U.S. Arising from World War I

Source: U.S. Treasury Department (Mar. 31, 1978)

| Country | Original indebtedness | Interest thru Mar. 31, 1978 | Total | Cumulative payments Principal | Interest | To outsta |
|---|---|---|---|---|---|---|
| Armenia. . . . . . | $11,959,917 | $35,016,459 | $46,976,377 | $32 | – | $46,9 |
| Austria[2] . . . . . | 26,843,149 | 11,412,543 | 38,255,692 | 862,668 | – | 37,3 |
| Belgium. . . . . . | 423,587,630 | 417,370,810 | 840,958,440 | 19,157,630 | $33,033,643 | 788,7 |
| Cuba . . . . . . | 10,000,000 | 2,286,752 | 12,286,752 | 10,000,000 | 2,286,752 | |
| Czechoslovakia . . | 185,071,023 | 208,600,165 | 393,671,188 | 19,829,914 | 304,178 | 373,5 |
| Estonia . . . . . | 16,958,373 | 28,500,844 | 45,459,217 | 11 | 1,248,432 | 44,2 |
| Finland . . . . . | 9,000,000 | 12,661,578 | 21,661,578 | [9]000,000 | [3]12,661,578 | |
| France . . . . . | 4,128,326,088 | 4,732,700,915 | 8,861,027,003 | 226,039,588 | 260,036,303 | 8,374,9 |
| Great Britain . . . | 4,933,701,642 | 8,738,741,018 | 13,672,442,659 | 434,181,642 | 1,590,672,656 | 11,647,5 |
| Greece[4] . . . . . | 34,319,844 | 5,984,106 | 40,303,950 | 1,784,375 | 5,960,559 | [5]32,5 |
| Hungary[6] . . . . . | 2,051,898 | 3,581,041 | [7]5,632,939 | 1,501,238 | 3,575,444 | 5 |
| Italy . . . . . . | 2,044,870,444 | 560,597,880 | 2,605,468,325 | 37,464,319 | 63,365,561 | 2,504,6 |
| Latvia . . . . . | 7,094,654 | 12,611,143 | 19,705,797 | 9,200 | 752,349 | 18,9 |
| Liberia. . . . . . | 26,000 | 10,472 | 36,742 | 26,000 | 10,472 | |
| Lithuania . . . . | 6,618,395 | 11,105,953 | 17,724,349 | 234,783 | 1,003,174 | 16,4 |
| Nicaragua[8] . . . . | 141,950 | 26,625 | 168,576 | 141,950 | 26,625 | |
| Poland . . . . . | 213,506,132 | 362,393,540 | 575,899,672 | [9]1,287,297 | 21,359,000 | 553,2 |
| Rumania . . . . | 68,359,192 | 87,319,483 | 155,678,675 | [10]4,498,632 | 292,375 | 150,8 |
| Russia. . . . . . | 192,601,297 | 579,626,069 | 972,227,366 | – | [11]8,750,312 | 763,4 |
| Yugoslavia . . . . | 63,577,714 | 49,107,709 | 112,685,423 | 1,952,713 | 636,059 | 110,0 |
| Total . . . . | 12,378,615,344 | 15,859,655,107 | 28,238,270,451 | 767,971,944 | 2,005,975,472 | 25,464,3 |

(1) Includes capitalized interest. (2) The Federal Republic of Germany has recognized liability for securities falling c tween March 12, 1938, and May 8, 1945. (3) $8,480,090 has been made available for educational exchange program Finland pursuant to 22 U.S.C. 2455(e). (4) Includes $13,155,921 refunded by the agreement of May 28, 1964 which w fied by Congress Nov. 5, 1966. (5) Includes $12,355,468 on agreement of May 28, 1964. (6) Interest payment from De 15, 1932, to June 15, 1937 were paid in pengo equivalent. (7) Includes $69,342 of principal and $120,535 of interest Moratorium Agreement of May 27, 1932. (8) The indebtedness of Nicaragua was canceled pursuant to the agreement o 14, 1938. (9) Excludes claim allowance of $1,813,429 dated December 15, 1969. (10) Excludes payment of $100,000 o 14, 1940, as a token of good faith. (11) Principally proceeds from liquidation of Russian assets in the United States.

## Major New U.S. Weapons Systems

Source: DMS, Inc., U.S. Defense Department

| s of June 31, 1978) Description | Estimated total cost (millions) | Estimated unit cost (thousands) | Number to be produced | Major contractors | Comment |
|---|---|---|---|---|---|
| cat | Swing-wing jet fighter, carrier-based, for fleet defense, strike escort. | $12,101.5 | $27,300 | 601 | Grumman | In production; 80 sold to Iran |
| e | Tactical jet fighter. Air Force. | 13,180.8 | 16,800 | 914 | McDonnell Douglas | In production; 25 for Israel, 100 for Japan, 60 for S. Arabia |
| lor | Supersonic, day-time fighter, defense. Air Force. | 15,036.8 | 9,300 | 1,736 | General Dynamics | In production; 348 for NATO, 700 additional may be sold abroad |
| et | All-weather fighter and attack plane. Fleet escort, Marine Corps ground support. | 14,299.9 | 13,500 | 800 for U.S. | McDonnell Douglas; Northrop | Advanced development; several hundred more may be sold abroad |
| 4 | Attack helicopter: anti-tank, air cavalry, escort. Army. | 4,139.3 | 6,200 | 536 | Hughes | Advanced development |
| nt | Nuclear-powered submarine carries 24 missiles with 4,000-mile range | 23,979.9 | Boat = 1,200,000 missile = 12,000 | 13 boats; 576 missiles | General Dynamics; Lockheed | Boats in production, missiles in development |
| -688 Ange- | Nuclear-powered attack submarines to destroy enemy shipping, subs. | 9,592.1 | 456,200 | 40 thru '82 | Newport News; General Dynamics | In production |
| -7 | Guided-missile frigate; anti-sub, anti-aircraft, attack and defense. | 13,874.3 | 147,500 | 71 thru '82 | Bath; Todd | In production |
| l | Patrol Combatant Missile (hydrofoil boat) | 391.7 | 65.2 | 6 | Boeing | In production |
| 1 ms | Main battle tank. Army. | 10,384.9 | 3,136 | 3,312 | Chrysler | Near production |
| 723 | Infantry or Cavalry fighting vehicle (IV or CFV) | 180.9 | 353 | (Unknown) | FMC Corp., Chrysler | Advanced development |
| per- d | Cannon-launched, laser-guided projectile; 10-12 mile range. Army and Navy. | 1,219.8[1] | About $1,000 per round | 100,000 (Army only) | Martin Marietta | Advanced development |
| ire | Missile for AH-64; may be laser-guided. | 804.8 | 10 | 28,000 | Rockwell | In development |
| ot M-D) | Surface-to-air missile for field air defense. | 6,234.0[2] | 49,800[2] | 125 batteries[2] | Martin Marietta, Raytheon | In engineering development |
| | Advanced ICBM to replace Minuteman. | (Unknown) | (Unknown) | 1,000 | Martin Marietta | In development |
| CM | Ground-launched, surface-to-surface cruise missile. | 1,527.2 | (Unknown) | (Unknown) | General Dynamics | In development |
| M | Air-launched, air-to-ground | 4,184.0 | 697 | 6,000(?) | Boeing | Advanced development |
| M | Sea-launched; strategic potential | 2,576.0 | 2,220 | 1,160 | Gen. Dynam., McDonnell Douglas | In development |

) Navy program estimated total cost is $713.8 million additional. (2) Batteries consist of 4 firing sections and fire control centers
n; the $49,800 unit cost is for firing sections and missiles only.
ome comparable costs: Total moon program, $30 billion, Bay Area Rapid Transit system, $1.6 billion; World Trade Center, land
uisition and construction, $1 billion; one manned moon shot, $400 million; February 1976 welfare payments to families with
endent children, $813 million; 1974-75 current elementary and secondary school expenditure in California, $3.6 billion; fiscal 1975
state budge outlays, $6.8 billion.

---

## Armed Services Senior Enlisted Adviser

he U.S. Army, Navy and Air Force in 1966-67 each cre-
a new position of senior enlisted adviser whose primary
is to represent the point of view of his services' enlisted
and women on matters of welfare, morale, and any
blems concerning enlisted personnel. The senior adviser
have direct access to the military chief of his branch of
ice and policy-making bodies.

The senior enlisted adviser for each Dept. is:
    **Army**-Sgt. Major of the Army William G. Bainbridge.
    **Navy**-Master Chief Petty Officer of the Navy Robert J. Walker.
    **Air Force**-Chief Master Sgt. of the AF R. D. Gaylor.
    **Marines**-Sgt. Major of the Marine Corps John. A Masaro.

# ASSOCIATIONS AND SOCIETIES

Source: World Almanac questionnaire

Arranged according to key words in titles. Founding year of organization in parentheses; last figure after ZIP code indicates membe

**Aaron Burr Assn.** (1946), TremonT, Inca Rd., Linden, VA 22642; 600.

**Abortion Federation, Natl.** (1977), 110 E. 59th St., Suite 1019, N.Y., NY 10022; 350.

**Abortion Rights Action League, Natl.** (1969), 825 15th St. NW, Wash., DC 20005; 30,000.

**Accountants, Amer. Institute of Certified Public** (1887), 1211 Ave. of the Americas, N.Y., N.Y. 10036; 136,000.

**Accountants, Natl. Assn. of** (1919), 919 Third Ave., N.Y., NY 10022; 86,000.

**Accountants, Natl. Society of Public** (1945), 1717 Pennsylvania Ave., NW, Wash., DC 20006; 16,000.

**Acoustical Society of America** (1929), 335 E. 45 St., N.Y., NY 10017; 5,300.

**Actors' Equity Assn.** (1913), 1500 Broadway, N.Y., NY 10036; 21,477.

**Actors' Fund of America** (1882), 1501 Broadway, N.Y., NY 10036; 4,179.

**Actuaries, Society of** (1949), 208 S. La Salle St., Chicago, Il. 60604; 6,125.

**Acupuncture Foundation of America** (1972), Box 1424, Nantucket, MA 02554.

**Adirondack Mountain Club** (1922), 172 Ridge St., Glens Falls, NY 12801; 9,300.

**Administrative Management Society** (1919), Maryland Rd., Willow Grove, PA 19090; 12,000.

**Adult Education Assn. of the U.S.A.** (1951), 810 18th St. NW, Wash., DC 20006; 5,000.

**Advertisers, Assn. of Natl.** (1910), 155 E. 44th St., N.Y., NY 10017; 425 cos.

**Advertising Agencies, Amer. Assn. of** (1917), 200 Park Ave., N.Y, NY 10017; 450 agencies.

**Aeronautic Assn., Natl.** (1922), 821 15th St. NW, Wash., DC 20005; 165,000.

**Aeronautics and Astronautics, Amer. Institute of** (1932), 1290 Ave. of the Americas, N.Y., NY 10019; 29,000.

**Aerospace Industries Assn. of America** (1919), 1725 De Sales St. NW, Wash., DC 20036; 61 cos.

**Aerospace Medical Assn.** (1929), Washington Natl. Airport, Wash., DC 20001; 3,500.

**Afro-American Life and History, Assn. for the Study of** (1915), 1401 14th St. NW, Wash., DC 20005; 2,500.

**Aging Assn., Amer.** (1970), Univ. of Nebraska Medical Center, 42d & Dewey Ave., Omaha, NE 68105; 500.

**Agricultural Chemicals Assn., Natl.** (1933), 1155 15th St. NW, Wash., DC 20005; 125 cos.

**Agricultural Economics Assn., Amer.** (1910), Univ. of Kentucky, Lexington, KY 40506; 7,200.

**Agricultural Engineers, Amer. Society of** (1907), 2950 Niles Rd., St. Joseph, MI 49085; 9,343.

**Agricultural History Society** (1919) ESCS, U.S. Dept. of Agriculture, Wash., DC 20250; 1,400.

**Agronomy, Amer. Society of** (1907), 677 S. Segoe Rd., Madison, WI 53711; 8,500.

**Ahepa, Order of** (1922), 1422 K St. NW, Wash., DC 20005; 26,000.

**Air, Citizens for Clean** (1965), 32 Broad St., N.Y., NY 10004; 2,000.

**Aircraft Assn., Experimental** (1953), 11311 W. Forest Home Ave., Franklin, WI 53132; 60,000.

**Aircraft Owners and Pilots Assn.** (1939), 7315 Wisconsin Ave., Bethesda, MD 20014; 205,000.

**Air Force Aid Society** (1942), 1117 N. 19th St., Arlington, VA 22209; 24,000.

**Air Force Assn.** (1946), 1750 Pennsylvania Ave. NW, Wash., DC 20006; 155,000.

**Air Force Sergeants Assn.** (1961), 4235 28th Ave., Marlow Heights, MD 20031; 107,202.

**Air Line Employees Assn., Intl.** (1952), 5600 S. Central Ave., Chicago, IL 60638; 10,000.

**Air Line Pilots Assn.** (1931), 1625 Massachusetts Ave. NW, Wash., DC 20036; 32,000.

**Air Pollution Control Assn.** (1907), P.O. Box 2861, Pittsburgh, PA 15230; 6,000.

**Airport Operators Council Intl.** (1948), 1700 K St. NW, Wash., DC 20006; 163.

**Air Transport Assn., Intl.** (1945), P.O. Box 550, Intl. Aviation Sq., Montreal, Quebec, Canada H3A 2R4; 107 airlines.

**Air Transport Assn. of America** (1936), 1709 New York Ave. NW, Wash., DC 20006; 26 airlines.

**Albert Schweitzer Fellowship** (1939), 866 UN Plaza, N.Y., NY 10017.

**Albert Schweitzer Friendship House** (1966), R.D. 1; Box 7,

Hurlburt Rd., Great Barrington, MA 01230; 5,000.

**Alcohol Problems, Amer. Council on** (1964), 119 Cc tion Ave. NE, Wash., DC 20002.

**Alcoholics Anonymous** (1935), 468 Park Ave. So., N. 10017; 1,000,000.

**Alcoholism, Natl. Council on** (1944), 733 Third Ave. NY 10017; 220 affiliates.

**Allergy, Amer. Academy of** (1943), 611 E. Wells St., M kee, WI 53202; 2,600.

**Alpine Club, Amer.** (1902), 113 E. 90th St., N.Y., NY 1,200.

**Altrusa Intl.** (1917), 332 S. Michigan Ave., Chicago, IL 19,800.

**Aluminum Assn.** (1933), 750 Third Ave., N.Y., NY 100 companies.

**American Federation of Labor & Congress of Ind Organizations (AFL-CIO)** (1955, by merging **American F ation of Labor** estab. 1881 and **Congress of Industrial nizations** estab. 1935), 815 16th St. NW, Wash., DC 13,500,000.

**Amer. Field Service** (1914), 313 E. 43d St., N.Y., NY 90,000.

**Amer. Indian Affairs, Assn. on** (1923), 432 Park Ave N.Y., NY, 10016; 50,000.

**American Legion, The** (1919), 700 N. Pennsylvania S1 anapolis, IN 46206; 2,713,962. **American Legion Au** (1919), 777 N. Meridian St., Indianapolis, IN 46204; 942,69

**Amer. States, Organization of** (1948), General Secre Wash., DC 20006; 26 countries.

**Amer. Veterans of World War II, Korea & Vi (AMVETS),** (1947), 1710 Rhode Island Ave. NW, Was 20036; 200,000. **AMVETS Auxiliary** (1946), Saco Rd., C chard Beach, ME 04064; 60,000.

**Amputation Foundation, Natl.** (1925), 12-45 150 Whitestone, NY 11357; 2,500.

**Animal Ecologist Society** (1977), P.O. Box 160371, mento, CA 95816; 50.

**Animal Protection Institute of America** (1968), 58 Land Park Dr., Sacramento, CA 95822; 100,000.

**Animal Welfare Institute** (1951), 1200 29th St. NW, DC 20007; 4,500.

**Animals, Amer. Society for Prevention of Cure (ASPCA)** (1866), 441 E. 92d St., N.Y., NY 10028; 3,000.

**Animals, Friends of** (1957), 11 W. 60th St., N.Y., NY 100,000.

**Animals, The Fund for** (1967), 140 W. 57th St., N. 10019; 100,000.

**Anthropological Assn., Amer.** (1902), 1703 New Harr Ave. NW, Wash., DC 20009; 10,000.

**Antiquarian Society, Amer.** (1812), 185 Salisbury St chester, MA 01609; 328.

**Anti-Vivisection Society, Amer.** (1883), 1903 Chestr Philadelphia, PA 19103; 12,500.

**Appalachian Mountain Club** (1876), 5 Joy St., Bosto 02108; 23,000.

**Appalachian Trial Conference** (1925), Box 236, H Ferry, WV 25425; 10,000.

**Appraisers, Amer. Society of** (1936), 11800 Sunrise Dr., Intl. Center, Reston, VA 22091; 5,017.

**Arbitration Assn., Amer.** (1926), 140 W. 51st St., N. 10020; 400.

**Arboriculture, Intl. Society of** (1924), P.O. Box 71, 5 L Sq., Urbana, IL 61801; 3,500.

**Archaeological Institute of America** (1879), 260 W. I way, N.Y., NY 10013; 7,500.

**Archaeology, Institute of Nautical** (1973), Drawer AL lege Station, TX 77840; 404.

**Archers Assn., Professional** (1961), P.O. Box 7609, F 48507; 300.

**Archery Assn. of the U.S., Natl.** (1879), 1951 Geralds Lancaster, PA 17601; 5,000.

**Architects, Amer. Institute of** (1857), 1735 New Yor NW, Wash., DC 20006; 28,500.

**Architectural Historians, Society of** (1940), 1700 \ St., Phila., PA 19103; 4,300.

**Archivists, Society of Amer.** (1936), P.O. Box 819 Library, Chicago, IL 60680; 3,534.

**Armed Forces Communications and Electronics** (1946), 5205 Leesburg Pike, Falls Church, VA 22041; 16,0(

**Army and Navy Union U.S.A.** (1886), 1391 Main St. more, OH 44250; 5,700.

**Army, Assn. of the United States** (1950), 1529 18th S Wash., DC 20036; 108,500.

**Art, Natl. Assn. of Schools of** (1944), 11250 Roger Bacon r., #5, Reston, VA 22090; 80 institutions.

**Arthritis Foundation** (1948), 475 Riverside Dr., N.Y., NY 0027; 73 chapters.

**Artists of America, Allied** (1914), 1083 Fifth Ave., N.Y., NY 0028; 350.

**Arts, Amer. Federation of** (1909), 41 E. 65th St., N.Y., NY 0021; 1,800.

**Arts, Associated Councils of the** (1969), 570 Seventh Ave., .Y., NY 10018; 2,000.

**Arts, Natl. Endowment for the** (1965), 2401 E. St. NW, 'ash., DC 20506.

**Arts and Letters, Amer. Academy and Institute of** (1898), 33 W. 155th St., N.Y., NY 10032; 238.

**Arts & Psychology, Assn. for the** (1976), P.O. Box 160371, acramento, CA 95816.

**Arts & Sciences, Amer. Academy of** (1780), 165 Allandale t., Jamaica Plain Sta., Boston, MA 02130; 2,500.

**Assistance League, Natl.** (1935), 5627 Fernwood Ave., Holwood, CA 90028; 11,346.

**Associated Press** (1848), 50 Rockefeller Plaza, N.Y., NY 0020; 1,265 newspapers & 3,400 broadcast stations.

**Astrologers, Amer. Federation of** (1938), P.O. Box 22040, empe, AZ 85282; 4,200.

**Astronautical Society, Amer.** (1953), 6060 Duke St., Alexndria, VA 22304; 700.

**Astronomical Society, Amer.** (1899), 211 FitzRandolph Rd., rinceton, NJ 08540; 3,500.

**Atheist Assn.** (1925), 3024 5th Ave., San Diego, CA 92112; 00.

**Atheists, Amer.** (1963), 2210 Hancock Dr., Austin, TX 78756; 0,000 families.

**Athletic Associations, Natl. Federation of State High** chool (1920), Federation Pl., Elgin, IL 60120; 61 assns.

**Athletic Conference, Eastern College** (1938), 1311 Craigille Beach Rd., Centerville, MA 02632; 212 schools.

**Athletic Union of the U.S., Amateur** (1888), 3400 W. 86th t., Indianapolis, IN 46268; 370,000.

**Attorneys General, Natl. Assn. of** (1907), P.O. Box 11910, ron Works Pike, Lexington, KY 40578; 55.

**Auctioneers Assn., Natl.** (1949), 135 Lakewood Dr., Lincoln, JE 68510; 5,200.

**Audubon Society, Natl.** (1905), 950 Third Ave., N.Y., NY 0022; 350,000.

**Authors and Composers, Amer. Guild of** (1931), 40 W. 7th St., N.Y., NY 10019; 3,500.

**Authors League of America** (1912), 234 W. 44th St., N.Y., JY 10036; 7,200.

**Automobile Assn., Amer.** (1902), 8111 Gatehouse Rd., Falls Church, VA 22042; 18.6 million.

**Automobile Club of America, Antique** (1935), 501 W. Govrnor Rd., Hershey, PA 17033; 40,000.

**Automobile Club, Natl.** (1924), 65 Battery St., San Francisco, CA 94111; 521,422.

**Automobile Dealers Assn., Natl.** (1917), 8400 Westpark Dr., McLean, VA 22101; 20,885.

**Automobile License Plate Collectors' Assn.** (1954), P.O. Box 399, Brattleboro, VT 05301; 1,111.

**Automotive Booster Clubs** (1921), 605 E. Algonquin Rd., Arlington Heights, IL 60005; 3,000.

**Automotive Organization Team** (1939), P.O. Box 1742, Midand, MI 48640; 2,700.

**Aviation Historical Society, Amer.** (1956), 3614 Pendleton St., Santa Ana, CA 92704; 4,076.

**Backpackers' Assn., Intl.** (1973), P.O. Box 85, Lincoln Cener, ME 04458; 6,021.

**Badminton Assn., U.S.** (1938), P.O. Box 237, Swartz Creek, MI 48473; 1,200.

**Ballplayers of America, Assn. of Professional** (1924), 337 E. San Antonio Dr., Suite 203, Long Beach, CA 90807; 10,000.

**Banker Assn., Intl.** (1968), 422 Washington Bldg., Wash., DC 20005; 1,500..

**Bankers Assn., Amer.** (1875), 1120 Connecticut Ave. NW, Wash., DC 20036; 13,700 banks.

**Bankers Assn. of America, Independent** (1930), 1168 S. Main St., Sauk Centre, MN 56378; 7,383 banks.

**Banks, Natl. Assn. of Mutual Savings** (1920), 200 Park Ave., N.Y., NY 10017; 467 banks.

**Bar Assn., Amer.** (1878), 1155 E. 60th St., Chicago, IL 60637; 226,000.

**Bar Assn., Federal** (1920), 1815 H St. NW, Wash., DC 20006; 15,400.

**Barber Shop Quartet Singing in America, Society for the Preservation & Encouragement of** (1938), 6315 Third Ave., Kenosha, WI 53141; 38,000.

**Baseball Congress, Amer. Amateur** (1935), 212 Plaza Bldg., 2855 W. Market St., P.O. Box 5332, Akron, OH 44313.

**Baseball Congress of America, Natl.** (1930), 338 S. Sycamore, Wichita, KS 67213; 6,750.

**Baseball Players of America, Assn. of Professional** (1924), 530 E. Wardlow Rd., Long Beach, CA 90807; 8,000.

**Basketball Assn., Natl.** (1946), 645 5th Ave., N.Y., NY 10022; 22 teams.

**Baton Twirling Assn. of America & Abroad, Intl.** (1967), Box 234, Waldwick, NJ 07463; 1,800.

**Battleship Assn., Amer.** (1963), P.O. Box 11247, San Diego, CA 92111; 1,200.

**Beer Can Collectors of America** (1970), 747 Merus Ct., St. Louis, MO 63026; 12,000.

**Beta Sigma Phi** (1931), 1800 W. 91st Pl., Kansas City, MO 64114; 241,570.

**Bible Society, Amer.** (1816), 1865 Broadway, N.Y., NY 10023; 450,000.

**Biblical Literature, Society of** (1880), Union Theological Seminary, 3401 Brook Rd., Richmond, VA 23227; 4,200.

**Bibliographical Society of America** (1904), P.O. Box 397, Grand Central Sta., N.Y., NY 10017; 1,625.

**Bicycle Manufacturers Assn.** (1965), 1101 15th St. NW, Wash., DC 20005; 6.

**Bide-A-Wee Home Assn.** (1903), 410 E. 38th St., N.Y., NY 10016; 8,500.

**Big Brothers/Big Sisters of America** (1977), 220 Suburban Station Bldg., Phila., PA 19103; 370 affiliates.

**Biological Chemists, Amer. Society of** (1906), 9650 Rockville Pike, Bethesda, MD 20014; 4,100.

**Biological Sciences, Amer. Institute of** (1947), 1401 Wilson Blvd., Arlington, VA 22209; 10,500.

**Blind, Amer. Foundation for the** (1921), 15 W. 16th St., N.Y., NY 10011.

**Blind, Natl. Federation of the** (1940), 1346 Connecticut Ave. NW, Suite 212, DuPont Circle Bldg., Wash., DC 20036; 50,000.

**Blind & Visually Handicapped, Natl. Accreditation Council for Agencies Serving the** (1967), 79 Madison Ave., N.Y., NY 10016; 64 agencies and schools.

**Blindness, Natl. Society for Prevention of** (1908), 79 Madison Ave., N.Y., NY 10016.

**Blindness, Research to Prevent** (1960), 598 Madison Ave., N.Y., NY 10022; 2,100.

**Blizzard Club, January 12th, 1888,** (1940), c/o Historian, 4827 Hillside Ave., Lincoln, NE 68506; 87.

**Blood Banks, Amer. Assn. of** (1947), 1828 L St. NW, Wash., DC 20036; 7,300.

**Blue Cross Assn.** (1948), 840 N. Lake Shore Dr., Chicago, IL 60611; 74 plans.

**Blue Shield Plans, Natl. Assn. of** (1946), 211 E. Chicago Ave., Chicago, IL 60611; 70 plans.

**Blueberry Council, No. Amer.** (1966), P.O. Box 166, Marmora, NJ 08223; 386 organizations.

**B'nai B'rith Intl.** (1843), 1640 Rhode Island Ave. NW, Wash., DC 20036; 500,000.

**Boat Owners Assn. of the U.S.** (1966), 880 S. Pickett St., Alexandria, VA 22304; 60,000.

**Book Manufacturers' Institute** (1933), 904 Ethan Allen Hwy., Ridgefield, CT 06877; 100 companies.

**Booksellers Assn., Amer.** (1900), 122 E. 42d St., N.Y., NY 10017; 5,300.

**Botanical Gardens & Arboreta, Amer. Assn. of** (1940), Dept. of Biology, 124 Botany Bldg., Univ. of Cal., Los Angeles, CA 90024; 646.

**Bottle Clubs, Federation of Historical** (1969), 5001 Queen Ave. N., Minneapolis, MN 55430; 130 clubs.

**Bowling Congress, Amer.** (1895), 5301 S. 76th St., Greendale, WI 53129; 4.3 million.

**Bowling Congress, Women's Internatl.** (1916), 503 S. 76th St., Greendale, WI 53129; 3,695,073.

**Boys' Brigades of America, United** (1893), P.O. Box 8406, Baltimore, MD 21234.

**Boys' Clubs of America** (1906), 771 First Ave., N.Y., NY 10017; 1,000,000+.

**Boy Scouts of America** (1910), North Brunswick, NJ 08902; 4,718,138.

**Brand Names Foundation** (1943), 477 Madison Ave., N.Y., NY 10022; 400.

**Brewers Assn., U.S.** (1862), 1750 K St., Wash., DC 20006.

**Brick Institute of America** (1934), 1750 Old Meadow Rd., McLean, VA 22101; 100 cos.

**Bridge, Tunnel and Turnpike Assn., Intl.** (1932), 1225 Connecticut Ave. NW, Suite 307, Wash., DC 20036; 200.

**Brith Sholom** (1905), 1235 Chestnut St., Phila., PA 19107; 20,000.

**Broadcasters, Natl. Assn. of** (1922), 1771 N St. NW, Wash., DC 20036; 5,000.

**Burroughs Bibliophiles, The** (1960), 454 Elaine Dr., Pittsburgh, PA 15236; 475.

**Bus Assn., Amer.** (1926), 1025 Connecticut Ave. NW, Wash., DC 20036; 600.

**Business Bureaus, Council of Better** (1970), 1150 17th St. NW, Wash., DC 20036; 650.

**Business Clubs, Natl. Assn. of Amer.** (1922), 3315 No. Main

St., High Point, NC 27260; 5,650.

**Business Communication Assn., Amer.** (1935), 317-B David Kinley Hall, Univ. of Illinois, Urbana, IL 61801; 1,400.

**Business Education Assn., Natl.** (1946), 1906 Association Dr., Reston, VA 22091; 23,000.

**Business Law Assn., Amer.** (1924), Georgia State Univ., University Plaza, Atlanta, GA 30303; 700.

**Business Press Editors, Amer. Society of** (1964), 2735 Central St., Evanston, IL 60201; 300.

**Business Professional Advertising Assn.** (1922), 205 E. 42d St., N.Y., NY 10017; 3,000.

**Button Society, Natl.** (1938), 353 Stockton St., Hightstown, NJ 08520; 1,931.

**Byron Society, The** (1971 England, 1973 in U.S.), 259 New Jersey Ave., Collingwood, NJ 08108; 275.

**CARE (Cooperative For American Relief Everywhere)** (1945), 660 First Ave., N.Y., NY 10016; 25 agencies.

**CORE (Congress of Racial Equality)** (1942), 200 W. 135th St., N.Y., NY 10030.

**Cable Television Assn., Natl.** (1952), 918 16th St. NW, Wash., DC 20006; 1,450.

**Campers & Hikers Assn., Natl.** (1949), 7172 Transit Rd., Buffalo, NY 14221; 55,000 families.

**Camp Fire Girls** (1910), 4601 Madison Ave., Kansas City, MO 64112; 750,000.

**Camping Assn., Amer.** (1910), Bradford Woods, Martinsville, IN 46151; 6,500.

**Cancer Council, United** (1963), 1803 N. Meridian St., Indianapolis, IN 46202; serves 30,000,000 people.

**Cancer Society, Amer.** (1913), 777 Third Ave., N.Y., NY 10017.

**Candy Brokers Assn. of America** (1956), P.O. Box 28325, Wash., DC 20005; 300.

**Canners Assn., Natl.** (1907), 1133 20th St. NW, Wash., DC 20036; 600 companies.

**Canoe Assn., U.S.** (1968), 606 Ross St., Middletown, OH 45042; 2,000.

**Captive European Nations, Assembly of** (1954), 29 W. 57th St., N.Y., NY 10019; 9 national committees.

**Carillonneurs in North America, Guild of** (1936), 3718 Settle Rd., Cincinnati, OH 45227; 345.

**Carnegie Hero Fund Commission** (1904), 1932 Oliver Bldg., Pittsburgh, PA 15222.

**Cartoonists Society, Natl.** (1946), 9 Ebony Ct., Brooklyn, NY 11229; 450.

**Cat Fanciers' Assn.** (1919), P.O. Box 430, 11 Globe Ct., Red Bank, NJ 07701; 550 clubs.

**Catch Society of America, The** (1968), Dept. of English, SUNY—Fredonia; Fredonia, NY 14063; 300.

**Catholic Bishops, Natl. Conference of/U.S. Catholic Conference** (1966), 1312 Massachusetts Ave. NW, Wash., DC 20015; 300.

**Catholic Charities, Natl. Conference of** (1910), 1346 Connecticut Ave. NW, Wash., DC 20036; 3,000.

**Catholic Church Extension Society of the U.S.A.** (1905), 1307 S. Wabash Ave., Chicago, IL 60605; 70,000.

**Catholic Daughters of America** (1903), 10 W. 71st St., N.Y., NY 10023; 180,000.

**Catholic Educational Assn., Natl.** (1904), One Dupont Circle NW, Wash., DC 20036; 14,000.

**Catholic Press Assn.** (1911), 119 N. Park Ave., Rockville Centre, NY 11570; 400.

**Catholic Rural Life Conference, Natl.** (1923), 3801 Grand Ave., Des Moines, IA 50312; 4,000.

**Catholic War Veterans of the U.S.A.** (1935), 2 Massachusetts Ave. NW, Wash., DC 20001; 75,000.

**Cemetery Assn., Amer.** (1887), 250 E. Broad St., Columbus, OH 43215; 1,100.

**Ceramic Society, Amer.** (1899), 65 Ceramic Dr., Columbus, OH 43214; 6,800.

**Cerebral Palsy Assns., United** (1949), 66 E. 34th St., N.Y., NY 10016; 276 affiliates.

**Chamber of Commerce of the U.S.A.** (1912), 1615 H St. NW, Wash., DC 20062; 67,127.

**Chamber Music Players, Amateur** (1948), P.O. Box 547, Vienna, VA 22180; 5,000.

**Chartered Life Underwriters, Amer. Society of** (1928), 270 Bryn Mawr Ave., Bryn Mawr, PA 19010; 20,100.

**Chartered Property & Casualty Underwriters, Society of** (1944), Providence & Sugartown Rds., Malvern, PA 19355; 8,800.

**Checks Anonymous, New Life Group of** (1963), Nebraska Penal and Correctional Complex, 14th and Pioneers Bldg., P.O. Box 81248, Lincoln, NE 68501; 50.

**Chemical Engineers, Amer. Institute of** (1908), 345 E. 47th St., N.Y., NY 10017; 39,000.

**Chemical Society, Amer.** (1876), 1155 16th St. NW, Wash., DC 20036; 111,000.

**Chemists, Amer. Institute of** (1923), 7315 Wisconsin Ave.,

Wash., DC 20014; 5,400.

**Chemists and Chemical Engineers, Assn. of Consulting** (1928), 50 E. 41st St., N.Y. NY 10017; 125.

**Chess Federation, U.S.** (1939), 186 Rte. 9W, New Windsor NY 12550; 50,000.

**Chief Warrant and Warrant Officers' Assn., USCG** (1929) 955 L'Enfant Plaza No. SW, Wash., DC 20024; 3,092.

**Childhood Education Intl., Assn. for** (1892), 3615 Wisconsin Ave. NW, Wash., DC 20016; 20,000.

**Child Study Assn. of America/Wel-Met** (1888), 50 Madison Ave., N.Y., NY 10010; 300.

**Child Welfare League of America** (1920), 67 Irving Pl., N.Y NY 10003; 387 agencies.

**Childbirth Without Pain League** (1964), P.O. Box 233, Dana Point, CA 92629; 200.

**Children of the Amer. Revolution, Natl. Society** (1895) 1776 D St. NW, Wash., DC 20006; 12,500.

**Children's Aid Society** (1853), 105 E. 22d St., N.Y., NY 10010.

**Children's Book Council** (1945), 67 Irving Pl., N.Y., NY 10003; 59 publishing houses.

**Chinese Women's Assn.** (1932), 13541 Emperor Dr., Santa Ana, CA 92705; 520.

**Chiropractic Assn., Amer.** (1964), 2200 Grand Ave., Des Moines, IA 50312; 12,141.

**Chiropractors Assn., Intl.** (1926), 741 Brady St., Davenport IA 52808; 6,100.

**Christian Culture Society** (1974), P.O. Box 325, Kokomo, IN 46901; 12,695.

**Christian Endeavor, Intl. Society of** (1881), 1221 E. Broad St., P.O. Box 1110, Columbus, OH 43216; 1,000,000.

**Christian Laity Counseling Board** (1970), 5901 Plainfield Dr., Charlotte, NC 28215; 5,001,000.

**Christians and Jews, Natl. Conference of** (1928), 43 W. 57th St., N.Y., NY 10019; 200,000.

**Churches, U.S. Conference for the World Council of** (1957), 475 Riverside Dr., N.Y., NY 10027.

**Church Women United in the U.S.A.** (1941), 475 Riverside Dr., N.Y., NY 10027; 2,000 units.

**Cincinnati, Society of the** (1783), 2118 Massachusetts Ave NW, Wash., DC 20008; 2,750.

**Circulation Managers Assn., Intl.** (1889), 11600 Sunrise Valley Dr., Reston, VA 22070; 1,325.

**Circulations, Audit Bureau of** (1914), 123 N. Wacker Dr Chicago, IL 60606; 3,965.

**Circus Fans Assn. of America** (1926), P.O. Box 69, 4 Center Dr., Camp Hill, PA 17011; 2,500.

**Circus Historical Society** (1939), 1325 Commercial St Atchison, KS 66002; 1,300.

**Cities, Natl. League of** (1924), 1620 Eye St. NW, Wash., DC 20006; 15,000 municipalities.

**Citizens Band Radio Patrol** (1976), 2000 P St. NW, Floor 615, Wash., DC 20036; 30,000.

**City Management Assn., Intl.** (1914), 1140 Connecticut Ave NW, Wash., DC 20036; 7,343.

**Civil Engineers, Amer. Society of** (1852), 345 E. 47th St N.Y., NY 10017; 74,000.

**Civil Liberties Union, Amer.** (1920), 22 E. 40th St., N.Y., NY 10016; 275,000.

**Civil Service League, Natl.** (1881), 917 15th St. NW, Wash DC 20005; 1,100.

**Civitan Internatl.** (1920), P.O. Box 2102, Birmingham, AL 35201; 50,000.

**Classical League, Amer.** (1919), Miami Univ., Oxford, OH 45056; 2,900.

**Clergy, Academy of Parish** (1968), P.O. Box 86, Princeton NJ 08540; 1,000.

**Clinical Pastoral Education, Assn. for** (1967), 475 Riverside Dr., N.Y., NY 10027 4,000.

**Clinical Pathologists, Amer. Society of** (1922), 2100 W Harrison St., Chicago, IL 60612; 20,395.

**Clowns of America** (1968), 2715 E. Fayette St., Baltimore MD 21224; 5,200.

**Coal Assn., Natl.** (1917), 1130 17th St. NW, Wash., DC 20036; 200 companies.

**Cocoa Exchange, New York** (1925), 127 John St., N.Y., NY 10038; 183.

**Collectors Assn., Amer.** (1939), 4040 W. 70th St., Minneapolis, MN 55435; 2,650.

**College Athletic Assn., Natl. Junior** (1938), 12 E. 2d, Box 1586, Hutchinson, KS 67501; 995.

**College Board, The** (1900), 888 Seventh Ave., N.Y., NY 10019; 2,412 institutions.

**College Physical Education Assn. for Men, Natl.** (1897), 108 Cooke Hall, Univ. of Minnesota, Minneapolis, MN 55455 1,200.

**College Placement Council** (1956), 65 E. Elizabeth Ave. Bethlehem, PA 18018; 1,700.

**Colleges, Assn. of Amer.** (1915), 1818 R St. NW, Wash., DC 20009; 600 institutions.

**Collegiate Athletic Assn., Natl.** (1906), P.O. Box 1906, Shawnee Mission, KS 66222; 831.

**Collegiate Schools of Business, Amer. Assembly of** (1916), 760 Office Parkway, St. Louis, MO 63141; 650 schools.

**Colonial Dames of America** (1890), 421 E. 61 St., N.Y., NY 10021; 2,000.

**Colonial Dames XVII Century, Natl. Society** (1915), 1300 New Hampshire Ave. NW, Wash., DC 20036; 9,000.

**Colonial Wars, General Society of** (1892), 840 Woodbine Ave., Glendale, OH 45246; 4,200.

**Colored Women's Clubs, Natl. Assn. of** (1896), 5808 16th St. NW, Wash., DC 20011; 50,000.

**Commercial Law League of America** (1895), 222 W. Adams St., Chicago, IL 60606; 6,200.

**Commercial Travelers of America, Order of United** (1888), 632 N. Park St., Columbus, OH 43215; 244,000.

**Common Cause** (1970), 2030 M St. NW, Wash., DC 20036; 253,000.

**Composers/USA, Natl. Assn. of** (1975), P.O. Box 49652, Barrington Sta., Los Angeles, CA 90049; 450.

**Composers, Authors & Publishers, Amer. Society of (ASCAP)** (1914), One Lincoln Plaza, N.Y., NY 10023; 20,000.

**Computing Machinery, Assn. for** (1947), 1133 Ave. of the Americas, N.Y., NY 10036; 36,500.

**Concrete Institute, Amer.** (1905), 22400 W. Seven Mile Rd., Detroit, MI 48219; 13,000.

**Conference Board, The** (1916), 845 Third Ave., N.Y., NY 10022; 4,000.

**Consairway** (1942), P.O. Box 1642, La Mesa, CA 92041; 500.

**Conscientious Objectors, Central Committee for** (1948), 2016 Walnut St., Phila., PA 19103.

**Conservation Engineers, Assn. of** (1961), Missouri Dept. of Conservation, P.O. Box 180, Jefferson City, MO 65101; 161.

**Conservation Foundation** (1948), 1717 Massachusetts Ave. NW, Wash., DC 20036.

**Construction Industry Manufacturers Assn.** (1903), 111 E. Wisconsin Ave., Milwaukee, WI 53202; 200 companies.

**Construction Specifications Institute** (1948), 1150 17th St. NW, Wash., DC 20036; 11,500.

**Consumer Credit Assn., Intl.** (1912), 375 Jackson Ave., St. Louis, MO 63130; 45,025.

**Consumer Federation of America** (1968), 1012 14th St. NW, Wash., DC 20005; 225 organizations.

**Consumer Interests, Amer. Council on** (1953), 162 Stanley Hall, Univ. of Missouri, Columbia, MO 65201; 3,240.

**Consumer Protection Council, Natl. Student** (1971), Villanova Univ., Bartley Hall, Villanova, PA 19085; 500.

**Consumers League, Natl.** (1899), 1785 Massachusetts Ave. NW, Wash., DC 20036; 20,000.

**Consumers Union of the U.S.** (1936), 256 Washington St., Mount Vernon, NY 10550; 1.8 million.

**Consumers Unions, Intl. Organization of** (1960), 9 Emmastraat, The Hague, Netherlands; 105 organizations.

**Contract Bridge League, Amer.** (1937), 2200 Democrat Rd., Memphis, TN 38116; 198,000.

**Cooperative League of the U.S.A.** (1916), 1828 L St. NW, Wash., DC 20036; 140 co-ops.

**Correctional Assn., Amer.** (1870), 4321 Hartwick Rd., Suite L-208, College Park, MD 20740; 11,000.

**Cosmopolitan Intl.** (1919), 7341 W. 80th St., Overland Park, KS 66210; 3,900.

**Cotton Council of America, Natl.** (1938), 1918 North Parkway, Memphis, TN 38112.

**Country Music Assn.** (1958), 7 Music Circle No., Nashville, TN 37203; 4,665.

**Creative Children and Adults, Natl. Assn. for** (1974), 8080 Springvalley Dr., Cincinnati, OH 45236; 500.

**Credit Management, Nat. Assn. of** (1896), 475 Park Ave. So., N.Y., NY 10016; 41,185.

**Credit Union Natl. Assn.** (1934), 1617 Sherman Ave., Madison, WI 53701; 51 state leagues.

**Crime and Delinquency, Natl. Council on** (1907), 411 Hackensack Ave., Hackensack, NJ 07601; 60,000.

**Criminology, Amer. Assn. of** (1953), P.O. Box 1115, North Marshfield, MA 02059; 2,500.

**Crop Science Society of America** (1955), 677 S. Segoe Rd., Madison, WI 53711; 4,035.

**Cryptogram Assn., Amer.** (1932) 9504 Forest Rd., Bethesda, MD 20014; 1,000.

**Cyprus, Sovereign Order of** (1192, 1964 in U.S.), 853 Seventh Ave., N.Y., NY 10019; 426.

**Dairy Council, Natl.** (1915), 6300 No. River Rd., Rosemont, IL 60018; 700.

**Dairy and Food Industries Supply Assn.** (1918), 5530 Wisconsin Ave., Wash., DC 20015; 400 organizations.

**Dairy Science Assn., Amer.** (1906), 113 N. Neil St., Champaign, IL 61820; 2,761.

**Dairylea Cooperative** (1919), One Blue Hill Plaza, Pearl River, NY 10965; 6,220.

**Data Processing Management Assn.** (1951), 505 Busse Highway, Park Ridge, IL 60068; 22,185.

**Daughters of the American Revolution, Natl. Society,** (1890), 1776 D St. NW, Wash., DC 20006; 206,264.

**Daughters of the Confederacy, United** (1894), 328 North Blvd., Richmond, VA 23220; 35,000.

**Daughters of 1812, Natl. Society, U.S.** (1892), 1461 Rhode Island Ave. NW, Wash., DC 20005; 4,350.

**Daughters of Union Veterans of the Civil War** (1885), 503 S. Walnut St., Springfield, IL 62704; 15,000.

**Deaf, Alexander Graham Bell Assn. for the** (1890), 3417 Volta Pl. NW, Wash., DC 20007; 7,000.

**Deaf, Conference of Executives of Amer. Schools for the** (1868), 5034 Wisconsin Ave. NW, Wash., DC 20016; 300.

**Deaf, Convention of Amer. Instructors of the** (1850), 5034 Wisconsin Ave. NW, Wash., DC 20016; 3,500.

**Deaf, Natl. Assn. of the** (1880), 814 Thayer Ave., Silver Spring, MD 20910; 17,000.

**Defense Preparedness Assn., Amer.** (1919), 740 15th St. NW, Wash., DC 20005; 32,000.

**Delta Kappa Gamma Society Intl.** (1929), P.O. Box 1589, Austin, TX 78767; 144,000.

**Deltiologists of America** (1960), 3709 Gradyville Rd., Newton Square, PA 19073; 1,850.

**Democratic Natl. Committee** (1848), 1625 Massachusetts Ave. NW, Wash., DC 20036; 360.

**DeMolay, Order of** (1919), 201 E. Armour Blvd., Kansas City, MO 64111; 2,700,000.

**Dental Assn., Amer.** (1859), 211 E. Chicago Ave., Chicago, IL 60611; 131,000.

**Dental Assn., Natl.** (1913), P.O. Box 197, Charlottesville, VA 22902; 1,500.

**Descendants of the Colonial Clergy, Society of the** (1933), 255 Madison St., Dedham, MA 02026; 1,100.

**Descendants of the Signers of the Declaration of Independence** (1907), 1300 Locust St., Phila., PA 19107; 1,050.

**Desert Protective Council** (1954), Box 4294, Palm Springs, CA 92262; 500.

**Diabetes Assn., Amer.** (1940), 600 Fifth Ave., N.Y., NY 10020; 3,000.

**Dialect Society, Amer.** (1889), c/o Dept. of English, Univ. of Western Ontario, London, Ontario N6A 3K7; 750.

**Dietetic Assn., Amer.** (1917), 430 N. Michigan Ave., Chicago, IL 60611; 35,000.

**Ding-A-Ling Club, Natl.** (1971), Box 2188, Glen Ellyn, IL 60137; 2,000.

**Direct Mail/Marketing Assn.** (1917), 6 E. 43d St., N.Y., NY 10017; 2,900 companies.

**Directors Guild of America** (1936), 7950 Sunset Blvd., Los Angeles, CA 90046; 4,737.

**Disabled Amer. Veterans** (1920), 3725 Alexandria Pike, Cold Spring, KY 41076; 562,000.

**Disabled Officers Assn.** (1919), 1612 K St. NW, Wash., DC 20006; 5,800.

**Divorce Reform, U.S.** (1961), P.O. Box 243, Kenwood, CA 95452; 6,000.

**Dowsers, Amer. Society of** (1961), Danville, VT 05328.

**Dracula Society, Count** (1962), 334 W. 54th St., Los Angeles, CA 90037; 250.

**Dragon, Imperial Order of the** (1900), P.O. Box 1707, San Francisco, CA 94101.

**Drug, Chemical and Allied Trades Assn.** (1891), 42-40 Bell Blvd., Suite 204, Bayside, NY 11361; 500 cos.

**Druggists, Natl. Assn. of Retail.** (1898), One E. Wacker Dr., Chicago, IL 60601; 32,000.

**Drum Corps Internatl.** (1971), 719 S. Main St., Lombard, IL 60148; 26.

**Ducks Unlimited** (1937), P.O. Box 66300, Chicago, IL 60666; 241,600.

**Dulcimer Assn., Southern Appalachian** (1974), Rte. 15, Box 1012, Birmingham, AL 35224; 150.

**Duodecimal Society of America** (1944), 5631 Trinette Ave., Garden Grove, CA 92645; 125.

**Dutch Settlers Soc. of Albany** (1924), 1088 Cortland St., Albany, NY 12203; 325.

**Eagles, Fraternal Order of** (1898), 2401 W. Wisconsin Ave., Milwaukee, WI 53233; 850,000.

**Earth, Friends of the** (1969), 124 Spear St., San Francisco, CA 94105; 20,000.

**Easter Seal Society for Crippled Children and Adults, Natl.** (1919), 2023 W. Ogden Ave., Chicago, IL 60612.

**Eastern Star, Order of the** (1876), 1618 New Hampshire Ave. NW, Wash., DC 20009; 2,500,000.

**Ecological Society of America** (1915), c/o Dr. E. J. Kormondy, Evergreen State College, Olympia, WA 98505; 5,700.

**Economic Assn., Amer.** (1885), 1313 21st Ave. So., Nashville, TN 37212; 23,600.

**Economic Development, Committee for** (1942), 477 Madison Ave., N.Y., NY 10022; 200.

**Edison Electric Institute** (1933), 90 Park Ave., N.Y., NY 10016.

**Educational Exchange, Council on Intl.** (1947), 777 United Nations Plaza, N.Y., NY 10017; 172 organizations.

**Education, Amer. Council on** (1918), One Dupont Circle NW, Wash., DC 20036; 1,400 schools.

**Education, Council for Advancement & Support of** (1974), One Dupont Circle NW, Wash., DC 20036; 1,800 schools.

**Education, Council for Basic** (1956), 725 15th St. NW, Wash., DC 20005; 5,100.

**Education, Natl. Committee for Citizens** (1973), 410 Wilde Lake Village Green, Columbia, MD 21044; 800.

**Education, Natl. Society for the Study of** (1902), 5835 Kimbark Ave., Chicago, IL 60637; 4,500.

**Education, Society for the Advancement of** (1939), 1860 Broadway, N.Y., NY 10023; 3,000.

**Education Assn., Natl.** (1857), 1201 16th St. NW, Wash., DC 20036; 1,700,000.

**Education Society, Comparative and Intl.** (1956), Grad. School of Education, Univ. of California at Los Angeles, Los Angeles, CA 90024; 2,450.

**Education of Young Children, Natl. Assn. for the** (1926), 1834 Connecticut Ave. NW, Wash., DC 20009; 28,000.

**Education Broadcasters, Natl. Assn. of** (1925), 1346 Connecticut Ave. NW, Wash., DC 20036; 3,500.

**Educational Research Assn., Amer.** (1915), 1126 16th St. NW, Wash., DC 20036; 13,000.

**Educators for World Peace, Intl. Assn. of** (1969), P.O. Box 3282, Blue Springs Sta., Huntsville, AL 35810; 12,500.

**Electric Railroaders Assn.** (1934), 4 W. 40th St., N.Y., NY 10018; 4,500.

**Electrical and Electronics Engineers, Institute of** (1884), 345 E. 47th St., N.Y., NY 10017; 175,000.

**Electrical Manufacturers Assn., Natl.** (1926), 2101 L St. NW, Wash., DC 20024; 550 companies.

**Electrochemical Society** (1902), P.O. Box 2071, Princeton, NJ 08540; 4,500.

**Electronic Industries Assn.** (1924), 2001 Eye St. NW, Wash., DC 20006; 280 firms.

**Electronic Service Dealers Assn., Natl.** (1963), 1715 Expo La., Indianapolis, IN 46224; 2,252.

**Electronics Technicians, Intl. Society of Certified** (1970), 1715 Expo Lane, Indianapolis, IN 46224.

**Electroplaters' Society, Amer.** (1909), 1201 Louisiana Ave., Winter Park, FL 32789; 8,000.

**Elks of the U.S.A., Benevolent and Protective Order of** (1868), 2750 N. Lake View Ave., Chicago, IL 60614; 1,611,139.

**Energy, Intl. Assn. for Hydrogen** (1974), P.O. Box 24866, Coral Gables, FL 33124; 1,100.

**Engine and Boat Manufacturers, Natl. Assn. of** (1904), 666 Third Ave., N.Y., NY 10017; 335 firms.

**Engineering, Natl. Academy of** (1964), 2101 Constitution Ave. NW, Wash., DC 20418; 685.

**Engineering Education, Amer. Society for** (1893), One Dupont Circle, Wash., DC 20036; 12,000.

**Engineering Society, Illuminating** (1906), 345 E. 47th St., N.Y., NY 10017; 9,500.

**Engineering Technicians, Amer. Society of Certified** (1964), 2029 K St. NW, Wash., DC 20006; 7,300.

**Engineering Trustees, United** (1904), 345 E. 47th St., N.Y., NY 10017.

**Engineers, Amer. Society of Lubrication** (1944), 838 Busse Hwy., Park Ridge, IL 60068; 3,200.

**Engineers, Natl. Society of Professional** (1934), 2029 K St. NW, Wash., DC 20006; 76,000.

**Engineers Joint Council** (1949), 345 E 47th St., N.Y., NY 10017; 500,000.

**Engineers, Assn. of Energy** (1977), 464 Armour Circle NE, Atlanta, GA 30324; 800.

**English Assn., College** (1939), English Dept., Oakland Univ., Rochester, MI 48063; 3,000.

**English-Speaking Union of the U.S.** (1920), 16 E. 69th St., N.Y., NY 10021; 33,500.

**Entomological Society of America** (1889), 4603 Calvert Rd., College Park, MD 20740; 7,068.

**Environmental Defense Fund** (1967), 475 Park Ave. So., N.Y., NY 10016; 45,000.

**Epilepsy Foundation of America** (1968), 1828 L St. NW, Wash., DC 20036; 161 chapters.

**Epsilon Pi Tau** (1929), Technology Bldg., Bowling Green State Univ., Bowling Green, OH 43403; 25,000.

**Esperanto Assn., Internatl. Catholic** (1910), Limbiate, Italy; U.S. rep., 7605 Winona Ln., Sebastopol, CA 95472; 1,600.

**Esperanto League for North America** (1952), P.O. Box 508, Burlingame, CA 94010; 750.

**Euthanasia Foundation, Amer.** (1972), 95 N. Birch Rd., Ft. Lauderdale, FL 33304; 20,000.

**Evangelicals, Natl. Assn. of** (1942), Box 28, Wheaton, IL 60187; 3,500,000.

**Evangelism Crusades, Intl.** (1959), 7970 Woodman Ave., Van Nuys, CA 91402; 100,000.

**Exchange Club, Natl.** (1911), 3050 Central Ave., Toledo, OH 43606; 50,000.

**Experiment in Internatl. Living** (1932), Kipling Rd., Brattleboro, VT 05301; 60,000.

**Eye-Bank Assn. of America** (1961), 3195 Maplewood Ave., Winston-Salem, NC 27103; 64.

**Eye-Bank for Sight Restoration** (1945), 3195 Maplewood Ave., Winston-Salem, NC 27103.

**Fairs & Expositions, Intl. Assn. of** (1919), 1010 Dixie Hwy., Chicago Heights, IL 60411; 180.

**Family Physicians, Amer. Academy of** (1947), 1740 W. 92d St., Kansas City, MO 64114; 37,000.

**Family Service Assn. of America** (1911), 44 E. 23d St., N.Y., NY 10010, 300 agencies.

**Farm Bureau Federation, Amer.** (1919), 225 Touhy Ave., Park Ridge, IL 60068; 2,900,000 families.

**Farmer Cooperatives, Natl. Council of** (1929), 1129 20th St. NW, Wash., DC 20036; 152 co-ops.

**Farmers of America, Future** (1928), 5630 Mt. Vernon Hwy., Alexandria, VA 22309; 509,735.

**Farmers Educational and Co-Operative Union of America** (1902), 12025 E. 45th Ave., Denver, CO 80201; 250,000 families.

**Fat Americans, Natl. Assn. to Aid (NAAFA)** (1969), P.O. Box 745, Westbury, NY 11590; 1,000.

**Federal Employees, Natl. Federation of** (1917), 1016 16th St. NW, Wash., DC 20036; 85,000.

**Federal Employees Veterans Assn.** (1954), P.O. Box 183, Merion Sta., PA 19066; 1,242.

**Federally Employed Women** (1968), 1249 Natl. Press Bldg., Wash., DC 20045; 6,000.

**Feline Society, Amer.** (1936), 41 Union Sq. W., N.Y., NY 10003; 425.

**Feminists for Life** (1972), P.O. Box 12726, Tucson, AZ 85732.

**Fencers League of America, Amateur** (1891), 601 Curtis St., Albany, CA 94706; 6,000.

**Fiddlers Assn., Amer. Old Time** (1965), 6141 Morrill Ave., Lincoln, NE 68507; 5,000.

**Film Library Assn., Educational** (1943), 17 W. 60 St., N.Y., NY 10023; 1,800.

**Financial Analysts Federation** (1947), 219 E. 42d St., N.Y., NY 10017; 14,700.

**Financial Executives Institute** (1931), 633 Third Ave., N.Y., NY 10017; 9,600.

**Fire Chiefs, Intl. Assn. of** (1873), 1329 18th St. NW, Wash., DC 20036; 7,332.

**Fire Fighters, Intl. Assn. of** (1918), 1750 New York Ave. NW, Wash., DC 20006; 175,000.

**Fire Marshals Assn. of No. America** (1906), 470 Atlantic Ave., Boston, MA 02210; 1,095.

**Fire Protection Assn., Natl.** (1896), 470 Atlantic Ave., Boston MA 02210; 32,000.

**Fire Protection Engineers, Society of** (1950), 60 Battery March St., Boston, MA 02110; 2,515.

**Fish Assn., Intl. Game** (1939), 3000 E. Las Olas Blvd., Ft. Lauderdale, FL 33316; 15,000.

**Fisheries Society, Amer.** (1870), 5410 Grosvenor Ln., Bethesda, MD 20014; 7,088.

**Fishing Institute, Sport** (1949), 608 13th St. NW, Wash., DC 20005; 24,500.

**Fishing Tackle Manufacturers Assn., Amer.** (1933), 20 N. Wacker Dr., Chicago, IL 60606; 400 companies.

**Flag Day Assn., Amer.** (1888), P.O. Box 1121, Denver, CO 80201.

**Flag Institute, The Amer.** (1976), 205 E. 78th St., N.Y., NY 10021; 350.

**Florists, Society of Amer.** (1884), 901 N. Washington St., Alexandria, VA 22314; 6,100.

**Fluid Power Society** (1957), 432 E. Kilbourn Ave., Milwaukee, WI 53202; 3,500.

**Folklore Society, Amer.** (1888), Center for Folklore & Ethnomusicology — SWB 306, Univ. of Texas, Austin, TX 78712; 2,800.

**Food Processing Machinery and Supplies Assn.** (1885), 7758 Wisconsin Ave., Wash., DC 20014; 405.

**Football Assn., U.S. Touch and Flag** (1976), 2705 Normandy Dr., Youngstown, OH 44511; 12,000.

**Footwear Industries Assn., Amer.** (1869), 1611 N. Kent St., Arlington, VA 22209; 400.

**Foreign Policy Assn.** (1918), 345 E. 46th St., N.Y., NY 10017.

**Foreign Press Assn.** (1918), 866 Second Ave., N.Y., NY 10017; 350.

**Foreign Relations, Council on** (1921), 58 E. 68th St., N.Y., NY 10021; 1,800.

**Foreign Student Affairs, Natl. Assn. for** (1948), 1860 19th

St. NW, Wash., DC 20009; 2,500.

**Foreign Study, Amer. Institute for** (1964), 102 Greenwich Ave., Greenwich, CT 06830; 110,000.

**Foreign Trade Council, Natl.** (1914), 10 Rockefeller Center, N.Y., NY 10020; 600 companies.

**Forensic Sciences, Amer. Academy of** (1948), 11400 Rockville Pike, Rockville, MD 20852.

**Forest Institute, Amer.** (1941), 1619 Massachusetts Ave. NW, Wash., DC 20036; 200 cos., 33,000 farmers.

**Forest Products Assn., Natl.** (1902), 1619 Massachusetts Ave. NW, Wash., DC 20036; 27.

**Forest Products Research Society** (1947), 2801 Marshall Ct., Madison, WI 53705; 4,500.

**Foresters, Society of Amer.** (1900), 5400 Grosvenor La., Wash., DC 20014; 22,000.

**Forestry Assn., Amer.** (1875), 1319 18th St. NW, Wash., DC 20036; 80,000.

**Fortean Organization, Intl.** (1967), 7317 Baltimore Ave., College Park, MD 20740; 800.

**Foundrymen's Society, Amer.** (1896), Golf & Wolf Rds., Des Plaines, IL 60016; 16,200.

**4-H Clubs** (1901-1905), Extension Service, U.S. Dept of Agriculture, Wash., DC 20250; 5.8 million.

**Franklin D. Roosevelt Philatelic Society** (1963), P.O. Box 150, Clinton Corners, NY 12514; 282.

**Freedom, Young Americans for** (1960), Woodland Rd., Sterling, VA 22170; 55,000.

**French Institute** (1911), 22 E. 60th St., N.Y., NY 10022; 24,000.

**Friends Service Committee, Amer.** (1917), 1501 Cherry St., Phila., PA 19102; 120,000.

**Frisbee Assn.** (1967), P.O. Box 970, San Gabriel, CA 91776; 107,000.

**Funeral and Memorial Services, Continental Assn.** (1963), 1828 L St. NW, Wash., DC 20036; 150 societies.

**GASP (Group Against Smokers' Pollution)** (1971), P.O. Box 632, College Park, MD 20740; 10,000.

**Gamblers Anonymous** (1957), 2705A W. 8th St., Los Angeles, CA 90005; 6,000.

**Garden Club of America** (1913), 598 Madison Ave., N.Y., NY 10022; 13,000.

**Garden Clubs, Natl. Council of State** (1929), 4401 Magnolia Ave., St. Louis, MO 63110; 365,000.

**Garden Clubs of America, Men's** (1932), 5560 Merle Hay Rd., Des Moines, IA 50323; 9,800.

**Gas Appliance Manufacturers Assn.** (1935), 1901 N. Ft. Myer Dr., Arlington, VA 22209; 275 companies.

**Gas Assn., Amer.** (1918), 1515 Wilson Blvd., Arlington, VA 22209; 5,000.

**Gay Task Force, Natl.** (1973), 80 Fifth Ave., N.Y., NY 10011; 8,000.

**Genealogical Society, Natl.** (1903), 1921 Sunderland Pl. NW, Wash., DC 20036; 4000.

**General Contractors of America, Associated** (1918), 1957 E St. NW, Wash., DC 20006; 8.300.

**Genetic Assn., Amer.** (1903), 1028 Connecticut Ave. NW, Wash., DC 20036; 1,483.

**Geographers, Assn. of Amer.** (1904), 1710 16th St. NW, Wash., DC 20009; 6,000.

**Geographic Education, Natl. Council for** (1914), 115 N. Marion St., Oak Park, IL 60301; 5,000.

**Geographic Society, Natl.** (1888), 1145 17th St. NW, Wash., DC 20036, 9,700,000.

**Geographical Society, Amer.** (1852), Broadway at 156th St., N.Y., NY 10032; 2,500.

**Geolinguistics, Amer. Society of** (1965), Bronx Community College, 120 E. 184th St., Bronx, NY 10453; 75.

**Geological Institute, Amer.** (1948), 5205 Leesburg Pike, Falls Church, VA 22041; 18 societies.

**Geological Society of America** (1888), 3300 Penrose Pl., Boulder, CO 80302; 12,569.

**Geologists, Assn. of Engineering** (1957), 8310 San Fernando Way, Dallas, TX 75218; 2,435.

**Geophysical Union, Amer.** (1919), 1909 K St. NW, Wash., DC 20036; 11,000.

**Geophysicists, Society of Exploration** (1930), 3707 E. 51st St., Tulsa, OK 74135; 11,000.

**George Smith Patton Jr. Historical Society** (1970), 11307 Vela Dr., San Diego, CA 92126.

**Geriatrics Society, Amer.** (1942), 10 Columbus Circle, N.Y., NY 10019; 6,000.

**Gideons Intl.** (1899), 2900 Lebanon Rd., Nashville, TN 37214; 59,000.

**Gifted Children, Amer. Assn. for** (1946), 15 Gramercy Park, N.Y., NY 10003.

**Gifted Children, Natl. Assn. for** (1954), 217 Gregory Dr., Hot Springs, AR 71901; 2,500.

**Girl Scouts of the U.S.A.** (1912), 830 Third Ave., N.Y., NY 10022; 3,160,000.

**Girls Clubs of America** (1945), 133 E. 62d St., N.Y., NY 10021; 200,000.

**Gladiolus Council, No. Amer.** (1945), 31 South Dr., E. Brunswick, NJ 08816; 1,400.

**Goat Assn., American Dairy** (1904), P.O. Box 865, Spindale, NC 28160; 8,500.

**Gold Star Mothers, Amer.** (1928), 2128 Leroy Pl. NW, Wash., DC 20008; 15,000.

**Golf Association, U.S.** (1894), Golf House, Far Hills, NJ 07931; 4,886 clubs.

**Golf Assn., Natl. Amputee** (1949), 24 Lakeview Terr., Watchung, NJ 07060; 500.

**Goose Island Bird & Girl Watching Society** (1960), 301 Arthur Ave., Park Ridge, IL 60068; 907.

**Gospel Music Assn.** (1964), 38 Music Sq. W., P.O. Box 23201, Nashville, TN 37203; 2,000.

**Governmental Research Assn.** (1938), P.O. Box 387, Ocean Gate, NJ 08740; 425.

**Graduate Schools in the U.S., Council of** (1961), One Dupont Circle NW, Wash., DC 20036; 361 institutions.

**Grandmother Clubs of America, Natl. Federation of** (1938), 203 N. Wabash Ave., Chicago, IL 60601; 15,500.

**Grange, Natl.** (1867), 1616 H St. NW, Wash., DC 20006; 600,000.

**Graphic Artists, Society of Amer.** (1915), 1083 Fifth Ave., N.Y., NY 10028; 200.

**Graphic Arts, Amer. Institute of** (1914), 1059 Third Ave., N.Y., NY 10021; 1,750.

**Gray Panthers** (1972), 3700 Chestnut, Phila., PA 19104.

**Greek-Amer. War Veterans in America, Natl. Legion** (1938), 739 W. 186th St., N.Y., NY 10033; 51.

**Grocers, Natl. Assn. of Retail** (1893), 11800 Sunrise Valley Dr., Reston, VA 22091; 38,000.

**Grocery Manufacturers of America** (1908), Dodge Center, Georgetown, Wash., DC 20003; 140 firms.

**Guide Dog Foundation for the Blind** (1946), 109-19 72d Ave., Forest Hills, NY 11375; 25,000.

**Gyro Intl.** (1912), 1096 Mentor Ave., Painesville, OH 44077; 6,000.

**HIAS (Hebrew Immigrant Aid Society)** (1884), 200 Park Ave. S, N.Y., NY 10003; 15,000.

**Hadassah, the Women's Zionist Organization of America** (1912), 50 W. 58th St., N.Y., NY 10019; 360,000.

**Handball Assn., U.S.** (1951), 4101 Dempster St., Skokie, IL 60076; 15,000.

**Handicapped, Federation of the** (1935), 211 W. 14th St., N.Y., NY 10011; 1,000.

**Handicapped, Natl. Assn. of the Physically** (1958), 6473 Granville, Detroit, MI 48228; 1,300.

**Hang Gliding Assn., U.S.** (1971), P.O. Box 66306, 11312 1/2 Venice Blvd., Los Angeles, CA 90066; 16,350.

**Health Council, Natl.** (1920), 1740 Broadway, N.Y., NY 10019; 83 agencies.

**Health Insurance Assn. of America** (1956), 1750 K St. NW, Wash., DC 20006; 320 companies.

**Health Insurance Institute** (1956), 1850 K St. NW, Wash., DC; 325 companies.

**Health, Physical Education & Recreation, Amer. Alliance for** (1885), 1201 16th St. NW, Wash., DC 20036; 45,000.

**Hearing Aid Society, Natl.** (1951), 20361 Middlebelt Rd., Livonia, MI 48152; 3,600.

**Hearing and Speech Action, Natl. Assn. for** (1919), 814 Thayer Ave., Silver Spring, MD 20910; 12,000.

**Heart Assn., Amer.** (1924), 7320 Greenville Ave., Dallas TX 75231; 115,000.

**Hearts, Mended** (1955), 721 Huntington Ave., Boston, MA 02115; 9,000.

**Heating, Refrigerating & Air Conditioning Engineers, Amer. Society of** (1894), 345 E. 47th St., N.Y., NY 10017; 32,000.

**Helicopter Assn. of America** (1948), 1156 15th St. NW, Wash., DC 20005; 576 companies.

**Helicopter Society, Amer.** (1943), 1325 18th St. NW, Wash., DC 20036; 3,200.

**High Twelve Internatl.** (1921), 3681 Lindell Blvd., St. Louis, MO 63108; 20,000.

**Hemispheric Affairs, Council on** (1975), 1735 New Hampshire Ave. NW, Suite 504, Wash., DC 20009.

**Historians, Organization of Amer.** (1907), 112 N. Bryan St., Bloomington, IN 47401; 11,832.

**Historians, The Society of Amer.** (1939), 610 Fayerweather Hall, Columbia Univ., N.Y., NY 10027; 200.

**Historic Preservation, Natl. Trust for** (1949), 740-748 Jackson Pl. NW, Wash., DC 20006; 116,000.

**Historical Assn., Amer.** (1884), 400 A St. SE, Wash., DC 20003; 15,000.

**Hockey Assn. of the U.S., Amateur** (1937), 10 Lake Circle, Colorado Springs, CO 80906; 11,000 teams.

**Hockey League, Natl.** (1917), 920 Sun Life Bldg., Montreal,

Quebec, Canada H3B 2W2; 18 clubs.

**Holiday Institute of Yonkers** (1969), Box 281, Yonkers, NY 10710.

**Holy Cross of Jerusalem, Order of** (1965), 853 Seventh Ave., N.Y., NY 10019; 1,073.

**Home Builders, Natl. Assn. of** (1942), 15th & M Sts. NW, Wash., DC 20005; 85,000 firms.

**Home Economics Assn., Amer.** (1909), 2010 Massachusetts Ave. NW, Wash., DC 20036; 53,000.

**Home Improvement Council, Natl.** (1956), 11 E. 44th St., N.Y., NY 10017; 1,750.

**Homemakers of America, Future** (1945), 2010 Massachusetts Ave. NW, Wash., DC 20036; 450,000.

**Homemakers Council, Natl. Extension** (1936), 95 Perry St., Harrisonburg, VA 22801; 546,505.

**Horatio Alger Society** (1961), 4907 Allison Dr., Lansing, MI 48910; 200.

**Horse Protection Assn., Amer.** (1966), 1312 18th St. NW, Wash., DC 20036; 10,000.

**Horse Show Assn. of America Ltd., Natl.** (1883), 527 Madison Ave., N.Y., NY 10022.

**Horse Shows Assn., Amer.** (1917), 598 Madison Ave., N.Y., NY 10022; 20,000.

**Hospital Assn., Amer.** (1898), 840 N. Lake Shore Dr., Chicago, IL 60611; 27,300.

**Hospital Public Relations, Amer. Society for** (1965), 840 N. Lake Shore Dr., Chicago, IL 60611; 1,069.

**Hotel & Motel Assn., Amer.** (1910), 888 Seventh Ave., N.Y., NY 10019; 7,000 hotels & motels.

**Hot Rod Assn., Natl.** (1951), 10639 Riverside Dr., N. Hollywood, CA 91602; 38,000.

**Humane Legislation, Committee for** (1967), 11 W. 60th St., N.Y., NY 10023; 100,000.

**Humane Society of the U.S.** (1954), 2100 L St. NW, Wash., DC 20037; 50,000.

**Humanics Foundation, Amer.** (1948), 912 Baltimore Ave., Kansas City, MO 64105; 5,000.

**Humanities, Natl. Endowment for the** (1965), 806 15th St. NW, Wash., DC 20506.

**Human Rights and Social Justice, Americans for** (1977), 109 Bent Bridge Rd., Greenville, SC 29611; 1,489.

**Iceland Veterans** (1948), 2101 Walnut St., Phila., PA 19103; 1,600.

**Identification, Intl. Assn. for** (1915), P.O. Box 139, Utica, NY 13503; 2,500.

**Illustrators, Society of** (1901), 128 E. 63d St., N.Y., NY 10021; 700.

**Immigration and Nationality Lawyers, Assn. of** (1946), 50 Court St., Brooklyn, NY 11201; 650.

**Indian Rights Assn.** (1882), 1505 Race St., Phila., PA 19102; 2,500.

**Indoor Sports Club** (1930), 1145 Highland St., Napoleon, OH 43545; 2,300.

**Industrial Democracy, League for** (1905), 275 Seventh Ave., N.Y., NY 10001; 15,000.

**Industrial Engineers, Amer. Institute of** (1948), 25 Technology Park, Norcross, GA 30092; 30,000.

**Industrial Health Foundation** (1935), 5231 Centre Ave., Pittsburgh, PA 15232; 140 companies.

**Industrial Management Society** (1937), 570 Northwest Hwy., Des Plaines, IL 60016; 1,000.

**Infant Death Syndrome (SIDS) Foundation, Natl. Sudden** (1962), 310 S. Michigan Ave., Chicago, IL 60604; 52 chapters.

**Information, Freedom of, Center** (1958), P.O. Box 858, Columbia, MO 65201; 1,050.

**Information Industry Assn.** (1968), 4720 Montgomery Ln., Bethesda, MD 20014; 108.

**Insurance Assn., Amer.** (1866), 85 John St., N.Y., NY 10038; 145 companies.

**Intelligence Officers, Assn. of Former** (1975), 6723 Whittier Ave., Suite 303A, McLean, VA 22101; 2,500.

**Intercollegiate Athletics, Natl. Assn. of** (1940), 1221 Baltimore Ave., Kansas City, MO 64105; 513 schools.

**Interfraternity Conference, Natl.** (1909), P.O. Box 40368, Indianapolis, IN 46240; 47 fraternities.

**Interior Designers, Amer. Society of** (1975), 730 Fifth Ave., N.Y., NY 10019; 16,550.

**Intl. Education, Institute of** (1919), 809 United Nations Plaza, N.Y., NY 10017.

**Intl. Educational Exchange, Council on** (1947), 777 United Nations Plaza, N.Y., NY 10017; 182 organizations.

**Intl. Law, Amer. Society of** (1906), 2223 Massachusetts Ave. NW, Wash., DC 20008; 5,500.

**Investment Clubs, Natl. Assn. of** (1951), 1515 E. Eleven Mile Rd., Royal Oak, MI 48067; 5,900 clubs.

**Iron Castings Society** (1975), 20611 Center Ridge Rd., Rocky River, OH 44116; 240 firms.

**Iron and Steel Engineers, Assn. of** (1907), Three Gateway Center, Pittsburgh, PA 15222; 12,800.

**Iron and Steel Institute, Amer.** (1908), 1000 16th St. NW, Wash., DC 20036; 2,500.

**Italian Historical Society of America** (1949), 111 Columbia Heights, Bklyn., NY 11201; 2,300.

**Italy-America Chamber of Commerce** (1887), 350 Fifth Ave., N.Y., NY 10001; 950.

**Izaak Walton League of America** (1922), 1800 N. Kent St., Arlington, VA 22304; 50,000.

**Jamestowne Society** (1936), P.O. Box 7389, Richmond, VA 23221; 1,500.

**Japanese Amer. Citizens League** (1930), 1765 Sutter St., San Francisco, CA 94115; 30,000.

**Jaycees, U.S.** (1920), P.O. Box 7, 4 W. 21st St., Tulsa, OK 74102; 355,000.

**Jewish Appeal, United** (1939), 1290 Ave. of the Americas, N.Y., NY 10019.

**Jewish Center Workers, Assn. of** (1918), 15 E. 26th St., N.Y., NY 10010; 950.

**Jewish Committee, Amer.** (1906), 165 E. 56th St., N.Y., NY 10022; 40,000.

**Jewish Congress, Amer.** (1918), 15 E. 84th St., N.Y., NY 10028; 50,000.

**Jewish Federations and Welfare Funds, Council of** (1932), 575 Lexington Ave., N.Y., NY 10022; 205 agencies.

**Jewish Historical Society, Amer.** (1892), 2 Thornton Rd., Waltham, MA 02154; 3,200.

**Jewish War Veterans of the U.S.A.** (1896), 1712 New Hampshire Ave. NW, Wash., DC 20009; 73,000.

**Jewish Welfare Board, Natl.** (1917), 15 E. 26th St., N.Y., NY 10010; serves 1,000,000.

**Jewish Women, Natl. Council of** (1893), 15 E. 26th St., N.Y., NY 10010; 100,000.

**Job's Daughters, Internatl. Order of** (1921), 1820 Douglas Masonic Temple, Omaha, NE 68102; 78,000.

**Jockey Club** (1894), 300 Park Ave., N.Y., NY 10022.

**Jogging Assn., Natl.** (1968), 919 18th St. NW, Suite 830, Wash., DC 20006; 22,000.

**John Birch Society** (1958), 395 Concord Ave., Belmont, MA 02178; 60,000 to 100,000.

**Journalists and Authors, Amer. Society of** (1948), 123 W. 43d St., N.Y., NY 10036; 475.

**Journalists, Society of Professional; Sigma Delta Chi** (1909), 35 E. Wacker Dr., Chicago, IL 60601; 70,000.

**Judaism, Amer. Council for** (1943), 307 Fifth Ave., N.Y., NY 10016; 15,000.

**Judicature Society, Amer.** (1913), 200 W. Monroe, Chicago, IL 60606; 33,000.

**Juggler's Assn., Intl.** (1948), 211 Forest St., Arlington, MA 02174; 550.

**Junior Achievement** (1918), 550 Summer St., Stamford, CT 06901; 275,000.

**Junior Colleges, Amer. Assn. of Community and** (1921), One Dupont Circle NW, Wash., DC 20036; 1,485.

**Junior Leagues, Assn. of** (1921), 825 Third Ave., N.Y., NY 10022; 119,000.

**Kailtone Adventure Society** (1907), P.O. Box 233, Dayton, NV 89403; 106.

**Kennel Club, Amer.** (1884), 51 Madison Ave., N.Y., NY 10010; 400 clubs.

**Key Club Intl.** (1925), 101 E. Erie St., Chicago, IL 60611; 80,000.

**Kitefliers Assn., Intl.** (1948), 321 E. 48th St., N.Y., NY 10017; 38,000.

**Kiwanis Intl.** (1915), 101 E. Erie St., Chicago, IL 60611; 289,731.

**Knights of Columbus** (1882), One Columbus Plaza, New Haven, CT 06510; 1,265,888.

**Knights of Equity** (1895), 16 Southern Pkwy., Rochester, NY 14618; 1,500.

**Knights Templar U.S.A., Grand Encampment** (1816), 14 E. Jackson Blvd., Chicago, IL 60604; 360,000.

**Labor Reform, Natl. Council for** (1969), 406 S. Plymouth Ct., Chicago, IL 60605; 5,000.

**Lacrosse Foundation** (1959), Newton H. White Athletic Ctr., Homewood, Baltimore, MD 21218; 750.

**La Leche League Intl.** (1956), 9616 Minneapolis, Franklin Park, IL 60131; 150,000.

**Lambs, The** (1874), 131 W. 56th St., N.Y., NY 10019; 400.

**Landscape Architects, Amer. Society of** (1899), 1750 Old Meadow Rd., McLean, VA 22101; 4,500.

**Law Enforcement Officers Assn., Amer.** (1976), 4005 Plaza Towers, New Orleans, LA 70113; 55,000.

**Law Institute, Amer.** (1923), 4025 Chestnut St., Phila., PA 19104; 2,043.

**Law Libraries, Amer. Assn. of** (1906), 53 W. Jackson Blvd., Chicago, IL 60604; 2,460.

**Law and Social Policy, Center for** (1969), 1751 N St. NW,

Wash., DC 20036.

**Lawn Bowls Assn., Amer.** (1915), 1033 Cheryl Dr., Sun City, AZ 85351; 9,500.

**Learned Societies, Amer. Council of** (1919), 345 E. 46th St., N.Y., NY 10017; 42 Societies.

**Lefthanders, League of** (1975), P.O. Box 89, New Milford, NJ 07646; 300.

**Lefthanders Intl.** (1975), 3601 SW 29th St., Topeka, KS 66614; 3,000.

**Legal Secretaries, Natl. Assn. of** (1950), 3005 E. Skelly Dr., Tulsa, OK 74105; 23,000.

**Legion of Valor of the U.S.A.** (1890), 621 S. Taylor St., Arlington, VA 22204; 850.

**Leonard Wood Memorial for the Eradication of Leprosy** (1928), 2430 Pennsylvania Ave. NW, Wash., DC 20037.

**Leprosy Missions, Amer.** (1906), 1262 Broad St., Bloomfield, NJ 07003; 50,000 donor members.

**Leukemia Society of America** (1949), 211 E. 43d St., N.Y., NY 10017; 1,340 trustees.

**Lewis Carroll Society of N. America** (1974), 617 Rockford Rd., Silver Spring, MD 20902; 350.

**Liberty Lobby** (1955), 300 Independence Ave. SE, Wash., DC 20003; 25,000.

**Libraries Assn., Special** (1909), 235 Park Ave. So., N.Y., NY 10003; 10,500.

**Library Assn., Amer.** (1876), 50 E. Huron St., Chicago, IL 60611; 35,000.

**Library Assn., Medical** (1898), 919 N. Michigan Ave., Chicago, IL 60611; 4,800.

**Life Insurance, Amer. Council of** (1976), 1850 K St. NW, Wash., DC 20006; 444 companies.

**Life Insurance Marketing & Research Assn.** (1916), 170 Sigoumey St., Hartford, CT 06105; 546.

**Life Office Management Assn.** (1924), 100 Park Ave., N.Y., NY 10017; 500.

**Life Underwriters, Natl. Assn. of** (1890), 1922 F St. NW, Nash., DC 20006; 135,000.

**Lifespan** (1970), 4274 N. Woodward, Royal Oak, MI 48073; 15,000.

**Lighter-Than-Air Society** (1952), 1800 Triplett Blvd., Akron, OH 44306; 1,200.

**Lions Clubs, Intl. Assn.** (1917), 300 22d St., Oak Brook, IL 60570; 1,224,144.

**Literacy Volunteers of America** (1962), 6th Fl., 700 E. Water St., Syracuse, NY 13210; 20,000.

**Little League Baseball** (1939), P.O. Box 1127, Williamsport, PA 17701; 12,500 leagues.

**Little People of America** (1960), Box 126, Owatonna, MN 55060; 5,000.

**Log Rolling Assn., Intl.** (1926), 143 S. 4th St., Bayport, MN 55003; 200.

**Lone Indian Fellowship** (1926), 1010 Huron Ave., Sheboygan, WI 53081; 850.

**Lung Assn., Amer.** (1904), 1740 Broadway, N.Y., NY 10019.

**Lutheran Education Assn.** (1942), 7400 Augusta St., River Forest, IL 60305; 2,525.

**Lutheran World Federation of the Lutheran World Ministries, U.S.A. Natl.**, 360 Park Ave. S., N.Y., NY 10010.

**Macaroni Manufacturers Assn., Natl.** (1904), 19 S. Bothwell, Box 336, Palatine, IL 60067; 95 firms.

**Magazine Publishers Assn.** (1919), 575 Lexington Ave., N.Y., NY 10022; 156 companies.

**Magicians, Intl. Brotherhood of** (1926), 28 N. Main St., Kenton, OH 43326; 11,000.

**Magicians, Society of Amer.** (1902), 66 Marked Tree Rd., Needham, MA 02192; 5,500.

**Magicians Guild of America** (1944), 20 W. 40th St., N.Y., NY 10018; 86.

**Male Nurse Assn., Natl.** (1975), 2309 State St. W., Saginaw, MI 48602; 4,396.

**Mammalogists, Amer. Society of** (1919), c/o Museum, Oklahoma State Univ., Stillwater, OK 74074; 3,700.

**Management, Amer. Institute of** (1948), 125 E. 38th St., N.Y., NY 10016; 5,000.

**Management Assns., Amer.** (1923), 135 W. 50th St., N.Y., NY 10020; 58,500.

**Management Consultants, Institute of** (1968), 347 Madison Ave., N.Y., NY 10017; 775.

**Management Engineers, Assn. of Consulting** (1933), 347 Madison Ave., N.Y., NY 10017; 45 firms.

**Management Systems Information, Society for** (1969), 10 W. 31st St., Chicago, IL 60616; 686.

**Manufacturers, Natl. Assn. of** (1895), 1776 F St. NW, Wash., DC 20006; 13,000 companies.

**Manufacturers' Agents Natl. Assn.** (1947), 2021 Business Center Dr., P.O. Box 16878, Irvine, CA 92713; 5,000.

**Manufacturing Chemists Assn.** (1872), 1825 Connecticut Ave. NW, Wash., DC 20009; 200 companies.

**Manufacturing Engineers, Society of** (1932), 20501 Ford Rd., Dearborn, MI 48128; 44,000.

**Man Watchers** (1975), 2865 State St., San Diego, CA 92103; 4,000.

**March of Dimes, Natl. Foundation—**(1938), 1275 Mamaroneck Ave., White Plains, NY 10605; 1,600 chapters.

**Marijuana Laws, Natl. Organization for the Reform of (NORML)** (1970), 2717 M St. NW, Wash., DC 20037; 25,000

**Marine Corps League** (1923), 933 N. Kenmore St., Arlington, VA 22201; 15,000.

**Marine Surveyors, Natl. Assn. of** (1960), P.O. Box 55, Peck Slip Sta., N.Y., NY 10038; 315.

**Marine Technology Society** (1963), 1730 M St. NW, Wash., DC 20036; 4,000.

**Marine Underwriters, Amer. Institute of** (1898), 99 John St., N.Y., NY 10038; 296.

**Marketing Assn., Amer.** (1937), 222 S. Riverside Plaza, Chicago, IL 60606; 17,969.

**Masonic Relief Assn. of U.S. and Canada** (1885), P.O. Box 468, Sioux Falls, SD 57101.

**Masonic Service Assn. of the U.S.** (1919), 8120 Fenton St., Silver Spring, MD 20910; 43 Grand Lodges.

**Masons, Ancient and Accepted Scottish Rite, Southern Jurisdiction, Supreme Council** (1801), 1733 16th St. NW, Wash., DC 20009; 647,500.

**Masons, Supreme Council 33°, Ancient and Accepted Scottish Rite, Northern Masonic Jurisdiction** (1813), 33 Marret Rd., Lexington, MA 02173; 507,940.

**Masons, Royal Arch, General Grand Chapter** (1797), 1084 New Circle Rd. NE, Lexington, KY 40505; 469,729.

**Masons of the State of N.Y., Grand Lodge of Free & Accepted** (1781), 71 W. 23d St., N.Y., NY 10010; 220,000.

**Mathematical Assn. of America** (1915), 1225 Connecticut Ave. NW, Wash., DC 20036; 18,500.

**Mathematical Society, Amer.** (1888), 201 Charles St., Providence, RI 02904; 16,403.

**Mathematical Statistics, Institute of** (1937), 1367 Laurel, San Carlos, CA 94070; 3,000.

**Mathematics, Society for Industrial and Applied** (1952), 33 S. 17th St., Phila., PA 19103; 4,400.

**Mayflower Descendants, General Society of** (1897), P.O. Box 297, Plymouth, MA 02360; 18,075.

**Mayors, U.S. Conference of** (1933), 1620 Eye St. NW, Wash., DC 20006; 750 cities.

**Mechanical Engineers, Amer. Society of** (1880), 345 E. 47th St., N.Y., NY 10017; 70,000.

**Mechanics, Amer. Academy of** (1969), Engineering Science and Mechanics Dept., Virginia Polytechnic Institute and State Univ., Blacksburg, VA 24061; 750.

**Mechanics, Assn. of Chairmen of Departments of** (1969), Dept. of Theoretical and Applied Mechanics, Univ. of Ill. at Urbana-Champaign, Urbana, IL 61801; 96.

**Mechanics, Junior Order of United Amer.** (1853), 170 Railway Rd., Crafton, VA 23692; 3,000.

**Mediaeval Academy of America** (1925), 1430 Massachusetts Ave., Cambridge, MA 02138; 4,000.

**Medical Assn., Amer.** (1847), 535 N. Dearborn St., Chicago, IL 60610; 215,000.

**Medical Assn., Natl.** (1895), 1720 Massachusetts Ave. NW, Wash., DC 20036; 6,400.

**Medical Colleges, Assn. of Amer.** (1876), One Dupont Circle NW, Wash., DC 20036; 2,149.

**Medical Record Assn., Amer.** (1928), 875 N. Michigan Ave., Chicago, IL 60611; 20,500.

**Medical Technologists, Amer.** (1939), 710 Higgins Rd., Park Ridge, IL 60068; 13,600.

**Medical Technologists, Amer. College of** (1942), 5608 Lane, Raytown, MO 64133; 368.

**Medical Women's Assn., Amer.** (1915), 1740 Broadway, N.Y., NY 10019, 6,000.

**Memorabilia Americana** (1973), 1211 Ave. I, Brooklyn, NY 11230; 600.

**Men Voters of the U.S., League of** (1969), 88 Arbol, Oroville, CA 95965.

**Mensa, Amer.** (1964), 1701 W. 3d St., Brooklyn, NY 11223; 24,000.

**Mental Health, Natl. Assn. for** (1909), 1800 N. Kent St., Arlington, VA 22209; 1,000,000.

**Mental Health Program Directors, Natl. Assn. of State** (1963), 1001 3d St. SW, Wash., DC 20024, 54.

**Merchant Marine Library Assn., Amer.** (1921), One World Trade Center, Suite 2601, N.Y., NY 10048.

**Merchants Assn., Natl. Retail** (1911), 100 W. 31st St., N.Y., NY 10001; 35,000 stores.

**Metal Finishers, Natl. Assn. of** (1951), 111 E. Wacker Dr., Chicago, IL 60601; 960.

**Metallurgy Institute, Amer. Powder** (1959), P.O. Box 2054, Princeton, NJ 08540; 2,000.

**Metals, Amer. Society for** (1913), Metals Park, OH 44073; 40,000.

**Meteorological Society, Amer.** (1919), 45 Beacon St., Boston, MA 02108; 9,000.

**Metric Assn., U.S.** (1916), Sugarloaf Star Rte., Boulder, CO 80302; 3,500.

**Microbiology, Amer. Society for** (1899), 1913 Eye St. NW, Wash. DC 20006; 24,000.

**Micrographics Assn., Natl.** (1943), 8728 Colesville Rd., Silver Spring, MD 20910; 8,000.

**Mideast Educational and Training Services, America—**, formerly **Amer. Friends of the Middle East** (1951), 1717 Massachusetts Ave. NW, Wash., DC 20036; 500.

**Military Chaplains Assn. of the U.S.A.** (1925), 7758 Wisconsin Ave. NW, Wash., DC 20014; 2,500.

**Military Engineers, Society of Amer.** (1920), 740 15th St. NW, Wash., DC 20005; 22,000.

**Military Order of the Loyal Legion of the U.S.A.** (1865), 1307 New Hampshire Ave. NW, Wash., DC 20036; 1,200.

**Military Order of the Purple Heart** (1782, by Gen. George Washington; reactivated Feb. 22, 1932, by President Herbert Hoover and Chief of Staff Douglas MacArthur), 1022 Wilson Blvd., Arlington, VA 22209; 15,000.

**Military Order of the World Wars** (1920), 1100 17th St. NW, Wash., DC 20036; 11,000.

**Military Surgeons of the U.S., Assn. of** (1891), 10605 Concord St., Kensington, MD 20795; 11,397.

**Mining, Metallurgical and Petroleum Engineers, Amer. Institute of** (1871), 345 E. 47th St., N.Y., NY 10017; 59,773.

**Mining and Metallurgical Society of America** (1910), 299 Park Ave., N.Y., NY 10017; 320.

**Ministerial Assn., Amer.** (1929), 446 Salem Ave., P.O. Box 1252, York, PA 17405; 18,179.

**Model Railroad Assn., Natl.** (1936), 7061 Twin Oaks Dr., Indianapolis, IN 46226; 30,157.

**Modern Language Assn. of America** (1883), 62 Fifth Ave., N.Y., NY 10011; 30,000.

**Modern Language Teachers Assns., Natl. Federation of** (1916), Dept. of Foreign Languages, Gannon Coll., Erie, PA 16501; 15 assns.

**Monopoly Assn., U.S.** (1963), 1866 City National Bank Bldg., Detroit, MI 48226; 450.

**Moose, Loyal Order of** (1888), Moosehart, IL 60539; 1,211,587.

**Mothers Committee, Amer.** (1935), Waldorf Astoria Hotel, 301 Park Ave., N.Y., NY 10022; 2,000.

**Mothers-in-Law Club Intl.** (1970), 739R Chestnut St., Cedarhurst, NY 11516; 5,000.

**Mothers of Twins Clubs, Natl. Organization of** (1960), 5402 Amberwood Ln., Rockville, MD 20853; 8,260.

**Motion Picture Arts & Sciences, Academy of** (1927), 8949 Wilshire Blvd., Beverly Hills, CA 90211; 4,000.

**Motion Picture Assn. of America** (1922), 522 Fifth Ave., N.Y., NY 10036.

**Motion Pictures, Natl. Board of Review of** (1909), 210 E. 68th St., N.Y., NY 10021; 150.

**Motion Picture & Television Engineers, Society of** (1916), 862 Scarsdale Ave., Scarsdale, NY 10583; 7,800.

**Motor Bus Owners, Natl. Assn. of** (1926), 1025 Connecticut Ave. NW, Wash., DC 20036; 450.

**Motor Car Club of America, Veteran** (1938), 15 Newton St., Brookline, MA 02146; 6,850.

**Motor Vehicle Administrators, Amer. Assn. of** (1933), 1201 Connecticut Ave. NW, Wash., DC 20036; 130.

**Motor Vehicle Manufacturers Assn.** (1913), 320 New Center Building, Detroit, MI 48202; 125.

**Motorcyclist Assn., Amer.** (1924), P.O. Box 141, 33 Collegeview Ave., Westerville, OH 43081; 130,000.

**Multiple Sclerosis Society, Natl.** (1946), 205 E. 42d St., N.Y., NY 10017; 250,000.

**Municipal Finance Officers Assn. of the U.S. & Canada** (1906), 180 N. Michigan Ave., Suite 800, Chicago, IL 60601; 7,200.

**Municipal League, Natl.** (1894), 47 E. 68th St., N.Y., NY 10021; 6,200.

**Mural Painters, Natl. Society of** (1895), 41 E. 65th St., N.Y., NY 10021; 150.

**Muscular Dystrophy Assn.** (1950), 810 Seventh Ave., N.Y., NY 10019, 28,000.

**Museums, Amer. Assn. of** (1906), 1055 Thomas Jefferson St. NW, Wash., DC 20007; 4,000.

**Music, Natl. Assn. of Schools of** (1924), 11250 Roger Bacon Dr. #5, Reston, VA 22090; 468 institutions.

**Music Center, Amer.** (1940), 250 W. 57th St., N.Y., NY 10019; 1,200.

**Music Clubs, Natl. Federation of** (1898), 310 S. Michigan Ave., Chicago, IL 60604; 500,000.

**Music Conference, Amer.** (1947), 1000 Skokie Blvd., Wilmette, IL 60091; 400.

**Music Council, Natl.** (1940), 250 W. 57th St., N.Y., NY 10019; 60.

**Music Educators Natl. Conference** (1907), 1902 Association Dr., Reston, VA 22091; 62,000.

**Musicians, Amer. Federation of** (1896), 1500 Broadway, N.Y., NY 10036; 330,000.

**Musicological Society, Amer.** (1934), 201 S. 34th St., Phila., PA 19104, 3,140.

**Music Publishers' Assn., Natl.** (1917), 110 E. 59th St., N.Y., NY 10022; 155.

**Music Scholarship Assn., Amer.** (1955), 1826 Carew Tower, Cincinnati, OH 45202; 2,000.

**Music Teachers Natl. Assn.** (1876), 408 Carew Tower, Cincinnati, OH 45202; 18,600.

**Mutual Savings Banks, Natl. Assn. of** (1920), 200 Park Ave., N.Y., NY 10017; 475 banks.

**Muzzle Loading Rifle Assn., Natl.** (1933), P.O. Box 67, Friendship, IN 47021; 22,500.

**Mystic Seaport** (1929), 30 Greenmanville Ave., Mystic, CT 06355; 14,000.


**NAACP (Natl. Assn. for the Advancement of Colored People** (1909), 1790 Broadway, N.Y., NY 10019, 500,000.

**Narcolepsy Assn., Amer.** (1975), P.O. Box 5846, Stanford, CA 94305; 2,500.

**Name Society, Amer.** (1951). English Dept., SUNY-Potsdam, Potsdam, NY 13676; 900.

**National Guard Assn. of the U.S.** (1878), One Massachusetts Ave. NW, Wash., DC 20001; 47,287.

**Nationalities Service, Amer. Council for** (1918), 20 W. 40th St., N.Y., NY 10018; 31 agencies.

**Natural Science for Youth Foundation** (1962), 763 Silvermine Rd., New Canaan, CT 06840; 600.

**Naturalists, Assn. of Interpretive** (1961), 6700 Needwood Rd., Derwood, MD 20855; 1,000.

**Nature Conservancy** (1951), 1800 N. Kent St., Arlington, VA 22209; 23,000.

**Nature & Natural Resources, Intl. Union for Conservation of** (1948), 1110 Morges, Switzerland; 398.

**Nature Study Society, Amer.** (1908), 4405 Paulsen St., Savannah, GA 31405; 950.

**Naval Architects & Marine Engineers, Society of** (1893), One World Trade Center, Suite 1369, N.Y., NY 10048; 11,500.

**Naval Engineers, Amer. Society of** (1888), 1012 14th St. NW, Wash., DC 20005; 4,000.

**Naval Institute, U.S.** (1873), U.S. Naval Academy, Annapolis, MD 21402; 64,374.

**Naval Reserve Assn.** (1954), 910 17th St. NW, Wash., DC 20006; 18,000.

**Navigation, Institute of** (1945), 815 15th St. NW, Wash., DC 20005; 3,000.

**Navy Club of the U.S.A.** (1940), 1602 Wells St., Fort Wayne, IN 46801; 3,000. **Navy Club of the U.S.A. Auxiliary** (1940), 216 W. Suttenfield, Fort Wayne, IN 46807; 1,000.

**Navy League of the U.S.** (1902); 818 18th St. NW, Wash., DC 20006; 40,356.

**Navy Wives Club of America** (1936), P.O. Box 6971, Wash., DC 20032; 3,000.

**Needlework Guild of America** (1885), 1736 Pine St., Phila., PA 19103; 400,000.

**Negro College Fund, United** (1944), 600 E. 62d St., N.Y., NY 10021; 41 institutions.

**Newspaper Editors, Amer. Society of** (1922), 1350 Sullivan Trail, Easton, PA 18042; 800.

**Newspaper Promotion Assn., Intl.** (1930), 11600 Sunrise Valley Dr., Reston, VA 22091; 1,200.

**Newspaper Publishers Assn., Amer.** (1887), 11600 Sunrise Valley Dr., Reston, VA 22091; 1,160 newspapers.

**Newspaper Publishers Assn., Natl.** (1940), 770 National Press Bldg., Wash., DC 20045; 300.

**Ninety-Nines (Internatl. Organization of Women Pilots)** (1929), P.O. Box 59964; Will Rogers World Airport, Oklahoma City, OK 73159, 5,000.

**Non-Commissioned Officers Assn.** (1960), 10635 IH 35 No., San Antonio, TX 78233; 150,000.

**Non-Parents, Natl. Organization for** (1972), 3 N. Liberty, Baltimore, MD 21201; 1,500.

**Notaries, Amer. Society of** (1965), 810 18th St. NW, Wash., DC 20006; 7,674.

**Nuclear Society, Amer.** (1954), 555 N. Kensington Ave., La Grange Park, IL 60525; 12,000.

**Numismatic Assn., Amer.** (1891), 818 N. Cascade Ave., Colorado Springs, CO 80903; 34,500.

**Numismatic Society, Amer.** (1858), Broadway at 155th St., N.Y., NY 10032; 1,814.

**Nurse Education and Service, Natl. Assn. for Practical** (1941), 122 E. 42d St., N.Y., NY 10017; 27,578.

**Nurses, Natl. Federation of Licensed Practical** (1949), 888 7th Ave., N.Y., NY 10019; 17,000.

**Nurses' Assn., Amer.** (1896), 2420 Pershing Rd., Kansas City, MO 64108; 190,000.

**Nursing, Natl. League for** (1952), 10 Columbus Circle, N.Y., NY 10019; 17,000.

**Nutrition, Amer. Institute of** (1928), 9650 Rockville Pike, Bethesda, MD 20014, 1,717.

**ORT Federation, Amer. (Org. for Rehabilitation through Training)** (1922), 817 Broadway, N.Y., NY 10013, 150,000.

**Occupational Therapy Assn., Amer.** (1917), 6000 Executive Blvd., Rockville, MD 20852; 25,841.

**Odd Fellows, Soverign Grand Lodge Independent Order of** (1819), 16 W. Chase St., Baltimore, MD 21201; 867,634.

**Old Crows, Assn. of** (1964), 2361 S. Jefferson Davis Hwy., Arlington, VA 22202; 8,000.

**Olympic Committee, U.S.** (1950), 57 Park Ave., N.Y., NY 10016; 92.

**Optical Society of America** (1916), 2000 L St. NW, Wash., DC 20036; 7,441.

**Optimist Internatl.** (1919), 4494 Lindell Blvd., St. Louis, MO 63108; 118,000.

**Optometric Assn., Amer.** (1898), 7000 Chippewa St., St. Louis, MO 63119.

**Oral and Maxillofacial Surgeons, Amer. Assn. of** (1918), 211 E. Chicago Ave., Chicago, IL 60611; 3,500.

**Organists, Amer. Guild of** (1896), 630 Fifth Ave., N.Y., NY 10020; 17,500.

**Oriental Society, Amer.** (1842), 329 Sterling Memorial Library, Yale Sta., New Haven, CT 06520, 1,500.

**Ornithologists' Union, Amer.** (1883), c/o National Museum of Natural History, Smithsonian Institution, Wash., DC 20560; 500.

**Osteopathic Assn., Amer.** (1897), 212 E. Ohio St., Chicago, 60611; 13,000.

**Ostomy Assn., United** (1962), 1111 Wilshire Blvd., Los Angeles, CA 90017; 29,000.

**Over-the-Counter Cos., Natl. Assn. of** (1973), Box 110, Jenkintown, PA 19046; 180 companies.

**Overeaters Anonymous** (1960), 2190 190th St., Torrance, 90254; 75,000.

**Paleontological Research Institution** (1932), 1259 Trumansburg Rd., Ithaca, NY 14850, 574.

**Paper Converters Assn.** (1934), 1619 Massachusetts Ave. NW, Wash., DC 20036; 30 companies.

**Paper Institute, Amer.** (1964), 260 Madison Ave., N.Y., NY 10016; 200 companies.

**Parasitologists, Amer. Society of** (1924), 1041 New Hampshire St., Box 368, Lawrence, KS 66044; 1,900.

**Parking Assn., Natl.** (1951), 1101 17th St. NW, Wash., DC 20036, 800 cos.

**PTA (Parents Teachers Assn.), Natl.** (1897), 700 N. Rush St., Chicago, IL 60611; 6.6 million.

**Parents Without Partners** (1957), 7910 Woodmont Ave. NW, Wash., DC 20014; 145,000.

**Parking Assn., Natl.** (1951), 1101 17th St. NW, Wash., DC 20036; 700 companies.

**Parkinson's Disease Foundation** (1957), Wm. Black Research Bldg., 640 W. 168th St., N.Y., NY 10032.

**Parks & Conservation Assn., Natl.** (1919), 1701 18th St. NW, Wash., DC 20009; 45,000.

**Pathologists & Bacteriologists, Amer. Assn. of** (1900), Dept. of Pathology, Box 3712, Duke Univ. Medical Center, Durham NC 27710; 1,271.

**Patriotism, Natl. Committee for Responsible** (1967), P.O. Box 5336, Grand Central Sta., N.Y., NY 10017; 150.

**Pearl Harbor Survivors Assn.** (1958). Drawer 00, McLean, VA 22101; 7,500.

**P.E.N. Amer. Center** (1922), 156 Fifth Ave. N.Y., NY 10010; 500.

**Pen Women, Natl. League of Amer.** (1897), 1300 17th St. NW, Wash., DC 20036; 6,234.

**Pennsylvania Society** (1899), Suite 594, Waldorf Astoria Hotel, 301 Park Ave., N.Y., NY 10022; 2,400.

**P.E.O (Philanthropic Educational Organization) Sisterhood** (1869), 3700 Grand Ave., Des Moines, IA 50312; 187,000.

**Performance Improvement, Amer. Society for** (1966), 790 Broad St., Newark, NJ 07102; 250.

**Personnel Administration, Amer. Society for** (1948), 19 Church St., Berea, OH 44017; 16,000.

**Personnel & Guidance Assn., Amer.** (1952), 1607 New Hampshire Ave. NW, Wash., DC 20009; 40,000.

**Petroleum Geologists, Amer. Assn. of** (1917), Box 979, 1444 S. Boulder, Tulsa, OK 74101; 18,734.

**Petroleum Institute, Amer.** (1919), 2101 L St. NW, Wash., DC 20037; 7,600.

**Petroleum Landmen, Amer. Assn. of** (1955), 2408 Continental Life Bldg., Fort Worth, TX 76102; 6,200.

**Pharmaceutical Assn., Amer.** (1852), 2215 Constitution Ave. NW, Wash., DC 20037; 54,000.

**Philatelic Americans, Society of** (1894), 58 W. Salisbury Dr., Wilmington, DE 19809; 8,122.

**Philatelic Society, Amer.** (1886), P.O. Box 800, 336 S. Fraser St., State College, PA 16801; 41,798.

**Philaticians, Society of** (1972), Salt Point Tpke., Clinton Corners, NY 12514; 240.

**Philharmonic Symphony Society of New York** (1842), Avery Fisher Hall, Lincoln Center, Broadway at 65th St., N.Y., NY 10023; 5,000.

**Philologocal Assn., Amer.** (1869), 431-432 N. Burrowes, Pennsylvania State Univ., University Park, PA 16802; 2,900.

**Philosophical Assn., Amer.** (1900), Univ. of Delaware, Newark, DE 19711; 6,000.

**Philosophical Society, Amer.** (1743), 104 S. 5th St., Phila., PA 19106; 600.

**Photographers of America, Professional** (1880), 1090 Executive Way, Des Plaines, IL 60018; 16,000.

**Photographic Society of Amer.** (1934), 2005 Walnut St., Phila. PA 19103; 18,600.

**Physical Society, Amer.** (1899), 335 E. 45th St., N.Y., NY 10017; 29,000.

**Physical Therapy Assn., Amer.** (1921), 1156 15th St. NW. Wash., DC 20005; 26,000.

**Physicians, Amer. Academy of Family** (1947), 1740 W. 92nd St., Kansas City, MO 64114; 40,000.

**Physicians, Amer. College of** (1915), 4200 Pine St., Phila., PA 19104; 20,000.

**Physics, Amer. Institute of** (1931), 335 E. 45th St., N.Y., NY 10017; 55,000.

**Physiological Society, Amer.** (1887), 9650 Rockville Pike, Bethesda, MD 20014; 5,200.

**Pilgrim Society** (1820), 75 Court St., Plymouth, MA 20360; 700.

**Pilgrims of the U.S.** (1903), 74 Trinity Pl., N.Y., NY 10006; 1,000.

**Pilot Club Intl.** (1921), 244 College St., Macon, GA 31201; 19,500.

**Pioneer Women, The Women's Labor Zionist Organization of America** (1925), 315 Fifth Ave., N.Y., NY 10016; 50,000.

**Planned Parenthood Federation of America** (1922), 810 Seventh Ave., N.Y., NY 10019; 189 affiliates.

**Planners, Amer. Institute of** (1917), 1776 Massachusetts Ave., NW, Wash., DC 20036; 11,838.

**Plastic Modelers Society, Intl.** (1964), P.O. Box 2555, Long Beach, CA 90801; 4,600.

**Plastics Engineers, Society of** (1942), 656 W. Putnam Ave., Greenwich, CT 06830; 18,500.

**Plastics Industry, Society of** (1937), 355 Lexington Ave., N.Y., NY 10017; 1,400 companies.

**Platform Assn., Intl.** (1831), 2564 Berkshire Rd., Cleveland Heights, OH 44106; 6,000.

**Podiatry Assn., Amer.** (1912), 20 Chevy Chase Circle NW, Wash., DC 20015; 7,000.

**Poetry Day Committee, Natl.** (1947), 1110 N. Venetian Dr., Miami Beach, FL 33139; 17,000.

**Poetry Society of America** (1910), 15 Gramercy Park So., N.Y., NY 10003; 850.

**Poets, Academy of Amer.** (1934), 1078 Madison Ave., N.Y., NY 10028; 93.

**Polar Society, Amer.** (1934), c/o Secretary, 98-20 62d Dr., Apt. 7H, Rego Park, NY 11374; 2,273.

**Police, Internatl. Assn. of Chiefs of** (1893), 11 Firstfield Rd., Gaithersburg, MD 20760; 11,106.

**Police Reserve Officers Assn., Natl.** (1967), 14600 S. Tamiami Trial N.P., Venice, FL 33595; 13,500.

**Polish Army Veterans Assn. of America** (1921), 19 Irving Pl., N.Y., NY 10003; 9,762.

**Polish Cultural Society of America** (1940), 55 W. 42d St., N.Y., NY 10036; 46,851.

**Polish Legion of American Veterans** (1920), 3024 N. Laramie Ave., Chicago, IL 60641; 150,000.

**Political Items Collectors, Amer.** (1945), 66 Golf St., Newington, CT 06111; 2,500.

**Political Science, Academy of** (1880), 2852 Broadway, N.Y., NY 10025; 10,000.

**Political Science Assn., Amer.** (1903), 1527 New Hampshire Ave. NW, Wash., DC 20036; 13,565.

**Political & Social Science, Amer. Academy of** (1889), 3937 Chestnut St., Phila., PA 19104; 16,000.

**Pollution Control, Internatl. Assn. for** (1970), 1625 Eye St. NW, Wash., DC 20006; 500.

**Polo Assn., U.S.** (1890), 1301 W. 22d St., Oak Brook, IL 60521; 1,500.

**Population Assn. of America** (1931), 806 15th St. NW, Wash., DC 20005; 2,600.

**Portuguese Continental Union of the U.S.A.** (1925), 899 Boylston St., Boston, MA 02115; 9,658.

**Postmasters of the U.S., Natl. Assn. of** (1936), 490 L'Enfant Plaza E., SW, Wash., DC 20024; 33,000.

**Postmasters of the U.S., Natl. League of** (1904), 955 L'Enfant Plaza SW, Wash., DC 20024; 19,500.

**Poultry Science Assn.** (1908), Illinois Bldg., Room 311, 113 N. Neil St., Champaign, IL 61820; 1,550.

**Power Boat Assn., Amer.** (1903), 22811 Greater Mack, St.

Clair Shores, MI 48080; 6,339.

**Power Squadrons, U.S.** (1914), P.O. Box 30423, Raleigh, NC 27612; 70,000.

**Precancel Collectors, Natl. Assn. of** (1950), 5121 Park Blvd., Wildwood, NJ 08260; 5,500.

**Press Club, Natl.** (1908), 529 14th St. NW, Wash., DC 20045; 5,000.

**Press Institute, Intl.** (1951), Lindenplatz 6, 8048 Zurich, Switzerland; 1,900.

**Press and Radio Club** (1948), P.O. Box 7023, Montgomery, AL 36107; 747.

**Press Women, Natl. Federation of** (1937), 1105 Main St., P.O. Box 99, Blue Springs, MD 64015; 4,250.

**Procrastinators' Club of America** (1956), 1111 Broad, Locust Bldg., Phila., PA 19102; 3,120.

**Production & Inventory Control Society, Amer.** (1957), 2600 Virginia Ave. NW, Wash., DC 20037; 14,750.

**Propeller Club of the U.S.** (1927), 1730 M St. NW, Wash., DC 20036; 14,000.

**Psychiatric Assn., Amer.** (1844), 1700 18th St. NW, Wash., DC 20009; 22,000.

**Psychical Research, Amer. Society for** (1907), 5 W. 73d St., N.Y., NY 10023; 2,500.

**Psychoanalytic Assn., Amer.** (1911), One E. 57th St., N.Y., NY 10022; 2,503.

**Psychological Assn., Amer.** (1892), 1200 17th St. NW, Wash., DC 20036; 45,000.

**Psychological Assn. for Psychoanalysis, Natl.** (1946), 150 W. 13th St., N.Y., NY 10011; 187.

**Psychological Minorities, Society for the Aid of** (1953), 4225 Hampton St., Elmhurst, NY 11373; 500.

**Psychotheatrics, Assn. for** (1976), P.O. Box 160371, Sacramento, CA 95816; 50.

**Psychotherapy Assn., Amer. Group** (1942), 1995 Broadway, N.Y., NY 10023; 3,000.

**Public Health Assn., Amer.** (1872), 1015 18th St. NW, Wash., DC 20036; 25,000.

**Public Relations Society of America** (1947), 845 Third Ave., N.Y., NY 10022; 8,400.

**Public Welfare Assn., Amer.** (1930), 1155 16th St. NW, Wash., DC 20036; 7,000.

**Publishers, Assn. of Amer.** (1970), One Park Ave., N.Y., NY 10016; 345.

**Quality Control, Amer. Society for** (1946), 161 W. Wisconsin Ave., Milwaukee, WI 53203; 26,000.

**Quint-A** (1954), 23219 Lincolnshire Dr., Bay Village, OH 44140; 7,033.

**Rabbinical Alliance of America** (1945), 156 5th Ave., N.Y., NY 10010; 500.

**Rabbinical Assembly** (1900), 3080 Broadway, N.Y., NY 10027; 1,100.

**Rabbis, Central Conference of Amer.** (1889), 790 Madison Ave., N.Y., NY 10021; 1,250.

**Racing Commissioners, Natl. Assn. of State** (1934), P.O. Box 4216, Lexington, KY 40504; 650.

**Racquetball Assn., U.S.** (1973), 4101 Dempster St., Skokie, IL 60076; 30,000.

**Radio Free Europe** (1949), 1201 Connecticut Ave. NW, Wash., DC 20036.

**Radio Relay League, Amer.** (1914), 225 Main St., Newington, CT 06111; 145,000.

**Radio and Television Society, Intl.** (1939), 420 Lexington Ave., N.Y., NY 10017; 1,100.

**Radio Union, Internatl. Amateur** (1925), P.O. Box AAA, Newington, CT 06111; 100 societies.

**Radiological Society of No. America** (1915), One MONY-Plaza, Syracuse, NY 13202; 7,560.

**Radio Relay League, Amer.** (1914), 225 Main St., Newington, CT 06111; 160,000.

**Railroad Passengers, Natl. Assn. of** (1967), 417 New Jersey Ave. SE, Wash., DC 20003; 5,500.

**Railroads, Assn. of Amer.** (1934), 1920 L St. NW, Wash., DC 20036; 158.

**Railway Historical Society, Natl.** (1937), P.O. Box 2051, Phila., PA 19103, 10,451.

**Railway Progress Institute** (1908), 801 N. Fairfax St., Alexandria, VA 22314; 145 companies.

**Rainbow for Girls, Supreme Assembly, Intl. Order of the** (1922) 315 E. Carl Albert Pkwy., McAlester, OK 74501; 175,000.

**Range Management, Society for** (1948), 2760 W. 5th Ave., Denver, CO 80204; 5,500.

**Rape, Feminist Alliance Against** (1974), P.O. Box 21033, Wash., DC 20009; 500.

**Real Estate Appraisers, Natl. Assn. of** (1967), 853 Broadway, N.Y., NY 10003; 1,000.

**Real Estate Investment Trusts, Natl. Assn. of** (1960), 1101 17th St. NW, Wash., DC 20036; 141 trusts, 223 associates.

**Realtors[n], Natl. Assn. of** (1908), 430 N. Michigan Ave., Chicago, IL 60611; 433,182.

**Reconciliation, Fellowship of** (1915), 523 N. Broadway, Nyack, NY 10960; 23,500.

**Recording Industry Assn. of America** (1952), One E. 57th St., N.Y., NY 10022; 58.

**Records Managers & Administrators, Assn. of** (1975), P.O. Box 281, Bradford, RI 02808; 3,900.

**Recreation and Park Assn., Natl.** (1965), 1601 N. Kent St., Arlington, VA 22209; 17,000.

**Red Cross, Amer. Natl.** (1881), 17th & D Sts. NW, Wash., DC 20006; 30,044,842.

**Red Men, Improved Order Of** (1765), 1525 West Ave., P.O. Box 683, Waco, TX 76707; 51,000.

**Redwoods League, Save-the-** (1918), 114 Sansome St., San Francisco, CA 94104; 55,000.

**Regional Plan Assn.** (1929), 235 E. 45th St., N.Y., NY 10017 3,000.

**Rehabilitation Assn., Natl.** (1925), 1522 K St. NW, Wash. DC 20005; 35,000.

**Religion, Amer. Academy of** (1909), 215 Williams Bldg. Florida State Univ., Tallahassee, FL 32306; 4,200.

**Renaissance Society of America** (1954), 1161 Amsterdam Ave., N.Y., NY 10027; 3,100.

**Rescue Committee, Intl.** (1933), 386 Park Ave. So., N.Y., NY 10016; 70.

**Reserve Officers Assn. of the U.S.** (1922), One Constitution Ave., NE, Wash., DC 20002; 105,000.

**Restaurant Assn., Natl.** (1919), Suite 2600, One IBM Plaza Chicago, IL 60611; 7,000 businesses.

**Retarded Citizens, Natl. Assn. for** (1950), P.O. Box 6109 2709 Ave. F East, Arlington, TX 76011; 219,000.

**Retired Federal Employees, Natl. Assn. of** (1926), 1533 New Hampshire Ave. NW, Wash., DC 20036; 260,000.

**Retired Officers Assn.** (1929), 1625 Eye St. NW, Wash., DC 20006; 221,545; 19,878 Auxiliary.

**Retired Persons, Amer. Assn. of** (1958), 1909 K St. NW Wash., DC 20049; 12,000,000.

**Retired Teachers Assn., Natl.** (1947), 1909 K St. NW. Wash., DC 20049; 500,000.

**Retreads (of World War I & II)** (1947), 40-07 154th St. Flushing, NY 11354; 1,500.

**Revolver Assn., U.S.** (1900), 59 Alvin St., Springfield, MA 01104; 1,250.

**Reye's Syndrome Foundation, Natl.** (1974), P.O. Box 829, Bryan, OH 43506; 2,000.

**Richard III Society** (1924), 534 Hudson Rd.; Sudbury, MA 01776; 650.

**Rifle Assn. of America, Natl.** (1871), 1600 Rhode Island Ave. NW, Wash., DC 20036; 1,000,000.

**Road Builders' Assn., Amer.** (1902), 525 School St. SW, Wash., DC 20024; 6,000.

**Rodeo Cowboys Assn., Professional** (1936), 2929 W. 19th Ave., Denver, CO 80204; 4,000.

**Roller Skating, U.S. Amateur Confederation of** (1973), 7700 A St., Lincoln, NE 68510; 25,000.

**Roller Skating Rink Operators Assn.** (1937), 7700 A St., Lincoln, NE 68510; 1,300.

**Rose Society, American** (1889), P.O. Box 30,000, Shreveport, LA 71130; 16,000.

**Rosicrucian Fraternity** (1614, Germany, 1861 in U.S.), R.D. No. 3, Box 220, Quakertown, PA 18951.

**Rosicrucian Order, AMORC** (1915), Rosicrucian Park, San Jose, CA 95191; 120,000.

**Rosicrucians, Society of** (1909), 321 W. 101st St., N.Y., NY 10025.

**Rotary Internatl.** (1905), 1600 Ridge Ave., Evanston, IL 60201; 803,000.

**Round Table Internatl., Knights of the** (1911), 61 E. Colorado Blvd., Pasadena, CA 91101; 1,900.

**Ruritan Natl.** (1928), P.O. Box 487, Dublin, VA 24084; 38,000.

**Russian Orthodox Clubs, Federated** (1927), 10 Downs Dr. (Plains), Wilkes-Barre, PA 18705; 5,000.

**Safety Council, Natl.** (1913), 444 N. Michigan Ave., Chicago, IL 60611; 15,000.

**Safety Engineers, Amer. Society of** (1911), 850 Busse Hwy., Park Ridge, IL 60068; 14,500.

**St. Dennis of Zante, Sovereign Greek Order of** (1096, 1953 in U.S.), 739 W. 186th St., N.Y., NY 10033; 816.

**St. Paul, Natl. Guild of** (1937), 601 Hill 'N Dale, Lexington, KY 40503.

**Salesmen, Natl. Assn. of Professional** (1970), 266 Tram Rd., Columbia, SC 29210; 20,000.

**Salt Institute** (1914), 206 N. Washington St., Alexandria, VA 22314; 25 cos.

**Sane World, A Citizen's Organization for a** (1957), 318 Massachusetts Ave. NW, Wash., DC 20002; 20,000.

**Savings & Loan League, Natl.** (1943), 1101 15th St. NW, Wash., DC 20005; 300.

**School Administrators, Amer. Assn. of** (1865), 1801 N. Moore St., Arlington, VA 22209; 19,000.

**School Boards Assn., Natl.** (1940), 1055 Thomas Jefferson St. NW, Wash., DC 20007; 52 boards.

**School Counselor Assn., Amer.** (1953), 1607 New Hampshire Ave. NW, Wash., DC 20015; 13,000.

**Schools of Art, Natl. Assn. of** (1944), 11250 Roger Bacon Dr., No. 5, Reston, VA 22090; 85 institutions.

**Schools & Colleges, Amer. Council on** (1927), 446 Salem Ave., P.O. Box 1252, York, PA 17405; 121 institutions.

**Science, Amer. Assn. for the Advancement of** (1848), 1515 Massachusetts Ave. NW, Wash., DC 20005; 128,000.

**Science Fiction Fantasy and Horror Films, Academy of** (1972), 334 W. 54th St., Los Angeles, CA 90037; 700.

**Science Service** (1921), 1719 N St. NW, Wash., DC 20036.

**Science Teachers Assn., Natl.** (1944), 1742 Connecticut Ave. NW, Wash., DC 20009; 40,000.

**Science Writers, Natl. Assn. of** (1934), Box H, Sea Cliff, NY 11579; 950.

**Sciences, Natl. Academy of** (1863), 2101 Constitution Ave. NW, Wash., DC 20418; 1,182.

**Sciences, New York Academy of** (1817), 2 E. 63d St., N.Y., NY 10021; 25,000.

**Scientific Apparatus Makers Assn.** (1918), 1140 Connecticut Ave. NW, Wash., DC 20036; 222 companies.

**Scientists, Federation of Amer.** (1946), 307 Massachusetts Ave. NE, Wash., DC 20002; 7,000.

**Screen Actors Guild** (1933), 7750 Sunset Blvd., Hollywood, CA 90046; 32,000.

**Sculpture Society, Natl.** (1893), 777 Third Ave., N.Y., NY 10017; 350.

**Seamen's Service, United** (1942), One World Trade Ctr., N.Y., NY 10048.

**Secondary School Principals, Natl. Assn. of** (1916), 1904 Association Dr., Reston, VA 22091; 35,000.

**Secularists of America, United** (1947), 377 Vernon St., Oakland, CA 94610.

**Securities Industry Assn.** (1972), 20 Broad St., N.Y., NY 10005; 575 firms.

**Security Industrial Assn., Natl.** (1944), 740 15th St. NW, Wash., DC 20005; 260 corporations.

**Seeing Eye, The** (1929), Morristown, NJ 07960; 26,000.

**Semantics, Institute of General** (1938), R.R. 1; Box 215, Lakeville, CT 06039; 500.

**Separation of Church & State, Americans United for** (1947), 8120 Fenton St., Silver Spring, MD 20910; 100,000.

**Sertoma Internatl.** (1912), 1900 E. Meyer Blvd., Kansas City, MO 64132; 33,883.

**Settlements & Neighborhood Centers, Natl. Federation of** (1911), 232 Madison Ave., N.Y., NY 10016; 175 agencies.

**Sex Information & Education Council of the U.S. (SIECUS)** (1964), 137 N. Franklin St., Hempstead, NY 11550.

**Shakespeare Assn. of America** (1973), Box 6328, Sta. B, Nashville, TN 37235; 500.

**Sheriff's Assn., Natl.** (1940), 1250 Connecticut Ave. NW, Wash., DC 20036; 60,000.

**Ship Society, World** (1946), 3319 Sweet Dr., Lafayette, CA 94549; 3,900.

**Shipbuilders Council of America** (1921), Watergate, 600 New Hampshire Ave. NW, Wash., DC 20037; 40 companies.

**Shoe Retailers Assn., Natl.** (1912), 200 Madison Ave., N.Y., NY 10016; 2,500.

**Shore & Beach Preservation Assn., Amer.** (1926), 412 O'Brien Hall, Univ. of California, Berkeley, CA 94720; 1,500.

**Shorthand Reporters Assn., Natl.** (1899), 2361 S. Jefferson Davis Hwy., Arlington, VA 22202; 11,000.

**Showmen's League of America** (1913), 300 W. Randolph St., Chicago, IL 60606; 1,650.

**Shrine, Ancient Arabic Order of the Nobles of the Mystic** (1872), 323 N. Michigan Ave., Chicago, IL 60601; 937,712.

**Shut-In Day Society, Natl.** (1970), 237 Franklin St., Reading, PA 19602; 5,000.

**Sierra Club** (1892), 530 Bush St., San Francisco, CA 94109; 183,698.

**Silurians, Society of the** (1924), 45 John St., N.Y., NY 10038; 780.

**Skating Union of the U.S., Amateur** (1927), 4423 W. Deming Pl., Chicago, IL 60639; 3,500.

**Skeet Shooting Assn., Natl.** (1946), P.O. Box 28188, San Antonio, TX 78228; 19,000.

**Ski Assn., U.S.** (1904), 1726 Champa St., Denver, CO 80202; 100,000.

**Small Business, Amer. Federation of** (1963), 407 S. Dearborn St., Chicago, IL 60605; 7,500.

**Small Business Assn., Natl.** (1937), 1604 K St. NW, Wash., DC 20006; 50,000.

**Smoking & Health, Natl. Clearinghouse for** (1965), Center for Disease Control, 1600 Clifton Road NE, Atlanta, GA 30333.

**Soaring Society of America** (1932), Box 66071, Los Angeles, CA 90066; 17,500.

**Soccer Federation, U.S.** (1913), 350 Fifth Ave., N.Y., NY 10001; 40 assns.

**Social Biology, Society for the Study of** (1926), Medical Dept., Brookhaven Natl. Laboratory, Upton, NY 11973; 440.

**Social Science Research Council** (1924), 605 Third Ave., N.Y., NY 10016.

**Social Sciences, Natl. Institute of** (1912), 150 Amsterdam Ave., N.Y., NY 10023; 1,000.

**Social Welfare, Intl. Council on** (1928), 345 E. 46th St., N.Y., NY 10017; 70 natl. committees.

**Social Welfare, Natl. Conference on** (1873), 22 W. Gay St., Columbus, OH 43215; 5,000.

**Social Work Education, Council on** (1952), 345 E. 46th St., N.Y., NY 10017; 4,500.

**Social Workers, Natl. Assn. of** (1955), 1425 H St. NW, Wash., DC 20005; 71,000.

**Sociological Assn., Amer.** (1905), 1722 N St. NW, Wash., DC 20036; 13,725.

**Softball Assn. of America, Amateur** (1933), 2801 N.E. 50th St., Okalhoma City, OK 73111; 1,500,000.

**Softball, Cinderella Natl.** (1958), 71 Bridge St., Corning, NY 14830.

**Soft Drink Assn., Natl.** (1919), 1101 16th St. NW, Wash., DC 20036; 1,600.

**Soil Conservation Society of America** (1945), 7515 N.E. Ankeny Rd., Ankeny, IA 50021; 15,000.

**Soil Science Society of America** (1936), 677 S. Segoe Rd., Madison, WI 53711; 4,595.

**Sojourners, Natl.** (1919), 8301 E. Boulevard Dr., Alexandria, VA 22308; 9,000.

**Soldier's, Sailor's and Airmen's Club** (1919), 283 Lexington Ave., N.Y., NY 10016.

**Sons of the Amer. Legion** (1932), P.O. Box 1055, Indianapolis, IN 46206; 31,000.

**Sons of the American Revolution, Natl. Society of** (1889), 2412 Massachusetts Ave. NW, Wash., DC 20008; 21,500.

**Sons of Confederate Veterans** (1896), Southern Sta., P.O. Box 5164, Hattiesburg, MS 39401; 5,000.

**Sons of Italy in America, Order** (1905), 1520 Locust St., Phila., PA 19102; 110,000.

**Sons of Norway** (1895), 1455 W. Lake St., Minneapolis, MN 55408; 100,150.

**Sons of Poland, Assn. of the** (1903), 655 Newark Ave., Jersey City, NJ 07306; 11,569.

**Sons of the Revolution in the State of New York** (1876), Fraunces Tavern, 54 Pearl St., N.Y., NY 10004; 1,400.

**Sons of St. Patrick, Society of the Friendly** (1784), 80 Wall St., N.Y., NY 10005; 1,300.

**Sons of Union Veterans of the Civil War** (1881), 2913 Main St., P.O. Box 6193, Lawrenceville, NJ 08648.

**Soroptimist Internatl. of the Americas** (1921), 1616 Walnut St., Phila., PA 19103; 32,000.

**Southern Christian Leadership Conference** (1957), 334 Auburn Ave. NE, Atlanta, GA 30303; 1,000,000.

**Southern Regional Council** (1944), 75 Marietta St. NW, Atlanta, GA 30303.

**Space Education Assoc., U.S.** (1973), 746 Turnpike Rd., Elizabethtown, PA 17022; 7 countries.

**Space Exploration Establishment** (1977), 3775 Hambletonian Dr., Florissant, MO 63033; 50.

**Spanish War Veterans, United** (1904), 810 Vermont Ave. NW, Wash., DC 20420; 328.

**Speech Communication Assn.** (1914), 5205 Leesburg Pike, Falls Church, VA 22041; 6,000.

**Speech & Hearing Assn., Amer.** (1925), 10801 Rockville Pike, Rockville, MD 20852; 27,500.

**Speleological Society, Natl.** (1941), Cave Ave., Huntsville, AL 35810; 4,500.

**Speleological Society of America** (1964), 1124 100th Ave. NE, Bellevue, WA 98004; 1,750.

**Sports Car Club of America** (1944), 1562 S. Parker Rd., Denver, CO 80231; 19,000.

**Sports Club, Indoor** (1930), 1145 Highland St., Napolean, OH 43545.

**Sports Philatelists Intl.** (1962), 3604 S. Home Ave., Berwyn, IL 60402; 1,112.

**Stamp Dealers' Assn., Amer.** (1914), 595 Madison Ave., N.Y., NY 10022; 1,200.

**Standards Institute, Amer. Natl.** (1918), 1430 Broadway, N.Y., NY 10018; 1,000.

**State Communities Aid Assn.** (1872), 105 E. 22d St., N.Y., NY 10010; 285.

**State Governments, Council of** (1933), P.O. Box 11910, Iron Works Pike, Lexington, KY 40511; 50 states.

**State High School Assns., Natl. Federation of** (1920), Federation Pl., Elgin, IL 60120; 50 states, 10 provinces.

**State & Local History, Amer. Assn. for** (1940), 1400 8th Ave. So., Nashville, TN 37203; 5,000.

**Statistical Assn., Amer.** (1839), 806 15th St. NW, Wash., DC 20005; 12,500.

**Steamship Historical Society of America** (1935), 414 Pelton Ave., Staten Island, NY 10310; 2,480.

**Steel Construction, Amer. Institute of** (1921), 1221 Ave. of the Americas, N.Y., NY 10020; 914.

**Steel Founders' Society of America** (1903), 20611 Center Ridge Rd., Rocky River, OH 44116; 120 companies.

**Steeplechase and Hunt Assn., Natl.** (1895), Box 308, Elmont, NY 11003; 3,000.

**Sterilization, Assn. for Voluntary** (1942), 708 Third Ave., N.Y., NY 10017; 2,000.

**Steuben Society of America** (1919) 369 Lexington Ave., N.Y. NY 10017.

**Stock Car Auto Racing, Natl. Assn. for (NASCAR)** (1948), 1801 Speedway Blvd., Daytona Beach, FL 32015; 17,000.

**Stock Exchange, American** (1911), 86 Trinity Pl., N.Y., NY 10006; 650.

**Stock Exchange, New York** (1792), 11 Wall St., N.Y., NY 10005; 1,366.

**Stock Exchange, Philadelphia-Baltimore-Washington** (1790), 17th St., Stock Exchange Pl., Phila., PA 19103; 448.

**Structural Stability Research Council** (1944), Fritz Engineering Laboratory No. 13, Lehigh Univ., Bethlehem, PA 18015; 200.

**Student Assn., Natl.** (1947), 2115 S St. NW, Wash., DC 20008; 3,478,000.

**Student Councils, Natl. Assn. of** (1931), 1904 Association Dr., Reston, VA 22091; 7,000 secondary schools.

**Students of German, Natl. Federation of** (1968), 339 Walnut St., Phila., PA 19106; 26,500.

**Stuttering Project, Natl.** (1976), Box 33, Walnut Creek, CA 94596.

**Sugar Brokers Assn., Amer.** (1903), 76 Beaver St., N.Y., NY 10005; 250.

**Sunbathing Assn., Amer.** (1929), 810 N. Mills Ave., Orlando, FL 32803; 20,000.

**Sunday League** (1933), 279 Highland Ave., Newark, NJ 07104; 25,000.

**Surfing Assn., Amer.** (1966), 2131 Kalakaua Ave., Honolulu, HI 96815; 500 teams.

**Surgeons, Amer. College of** (1913), 55 E. Erie St., Chicago IL 60611; 40,000.

**Surgeons, Intl. College of** (1935), 1516 N. Lake Shore Dr., Chicago IL 60610; 14,000.

**Surveying & Mapping, Amer. Congress on** (1941), 210 Little Falls, Falls Church, VA 22046; 7,500.

**Symphony Orchestra League, Amer.** (1942), P.O. Box 669, Vienna, VA 22180; 3,800.

**Systems Management, Assn. for** (1947), 24587 Bagley Rd., Cleveland, OH 44138; 9,000.

**Table Tennis Assn., U.S.** (1933), 3466 Bridgeland Dr. #209, St. Louis, MO 63044; 5,100.

**Tall Buildings and Urban Habitat, Council on** (1969), Fritz Engineering Laboratory No. 13, Lehigh Univ., Bethlehem, PA 18015; 1,500.

**Tattoo Club of America** (1974), 112 W. First St., Mt. Vernon, NY 10550; 5,500.

**Tax Accountants, Natl. Assn. of Enrolled Federal** (1960), 6108 N. Harding Ave., Chicago, IL 60659; 500.

**Tax Administrators, Federation of** (1937), 444 N. Capitol St., Wash., DC 20001; 51 revenue departments.

**Tax Assn.-Natl. Tax Institute of America** (1907), 21 E. State St., Columbus, OH 43215; 2,200.

**Tax Foundation** (1937), 50 Rockefeller Plaza, N.Y., NY 10020; 1,573.

**Tea Assn. of the U.S.A.** (1899), 230 Park Ave., N.Y., NY 10017; 160.

**Teachers, Amer. Federation of** (1916), 11 Dupont Circle NW, Wash., DC 20036; 475,000.

**Teachers of English, Natl. Council of** (1911), 1111 Kenyon Rd., Urbana, IL 61801; 38,000.

**Teachers of French, Amer. Assn. of** (1927), 57 E. Armory Ave., Champaign, IL 61820; 10,800.

**Teachers of German, Amer. Assn. of** (1926), 339 Walnut St., Phila., PA 19106; 7,600.

**Teachers of Singing, Natl. Assn. of** (1944), 250 W. 57th St., N.Y., NY 10019; 3,100.

**Teachers of Spanish & Portuguese, Amer. Assn. of** (1917), Holy Cross Coll., Worcester, MA 01610; 13,000.

**Technical Communication, Society for** (1958), 1010 Vermont Ave. NW, Wash., DC 20005; 3,300.

**Television Arts & Sciences, Natl. Academy of** (1947), 291 S. La Cienega Blvd., Beverly Hills, CA 90211; 11,000.

**Television Bureau of Advertising** (1954), 1350 Ave. of the Americas, N.Y., NY 10019; 35,000.

**Television & Radio Artists, Amer. Federation of** (1937), 1350 Ave. of the Americas; N.Y., NY 10019; 30,000.

**Telluride Assn.** (1910), 217 West Ave., Ithaca, NY 14850; 69.

**Tennis Assn., U.S.** (1881), 51 E. 42d St., N.Y., NY 10017; 100,000.

**Tennis League, Youth** (1968), 1701 Vandalia, Collinsville, Il 62234; 850.

**Terrain Vehicle Owners Assn., Natl.** (1972), P.O. Box 574 Feasterville, PA 19047; 701.

**Testing & Materials, Amer. Society for** (1898), 1916 Race St., Phila., PA 19103; 26,000.

**Textile Assn., Northern** (1854), 211 Congress St., Boston MA 02110; 350.

**Textile Manufacturers Institute, Amer.** (1949), 2124 Wachovia Ctr., Charlotte, NC 28285; 250 companies.

**Theatre & Academy, Amer. Natl.** (1935), 245 W. 52d St. N.Y., NY 10019; 1,000.

**Theatre Assn., Amer.** (1936), 1029 Vermont Ave. NW Wash., DC 20005; 7,000.

**Theatre Organ Society, Amer.** (1955), P.O. Box 1002, Middleburg, VA 22117; 6,200 families.

**Theatre Owners, Natl. Assn. of** (1924), 1501 Broadway N.Y., NY 10036; 8,000.

**Theodore Roosevelt Assn.** (1919), P.O. Box 720, Oyster Bay, NY 11771; 500.

**Theological Library Assn., Amer.** (1947), Lutheran Theological Seminary, 7301 Germantown Ave., Phila., PA 19119; 568.

**Theological Schools, Amer. Assn. of** (1936), P.O. Box 396 Vandalia, OH 45377; 198 schools.

**Theosophical Society** (1875), 1926 N. Main St., Wheaton, IL 60187; 5,500.

**Thoreau Society** (1941), SUNY-Geneseo, Geneseo, NY 14454; 1,100.

**Thoroughbred Racing Assn. of North America** (1942) 8000 Marcus Ave., Lake Success, NY 11040; 53 racetracks.

**Titanic Historical Society** (1963), P.O. Box 53, Indian Orchard, MA 01151; 1,575.

**Toastmasters Intl.** (1924), 2200 N. Grand Ave., Santa Ana, CA 92711; 62,000.

**Toastmistress Clubs, Intl.** (1938), 9068 E. Firestone Blvd. Downey CA 90241; 21,429.

**Topical Assn., Amer.** (1949), 3306 N. 50th St., Milwaukee WI 53216; 10,000.

**Torch Clubs, Internatl. Assn. of** (1924), P.O. Box 81890, Lincoln, NE 68501; 5,000.

**Toy Manufacturers of America** (1916), 200 Fifth Ave., N.Y., NY 10010; 250.

**Trade Relations Council of the U.S.** (1885), 1001 Connecticut Ave. NW, Wash., DC 20036; 50 companies.

**Traffic and Transportation, Amer. Society of** (1946), 547 W. Jackson Blvd., Chicago, IL 60606; 2,800.

**Training Corps, Amer.** (1961), 107-12 Jamaica Ave., Richmond Hill, NY 11418; 350.

**Training & Development, Amer. Society for** (1943), P.O. Box 5307, Madison, WI 53705; 12,000.

**Transit Assn., Amer. Public** (1974), 1100 17th St. NW, Wash., DC 20036; 750.

**Translators Assn., Amer.** (1959), P.O. Box 129, Croton-on-Hudson, NY 10520; 1,100.

**Transportation Assn. of America** (1935), 1100 17th St. NW, Wash., DC 20036; 600 companies.

**Transportation Engineers, Institute of** (1930), 1815 N. Ft. Meyer Dr., Arlington, VA 22209; 5,745.

**Trapshooting Assn., Amateur** (1923), 601 W. National Rd. Vandalia, OH 45377; 80,000.

**Travel Agents, Amer. Society of** (1931), 711 Fifth Ave., N.Y., NY 10022; 15,000.

**Travel Organizations, Discover America** (1969), 1100 Connecticut Ave. NW, Wash., DC 20036; 950.

**Travelers Aid-Intl. Social Service of America** (1972), 345 E. 46th St., N.Y., NY 10017; 1,010 U.S. & foreign agencies.

**Trucking Assn., Amer.** (1933), 1616 P St. NW, Wash., DC 20036; 51 assns.

**True Sisters, United Order** (1846), 150 W. 85th St., N.Y., NY 10024; 11,000.

**Turners, Amer.** (1848), 1550 Clinton Ave. N., Rochester, NY 14621; 17,000.

**UNICEF, U.S. Committee for** (1947), 331 E. 38th St., N.Y., NY 10016.

**UFOs (Unidentified Flying Objects), Natl. Investigations Commitee on** (1967), 7970 Woodman Ave., Van Nuys, CA 91402; 1,300.

**Uniformed Services, Natl. Assn. for** (1968), 956 N. Monroe St., Arlington, VA 22201; 25,343.

**United Nations Assn. of the U.S.A.** (1923, as League of Nations Assn.) 300 E. 42d St., N.Y., NY 10017; 27,200.

**United Press Intl.** (1907), 220 E. 42d St., N.Y., NY 10017.

**United Service Organizations (USO)** (1941), 237 E. 52d St., N.Y., NY 10022.

**United Way of America** (1932), 801 N. Fairfax St., Alexandria, VA 22314; 1,148.

**Universities, Assn. of Amer.** (1900), One Dupont Circle NW, Wash., DC 20036; 50 institutions.

**Universities & Colleges, Assn. of Governing Boards of**

921), One Dupont Circle NW, Wash., DC 20036; 17,000.

**University Extension Assn., Natl.** (1915), One Dupont Circle W, Wash., DC 20036; 1,375.

**University Foundation, Intl.** (1973), 501 E. Armour Blvd., ansas City, MO 64109; 692.

**University Professors, Amer. Assn. of** (1915), One Dupont rcle NW, Wash., DC 20036; 74,473.

**University Women, Amer. Assn. of** (1882), 2401 Virginia ve. NW, Wash., DC 20037; 190,000.

**Urban Coalition, Natl.** (1968), 1201 Connecticut Ave. NW, ʼash., DC 20024.

**Urban League, Natl.** (1910), 500 E. 62d St., N.Y., NY 10021.

**Utility Commissioners, Natl. Assn. of Regulatory** (1889), 102 ICC Bldg., P.O. Box 684, Wash., DC 20044; 308.

**Valley Forge, Society of the Descendants of Washington's Army at** (1976), Valley Forge Military Academy and Jr. ollege, Wayne, PA 19087; 206.

**Variety Clubs Intl.** (1928), 58 W. 58th St., N.Y., NY 10019; 1,000.

**VASA Order of America** (1896), 3720 Daryl Dr., Landisville, A 17538; 35,000.

**Veterans Assn., Blinded** (1945), 1735 DeSales St. NW, ʼash., DC 20036; 2,500.

**Veterans Committee, Amer.** (1948), 1333 Connecticut Ave. ⁣W, Wash., DC 20036; 10,000.

**Veterans of Foreign Wars of the U.S.** (1899) **& Ladies uxiliary** (1914), 406 W. 34th St., Kansas City, MO 64111; ,850,000 & 540,000.

**Veterans of World War I of the U.S.A.** (1953), 916 Prince t., Alexandria, VA 22314; 99,000.

**Veterinary Medical Assn., Amer.** (1863), 930 N. Meacham ⁣d., Schaumburg, IL 60196; 27,500.

**Victorian Society in America** (1966), The Athenaeum, East ʼashington Sq., Phila., PA 19106; 3,500.

**Vocational Assn., Amer.** (1925), 1510 H St. NW, Wash., DC 005; 55,000.

**Volleyball Assn., U.S.** (1928), P.O. Box 77065, San Fran⁣isco, CA 94107; 14,350.

**Walking Assn.** (1976), 4113 Lee Hwy., Arlington, VA 22207; 12.

**War of 1812, General Society of the** (1814), 1307 New ⁣lampshire Ave. NW, Wash., DC 20036; 1,800.

**War Mothers, Amer.** (1917), 2615 Woodley Pl. NW, Wash., ⁣C 20008; 11,000.

**Warrant and Warrant Officers' Assn., U.S. Coast Guard** ⁣hief (1929), 955 L'Enfant Plaza N., SW, Wash., DC 20024; ,138.

**Watch & Clock Collectors, Natl. Assn. of** (1943), 514 Popu⁣ar St., Columbia, PA 17512; 30,500.

**Watercolor Society, Amer.** (1866), 1083 Fifth Ave., N.Y., NY 0028; 575.

**Water Pollution Control Federation** (1928), 2626 Pennsyl⁣ania Ave. NW, Wash., DC 20037; 26,000.

**Water Resources Assn., Amer.** (1964), St. Anthony Falls ⁣lydraulic Lab, Mississippi River at 3d Ave. SE, Minneapolis, MN ⁣5414; 1,523.

**Water Ski Assn., Amer.** (1939), State Rte. 550 at Carl Floyd ⁣Id., Winter Haven, FL 33880; 15,000.

**Water Well Assn., Natl.** (1948), 500 W. Wilson Bridge Rd., ʼorthington, OH 43085; 5,291.

**Water Works Assn., Amer.** (1881), 6666 W. Quincy Ave., ⁣enver, OH 80235; 26,000.

**Weather Modification Assn.** (1950), P.O. Box 8116, Fresno, ⁣A 93727; 300.

**Welding Society, Amer.** (1919), 2501 NW 7th St., Miami, FL ⁣3125; 30,560.

**Wheelchair Athletic Assn., Natl.** (1958), 40-24 62d St., ⁣Woodside, NY 11377; 2,500.

**Wilderness Society** (1935), 1901 Pennsylvania Ave. NW, ʼash., DC 20006; 75,000.

**Wild Horse Organized Assistance (WHOA!)** (1971), 63 ⁣Keyston, P.O. Box 555, Reno, NV 89504; 12,000.

**Wildlife, Defenders of** (1925), 1244 19th St. NW, Wash., DC ⁣20036; 35,000.

**Wildlife Federation, Natl.** (1936), 1412 16th St. NW, Wash., ⁣C 20036; 3,500,000.

**Wildlife Foundation, No. Amer.** (1935), 1000 Vermont Ave. ⁣W, Wash., DC 20005.

**Wildlife Fund—U.S., World** (1961), 1319 18th St. NW, ʼash., DC 20036; 50,000.

**Wildlife Management Institute** (1911), 1000 Vermont Ave. ⁣W, Wash., DC 20005.

**Wildlife Society** (1937), 7101 Wisconsin Ave. NW, Wash., ⁣C 20014; 7,500.

**William Penn Assn.** (1886), 429 Forbes Ave., Pittsburgh, PA 15219; 66,902.

**Wireless Pioneers, Society of** (1967), P.O. Box 530, 3366—15 Mendocino Ave., Santa Rosa, CA 95401; 3,267.

**Wizard of Oz Club, Internatl.** (1957), Box 95, Kinderhook, IL 62345; 1,628.

**Woman's Assn., Amer.** (1914), 1271 Ave. of the Americas, N.Y., NY 10020; 250.

**Woman's Christian Temperance Union, Natl.** (1874), 1730 Chicago Ave., Evanston, IL 60201; 250,000.

**Women Artists, Natl. Assn.** (1889), 41 Union Sq., N.Y., NY 10003.

**Women, Natl. Organization for (NOW)** (1966), 425 13th St. NW, Wash., DC 20004; 85,000.

**Women Engineers, Society of** (1950), 345 E. 47th St., N.Y., NY 10017; 3,800.

**Women Geographers, Society of** (1925), 1619 New Hampshire Ave. NW, Wash., DC 20009; 460.

**Women Marines Assn.** (1960), 5403 Oakhurst Dr. N., Seminole, FL 33542; 2,700.

**Women, Rural American** (1977), 1522 K St. NW, Wash., DC 20037.

**Women Strike for Peace** (1961), 145 S. 13th St., Phila., PA 19107; 10,000.

**Women of the U.S.A., Natl. Council of** (1888), 345 E. 46th St., N.Y., NY 10017; 22,000,000.

**Women Voters of the U.S., League of** (1920), 1730 M St. NW, Wash., DC 20036; 140,000.

**Women World War Veterans** (1919), 237 Madison Ave., N.Y., NY 10016; 145,000.

**Women's Army Corps Veterans Assn.** (1946), 3839-37 Vista Campana So., Oceanside, CA 92054; 1,905.

**Women's Clubs, General Federation of** (1890), 1734 N St. NW, Wash., DC 20036; 10,000,000.

**Women's Clubs, Natl. Federation of Business & Professional** (1919), 2012 Massachusetts Ave. NW, Wash., DC 20036; 170,000.

**Women's Educational & Industrial Union** (1877), 356 Boylston St., Boston, MA 02116; 2,500.

**Women's Internatl. League for Peace & Freedom** (1915), 1213 Race St., Phila., PA 19118; 10,000.

**Women's Overseas Service League** (1921), P.O. Box 39033, Friendship Sta., Wash., DC 20016; 5,000.

**Women's Veterinary Medical Assn.** (1947), c/o Dr. Judith Spurling, 6246 S. Ash Circle E., Littleton, CO 81001.

**Woodmen of America, Modern** (1883), 1701 First Ave., Rock Island, IL 61201; 500,000.

**Woodmen of the World** (1890), 1450 Speer Blvd., Denver, CO 80204; 28,954.

**Wool Growers Assn., Natl.** (1865), 336 Southern Bldg., 805 15th St. NW, Wash., DC 20005; 24 state assns.

**Workmen's Circle** (1900), 45 E. 33d St., N.Y., NY 10016; 55,000.

**World Federalists, World Assn. of** (1946), Leliegracht 21, Amsterdam, Netherlands; 40,000.

**World Future Society** (1966), 4916 St. Elmo Ave., Wash., DC 20014; 24,000.

**World Health, Amer. Assn. for** (1951), 777 United Nations Plaza, N.Y., NY 10017; 1,031.

**Writers, Amer. Society of** (1975), 890 National Press Bldg., Wash., DC 20045; 1,300.

**Writers of America, Western** (1952), 1505 W. D St., North Platte, NE 69101; 325.

**Writers Assn. of America, Outdoor** (1927), 4141 W. Bradley Rd., Milwaukee, WI 53209; 1,400.

**Writers Guild of America, West** (1932), 8955 Beverly Blvd., Los Angeles, CA 90048; 4,800.

**Yeoman F. Natl.** (1936), 223 El Camino Real, Vallejo, CA 94590; 800.

**Young Americans for Freedom** (1960), Woodland Rd., Sterling, VA 22170; 55,000.

**Young Men's Christian Assns. of the U.S.A., Natl. Council of** (1851), 291 Broadway, N.Y., NY 10007; 9,000,000.

**Youth Allied** (1936), 933 N. Kenmore St., Arlington, VA 22201; 10,000.

**YM-YWHAs of Greater New York, Associated** (1957), 130 E. 59th St., N.Y., NY 10022; 60,000.

**Young Women's Christian Assn. of the U.S.A.** (1858), 600 Lexington Ave., N.Y., NY 10022; 2,471,000.

**Youth Hostels, Amer.** (1934), Natl. Campus, Delaplane, VA 22025; 70,000.

**Zero Population Growth** (1968), 1346 Connecticut Ave. NW, Wash., DC 20036; 8,000.

**Ziegfeld Club** (1936), 55 W. 42d St., N.Y., NY 10036; 347.

**Zionist Organization of America** (1897), 4 E. 34th St., N.Y., NY 10016; 130,000.

**Zonta Intl.** (1919), 59 E. Van Buren St., Chicago, IL 60605; 30,000.

**Zoological Parks & Aquariums, Amer. Assn. of** (1924), Oglebay Park, Wheeling, WV 26003; 2,500.

**Zoologists, Amer. Society of** (1913), Box 2739, California Lutheran College, Thousand Oaks, CA 91360; 4,600.

# RELIGIOUS INFORMATION
## Census of Religious Groups in the U.S.

Source: World Almanac questionnaire and 1978 Yearbook of American and Canadian Churches

Membership figures in the following table are the latest available. Some denominations submitted carefully compiled data while others approached the task more casually. The number of churches is given in parentheses. Asterisk (*) indicates church declines to publish membership figures.

| Denomination | Members |
|---|---|
| **Adventist churches:** | |
| Advent Christian Ch. (375) | 31,188 |
| Primitive Advent Christian Ch. (10) | 514 |
| Seventh-day Adventists (3,742) | 551,884 |
| **American Rescue Workers (14)** | 750 |
| **Anglican Orthodox Church (40)** | * |
| **Baha'i Faith (5,500)** | * |
| **Baptist churches:** | |
| Amer. Baptist Chs. in U.S.A. (5,876) | 1,584,517 |
| Baptist General Conference (624) | 113,163 |
| Baptist Missionary Assn. of America (1,478) | 216,471 |
| Conservative Baptist Assn. of America (1,111) | 300,000 |
| Duck River (and Kindred) Assn. of Baptists (85) | 8,632 |
| Free Will Baptists (2,408) | 229,480 |
| Gen. Assn. of General Baptists (867) | 72,030 |
| Gen. Assn. of Regular Baptist Chs. (1,542) | 235,918 |
| Natl. Primitive Baptist Convention (606) | 250,000 |
| No. Amer. Baptist Conference (251) | 42,745 |
| Seventh Day Baptist General Conference (60) | 5,156 |
| Southern Baptist Convention (35,255) | 13,083,199 |
| **Brethren (German Baptists):** | |
| Brethren Ch. (Ashland, Ohio) (124) | 15,619 |
| Ch. of the Brethren (1,041) | 178,157 |
| Fellowship of Grace Brethren Chs. (249) | 37,727 |
| Old German Baptist Brethren (50) | 4,900 |
| **Brethren, River:** | |
| Brethren in Christ Ch. (162) | 11,915 |
| **Buddhist Churches of America (159)** | 11,375 |
| **Calvary Grace Christian Churches of Faith (350).** | * |
| **Calvary Grace Church of Faith, Inc. (100)** | 10,000 |
| **Christadelphians (100)** | 5,000 |
| **The Christian and Missionary Alliance (1,561).** | 112,867 |
| **Christian Catholic Church (6)** | 2,500 |
| **Christian Church (Disciples of Christ) (4,376).** | 1,256,849 |
| **Christian Churches and Chuches of Christ (5,436)** | 1,040,856 |
| **Christian Nation Church U.S.A. (12)** | 800 |
| **Christian Union (104)** | 4,590 |
| **Churches of Christ (17,000)** | 2,500,000 |
| **Churches of Christ in Christian Union (250)** | 10,177 |
| **Churches of God:** | |
| Chs. of God, General Conference (347) | 36,359 |
| Church of God (2,274) | 171,947 |
| Ch. of God (Anderson, Ind.) (2,270) | 170,285 |
| Ch. of God (Seventh Day), Denver, Col. (104). | 8,000 |
| **Church of Christ, Scientist (3,000)** | * |
| **The Church of God by Faith (105)** | 4,500 |
| **Church of the Nazarene (4,730)** | 455,648 |
| **Church of Revelation (8)** | 750 |
| **National Council of Community Churches (185).** | 125,000 |
| **Natl. Assn. of Congregational Christian Churches (383)** | 100,000 |
| **Conservative Congregational Christian Conference (130)** | 21,977 |
| **Eastern Orthodox churches:** | |
| Albanian Orth. Diocese of America (10) | 5,235 |
| American Carpatho-Russian Orth. Greek Catholic Ch. (70) | 100,000 |
| Antiochian Orth. Christian Archdiocese of No. Amer. (114) | 150,000 |
| Diocese of the Armenian Ch. of America (51) | 1,700,000 |
| Bulgarian Eastern Orth. Ch. (15) | 4,000 |
| Coptic Orthodox Ch. (14). | 40,000 |
| Greek Orth. Archdiocese of N. and S. America (535). | 1,950,000 |
| Orthodox Ch. in America (425) | 1,000,000 |
| Romanian Orth. Episcopate of America (34). | 40,000 |
| Patriarchal Parishes of the Russian Orth. Ch. in the U.S.A. (41) | 51,500 |
| Serbian Eastern Orth. Ch. (47) | 20,000 |
| Syrian Orth. Ch. of Antioch (Archdiocese of | |

| Denomination | Members |
|---|---|
| the U.S.A. and Canada) (9) | 25,000 |
| Ukrainian Orth. Ch. in America (Ecumenical Partriarchate) (21) | 25,000 |
| **The Episcopal Church in the U.S.A. (7,494)** | 3,070,349 |
| **American Ethical Union (Ethical Culture Movement) (23)** | 5,000 |
| **Evangelical Christian Churches (129)** | 25,080 |
| **Evangelical Christian Churches, California Synod (142)** | 59,494 |
| **Evangelical Church of North America (127)** | 11,502 |
| **Evangelical Congregational Church (161)** | 28,840 |
| **The Evangelical Covenant Church of America (515).** | 74,060 |
| **Evangelical Free Church of America (621).** | 75,000 |
| **Evangelical associations:** | |
| Apostolic Christian Chs. of America (80) | 17,888 |
| Apostolic Christian Ch. (Nazarean) (43) | 2,428 |
| Christian Congregation (1,120) | 80,411 |
| **Friends:** | |
| Evangelical Friends Alliance (256) | 25,755 |
| Friends General Conference | 26,652 |
| Friends United Meeting (526) | 63,552 |
| Religious Society of Friends (Conservative) (27) | 1,728 |
| Religious Society of Friends (Unaffiliated Meetings) (87) | 5,69 |
| **Independent Fundamental Churches of America (665)** | 1,354 |
| **Grace Gospel Fellowship (43)** | 3,200 |
| **Jehovah's Witnesses (7,451)** | 505,592 |
| **Jewish congregations:** | |
| Agudath Israel of America (Orthodox) (40) | 100,000 |
| Union of Amer. Hebrew Congregations (Reformed) (720) | 1,100,000 |
| Natl. Council of Young Israel (Orthodox) | 200,000 |
| Union of Orthodox Jewish Congregations of America (500) | 250,000 |
| United Synagogue of America (Conservative) (830) | 225,000 families |
| **Latter-day Saints:** | |
| Ch. of Jesus Christ (Bickertonites) (41) | 2,500 |
| Ch. of Jesus Christ of Latter-day Saints (Mormon) (5,917) | 2,486,261 |
| Reorganized Ch. of Jesus Christ of Latter Day Saints (1,053) | 185,839 |
| **Lutheran churches:** | |
| American Lutheran Ch. (4,832) | 4,160,955 |
| Ch. of the Lutheran Brethren (100) | 9,630 |
| Ch. of the Lutheran Confession (72) | 9,684 |
| Assn. of Evangelical Lutheran Chs. (245) | 100,000 |
| Evangelical Lutheran Synod (106) | 19,571 |
| Assn. of Free Lutheran Congregations (131). | 14,000 |
| Latvian Evangelical Lutheran Church in America (59) | 13,247 |
| Lutheran Ch. in America (5,740) | 2,963,212 |
| Lutheran Ch.-Missouri Synod (5,722) | 2,681,620 |
| Protestant Conference (Lutheran) (9) | 2,660 |
| Wisconsin Evangelical Lutheran Synod (1,097) | 402,573 |
| **Mennonite churches:** | |
| Beachy Amish Mennonite Chs. (74) | 4,563 |
| Evangelical Mennonite Ch. (21) | 3,484 |
| General Conference of Mennonite Brethren Chs. (121) | 16,956 |
| The General Conference Mennonite Ch. (188) | 36,400 |
| Hutterian Brethren (63) | 8,954 |
| Mennonite Ch. (1,074) | 96,609 |
| Old Order Amish Ch. (497) | 32,305 |
| Old Order (Wisler) Mennonite Ch. (60) | 8,400 |

| Denomination | Members |
|---|---|
| **Methodist churches:** | |
| African Methodist Episcopal Ch. (3,987) | 2,000,000 |
| African Methodist Episcopal Zion Ch. (6,000) | 1,083,391 |
| Evangelical Methodist Ch. (133) | 10,178 |
| Free Methodist Ch. of North America (1,036) | 69,134 |
| Fundamental Methodist Ch. (15) | 745 |
| Primitive Methodist Chs., U.S.A. (89) | 10,329 |
| Reformed Methodist Union Episcopal Ch. (20) | 4,500 |
| Southern Methodist Ch. (169) | 10,500 |
| United Methodist Ch. (38,744) | 9,785,534 |
| Univeral Fellowship of Metropolitan Community Chs. (95) | 21,000 |
| **Moravian churches:** | |
| Moravian Ch. in America (Unitas Fratrum), Northern Province (95) | 32,497 |
| Moravian Ch. in America (Unitas Fratrum), Southern Province (50) | 20,957 |
| Unity of the Brethren (26) | * |
| **Muslims** | **2,000,000** |
| **New Apostolic Church of North America (327)** | **24,361** |
| **North American Old Roman Catholic Church (5)** | **1,525** |
| **Old Catholic churches:** | |
| American Catholic Ch. (Syro-Antiochean) (3) | 495 |
| Christ Catholic Ch. (7) | 2,537 |
| Mariavite Old Cath. Ch. Province of North America (157) | 350,542 |
| No. Amer. Old Roman Cath. Ch. (Schweikert) (161) | 61,300 |
| **Pentecostal churches:** | |
| Apostolic Faith (45) | 4,100 |
| Assemblies of God (9,208) | 1,302,318 |
| Bible Church of Christ (5) | 1,800 |
| Bible Way Church of Our Lord Jesus Christ World Wide (100) | 100,000 |
| Church of God (Cleveland, Tenn.) (4,783) | 380,683 |
| Church of God of Prophecy (1,791) | 65,801 |
| Congregational Holiness Ch. (175) | 5,925 |
| Gen. Conference, Christian Ch. of No. Amer. (111) | 12,000 |
| Intl. Ch. of the Foursquare Gospel (789) | 127,205 |
| Open Bible Standard Chs. (274) | 30,000 |
| Pentecostal Assemblies of the World (150) | 15,000 |

| Denomination | Members |
|---|---|
| Pentecostal Church of Christ (50) | 1,659 |
| Pentecostal Church of God of America (1,300) | 135,000 |
| United Pentecostal Ch. (2,950) | 440,000 |
| Pentecostal Free-Will Baptist Ch. (136) | 10,000 |
| **Plymouth Brethren (745)** | **74,000** |
| **Presbyterian churches:** | |
| Associate Reformed Presbyterian Ch. (Gen. Synod) (156) | 31,854 |
| Cumberland Presbyterian Ch. (857) | 88,352 |
| Orthodox Presbyterian Ch. (151) | 15,536 |
| Presbyterian Ch. in America (428) | 73,899 |
| Presbyterian Ch. in the U.S. (4,036) | 877,664 |
| Reformed Presbyterian Ch., Evangelical Synod (142) | 24,248 |
| Reformed Presbyterian Ch. of No. Amer. (71) | 5,151 |
| United Presbyterian Ch. in the U.S.A. (8,656) | 2,569,437 |
| **Reformed churches:** | |
| Christian Reformed Ch. (610) | 210,088 |
| Hungarian Reformed Ch. in America (28) | 11,679 |
| Protestant Reformed Chs. in America (21) | 3,871 |
| Reformed Ch. in America (916) | 215,188 |
| Reformed Ch. in the U.S. (26) | 3,861 |
| **The Roman Catholic Church (18,572)** | **49,325,752** |
| **The Salvation Army (1,178)** | **380,618** |
| **The Schwenkfelder Church (5)** | **2,748** |
| **Social Brethren (30)** | **1,784** |
| **Natl. Spiritualist Assn. of Churches (164)** | **5,168** |
| **Gen. Convention The Swedenborgian Church (35)** | **3,500** |
| **Unitarian Universalist Assn. (1,000)** | **186,153** |
| **United Brethren:** | |
| Ch. of the United Brethren in Christ (281) | 28,035 |
| United Christian Ch. (11) | 430 |
| **United Church of Christ (6,510)** | **1,778,000** |
| **Vedanta Society of N.Y. (12)** | **1,000** |
| **Volunteers of America (572)** | **31,786** |
| **The Wesleyan Church (1,808)** | **102,482** |
| **Worldwide Church of God (306)** | **66,529** |

## Religious Population of the World

Source: The 1978 Encyclopaedia Britannica Book of the Year

| Religion | N. America[1] | S. America | Europe[2] | Asia | Africa | Oceania[3] | Totals |
|---|---|---|---|---|---|---|---|
| Total Christian | 231,099,700 | 158,980,000 | 348,059,300 | 89,909,000 | 137,460,300 | 18,112,600 | 983,620,900 |
| Roman Catholic | 131,631,500 | 147,280,000 | 182,514,300 | 47,046,000 | 53,740,000 | 4,475,000 | 566,686,800 |
| Eastern Orthodox | 4,189,000 | 552,000 | 50,545,000 | 1,894,000 | 15,255,000[4] | 380,000 | 72,815,000 |
| Protestant[5] | 95,279,200 | 11,148,000 | 115,000,000 | 40,969,000 | 68,465,300[6] | 13,257,600 | 344,119,100 |
| Jewish | 6,641,118 | 727,000 | 4,082,400 | 3,203,460 | 294,400 | 84,000 | 15,032,378 |
| Moslem | 249,200 | 238,300 | 8,283,500 | 433,001,000 | 134,285,200 | 103,000 | 576,160,200 |
| Zoroastrian | 250 | 2,000 | 6,000 | 224,700 | 600 | — | 233,550 |
| Shinto | 60,000 | 92,000 | — | 55,004,000 | — | — | 55,156,000 |
| Taoist[7] | 16,000 | 12,000 | — | 31,088,100 | — | — | 31,116,100 |
| Confucian[7] | 96,100 | 85,150 | 25,000 | 173,940,250 | 500 | 42,200 | 174,189,200 |
| Buddhist | 155,250 | 195,300 | 200,000 | 260,117,000 | 2,000 | 16,000 | 260,685,550 |
| Hindu | 81,000 | 782,300 | 260,000 | 515,449,500 | 483,650 | 841,000 | 517,897,450 |
| Totals | 238,398,618 | 161,114,050 | 360,916,200 | 1,561,937,010 | 272,526,650 | 19,198,800 | 2,614,091,328 |
| Population[8] | 353,560,000 | 230,139,000 | 738,746,000 | 2,355,700,000 | 423,655,000 | 22,157,000 | 4,123,957,000 |

(1) Includes Central America and the West Indies. (2) Includes communist countries where it is difficult to determine religious affiliation. (3) Includes Australia, New Zealand, and islands of the South Pacific. (4) Includes Coptic christians. (5) Protestant figures outside Europe usually include "full members" rather than all baptized persons and are not comparable to those of ethnic religions or churches counting all adherents. (6) Including many new sects and cults among African christians. (7) Statistics for Confucianism and Taoism are undeterminable in China since the Maoist-Marxist revolution. (8) Continental total populations are United Nations data.

## National Council of Churches

The National Council of the Churches of Christ in the U.S.A. is a cooperative federation of 31 Protestant and Orthodox churches which seeks to advance programs and policies of mutual interest to its members. The NCC was formed in 1950 by the merger of 12 inter-denominational agencies. The Council's member churches now have an aggregate membership totaling approximately 40 million. The NCC is not a governing body and has no control over the policies or operations of any church belonging to it. The work of the Council is divided into 3 divisions — Church and Society; Education and Ministry; Overseas Ministries — and 5 commissions — Faith and Order; Regional and Local Ecumenism; Communication; Stewardship; and Justice, Liberation, and Human Fulfillment. The chief administrative officer of the NCC is Dr. Claire Randall, 475 Riverside Drive, N.Y., NY 10027.

# Headquarters, Leaders of U.S. Religious Groups

See Associations and Societies section for religious organizations. (year organized in parentheses)

*Adventist churches:*
**Advent Christian Church** (1854) — Pres., Joe Tom Tate; exec. v.p., Rev. Adrian B. Shepard, Box 23152, Charlotte, NC 28212.

**Seventh-day Adventists** (1863) — Pres., Robert H. Pierson; sec., C.O. Franz, 6840 Eastern Ave. NW, Wash., DC 20012.

**Baha'i Faith** — Chpsn., Dr. Daniel C. Jordan; sec., Glenford E. Mitchell, 536 Sheridan Rd., Wilmette, IL 60091.

*Baptist churches:*
**American Baptist Assn.** (1905) — Pres., Dr. I K. Cross; rec. clk., W E. Norris, 4605 N. State Line, Texarkana, TX 75501.

**American Baptist Churches in the U.S.A.** (1907) — Pres., Mrs. Cora Sparrowk; gen. sec., Rev. Dr. Robert C. Campbell, Valley Forge, PA 19481.

**Baptist General Conference** (1879) — Gen. sec., Warren Magnuson, 1233 Central St., Evanston, IL 60201.

**Baptist Missionary Assn. of America** (formerly **North American Baptist Assn.**) (1950) — Pres., Rev. Ray Thornton; rec. sec., Rev. Ralph Cottrell, Box 2866, Texarkana, AR 75501.

**Conservative Baptist Assn. of America** (1947) — Pres., Dr. Lee W. Toms; sec., Rev. C. E. Abrahamsen Jr., Genva Rd., Box 66, Wheaton, IL 60187.

**Free Will Baptists** (1727) — Mod., Rev. Robert Jackson; exec. sec., Rufus Coffey, Box 1088, Nashville, TN 37202.

**General Assn. of General Baptists** (1823) — Mod., Dr. Kenneth Kennedy; exec. sec., Rev. Glen Spence, Box 537, Poplar Bluff, MO 63901.

**General Assn. of Regular Baptist Churches** (1932) — Chpsn., Dr. Mark Jackson; natl. rep., Dr. Joseph M. Stowell, 1300 N. Meacham Rd., Schaumburg, IL 60195.

**North American Baptist Conference** (1865) — Mod., Rev. Kenneth L. Fischer; exec. sec., Dr. Gideon K. Zimmerman, 1 S. 210 Summit Ave., Oakbrook Terrace, IL 60181.

**Southern Baptist Convention** (1945) — Pres., Jimmy Allen; exec. sec., Dr. Porter Routh, 460 James Robertson Pkwy., Nashville, TN 37219.

**United Free Will Baptist Church** (1870) — Vice-mod., Rev. O.L. Williams; gen. rec. sec., Rev. J.H. O'Neal, Kinston College, 1000 University St., Kinston, NC 28501.

**Brethren in Christ Church** (1798) — Mod., Bishop R. Donald Shafer; sec., Dr. Arthur M. Climenhaga, 4200 SE Jennings Ave., Portland, OR 97222.

*Brethren (German Baptists):*
**Brethren Church (Ashland, Oh.)** (1708) — Mod., James R. Black; exec. sec., Rev. Smith F. Rose, 524 College Ave., Ashland, OH 44805.

**Church of the Brethren** (1719) — Mod., Warren Groff; gen. sec., Robert Neff, 1451 Dundee Ave., Elgin, IL

**Buddhist Churches of America** (1899) — Bishop, Rt. Rev. Kenryu Tsuji, 1710 Octavia St., San Francisco, CA 94109.

**Calvary Grace Christian Church of Faith** (1898) — Intl. gen. supt., Rev. Dr. Herman Keck Jr., 5610 Tennessee Ave., Chattanooga, TN 37409.

**Calvary Grace Church of Faith** (1874) — Intl. gen. supt., Rev. A.C. Spern, Box 333, Rillton, PA 15678.

**The Christian and Missionary Alliance** (1887) — Pres., Dr. Nathan Bailey; sec., Dr. R.W. Battles, 350 N. Highland Ave., Nyack, NY 10960.

**Christian Church (Disciples of Christ)** (1809) — Gen. minister and pres., Dr. Kenneth L. Teegarden, 222 S. Downey Ave., Box 1986, Indianapolis, IN 46206.

**The Christian Congregation** (1887) — Gen. supt., Rev. Ora Wilbert Eads, 804 W. Hemlock St., LaFollette, TN 37766.

**Churches of Christ in Christian Union** (1909) — Gen. supt., Rev. Donovan Humble; adm., Rev. Paul Dorsey, Box 30, Circleville, OH 43113.

*Churches of God:*
**Churches of God, General Conference** (1825) — Pres., Lloyd Harlan; sec., Rev. Harry Cadamore, 2200 Jennifer La., Box 926, Findlay, OH 45840.

**Church of God (Anderson, Ind.)** (1880) — Chpsn., Paul L. Hart; exec. sec., W.E. Reed, Box 2420, Anderson, IN 46011.

**Church of Christ, Scientist** (1879) — Pres., John R. Peterson; clerk, Corinne LaBarre, Christian Science Center, Boston, MA 02115.

**Church of the Nazarene** (1908) — Gen. sec., B. Edgar Johnson, 6401 The Paseo, Kansas City, MO 64131.

**National Association of Congregational Christian Churches** (1955) — Mod., John A. Strom; exec. sec., Rev. Dr. Erwin A Britton, Box 1620, Oak Creek, WI 53154.

*Eastern Orthodox churches:*
**Antiochian Orthodox Christian Archdiocese of North America** (formerly **Syrian Antiochian Orthodox Church**) (1894) — Primate, Metropolitan Archbishop Philip (Saleba); aux. Archbishop Michael Shaheen, 358 Mountain Rd., Englewood, NJ 07631.

**Diocese of the Armenian Church of America** (1889) — Primate, His Eminence Archbishop Torkom Manoogian; sec., V Rev. Paren Avedikian, 630 2d Ave., N.Y., NY 10016.

**Coptic Orthodox Ch.** — Correspnt., Archpriest Fr. Gabrie Abdelsayed, 427 West Side Ave., Jersey City, NJ 07304.

**Greek Orthodox Archdiocese of North and South America** (1864) — Primate, Archbishop Iakovos; chan., V. Rev George Bacopulos, 8-10 E. 79th St., N.Y., NY 10021.

**Orthodox Church in America** (formerly **Russian Orthodox Greek Catholic Church of North America**) (1794) — Primate Metropolitan Theodosius; chan., V. Rev. Daniel Hubiak, Rt. 25A Box 675, Syosset, NY 11791.

**Romanian Orthodox Episcopate of America** (1929) — Bishop, Archbishop Valerian D. Trifa; sec., Rev. Laurence C Lazar, 2522 Grey Tower Rd., Jackson, MI 49201.

**Serbian Orthodox Diocese for the U.S.A. and Canada** Bishops, Most Rev. Dionisije and Iriney; sec., V. Rev. Aleksand Ivanovich, St. Sava Monastery, Libertyville, IL 60048.

**Syrian Orthodox Church of Antioch, Archdiocese of the U.S.A. and Canada** (1957) — Primate, Archbishop MarA thanasius Y. Samuel; gen. sec., Rev. Fr. John Meno, 293 Hamil ton Pl., Hackensack, NJ 07601.

**Ukrainian Orthodox Church of America (Ecumenical Patri archate)** (1928) — Primate, Most. Rev. Bishop Andrei Kuschak chan., V. Rev. H. Wroblewsky, 90-34 139th St., Jamaica, N 11435.

**Ukrainian Orthodox Church in the U.S.A.** (1919) — Metro politan, Most Rev. Mstyslav S. Skrypnyk, Box 495, South Boune Brook, NJ 08880.

**The Episcopal Church** (1789) — Presiding bishop, Rt. Rev John M. Allin; exec. sec., Rev. James R. Gundrum, 815 2d Ave N.Y., NY 10017.

**Evangelical Christian Churches** (1966) — Pres., Rev. Joh Wahnert, 2075-AN, John Russell Circle, Elkins Park, PA 19117.

**Evangelical Christian Churches, California Synod** (1966) — Pres.-Treas., Dr. Richard W. Hart Sr., Box 399, Huntington Park CA 90255.

**The Evangelical Covenant Church of America** (1885) — Pres., Dr. Milton B. Engebretson; sec., Rev. Clifford Bjorklund 5101 N. Francisco Ave., Chicago, IL 60625.

*Friends:*
**Evangelical Friends Alliance** (1965) — Pres., Norval Hadley Box 190, Newberg, OR 97132.

**Friends General Conference** (1900) — Chmn. Stephen L Angell Jr.; exec. dir., Dwight L. Wilson, 1520-B Race St., Phila. PA 19102.

**Friends United Meeting** (formerly **Five Years Meeting of Friends**) (1902) — Presiding clerk, J. Binford Farlow; gen. sec. Lorton G. Heusel, 101 Quaker Hill Dr., Richmond, IN 47374.

**Independent Fundamental Churches of America** (1930) — Exec. dir., Rev. Bryan J. Jones, 1860 S. Mannheim Rd., Box 250, Westchester, IL 60153.

**Islamic Center of Washington** — 2551 Massachusetts Ave. NW, Washington, DC 20008.

**Jehovah's Witnesses** (1884) — Pres., F.W. Franz, 124 Columbia Heights, Brooklyn, NY 11201.

*Jewish congregations:*
**Union of American Hebrew Congregations** (Reform) — Pres., Rabbi Alexander M. Schindler, 838 5th Ave., N.Y., NY 10021.

**National Council of Young Israel** (Orthodox) (1912) —

es., Herman Rosenbaum; exec. v.p., Rabbi Ephraim H. Sturm,
W. 16th St:, N.Y., NY 10011.
**Union of Orthodox Jewish Congregations of America** —
res., Harold Jacobs, 116 E. 27th St., N.Y., NY 10016.
**United Synagogue of America** (Conservative) — Pres., Ar-
ur Levine, 155 5th Ave., N.Y., NY 10010.

**atter-day Saints:**
**The Church of Jesus Christ of Latter-day Saints (Mor-**
on) (1830) — Pres., Spencer W. Kimball; recorder, Leonard L.
rrington, 50 E. North Temple St., Salt Lake City, UT 84111.
**Reorganized Church of Jesus Christ of Latter Day Saints**
830) — Pres., W. Wallace Smith; pub. info., Elroy E. Hanton,
aints Auditorium, Independence, MO 64051.

**utheran churches:**
**The American Lutheran Church** (1961) — Pres., Dr. David
. Preus; gen. sec., Dr. A.R. Mickelson, 422 S. 5th St., Minneap-
is, MN 55415.
**Church of the Lutheran Brethren** (1900) — Pres., Rev. E.
Strom; sec., Rev. Robert M. Sletta, 1007 Westside Dr., Box
55, Fergus Falls, MN 56537.
**Church of the Lutheran Confession** (1961) — Pres., Rev.
gbert Albrecht; sec., Rev. Paul Nolting, Rt. 2, Markesan, WI
3946.
**Assn. of Evangelical Lutheran Churches** (1976) — Pres.,
r. William H. Kohn; exec. sec., Elwyn Ewald, 12015 Manches-
r Rd., St. Louis, MO 63131.
**Evangelical Lutheran Synod** (1853) — Pres., Rev. W.W. Pe-
rsen; sec., Rev. Alf Merseth, 106 13th St. S., Northwood, IA
0459.
**Assn. of Free Lutheran Congregations** (1962) — Pres.,
ev. John P. Strand; sec. Rev. Einar Unseth, 3110 E. Medicine
ake Blvd., Minneapolis, MN 55441.
**Lutheran Church in America** (1962) — Pres., Rev. Dr.
ames R. Crumley; sec., Rev. Dr. Reuban T. Swanson, 231
adison Ave., N.Y. NY 10016.
**Lutheran Church — Missouri Synod** (1847) — Pres., Dr.
.O. Preus; sec., Rev. Herbert A. Mueller, 500 N. Broadway,
t. Louis, MO 63102.
**Wisconsin Evangelical Lutheran Synod** (1850) — Pres.,
ev. Oscar Naumann; sec., Heinrich J. Vogel, 11757 N. Semi-
ary Dr., 65W, Mequon, WI 53092.

**Mennonite churches:**
**The General Conference Mennonite Church** (1860) —
res. Elmer Neufeld; gen. sec., Heinz Janzen, 722 Main, Box
47, Newton, KS 67114.
**Mennonite Church** (1690) — Mod., Willis L. Breckbill; sec.,
an J. Kauffmann, 528 E. Madison St., Lombard, IL 60148.

**Methodist churches:**
**African Methodist Episcopal Zion Church** (1796) — Sr.
ishop, Herbert Shaw; gen. sec.-aud., Rev. Herman L. Ander-
on, Box 1401, Charlotte, NC 28232.
**Evangelical Methodist Church** (1946) — Gen. supt., John F.
unkle; gen. sec., Rev. R.D. Driggers, Box 4309, Wichita, KS
7204.
**Free Methodist Church of North America** (1860) — Bishop,
onald N. Bastian; gen. conf. sec., C.T. Denbo, 901 College
ve., Winona Lake, IN 46590.
**The United Methodist Church** (1968) — Pres., Bishop Mar-
n Stuart; sec., Bishop James K. Mathews, 100 Maryland Ave.
IE, Wash., DC 20002.
**Universal Fellowship of Metropolitan Community Churches**
–Mod., Rev. Troy Perry; exec. sec., Frank K. Zerilli, Box 5570,
os Angeles, CA 90055.
**Moravian Church in America (Unitas Fratum)** (1740) North-
rn Province — Pres., Dr. J.S. Groenfeldt, 69 W. Church St.,
ox 1245, Bethlehem, PA 18018. **Southern Province** — Pres.,
r. Richard F. Amos, 459 S. Church St., Winston-Salem, NC
7101.

**Old Catholic churches:**
**Mariavite Old Catholic Church-Province of North America**
1932) — Prime bishop, Most Rev. Archbishop Robert R.J.M.
aborowski; chan., Rev. Fr. A.E. Giles Maria Solochier, 2803
0th St., Wyandotte, MI 48192.
**North American Old Roman Catholic Church** (1915) —
rchbishop, Most Rev. J.E. Schweikert, 4200 N. Kedvale Ave.,
hicago, IL 60641.

**Pentecostal churches:**
**Assemblies of God** (1914) — Gen. supt., Thomas F. Zim-
herman; gen. sec., Joseph R. Flower, 1445 Boonville Ave.,
pringfield, MO 65802.
**Bible Way Church of Our Lord Jesus Christ World Wide**
1927) — Presiding bishop, Dr. Smallwood E. Williams, 1100
ew Jersey Ave. NW, Wash., DC 20001.

**Gen. Council, Christian Church of No. America** (1948) —
Gen. overseer; Rev. Dr. Carmine Saginario; gen. sec., Rev.
Richard Tedesco, Box 801, 1818 State St., Sharon, PA 16146.
**The Church of God** (1903) — Gen. overseer, Bishop Voy M.
Bullen, 2504 Arrow Wood Dr. SE, Huntsville, AL 35803.
**Church of God (Cleveland, Tenn.)** (1886) — Gen. overseer,
Dr. Cecil B. Knight; gen. sec. Floyd Timmerman, Keith at 25th St.
NW, Cleveland, TN 37311.
**International Church of the Foursquare Gospel** (1927) —
Pres., Dr. Rolf K. McPherson; sec., Dr. Leland B. Edwards, 1100
Glendale Blvd., Los Angeles, CA 90026.
**Open Bible Standard Churches** (1919) — Gen. supt., Frank
W. Smith; sec.-treas., O. Ralph Isbill, 2020 Bell Ave., Des
Moines, IA 50315.
**Pentecostal Church of God of America** (1919) — Gen.
supt., Rev. Roy M. Chappell; sec.-treas., Rev. O. Lawrence Per-
kins, Messenger Plaza, 221 Main St., Joplin, MO 64801.
**United Pentecostal Church International** (1945) — Gen.
supt., Nathaniel A. Urshan; gen. sec., Robert L. McFarland, 8855
Dunn Rd., Hazelwood, MO 63042.
**Pentecostal Free Will Baptist Church** (1959) — Gen. supt.,
Rev. Herbert Carter; gen. sec., Rev. Don Sauls, Box 1081,
Dunn, NC 28334.

**Presbyterian churches:**
**Cumberland Presbyterian Church** (1810) — Mod., Fred
Bryson; stated clerk, T.V. Warnick, 1978 Union Ave., Memphis,
TN 38104.
**The Orthodox Presbyterian Church** (1936) — Mod. Wen-
dell L. Rockey Jr., stated clerk, Richard A. Barker, 7401 Old
York Rd., Phila., PA 19126.
**Presbyterian Church in America** (1973) — Mod. John T.
Clark; stated clerk, Rev. Morton H. Smith, Box 256, Clinton, MS
39056.
**Presbyterian Church in the U.S.** (1865) — Mod., Sara B.
Moseley; stated clerk, James E. Andrews, 341 Ponce de Leon
Ave. NE, Atlanta, GA 30308.
**Reformed Presbyterian Church, Evangelical Synod** (1965)
— Mod., Dr. L.E. Kilpatrick; stated clerk, Dr. Paul R. Gilchrist,
107 Hardy Rd., Lookout Mountain, TN 37350.
**United Presbyterian Church in the U.S.A.** (1958) — Mod.,
William P. Lytle; stated clerk, William P. Thompson, 475 River-
side Dr., N.Y., NY 10027.

**Reformed Episcopal Church** (1873) — Pres., Rev. Theophilos
J. Herter; sec., Rev. D. Ellsworth Raudenbush, 560 Fountain St.,
Havre de Grace, MD 21078.

**Reformed churches:**
**Christian Reformed Church in North America** (1847) —
Stated clerk, Rev. William P. Brink, 2850 Kalamazoo Ave., SE,
Grand Rapids, MI 49560.
**Reformed Church in America** (1628) — Pres., Rev. Albertus
G. Bossenbroek; gen. sec., Rev. Arie R. Brouwer, 475 Riverside
Dr., N.Y., NY 10027.

**Roman Catholic Church** — National Conference of Catholic
Bishops. Pres., Archbishop John R. Quinn; sec., Bishop Thomas
C. Kelly, O.P., 1312 Massachusetts Ave. NW, Wash., DC 20005.

**The Salvation Army** (1880) — Natl. cmdr., Paul S. Kaiser; natl.
chief sec., Col. Orval A. Taylor, 120-130 W. 14th St., N.Y., NY
10011.

**Sikh** (1972) — Chief adm., Siri Singh Sahib, Harbhajan Singh
Khalsa Yogiji; sec. gen., Mukhia Sardarni Sahiba, Sardarni
Premka Kaur Khalsa, 1649 S. Robertson Blvd., Los Angeles, CA
90035.

**Unitarian Universalist Assn.** (1961) — Pres., Dr. Paul Carnes;
sec., Lori Pederson, 25 Beacon St., Boston, MA 02108.

**United Brethren in Christ** (1789) — Chpsn., Bishop C. Ray
Miller; admin. asst., David G. Jackson, 302 Lake St., Box 650,
Huntington, IN 46750.

**United Church of Christ** (1957) — Pres., Rev. Avery D. Post;
sec., Rev. Joseph H. Evans, 297 Park Ave. S., N.Y., NY 10010.

**Volunteers of America** (1896) — Cmdr.-in-chief, Gen. John F.
McMahon; natl. field sec., Lt. Col. Belle Leach, 340 W. 85th St.,
N.Y., NY 10024.

**The Wesleyan Church** (1968) — Gen. supt., Dr. Robert W. Mc-
Intyre; sec., D. Wayne Brown, Box 2000, Marion, IN 46952.

**Worldwide Church of God** (1934) — Pastor gen., Herbert W.
Armstrong; adm., Garner Ted Armstrong, 300 W. Green St.,
Pasadena, CA 91123.

# Headquarters of Religious Groups in Canada

(year organized in parentheses)

**Anglican Church of Canada** (creation of General Synod 1893) - Primate, Most Rev. E.W. Scott; Gen. Sec. of the General Synod, The Ven. E.S. Light, 600 Jarvis St., Toronto, Ont. M4Y 2J6.

**Antiochian Orthodox Christian Church (Syrian)** - Rev. Anthony Gabriel, 555-575 Jean Talon E., Montreal, P.Q. H2R 1T8.

**Apostolic Church in Canada** - H.O. 27 Castlefield Ave., Toronto, Ont. M4R 1G3, Pres., Rev. D.S. Morris, 388 Gerald St., La Salle, P.Q.

**Baha'is of Canada, The National Spiritual Assembly of the** (1949) - Gen. Sec. J.D. Martin, 7200 Leslie St., Thornhill, Ont. L3T 2A1.

**Baptist Federation of Canada** - Pres., David Simmonds; Gen. Sec.-Treasurer, Rev. R. Fred Bullen, 91 Queen St., Brantford, Ont. N3T 5T6.

**Bible Holiness Movement, The** (1949) - Pres., Evangelist Wesley H. Wakefield, Box 223, Stn. A, Vancouver, B.C. V6C 2M3.

**Buddhist Churches of Canada** (1945) - Bishop, Rev. Seimoka Kosaka, 918 Bathurst St., Toronto, Ont. M5R 3G5.

**Canadian Council of Churches, The** (1938) - Pres., Rev. Lois Wilson, 40 St. Clair Ave. E., Toronto, Ont. M4T 1M9.

**Christian and Missionary Alliance in Canada, The** (1889) - Pres., Rev. W.J. Newell, 125 Panin Rd., Burlington, Ont. L7T 1N0.

**Christian Chu. ⅔ (Disciples of Christ)** (All Canada Committee formed 1922) - Exec. Min. Robert K. Leland, 39 Arkell Rd., R.R. 2, Guelph, Ont. N1H 6H8.

**Christian Science in Canada** - Mr. J.D. Fulton, 696 Yonge St., Ste. 403, Toronto, Ont. M4Y 2A7.

**Church of Jesus Christ of Latter Day Saints (Mormons)** (1830) - Pres. Calgary Stake, R.H. Walker, 930 Prospect Ave. S.W., Calgary Alta. T2T 0W5. Pres. Edmonton Stake, Warren S. Wilde, 5108-112 St. Edmonton, Alta. T6H 3J2. Pres. Toronto Stake, C.L. Merkley, 2 The Outlook, Islington, Ont. M9B 2X6. Pres. Vancouver Stake, R.W. Komm, 1384 Chartwell Dr., West Vancouver, B.O. V7S 2R5.

**Church of Jesus Christ of Latter Day Saints, The Reorganized** (1830) - Bishop of Canada and Regional Bishop Kenneth G. Fisher; Regional Pres. A. Alex Kahtava, Box 38, Guelph, Ont. N1H 6J6.

**Church of the Nazarene** (1902) - Dist. Superintendent of Canada Central District, Rev. N. Hightower, 38 Riverhead Dr., Rexdale, Ont.; Chairman of Exec. Board, Rev. Alexander Ardrey, 2236 Capitol Hill Crescent, N.W., Calgary, Alta. T2M 4B9.

**Fellowship of Evangelical Baptist Churches in Canada** (1953) - Gen. Sec. Rev. Roy W. Lawson, 74 Sheppard Ave. W., Willowdale, Ont. M2N 1M3.

**Free Methodist Church in Canada** (1880) - Pres. Bishop D.N. Bastian, 3 Harrowby St., Islington, Ont. M9B 3H3; Sec.,

Rev. C.A. Horton, 833 D Upper James St., Hamilton, Ont. L9 3A3.

**Greek Orthodox Church** - Ninth Archdiocese District, Cai ada, Titular bishop of Constantia, His Grace Sotirios, 27 Te dington Park Ave., Toronto, Ont. M4N 2C4.

**Jehovah's Witnesses** (Branch Office estab. in Winnip 1918) - Branch Overseer, Mr. Kenneth A. Little, 150 Bridgelar Ave., Toronto, Ont. M6A 1Z5.

**Jewish Congress** (1919) Exec. Vice-Pres., Alan Rose, 155 McGregor Ave., Montreal, P.Q. H3G 1C5.

**Lutheran Council in Canada** (a joint body of The Evange cal Lutheran Church of Canada, Lutheran Church-Canad and Lutheran Church in America - Canada Section) - Pres. Roger Nostibakken, Exec. Dir. W.A. Schultz, 500-365 Hargrav St., Winnipeg, Man. R3B 2K3.

**Mennonite Brethren Churches of North America. Can dian Conference** (inc. 1945) - Mod. Frank C. Peters, Wilfr Laurier Univ., Waterloo, Ont. N2L 3C5.

**Mennonites in Canada, Conference of** - Mod. Jake Harme 767 Buckingham Rd., Winnipeg, Man. R3R 1C3.

**Pentecostal Assemblies of Canada, The** (inc. 1919) - Ge Supt., Rev. Robert W. Taitinger, 10 Overlea Blvd., Toronto, Or M4H 1A5.

**Presbyterian Church in Canada, The** (1875) - 50 Wynfor Dr., Don Mills, Ont. M3C 1J7; Mod. Rev. DeCourcy H. Rayner.

**Religious Society of Friends (Quakers),** (Canadian Year Meeting of the Religious Society of Friends formed 1955) - Pr siding Clerk, Vivien Abbott, 60 Lowther Ave., Toronto, Ont. M5 1C7.

**Roman Catholic Church in Canada** - Apostolic Pro Nuncie His Exellency the Most Reverend Angelo Palmas; Sec. to th Apostolic Nunciature, Robert Robidoux, S.S.; Apostolic Nunci ture, 724 Manor Ave., Rockcliffe Park, Ottawa, Ont. K1M 0E3

**Salvation Army, The** (1882) - Territorial Commander, C missioner Arnold Brown, 20 Albert St., Toronto, Ont. M5G 1A6.

**Seventh-day Adventist Church in Canada** - Pres., L.N Reile, Sec. A.N. How; 1148 King St. E., Oshawa, Ont. L1H 1H8

**Ukrainian Greek Orthodox Church in Canada** - Primate Metropolitan of Winnipeg and of all Canada, His Beatitude Me ropolitan Andrew (Metiuk), 9 St. Johns Ave., Winnipeg, Mar R2W 0T9.

**Union of Spiritual Communities of Christ (Orthodox Dou khobors in Canada)** (1938) - Honorary Chmn. of the Exec Comm., John J. Verigin, Box 760, Grand Forks, B.C.

**Unitarian Church, Canadian** (1842) - Pres. Brian Reic Admin. Sec. Ms. Barbara Arnott, Canadian Unitarian Counci 175 St. Clair Ave. W., Toronto, Ont. M4V 1P7.

**United Church of Canada, The** (1925) - Mod. Rt. Rev George Tuttle; Sec. of General Council, Rev. Donald Ray, 85 S Clair Ave. E., Toronto, Ont. M4T 1M8.

---

# Protestant Episcopal Calendar and Altar Colors

**White**—from Christmas Day through the Epiphany; First Sunday after Epiphany; Maundy Thursday (at the Eucharist); from the Vig of Easter to Whitsunday; Trinity Sunday; Feasts of the Lord (except Holy Cross Day); St. Joseph; St. Mary Magdalene, St. Mary the Vi gin, and St. Michael and All Angels. **Red**—Pentecost (Whitsunday); Holy Cross Day; all feasts of apostles, evangelists, and martyrs. V olet—Advent, Lent, Ember days, and Holy Innocents' Day. Optional color scheme for Lent: **Lenten White** from Ash Wednesday to Pal Sunday; **Crimson** during Holy Week. **Green**—Epiphany season and season after Pentecost. **Black**—optional for Good Friday and funerals.

| Days, etc. | 1978 | | 1979 | | 1980 | | 1981 | | 1982 | | 1983 | |
|---|---|---|---|---|---|---|---|---|---|---|---|---|
| Golden Number | 3 | | 4 | | 5 | | 6 | | 7 | | 8 | |
| Sunday Letter | A | | G | | FE | | D | | C | | B | |
| Sundays after Epiphany* | 2 | | 5 | | 3(6) | | 5(8) | | 4(7) | | 3(6) | |
| Septuagesima** | Jan. | 22 | Feb. | 11 | Feb. | 3 | Feb. | 15 | Feb. | 7 | Jan. | 3 |
| Ash Wednesday | Feb. | 8 | Feb. | 28 | Feb. | 20 | Mar. | 4 | Feb. | 24 | Feb. | 1 |
| First Sunday in Lent | Feb. | 12 | Mar. | 4 | Feb. | 24 | Mar. | 8 | Feb. | 28 | Feb. | 2 |
| Passion Sunday** | Mar. | 12 | Apr. | 1 | Mar. | 23 | Apr. | 5 | Mar. | 28 | Mar. | 2 |
| Palm Sunday | Mar. | 19 | Apr. | 8 | Mar. | 30 | Apr. | 12 | Apr. | 4 | Mar. | 2 |
| Good Friday | Mar. | 24 | Apr. | 13 | Apr. | 4 | Apr. | 17 | Apr. | 9 | Apr. | |
| Easter Day | Mar. | 26 | Apr. | 15 | Apr. | 6 | Apr. | 19 | Apr. | 11 | Apr. | |
| Rogation Sunday** | Apr. | 30 | May | 20 | May | 11 | May | 24 | May | 16 | May | |
| Ascension Day | May | 4 | May | 24 | May | 15 | May | 28 | May | 20 | May | 1 |
| Whitsunday | May | 14 | June | 3 | May | 18 | June | 7 | May | 30 | May | 2 |
| Trinity Sunday | May | 21 | June | 10 | May | 25 | June | 14 | June | 6 | May | 2 |
| Sundays after Trinity*** | 27 | | 24 | | 25(26) | | 23(24) | | 24(25) | | 25(26) | |
| First Sunday in Advent | Dec. | 3 | Dec. | 2 | Nov. | 30 | Nov. | 29 | Nov. | 28 | Nov. | 2 |

In the Protestant Episcopal Church the days of fasting are Ash Wednesday and Good Friday. Other days of abstinence are the 40 day of Lent, the Ember Days, and all Fridays of the year except those in the Christmas and Easter seasons. Ember Days (optional) are days c abstinence and prayer for ordinands and the increase of the ministry. They fall on the Wednesday, Friday, and Saturday after the first Sun day in Lent, the Feast of Pentecost (Whitsunday), Sept. 14, and Dec. 13. Rogation Days (also optional) are the three days before Ascensio Day, and are days of solemn supplication for God's blessing upon the fields and harvests of the world.

The Episcopal Church has given first constitutional approval to a revised calendar. If adopted in 1979, the following changes in the fore going table will obtain: *The number of Sundays after Epiphany will be increased by three. **These Sundays will no longer be listed ***These Sundays will be identified as "Sundays after Pentecost" and will be one more in number than the former "Sundays after Trinity"

## Ash Wednesday and Easter Sunday

| Year | Ash Wed. | Easter Sunday | Year | Ash Wed. | Easter Sunday | Year | Ash Wed. | Easter Sunday | Year | Ash Wed. | Easter Sunday |
|---|---|---|---|---|---|---|---|---|---|---|---|
| 901 | Feb. 20 | Apr. 7 | 1951 | Feb. 7 | Mar. 25 | 2001 | Feb. 28 | Apr. 15 | 2051 | Feb. 15 | Apr. 2 |
| 902 | Feb. 12 | Mar. 30 | 1952 | Feb. 27 | Apr. 13 | 2002 | Feb. 13 | Mar. 31 | 2052 | Mar. 6 | Apr. 21 |
| 903 | Feb. 25 | Apr. 12 | 1953 | Feb. 18 | Apr. 5 | 2003 | Mar. 5 | Apr. 20 | 2053 | Feb. 19 | Apr. 6 |
| 904 | Feb. 17 | Apr. 3 | 1954 | Mar. 3 | Apr. 18 | 2004 | Feb. 25 | Apr. 11 | 2054 | Feb. 11 | Mar. 29 |
| 905 | Mar. 8 | Apr. 23 | 1955 | Feb. 23 | Apr. 10 | 2005 | Feb. 9 | Mar. 27 | 2055 | Mar. 3 | Apr. 18 |
| 906 | Feb. 28 | Apr. 15 | 1956 | Feb. 15 | Apr. 1 | 2006 | Mar. 1 | Apr. 16 | 2056 | Feb. 16 | Apr. 2 |
| 907 | Feb. 13 | Mar. 31 | 1957 | Mar. 6 | Apr. 21 | 2007 | Feb. 21 | Apr. 8 | 2057 | Mar. 7 | Apr. 22 |
| 908 | Mar. 4 | Apr. 19 | 1958 | Feb. 19 | Apr. 6 | 2008 | Feb. 6 | Mar. 23 | 2058 | Feb. 27 | Apr. 14 |
| 909 | Feb. 24 | Apr. 11 | 1959 | Feb. 11 | Mar. 29 | 2009 | Feb. 25 | Apr. 12 | 2059 | Feb. 12 | Mar. 30 |
| 910 | Feb. 9 | Mar. 27 | 1960 | Mar. 2 | Apr. 17 | 2010 | Feb. 17 | Apr. 4 | 2060 | Mar. 3 | Apr. 18 |
| 911 | Feb. 1 | Apr. 16 | 1961 | Feb. 15 | Apr. 2 | 2011 | Mar. 9 | Apr. 24 | 2061 | Feb. 23 | Apr. 10 |
| 912 | Feb. 21 | Apr. 7 | 1962 | Mar. 7 | Apr. 22 | 2012 | Feb. 22 | Apr. 8 | 2062 | Feb. 8 | Mar. 26 |
| 913 | Feb. 5 | Mar. 23 | 1963 | Feb. 27 | Apr. 14 | 2013 | Feb. 13 | Mar. 31 | 2063 | Feb. 28 | Apr. 15 |
| 914 | Feb. 25 | Apr. 12 | 1964 | Feb. 12 | Mar. 29 | 2014 | Mar. 5 | Apr. 20 | 2064 | Feb. 20 | Apr. 6 |
| 915 | Feb. 17 | Apr. 4 | 1965 | Mar. 3 | Apr. 18 | 2015 | Feb. 18 | Apr. 5 | 2065 | Feb. 11 | Mar. 29 |
| 916 | Mar. 8 | Apr. 23 | 1966 | Feb. 23 | Apr. 10 | 2016 | Feb. 10 | Mar. 27 | 2066 | Feb. 24 | Apr. 11 |
| 917 | Feb. 21 | Apr. 8 | 1967 | Feb. 8 | Mar. 26 | 2017 | Mar. 1 | Apr. 16 | 2067 | Feb. 16 | Apr. 3 |
| 918 | Feb. 13 | Mar. 31 | 1968 | Feb. 28 | Apr. 14 | 2018 | Feb. 14 | Apr. 1 | 2068 | Mar. 7 | Apr. 22 |
| 919 | Feb. 5 | Apr. 20 | 1969 | Feb. 19 | Apr. 6 | 2019 | Mar. 6 | Apr. 21 | 2069 | Feb. 27 | Apr. 14 |
| 920 | Feb. 18 | Apr. 4 | 1970 | Feb. 11 | Mar. 29 | 2020 | Feb. 26 | Apr. 12 | 2070 | Feb. 12 | Mar. 30 |
| 921 | Feb. 9 | Mar. 27 | 1971 | Feb. 24 | Apr. 11 | 2021 | Feb. 17 | Apr. 4 | 2071 | Mar. 4 | Apr. 19 |
| 922 | Feb. 1 | Apr. 16 | 1972 | Feb. 16 | Apr. 2 | 2022 | Mar. 2 | Apr. 17 | 2072 | Feb. 24 | Apr. 10 |
| 923 | Feb. 14 | Apr. 1 | 1973 | Mar. 7 | Apr. 22 | 2023 | Feb. 22 | Apr. 9 | 2073 | Feb. 8 | Mar. 26 |
| 924 | Feb. 5 | Apr. 20 | 1974 | Feb. 27 | Apr. 14 | 2024 | Feb. 14 | Mar. 31 | 2074 | Feb. 28 | Apr. 15 |
| 925 | Feb. 25 | Apr. 12 | 1975 | Feb. 12 | Mar. 30 | 2025 | Mar. 5 | Apr. 20 | 2075 | Feb. 20 | Apr. 7 |
| 926 | Feb. 17 | Apr. 4 | 1976 | Mar. 3 | Apr. 18 | 2026 | Feb. 18 | Apr. 5 | 2076 | Mar. 4 | Apr. 19 |
| 927 | Mar. 2 | Apr. 17 | 1977 | Feb. 23 | Apr. 10 | 2027 | Feb. 10 | Mar. 28 | 2077 | Feb. 24 | Apr. 11 |
| 928 | Feb. 22 | Apr. 8 | 1978 | Feb. 8 | Mar. 26 | 2028 | Mar. 1 | Apr. 16 | 2078 | Feb. 16 | Apr. 3 |
| 929 | Feb. 13 | Mar. 31 | 1979 | Feb. 28 | Apr. 15 | 2029 | Feb. 14 | Apr. 1 | 2079 | Mar. 8 | Apr. 23 |
| 930 | Mar. 5 | Apr. 20 | 1980 | Feb. 20 | Apr. 6 | 2030 | Mar. 6 | Apr. 21 | 2080 | Feb. 21 | Apr. 7 |
| 931 | Feb. 18 | Apr. 5 | 1981 | Mar. 4 | Apr. 19 | 2031 | Feb. 26 | Apr. 13 | 2081 | Feb. 12 | Mar. 30 |
| 932 | Feb. 10 | Mar. 27 | 1982 | Feb. 24 | Apr. 11 | 2032 | Feb. 11 | Mar. 28 | 2082 | Mar. 4 | Apr. 19 |
| 933 | Mar. 1 | Apr. 16 | 1983 | Feb. 16 | Apr. 3 | 2033 | Mar. 2 | Apr. 17 | 2083 | Feb. 17 | Apr. 4 |
| 934 | Feb. 14 | Apr. 1 | 1984 | Mar. 7 | Apr. 22 | 2034 | Feb. 22 | Apr. 9 | 2084 | Feb. 9 | Mar. 26 |
| 935 | Mar. 6 | Apr. 21 | 1985 | Feb. 20 | Apr. 7 | 2035 | Feb. 7 | Mar. 25 | 2085 | Feb. 28 | Apr. 15 |
| 936 | Feb. 26 | Apr. 12 | 1986 | Feb. 12 | Mar. 30 | 2036 | Feb. 27 | Apr. 13 | 2086 | Feb. 13 | Mar. 31 |
| 937 | Feb. 10 | Mar. 28 | 1987 | Mar. 4 | Apr. 19 | 2037 | Feb. 18 | Apr. 5 | 2087 | Mar. 5 | Apr. 20 |
| 938 | Mar. 2 | Apr. 17 | 1988 | Feb. 17 | Apr. 3 | 2038 | Mar. 10 | Apr. 25 | 2088 | Feb. 25 | Apr. 11 |
| 939 | Feb. 22 | Apr. 9 | 1989 | Feb. 8 | Mar. 26 | 2039 | Feb. 23 | Apr. 10 | 2089 | Feb. 16 | Apr. 3 |
| 940 | Feb. 7 | Mar. 24 | 1990 | Feb. 28 | Apr. 15 | 2040 | Feb. 15 | Apr. 1 | 2090 | Mar. 1 | Apr. 16 |
| 941 | Feb. 26 | Apr. 13 | 1991 | Feb. 13 | Mar. 31 | 2041 | Mar. 6 | Apr. 21 | 2091 | Feb. 21 | Apr. 8 |
| 942 | Feb. 18 | Apr. 5 | 1992 | Mar. 4 | Apr. 19 | 2042 | Feb. 19 | Apr. 6 | 2092 | Feb. 13 | Mar. 30 |
| 943 | Mar. 10 | Apr. 25 | 1993 | Feb. 24 | Apr. 11 | 2043 | Feb. 11 | Mar. 29 | 2093 | Feb. 25 | Apr. 12 |
| 944 | Feb. 23 | Apr. 9 | 1994 | Feb. 16 | Apr. 3 | 2044 | Mar. 2 | Apr. 17 | 2094 | Feb. 17 | Apr. 4 |
| 945 | Feb. 14 | Apr. 1 | 1995 | Mar. 1 | Apr. 16 | 2045 | Feb. 22 | Apr. 9 | 2095 | Mar. 9 | Apr. 24 |
| 946 | Mar. 6 | Apr. 21 | 1996 | Feb. 21 | Apr. 7 | 2046 | Feb. 7 | Mar. 25 | 2096 | Feb. 29 | Apr. 15 |
| 947 | Feb. 19 | Apr. 6 | 1997 | Feb. 12 | Mar. 30 | 2047 | Feb. 27 | Apr. 14 | 2097 | Feb. 13 | Mar. 31 |
| 948 | Feb. 11 | Mar. 28 | 1998 | Feb. 25 | Apr. 12 | 2048 | Feb. 19 | Apr. 5 | 2098 | Mar. 5 | Apr. 20 |
| 949 | Mar. 2 | Apr. 17 | 1999 | Feb. 17 | Apr. 4 | 2049 | Mar. 3 | Apr. 18 | 2099 | Feb. 25 | Apr. 12 |
| 950 | Feb. 22 | Apr. 9 | 2000 | Mar. 8 | Apr. 23 | 2050 | Feb. 23 | Apr. 10 | 2100 | Feb. 10 | Mar. 28 |

A lengthy dispute over the date for the celebration of Easter was settled by the first Council of the Christian Churches at Nicaea, in Asia Minor, in 325 A.D. The Council ruled that Easter would be observed on the first Sunday following the 14th day of the Paschal Moon, referred to as the Paschal Full Moon. The Paschal Moon is the first moon whose 14th day comes on or after March 21. Dates of the Paschal Full Moon, which are not necessarily the same as those of the real or astronomical full moon, are listed in the table below with an explanation of how to compute the date of Easter.

If the Paschal Full Moon falls on a Sunday, then Easter is the following Sunday. The earliest date on which Easter can fall is March 22; it fell on that date in 1761 and 1818 but will not do so in the 20th or 21st century. The latest possible date for Easter is April 25; it fell on that date in 1943 and will again in 2038.

For western churches Lent begins on Ash Wednesday, which comes 40 days before Easter Sunday, not counting Sundays. Originally it was a period of but 40 hours. Later it comprised 30 days of fasting, omitting all the Sundays and also all the Saturdays except one. Pope Gregory (590-604) added Ash Wednesday to the fast, together with the remainder of that week.

The last seven days of Lent constitute Holy Week, beginning with Palm Sunday. The last Thursday — Maundy Thursday — commemorates the institution of the Eucharist. The following day, Good Friday, commemorates the day of the Crucifixion.

Easter is the chief festival of the Christian year, commemorating the Resurrection of Christ. It occurs about the same time as the ancient Roman celebration of the Vernal Equinox, the arrival of spring. In the second century, A.D., Easter Day among Christians in Asia Minor was the 14th Nisan, the seventh month of the Jewish calendar. The Christians in Europe observed the nearest Sunday.

## Date of Paschal Full Moon, 1900-2199

The Golden Number, used in determining the date of Easter, is greater by unity (one) than the remainder obtained upon dividing the given year by 19. For example, when dividing 1979 by 19, one obtains a remainder of 3. Adding 1 gives 4 as the Golden Number for the year 1979. From the table then the date of the Paschal Full Moon is Apr. 11, 1979. This being a Wednesday, the date of Easter is the following Sunday Apr. 15.

| Golden Number | Date | Golden Number | Date | Golden Number | Date | Golden Number | Date |
|---|---|---|---|---|---|---|---|
| 1 | Apr. 14 | 6 | Apr. 18 | 11 | Mar. 25 | 16 | Mar. 30 |
| 2 | Apr. 3 | 7 | Apr. 8 | 12 | Apr. 13 | 17 | Apr. 17 |
| 3 | Mar. 23 | 8 | Mar. 28 | 13 | Apr. 2 | 18 | Apr. 7 |
| 4 | Apr. 11 | 9 | Apr. 16 | 14 | Mar. 22 | 19 | Mar. 27 |
| 5 | Mar. 31 | 10 | Apr. 5 | 15 | Apr. 10 | | |

## Jewish Holy Days, Festivals, and Fasts

**Source:** Synagogue Council of America

| Festivals and fasts | Hebrew date | 5739 (1978-1979) | 5740 (1979-1980) | 5741 (1980-1981) | 5742 (1981-198 |
|---|---|---|---|---|---|
| Rosh Hashana (New Year)[1] | Tishri 1 | Oct. 2 Mo | Sept. 22 Sa | Sept. 11 Th | Sept. 29 T |
| Fast of Gedalia | Tishri 3 | Oct. 4 We | Sept. 24 Mo | .......... | Oct 1 T |
| Fast of Gedalia | Tishri 4 | .......... | .......... | Sept. 14 Su | .......... |
| Yom Kippur (Day of Atonement) | Tishri 10 | Oct. 11 We | Oct. 1 Mo | Sept. 20 Sa | Oct. 8 T |
| Sukkoth (Feast of Tabernacles), 1st Day[1] | Tishri 15 | Oct. 16 Mo | Oct. 6 Sa | Sept. 25 Th | Oct. 13 T |
| Sukkoth, 8th Day of Assembly (Shemini Atzereth) | Tishri 22 | Oct. 23 Mo | Oct. 13 Sa | Oct. 2 Th | Oct. 20 T |
| Simchat Torah (Rejoicing of the Law) | Tishri 23 | Oct. 24 Tu | Oct. 14 Su | Oct. 3 Fr | Oct. 21 V |
| Chanukah (Feast of Lights) | Kislev 25 | Dec. 25 Mo | Dec. 15 Sa | Dec. 3 We | Dec. 21 N |
| Fast of Tebet[2] | Tebet 10 | Jan. 9 Tu | Dec. 30 Su | Dec. 17 We | Jan. 5 T |
| Fast of Esther[2] | Adar 13 | Mar. 12 Mo | .......... | .......... | Mar. 8 N |
| Fast of Esther[2] | Adar II 13 | .......... | Feb. 28 Th | Mar. 19 Th | .......... |
| Purim (Feast of Lots) | Adar 14 | Mar. 13 Tu | Mar. 2 Su | .......... | Mar. 9 T |
| Purim | Adar II 14 | .......... | .......... | Mar. 20 Fr | .......... |
| Pesach (Passover), 1st Day[1] | Nisan 15 | Apr. 12 Th | Apr. 1 Tu | Apr. 19 Su | Apr. 8 T |
| Pesach, 7th Day[1] | Nisan 21 | Apr. 18 We | Apr. 7 Mo | Apr. 25 Sa | Apr. 14 V |
| Lag B'Omer | Iyar 18 | May 15 Tu | May 4 Su | May 22 Fr | May 11 T |
| Shavuoth (Feast of Weeks)[1] | Sivan 6 | June 1 Fr | May 21 We | June 8 Mo | May 28 F |
| Fast of Tammuz[2] | Tammuz 17 | July 12 Th | July 1 Tu | July 19 Su | July 8 |
| Tisha B'Av (Fast of Av)[2] | Av 9 | Aug. 2 Th | July 22 Tu | Aug. 9 Su | July 29 |

**The months of the Jewish year are:** 1) Tishri; 2) Cheshvan (also Marcheshvan); 3) Kislev; 4) Tebet (also Tebeth); 5) Shebat (a Shebhat); 6) Adar; 6a) Adar Sheni (II) added in leap years; 7) Nisan; 8) Iyar; 9) Sivan; 10) Tammuz; 11) Av (also Abh); 12) Elul. Jewish holy days, etc., begin at sunset on the day previous. (1) Also observed the following day. (2) Hebrew date varies to avoid c flict with Sabbath.

---

## Greek Orthodox Church Calendar, 1979

| Date | | Holy Days | Date | | Holy Days |
|---|---|---|---|---|---|
| Jan. | 1 | The Circumcision of Jesus Christ; feast day of St. Basil | *May | 31 | The Ascension of Jesus Christ |
| Jan. | 6 | The Epiphany: The Baptism of Jesus Christ - The Santification of the Waters | *June | 10 | Sunday of Pentecost |
| | | | June | 29 | Feast day of Sts. Peter and Paul |
| Jan. | 7 | Feast day of St. John the Baptist | June | 30 | Feast day of the Twelve Apostles of Jes Christ |
| Jan. | 30 | Feast day of the Three Hierarchs: St. Basil the Great, St. Gregory the Theologian, and St. John Chrysostom | Aug. | 6 | The Transfiguration of Jesus Christ |
| | | | Aug. | 15 | The Dormition of the Virgin Mary |
| | | | Aug. | 29 | The Beheading of St. John the Baptist |
| Feb. | 2 | Presentation of Jesus Christ in the Temple | Sept. | 1 | The beginning of the Church Year |
| *Mar. | 5 | Easter Lent begins | Sept. | 8 | Nativity of the Virgin Mary |
| *Mar. | 11 | Sunday of Orthodoxy (1st Sun. of Lent) | Sept. | 14 | The Elevation of the Holy Cross |
| Mar. | 25 | The Annunciation of the Virgin Mary | Oct. | 23 | Feast day of St. James |
| *Apr. | 15 | Palm Sunday | Oct. | 26 | Feast day of St. Demetrios the Martyr |
| *Apr. | 16-22 | Holy Week | Nov. | 15 | Christmas Lent begins |
| *Apr. | 20 | Holy (Good) Friday: The Burial of Jesus Christ | Nov. | 21 | Presentation of the Virgin Mary |
| *Apr. | 22 | Easter Sunday: The Resurrection of Jesus Christ | Nov. | 30 | Feast day of St. Andrew the Apostle |
| | | | Dec. | 6 | Feast day of St. Nicholas, Bishop of Myra |
| *Apr. | 23 | Feast day of St. George | Dec. | 25 | Christmas Day: Nativity of Jesus Christ |
| May | 21 | Feast day of Sts. Constantine and Helen | | | |

*Movable holy days dependent upon the date of Easter. (The feast day of St. George is normally celebrated Apr. 23. If this day arrives du ing Lent, it is then celebrated the day after Easter.) The Greek Orthodox Church celebrates holy days in accordance with the Gregori Calendar. Some Eastern Orthodox Churches still adhere to the Julian Calendar and observe the holy days (with the exception of the East cycle) 13 days later.

---

## Islamic (Moslem) Calendar 1978-1980

The Islamic Calendar, often referred to as Mohammedan, is a lunar reckoning from the year of the *hegira*, 622 A.D., when Mohamm moved to Medina from Mecca. It runs in cycles of 30 years, of which the 2d, 5th, 7th, 10th, 13th, 16th, 18th, 21st, 24th, 26th, and 29th a leap years; 1399 and 1400 are the 19th and 20th years, respectively, of the cycle. Common years have 354 days, leap years 355, the ext day being added to the last month, Zu'lhijjah. Except for this case, the 12 months beginning with Muharram have alternately 30 and days.

| Year | Name of month | Month begins | Year | Name of Month | Month begir |
|---|---|---|---|---|---|
| 1399 | Muharram (New Year) | Dec. 2, 1978 | 1400 | Muharram (New Year) | Nov. 21, 197 |
| 1399 | Safar | Jan. 1, 1979 | 1400 | Safar | Dec. 21, 197 |
| 1399 | Rabia I. | Jan. 30, 1979 | 1400 | Rabia I. | Jan. 19, 198 |
| 1399 | Rabia II. | Mar. 1, 1979 | 1400 | Rabia II. | Feb. 18, 198 |
| 1399 | Jumada I | Mar. 30, 1979 | 1400 | Jumada I | Mar. 18, 198 |
| 1399 | Jumada II | Apr. 29, 1979 | 1400 | Jumada II | Apr. 17, 198 |
| 1399 | Rajab | May 28, 1979 | 1400 | Rajab | May 16, 198 |
| 1399 | Shaban | June 27, 1979 | 1400 | Shaban | June 15, 198 |
| 1399 | Ramadan | July 26, 1979 | 1400 | Ramadan | July 14, 198 |
| 1399 | Shawwai | Aug. 25, 1979 | 1400 | Shawwai | Aug. 13, 198 |
| 1399 | Zu'lkadah | Sept. 23, 1979 | 1400 | Zu'lkadah | Sept. 11, 198 |
| 1399 | Zu'lhijjah | Oct. 23, 1979 | 1400 | Zu'lhijjah | Oct. 11, 198 |

# The Major World Religions

## Buddhism

**Founded:** About 525 BC, reportedly near Benares, India.

**Founder:** Gautama Siddhartha (ca. 563-480), the Buddha, who achieved enlightenment through intense meditation.

**Sacred Texts:** The *Tripitaka*, a collection of the Buddha's teachings, rules of monastic life, and philosophical commentaries on the teachings; also a vast body of Buddhist teachings and commentaries, many of which are called *sutras*.

**Organization:** The basic institution is the *sangha* or monastic order through which the traditions are passed to each generation. Monastic life tends to be democratic and anti-authoritarian. Large lay organizations have developed in some sects.

**Practice:** Varies widely according to the sect and ranges from austere meditation to magical chanting and elaborate temple rites. Many practices, such as exorcism of devils, reflect pre-Buddhist beliefs.

**Divisions:** A wide variety of sects grouped into 3 primary branches: Therevada (sole survivor of the ancient Hinayana schools) which emphasizes the importance of pure thought and deed; Mahayana, which includes Zen and Soka-gakkai, ranges from philosophical schools to belief in the saving grace of higher beings or ritual practices, and to practical meditative disciplines; and Tantrism, and unusual combination of belief in ritual magic and sophisticated philosophy.

**Location:** Throughout Asia, from Ceylon to Japan. Zen and Soka-gakkai have several thousand adherents in the U.S.

**Beliefs:** Life is misery and decay, and there is no ultimate reality in it or behind it. The cycle of endless birth and rebirth continues because of desire and attachment to the unreal "self". Right meditation and deeds will end the cycle and achieve Nirvana, the Void, nothingness.

## Hinduism

**Founded:** Ca. 1500 BC by Aryan invaders of India where their Vedic religion intermixed with the practices and beliefs of the natives.

**Sacred texts:** The *Veda*, including the *Upanishads*, a collection of rituals and mythological and philosophical commentaries; a vast number of epic stories about gods, heroes and saints, including the *Bhagavadgita*, a part of the *Mahabharata*, and the *Ramayana;* and a great variety of other literature.

**Organization:** None, strictly speaking. Generally, rituals should be performed or assisted by Brahmins, the priestly caste, but in practice simpler rituals can be performed by anyone. Brahmins are the final judges of ritual purity, the vital element in Hindu life. Temples and religious organizations are usually presided over by Brahmins.

**Practice:** A variety of private rituals, primarily passage rites (eg. initiation, marriage, death, etc.) and daily devotions, and a similar variety of public rites in temples. Of the latter, the *puja*, a ceremonial dinner for a god, is the most common.

**Divisions:** There is no concept of orthodoxy in Hinduism, which presents a bewildering variety of sects, most of them devoted to the worship of one of the many gods. The 3 major living traditions are those devoted to the gods Vishnu and Shiva and to the goddess Shakti; each of them divided into further sub-sects. Numerous folk beliefs and practices, often in amalgamation with the above groups, exist side-by-side with sophisticated philosophical schools and exotic cults.

**Location:** Confined to India, except for the missionary work of Vedanta, the Krishna Consciousness society, and individual *gurus* (teachers) in the West.

**Beliefs:** There is only one divine principle; the many gods are only aspects of that unity. Life in all its forms is an aspect of the divine, but it appears as a separation from the divine, a meaningless cycle of birth and rebirth (*samsara*) determined by the purity or impurity of past deeds (*karma*). To improve one's *karma* or escape *samsara* by pure acts, thought, and/or devotion is the aim of every Hindu.

## Islam (submission)

**Founded:** 622 AD in Medina, Arabian peninsula.

**Founder:** Mohammed (ca. 570-632), the Prophet, as a result of visions.

**Sacred texts:** *Koran*, the words of God, delivered to Mohammed by the angel Gabriel; *Hadith*, collections of the sayings of the Prophet.

**Organization:** Theoretically the state and religious community are one, administered by a caliph. In practice, Islam is a loose collection of congregations united by a very conservative tradition. Islam is basically egalitarian and non-authoritarian.

**Practice:** Every Moslem is supposed to make the profession of faith ("There is no god but Allah . . ."), pray 5 times a day, give a regular portion of his goods to charity, fast during the day in the month of Ramadan, and make at least one pilgrimage to Mecca if possible. Additionally saints' days are celebrated and pilgrimages made to shrines.

**Divisions:** The 2 major sects of Islam are the Sunni (orthodox) and the Shi'ah. The Shi'ah believe in 12 *imams*, perfect teachers, who still guide the faithful from Paradise. Shi'ah practice tends toward the ecstatic, while the Sunni is staid and simple. The Shi'ah sect affirms man's free will; the Sunni is deterministic. The mystic tradition in Islam is Sufism. A Sufi adept believes he has acquired a special inner knowledge direct from Allah.

**Location:** From the west coast of Africa to the Philipines across a broad band that includes Tanzania, southern USSR and western China, India, Malaysia and Indonesia. Islam has perhaps 100,000 adherents among American blacks.

**Beliefs:** Strictly monotheistic. God is creator of the universe, omnipotent, just, and merciful. Man is God's highest creation, but limited and sinful. He is misled by Satan, a prideful angel. God gave the *Koran* to Mohammed to guide men to the truth. Those who repent and sincerely submit to God return to a state of sinlessness. In the end, the sinless go to Paradise, a place of physical and spiritual pleasure, and the wicked burn in Hell.

## Judaism

**Founded:** About 1300 BC, reportedly at Mt. Sinai.

**Founder:** Moses, probably an historical person.

**Sacred Texts:** Torah, or divine teaching, found particularly in the first 5 books of the Bible; Talmud and Midrash, commentaries on Torah.

**Organization:** Originally theocratic, Judaism has evolved a congregational polity. The basic institution is the local synagogue, operated by the congregation and led by a rabbi of their choice. Chief Rabbis in France and Great Britain have authority only over those who accept it; in Israel, the 2 Chief Rabbis have civil authority in family law.

**Practice:** Among the very conservative, prayers accompany almost every action of daily life. Synagogue services center around the Torah reading. The chief annual observances are Passover, celebrating the liberation of the Israelites from Egypt and marked by the ritual Seder meal in the home, and the 10 days from Rosh Hashana (New Year) to Yom Kippur (Day of Atonement), a period of fasting and penitence.

**Divisions:** Judaism is an unbroken spectrum from ultra-conservative to ultra-liberal. Distinctions depend primarily on the care taken to observe the many prescribed duties and prohibitions in daily life, particularly the dietary and Sabbath regulations, and whether these are seen as binding or optional. The amount of Hebrew used in services distinguishes groups on the liberal end of the spectrum. Hasidism is a pietistic movement which emphasizes joyful devotion and the charismatic power of individual Hasidic leaders.

**Location:** Almost world-wide, with concentrations in Israel and the U.S.

**Beliefs:** Strictly monotheistic. God is the creator and absolute ruler of the universe. Men are free to choose to rebel against God's rule. God established a particular relationship with the Hebrew people: by obeying the divine law God gave them they would be a special witness to God's mercy and justice. The emphasis in Judaism is on ethical behavior (and, among the conservative, careful ritual obedience) as the true worship of God.

## Major Christian Denomination

*Italics* indicate that area which, generally speaking, mo

| Denomination | Origins | Organization | Authority | Special rites |
|---|---|---|---|---|
| Baptists | In radical Reformation objections to infant baptism, demands for church-state separation; John Smyth, English Separatist in 1609; Roger Williams, 1638, Providence, R.I. | Congregational, *i.e.,* each local church is autonomous. | Scripture; some Baptists, particularly in the South, interpret the Bible literally. | Baptism, after about age 12, by total immersion; Lord's Supper. |
| Church of Christ (Disciples) | Among evangelical Presbyterians in Ky. (1804) and Penn. (1809), in distress over Protestant factionalism and decline of fervor. Organized 1832. | Congregational. | *"Where the Scriptures speak, we speak; where the Scriptures are silent, we are silent."* | Adult baptism, Lord's Supper (weekly). |
| Episcopalians | Henry VIII separated English Catholic Church from Rome, 1534, for political reasons. Protestant Episcopal Church in U.S. founded 1789. | *Bishops, in apostolic succession, are elected by diocesan representatives; part of Anglican Communion symbolically headed by Archbishop of Canterbury.* | Scripture as interpreted by tradition, esp. *39 Articles* (1563); not dogmatic. Tri-annual convention of bishops, priests, and laymen. | Infant baptism, Holy Communion, others. Sacrament is symbolic, but has real spiritual effect. |
| Lutherans | Martin Luther in Wittenberg, Germany, 1517, objected to Catholic doctrine of salvation by merit and sale of indulgences; break complete by 1519. | Varies from congregational to episcopal; in U.S. a combination of regional synods and congregational polities is most common. | *Scripture, and tradition as spelled out in Augsburg Confession (1530) and other creeds. These confessions of faith are binding although interpretations vary.* | Infant baptism, Lord's Supper. Bread and wine in Supper is less than actually physical body and blood of Christ, but more than simply symbolic. |
| Methodists | Rev. John Wesley began movement, 1738, to infuse pietist enthusiasm into Church of England formalism. First U.S. conference, 1773. | *Bishops (not a priestly order, only an office) are elected for life, appoint district superintendants and local ministers.* | Scripture as interpreted by tradition, reason, and personal insight. | Infant baptism, Lord's Supper. |
| Mormons | In visions of the Angel Moroni by Joseph Smith, 1820, in New York, in which he received a new revelation on golden tablets: *The Book of Mormon.* | Theocratic; all male adults are in priesthood which culminates in Council of 12 Apostles and 1st Presidency (1st President, 2 counselors). | *The Bible (Mormon translation), Book of Mormon and other revelations to Smith, and certain pronouncements of the 1st Presidency.* | Adult baptism, laying on of hands (which grants gifts of the Spirit), Lord's Supper. Temple rites: baptism for the dead, marriage for eternity, others. |
| Orthodox | Original Christian proselytizing in 1st century; broke with Rome, 1054, over a fine point of doctrine after centuries of disputes and diverging traditions. | Synods of bishops in autonomous, usually national, churches elect a patriarch, archbishop or metropolitan. These men, as a group, are the heads of the church. | Scripture, tradition, and the first 7 church councils up to Nicaea II in 787. Bishops in council have authority in doctrine and policy. | Seven sacraments: infant baptism and anointing, Eucharist (both bread and wine), ordination, penance, anointing of the sick, marriage. |
| Pentacostal | In Topeka, Kansas (1901), and Los Angeles (1906) in reaction to loss of evangelical fervor among Methodists and other denominations. | Originally a movement, not a formal organization, Pentacostalism now has a variety of organized forms and continues also as a movement. | Scripture, individual charismatic leaders, the teachings of the Holy Spirit. | *Spirit baptism, esp. as shown in "speaking in tongues"; healing and sometimes exorcism; adult baptism, Lord's Supper.* |
| Presbyterians | In Calvinist Reformation in 1500s; differed with Lutherans over sacraments, church government. John Knox founded Scotch Presbyterian church about 1560. | *Highly structured representational system of ministers and laypersons (presbyters) in local, regional and national bodies. (synods).* | Scripture. | Infant baptism, Lord's Supper; bread and wine symbolize Christ's spiritual presence. |
| Roman Catholics | Traditionally, by Jesus who named St. Peter the 1st Vicar; historically, in early Christian proselytizing and the conversion of imperial Rome in the 4th century. | Hierarchy with supreme power vested in Pope elected by cardinals. Councils of Bishops may advise on matters of doctrine and policy. | *The Pope when speaking for the whole church in matters of faith and morals, and tradition, which is partly recorded in scripture.* | Seven sacraments: baptism, contrition and penance, confirmation, Eucharist (bread only), marriage, ordination, and anointing of the sick (unction). |
| United Church of Christ | *By ecumenical union, 1957, of Congregationalists and Evangelical & Reformed, representing both Calvinist and Lutheran traditions.* | Congregational; a General Synod, representative of all congregations, sets general policy. | Scripture. | Infant baptism, Lord's Supper. |

# How Do They Differ?

...distinguishes that denomination from any other.

| Practice | Ethics | Doctrine | Other | Denomination |
|---|---|---|---|---|
| Worship style varies from staid to evangelistic. Extensive missionary activity. | Usually opposed to alcohol and tobacco; sometimes tends toward Holiness (a perfectionist ethical standard). | *No creed; true church is of believers only, who are all equal.* | Since no authority can stand between the believer and God, the Baptists are strong supporters of church-state separation. | Baptists |
| Tries to avoid any rite or doctrine not explicitly part of the 1st century church. Some congregations may reject instrumental music. | Some tendency toward Holiness; increasing interest in social action programs. | Simple New Testament faith; avoids any elaboration not firmly based on Scripture. | Highly tolerant in doctrinal and religious matters; strongly supportive of scholarly education. | Church of Christ (Disciples) |
| Formal, based on *Book of Common Prayer* (1549); services range from austerely simple to highly elaborate. | Tolerant; sometimes permissive; some social action programs. | *Apostle's Creed* is basic; otherwise, considerable variation ranges from rationalist and liberal to acceptance of most Roman Catholic dogma. | Strongly ecumenical, holding talks with all other branches of Christendom. | Episcopalians |
| Relatively simple formal liturgy with emphasis on the sermon. | Generally, conservative in personal and social ethics; doctrine of "2 kingdoms" (worldly and holy) supports conservatism in secular affairs. | Salvation by faith alone through grace. Lutheranism has made major contributions to Protestant theology. | Though still somewhat divided along ethnic lines (German, Swede, etc.), main divisions are between fundamentalists and liberals. | Lutherans |
| Worship style varies; ... staid, some-...es evangelistic. | Originally pietist and perfectionist with a tendency to withdraw from secular affairs; now with strong social activist elements. | No distinctive theological development; *25 Articles,* abridged from Church of England's 39, not binding. | In 1968, the United Methodist Church was formed by the union of the major Methodist church and the 1946 union of Evangelical and United Brethren churches. | Methodists |
| Staid service with hymns, sermon. Secret temple ceremonies may be more elaborate. Strong missionary activity. | Temperance; strict tithing. Combine a strong work ethic with communal self-reliance. | God is a material being; the universe always existed, God did not create it; all persons will be saved and many will become divine. Most other beliefs are Christian. | Mormons regard mainline churches as apostate, corrupt. Splinter group, Reorganized Church, rejects most Mormon doctrine and practice except Book of Mormon. | Mormons |
| *Elaborate liturgy, usually in the vernacular, though extremely traditional. The liturgy is the essence of Orthodoxy. Veneration of icons.* | Tolerant; very little social action; divorce, remarriage permitted in some cases. Priests need not be celibate; bishops are. | Emphasizes on Christ's divinity and resurrection, rather than crucifixion, and on 3 persons of God, rather than the unity. Rejects Roman dogmas of Immaculate Conception of Mary, purgatory. | Orthodox Church in America, originally under Patriarch of Moscow, was granted autonomy in 1970. Greek Orthodox do not recognize this autonomy. | Orthodox |
| Loosely structured service with rousing hymns and sermons, culminating in spirit baptism. | Usually, emphasis on Holiness with varying degrees of tolerance. | Simple traditional beliefs, usually Protestant, with emphasis on the immediate presence of God in the Holy Spirit | Once confined to lower-class "holy rollers," Pentacostalism now appears in mainline churches and has established middle-class congregations. | Pentacostal |
| A simple, sober service in which the sermon is central. | Traditionally, a tendency toward strictness with firm church- and self-discipline; otherwise tolerant. | Emphasizes the sovereignty and justice of God; no longer doctrinaire. | While traces of belief in predestination (that God has foreordained salvation for the "elect") remain, this idea is no longer a central element in Presbyterianism. | Presbyterians |
| Relatively elaborate ritual; wide variety of public and private rites, eg., rosary recitation, processions, novenas. | Theoretically very strict; tolerant in practice on most issues. Divorce and remarriage not accepted. Celibate clergy. | Highly elaborated. Salvation by merit gained through faith. Unusual development of doctrines surrounding Mary. Dogmatic. | Roman Catholicism is presently in a period of relatively rapid change as a result of Vatican Councils I and II. | Roman Catholics |
| Usually simple services with emphasis on the sermon. | Tolerant; some social action emphasis. | Standard Protestant; *Statement of Faith* (1959) is not binding. | The 2 main churches in the 1957 union represented earlier unions with small groups of almost every Protestant denomination. | United Church of Christ |

# Roman Catholic Hierarchy

Source: Apostolic Delegation, Washington, D.C.

## Supreme Pontiff

At the head of the Roman Catholic Church is the Supreme Pontiff, Paul VI, Giovanni Battista Montini, born at Concesi Italy, Sept. 26, 1897, ordained priest May 29, 1920, enthroned archbishop of Milan Jan. 6, 1955, proclaimed cardinal De 15, 1958; elected Pope as successor of John XXIII, June 21, 1963; crowned June 30, 1963.

## Cardinals

| Name | Office | Nationality | Born | Name |
|---|---|---|---|---|
| Alfrink, Bernard | | Dutch | 1900 | 196 |
| Antonelli, Ferdinando | | Italian | 1896 | 197 |
| Aponte Martinez, Luis | Archbishop of San Juan in Puerto Rico | American | 1922 | 197 |
| Aramburu, Juan | Archbishop of Buenos Aires | Argentinian | 1912 | 197 |
| Arns, Paulo | Archbishop of San Paulo | Brazilian | 1921 | 197 |
| | | | | |
| Bafile, Corrado | Prefect of the Sacred Congregation for the Causes of Saints | Italian | 1903 | 197 |
| Baggio, Sebastiano | Prefect of the Sacred Congregation for the Bishops | Italian | 1913 | 196 |
| Barbieri, Antonio Maria | | Uruguayan | 1892 | 195 |
| Baum, William | Archbishop of Washington | American | 1926 | 197 |
| Benelli, Giovanni | Archbishop of Florence | Italian | 1921 | 197 |
| Bengsch, Alfred | Archbishop-Bishop of Berlin | German | 1921 | 196 |
| Beras Rojas, Octavio | Archbishop of Santo Domingo | San Domingan | 1906 | 197 |
| Bertoli, Paolo | | Italian | 1908 | 196 |
| Brandao Vilela, Avela | Archbishop of Sao Salvador da Bahia | Brazilian | 1912 | 197 |
| Bueno y Monreal, Jose M. | Archbishop of Seville | Spanish | 1904 | 195 |
| | | | | |
| Caggiano, Antonio | | Argentinian | 1889 | 194 |
| Carberry, John | Archbishop of St. Louis | American | 1904 | 196 |
| Carpino, Francesco | | Italian | 1905 | 196 |
| Casariego, Mario | Archbishop of Guatemala | Guatemalan | 1909 | 196 |
| Ciappi, O.P., Mario Luigi | Pro-Theologian of Pontifical Household | Italian | 1909 | 1 |
| Cody, John P. | Archbishop of Chicago | American | 1907 | 196 |
| Colombo, Giovanni | Archbishop of Milan | Italian | 1902 | 196 |
| Confalonieri, Carlo | Dean of the Sacred College | Italian | 1893 | 195 |
| Cooke, Terence | Archbishop of New York | American | 1921 | 196 |
| Cooray, Thomas B. | | Ceylonese | 1901 | 196 |
| Cordeiro, Joseph | Archbishop of Karachi | Pakistanian | 1918 | 197 |
| | | | | |
| Darmojuwono, Justin | Archbishop of Semarang | Indonesian | 1914 | 196 |
| de Araujo Sales, Eugenio | Archbishop of St. Sebastian of Rio de Janeiro | Brazilian | 1920 | 196 |
| Dearden, John | Archbishop of Detroit | American | 1907 | 196 |
| de Furstenberg, Maximilian | | Belgian | 1904 | 196 |
| Delargey, Reginald | Archbishop of Wellington | New Zealander | 1914 | 197 |
| Di Jorio, Alberto | | Italian | 1884 | 195 |
| Duval, Leon-Etienne | Archbishop of Algiers | Algerian | 1903 | 196 |
| | | | | |
| Ekandem, Dominic | Bishop of Ikot Ekpene | Nigerian | 1917 | 197 |
| Enrique y Tarancon, Vincenzo | Archbishop of Madrid | Spanish | 1907 | 196 |
| | | | | |
| Felici, Pericle | President of Pontifical Commission for the Revision of Code of Canon Law, Prefect of Supreme Tribunal of Apostolic Signatura | Italian | 1911 | 196 |
| Filipiak, Boleslaw | | Polish | 1901 | 197 |
| Flahiff, George | Archbishop of Winnipeg | Canadian | 1905 | 196 |
| Florit, Ermenegildo | | Italian | 1901 | 196 |
| Freeman, James | Archbishop of Sydney | Australian | 1907 | 197 |
| Frings, Joseph | | German | 1887 | 194 |
| | | | | |
| Gantin, Bernardin | President, Pontifical Commission "Justitia et Pax" | Benin | 1922 | 197 |
| Garrone, Gabriele M. | Prefect of the Sacred Congregation for Catholic Education | French | 1901 | 196 |
| Gonzalez Martin, Marcelo | Archbishop of Toledo | Spanish | 1918 | 197 |
| Gouyon, Paul | Archbishop of Rennes | French | 1910 | 196 |
| Gracias, Valerian | Archbishop of Bombay | Indian | 1900 | 195 |
| Gray, Gordon | Archbishop of St. Andrews and Edinburgh | Scottish | 1910 | 196 |
| Guerri, Sergio | Pro-President of the Pontifical Comm. for Vatican City State | Italian | 1905 | 196 |
| Guyot, Jean | Archbishop of Toulouse | French | 1905 | 197 |
| | | | | |
| Hoffner, Joseph | Archbishop of Cologne | German | 1906 | 196 |
| Hume, Basil | Archbishop of Westminster | English | 1923 | 197 |
| | | | | |
| Jubany Arnau, Narciso | Archbishop of Barcelona | Spanish | 1913 | 197 |
| | | | | |
| Kim Sou Hwan, Stephan | Archbishop of Seoul | Korean | 1922 | 196 |
| Knox, James | Prefect of the Sacred Congregations of the Sacraments and of Divine Worship | Australian | 1914 | 197 |
| Koenig, Franz | Archbishop of Vienna | Austrian | 1905 | 195 |
| Krol, John | Archbishop of Philadelphia | American | 1910 | 196 |
| | | | | |
| Landazuri, Ricketts Juan | Archbishop of Lima | Peruvian | 1913 | 196 |
| Leger, Paul | | Canadian | 1904 | 195 |
| Lekai, Laszlo | Archbishop of Esztergom | Hungarian | 1910 | 197 |
| Lorscheider, Aloisio | Archbishop of Fortaleza | Brazilian | 1924 | 197 |
| Luciani, Albino | Patriarch of Venice | Italian | 1912 | 197 |

| Name | Office | Nationality | Born | Named |
|------|--------|-------------|------|-------|
| Malula, Joseph | Archbishop of Kinshasa | Congolese | 1917 | 1969 |
| Manning, Timothy | Archbishop of Los Angeles | American | 1909 | 1973 |
| Marella, Paolo | | Italian | 1895 | 1959 |
| Marty, Francis | Archbishop of Paris | French | 1904 | 1969 |
| Maurer, Jose | Archbishop of Sucre | Bolivian | 1900 | 1967 |
| McCann, Owen | Archbishop of Cape Town | S. African | 1907 | 1965 |
| McIntyre, James | | American | 1886 | 1953 |
| Medeiros, Humberto | Archbishop of Boston | American | 1915 | 1973 |
| Miranda y Gomez, Miguel | | Mexican | 1895 | 1969 |
| Motta, Carlos Carmelo de Vasconcellos | Archbishop of Aparecida | Brazilian | 1890 | 1946 |
| Mozzoni, Umberto | | Italian | 1904 | 1973 |
| Munoz Duque, Anibal | Archbishop of Bogota | Colombian | 1908 | 1973 |
| Munoz Vega, Paolo | Archbishop of Quito | Ecuadorian | 1903 | 1969 |
| Nasalli Rocca Di Corneliano, Mario | | Italian | 1903 | 1969 |
| Nsubuga, Emmanuel | Archbishop of Kampala | Ugandan | 1914 | 1976 |
| O'Boyle, Patrick | | American | 1896 | 1967 |
| Oddi, Silvio | | Italian | 1910 | 1969 |
| Ottaviani, Alfredo | | Italian | 1890 | 1953 |
| Otunga, Maurice | Archbishop of Nairobi | Kenyan | 1923 | 1973 |
| Palazzini, Pietro | | Italian | 1912 | 1973 |
| Pappalardo, Salvatore | Archbishop of Palermo | Italian | 1918 | 1973 |
| Parecattil, Joseph | Archbishop of Ernakulam | Indian | 1912 | 1969 |
| Parente, Pietro | | Italian | 1891 | 1967 |
| Paupini, Giuseppe | Grand Penitentiary | Italian | 1907 | 1969 |
| Pellegrino, Michele | | Italian | 1903 | 1967 |
| Philippe, Paul | Prefect of the Sacred Congregation for the Oriental Churches | French | 1905 | 1973 |
| Picachy, Lawrence | Archbishop of Calcutta | Indian | 1916 | 1976 |
| Pignedoli, Sergio | President of the Secretariat for Non-Christians | Italian | 1910 | 1973 |
| Pironio, Eduardo | Prefect of the Sacred Congregation for Religious and for Secular Institutes | Argentinian | 1920 | 1976 |
| Poletti, Ugo | Vicar General of His Holiness for the City of Rome | Italian | 1914 | 1973 |
| Poma, Antonio | Archbishop of Bologna | Italian | 1910 | 1969 |
| Primatesta, Francisco | Archbishop of Cordova | Argentinian | 1919 | 1973 |
| Quintero, Jose | Archbishop of Caracas | Venezuelan | 1902 | 1961 |
| Ratzinger, Joseph | Archbishop of Munich | German | 1927 | 1977 |
| Razafimahatratra, Victor | Archbishop of Tananarive | Madagascan | 1921 | 1976 |
| Renard, Alexandre | Archbishop of Lyon | French | 1906 | 1967 |
| Ribeiro, Antonio | Patriarch of Lisbon | Portuguese | 1928 | 1973 |
| Roberti, Francesco | | Italian | 1889 | 1958 |
| Rosales, Julio | Archbishop of Cebu | Filipino | 1906 | 1969 |
| Rossi, Angelo | Prefect of the Sacred Congregation for the Evangelization of Peoples | Brazilian | 1913 | 1965 |
| Rossi, Opilio | | Italian | 1910 | 1976 |
| Roy, Maurice | Archbishop of Quebec | Canadian | 1905 | 1965 |
| Rugambwa, Laurean | Archbishop of Dar-es-Salaam | Tanzanian | 1912 | 1960 |
| Salazar Lopez, Jose | Archbishop of Guadalajara | Mexican | 1910 | 1973 |
| Samore, Antonio | Archivist of Holy Roman Church | Italian | 1905 | 1967 |
| Scherer, Alfred | Archbishop of Porto Alegre | Brazilian | 1903 | 1969 |
| Schroffer, Joseph | | German | 1903 | 1976 |
| Sensi, Giuseppe | | Italian | 1907 | 1976 |
| Seper, Franjo | Prefect of Sacred Congregation for the Doctrine of the Faith | Yugoslav | 1905 | 1965 |
| Shehan, Lawrence | | American | 1898 | 1965 |
| Sidarouss, Stephanos | Coptic Patriarch of Alexandria | Egyptian | 1904 | 1965 |
| Silva Henriquez, Raul | Archbishop of Santiago | Chilean | 1907 | 1962 |
| Sin, Jaime | Archbishop of Manila | Filipino | 1928 | 1976 |
| Siri, Giuseppe | Archbishop of Genoa | Italian | 1906 | 1953 |
| Slipyj, Josyf | Ukrainian Archbishop of Lwow | Ukrainian | 1892 | 1965 |
| Suenens, Leo | Archbishop of Malines Brussels | Belgian | 1904 | 1962 |
| Taofinu'u, Pio | Bishop of Samoa and Tokelau | Samoan | 1923 | 1973 |
| Thiandoum, Hyacinthe | Archbishop of Dakar | Senegalese | 1921 | 1976 |
| Tomasek, Frantisek | Archbishop of Prague | Czechoslovakian | 1899 | 1977 |
| Trin Nhu Khue, Joseph | Archbishop of Hanoi | Vietnamese | 1899 | 1976 |
| Ursi, Corrado | Archbishop of Naples | Italian | 1908 | 1967 |
| Vagnozzi, Edigio | Pres. of the Prefecture of the Holy See's Economic Affairs | Italian | 1906 | 1967 |
| Villot, Jean | Secretary of State of His Holiness | French | 1905 | 1965 |
| Volk, Hermann | Bishop of Mainz | German | 1903 | 1973 |
| Willebrands, John | President of Secretariat for the Union of Christians Archbishop of Utrecht | Dutch | 1909 | 1969 |
| Wojtyla, Karol | Archbishop of Krakow | Polish | 1920 | 1967 |
| Wright, John | Prefect of the Sacred Congregation for the Clergy | American | 1909 | 1969 |
| Wyszynski, Stefan | Archbishop of Gniezno-Warsaw | Polish | 1901 | 1953 |
| Yu Pin, Paul | Archbishop of Nanking | Chinese | 1901 | 1969 |
| Zoungrana, Paul | Archbishop of Ouagadougou | Upper Voltan | 1917 | 1965 |

# NOTED PERSONALITIES

## Widely Known Americans of the Present

Statesmen, authors, military men, and other prominent persons not listed in other categories.

| Name (Birthplace) | Birthdate | Name (Birthplace) | Birthdate |
|---|---|---|---|
| Abel, I. W. (Magnolia, Oh.) | 8/11/08 | Cranston, Alan (Palo Alto, Cal.) | 6/19/14 |
| Abernathy, Ralph (Linden, Ala.) | 3/11/26 | Cronkite, Walter (St. Joseph, Mo.) | 11/4/16 |
| Abzug, Bella (New York, N.Y.) | 7/24/20 | Curtis, Charlotte (Chicago, Ill.) | 1929 |
| Adams, Brockman (Atlanta, Ga.) | 1/13/27 | | |
| Agnew, Spiro (Baltimore, Md.) | 11/9/18 | Davis, Angela (Birmingham, Ala.) | 1/26/44 |
| Albert, Carl (McAlester, Okla.) | 5/10/08 | Denenberg, Herbert (Omaha, Neb.) | 10/20/29 |
| Aldrin, Edwin E. Jr. (Buzz) (Glen Ridge, N.J.) | 1/20/30 | Dole, Robert (Russell, Kan.) | 7/22/23 |
| Alsop, Joseph W. Jr. (Avon, Conn.) | 10/11/10 | Doolittle, James H. (Alameda, Cal.) | 12/14/96 |
| Anderson, Jack (Long Beach, Cal.) | 10/19/22 | Douglas, William O. (Maine, Minn.) | 10/16/98 |
| Andrus, Cecil (Hood River, Ore.) | 8/25/31 | Dubinsky, David (Brest-Litovsk, Poland) | 2/22/92 |
| Armstrong, Neil (Wapakoneta, Oh.) | 8/5/30 | | |
| Askew, Reubin (Muskogee, Okla.) | 9/11/28 | Eagleton, Thomas (St. Louis, Mo.) | 9/4/29 |
| | | Eastland, James O. (Doddsville, Miss.) | 11/28/04 |
| Bailey, F. Lee (Waltham, Mass.) | 6/10/33 | Ehrlichman, John (Tacoma, Wash.) | 3/20/25 |
| Baker, Howard (Huntsville, Tenn.) | 11/15/25 | Eisenhower, Mamie (Boone, la.) | 11/14/96 |
| Baker, Russell (Loudoun Co., Va.) | 8/14/25 | Eisenhower, Milton S. (Abilene, Kan.) | 9/15/99 |
| Baldwin, James (New York, N.Y.) | 8/2/24 | Eizenstat, Stuart E. (Chicago, Ill.) | 1943 |
| Ball, George (Des Moines, la.) | 12/21/09 | Ervin, Sam (Morganton, N.C.) | 9/27/96 |
| Bayh, Birch (Terre Haute, Ind.) | 1/22/28 | Farmer, James (Marshall, Tex.) | 1/12/20 |
| Bell, Griffin (Americus, Ga.) | 10/31/18 | Fischer, Bobby (Chicago, Ill.) | 3/9/43 |
| Belli, Melvin (Sonora, Cal.) | 7/29/07 | Fitzsimmons, Frank (Jeannette, Pa.) | 4/7/08 |
| Bentsen, Lloyd (Mission, Tex.) | 2/11/21 | Flynt, Larry (Salyersville, Ky.) | 11/1/42 |
| Bergland, Bob (Roseau, Minn.) | 7/22/28 | Fong, Hiram (Honolulu, Ha.) | 10/1/07 |
| Blackmun, Harry (Nashville, Ill.) | 11/12/08 | Ford, Elizabeth (Mrs. Gerald) (Chicago, Ill.) | 4/8/18 |
| Blumenthal, W. Michael (Berlin, Germany) | 1/3/26 | Ford, Gerald R. (Omaha, Neb.) | 7/14/13 |
| Bok, Derek (Ardmore, Pa.) | 3/22/30 | Fraser, Douglas A. (Glasgow, Scotland) | 12/18/16 |
| Bond, Julian (Nashville, Tenn.) | 1/14/40 | Friedan, Betty (Peoria, Ill.) | 2/4/21 |
| Borman, Frank (Gary, Ind.) | 3/14/28 | Friedman, Milton (Brooklyn, N.Y.) | 7/31/12 |
| Bowles, Chester (Springfield, Mass.) | 4/5/01 | Fulbright, J. William (Sumner, Mo.) | 4/9/05 |
| Bradley, Omar N. (Clark, Mo.) | 2/12/93 | | |
| Bradley, Thomas (Calvert, Tex.) | 12/29/17 | Galbraith, John Kenneth (Ontario, Can.) | 10/15/08 |
| Brennan, William J. (Newark, N.J.) | 4/25/06 | Gardner, John (Los Angeles, Cal.) | 10/8/12 |
| Brewster, Kingman (Longmeadow, Mass.) | 6/17/19 | Glenn, John (Cambridge, Oh.) | 7/18/21 |
| Brinkley, David (Wilmington, N.C.) | 7/10/20 | Goheen, Robert F. (Vengurla, India) | 8/15/19 |
| Brooke, Edward (Washington, D.C.) | 10/26/19 | Goldberg, Arthur J. (Chicago, Ill.) | 8/8/08 |
| Brooks, Jack (Crowley, La.) | 12/18/22 | Goldwater, Barry M. (Phoenix, Ariz.) | 1/1/09 |
| Brown, Edmund G. Jr. (San Francisco, Cal.) | 4/7/38 | Goodpaster, Andrew J. (Granite City, Ill.) | 2/12/15 |
| Brown, George S. (Montclair, N.J.) | 8/17/18 | Graham, Billy (Charlotte, N.C.) | 11/7/18 |
| Brown, Harold (New York, N.Y.) | 9/19/27 | Graham, Katharine (New York, N.Y.) | 6/16/17 |
| Brown, Helen Gurley (Green Forest, Ark.) | 2/18/22 | Grasso, Ella (Windsor Locks, Conn.) | 5/10/19 |
| Brown, Samuel (Council Bluffs, la.) | 7/27/43 | Greenspan, Alan (New York, N.Y.) | 3/6/26 |
| Brzezinski, Zbigniew (Warsaw, Poland) | 3/28/28 | Griffin, Robert P. (Traverse City, Mich.) | 11/6/23 |
| Buchwald, Art (Mt. Vernon, N.Y.) | 10/20/25 | | |
| Buckley, William F. (New York, N.Y.) | 11/24/25 | Haig, Alexander (Philadelphia, Pa.) | 12/2/24 |
| Bundy, McGeorge (Boston, Mass.) | 3/30/19 | Hanks, Nancy (Miami Beach, Fla.) | 12/31/27 |
| Bunker, Ellsworth (Yonkers, N.Y.) | 5/11/94 | Harriman, W. Averell (New York, N.Y.) | 11/15/91 |
| Burger, Warren (St. Paul, Minn.) | 9/17/07 | Harris, Fred (Walters, Okla.) | 11/13/30 |
| Burns, Arthur F. (Stanislau, Aust.) | 4/27/04 | Harris, Patricia Roberts (Mattoon, Ill.) | 5/31/24 |
| Burton, Phillip (Cincinnati, Oh.) | 6/1/26 | Hatfield, Mark O. (Dallas, Ore.) | 7/12/22 |
| Bush, George (Milton, Mass.) | 6/12/24 | Hayakawa, S.I. (Vancouver, British Columbia) | 7/18/06 |
| Byrd, Robert (N. Wilkesboro, N.C.) | 1/15/18 | Hefner, Hugh (Chicago, Ill.) | 4/9/26 |
| | | Heller, Walter (Buffalo, N.Y.) | 8/27/15 |
| Califano, Joseph A. Jr. (Brooklyn, N.Y.) | 3/15/21 | Helms, Richard (St. Davids, Pa.) | 3/30/13 |
| Carey, Hugh (Brooklyn, N.Y.) | 4/11/19 | Hershey, Lenore (New York, N.Y.) | 3/20/20 |
| Carter, Amy (Plains, Ga.) | 10/19/67 | Hesburgh, Theodore (Syracuse, N.Y.) | 5/25/17 |
| Carter, Billy (Plains, Ga.) | 3/29/37 | Hills, Carla (Los Angeles, Cal.) | 1/3/34 |
| Carter, Donnel Jeffrey "Jeff" (New London, Conn.) | 8/18/52 | Hiss, Alger (Baltimore, Md.) | 11/11/04 |
| Carter, James Earl III "Chip" (Honolulu, Ha.) | 4/12/50 | Hughes, Harold (Ida Grove, la.) | 2/10/22 |
| Carter, Jimmy (Plains, Ga.) | 10/1/24 | | |
| Carter, John William "Jack" (Portsmouth, Va.) | 7/3/47 | Inouye, Daniel (Honolulu, Ha.) | 9/7/24 |
| Carter, Lillian (Richland, Ga.) | 8/15/98 | | |
| Carter, Rosalynn (Plains, Ga.) | 8/18/27 | Jackson, Henry (Everett, Wash.) | 5/31/12 |
| Case, Clifford (Franklin Park, N.J.) | 4/16/04 | Jackson, Jesse (Greenville, N.C.) | 10/8/41 |
| Chancellor, John (Chicago, Ill.) | 7/14/27 | Jackson, Maynard (Dallas, Tex.) | 3/23/38 |
| Chandler, Otis (Los Angles, Cal.) | 11/23/27 | Javits, Jacob K. (New York, N.Y.) | 5/18/04 |
| Chavez, Cesar (Yuma, Ariz.) | 3/31/27 | Johnson, Lady Bird (Mrs. Lyndon) (Karnack, Tex.) | 12/22/12 |
| Chisholm, Shirley (Brooklyn, N.Y.) | 11/30/24 | Jones, David C. (Aberdeen, S.D.) | 7/9/21 |
| Church, Frank (Boise, Ida.) | 7/25/24 | Jordan, Barbara (Houston, Tex.) | 2/21/36 |
| Cleland, J. Maxwell (Atlanta, Ga.) | 8/24/42 | Jordan, Hamilton (Charlotte, N.C.) | 9/21/44 |
| Commager, Henry Steele (Pittsburgh, Pa.) | 10/25/02 | Jordan, Vernon (Atlanta, Ga.) | 8/15/35 |
| Commoner, Barry (Brooklyn, N.Y.) | 5/28/17 | | |
| Conant, James B. (Dorchester, Mass.) | 3/26/93 | Kennedy, Edward M. (Brookline, Mass.) | 2/22/32 |
| Connally, John B. (Floresville, Tex.) | 2/28/17 | Kennedy, Rose (Mrs. Joseph P.) (Boston, Mass.) | 7/22/90 |
| Cooke, Terence Cardinal (New York, N.Y.) | 3/1/21 | Kerr, Walter (Evanston, Ill.) | 7/8/13 |
| Cooney, Joan Ganz (Phoenix, Ariz.) | 10/30/29 | King, Coretta (Mrs. Martin L.) (Marion, Ala.) | 4/27/27 |
| Cosell, Howard (Winston-Salem, N.C.) | 1920 | Kirbo, Charles (Bainbridge, Ga.) | 3/15/17 |
| Costanza, Margaret (Le Roy, N.Y.) | 11/28/32 | Kirkland, Lane (Camden, S.C.) | 3/12/22 |
| Costle, Douglas M. (Long Beach, Cal.) | 7/27/39 | Kissinger, Henry (Fuerth, Germany) | 5/27/23 |
| Cousins, Norman (Union Hill, N.J.) | 6/24/12 | Koch, Edward I. (New York, N.Y.) | 12/12/24 |
| Cox, Archibald (Plainfield, N.J.) | 5/17/12 | Kreps, Juanita M. (Lynch, Ky.) | 1/11/21 |

| Name (Birthplace) | Birthdate | Name (Birthplace) | Birthdate |
|---|---|---|---|
| Laird, Melvin (Omaha, Neb.) | 9/1/22 | Rusk, Dean (Cherokee Co., Ga.) | 2/9/09 |
| Lance, Thomas B. "Bert" (Young Harris, Ga.) | 6/3/31 | | |
| Landers, Ann (Sioux City, Ia.) | 3/27/17 | Safer, Morley (Toronto, Ontario) | 11/8/31 |
| Landon, Alfred (West Middlesex, Pa.) | 9/9/87 | Safire, William (New York, N.Y.) | 12/17/29 |
| LeMay, Curtis (Ohio) | 11/15/06 | Sagan, Carl (New York, N.Y.) | 11/9/34 |
| Lemnitzer, Lyman L. (Honesdale, Pa.) | 8/29/99 | Salk, Jonas (New York, N.Y.) | 10/28/14 |
| Levi, Edward (Chicago, Ill.) | 6/26/11 | Samuelson, Paul A. (Gary, Ind.) | 5/15/15 |
| Lipshutz, Robert J. (Atlanta, Ga.) | 12/27/21 | Schlafly, Phyllis (St. Louis, Mo.) | 8/15/24 |
| Lodge, Henry Cabot (Nahant, Mass.) | 7/5/02 | Schlesinger, Arthur Jr. (Columbus, Oh.) | 10/15/17 |
| Long, Russell B. Shreveport, La.) | 11/3/18 | Schlesinger, James R. (New York, N.Y.) | 2/15/29 |
| Luce, Clare Boothe (New York, N.Y.) | 4/10/03 | Schultze, Charles (Alexandria, Va.) | 12/22/24 |
| | | Scott, Hugh (Fredericksburg, Va.) | 11/11/00 |
| Maddox, Lester (Atlanta, Ga.) | 9/30/15 | Scranton, William W. (Madison, Conn.) | 7/19/17 |
| Mansfield, Mike (New York, N.Y.) | 3/16/03 | Seaborg, Glenn T. (Ishpeming, Mich.) | 4/19/12 |
| Marshall, Freddie Ray (Oak Grove, La.) | 8/22/28 | Sevareid, Eric (Velva, N.D.) | 11/26/12 |
| Marshall, Thurgood (Baltimore, Md.) | 7/2/08 | Shanker, Albert (New York, N.Y.) | 9/14/28 |
| McCarthy, Eugene (Watkins, Minn.) | 3/29/16 | Sheen, Fulton J. (El Paso, Ill.) | 5/8/95 |
| McCormack, John W. (Boston, Mass.) | 12/21/91 | Shirer, William L. (Chicago, Ill.) | 2/23/04 |
| McClellan, John J. (Sheridan, Ark.) | 2/25/96 | Shriver, R. Sargent (Westminster, Md.) | 11/9/15 |
| McCloskey, Paul (San Bernardino, Cal.) | 9/29/27 | Shultz, George (New York, N.Y.) | 12/13/20 |
| McCree, Wade H. Jr. (Des Moines, Ia.) | 7/3/20 | Simon, William (Paterson, N.J.) | 1927 |
| McGovern, George (Avon, S.D.) | 7/19/22 | Sirica, John J. (Waterbury, Conn.) | 3/19/04 |
| McNamara, Robert S. (San Francisco, Cal.) | 6/9/16 | Smeal, Eleanor (Ashtabula, Oh.) | 7/30/39 |
| Mead, Margaret (Philadelphia, Pa.) | 12/16/01 | Smith, Howard K. (Ferriday, La.) | 5/12/14 |
| Meany, George (New York, N.Y.) | 8/16/94 | Smith, Margaret Chase (Skowhegan, Me.) | 12/14/97 |
| Miller, Arnold (Leewood, W. Va.) | 4/25/23 | Snyder, Tom (Milwaukee, Wisc.) | 5/12/36 |
| Miller, G. William (Sapulpa, Okla.) | 3/9/25 | Spock, Benjamin (New Haven, Conn.) | 5/2/03 |
| Millett, Kate (St. Paul, Minn.) | 9/14/34 | Stassen, Harold (West St. Paul, Minn.) | 4/13/07 |
| Milliken, William (Traverse City, Mich.) | 3/26/22 | Steinem, Gloria (Toledo, Oh.) | 3/25/34 |
| Mitchell, John (Detroit, Mich.) | 9/15/13 | Stennis, John (Kamper City, Miss.) | 8/3/01 |
| Mondale, Joan (Eugene, Ore.) | 8/8/30 | Stevens, John Paul (Chicago, Ill.) | 4/20/20 |
| Mondale, Walter (Ceylon, Minn.) | 1/5/28 | Stevenson 3d, Adlai (Chicago, Ill.) | 10/10/30 |
| Morgan, Marabel (Crestline, Oh.) | 6/25/37 | Stewart, Potter (Jackson, Mich.) | 1/23/15 |
| Moses, Robert (New Haven, Conn.) | 12/18/88 | Stokes, Carl (Cleveland, Oh.) | 6/21/27 |
| Moynihan, Daniel P. (Tulsa, Okla.) | 3/16/27 | Strauss, Robert S. (Lockhart, Tex.) | 10/19/18 |
| Mudd, Roger (Washington, D.C.) | 2/9/28 | Sulzberger, Arthur Ochs (New York, N.Y.) | 2/5/26 |
| Muskie, Edmund (Rumford, Me.) | 3/28/14 | Symington, Stuart (Amherst, Mass.) | 6/26/01 |
| Nader, Ralph (Winsted, Conn.) | 2/27/34 | Taft, Robert Jr. (Cincinnati, Oh.) | 2/26/17 |
| Nixon, Julie (Mrs. David Eisenhower) | | Talmadge, Herman (Lovejoy, Ga.) | 8/9/13 |
| (Wash., D.C.) | 7/5/48 | Taylor, Maxwell D. (Keytesville, Mo.) | 8/26/01 |
| Nixon, Pat (Mrs. Richard) (Ely, Nev.) | 3/16/12 | Thomas, Helen (Winchester, Ky.) | 8/4/20 |
| Nixon, Richard (Yorba Linda, Cal.) | 1/9/13 | Thomas, Lowell (Woodington, Oh.) | 4/6/92 |
| Nixon, Tricia (Mrs. Edward Cox) (Cal.) | 2/21/46 | Thompson, James R. (Chicago, Ill.) | 5/8/36 |
| Nizer, Louis (London, England) | 2/6/02 | Thurmond, J. Strom (Edgefield, S.C.) | 12/5/02 |
| Norton, Eleanor Holmes (Washington, D.C.) | 6/13/37 | Tower, John (Houston, Tex.) | 9/29/25 |
| | | Truman, Mrs. Harry (Independence, Mo.) | 2/13/85 |
| O'Brien, Lawrence F. (Springfield, Mass.) | 7/7/17 | Truman, Margaret (Mrs. Clifton Daniel) | |
| Onassis, Jacqueline (Southampton, N.Y.) | 7/28/29 | (Independence, Mo.) | 2/17/24 |
| O'Neill, Thomas P. (Cambridge, Mass.) | 12/9/12 | Tuchman, Barbara (New York, N.Y.) | 1/30/12 |
| | | Turner, Stansfield (Chicago, Ill.) | 2/1/33 |
| Paley, William S. (Chicago, Ill.) | 9/28/01 | | |
| Pauling, Linus (Portland, Ore.) | 2/28/01 | Udall, Morris K. (St. Johns, Ariz.) | 6/15/22 |
| Peale, Norman Vincent (Bowersville, Oh.) | 5/31/98 | Ullman, Al (Great Falls, Mont.) | 3/9/14 |
| Percy, Charles H. (Pensacola, Fla.) | 9/27/19 | | |
| Powell, Jody (Cordele, Ga.) | 9/30/43 | Van Buren, Abigail (Sioux City, Ia.) | 7/4/18 |
| Powell, Lewis F. (Suffolk, Va.) | 9/19/07 | Vance, Cyrus R. (Clarksburg, W. Va.) | 3/27/17 |
| Proxmire, William (Lake Forest, Ill.) | 1/11/15 | Vanderbilt, Alfred G. (London, England) | 9/22/12 |
| | | Veeck, Bill (Chicago, Ill.) | 2/9/14 |
| Randolph, A. Philip (Crescent City, Fla.) | 4/15/89 | | |
| Ray, Dixy Lee (Tacoma, Wash.) | 9/3/14 | Wallace, George (Clio, Ala.) | 8/25/19 |
| Reagan, Ronald (Tampico, Ill.) | 2/6/11 | Wallace, Mike (Brookline, Mass.) | 5/9/18 |
| Reasoner, Harry (Dakota City, Ia.) | 4/17/23 | Walters, Barbara (Boston, Mass.) | 9/25/31 |
| Rehnquist, William (Milwaukee, Wis.) | 10/1/24 | Warnke, Paul (Webster, Mass.) | 1/31/20 |
| Reston, James (Clydebank, Scotland) | 11/3/09 | Washington, Walter E. (Dawson, Ga.) | 4/15/15 |
| Rhodes, John (Council Grove, Kan.) | 9/18/16 | Webster, William H. (St. Louis, Mo.) | 3/6/24 |
| Ribicoff, Abe (New Britain, Conn.) | 4/9/10 | Weicker, Lowell (Paris, France) | 5/16/31 |
| Richardson, Elliot L. (Boston, Mass.) | 7/20/21 | Westmoreland, William (Spartanburg, S.C.) | 3/26/14 |
| Rickover, Hyman (Makowa, Poland) | 1/27/00 | White, Byron R. (Ft. Collins, Col.) | 6/8/17 |
| Rizzo, Frank (Philadelphia, Pa.) | 10/23/20 | White, Theodore (Boston, Mass.) | 5/6/15 |
| Rockefeller, David (New York, N.Y.) | 6/12/15 | Wicker, Tom (Hamlet, N.C.) | 6/18/26 |
| Rockefeller, John D. 4th "Jay" (New York, N.Y.) | 6/18/37 | Wilkins, Roy (St. Louis, Mo.) | 8/30/01 |
| Rockefeller, Laurance S. (New York, N.Y.) | 5/26/10 | Williams, Edward Bennett (Hartford, Conn.) | 5/31/20 |
| Rockefeller, Nelson A. (Bar Harbor, Me.) | 7/8/08 | Woodcock, Leonard (Providence, R.I.) | 2/15/11 |
| Rockwell, Norman (New York, N.Y.) | 2/3/94 | Wright, James C. Jr. (Ft. Worth, Tex.) | 12/22/22 |
| Rodino, Peter (Newark, N.J.) | 6/7/09 | Wriston, Walter B. (Middletown, Conn.) | 8/3/19 |
| Romney, George W. (Chihuahua, Mexico) | 7/8/07 | Wurf, Jerry (New York, N.Y.) | 5/18/19 |
| Roosevelt, Elliot (New York, N.Y.) | 9/23/10 | | |
| Roosevelt, Franklin D. Jr. (Canada) | 8/17/14 | Young, Andrew (New Orleans, La.) | 3/12/22 |
| Ruckelshaus, William (Indianapolis, Ind.) | 7/24/32 | | |
| Rumsfeld, Donald (Chicago, Ill.) | 7/9/32 | Zumwalt, Elmo (San Francisco, Cal.) | 11/29/20 |

## Noted Black Americans

Names of black athletes and entertainers are not included here as they are listed elsewhere in The World Almanac.

**The Rev. Dr. Ralph David Abernathy,** b. 1926, organizer, 1957, and president, 1968, of the Southern Christian Leadership Conference.

**Crispus Attucks,** c. 1723-1770, agitator led group which precipitated the "Boston Massacre," Mar. 5, 1770.
**James Baldwin,** b. 1924, author, playwright; Another Country,

The Fire Next Time, Blues for Mister Charlie.

**Benjamin Banneker**, 1731-1806, inventor, astronomer, mathematician, and gazeteer; served on commission which surveyed and laid out Washington, D. C.

**Imamu Amiri Baraka**, b. LeRoi Jones, 1934, poet, playwright.

**James P. Beckwourth**, 1798-c. 1867, western fur-trader, scout, after whom Beckwourth Pass in northern California is named.

**Dr. Mary McCleod Bethune**, 1875-1955, adviser to presidents F. D. Roosevelt and Truman; division administrator, National Youth Administration, 1935; founder, president of Bethune-Cookman College.

**Henry Blair**, 19th century, obtained patents (believed the first issued to a black) for a corn-planter, 1834, and for a cotton-planter, 1836.

**Julian Bond**, b. 1940, civil rights leader first elected to the Georgia state legislature, 1965; helped found Student Nonviolent Coordinating Committee.

**Edward Bouchet**, 1852-1918, first black to earn a Ph.D., Yale, 1876, at a U. S. university; first black to be elected to Phi Beta Kappa.

**Thomas Bradley**, b. 1917, elected mayor of Los Angeles, 1973.

**Andrew F. Brimmer**, b. 1926, first black member, 1966, Federal Reserve Board.

**Edward W. Brooke**, b. 1919, attorney general, 1962, of Massachusetts; first black elected to U. S. Senate, 1967, since 19th century Reconstruction.

**Gwendolyn Brooks**, b. 1917, poet, novelist; first black to win a Pulitzer Prize, 1950, for Annie Allen.

**William Wells Brown**, 1815-1884, novelist, dramatist; first American black to publish a novel.

**Dr. Ralph Bunche**, 1904-1971, first black to win the Nobel Peace Prize, 1950; undersecretary of the UN, 1950.

**George E. Carruthers**, b. 1940, physicist developed the Apollo 16 lunar surface ultraviolet camera/spectograph.

**George Washington Carver**, 1861-1943, botanist, chemurgist, and educator; his extensive experiments in soil building and plant diseases revolutionized the economy of the South.

**Charles Waddell Chestnutt**, 1858-1932, author known primarily for his short stories, including The Conjure Woman.

**Shirley Chisholm**, b. 1924, first black woman elected to House of Representatives, Brooklyn, N. Y., 1968.

**Countee Cullen**, 1903-1946, poet, winner of numerous literary prizes.

**Lt. Gen. Benjamin O. Davis Jr.** b. 1912, West Point, 1936, first black Air Force general, 1954.

**Brig. Gen. Benjamin O. Davis Sr.**, 1877-1970, first black general, 1940, in U. S. Army.

**William L. Dawson**, 1886-1970, Illinois congressman, first black chairman of a major House of Representatives committee.

**Isaiah Dorman**, 19th century, U. S. Army interpreter, killed with Custer, 1876, at Battle of the Little Big Horn.

**Frederick Douglass**, 1817-1895, author, editor, orator, diplomat; edited the abolitionist weekly, The North Star, in Rochester, N. Y.; U.S. minister and counsul general to Haiti.

**Dr. Charles Richard Drew**, 1904-1950, pioneer in development of blood plasma; director of American Red Cross blood donor project in World War II.

**William Edward Burghardt Du Bois**, 1868-1963, historian, sociologist; a founder of the National Association for the Advancement of Colored People (NAACP), 1909, and founder of its magazine The Crisis; author, The Souls of Black Folk.

**Paul Laurence Dunbar**, 1872-1906, poet, novelist; won fame with Lyrics of Lowly Life, 1896.

**Jean Baptiste Point du Sable**, c. 1750-1818, pioneer trader and first settler of Chicago, 1779.

**Ralph Ellison**, b. 1914, novelist, winner of 1952 National Book Award, for Invisible Man.

**Estevanico** explorer led Spanish expedition of 1538 into the American Southwest.

**James Farmer**, b. 1920, a founder of the Congress of Racial Equality, 1942; asst. secretary, Dept. of HEW, 1969.

**Henry O. Flipper**, 1856-1940, first black to graduate, 1877, from West Point.

**Marcus Garvey**, 1887-1940, founded Universal Negro Improvement Assn., 1911.

**Kenneth Gibson**, b. 1932, elected mayor of Newark, N.J., 1970.

**Charles Gordone**, b. 1925, won 1970 Pulitzer Prize in Drama, with No Place to Be Somebody.

**Vice Adm. Samuel L. Gravely Jr.** b. 1922, first black admiral, 1971, served in World War II, Korea, and Vietnam; commander, Third Fleet.

**Alex Haley**, b. 1921, Pulitzer Prize-winning author; Roots, The Autobiography of Malcolm X.

**Jupiter Hammon**, c. 1720-1800, poet; the first black American to have his works published, 1761.

**Lorraine Hansberry**, 1930-1965, playwright; won N. Y. Drama Critics Circle Award, 1959, with Raisin in the Sun.

**Patricia Roberts Harris**, b. 1924, U. S. ambassador to Luxembourg, 1965-67, secretary, Dept. of HUD, 1977.

**William H. Hastie**, b. 1904, first black federal judge, appointed 1937; governor of Virgin Islands, 1946-49; judge, U.S. Circuit Court of Appeals, 1949.

**Matthew A. Henson**, 1866-1955, member of Peary's 1909 expedition to the North Pole; placed U.S. flag at the Pole.

**Dr. William A. Hinton**, 1883-1959, developed the Hinton and Davies-Hinton tests for detection of syphilis; first black professor, 1949, at Harvard Medical School.

**Benjamin L. Hooks**, b. 1925, first black member, 1972-1979, Federal Communications Comm.; exec. dir., 1977, NAACP.

**Langston Hughes**, 1902-1967, poet; also author of stories and song lyrics.

**The Rev. Jesse Jackson**, b. 1941, national director, Operation Bread Basket, and major community leader in Chicago.

**Maynard Jackson**, b. 1938, elected mayor of Atlanta, 1973.

**Gen. Daniel James Jr.** 1920-1978, first black 4-star general, 1975; Commander, North American Air Defense Command.

**Pvt. Henry Johnson**, 1897-1929, the first American decorated by France in World War I with the Croix de Guerre.

**James Weldon Johnson**, 1871-1938, poet, lyricist, novelist; first black admitted to Florida bar; U.S. consul in Venezuela and Nicaragua.

**Barbara Jordan**, b. 1936, congresswoman from Texas; member, House Judiciary Committee.

**Vernon E. Jordan**, b. 1935, executive director, National Urban League, 1972.

**Ernest E. Just**, 1883-1941, marine biologist studied egg development; author, Biology of Cell Surfaces, 1941.

**The Rev. Dr. Martin Luther King Jr.,** 1929-1968, led 382-day, Montgomery, Ala., boycott which brought 1956 U.S. Supreme Court decision holding segregation on buses unconstitutional; founder, president of the Southern Christian Leadership Conference, 1957; won Nobel Peace Prize, 1964.

**Lewis H. Latimer**, 1848-1928, associate of Edison; supervised installation of first electric street lighting in N.Y.C.

**Malcom X**, 1925-1965, leading spokesman for black pride, founded, 1965, Organization of Afro-American Unity.

**Thurgood Marshall**, b. 1908, first black U.S. solicitor general 1965; first black justice of the U. S. Supreme Court, 1967; as a lawyer led the legal battery which won the historic decision from the Supreme Court declaring racial segregation of public schools unconstitutional, 1954.

**Jan Matzeliger**, 1852-1889, invented lasting machine, patented 1883, which revolutionized the shoe industry.

**Wade H. McCree Jr.,** b. 1920, solicitor general of the U.S.

**Dorie Miller**, 1919-1943, Navy hero of Pearl Harbor attack; awarded the Navy Cross.

**Ernest N. Morial**, b. 1929, elected first black mayor of New Orleans, 1977.

**Willard Motley**, 1912-1965, novelist; Knock on Any Door.

**Elijah Muhammand**, 1897-1975, founded the Nation of Islam, or Black Muslims, 1931.

**Pedro Alonzo Nino**, navigator of the Nina, one of Columbus' 3 ships on his first voyage of discovery to the New World, 1492.

**Adam Clayton Powell**, 1908-1972, early civil rights leader, congressman, 1945-1969; chairman, House Committee on Education and Labor, 1960-1967.

**Joseph H. Rainey**, 1832-1887, first black elected to House of Representatives, 1869, from South Carolina.

**A. Philip Randolph**, b. 1889, organized the Brotherhood of Sleeping Car Porters, 1925; organizer of 1941 and 1963 March on Washington movements; vice president, AFL-CIO.

**Charles Rangel**, b. 1930, congressman from N.Y.C., 1970; chairman, Congressional Black Caucus.

**Hiram R. Revels**, 1822-1901, first black U.S. senator, elected in Mississippi, served 1870-1871.

**Wilson C. Riles**, b. 1917, elected, 1970, California State Superintendent of Public Instruction.

**Norbert Rillieux**, 1806-1894; invented a vacuum pan evaporator, 1846, revolutionizing the sugar-refining industry.

**Carl T. Rowan**, b. 1925, prize-winning journalist; director of the U.S. Information Agency, 1964, the first black to sit on the National Security Council; U. S. ambassador to Finland, 1963.

**John B. Russwurm**, 1799-1851, with **Samuel E. Cornish**, 1793-1858, founded, 1827, the nation's first black newspaper, Freedom's Journal, in N.Y.C.

**Bayard Rustin**, b. 1910, organizer of the 1963 March on Washington; executive director, A. Philip Randolph Institute.

**Peter Salem**, at the Battle of Bunker Hill, June 17, 1775, shot and killed British commander Maj. John Pitcairn.

**Bishop Stephen Spottswood**, 1897-1974, board chairman of NAACP from 1966.

**Willard Townsend**, 1895-1957, organized the United Transport Service Employees, 1935 (redcaps, etc.); vice president, AFL-CIO.

**Sojourner Truth**, 1797-1883, born Isabella Baumfree; preacher, abolitionist; raised funds for Union in Civil War; worked for black educational opportunities.

**Harriet Tubman,** 1823-1913, Underground Railroad conductor served as nurse and spy for Union Army in the Civil War.

**Nat Turner,** 1800-1831, leader of the most significant of over 200 slave revolts in U.S. history, in Southampton, Va.; he and 16 others were hanged.

**Booker T. Washington,** 1856-1915, founder, 1881, and first president of Tuskegee Institute; author, Up From Slavery.

**Dr. Robert C. Weaver,** b. 1907, first black member of the U.S. Cabinet, secretary, Dept. of HUD, 1966.

**Phillis Wheatley,** c. 1753-1784, poet; 2d American woman and first black woman to have her works published, 1770.

**Walter White,** 1893-1955, exec. secretary, NAACP, 1931-1955.

**Roy Wilkins,** b. 1901, executive director, NAACP, 1955-1977.

**Dr. Daniel Hale Williams,** 1858-1931, performed one of first 2 open-heart operations, 1893; founded Provident, Chicago's first Negro hospital; first black elected a fellow of the American College of Surgeons.

**Granville T. Woods,** 1856-1910, invented the third-rail system now used in subways, a complex railway telegraph device that helped reduce train accidents, and an automatic air brake.

**Richard Wright,** 1908-1960, novelist; Native Son, Black Boy.

**Dr. Carter G. Woodson,** 1875-1950, historian; founded Assn. for the Study of Negro Life and History, 1915, and Journal of Negro History, 1916.

**Frank Yerby,** b. 1916, most successful of American black novelists; The Foxes of Harrow, Vixen.

**Andrew Young,** b. 1932, civil rights leader, congressman from Georgia, U.S. ambassador to the United Nations, 1977.

**Whitney M. Young Jr.,** 1921-1971, exec. director, 1961, National Urban League; author, lecturer, newspaper columnist.

About 5,000 blacks served in the Continental Army during the **American Revolution,** mostly in integrated units, some in all-black combat units. Some 200,000 blacks served in the Union Army during the **Civil War;** 38,000 gave their lives; 22 won the Medal of Honor, the nation's highest award. Of 367,000 blacks in the armed forces during **World War I,** 100,000 served in France. More than 1,000,000 blacks served in the armed forces during **World War II;** all-black fighter and bomber AAF units and infantry divisions gave distinguished service. In 1954 the policy of all-black units was finally abolished. Of 274,937 blacks who served in the armed forces during the **Vietnam War** (1965-1974), 5,681 were killed in combat.

As of July, 1978, there were 171 black mayors, 1,620 members of municipal governing bodies, 410 county officers, 56 state senators, 238 state representatives, one U.S. senator, and 16 U.S. representatives. There are now 4,503 blacks holding elected office in the U.S., an increase of 4.5% over the previous year, according to a survey by the Joint Center for Political Studies, Washington, D.C.

## Notable American Fiction Writers and Playwrights

| Name (Birthplace) | Birthdate |
| --- | --- |
| Abbott, George (Forestville, N.Y.) | 6/25/87 |
| Albee, Edward (Washington, D.C.) | 3/12/28 |
| Algren, Nelson (Detroit, Mich.) | 3/28/09 |
| Asimov, Isaac (Petrovichi, Russia) | 1/2/20 |
| Auchincloss, Louis (Lawrence, N.Y.) | 9/27/17 |
| Baldwin, James (New York, N.Y.) | 8/2/24 |
| Barth, John (Cambridge, Md.) | 5/27/30 |
| Barthelme, Donald (Philadelphia, Pa.) | 1931 |
| Bellow, Saul (Quebec, Canada) | 7/10/15 |
| Benchley, Nathaniel (Newton, Mass.) | 11/13/15 |
| Benchley, Peter (New York, N.Y.) | 5/8/40 |
| Berger, Thomas (Cincinnati, Oh.) | 7/20/24 |
| Bishop, Jim (Jersey City, N.J.) | 11/21/07 |
| Bradbury, Ray (Waukegan, Ill.) | 8/22/20 |
| Breslin, Jimmy (Jamaica, N.Y.) | 10/17/30 |
| Brooks, Gwendolyn (Topeka, Kan.) | 6/7/17 |
| Burrows, Abe (New York, N.Y.) | 12/18/10 |
| Caldwell, Erskine (Coweta Co., Ga.) | 12/17/03 |
| Caldwell, Taylor (London, England) | 1900 |
| Calisher, Hortense (New York, N.Y.) | 12/20/11 |
| Capote, Truman (New Orleans, La.) | 9/30/24 |
| Chase, Mary (Denver, Col.) | 2/25/07 |
| Chayefsky, Paddy (New York, N.Y.) | 1/29/23 |
| Cheever, John (Quincy Mass.) | 5/27/12 |
| Clavell, James (England) | 10/10/24 |
| Connelly, Marc (McKeesport, Pa.) | 12/13/90 |
| Cozzens, James Gould (Chicago, Ill.) | 8/19/03 |
| Crews, Harry (Alma, Ga.) | 6/6/35 |
| Crichton, Michael (Chicago, Ill.) | 10/23/42 |
| De Vries, Peter (Chicago, Ill.) | 2/27/10 |
| Dickey, James (Atlanta, Ga.) | 2/2/23 |
| Didion, Joan (Sacramento, Cal.) | 12/5/34 |
| Doctorow, E. L. (New York, N.Y.) | 1/6/31 |
| Drury, Allen (Houston, Tex.) | 9/2/18 |
| Elkin, Stanley (New York, N.Y.) | 5/11/30 |
| Ellison, Ralph (Oklahoma City, Okla.) | 3/1/14 |
| Farrell, James T. (Chicago, Ill.) | 2/27/04 |
| Fox, Paula (New York, N.Y.) | 11/22/23 |
| Gaddis, William (New York, N.Y.) | 1922 |
| Gann, Ernest K. (Lincoln, Neb.) | 10/13/10 |
| Gardner, John (Batavia, N.Y.) | 7/21/33 |
| Gibson, William (New York, N.Y.) | 11/13/14 |
| Gilroy, Frank (New York, N.Y.) | 10/13/25 |
| Goldman, William (Chicago, Ill.) | 8/12/31 |
| Grau, Shirley Ann (New Orleans, La.) | 7/8/29 |
| Hailey, Arthur (Luton, England) | 4/5/20 |
| Haley, Alex (Ithaca, N.Y.) | 8/11/21 |
| Hawkes, John (Stamford, Conn.) | 8/17/25 |
| Heinlein, Robert (Butler, Mon.) | 7/7/07 |
| Heller, Joseph (Brooklyn, N.Y.) | 5/1/23 |
| Hellman, Lillian (New Orleans, La.) | 6/20/07 |
| Hersey, John (Tientsin, China) | 6/17/14 |
| Himes, Chester (Jefferson City, Mo.) | 7/29/09 |
| Jong, Erica (New York, N.Y.) | 4/26/42 |
| Kazan, Elia (Constantinople, Turkey) | 9/7/09 |
| Kerr, Jean (Scranton, Pa.) | 7/?/23 |
| Kesey, Ken (La Hunta, Col.) | 9/17/35 |
| Kingsley, Sidney (New York, N.Y.) | 10/22/06 |
| Knowles, John (Fairmont, W. Va.) | 9/16/26 |
| L'Amour, Louis (Jamestown, N.D.) | — |
| Lee, Harper (Alabama) | 1926 |
| LeGuin, Ursula (Berkeley, Cal.) | 10/21/29 |
| Levin, Ira (New York, N.Y.) | 8/27/29 |
| Lindbergh, Ann Morrow (Englewood, N.J.) | 1906 |
| Loos, Anita (Sisson, Cal.) | 4/26/93 |
| Ludlum, Robert (New York, N.Y.) | 5/25/27 |
| MacDonald, John D. (Sharon, Pa.) | 7/24/16 |
| MacDonald, Ross (Los Gatos, Cal.) | 12/13/15 |
| MacInnes, Helen (Glasgow, Scotland) | 10/7/07 |
| Mailer, Norman (Long Branch, N.J.) | 1/31/23 |
| Malamud, Bernard (Brooklyn, N.Y.) | 4/26/14 |
| Mayer, Martin (New York, N.Y.) | 1/14/28 |
| McCarthy, Mary (Seattle, Wash.) | 6/21/12 |
| McMurtry, Larry (Wichita Falls, Tex.) | 6/3/36 |
| Michener, James A. (New York, N.Y.) | 2/3/07 |
| Miller, Arthur (New York, N.Y.) | 10/17/15 |
| Morris, Willie (Jackson, Miss.) | 11/29/34 |
| Oates, Joyce Carol (Lockport, N.Y.) | 6/16/38 |
| Patrick, John (Louisville, Ky.) | 5/17/05 |
| Percy, Walker (Birmingham, Ala.) | 5/28/16 |
| Perelman, S. J. (Brooklyn, N.Y.) | 2/1/04 |
| Porter, Katherine Ann (Indian Creek, Tex.) | 5/15/90 |
| Potok, Chaim (New York, N.Y.) | 2/17/29 |
| Puzo, Mario (New York, N.Y.) | 10/15/20 |
| Pynchon, Thomas (Glen Cove, N.Y.) | 5/8/37 |
| Rand, Ayn (St. Petersburg, Russia) | 1905 |
| Reed, Ishmael (Chattanooga, Tenn.) | 2/22/38 |
| Robbins, Harold (New York, N.Y.) | 5/21/12 |
| Rossner, Judith (New York, N.Y.) | 3/31/35 |
| Roth, Henry (Austria-Hungary) | 2/8/06 |
| Roth, Philip (Newark, N.J.) | 3/19/33 |
| Salinger, J. D. (New York, N.Y.) | 1/1/19 |
| Saroyan, William (Fresno, Cal.) | 8/31/08 |
| Schary, Dore (Newark, N.J.) | 8/31/05 |
| Schisgal, Murray (New York, N.Y.) | 11/25/26 |
| Schulberg, Budd (New York, N.Y.) | 3/27/14 |
| Segal, Erich (Brooklyn, N.Y.) | 6/16/37 |
| Shaw, Irwin (New York, N.Y.) | 2/27/13 |
| Shirer, William L. (Chicago, Ill.) | 2/23/04 |
| Simon, Neil (New York, N.Y.) | 7/4/27 |
| Singer, Isaac Bashevis (Radzymin, Poland) | 7/14/04 |
| Slaughter, Frank (Washington, D.C.) | 2/25/08 |

| Name, (Birthplace) | Birthdate | Name (Birthplace) | Birthdate |
|---|---|---|---|
| Spillane, Mickey (Brooklyn, N.Y.) | 3/9/18 | Vonnegut, Kurt Jr. (Indianapolis, Ind.) | 11/11/22 |
| Stafford, Jean (Covina, Cal.) | 7/1/15 | Wallace, Irving (Chicago, Ill.) | 3/18/16 |
| Stone, Irving (San Francisco, Cal.) | 7/14/03 | Wambaugh, Joseph (East Pittsburgh, Pa.) | 1/22/37 |
| Styron, William (Newport News, Va.) | 6/11/25 | Warren, Robert Penn (Guthrie, Ky.) | 4/24/05 |
| | | Welty, Eudora (Jackson, Miss.) | 4/13/09 |
| Taylor, Samuel A. (Chicago, Ill.) | 6/13/12 | Williams, Tennessee (Columbus, Miss.) | 3/26/11 |
| Tryon, Thomas (Hartford, Conn.) | 1/14/26 | Willingham, Calder (Atlanta, Ga.) | 12/23/22 |
| | | Wolfe, Tom (Richmond, Va.) | 3/2/31 |
| Updike, John (Shillington, Pa.) | 3/18/32 | Wouk, Herman (New York, N.Y.) | 5/27/15 |
| Uris, Leon (Baltimore, Md.) | 8/3/24 | | |
| | | Yerby, Frank (Augusta, Ga.) | 9/5/16 |
| Vidal, Gore (West Point, N.Y.) | 10/3/25 | | |

## American Architects and Some of Their Achievements

**Max Abramovitz**, b. 1908, Avery Fisher Hall, Lincoln Center, N.Y.C.

**Henry Bacon**, 1866-1924, Lincoln Memorial.

**Pietro Belluschi**, b. 1899, Julliard School of Music, Lincoln Center, N.Y.C.

**Marcel Breuer**, b. 1902, Whitney Museum of American Art, N.Y.C. (with Hamilton Smith).

**Charles Bulfinch**, 1763-1844, State House, Boston; Capitol, Wash. D.C., (part).

**Daniel H. Burnham**, 1846-1912, Union Station, Wash. D.C.; Flatiron, N.Y.C.

**Ralph Adams Cram**, 1863-1942, Cathedral of St. John the Divine, N.Y.C.; U.S. Military Academy (part).

**R. Buckminster Fuller**, b. 1895, U.S. Pavilion, Expo 67, Montreal (geodesic domes).

**Cass Gilbert**, 1859-1934, Custom House, Woolworth Bldg., N.Y.C.; Supreme Court bldg., Wash., D.C.

**Bertram G. Goodhue**, 1869-1924, Capitol, Lincoln, Neb.; St. Thomas, St. Bartholomew, N.Y.C.

**Walter Gropius**, 1883-1969, Pan Am Building, N.Y.C. (with Pietro Belluschi).

**Peter Harrison**, 1716-1775, Touro Synagogue, Redwood Library, Newport, R.I.

**Wallace K. Harrison**, b. 1895, Metropolitan Opera House, Lincoln Center, N.Y.C.

**Thomas Hastings**, 1860-1929, Public Library, Frick Mansion, N.Y.C.

**James Hoban**, 1762-1831, The White House.

**William Holabird**, 1854-1923, Crerar Library, City Hall, Chicago.

**Raymond Hood**, 1881-1934, Rockefeller Center, N.Y.C. (part); Daily News, N.Y.C.; Tribune, Chicago.

**Richard M. Hunt**, 1827-1895, Metropolitan Museum, N.Y.C. (part); Natl. Observatory, Wash., D.C.

**William Le Baron Jenney**, 1832-1907, Home Insurance, Chicago (demolished 1931).

**Philip C. Johnson**, b. 1906, N.Y. State Theater, Lincoln Center, N.Y.C.

**Albert Kahn**, 1869-1942, Athletic Club Bldg., General Motors Bldg., Detroit.

**Louis Kahn**, 1901-1974, Salk Laboratory, La Jolla, Cal.; Yale Art Gallery.

**Christopher Grant LaFarge**, 1862-1938, Roman Catholic Chapel, West Point.

**Benjamin H. Latrobe**, 1764-1820, U.S. Capitol (part).

**William Lescaze**, 1896-1969, Philadelphia Savings Fund Society; Borg-Warner Bldg., Chicago.

**Charles F. McKim**, 1847-1909, Public Library, Boston, Columbia Univ., N.Y.C. (part).

**Charles M. McKim**, b. 1920, KUHT-TV Transmitter Building, Houston; Lutheran Church of the Redeemer, Houston.

**Ludwig Mies van der Rohe**, 1886-1969, Seagram Building, N.Y.C. (with Philip C. Johnson); National Gallery, Berlin.

**Robert Mills**, 1781-1855, Washington Monument.

**Richard J. Neutra**, 1892-1970, Mathematics Park, Princeton; Orange Co. Courthouse, Santa Ana, Cal.

**Gyo Obata**, b. 1923, Natl. Air & Space Mus., Smithsonian Institution; Dallas-Ft. Worth Airport.

**Frederick L. Olmsted**, 1822-1903, Central Park, N.Y.C.; Fairmount Park, Philadelphia.

**Ieoh Ming Pei**, b. 1917, National Center for Atmospheric Research, Boulder, Col.

**William Pereira**, b. 1909, Cape Canaveral; Transamerica Bldg., San Francisco.

**John Russell Pope**, 1874-1937, National Gallery.

**John Portman**, b. 1924, Peachtree Center, Atlanta.

**James Renwick Jr.**, 1818-1895, Grace Church, St. Patrick's Cathedral, N.Y.C.; Smithsonian, Corcoran Galleries, Wash., D.C.

**Henry H. Richardson**, 1838-1886, Trinity Church, Boston.

**Kevin Roche**, b. 1922, Oakland Cal. Museum; Fine Arts Center, U. of Mass.

**James Gamble Rogers**, 1867-1947, Columbia-Presbyterian Medical Center, N.Y.C.; Northwestern Univ., Chicago.

**John Weldon Root**, b. 1887, Palmolive Building, Chicago; Hotel Statler, Washington; Hotel Tamanaco, Caracas.

**Paul Rudolph**, b. 1918, Jewitt Art Center, Wellesley College; Art & Architecture Bldg., Yale.

**Eero Saarinen**, 1910-1961, Gateway to the West Arch, St. Louis; Trans World Flight Center, N.Y.C.

**Louis Skidmore**, 1897-1962, AEC town site, Oak Ridge, Tenn.; Terrace Plaza Hotel, Cincinnati.

**Clarence S. Stein**, b. 1882, Temple Emanu-El, N.Y.C.

**Edward Durell Stone**, b. 1902, U.S. Embassy, New Delhi, India; (H. Hartford) Gallery of Modern Art, N.Y.C.

**Louis H. Sullivan**, 1856-1924, Auditorium, Chicago.

**Richard Upjohn**, 1802-1878, Trinity Church, N.Y.C.

**Ralph T. Walker**, 1889-1973, N.Y. Telephone Hdqrs., N.Y.C.; IBM Research Lab., Poughkeepsie, N.Y.

**Roland A. Wank**, 1898-1970, Cincinnati Union Terminal; head architect TVA, 1933-44.

**Stanford White**, 1853-1906, Washington Arch; first Madison Square Garden, N.Y.C.

**Frank Lloyd Wright**, 1869-1959, Imperial Hotel, Tokyo; Guggenheim Museum, N.Y.C.

**William Wurster**, b. 1895, Ghirardelli Sq., San Francisco; Cowell College, U. Cal., Berkeley.

**Minoru Yamasaki**, b. 1912, World Trade Center, N.Y.C.

## Noted American Cartoonists

**Charles Addams**, b. 1912, noted for macabre cartoons.

**Peter Arno**, 1904-1968, noted for urban characterizations.

**George Baker**, 1915-1975, The Sad Sack.

**C. C. Beck**, b. 1910, Captain Marvel.

**Herb Block (Herblock)**, b. 1909, leading political cartoonist.

**Clare Briggs**, 1875-1930, Mr. & Mrs.

**Ernie Bushmiller**, b. 1905, Nancy.

**Milton Caniff**, b. 1907, Terry & the Pirates; Steve Canyon.

**Al Capp**, b. 1909, Li'l Abner.

**Roy Crane**, 1901-1977, Captain Easy; Buz Sawyer.

**Jay N. Darling (Ding)**, 1876-1962, political cartoonist.

**Billy DeBeck**, 1890-1942, Barnie Google.

**Rudolph Dirks**, 1877-1968, The Katzenjammer Kids.

**Walt Disney**, 1901-1966, producer of animated cartoons created Mickey Mouse & Donald Duck.

**Jules Feiffer**, b. 1929, satirical *Village Voice* cartoonist.

**Bud Fisher**, 1884-1954, Mutt & Jeff.

**Ham Fisher**, 1900-1955, Joe Palooka.

**James Montgomery Flagg**, 1877-1960, illustrator created the famous Uncle Sam recruiting poster during WWI.

**Hal Foster**, b. 1892, Tarzan; Prince Valiant.

**Fontaine Fox**, 1884-1964, Toonerville Folks.

**Rube Goldberg**, 1883-1970, Boob McNutt.

**Chester Gould**, b. 1900, Dick Tracy.

**Harold Gray**, 1894-1968, Little Orphan Annie.

**Jimmy Hatlo**, 1898-1963, They'll Do It Everytime, Little Iodine.

**John Held Jr.**, 1889-1958, "Jazz Age" cartoonist.

**George Herriman**, 1881-1944, Krazy Kat.

**Harry Hershfield**, 1885-1974, Abie the Agent.

**Burne Hogarth**, b. 1911, Tarzan.

**Helen Hokinson**, 1900-1949, known for satirical drawings of plump, bewildered suburban matrons and clubwomen.

**Walt Kelly**, 1913-1973, Pogo.

**Hank Ketcham**, b. 1920, Dennis the Menace.

**Ted Key**, b. 1912 Hazel.

**Frank King**, 1883-1969, Gasoline Alley.

**Jack Kirby**, b. 1917, Captain America.

**Rollin Kirby,** 1875-1952, political cartoonist.

**Bill Mauldin,** b. 1921, depicted squalid life of the G.I. in WWII.

**Winsor McCay,** 1872-1934, Little Nemo.

**John T. McCutcheon,** 1870-1949, noted for cartoons of mid-western rural life.

**George McManus,** 1884-1954, Bringing Up Father (Maggie & Jiggs).

**Dale Messick,** b. 1906, Brenda Starr.

**Bob Montana,** 1920-1975, Archie.

**Willard Mullin,** b. 1902, sports cartoonist created the Dodgers "Bum" and the Mets "Kid".

**Thomas Nast,** 1840-1902, political cartoonist instrumental in breaking the corrupt Boss Tweed ring in N.Y. Created the Democratic donkey and Republican elephant.

**Frederick Burr Opper,** 1857-1937, Happy Hooligan.

**Richard Outcault,** 1863-1928, Yellow Kid; Buster Brown.

**Alex Raymond,** 1909-1956, Flash Gordon; Jungle Jim.

**Charles Schulz,** b. 1922, Peanuts.

**Elzie C. Segar,** 1894-1938, Popeye.

**Sydney Smith,** 1887-1935, The Gumps.

**Otto Soglow,** 1900-1975, The Little King; The Canyon Kiddies.

**James Swinnerton,** 1875-1974, Little Jimmy.

**James Thurber,** 1894-1961, *New Yorker* cartoonist of the smugly childish line coupled with the sophisticated caption.

**Mort Walker,** b. 1923, Beetle Bailey.

**Russ Westover,** 1887-1966, Tillie the Toiler.

**Frank Willard,** 1893-1958, Moon Mullins.

**J. R. Williams,** 1888-1957, The Willets Family; Out Our Way.

**Gahan Wilson,** b. 1930, cartoonist of the macabre.

**Art Young,** 1866-1943, political radical and satirist.

**Chic Young,** 1901-1973, Blondie.

## Business Hall of Fame

Established and supported by Junior Achievement Inc. Laureates selected by *Fortune* board of editors.

| | | | |
|---|---|---|---|
| William M. Allen | Amadeo P. Giannini | Charles E. Merrill | Cyrus R. Smith |
| Stephen D. Bechtel Sr. | Florence Nightingale Graham | John J. McCloy | Alexander T. Stewart |
| William Blackie | Joyce Clyde Hall | Cyrus H. McCormick | J. Edgar Thomson |
| Andrew Carnegie | H.J. Heinz | J. Irwin Miller | Theodore N. Vail |
| Harry B. Cunningham | James J. Hill | George S. Moore | George Washington |
| Arthur Vining Davis | Conrad N. Hilton | J. Pierpont Morgan | Thomas J. Watson Jr. |
| Walter E. Disney | J. Erik Jonsson | James Cash Penney | Frederick W. Weyerhaeuser |
| Donald W. Douglas | Henry John Kaiser | William C. Procter | Eli Whitney |
| George Eastman | Albert D. Lasker | M.J. Rathbone | Robert W. Woodruff |
| Thomas A. Edison | Royal Little | John D. Rockefeller | |
| Henry Ford | Francis Cabot Lowell | David Sarnoff | |
| Benjamin Franklin | Henry R. Luce | Alfred P. Sloan Jr. | |

## Noted Political Leaders of the Past

(Excluding U.S. presidents and most U.S. vice presidents, Supreme Court justices and signers of the Declaration of Independence; listed elsewhere.)

**Abu Bakr,** 573-634, Mohammedan leader, first caliph, chosen successor to Mohammed.

**Dean Acheson,** 1893-1971, (U.S.) secretary of state, chief architect of cold war foreign policy.

**Samuel Adams,** 1722-1803, (U.S.) patriot, firebrand of the Boston Tea Party.

**Konrad Adenauer,** 1876-1967, (G.) West German chancellor.

**Emilio Aguinaldo,** 1869-1964, (Philip.) revolutionary, fought against Spain and the U.S.

**Akbar,** 1542-1605, greatest Mogul emperor of India.

**Salvador Allende Gossens,** 1908-1973, (Chil.) president, advocate of democratic socialism.

**Herbert H. Asquith,** 1852-1928, (Br.) Liberal prime minister, instituted an advanced program of social reform.

**Atahualpa,** ?-1533, Inca (ruling chief) of Peru, executed by Pizarro.

**Kemal Atatürk,** 1881-1938, (Turk.) founder of modern Turkey.

**Clement Attlee,** 1883-1967, (Br.) Labour party leader, prime minister, enacted national health, nationalized gas, electric, coal, iron, steel industries.

**Stephen F. Austin,** 1793-1836, (U.S.) leader of colonization of Texas.

**Mikhail Bakunin,** 1814-1876, (R.) revolutionary, leading exponent of anarchism.

**Arthur J. Balfour,** 1848-1930, (Br.) as foreign secretary under Lloyd George issued Balfour Declaration expressing official British approval of Zionism.

**Bernard M. Baruch,** 1870-1965, (U.S.) financier and government adviser.

**Fulgencio Batista y Zaldívar,** 1901-1973, (Cub.) dictator overthrown by Castro.

**Lord Beaverbrook,** 1879-1964, (Br.) financier, statesman, newspaper owner (Daily and Sunday Express, Evening Standard).

**Eduard Benes,** 1884-1948, (Czech.) president during interwar and post-WW II eras.

**David Ben-Gurion,** 1886-1973, (Isr.) first premier of Israel.

**Thomas Hart Benton,** 1782-1858, (U.S.) Missouri senator, championed agrarian interests and westward expansion.

**Lavrenti Beria,** 1899-1953, (USSR) Communist leader prominent in political purges under Stalin.

**Aneurin Bevan,** 1897-1960, (Br.) Labour party leader, developed socialized medicine system.

**Ernest Bevin,** 1881-1951, (Br.) Labour party leader, foreign minister, helped lay foundation for NATO.

**Otto von Bismarck,** 1815-1898, (G.) statesman known as the Iron Chancellor, uniter of Germany, 1870.

**James G. Blaine,** 1830-1893, (U.S.) Republican politician,

diplomat, influential in launching Pan-American movement.

**Léon Blum,** 1872-1950, (F.) socialist leader, writer, headed first Popular Front government.

**Simón Bolívar,** 1783-1830, (Venez.) South American revolutionary who liberated much of the continent from Spanish rule.

**William E. Borah,** 1865-1940, (U.S.) isolationist senator, instrumental in blocking U.S. membership in League of Nations and the World Court.

**Cesare Borgia,** 1476-1507, (It.) soldier, politician, an outstanding figure of the Italian Renaissance.

**Aristide Briand,** 1862-1932, (F.) foreign minister, chief architect of Locarno Pact and anti-war Kellogg-Briand Pact.

**William Jennings Bryan,** 1860-1925, (U.S.) Democratic, populist leader, orator, 3 times lost race for presidency.

**Nikolai Bukharin,** 1888-1938, (USSR) communist leader and theoretician.

**William C. Bullitt,** 1891-1967, (U.S.) diplomat, first ambassador to USSR, ambassador to France.

**Ralph Bunche,** 1904-1971, (U.S.) a founder and key diplomat of United Nations for more than 20 years.

**John C. Calhoun,** 1782-1850, (U.S.) political leader, champion of states' rights and a symbol of the Old South.

**Robert Castlereagh,** 1769-1822, (Br.) foreign secretary, guided Grand Alliance against Napoleon, major figure at the Congress of Vienna, 1814-15.

**Camillo Benso Cavour,** 1810-1861, (It.) statesman, largely responsible for uniting Italy under the House of Savoy.

**Austen Chamberlain,** 1863-1937, (Br.) Conservative party leader, largely responsible for Locarno Pact of 1925.

**Neville Chamberlain,** 1869-1940, (Br.) Conservative prime minister whose appeasement of Hitler led to Munich Pact.

**Salmon P. Chase,** 1808-1873, (U.S.) public official, abolitionist, jurist, 6th Supreme Court chief justice.

**Chiang Kai-shek,** 1887-1975, (Chin.) Nationalist Chinese president whose government was driven from mainland to Taiwan.

**Chou En-lai,** 1898-1976, (Chin.) diplomat, prime minister, a leading figure of the Chinese Communist party.

**Winston Churchill,** 1874-1965, (Br.) prime minister, soldier, author, guided Britain through WW II.

**Galeazzo Ciano,** 1903-1944, (It.) fascist foreign minister, helped create Rome-Berlin Axis, executed by Mussolini.

**Henry Clay,** 1777-1852, (U.S.) "The Great Compromiser," one of most influential pre-Civil War political leaders.

**Georges Clemenceau,** 1841-1929, (F.) twice premier, Wilson's chief antagonist at Paris Peace Conference after WW I.

**DeWitt Clinton,** 1769-1828, (U.S.) political leader, responsible for promoting idea of the Erie Canal.

**Robert Clive,** 1725-1774, (Br.) first administrator of Bengal, laid foundation for British Empire in India.

**Jean Baptiste Colbert,** 1619-1683, (F.) statesman, influential under Louis XIV, created the French navy.

**James M. Cox,** 1870-1957, (U.S.) newspaper publisher and reformist Ohio governor.

**Oliver Cromwell,** 1599-1658, (Br.) Lord Protector of England, led parliamentary forces during Civil War.

**Curzon of Kedleston,** 1859-1925, (Br.) viceroy of India, foreign secretary, major force in dealing with post-WW I problems in Europe and Far East.

**Édouard Daladier,** 1884-1970, (F.) radical socialist politician, arrested by Vichy, interned by Germans until liberation in 1945.

**Georges Danton,** 1759-1794, (F.) a leading figure in the French Revolution.

**Jefferson Davis,** 1808-1889, (U.S.) president of the Confederate States of America.

**Charles G. Dawes,** 1865-1951, (U.S.) statesman, banker, advanced Dawes Plan to stabilize post-WW I German finances.

**Alcide De Gasperi,** 1881-1954, (It.) premier, founder of the Christian Democratic party.

**Charles DeGaulle,** 1890-1970, (F.) general, statesman, and president of the Fifth Republic.

**Thomas E. Dewey,** 1902-1971, (U.S.) New York governor, twice loser in try for presidency.

**Ngo Dinh Diem,** 1901-1963, (Viet.) South Vietnamese president, assassinated in government take-over.

**Everett M. Dirksen,** 1896-1969, (U.S.) Senate Republican minority leader, orator.

**Benjamin Disraeli,** 1804-1881, (Br.) prime minister, considered founder of modern Conservative party.

**Engelbert Dollfuss,** 1892-1934, (Aus.) chancellor, assassinated by Austrian Nazis.

**Andrea Doria,** 1466-1560, (It.) Genoese admiral, statesman, called "Father of Peace" and "Liberator of Genoa."

**Stephen A. Douglas,** 1813-1861, (U.S.) Democratic leader, orator, opposed Lincoln for the presidency.

**John Foster Dulles,** 1888-1959, (U.S.) secretary of state under Eisenhower, cold war policy maker.

**Friedrich Ebert,** 1871-1925, (G.) Social Democratic movement leader, instrumental in bringing about Weimar constitution.

**Sir Anthony Eden,** 1897-1977, (Br.) foreign secretary, prime minister during Suez invasion of 1956.

**Ludwig Erhard,** 1897-1977, (G.) economist, West German chancellor, led nation's economic rise after WW II.

**Hamilton Fish,** 1808-1893, (U.S.) secretary of state, successfully mediated disputes with Great Britain, Latin America.

**James V. Forrestal,** 1892-1949, (U.S.) secretary of navy, first secretary of defense.

**Francisco Franco,** 1892-1975, (Sp.) leader of rebel forces during Spanish Civil War and dictator of Spain.

**Benjamin Franklin,** 1706-1790, (U.S.) printer, publisher, author, inventor, scientist, diplomat.

**Louis de Frontenac,** 1620-1698, (F.) governor of New France (Canada) where he encouraged explorations and fought Iroquois.

**Hugh Gaitskell,** 1906-1963, (Br.) Labour party leader, major force in reversing its stand for unilateral disarmament.

**Albert Gallatin,** 1761-1849, (U.S.) second secretary of treasury, instrumental in negotiating end of War of 1812.

**Léon Gambetta,** 1838-1882, (F.) statesman, politician, one of the founders of the Third Republic.

**Mohandas K. Gandhi,** 1869-1948, (Ind.) political leader, ascetic, led nationalist movement against British rule.

**Giuseppe Garibaldi,** 1807-1882, (It.) patriot, soldier, a leading figure in the Risorgimento, the Italian unification movement.

**Genghis Khan,** c. 1167-1227, brilliant Mongol conqueror, ruler of vast Asian empire.

**William E. Gladstone,** 1809-1898, (Br.) prime minister 4 times, dominant force of Liberal party from 1868 to 1894.

**Paul Joseph Goebbels,** 1897-1945, (G.) Nazi propagandist, master of mass psychology.

**Hermann Goering,** 1893-1946, (G.) Nazi leader, founded and headed Gestapo.

**Klement Gottwald,** 1896-1953, (Czech.) communist leader ushered communism into his country.

**Che (Ernesto) Guevara,** 1928-1967, (Arg.) guerilla leader, prominent in Cuban revolution, killed in Bolivia.

**Haile Selassie,** 1891-1975, (Eth.) emperor, maintained traditional monarchy in face of foreign invasion, occupation, and internal resistance.

**Alexander Hamilton,** 1755-1804, (U.S.) first treasury secretary, champion of strong central government.

**Dag Hammarskjold,** 1905-1961, (Swed.) statesman, UN secretary general.

**John Hancock,** 1737-1793, (U.S.) revolutionary leader, first signer of Declaration of Independence.

**John Hay,** 1838-1905, (U.S.) secretary of state, primarily associated with Open Door Policy toward China.

**Patrick Henry,** 1736-1799, (U.S.) major revolutionary figure, remarkable orator.

**Édouard Herriot,** 1872-1957, (F.) radical socialist leader, twice premier, president of National Assembly.

**Theodor Herzl,** 1860-1904, (Aus.) founder of modern Zionism.

**Heinrich Himmler,** 1900-1945, (G.) chief of Nazi SS and Gestapo, primarily responsible for the Holocaust.

**Paul von Hindenburg,** 1847-1934, (G.) field marshal, president.

**Adolf Hitler,** 1889-1945, (G.) dictator, founder of National Socialism.

**Ho Chi Minh,** 1890-1969, (Viet.) North Vietnamese president, Vietnamese Communist leader, national hero.

**Harry L. Hopkins,** 1890-1946, (U.S.) New Deal administrator, closest adviser to FDR during WW II.

**Edward M. House,** 1858-1938, (U.S.) diplomat, confidential adviser to Woodrow Wilson.

**Samuel Houston,** 1793-1863, (U.S.) leader of struggle to win control of Texas from Mexico.

**Cordell Hull,** 1871-1955, (U.S.) secretary of state, initiated reciprocal trade to lower tariffs, helped organize UN.

**Hubert H. Humphrey,** 1911-1978, (U.S.) Minnesota Democrat, senator, vice president, spent 32 years in public service.

**Ibn Saud,** c. 1888-1953, (S. Arab.) founder of Saudi Arabia and its first king.

**Benito Juarez,** 1806-1872, (Mex.) national hero, rallied countrymen against foreign threats, sought to create democatic, federal republic.

**Frank B. Kellogg,** 1856-1937, (U.S.) secretary of state, negotiated Kellogg-Briand Pact to outlaw war.

**Robert F. Kennedy,** 1925-1968, (U.S.) attorney general, senator, assassinated while seeking presidential nomination.

**Aleksandr Kerensky,** 1881-1970, (R.) revolutionary, served as premier after Feb. 1917 revolution until Bolshevik overthrow.

**Nikita Khrushchev,** 1894-1971, (USSR) communist leader, premier, first secretary of Communist party, initiated de-Stalinization.

**Pyotr Kropotkin,** 1842-1921, (R.) anarchist, championed the peasants but opposed Bolshevism.

**Kublai Khan,** c. 1215-1294, Mongol emperor, founder of Yüan dynasty in China.

**Béla Kun,** 1886-c.1939, (Hung.) communist dictator, member of 3d International, tried to foment worldwide revolution.

**Robert M. LaFollette,** 1855-1925, (U.S.) Wisconsin public official, leader of progressive movement.

**Pierre Laval,** 1883-1945, (F.) politician, Vichy foreign minister, executed for treason.

**Andrew Bonar Law,** 1858-1923, (Br.) Conservative party politician, led opposition to Irish home rule.

**Vladimir Ilyich Lenin (Ulyanov),** 1870-1924, (USSR) revolutionary, founder of Bolshevism, Soviet leader 1917-1924.

**Ferdinand de Lesseps,** 1805-1894, (F.) diplomat, engineer, conceived idea of Suez Canal.

**Liu Shao-ch'i,** c.1898-1974, (Chin.) communist leader, fell from grace during "cultural revolution."

**Maxim Litvinov,** 1876-1951, (USSR) revolutionary, commissar of foreign affairs, proponent of cooperation with western powers.

**David Lloyd George,** 1863-1945, (Br.) Liberal party prime minister, laid foundations for the modern welfare state.

**Henry Cabot Lodge,** 1850-1924, (U.S.) conservative Republican senator, led opposition to participation in League of Nations.

**Huey P. Long,** 1893-1935, (U.S.) Louisiana political demagogue, governor, assassinated.

**Rosa Luxemburg,** 1871-1919, (G.) revolutionary, leader of the German Social Democratic party and Spartacus party.

**J. Ramsay MacDonald,** 1866-1937, (Br.) first Labour party prime minister of Great Britain.

**Joseph R. McCarthy,** 1908-1957, (U.S.) senator notorious for his witch hunt for communists in the government.

**Makarios III,** 1913-1977, (Cypr.) Greek Orthodox archbishop, first president of Cyprus.

**Malcolm X** (Malcolm Little), 1925-1965, (U.S.) black separatist leader, assassinated.

**Mao Tse-tung,** 1893-1976, (Chin.) chief Chinese Marxist theorist, soldier, lead Chinese revolution establishing his nation as an important communist state.

**Jean Paul Marat,** 1743-1793, (F.) revolutionary politician, identified with radical Jacobins, assassinated by Charlotte Corday.

**José Martí,** 1853-1895, (Cub.) patriot, poet, leader of Cuban struggle for independence.

**Jan Masaryk,** 1886-1948, (Czech.) foreign minister, died by mysterious suicide following communist coup.

**Thomas G. Masaryk,** 1850-1937, (Czech.) statesman, philosopher, first president of Czechoslovakia Republic.

**Jules Mazarin,** 1602-1661, (F.) cardinal, statesman, prime minister under Louis XIII and queen regent Anne of Austria.

**Tom Mboya,** 1930-1969, (Kenyan) political leader, instrumenal in securing independence for his country.

**Cosimo I de' Medici,** 1519-1574 (It.) Duke of Florence, grand uke of Tuscany.

**Lorenzo de' Medici,** the Magnificent, 1449-1492, (It.) merchant prince, a towering figure in Italian Renaissance.

**Catherine de Medicis,** 1519-1589, (F.) queen consort of Henry II, regent of France, influential in Catholic-Huguenot wars.

**Klemens W.N.L. Metternich,** 1773-1859, (Aus.) statesman, arbiter of post-Napoleonic Europe.

**Guy Mollet,** 1905-1975, (F.) socialist politician, resistance leader.

**Henry Morgenthau Jr.,** 1891-1967, (U.S.) secretary of treasury, raised funds to finance New Deal and U.S. WW II activities.

**Gouverneur Morris,** 1752-1816, (U.S.) statesman, diplomat, financial expert who helped plan decimal coinage system.

**Wayne Morse,** 1900-1974, (U.S.) senator, long-time critic of Vietnam War.

**Muhammad Ali,** 1769?-1849, (Egypt), pasha, founder of dynasty that encouraged emergence of modern Egyptian state.

**Benito Mussolini,** 1883-1945, (It.) dictator and leader of the Italian fascist movement.

**Imre Nagy,** c. 1895-1958, (Hung.) communist premier, assassinated after Soviets crushed 1958 uprising.

**Gamel Abdel Nasser,** 1918-1970, (Egypt.) leader of Arab unification, first Egyptian president.

**Jawaharlal Nehru,** 1889-1964, (Ind.) prime minister, guided India through its early years of independence.

**Kwame Nkrumah,** 1909-1972, (Ghan.) dictatorial prime minister, deposed in 1966.

**Frederick North,** 1732-1792, (Br.) prime minister, his inept policies led to loss of American colonies.

**Daniel O'Connell,** 1775-1847, (Ir.) political leader, known as the Liberator.

**Omar,** c.581-644, Mohammedan leader, 2d caliph, led Islam to become an imperial power.

**Ignace Paderewski,** 1860-1941, (Pol.) statesman, pianist, composer, briefly prime minister, an ardent patriot.

**Viscount Palmerston,** 1784-1865, (Br.) Whig-Liberal prime minister, foreign minister, embodied British nationalism.

**George Papandreou,** 1888-1968, (Gk.) Republican politician, served three times as prime minister.

**Franz von Papen,** 1879-1969, (G.) politician, played major role in overthrow of Weimar Republic and rise of Hitler.

**Charles Stewart Parnell,** 1846-1891, (Ir.) nationalist leader, "uncrowned king of Ireland."

**Lester Pearson,** 1897-1972, (Can.) diplomat, Liberal party leader, prime minister.

**Robert Peel,** 1788-1850, (Br.) reformist prime minister, founder of the Conservative party.

**Juan Perón,** 1895-1974, (Arg.) president, dictator.

**Joseph Pilsudski,** 1867-1935, (Pol.) statesman, instrumental in re-establishing Polish state in the 20th century.

**Charles Pinckney,** 1757-1824, (U.S.) founding father, his Pinckney plan was largely incorporated into constitution.

**William Pitt,** the Elder, 1708-1778, (Br.) statesman, called the "Great Commoner," transformed Britain into imperial power.

**William Pitt,** the Younger, 1759-1806, (Br.) prime minister during the French Revolutionary wars.

**Georgi Plekhanov,** 1857-1918, (R.) revolutionary, social philosopher, called "father of Russian Marxism."

**Raymond Poincaré,** 1860-1934, (F.) 9th president of the Republic, advocated harsh punishment of Germany after WW I.

**Georges Pompidou,** 1911-1974, (F.) Gaullist political leader, president from 1969 to 1974.

**Grigori Potemkin,** 1739-1791, (R.) field marshal, favorite of Catherine II.

**Edmund Randolph,** 1753-1813, (U.S.) attorney, prominent in drafting, ratification of constitution, senior counsel to Burr in his treason trial.

**John Randolph,** 1773-1833, (U.S.) southern planter, strong advocate of states' rights.

**Jeanette Rankin,** 1880-1973, (U.S.) pacifist, first woman member of U.S. Congress.

**Walter Rathenau,** 1867-1922, (G.) industrialist, social theorist, statesman.

**Sam Rayburn,** 1882-1961, (U.S.) Democratic leader, representative for 47 years, House speaker for 17.

**Paul Reynaud,** 1878-1966, (F.) statesman, premier in 1940 at the time of France's defeat by Germany.

**Syngman Rhee,** 1875-1965, (Kor.) first president of the Republic of Korea.

**Cecil Rhodes,** 1853-1902, (Br.) imperialist, industrial magnate, established Rhodes scholarships in his will.

**Cardinal de Richelieu,** 1585-1642, (F.) statesman, known as "red eminence," chief minister to Louis XIII.

**Maximilien Robespierre,** 1758-1794, (F.) leading figure of French Revolution, responsible for much of Reign of Terror.

**Eleanor Roosevelt,** 1884-1962, (U.S.) humanitarian, United Nations diplomat.

**Elihu Root,** 1845-1937, (U.S.) lawyer, statesman, diplomat,

leading Republican supporter of the League of Nations.

**John Russell,** 1792-1878, (Br.) Liberal prime minister during the Irish potato famine.

**Antônio de O. Salazar,** 1899-1970, (Port.) statesman, longtime dictator.

**José de San Martín,** 1778-1850, South American revolutionary, protector of Peru.

**Eisaku Sato,** 1901-1975, (Jap.) prime minister, presided over Japan's post-WW II emergence as major world power.

**Philipp Scheidemann,** 1865-1939, (G.) Social Democratic leader, first chancellor of the German republic.

**Robert Schuman,** 1886-1963, (F.) statesman, founded European Coal and Steel Community, strove for a "United States of Europe."

**Carl Schurz,** 1829-1906, (U.S.) German-American political leader, journalist, orator, dedicated reformer.

**Kurt Schuschnigg,** 1897-1977, (Aus.) chancellor, unsuccessful in stopping his country's annexation by Germany.

**William H. Seward,** 1801-1872, (U.S.) anti-slavery activist, as Lincoln's secretary of state purchased Alaska.

**Carlo Sforza,** 1872-1952, (It.) foreign minister, prominent Italian anti-fascist.

**Alfred E. Smith,** 1873-1944, (U.S.) New York Democratic governor, first Roman Catholic to run for presidency.

**Jan C. Smuts,** 1870-1950, (S.Af.) statesman, philosopher, soldier, prime minister.

**Paul Henri Spaak,** 1899-1972, (Belg.) statesman, socialist leader.

**Joseph Stalin,** 1879-1953, (USSR) Soviet dictator from 1924 to 1953.

**Edwin M. Stanton,** 1814-1869, (U.S.) Lincoln's secretary of war during the Civil War.

**Edward R. Stettinius Jr.,** 1900-1949, (U.S.) industrialist, secretary of state who coordinated aid to WW II allies.

**Adlai E. Stevenson,** 1900-1965, (U.S.) Democratic leader, diplomat, Illinois governor, presidential candidate.

**Henry L. Stimson,** 1867-1950, (U.S.) statesman, served in 5 administrations, deeply influenced foreign policy in 1930s and 1940s.

**Gustav Stresemann,** 1878-1929, (G.) chancellor, foreign minister, dedicated to regaining world friendship for post-WW I Germany.

**Sukarno,** 1901-1970, (Indon.) dictatorial first president of the Indonesian republic.

**Sun Yat-sen,** 1866-1925, (Chin.) revolutionary, leader of Kuomintang, regarded as the father of modern China.

**Robert A. Taft,** 1889-1953, (U.S.) conservative Senate leader, called "Mr. Republican."

**Charles de Talleyrand,** 1754-1838, (F.) statesman, diplomat, the major force of the Congress of Vienna of 1814-15.

**U Thant,** 1909-1974, (Bur.) statesman, UN secretary-general.

**Norman A. Thomas,** 1884-1968, (U.S.) social reformer, 6 times unsuccessful Socialist party presidential candidate.

**Palmiro Togliatti,** 1893-1964, (It.) founder and leader of Italian Communist party.

**Hideki Tojo,** 1885-1948, (Jap.) statesman, soldier, prime minister during most of WW II.

**François Toussaint L'Ouverture,** c. 1744-1803, (Hait.) patriot, martyr, thwarted French colonial aims.

**Leon Trotsky,** 1879-1940, (USSR) revolutionary, communist leader, founded Red Army, expelled from party in conflict with Stalin.

**Rafael L. Trujillo Molina,** 1891-1961, (Dom.) absolute dictator, assassinated.

**Moise K. Tshombe,** 1919-1969, (Cong.) politician, president of secessionist Katanga, premier of Repubic of Congo (Zaire).

**William M. Tweed,** 1823-1878, (U.S.) politician, absolute leader of Tammany Hall, NYC's Democratic political machine, called "Boss" Tweed.

**Walter Ulbricht,** 1893-1973, (G.) communist leader of German Democratic Republic.

**Arthur H. Vandenberg,** 1884-1951, (U.S.) senator, major proponent of anti-communist bipartisan foreign policy after WW II.

**Eleutherios Venizelos,** 1864-1936, (Gk.) most prominent Greek statesman in early 20th century, considerably expanded Greek territory through his diplomacy.

**Hendrik F. Verwoerd,** 1901-1966, (S.Af.) prime minister, rigorously applied apartheid policy despite protest.

**Robert Walpole,** 1676-1745, (Br.) statesman, generally considered Britain's first prime minister.

**Daniel Webster,** 1782-1852, (U.S.) orator, politician, enthusiastic nationalist, advocate of business interests during Jacksonian agrarianism.

**Chaim Weizmann,** 1874-1952, Zionist leader, scientist, first Israeli president.

**Wendell L. Willkie,** 1892-1944, (U.S.) Republican who tried to unseat FDR when he ran for his 3d term.

**Emiliano Zapata,** c. 1879-1919, (Mex.) revolutionary, major influence on modern Mexico.

## Notable Military and Naval Leaders of the Past

**Creighton Abrams,** 1914-1974, (U.S.) commanded forces in Vietnam, 1968-72.

**Harold Alexander,** 1891-1969, (Br.) led Allied invasion of Italy, 1943.

**Ethan Allen,** 1738-1789, (U.S.) headed Green Mountain Boys; captured Ft. Ticonderoga, 1775.

**Edmund Allenby,** 1861-1936, (Br.) in Boer War, WW1; led Egyptian expeditionary force, 1917-18.

**Benedict Arnold,** 1741-1801, (U.S.) victorious at Saratoga; tried to betray West Point to British.

**Henry "Hap" Arnold,** 1886-1950, (U.S.) commanded Army Air Force in WW2.

**Petr Bagration,** 1765-1812, (R.) hero of Napoleonic wars.

**John Barry,** 1745-1803, (U.S.) won numerous sea battles during revolution.

**Pierre Beauregard,** 1818-1893, (U.S.) Confederate general ordered bombardment of Ft. Sumter that began the Civil War.

**Gebhard v. Blücher,** 1742-1819, (G.) helped defeat Napoleon at Waterloo.

**Napoleon Bonaparte,** 1769-1821, (F.) defeated Russia and Austria at Austerlitz, 1805; invaded Russia, 1812; defeated at Waterloo, 1815.

**Edward Braddock,** 1695-1755, (Br.) commanded forces in French and Indian War.

**John Burgoyne,** 1722-1792, (Br.) defeated at Saratoga.

**Claire Chennault,** 1890-1958, (U.S.) headed Flying Tigers in WW2.

**Karl v. Clausewitz,** 1780-1831, (G.) wrote books on military theory.

**Henry Clinton,** 1738-1795, (Br.) commander of forces in America, 1778-81.

**Lucius D. Clay,** 1897-1978, (U.S.) led Berlin airlift, 1948-49.

**Charles Cornwallis,** 1738-1805, (Br.) victorious at Brandywine, 1777; surrendered at Yorktown.

**Crazy Horse,** 1849-1877, (U.S.) Sioux war chief victorious at Little Big Horn.

**George A. Custer,** 1839-1876, (U.S.) defeated and killed at Little Big Horn.

**Stephen Decatur,** 1779-1820, (U.S.) naval hero of Barbary wars, War of 1812.

**Anton Denikin,** 1872-1947, (R.) led White forces in Russian civil war.

**George Dewey,** 1837-1917, (U.S.) destroyed Spanish fleet at Manila, 1898.

**Hugh C. Dowding,** 1883-1970, (Br.) headed RAF, 1936-40.

**Jubal Early,** 1816-1894, (U.S.) Confederate general led raid on Washington, 1864.

**Dwight D. Eisenhower,** 1890-1969, (U.S.) commanded Allied forces in Europe, WW2.

**David Farragut,** 1801-1870, (U.S.) Union admiral captured New Orleans, Mobile Bay.

**Ferdinand Foch,** 1851-1929, (F.) headed victorious Allied armies, 1918.

**Nathan Bedford Forrest,** 1821-1877, (U.S.) Confederate general led cavalry raids against Union supply lines.

**Frederick the Great,** 1712-1786, (G.) led Prussia in The Seven Years War.

**Charles G. Gordon,** 1833-1885, (Br.) led forces in China; killed at Khartoum.

**Horatio Gates,** 1728-1806, (U.S.) commanded army at Saratoga.

**Ulysses S. Grant,** 1822-1885, (U.S.) headed Union army, 1864-65; forced Lee's surrender, 1865.

**Heinz Guderian,** 1888-1953, (G.) tank theorist led panzer forces in Poland, France, Russia.

**Douglas Haig,** 1861-1928, (Br.) led British armies in France, 1915-18.

**William F. Halsey,** 1882-1959, (U.S.) defeated Japanese fleet at Leyte Gulf, 1944.

**Richard Howe,** 1726-1799, (Br.) commanded navy in America, 1776-78; first of June victory against French, 1794.

**William Howe,** 1729-1814, (Br.) commanded forces in America, 1776-78.

**Isaac Hull,** 1773-1843, (U.S.) sunk British frigate Guerriere, 1812.

**Thomas (Stonewall) Jackson,** 1824-1863, (U.S.) Confederate general led forces in the Shenandoah Valley campaign; killed at Chancellorsville.

**Joseph Joffre,** 1852-1931, (F.) headed Allied armies, won Battle of the Marne, 1914.

**John Paul Jones,** 1747-1792, (U.S.) raided British coast; commanded Bonhomme Richard in victory over Serapis, 1779.

**Stephen Kearny,** 1794-1848, (U.S.) headed Army of the West in Mexican War.

**Ernest J. King,** 1878-1956, (U.S.) chief naval strategist in WW2.

**Horatio H. Kitchener,** 1850-1916, (Br.) led forces in Boer War; victorious at Khartoum; organized army in WW1.

**Lavrenti Kornilov,** 1870-1918, (R.) Commander-in-Chief 1917; led counter-revolutionary march on Petrograd.

**Thaddeus Kosciusko,** 1746-1817, (P.) aided American cause in revolution.

**Mikhail Kutuzov,** 1745-1813, (R.) fought French at Borodino 1812; abandoned Moscow; forced French retreat.

**Marquis de Lafayette,** 1757-1834, (F.) aided American cause in the revolution.

**Thomas E. Lawrence (of Arabia),** 1888-1935, (Br.) organized revolt of Arabs against Turks in WW1.

**Henry (Light-Horse Harry) Lee,** 1756-1818, (U.S.) cavalry officer in revolution.

**Robert E. Lee,** 1807-1870, (U.S.) Confederate general defeated at Gettysburg; surrendered to Grant, 1865.

**James Longstreet,** 1821-1904, (U.S.) aided Lee at Gettysburg.

**Erich Ludendorff,** 1865-1937, (G.) victorious at Tannenberg; supreme commander in East, 1916-18.

**William D. Leahy,** 1875-1959, (U.S.) personal chief of staff to Roosevelt during WW2.

**Douglas MacArthur,** 1880-1964, (U.S.) commanded forces in SW Pacific in WW2; headed occupation forces in Japan, 1945-50; UN commander in Korean War.

**Francis Marion,** 1733-1795, (U.S.) led guerrilla actions in S.C. during revolution.

**Duke of Marlborough,** 1650-1722, (Br.) led forces against Louis XIV in War of the Spanish Sucession.

**George C. Marshall,** 1880-1959, (U.S.) chief of staff in WW2, authored Marshall Plan.

**George B. McClellan,** 1826-1885, (U.S.) Union general commanded Army of the Potomac, 1861-62.

**George Meade,** 1815-1872, (U.S.) commanded Union forces at Gettysburg.

**Billy Mitchell,** 1879-1936, (U.S.) air-power advocate; court-martialed for insubordination, later vindicated.

**Helmuth v. Moltke,** 1800-1891, (G.) victorious in Austro-Prussian, Franco-Prussian wars.

**Louis de Montcalm,** 1712-1759, (F.) headed troops in Canada; defeated at Quebec, 1759.

**Bernard Law Montgomery,** 1887-1976, (Br.) stopped German offensive at Alamein, 1942; helped plan Normandy invasion.

**Daniel Morgan,** 1736-1802, (U.S.) victorious at Cowpens, 1781.

**Joachim Murat,** 1767-1815, (F.) leader of cavalry at Marengo, 1800; Austerlitz, 1805; and Jena, 1806.

**Horatio Nelson,** 1758-1805, (Br.) naval commander destroyed French fleet at Trafalgar.

**Michel Ney,** 1769-1815, (F.) commanded forces in Switzerland, Austria, Russia; defeated at Waterloo.

**Chester Nimitz,** 1885-1966, (U.S.) commander of naval forces in Pacific in WW2.

**George S. Patton,** 1885-1945, (U.S.) led assault on Sicily, 1943; headed 3d Army invasion of German-occupied Europe.

**Oliver Perry,** 1785-1819, (U.S.) won Battle of Lake Erie in War of 1812.

**John Pershing,** 1860-1948, (U.S.) commanded Mexican border campaign, 1916; American expeditionary forces in WW1.

**Henri Philippe Pétain,** 1856-1951, (F.) defended Verdun, 1916; headed Vichy government in WW2.

**George E. Pickett,** 1825-1875, (U.S.) Confederate general famed for "charge" at Gettysburg.

**Erwin Rommel,** 1891-1944, (G.) headed Afrika Korps in WW2.

**Karl v. Rundsteor,** 1875-1953, (G.) supreme commander in West, 1943-45.

**Aleksandr Samsonov,** 1859-1914, (R.) led invasion of E. Prussia, defeated at Tannenberg, 1914.

**Winfield Scott,** 1786-1866, (U.S.) hero of War of 1812; headed forces in Mexican war, took Mexico City.

**Philip Sheridan,** 1831-1888, (U.S.) Union cavalry officer headed Army of the Shenandoah, 1864-65.

**William T. Sherman,** 1820-1891, (U.S.) Union general sacked Atlanta during "march to the sea," 1864.

**Carl Spaatz,** 1891-1974, (U.S.) directed strategic bombing against Germany, later Japan, in WW2.

**Raymond Spruance,** 1886-1969, (U.S.) victorious at Midway Island, 1942.

**Joseph W. Stilwell,** 1883-1946, (U.S.) headed forces in the China, Burma, India theater in WW2.

**J.E.B. Stuart,** 1833-1864, (U.S.) Confederate cavalry commander.

**George H. Thomas,** 1816-1870, (U.S.) saved Union army at Chattanooga, 1863; victorious at Nashville, 1864.

**Semyon Timoshenko,** 1895-1970, (USSR) defended Moscow, Stalingrad; led winter offensive, 1942-43.

**Alfred v. Tirpitz,** 1849-1930, (G.) responsible for submarine ockade in WW1.
**Jonathan M. Wainwright,** 1883-1953, (U.S.) forced to surrender on Corregidor, 1942.
**George Washington,** 1732-1799, (U.S.) led Continental my, 1775-83.
**Archibald Wavell,** 1883-1950, (Br.) commanded forces in N. d E. Africa, and SE Asia in WW2.

**Anthony Wayne,** 1745-1796, (U.S.) captured Stony Point, 1779; defeated Indians at Fallen Timbers, 1794.
**Duke of Wellington,** 1769-1852, (Br.) defeated Napoleon at Waterloo.
**James Wolfe,** 1727-1759, (Br.) captured Quebec from French, 1758.
**Georgi Zhukov,** 1895-1974, (USSR) defended Moscow, 1941; led assault on Berlin.

## Noted Writers of the Past

**Henry Adams,** 1838-1918, (U.S.) historian, philosopher. *The ducation of Henry Adams.*
**George Ade,** 1866-1944, (U.S.) humorist, dramatist. *Fables in lang.*
**Conrad Aiken,** 1889-1973,(U.S.) poet, critic.*Collected Poems.*
**Louisa May Alcott,** 1832-1888, (U.S.) novelist. *Little Women.*
**Sholom Aleichem,** 1859-1916. (R.) Yiddish writer. *Tevye's aughter, The Great Fair.*
**Horatio Alger,** 1832-1899, (U.S.) author of "rags-to-riches" ys' books.
**Maxwell Anderson,** 1888-1959, (U.S.) playwright. *What Price lory?, High Tor, Winterset, Key Largo.*
**Sherwood Anderson,** 1876-1941, (U.S.) author. *Winesburg, hio.*
**Matthew Arnold,** 1822-1888, (Br.) poet, critic. "Thrysis," "Dor Beach."
**Jane Austen,** 1775-1817, (Br.) novelist. *Pride and Prejudice, ense and Sensibility, Emma, Mansfield Park.*
**Isaac Babel,** 1894-1941, (R.) short-story writer, playwright. dessa Tales, Red Cavalry.
**James M. Barrie,** 1860-1937, (Br.) playwright, novelist. *Peter an, Dear Brutus, What Every Woman Knows.*
**Honoré de Balzac,** 1799-1850, (F.) novelist. Le Père Goriot, ousin Bette, Eugénie Grandet, The Human Comedy.
**Charles Baudelaire,** 1821-1867, (Fr.) symbolist poet. *Les leurs du Mal.*
**Brendan Behan,** 1923-1964, (Ir.) playwright. *The Quare Felw, The Hostage, Borstal Boy.*
**Stephen Vincent Benét,** 1898-1943, (U.S.) poet, novelist. ohn Brown's Body.
**John Berryman,** 1914-1972, (U.S.) poet. *Homage to Mistress radstreet.*
**Ambrose Bierce,** 1842-1914, (U.S.) short-story writer, journalist. *In the Midst of Life, The Devil's Dictionary.*
**William Blake,** 1757-1827, (Br.) poet, mystic, artist. *Songs of nocence, Songs of Experience.*
**Giovanni Boccaccio,** 1313-1375, (It.) poet, storyteller. ecameron, Filostrato.
**James Boswell,** 1740-1795, (Sc.) author. *The Life of Samuel ohnson.*
**Bertolt Brecht,** 1898-1956, (G.) dramatist, poet. *The Threeenny Opera, Mother Courage and Her Children.*
**Charlotte Brontë,** 1816-1855, (Br.) novelist. *Jane Eyre.*
**Emily Brontë,** 1818-1848, (Br.) novelist. *Wuthering Heights.*
**Elizabeth Barrett Browning,** 1806-1861, (Br.) poet. *Sonnets om the Portuguese.*
**Robert Browning,** 1812-1889, (Br.) poet. "My Last Dutness," "Soliloquy of the Spanish Cloister."
**Pearl Buck,** 1892-1973, (U.S.) novelist. *The Good Earth.*
**Mikhail Bulgakov,** 1891-1940, (R.) novelist, playwright. *The leart of a Dog, The Master and Margarita.*
**John Bunyan,** 1628-1688, (Br.) writer. *Pilgrim's Progress.*
**Robert Burns,** 1759-1796, (Sc.) poet. "Flow Gently, Sweet fton," "My Heart's in the Highlands," "Auld Lang Syne."
**Edgar Rice Burroughs,** 1875-1950, (U.S.) novelist. *Tarzan of e Apes.*
**George Gordon Lord Byron,** 1788-1824, (Br.) poet. *Don uan, Childe Harold.*
**Albert Camus,** 1913-1960, (F.) novelist. *The Plague, The tranger, Caligula, The Fall.*
**Lewis Carroll,** 1832-1898, (Br.) writer, mathematician. *Alice's dventures in Wonderland, Through the Looking Glass.*
**Karel Capek,** 1890-1938, (Czech.) playwright, novelist, essayt. *R.U.R. (Rossum's Univeral Robots).*
**Giacomo Casanova,** 1725-1798, (It.) Venetian adventurer, uthor, world famous for his memoirs.
**Willa Cather,** 1876-1947, (U.S.) novelist, essayist. *O Pioeers!, My AAntonia.*
**Miguel de Cervantes Saavedra,** 1547-1616, (Sp.) novelist, ramatist, poet. *Don Quixote de la Mancha.*
**Raymond Chandler,** 1888-1959, (U.S.) writer of detective ction. Philip Marlowe series.
**Geoffrey Chaucer,** c. 1340-1400, (Br.) poet. *The Canterbury ales.*
**Anton Chekhov,** 1860-1904, (R.) short-story writer, dramast. *Uncle Vanya, The Cherry Orchard, The Three Sisters.*
**G.K. Chesterton,** 1874-1936, (Br.) author, created Father rown.

**Agatha Christie,** 1891-1976, (Br.) mystery writer. *And Then There Were None, Murder on the Orient Express.*
**Jean Cocteau,** 1889-1963, (F.) writer, visual artist, filmmaker. *The Beauty and the Beast, Enfants Terribles.*
**Samuel Taylor Coleridge,** 1772-1834, (Br.) poet, man of letters. "Kubla Khan," "The Rime of the Ancient Mariner."
**Sidonie Colette,** 1873-1954, (F.) novelist. *Claudine, The Vagrant, Gigi, Chéri.*
**Joseph Conrad,** 1857-1924, (Br.) novelist. *Lord Jim, Heart of Darkness, The Nigger of the Narcissus.*
**James Fenimore Cooper,** 1789-1851, (U.S.) novelist. *Leather-Stocking Tales, Drums Along the Mohawk.*
**Pierre Corneille,** 1606-1684, (F.) Dramatist. *Medea, El Cid, Horace, Cinna, Polyeucte.*
**Stephen Crane,** 1871-1900, (U.S.) novelist. *The Red Badge of Courage.*
**e.e. cummings,** 1894-1962, (U.S.) poet. *Tulips and Chimneys, Is 5, 95 Poems, The Enormous Room.*
**Gabriele D'Annunzio,** 1863-1938, (It.) poet, novelist, dramatist. *The Child of Pleasure, The Intruder, The Victim.*
**Dante Alighieri,** 1265-1321, (It.) poet. *The Divine Comedy.*
**Alphonse Daudet,** 1840-1897, (F.) writer. *Letters from My Mill, Tartarin de Tarascon, Le Petit Chose.*
**Daniel Defoe,** 1660-1731, (Br.) writer. *Robinson Crusoe, Moll Flanders, Journal of the Plague Year.*
**Charles Dickens,** 1812-1870, (Br.) novelist. *David Copperfield, Oliver Twist, Great Expectations, The Pickwick Papers.*
**Emily Dickinson,** 1830-1886, (U.S.) poet.
**Isak Dinesen** (Karen Blixen), 1885-1962, (Dan.) author. *Out of Africa, Seven Gothic Tales, Winter's Tales.*
**John Donne,** 1573-1631, (Br.) poet. *Songs and Sonnets, Holy Sonnets,* "Death Be Not Proud."
**Hilda Doolittle** (H.D.), 1886-1961, (U.S.) poet. *Sea Garden, Red Shoes for Bronze, Bid Me to Live.*
**John Dos Passos,** 1896-1970, (U.S.) author. *U.S.A., Midcentury.*
**Fyodor Dostoyevsky,** 1821-1881, (R.) author. *Crime and Punishment, The Brothers Karamazov, The Possessed, The Idiot.*
**Arthur Conan Doyle,** 1859-1930, (Br.) author, created Sherlock Holmes.
**Theodore Dreiser,** 1871-1945, (U.S.) novelist. *An American Tragedy, Sister Carrie.*
**John Dryden,** 1631-1700, (Br.) poet, dramatist, critic. *Fables, Ancient and Modern.*
**Alexandre Dumas,** 1802-1870, (F.) novelist, dramatist. *The Three Musketeers, The Count of Monte Cristo.*
**Alexandre Dumas** (fils), 1824-1895, (F.) dramatist, novelist. *La Dame aux camélias, Le Demi-Monde.*
**Ilya G. Ehrenburg,** 1891-1967, (R.) novelist, journalist. *The Thaw.*
**George Eliot,** 1819-1880, (Br.) novelist. *Adam Bede, Silas Marner, The Mill and the Floss.*
**T.S. Eliot,** 1888-1965, (Br.) poet, critic. *The Wasteland,* "The Lovesong of J. Alfred Prufrock," *Murder in the Cathedral.*
**Ralph Waldo Emerson,** 1803-1882, (U.S.) poet, essayist. "The Concord Hymn," "Brahma," "The Rhodora."
**William Faulkner,** 1897-1962, (U.S.) novelist. *Sanctuary, Light in August, The Sound and the Fury, Absalom, Absalom!*
**Edna Ferber,** 1885-1968, (U.S.) novelist, dramatist. *Show Boat, Saratoga Trunk, Giant, Dinner at Eight.*
**Henry Fielding,** 1707-1754, (Br.) novelist, dramatist. *Tom Jones.*
**F. Scott Fitzgerald,** 1896-1940, (U.S.) short-story writer, novelist. *The Great Gatsby, Tender is the Night.*
**Gustave Flaubert,** 1821-1880, (F.) novelist. *Madame Bovary, Salammbô.*
**C.S. Forester,** 1899-1966, (Br.) novelist. Horatio Hornblower series.
**E.M. Forster,** 1879-1970, (Br.) novelist. *A Passage to India, Where Angels Fear to Tread, Maurice.*
**Anatole France,** 1844-1924. (F.) writer. *Penguin Island, My Friend's Book, Le Crime de Sylvestre Bonnard.*
**Robert Frost,** 1874-1963, (U.S.) poet. *A Boy's Will,* "Birches," "Fire and Ice," "Stopping by Woods on a Snowy Evening."
**John Galsworthy,** 1867-1923, (Br.) novelist, dramatist. *The Forsythe Saga, A Modern Comedy.*

**Erle Stanley Gardner,** 1889-1970, (U.S.) author, lawyer. Perry Mason series.

**André Gide,** 1869-1951, (F.) writer, *The Immoralist, The Pastoral Symphony, Strait is the Gate.*

**Jean Giraudoux,** 1882-1944, (F.) novelist, dramatist. *Electra, The Madwoman of Chaillot, Ondine, Tiger at the Gate.*

**Johann W. von Goethe,** 1749-1832, (G.) poet, dramatist, novelist. *Faust.*

**Nikolai Gogol,** 1809-1852, (R.) short-story writer, dramatist, novelist. *Dead Souls, The Inspector General.*

**Oliver Goldsmith,** 1730?-1774, (Br.-Ir.) writer. *The Vicar of Wakefield, She Stoops to Conquer.*

**Maxim Gorky,** 1868-1936, (R.) writer, founder of Soviet realism. *Mother, The Lower Depths.*

**Thomas Gray,** 1716-1771, (Br.) poet. "Elegy Written in a Country Churchyard."

**Zane Grey,** 1875-1939, (U.S.) writer of western stories.

**Jakob Grimm,** 1785-1863, (G.) philologist, folklorist. *German Methodology, Grimm's Fairy Tales.*

**Wilhelm Grimm,** 1786-1859, (G.) philologist, folklorist. *Grimm's Fairy Tales.*

**Edgar A. Guest,** 1881-1959, (U.S.) poet. *A Heap of Livin!*

**Dashiell Hammett,** 1894-1961, (U.S.) writer of detective fiction, created Sam Spade.

**Lorraine Hansberry,** 1930-1965, (U.S.) playwright. *A Raisin in the Sun.*

**Thomas Hardy,** 1840-1928, (Br.) novelist, poet. *The Return of the Native, Tess of the D'Urbervilles, Jude the Obscure.*

**Joel Chandler Harris,** 1848-1908, (U.S.) short-story writer. Uncle Remus series.

**Moss Hart,** 1904-1961, (U.S.) playwright. *Once in a Lifetime, You Can't Take It With You.*

**Bret Harte,** 1836-1902, (U.S.) short-story writer, poet. *The Luck of Roaring Camp.*

**Jaroslav Hasek,** 1883-1923, (Czech) writer. *The Good Soldier Schweik.*

**Heinrich Heine,** 1797-1856, (G.) poet. *Book of Songs.*

**Ernest Hemingway,** 1899-1961, (U.S.) novelist, short-story writer. *A Farewell to Arms, For Whom the Bell Tolls.*

**O. Henry** (W.S. Porter), 1862-1910, (U.S.) short-story writer. "The Gift of the Magi."

**Hermann Hesse,** 1877-1962, (G.) novelist, poet. *Death and the Lover, Steppenwolf, Siddhartha.*

**Oliver Wendell Holmes,** 1809-1894, (U.S.) poet, novelist. *The Autocrat of the Breakfast-Table.*

**Alfred E. Housman,** 1859-1936, (Br.) poet. *A Shropshire Lad.*

**Elbert Hubbard,** 1856-1916, (U.S.) author, editor. "A Message to Garcia."

**Langston Hughes,** 1902-1967, (U.S.) poet, playwright. *The Weary Blues, One-Way Ticket, Shakespeare in Harlem.*

**Victor Hugo,** 1802-1885, (F.) poet, dramatist, novelist. *Notre Dame de Paris, Les Misérables.*

**Aldous Huxley** 1894-1963, (Br.) author. *Point Counter Point, Brave New World.*

**Henrik Ibsen,** 1828-1906, (Nor.) dramatist, poet. *A Doll's House, Ghosts, The Wild Duck, Hedda Gabler.*

**William Inge,** 1913-1973, (U.S.) playwright. *Come Back Little Sheba, Bus Stop, The Dark at the Top of the Stairs.*

**Washington Irving,** 1783-1859, (U.S.) essayist, author. "Rip Van Winkle," "The Legend of Sleepy Hollow."

**Shirley Jackson,** 1919-1965, (U.S.) writer. *The Lottery, The Haunting of Hill House, We Have Always Lived in the Castle.*

**Henry James,** 1843-1916, (U.S.) novelist, critic. *Washington Square, Portrait of a Lady, The American.*

**Robinson Jeffers,** 1887-1962, (U.S.) poet, dramatist. *Tamar and Other Poems, Medea.*

**Samuel Johnson,** 1709-1784, (Br.) author, scholar, critic. *Dictionary of the English Language.*

**Ben Jonson,** 1572-1637, (Br.) dramatist, poet. *The Alchemist, Volpone.*

**James Joyce,** 1882-1941, (Ir.) novelist. *Ulysses, A Portrait of the Artist as a Young Man, Finnegan's Wake.*

**Franz Kafka,** 1883-1924, (G.) novelist, short-story writer. *The Trial, Amerika, The Castle.*

**George S. Kaufman,** 1889-1961, (U.S.) playwright. *The Man Who Came to Dinner, You Can't Take It With You, Stage Door.*

**Nikos Kazantzakis,** 1883?-1957, (Gk.) novelist. *Zorba the Greek, A Greek Passion.*

**Joyce Kilmer,** 1886-1918, (U.S.) poet. "Trees."

**Rudyard Kipling,** •1865-1936, (Br.) author, poet. "The White Man's Burden," "Gunga Din," *The Jungle Book.*

**Heinrich von Kleist,** 1777-1811, (G.) dramatic poet. *The Prince of Homburg, The Broken Pitcher, Amphitryon.*

**Oliver La Farge,** 1901-1963, (U.S.) novelist. *Laughing Boy.*

**Jean de la Fontaine,** 1621-1695, (F.) poet. *Fables choisies.*

**Pär Lagerkvist,** 1891-1974, (Swed.) poet, dramatist, novelist. *Barabbas, The Sybil.*

**Selma Lagerlöf,** 1858-1940, (Swed.) novelist. *Jerusalem, The Ring of the Lowenskolds.*

**Alphonse de Lamartine,** 1790-1869, (F.) poet, novelist,

statesman. *Méditations poétiques.*

**Charles Lamb,** 1775-1834, (Br.) essayist. *Specimens of English Dramatic Poets, Essays of Elia.*

**Giuseppe di Lampedusa,** 1896-1957,(It.)novelist.*The Leopar*

**David H. Lawrence,** 1885-1930, (Br.) novelist. *Women Love, Lady Chatterly's Lover, Sons and Lovers.*

**Mikhail Lermontov,** 1814-1841, (R.) novelist, poet. "Demon, *Hero of Our Time.*

**Alain-René Lesage,** 1668-1747, (F.) novelist. *Gil Blas c Santillane.*

**Gotthold Lessing,** 1729-1781, (G.) dramatist, philosophe critic. *Miss Sara Sampson, Minna von Barnhelm.*

**Sinclair Lewis,** 1885-1951, (U.S.) novelist, playwright. *Babb Arrowsmith, Dodsworth.*

**Vachel Lindsay,** 1879-1931, (U.S.) poet. *General Willia Booth Enters into Heaven, The Congo.*

**Jack London,** 1876-1916, (U.S.) novelist, journalist. *Call the Wild, The Sea-Wolf.*

**Henry Wadsworth Longfellow,** 1807-1882, (U.S.) poe "The Wreck of the Hesperus,"*Evangeline,The Song of Hiawath*

**Amy Lowell,** 1874-1925, (U.S.) poet, critic. *A Dome of Many Colored Glass,* "Patterns," "Lilacs."

**James Russell Lowell,** 1819-1891, (U.S.) poet, editor. *Pi ems, The Bigelow Papers.*

**Robert Lowell,**1917-1977,(U.S.) poet."Lord Weary's Castle.

**Emil Ludwig,** 1881-1948, (G.) biographer. *Goethe, Bee thoven, Napoleon, Bismarck.*

**Niccolò Machiavelli,** 1469-1527, (It.) author, statesman. *Th Prince, Discourses on Livy.*

**Stéphane Mallarmé,** 1842-1898, (F.) poet. *The Afternoon a Faun.*

**Thomas Malory,** ?-1471, (Br.) writer. *Morte d'Arthur.*

**Andre Malraux,** 1901-1976, (F.) novelist. *Man's Fate, Th Voices of Silence.*

**Osip Mandelstam,** 1891-1938, (R.) Acmeist poet.

**Thomas Mann,** 1875-1955, (G.) novelist, essayist. *Budder brooks, Death in Venice, The Magic Mountain.*

**Katherine Mansfield,** 1888-1923, (Br.) author, master o short story. *Bliss, The Garden Party.*

**Christopher Marlowe,** 1564-1593, (Br.) dramatist, poet *Tamburlaine the Great, Dr. Faustus, The Jew of Malta.*

**John Masefield,** 1878-1967, (Br.) poet. "Sea Fever," "Car goes," *Salt Water Ballads.*

**Edgar Lee Masters,** 1869-1950, (U.S.) poet, biographe *Spoon River Anthology.*

**W. Somerset Maugham,** 1874-1965, (Br.) author. *Of Huma Bondage, The Razor's Edge, The Moon and Sixpence.*

**Guy de Maupassant,** 1850-1893, (F.) novelist, short-stor writer. *A Life, Bel-Ami,* "The Necklace."

**Vladimir Mayakovsky,** 1893-1930, (R.) poet, dramatist. *Th Cloud in Trousers.*

**Carson McCullers,** 1917-1967, (U.S.) novelist. *The Heart is Lonely Hunter, Member of the Wedding.*

**Herman Melville,** 1819-1891, (U.S.) novelist, poet. *Mob Dick, Typee, Billy Budd, Omoo.*

**H.L. Mencken,** 1880-1956, (U.S.) author, critic, editor. *Prejud ces, The American Language.*

**George Meredith,** 1828-1909, (Br.) novelist, poet. *The Or deal of Richard Feverel, The Egoist.*

**Prosper Mérimée,** 1803-1870, (F.) author. *Carmer Colomba.*

**Edna St. Vincent Millay,** 1892-1950, (U.S.) poet. *The Har Weaver and Other Poems, A Few Figs from Thistles.*

**A.A. Milne,** 1882-1956, (Br.) author. *When We Were Ver Young, Winnie-the-Pooh, The House at Pooh Corner.*

**John Milton,** 1608-1674, (Br.) poet. *Paradise Lost, Samso Agonistes.*

**Gabriela Mistral,** 1889-1957, (Chil.) poet. *Sonnets of Deatl Desolación, Tala, Lagar.*

**Margaret Mitchell,** 1900-1949, (U.S.) novelist. *Gone With th Wind.*

**Jean Baptiste Molière,** 1622-1673, (F.) dramatist. *Le Ta tuffe, Le Misanthrope, Le Bourgeois Gentilhomme.*

**Ferenc Molnár,** 1878-1952, (Hung.) dramatist, novelist *Liliom, The Guardsman, The Swan.*

**Michel de Montaigne,** 1533-1592, (F.) essayist. *Essais.*

**Clement C. Moore,** 1779-1863, (U.S.) poet, educator. "A Vis from Saint Nicholas."

**Marianne Moore,** 1887-1972, (U.S.) poet. *Observations, O f Be a Dragon.*

**Thomas More,** 1478-1535, (Br.) author. *Utopia.*

**H.H. Munro** (Saki), 1870-1916, (Br.) author. *Reginald, Th Chronicles of Clovis, Beasts and Super-Beasts.*

**Alfred de Musset,** 1810-1857, (F.) poet, dramatist. *Confes sion d'un enfant du siécle.*

**Vladimir Nabokov,** 1899-1977, (U.S.) author. *Lolita, Ada.*

**Ogden Nash,** 1902-1971, (U.S.) poet. *Hard Lines, I'm Stranger Here Myself, The Private Dining Room.*

**Pablo Neruda,** 1904-1973, (Chil.) poet. *Twenty Love Poem and One Song of Despair, Toward the Splendid City.*

**ean O'Casey**, 1884-1964, (Ir.) dramatist. *Juno and the Pay-ck, The Plough and the Stars.*

**clifford Odets**, 1906-1963, (U.S.) playwright. *Waiting for ty, Awake and Sing, Golden Boy, The Country Girl.*

**ohn O'Hara**, 1905-1970, (U.S.) novelist. *Butterfield 8, Ten rth Frederick, From the Terrace.*

**·mar Khayyam**, c. 1028-1122, (Per.) poet, mathematician. *biyat.*

**ugene O'Neill**, 1888-1953, (U.S.) playwright. *Emperor nes, Anna Christie, Long Day's Journey into Night, Desire Un-· the Elms, Mourning Becomes Electra.*

**·eorge Orwell**, 1903-1950, (Br.) novelist, essayist. *Animal m, Nineteen Eighty-Four.*

**·homas (Tom) Paine**, 1737-1809, (U.S.) author, political the-·t. *Common Sense.*

**·orothy Parker**, 1893-1967, (U.S.) poet, short-story writer. *·ugh Rope, Laments for the Living.*

**·oris Pasternak**, 1890-1960, (R.) poet, novelist. *Doctor ·vago, My Sister, Life.*

**·amuel Pepys**, 1633-1703, (Br.) public offical, author of the ·atest diary in the English language.

**·rancesco Petrarca**, 1304-1374, (It.) poet, humanist. *Africa, ·onfi, Canzoniere, On Solitude.*

**·uigi Pirandello**, 1867-1936, (It.) novelist, dramatist. *Six ·aracters in Search of an Author.*

**·dgar Allen Poe**, 1809-1849, (U.S.) poet, short-story writer, ·ic. "Annabel Lee," "The Raven," "The Purloined Letter."

**·lexander Pope**, 1688-1744, (Br.) poet. *The Rape of the ·ck, An Essay on Man.*

**·zra Pound**, 1885-1972, (U.S.) poet. *Cantos.*

**·arcel Proust**, 1871-1922, (F.) novelist. *A la recherche du ·mps perdu (Remembrance of Things Past).*

**·leksandr Pushkin**, 1799-1837, (R.) poet, prose writer. *Boris ·donov, Eugene Onegin, The Bronze Horseman.*

**·rançois Rabelais**, 1495-1553, (F.) writer, physician. *Gargan-·, Pantagruel.*

**·ean Racine**, 1639-1699, (F.) dramatist. *Andromaque, ·èdre, Bérénice, Britannicus.*

**·rich Maria Remarque**, 1898-1970, (U.S.) novelist. *All Quiet ·· the Western Front.*

**·amuel Richardson**, 1689-1761, (Br.) novelist. *Clarissa Har-·we, Pamela; or, Virtue Rewarded.*

**·ames Whitcomb Riley**, 1849-1916, (U.S.) poet. "When the ·ost is on the Pumpkin," "Little Orphant Annie."

**·ainer Maria Rilke**, /1875-1926, (G.) poet. *Life and Songs, ·vine Elegies, Sonnets to Orpheus.*

**·rthur Rimbaud**, 1854-1891, (F.) *A Season in Hell*, "Le Ba-·au ivre."

**·dwin Arlington Robinson**, 1869-1935, (U.S.) poet. "Richard ·ory," "Miniver Cheevy."

**·heodore Roethke**, 1908-1963, (U.S.) poet. *Open House, ·e Waking, The Far Field.*

**·omain Rolland**, 1866-1944, (F.) novelist, biographer. *Jean-·hristophe.*

**·ierre de Ronsard**, 1524-1585, (F.) poet. *Sonnets pour Hé-·ne.*

**·dmond Rostand**, 1868-1918, (F.) poet, dramatist. *Cyrano ·· Bergerac.*

**·amon Runyon**, 1884-1946, (U.S.) short-story writer, journal-·· *Guys and Dolls, Blue Plate Special.*

**·ohn Ruskin**, 1819-1900, (Br.) critic, social theorist. *Modern ·ainters, The Seven Lamps of Architecture.*

**·ntoine de Saint-Exupery**, 1900-1944, (F.) writer, aviator. *·ind, Sand and Stars, Le Petit Prince.*

**·eorge Sand**, 1804-1876, (F.) novelist. *Consuelo, The ·aunted Pool, Les Maitres sonneurs.*

**·arl Sandburg**, 1878-1967, (U.S.) poet. *Chicago Poems, ·moke and Steel, Harvest Poems.*

**·eorge Santayana**, 1863-1952, (U.S.) poet, essayist, philos-·pher. *The Sense of Beauty, The Realms of Being.*

**·riedrich von Schiller**, 1759-1805, (G.) dramatist, poet, histo-·an. *Don Carlos, Maria Stuart, Wilhelm Tell.*

**·ir Walter Scott**, 1771-1832, (Sc.) novelist, poet. *Ivanhoe, ·ob Roy, The Bride of Lammermoor.*

**·illiam Shakespeare**, 1564-1616, (Br.) dramatist, poet. *Ro-·eo and Juliet, Hamlet, King Lear, The Merchant of Venice.*

**·eorge Bernard Shaw**, 1856-1950, (Ir.) playwright, critic. *St. ·oan, Pygmalion, Major Barbara, Man and Superman.*

**·ary Wollstonecraft Shelley**, 1797-1851, (Br.) author. *Fran-·enstein.*

**·ercy Bysshe Shelly**, 1792-1822, (Br.) poet. *Prometheus ·Inbound, Adonais,* "Ode to the West Wind," "To a Skylark."

**·ichard B. Sheridan**, 1751-1816, (Br.) dramatist. *The Rivals, ·chool for Scandal.*

**·obert Sherwood**, 1896-1955, (U.S.) playwright. *The Petri-·ed Forest, Abe Lincoln in Illinois, Reunion in Vienna.*

**·pton Sinclair**, 1878-1968, (U.S.) novelist. *The Jungle, Drag-·n's Teeth.*

**·dmund Spenser**, 1552-1599, (Br.) poet. *The Faerie Queen.*

**·ichard Steele**, 1672-1729, (Br.) essayist, playwright, began ·e Tatler and Spectator. *The Conscious Lovers.*

**Lincoln Steffens**, 1866-1936, (U.S.) editor, author. *The Shame of the Cities.*

**Gertrude Stein**, 1874-1946, (U.S.) author. *Three Lives.*

**John Steinbeck**, 1902-1968, (U.S.) novelist. *Grapes of Wrath, Of Mice and Men, Winter of Our Discontent.*

**Stendhal** (Marie Henri Beyle), 1783-1842, poet, novelist. *The Red and the Black, The Charterhouse of Parma.*

**Laurence Sterne**, 1713-1768, (Br.) novelist. *Tristram Shandy.*

**Wallace Stevens**, 1879-1955, (U.S.) poet. *Harmonium, The Man With the Blue Guitar, Transport to Summer.*

**Robert Louis Stevenson**, 1850-1894, (Br.) novelist, poet, essayist. *Treasure Island, A Child's Garden of Verses.*

**Rex Stout**, 1886-1975, (U.S.) mystery novelist, created Nero Wolfe.

**Harriet Beecher Stowe**, 1811-1896, (U.S.) novelist. *Uncle Tom's Cabin.*

**Lytton Strachey**, 1880-1932, (Br.) biographer, critic. *Eminent Victorians, Queen Victoria, Elizabeth and Essex.*

**August Strindberg**, 1849-1912, (Swed.) dramatist, novelist. *The Father, Miss Julie, The Creditors.*

**Jacqueline Susann**, 1921-1974, (U.S.) novelist. *Valley of the Dolls.*

**Jonathan Swift**, 1667-1745, (Br.) author. *Gulliver's Travels.*

**Algernon C. Swinburne**, 1837-1909, (Br.) poet, critic. *Songs Before Sunrise.*

**John M. Synge**, 1871-1909, (Ir.) poet, dramatist. *Riders to the Sea, The Playboy of the Western World.*

**Rabindranath Tagore**, 1861-1941, (Ind.), author, poet. *Sad-hana, The Realization of Life, Gitanjali.*

**Booth Tarkington**, 1869-1946, (U.S.) novelist. *Seventeen, Alice Adams, Penrod.*

**Sara Teasdale**, 1884-1933, (U.S.) poet. *Helen of Troy and Other Poems, Rivers to the Sea, Flame and Shadow.*

**Alfred Lord Tennyson**, 1809-1892, (Br.) poet. *Idylls of the King, In Memoriam,* "The Charge of the Light Brigade."

**Albert Payson Terhune**, 1872-1942, (U.S.) novelist, journal-ist. *Lad: A Dog.*

**William Makepeace Thackeray**, 1811-1863, (Br.) novelist. *Vanity Fair.*

**Dylan Thomas**, 1914-1953, (Welsh) poet. *Under Milk Wood, A Child's Christmas in Wales.*

**James Thurber**, 1894-1961, (U.S.) humorist, artist. *The New Yorker, The Owl in the Attic, Thurber Carnival.*

**J.R.R. Tolkien**, 1892-1973, (Br.) author. *The Hobbit, Lord of the Rings.*

**Lev Tolstoy**, 1828-1910, (R.) novelist. *War and Peace, Anna Karenina.*

**Anthony Trollope**, 1815-1882, (Br.) novelist. *The Warden, Barchester Towers, The Palliser novels.*

**Ivan Turgenev**, 1818-1883, (R.) novelist, short-story writer. *Fathers and Sons, First Love, A Month in the Country.*

**Mark Twain** (Samuel Clemens), 1835-1910, (U.S.) novelist, humorist. *The Adventures of Huckleberry Finn, Tom Sawyer.*

**Sigrid Undset**, 1881-1949, (Nor.) novelist, poet. Kristin Lav-ransdatter.

**Paul Valéry**, 1871-1945, (F.) poet, critic. *La Jeune Parque, The Graveyard by the Sea.*

**Jules Verne**, 1828-1905, (F.) novelist, originator of modern science fiction. *Twenty Thousand Leagues Under the Sea.*

**François Villon**, 1431-1463?, (F.) poet. *Le petit et le Grand, Testament.*

**Evelyn Waugh**, 1903-1966, (Br.) satirist. *Brideshead Revi-sited, The Loved One.*

**H.G. Wells**, 1866-1946, (Br.) author. *The Time Machine, The Invisible Man, The War of the Worlds.*

**Edith Wharton**, 1862-1937, (U.S.) novelist. *The Age of Inno-cence, The House of Mirth.*

**T.H. White**, 1906-1964, (Br.) author. *The Once and Future King.*

**Walt Whitman**, 1819-1892, (U.S.) poet. *Leaves of Grass.*

**John Greenleaf Whittier**, 1807-1892, (U.S.) poet, journalist. *Snow-bound.*

**Oscar Wilde**, 1856-1900, (Ir.) author, wit. *The Picture of Dorian Gray, The Importance of Being Earnest.*

**Thornton Wilder**, 1897-1975, (U.S.) playwright. *Our Town, The Skin of Our Teeth, The Matchmaker.*

**William Carlos Williams**, 1883-1963, (U.S.) poet, physician. *Tempers, Al Que Quiere!, Paterson.*

**Edmund Wilson**, 1895-1972, (U.S.) author, literary and social critic. *Axel's Castle, To the Finland Station.*

**P.G. Wodehouse**, 1881-1975, (U.S.) poet, dramatist. The "Jeeves" novels, *Anything Goes.*

**Thomas Wolfe**, 1900-1938, (U.S.) novelist. *Look Homeward, Angel, You Can't Go Home Again, Of Time and the River.*

**Virginia Woolf**, 1882-1941, (Br.) novelist, essayist. *Mrs. Dal-loway, To the Lighthouse, The Waves.*

**William Wordsworth**, 1770-1850, (Br.) poet. "Tintern Ab-bey," "Ode: Intimations of Immortality."

**William Butler Yeats**, 1865-1939, (Ir.) poet, playwright. *The Wild Swans at Coole, The Tower, Last Poems.*

**Émile Zola**, 1840-1902, (F.) novelist. *Nana, The Dram Shop, Germinal.*

## Poets Laureate of England

There is no authentic record of the origin of the office of Poet Laureate of England. According to Warton, there was a Versificator Regis, or King's Poet, in the reign of Henry III (1216-1272), and he was paid 100 shillings a year. Geoffrey Chaucer (1340-1400) assumed the title of Poet Laureate, and in 1389 got a royal grant of a yearly allowance of wine. In the reign of Edward IV (1461-1483), John Kay held the post. Under Henry VII (1485-1509), Andrew Bernard was the Poet Laureate, and was succeeded under Henry VIII (1509-1547) by John Skelton. Next came Edmund Spenser, who died in 1599; then Samuel Daniel, appointed 1599, and then Ben Jonson, 1619. Sir William D'Avenant was appointed in 1637. He was a godson of William Shakespeare.

Others were John Dryden, 1670; Thomas Shadwell, 1688; Nahum Tate, 1692; Nicholas Rowe, 1715; the Rev. Laurence Eusden, 1718; Colley Cibber, 1730; William Whitehead, 1757, on the refusal of Gray; Rev. Thomas Warton 1785, on the refusal of Mason; Henry J. Pye, 1790; Robert Southey, 1813, on the refusal of Sir Walter Scott; William Wordsworth, 1843; Alfred, Lord Tennyson, 1850; Alfred Austin, 1896; Robert Bridges, 1913; John Masefield, 1930; Cecil Day Lewis, 1967; Sir John Betjeman, 1972.

## Noted Artists and Sculptors of the Past

Artists are painters unless otherwise indicated.

**Washington Allston,** 1779-1842, landscapist. The Deluge.
**Albrecht Altdorfer,** 1480-1538, landscapist. Birth of the Virgin.
**Andrea del Sarto,** 1486-1530, frescoes. Madonna of the Harpies.
**Fra Angelico,** 1387-1455, Renaissance muralist. Madonna of the Linen Drapers' Guild.
**Aleksandr Archipenko,** 1887-1967, Boxing Match, Medranos.
**John James Audubon,** 1785-1851, Birds of America.
**Hans Baldun-Grien,** 1484-1545, Todentanz.
**Ernst Barlach,** 1870-1938, Expressionist sculptor. Man Drawing a Sword.
**Frederic-Auguste Bartholdi,** 1834-1904, Liberty Enlightening the World, Lion c. Belfort.
**Fra Bartolommeo,** 1472-1517, Vision of St. Bernard.
**Aubrey Beardsley,** 1872-1898, illustrator. Salome, Lysistrata.
**Max Beckmann,** 1884-1950, Expressionist. The Descent from the Cross.
**Gentile Bellini,** 1426-1507, Renaissance. Procession in St. Mark's Square.
**Giovanni Bellini,** 1428-1516, St. Francis in Ecstasy.
**Jacopo Bellini,** 1400-1470, Crucifixion.
**George W. Bellows,** 1882-1925, sports artist. Stag at Sharkey's.
**Thomas Hart Benton,** 1889-1975, American regionalist. Threshing Wheat, Arts of the West.
**Gian Lorenzo Bernini,** 1598-1680, Baroque reliefs. The Assumption.
**Albert Bierstadt,** 1830-1902, landscapist. The Rocky Mountains, Mount Corcoran.
**George Caleb Bingham,** 1811-1879, Fur Traders Descending the Missouri.
**William Blake,** 1752-1827, engraver. Book of Job, Songs of Innocence, Songs of Experience.
**Rosa Bonheur,** 1822-1899, The Horse Fair.
**Pierre Bonnard,** 1867-1947, Intimist. The Breakfast Room.
**Paul-Emile Borduas,** 1905-1960, Abstractionist. Leeward of the Island, Enchanted Shields.
**Gutzon Borglum,** 1871-1941, Mt. Rushmore Memorial.
**Hieronymus Bosch,** 1450-1516, religious allegories. The Crowning with Thorns.
**Sandro Botticelli,** 1444-1510, Renaissance. Birth of Venus.
**Constantin Brancusi,** 1876-1957, Abstract sculptor. Flying Turtle, The Kiss.
**Georges Braque,** 1882-1963, Cubist. Violin and Palette.
**Pieter Bruegel the Elder,** 1525-1569, Flemish landscapist. The Peasant Dance.
**Pieter Bruegel the Younger,** 1564-1638, Village Fair, The Crucifixon.
**Edward Burne-Jones,** 1833-1898, Pre-Raphaelite artist-craftsman. The Mirror of Venus.
**Alexander Calder,** 1898-1976, sculptor. Lobster Trap and Fish Tail.
**Caravaggio,** 1573-1610, Baroque. The Supper at Emmaus.
**Emily Carr,** 1871-1945, landscapist. Blunden Harbour, Big Raven.
**Carlo Carra,** 1881-1966, Metaphysical school. Lot's Daughters.
**Mary Cassatt,** 1845-1926, Impressionist. Woman Bathing.
**George Catlin,** 1796-1872, American Indian life. Gallery of Indians.
**Benvenuto Cellini,** 1500-1571, Mannerist sculptor, goldsmith. Perseus.
**Paul Cezanne,** 1839-1906, early Cubist. Card Players, Mont-Sainte-Victoire with Large Pine Trees.
**Jean-Baptiste-Simeon-Chardin,** 1699-1779, still lifes. The Kiss, The Grace.
**Frederick Church,** 1826-1900, Hudson River school. Niagara, Andes of Ecuador.
**Cimabue,** 1240-1302, Byzantine mosaicist. Madonna Enthroned with St. Francis.
**Claude Lorrain,** 1600-1682, ideal-landscapist. The Enchanted Castle.
**Thomas Cole,** 1801-1848, Hudson River school. The Ox Bow.
**John Constable,** 1776-1837, landscapist. Salisbury Cathedral from the Bishop's Grounds.
**John Singleton Copley,** 1738-1815, portraitist. Samuel Adams, Watson and the Shark.
**Lovis Corinth,** 1858-1925, Expressionist. Apocalypse.
**Jean-Baptiste-Camille Corot,** 1796-1875, landscapist. Souvenir de Mortefontaine, Pastorale.
**Correggio,** 1494-1534, Renaissance muralist. Mystic Marriage of St. Catherine.
**Gustave Courbet,** 1819-1877, Realist. The Artist's Studio.
**Lucas Cranach the Elder,** 1472-1553, Protestant Reformation portraitist. Luther.
**Nathaniel Currier,** 1813-1888, and **James M. Ives** 1824-1895, lithographers. A Midnight Race on the Mississippi.
**Honore Daumier,** 1808-1879, caricaturist. The Third-Class Carriage.
**Jacques-Louis David,** 1748-1825, Neoclassicist. The Oath of the Horatii.
**Arthur Davies,** 1862-1928, Romantic landscapist. Unicorns.
**Edgar Degas,** 1834-1917, The Ballet Class.
**Eugene Delacroix,** 1798-1863, Romantic. Massacre at Chios.
**Paul Delaroche,** 1797-1859, historical themes. Children of Edward.
**Luca Della Robbia,** 1400-1482, Renaissance terracotta artist. Cantoria (singing gallery), Florence cathedral.
**Donato Donatello,** 1386-1466, Renaissance sculptor. David, Gattamelata.
**Raoul Dufy,** 1877-1953, Fauvist. Chateau and Horses.
**Asher Brown Durand,** 1796-1886, Hudson River school. Kindred Spirits.
**Albrecht Durer,** 1471-1528, Renaissance engraver, woodcuts. St. Jerome in His Study, Melancholia I, Apocalypse.
**Thomas Eakins,** 1844-1916, Realist. The Gross Clinic.
**Jacob Epstein,** 1880-1959, religious and allegorical sculptor. Genesis, Ecce Homo.
**Jan Van Eyck,** 1366-1440, naturalistic panels. Adoration of the Lamb.
**Anselm Feuerbach,** 1829-1880, Romantic Classicist. Judgement of Paris, Iphigeneia.
**John Bernard Flannagan,** 1895-1942, primitive animal sculptor. Triumph of the Egg.
**Jean-Honore Fragonard,** 1732-1806, Rococo. The Swing.
**Daniel C. French,** 1850-1931, The Minute Man of Concord, seated Lincoln, Lincoln Memorial, Washington, D.C.
**Caspar Daniel Friedrich,** 1774-1840, Romantic landscapist. Man and Woman Gazing at the Moon.
**Thomas Gainsborough,** 1727-1788, portraitist. The Blue Boy.
**Paul Gauguin,** 1848-1903, Post-impressionist. The Tahitians.
**Lorenzo Ghiberti,** 1378-1455, Renaissance sculptor. Gates of Paradise baptistry doors, Florence.
**Alberto Giacometti,** 1901-1966, attenuated sculptures of solitary figures. Man Pointing.
**Giorgione,** 1477-1510, Renaissance. The Tempest.
**Giotto,** 1276-1337, Renaissance. Presentation of Christ in the Temple.
**Francois Girardon,** 1628-1715, Baroque sculptor of classical themes. Apollo Tended by the Nymphs.

Vincent van Gogh, 1853-1890, The Starry Night, L'Arlsienne.

Arshile Gorky, 1905-1948, Surrealist. The Liver Is the Cock's Comb.

Francisco de Goya y Lucientes, 1746-1828, The Naked Maya, The Disasters of War (etchings).

El Greco, 1541-1614, View of Toledo, Burial of the Count of Orgaz.

Horatio Greenough, 1805-1852, Neo-classical sculptor. George Washington.

Matthias Grünewald, 1480-1528, mystical religious themes. The Resurrection.

Franz Hals, 1580-1666, portraitist. Laughing Cavalier, Gypsy Girl.

Childe Hassam, 1859-1935, Impressionist. Southwest Wind.

Edward Hicks, 1780-1849, primitive folk painter. The Peaceable Kingdom.

Hans Hofmann, 1880-1966, early Abstract Expressionist. Spring. The Gate.

William Hogarth, 1697-1764, caricaturist. The Rake's Progress.

Katsushika Hokusai, 1760-1849, printmaker. Crabs.

Hans Holbein the Elder, 1460-1524, late Gothic. Presentation of Christ in the Temple.

Hans Holbein the Younger, 1497-1543, portraitist. Henry VIII.

Winslow Homer, 1836-1910, marine themes. Marine Coast, High Cliff.

Edward Hopper, 1882-1967, realistic urban scenes. Sunlight in a Cafeteria.

Jean-Auguste-Dominique Ingres, 1780-1867, Classicist. Valpincon Bather.

George Innes, 1825-1894, luminous landscapist. Delaware Water Gap.

Vasily Kandinsky, 1866-1944, Abstractionist. Capricious Forms.

Paul Klee, 1879-1940, Abstractionist. Twittering Machine.

Kathe Kollwitz, 1867-1945, printmaker, social justice themes. The Peasant War.

Gaston Lachaise, 1882-1935, figurative sculptor. Standing Woman.

John La Farge, 1835-1910, muralist. Red and White Peonies.

Fernand Leger, 1881-1955, machine art. The Cyclists, Adam and Eve.

Leonardo da Vinci, 1452-1519, Mona Lisa, Last Supper, The Annunciation.

Emanuel Leutz, 1816-1868, historical themes. Washington Crossing the Delaware.

Jacques Lipchitz, 1891-1973, Cubist sculptor. Harpist.

Filippino Lippi, 1457-1504, Renaissance. The Vision of St. Bernard.

Fra Filippo Lippi, 1406-1469, Renaissance. Coronation of the Virgin.

Aristide Maillol, 1861-1944, sculptor. Night, The Mediterranean.

Edouard Manet, 1832-1883, forerunner of Impressionism. Luncheon on the Grass, Olympia.

Andrea Mantegna, 1431-1506, Renaissance frescoes. Triumph of Caesar.

Franz Marc, 1880-1916, Expressionist. Blue Horses.

John Marin, 1870-1953, expressionist seascapes. Maine Island.

Reginald Marsh, 1898-1954, satirical artist. Tattoo and Haircut.

Tommaso Masaccio, 1401-1428, Renaissance. The Tribute Money.

Henri Matisse, 1869-1954, Fauvist. Woman with the Hat.

Michelangelo Buonarroti, 1475-1564, Pieta, David, Moses, Battle of Cascina, The Last Judgment.

Carl Milles, 1875-1955, expressive rhythmic sculptor. Playing Bears.

Jean-Francois Millet, 1814-1875, painter of peasant subjects. The Gleaners, The Man with a Hoe.

David Milne, 1882-1953, landscapist. Boston Corner, Berkshire Hills.

Amadeo Modigliani, 1884-1920, Reclining Nude.

Piet Mondrian, 1872-1944, Abstractionist. Composition.

Claude Monet, 1840-1926, Impressionist. The Bridge at Arnteuil, Haystacks.

Gustave Moreau, 1826-1898, Symbolist. The Apparition, Dance of Salome.

James Wilson Morrice, 1865-1924, landscapist. The Ferry, Quebec, Venice, Looking Over the Lagoon.

Grandma Moses, 1860-1961, primitive folk painter. Out for Christmas Trees.

Edvard Munch, 1863-1944, Expressionist death themes. The Cry.

Bartolome Murillo, 1618-1682, Baroque religious artist. Vision of St. Anthony. The Two Trinities.

Barnett Newman, 1905-1970, Abstract Expressionist. Stations of the Cross.

Jose Clemente Orozco, 1883-1949, frescoes. House of Tears.

Charles Willson Peale, 1741-1827, American Revolutionary portraitist. Washington, Franklin, Jefferson, John Adams.

Rembrandt Peale, 1778-1860, post-Revolutionary portraitist. Thomas Jefferson.

Pietro Perugino, 1446-1523, Renaissance. Delivery of the Keys to St. Peter.

Pablo Picasso, 1881-1973, Guernica, Dove, Head of a Woman.

Piero della Francesca, 1420-1492, Renaissance. Duke of Urbino, Flagellation of Christ.

Camille Pissarro, 1830-1903, Impressionist. Morning Sunlight.

Jackson Pollock, 1912-1956, Abstract Expressionist. Autumn Rhythm.

Nicholas Poussin, 1594-1665, Baroque pictorial classicism. St. John on Patmos.

Maurice B. Prendergast, 1861-1924, Post-impressionist water colorist. Umbrellas in the Rain.

Pierre-Paul Prud'hon, 1758-1823, Romanticist. Crime pursued by Vengeance and Justice.

Puvis de Chavannes, 1824-1898, muralist. The Poor Fisherman.

Raphael, 1483-1520, Renaissance. Disputa, School of Athens.

Man Ray, 1890-1976, Dadaist. Observing Time, The Lovers.

Odilon Redon, 1840-1916, Symbolist lithographer. In the Dream.

Rembrandt van Rijn, 1606-1669, The Bridal Couple, The Night Watch.

Frederic Remington, 1861-1909, portrayal of the American West. Bronco Buster, Cavalry Charge on the Southern Plains.

Pierre-Auguste Renoir, 1841-1919, Impressionist. The Luncheon of the Boating Party.

Ilya Repin, 1844-1918, historical canvases. Zaporozhye Cossacks.

Joshua Reynolds, 1723-1792, portraitist. Mrs. Siddons as the Tragic Muse.

Diego Rivera, 1886-1957, frescoes. The Fecund Earth.

Auguste Rodin, 1840-1917, The Thinker, The Burghers of Calais.

Mark Rothko, 1903-1970, Abstract Expressionist. Light, Earth and Blue.

Georges Rouault, 1871-1958, Expressionist. The Old King.

Henri Rousseau, 1844-1910, primitive exotic themes. The Snake Charmer.

Theodore Rousseau, 1812-1867, landscapist. Under the Birches, Evening.

Peter Paul Rubens, 1577-1640, Baroque. Mystic Marriage of St. Catherine.

Andrey Rublyov, 1370-1430, iconographer. Old Testament Trinity.

Albert Pinkham Ryder, 1847-1917, seascapes and allegories. Toilers of the Sea.

Augustus Saint-Gaudens, 1848-1901, memorial statues. Farragut, Mrs. Henry Adams (Grief).

Andrea Sansovino, 1460-1529, Renaissance sculptor. Baptism of Christ.

Jacopo Sansovino, 1486-1570, Renaissance sculptor. St. John the Baptist.

John Singer Sargent, 1856-1925, Edwardian society portraitist. The Wyndham Sisters, Madam X.

Johann Gottfried Schadow, 1764-1850, monumental sculptor. Quadriga, Bradenburg Gate.

Georges Seurat, 1859-1891, Pointillist. Sunday Afternoon on the Island of Grande Jatte.

Gino Severini, 1883-1891, Futurist and Cubist. Dynamic Hieroglyph of the Bal Tabarin.

Ben Shahn, 1898-1969, social and political themes. Sacco and Vanzetti series, Seurat's Lunch, Handball.

Charles Sheeler, 1883-1965, Abstractionist. Upper Deck, Rolling Power.

David Alfaro Siqueiros, 1896-1974, political muralist. March of Humanity.

John F. Sloan, 1871-1951, depictions of New York City. Wake of the Ferry.

David Smith, 1906-1965, welded metal sculpture. Hudson River Landscape, Zig, Cubi series.

Gilbert Stuart, 1755-1828, portraitist. George Washington.

Thomas Sully, 1783-1872, portraitist. Col. Thomas Handasyd Perkins, The Passage of the Delaware.

Yves Tanguy, 1900-1955, Surrealist. Rose of the Four Winds.

Thomas J. Thomson, 1877-1918, landscapist. Spring Ice.

Giovanni Battista Tiepolo, 1696-1770, Rococo frescoes. The Crucifixion.

Tintoretto, 1518-1594, Mannerist. The Last Supper.

Titian, 1477-1576, Renaissance. Venus and the Lute Player,

The Bacchanal.
**Henri de Toulouse-Lautrec,** 1864-1901, At the Moulin Rouge.
**John Trumbull,** 1756-1843, historical themes. The Declaration of Independence.
**J.M.W. Turner,** 1755-1851, Romantic landscapist. Snow Storm.
**Paolo Uccello,** 1397-1475, Gothic-Renaissance. The Rout of San Romano.
**Maurice Utrillo,** 1883-1955, Impressionist. Sacre-Coeur de Montmartre.
**John Vanderlyn,** 1775-1852, Neo-classicist. Ariadne Asleep on the Island of Naxos.
**Anthony Van Dyck,** 1599-1641, Baroque portraitist. Portrait of Charles I Hunting.
**Diego Velazquez,** 1599-1660, Baroque. Las Meninas, Portrait of Juan de Pareja.
**Jan Vermeer,** 1632-1675, interior genre subjects. Young Woman with a Water Jug.

**Paolo Veronese,** 1528-1588, devotional themes, vastly pe‑ pled canvases. The Temptation of St. Anthony.
**Andrea del Verrocchio,** 1435-1488, Florentine sculptor. Co leoni.
**Maurice de Vlaminck,** 1876-1958, Fauvist landscapist. Th Storm.
**Antoine Watteau,** 1684-1721, Rococo painter of "scenes gallantry". The Embarkation for Cythera.
**George Frederic Watts,** 1817-1904, painter and sculptor grandiose allegorical themes. Hope, Physical Energy.
**Benjamin West,** 1738-1820, realistic historical themes. Dea of General Wolfe.
**James Abbott McNeill Whistler,** 1834-1903, Arrangement Grey and Black, No. 1: The Artist's Mother.
**Archibald M. Willard,** 1836-1918, The Spirit of '76.
**Grant Wood,** 1891-1942, Midwestern regionalist. America Gothic, Daughters of Revolution.
**Osip Zadkine,** 1890-1967, School of Paris sculptor. The D stroyed City, Musicians, Christ.

## Noted Philosophers and Religionists of the Past

**Lyman Abbott,** 1835-1922, (U.S.) clergyman, reformer; advocate of Christian Socialism.
**Pierre Abelard,** 1079-1142, (F.) philosopher, theologian, and teacher, used dialectic method to support Christian dogma.
**Felix Adler,** 1851-1933, (U.S.) German-born founder of the Ethical Culture Society.
**St. Augustine,** 354-430, Latin bishop considered the four der of formalized Christian theology.
**Averroes,** 1126-1198, (Sp.) Islamic philosopher.
**Roger Bacon,** c.1214-1294, (Br.) philosopher and scientist.
**Karl Barth,** 1886-1968, (Sw.) theologian, a leading force in 20th-century Protestantism.
**St. Benedict,** c.480-547, (It.) founded the Benedictines.
**Jeremy Bentham,** 1748-1832, (Br.) philosopher, reformer, founder of Utilitarianism.
**Henri Bergson,** 1859-1941, (F.) philosopher of evolution.
**George Berkeley,** 1685-1753, (Ir.) philosopher, churchman.
**John Biddle,** 1615-1662, (Br.) founder of English Unitarianism.
**Jakob Boehme,** 1575-1624, (G.) theosophist and mystic.
**William Brewster,** 1567-1644, (Br.) headed Pilgrims, signed Mayflower Compact.
**Emil Brunner,** 1889-1966, (Sw.) theologian.
**Giordano Bruno,** 1548-1600, (It.) philosopher.
**Martin Buber,** 1878-1965, (G.) Jewish philosopher, theologian, wrote I and Thou.
**Buddha (Siddhartha Gautama),** c.563-c.483 BC, (Ind.) philosopher, founded Buddhism.
**John Calvin,** 1509-1564, (F.) theologian, a key figure in the Protestant Reformation.
**Rudolph Carnap,** 1891-1970, (U.S.) German-born philosopher, a founder of logical positivism.
**William Ellery Channing,** 1780-1842, (U.S.) clergyman, early spokesman for Unitarianism.
**Auguste Comte,** 1798-1857, (F.) philosopher, the founder of positivism.
**Confucius,** 551-479 BC, (Chin.) founder of Confucianism.
**John Cotton,** 1584-1652, (Br.) Puritan theologian.
**Thomas Cranmer,** 1489-1556, (Br.) churchman, wrote much of the first Book of Common Prayer; promoter of the English Reformation.
**René Descartes,** 1596-1650, (F.) philosopher, mathematician.
**John Dewey,** 1859-1952, (U.S.) philosopher, educator; helped inaugurate the progressive education movement.
**Denis Diderot,** 1713-1784, (F.) philosopher, creator of first modern encyclopedia.
**Mary Baker Eddy,** 1821-1910, (U.S.) founder of Christian Science.
**Jonathan Edwards,** 1703-1758, (U.S.) preacher, theologian.
**(Desiderius) Erasmus,** c.1466-1536, (Du.) Renaissance humanist.
**Johann Fichte,** 1762-1814, (G.) philosopher, the first of the Transcendental Idealists.
**George Fox,** 1624-1691, (Br.) founder of the Quakers.
**St. Francis of Assisi,** 1182-1226, (It.) founded the Franciscans.
**al Ghazali,** 1058-1111, Islamic philosopher.
**Georg W. Hegel,** 1770-1831, (G.) Idealist philosopher.
**Martin Heidegger,** 1889-1976, (G.) existentialist philosopher, affected fields ranging from physics to literary criticism.
**Johann G. Herder,** 1744-1803, (G.) philosopher, cultural historian; a founder of German Romanticism.
**David Hume,** 1711-1776, (Sc.) philosopher, historian.
**Jan Hus,** 1369-1415, (Czech.) religious reformer.
**Edmund Husserl,** 1859-1938, (G.) philosopher, founded the

Phenomenological movement.
**Thomas Huxley,** 1825-1895, (Br.) agnostic philosopher, ed cator.
**Ignatius of Loyola,** 1491-1556, (Sp.) founder of the Jesuits.
**William Inge,** 1860-1954, (Br.) theologian, explored the myst aspects of Christianity.
**William James,** 1842-1910, (U.S.) philosopher, psychologis advanced theory of the pragmatic nature of truth.
**Karl Jaspers,** 1883-1969, (G.) existentialist philosopher.
**Immanuel Kant,** 1724-1804, (G.) metaphysician, preemine founder of modern critical philosophy.
**Soren Kierkegaard,** 1813-1855, (Du.) philosopher, consi ered the father of Existentialism.
**John Knox,** 1505-1572, (Sc.) leader of the Protestant Refo mation in Scotland.
**Lao-Tzu,** 604-531 BC, (Chin.) philosopher, considered th founder of the Taoist religion.
**Gottfried von Leibniz,** 1646-1716, (G.) philosopher, math matician.
**Martin Luther,** 1483-1546, (G.) leader of the Protestant R formation, founded Lutheran church.
**Maimonides,** 1135-1204, (Sp.) Jewish physician and philos pher.
**Jacques Maritain,** 1882-1973, (F.) Neo-Thomist philosopher
**Cotton Mather,** 1663-1728, (U.S.) defender of orthodox Pu tanism; founded Yale, 1703.
**Aimee Semple McPherson,** 1890-1944, (U.S.) evangelist.
**Philipp Melanchthon,** 1497-1560, (G.) theologian, humanis an important voice in the Reformation.
**Mohammed,** c.570-632, Arab prophet of the religion of Islam
**Dwight Moody,** 1837-1899, (U.S.) evangelist.
**George E. Moore,** 1873-1958, (Br.) ethical theorist.
**Elijah Muhammad,** 1897-1975, (U.S.) leader of the Blac Muslim sect.
**Heinrich Muhlenberg,** 1711-1787, (G.) organized the L theran Church in America.
**John H. Newman,** 1801-1890, (Br.) Roman Catholic cardina led Oxford Movement.
**Reinhold Niebuhr,** 1892-1971, (U.S.) Protestant theologia social and political critic.
**Friedrich Nietzsche,** 1844-1900, (G.) moral philosopher.
**Blaise Pascal,** 1623-1662, (F.) philosopher and mathema can.
**St. Patrick,** c.389-c.461, brought Christianity to Ireland.
**St. Paul,** ?-c.67, a founder of the Christian religion.
**Charles S. Peirce,** 1839-1914, (U.S.) philosopher, logicia originated concept of Pragmatism, 1878.
**Josiah Royce** 1855-1916, (U.S.) Idealist philosopher.
**Charles T. Russell,** 1852-1916, (U.S.) founder of Jehova Witnesses.
**Fredrich von Schelling,** 1775-1854, (G.) philosopher.
**Friedrich Schleiermacher,** 1768-1834, (G.) theologian, founder of modern Protestant theology.
**Arthur Schopenhauer,** 1788-1860, (G.) philosopher.
**Joseph Smith,** 1805-1844, (U.S.) founded Morman Churc 1830.
**Herbert Spencer,** 1820-1903, (Br.) philosopher of evolution.
**Baruch Spinoza,** 1632-1677, (Du.) rationalist philosopher.
**Billy Sunday,** 1862-1935, (U.S.) evangelist.
**Daisetz Teitaro Suzuki,** 1870-1966, (Jap.) Buddhist scholar
**Emanuel Swedenborg,** 1688-1722, (Swed.) philosophe mystic.
**Thomas à Becket,** 1118-1170, (Br.) archbishop of Cante bury, opposed Henry II.
**Thomas à Kempis,** c.1380-1471, (G.) theologian probab

te *Imitation of Christ*.

**Thomas Aquinas,** 1225-1274, (It.) theologian and philosopher.

**Paul Tillich,** 1886-1965, (U.S.) German-born philosopher and theologian.

**John Wesley,** 1703-1791, (Br.) theologian, evangelist; founded Methodism.

**Alfred North Whitehead,** 1861-1947, (Br.) philosopher, mathematician.

**William of Occam,** c.1285-c.1349 (Br.) philosopher.

**Roger Williams,** c.1603-1683, (U.S.) clergyman, championed religious freedom and separation of church and state.

**Ludwig Wittgenstein,** 1889-1951, (Aus.) philosopher.

**John Wycliffe,** 1320-1384, (Br.) theologian, reformer.

**Brigham Young,** 1801-1877, (U.S.) Mormon leader, colonized Utah.

**Huldrych Zwingli,** 1484-1531, (Swi.) theologian, led Swiss Protestant Reformation.

## Noted Social Reformers and Educators of the Past

**Jane Addams,** 1860-1935, (U.S.) co-founder of Hull House; won Nobel Peace Prize, 1931.

**Susan B. Anthony,** 1820-1906, (U.S.) a leader in temperance, anti-slavery, and women's suffrage movements.

**Henry Barnard,** 1811-1900, (U.S.) public school reformer.

**Thomas Barnardo,** 1845-1905, (Br.) social reformer, pioneered in the care of destitute children.

**Clara Barton,** 1821-1912, (U.S.) organizer of the American Red Cross.

**Henry Ward Beecher,** 1813-1887, (U.S.) clergyman, abolitionist.

**Amelia Bloomer,** 1818-1894, (U.S.) social reformer, women's rights advocate.

**William Booth,** 1829-1912, (Br.) founded the Salvation Army.

**Nicholas Murray Butler,** 1862-1947, (U.S.) educator headed Columbia Univ., 1902-45; won Nobel Peace Prize, 1931.

**Francis X. (Mother) Cabrini,** 1850-1917, (U.S.) Italian-born founded numerous charitable institutions; first American to be canonized.

**Carrie Chapman Catt,** 1859-1947, (U.S.) suffragette, helped passage of the 19th amendment.

**Eugene V. Debs,** 1855-1926, (U.S.) labor leader, led Pullman strike, 1894; 4-time Socialist presidential candidate.

**Melvil Dewey,** 1851-1931, (U.S.) devised decimal system of library-book classification.

**Dorothea Dix,** 1802-1887, (U.S.) crusader for humane care of mentally ill.

**Frederick Douglass,** 1817-1895, (U.S.) abolitionist.

**W.E.B. DuBois,** 1868-1963, (U.S.) Negro-rights leader, educator, and writer.

**William Lloyd Garrison,** 1805-1879, (U.S.) abolitionist, reformer.

**Giovanni Gentile,** 1875-1944, (It.) philosopher, educator; reformed Italian educational system.

**Samuel Gompers,** 1850-1924, (U.S.) labor leader; a founder president of AFL.

**William Green,** 1873-1952, (U.S.) president of AFL, 1924-52.

**Sidney Hillman,** 1887-1946, (U.S.) labor leader, helped organize CIO.

**Samuel G. Howe,** 1801-1876, (U.S.) social reformer, changed public attitudes toward the handicapped.

**Helen Keller,** 1880-1968, (U.S.) crusader for better treatment of the handicapped.

**Martin Luther King Jr.,** 1929-1968, (U.S.) civil rights leader; won Nobel Peace Prize, 1964.

**John L. Lewis,** 1880-1969, (U.S.) labor leader, headed United Mine Workers, 1920-60.

**Horace Mann,** 1796-1859, (U.S.) pioneered modern public school system.

**William H. McGuffey,** 1800-1873, (U.S.) author of *Reader* the mainstay of 19th century U.S. public education.

**Alexander Meiklejohn,** 1872-1964, (U.S.) British-born educator, championed academic freedom and experimental curricula.

**Lucretia Mott,** 1793-1880, (U.S.) reformer, pioneer feminist.

**Philip Murray,** 1886-1952, (U.S.) Scotch-born labor leader.

**Florence Nightingale,** 1820-1910, (Br.) founder of modern nursing.

**Emmeline Pankhurst,** 1858-1928, (Br.) woman suffragist.

**Elizabeth P. Peabody,** 1804-1894, (U.S.) education pioneer, founded 1st kindergarten in U.S., 1860.

**Walter Reuther,** 1907-1970, (U.S.) labor leader, headed UAW.

**Jacob Riis,** 1849-1914, (U.S.) crusader for urban reforms.

**Margaret Sanger,** 1883-1966, (U.S.) social reformer, pioneered the birth control movement.

**Elizabeth Seton,** 1774-1821, (U.S.) established parochial school education in U.S.

**Earl of Shaftesbury (A.A. Cooper),** 1801-1885, (Br.) social reformer.

**Elizabeth Cady Stanton,** 1815-1902, (U.S.) women's suffrage pioneer.

**Lucy Stone,** 1818-1893, (U.S.) feminist, abolitionist.

**Harriet Tubman,** c.1820-1913, (U.S.) abolitionist, ran Underground Railroad.

**Booker T. Washington,** 1856-1915, (U.S.) educator, reformer; championed vocational training for blacks.

**Walter F. White,** 1893-1955, (U.S.) headed NAACP, 1931-55.

**William Wilberforce,** 1759-1833, (Br.) social reformer, prominent in struggle to abolish the slave trade.

**Emma Hart Willard,** 1787-1870, (U.S.) pioneered higher education for women.

**Frances E. Willard,** 1839-1898, (U.S.) temperance, woman's rights leader.

**Whitney M. Young Jr.,** 1921-1971, (U.S.) civil rights leader, headed National Urban League, 1961-71.

## Noted Historians, Economists, and Social Scientists of the Past

**Brooks Adams,** 1848-1927, (U.S.) historian, political theoretician.

**Francis Bacon,** 1561-1626, (Br.) philosopher, essayist, and statesman.

**George Bancroft,** 1800-1891, (U.S.) historian, wrote 10-volume *History of the United States*.

**Charles A. Beard,** 1874-1948, (U.S.) historian, attacked motives of the Founding Fathers.

**Bede (the Venerable),** c.673-735, (Br.) scholar, historian.

**Ruth Benedict,** 1887-1948, (U.S.) anthropologist, studied Indian tribes of the Southwest.

**Louis Blanc,** 1811-1882, (F.) Socialist leader and historian whose ideas were a link between utopian and Marxist socialism.

**Franz Boas,** 1858-1942, (U.S.) German-born anthropologist, studied American Indians.

**Van Wyck Brooks,** 1886-1963, (U.S.) cultural historian, critic.

**Edmund Burke,** 1729-1797, (Ir.) British parliamentarian and political philosopher; influenced many Federalists.

**Thomas Carlyle,** 1795-1881, (Sc.) philosopher, historian, and critic.

**Edward Channing,** 1856-1931, (U.S.) historian wrote 6-volume *A History of the United States*.

**John R. Commons,** 1862-1945, (U.S.) economist, labor historian.

**Benedetto Croce,** 1866-1952, (It.) philosopher, statesman, historian.

**Bernard A. De Voto,** 1897-1955, (U.S.) historian, won Pulitzer prize in 1948 for *Across the Wide Missouri*.

**Émile Durkheim,** 1858-1917, (F.) a founder of modern sociology.

**Friedrich Engels,** 1820-1895, (G.) political writer, with Marx wrote the *Communist Manifesto*.

**Irving Fisher,** 1867-1947, (U.S.) economist, contributed to the development of modern monetary theory.

**John Fiske,** 1842-1901, (U.S.) historian and lecturer, popularized Darwinian theory of evolution.

**Charles Fourier,** 1772-1837, (F.) utopian socialist.

**Henry George,** 1839-1897, (U.S.) economist, reformer, led single-tax movement.

**Edward Gibbon,** 1737-1794, (Br.) historian, wrote *The History of the Decline and Fall of the Roman Empire*.

**Francesco Guicciardini,** 1483-1540, (It.) historian, wrote *Storia d'Italia*, principal historical work of the 16th-century.

**Alvin Hansen,** 1887-1975, (U.S.) economist.

**Thomas Hobbes,** 1588-1679, (Br.) social philosopher.

**Richard Hofstadter,** 1916-1970, (U.S.) historian, wrote *The Age of Reform*.

**John Maynard Keynes,** 1883-1946, (Br.) economist, principal advocate of deficit spending.

**Alfred L. Kroeber,** 1876-1960, (U.S.) cultural anthropologist, studied Indians of North and South America.

**James L. Laughlin,** 1850-1933, (U.S.) economist, helped establish Federal Reserve System.

**Lucien Lévy-Bruhl,** 1857-1939, (F.) philosopher, studied the psychology of primitive societies.

**Kurt Lewin,** 1890-1947, (U.S.) German-born psychologist, studied human motivaion and group dynamics.

**John Locke,** 1632-1704, (Br.) political philosopher.

**Thomas B. Macauley,** 1800-1859, (Br.) historian, statesman.

**Bronislaw Malinowski,** 1884-1942, (Pol.) anthropologist, considered the father of social anthropology.

**Thomas R. Malthus,** 1766-1834, (Br.) economist, famed for *Essay on the Principal of Population.*

**Karl Mannheim,** 1893-1947, (Hung.) sociologist, historian.

**Karl Marx,** 1818-1883, (G.) political philosopher, proponent of modern communism.

**Giuseppe Mazzini,** 1805-1872, (It.) political philosopher.

**George H. Mead,** 1863-1931, (U.S.) philosopher and social psychologist.

**James Mill,** 1773-1836, (Sc.) philosopher, historian, and economist; a proponent of Utilitarianism.

**John Stuart Mill,** 1806-1873, (Br.) philosopher, political economist.

**Perry G. Miller,** 1905-1963, (U.S.) historian, interpreted 17th-century New England.

**Theodor Mommsen,** 1817-1903, (G.) historian, wrote *The History of Rome.*

**Charles-Louis Montesquieu,** 1689-1755, (F.) social philosopher.

**Samuel Eliot Morison,** 1887-1976, (U.S.) historian, chronicled voyages of early explorers.

**Allen Nevins,** 1890-1971, (U.S.) historian, biographer; twice won Pulitzer prize.

**Jose Ortega y Gasset,** 1883-1955, (Sp.) philosopher and humanist; advocated control by an elite.

**Robert Owen,** 1771-1858, (Br.) political philosopher, reformer.

**Vilfredo Pareto,** 1848-1923, (It.) economist, sociologist.

**Francis Parkman,** 1823-1893, (U.S.) historian, wrote 8-volume *France and England in North America, 1851-92.*

**Marco Polo,** c.1254-1324, (It.) narrated an account of his travels to China.

**William Prescott,** 1796-1859, (U.S.) early American historian.

**Pierre Joseph Proudhon,** 1809-1865, (F.) social theorist, regarded as the father of anarchism.

**Francois Quesnay,** 1694-1774, (F.) economic theorist, demonstrated the circular flow of economic activity throughout society.

**David Ricardo,** 1772-1823, (Br.) economic theorist, advocated free international trade.

**James H. Robinson,** 1863-1936, (U.S.) historian, educator.

**Jean-Jacques Rousseau,** 1712-1778, (F.) social philosophy author.

**Bertrand Russell,** 1872-1970, (Br.) political philosophy mathematician; wrote *Principia Mathematica.*

**Hjalmar Schacht,** 1877-1970, (G.) economist.

**Joseph Schumpeter,** 1883-1950, (U.S.) Czech.-born economist, championed big business, capitalism.

**Albert Schweitzer,** 1875-1965, (Alsatian) social philosopher theologian, and humanitarian.

**George Simmel,** 1858-1918, (G.) sociologist, philosopher.

**Adam Smith,** 1723-1790, (Br.) economist, advocated laissez-faire economy and free trade.

**Jared Sparks,** 1789-1866, (U.S.) historian, among first to research from original documents.

**Oswald Spengler,** 1880-1936, (G.) philosopher and historian wrote *The Decline of the West.*

**William G. Sumner,** 1840-1910, (U.S.) social scientist, economist; championed laissez-faire economy, Social Darwinism.

**Hippolyte Taine,** 1828-1893, (F.) historian.

**Frank W. Taussig,** 1859-1940, (U.S.) economist, educator

**Alexis de Tocqueville,** 1805-1859, (F.) political scientist, torian.

**Francis E. Townsend,** 1897-1960, (U.S.) author of old-pension plan.

**Arnold Toynbee,** 1889-1975, (Br.) historian, wrote 10-vol *A Study of History.*

**Heinrich von Treitschke,** 1834-1896, (G.) historian, political writer.

**George Trevelyan,** 1838-1928, (Br.) historian, statesman.

**Frederick J. Turner,** 1861-1932, (U.S.) historian, educator

**Thorstein B. Veblen,** 1857-1929, (U.S.) economist, social philosopher.

**Giovanni Vico,** 1668-1744, (It.) historian, philosopher.

**Voltaire (F.A. Arouet),** 1694-1778, (F.) philosopher, historian and poet.

**Izaak Walton,** 1593-1683, (Br.) author, wrote first biographical works in English literature.

**Sidney J.,** 1859-1947, and wife **Beatrice,** 1858-1943, Webb (Br.) leading figures in Fabian Society and British Labour Party

**Walter P. Webb,** 1888-1963, (U.S.) historian of the West.

**Max Weber,** 1864-1920, (G.) sociologist.

## Noted Scientists of the Past

**Howard H. Aiken,** 1900-1973, (U.S.) mathematician, designed world's first large-scale digital computer (Mark I) for IBM.

**Albertus Magnus,** 1193-1280, (G.) theologian, philosopher, scientist, established medieval Christian study of natural science.

**Andre-Marie Ampère,** 1775-1836, (F.) scientist known for contributions to electrodynamics.

**Amedeo Avogadro,** 1776-1856, (It.) chemist, physicist, advanced important theories on properties of gases.

**A.C. Becquerel,** 1788-1878, (F.) physicist, pioneer in electrochemical science.

**A.H. Becquerel,** 1852-1908, (F.) physicist, discovered radioactivity in uranium.

**Daniel Bernoulli,** 1700-1782, (Swiss) mathematician, advanced kinetic theory of gases and fluids.

**Jöns Jakob Berzelius,** 1779-1848, (Swed.) chemist, developed modern chemical symbols and formulas.

**Henry Bessemer,** 1813-1898, (Br.) engineer, invented Bessemer steel-making process.

**Louis Blériot,** 1872-1936, (F.) engineer, pioneer aviator, invented and constructed monoplanes.

**Niels Bohr,** 1885-1962, (Dan.) physicist, leading figure in the development of quantum theory.

**Max Born,** 1882-1970, (G.) physicist known for research in quantum mechanics.

**Robert Bunsen,** 1811-1899, (G.) chemist, invented Bunsen burner.

**Luther Burbank,** 1849-1926, (U.S.) plant breeder whose work developed plant breeding into a modern science.

**Vannevar Bush,** 1890-1974, (U.S.) electrical engineer, developed differential analyzer, first electronic analogue computer.

**Alexis Carrel,** 1873-1944, (F.) surgeon, biologist, developed methods of suturing blood vessels and transplanting organs.

**George Washington Carver,** 1860?-1943, (U.S.) agricultural chemist, experimenter, benefactor of South, a black hero.

**Henry Cavendish,** 1731-1810, (Br.) chemist, physicist, discovered hydrogen.

**James Chadwick,** 1891-1974, (Br.) physicist, discovered the neutron.

**Jean M. Charcot,** 1825-1893, (F.) neurologist known for work on hysteria, hypnotism, sclerosis.

**John D. Cockcroft,** 1897-1967, (Br.) nuclear physicist, constructed first atomic particle accelerator with E.T.S. Walton.

**William Crookes,** 1832-1919, (Br.) physicist, chemist, discovered thallium, invented a cathode-ray tube, radiometer.

**Marie Curie,** 1867-1934, (Pol.) physical chemist known for work on radium and its compounds.

**Pierre Curie,** 1859-1906, (F.) physical chemist known for work with his wife on radioactivity.

**Gottlieb Daimler,** 1834-1900, (G.) engineer, inventor, pioneer automobile manufacturer.

**John Dalton,** 1766-1844, (Br.) chemist, physicist, formulated atomic theory, made first table of atomic weights.

**Charles Darwin,** 1809-1882, (Br.) naturalist, established theory of organic evolution.

**Humphry Davy,** 1778-1829, (Br.) chemist, research in electrochemistry led to isolation of potassium, sodium, calcium, ium, boron, magnesium, and strontium.

**Lee De Forest,** 1873-1961, (U.S.) inventor, pioneer in development of wireless telegraphy, sound pictures, television.

**Rudolf Diesel,** 1858-1913, (G.) mechanical engineer, invented Diesel engine.

**Thomas Dooley,** 1927-1961, (U.S.) "jungle doctor," noted efforts to supply medical aid to underdeveloped countries.

**Christian Doppler,** 1803-1853, (Aus.) physicist, demonstrated Doppler effect (change in energy wavelengths caused motion).

**Thomas A. Edison,** 1847-1931, (U.S.) inventor, held 1,000 patents, including incandescent electric lamp, phonograph

**Paul Ehrlich,** 1854-1915, (G.) bacteriologist, pioneer in modern immunology and bacteriology.

**Albert Einstein,** 1879-1955, (U.S.) theoretical physicist known for formulation of relativity theory.

**Gabriel Fahrenheit,** 1686-1736, (G.) physicist, introduced Fahrenheit scale for thermometers.

**Michael Faraday,** 1791-1867, (Br.) chemist, physicist, known for work in field of electricity.

**Pierre de Fermat,** 1601-1665, (F.) mathematician, discovered analytic geometry, founded modern theory of numbers and calculus of probabilities.

**Enrico Fermi,** 1901-1954, (It.) physicist, one of chief architects of the nuclear age.

**Galileo Ferraris,** 1847-1897, (It.) physicist, electrical engineer, discovered principle of rotary magnetic field.

**Camille Flammarion,** 1842-1925, (F.) astronomer, popularized study of astronomy.

**Alexander Fleming,** 1881-1955, (Br.) bacteriologist, discovered penicillin.

ean B.J. Fourier, 1768-1830, (F.) mathematician, discovered orem governing periodic oscillation.

ames Franck, 1882-1964, (G.) physicist, proved value of intum theory.

igmund Freud, 1856-1939, (Aus.) psychiatrist, founder of choanalysis.

Galileo Galilei, 1564-1642, (It.) astronomer, physicist, a nder of the experimental method.

uigi Galvani, 1737-1798, (It.) physician, physicist, known as nder of galvanism.

oseph Gay-Lussac, 1778-1850, (F.) chemist, physicist, intigated behavior of gases, discovered law of combining voles.

osiah W. Gibbs, 1839-1903, (U.S.) theoretical physicist, mist, founded chemical thermodynamics.

George W. Goethals, 1858-1928, (U.S.) army engineer, built Panama Canal.

William C. Gorgas, 1854-1920, (U.S.) sanitarian, U.S. army geon-general, his work to prevent yellow fever, malaria ped insure construction of Panama Canal.

Ernest Haeckel, 1834-1919, (G.) zoologist, evolutionist, a ong proponent of Darwin.

Otto Hahn, 1879-1968, (G.) chemist, worked on atomic fisn.

N.B.S. Haldane, 1892-1964, (Sc.) scientist, known for work as neticist and application of mathematics to science.

James Hall, 1761-1832, (Br.) geologist, chemist, founded experimental geology, geochemistry.

Edmund Halley, 1656-1742, (Br.) astronomer, calculated the its of many planets.

William Harvey, 1578-1657, (Br.) physician, anatomist, disered circulation of the blood.

Hermann v. Helmholtz, 1821-1894, (G.) physicist, anatomist, vsiologist, made fundamental contributions to physiology, op-, electrodynamics, mathematics, meteorology.

William Herschel, 1738-1822, (Br.) astronomer, discovered anus.

Heinrich Hertz, 1857-1894, (G.) physicist, his discoveries led wireless telegraphy.

David Hilbert, 1862-1943, (G.) mathematician, formulated t satisfactory set of axioms for modern Euclidean geometry.

Edwin P. Hubble, 1889-1953, (U.S.) astronomer, produced t observational evidence of expanding universe.

Alexander v. Humboldt, 1769-1859, (G.) explorer, naturalist, opagator of earth sciences, originated ecology, geophysics.

Julian Huxley, 1887-1975, (Br.) biologist, a gifted exponent d philosopher of science.

Edward Jenner, 1749-1823, (Br.) physician, discovered vaccation.

William Jenner, 1815-1898, (Br.) physician, pathological anatist.

Frederic Joliot-Curie, 1900-1958, (F.) physicist, with his wife ntinued work of Curies on radioactivity.

Irene Joliot-Curie, 1897-1956, (F.) physicist, continued work Curies in radioactivity.

James P. Joule, 1818-1889, (Br.) physicist, determined relanship between heat and mechanical energy (conservation of ergy).

Carl Jung, 1875-1961, (Sw.) psychiatrist, founder of analytical ychology.

Wm. Thomas Kelvin, 1824-1907, (Br.) mathematician, physist, known for work on heat and electricity.

Sister Elizabeth Kenny, 1886-1952, (Austral.) nurse, develed method of treatment for polio.

Johannes Kepler, 1571-1630, (G.) astronomer, discovered portant laws of planetary motion.

Joseph Lagrange, 1736-1813, (F.) geometer, astronomer, rked in all fields of analysis, and number theory, and analytiand celestial mechanics.

Jean B. Lamarck, 1744-1829, (F.) naturalist, forerunner of rwin in evolutionary theory.

Irving Langmuir, 1881-1957, (U.S.) physical chemist, his dies of molecular films on solid and liquid surfaces opened w fields in colloid research and biochemistry.

Pierre S. Laplace, 1749-1827, (F.) astronomer, physicist, put th nebular hypothesis of orgin of solar system.

Antonie Lavoisier, 1743-1794, (F.) chemist, founder of modn chemistry.

Ernest O. Lawrence, 1901-1958, (U.S.) physicist, invented the cyclotron.

Louis Leakey, 1903-1972, (Br.) anthropologist, discovered important fossils, remains of early hominids.

Anton van Leeuwenhoek, 1632-1723, (Du.) microscopist, father of microbiology.

Gottfried Wilhelm Leibniz, 1646-1716, (G.) mathematician, developed theories of differential and integral calculus.

Justus von Liebig, 1803-1873, (G.) chemist, established quantitative organic chemical analysis.

Percival Lowell, 1855-1961, (U.S.) astronomer, predicted the existence of Pluto.

Guglielmo Marconi, 1874-1937, (It.) physicist, known for his development of wireless telegraphy.

James Clerk Maxwell, 1831-1879, (Sc.) physicist, known especially for his work in electricity and magnetism.

Maria Goeppert Mayer, 1906-1972, (G.-U.S.) physicist, independently developed theory of structure of atomic nuclei.

Lise Meitner, 1878-1968, (Aus.) physicist whose work contributed to the development of the atomic bomb.

Gregor J. Mendel, 1822-1884, (Aus.) botanist, known for his experimental work on heredity.

Franz Mesmer, 1734-1815, (G.) physician, developed theory of animal magnetism.

Albert A. Michelson, 1852-1931, (U.S.) physicist, established speed of light as a fundamental constant.

Robert A. Millikan, 1868-1953, (U.S.) physicist, noted for study of elementary electronic charge and photoelectric effect.

Thomas Hunt Morgan, 1866-1945, (U.S.) geneticist, embryologist, researched fruit fly, established chromosome theory of heredity.

Isaac Newton, 1642-1727, (Br.) natural philosopher, mathematician, discovered law of gravitation, laws of motion.

J. Robert Oppenheimer, 1904-1967, (U.S.) theoretical physicist, director of Los Alamos during development of the atomic bomb.

Wilhelm Ostwald, 1853-1932, (G.) physical chemist, philosopher, chief founder of physical chemistry.

Louis Pasteur, 1822-1895, (F.) chemist, originated process of pasteurization.

Max Planck, 1858-1947, (G.) physicist, originated and developed quantum theory.

Henri Poincaré, 1854-1912, (F.) mathematician, physicist, influenced cosmology, relativity, and topology.

Joseph Priestley, 1733-1804, (Br.) chemist, one of the discoverers of oxygen.

Walter S. Reed, 1851-1902, (U.S.) army pathologist, bacteriologist, proved mosquitos transmit yellow fever.

Wilhelm Roentgen, 1845-1923, (G.) physicist, discovered X-rays.

Ernest Rutherford, 1871-1937, (Br.) physicist, discovered the atomic nucleus.

Giovanni Schiaparelli, 1835-1910, (It.) astronomer, hypothesized canals on the surface of Mars.

Angelo Secchi, 1818-1878, (It.) astronomer, pioneer in classifying stars by their spectra.

Harlow Shapley, 1885-1972, (U.S.) astronomer, noted for his studies of the galaxy.

Charles P. Steinmetz, 1865-1923, (U.S.) electrical engineer, developed fundamental ideas on alternating current systems.

Leo Szilard, 1898-1964, (U.S.) physicist, helped create first sustained nuclear reaction.

Rudolf Virchow, 1821-1902, (G.) pathologist, a founder of cellular pathology.

Alessandro Volta, 1745-1827, (It.) physicist, pioneer in electricity.

Alfred Russell Wallace, 1823-1913, (Br.) naturalist, proposed concept of evolution similar to Darwin.

August v. Wasserman, 1866-1925, (G.) bacteriologist, discovered reaction used as test for syphilis.

James E. Watt, 1736-1819, (Sc.) mechanical engineer, inventor, invented modern steam condensing engine.

Alfred L. Wegener, 1880-1930, (G.) meteorologist, geophysicist, postulated theory of continental drift.

Norbert Wiener, 1894-1964, (U.S.) mathematician, founder of the science of cybernetics.

Ferdinand v. Zeppelin, 1838-1917 (G.) soldier, aeronaut, airship designer.

## Noted Business Leaders, Industrialists, and Philanthropists of the Past

Elizabeth Arden (F.N. Graham), 1884-1966, (U.S.) Canadi-born businesswoman founded and headed cosmetics empire.

Philip D. Armour, 1832-1901, (U.S.) industrialist, streamlined eat packing.

John Jacob Astor, 1763-1848, (U.S.) German-born fur der, banker, real estate magnate; richest man in U.S. at his ath.

Francis W. Ayer, 1848-1923, (U.S.) advertising industry pioneer.

August Belmont, 1816-1890, (U.S.) German-born financier.

James B. (Diamond Jim) Brady, 1856-1917, (U.S.) financier, philanthropist, legendary bon vivant.

Adolphus Busch, 1839-1913, (U.S.) German-born businessman, established brewery empire.

Asa Candler, 1851-1929, (U.S.) founded Coca-Cola Co.

Andrew Carnegie, 1835-1919, (U.S.) Scots-born industrialist, founded U.S. Steel; financed over 2,800 libraries.

**William Colgate,** 1783-1857, (U.S.) British-born businessman, philanthropist; founded soap-making empire.

**Jay Cooke,** 1821-1905, (U.S.) financier, sold $1 billion in Union bonds during Civil War.

**Peter Cooper,** 1791-1883, (U.S.) industrialist, inventor, philanthropist.

**Ezra Cornell,** 1807-1874, (U.S.) businessman, philanthropist; headed Western Union, established univ.

**Erastus Corning,** 1794-1872, (U.S.) financier, headed N.Y. Central.

**Charles Crocker,** 1822-1888, (U.S.) railroad builder, financier.

**Samuel Cunard,** 1787-1865, (Can.) pioneered trans-Atlantic steam navigation.

**Marcus Daly,** 1841-1900, (U.S.) Irish-born copper magnate.

**Walt Disney,** 1901-1966, (U.S.) pioneer in cinema animation, built entertainment empire.

**Herbert H. Dow,** 1866-1930, (U.S.) Canadian-born founder of chemical co.

**James Duke,** 1856-1925, (U.S.) founded American Tobacco, Duke Univ.

**Eleuthere I. du Pont,** 1771-1834, (U.S.) French-born gunpowder manufacturer; founded one of world's largest business empires.

**Thomas C. Durant,** 1820-1885, (U.S.) railroad official, financier.

**William C. Durant,** 1861-1947, (U.S.) industrialist, formed General Motors.

**George Eastman,** 1854-1932, (U.S.) inventor, manufacturer of photographic equipment.

**Marshall Field,** 1834-1906, (U.S.) merchant, founded Chicago's largest department store.

**Harvey Firestone,** 1868-1938, (U.S.) industrialist, founded tire co.

**Henry M. Flagler,** 1830-1913, (U.S.) financier, helped form Standard Oil; developed Florida as resort state.

**Henry Ford,** 1863-1947, (U.S.) auto maker developed first popular low-priced car.

**Henry C. Frick,** 1849-1919, (U.S.) industrialist, helped organize U.S. Steel.

**Jakob Fugger (Jakob the Rich),** 1459-1525, (G.) headed foremost banking house and trading concern in 16th-century Europe.

**Alfred C. Fuller,** 1885-1973, (U.S.) Canadian-born businessman, founded brush co.

**Elbert H. Gary,** 1846-1927, (U.S.) headed U.S. Steel, 1903-27.

**Amadeo P. Giannini,** 1870-1949, (U.S.) founded Bank of America.

**Stephen Girard,** 1750-1831, (U.S.) French-born financier, philanthropist; richest man in U.S. at his death.

**Jean Paul Getty,** 1892-1976, (U.S.) founded oil empire.

**Jay Gould,** 1836-1892, (U.S.) railroad magnate, financier, speculator.

**Hetty Green,** 1834-1916, (U.S.) financier, the "witch of Wall St."; richest woman in U.S in her day.

**William Gregg,** 1800-1867, (U.S.) launched textile industry in the South.

**Meyer Guggenheim,** 1828-1905, (U.S.) Swiss-born merchant, philanthropist; built merchandising, mining empires.

**Edward H. Harriman,** 1848-1909, (U.S.) railroad financier, administrator; headed Union Pacific.

**Henry J. Heinz,** 1844-1919, (U.S.) founded food empire.

**James J. Hill,** 1838-1916, (U.S.) Canadian-born railroad magnate, financier; founded Great Northern Railway.

**Howard Hughes,** 1905-1976, (U.S.) industrialist, financier, movie maker.

**H.L. Hunt,** 1889-1974, (U.S.) oil magnate.

**Collis P. Huntington,** 1821-1900, (U.S.) railroad magnate.

**Henry E. Huntington,** 1850-1927, (U.S.) railroad builder, philanthropist.

**Howard Johnson,** 1896-1972, (U.S.) founded restaurant chain.

**Henry J. Kaiser,** 1882-1967, (U.S.) industrialist, built empire in steel, aluminum.

**Minor C. Keith,** 1848-1929, (U.S.) railroad magnate; founded United Fruit Co.

**Will K. Kellogg,** 1860-1951, (U.S.) businessman, philanthropist, founded breakfast food co.

**Richard King,** 1825-1885, (U.S.) cattleman, founded million acre King Ranch in Texas.

**William S. Knudsen,** 1879-1948, (U.S.) Danish-born auto industry executive.

**Samuel H. Kress,** 1863-1955, (U.S.) businessman, art collector, philanthropist; founded "dime store" chain.

**Alfred Krupp,** 1812-1887, (G.) armaments magnate.

**Albert Lasker,** 1880-1952, (U.S.) businessman, philanthropist.

**Thomas Lipton,** 1850-1931, (Ir.) merchant, built tea empire.

**James McGill,** 1744-1813, (Can.) Scots-born fur trader, founded univ.

**Andrew W. Mellon,** 1855-1937, (U.S.) financier, industrialist, benefactor of National Gallary of Art.

**Charles E. Merrill,** 1885-1956, (U.S.) financier, developed firm of Merrill Lynch.

**John Pierpont Morgan,** 1837-1913, (U.S.) most powerful figure in finance and industry at the turn-of-the-century.

**Aristotle Onassis,** 1900-1975, (Gr.) shipping magnate.

**George Peabody,** 1795-1869, (U.S.) merchant, financier, philanthropist.

**James C. Penney,** 1875-1971, (U.S.) businessman, developed department store chain.

**William C. Procter,** 1862-1934, (U.S.) headed soap company.

**John D. Rockefeller,** 1839-1937, (U.S.) industrialist, established Standard Oil; became world's wealthiest person.

**John D. Rockefeller Jr.,** 1874-1960, (U.S.) philanthropist, established foundation; provided land for United Nations.

**Meyer A. Rothschild,** 1743-1812, (G.) founded international banking house.

**Thomas Fortune Ryan,** 1851-1928, (U.S.) financier, dominated N.Y. City public transportation; helped found American Tobacco.

**Russell Sage,** 1816-1906, (U.S.) financier.

**David Sarnoff,** 1891-1971, (U.S.) broadcasting pioneer, established first radio network, NBC.

**Richard W. Sears,** 1863-1914, (U.S.) businessman, founded mail-order co.

**(Ernst) Werner von Siemens,** 1816-1892, (G.) industrialist, inventor.

**Alfred P. Sloan,** 1875-1966, (U.S.) industrialist, philanthropist, headed General Motors.

**A. Leland Stanford,** 1824-1893, (U.S.) railroad official, philanthropist; founded univ.

**Nathan Strauss,** 1848-1931, (U.S.) German-born merchant, philanthropist; headed Macy's.

**Levi Strauss,** c.1829-1902, (U.S.) pants manufacturer.

**Clement Studebaker,** 1831-1901, (U.S.) wagon, carriage manufacturer.

**Gustavus Swift,** 1839-1903, (U.S.) pioneer meat-packer; promoted refrigerated railroad cars.

**Gerard Swope,** 1872-1957, (U.S.) industrialist, economist, headed General Electric.

**James Walter Thompson,** 1847-1928, (U.S.) advertising executive.

**Theodore N. Vail,** 1845-1920, (U.S.) organized Bell Telephone system, headed ATT.

**Cornelius Vanderbilt,** 1794-1877, (U.S.) financier, established steamship, railroad empires.

**Henry Villard,** 1835-1900, (U.S.) German-born railroad executive, financier.

**Charles R. Walgreen,** 1873-1939, (U.S.) founded drugstore chain.

**John Wanamaker,** 1838-1922, (U.S.) pioneered department store merchandising.

**Aaron Montgomery Ward,** 1843-1913, (U.S.) established first mail-order firm.

**Thomas J. Watson,** 1874-1956, (U.S.) headed IBM, 1924.

**Charles E. Wilson,** 1890-1961, (U.S.) auto industry executive, public official.

**Frank W. Woolworth,** 1852-1919, (U.S.) created chain of 10s.

**William Wrigley Jr.,** 1861-1932, (U.S.) founded chewing co.

## Composers of the Western World

**Carl Philipp Emanuel Bach,** 1714-1788, (G.) Prussian and Wurtemberg Sonatas.

**Johann Christian Bach,** 1735-1782, (G.) Concertos; sonatas.

**Johann Sebastian Bach,** 1685-1750, (G.) St. Matthew Passion, The Well-Tempered Clavichord.

**Samuel Barber,** b. 1910, (U.S.) Adagio for Strings, Vanessa.

**Bela Bartok,** 1881-1945, (Hung.) Concerto for Orchestra, The Miraculous Mandarin.

**Ludwig Van Beethoven,** 1770-1827, (G.) Concertos (Emperor); sonatas (Moonlight, Pastorale, Pathetique); symphonies (Eroica).

**Vincenzo Bellini,** 1801-1835, (It.) La Sonnambula, Norma, Puritani.

**Alban Berg,** 1885-1935, (Aus.) Wozzeck, Lulu.

**Hector Berlioz,** 1803-1869, (F.) Damnation of Faust, Symphonie Fantastique, Requiem.

**Leonard Bernstein,** b. 1918, (U.S.) Jeremiah, West Side Story.

**eorges Bizet,** 1838-1875, (F.) Carmen, Pearl Fishers.

**nest Bloch,** 1880-1959, (Swiss) Schelomo, Voice in the erness, Sacred Service.

**iigi Boccherini,** 1743-1805, (It.) Cello Concerto in B Flat, phony in C.

**exander Borodin,** 1834-1887, (R.) Prince Ignor, In the pes of Central Asia.

**hannes Brahms,** 1833-1897, (G.) Liebeslieder Waltzes, psody in E Flat Major, Opus 119 for Piano, Academic Festi-Overture; symphonies; quartets.

**njamin Britten,** 1913-1976, (Br.) Peter Grimes, Turn of the w, Ceremony of Carols.

**nton Bruckner,** 1824-1896, (Aus.) Symphonies (Romantic), mezzo for String Quintet.

**erruccio Busoni,** 1866-1924, (It.) Doctor Faust, Comedy rture.

**ietrich Buxtehud,** 1637-1707, (D.) Cantatas, trio sonatas.

**illiam Byrd,** 1543-1623, (Br.) Masses, sacred songs.

**lexis Emmanuel Chabrier,** 1841-1894, (Fr.) Le Roi Malgre Espana.

**ustave Charpentier,** 1860-1956, (F.) Louise.

**ederic Chopin,** 1810-1849, (P.) Concertos, Polonaise No. 6 Flat Major (Heroic); sonatas.

**aron Copland,** b. 1900, (U.S.) Appalachian Spring.

**aude Achille Debussy,** 1862-1918, (F.) Pelleas et Mel-de, La Mer, Prelude to the Afternoon of a Faun.

**P. Leo Delibes,** 1836-1891, (Fr.) Lakme, Coppelia, Sylvia.

**orman Dello Joio,** b. 1913, (U.S.), Triumph of St. Joan, m of David.

**aetano Donizetti,** 1797-1848, (It.) Elixir of Love, Lucia de mermoor, Daughter of the Regiment.

**aul Dukas,** 1865-1935, (Fr.) Sorcerer's Apprentice.

**ntonin Dvorak,** 1841-1904, (C.) Symphony in E Minor m the New World).

**dward Elgar,** 1857-1934, (Br.) Pomp and Circumstance.

**anuel de Falla,** 1876-1946, (Sp.) La Vide Breve, El Amor o.

**abriel Faure,** 1845-1924, (Fr.) Requiem, Ballade.

**riedrich von Flotow,** 1812-1883, (G.) Martha.

**esar Franck,** 1822-1890, (Belg.) D Minor Symphony.

**eorge Gershwin,** 1898-1937, (U.S.) Rhapsody in Blue, erican in Paris, Porgy and Bess.

**mberto Giordano,** 1867-1948, (It.) Andrea Chenier.

**lex K. Glazunoff,** 1865-1936, (R.) Symphonies, Stenka Ra-

**ikhail Glinka,** 1804-1857, (R.) Ruslan & Ludmilla.

**hristoph W. Gluck,** 1714-1787, (G.) Alceste, Iphigenie en ride.

**harles Gounod,** 1818-1893, (F.) Faust, Romeo and Juliet.

**dvard Grieg,** 1843-1907, (Nor.) Peer Gynt Suite, Concerto Minor.

**eorge Frederick Handel,** 1685-1759, (G., Br.) Messiah, xes, Berenice.

**oward Hanson,** b. 1896, (U.S.) Symphonies No. 1 (Nordic) 2 (Romantic).

**oy Harris,** b. 1898, (U.S.) Symphonies, Amer. Portraits.

**oseph Haydn,** 1732-1809, (Aus.) Symphonies (Clock); ora-s; chamber music.

**aul Hindemith,** 1895-1963, (U.S.) Mathis Der Maler.

**ustav Holst,** 1874-1934, (Br.) The Planets.

**rthur Honegger,** 1892-1955, (Swiss) Judith, Le Roi David, fic 231.

**lan Hovhaness,** b. 1911, (U.S.) Symphonies, Magnificat.

**ngelbert Humperdinck,** 1854-1921, (G.) Hansel and Gretel.

**harles Ives,** 1874-1954, (U.S.) Third Symphony.

**ram Khachaturian,** 1903-1978, (R.) Gayane (ballet), sym-nies.

**oltan Kodaly,** 1882-1967, (Hung.) Hary Janos, Psalmus garicus.

**ritz Kreisler,** 1875-1962, (Aus.) Caprice Viennois, Tambou-hinois.

**odolphe Kreutzer,** 1766-1831, (F.) 40 etudes for violin.

**Edouard V.A. Lalo,** 1823-1892, (F.) Symphonie Espagnole.

**Ruggiero Leoncavallo,** 1858-1919, (It.) I Pagliacci.

**Franz Liszt,** 1811-1886, (Hung.) 20 Hungarian rhapsodies; symphonic poems.

**Edward MacDowell,** 1861-1908, (U.S.) To a Wild Rose.

**Gustav Mahler,** 1860-1911, (Aus.) Lied von der Erde.

**Pietro Mascagni,** 1863-1945, (It.) Cavalleria Rusticana.

**Jules Massenet,** 1842-1912, (F.) Manon, Le Cid, Thais.

**Mendelssohn-Bartholdy,** 1809-1847, (G.) Midsummer Night's Dream, Songs Without Words.

**Gian-Carlo Menotti,** b. 1911, (It.-U.S.) The Medium, The Con-sul, Amahl and the Night Visitors.

**Claudio Monteverdi,** 1567-1643, (It.) Opera; masses; madri-gals.

**Wolfgang Amadeus Mozart,** 1756-1791, (Aus.) Magic Flute, Marriage of Figaro; concertos; symphonies, etc.

**Modest Moussorgsky,** 1835-1881, (R.) Boris Godunov, Pic-tures at an Exhibition.

**Jacques Offenbach,** 1819-1880, (F.) Tales of Hoffman.

**Karl Orff,** b. 1895, (G.) Carmina Burana.

**Ignace Paderewski,** 1860-1941, (P.) Minuet in G.

**Giovanni P. da Palestrina,** 1524-1594, (It.) Masses; madri-gals.

**Amilcare Ponchielli,** 1834-1886, (It.) La Gioconda.

**Francis Poulenc,** 1899-1963, (Fr.) Dialogues des Carmelites.

**Serge Prokofiev,** 1891-1953, (R.) Love for Three Oranges, Lt. Kije, Peter and the Wolf.

**Giacomo Puccini,** 1858-1924, (It.) La Boheme, Manon Les-caut, Tosca, Madame Butterfly.

**Sergei Rachmaninov,** 1873-1943, (R.) Prelude in C Sharp Minor.

**Maurice Ravel,** 1875-1937, (Fr.) Bolero, Daphne et Chloe, Rapsodie Espagnole.

**Nikolai Rimsky-Korsakov,** 1844-1908, (R.) Golden Cockerel, Cappriccio Espagnol, Scheherazade, Russian Easter Overture.

**Gioacchino Rossini,** 1792-1868, (It.) Barber of Seville, Semiramide, William Tell.

**Chas. Camille Saint-Saens,** 1835-1921, (F.) Samson and Delilah, Danse Macabre.

**Alessandro Scarlatti,** 1659-1725, (It.) Cantatas; concertos.

**Arnold Schoenberg,** 1874-1951, (Aus.) Pelleas and Meli-sande, Transfigured Night, De Profundis.

**Franz Schubert,** 1797-1828, (A.) Lieder; symphonies (Unfin-ished); overtures (Rosamunde).

**William Schuman,** b. 1910, (U.S.) Credendum, New England Triptych.

**Robert Schumann,** 1810-1856, (G.) Symphonies, songs.

**Aleksandr Scriabin,** 1872-1915, (R.) Prometheus.

**Dimitri Shostakovich,** b. 1906-1975, (R.) Symphonies, Lady Macbeth of Minsk, The Nose.

**Jean Sibelius,** 1865-1957, (Finn.) Finlandia, Karelia.

**Bedrich Smetana,** 1824-1884, (Cz.) The Bartered Bride.

**Karlheinz Stockhausen,** b. 1928, (G.) Kontrapunkte, Kon-takte.

**Richard Strauss,** 1864-1949, (G.) Salome, Elektra, Der Rosenkavalier, Thus Spake Zarathustra.

**Igor F. Stravinsky,** 1882-1971, (R.-U.S.) Oedipus Rex, Le Sacre du Printemps, Petrushka.

**Peter I. Tchaikovsky,** 1840-1893, (R.) Nutcracker Suite, Swan Lake, Eugen Onegin.

**Ambroise Thomas,** 1811-1896, (F.) Mignon.

**Virgil Thomson,** b. 1896, (U.S.) Opera, ballet; Four Saints in Three Acts.

**Ralph Vaughan Williams,** 1872-1958, (Br.) Job, London Sym-phony, Symphony No. 7 (Antarctica).

**Giuseppe Verdi,** 1813-1901, (It.) Aida, Rigoletto, Don Carlo, Il Trovatore, La Traviata, Falstaff, Macbeth.

**Hector Villa Lobos,** 1887-1959, (Brazil) Choros:

**Antonio Vivaldi,** 1678-1741, (It.) Concerti, The Four Seasons.

**Richard Wagner,** 1813-1883, (G.) Rienzi, Tannhauser, Lohen-grin, Tristan und Isolde.

**Karl Maria von Weber,** 1786-1826, (G.) Der Freischutz.

---

## Composers of Operettas, Musicals, and Popular Music

**ilton Ager,** b. 1919, (U.S.) I Wonder What's Become of y; Hard Hearted Hannah.

**eroy Anderson,** 1908-1975, (U.S.) Syncopated Clock; Blue go; Sleigh Ride.

**arold Arlen,** b. 1905, (U.S.) Stormy Weather; Over the Rain-; Blues in the Night; That Old Black Magic.

**urt Bacharach,** b. 1928, (U.S.) Raindrops Keep Fallin' on Head; Walk on By; What the World Needs Now is Love.

**rnest Ball,** 1878-1927, (U.S.) Mother Machree; When Irish s Are Smiling.

**ving Berlin,** b. 1888, (U.S.) *This is the Army; Annie Get Your ; Call Me Madam;* God Bless America; White Christmas.

**Jerry Bock,** b. 1928, (U.S.) *Mr. Wonderful; Fiorello; Fiddler on the Roof; The Rothschilds.*

**Carrie Jacobs Bond,** 1862-1946, (U.S.) I Love You Truly.

**Nacio Herb Brown,** 1896-1964, (U.S.) Singing in the Rain; You Were Meant for Me; All I Do Is Dream of You.

**Hoagy Carmichael,** b. 1899, (U.S.) Stardust; Georgia on My Mind; Old Buttermilk Sky.

**George M. Cohan,** 1878-1942, (U.S.) Give My Regards to Broadway; You're A Grand Old Flag; Over There.

**Noel Coward,** 1899-1973 (Br.) *Bitter Sweet;* Mad Dogs and Englishmen; Mad About the Boy.

**Walter Donaldson,** 1893-1947, (U.S.) My Buddy; Carolina in the Morning; You're Driving Me Crazy; Makin' Whoopee.

**Vernon Duke,** 1903-1969, (U.S.) April in Paris.

**Gus Edwards,** 1879-1945, (U.S.) School Days; By the Light of the Silvery Moon; In My Merry Oldsmobile.

**Sherman Edwards,** b. 1919, (U.S.) See You in September; Wonderful! Wonderful!

**Sammy Fain,** b. 1902, Wedding Bells Are Breaking Up That Old Gang of Mine; Let a Smile Be Your Umbrella.

**Fred Fisher,** 1875-1942, (U.S.) Peg O' My Heart; Chicago; Dardenella.

**Stephen Collins Foster,** 1826-1864, (U.S.) My Old Kentucky Home; Old Folks At Home.

**Rudolf Friml,** 1879-1972, (naturalized U.S.) The Firefly; Rose Marie; Vagabond King; Bird of Paradise.

**John Gay,** 1685-1732, (Br.) The Beggar's Opera.

**Edwin F. Goldman,** 1878-1956, (U.S.) marches.

**Percy Grainger,** 1882-1961, (Br.) Country Gardens.

**John Green,** b. 1908, (U.S.) Body and Soul; Out of Nowhere; I Cover the Waterfront.

**Ferde Grofe,** 1892-1972, (U.S.) Grand Canyon Suite.

**W. C. Handy,** 1873-1958, (U.S.) St. Louis Blues.

**Ray Henderson,** 1896-1970, (U.S.) George White's Scandals; That Old Gang of Mine; Five Foot Two, Eyes of Blue.

**Victor Herbert,** 1859-1924, (Ir.-U.S.) Mlle. Modiste; Babes in Toyland; The Red Mill; Naughty Marietta; Sweethearts.

**Jerry Herman,** b. 1932, (U.S.) Milk and Honey; Hello Dolly; Mame; Dear World.

**Al Hoffman,** 1902-1960, (U.S.) Heartaches, Mairzy Doats.

**Scott Joplin,** 1868-1917, (U.S.) Treemonisha.

**John Kander,** b. 1927, (U.S.) Cabaret; Chicago; Funny Lady.

**Jerome Kern,** 1885-1945, (U.S.) Sally; Sunny; Show Boat; Cat and the Fiddle; Music in the Air; Roberta.

**Burton Lane,** b. 1912, (U.S.) Three's a Crowd; Finnian's Rainbow; On A Clear Day You Can See Forever.

**Franz Lehar,** 1870-1948, (Hung.) Merry Widow.

**Mitch Leigh,** b. 1928, (U.S.) Man of La Mancha.

**Frank Loesser,** 1910-1969, (U.S.) Guys and Dolls; Where's Charley?; The Most Happy Fella.

**Frederick Loewe,** b. 1901, (Aust.-U.S.) The Day Before Spring; Brigadoon; Paint Your Wagon; My Fair Lady; Camelot.

**Henry Mancini,** b. 1924, (U.S.) Moon River; Days of Wine and Roses; Pink Panther Theme.

**Jimmy McHugh,** 1894-1969, (U.S.) I Can't Give You Anything But Love; I Feel a Song Coming On.

**Joseph Meyer,** b. 1894, (U.S.) If You Knew Susie; California, Here I Come; Crazy Rhythm.

**Chauncey Olcott,** 1858-1932, (U.S.) Mother Machree; My Wild Irish Rose.

**Cole Porter,** 1893-1964, (U.S.) Anything Goes; Jubilee; DuBarry Was a Lady; Panama Hattie; Mexican Hayride; Kiss Me Kate; Can Can; Silk Stockings.

**Andre Previn,** b. 1929, (U.S.) Coco.

**Richard Rodgers,** b. 1902, (U.S.) Garrick Gaieties; Connecticut Yankee; America's Sweetheart; On Your Toes; Babes in Arms; The Boys from Syracuse; Oklahoma!; Carousel; South Pacific; The King and I; Flower Drum Song; The Sound of Music.

**Sigmund Romberg,** 1887-1951, (Hung.) Maytime; The Student Prince; Desert Song; Blossom Time.

**Harold Rome,** b. 1908, (U.S.) Pins and Needles; Call Me Mister; Wish You Were Here; Fanny; Destry Rides Again.

**Vincent Rose,** b. 1880-1944, (U.S.) Avalon; Whispering; Blueberry Hill.

**Harry Ruby,** 1895-1974, (U.S.) Three Little Words; Who's Sorry Now?

**Arthur Schwartz,** b. 1900, (U.S.) The Band Wagon; Inside U.S.A.; A Tree Grows in Brooklyn.

**Stephen Sondheim,** b. 1930, (U.S.) A Little Night Music.

**John Philip Sousa.** 1854-1932, (U.S.) El Capitan; Stars Stripes Forever.

**Oskar Straus,** 1870-1954, (Aus.) Chocolate Soldier.

**Johann Strauss,** 1825-1899, (Aus.) Gypsy Baron; Die Fle maus; waltzes: Blue Danube, Artist's Life.

**Charles Strouse,** b. 1928, (U.S.) Bye Bye, Birdie; All A can; Golden Boy; Applause.

**Jule Styne,** b. 1905, (b. London-U.S.) Gentlemen P Blondes; Bells Are Ringing; Gypsy; Funny Girl.

**Arthur S. Sullivan,** 1842-1900, (Br.) H.M.S. Pinafore, Pi of Penzance; The Mikado.

**Deems Taylor,** 1885-1966, (U.S.) Peter Ibbetson.

**Egbert van Alstyne,** 1882-1951, (U.S.) In the Shade o Old Apple Tree; Memories; Pretty Baby.

**James Van Heusen,** b. 1913, (U.S.) Moonlight Becomes Swinging on a Star.

**Albert von Tilzer,** 1878-1956, (U.S.) I'll Be With You in A Blossom Time; Take Me Out to the Ball Game.

**Harry von Tilzer,** 1872-1946, (U.S.) Only a Bird in a G Cage; On a Sunday Afternoon.

**Harry Warren,** b. 1893, (U.S.) You're My Everything; We' the Money; I Only Have Eyes for You; September in the Rair

**Kurt Weill,** 1900-1950, (G.-U.S.) Threepenny Opera; La the Dark; Knickerbocker Holiday; One Touch of Venus.

**Percy Wenrich,** 1887-1952, (U.S.) When You Wore a T Moonlight Bay; Put On Your Old Gray Bonnet.

**Richard A. Whiting,** 1891-1938, (U.S.) Till We Meet A Sleepytime Gal; Beyond the Blue Horizon.

**Meredith Willson,** b. 1902, (U.S.) The Music Man.

**Vincent Youmans,** 1898-1946, (U.S.) Two Little Girls in Wildflower; No, No, Nanette; Hit the Deck; Rainbow; Smiles.

## Lyricists

**Sammy Cahn,** b. 1913, (U.S.) High Hopes; Love and riage; The Second Time Around.

**Buddy De Sylva,** 1895-1950, (U.S.) When Day is Done; for the Silver Lining; April Showers; The Best Things in Life Free.

**Howard Dietz,** b. 1896, (U.S.) Dancing in the Dark; You the Night and the Music.

**Al Dubin,** 1891-1945, (U.S.) Tiptoe Through the Tulips; A versary Waltz; Lullaby of Broadway.

**Dorothy Fields,** 1905-1974, (U.S.) On the Sunny Side o Street; Don't Blame Me; The Way You Look Tonight.

**Ira Gershwin,** b. 1896, (U.S.) The Man I Love; Fascina Rhythm; S'Wonderful; Embraceable You.

**Wm. S. Gilbert,** 1836-1911. (Br.) The Mikado; H.M.S. afore.

**Oscar Hammerstein II,** 1895-1960, (U.S.) Ol' Man River; lahoma; Carousel.

**E. Y. (Yip) Harburg,** b. 1898, (U.S.) Brother, Can You Spa Dime; April in Paris; Over the Rainbow.

**Lorenz Hart,** 1895-1943, (U.S.) With a Song in My Heart; It Romantic; Blue Moon; Lover.

**DuBose Heyward,** 1885-1940, (U.S.) Summertime Woman Is A Sometime Thing.

**Gus Kahn,** 1886-1941, (U.S.) Memories; Ain't We Got Pretty Baby.

**Johnny Mercer,** 1909-1976, (U.S.) Days of Wine and Ro Come Rain or Come Shine; Laura; That Old Black Magic.

**Jack Norworth,** 1879-1959, (U.S.) Take Me Out to the Game; Shine On Harvest Moon.

**Jack Yellen,** b. 1892, (U.S.) Down by the O-Hi-O; Ain't Sweet; Happy Days Are Here Again.

---

# Noted Jazz Artists

Jazz has been called America's only completely unique contribution to Western culture. The following individuals made major contributions in this field:

**Julian "Cannonball" Adderley,** 1928-1975: alto sax.

**Henry "Red" Allen,** 1908-1967: trumpet.

**Albert Ammons,** 1907-1949: boogie-woogie pianist.

**Louis "Satchmo" Armstrong,** 1900-1971: trumpet, singer; originated the "scat" vocal.

**Mildred Bailey,** 1907-1951: blues singer.

**Count Basie,** b. 1904: orchestra leader, piano.

**Sidney Bechet,** 1897-1950: early innovator on the soprano sax.

**Bix Beiderbecke,** 1903-1931: cornet, piano, composer.

**Bunny Berrigan,** 1909-1942: trumpet, singer, "I Can't Get Started With You".

**Art Blakey,** b. 1919: drums, leader.

**Jimmy Blanton,** 1921-1942: bass.

**Charles "Buddy" Bolden,** 1868-1931: cornet; formed the first jazz band in the 1890s.

**Big Bill Broonzy,** 1893-1958: blues singer, guitar.

**Dave Brubeck,** b. 1920: piano, combo leader.

**Harry Carney,** 1910-1975: baritone sax.

**Benny Carter,** b. 1907: alto sax, trumpet, clarinet.

**Sidney Catlett,** 1910-1951: drums.

**Charlie Christian,** 1919-1942: guitar; often given credit fo term "bebop".

**Buck Clayton,** b. 1911: trumpet, arranger.

**Al Cohn,** b. 1925: tenor sax, composer.

**Cozy Cole,** b. 1909: drums.

**Ornette Coleman,** b. 1930: saxophonist noted for his unor dox style.

**John Coltrane,** 1926-1967: tenor sax innovator.

**Eddie Condon,** 1904-1973: guitar, band leader; promote Dixieland.

**Miles Davis,** b. 1926: trumpet; pioneer of cool jazz.

**Buddy De Franco,** b. 1933: clarinet.

**Paul Desmond,** 1924-1977: alto sax.

**Warren "Baby" Dodds,** 1898-1959: Dixieland drummer.

**Johnny Dodds,** 1892-1940: clarinet.

**Jimmy Dorsey,** 1904-1957: clarinet, alto sax; band lead the swing era.

ommy Dorsey, 1905-1956: trombone; band leader in swing

oy Eldridge, b. 1911: trumpet, drums, singer.
uke Ellington, 1899-1974: piano, orchestra leader, composer.
ill Evans, b. 1929: piano.
lla Fitzgerald, b. 1918: singer.
rroll Garner, 1921-1977: piano, composer, "Misty".
tan Getz, b. 1927: tenor sax.
erry Gibbs, b. 1924: vibes.
ohn "Dizzy" Gillespie, b. 1917: trumpet, composer; a deoper of bop.
lenny Goodman, b. 1909: clarinet, band and combo leader.
lobby Hackett, 1915-1976: trumpet, cornet.
lonel Hampton, b. 1913: vibes, drums, piano, combo leader.
V. C. Handy, 1873-1958: composer, "St. Louis Blues", emphis Blues".
ill Harris, 1916-1973: trombone.
Coleman Hawkins, 1904-1969: tenor sax; 1939 recording of ody and Soul", a classic.
letcher Henderson, 1898-1952: orchestra leader, arranger; : jazz man to use written arrangements pioneering the regimted jazz and dance bands of the 30s.
Voody Herman, b. 1913: clarinet, alto sax, band leader.
lay C. Higginbotham, 1906-1973: trombone.
lertha "Chippie" Hill, 1905-1950: blues singer.
larl "Fatha" Hines, b. 1905: piano, songwriter.
ohnny Hodges, b. 1906: alto sax.
lillie Holiday, 1915-1959: blues singer, "Strange Fruit", od Bless the Child".
lam "Lightnin' " Hopkins, b. 1912: blues singer, guitar.
lahalia Jackson, 1911-1972: gospel singer; and example of link between the religious and secular roots of jazz.
lilt Jackson, b. 1923: vibes, piano, guitar.
llind Lemon Jefferson, 1897-1930: blues singer, guitar.
lunk Johnson, 1879-1949: cornet, trumpet.
lames P. Johnson, 1891-1955: piano, composer.
l. J. Johnson, b. 1924: trombone, composer.
luincy Jones, b. 1933: arranger.
cott Joplin, 1868-1917: ragtime composer, "Maple Leaf g".
tan Kenton, b. 1912: orchestra leader, composer, piano.
reddie Keppard, 1899-1933: trumpet.
lohn Kirby, 1908-1952: major combo leader of the 30s.
.ee Konitz, b. 1927: alto sax.
lene Krupa, 1909-1973: drums, band and combo leader.
ommy Ladnier, 1900-1939: trumpet.
ddie Lang, 1904-1933: guitar.
luddie Ledbetter (Leadbelly), 1888-1949: blues singer, gui-

lohn Lewis, b. 1920: composer, piano, combo leader.
limmie Lunceford, 1902-1947: band leader, sax.
hhelly Manne, b. 1920: drums.
limmy McPartland, b. 1907: trumpet.
lenn Miller, 1904-1944: trombone, dance band leader.
Charles Mingus, b. 1922: bass, composer, combo leader.
helonious Monk, b. 1920: piano, composer, combo leader; eveloper of bop.
Ves Montgomery, 1925-1971: guitar.
erdinand "Jelly Roll" Morton, 1885-1941: composer, pi-ò, singer.
lennie Moten, 1894-1935: piano; an early organizer of large z orchestras.
lerry Mulligan, b. 1927: baritone sax, arranger, leader.
urk Murphy, b. 1915: trombone, band leader.
heodore "Fats" Navarro, 1923-1950: trumpet.

Red Nichols, 1905-1965: cornet, combo leader.
Jimmie Noone, 1895-1944: clarinet, leader.
Red Norvo, b. 1908: vibes, band leader.
Anita O'Day, b. 1919: singer.
King Oliver, 1885-1938: cornet, band leader; teacher of Louis Armstrong.
Kid Ory, 1886-1973: trombone, composer, "Muskrat Ramble".
Charlie "Bird" Parker, 1920-1955: alto sax, composer; rated by many as the greatest jazz improviser.
Oscar Peterson, b. 1925: piano, composer, combo leader.
Oscar Pettiford, 1922-1960: a leading bassist in the bop era.
Bud Powell, 1924-1966: piano, composer; modern jazz pioneer.
Gertrude "Ma" Rainey, 1886-1939: first of the great blues singers; teacher of Bessie Smith.
Don Redman, 1900-1964: composer, arranger; pioneer in the evolution of the large orchestra.
Django Reinhardt, 1910-1953: guitar; Belgian gypsy, first European to influence American jazz.
Buddy Rich, b. 1917: drums, band leader.
Max Roach, b. 1925: drums.
Shorty Rogers, b. 1924: composer, trumpet, band leader: a founder of the West coast school of jazz.
Sonny Rollins, b. 1929: tenor sax.
Pete Rugolo, b. 1915: composer, orchestra leader.
Jimmy Rushing, 1903-1972: blues singer.
Pee Wee Russell, 1906-1969: clarinet.
Artie Shaw, b. 1910: clarinet, combo leader: 1939 recording of "Begin the Beguine", a classic.
George Shearing, b. 1919: piano, composer, "Lullaby of Birdland".
Horace Silver, b. 1928: piano, combo leader.
Zoot Sims, b 1925: tenor, alto sax; clarinet.
Zutty Singleton, 1898-1975: Dixieland drummer.
Bessie Smith, 1894-1937: blues singer.
Clarence "Pinetop" Smith, 1904-1929: piano, singer; pioneer of boogie woogie.
Joe Smith, 1902-1937: trumpet.
Willie "The Lion" Smith, 1897-1973: stride style pianist.
Muggsy Spanier, 1906-1967: cornet, band leader.
Sonny Stitt, b. 1924: alto, tenor sax.
Art Tatum, 1910-1956: piano; considered one of the great technical virtuosos in jazz.
Billy Taylor, b. 1921: piano.
Jack Teagarden, 1905-1964: trombone, singer.
Dave Tough, 1908-1948: drums.
Lennie Tristano, b. 1919: piano, composer.
Joe Turner, b. 1911: blues singer.
Joe Turner, b. 1907: stride piano.
Sarah Vaughan, b. 1924: singer.
Thomas "Fats" Waller, 1904-1943: pinao, singer, composer, "Ain't Misbehavin' ".
Dinah Washington, 1924-1963: singer.
Teddy Weatherford, 1903-1945: piano.
Chick Webb, 1902-1939: band leader, drums; generally credited with laying the foundations for jazz percussion.
Paul Whiteman, 1890-1967: orchestra leader; a major figure in the introduction of jazz to a large audience.
Charles "Cootie" Williams, b. 1908: trumpet, band leader.
Mary Lou Williams, b. 1910: singer.
Teddy Wilson, b. 1912: piano, composer.
Kai Winding, b. 1922: trombone, composer.
Jimmy Yancey, 1894-1951: piano.
Lester "Pres" Young, 1909-1959: tenor sax, composer: a bop pioneer.

---

## Popular American Songs

(m-music; w-words)

After You've Gone: Turner Layton(m); Henry Creamer(w); 16; popularized by Al Jolson, Sophie Tucker.
Ain't She Sweet: Milton Ager(m); Jack Yellen(w); 1927; inducted by Paul Ash orch., Oriental Theater, Chicago.
Alexander's Ragtime Band: Irving Berlin(m,w); 1911.
Always (I'll Be Loving You): Irving Berlin(m,w); 1925.
April In Paris: Vernon Duke(m); E. Y. Harburg(w); 1932; sung Evelyn Hoey in revue Walk a Little Faster.
April Showers: Louis Silvers(m); Buddy De Sylva(w); 1921; roduced by Al Joslon in musical Bombo.
As Time Goes By: Herman Hupfield(m,w); 1931, in musical erbody's Welcome, also movie Casablanca, in 1942.
Baby Face: Harry Akst(m); Benny Davis(w); 1926; introduced Jan Garber on RCA Victor record.
The Band Played On: C. B. Ward(m); J. E. Palmer(w); 1895; ng owned and promoted by newspaper, New York World.
Beer Barrel Polka: J. Vejvoda and Lew Brown(w); 1934(w); sic was a Czech popular song.
The Best Things In Life Are Free: Ray Henderson(m);

Buddy De Sylva and Lew Brown(w); 1927; in musical Good News.
Beyond the Blue Horizon: R. A. Whiting(m); Leo Robin(w); 1930; introduced by Jeanette MacDonald in movie Monte Carlo.
Blue Skies: Irving Berlin(m,w); 1926; introduced by Belle Baker in musical Betsy.
Body and Soul: John Green(m); E. Heyton, R. Sour, F. Eyton(w); 1930; introduced by Gertrude Lawrence on BBC.
Bye, Bye Blackbird: R. Henderson(m); Mort Dixon(w); 1926; popularized by Eddie Cantor.
By the Beautiful Sea: Harry Carroll(m); Harold Atteridge(w); 1914; vaudeville.
By the Light of the Silvery Moon: Gus Edwards(m); Edward Madden(w); 1909; in revue School Boys and Girls.
Chicago: Fred Fisher(m,w); 1922; vaudeville.
California, Here I Come: Joseph Meyer(m); Al Jolson, Buddy De Sylva(w); 1923; by Al Jolson in road tour of Bombo.
Daisy Bell (Bicycle Built for Two): Harry Dacre(m,w); circa 1892; London tune popularized in U.S. by Tony Pastor.

**Dancing in the Dark:** Arthur Schwartz(m); Howard Dietz(w); 1931; in revue *The Band Wagon*.

**Down by the Old Mill Stream:** Tell Taylor(m,w); 1910.

**Easter Parade:** Irving Berlin(m,w); 1933; introduced by Clifton Webb and Marilyn Miller in musical *As Thousands Cheer.*

**For Me and My Gal:** G. W. Meyer(m); Edgar Leslie, E. R. Goetz(w); 1917; sung by Jolson, Cantor, Sophie Tucker, others.

**Give My Regards to Broadway:** George M. Cohan(m,w); 1904; in musical *Little Johnny Jones.*

**Good Night Irene:** Huddie Ledbetter(m,w); 1936; found by John Lomax in Louisiana State Prison, Angola, La.

**Hail, Hail, the Gang's All Here:** Arthur S. Sullivan(m); T. A. Morse(w), under pseudonym. D. A. Esrom; 1917.

**Happy Days Are Here Again:** Milton Ager(m); Jack Yellen(w); 1929; introduced on Black Thursday (10-24-29) at Penn Hotel, N.Y.C.

**Heartaches:** Al Hoffman(m); John Klenner(w); 1931; popularized by Ted Weems.

**Home on the Range:** Daniel E. Kelly?(m); Brewster (Bruce) Higley (w,m), 1904, called Arizona Home(w) 1873; composer and author uncertain.

**Hot Time in the Old Town Tonight:** T. M. Metz(m); Joe Hayden(w); 1896; minstrel show.

**I Can't Give You Anything But Love:** Jimmy McHugh(m); Dorothy Fields(w); 1928; in revue *Delmar's Revels.*

**I Could Have Danced All Night:** F. Loewe(m); A. J. Lerner(w); 1956; by Julie Andrews in *My Fair Lady.*

**I Don't Know Why I Love You Like I Do:** F. E. Ahlert(m); Roy Turk(w); 1931.

**If You Knew Susie:** Bud De Sylva and Joseph Meyer(w,m); 1925; by Al Jolson in *Big Boy.*

**I Got Plenty o'Nothin':** G. Gershwin(m); I. Gershwin, DuBose Heyward(w); 1935; in *Porgy and Bess.*

**I'll Be Seeing You:** Sammy Fain(m); Irving Kahal(w); 1938; popularized by Sinatra, Hildegarde, in 1943.

**I'll See You in My Dreams:** Isham Jones(m); Gus Kahn(w); 1924.

**I Love You Truly:** Carrie Jacobs Bond(m,w); 1901; originally an art song, later picked up by vaudeville.

**I'm in the Mood for Love:** J. McHugh(m); Dorothy Fields(w); 1935; by Alice Faye in movie *Every Night at Eight.*

**I'm Sitting on Top of the World:** Ray Henderson(m); Sam M. Lewis, Joe Young(w); 1925; popularized by Jolson in 1929 movie *The Singing Fool.*

**In the Good Old Summertime:** George Evans(m); Ren Shields(w); 1902.

**In the Shade of the Old Apple Tree:** Egbert van Alstyne(m); Harry H. Williams(w); 1905.

**I Only Have Eyes for You:** Harry Warren(m); Al Dubin(w); 1934; by Dick Powell in movie *Dames.*

**It Had To Be You:** Isham Jones(m); Gus Kahn(w); 1924.

**It's Been a Long, Long Time:** Julie Styne(m); Sammy Cahn(w); 1945.

**It Was a Very Good Year:** Ervin Drake(m,w); 1965; introduced by Kingston Trio on record; popularized by Sinatra in 1965.

**I've Got You Under My Skin:** Cole Porter(m,w); 1936; by Virginia Bruce in movie *Born to Dance.*

**I Want a Girl Just Like the Girl:** Harry von Tilzer(m); Wiliam Dillion(w); 1911.

**I Wonder Who's Kissing Her Now:** J. E. Howard, H. Orlob(m); Wm. M. Hough, F. R. Adams(w); 1909.

**Jeannie With the Light Brown Hair:** Stephen Foster(m,w); 1854.

**June is Busting Out All Over:** R. Rodgers(m); O. Hammerstein II(w); 1945; in *Carousel.*

**Lazy River:** S. Arodin, Hoagy Carmichael(m,w); 1931; on record by Carmichael with band including both Dorseys, Teagarden, Krupa, Goodman, Venuti, and Beiderbecke.

**Let Me Call You Sweetheart:** Leo Friedman(m); Beth Slater Whitson(w); 1910.

**Lover:** R. Rodgers(m); Lorenz Hart(w); 1933; by Jeanette MacDonald in movie *Love Me Tonight.*

**Lullaby of Broadway:** Harry Warren(m); Al Dubin(w); 1935; in movie *Gold Diggers of Broadway.*

**Memories:** Egbert van Alstyne(m); Gus Kahn(w); 1915.

**Moonlight and Roses:** Neil Moret, Ben Black(m,w); 1925; music based on Lamare's *Andantino;* sung by Betty Grable in 1943 movie *Tin Pan Alley.*

**Moon River:** Henry Mancini(m); Johnny Mercer(w); 1961; by Andy Williams under title for movie *Breakfast at Tiffany's.*

**Moonlight Bay:** Percy Wenrich(m); Edward Madden(w); 1912; vaudeville.

**My Blue Heaven:** Walter Donaldson(m); George Whiting(w); 1927; Tommy Lyman radio theme song.

**Melancholy Baby;** Ernie Burnett(m); George A. Norton(w); 1912; vaudeville.

**My Wild Irish Rose:** Chauncey Olcott(m,w); 1899; in musical *A Romance of Athlone.*

**Night and Day:** Cole Porter(m,w); 1932; by Fred Astaire and Claire Luce in musical *Gay Divorce;* title of Porter film biograp

**Now Is The Hour:** Kaihan, Scott, Stewart(m,w); originate Austria in 1913; American version, 1946.

**Oh, What a Beautiful Mornin':** R. Rodgers(m); O. Hamm stein II(w); 1943; by Alfred Drake in *Oklahoma!*

**Oh! You Beautiful Doll:** Nat D. Ayer(m); A. Seym Brown(w); 1911; vaudeville.

**Old Folks at Home** (Swanee River): Stephen Foster(m 1851; minstrel show.

**Ol' Man River:** Jerome Kern(m); O. Hammerstein II(w); 19 by Jules Bledsoe in *Show Boat.*

**On the Sunny Side of the Street:** J. McHugh(m); Dorc Fields(w); 1930; in *International Revue* with Gertrude Lawrenc

**Over The Rainbow:** Harold Arlen(m); E. Y. Harburg(w); by fourteen-year-old Judy Garland in *Wizard of Oz.*

**Peg O'My Heart:** Fred Fisher(m); Alfred Bryan(w); in *Zieg Follies of 1913.*

**Pennies From Heaven:** Arthur Johnston(m); Johnny E ke(w); 1936; by Bing Crosby in movie of same name.

**Pretty Baby:** F. van Alstyne, Tony Jackson(m); Gus Kahn(m) 1916; by Dolly Hackett in musical *The Passing Show.*

**A Pretty Girl Is Like a Melody:** Irving Berlin(m,w); in *Zieg Follies of 1919;* became Follies theme song.

**Put On Your Old Gray Bonnet:** Percy Wenrich(m); Star Murphy(w); 1909.

**Put Your Arms Around Me, Honey:** Albert von Tilzer( Junie McCree(w); 1910; vaudeville.

**Rudolph, the Red-Nosed Reindeer:** Johnny Marks(m 1949; by Gene Autry on Columbia record.

**School Days:** Gus Edwards(m); Will D. Cobb(w); 19 vaudeville.

**September Song:** Kurt Weill(m); Maxwell Anderson(w); 19 by Walter Huston in play *Knickerbocker Holiday.*

**Shine On Harvest Moon:** Nora Bayes, Jack Norworth( Norworth(w); introduced by Nora Bayes in *Ziegfeld Follies* 1908.

**Sidewalks of New York:** J. W. Blake, C. B. Lawlor(m 1894; by Lottie Gilson at Old London Theatre on the Bowery.

**Singing in the Rain:** Nacio Herb Brown(m); Arthur Freed 1929; by Cliff Edwards in movie *Hollywood Revue of 1929.*

**Smoke Gets in Your Eyes:** Jerome Kern(m); Otto F bach(w); 1933; by Tamara in musical *Roberta.*

**Somebody Loves Me:** G. Gershwin(m); B. DeSylva, B. M Donald(w); 1929; *George White's Scandals of 1924.*

**Some Enchanted Evening:** R. Rodgers(m); O. Hammers II(w); 1949; by Ezio Pinza in *South Pacific.*

**Stardust:** Hoagy Carmichael(m); Michell Parish(w); 1929.

**Stormy Weather:** Harold Arlen(m); Ted Koehler(w); 19 popularized by Ethel Waters.

**Strike Up the Band:** George Gershwin(m); Ira Gershwin 1930; in musical of the same name.

**Summertime:** George Gershwin(m); DuBose Heyward 1935; by Abbie Mitchell opening *Porgy and Bess.*

**Sweet Georgia Brown:** Ben Bernie, M. Pinkard, K. sey(m,w); 1925.

**Sweethearts:** Victor Herbert(m); R. B. Smith(w); 1913; in sical of the same name.

**Take Me Out to the Ball Game:** Albert von Tilzer(m); J Norworth(w); 1908; vaudeville.

**Tea for Two:** Vincent Youmans(m); Irving Ceasar(w); 19 by Louise Groody, John Barker, in *No, No, Nanette.*

**Tennessee Waltz:** Redd Stewart, Pee Wee King(m,w); 19 popularized by Patti Page.

**Thanks for the Memory:** R. Rainger(m); Leo Robin(w); 19 by Bob Hope in his debut film, *The Big Broadcast of 1938.*

**That Old Black Magic:** Harold Arlen(m); Johnny Mercer 1942; in movie *Star Spangled Rhythm.*

**There's a Long, Long Trail:** Z. Elliott(m); Stoddard King 1913; written for their Yale frat, became popular at end of W War I.

**Three Little Words:** Harry Ruby(m); Bert Kalmar(w); 19 by Bing Crosby in Amos & Andy movie *Check and Do Check.*

**Toot, Toot, Tootsie, Goodbye:** Dan Russo(m); Gus Ka Ernie Erdman(w); 1922; by Jolson in *Bombo;* later in first tai *The Jazz Singer.*

**When Irish Eyes Are Smiling:** Ernest R. Ball(m); C. Olc G. Graff(w); 1912; by Olcott in musical *Isle of Dreams.*

**When Johnny Comes Marching Home:** Louis L bert(m,w); 1863; Lambert believed to be a pen-name for Pat S. Gilmore.

**When You're Smiling:** M. Fisher, J. Goodwin, L. Shay(m 1928.

**When You Wish Upon A Star:** Leigh Harline(m); Ned V shington(w); 1940; by Cliff Edwards in animated *Pinocchio.*

**When You Wore a Tulip:** Percy Wenrich(m); Jack Ma ney(w); 1914; vaudeville.

**Whispering:** John Schonberger, Vincent Rose(m); Rich Coburn(w); 1920; introduced by Paul Whiteman.

**White Christmas:** Irving Berlin(m,w); 1942; by Bing Crosby *ie Holiday Inn.*

**ith a Song in My Heart:** R. Rodgers(m); Lorenz Hart(w); **?**; in musical *Spring Is Here.*

**ithout a Song:** Vincent Youmans(m); Billy Rose, E. Elis-**?**); 1929; in musical *Great Day.*

**ellow Rose of Texas:** nothing is known of the songwriter initials "J. K."; 1853; minstrel show.

**es, Sir, That's My Baby:** Walter Donaldson(m); Gus

Kahn(w); 1925; popularized by Eddie Cantor.

**You and the Night and the Music:** Arthur Schwartz(m); Howard Dietz(w); 1934; in musical play *Revenge With Music.*

**You Are My Sunshine:** Jimmie Davis(m); C. Mitchell(w); 1940; in Tex Ritter movie *Take Me Back to Oklahoma.* Davis governor of Louisiana, 1944-48.

**You Made Me Love You:** J. V. Monaco(m); Joe McCarthy(w); 1913; by Al Jolson in musical *Honeymoon Express.*

---

# Entertainment Personalities — Where and When Born

### Actors, Actresses, Dancers, Musicians, Producers, Radio-TV Performers, Singers

| e | Birthplace | Born | Name | Birthplace | Born |
|---|---|---|---|---|---|
| ott, George | Forestville, N.Y. | 6/25/87 | Astaire, Fred | Omaha, Neb. | 5/10/99 |
| , Walter | St. Paul, Minn. | 6/6/98 | Astin, John | Baltimore, Md. | 3/30/30 |
| ermann, Bettye | Cottageville, S.C. | 2/28/28 | Astor, Mary | Quincy, Ill. | 5/3/06 |
| f, Roy | Maynardsville, Tenn. | 9/15/03 | Atkins, Chet | Luttrell, Tenn. | 6/20/24 |
| ns, Don | New York, N.Y. | 4/19/27 | Attenborough, Richard | Cambridge, England | 8/29/23 |
| ns, Edie | Kingston, Pa. | 4/16/29 | Aumont, Jean-Pierre | Paris, France | 1/5/13 |
| ns, Joey | New York, N.Y. | 1/6/11 | Autry, Gene | Tioga, Tex. | 9/29/07 |
| ns, Julie | Waterloo, Ia. | 1926 | Avalon, Frankie | Philadelphia, Pa. | 9/8/40 |
| ams, Dawn | Suffolk, England | 9/21/30 | Ayres, Lew | Minneapolis, Minn. | 12/28/08 |
| ir, Larry | Baltimore, Md. | 2/10/14 | Aznavour, Charles | Paris, France | 5/22/24 |
| ir, Luther | New York, N.Y. | 5/4/03 | | | |
| r, John | Chicago, Ill. | 1/31/21 | | | |
| rne, Brian | Worcestershire, England. | 5/2/02 | Bacall, Lauren | New York, N.Y. | 9/16/24 |
| ee, Anouk | Paris, France | 1932 | Backus, Jim | Cleveland, Oh. | 2/25/13 |
| s, Claude | Bedford, Ind. | 1918 | Baddeley, Hermione | Shropshire, England | 1906 |
| anese, Licia | Bari, Italy | 7/22/13 | Baer, Max Jr. | Oakland, Cal. | 1937 |
| orghetti, Anna Maria. | Pesaro, Italy | 5/15/36 | Baez, Joan | Staten Island, N.Y. | 1/9/41 |
| irt, Eddie | Rock Island, Ill. | 4/22/08 | Bailey, Pearl | Newport News, Va. | 3/29/18 |
| irt, Edward | Los Angeles, Cal. | 2/20/51 | Bailey, Raymond | San Francisco, Cal. | 1904 |
| ertson, Jack | Malden, Mass. | 6/16/10 | Bain, Barbara | Chicago, Ill. | 1934 |
| ight, Lola | Akron, Oh. | 7/20/25 | Bain, Conrad | Lethbridge, Alta. | 2/4/23 |
| a, Alan | New York, N.Y. | 1/28/36 | Baird, Bil | Grand Island, Neb. | 8/15/04 |
| a, Robert | New York, N.Y. | 2/26/14 | Baker, Carroll | Johnstown, Pa. | 5/28/31 |
| xander, Jane | Boston, Mass. | 10/28/39 | Baker, Diane | Hollywood, Cal. | 1938 |
| xander, Katherine | Arkansas | 1901 | Baker, Kenny | Monrovia, Cal. | 9/30/12 |
| n, Elizabeth | England | 1920 | Baker, Stanley | Glamorgan, Wales | 2/28/28 |
| ritton, Louise | Oklahoma City, Okla. | 1920 | Bakewell, William | Hollywood, Cal. | 1908 |
| n, Mel | Birmingham, Ala. | 2/14/13 | Balanchine, George | St. Petersburg, Russia | 1/9/04 |
| n, Steve | New York, N.Y. | 12/26/21 | Ball, Lucille | Jamestown, N.Y. | 8/6/11 |
| n, Woody | Brooklyn, N.Y. | 12/1/35 | Ballard, Kaye | Cleveland, Oh. | 11/20/26 |
| on, Fran | LaPorte City, Ia. | — | Balsam, Martin | New York, N.Y. | 11/4/19 |
| rson, June | Lucerne, N.Y. | 10/7/23 | Bampton, Rose | Cleveland, Oh. | 1909 |
| ert, Herb | Los Angeles, Cal. | 3/31/35 | Bancroft, Anne | New York, N.Y. | 9/17/31 |
| xian, Robert | Kansas City, Mo. | 2/20/25 | Bannon, Ian | Airdrie, Scotland | 1928 |
| oche, Don | Kenosha, Wis. | 5/31/08 | Barber, Red | Columbus, Miss. | 2/17/08 |
| es, Ed | Boston, Mass. | 1929 | Bardot, Brigitte | Paris, France | 1934 |
| es, Leon | Portland, Ind. | 1/20/03 | Bari, Lynn | Roanoke, Va. | 1917 |
| es, Nancy | Washington, D.C. | 1937 | Barrault, Jean-Louis | Le Vesinet, France | 1919 |
| os (F.F. Gosden). | Richmond, Va. | 5/5/99 | Barrie, Mona | London, England | 12/18/09 |
| es, John | Newark, N.J. | — | Barris, Chuck | Philadelphia, Pa. | 6/3/29 |
| sterdam, Morey | Chicago, Ill. | 12/14/14 | Barry, Gene | New York, N.Y. | 6/4/22 |
| erson, Ian | Scotland | 8/10/47 | Barry, Jack | Lindenhurst, N.Y. | 3/20/18 |
| erson, Judith | Adelaide, Australia | 2/10/98 | Barrymore, John Jr. | Beverly Hills, Cal. | 6/4/32 |
| erson, Lynn | Grand Forks, N.D. | 9/26/47 | Bartholomew, Freddie | London, England | 3/28/24 |
| erson, Marian | Philadelphia, Pa. | 2/17/02 | Bartok, Eva | Budapest, Hungary | 1929 |
| erson, Mary | Birmingham, Ala. | 1922 | Baryshnikov, Mikhail | Riga, Latvia | 1/27/48 |
| erson, Melissa Sue | Berkeley, Cal. | 9/26/62 | Basehart, Richard | Zanesville, Oh. | 8/31/14 |
| erson, Michael Jr. | London, England | 1943 | Basie, Count (Wm.) | Red Bank, N.J. | 8/21/04 |
| erson, Richard | Long Branch, N.J. | 8/8/26 | Bassey, Shirley | Cardiff, Wales | 1937 |
| ersson, Bibi | Stockholm, Sweden | 11/11/35 | Bates, Alan | Allestree, England | 2/17/34 |
| ress, Ursula | Switzerland | 1936 | Baum, Kurt | Cologne, Germany | 1908 |
| rews, Dana | Collins, Miss. | 1909 | Bavier, Frances | New York, N.Y. | 1905 |
| rews, Edward | Griffin, Ga. | 10/9/15 | Baxter, Anne | Michigan City, Ind. | 5/7/23 |
| rews, Julie | Walton, England | 10/1/35 | Beal, John | Joplin, Mo. | 8/13/09 |
| rews, Maxene | Minneapolis, Minn. | 1918 | Bean, Orson | Burlington, Vt. | 7/22/28 |
| rews, Patty | Minneapolis, Minn. | 1920 | Beatty, Robert | Hamilton, Ont. | 10/19/09 |
| gel, Heather | Oxford, England | 2/9/09 | Beatty, Warren | Richmond, Va. | 3/30/38 |
| a, Paul | Ottawa, Ont. | 7/30/41 | Becker, Sandy | New York, N.Y. | 1922 |
| -Margret | Stockholm, Sweden | 4/28/41 | Bedelia, Bonnie | New York, N.Y. | 1948 |
| abella | Paris, France | 1912 | Bee Gees | | |
| ara, Michael | Lowell, Mass. | 1927 | Gibb, Barry | Manchester, England. | 1946 |
| en, Eve | Mill Valley, Cal. | 4/30/12 | Gibb, Robin | " " | 1949 |
| n, Alan | New York, N.Y. | 3/26/34 | Gibb, Maurice | " " | 1949 |
| az, Desi | Santiago, Cuba | 3/2/17 | Beery, Noah Jr. | New York, N.Y. | 8/10/16 |
| az, Desi Jr. | Los Angeles, Cal. | 1953 | Belafonte, Harry | New York, N.Y. | 3/1/27 |
| az, Lucie | Hollywood, Cal. | 1951 | Bel Geddes, Barbara | New York, N.Y. | 10/31/22 |
| ess, James | Minneapolis, Minn. | 5/26/23 | Bellamy, Ralph | Chicago, Ill. | 6/17/04 |
| old, Eddy | Henderson, Tenn. | 5/15/18 | Belmondo, Jean-Paul | Neuilly-sur-Seine, France | 4/9/33 |
| au, Claudio | Chillau, Chile | 1903 | Benjamin, Richard | New York, N.Y. | 5/22/38 |
| oyo, Martina | New York, N.Y. | 1937 | Bennett, Joan | Palisades, N.J. | 2/27/10 |
| ur, Beatrice | New York, N.Y. | 5/13/26 | Bennett, Michael | Buffalo, N.Y. | 4/8/43 |
| ur, Jean | New York, N.Y. | 10/17/08 | Bennett, Tony | Astoria, N.Y. | 8/3/26 |
| ley, Elizabeth | Ocala, Fla. | 8/30/39 | Benson, Robby | Dallas, Tex. | 1957 |
| er, Edward | Kansas City, Kan. | 11/15/29 | Bentley, John | Warwickshire, England. | 12/2/16 |

| Name | Birthplace | Born |
|---|---|---|
| Bergen, Candice | Beverly Hills, Cal. | 5/9/46 |
| Bergen, Edgar | Chicago, Ill. | 2/16/03 |
| Bergen, Polly | Knoxville, Tenn. | 7/14/30 |
| Berger, Senta | Vienna, Austria | 1941 |
| Bergerac, Jacques | Biarritz, France | 5/26/27 |
| Bergman, Ingmar | Uppsala, Sweden | 7/14/18 |
| Bergman, Ingrid | Stockholm, Sweden | 8/29/15 |
| Bergner, Elisabeth | Vienna, Austria | 1900 |
| Berle, Milton | New York, N.Y. | 7/12/08 |
| Berlinger, Warren | Brooklyn, N.Y. | 8/31/37 |
| Berman, Shelley | Chicago, Ill. | 2/3/26 |
| Bernardi, Herschel | New York, N.Y. | 1923 |
| Bernstein, Elmer | New York, N.Y. | 4/4/22 |
| Bernstein, Leonard | Lawrence, Mass. | 8/25/18 |
| Berry, Chuck | St. Louis, Mo. | 10/18/26 |
| Berry, Ken | Moline, Ill. | — |
| Bessell, Ted | Flushing, N.Y. | 1936 |
| Bikel, Theodore | Vienna, Austria | 5/2/24 |
| Birney, David | Washington, D.C. | 1940 |
| Bishop, Joey | Bronx, N.Y. | 2/3/18 |
| Bisoglio, Val | New York, N.Y. | 5/7/26 |
| Bisset, Jacqueline | Weybridge, England | 9/13/46 |
| Bixby, Bill | San Francisco, Cal. | 1/22/34 |
| Black, Karen | Park Ridge, Ill. | 7/1/42 |
| Blaine, Vivian | Newark, N.J. | 11/21/24 |
| Blair, Janet | Altoona, Pa. | 4/23/21 |
| Blair, Linda | Westport, Conn. | 1959 |
| Blake, Amanda | Buffalo, N.Y. | 2/20/31 |
| Blake, Robert | Nutley, N.J. | 9/18/38 |
| Blakeley, Ronee | Idaho | 1946 |
| Blakely, Susan | Germany | — |
| Blanc, Mel | San Francisco, Cal. | 5/30/08 |
| Bloch, Ray | Alsace-Lorraine | 1902 |
| Blondell, Joan | New York, N.Y. | 8/30/12 |
| Bloom, Claire | London, England | 2/15/31 |
| Blyth, Ann | Mt. Kisco, N.Y. | 8/16/28 |
| Bohm, Karl | Graz, Austria | 8/28/94 |
| Bogarde, Dirk | London, England | 3/28/21 |
| Bogdanovich, Peter | Kingston, N.Y. | 7/30/39 |
| Bolger, Ray | Boston, Mass. | 11/10/04 |
| Bondi, Beulah | Chicago, Ill. | 5/3/82 |
| Bono, Sonny | Detroit, Mich. | 2/16/40 |
| Boone, Pat | Jacksonville, Fla. | 6/1/34 |
| Boone, Richard | Los Angeles, Cal. | 6/18/17 |
| Booth, Shirley | New York, N.Y. | 8/30/09 |
| Borge, Victor | Copenhagen, Denmark | 1/30/09 |
| Borgnine, Ernest | Hamden, Conn. | 1/24/17 |
| Bosley, Tom | Chicago, Ill. | 10/1/27 |
| Bottoms, Timothy | Santa Barbara, Cal. | 1951 |
| Bowie, David | London, England | 1947 |
| Bowman, Lee | Cincinnati, Oh. | 12/28/14 |
| Boyer, Charles | Figeac, France | 8/28/99 |
| Boyle, Peter | Philadelphia, Pa. | 1933 |
| Bracken, Eddie | Astoria, N.Y. | 2/7/20 |
| Brand, Neville | Kewanee, Ill. | 8/13/21 |
| Brando, Marlon | Omaha, Neb. | 4/3/24 |
| Brasselle, Keefe | Elyria, Oh. | 2/7/23 |
| Brazzi, Rossano | Bologna, Italy | 9/18/16 |
| Brennan, Eileen | Los Angeles, Cal. | 1937 |
| Brenner, David | Philadelphia, Pa. | 1945 |
| Brent, George | Dublin, Ireland. | 3/15/04 |
| Brewer, Teresa | Toledo, Oh. | 5/7/31 |
| Brian, David | New York, N.Y. | 8/5/14 |
| Bridges, Beau | Hollywood, Cal. | 12/9/41 |
| Bridges, Jeff | Los Angeles, Cal. | 1950 |
| Bridges, Lloyd | San Leandro, Cal. | 1/15/13 |
| Britton, Barbara | Long Beach, Cal. | 1923 |
| Brolin, James | Los Angeles, Cal. | 1942 |
| Bronson, Charles | Scooptown, Pa. | 11/3/21 |
| Brooks, Louise | Cherryvale, Kan. | 1906 |
| Brooks, Mel | New York, N.Y. | 1926 |
| Brooks, Stephen | Columbus, Oh. | 1942 |
| Brown, James | Augusta, Ga. | 5/3/33 |
| Brown, Jimmy | St. Simons Island, Ga. | 2/17/36 |
| Brown, Les | Reinerton, Pa. | 1912 |
| Brown, Tom | New York, N.Y. | 1/6/13 |
| Brown, Vanessa | Vienna, Austria | 1928 |
| Bruce, Carol | Great Neck, N.Y. | 1919 |
| Bruce, Virginia | Minneapolis, Minn. | 1910 |
| Bryant, Anita | Barnsdale, Okla. | 3/25/40 |
| Brynner, Yul | Sakhalin, Japan | 7/11/20 |
| Bubbles, John | Louisville, Ky. | 1903 |
| Buchanan, Edgar | Humansville, Mo. | 1903 |
| Bucholz, Horst | Berlin, Germany | 12/4/33 |
| Bujold, Genevieve | Montreal, Que. | 7/1/42 |
| Buono, Victor | Los Angeles, Cal. | 1938 |
| Burghoff, Gary | Bristol, Conn. | 8/6/— |
| Burke, Paul | New Orleans, La. | 7/21/26 |

| Name | Birthplace | B |
|---|---|---|
| Burnett, Carol | San Antonio, Tex. | 4/2 |
| Burns, George | New York, N.Y. | 1/2 |
| Burr, Raymond | New Westminster, B.C. | 5/21 |
| Burstyn, Ellen | Detroit, Mich. | 12/7 |
| Burton, Richard | South Wales | 11/1 |
| Bushell, Anthony | Kent, England | |
| Buttons, Red | New York, N.Y. | 2/5 |
| Buzzi, Ruth | Wequetequock, Conn. | 7/24 |
| Caan, James | New York, N.Y. | 3/26 |
| Caesar, Sid | Yonkers, N.Y. | 9/18 |
| Cagney, James | New York, N.Y. | 7/17 |
| Caine, Michael | London, England | 3/14 |
| Caldwell, Sarah | Maryville, Mo. | |
| Caldwell, Zoe | Melbourne, Australia | 9/14 |
| Calhoun, Rory | Los Angeles, Cal. | 8/8 |
| Callan, Michael | Philadelphia, Pa. | |
| Callas, Charlie | Brooklyn, N.Y. | 12/ |
| Calloway, Cab | Rochester, N.Y. | 12/25 |
| Calvert, Phyllis | London, England | 2/18 |
| Calvet, Corinne | Paris, France | 4/30 |
| Cameron, Rod | Calgary, Canada | 12/7 |
| Campbell, Glen | Billstown, Ark. | 4/22 |
| Canary, David | Elwood, Ind. | |
| Cannon, Dyan | Tacoma, Wash. | 1/4 |
| Canova, Judy | Starke, Fla. | 11/20 |
| Cantinflas | Mexico City, Mex. | |
| Cantrell, Lana | Sydney, Australia | 8/7 |
| Capra, Frank | Palermo, Italy | 5/18 |
| Cardinale, Claudia | Tunisia | |
| Carey, Macdonald | Sioux City, Ia. | 3/15 |
| Carey, Phil | Hackensack, N.J. | 7/15 |
| Carle, Frankie | Providence, R.I. | 1 |
| Carlisle, Kitty | New Orleans, La | 1 |
| Carmichael, Hoagy | Bloomington, Ind | 11/22 |
| Carmichael, Ian | Hull, England | 6/18 |
| Carne, Judy | Northampton, England | 1 |
| Carney, Art | Mt. Vernon, N.Y. | 11/4 |
| Carnovsky, Morris | St. Louis, Mo. | 9/5 |
| Caron, Leslie | Boulogne, France | 7/1 |
| Carpenter, Karen | New Haven, Conn. | 3/2 |
| Carpenter, Richard | New Haven, Conn. | 10/15 |
| Carr, Vikki | El Paso, Tex. | 7/19 |
| Carradine, David | Hollywood, Cal. | 1 |
| Carradine, John | New York, N.Y. | 2/5 |
| Carradine, Keith | San Mateo, Cal. | 1 |
| Carroll, Diahann | Bronx, N.Y. | 7/17 |
| Carroll, Madeleine | W. Bromwich, England. | 2/26 |
| Carroll, Pat | Shreveport, La. | 5/5 |
| Carson, Johnny | Corning, Ia. | 10/29 |
| Carter, Jack | New York, N.Y. | 6/24 |
| Carter, June | Maces Spring, Va. | 6/23 |
| Carter, Lynda | Phoenix, Ariz. | |
| Casadesus, Gaby | Marseilles, France | 1 |
| Cash, Johnny | Kingsland, Ark. | 2/26 |
| Cass, Peggy | Boston, Mass. | 5/21 |
| Cassavetes, John | New York, N.Y. | 12/9 |
| Cassidy, David | New York, N.Y. | 4/12 |
| Cassidy, Ted | Pittsburgh, Pa. | 1 |
| Castellano, Richard | New York, N.Y. | 9/3 |
| Caulfield, Joan | West Orange, N.J. | 6/1 |
| Cavallaro, Carmen | New York, N.Y. | |
| Cavett, Dick | Gibbon, Neb. | 11/19 |
| Chamberlain, Richard | Beverly Hills, Cal. | 3/31 |
| Champion, Gower | Geneva, Ill. | 6/22 |
| Champion, Marge | Los Angeles, Cal. | 9/2 |
| Channing, Carol | Seattle, Wash. | 1/31 |
| Chaplin, Geraldine | Santa Monica, Cal. | 1 |
| Chaplin, Sydney | Beverly Hills, Cal. | 3/31 |
| Charisse, Cyd | Amarillo, Tex. | 3/8 |
| Charles, Ray | Albany, Ga. | 9/23 |
| Chase, Chevy | New York, N.Y. | 1 |
| Checker, Chubby | Philadelphia, Pa. | 10/3 |
| Cher | El Centro, Cal. | 5/20 |
| Christian, Linda | Tampico, Mexico | 11/13 |
| Christie, Audrey | Chicago, Ill. | 1 |
| Christie, Julie | Chukur, India | 4/14 |
| Christopher, Jordon | Youngstown, Oh. | 1 |
| Christy, June | Springfield, Ill. | 1 |
| Cilento, Diane | Queensland, Australia | 1 |
| Claire, Ina | Washington, D.C. | 1 |
| Clapton, Eric | Surrey, England. | 3/30 |
| Clark, Dane | New York, N.Y. | 2/18 |
| Clark, Dick | Mt. Vernon, N.Y. | 11/30 |
| Clark, Petula | Ewell, Surrey, England. | 11/15 |
| Clark, Roy | Meherrin, Va. | 4/15 |
| Clayton, Jan | Tularosa, N.M. | 1 |
| Cliburn, Van | Shreveport, La. | 7/12 |

| Name | Birthplace | Born | Name | Birthplace | Born |
|---|---|---|---|---|---|
| oney, Rosemary | Maysville, Ky. | 5/23/28 | Davidson, John | Pittsburgh, Pa. | 1941 |
| urn, James | Laurel, Neb. | 8/31/28 | Davis, Ann B. | Schenectady, N.Y. | 5/5/26 |
| a, Imogene | Philadelphia, Pa. | 11/18/08 | Davis, Bette | Lowell, Mass. | 4/5/08 |
| o, James | New York, N.Y. | 3/21/30 | Davis, Clifton | Chicago, Ill. | 1945 |
| en, Myron | Grodno, Poland | 1902 | Davis, Mac | Lubbock, Tex. | 1942 |
| ert, Claudette | Paris, France | 9/18/07 | Davis, Ossie | Cogdell, Ga. | 12/18/17 |
| e, Dennis | Detroit, Mich. | 1943 | Davis, Sammy Jr. | New York, N.Y. | 12/8/25 |
| e, Michael | Madison, Wis. | 1945 | Dawn, Hazel | Ogden, Ut. | 1898 |
| e, Tina | Hollywood, Cal. | 1943 | Dawson, Richard | Hampshire, England | 11/20/- |
| ins, Dorothy | Windsor, Ont. | 11/18/26 | Day, Dennis | New York, N.Y. | 1917 |
| ins, Joan | London, England | 5/23/33 | Day, Doris | Cincinnati, Oh. | 4/3/24 |
| ins, Judy | Seattle, Wash. | 5/1/39 | Day, Laraine | Roosevelt, Ut. | 10/13/20 |
| onna, Jerry | Boston, Mass. | 1903 | Dean, James | Plainview, Tex. | 8/10/28 |
| nden Betty | Brooklyn, N.Y. | 5/3/19 | De Camp, Rosemary | Prescott, Ariz. | 1913 |
| no, Perry | Canonsburg, Pa. | 5/18/12 | DeCarlo, Yvonne | Vancouver, B.C. | 9/1/24 |
| nner, Nadine | Compton, Cal. | 1913 | Dee, Frances | Los Angeles, Cal. | 1907 |
| nnery, Sean | Edinburgh, Scotland | 8/25/30 | Dee, Joey | Passaic, N.J. | 1940 |
| nniff, Ray | Attleboro, Mass. | 11/6/16 | Dee, Ruby | Cleveland, Oh. | 10/27/24 |
| nnors, Chuck | Brooklyn, N.Y. | 4/10/21 | Dee, Sandra | Bayonne, N.J. | 4/23/42 |
| nnors, Michael | Fresno, Cal. | 8/15/25 | Defore, Don | Cedar Rapids, Ia. | 8/25/17 |
| nrad, Robert | Chicago, Ill. | 3/1/35 | DeHaven, Gloria | Los Angeles, Cal. | 1925 |
| nrad, William | Louisville, Ky. | 9/27/20 | de Havilland, Olivia | Tokyo, Japan | 7/1/16 |
| nried, Hans | Baltimore, Md. | 4/15/17 | De Niro, Robert | New York, N.Y. | 1945 |
| nstantine, Michael | Reading, Pa. | 5/22/27 | Del Rio, Dolores | Durango, Mexico | 8/3/08 |
| nverse, Frank | St. Louis, Mo. | 1938 | Dell, Gabriel | Brooklyn, N.Y. | 1921 |
| nway, Gary | Boston, Mass. | 1938 | Della Chiesa, Vivienne | Chicago, Ill. | 1920 |
| nway, Shirl | Franklinville, N.Y. | 6/13/16 | Delon, Alain | France | 11/8/35 |
| nway, Tim | Willoughby, Oh. | 12/15/33 | DeLuise, Dom | Brooklyn, N.Y. | 8/1/33 |
| ogan, Jackie | Los Angeles, Cal. | 10/26/14 | Demarest, William | St. Paul, Minn. | 2/27/92 |
| ok, Barbara | Atlanta, Ga. | 10/25/27 | De Mille, Agnes | New York, N.Y. | 1905 |
| oke, Alistair | England | 11/20/08 | Dempster, Carol | Duluth, Minn. | 1901 |
| oper, Alice | Detroit, Mich. | 2/4/48 | Deneuve, Catherine | Paris, France | 10/22/43 |
| oper, Jackie | Los Angeles, Cal. | 9/15/22 | Denning, Richard | Poughkeepsie, N.Y. | 1914 |
| oppola, Francis Ford | Detroit, Mich. | 4/7/39 | Dennis, Sandy | Hastings, Neb. | 4/27/37 |
| rby, Ellen | Racine, Wis. | 1913 | Denver, Bob | New Rochelle, N.Y. | 1935 |
| rey, Jeff | New York, N.Y. | 8/10/14 | Denver, John | Roswell, N.M. | 12/31/43 |
| sby, Bill | Philadelphia, Pa. | 7/12/37 | Derek, John | Hollywood, Cal. | 1926 |
| stello, Dolores | Pittsburgh, Pa. | 1905 | Dern, Bruce | Chicago, Ill. | 6/4/36 |
| tsworth, Staats | Oak Park, Ill. | 2/17/08 | Desmond, Johnny | Detroit, Mich. | 11/14/21 |
| tten, Joseph | Petersburg, Va. | 1905 | Devane, William | Albany, N.Y. | 1937 |
| urtenay, Tom | Hull, England | 2/25/37 | Dewhurst, Colleen | Montreal, Que. | 6/3/26 |
| abbe, Buster | Oakland, Cal. | 2/07/08 | DeWitt, Joyce | Wheeling, W.Va. | 4/23/- |
| ain, Jeanne | Barstow, Cal. | 5/25/25 | Dey, Susan. | Pekin, Ill. | 12/10/52 |
| awford, Broderick. | Philadelphia, Pa. | 12/9/11 | Diamond, Neil | Brooklyn, N.Y. | 1/24/41 |
| awford, Michael | Salisbury, England | 1942 | Dickinson, Angie | Kulm, N.D. | 9/30/36 |
| enna, Richard | Los Angeles, Cal. | 11/30/27 | Dierkop, Charles. | La Crosse, Wis. | 9/11/36 |
| stal, Linda | Argentina | 1936 | Dietrich, Marlene | Berlin, Germany | 1901 |
| onyn, Hume | London, Ont. | 7/18/11 | Diller, Phyllis | Lima, Oh. | 7/17/17 |
| osby, Bob | Spokane, Wash. | 8/23/13 | Dillman, Bradford | San Francisco, Cal. | 4/14/30 |
| osby, David | Los Angeles, Cal. | 8/14/41 | Dixon, Ivan | New York, N.Y. | 4/6/31 |
| owley, Pat | Scranton, Pa. | 1929 | Domingo, Placido | Madrid, Spain | 1/21/41 |
| uz, Brandon | Bakersfield, Cal. | 1962 | Domino, Fats. | New Orleans, La. | 2/26/28 |
| ystal, Billy | New York, N.Y. | 1947 | Donahue, Troy | New York, N.Y. | 1/27/36 |
| gat, Xavier | Barcelona, Spain | 1/1/00 | Donald, James | Aberdeen, Scotland | 5/18/17 |
| llen, Bill | Pittsburgh, Pa. | 2/18/20 | Donald, Peter | Bristol, England | 1918 |
| llum, John | Knoxville, Tenn. | 1930 | Donnelly, Ruth | Trenton, N.J. | 1896 |
| lp, Robert | Oakland, Cal. | 8/16/30 | Donovan | Glasgow, Scotland | 5/10/46 |
| mmings, Constance | Seattle, Wash. | 5/15/10 | Dors, Diana | Swindon, England | 10/23/31 |
| mmings, Robert | Joplin, Mo. | 6/9/10 | d'Orsay, Fifi | Montreal, Que. | 1908 |
| rtin, Phyllis | Clarksburg, W.Va. | 1930 | Douglas, Donna | Baywood, La. | 1939 |
| rtis, Ken | Lamar, Col. | 1916 | Douglas, Kirk | Amsterdam, N.Y. | 12/9/18 |
| rtis, Tony | New York, N.Y. | 6/3/25 | Douglas, Melvyn | Macon, Ga. | 4/5/01 |
| sack, Cyril. | Durban, S. Africa | 11/26/10 | Douglas, Michael | New Brunswick, N.J. | 1945 |
| shing, Peter | Surrey, England. | 5/26/13 | Douglas, Mike | Chicago, Ill. | 8/11/25 |
| | | | Downey, Morton | Wallingford, Conn. | 11/14/01 |
| gmar (Egnor) | Huntington, W.Va. | 1926 | Downs, Hugh | Akron, Oh. | 2/14/21 |
| hl, Arlene | Minneapolis, Minn. | 8/11/27 | Dragonette, Jessica | Calcutta, India. | — |
| iley, Dan | New York, N.Y. | 12/14/17 | Drake, Alfred. | Bronx, N.Y. | 10/7/14 |
| lrymple, Jean | Morristown, N.J. | 9/2/10 | Drake, Betsy | Paris, France | 1923 |
| lton, Abby | Las Vegas, Nev. | 1935 | Drew, Ellen | Kansas City, Mo. | 11/23/15 |
| ly, James | Wisconsin Rapids, Wis. | 10/23/18 | Dreyfuss, Richard | Brooklyn, N.Y. | 1947 |
| ly, John | Johannesburg, S. Africa | 2/20/14 | Dru, Joanne | Logan, W.Va. | 1/31/23 |
| mita, Lili | Paris, France | 1907 | Drury, James | New York, N.Y. | 1934 |
| mone, Vic | Brooklyn, N.Y. | 6/12/28 | Duchin, Peter | New York, N.Y. | 7/28/37 |
| na, Bill | Quincy, Mass. | 1924 | Duff, Howard. | Bremerton, Wash. | 11/24/17 |
| ngerfield, Rodney | Babylon, N.Y. | 1921 | Duffy, Patrick | Townsend, Mont. | 3/17/49 |
| niels, William | Brooklyn, N.Y. | 3/31/27 | Dufour, Val | New Orleans, La. | 2/5/27 |
| nilova, Alexandra | Peterhof, Russia | 1907 | Duke, Patty | New York, N.Y. | 12/14/46 |
| nner, Blythe | Philadelphia, Pa. | — | Dullea, Keir | Cleveland, Oh. | 5/30/36 |
| nton, Ray | New York, N.Y. | 9/19/31 | Dunaway, Faye | Bascom, Fla. | 1/14/41 |
| arby, Kim | Hollywood, Cal. | 7/8/48 | Duncan, Sandy | Henderson, Tex. | 2/20/46 |
| arcel, Denise | Paris, France | 9/8/25 | Duncan, Todd | Danville, Ky. | 1900 |
| arren, James | Philadelphia, Pa. | 6/8/36 | Duncan, Vivian | Los Angeles, Cal. | 1902 |
| arrieux, Danielle | Bordeaux, France | 5/1/17 | Dunham, Katherine | Chicago, Ill. | 1910 |
| arrow, Henry | New York, N.Y. | 1933 | Dunne, Irene | Louisville, Ky. | 12/20/04 |
| a Silva, Howard | Cleveland, Oh. | 5/4/09 | Dunnock, Mildred | Baltimore, Md. | 1/25/06 |
| assin, Jules | Middletown, Conn. | 12/18/11 | Durante, Jimmy | New York, N.Y. | 2/10/93 |
| auphin, Claude | Corbeil, France | 8/19/05 | Durbin, Deanna | Winnipeg, Man. | 12/4/22 |

| Name | Birthplace | Born |
|---|---|---|
| Duvall, Robert | San Diego, Cal. | 1931 |
| Duvall, Shelly | Houston, Tex. | — |
| Dvorak, Ann | New York, N.Y. | 1912 |
| Dylan, Bob | Duluth, Minn. | 5/24/41 |
| Eastwood, Clint | San Francisco, Cal. | 5/31/30 |
| Eaton, Shirley | London, England | 1937 |
| Ebsen, Buddy | Belleville, Ill. | 4/2/08 |
| Eckstine, Billy | Pittsburgh, Pa. | 7/8/14 |
| Edelman, Herb | Brooklyn, N.Y. | 11/5/33 |
| Eden, Barbara | Tucson, Ariz. | 1934 |
| Edwards, Ralph | Merino, Col. | 1913 |
| Edwards, Vincent | Brooklyn, N.Y. | 7/7/28 |
| Egan, Richard | San Francisco, Cal. | 7/29/23 |
| Eggar, Samantha | London, England | 1940 |
| Ekberg, Anita | Malmo, Sweden | 9/29/31 |
| Ekland, Britt | Stockholm, Sweden | 1942 |
| Elam, Jack | Phoenix, Ariz. | — |
| Eldridge, Florence | Brooklyn, N.Y. | 1901 |
| Elgart, Larry | New London, Conn. | 1922 |
| Elgart, Les | New Haven, Conn. | 1918 |
| Elliott, Bob | Boston, Mass. | 1923 |
| Emerson, Faye | Elizabeth, La. | 1917 |
| Erickson, Leif | Alameda, Cal. | 10/27/11 |
| Esmond, Jill | London, England | 1908 |
| Etting, Ruth | David City, Neb. | 1896 |
| Evans, Dale | Uvalde, Tex. | 10/31/12 |
| Evans, Gene | Holbrook, Ariz. | 7/11/24 |
| Evans, Maurice | Dorchester, England | 6/3/01 |
| Evans, Robert | New York, N.Y. | 6/29/30 |
| Everett, Chad | South Bend, Ind. | 6/11/37 |
| Everly, Don | Brownie, Ky. | 2/1/37 |
| Everly, Phil | Brownie, Ky. | 1/19/38 |
| Evers, Jason | New York, N.Y. | 1/2/27 |
| Ewell, Tom | Owensboro, Ky. | 4/29/09 |
| Fabares, Shelley | Santa Monica, Cal. | 1944 |
| Fabian (Forte) | Philadelphia, Pa. | 2/6/43 |
| Fabray, Nanette | San Diego, Cal. | 10/27/20 |
| Fadiman, Clifton | Brooklyn, N.Y. | 5/15/04 |
| Fairbanks, Douglas Jr. | New York, N.Y. | 12/9/09 |
| Falk, Peter | New York, N.Y. | 9/16/27 |
| Farber, Barry | Baltimore, Md. | 1930 |
| Farentino, James | Brooklyn, N.Y. | 2/24/38 |
| Fargo, Donna | Mt. Airy, N.C. | 11/10/45 |
| Farrell, Charles | Onset Bay, Mass. | 8/9/01 |
| Farrell, Eileen | Willimantic, Conn. | 2/13/20 |
| Farrell, Mike | St. Paul, Minn. | 2/6/- |
| Farrow, Mia | Los Angeles, Cal. | 2/9/45 |
| Fawcett-Majors, Farrah. | Houston, Tex. | 2/2/47 |
| Faye, Alice | New York, N.Y. | 5/5/15 |
| Feld, Fritz | Berlin, Germany | 10/15/00 |
| Feldman, Marty | England | 1933 |
| Feldon, Barbara | Pittsburgh, Pa. | 3/12/41 |
| Feliciano, Jose | Puerto Rico | 9/10/45 |
| Fellini, Federico | Rimini, Italy | 1/20/20 |
| Fellows, Edith | Boston, Mass. | 1923 |
| Ferrer, Jose | Santurce, P.R. | 1/8/12 |
| Ferrer, Mel | Elberon, N.J. | 8/25/17 |
| Ferris, Barbara | London, England | 1942 |
| Fetchit, Stepin | Key West, Fla. | 1902 |
| Fiedler, Arthur | Boston, Mass. | 12/10/94 |
| Field, Sally | Pasadena, Cal. | 1946 |
| Fields, Gracie | Rochdale, England | 1/9/98 |
| Fields, Totie | Hartford, Conn. | 1931 |
| Finney, Albert | Salford, England | 5/9/36 |
| Firkusny, Rudolf | Napajedla, Czechoslovakia | 2/11/12 |
| Fisher, Carrie | Beverly Hills, Cal. | 1956 |
| Fisher, Eddie | Philadelphia, Pa. | 8/10/28 |
| Fisher, Gail | Orange, N.J. | — |
| Fitzgerald, Ella | Newport News, Va. | 4/25/18 |
| Fitzgerald, Geraldine | Dublin, Ireland | 11/24/14 |
| Fitzgerald, Pegeen | Norcatur, Kan. | 1910 |
| Fix, Paul | Dobbs Ferry, N.Y. | 3/13/02 |
| Flack, Roberta | Black Mountain, N.C. | 2/10/40 |
| Flatt, Lester | Overton County, Tenn. | 6/19/14 |
| Fleming, Rhonda | Hollywood, Cal. | 1923 |
| Fletcher, Louise | Birmingham, Ala. | 1935 |
| Foch, Nina | Leyden, Netherlands | 4/20/24 |
| Fonda, Henry | Grand Island, Neb. | 5/16/05 |
| Fonda, Jane | New York, N.Y. | 12/21/37 |
| Fonda, Peter | New York, N.Y. | 2/23/39 |
| Fontaine, Frank | Cambridge, Mass. | 1920 |
| Fontaine, Joan | Tokyo, Japan | 10/22/17 |
| Fontanne, Lynn | London, England | 1887 |
| Fonteyn, Margot | Reigate, England | 5/18/19 |
| Foran, Dick | Flemington, N.J. | 6/18/10 |

| Name | Birthplace | Bo |
|---|---|---|
| Forbes, Bryan | London, England | 7/22/ |
| Ford (Tenn.), Ernie | Bristol, Tenn. | 2/13/ |
| Ford, Glenn | Quebec, Canada | 5/1/ |
| Ford, Ruth | Hazelhurst, Miss. | 19 |
| Forrest, Steve | Huntsville, Tex. | 9/29/ |
| Forster, Robert | Rochester, N.Y. | 19 |
| Forsythe, John | Penns Grove, N.J. | 1/29/ |
| Fosse, Bob | Chicago, Ill. | 6/23/ |
| Foster, Jodie | Los Angeles, Cal. | 19 |
| Foster, Phil | Brooklyn, N.Y. | 3/29/ |
| Fox, James | London, England | 19 |
| Foxx, Redd | St. Louis, Mo. | 12/9/ |
| Foy, Eddie Jr. | New Rochelle, N.Y. | 2/4/ |
| Frampton, Peter | Kent, England | 4/22/ |
| Francescatti, Zino | Marseilles, France | 8/9/ |
| Franciosa, Anthony | New York, N.Y. | 10/25/ |
| Francis, Ann | Ossining, N.Y. | |
| Francis, Arlene | Boston, Mass. | 19 |
| Francis, Connie | Newark, N.J. | 12/12/ |
| Franciscus, James | Clayton, Mo. | 1/31/ |
| Frankenheimer, John | Malba, N.Y. | 2/19/ |
| Franklin, Aretha | Memphis, Tenn. | 3/25/ |
| Franklin, Bonnie | Santa Monica, Cal. | 1/ |
| Franklin, Joe | New York, N.Y. | 19 |
| Franz, Arthur | Perth Amboy, N.J. | 2/29/ |
| Freberg, Stan | Pasadena, Cal. | 8/7/ |
| Freed, Bert | New York, N.Y. | 11/3/ |
| Freeman, Mona | Baltimore, Md. | 19 |
| Froman, Jane | St. Louis, Mo. | 19 |
| Frost, David | Tenterden, England | 4/7/ |
| Frye, David | Brooklyn, N.Y. | 19 |
| Funicello, Annette | Utica, N.Y. | 19 |
| Funt, Allen | New York, N.Y. | 9/16/ |
| Furness, Betty | New York, N.Y. | 1/3/ |
| Gabel, Martin | Philadelphia, Pa. | 19 |
| Gabor, Eva | Hungary | 19 |
| Gabor, Zsa Zsa | Hungary | 19 |
| Gahagan, Helen | Boonton, N.J. | 19 |
| Galloway, Don | Brooksville, Ky. | 19 |
| Gam, Rita | Pittsburgh, Pa. | 19 |
| Gambling, John | New York, N.Y. | 19 |
| Garagiola, Joe | St. Louis, Mo. | 2/12/ |
| Garbo, Greta | Stockholm, Sweden | 9/18/ |
| Gardenia, Vincent | Naples, Italy | 1/7/ |
| Gardiner, Reginald | Wimbledon, England | 19 |
| Gardner, Ava | Smithfield, N.C. | 12/24/ |
| Garfunkel, Art | New York, N.Y. | 10/13/ |
| Gargan, William | Brooklyn, N.Y. | 7/17/ |
| Garland, Beverly | Santa Cruz, Cal. | 10/17/ |
| Garner, James | Norman, Okla. | 4/7/ |
| Garner, Peggy Ann | Canton, Oh. | 2/3/ |
| Garrett, Betty | St. Joseph, Mo. | 5/23/ |
| Garroway, Dave | Schenectady, N.Y. | 7/13/ |
| Garson, Greer | Co. Down, N. Ireland | 19 |
| Gary, John | Watertown, N.Y. | 11/29/ |
| Gavin, John | Los Angeles, Cal. | 4/8/ |
| Gaye, Marvin | Washington, D.C. | 4/2/ |
| Gaynor, Janet | Philadelphia, Pa. | 10/6/ |
| Gaynor, Mitzi | Chicago, Ill. | 9/4/ |
| Gazzara, Ben | New York, N.Y. | 8/28/ |
| Gedda, Nicolai | Sweden | 19 |
| Geeson, Judy | Sussex, England | 9/10/ |
| Gennaro, Peter | Metairie, La. | 19 |
| Gentry, Bobby | Chickasaw Co., Miss. | 7/27/ |
| Ghostley, Alice | Eve, Mo. | 19 |
| Gibb, Andy | Manchester, England | 3/5/ |
| Gibson, Henry | Germantown, Pa. | 19 |
| Gielgud, John | London, England | 4/14/ |
| Gilbert, Melissa | Los Angeles, Cal. | 5/8/ |
| Gilford, Jack | New York, N.Y. | 190 |
| Gillette, Anita | Baltimore, Md. | 193 |
| Gingold, Hermione | London, England | 12/9/ |
| Gish, Lillian | Springfield, Oh. | 10/14/ |
| Givot, George | Omaha, Neb. | 190 |
| Gleason, Jackie | Brooklyn, N.Y. | 2/26/ |
| Gobel, George | Chicago, Ill. | 5/20/ |
| Godard, Jean Luc | Paris, France | 193 |
| Goddard, Paulette | Great Neck, N.Y. | 6/3/ |
| Godfrey, Arthur | New York, N.Y. | 8/31/ |
| Goldsboro, Bobby | Marianne, Fla. | 1/18/ |
| Goodman, Benny | Chicago, Ill. | 5/30/ |
| Goodman, Dody | Columbus, Oh. | 192 |
| Gordon, Gale | New York, N.Y. | 2/2/ |
| Gordon, Max | New York, N.Y. | 189 |
| Gordon, Ruth | Wollaston, Mass. | 10/30/ |
| Gorin, Igor | Ukraine, Russia | 190 |
| Gorme, Eydie | Bronx, N.Y. | 193 |

| me | Birthplace | Born | Name | Birthplace | Born |
|---|---|---|---|---|---|
| shin, Frank | Pittsburgh, Pa. | 4/5/34 | Hayes, Isaac | Covington, Tenn. | 8/20/42 |
| tner, Marjoe | Long Beach, Cal. | 1945 | Hayes, Peter Lind | San Francisco, Cal. | 6/25/15 |
| den, Freeman | | | Haymes, Dick | Buenos Aires, Argentina | 1918 |
| (Amos) | Richmond, Va. | 5/5/99 | Haynes, Lloyd | South Bend, Ind. | 1934 |
| ld, Elliott | Brooklyn, N.Y. | 8/29/38 | Hayward, Louis | Johannesburg, S. Africa | 1909 |
| ld, Morton | Richmond Hill, N.Y. | 12/10/13 | Hayworth, Rita | New York, N.Y. | 10/17/18 |
| lding, Ray | Lowell, Mass. | 3/20/22 | Healy, Mary | New Orleans, La. | 4/14/18 |
| let, Robert | Lawrence, Mass. | 11/26/33 | Heatherton, Joey | Rockville Centre, N.Y. | 9/14/44 |
| vdy, Curt | Green River, Wyo. | 1919 | Heckart, Eileen | Columbus, Oh. | 3/29/19 |
| dy, Don | San Diego, Cal. | 1944 | Hefner, Hugh. | Chicago, Ill. | 4/9/26 |
| ham, Martha | Pittsburgh, Pa. | 5/11/94 | Heifetz, Jascha | Vilna, Russia | 2/2/01 |
| ham, Virginia | Chicago, Ill. | 7/4/12 | Helpmann, Robert. | Mt. Gambier, Australia | 4/9/09 |
| ahame, Gloria | Los Angeles, Cal. | 11/28/29 | Hemmings, David | Guilford, England | 11/2/41 |
| ahame, Margot | Canterbury, England | 1911 | Hemsley, Sherman | Philadelphia, Pa. | 2/1/- |
| anger, Farley | San Jose, Cal. | 7/1/25 | Henderson, Florence | Dale, Ind. | 2/14/34 |
| anger, Stewart | London, England | 5/6/13 | Henderson, Marcia | Andover, Mass. | 1932 |
| anville, Bonita | New York, N.Y. | 1923 | Henderson, Skitch | Halstad, Minn. | 1/27/18 |
| ant, Cary | Bristol, England | 1/18/04 | Henreid, Paul | Trieste, Italy | 1/10/08 |
| ant, Kathryn | Houston, Tex. | 1933 | Henson, Jim | Greenville, Miss. | 9/24/36 |
| ant, Lee | New York, N.Y. | 10/31/31 | Hepburn, Audrey | Brussels, Belgium | 5/4/29 |
| aves, Peter | Minneapolis, Minn. | 3/18/26 | Hepburn, Katharine | Hartford, Conn. | 11/8/09 |
| ay, Coleen | Staplehurst, Neb. | 10/23/22 | Herbert, Evelyn | Philadelphia, Pa. | 1898 |
| ay, Dolores | Chicago, Ill. | 1924 | Heston, Charlton | Evanston, Ill. | 10/4/24 |
| ayson, Kathryn | Winston-Salem, N.C. | 2/9/23 | Heywood, Anne | Birmingham, England. | 1937 |
| aziano, Rocky | New York, N.Y. | 6/7/22 | Hickman, Darryl | Los Angeles, Cal. | 1931 |
| co, Buddy | Philadelphia, Pa. | 8/14/26 | Hickman, Dwayne | Los Angeles, Cal. | 1934 |
| co, Jose | Abruzzi, Italy | 12/23/18 | Hildegarde | Adell, Wis. | 2/1/06 |
| een, Adolph | New York, N.Y. | 12/2/15 | Hill, Arthur | Melfort, Sask. | 1922 |
| een, Al | Forest City, Ark. | 4/13/46 | Hiller, Wendy | Stockport, England | 8/15/12 |
| eene, Lorne | Ottawa, Ont. | 2/12/15 | Hines, Earl (Fatha) | Duquesne, Pa. | 12/28/05 |
| eene, Richard | England | 1918 | Hines, Jerome | Hollywood, Cal. | 11/8/21 |
| eenwood, Joan | London, England | 3/4/21 | Hines, Mimi. | Vancouver, B.C. | 1933 |
| eer, Jane | Washington, D.C. | 9/9/24 | Hingle, Pat | Denver, Col. | 7/19/24 |
| egory, Dick | St. Louis, Mo. | 10/12/32 | Hirt, Al | New Orleans, La. | 11/7/22 |
| ey, Joel | Cleveland, Oh. | 4/11/32 | Hitchcock, Alfred | London, England | 8/13/99 |
| ffin, Merv | San Mateo, Cal. | 7/6/25 | Ho, Don. | Kakaako, Oahu, Ha. | 1930 |
| ffith, Andy | Mount Airy, N.C. | 6/1/26 | Hobart, Rose. | New York, N.Y. | 1906 |
| ffith, Hugh | Wales | 5/30/12 | Hoffman, Dustin | Los Angeles, Cal. | 8/8/37 |
| mes, Gary. | San Francisco, Cal. | 1955 | Holbrook, Hal | Cleveland, Oh. | 2/17/25 |
| mes, Tammy | Lynn, Mass. | 1/30/36 | Holden, William | O'Fallon, Ill. | 4/17/18 |
| zzard, George | Roanoke Rapids, N.C. | 4/1/28 | Holder, Geoffrey. | Trinidad | 8/1/30 |
| odin, Charles | Pittsburgh, Pa. | 4/21/35 | Holliman, Earl | Delhi, La. | 9/11/28 |
| ardino, Harry | New York, N.Y. | 12/23/25 | Holloway, Stanley. | London, England | 10/1/90 |
| inness, Alec | London, England | 4/2/14 | Holloway, Sterling | Cedartown, Ga. | 1905 |
| nn, Moses. | St. Louis, Mo. | 10/2/29 | Holm, Celeste | New York, N.Y. | 4/29/19 |
| thrie, Arlo | New York, N.Y. | 7/10/47 | Holtz, Lou | San Francisco, Cal. | 1893 |
| | | | Homeier, Skip | Chicago, Ill. | 10/5/30 |
| ckett, Buddy | Brooklyn, N.Y. | 8/31/24 | Hooks, Robert | Washington, D.C. | 4/18/37 |
| ckett, Joan | New York, N.Y. | 1933 | Hope, Bob | London, England | 5/29/03 |
| ckman, Gene | San Bernardino, Cal. | 1/30/31 | Hopkin, Mary. | Wales | 1950 |
| agen, Uta. | Gottingen, Germany | 6/12/19 | Hopkins, Anthony | England | 1941 |
| aggard, Merle | Bakersfield, Cal. | 4/6/37 | Hopkins, Bo | Greenwood, S.C. | — |
| agman, Larry | Ft. Worth, Tex. | 1931 | Hopper, Dennis | Dodge City, Kan. | 5/17/36 |
| ale, Barbara | DeKalb, Ill. | 1922 | Horne, Lena | Brooklyn, N.Y. | 6/30/17 |
| aley, Bill | Detroit, Mich. | 1927 | Horowitz, Vladimir. | Kiev, Russia | 10/1/04 |
| aley, Jack | Boston, Mass. | 1899 | Horton, Robert. | Los Angeles, Cal. | 7/29/24 |
| all, Huntz | New York, N.Y. | 1920 | Houseman, John | Bucarest, Romania | 9/22/02 |
| all, Monty | Winnipeg, Man. | 1925 | Howard, Clint | Burbank, Cal. | 1959 |
| all, Tom T. | Olive Hill, Ky. | 5/25/36 | Howard, Ken | El Centro, Cal. | 3/28/44 |
| amilton, George | Memphis, Tenn. | 8/12/39 | Howard, Ron. | Duncan, Okla. | 3/1/54 |
| amilton, Margaret | Cleveland, Oh. | 9/12/02 | Howard, Trevor | Kent, England | 8/29/16 |
| amilton, Neil | Lynn, Mass | 1899 | Howes, Sally Ann | London, England | 7/20/34 |
| ampshire, Susan. | London, England | 5/12/42 | Hudson, Rock | Winnetka, Ill. | 11/17/25 |
| ampton, Lionel | Birmingham, Ala. | 4/20/14 | Humperdinck, Engelbert | Madras, India | 5/2/36 |
| ampton, Ruth. | Throop, Pa. | 1932 | Hunnicutt, Arthur | Gravelly, Ark. | 2/17/11 |
| arding, Ann | Ft. Sam Houston, Tex. | 1904 | Hunt, Lois | York, Pa. | 11/26/25 |
| arper, Ron | Turtle Creek, Pa. | 1935 | Hunt, Marsha | Chicago, Ill. | 10/17/17 |
| arper, Valerie | Suffern, N.Y. | 8/22/40 | Hunter, Kim | Detroit, Mich. | 11/12/22 |
| arrington, Pat Jr. | New York, N.Y. | 8/13/29 | Hunter, Ross | Cleveland, Oh. | 5/6/26 |
| arris, Barbara | Evanston, Ill. | 1935 | Hunter, Tab | New York, N.Y. | 7/11/31 |
| arris, Emmy Lou | Birmingham, Ala. | 1947 | Hussey, Olivia | Buenos Aires, Argentina | 1952 |
| arris, Julie | Grosse Pte. Park, Mich. | 12/2/25 | Hussey, Ruth | Providence, R.I. | 10/30/17 |
| arris, Phil | Linton, Ind. | 6/24/06 | Huston, John. | Nevada, Mo. | 8/5/06 |
| arris, Richard. | Co. Limerick, Ireland | 10/1/33 | Hutchinson, Josephine | Seattle, Wash. | 1916 |
| arris, Rosemary | Ashby, England | 9/19/30 | Hutton, Betty | Battle Creek, Mich. | 2/26/21 |
| arrison, George | Liverpool, England | 2/25/43 | Hutton, Ina Ray | Chicago, Ill. | 1918 |
| arrison, Noel | London, England | 1933 | Hutton, Lauren | Charleston, S.C. | 1944 |
| arrison, Rex | Huyton, England | 3/5/08 | Hyde-White, Wilfrid | England | 1903 |
| artman, David | Pawtucket, R.I. | 5/19/35 | Hyer, Martha | Fort Worth, Tex. | 1929 |
| asso, Signe. | Stockholm, Sweden | 8/15/15 | Hyman, Earle | Rocky Mt., N.C. | 1926 |
| aver, June | Rock Island, Ill. | 1926 | | | |
| avoc, June | Vancouver, B.C. | 1916 | Ian, Janis | New York, N.Y. | 5/7/51 |
| awn, Goldie | Washington, D.C. | 11/21/45 | Inescort, Frieda | Edinburgh, Scotland | 1901 |
| aworth, Jill | Sussex, England | 1945 | Ingels, Marty | Brooklyn, N.Y. | 3/9/36 |
| ayden, Melissa | Toronto, Ont. | 4/25/23 | Ireland, Jill | London, England | 4/24/36 |
| ayden, Russell | Chico, Cal. | 6/12/12 | Ireland, John | Vancouver, B.C. | 1/30/15 |
| ayden, Sterling | Montclair, N.Y. | 1916 | Iturbi, Jose | Valencia, Spain | 11/28/95 |
| ayes, Helen | Washington, D.C. | 10/10/00 | Ives, Burl | Hunt, Ill. | 6/14/09 |

| Name | Birthplace | Born | Name | Birthplace | Bo |
|------|-----------|------|------|-----------|-----|
| Jackson, Anne | Allegheny, Pa. | 9/3/26 | Klein, Robert | New York, N.Y. | 19- |
| Jackson, Glenda | Cheshire, England | 5/9/36 | Klugman, Jack | Philadelphia, Pa. | 4/27/ |
| Jackson, Kate | Birmingham, Ala. | 10/29/49 | Knight, Gladys | Atlanta, Ga. | 5/28/ |
| Jackson, Michael | Gary, Ind. | 8/29/58 | Knight, Ted | Terryville, Conn. | |
| Jaeckel, Richard | Long Beach, Cal. | 1926 | Knotts, Don | Morgantown, W. Va. | 7/21/ |
| Jaffe, Sam | New York, N.Y. | 3/10/91 | Knowles, Patric | Horsforth, England | 11/11/ |
| Jagger, Dean | Columbus Grove, Oh. | 11/7/05 | Knox, Alexander | Strathroy, Canada | 1/16/ |
| Jagger, Mick | Dartford, England | 7/26/44 | Korjus, Miliza | Warsaw, Poland | 19 |
| James, Dennis | Jersey City, N.J. | 8/24/17 | Korman, Harvey | Chicago, Ill. | 2/15/ |
| James, Harry | Albany, Ga. | 3/15/16 | Kostelanetz, Andre | St. Petersburg, Russia | 12/22/ |
| Janssen, David | Naponee, Neb. | 3/27/30 | Kramer, Stanley | New York, N.Y. | 9/29/ |
| Jason, Rick | New York, N.Y. | 5/21/26 | Kristofferson, Kris | Brownsville, Tex. | 6/22/ |
| Jeanmaire, Renee | Paris, France | 4/29/24 | Kruger, Hardy | Berlin, Germany | 4/12/ |
| Jeffreys, Anne | Goldsboro, N.C. | 1923 | Kubelik, Rafael | Bychori, Czechoslovakia | 6/29/ |
| Jeffries, Fran | San Jose, Cal. | 1939 | Kubrick, Stanley | Bronx, N.Y. | 7/26/ |
| Jeffries, Lionel | England | 1926 | Kulp, Nancy | Harrisburg, Pa. | 8/28/ |
| Jennings, Waylon | Littlefield, Tex. | 6/15/37 | Kwan, Nancy | Hong Kong | 193 |
| Jens, Salome | Milwaukee, Wis. | 1935 | Kyser, Kay | Rocky Mount, N.C. | 190 |
| Jepson, Helen | Titusville, Pa. | 1907 | | | |
| Jessel, George | New York, N.Y. | 4/3/98 | Ladd, Cheryl | Huron, S.D. | 7/2/ |
| John, Elton | Middlesex, England | 3/25/47 | Laine, Frankie | Chicago, Ill. | 3/30/ |
| Johns, Glynis | Durban, S. Africa | 10/5/23 | Lamarr, Hedy | Vienna, Austria | 191 |
| Johnson, Ben | Foraker, Okla. | 1918 | Lamas, Fernando | Buenos Aires, Argentina | 1/9/ |
| Johnson, Van | Newport, R.I. | 8/20/16 | Lamb, Gil | Minneapolis, Minn. | 6/14/ |
| Johnston, Johnny | St. Louis, Mo. | 1916 | Lamour, Dorothy | New Orleans, La. | 10/10/ |
| Jones, Allan | Scranton, Pa. | 1907 | Lancaster, Burt | New York, N.Y. | 11/2/ |
| Jones, Carolyn | Amarillo, Tex. | 4/28/33 | Lanchester, Elsa | London, England | 10/28/ |
| Jones, Chris | Jackson, Tenn. | 1941 | Landau, Martin | Brooklyn, N.Y. | 193 |
| Jones, Dean | Morgan Co., Ala. | 1/25/35 | Landon, Michael | Forest Hills, N.Y. | - |
| Jones, Grandpa | Niagara, Ky. | 10/20/13 | Lane, Abbe | Brooklyn, N.Y. | 193 |
| Jones, Henry | Philadelphia, Pa. | 8/1/12 | Lane, Lola | Macy, Ind. | 190 |
| Jones, Jack | Hollywood, Cal. | 1938 | Lane, Priscilla | Indianola, Ia. | 191 |
| Jones, James Earl | Tate Co., Miss. | 1/17/31 | Lane, Sara | New York, N.Y. | 194 |
| Jones, Jennifer | Tulsa, Okla. | 3/2/19 | Lange, Hope | Redding Ridge, Conn. | 11/28/ |
| Jones, Shirley | Smithton, Pa. | 3/31/34 | Langella, Frank | Bayonne, N.J. | 194 |
| Jones, Tom | Pontypridd, Wales | 6/7/40 | Langford, Frances | Lakeland, Fla. | 4/4/1 |
| Jory, Victor | Dawson, Yukon, Canada | 1902 | Lansbury, Angela | London, England | 10/16/ |
| Joslyn, Allyn | Milford, Pa. | 7/21/05 | Lansing, Robert | San Diego, Cal. | 6/5/2 |
| Jourdan, Louis | Marseilles, France | 6/19/21 | Lanson, Snooky (Roy) | Memphis, Tenn. | 191 |
| Jurado, Katy | Guadalajara, Mexico | 1927 | LaPlante, Laura | St. Louis, Mo. | 190 |
| | | | La Rosa, Julius | Brooklyn, N.Y. | 193 |
| | | | La Rue, Jack | New York, N.Y. | |
| Kahn, Madeline | Boston, Mass. | 9/29/42 | Lasser, Louise | New York N.Y. | 194 |
| Kaminska, Ida | Odessa, Russia | 1899 | Laughlin, Tom | Minneapolis, Minn. | 193 |
| Kaplan, Gabe | Brooklyn, N.Y. | 3/31/45 | Laurie, Piper | Detroit, Mich. | 1/22/3 |
| Kasznar, Kurt | Vienna, Austria | 8/12/13 | Lavin, Linda | Portland, Ore. | - |
| Kaye, Danny | Brooklyn, N.Y. | 1/18/13 | Lawford, Peter | London, England | 9/7/2 |
| Kaye, Sammy | Lakewood, Oh. | 3/13/13 | Lawrence, Barbara | Carnegie, Okla. | 2/24/3 |
| Kazan, Elia | Constantinople, Turkey | 9/7/09 | Lawrence, Carol | Melrose Park, Ill. | 9/5/3 |
| Kazan, Lainie | New York, N.Y. | 5/16/40 | Lawrence, Marjorie | Victoria, Australia | 2/17/0 |
| Keach, Stacy | Savannah, Ga. | 6/2/41 | Lawrence, Steve | Brooklyn, N.Y. | 7/8/3 |
| Keaton, Diane | Santa Ana, Cal. | 1949 | Lawrence, Vicki | Inglewood, Cal. | 3/26/4 |
| Keel, Howard | Gillespie, Ill. | 4/13/19 | Leachman, Cloris | Des Moines, Ia. | 192 |
| Keeler, Ruby | Halifax, N.S. | 8/25/10 | Lean, David | Croydon, England | 3/25/0 |
| Keeshan, Bob | Lynbrook, N.Y. | 6/27/27 | Lear, Norman | New Haven, Conn. | 7/27/2 |
| Keitel, Harvey | Brooklyn, N.Y. | 1941 | Learned, Michael | Washington, D.C. | 193 |
| Keith, Brian | Bayonne, N.J. | 11/14/21 | Lederer, Francis | Prague, Czechoslovakia | 11/6/0 |
| Keller, Marthe | Switzerland | 1946 | Lee, Brenda | Atlanta, Ga. | 12/11/4 |
| Kellerman, Sally | Long Beach, Cal. | 6/2/37 | Lee, Christopher | London, England | 5/27/2 |
| Kelley, DeForrest | Atlanta, Ga. | 1920 | Lee, Michele | Los Angeles, Cal. | 194 |
| Kelly, Emmett | Sedan, Kan. | 12/8/98 | Lee, Peggy | Jamestown, N.D. | 5/26/2 |
| Kelly, Gene | Pittsburgh, Pa. | 8/23/12 | Lee, Pinky | St. Paul, Minn. | - |
| Kelly, Grace | Philadelphia, Pa. | 11/12/29 | Le Gallienne, Eva | London, England | 1/11/9 |
| Kelly, Jack | Astoria, N.Y. | 1927 | Legrand, Michel | Paris, France | 193 |
| Kelly, Nancy | Lowell, Mass. | 3/25/21 | Leigh, Janet | Merced, Cal. | 7/6/2 |
| Kelly, Patsy | Brooklyn, N.Y. | 1/12/10 | Leinsdorf, Erich | Vienna, Austria | 2/4/1 |
| Kennedy, Arthur | Worcester, Mass. | 2/17/14 | Lembeck, Harvey | New York, N.Y. | 192 |
| Kennedy, George | New York, N.Y. | 2/18/26 | Lemmon, Jack | Boston, Mass. | 2/8/2 |
| Kennedy, Madge | Chicago, Ill. | — | Lennon, Dianne | Los Angeles, Cal. | 1939 |
| Kent, Allegra | Los Angeles, Cal. | 8/11/38 | Lennon, Janet | Culver City, Cal. | 1946 |
| Kenyon, Doris | Syracuse, N.Y. | 1897 | Lennon, John | Liverpool, England | 10/9/4 |
| Kerr, Deborah | Helensburgh, Scotland. | 9/30/21 | Lennon, Kathy | Santa Monica, Cal. | 194 |
| Kerr, John | New York, N.Y. | 11/5/31 | Lennon, Peggy | Los Angeles, Cal. | 194 |
| Kert, Larry | Los Angeles, Cal. | 1930 | Leonard, Sheldon | New York, N.Y. | 2/22/0 |
| Keyes, Evelyn | Port Arthur, Tex. | 1925 | Leontovich, Eugenie | Moscow, Russia | 189 |
| Kiley, Richard | Chicago, Ill. | 3/21/22 | LeRoy, Mervyn | San Francisco, Cal. | 10/15/0 |
| Kilian, Victor | Jersey City, N.J. | 3/6/98 | Leslie, Joan | Detroit, Mich. | 1/26/2 |
| King, Alan | Brooklyn, N.Y. | 12/26/27 | Lester, Jerry | Chicago, Ill. | 191 |
| King, B. B. | Itta Bena, Miss. | 9/16/25 | Lester, Mark | Richmond, England. | -1958 |
| King, Carole | Brooklyn, N.Y. | 2/9/41 | Levene, Sam | Russia | 8/28/0 |
| King, Walter Woolf | San Francisco, Cal. | 1899 | Levenson, Sam | New York, N.Y. | 12/28/1 |
| King, Wayne | Savannah, Ill. | 1901 | Lewis, Jerry | Newark, N.J. | 3/16/2 |
| Kirby, Durward | Covington, Ky. | 8/24/12 | Lewis, Jerry Lee | Ferriday, La. | 9/29/3 |
| Kirk, Lisa | Brownsville, Pa. | 1925 | Lewis, Monica | Chicago, Ill. | 5/5/2 |
| Kirk, Phyllis | Plainfield, N.J. | 9/18/30 | Lewis, Robert Q. | New York, N.Y. | 1924 |
| Kirsten, Dorothy | Montclair, N.J. | 7/6/19 | Lewis, Shari | New York, N.Y. | 1/17/3 |
| Kitt, Eartha | North, S.C. | 1/26/28 | Liberace | West Allis, Wis. | 5/16/1 |
| Klemperer, Werner | Cologne, Germany | 3/22/20 | Lillie, Beatrice | Toronto, Ont. | 189 |

| me | Birthplace | Born | Name | Birthplace | Born |
|---|---|---|---|---|---|
| coln, Abbey | Chicago, Ill. | 1930 | Martino, Al | Philadelphia, Pa. | 1927 |
| den, Hal | New York, N.Y. | 3/20/31 | Marvin, Lee | New York, N.Y. | 2/19/24 |
| ffors, Viveca | Uppsala, Sweden | 12/29/20 | Marx, Herbert (Zeppo) | New York, N.Y. | 1901 |
| dsay, Margaret | Dubuque, Ia. | 1910 | Mason, Jackie | Sheboygan, Wis. | 1931 |
| dsey, Mort | Newark, N.J. | 1923 | Mason, James | Huddersfield, England | 5/15/09 |
| kletter, Art | Saskatchewan, Canada | 7/17/12 | Mason, Marsha | St. Louis, Mo. | 4/3/42 |
| ton, Peggy | Lawrence, N.Y. | 1948 | Mason, Pamela | London, England | 3/10/22 |
| , Virna | Italy | 1937 | Massey, Curt | Midland, Tex. | — |
| e, Cleavon | Chickasha, Okla. | 6/1/39 | Massey, Raymond | Toronto, Ont. | 8/30/96 |
| e, Rich | Ottawa, Ont. | 11/26/38 | Massine, Leonide | Moscow, Russia | 8/9/96 |
| e Richard | Macon, Ga. | 1935 | Mastroianni, Marcello | Rome, Italy | 9/28/24 |
| ngston, Barry | Los Angeles, Cal. | 1953 | Mathieu, Mireille | Avignon, France | 1946 |
| ngston, Stanley | Los Angeles, Cal. | 1950 | Mathis, Johnny | San Francisco, Cal. | 9/30/35 |
| ngstone, Mary | Seattle, Wash. | 1909 | Matthau, Walter | New York, N.Y. | 10/1/20 |
| ckhart, June | New York, N.Y. | 6/25/25 | Mature, Victor | Louisville, Ky. | 1/19/16 |
| ckwood, Margaret | Karachi, India | 9/15/16 | May, Billy | Pittsburgh, Pa. | 1916 |
| den, Barbara | Marion, N.C. | 1937 | May, Elaine | Philadelphia, Pa. | 4/21/32 |
| der, John | London, England | 1898 | Mayehoff, Eddie | Baltimore, Md. | 7/7/14 |
| gan, Joshua | Texarkana, Tex. | 10/5/08 | Mayo, Virginia | St. Louis, Mo. | 1920 |
| lobrigida, Gina | Subiaco, Italy | 7/4/28 | Mazurki, Mike | Austria | 12/25/09 |
| m, Herbert | Prague, Czechoslovakia | 1917 | McArdle, Andrea | Philadelphia, Pa. | 11/4/63 |
| ndon, Julie | Santa Rosa, Cal. | 9/26/26 | McBride, Patricia | Teaneck, N.J. | 8/23/42 |
| nget, Claudine | France | 1/29/42 | McCallum, David | Glasgow, Scotland | 9/19/33 |
| pez, Trini | Dallas, Tex. | 5/15/37 | McCambridge, | | |
| rd, Jack | New York, N.Y. | — | Mercedes | Joliet, Ill. | 3/17/18 |
| ren, Sophia | Rome, Italy | 9/20/34 | McCarthy, Kevin | Seattle, Wash. | 1915 |
| ring, Gloria | New York, N.Y. | 1946 | McCartney, Paul | Liverpool, England | 6/18/42 |
| udon, Dorothy | Boston, Mass. | 9/17/33 | McClure, Doug. | Glendale, Cal. | 5/11/38 |
| uise, Tina | New York, N.Y. | 1934 | McCord, Kent | Los Angeles, Cal. | 1942 |
| ve, Bessie | Midland, Tex. | 9/10/98 | McCrary, Tex (John) | Calvert, Tex. | 1910 |
| y, Myrna | Helena, Mon. | 8/2/05 | McCrea, Joel | Los Angeles, Cal. | 11/5/05 |
| cas, Nick | New Jersey | 1897 | McDonough, Mary | Los Angeles, Cal. | 5/4/61 |
| ckinbill, Laurence | Ft. Smith, Ark. | 11/21/34 | McDowall, Roddy | London, England | 9/17/28 |
| dwig, Christa | Berlin, Germany | 1928 | McDowell, Malcolm | Leeds, England | 6/19/43 |
| ke, Keye | Canton, China | 1904 | McEachin, James | Pennert, N.C. | 1930 |
| lu | Glasgow, Scotland | 1948 | McFarland, George | | |
| met, Sidney | Philadelphia, Pa. | 6/25/24 | (Spanky) | Dallas, Tex. | 1928 |
| nd, John | Rochester, N.Y. | 1913 | McGavin, Darren | San Joaquin, Cal. | 5/7/22 |
| pino, Ida | London, England | 2/4/18 | McGee, Fibber | Peoria, Ill. | 1896 |
| nde, Paul | Mt. Vernon, Oh. | 6/13/26 | McGoohan, Patrick | Astoria, N.Y. | 3/19/28 |
| nley, Carol | New York, N.Y. | 2/13/42 | McGuire, Dorothy | Omaha, Neb. | 6/14/19 |
| nn, Jeffrey | Auburn, Mass. | 1909 | McGuire Sisters: | | |
| nn, Loretta | Butcher Hollow, Ky. | 1/14/32 | Christine | Middletown, Oh. | 1928 |
| on, Ben | Atlanta, Ga. | 2/6/01 | Dorothy | Middletown, Oh. | 1930 |
| on, Sue | Davenport, Ia. | 7/10/46 | Phyllis | Middletown, Oh. | 1931 |
| | | | McHugh, Frank | Homestead, Pa. | 5/23/99 |
| azel, Lorin | Paris, France | 3/6/30 | McIntire, John | Spokane, Wash. | 6/27/07 |
| acArthur, James | Los Angeles, Cal. | 12/8/37 | McKechnie, Donna | Detroit, Mich. | 1940 |
| acGraw, Ali | Pound Ridge, N.Y. | 4/1/39 | McKenna, Siobhan | Belfast, Ireland | 5/24/23 |
| acKay, Jim | Philadelphia, Pa. | 1921 | McLean, Don | New Rochelle, N.Y. | 10/2/45 |
| acKenzie, Gisele | Winnipeg, Man. | 1/10/27 | McLerie, Allyn | Grand Mere, Que. | 12/1/26 |
| acLaine, Shirley | Richmond, Va. | 4/24/34 | McMahon, Ed | Detroit, Mich. | 3/6/23 |
| acMurray, Fred | Kankakee, Ill. | 8/30/08 | McNair, Barbara | Chicago, Ill. | 1939 |
| acRae, Gordon | East Orange, N.J. | 3/12/21 | McQueen, Butterfly | Tampa, Fla. | 1/7/11 |
| acRae, Meredith | Houston, Tex. | 1945 | McQueen, Steve | Indianapolis, Ind. | 1930 |
| acRae, Sheila | London, England | 1924 | Meadows, Audrey | Wu Chang, China | 1924 |
| acy, Bill | Revere, Mass. | 5/18/22 | Meadows, Jayne | Wu Chang, China | 9/27/26 |
| adison, Guy | Bakersfield, Cal. | 1/19/22 | Meara, Anne | New York, N.Y. | 1929 |
| ajors, Lee | Wyandotte, Mich. | 4/23/40 | Medford, Kay | New York, N.Y. | 1920 |
| akarova, Natalia | Leningrad, USSR | 11/21/40 | Meeker, Ralph | Minneapolis, Minn. | 11/21/20 |
| albin, Elaine | New York, N.Y. | 1932 | Melanie | New York, N.Y. | 1/3/47 |
| alden, Karl | Chicago, Ill. | 6/22/13 | Melton, Sid | Brooklyn, N.Y. | 1920 |
| alone, Dorothy | Chicago, Ill. | 1/30/25 | Menuhin, Yehudi | New York, N.Y. | 4/22/16 |
| alone, Nancy | New York, N.Y. | 1935 | Mercouri, Melina | Athens, Greece | 10/18/25 |
| anchester, Melissa | Bronx, N.Y. | 2/15/51 | Meredith, Burgess | Cleveland, Oh. | 11/16/09 |
| ancini, Henry | Cleveland, Oh. | 4/16/24 | Merkel, Una | Covington, Ky. | 12/10/03 |
| andrell, Barbara | Houston, Tex. | 12/25/48 | Merman, Ethel | Astoria, N.Y. | 1/16/09 |
| anilow, Barry | New York, N.Y. | 6/17/46 | Merrick, David | Hong Kong | 11/27/12 |
| ann, Herbie | New York, N.Y. | 1930 | Merrill, Dina | New York, N.Y. | 12/9/25 |
| anning, Irene | Cincinnati, Oh. | 1918 | Merrill, Gary | Hartford, Conn. | 1915 |
| antovani, Annuzio | Venice, Italy | 1905 | Merrill, Robert | Brooklyn, N.Y. | 6/4/19 |
| arceau, Marcel | France | 3/22/23 | Middleton, Ray | Chicago, Ill. | 1907 |
| argo | Mexico City, Mexico | 1918 | Midler, Bette | New Jersey | 1945 |
| argolin, Janet | New York, N.Y. | 1943 | Milanov, Zinka | Zagreb, Yugoslavia | 5/17/08 |
| arkova, Alicia | London, England | 12/1/10 | Miles, Sarah | Ingatestone, England | 12/31/43 |
| arlowe, Hugh | Philadelphia, Pa. | 1914 | Miles, Vera | near Boise City, Okla. | 11/23/30 |
| arsh, Jean | London, England | 7/1/34 | Milland, Ray | Neath, Wales | 1/3/08 |
| arshall, Brenda | Philippines | 1915 | Miller, Ann | Houston, Tex. | 4/12/23 |
| arshall, E. G. | Awatonna, Minn. | 6/18/10 | Miller, Cheryl | Sherman Oaks, Cal. | 2/4/43 |
| arshall, Penny | New York, N.Y. | — | Miller, Jason | Scranton, Pa. | 4/22/40 |
| arshall, William | Chicago, Ill. | 10/12/17 | Miller, Mitch | Rochester, N.Y. | 7/4/11 |
| artin, Dean | Steubenville, Oh. | 6/17/17 | Miller, Roger | Ft. Worth, Tex. | 1/2/36 |
| artin, Dick | Detroit, Mich. | 1922 | Mills, Hayley | London, England | 4/18/46 |
| artin, Mary | Weatherford, Tex. | 12/1/13 | Mills, John | Suffolk, England | 2/22/08 |
| artin, Ross | Poland | 3/22/20 | Mills, Juliet | London, England | 1941 |
| artin, Strother | Kokomo, Ind. | 1919 | Milner, Martin | Detroit, Mich. | — |
| artin, Tony | San Francisco, Cal. | 12/25/13 | Milnes, Sherrill | Downers Grove, Ill. | 1/10/35 |
| | | | Milsap, Ronnie | Robinsville, N.C. | — |

| Name | Birthplace | Born | Name | Birthplace | Bo |
|---|---|---|---|---|---|
| Milstein, Nathan | Odessa, Russia | 12/31/04 | Novak, Kim | Chicago, Ill. | 2/18/3 |
| Mimieux, Yvette | Hollywood, Cal. | 1/8/42 | Nugent, Elliott | Dover, Oh. | 9/20/9 |
| Minnelli, Liza | Los Angeles, Cal. | 3/12/46 | Nureyev, Rudolf | Russia | 3/17/3 |
| Mitchell, Cameron | Dallastown, Pa. | 4/11/18 | Nuyen, France | Marseilles, France | 7/31/3 |
| Mitchell, Guy | Detroit, Mich. | 2/22/25 | | | |
| Mitchell, Joni | McLeod, Alta. | 11/7/43 | Oakland, Simon | New York, N.Y. | 192 |
| Mitchum, Robert | Bridgeport, Conn. | 8/6/17 | Oberon, Merle | Tasmania, Australia | 2/19/1 |
| Moffo, Anna | Wayne, Pa. | 6/27/34 | O'Brian, Hugh | Rochester, N.Y. | 4/19/3 |
| Montalban, Ricardo | Mexico City, Mexico | 11/25/20 | O'Brien, Edmond | New York, N.Y. | 9/10/1 |
| Montand, Yves | Monsummano, Italy. | 10/31/21 | O'Brien, George | San Francisco, Cal. | 190 |
| Montgomery, Elizabeth | Hollywood, Cal. | 4/15/33 | O'Brien, Margaret | San Diego, Cal. | 1/15/3 |
| Montgomery, George | Brady, Mon. | 8/29/16 | O'Brien, Pat | Milwaukee, Wis. | 11/11/ |
| Montgomery, Robert | Beacon, N.Y. | 5/21/04 | O'Connell, Arthur | New York, N.Y. | 3/29/ |
| Moore, Colleen | Port Huron, Mich. | 1902 | O'Connell, Helen | Lima, Oh. | 19. |
| Moore, Constance | Sioux City, Ia. | 1/18/22 | O'Connor, Carroll | New York, N.Y. | 8/2/ |
| Moore, Dickie | Los Angeles, Cal. | 9/12/25 | O'Connor, Donald | Chicago, Ill. | 8/28/ |
| Moore, Garry | Baltimore, Md. | 1/31/15 | Odetta | Birmingham, Ala. | 12/31/3 |
| Moore, Mary Tyler | Brooklyn, N.Y. | 12/29/37 | O'Driscoll, Martha | Tulsa, Okla. | 192 |
| Moore, Melba | New York, N.Y. | 10/29/45 | O'Hara, Jill | Warren, Pa. | 194 |
| Moore, Roger | London, England | 10/14/27 | O'Hara, Maureen | Dublin, Ireland. | 8/17/2 |
| Moore, Terry | Los Angeles, Cal. | 1/1/32 | O'Herlihy, Dan. | Wexford, Ireland | 191 |
| Moreau, Jeanne | Paris, France | 1929 | O'Keefe, Walter | Hartford, Conn. | 190 |
| Moreno, Rita | Humacao, P.R. | 12/11/31 | Olivier, Laurence | Dorking, England. | 5/22/0 |
| Morgan, Dennis | Prentice, Wis. | 1910 | O'Malley, J. Pat | Burnley, England | 190 |
| Morgan, Harry | Detroit, Mich. | 4/10/15 | O'Neal, Patrick | Ocala, Fla. | 192 |
| Morgan, Henry | New York, N.Y. | 3/31/15 | O'Neal, Ryan | Los Angeles, Cal. | 4/20/4 |
| Morgan, Jane | Boston, Mass. | 1920 | O'Neal, Tatum | Los Angeles, Cal. | 196 |
| Morgana, Nina | Buffalo, N.Y. | 1895 | O'Neill, Jennifer | Brazil. | 2/20/4 |
| Moriarty, Michael | Detroit, Mich. | 4/5/41 | Opatoshu, David | New York, N.Y. | 1/30/1 |
| Morini, Erika | Vienna, Austria | 1/5/10 | Orbach, Jerry | New York, N.Y. | 10/20/3 |
| Morison, Patricia | New York, N.Y. | 1915 | Orlando, Tony | New York, N.Y. | 194 |
| Morley, Robert. | Wiltshire, England | 5/26/08 | Ormandy, Eugene | Budapest, Hungary. | 11/18/9 |
| Morris, Greg | Cleveland, Oh. | 1934 | Osmond, Donny | Ogden, Ut. | 12/9/5 |
| Morris, Howard | New York, N.Y. | 9/4/25 | Osmond, Marie | Odgen, Ut. | 10/13/5 |
| Morrow, Vic | Bronx, N.Y. | 2/14/32 | O'Sullivan, Maureen | Boyle, Ireland | 5/17/1 |
| Morse, Robert | Newton, Mass. | 5/18/31 | O'Toole, Peter | Connemara, Ireland | 193 |
| Moss, Arnold | Brooklyn, N.Y. | 1/28/11 | Owens, Buck | Sherman, Tex. | 8/12/2 |
| Mulhall, Jack | Wappingers Falls, N.Y. | 10/7/94 | Owens, Gary | Mitchell, S.D. | 193 |
| Mulhare, Edward | Ireland | 1923 | | | |
| Munsel, Patrice | Spokane, Wash. | 5/14/25 | Paar, Jack | Canton, Oh. | 5/1/1 |
| Murphy, George | New Haven, Conn. | 7/4/02 | Pacino, Al | New York, N.Y. | 4/25/4 |
| Murray, Anne | Springhill, Nova Scotia | — | Page, Geraldine | Kirksville, Mo. | 11/22/2 |
| Murray, Arthur | New York, N.Y. | 4/4/95 | Page, LaWanda | Cleveland, Oh. | 10/19/2 |
| Murray, Don | Hollywood, Cal. | 7/31/29 | Page, Patti | Claremore, Okla. | 11/8/2 |
| Murray, Jan | New York, N.Y. | 1917 | Paige, Janis | Tacoma, Wash. | 9/16/2 |
| Murray, Kathryn | Jersey City, N.J. | 9/15/06 | Palance, Jack | Lattimer, Pa. | 2/18/2 |
| Murray, Ken | New York, N.Y. | 7/14/03 | Palillo, Ron | New Haven, Conn. | 4/2. |
| Musante, Tony | Bridgeport, Conn. | 1941 | Palmer, Betsy | East Chicago, Ind. | 11/1/2 |
| | | | Palmer, Lilli. | Posen, Germany | 5/24/1 |
| Nabors, Jim | Sylacauga, Ala. | 6/12/33 | Papas, Irene | Greece. | 192 |
| Natwick, Mildred | Baltimore, Md. | 6/19/08 | Papp, Joseph | Brooklyn, N.Y. | 6/22/2 |
| Neal, Patricia | Packard, Ky. | 1/20/26 | Parker, Eleanor | Cedarville, Oh. | 6/26/2 |
| Neff, Hildegarde | Ulm, Germany | 12/28/25 | Parker, Fess | Ft. Worth, Tex. | 8/16/2 |
| Negri, Pola | Lipno, Poland | 1899 | Parker, Frank | New York, N.Y. | 190 |
| Nelson, Barry | San Francisco, Cal. | 1920 | Parker, Jean | Deer Lodge, Mon. | 191 |
| Nelson, David | New York, N.Y. | 10/24/36 | Parker, Suzy | San Antonio, Tex. | 10/28/3 |
| Nelson, Ed | New Orleans, La. | 1928 | Parkins, Barbara | Vancouver, B.C. | 194 |
| Nelson, Gene | Seattle, Wash. | 3/24/20 | Parks, Bert | Atlanta, Ga. | 12/30/1 |
| Nelson, Harriet (Hilliard) | Des Moines, Ia. | 1914 | Parsons, Estelle | Lynn, Mass. | 11/20/2 |
| Nelson, Ricky | Teaneck, N.J. | 5/8/40 | Parton, Dolly | Sevierville, Tenn. | 1/19/4 |
| Nelson, Willie | Waco, Tex. | 4/30/33 | Pasternak, Joseph | Hungary | 9/19/0 |
| Nero, Peter | New York, N.Y. | 5/22/34 | Patterson, Neva | Nevada, Ia. | 192 |
| Nesbit, Cathleen | Cheshire, England | 1889 | Paulsen, Pat | South Bend, Wash. | — |
| Newhart, Bob | Oak Park, Ill. | 9/5/29 | Pavan, Marisa | Cagliari, Sardinia | 6/19/3 |
| Newley, Anthony | Hackney, England | 9/24/31 | Pavarotti, Luciano | Modena, Italy | 10/12/3 |
| Newman, Barry | Boston, Mass. | 11/7/38 | Payne, John | Roanoke, Va. | 191 |
| Newman, Paul | Cleveland, Oh. | 1/29/25 | Pearl, Jack | New York, N.Y. | 189 |
| Newman, Phyllis | Jersey City, N.J. | 1935 | Pearl, Minnie | Centerville, Tenn. | 10/25/1 |
| Newman, Randy | Los Angeles, Cal. | 11/28/43 | Peck, Gregory | La Jolla, Cal. | 4/5/1 |
| Newmar, Julie | Los Angeles, Cal. | 1935 | Peckinpah, Sam | Fresno, Cal. | 2/21/2 |
| Newton, Wayne | Roanoke, Va. | 4/3/42 | Peerce, Jan | New York, N.Y. | 190 |
| Newton-John, Oliva | Cambridge, England | 9/26/48 | Penn, Arthur | Philadelphia, Pa. | 9/27/2 |
| Nicholas, Denise | Detroit, Mich. | | Peppard, George | Detroit, Mich. | 10/1/2 |
| Nichols, Mike | Berlin, Germany | 11/6/31 | Perkins, Anthony | New York, N.Y. | 4/4/3 |
| Nicholson, Jack | Neptune, N.J. | 4/22/37 | Perrine, Valerie | Galveston, Tex. | 9/3/4 |
| Nielsen, Leslie | Regina, Sask | 2/11/26 | Persoff, Nehemiah | Jerusalem | 8/14/2 |
| Nilsson, Birgit | W. Karop, Sweden | 1918 | Peters, Bernadette | Queens, N.Y. | 2/28/4 |
| Nimoy, Leonard | Boston, Mass. | 3/26/31 | Peters, Brock | New York, N.Y. | 7/2/2 |
| Niven, David | Kirriemuir, Scotland | 3/1/10 | Peters, Jean | Canton, Oh. | 10/15/2 |
| Nolan, Doris | New York, N.Y. | 1916 | Peters, Roberta | New York, N.Y. | 5/4/3 |
| Nolan, Jeannette | Los Angeles, Cal. | 1911 | Petit, Pascale | France. | 193 |
| Nolan, Kathy | St. Louis, Mo. | 1934 | Pettet, Joanna | London, England | 192 |
| Nolan, Lloyd | San Francisco, Cal. | 8/11/02 | Piazza, Marguerite | New Orleans, La. | 5/6/2 |
| Nolte, Nick | Omaha, Neb. | 1940 | Phillips, Michelle | Long Beach, Cal. | 4/6/4 |
| North, Jay | Hollywood, Cal. | 1953 | Pickens, Jane | Macon, Ga. | |
| North, John Ringling | Baraboo, Wis. | 8/14/03 | Pickens, Slim | Kingsberg, Cal. | 191 |
| North, Sheree | Los Angeles, Cal. | 1/17/33 | Pickford, Mary | Toronto, Canada | 4/9/9 |
| Norton, Judy | Santa Monica, Cal. | 1/29/58 | Picon, Molly | New York, N.Y. | 6/1/9 |

| Name | Birthplace | Born | Name | Birthplace | Born |
|---|---|---|---|---|---|
| geon, Walter | E. St. John, N.B. | 9/23/98 | Robards, Jason Jr. | Chicago, Ill. | 7/22/22 |
| asance, Donald | Worksop, England | 10/5/19 | Robbins, Jerome | New York, N.Y. | 10/11/18 |
| shette, Suzanne | New York, N.Y. | 1/31/37 | Robbins, Marty | Glendale, Ariz. | 9/26/25 |
| wright, Joan | Brigg, England | 10/28/29 | Robertson, Cliff | La Jolla, Cal. | 9/9/25 |
| mmer, Christopher. | Toronto, Ont. | 12/13/29 | Robertson, Dale | Oklahoma City, Okla. | 7/14/23 |
| itier, Sidney | Miami, Fla. | 2/20/27 | Robinson, Jay | New York, N.Y. | 1930 |
| lanski, Roman | Paris, France | 8/18/33 | Robson, Flora | South Shields, England | 3/28/02 |
| llard, Michael | Passaic, N.J. | 5/30/39 | Rodgers, Jimmie | Camas, Wash. | 1933 |
| nselle, Carmela. | Schenectady, N.Y. | 1892 | Rodriquez, Johnny | Sabinal, Tex. | 12/10/51 |
| nselle, Rosa. | Meriden, Conn. | 1897 | Rogers, Chas. (Buddy) | Olathe, Kan. | 8/13/04 |
| nti, Carlo | Milan, Italy | 12/11/13 | Rogers, Ginger | Independence, Mo. | 7/16/11 |
| ston, Tom | Columbus, Oh. | 10/17/27 | Rogers, Roy | Cincinnati, Oh. | 11/5/12 |
| well, Eleanor | Springfield, Mass. | 11/21/12 | Roland, Gilbert. | Juarez, Mexico | 12/11/05 |
| well, Jane | Portland, Ore. | 4/1/29 | Rolle, Esther | Pompano Beach, Fla. | — |
| well, William. | Pittsburgh, Pa. | 7/29/92 | Roman, Ruth. | Boston, Mass. | 12/23/24 |
| wers, Mala | San Francisco, Cal. | 1931 | Romero, Cesar | New York, N.Y. | 2/15/07 |
| wers, Stefanie | Hollywood, Cal. | 11/12/42 | Ronstadt, Linda | Tucson, Ariz. | 7/15/46 |
| eminger, Otto | Vienna, Austria | 12/5/06 | Rooney, Mickey | Brooklyn, N.Y. | 9/23/20 |
| entiss, Paula. | San Antonio, Tex. | 3/4/39 | Rose Marie. | New York, N.Y. | — |
| eston, Robert | Newton, Mass. | 6/8/18 | Ross, David | St. Paul, Minn. | 1924 |
| evin, Andre | Berlin, Germany | 4/6/29 | Ross, Diana | Detroit, Mich. | 3/26/44 |
| ice, Leontyne | Laurel, Miss. | 2/10/27 | Ross, Katharine | Hollywood, Cal. | 1/29/43 |
| ice, Ray | Perryville, Tex. | 1/12/26 | Ross, Lanny | Seattle, Wash. | 1/19/06 |
| ice, Roger | Charleston, W.Va. | 3/6/20 | Roth, Lillian. | Boston, Mass. | 12/13/10 |
| ice, Vincent | St. Louis, Mo. | 5/27/11 | Roundtree, Richard | New Rochelle, N.Y. | 7/9/42 |
| ide, Charlie | Sledge, Miss. | 3/18/38 | Rowan, Dan | Beggs, Okla. | 7/2/22 |
| ima, Louis | New Orleans, La. | 12/7/12 | Rowlands, Gena | Cambria, Wis. | 6/19/36 |
| ince, William. | Nichols, N.Y. | 1/26/13 | Rubin, Benny | Boston, Mass. | 1899 |
| ovine, Dorothy. | Deadwood, S.D. | 1/20/37 | Rubinoff, David | Grodno, Russia | 1897 |
| owse, Juliet | Bombay, India. | 1937 | Rubinstein, Arthur | Lodz, Poland | 1/28/89 |
| yor, Richard | Peoria, Ill. | 12/1/40 | Rudolf, Max | Frankfurt, Germany | 6/15/02 |
| le, Denver | Bethune, Col. | 5/11/20 | Rule, Janice | Norwood, Oh. | 8/15/31 |
| ualen, John. | Vancouver, B.C. | 1899 | Rush, Barbara | Denver, Col. | 1/4/30 |
| ayle, Anthony | Lancashire, England | 9/7/13 | Russell, Jane | Bemidji, Minn. | 6/21/21 |
| illan, Eddie | Philadelphia, Pa. | 3/31/07 | Russell, Ken | Southampton, England. | 7/3/27 |
| uinn, Anthony | Chihuahua, Mexico | 4/21/16 | Russell, Nipsey | Atlanta, Ga. | 1924 |
| affin, Deborah | Los Angeles, Cal. | 1953 | Rutherford, Ann | Toronto, Ont. | 1924 |
| aft, George | New York, N.Y. | 1895 | Ryan, Peggy | Long Beach, Cal. | 8/28/24 |
| ainer, Luise | Vienna, Austria | 1912 | Rydell, Bobby | Philadelphia, Pa. | 1942 |
| aines, Ella | Snoqualmie Falls, Wash. | 8/6/21 | Sahl, Mort | Montreal, Que. | 5/11/27 |
| aitt, John | Santa Ana, Cal. | 1/29/17 | Saint, Eva Marie | Newark, N.J. | 7/4/24 |
| alston, Esther | Bar Harbor, Me. | 1902 | St. James, Susan | Los Angeles, Cal. | 8/14/46 |
| alston, Vera | Prague, Czechoslovakia | 1921 | St. John, Jill | Los Angeles, Cal. | 8/19/40 |
| andall, Tony | Tulsa, Okla. | 2/26/20 | Sainte-Marie, Buffy | Maine | 2/20/41 |
| awls, Lou | Chicago, Ill. | 12/1/35 | Saks, Gene | New York, N.Y. | 11/8/21 |
| y, Aldo. | Pen Argyl, Pa. | 9/25/26 | Sales, Soupy | Franklinton, N.C. | 1926 |
| ay, Johnnie | Dallas, Ore. | 1927 | Sand, Paul | Los Angeles, Cal. | 1941 |
| yburn, Gene | Christopher, Ill. | 12/17/17 | Sands, Tommy | Chicago, Ill. | 8/27/37 |
| aye, Martha | Butte, Mon. | 8/27/16 | Sargent, Dick | Carmel, Cal. | 1933 |
| aymond, Gene | New York, N.Y. | 8/13/08 | Sarnoff, Dorothy | New York, N.Y. | 1919 |
| eddy, Helen | Melbourne, Australia | 10/25/41 | Sarrazin, Michael | Quebec City, Que. | 5/22/40 |
| edford, Robert | Santa Monica, Cal. | 8/18/37 | Savalas, Telly | Garden City, N.Y. | 1/21/27 |
| edgrave, Lynn | London, England | 3/8/43 | Saxon, John | Brooklyn, N.Y. | 8/5/35 |
| edgrave, Michael | Bristol, England | 3/20/08 | Sayao, Bidu | Rio de Janeiro, Brazil | 1908 |
| edgrave, Vanessa. | London, England | 1/30/37 | Sayer, Leo | Sussex, England | 5/21/48 |
| eed, Donna | Denison, Ia. | 1/27/21 | Schallert, William | Los Angeles, Cal. | 7/6/22 |
| eed, Jerry | Atlanta, Ga. | 3/20/37 | Schary, Dore. | Newark, N.J. | 8/31/05 |
| eed, Rex | Ft. Worth, Tex. | 10/2/38 | Scheider, Roy | Orange, N.J. | 1934 |
| eed, Robert | Highland Park, Ill. | 1932 | Schell, Maria | Vienna, Austria | 1926 |
| eese, Della | Detroit, Mich. | 7/6/32 | Schell, Maximilian | Vienna, Austria | 12/8/30 |
| egan, Phil. | Brooklyn, N.Y. | 5/28/06 | Schenkel, Chris | Bippus, Ind. | 1924 |
| eid, Kate | London, England | 1930 | Scherman, Thomas | New York, N.Y. | 2/12/17 |
| eilly, Charles Nelson | New York, N.Y. | 1/13/31 | Schnabel, Artur | Berlin, Germany | 2/2/12 |
| einer, Carl | Bronx, N.Y. | 3/20/22 | Schneider, Alexander | Vilna, Poland | 10/21/08 |
| einer, Rob | Bronx, N.Y. | 3/6/45 | Schneider, Romy | Austria | 9/23/38 |
| emick, Lee | Boston, Mass. | 12/14/35 | Schreiber, Avery | Chicago, Ill. | 1935 |
| enaldo, Duncan | Camden, N.J. | 4/23/04 | Schwarzkopf, Elisabeth | Jarotschin, Poland | 12/9/15 |
| esnik, Regina. | New York, N.Y. | 8/30/24 | Scofield, Paul | Hurst, Pierpont, England. | 1/21/22 |
| ey, Alejandro. | Buenos Aires, Argentina. | 2/8/30 | Scott, George C. | Wise, Va. | 10/18/27 |
| eynolds, Burt. | Waycross, Ga. | 2/11/36 | Scott, Hazel | Trinidad | 1920 |
| eynolds, Debbie. | El Paso, Tex. | 4/1/32 | Scott, Lizabeth | Scranton, Pa. | 1923 |
| eynolds, Marjorie | Buhl, Ida. | 8/12/21 | Scott, Martha | Jamesport, Mo. | 9/22/14 |
| eynolds, William | Los Angeles, Cal. | 1931 | Scott, Randolph | Orange Co., Va. | 1/23/03 |
| odes, Hari | Cincinnati, Oh. | 1932 | Scourby, Alexander | New York, N.Y. | 1913 |
| ch, Charlie | Forest City, Ark. | 12/14/32 | Sebastian, John | New York N.Y. | 3/17/44 |
| ch, Irene | Buffalo, N.Y. | 10/13/97 | Seberg, Jean | Marshalltown, Ia. | 11/13/38 |
| chardson, Ralph. | Cheltenham, England | 12/19/02 | Sedaka, Neil | New York, N.Y. | 3/13/39 |
| chardson, Tony | Shipley, England | 6/5/28 | Seeger, Pete | New York, N.Y. | 5/3/19 |
| ckles, Don | New York, N.Y. | 9/8/26 | Segal, George | Great Neck, N.Y. | 2/13/34 |
| ddle, Nelson | Hackensack, N.J. | 6/1/21 | Segal, Vivienne | Philadelphia, Pa. | 1897 |
| gg, Diana. | Doncaster, England | 7/20/38 | Segovia, Andres | Linares, Spain. | 2/21/93 |
| ter, John. | Burbank, Cal. | 9/17/- | Sellers, Peter | Southsea, England | 9/8/25 |
| z, Harry | Newark, N.J. | 1908 | Serkin, Rudolf | Eger, Austria | 3/28/03 |
| z, Jimmy | Newark, N.J. | 1905 | Severinsen, Doc. | Arlington, Ore. | 7/7/27 |
| vera, Chita | Washington, D.C. | 1933 | Shankar, Ravi | India | 4/7/20 |
| vers, Joan | Brooklyn, N.Y. | 1937 | Sharif, Omar | Alexandria, Egypt. | 4/10/32 |
| | | | Shatner, William | Montreal, Que. | 3/22/31 |

| Name | Birthplace | Born |
|---|---|---|
| Shaw, Robert | Red Bluff, Cal. | 4/30/16 |
| Shaw, Robert | West Houghton, England | 8/9/27 |
| Shaw, Winfred | San Francisco, Cal. | 1899 |
| Shawn, Dick | Buffalo, N.Y. | 12/1/29 |
| Shearer, Moira | Scotland | 1/17/26 |
| Shearer, Norma | Montreal Que. | 1904 |
| Sheen, Martin | Dayton, Oh. | 8/3/40 |
| Sheldon, Jack | Jacksonville, Fla. | 1931 |
| Shepherd, Cybill | Memphis, Tenn. | 1950 |
| Shepherd, Jean | Chicago, Ill. | 7/26/29 |
| Sherman, Bobby | Santa Monica, Cal. | 1945 |
| Sherwood, Roberta | St. Louis, Mo. | 1913 |
| Shire, Talia | New York, N.Y. | 1947 |
| Shirley, Ann | New York, N.Y. | 1918 |
| Shore, Dinah | Winchester, Tenn. | 3/1/21 |
| Short, Bobby | Danville, Ill. | 1936 |
| Sidney, Sylvia | New York, N.Y. | 8/8/10 |
| Siepi, Cesare | Milan, Italy | 2/10/23 |
| Signoret, Simone | Wiesbaden, Germany | 3/25/21 |
| Sills, Beverly | Brooklyn, N.Y. | 5/25/29 |
| Silvers, Phil | Brooklyn, N.Y. | 5/11/12 |
| Simmons, Jean | London, England | 1/31/29 |
| Simon, Carly | New York, N.Y. | 6/25/45 |
| Simon, Paul | Newark, N.J. | 11/13/42 |
| Simon, Simone | Marseilles, France | 4/23/14 |
| Simone, Nina | Tyron, N.C. | 2/21/33 |
| Sinatra, Frank | Hoboken, N.J. | 12/12/15 |
| Sinatra, Frank Jr. | Jersey City, N.J. | 1944 |
| Sinatra, Nancy | Jersey City, N.J. | 6/8/40 |
| Skelton, Red (Richard) | Vincennes, Ind. | 7/18/13 |
| Skinner, Cornelia Otis | Chicago, Ill. | 1903 |
| Slezak, Walter | Vienna, Austria | 5/3/02 |
| Slick, Grace | Chicago, Ill. | 10/30/39 |
| Smith, Alexis | Penticton, B.C. | 6/8/21 |
| Smith, Bob | Buffalo, N.Y. | 1917 |
| Smith, Connie | Elkhart, Ind. | 1941 |
| Smith, Ethel | Pittsburgh, Pa. | 1921 |
| Smith, Jaclyn | Houston, Tex. | 10/26/48 |
| Smith, Kate | Greenville, Va. | 5/1/09 |
| Smith, Keeley | Norfolk, Va. | 3/9/35 |
| Smith, Loring | Stratford, Conn. | 1900 |
| Smith, Maggie | Ilford, England | 12/28/34 |
| Smith, Patti | Chicago, Ill. | 1946 |
| Smith, Roger | South Gate, Cal. | 1934 |
| Smothers, Dick | New York, N.Y. | 11/20/39 |
| Smothers, Tom | New York, N.Y. | 2/2/37 |
| Snodgress, Carrie | Park Ridge, Ill. | 10/27/45 |
| Snow, Hank | Nova Scotia, Canada | 5/9/14 |
| Solti, Georg | Budapest, Hungary | 10/21/12 |
| Somes, Michael | nr. Stroud, England | 1917 |
| Somers, Suzanne | San Bruno, Cal. | 10/16/46 |
| Sommer, Elke | Berlin, Germany | 11/5/41 |
| Sorvino, Paul | Brooklyn, N.Y. | 1939 |
| Sothern, Ann | Valley City, N.D. | 1/22/12 |
| Spacek, Sissy | Quitman, Tex. | 1950 |
| Spencer, Danielle | Bronx, N.Y. | 6/24/65 |
| Spewack, Bella | Hungary | 1899 |
| Spivak, Lawrence | Brooklyn, N.Y. | 6/11/00 |
| Stack, Robert | Los Angeles, Cal. | 1/13/19 |
| Stafford, Jo | Coalinga, Cal. | 1918 |
| Stallone, Sylvester | New York, N.Y. | 1946 |
| Stamp, Terence | London, England | 1940 |
| Stang, Arnold | Chelsea, Mass. | 1925 |
| Stanley, Kim | Tularosa, N.M. | 2/11/25 |
| Stanwyck, Barbara | Brooklyn, N.Y. | 7/16/07 |
| Stapleton, Jean | New York, N.Y. | 1/19/23 |
| Stapleton, Maureen | Troy, N.Y. | 6/21/25 |
| Starr, Kay | Dougherty, Okla. | 1924 |
| Starr, Ringo | Liverpool, England | 7/7/40 |
| Steber, Eleanor | Wheeling, W. Va. | 7/17/16 |
| Steele, Bob | Pendleton, Ore. | 1907 |
| Steele, Karen | Hawaii | 1934 |
| Steele, Tommy | London, England | 12/17/36 |
| Steiger, Rod | W. Hampton, N.Y. | 4/14/25 |
| Steinberg, David | Winnipeg, Man. | 8/9/42 |
| Sterling, Jan | New York, N.Y. | 4/3/23 |
| Sterling, Robert | New Castle, Pa. | 11/13/17 |
| Stern, Isaac | Kreminiecz, Russia | 7/21/20 |
| Stevens, Cat | London, England | 1947 |
| Stevens, Connie | Brooklyn, N.Y. | 8/8/38 |
| Stevens, Kaye | Pittsburgh, Pa. | 1935 |
| Stevens, Mark | Cleveland, Oh. | 12/13/22 |
| Stevens, Rise | New York, N.Y. | 6/11/13 |
| Stevens, Stella | Yazoo City, Miss. | 10/1/36 |
| Stevens, Warren | Clark's Summit, Pa. | 11/2/19 |
| Stewart, James | Indiana, Pa. | 5/20/08 |
| Stewart, Rod | London, England | 1/10/45 |
| Stickney, Dorothy | Dickinson, N.D. | 1903 |

| Name | Birthplace | Bo |
|---|---|---|
| Stiers, David Ogden | Peoria, Ill. | 10/31/ |
| Stills, Stephen | Dallas, Tex. | 1/3/ |
| Stockwell, Dean | Hollywood, Cal. | 3/5/ |
| Stone, Carol | New York, N.Y. | 19 |
| Stone, Dorothy | Bensonhurst, N.Y. | 19 |
| Stone, Ezra | New Bedford, Mass. | 12/2/ |
| Stone, Milburn | Burton, Kan. | 19 |
| Stone, Paula | New York, N.Y. | 19 |
| Storch, Larry | New York, N.Y. | 1/8/ |
| Storm, Gale | Bloomington, Tex. | 4/5/ |
| Storrs, Suzanne | Salt Lake City, Ut. | 19 |
| Straight, Beatrice | Old Westbury, N.Y. | 19 |
| Strasberg, Susan | New York, N.Y. | 5/22/ |
| Strauss, Peter | New York, N.Y. | 19 |
| Streisand, Barbra | Brooklyn, N.Y. | 4/24/ |
| Stritch, Elaine | Detroit, Mich. | 2/2/ |
| Strode, Woody | Los Angeles, Cal. | 19 |
| Struthers, Sally | Portland, Ore. | 7/28/ |
| Sullivan, Barry | New York, N.Y. | 8/29/ |
| Sumac, Yma | Ichocan, Peru | 19 |
| Susskind, David | New York, N.Y. | 12/19/ |
| Sutherland, Donald | St. John, New Brunswick | 7/17/ |
| Sutherland, Joan | Sydney, Australia | 11/7/ |
| Suzuki, Pat | Cressey, Cal | 193 |
| Swanson, Gloria | Chicago, Ill. | 3/27/9 |
| Sweet, Blanche | Chicago, Ill. | 189 |
| Swit, Loretta | Passaic, N.J. | |
| Talbot, Lyle | Pittsburgh, Pa. | 190 |
| Talbot, Nita | New York, N.Y. | 193 |
| Tallchief, Maria | Fairfax, Okla. | 1/24/2 |
| Tamblyn, Russ | Los Angeles, Cal. | 12/30/3 |
| Tandy, Jessica | London, England | 6/7/ |
| Taylor, Elizabeth | London, England | 2/27/3 |
| Taylor, James | Boston, Mass. | 3/12/ |
| Taylor, Kent | Nashua, Ia. | 5/11/ |
| Taylor, Rod | Sydney, Australia | 1/11/3 |
| Tebaldi, Renata | Pesaro, Italy | 1/2/2 |
| Temple, Shirley | Santa Monica, Cal. | 4/23/2 |
| Terris, Norma | Columbus, Kan. | 190 |
| Terry-Thomas | London, England | 7/14/1 |
| Thaxter, Phyllis | Portland, Me. | 11/20/2 |
| Thebom, Blanche | Monessen, Pa. | 9/19/1 |
| Thibault, Conrad | Northbridge, Mass. | 11/13/0 |
| Thinnes, Roy | Chicago, Ill. | 193 |
| Thomas, B.J. | Houston, Tex. | 194 |
| Thomas, Danny | Deerfield, Mich. | 1/6/1 |
| Thomas, Lowell | Woodrington, Oh. | 4/6/ |
| Thomas, Marlo | Detroit, Mich. | 11/21/4 |
| Thomas, Richard | New York, N.Y. | 195 |
| Thompson, Marshall | Peoria, Ill. | 11/27/2 |
| Thompson, Sada | Des Moines, Ia. | 9/27/2 |
| Thulin, Ingrid | Sweden | 1/27/2 |
| Tierney, Gene | Brooklyn, N.Y. | 11/20/2 |
| Tierney, Lawrence | Brooklyn, N.Y. | 3/15/1 |
| Tiffin, Pamela | Oklahoma City, Okla. | 10/13/4 |
| Tillis, Mel | Tampa, Fla. | 8/8/3 |
| Tillstrom, Burr | Chicago, Ill. | 10/13/1 |
| Tiny Tim | New York, N.Y. | |
| Tobias, George | New York, N.Y. | 190 |
| Todd, Richard | Dublin, Ireland | 6/11/1 |
| Tomlin, Lily | Detroit, Mich. | 193 |
| Tomlinson, David | Scotland | 5/17/1 |
| Toomey, Regis | Pittsburgh, Pa. | 8/13/0 |
| Torme, Mel | Chicago, Ill. | 9/13/2 |
| Torn, Rip | Temple, Tex. | 2/6/3 |
| Totter, Audrey | Joliet, Ill. | 12/20/2 |
| Tracy, Arthur | Kamenetz, Podolsk, Russia | 6/25/0 |
| Travers, Mary | Louisville, Ky. | 11/9/3 |
| Travolta, John | Englewood, N.J. | 195 |
| Trevor, Claire | New York, N.Y. | 190 |
| Truffaut, Francois | Paris, France | 2/6/3 |
| Tucker, Forrest | Plainfield, Ind. | 2/12/1 |
| Tucker, Orrin | St. Louis, Mo. | 191 |
| Tucker, Tanya | Seminole, Tex. | 195 |
| Tucker, Tommy | Souris, N.D. | 190 |
| Turner, Ike | Clarksdale, Miss. | 11/5/3 |
| Turner, Lana | Wallace, Ida. | 2/8/2 |
| Turner, Tina | Brownsville, Tex. | 11/25/4 |
| Tushingham, Rita | Liverpool, England | 194. |
| Twiggy (Leslie Hornby) | London, England | 9/19/4 |
| Twitty, Conway | Friar's Point, Miss. | 9/1/3 |
| Tyrell, Susan | New Canaan, Conn. | 194 |
| Tyson, Cicely | New York, N.Y. | — |
| Uggams, Leslie | New York, N.Y. | 5/25/4 |
| Ullmann, Liv | Tokyo, Japan | 12/16/3 |

| ame | Birthplace | Born | Name | Birthplace | Born |
|---|---|---|---|---|---|
| meki, Miyoshi | Hokkaido, Japan | 1929 | West, Mae | Brooklyn, N.Y. | 8/17/92 |
| stinov, Peter | London, England | 4/16/21 | Whitaker, Johnny | Van Nuys, Cal. | 1959 |
| | | | White, Barry | Galveston, Tex. | 1944 |
| accaro, Brenda | Brooklyn, N.Y. | 11/18/39 | White, Betty | Oak Park, Ill. | 1/17/- |
| ale, Jerry | New York, N.Y. | 1931 | White, Jesse | Buffalo, N.Y. | 1/8/19 |
| alente, Caterina | Italy | 1931 | Whiting, Margaret | Detroit, Mich. | 1924 |
| alentine, Karen | Santa Rosa, Cal. | 1947 | Whitman, Stuart | San Francisco, Cal. | — |
| allee, Rudy | Island Pond, Vt. | 7/28/01 | Whitmore, James | White Plains, N.Y. | 10/1/21 |
| alli, Alida | Pola, Italy | 5/31/21 | Widmark, Richard | Sunrise, Minn. | 12/26/14 |
| alli, Frankie | Newark, N.J. | 5/3/37 | Wilcoxon, Henry | British West Indies | 1905 |
| ance, Vivian | Cherryvale, Kan. | 7/26/12 | Wilde, Cornel | New York, N.Y. | 10/13/18 |
| an Cleef, Lee | Somerville, N.J. | 1/9/25 | Wilder, Billy | Vienna, Austria | 6/22/06 |
| an Doren, Mamie | Rowena, S.D. | 2/6/33 | Wilder, Gene | Milwaukee, Wis. | 6/11/35 |
| an Dyke, Dick | West Plains, Mo. | 12/13/25 | Wilding, Michael | Essex, England | 7/28/12 |
| an Dyke, Jerry | Danville, Ill. | 1932 | Williams, Andy | Wall Lake, Ia. | 12/3/30 |
| an Fleet, Jo | Oakland, Cal. | 1922 | Williams, Cindy | Van Nuys, Cal. | — |
| an Patten, Dick | New York, N.Y. | 12/9/28 | Williams, Clarence | New York, N.Y. | 8/21/39 |
| an Vooren, Monique | Brussels, Belgium | 4/17/33 | Williams, Emlyn | Mostyn, Wales | 11/26/05 |
| andervere, Tish | Tenafly, N.J. | 1945 | Williams, Esther | Los Angeles, Cal. | 8/8/23 |
| arnay, Astrid | Stockholm, Sweden | 1918 | Williams, Joe | Cordele, Ga. | 1918 |
| arsi, Diane | San Francisco, Cal. | 1938 | Williams, Mason | Abilene, Tex. | 1938 |
| aughan, Sarah | Newark, N.J. | 3/27/24 | Williams, Paul | Omaha, Neb. | 9/19/40 |
| aughn, Robert | New York, N.Y. | 11/22/32 | Williams, Roger | Omaha, Neb. | 1926 |
| enuta, Benay | San Francisco | 1911 | Williamson, Fred | Gary, Ind. | 1937 |
| era-Ellen | Cincinnati, Oh. | 1926 | Williamson, Nicol | Hamilton, Scotland | 1936 |
| erdon, Gwen | Los Angeles, Cal. | 1/13/25 | Wills, Chill | Seagoville, Tex. | 1903 |
| ereen, Ben | Miami, Fla. | 10/10/46 | Wilson, Demond | Valdosta, Ga. | — |
| ernon, Jackie | New York, N.Y. | 1924 | Wilson, Dolores | Philadelphia, Pa. | 1929 |
| idor, King Wallis | Galveston, Tex. | 2/8/95 | Wilson, Don | Lincoln, Neb. | 1900 |
| igoda, Abe | New York, N.Y. | 2/24/22 | Wilson, Flip | Jersey City, N.J. | 12/8/33 |
| illella, Edward | Long Island, N.Y. | 10/1/36 | Wilson, Julie | Omaha, Neb. | 1924 |
| incent, Jan-Michael | Ventura, Cal. | 1944 | Wilson, Nancy | Chillicothe, Oh. | 2/20/37 |
| inson, Helen | Beaumont, Tex. | 1907 | Winchell, Paul | New York, N.Y. | 12/21/22 |
| inton, Bobby | Canonsburg, Pa. | 4/16/35 | Windom, William | New York, N.Y. | 9/28/23 |
| ogel, Mitch | Alhambra, Cal. | 1956 | Winkler, Henry | New York, N.Y. | 10/30/45 |
| oight, Jon | Yonkers, N.Y. | 12/29/38 | Winters, Jonathan | Dayton, Oh. | 11/11/25 |
| on Furstenberg, Betsy | Neihem Heusen, Germany | 8/16/32 | Winters, Shelley | St. Louis, Mo. | 8/18/22 |
| on Sydow, Max | Lund, Sweden | 4/10/29 | Winwood, Estelle | Lee, England | 1884 |
| on Zell, Harry | Indianapolis, Ind. | 7/11/06 | Wiseman, Joseph | Montreal, Que. | 1918 |
| oorhees, Donald | Allentown, Pa. | 7/26/03 | Withers, Jane | Atlanta, Ga. | 1927 |
| | | | Wonder, Stevie | Saginaw, Mich. | 5/13/50 |
| | | | Wood, Helen | Clarksville, Tenn. | 1937 |
| Vaggoner, Lyle | Kansas City, Kan. | 1935 | Wood, Natalie | San Francisco, Cal. | 7/20/38 |
| Vagner, Lindsay | Los Angeles, Cal. | 6/22/49 | Woodward, Joanne | Thomasville, Ga. | 2/27/30 |
| Vagner, Robert | Detroit, Mich. | 2/10/30 | Worley, Jo Anne | Lowell, Ind. | 9/6/37 |
| Vagoner, Porter | West Plains, Mo. | 8/12/27 | Worth, Irene | Nebraska | 6/23/16 |
| Vain, Bea | Bronx, N.Y. | 1917 | Wray, Fay | Alberta, Canada | 9/10/07 |
| Vaite, Ralph | White Plains, N.Y. | 6/22/28 | Wright, Martha | Seattle, Wash. | 1926 |
| Valker, Clint | Hartford, Ill. | 5/30/27 | Wright, Teresa | New York, N.Y. | 10/27/18 |
| Valker, Jimmy | New York, N.Y. | — | Wrightson, Earl | Baltimore, Md. | 1916 |
| Valker, Nancy | Philadelphia, Pa. | 5/10/21 | Wyatt, Jane | Campgaw, N.J. | 8/12/12 |
| Vallach, Eli | Brooklyn, N.Y. | 12/7/15 | Wyler, William | Mulhouse, France | 7/1/02 |
| Vallenstein, Alfred | Chicago, Ill. | 10/7/98 | Wyman, Jane | St. Joseph, Mo. | 1/4/14 |
| Vallis, Hal | Chicago, Ill. | 9/14/99 | Wynette, Tammy | Red Bay, Ala. | 5/5/42 |
| Vard, Burt | Los Angeles, Cal. | 1946 | Wynn, Keenan | New York, N.Y. | 7/27/16 |
| Vard, Simon | London, England | 1941 | Wynter, Dana | London, England | 6/8/30 |
| Varden, Jack | Newark, N.J. | 1920 | | | |
| Varfield, William | W. Helena, Ark. | 1/22/20 | Yarborough, Glenn | Milwaukee, Wis. | 1930 |
| Varhol, Andy | Pittsburgh, Pa. | 8/6/27 | Yarrow, Peter | New York, N.Y. | 5/31/38 |
| Varing, Fred | Tyrone, Pa. | 6/9/00 | York, Dick | Ft. Wayne, Ind. | 9/4/28 |
| Varwick, Dionne | E. Orange, N.J. | 12/12/41 | York, Michael | Fulmer, England | 3/27/42 |
| Vayne, David | Traverse City, Mich. | 1/30/14 | York, Susannah | London, England | 1/9/41 |
| Vayne, John | Winterset, Ia. | 5/26/07 | Young, Alan | Northumberland, England | 11/19/19 |
| Veaver, Dennis | Joplin, Mo. | 6/4/25 | Young, Gig | St. Cloud, Minn. | 11/4/17 |
| Veaver, Fritz | Pittsburgh, Pa. | 1/19/26 | Young, Loretta | Salt Lake City, Ut. | 1/6/13 |
| Vebb, Jack | Santa Monica, Cal. | 4/2/20 | Young, Neil | Toronto, Ont. | 11/12/45 |
| Veissmuller, Johnny | Windber, Pa. | 6/2/04 | Young, Robert | Chicago, Ill. | 2/22/07 |
| Velch, Raquel | Chicago, Ill. | 9/5/42 | Young, Stephen | Toronto, Ont. | 1939 |
| Veld, Tuesday | New York, N.Y. | 8/27/43 | Youngman, Henny | Liverpool, England | 1906 |
| Velk, Lawrence | nr. Strasburg, N.D. | 3/11/03 | | | |
| Velles, Orson | Kenosha, Wis. | 5/16/15 | Zanuck, Darryl F. | Wahoo, Neb. | 9/5/02 |
| Vells, Kitty | Nashville, Tenn. | 8/30/19 | Zimbalist, Efrem | Rostov, Russia | 4/9/89 |
| Verner, Oskar | Vienna, Austria | 11/13/22 | Zimbalist, Efrem Jr. | New York, N.Y. | 11/30/23 |
| Vest, Adam | Walla Walla, Wash. | 1929 | Zimmer, Norma | Larsen, Ida | — |
| | | | Zorina, Vera | Berlin, Germany | 1917 |

## Entertainment Personalities of the Past

| Born | Died | Name | Born | Died | Name | Born | Died | Name |
|---|---|---|---|---|---|---|---|---|
| 1896 | 1974 | Abbott, Bud | 1894 | 1956 | Allen, Fred | 1933 | 1971 | Angeli, Pier |
| 1872 | 1953 | Adams, Maude | 1906 | 1964 | Allen, Gracie | 1876 | 1958 | Anglin, Margaret |
| 1931 | 1968 | Adams, Nick | 1883 | 1950 | Allgood, Sara | 1887 | 1933 | Arbuckle, Fatty (Roscoe) |
| 1855 | 1926 | Adler, Jacob P. | 1882 | 1971 | Anderson, Gilbert | 1900 | 1976 | Arlen, Richard |
| 1898 | 1933 | Adoree, Renee | | | (Bronco Billy) | 1868 | 1946 | Arliss, George |
| 1909 | 1964 | Albertson, Frank | 1886 | 1954 | Anderson, John Murray | 1900 | 1971 | Armstrong, Louis |
| 1885 | 1952 | Alda, Frances | 1915 | 1967 | Andrews, Laverne | 1890 | 1956 | Arnold, Edward |

| Born | Died | Name | Born | Died | Name | Born | Died | Name |
|---|---|---|---|---|---|---|---|---|
| 1905 | 1974 | Arquette, Cliff (Charlie Weaver) | 1896 | 1956 | Burns, Bob | 1878 | 1968 | Currie, Finlay |
| 1885 | 1946 | Atwill, Lionel | 1902 | 1971 | Burns, David | 1816 | 1876 | Cushman, Charlotte |
| 1845 | 1930 | Auer, Leopold | 1882 | 1941 | Burr, Henry | | | |
| 1905 | 1967 | Auer, Mischa | 1883 | 1966 | Bushman, Francis X. | 1924 | 1965 | Dandridge, Dorothy |
| 1900 | 1972 | Austin, Gene | 1896 | 1946 | Butterworth, Charles | 1869 | 1941 | Danforth, William |
| 1898 | 1940 | Ayres, Agnes | 1893 | 1971 | Byington, Spring | 1894 | 1963 | Daniell, Henry |
| | | | | | | 1901 | 1971 | Daniels, Bebe |
| 1864 | 1922 | Bacon, Frank | 1905 | 1972 | Cabot, Bruce | 1860 | 1935 | Daniels, Frank |
| 1903 | 1951 | Bailey, Mildred | 1918 | 1977 | Cabot, Sebastian | 1936 | 1973 | Darin, Bobby |
| 1893 | 1968 | Bainter, Fay | 1895 | 1956 | Calhern, Louis | 1921 | 1965 | Darnell, Linda |
| 1895 | 1957 | Baker, Belle | 1923 | 1977 | Callas, Maria | 1879 | 1967 | Darwell, Jane |
| 1906 | 1975 | Baker, Josephine | 1853 | 1942 | Calve, Emma | 1866 | 1949 | Davenport, Harry |
| 1898 | 1963 | Baker, Phil | 1933 | 1976 | Cambridge, Godfrey | 1900 | 1961 | Davies, Marion |
| 1882 | 1956 | Bancroft, George | 1865 | 1940 | Campbell, Mrs. Patrick | 1908 | 1961 | Davis, Joan |
| 1903 | 1968 | Bankhead, Tallulah | 1892 | 1964 | Cantor, Eddie | 1931 | 1955 | Dean, James |
| 1890 | 1952 | Banks, Leslie | 1878 | 1947 | Carey, Harry | 1881 | 1950 | DeCordoba, Pedro |
| 1897 | 1950 | Banks, Monty | 1876 | 1941 | Carle, Richard | 1905 | 1968 | Dekker, Albert |
| 1890 | 1955 | Bara, Theda | 1897 | 1954 | Carney, "Uncle Don" | 1898 | 1965 | Demarco, Tony |
| 1810 | 1891 | Barnum, Phineas T. | 1880 | 1961 | Carrillo, Leo | 1881 | 1959 | DeMille, Cecil B. |
| 1912 | 1978 | Barrie, Wendy | 1892 | 1972 | Carroll, Leo G. | 1891 | 1967 | Denny, Reginald |
| 1879 | 1959 | Barrymore, Ethel | 1905 | 1965 | Carroll, Nancy | 1902 | 1974 | DeSica, Vittorio |
| 1882 | 1942 | Barrymore, John | 1910 | 1963 | Carson, Jack | 1878 | 1949 | Desmond, William |
| 1878 | 1954 | Barrymore, Lionel | 1862 | 1937 | Carter, Mrs. Leslie | 1878 | 1930 | Destinn, Emmy |
| 1848 | 1905 | Barrymore, Maurice | 1873 | 1921 | Caruso, Enrico | 1905 | 1977 | Devine, Andy |
| 1897 | 1963 | Barthelmess, Richard | 1876 | 1973 | Casals, Pablo | 1942 | 1972 | De Wilde, Brandon |
| 1890 | 1962 | Barton, James | 1894 | 1969 | Castle, Irene | 1907 | 1974 | De Wolfe, Billy |
| 1873 | 1951 | Bauer, Harold | 1887 | 1918 | Castle, Vernon | 1865 | 1950 | De Wolfe, Elsie |
| 1893 | 1951 | Baxter, Warner | 1889 | 1960 | Catlett, Walter | 1879 | 1947 | Digges, Dudley |
| 1880 | 1928 | Bayes, Nora | 1874 | 1944 | Cavalieri, Lina | 1890 | 1944 | Dinehart, Alan |
| 1904 | 1965 | Beatty, Clyde | 1887 | 1950 | Cavanaugh, Hobart | 1901 | 1966 | Disney, Walt |
| 1904 | 1962 | Beavers, Louise | 1873 | 1938 | Chaliapin, Feodor | 1895 | 1949 | Dix, Richard |
| 1887 | 1955 | Beecher, Janet | 1919 | 1961 | Chandler, Jeff | 1856 | 1924 | Dockstader, Lew |
| 1884 | 1946 | Beery, Noah | 1883 | 1930 | Chaney, Lon | 1892 | 1941 | Dolly, Jennie |
| 1889 | 1949 | Beery, Wallace | 1906 | 1973 | Chaney Jr., Lon | 1892 | 1970 | Dolly, Rosie |
| 1901 | 1970 | Begley, Ed | 1889 | 1977 | Chaplin, Charles | 1905 | 1958 | Donat, Robert |
| 1854 | 1931 | Belasco, David | 1893 | 1940 | Chase, Charlie | 1903 | 1972 | Donlevy, Brian |
| 1906 | 1968 | Benaderet, Bea | 1893 | 1961 | Chatterton, Ruth | 1907 | 1959 | Douglas, Paul |
| 1906 | 1964 | Bendix, William | 1888 | 1971 | Chevalier, Maurice | 1889 | 1956 | Draper, Ruth |
| 1905 | 1965 | Bennett, Constance | 1888 | 1960 | Clark, Bobby | 1881 | 1965 | Dresser, Louise |
| 1873 | 1944 | Bennett, Richard | 1914 | 1968 | Clark, Fred | 1869 | 1934 | Dressler, Marie |
| 1894 | 1974 | Benny, Jack | 1920 | 1966 | Clift, Montgomery | 1820 | 1897 | Drew, Mrs. John |
| 1924 | 1970 | Benzell, Mimi | 1932 | 1963 | Cline, Patsy | 1853 | 1927 | Drew, John (son) |
| 1867 | 1944 | Beresford, Harry | 1900 | 1937 | Clive, Colin | 1879 | 1920 | Drew, Sydney |
| 1899 | 1966 | Berg, Gertrude | 1892 | 1967 | Clyde, Andy | 1909 | 1951 | Duchin, Eddy |
| 1895 | 1976 | Berkeley, Busby | 1911 | 1976 | Cobb, Lee J. | 1890 | 1965 | Dumont, Margaret |
| 1863 | 1927 | Bernard, Sam | 1877 | 1961 | Coburn, Charles | 1877 | 1927 | Duncan, Isadora |
| 1844 | 1923 | Bernhardt, Sarah | 1887 | 1934 | Cody, Lew | 1905 | 1967 | Dunn, James |
| 1893 | 1943 | Bernie, Ben | 1878 | 1942 | Cohan, George M. | 1873 | 1947 | Dupree, Minnie |
| 1889 | 1967 | Bickford, Charles | 1876 | 1916 | Cohan, Josephine | 1907 | 1968 | Duryea, Dan |
| 1911 | 1960 | Bjoerling, Jussi | 1919 | 1965 | Cole, Nat (King) | 1859 | 1924 | Duse, Eleanora |
| 1898 | 1973 | Blackmer, Sidney | 1878 | 1955 | Collier, Constance | | | |
| 1882 | 1951 | Blaney, Charles E. | 1866 | 1944 | Collier, William Sr. | 1894 | 1929 | Eagles, Jeanne |
| 1900 | 1943 | Bledsoe, Jules | 1890 | 1965 | Collins, Ray | 1896 | 1930 | Eames, Clare |
| 1928 | 1972 | Blocker, Dan | 1891 | 1958 | Colman, Ronald | 1865 | 1952 | Eames, Emma |
| 1888 | 1959 | Blore, Eric | 1908 | 1934 | Columbo, Russ | 1901 | 1967 | Eddy, Nelson |
| 1901 | 1975 | Blue, Ben | 1907 | 1944 | Compton, Betty | 1894 | 1971 | Edwards, Cliff |
| 1899 | 1957 | Bogart, Humphrey | 1887 | 1940 | Connolly, Walter | 1879 | 1945 | Edwards, Gus |
| 1885 | 1965 | Boland, Mary | 1855 | 1909 | Conried, Henrich | 1899 | 1974 | Ellington, Duke |
| 1897 | 1969 | Boles, John | 1918 | 1975 | Conte, Richard | 1941 | 1974 | Elliot, Cass |
| 1903 | 1960 | Bond, Ward | 1904 | 1967 | Conway, Tom | 1871 | 1940 | Elliott, Maxine |
| 1833 | 1893 | Booth, Edwin | 1901 | 1961 | Cook, Donald | 1891 | 1967 | Elman, Mischa |
| 1796 | 1852 | Booth, Junius Brutus | 1890 | 1959 | Cook, Joe | 1881 | 1951 | Errol, Leon |
| 1894 | 1953 | Bordoni, Irene | 1893 | 1958 | Cook, Phil | 1903 | 1967 | Erwin, Stuart |
| 1888 | 1960 | Bori, Lucrezia | 1901 | 1961 | Cooper, Gary | 1888 | 1976 | Evans, Edith |
| 1867 | 1943 | Bosworth, Hobart | 1891 | 1971 | Cooper, Gladys | 1913 | 1967 | Evelyn, Judith |
| 1905 | 1965 | Bow, Clara | 1896 | 1973 | Cooper, Melville | | | |
| 1874 | 1946 | Bowes, Maj. Edward | 1914 | 1968 | Corey, Wendell | 1883 | 1939 | Fairbanks, Douglas |
| 1895 | 1972 | Boyd, William | 1893 | 1974 | Cornell, Katherine | 1915 | 1970 | Farmer, Frances |
| 1893 | 1939 | Brady, Alice | 1890 | 1972 | Correll, Charles (Andy) | 1870 | 1929 | Farnum, Dustin |
| 1863 | 1950 | Brady, William A. | 1876 | 1951 | Cossart, Ernest | 1876 | 1953 | Farnum, William |
| 1871 | 1936 | Breese, Edmund | 1904 | 1957 | Costello, Helene | 1882 | 1967 | Farrar, Geraldine |
| 1898 | 1964 | Brendel, El | 1906 | 1959 | Costello, Lou | 1904 | 1971 | Farrell, Glenda |
| 1901 | 1948 | Breneman, Tom | 1877 | 1950 | Costello, Maurice | 1868 | 1940 | Faversham, William |
| 1894 | 1974 | Brennan, Walter | 1899 | 1973 | Coward, Noel | 1861 | 1939 | Fawcett, George |
| 1875 | 1948 | Brian, Donald | 1890 | 1950 | Cowl, Jane | 1897 | 1960 | Fay, Frank |
| 1891 | 1951 | Brice, Fanny | 1924 | 1973 | Cox, Wally | 1895 | 1962 | Fazenda, Louise |
| 1891 | 1959 | Broderick, Helen | 1847 | 1924 | Crabtree, Lotta | 1918 | 1973 | Field, Betty |
| 1904 | 1951 | Bromberg, J. Edward | 1875 | 1945 | Craven, Frank | 1867 | 1941 | Fields, Lew |
| 1892 | 1973 | Brown, Joe E. | 1903 | 1977 | Crawford, Joan | 1879 | 1946 | Fields, W.C. |
| 1926 | 1966 | Bruce, Lenny | 1916 | 1944 | Cregar, Laird | 1916 | 1977 | Finch, Peter |
| 1895 | 1953 | Bruce, Nigel | 1880 | 1942 | Crews, Laura Hope | 1902 | 1975 | Fine, Larry |
| 1891 | 1957 | Buchanan, Jack | 1830 | 1974 | Crisp, Donald | 1865 | 1932 | Fiske, Minnie Maddern |
| 1836 | 1957 | Buck, Gene | 1943 | 1973 | Croce, Jim | 1888 | 1961 | Fitzgerald, Barry |
| 1904 | 1965 | Bunce, Alan | 1910 | 1960 | Cromwell, Richard | 1874 | 1941 | Fitzgerald, Cissy |
| 1863 | 1915 | Bunny, John | 1903 | 1977 | Crosby, Bing | 1895 | 1962 | Flagstad, Kirsten |
| 1885 | 1970 | Burke, Billie | 1897 | 1975 | Cross, Milton | 1900 | 1971 | Flippen, Jay C. |
| 1912 | 1967 | Burnette, Smiley | 1893 | 1966 | Crouse, Russell | 1909 | 1959 | Flynn, Errol |
| | | | | | | 1925 | 1974 | Flynn, Joe |

| Born | Died | Name | Born | Died | Name | Born | Died | Name |
|------|------|------|------|------|------|------|------|------|
| 1890 | 1977 | Marx, Julius (Groucho) | 1898 | 1943 | O'Connell, Hugh | 1877 | 1968 | St. Denis, Ruth |
| 1887 | 1961 | Marx, Leonard (Chico) | 1881 | 1959 | O'Connor, Una | 1884 | 1955 | Sakall, S.Z. |
| 1862 | 1951 | Maude, Cyril | 1878 | 1945 | O'Hara, Fiske | 1885 | 1936 | Sale (Chic), Charles |
| 1922 | 1972 | Maxwell, Marilyn | 1908 | 1968 | O'Keefe, Dennis | 1906 | 1972 | Sanders, George |
| 1879 | 1948 | May, Edna | 1880 | 1938 | Oland, Warner | 1934 | 1973 | Sands, Diana |
| 1885 | 1957 | Mayer, Louis B. | 1860 | 1932 | Olcott, Chauncey | 1896 | 1960 | Savo, Jimmy |
| 1895 | 1973 | Maynard, Ken | 1885 | 1942 | Oliver, Edna May | 1879 | 1954 | Scheff, Fritzi |
| 1884 | 1945 | McCormack, John | 1892 | 1963 | Olsen, Ole | 1892 | 1930 | Schenck, Joe |
| 1907 | 1962 | McCormick, Myron | 1847 | 1920 | O'Neill, James | 1895 | 1964 | Schildkraut, Joseph |
| 1888 | 1931 | McCoy, Bessie | 1887 | 1949 | Ouspenskaya, Maria | 1865 | 1930 | Schildkraut, Rudolph |
| 1883 | 1936 | McCullough, Paul | 1887 | 1972 | Owen, Reginald | 1889 | 1965 | Schipa, Tito |
| 1895 | 1952 | McDaniel, Hattie | | | | 1882 | 1951 | Schnabel, Artur |
| 1924 | 1965 | McDonald, Marie | 1860 | 1941 | Paderewski, Ignace | 1910 | 1949 | Schumann, Henrietta |
| 1913 | 1975 | McGiver, John | 1889 | 1954 | Pallette, Eugene | 1861 | 1936 | Schumann-Heink, E. |
| 1879 | 1949 | McIntyre, Frank J. | 1894 | 1958 | Pangborn, Franklin | 1866 | 1945 | Scott, Cyril |
| 1857 | 1937 | McIntyre, James | 1914 | 1975 | Parks, Larry | 1914 | 1965 | Scott, Zachary |
| 1879 | 1937 | McKinley, Mabel | 1881 | 1972 | Parsons, Louella | 1843 | 1896 | Scott-Siddons, Mrs. |
| 1886 | 1959 | McLaglen, Victor | 1881 | 1940 | Pasternack, Josef A. | 1892 | 1974 | Seeley, Blossom |
| 1907 | 1971 | McMahon, Horace | 1837 | 1908 | Pastor, Tony | 1902 | 1965 | Selznick, David O. |
| 1880 | 1946 | Meek, Donald | 1843 | 1919 | Patti, Adelina | 1858 | 1935 | Sembrich, Marcella |
| 1879 | 1936 | Meighan, Thomas | 1840 | 1889 | Patti, Carlotta | 1884 | 1960 | Sennett, Mack |
| 1861 | 1931 | Melba, Nellie | 1885 | 1831 | Pavlova, Anna | 1881 | 1951 | Shattuck, Arthur |
| 1890 | 1973 | Melchior, Lauritz | 1899 | 1973 | Paxinou, Katina | 1860 | 1929 | Shaw, Mary |
| 1904 | 1961 | Melton, James | 1917 | 1966 | Pearce, Alice | 1891 | 1972 | Shawn, Ted |
| 1890 | 1963 | Menjou, Adolphe | 1885 | 1950 | Pemberton, Brock | 1868 | 1949 | Shean, Al |
| 1902 | 1966 | Menken, Helen | 1899 | 1967 | Pendleton, Nat | 1915 | 1967 | Sheridan, Ann |
| 1882 | 1939 | Mercer, Beryl | 1904 | 1941 | Penner, Joe | 1924 | 1973 | Sherman, Allan |
| 1880 | 1946 | Merivale, Phillip | 1892 | 1937 | Perkins, Osgood | 1885 | 1934 | Sherman, Lowell |
| 1904 | 1944 | Miller, Glenn | 1893 | 1956 | Peters, Brandon | 1918 | 1970 | Shriner, Herb |
| 1860 | 1926 | Miller, Henry | 1915 | 1963 | Piaf, Edith | 1883 | 1953 | Shubert, Lee |
| 1898 | 1936 | Miller, Marilyn | 1893 | 1957 | Pinza, Ezio | 1755 | 1831 | Siddons, Mrs. Sarah |
| 1895 | 1927 | Mills, Florence | 1900 | 1963 | Pitts, Zasu | 1882 | 1930 | Sills, Milton |
| 1939 | 1976 | Mineo, Sal | 1904 | 1976 | Pons, Lili | 1914 | 1970 | Silvera, Frank |
| 1903 | 1955 | Minnevitch, Borrah | 1903 | 1969 | Portman, Eric | 1900 | 1976 | Sim, Alastair |
| 1917 | 1955 | Miranda, Carmen | 1904 | 1963 | Powell, Dick | 1878 | 1946 | Sis Hopkins (Melville) |
| 1875 | 1957 | Mitchell, Grant | 1869 | 1931 | Power, F. Tyrone | 1891 | 1934 | Skelly, Hal |
| 1892 | 1962 | Mitchell, Thomas | 1914 | 1958 | Power, Tyrone E. | 1858 | 1942 | Skinner, Otis |
| 1880 | 1940 | Mix, Tom | 1872 | 1935 | Powers, Eugene | 1870 | 1952 | Skipworth, Alison |
| 1845 | 1909 | Modjeska, Helena | 1935 | 1977 | Presley, Elvis | 1892 | 1970 | Skulnik, Menasha |
| 1926 | 1962 | Monroe, Marilyn | 1900 | 1964 | Price, George E. | 1863 | 1948 | Smith, C. Aubrey |
| 1912 | 1973 | Monroe, Vaughn | 1856 | 1919 | Primrose, George | 1826 | 1881 | Sothern, Edward A. |
| 1875 | 1964 | Monteux, Pierre | 1954 | 1977 | Prinze, Freddie | 1859 | 1933 | Sothern, Edward H. |
| 1824 | 1861 | Montez, Lola | 1879 | 1956 | Prouty, Jed | 1884 | 1957 | Sothern, Harry |
| 1919 | 1951 | Montez, Maria | 1871 | 1942 | Pryor, Arthur | 1854 | 1932 | Sousa, John Philip |
| 1903 | 1947 | Moore, Grace | 1925 | 1970 | Pyne, Joe | 1884 | 1957 | Sparks, Ned |
| 1885 | 1955 | Moore, Tom | | | | 1876 | 1948 | Speaks, Oley |
| 1876 | 1962 | Moore, Victor | 1906 | 1946 | Ragland, John (Rags) | 1890 | 1970 | Spitalny, Phil |
| 1906 | 1974 | Moorehead, Agnes | 1890 | 1967 | Rains, Claude | 1873 | 1937 | Standing, Guy |
| 1882 | 1949 | Moran, George | 1889 | 1970 | Rambeau, Marjorie | 1871 | 1956 | Stephenson, Henry |
| 1884 | 1952 | Moran, Polly | 1900 | 1947 | Rankin, Arthur | 1900 | 1941 | Stephenson, James |
| 1890 | 1949 | Morgan, Frank | 1892 | 1967 | Rathbone, Basil | 1883 | 1939 | Sterling, Ford |
| 1900 | 1941 | Morgan, Helen | 1897 | 1960 | Ratoff, Gregory | 1882 | 1928 | Stevens, Emily A. |
| 1888 | 1956 | Morgan, Ralph | 1883 | 1953 | Rawlinson, Herbert | 1934 | 1970 | Stevens, Inger |
| 1901 | 1970 | Morris, Chester | 1891 | 1943 | Ray, Charles | 1896 | 1961 | Stewart, Anita |
| 1849 | 1925 | Morris, Clara | 1941 | 1967 | Redding, Otis | 1882 | 1977 | Stokowski, Leopold |
| 1914 | 1959 | Morris, Wayne | 1860 | 1916 | Rehan, Ada | 1873 | 1959 | Stone, Fred |
| 1943 | 1971 | Morrison, Jim | 1893 | 1923 | Reid, Wallace | 1879 | 1953 | Stone, Lewis |
| 1915 | 1977 | Mostel, Zero | 1873 | 1943 | Reinhardt, Max | 1871 | 1954 | Straus, Oskar |
| 1897 | 1969 | Mowbray, Alan | 1909 | 1971 | Rennie, Michael | 1911 | 1960 | Sullavan, Margaret |
| 1897 | 1967 | Muni, Paul | 1870 | 1940 | Richman, Charles | 1902 | 1974 | Sullivan, Ed |
| 1894 | 1953 | Munn, Frank | 1895 | 1972 | Richman, Harry | 1903 | 1956 | Sullivan, Francis L. |
| 1906 | 1955 | Munson, Ona | 1872 | 1961 | Ring, Blanche | 1892 | 1946 | Summerville, Slim |
| 1924 | 1971 | Murphy, Audie | 1888 | 1958 | Risdon, Elizabeth | 1904 | 1969 | Swarthout, Gladys |
| 1885 | 1965 | Murray, Mae | 1898 | 1977 | Ritchard, Cyril | | | |
| | | | 1907 | 1974 | Ritter, Tex | | | |
| 1897 | 1970 | Nagel, Conrad | 1905 | 1969 | Ritter, Thelma | 1897 | 1957 | Talmadge, Norma |
| 1900 | 1973 | Naish, J. Carroll | 1903 | 1966 | Ritz, Al | 1917 | 1968 | Talman, William |
| 1898 | 1961 | Naldi, Nita | 1898 | 1976 | Robeson, Paul | 1900 | 1972 | Tamiroff, Akim |
| 1888 | 1950 | Nash, Florence | 1878 | 1949 | Robinson, Bill | 1878 | 1947 | Tanguay, Eva |
| 1865 | 1945 | Nash, George | 1893 | 1973 | Robinson, Edward G. | 1899 | 1934 | Tashman, Lilyan |
| 1879 | 1945 | Nazimova, Alla | 1865 | 1942 | Robson, May | 1885 | 1966 | Taylor, Deems |
| 1846 | 1905 | Neilson, Ada | 1905 | 1977 | Rochester (E. Anderson) | 1899 | 1958 | Taylor, Estelle |
| 1848 | 1880 | Neilson, Adelaide | 1897 | 1933 | Rodgers, Jimmy | 1887 | 1946 | Taylor, Laurette |
| 1868 | 1957 | Neilson-Terry, Julia | 1894 | 1958 | Rodzinsky, Artur | 1911 | 1969 | Taylor, Robert |
| 1907 | 1975 | Nelson, Ozzie | 1879 | 1935 | Rogers, Will | 1878 | 1938 | Tearle, Conway |
| 1885 | 1967 | Nesbit, Evelyn | 1897 | 1937 | Roland, Ruth | 1884 | 1953 | Tearle, Godfrey |
| 1870 | 1951 | Nethersole, Olga | 1880 | 1962 | Rooney, Pat | 1892 | 1937 | Tell, Alma |
| 1905 | 1956 | Newton, Robert | 1899 | 1966 | Rose, Billy | 1881 | 1934 | Tellegen, Lou |
| 1874 | 1948 | Niblo, Fred | 1882 | 1936 | Rothafel, S. L. (Roxy) | 1864 | 1942 | Tempest, Marie |
| 1890 | 1950 | Nijinsky, Vaslav | 1878 | 1953 | Ruffo, Titta | 1910 | 1963 | Templeton, Alec |
| 1893 | 1974 | Nilsson, Anna Q. | 1892 | 1970 | Ruggles, Charles | 1848 | 1928 | Terry, Ellen |
| 1898 | 1930 | Normand, Mabel | 1864 | 1936 | Russell, Annie | 1874 | 1940 | Tetrazzini, Luisa |
| 1879 | 1959 | Norworth, Jack | 1924 | 1961 | Russell, Gail | 1899 | 1936 | Thalberg, Irving |
| 1905 | 1968 | Novarro, Ramon | 1861 | 1922 | Russell, Lillian | 1857 | 1914 | Thomas, Brandon |
| 1893 | 1951 | Novello, Ivor | 1911 | 1976 | Russell, Rosalind | 1892 | 1960 | Thomas, John Charles |
| | | | 1892 | 1972 | Rutherford, Margaret | 1882 | 1976 | Thorndike, Sybil |
| 1903 | 1978 | Oakie, Jack | 1902 | 1973 | Ryan, Irene | 1869 | 1936 | Thurston, Howard |
| 1860 | 1926 | Oakley, Annie | 1909 | 1973 | Ryan, Robert | 1896 | 1960 | Tibbett, Lawrence |

| Born | Died | Name | Born | Died | Name | Born | Died | Name |
|------|------|------|------|------|------|------|------|------|
| 1887 | 1940 | Tinney, Frank | 1886 | 1957 | Von Stroheim, Erich | 1889 | 1938 | White, Pearl |
| 1909 | 1958 | Todd, Michael | 1887 | 1969 | Walburn, Raymond | 1890 | 1967 | Whiteman, Paul |
| 1906 | 1935 | Todd, Thelma | 1874 | 1964 | Waldron, Charles D. | 1882 | 1943 | Whiting, George |
| 1874 | 1947 | Toler, Sidney | 1904 | 1966 | Walker, June | 1865 | 1948 | Whitty, Dame May |
| 1905 | 1968 | Tone, Franchot | 1919 | 1951 | Walker, Robert | 1906 | 1966 | Whorf, Richard |
| 1878 | 1933 | Torrence, Ernest | 1876 | 1962 | Walter, Bruno | 1895 | 1948 | William, Warren |
| 1867 | 1957 | Toscanini, Arturo | 1878 | 1936 | Walthall, Henry B. | 1877 | 1922 | Williams, Bert |
| 1898 | 1968 | Tracy, Lee | 1872 | 1952 | Ward, Fannie | 1867 | 1918 | Williams, Evan |
| 1900 | 1967 | Tracy, Spencer | 1866 | 1951 | Warfield, David | 1923 | 1953 | Williams, Hank |
| 1903 | 1972 | Traubel, Helen | 1876 | 1958 | Warner, H. B. | 1917 | 1972 | Wilson, Marie |
| 1894 | 1975 | Treacher, Arthur | 1878 | 1964 | Warwick, Robert | 1884 | 1969 | Winninger, Charles |
| 1853 | 1917 | Tree, Herbert Beerbohm | 1924 | 1963 | Washington, Dinah | 1904 | 1959 | Withers, Grant |
| 1890 | 1973 | Truex, Ernest | 1900 | 1977 | Waters, Ethel | 1881 | 1931 | Wolheim, Louis |
| 1883 | 1942 | Tucker, Richard | 1867 | 1945 | Watson, Billy | 1907 | 1961 | Wong, Anna May |
| 1915 | 1975 | Tucker, Richard | 1879 | 1962 | Watson, Lucille | 1892 | 1978 | Wood, Peggy |
| 1884 | 1966 | Tucker, Sophie | 1890 | 1965 | Watson, Minor | 1888 | 1963 | Woolley, Monty |
| 1911 | 1970 | Tufts, Sonny | 1896 | 1966 | Webb, Clifton | 1889 | 1938 | Woolsey, Robert |
| 1874 | 1940 | Turpin, Ben | 1867 | 1942 | Weber, Joe | 1881 | 1956 | Wycherty, Margaret |
| 1908 | 1959 | Twelvetrees, Helen | 1905 | 1973 | Webster, Margaret | 1886 | 1966 | Wynn, Ed |
|      |      |              | 1876 | 1926 | Welch, Ben | 1906 | 1964 | Wynyard, Diana |
| 1894 | 1970 | Ulric, Lenore | 1873 | 1918 | Welch, Joe |      |      |              |
| 1933 | 1975 | Ure, Mary | 1896 | 1975 | Wellman, William | 1891 | 1960 | Young, Clara Kimball |
| 1895 | 1926 | Valentino, Rudolph | 1883 | 1953 | Werrenrath, Reinald | 1887 | 1953 | Young, Roland |
| 1870 | 1950 | Van, Billy B. | 1879 | 1942 | Westley, Helen | 1869 | 1932 | Ziegfeld, Florenz |
| 1894 | 1943 | Veidt, Conrad | 1895 | 1968 | Wheeler, Bert | 1873 | 1976 | Zukor, Adolph |

## Ancient Greeks and Latins

### Greeks

Aeschines, orator, 389-314BC.
Aeschylus, dramatist, 525-456BC.
Aesop, fableist, c620-c560BC.
Anacreon, poet, c582-c485BC.
Anaxagoras, philosopher, c500-428BC.
Archimedes, math. c287-212BC.
Aristophanes, dramatist, c448-380BC.
Aristotle, philosopher, 384-322BC.
Athenaeus, scholar, fl.c200.
Callicrates, architect, fl.5th cent.BC.
Callimachus, poet, c305-240BC.
Democritus, philosopher, c460-370BC.
Demosthenes, orator, 384-322BC.
Diodorus, historian, fl.20BC.
Diogenes, philosopher, c372-c287BC.

Dionysius, historian, d.c7BC.
Empedocles, philosopher, c490-430BC.
Epictetus, philosopher, c55-c135.
Epicurus, philosopher, 341-270BC.
Euclid, mathematician, fl.c300BC.
Euripides, dramatist, c484-406BC.
Heraclitus, philosopher, c535-c475BC.
Herodotus, historian, c484-420BC.
Hesiod, poet, 8th cent. BC.
Hippocrates, physician, c460-377BC.
Homer, poet, believed lived c850BC.
Menander, dramatist, 342-292BC.
Pindar, poet, c518-c438BC.
Plato, philosopher, c428-c347BC.
Plutarch, biographer, c46-120.

Polybius, historian, c200-c118BC.
Pythagoras, phil., math., c580-c500BC.
Sappho, poet, c610-c580BC.
Simonides, poet, 556-c468BC.
Socrates, philosopher, c470-399BC.
Sophocles, dramatist, C496-406BC.
Strabo, geographer, c63BC-AD24.
Thales, philosopher, c634-c546BC.
Themistocles, politician, c524-c460BC.
Theocritus, poet, c310-250BC.
Theophrastus, phil. c372-c287BC.
Thucydides, historian, fl.5th cent.BC.
Timon, philosopher, c320-c230BC.
Xenophon, historian, c434-c355BC.
Zeno, philospher, c495-c430BC.

### Latins

Ammianus, historian, c330-395.
Apuleius, satirist, c124-c170.
Boethius, scholar, c480-524.
Caesar, Julius, general, 100-44BC.
Cato (Elder), statesman, 234-149BC.
Catullus, poet, c84-54BC.
Cicero, orator, 106-43BC.
Claudian, poet, c370-c404.
Gellius, author, c130-c165.
Horace, poet, 65-8BC.
Juvenal, satirist, c60-c127.

Livy, historian, 59BC-AD17.
Lucan, poet, 39-65.
Lucilius, poet, c180-c102BC.
Lucretius, poet, c99-c55BC.
Martial, epigrammatist, c38-c103.
Nepos, historian, c100-c25BC.
Ovid, poet, 43BC-AD17.
Persius, satirist, 34-62.
Plautus, dramatist, c254-c184BC.
Pliny, scholar, 23-79.
Pliny (Younger), author, 62-113.

Quintilian, rhetorician, c35-c97.
Sallust, historian, 86-34BC.
Seneca, philosopher, 4BC-AD65.
Silius, poet, c25-101.
Statius, poet, c45-c96.
Suetonius, biographer, c69-c122.
Tacitus, historian, c56-c120.
Terence, dramatist, 185-c159BC.
Tibullus, poet, c55-c19BC.
Virgil, poet, 70-19BC.
Vitruvius, architect, fl.1st cent.BC.

## Rulers of England and Great Britain

| Name | England | Began | Died | Age | Rgd |
|------|---------|-------|------|-----|-----|
| | **Saxons and Danes** | | | | |
| Egbert | King of Wessex, won allegiance of all English | 829 | 839 | — | 10 |
| Ethelwulf | Son, King of Wessex, Sussex, Kent, Essex | 839 | 858 | — | 19 |
| Ethelbald | Son of Ethelwulf, displaced father in Wessex | 858 | 860 | — | 2 |
| Ethelbert | 2d son of Ethelwulf, united Kent and Wessex | 860 | 866 | — | 6 |
| Ethelred I | 3d son, King of Wessex, fought Danes | 866 | 871 | — | 5 |
| Alfred | The Great, 4th son, defeated Danes, fortified London | 871 | 899 | 52 | 28 |
| Edward | The Elder, Alfred's son, united English, claimed Scotland | 899 | 924 | 55 | 25 |
| Athelstan | The Glorious, Edward's son, King of Mercia, Wessex | 924 | 940 | 45 | 16 |
| Edmund I | 3d son of Edward, King of Wessex, Mercia | 940 | 946 | 25 | 6 |
| Edred | 4th son of Edward | 946 | 955 | 32 | 9 |
| Edwy | The Fair, eldest son of Edmund, King of Wessex | 955 | 959 | 18 | 3 |
| Edgar | The Peaceful, 2d son of Edmund, ruled all English | 959 | 975 | 32 | 17 |
| Edward | The Martyr, eldest son of Edgar, murdered by stepmother | 975 | 978 | 17 | 4 |
| Ethelred II | The Unready, 2d son of Edgar, married Emma of Normandy | 978 | 1016 | 48 | 37 |
| Edmund II | Ironside, son of Ethelred II, King of London | 1016 | 1016 | 27 | 0 |
| Canute | The Dane, gave Wessex to Edmund, married Emma | 1016 | 1035 | 40 | 19 |
| Harold I | Harefoot, natural son of Canute | 1035 | 1040 | — | 5 |
| Hardecanute | Son of Canute by Emma, Danish King | 1040 | 1042 | 24 | 2 |
| Edward | The Confessor, son of Ethelred II (Canonized 1161) | 1042 | 1066 | 62 | 24 |
| Harold II | Edward's brother-in-law, last Saxon King | 1066 | 1066 | 44 | 0 |
| | **House of Normandy** | | | | |
| William I | The Conqueror, defeated Harold at Hastings | 1066 | 1087 | 60 | 21 |
| William II | Rufus, 3d son of William I, killed by arrow | 1087 | 1100 | 43 | 13 |
| Henry I | Beauclerc, youngest son of William I | 1100 | 1135 | 67 | 35 |

### House of Blois

|  |  | | | | |
|---|---|---|---|---|---|
| Stephen | Son of Adela, daughter of William I, and Count of Blois | 1135 | 1154 | 50 | 19 |

### House of Plantagenet

|  |  | | | | |
|---|---|---|---|---|---|
| Henry II | Son of Goeffrey Plantagenet (Angevin) by Matilda, dau. of Henry I | 1154 | 1189 | 56 | 35 |
| Richard I | Coeur de Lion, son of Henry II, crusader | 1189 | 1199 | 42 | 10 |
| John | Lackland, son of Henry II, signed Magna Carta, 1215 | 1199 | 1216 | 50 | 17 |
| Henry III | Son of John, acceded at 9, under regency until 1227 | 1216 | 1272 | 65 | 56 |
| Edward I | Longshanks, son of Henry III | 1272 | 1307 | 68 | 35 |
| Edward II | Son of Edward I, deposed by Parliament, 1327 | 1307 | 1327 | 43 | 20 |
| Edward III | Of Windsor, son of Edward II | 1327 | 1377 | 65 | 50 |
| Richard II | Grandson of Edw. III, minor until 1389, deposed 1399 | 1377 | 1400 | 34 | 22 |

### House of Lancaster

|  |  | | | | |
|---|---|---|---|---|---|
| Henry IV | Son of John of Gaunt, Duke of Lancaster, son of Edw. III | 1399 | 1413 | 47 | 13 |
| Henry V | Son of Henry IV, victor of Agincourt | 1413 | 1422 | 34 | 9 |
| Henry VI | Son of Henry V, deposed 1461, died in Tower | 1422 | 1471 | 49 | 39 |

### House of York

|  |  | | | | |
|---|---|---|---|---|---|
| Edward IV | Great-great-grandson of Edward III, son of Duke of York | 1461 | 1483 | 41 | 22 |
| Edward V | Son of Edward IV, murdered in Tower of London | 1483 | 1483 | 13 | 0 |
| Richard III | Crookback, bro. of Edward IV, fell at Bosworth Field | 1483 | 1485 | 35 | 2 |

### House of Tudor

|  |  | | | | |
|---|---|---|---|---|---|
| Henry VII | Son of Edmund Tudor, Earl of Richmond, whose father had married the widow of Henry V; descended from Edward III through his mother, Margaret Beaufort via John of Gaunt. By marriage with dau. of Edward IV he united Lancaster and York | 1485 | 1509 | 53 | 24 |
| Henry VIII | Son of Henry VII by Elizabeth, dau. of Edward IV | 1509 | 1547 | 56 | 38 |
| Edward VI | Son of Henry VIII, by Jane Seymour, his 3d queen. Ruled under regents. Was forced to name Lady Jane Grey his successor. Council of State proclaimed her queen July 10, 1553. Mary Tudor won Council, was proclaimed queen July 19, 1553. Mary had Lady Jane Grey beheaded for treason, Feb., 1554 | 1547 | 1553 | 16 | 6 |
| Mary I | Daughter of Henry VIII, by Catherine of Aragon | 1553 | 1558 | 43 | 5 |
| Elizabeth I | Daughter of Henry VIII, by Anne Boleyn | 1558 | 1603 | 69 | 44 |

## Great Britain

### House of Stuart

|  |  | | | | |
|---|---|---|---|---|---|
| James I | James VI of Scotland, son of Mary, Queen of Scots. *First to call himself King of Great Britain. This became official with the Act of Union, 1707* | 1603 | 1625 | 59 | 22 |
| Charles I | Only surviving son of James I; beheaded Jan. 30, 1649 | 1625 | 1649 | 48 | 24 |

### Commonwealth, 1649-1660
Council of State, 1649; Protectorate, 1653

|  |  | | | | |
|---|---|---|---|---|---|
| The Cromwells | Oliver Cromwell, Lord Protector | 1653 | 1658 | 59 | — |
| | Richard Cromwell, son, Lord Protector, resigned May 25, 1659 | 1658 | 1712 | 86 | — |

### House of Stuart (Restored)

|  |  | | | | |
|---|---|---|---|---|---|
| Charles II | Eldest son of Charles I, died without issue | 1660 | 1685 | 55 | 25 |
| James II | 2d son of Charles I. Deposed 1688. Interregnum Dec. 11, 1688, to Feb. 13, 1689 | 1685 | 1701 | 68 | 3 |
| William III | Son of William, Prince of Orange, by Mary, dau. of Charles I | 1689 | 1702 | 51 | 13 |
| and Mary II | Eldest daughter of James II and wife of William III | | 1694 | 33 | 6 |
| Anne | 2d daughter of James II | 1702 | 1714 | 49 | 12 |

### House of Hanover

|  |  | | | | |
|---|---|---|---|---|---|
| George I | Son of Elector of Hanover, by Sophia, grand-dau. of James I | 1714 | 1727 | 67 | 13 |
| George II | Only son of George I, married Caroline of Brandenburg | 1727 | 1760 | 77 | 33 |
| George III | Grandson of George II, married Charlotte of Mecklenburg | 1760 | 1820 | 81 | 59 |
| George IV | Eldest son of George III, Prince Regent, from Feb., 1811 | 1820 | 1830 | 67 | 10 |
| William IV | 3d son of George III, married Adelaide of Saxe-Meiningen | 1830 | 1837 | 71 | 7 |
| Victoria | Dau. of Edward, 4th son of George III; married (1840) Prince Albert of Saxe-Coburg and Gotha, who became Prince Consort | 1837 | 1901 | 81 | 63 |

### House of Saxe-Coburg and Gotha

|  |  | | | | |
|---|---|---|---|---|---|
| Edward VII | Eldest son of Victoria, married Alexandra, Princess of Denmark | 1901 | 1910 | 68 | 9 |

### House of Windsor
*Name Adopted July 17, 1917*

|  |  | | | | |
|---|---|---|---|---|---|
| George V | 2d son of Edward VII, married Princess Mary of Teck | 1910 | 1936 | 70 | 25 |
| Edward VIII | Eldest son of George V; acceded Jan. 20, 1936, abdicated Dec. 11 | 1936 | 1972 | 77 | 1 |
| George VI | 2d son of George V; married Lady Elizabeth Bowes-Lyon | 1936 | 1952 | 56 | 15 |
| Elizabeth II | Elder daughter of George VI, acceded Feb. 6, 1952 | 1952 | — | — | — |

## Rulers of Scotland

The Romans gave the name of Caledonia to present-day Scotland. The Scots, a Celtic race that spoke Gaelic, came from Ireland, then called Scotia.

Kenneth I MacAlpin was the first Scot to rule both Scots and Picts, 846 AD.

Duncan I was the first general ruler, 1034. Macbeth seized the kingdom 1040, but was slain by Duncan's son, Malcolm III MacDuncan (Canmore), 1057.

Malcolm married Margaret, Saxon princess who had fled from the Normans. Queen Margaret introduced English language and English monastic customs. She was canonized, 1250. Her son Edgar, 1097, moved the court to Edinburgh. His brothers Alexander I and David I succeeded. Malcolm IV, the Maiden, 1153, grandson of David I, was followed by his brother, William the Lion, 1165, whose son was Alexander II, 1214. The latter's son, Alexander III, 1249, defeated the Norse and regained the Hebrides. When he died, 1286, his granddaughter, Margaret, child of Eric of Norway and grandniece of Edward I of England, known as the Maid of Norway, was chosen ruler, but died 1290, aged 8.

John Baliol, 1292-1296. (Interregnum, 10 years).

Robert Bruce (The Bruce), 1306-1329, victor at Bannockburn, 1314.

David II, only son of Robert Bruce, ruled 1329-1371.

Robert II, 1371-1390, grandson of Robert Bruce, son of Walter, the Steward of Scotland, was called The Steward, first of the so-called Stuart line.

Robert III, son of Robert II, 1390-1406.
James I, son of Robert III, 1406-1437.
James II, son of James I, 1437-1460.
James III, eldest son of James II, 1460-1488.
James IV, eldest son of James III, 1488-1513.
James V, eldest son of James IV, 1513-1542.

Mary, daughter of Jame V, born 1542, became queen when 1 week old; was crowned 1543. Married, 1558, Francis, son of Henry II of France, who became king 1559, died

1560. Mary ruled Scots 1561 until abdication, 1567. She also married (2) Henry Stewart, Lord Darnley, and (3) James, Earl of Bothwell. Imprisoned by Elizabeth I, Mary was beheaded 1587.

James VI, 1567-1625, son of Mary and Lord Darnley, became King of England on death of Elizabeth in 1603. Although the thrones were thus united, the legislative union of Scotland and England was not effected until the Act of Union, May 1, 1707.

# Rulers of France: Kings, Queens, Presidents

## Caesar to Charlemagne

Julius Caesar subdued the Gauls, native tribes of Gaul (France) 57 to 52 BC. The Romans ruled 500 years. The Franks, a Teutonic tribe, reached the Somme from the East ca. 250 AD. By the 5th century the Merovingian Franks ousted the Romans. In 451 AD, with the help of Visigoths, Burgundians and others, they defeated Attila and the Huns at Chalons-sur-Marne.

Childeric I became leader of the Merovingians 458 AD. His son Clovis I (Chlodwig, Ludwig, Louis), crowned 481, founded the dynasty. After defeating the Alemanni (Germans) 496, he was baptized a Christian and made Paris his capital. His line ruled until Childeric III was deposed, 751.

The West Merovingians were called Neustrians, the eastern Austrasians. Pepin of Herstal (687-714) major domus, or head of the palace, of Austrasia, took over Neustria as dux (leader) of the Franks. Pepin's son, Charles, called Martel (the Hammer) defeated the Saracens at Tours-Poitiers, 732; was succeeded by his son, Pepin the Short, 741, who deposed Childeric III and ruled as king until 768.

His son, Charlemagne, or Charles the Great (742-814) became king of the Franks, 768, with his brother Carloman, who died 771. He ruled France, Germany, parts of Italy, Spain, Austria, and enforced Christianity. Crowned Emperor of the Romans by Pope Leo III in St. Peter's, Rome, Dec. 25, 800 AD. Succeeded by son, Louis I the Pious, 814. At death, 840, Louis left empire to sons, Lothair (Roman emperor); Pepin I (king of Aquitaine); Louis II (of Germany); Charles the Bald (France). They quarreled and by the peace of Verdun, 843, divided the empire.

**AD  Name, year of accession**

### The Carolingians

843  Charles I (the Bald), Roman Emperor, 875
877  Louis II (the Stammerer), son
879  Louis III (died 882) and Carloman, brothers
885  Charles II (the Fat), Roman Emperor, 881
888  Eudes (Odo) elected by nobles
898  Charles III (the Simple), son of Louis II, defeated by
922  Robert, brother of Eudes, killed in war
923  Rudolph (Raoul) Duke of Burgundy
936  Louis IV, son of Charles III
954  Lothair, son, aged 13, defeated by Capet
986  Louis V (the Sluggard), left no heirs

### The Capets

987  Hugh Capet, son of Hugh the Great
996  Robert II (the Wise), his son
1031  Henry I, his son, last Norman
1060  Philip I (the Fair), son
1108  Louis VI (the Fat), son
1137  Louis VII (the Younger), son
1180  Philip II (Augustus), son, crowned at Reims
1223  Louis VIII (the Lion), son
1226  Louis IX, son, crusader; Louis IX (1214-1270) reigned 44 years, arbitrated disputes with English King Henry III; led crusades, 1248 (captured in Egypt 1250) and 1270, when he died of plague in Tunis. Canonized 1297 as St. Louis.
1270  Philip III (the Hardy), son
1285  Philip IV (the Fair), son, king at 17
1314  Louis X (the Headstrong), son. His posthumous son, John I, lived only 7 days
1316  Philip V (the Tall), brother of Louis X
1322  Charles IV (the Fair), brother of Louis X

### House of Valois

1328  Philip VI (of Valois), grandson of Philip III
1350  John II (the Good), his son, retired to England
1364  Charles V (the Wise), son
1380  Charles VI (the Beloved), son
1422  Charles VII (the Victorious), son. In 1429 Joan of Arc (Jeanne d'Arc) promised Charles to oust the English, who occupied northern France. Joan won at Orleans and Patay and had Charles crowned at Reims July 17, 1429. Joan was captured May 24, 1430, and executed May 30, 1431, at Rouen for heresy. Charles ordered her rehabilitation, effected 1455.
1461  Louis XI (the Cruel), son, civil reformer

1483  Charles VIII (the Affable), son
1498  Louis XII, great-grandson of Charles V
1515  Francis I, of Angouleme, nephew, son-in-law. Francis I (1494-1547) reigned 32 years, fought 4 big wars, was patron of the arts, aided Cellini, del Sarto, Leonardo da Vinci, Rabelais, Embellished Fontainebleau.
1547  Henry II, son, killed at a joust in a tournament. He was the husband of Catherine de Medicis (1519-1589) and the lover of Diane de Poitiers (1499-1566). Catherine was born in Florence, daughter of Lorenzo de Medicis. By her marriage to Henry II she became the mother of Francis II, Charles IX, Henry III and Queen Margaret (Reine Margot) wife of Henry IV. She persuaded Charles IX to order the massacre of Huguenots on the Feast of St. Bartholomew, Aug. 24, 1572, the day her daughter was married to Henry of Navarre.
1559  Francis II, son. In 1548, Mary, Queen of Scots since infancy, was betrothed to Henry II she became the mother of Francis II. They were married 1558. Francis died 1560, aged 16; Mary ruled Scotland, abdicated 1567.
1560  Charles IX, brother
1574  Henry III, brother, assassinated

### House of Bourbon

1589  Henry IV, of Navarre, assassinated. Henry IV made enemies when he gave tolerance to Protestants by Edict of Nantes, 1598. He was grandson of Queen Margaret of Navarre, literary patron. He married Margaret of Valois, daughter of Henry II and Catherine de Medicis; was divorced; in 1600 married Marie de Medicis, who became Regent of France, 1610-17 for her son, Louis XIII, but was exiled by Richelieu, 1631.
1610  Louis XIII (the Just), son. Louis XIII (1601-1643) married Anne of Austria. His ministers were Cardinals Richelieu and Mazarin.
1643  Louis XIV (The Grand Monarch), son. Louis XIV was king 72 years. He exhausted a prosperous country in wars for thrones and territory. By revoking the Edict of Nantes (1685) he caused the emigration of the Huguenots. He said: "I am the state."
1715  Louis XV, great-grandson. Louis XV married a Polish princess; lost Canada to the English. His favorites, Mme. Pompadour and Mme. Du Barry, influenced policies. Noted for saying "After me, the deluge".
1774  Louis XVI, grandson; married Marie Antoinette, daughter of Empress Maria Therese of Austria. King and queen beheaded by Revolution, 1793. Their son, called Louis XVII, died in prison, never ruled.

### First Republic

1792  National Convention of the French Revolution
1795  Directory, under Barras and others
1799  Consulate, Napoleon Bonaparte, first consul. Elected consul for life, 1802.

### First Empire

1804  Napoleon I, emperor. Josephine (de Beauharnais) empress, 1804-09; Marie Louise, empress, 1810-1814. Her son, Francois (1811-1832), titular King of Rome, later Duke de Reichstadt and "Napoleon II," never ruled. Napoleon abdicated 1814, died 1821.

### Bourbons Restored

1814  Louis XVIII king; brother of Louis XVI.
1824  Charles X, brother; reactionary; deposed by the July Revolution, 1830.

### House of Orleans

1830  Louis-Philippe, the "citizen king."

### Second Republic

1848  Louis Napoleon Bonaparte, president, nephew of Napoleon I. He became:

### Second Empire

1852  Napoleon III, emperor; Eugenie (de Montijo) empress. Lost Franco-Prussian war, deposed 1870. Son, Prince

Imperial (1856-79), died in Zulu War. Eugenie died 1920.

## Third Republic—Presidents

**1871** Thiers, Louis Adolphe (1797-1877)
**1873** MacMahon, Marshall Patrice M. de (1808-1893)
**1879** Grevy, Paul J. (1807-1891)
**1887** Sadi-Carnot, M. (1837-1894), assassinated
**1894** Casimir-Perier, Jean P. P. (1847-1907)
**1895** Faure, Francois Felix (1841-1899)
**1899** Loubet, Emile (1838-1929)
**1906** Fallieres, C. Armand (1841-1931)
**1913** Poincare, Raymond (1860-1934)
**1920** Deschanel, Paul (1856-1922)
**1920** Millerand, Alexandre (1859-1943)
**1924** Doumergue, Gaston (1863-1937)
**1931** Doumer, Paul (1857-1932), assassinated

**1932** Lebrun, Albert (1871-1950), resigned 1940
**1940** **Vichy govt.** under German armistice: Henri Philippe Petain (1856-1951) Chief of State, 1940-1944.
**Provisional govt.** after liberation: Charles de Gaulle (1890-1970) Oct. 1944-Jan. 21, 1946; Felix Gouin (1884-1977) Jan. 23, 1946; Georges Bidault (1899-     ) June 24, 1946.

## Fourth Republic—Presidents

**1947** Auriol, Vincent (1884-1966)
**1954** Coty, Rene (1882-1962)

## Fifth Republic—Presidents

**1959** de Gaulle, Charles Andre J. M. (1890-1970)
**1969** Pompidou, Georges (1911-1974)
**1974** Giscard d'Estaing, Valery (1926-     )

# Rulers of Middle Europe; Rise and Fall of Dynasties

## Carolingian Dynasty

Charles the Great, or Charlemagne, ruled France, Italy, and Middle Europe; established Ostmark (later Austria); crowned Roman emperor by pope in Rome, 800 AD; died 814.

Louis I (Ludwig) the Pious, son; crowned by Charlemagne 814, d. 840.

Louis II, the German, son; succeeded to East Francia (Germany) 843-876.

Charles the Fat, son; inherited East Francia and West Francia (France) 876, reunited empire, crowned emperor by pope, 881, deposed 887.

Arnulf, nephew, 887-899. Partition of empire.

Louis the Child, 899-911, last direct descendant of Charlemagne.

Conrad I, duke of Franconia, first elected German king, 911-918, founded House of Franconia.

## Saxon Dynasty; First Reich

Henry I, the Fowler, duke of Saxony, 919-936.

Otto I, the Great, 936-973, son; crowned Holy Roman Emperor by pope, 962.

Otto II, 973-983, son; failed to oust Greeks and Arabs from Sicily.

Otto III, 983-1002, son; crowned emperor at 16.

Henry II, the Saint, duke of Bavaria, 1002-1024, great-grandson of Otto the Great.

## House of Franconia

Conrad II, 1024-1039, elected king of Germany.

Henry III, the Black, 1039-1056, son; deposed 3 popes; annexed Burgundy.

Henry IV, 1056-1106, son; regency by his mother, Agnes of Poitou. Banned by Pope Gregory VII, he did penance at Canossa.

Henry V, 1106-1125, son; last of Salic House.

Lothair, duke of Saxony, 1125-1137. Crowned emperor in Rome, 1134.

## House of Hohenstaufen

Conrad III, duke of Suabia, 1138-1152. In 2d Crusade.

Frederick I, Barbarossa, 1152-1190; Conrad's nephew.

Henry VI, 1190-1196, took lower Italy from Normans. Son became king of Sicily.

Philip of Suabia, 1198-1208, brother.

Otto IV, of House of Welf, 1198-1215; deposed.

Frederick II, 1215-1250, son of Henry VI; king of Sicily; crowned king of Jerusalem; in 5th Crusade.

Conrad IV, 1250-1254, son; lost lower Italy to Charles of Anjou.

Conradin (1252-1268) son, king of Jerusalem and Sicily, beheaded. Last Hohenstaufen.

Interregnum, 1254-1273, Rise of the Electors.

## Transition

Rudolph I of Hapsburg, 1273-1291, defeated King Ottocar II of Bohemia. Bequeathed duchy of Austria to eldest son, Albert.

Adolph of Nassau, 1292-1298, killed in war with Albert of Austria.

Albert I, king of Germany, 1298-1308, son of Rudolph.

Henry VII, of Luxemburg, 1308-1313, crowned emperor in Rome. Seized Bohemia, 1310.

Louis IV of Bavaria (Wittelsbach), 1314-1347. Also elected was Frederick of Austria, 1314-1330 (Hapsburg). Abolition of papal sanction for election of Holy Roman Emperor.

Charles IV, of Luxemburg, 1347-1378, grandson of Henry VII, German emperor and king of Bohemia, Lombardy, Burgundy; took Mark of Brandenburg.

Wenceslaus, 1378-1400, deposed.

Rupert, Duke of Palatine, 1400-1410.

## Hungary

Stephen I, house of Arpad, 997-1038. Crowned king 1000; converted Magyars; canonized 1083. After several centuries of feuds Charles Robert of Anjou became Charles I, 1308-1342.

Louis I, the Great, son, 1342-1382; joint ruler of Poland with Casimir III, 1370. Defeated Turks.

Mary, daughter, 1382-1395, ruled with husband. Sigismund of Luxemburg, 1387-1437, also king of Bohemia. As bro. of Wenceslaus he succeeded Rupert as Holy Roman Emperor, 1410.

Albert II, 1438-1439, son-in-law of Sigismund; also Roman emperor. (see under Hapsburg.)

Ladislas V of Poland, 1440-1444.

Ladislaus V, posthumous son, 1444-1457. John Hunyadi (Hunyadi Janos) guardian, fought Turks, Czechs; died 1456.

Matthias I (Corvinus) son of Hunyadi, 1458-1490. Shared rule of Bohemia, captured Vienna, 1485, annexed Austria, Styria, Carinthia.

Ladislas II (king of Bohemia), 1490-1516.

Louis II, son, aged 10, 1516-1526. Wars with Suleiman, Turk. In 1527 Hungary was split between Ferdinand I, Archduke of Austria, bro.-in-law of Louis II, and John Zapolya of Transylvania. After Turkish invasion, 1547, Hungary was split between Ferdinand, Prince John Sigismund (Transylvania) and the Turks.

## House of Hapsburg

Albert V of Austria, Hapsburg, crowned king of Hungary, Jan. 1438, Roman emperor, March, 1438, as Albert II; died 1439.

Frederick III, cousin, 1440-1493. Fought Turks.

Maximilian I, son, 1493-1519. Assumed title of Holy Roman Emperor (German), 1493.

Charles V, grandson, 1519-1556. King of Spain with mother co-regent; crowned Roman emperor at Aix, 1520. Confronted Luther at Worms; attempted church reform and religious conciliation; abdicated 1556.

Ferdinand I, king of Bohemia, 1526, of Hungary, 1527; disputed. German king, 1531. Crowned Roman emperor on abdication of brother Charles V, 1556.

Maximilian II, son, 1564-1576.

Rudolph II, son, 1576-1612.

Matthias, brother, 1612-1619, king of Bohemia and Hungary.

Ferdinand II of Styria, king of Bohemia, 1617, of Hungary, 1618, Roman emperor, 1619. Bohemian Protestants deposed him, elected Frederick V of Palatine, starting Thirty Years War.

Ferdinand III, son, king of Hungary, 1625, Bohemia, 1627, Roman emperor, 1637. Peace of Westphalia, 1648, ended war. Leopold I, 1658-1705; Joseph I, 1705-1711; Charles VI, 1711-1740.

Maria Theresa, daughter, 1740-1780. Archduchess of Austria, queen of Hungary; ousted pretender, Charles VII, crowned 1742; in 1745 obtained election of her husband Francis I as Roman emperor and co-regent (d. 1765). Fought Seven Years' War with Frederick II (the Great) of Prussia. Mother of Marie Antoinette, Queen of France.

Joseph II, son 1765-1790, Roman emperor, reformer; powers restricted by Empress Maria Theresa until her death, 1780. First partition of Poland. Leopold II, 1790-1792.

Francis II, son, 1792-1835. Fought Napoleon. Proclaimed first hereditary emperor of Austria, 1806. Forced to abdicate as Roman emperor, 1806; last use of title. Ferdinand I, son, 1835-1848, abdicated during revolution.

## Austro-Hungarian Monarchy

Francis Joseph I, nephew, 1848-1916, emperor of Austria, king of Hungary. Dual monarchy of Austria-Hungary formed, 1867. After assassination of heir, Archduke Francis Ferdinand, June 28, 1914, Austrian diplomacy precipitated World War I.

Charles I, grand-nephew, 1916-1918, last emperor of Austria and king of Hungary. Abdicated Nov. 11-13, 1918, died 1922.

## Rulers of Prussia

Nucleus of Prussia was the Mark of Brandenburg. First margrave was Albert the Bear (Albrecht), 1134-1170. First Hohenzollern margrave was Frederick, burggrave of Nuremberg, 1417-1440.

Frederick William, 1640-1688, the Great Elector. Son, Frederick III, 1688-1713, was crowned King Frederick of Prussia, 1701.

Frederick William I, son, 1713-1740.

Frederick II, the Great, son, 1740-1786, annexed Silesia part of Austria.

Frederick William II, nephew, 1786-1797.

Frederick William III, son, 1797-1840. Napoleonic wars.

Frederick William IV, son, 1840-1861. Uprising of 1848 and first parliament and constitution.

### Second and Third Reich

William I, 1861-1888, brother. Annexation of Schleswig and Hanover; Franco-Prussian war, 1870-71, proclamation of German Reich, Jan. 18, 1871, at Versailles; William, German emperor (Deutscher Kaiser), Bismarck, chancellor.

Frederick III, son, 1888.

William II, son, 1888-1918. Led Germany in World War I, abdicated as German emperor and king of Prussia, Nov. 9, 1918. Died in exile in Netherlands June 4, 1941. Minor rulers of Bavaria, Saxony, Wurttemberg also abdicated.

Germany proclaimed a republic at Weimar, July 1, 1919. Presidents: Frederick Ebert, 1919-1925, Paul von Hindenburg-Beneckendorff, 1925, reelected 1932, d. Aug. 2, 1934. Adolf Hitler, chancellor, chosen successor as Leader-Chancellor (Fuehrer & Reichskanzler) of Third Reich. Annexed Austria, March, 1938. Precipitated World War II, 1939-1945. Committed suicide April 30, 1945.

## Rulers of Denmark, Sweden, Norway

### Denmark

Earliest rulers invaded Britain; King Canute, who ruled in London 1016-1035, was most famous. The Valdemars furnished kings until the 15th century. In 1282 the Danes won the first national assembly, Danehof, from King Erik V.

Most redoubtable medieval character was Margaret, daughter of Valdemar IV, born 1353, married at 10 to King Haakon VI of Norway. In 1376 she had her first infant son Olaf made king of Denmark. After his death, 1387, she was regent of Denmark and Norway. In 1388 Sweden accepted her as sovereign. In 1389 she made her grand-nephew, Duke Erik of Pomerania, titular king of Denmark, Sweden, and Norway, with herself as regent. In 1397 she effected the Union of Kalmar of the three kingdoms and had Erik VII crowned. In 1439 the three kingdoms deposed him and elected, 1440, Christopher of Bavaria king (Christopher III). On his death, 1448, the union broke up.

Succeeding rulers were unable to enforce their claims as rulers of Sweden until 1520, when Christian II conquered Sweden. He was thrown out 1522, and in 1523 Gustavus Vasa united Sweden. Denmark continued to dominate Norway until the Napoleonic wars, when Frederick VI, 1808-1839, joined the Napoleonic cause after Britain had destroyed the Danish fleet, 1807. In 1814 he was forced to cede Norway to Sweden and Helgoland to Britain, receiving Lauenburg. Successors Christian VIII, 1839; Frederick VII, 1848; Christian IX, 1863; Frederick VIII, 1906; Christian X, 1912; Frederick IX, 1947; Margrethe II, 1972.

### Sweden

Early kings ruled at Uppsala, but did not dominate the country. Sverker, c1130-c1156, united the Swedes and Goths. In 1435 Sweden obtained the Riksdag, or parliament. After the Union of Kalmar, 1379, the Danes either ruled or harried the country until Christian II of Denmark conquered it anew, 1520. This led to a rising under Gustavus Vasa, who ruled Sweden 1523-1560, and established an independent kingdom. Charles IX, 1599-1611, crowned 1604, conquered Moscow. Gustavus II Adolphus, 1611-1632, was called the Lion of the North. Later rulers: Christina, 1632; Charles X, Gustavus 1654; Charles XI, 1660; Charles XII (invader of Russia and Poland, defeated at Poltava, June 28, 1709), 1697; Ulrika Eleanora, sister, elected queen 1718; Frederick I (of Hesse), her husband, 1720; Adolphus Frederick, 1751; Gustavus III, 1771; Gustavus IV Adolphus, 1792; Charles XIII, 1809. (Union with Norway began 1814.) Charles XIV John, 1818. He was Jean Bernadotte, Napoleon's Prince of Ponte Corvo, elected 1810 to succeed Charles XIII. He founded the present dynasty: Oscar I, 1844, Charles XV, 1859; Oscar II, 1872; Gustavus V, 1907; Gustav VI Adolf, 1950; Carl XVI Gustaf, 1973.

### Norway

Overcoming many rivals, Harald Haarfager, 872-930, conquered Norway, Orkneys, and Shetlands; Olaf I, great-grandson, 995-1000, brought Christianity into Norway, Iceland, and Greenland. In 1035 Magnus the Good also became king of Denmark. Haakon V, 1299-1319, had married his daughter to Erik of Sweden. Their son, Magnus became ruler of Norway and Sweden at 6. His son, Haakon VI, married Margaret of Denmark; their son Olaf IV became king of Norway and Denmark, followed by Margaret's regency and the Union of Kalmar, 1397.

In 1450 Norway became subservient to Denmark. Christian IV, 1588-1648, founded Christiania, now Oslo. After Napoleonic wars, when Denmark ceded Norway to Sweden, a strong nationalist movement forced recognition of Norway as an independent kingdom united with Sweden under the Swedish kings, 1814-1905. In 1905 the union was dissolved and Prince Carl of Denmark became Haakon VII. He died Sept. 21, 1957, aged 85; succeeded by son, Olav V, b. July 2, 1903.

## Rulers of the Netherlands and Belgium

### The Netherlands (Holland)

William Frederick, Prince of Orange, led a revolt against French rule, 1813, and was crowned King of the Netherlands, 1815. Belgium seceded Oct. 4, 1830, after a revolt, and formed a separate government. The change was ratified by the two kingdoms by treaty Apr. 19, 1839.

Succession: William II, son, 1840; William III, son, 1849; Wilhelmina, daughter of William III and his 2d wife Princess Emma of Waldeck, 1890; Wilhelmina abdicated, Sept. 4, 1948, in favor of daughter, Juliana.

### Belgium

A national congress elected Prince Leopold of Saxe-Coburg King; he took the throne July 21, 1831, as Leopold I. Succession: Leopold II, son 1865; Albert I, nephew of Leopold II, 1909; Leopold III, son of Albert, 1934; Prince Charles, Regent 1944; Leopold returned 1950, yielded powers to son Baudouin, Prince Royal, Aug. 6, 1950, abdicated July 16, 1951. Baudouin I took throne July 17, 1951.

*For political history prior to 1830 see articles on the Netherlands and Belgium.*

## Roman Rulers

From Romulus to the end of the Empire in the West. Rulers of the Roman Empire in the East sat in Constantinople and for a brief period in Nicaea, until the capture of Constantinople by the Turks in 1453, when Byzantium was succeeded by the Ottoman Empire.

| BC | Name | BC | Name | AD | Name |
|---|---|---|---|---|---|
| | **The Kingdom** | 366 | Praetorship established | | Caesar Octavianus) |
| 753 | Romulus (Quirinus) | 366 | Curule Aedileship crested | 14 | Tiberius I |
| 716 | Numa Pompilius | 362 | Military Tribunate elective | 37 | Gaius Caesar (Caligula) |
| 673 | Tullus Hostilius | 326 | Proconsulate introduced | 41 | Claudius I |
| 640 | Ancus Marcius | 311 | Naval Duumvirate elective | 54 | Nero |
| 616 | L. Tarquinius Priscus | 217 | Dictatorship of Fabius Maximus | 68 | Galba |
| 578 | Servius Tullius | 133 | Tribunate of Tiberius Gracchua | 69 | Galba; Otho, Vitellius |
| 534 | L. Tarquinius Superbus | 123 | Tribunate of Gaius Gracchus | 69 | Vespasianus |
| | **The Republic** | 82 | Dictatorship of Sulla | 79 | Titus |
| 509 | Consulate established | 60 | First Triumvirate formed | 81 | Domitianus |
| 509 | Quaestorship instituted | | (Caesar, Pompeius, Crassus) | 96 | Nerva |
| 498 | Dictatorship introduced | 46 | Dictatorship of Caesar | 98 | Trajanus |
| 494 | Plebeian Tribunate created | 43 | Second Triumvirate formed | 117 | Hadrianus |
| 494 | Plebeian Aedileship created | | (Octavianus, Antonius, Lepidus) | 138 | Antoninus Pius |
| 444 | Consular Tribunate organized | | **The Empire** | 161 | Marcus Aurelius and Lucius Verus |
| 435 | Censorship instituted | 27 | Augustus (Gaius Julius | 169 | Marcus Aurelius (alone) |

| | | |
|---|---|---|
| 180 | Commodus | |
| 193 | Pertinax; Julianus I | |
| 193 | Septimius Severus | |
| 211 | Caracalla and Geta | |
| 212 | Caracalla (alone) | |
| 217 | Macrinus | |
| 218 | Elagabalus (Heliogabalus) | |
| 222 | Alexander Severus | |
| 235 | Maximinus I (the Thracian) | |
| 238 | Gordianus I and Gordianus II; Pupienus and Balbinus | |
| 238 | Gordianus III | |
| 244 | Philippus (the Arabian) | |
| 249 | Decius | |
| 251 | Gallus and Volusianus | |
| 253 | Aemilianus | |
| 253 | Valerianus and Gallienus | |
| 258 | Gallienus (alone) | |
| 268 | Claudius II (the Goth) | |
| 270 | Quintillus | |
| 270 | Aurelianus | |
| 275 | Tacitus | |
| 276 | Florianus | |
| 276 | Probus | |
| 282 | Carus | |
| 283 | Carinus and Numerianus | |
| 284 | Diocletianus | |
| 286 | Diocletianus and Maximianus | |
| 305 | Galerius and Constantius I | |
| 306 | Galerius, Maximinus II, Severus I | |
| 307 | Galerius, Maximinus II, Constantinus I, Licinius, Maxentius | |
| 311 | Maximinus II, Constantinus I, Licinius, Maxentius | |
| 314 | Maximinus II, Constantinus I, Licinius | |
| 314 | Constantinus I and Licinius | |
| 324 | Constantinus I (the Great) | |
| 337 | Constantinus II, Constans I, Constantius II | |
| 340 | Constantius II and Constans I | |
| 350 | Constantius II | |
| 361 | Julianus II (the Apostate) | |
| 363 | Jovianus | |

**West (Rome) and East (Constantinople)**

| | | |
|---|---|---|
| 364 | Valentinianus I (West) and Valens (East) | |
| 367 | Valentinianus I with Gratianus (West) and Valens (East) | |
| 375 | Gratianus with Valentinianus II (West) and Valens (East) | |
| 378 | Gratianus with Valentinianus II (West) Theodosius I (East) | |
| 383 | Valentinianus II (West) and Theodosius I (East) | |
| 394 | Theodosius I (the Great) | |
| 395 | Honorius (West) and Arcadius (East) | |
| 408 | Honorius (West) and Theodosius II (East) | |
| 423 | Valentinianus III (West) and Theodosius II (East) | |
| 450 | Valentinianus III (West) and Marcianus (East) | |
| 455 | Maximus (West), Avitus (West); Marcianus (East) | |
| 456 | Avitus (West), Marcianus (East) | |
| 457 | Majorianus (West), Leo I (East) | |
| 461 | Severus II (West), Leo I (East) | |
| 467 | Anthemius (West), Leo I (East) | |
| 472 | Olybrius (West), Leo I (East) | |
| 473 | Glycerius (West), Leo I (East) | |
| 474 | Julius Nepos (West), Leo II (East) | |
| 475 | Romulus Augustulus (West) and Zeno (East) | |
| 476 | End of Empire in West; Odovacar, King, drops title of Emperor; murdered by King Theodoric of Ostrogoths 493 AD | |

## Rulers of Modern Italy

After the fall of Napoleon in 1814, the Congress of Vienna, 1815, restored Italy as a political patchwork, comprising the Kingdom of Naples and Sicily, the Papal States, and smaller units. Piedmont and Genoa were awarded to Sardinia, ruled by King Victor Emmanuel I of Savoy.

United Italy emerged under the leadership of Camillo, Count di Cavour (1810-1861), Sardinian prime minister. Agitation was led by Giuseppe Mazzini (1805-1872) and Giuseppe Garibaldi (1807-1882), soldier. Victor Emmanuel I abdicated 1821. After a brief regency for a brother, Charles Albert was King 1831-1849, abdicating when defeated by the Austrians at Novara. Succeeded by Victor Emmanuel II, 1849-1861.

In 1859 France forced Austria to cede Lombardy to Sardinia, which gave rights to Savoy and Nice to France. In 1860 Garibaldi led 1,000 volunteers in a spectacular campaign, took Sicily and expelled the King of Naples. In 1860 the House of Savoy annexed Tuscany, Parma, Moderna, Romagna, the Two Sicilies, the Marches, and Umbria. Victor Emmanuel assumed the title of King

of Italy at Turin Mar. 17, 1861. In 1866 he joined Prussia and Austria in the Triple Alliance and received Venetia from Austria. On Sept. 20, 1870, his troops under Gen. Raffaele Cardorna entered Rome and took over the Papal States, ending the temporal power of the Roman Catholic Church.

Succession: Umberto I; 1878, assassinated 1900; Victor Emmanuel III, 1900, abdicated 1946, died 1947; Umberto II, 1946, ruled a month. In 1921 Benito Mussolini (1883-1945) formed the Fascist party and became prime minister Oct. 31, 1922. He made the King Emperor of Ethiopia, 1937; entered World War II as ally of Hitler. He was deposed July 25, 1943.

At a plebiscite June 2, 1946, Italy voted for a republic; Premier Alcide de Gasperi became chief of state June 13, 1946. On June 28, 1946, the Constituent Assembly elected Enrico de Nicola, Liberal, provisional president. Successive presidents: Luigi Einaudi, elected May 11, 1948; Giovanni Gronchi, Apr. 29, 1955; Antonio Segni, May 6, 1962; Giuseppe Saragat, Dec. 28, 1964; Giovanni Leone, Dec. 29, 1971; Sandro Pertini, July 8, 1978.

## Rulers of Spain

From 8th to 11th centuries Spain was dominated by the Moors (Arabs and Berbers). The Christian reconquest established small competing kingdoms of the Asturias, Aragon, Castile, Catalonia, Leon, Navarre, and Valencia. In 1474 Isabella (Isabel), b. 1451, became Queen of Castile & Leon. Her husband, Ferdinand, b. 1452, inherited Aragon 1479, with Catalonia, Valcencia, and the Balearic Islands, became Ferdinand V of Castile. By Isabella's request Pope Sixtus IV established the Inquisition, 1478. Last Moorish kingdom, Granada, fell 1492. Columbus opened New World of colonies, 1492. Isabella died 1504, succeeded her daughter, Juana "the Mad," but Ferdinand ruled until his death 1516.

Charles I, b. 1500, son of Juana and grandson of Ferdinand and Isabella, and of Maximilian I of Hapsburg; succeeded later as Holy Roman Emperor, Charles V, 1520; abdicated 1556. Philip II, son, 1556-1598, inherited only Spanish throne; conquered Portugal, fought Turks, persecuted non-Catholics, sent Armada vs. England. Was briefly married to Mary I of England, 1554-1558. Succession: Philip III, 1598-1621; Philip IV, 1621-1665; Charles II, 1665-1700, left Spain to Philip of Anjou, grandson of Louis XIV, who as Philip V, 1700-1746, founded Bourbon dynasty. Ferdinand VI, 1746-1759; Charles III, 1759-1788; Charles IV, 1788-1808, abdicated.

Napoleon now dominated politics and made his brother Joseph King of Spain 1808, but the Spanish ousted him finally in 1813. Ferdinand VII, 1808, 1814-1833, lost American colonies; succeeded by daughter Isabella II, aged 3, with wife Maria Christina of Na-

ples regent until 1843. Isabella deposed by revolution 1868. Elected king by the Cortes, Amadeo of Savoy, 1870; abdicated 1873. First republic, 1873-1874. Alphonso XII, son of Isabella, 1875-1885. His posthumous son was Alphonso XIII, with his mother, Queen Maria Christina regent; Spanish-American war, Spain lost Cuba, gave up Puerto Rico, Philippines, Sulu Is., Marianas. Alphonso took throne 1902, aged 16, married British Princess Victoria Eugenia of Battenberg. The dictatorship of Primo de Rivera, 1923-30, precipitated the revolution of 1931. Alphonso agreed to leave without formal abdication. The monarchy was abolished and the second republic established, with strong socialist backing. Presidents were Niceto Alcala Zamora, to 1936, when Manuel Anzana was chosen.

In July, 1936, the army in Morocco revolted against the government and General Francisco Franco led the troops into Spain. The revolution succeeded by Feb., 1939, when Anzana resigned. Franco became chief of state, with provisions that if he was incapacitated the Regency Council by two-thirds vote may propose a king to the Cortes, which must have a two-thirds majority to elect him.

Alphonso XIII died in Rome Feb. 28, 1941, aged 54. His property and citizenship had been restored.

A succession law restoring the monarchy was approved in a 1947 referendum. Prince Juan Carlos, son of the pretender to the throne, was designated by Franco and the Cortes in 1969 as the future king and chief of state. Upon Franco's death, Nov. 20, 1975, Juan Carlos was proclaimed king, Nov. 22, 1975.

## Leaders in the South American Wars of Liberation

Simon Bolivar (1783-1830), Jose Francisco de San Martin (1783-1850), and Francisco Antonio Gabriel Miranda (1750-1816), are among the heroes of the early 19th century struggles of South American nations to free themselves from Spain. All three, and their contemporaries, operated in periods of intense factional strife, during which soldiers and civilians suffered.

Miranda, a Venezuelan, who had served with the French in the American Revolution and commanded parts of the French Revolu-

tionary armies in the Netherlands, attempted to start a revolt in Venezuela in 1806 and failed. In 1810, with British and American backing, he returned and was briefly a dictator, until the British withdrew their support. In 1812 he was overcome by the royalists in Venezuela and taken prisoner, dying in a Spanish prison in 1816.

San Martin was born in Argentina and during 1789-1811 served in campaigns of the Spanish armies in Europe and Africa. He first joined the independence movement in Argentina in 1812 and then in 1817 invaded Chile with 4,000 men over the high mountain passes. Here he and General Bernardo O'Higgins (1778-1842) defeated the Spaniards at Chacabuco, 1817, and O'Higgins was named Liberator and became first director of Chile, 1817-1823. In 1821 San Martin occupied Lima and Callao, Peru, and became protector of Peru.

Bolivar, the greatest leader of South American liberation from Spain, was born in Venezuela, the son of an aristocratic family. His organizing and administrative abilities were superior and he foresaw many of the political difficulties of the future. He first served under Miranda in 1812 and in 1813 captured Caracas, where he was named Liberator. Forced out next year by civil strife, he led a campaign that captured Bogota in 1814. In 1817 he was again in control of Venezuela and was named dictator. He organized Nueva Granada with the help of General Francisco de Paula Santander (1792-1840). By joining Nueva Granada, Venezuela, and the present terrain of Panama and Ecuador, the republic of Colombia was formed with Bolivar president. After numerous setbacks he deci-

sively defeated the Spaniards in the second battle of Carabobo, Venezuela, June 24, 1821.

In May, 1822, Gen. Antonio Jose de Sucre, Bolivar's trusted lieutenant, took Quito. Bolivar went to Guayaquil to confer with San Martin, who resigned as protector of Peru and withdrew from politics. With a new army of Colombians and Peruvians Bolivar defeated the Spaniards in a saber battle at Juin in 1824 and cleared Peru.

De Sucre organized Charcas (Upper Peru) as Republica Bolivar (now Bolivia) and acted as president in place of Bolivar, who wrote its constitution. De Sucre defeated the Spanish faction of Peru at Ayacucho, Dec. 19, 1824.

Continued civil strife finally caused the Colombian federation to break apart. Santander turned against Bolivar, but the latter defeated him and banished him. In 1828 Bolivar gave up the presidency he had held precariously for 14 years. He became ill from tuberculosis and died Dec. 17, 1830. He was honored as the great liberator and is buried in the national pantheon in Caracas.

## Rulers of Russia; Premiers of the USSR

First ruler to consolidate Slavic tribes was Rurik, leader of the Russians who established himself at Novgorod, 862 A.D. He and his immediate successors had Scandinavian affiliations. They moved to Kiev after 972 AD and ruled as Dukes of Kiev. In 988 Vladimir was converted and adopted the Byzantine Greek Orthodox service, later modified by Slav influences. Important as organizer and lawgiver was Yaroslav, 1019-1054, whose daughters married kings of Norway, Hungary, and France. His grandson, Vladimir II (Monomarchos), 1113-1125, was progenitor of several rulers, but in 1169 Andrew Bogolubski overthrew Kiev and began the line known as Grand Dukes of Vladimir.

Of the Grand Dukes of Vladimir, Alexander Nevsky, 1246-1263, had a son, Daniel, first to be called Duke of Muscovy (Moscow) who ruled 1294-1303. His successors became Grand Dukes of Muscovy. After Dmitri III Donskoi defeated the Tartars in 1380, they also became Grand Dukes of all Russia. Independence of the Tartars and considerable territorial expansion were achieved under Ivan III, 1462-1505.

Tsars of Muscovy—Ivan III was referred to in church ritual as Tsar. He married Sofia, niece of the last Byzantine emperor. His successor, Basil III, died in 1533 when Basil's son Ivan was only 3. He became Ivan IV, "the Terrible"; crowned 1547 as Tsar of all the Russias, ruled till 1584. Under the weak rule of his son, Feodor I, 1584-1598, Boris Godunov had control. The dynasty died, and after years of tribal strife and intervention by Polish and Swedish armies, the Russians united under 17-year-old Michael Romanov, distantly related to the first wife of Ivan IV. He ruled 1613-1645 and established the Romanov line. Fourth ruler after Michael was Peter I.

Tsars, or Emperors of Russia (Romanovs)—Peter I, 1682-1725, known as Peter the Great, took title of Emperor in 1721. His successors and dates of accession were: Catherine, his widow, 1725; Peter II, his grandson, 1727-1730; Anne, Duchess of Courland, 1730, daughter of Peter the Great's brother, Tsar Ivan V; Ivan VI,

1740-1741, great-grandson of Ivan V, child, kept in prison and murdered 1764; Elizabeth, daughter of Peter I, 1741; Peter III, grandson of Peter I, 1761, deposed 1762 for his consort, Catherine II, former princess of Anhalt Zerbst (Germany) who is known as Catherine the Great, 1762-1796; Paul I, her son, 1796, killed 1801; Alexander I, son of Paul, 1801-1825, defeated Napoleon; Nicholas I, his brother, 1825; Alexander II, son of Nicholas, 1855, assassinated 1881 by terrorists; Alexander III, son, 1881-1894.

Nicholas II, son, 1894-1917, last Tsar of Russia, was forced to abdicate by the Revolution that followed losses to Germany in WWI. The Tsar, the Empress, the Tsesarevich (Crown Prince) and the Tsar's 4 daughters were murdered by the Bolsheviks in Ekaterinburg, July 16, 1918.

Provisional Government—Prince Georgi Lvov and Alexander Kerensky, premiers, 1917.

### Union of Soviet Socialist Republics

Bolshevik Revolution, Nov. 7, 1917, displaced Kerensky; council of People's Commissars formed, Lenin (Vladimir Ilyich Ulyanov), premier. Lenin died Jan. 21, 1924. Aleksei Rykov (executed 1938) and V. M. Molotov held the office, but actual ruler was Joseph Stalin (Joseph Vissarionovich Djugashvili), general secretary of the Central Committee of the Communist Party. Stalin became president of the Council of Ministers (premier) May 7, 1941, died Mar. 5, 1953. Succeeded by Georgi M. Malenkov, as head of the Council and premier and Nikita S. Khrushchev, first secretary of the Central Committee. Malenkov resigned Feb. 8, 1955, became deputy premier, was dropped July 3, 1957. Marshal Nikolai A. Bulganin became premier Feb. 8, 1955; was demoted and Khrushchev became premier Mar. 27 1958. Khrushchev was ousted Oct. 14-15, 1964, replaced by Leonid I. Brezhnev as first secretary of the party and by Aleksei N. Kosygin as premier. On June 16, 1977, Brezhnev took office as president.

## Governments of China

(Until 221 BC and frequently thereafter, China was not a unified state. Where dynastic dates overlap, the rulers or events referred to appeared in different areas of China.)

| | | |
|---|---|---|
| Hsia | c1994BC | c1523BC |
| Shang | c1523 | c1028 |
| Western Chou | c1027 | 770 |
| Eastern Chou | 770 | 256 |
| Warring States | 403 | 222 |
| Ch'in (first unified empire) | 221 | 206 |
| Han | 202BC | 220AD |
| Western Han (expanded Chinese state beyond the Yellow and Yangtze River valleys) | 202BC | 9AD |
| Hsin (Wang Mang, usurper) | 9AD | 23AD |
| Eastern Han (expanded Chinese state into Indo-China and Turkestan) | 25 | 220 |
| Three Kingdoms (Wei, Shu, Wu) | 220 | 265 |
| Chin (western) | 265 | 317 |
| (eastern) | 317 | 420 |
| Northern Dynasties (followed several short-lived governments by Turks, Mongols, etc.) | 386 | 581 |
| Southern Dynasties (capital: Nanking) | 420 | 589 |
| Sui (reunified China) | 581 | 618 |
| Tang (a golden age of Chinese culture; capital: Sian) | 618 | 906 |
| Five Dynasties (Yellow River basin) | 902 | 960 |
| Ten Kingdoms (southern China) | 907 | 979 |
| Liao (Khitan Mongols; capital: Peking) | 947 | 1125 |
| Sung | 960 | 1279 |
| Northern Sung (reunified central and southern China) | 960 | 1126 |
| Western Hsai (non-Chinese rulers in northwest) | 990 | 1227 |
| Chin (Tartars; drove Sung out of central China) | 1115 | 1234 |
| Yuan (Mongols; Kublai Khan made Peking his capital in 1267) | 1271 | 1368 |
| Ming (China reunified under Chinese rule; capital: Nanking, then Peking in 1420) | 1368 | 1644 |
| Ch'ing (Manchus, descendents of Tartars) | 1644 | 1911 |
| Republic (disunity; provincial rulers, warlords) | 1912 | 1949 |
| People's Republic of China (Nationalist China established on Taiwan) | 1949 | — |

## Chronological List of Popes

Source: Annuario Pontifici Table lists year of coronation of each Pope.

The Roman Catholic Church names the Apostle Peter as founder of the Church in Rome. He arrived there c. 42, was martyred there c. 67, and raised to sainthood.

**The Pope's temporal title is:** Sovereign of the State of Vatican City.

**The Pope's spirital titles are:** Bishop of Rome, Vicar of Jesus Christ, Successor of St. Peter, Prince of the Apostles, Supreme Pontiff of the Universal Church, Patriarch of the West, Primate of Italy, Archbishop and Metropolitan of the Roman Province and Sovereign of the State of Vatican City.

**Anti-Popes** are in *Italics*. Anti-Popes were illegitimate claimants of or pretenders to the papal throne.

| Year | Name of Pope | Year | Name of Pope | Year | Name of Pope | Year | Name of Pope |
|---|---|---|---|---|---|---|---|
| See above | St. Peter | 615 | St. Deusdedit or Adeodatus | 974 | Benedict VII | 1305 | Clement V |
| 67 | St. Linus | 619 | Boniface V | 983 | John XIV | 1316 | John XXII |
| 76 | St. Anacletus or Cletus | 625 | Honorius I | 985 | John XV | *1328* | *Nicholas V* |
| 88 | St. Clement I | 640 | Severinus | 996 | Gregory V | 1334 | Benedict XII |
| 97 | St. Evaristus | 640 | John IV | *997* | *John XVI* | 1342 | Clement VI |
| 105 | St. Alexander I | 642 | Theodore I | 999 | Sylvester II | 1352 | Innocent VI |
| 115 | St. Sixtus I | 649 | St. Martin I, Martyr | 1003 | John XVII | 1362 | Bl. Urban V |
| 125 | St. Telesphorus | 654 | St. Eugene I | 1004 | John XVIII | 1370 | Gregory XI |
| 136 | St. Hyginus | 657 | St. Vitalian | 1009 | Sergius IV | 1378 | Urban VI |
| 140 | St. Pius I | 672 | Adeodatus II | 1012 | Benedict VIII | *1378* | *Clement VII* |
| 155 | St. Anicetus | 676 | Donus | *1012* | *Gregory* | 1389 | Boniface IX |
| 166 | St. Soter | 678 | St. Agatho | 1024 | John XIX | *1394* | *Benedict XIII* |
| 175 | St. Eleutherius | 682 | St. Leo II | 1032 | Benedict IX | 1404 | Innocent VII |
| 189 | St. Victor I | 684 | St. Benedict II | 1045 | Sylvester III | 1406 | Gregory XII |
| 199 | St. Zephyrinus | 685 | John V | 1045 | Benedict IX | *1409* | *Alexander V* |
| 217 | St. Callistus I | 686 | Conon | 1045 | Gregory VI | *1410* | *John XXIII* |
| *217* | *St. Hippolytus* | *687* | *Theodore* | 1046 | Clement II | 1417 | Martin V |
| 222 | St. Urban I | *687* | *Paschal* | 1047 | Benedict IX | 1431 | Eugene IV |
| 230 | St. Pontian | 687 | St. Sergius I | 1048 | Damasus II | *1439* | *Felix V* |
| 235 | St. Anterus | 701 | John VI | 1049 | St. Leo IX | 1447 | Nicholas V |
| 236 | St. Fabian | 705 | John VII | 1055 | Victor II | 1455 | Callistus III |
| 251 | St. Cornelius | 708 | Sisinnius | 1057 | Stephen IX (X) | 1458 | Pius II |
| *251* | *Novatian* | 708 | Constantine | *1058* | *Benedict X* | 1464 | Paul II |
| 253 | St. Lucius I | 715 | St. Gregory II | 1059 | Nicholas II | 1471 | Sixtus IV |
| 254 | St. Stephen I | 731 | St. Gregory III | 1061 | Alexander II | 1484 | Innocent VIII |
| 257 | St. Sixtus II | 741 | St. Zachary | *1061* | *Honorius II* | 1492 | Alexander VI |
| 259 | St. Dionysius | 752 | Stephen II (III) | 1073 | St. Gregory VII | 1503 | Pius III |
| 269 | St. Felix I | 757 | St. Paul I | *1080* | *Clement III* | 1503 | Julius II |
| 275 | St. Eutychian | *767* | *Constantine* | 1086 | Bl. Victor III | 1513 | Leo X |
| 283 | St. Caius | *768* | *Philip* | 1088 | Bl. Urban II | 1522 | Adrian VI |
| 296 | St. Marcellinus | 768 | Stephen III (IV) | 1099 | Paschal II | 1523 | Clement VII |
| 308 | St. Marcellus I | 772 | Adrian I | *1100* | *Theodoric* | 1534 | Paul III |
| 309 | St. Eusebius | 795 | St. Leo III | *1102* | *Albert* | 1550 | Julius III |
| 311 | St. Melchiades | 816 | Stephen IV (V) | *1105* | *Sylvester IV* | 1555 | Marcellus II |
| 314 | St. Sylvester I | 817 | St. Paschal I | 1118 | Gelasius II | 1555 | Paul IV |
| 336 | St. Marus | 824 | Eugene II | *1118* | *Gregory VIII* | 1559 | Pius IV |
| 337 | St. Julius I | 827 | Valentine | 1119 | Callistus II | 1566 | St. Pius V |
| 352 | Liberius | 827 | Gregory IV | 1124 | Honorius II | 1572 | Gregory XIII |
| *355* | *Felix II* | *844* | *John* | *1124* | *Celestine II* | 1585 | Sixtus V |
| 366 | St. Damasus I | 844 | Sergius II | 1130 | Innocent II | 1590 | Urban VII |
| *366* | *Ursinus* | 847 | St. Leo IV | *1130* | *Anacletus II* | 1590 | Gregory XIV |
| 384 | St. Siricius | 855 | Benedict III | *1138* | *Victor IV* | 1591 | Innocent IX |
| 399 | St. Anastasius I | *855* | *Anastasius* | 1143 | Celestine II | 1592 | Clement VIII |
| 401 | St. Innocent I | 858 | St. Nicholas I | 1144 | Lucius II | 1605 | Leo XI |
| 417 | St. Zozimus | 867 | Adrian II | 1145 | Bl. Eugene III | 1605 | Paul V |
| 418 | St. Boniface I | 872 | John VIII | 1153 | Anastasius IV | 1621 | Gregory XV |
| *418* | *Eulalius* | 882 | Marinus I | 1154 | Adrian IV | 1623 | Urban VIII |
| 422 | St. Celestine I | 884 | St. Adrian III | 1159 | Alexander III | 1644 | Innocent X |
| 432 | St. Sixtus III | 885 | Stephen V (VI) | *1159* | *Victor IV* | 1655 | Alexander VII |
| 440 | St. Leo I | 891 | Formosus | *1164* | *Paschal III* | 1667 | Clement IX |
| 461 | St. Hilary | 896 | Boniface VI | *1168* | *Callistus III* | 1670 | Clement X |
| 468 | St. Simplicius | 896 | Stephen VI (VII) | *1179* | *Innocent III* | 1676 | Bl. Innocent XI |
| 483 | St. Felix III (II) | 897 | Romanus | 1181 | Lucius III | 1689 | Alexander VIII |
| 492 | St. Gelasius I | 897 | Theodore II | 1185 | Urban III | 1691 | Innocent XII |
| 496 | Anastasius II | 898 | John IX | 1187 | Gregory VIII | 1700 | Clement XI |
| 498 | St. Symmachus | 900 | Benedict IV | 1187 | Clement III | 1721 | Innocent XIII |
| *498* | *Lawrence (501-505)* | 903 | Leo V | 1191 | Celestine III | 1724 | Benedict XIII |
| 514 | St. Hormisdas | *903* | *Christopher* | 1198 | Innocent III | 1730 | Clement XII |
| 523 | St. John I, Martyr | 904 | Sergius III | 1216 | Honorius III | 1740 | Benedict XIV |
| 526 | St. Felix IV (III) | 911 | Anastasius III | 1227 | Gregory IX | 1758 | Clement XIII |
| 530 | Boniface II | 913 | Landus | *1241* | *Celestine IV* | 1769 | Clement XIV |
| *530* | *Dioscorus* | 914 | John X | 1243 | Innocent IV | 1775 | Pius VI |
| 533 | John II | 928 | Leo VI | 1254 | Alexander IV | 1800 | Pius VII |
| 535 | St. Agapitus I | 928 | Stephen VII (VIII) | 1261 | Urban IV | 1823 | Leo XII |
| 536 | St. Silverius, Martyr | 931 | John XI | 1265 | Clement IV | 1829 | Pius VIII |
| 537 | Vigilius | 936 | Leo VII | 1271 | Bl. Gregory X | 1831 | Gregory XVI |
| 556 | Pelagius I | 939 | Stephen VIII (IX) | 1276 | Bl. Innocent V | 1846 | Pius IX |
| 561 | John III | 942 | Marinus II | 1276 | Adrian V | 1878 | Leo XIII |
| 575 | Benedict I | 946 | Agapitus II | 1276 | John XXI | 1903 | St. Pius X |
| 579 | Pelagius II | 955 | John XII | 1277 | Nicholas III | 1914 | Benedict XV |
| 590 | St. Gregory I | 963 | Leo VIII | 1281 | Martin IV | 1922 | Pius XI |
| 604 | Sabinian | 964 | Benedict V | 1285 | Honorius IV | 1939 | Pius XII |
| 606 | Boniface III | 965 | John XIII | 1288 | Nicholas IV | 1958 | John XXIII |
| 608 | St. Boniface IV | 973 | Benedict VI | 1294 | St. Celestine V | 1963 | Paul VI |
| | | *974* | *Boniface VII* | 1294 | Boniface VIII | | |
| | | | | 1303 | Bl. Benedict XI | | |

# AWARDS — MEDALS — PRIZES

## The Alfred B. Nobel Prize Winners

Alfred B. Nobel, inventor of dynamite, bequeathed $9,000,000, the interest to be distributed yearly to those who had most benefited mankind in physics, chemistry, medicine-physiology, literature, and peace. The first Nobel Prize in Economics was awarded in 1969. No awards given for years omitted. In 1977, each prize was worth $145,000.

### Physics

1977 John H. Van Vleck, Philip W. Anderson, both U.S.; Nevill F. Mott, British
1976 Burton Richter, U.S.; Samuel C.C. Ting, U.S.
1975 James Rainwater, U.S.; Ben Mottelson, U.S.-Danish, Aage Bohr, Danish
1974 Martin Ryle, British; Antony Hewish, British
1973 Ivar Giaever, U.S.; Leo Esaki, U.S.; Brian D. Josephson, British
1972 John Bardeen, U.S.; Leon N. Cooper, U.S.; John R. Schrieffer, U.S.
1971 Dennis Gabor, British
1970 Louis Neel, French; Hannes Alfven, Swedish
1969 Murray Gell-Mann, U.S.
1968 Luis W. Alvarez, U.S.
1967 Hans A. Bethe, U.S.
1966 Alfred Kastler, French
1965 Richard P. Feynman, U.S.; Julian S. Schwinger, U.S.; Shinichiro Tomanaga, Japanese
1964 Nikolai G. Basov, USSR; Aleksander M. Prochorov, USSR; Charles H. Townes, U.S.
1963 Maria Goeppert-Mayer, U.S.; J. Hans D. Jensen, German; Eugene P. Wigner, U.S.
1962 Lev. D. Landau, USSR
1961 Robert Hofstadter, U.S.; Rudolf L. Mossbauer, German
1960 Donald A. Glaser, U.S.
1959 Owen Chamberlain, U.S.

Emilio G. Segre, U.S.
1958 Paval Cerenkov, Ilya Frank, Igor J. Tamm, all USSR
1957 Tsung-Dao Lee, Chen Ning Yang, both U.S.
1956 John Bardeen, U.S.; Walter H. Brattain, U.S.; William Shockley, U.S.
1955 Polykarp Kusch, U.S.; Willis E. Lamb, U.S.
1954 Max Born, British; Walter Bothe, German
1953 Frits Zernike, Dutch
1952 Felix Bloch, U.S.; Edward M. Purcell, U.S.
1951 Sir John D. Cockroft, British; Ernest T. S. Walton, Irish
1950 Cecil F. Powell, British
1949 Hideki Yukawa, Japanese
1948 Patrick M. S. Blackett, British
1947 Sir Edward V. Appleton, British
1946 Percy Williams Bridgman, U.S.
1945 Wolfgang Pauli, U.S.
1944 Isidor Isaac Rabi, U.S.
1943 Otto Sern, U.S.
1939 Ernest O. Lawrence, U.S.
1938 Enrico Fermi, U.S.
1937 Clinton J. Davisson, U.S.; George P. Thomson, British
1936 Carl D. Anderson, U.S.; Victor F. Hess, Austrian
1935 James Chadwick, British
1933 Paul A. M. Dirac, British; Erwin Schrodinger, Austrian
1932 Werner Heisenberg, German
1930 Sir Chandrasekhara V. Raman, Indian

1929 Prince Louis-Victor de Broglie, French
1928 Owen W. Richardson, British
1927 Arthur H. Compton, U.S.; Charles T. R. Wilson, British
1926 Jean B. Perrin, French
1925 James Franck, Gustav Hertz, both German
1924 Karl M. G. Siegbahn, Swedish
1923 Robert A. Millikan, U.S.
1922 Niels Bohr, Danish
1921 Albert Einstein, Ger.-U.S.
1920 Charles E. Guillaume, French
1919 Johannes Stark, German
1918 Max K. E. L. Planck, German
1917 Charles G. Barkla, British
1915 Sir William H. Bragg, British; William L. Bragg, British
1914 Max von Laue, German
1913 Heike Kamerlingh-Onnes, Dutch
1912 Nils G. Dalen, Swedish
1911 Wilhelm Wein, German
1910 Johannes D. van der Waals, Dutch
1909 Carl F. Braun, German; Guglielmo Marconi, Italian
1908 Gabriel Lippmann, French
1907 Albert A. Michelson, U.S.
1906 Sir Joseph J. Thomson, British
1905 Philipp E. A. von Lenard, Ger.
1904 Rayleigh, Lord (John W. Strutt), British
1903 Antoine Henri Becquerel, Marie and Pierre Curie, all French
1902 Hendrik A. Lorentz, Pieter Zeeman, both Dutch
1901 Wilhelm C. Roentgen, German

### Chemistry

1977 Ilya Prigogine, Belgian
1976 William L. Lipscomb, U.S.
1975 John Cornforth, Austral.-Brit., Vladimir Prelog, Yugo.-Switz.
1974 Paul J. Flory, U.S.
1973 Ernst Otto Fischer, W. German; Geoffrey Wilkinson, British
1972 Christian B. Anfinsen, U.S.; Stanford Moore, U.S.; William H. Stein, U.S.
1971 Gerhard Herzberg, Canadian
1970 Luis A. Leloir, Arg.
1969 Derek H. R. Barton, British; Odd Hassel, Norwegian
1968 Lars Onsager, U.S.
1967 Manfred Eigen, German; Ronald G. W. Norrish, British; George Porter, British
1966 Robert S. Mulliken, U.S.
1965 Robert B. Woodward, U.S.
1964 Dorothy C. Hodgkin, British
1963 Giulio Natta, Italian; Karl Ziegler, German
1962 John C. Kendrew, British; Max F. Perutz, British
1961 Melvin Calvin, U.S.
1960 Willard F. Libby, U.S.
1959 Jaroslav Heyrovsky, Czech
1958 Frederick Sanger, British
1957 Sir Alexander R. Todd, British

1956 Sir Cyril N. Hinshelwood, British; Nikolai N. Semenov, USSR
1955 Vincent du Vigneaud, U.S.
1954 Linus C. Pauling, U.S.
1953 Hermann Staudinger, German
1952 Archer J. P. Martin, British; Richard L. M. Synge, British
1951 Edwin M. McMillan, U.S.; Glenn T. Seaborg, U.S.
1950 Kurt Adler, German; Otto P. H. Diels, German
1949 William F. Glauque, U.S.
1948 Arne W. K. Tiselius, Swedish
1947 Sir Robert Robinson, British
1946 James B. Sumner, John H. Northrop, Wendell M. Stanley, all U.S.
1945 Artturi I. Virtanen, Finnish
1944 Otto Hahn, German
1943 Georg de Hevesy, Hungarian
1939 Adolf F. J. Butenandt, German; Leopold Ruzicka, Swiss
1938 Richard Kuhn, German
1937 Walter N. Haworth, British; Paul Karrer, Swiss
1936 Peter J. W. Debye, Dutch
1935 Frederic Joliot-Curie, French; Irene Joliot-Curie, French
1934 Harold C. Urey, U.S.
1932 Irving Langmuir, U.S.

1931 Friedrich Bergius, German; Carl Bosch, German
1930 Hans Fischer, German
1929 Arthur Harden, British; Hans von Euler-Chelpin, Swed.
1928 Adolf O. R. Windaus, German
1927 Heinrich O. Wieland, German
1926 Theodor Svedberg, Swedish
1925 Richard A. Zsigmondy, German
1923 Fritz Pregl, Austrian
1922 Francis W. Aston, British
1921 Frederick Soddy, British
1920 Walther H. Nernst, German
1918 Fritz Haber, German
1915 Richard M. Willstatter, German
1914 Theodore W. Richards, U.S.
1913 Alfred Werner, Swiss
1912 Victor Grignard, French; Paul Sabatier, French
1911 Marie Curie, French
1910 Otto Wallach, German
1909 Wilhelm Ostwald, German
1908 Ernest Rutherford, British
1907 Eduard Buchner, German
1906 Henri Moissan, French
1905 Adolf von Baeyer, German
1904 Sir William Ramsay, British
1903 Svante A. Arrhenius, Swedish
1902 Emil Fischer, German
1901 Jacobus H. van't Hoff, Dutch

### Physiology or Medicine

1977 Rosalyn S. Yalow, Roger C.L. Guillemin, Andrew V. Schally, all U.S.
1976 Baruch S. Blumberg, U.S.; Daniel Carleton Gajdusek, U.S.

1975 David Baltimore, Howard Temin, both U.S.; Renato Dulbecco, Ital.-U.S.
1974 Albert Claude, Lux.-U.S.; George Emil Palade, Rom.-U.S.; Christian

Rene de Duve, Belg.
1973 Karl von Frisch, Ger.; Konrad Lorenz, Ger.-Austrian; Nikolaas Tinbergen, Brit.
1972 Gerald M. Edelman, U.S.

Rodney R. Porter, British
1971 Earl W. Sutherland Jr., U.S.
1970 Julius Axelrod, U.S.
     Sir Bernard Katz, British
     Ulf von Euler, Swedish
1969 Max Delbruck,
     Alfred D. Hershey,
     Salvador Luria, all U.S.
1968 Robert W. Holley,
     H. Gobind Khorana,
     Marshall W. Nirenberg, all U.S.
1967 Ragnar Granit, Swedish
     Haldan Keffer Hartline, U.S.
     George Wald, U.S.
1966 Charles B. Huggins,
     Francis Peyton Rous, both U.S.
1965 Francois Jacob, Andre Lwoff,
     Jacquest Monod, all French
1964 Konrad E. Bloch, U.S.
     Feodor Lynen, German
1963 Sir John C. Eccles, Australian
     Alan L. Hodgkin, British
     Andrew F. Huxley, British
1962 Francis H. C. Crick, British
     James D. Watson, U.S.
     Maurice H. F. Wilkins, British
1961 Georg von Bekesy, U.S.
1960 Sir F. MacFarlane Bumet, Australian
     Peter B. Medawar, British
1959 Arthur Kornberg, U.S.
     Severo Ochoa, U.S.
*958 George W. Beadle, U.S.
     Edward L. Tatum, U.S.
     Joshua Lederberg, U.S.

1957 Daniel Bovet, Italian
1956 Andre F. Cournand, U.S.
     Werner Forssmann, German
     Dickinson W. Richards, Jr., U.S.
1955 Alex H. T. Theorell, Swedish
1954 John F. Enders,
     Frederick C. Robbins,
     Thomas H. Weller, all U.S.
1953 Hans A. Krebs, British
     Fritz A. Lipmann, U.S.
1952 Selman A. Waksman, U.S.
1951 Max Theiler, U.S.
1950 Philip S. Hench,
     Edward C. Kendall, both U.S.
     Tadeus Reichstein, Swiss
1949 Walter R. Hess, Swiss
     Antonio Moniz, Portuguese
1948 Paul H. Muller, Swiss
1947 Carl F. Cori,
     Gerty T. Cori, both U.S.
     Bernardo A. Houssay, Arg.
1946 Hermann J. Muller, U.S.
1945 Ernst B. Chain, British
     Sir Alexander Fleming, British
     Sir Howard W. Florey, British
1944 Joseph Erlanger,
     Herbert S. Gasser, U.S.
1943 Henrik C. P. Dam, Danish
     Edward A. Doisy, U.S.
1939 Gerhard Domagk, German
1938 Corneille J. F. Heymans, Belg.
1937 Albert Szent-Gyorgyi, U.S.
1936 Sir Henry H. Dale, British
     Otto Loewi, U.S.
1935 Hans Spemann, German

1934 George R. Minot, Wm. P. Murphy,
     G. H. Whipple, all U.S.
1933 Thomas H. Morgan, U.S.
1932 Edgard D. Adrian, British
     Sir Charles S. Sherrington, Brit.
1931 Otto H. Warburg, German
1930 Karl Landsteiner, U.S.
1929 Christiaan Eijkman, Dutch
     Sir Frederick G. Hopkins, British
1928 Charles J. H. Nicolle, French
1927 Julius Wagner-Jauregg, Aus.
1926 Johannes A. G. Fibiger, Danish
1924 Willem Einthoven, Dutch
1923 Frederick G. Banting, Canadian
     John J. R. Macleod, Canadian
1922 Archibald V. Hill, British
     Otto F. Meyerhof, German
1920 Schack A. S. Krogh, Danish
1919 Jules Bordet, Belgian
1914 Robert Barany, Austrian
1913 Charles R. Richet, French
1912 Alexis Carrel, U.S.
1911 Allvar Gullstrand, Swedish
1910 Albrecht Kossel, German
1909 Emil T. Kocher, Swiss
1908 Paul Ehrlich, German
     Elie Metchnikoff, French
1907 Charles L. A. Laveran, French
1906 Camillo Golgi, Italian
     Santiago Roman y Cajal, Sp.
1905 Robert Koch, German
1904 Ivan P. Pavlov, Russian
1903 Niels R. Finsen, Danish
1902 Sir Ronald Ross, British
1901 Emil A. von Behring, German

## Literature

1977 Vicente Aleixandre, Spanish
1976 Saul Bellow, U.S.
1975 Eugenio Montale, Ital.
1974 Eyvvind Johnson, Harry Edmund
     Martinson, both Swedish
1973 Patrick White, Australian
1972 Heinrich Boll, W. German
1971 Pablo Neruda, Chilean
1970 Aleksandr I. Solzhenitsyn, Russ.
1969 Samuel Beckett, Irish
1968 Yasunari Kawabata, Japanese
1967 Miguel Angel Asturias, Guate.
1966 Samuel Joseph Agnon, Israeli
     Nelly Sachs, Swedish
1965 Mikhail Sholokhov, Russian
1964 Jean Paul Sartre, French
     (Prize declined)
1963 Giorgos Seferis, Greek
1962 John Steinbeck, U.S.
1961 Ivo Andric, Yugoslavian
1960 Saint-John Perse, French
1959 Salvatore Quasimodo, Italian
1958 Boris L. Pasternak, Russian
     (Prize declined)
1957 Albert Camus, French
1956 Juan Ramon Jimenez,

Puerto Rican-Span.
1955 Halldor K. Laxness, Icelandic
1954 Ernest Hemingway, U.S.
1953 Sir Winston Churchill, British
1952 Francois Mauriac, French
1951 Par F. Lagerkvist, Swedish
1950 Bertrand Russell, British
1949 William Faulkner, U.S.
1948 T.S. Eliot, British
1947 Andre Gide, French
1946 Hermann Hesse, Swiss
1945 Gabriela Mistral, Chilean
1944 Johannes V. Jensen, Danish
1939 Frans E. Sillanpaa, Finnish
1938 Pearl S. Buck, U.S.
1937 Roger Martin du Gard, French
1936 Eugene O'Neill, U.S.
1934 Luigi Pirandello, Italian
1933 Ivan A. Bunin, French
1932 John Galsworthy, British
1931 Erik A. Karlfeldt, Swedish
1930 Sinclair Lewis, U.S.
1929 Thomas Mann, German
1928 Sigrid Undset, Norwegian
1927 Henri Bergson, French
1926 Grazia Deledda, Italian

1925 George Bernard Shaw, British
1924 Wladyslaw S. Reymont, Polish
1923 William Butler Yeats, Irish
1922 Jacinto Benavente, Spanish
1921 Anatole France, French
1920 Knut Hamsun, Norwegian
1919 Carl F. G. Spitteler, Swiss
1917 Karl A. Gjellerup, Danish
     Henrik Pontoppidan, Danish
1916 Verner von Heidenstam, Swed.
1915 Romain Rolland, French
1913 Rabindranath Tagore, Indian
1912 Gerhart Hauptmann, German
1911 Maurice Maeterlinck, Belgian
1910 Paul J. L. Heyse, German
1909 Seima Lagerlof, Swedish
1908 Rudolf C. Eucken, German
1907 Rudyard Kipling, British
1906 Giosue Carducci, Italian
1905 Henryk Sienkiewicz, Polish
1904 Frederic Mistral, French
     Jose Echegaray, Spanish
1903 Bjornstjerne Bjornson, Norw.
1902 Theodor Mommsen, German
1901 Rene F. A Sully Prudhomme,
     French

## Peace

1977 Amnesty International
1976 Mairead Corrigan, Betty Williams,
     N. Irish
1975 Andrei Sakharov, USSR
1974 Eisaku Sato, Jap., Sean MacBride,
     Irish
1973 Henry Kissinger, U.S.
     Le Duc Tho, N. Vietnamese
     (Tho declined)
1971 Willy Brandt, W. German
1970 Norman E. Borlaug, U.S.
1969 Intl. Labor Organization
1968 Rene Cassin, French
1965 U.N. Children's Fund (UNICEF)
1964 Martin Luther King Jr., U.S.
1963 International Red Cross,
     League of Red Cross Societies
1962 Linus C. Pauling, U.S.
1961 Dag Hammarskjold, Swedish
1960 Albert J. Luthuli, South African
1959 Philip J. Noel-Baker, British
1958 Georges Pire, Belgian
1957 Lester B. Pearson, Canadian

1954 Office of the UN High
     Commissioner for Refugees
1953 George C. Marshall, U.S.
1952 Albert Schweitzer, French
1951 Leon Jouhaux, French
1950 Ralph J. Bunche, U.S.
1949 Lord John Boyd Orr of Brechin
     Mearns, British
1947 Friends Service Council, Brit.
     Amer. Friends Service Com.
1946 Emily G. Balch,
     John R. Mott, both U.S.
1945 Cordell Hull, U.S.
1944 International Red Cross
1938 Nansen International Office
     for Refugees
1937 Viscount Cecil of Chelwood, Brit.
1936 Carlos de Saavedra Lamas, Arg.
1935 Carl von Ossietzky, German
1934 Arthur Henderson, British
1933 Sir Norman Angell, British
1931 Jane Addams, U.S.
     Nicholas Murray Butler, U.S.

1930 Nathan Soderblom, Swedish
1929 Frank B. Kellogg, U.S.
1927 Ferdinand E. Buisson, French
     Ludwig Quidde, German
1926 Aristide Briand, French
     Gustav Stresemann, German
1925 Sir J. Austen Chamberlain, Brit.
     Charles G. Dawes, U.S.
1922 Fridtjof Nansen, Norwegian
1921 Karl H. Branting, Swedish
     Christian L. Lange, Norwegian
1920 Leon V.A. Bourgeois, French
1919 Woodrow Wilson, U.S.
1917 International Red Cross
1913 Henri La Fontaine, Belgian
1912 Elihu Root, U.S.
1911 Tobias M.C. Asser, Dutch
     Alfred H. Fried, Austrian
1910 Permanent International Peace
     Bureau
1909 Auguste M. F. Beernaert, Belg.
     Paul H. B. B. d'Estournells de
     Constant, French

1908 Klas P. Arnoldson, Swedish
Fredrik Bajer, Danish
1907 Ernesto T. Moneta, Italian
Louis Renault, French
1906 Theodore Roosevelt, U.S.

1905 Baroness Bertha von Suttner,
Austrian
1904 Institute of International Law
1903 Sir William R. Cremer, British
1902 Elie Ducommun,

Charles A. Gobat, both Swiss
1901 Jean H. Dunant, Swiss
Frederic Passy, French

## Economics

1977 Bertil Ohlin, Swedish
James E. Meade, British
1976 Milton Friedman, U.S.
1975 Tjalling Koopmans, Dutch-U.S.,
Leonid Kantorovich, USSR

1974 Gunnar Myrdal, Swed.,
Friedrich A. von Hayek, Austrian
1973 Wassily Leontief, U.S.
1972 Kenneth J. Arrow, U.S.
John R. Hicks, British

1971 Simon Kuznets, U.S.
1970 Paul A. Samuelson, U.S.
1969 Ragnar Frisch, Norwegian
Jan Tinbergen, Dutch

---

# Pulitzer Prizes in Journalism, Letters, and Music

The Pulitzer Prizes were endowed by Joseph Pulitzer (1847-1911), publisher of The World, New York, N.Y., in a bequest to Columbia University, New York, N.Y., and are awarded annually by the president of the university on recommendation of the Advisory Board on Pulitzer Prizes for work done during the preceding year. The administrator is Prof. Richard T. Baker of Columbia Univ. All prizes are $1,000 (originally $500) in each category, except Meritorious Public Service for which a gold medal is given.

For journalism awards from 1917 to 1940, consult the 1978 or earlier editions of The World Almanac. No awards given for later years omitted.

## Journalism

### Meritorious Public Service

For distinguished and meritorious public service by a United States newspaper.
1940—Waterbury (Conn.) Republican and American.
1941—St. Louis Post-Dispatch.
1942—Los Angeles Times.
1943—Omaha World Herald.
1944—New York Times.
1945—Detroit Free Press.
1946—Scranton (Pa.) Times.
1947—Baltimore Sun.
1948—St. Louis Post-Dispatch.
1949—Nebraska State Journal.
1950—Chicago Daily News; St. Louis Post-Dispatch.
1951—Miami (Fla.) Herald and Brooklyn Eagle.
1952—St. Louis Post-Dispatch.
1953—Whiteville (N.C.) News Reporter; Tabor City (N.C.) Tribune.
1954—Newsday (Long Island, N.Y.)
1955—Columbus (Ga.) Ledger and Sunday Ledger-Enquirer.
1956—Watsonville (Cal.) Register-Pajaronian.
1957—Chicago Daily News.
1958—Arkansas Gazette, Little Rock.
1959—Utica (N.Y.) Observer-Dispatch and Utica Daily Press.
1960—Los Angeles Times.
1961—Amarillo (Tex.) Globe-Times.
1962—Panama City (Fla.) News-Herald.
1963—Chicago Daily News.
1964—St. Petersburg (Fla.) Times.
1965—Hutchinson (Kan.) News.
1966—Boston Globe.
1967—The Louisville Courier-Journal; The Milwaukee Journal.
1968—Riverside (Cal.) Press-Enterprise.
1969—Los Angeles Times.
1970—Newsday (Long Island, N.Y.).
1971—Winston Salem (N.C.) Journal & Sentinel.
1972—New York Times.
1973—Washington Post.
1974—Newsday (Long Island, N.Y.).
1975—Boston Globe.
1976—Anchorage Daily News.
1977—Lufkin (Tex.) News.
1978—Philadelphia Inquirer.

### Reporting

This category originally embraced all fields, local, national, and international. Later separate categories were created for the different fields of reporting.
1940—S. Burton Heath, New York World-Telegram.
1941—Westbrook Pegler, New York World-Telegram.
1942—Stanton Delaplane, San Francisco Chronicle.
1943—George Weller, Chicago Daily News.
1944—Paul Schoenstein, N.Y. Journal-American.
1945—Jack S. McDowell, San Francisco Call-Bulletin.
1946—William L. Laurence, New York Times.
1947—Frederick Woltman, N.Y. World-Telegram.
1948—George E. Goodwin, Atlanta Journal.
1949—Malcolm Johnson, New York Sun.

1950—Meyer Berger, New York Times.
1951—Edward S. Montgomery, San Francisco Examiner.
1952—Geo. de Carvalho, San Francisco Chronicle.
*(1) General or Spot; (2) Special or Investigative*
1953—(1) Providence (R.I.) Journal and Evening Bulletin; (2) Edward J. Mowery, N.Y. World-Telegram & Sun.
1954—(1) Vicksburg (Miss.) Sunday Post-Herald; (2) Alvin Scott McCoy, Kansas City (Mo.) Star.
1955—(1) Mrs. Caro Brown, Alice (Tex.) Daily Echo; (2) Roland K. Towery, Cuero (Tex.) Record.
1956—(1) Lee Hills, Detroit Free Press; (2) Arthur Daley, New York Times.
1957—(1) Salt Lake Tribune, Salt Lake City, Ut.; (2) Wallace Turner and William Lambert, Portland Oregonian.
1958—(1) Fargo, (N.D.) Forum; (2) George Beveridge, Evening Star, Washington, D.C.
1959—(1) Mary Lou Werner, Washington Evening Star; (2) John Harold Brislin, Scranton (Pa.) Tribune, and The Scrantonian.
1960—(1) Jack Nelson, Atlanta Constitution; (2) Miriam Ottenberg, Washington Evening Star.
1961—(1) Sanche de Gramont, N.Y. Herald Tribune; (2) Edgar May, Buffalo Evening News.
1962—(1) Robert D. Mullins, Deseret News, Salt Lake City; (2) George Bliss, Chicago Tribune.
1963—(1) Shared by Sylvan Fox, William Longgood, and Anthony Shannon, N.Y. World-Telegram & Sun; (2) Oscar Griffin, Jr., Pecos (Tex.) Independent and Enterprise.
*(1) General Reporting; (2) Special Reporting.*
1964—(1) Norman C. Miller, Wall Street Journal; (2) Shared by James V. Magee, Albert V. Gaudiosi, and Frederick A. Meyer, Philadelphia Bulletin.
1965—(1) Melvin H. Ruder, Hungry Horse News (Columbia Falls, Mon.); (2) Gene Goltz, Houston Post.
1966—(1) Los Angeles Times Staff; (2) John A. Frasca, Tampa (Fla.) Tribune.
1967—(1) Robert V. Cox, Chambersburg (Pa.) Public Opinion; (2) Gene Miller, Miami Herald.
1968—Detroit Free Press Staff; (2) J. Anthony Lukas, N.Y. Times.
1969—(1) John Fetterman, Louisville Courier-Journal and Times; (2) Albert L. Delugach, St. Louis Globe Democrat, and Denny Walsh, Life.
1970—(1) Thomas Fitzpatrick, Chicago Sun-Times; (2) Harold Eugene Martin, Montgomery Advertiser & Alabama Journal.
1971—(1) Akron Beacon Journal Staff, (2) William Hugh Jones, Chicago Tribune.
1972—(1) Richard Cooper and John Machacek, Rochester Times-Union; (2) Timothy Leland, Gerard M. O'Neill, Stephen Kurkjian and Anne De Santis, Boston Globe.
1973—(1) Chicago Tribune; (2) Sun Newspapers of Omaha.
1974—(1) Hugh F. Hough, Arthur M. Petacque, Chicago Sun-Times; (2) William Sherman, N.Y. Daily News.
1975—(1) Xenia (Oh.) Daily Gazette; (2) Indianapolis Star.
1976—(1) Gene Miller, Miami Herald; (2) Chicago Tribune.
1977—(1) Margo Huston, Milwaukee Journal; (2) Acel Moore, Wendell Rawls Jr., Philadelphia Inquirer.
1978—(1) Richard Whitt, Louisville Courier-Journal; (2) Anthony R. Dolan, Stamford (Conn.) Advocate.

## Criticism or Commentary

*(1) Criticism; (2) Commentary*

**1970**—(1) Ada Louise Huxtable, N.Y. Times; (2) Marquis W. Childs, St. Louis Post-Dispatch.
**1971**—(1) Harold C. Schonberg, N.Y. Times; (2) William A. Caldwell, The Record, Hackensack, N.J.
**1972**—(1) Frank Peters Jr., St. Louis Post-Dispatch; (2) Mike Royko, Chicago Daily News.
**1973**—(1) Ronald Powers, Chicago Sun-Times; (2) David S. Broder, Washington Post.
**1974**—(1) Emily Genauer, Newsday, (N.Y.); (2) Edwin A. Roberts, Jr., National Observer.
**1975**—(1) Roger Ebert, Chicago Sun Times; (2) Mary McGrory, Washington Star.
**1976**—(1) Alan M. Kriegsman, Washington Post; (2) Walter W. (Red) Smith, N.Y. Times.
**1977**—(1) William McPherson, Washington Post; (2) George F. Will, Wash. Post Writers Group.
**1978**—(1) Walter Kerr, New York Times; (2) William Safire, New York Times.

## National Reporting

**1942**—Louis Stark, New York Times.
**1944**—Dewey L. Fleming, Baltimore Sun.
**1945**—James B. Reston, New York Times.
**1946**—Edward A. Harris, St. Louis Post-Dispatch.
**1947**—Edward T. Folliard, Washington Post.
**1948**—Bert Andrews, New York Herald Tribune; Nat S. Finney, Minneapolis Tribune.
**1949**—Charles P. Trussell, New York Times.
**1950**—Edwin O. Guthman, Seattle Times.
**1952**—Anthony Leviero, New York Times.
**1953**—Don Whitehead, Associated Press.
**1954**—Richard Wilson, Cowles Newspapers.
**1955**—Anthony Lewis, Washington Daily News.
**1956**—Charles L. Bartlett, Chattanooga Times.
**1957**—James Reston, New York Times.
**1958**—Relman Morin, AP; Clark Mollenhoff, Des Moines Register & Tribune.
**1959**—Howard Van Smith, Miami (Fla.) News.
**1960**—Vance Trimble, Scripps-Howard, Washington, D.C.
**1961**—Edward R. Cony, Wall Street Journal.
**1962**—Nathan G. Caldwell and Gene S. Graham, Nashville Tennessean.
**1963**—Anthony Lewis, New York Times.
**1964**—Merriman Smith, UPI.
**1965**—Louis M. Kohlmeier, Wall Street Journal.
**1966**—Haynes Johnson, Washington Evening Star.
**1967**—Monroe Karmin and Stanley Penn, Wall Street Journal.
**1968**—Howard James, Christian Science Monitor; Nathan K. Kotz, Des Moines Register.
**1969**—Robert Cahn, Christian Science Monitor.
**1970**—William J. Eaton, Chicago Daily News.
**1971**—Lucinda Franks & Thomas Powers, UPI.
**1972**—Jack Anderson, United Features.
**1973**—Robert Boyd and Clark Hoyt, Knight Newspapers.
**1974**—James R. Polk, Washington Star-News; Jack White, Providence Journal-Bulletin.
**1975**—Donald L. Barlett and James B. Steele, Philadelphia Inquirer.
**1976**—James Risser, Des Moines Register.
**1977**—Walter Mears, Associated Press.
**1978**—Gaylord D. Shaw, Los Angeles Times.

## International Reporting

**1942**—Laurence Edmund Allen, Associated Press.
**1943**—Ira Wolfert, No. Am. Newspaper Alliance.
**1944**—Daniel DeLuce, Associated Press.
**1945**—Mark S. Watson, Baltimore Sun.
**1946**—Homer W. Bigart, New York Herald Tribune.
**1947**—Eddy Gilmore, Associated Press.
**1948**—Paul W. Ward, Baltimore Sun.
**1949**—Price Day, Baltimore Sun.
**1950**—Edmund Stevens, Christian Science Monitor.
**1951**—Keyes Beech and Fred Sparks, Chicago Daily News; Homer Bigart and Marguerite Higgins, New York Herald Tribune; Relman Morin and Don Whitehead, AP.
**1952**—John M. Hightower, Associated Press.
**1953**—Austin C. Wehrwein, Milwaukee Journal.
**1954**—Jim G. Lucas, Scripps-Howard Newspapers.
**1955**—Harrison Salisbury, New York Times.
**1956**—William Randolph Hearst, Jr., Frank Conniff, Hearst Newspapers; Kingsbury Smith, INS.
**1957**—Russell Jones, United Press.
**1958**—New York Times.
**1959**—Joseph Martin and Philip Santora, N.Y. News.
**1960**—A.M. Rosenthal, New York Times.

**1961**—Lynn Heinzerling, Associated Press.
**1962**—Walter Lippmann, N.Y. Herald Tribune Synd.
**1963**—Hal Hendrix, Miami (Fla.) News.
**1964**—Malcolm W. Browne, AP; David Halberstam, N.Y. Times.
**1965**—J.A. Livingston, Philadelphia Bulletin.
**1966**—Peter Arnett, AP.
**1967**—R. John Hughes, Christian Science Monitor.
**1968**—Alfred Friendly, Washington Post.
**1969**—William Tuohy, L.A. Times.
**1970**—Seymour M. Hersh, Dispatch News Service.
**1971**—Jimmie Lee Hoagland, Washington Post.
**1972**—Peter R. Kann, Wall Street Journal.
**1973**—Max Frankel, N.Y. Times.
**1974**—Hedrick Smith, N.Y. Times.
**1975**—William Mullen and Ovie Carter, Chicago Tribune.
**1976**—Sydney H. Schanberg, N.Y. Times.
**1978**—Henry Kamm, N.Y. Times.

## Correspondence

For Washington or foreign correspondence. Category was merged with those in national and international reporting in 1948.

**1940**—Otto D. Tolischus, New York Times.
**1941**—Bronze plaque to commemorate work of American correspondents on war fronts.
**1942**—Carlos P. Romulo, Philippines Herald.
**1943**—Hanson W. Baldwin, New York Times.
**1944**—Ernest Taylor Pyle, Scripps-Howard Newspaper Alliance.
**1945**—Harold V. (Hal) Boyle, Associated Press.
**1946**—Arnaldo Cortesi, New York Times.
**1947**—Brooks Atkinson, New York Times.

## Editorial Writing

**1940**—Bart Howard, St. Louis Post-Dispatch.
**1941**—Reuben Maury, Daily News, N.Y.
**1942**—Geoffrey Parsons, New York Herald Tribune.
**1943**—Forrest W. Seymour, Des Moines (la.) Register and Tribune.
**1944**—Henry J. Haskell, Kansas City (Mo.) Star.
**1945**—George W. Potter, Providence (R.I.) Journal-Bulletin.
**1946**—Hodding Carter, Greenville (Miss.) Delta Democrat-Times.
**1947**—William H. Grimes, Wall Street Journal.
**1948**—Virginius Dabney, Richmond (Va.) Times-Dispatch.
**1949**—John H. Crider, Boston (Mass.) Herald, Herbert Elliston, Washington Post.
**1950**—Carl M. Saunders, Jackson (Mich.) Citizen-Patriot.
**1951**—William H. Fitzpatrick, New Orleans States.
**1952**—Louis LaCoss, St. Louis Globe Democrat.
**1953**—Vermont C. Royster, Wall Street Journal.
**1954**—Don Murray, Boston Herald.
**1955**—Royce Howes, Detroit Free Press.
**1956**—Lauren K. Soth, Des Moines (la.) Register and Tribune.
**1957**—Buford Boone, Tuscaloosa (Ala.) News.
**1958**—Harry S. Ashmore, Arkansas Gazette.
**1959**—Ralph McGill, Atlanta Constitution.
**1960**—Lenoir Chambers, Norfolk Virginian-Pilot.
**1961**—William J. Dorvillier, San Juan (Puerto Rico) Star.
**1962**—Thomas M. Storke, Santa Barbara (Cal.) News-Press.
**1963**—Ira B. Harkey, Jr., Pascagoula (Miss.) Chronicle.
**1964**—Hazel Brannon Smith, Lexington (Miss.) Advertiser.
**1965**—John R. Harrison, The Gainesville (Fla.) Sun.
**1966**—Robert Lasch, St. Louis Post-Dispatch.
**1967**—Eugene C. Patterson, Atlanta Constitution.
**1968**—John S. Knight, Knight Newspapers.
**1969**—Paul Greenberg, Pine Bluff (Ark.) Commercial.
**1970**—Philip L. Geyelin, Washington Post.
**1971**—Horance G. Davis, Jr., Gainesville (Fla.) Sun.
**1972**—John Strohmeyer, Bethlehem (Pa.) Globe-Times.
**1973**—Rober B. Linscott, Berkshire Eagle, Pittsfield, Mass.
**1974**—F. Gilman Spencer, Trenton (N.J.) Trentonian.
**1975**—John D. Maurice, Charleston (W. Va.) Daily Mail.
**1976**—Philip Kerby, Los Angeles Times.
**1977**—Warren L. Lerude, Foster Church, and Norman F. Cardoza, Reno (Nev.) Evening Gazette and Nevada State Journal.
**1978**—Meg Greenfield, Washington Post.

## Editorial Cartooning

**1940**—Edmund Duffy, Baltimore Sun.
**1941**—Jacob Burck, Chicago Times.
**1942**—Herbert L. Block, Newspaper Enterprise Assn.
**1943**—Jay N. Darling, New York Herald Tribune.
**1944**—Clifford K. Berryman, Washington Star.
**1945**—Bill Mauldin, United Feature Syndicate.
**1946**—Bruce Alexander Russell, Los Angeles Times.
**1947**—Vaughn Shoemaker, Chicago Daily News.
**1948**—Reuben L. (Rube) Goldberg, N. Y. Sun.

'49—Lute Pease, Newark (N.J.) Evening News.
'50—James T. Berryman, Washington Star.
'51—Reginald W. Manning, Arizona Republic.
'52—Fred L. Packer, New York Mirror.
'53—Edward D. Kuekes, Cleveland Plain Dealer.
'54—Herbert L. Block, Washington Post & Times-Herald.
'55—Daniel R. Fitzpatrick, St. Louis Post-Dispatch.
'56—Robert York, Louisville (Ky.) Times.
'57—Tom Little, Nashville Tennessean.
'58—Bruce M. Shanks, Buffalo Evening News.
'59—Bill Mauldin, St. Louis Post-Dispatch.
'61—Carey Orr, Chicago Tribune.
'62—Edmund S. Valtman, Hartford Times.
'63—Frank Miller, Des Moines Register.
'64—Paul Conrad, Denver Post.
'66—Don Wright, Miami News.
'67—Patrick B. Oliphant, Denver Post.
'68—Eugene Gray Payne, Charlotte Observer.
'69—John Fischetti, Chicago Daily News.
'70—Thomas F. Darcy, Newsday.
'71—Paul Conrad, L. A. Times.
'72—Jeffrey K. MacNelly, Richmond News-Leader.
'74—Paul Szep, Boston Globe.
'75—Garry Trudeau, Universal Press Syndicate.
'75—Tony Auth, Philadelphia Inquirer.
'77—Paul Szep, Boston Globe.
'78—Jeffrey K. MacNelly, Richmond News Leader.

1953—William M. Gallagher, Flint (Mich.) Journal.
1954—Mrs. Walter M. Schau, amateur.
1955—John L. Gaunt, Jr., Los Angeles Times.
1956—New York Daily News.
1957—Harry A. Trask, Boston Traveler.
1958—William C. Beall, Washington Daily News.
1959—William Seaman, Minneapolis Star.
1960—Andrew Lopez, UPI.
1961—Yasushi Nagao, Mainichi Newspapers, Tokyo.
1962—Paul Vathis, Associated Press.
1963—Hector Rondon, La Republica, Caracas, Venezuela.
1964—Robert H. Jackson, Dallas Times-Herald.
1965—Horst Faas, Associated Press.
1966—Kyoichi Sawada, UPI.
1967—Jack R. Thornell, Associated Press.
1968—Rocco Morabito, Jacksonville Journal.
1969—Edward Adams, AP.
1970—Steve Starr, AP.
1971—John Paul Filo, Valley Daily News & Daily Dispatch of Tarentum & New Kensington, Pa.
1972—Horst Faas and Michel Laurent, AP.
1973—Huynh Cong Ut, AP.
1974—Anthony K. Roberts, AP.
1975—Gerald H. Gay, Seattle Times.
1976—Stanley Forman, Boston Herald American.
1977—Neal Ulevich, Associated Press; Stanley Forman, Boston Herald American.
1978—Jim Schweiker, UPI.

## Spot News Photography

'42—Milton Brooks, Detroit News.
'43—Frank Noel, Associated Press.
'44—Frank Filan, AP; Earl L. Bunker, Omaha World-Herald.
'45—Joe Rosenthal, Associated Press, for photograph of planting American flag on Iwo Jima.
'47—Arnold Hardy, amateur, Atlanta, Ga.
—Frank Cushing, Boston Traveler.
—Nathaniel Fein, New York Herald Tribune.
'50—Bill Crouch, Oakland (Cal.) Tribune.
'51—Max Desfor, Associated Press.
'52—John Robinson and Don Ultang, Des Moines Register and Tribune.

## Feature Photography

1968—Toshio Sakai, UPI.
1969—Moneta Sleet, Jr., Ebony.
1970—Dallas Kinney, Palm Beach Post.
1971—Jack Dykinga, Chicago Sun-Times.
1972—Dave Kennerly, UPI.
1973—Brian Lanker, Topeka Capitol-Journal.
1974—Slava Veder, AP.
1975—Matthew Lewis, Washington Post.
1976—Louisville Courier-Journal and Louisville Times.
1977—Robin Hood, Chattanooga News-Free Press.
1978—J. Ross Baughman, AP.

## Special Citation

'41—New York Times.
'44—Byron Price and Mrs. William Allen White. Also to Richard Rodgers and Oscar Hammerstein 2d, for musical, Oklahoma!
'45—Press cartographers for war maps.
'47—(Pulitzer centennial year.) Columbia Univ. and the Graduate School of Journalism, and St. Louis Post-Dispatch.
'48—Dr. Frank Diehl Fackenthal.
'51—Cyrus L. Sulzberger, New York Times.
'52—Max Kase, New York Journal-American.
'53—The New York Times; Lester Markel.
'57—Kenneth Roberts, for his historical novels.

1958—Walter Lippmann, New York Herald Tribune.
1960—Garrett Mattingly, for The Armada.
1961—American Heritage Picture History of the Civil War.
1964—The Gannett Newspapers.
1973—James T. Flexner, for "George Washington," a four-volume biography.
1976—John Hohenberg, for services to American journalism.
1977—Alex Haley, for Roots, $1,000.
1978—Richard Lee Strout, Christian Science Monitor and New Republic.
—E.B. White, for his work.

## Letters

### Fiction

For fiction in book form by an American author, preferably dealing with American life.

'18—Ernest Poole, His Family.
'19—Booth Tarkington, The Magnificent Ambersons.
'21—Edith Wharton, The Age of Innocence.
'22—Booth Tarkington, Alice Adams.
'23—Willa Cather, One of Ours.
'24—Margaret Wilson, The Able McLaughlins.
'25—Edna Ferber, So Big.
'26—Sinclair Lewis, Arrowsmith. (Refused prize.)
'27—Louis Bromfield, Early Autumn.
'28—Thornton Wilder, Bridge of San Luis Rey.
'29—Julia M. Peterkin, Scarlet Sister Mary.
'30—Oliver LaFarge, Laughing Boy.
'31—Margaret Ayer Barnes, Years of Grace.
'32—Pearl S. Buck, The Good Earth.
'33—T. S. Stribling, The Store.
'34—Caroline Miller, Lamb in His Bosom.
'35—Josephine W. Johnson, Now in November.
'36—Harold L. Davis, Honey in the Horn.
'37—Margaret Mitchell, Gone with the Wind.
'38—John P. Marquand, The Late George Apley.
'39—Marjorie Kinnan Rawlings, The Yearling.
'40—John Steinbeck, The Grapes of Wrath.
'42—Ellen Glasgow, In This Our Life.
'43—Upton Sinclair, Dragon's Teeth.

1944—Martin Flavin, Journey in the Dark.
1945—John Hersey, A Bell for Adano.
1947—Robert Penn Warren, All the King's Men.
1948—James A Michener, Tales of the South Pacific.
1949—James Gould Cozzens, Guard of Honor.
1950—A. B. Guthrie Jr., The Way West.
1951—Conrad Richter, The Town.
1952—Herman Wouk, The Caine Mutiny.
1953—Ernest Hemingway, The Old Man and the Sea.
1955—William Faulkner, A Fable.
1956—MacKinlay Kantor, Andersonville.
1958—James Agee, A Death in the Family.
1959—Robert Lewis Taylor, The Travels of Jaimie McPheeters.
1960—Allen Drury, Advise and Consent.
1961—Harper Lee, To Kill a Mockingbird.
1962—Edwin O'Connor, The Edge of Sadness.
1963—William Faulkner, The Reivers.
1965—Shirley Ann Grau, The Keepers of the House.
1966—Katherine Anne Porter, Collected Stories of Katherine Anne Porter.
1967—Bernard Malamud, The Fixer.
1968—William Styron, The Confessions of Nat Turner.
1969—N. Scott Momaday, House Made of Dawn.
1970—Jean Stafford, Collected Stories.
1972—Wallace Stegner, Angle of Repose.
1973—Eudora Welty, The Optimist's Daughter.
1975—Michael Shaara, The Killer Angels.
1976—Saul Bellow, Humboldt's Gift.
1978—James Alan McPherson, Elbow Room.

## Drama

For an American play, preferably original and dealing with American life.

1918—Jesse Lynch Williams, Why Marry?
1920—Eugene O'Neill, Beyond the Horizon.
1921—Zona Gale, Miss Lulu Bett.
1922—Eugene O'Neill, Anna Christie.
1923—Owen Davis, Icebound.
1924—Hatcher Hughes, Hell-Bent for Heaven.
1925—Sidney Howard, They Knew What They Wanted.
1926—George Kelly, Craig's Wife.
1927—Paul Green, In Abraham's Bosom.
1928—Eugene O'Neill, Strange Interlude.
1929—Elmer Rice, Street Scene.
1930—Marc Connelly, The Green Pastures.
1931—Susan Glaspell, Alison's House.
1932—George S. Kaufman, Morrie Ryskind and Ira Gershwin, Of Thee I Sing.
1933—Maxwell Anderson, Both Your Houses.
1934—Sidney Kingsley, Men in White.
1935—Zoe Akins, The Old Maid.
1936—Robert E. Sherwood, Idiot's Delight.
1937—George S. Kaufman and Moss Hart, You Can't Take It With You.
1938—Thornton Wilder, Our Town.
1939—Robert E. Sherwood, Abe Lincoln in Illinois.
1940—William Saroyan, The Time of Your Life.
1941—Robert E. Sherwood, There Shall Be No Night.
1943—Thornton Wilder, The Skin of Our Teeth.
1945—Mary Chase, Harvey.
1946—Russel Crouse and Howard Lindsay, State of the Union.
1948—Tennessee Williams, A Streetcar Named Desire.
1949—Arthur Miller, Death of a Salesman.
1950—Richard Rodgers, Oscar Hammerstein 2d, and Joshua Logan, South Pacific.
1952—Joseph Kramm, The Shrike.
1953—William Inge, Picnic.
1954—John Patrick, Teahouse of the August Moon.
1955—Tennessee Williams, Cat on a Hot Tin Roof.
1956—Frances Goodrich and Albert Hackett, The Dairy of Anne Frank.
1957—Eugene O'Neill, Long Day's Journey Into Night.
1958—Ketti Frings, Look Homeward, Angel.
1959—Archibald MacLeish, J. B.
1960—George Abbott, Jerome Weidman, Sheldon Harnick and Jerry Bock, Fiorello.
1961—Tad Mosel, All the Way Home.
1962—Frank Loesser and Abe Burrows, How To Succeed In Business Without Really Trying.
1965—Frank D. Gilroy, The Subject Was Roses.
1967—Edward Albee, A Delicate Balance.
1969—Howard Sackler, The Great White Hope.
1970—Charles Gordone, No Place to Be Somebody.
1971—Paul Zindel, The Effect of Gamma Rays on Man-in-the-Moon Marigolds.
1973—Jason Miller, That Championship Season.
1975—Edward Albee, Seascape.
1976—Michael Bennett, James Kirkwood, Nicholas Dante, Marvin Hamlisch, Edward Kleban, A Chorus Line.
1977—Michael Cristofer, The Shadow Box.
1978—Donald L. Coburn, The Gin Game.

## History

For a book on the history of the United States.
1917—J. J. Jusserand, With Americans of Past and Present Days.
1918—James Ford Rhodes, History of the Civil War.
1920—Justin H. Smith, The War with Mexico.
1921—William Snowden Sims, The Victory at Sea.
1922—James Truslow Adams, The Founding of New England.
1923—Charles Warren, The Supreme Court in United States History.
1924—Charles Howard McIlwain, The American Revolution: A Constitutional Interpretation.
1925—Frederick L. Paxton, A History of the American Frontier.
1926—Edward Channing, A History of the U.S.
1927—Samuel Flagg Bemis, Pinckney's Treaty.
1928—Vernon Louis Parrington, Main Currents in American Thought.
1929—Fred A. Shannon, The Organization and Administration of the Union Army, 1861-65.
1930—Claude H. Van Tyne, The War of Independence.
1931—Bernadotte E. Schmitt, The Coming of the War, 1914.
1932—Gen. John J. Pershing, My Experiences in the World War.
1933—Frederick J. Turner, The Significance of Sections in American History.
1934—Herbert Agar, The People's Choice.
1935—Charles McLean Andrews, The Colonial Period of American History.
1936—Andrew C. McLaughlin, The Constitutional History of th United States.
1937—Van Wyck Brooks, The Flowering of New England.
1938—Paul Herman Buck, The Road to Reunion, 1865-1900.
1939—Frank Luther Mott, A History of American Magazines.
1940—Carl Sandberg, Abraham Lincoln: The War Years.
1941—Marcus Lee Hansen, The Atlantic Migration, 1607-1860.
1942—Margaret Leech, Reveille in Washington.
1943—Esther Forbes, Paul Revere and the World He Lived In.
1944—Merle Curti, The Growth of American Thought.
1945—Stephen Bonsal, Unfinished Business.
1946—Arthur M. Schlesinger Jr., The Age of Jackson.
1947—James Phinney Baxter 3d, Scientists Against Time.
1948—Bernard De Voto, Across the Wide Missouri.
1949—Roy F. Nichols, The Disruption of American Democracy.
1950—O. W. Larkin, Art and Life in America.
1951—R. Carlyle Buley, The Old Northwest: Pioneer Perioc 1815-1840.
1952—Oscar Handlin, The Uprooted.
1953—George Dangerfield, The Era of Good Feelings.
1954—Bruce Catton, A Stillness at Appomattox.
1955—Paul Horgan, Great River: The Rio Grande in North American History.
1956—Richard Hofstadter, The Age of Reform.
1957—George F. Kennan, Russia Leaves the War.
1958—Bray Hammond, Banks and Politics in America—Fron the Revolution to the Civil War.
1959—Leonard D. White and Jean Schneider, The Republica Era; 1869-1901.
1960—Margaret Leech, In the Days of McKinley.
1961—Herbert Feis, Between War and Peace: The Potsdan Conference.
1962—Lawrence H. Gibson, The Triumphant Empire: Thunder clouds Gather in the West.
1963—Constance McLaughlin Green, Washington: Village anc Capital, 1800-1878.
1964—Summer Chilton Powell, Puritan Village: The Formation of A New England Town.
1965—Irwin Unger, The Greenback Era.
1966—Perry Miller, Life of the Mind in America.
1967—William H. Goetzmann, Exploration and Empire: the Explorer and Scientist in the Winning of the American West.
1968—Bernard Bailyn, The Ideological Origins of the Americar Revolution.
1969—Leonard W. Levy, Origin of the Fifth Amendment.
1970—Dean Acheson, Present at the Creation: My Years in the State Department.
1971—James McGregor Burns, Roosevelt: The Soldier of Freedom.
1972—Carl N. Degler, Neither Black Nor White.
1973—Michael Kammen, People of Paradox: An Inquiry Concerning the Origins of American Civilization.
1974—Daniel J. Boorstin, The Americans: The Democratic Experience.
1975—Dumas Malone, Jefferson ànd His Time.
1976—Paul Horgan, Lamy of Santa Fe.
1977—David M. Potter, The Impending Crisis.
1978—Alfred D. Chandler, Jr., The Visible Hand: The Managerial Revolution in American Business.

## Biography or Autobiography

For a distinguished biography or autobiography by an American author, preferably on an American subject.
1917—Laura E. Richards and Maude Howe Elliott, assisted by Florence Howe Hall, Julia Ward Howe.
1918—William Cabell Bruce, Benjamin Franklin, Self-Revealed.
1919—Henry Adams, The Education of Henry Adams.
1920—Albert J. Beveridge, The Life of John Marshall.
1921—Edward Bok, The Americanization of Edward Bok.
1922—Hamlin Garland, A Daughter of the Middle Border.
1923—Burton J. Hendrick, The Life and Letters of Walter H. Page.
1924—Michael Pupin, From Immigrant to Inventor.
1925—M. A. DeWolfe Howe, Barrett Wendell and His Letters.
1926—Harvey Cushing, Life of Sir William Osler.
1927—Emory Holloway, Whitman: An Interpretation in Narrative.
1928—Charles Edward Russell, The American Orchestra and Theodore Thomas.
1929—Burton J. Hendrick, The Training of an American: The Earlier Life and Letters of Walter H. Page.
1930—Marquis James, The Raven (Sam Houston).
1931—Henry James, Charles W. Eliot.
1932—Henry F. Pringle, Theodore Roosevelt.
1933—Allan Nevins, Grover Cleveland.
1934—Tyler Dennett, John Hay.
1935—Douglas Southall Freeman, R. E. Lee.
1936—Ralph Barton Perry, The Thought and Character of William James.

37—Allan Nevins, Hamilton Fish: The Inner History of the Grant Administration.
'38—Divided between Odell Shepard, Pedlar's Progress; Marquis James, Andrew Jackson.
'39—Carl Van Doren, Benjamin Franklin.
'40—Ray Stannard Baker, Woodrow Wilson, Life and Letters.
'41—Ola Elizabeth Winslow, Jonathan Edwards.
'42—Forrest Wilson, Crusader in Crinoline.
'43—Samuel Eliot Morison, Admiral of the Ocean Sea (Columbus).
'44—Carleton Mabee, The American Leonardo: The Life of Samuel F. B. Morse.
'45—Russell Blaine Nye, George Bancroft; Brahmin Rebel.
'46—Linny Marsh Wolfe, Son of the Wilderness.
'47—William Allen White, The Autobiography of William Allen White.
'48—Margaret Clapp, Forgotten First Citizen: John Bigelow.
'49—Robert E. Sherwood, Roosevelt and Hopkins.
'50—Samuel Flag Bemis, John Quincy Adams and the Foundations of American Foreign Policy.
'51—Margaret Louise Colt, John C. Calhoun: American Portrait.
'52—Merlo J. Pusey, Charles Evans Hughes.
'53—David J. Mays, Edmund Pendleton, 1721-1803.
'54—Charles A. Lindberg, The Spirit of St. Louis.
'55—William S. White, The Taft Story.
'56—Talbot F. Hamlin, Benjamin Henry Latrobe.
'57—John F. Kennedy, Profiles in Courage.
'58—Douglas Southall Freeman (decd. 1953), George Washington, Vols. I-VI: John Alexander Carroll and Mary Wells Ashworth, Vol. VII.
'59—Arthur Walworth, Woodrow Wilson: American Prophet.
'60—Samuel Eliot Morison, John Paul Jones.
'61—David Donald, Charles Sumner and The Coming of the Civil War.
'63—Leon Edel, Henry James: Vol. II. The Conquest of London, 1870-1881; Vol. III, The Middle Years, 1881-1895.
'64—Walter Jackson Bate, John Keats.
'65—Ernest Samuels, Henry Adams.
'66—Arthur M. Schlesinger, Jr., A Thousand Days.
'67—Justin Kaplan, Mr. Clemens and Mark Twain.
'68—George F. Kennan, Memoirs (1925-1950).
'69—B. L. Reid, The Man from New York: John Quinn and his Friends.
'70—T. Harry Williams, Huey Long.
'71—Lawrence Thompson, Robert Frost: The Years of Triumph, 1915-1938.
'72—Joseph P. Lash, Eleanor and Franklin.
'73—W. A. Swanberg, Luce and His Empire.
'74—Louis Sheaffer, O'Neill, Son and Artist.
'75—Robert A. Caro, The Power Broker: Robert Moses and the Fall of New York.
'76—R.W.B. Lewis, Edith Wharton: A Biography.
'77—John E. Mack, A Prince of Our Disorder, The Life of T.E. Lawrence.
'78—Walter Jackson Bate, Samuel Johnson.

## American Poetry

Before this prize was established in 1922, awards were made from gifts provided by the Poetry Society: 1918—Love Songs, by Sara Teasdale. 1919—Old Road to Paradise, by Margaret Widemer; Corn Huskers, by Carl Sandburg.

'22—Edwin Arlington Robinson, Collected Poems.
'23—Edna St. Vincent Millay, The Ballad of the Harp-Weaver; A Few Figs from Thistles; Eight Sonnets in American Poetry, 1922; A Miscellany.
'24—Robert Frost, New Hampshire: A Poem with Notes and Grace Notes.
'25—Edwin Arlington Robinson, The Man Who Died Twice.
'26—Amy Lowell, What's O'Clock.
'27—Leonora Speyer, Fiddler's Farewell.
'28—Edwin Arlington Robinson, Tristram.
'29—Stephen Vincent Benet, John Brown's Body.
'30—Conrad Aiken, Selected Poems.

1931—Robert Frost, Collected Poems.
1932—George Dillon, The Flowering Stone.
1933—Archibald MacLeish, Conquistador.
1934—Robert Hillyer, Collected Verse.
1935—Audrey Wurdemann, Bright Ambush.
1936—Robert P. Tristram Coffin, Strange Holiness.
1937—Robert Frost, A Further Range.
1938—Marya Zaturenska, Cold Morning Sky.
1939—John Gould Fletcher, Selected Poems.
1940—Mark Van Doren, Collected Poems.
1941—Leonard Bacon, Sunderland Capture.
1942—William Rose Benet, The Dust Which Is God.
1943—Robert Frost, A Witness Tree.
1944—Stephen Vincent Benet, Western Star.
1945—Karl Shapiro, V-Letter and Other Poems.
1947—Robert Lowell, Lord Weary's Castle.
1948—W. H. Auden, The Age of Anxiety.
1949—Peter Viereck, Terror and Decorum.
1950—Gwendolyn Brooks, Annie Allen.
1951—Carl Sandburg, Complete Poems.
1952—Marianne Moore, Collected Poems.
1953—Archibald MacLeish, Collected Poems.
1954—Theodore Roethke, The Waking.
1955—Wallace Stevens, Collected Poems.
1956—Elizabeth Bishop, Poems, North and South.
1957—Richard Wilbur, Things of This World.
1958—Robert Penn Warren, Promises: Poems 1954-1956.
1959—Stanley Kunitz, Selected Poems 1928-1958.
1960—W. D. Snodgrass, Heart's Needle.
1961—Phyllis McGinley, Times Three: Selected Verse from Three Decades.
1962—Alan Dugan, Poems.
1963—William Carlos Williams, Picturés From Breughel.
1964—Louis Simpson, At the End of the Open Road.
1965—John Berryman, 77 Dream Songs.
1966—Richard Eberhart, Selected Poems.
1967—Anne Sexton, Live or Die.
1968—Anthony Hecht, The Hard Hours.
1969—George Oppen, Of Being Numerous.
1970—Richard Howard, Untitled Subjects.
1971—William S. Merwin, The Carrier of Ladders.
1972—James Wright, Collected Poems.
1973—Maxine Winokur Kumin, Up Country.
1974—Robert Lowell, The Dolphin.
1975—Gary Snyder, Turtle Island.
1976—John Ashbery, Self-Portrait in a Convex Mirror.
1977—James Merrill, Divine Comedies.
1978—Howard Nemerov, Collected Poems.

## General Non-Fiction

For best book by an American, not eligible in any other category.
1962—Theodore H. White, The Making of the President 1960.
1963—Barbara W. Tuchman, The Guns of August.
1964—Richard Hofstadter, Anti-Intellectualism in American Life.
1965—Howard Mumford Jones, O Strange New World.
1966—Edwin Way Teale, Wandering Through Winter.
1967—David Brion Davis, The Problem of Slavery in Western Culture.
1968—Will and Ariel Durant, Rousseau and Revolution.
1969—Norman Mailer, The Armies of the Night; and Rene Jules Dubos, So Human an Animal: How We Are Shaped by Surroundings and Events.
1970—Eric H. Erikson, Gandhi's Truth.
1971—John Toland, The Rising Sun.
1972—Barbara W. Tuchman, Stilwell and the American Experience in China, 1911-1945.
1973—Frances FitzGerald, Fire in the Lake: The Vietnamese and the Americans in Vietnam; and Robert Coles, Children of Crisis, Volumes II and III.
1974—Ernest Becker, The Denial of Death.
1975—Annie Dillard, Pilgrim at Tinker Creek.
1976—Robert N. Butler, Why Survive? Being Old in America.
1977—William W. Warner, Beautiful Swimmers.
1978—Carl Sagan, The Dragons of Eden.

## Music

For composition by an American (before 1977, by a composer resident in the U.S.), in the larger forms of chamber, orchestra or choral music or for an operatic work including ballet. A special posthumous award was granted in 1976 to Scott Joplin.
'43—William Schuman, Secular Cantata No. 2, A Free Song.
'44—Howard Hanson, Symphony No. 4, Op. 34.
'45—Aaron Copland, Appalachian Spring.
'46—Leo Sowerby, The Canticle of the Sun.
'47—Charles E. Ives, Symphony No. 3.
'48—Walter Piston, Symphony No. 3.
'49—Virgil Thomson, Louisiana Story.

1950—Gian-Carlo Menotti, The Consul.
1951—Douglas Moore, Giants in the Earth.
1952—Gail Kubil, Symphony Concertante.
1954—Quincy Porter, Concerto for Two Pianos and Orchestra.
1955—Gian-Carlo Menotti, The Saint of Bleecker Street.
1956—Ernest Toch, Symphony No. 3.
1957—Norman Dello Joio, Meditations on Ecclesiastes.
1958—Samuel Barber, Vanessa.
1959—John La Montaine, Concerto for Piano and Orchestra.
1960—Elliott Carter, Second String Quartet.
1961—Walter Piston, Symphony No. 7.

**1962**—Robert Ward, The Crucible.
**1963**—Samuel Barber, Piano Concerto No. 1.
**1966**—Leslie Bassett, Variations for Orchestra.
**1967**—Leon Kirchner, Quartet No. 3.
**1968**—George Crumb, Echoes of Time and The River.
**1969**—Karel Husa, String Quartet No. 3.
**1970**—Charles W. Wuorinen, Time's Encomium.
**1971**—Mario Davidovsky, Synchronisms No. 6.

**1972**—Jacob Druckman, Windows.
**1973**—Elliott Carter, String Quartet No. 3.
**1974**—Donald Martino, Notturno. (Special citation) Roger Sessions.
**1975**—Dominick Argento, From the Diary of Virginia Woolf.
**1976**—Ned Rorem, Air Music.
**1977**—Richard Wernick, Visions of Terror and Wonder.
**1978**—Michael Colgrass, Deja Vu for Percussion and Orchestra.

## Special Awards

Awarded in 1978 unless otherwise designated

### Books, Allied Arts

**Academy of American Poets Fellow,** for distinguished achievement, (1977) $10,000: Louis Coxe.

**American Academy and Institute of Arts and Letters Awards:** Gold Medal for History: Barbara W. Tuchman; Gold Medal for the Short Story: Peter Taylor; Award for Distinguished Service to the Arts: Congressman John Brademas; Rosenthal Award, $4,000: Douglas Day; Zabel Award, $2,500: Joan Didion; Academy-Institute Awards in Literature, $3,000: Renata Adler, William Arrowsmith, Lerone Bennett Jr., Terrence Des Pres, Leslie Epstein, Michael Herr, Murray Kempton, Alison Lurie, Toni Morrison, Page Smith.

**American Historical Association Prizes:** Herbert B. Adams Prize: Charles Maier, Recasting Bourgeois Europe; George L. Beer Prize: Stephen A. Schuker, The End of French Predominance in Europe; Albert J. Beveridge Award: Henry F. May, The Enlightenment in America; John K. Fairbank Prize: Gail L. Bernstein, Japanese Marxist; Leo Gershoy Award: Simon Schama, Patriots and Liberators; Howard R. Marraro Prize: Gene A. Brucker, The Civic World of Early Renaissance Florence.

**American Institute of Physics Science-Writing Award** in Physics and Astronomy: Timothy Ferris, The Red Limit: The Search for the Edge of the Universe.

**American Printing History Association Award:** Joseph Blumenthal, Spiral Press.

**Bancroft Prizes,** for American history, by Columbia Univ., $4,000: Alfred D. Chandler, The Visible Hand: The Managerial Revolution in American Business; Morton J. Horwitz, The Transformation of American Law: 1780-1860.

**Irma Simonton Black Award,** by Bank Street College, for children's literature: Steven Kellogg, Mysterious Tadpole.

**Burroughs Medal,** for natural history book: Aldo Leopold, Sand County Almanac.

**Caldecott Medal,** by American Library Association, for children's book illustration: Peter Spier, Noah's Ark.

**Canada Council Children's Literature Prizes** (1977), $5,000: Jean Little, Listen for the Singing; $5,000 (shared): Denise Houle, Lune de neige (text); Claude Lafortune, L'Evangile en paper (illustration).

**Canada Council Translation Prizes** (1977), $5,000 each: Frank Scott, Poems of French Canada; Jean Paré, Un homme de week-end.

**Canadian Governor General's Literary Awards,** $5,000 each (1977): Timothy Findley, The Wars; Gabrielle Roy, Ces enfants de ma vie; Frank Scott, Essays on the Constitution; Denis Monière, Le développement des idéologies au Québec des origines à nos jours; D. G. Jones, Under the Thunder the Flowers Light up the Earth; Michel Garneau, Les Célébrations and Adidou Adidouce.

**Canadian Library Association Children's Book Awards:** English language book: Dennis Lee, Garbage Delight; illustration: Elizabeth Cleaver, The Loon's Necklace.

**Carey-Thomas Award,** for distinguished book publishing project, by Publishers Weekly: Horizon Press, Frank Lloyd Wright's Autobiography.

**Christopher Awards,** by the Christophers, for affirmation of human spirit: adult books: Richard K. Taylor, Blockade; Will D. Campbell, Brother to a Dragonfly; Archie Hill, Closed World of Love; John McPhee, Coming Into the Country; Peter Forbath, The River Congo; Stephen B. Oates, With Malice Toward None: The Life of Abraham Lincoln.

**Commonwealth Club of Calif. Literature Awards:** Ferol Egan for Fremont, Explorer for a Restless Nation; Ingrid

Rimland for The Wanderers; Ann Stanford for In Mediterranean Air; Louis Irigaray, Theodore Taylor for A Shepherd Watches, A Shepherd Sings; Henry Evans for Botanical Prints; Brooke Hayward for Haywire.

**Delta Kappa Gamma Society Educator's Award:** Kate Long, Johnny's Such a Bright Boy, What a Shame He's Retarded.

**Ralph Waldo Emerson Award,** by Phi Beta Kappa, for interpretive synthesis in humane studies (1977), $2,500: Eugen Weber, Peasants into Frenchmen: The Modernization of Rural France.

**Emerson-Thoreau Medal,** by American Academy of Arts and Sciences (1977), $1,000: Saul Bellow.

**Dorothy Canfield Fisher Children's Book Award:** Lois Duncan, Summer of Fear.

**George Freedley Award,** for book on theater, by Theatre Library Assoc.: George C. Izenour, Theater Design.

**Christian Gauss Award,** by Phi Beta Kappa, for literary scholarship (1977), $2,500: Joseph Frank, Dostoevsky: the Seeds of Revolt.

**Gay Book Awards,** by American Library Association: Harold Brown, Familiar Faces, Hidden Lives.

**Goethe House—P.E.N. Translation Prize,** by American P.E.N.: Joachim Neugroschel.

**Golden Kite Award,** by Society of Children's Book Writers: Berniece Rabe, The Girl Who Had No Name; Robert McClung, Peeper, First Voice of Spring.

**Haskins Medal,** by Mediaeval Academy of America: George Kane, E. Talbot Donaldson, Piers Plowman.

**Ernest Hemingway Foundation Award,** for first book of fiction, $6,000: Darcy O'Brien, A Way of Life, Like Any Other.

**Sidney Hillman Foundation Awards;** public service: Andrew Young; communications: Philip Caputo, A Rumor of War; Eliot Marshall, "Anatomy of Health Care Costs"; Stan Swofford, "The Untold Story of the Wilmington Ten."

**Hugo Award,** for science fiction (1977): Kate Wilhelm, Where Late the Sweet Birds Sang.

**International Reading Association Children's Book Award,** for promising writer, $1,000: Lois Lowry, A Summer to Die.

**Iowa School of Letters Award for Short Fiction,** $1,000: Lon Otto, A Nest of Hooks.

**Lamont Poetry Selection,** by Academy of American Poets (1977): Gerald Stern, Lucky Life.

**Landon Award,** by Academy of American Poets, $1,000: Galway Kinnell, The Poems of Francois Villon; Howard Norman, The Wishing Bone Cycle.

**Man in his Environment Book Award,** by E.P. Dutton, $10,000 advance: Richard E. Leakey, Robert Lewin: Origins.

**Lenore Marshall Poetry Prize,** by Saturday Review and New Hope Foundation (1977), $5,000: Philip Levine, The Names of the Lost.

**Lucille J. Medwick Award,** by Poetry Society of America, humanitarian poem, $500: David R. Godine, Godine Press.

**Mitchell Prize,** by Mitchell Foundation, for writing on visual arts (1977), $10,000: Francis J. H. Haskell, Rediscoveries in Art.

**National Arts Club Medal of Honor for Literature:** Saul Bellow.

**National Book Awards,** administered by American Academy and Institute of Arts and Letters, $1,000: contemporary thought: Gloria Emerson, Winners and Losers: Battles, Retreats, Gains, Losses and Ruins From a Long War; fiction:

Mary Lee Settle, *Blood Tie*; translation: Richard and Clara Winston, Uwe George's *In the Deserts of This Earth*; biography: W. Jackson Bate, *Samuel Johnson*; poetry: Howard Nemerov, *The Collected Poems*; children's literature: Judith and Herbert Kohl, *The View from the Oak: The Private Worlds of Other Creatures*; history: David McCullough, *The Path Between the Seas: The Creation of the Panama Canal, 1870-1914*; Special Achievement Medal: S.J. Perelman.

**National Book Critics Circle Awards:** fiction: Toni Morrison, *Song of Solomon*; poems: Robert Lowell, *Day by Day*; nonfiction: W. Jackson Bate, *Samuel Johnson*; criticism: Susan Sontag, *On Photography*.

**National Jewish Book Awards,** by Jewish Book Council: juvenile: Milton Meltzer, *Never to Forget: The Jews of the Holocaust*; fiction: Chaim Grade, *The Yeshiva*; history: Celia S. Heller, *On the Edge of Destruction*; holocaust: Terence Des Pres, *The Survivor: An Anatomy of Life in the Death Camp*; poetry: T. Carmi, *El Eretz Aheret (To Another Land)*; Israel: Hillel Halkin, *Letters to an American Jewish Friend*; thought: Raphael Patai, *The Jewish Mind*.

**National Media Award,** by American Psychological Foundation, $1,000: Robert M. Stern, William J. Ray, *Biofeedback*.

**National Religious Book Awards,** by *Religious Media Today*: theology: Avery Dulles, *The Resilient Church*; John T. Robinson, *Redating the New Testament*; Nicholas Wolterstorff, *Reason Within the Bounds of Religion*; scripture: Raymond Brown, *The Birth of the Messiah*; Joseph Jenkinsopp, *Prophecy and Canon*; E.P. Sanders, *Paul and Palestinian Judaism*; J.M. Robinson, *The Nag Hammadi Documents*.

**Nebula Award,** by Science Fiction Writers of America, for novel: Frederik Pohl, *Gateway*.

**Newberry Medal,** by American Library Association, for children's literature: Katherine Paterson, *Bridge to Terabithia*.

**N.Y. Academy of Sciences Children's Science Book Awards:** Irene Brady, *Wild Mouse*; Elizabeth Burton Brown, *Grains*.

**O'Henry Prize Stories,** by Doubleday: Woody Allen, "The Kugelmass Episode"; Mark Shorer, "A Lamp"; Robert Henson, "The Upper and the Lower Millstone."

**Phi Beta Kappa Science Award,** for the literature of science (1977), $2,500: Gerard K. O'Neill, *The High Frontier:*

*Human Colonies in Space.*

**P.E.N. Translation Prize,** by American P.E.N.: Adrienne Foulke, *One Way or Another.*

**Edgar Allen Poe Awards,** by Mystery Writers of America: best novel: William H. Hallahan, *Catch Me: Kill Me*; first novel: Robert Ross, *A French Finish*; paperback: Mike John, *The Quark Maneuver*; juvenile: Eloise Jarvis McGraw, *A Really Weird Summer*; critical/biographical: John McAleer, *Rex Stout*; fact crime book: George Jones and Barbara Amiel, *By Persons Unknown.*

**Poetry Society of America Awards:** Shelly Award, $2,200: Jane Cooper, William Everson; Melville Cane Award, $500: Michael Harper for *Images of Kin*; Castagnola Award, $2,000: Carol Muske for *Skylight*; Lucille Medwick Award, $500: Willis Barnstone for "Miklos Radnotti"; Masefield Award, $500: Dorothy Foltz-Gray for "Schooling on a Georgia Farm"; Gustav Davidson Award, $500: Norma Farber for "To Live as Marsh."

**Sir Walter Raleigh Award,** by Historical Book Club of N. Carolina: Sylvia Wilkinson, *Shadow of the Mountain.*

**Regina Medal,** by Catholic Library Association, for children's literature, silver medal: Scott O'Dell.

**Society for Animal Rights Awards:** Peter Singer, *Animal Liberation*; Hans Ruesch, *Slaughter of the Innocent.*

**Southwestern Library Assoc. Award:** Angie Debo for *Geronimo: The Man, His Time, His Place.*

**Spur Award,** by Western Writers of America, for young people's western (1977): Philip H. Ault, *All Aboard.*

**Deems Taylor Awards,** by Amer. Society of Composers, Authors and Publishers, for books on music, $500 each: John Hammond, *John Hammond on Record*; Edward Lowinsky, *Josquin des Prez*; Howard E. Smither, *A History of the Oratorio*; Maynard Solomon, *Beethoven*; Jeff Todd Titon, *Early Downhome Blues.*

**Theatre Library Association Award,** book on recorded performance: Mira Liehm, Antonin Liehm, *The Most Important Art: East European Film After 1945.*

**Irita Van Doren Book Award:** Barbara A. Bannon, *Publisher's Weekly.*

**Edward Lewis Wallant Award** (1977): Curt Leviant for *The Yemenite Girl.*

**Walt Whitman Award,** by Academy of American Poets, $1,000: Karen Snow for *Wonders.*

# Journalism Awards

**American Legion's Fourth Estate Awards,** for writing on the American way of life: Jess Gorkin, *Parade Magazine*; Columbus (O.) *Dispatch.*

**Claude Bernard Science Journalism Award,** by National Society for Medical Research: Donald C. Drake, *Philadelphia Inquirer*; Arthur Fisher, "Slow viruses: biological time bombs."

**Worth Bingham Prize,** by White House Correspondents Assoc., for national reporting, $1,000: Richard E. Meyer, Michael J. Sniffen, Associated Press.

**National Association of Engine and Boat Mfrs. Director's Award and Press Prize:** (1977): Bill Seibel, St. Louis *Globe Democrat.*

**Heywood Broun Award,** by the Newspaper Guild, for concern for the underdog, $1,000: Fredric N. Tulsky, David Phelps, *Jackson* (Miss.) *Clarion-Ledger.*

**Canadian National Newspaper Awards,** by Toronto Press Club, $500 each: spot news: Gerald Utting, *Toronto Star*; criticism: William French, *Toronto Globe*; feature story: Brenda Zosky, *Toronto Star*; editorials: David Ablett, *Vancouver Sun*; sports: Brodie Snyder, Dick Bacon, *Montreal Gazette*; spot news photo: Douglas Ball, Canadian Press; feature photo: Boris Spremo, *Toronto Star*; cartoon: Terry Mosher, *Montreal Gazette.*

**Cartoonist of the Year,** by International Pavilion of Humor: Charles Schulz, "Peanuts."

**Catholic Press Association Awards,** general excellence: *National Catholic Reporter;* Portland (Me.) *Church World; Muenster* (Sask.) *Prairie Messenger; Chicago Catholic.*

**Russell L. Cecil Awards,** by Arthritis Foundation: Susan Leitner, Longview (Tex.) *Morning Journal;* Ruth Winter.

**Eugene Cervi Award,** by International Society of Weekly Newspaper Editors, for local government reporting: Tom Leathers, Squire Newspapers.

**CIBA-Geigy Agricultural Writing Award:** (1977): newspapers: Mick Cochran, *Springfield* (Ill.) *State Journal & Register.*

**Raymond Clapper Award,** by White House Correspondents Association, government reporting, $1,000: James V. Risser, George P. Anthan, *Des Moines Register and Tribune.*

**Clarion Awards,** by Women in Communications: magazines: Jim Atkinson, *D Magazine*; Frederic Golden, *Time*; Harry F. Waters, *Newsweek*; Loretta Schwartz, Ann Northrop, *Ms.*; John Mack Carter, *Good Housekeeping*; Judy Langford Carter, Frances Ruffin, *Redbook*; newspapers: Gail Marks Jarvis, *National Catholic Reporter*; Linda M. Daniel, Seattle *Times*; Gloria Hochman, Philadelphia *Inquirer*; Andrew Feinberg, Philadelphia *Inquirer*; Carolyn Robbins-Chipkin, *Union-Republican*, Springfield, Mass; Carolyn Kortge, *Wichita* (Kan.) *Eagle and Beacon*; Cynthia Parsons, *Christian Science Monitor.*

**Institute of Collective Bargaining Award,** $1,000 (1977): A.H. Raskin, *New York Times.*

**Dog Writers' Association of America Awards** (1977): newspapers: Walter R. Fletcher, New York *Times*; Randy White, *Fort Meyers* (Fla.) *News-Press*; Sherry Carpenter, *Grit*; Frances I. Reid, *From the Kennels.*

**E.P. Dutton Best Sport Stories:** coverage: Tom Boswell, *Washington Post*; feature: Dave Klein, *Newark Star Ledger*; magazine: A. Bartlett Giametti, *Harpers*; action photo: Charles R. Pugh Jr., *Atlanta Journal-Constitution*; feature photo: George D. Waldman, *Detroit News.*

**Elliott Prize,** by Mediaeval Academy of America: Norman Roth, "The Jews and Muslim Conquest of Spain."

**American Academy of Family Physicians Awards,** $1,000: Norman Lobsenz, "Coping with a Killer: Hypertension;" $750: Kate Keating, *Better Homes and Gardens*; $250: Abigail Brett, *U.S. News and World Report.*

**International Association of Firefighters Awards:** Lucille Storen, *Mount Vernon* (N.Y.) *Daily Argus;* Richard Haynes, Ray Hill, *Buffalo* (N.Y.) *Evening News;* Dick Floyd, *Cranbrook* (B.C.) *Daily Townsman;* Stanley Forman, *Boston Herald American.*

**Garber Award,** for woman sportswriter: Kathleen Maxa, *Washington Star.*

**James T. Grady Award,** for chemistry journalism, by American Chemical Society, $2,000: Michael Woods.

**Great Lakes Colleges Awards,** for new writers: Jonathan Penner, *Going Blind;* Eugene Ruggles, *The Lifeguard in the Snow.*

**Hancock Awards,** for business and finance writing, by John Hancock Mutual Life: Brooks Jackson, Evans Witt, Associated Press; William Tucker, *Harper's;* Chris Welles, *Institutional Investor;* Harry Nelson, Paul Steiger, S.J. Diamond, Alexander Auerback, *Los Angeles Times;* Philip Moeller, Larry Werner, Phil Norman, Ben Hershberg, Jim Thompson, Dan Kauffman, *Louisville Courier-Journal;* Jeff Kosnett, *Charlestown* (W.Va.) *Daily Mail.*

**Roy W. Howard Public Service Awards,** by Scripps-Howard Foundation, first prize, $2,500: *Philadelphia Inquirer;* second prize, $1,000: *Advocate,* Stamford, Conn.; special mention: *Clarion-Ledger,* Jackson, Miss.; *Newsday; Boston Globe.*

**Robert F. Kennedy Awards:** print journalism, $1,000: Jonathan Neumann, Bill Marimow, *Philadelphia Inquirer;* photojournalism, $1,000: Michael O'Brien, *Miami News,* Peter A. Silva, *Corpus Christi Caller.*

**Gerald Loeb Awards,** for distinguished business and financial journalism, $1,000 each: large newspapers: Paul Steiger, Robert Rosenblatt, Ronald Soble, Murray Seeger, Sam Jameson, *Los Angeles Times* for "The Dollar: Its History and Current Woes"; smaller newspapers: Harold Chucker, *Minneapolis Star* for "Where's the Money?"; national magazines; Lewis Lapham, *Harper's* for "The Energy Debacle"; column/editorial: Hobart Rowen, *Washington Post* for "IMF, World Bank Face Grave Issues."

**Elijah Parrish Lovejoy Award,** for courage in journalism, by Southern Ill. Univ. — Carbondale School of Journalism: Wilson F. Minor, *Jackson* (Miss.) *Capital Reporter.*

**National Magazine Awards,** by Columbia University School of Journalism: visual excellence: *Architectural Digest;* essays and criticism: *Esquire;* public service: *Mother Jones;* service to the individual: *Newsweek;* fiction and reporting excellence: *New Yorker;* specialized journalism: *Scientific American.*

**Edward J. Meeman Conservation Awards,** by Scripps-Howard Foundation, $2,500: Bruce Ingersoll, *Chicago Sun-Times;* first prizes, $2,000: Kathy Warbelow, Ellen Grzech, Robert Calverley, *Detroit Free Press;* Jim Detjen, *Poughkeepsie* (N.Y.) *Journal;* second prize, $1,000: Cornelia Carrier, *Times Picayune,* New Orleans.

**Charles Stewart Mott Awards,** by Education Writers Assoc. (1977): grand prize $1,500: Lou Antosh, *Philadelphia Evening Bulletin.*

**Frank Luther Mott Award,** by Kappa Tau Alpha, for research in journalism, $250: Chalmers M. Roberts, *The Washington Post: The First 100 Years.*

**Multiple Sclerosis Public Education Award** (1977), $1,000: Al Allen, *Louisville Courier Journal & Times.*

**Overseas Press Club:** photos requiring courage: Eddie Adams, Associated Press; daily reporting: Robert C. Toth, *Los Angeles Times;* interpretation: Jim Hoagland, *Washington Post;* photos: James P. Blair, *National Geographic;* magazine reporting: James Pringle, Elizabeth Peet, Arnaud de Borchgrave, Kim Willenson, *Newsweek;* magazine interpre-

tation: Joseph B. Treaster, *Atlantic Monthly;* cartoon: E Fischer, *Omaha World-Herald;* business: Cary Reich, *Ins tutional Investor.*

**American Penal Press Contest and Charles C. Clayt Award:** Wilbert Rideau, Tommy R. Mason, eds., *Angoli Louisiana State Penitentiary,* Angola.

**Penney-Missouri Awards** (1977), $1,000 each: newsp pers: reporting: Richard Severo, *New York Times;* Mar Huston, *Milwaukee Journal;* consumer affairs: Jane Brody, *New York Times;* fashion and clothing: Eva Hodge *Denver Post;* magazines: contemporary living: Susan Edmi ton, *Woman's Day;* consumerism: Bil Gilbert, *Sports Illu trated;* health: Gerald Jonas, *The New Yorker;* person lifestyle: Judith Ramsey, *Family Circle;* expanding opport nities: William Broyles, *Texas Monthly;* smaller magazine Sam Merrill, *New Times,* Loretta Schwartz, *Philadelphia.*

**Photographer of the Year Award,** by White House New Photographers Association (1977): Frank Johnston, *Wa ington Post.*

**George Polk Awards:** foreign reporting: Robert C. To *Los Angeles Times;* national reporting: Walter Pincu *Washington Post;* local reporting: Len Ackland, *Des Moin Register;* magazine reporting: Daniel Lang, *New Yorke* science reporting: *New England Journal of Medicine;* crit cism: Peter S. Prescott, *Newsweek;* commentary: Red Smit *New York Times;* editorial cartoons, Jeff MacNelly, *Ric mond News Leader;* news photography: Eddie Adams, A sociated Press; Special Award: Carey McWilliams.

**Ernie Pyle Memorial Awards,** by Scripps-Howard Fou dation, $1000: Stephen Smith, *Boston Globe;* second priz $500: Bert Lindler, *Great Falls* (Mont.) *Tribune.*

**Recycling Industry Media Awards** (1977), $1,000 eac Sylvia Porter, Field Newspaper Syndicate; $1,000 (share Claudia Deutsch, Bob Yaeger, *Business Week;* $500 eac UPI, Business News Dept.; *American Metal Market;* T.( DuMond, *Iron Age;* Kevin Priscu-Lynch, *Solid Waste Ma agement.*

**National Association for Retarded Citizens Award:** ove all media: Peg Meier, *Minneapolis Tribune.*

**Reuben Award,** by National Cartoonists Society: Chest Gould.

**Science Writers Award,** by American Dental Associatic (1977), $1,000: newspapers: Lucy Eckberg, *Winona* (Minn *Daily News;* magazines: Annette Stec, *Exploring.*

**National Association of Science Writers Awards,** $1,00 John Douglas, *Science News;* Philip Boffey, *New Yo Times.*

**Edward Willis Scripps First Amendment Award,** b Scripps-Howard Foundation, $2,500: Sun Enterprise New papers, Monmouth, Ore.; special mention: *Bethlehem* (Pa *Globe Times;* Daily Oklahoman and *Oklahoma City Time* Oklahoma City.

**Walker Stone Awards for Editorial Writing,** by Scripp Howard Foundation, $1,000: Michael Pakenham, *Philade phia Inquirer;* second prize, $500: Edwin Yoder Jr., *Was ington Star.*

**Suburban Journalist of the Year** (1977), by Suburba Newspapers of America: Jack W. Hoffman, *Northvi* (Mich.) *Record.*

**Deems Taylor Awards,** by Amer. Society of Composer Authors and Publishers, for music journalism, $500 eac Martin Bernheimer, *Los Angeles Times;* Andrew Porte *New Yorker;* David Burge, "Contemporary Piano;" Georg Perle, "Secret Program of the Lyric Suite;" Douglass M Green, "Berg's De Profundis;" Gene Lees, *High Fidelit* Joe Klein, "Notes on a Native Son."

**Westinghouse Science Writing Awards,** by American A sociation for the Advancement of Science, $1,000: Robert ( Cowen, *Christian Science Monitor;* Lee Hotz, Lee Bowma Jr., *Waynesboro* (Va.) *News-Virginian;* William Bennett, Jo Gurin, "The Great Debate Over DNA."

**John Peter Zenger Award,** by University of Arizona, fc freedom of the press, $500: Robert W. Greene, *Newsday.*

## Broadcasting and Theater Awards

**Clarion Awards,** by Women in Communications: TV: ABC, Stan Margulies, *Roots;* Joan Konner, NBC News, "Danger: Radioactive Waste"; CBS News, CBS Reports,

"The Fire Next Door," Howard Stringer, Tom Spain, B Moyers; Beverly Williams, Cliff Abromats, KYW-T Phila., "Police Brutality"; Perry Miller Adato, WNET, Ne ork, "Georgia O'Keefe"; Susan Silk, Garry Armstrong, WNAC-TV, Boston, "Sirens"; radio: Gale Cunningham, KXL, Portland, Ore., "Rights in Conflict-The Gay Movement 1977"; Bill Cusack, WBZ, Boston, "BZ Living"; Susan Stamberg, Natl. Public Radio, Wash., D.C. "Interviews of Susan Stamberg."

**New York Drama Critics Circle Awards:** best play: *Da*; best musical: *Ain't Misbehavin'*.

**Dupont-Columbia Broadcast Journalism Awards:** Walter Cronkite, CBS; NBC News, "Human Rights: A Soviet-American Debate"; WNET, New York, WETA, Arlington, Va., "MacNeil/Lehrer Report"; Susan and Alan Raymond, WNET, New York, "The Police Tapes"; Westinghouse Broadcasting, "Six American Families"; WBBM-TV, Chicago, "Once a Priest"; KCET-TV, Los Angeles; KGW-TV, Portland, Ore., "The Timber Farmers"; WFAA-TV, Dallas, energy, racial issues.

**Sidney Hillman Foundation Awards:** Bill Moyers, CBS-TV, "The Fire Next Door"; ABC, "Roots."

**Roy W. Howard Public Service Award,** by Scripps-Howard Foundation, first prize, $2,500: KOY radio, Phoenix, Ariz.; second prizes, $1,000 each: WBMM-TV, Chicago; KNX/FM Radio, Los Angeles.

**Obie Awards,** for Off-Broadway theater: distinguished performance: Richard Bauer; Nell Carter; Alma Cuervo; Swoosie Kurtz; Kaiulani Lee; Bruce Myers; Lee S. Wilkof; distinguished direction: Robert Allan Ackerman, *Prayer for My Daughter*; Thomas Bullard, *Statements After an Arrest Under the Immorality Act*; Elizabeth Swados, *Runaway*; distinguished design: Garland Wright, John Arnone, *K*; Robert Yodice, *Museum.*

**Overseas Press Club:** TV interpretation: Barbara Walters, ABC News; radio spot news: Reid Collins, Tom Fenton, Christopher Glenn, Mike Lee, Bob McNamara, Bert Quint, John Shearhan, Bob Simon, Doug Tunnell, Bruno Wasserneil, CBS News; radio interpretation: Clark Todd, NBC.

**George Foster Peabody Awards,** by Univ. of Georgia, for public service: radio: WXYZ, Detroit, "Winter's Fear"; Paul Hume, WGMS, Rockville, Md., "A Variable Feast"; WHA, Madison, Wis., "Earplay"; KSJN, Saint Paul, Minn., "The Prairie Was Quiet"; KPFA, Berkeley, Cal., "Science Story"; National Public Radio, Washington, "Crossroads"; WHLN, Harlan, Ky., 1977 flood coverage; television: KABC-TV, Los Angeles, "Police Accountability"; KCMO-TV, Kansas City, "Where Have All the Flood Cars Gone?"; WNET, New York, WETA, Arlington, Va., "MacNeil/Lehrer Report"; WBTV, Charlotte, N.C., "The Rowe String Quartet"; Lorimar Productions, "Green Eyes"; David Wolper, ABC-TV, "Roots"; Norman Lear, "All in the Family"; London Weekend Television, "Upstairs, Downstairs"; MTM Productions, "Mary Tyler Moore Show"; Steve Allen, "Meeting of Minds"; NBC-TV, New York, "Tut: the Boy King"; Metropolitan Opera Assoc., "Live From the Met"; WNET, New York, "A Good Dissonance Like a Man"; WNBC-TV, New York, "F.I.N.D. Investigative Reports"; Multimedia Program Productions, "Joshua's Confusion"; NBC-TV, Arthur Rankin, and Jules Bass, "The Hobbit"; WCBS-TV, New York "Camera Three"; New York, "The Lifer's Group"; WNBC-TV, New York, "Buyline: Betty Furness"; WNET, New York, "Police Tapes."

**Antoinette Perry Awards (Tonys):** play: *Da*; musical: *Ain't Misbehavin'*; actress: Jessica Tandy, *The Gin Game*; actor: Barnard Hughes, *Da*; director: Melvin Bernhardt, *Da*; director, musical: Richard Maltby Jr., *Ain't Misbehavin'*; book: Betty Comden, Adolph Green, *On the Twentieth Century*; score: Cy Coleman, Betty Comden, Adolph Green, *On the Twentieth Century*; musical actress: Liza Minelli, *The Act*; musical actor: John Cullum, *On the Twentieth Century*; revival: *Dracula*; choreographer: Bob Fosse, *Dancin'*; scenic design: Robin Wagner, *On the Twentieth Century*; lighting: Jules Fisher, *Dancin'*; costume: Edward Gorey, *Dracula*; featured actor: Lester Rawlins, *Da*; featured actress: Ann Wedgeworth, *Chapter Two*; featured actor, musical: Kevin Klein, *On the Twentieth Century*; featured actress: Nell Carter, *Ain't Misbehavin'*; lifetime achievement: Irving Berlin.

## Miscellaneous Awards

**American Academy and Institute of Arts and Letters Awards:** Arnold W. Brunner Memorial Prize in Architecture: Cesar Pelli; Award of Merit Medal for Sculpture: Tony Smith; Academy-Institute Awards, $3,000: art: William Dole, Daniel Maloney, Herman Maril, Richard McDermott Miller, Sara Roszak, Reuben Tam, Ulfert Wilke; music: Wallace Berry, Curtis O.B. Curtis-Smith, Elie Siegmeister, Richard Swift; Rosenthal Award in art, $4,000: Clifford Ross; Waite Award in music, $1,500: Dane Rudhyar; Ives Scholarships in music, $4,000: Daniel Brew-Baker, Justin Dello Joio, Lee Scott Goldstein, Arthur W. Gottschalk, Thomas Mountain, David Olan.

**Boy of the Year,** by Boys Club of America, $5,000: Ray Anthony Owens.

**Louis Dembitz Brandeis Medal,** by Brandeis Univ., for distinguished legal services: Edward M. Levi.

**Bristol Meyers Award,** for cancer research, $25,000:

James Miller, Elizabeth Miller.

**Capezio Foundation Dance Award,** $1,000: Hanya Holm.

**Albert Lasker Awards** in medicine, $15,000 each (1977): Inge G. Edler, Univ. Hospital, Lund, Sweden; C. Hellmuth Hertz, Lund Institute of Technology; K. Sune D. Bergstrom and Bengt Samuelsson, Kaarolinska Institute, Sweden; John R. Vane, Wellcome Research Labs, England.

**National Association for Retarded Citizens Awards:** employer of the year: F. Wolkow and Sons, Louisville; educator of the year: H.D. Frederick, Oregon College of Education, Monmouth, Ore.; teacher of the year: Beverly Bieniek, Arthurdale Elementary School, Arthurdale, W. Va.

**Vetlesen Prize,** in earth sciences, by Columbia Univ., $50,000: J. Tuzo Wilson.

**Theodore Weicker Award,** by American Society of Pharmacology and Experimental Therapeutics, $10,000: Ernest Bueding.

## Motion Picture Academy Awards (Oscars)

**1927-28**
Actor: Emil Jennings, The Way of All Flesh.
Actress: Janet Gaynor, Seventh Heaven.
Picture: Wings, Paramount.

**1928-29**
Actor: Warner Baxter, In Old Arizona.
Actress: Mary Pickford, Coquette.
Picture: Broadway Melody, MGM.

**1929-30**
Actor: George Arliss, Disraeli.
Actress: Norma Shearer, The Divorcee.
Picture: All Quiet on the Western Front, Univ.

**1930-31**
Actor: Lionel Barrymore, Free Soul.
Actress: Marie Dressler, Min and Bill.
Picture: Cimarron, RKO.

**1931-32**
Actor: Fredric March, Dr. Jekyll and Mr. Hyde; Wallace Beery, The Champ (tie).

Actress: Helen Hayes, Sin of Madelon Claudet.
Picture: Grand Hotel, MGM.
Special: Walt Disney, Mickey Mouse.

**1932-33**
Actor: Charles Laughton, Private Life of Henry VIII.
Actress: Katharine Hepburn, Morning Glory.
Picture: Cavalcade, Fox.

**1934**
Actor: Clark Gable, It Happened One Night.
Actress: Claudette Colbert, same.
Picture: It Happened One Night, Columbia.

**1935**
Actor: Victor McLaglen, The Informer.
Actress: Bette Davis, Dangerous.
Picture: Mutiny on the Bounty, MGM.

**1936**
Actor: Paul Muni, Story of Louis Pasteur.
Actress: Luise Rainer, The Great Ziegfeld.
Picture: The Great Ziegfeld, MGM.

**1937**
Actor: Spencer Tracy, Captains Courageous.
Actress: Luise Rainer, The Good Earth.
Picture: Life of Emile Zola, Warner.

**1938**
Actor: Spencer Tracy, Boys Town.
Actress: Bette Davis, Jezebel.
Picture: You Can't Take It With You, Columbia.

**1939**
Actor: Robert Donat, Goodbye Mr. Chips.
Actress: Vivien Leigh, Gone With the Wind.
Picture: Gone With the Wind, Selznick International.

**1940**
Actor: James Stewart, The Philadelphia Story.
Actress: Ginger Rogers, Kitty Foyle.
Picture: Rebecca, Selznick International.

**1941**
Actor: Gary Cooper, Sergeant York.
Actress: Joan Fontaine, Suspicion.
Picture: How Green Was My Valley, 20th Cent.-Fox.

**1942**
Actor: James Cagney, Yankee Doodle Dandy.
Actress: Greer Garson, Mrs. Miniver.
Picture: Mrs. Miniver, MGM.

**1943**
Actor: Paul Lukas, Watch on the Rhine.
Actress: Jennifer Jones, The Song of Bernadette.
Picture: Casablanca, Warner.

**1944**
Actor: Bing Crosby, Going My Way.
Actress: Ingrid Bergman, Gaslight.
Picture: Going My Way, Paramount.

**1945**
Actor: Ray Milland, The Lost Weekend.
Actress: Joan Crawford, Mildred Pierce.
Picture: The Lost Weekend, Paramount.

**1946**
Actor: Fredric March, Best Years of Our Lives.
Actress: Olivia de Havilland, To Each His Own.
Picture: The Best Years of Our Lives, Goldwyn, RKO.

**1947**
Actor: Ronald Colman, A Double Life.
Actress: Loretta Young, The Farmer's Daughter.
Picture: Gentleman's Agreement, 20th Cent.-Fox.

**1948**
Actor: Laurence Olivier, Hamlet.
Actress: Jane Wyman, Johnny Belinda.
Picture: Hamlet, Two Cities Film, Universal International

**1949**
Actor: Broderick Crawford. All the King's Men.
Actress: Olivia de Havilland, The Heiress.
Picture: All the King's Men, Columbia.

**1950**
Actor: Jose Ferrer, Cyrano de Bergerac.
Actress: Judy Holliday, Born Yesterday.
Picture: All About Eve, 20th Century-Fox.

**1951**
Actor: Humphrey Bogart, The African Queen.
Actress: Vivien Leigh, A Streetcar Named Desire.
Picture: An American in Paris, MGM.

**1952**
Actor: Gary Cooper, High Noon.
Actress: Shirley Booth, Come Back, Little Sheba.
Picture: Greatest Show on Earth, C.B. DeMille, Paramount.

**1953**
Actor: William Holden, Stalag 17.
Actress: Audrey Hepburn, Roman Holiday.
Picture: From Here to Eternity, Columbia.

**1954**
Actor: Marlon Brando, On the Waterfront.
Actress: Grace Kelly, The Country Girl.
Picture: On the Waterfront, Horizon-American, Colum.

**1955**
Actor: Ernest Borgnine, Marty.
Actress: Anna Magnani, The Rose Tattoo.
Picture: Marty, Hecht and Lancaster's Steven Prods., U.A.

**1956**
Actor: Yul Brynner, The King and I.
Actress: Ingrid Bergman, Anastasia.
Picture: Around the World in 80 Days, Michael Todd, U.A.

**1957**
Actor: Alec Guinness, The Bridge on the River Kwai.
Actress: Joanne Woodward, The Three Faces of Eve.
Picture: The Bridge on the River Kwai, Columbia.

**1958**
Actor: David Niven, Separate Tables.
Actress: Susan Hayward, I Want to Live.

Picture: Gigi, Arthur Freed Production, MGM.

**1959**
Actor: Charlton Heston, Ben-Hur.
Actress: Simone Signoret, Room at the Top.
Picture: Ben-Hur, MGM.

**1960**
Actor: Burt Lancaster, Elmer Gantry.
Actress: Elizabeth Taylor, Butterfield 8.
Picture: The Apartment, Mirisch Co., U.A.

**1961**
Actor: Maximilian Schell, Judgment at Nuremberg.
Actress: Sophia Loren, Two Women.
Picture: West Side Story, United Artists.

**1962**
Actor: Gregory Peck, To Kill a Mockingbird.
Actress: Anne Bancroft, The Miracle Worker.
Picture: Lawrence of Arabia, Columbia.

**1963**
Actor: Sidney Poitier, Lilies of the Field.
Actress: Patricia Neal, Hud.
Picture: Tom Jones, Woodfall Prod., UA-Lopert Pictures.

**1964**
Actor: Rex Harrison, My Fair Lady.
Actress: Julie Andrews, Mary Poppins.
Picture: My Fair Lady, Warner Bros.

**1965**
Actor: Lee Marvin, Cat Ballou.
Actress: Julie Christie, Darling.
Picture: The Sound of Music, 20th Century-Fox.

**1966**
Actor: Paul Scofield, A Man for All Seasons.
Actress: Elizabeth Taylor, Who's Afraid of Virginia Woolf?
Picture: A Man for All Seasons, Columbia.

**1967**
Actor: Rod Steiger, In the Heat of the Night.
Actress: Katharine Hepburn, Guess Who's Coming to Dinner.
Picture: In the Heat of the Night.

**1968**
Actor: Cliff Robertson, Charly.
Actress: Katharine Hepburn, The Lion in Winter, Barbra Streisand, Funny Girl (tie).
Picture: Oliver.

**1969**
Actor: John Wayne, True Grit.
Actress: Maggie Smith, The Prime of Miss Jean Brodie.
Picture: Midnight Cowboy.

**1970**
Actor: George C. Scott, Patton (refused).
Actress: Glenda Jackson, Women in Love.
Picture: Patton.

**1971**
Actor: Gene Hackman, The French Connection.
Actress: Jane Fonda, Klute.
Picture: The French Connection.

**1972**
Actor: Marlon Brando, The Godfather (refused).
Actress: Liza Minnelli, Cabaret.
Picture: The Godfather.

**1973**
Actor: Jack Lemmon, Save the Tiger.
Actress: Glenda Jackson, A Touch of Class.
Picture: The Sting.

**1974**
Actor: Art Carney, Harry and Tonto.
Actress: Ellen Burstyn, Alice Doesn't Live Here Anymore.
Picture: The Godfather, Part II.

**1975**
Actor: Jack Nicholson, One Flew Over the Cuckoo's Nest.
Actress: Louise Fletcher, same.
Picture: One Flew Over the Cuckoo's Nest.

**1976**
Actor: Peter Finch, Network.
Actress: Faye Dunaway, same.
Picture: Rocky.

**1977**
Actor: Richard Dreyfuss, The Goodbye Girl.
Actress: Diane Keaton, Annie Hall.
Picture: Annie Hall.
Foreign Film: Madame Rosa.
Director: Woody Allen, Annie Hall.
Supporting Actor: Jason Robards, Julia.
Supporting Actress: Vanessa Redgrave, Julia.
Screenplay (original): Woody Allen, Marshall Brickman, Annie Hall; (adapted): Alvin Sargent, Julia.
Cinematography: Vilmos Zsigmond, Close Encounters of the Third Kind.
Editing: Paul Hirsch, Marcia Lucas, Richard Cheu, Star Wars.

core (original): John Williams, Star Wars. (adapted): Jonathan Tunick, A Little Night Music.
ong: Joseph Brooks, You Light Up My Life.
rt Direction: John Barry, Norman Reynolds, Leslie Dilley, Star Wars.
Costumes: John Mollo, Star Wars.
ound: Don MacDougall, Ray West, Bob Minkler, Derek Ball, Star Wars.
hort Subject (animated): Sand Castle, Co Hoedeman; (live):

I'll Find a Way, Beverly Shaffer, Yuki Yoshida.
Documentary (feature): Who are the DeBolts? And Where Did They Get Nineteen Kids? Dan McCann, Warren L. Lockhart; (short): Gravity Is My Enemy, John Joseph, Jan Stussy.
Irving Thalberg Award: Walter Mirisch.
Gene Hersholt Humanitarian Award: Charlton Heston.
Special Award, Sound Effects Editing: Frank E. Warner, Close Encounters of the Third Kind.
Special Award, Sound Effects: Benjamin Burtt Jr., Star Wars.

## Canadian Film Awards

### Source: Canadian Film Institute

**1968**
Actor: Gerard Parkes, Isabel
Actress: Genevieve Bujold, Isabel
Picture: A Place to Stand
**1969**
Actor: Chris Wiggins, The Best Damn Fiddler From Calabogie to Kaladar
Actress: Jackie Burroughs, Dulcima
Picture: The Best Damn Fiddler from Calabogie to Kaladar
**1970**
Actor: Doug McGrath and Paul Bradley (tied), Goin' Down the Road
Actress: Genevieve Bujold, Act of the Heart
Picture: Psychocratie
**1971**
Actor: Jean Duceppe, Mon oncle Antoine
Actress: Ann Knox, The Only Thing You Know
Picture: Mon oncle Antoine
**1972**
Actor: Gordon Pinsent, The Rowdyman
Actress: Micheline Lanctot, Vrai nature de Bernadette
Picture: Wedding in White

**1973**
Actor: Jacques Godin, O.K. Laliberte
Actress: Genevieve Bujold, Kamouraska
Picture: Slipstream
**1974**
No awards
**1975**
Actor: Stuart Gillard, Why Rock the Boat?
Actress: Margot Kidder, Black Christmas and A Quiet Day in Belfast
Picture: Les Ordres
Film of the Year: The Apprenticeship of Duddy Kravitz
**1976**
Actor: Andre Melancon, Partis pur la gloire
Actress: Marilyn Lightstone, Lies My Father Told Me
Picture: Lies My Father Told Me
**1977**
Actor: Len Cariou, One Man
Actress: Monique Mercure, J.A. Martin: Photographe
Picture: J.A. Martin: Photographe

## The Spingarn Medal

The Spingarn Medal has been awarded annually since 1914 by the National Association for the Advancement of Colored People for the highest achievement by a black American.

| | | | | | |
|---|---|---|---|---|---|
| 1946 | Dr. Percy L. Julian | 1957 | Mrs. Daisy Bates and the Little Rock Nine | 1967 | Sammy Davis, Jr. |
| 1947 | Channing H. Tobias | | | 1968 | Clarence M. Mitchell, Jr. |
| 1948 | Ralph J. Bunche | 1958 | Edward Kennedy (Duke) Ellington | 1969 | Jacob Lawrence |
| 1949 | Charles Hamilton Houston | 1959 | Langston Hughes | 1970 | Leon Howard Sullivan |
| 1950 | Mabel Keaton Staupers | 1960 | Kenneth B. Clark | 1971 | Gordon Parks |
| 1951 | Harry T. Moore | 1961 | Robert C. Weaver | 1972 | Wilson C. Riles |
| 1952 | Paul R. Williams | 1962 | Medgar Wiley Evers | 1973 | Damon Keith |
| 1953 | Theodore K. Lawless | 1963 | Roy Wilkins | 1974 | Henry (Hank) Aaron |
| 1954 | Carl Murphy | 1964 | Leontyne Price | 1975 | Alvin Ailey |
| 1955 | Jack Roosevelt Robinson | 1965 | John H. Johnson | 1976 | Alex Haley |
| 1956 | Martin Luther King, Jr. | 1966 | Edward W. Brooke | | |

## National Teacher of the Year Award

Awarded by the Council of Chief State School Officers, Encyclopaedia Britannica, and the Ladies' Home Journal for service in elementary and secondary schools.

**1965** Richard E. Klinck, sixth grade, Reed Street Elementary, Wheat Ridge, Col.
**1966** Mona Dayton, first grade, Walter Douglas Elementary, Tucson, Ariz.
**1967** Roger Tenney, music, Owatonna Junior-Senior H.S., Owatonna, Minn.
**1968** David E. Graf, vocational education & industrial arts, Sandwich Comm. H.S., Sandwich, Ill.
**1969** Barbara Goleman, language arts, Miami Jackson H.S., Miami, Fla.
**1970** Johnnie T. Dennis, physics, math analysis, Walla Walla H.S., Walla Walla, Wash.
**1971** Martha Marion Stringfellow, first grade, Lewisville Elementary, Chester Co., S.C.
**1972** James Marshall Rogers, American history & Black studies, Durham H.S., Raleigh, N.C.
**1973** John A. Ensworth, sixth grade, Kenwood school, Bend, Ore.
**1974** Vivian Tom, social studies, Lincoln H.S. Yonkers, N.Y.
**1975** Robert G. Heyer, science, Johanna Junior H.S., St. Paul, Minn.
**1976** Ruby S. Murchison, social studies, Washington Drive J.H.S., Fayetteville, N.C.
**1977** Myrra Leonore Lee, social studies, Helix H.S., La Mesa, Cal.
**1978** Elaine Barbour, Coal Creek Elementary, Montrose, Col.

## The Molson Prize

The Molson Prizes have been given annually to recognize and encourage outstanding contributions in the arts, humanities, or social sciences. They are financed from the interest on a gift to the Canada Council by the Molson Foundation. The value of each prize is $20,000.

1964  No awards made.
1965  Jean Gascon; Frank Scott
1966  Rev. Georges-Henri Levesque; H. McLennan
1967  Arthur Erickson; Anne Hebert; Marshall McLuhan
1968  Glenn Gould; Jean Le Moyne
1969  Jean-Paul Audet; Morley Callaghan; Arnold Spohr
1970  Northrop Frye; Duncan Macpherson; Yves Pheriault
1971  Maureen Forrester; Rina Lasnier; Norman McLaren

1972  John Deutsch; Alfred Pellan; George Woodcock
1973  W.A.C.H. Dobson; Celia Franca; Jean-Paul Lemieux
1974  Alex Colville, Margaret Laurence; Pierre Dansereau
1975  Jon Vickers; Denise Pelletier; the Orford String Quartet; Andrew Dawes; Terrence Helmer; Kenneth Perkins and Marcel St-Cyr
1976  John Hirsch; Bill Reid; Jean-Louis Roux
1977  Gabrielle Roy; Jack Shadbolt; George Story

# ARTS AND MEDIA

## Notable New York Theater Openings, 1977-78 Season

**A History of the American Film,** play by Christopher Durang; with April Shawhan, Swoosie Kurtz, Gary Bayer, and Ben Halley Jr.

**A Touch of the Poet,** revival of the Eugene O'Neill play; with Jason Robards, Geraldine Fitzgerald, and Milo O'-Shea.

**Ain't Misbehavin',** musical salute to Fats Waller; directed by Richard Maltby Jr.

**American Dance Machine,** theater piece re-creating outstanding dance numbers from past Broadway musicals.

**An Almost Perfect Person,** comedy by Judith A. Ross about the aftermath of a political campaign by a female politician; with Colleen Dewhurst.

**Angel,** musical by Gary Geld based on the Ketti Frings adaptation of Thomas Wolfe's *Look Homeward Angel;* with Fred Gwynne and Frances Sternhagen.

**Chapter Two,** comedy by Neil Simon; with Judd Hirsch, Cliff Gorman, Anita Gillette, and Ann Wedgeworth.

**Cheaters,** comedy by Michael Jacobs; with Rosemary Murphy, Lou Jacobi, and Jack Weston.

**Cold Storage,** play by Ronald Ribman; with Martin Balsam and Len Cariou.

**Da,** play by Hugh Leonard about a son's need to come to terms with his father; with Barnard Hughes and Brian Murray.

**Dancin',** musical entertainment directed and choreographed by Bob Fosse; featuring the music of Bach, Cat Stevens, Neil Diamond, and John Philip Sousa.

**Deathtrap,** comedy-thriller by Ira Levin; with John Wood.

**Diversions and Delights,** play by John Gay; with Vincent Price as Oscar Wilde.

**Do You Turn Somersaults?,** play by Aleksei Arbuzov; with Mary Martin and Anthony Quayle.

**Dracula,** 1927 play by John Balderston and Hamilton Dean based on the Bram Stoker novel; with Frank Langella.

**Golda,** play by William Gibson based on the life of Golda Meir; with Anne Bancroft.

**Hello, Dolly!,** revival of the popular Jerry Herman musical; with Carol Channing and Eddie Bracken.

**Man of La Mancha,** revival of the Dale Wasserman Mitch Leigh, Joe Darion musical; with Richard Kiley.

**Miss Margarida's Way,** play by Roberto Athayde; with Estelle Parsons.

**On the Twentieth Century,** musical by Betty Comden and Adolph Green that takes place aboard a Chicago-New York train in 1930; with Imogene Coca, John Cullum, Madeline Kahn, and Judy Kaye.

**Once in a Lifetime,** revival of the Moss Hart, George S Kaufman comedy; with Jayne Meadows, George S. Irving and John Lithgow.

**Paul Robeson,** play by Phillip Hayes Dean based on the life of the singer, actor, and political activist; with James Earl Jones.

**Runaways,** musical by Elizabeth Swados about young people estranged from their families and searching for themselves.

**Saint Joan,** revival of the George Bernard Shaw play about Joan of Arc; with Lynn Redgrave.

**Some of My Best Friends,** comedy by Stanley Hart; with Ted Knight.

**The Act,** musical by John Kanders and Fred Ebb; with Liza Minnelli and Barry Nelson.

**The Best Little Whorehouse in Texas,** musical by Carol Hall about the furor created by the closing of a brothel in a small Texas town; with Henderson Forsythe.

**The 5th of July,** comedy by Lanford Wilson about the 1960s.

**The Gin Game,** play by D. L. Coburn about 2 elderly people who meet in a convalescent home; with Hume Cronyn and Jessica Tandy; won Pulitzer Prize.

**13 Rue de L'Amour,** George Feydeau's marital farce adapted by Mawby Green and Ed Feilbert; with Louis Jourdan, Patricia Elliott, Bernard Fox, and Kathleen Freeman.

**Timbuktu!,** all-black musical by Robert Wright and George Forrest adapted from *Kismet;* with Eartha Kitt, Melba Moore, and Ira Hawkins.

**Tribute,** play by Bernard Slade; with Jack Lemmon.

## Record Long Run Broadway Plays *Still Running June 28, 1978

| | | | | | |
|---|---|---|---|---|---|
| Fiddler on the Roof | 3,242 | Voice of the Turtle | 1,557 | The King and I | 1,246 |
| Life With Father | 3,224 | Barefoot in the Park | 1,532 | Cactus Flower | 1,234 |
| Tobacco Road | 3,182 | Mame | 1,508 | Sleuth | 1,222 |
| Hello Dolly | 2,844 | Arsenic and Old Lace | 1,444 | "1776" | 1,217 |
| My Fair Lady | 2,717 | The Sound of Music | 1,443 | Equus | 1,207 |
| *Grease | 2,629 | How To Succeed in Business | | Guys and Dolls | 1,200 |
| Man of La Mancha | 2,329 | Without Really Trying | 1,417 | *Chorus Line | 1,185 |
| Abie's Irish Rose | 2,327 | *The Wiz | 1,413 | Cabaret | 1,166 |
| Oklahoma! | 2,212 | Hellzapoppin | 1,404 | Mister Roberts | 1,157 |
| Pippin | 1,900 | The Music Man | 1,375 | Annie Get Your Gun | 1,147 |
| Harvey | 1,775 | *Same Time, Next Year | 1,364 | Butterflies Are Free | 1,128 |
| Hair | 1,742 | Funny Girl | 1,348 | Pins and Needles | 1,108 |
| South Pacific | 1,694 | Oh! Calcutta! | 1,316 | Plaza Suite | 1,097 |
| *Magic Show | 1,660 | Angel Street | 1,295 | Kiss Me Kate | 1,070 |
| Born Yesterday | 1,643 | Lightnin' | 1,291 | | |
| Mary, Mary | 1,572 | Promises, Promises | 1,281 | | |

## Plays in London *Still running June 27, 1978

| | | | | | |
|---|---|---|---|---|---|
| *The Mousetrap | 10,634 | The Boy Friend | 2,084 | The Beggar's Opera | 1,463 |
| Black and White Minstrels | 4,354 | Canterbury Tales | 2,082 | Simple Spymen | 1,404 |
| *Oh! Calcutta! | 3,263 | Boeing Boeing | 2,036 | Our Boys | 1,362 |
| *No Sex Please, We're British | 2,941 | Fiddler on the Roof | 2,030 | Knights of Madness | 1,361 |
| Oliver | 2,811 | Blithe Spirit | 1,997 | Maid of the Mountains | 1,352 |
| There's a Girl in my Soup | 2,547 | Worms Eye View | 1,745 | Arsenic and Old Lace | 1,337 |
| Pyjama Tops | 2,498 | Me and My Girl | 1,646 | The Farmer's Wife | 1,329 |
| *Jesus Christ Superstar | 2,461 | Reluctant Heroes | 1,610 | Annie Get Your Gun | 1,304 |
| Sound of Music | 2,385 | Together Again | 1,566 | The Little Hut | 1,261 |
| Salad Days | 2,283 | Seagulls over Sorrento | 1,551 | A Little Bit of Fluff | 1,241 |
| My Fair Lady | 2,281 | Oklahoma! | 1,543 | Sailor Beware | 1,231 |
| Sleuth | 2,258 | Irma La Douce | 1,512 | One for the Pot | 1,221 |
| Hair | 2,239 | Dry Rot | 1,475 | Beyond the Fringe | 1,184 |
| Chu Chin Chow | 2,238 | Charley's Aunt | 1,466 | | |
| The Man Most Likely To | 2,213 | The Secretary Bird | 1,463 | | |

# Symphony Orchestras of the U.S. and Canada

Source: American Symphony Orchestra League
(as of July 20, 1978)

*Classifications are based on annual incomes or budgets of orchestras.*

## Major Symphony Orchestras | Conductor

| | | Conductor |
|---|---|---|
| tlanta Symphony | 1280 Peachtree St., NE, Atlanta, GA 30309 | Robert Shaw |
| altimore Symphony | 5204 Roland Avenue, Baltimore, MD 21210 | Sergiu Comissiona |
| oston Symphony | Symphony Hall, Boston, MA 02115 | Seiji Ozawa |
| uffalo Philharmonic | 26 Richmond Ave., Buffalo, NY 14222 | Michael Thomas |
| hicago Symphony | 220 S. Michigan Ave., Chicago, IL 60604 | Sir Georg Solti |
| incinnati Symphony | 1241 Elm St., Cincinnati, OH 45210 | Walter Susskind |
| leveland Orchestra | 11001 Euclid Ave., Cleveland, OH 44106 | Lorin Maazel |
| allas Symphony | P.O. Box 26207, Dallas, TX 75226 | Eduardo Mata |
| enver Symphony | 1615 California St., Denver, CO 80202 | Sixten Ehrling |
| etroit Symphony | 20 Auditorium Dr., Detroit, MI 48226 | Antel Dorati |
| onolulu Symphony | 1000 Bishop St., Honolulu, HA 96813 | Robert LaMarchina |
| ouston Symphony | 615 Louisiana, Houston, TX 77002 | Lawrence Foster |
| dianapolis Symphony | 4600 Sunset Ave., Indianapolis, IN 46208 | John Nelson |
| ansas City Philharmonic | 200 W. 19th Street, Kansas City, MO 64105 | Maurice Peress |
| os Angeles Philharmonic | 135 North Grand, Los Angeles, CA 90012 | Carlo Giulini |
| ilwaukee Symphony | 929 N. Water St., Milwaukee, WI 53202 | Kenneth Schermerhorn |
| innesota Orchestra | 1111 Nicollet Mall, Minneapolis, MN 55403 | S. Skrowaczewski |
| ontreal Symphony | Place des Arts, Montreal, Que. H2X1Y9 | Charles Dutoit |
| ational Arts Centre Orchestra | Box 1534, Station B., Ottawa, Ont. K1P5W1 | Mario Bernardi |
| ational Symphony | JFK Center for the Performing Arts, Wash., DC 20566 | Mstislav Rostropovich |
| ew Jersey Symphony | 213 Washington St., Newark, NJ 07101 | Thomas Michalak |
| ew Orleans Philharmonic | 203 Carondelet St., New Orleans, LA 70130 | Leonard Slatkin |
| ew York Philharmonic | Avery Fisher Hall, New York, NY 10023 | Zubin Mehta |
| orth Carolina Symphony | P.O. Box 28026, Raleigh, NC 27611 | John Gosling |
| hiladelphia Orchestra | 1420 Locust St., Philadelphia, PA 19102 | Eugene Ormandy |
| ittsburgh Symphony | 600 Penn Ave., Pittsburgh, PA 15222 | Andre Previn |
| ochester Philharmonic | 20 Grove Pl., Rochester, NY 14605 | David Zinman |
| . Louis Symphony | 718 N. Grand Blvd., St. Louis, MO 63103 | Jerzy Semkow |
| an Antonio Symphony | 109 Lexington Ave., San Antonio, TX 78205 | François Huybrechts |
| an Francisco Symphony | 107 War Memorial Veterans' Bldg., San Fran., CA 94102 | Edo de Waart |
| eattle Symphony | 305 Harrison St., Seattle, WA 98109 | Rainer Miedel |
| yracuse Symphony | 411 Montgomery St., Syracuse, NY 13202 | Christopher Keene |
| oronto Symphony | 215 Victoria St., Toronto, Ont. M5B 1V1 | Andrew Davis |
| tah Symphony | 55 W. 1st So. St., Salt Lake City, UT 84101 | Maurice Abravanel |
| ancouver Symphony | 873 Beatty St., Vancouver, B.C. V6B 2M6 | Kazuyoshi Akiyama |

## Regional Orchestras

| | | |
|---|---|---|
| merican Symphony | 119 W. 57th St., New York, NY 10019 | Kazuyoshi Akiyama |
| irmingham Symphony | 2133 7th Ave. N., Birmingham, AL 35203 | Amerigo Marino |
| algary Philharmonic | 300-330 9th Ave. SW, Calgary, Alta. T2P 1K6 | Arpad Joo |
| harlotte Symphony | 110 E. 7th Street, Charlotte, NC 28202 | Leo Driehuys |
| olumbus Symphony | 101 E. Town St., Columbus, OH 43215 | Evan Whallon |
| dmonton Symphony Society | 11712 87 Avenue, Edmonton, Alta. T6G 0Y3 | Pierre Hetu |
| lorida Philharmonic | 150 S.E. 2d Ave., Miami, FL 33131 | Brian Priestman |
| lorida Symphony | P.O. Box 782, Orlando, FL 32802 | Pavle Despali |
| ort Worth Symphony | 4401 Trial Lake Dr., Fort Worth, TX 76109 | John Giordano |
| rand Rapids Symphony | Exhibitors Bldg., Grand Rapids, MI 49501 | Theo Alcantara |
| artford Symphony | 470-Capitol Ave., Hartford, CT 06106 | Arthur Winograd |
| udson Valley Philharmonic | Box 191, Poughkeepsie, NY 12602 | Imre Pallo |
| acksonville Symphony | 333 Laura St., Jacksonville, FL 32202 | Willis Page |
| ouisville Orchestra | 333 W. Broadway, Louisville, KY 40202 | Jorge Mester |
| emphis Symphony | 1503 Monroe Avenue, Memphis, TN 38104 | Vincent de Frank |
| ashville Symphony | 1805 West End Ave., Nashville, TN 37203 | Michael Charry |
| akland Symphony | 2025 Broadway, Oakland, CA 94612 | Harold Farberman |
| klahoma Symphony | 512 Civic Center Music Hall, Oklahoma City, OK 73102 | Vacant |
| regon Symphony | 1119 SW Park Ave., Portland, OR 97205 | Lawrence Smith |
| hoenix Symphony | 6328 N. 7th St., Phoenix, AZ 85014 | Vacant |
| uerto Rico Symphony | P.O. Box 2350, San Juan, PR 00936 | Victor Tevah |
| ichmond Symphony | 15 S. Fifth St., Richmond, VA 23219 | Jacques Houtmann |
| an Diego Symphony | P.O. Box 3175, San Diego, CA 92103 | Peter Eros |
| an Jose Symphony | 170 Park Center Plaza, San Jose, CA 95113 | George Cleve |
| oledo Symphony | 1 Stranahan Sq., Toledo, OH 43604 | Serge Fournier |
| ulsa Philharmonic | 2210 South Main, Tulsa, OK 74114 | Murry Sidlin |
| ictoria Symphony | 30-B Centennial Square, Victoria, BC V8W 1P7 | Laszlo Gati |
| innipeg Symphony | 555 Main St., Winnipeg, Man. R3B 1C3 | Piero Gamba |

## Metropolitan Orchestras

| | | |
|---|---|---|
| kron Symphony | Thomas Hall, Hill & Center Sts., Akron, OH 44325 | Louis Lane |
| lbany Symphony | 19 Clinton Ave., Albany, NY 12207 | Julius Hegyi |
| marillo Symphony | P.O. Box 2552, Amarillo, TX 79105 | Thomas Conlin |
| rkansas Orchestra Society | 604 E. 6th St., Little Rock, AR 72202 | Kurt Klippstatter |
| ustin Symphony | 1101 Red River St., Austin, TX 78701 | Akiro Endo |
| .C. Pops Orchestra | 435 Main St., Johnson City, NY 13790 | David L. Agard |
| aton Rouge Symphony | Box 103, Baton Rouge, LA 70821 | James Yestadt |
| (Greater) Bridgeport Symphony | Univ. of Bridgeport, Bridgeport, CT 06602 | Gustav Meier |
| rooklyn Philharmonia | 30 Lafayette Ave., Brooklyn, NY 11217 | Lukas Foss |
| California Chamber Orchestra | 6380 Wilshire Blvd., Los Angeles, CA 90048 | Henri Temianka |
| Canton Symphony | 1001 Market Ave. N., Canton, OH 44702 | Thomas Michalak |
| Cedar Rapids Symphony | 223 Dows Bldg., Cedar Rapids, IA 52401 | Richard D. Williams |

| | | |
|---|---|---|
| CETA Symphony | 155 Montgomery, San Francisco, CA 94104 | Jonathan Khuner |
| Charleston Symphony | Box 2292, Charleston, WV 25328 | Ronald Dishinger |
| Chattanooga Symphony | 730 Cherry St., Chattanooga, TN 37402 | Richard Cormier |
| Chautauqua Symphony | Chautauqua Institution, Chautauqua, NY 14722 | Sergiu Commissiona |
| Chicago Pops Orchestra | 100 N. LaSalle St., Chicago, IL 60602 | Vacant |
| Clarion Music Society | 415 Lexington Ave., New York, NY 10017 | Newell Jenkins |
| Colorado Springs Symphony | P.O. Box 1692, Colorado Springs, CO 80901 | Charles Ansbacher |
| Concerto Soloists of Philadelphia | 130 S. 18th St., Philadelphia, PA 19103 | Marc Mostovoy |
| Corpus Christi Symphony | P.O. Box 495, Corpus Christi, TX 78403 | Cornelius Eberhardt |
| County Symphony of Westchester | Box 333, Scarsdale, NY 10583 | Stephen Simon |
| Dayton Philharmonic | 210 N. Main St., Dayton, OH 45402 | C. Wendelken-Wilson |
| Des Moines Symphony | 702 Employees Mutual Bldg., Des Moines, IA 50309 | Yuri Krasnapolsky |
| Duluth-Superior Symphony | 506 W. Michigan St., Duluth, MN 55802 | Taavo Virkhaus |
| Eastern Music Festival | 712 Summit Ave., Greensboro, NC 27405 | Sheldon Morgenstern |
| El Paso Philharmonic | P.O. Box 180, El Paso, TX 79942 | Abraham Chavez Jr. |
| Erie Philharmonic | 720 G. Daniel Baldwin Bldg., Erie, PA 16501 | Walter Hendl |
| Evansville Philharmonic | P.O. Box 84, Evansville, IN 47701 | Minas Christian |
| Flint Symphony | 1025 E. Kearsley St., Flint, MI 48503 | John Covelli |
| Florida Gulf Coast Symphony | P.O. Box 569, St. Petersburg, FL 33731 | Irwin Hoffman |
| Florida West Coast Symphony | 709 N. Tamiami Trail, Sarasota, FL 33577 | Paul C. Wolfe |
| Fort Lauderdale Symphony | 1430 N. Federal Hwy., Fort Lauderdale, FL 33304 | Emerson Buckley |
| Fort Wayne Philharmonic | 227 E. Washington Blvd., Fort Wayne, IN 46802 | Ronald Ondrejka |
| Fresno Philharmonic | 1362 N. Fresno St., Fresno, CA 93703 | Guy Taylor |
| Glendale Symphony | 401 N. Brand Blvd., Glendale, CA 91203 | Carmen Dragon |
| Hamilton Philharmonic | 50 Main St., W. Hamilton, Ont. L8P 1H3 | Boris Brott |
| Harrisburg Symphony | 16 N. 2nd Street, Harrisburg, PA 17101 | Larry Newland |
| Hartford Chamber Orchestra | 179 Allyn St., Hartford, CT 06103 | Daniel Parker |
| Jackson Symphony | P.O. Box 4584, Jackson, MS 39216 | Lewis Dalvit |
| Kalamazoo Symphony | 426 S. Park St., Kalamazoo, MI 49007 | Yoshimi Takeda |
| Kern Philharmonic | 400 Truxtun Ave., Bakersfield, CA 93301 | John Farrer |
| Kitchener-Waterloo Symphony | Box 2, Waterloo, Ont., N2J 3Z6 | Raffi Armenian |
| Knoxville Symphony | 618 Gay St., Knoxville, TN 37902 | Zoltan Rozsnyai |
| Lansing Symphony | 230 N. Washington Sq., Lansing, MI 48933 | Dr. A. Clyde Roller |
| Lexington Philharmonic | P.O. Box 838, Lexington, KY 40501 | George Zack |
| Lincoln Symphony | 1315 Sharp Bldg., Lincoln, Neb. 68508 | Robert Emile |
| London Symphony | 520 Wellington St., London, Ont. N6A-3R2 | Clifford Evens |
| Long Beach Symphony | 121 Linden Ave., Long Beach, CA 90802 | Alberto Bolet |
| Long Island Symphony | P.O. Box 315, Huntington, NY 11743 | Seymour Lipkin |
| Los Angeles Chamber Orchestra | 1777 N. Vine St., Hollywood, CA 90028 | Neville Marriner |
| Lubbock Symphony | 1721 Broadway, Lubbock, TX 79401 | William A. Harrod |
| Madison Symphony | 211 N. Carroll St., Madison, WI 53703 | Roland Johnson |
| Miami Beach Symphony | 420 Lincoln Rd. Mall, Miami Beach, FL 33139 | Barnett Breeskin |
| Midland Odessa Symphony | P.O. Box 6266, Midland, TX 79701 | Thomas Hohstadt |
| Monterey County Symphony | P.O. Box 3965, Carmel, CA 93921 | Haymo Taeuber |
| Municipal Concerts | 50 E. 42nd St., New York, NY 10017 | Julius Grossman |
| Music for Westchester Symphony | Box 35, Gedney Station, White Plains, NY 10605 | Siegfried Landau |
| New Haven Symphony | 33 Whitney Ave., New Haven, CT 06511 | Murry Sidlin |
| New Mexico Symphony | 120 Madeira Dr. NE, Albuquerque, NM 87108 | Yoshima Takeda |
| Norfolk Symphony | P.O. Box 26, Norfolk, VA 23501 | Russell Stanger |
| Northeastern Pennsylvania Phil. | P.O. Box 71, Avoca, PA 18641 | Thomas Michalak |
| Omaha Symphony | 478 Aquila Ct., Omaha, NE 68102 | Thomas Bricetti |
| Orchestra da Camera | 129 East Dr., N. Massapequa, NY 11758 | Herbert Grossman |
| (Greater) Palm Beach Symphony | P.O. Box 996, Palm Beach, FL 33480 | John Inele |
| Pasadena Symphony | 300 E. Green St., Pasadena, CA 91101 | Daniel Lewis |
| Peoria Symphony | 416 Hamilton, Peoria, IL 61602 | Robert Kreis |
| Portland Symphony | 30 Myrtle St., Portland, ME 04111 | Bruce Hangen |
| Quebec Symphony | 116 Côte de la Montagne, Quebec, Que. G1K 4E5 | James De Preist |
| Queens Symphony | 1 Station Sq., Forest Hills, NY 11375 | David Katz |
| Regina Symphony | 200 Lakeshore Dr., Regina, Sask. S4S 0A4 | Gregory Millar |
| Rhode Island Philharmonic | 334 Westminster Mall, Providence, RI 02903 | Vacant |
| Rockford Symphony | 415 N. Church St., Rockford, IL 61103 | Crawford Gates |
| Sacramento Symphony | 451 Parkfair Dr., Sacramento, CA 95825 | Vacant |
| Saginaw Symphony | P.O. Box 415, Saginaw, MI 48606 | Gideon Grau |
| Santa Barbara Symphony | 1525 State St., Santa Barbara, CA 93101 | Ronald Ondrejka |
| Savannah Symphony | P.O. Box 9505, Savannah, GA 31402 | Christian Badea |
| Shreveport Symphony | P.O. Box 4057, Shreveport, LA 71104 | John Shenaut |
| South Bend Symphony | 215 W. North Shore Drive, South Bend, IN 46617 | Herbert Butler |
| Spokane Symphony | W. 245 Spokane Falls Blvd., Spokane, WA 99201 | Donald Thulean |
| Springfield (Mass.) Symphony | 284 State St., Springfield, MA 01105 | Robert Gutter |
| Springfield (Ohio) Symphony | Box 1374, Springfield, OH 45501 | John E. Ferritto |
| Stockton Symphony | Box 4273, Stockton, CA 95204 | Kyung-Soo Won |
| Symphony of the New World | Carnegie Hall, New York, NY 10019 | Everett Lee |
| Tacoma Symphony | P.O. Box 19, Tacoma, WA 98401 | Edward Sefarian |
| Thunder Bay Symphony | P.O. Box 2004, Station P, Thunder Bay, Ont. P7B 5E7 | Dwight Bennett |
| Tri-City Symphony | P.O. Box 67, Davenport, IA 52805 | James Dixon |
| Tucson Symphony | 443 So. Stone Ave., Tucson, AZ 85701 | George Trautwein |
| Vermont Symphony | 163 Willard St., Burlington, VT 05401 | Efrain Guigui |
| Wheeling Symphony | 51 16th St., Wheeling, WV 26003 | Jeff Holland Cook |
| Wichita Symphony | 225 W. Douglas, Wichita, KS 67202 | Michael Palmer |
| Winston-Salem Symphony | 610 Coliseum Dr., Winston-Salem, NC 27106 | Vacant |
| Youngstown Symphony | 260 Federal Plaza West, Youngstown, OH 44503 | Franz Bibo |

# Major U.S. and Canadian Opera Companies

Source: Central Opera Service, New York, N.Y.

Arizona Opera Company (Tucson); Jim Sullivan, gen. dir.

Artists Internationale (Providence, R.I.); Marguerite Ruffino, art. dir.

Asolo Opera Company (Sarasota); Philip Hall, exec. dir.

Baltimore Opera Company; Robert J. Collinge, gen. mgr.

Canadian Opera Company (Toronto); Lotfi Mansouri, gen. dir.

Central City Opera House Assn. (Colo.); Robert Darling, art. dir.

Charlotte Opera Assn.; Richard Marshall, gen. dir.

Chautauqua Opera (N.Y.); Leonard Treash, dir.

Cincinnati Opera Assn.; James DeBlasis, gen. mgr.

Civic Opera of the Palm Beaches (Fla.); Paul Csonka, art. dir.

Colorado Opera Festival (Colorado Springs); Donald Jenkins, art. dir.

Columbus Opera Symphony (O.); Evan Whallon, mus. dir.

Connecticut Opera Assn. (Hartford); Wm. Warden, gen. mgr.

Dallas Civic Opera; Plato Karayanis, gen. dir.

Dayton Opera Assn.; Lester Freedman, gen. dir.

Edmonton Opera Assn.; Lorin J. Moore, gen. mgr.

Florentine Opera Company (Milwaukee, Wis.); Alan J. Bellamente, gen. mgr.

Fort Worth Opera Assn.; Rudolf Kruger, gen. mgr.

Goldovsky Opera Institute and Theatre (N.Y., N.Y.); Boris Goldovsky, art. dir.

Greater Miami Opera Assn.; Robert Herman, gen. mgr.

Hawaii Opera Theatre (Honolulu); Robert C. Bickley, gen. mgr.

Hidden Valley Music Seminar (Carmel Valley, Cal.); Peter Meckel, dir.

Houston Grand Opera; David Gockley, gen. dir.

Kentucky Opera Assn. (Louisville); Moritz Bomhard, dir.

Lake George Opera Festival (Glens Falls, N.Y.); David Lloyd, gen. dir.

Lyric Opera of Chicago; Carol Fox, gen. mgr.

Lyric Opera of Kansas City (Mo.); Russell Patterson, gen. mgr.

Manitoba Opera Assn. (Winnipeg); Irving Guttman, art. dir.

Memphis Opera Theatre; Kenneth Caswell, gen. dir.

Metropolitan Opera Assn. (N.Y., N.Y.); Anthony A. Bliss, exec. dir.

Michigan Opera Theatre (Detroit); David DiChiera, gen. dir.

Minnesota Opera Company (St. Paul); Charles Fullmer, mgr.

Music Theatre of Wichita; James Miller, dir.

National Opera Assn. (Raleigh, N.C.); A.J. Fletcher, prod.

Nevada Opera Guild (Reno); Ted Puffer, dir.

New Jersey State Opera (Newark); Alfred Silipigni, art. dir.

New Orleans Opera Assn.; Arthur Cosenz, gen. dir.

New York City Opera Company; Julius Rudel, gen. dir.

Opera Company of Philadelphia; Edward Corn, gen. dir.

Opera Company of Boston; Sarah Caldwell, art. dir.

Opera/Omaha; Martha Elsberry, gen. dir.

Opera Orchestra of New York (NYC); Eve Queler, dir.

Opera/South (Jackson, Miss.); Dolores Ardoyno, gen. mgr.

Opera Theatre of St. Louis; Richard Gaddes, gen. mgr.

Opera Theatre of Syracuse; Robert Driver, gen. mgr.

Ottawa Festival Opera; Andree Gringas, adm.

Pittsburgh Opera; Barbara Karp, dir.

Portland Opera Assn. (Ore.) Stefan Minde, gen. dir.

San Antonio Opera and Symphony; Nat Greenberg, mgr.

San Diego Opera; Tito Capobianco, gen. dir.

San Francisco Opera Assn.; Kurt Herbert Adler, gen. dir.

Santa Fe Opera/Opera Assn. of New Mexico; John Crosby, gen. dir.

Seattle Opera Assn.; Glynn Ross, gen. dir.

Skylight Theatre (Milwaukee, Wis.); Clair Richardson, Mng. dir.

Southern Alberta Opera Assn. (Calgary); Brian Hanson, gen. mgr.

Spoleto Festival (Charleston, S.C.); Christine Reed, gen. mgr.

Spring Opera Theatre of San Francisco; Kurt Herbert Adler, gen. dir.

Texas Opera Theatre (Houston); Terrell Miller, mgr.

Toledo Opera Assn.; Lester Freedman, gen. dir.

Tri-Cities Opera Company (Binghampton, N.Y.); Peyton Hibbitt and Carmen Savoca, dirs.

Tulsa Opera; Edward Parrington, gen. mgr.

Virginia Opera Assn. (Norfolk); Peter Mark, art. dir.

Vancouver Opera Assn.; Hamilton McClymont, gen. mgr.

The Washington Opera, (D.C.); George London, gen. dir.

Western Opera Theater (San Francisco); Robert Bailey, mgr.

Wilmington Opera Society; I. Duncan, pres.

Wolf Trap Company (Vienna, Va.); Carol Harford, exec. dir.

---

# Recordings

## Disc and Tape Sales Set Records; Revenues, Volume Both Up

Manufacturers' sales of phonograph records and prerecorded discs jumped by 28% in 1977 to a new high of $3.5 billion, according to the Recording Industry Association of America. Unit sales rose to 698.2 million, an increase of 18% over 1976. Sales of long-play albums went up 32% to $2.2 billion; singles remained steady at 245.1 million; 8-track cartridge tapes were up 19.6% to $18 million; cassette tapes skyrocketed 71.3% to $249.6 billion. The RIAA confers Gold Record awards on single records which sell one million units, Platinum Awards to those selling 2 million, Gold Awards to L-P albums and their tape equivalents which sell 500,000 units, Platinum Awards to those selling one million. Recordings winning awards in 1977-78 follow (most Platinum Award winners also won Gold Awards):

### Artists and Recording Titles

A-album, S-single, G-gold, P-platinum

**Aug. 1977**

Heart; *Little Queen;* A, P.

Brothers Johnson; *Right on Time;* A, P.

Barbra Streisand; *Superman;* A, P.

Foreigner; *Foreigner;* A, P.

Natalie Cole; *Unpredictable;* A, P.

The Beatles; *The Beatles at the Hollywood Bowl;* A, P.

Original Soundtrack; *Star Wars;* A, P.

Crosby, Stills and Nash; *CSN;* A, P.

Waylon Jennings; *Are You Ready for the Country;* A, G.

Maze; *Maze, Featuring Frankie Beverly;* A, G.

Yes; *Going For the One;* A, G.

Supertramp; *Crime of the Century;* A, G.

Dan Fogelberg; *Nether Lands,* A, G.

REO Speedwagon; *You Get What You Play For;* A, G.

Kenny Rogers; *Kenny Rogers;* A, G.

War, *Platinum Jazz;* A, G.

Marshall Tucker Band; *A New Life;* A, G.

Bay City Rollers; *It's A Game,* A, G.

Pablo Cruise; *A Place in the Sun;* A, G.

Styx; *Equinox;* A, G.

Emotions; *Best of My Love;* S, G.

Andy Gibb; *I Just Want to be Your Everything;* S, G.

Ricky Nelson; *Travelin' Man;* S, G.

Peter McCann; *Do You Wanna Make Love;* S, G.

The Floaters; *Float On;* S, G.

Rita Coolidge; *(Your Love Has Lifted Me) Higher and Higher;* S, G.

## Sept. 1977

Emotions; *Rejoice;* A, P.
James Taylor; *J.T.;* A, P.
Elvis Presley; *Moody Blue;* A, P.
Leo Sayer; *Endless Flight;* A, P.
Shaun Cassidy; *Shaun Cassidy;* A, P.
Ted Nugent; *Cat Scratch Fever;* A, P.
Ted Nugent; *Free For All;* A, P.
Ozark Mountain Daredevils; *Ozark Mountain Daredevils;* A, G.
Elvis Presley; *Pure Gold;* A, G.
Doobie Brothers; *Livin' On the Fault Line;* A, G.
Alan Parsons; *I Robot;* A, G.
Daryl Hall and John Oates; *Beauty on a Back Street;* A, G.
Kenny Loggins; *Celebrate Me Home;* A, G.
The Outlaws; *The Outlaws;* A, G.
Carole King; *Simple Things;* A, G.
Elvis Presley; *Welcome to My World;* A, G.
Barry Manilow; *Looks Like We Made It;* S, G.
Ronnie McDowell; *The King is Gone;* S, G.
Elvis Presley; *Way Down;* S, G.
Fleetwood Mac; *Dreams;* S, G.
Electric Light Orchestra; *Telephone Line;* S, G.

## Oct. 1977

George Benson; *In Flight;* A, P.
The Floaters; *The Floaters;* A, P.
Waylon Jennings; *Ol' Waylon;* A, P.
Chicago; *Chicago XI;* A, P.
Linda Ronstadt; *Simple Dreams;* A, P.
Elvis Presley; *In Concert;* A, P.
Rita Coolidge; *Anytime. . .Anywhere;* A, P.
Firefall; *Luna Sea;* A, G.
Rolling Stones; *Love You Live;* A, G.
Glen Campbell; *Southern Nights;* A, G.
Elvis Presley; *From Elvis Presley Boulevard, Memphis, Tennessee;* A, G.
Neil Young; *American Stars 'N Bars;* A, G.
Thin Lizzy; *Jailbreak;* A, G.
The Beatles; *Love Songs;* A, G.
Elvis Presley; *Elvis - A Legendary Performer, Vol. II;* A, G.
Johnny Cash; *The Johnny Cash Portrait/His Greatest Hits, Vol. II;* A, G.
Bay City Rollers; *Rock & Roll Love Letter;* A, G.
Eric Carmen; *Eric Carmen;* A, G.
Shaun Cassidy; *That's Rock 'N Roll;* S, G.
Barry White; *It's Ecstasy When You Lay Down Next to Me;* S, G.
Brothers Johnson; *Strawberry Letter 23;* S, G.
Meri Wilson; *Telephone Man;* S, G.

## Nov. 1977

Elton John; *Elton John's Greatest Hits, Vol. II;* A, P.
Electric Light Orchestra; *Out of the Blue;* A, P.
Barry White; *Barry White Sings For Someone You Love;* A, P.
James Taylor; *James Taylor's Greatest Hits;* A, P.
Bee Gees; *Here at Last. . .Bee Gees. . .Live;* A, P.
Kiss; *Kiss Alive II;* A, P.
Kansas; *Point of Know Return;* A, P.
Debby Boone; *You Light Up My Life;* S, P.
Original Soundtrack; *You Light Up My Life;* A, G.
Dan Fogelberg; *Captured Angel;* A, G.
Dave Mason; *Let It Flow;* A, G.
Steve Miller Band; *Anthology;* A, G.
L.T.D.; *Something to Love;* A, G.
Electric Light Orchestra; *Out of the Blue;* A, G.
Rush; *2112;* A, G.
Rush; *A Farewell to Kings;* A, G.
Rush; *All the World's A Stage;* A, G.
Robin Trower; *In City Dreams;* A, G.
Original Soundtrack; *Saturday Night Fever;* A, G.
Andy Gibb; *Flowing Rivers;* A, G.
Bay City Rollers; *Dedication;* A, G.
Kiss; *Kiss Alive II;* A, G.
War; *Galaxy;* A, G.
John Mayall; *The Turning Point;* A, G.

Carly Simon; *Nobody Does It Better;* S, G.
Donna Summer; *I Feel Love;* S, G.
Crystal Gayle; *Don't It Make My Brown Eyes Blue;* S, G.
Johnny Rivers; *Swayin' to the Music;* S, G.

## Dec. 1977

Elvis Presley; *Elvis Sings The Wonderful World of Christmas;* A, P.
Rose Royce; *In Full Bloom;* A, P.
Boz Scaggs; *Down Two Then Left;* A, P.
Earth, Wind & Fire; *All 'N' All;* A, P.
Lynyrd Skynyrd; *Street Survivors;* A, P.
Neil Diamond; *I'm Glad You're Here With Me Tonight;* A, P.
Aerosmith; *Draw the Line;* A, P.
Debby Boone; *You Light Up My Life;* A, P.
Shaun Cassidy; *Born Late;* A, P.
Jimmy Buffett; *Changes in Latitudes, Changes in Attitudes;* A, P.
Olivia Newton-John; *Greatest Hits;* A, P.
Bob Seger & The Silver Bullet Band; *'Live' Bullet;* A, P.
Foghat; *Foghat Live;* A, P.
Rod Stewart; *Foot Loose & Fancy Free;* A, P.
Heatwave; *Too Hot to Handle;* A, P.
Styx; *The Grand Illusion;* A, P.
Steely Dan; *Aja;* A, P.
Queen; *News of the World;* A, P.
Heatwave; *Boogie Nights;* S, P.
Santana; *Moonflower;* A, G.
Elvis Presley; *His Hand in Mine;* A, G.
Elvis Presley; *Elvis Country;* A, G.
Original Cast; *The Story of Star Wars;* A, G.
Bay City Rollers; *Bay City Rollers/Greatest Hits;* A, G.
Donna Summer; *Once Upon A Time;* A, G.
Ronnie Laws; *Friends & Strangers;* A, G.
Captain & Tennille; *Greatest Hits;* A, G.
Van Morrison; *Tupelo Honey;* A, G.
Kenny Rogers; *Daytime Friends;* A, G.
Jerry Jeff Walker; *Viva Terlingua;* A, G.
Kansas; *Masque;* A, G.
Original Cast; *A Chorus Line;* A, G.
Millie Jackson; *Feelin' Bitchy;* A, G.
Blackbyrds; *Action;* A, G.
Emerson, Lake & Palmer; *Works, Vol. II;* A, G.
Z.Z. Top; *Best of Z.Z. Top;* A, G.
Paul Nicholas; *Heaven on the 7th Floor;* S, G.
Bee Gees; *How Deep Is Your Love;* S, G.
L.T.D.; *(Everytime I Turn Around) Back in Love Again;* S, G.

## Jan. 1978

Bee Gees; *Saturday Night Fever;* A, P.
Billy Joel; *The Stranger;* A, P.
Bee Gees; *Bee Gees Gold;* A, G.
Brass Construction; *Brass Construction III;* A, G.
Original Soundtrack; *Close Encounters of a Third Kind;* A, G.
Little River Band; *Diamantina Cocktail;* A, G.
Donny & Marie Osmond; *New Season;* A, G.
Waylon Jennings; *Waylon Live;* A, G.
George Duke; *Reach For It;* A, G.
Blue Oyster Cult; *Spectres;* A, G.
Randy Newman; *Little Criminals;* A, G.
Leif Garrett; *Leif Garrett;* A, G.
Player; *Baby Come Back;* S, G.
Elvis Presley; *My Way;* S, G.
Shaun Cassidy; *Hey Deanie;* S, G.
Randy Newman; *Short People;* S, G.
Linda Ronstadt; *Blue Bayou;* S, G.

## Feb. 1978

Paul Simon; *Greatest Hits, Etc.;* A, P.
Crystal Gayle; *We Must Believe in Magic;* A, P.
Barry Manilow; *Even Now;* A, P.
Jackson Browne; *Running on Empty;* A, P.
Ronnie Milsap; *It Was Almost Like a Song;* A, G.
Joni Mitchell; *Don Juan's Reckless Daughter;* A, G.
Lou Rawls; *When You Hear Lou, You've Heard It All;* A, G.
Rufus; *Street Player;* A, G.

oberta Flack; *Blue Lights in the Basement;* A, G.
Dolly Parton; *Here You Come Again;* S, G.
Lita Coolidge; *We're All Alone;* S, G.
Rod Stewart; *You're in My Heart;* S, G.
Andy Gibb; *Love is Thicker Than Water;* S, G.
Chic; *Dance, Dance, Dance (Yowsah, Yowsah, Yowsah);* S, G.
Dan Hill; *Sometimes When We Touch;* S, G.

**Mar. 1978**

Eric Clapton; *Slowhand;* A, P.
Paul McCartney & Wings; *London Town;* A, P.
Bee Gees; *Stayin' Alive;* S, P.
Art Garfunkel; *Watermark;* A, G.
Steely Dan; *Countdown to Ecstasy;* A, G.
Bootsy's Rubber Band; *Bootsy? Player of the Year;* A, G.
Maze; *Golden Time of Day;* A, G.
Manhattans; *It Feels So Good;* A, G.
Abba; *ABBA-The Album;* A, G.
Dan Hill; *Longer Fuse;* A, G.
Samantha Sang; *Emotion;* A, G.
Chic; *Chic;* A, G.
Billy Joel; *Just the Way You Are;* S, G.
Heatwave; *Always and Forever;* S, G.

**Apr. 1978**

Waylon Jennings & Willie Nelson; *Waylon & Willie;* A, P.
Dolly Parton; *Here You Come Again;* A, P.
Samantha Sang; *Emotion;* S, P.
Queen; *We Are the Champions;* S, P.
Carole King; *Carole King. . .Her Greatest Hits;* A, G.
Isley Brothers; *Showdown;* A, G.
Atlanta Rhythm Section; *Champagne Jam;* A, G.
Jethro Tull; *Heavy Horses;* A, G.
Warren Zevon; *Excitable Boy;* A, G.
Gordon Lightfoot; *Endless Wire;* A, G.
Natalie Cole; *Our Love;* S, G.
Barry Manilow; *Can't Smile Without You;* S, G.
Eric Clapton; *Lay Down Sally;* S, G.
Parliament; *Flash Light;* S, G.
Raydio; *Jack and Jill;* S, G.

**May 1978**

Bob Welch; *French Kiss;* A, P.
Isley Brothers; *Showdown;* A, P.
Jethro Tull; *M.U. The Best of Jethro Tull;* A, P.
George Benson; *Weekend in L.A.;* A, P.
Parliament; *Funkentelechy vs. The Placebo Syndrome;* A, P.
Jefferson Starship; *Earth;* A, P.
Original Soundtrack; *Grease;* A, P.
Steve Martin; *Let's Get Small;* A, P.
Movie Soundtract; *FM;* A, P.
Jimmy Buffett; *Son of a Son of a Sailor;* A, P.
John Denver; *I Want to Live;* A, P.
Kiss; *Double Platinum;* A, P.
Chuck Mangione; *Feels So Good;* A, P.
Marshall Tucker Band; *Carolina Dreams;* A, P.
Bob Seger & The Silver Bullet Band; *Stranger in Town;* A, P.
O'Jays; *So Full of Love;* A, P.
Bee Gees; *Night Fever;* S, P.
Lou Reed; *Rock 'n' Animal;* A, G.
Marshall Tucker Band; *Together Forever;* A, G.
Journey; *Infinity;* A, G.
Willie Nelson; *The Sound in Your Mind;* A, G.
Secrets; *Con Funk Shun;* A, G.
Bar-Kays; *Flying High on Your Love;* A, G.
Carly Simon; *Boys in the Trees;* A, G.
Average White Band; *Warmer Communications;* A, G.
Bill Withers; *Menagerie;* A, G.
Meat Loaf; *Bat Out of Hell;* A, G.
Van Halen; *Van Halen;* A, G.

Rod Stewart; *The Best of Rod Stewart;* A, G.
Genesis; *And Then There Were Three;* A, G.
Trammps; *Disco Inferno;* A, G.
Barbra Streisand; *Songbird;* A, G.
Joe Walsh; *But Seriously, Folks;* S, G.
Roberta Flack and Donny Hathaway; *The Closer I Get To You;* S, G.
Yvonne Elliman; *If I Can't Have You;* S, G.
Johnny Mathis and Deniece Williams; *Too Much, Too Little, Too Late;* S, G.

**June 1978**

Heart; *Magazine;* A, P.
Meco; *Star Wars and Other Galactic Funk;* A, P.
Original Soundtrack; *Thank God It's Friday;* A, G.
Andy Gibb; *Shadow Dancing;* A, P.
Gerry Rafferty; *City to City;* A, P.
Foreigner; *Double Vision;* A, P.
Heatwave; *Central Heating;* A, P.
Rolling Stones; *Some Girls;* A, P.
Teddy Pendergrass; *Teddy Pendergrass;* A, P.
Natalie Cole; *Thankful;* A, P.
Bruce Springsteen; *Darkness on the Edge of Town;* A, P.
Meco; *Star Wars Theme/Catina Band;* S, P.
Harry Chapin; *Greatest Stories Live;* A, G.
Santa Esmeralda; *Don't Let Me Be Misunderstood;* A, G.
Rolling Stones; *Some Girls;* A, G.
Dolly Parton; *The Best of Dolly Parton;* A, G.
Teddy Pendergrass; *Life is a Song Worth Singing;* A, G.
Moody Blues; *Octave;* A, G.
Foghat; *Stone Blue;* A. G.
Ashford & Simpson; *Send It;* A, G.
LTD; *Togetherness;* A, G.
Quincy Jones; *Sounds. . .And Stuff Like That;* A, G.
Rita Coolidge; *Love Me Again;* A, G.
Pablo Cruise; *Worlds Away;* A, G.
Reo Speedwagon; *You Can Tuna a Piano, But You Can't Tuna Fish;* A, G.
O'Jays; *Us Ta Be My Girl;* S, G.
Bonnie Tyler; *It's a Heartache;* S, G.

**July 1978**

Johnny Mathis; *You Light Up My Life;* A, P.
Blue Oyster Cult, *Agents of Fortune;* A, P.
Original Soundtrack; *Sgt. Pepper's Lonely Hearts Club Band,* A, P.
Kenny Rogers; *Ten Years of Gold;* A, P.
Abba; *Greatest Hits;* A, P.
Ted Nugent; *Double Live Gonzo;* A, P.
Doobie Brothers, *Takin' It To the Streets;* A, P.
Eddie Money; *Eddie Money;* A, G.
Tom Petty and the Heartbreakers; *You're Gonna Get It;* A, G.
Natalie Cole; *Natalie Live;* A, G.
Johnny Mathis and Deniece Williams; *That's What Friends Are For;* A, G.
Willie Nelson; *Stardust;* A, G.
Alan Parsons Project; *Pyramid;* A, G.
Emmylou Harris; *Elite Hotel;* A, G.
Andy Gibb; *Shadow Dancing;* A, G.
John Travolta and Olivia Newton-John; *You're The One That I Want;* S, P.
Kansas; *Dust in the Wind;* S, G.
Heatwave; *The Groove Line;* S, G.
Gerry Rafferty; *Baker Street;* S, G.
Donna Summer; *Last Dance;* S, G.
Meat Loaf; *Two Out of Three Ain't Bad;* S, G.
Rolling Stones; *Miss You;* S, G.
Frankie Valli; *Grease;* S, G.

## Recent Miss America Winners

1959  Mary Ann Mobley, Brandon, Miss. (21).
1960  Lynda Lee Mead, Natchez, Miss. (20).
1961  Nancy Fleming, Montague, Mich. (18).
1962  Maria Fletcher, Asheville, N.C. (19).

1963  Jacquelyn Mayer, Sandusky, Oh. (20).
1964  Donna Axum, El Dorado, Ark. (21).
1965  Vonda Kay Van Dyke, Phoenix, Ariz. (21).
1966  Deborah Irene Bryant, Overland Park, Kan. (19).

1967   Jane Anne Jayroe, Laverne, Okla. (19).
1968   Debra Dene Barnes, Moran, Kan. (20).
1969   Judith Anne Ford, Belvidere, Ill. (18).
1970   Pamela Anne Eldred, Birmingham, Mich. (21).
1971   Phyllis Ann George, Denton, Tex. (21).
1972   Laurie Lea Schaefer, Columbus, Oh. (22).

1973   Terry Anne Meeuwsen, DePere, Wis. (23).
1974   Rebecca Ann King, Denver, Col. (23).
1975   Shirley Cothran, Fort Worth, Tex. (21).
1976   Tawney Elaine Godin, Yonkers, N.Y. (18).
1977   Dorothy Kathleen Benham, Edina, Minn. (20).
1978   Susan Perkins, Columbus, Oh. (23).

## America's Favorite Television Programs

Source: A.C. Nielsen estimates

### Network Programs, Oct.-Dec. 1977

| Program | % of TV Households | % of Women | % of Men | % of Teens | % of Children |
|---|---|---|---|---|---|
| Laverne and Shirley | 32.1 | 24.9 | 18.8 | 31.1 | 35.2 |
| Happy Days | 31.4 | 23.3 | 18.7 | 30.7 | 37.1 |
| Three's Company | 27.6 | 21.8 | 16.6 | 26.8 | 20.7 |
| All in the Family | 25.2 | 21.4 | 18.2 | 15.6 | — |
| Charlie's Angels | 24.6 | 18.5 | 14.7 | 22.4 | — |
| 60 Minutes | 24.5 | 19.6 | 20.5 | — | — |
| Alice | 24.1 | 20.1 | 17.3 | — | — |
| Eight is Enough | 22.9 | 17.9 | — | 21.8 | 21.3 |
| NBC Mon. Night Movie | 22.8 | 19.5 | — | — | — |
| Little House. . . | 22.8 | 19.4 | — | — | — |
| On Our Own | 22.4 | 18.4 | 16.0 | — | — |
| Rhoda | 21.9 | 18.5 | 15.3 | — | — |
| Soap | 21.7 | — | — | 16.0 | — |
| NFL Mon. Night Football | 21.7 | — | 20.6 | — | — |
| One Day at a Time | 21.6 | — | — | 17.8 | — |
| The Waltons | — | 18.1 | — | — | — |
| Family | — | 17.2 | — | — | — |
| Big Event | — | 17.1 | 15.6 | — | — |
| ABC Sun. Night Movie | — | 16.7 | — | — | — |
| $6 Million Man | — | — | 15.5 | — | 26.0 |
| What's Happening | — | — | — | 20.0 | 19.6 |
| Love Boat | — | — | — | 19.4 | — |
| Hardy Boys/ Nancy Drew | — | — | — | 18.0 | 21.7 |
| Donny & Marie | — | — | — | 15.0 | 24.0 |
| Wonderful World of Disney | — | — | — | — | 23.2 |
| Wonder Woman | — | — | — | — | 20.7 |

### Syndicated Programs

(Average Designated Market Area rating)

| Program | % of TV Households | % of Women | % of Men | % of Children |
|---|---|---|---|---|
| Lawrence Welk | 14.8 | 12.7 | 8.9 | — |
| Hee Haw | 14.5 | 11.1 | 11.0 | — |
| Muppets | 14.0 | 9.4 | 8.4 | 20.7 |
| Name That Tune | 13.9 | 11.5 | 8.4 | — |
| Price Is Right | 13.8 | 11.0 | 8.5 | — |
| Match Game PM | 13.7 | 11.0 | 8.3 | — |
| Hollywood Squares | 13.5 | 10.6 | 8.5 | — |
| Gong Show | 12.7 | 9.2 | 8.7 | 11.5 |
| Family Feud PM | 12.7 | 10.4 | 7.6 | — |
| $25,000 Pyramid | 12.4 | 10.1 | 7.4 | — |
| Wild Wild World | 12.2 | 8.6 | 8.8 | — |
| Candid Camera | 12.1 | 8.9 | 8.1 | — |
| Wild Kingdom | 11.7 | — | 8.6 | — |
| All-Star Anything Goes | 11.2 | — | 7.2 | 10.9 |
| Bowling For Dollars | 10.8 | 8.6 | 7.2 | — |
| Let's Go To The Races | 10.8 | 8.4 | — | — |
| $128,000 Question | — | 8.4 | — | — |
| Brady Bunch | — | — | — | 16.3 |
| Tom and Jerry | — | — | — | 13.7 |
| Wonderama | — | — | — | 12.5 |
| Gilligan's Island | — | — | — | 12.1 |
| Fred Flintstone & Friends | — | — | — | 11.9 |
| The Flintstones | — | — | — | 11.8 |
| New Mickey Mouse | — | — | — | 11.6 |
| Bugs Bunny | — | — | — | 11.0 |
| Sha Na Na | — | — | — | 10.3 |

## Network TV Program Ratings

Source: A. C. Nielson, November, 1977

| Program type | TV households Rating | TV households No. (000) | Men% 18-34 | Men% 25-54 | Men% 55+ | Women% 18-34 | Women% 25-54 | Women% 55+ | Women% Working | % Teens 12-17 | % Children 6-11 |
|---|---|---|---|---|---|---|---|---|---|---|---|
| Today (7:30-8:00 am) | 4.2 | 3,060 | 1.0 | 1.3 | 3.6 | 1.9 | 2.3 | 5.2 | 2.4 | * | * |
| CBS Morning News (7:15-8:00) | 2.3 | 1,680 | * | * | 1.2 | * | 1.4 | 1.9 | * | * | 1.0 |
| Daytime | | | | | | | | | | | |
| Drama | 7.1 | 5,210 | 1.0 | 1.1 | 2.9 | 6.2 | 5.8 | 7.3 | 2.9 | 1.8 | * |
| Quiz & Aud. Part. | 5.3 | 3,870 | 1.3 | 1.2 | 3.2 | 3.5 | 3.2 | 5.5 | 1.7 | 1.5 | 1.1 |
| All 10 am-4:30 pm | 6.3 | 4,580 | 1.2 | 1.2 | 3.0 | 4.9 | 4.5 | 6.3 | 2.3 | 1.7 | * |
| Evening Info. | 13.0 | 9,450 | 5.5 | 7.2 | 15.1 | 6.2 | 8.0 | 15.2 | 7.4 | 3.5 | 3.9 |
| Evening | | | | | | | | | | | |
| General Drama | 16.8 | 12,280 | 8.7 | 9.0 | 13.7 | 11.9 | 12.4 | 16.6 | 11.5 | 9.2 | 8.0 |
| Susp. & Mystery | 17.9 | 13,040 | 10.0 | 11.6 | 15.2 | 12.2 | 14.0 | 14.0 | 12.1 | 10.5 | 9.7 |
| Sit. Com. | 20.1 | 14,670 | 12.7 | 12.2 | 14.4 | 15.5 | 15.3 | 15.2 | 14.6 | 15.0 | 15.3 |
| Variety | 17.0 | 12,360 | 10.5 | 9.9 | 12.0 | 11.5 | 11.6 | 14.1 | 11.1 | 11.6 | 14.4 |
| Feature Film | 19.8 | 14,470 | 13.8 | 15.0 | 14.2 | 15.9 | 16.7 | 13.9 | 14.8 | 10.3 | 6.8 |
| All 7-11 pm regular | 19.0 | 13,880 | 12.4 | 13.1 | 14.9 | 13.9 | 14.5 | 14.4 | 13.2 | 11.6 | 11.1 |

*Less than 1.0 rating.

## All-time Top Television Programs

Source: A.C. Nielsen estimates

| Program | Date | Network | Avg. Audience | Program | Date | Network | Avg. Audience |
|---|---|---|---|---|---|---|---|
| Roots | 1/30/77 | ABC | 36,380,000 | Super Bowl X | 1/18/76 | CBS | 29,440,000 |
| Super Bowl XII | 1/15/78 | CBS | 34,410,000 | Super Bowl IX | 1/12/75 | NBC | 29,040,000 |
| Gone With The Wind, Pt. 1 | 11/7/76 | NBC | 33,960,000 | Roots | 1/23/77 | ABC | 28,840,000 |
| | | | | Airport (movie) | 11/11/73 | ABC | 28,000,000 |
| Gone With The Wind, Pt. 2 | 11/8/76 | NBC | 33,750,000 | Super Bowl VII | 1/14/73 | NBC | 27,670,000 |
| Roots | 1/28/77 | ABC | 32,680,000 | World Series Game 7 | 10/22/75 | NBC | 27,560,000 |
| Roots | 1/27/77 | ABC | 32,540,000 | Super Bowl VIII | 1/13/74 | CBS | 27,540,000 |
| Roots | 1/25/77 | ABC | 31,900,000 | Super Bowl VI | 1/16/72 | CBS | 27,450,000 |
| Super Bowl XI | 1/9/77 | NBC | 31,610,000 | Love Story (movie) | 10/1/72 | ABC | 27,410,000 |
| Roots | 1/24/77 | ABC | 31,400,000 | Laverne & Shirley | 1/10/78 | ABC | 27,410,000 |
| Roots | 1/26/77 | ABC | 31,190,000 | All In The Family | 1/5/76 | CBS | 27,350,000 |
| Roots | 1/29/77 | ABC | 30,120,000 | Bob Hope Christmas Show | 1/15/1970 | NBC | 27,260,000 |

## Average Television Viewing Time

Source: A.C. Nielsen estimates, Nov. 1977 (hours: minutes, per week)

| | | Total | Mon.-Fri. 10am-4:30pm | Mon.-Fri. 4:30-7:30pm | Mon.-Sat. 8-11pm Sun. 7-11pm | Sat. 7am-8pm Sun. 7am-7pm | Mon.-Sun. 11pm-1am | All other times |
|---|---|---|---|---|---|---|---|---|
| Avg. all persons | | 27:19 | 3:49 | 4:06 | 9:17 | 4:39 | 2:27 | 3:00 |
| Women | 18-24 | 29:22 | 6:10 | 3:49 | 9:41 | 4:07 | 2:39 | 2:56 |
| | 25-54 | 29:44 | 5:03 | 3:52 | 10:42 | 3:52 | 2:58 | 3:16 |
| | 55+ | 35:01 | 7:02 | 5:57 | 10:51 | 4:33 | 2:48 | 3:51 |
| Men | 18-24 | 20:12 | 1:37 | 2:37 | 7:41 | 3:50 | 2:13 | 2:13 |
| | 25-54 | 24:29 | 1:43 | 2:56 | 9:33 | 4:54 | 2:56 | 2:27 |
| | 55+ | 31:57 | 3:50 | 5:26 | 11:11 | 5:45 | 2:53 | 2:53 |
| Teens | Female | 21:25 | 3:00 | 3:51 | 7:56 | 3:38 | 1:17 | 1:43 |
| | Male | 22:42 | 2:03 | 3:38 | 8:10 | 5:00 | 1:49 | 2:03 |
| Children | 2-5 | 27:35 | 5:31 | 5:31 | 6:04 | 6:04 | 0:17 | 4:08 |
| | 6-11 | 24:26 | 2:12 | 5:08 | 8:04 | 5:52 | 0:29 | 2:41 |

## U.S. Television Sets and Stations Received

**Set Ownership**
(Nielsen est. as of Sept. 1977)

| | | |
|---|---|---|
| Total TV homes | 72,900,000 | 100% |
| (98% of U.S. homes own at least one TV set) | | |
| Homes with: | | |
| Color TV sets | 56,862,000 | 78% |
| B&W only | 16,038,000 | 22 |
| 2 or more sets | 33,534,000 | 46 |
| One set | 39,366,000 | 54 |
| CATV (May, 1978) | 12,705,960 | 17.4 |

**Number of Stations**
(FCC, Jan., 1978)

| | |
|---|---|
| Commercial | 727 |
| VHF | 516 |
| UHF | 211 |
| Educational | 269 |
| VHF | 111 |
| UHF | 159 |
| **Total** | **996** |

**Stations Receivable**
(Nielsen, Sept. 1977)

% of TV homes receiving:

| | |
|---|---|
| 1-3 stations | 4% |
| 4 | 8 |
| 5 | 12 |
| 6 | 11 |
| 7 | 13 |
| 8 | 9 |
| 9 | 10 |
| 10+ | 33 |

## Television Network Addresses

**American Broadcasting Company (ABC)**
1330 Avenue of Americas
New York, NY 10019

**Columbia Broadcasting System (CBS)**
51 W. 52nd St.
New York, NY 10019

**National Broadcasting Company (NBC)**
30 Rockefeller Plaza
New York, NY 10020

**Westinghouse Broadcasting (Group W)**
90 Park Ave.
New York, NY 10016

**Metromedia**
277 Park Ave.
New York, NY 10017

**Public Broadcasting Service (PBS)**
15 W. 51st St.
New York, NY 10020

**Canadian Broadcasting Corp. (CBC)**
1500 Bronson Ave.
Ottawa, Ontario, Canada K1G 3J5

## Best-Selling Books of 1977-78

Listed according to frequency of citation on best seller reports from Aug. 1977 to July 1978.
Numbers in parentheses show rank on top ten list for calendar year 1977, according to *Publishers Weekly*.

### Hardcover Fiction

The Thorn Birds, Colleen McCullough (2).
The Silmarillion, J.R.R. Tolkien (1).
Bloodline, Sidney Sheldon.
Illusions: The Adventures of a Reluctant Messiah, Richard Bach (3).
The Honorable Schoolboy, John le Carré (4).
Scruples, Judith Krantz.
The Holcroft Covenant, Robert Ludlum.
Daniel Martin, John Fowles (10).
The Human Factor, Graham Greene.

10. Delta of Venus: Erotica, Anais Nin (9).
11. The Crash of '79, Paul E. Erdman.
12. Beggarman, Thief, Irwin Shaw.
13. The Women's Room, Marilyn French.
14. The Black Marble, Joseph Wambaugh.
15. Dynasty, Robert S. Elegant.
16. Stained Glass, William F. Buckley Jr.
17. Dreams Die First, Harold Robbins.
18. The Immigrants, Howard Fast.
19. Whistle, James Jones.
20. The Book of Merlyn, Terence H. White.

21. The World According to Garp, John Irving.
22. Coma, Robin Cook.
23. Full Disclosure, William Safire.
24. The Second Deadly Sin, Lawrence Sanders.
25. Oliver's Story, Erich Segal (5).

### Hardcover Nonfiction

1. All Things Wise and Wonderful, James Herriot (3).
2. The Complete Book of Running, James F. Fixx.
3. Looking Out for #1, Robert Ringer (2).
4. The Book of Lists, David Wallechinsky, Irving Wallace, and Amy Wallace (5).
5. Gnomes, Will Huygen, Rien Poortvliet.
6. My Mother/My Self, Nancy Friday.
7. The Amityville Horror, Jay Anson (10).
8. If Life is a Bowl of Cherries — What Am I Doing in the Pits?, Erma Bombeck.
9. The Dragons of Eden, Carl Sagan (7).
10. Your Erroneous Zones, Dr. Wayne W. Dyer (4).
11. The Camera Never Blinks, Dan Rather with Mickey Herskowitz.
12. The Second Ring of Power, Carlos Castaneda (8).
13. Pulling Your Own Strings, Dr. Wayne W. Dyer.
14. RN: The Memoirs of Richard Nixon, Richard Nixon.
15. Six Men, Alistair Cooke.
16. The Ends of Power, H.R. Haldeman with Joseph DiMona.
17. Adrien Arpel's Three-Week Crash Makeover, Shapeover Beauty Program, Adrien Arpel with Ronnie Sue Ebenstein.
18. Coming Into the Country, John McPhee.
19. It Didn't Start with Watergate, Victor Lasky.
20. Running and Being, George A. Sheehan.
21. Vivien Leigh, Anne Edwards.
22. The Country Diary of an Edwardian Lady, Edith Holden.
23. Metropolitan Life, Fran Lebowitz.
24. The Only Investment Guide You'll Ever Need, Andrew Tobias.
25. The Path Between the Seas, David McCullough.

### Mass Market Paperback

1. Your Erroneous Zones, Wayne W. Dyer.
2. Coma, Robin Cook.
3. Passages, Gail Sheehy.
4. Trinity, Leon Uris.
5. Close Encounters of the Third Kind, Steven Spielberg.
6. The Lawless, John Jakes.
7. The Crash of '79, Paul E. Erdman.

8. Jaws 2, Hank Searls.
9. The Grass Is Always Greener Over the Septic Tank, Erma Bombeck.
10. Star Wars, George Lucas.
11. The Book of Lists, David Wallechinsky, Irving Wallace, and Amy Wallace.
12. The Shining, Stephen King.
13. Roots, Alex Haley.
14. Raise the Titanic!, Clive Cussler.
15. The Thorn Birds, Colleen McCullough.
16. The Ghost of Flight 401, John G. Fuller.
17. The Investigation, Dorothy Uhnak.
18. Elvis: What Happened?, Steve Dunleavy.
19. Looking for Mr. Goodbar, Judith Rossner.
20. The Lincoln Conspiracy, David Balsiger and Charles E. Sellier Jr.
21. Twins, Bari Wood and Jack Geasland.
22. The Dragons of Eden, Carl Sagan.
23. Oliver's Story, Erich Segal.
24. Condominium, Jack D. MacDonald.
25. Dare To Love, Jennifer Wilde.

### Best Sellers, Calendar Year 1977
### Hardcover Fiction

1. The Silmarillion, J.R.R. Tolkien.
2. The Thorn Birds, Colleen McCullough.
3. Illusions: The Adventures of a Reluctant Messiah, Richard Bach.
4. The Honorable Schoolboy, John le Carre.
5. Oliver's Story, Erich Segal.
6. Dreams Die First, Harold Robbins.
7. Beggarman, Thief, Irwin Shaw.
8. How to Save Your Own Life, Erica Jong.
9. Delta of Venus: Erotica, Anais Nin.
10. Daniel Martin, John Fowles.

### Hardcover Nonfiction

1. Roots, Alex Haley.
2. Looking Out for #1, Robert Ringer.
3. All Things Wise and Wonderful, James Herriot.
4. Your Erroneous Zones, Dr. Wayne W. Dyer.
5. The Book of Lists, David Wallechinsky, Irving Wallace, and Amy Wallace.
6. The Possible Dream: A Candid Look at Amway, Charles Paul Conn.
7. The Dragons of Eden, Carl Sagan.
8. The Second Ring of Power, Carlos Castaneda.
9. The Grass Is Always Greener over the Septic Tank, Erma Bombeck.
10. The Amityville Horror, Jay Anson.

## Selected U.S. Daily Newspapers' Circulation

**Source:** Audit Bureau of Circulations' FAS-FAX Report. Average paid circulation for 6 months to Mar. 31, 1978. †3 months. For the 6 months up to Sept. 30, 1977, 1,759 English language dailies in the U.S. (339 morning, 1,403 evening, 17 all day) had an average audited circulation of 61,711,861. Sunday papers included 668 with audited average circulation of 52,078,543. (m) morning; (e) evening; *Mon.-Fri. average. Includes all ABC newspapers with daily circulation over 100,000.

| Newspaper | Daily | Sunday | Newspaper | Daily | Sunday |
|---|---|---|---|---|---|
| Albany, N.Y. Times-Union (m) | 79,177 | 139,980 | Cincinnati Enquirer (m) | 185,523 | 288,831 |
| Albany, N.Y. Knickerbocker News (e) | 58,059 | | Cincinnati Post (e) | 187,096 | |
| | | | Cleveland Plain Dealer (m) | 379,615 | 453,840 |
| Akron Beacon Journal (e) | 167,040 | 215,559 | Cleveland Press (e) | 320,346 | |
| Allentown Call (m) | *103,071 | 157,359 | Columbia, S.C. State (m) | 103,694 | 120,777 |
| Asbury Park Press (e) | 96,749 | 126,834 | Columbia, S.C. Record (e) | 33,333 | |
| Atlanta Constitution (m) | 216,532 | | Columbus, Ga. Enquirer (m) | *34,992 | 69,749 |
| Atlanta Journal (e) | 221,292 | 54,444 | Columbus, Ga. Ledger (e) | *31,831 | |
| Baltimore News-American (e) | *163,187 | 245,650 | Columbus, O. Citizen-Journal (m) | 111,042 | |
| Baltimore Sun (m&e) | *348,555 | 368,675 | Columbus, O. Dispatch (e) | 202,474 | 338,447 |
| Bergen Co. (N.J.) Record (e) | †154,677 | †206,726 | Dallas News (m) | 282,751 | 352,257 |
| Birmingham News (e) | *179,008 | 226,045 | Dallas Time Herald (e) | *250,505 | 344,601 |
| Birmingham Post-Herald (m) | *60,169 | | Dayton Journal-Herald (m) | 100,746 | |
| Boston Globe (m&e) | 466,783 | 660,428 | Dayton News (e) | 149,323 | 222,552 |
| Boston Herald American (m) | *273,716 | 388,255 | Denver Post (e) | *262,952 | 347,466 |
| Buffalo Courier-Express (m) | 124,061 | 261,398 | Denver: Rocky Mountain News (m) | 255,270 | 275,487 |
| Buffalo News (e) | *273,535 | 163,004 | Des Moines Register (m) | 224,393 | 423,241 |
| Camden (N.J.) Courier-Post (e) | †123,755 | | Des Moines Tribune (e) | 89,972 | |
| Charlotte News (e) | 55,696 | | Detroit Free Press (m) | *608,987 | 716,107 |
| Charlotte Observer (m) | 171,952 | 240,777 | Detroit News (e) | *633,708 | 826,111 |
| Chicago Sun-Times (m&e) | *611,135 | 704,358 | Flint Journal (e) | †105,903 | †105,983 |
| Chicago Tribune (m&e) | *762,810 | 1,155,687 | Fort Lauderdale News (e) | *112,787 | 167,310 |
| Christian Science Monitor (m) | *175,179 | | Ft. Worth Star-Telegram (m&e) | 230,344 | 233,464 |

| Newspaper | Daily | Sunday | Newspaper | Daily | Sunday |
|---|---|---|---|---|---|
| Fresno Bee (m) | 125,548 | 144,999 | Pittsburgh Press (e) | *266,077 | 675,356 |
| Grand Rapids Press (e) | †125,055 | 139,922 | Portland, Me. Press-Herald (m) | 52,710 | |
| Hartford Courant (m) | 211,016 | 281,890 | Portland, Me. Express (e) & Maine | | |
| Honolulu Advertiser (m) | 81,436 | | Sunday Telegram | 30,085 | 112,270 |
| Honolulu Star-Bulletin (e) | 120,311 | 198,046 | Portland Oregonian (m) | 241,264 | 413,229 |
| Houston Chronicle (m) | *322,762 | 413,934 | Portland: Oregon Journal (e) | *106,628 | |
| Houston Post (e) | *303,447 | 360,603 | Providence Bulletin (e) | *142,501 | |
| Indianapolis News (e) | †154,648 | | Providence Journal (m) | *69,280 | 218,873 |
| Indianapolis Star (m) | †214,979 | †354,602 | Raleigh News & Observer (m) | †128,887 | †162,640 |
| Jacksonville Journal (e) | *52,533 | | Raleigh Times (e) | †33,239 | |
| Jacksonville: Fla. Times Union (m) | 183,504 | 188,736 | Richmond News Leader (e) | 116,234 | |
| Kansas City Star (e) | 295,606 | 403,851 | Richmond Times Dispatch (m) | 136,266 | 214,092 |
| Kansas City Times (m) | 322,800 | | Rochester Democrat-Chronicle (m) | 125,601 | 229,149 |
| Knoxville News-Sentinel (m) | 103,666 | 157,882 | Rochester Times-Union (e) | 126,035 | |
| Little Rock: Ark. Democrat (e) | *55,520 | 101,550 | Sacramento Bee (m) | *186,300 | 216,048 |
| Little Rock: Ark. Gazette (m) | *129,725 | 153,790 | Sacramento Union (m) | *94,401 | 95,020 |
| Long Beach Independent (m) | *64,593 | 138,079 | St. Louis Globe-Democrat (m) | *271,755 | 270,801 |
| Long Beach Press (e) | *80,318 | | St. Louis Post-Dispatch (e) | *262,707 | 452,169 |
| Long Island, N.Y. Newsday (e) | 478,354 | 506,821 | St. Paul Dispatch (e) | *117,985 | |
| Los Angeles Herald-Examiner (e) | *322,143 | 325,426 | St. Paul Pioneer Press (m) | *100,439 | 240,696 |
| Los Angeles Times (m) | *1,020,208 | 1,315,051 | St. Petersburg Independent (e) | 39,923 | |
| Louisville Courier-Journal (m) | 205,430 | 348,667 | St. Petersburg Times (m) | 210,835 | 260,187 |
| Louisville Times (e) | 160,637 | | Salt Lake City Tribune (m) | 110,945 | 18,110 |
| Madison, Wis. State Journal | 73,435 | 119,643 | Salt Lake City Deseret News (e) | 76,908 | |
| Memphis Commercial Appeal (m) | 208,971 | 287,994 | San Antonio Express (m) | *82,511 | 176,057 |
| Memphis Press Scimitar (e) | 105,092 | | San Antonio News (e) | *75,971 | |
| Miami Herald (m) | 447,057 | 551,593 | San Antonio Light (e) | *124,091 | 180,976 |
| Miami News (e) | 71,743 | | San Diego Union (m) | †198,351 | †325,055 |
| Milwaukee Journal (e) | 334,167 | 532,692 | San Diego Tribune (e) | †131,374 | |
| Milwaukee Sentinel (m) | 161,310 | | San Francisco Examiner (e) | *156,083 | |
| Minneapolis Star (e) | *233,110 | | San Francisco Chronicle (m) | *488,782 | 668,550 |
| Minneapolis Tribune (m) | *203,843 | 607,194 | San Jose Mercury (m) | *144,745 | 252,966 |
| Nashville Banner (e) | 83,340 | | San Jose News (e) | *67,859 | |
| Newark Star-Ledger (m) | *†406,282 | †572,847 | Seattle Post-Intelligencer (m) | *187,015 | 233,404 |
| New Haven Register (e) | 101,911 | 139,428 | Seattle Times (e) | *245,614 | 327,818 |
| New Haven Journal-Courier (m) | *32,018 | | Shreveport Times (m) | †91,528 | †127,730 |
| New Orleans Times-Picayune (m) | †213,275 | †318,132 | South Bend Tribune (e) | 109,630 | 126,134 |
| New Orleans States-Item (e) | *†117,582 | | Spokane Chronicle (e) | 62,631 | |
| New York News (m) | *1,824,836 | 2,656,981 | Spokane Spokesman-Review (m) | 73,468 | 123,077 |
| New York Post (e) | *621,564 | | Springfield, Ill. State Journal-Register | | |
| New York Times (m) | *878,714 | 1,486,662 | (m&e) | 72,028 | 73,058 |
| Norfolk Ledger-Star (e) | †95,658 | | Springfield, Mass. Union (m) | 73,770 | |
| Norfolk Virginia-Pilot (m) | †126,523 | †196,603 | Springfield, Mass. News (e) & | | |
| Oakland Tribune (e) | *164,525 | 190,763 | Sunday Republican | 77,689 | 143,709 |
| Oklahoma City Oklahoman (m) | *181,562 | 290,083 | Syracuse Herald-Journal (e) | 121,876 | 236,465 |
| Oklahoma City Times (e) | *91,512 | | Syracuse Post-Standard (m) | 84,854 | |
| Omaha World-Herald (m&e) | *237,138 | 282,093 | Tacoma News Tribune (e) | 103,417 | 104,215 |
| Orange Co. (Cal.) Register (m&e) | *208,398 | 237,680 | Toledo Blade (e) | 170,107 | 209,663 |
| Orlando Sentinel-Star (m&e) | *192,868 | 219,438 | Tucson Daily Star (m) | †70,833 | †128,091 |
| Palm Beach Post (m) | *83,076 | 125,002 | Tulsa Tribune (e) | †77,272 | |
| Palm Beach Times (e) | *31,510 | | Tulsa World (m) | †122,560 | †209,586 |
| Peoria Journal Star (m&e) | 104,992 | 121,136 | Wall St. Journal (m) (total) | *1,519,805 | |
| Philadelphia Bulletin (e) | *516,872 | 610,898 | Washington, D.C. Post (m) | *567,640 | 801,035 |
| Philadelphia Inquirer (m) | *413,200 | 842,119 | Washington, D.C. Star (e) | *329,147 | 315,763 |
| Philadelphia News (e) | *230,663 | | Wichita Eagle (m) | 125,288 | 179,683 |
| Phoenix Republic (m) | †251,055 | †377,363 | Wichita Beacon (e) | 43,699 | |
| Phoenix Gazette (e) | †112,247 | | Winston-Salem Journal (m) | 73,046 | 98,212 |
| Pittsburgh Post Gazette (m) | *190,812 | | Winston-Salem Sentinel (e) | 40,812 | |
| | | | Youngstown Vindicator (e) | †101,325 | †150,951 |

## Circulation of Leading U.S. Magazines

Source: Audit Bureau of Circulations' FAS-FAX Report

General magazines, exclusive of groups and comics. Based on total average paid circulation during the 6 months prior to Dec. 31, 1977.

| | | | | | |
|---|---|---|---|---|---|
| TV Guide | 20,443,254 | Sports Illustrated | 2,263,148 | Sunset | 1,365,509 |
| Reader's Digest | 18,371,000 | American Home | 2,217,510 | Sport | 1,305,429 |
| Nat'l. Geographic | | U.S. News-World Report | 2,040,589 | Ebony | 1,255,077 |
| Magazine | 9,756,312 | Field & Stream | 2,033,135 | Psychology Today | 1,163,248 |
| Family Circle | 8,498,517 | Popular Science | 1,828,600 | Nation's Business | 1,155,620 |
| Woman's Day | 8,404,618 | Hustler | 1,799,650 | Grit | 1,145,340 |
| Better Homes & Gar. | 8,056,355 | True Story | 1,797,127 | House & Garden | 1,042,078 |
| McCall's | 6,512,186 | Outdoor Life | 1,795,598 | Esquire | 1,007,101 |
| Ladies' Home Jour. | 6,004,334 | V.F.W. Magazine | 1,793,529 | Qui | 1,001,329 |
| National Enquirer | 5,208,375 | Glamour | 1,755,775 | Jr. Scholastic | 962,589 |
| Good Housekeeping | 5,170,007 | Workbasket | 1,731,450 | Teen | 961,733 |
| Playboy | 4,970,753 | Midnight Globe | 1,706,746 | Scouting | 951,729 |
| Redbook | 4,613,908 | Today's Education | 1,666,689 | Photoplay | 949,104 |
| Penthouse | 4,606,134 | Popular Mechanics | 1,661,568 | Discovery | 928,178 |
| Time | 4,273,962 | Mechanix Illustrated | 1,640,116 | Family Health | 926,450 |
| Newsweek | 2,947,406 | Elks Magazine | 1,609,220 | Vogue | 925,451 |
| Sr. Scholastic | 2,927,108 | Smithsonian | 1,585,318 | Mademoiselle | 882,645 |
| Star | 2,708,495 | Boy's Life | 1,529,252 | Golf Digest | 877,217 |
| American Legion | 2,616,027 | Parents' Magazine | 1,511,065 | Moneysworth | 861,428 |
| Cosmopolitan | 2,581,157 | Seventeen | 1,496,676 | New Woman | 840,741 |
| People | 2,394,979 | Southern Living | 1,433,620 | Co-Ed | 830,598 |

| Magazine | Circulation | Magazine | Circulation | Magazine | Circulation |
|---|---|---|---|---|---|
| Hot Rod | 810,545 | Forbes | 658,828 | Road & Track | 529,08 |
| Apartment Life | 809,457 | Bon Appetit | 656,418 | Saturday Review | 528,83 |
| House Beautiful | 804,717 | Sports Afield | 652,610 | Workbench | 520,23 |
| Popular Photo'y | 784,121 | Gourmet | 650,169 | Ms. Magazine | 514,09 |
| Weight Watchers Magazine | 773,271 | Sphere Magazine | 649,582 | Soap Opera Digest | 499,37 |
| | | Jet | 633,536 | New Yorker | 494,12 |
| Business Week | 761,295 | National Lampoon | 631,996 | Mother Earth News | 491,94 |
| Playgirl | 755,166 | Signature | 630,979 | Skiing Magazine | 474,60 |
| 1,001 Decorat. Ideas | 750,400 | Fortune | 629,046 | Saturday Eve. Post | 467,47 |
| Book Digest | 749,787 | Club | 620,936 | Modern Screen | 466,07 |
| Car and Driver | 749,426 | American Girl | 602,984 | Stereo Review | 465,27 |
| Gallery | 740,041 | Flower & Garden Magazine | 576,956 | Rotarian | 450,04 |
| Penthouse Forum | 737,657 | Carte Blanche | 574,139 | Guns & Ammo | 452,02 |
| Yankee | 735,527 | Harper's Bazaar | 571,629 | Westways | 447,77 |
| Motor Trend | 733,311 | Tiger Beat | 570,135 | Ski | 444,02 |
| Money | 708,572 | Lutheran | 562,311 | Natural History | 439,97 |
| Family Handyman | 706,712 | Simplic. Home Catalog | 560,871 | Cycle | 433,59 |
| Decorating & Craft | 684,806 | Modern Photo'y | 555,845 | Capper's Weekly | 423,40 |
| Scientific American | 680,724 | Rolling Stone | 553,650 | Flying | 420,06 |
| Golf | 670,134 | Catholic Digest | 550,682 | Tennis | 417,03 |
| Eagle | 666,688 | Essence | 550,264 | Genesis | 406,98 |
| Lion Magazine | 660,658 | | | Popular Electronics | 401,23 |

## Sunday Magazines Weekly Circulation

Family Weekly (342 papers) .......... 12,600,000     Parade (125 papers) .......... 21,035,92

---

## Selected Canadian Daily Newspaper Circulation

**Source:** Audit Bureau of Circulations' FAS-FAX Report of average paid circulation for 6 months ending Mar. 31, 1978.

For the 6 months up to Sept. 30, 1977. 120 daily newspapers in Canada (23 morning; 96 evening, 1 all day) had an average audited circ lation of 5,034,129; 10 Sunday newspapers had an average circulation of 1,060,722.

| Newspaper | Daily | Saturday | Newspaper | Daily | Saturda |
|---|---|---|---|---|---|
| Calgary Albertan (m) | 41,716 | ....... | Regina Leader Post (e) | 67,239 | |
| Calgary Herald (e) | *122,239 | 152,185 | St. Catharines Standard (e) | 42,392 | |
| Edmonton Journal (e) | *175,256 | 216,221 | St. John's Telegram (e) | *33,745 | 49,6 |
| Halifax Chronicle-Herald (m) | 70,627 | ....... | Saint John Telegraph-Journal (m) | *32,612 | 65,97 |
| Halifax Mail-Star (e) | 54,675 | ....... | Saint John Times Globe (e) | *30,654 | .... |
| Hamilton Spectator (e) | †142,928 | ....... | Saskatoon Star-Phoenix (e) | 53,099 | .... |
| Kingston Whig-Standard (e) | †36,095 | ....... | Sherbrooke: La Tribune (e) | *41,737 | 44,13 |
| Kitchener-Waterloo Record (e) | †68,391 | ....... | Sudbury Star (e) | 34,674 | .... |
| London Free Press (m & e) | 131,553 | 136,420 | Sydney: Cape Breton Post (e) | 30,296 | .... |
| Montreal Gazette (m) | *113,592 | 126,428 | Toronto Globe and Mail (m) | 259,740 | .... |
| Montreal: La Presse (e)' | *180,972 | 281,793 | Toronto Star (e) | *491,454 | 784,25 |
| Montreal: Le Devoir (m)' | *41,017 | 37,272 | Toronto Sun (m) | *164,490 | *306,87 |
| Montreal: Le Journal de Montreal (m) | *288,471 | **294,952 | Trois Rivieres Nouvelliste (e) | *50,368 | 50,88 |
| Montreal-Matin (m)' | *140,916 | **116,541 | Vancouver Province (e) | 130,920 | .... |
| Montreal Star (e) | *169,681 | 238,934 | Vancouver Sun (e) | 240,453 | .... |
| Ottawa Citizen (e) | *112,807 | 142,908 | Victoria Colonist (m) | 39,982 | **45,22 |
| Ottawa Journal (e) | *69,145 | 82,826 | Victoria Times (e) | 30,695 | .... |
| Ottawa: Le Droit (e) | *46,845 | 50,992 | Windsor Star (e) | 89,663 | .... |
| Quebec: Le Journal de Quebec (m) | *115,060 | 48,689 | Winnipeg Free Press (e) | *138,770 | 163,85 |
| Quebec: Le Soleil (e)' | *142,899 | 148,561 | Winnipeg Tribune (e) | 102,011 | .... |

(1) 1977 estimate. (m) Morning; (e) Evening; * Based on Monday to Friday average; **Sunday. (†) Indicates 3 month circulation average.

---

## Circulation of Leading Canadian Magazines

**Source:** Audit Bureau of Circulations' FAS-FAX Report.

General magazines, exclusive of groups and comics. Statistics based on average paid circulation during the 6 months prior to Dec. 31, 1977.

| Magazine | Circulation | Magazine | Circulation | Magazine | Circulatior |
|---|---|---|---|---|---|
| Reader's Digest (Eng.-Fr.) | 1,543,761 | MacLean's Magazine | 666,383 | Chatelaine (French) | 272,964 |
| Chatelaine (English-French) | 1,279,499 | Legion Magazine | 474,331 | L'Actualite | 240,524 |
| Reader's Digest (English) | 1,234,179 | T.V. Hebdo | 348,871 | Madame | 184,515 |
| TV Guide (English-French) | 1,030,435 | Selection du Reader's Digest | 309,582 | Alberta Motorist | 179,609 |
| Chatelaine (English) | 1,001,535 | Time Canada | 309,372 | Canadian Motorist | 157,577 |

---

## 50 Leading U.S. Advertisers, 1977

Reprinted by permission of Advertising Age, Aug. 28, 1978
Copyright © Crain Communications Inc. (1978)

| Rank | Company | Ad Costs (000) | Sales (000) | Ads as % sales | Rank | Company | Ad Costs (000) | Sales (000) | Ads as % sales |
|---|---|---|---|---|---|---|---|---|---|
| | **Soaps, cleansers** | | | | 23 | Colgate-Palmolive Co. | 120,000 | 3,837,204 | 3.1 |
| 1 | Procter & Gamble | $460,000 | $ — | — | | **Automobiles** | | | |
| 14 | Unilever | 145,000 | 1,355,072 | 10.7 | 2 | General Motors Corp. | 312,000 | 54,961,300 | 0.5 |

| Rank | Company | Ad Costs (000) | Sales (000) | Ads as % sales |
|---|---|---|---|---|
| 8 | Ford Motor Co. | 184,000 | 37,841,000 | 0.4 |
| 17 | Chrysler Corp. | 127,100 | 16,708,000 | 0.7 |
| **Food** | | | | |
| 3 | General Foods Corp. | 300,000 | 5,380,000 | 5.6 |
| 12 | General Mills | 160,500 | 3,243,000 | 4.9 |
| 17 | Norton Simon Inc. | 127,115 | 1,755,958 | 7.2 |
| 21 | Beatrice Foods Co. | 123,000 | 6,313,888 | 1.9 |
| 22 | McDonald's Corp. | 122,158 | 3,241,477 | 3.8 |
| 30 | Kraft Inc. | 99,000 | 5,238,807 | 1.9 |
| 31 | Nabisco Inc. | 96,400 | 2,073,278 | 4.6 |
| 39 | Pillsbury Co. | 85,800 | 1,700,000 | 5.0 |
| 42 | Ralston Purina Co. | 80,674 | 3,760,000 | 2.1 |
| 47 | Nestle Enterprises | 71,300 | 1,250,000 | 5.7 |
| 48 | Kellogg Co. | 69,804 | 1,533,442 | 4.6 |
| **Retail chains** | | | | |
| 4 | Sears, Roebuck & Co.[1] | 290,000 | 17,224,033 | 1.7 |
| 5 | K Mart | 210,000 | 9,941,398 | 2.1 |
| 29 | J.C. Penny Co. | 100,000 | 9,369,000 | 1.1 |
| **Drugs and cosmetics** | | | | |
| 6 | Bristol-Myers Co. | 203,000 | 2,191,433 | 9.3 |
| 7 | Warner-Lambert Co. | 201,000 | 2,547,728 | 7.9 |
| 10 | Amer. Home Products Corp. | 171,000 | 1,972,000 | 8.7 |
| 13 | Richardson-Merrell | 148,771 | 836,004 | 17.8 |
| 35 | Johnson & Johnson | 91,800 | 1,713,583 | 5.3 |
| 37 | Gillette Co. | 90,044 | 1,587,209 | 5.7 |
| 43 | Revlon Inc. | 80,000 | 809,810 | 9.9 |
| 46 | Sterling Drug | 72,000 | 687,853 | 10.5 |
| 50 | Chesebrough-Pond's | 67,260 | 807,997 | 8.3 |

| Rank | Company | Ad Costs (000) | Sales (000) | Ads as % sales |
|---|---|---|---|---|
| **Tobacco** | | | | |
| 9 | Philip Morris Inc. | 184,000 | 5,201,977 | 3.5 |
| 11 | R.J. Reynolds Industries | 164,686 | 6,363,100 | 2.6 |
| 36 | B.A.T. Industries | 91,253 | 1,478,778 | 6.2 |
| 41 | American Brands | 83,921 | 4,616,390 | 1.8 |
| 49 | Liggett Group | 68,357 | 943,248 | 7.2 |
| **Oil** | | | | |
| 15 | Mobil Corp. | 142,772 | 34,442,935 | 0.4 |
| **Telephone service, equipment** | | | | |
| 16 | American T & T | 131,968 | 36,494,806 | 0.4 |
| 27 | International T & T | 104,699 | 16,688,000 | 0.6 |
| **Appliances, TV, radio** | | | | |
| 19 | RCA Corp. | 124,000 | 5,100,000 | 2.4 |
| 25 | General Electric Co. | 112,210 | 17,518,800 | 0.6 |
| **Soft drinks** | | | | |
| 19 | PepsiCo Inc. | 124,000 | 3,545,714 | 3.5 |
| 38 | Coca-Cola Co. | 88,982 | 1,993,544 | 4.5 |
| **Beer and liquor** | | | | |
| 26 | Heublein Inc. | 106,459 | 1,620,112 | 6.6 |
| 44 | Seagram Co. | 78,000 | 2,184,263 | 3.6 |
| 45 | Anheuser-Busch | 75,437 | 2,231,230 | 3.4 |
| **Chemicals** | | | | |
| 33 | American Cyanamid Co. | 96,000 | 1,600,000 | 6.0 |
| **Photographic equipment** | | | | |
| 40 | Eastman Kodak Co. | 85,472 | 4,763,500 | 1.8 |
| **Miscellaneous** | | | | |
| 24 | U.S. Government | 116,236 | — | — |
| 28 | Gulf & Western Industries | 100,611 | 3,642,998 | 2.8 |
| 31 | CBS Inc. | 96,379 | 2,776,311 | 3.5 |
| 34 | Goodyear Tire & Rubber Co. | 93,863 | 6,627,800 | 1.4 |

) Percentage shown would be more than doubled if Sears' $360,000,000 in local advertising were added to the $290,000,000 ional total. The ad totals for the other retail chains also do not include local spending.

Note: All ad totals are domestic. Whenever possible, AA has reported the company's domestic sales figure in this table, although only a worldwide sales total was available for some companies.

## Estimated Advertising Expenditures in the U.S.

Source: Advertising Age; prepared by Robert J. Coen of McCann-Erickson, Inc.

| Medium | 1974 Dollars (millions) | 1974 Per cent of total | 1975 Dollars (millions) | 1975 Per cent of total | 1976 Dollars (millions) | 1976 Percent of total | 1977 Dollars (millions) | 1977 Percent of total | % change '77 vs. '76 |
|---|---|---|---|---|---|---|---|---|---|
| **Newspapers** | | | | | | | | | |
| Total | $ 8,001 | 29.8 | $ 8,442 | 29.9 | $ 9,910 | 29.4 | $11,132 | 29.2 | +12.3 |
| National | 1,194 | 4.5 | 1,221 | 4.3 | 1,502 | 4.5 | 1,677 | 4.4 | +11.7 |
| Local | 6,807 | 25.4 | 7,221 | 25.6 | 8,408 | 4.9 | 9,455 | 24.8 | +12.5 |
| **Magazines** | | | | | | | | | |
| Total | 1,504 | 5.6 | 1,465 | 5.2 | 1,789 | 5.3 | 2,162 | 5.7 | +20.8 |
| Weeklies | 630 | 2.3 | 612 | 2.2 | 748 | 2.2 | 903 | 2.4 | +20.7 |
| Women's | 372 | 1.4 | 368 | 1.3 | 457 | 1.4 | 565 | 1.5 | +23.6 |
| Monthlies | 502 | 1.9 | 485 | 1.7 | 584 | 1.7 | 694 | 1.8 | +18.8 |
| **Farm publications** | 72 | 0.3 | 74 | 0.3 | 86 | 0.3 | 90 | 2.4 | + 0.5 |
| **Television** | | | | | | | | | |
| Total | 4,851 | 18.1 | 5,263 | 18.6 | 6,721 | 19.9 | 7,612 | 20.0 | +13.3 |
| Network | 2,145 | 8.0 | 2,306 | 8.2 | 2,857 | 8.5 | 3,460 | 9.1 | +21.1 |
| Spot | 1,495 | 5.6 | 1,623 | 5.7 | 2,154 | 6.4 | 2,204 | 5.8 | + 2.3 |
| Local | 1,211 | 4.5 | 1,334 | 4.7 | 1,710 | 5.0 | 1,948 | 5.1 | +13.9 |
| **Radio** | | | | | | | | | |
| Total | 1,837 | 6.9 | 1,980 | 7.0 | 2,330 | 6.9 | 2,586 | 6.8 | +11.0 |
| Network | 69 | 0.3 | 83 | 0.3 | 105 | 0.3 | 137 | 0.4 | +30.5 |
| Spot | 405 | 1.5 | 436 | 1.5 | 518 | 1.5 | 571 | 1.5 | +10.2 |
| Local | 1,363 | 5.1 | 1,461 | 5.2 | 1,707 | 5.1 | 1,878 | 4.9 | +10.0 |
| **Direct Mail** | 3,986 | 14.9 | 4,181 | 14.8 | 4,813 | 14.3 | 5,333 | 14.0 | +10.8 |
| **Business publications** | 900 | 3.4 | 919 | 3.3 | 1,035 | 3.1 | 1,221 | 3.2 | +18.0 |
| **Outdoor** | | | | | | | | | |
| Total | 309 | 1.2 | 335 | 1.2 | 383 | 1.1 | 418 | 1.1 | + 9.1 |
| National | 203 | 0.8 | 220 | 0.8 | 252 | 0.7 | 290 | 0.8 | +15.1 |
| Local | 106 | 0.4 | 115 | 0.4 | 131 | 0.4 | 128 | 0.3 | − 2.3 |
| **Miscellaneous** | | | | | | | | | |
| Total | 5,270 | 19.7 | 5,571 | 19.7 | 6,653 | 19.7 | 7,506 | 19.7 | +12.8 |
| National | 2,752 | 10.3 | 2,882 | 10.2 | 3,474 | 10.3 | 3,945 | 10.4 | +13.6 |
| Local | 2,518 | 9.4 | 2,689 | 9.5 | 3,179 | 9.4 | 3,561 | 9.3 | +12.0 |
| **Total** | | | | | | | | | |
| National | 14,725 | 55.1 | 15,410 | 54.6 | 18,585 | 55.1 | 21,090 | 55.4 | +13.5 |
| Local | 12,005 | 44.9 | 12,820 | 45.4 | 15,135 | 44.9 | 16,970 | 44.6 | +12.1 |
| **Grand total** | 26,730 | 100.0 | 28,230 | 100.0 | 33,720 | 100.0 | 38,060 | 100.0 | +12.9 |

## Movies of the Year (Sept. 1, 1977 to Sept. 1, 1978)

Listed below, alphabetically, are some of the major films rated by the New York Daily News star system: ★★★★ is fo excellent, ★★★½ very good, ★★★ good, ★★½ fair, ★★ mediocre, ★½poor, ★very poor, 0★ not worth rating. Be cause of the newspaper strike in New York, some films were not rated by the Daily News.

**Kathleen Carroll, N. Y. Daily News Movie Editor and Critic**

| Movie | Star rating | Stars | Director |
|---|---|---|---|
| Animal House | ★★★ | John Belushi, Verna Bloom | John Landis |
| The Betsy | ★ | Robert Duvall, Katherine Ross | Daniel Petrie |
| The Big Sleep | ★★ | Robert Mitchum, Sarah Miles | Michael Winner |
| Blue Collar | ★★★ | Richard Pryor, Harvey Keitel | Paul Schrader |
| Bobby Deerfield | ★★½ | Al Pacino, Marthe Keller | Sydney Pollack |
| The Boys in Company C | ★★ | Stan Shaw, Andrew Stevens | Sidney J. Furie |
| The Buddy Holly Story | ★★★ | Gary Busey, Don Stroud | Steve Rash |
| Cat & Mouse | ★★★ | Michele Morgan, Serge Reggiani | Claude Lelouch |
| The Cheap Detective | ★★★ | Peter Falk, Ann-Margaret | Robert Moore |
| The Choirboys | ★★ | Randy Quaid, Charles Durning | Robert Aldrich |
| Close Encounters of the Third Kind | ★★★ | Richard Dreyfuss, Melinda Dillion | Steven Spielberg |
| Coma | ★★½ | Genevieve Bujold, Michael Douglas | Michael Crichton |
| Coming Home | ★★★½ | Jane Fonda, Jon Voight | Hal Ashby |
| Convoy | ★★½ | Kris Kristofferson, Ali MacGraw | Sam Peckinpah |
| Corvette Summer | ★★½ | Mark Hamill, Annie Potts | Matthew Robbins |
| Crossed Swords | ★★★ | Oliver Reed, Raquel Welsh | Richard Fleischer |
| Damien Omen II | ★★½ | William Holden, Lee Grant | Don Taylor |
| Dear Detective | ★★★ | Annie Girardot, Philippe Noret | Philippe de Broca |
| Dersu Uzala . . . The Hunter | ★★★½ | Maxim Munzuk, Yuri Solomon | Akira Kurosawa |
| Dona Flor & Her Two Husbands | ★★★½ | Sonia Braga, Jose Wilker | Bruno Barreto |
| The Duellists | ★★½ | Keith Carradine, Harvey Keitel | Ridley Scott |
| The End | ★★½ | Burt Reynolds, Dom DeLuise | Burt Reynolds |
| Equus | ★★½ | Richard Burton, Peter Firth | Sidney Lumet |
| Eyes of Laura Mars | ★★ | Faye Dunaway, Tommy Lee Jones | Irvin Kershner |
| Final Chapter Walking Tall | ★★½ | Bo Svenson, Margaret Blye | Jack Starrett |
| Fingers | ★★½ | Harvey Keitel, Jim Brown | James Toback |
| First Love | ★★ | William Katt, Susan Dey | Joan Darling |
| F·I·S·T | ★★½ | Sylvester Stallone, Rod Steiger | Norman Jewison |
| Foul Play | ★★★ | Chevy Chase, Goldie Hawn | Colin Higgins |
| The Fury | ★★★ | Kirk Douglas, Carrie Snodgrass | Brian DePalma |
| Girlfriends | ★★★½ | Anita Skinner, Melanie Mayron | Claudia Weill |
| The Goodbye Girl | ★★★ | Richard Dreyfuss, Marsha Mason | Herbert Ross |
| Grease | ★★★ | John Travolta, Olivia Newton-John | Randal Kleiser |
| The Greek Tycoon | ★★½ | Anthony Quinn, Jacqueline Bisset | J. Lee Thompson |
| Heaven Can Wait | ★★★ | Warren Beatty, Julie Christie | W. Beatty, Buck Henry |
| A Hero Ain't Nothin' | ★★½ | Cicely Tyson, Paul Winfield | Ralph Nelson |
| Heroes | ★★★ | Henry Winkler, Sally Field | Jeremy Paul Kagan |
| High Anxiety | ★★★ | Mel Brooks, Madeline Kahn | Mel Brooks |
| Hooper | ★★★ | Burt Reynolds, Sally Field | Hal Needham |
| House Calls | ★★½ | Walter Matthau, Glenda Jackson | Howard Zieff |
| Interiors | ★★★½ | Diane Keaton, E. G. Marshall | Woody Allen |
| International Velvet | ★★½ | Tatum O'Neal, Christopher Plummer | Bryan Forbes |
| Iphigenia | ★★★½ | Irene Papas, Tatiana Papamoskou | Michael Cacoyannis |
| Jaws 2 | ★★½ | Roy Scheider, Lorraine Gary | Jeannot Szware |
| Joseph Andrews | ★★½ | Ann-Margret, Peter Firth | Tony Richardson |
| Julia | ★★★★ | Jane Fonda, Vanessa Redgrave | Fred Zinnemann |
| The Lacemaker | ★★★ | Isabelle Huppert, Yves Beneyton | Claude Goretta |
| La Grande Bourgeoise | ★★★ | Catherine Deneuve, G. Giannini | Mauro Bolognini |
| The Last Waltz | ★★★½ | Neil Diamond, Bob Dylan | Martin Scorsese |
| A Little Night Music | ★★½ | Elizabeth Taylor, Diana Rigg | Harold Prince |
| Looking For Mr. Goodbar | ★★★½ | Diane Keaton, William Atherton | Richard Brooks |
| Madame Rosa | ★★★ | Simone Signoret, Claude Dauphin | Moshe Mizrahi |
| The Man Who Loved Women | ★★★ | Charles Denner, Leslie Caron | Francois Truffaut |
| Mr. Klein | ★★★ | Alain Delon, Jeanne Moreau | Joseph Losey |
| A Night Full of Rain | ★★ | Giancarlo Giannini, Candice Bergen | Lina Wertmuller |
| 1900 | ★★½ | Donald Sutherland, Burt Lancaster | Bernardo Bertolucci |
| Nunzio | ★★★ | David Provial, Morgana King | Paul Williams |
| Oh, God | ★★½ | George Burns, John Denver | Carl Reiner |
| The One and Only | ★★½ | Henry Winkler, Kim Darby | Carl Reiner |
| Pete's Dragon | ★★★ | Helen Reddy, Jim Dale | Don Chaffey |
| A Piece of the Action | ★★★ | Sidney Poitier, Bill Cosby | Sidney Poitier |
| Pretty Baby | ★★½ | Keith Carradine, Susan Sarandon | Louis Malle |
| Revenge of the Pink Panther | ★★½ | Peter Sellers, Herbert Lom | Blake Edwards |
| Roseland | ★★★ | Geraldine Chaplin, Lou Jacobi | James Ivory |
| Saturday Night Fever | ★★★ | John Travolta, Karen Lynn Gorney | John Badham |
| Semi-Tough | ★★★ | Burt Reynolds, Jill Claybourgh | Michael Ritchie |
| The Serpent's Egg | ★★½ | Liv Ullmann, David Carradine | Ingmar Bergman |
| Sgt. Pepper's Lonely Hearts | ★★ | The Bee Gees, Peter Frampton | Michael Schultz |
| Sinbad and the Eyes of the Tiger | ★★ | Patrick Wayne, Taryn Power | Sam Wanamaker |
| A Special Day | ★★½ | Sophia Loren, M. Mastroianni | Ettore Scola |
| Straight Time | ★★★ | Dustin Hoffman, Harry D. Stanton | Ulu Crossbard |
| The Swarm | ★½ | Richard Widmark, Patty Duke Astin | Irwin Allen |
| That Obscure Object of Desire | ★★★½ | Fernando Rey, Carole Bouquet | Luis Buenel |
| The Turning Point | ★★★½ | Anne Bancroft, Shirley MacLaine | Herbert Ross |
| An Unmarried Woman | ★★★★ | Jill Claybourgh, Alan Bates | Paul Mazursky |
| Valentino | ★★½ | Rudolph Nureyev, Leslie Caron | Ken Russel |
| Viva Italia! | ★★½ | Alberto Sordi, Ugo Tognazzi | Monicello, Risi, Scola |
| We Will All Meet in Paradise | ★★★ | Jean Rochefort, Claude Brasseur | Yves Robert |
| Which Way Is Up? | ★★½ | Richard Pryor, Margaret Avery | Michael Schultz |
| Who'll Stop the Rain | | Nick Nolte, Tuesday Weld | Karel Reisz |
| The World's Greatest Lover | ★★ | Gene Wilder, Carol Kane | Gene Wilder |

1778 — James Cook (Britain). Through Bering Strait to Icy [Ca]pe, Alaska, and North Cape, Siberia.

1789 — Alexander Mackenzie (North West Co., Britain). Mon[tre]al to mouth of Mackenzie River.

1806 — William Scoresby (Britain). North of Spitsbergen to 81°

1820-3 — Ferdinand von Wrangel (Russia). Completed a survey [of] Siberian Arctic coast. His exploration joined that of James Cook [at] North Cape, confirming separation of the continents.

1845 — Sir John Franklin (Britain) was one of many to seek the [No]rthwest Passage—an ocean route connecting the Atlantic and [Pa]cific via the Arctic. His 2 ships (the Erebus and Terror) were last [see]n entering Lancaster Sound July 26.

1888 — Fridtjof Nansen (Norway) crossed Greenland's icecap, [189]3-96 — Nansen in Fram drifted from New Siberian Is. to Spits[ber]gen; tried polar dash in 1895, reached Franz Josef Land.

1896 — Salomon A. Andree (Sweden) and companion, in June, [ma]de first attempt to reach North Pole by balloon; failed and re[turned] in August. On July 11, 1897, Andree and 2 others started in [ba]loon from Danes, Is., Spitsbergen, to drift across pole to Amer[ica], and disappeared. Over 33 years later, Aug. 6, 1930, Dr. Gun[na]r Horn (Norway) found their frozen bodies on White Is., 82° 57' 29' 52' E.

1903-06 — Roald Amundsen (Norway) first sailed Northwest [Pa]ssage.

## Discovery of North Pole

Robert E. Peary began exploring in 1886 on Greenland, when he [wa]s 30. With his hq. at McCormick Bay he explored Greenland's [co]ast 1891-92, tried for North Pole 1893, returned with large mete[ori]tes. In 1900 he reached northern limit of Greenland and 83° 50' [N;] in 1902 he reached 84° 06' N; in 1906 he went from Ellesmere [Is.] to 87° 06' N. He sailed in the Roosevelt, July, 1908, to winter [at] Cape Meridian, Grant Land. The dash for the North Pole began [Ma]r. 1 from Cape Columbia, Ellesmere Land. Peary reached the [Pol]e, 90° N, Apr. 6, 1909.

Peary had several supporting groups carrying supplies until the [last] group, under Capt. Robt. A. Bartlett, turned back at 87° 47' [N.] Peary, Matthew Henson, and 4 eskimos proceeded with dog [tea]ms and sleds. They crossed the pole several times, finally built [an] igloo at 90°, remained 36 hours. Started south Apr. 7 at 4 p.m. [for] Cape Columbia. Eskimos were Coqueeh, Ootah, Eginwah, and [See]gloo. Adm. Peary died Feb. 20, 1920. Henson, a Negro, born [Au]g. 8, 1866, died in New York, N.Y., Mar. 9, 1955, aged 88. [O]tah, the last survivor, died near Thule, Greenland, May, 1955, aged 80.

1914 — Donald Macmillan (U.S.). Northwest, 200 miles, from Axel Hieberg Island to seek Peary's Crocker Land.

1915-17 — Vihjalmur Stefansson (Canada) discovered Borden, Brock, Meighen, and Lougheed Islands.

1918-20 — Amundsen sailed Northeast Passage.

1926 — Richard E. Byrd and Floyd Bennett (U.S.) reached 87° 44' N in attempt to fly to North Pole from Spitsbergen.

1926 — Richard E. Byrd and Floyd Bennett (U.S.) first over North Pole by air, May 9.

1926 — Amundsen, Ellsworth, and Umberto Nobile (Italy) flew from Spitsbergen over North Pole May 12, to Teller, Alaska, in dirigible Norge.

1928 — Nobile crossed North Pole in airship Italia May 24, crashed May 25. Amundsen lost while trying to effect rescue by plane.

1928 — Sir Hubert Wilkins and Eielson from Point Barrow to Spitsbergen, 84° N.

## North Pole Exploration Records

On Aug. 3, 1958, the Nautilus, under Comdr. William R. Anderson, became the first ship to cross the North Pole beneath the Arctic ice.

On Aug. 12, 1958, the nuclear submarine Skate, Comdr. James F. Calvert, became the 2d ship to make an underwater crossing of the North Pole.

In March, 1959, the Skate returned to the Arctic and on its 3d attempt, broke through at the North Pole, the first time any ship had been on the surface at 90° N.

The nuclear-powered U.S. submarine Seadragon, Comdr. George P. Steele 2d, made the first east-west underwater transit through the Northwest Passage during August, 1960. It sailed from Portsmouth N.H., headed between Greenland and Labrador through Baffin Bay, then west through Lancaster Sound and McClure Strait to the Beaufort Sea. Traveling submerged for the most part, the submarine made 850 miles from Baffin Bay to the Beaufort Sea in 6 days.

On Aug. 16, 1977, according to press dispatches from Moscow, the Soviet nuclear icebreaker Arktika reached the North Pole and became the first surface ship to break through the Arctic ice pack to the top of the world.

On April 30, 1978, Naomi Uemura, a Japanese explorer, became the first man to reach the North Pole alone by dog sled. During the 54-day, 600-mile trek over the frozen Arctic, Uemura survived attacks by a marauding polar bear.

# Antarctic Exploration

## Early History

Antarctica has been approached since 1773-75, when Capt. Jas. [Co]ok (Britain) reached 71° 10' S. Many sea and landmarks bear [na]mes of early explorers. Bellingshausen (Russia) discovered Peter [and] Alexander I Islands, 1819-21. Nathaniel Palmer (U.S.) dis[co]vered Palmer Peninsula, 60° W, 1820, without realizing that this [wa]s a continent. Jas. Weddell (Britain) found Weddell Sea, 74° 15' [S] 1823.

First to announce existence of the continent of Antarctica was [Ch]arles Wilkes (U.S.), who followed the coast for 1,500 mi., 1840. [A]delie Coast, 140° E, was found by Dumont d'Urville (France), [18]40. Ross Ice Shelf was found by Jas. Clark Ross (Britain), [18]41-42.

1895 — Leonard Kristensen, Norwegian whaling captain, [la]nded a party on the coast of Victoria Land in Jan. 1895. They [we]re the first ashore on the main continental mass. C.E. Borch[gr]evink, a member of that party, returned in 1899 with a British [ex]pedition, first to winter on Antarctica.

1902-04 — Robert F. Scott (Britain) discovered Edward VII [Pe]ninsula. In 1902 he reached 82° 17' S, 146° 33' E from McMurdo [So]und.

1908-09 — Ernest Shackleton, in 1908, introduced the use of [Ma]nchurian ponies in Antarctic sledging. In 1909 he reached 88° [2]' S, discovering a route on to the plateau by way of the Beard[m]ore Glacier and pioneering the way to the pole.

## Discovery of South Pole

1911 — Roald Amundsen (Norway) with 4 men and dog teams [re]ached the pole Dec. 14, 1911.

1912 — Capt. Scott reached the pole from Ross Island Jan. 18, [19]12, with 4 companions, where they found Amundsen's tent. [N]one of Scott's party survived. They were found Nov. 12, 1912.

1928 — First man to use an airplane over Antarctica was Hu[be]rt Wilkins (Britain).

1929 — Richard E. Byrd (U.S.) established Little America on [Ba]y of Whales. On 1600-mi. airplane flight begun Nov. 28 he [cr]ossed South Pole Nov. 29 with his pilot, a radio operator, and a [ph]otographer. Dropped U.S. flag over pole, temp. 16° below zero.

1934-35 — Richard E. Byrd (U.S.) led 2d expedition to Little [A]merica, which explored 450,000 sq. mi. Byrd remained alone at an [a]dvance weather station in 80° 08' S.

1934-37 — John Rymill led British Graham Land expedition of

1934-37; discovered that Palmer Peninsula is part of Antarctic mainland.

1935 — Lincoln Ellsworth (U.S.) flew south along Palmer Peninsula's east coast, then crossed continent to Little America, making 4 landings on unprepared terrain in bad weather, a new feat.

1939-41 — U.S. Antarctic Service built West Base on Ross Ice Shelf under Paul Siple, and East Base on Palmer Peninsula under Richard Black. U.S. Navy plane flights discovered about 150,000 sq. miles of new land.

1940 — Richard E. Byrd (U.S.) charted most of coast between Ross Sea and Palmer Peninsula.

1946-47 — U.S. Navy undertook Operation High-jump under Rear Admiral Byrd. Expedition included 13 ships and 4,000 men. Twenty-nine land-based flights from Little America and 35 by seaplanes from tenders photomapped coastline and penetrated beyond pole.

1946-48 — Ronne Antarctic Research Expedition, Comdr. Finn Ronne, USNR, determined the Antarctic to be only one continent with no strait between Weddell Sea and Ross Sea; discovered 250,000 sq. miles of land by flights to 79° S Lat., and made 14,000 aerial photographs over 450,000 sq. miles of land. Mrs. Ronne and Mrs. H. Darlington, who accompanied their husbands, were the first women to winter on Antarctica.

1955-57 — U.S. Navy's Operation Deep Freeze led by Adm. Richard E. Byrd. Supporting U.S. scientific efforts for the International Geophysical Year, the operation was commanded by Rear Adm. George Dufek. It established 5 coastal stations fronting the Indian, Pacific, and Atlantic Oceans and also 3 interior stations; explored more than 1,000,000 sq. miles in Wilkes Land. Seven Navy men under Adm. Dufek landed by plane at the Pole Oct. 31, 1956, and landed radar reflectors.

1957-58 — During the International Geophysical year, July, 1957, through Dec. 1958, scientists from 12 countries conducted ambitious programs of Antarctic research. A network of some 60 stations on the continent and sub-Arctic islands studied oceanography, glaciology, meteorology, seismology, geomagnetism, the ionosphere, cosmic rays, aurora, and airglow. A party from Ellsworth IGY station (U.S.) south of Weddell Sea under the direction of Captain Finn Ronne explored beyond 1947 flight and delineated Berkner Island imbedded in the Filchner Ice Shelf.

Dr. V.E. Fuchs led a 12-man Trans-Antarctic Expedition on the first land crossing of Antarctica. Starting from the Weddell Sea, they reached Scott Station Mar. 2, 1958, after traveling 2,158 miles in 98 days.

**1958** — A group of 5 U.S. scientists led by Edward C. Thiel, seismologist, moving by tractor from Ellsworth Station on Weddell Sea, identified a huge mountain range, 5,000 ft. above the ice sheet and 9,000 ft. above sea level. The range, originally seen by a Navy plane, was named the Dufek Massif, for Rear Adm. George Dufek.

**1959** — Twelve nations — Argentina, Australia, Belgium, Chile, France, Japan, New Zealand, Norway, South Africa, the Soviet Union, the United Kingdom, and the U.S. — signed a treaty suspending any territorial claims for 30 years and reserving the continent for research.

**1961-62** — Scientists discovered a trough, the Bentley Trench, running from Ross Ice Shelf, Pacific, into Marie Byrd Land, around the end of the Ellsworth Mtns., toward the Weddell Sea, which may be the long-suspected link between the Atlantic and Pacific Oceans.

**1962** — First nuclear power plant began operation at McMur Sound.

**1963** — On Feb. 22 a U.S. plane made the longest nonstop fli ever made in the S. Pole area, covering 3,600 miles in 10 hours. flight was from McMurdo Station south past the geographical Pole to Shackleton Mtns., southeast to the "Area of Inaccessib ity" and back to McMurdo Station.

**1963** — Three turbine-powered helicopters made the first cop landings on the S. Pole.

**1964** — A British survey team was landed by helicopter on Co Island, the first recorded visit since its discovery in 1775.

**1964** — New Zealanders completed one of the last and most i portant surveys when they mapped the mountain area from Ca Adare west some 400 miles to Pennell Glacier.

**1966-67** — Fifteen Antarctic areas set aside as Specially P. tected Areas for the conservation of flora and fauna.

# Volcanoes of the World

Source: The Center for Short-Lived Phenomena, Cambridge, Mass.
Year of last eruption in parentheses.

More than 75 per cent of the world's 850 active volcanoes lie within the "Ring of Fire," a zone running along the we coast of the Americas from Chile to Alaska and down the east coast of Asia from Siberia to New Zealand. Twenty per cent these volcanoes are located in Indonesia. Other prominent groupings are located in Japan, the Aleutian Islands, and Cent America. Almost all active volcanic regions are found at the boundaries of the large moving plates which comprise the earth surface. The "Ring of Fire" marks the boundary between the plates underlying the Pacific Ocean and those underlying t surrounding continents. Other active volcanic regions, such as the Mediterranean Sea and Iceland, are located on pla boundaries.

### Major Historical Eruptions

Approximately 7,000 years ago, Mazama, a 3,000-meter-high volcano in southern Oregon, erupted violently, ejecting abo 40 cubic kilometers of ash and lava. The ash spread over the entire northwestern United States and as far away as Saskatch wan, Canada. During the eruption, the top of the mountain collapsed, leaving a caldera 10 kilometers across and about o kilometer deep, which filled with rain water to form what is now called Crater Lake.

In 79 A.D., Vesuvio, a 1281-meter-high volcano оʃ king Naples Bay, became active after several centuries of q cence. On October 26 of that year, a heated mud and ash flow swept down the mountain, engulfing the cities of Pomp Herculaneum, and Stabiae with debris up to 15 meters deep. Virtually all residents of the 3 towns were killed.

The largest eruptions in recent centuries have been in Indonesia. In 1883, an eruption similar to the Mazama eruption curred on the island of Krakatau. On August 27, the 800-meter-high peak of the volcano collapsed to 300 meters below s level, leaving only a small portion of the island standing above the sea. Ash from the eruption covered nearly 1,000,0 square kilometers and colored sunsets around the world for 2 years. A tsunami ("tidal wave") generated by the collap killed 36,000 people in nearby Java and Sumatra and eventually reached England. A similar, but even more powerful, eru tion had taken place 68 years earlier at Tambora volcano on the Indonesian island of Sumbawa.

### Major Eruptions 1977-78

From May 1, 1977 to May 1, 1978, significant eruptive activity reportedly occurred at 31 volcanoes around the world. M Etna on Sicily erupted on several occasions from mid-1977 through May 1978. A major eruption at Mt. Usu in Japan beg on August 7, 1977. Ashfall from Mt. Usu forced the evacuation of 20,000 tourists and 7,000 residents from nearby towns an caused serious crop damage. Westdahl Volcano in the Aleutian Islands erupted in February 1978, sending ash into the strat sphere. Ash accumulation totalled one meter on Scotch Cap, a U.S. Coast Guard station 15 kilometers from the volcano.

Intermittent eruptive activity at Fuego in Guatemala began in September 1977 and culminated in late January 1978, in t largest eruption since 1974. This was followed by a lava flow in February 1978, an uncommon event at Fuego. Sin Fuego's first recorded eruption in 1524, less than one in 4 eruptions have been accompanied by lava flows.

| Name | Location | Meters | Name | Location | Mete |
|---|---|---|---|---|---|
| **Africa** | | | Shiveluch (1964) | USSR | 3,3 |
| Kilimanjaro | Tanzania | 5,895 | Ardjuno-Welirang | Java | 3,3 |
| Cameroon | Cameroons | 4,070 | Raung (1945) | Java | 3,3 |
| Teide (Tenerife) (1909) | Canary Is. | 3,713 | Dempo (1940) | Sumatra | 3,1 |
| Nyirangongo (1977) | Zaire | 3,465 | Sundoro (1906) | Java | 3,1 |
| Nyamuragira (1977) | Zaire | 3,056 | Agung (1964) | Bali | 3,1 |
| Ol Doinyo Lengai (1960) | Tanzania | 2,886 | Piosky Tolbachik (1976) | USSR | 3,0 |
| Fogo (1951) | Cape Verde Is. | 2,829 | Tjiremai (1938) | Java | 3,0 |
| Piton de la Fournaise (1977) | Reunion | 2,631 | Ontake | Japan | 3,0 |
| Palma (1971) | Canary Is. | 2,423 | Mayon (1978) | Philippines | 2,9 |
| Karthala (1977) | Comoro Is. | 2,361 | Gede (1949) | Java | 2,9 |
| Erta-Ale (1973) | Ethiopia | 615 | Zhupanovsky (1959) | USSR | 2,9 |
| **Antarctica** | | | Apo | Philippines | 2,9 |
| Erebus (1975) | Ross Island | 3,743 | Merapi (1976) | Java | 2,9 |
| Big Ben (1960) | Heard Island | 2,745 | Marapi (1949) | Sumatra | 2,8 |
| Melbourne | Victoria Land | 2,590 | Tambora (1913) | Indonesia | 2,8 |
| Darnley (1956) | South Sandwich Islands | 1,100 | Bezymianny (1977) | USSR | 2,8 |
| | | | Ruapehu (1975) | New Zealand | 2,7 |
| Deception Island (1970) | South Shetland Islands | 602 | Peuetsagoe (1921) | Sumatra | 2,7 |
| **Asia-Oceania** | | | Avachinskaya (1945) | USSR | 2,7 |
| Klyuchevskaya (1974) | USSR | 4,850 | Papandajan (1925) | Java | 2,6 |
| Kerintji (1968) | Sumatra | 3,805 | Balbi | Solomon Is. | 2,5 |
| Fuji | Japan | 3,776 | Geureudong | Sumatra | 2,5 |
| Rindjani (1966) | Indonesia | 3,726 | Asama (1973) | Japan | 2,5 |
| Semeru (1976) | Java | 3,676 | Sumbing (1921) | Sumatra | 2,5 |
| Ichinskaya | USSR | 3,631 | Canlaon (1969) | Philippines | 2,4 |
| Kronotskaya (1923) | USSR | 3,528 | Sinabung | Sumatra | 2,4 |
| Koryakskaya (1957) | USSR | 3,456 | Yake Dake (1963) | Japan | 2,4 |
| Slamet (1967) | Java | 3,432 | Tandikat (1914) | Sumatra | 2,4 |
| | | | Niigata Yakeyama (1974) | Japan | 2,4 |

| Name | Location | Meters |
|---|---|---|
| jen (1936) | Java | 2,386 |
| aid (1972) | Kuril Is. | 2,339 |
| romo (1950) | Java | 2,329 |
| awun (1973) | New Britain | 2,300 |
| gauruhoe (1975) | New Zealand | 2,291 |
| untur | Java | 2,249 |
| amus | New Britain | 2,248 |
| hokai (1974) | Japan | 2,230 |
| utak Petarangan (1939) | Java | 2,222 |
| ibajak | Sumatra | 2,212 |
| alunggung (1918) | Java | 2,168 |
| orikmerapi (1917) | Sumatra | 2,145 |
| mburombu (1969) | Indonesia | 2,124 |
| angkuban Prahu (1967) | Java | 2,084 |
| okachi (1962) | Japan | 2,077 |
| zuma (1978) | Japan | 2,024 |
| ongariro | New Zealand | 1,978 |
| heltovskaya (1923) | USSR | 1,953 |
| aba (1941) | Sumatra | 1,952 |
| angeang Api (1966) | Indonesia | 1,949 |
| asu (1977) | Japan | 1,917 |
| Manam (1977) | Papua New Guinea | 1,830 |
| iatia (1973) | Kuril Islands | 1,822 |
| iau (1976) | Indonesia | 1,784 |
| oputan (1968) | Celebes | 1,784 |
| amington (1952) | Papua New Guinea | 1,780 |
| elud (1967) | Java | 1,731 |
| atur (1968) | Bali | 1,717 |
| ernate (1963) | Indonesia | 1,715 |
| ewotobi (1935) | Indonesia | 1,703 |
| agana (1960) | Solomon Islands | 1,702 |
| irishima (1956) | Japan | 1,700 |
| Boleng (1950) | Indonesia | 1,659 |
| alinao | Philippines | 1,657 |
| mongan | Java | 1,651 |
| li Mutu (1968) | Indonesia | 1,640 |
| kita Komaga take (1970) | Japan | 1,637 |
| iamkunoro (1949) | Indonesia | 1,635 |
| so (1978) | Japan | 1,592 |
| ewotobi Laki-Laki (1968) | Indonesia | 1,584 |
| okon-Empung (1970) | Celebes | 1,579 |
| ulusan (1933) | Philippines | 1,559 |
| le-akan (1966) | Japan | 1,503 |
| Karkar (1975) | Papua New Guinea | 1,500 |
| arycheva (1976) | Kuril Islands | 1,497 |
| arymskaya (1976) | USSR | 1,486 |
| opevi (1960) | New Hebrides | 1,447 |
| ou (1911) | Indonesia | 1,340 |
| mbrim (1953) | New Hebrides | 1,334 |
| atarman (1952) | Philippines | 1,332 |
| ahawu | Celebes | 1,331 |
| wu (1968) | Indonesia | 1,320 |
| i Lewotolo (1920) | Indonesia | 1,319 |
| angila (1973) | New Britain | 1,189 |
| ongkoko | Celebes | 1,149 |
| omaga take (1942) | Japan | 1,140 |
| akurajima (1978) | Japan | 1,118 |
| ukono (1971) | Indonesia | 1,087 |
| angum | New Britain | 1,052 |
| i Werung (1948) | Indonesia | 1,018 |
| olobau (1905) | New Britain | 932 |
| uwanosezima (1977) | Japan | 799 |
| O-Sima (1977) | Japan | 758 |
| su (1978) | Japan | 725 |
| hite Island (1978) | New Zealand | 321 |
| aal (1977) | Philippines | 300 |
| **Central America—Caribbean** | | |
| ajumulco | Guatemala | 4,220 |
| acana | Guatemala | 4,092 |
| catenango (1972) | Guatemala | 3,976 |
| antiaguito (Santa Maria) (1977) | Guatemala | 3,772 |
| Fuego (1978) | Guatemala | 3,736 |
| titlan | Guatemala | 3,537 |
| razu (1967) | Costa Rica | 3,432 |
| oas (1977) | Costa Rica | 2,704 |
| acaya (1977) | Guatemala | 2,552 |
| San Miguel (1976) | El Salvador | 2,130 |
| zalco (1966) | El Salvador | 1,965 |
| incon de la Vieja (1968) | Costa Rica | 1,806 |
| El Viejo (San Cristobal) (1977) | Nicaragua | 1,745 |
| Ometepe (Concepcion) (1978) | Nicaragua | 1,610 |
| Arenal (1977) | Costa Rica | 1,552 |
| a Soufrière | Guadeloupe | 1,467 |

| Name | Location | Meters |
|---|---|---|
| Pelée (1932) | Martinique | 1,397 |
| Conchagua (1947) | El Salvador | 1,250 |
| Momotombo (1905) | Nicaragua | 1,191 |
| Soutriere (1972) | St. Vincent | 1,178 |
| Telica (1976) | Nicaragua | 1,010 |
| Masaya (1978) | Nicaragua | 635 |
| **South America** | | |
| Guallatiri (1960) | Chile | 6,060 |
| Cotopaxi (1975) | Ecuador | 5,897 |
| El Misti | Peru | 5,825 |
| Ubinas (1969) | Peru | 5,672 |
| Lascar (1968) | Chile | 5,641 |
| Tupungato (1964) | Chile | 5,640 |
| Tolima (1943) | Colombia | 5,525 |
| Sangay (1976) | Ecuador | 5,230 |
| Tungurahua (1944) | Ecuador | 5,016 |
| Pichincha | Ecuador | 4,787 |
| Purace (1977) | Colombia | 4,600 |
| Reventador (1976) | Ecuador | 3,485 |
| Lautaro (1960) | Chile | 3,380 |
| Llaima (1957) | Chile | 3,124 |
| Villarrica (1971) | Chile | 2,840 |
| Hudson (1973) | Chile | 2,600 |
| Rinihue | Chile | 2,430 |
| Puyehue (1960) | Chile | 2,240 |
| Calbuco (1961) | Chile | 2,015 |
| Fernandina (1977) | Galapagos Is. | 1,546 |
| Alcedo (1954) | Galapagos Is. | 1,127 |
| **Mid-Pacific** | | |
| Mauna Kea | Hawaii | 4,206 |
| Mauna Loa (1978) | Hawaii | 4,170 |
| Haleakala | Hawaii | 3,055 |
| Kilauea (1977) | Hawaii | 1,222 |
| **Mid-Atlantic Ridge** | | |
| Beerenberg (1970) | Jan Mayen Is. | 2,277 |
| Tristan da Cunha (1962) | Tristan da Cunha Is. | 2,060 |
| Askja (1961) | Iceland | 1,510 |
| Hekla (1970) | Iceland | 1,491 |
| Faial (1968) | Azores | 1,043 |
| Katla (1918) | Iceland | 900 |
| Leirhnukur (1975) | Iceland | 650 |
| Krafla (1977) | Iceland | 650 |
| Helgatell (1973) | Iceland | 226 |
| Surtsey (1967) | Iceland | 174 |
| **Europe** | | |
| Etna (1978) | Italy | 3,290 |
| Vesuvio (1944) | Italy | 1,281 |
| Stromboli (1975) | Italy | 926 |
| Vulcano | Italy | 500 |
| Santorini (1950) | Greece | 130 |
| **North America** | | |
| Citlaltepec | Mexico | 5,676 |
| Popocatepetl (1920) | Mexico | 5,452 |
| Rainier | Washington | 4,395 |
| Wrangell | Alaska | 4,320 |
| Colima (1975) | Mexico | 3,960 |
| Spurr (1953) | Alaska | 3,375 |
| Baker | Washington | 3,316 |
| Lassen (1915) | California | 3,186 |
| Paricutin (1952) | Mexico | 3,170 |
| Redoubt (1966) | Alaska | 3,110 |
| Iliamna | Alaska | 3,073 |
| Shishaldin (1978) | Aleutian Is. | 2,858 |
| Pavlof (1977) | Aleutian Is. | 2,715 |
| Veniaminof | Alaska | 2,560 |
| Chiginagak | Alaska | 2,420 |
| Douglas | Alaska | 2,328 |
| Pogromni | Alaska | 2,286 |
| Katmai (1931) | Alaska | 2,285 |
| Mageik (1912) | Alaska | 2,210 |
| Tanaga | Aleutian Is. | 2,125 |
| Trident (1963) | Alaska | 2,070 |
| Kukak | Alaska | 2,046 |
| Makushin | Aleutian Is. | 2,036 |
| Martin (1912) | Alaska | 1,830 |
| Great Sitkin (1974) | Aleutian Is. | 1,750 |
| Cleveland (1951) | Aleutian Is. | 1,730 |
| Gareloi | Aleutian Is. | 1,627 |
| Westdahl (1978) | Aleutian Is. | 1,532 |
| Korovin | Aleutian Is. | 1,480 |
| Kanaga | Aleutian Is. | 1,348 |
| Aniakchak | Alaska | 1,348 |
| Akutan (1977) | Aleutian Is. | 1,293 |
| Kiska (1969) | Aleutian Is. | 1,220 |
| Augustine (1976) | Alaska | 1,210 |
| Little Sitkin | Aleutian Is. | 1,195 |
| Okmok (1945) | Aleutian Is. | 1,072 |
| Seguam (1977) | Alaska | 1,050 |

## Continental Drift: Lithospheri

(Illustrations adapted from U

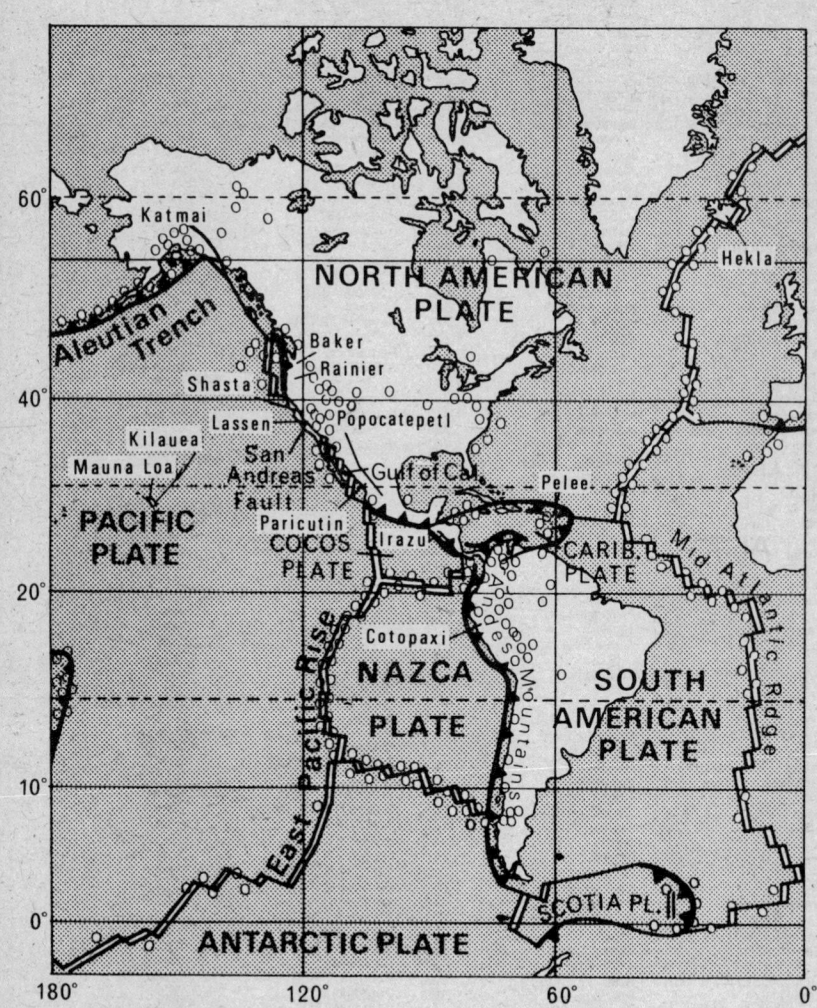

The earth's crust is broken into moving plates of "lithosphere" (litho=rock). There are 7 major plates and at least 12 minor ones (not all of which are shown above). Each plate is more than 50 miles thick and has at least 2 levels. On top, a relatively shallow part can be deformed by brittle breaking or by bending. The deeper bottom part yields to pressure like firm clay. The plates rest on and slide over a layer of viscous material.

### Map Symbols

The plate boundaries shown above are those that are presently active. The *double line* indicates a zone of spreading where plates are moving away from each other. A *single line* represents a slip-strike fault, along which plates are sliding by each other (the San Andreas fault in California and the long line stretching from the western Himalayas toward Africa). A *barbed line* marks subduction zone, an area where one plate is being pushe down under another; the barbs show the direction of m tion of the overriding plate.

Volcanoes and earthquakes tend to occur along pla boundaries, although there are notable exceptions suc as the volcanoes of Hawaii. The *white circles* in the map indicate areas of strong earthquakes, while 20 volcanoe are indicated by name.

Earthquakes are caused by the grinding of the litho pheric plates against each other and by the extensive d formations of the earth's surface that can occur thou sands of miles away from a zone where one plate is ridin over another. Volcanoes are caused by the upwelling material from deep within the lithosphere which break through the thinner plate material of the ocean floor

## lates, Earthquakes and Volcanoes

ological Survey Annual Report 1976).

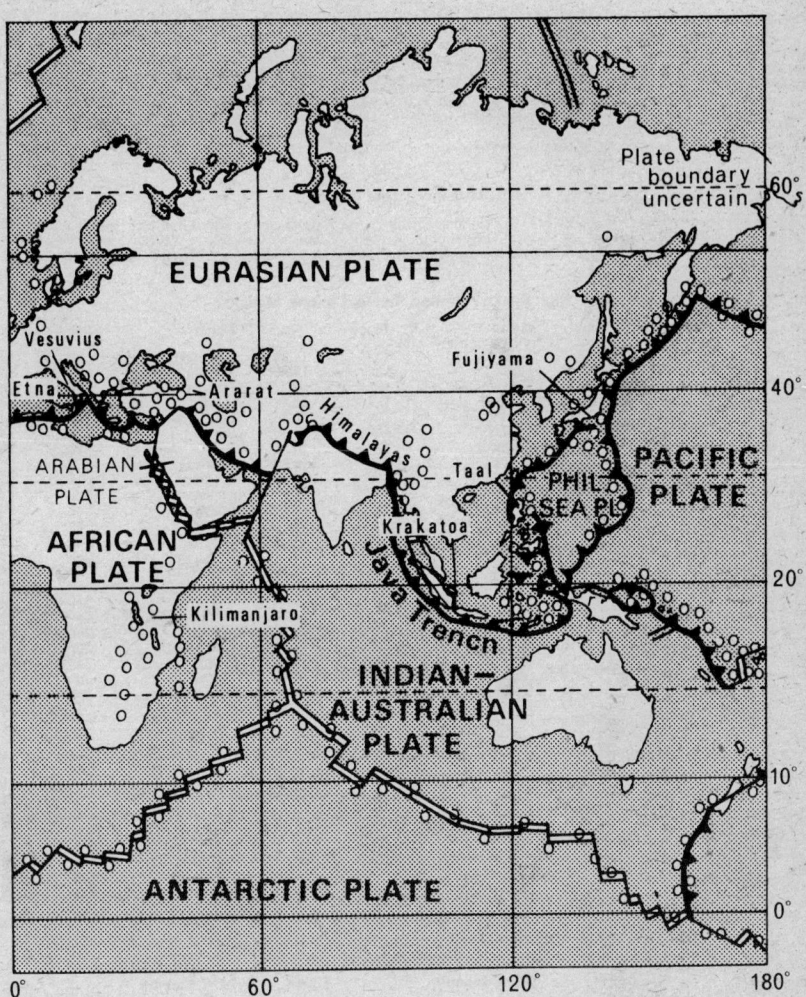

rough weakened plates along the overriding edge of ubduction zones.

Undersea volcanic activity along the Mid-Atlantic Ridge nd East Pacific Rise has broken the once solid litho- phere into plates and is pushing the plates apart at rates stimated at one-half inch to as much as 8 inches a year.

Hawaii, volcanic activity has not been strong enough or idespread enough to break the lithosphere into separate lates.

### Wegener's Hypothesis

The theory of continental drift was first systematically roposed early in the 20th century, although laymen and cientists, noting the close fit between the bulge of South merica and the bight of west Africa, had suggested the ea as early as 1620. In 1912, a German meteorologist

and astronomer, Anton Wegener, postulated that all the earth's continents had once formed a single large land mass that began to break up about 40 million years ago (the breakup is now dated to 190 million years ago).

Wegener's hypothesis was roundly attacked from all sides, particularly because no force was known to be strong enough to break up the original continent and set its pieces adrift. After some 15 years of bitter controversy, Wegener's idea was disregarded by most scientists. Then in the 1960s new data, particularly oceanographic studies that confirmed sea-floor spreading along the Mid-Atlantic Ridge, brought strong support to the theory. Today the idea of continental drift is widely accepted because of a variety of convincing evidence, even though the nature of the powerful forces that cause the drift has yet to be un- derstood.

## Highest and Lowest Continental Altitudes

Source: National Geographic Society, Washington, D.C.

| Continent | Highest point | Feet elevation | Lowest point | Feet below sea level |
|---|---|---|---|---|
| Asia | Mount Everest, Nepal-Tibet | 29,028 | Dead Sea, Israel-Jordan | 1,3 |
| South America | Mount Aconcagua, Argentina | 22,834 | Valdes Peninsula, Argentina | 1 |
| North America | Mount McKinley, Alaska | 20,320 | Death Valley, California | 2 |
| Africa | Kilimanjaro, Tanzania | 19,340 | Lake Assal, Djibouti | 5 |
| Europe | Mount El'brus USSR Caucasus Mts | 18,510 | Caspian Sea, USSR | |
| Antarctica | Vinson Massif | 16,860 | Unknown | |
| Australia | Mount Kosciusko, New South Wales | 7,310 | Lake Eyre, South Australia | |

### Height of Mount Everest

Mt. Everest was considered to be 29,002 ft. tall when Edmund Hillary and Tenzing Norgay scaled it in 1953. This triangulation fig had been accepted since 1850. In 1954 the Surveyor General of the Republic of India set the height at 29,028 ft., plus or minus 10 ft. cause of snow. The National Geographic Society accepts the new figure, but many mountaineering groups still use 29,002 ft.

### High Peaks in United States, Canada, Mexico

| Name | Place | Feet | Name | Place | Feet | Name | Place | Fee |
|---|---|---|---|---|---|---|---|---|
| McKinley | Alas | 20,320 | Crestone | Col | 14,294 | Columbia | Col | 14,0 |
| Logan | Can | 19,850 | Lincoln | Col | 14,286 | Augusta | Alas-Can | 14,0 |
| Citlaltepec (Orizaba) | Mexico | 18,700 | Grays | Col | 14,270 | Missouri | Col | 14,0 |
| St. Elias | Alas-Can | 18,008 | Antero | Col | 14,269 | Humboldt | Col | 14,0 |
| Popocatepetl | Mexico | 17,887 | Torreys | Col | 14,267 | Bierstadt | Col | 14,0 |
| Foraker | Alas | 17,400 | Castle | Col | 14,265 | Sunlight | Col | 14,0 |
| Iztaccihuatl | Mexico | 17,343 | Quandary | Col | 14,265 | Split | Cal | 14,0 |
| Lucania | Can | 17,147 | Evans | Col | 14,264 | Nauhcampatepetl | | |
| King | Can | 16,971 | Longs | Col | 14,256 | (Cofre de Perote) | Mexico | 14,0 |
| Steele | Can | 16,644 | McArthur | Can | 14,253 | Handies | Col | 14, |
| Bona | Alas | 16,550 | Wilson | Col | 14,246 | Culebra | Col | 14, |
| Blackburn | Alas | 16,390 | White | Cal | 14,246 | Langley | Cal | 14,0 |
| Kennedy | Alas | 16,286 | North Palisade | Col | 14,242 | Lindsey | Col | 14,0 |
| Sanford | Alas | 16,237 | Shavano | Col | 14,229 | Middle Palisade | Cal | 14,0 |
| South Buttress | Alas | 15,885 | Belford | Col | 14,197 | Little Bear | Col | 14,0 |
| Wood | Can | 15,885 | Princeton | Col | 14,197 | Sherman | Col | 14,0 |
| Vancouver | Alas-Can | 15,700 | Crestone Needle | Col | 14,197 | Redcloud | Col | 14,0 |
| Churchill | Alas | 15,638 | Yale | Col | 14,196 | Tyndall | Cal | 14,0 |
| Fairweather | Alas | 15,300 | Bross | Col | 14,172 | Pyramid | Col | 14,0 |
| Zinantecatl (Toluca) | Mexico | 15,016 | Kit Carson | Col | 14,165 | Wilson Peak | Col | 14,0 |
| Hubbard | Alas-Can | 15,015 | Wrangell | Alas | 14,163 | Muir | Cal | 14,0 |
| Bear | Alas | 14,831 | Shasta | Cal | 14,162 | Wetterhorn | Col | 14,0 |
| Walsh | Can | 14,780 | Sill | Cal | 14,162 | North Maroon | Col | 14,0 |
| East Buttress | Alas | 14,730 | El Diente | Col | 14,159 | San Luis | Col | 14,0 |
| Matlalcueyetl | Mexico | 14,636 | Maroon | Col | 14,156 | Huron | Col | 14,0 |
| Hunter | Alas | 14,573 | Tabeguache | Col | 14,155 | Holy Cross | Col | 14,0 |
| Alverstone | Alas-Can | 14,565 | Oxford | Col | 14,153 | Colima | Mexico | 14,0 |
| Browne Tower | Alas | 14,530 | Sneffels | Col | 14,150 | Sunshine | Col | 14,0 |
| Whitney | Cal | 14,494 | Point Success | Wash | 14,150 | Grizzly | Col | 14,0 |
| Elbert | Col | 14,433 | Democrat | Col | 14,148 | Barnard | Cal | 13,9 |
| Massive | Col | 14,421 | Capitol | Col | 14,130 | Stewart | Cal | 13,98 |
| Harvard | Col | 14,420 | Liberty Cap | Wash | 14,112 | Keith | Cal | 13,97 |
| Rainier | Wash | 14,410 | Pikes Peak | Col | 14,110 | Ouray | Col | 13,97 |
| Williamson | Cal | 14,375 | Snowmass | Col | 14,092 | Le Conte | Cal | 13,96 |
| Blanca | Col | 14,345 | Windom | Col | 14,087 | Meeker | Col | 13,91 |
| La Plata | Col | 14,336 | Russell | Col | 14,086 | Kennedy | Can | 13,90 |
| Uncompahgre | Col | 14,309 | Eolus | Col | 14,084 | | | |

### South America

| Peak, Country | Feet | Peak, Country | Feet | Peak, Country | Feet |
|---|---|---|---|---|---|
| Aconcagua, Argentina | 22,834 | Laudo, Argentina | 20,997 | Polleras, Argentina | 20,456 |
| Ojos del Salado, Arg.-Chile | 22,572 | Ancohuma, Bolivia | 20,958 | Pular, Chile | 20,423 |
| Bonete, Argentina | 22,546 | Ausangate, Peru | 20,945 | Chani, Argentina | 20,341 |
| Tupungato, Argentina-Chile | 22,310 | Toro, Argentina-Chile | 20,932 | Aucanquilcha, Chile | 20,295 |
| Pissis, Argentina | 22,241 | Illampu, Bolivia | 20,873 | Juncal, Argentina-Chile | 20,276 |
| Mercedario, Argentina | 22,211 | Tres Cruces, Argentina-Chile | 20,853 | Negro, Argentina | 20,184 |
| Huascaran, Peru | 22,205 | Huandoy, Peru | 20,852 | Quela, Argentina | 20,128 |
| Llullaillaco, Argentina-Chile | 22,057 | Parinacota, Bolivia-Chile | 20,768 | Condoriri, Bolivia | 20,095 |
| El Libertador, Argentina | 22,047 | Tortolas, Argentina-Chile | 20,745 | Palermo, Argentina | 20,079 |
| Cachi, Argentina | 22,047 | Ampato, Peru | 20,702 | Solimana, Peru | 20,068 |
| Yerupaja, Peru | 21,709 | Condor, Argentina | 20,669 | San Juan, Argentina-Chile | 20,049 |
| Galan, Argentina | 21,654 | Salcantay, Peru | 20,574 | Sierra Nevada, Arg.-Chile | 20,023 |
| El Muerto, Argentina-Chile | 21,457 | Chimborazo, Ecuador | 20,561 | Antofalla, Argentina | 20,013 |
| Sajama, Bolivia | 21,391 | Huancarhuas, Peru | 20,531 | Marmolejo, Argentina-Chile | 20,013 |
| Nacimiento, Argentina | 21,302 | Famatina, Argentina | 20,505 | Chachani, Peru | 19,931 |
| Illimani, Bolivia | 21,201 | Pumasillo, Peru | 20,492 | Licancabur, Argentina-Chile | 19,425 |
| Coropuna, Peru | 21,083 | Solo, Argentina | 20,492 | | |

The highest point in the West Indies is in the Dominican Republic, Pico Duarte (10,417 ft.)

## Africa, Australia, and Oceania

| Peak, country | Feet | Peak, country | Feet | Peak, country | Feet |
|---|---|---|---|---|---|
| imanjaro, Tanzania | 19,340 | Meru, Tanzania | 14,979 | Toubkal, Morocco | 13,665 |
| nya, Kenya | 17,058 | Wilhelm, New Guinea | 14,793 | Kinabalu, Malaysia | 13,455 |
| argherita Pk., Uganda-Zaire | 16,763 | Karisimbi, Zaire-Rwanda | 14,787 | Kerinci, Sumatra | 12,467 |
| ja, New Guinea | 16,500 | Elgon, Kenya-Uganda | 14,178 | Cook, New Zealand | 12,349 |
| ikora, New Guinea | 15,585 | Batu, Ethiopia | 14,131 | Teide, Canary Islands | 12,198 |
| andala, New Guinea | 15,420 | Guna, Ethiopia | 13,881 | Semeru, Java | 12,060 |
| as Dashan, Ethiopia | 15,158 | Gughe, Ethiopia | 13,780 | Kosciusko, Australia | 7,310 |

## Europe

### Alps

| Peak, country | Feet | Peak, county | Feet | Peak, country | Feet |
|---|---|---|---|---|---|
| ont Blanc, Fr. It. | 15,771 | Breithorn, It., Switz. | 13,665 | Scerscen, Switz. | 13,028 |
| onte Rosa (highest peak of group), Switz. | 15,203 | Bishorn, Switz. | 13,645 | Eiger, Switz. | 13,025 |
| m, Switz. | 14,911 | Jungfrau, Switz. | 13,642 | Jagerhorn, Switz. | 13,024 |
| skamm, It., Switz. | 14,852 | Ecrins, Fr. | 13,461 | Rottalhorn, Switz. | 13,022 |
| eisshorn, Switz. | 14,780 | Monch, Switz. | 13,448 | | |
| schhorn, Switz. | 14,733 | Pollux, Switz. | 13,422 | | |
| atterhorn, Switz. | 14,690 | Schreckhorn, Switz. | 13,379 | | |
| ent Blanche, Switz. | 14,293 | Ober Gabelhorn, Switz. | 13,330 | | |
| adelhorn, Switz. | 14,196 | Gran Paradiso, It. | 13,323 | | |
| and Combin, Switz. | 14,154 | Bernina, It., Switz. | 13,284 | | |
| nzpitze, Switz. | 14,088 | Fiescherhorn, Switz. | 13,283 | | |
| nsteraarhorn, Switz. | 14,022 | Grunhorn, Switz. | 13,266 | | |
| astor, Switz. | 13,865 | Lauteraarhorn, Switz. | 13,261 | | |
| nalrothorn, Switz. | 13,849 | Durrenhorn, Switz. | 13,238 | | |
| ohberghorn, Switz. | 13,842 | Allalinhorn, Switz. | 13,213 | | |
| phubel, Switz. | 13,799 | Weissmies, Switz. | 13,199 | | |
| mpfischhorn, Switz. | 13,776 | Lagginhorn, Switz. | 13,156 | | |
| schorn, Switz. | 13,763 | Zupo, Switz. | 13,120 | | |
| hlhorn, Switz. | 13,747 | Fletschhorn, Switz. | 13,110 | | |
| D'Herens, Switz. | 13,686 | Adlerhorn, Switz. | 13,081 | | |
| | | Gletscherhorn, Switz. | 13,068 | | |
| | | Schalihorn, Switz. | 13,040 | | |

#### Pyrenees

| Peak, country | Feet |
|---|---|
| Aneto, Sp. | 11,168 |
| Posets, Sp. | 11,073 |
| Perdido, Sp. | 11,007 |
| Vignemale, Fr., Sp. | 10,820 |
| Long, Sp. | 10,479 |
| Estats, Sp. | 10,304 |
| Montcalm, Sp. | 10,105 |

#### Caucasus (Europe-Asia)

| Peak, country | Feet |
|---|---|
| El'brus, USSR | 18,510 |
| Shkara, USSR | 17,064 |
| Dykh Tau, USSR | 17,054 |
| Kashtan Tau, USSR | 16,877 |
| Dzhangi Tau, USSR | 16,565 |
| Kazbek, USSR | 16,558 |

## Asia

| Peak | Country | Feet | Peak | Country | Feet | Peak | Country | Feet |
|---|---|---|---|---|---|---|---|---|
| verest | Nepal-Tibet | 29,028 | Kungur | Sinkiang | 25,325 | Badrinath | India | 23,420 |
| 2 (Godwin Austen) | Kashmir | 28,250 | Tirich Mir | Pakistan | 25,230 | Nunkun | Kashmir | 23,410 |
| anchenjunga | India-Nepal | 28,208 | Makalu II | Nepal-Tibet | 25,120 | Lenina Peak | USSR | 23,405 |
| otse I (Everest) | Nepal-Tibet | 27,923 | Minya Konka | China | 24,900 | Pyramid | India-Nepal | 23,400 |
| akalu I | Nepal-Tibet | 27,824 | Kula Gangri | Bhutan-Tibet | 24,784 | Api | Nepal | 23,399 |
| otse II (Everest) | Nepal-Tibet | 27,560 | Changtzu (Everest) | Nepal-Tibet | 24,780 | Pauhunri | India-Tibet | 23,385 |
| haulagiri | Nepal | 26,810 | Muz Tagh Ata | Sinkiang | 24,757 | Trisul | India | 23,360 |
| anaslu I | Nepal | 26,760 | Skyang Kangri | Kashmir | 24,750 | Kangto | India-Tibet | 23,260 |
| ho Oyu | Nepal-Tibet | 26,750 | Communism Peak | USSR | 24,590 | Nyenchhen Thanglha | Tibet | 23,255 |
| anga Parbat | Kashmir | 26,660 | Jongsang Peak | India-Nepal | 24,472 | Trisuli | India | 23,210 |
| nnapurna I | Nepal | 26,504 | Pobedy Peak | Sinkiang-USSR | 24,406 | Pumori | Nepal-Tibet | 23,190 |
| asherbrum | Kashmir | 26,470 | Sia Kangri | Kashmir | 24,350 | Dunagiri | India | 23,184 |
| road | Kashmir | 26,400 | Haramosh Peak | Pakistan | 24,270 | Lombo Kangra | Tibet | 23,165 |
| osainthan | Tibet | 26,287 | Istoro Nal | Pakistan | 24,240 | Saipal | Nepal | 23,100 |
| nnapurna II | Nepal | 26,041 | Tent Peak | India-Nepal | 24,165 | Macha Pucchare | Nepal | 22,958 |
| wachung Kang | Nepal-Tibet | 25,910 | Chomo Lhari | Bhutan-Tibet | 24,040 | Numbar | Nepal | 22,817 |
| steghil Sar | Kashmir | 25,868 | Chamlang | Nepal | 24,012 | Kanjiroba | Nepal | 22,580 |
| malchuli | Nepal | 25,801 | Kabru | India-Nepal | 24,002 | Ama Dablam | Nepal | 22,350 |
| uptse (Everest) | Nepal-Tibet | 25,726 | Alung Gangri | Tibet | 24,000 | Cho Polu | Nepal | 22,093 |
| asherbrum | Kashmir | 25,660 | Baltoro Kangri | Kashmir | 23,990 | Lingtren | Nepal-Tibet | 21,972 |
| anda Devi | India | 25,645 | Mussu Shan | Sinkiang | 23,890 | Khumbutse | Nepal-Tibet | 21,785 |
| akaposhi | Kashmir | 25,550 | Mana | India | 23,860 | Hlako Gangri | Tibet | 21,266 |
| amet | India-Tibet | 25,447 | Baruntse | Nepal | 23,688 | Mt. Grosvenor | China | 21,190 |
| amcha Barwa | Tibet | 25,445 | Nepal Peak | India-Nepal | 23,500 | Thagchhab Gangri | Tibet | 20,970 |
| urla Mandhata | Tibet | 25,355 | Amne Machin | China | 23,490 | Damavand | Iran | 18,606 |
| ugh Muz Tagh | Sinkiang-Tibet | 25,340 | Gauri Sankar | Nepal-Tibet | 23,440 | Ararat | Turkey | 16,946 |

## Antarctica

| Peak | Feet | Peak | Feet | Peak | Feet | Peak | Feet |
|---|---|---|---|---|---|---|---|
| nson Massif | 16,860 | Andrew Jackson | 13,750 | Shear | 13,100 | Campbell | 12,434 |
| yree | 16,290 | Sidley | 13,720 | Odishaw | 13,008 | Don Pedro Christophersen | 12,355 |
| hinn | 15,750 | Ostenso | 13,710 | Donaldson | 12,894 | Lysaght | 12,326 |
| ardner | 15,375 | Minto | 13,668 | Ray | 12,804 | Huggins | 12,247 |
| pperly | 15,100 | Miller | 13,650 | Sellery | 12,779 | Sabine | 12,200 |
| rkpatrick | 14,855 | Long Gables | 13,620 | Waterman | 12,730 | Astor | 12,175 |
| izabeth | 14,698 | Dickerson | 13,517 | Anne | 12,703 | Mohl | 12,172 |
| arkham | 14,290 | Giovinetto | 13,412 | Press | 12,566 | Frankes | 12,064 |
| ell | 14,117 | Wade | 13,400 | Falla | 12,549 | Jones | 12,040 |
| ackellar | 14,098 | Fisher | 13,386 | Rucker | 12,520 | Gjelsvik | 12,008 |
| nderson | 13,957 | Fridtjof Nansen | 13,350 | Goldthwait | 12,510 | Coman | 12,000 |
| entley | 13,934 | Wexler | 13,202 | Morris | 12,500 | | |
| aplan | 13,878 | Lister | 13,200 | Erebus | 12,450 | | |

# How Deep Is the Ocean?

Principal ocean depths. Source: Defense Mapping Agency Hydrographic/Topographic Center

| Name of area | Location | | Meters | Depth Fathoms | Feet | Ship and/or country | Ye |
|---|---|---|---|---|---|---|---|
| **Pacific Ocean** | | | | | | | |
| Mariana Trench | 11°21′N, | 142°12′E | 11,034 | 6,033 | 36,198 | Vityaz (USSR) | 19 |
| Tonga Trench | 23°15.3′S, | 174°44.7′W | 10,882 | 5,950 | 35,702 | Vityaz (USSR) | 19 |
| Kuril Trench | 44°15.2′N, | 150°34.2′E | 10,542 | 5,764 | 34,587 | Vityaz (USSR) | 19 |
| Philippine Trench | 10°24′N, | 126°40′E | 10,539 | 5,763 | 34,578 | Galathea (Danish) | 19 |
| Izu Trench | 30°32′N, | 142°31′E | 10,374 | 5,673 | 34,033 | USS Ramapo | 19 |
| Kermadec Trench | 31°52.8′S, | 177°20.6′W | 10,047 | 5,494 | 32,964 | Vityaz (USSR) | 19 |
| Bonin Trench | 24°30′N, | 143°24′E | 9,156 | 5,005 | 30,032 | Vityaz (USSR) | 19 |
| New Britain Trench | 06°34′S, | 153°55′E | 9,140 | 4,998 | 29,988 | Planet (German) | 19 |
| Yap Trench | 08°33′N, | 138°02′E | 8,527 | 4,662 | 27,976 | Vityaz (USSR) | 19 |
| Japan Trench | 36°08′N, | 142°43′E | 8,412 | 4,597 | 27,591 | Bathymetric Map (USSR) | 19 |
| Palau Trench | 07°40′N, | 135°04′E | 8,138 | 4,449 | 26,693 | Stefan (Germany) | 19 |
| Aleutian Trench | 50°53′N, | 176°23′E | 8,100 | 4,429 | 26,574 | USCGC Bering Strait | 19 |
| Peru Chile Trench | 23°18′S, | 71°41′W | 8,064 | 4,409 | 26,454 | R/V Spencer F. Baird | 19 |
| (Atacama Trench) | 23°27′S, | 71°21′W | 8,064 | 4,409 | 26,454 | IGY | |
| New Hebrides Trench | 20°36′S, | 168°37′E | 7,570 | 4,138 | 24,830 | Planet (Germany) | 19 |
| Ryukyu Trench | 25°15′N, | 128°32′E | 7,507 | 4,105 | 24,629 | Mansyu (Japan) | 19 |
| Mid. America Trench | 14°02′N, | 93°39′W | 6,669 | 3,642 | 21,852 | USS Epce | 19 |
| **Atlantic Ocean** | | | | | | | |
| Puerto Rico Trench | 19°35′N, | 68°17′W | 8,648 | 4,729 | 28,374 | SS Archerfish | 19 |
| Cayman Trench | 19°12′N, | 80°00′W | 7,535 | 4,120 | 24,720 | R/V Vema (U.S.) | 19 |
| So. Sandwich Trench | 55°14′S, | 26°29′W | 8,252 | 4,512 | 27,072 | USS Eltanin | 19 |
| Romanche Gap | 00°16′S, | 18°35′W | 7,864 | 4,300 | 25,800 | R/V Vema | 19 |
| Brazil Basin | 09°10′S, | 23°02′W | 6,119 | 3,346 | 20,076 | R/V Vema (U.S.) | 19 |
| **Indian Ocean** | | | | | | | |
| Java Trench | 10°15′S, | 109°E′(approx.) | 7,725 | 4,224 | 25,344 | Natl Geographic | 1 |
| Ob Trench | (no position) | | 6,874 | 3,759 | 22,553 | Nat'l Geographic | 1 |
| Vema Trench | (no position) | | 6,402 | 3,501 | 21,004 | Nat'l Geographic | 1 |
| Agulhas Basin | (no position) | | 6,195 | 3,388 | 20,325 | Nat'l Geographic | 1 |
| Diamantina Trench | 35°00′S, | 105°35′E | 6,062 | 3,315 | 19,800 | Nat'l Geographic | 19 |
| **Arctic Ocean** | | | | | | | |
| Eurasia Basin | 82°23′N, | 19°31′E | 5,450 | 2,980 | 17,880 | Fidor Lithke (USSR) | 19 |
| **Mediterranean Sea** | | | | | | | |
| Ionian Basin | 36°32′N, | 21°06′E | 5,150 | 2,816 | 16,896 | USS Tanner, | 19 |

## Ocean Areas and Average Depths

Four major bodies of water are recognized by geographers and mapmakers. They are: the Pacific, Atlantic, Indian, an Arctic oceans. The Atlantic and Pacific oceans are considered divided at the equator into the No. and So. Atlantic; the N and So. Pacific. The Arctic Ocean is the name for waters north of the continental land masses in the region of the Arctic C cle.

| | Sq. miles | Avg. depth in feet | | Sq. miles | Avg. dept in fee |
|---|---|---|---|---|---|
| Pacific Ocean | 64,186,300 | 13,739 | Hudson Bay | 281,900 | 30 |
| Atlantic Ocean | 33,420,000 | 12,257 | East China Sea | 256,600 | 62 |
| Indian Ocean | 28,350,500 | 12,704 | Andaman Sea | 218,100 | 3,66 |
| Arctic Ocean | 5,105,700 | 4,362 | Black Sea | 196,100 | 3,90 |
| South China Sea | 1,148,500 | 4,802 | Red Sea | 174,900 | 1,76 |
| Caribbean Sea | 971,400 | 8,448 | North Sea | 164,900 | 30 |
| Mediterranean Sea | 969,100 | 4,926 | Baltic Sea | 147,500 | 18 |
| Bering Sea | 873,000 | 4,893 | Yellow Sea | 113,500 | 12 |
| Gulf of Mexico | 582,100 | 5,297 | Persian Gulf | 88,800 | 32 |
| Sea of Okhotsk | 537,500 | 3,192 | Gulf of California | 59,100 | 2,37 |
| Sea of Japan | 391,100 | 5,468 | | | |

The Malayan Sea is not considered a geographical entity but a term used for convenience for waters between the South Pa cific and the Indian Ocean.

## Continental Statistics

Source: National Geographic Society, Washington, D.C.

| Continents | Area (sq. mi.) | % of Earth | Population (est.) | % World total | Highest point (in feet) | Lowest point |
|---|---|---|---|---|---|---|
| Asia | 16,988,000 | 29.5 | 2,499,700,000 | 59.2 | Everest, 29,028 | Dead Sea, −1,302 |
| Africa | 11,506,000 | 20.0 | 436,000,000 | 10.3 | Kilimanjaro, 19,340 | Lake Assal, −512 |
| North America | 9,390,000 | 16.3 | 357,000,000 | 8.5 | McKinley, 20,320 | Death Valley, −282 |
| South America | 6,795,000 | 11.8 | 228,000,000 | 5.4 | Aconcagua, 22,834 | Valdes Penin., −131 |
| Europe | 3,745,000 | 6.5 | 674,300,000 | 16.0 | El'brus, 18,510 | Caspian Sea, −92 |
| Australia | 2,968,000 | 5.2 | 14,300,000 | 0.3 | Kosciusko, 7,310 | Lake Eyre, −52 |
| Antarctica | 5,500,000 | 9.6 | — | — | Vinson Massif, 16,860 | Not Known |
| **Est. World Population** | | | 4,219,000,000 | | | |

## Important Islands and Their Areas

**Source:** National Georgraphic Society, Washington, D.C.

Figure in parentheses shows rank among the world's 10 largest islands, some islands have not been surveyed accurately; in h cases estimated areas are shown.

### Location-Ownership
#### Area in square miles

### Arctic Ocean
#### Canadian

| | |
|---|---|
| el Heiberg | 16,671 |
| ffin (5) | 195,928 |
| nks | 27,038 |
| thurst | 6,194 |
| von | 21,331 |
| esmere (10) | 75,767 |
| Iville | 16,274 |
| nce of Wales | 12,872 |
| merset | 9,570 |
| uthampton | 15,913 |
| toria (9) | 83,896 |

#### USSR

| | |
|---|---|
| anz Josef Land | 8,000 |
| vaya Zemlya (two is.) | 35,000 |
| angel | 2,800 |

#### Norwegian

| | |
|---|---|
| albard | 23,940 |
| Nordaustlandet | 5,410 |
| Spitsbergen | 15,060 |

### Atlantic Ocean

| | |
|---|---|
| icosti, Canada | 3,066 |
| ension, UK | 34 |
| es, Portugal | 902 |
| aial | 67 |
| Sao Miguel | 291 |
| hamas | 5,380 |
| rmuda Is., UK | 20 |
| ck, Rhode Island | 10 |
| nary Is., Spain | 2,808 |
| Fuerteventura | 668 |
| Gran Canaria | 592 |
| Tenerife | 795 |
| pe Breton, Canada | 3,981 |
| pe Verde Is. | 1,557 |
| eroe Is., Denmark | 540 |
| lkland Is., UK | 4,618 |
| rnando de Noronha | |
| Archipelago, Brazil | 7 |
| eenland, Denmark (1) | 840,000 |
| land | 39,768 |
| ng Island, N.Y. | 1,396 |
| arcias Nguema Biyogo, | |
| uatorial Guinea | 785 |
| adeira Is., Portugal | 307 |
| arajo, Brazil | 15,528 |
| artha's Vineyard, Mass. | 91 |
| unt Desert, Me. | 108 |
| ntucket, Mass. | 46 |
| wfoundland, Canada | 42,031 |
| nce Edward, Canada | 2,184 |
| . Helena, UK | 47 |
| uth Georgia, UK | 1,450 |
| erra del Fuego, Chile | |
| and Argentina | 17,800 |
| stan da Cunha, UK | 40 |

#### British Isles

| | |
|---|---|
| eat Britain, mainland (8) | 84,186 |
| annel Islands | 75 |
| Guernsey | 24 |
| Jersey | 45 |
| Sark | 2 |
| brides | 2,744 |
| land | 32,598 |
| rish Republic | 27,136 |
| Northern Ireland | 5,462 |

| | |
|---|---|
| Man | 227 |
| Orkney Is. | 390 |
| Scilly Is. | 6 |
| Shetland Is. | 567 |
| Skye | 670 |
| Wight | 147 |

### Baltic Sea

| | |
|---|---|
| Aland Is., Finland | 581 |
| Bornholm, Denmark | 227 |
| Gotland, Sweden | 1,164 |

### Caribbean Sea

| | |
|---|---|
| Antigua, UK | 108 |
| Aruba, Netherlands | 75 |
| Barbados | 166 |
| Cuba | 44,218 |
| Isle of Pines | 1,182 |
| Curacao, Netherlands | 171 |
| Dominica, UK | 290 |
| Guadeloupe, France | 687 |
| Hispaniola, Haiti and | |
| Dominican Republic | 29,530 |
| Jamaica | 4,232 |
| Martinique, France | 425 |
| Puerto Rico, U.S. | 3,4?5 |
| Tobago | ? |
| Trinidad | 1 |
| Virgin Is., UK | ? |
| Virgin Is., U.S. | 1?3 |

### Indian Ocean

| | |
|---|---|
| Andaman Is., India | 2,500 |
| Madagascar (4) | 226,657 |
| Mauritius | 720 |
| Pemba, Tanzania | 380 |
| Reunion, France | 969 |
| Seychelles | 107 |
| Sri Lanka | 25,332 |
| Zanzibar, Tanzania | 640 |

### Persian Gulf

| | |
|---|---|
| Bahrain | 231 |

### Mediterranean Sea

| | |
|---|---|
| Balearic Is., Spain | 1,936 |
| Corfu, Greece | 229 |
| Corsica, France | 3,365 |
| Crete, Greece | 3,186 |
| Cyprus | 3,572 |
| Elba, Italy | 86 |
| Euboea, Greece | 1,409 |
| Malta | 122 |
| Rhodes, Greece | 542 |
| Sardinia, Italy | 9,262 |
| Sicily, Italy | 9,822 |

### Pacific Ocean

| | |
|---|---|
| Aleutian Is., U.S. | 6,821 |
| Adak | 289 |
| Amchitka | 121 |
| Attu | 388 |
| Kanaga | 135 |
| Kiska | 110 |
| Tanaga | 209 |
| Umnak | 675 |
| Unalaska | 1,064 |
| Unimak | 1,600 |
| Canton, U.S., UK* | 4 |
| Caroline Is., U.S. trust terr. | 463 |
| Christmas, U.S., UK* | 94 |
| Diomede, Big, USSR. | 11 |

| | |
|---|---|
| Diomede, Little, U.S. | 2 |
| Easter, Chile | 68 |
| Fiji | 7,055 |
| Vanua Levi | 2,242 |
| Viti Levu. | 4,109 |
| Funafuti, UK, U.S.* | 2 |
| Galapagos Is., Ecuador | 3,043 |
| Guadalcanal, UK | 2,500 |
| Hainan, China. | 13,000 |
| Hawaiian Is., U.S. | 6,450 |
| Hawaii. | 4,037 |
| Oahu | 593 |
| Hong Kong, UK | 29 |
| Japan | 143,750 |
| Hokkaido | 30,100 |
| Honshu (7) | 87,804 |
| Iwo Jima | 9 |
| Kyushu | 14,154 |
| Okinawa | 460 |
| Shikoku | 7,053 |
| Kodiak, U.S. | 3,670 |
| Mariana Is., U.S. trust terr. | |
| excluding Guam | 182 |
| Guam, U.S. | 209 |
| Marquesas Is., France | 492 |
| Marshall Is., U.S. trust terr. | 69 |
| Bikini* | 2 |
| Nauru | 8 |
| New Caledonia, France | 6,530 |
| New Guinea (2) | 305,577 |
| New Hebrides, UK, Fr. | 5,700 |
| New Zealand | 103,747 |
| Chatham | 372 |
| North | 44,190 |
| South | 58,192 |
| Stewart | 674 |
| Philippines | 115,830 |
| Leyte | 2,787 |
| Luzon | 40,880 |
| Mindanao | 36,775 |
| Mindoro | 3,790 |
| Negros | 4,907 |
| Palawan | 4,554 |
| Panay | 4,446 |
| Samar. | 5,050 |
| Quemoy, Taiwan | 56 |
| Sakhalin, USSR | 29,500 |
| Samoa Is. | 1,177 |
| American Samoa | 76 |
| Tutuila | 52 |
| Western Samoa | 1,101 |
| Savaii. | 670 |
| Upolu. | 429 |
| Santa Catalina, U.S. | 72 |
| Tahiti, France | 402 |
| Taiwan. | 13,812 |
| Tasmania, Australia | 26,383 |
| Tonga Is. | 270 |
| Vancouver, Canada | 12,079 |

### East Indies

| | |
|---|---|
| Bali, Indonesia | 2,147 |
| Borneo, Indonesia- | |
| Malaysia, UK (3) | 280,107 |
| Celebes, Indonesia | 69,255 |
| Java, Indonesia | 48,763 |
| Madura, Indonesia | 2,113 |
| Moluccas, Indonesia | 28,766 |
| New Britain, Papua New | |
| Guinea | 14,050 |
| New Ireland, Papua New | |
| Guinea | 2,700 |
| Sumatra, Indonesia (6). | 182,860 |
| Timor | 11,570 |

*Atolls: Bikini (lagoon area, 230 sq. mi., land area 2 sq. mi.), U.S. Trust Territory of the Pacific Islands; Canton (lagoon 20 sq. mi., land sq. mi.), U.S. and UK; Christmas (lagoon 140 sq. mi., land 94 sq. mi.), U.S. and UK; Funafuti (lagoon 84 sq. mi., land 2 sq. mi.), U.S. d UK.

**Australia**, often called an island, is a continent. Its mainland area is 2,941,526 sq. mi.

**Islands in minor waters**; Manhattan (23 sq. mi.) Staten (58 sq. mi.) and Governors (173 acres), all in New York Harbor, U.S.; Isle Royale 09 sq. mi.), Lake Superior, U.S.; Manitoulin (1,068 sq. mi.), Lake Huron, Canada; Pinang (110 sq. mi.), Strait of Malacca, Malaysia; agapore (224 sq. mi.), Singapore Strait, Singapore.

## Major Rivers in North America
Source: U.S. Geological Survey

| River | Source or Upper Limit of Length | Outflow | Mile |
|---|---|---|---|
| Alabama | Gilmer County, Ga. | Mobile River | 7 |
| Albany | Lake St. Joseph, Ont., Can. | James Bay | 3 |
| Allegheny | Potter County, Pa. | Ohio River | 3 |
| Altamaha-Ocmulgee | Junction of Yellow and South Rivers, Newton County, Ga. | Atlantic Ocean | 3 |
| Apalachicola-Chattahoochee | Towns County, Ga. | Gulf of Mexico, Fla. | 5 |
| Arkansas | Lake County, Col. | Mississippi River, Ark. | 1,4 |
| Assiniboine | Eastern Saskatchewan | Red River | 4 |
| Attawapiskat | Attawapiskat, Ont., Can. | James Bay | 4 |
| Big Black (Miss.) | Webster County, Miss. | Mississippi River | 3 |
| Big Horn | Junction of Wind and Popo Agie Rivers, Fremont County, Wyo. | Yellowstone River, Mon. | 3 |
| Black (N.W.T.) | Contwoyto Lake | Chantrey Inlet | 6 |
| Brazos | Junction of Salt and Double Mountain Forks, Stonewall County, Tex. | Gulf of Mexico | 8 |
| Canadian | Las Animas County, Col. | Arkansas River, Okla. | 9 |
| Cedar (Iowa) | Dodge County, Minn. | Iowa River, Ia. | 3 |
| Cheyenne | Junction of Antelope Creek and Dry Fork, Converse County, Wyo. | Missouri River | 2 |
| Churchill | Methy Lake | Hudson Bay | 1,0 |
| Cimarron | Colfax County, N.M. | Arkansas River, Okla. | 6 |
| Clark Fork-Pend Oreille | Silver Bow County, Mon. | Columbia River, B.C. | 5 |
| Colorado (Ariz.) | Rocky Mountain National Park, Col. (90 miles in Mexico) | Gulf of Cal., Mexico | 1,4 |
| Colorado (Texas) | West Texas | Matagorda Bay | 8 |
| Columbia | Columbia Lake, British Columbia | Pacific Ocean, bet. Ore. and Wash. | 1,2 |
| Columbia, Upper | Columbia Lake, British Columbia | To mouth of Snake River | 8 |
| Connecticut | Third Connecticut Lake, N.H. | L.I. Sound, Conn. | 4 |
| Coppermine (N.W.T.) | Lac de Gras | Coronation Gulf (Atlantic Ocean) | 5 |
| Cumberland | Letcher County, Ky. | Ohio River | 7 |
| Delaware | Schoharie County, N.Y. | Liston Point, Delaware Bay | 3 |
| Fraser | Near Mount Robson (on Continental Divide) | Strait of Georgia | |
| Gila | Catron County, N.M. | Colorado River, Ariz. | |
| Green (Ut.-Wyo.) | Junction of Wells and Trail Creeks, Sublette County, Wyo. | Colorado River, Ut. | 7 |
| Hamilton (Lab.) | Lake Ashuanipi | Atlantic Ocean | 6 |
| Hudson | Henderson Lake, Essex County, N.Y. | Upper N.Y. Bay, N.Y.,-N.J. | 3 |
| Illinois | St. Joseph County, Ind. | Mississippi River | 4 |
| James (N.D.-S.D.) | Wells County, N.D. | Missouri River, S.D. | 7 |
| James (Va.) | Junction of Jackson and Cowpasture Rivers, Botetourt County, Va. | Hampton Roads | 3 |
| Kanawha-New | Junction of North and South Forks of New River, N.C. | Ohio River | 3 |
| Kentucky | Junction of North and Middle Forks, Lee County, Ky. | Ohio River | 2 |
| Klamath | Lake Ewauna, Klamath Falls, Ore. | Pacific Ocean | 2 |
| Koyukuk | Endicott Mountains, Alaska | Yukon River | 4 |
| Kuskokwim | Alaska Range | Kuskokwim Bay | 6 |
| Liard | Southern Yukon, Alaska | Mackenzie River | 6 |
| Little Missouri | Crook County, Wyo. | Missouri River | 5 |
| Mackenzie | Great Slave Lake | Arctic Ocean | 9 |
| Milk | Junction of North and South Forks, Alberta Province | Missouri River, Mon. | 6 |
| Minnesota | Big Stone Lake, Minn. | Mississippi River, St. Paul, Minn. | 3 |
| Mississippi | Lake Itasca, Minn. | Mouth of Southwest Pass | 2,3 |
| Mississippi, Upper | Lake Itasca, Minn. | To mouth of Missouri R. | 1,1 |
| Mississippi-Missouri-Red Rock | Source of Red Rock, Beaverhead Co., Mon. | Mouth of Southwest Pass | 3,7 |
| Missouri | Junction of Jefferson, Madison, and Gallatin Rivers, Madison County, Mon. | Mississippi River | 2,3 |
| Missouri-Red Rock | Source of Red Rock, Beaverhead Co., Mon. | Mississippi River | 2,5 |
| Mobile-Alabama-Coosa | Gilmer County, Ga. | Mobile Bay | 7 |
| Nelson (Manitoba) | Lake Winnipeg | Hudson Bay | 4 |
| Neosho | Morris County, Kan. | Arkansas River, Okla. | 4 |
| Niobrara | Niobrara County, Wyo. | Missouri River, Neb. | 4 |
| North Canadian | Union County, N.M. | Canadian River, Okla. | 7 |
| North Platte | Junction of Grizzly and Little Grizzly Creeks, Jackson County, Col. | Platte River, Neb. | 6 |
| Ohio | Junction of Allegheny and Monongahela Rivers, Pittsburgh, Pa. | Mississippi River, Ill.-Ky. | 9 |
| Ohio-Allegheny | Potter County, Pa. | Mississippi River | 1,3 |
| Osage | East-central Kansas | Missouri River, Mo. | 5 |
| Ottawa | Lake Capimitchigama | St. Lawrence | 7 |
| Ouachita | Polk County, Ark. | Red River, La. | 6 |
| Peace | Stikine Mountains, B.C. | Slave River | 1,1 |
| Pearl | Neshoba County, Miss. | Gulf of Mexico, Miss.-La. | 4 |
| Pecos | Mora County, N.M. | Rio Grande, Tex. | 7 |
| Pee Dee-Yadkin | Watauga County, N.C. | Winyah Bay, S.C. | 4 |
| Pend Oreille | Near Butte, Mon. | Columbia River | 4 |
| Platte | Junction of North and South Platte Rivers, Neb. | Missouri River, Neb. | 3 |
| Porcupine | Ogilvie Mountains, Alaska | Yukon River, Alaska | 4 |
| Potomac | Garrett County, Md. | Chesapeake Bay | 3 |
| Powder | Junction of South and Middle Forks, Wyo. | Yellowstone River, Mon. | 3 |

| River | Source or Upper Limit of Length | Outflow | Miles |
|---|---|---|---|
| Red (Okla.-Tex.-La.) | Curry County, N.M. | Mississippi River | 1,270 |
| Red River of the North | Junction of Otter Tail and Bois de Sioux Rivers, Wilkin County, Minn. | Lake Winnipeg, Manitoba | 545 |
| Republican | Junction of North Fork and Arikaree River, Neb. | Kansas River, Kan. | 445 |
| Rio Grande | San Juan County, Col. | Gulf of Mexico | 1,885 |
| Roanoke | Junction of North and South Forks, Montgomery County, Va. | Albemarle Sound, N.C. | 380 |
| Rock (Ill.-Wis.) | Dodge County, Wis. | Mississippi River, Ill. | 300 |
| Sabine | Junction of South and Caddo Forks, Hunt County, Tex. | Sabine Lake, Tex.-La. | 380 |
| Sacramento | Siskiyou County, Cal. | Suisun Bay | 377 |
| St. Francis | Iron County, Mo. | Mississippi River, Ark. | 425 |
| St. Lawrence | Lake Ontario | Gulf of St. Lawrence (Atlantic Ocean) | 800 |
| Salmon (Idaho) | Custer County, Ida. | Snake River, Ida. | 420 |
| San Joaquin | Junction of South and Middle Forks, Madera County, Cal. | Suisun Bay | 350 |
| San Juan | Silver Lake, Archuleta County, Col. | Colorado River, Ut. | 360 |
| Santee-Wateree-Catawba | McDowell County, N.C. | Atlantic Ocean, S.C. | 538 |
| Saskatchewan, North | Rocky Mountains | Lake Winnipeg | 1,100 |
| Saskatchewan, South | Rocky Mountains | Lake Winnipeg | 1,205 |
| Savannah | Junction of Seneca and Tugaloo Rivers, Anderson County, S.C. | Atlantic Ocean, Ga.-S.C. | 314 |
| Severn (Ontario) | Sandy Lake | Hudson Bay | 610 |
| Smoky Hill | Cheyenne County, Col. | Kansas River, Kan. | 540 |
| Snake | Teton County, Wyo. | Columbia River, Wash. | 1,038 |
| South Platte | Junction of South and Middle Forks, Park County, Col. | Platte River, Neb. | 424 |
| Susitna | Alaska Range | Cook Inlet | 300 |
| Susquehanna | Otsego Lake, Otsego County, N.Y. | Chesapeake Bay, Md. | 444 |
| Tallahatchie | Tippah County, Miss. | Yazoo River, Miss. | 301 |
| Tanana | Wrangell Mountains | Yukon River, Alaska | 620 |
| Tennessee | Junction of French Broad and Holston Rivers | Ohio River, Ky. | 652 |
| Tennessee-French Broad | Bland County, Va. | Ohio River | 900 |
| Tombigbee | Prentiss County, Miss. | Mobile River, Ala. | 525 |
| Trinity | North of Dallas, Tex. | Galveston Bay, Tex. | 360 |
| Wabash | Darke County, Oh. | Ohio River, Ill.-Ind. | 529 |
| Washita | Hemphill County, Tex. | Red River, Okla. | 500 |
| White (Ark.-Mo.) | Madison County, Ark. | Mississippi River | 720 |
| Willamette | Douglas County, Ore. | Columbia River | 270 |
| Wisconsin | LeVieux Desert, Vilas County, Wis. | Mississippi River | 430 |
| Yellowstone | Park County, Wyo. | Missouri River, N.D. | 671 |
| Yukon | Junction of Lewes and Pelly Rivers, Yukon | Bering Sea, Alaska | 1,770 |

## Flows of Largest U.S. Rivers

Source: U.S. Geological Survey (average discharges for the period 1941-70). Ranked according to average discharge in cubic feet per second (cfs) at mouth.

| Rank | River | Average discharge | Length[a] (miles) | Drainage area | Most distant source | Maximum discharge at gauging station farthest downstream | Date |
|---|---|---|---|---|---|---|---|
| 1 | Mississippi | [b]640,000 | [c]3,710 | [d]1,247,300 | Beaverhead Co., Mont. | 2,080,000 | 2-17-37 |
| 2 | Columbia | 262,000 | 1,243 | 258,000 | Columbia Lake, B.C. | 1,240,000 | June 1894 |
| 3 | Ohio | 258,000 | 1,306 | 203,900 | Potter Co., Pa. | 1,850,000 | 2-1-37 |
| 4 | St. Lawrence | [e]243,000 | — | [e]302,000 | | [f]350,000 | July 1973 |
| 5 | Yukon | [g]240,000 | 1,770 | 327,600 | Coast Mountains, B.C. | 1,030,000 | 6-22-64 |
| 6 | [h]Atchafalaya | 183,000 | 135 | 95,105 | Curry Co., N. Mex. | | |
| 7 | Missouri | 76,300 | 2,533 | 529,400 | Beaverhead Co., Mont. | 892,000 | June 1844 |
| 8 | Tennessee | [m]64,000 | 900 | 40,910 | Bland Co., Va. | 500,000 | 2-17-48 |
| 9 | Red | 62,300 | 1,270 | 93,244 | Curry Co., N. Mex. | 233,000 | 4-17-45 |
| 10 | Kuskokwim | 62,000 | 680 | 49,000 | Alaska Range, Alas. | 392,000 | 6-5-64 |
| 11 | Mobile | 61,400 | 780 | 43,800 | Gilmer, Co., Ga. | | |
| 12 | Snake | 50,000 | 1,038 | 109,000 | Teton Co., Wyo. | 409,000 | June 1894 |
| 13 | Arkansas | 45,100 | 1,459 | 160,600 | Lake Co., Col. | 536,000 | 5-27-43 |
| 14 | Copper | [j]43,000 | 280 | 24,000 | Alaska Range, Alas. | 265,000 | 7-15-71 |
| 15 | Tanana | [k]41,000 | 620 | ~44,000 | Wrangell Mtn., Alas. | 186,000 | 8-18-67 |
| 16 | Susitna | [l]40,000 | 300 | 20,000 | Alaska Range, Alas. | 173,000 | 7-1-75 |
| 17 | Susquehanna | 37,190 | 444 | 27,570 | Otsego Co., N.Y. | 1,080,000 | 6-23-72 |
| 18 | Willamette | 35,660 | 270 | 11,200 | Douglas Co., Ore. | 500,000 | 12-4-1861 |
| 19 | Alabama | 32,400 | 735 | 22,600 | Gilmer Co., Ga. | 267,000 | 3-7-61 |
| 20 | White | 32,100 | 720 | 28,000 | Madison Co., Ark. | 343,000 | 4-17-45 |
| 21 | Wabash | 30,400 | 529 | 33,150 | Darke Co., Oh. | 428,000 | 3-30-13 |
| 22 | Pend Oreille | 29,900 | 490 | 25,820 | Near Butte, Mont. | 171,300 | 6-13-48 |
| 23 | Tombigbee | 27,300 | 525 | 20,100 | Prentiss Co., Miss. | 280,000 | 1874 and 1900 |
| 24 | Cumberland | [n]26,900 | 720 | 18,080 | Letcher Co., Ky. | 201,000 | 2-18-50 |
| 25 | Stikine | [n]26,000 | 310 | 20,000 | Stikine Range, B.C. | 120,000 | 6-26-55 |
| 26 | Sacramento | — | 377 | 27,100 | Siskiyou Co., Cal. | [o]332,000 | 12-25-64 |
| 27 | Apalachicola | 24,700 | 524 | 19,600 | Towns Co., Ga. | 293,000 | 3-20-29 |
| 28 | Illinois | 22,800 | 420 | 27,900 | St. Joseph Co., Ind. | 123,000 | May 1943 |
| 29 | Koyukuk | [p]22,000 | 470 | 32,400 | Endicott Mtns., Alas. | 266,000 | 6-6-64 |
| 30 | Porcupine | [q]20,000 | 460 | 45,000 | Ogilvie Mtns., Alas. | 299,000 | 5-24-73 |
| 31 | Hudson | 19,500 | 306 | 13,370 | Essex Co., N.Y. | 215,000 | 3-19-36 |
| 32 | Allegheny | 19,290 | 325 | 11,700 | Potter Co., Pa. | 365,000 | 3-18-36 |
| 33 | Delaware | [r]17,200 | 390 | 11,440 | Schoharie Co., N.Y. | 329,000 | 8-20-55 |

(a) Because river lengths and methods of measurement may change from time to time, the length figures given are subject to revision; (b) about 25 percent of flow occurs in the Atchafalaya River; (c) the length from mouth to source of the Mississippi River in Minnesota is 2,348 miles; (d) at Baptiste Collete Bayou, Louisiana; (e) at international boundary lat. 45°; (f) maximum monthly discharge; (g) period

1957-70; (h) continuation of Red River; (i) flow of Ouachita River added; (j) period 1956-69; (k) period 1962-69; (l) based on records of Chulitna, Talkeetna, and Yetna rivers; (m) period 1931-60; (n) period 1954-63; summer records only; (o) discharge of American River not included (p) period 1960-69; (q) period 1964-69; (r) at Liston Point on Delaware Bay.

## Large Rivers in Canada

Source: "Inland Waters Directorate," Department of Fisheries and the Environment.
(Ranked according to average discharge in cubic feet per second (cfs). Figures indicate discharge and drainage to river mouths.

| Rank | River | Average discharge | Length (miles | Drainage area (sq. mi.) |
|---|---|---|---|---|
| 1 | St. Lawrence (to Nicolet) | 355,000 | 1,900 | 396,000[1] |
| 2 | Mackenzie | 350,000 | 2,635 | 690,000 |
| 3 | Fraser | 128,000 | 850 | 89,900[2] |
| 4 | Columbia (International Boundary) | 102,000 | 498 | 59,700[3] |
| 5 | Nelson | 100,000 | 1,600 | 437,000[4] |
| 6 | Kokosak | 85,500 | 543 | 51,500 |
| 7 | Yukon (International Boundary) | 83,000 | 714 | 115,000[5] |
| 8 | Ottawa | 70,500 | 790 | 56,500 |
| 9 | Saguenay (to head of Peribonea) | 62,200 | 434 | 34,000 |
| 10 | Skeena | 62,100 | 300 | 21,200 |

(1) Including 195,000 sq. mi. in U.S. (2) Including diversion. (3) Including 20,000 sq. mi. in U.S. (4) Including 69,500 sq. mi. in U.S. (5) Including 9,000 sq. mi. in U.S.

## Principal World Rivers

Source: National Geographic Society, Washington, D.C. (length in miles)

| River | Outflow | Lgth | River | Outflow | Lgth | River | Outflow | Lgth |
|---|---|---|---|---|---|---|---|---|
| Albany | James Bay | 610 | Irrawaddy | Bay of Bengal | 1,300 | Rhine | North Sea | 820 |
| Amazon | Atlantic Ocean | 4,000 | Japura | Amazon River | 1,750 | Rhone | Gulf of Lions | 505 |
| Amu | Aral Sea | 1,578 | Jordan | Dead Sea | 200 | Rio de la Plata | Atlantic Ocean | 150 |
| Amur | Tatar Strait | 2,700 | Kootenay | Columbia River | 485 | Rio Grande | Gulf of Mexico | 1,885 |
| Angara | Yenisey River | 1,151 | Lena | Laptev Sea | 2,680 | Rio Roosevelt | Aripuana | 400 |
| Arkansas | Mississippi | 1,459 | Loire | Bay of Biscay | 634 | Saguenay | St. Lawrence R. | 434 |
| Back | Arctic Ocean | 605 | Mackenzie | Arctic Ocean | 2,635 | St. John | Bay of Fundy | 418 |
| Brahmaputra | Bay of Bengal | 1,800 | Madeira | Amazon River | 2,013 | St. Lawrence | Gulf of St. Law. | 800 |
| Bug, Southern | Dnieper River | 532 | Magdalena | Caribbean Sea | 956 | Salween | Andaman Sea | 1,500 |
| Bug, Western | Wisla River | 481 | Marne | Seine River | 326 | Sao Francisco | Atlantic Ocean | 1,988 |
| Canadian | Arkansas River | 906 | Mekong | S. China Sea | 2,600 | Saskatchewan | Lake Winnipeg | 1,205 |
| Churchill, Man. | Hudson Bay | 1,000 | Meuse | North Sea | 580 | Seine | English Chan. | 482 |
| Churchill, Que. | Atlantic Ocean | 532 | Mississippi | Gulf of Mexico | 2,348 | Shannon | Atlantic Ocean | 230 |
| Colorado | Gulf of Calif. | 1,450 | Missouri | Mississippi | 2,533 | Snake | Columbia River | 1,038 |
| Columbia | Pacific Ocean | 1,243 | Murray-Darling | Indian Ocean | 2,310 | Sungari | Amur River | 1,150 |
| Congo | Atlantic Ocean | 2,718 | Negro | Amazon | 1,400 | Syr | Aral Sea | 1,370 |
| Danube | Black Sea | 1,776 | Nelson | Hudson Bay | 1,600 | Tajo, Tagus | Atlantic Ocean | 626 |
| Dnieper | Black Sea | 1,420 | Niger | Gulf of Guinea | 2,600 | Tennessee | Ohio River | 900 |
| Dniester | Black Sea | 877 | Nile | Mediterranean | 4,145 | Thames | North Sea | 215 |
| Don | Sea of Azov | 1,224 | Ob-Irtysh | Gulf of Ob | 3,460 | Tiber | Tyrrhenian Sea | 252 |
| Drava | Danube River | 447 | Oder | Baltic Sea | 567 | Tigris | Euphrates | 1,180 |
| Dvina, North | White Sea | 824 | Ohio | Mississippi | 1,306 | Tisza | Danube River | 600 |
| Dvina, West | Gulf of Riga | 634 | Orange | Atlantic Ocean | 1,300 | Tocantins | Para River | 1,677 |
| Ebro | Mediterranean | 565 | Orinoco | Atantic Ocean | 1,600 | Ural | Caspian Sea | 1,575 |
| Elbe | North Sea | 724 | Ottawa | St. Lawrence R. | 790 | Uruguay | Rio de la Plata | 1,000 |
| Euphrates | Persian Gulf | 2,235 | Paraguay | Parana River | 1,584 | Volga | Caspian Sea | 2,290 |
| Fraser | Str. of Georgia | 850 | Parana | Rio de la Plata | 2,500 | Weser | North Sea | 454 |
| Gambia | Atlantic Ocean | 700 | Peace | Slave River | 1,195 | Wisla | Bay of Danzig | 675 |
| Ganges | Bay of Bengal | 1,560 | Pilcomayo | Paraguay River | 1,000 | Yangtze | E. China Sea | 3,400 |
| Garonne | Bay of Biscay | 357 | Po | Adriatic Sea | 405 | Yellow (See Huang) | | |
| Hsi | S. China Sea | 1,200 | Purus | Amazon River | 2,100 | Yenisey | Kara Sea | 2,566 |
| Huang | Yellow Sea | 2,900 | Red | Mississippi | 1,270 | Yukon | Bering Sea | 1,979 |
| Indus | Arabian Sea | 1,800 | Red River of N. | Lake Winnipeg | 545 | Zambezi | Indian Ocean | 1,700 |

## Famous Waterfalls

Source: National Geographic Society, Washington, D.C.

The earth has thousands of waterfalls, some of considerable magnitude. Their importance is determined not only by height but volume of flow, steadiness of flow, crest width, whether the water drops sheerly or over a sloping surface, and in one leap or a succession of leaps. A series of low falls flowing over a considerable distance is known as a cascade.

Sete Quedas or Guaira is the world's greatest waterfall when its mean annual low (estimated at 470,000 cusecs, cubic feet per second) is combined with height. A greater volume of water passes over Boyoma Falls (Stanley Falls), though not one of its seven cataracts, spread over nearly 60 miles of the Congo River, exceeds 10 feet.

Estimated mean annual flow, in cusecs, of other major waterfalls are: Niagara, 212,200; Paulo Afonso, 100,000; Urubupunga, 97,000; Iguazu, 61,000; Patos-Maribondo, 53,000; Victoria, 38,400; and Kaieteur, 23,400.

Height = total drop in feet in one or more leaps. † = falls of more than one leap; * = falls that diminish greatly seasonally; ** = falls that reduce to a trickle or are dry for part of each year. If river names not shown, they are same as the falls. R. = river; L. = lake; (C) = cascade type.

| Name and location | Ht. | Name and location | Ht. | Name and location | Ht. |
|---|---|---|---|---|---|
| **Africa** | | Tesissat, Blue Nile R. | 140 | **Tanzania-Zambia** | |
| **Angola** | | **Lesotho** | | *Kalambo | 726 |
| Duque de Braganca, Lucala R. | 344 | *Maletsunyane | 630 | **Uganda** | |
| Ruacana, Cuene R. | 406 | **Rhodesia-Zambia** | | Kabalega (Murchison) Victoria Nile R. | 130 |
| **Ethiopia** | | *Victoria, Zambezi R. | 355 | | |
| Dal Verme, Dorya R. | 98 | **South Africa** | | **Asia** | |
| | | *Augrabies, Orange R. | 480 | **India**—*Cauvery | 330 |
| | | Howick, Umgeni R. | 364 | *Gokak, Ghataprabha R. | 170 |
| Fincha | 508 | † Tugela | 2,014 | *Jog (Gersoppa), Sharavathi R. | 830 |
| | | Highest fall | 597 | | |

| Name and location | Ht. |
|---|---|
| **Japan** | |
| *Kegon, Daiya R. | 330 |
| **Laos** | |
| Khon Cataracts, | |
| Mekong R. (C) | 70 |

## Australasia

| Name and location | Ht. |
|---|---|
| **Australia** | |
| New South Wales | |
| † Wentworth | 614 |
| Highest fall | 360 |
| Wollomombi | 1,100 |
| Queensland | |
| Coomera | 210 |
| Tully | 885 |
| † Wallaman, Stony Cr. | 1,137 |
| Highest fall | 937 |
| **New Zealand** | |
| Bowen | 540 |
| Helena | 890 |
| Stirling | 505 |
| † Sutherland, Arthur R. | 1,904 |
| Highest fall | 815 |

## Europe

| Name and location | Ht. |
|---|---|
| **Austria**—† Gastein | 492 |
| Highest fall | 280 |
| † *Golling, Schwarzbach R. | 250 |
| † Krimml | 1,312 |
| **France**—*Gavarnie | 1,385 |
| **Great Britain**—Scotland | |
| Glomach | 370 |
| Wales | |
| Cain | 150 |
| Rhaiadr | 240 |
| **Iceland**—Detti | 144 |
| † Gull, Hvita R. | 105 |
| **Italy**—Frua, Toce R. (C). | 470 |
| **Norway** | |
| Mardalsfossen (Northern) | 1,535 |
| † Mardalsfossen (Southern) | 2,150 |
| † **Skjeggedal, Nybuai R. | 1,378 |
| **Skykje | 984 |
| Vetti, Morka-Koldedola R. | 900 |
| Voring, Bjoreio R. | 597 |
| **Sweden** | |
| † Handol | 427 |
| † Tannforsen, Are R. | 120 |
| **Switzerland** | |
| † Diesbach | 394 |
| Giessbach (C) | 1,982 |
| Handegg, Aare R. | 150 |

| Name and location | Ht. |
|---|---|
| Iffigen | 120 |
| Pissevache, Salanfe R. | 213 |
| † Reichenbach | 656 |
| Rhine | 79 |
| † Simmen | 459 |
| Staubbach | 984 |
| † Trummelbach | 1,312 |

## North America

| Name and location | Ht. |
|---|---|
| **Canada** | |
| Alberta | |
| Panther, Nigel Cr. | 600 |
| British Columbia | |
| † Della | 1,443 |
| † Takakkaw, Daly Glacier | 1,200 |
| Northwest Territories | |
| Virginia, S. Nahanni R. | 294 |
| Quebec | |
| Montmorency | 274 |
| **Canada—United States** | |
| Niagara: American | 193 |
| Horseshoe | 186 |
| **United States** | |
| California | |
| *Feather, Fall R. | 640 |
| Yosemite National Park | |
| *Bridalveil | 620 |
| *Illilouette | 370 |
| *Nevada, Merced R. | 594 |
| **Ribbon | 1,612 |
| **Silver Strand, Meadow Br. | 1,170 |
| *Vernal, Merced R. | 317 |
| † **Yosemite | 2,425 |
| Yosemite (upper) | 1,430 |
| Yosemite (lower) | 320 |
| Yosemite (middle) (C) | 675 |
| Colorado | |
| † Seven, South Cheyenne Cr. | 300 |
| Hawaii | |
| Akaka, Kolekole Str. | 442 |
| Idaho | |
| **Shoshone, Snake R. | 212 |
| Twin, Snake R. | 120 |
| Kentucky | |
| Cumberland | 68 |
| Maryland | |
| *Great, Potomac R. (C) | 71 |
| Minnesota | |
| **Minnehaha | 53 |
| New Jersey | |
| Passaic | 70 |

| Name and location | Ht. |
|---|---|
| New York | |
| *Taughannock | 215 |
| Oregon | |
| † Multnomah | 620 |
| Highest fall | 542 |
| Tennessee | |
| Fall Creek | 256 |
| Washington | |
| Mt. Rainier Natl. Park | |
| Narada, Paradise R. | 168 |
| Sluiskin, Paradise R. | 300 |
| Palouse | 197 |
| **Snoquaimie | 268 |
| Wisconsin | |
| *Big Manitou, Black R. (C). | 165 |
| Wyoming | |
| Yellowstone Natl. Pk. Tower | 132 |
| *Yellowstone (upper) | 109 |
| *Yellowstone (lower) | 308 |
| **Mexico** | |
| El Salto | 218 |
| **Juanacatlan, Santiago R. | 72 |

## South America

| Name and location | Ht. |
|---|---|
| **Argentina-Brazil** | |
| Iguazu | 230 |
| **Brazil** | |
| Glass | 1,325 |
| Patos-Maribondo, Grande R. | 115 |
| Paulo Afonso, Sao Francisco R. | 275 |
| Urubupunga, Parana R. | 40 |
| **Brazil-Paraguay** | |
| Sete Quedas | |
| Parana R. | 130 |
| **Colombia** | |
| Catarata de Candelas, | |
| Cusiana R. | 984 |
| *Tequendama, Bogota R. | 427 |
| **Ecuador** | |
| *Agoyan, Pastaza R. | 200 |
| **Guyana** | |
| Kaieteur, Potaro R. | 741 |
| King George VI, Kamarang R. | 1,600 |
| † Marina, Ipobe R. | 500 |
| Highest fall | 300 |
| **Venezuela**— | |
| † *Angel | 3,212 |
| Highest fall | 2,648 |
| Cuquenan | 2,000 |

---

# Notable Deserts of the World

**Arabian (Eastern),** 70,000 sq. mi. in Egypt between the Nile river and Red Sea, extending southward into Sudan.

**Atacama,** 600 mi. long area rich in nitrate and copper deposits in N. Chile.

**Black Rock,** 1,000 sq. mi. barren plain in NW Nev.

**Death Valley,** 2,936 sq. mi. in E. Cal. and SW Nev. Contains lowest point below sea level (282 ft.) in western hemisphere.

**Gibson,** 250,000 sq. mi. in the interior of W. Australia.

**Gobi,** 500,000 sq. mi. in Mongolia and China.

**Great Sandy,** 150,000 sq. mi. in W. Australia.

**Great Victoria,** 250,000 sq. mi. in W. and S. Australia.

**Kalahari,** 225,000 sq. mi. in southern Africa.

**Kara-Kum,** 110,000 sq. mi. in Turkman, SSR.

**Kavir (Dasht-e-Kavir),** great salt waste in central Iran some 400 mi. long.

**Kyzyl-Kum,** 100,000 sq. mi. in Kazakh and Uzbuk, SSR.

**Libyan,** 600,000 sq. mi. in the Sahara extending from Lybia through SW Egypt into Sudan.

**Lut (Dasht-e-Lut),** 20,000 sq. mi. in E. Iran.

**Mojave,** 15,000 sq. mi. in S. Cal.

**Nafud (An Nafud),** 50,000 sq. mi. near Jawf in Saudi Arabia.

**Namib,** long narrow area extending 800 miles along SW coast of Africa.

**Nubian,** 120,000 sq. mi. in the Sahara in NE Sudan.

**Painted Desert,** section of high plateau in N. Ariz. extending 150 mi.

**Rub al-Khali (Empty Quarter),** 250,000 sq. mi. in the south Arabian Peninsula. World's largest continuous sand area.

**Sahara,** 3,320,000 sq. mi. in N. Africa extending westward to the Atlantic. Largest tropical and climatic desert in the world.

**Simpson,** 50,000 sq. mi. in central Australia.

**Sonoran,** 120,000 sq. mi. in SW Ariz. and SE Cal. extending into Mexico.

**Syrian,** 100,000 sq. mi. arid wasteland extending over much of N. Saudi Arabia, E. Jordan, S. Syria, and W. Iraq.

**Taklamakan,** 125,000 sq. mi. in Sinkiang Province, China.

**Thar (Great Indian),** 100,000 sq. mi. arid area extending 400 mi. along India-Pakistan border.

---

# The Great Lakes

**Source:** National Ocean Survey, U.S. Commerce Department

The Great Lakes form the largest body of fresh water in the world and with their connecting waterways are the largest inland water transportation unit. Draining the great North Central basin of the U.S., they enable shipping to reach the Atlantic via their outlet, the St. Lawrence R., and also the Gulf of Mexico via the Illinois Waterway, from Lake Michigan to the Mississippi R. A third outlet connects with the Hudson R. and thence the Atlantic via the N. Y. State Barge Canal System.

Only one of the lakes, Lake Michigan, is wholly in the United States; the others are shared with Canada. Ships carrying grain, lumber and iron ore move from the shores of Lake Superior to Whitefish Bay at the east end of the lake, thence through the Soo (Sault Ste. Marie) locks, through the St. Mary's River and into Lake Huron. To reach the steel mills at Gary, and Port of Indiana and South Chicago, Ill., ore ships move west from Lake Huron to Lake Michigan through the Straits of Mackinac.

Lake Huron discharges its waters into Lake Erie through a narrow waterway, the St. Clair R., Lake St. Clair (both included in the drainage basin figures) and the Detroit R. Lake St. Clair, a marshy basin, is 26 miles long and 24 miles wide at its maximum. A ship channel has been dredged through the lake.

Lake Superior is 600 feet above mean water level at Father Point, Quebec, on the International Great Lakes Datum (1955). From Duluth, Minn., to the eastern end of Lake Ontario is 1,156 mi.

| | Superior | Michigan | Huron | Erie | Ontario |
|---|---|---|---|---|---|
| Length in miles | 350 | 307 | 206 | 241 | 193 |
| Breadth in miles | 160 | 118 | 183 | 57 | 53 |
| Deepest soundings in feet | 1,330 | 923 | 750 | 210 | 802 |
| Volume of water in cubic miles | 2,900 | 1,180 | 849 | 116 | 393 |
| Area (sq. miles) water surface—U.S. | 20,600 | 22,300 | 9,100 | 4,980 | 3,560 |
| Canada | 11,100 | ..... | 13,900 | 4,930 | 3,990 |
| Area (sq. miles) entire drainage basin—U.S. | 16,900 | 45,600 | 16,000 | 18,000 | 15,200 |
| Canada | 32,400 | ..... | 34,700 | 4,720 | 12,100 |
| **Total Area (sq. miles) U.S. and Canada** | **81,000** | **67,900** | **73,700** | **32,630** | **34,850** |
| Mean surface above mean water level at Father Point, Quebec, aver. level in feet (112 yrs.) | 600.42 | 578.74 | 578.74 | 570.48 | 244.80 |
| Latitude, North | {46° 25' {49° 00' | 41° 37' | 43° 00' | 41° 23' | 43° 11' |
| | | 46° 06' | 46° 17' | 42° 52' | 44° 15' |
| Longitude, West | {84° 22' {92° 06' | 84° 45' | 79° 43' | 78° 51' | 76° 03' |
| | | 88° 02' | 84° 45' | 83° 29' | 79° 53' |
| National boundary line in miles | 282.8 | None | 260.8 | 251.5 | 174.6 |
| United States shore line (mainland only) miles | 863 | 1,400 | 580 | 431 | 300 |

## Largest Lake in Each Province of Canada

Source: "Inland Waters Directorate" and others.

| Province | Largest within: | Largest partly in: | Shared with: | Origin | Area (sq. miles) | Ft. above sea level |
|---|---|---|---|---|---|---|
| Alberta | Claire | | | Natural | 555 | 700 |
| | | Athabasca | Saskatchewan | Natural | 3,066 | 700 |
| British Columbia | Williston | | | Natural | 640 | 2,180 |
| Manitoba | Winnipeg | | | Manmade | 9,417 | 713 |
| Newfoundland | Smallwood Reservoir | | | Natural | 2,520 | S.L. |
| New Brunswick | Grand | | | Manmade | 70 | 4 |
| Northwest Territories | Great Bear | | | Natural | 12,096 | 512 |
| Nova Scotia | Bras d'Or | | | Natural | 424 | Tidal |
| Ontario | Nipigon | | | Natural | 1,872 | 1,050 |
| Prince Edward Island | Forest Hill Pond | | | Natural | 15,241 | 580 |
| | | Huron | U.S. | Natural | .7 | 50 |
| Quebec | Mistassini | | | Manmade | 902 | 1,230 |
| Saskatchewan | Wollaston | | | Natural | 1,035 | 1,306 |
| | | Athabasca | Alberta | Natural | 3,066 | 700 |

## Lakes of the World

Source: National Geographic Society, Washington, D.C.

A lake is a body of water surrounded by land. Although some lakes are called seas, they are lakes by definition. The Caspian Sea is bounded by the Soviet Union and Iran and is fed by eight rivers.

| Name | Continent | Area sq. mi. | Length mi. | Depth feet | Elev. feet |
|---|---|---|---|---|---|
| Caspian Sea | Asia-Europe | 143,550 | 760 | 3,264 | −92 |
| Superior | North America | 31,700 | 350 | 1,330 | 600 |
| Victoria | Africa | 26,828 | 250 | 265 | 3,720 |
| Aral Sea | Asia | 25,300 | 280 | 223 | 174 |
| Huron | North America | 23,000 | 206 | 750 | 579 |
| Michigan | North America | 22,300 | 307 | 923 | 579 |
| Tanganyika | Africa | 12,700 | 420 | 4,650 | 2,534 |
| Great Bear | North America | 12,096 | 192 | 1,356 | 512 |
| Baykal | Asia | 11,780 | 395 | 5,315 | 1,493 |
| Nyasa | Africa | 11,430 | 360 | 2,226 | 1,550 |
| Great Slave | North America | 11,031 | 298 | 2,015 | 513 |
| Erie | North America | 9,910 | 241 | 210 | 570 |
| Winnipeg | North America | 9,417 | 266 | 60 | 713 |
| Ontario | North America | 7,550 | 193 | 802 | 245 |
| Ladoga | Europe | 6,835 | 124 | 738 | 13 |
| Balkhash | Asia | 7,115 | 376 | 85 | 1,115 |
| Chad | Africa | 6,300 | 175 | 24 | 787 |
| Maracaibo | South America | 5,217 | 133 | 115 | Sea level |
| Onega | Europe | 3,710 | 145 | 328 | 108 |
| Volta | Africa | 3,276 | 250 | .... | |
| Titicaca | South America | 3,200 | 122 | 922 | 12,500 |
| Athabasca | North America | 3,064 | 208 | 407 | 700 |
| Nicaragua | North America | 3,100 | 102 | 230 | 102 |
| Eyre | Australia | 3,600 | 90 | 4 | −52 |
| Rudolf | Africa | 2,473 | 154 | 240 | 1,230 |
| Reindeer | North America | 2,568 | 143 | .... | 1,106 |
| Issyk Kul | Asia | 2,355 | 115 | 2,303 | 5,279 |
| Torrens | Australia | 2,230 | 130 | .... | 92 |
| Vanern | Europe | 2,156 | 91 | 328 | 144 |
| Winnipegosis | North America | 2,075 | 141 | 38 | 830 |
| Albert | Africa | 2,075 | 100 | 168 | 2,030 |
| Kariba | Africa | 2,050 | 175 | 390 | 1,590 |
| Nettilling | North America | 2,140 | 67 | Sea level | 95 |
| Nipigon | North America | 1,872 | 72 | 540 | 855 |
| Gairdner | Australia | 1,840 | 90 | .... | 112 |
| Manitoba | North America | 1,799 | 140 | 12 | 813 |
| Urmia | Asia | 1,815 | 90 | 49 | 4,180 |

## Largest Lake in Each State of the U.S.

Source: National Geographic Society, Washington, D.C.
*indicates reservoir

| State | Largest entirely within state | Largest partly in another state | Shared with | Origin | Total area (square miles) | Feet above sea level | Maxi-mum depth (feet) | Shore-line length (miles) |
|---|---|---|---|---|---|---|---|---|
| Ala... | Guntersville | | | Man-made | 108 | 595 | 94 | 962 |
| | | Walter F. George | Ga. | Man-made | 71 | 190 | 90 | 640 |
| Alas. | illiamna | | | Natural | 1,150 | 150 | 1,289 | 230 |
| Ariz. | Theodore Roosevelt | | | Man-made | 27 | 2,136 | 280 | 88 |
| | | Powell | Ut. | Man-made | 252 | 3,700 | 580 | 1,800 |
| Ark. | Ouachita | | | Man-made | 63 | 578 | 179 | 690 |
| | | Bull Shoals | Mo. | Man-made | 71 | 654 | 175 | 740 |
| Cal. | Salton Sea | | | Natural | 360 | -235 | 48 | — |
| | | Tahoe | Nev. | Natural | 192 | 6,229 | 1,644 | 71 |
| Col. | Blue Mesa* | | | Man-made | 14 | 7,519 | 325 | 150 |
| | | Navajo* | N.M. | Man-made | 24 | 6,085 | 382 | 95 |
| Conn. | Candlewood | | | Man-made | 8 | 429 | 85 | 75 |
| Del... | Lum's Pond | | | Man-made | .34 | 44 | 22 | 5 |
| Fla. | Okeechobee | | | Natural | 700 | 14 | 15 | 96 |
| Ga. | Sidney Lanier | | | Man-made | 59 | 1,070 | 156 | 540 |
| | | Clark Hill | S.C. | Man-made | 109 | 330 | 150 | 1,200 |
| Ha. | Waita* | | | Man-made | .66 | 242 | — | 4 |
| Ida. | Pend Oreille | | | Natural | 136 | 2,063 | 1,200 | 127 |
| Ill. | Carlyle* | | | Man-made | 41 | 445 | 40 | 83 |
| | | Michigan | Wis., Ind., Mich. | Natural | 22,300 | 579 | 923 | 1,660 |
| Ind. | Monroe* | | | Man-made | 29 | 556 | 75 | 100 |
| | | Michigan | Wis., Ill., Mich. | Natural | 22,300 | 579 | 923 | 1,660 |
| Ia. | Rathbun* | | | Man-made | 18 | 904 | 55 | 180 |
| Kan. | Tuttle Creek* | | | Man-made | 25 | 1,079 | 90 | 112 |
| Ky. | Cumberland | | | Man-made | 79 | 760 | 183 | 1,255 |
| | | Kentucky | Tenn. | Man-made | 250 | 359 | 90 | 2,380 |
| La... | Pontchartrain | | | Natural | 621 | sea lev. | 18 | 112 |
| Me... | Moosehead | | | Natural | 117 | 1,042 | 246 | 190 |
| Md. | Deep Creek | | | Man-made | 6 | 2,462 | 72 | 62 |
| | | Conowingo* | Pa. | Man-made | 13 | 109 | 110 | 38 |
| Mass. | Quabbin* | | | Man-made | 39 | 524 | 150 | 104 |
| Mich. | Houghton | | | Natural | 31 | 1,138 | 20 | 30 |
| | | Superior | Wis., Minn., Ont. | Natural | 31,700 | 600 | 1,330 | 2,980 |
| Minn. | Red | | | Natural | 452 | 1,172 | — | — |
| | | Superior | Wis., Mich., Ont. | Natural | 31,700 | 600 | 1,330 | 2,980 |
| Miss. | Grenada | | | Man-made | 100 | 231 | 102 | 282 |
| Mo... | Lake of the Ozarks | | | Man-made | 93 | 659 | 148 | 1,300 |
| Mon. | Fort Peck* | | | Man-made | 375 | 2,246 | 220 | 1,540 |
| Neb. | McConaughty | | | Man-made | 50 | 3,260 | 130 | 105 |
| Nev. | Pyramid | | | Natural | 169 | 3,789 | 330 | 66 |
| | | Mead | Ariz. | Man-made | 247 | 1,221 | 432 | 550 |
| N.H. | Winnipesaukee | | | Natural | 70 | 504 | 169 | 240 |
| N.J... | Hopatcong | | | Natural | 4 | 924 | 58 | 32 |
| N.M. | Elephant Butte* | | | Man-made | 57 | 4,450 | 176 | 201 |
| N.Y. | Oneida | | | Natural | 80 | 369 | 55 | 63 |
| | | Erie | Mich., Pa., Ont., Oh. | Natural | 9,910 | 570 | 210 | 856 |
| N.C. | Mattamuskeet | | | Natural | 67 | 3 | 5 | — |
| | | John H. Kerr* | Va. | Man-made | 76 | 300 | 99 | 800 |
| N.D. | Sakakawea | | | Man-made | 575 | 1,850 | 180 | 1,600 |
| | | Oahe* | S.D. | Man-made | 556 | 1,617 | 200 | 2,250 |
| Oh. | Lake St. Mary's | | | Man-made | 17 | 869 | 10 | 60 |
| | | Erie | Mich., Pa., N.Y., Ont. | Natural | 9,910 | 570 | 210 | 856 |
| Okla. | Eufaula | | | Man-made | 160 | 585 | 87 | 600 |
| Ore... | Klamath | | | Natural | 143 | 4,143 | 50 | 165 |
| | | Goose Lake | Cal. | Natural | 194 | 4,716 | 24 | 90 |
| Pa... | Raystown* | | | Man-made | 13 | 786 | 185 | 110 |
| | | Erie | Mich., N.Y., Oh., Ont. | Natural | 9,910 | 570 | 210 | 856 |
| R.I. | Scituate | | | Man-made | 5 | 284 | 94 | 38 |
| S.C. | Marion | | | Man-made | 173 | 75 | 55 | 300 |
| S.D. | Francis Case | | | Man-made | 159 | 1,375 | 140 | 540 |
| | | Oahe* | N.D. | Man-made | 556 | 1,617 | 200 | 2,250 |
| Tenn. | Watts Bar | | | Man-made | 61 | 741 | 75 | 783 |
| | | Kentucky | Ky. | Man-made | 250 | 359 | 90 | 2,380 |
| Tex. | Sam Rayburn* | | | Man-made | 179 | 164 | 74 | — |
| | | Toledo Bend* | La. | Man-made | 284 | 172 | 92 | — |
| Ut. | Great Salt Lake | | | Natural | 1,438 | 4,200 | 36 | 334 |
| Vt. | Bomoseen | | | Natural | 4 | 413 | — | — |
| | | Champlain | N.Y., Que. | Natural | 437 | 95 | 400 | 379 |
| Va. | Smith Mountain | | | Man-made | 31 | 795 | 200 | 500 |
| | | John H. Kerr* | N.C. | Man-made | 76 | 300 | 99 | 800 |
| Wash. | F.D. Roosevelt | | | Man-made | 123 | 1,288 | 375 | 325 |
| W. Va. | Summersville | | | Man-made | 4 | 1,652 | 267 | 65 |
| Wis... | Winnebago | | | Natural | 215 | 747 | 21 | 78 |
| | | Superior | Minn., Mich., Ont. | Natural | 31,700 | 600 | 1,330 | 2,980 |
| Wyo... | Yellowstone | | | Natural | 137 | 7,733 | 309 | 110 |
| | | Flaming Gorge* | Utah | Man-made | — | 6,040 | 437 | — |

## Notable Bridges in North America

Source: State Highway Engineers; Canadian Civil Engineering — ASCE

Asterisk (*) designates railroad bridge. Span of a bridge is distance (in feet) between its supports.

### Suspension

| Year | Bridge | Location | Longest span |
|---|---|---|---|
| 1964 | Verrazano-Narrows | New York, N.Y. | 4,260 |
| 1937 | Golden Gate | San Fran. Bay, Cal. | 4,200 |
| 1957 | Mackinac | Sts. of Mackinac | 3,800 |
| 1931 | Geo. Washington | Hudson River | 3,500 |
| 1952 | Tacoma | Washington | 2,800 |
| 1939 | Lions Gate | Burrard Inlet, B.C. | 2,778 |
| 1936 | ¹Transbay | San Fran. Bay, Cal. | 2,310 |
| 1939 | Bronx-Whitestone | East R., N.Y.C. | 2,300 |
| 1970 | Quebec Road | Quebec | 2,190 |
| 1951 | Del. Memorial | Wilmington, Del. | 2,150 |
| 1968 | Del. Mem. (new) | Wilmington, Del. | 2,150 |
| 1957 | Walt Whitman | Phila., Pa. | 2,000 |
| 1929 | Ambassador | Detroit-Canada | 1,850 |
| 1961 | Throgs Neck | Long Is. Sound | 1,800 |
| 1926 | Benjamin Franklin | Philadelphia | 1,750 |
| 1924 | Bear Mt., N.Y. | Hudson River | 1,632 |
| 1952 | ²Wm. Preston Lane Mem. | Sandy Point, Md. | 1,600 |
| 1903 | Williamsburg | East R., N.Y.C. | 1,600 |
| 1969 | Newport | Narragansett Bay, R.I. | 1,600 |
| 1883 | Brooklyn | East R., N.Y.C. | 1,595 |
| 1930 | Mid-Hudson, N.Y. | Poughkeepsie | 1,500 |
| 1964 | Vincent Thomas | Los Angeles Harbor | 1,500 |
| 1909 | Manhattan | East R., N.Y.C. | 1,470 |
| 1936 | Triborough | East R., N.Y.C. | 1,380 |
| 1931 | St. Johns | Portland, Ore. | 1,207 |
| 1929 | Mount Hope | Rhode Island | 1,200 |
| 1939 | Deer Isle | Maine | 1,080 |
| 1931 | Maysville (Ky.) | Ohio River | 1,060 |
| 1867 | Cincinnati | Ohio River | 1,057 |
| 1971 | Dent. | Clearwater Co., Ida. | 1,050 |
| 1900 | Miampimi | Mexico | 1,030 |
| 1849 | Wheeling, W. Va. | Ohio River | 1,010 |

### Cantilever

| Year | Bridge | Location | Longest span |
|---|---|---|---|
| 1917 | *Quebec (Railway) | Quebec | 1,800 |
| 1970 | Chester, Pa. | Delaware River | 1,644 |
| 1958 | New Orleans, La. | Mississippi R. | 1,575 |
| 1936 | Transbay | San Fran. Bay | 1,400 |
| 1968 | Baton Rouge, La. | Mississippi R. | 1,235 |
| 1955 | Nyack-Tarrytown | Hudson River | 1,212 |
| 1930 | Longview, Wash. | Columbia River | 1,200 |
| 1909 | Queensboro | East R., N.Y.C. | 1,182 |
| 1927 | Carquinez Strait | California | 1,100 |
| 1958 | Parallel Span | " | 1,100 |
| 1930 | Jacques Cartier | Montreal, P.Q. | 1,097 |
| 1968 | Isaiah D. Hart | Jacksonville, Fla. | 1,088 |
| 1957 | ³Richmond | San Fran. Bay, Cal. | 1,070 |
| 1929 | Grace Memorial | Charleston, S.C. | 1,050 |
| 1963 | Newburgh-Beacon | Hudson R., N.Y. | 1,000 |
| 1975 | Caruthersville, Mo. | Mississippi R. | 920 |
| 1969 | Ohio River | Pt. Pleasant, W. Va. | 900 |
| 1940 | Natchez | Mississippi R. | 875 |
| 1938 | Blue Water | Pt. Huron, Mich. | 871 |
| 1972 | Vicksburg | Mississippi River. | 870 |
| 1954 | Sunshine Skyway | St. Petersburg, Fla. | 864 |
| 1940 | *Baton Rouge | Mississippi R. | 848 |
| 1899 | *Cornwall | St. Lawrence R. | 843 |
| 1940 | Greenville | Mississippi R. | 840 |
| 1961 | Helena, Ark. | Mississippi R. | 840 |
| 1963 | Brent Spence | Covington, Ky. | 831 |
| 1963 | Cincinnati, Oh. | Ohio River | 830 |
| 1956 | Earl C. Clements | Ohio R., Ill-Ky. | 825⁸ |
| 1930 | *Vicksburg | Mississippi R. | 825 |
| 1929 | Louisville | Ohio River | 820 |
| 1961 | Campbellton-Cross Point | New Brunswick-Quebec | 815 |
| 1943 | Jeff'rson Barr'ks, Mo. | Mississippi R. | 804 |
| 1950 | Maurice J. Tobin | Boston, Mass. | 800 |
| 1935 | Rip Van Winkle | Catskill, N.Y. | 800 |
| 1938 | Cairo | Ohio River, Ill.-Ky. | 800 |
| 1940 | Ludlow Ferry | Potomac R. | 800 |
| 1932 | Washington Mem. | Seattle, Wash. | 800 |
| 1936 | North Bend, Ore. | Coos Bay | 793 |
| 1936 | McCullough | Coos Bay, Ore. | 793 |
| 1935 | *Huey P Long | New Orleans | 790 |
| 1916 | *Memphis (Harahan) | Mississippi R. | 790 |
| 1892 | *Memphis | Mississippi R. | 790 |
| 1949 | Memphis-Arkansas | Mississippi R. | 790 |
| 1904 | *Mingo Jct., W. Va. | Ohio River | 769 |

| Year | Bridge | Location | Longest span |
|---|---|---|---|
| 1910 | *Beaver, Pa. | Ohio River | 767 |
| 1966 | ⁵S.N. Pearman | Charleston, S.C. | 760 |
| 1940 | Owensboro. | Ohio River | 750 |
| 1911 | Sewickley, Pa. | Ohio River | 750 |
| 1928 | Outerbridge, N.Y.-N.J. | Arthur Kill | 750 |
| 1964 | Sunshine, Don'ville | Mississippi, La. | 750 |

### Simple Truss

| Year | Bridge | Location | Longest span |
|---|---|---|---|
| 1917 | *Metropolis | Ohio River | 720 |
| 1929 | Irvin S. Cobb | Ohio River-Ill.-Ky. | 716 |
| 1922 | *Tanana River | Nenana, Alaska | 700 |
| 1933 | *Henderson | Ohio River-Ind.-Ky. | 665 |
| 1967 | I-77, Ohio River | Marietta, Oh. | 650 |
| 1917 | MacArthur, Ill.-Mo. | St. Louis | 647 |
| 1919 | Louisville | Ohio River | 644 |
| 1933 | Atchafalaya | Morgan City, La. | 608 |
| 1924 | *Castleton | Hudson River | 598 |
| 1906 | Elizabethtown | Great Miami R., Oh. | 586 |
| 1889 | *Cincinnati | Ohio River | 542 |
| 1951 | Allegheny River | Allegheny Co., Pa. | 533 |
| 1914 | Pittsburgh | Allegheny R. | 531 |
| 1930 | *Martinez | California. | 528 |
| 1967 | Tanana River | Alaska | 500 |
| 1963 | 216 Nenana River | Rex, Alaska | 406 |

### Steel Truss

| Year | Bridge | Location | Longest span |
|---|---|---|---|
| 1940 | Gov. Nice Mem. | Potomac River, Md. | 800 |
| 1975 | I-24 | Tenn.-Ky. | 720 |
| 1938 | US-62, Ky. | Green River | 700 |
| 1952 | US-62, Ky. | Cumberland River. | 700 |
| 1940 | Jamestown | Jamestown, R.I. | 640 |
| 1940 | Greenville | Mississippi R., Ark. | 640 |
| 1949 | Memphis | Mississippi R., Ark. | 621 |
| 1938 | US-22 | Delaware River, N.J. | 540 |
| 1972 | Mississippi River | Muscatine, Ia. | 512 |
| 1896 | Newport | Ohio River, Ky. | 511 |
| 1931 | US-60. | Cumberland R., Ky. | 500 |
| 1958 | Lake Oahe | Mobridge, S.D. | 500 |
| 1958 | Lake Oahe | Gettysburg, S.D. | 500 |
| 1910 | McKinley, St. Louis | Mississippi River. | 500 |
| 1963 | Millard E. Tydings | Susquehanna R., Md. | 490 |
| 1955 | Four Bears | Missouri R., N.D. | 475 |
| 1930 | Lake Champlain | Lake Champlain, N.Y. | 434 |
| 1947 | Mayo | Suwanee R., Fla. | 420 |
| 1929 | Clarendon | White River, Ark. | 400 |
| 1931 | US-60. | Tennessee R., Ky. | 400 |

### Continuous Truss

| Year | Bridge | Location | Longest span |
|---|---|---|---|
| 1966 | Astoria, Ore. | Columbia R. | 1,232 |
| 1966 | Marquam | Willamette R., Ore. | 1,044 |
| 1969 | Miss. R. | Dyersburg, Tenn. | 900 |
| 1969 | Irondequoit Bay | Rochester, N.Y. | 891 |
| 1943 | Dubuque, Ia. | Mississippi R. | 845 |
| 1953 | John E. Mathews | Jacksonville, Fla. | 810 |
| 1957 | Kingston-Rhinecliff | Hudson R., N.Y. | 800 |
| 1918 | *Sciotoville | Ohio River | 775 |
| 1929 | Madison-Milton | Ohio River | 727 |
| 1966 | Matthew E. Welsh | Mauckport | 707⁵ |
| 1962 | Champlain | Montreal, P.Q. | 707 |
| 1975 | Girard Point | Philadelphia, Pa. | 700 |
| 1929 | Chain of Rocks | Mississippi R. | 699 |
| 1966 | Braga | Taunton R., Mass. | 682 |
| 1938 | Port Arthur-Orange | Texas. | 680 |
| 1929 | *Cincinnati | Ohio River | 675 |
| 1928 | Cape Girardeau, Mo. | Mississippi R. | 672 |
| 1946 | Chester, Ill. | Mississippi R. | 670 |
| 1930 | Quincy, Ill. | Mississippi R. | 628 |
| 1934 | Bourne | Cape Cod Canal | 616 |
| 1935 | Sagamore | Cape Cod Canal | 616 |
| 1965 | Clarion River | Clarion Co., Pa. | 612 |
| 1965 | Rio Grande Gorge | Taos, N.M. | 600 |
| 1941 | Columbia River | Kettle Falls, Wash. | 600 |
| 1954 | Columbia River | Umatilla, Ore. | 600 |
| 1954 | Columbia River | The Dalles, Ore. | 576 |
| 1962 | W. Br. Feather River | Oroville, Cal. | 576 |
| 1936 | Meredosia | Illinois River | 567 |
| 1936 | Mark Twain Mem. | Hannibal, Mo. | 560 |
| 1957 | Mackinac | Mackinac Straits, Mich. | 560 |
| 1937 | Homestead. | Pittsburgh | 553 |
| 1961 | Ship Canal | Seattle, Wash. | 552 |
| 1932 | Pulaski Skyway | Passaic R., N.J. | 550 |
| 1973 | I-95, Thames River | New London, Conn. | 540 |
| 1927 | Ross Island | Portland, Ore. | 535 |

| Year | Bridge | Location | Longest span |
|---|---|---|---|
| 1936 | South Omaha | Missouri R, Neb.-Ia. | 525 |
| 1932 | Savanna, Ill.-Sabula. | Mississippi R. | 520 |
| 1962 | Columbia River | Beebe, Wash. | 520 |
| 1970 | Snake River | Central Ferry, Wash. | 520 |
| 1954 | Columbia River | Pasco, Wash. | 520 |
| 1962 | Columbia River | Vantage, Wash. | 520 |
| 1974 | New Lyons Fulton | Mississippi R. (Ia.-Ill.) | 500 |
| 1958 | Stevenson, Ala. | Tennessee R. | 500 |

## Continuous Box and Plate Girder

| Year | Bridge | Location | Longest span |
|---|---|---|---|
| 1953 | Neches River | Orange County, Tex. | 850 |
| 1967 | San Mateo-Hayward No. 2. | San Fran. Bay, Cal. | 750 |
| 1963 | Gunnison River | Gunnison, Col. | 720 |
| 1969 | San Diego-Coronado | San Diego Bay, Cal. | 660[7] |
| 1972 | Ship Channel | Houston, Tex. | 630 |
| 1967 | Poplar St. | St. Louis, Mo. | 600 |
| 1965 | McDonald-Cartier | Ottawa, Ont. | 520 |
| 1971 | Lake Koocanusa | Lincoln Co., Mon. | 500 |
| 1967 | Mississippi R. | LaCrescent, Minn. | 450 |
| 1972 | Sitka Harbor | Sitka, Alaska | 450 |
| 1974 | I-430 | Arkansas R. | 430 |
| 1972 | Kansas City | Missouri R., Kan.-Mo. | 425 |
| 1967 | Chattanooga | Tennessee R., Tenn. | 420 |
| 1975 | Yukon River | Taylor Highway, Alaska | 410 |
| 1972 | I-75, Tennessee River. | Loudon, Co., Tenn | 400 |
| 19.. | isquehanna | Susquehanna R., Md. | 400 |
| 1963 | Lake Charles B'Pass | Louisiana | 399 |
| 1971 | St. Croix River | Hudson, Minn. | 390 |
| 1957 | Conn. Turnpike | Quinnipiac R. | 387 |
| 1960 | Route 34 | New Haven, Conn. | 379 |
| 1971 | S.H. No. 1 | Pendleton, Ark. | 377 |
| 1960 | Tennessee River | Chattanooga, Tenn. | 375 |
| 1966 | I-80, LeClaire, Ia. | Mississippi | 370 |
| 1971 | Sacramento R. | Bryte, Cal. | 370 |
| 1963 | I-40, Tennessee River. | Benton Co., Tenn. | 365 |
| 1967 | San Mateo Creek | Hillsborough, Cal. | 360 |
| 1950 | US-62, Kentucky Dam | Tennessee R., Ky. | 350 |
| 1961 | Whiskey Creek | Trinity Co., Cal. | 350 |
| 1972 | Franklin Falls. | Snoq'Imie Pass, Wash. | 350 |
| 1971 | Don Pedro Reserv | Tuolumne Co., Cal. | 350 |

## Continuous Plate

| Year | Bridge | Location | Longest span |
|---|---|---|---|
| 1965 | New Chain of Rocks | Mississippi R., Ill. | 5,411[9] |
| 1973 | Great Congress Gty. | Schenectady, N.Y. | 1,870 |
| 1971 | Congress St. | Troy, N.Y. | 1,420 |
| 1966 | I-480 | Missouri R., a.-Neb. | 425 |
| 1970 | I-435 | Missouri R., Mo. | 425 |
| 1972 | I-80 | Missouri R., Ia.-Neb. | 425 |
| 1970 | Green River | Hendersonville, N.C. | 350 |
| 1969 | Fort Smith | Arkansas River | 340 |
| 1971 | Audubon Pkwy. | Green R., Ky. | 330 |
| 1974 | Green River Pkwy. | Green R., Ky. | 330 |
| 1974 | Camp Nelson | Kentucky, R. | 330 |
| 1974 | Queen Isabella Cswy. | Port Isabel, Tex. | 310 |

## I-Beam Girder

| Year | Bridge | Location | Longest span |
|---|---|---|---|
| 1941 | US-31E | Rolling Fork R., Ky. | 340 |
| 1948 | US-27. | Licking River, Ky. | 316 |
| 1947 | US-31E | Green River, Ky. | 316 |
| 1941 | US-62. | Rolling Fork R., Ky. | 240 |
| 1942 | Licking River. | Owingsville, Ky. | 240 |
| 1954 | Fuller Warren | Jacksonville, Fla. | 224 |

## Steel Arch

| Year | Bridge | Location | Longest span |
|---|---|---|---|
| 1931 | Bayonne, N.J. | Kill Van Kull | 1,652 |
| 1972 | Fremont | Portland, Ore. | 1,255 |
| 1964 | Port Mann | British Columbia. | 1,200 |
| 1959 | Glen Canyon | Colorado River | 1,028 |
| 1967 | Trois-Rivieres | St. Lawrence R., P.Q. | 1,100 |
| 1962 | Lewiston-Queenston | Niagara River, Ont. | 1,000 |
| 1976 | Perrine | Twin Falls, Ida. | 993 |
| 1917 | *Hell Gate | East R., N.Y.C. | 977 |
| 1941 | Rainbow | Niagara Falls | 950 |
| 1972 | I-40, Mississippi R. | Memphis, Tenn. | 900[10] |
| 1970 | Lake Quinsigamond. | Worcester, Mass. | 849 |
| 1966 | Charles Braga | Somerset, Mass. | 840 |
| 1967 | Lincoln Trail | Ohio R., Ind.-Ky. | 825 |
| 1961 | Sherman Minton | Louisville, Ky. | 800 |
| 1936 | Henry Hudson | Harlem River | 800 |
| 1936 | French King | Conn. R. (Rt. 2, Mass.) | 782 |
| 1931 | West End. | Pittsburgh | 778 |
| 1972 | Piscataqua R. | I-95, N.H.-Me. | 756 |
| 1963 | Cold Spring Canyon. | Santa Barbara, Cal. | 700 |

| Year | Bridge | Location | Longest span |
|---|---|---|---|
| 1973 | I-24, Paducah, Ky. | Ohio River | 700 |

## Concrete Arch

| Year | Bridge | Location | Longest span |
|---|---|---|---|
| 1934 | New River | Ripplemead, Va. | 1,321[9] |
| 1932 | Clark Memorial | Wabash River | 1,033[9] |
| 1971 | Selah Creek (twin) | Selah, Wash. | 549 |
| 1968 | Cowlitz River. | Mossyrock, Wash. | 520 |
| 1931 | Westinghouse | Pittsburgh | 425 |
| 1923 | Cappelen | Minneapolis | 400 |
| 1930 | Jack's Run | Pittsburgh | 400 |
| 1973 | Elwha River | Port Angeles, Wash. | 380 |
| 1931 | Bixby Creek | Monterey Coast, Cal. | 330 |
| 1953 | Arroyo Seco | Pasadena, Cal. | 320 |
| 1927 | Mendota | Ft. Snelling, Minn. | 304 |

## Twin Concrete Trestle

| Year | Bridge | Location | Longest span |
|---|---|---|---|
| 1963 | Slidell, La. | L. Pontchartrain | 28,547[5] |

## Concrete Slab Dam

| Year | Bridge | Location | Longest span |
|---|---|---|---|
| 1927 | Conowingo Dam. | Maryland | 4,611 |
| 1952 | John H. Kerr Dam. | Roanoke River, Va. | 2,785 |
| 1936 | Hoover Dam. | Boulder City, Nev. | 1,324 |

## Drawbridges

### Vertical Lift

| Year | Bridge | Location | Longest span |
|---|---|---|---|
| 1959 | *Arthur Kill | N.Y.-N.J. | 558 |
| 1935 | *Cape Cod Canal | Massachusetts | 544 |
| 1960 | *Delair, N.J. | Delaware River | 542 |
| 1937 | Marine Parkway | New York City | 540 |
| 1931 | Burlington, N.J. | Delaware R. | 534 |
| 1912 | *A-S-B Fratt | Kansas City | 428 |
| 1945 | *Harry S. Truman | Kansas City | 427 |
| 1932 | *M-K-T R.R. | Missouri R. | 414 |
| 1969 | Wilm'gton Mem. | Wilmington, N.C. | 408 |
| 1930 | Duluth | Minnesota | 386 |
| 1941 | Main St. | Jacksonville, Fla. | 386 |
| 1962 | Burlington | Ontario | 370 |
| 1922 | *Cincinnati | Ohio River | 365 |
| 1967 | Benj. Harrison Mem. | James River, Va. | 363 |
| 1961 | Corpus Christi Harbor. | Corpus Christi, Tex. | 344[4] |
| 1962 | Sand Island Access. | Oahu, Hawaii | 340 |
| 1941 | U.S. 1&9, Passaic R. | Newark, N.J. | 332 |
| 1929 | Carlton | Bath-Woolwich, Me. | 328 |
| 1930 | *Martinez | California. | 328 |
| 1960 | St. Andrews Bay. | Panama City, Fla. | 327 |
| 1929 | *Penn-Lehigh | Newark Bay | 322 |
| 1920 | *Chattanooga | Tennessee R. | 310 |
| 1936 | Triboro, N.Y.C. | Harlem River | 310 |
| 1936 | Hardin | Illinois River | 309 |
| 1960 | Sacramento River. | Rio Vista, Cal. | 306 |
| 1957 | Claiborne Ave. | New Orleans | 305 |
| 1927 | Cochrane | Mobile, Ala. | 300 |
| 1928 | James River | Newport News | 300 |
| 1929 | San Mateo | California. | 300 |
| 1926 | *Missouri Pacific | Kragen, Ark. | 300 |

### Bascule

| Year | Bridge | Location | Longest span |
|---|---|---|---|
| 1926 | Fort Madison | Mississippi R. | 525[4] |
| 1969 | Pearl River | Slidell, La. | 482 |
| 1916 | Keokuk Municipal | Mississippi R., Ia. | 377 |
| 1917 | SR-8, Tennessee River | Chattanooga, Tenn. | 306 |
| 1940 | Lorain, Ohio | Black River | 295 |
| 1958 | Morrison | Portland, Ore. | 285 |
| 1969 | Elizabeth River. | Chesapeake, Va. | 281 |
| 1957 | Craig Memorial | I-280, Toledo, Oh. | 271 |
| 1952 | Downtown | Norfolk, Va. | 230 |

### Swing Bridges

| Year | Bridge | Location | Longest span |
|---|---|---|---|
| 1950 | Douglass Memorial | Anac'tia R., Wash. D.C. | 386 |
| 1945 | Lord Delaware | Mattaponi River, Va. | 252 |
| 1957 | Eltham | Pamunkey River, Va. | 237 |
| 1939 | Chickahominy River. | Route 5, Va. | 222 |
| 1930 | Nansemond River. | Route 125, Va. | 200 |

### Swing Span

| Year | Bridge | Location | Longest span |
|---|---|---|---|
| 1908 | *Willamette R. | Portland, Ore. | 521 |
| 1903 | *East Omaha | Missouri R. | 519 |
| 1952 | Yorktown | York River, Va. | 500 |
| 1897 | *Duluth, Minn. | St. Louis Bay | 486 |
| 1899 | *C.M.&N.R.R. | Chicago | 474 |
| 1897 | Sioux City, Ia. | Missouri R. (Nebr.-Ia.) | 470 |
| 1914 | *Coos Bay | Oregon | 458 |

### Floating Pontoon

| Year | Bridge | Location | Longest span |
|---|---|---|---|
| 1963 | Evergreen Pt. | Seattle, Wash. | 7,518 |
| 1940 | Lacey V. Murrow | Seattle | 6,561 |
| 1961 | Hood Canal | Pt. Gamble, Wash. | 6,471 |

(1) The Transbay Bridge has 2 spans of 2,310 ft. each. (2) A second bridge in parallel will be completed. (3) The Richmond Bridge has twin spans, 1,070 ft. each. (4) Railroad and vehicular bridge. (5) Two spans each 760 ft. (6) Two spans each 707 ft. (7) Two spans each 660 ft. (8) Two spans each 825 ft. (9) Total length of bridge. (10) Two spans each 900 ft.

## Construction Details of Large and Unusual Bridges

**Verrazano-Narrows Bridge**, between Staten Island and Brooklyn, N.Y., has a suspension span of 4,260 ft., longest in the world and exceeding the Golden Gate Bridge, San Francisco, by 60 ft. One level in use Nov., 1964, second opened Jun. 28, 1969. The name is a compromise; it spans the Narrows and commemorates a visit to New York Harbor in Apr., 1524, deduced from certain notes left by Giovanni da Verrazano, Italian navigator sailing for Francis I of France.

**Allegheny River Bridge** (Interstate 80) near Emlenton, Pa., 270 ft. above the water, tallest in eastern U.S., a continuous truss, 688 ft. long, 1968.

**Angostura,** suspension type, span 2,336 feet, 1967 at Ciudad Bolivar, Venezuela. Total length, 5,507.

**Charles Braga Bridge** over Taunton River between Fall River and Somerset, Mass. It is 5,780 feet long.

**Bendorf Bridge** on the Rhine River, 5 mi. n. of Coblenz, completed 1965, is a 3-span cement girder bridge, 3,378 ft. overall length, 101 ft. wide; with the main span 682 ft.

**Burro Creek Bridge** with 4 spans over Burro Creek on highway 93 near Kingman, Ariz. Main span steel truss 680 ft. Others plate girder, 110 and 2 of 85 ft. 1966.

**Champlain Bridge** at Montreal crossing the St. Lawrence River was opened 1962. It is 4 miles long.

**Chesapeake Bay Bridge-Tunnel,** opened Apr. 15, 1964 on US-13, connects Virginia Beach-Norfolk with the Eastern Shore of Virginia. Shore to shore, 17.6 miles. Twelve miles of trestles, 4 man-made islands, 2 mile-long tunnels, and 2 bridges.

**Cross Bay Parkway Bridge** (N.Y.), 3,000 feet long with 6 traffic lanes, 11 eight foot wide precast, prestressed concrete T girders to support spans 130 feet long each with main span 275 feet.

**Delaware Memorial Bridge** over Delaware River near Wilmington. A twin suspension bridge paralleling the original 250 ft. upstream has a 2,150-ft. main span suspended from 440-ft. towers.

**Eads Bridge** across the Mississippi R. between St. Louis and E. St. Louis, built in 1874 has 4 main spans 1,520 ft., 2,502 ft. and 1,118 ft. crossing Miss. R., a railroad and a road.

**Evergreen Point Bridge,** Wash. consists of 33 floating concrete pontoons weighing 4,700 tons each, held in place by 77 ton crete anchors. Pontoon structure is 6,561 ft. long; with approaches bridge is 12,596 ft. long.

**Fremont Bridge.** Part of Stadium Freeway, Portland, Ore., crossing Willamette R. 1,255 ft. steel arch span with two 452 ft. flanking steel arch spans. 1971.

**Frontenac Bridge,** Quebec, suspension, span 2,190 ft., open 1970.

**Gladesville Bridge** at Sydney, Australia, has the longest concrete arch in the world (1,000 ft. span).

**George Washington Bridge,** New York City, 4th longest suspension bridge in the world, spans the Hudson River between W. 178th St., Manhattan, and Ft. Lee, N.J.; 4,760 ft. between anchorages, two levels, 14 traffic lanes. Triborough Bridge connects Manhattan, the Bronx, and Queens; project comprises a suspension bridge, a vertical lift bridge, and a fixed bridge, all connected by long viaducts. The famous Brooklyn Bridge over the East River, connecting Manhattan and Brooklyn, was completed in 1883, breaking all previous records by spanning 1,595 ft.

**Golden Gate Bridge,** crossing San Francisco Bay, has the second longest single span, 4,200 ft.

**Hampton Roads Bridge-Tunnel,** Va. A crossing completed in 1957 consisting of 2 man-made islands, 2 concrete trestle bridges, and one tunnel, under Hampton Roads with a length of 7,479 ft. A parallel facility with a 7,315 ft. tunnel is now open to traffic.

**Hood Canal Floating Bridge,** Wash. 23 floating concrete pontoons 4,980 tons each. Roadway is supported on crete T-beam sections mounted on pontoons 20 feet above canal. Floating section is 6,471 ft. long, overall 7,866 ft.

**International Bridge,** a series of 8 arch and truss bridges crossing St. Mary's and the Soo Locks between Mich. and Ontario. Two-mile toll completed 1962.

**Lacy V. Murrow Floating Bridge,** Wash. 25 floating pontoons of 4,558 tons each. Bridge with approaches is 8,583 ft.

**Lake Pontchartrain Twin Causeway,** a twin-span crete trestle bridge and 24-mile link within metropolitan New Orleans that connects the north and south shore. First span opened 1956, second 1969.

**Lavaca Bay Causeway,** Tex., 2.2 miles long, consisting of one 260 ft. continuous plate girder unit and 194 precast, prestressed concrete spans of 60 ft. length. 1961.

**Newport Bridge** between Newport and Jamestown, R.I. Total length 11,248 ft., a main suspension span of 1,600 feet, 2 side spans each 688 feet long. It has U.S.A.'s first prefabricated wire strands.

**New York City bridges,** *see Verrazano-Narrows Bridge and George Washington Bridge above.*

**Ogdensburg-Prescott Internat'l Bridge** across the St. Lawrence River from Ogdensburg, N.Y., to Johnston, Ont., opened 1970, is 13,510 ft. long with approaches and 7,260 ft. between abutments.

**Oland Island Bridge** in Sweden was completed in 1972. It is 19,882 feet long, Europe's longest.

**Oosterscheldebrug,** opened Dec. 15, 1965, is a 3.125-mile causeway for automobiles over a sea arm in Zeeland, the Netherlands. It completes a direct connection between Flushing and Rotterdam.

**Poplar St. Bridge** over the Mississippi at St. Louis, a 5-span continuous orthotropic deck plate girder bridge, longest span 600 ft. Eight lanes, 2,165 ft. long.

**Quebec Road,** suspension, span 2,190 feet, 1969, Quebec, Canada.

**Rio-Niteroi,** Guanabara Bay, Brazil, under construction, will be world's longest continuous box and plate girder bridge, 8 miles, 3,363 feet long, with a center span of 984 feet and a span on each side of 656 feet.

**Robert Opie Norris Bridge,** Rappahannock R. between Greys Pt. and White Stone, Va. 9,989 ft. long. Main spans are two 144 foot cantilever truss spans with a 360 foot truss span suspended between them.

**Rockville Bridge,** world's longest 4-track stone arch bridge, 3,810 ft., with 48 arches. Part of the Penn-Central RR system west of Harrisburg, Pa. It contains 440 million lbs. of stone, 100,000 cubic yds. of masonry and crosses the Susquehanna Riv. to Rockville, Pa.

**Royal Gorge Bridge,** 1,053 ft. above the Arkansas River in Colorado, is the highest bridge above water. Opened Dec. 8, 1929, it is 1,260 ft. long with a main span of 880 ft., width 18 ft.

**San Mateo-Hayward Bridge** across San Francisco Bay is first major orthotropic bridge in U.S. It is 6.7 miles long, 4.9 mile low-level concrete trestle and 1.8 miles high-level steel bridge.

**Seven Mile Bridge** is the longest of an expanse of bridges connecting the Florida Keys. It was built by the Florida East Coast Railway between 1904 and 1916, now a state highway.

**Shenandoah River Bridges,** one spans the south fork, 1,924 ft. long, the other north fork, 1,090 ft. long. Warren County, Va.

**Straits of Mackinac Bridge,** completed in 1957, is the longest suspension bridge between anchorages and with approaches extends nearly 5 mi. between Mackinaw City and St. Ignace, Mich.

**Sunshine Skyway,** a 15-mile long bridge-causeway with twin roadbeds that crosses Tampa Bay at St. Petersburg, Fla., a system of twin bridges 864 feet long and 4 smaller bridges with 6 causeways.

**Tagus River Bridge** near Lisbon, Portugal, longest suspension bridge outside the United States, has a 3,323-ft. main span. Opened Aug. 6, 1966, it was named Salazar Bridge for the former premier.

**Thomas A. Edison Memorial Bridge** (causeway) across Sandusky Bay between Martin Point and Danbury, Oh., is 2.67 miles long. The main bridge is 2,044 feet long.

**Thousand Island Bridge,** St. Lawrence River. American span 800 ft.; Canadian 750 ft.

**Union St. Bridge** in Woodstock, Vt., a timber lattice truss with a span of 122 feet built in 1969 using old time procedure of hand drilled holes and wooden pegs.

**Vancouver Bridge,** Canada's longest railway lift span connecting Vancouver and North Vancouver over Burrard Inlet. It is in 3 sections, the longest 493 ft. Spans are part of a project that includes a 2-mile tunnel under Vancouver Hts.

**Woodrow Wilson Memorial Bridge** across the Potomac River at Alexandria, Va., is over a mile long.

**Zoo Bridge** across the Rhine at Cologne, with steel box girders, has a single main span of 850 ft.

**The Interstate Highway 610** crossing the Houston Ship Channel in Texas is 6,300 feet in length and consists of various lengths of prestressed concrete beam and slab approach spans and a 1,233 foot main unit of two 471'6" plate girder units and one 290 ft. simple span.

## Underwater Vehicular Tunnels in North America

(3,000 feet in length or more)

| Name | Location | Waterway | Lgth. Ft. |
|---|---|---|---|
| Bart Trans-Bay Tubes (Rapid Transit) | San Francisco, Cal. | S.F. Bay | 3.6 miles |
| Brooklyn-Battery | New York, N.Y. | East River | 9,117 |
| Holland Tunnel | New York, N.Y. | Hudson River | 8,557 |
| Lincoln Tunnel | New York, N.Y. | Hudson River | 8,216 |
| Baltimore Harbor Tunnel | Baltimore, Md. | Patapsco River | 7,650 |
| Hampton Roads | Norfolk, Va. | Hampton Roads | 7,479 |
| Queens Midtown | New York, N.Y. | East River | 6,414 |
| Thimble Shoal Channel | Cape Henry, Va. | Chesapeake Bay | 5,738 |
| Sumner Tunnel | Boston, Mass. | Boston Harbor | 5,650 |
| Chesapeake Channel | Cape Charles, Va. | Chesapeake Bay | 5,450 |
| Louis-Hippolyte Lafontaine Tunnel | Montreal, Que. | St. Lawrence River | 5,280 |
| Detroit-Windsor | Detroit, Mich. | Detroit River | 5,135 |
| Callahan Tunnel | Boston, Mass. | Boston Harbor | 5,046 |
| Midtown Tunnel | Norfolk, Va. | Elizabeth River | 4,194 |
| Baytown Tunnel | Baytown, Tex. | Houston Ship Channel | 4,111 |
| Posey Tube | Oakland, Cal. | Oakland Estuary | 3,500 |
| Downtown Tunnel | Norfolk, Va. | Elizabeth River | 3,350 |
| Webster St. | Alameda, Cal. | Oakland Estuary | 3,350 |
| Bankhead Tunnel | Mobile, Ala. | Mobile River | 3,109 |
| I-10 Twin Tunnel | Mobile, Ala. | Mobile River | 3,000 |

## Land Vehicular Tunnels in U.S.

(over 1,000 feet in length.)

| Name | Location | Lgth. Ft. | Name | Location | Lgth. Ft. |
|---|---|---|---|---|---|
| Eisenhower Memorial | Route 70, Col. | 8,941 | Battery Park | N.Y.C. | 2,300 |
| Copperfield | Copperfield, Ut. | 6,989 | Battery St. | Seattle, Wash. | 2,140 |
| Allegheny (twin) | Penna. Turnpike | 6,070 | Big Oak Flat | Yosemite Natl. Park | 2,083 |
| Liberty Tubes | Pittsburgh, Pa. | 5,920 | Carlin | I-80, Nev. | 1,993 |
| Zion Natl. Park | Rte. 1, Utah. | 5,766 | Prudential | Boston, Mass. | 1,980 |
| East River Mt. (twin) | Interstate 77, W. Va.-Va. | 5,661 | Internatl. Underpass | Los Angeles, Cal. | 1,910 |
| Tuscarora (twin) | Penna. Turnpike | 5,326 | Street-Car | Providence, R.I. | 1,793 |
| Kittatinny (twin) | Penna. Turnpike | 4,727 | Broadway | San Francisco, Cal. | 1,616 |
| Lehigh | Penna. Turnpike | 4,379 | 9th Street Expy. | Washington, D.C. | 1,610 |
| Blue Mountain (twin) | Penna. Turnpike | 4,339 | F.D. Roosevelt Dr. | 42-48 Sts. N.Y.C. | 1,600 |
| Wawona | Yosemite Natl. Park | 4,233 | Lowry Hill | Minneapolis | 1,496 |
| Squirrel Hill | Pittsburgh, Pa. | 4,225 | Wheeling | Interstate 70, W. Va. | 1,490 |
| Big Walker Mt. | Route I-77, Va. | 4,200 | Mt. Baker Ridge (3) | Seattle, Wash. | 1,466 |
| Fort Pitt | Pittsburgh, Pa. | 3,560 | Knowls Creek | Lane County, Ore. | 1,430 |
| Mall Tunnel | Dist. of Columbia | 3,400 | Mule Pass | Near Bisbee, Ariz. | 1,400 |
| Caldecott | Oakland, Cal. | 3,371 | Arch Cape | Oregon Coast Hwy. 9 | 1,228 |
| Kalihi | Honolulu, Ha. | 2,780 | Queen Creek | Superior, Ariz. | 1,200 |
| Memorial | W. Va. Tpke. (I-77) | 2,669 | West Rock | New Haven, Conn. | 1,200 |
| Cross-Town | 178 St. N.Y.C. | 2,414 | Green River | Route I-80, Wyo. | 1,135 |
| F.D. Roosevelt Dr. | 81-89 Sts. N.Y.C. | 2,400 | Nouanu Pali | Koolau Mt. Oahu, Ha. | 1,080 |
| Dewey Sq. | Boston, Mass. | 2,400 | Elk Creek | Umpqua Hwy. 45, Ore. | 1,080 |

## World's Longest Railway Tunnels

**Source:** Railway Directory & Year Book. Tunnels over 4 miles in length.

| Tunnel | Date | Miles | Yds | Operating railway | Country |
|---|---|---|---|---|---|
| Simplon No. 1 and 11 | 1922 | 12 | 559 | Swiss Fed. & Italian St. | Switz.-Italy |
| Apennine | 1934 | 11 | 892 | Italian State | Italy |
| Cotthard | 1882 | 9 | 562 | Swiss Federal | Switzerland |
| Lotschberg | 1913 | 9 | 140 | Bern-Lotschberg-Simplon | Switzerland |
| Hokuriku | 1962 | 8 | 1,089 | Japanese National | Japan |
| Mont Cenis (Frejus) | 1871 | 8 | 855 | Italian State | France-Italy |
| Cascade | 1929 | 7 | 1,397 | Great Northern | U.S. |
| Flathead Tunnel Mont | 1970 | 6 | 1,758 | Great Northern | U.S. |
| Arlberg | 1884 | 6 | 650 | Austrian Federal | Austria |
| Moffat | 1928 | 6 | 373 | Denver & Rio Grande | U.S. |
| Shimizu | 1931 | 6 | 50 | Japanese National | Japan |
| Kvineshei | 1943 | 5 | 1,112 | Norwegian State | Norway |
| Rimutaka | 1955 | 5 | 821 | New Zealand Gov. | New Zealand |
| Ricken | 1910 | 5 | 608 | Swiss Federal | Switzerland |
| Grenchenberg | 1915 | 5 | 581 | Swiss Federal | Switzerland |
| Otira | 1923 | 5 | 564 | New Zealand Gov. | New Zealand |
| Tauern | 1909 | 5 | 551 | Austrian Federal | Austria |
| Haegebostad | 1943 | 5 | 467 | Norwegian State | Norway |
| Ronco | 1889 | 5 | 277 | Italian State | Italy |
| Hauenstein (Lower) | 1916 | 5 | 95 | Swiss Federal | Switzerland |
| Connaught | 1916 | 5 | 39 | Canadian Pacific | Canada |
| Karawanken | 1906 | 4 | 1,683 | Austrian Federal | Austria-Yugo. |
| New Tanna | 1964 | 4 | 1,663 | Japanese National | Japan |
| Somport | 1928 | 4 | 1,572 | French National | France-Spain |
| Tanna | 1934 | 4 | 1,493 | Japanese National | Japan |
| Ulrikken | 1964 | 4 | 1,338 | Norwegian State | Norway |
| Hoosac | 1875 | 4 | 1,230 | Boston & Maine | U.S. |
| Monte Orso | 1927 | 4 | 1,230 | Italian State | Italy |
| Lupacino | 1958 | 4 | 1,178 | Italian State | Italy |
| Vivola | 1927 | 4 | 1,004 | Italian State | Italy |
| Monte Adone | 1934 | 4 | 760 | Italian State | Italy |
| Jungfrau | 1912 | 4 | 750 | Jungfrau | Switzerland |
| Borgallo | 1884 | 4 | 700 | Italian State | Italy |
| Severn | 1886 | 4 | 628 | Western Region | Great Britain |
| Lusse (Vosges) | 1937 | 4 | 474 | French National | France |

## Major World Dams

Source: Bureau of Reclamation, U.S. Interior Department. *Replaces existing dam.
**Volume** in cubic yards. **Capacity** (gross) in acre feet. Year of completion. U.C. under construction.
Type: A—Arch. B—Buttress. E—Earthfill. G—Gravity. R—Rockfill. MA—Multi-arch.

| Name of dam | Type | Year | River and basin | Country | Height Feet | Crest Length Feet | Volume (1,000 C.Y.) | Res. cap. (1,000 A.F.) |
|---|---|---|---|---|---|---|---|---|
| Afsluitdijk | E | 1932 | Zuider Zee | Netherlands | 62 | 10,500 | 82,927 | 4,864 |
| Akosombo-Main | R | 1965 | Volta | Ghana | | | | |
| Almendra | A | 1970 | Turmes-Douro | Spain | 463 | 2,100 | 10,400 | 120,000 |
| Alpe Gera | G | 1965 | Comor-Adda-Po | Italy | 662 | 1,860 | 2,188 | 2,148 |
| Bagdad Tailings | E | 1973 | Maroney Gulch | U.S. | 121 | 1,710 | 2,252 | 53 |
| Beas | E | 1975 | Beas-Indus | India | 435 | 2,601 | 37,304 | 40 |
| W.A.C. Bennett* | E | 1967 | Peace-Mackenzie | Canada | 600 | 6,400 | 45,800 | 6,600 |
| Bhakra | G | 1963 | Sutlend-Indus | India | 742 | 1,700 | 5,400 | 57,006 |
| Bratsk | GE | 1964 | Angara | USSR | 410 | 16,864 | 18,283 | 137,220 |
| Brouwershavensche Gat | E | 1972 | | Netherlands | 118 | 20,341 | 35,316 | 466 |
| Castaic | E | 1973 | Castaic Cr. | U.S. | 340 | 5,200 | 44,000 | 432 |
| Charvak | A | 1970 | Chirchik-Sir Darya | USSR | 551 | 2,483 | 24,983 | 1,620 |
| Chirkey | A | 1975 | Sulak-Caspian Sea. | USSR | 764 | 1,109 | 1,602 | 2,252 |
| Chivor | R | 1975 | Bata | Colombia | 778 | 919 | 14,126 | 661 |
| Cochiti | E | 1975 | Rio Grande | U.S. | 253 | 26,891 | 64,631 | 513 |
| Copper Cities Tailing 2 | E | 1973 | Tinhorn Wash. | U.S. | 325 | 7,598 | 30,003 | 4 |
| Cougar | R | 1964 | S.F. McKenzie | U.S. | 519 | 1,600 | 13,000 | 219 |
| Dartmouth | R | | Mitta-Mitta. | Australia | 591 | 2,264 | 20,012 | 5,232 |
| Dneprodzerzhinsk | GE | 1964 | Dnieper | USSR | 112 | 118,090 | 28,503 | 1,994 |
| Don Pedro* | ER | 1971 | Tuolume-San Joaquin | U.S. | 585 | 1,900 | 16,760 | 2,030 |
| Dworshak | G | 1974 | N. Fork Clearwater. | U.S. | 717 | 3,287 | 6,500 | 3,453 |
| El Chocon | E | 1974 | Limay | Argentina | 282 | 7,546 | 17,004 | 17,025 |
| Emosson | A | 1974 | Barberine | Switz. | 590 | 1,818 | 1,400 | 182 |
| Esperanza Tailings | E | 1973 | Santa Cruz | U.S. | 121 | 10,600 | 39,704 | 5 |
| Fort Peck | E | 1940 | Missouri | U.S. | 250 | 21,026 | 125,612 | 19,133 |
| Fort Randall | E | 1956 | Missouri | U.S. | 165 | 10,700 | 50,205 | 5,701 |
| Gardiner* | E | 1968 | South Saskatchewan | Canada | 223 | 16,700 | 85,743 | 8,000 |
| Garrison | E | 1956 | Missouri | U.S. | 203 | 11,300 | 66,506 | 24,321 |
| Gepatsch | R | 1965 | Faggenbach-Inn | Austria | 500 | 1,908 | 9,810 | 113 |
| Glen Canyon | A | 1964 | Colorado | U.S. | 710 | 1,560 | 4,901 | 27,000 |
| Goscheneralp | G | 1960 | Goschener | Switz. | 508 | 1,771 | 12,230 | 61 |
| Grand Coulee | G | 1942 | Columbia | U.S. | 550 | 4,173 | 10,585 | 9,724 |
| Grande Dixence | G | 1962 | Dixence-Rhone. | Switz. | 935 | 2,280 | 7,792 | 324 |
| Guri | GER | 1968 | Caroni-Orinoco | Venezuela | 348 | 2,264 | 4,917 | 14,349 |
| Haringvliet | E | 1970 | Haringvliet. | Netherlands | 79 | 18,044 | 26,160 | 527 |
| High Aswan (Saad-El-Aali) | ER | 1970 | Nile. | Egypt | 364 | 12,565 | 57,203 | 137,000 |
| Hirakud | GE | 1956 | Mahandi | India | 202 | 15,748 | 25,100 | 6,600 |
| Hoover | A | 1936 | Colorado | U.S. | 726 | 1,244 | 4,400 | 29,755 |
| Hungry Horse | A | 1953 | S. Fork Flathead | U.S. | 564 | 2,115 | 3,086 | 3,468 |
| Ilha Solteira | EG | 1973 | Parana Rio de la Plata | Brazil | 295 | 20,308 | 29,454 | 27,730 |
| Irkutsk | GE | 1956 | Angara | USSR | 144 | 8,989 | 16,219 | 37,290 |
| Ivankova | EG | 1937 | Volga-Caspian S. | USSR | 98 | 31,398 | 20,207 | 908 |
| Jari | E | 1967 | Jari | Pakistan | 234 | 5,700 | 22,400 | 400 |
| Daniel Johnson* | MA | 1968 | Manicouagan-St. Lawrence. | Canada | 703 | 4,311 | 2,950 | 115,000 |
| Kakhovka | EG | 1955 | Dnieper | USSR | 121 | 5,380 | 46,617 | 14,755 |
| Kanev | E | 1974 | Dnieper | USSR | 82 | 52,950 | 49,520 | 2,125 |
| Kapchagay | E | 1970 | Ili | USSR | 164 | 1,542 | 5,078 | 22,813 |
| Kariba | A | 1959 | Zambesi | Rhodesia-Zambia | 420 | 2,025 | 1,350 | 130,000 |
| Keban | RG | 1974 | First (Euphrates) | Turkey | 679 | 3,881 | 20,900 | 25,110 |
| Kiev | E | 1964 | Dnieper | USSR | 72 | 177,448 | 57,552 | 3,021 |
| King Paul (Kremasta) | ER | 1965 | Acheloos | Greece | 541 | 1,510 | 10,686 | 3,850 |
| Kremenchug | GE | 1961 | Dnieper | USSR | 108 | 39,844 | 41,192 | 10,945 |
| Kurobegawa No. 4 | A | 1964 | Kurobe. | Japan | 610 | 1,603 | 1,782 | 162 |
| Lauwerszee | E | 1969 | Lauwerszee. | Netherlands | 75 | 42,650 | 46,532 | 40 |
| Ludington | E | 1973 | Lake Michigan | U.S. | 170 | 29,301 | 37,703 | 83 |
| Luzzone | A | 1963 | Brenno di Luzzone | Switz. | 682 | 1,738 | 1,739 | 70 |
| Mangla | E | 1967 | Jhelum. | Pakistan | 380 | 11,000 | 85,872 | 5,150 |
| Marimbondo | E | 1975 | Grande | Brazil | 295 | 12,297 | 24,328 | 5,184 |
| Mauvoisin | A | 1957 | Drance de Bagnes. | Switz. | 777 | 1,706 | 2,655 | 146 |
| Mica | R | 1974 | Columbia | Canada | 794 | 2,600 | 42,000 | 20,000 |
| Mingechaur | E | 1953 | Kura | USSR | 262 | 5,085 | 20,400 | 12,970 |
| Navajo | E | 1963 | San Juan | U.S. | 407 | 3,648 | 26,841 | 1,709 |
| New Bullards Bar | A | 1970 | North Yuba-Sacramento. | U.S. | 637 | 2,200 | 2,700 | 960 |
| New Cornelia Tailings | E | 1973 | Ten Mile Wash, Ariz. | U.S. | 98 | 35,600 | 274,026 | 20 |
| New Melones | E | 1975 | Stanislaus-San Joaquin | U.S. | 625 | 1,600 | 15,970 | 2,400 |
| Oahe | E | 1963 | Missouri | U.S. | 245 | 9,300 | 92,008 | 23,591 |
| Okutadami | G | 1961 | Tadami. | Japan | 515 | 1,575 | 2,145 | 487 |
| Oroville | E | 1968 | Feather-Sacramento. | U.S. | 770 | 6,920 | 78,008 | 3,538 |
| Owen Falls | G | 1954 | Lake Victoria-Nile. | Uganda | 100 | 2,725 | | 166,000 |
| Place Moulin | AG | 1965 | Buthier-Dora Baltea | Italy | 502 | 2,181 | 1,962 | 81 |
| Reza Shah Kabir | A | 1975 | Karoun. | Iran | 656 | 1,247 | 1,570 | 2,351 |
| Rybinsk | GE | 1941 | Volga-Caspian S. | USSR | 98 | 2,060 | 3,329 | 20,590 |
| Sakuma | G | 1956 | Tenryu. | Japan | 510 | 963 | 1,465 | 265 |
| San Luis | E | 1967 | San Luis-San Joaquin | U.S. | 382 | 18,600 | 77,666 | 2,039 |
| Saratov | E | 1967 | Volga-Caspian S. | USSR | 131 | 37,204 | 52,843 | 10,458 |
| Shasta | G | 1945 | Sacramento. | U.S. | 602 | 3,460 | 8,711 | 4,552 |
| Swift | E | 1958 | Lewis-Columbia. | U.S. | 610 | 2,100 | 15,800 | 756 |
| Tabka | E | 1975 | Euphrates | Syria | 197 | 14,764 | 60,168 | 11,350 |
| Talbingo | R | 1971 | Tumut | Australia | 530 | 2,300 | 18,950 | 747 |
| Tarbela | ER | 1975 | Indus | Pakistan | 486 | 9,000 | 186,000 | 11,100 |
| Trinity | E | 1962 | Trinity-Klamath | U.S. | 537 | 2,600 | 29,252 | 2,448 |
| Tsimlyansk | EG | 1952 | Don | USSR | 128 | 43,411 | 44,323 | 17,715 |
| Tuttle Creek | E | 1962 | Big Blue-Missouri | U.S. | 154 | 7,500 | 22,987 | 413 |
| Twin Buttes | E | 1963 | Concho-Colorado, Texas | U.S. | 134 | 42,463 | 21,442 | 641 |
| Twin Buttes Tailings | E | 1973 | Santa Cruz. | U.S. | 239 | 11,299 | 38,604 | 209 |
| Vilyui | ER | 1967 | Vilyui. | USSR | 246 | 2,297 | 3,793 | 29,104 |
| Volga-22d congress USSR | ERG | 1958 | Volga-Caspian S. | USSR | 144 | 13,108 | 33,020 | 27,160 |
| Volga-V.I. Lenin | EG | 1955 | Volga-Caspian S. | USSR | 148 | 12,405 | 44,298 | 47,020 |
| Yellowtail | A | 1966 | Bighorn-Missouri | U.S. | 525 | 1,480 | 1,456 | 1,375 |
| Zeya | G | 1975 | Zeya | USSR | 369 | 2,343 | 3,139 | 55,452 |

## Major U.S. Public and Private Dams and Reservoirs

Source: Corps of Engineers, U.S. Army

Heights over 330 feet.

**Height**—Difference in elevation in feet, between lowest point in foundation and top of dam, exclusive of parapet or other projections. **Length**—Overall length of barrier in feet, main dam and its integral features as located between natural abutments. **Volume**—Total volume in cubic yards of all material in main dam and its appurtenant works. **Year**—Date structure was originally completed for use. (UC) Under construction subject to revision. **River**—Mainstream. **Purpose**—I-Irrigation; C-Flood Control; H-Hydroelectric; N-Navigation; S-Water Supply; R-Recreation; D-Debris Control; O-Other. **Parentheses** after name indicate type of dam as follows: (RE)-Earth; (PG)-Gravity; (ER)-Rockfill; (CB)-Buttress; (VA)-Arch; (MV)-Multi-arch; (OT)-Other. †Replacing existing dam.

| Name of dam | State | River | Ht. | Lgth. | Vol. (1,000) | Purpose | Year |
|---|---|---|---|---|---|---|---|
| Oroville (RE) | Cal. | Feather River | 742 | 6800 | 78000 | IR | 1968 |
| Hoover (VA) | Nev. | Colorado River | 726 | 1242 | 4400 | IHCO | 1936 |
| Dworshak (PG) | Ida. | North Fork of Clearwater | 717 | 3287 | 6500 | HCR | 1972 |
| Glen Canyon (VA) | Ariz. | Colorado River | 710 | 1560 | 4901 | HCSR | 1964 |
| Auburn (PG) | Cal. | North Fork American | 680 | 3500 | 6000 | ISCH | UC |
| New Bullards Bar (VA) | Cal. | North Yuba River | 635 | 2200 | 2600 | SD | 1970 |
| New Melones (ER) | Cal. | Stanislaus River | 625 | 1600 | 15970 | IH | UC |
| Swift Dam (RE) | Wash. | North Fork Lewis River | 610 | 2100 | 15800 | HR | 1958 |
| Mossyrock Dam (VA) | Wash. | Cowlitz River | 605 | 1300 | 1231 | HCR | 1968 |
| Shasta (PG) | Cal. | Sacramento River | 602 | 3460 | 8711 | ISHN | 1945 |
| Kopperston No. 3 Refuse Bank (OT) | W.Va. | Jones Br. of Toney Cr. | 580 | 1100 | | O | 1963 |
| Don Pedro (RE) | Cal. | Tuolumne River | 568 | 1800 | 16000 | HI | 1971 |
| Hungry Horse (VA) | Mon. | South Fork of Flathead River | 564 | 2115 | 3086 | IHCN | 1953 |
| Grand Coulee (PG) | Wash. | Columbia River | 550 | 4173 | 10585 | IHCN | 1942 |
| Ross Dam (VA) | Wash. | Skagit River | 540 | 1235 | 905 | HR | 1949 |
| Trinity (RE) | Cal | Trinity River | 537 | 2600 | 29410 | IHCR | 1962 |
| Yellowtail (VA) | Mon. | Bighorn River | 525 | 1480 | 1546 | ICHR | 1966 |
| Cougar (ER) | Ore. | South Fork McKenzie River | 519 | 1600 | 13000 | HCIR | 1964 |
| Flaming Gorge (VA) | Ut. | Green River | 502 | 1285 | 987 | HCSR | 1964 |
| Fontana Dam (PG) | N.C. | Little Tennessee River | 480 | 2365 | 3576 | H | 1944 |
| New Exchequer (ER) | Cal. | Merced River | 479 | 1240 | 5169 | HI | 1926 |
| Morrow Point (VA) | Col. | Gunnison River | 468 | 741 | 365 | HCRO | 1968 |
| Carters Main Dam (ER,RE) | Ga. | Coosawattee River | 464 | 1950 | 15000 | CHR | 1974 |
| Detroit (PG) | Ore. | North Santiam River | 463 | 1580 | 1500 | HCRI | 1953 |
| Anderson Ranch (RE) | Ida. | South Fork Boise River | 456 | 1350 | 9653 | IHCR | 1950 |
| Union Valley (RE) | Cal. | Silver Creek | 453 | 1800 | 10000 | SH | 1963 |
| Elmore Mine Refuse Dump (OT) | W.Va. | Tr-Guyandotte River | 447 | 1975 | | O | 1973 |
| Round Butte Dam (RE,ER) | Ore. | Deschutes River | 440 | 1450 | 9600 | HR | 1964 |
| Pine Flat Lake (PG) | Cal. | Kings River | 440 | 1840 | 2400 | CIRH | 1954 |
| Kopperston No. 4 Dam (OT) | W.Va. | Crane Fork of Clear Fork | 435 | 1100 | | O | 1963 |
| Jocassee (ER) | S.C. | Keowee River | 435 | 1800 | 11600 | H | 1973 |
| Mud Mountain Dam (ER) | Wash. | White River | 425 | 700 | 2300 | C | 1948 |
| Libby Dam (PG) | Mon. | Kootenai River | 420 | 3055 | 13760 | HC | 1973 |
| Owyhee Dam (VA) | Ore. | Owyhee River | 417 | 833 | 538 | ICR | 1932 |
| Lower Hell Hole (ER) | Cal. | Rubicon River | 410 | 1550 | 8315 | SD | 1966 |
| Mammoth Pool (RE) | Cal. | San Joaquin River | 406 | 820 | 5355 | HS | 1960 |
| Navajo (RE) | N.M. | San Juan River | 402 | 3648 | 26840 | IR | 1963 |
| Stirrat No. 15 Embankment (OT) | W.Va. | Rockhouse Br. of Island Cr. | 400 | 1200 | | O | 1972 |
| Toxaway Lake (RE) | S.C. | Jocassee River | 400 | 1000 | | H | 1930 |
| Diablo Dam (VA) | Wash. | Skagit River | 400 | 1142 | 350 | HR | 1906 |
| Trout Lake Dam (RE) | Col. | Lake Fork San Miguel River | 395 | 870 | | H | 1906 |
| Brownlee Dam (ER) | Ida. | Snake River | 395 | 1380 | 6700 | H | 1959 |
| Summersville Dam (ER) | W.Va. | Cauley River | 393 | 2280 | 13565 | CRSO | 1965 |
| Blue Mesa (RE) | Col. | Gunnison River | 390 | 785 | 3093 | HCRO | 1966 |
| Pyramid (ER) | Cal. | Piru Creek | 386 | 1080 | 6952 | IR | 1973 |
| Boundary Dam (VA) | Wash. | Pend Oreille River | 385 | 740 | 240 | HR | 1967 |
| San Luis (RE) | Cal. | San Luis Creek | 382 | 18000 | 77664 | ISHR | 1967 |
| Green Peter (PG) | Ore. | Middle Santiam River | 378 | 1517 | 1142 | CHRI | 1967 |
| Pacoima (VA) | Cal. | Pacoima Creek | 365 | 640 | 226 | C | 1929 |
| Yale Dam (RE) | Wash. | Lewis River | 357 | 1600 | 4200 | HR | 1952 |
| Abiquiu Dam (RE) | N.M. | Rio Chama | 354 | 1540 | 11793 | CD | 1963 |
| Arrowrock (VA) | Ida. | Boise River | 350 | 1150 | 636 | IC | 1915 |
| Pardee (PG) | Cal. | Mokelumne River | 345 | 1337 | 615 | S | 1929 |
| Hills Creek (RE) | Ore. | Middle Fork Willamette River | 341 | 2306 | 10800 | CHIS | 1962 |
| Folsom (PG) | Cal. | American River | 340 | 10200 | 8980 | ISHC | 1956 |
| Whitman Cr. Embankment (OT) | W.Va. | Whitman Cr. of Coopers Fk. | 340 | 625 | | O | 1952 |
| Reservoir No. 22 (VA) | Col. | Boulder Creek | 340 | 1090 | | S | 1953 |
| Gross Dam (PG) | Col. | South Boulder Creek | 340 | 1050 | 592 | S | 1955 |
| Castaic (RE) | Cal. | Castaic Creek | 340 | 5200 | 44000 | IR | 1973 |
| Casitas (RE) | Cal. | Coyote Creek | 334 | 2000 | 9112 | ISC | 1959 |
| Smith Dam (RE) | Ore. | Smith River | 333 | 1150 | 2500 | H | 1962 |
| Upper Baker Dam (PG) | Wash. | Baker River | 332 | 1220 | 628 | HR | 1961 |

## World's Largest Dams

Source: Bureau of Reclamation, U.S. Interior Department

Based on total volume of structure. All dams listed are predominantly earthfill or rockfill and may contain concrete section. UC—Under Construction.

| Name of dam | Cubic yards | Completed | Name of dam | Cubic yards | Completed |
|---|---|---|---|---|---|
| New Cornelia Tailings, U.S. | 274,026,000 | 1973 | Kiev, USSR | 57,552,000 | 1964 |
| Tarbela, Pakistan | 186,000,000 | 1975 | W.A.C. Bennett, Canada | 57,203,000 | 1967 |
| Fort Peck, U.S. | 125,612,000 | 1940 | High Aswan Saad-El-Aili, Egypt | 57,203,000 | 1970 |
| Oahe, U.S. | 92,008,000 | 1963 | Saratov, U.S.S.R. | 52,843,000 | 1967 |
| Mangla, Pakistan | 85,872,000 | 1967 | Mission Tailings, No. 2, U.S. | 52,435,000 | 1973 |
| Gardiner, Canada | 85,743,000 | 1968 | Fort Randall, U.S. | 50,205,000 | 1956 |
| Afsluitdijk, Netherlands | 82,927,000 | 1932 | Kanev, USSR | 49,520,000 | 1974 |
| Orville, U.S. | 78,008,000 | 1968 | Kakhovka, USSR | 46,617,000 | 1955 |
| San Luis, U.S. | 77,666,000 | 1967 | Volga, V.I. Lenin, USSR | 44,298,000 | 1955 |
| Garrison, U.S. | 66,506,000 | 1956 | Castaic, U.S. | 44,000,000 | 1971 |
| Cochiti, U.S. | 64,631,000 | 1975 | Jari, Pakistan | 42,400,000 | 1967 |
| Tabka, Syria | 60,168,000 | 1975 | Kremenchug, USSR | 41,192,000 | 1961 |

## Superlative U.S. Statistics

Source: National Geographic Society, Washington, D.C.

| | | |
|---|---|---|
| Area for 50 states | Total | 3,615,122 sq. mi. |
| | Land 3,536,855 sq. mi.—Water 78,267 sq. mi. | |
| Largest state | Alaska | 586,412 sq. mi. |
| Smallest state | Rhode Island | 1,214 sq. mi. |
| Largest county | San Bernardino County, California | 20,119 sq. mi. |
| Smallest county | New York, New York | 23 sq. mi. |
| Northernmost city | Barrow, Alaska | 71°17'N. |
| Northernmost point | Point Barrow, Alaska | 71°23'N. |
| Southernmost city | Hilo, Island of Hawaii | 19°43'N. |
| Southernmost town | Naalehu, Island of Hawaii | 19°03'N. |
| Southernmost point | Ka Lae (South Cape), Island of Hawaii. | 18°56'N. (155°41'W.) |
| Easternmost city | Eastport, Maine | 66°59'02"W |
| Easternmost town | Lubec, Maine | 66°58'49"W |
| Easternmost point | West Quoddy Head, Maine | 66°57'W. |
| Westernmost city | Lihue, Island of Kauai, Hawaii | 159°22'W. |
| Westernmost town | Adak, Aleutians, Alaska | 176°45'W. |
| Westernmost point | Cape Wrangell, Attu Island, Aleutians, Alaska | 172°27'E |
| Highest city | Leadville, Colorado | 10,200 ft. |
| Lowest town | Calipatria, California | -184 ft. |
| Highest point on Atlantic coast. | Cadillac Mountain, Mount Desert Is., Maine | 1,530 ft. |
| Largest and oldest national park | Yellowstone National Park (1872), Wyoming, Montana, Idaho. | 3,468 sq. mi. |
| Largest national monument | Glacier Bay, Alaska | 4,383 sq. mi. |
| Highest waterfall | Yosemite Falls—Total in three sections | 2,425 ft. |
| | Upper Yosemite Fall | 1,430 ft. |
| | Cascades in middle section | 675 ft. |
| | Lower Yosemite Fall | 320 ft. |
| Longest river. | Mississippi-Missouri | 3,710 mi. |
| Highest mountain | Mount McKinley, Alaska | 20,320 ft. |
| Lowest point | Death Valley, California | -282 ft. |
| Deepest lake. | Crater Lake, Oregon | 1,932 ft. |
| Rainiest spot | Mt. Waialeale, Hawaii | Annual aver. rainfall 460 inches |
| Largest gorge | Grand Canyon, Colorado River, Arizona | 277 miles long, 1 to 20 miles wide, 1 mile deep |
| Deepest gorge. | Hell's Canyon, Snake River, Idaho | 7,900 ft. |
| Strongest surface wind | Mount Washington, New Hampshire recorded 1934 | 231 mph |
| Biggest dam . | New Cornelia Tailings, Ten Mile Wash, Arizona | 274,026,000 cu. yds. material used |
| Tallest building. | Sears Tower, Chicago, Illinois | 1,454 ft. |
| Largest building | Boeing 747 Manufacturing Plant, Everett, Washington | 205,600,000 cu. ft.; covers 47 acres. |
| Tallest structure. | TV tower, Blanchard, North Dakota | 2,063 ft. |
| Longest bridge span | Verrazano-Narrows, New York | 4,260 ft. |
| Highest bridge | Royal Gorge, Colorado | 1,053 ft. above water |
| Deepest well | Gas well, Washita County, Oklahoma | 31,441 ft. |

### The 49 States, Including Alaska

| | | |
|---|---|---|
| Area for 49 states | Total | 3,608,672 sq. mi. |
| | Land 3,530,430 sq. mi.—Water 78,242 sq. mi. | |

### .The 48 Contiguous States

| | | |
|---|---|---|
| Area for 48 states | Total | 3,022,260 sq. mi. |
| | Land 2,963,998 sq. mi.—Water 58,262 sq. mi. | |
| Largest state | Texas | 267,338 sq. mi |
| Northernmost town | Angle Inlet, Minnesota | 49°22'N. |
| Northernmost point | Northwest Angle, Minnesota | 49°23'N. |
| Southernmost city | Key West, Florida | 24°33'N. |
| Southernmost mainland city | Florida City, Florida | 25°27'N. |
| Southernmost point | Key West, Florida | 24°33'N. |
| Westernmost town | La Push, Washington | 124°38'W. |
| Westernmost point | Cape Alava, Washington | 124°44'W. |
| Highest mountain | Mount Whitney, California | 14,494 ft. |

Note to users: The distinction between cities and towns varies from state to state. In this table the U.S. Bureau of the Census usage was followed.

---

## Geodetic Datum Point of North America

The geodetic datum point of the U.S. is the National Ocean Survey's triangulation station Meades Ranch in Osborne County, Kansas, at latitude 39° 13'26". 686 N and longitude 98° 32'30". 506 W. This geodetic datum point is a fundamental point from which all latitude and longitude computations originate for North America and Central America.

## Statistical Information about the U.S.

In the *Statistical Abstract of the United States* the Bureau of the Census, U.S. Dept. of Commerce, annually publishes a summary of social, political, and economic information. A book of more than 1,000 pages, it presents in 33 sections comprehensive data on population, housing, health, education, employment, income, prices, business, banking, energy, science, defense, trade, government finance, foreign country comparison, and other subjects. Special features include an appendix on statistical methodology and reliability and a summary of recent trends. The book is prepared under the direction of William Lerner, Data User Services Division, Bureau of the Census. Supplements to the *Statistical Abstract* are *Pocket Data Book USA, 1976; County and City Data Book, 1972* (1977 edition is in preparation); *Congressional District Data Book, 93rd Congress with supplements for the 3 states that redistricted for the 94th Congress; Historical Statistics of the United States, Colonial Times to 1970.* Information concerning these and other publications may be obtained from the Supt. of Documents, Government Printing Office, Wash., D.C. 20402, or from the U.S. Bureau of the Census, Data User Services Division, Wash., D.C. 20233.

## Highest and Lowest Altitudes in the U.S. and Territories

**Source:** Geological Survey, U.S. Interior Department. (Minus sign means below sea level; elevations are in feet.)

| State | Highest Point Name | County | Elev. | Lowest Point Name | County | Elev. |
|---|---|---|---|---|---|---|
| Alabama | Cheaha Mountain | Cleburne | 2,407 | Gulf of Mexico | | Sea level |
| Alaska | Mount McKinley | | 20,320 | Pacific Ocean | | Sea level |
| Arizona | Humphreys Park | Coconino | 12,633 | Colorado R. | Yuma | 70 |
| Arkansas | Magazine Mountain | Logan | 2,753 | Ouachita R. | Ashley Union | 55 |
| California | Mount Whitney | Inyo-Tulare | 14,494 | Death Valley | Inyo | −282 |
| Canal Zone | Cerro Galera | Balboa District | 1,205 | Atlantic Ocean | | Sea level |
| Colorado | Mount Elbert | Lake | 14,433 | Arkansas R. | Prowers | 3,350 |
| Connecticut | Mount Frissell | Litchfield | 2,380 | L.I. Sound | | Sea level |
| Delaware | On Ebright Road | New Castle | 442 | Atlantic Ocean | | Sea level |
| Dist. of Col. | Tenleytown | N. W. part | 410 | Potomac R. | | 1 |
| Florida | West boundary | Walton | 345 | Atlantic Ocean | | Sea level |
| Georgia | Brasstown Bald | Towns-Union | 4,784 | Atlantic Ocean | | Sea level |
| Guam | Mount Lamlam | Agat District | 1,329 | Pacific Ocean | | Sea level |
| Hawaii | Mauna Kea | Hawaii | 13,796 | Pacific Ocean | | Sea level |
| Idaho | Borah Peak | Custer | 12,662 | Snake R. | Nez Perce | 710 |
| Illinois | Charles Mound | Jo Daviess | 1,235 | Mississippi R. | Alexander | 279 |
| Indiana | Franklin Township | Wayne | 1,257 | Ohio R. | Posey | 320 |
| Iowa | NE of Sibley | Osceola | 1,670 | Mississippi R. | Lee | 480 |
| Kansas | Mount Sunflower | Wallace | 4,039 | Verdigris R. | Montgomery | 680 |
| Kentucky | Black Mountain | Harlan | 4,145 | Mississippi R. | Fulton | 257 |
| Louisiana | Driskill Mountain | Bienville | 535 | New Orleans | Orleans | −5 |
| Maine | Mount Katahdin | Piscataquis | 5,268 | Atlantic Ocean | | Sea level |
| Maryland | Backbone Mountain | Garrett | 3,360 | Atlantic Ocean | | Sea level |
| Massachusetts | Mount Greylock | Berkshire | 3,491 | Atlantic Ocean | | Sea level |
| Michigan | Mount Curwood | Baraga | 1,980 | Lake Erie | | 572 |
| Minnesota | Eagle Mountain | Cook | 2,301 | Lake Superior | | 602 |
| Mississippi | Woodall Mountain | Tishomingo | 806 | Gulf of Mexico | | Sea level |
| Missouri | Taum Sauk Mt. | Iron | 1,772 | St. Francis R. | Dunklin | 230 |
| Montana | Granite Peak | Park | 12,799 | Kootenai R. | Lincoln | 1,800 |
| Nebraska | Johnson Township | Kimball | 5,426 | S.E. cor. State | Richardson | 840 |
| Nevada | Boundary Peak | Esmeralda | 13,143 | Colorado R. | Clark | 470 |
| New Hamp. | Mt. Washington | Coos | 6,288 | Atlantic Ocean | | Sea level |
| New Jersey | High Point | Sussex | 1,803 | Atlantic Ocean | | Sea level |
| New Mexico | Wheeler Peak | Taos | 13,161 | Red Bluff Res. | Eddy | 2,817 |
| New York | Mount Marcy | Essex | 5,344 | Atlantic Ocean | | Sea level |
| North Carolina | Mount Mitchell | Yancey | 6,684 | Atlantic Ocean | | Sea level |
| North Dakota | White Butte | Slope | 3,506 | Red R. | Pembina | 750 |
| Ohio | Campbell Hill | Logan | 1,550 | Ohio R. | Hamilton | 433 |
| Oklahoma | Black Mesa | Cimarron | 4,973 | Little R. | McCurtain | 287 |
| Oregon | Mount Hood | Clackamas-Hood R. | 11,235 | Pacific Ocean | | Sea level |
| Pennsylvania | Mt. Davis | Somerset | 3,213 | Delaware R. | Delaware | Sea level |
| Puerto Rico | Cerro de Punta | Ponce | 4,389 | Atlantic Ocean | | Sea level |
| Rhode Island | Jerimoth Hill | Providence | 812 | Atlantic Ocean | | Sea level |
| Samoa | Lata Mountain | Tau Island | 3,160 | Pacific Ocean | | Sea level |
| South Carolina | Sassafras Mountain | Pickens | 3,560 | Atlantic Ocean | | Sea level |
| South Dakota | Harney Peak | Pennington | 7,242 | Big Stone Lake | Roberts | 962 |
| Tennessee | Clingmans Dome | Sevier | 6,643 | Mississippi R. | Shelby | 182 |
| Texas | Guadalupe Peak | Culberson | 8,751 | Gulf of Mexico | | Sea level |
| Utah | Kings Peak | Duchesne | 13,528 | Beaverdam Cr. | Washington | 2,000 |
| Vermont | Mount Mansfield | Lamoille | 4,393 | Lake Champlain | Franklin | 95 |
| Virginia | Mount Rogers | Grayson-Smyth | 5,729 | Atlantic Ocean | | Sea level |
| Virgin Islands | Crown Mountain | Is. St. Thomas | 1,556 | Atlantic Ocean | | Sea level |
| Washington | Mount Rainier | Pierce | 14,410 | Pacific Ocean | | Sea level |
| West Virginia | Spruce Knob | Pendleton | 4,863 | Potomac R. | Jefferson | 240 |
| Wisconsin | Timms Hill | Price | 1,952 | Lake Michigan | | 581 |
| Wyoming | Gannett Peak | Fremont | 13,804 | B. Fourche R. | Crook | 3,100 |

## U.S. Coastline by States

**Source:** NOAA, U.S. Commerce Department
(statute miles)

| State | Coastline[1] | Shoreline[2] | State | Coastline[1] | Shoreline[2] |
|---|---|---|---|---|---|
| **Atlantic coast** | **2,069** | **28,673** | Virginia | 112 | 3,315 |
| Connecticut | 0 | 618 | **Gulf coast** | **1,631** | **17,141** |
| Delaware | 28 | 381 | Alabama | 53 | 607 |
| Florida | 580 | 3,331 | Florida | 770 | 5,095 |
| Georgia | 100 | 2,344 | Louisiana | 397 | 7,721 |
| Maine | 228 | 3,478 | Mississippi | 44 | 359 |
| Maryland | 31 | 3,190 | Texas | 367 | 3,359 |
| Massachusetts | 192 | 1,519 | **Pacific coast** | **7,623** | **40,298** |
| New Hampshire | 13 | 131 | Alaska | 5,580 | 31,383 |
| New Jersey | 130 | 1,792 | California | 840 | 3,427 |
| New York | 127 | 1,850 | Hawaii | 750 | 1,052 |
| North Carolina | 301 | 3,375 | Oregon | 296 | 1,410 |
| Pennsylvania | 0 | 89 | Washington | 157 | 3,026 |
| Rhode Island | 40 | 384 | **Arctic coast, Alaska** | **1,060** | **2,521** |
| South Carolina | 187 | 2,876 | **United States** | **12,383** | **88,633** |

(1) Figures are lengths of general outline of seacoast. Measurements were made with a unit measure of 30 minutes of latitude on charts as near the scale of 1:1,200,000 as possible. Coastline of sounds and bays is included to a point where they narrow to width of unit measure, and includes the distance across at such point. (2) Figures obtained in 1939-40 with a recording instrument on the largest-scale charts and maps then available. Shoreline of outer coast, offshore islands, sounds, bays, rivers, and creeks is included to the head of tidewater or to a point where tidal waters narrow to a width of 100 feet.

## States: Settled, Capitals, Entry into Union, Area, Rank

The original 13 states—The 13 colonies that seceded from Great Britain and fought the War of Independence (American Revolution) became the 13 original states. They were: Delaware, Pennsylvania, New Jersey, Georgia, Connecticut, Massachusetts, Maryland, South Carolina, New Hampshire, Virginia, New York, North Carolina, and Rhode Island. The order for the original 13 states is the order in which they ratified the Constitution.

| State | Set-tled* | Capital | Entered Union Date | Order | Extent in miles (approx. mean) Long | Wide | Area in square miles Land | Inland water | Total | Rank in area |
|---|---|---|---|---|---|---|---|---|---|---|
| Ala. | 1702 | Montgomery | Dec. 14, 1819 | 22 | 330 | 190 | 50,708 | 901 | 51,609 | 29 |
| Alas. | 1784 | Juneau | Jan. 3, 1959 | 49 | (a)1,480 | 810 | 566,432 | 19,980 | 586,412 | 1 |
| Ariz. | 1776 | Phoenix | Feb. 14, 1912 | 48 | 400 | 310 | 113,417 | 492 | 113,909 | 6 |
| Ark. | 1785 | Little Rock | June 15, 1836 | 25 | 260 | 240 | 51,945 | 1,159 | 53,104 | 27 |
| Cal. | 1769 | Sacramento | Sept. 9, 1850 | 31 | 770 | 250 | 156,361 | 2,332 | 158,693 | 3 |
| Col. | 1858 | Denver | Aug. 1, 1876 | 38 | 380 | 280 | 103,766 | 481 | 104,247 | 8 |
| Conn. | 1635 | Hartford | Jan. 9, 1788 | 5 | 110 | 70 | 4,862 | 147 | 5,009 | 48 |
| Del. | 1683 | Dover | Dec. 7, 1787 | 1 | 100 | 30 | 1,982 | 75 | 2,057 | 49 |
| D.C. | | Washington | | | ... | ... | 61 | 6 | 67 | 51 |
| Fla. | 1565 | Tallahassee | Mar. 3, 1845 | 27 | 500 | 160 | 54,090 | 4,470 | 58,560 | 22 |
| Ga. | 1733 | Atlanta | Jan. 2, 1788 | 4 | 300 | 230 | 58,073 | 803 | 58,876 | 21 |
| Ha. | | Honolulu | Aug. 21, 1959 | 50 | ... | ... | 6,425 | 25 | 6,450 | 47 |
| Ida. | 1842 | Boise | July 3, 1890 | 43 | 570 | 300 | 82,677 | 880 | 83,557 | 13 |
| Ill. | 1720 | Springfield | Dec. 3, 1818 | 21 | 390 | 210 | 55,748 | 652 | 56,400 | 24 |
| Ind. | 1733 | Indianapolis | Dec. 11, 1816 | 19 | 270 | 140 | 36,097 | 194 | 36,291 | 38 |
| Ia. | 1788 | Des Moines | Dec. 28, 1846 | 29 | 310 | 200 | 55,941 | 349 | 56,290 | 25 |
| Kan. | 1727 | Topeka | Jan. 29, 1861 | 34 | 400 | 210 | 81,787 | 477 | 82,264 | 14 |
| Ky. | 1774 | Frankfort | June 1, 1792 | 15 | 380 | 140 | 39,650 | 745 | 40,395 | 37 |
| La. | 1699 | Baton Rouge | Apr. 30, 1812 | 18 | 380 | 130 | 44,930 | 3,593 | 48,523 | 31 |
| Me. | 1624 | Augusta | Mar. 15, 1820 | 23 | 320 | 190 | 30,920 | 2,295 | 33,215 | 39 |
| Md. | 1634 | Annapolis | Apr. 28, 1788 | 7 | 250 | 90 | 9,891 | 686 | 10,577 | 42 |
| Mass. | 1620 | Boston | Feb. 6, 1788 | 6 | 190 | 50 | 7,826 | 431 | 8,257 | 45 |
| Mich. | 1668 | Lansing | Jan. 26, 1837 | 26 | 490 | 240 | 56,817 | 1,399 | 58,216 | 23 |
| Minn. | 1805 | St. Paul | May 11, 1858 | 32 | 400 | 250 | 79,289 | 4,779 | 84,068 | 12 |
| Miss. | 1699 | Jackson | Dec. 10, 1817 | 20 | 340 | 170 | 47,296 | 420 | 47,716 | 32 |
| Mo. | 1735 | Jefferson City | Aug. 10, 1821 | 24 | 300 | 240 | 68,995 | 691 | 69,686 | 19 |
| Mon. | 1809 | Helena | Nov. 8, 1889 | 41 | 630 | 280 | 145,587 | 1,551 | 147,138 | 4 |
| Neb. | 1847 | Lincoln | Mar. 1, 1867 | 37 | 430 | 210 | 76,483 | 744 | 77,227 | 15 |
| Nev. | 1850 | Carson City | Oct. 31, 1864 | 36 | 490 | 320 | 109,889 | 651 | 110,540 | 7 |
| N.H. | 1623 | Concord | June 21, 1788 | 9 | 190 | 70 | 9,027 | 277 | 9,304 | 44 |
| N.J. | 1664 | Trenton | Dec. 18, 1787 | 3 | 150 | 70 | 7,521 | 315 | 7,836 | 46 |
| N.M. | 1605 | Santa Fe | Jan. 6, 1912 | 47 | 370 | 343 | 121,412 | 254 | 121,666 | 5 |
| N.Y. | 1614 | Albany | July 26, 1788 | 11 | 330 | 283 | 47,831 | 1,745 | 49,576 | 30 |
| N.C. | 1650 | Raleigh | Nov. 21, 1789 | 12 | 500 | 150 | 48,798 | 3,788 | 52,586 | 28 |
| N.D. | 1766 | Bismarck | Nov. 2, 1889 | 39 | 340 | 211 | 69,273 | 1,392 | 70,665 | 17 |
| Oh. | 1788 | Columbus | Mar. 1, 1803 | 17 | 220 | 220 | 40,975 | 247 | 41,222 | 35 |
| Okla. | 1889 | Oklahoma City | Nov. 16, 1907 | 46 | 400 | 220 | 68,782 | 1,137 | 69,919 | 18 |
| Ore. | 1811 | Salem | Feb. 14, 1859 | 33 | 360 | 261 | 96,184 | 797 | 96,981 | 10 |
| Pa. | 1682 | Harrisburg | Dec. 12, 1787 | 2 | 283 | 160 | 44,966 | 367 | 45,333 | 33 |
| R.I. | 1636 | Providence | May 29, 1790 | 13 | 40 | 30 | 1,049 | 165 | 1,214 | 50 |
| S.C. | 1670 | Columbia | May 23, 1788 | 8 | 260 | 200 | 30,225 | 830 | 31,055 | 40 |
| S.D. | 1856 | Pierre | Nov. 2, 1889 | 40 | 380 | 210 | 75,955 | 1,092 | 77,047 | 16 |
| Tenn. | 1757 | Nashville | June 1, 1796 | 16 | 440 | 120 | 41,328 | 916 | 42,244 | 34 |
| Tex. | 1691 | Austin | Dec. 29, 1845 | 28 | 790 | 660 | 262,134 | 5,204 | 267,338 | 2 |
| Ut. | 1847 | Salt Lake City | Jan. 4, 1896 | 45 | 350 | 270 | 82,096 | 2,820 | 84,916 | 11 |
| Vt. | 1724 | Montpelier | Mar. 4, 1791 | 14 | 160 | 80 | 9,267 | 342 | 9,609 | 43 |
| Va. | 1607 | Richmond | June 25, 1788 | 10 | 430 | 200 | 39,780 | 1,037 | 40,817 | 36 |
| Wash. | 1811 | Olympia | Nov. 11, 1889 | 42 | 360 | 240 | 66,570 | 1,622 | 68,192 | 20 |
| W.Va. | 1727 | Charleston | June 20, 1863 | 35 | 240 | 130 | 24,070 | 111 | 24,181 | 41 |
| Wis. | 1766 | Madison | May 29, 1848 | 30 | 310 | 260 | 54,464 | 1,690 | 56,154 | 26 |
| Wy. | 1834 | Cheyenne | July 10, 1890 | 44 | 360 | 280 | 97,203 | 711 | 97,914 | 9 |

*First European permanent settlement. (a) Aleutian Islands and Alexander Archipelago are not considered in these lengths.

---

## The Continental Divide

**Source:** Geological Survey, U.S. Interior Department

Continental Divide: watershed, created by mountain ranges or table-lands of the Rocky Mountains, from which the drainage is easterly or westerly; the easterly flowing waters reaching the Atlantic Ocean chiefly through the Gulf of Mexico, and the westerly flowing waters reaching the Pacific Ocean through the Columbia River, or through the Colorado River, which flows into the Gulf of California.

The location and route of the Continental Divide across the United States may briefly be described as follows:

Beginning at point of crossing the United States-Mexican boundary, near long. 108°45'W., the Divide, in a northerly direction, crosses New Mexico along the western edge of the Rio Grande drainage basin, entering Colorado near long. 106°41'W.

Thence by a very irregular route northerly across Colorado along the western summits of the Rio Grande and of the Arkansas, the South Platte, and the North Platte River basins, and across Rocky Mountain National Park, entering Wyoming near long. 106°52'W.

Thence in a northwesterly direction, forming the western rims of the North Platte, Big Horn, and Yellowstone River basins, crossing the southwestern portion of Yellowstone National Park.

Thence in a westerly and then a northerly direction forming the common boundary of Idaho and Montana, to a point on said boundary near long. 114°00'W.

Thence northeasterly and northwesterly through Montana and the Glacier National Park, entering Canada near long. 114°04'W.

## Chronological List of Territories

Source: National Archives and Records Service

| Name of territory | Date of Organic Act | Organic Act effective | Admission as state | Yrs. terr. |
|---|---|---|---|---|
| rthwest Territory(a) | July 13, 1787 | No fixed date | Mar. 1, 1803(b) | 16 |
| rritory southwest of River Ohio | May 26, 1790 | No fixed date | June 1, 1796(c) | 6 |
| sissippi | Apr. 7, 1798 | When president acted | Dec. 10, 1817 | 19 |
| iana | May 7, 1800 | July 4, 1800 | Dec. 11, 1816 | 16 |
| eans | Mar. 26, 1804 | Oct. 1, 1804 | Apr. 30, 1812(d) | 7 |
| higan | Jan. 11, 1805 | June 30, 1805 | Jan. 26, 1837 | 31 |
| uisiana-Missouri(e) | Mar. 3, 1805 | July 4, 1805 | Aug. 10, 1821 | 16 |
| ois | Feb. 3, 1809 | Mar. 1, 1809 | Dec. 3, 1818 | 9 |
| abama | Mar. 3, 1817 | When Miss. became a state | Dec. 14, 1819 | 2 |
| ansas | Mar. 2, 1819 | July 4, 1819 | June 15, 1836 | 17 |
| rida | Mar. 30, 1822 | No fixed date | Mar. 3, 1845 | 23 |
| sconsin | Apr. 20, 1836 | July 3, 1836 | May 29, 1848 | 12 |
| a | June 12, 1838 | July 3, 1838 | Dec. 28, 1846 | 7 |
| egon | Aug. 14, 1848 | Date of act | Feb. 14, 1859 | 10 |
| nnesota | Mar. 3, 1849 | Date of act | May 11, 1858 | 9 |
| w Mexico | Sept. 9, 1850 | On president's proclamation | Jan. 6, 1912 | 61 |
| ah | Sept. 9, 1850 | Date of act | Jan. 4, 1896 | 44 |
| shington | Mar. 2, 1853 | Date of act | Nov. 11, 1889 | 36 |
| braska | May 30, 1854 | Date of act | Mar. 1, 1867 | 12 |
| nsas | May 30, 1854 | Date of act | Jan. 29, 1861 | 6 |
| lorado | Feb. 28, 1861 | Date of act | Aug. 1, 1876 | 15 |
| vada | Mar. 2, 1861 | Date of act | Oct. 31, 1864 | 3 |
| kota | Mar. 2, 1861 | Date of act | Nov. 2, 1889 | 28 |
| zona | Feb. 24, 1863 | Date of act | Feb. 14, 1912 | 49 |
| ho | Mar. 3, 1863 | Date of act | July 3, 1890 | 27 |
| ntana | May 26, 1864 | Date of act | Nov. 8, 1889 | 25 |
| roming | July 25, 1868 | When officers were qualified | July 10, 1890 | 22 |
| aska | May 17, 1884 | No fixed date | Jan. 3, 1959 | 75 |
| lahoma | May 2, 1890 | Date of act | Nov. 16, 1907 | 17 |
| waii | Apr. 30, 1900 | June 14, 1900 | Aug. 21, 1959 | 59 |

(a) Included Ohio, Indiana, Illinois, Michigan, Wisconsin, eastern Minnesota; (b) as the state of Ohio; (c) as the state of nnessee; (d) as the state of Louisiana; (e) organic act for Missouri Territory of June 4 1812, became effective Dec. 7, 1812.

## Geographic Centers, U.S. and Each State

Source: Geological Survey, U.S. Interior Department

ited States, including Alaska and Hawaii — South Dakota; Butte County, 17 miles W of Castle Rock, 14 miles E of junction of borders of South Dakota, Montana, and Wyoming. Approx. lat. 44°58'N. long. 103°46'W.

ntiguous U. S. (48 states) — Near Lebanon, Smith Co., Kansas, lat. 39°50'N. long. 98°35'W.

rth American continent — The geographic center is in Pierce County, North Dakota, 6 miles W of Balta, latitude 48°10', longitude 100°10'W.

### State—county, locality

abama—Chilton, 12 miles SW of Clanton.
aska—lat. 63°50'N. long. 152°W. Approx. 60 mi. NW of Mt. McKinley.
izona—Yavapai, 55 miles ESE of Prescott.
kansas—Pulaski, 12 miles NW of Little Rock.
lifornia—Madera, 38 miles E of Madera.
olorado—Park, 30 miles NW of Pikes Peak.
onnecticut—Hartford, at East Berlin.
elaware—Kent, 11 miles S of Dover.
strict of Columbia—Near Fourth and "L" Streets, NW.
orida—Hernando, 12 miles NNW of Brooksville.
eorgia—Twiggs, 18 miles SE of Macon.
waii—Hawaii, 20°15'N, 156°20'W, off Maui Island.
aho—Custer, at Custer, SW of Challis.
nois—Logan, 28 miles NE of Springfield.
diana—Boone, 14 miles NNW of Indianapolis.
wa—Story, 5 miles NE of Ames.
ansas—Barton, 15 miles NE of Great Bend.
entucky—Marion, 3 miles NNW of Lebanon.
uisiana—Avoyelles, 3 miles SE of Marksville.
aine—Piscataquis, 18 miles north of Dover.

Maryland—Prince Georges, 4.5 miles NW of Davidsonville.
Massachusetts—Worcester, north part of city.
Michigan—Wexford, 5 miles NNW of Cadillac.
Minnesota—Crow Wing, 10 miles SW of Brainerd.
Mississippi—Leake, 9 miles WNW of Carthage.
Missouri—Miller, 20 miles SW of Jefferson City.
Montana—Fergus, 12 miles west of Lewistown.
Nebraska—Custer, 10 miles NW of Broken Bow.
Nevada—Lander, 26 miles SE of Austin.
New Hampshire—Belknap, 3 miles E of Ashland.
New Jersey—Mercer, 5 miles SE of Trenton.
New Mexico—Torrance, 12 miles SSW of Willard.
New York—Madison, 12 miles S of Oneida and 26 miles SW of Utica.
North Carolina—Chatham, 10 miles NW of Sanford.
North Dakota—Sheridan, 5 miles SW of McClusky.
Ohio—Delaware, 25 miles NNE of Columbus.
Oklahoma—Oklahoma, 8 miles N of Oklahoma City.
Oregon—Crook, 25 miles SSE of Prineville.
Pennsylvania—Centre, 2.5 miles SW of Bellefonte.
Rhode Island—Kent, 1 mile SSW of Crompton.
South Carolina—Richland, 13 miles NE of Columbia.
South Dakota—Hughes, 8 miles NE of Pierre.
Tennessee—Rutherford, 5 mi. NE of Murfreesboro.
Texas—McCulloch, 15 miles NE of Brady.
Utah—Sanpete, 3 miles N of Manti.
Vermont—Washington, 3 miles E of Roxbury.
Virginia—Buckingham, 5 miles SW of Buckingham.
Washington—Chelan, 10 mi. WSW of Wenatchee.
West Virginia—Braxton, 4 miles E of Sutton.
Wisconsin—Wood, 9 miles SE of Marshfield.
Wyoming—Fremont, 58 miles ENE of Lander.

There is no generally accepted definition of geographic center, and no satisfactory method for determining it. The geographic center an area may be defined as the center of gravity of the surface, or that point on which the surface of the area would balance if it re a plane of uniform thickness.
No marked or monumented point has been established by any government agency as the geographic center of either the 50 states, e contiguous United States, or the North American continent. A monument was erected in Lebanon, Kan., contiguous U.S. center, by group of citizens.

## International Boundary Lines of the U.S.

The length of the northern boundary of the contiguous U.S. — the U.S.-Canadian border, excluding Alaska — is 3,987 miles according the U.S. Geological Survey, Dept. of the Interior. The length of the Alaskan-Canadian border is 1,538 miles. The length of the U.S.-exican border, from the Gulf of Mexico to the Pacific Ocean, is approximately 1,933 miles (1963 boundary agreement).

# Origin of the Names of U.S. States

Source: State officials, the Smithsonian Institution, and the Topographic Division, U.S. Geological Survey.

**Alabama**—Indian for tribal town, later a tribe (Alabamas or Alibamons) of the Creek confederacy.

**Alaska**—Russian version of Aleutian (Eskimo) word, alakshak, for "peninsula" or "great lands."

**Arizona**—Spanish version of Pima Indian word for "little spring place," or Aztec arizuma, meaning "silver-bearing."

**Arkansas**—French variant of Kansas, a Sioux Indian name for "south wind people."

**California**—Bestowed by the Spanish conquistadors (possibly by Cortez). It was the name of an imaginary island, an earthly paradise, in "Las Serges de Esplandian," a Spanish romance written by Montalvo in 1510. Baja California (Lower California, in Mexico) was first visited by Spanish in 1533. The present U.S. state was called Alta (Upper) California.

**Colorado**—Spanish, red, first applied to Colorado River.

**Connecticut**—From Mohican and other Algonquin words meaning "long river place."

**Delaware**—Named for Lord De La Warr, early governor of Virginia; first applied to river, then to Indian tribe (Lenni-Lenape), and the state.

**District of Columbia**—For Columbus, 1791.

**Florida**—Named by Ponce de Leon on Pascua Florida, "Flowery Easter," on Easter Sunday, 1513.

**Georgia**—For King George II of England by James Oglethorpe, colonial administrator, 1732.

**Hawaii**—Possibly derived from native world for homeland, Hawaiki or Owhyhee.

**Idaho**—A coined name with an invented Indian meaning "gem of the mountains;" originally suggested for the Pike's Peak mining territory (Colorado), then applied to the new mining territory of the Pacific Northwest.

**Illinois**—French for Illini or land of Illini, Algonquin word meaning men or warriors.

**Indiana**—Means "land of the Indians."

**Iowa**—Indian word variously translated as "one who puts to sleep" or "beautiful land."

**Kansas**—Sioux word for "south wind people."

**Kentucky**—Indian word variously translated as "dark and bloody ground," "meadow land" and "land of tomorrow."

**Louisiana**—Part of territory called Louisiana by Sieur de La Salle for French King Louis XIV.

**Maine**—From Maine, ancient French province.

**Maryland**—For Queen Henrietta Maria, wife of Charles I of England.

**Massachusetts**—From Indian tribe named after "large hill place" identified by Capt. John Smith as near Milton, Mass.

**Michigan**—From Chippewa words mici gama meaning "great water," after the lake of the same name.

**Minnesota**—From Dakota Sioux word meaning "cloudy water" or "sky-tinted water" of the Minnesota River.

**Mississippi**—Probably Chippewa; mici zibi, "great river" or "gathering-in of all the waters."

**Missouri**—Indian tribe named after Missouri River, meaning "muddy water."

**Montana**—Latin or Spanish for "mountainous."

**Nebraska**—From Omaha or Otos Indian word meaning "broad water" or "flat river," describing the Platte River.

**Nevada**—Spanish, meaning snow-clad.

**New Hampshire**—Named 1629 by Capt. John Mason of Plymouth Council for county in England.

**New Jersey**—The Duke of York, 1664, gave a patent to John Berkeley and Sir George Carteret to be called Nova Caesaria New Jersey, after England's Isle of Jersey.

**New Mexico**—Spaniards in Mexico applied term to land n‹ and west of Rio Grande in the 16th century.

**New York**—For Duke of York and Albany who received pa to New Netherland from his brother Charles II and sent an exp‹ tion to capture it, 1664.

**North Carolina**—In 1619 Charles I gave a large patent to Robert Heath to be called Province of Carolana, from Car‹ Latin name for Charles. A new patent was granted by Charles ‹ Earl of Clarendon and others. Divided into North and South C‹ lina, 1710.

**North Dakota**—Dakota is Sioux for friend or ally.

**Ohio**—Iroquois word for "fine or good river."

**Oklahoma**—Choctaw coined word meaning red man, prop‹ by Rev. Allen Wright, Choctaw-speaking Indian.

**Oregon**—Origin unknown.

**Pennsylvania**—William Penn, the Quaker, who was made proprietor by King Charles II in 1681, suggested Sylvania, woodland, for his tract. The king's government owed Penn's fat‹ Admiral William Penn, £16,000, and the land being granted in ‹ settlement, the king added the Penn to Sylvania, against the des‹ of the modest proprietor, in honor of the admiral.

**Puerto Rico**—Spanish for Rich Port.

**Rhode Island**—Named Roode Eylandt by Adriaen Block, D‹ explorer, because of its red clay. Name of Roger Williams' se‹ ment was added to give the small state its long, official title: S‹ of Rhode Island and Providence Plantations.

**South Carolina**—See North Carolina.

**South Dakota**—See North Dakota.

**Tennessee**—Tanasi was the name of Cherokee villages on Little Tennessee River. From 1784 to 1788 this was the State Franklin, or Frankland.

**Texas**—Variant of word used by Caddo and other Indi‹ meaning friends or allies, and applied to them by the Spanish eastern Texas. Also written texias, tejas, teysas.

**Utah**—From a Navajo word meaning upper, or higher up, applied to a Shoshone tribe called Ute. Spanish form is Yutta, ‹ glish Uta or Utah. Proposed name Deseret, "land of honeybe‹ from Book of Mormon, was rejected by Congress.

**Vermont**—From French words vert, green, and mont, mount‹ The Green Mountains were said to have been named by Samuel Champlain. The Green Mountain Boys were Gen. Stark's men the Revolution. When the state was formed, 1777, Dr. Thom Young suggested combining vert and mont into Vermont.

**Virginia**—Named by Sir Walter Raleigh, who fitted out the pedition of 1584, in honor of Queen Elizabeth, the Virgin Queen England.

**Washington**—Named after George Washington. When the ‹ creating the Territory of Columbia was introduced in the 32d C‹ gress, the name was changed to Washington because of the e‹ tence of the District of Columbia.

**West Virginia**—So named when western counties of Virgi‹ refused to secede from the United States, 1863.

**Wisconsin**—An Indian name, spelled Ouisconsin and Misco‹ ing by early chroniclers. Believed to mean "grassy place" in Ch‹ pewa. Congress made it Wisconsin.

**Wyoming**—The word was taken from Wyoming Valley, ‹ which was the site of an Indian massacre and became wid‹ known by Campbell's poem, "Gertrude of Wyoming." In Alg‹ quin it means "large prairie place."

---

# Accession of Territory by the U.S.

Source: Statistical Abstract of the United States

| Division | Year | Sq. mi.[1] | Division | Year | Sq. mi.[1] | Division | Year | Sq. mi.[1] |
|---|---|---|---|---|---|---|---|---|
| **Total U.S. (1970)** . | | **3,628,066** | Oregon . . . . . . . | 1846 | 285,580 | American Samoa . . | 1900 | |
| 50 states & D.C. . . | | 3,615,122 | Mexican Cession . . | 1848 | 529,017 | Canal Zone[4] . . . . . | 1904 | 5 |
| Territory in 1790[2] . . . | | 888,685 | Gadsden Purchase . | 1853 | 29,640 | Corn Islands[5] . . . . | 1914 | |
| Louisiana Purchase . | 1803 | 827,192 | Alaska . . . . . . . . | 1867 | 586,412 | Virgin Islands, U.S.. . | 1917 | |
| By treaty with Spain: | | | Hawaii. . . . . . . . | 1898 | 6,450 | Trust Territory of | | |
|   Florida . . . . . . . | 1819 | 58,560 | The Philippines[3] . . | 1898 | 115,600 |   the Pacific is.. . . | 1947 | 8,4 |
|   Other areas . . . . | 1819 | 13,443 | Puerto Rico. . . . . . | 1899 | 3,435 | All other[6] . . . . . . . . . | | . . . . |
| Texas . . . . . . . . . | 1845 | 390,143 | Guam . . . . . . . . | 1899 | 212 | | | |

(1) Gross area (land and water). (2) Includes drainage basin of Red River on the north, south of 49th parallel sometimes consider‹ a part of the Louisiana Purchase. (3) Area not included in total; became Republic of the Philippines July 4, 1946. (4) Under U.S. ju‹ diction by treaty with Panama. (5) Leased from Nicaragua for 99 years but returned Apr. 25, 1971; area not included in total. (6) S‹ index for Outlying Areas, U.S.

## Public Lands of the U. S.

**Source:** Bureau of Land Management, U.S. Interior Department

### Acquisition of the Public Domain 1781-1867

| Acquisition | Area* (acres) Land | Water | Total | Cost[1] |
|---|---|---|---|---|
| State Cessions (1781-1802) | 233,415,680 | 3,409,920 | 236,825,600 | [2]$6,200,000 |
| Louisiana Purchase (1803)[3] | 523,446,400 | 6,465,280 | 529,911,680 | 23,213,568 |
| Red River Basin[4] | 29,066,880 | 535,040 | 29,601,920 | |
| Cession from Spain (1819) | 43,342,720 | 2,801,920 | 46,144,640 | 6,674,057 |
| Oregon Compromise (1846) | 180,644,480 | 2,741,760 | 183,386,240 | |
| Mexican Cession (1848) | 334,479,360 | 4,201,600 | 338,680,960 | 16,295,149 |
| Purchase from Texas (1850) | 78,842,880 | 83,840 | 78,926,720 | 15,496,448 |
| Gadsden Purchase (1853) | 18,961,920 | 26,880 | 18,988,800 | 10,000,000 |
| Alaska Purchase (1867) | 362,516,480 | 12,787,200 | 375,303,680 | 7,200,000 |
| **Total** | **1,804,716,800** | **33,053,440** | **1,837,770,240** | **$85,079,222** |

*All areas except Alaska were computed in 1912, and have not been adjusted for the recomputation of the area of the United States which was made for the 1950 Decennial Census. (1) Cost data for all except "State Cessions" obtained from U.S. Geological Survey. (2) Paid by federal government for Georgia cession, 1802 (56,689,920 acres). (3) Excludes areas eliminated by Treaty of 1819 with Spain. (4) Basin of the Red River of the North, south of the 49th parallel.

### Disposition of Public Lands 1781 to 1970

| Disposition by methods not elsewhere classified[1] | Acres | Granted to states for: | Acres |
|---|---|---|---|
| | 303,500,000 | Support of common schools | 77,600,000 |
| Granted or sold to homesteaders | 287,500,000 | Reclamation of swampland | 64,900,000 |
| Granted to railroad corporations | 94,300,000 | Construction of railroads | 37,100,000 |
| Granted to veterans as military bounties | 61,100,000 | Support of misc. institutions[6] | 21,700,000 |
| Confirmed as private land claims[2] | 34,000,000 | Purposes not elsewhere classified[7] | 117,500,000 |
| Sold under timber and stone law[3] | 13,900,000 | Canals and rivers | 6,100,000 |
| Granted or sold under timber culture law[4] | 10,900,000 | Construction of wagon roads | 3,400,000 |
| Sold under desert land law[5] | 10,700,000 | **Total granted to states** | **328,300,000** |

**Grand Total** . . . . . . . . . . . . . . . . . **1,144,200,000**

(1) Chiefly public, private, and preemption sales, but includes mineral entries, script locations, sales of townsites and townlots. (2) The Government has confirmed title to lands claimed under valid grants made by foreign governments prior to the acquisition of the public domain by the United States. (3) The law provided for the sale of lands valuable for timber or stone and unfit for cultivation. (4) The law provided for the granting of public lands to settlers on condition that they plant and cultivate trees on the lands granted. (5) The law provided for the sale of arid agricultural public lands to settlers who irrigate them and bring them under cultivation. (6) Universities, hospitals, asylums, etc. (7) For construction of various public improvements (individual items not specified in the granting act) reclamation of desert lands, construction of water reservoirs, etc.

### Land Owned by the Federal Government

(acres)

| Agency (June 30, 1975) | Public domain | Acquired | Total |
|---|---|---|---|
| Bureau of Land Management | 467,817,798 | 2,356,519 | 470,174,318 |
| U.S. Forest Service | 160,202,013 | 27,305,957 | 187,507,970 |
| U.S. Fish and Wildlife Service | 26,251,564 | 4,029,626 | 30,281,190 |
| U.S. Park Service | 19,765,785 | 5,318,965 | 25,084,750 |
| U.S. Army | 7,066,789 | 3,955,894 | 11,022,683 |
| Bureau of Reclamation | 5,659,928 | 1,891,661 | 7,551,589 |
| U.S. Air Force | 6,921,141 | 1,415,909 | 8,337,050 |
| Corps of Engineers | 724,851 | 7,158,999 | 7,883,850 |
| Bureau of Indian Affairs | 4,204,849 | 763,121 | 4,967,971 |
| U.S. Navy | 2,262,766 | 1,254,517 | 3,517,283 |
| Nuclear Regulatory Commission | 1,438,510 | 670,405 | 2,108,915 |
| Other | 550,741 | 1,426,495 | 1,977,237 |
| **Total** | **702,866,735** | **57,548,072** | **760,414,810** |

Total land holdings in foreign countries 637,414.4 acres.

## The Homestead Act; Sale of Public Land

On October 21, 1976 Congress repealed the Homestead Act of 1862 for all states except Alaska. At the present time the exception for Alaska has little meaning since homesteading along with all disposal laws had been suspended from operation by the Alaska Native Claims Settlement Act. The suspension which was first imposed by Secretarial order in 1969, will remain in effect until all claims for Federal land by Alaska's native Eskimos, Indians and Aleuts have been satisfied. The Homestead Act is scheduled to expire in Alaska in 1986.

The Homestead Act was repealed because there was no longer any land in the public domain suitable for cultivation. The law had been in effect for 114 years. During that time it had exerted a profound influence on the settlement of the west. Under the authority of the Homestead Act more than 1.6 million settlers claimed more than 270 million acres of public lands. The influx of settlers into the west in pursuit of homestead land made such states as Oklahoma, Kansas, Nebraska, and North and South Dakota a reality and brought substantial numbers of settlers into many other western states.

### Public Land Sale

From time to time the Bureau of Land Management sells public land to private individuals. Public land is always sold for its fair market value as determined by public auction. The Federal Govt. offers no free land. Persons wishing to purchase public land should contact the Bureau of Land Management, Wash., DC 20240, or one of the Bureau's Land Offices in the public land states.

The Bureau stresses that it is the only authoritative source of information on the sale of land under its jurisdiction.

# National Parks, Other Areas Administered by Nat'l Park Service

Figures given are date area was set aside by Congress or proclaimed by president, and gross area in acres Dec. 31, 1977.

## National Parks

**Acadia,** Me. (1916) 38,522. Includes Mount Desert Island, half of Isle au Haut, Schoodic Point on mainland. Highest elevation on Eastern seaboard.

**Arches,** Ut. (1929) 73,379. Contains giant red sandstone arches and other products of erosion.

**Big Bend,** Tex. (1935) 708,118. Rio Grande, Chisos Mts.

**Bryce Canyon,** Ut. (1923) 35,835. Spectacularly colorful and unusual display of erosion effects.

**Canyonlands,** Ut. (1964) 337,570. At junction of Colorado and Green rivers, extensive evidence of prehistoric Indians.

**Capitol Reef,** Ut. (1937) 241,874. A 70-mile uplift of sandstone cliffs dissected by high-walled gorges.

**Carlsbad Caverns,** N.M. (1923) 46,755. Largest known underground caverns, not yet fully explored.

**Crater Lake,** Ore. (1902) 160,290. Extraordinary blue lake in crater of extinct volcano encircled by lava walls 500 to 2,000 feet high.

**Everglades,** Fla. (1934) 1,398,800. Largest remaining subtropical wilderness in Continental U.S.

**Glacier,** Mon. (1910) 1,013,595. Superb Rocky Mountain scenery, numerous glaciers and glacial lakes. Part of Waterton-Glacier International Peace Park established by U.S. and Canada in 1932.

**Grand Canyon,** Ariz. (1908) 1,218,375. Most spectacular part of Colorado River's greatest canyon.

**Grand Teton,** Wy. (1929) 310,516. Most impressive part of the Teton Mountains, winter feeding ground of largest American elk herd.

**Great Smoky Mountains,** N.C.-Tenn. (1926) 517,368. Largest eastern mountain range, magnificent forests.

**Guadalupe Mountains,** Tex. (1966) 76,293. Extensive Permian limestone fossil reef; tremendous earth fault.

**Haleakala,** Ha. (1960) 28,660. 10,023 foot dormant volcano on Maui.

**Hawaii Volcanoes,** Ha. (1916) 229,177. Contains Kilauea and Mauna Loa, active volcanoes.

**Hot Springs,** Ark. (1832) 5,801. Government supervised bath houses use waters of 45 of the 47 natural hot springs.

**Isle Royale,** Mich. (1931) 571,796. Largest island in Lake Superior, noted for its wilderness area and wildlife.

**Kings Canyon,** Cal. (1890) 460,136. Mountain wilderness, dominated by Kings River Canyons and High Sierra; contains giant sequoias.

**Lassen Volcanic,** Cal. (1907) 106,372. Contains Lassen Peak, most recently active volcano in continental U.S., and other volcanic phenomena.

**Mammoth Cave,** Ky. (1926) 52,129. 144 miles of surveyed underground passages, beautiful natural formations, river 360 feet below surface.

**Mesa Verde,** Col. (1906) 52,036. Most notable and best preserved prehistoric cliff dwellings in the United States.

**Mount McKinley,** Alas. (1917) 1,939,493. Highest mountain in North America, large glaciers, and unusual wildlife.

**Mount Rainier,** Wash. (1899) 235,404. Greatest single-peak glacial system in the U.S. radiates from this dormant volcano.

**North Cascades,** Wash. (1968) 504,780. Spectacular mountainous region with many glaciers, lakes.

**Olympic,** Wash. (1909) 908,692. Mountain wilderness containing finest remnant of Pacific Northwest rain forest, active glaciers, Pacific shoreline, rare elk.

**Petrified Forest,** Ariz. (1906) 93,493. Extensive petrified wood and Indian artifacts. Contains part of Painted Desert.

**Redwood,** Cal. (1968) 62,211. Forty miles of Pacific coastline, groves of ancient redwoods.

**Rocky Mountain,** Col. (1915) 263,793. On the continental divide, includes 107 named peaks over 11,000 feet.

**Sequoia,** Cal. (1890) 386,823. Groves of giant sequoias, highest mountain in contiguous United States — Mount Whitney (14,494 feet).

**Shenandoah,** Va. (1926) 190,591. Portion of the Blue Ridge Mountains; overlooks Shenandoah Valley.

**Virgin Islands,** V.I. (1956) 14,490. Covers 75% of St. John Island, lush growth, lovely beaches, Indian relics, evidence of colonial Danes.

**Voyageurs,** Minn. (1971) 219,128. Abundant lakes, forests, wildlife, canoeing, boating.

**Wind Cave,** S.D. (1903) 28,060. Limestone Caverns in Black Hills. Extensive wildlife includes a herd of bison.

**Yellowstone,** Ida., Mon., Wy., (1872) 2,219,823. Oldest and largest national park. World's greatest geyser area has about 3,000 geysers and hot springs; spectacular falls and impressive canyons of the Yellowstone River, grizzly bear, moose, bison, other wildlife are major attractions.

**Yosemite,** Cal. (1890) 760,917. Yosemite Valley, the natio highest waterfall, 3 groves of giant sequoias, and mountain terrain.

**Zion,** Ut. (1909) 146,547. Unusual shapes and landsca have resulted from the effects of erosion and faulting acti Zion Canyon, with sheer walls ranging up to 2,500 feet, is rea accessible.

## National Historical Parks

**Appomattox Court House,** Va. (1930) 1,319. Where surrendered to Grant.

**Boston,** Mass. (1974) 35. Includes Faneuil Hall, Old Nc Church, Bunker Hill, Paul Revere House.

**Chalmette,** La. (1907) 143. Scene of part of the Battle of N Orleans.

**Chesapeake and Ohio Canal,** Md.-W.Va.-D.C. (19 20,239. 185 mile historic canal; D.C. to Cumberland, Md.

**City of Refuge,** Ha. (1955) 182. Until 1819, a sanctuary Hawaiians vanquished in battle, and those guilty of crimes breaking taboos.

**Colonial,** Va. (1930) 9,834. Includes most of Jamestown land, site of first successful English colony; Yorktown, site Cornwallis' surrender to George Washington; Cape Henry N morial, approximate site of the first landing of the Jamestc colonists; and the Colonial Parkway.

**Cumberland Gap,** Ky.-Tenn.-Va. (1940) 20,274. Mount pass of the Wilderness Road which carried the first great mic tion of pioneers into America's interior.

**George Rogers Clark,** Vincennes, Ind. (1966) 24. Comme orates American defeat of British in west during Revolution.

**Harpers Ferry,** Md., W. Va. (1944) 1,909. At the confluen of the Shenandoah and Potomac rivers, the site of John Brow 1859 raid on the Army arsenal. Scene of several Civil War r neuvers.

**Independence,** Pa. (1948) 37. Contains several propertie Philadelphia associated with the Revolutionary War and founding of the U.S.

**Klondike Gold Rush,** Alas.-Wash. (1976) 13,270. Skagw Alaskan Trails in 1898 Gold Rush. Museum in Seattle.

**Minute Man,** Mass. (1959) 745. Where the colonial Min Men battled the British, April 19, 1775. Also contains Natha Hawthorne's home.

**Morristown,** N.J. (1933) 1,677. Sites of important military campments during the Revolutionary War; Washington's hea quarters 1777, 1779-80.

**Nez Perce,** Ida. (1965) 2,114. Illustrates the history and c ture of the Nez Perce Indian country. 22 separate sites.

**San Juan Island,** Wash. (1966) 1,752. Commemora peaceful relations of the U.S., Canada and Great Britain sir the 1872 boundary disputes.

**Saratoga,** N.Y. (1938) 2,455. Scene of a major battle wh became a turning point in the War of Independence.

**Sitka,** Alas. (1910) 108. Scene of last major resistance of Tlingit Indians to the Russians, 1804.

**Valley Forge,** Pa. (1976) 2,466. Continental Army campsite 1777-78 winter.

## National Memorial Park

**Theodore Roosevelt,** N.D. (1947) 70,409. Part of T.R.'s E horn Ranch along the Little Missouri River. Has bison and so original prairie.

## National Battlefields

**Big Hole,** Mon. (1910) 656. Site of major battle with N Perce Indians.

**Cowpens,** S.C. (1929) 843. Revolutionary War battlefield.

**Fort Necessity,** Pa. (1931) 901. First battle of French a Indian War.

**Monocacy,** Md. (1976) 633.

**Petersburg,** Va. (1926) 1,515. Scene of 10-month Uni campaign 1864-65.

**Stones River,** Tenn. (1927) 331. Civil War battle leading Sherman's "March to the Sea."

**Tupelo,** Miss. (1929) 1. Crucial battle over Sherman's supp line.

**Wilson's Creek,** Mo. (1960) 1,750. Civil War battle for cont of Missouri.

## National Battlefield Parks

**Kennesaw Mountain,** Ga. (1917) 2,884. Two major battles Atlanta campaign in Civil War.

**Manassas,** Va. (1940) 3,109. Two early Civil War battles.
**Richmond,** Va. (1936) 769. Site of battles defending Confederate capital.

## National Battlefield Sites

**Antietam,** Md. (1890) 1,800. End of first Confederate invasion North.
**Brices Cross Roads,** Miss. (1929) 1. Civil War battlefield.

## National Military Parks

**Chickamauga and Chattanooga,** Ga.-Tenn. (1890) 8,095. Civil War battlefields.
**Fort Donelson,** Tenn. (1928) 544. Site of first major Union victory.
**Fredericksburg and Spotsylvania County,** Va. (1927) 5,887. Sites of several major Civil War battles and campaigns.
**Gettysburg,** Pa. (1895) 3,862. Site of decisive Confederate defeat in North. Gettysburg Address.
**Guilford Courthouse,** N.C. (1917) 220. Revolutionary War battle site.
**Horseshoe Bend,** Ala. (1956) 2,040. On Tallapoosa River, where Gen. Andrew Jackson broke the power of the Creek Indian Confederacy.
**Kings Mountain,** S.C. (1931) 3,945. Revolutionary War battle.
**Moores Creek,** N.C. (1926) 84. Pre-Revolutionary War battle.
**Pea Ridge,** Ark. (1956) 4,300. Civil War battle.
**Shiloh,** Tenn. (1894) 3,762. Major Civil War battle; site includes some well-preserved Indian burial mounds.
**Vicksburg,** Miss. (1899) 1,741. Union victory gave North control of the Mississippi and split the Confederacy in two.

## National Memorials

**Arkansas Post,** Ark. (1960) 389. First permanent French settlement in the lower Mississippi River valley.
**Chamizal,** El Paso, Tex. (1966) 55. Commemorates 1963 settlement of 99-year border dispute with Mexico.
**Coronado,** Ariz. (1952) 2,834. Commemorates first European exploration of the Southwest.
**DeSoto,** Fla. (1948) 30. Commemorates 16th-century Spanish explorations.
**Federal Hall,** N.Y. (1939) 0.45. First seat of U.S. government under the Constitution.
**Fort Caroline,** Fla. (1950) 129. On St. Johns River, overlooks site of second attempt by French Huguenots to colonize North America.
**Fort Clatsop,** Ore. (1958) 125. Lewis and Clark encampment 1805-06.
**General Grant,** N.Y. (1958) 0.76. Tombs of Pres. and wife.
**Hamilton Grange,** N.Y. (1962) 0.71. Home of Alexander Hamilton.
**John F. Kennedy Center for the Performing Arts,** D.C. (1972) 18.
**Johnstown Flood,** Pa. (1964) 106. Commemorates tragic flood of 1889.
**Lincoln Boyhood,** Ind. (1962) 198. Lincoln grew up here.
**Lincoln Memorial,** D.C. (1911) 164.
**Lyndon B. Johnson Grove on the Potomac,** D.C. (1973)
**Mount Rushmore,** S.D. (1925) 1,278. World famous sculpture of 4 presidents.
**Perry's Victory and International Peace Memorial,** Oh. (1936) 26. American naval victory, War of 1812.
**Roger Williams,** R.I. (1965) 5. Memorial to founder of Rhode Island.
**Thaddeus Kosciuszko,** Pa. (1972) 0.02. Memorial to Polish hero of American Revolution.
**Theodore Roosevelt Island,** D.C. (1947) 89.
**Thomas Jefferson Memorial,** D.C. (1943) 18.
**Washington Monument,** D.C. (1848) 106.
**Wright Brothers,** N.C. (1927) 431. Site of first powered flight.

## National Historic Sites

**Abraham Lincoln Birthplace,** Hodgenville, Ky. (1916) 117.
**Adams,** Quincy, Mass. (1946) 8. Home of Presidents John Adams, John Quincy Adams, and celebrated descendants.
**Allegheny Portage Railroad,** Pa. (1964) 760. Part of the Pennsylvania Canal system.
**Andersonville,** Andersonville, Ga. (1970) 478. Noted Civil War prison.
**Andrew Johnson,** Greeneville, Tenn. (1935) 17. Home of the president.
**Bent's Old Fort,** Col. (1960) 178. Old West fur-trading post.
**Carl Sandburg Home,** N.C. (1968) 247. Poet's farm home.
**Christiansted,** St. Croix; V.I. (1952) 27. Commemorates Danish colony.
**Clara Barton,** Md. (1974) 9. Home of founder of American Red Cross.
**Edison,** West Orange, N.J. (1955) 21. Home and laboratory.
**Eisenhower,** Gettysburg, Pa. (1967) 493. Home of 34th president. Not open to public.
**Eleanor Roosevelt,** Hyde Park, N.Y. (1977) 175.
**Ford's Theatre,** Washington, D.C. (1866) 0.29. Includes theater, now restored, where Lincoln was assassinated, house where he died, and Lincoln Museum.
**Fort Bowie,** Ariz. (1964) 1,000. Focal point of operations against Geronimo and the Apaches.
**Fort Davis,** Tex. (1961) 460. Frontier outpost battled Comanches and Apaches.
**Fort Laramie,** Wy. (1938) 571. Military post on Oregon Trail.
**Fort Larned,** Kan. (1964) 718. Military post on Sante Fe Trail.
**Fort Point,** San Francisco, Cal. (1970) 29. Largest West Coast fortification.
**Fort Raleigh,** N.C. (1941) 160. First English settlement.
**Fort Smith,** Ark. (1961) 67. Active post from 1817 to 1890.
**Fort Union Trading Post,** Mon., N.D. (1966) 398. Principal fur-trading post on upper Missouri, 1828-1867.
**Fort Vancouver,** Wash. (1948) 209. Hdqts. for Hudson's Bay Company in 1825. Early military and political seat.
**Golden Spike,** Utah (1957) 2,203. Commemorates completion of first transcontinental railroad in 1869.
**Grant-Kohrs Ranch,** Mon. (1972) 1,528. Ranch house and part of 19th century ranch.
**Hampton,** Md. (1948) 45. 18th-century Georgian mansion.
**Herbert Hoover,** West Branch, Ia. (1965) 187. Birthplace and boyhood home of 31st president.
**Home of Franklin D. Roosevelt,** Hyde Park, N.Y. (1944) 264. Birthplace, home and "Summer White House".
**Hopewell Village,** Pa. (1938) 848. 19th-century iron making village.
**Hubbell Trading Post,** Ariz. (1965) 160. Indian trading post.
**Jefferson National Expansion Memorial,** St. Louis, Mo. (1935) 91. Commemorates westward expansion with park and memorial arch.
**John Fitzgerald Kennedy,** Brookline, Mass. (1967) .09. Birthplace and childhood home of the President.
**John Muir,** Martinez, Cal. (1964) 9. Home of early conservationist and writer.
**Knife River Indian Villages,** N.D. (1974) 1,310. Remnants of 5 Hidatsa villages.
**Lincoln Home,** Springfield, Ill. (1971) 12. Lincoln's residence when he was elected President, 1860.
**Longfellow,** Cambridge, Mass. (1972) 2. Longfellow's home, 1837-82, and Washington's hq. during Boston Siege, 1775-76. **No federal facilities.**
**Lyndon B. Johnson,** Johnson City, Tex. (1969) 241. Birthplace and boyhood home of the 36th President.
**Mar-A-Largo,** Fla. (1969) 17. Mansion expresses the affluent Palm Beach life of the 1920s. Not open to public.
**Martin Van Buren,** N.Y. (1974) 40. Lindenwald, home of 8th president, near Kinderhook.
**Ninety Six,** S.C. (1976) 1,115.
**Puukohola Heiau,** Ha. (1972) 77. Ruins of temple built by King Kamehameha.
**Sagamore Hill,** Oyster Bay, N.Y. (1962) 85. Home of President Theodore Roosevelt from 1885 until his death in 1919.
**Saint-Gaudens,** Cornish, N.H. (1964) 149. Home, studio and gardens of American sculptor Augustus Saint-Gaudens.
**Salem Maritime,** Mass. (1938) 9. Only port never seized from the patriots by the British. Major fishing and whaling port.
**San Juan,** P.R. (1949) 53. 16th-century Spanish fortifications.
**Saugus Iron Works,** Mass. (1968) 9. Reconstructed 17th-century colonial ironworks.
**Sewall-Belmont House,** D.C. (1974) 0.35. National Women's Party headquarters 1929-74.
**Springfield Armory,** Mass. (1974) 55. Small arms manufacturing center for nearly 200 years.
**Theodore Roosevelt Birthplace,** N.Y., N.Y. (1962) 0.11.
**Theodore Roosevelt Inaugural,** Buffalo, N.Y. (1966) 1. Wilcox House where he took oath of office, 1901.
**Tuskegee Institute,** Ala. (1974) 74. College founded by Booker T. Washington in 1881 for blacks, includes student-made brick buildings.
**Vanderbilt Mansion,** Hyde Park, N.Y. (1940) 212. Mansion of 19th-century financier.
**Whitman Mission,** Wash. (1936) 98. Site where Dr. and Mrs. Marcus Whitman ministered to the Indians until slain by them in 1847.
**William Howard Taft,** Cincinnati, Oh. (1969) 0.83. Birthplace and early home of the 27th president.

## National Capital Parks

**District of Columbia — Maryland — Virginia** (1790) 6,471. Comprises 346 units.

## White House

**Washington,** D.C. (1792) 18. Presidential residence since November 1800.

| Name | State | Year | Acreage |
|---|---|---|---|
| **National Monuments** | | | |
| Agate Fossil Beds | Neb. | 1965 | 3,054 |
| Alibates Flint Quarries and Texas Panhandle Pueblo Culture | Tex. | 1965 | 93 |
| Aztec Ruins | N.M. | 1923 | 27 |
| Badlands | S.D. | 1929 | 243,302 |
| Bandelier | N.M. | 1916 | 36,971 |
| Biscayne | Fla. | 1968 | 103,643 |
| Black Canyon of the Gunnison | Col. | 1933 | 13,672 |
| Booker T. Washington | Va. | 1956 | 224 |
| Buck Island Reef | V.I. | 1961 | 880 |
| Cabrillo | Cal. | 1913 | 144 |
| Canyon de Chelly | Ariz. | 1931 | 83,840 |
| Capulin Mountain | N.M. | 1916 | 775 |
| Casa Grande Ruins | Ariz. | 1892 | 473 |
| Castillo de San Marcos | Fla. | 1924 | 20 |
| Castle Clinton | N.Y. | 1946 | 1 |
| Cedar Breaks | Ut. | 1933 | 6,155 |
| Chaco Canyon | N.M. | 1907 | 21,509 |
| Channel Islands | Cal. | 1938 | 18,388 |
| Chiricahua | Ariz. | 1924 | 10,648 |
| Colorado | Col. | 1911 | 20,445 |
| Congaree Swamp | S.C. | 1976 | 15,200 |
| Craters of the Moon | Ida. | 1924 | 53,545 |
| Custer Battlefield | Mon. | 1879 | 765 |
| Death Valley | Cal.-Nev. | 1933 | 2,067,795 |
| Devils Postpile | Cal. | 1911 | 798 |
| Devils Tower | Wy. | 1906 | 1,347 |
| Dinosaur | Col.-Ut. | 1915 | 211,051 |
| Effigy Mounds | Ia. | 1949 | 1,475 |
| El Morro | N.M. | 1906 | 1,279 |
| Florissant Fossil Beds** | Col. | 1969 | 5,992 |
| Fort Frederica | Ga. | 1936 | 215 |
| Fort Jefferson | Fla. | 1935 | 47,125 |
| Fort Matanzas | Fla. | 1924 | 299 |
| Fort McHenry National Monument and Historic Shrine | Md. | 1925 | 43 |
| Fort Pulaski | Ga. | 1924 | 5,616 |
| Fort Stanwix | N.Y. | 1935 | 16 |
| Fort Sumter | S.C. | 1948 | 64 |
| Fort Union | N.M. | 1954 | 721 |
| Fossil Butte | Wy. | 1972 | 8,178 |
| G. Washington Birthplace | Va. | 1930 | 456 |
| George Washington Carver | Mo. | 1943 | 210 |
| Gila Cliff Dwellings | N.M. | 1907 | 533 |
| Glacier Bay | Alas. | 1925 | 2,805,269 |
| Grand Portage | Minn. | 1951 | 710 |
| Gran Quivira | N.M. | 1909 | 611 |
| Great Sand Dunes | Col. | 1932 | 36,827 |
| Hohokam Pima* | Ariz. | 1972 | 1,690 |
| Homestead Nat'l. Monument of America | Neb. | 1936 | 195 |
| Hovenweep | Col.-Ut. | 1923 | 785 |
| Jewel Cave | S.D. | 1908 | 1,275 |
| John Day Fossil Beds | Ore. | 1974 | 14,402 |
| Joshua Tree | Cal. | 1936 | 559,960 |
| Katmai | Alas. | 1918 | 2,792,151 |
| Lava Beds | Cal. | 1925 | 46,821 |
| Lehman Caves | Nev. | 1922 | 640 |
| Montezuma Castle | Ariz. | 1906 | 842 |
| Mound City Group | Oh. | 1923 | 68 |
| Muir Woods | Cal. | 1908 | 554 |
| Natural Bridges | Ut. | 1908 | 7,779 |
| Navajo | Ariz. | 1909 | 360 |
| Ocmulgee | Ga. | 1934 | 683 |
| Oregon Caves | Ore. | 1909 | 466 |
| Organ Pipe Cactus | Ariz. | 1937 | 330,689 |
| Pecos | N.M. | 1965 | 365 |
| Pinnacles | Cal. | 1908 | 16,216 |
| Pipe Spring | Ariz. | 1923 | 40 |
| Pipestone | Minn. | 1937 | 282 |
| Rainbow Bridge | Ut. | 1910 | 160 |
| Russell Cave | Ala. | 1961 | 310 |
| Saguaro | Ariz. | 1933 | 83,576 |
| Saint Croix Island** | Me. | 1949 | 35 |
| Scotts Bluff | Neb. | 1919 | 2,988 |
| Statue of Liberty | N.J.-N.Y. | 1924 | 58 |
| Sunset Crater | Ariz. | 1930 | 3,040 |
| Timpanogos Cave | Ut. | 1922 | 250 |
| Tonto | Ariz. | 1907 | 1,120 |
| Tumacacori | Ariz. | 1908 | 10 |
| Tuzigoot | Ariz. | 1939 | 58 |
| Walnut Canyon | Ariz. | 1915 | 2,249 |
| White Sands | N.M. | 1933 | 145,335 |
| Wupatki | Ariz. | 1924 | 35,253 |
| Yucca House* | Col. | 1919 | 10 |

| Name | State | Year | Acre |
|---|---|---|---|
| **National Preserves** | | | |
| Big Cypress | Fla. | 1974 | 570 |
| Big Thicket | Tex. | 1974 | 84 |
| **National Seashores** | | | |
| Assateague Island | Md.-Va. | 1965 | 39 |
| Canaveral | Fla. | 1975 | 57 |
| Cape Cod | Mass. | 1961 | 44 |
| Cape Hatteras | N.C. | 1937 | 30 |
| Cape Lookout** | N.C. | 1966 | 28 |
| Cumberland Island | Ga. | 1972 | 36 |
| Fire Island | N.Y. | 1964 | 19 |
| Gulf Islands | Fla.-Miss. | 1971 | 139 |
| Padre Island | Tex. | 1962 | 133 |
| Point Reyes | Cal. | 1962 | 65 |
| **National Parkways** | | | |
| Blue Ridge | Va.-N.C. | 1936 | 81, |
| George Washington Memorial | Va.-Md. | 1930 | 7 |
| John D. Rockefeller Jr. Mem. | Wy. | 1972 | 23, |
| Natchez Trace | Ala.-Miss.-Tenn. | 1938 | 48 |
| **National Lakeshores** | | | |
| Apostle Islands | Wis. | 1970 | 42, |
| Indiana Dunes | Ind. | 1966 | 12, |
| Pictured Rocks | Mich. | 1966 | 70, |
| Sleeping Bear Dunes | Mich. | 1970 | 71, |
| **National River** | | | |
| Buffalo | Ark. | 1972 | 94, |
| **National Scenic Rivers and Riverways** | | | |
| Big South Fork | Ky.-Tenn. | 1976 | 122, |
| Lower Saint Croix** | Minn.-Wis. | 1972 | 7, |
| Obed Wild | Tenn. | 1976 | 6, |
| Ozark | Mo. | 1964 | 79, |
| Saint Croix** | Minn.-Wis. | 1968 | 62, |
| **Parks** (no other classification) | | | |
| Arlington House, The Robert E. Lee Memorial | Va. | 1925 | |
| Catoctin Mountain | Md. | 1954 | 5, |
| Fort Benton | Mon. | 1976 | |
| Fort Washington | Md. | 1930 | |
| Frederick Douglass Home | D.C. | 1962 | |
| Greenbelt | Md. | 1933 | 1,0 |
| Piscataway | Md. | 1961 | 4,2 |
| Prince William Forest | Va. | 1948 | 18,8 |
| Rock Creek | D.C. | 1890 | 1, |
| Wolf Trap Farm Park for the Performing Arts | Va. | 1966 | |
| **National Recreation Areas** | | | |
| Amistad | Tex. | 1965 | 62,4 |
| Bighorn Canyon | Mon.-Wy. | 1964 | 120,1 |
| Chickasaw | Okla. | 1976 | 9,6 |
| Coulee Dam | Wash. | 1946 | 100,0 |
| Curecanti | Col. | 1965 | 42,1 |
| Cuyahoga Valley | Oh. | 1974 | 30,0 |
| Delaware Water Gap | N.J.-Pa. | 1965 | 47,6 |
| Gateway | N.Y.-N.J. | 1972 | 26,1 |
| Glen Canyon | Ariz.-Ut. | 1958 | 1,236,8 |
| Golden Gate | Cal. | 1972 | 34,9 |
| Lake Chelan | Wash. | 1968 | 61,8 |
| Lake Mead | Ariz.-Nev. | 1936 | 1,496,6 |
| Lake Meredith | Tex. | 1965 | 45,9 |
| Ross Lake | Wash. | 1968 | 117,5 |
| Shadow Mountain | Col. | 1952 | 19,0 |
| Whiskeytown-Shasta-Trinity | Cal. | 1962 | 42,4 |
| **National Mall** | D.C. | 1933 | |
| **National Visitor Center** | D.C. | 1968 | |
| **National Scenic Trail** | | | |
| Appalachian | Me. to Ga. | 1968 | 52,0 |

*Not open to the public
**No federal facilities

## Federal and State Indian Reservations

Source: U.S. Commerce Department (data as of circa Dec., 1972)

| te | No. of reservations[1] | Tribally-owned acreage[1] | Allotted acreage[1] | No. of tribes[3] | No. of persons[4] | Avg. unemp. rate%[5] | Major tribes |
|---|---|---|---|---|---|---|---|
| ska | 13[2] | (2) | (2) | 6 | 35,817 | NA | Eskimo, Tlingit, Haida, Aleut, Athapascan[6] |
| zona | 17 | 23,467,727 | 892,917 | 13 | 173,412 | 41 | Navaho, Apache, Papago, Hopi, Pima |
| ifornia | 76 | 386,954 | 67,390 | (7) | 6,905 | 45 | Quechan, Hoopa, Paiute, mission bands[7] |
| orado | 2 | 888,155 | 14,425 | 1 | 2,144 | 37 | Ute |
| nnecticut | 4 | 795 | — | 3 | 25 | NA | Pequot, Mohegan[8] |
| rida | 5 | 183,319 | — | 2 | 1,511 | 31 | Seminole, Miccosukee[9] |
| ho | 4 | 274,428 | 36,723 | 5 | 4,849 | 36 | Shoshone, Bannock, Nez Perce |
| a | 1 | 3,476 | — | 1 | 561 | 35 | Sac and Fox[10] |
| nsas | 4 | 2,436 | 24,030 | 5 | 3,009 | 10 | Potawatomi, Kickapoo, Iowa |
| uisiana | 1 | 262 | — | 1 | 268 | NA | Chitimacha |
| ine | 3 | 27,546 | — | 2 | 1,077 | 45 | Passamaquoddy, Penobscot |
| ssachusetts | 1 | 12 | — | 1 | 1 | 0 | Hassanamisco-Nipmuk[11] |
| higan | 5 | 4,425 | 12,210 | 2 | 2,069 | 38 | Chippewa, Potawatami |
| nesota | 11 | 682,534 | 50,935 | 2 | 10,739 | 40 | Chippewa, Sioux |
| sissippi | 1 | 17,381 | 209 | 1 | 3,294 | 10 | Choctaw |
| ntana | 7 | 1,792,383 | 3,279,926 | 10 | 24,137 | 38 | Blackfeet, Sioux, Crow, Assiniboine, Cheyenne |
| oraska | 3 | 27,193 | 45,467 | 3 | 2,601 | 62 | Omaha, Winnebago, Santee Sioux |
| vada | 23 | 1,133,529 | 32,691 | 3 | 4,784 | 46 | Paiute, Shoshone, Washoe |
| w Mexico | 24 | 3,329,270 | 119,877 | 7 | 30,125 | 43 | Keresan, Zuni, Apache, Tanoan, Navaho[12] |
| w York | 9 | 88,158 | — | 7 | 11,616 | 27 | Seneca, Mohawk, Onondaga, Oneida[13] |
| rth Carolina | 1 | 56,573 | — | 1 | 4,880 | 21 | Cherokee |
| rth Dakota | 4 | 375,936 | 996,744 | 5 | 16,735 | 41 | Chippewa, Sioux, Mandan, Arikara Hidatsa |
| ahoma[14] | — | 56,741 | 991,715 | 27 | 80,994 | 24 | Cherokee, Creek, Choctaw, Chicasaw, Cheyenne, Arapaho[14] |
| egon | 4 | 495,842 | 165,778 | 8 | 2,718 | 41 | Warm Springs, Wasco, Paiute, Umatilla |
| uth Dakota | 8 | 1,807,623 | 2,371,427 | 1 | 29,119 | 37 | Sioux |
| xas | 2 | 4,400 | — | 3 | 1,000 | 30 | Tigua (Peublo), Alabama, Coushatta |
| h | 4 | 1,095,531 | 48,095 | 3 | 1,961 | 36 | Ute, Southern Paiute, Goshute |
| ginia | 2 | 925 | — | 1 | 110 | NA | Algonquian |
| shington | 22 | 1,920,850 | 537,876 | 20 | 18,138 | 45 | Yakima, Confederated, Lummi, Quinault |
| sconsin | 10 | 61,931 | 82,977 | 6 | 7,497 | 38 | Chippewa, Oneida, Winnebago |
| oming | 1 | 1,776,136 | 109,344 | 2 | 4,435 | 47 | Shoshone, Arapaho |

1) Approximations. Ownership of reservation land is very complex. Most tribally-owned land listed here is owned by tribal organizations, but some of it is held in trust by the government and some is leased to or occupied by non-Indians. Government-owned land, in that held for the exclusive use of Indians, and non-Indian land formally included in reservations is not counted here. Allotted land was land held by Indian individuals or families. The Department of Commerce data is not clear on whether all land ed as allotted is still securely held by Indians.

2) Alaskan Indian affairs are handled under the Native Claims Settlement Act (Dec. 18, 1971). The act provides for the establishment of regional and village corporations to conduct business for profit. There are 12 regional corporations. Within each regional corporation, village corporations must be organized. These village corporations then receive title to lands previously held in reservations. re were approximately 2.5 million acres in reservations subject to the Settlement Act. Another 86,471 acres remain outside the in the Annette Island Reserve. Latest figures show that 5,687 acres have been assigned to village corporations, while an additional 490 acres have been surveyed but not yet assigned.

3) The concept of "tribe" is, in many cases, a white man's invention and, at first, was used to define loosely associated Indians with ural similarities. Today, "tribe" is a formal status of Indians organized by law. Some present day "tribes" such as the Blackfeet are ly confederacies of smaller groups. The Alaskan natives are organized, on paper, into general linguistic groups.

4) Number of Indians living on or adjacent to reservations. When these figures are compared to 1970 census figures, it appears nearly 64% of Indians are living on or near reservations.

5) Unemployment rate of Indian labor force living on or adjacent to reservations.

6) Aleuts and Eskimos are racially and linguistically related. Athapascans are related to the Navaho and Apache Indians.

7) Many California Indians are historically associated with groups which settled near Spanish missions where much of the tradial culture was destroyed. Many of these bands, however, still retain some of their Indian language and customs. Excluding the ds, there are 22 tribes represented on California reservations.

8) The Mohegan or Mohican are a branch of the Pequot.

9) "Seminole" means "runaways" and these Indians from various tribes were originally refugees from whites in the Carolinas and orgia. Later joined by runaway slaves, the Seminole were united by their hostility to the United States. Formal peace with the Semies in Florida was not achieved until 1934. The Miccosukee are a branch of the Seminole; they retain their Indian religion and have made formal peace with the U.S.

10) Once two tribes, the Sac and Fox formed a political alliance in 1734.

11) Reservation prior to 1728 consisted of 8,000 acres. The land was sold to whites who put the Indians' money in a bank. Over years the money was "lost" or "borrowed." In 1848, the state granted 11.9 acres to one Indian family of which there are about 20 ct descendants today.

12) Tanoan, Keresan, and Zuni are all pueblo-dwelling Indians.

13) These 4 tribes along with the Cayuga and Tuscarora made up the Iroquois League, which ruled large portions of New York, w England, and Pennsylvania and ranged into the Mid-West and South. The Onondaga, who traditionally provide the president of League, maintain that they are a foreign nation within New York and the U.S.

14) Indian land status in Oklahoma is unique and there are no reservations in the sense that the term is used elsewhere in the U.S. ewise, many of the Oklahoma tribes are unique in their high degree of assimilation to the white culture.

## Declaration of Independence

The Declaration of Independence was adopted by the Continental Congress in Philadelphia, on July 4, 1776. John H
cock was president of the Congress and Charles Thomson was secretary. A copy of the Declaration, engrossed on parchme
was signed by members of Congress on and after Aug. 2, 1776. On Jan. 18, 1777, Congress ordered that "authenticated c
ies, with the names of the members of Congress subscribed the same, be sent to each of the United States, and that they
desired to have same put upon record." Authenticated copies were printed in broadside form in Baltimore, where the Co
nental Congress was then in session. The following text is that of the original printed by John Dunlap at Philadelphia for
Continental Congress.

# IN CONGRESS, July 4, 1776.

## A DECLARATION

### By the REPRESENTATIVES of the

# UNITED STATES OF AMERICA,

### In GENERAL CONGRESS assembled

When in the Course of human Events, it becomes necessary for one People to dissolve the Political Bands which have connected them with another, and to assume among the Powers of the Earth, the separate and equal Station to which the Laws of Nature and of Nature's God entitle them, a decent Respect to the Opinions of Mankind requires that they should declare the causes which impel them to the Separation.

We hold these Truths to be self-evident, that all Men are created equal, that they are endowed by their Creator with certain unalienable Rights, that among these are Life, Liberty, and the Pursuit of Happiness—That to secure these Rights, Governments are instituted among Men, deriving their just Powers from the Consent of the Governed, that whenever any Form of Government becomes destructive of these Ends, it is the Right of the People to alter or to abolish it, and to institute new Government, laying its Foundation on such Principles, and organizing its Powers in such Form, as to them shall seem most likely to effect their Safety and Happiness. Prudence, indeed, will dictate that Governments long established should not be changed for light and transient Causes; and accordingly all Experience hath shewn, that Mankind are more disposed to suffer, while Evils are sufferable, than to right themselves by abolishing the Forms to which they are accustomed. But when a long Train of Abuses and Usurpations, pursuing invariably the same Object, evinces a Design to reduce them under absolute Depotism, it is their Right, it is their Duty, to throw off such Government, and to provide new Guards for their future Security. Such has been the patient Sufferance of these Colonies; and such is now the Necessity which constrains them to alter their former Systems of Government. The History of the present King of Great-Britain is a History of repeated Injuries and Usurpations, all having in direct Object the Establishment of an absolute Tyranny over these States. To prove this, let Facts be submitted to a candid World.

He has refused his Assent to Laws, the most wholesome and necessary for the public Good.

He has forbidden his Governors to pass Laws of immediate and pressing Importance, unless suspended in their Operation till his Assent should be obtained; and when so suspended, he has utterly neglected to attend to them.

He has refused to pass other Laws for the Accommodation of large Districts of People, unless those People would relinquish the Right of Representation in the Legislature, a Right inestimable to them, and formidable to Tyrants only.

He has called together Legislative Bodies at Places unusual, uncomfortable, and distant from the Depository of their Public Records, for the sole Purpose of fatiguing them into Compliance with his Measures.

He has dissolved Representative Houses repeatedly, for opposing with manly Firmness his Invasions on the Rights of the People.

He has refused for a long Time, after such Dissolutions, to cause others to be elected; whereby the Legislative Powers, incapable of Annihilation, have returned to the People

at large for their exercise; the State remaining in the me
time exposed to all the Dangers of Invasion from withc
and Convulsions within.

He has endeavoured to prevent the Population of th
States; for that Purpose obstructing the Laws for Natu
ization of Foreigners; refusing to pass others to encoura
their Migrations hither, and raising the Conditions of n
Appropriations of Lands.

He has obstructed the Administration of Justice, by re
ing his Assent to Laws for establishing Judiciary Powers.

He has made Judges dependent on his Will alone, for
Tenure of their Offices, and the Amount and payment
their Salaries.

He has erected a Multitude of new Offices, and sent hit
Swarms of Officers to harrass our People, and eat out th
Substance.

He has kept among us, in Time of Peace, Standing A
mies, without the consent of our Legislatures.

He has affected to render the Military independent of, a
superior to the Civil Power.

He has combined with others to subject us to a Jurisd
tion foreign to our Constitution, and unacknowledged
our Laws; giving his Assent to their Acts of pretended L
islation:

For quartering large Bodies of Armed Troops among us

For protecting them, by a mock Trial, from Punishme
for any Murders which they should commit on the Inha
tants of these States:

For cutting off our Trade with all Parts of the World:

For imposing Taxes on us without our Consent:

For depriving us, in many Cases, of the Benefits of T
by Jury:

For transporting us beyond Seas to be tried for pretend
Offences:

For abolishing the free System of English Laws in
neighbouring Province, establishing therein an arbitra
Government, and enlarging its Boundaries, so as to rende
at once an Example and fit Instrument for introducing
same absolute Rule into these Colonies:

For taking away our Charters, abolishing our most va
able Laws, and altering fundamentally the Forms of c
Governments:

For suspending our own Legislatures, and declari
themselves invested with Power to legislate for us in
Cases whatsoever.

He has abdicated Government here, by declaring us c
of his Protection and waging War against us.

He has plundered our Seas, ravaged our Coasts, burnt c
towns, and destroyed the Lives of our People.

He is, at this Time, transporting large Armies of forei
Mercenaries to compleat the works of Death, Desolati
and Tyranny, already begun with circumstances of Crue
and Perfidy, scarcely paralleled in the most barbarous Ag
and totally unworthy the Head of a civilized Nation.

He has constrained our fellow Citizens taken Captive
the high Seas to bear Arms against their Country, to beco
the Executioners of their Friends and Brethren, or to
themselves by their Hands.

He has excited domestic Insurrections amongst us, a
has endeavoured to bring on the Inhabitants of our Fro
tiers, the merciless Indian Savages, whose known Rule
Warfare, is an undistinguished Destruction, of all Ag
Sexes and Conditions.

In every stage of these Oppressions we have Petitioned
Redress in the most humble Terms: Our repeated Petitio
have been answered only by repeated Injury. A Prin
whose Character is thus marked by every act which may

Tyrant, is unfit to be the Ruler of a free People.
 r have we been wanting in Attentions to our British
 ren. We have warned them from Time to Time of At-
 ts by their Legislature to extend an unwarrantable Ju-
 tion over us. We have reminded them of the Circum-
 es of our Emigration and Settlement here. We have
 led to their native Justice and Magnanimity, and we
 conjured them by the Ties of our common Kindred to
 ow these Usurpations, which, would inevitably inter-
 our Connections and Correspondence. They too have
 deaf to the Voice of Justice and of Consanguinity. We
 , therefore, acquiesce in the Necessity, which denounces
 eparation, and hold them, as we hold the rest of Man-
 Enemies in War, in Peace, Friends.
 e, therefore, the Representatives of the UNITED
 TES OF AMERICA, in General Congress, Assembled,
 aling to the Supreme Judge of the World in the Recti-
 of our Intentions, do, in the Name, and by Authority

of the good People of these Colonies, solemnly Publish and
Declare, That these United Colonies are, and of Right ought
to be, Free and Independent States; that they are absolved
from all Allegiance to the British Crown, and that all political Connection between them and the State of Great-Britain,
is and ought to be totally dissolved; and that as Free and
Independent States, they have full Power to levy War, conclude Peace, contract Alliances, establish Commerce, and to
do all other Acts and Things which Independent States may
of right do. And for the support of this declaration, with a
firm Reliance on the Protection of divine Providence, we
mutually pledge to each other our lives, our Fortunes, and
our sacred Honor.

**JOHN HANCOCK, President**

Attest.
**CHARLES THOMSON, Secretary.**

## Signers of the Declaration of Independence

| Delegate and state | Vocation | Birthplace | Born | Died |
| --- | --- | --- | --- | --- |
| ms, John (Mass.) | Lawyer | Braintree (Quincy), Mass. | Oct. 30, 1735 | July 4, 1826 |
| ms, Samuel (Mass.) | Political leader | Boston, Mass. | Sept. 27, 1722 | Oct. 2, 1803 |
| ett, Josiah (N.H.) | Physician, judge | Amesbury, Mass. | Nov. 21, 1729 | May 19, 1795 |
| ton, Carter (Va.) | Farmer | Newington Plantation, Va. | Sept. 10, 1736 | Oct. 10, 1797 |
| oll, Chas. of Carrollton (Md.) | Lawyer | Annapolis, Md. | Sept. 19, 1737 | Nov. 14, 1832 |
| se, Samuel (Md.) | Judge | Princess Anne, Md. | Apr. 17, 1741 | June 19, 1811 |
| k, Abraham (N.J.) | Surveyor | Roselle, N.J. | Feb. 15, 1726 | Sept. 15, 1794 |
| ner, George (Pa.) | Merchant | Philadelphia, Pa. | Mar. 16, 1739 | Jan. 23, 1813 |
| y, William (R.I.) | Lawyer | Newport, R.I. | Dec. 22, 1727 | Feb. 15, 1820 |
| d, William (N.Y.) | Soldier | Brookhaven, N.Y. | Dec. 17, 1734 | Aug. 4, 1821 |
| klin, Benjamin (Pa.) | Printer, publisher. | Boston, Mass. | Jan. 17, 1706 | Apr. 17, 1790 |
| y, Elbridge (Mass.) | Merchant | Marblehead, Mass. | July 17, 1744 | Nov. 23, 1814 |
| nnett, Button (Ga.) | Merchant | Down Hatherly, England. | c. 1735 | May 19, 1777 |
| , Lyman (Ga.) | Physician | Wallingford, Conn. | Apr. 12, 1724 | Oct. 19, 1790 |
| cock, John (Mass.) | Merchant | Braintree (Quincy), Mass. | Jan. 12, 1737 | Oct. 8, 1793 |
| rison, Benjamin (Va.) | Farmer | Berkeley, Va. | Apr. 5, 1726 | Apr. 24, 1791 |
| t, John (N.J.) | Farmer | Stonington, Conn. | c. 1711 | May 11, 1779 |
| es, Joseph (N.C.) | Merchant | Princeton, N.J. | Jan. 23, 1730 | Nov. 10, 1779 |
| ward, Thos. Jr. (S.C.) | Lawyer, farmer. | St. Luke's Parish, S.C. | July 28, 1746 | Mar. 6, 1809 |
| per, William (N.C.) | Lawyer | Boston, Mass. | June 28, 1742 | Oct. 14, 1790 |
| kins, Stephen (R.I.) | Judge, educator | Providence, R.I. | Mar. 7, 1707 | July 13, 1785 |
| kinson, Francis (N.J.) | Judge, author. | Philadelphia, Pa. | Sept. 21, 1737 | May 9, 1791 |
| tington, Samuel (Conn.) | Judge | Windham County, Conn. | July 3, 1731 | Jan. 5, 1796 |
| erson, Thomas (Va.) | Lawyer | Shadwell, Va. | Apr. 13, 1743 | July 4, 1826 |
| Francis Lightfoot (Va.) | Farmer | Westmoreland County, Va. | Oct. 14, 1734 | Jan. 11, 1797 |
| Richard Henry (Va.) | Farmer | Westmoreland County, Va. | Jan. 20, 1732 | June 19, 1794 |
| is, Francis (N.Y.) | Merchant | Llandaff, Wales | Mar., 1713 | Dec. 31, 1802 |
| ngston, Philip (N.Y.) | Merchant | Albany, N.Y. | Jan. 15, 1716 | June 12, 1778 |
| ch, Thomas Jr. (S.C.) | Farmer | Winyah, S.C. | Aug. 5, 1749 | (at sea) 1779 |
| Kean, Thomas (Del.) | Lawyer | New London, Pa. | Mar. 19, 1734 | June 24, 1817 |
| rris, Lewis (N.Y.) | Farmer | Morrisania (Bronx County), N.Y. | Apr. 8, 1726 | Jan. 22, 1798 |
| rris, Robert (Pa.) | Merchant | Liverpool, England | Jan. 20, 1734 | May 9, 1806 |
| rton, John (Pa.) | Judge | Ridley, Pa. | 1724 | Apr., 1777 |
| son, Thos. Jr. (Va.) | Farmer | Yorktown, Va. | Dec. 26, 1738 | Jan. 4, 1789 |
| a, William (Md.) | Judge | Abingdon, Md. | Oct. 31, 1740 | Oct. 23, 1799 |
| ne, Robert Treat (Mass.) | Judge | Boston, Mass. | Mar. 11, 1731 | May 12, 1814 |
| n. John (N.C.) | Lawyer | Near Port Royal, Va. | May 17, 1741 | Sept. 14, 1788 |
| d, George (Del.) | Judge | Near North East, Md. | Sept. 18, 1733 | Sept. 21, 1798 |
| dney, Caesar (Del.) | Judge | Dover, Del. | Oct. 7, 1728 | June 29, 1784 |
| s, George (Pa.) | Judge | New Castle, Del. | May 10, 1730 | July 14, 1779 |
| h, Benjamin (Pa.) | Physician | Byberry, Pa. (Philadelphia). | Dec. 24, 1745 | Apr. 19, 1813 |
| ledge, Edward (S.C.) | Lawyer | Charleston, S.C. | Nov. 23, 1749 | Jan. 23, 1800 |
| rman, Roger (Conn.) | Lawyer | Newton, Mass. | Apr. 19, 1721 | July 23, 1793 |
| th, James (Pa.) | Lawyer | Dublin, Ireland. | c. 1719 | July 11, 1806 |
| ckton, Richard (N.J.) | Lawyer | Near Princeton, N.J. | Oct. 1, 1730 | Feb. 28, 1781 |
| ne, Thomas (Md.) | Lawyer | Charles County, Md. | 1743 | Oct. 5, 1787 |
| lor, George (Pa.) | Ironmaster | Ireland. | 1716 | Feb. 23, 1781 |
| rnton, Matthew (N.H.) | Physician | Ireland. | 1714 | June 24, 1803 |
| ton, George (Ga.) | Judge | Prince Edward County, Va. | 1741 | Feb. 2, 1804 |
| pple, William (N.H.) | Merchant, judge | Kittery, Me. | Jan. 14, 1730 | Nov. 28, 1785 |
| iams, William (Conn.) | Merchant | Lebanon, Conn. | Apr. 23, 1731 | Aug. 2, 1811 |
| son James (Pa.) | Judge | Carskerdo, Scotland | Sept. 14, 1742 | Aug. 28, 1798 |
| herspoon, John (N.J.) | Educator | Gifford, Scotland | Feb. 5, 1723 | Nov. 15, 1794 |
| cott, Oliver (Conn.) | Judge | Windsor, Conn. | Dec. 1, 1726 | Dec. 1, 1797 |
| the, George (Va.) | Lawyer | Elizabeth City Co. (Hampton), Va. | 1726 | June 8, 1806 |

# Constitution of the United States
## The Original 7 Articles

### PREAMBLE

We, the people of the United States, in order to form a more perfect Union, establish justice, insure domestic tranquility, provide for the common defense, promote the general welfare, and secure the blessings of liberty to ourselves and our posterity do ordain and establish this Constitution for the United States of America.

### ARTICLE I.

#### Section 1—Legislative powers; in whom vested:

All legislative powers herein granted shall be vested in a Congress of the United States, which shall consist of a Senate and House of Representatives.

#### Section 2—House of Representatives, how and by whom chosen. Qualifications of a Representative. Representatives and direct taxes, how apportioned. Enumeration. Vacancies to be filled. Power of choosing officers, and of impeachment.

1. The House of Representatives shall be composed of members chosen every second year by the people of the several States, and the electors in each State shall have the qualifications requisite for electors of the most numerous branch of the State Legislature.

2. No person shall be a Representative who shall not have attained to the age of twenty-five years, and been seven years a citizen of the United States, and who shall not, when elected, be an inhabitant of that State in which he shall be chosen.

3. *(Representatives and direct taxes shall be apportioned among the several States which may be included within this Union, according to their respective numbers, which shall be determined by adding to the whole number of free persons, including those bound to service for a term of years, and excluding Indians not taxed, three-fifths of all other persons.) (The previous sentence was superseded by Amendment XIV, section 2.)* The actual enumeration shall be made within three years after the first meeting of the Congress of the United States, and within every subsequent term of ten years, in such manner as they shall by law direct. The number of Representatives shall not exceed one for every thirty thousand, but each State shall have at least one Representative; and until such enumeration shall be made, the State of New Hampshire shall be entitled to choose three, Massachusetts eight, Rhode Island and Providence Plantations one, Connecticut five, New York six, New Jersey four, Pennsylvania eight, Delaware one, Maryland six, Virginia ten, North Carolina five, South Carolina five, and Georgia three.

4. When vacancies happen in the representation from any State, the Executive Authority thereof shall issue writs of election to fill such vacancies.

5. The House of Representatives shall choose their Speaker and other officers; and shall have the sole power of impeachment.

#### Section 3—Senators, how and by whom chosen. How classified. Qualifications of a Senator. President of the Senate, his right to vote. President pro tem., and other officers of the Senate, how chosen. Power to try impeachments. When President is tried, Chief Justice to preside. Sentence.

1. The Senate of the United States shall be composed of two Senators from each State. *(chosen by the Legislature thereof), (The preceding five words were superseded by Amendment XVII, section I.)* for six years; and each Senator shall have one vote.

2. Immediately after they shall be assembled in consequence of the first election, they shall be divided as equally as may be into three classes. The seats of the Senators of the first class shall be vacated at the expiration of the second year, of the second class at the expiration of the fourth year, and of the third class at the expiration of the sixth year, so that one-third may be chosen every second year; *(and if vacancies happen by resignation, or otherwise, during the recess of the Legislature of any State, the Executive thereof may make temporary appointments until the next meeting of the Legislature, which shall then fill such vacancies.) (The words*

*in parentheses were superseded by Amendment XVII, se 2.)*

3. No person shall be a Senator who shall not have tained to the age of thirty years, and been nine years a zen of the United States, and who shall not, when electe an inhabitant of that State for which he shall be chosen.

4. The Vice President of the United States shall be P dent of the Senate, but shall have no vote, unless the equally divided.

5. The Senate shall choose their other officers, and a President pro tempore, in the absence of the Vice Presi or when he shall exercise the office of President of United States.

6. The Senate shall have the sole power to try all impe ments. When sitting for that purpose, they shall be on or affirmation. When the President of the United Stat tried, the Chief Justice shall preside: and no person sha convicted without the concurrence of two-thirds of members present.

7. Judgment in cases of impeachment shall not extend ther than to removal from office, and disqualificatio hold and enjoy any office of honor, trust or profit unde United States: but the party convicted shall nevertheles liable and subject to indictment, trial, judgment and pu ment, according to law.

#### Section 4—Times, etc., of holding elections, how pr scribed. One session each year.

1. The times, places and manner of holding election Senators and Representatives, shall be prescribed in State by the Legislature thereof; but the Congress ma any time by law make or alter such regulations, except the places of choosing Senators.

2. The Congress shall assemble at least once in every and such meeting shall *(be on the first Monday in Decem (The words in parentheses were superseded by Amend XX, section 2).* unless they shall by law appoint a diff day.

#### Section 5—Membership, quorum, adjournmen rules. Power to punish or expel. Journal. Time of a journments, how limited, etc.

1. Each House shall be the judge of the elections, ret and qualifications of its own members, and a majori each shall constitute a quorum to do business; but a sm number may adjourn from day to day, and may be au rized to compel the attendance of absent members, in manner, and under such penalties as each House may vide.

2. Each House may determine the rules of its proceed punish its members for disorderly behavior, and, with concurrence of two-thirds, expel a member.

3. Each House shall keep a journal of its proceedings, from time to time publish the same, excepting such par may in their judgment require secrecy; and the yeas nays of the members of either House on any question s at the desire of one-fifth of those present, be entered o journal.

4. Neither House, during the session of Congress, s without the consent of the other, adjourn for more three days, nor to any other place than that in which two Houses shall be sitting.

#### Section 6—Compensation, privileges, disqualific tions in certain cases.

1. The Senators and Representatives shall receive a pensation for their services, to be ascertained by law, paid out of the Treasury of the United States. They sha all cases, except treason, felony and breach of the peac privileged from arrest during their attendance at the se of their respective Houses, and in going to and retur from the same; and for any speech or debate in e House, they shall not be questioned in any other place.

2. No Senator or Representative shall, during the tim which he was elected, be appointed to any civil office u the authority of the United States, which shall have created, or the emoluments whereof shall have beer creased during such time; and no person holding any o under the United States, shall be a member of either H

uring his continuance in office.

**Section 7—House to originate all revenue bills. Veto. Bill may be passed by two-thirds of each House, notwithstanding, etc. Bill, not returned in ten days, to become a law. Provisions as to orders, concurrent resolutions, etc.**

1. All bills for raising revenue shall originate in the House of Representatives; but the Senate may propose or concur with amendments as on other bills.

2. Every bill which shall have passed the House of Representatives and the Senate, shall, before it becomes a law, be resented to the President of the United States; if he approves he shall sign it, but if not he shall return it, with his objections to that House in which it shall have originated, who shall enter the objections at large on their journal, and proceed to reconsider it. If after such reconsideration two-thirds of that House shall agree to pass the bill, it shall be sent, together with the objections, to the other House, by which it shall likewise be reconsidered, and if approved by two-thirds of that House, it shall become a law. But in all such cases the votes of both Houses shall be determined by yeas and nays, and the names of the persons voting for and against the bill shall be entered on the journal of each House respectively. If any bill shall not be returned by the President within ten days (Sundays excepted) after it shall have been presented to him, the same shall be a law, in like manner as if he had signed it, unless the Congress by their adjournment prevent its return, in which case it shall not be a law.

3. Every order, resolution, or vote to which the concurrence of the Senate and House of Representatives may be necessary (except on a question of adjournment) shall be presented to the President of the United States; and before the same shall take effect, shall be approved by him, or being disapproved by him, shall be repassed by two-thirds of the Senate and House of Representatives, according to the rules and limitations prescribed in the case of a bill.

**Section 8—Powers of Congress.**

The Congress shall have power

1. To lay and collect taxes, duties, imposts and excises, to pay the debts and provide for the common defense and general welfare of the United States; but all duties, imposts and excises shall be uniform throughout the United States;

2. To borrow money on the credit of the United States;

3. To regulate commerce with foreign nations, and among the several States, and with the Indian tribes;

4. To establish a uniform rule of naturalization, and uniform laws on the subject of bankruptcies throughout the United States;

5. To coin money, regulate the value thereof, and of foreign coin, and fix the standard of weights and measures;

6. To provide for the punishment of counterfeiting the securities and current coin of the United States;

7. To establish post-offices and post-roads;

8. To promote the progress of science and useful arts, by securing for limited times to authors and inventors the exclusive right to their respective writings and discoveries;

9. To constitute tribunals inferior to the Supreme Court;

10. To define and punish piracies and felonies committed on the high seas, and offenses against the law of nations;

11. To declare war, grant letters of marque and reprisal, and make rules concerning captures on land and water;

12. To raise and support armies, but no appropriation of money to that use shall be for a longer term than two years;

13. To provide and maintain a navy;

14. To make rules for the government and regulation of the land and naval forces;

15. To provide for calling forth the militia to execute the laws of the Union, suppress insurrections and repel invasions;

16. To provide for organizing, arming, and disciplining the militia, and for governing such part of them as may be employed in the service of the United States, reserving to the States respectively, the appointment of the officers, and the authority of training and militia according to the discipline prescribed by Congress;

17. To exercise exclusive legislation in all cases whatsoever, over such district (not exceeding ten miles square) as may, by cession of particular States, and the acceptance of Congress, become the seat of the Government of the United States, and to exercise like authority over all places purchased by the consent of the Legislature of the State in which the same shall be, for the erection of forts, magazines, arsenals, dockyards, and other needful buildings;—And

18. To make all laws which shall be necessary and proper for carrying into execution the foregoing powers, and all other powers vested by this Constitution in the Government of the United States, or in any department or officer thereof.

**Section 9—Provision as to migration or importation of certain persons. Habeas corpus, bills of attainder, etc. Taxes, how apportioned. No export duty. No commercial preference. Money, how drawn from Treasury, etc. No titular nobility. Officers not to receive presents, etc.**

1. The migration or importation of such persons as any of the States now existing shall think proper to admit, shall not be prohibited by the Congress prior to the year one thousand eight hundred and eight, but a tax or duty may be imposed on such importation, not exceeding ten dollars for each person.

2. The privilege of the writ of habeas corpus shall not be suspended, unless when in cases of rebellion or invasion the public safety may require it.

3. No bill of attainder or ex post facto law shall be passed.

4. No capitation, or other direct, tax shall be laid, unless in proportion to the census or enumeration herein before directed to be taken. *(Modified by Amendment XVI.)*

5. No tax or duty shall be laid on articles exported from any State.

6. No preference shall be given by any regulation of commerce or revenue to the ports of one State over those of another: nor shall vessels bound to, or from, one State, be obliged to enter, clear, or pay duties in another.

7. No money shall be drawn from the Treasury, but in consequence of appropriations made by law; and a regular statement and account of the receipts and expenditures of all public money shall be published from time to time.

8. No title of nobility shall be granted by the United States: and no person holding any office of profit or trust under them, shall, without the consent of the Congress, accept of any present, emolument, office, or title, of any kind whatever, from any king, prince, or foreign state.

**Section 10—States prohibited from the exercise of certain powers.**

1. No State shall enter into any treaty, alliance, or confederation; grant letters of marque and reprisal; coin money; emit bills of credit; make anything but gold and silver coin a tender in payment of debts; pass any bill of attainder, ex post facto law, or law impairing the obligation of contracts, or grant any title of nobility.

2. No State shall, without the consent of the Congress, lay any imposts or duties on imports or exports, except what may be absolutely necessary for executing its inspection laws: and the net produce of all duties and imposts, laid by any State on imports or exports, shall be for the use of the Treasury of the United States; and all such laws shall be subject to the revision and control of the Congress.

3. No State shall, without the consent of Congress, lay any duty of tonnage, keep troops, or ships of war in time of peace, enter into any agreement or compact with another State, or with a foreign power, or engage in war, unless actually invaded, or in such imminent danger as will not admit of delay.

### ARTICLE II.

**Section 1—President: his term of office. Electors of President; number and how appointed. Electors to vote on same day. Qualification of President. On whom his duties devolve in case of his removal, death, etc. President's compensation. His oath of office.**

1. The Executive power shall be vested in a President of the United States of America. He shall hold his office during the term of four years, and together with the Vice President, chosen for the same term, be elected as follows

2. Each State shall appoint, in such manner as the Legis-

lature thereof may direct, a number of electors, equal to the whole number of Senators and Representatives to which the State may be entitled in the Congress: but no Senator or Representative, or person holding an office of trust or profit under the United States, shall be appointed an elector.

*(The electors shall meet in their respective States, and vote by ballot for two persons, of whom one at least shall not be an inhabitant of the same State with themselves. And they shall make a list of all the persons voted for, and of the number of votes for each; which list they shall sign and certify, and transmit sealed to the seat of the Government of the United States, directed to the President of the Senate. The President of the Senate shall, in the presence of the Senate and House of Representatives, open all the certificates, and the votes shall then be counted. The person having the greatest number of votes shall be the President, if such number be a majority of the whole number of electors appointed; and if there be more than one who have such majority, and have an equal number of votes, then the House of Representatives shall immediately choose by ballot one of them for President; and if no person have a majority, then from the five highest on the list the said House shall in like manner choose the President. But in choosing the President, the votes shall be taken by States, the representation from each State having one vote; a quorum for this purpose shall consist of a member or members from two-thirds of the States, and a majority of all the States shall be necessary to a choice. In every case, after the choice of the President, the person having the greatest number of votes of the electors shall be the Vice President. But if there should remain two or more who have equal votes, the Senate shall choose from them by ballot the Vice President.)*

*(This clause was superseded by Amendment XII.)*

3. The Congress may determine the time of choosing the electors, and the day on which they shall give their votes; which day shall be the same throughout the United States.

4. No person except a natural born citizen, or a citizen of the United States, at the time of the adoption of this Constitution, shall be eligible to the office of President; neither shall any person be eligible to that office who shall not have attained to the age of thirty-five years, and been fourteen years a resident within the United States.

*(For qualification of the Vice President, see Amendment XII.)*

5. In case of the removal of the President from office, or of his death, resignation, or inability to discharge the powers and duties of the said office, the same shall devolve on the Vice President, and the Congress may by law provide for the case of removal, death, resignation or inability, both of the President and Vice President, declaring what officer shall then act as President, and such officer shall act accordingly, until the disability be removed, or a President shall be elected.

*(This clause has been modified by Amendments XX and XXV.)*

6. The President shall, at stated times, receive for his services, a compensation, which shall neither be increased nor diminished during the period for which he shall have been elected, and he shall not receive within that period any other emolument from the United States, or any of them.

7. Before he enter on the execution of his office, he shall take the following oath or affirmation:

"I do solemnly swear (or affirm) that I will faithfully execute the office of President of the United States, and will to the best of my ability, preserve, protect and defend the Constitution of the United States."

### Section 2—President to be Commander-in-Chief. He may require opinions of cabinet officers, etc., may pardon. Treaty-making power. Nomination of certain officers. When President may fill vacancies.

1. The President shall be Commander-in-Chief of the Army and Navy of the United States, and of the militia of the several States, when called into the actual service of the United States; he may require the opinion, in writing, of the principal officer in each of the executive departments, upon any subject relating to the duties of their respective offices, and he shall have power to grant reprieves and pardons for offenses against the United States, except in cases of impeachment.

2. He shall have power, by and with the advice and con-

sent of the Senate, to make treaties, provided two-thirds of the Senators present concur; and he shall nominate, and by and with the advice and consent of the Senate, shall appoint ambassadors, other public ministers and consuls, judges of the Supreme Court, and all other officers of the United States, whose appointments are not herein otherwise provided for, and which shall be established by law: but the Congress may by law vest the appointment of such inferior officers, as they think proper, in the President alone, in the courts of law, or in the heads of departments.

3. The President shall have power to fill up all vacancies that may happen during the recess of the Senate, by granting commissions, which shall expire at the end of their next session.

### Section 3—President shall communicate to Congress. He may convene and adjourn Congress, in case of disagreement, etc. Shall receive ambassadors, execute laws, and commission officers.

He shall from time to time give to the Congress information of the state of the Union, and recommend to their consideration such measures as he shall judge necessary and expedient; he may, on extraordinary occasions, convene both Houses, or either of them, and in case of disagreement between them, with respect to the time of adjournment, he may adjourn them to such time as he shall think proper; he shall receive ambassadors and other public ministers; he shall take care that the laws be faithfully executed, and shall commission all the officers of the United States.

### Section 4—All civil offices forfeited for certain crimes.

The President, Vice President, and all civil officers of the United States, shall be removed from office on impeachment for, and conviction of, treason, bribery, or other high crimes and misdemeanors.

## ARTICLE III.

### Section 1—Judicial powers, Tenure, Compensation.

The judicial power of the United States, shall be vested in one Supreme Court, and in such inferior courts as the Congress may from time to time ordain and establish. The judges, both of the Supreme and inferior courts, shall hold their offices during good behavior, and shall at stated times, receive for their services, a compensation, which shall not be diminished during their continuance in office.

### Section 2—Judicial power; to what cases it extends. Original jurisdiction of Supreme Court; appellate jurisdiction. Trial by jury, etc. Trial, where.

1. The judicial power shall extend to all cases, in law and equity, arising under this Constitution, the laws of the United States, and treaties made, or which shall be made, under their authority; to all cases affecting ambassadors, other public ministers and consuls; to all cases of admiralty and maritime jurisdiction; to controversies to which the United States shall be a party; to controversies between two or more States; between a State and citizens of another State; between citizens of different States, between citizens of the same State claiming lands under grants of different States, and between a State, or the citizens thereof, and foreign states, citizens or subjects.

*(This section is modified by Amendment XI.)*

2. In all cases affecting ambassadors, other public ministers and consuls, and those in which a State shall be party, the Supreme Court shall have original jurisdiction. In all the other cases before mentioned, the Supreme Court shall have appellate jurisdiction, both as to law and fact, with such exceptions, and under such regulations as the Congress shall make.

3. The trial of all crimes, except in cases of impeachment, shall be by jury; and such trial shall be held in the State where the said crimes shall have been committed; but when not committed within any State, the trial shall be at such place or places as the Congress may by law have directed.

### Section 3—Treason Defined, Proof of, Punishment of.

1. Treason against the United States, shall consist only in levying war against them, or in adhering to their enemies,

ving them aid and comfort. No person shall be convicted treason unless on the testimony of two witnesses to the me overt act, or on confession in open court.

2. The Congress shall have power to declare the punishent of treason, but no attainder of treason shall work corption of blood, or forfeiture except during the life of the rson attainted.

### ARTICLE IV.

**Section 1—Each State to give credit to the public acts, etc., of every other State.**

Full faith and credit shall be given in each State to the ublic acts, records, and judicial proceedings of every other tate. And the Congress may by general laws prescribe the anner in which such acts, records and proceedings shall be roved, and the effect thereof.

**Section 2—Privileges of citizens of each State. Fugitives from justice to be delivered up. Persons held to service having escaped, to be delivered up.**

1. The citizens of each State shall be entitled to all priviges and immunities of citizens in the several States.

2. A person charged in any State with treason, felony, or ther crime, who shall flee from justice, and be found in anther State, shall on demand of the Executive authority of he State from which he fled, be delivered up, to be removed  the State having jurisdiction of the crime.

*(3. No person held to service or labor in one State, under he laws thereof, escaping into another, shall in consequence of ny law or regulation therein, be discharged from such service r labor, but shall be delivered up on claim of the party to whom such service or labor may be due.) (This clause was superseded by Amendment XIII.)*

**Section 3—Admission of new States. Power of Congress over territory and other property.**

1. New States may be admitted by the Congress into this Union; but no new State shall be formed or erected within he jurisdiction of any other State; nor any State be formed y the junction of two or more States, or parts of States, without the consent of the Legislatures of the States concerned as well as of the Congress.

2. The Congress shall have power to dispose of and make ll needful rules and regulations respecting the territory or ther property belonging to the United States; and nothing n this Constitution shall be so construed as to prejudice any laims of the United States, or of any particular State.

**Section 4—Republican form of government guaranteed. Each state to be protected.**

The United States shall guarantee to every State in this Union a Republican form of government, and shall protect ach of them against invasion; and on application of the Legislature, or of the Executive (when the Legislature cannot be convened) against domestic violence.

### ARTICLE V.

**Constitution: how amended; proviso.**

The Congress, whenever two-thirds of both Houses shall deem it necessary, shall propose amendments to this Constiution, or, on the application of the Legislatures of twohirds of the several States, shall call a convention for proposing amendments, which, in either case, shall be valid to all intents and purposes, as part of this Constitution, when ratified by the Legislatures of three-fourths of the several States, or by conventions in three-fourths thereof, as the one

or the other mode of ratification may be proposed by the Congress; provided that no amendment which may be made prior to the year one thousand eight hundred and eight shall in any manner affect the first and fourth clauses in the Ninth Section of the First Article; and that no State, without its consent, shall be deprived of its equal suffrage in the Senate.

### ARTICLE VI.

**Certain debts, etc., declared valid. Supremacy of Constitution, treaties, and laws of the United States. Oath to support Constitution, by whom taken. No religious test.**

1. All debts contracted and engagements entered into, before the adoption of this Constitution, shall be as valid against the United States under this Constitution, as under the Confederation.

2. This Constitution, and the laws of the United States which shall be made in pursuance thereof; and all treaties made, or which shall be made, under the authority of the United States, shall be the supreme law of the land; and the judges in every State shall be bound thereby, any thing in the Constitution or laws of any State to the contrary notwithstanding.

3. The Senators and Representatives before mentioned, and the members of the several State Legislatures, and all executive and judicial officers, both of the United States and of the several States, shall be bound by oath or affirmation, to support this Constitution; but no religious test shall ever be required as a qualification to any office or public trust under the United States.

### ARTICLE VII.

**What ratification shall establish Constitution.**

The ratification of the Conventions of nine States, shall be sufficient for the establishment of this Constitution between the States so ratifying the same.

Done in convention by the unanimous consent of the States present the Seventeenth day of September in the year of our Lord one thousand seven hundred and eighty seven, and of the independence of the United States of America the Twelfth. In witness whereof we have hereunto subscribed our names.

George Washington, President and deputy from Virginia.

New Hampshire—John Langdon, Nicholas Gilman.

Massachusetts—Nathaniel Gorham, Rufus King.

Connecticut—Wm. Saml. Johnson, Roger Sherman.

New York—Alexander Hamilton.

New Jersey—Wil: Livingston, David Brearley, Wm. Paterson, Jona: Dayton.

Pennsylvania—B. Franklin, Thomas Mifflin, Robt. Morris, Geo. Clymer, Thos. FitzSimons, Jared Ingersoll, James Wilson, Gouv. Morris.

Delaware—Geo: Read, Gunning Bedford Jun., John Dickinson, Richard Bassett, Jaco: Broom.

Maryland—James McHenry, Daniel of Saint Thomas' Jenifer, Danl. Carroll.

Virginia—John Blair, James Madison Jr.

North Carolina—Wm. Blount, Rich'd. Dobbs Spaight, Hugh Williamson.

South Carolina—J. Rutledge, Charles Cotesworth Pinckney, Charles Pinckney, Pierce Butler.

Georgia—William Few, Abr. Baldwin.

Attest: William Jackson, Secretary.

## Ten Original Amendments: The Bill of Rights
In force Dec. 15, 1791

*(The First Congress, at its first session in the City of New York, Sept. 25, 1789, submitted to the states 12 amendments to clarify certain individual and state rights not named in the Constitution. They are generally called the Bill of Rights.*

*(Influential in framing these amendments was the Declaration of Rights of Virginia, written by George Mason (1725-1792) in 1776. Mason, a Virginia delegate to the Constitutional Convention, did not sign the Constitution and opposed its ratification on the ground that it did not sufficiently oppose slavery or safeguard individual rights.*

*(In the preamble to the resolution offering the proposed amendments, Congress said: "The conventions of a number of the States having at the time of their adopting the Constitution, expressed a desire, in order to prevent misconstruction or abuse of its powers, that further declaratory and restrictive clauses should be added, and as extending the ground of public confidence in the government will best insure the beneficent ends of its institution, be it resolved," etc.*

*(Ten of these amendments now commonly known as one to 10 inclusive, but originally 3 to 12 inclusive, were ratified by the states as follows: New Jersey, Nov. 20, 1789; Maryland, Dec. 19, 1789; North Carolina, Dec. 22, 1789; South Carolina, Jan. 19, 1790; New Hampshire, Jan 25, 1790; Delaware, Jan 28, 1790; New York, Feb. 24, 1790; Pennsylvania, Mar. 10, 1790; Rhode*

*Island, June 7, 1790; Vermont, Nov 3, 1791; Virginia, Dec. 15, 1791; Massachusetts, Mar. 2, 1939; Georgia, Mar. 8, 1939; Co necticut, Apr. 19, 1939. These original 10 ratified amendments follow as Amendments I to X inclusive.*

*(Of the two original proposed amendments which were not ratified by the necessary number of states, the first related to appo tionment of Representatives; the second, to compensation of members.)*

## AMENDMENT I.
### Religious establishment prohibited. Freedom of speech, of the press, and right to petition.

Congress shall make no law respecting an establishment of religion, or prohibiting the free exercise thereof; or abridging the freedom of speech, or of the press; or the right of the people peaceably to assemble, and to petition the Government for a redress of grievances.

## AMENDMENT II.
### Right to keep and bear arms.

A well-regulated militia, being necessary to the security of a free State, the right of the people to keep and bear arms, shall not be infringed.

## AMENDMENT III.
### Conditions for quarters for soldiers.

No soldier shall, in time of peace be quartered in any house, without the consent of the owner, nor in time of war, but in a manner to be prescribed by law.

## AMENDMENT IV.
### Right of search and seizure regulated.

The right of the people to be secure in their persons, houses, papers, and effects, against unreasonable searches and seizures, shall not be violated, and no warrants shall issue, but upon probable cause, supported by oath or affirmation, and particularly describing the place to be searched, and the persons or things to be seized.

## AMENDMENT V.
### Provisions concerning prosecution. Trial and punishment—private property not to be taken for public use without compensation.

No person shall be held to answer for a capital, or otherwise infamous crime, unless on a presentment or indictment of a Grand Jury, except in cases arising in the land and naval forces, or in the militia, when in actual service in time of war or public danger; nor shall any person be subject for the same offense to be twice put in jeopardy of life or limb; nor shall be compelled in any criminal case to be a witne against himself, nor be deprived of life, liberty, or propert without due process of law; nor shall private property b taken for public use without just compensation.

## AMENDMENT VI.
### Right to speedy trial, witnesses, etc.

In all criminal prosecutions, the accused shall enjoy th right to a speedy and public trial, by an impartial jury of th State and district wherein the crime shall have been commi ted, which district shall have been previously ascertained b law, and to be informed of the nature and cause of the acc sation; to be confronted with the witnesses against him; t have compulsory process for obtaining witnesses in his fa vor, and to have the assistance of counsel for his defense.

## AMENDMENT VII.
### Right of trial by jury.

In suits at common law, where the value in controvers shall exceed twenty dollars, the right of trial by jury shall b preserved, and no fact tried by a jury shall be otherwise r examined in any court of the United States, than accordin to the rules of the common law.

## AMENDMENT VIII.
### Excessive bail or fines and cruel punishment prohibited.

Excessive bail shall not be required, nor excessive fine imposed, nor cruel and unusual punishments inflicted.

## AMENDMENT IX.
### Rule of construction of Constitution.

The enumeration in the Constitution, of certain rights shall not be construed to deny or disparage others retaine by the people.

## AMENDMENT X.
### Rights of States under Constitution.

The powers not delegated to the United States by th Constitution, nor prohibited by it to the States, are reserve to the States respectively, or to the people.

# Amendments Since the Bill of Rights

## AMENDMENT XI.
### Judicial powers construed.

The judicial power of the United States shall not be construed to extend to any suit in law or equity, commenced or prosecuted against one of the United States by citizens of another State, or by citizens or subjects of any foreign state.

*(This amendment was proposed to the Legislatures of the several States by the Third Congress on March 4, 1794, and was declared to have been ratified in a message from the President to Congress, dated Jan. 8, 1798.*

*(It was on Jan 5, 1798, that Secretary of State Pickering received from 12 of the States authenticated ratifications, and informed President John Adams of that fact.*

*(As a result of later research in the Department of State, it is now established that Amendment XI became part of the Constitution on Feb. 7, 1795, for on that date it had been ratified by 12 States as follows:*

*(1. New York, Mar. 27, 1794. 2. Rhode Island, Mar. 31, 1794. 3. Connecticut, May 8, 1794. 4. New Hampshire, June 16, 1794. 5. Massachusetts, June 26, 1794. 6. Vermont, between Oct 9, 1794, and Nov. 9, 1794. 7. Virginia, Nov. 18, 1794. 8. Georgia, Nov. 29, 1794. 9. Kentucky, Dec. 7, 1794. 10. Maryland, Dec. 26, 1794. 11. Delaware, Jan 23, 1795. 12. North Carolina, Feb. 7, 1795.*

*(On June 1, 1796, more than a year after Amendment XI had become a part of the Constitution (but before anyone was officially aware of this), Tennessee had been admitted as a State; but not until Oct. 16, 1797, was a certified copy of the resolution of Congress proposing the amendment sent to the Governor of Tennessee (John Sevier) by Secretary of State Pickering, whose office was then at Trenton, New Jersey, because* of the epidemic of yellow fever at Philadelphia; it seems, however, that the Legislature of Tennessee took no action on Amendment XI, owing doubtless to the fact that public announcement of its adoption was made soon thereafter.*

*(Besides the necessary 12 States, one other, South Carolina, ratified Amendment XI, but this action was not taken until Dec. 4, 1797; the two remaining States, New Jersey and Pennsylvania, failed to ratify.)*

## AMENDMENT XII.
### Manner of choosing President and Vice-President.

*(Proposed by Congress Dec. 9, 1803; ratification completed June 15, 1804.)*

The Electors shall meet in their respective States and vote by ballot for President and Vice-President, one of whom, at least, shall not be an inhabitant of the same State with themselves; they shall name in their ballots the person voted for as President, and in distinct ballots the person voted for as Vice-President, and they shall make distinct lists of all persons voted for as President, and of all persons voted for as Vice-President, and of the number of votes for each, which lists they shall sign and certify, and transmit sealed to the seat of the Government of the United States, directed to the President of the Senate; the President of the Senate shall, in the presence of the Senate and House of Representatives, open all the certificates and the votes shall then be counted;—The person having the greatest number of votes for President, shall be the President, if such number be a majority of the whole number of Electors appointed; and if no person have such majority, then from the persons having the highest numbers not exceeding three on the list of those voted for as President, the House of Representatives shall oose immediately, by ballot, the President. But in choosing the President, the votes shall be taken by States, the representation from each State having one vote; a quorum for is purpose shall consist of a member or members from vo-thirds of the States, and a majority of all the States all be necessary to a choice. *(And if the House of Representatives shall not choose a President whenever the right of hoice shall devolve upon them, before the fourth day of March next following, then the Vice-President shall act as resident, as in the case of the death or other constitutional isability of the President.) (The words in parentheses were perseded by Amendment XX, section 3.)* The person having e greatest number of votes as Vice-President, shall be the ice-President, if such number be a majority of the whole umber of Electors appointed, and if no person have a majority, then from the two highest numbers on the list, the enate shall choose the Vice-President; a quorum for the urpose shall consist of two-thirds of the whole number of enators, and a majority of the whole number shall be necessary to a choice. But no person constitutionally ineligible o the office of President shall be eligible to that of Vice-resident of the United States.

## THE RECONSTRUCTION AMENDMENTS

*(Amendments XIII, XIV, and XV are commonly known as the Reconstruction Amendments, inasmuch as they followed the Civil War, and were drafted by Republicans who were bent on imposing their own policy of reconstruction on the South. Post-bellum legislatures there—Mississippi, South Carolina, Georgia, for example—had set up laws which, it was charged, were contrived to perpetuate Negro slavery under other names.)*

### AMENDMENT XIII.

#### Slavery abolished.

*(Proposed by Congress Jan. 31, 1865; ratification completed Dec. 18, 1865. The amendment, when first proposed by a resolution in Congress, was passed by the Senate, 38 to 6, on Apr. 8, 1864, but was defeated in the House, 95 to 66 on June 15, 1864. On reconsideration by the House, on Jan. 31, 1865, the resolution passed, 119 to 56. It was approved by President Lincoln on Feb. 1, 1865, although the Supreme Court had decided in 1798 that the President has nothing to do with the proposing of amendments to the Constitution, or their adoption.)*

1. Neither slavery nor involuntary servitude, except as a punishment for crime whereof the party shall have been duly convicted, shall exist within the United States or any place subject to their jurisdiction.

2. Congress shall have power to enforce this article by appropriate legislation.

### AMENDMENT XIV.

#### Citizenship rights not to be abridged.

*(The following amendment was proposed to the Legislatures of the several states by the 39th Congress, June 13, 1866, and was declared to have been ratified in a proclamation by the Secretary of State, July 28, 1868.*

*(The 14th amendment was adopted only by virtue of ratification subsequent to earlier rejections. Newly constituted legislatures in both North Carolina and South Carolina (respectively July 4 and 9, 1868), ratified the proposed amendment, although earlier legislatures had rejected the proposal. The Secretary of State issued a proclamation, which, though doubtful as to the effect of attempted withdrawals by Ohio and New Jersey, entertained no doubt as to the validity of the ratification by North and South Carolina. The following day July 21, 1868, Congress passed a resolution which declared the 14th Amendment to be a part of the Constitution and directed the Secretary of State so to promulgate it. The Secretary waited, however, until the newly constituted Legislature of Georgia had ratified the amendment, subsequent to an earlier rejection, before the promulgation of the ratification of the new amendment.)*

1. All persons born or naturalized in the United States, nd subject to the jurisdiction thereof, are citizens of the United States and of the State wherein they reside. No State hall make or enforce any law which shall abridge the privieges or immunities of citizens of the United States; nor shall any State deprive any person of life, liberty, or property, without due process of law; nor deny to any person within its jurisdiction the equal protection of the laws.

2. Representatives shall be apportioned among the several States according to their respective numbers, counting the whole number of persons in each State, excluding Indians not taxed. But when the right to vote at any election for the choice of Electors for President and Vice-President of the United States, Representatives in Congress, the executive and judicial officers of a State, or the members of the Legislature thereof, is denied to any of the male inhabitants of such State, being twenty-one years of age, and, citizens of the United States, or in any way abridged, except for participation in rebellion, or other crime, the basis of representation therein shall be reduced in the proportion which the number of such male citizens shall bear to the whole number of male citizens twenty-one years of age in such State.

3. No person shall be a Senator or Representative in Congress, or Elector of President and Vice-President, or hold any office, civil or military, under the United States, or under any State, who, having previously taken an oath, as a member of Congress, or as an officer of the United States, or as a member of any State Legislature, or as an executive or judicial officer of any State, to support the Constitution of the United States, shall have engaged in insurrection or rebellion against the same, or given aid or comfort to the enemies thereof. But Congress may by a vote of two-thirds of each House, remove such disability.

4. The validity of the public debt of the United States, authorized by law, including debts incurred for payment of pensions and bounties for services in suppressing insurrection or rebellion, shall not be questioned. But neither the United States nor any State shall assume or pay any debt or obligation incurred in aid of insurrection or rebellion against the United States, or any claim for the loss or emancipation of any slave; but all such debts, obligations and claims, shall be held illegal and void.

5. The Congress shall have power to enforce, by appropriate legislation, the provisions of this article.

### AMENDMENT XV.

#### Race no bar to voting rights.

*(The following amendment was proposed to the legislatures of the several States by the 40th Congress, Feb. 26, 1869, and was declared to have been ratified in a proclamation by the Secretary of State, Mar. 30, 1870.)*

1. The right of citizens of the United States to vote shall not be denied or abridged by the United States or by any State on account of race, color, or previous condition of servitude.

2. The Congress shall have power to enforce this article by appropriate legislation.

### AMENDMENT XVI.

#### Income taxes authorized.

*(Proposed by Congress July 12, 1909; ratification declared by the Secretary of State Feb. 25, 1913.)*

The Congress shall have power to lay and collect taxes on incomes, from whatever sources derived, without apportionment among the several States, and without regard to any census or enumeration.

### AMENDMENT XVII.

#### United States Senators to be elected by direct popular vote.

*(Proposed by Congress May 13, 1912; ratification declared by the Secretary of State May 31, 1913.)*

1. The Senate of the United States shall be composed of two Senators from each State, elected by the people thereof, for six years; and each Senator shall have one vote. The electors in each State shall have the qualifications requisite for electors of the most numerous branch of the State Legislatures.

2. When vacancies happen in the representation of any State in the Senate, the executive authority of such State shall issue writs of election to fill such vacancies: Provided, That the Legislature of any State may empower the Executive thereof to make temporary appointments until the peo-

ple fill the vacancies by election as the Legislature may direct.

3. This amendment shall not be so construed as to affect the election or term of any Senator chosen before it becomes valid as part of the Constitution.

### AMENDMENT XVIII.

#### Liquor prohibition amendment.

*(Proposed by Congress Dec. 18, 1917; ratification completed Jan. 16, 1919. Repealed by Amendment XXI, effective Dec. 5, 1933.)*

(1. After one year from the ratification of this article the manufacture, sale, or transportation of intoxicating liquors within, the importation thereof into, or the exportation thereof from the United States and all territory subject to the jurisdiction thereof for beverage purposes is hereby prohibited.

(2. The Congress and the several States shall have concurrent power to enforce this article by appropriate legislation.

(3. This article shall be inoperative unless it shall have been ratified as an amendment to the Constitution by the Legislatures of the several States, as provided in the Constitution, within seven years from the date of the submission hereof to the States by the Congress.)

*(The total vote in the Senates of the various States was 1,310 for, 237 against—84.6% dry. In the lower houses of the States the vote was 3,782 for, 1,035 against—78.5% dry.*

*(The amendment ultimately was adopted by all the States except Connecticut and Rhode Island.)*

### AMENDMENT XIX.

#### Giving nationwide suffrage to women.

*(Proposed by Congress June 4, 1919; ratification certified by Secretary of State Aug. 26, 1920.)*

1. The right of citizens of the United States to vote shall not be denied or abridged by the United States or by any State on account of sex.

2. Congress shall have power to enforce this Article by appropriate legislation.

### AMENDMENT XX.

#### Terms of President and Vice President to begin on Jan. 20; those of Senators, Representatives, Jan. 3.

*(Proposed by Congress Mar. 2, 1932; ratification completed Jan. 23, 1933.)*

1. The terms of the President and Vice President shall end at noon on the 20th day of January, and the terms of Senators and Representatives at noon on the 3rd day of January, of the years in which such terms would have ended if this article had not been ratified; and the terms of their successors shall then begin.

2. The Congress shall assemble at least once in every year, and such meeting shall begin at noon on the 3rd day of January, unless they shall by law appoint a different day.

3. If, at the time fixed for the beginning of the term of the President, the President elect shall have died, the Vice President elect shall become President. If a President shall not have been chosen before the time fixed for the beginning of his term, or if the President elect shall have failed to qualify, then the Vice President elect shall act as President until a President shall have qualified; and the Congress may by law provide for the case wherein neither a President elect nor a Vice President elect shall have qualified, declaring who shall then act as President, or the manner in which one who is to act shall be selected, and such person shall act accordingly until a President or Vice President shall have qualified.

4. The Congress may by law provide for the case of the death of any of the persons from whom the House of Representatives may choose a President whenever the right of choice shall have devolved upon them, and for the case of the death of any of the persons from whom the Senate may choose a Vice President whenever the right of choice shall have devolved upon them.

5. Sections 1 and 2 shall take effect on the 15th day of October following the ratification of this article (Oct., 1933).

6. This article shall be inoperative unless it shall have been ratified as an amendment to the Constitution by the Legislatures of three-fourths of the several States within seven years from the date of its submission.

### AMENDMENT XXI.

#### Repeal of Amendment XVIII.

*(Proposed by Congress Feb. 20, 1933; ratification completed Dec. 5, 1933.)*

1. The eighteenth article of amendment to the Constitution of the United States is hereby repealed.

2. The transportation or importation into any State, Territory, or Possession of the United States for delivery or use therein of intoxicating liquors, in violation of the laws thereof, is hereby prohibited.

3. This article shall be inoperative unless it shall have been ratified as an amendment to the Constitution by conventions in the several States, as provided in the Constitution, within seven years from the date of the submission hereof to the States by the Congress.

### AMENDMENT XXII.

#### Limiting Presidential terms of office.

*(Proposed by Congress Mar. 24, 1947; ratification completed Feb. 27, 1951.)*

1. No person shall be elected to the office of the President more than twice, and no person who has held the office of President, or acted as President, for more than two years of a term to which some other person was elected President shall be elected to the office of the President more than once. But this Article shall not apply to any person holding the office of President when this Article was proposed by the Congress, and shall not prevent any person who may be holding the office of President, or acting as President, during the term within which this Article becomes operative from holding the office of President or acting as President during the remainder of such term.

2. This article shall be inoperative unless it shall have been ratified as an amendment to the Constitution by the Legislatures of three-fourths of the several States within seven years from the date of its submission to the States by the Congress.

### AMENDMENT XXIII.

#### Presidential vote for District of Columbia.

*(Proposed by Congress June 17, 1960; ratification completed Mar. 29, 1961.)*

1. The District constituting the seat of Government of the United States shall appoint in such manner as the Congress may direct:

A number of electors of President and Vice President equal to the whole number of Senators and Representatives in Congress to which the District would be entitled if it were a State, but in no event more than the least populous State; they shall be in addition to those appointed by the States, but they shall be considered, for the purposes of the election of President and Vice President, to be electors appointed by a State; and they shall meet in the District and perform such duties as provided by the twelfth article of amendment.

2. The Congress shall have power to enforce this article by appropriate legislation.

### AMENDMENT XXIV.

#### Barring poll tax in federal elections.

*(Proposed by Congress Aug. 27, 1962; ratification completed Jan. 23, 1964.)*

1. The right of citizens of the United States to vote in any primary or other election for President or Vice President, for electors for President or Vice President, or for Senator or Representative in Congress, shall not be denied or abridged by the United States or any State by reason of failure to pay any poll tax or other tax.

2. The Congress shall have power to enforce this article by appropriate legislation.

### AMENDMENT XXV.

#### Presidential disability and succession.

*(Proposed by Congress July 6, 1965; ratification completed Feb. 10, 1967.)*

1. In case of the removal of the President from office or of

s death or resignation, the Vice President shall become resident.

2. Whenever there is a vacancy in the office of the Vice resident, the President shall nominate a Vice President who all take office upon confirmation by a majority vote of th houses of Congress.

3. Whenever the President transmits to the President pro mpore of the Senate and the Speaker of the House of Representatives his written declaration that he is unable to disharge the powers and duties of his office, and until he ansmits to them a written declaration to the contrary, such owers and duties shall be discharged by the Vice President s Acting President.

4. Whenever the Vice President and a majority of either te principal officers of the executive departments or of such ther body as Congress may by law provide, transmit to the resident pro tempore of the Senate and the Speaker of the ouse of Representatives their written declaration that the resident is unable to discharge the powers and duties of his fice, the Vice President shall immediately assume the pows and duties of the office as Acting President.

Thereafter, when the President transmits to the President ro tempore of the Senate and the Speaker of the House of epresentatives his written declaration that no inability exts, he shall resume the powers and duties of his office unss the Vice President and a majority of either the principal fficers of the executive department or of such other body as ongress may by law provide, transmit within four days to te President pro tempore of the Senate and the Speaker of te House of Representatives their written declaration that te President is unable to discharge the powers and duties of is office. Thereupon Congress shall decide the issue, assemling within forty-eight hours for that purpose if not in ses-

sion. If the Congress, within twenty-one days after receipt of the latter written declaration, or, if Congress is not in session, within twenty-one days after Congress is required to assemble, determines by two-thirds vote of both houses that the President is unable to discharge the powers and duties of his office, the Vice President shall continue to discharge the same as Acting President; otherwise, the President shall resume the powers and duties of his office.

### AMENDMENT XXVI.

#### Lowering voting age to 18 years.

*(Proposed by Congress Mar. 8, 1971; ratification completed July 1, 1971.)*

1. The right of citizens of the United States, who are 18 years of age or older, to vote shall not be denied or abridged by the United States or any state on account of age.

2. The Congress shall have the power to enforce this article by appropriate legislation.

### PROPOSED EQUAL RIGHTS AMENDMENT

*(Proposed by Congress Mar. 22, 1972; ratification completed, as of mid-1978, by 35 states, not ratified by 6, defeated in 9; needed total of 38 for adoption before deadline, Mar. 22, 1979.)*

1. Equality of rights under the law shall not be denied or abridged by the United States or by any State on account of sex.

2. The Congress shall have the power to enforce, by appropriate legislation, the provisions of this article.

3. This amendment shall take effect two years after the date of ratification.

## Origin of the Constitution

The War of Independence was conducted by delegates om the original 13 states, called the Congress of the nited States of America and generally known as the Contiental Congress. In 1777 the Congress submitted to the leglatures of the states the Articles of Confederation and Peretual Union, which were ratified by New Hampshire, Massachusetts, Rhode Island, Connecticut, New York, New ersey, Pennsylvania, Delaware, Virginia, North Carolina, outh Carolina, and Georgia, and finally, in 1781, by Marynd.

The first article of the instrument read: "The stile of this onfederacy shall be the United States of America." This did ot signify a sovereign nation, because the states delegated nly those powers they could not handle individually, such s power to wage war, establish a uniform currency, make eaties with foreign nations and contract debts for general xpenses (such as paying the army). Taxes for the payment f such debts were levied by the individual states. The presient under the Articles signed himself "President of the nited States in Congress assembled," but here the United tates were considered in the plural, a cooperating group. anada was invited to join the union on equal terms but did ot act.

When the war was won it became evident that a stronger ederal union was needed to protect the mutual interests of te states. The Congress left the initiative to the legislatures. irginia in Jan. 1786 appointed commissioners to meet with epresentatives of other states, with the result that delegates om Virginia, Delaware, New York, New Jersey, and Pennylvania met at Annapolis. Alexander Hamilton prepared or their call by asking delegates from all states to meet in hiladelphia in May 1787 "to render the Constitution of the ederal government adequate to the exigencies of the unon." Congress endorsed the plan Feb. 21, 1787. Delegates

were appointed by all states except Rhode Island.

The convention met May 14, 1787. George Washington was chosen president (presiding officer). The states certified 65 delegates, but 10 did not attend. The work was done by 55, not all of whom were present at all sessions. Of the 55 attending delegates, 16 failed to sign, and 39 actually signed Sept. 17, 1787, some with reservations. Some historians have said 74 delegates (9 more than the 65 actually certified) were named and 19 failed to attend. These 9 additional persons refused the appointment, were never delegates and never counted as absentees. Washington sent the Constitution to Congress with a covering letter and that body, Sept. 28, 1787, ordered it sent to the legislatures, "in order to be submitted to a convention of delegates chosen in each state by the people thereof."

The Constitution was ratified by votes of state conventions as follows: Delaware, Dec. 7, 1787, unanimous; Pennsylvania, Dec. 12, 1787, 43 to 23; New Jersey, Dec. 18, 1787, unanimous; Georgia, Jan 2, 1788, unanimous; Connecticut, Jan. 9, 1788, 128 to 40; Massachusetts, Feb. 6, 1788, 187 to 168; Maryland, Apr. 28, 1788, 63 to 11; South Carolina, May 23, 1788, 149 to 73; New Hampshire, June 21, 1788, 57 to 46; Virginia, June 25, 1788, 89 to 79; New York, July 26, 1788, 30 to 27. Nine states were needed to establish the operation of the Constitution "between the states so ratifying the same" and New Hampshire was the 9th state. The government did not declare the Constitution in effect until the first Wednesday in Mar. 1789 which was Mar. 4. After that North Carolina ratified it Nov. 21, 1789, 197 to 77; and Rhode Island, May 29, 1790, 34 to 32. Vermont in convention ratified it Jan. 10, 1791, and by act of Congress approved Feb. 19, 1791, was admitted into the Union as the 14th state, Mar. 4, 1791.

## How the Declaration of Independence Was Adopted

On June 7, 1776, Richard Henry Lee, who had issued the rst call for a congress of the colonies, introduced in the ontinental Congress at Philadelphia a resolution declaring that these United Colonies are, and of right ought to be, ee and independent states, that they are absolved from al-

legiance to the British Crown, and that all political connection between them and the state of Great Britain is, and ought to be, totally dissolved."

The resolution, seconded by John Adams on behalf of the Massachusetts delegation, came up again June 10 when a committee of 5, headed by Thomas Jefferson, was appointed to express the purpose of the resolution in a declaration of independence. The others on the committee were John Adams, Benjamin Franklin, Robert R. Livingston, and Roger Sherman.

Drafting the Declaration was assigned to Jefferson, who worked on a portable desk of his own construction in a room at Market and 7th Sts. The committee reported the result June 28, 1776. The members of the Congress suggested a number of changes, which Jefferson called "deplorable." They didn't approve Jefferson's arraignment of the British people and King George III for encouraging and fostering the slave trade, which Jefferson called "an execrable commerce." They made 86 changes, eliminating 480 words and leaving 1,337. In the final form capitalization was erratic. Jefferson had written that men were endowed with "inalienable" rights; in the final copy it came out as "unalienable" and has been thus ever since.

The Lee-Adams resolution of independence was adopted by 12 yeas July 2 — the actual date of the act of independence. The Declaration, which explains the act, was adopted July 4, in the evening.

After the Declaration was adopted, July 4, 1776, it was turned over to John Dunlap, printer, to be printed on broadsides. The original copy was lost and one of his broadsides was attached to a page in the journal of the Congress. It was read aloud July 8 in Philadelphia, Easton, Pa., and Trenton, N.J. On July 9 at 6 p.m. it was read by order of Gen. George Washington to the troops assembled on the Common in New York City (City Hall Park).

The Continental Congress of July 19, 1776, adopted following resolution:

"Resolved, That the Declaration passed on the 4th, fairly engrossed on parchment with the title and stile "The Unanimous Declaration of the thirteen United Sta of America' and that the same, when engrossed, be sign by every member of Congress."

Not all delegates who signed the engrossed Declarati were present on July 4. Robert Morris (Pa.), William W liams (Conn.) and Samuel Chase (Md.) signed on Aug. Oliver Wolcott (Conn.), George Wythe (Va.), Richa Henry Lee (Va.) and Elbridge Gerry (Mass.) signed in A gust and September, Matthew Thronton (N. H.) joined Congress Nov. 4 and signed later. Thomas McKean (De rejoined Washington's Army before signing and said la that he signed in 1781.

Charles Carroll of Carrollton was appointed a delegate Maryland on July 4, 1776, presented his credentials July and signed the engrossed Declaration Aug. 2. Born Sept. 1737, he was 95 years old and the last surviving signer wh he died Nov. 14, 1832.

Two Pennsylvania delegates who did not support the D laration on July 4 were replaced.

The 4 New York delegates did not have authority fr their state to vote on July 4. On July 9 the New York sta convention authorized its delegates to approve the Decla tion and the Congress was so notified on July 15, 1776. T 4 signed the Declaration on Aug. 2.

The original engrossed Declaration is preserved in the N tional Archives Building in Washington.

## The Liberty Bell: Its History and Significance

The Liberty Bell, in Independence Hall, Philadelphia, is an object of great reverence to Americans because of its association with the historic events of the War of Independence.

The original Province bell, ordered to commemorate the 50th anniversary of the Commonwealth of Pennsylvania, was cast by Thomas Lister, Whitechapel, London, and reached Philadelphia in Aug. 1752. It bore an inscription from Leviticus XXV, 10: "Proclaim liberty throughout all the land unto all the inhabitants thereof."

The bell was cracked by a stroke of its clapper in Sept. 1752 while it hung on a truss in the State House yard for testing. Pass & Stow, Philadelphia founders, recast the bell, adding 1 1/2 ounces of copper to a pound of the original metal to reduce brittleness. It was found that the bell contained too much copper, injuring its tone, so Pass & Stow recast it again, this time successfully.

In June 1753 the bell was hung in the wooden steeple of the State House, erected on top of the brick tower. In use while the Continental Congress was in session in the State House, it rang out in defiance of British tax and trade restrictions, and proclaimed the Boston Tea Party and the first public reading of the Declaration of Independence.

On Sept. 18, 1777, when the British Army was about to occupy Philadelphia, the bell was moved in a baggage train of the American Army to Allentown, Pa. where it was hidden in the Zion Reformed Church until June 27, 1778. It was moved back to Philadelphia after the British left.

In July 1781 the wooden steeple became insecure and h to be taken down. The bell was lowered into the brick se tion of the tower. Here it was hanging in July, 1835, when cracked while tolling for the funeral of John Marshall, ch justice of the United States. Because of its association wi the War of Independence it was not recast but remain mute in this location until 1846, the year of the Mexic War, when it was placed on exhibition in the Declarati Chamber of Independence Hall.

In 1876, when many thousands of Americans visited Ph adelphia for the Centennial Exposition, it was placed in old walnut frame in the tower hallway. In 1877 it was hu from the ceiling of the tower by a chain of 13 links. It w returned again to the Declaration Chamber and in 18 taken back to the tower hall, where it occupied a glass ca In 1915 the case was removed so that the public mig touch it. On Jan. 1, 1976, just after midnight to mark t opening of the Bicentennial Year, the bell was moved to new glass and steel pavilion behind Independence Hall f easier viewing by the larger number of visitors expected du ing the year.

The measurements of the bell follow: circumferen around the lip, 12 ft.; circumference around the crown, 7 6 in.; lip to the crown, 3 ft.; height over the crown, 2 ft. in.; thickness at lip, 3 in.; thickness at crown, 1 1/4 in weight, 2080 lbs.; length of clapper, 3 ft. 2 in.; cost, £60 1 5d.

## Confederate States and Secession

The American Civil War, 1861-65, grew out of sectional disputes over the continued existence of slavery in the South and the contention of Southern legislators that the states retained many sovereign rights, including the right to secede from the Union.

The war was not fought by state against state but by one federal regime against another, the Confederate government in Richmond assuming control over the economic, political, and military life of the South, under protest from Georgia and South Carolina.

South Carolina voted an ordinance of secession from the Union, repealing its 1788 ratification of the U.S. Constitu-

tion on Dec. 20, 1860, to take effect Dec. 24. Other stat seceded in 1861. Their votes in conventions were:

Mississippi, Jan. 9, 84-15; Florida, Jan. 10, 62-7; Al bama, Jan. 11, 61-39; Georgia, Jan. 19, 208-89; Louisian Jan. 26, 113-17; Texas, Feb. 1, 166-7, ratified by popul vote Feb. 23 (for 34,794, against 11,325); Virginia, Apr. 1 88-55, ratified by popular vote May 23 (for 128,884; again 32,134); Arkansas, May 6, 69-1; Tennessee, May 7, ratifie by popular vote June 8 (for 104,019, against 47,238); Nor Carolina, May 21.

Missouri Unionists stopped secession in conventions Fe 28 and Mar. 9. The legislature condemned secession Mar.

nder the protection of Confederate troops, secessionist embers of the legislature adopted a resolution of secession Neosho, Oct. 31. The Confederate Congress seated the cessionists' representatives.

Kentucky did not secede and its government remained nionist. In a part occupied by Confederate troops, Kenckians approved secession and the Confederate Congress mitted their representatives.

The Maryland legislature voted against secession Apr. 27, 3-13. Delaware did not secede. Western Virginia held con-ntions at Wheeling, named a pro-Union governor June 11, 61; admitted to Union as West Virginia June 30, 1863; its nstitution provided for gradual abolition of slavery.

## Confederate Government

Forty-two delegates from South Carolina, Georgia, Ala-

bama, Mississippi, Louisiana, and Florida met in convention at Montgomery, Ala., Feb. 4, 1861. They adopted a provisional constitution of the Confederate States of America, and elected Jefferson Davis (Miss.) provisional president, and Alexander H. Stephens (Ga.) provisional vice president.

A permanent constitution was adopted Mar. 11; it abolished the African slave trade. The Congress moved to Richmond, Va. July 20. Davis was elected president in October, and was inaugurated Feb. 22, 1862.

The Congress adopted a flag, consisting of a red field with a white stripe, and a blue jack with a circle of white stars. Later the more popular flag was the red field with blue diagonal cross bars that held 13 white stars. The stars represented the 11 states actually in the Confederacy plus Kentucky and Missouri.

(See also Civil War, U.S., in Index)

## Dixie

The name Dixie popularly refers to the southern states. It has several possible origins.

One is said to be French word dix (ten) which was printed on $10 bills used in early Louisiana which were called "dixies" y Americans. Louisiana became known as "Dix's Land" of "Land of the Dixies."

Some sources suggest that the name originated from a kind-hearted Dutch farmer, Dixie (Dixye), who unsuccessfully tried cultivate tobacco in Harlem, N.Y., in the late 1700s. When he sold his slaves to a farmer in Piedmont County, S.C., they e said to have longed to return to Dixie's farm and sang of its joys.

Many consider Dixie a derivation from the "Mason-Dixon Line" which divided the free and slave states.

## Lincoln's Address at Gettysburg, 1863

Fourscore and seven years ago our fathers brought forth on this continent a new nation, conceived in liberty and dedicated the proposition that all men are created equal.

Now we are engaged in a great civil war, testing whether that nation or any nation so conceived and so dedicated can long ndure. We are met on a great battle field of that war. We have come to dedicate a portion of that field, as a final restinglace for those who here gave their lives that that nation might live. It is altogether fitting and proper that we should do this.

But, in a larger sense, we can not dedicate — we can not consecrate — we can not hallow — this ground. The brave men, ving and dead, who struggled here, have consecrated it, far above our poor power to add or detract. The world will little ote, nor long remember, what we say here, but it can never forget what they did here. It is for us the living, rather, to be edicated here to the unfinished work which they who fought here have thus far so nobly advanced. It is rather to us to be ere dedicated to the great task remaining before us — that from these honored dead we take increased devotion to that ause for which they gave the last full measure of devotion — that we here highly resolve that these dead shall not have died n vain — that this nation, under God, shall have a new birth of freedom — and that government of the people, by the peo-le, for the people, shall not perish from the earth.

### History of the Address

President Lincoln delivered his address at the dedication of the military cemetery at Gettysburg, Pa., Nov. 19, 1863. The battle ad been fought July 1-3, 1863. He was preceded by Edward Ever-tt, former president of Harvard, secretary of state and senator om Massachusetts, then 69 and one of the nation's great orators. verett gave a full resume of the battle, Lincoln's speech was so hort that the photographer did not get his camera adjusted in ime. The report that newspapers ignored Lincoln's address is not ntirely accurate; Everett's address swamped their columns, but the greatness of Lincoln's speech was immediately recognized. Everett wrote him: "I should be glad if I could flatter myself that I came as ear the central idea of the occasion in 2 hours as you did in 2 min-tes."

Five copies of the Gettysburg address in Lincoln's hand are ex-

tant. The first and 2d drafts, prepared in Washington and Gettysburg just before delivery, are in the Library of Congress. The 3d draft, written at the request of Everett to be sold at a fair in New York for the benefit of soldiers, was given the Illinois State Historical Library by public subscription.

The 4th copy was written out by Lincoln for George Bancroft, the historian, and remained in custody of the Bancroft family until 1929, when it was acquired by Mrs. Nicholas H. Noyes, of Indianapolis, Ind. In 1949 Mrs. Noyes presented this copy to the Cornell University Library, Ithaca, N.Y. The 5th copy, usually described as the clearest and best, was also written by Lincoln for George Bancroft. It is in the Lincoln Room of the White House, where it was placed in Mar. 1959. Lincoln's spelling of battle field and can not as separated words in that version is reproduced above.

## The National Anthem — The Star-Spangled Banner

The Star-Spangled Banner was ordered played by the military and naval services by President Woodrow Wilson in 916. It was designated the National Anthem by Act of Congress, Mar. 3, 1931. It was written by Francis Scott Key, of Georgetown, D. C., during the bombardment of 'ort McHenry, Baltimore, Md., Sept. 13-14, 1814. Key was a lawyer, a graduate of St. John's College, Annapolis, and a olunteer in a light artillery company. When a friend, Dr. Beanes, a physician of Upper Marlborough, Md., was taken board Admiral Cockburn's British squadron for interfering with ground troops, Key and J. S. Skinner, carrying a note rom President Madison, went to the fleet under a flag of ruce on a cartel ship to ask Beanes' release. Admiral Cock-urn consented, but as the fleet was about to sail up the Pa-apsco to bombard Fort McHenry he detained them, first on H. M. S. Surprise, and then on a supply ship.

Key witnessed the bombardment from his own vessel. It began at 7 a.m., Sept. 13, 1814, and lasted, with intermis-sions, for 25 hours. The British fired over 1,500 shells, each weighing as much as 220 lbs. They were unable to approach closely because the Americans had sunk 22 vessels in the

channel. Only four Americans were killed and 24 wounded. A British bomb-ship was disabled.

During the bombardment Key wrote a stanza on the back of an envelope. Next day at Indian Queen Inn, Baltimore, he wrote out the poem and gave it to his brother-in-law, Judge J. H. Nicholson. Nicholson suggested the tune, Anacreon in Heaven, and had the poem printed on broadsides, of which two survive. On Sept. 20 it appeared in the "Baltimore American." Later Key made 3 copies; one is in the Library of Congress and one in the Pennsylvania Historical Society.

The copy that Key wrote in his hotel Sept. 14, 1814, re-mained in the Nicholson family for 93 years. In 1907 it was sold to Henry Walters of Baltimore. In 1934 it was bought at auction in New York from the Walters estate by the Wal-ters Art Gallery, Baltimore, for $26,400. The Walters Gal-lery in 1953 sold the manuscript to the Maryland Historical Society for the same price.

The flag that Key saw during the bombardment is pre-served in the Smithsonian Institution, Washington. It is 30 by 42 ft., and has 15 alternate red and white stripes and 15 stars, for the original 13 states plus Kentucky and Vermont.

It was made by Mary Young Pickersgill. The Baltimore Flag House, a museum, occupies her premises, which were restored in 1953.

## The Star-Spangled Banner

### I

Oh, say can you see by the dawn's early light
  What so proudly we hailed at the twilight's last gleaming?
Whose broad stripes and bright stars thru the perilous fight,
  O'er the ramparts we watched were so gallantly streaming?
And the rocket's red glare, the bombs bursting in air,
  Gave proof through the night that our flag was still there.
Oh, say does that star-spangled banner yet wave
  O'er the land of the free and the home of the brave?

### II

On the shore, dimly seen through the mists of the deep,
  Where the foe's haughty host in dread silence reposes,
What is that which the breeze, o'er the towering steep,
  As it fitfully blows, half conceals, half discloses?
Now it catches the gleam of the morning's first beam,
  In full glory reflected now shines on the stream:

'Tis the star-spangled banner! Oh long may it wave
  O'er the land of the free and the home of the brave!

### III

And where is that band who so vauntingly swore
  That the havoc of war and the battle's confusion,
A home and a country should leave us no more!
  Their blood has washed out their foul footsteps' pollution
No refuge could save the hireling and slave
  From the terror of flight, or the gloom of the grave:
And the star-spangled banner in triumph doth wave
  O'er the land of the free and the home of the brave!

### IV

Oh! thus be it ever, when freemen shall stand
  Between their loved homes and the war's desolation!
Blest with victory and peace, may the heav'n rescued land
  Praise the Power that hath made and preserved us a nation.
Then conquer we must, when our cause it is just,
  And this be our motto: "In God is our trust."
And the star-spangled banner in triumph shall wave
  O'er the land of the free and the home of the brave!

# Statue of Liberty National Monument

Since 1886, the Statue of Liberty Enlightening the World has stood as a symbol of freedom in New York harbor. It also commemorates French-American friendship for it was given by the people of France, designed by Frederic Auguste Bartholdi (1834-1904). A $2.5 million building housing the American Museum of Immigration was opened by Pres. Nixon Sept. 26, 1972, at the base of the statue. It houses a permanent exhibition of photos, posters, and artifacts tracing the history of American immigration. In addition, there is a small immigration library. The Monument is administered by the National Park Service.

Nearby Ellis Island, gateway to America for more than 12 million immigrants between 1892 and 1954, was proclaimed part of the National Monument in 1965 by Pres. Johnson. It can be visited between May and October.

Edouard de Laboulaye, French historian and admirer of American political institutions, suggested that the French present a monument to the United States, the latter to provide pedestal and site. Bartholdi visualized a colossal statue at the entrance of New York harbor, welcoming the peoples of the world with the torch of liberty.

The French approved the idea and formed the Franco-American Union to raise funds, which eventually reached $250,000. Bartholdi began work about 1874 in Paris.

On Washington's birthday, Feb. 22, 1877, Congress approved the use of a site on Bedloe's Island suggested by Bartholdi. This island of 12 acres had been owned in the 17th century by a Walloon named Isaac Bedloe. It was called Bedloe's until Aug. 3, 1956, when Pres. Eisenhower approved a resolution of Congress changing the name to Liberty Island.

The statue was finished May 21, 1884, and formally presented to U.S. Minister Morton July 4, 1884, by Ferdinand de Lesseps, head of the Franco-American Union, promoter of the Panama Canal, and builder of the Suez Canal.

On Aug. 5, 1884, the Americans laid the cornerstone for the pedestal. This was to be built on the foundations of Fort Wood, which had been erected by the Government in 1811. The American committee had raised $125,000, but this was found to be inadequate. Joseph Pulitzer, owner of the New York World, appealed on Mar. 16, 1885, for general donations. By Aug. 11, 1885, he had raised $100,000.

The statue arrived dismantled, in 214 packing cases, from Rouen, France, in June, 1885. The last rivet of the statue was driven Oct. 28, 1886, when Pres. Grover Cleveland dedicated the monument.

The statue weighs 450,000 lbs. or 225 tons. The copper sheeting weighs 200,000 lbs. There are 167 steps from the land level to the top of the pedestal, 168 steps inside the statue to the head, and 54 rungs on the ladder leading to the arm that holds the torch.

| Dimensions of the Statue | Ft. | In. |
|---|---|---|
| Height from base to torch (45.3 meters) | 151 | |
| Foundation of pedestal to torch (91.5 meters) | 305 | |
| Heel to top of head | 111 | |
| Length of hand | 16 | |
| Index finger | 8 | |
| Circumference at second joint | 3 | |
| Size of finger nail | 13x10 in. | |
| Head from chin to cranium | 17 | |
| Head thickness from ear to ear | 10 | |
| Distance across the eye | 2 | |
| Length of nose | 4 | |
| Right arm, length | 42 | |
| Right arm, greatest thickness | 12 | |
| Thickness of waist | 35 | |
| Width of mouth | 3 | |
| Tablet, length | 23 | |
| Tablet, width | 13 | |
| Tablet, thickness | 2 | |

### Emma Lazarus' Famous Poem

A poem by Emma Lazarus is graven on a tablet within the pedestal on which the statue stands.

#### The New Colossus

*Not like the brazen giant of Greek fame,*
*With conquering limbs astride from land to land;*
*Here at our sea-washed, sunset gates shall stand*
*A mighty woman with a torch, whose flame*
*Is the imprisoned lightning, and her name*
*Mother of Exiles. From her beacon-hand*
*Glows world-wide welcome; her mild eyes command*
*The air-bridged harbor that twin cities frame.*
*"Keep ancient lands, your storied pomp!" cries she*
*With silent lips. "Give me your tired, your poor,*
*Your huddled masses yearning to breathe free,*
*The wretched refuse of your teeming shore.*
*Send these, the homeless, tempest-tost to me,*
*I lift my lamp beside the golden door!"*

# Forms of Address for Persons of Rank and Public Office

In these examples John Smith is used as a representative American name. The salutation Dear Sir or Dear Madam is always permissible when addressing a person not known to the writer.

### President of the United States

**Address:** The President, The White House, Washington, DC 20500. Also, The President and Mrs. ____.

**Salutation:** Dear Sir or Mr. President or Dear Mr. President. More intimately: My dear Mr. President. Also: Dear Mr. President and Mrs. ____.

The vice president takes the same forms.

### Cabinet Officers

**Address:** Mr. John Smith, Secretary of State, Washington D.C. or The Hon. John Smith. Similar addresses for other members of the cabinet. Also: Secretary and Mrs. John Smith.

**Salutation:** Dear Sir, or Dear Mr. Secretary. Also: Dear Mr. and Mrs. Smith.

### The Bench

**Address:** The Hon. John Smith, Chief Justice of the United States. The Hon. John Smith, Associate Justice of the Supreme Court of the United States. The Hon. John Smith, Associate Judge, U.S. District Court.

**Salutation:** Dear Sir, or Dear Mr. Chief Justice. Dear Mr. Justice. Dear Judge Smith.

### Members of Congress

**Address:** The Hon. John Smith, United States Senate, Washington, DC 20510, or Sen. John Smith, etc. Also The Hon. John Smith, House of Representatives, Washington, DC 20515, or Rep. John Smith, etc.

**Salutation:** Dear Mr. Senator or Dear Mr. Smith; for Representative, Dear Mr. Smith.

### Officers of Armed Forces

**Address:** Careful attention should be given to the precise rank, thus: General of the Army John Smith, Fleet Admiral John Smith. The rules for Air Force are same as Army.

**Salutation:** Dear Sir, or Dear General. All general officers, whatever rank, are entitled to be addressed as generals. Likewise a lieutenant colonel is addressed as colonel and first and second lieutenants are addressed as lieutenant.

Warrant officers and flight officers are addressed as Mister. Chaplains are addressed as Chaplain. A Catholic chaplain may be addressed as Father. Cadets of the United States Military Academy and Air Force Academy are addressed as Cadet. Noncommissioned officers are addressed by their titles. In the U. S. Navy all men from midshipman at Annapolis up to and including lieutenant commander are addressed as Mister.

### Ambassador, Governor, Mayor

**Address:** The Hon. John Smith, followed by his title. He can be addressed either at his embassy, or at the Department of State, Washington, D.C. An ambassador from a foreign nation may be addressed as His Excellency. An American is not to be so addressed.

**Salutation:** Dear Mr. Ambassador. An ambassador from a foreign nation may be called Your Excellency.

Governors and mayors are often addressed as The Hon. John Smith, Governor of _____, or The Hon. John Smith, Mayor of _____; also Governor John Smith, State House, Albany, N.Y., or Mayor John Smith, City Hall, Erie, Pa.

### The Clergy

**Address:** His Holiness, the Pope, or His Holiness Pope (name), State of Vatican City, Italy.

**Salutation:** Your Holiness or Most Holy Father.

Also: His Eminence, John, Cardinal Smith; salutation: Your Eminence. An archbishop or a bishop is addressed The Most Reverend, and the salutation is Your Excellency. A monsignor who is a papal chamberlain is The Very Reverend Monsignor and the salutation is Dear Sir or Very Reverend Monsignor; a monsignor who is a domestic prelate is The Right Reverend Monsignor and salutation is Right Reverend Monsignor. A priest is addressed Reverend John Smith. A brother of an order is addressed Brother —. A sister takes the same form.

A bishop of the Protestant Episcopal Church is The Right Reverend John Smith; salutation is Right Reverend Sir, or Dear Bishop Smith. If a clergyman is a doctor of divinity, he is addressed: The Reverend John Smith, D.D., and the salutation is Reverend Sir, or Dear Dr. Smith. When a clergyman does not have the degree the salutation is Dear Mr. Smith.

A bishop of the Methodist Church is addressed Bishop John Smith with titles following.

### Royalty and Nobility

An emperor is to be addressed in a letter as Sir, or Your Imperial Majesty.

A king or queen is addressed as His Majesty (Name), King of (Name), or Her Majesty (Name), Queen of (Name), Salutation: Sir, or Madam, or May it please Your Majesty.

Princes and princesses and other persons of royal blood are addressed as His (or Her) Royal Highness, and saluted with May it please Your Royal Highness.

A duke or marquis is My Lord Duke (or Marquis), a duke is His (or Your) Grace.

---

## Code of Etiquette for Display and Use of the U.S. Flag

Although the Stars and Stripes originated in 1777, it was not til 146 years later that there was a serious attempt to establish a uniform code of etiquette for the U.S. flag. The War Department issued Feb. 15, 1923, a circular on the rules of flag usage. These were adopted almost in their entirety June 14, 1923, by a conference of 68 patriotic organizations in Washington. Finally, on June 1942, a joint resolution of Congress codified "existing rules and customs pertaining to the flag for civilians."

**When to Display the Flag**—The flag should be displayed on all days when the weather permits, especially on legal holidays and other special occasions, on official buildings when in use, in or near polling places on election days, and in or near schools when in session. A citizen may fly the flag at any time he wishes. It is customary to display the flag only from sunrise to sunset on buildings and stationary flagstaffs in the open. However, it may be displayed night on special occasions, preferably lighted. In Washington, the flag now flies over the White House both day and night. It flies over the Senate wing of the Capitol when the Senate is in session and over the House wing when that body is in session. It flies day and night over the east and west fronts of the Capitol, without floodlights at night but receiving light from the illuminated Capitol dome. It flies 24 hours a day at several other places, including the Fort McHenry Nat'l Monument in Baltimore, where it inspired Francis Scott Key to write The Star Spangled Banner.

**How to Fly the Flag**—The flag should be hoisted briskly and lowered ceremoniously, and should never be allowed to touch the ground or the floor. When hung over a sidewalk from a rope extending from a building to a pole, the union should be away from the building. When hung over the center of a street it should have the union to the north in an east-west street and to the east in a north-south street. No other flag may be flown above or, if on the same level, to the right of the U.S. flag, except that at the United Nations Headquarters the UN flag may be placed above flags of all member nations and other national flags may be flown with equal prominence or honor with the flag of the U.S. At services by Navy chaplains at sea, the church pennant may be flown above the flag. When two flags are placed against a wall with crossed staffs, the U.S. flag should be at right—its own right, and its staff should be in front of the staff of the other flag; when a number of flags are grouped and displayed from staffs, it should be at the center and highest point of the group.

**Church and Platform Use**—In an auditorium, the flag may be displayed flat, above and behind the speaker. When displayed from a staff in a church or public auditorium, the flag should hold the position of superior prominence, in advance of the audience, and in the position of honor at the clergyman's or speaker's right as he faces the audience. Any other flag so displayed should be placed on the left of the clergyman or speaker or to the right of the audience.

When the flag is displayed horizontally or vertically against a wall, the stars should be at the observer's left.

**When to Salute the Flag**—All persons present should face the flag, stand at attention and salute on the following occasions: (1) When the flag is passing in a parade or in a review, (2) During the ceremony of hoisting or lowering, (3) When the National Anthem is played and the flag is displayed, and (4) During the Pledge of Allegiance. Those present in uniform should render the military salute. When not in uniform, men should remove the hat with the right hand holding it at the left shoulder, the hand being over the heart. Men without hats should salute in the same manner. Aliens should stand at attention. Women should salute by placing the right hand over the heart.

On Memorial Day, the flag should fly at half-staff until noon, then be raised to the peak.

As provided by Presidential proclamation the flag should fly at half-staff for 30 days from the day of a death of a president or former president; for 10 days from the day of death of a vice president, chief justice or retired chief justice of the U.S., or speaker of the House of Representatives; from day of death until burial of an associate justice of the Supreme Court, cabinet member, former vice president, or Senate president pro tempore, majority or minority Senate leader, or majority or minority House leader; for a U.S. senator, representative, territorial delegate, or the resident commissioner of Puerto Rico, on day of death and the following day within the metropolitan area of the District of Columbia and from day of death until burial within the decedent's state, congressional district, territory or commonwealth; and for the death of the governor of a state, territory, or possession of the U.S., from day of death until burial within that state, territory, or possession.

When used to cover a casket, the flag should be placed so that the union is at the head and over the left shoulder. It should not be lowered into the grave nor touch the ground.

**Prohibited Uses of the Flag**—The flag should not be dipped to any person or thing. It should never be displayed with the union down-save as a distress signal. It should never be carried flat or horizontally, but always aloft and free.

It should not be displayed on a float, motor car or boat except from a staff.

It should never be used as a covering for a ceiling, nor have placed upon it any word, design, or drawing. It should never be used as a receptacle for carrying anything. It should not be used to cover a statue or a monument.

The flag should never be used for advertising purposes, nor be embroidered on such articles as cushions or hankerchiefs, printed or otherwise impressed on boxes or used as a costume or athletic uniform. Advertising signs should not be fastened to its staff or halyard.

The flag should never be used as drapery of any sort, never festooned, drawn back, nor up, in folds, but always allowed to fall free. Bunting of blue, white and red always arranged with the blue above and the white in the middle, should be used for covering a speaker's desk, draping the front of a platform, and for decoration in general.

An Act of Congress approved Feb. 8, 1917, provided certain penalties for the desecration, mutilation or improper use of the flag within the District of Columbia. A 1968 federal law provided penalties of up to a year's imprisonment or a $1,000 fine or both, for

publicly burning or otherwise desecrating any flag of the Uni States. In addition, many states have laws against flag desecratic

**How to Dispose of Worn Flags**—The flag, when it is in s condition that it is no longer a fitting emblem for display, sho be destroyed in a dignified way, preferably by burning in private

## Pledge of Allegiance to the Flag

*I pledge allegiance to the flag of the United States of America to the republic for which it stands, one nation under God, indivis with liberty and justice for all.*

This, the current official version of the Pledge of Allegiance, developed from the original pledge, which was first published the Sept. 8, 1892, issue of the Youth's Companion, a weekly ma zine then published in Boston. The original pledge contained phrase "my flag," which was changed more than 30 years later "flag of the United States of America." An act of Congress in 19 added the words "under God."

The authorship of the pledge has been in dispute for many yea The Youth's Companion stated in 1917 that the original draft v written by James B. Upham, an executive of the magazine w died in 1910. A leaflet circulated by the magazine later named b ham as the originator of the draft "afterwards condensed and p fected by him and his associates of the Companion force."

Francis Bellamy, a former member of the Youth's Compan editorial staff, publicly claimed authorship of the pledge in 19 The United States Flag Assn., acting on the advice of a commit named to study the controversy, upheld in 1939 the claim of E lamy, who had died 8 years earlier. The Library of Congress issu in 1957 a report attributing the authorship to Bellamy.

---

# The Flag of the U.S.—The Stars and Stripes

The 50-star flag of the United States was raised for the first time officially at 12:01 a.m. on July 4, 1960, at Fort McHenry National Monument in Baltimore, Md. The 50th star had been added for Hawaii; a year earlier the 49th, for Alaska. Before that, no star had been added since 1912, when N.M. and Ariz. were admitted to the Union.

## History of the Flag

The true history of the Stars and Stripes has become so cluttered by a volume of myth and tradition that the facts are difficult, and in some cases impossible, to establish. For example, it is not certain who designed the Stars and Stripes, who made the first such flag, or even whether it ever flew in any sea fight or land battle of the American Revolution.

One thing all agree on is that the Stars and Stripes originated as the result of a resolution offered by the Marine Committee of the Second Continental Congress at Philadelphia and adopted June 14, 1777. It read:

*Resolved: that the flag of the United States be thirteen stripes, alternate red and white; that the union be thirteen stars, white in a blue field, representing a new constellation.*

Congress gave no hint as to the designer of the flag, no instructions as to the arrangement of the stars, and no information on its appropriate uses. Historians have been unable to find the original flag law.

The resolution establishing the flag was not even published until Sept. 2, 1777. Despite repeated requests, Washington did not get the flags until 1783, after the Revolutionary War was over. And there is no certainty that they were the Stars and Stripes.

## Early Flags

Although it was never officially adopted by the Continental Congress, many historians consider the first flag of the United States to have been the Grand Union (sometimes called Great Union) flag. This was a modification of the British Meteor flag, which had the red cross of St. George and the white cross of St. Andrew combined in the blue canton. For the Grand Union flag, 6 horizontal stripes were imposed on the red field, dividing it into 13 alternate red and white stripes. On Jan. 1, 1776, when the Continental Army came into formal existence, this flag was unfurled on Prospect Hill, Somerville, Mass. Washington wrote that "we hoisted the Union Flag in compliment to the United Colonies."

One of several flags about which controversy has raged for years is at Easton, Pa. Containing the devices of the national flag in reversed order, this has been in the public library at Easton for over 150 years. Some contend that this flag was actually the first Stars and Stripes, first displayed on July 8, 1776. This flag has 13 red and white stripes in the canton, 13 white stars centered in a blue field.

A flag was hastily improvised from garments by the defenders of Fort Schuyler at Rome, N.Y., Aug. 3-22, 1777. Historians believe it was the Grand Union Flag.

The Sons of Liberty had a flag of 9 red and white stripes, to signify 9 colonies, when they met in New York in 1765 to oppose the Stamp Tax. By 1775, the flag had grown to 13 red and white stripes, with a rattlesnake on it.

At Concord, Apr. 19, 1775, the minute men from Bedford, Mass., are said to have carried a flag having a silver arm with

sword on a red field.

At Cambridge, Mass., the Sons of Liberty used a plain red fl with a green pine tree on it.

In June 1775, Washington went from Philadelphia to Boston take command of the army, escorted to New York by the Philad phia Light Horse Troop. It carried a yellow flag which had elaborate coat of arms — the shield charged with 13 knots, t motto "For These We Strive" — and a canton of 13 blue and silv stripes.

In Feb., 1776, Col. Christopher Gadsden, member of the Con nental Congress, gave the South Carolina Provincial Congress flag "such as is to be used by the commander-in-chief of the Am ican Navy." It had a yellow field, with a rattlesnake about to stri and the words "Don't Tread on Me."

At the battle of Bennington, Aug. 16, 1777, patriots used a fl of 7 white and 6 red stripes with a blue canton extending down strips and showing an arch of 11 white stars over the figure 76 ar a star in each of the upper corners. The stars are seven-pointe This flag is preserved in the Historical Museum at Bennington, V

At the Battle of Cowpens, Jan. 17, 1781, the 3d Maryland Reg is said to have carried a flag of 13 red and white stripes, with a bl canton containing 12 stars in a circle around one star.

## Legends about the Flag

**Who Designed the Flag?** No one knows for a certainty. Fran Hopkinson, designer of a naval flag, declared he also had design the flag and in 1781 asked Congress to reimburse him for his se vices. Congress did not do so. Dumas Malone of Columbia Uni wrote: "This talented man . . . designed the American flag."

**Who Called the Flag Old Glory?** — The flag is said to have bee named Old Glory by William Driver, a sea captain of Salem, Mas One legend has it that when he raised the flag on his brig, t Charles Doggett, in 1824, he said: "I name thee Old Glory." B his daughter, who presented the flag to the Smithsonian Instit tion, said he named it at his 21st birthday celebration Mar. 1 1824, when his mother presented the homemade flag to him.

**The Betsy Ross Legend** — The widely publicized legend th Mrs. Betsy Ross made the first Stars and Stripes in June 1776, the request of a committee composed of George Washington, R bert Morris, and George Ross, an uncle, was first made public 1870, by a grandson of Mrs. Ross. Historians have been unable find a historical record of such a meeting or committee.

## Adding New Stars

The flag of 1777 was used until 1795. Then, on the admission Vermont and Kentucky to the Union, Congress passed and Pre Washington signed an act that after May 1, 1795, the flag shoul have 15 stripes, alternate red and white, and 15 stars on a blue fiel in the union.

When new states were admitted it became evident that the fla would become burdened with stripes. Congress thereupon ordere that after July 4, 1818, the flag should have 13 stripes, symbolizin the 13 original states; that the union have 20 stars, and that whe ever a new state was admitted a new star should be added on th July 4 following admission. No law designates the permanent a rangement of the stars. However, since 1912 when a new state ha been admitted, the new design has been announced by executiv order. No star is specifically identified with any state.

# WORLD FLAGS AND MAPS

481

 GHANISTAN
 ALBANIA
 ALGERIA
 ANDORRA
 ANGOLA

 ARGENTINA
 AUSTRALIA
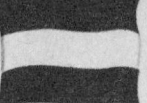 AUSTRIA
 BAHAMAS
 BAHRAIN

 ANGLADESH
 BARBADOS
 BELGIUM
 BENIN
 BHUTAN

 BOLIVIA
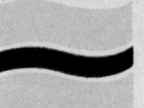 BOTSWANA
 BRAZIL
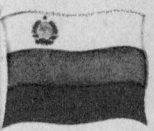 BULGARIA
 BURMA

 BURUNDI
 CAMBODIA
 CAMEROON
 CANADA
 CAPE VERDE

 NTRAL AFRICAN EMPIRE
 CHAD
 CHILE
 CHINA (MAINLAND)
 CHINA (TAIWAN)

 COLOMBIA
 COMORO ISLANDS
 CONGO
 COSTA RICA
 CUBA

 CYPRUS
 CZECHOSLOVAKIA
 DENMARK
 DJIBOUTI
 DOMINICAN REPUBLIC

Flags shown are *national* flags in common use and vary slightly from official *state* flags, most particularly by omitting coats of arms in some cases.

| | | | | |
|---|---|---|---|---|
| ECUADOR |  EGYPT | 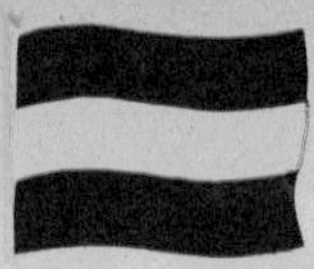 EL SALVADOR |  EQUATORIAL GUINEA |  ETHIOPIA |
|  FIJI | FINLAND |  FRANCE |  GABON | 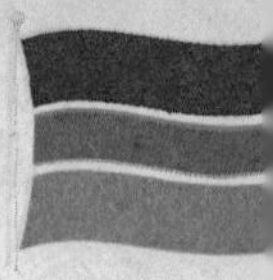 GAMBIA |
|  GERMAN DEM. REP. |  GERMANY, FED. REP. OF |  GHANA |  GREECE |  GRENADA |
|  GUATEMALA |  GUINEA |  GUINEA-BISSAU |  GUYANA |  HAITI |
|  HONDURAS |  HUNGARY |  ICELAND | 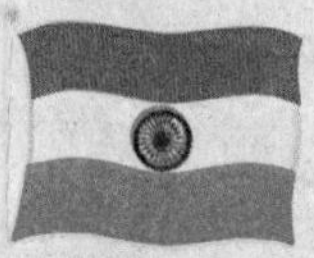 INDIA |  INDONESIA |
| IRAN |  IRAQ | IRELAND | ISRAEL | ITALY |
| IVORY COAST | JAMAICA | JAPAN | JORDAN | 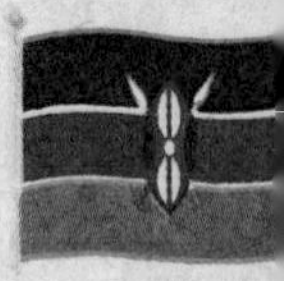 KENYA |
| KOREA, NORTH | KOREA, SOUTH | KUWAIT | LAOS | LEBANON |

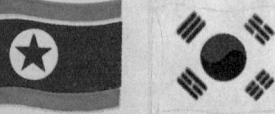

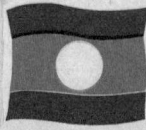

483

| | | | | |
|---|---|---|---|---|
| LESOTHO | LIBERIA | LIBYA | LIECHTENSTEIN | LUXEMBOURG |
| ADAGASCAR | MALAWI | MALAYSIA | MALDIVES | MALI |
| MALTA | MAURITANIA | MAURITIUS | MEXICO | MONACO |
| MONGOLIA | MOROCCO | MOZAMBIQUE | NAURU | NEPAL |
| ETHERLANDS | NEW ZEALAND | NICARAGUA | NIGER | NIGERIA |
| NORWAY | OMAN | PAKISTAN | PANAMA | PAPUA NEW GUINEA |
| PARAGUAY | PERU | PHILIPPINES | POLAND | PORTUGAL |
| QATAR | ROMANIA | RWANDA | SAN MARINO | SAO TOME & PRINCIPE |

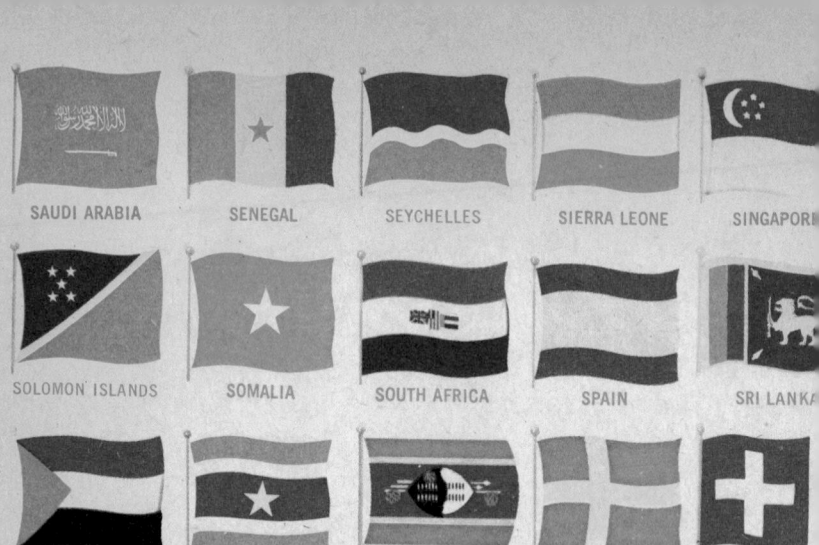

SAUDI ARABIA

SENEGAL

SEYCHELLES

SIERRA LEONE

SINGAPORE

SOLOMON ISLANDS

SOMALIA

SOUTH AFRICA

SPAIN

SRI LANKA

SUDAN

SURINAM

SWAZILAND

SWEDEN

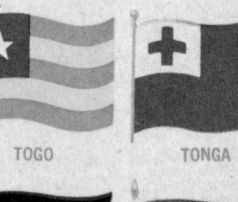

SWITZERLAND

SYRIA

TANZANIA

THAILAND

TOGO

TONGA

TRINIDAD & TOBAGO

TUNISIA

TURKEY

UGANDA

U.S.S.R.

UNITED ARAB
EMIRATES

UNITED KINGDOM

UNITED STATES

UPPER VOLTA

URUGUAY

VATICAN CITY

VENEZUELA

VIETNAM

WESTERN SAMOA

YEMEN

YEMEN, P.D.R. OF

YUGOSLAVIA

ZAIRE

ZAMBIA

ZIMBABWE

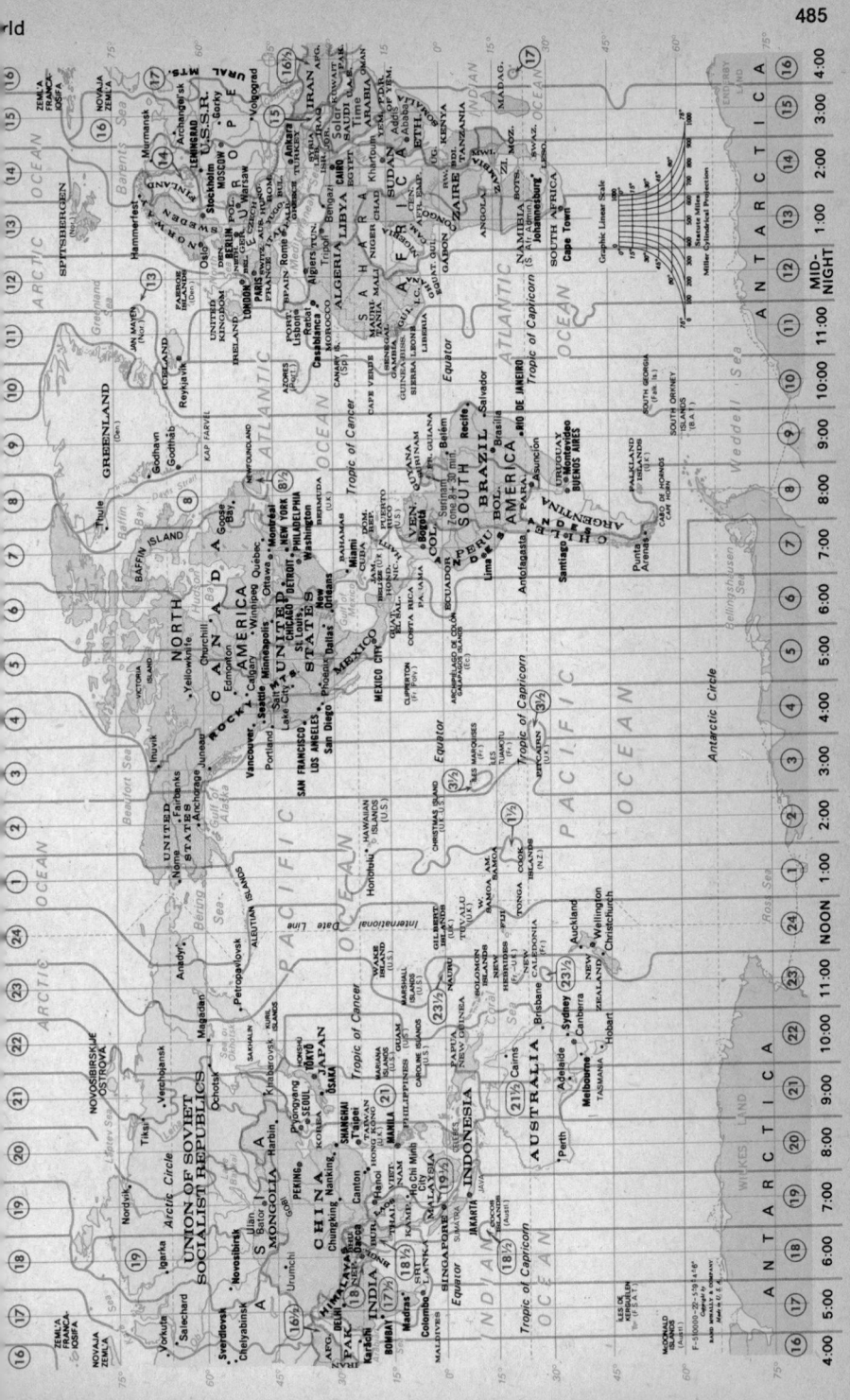

## INDEX

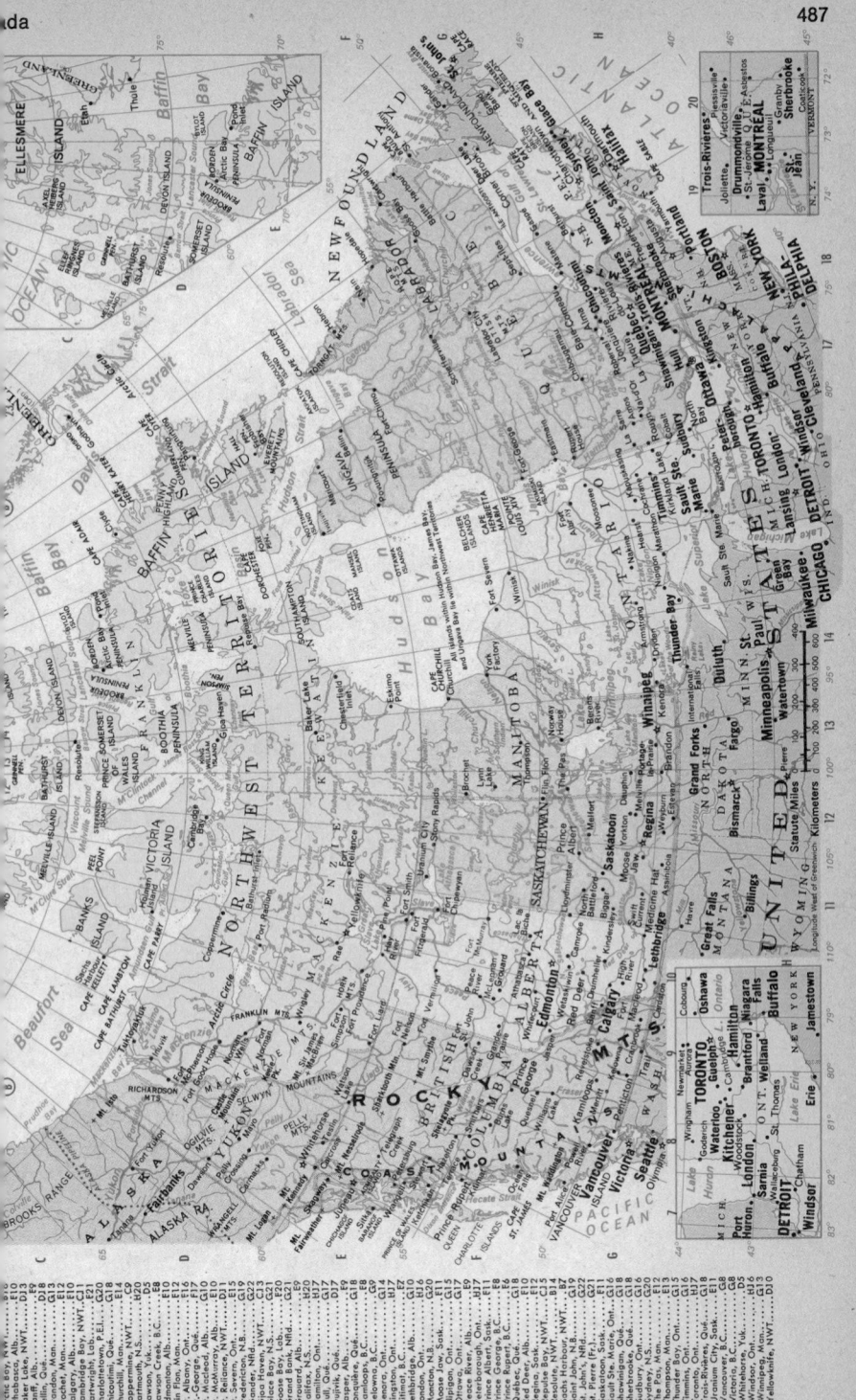

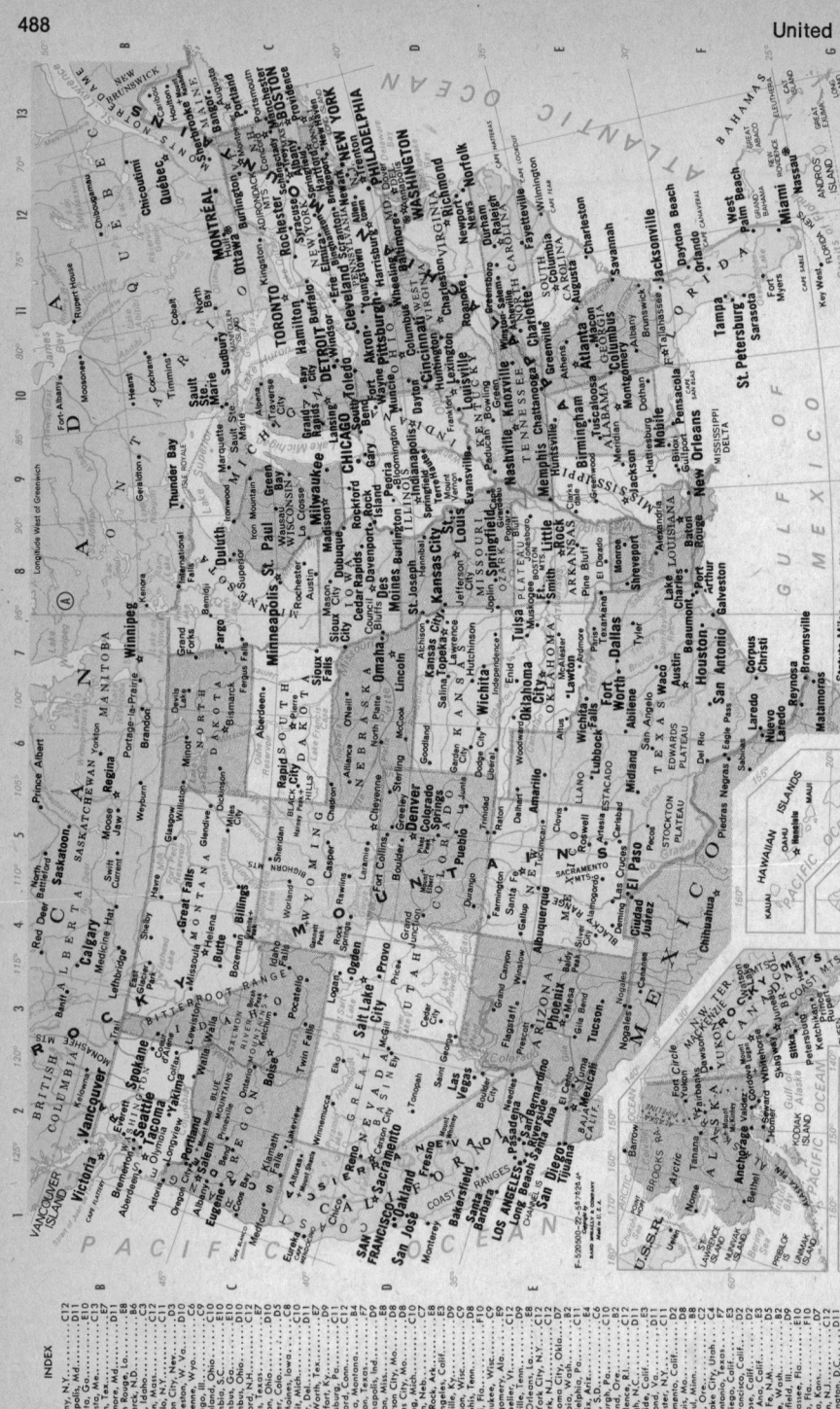

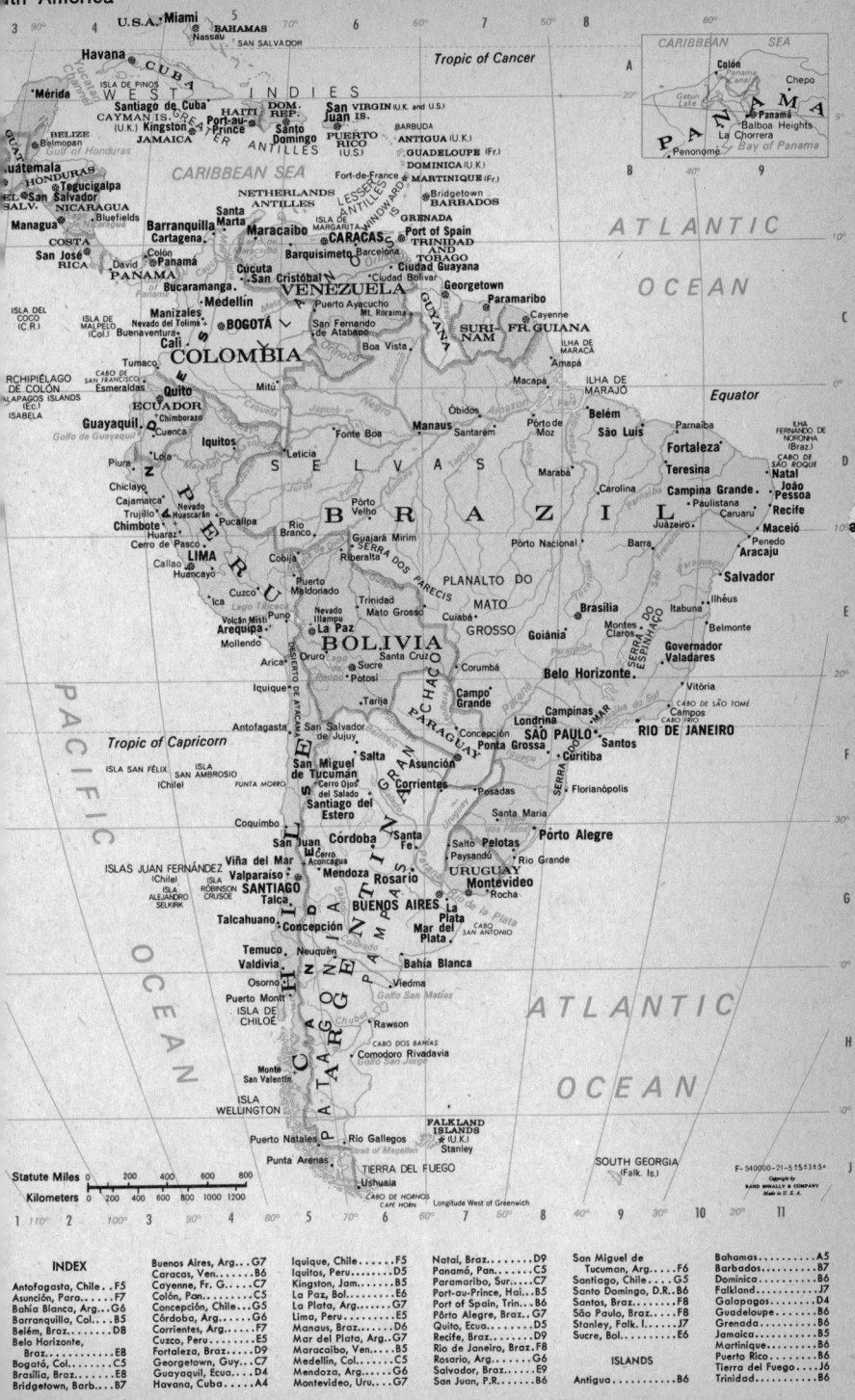

---

# South America

489

**Scale**

Statute Miles: 0 200 400 600 800
Kilometers: 0 200 400 600 800 1000 1200

F- 540000-21-5 55 53 65 54
Copyright by
RAND McNALLY & COMPANY
Made in U.S.A.

## INDEX

Antofagasta, Chile . . . F5
Asunción, Para. . . . . F7
Bahía Blanca, Arg. . . G6
Barranquilla, Col. . . . B5
Belém, Braz. . . . . . . D8
Belo Horizonte,
  Braz. . . . . . . . . . E8
Bogotá, Col. . . . . . . C5
Brasília, Braz. . . . . . E8
Bridgetown, Barb. . . B7

Buenos Aires, Arg. . . G7
Caracas, Ven. . . . . . B6
Cayenne, Fr. G. . . . . C7
Colón, Pan. . . . . . . . C5
Concepción, Chile . . G5
Córdoba, Arg. . . . . . G6
Corrientes, Arg. . . . . F7
Cuzco, Peru . . . . . . E5
Fortaleza, Braz. . . . . D9
Georgetown, Guy. . . C7
Guayaquil, Ecua. . . . D4
Havana, Cuba . . . . . A4

Iquique, Chile . . . . . F5
Iquitos, Peru . . . . . . D5
Kingston, Jam. . . . . B5
La Paz, Bol. . . . . . . E6
La Plata, Arg. . . . . . G7
Lima, Peru . . . . . . . E5
Manaus, Braz. . . . . . D6
Mar del Plata, Arg. . G7
Maracaibo, Ven. . . . B5
Medellín, Col. . . . . . C5
Mendoza, Arg. . . . . . G6
Montevideo, Uru. . . . G7

Natal, Braz. . . . . . . D9
Panamá, Pan. . . . . . C5
Paramaribo, Sur. . . . C7
Port-au-Prince, Hai. . B5
Port of Spain, Trin. . B6
Pôrto Alegre, Braz. . G7
Quito, Ecua. . . . . . . D5
Recife, Braz. . . . . . . D9
Rio de Janeiro, Braz. F8
Rosario, Arg. . . . . . . G6
Salvador, Braz. . . . . E9
San Juan, P.R. . . . . . B6

San Miguel de
  Tucuman, Arg. . . . F6
Santiago, Chile . . . . G5
Santo Domingo, D.R. . B6
Santos, Braz. . . . . . . F8
São Paulo, Braz. . . . F8
Stanley, Falk. I. . . . . J7
Sucre, Bol. . . . . . . . E6

Bahamas . . . . . . . . . A5
Barbados . . . . . . . . B7
Dominica . . . . . . . . B6
Falkland . . . . . . . . . J7
Galapagos . . . . . . . D4
Guadeloupe . . . . . . B6
Grenada . . . . . . . . . B6
Jamaica . . . . . . . . . B5
Martinique . . . . . . . B6
Puerto Rico . . . . . . . B6
Tierra del Fuego . . . J6
Trinidad . . . . . . . . . B6

## ISLANDS

Antigua . . . . . . . . . B6

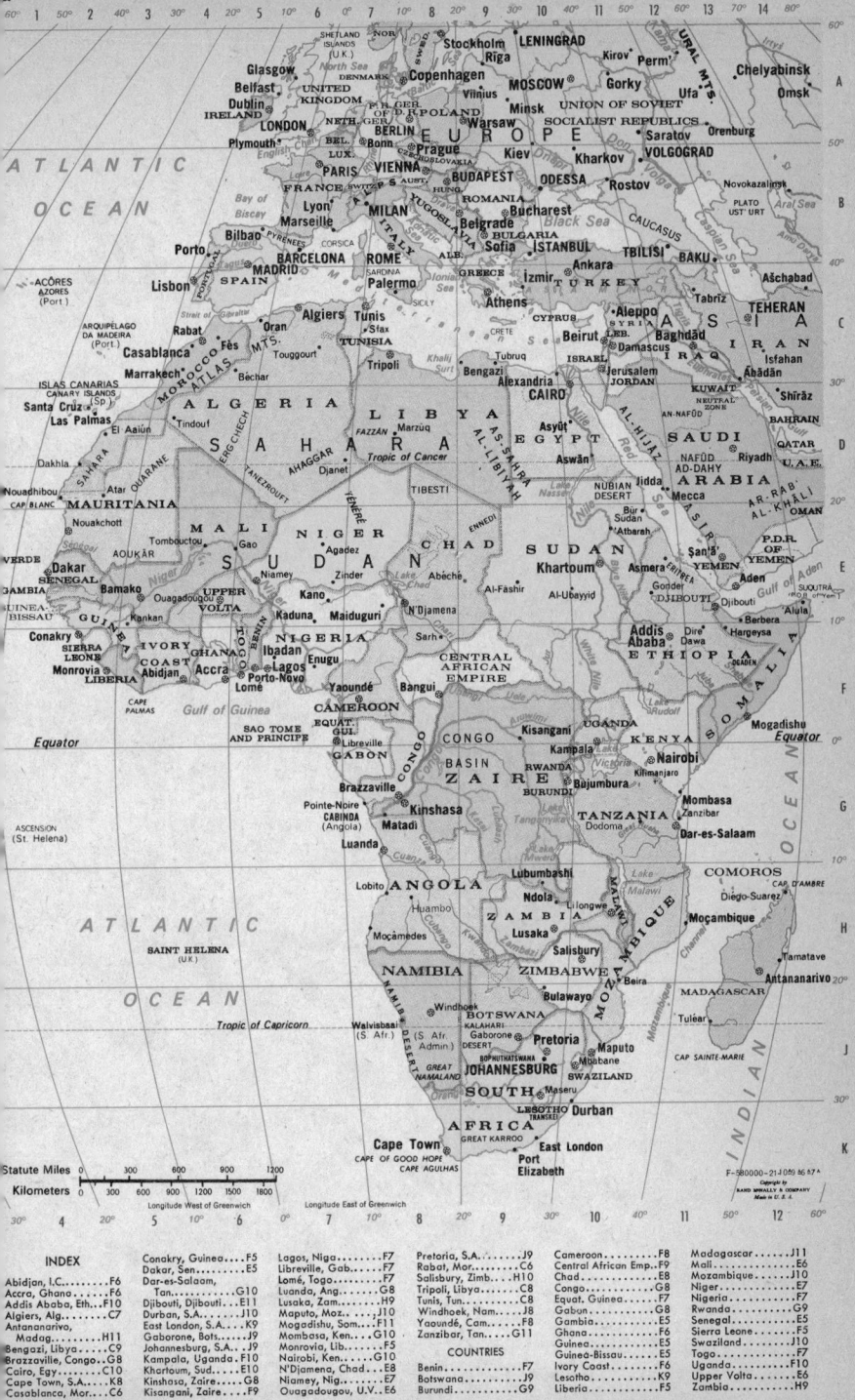

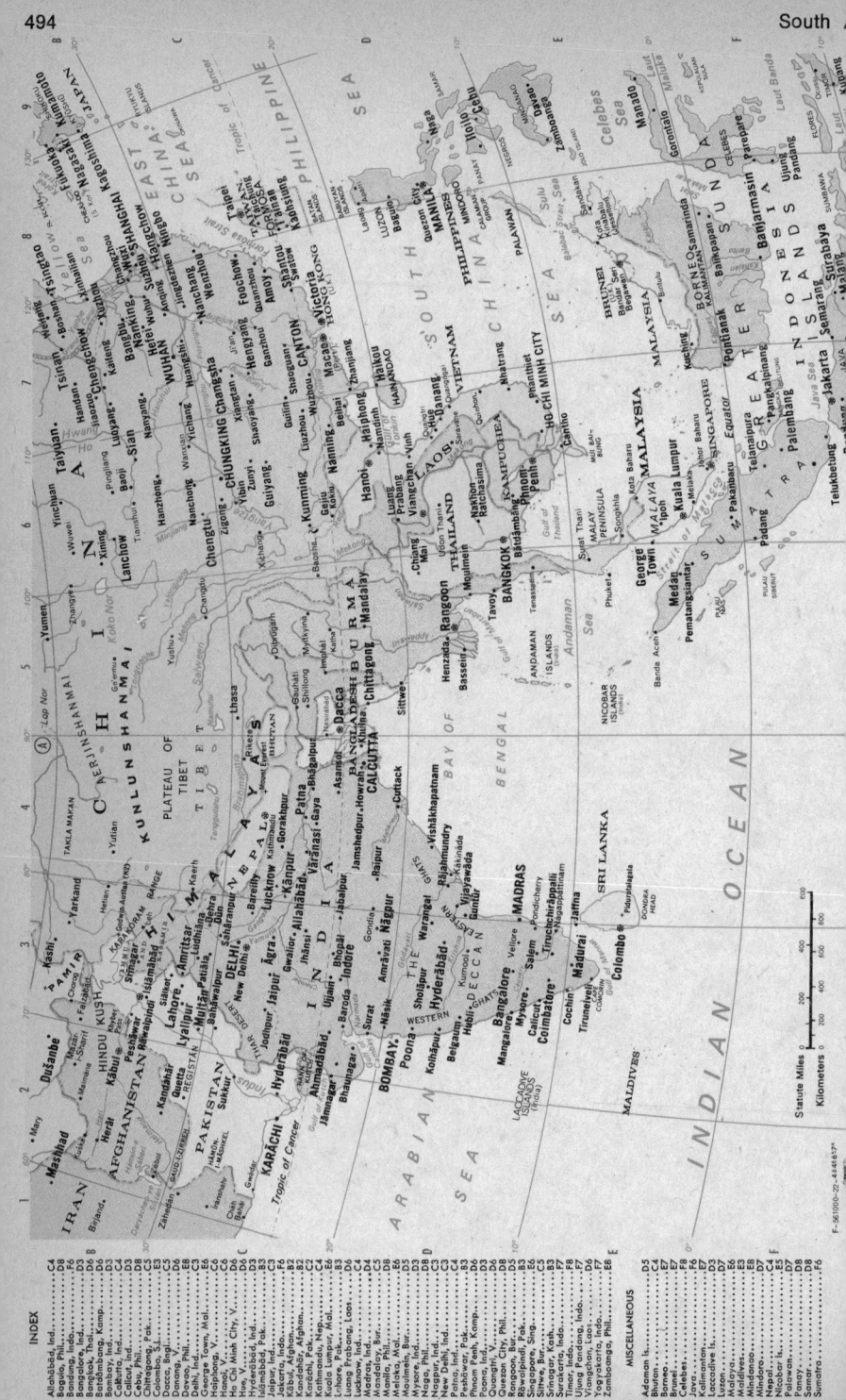

Send a copy of the popular **WORLD ALMANAC** to a relative, friend, student. You may want to order some other books the easy way, by mail. See additional reference books at special prices on other side. Indicate your choice(s) in the appropriate box and mail with check or money order.

| | Price | | Number of Copies | Shipping Each Copy | Total Amount |
|---|---|---|---|---|---|
| | Hard Cover | Soft Cover | | | |
| **THE 1979 WORLD ALMANAC** the most popular single volume reference available. | $6.95 | $3.95 | | $.85 | |
| **THE 1868 WORLD ALMANAC** authentic reproduction of the first edition. | | $2.50 | | $.60 | |
| **THE 1929 WORLD ALMANAC** special reprint of the complete record of 1928 — last of the great years. | | $3.00 | | $.85 | |
| **THE WORLD ALMANAC WHOLE HEALTH GUIDE —** consumer's guide to health care. | | $4.95 | | $.60 | |
| **BEAT THE BUREAUCRACY —** get your tax dollars worth of federal benefits! The best ways to get help from the government. | | $2.25 | | $.60 | |
| **PARENT POWER —** no-nonsense guide to help your child to a better education. | | $1.75 | | $.60 | |
| Shipping charges on all orders of $15.00 or more are 7% of total order. | | | | TOTAL | |

Enclosed is my check or money order for _____

Send books to: _____

Name _____

Address _____

City _____ State _____ Zip _____

Please allow four weeks for delivery.

**Your satisfaction is guaranteed on all WORLD ALMANAC books. If you are not completely satisfied, just return the books to us within 30 days and your money will be promptly refunded.**

| | Price | Number of Copies | Shipping Each Copy | Total Amount |
|---|---|---|---|---|
| **WEBSTER'S COLLE-GIATE DICTIONARY** No. 1 in word reference, deluxe, hard cover, thumb-indexed. | $9.95 | | $1.02 | |
| **WEBSTER'S COLLE-GIATE THESAURUS** guides you to right words in seconds. | $8.95 | | $1.02 | |
| **BARTLETT'S QUO-TATIONS** — over a century old but always up to date. Indexed by name, subject, word. | $13.95 | | $1.02 | |
| **RAND-McNALLY WORLD ATLAS EXPLORER EDITION** — ideal for the home with perspective, political and physical maps — population, physical data. | $10.50 | | $1.02 | |

**Order all four of the above books PLUS the hard cover WORLD ALMANAC for a complete home reference library at the special price of only $45.00 including all shipping charges.**

**Don't forget to complete other side and include your check or money order. If more than one book is ordered, shipping charges are 10 percent of total order.**

*Mail this card to:*

# THE WORLD ALMANAC

P.O. Box 91428
Cleveland, Ohio 44101

**(Please allow four weeks for delivery.)**

# CANADA

See Index for Calgary, Edmonton, Halifax, Hamilton, Kitchener-Waterloo, Lethbridge, Montreal, Ottawa, Quebec, Re-
a, Saskatoon, Toronto, Vancouver, Windsor, Winnipeg.

**Capital: Ottawa. Area: 3,851,809 sq. mi. Population (Govt. est., Jan. 1978): 23,444,200. Monetary unit: Canadian dollar.**

## The Land

The world's second largest country in land size, Canada
etches 3,223 miles from east to west and extends south-
rd from the North Pole to the U.S. border. Its seacoast
ludes 17,860 miles of mainland and 41,810 miles of is-
ads, including the Arctic islands almost from Greenland
near the Alaskan border.

Canada's continental climate, while generally temperate,
ries from freezing winter cold to blistering summer heat -
ange beyond 100 degrees Fahrenheit.

Major cities, industrial centres, agricultural regions, and
e vast majority of the population are situated along a thin,
uthern fringe bordering the United States. To the north lie
st expanses of varied, virgin land. The remote north, due
extreme cold, is virtually uninhabitable.

Fragmented by history, geography, and economic factors,
e country is as diverse as it is large. Regionally, Canada's
provinces can be put into 5 groups: the industrially-poor
lantic Provinces of New Brunswick, Newfoundland, Nova
otia, and Prince Edward Island; predominantly French-
eaking Quebec; Ontario, financial and governmental
artland of the nation; the Prairies, including Manitoba,
skatchewan, and oil-rich Alberta; and British Columbia,
parated from the rest of the country by the Rocky Moun-
ns.

Despite continuing problems of regional disparity in polit-
al, economic, and cultural outlook, Canada has survived as
nation by accepting the need to recognize and tolerate dif-
ences. Unlike the U.S., Canada has never been a melting
t, nor has it strived to become one.

## History

French explorer Jacques Cartier, who discovered the Gulf
St. Lawrence in 1534, is generally regarded as the founder
Canada. But English seaman John Cabot sighted New-
undland 37 years earlier, in 1547, and Vikings are believed
have reached the Atlantic coast centuries before either
plorer.

Canadian settlement was pioneered by the French who
tablished Quebec City (1608) and Montreal (1642) and
clared New France a colony in 1663.

Britain, as part of its American expansion, acquired Aca-
a (later Nova Scotia) in 1717 and, through military victory
er French forces in Canada (an extension of a European
nflict between the 2 powers), captured Quebec (1759) and
tained control of the rest of New France in 1763. The
ench, through the Quebec Act of 1774, retained the rights
their own language, religion, and civil law.

The British presence in Canada increased during the
merican Revolution when many colonials, proudly calling
emselves United Empire Loyalists, moved north to Can-
a.

Fur traders and explorers led Canadians westward across
e continent. Sir Alexander Mackenzie reached the Pacific
1793 and scrawled on a rock by the ocean, "from Canada
y land."

In Upper and Lower Canada (later called Ontario and
uebec) and in the Maritimes, legislative assemblies ap-
eared in the 18th century and reformers called for responsi-
e government. But the War of 1812 intervened. The war, a
nflict between Great Britain and the United States fought
ainly in Upper Canada, ended in a stalemate in 1814.

In 1837 political agitation for more democratic govern-
nt culminated in rebellions in Upper and Lower Canada.
ritain sent Lord Durham to investigate and, in a famous
port (1839), he recommended union of the 2 parts into one
lony called Canada. The union lasted until Confederation,

July 1, 1867, when proclamation of the British North America (BNA) Act launched the Dominion of Canada, consisting of Ontario, Quebec, and the former colonies of Nova
Scotia and New Brunswick.

Since 1840 the Canadian colonies had held the right to
internal self-government. The BNA act, which became the
country's written constitution, established a federal system
of government on the model of a British parliament and cabinet structure under the crown. Canada was proclaimed a
self-governing Dominion within the British Empire in 1931.
Empire has given way to Commonwealth, of which Canada
is an independent member.

## The Government

Canada is a constitutional monarchy with a parliamentary
system of government. It is also a federal state. Official head
of state remains England's Queen Elizabeth, represented by
a resident governor-general. But in practice the nation is
governed by the Prime Minister, leader of the party able to
command the support of a majority of members of the
House of Commons, dominant chamber of Canada's bicameral Parliament.

The Commons' 264 members (increased to 282 with the
next election) are elected at least every 5 years - sooner if the
Prime Minister so chooses or if the government is defeated
in Parliament. This can occur either through passage of a
motion of nonconfidence in the government or by defeat of a
major piece of government legislation.

The upper house of Canada's Parliament is the Senate,
comprised of 104 members traditionally appointed by party
patronage and serving to age 75.

Legislation becomes law by receiving 3 "readings" in the
Commons, passing in the Senate and obtaining assent from
the governor-general. The latter 2 steps are, in practice, mere
formality.

The Prime Minister heads the executive branch of government composed of the cabinet and governor-general. The
cabinet is chosen by the Prime Minister, almost always from
among members of his party holding seats in the House of
Commons.

Provincial governments follow a modified version of the
Ottawa pattern, with a unicameral legislature and an executive head usually referred to as the Premier.

In June, 1978, Prime Minister Pierre Elliott Trudeau introduced his plan for a new Canadian constitution to replace
the outmoded British North America Act. The main point
in the proposal, which Trudeau hopes will become law by
July 1, 1979, calls for replacement of the Senate by a slightly
more powerful 118-seat House of Federation charged with
representing and protecting regional, provincial and language rights. Half the members would be appointed by the
provinces and half by the federal political parties. The
House would have the power to delay but not veto legislation.

## Politics

National unity remained Canada's foremost political issue
in 1978, as it has since the election of a separatist Parti Quebecois (PQ) government in the November, 1976, Quebec
provincial election. It is not known to what extent the PQ's
ouster of the unpopular and corrupt Liberal regime of Premier Robert Bourassa indicated a vote for separation or simply a desire for change in government. This question should
be answered sometime in 1979 when an anticipated provincial referendum places the separation question before Quebec voters.

Parti Quebecois leader and Quebec Premier Rene Levesque, an articulate spokesman for independence, has made it clear he is not interested in any compromise solutions granting Quebec greater autonomy; his party is pledged to remove the province from Canada. A strong rival for Levesque's popularity with Quebec voters has emerged with the election of Claude Ryan as new provincial Liberal leader. Ryan, formerly the influential publisher of the French-language newspaper *Le Devoir*, would keep Quebec within Canada - though not necessarily on those terms favored by the federal government.

If Quebec does separate, the economic and political effect on Canada would be staggering. The province is the country's largest in size, 2d in population (27% of the nation's total), 2d in manufacturing output and shipments, and 3rd both in energy and mineral production. Further, Quebec separation would create an enormous geographical barrier between the rest of Canada and the already isolated Atlantic provinces. The continued feasability of Confederation might be questioned as rumblings of discontent from other provinces would likely grow louder and stronger. The loss of Quebec could also significantly alter the federal political makeup; the ability of the federal Liberal party to remain in power through much of this century has depended to a large extent on overwhelming support from Quebec.

In June, 1978, the federal government formally entered the constitutional fray with a draft proposal for a "renewal of the Canadian Federation" aimed in part at easing contentious federal-provincial relationships. The proposal, outlining plans for a new Canadian constitution to replace the antiquated British North America Act, sets as its goal the difficult task of strengthening national unity while encouraging regional self-development and the preservation of local lifestyles and cultural traditions.

Coinciding with other dramatically unfolding political events, Canada faces a federal election by July, 1979. With popular support for the Liberal government and opposition Conservative party see-sawing in successive opinion polls, the outcome of this contest too remains much in doubt.

## The Economy

The Canadian economy continued to perform poorly through the first half of 1978 with no immediate improvement anticipated. The Gross National Product, a measure of all goods and services produced in the country, grew a meagre 2.5% in 1977; growth for the first quarter of 1978 was only 0.7%.

With the labor force expanding faster than the economy could provide new jobs, unemployment, already at 8.1% for 1977, rose to 8.6% by the summer of 1978. At the same time, the rate of inflation as measured by the consumer price index was running at 9.2% - despite more than 2 years of wage and price controls, limiting pay increases to 6%. The controls were due to be phased out by the end of 1978, and Finance Minister Jean Chretien warned Canadians that the economy could not support wage and salary hikes in line with increases in the cost of living.

The Canadian dollar hit a 45-year low of less than .87 U.S. in April 1978, compared with 1.03 U.S. 18 months earlier. By July it had levelled at .89 U.S. One bright note was that the lower dollar value was improving the nation's balance of trade by making the price of Canadian export commodities more competitive.

Principal Canadian industries are motor vehicle manufacturing, petroleum refining, pulp and paper production, slaughtering and meat processing, iron and steel production, the manufacture of miscellaneous machinery and equipment, sawmill and planing mill industries, and smelting and refining.

In Canada, an historical tradition of state aid necessitated by a harsh climate and sparse population has fostered development of a mixed economic system in which publicly-owned corporations exist alongside - and sometimes compete with - private enterprise. Most hydroelectric and many transportation and communication facilities are owned by either federal, provincial, or municipal governments. Canada and the Canadian National Railways, both la federal crown corporations, compete with the private owned Canadian Pacific, Ltd., whose 1977 assets were largest of any company in Canada. The Canadian Broacasting Corp., publicly owned though independently ma aged, shares airwaves with a string of private radio cha and television networks.

## Social Security

Responsibility for health and welfare programs was i tially assigned to the provinces, and they retain jurisdicti over a variety of social services with subsidies of up to 5 from Ottawa. But constitutional ammendments in rec decades have given the federal government authority o large-scale social insurance programs: Unemployment Ins ance; Family Allowances; a Guaranteed Income Suppleme for the aged; the Canada and Quebec Pension Plans; Vet ans' Benefits; and shared-cost provincial Welfare Assista plans. Payments under almost all these schemes are adjus to the cost-of-living index.

Universal and compulsory medical care was fully imp mented in 1968. Financial arrangements for medicare w altered in 1977 to allow the provinces more flexibility in c erating their programs.

## Foreign Relations

Canada's most important foreign relation remains United States with whom she shares a broad and mutua beneficial range of ties. A "warm and open personal ra port" has been established between the Trudeau and Car administrations, according to External Affairs Minister D Jamieson, and agreements have been concluded on a nor ern gas pipeline, St. Lawrence Seaway tolls, and peace nuclear exchanges. Sources of disagreement between the neighbors are maritime boundaries and trans-boundary en ronmental matters. In June, 1978, Canada suspended U commercial fishing in Canadian waters after a deadlock lengthy discussions on catch quotas and conservation co cerns. The U.S. responded with similar action.

As part of a "Third Option" policy adopted in 1972 w the aim of reducing vulnerability to U.S. interests, Cana has recently expanded relations with the European Ec nomic Community and Japan. The Prime Minister's visits both these areas in 1976 culminated in the signing of sep rate framework agreements for economic co-operation. T agreement with Japan also provided for annual high-lev meetings between the 2 countries beginning in June, 19 Canada seeks a balanced economic exchange with Euro and Japan through easier access to their markets for mc Canadian processed and manufactured goods.

Canada remains committed to the principle of detente a supports multilateral efforts to reduce East-West tensio and promote disarmament. Prime Minister Trudeau reite ated these policies during 1978 in an address before t United Nations conference on disarmament and in tal with Western leaders at a summit meeting of the North A lantic Treaty Organization to which Canada belongs.

As an important exporter of uranium and nuclear rea tors, Canada, in December 1977, adopted strict safeguar designed to allow it to provide nuclear technology whi minimizing the risk of proliferating nuclear weapons. Shi ments are restricted to countries that ratify the No Proliferation Treaty or otherwise accept international sa guards on their entire nuclear programs. Canada will e nuclear shipments to any non-nuclear-weapon state that e plodes a nuclear device.

To register its abhorrence of South Africa's apartheid p icy, the Canadian government, in December 1977, a nounced economic and diplomatic measures against the r tion. The Canadian trade office in South Africa was clos and legislation was enacted requiring citizens of that coun to obtain visas to enter Canada.

## Canada's Native Peoples

Canada's native population consists of 2 groups, the Indian and Inuit (Eskimo). Both are thought to have crossed from Asia via the Bering Sea several thousand years before the arrival of Europeans in North America.

Most populous are the Indians, of whom approximately 300,000 are registered under the Indian Act. The number of non-registered Indians is unknown. Of those registered, 73% live on one of 2,230 federal reserves or on other government land; 82% of the total live in Ontario and the 4 western provinces. Only Newfoundland has no registered Indian population.

Registered Indians or those entitled to be registered receive a broad range of government benefits administered through the federal Department of Indian Affairs and Northern Development. Those living on reserves are eligible for direct federal assistance in such areas as education, housing, social services and community development.

More than 75% of Canada's approximately 19,000 Inuit (meaning "the people" in their language, Inuktitut; Eskimo is an Indian word adopted by European settlers) live in the Northwest Territories, the remainder in Arctic Quebec and northern Labrador.

Due to the remoteness of their settlements close to the northern coasts where sea mammals provided the chief source of food, fuel and clothing, the Inuit lifestyle was affected later and less directly than that of the Indian by the encroachment of western civilization. Many Inuit still live by their traditional skills of hunting, trapping and fishing as well as through the production and sale of artwork. But increasing numbers now find work outside their communities, particularly since the search for oil, gas and minerals has brought more jobs to the north. Through the Indian and Inuit Affairs Program the federal government aims to provide equality of opportunity for all native peoples whether they choose a traditional or contemporary lifestyle. In either case communities and individuals are encouraged to strive for self-reliance.

The Inuit are eligible for a range of benefits similar to those available to registered Indians. These are provided through the provincial and territorial governments as well as the federal Department of Indian Affairs and Northern Development.

To represent Inuit cultural and legal interests in Ottawa, the Inuit Tapirisat (Eskimo Brotherhood) was founded in 1971 with financial aid from the Department of the Secretary of State. A major Tapirisat task is the presentation of native land claims.

Approximately half the registered Indians in Canada (mainly those living in Ontario and the 3 Prairie provinces) are entitled to payments as a result of treaties between their ancestors and the Crown. In remote northern areas, however, no such legal settlements were made, and recently Indian and Inuit groups have pressed claims to aboriginal rights to vast areas of land in northern British Columbia, the Yukon and Northwest Territories, and northern Quebec and Labrador.

In 1973 the federal government agreed to consider native claims. Thus far 2 settlements have been reached: In 1975 the Inuit and Cree in the James Bay area surrendered claim to 400,000 sq. mi. in return for $225 million and a range of rights and privileges. In July, 1978, the Inuit of the western Arctic and the government reached a tentative settlement of claims to 168,000 sq. mi. The agreement includes payment, over 14 years, of $18,000 to each of the 2,500 Inuit living in the area and a clear grant to the Inuit of ownership of 37,000 sq. mi. of land.

## Provinces of Canada

### Alberta

**People. Population** (Jan. 1978): 1,936,200; **rank:** 4. **Pop. density:** 7.8 per sq. mi. **Urban** (1976) 75%. **Ethnic distrib.** (1976): English 80.7%; German 4.3%; Ukrainian 3.5%; French 2.4%. **Net migration** (1971-76) +112,642.

**Geography: Total area:** 255,285 sq. mi.; **rank:** 4. **Land area:** 248,800 sq. mi. **Acres forested land:** 68,341,000. **Location:** Canada's 2d most westerly province, bounded to the W by British Columbia, to the E by Saskatchewan, to the N by the Northwest Territories, and to the S by Montana. **Climate:** great variance in temperatures between regions and seasons; summer highs can range between 16°C and 32°C; winter temperatures can drop as low as −45°C; mean Jan. temperature in Edmonton is −14°C. **Topography:** ranges from the Rocky Mountains in the SW to flat prairie in the SE; the far north is a wilderness of forest and muskeg.

**Economy. Principal industries:** mining, oil production, agriculture, manufacturing, construction. **Principal manufactured goods:** foods and beverages, wood products, fabricated metal, transportation equipment, refined petroleum. **Value added by manufacture** (1975): $1.64 billion. **Gross Domestic Product** (1976): $20.91 billion. **Agriculture: Chief crops:** wheat, barley, rapeseed, sugar beets, flaxseed. **Livestock** (1976): 4,603,056 cattle; 876,283 pigs; 7,897,075 sheep; 8,884,727 poultry. **Forestry production** (1976): $23.9 million. **Mineral production** 1977): total value, $8.53 billion; fuels, $8.32 billion (85% of national production of petroleum, 87% of natural gas); metals, structural materials, $119 million; elemental sulphur, $71.8 million (99% of national total). **Commercial fishing:** (1976) $1.1 million. **Value of construction** 1977): $6.2 billion. **Employment distribution** (1977): 7.9% agriculture; 9% manufacturing; 27.4% services; 8.9% trade; 9.9% construction; 6.5% public administration. **Per capita income** (1976): $6,999. **Unemployment** (1977): 4.4%.

**Finance: No. banks** 686; **No. credit unions, caisses populaires** 187.

**International airports:** Edmonton, Calgary.

**Federal government: No. federal employees** (1977): 29,415; **Federal payroll** (1977): $406.1 million.

**Energy. Electricity production,** by mwh, (1977): mineral, 16,236,664; hydroelectric, 1,519,704.

**Education. No schools:** 1,225 elementary; 159 secondary; 25 higher education. **Avg. salary, public school teachers** (1976-77): $15,813.

**Provincial data. Motto:** none. **Flower:** The Wild Rose. **Bird:** Great horned owl. **Date entered Confederation:** 1905. **Capital:** Edmonton.

**Politics. Premier:** Peter Lougheed (Progressive Conservative). **Leaders, opposition parties:** Robert Clark (Social Credit), Grant Notley (New Democratic), Nick Taylor (Liberal). **Composition of legislature** (May, 1978): PC 69; SC 4; NDP 1; Independent 1. **Date of last election:** Mar. 26, 1975.

**Tourist attractions:** Banff, Jasper, and Waterton Lakes national parks; resorts at Banff, Jasper and Lake Louise; spectacular skiing, hiking, trail riding and camping in the Canadian Rockies; the Badlands near Drumheller; Elk Island National Park and Alberta Game Farm (both near Edmonton).

### British Columbia

**People. Population** (Jan. 1978): 2,523,400; **rank:** 3. **Pop. density:** 10.1 per sq. mi. **Urban** (1976) 76.9%. **Ethnic distrib.** (1976): English 82.6%; German 3.3%; Chinese 1.9%; French 1.6%; Italian 1.1%. **Net migration** (1971-76) +201,025.

**Geography. Total area:** 255,285 sq. mi.; **rank:** 3. **Land area:** 248,800 sq. mi. **Acres forested land:** 134,652,000. **Location:** bounded to the N by the Yukon and Northwest

Territories, to the NW by the Alaskan panhandle, to the W by the Pacific Ocean, to the E by Alberta, and to the S by Washington, Idaho and Montana. **Climate:** maritime with mild termperatures and abundant rainfall in the coastal areas; continental climate with temperature extremes in the interior and northeast. **Topography:** mostly mountainous except for the NE corner which is an extension of the Great Plains.

**Economy. Principal industries:** forestry, mining, tourism, agriculture, fishing, manufacturing. **Principal manufactured goods:** paper and allied products, wood products, mineral products and associated machinery, food and beverages, transportation equipment, chemicals. **Value added by manufacture** (1975): $3.38 billion. **Gross Domestic Product** (1976): $22.65 billion (including GDP for Yukon and NWT). **Agriculture:** Chief crops: fruits and vegetables, barley, oats. **Livestock** (1976): 667,320 cattle; 53,014 pigs; 37,938 sheep; 10,369,167 poultry. **Forestry production** (1976): $460.1 million. **Mineral production** (1977): total value, $1.89 billion; fuels, $900.5 million; metals, $809.9 million; structural materials, $107.6 million. **Commercial fishing:** (1976) $141.8 million. **Value of construction** (1977) $4.95 billion. **Employment distribution** (1977): 2% agriculture; 16.1% manufacturing; 28.3% services; 18.5% trade; 8% construction; 6.9% public administration. **Per capita income** (1976): $7,318. **Unemployment** (1977): 8.5%.

**Finance: No. banks** 867; **No. credit unions, caisses populaires** 175.

**International airports:** Vancouver, Victoria.

**Federal government: No. federal employees** (1977): 40,687. **Federal payroll** (1977): $596.8 million.

**Energy. Electricity production,** by mwh, (1977): mineral, 1,842,995; hydroelectric, 41,280,738.

**Education. No schools:** 1,452 elementary; 324 secondary; 28 higher education. **Avg. salary, public school teachers** (1976-77): $16,279.

**Provincial data. Motto:** Splendor Sine Occasu (Spendor Without Diminishment). **Flower:** Dogwood. **Bird:** None. **Date entered Confederation:** 1871. **Capital:** Victoria.

**Politics. Premier:** William R. Bennett (Social Credit). **Leaders, opposition parties:** Dave Barrett (New Democratic), Gordon Gibson (Liberal), Victor Stephens (Progressive Conservative). **Composition of legislature** (May, 1978): SC 35; NDP 17; Lib. 1; PC 1; 1 vacant. **Date of last election:** Dec. 12, 1976.

**Tourist attractions.** Victoria: Butchart Gardens, Provincial Museum, Parliament Buildings; Vancouver Island: Long Beach, Campbell River; Vancouver: Public Aquarium, Grouse Mountain, Planetarium; also Gulf Islands, Okanagan Valley, Yellowhead Highway, Totem Triangle Tour.

## Manitoba

**People. Population** (Jan. 1978): 1,034,700; **rank:** 5. **Pop. density:** 4.9 per sq. mi. **Urban** (1976) 69.9%. **Ethnic distrib.** (1976): English 71.2%; German 7.2%; Ukrainian 5.9%; French 5.4%; Native Indians 2.4%. **Net migration** (1971-76): +434.

**Geography. Total area:** 251,000 sq. mi.; **rank:** 6. **Land area:** 211,755 sq. mi. **Acres forested land:** 33,476,000. **Location:** bounded to the N by the Northwest Territories, to the S by Minnesota and North Dakota, to the E by Ontario and Hudson Bay, to the W by Saskatchewan. **Climate:** continental, with seasonal extremes: Winnipeg avg. Jan. low −23°C, avg. July high 26°C. **Topography:** the land rises gradually S and W from Hudson Bay; most of the province is between 500 and 1,000 feet above sea level.

**Economy. Principal industries:** manufacturing, agriculture, slaughtering and meat processing, mining. **Principal manufactured goods:** agricultural implements, processed food, machinery, transportation equipment, clothing. **Value added by manufacture** (1975): $1.08 billion. **Gross Domestic Product** (1976): $7.95 billion. **Agriculture:** Chief crops: cereal grains, sunflower seeds, rape, flax, sugarbeets. **Livestock** (1976): 1,392,974 cattle; 624,951 pigs; 20,534 sheep; 6,825,966 poultry. For-

estry production (1976): $19.9 million. **Mineral production** (1977): total value, $532.8 million; fuels, $40.8 million; metals, $419.4 million; structural materials, $67.5 million. **Commercial fishing:** (1976) $7.7 million. **Value of construction** (1977): $1.39 billion. **Employment distribution** (1977): 9.3% agriculture; 12.8% manufacturing; 27.8% services; 17.8% trade; 6% construction; 7.6% public administration. **Per capita income** (1976): $6,357. **Unemployment** (1977): 5.9%.

**Finance: No. banks** 351; **No. credit unions, caisses populaires** 177.

**International airports:** Winnipeg.

**Federal Government: No. federal employees** (1977) 19,491. **Federal payroll** (1977): $278 million.

**Energy. Electricity production,** by mwh, (1977): mineral, 1,367,825; hydroelectric, 11,143,797.

**Education. No. schools:** 700 elementary; 119 secondary; 15 higher education. **Avg. salary, public school teachers** (1976-77): $13,522.

**Provincial data. Motto:** None. **Flower:** Prairie crocus. **Bird:** none. **Date entered Confederation:** July 15, 1870. **Capital:** Winnipeg.

**Politics. Premier:** Sterling Lyon (Progressive Conservative). **Leaders, opposition parties:** Edward Schreyer (New Democratic), Lloyd Axworthy (Liberal). **Composition of legislature** (May, 1978): PC 33; NDP 23; Lib. **Date of last election:** Oct. 1977.

**Tourist attractions.** Museum of Man and Nature (Winnipeg), Lower Fort Garry (near Lockport), Red River cruises, Riding Mountain National Park, canoeing, fishing and camping on northern lakes.

## New Brunswick

**People. Population** (Jan. 1978): 691,900; **rank:** 8. **Pop. density:** 24.9 per sq. mi. **Urban** (1976) 52.3%. **Ethnic distrib.** (1976): English 64.4%; French 33%. **Net migration** (1971-76) +19,847.

**Geography. Total area:** 28,354 sq. mi.; **rank:** 8. **Land area:** 27,835 sq. mi. **Acres forested land:** 15,594,000. **Location:** bounded by Quebec to the N, Nova Scotia and the Bay of Fundy to the S, the Gulf of St. Lawrence and Northumberland Strait to the E, and Maine to the W. **Climate:** humid continental climate except along the shore where there is a marked maritime effect; avg. Jan. low Fredericton is −14°C, avg. July high 22°C. **Topography:** upland, lowland and plateau regions throughout the province.

**Economy. Principal industries:** manufacturing, mining, forestry, pulp and paper. **Principal manufactured goods:** paper and allied products, wood products, fish products, semi-processed mineral products. **Value added by manufacture** (1975): $610 million. **Gross Domestic Product** (1976): $3.68 billion. **Agriculture:** Chief crops: potatoes, apples, blueberries, oats. **Livestock** (1976) 111,061 cattle; 39,317 pigs; 11,640 sheep; 2,098,515 poultry. **Forestry production** (1976): $64 million. **Mineral production** (1977): total value, $267.8 million; fuels, $6 million; metals, $224.2 million; structural materials, $28 million. **Commercial fishing:** (1976) $25 million. **Value of construction** (1977): $883.7 million. **Employment distribution** (1977): 2.2% agriculture; 15.3% manufacturing; 26.9% services; 19% trade; 9% construction; 7.5% public administration. **Per capita income** (1976): $5,064. **Unemployment** (1977): 13.4%.

**Finance: No. banks** 170; **No. credit unions, caisses populaires** 149.

**International airports:** none.

**Federal Government: No. federal employees** (1977) 13,904. **Federal payroll** (1977): $195.5 million.

**Energy. Electricity production,** by mwh, (1977): mineral, 5,135,464; hydroelectric, 3,019,129.

**Education. No. schools:** 445 elementary; 67 secondary; 12 higher education. **Avg. salary, public school teachers** (1976-77): $14,076.

**Provincial Data. Motto:** Spem Reduxit (Hope Restored). **Flower:** Purple violet. **Bird:** none. **Date entered Confederation:** 1867. **Capital:** Fredericton.

**Politics. Premier:** Richard Hatfield (Progressive Conservative). **Leaders, opposition parties:** Joseph Daigle

Liberal). **Composition of legislature** (May, 1978): P.C. 3; Lib. 24; 1 vacant. **Date of last election:** Nov. 18, 1974.

**Tourist attractions:** Roosevelt-Campobello International Memorial Park; the tidal bore at Chignacto Bay (Moncton); Magnetic Hill (Moncton); sport salmon fishing n the Miramichi River; 108 covered bridges including the world's longest at Hartland.

## Newfoundland

**People. Population** (Jan. 1978): 564,800; **rank:** 9. **Pop. density:** 3.8 per sq. mi. **Urban** (1976) 58.9%. **Ethnic distrib.** (1976): English 98%. **Net migration** 1971-76) —10,052.

**Geography. Total area:** 156,185 sq. mi.; **rank:** 7. **Land area:** 143,045 sq. mi. **Acres forested land:** 31,504,000. **Location:** 2 parts: a 43,359 sq. mi. Atlantic island and 112,826 sq. mi. mainland Labrador, bordered to the E by northern Quebec and to the W by the Atlantic Ocean. **Climate:** ranges from subarctic in Labrador and northern tip of island to humid continental with cool summers and heavy precipitation. **Topography:** highlands of the Long Range (max. elev. 2,673 ft.) along the western coast; central plateau contains uplands descending to lowlands towards the northeast; interior barren and rocky with many lakes and bogs; Labrador is part of the Canadian Shield.

**Economy. Principal industries:** mining, manufacturing, fishing, pulp and paper, electricity production. **Principal manufactured goods:** fish products, paper products. **Value added by manufacture** (1975): $224.1 million. **Gross Domestic Product** (1976): $2.51 billion. **Agriculture:** Livestock (1976): 5,839 cattle; 15,703 pigs; 4,816 sheep; 913,520 poultry. **Forestry production** (1976): $36.6 million. **Mineral production** (1977): total value, $845.5 million; metals, $781.5 million; asbestos, $35 million. **Commercial fishing:** (1976) $67.4 million. **Value of construction** (1977): $593.3 million. **Employment distribution** (1977): less than 1% agriculture; 11.5% manufacturing; 28% services; 16.7% trade; 9.4% construction; 3.6% public administration. **Per capita income** (1976): $4,603. **Unemployment** (1977): 15.9%.

**Finance: No. banks** 137; **no. credit unions, caisses populaires** 15.

**International airports:** Gander.

**Federal Government: No. federal employees** (1977): 8,099. **Federal payroll** (1977): $113.6 million.

**Energy. Electricity production,** by mwh, (1977): mineral, 427,803; hydroelectric, 40,593,708.

**Education. No. schools:** 570 elementary; 144 secondary; 7 higher education. **Avg. salary, public school teachers** (1976-77): $14,814.

**Provincial data. Motto:** Quaerite prime regnum Dei (Seek ye first the kingdom of God). **Flower:** Pitcher plant. **Bird:** none. **Date entered Confederation:** 1949. **Capital:** St. John's.

**Politics. Premier:** Frank Moores (Progressive Conservative). **Leaders, opposition parties:** William Rowe (Liberal). **Composition of legislature** (May, 1978): PC 29; Lib. 20; Independent Lib. 1; 1 vacant. **Date of last election:** Aug. 1975.

**Tourist attractions:** numerous picturesque "outport" fishing villages; Signal Hill National Historical Park (St. John's); the Aviation Museum at Gander International Airport; Witless Bay Island Seabird Sanctuary.

## Nova Scotia

**People. Population** (Jan. 1978): 839,600; **rank:** 7. **Pop. density:** 41.2 per sq. mi. **Urban** (1976) 55.8%. **Ethnic distrib.** (1976): English 92.7%; French 4.4%. **Net migration** (1971-76) +14,919.

**Geography. Total area:** 21,425 sq. mi.; **rank:** 9. **Land area:** 20,402 sq. mi. **Acres forested land:** 10,982,000. **Location:** connected to New Brunswick by a 17-mi. isthmus, otherwise surrounded by water - the Gulf of St. Lawrence, Atlantic Ocean and Bay of Fundy. **Climate:** humid continental, with some moderating effects due to the province's maritime location; avg. July temperature high in

Halifax is 23°C, avg. Jan. low —10°C. **Topography:** the Atlantic Uplands in the southern half of the province descend to lowlands in the northern portion; 6,409 mi. of coastline, 3,000 lakes, hundreds of rivers.

**Economy. Principal industries:** manufacturing, fishing, mining, tourism, agriculture, petroleum refining. **Principal manufactured goods:** paper and allied products, fish products, dairy products, ships. **Value added by manufacture** (1975): $700 million. **Gross Domestic Product** (1976): $4.72 billion. **Agriculture: Chief crops:** apples, blueberries, strawberries, oats, potatoes. **Livestock** (1976): 125,445 cattle; 72,714 pigs; 34,483 sheep; 3,110,769 poultry. **Forestry production** (1976): $20.4 million. **Mineral production** (1977): total value, $151.9 million; fuels, $80.5 million; structural materials, $32.5 million; gypsum $18.6 million. **Commercial fishing:** (1976) $106.3 million. **Value of construction** (1977): $908 million. **Employment distribution** (1977): 2.4% agriculture; 14.4% manufacturing; 28.8% services; 18.3% trade; 7.5% construction; 9.6% public administration. **Per capita income** (1976): $5,313. **Unemployment** (1977): 10.7%.

**Finance: No. banks** 231; **No. credit unions, caisses populaires** 124

**International airports:** Halifax.

**Federal Government: No. federal employees** (1977): 35,923. **Federal payroll** (1977): $500.6 million.

**Energy. Electricity production,** by mwh, (1977): mineral, 4,965,152; hydroelectric, 793,859.

**Education. No. schools:** 538 elementary; 88 secondary; 24 higher education. **Avg. salary, public school teachers** (1976-77): $14,938.

**Provincial Data. Motto:** Munit Haec et Altera Vincit (One Defends and the Other Conquers). **Flower:** Trailing arbutus. **Bird:** None. **Date entered Confederation:** 1867. **Capital:** Halifax.

**Politics. Premier:** Gerald A. Regan (Liberal). **Leaders, opposition parties:** John M. Buchanan (Progressive Conservative), Jeremy Akerman (New Democratic). **Composition of legislature** (May, 1978): Lib. 30; P.C. 12; NDP 3; 1 vacant. **Date of last election:** 1974.

**Tourist attractions:** Cabot Trail around Cape Breton Island; Fortress Louisbourg; Peggy's Cove; Alexander Graham Bell Museum (Baddeck); the Miners' Museum (Glace Bay).

## Ontario

**People. Population** (Jan. 1978): 8,441,100; **rank:** 1. **Pop. density:** 24.5 per sq. mi. **Urban** (1976) 81.2% **Ethnic distrib.** (1976): English 78.1%; French 5.6%; German 1.9%; Portuguese 1%. **Net migration** (1971-76) +321,940.

**Geography. Total area:** 412,582 sq. mi.; **rank:** 2. **Land area:** 344,092 sq. mi. **Acres forested land:** 106,806,000. **Location:** Canada's most centrally-situated province, with Quebec on the E and Manitoba to the W; extends N to shores of James and Hudson Bays; southern boundary with New York, Michigan, Minnesota, and 4 great Lakes. **Climate:** ranges from humid continental in southern regions to subarctic in the far north, westerly winds bring winter storms; the Great lakes moderate winter temperatures. **Topography:** 2/3 of province is Precambrian rock of the Canadian Shield; lowland areas lie along the shores of Hudson Bay, the St. Lawrence River and the southern Great Lakes region.

**Economy. Principal industries:** manufacturing. **Principal manufactured goods:** motor vehicles, iron and steel, motor vehicle parts and accessories, foods and beverages, paper and allied products. **Value added by manufacture** (1975): $20.12 billion. **Gross Domestic Product** (1976): $75.61 billion. **Agriculture: Chief crops:** corn, wheat, oats, barley, rye, tobacco, tree fruits. **Livestock** (1976): 3,121,898 cattle; 1,904,446 pigs; 133,957 sheep; 34,121,866 poultry. **Forestry production** (1976): $176.2 million. **Mineral production** (1977): total value, $2.71 billion; fuels, $13.4 million; metals, $2.19 billion; structural materials, $415.9 million. **Commercial fishing:** (1976) $12.6 million. **Value of construction** (1977): $10.48 billion. **Employment distribution** (1977): 3.3% agriculture; 24.4% manufacturing; 27.4% services; 16.5% trade;

7.2% construction; 6.8% public administration. **Per capita income** (1976): $7,367. **Unemployment** (1977): 7.0%.

**Finance: No. banks** 2,858; **No credit unions, caisses populaires** 1,187

**International airports:** Toronto, Ottawa.

**Federal Government: No. federal employees** (1977): 181,371. **Federal payroll** (1977): $2.75 billion.

**Energy. Electricity production,** by mwh, (1977): mineral, 34,597,899; hydroelectric, 36,421,046; nuclear, 24,674,040.

**Education. No. schools:** 4,376 elementary; 771 secondary; 52 higher education. **Avg. salary, public school teachers** (1976-77): $15,318. **Provincial data. Motto:** Ut Incepit Fidelis Sic Permanet (Loyal she began, loyal she remains). **Flower:** White trillium. **Bird:** none. **Date entered Confederation:** 1867. **Capital:** Toronto.

**Politics. Premier:** William (Bill) Davis (Progressive Conservative), **Leaders, opposition parties:** Dr. Stuart Smith (Liberal) Michael Cassidy (New Democratic). **Composition of legislature** (May 1978): PC 58; Lib. 34; NDP 33. **Date of last election:** June 9, 1977.

**Tourist attractions.** Toronto C.N. Tower, Ontario Science Centre, Ontario Place, Metro Toronto Zoo, McLaughlin Planetarium, Black Creek Pioneer Village, Canadian Nation Exhibition (mid Aug. to Labor Day); Ottawa's Parliament buildings; Niagara Falls; Polar Bear Express and Agawa Canyon train rides into northern Ontario.

## Prince Edward Island

**People. Population** (Jan. 1978): 120,900; **rank:** 10. **Pop. density:** 55.8 per sq. mi. **Urban** (1976) 37.1% **Ethnic distrib.** (1976): English 92.7%; French 5.5%. **Net migration** (1971-76) +3,963.

**Geography. Total area:** 2,184 sq. mi.; **rank:** 10. **Land area:** 2,184 sq. mi. **Acres forested land:** 619,000. **Location:** an island 140 mi. long, between 40 and 140 mi. wide, situated in the Gulf of St. Lawrence approx. 10 mi. from the coasts of Nova Scotia and New Brunswick. **Climate:** humid continental with temperatures moderated by maritime location; avg. Jan. low in Charlottetown is −11°C, avg. July high 23°C. **Topography:** gently rolling hills; sharply indented coastline; many streams but only small rivers and lakes.

**Economy. Principal industries:** agriculture, tourism, fisheries, light manufacturing. **Principal manufactured goods:** paint, farm vehicles, metal products, electronic equipment. **Value added by manufacture** (1975): $36.7 million. **Gross Domestic Product (1976):** $532.5 million. **Agriculture: Chief crops:** potatoes, mixed grains, oats, barley. **Livestock** (1976): 106,991 cattle; 78,124 pigs; 5,651 sheep; 266,236 poultry. **Mineral production** (1977): total value, $1.8 million, all from structural materials. **Commercial fishing:** (1976) $12.7 million. **Value of construction** (1977): $123.8 million. **Employment distribution** (1977): 12% agriculture; 8% manufacturing; 28% services; 16% trade; 10% construction; 10% public administration. **Per capita income** (1976): $4,650. **Unemployment** (1977): 10%.

**Finance: No. banks** 32; **No. credit unions, caisses populaires** 13.

**International airports:** none. **Federal Government: No. federal employees** (1977): 2,782. **Federal payroll:** (1977): $40.6 million.

**Energy.** Electricity production, by mwh, (1977): mineral, 385,012.

**Education. No. schools:** 60 elementary; 14 secondary; 3 higher education. **Avg. salary, public school teachers** (1976-77): $14,714.

**Provincial Data. Motto:** Parva Sub Ingenti (The small under the protection of the large). **Flower:** Lady's slipper. **Bird:** Blue jay. **Date entered Confederation:** 1873. **Capital:** Charlottetown.

**Politics. Premier:** Alex B. Campbell (Liberal). **Leaders, opposition parties:** Angus MacLean (Progressive Conservative), Aquinas Ryan (New Democratic). **Composition of legislature** (May, 1978): Lib. 17; P.C. 15. **Date of last election:** Apr. 24, 1978.

**Tourist attractions:** P.E.I. National Park; beaches all along the coastline; 9 golf courses; 70 campgrounds; Summerside Lobster Carnival, 3d wk. in July; Charlottetown Confederation Centre; Woodleigh Replicas (Burlington).

## Quebec

**People. Population** (Jan. 1978): 6,280,900; **rank:** 2. **Pop. density:** 12 per sq. mi. **Urban** (1976) 79.1%. **Ethnic distrib.** (1976): French 80%; English 12.8%; Italian 2%. **Net migration** (1971-76) −9,940.

**Geography. Total area:** 594,860 sq. mi.; **rank:** 1. **Land area:** 523,860 sq. mi. **Acres forested land:** 171,998,000. **Location:** borders Ontario on the W and Labrador and New Brunswick on the E; extends N to Hudson Strait and NW to James and Hudson Bays; the southern border touches New York, Vermont, New Hampshire and Maine. **Climate:** varies from subarctic in the northern half of the province to continental in the southern populated regions; avg. Jan. low in Montreal is −14°C, avg. Jan. High 26°C. **Topography:** half a million sq. mi. of Quebec consists of the Laurentian Uplands, part of the Canadian Shield; Appalachian Highlands are in southeastern Quebec; lowlands form a small area along the shore of the St. Lawrence River.

**Economy. Principal industries:** manufacturing, agriculture, electrical production, mining, meat processing, petroleum refining. **Principal manufactured goods:** foods and beverages, clothing, textiles, paper and paper products, furniture. **Value added by manufacture** (1975): $10.46 billion. **Gross Domestic Product** (1976): $45.84 billion. **Agriculture: Chief crops:** oats, corn grains, potatoes, mixed grains, tame hay, apples. **Livestock** (1976): 1,706,913 cattle; 1,613,139 pigs; 45,688 sheep; 24,866,354 poultry. **Forestry production** (1976): $308.4 million. **Mineral production** (1977): total value, $1.63 billion; metals; $759.8 million; asbestos; $430.8 million; structural materials; $342.5 million. **Commercial fishing:** (1976) $15.9 million. **Value of construction** (1977): $8.68 billion. **Employment distribution** (1977): 2.7% agriculture; 22.6% manufacturing; 28% services; 17% trade; 6.4% construction; 7.1% public administration. **Per capita income** (1976): $6,253. **Unemployment** (1977): 10.3%.

**Finance: No. banks** 1,609; **no. credit unions, caisses populaires** 1,566.

**International airports:** Dorval, Mirabel (both near Montreal).

**Federal Government: No. federal employees** (1977): 69,413. **Federal payroll** (1977): $996 million.

**Energy.** Electricity production, by mwh, (1977): mineral, 251,612; hydroelectric, 82,742,583; nuclear, 21,987.

**Education. No. schools:** n.a. elementary; n.a. secondary; 83 higher education. **Avg. salary, public school teachers** (1976-77): $n.a.

**Provincial Data.** Motto Je me souviens (I remember). **Flower:** Fleur de Lys. **Birds:** Alouette (lark). **Date entered Confederation:** 1867. **Capital:** Quebec City.

**Politics. Premier:** Rene Levesque (Parti Quebecois). **Leaders, opposition parties:** Claude Ryan (Liberal), Rodrique Biron (Union Nationale). Composition of legislature (May, 1978): PQ 71; Lib. 25; UN 11; 2 independent; 1 vacant. **Date of last election:** Nov. 15, 1976.

**Tourist attractions:** Quebec City, often described as North America's "most European city", and sophisticated Montreal each offer numerous attractions; the north shore of the St. Lawrence River and the Gaspé Peninsula are picturesque.

## Saskatchewan

**People. Population** (Jan. 1978): 1,034,700; **rank:** 5. **Pop. density:** 4.7 per sq. mi. **Urban** (1976) 55.5% **Ethnic distrib.** (1976): English 77.7%; German 6.6%; Ukrainian 5%; French 2.9%; Native Indian 2.3% **Net migration** (1971-76) -34,615.

**Geography. Total area:** 251,700 sq. mi.; **rank:** 5. **Land area:** 220,182 sq. mi. **Acres forested land:** 31,678,000. **Location:** borders on the Northwest Territories to the N,

anitoba to the E, Alberta to the W, and Montana and
orth Dakota to the S. **Climate:** continental, with cold win-
rs (Jan. avg. low in Regina is −23°C) and hot summers
uly avg. high in Regina is 26°C). **Topography:** southern
3ds of province are plains and grassland; northern 3d is
anadian Shield.

**Economy. Principal industries:** agriculture, mining of
tash, meat processing, electricity production, petroleum
fining. **Principal manufactured goods:** foods and bev-
ages, agricultural implements, fabricated metals, non-
etallic mineral products. **Value added by manufacture**
975): $455.2 million. **Gross Domestic product** (1976):
.98 billion. **Agriculture:** Chief crops: wheat (63% of
ational total), barley, oats, mustard seed, rye, flax. Live-
ock (1976): 3,127,951 cattle; 490,388 pigs; 83,361
eep; 4,591,875 poultry. **Forestry production** (1976):
6 million. **Mineral production** (1977): total value,
.12 billion; fuels, $614.7 million; metals, $22.6 million;
tash, $421.3 million. **Commercial fishing:** (1976) $2.8
lion. **Value of construction** (1977): $1.56 billion. **Em-
oyment distribution** (1977): 24% agriculture; 5.9%
anufacturing; 25.4% services; 16.4% trade, 6.9% con-
ruction; 6.9% public administration. **Per capita income**

(1976): $6,709. **Unemployment** (1977): 4.5%.
**Finance: No. banks** 367; **No. credit unions, caisses
populaires** 242.
**International airports:** none.
**Federal Government: No. Federal employees**
(1977): 12,906. **Federal payroll** (1977): $190.7 million.
**Energy. Electricity production,** by mwh, (1977): min-
eral, 6,288,711; hydroelectric, 2,101,652.
**Education. No. schools:** 896 elementary; 146 second-
ary; 6 higher education. **Avg. salary, public school
teachers** (1976-77); $14,404.
**Provincial Data. Motto:** none. **Flower:** Red prairie lily.
**Bird:** Prairie sharp-tailed grouse. **Date entered Confed-
eration:** 1905. **Capital:** Regina.
**Politics. Premier:** Allan Blakeney (New Democratic).
**Leaders, opposition parties:** Edward (Ted) Malone (Liberal), Richard (Dick) Collver (Progressive Conservative).
**Composition of legislature** (May, 1978): NDP 39; Lib.
11; PC 11. **Date of last election:** June 11, 1975.
**Tourist attractions:** Regina: RCMP Museum, Museum
of Natural History, Wascana Centre; Western Develop-
ment Museums located at Saskatoon, Yorkton, North
Battleford, Moose Jaw.

# Territories of Canada

In addition to its 10 provinces Canada contains the Yu-
on and Northwest Territories making up more than a third
f the nation's land area but a minuscule amount of its pop-
ation. Each territory is administered by a resident commis-
oner appointed by the federal government which retains
ontrol over all natural resources excluding fish and wildlife.
n elected council in each territory exercises jurisdiction
ver such matters as education, housing and social services.
echnically, the commissioner is not obliged to follow the
rections of council. Each territory is represented federally
y one member in both the House of Commons and Senate.
There is substantial support in both territories for in-
eased autonomy or provincial status. The federal position
as been that the territories are not developed enough to be-
ome provinces. In 1978, however, Ottawa appointed a spe-
al representative to examine constitutional development in
e Northwest Territories.

## The Yukon

*Data applies to both Territories.

**People. Population** (Jan. 1978): 22,000; **Pop. density:**
1 per sq. mi. **Urban** (1976) 61%. **Ethnic distrib. by
other tongue** (1976): English 86.7%; French 2.4%; Nave Indian 2.3%; German 1.9%. (Using other criteria Nave Indians make up 19% of the population). **Net migra-
on** (1971-76) 4,260*.
**Geography. Total area:** 1,304,903 sq. mi. **Land area:**
253,438 sq. mi. **Acres forested land:** 57,417,000. **Lo-
ation:** extreme northwestern area of mainland Canada;
ounded on the N by the Beaufort Sea, on the S by British
olumbia, on the E by the Mackenzie District of the North-
est Territories, and on the W by Alaska. **Climate:** great
ariance in temperatures; warm summers, very cold win-
rs; low precipitation. **Topography:** main feature is the
ukon plateau with 21 peaks exceeding 10,000 ft.; open
ndra in the far north.
**Economy. Principal industries:** mining, tourism. **Prin-
pal manufactured goods:** small amount of outdoor
creation equipment. **Value added by manufacture**
975): $5.9 million*. **Agriculture:** hay, oats, vegetable
ardens for local use. **Mineral production** (1977): total
alue, $210.3 million; fuels, $.5 million; Metals, $172.6 mil-
on; asbestos, $37.2 million. **Commercial fishing:** (1976)
66,000. **Per capita income** (1976): $6,780*. **No. of
anks** 16.
**Federal Government: No. federal employees** (1977):
,450. **Federal payroll** (1977): $19.5 million.
**Energy. Electricity production,** by mwh, (1977): min-
rals, 42,811; hydroelectric, 324,281.
**Education. No. schools:** 22 elementary; 1 secondary;

0 higher education. **Avg. salary, public school teachers**
(1976-77): $19,466.
**Territorial Data. Flower:** Fireweed. **Date established:**
June 13, 1898. **Capital:** Whitehorse. **Commissioner:** Art
Pearson. **Council:** 12 independent elected representa-
tives.

**Tourist attractions:** Whitehorse, Dawson City, the
Klondike area, Miles Canyon.

## The Northwest Territories

**People. Population** (Jan. 1978): 43,700; **Pop. density:**
0.03 per sq. mi. **Urban** (1976) 49.7% **Ethnic distrib. by
mother tongue** (1976): English 54.2%; Inuit 26.7%; Native Indian 9.7%; French 2.6%. (Using other criteria the
Inuit make up 35% of the population, Native Indians 17%.)
**Net migration** (1971-76) See Yukon.
**Geography. Total area:** 207,076 sq. mi. **Land area:**
205,346 sq. mi. **Acres forested land:** 135,194,000 **Location:** all land north of the 60th parallel between the Yukon
Territory and Hudson Bay and all northern islands east to
Greenland; land area bounded by the Yukon Territory to
the W, Hudson Bay to the E, the Beaufort Sea to the N
and B.C, Alta., Sask. and Man. to S. **Climate:** extreme
temperatures and low precipitation; Arctic and sub-Arctic.
**Topography:** mostly tundra plains formed on the rocks of
the Canadian shield; the Mackenzie Lowland is a continuation of the Great Plains; the Mackenzie River Valley is
forested.
**Economy. Principal industries:** mining, mineral and
hydrocarbon exploration; oil refining. **Value added by
manufacture** (1975): See Yukon. **Agriculture:** scattered
market gardening in the southern Mackenzie district only.
**Mineral production** (1977): total value, $250.4 million;
fuels, $32.5 million; metals, $217.9 million. **Commercial
fishing:** (1976) $871,000. **Per capita income** (1976): see
Yukon. **No. of banks** 23.
**Federal Government: No. federal employees** (1977):
2,462. **Federal payroll** (1977); $34.5 million.
**Energy. Electricity production,** by mwh, (1977): mineral, 104,257; hydroelectric, 266,074.
**Education. No. schools:** 60 elementary; 7 secondary;
0 higher education. **Avg. salary, public school teachers**
(1976-77): $17,730.
**Territorial Data. Flower:** Mountain avens. **Date Established:** June 22, 1869. **Capital:** Yellowknife. **Commissioner:** Stuart M. Hodgson. **Council:** 15 independent
elected representatives.

**Tourist attractions:** Wood Buffalo, Auyuittuq, and
Nahanni National Parks; Mackenzie River and Delta; annual Midnight Golf Tournament in Yellowknife July 21.

## Head of State and Cabinet

Queen Elizabeth, succeeded to the throne in 1952, is represented by Governor-General Rt. Hon. Jules Leger, appoin 1974. Titles: Minister unless otherwise stated or *Minister of State.

(listed according to precedence) (Sept 16, 1977)

Prime Minister — Pierre Elliott Trudeau
Deputy Prime Minister, President of the Queen's Privy Council for Canada and House Leader — Allan J. MacEachen
Finance — Jean Chretien
Labor — John Carr Munro
Justice and Attorney General — Stanley R. (Ron) Basford
Secretary of State for External Affairs — Donald Jamieson
President of Treasury Board — Robert K. Andras
Transport — Otto E. Lang
Supply and Services — Jean-Pierre Goyer
Energy, Mines and Resources — Alastair W. Gillespie
Agriculture — Eugene F. Whelan
Corporate and Consumer Affairs — W. Warren Allmand
Indian Affairs and Northern Development — James H. (Hugh) Faulkner
*Urban Affairs — Andre Ouellet
Veteran Affairs — Daniel J. MacDonald
*Federal-Provincial Relations and Status of Women — Marc Lalonde

Communications — Jeanne Sauve
Leader of the Government in the Senate — Raymone Perrault
National Defence — Barnett (Barney) J. Danson
Public Works — J. Judd Buchanan
*Science and Technology — J. Judd Buchanan
Fisheries and Environment — Romeo LeBlanc
Regional Economic Expansion — Marcel Lessard
Employment and Immigration — Jack (Bud) Cullen
*Environment — Leonard (Len) S. Marchand
Secretary of State — John Roberts
National Health and Welfare — Monique Begin
Solicitor General and Deputy House Leader — Je Jacques Blais
*Small Business — Anthony (Tony) C. Abbott
*Fitness and Sport — Iona Campagnolo
National Revenue — Joseph-Philippe (Joe) Guay
Industry, Trade, and Commerce — Jack H. Horner
*Multiculturism — Norman Cafik
Postmaster General — Giles Lamontagne

## Governors-General of Canada Since Confederation, 1867

| Name | Term | Name | Terr |
|---|---|---|---|
| The Viscount Monck of Ballytrammon | 1867-1868 | General The Baron Byng of Vimy | 1921-19 |
| The Baron Lisgar of Lisgar and Bailieborough | 1869-1872 | The Viscount Willingdon of Ratton | 1926-19 |
| The Earl of Dufferin | 1872-1878 | The Earl of Bessborough | 1931-19 |
| The Marquis of Lorne | 1878-1883 | The Baron Tweedsmuir of Elsfield | 1935-19 |
| The Marquis of Lansdowne | 1883-1888 | Major General The Earl of Athlone | 1940-19 |
| The Baron Stanley of Preston | 1888-1893 | Field Marshall The Viscount Alexander of Tunis | 1946-19 |
| The Earl of Aberdeen | 1893-1898 | The Right Hon. Vincent Massey | 1952-19 |
| The Earl of Minto | 1898-1904 | General The Right Hon. | |
| The Earl Grey | 1904-1911 | Georges P. Vanier | 1959-19 |
| Field Marshall H.R.H. The Duke of Connaught | 1911-1916 | The Right Hon. Roland Michener | 1967-19 |
| The Duke of Devonshire | 1916-1921 | The Right Hon. Jules Leger | 1974- |

## Fathers of Confederation

Union of the British North American colonies into the Dominion of Canada was discussed and its terms negotiated a confederation conferences held at Charlottetown (C), Sept. 1, 1864; Quebec (Q), Oct. 10, 1864; and London (L), Dec. 4, 18 The names of delegates are followed by the provinces they represented. Canada refers to what are now the provinces of tario and Quebec.

| | | | |
|---|---|---|---|
| Adams G. Archibald, N.S. | (C,Q,L) | Hector L. Langevin, Canada | (C,C |
| George Brown, Canada | (C,Q) | Jonathan McCully, N.S. | (C,C |
| Alexander Campbell, Canada | (C,Q) | A.A. Macdonald, P.E.I. | (C |
| Frederick B.T. Carter, Nfld. | (Q) | John A. Macdonald, Canada. | (C,C |
| George-Etienne Cartier, Canada | (C,Q,L) | William McDougall, Canada | (C,C |
| Edward B. Chandler, N.B. | (C,Q) | Thomas D'Arcy McGee, Canada | (C |
| Jean-Charles Chapais, Canada | (Q) | Peter Mitchell, N.B. | (C |
| James Cockburn, Canada | (Q) | Oliver Mowat, Canada | |
| George H. Coles, P.E.I. | (C,Q) | Edward Palmer, P.E.I. | (C |
| Robert B. Dickey, N.S. | (Q) | William H. Pope, P.E.I. | (C |
| Charles Fisher, N.B. | (Q,L) | John W. Ritchie, N.S. | |
| Alexander T. Galt, Canada | (C,Q,L) | J. Ambrose Shea, Nfld. | |
| John Hamilton Gray, N.B. | (C,Q) | William H. Steeves, N.B. | (C |
| John Hamilton Gray, P.E.I. | (C,Q) | Sir Etienne-Paschal Tache, Canada | |
| Thomas Heath Haviland, P.E.I. | (Q) | Samuel Leonard Tilley, N.B. | (C,C |
| William A. Henry, N.S. | (C,Q,L) | Charles Tupper, N.S. | (C,C |
| William P. Howland, Canada | (L) | Edward Whelan, P.E.I. | |
| John M. Johnson, N.B. | (C,Q,L) | R.D. Wilmot, N.B. | |

## The Political Parties

Canadian parties, from whatever point in the political spectrum they begin, gravitate toward the middle of the road where most of the votes lie. Despite variations in outlook and official policy, all 4 major parties tend to adopt a

practical rather than dogmatic line on most issues.
Conservatives — The oldest party, they have adopted prefix "Progressive" and moved to the left, advocating fa support programs and endorsing an extension of social v

are. Their support comes from older voters, Protestants, and English-speaking rural residents—especially in western Canada. **Leader:** Joe Clark.

**Liberals** — Originally the Canadian equivalent of the American Jacksonian Democrats, favoring strict representation by population and the rural pioneer against the urban elite, they now get most of their electoral support from the middle and upper classes in cities, from ethnic voters, and among French-speaking Canadians. Liberals are cautious about extending the welfare state. **Leader:** Pierre Elliott Trudeau.

**New Democratic Party** — Successor to the Cooperative Commonwealth Federation, which combined the agrarian protest movement in western Canada with a democratic socialism of the British Labor Party variety, the NDP was founded in 1961. It now attempts to attract the vote of middle-class Canadians and fuse it with the party's labor support. **Leader:** Ed Broadbent.

**Social Credit** — adopting in diluted form the unorthodox monetary theories of the movement's English founder, Major C.H. Douglas, Social Credit has appealed to the have-nots. Originally based in western Canada where it still forms the government in some provinces, the party now relies on rural Quebec for most of its federal support. **Leader:** Lorne Reznowski.

Political power in Canada has been dominated by the Progressive Conservative and Liberal parties which, since Confederation, have alternated in forming the government. Of 30 federal elections since 1867 the Conservatives have won 12, holding power for 47 years; the Liberals have gained office 18 times, governing for 64 years. As a measure of traditional Liberal strength, all but one (Edward Blake, 1800-1887) of the party's 7 leaders has been elected Prime Minister—though not always on the first attempt.

Despite the overwhelming dominance of political life by the Liberals and Conservatives, the role of 3d parties has been significant, particularly in recent decades when several elections have resulted in failure of the major parties to form a parliamentary majority. At such times the governing party is able to maintain power and pass legislation only with the support of one or both of the minor parties.

Although its success at the polls has been unspectacular—31 of 264 seats in 1972 is its best showing thus far—the NDP has been the most influential and persistent of the 3d parties. Pressure from the NPD on the left has influenced policy decisions by both major parties.

The Socreds, to the far right of the other 3 parties, came into national prominence in the 1962 election with a sudden gain in support in the province of Quebec where the party captured 26 of 75 seats (giving it 30 seats nationally). Since then the party's fortunes have declined considerably. In 1974 it received only 11 seats and captured a mere 5% of the popular vote.

## Party Representation by Regions, 1949-1974

| Canada[1] | 1949 | 1953 | 1957 | 1958 | 1962 | 1963 | 1965 | 1968 | 1972 | 1974 |
|---|---|---|---|---|---|---|---|---|---|---|
| Liberal | 193 | 171 | 105 | 40 | 100 | 129 | 131 | 155 | 109 | 141 |
| Conservative | 41 | 51 | 112 | 208 | 116 | 95 | 97 | 72 | 107 | 95 |
| New Democratic | 13 | 23 | 25 | 8 | 19 | 17 | 21 | 22 | 31 | 16 |
| Social Credit | 10 | 15 | 19 | — | 30 | 24 | 14 | 14 | 15 | 11 |
| Other | 5 | 5 | 4 | — | — | — | 2 | 1 | 2 | 1 |
| **Ontario** | | | | | | | | | | |
| Liberal | 56 | 51 | 21 | 15 | 44 | 52 | 51 | 64 | 36 | 55 |
| Conservative | 25 | 33 | 61 | 67 | 35 | 27 | 25 | 17 | 40 | 25 |
| New Democratic | 1 | 1 | 3 | 3 | 6 | 6 | 9 | 6 | 11 | 8 |
| **Quebec** | | | | | | | | | | |
| Liberal | 68 | 66 | 62 | 25 | 35 | 47 | 56 | 56 | 56 | 60 |
| Conservative | 2 | 4 | 9 | 50 | 14 | 8 | 8 | 4 | 2 | 3 |
| Social Credit | — | — | — | — | 26 | 20 | 9 | 14 | 15 | 11 |
| **Atlantic** | | | | | | | | | | |
| Liberal | 26 | 27 | 12 | 8 | 14 | 20 | 15 | 7 | 10 | 13 |
| Conservative | 7 | 5 | 21 | 25 | 18 | 13 | 18 | 25 | 22 | 17 |
| New Democratic | 1 | 1 | — | — | 1 | — | — | — | — | 1 |
| **Western** | | | | | | | | | | |
| Liberal | 43 | 27 | 10 | 1 | 7 | 10 | 9 | 27 | 7 | 13 |
| Conservative | 7 | 9 | 21 | 66 | 49 | 47 | 46 | 25 | 42 | 49 |
| New Democratic | 11 | 21 | 22 | 5 | 12 | 11 | 12 | 16 | 19 | 6 |
| Social Credit | 10 | 15 | 19 | — | 4 | 4 | 5 | — | — | — |

1) Total seats in 1968, 1972, and 1974 elections include one each for Yukon and Northwest Territories.

## Canadian Armed Forces

In Feb., 1968, Canada carried out the unification of its traditionally separate services: the Royal Canadian Navy, the Canadian Army, and the Royal Canadian Air Force. The first step towards a unified force was taken in 1964 when the 3 services were brought together under one control with common logistics and supply and training systems, but retaining their separate legal entities. The positions of Chairman of the Chiefs of Staff and Chiefs of the Navy, Army, and Air Force were abolished and replaced by the Chief of the Defense Staff. On Feb. 1, 1968, the 3 services ceased to exist. They were unified into the Canadian Armed Forces in which all officers, men, and women are managed within a single body, with a common uniform.

### Chief of the Defense Staff: Admiral R. H. Falls
### Vice Chief of the Defense Staff: Lieut. Gen. R. M. Withers

Maritime Command — Vice Admiral A. L. Collier
Mobile Command — Lieut. Gen. J. J. Paradis
Air Command — Lieut. Gen. G. A. Mackenzie

Communications Command — Brig. Gen. R. N. Senior
Canadian Forces Europe — Maj. Gen. C. H. Belzile

## Regular Forces Strength

(as of March 31)

| Year | Navy | Army | Air Force | Total | Year | Navy | Army | Air Force | Total |
|---|---|---|---|---|---|---|---|---|---|
| 1945 | 92,529 | 494,258 | 174,254 | 761,041 | 1974 | .... | .... | .... | 80,639 |
| 1955 | 19,207 | 49,409 | 49,461 | 118,077 | 1975 | .... | .... | .... | 78,448 |
| 1965 | 19,756 | 46,264 | 48,144 | 114,164 | 1976 | .... | .... | .... | 78,394 |
| 1972 | .... | .... | .... | 82,879 | 1977 | .... | .... | .... | 78,091 |
| 1973 | .... | .... | .... | 81,443 | 1978 | .... | .... | .... | 79,656 |

## Canadian Military Participation in Major Conflicts

**Northwest Rebellion (1885)**[1]
Participants—3,323
Killed—38
Last veteran died at the age of 104 in 1971.
**South African War (1899-1902)**
Participants—7,368[2]
Killed—89
Living Veterans—less than 50
**First World War (1914-1918)**
Participants—626,636[3]

Killed—61,332[4]
Living Veterans—96,900
**Second World War (1939-1945)**
Participants—1,086,343 (inc. 45,423 women)
Killed—37,714 (inc. 8 women)
Living Veterans—801,000
**Korean War (1950-1953)**
Participants—25,583
Killed—314
Living Veterans—25,000

(1) First battle in history to be fought entirely by Canadian troops. (2) Includes Canadians in the South African constabulary and 8 nursing sisters. (3) Includes 2,854 nursing sisters. (4) Includes 21 nursing sisters and 1,563 airmen serving with the British air forces.

## Canadian World War II Winners of the Victoria Cross

The Victoria Cross is Britain's highest military honor. It has been accorded to 94 Canadians since its inception in 1856. The cross was originally cast from metal of a Russian cannon captured during the Crimean War.

| Name | Unit | Theater of war & date |
|---|---|---|
| Sgt. Mjr. J. R. Osborn | Winnipeg Grenadiers | Hong Kong, Dec. 19, 1941 |
| Lt. Col. C. E. Merritt | S. Sask. Regiment | Dieppe, Aug. 19, 1942 |
| Capt. J. W. Foote | Royal Hamilton Light Infantry | Dieppe, Aug. 19, 1942 |
| Capt. F. T. Peters | Royal Navy | Oran, North Africa, Nov. 8, 1942 |
| Capt. Paul Triquet | Royal 22d Regiment | Casa Berardi, Dec. 14, 1943 |
| Maj. C. F. Hoey | Lincolnshire Regiment | Burma, Feb. 16, 1944 |
| Maj. John K. Mahoney | Westminster Regiment | Melfa River, May 24, 1944 |
| P.O.A.C. Mynarksi | RCAF | Camria, France, June 12, 1944 |
| Flt. Lieut. D. E. Hornell | RCAF | "Northern waters", June 25, 1944 |
| Sqd. Ldr. Ian Bazalgette | RCAF | Trossy St. Maximin, Aug. 4, 1944 |
| Maj. D. V. Currie | South Alberta Regiment | Normandy, Aug. 20, 1944 |
| Pvt. E. A. Smith | Seaforth Highlanders | Savio River, Italy, Oct. 22, 1944 |
| Sgt. Aubrey Cosens | Queen's Own Rifles | Holland, Feb. 26, 1945 |
| Maj. F. A. Tilston | Essex Scottish | Hochwald Forest, Mar. 1, 1945 |
| Cpl. F. G. Topham | 1st Canadian Parachute Battalion | Germany, Mar. 24, 1945 |
| Lt. R. H. Gray | Royal Canadian Navy | Pacific, Aug. 9, 1945 |

## Canadian Peacekeeping Operations

Canada has played a major role in the United Nations' efforts to preserve peace and promote international security, participating in almost all UN peacekeeping operations to date - in Egypt, Israel, Syria, Lebanon, Cyprus, Korea, India, Pakistan, West New Guinea, the Congo, Yemen and Nigeria.

Nearly 900 Canadian soldiers served in the Gaza Strip following the Israeli-Egyptian crisis of 1956 until the peacekeeping force there was disbanded in 1967.

In the Congo, a 300-man signals unit provided communications for the UN force from 1960 to 1964.

Canadian participation in the International Commission for Control and Supervision in Vietnam and Laos began in 1954, and, at its height following U.S. military withdrawal from Vietnam in 1973, involved 245 Canadian Forces personnel. The Canadian Vietnam supervisory contingent was withdrawn in July 1973, the Laos mission in the spring of 1974.

Canada's largest peacekeeping commitment as of mid-1978 was in the Middle East where 850 Canadians are serving in the United Nations Emergency Force and another 150 with the United Nations Disengagement Observer Force. An additional 115 Canadian Forces communications personnel were stationed with the United Nations Interim Force in Lebanon in March 1978.

Some 515 Canadians currently serve in the UN Peacekeeping Force in Cyprus where Canadian participation began in 1964 and was augmented in 1974.

Other Canadian peacekeeping operations in 1978 were as follows:

- 9 Canadian Forces personnel with UN Military Observer Group, India-Pakistan.

- 20 Canadian officers with the UN Truce Supervisory Organization, Israel.

- 2 Canadian Forces personnel in Korea with the UN Military Armistice Commission.

## Canadian Legal or Public Holidays, 1979

Legal public holidays in all provinces are: New Year's Day, Good Friday, Easter Monday, Victoria Day, Dominion Day, Labor Day, Remembrance Day and Christmas Day. Additional holidays may be proclaimed provincially by the Lieutenant-Governor of that province and in municipalities by an order of the local council. For some holidays government and business closing practices vary. In most provinces the provincial Ministry or Department of Labor can provide details of holiday closings.

### Chief Legal or Public Holidays

Jan. 1 (Monday) - New Year's Day. All provinces.
Apr. 13 - Good Friday. All provinces.
Apr. 16 - Easter Monday. N.S., Que. (businesses remain open in other provinces)
May 21 (the Monday preceding May 25) - Victoria Day. All provinces.

*July 1 (Sunday) - Dominion Day. All provinces.
Aug. 6 (1st Monday in Aug.) - Civic Holiday. Ont. Man.
Sept. 3 (1st Monday in Sept.) - Labor Day. All provinces.
Oct. 8 (2d Monday in Oct.) - Thanksgiving. All provinces.
Nov. 11 (Sunday) - Remembrance Day. Observed in all

provinces but most businesses remain open.
**Dec. 25 (Tuesday) - Christmas Day.** All provinces.

**Dec. 26 (Wednesday) - Boxing Day.** All provinces except Que.

## Other Legal or Public Holidays

**Jan. 6** (Saturday) - **Epiphany.** Que.
**Jan. 11** (Thursday) - **Sir John A. Macdonald's Birthday.**
Schools closed in some provinces.
**Feb. 28** - **Ash Wednesday.** Que.
**Mar. 17** (Saturday) - **St. Patrick's Day.** Nfld.
**Apr. 23** (Monday) - **St. George's Day.** Nfld.
**June 24** (Sunday) - **St. John the Baptist's Day.** Que.

**June 26** (Tuesday) - **Discovery Day (Nfld.).** Nfld.
**July 3** (Tuesday) - **Memorial Day.** Nfld.
**July 12** (Thursday) - **Orangemen's Day.** Nfld.
**July 15** (Sunday) - **Natal Day.** N.W.T.
**Aug. 17** (Friday) - **Discovery Day (Yukon).** Yukon.
**Nov. 1** (Thursday) - **All Saints Day.** Que.
**Dec. 8** (Saturday) - **Conception Day.** Que.

## Superlative Canadian Statistics

| | | |
|---|---|---|
| Area | Total: Land 3,560,238 sq. mi.; Water 291,571 sq. mi. | 3,851,809 sq. mi. |
| Largest city in area | Whitehorse | 162 sq. mi. |
| Smallest city in area (east). | Thetford Mines, Que. | 7 sq. mi. |
| Smallest city in area (west) | Prince George, B.C. | 17 sq. mi. |
| Northernmost point | Cape Columbia, N.W.T. | 83°07′N. |
| Northernmost town | Inuvik, N.W.T. | 68°21′N. |
| Southernmost point | Middle Island (Lake Erie), Ont. | 42°41′N. |
| Southernmost town | Kingsville, Ont. | 42°02′N. |
| Westernmost point | Mount St. Elias, Yukon | 141°W. |
| Westernmost town | Dawson, Yukon | 139°25′W. |
| Easternmost point. | Cape Spear, Nfld. | 52°37′W. |
| Easternmost town. | St. John's, Nfld. | 52°43′W. |
| Highest City | Rossland, B.C. at R.R. Stn. (49°05′N117°47′W) | 3,465 ft. |
| Highest town. | Lake Louise, Alta. | 5,051 ft. |
| Highest waterfall | Takakkaw Falls, B.C. (51°30′N116°29′W) | 1,650 ft. |
| Longest river. | Mackenzie (from head of Finlay R.) | 2,635 mi. |
| Highest mountain | Mt. Logan | 19,850 ft. |
| Rainiest spot. | Henderson Lake, Vancouver Is. yrly. avg. rainfall. | 262.0 inches |
| Highest lake | Chilco Lake (51°20′N124°05′W) 75.1 sq. mi. | 3,842 ft. |

## Population and Area of Canada by Provinces

Source: Statistics Canada

| Province, territory | Capital | Area in square miles | | | Population | | |
|---|---|---|---|---|---|---|---|
| | | Land | Fresh water | Total | 1966 census | 1976 census | Jan. 1978 estimate |
| Newfoundland | St. John's | 143,045 | 13,140 | 156,185 | 493,396 | 557,725 | 564,800 |
| Prince Edward Island | Charlottetown. | 2,184 | | 2,184 | 108,645 | 118,229 | 121,900 |
| Nova Scotia | Halifax | 20,402 | 1,023 | 21,425 | 756,039 | 828,571 | 839,600 |
| New Brunswick | Fredericton | 27,385 | 519 | 28,345 | 616,788 | 677,250 | 691,900 |
| Quebec. | Quebec | 523,860 | 71,000 | 594,860 | 5,780,845 | 6,234,445 | 6,280,900 |
| Ontario | Toronto | 344,092 | 68,490 | 412,582 | 6,960,870 | 8,264,465 | 8,441,100 |
| Manitoba | Winnipeg | 211,775 | 39,225 | 251,000 | 963,066 | 1,021,506 | 1,034,700 |
| Saskatchewan | Regina | 220,182 | 31,518 | 251,700 | 955,344 | 921,323 | 944,000 |
| Alberta | Edmonton | 248,800 | 6,485 | 255,285 | 1,463,203 | 1,838,037 | 1,936,200 |
| British Columbia | Victoria | 359,279 | 6,976 | 366,255 | 1,873,674 | 2,466,608 | 2,523,400 |
| Northwest Territories | Yellowknife | 1,253,438 | 51,465 | 1,304,903 | 28,738 | 42,609 | 43,700 |
| Yukon Territory | Whitehorse | 205,345 | 1,730 | 207,076 | 14,382 | 21,836 | 22,000 |
| **Total** | | **3,560,238** | **291,571** | **3,851,809** | **20,014,880** | **22,992,604** | **23,444,200** |

## Births and Deaths in Canada by Province

Source: Statistics Canada

| Province | Births 1976 | 1977 | Deaths 1976 | 1977 | Province | Births 1976 | 1977 | Deaths 1976 | 1977 |
|---|---|---|---|---|---|---|---|---|---|
| Newfoundland | 11,320 | 11,210 | 3,230 | 3,290 | Saskatchewan | 15,570 | 15,670 | 7,560 | 7,520 |
| Prince Edward Island | 1,900 | 1,870 | 1,060 | 1,080 | Alberta | 33,000 | 32,490 | 11,320 | 11,490 |
| Nova Scotia | 13,200 | 12,610 | 6,860 | 6,980 | British Columbia | 38,590 | 37,620 | 19,100 | 19,190 |
| New Brunswick | 12,060 | 12,230 | 5,160 | 5,300 | Yukon | 450 | 430 | 130 | 120 |
| Quebec | 95,420 | -95,560 | 42,750 | 43,830 | Northwest Territories | 1,110 | 1,010 | 200 | 170 |
| Ontario | 124,770 | 123,630 | 60,710 | 61,380 | **Total** | **364,630** | **360,340** | **166,490** | **169,040** |
| Manitoba | 17,240 | 17,010 | 8,410 | 8,690 | | | | | |

## Marriages, Divorces in Canada

Source: Statistics Canada
(Rates per 1,000 population)

| Year | Marriages No. | Rate | Divorces No. | Rate | Year | Marriages No. | Rate | Divorces No. | Rate |
|---|---|---|---|---|---|---|---|---|---|
| 1940. | 125,709 | 10.8 | 2,416 | 0.21 | 1973. | 199,064 | 9.0 | 36,704 | 1.66 |
| 1950. | 125,083 | 9.1 | 5,386 | 0.39 | 1974. | 198,824 | 8.9 | 45,019 | 2.00 |
| 1960. | 130,338 | 7.3 | 6,980 | 0.39 | 1975. | 197,585 | 8.7 | 50,611 | 2.22 |
| 1970. | 188,428 | 8.8 | 29,775 | 1.39 | 1976. | 198,020 | 8.6 | 54,207 | 2.36 |

## Canadian Cities with Metropolitan Populations Over 100,000

Source: Statistics Canada

Census Metropolitan Areas. All figures shown are for the 1976 Census.

| | Metro Area | City | | Metro Area | City |
|---|---|---|---|---|---|
| Toronto, Ontario | 2,803,101 | 633,318 | Halifax, Nova Scotia | 267,991 | 117,88 |
| Montreal, Quebec | 2,802,485 | 1,080,546 | Windsor, Ontario | 247,582 | 196,52 |
| Vancouver, British Columbia | 1,166,348 | 410,188 | Victoria, British Columbia | 218,250 | 62,55 |
| Ottawa-Hull, Ontario, Quebec | 693,288 | 304,462 | Quebec (part) Quebec | 171,947 | — |
| Winnipeg, Manitoba | 578,217 | 560,874 | Sudbury, Ontario | 157,030 | 97,60 |
| Edmonton, Alberta | 554,228 | 461,361 | Regina, Saskatchewan | 151,191 | 149,59 |
| Quebec, Quebec | 542,158 | 177,082 | St. John's, Newfoundland | 143,390 | 86,57 |
| Hamilton, Ontario | 529,371 | 312,003 | Oshawa, Ontario | 135,196 | 107,02 |
| Ontario (part) Ontario | 521,341 | — | Saskatoon, Saskatchewan | 133,750 | 133,75 |
| Calgary, Alberta | 469,917 | 469,917 | Chicoutimi-Jonquiere, Quebec | 128,643 | 57,73 |
| St. Catharines-Niagara, Ontario | 301,921 | 123,351 | Thunder Bay, Ontario | 119,253 | 111,47 |
| Kitchener, Ontario | 272,158 | 131,870 | Saint John, New Brunswick | 112,974 | 85,95 |
| London, Ontario | 270,383 | 240,392 | | | |

## Canadian Population by Mother Tongue, 1976

Source: Statistics Canada

| Province | English | French | Italian | German | Ukrain-ian | Indian, Eskimo | Chinese | Portu-guese | Other |
|---|---|---|---|---|---|---|---|---|---|
| Newfoundland | 545,340 | 2,760 | 170 | 450 | 40 | 1,555 | 535 | 210 | 6,66 |
| Prince Edward Island | 109,745 | 6,545 | 30 | 145 | 30 | 70 | 55 | — | 1,61 |
| Nova Scotia | 768,070 | 36,870 | 1,135 | 1,555 | 570 | 2,340 | 800 | 185 | 17,04 |
| New Brunswick | 435,975 | 223,780 | 550 | 1,020 | 170 | 1,695 | 495 | 110 | 13,45 |
| Quebec | 800,680 | 4,989,245 | 124,575 | 22,630 | 10,975 | 18,375 | 10,680 | 19,150 | 238,13 |
| Ontario | 6,457,645 | 462,070 | 309,810 | 154,625 | 76,035 | 21,285 | 51,660 | 88,495 | 642,84 |
| Manitoba | 727,240 | 54,745 | 5,875 | 73,375 | 60,250 | 24,855 | 3,705 | 5,455 | 66,01 |
| Saskatchewan | 715,685 | 26,710 | 1,260 | 61,250 | 45,920 | 20,860 | 3,390 | 220 | 46,03 |
| Alberta | 1,482,725 | 44,440 | 13,745 | 79,925 | 64,960 | 17,690 | 14,430 | 3,445 | 116,68 |
| British Columbia | 2,037,645 | 38,430 | 26,715 | 80,970 | 22,775 | 8,245 | 46,655 | 9,245 | 195,93 |
| Yukon | 18,940 | 525 | 45 | 405 | 140 | 510 | 45 | — | 1,23 |
| Northwest Territories | 23,085 | 1,095 | 135 | 365 | 195 | 15,525 | 120 | 25 | 2,06 |
| Total | 14,122,770 | 5,887,205 | 484,050 | 476,715 | 282,060 | 133,005 | 132,560 | 126,535 | 1,347,69 |

## Population by Religious Denomination

Source: Statistics Canada

| Denomination | 1961 | 1971 | Denomination | 1961 | 197 |
|---|---|---|---|---|---|
| Adventist | 25,999 | 28,590 | Lutheran | 662,744 | 715,74 |
| Anglican | 2,409,068 | 2,543,180 | Mennonite(2) | 152,452 | 168,15 |
| Baptist | 593,553 | 667,245 | Mormon | 50,016 | 66,63 |
| Buddhist | 11,611 | 16,175 | Orthodox(3) | 239,766 | 316,60 |
| Chr. & Miss'nary Alliance | 18,006 | 23,630 | Pentecostal | 143,877 | 220,39 |
| Christian Reformed | 62,257 | 83,390 | Presbyterian | 818,588 | 872,33 |
| Ch. of Christ, Disciples | 19,512 | 16,405 | Roman Catholic | 8,342,826 | 9,974,89 |
| Confucian | 5,089 | 2,165 | Salvation Army | 92,054 | 119,66 |
| Doukhobor | 13,234 | 9,107 | Ukrainian Catholic(4) | 189,653 | 227,73 |
| Free Methodist | 14,245 | 19,125 | Unitarian | 15,062 | 20,99 |
| Hutterite | (1) | 13,650 | United Church | 3,664,008 | 3,768,80 |
| Jehovah's Witnesses | 68,018 | 174,810 | Other | 277,508 | 293,24 |
| Jewish | 254,368 | 276,025 | No religion | 94,763 | 929,57 |

(1) Included with Mennonite. (2) Includes Hutterites in 1961. (3) Those churches which observe the Eastern Orthodox rite, includin Greek, Russian, Ukrainian, and Syrian Orthodox. (4) Includes other "Greek Catholic."

## Immigration to Canada, by Country of Last Permanent Residence

Source: Canadian Statistical Review, May 1977

| Year | Total | UK and Ireland | France | Germany | Nether-lands | Greece | Italy |
|---|---|---|---|---|---|---|---|
| 1974 | 218,465 | 39,748 | 4,232 | 3,621 | 2,103 | 5,632 | 5,22 |
| 1975 | 187,881 | 36,076 | 3,891 | 3,469 | 1,448 | 4,062 | 5,07 |
| 1976 | 149,429 | 22,187 | 3,251 | 2,672 | 1,359 | 2,487 | 4,53 |
| 1977 | 114,914 | 18,568 | 2,757 | 2,254 | 1,247 | 1,960 | 3,41 |

| Year | Portugal | Other Europe | Asia | Austral-asia | United States | West Indies | All Othe |
|---|---|---|---|---|---|---|---|
| 1974 | 16,333 | 11,799 | 50,566 | 2,594 | 26,541 | 23,670 | 26,40 |
| 1975 | 8,547 | 10,327 | 47,382 | 2,174 | 20,155 | 17,800 | 27,47 |
| 1976 | 5,344 | 8,078 | 44,328 | 1,886 | 17,315 | 14,723 | 21,26 |
| 1977 | 3,579 | 6,972 | 31,368 | 1,545 | 12,888 | 12,022 | 16,34 |

## Immigration to Canada, by Province of Intended Destination

Source: Canadian Statistical Review

| ar | Canada | Nfld. | P.E.I. | N.S. | N.B. | Que. | Ont. | Man. | Sask. | Alta. | B.C. | N.W.T. Yukon |
|---|---|---|---|---|---|---|---|---|---|---|---|---|
| 72 | 122,006 | 686 | 175 | 1,872 | 1,301 | 18,592 | 63,805 | 5,262 | 1,511 | 8,390 | 20,107 | 305 |
| 73 | 184,200 | 984 | 273 | 2,548 | 1,729 | 26,871 | 103,187 | 6,621 | 1,866 | 11,904 | 27,949 | 268 |
| 74 | 218,465 | 1,036 | 311 | 2,601 | 2,207 | 33,458 | 120,115 | 7,423 | 2,244 | 14,289 | 34,481 | 300 |
| 75 | 187,881 | 1,106 | 235 | 2,124 | 2,093 | 28,042 | 98,471 | 7,134 | 2,837 | 16,277 | 29,272 | 290 |
| 76 | 149,429 | 725 | 235 | 1,942 | 1,752 | 29,282 | 72,031 | 5,509 | 2,323 | 14,896 | 20,484 | 250 |
| 77 | 114,914 | 583 | 192 | 1,587 | 1,158 | 19,248 | 56,594 | 5,058 | 2,231 | 12,694 | 15,395 | 174 |

## Noted Canadian Personalities of the Past

| rn | Died | Name | Born | Died | Name | Born | Died | Name |
|---|---|---|---|---|---|---|---|---|
| | | **Statesmen** | 1876 | 1935 | Macleod, John J.R. | 1874 | 1942 | Montgomery, Lucy |
| 8 | 1943 | Aberhart, William | 1908 | 1978 | McDougald, John (Bud) | 1803 | 1885 | Moodie, Susanna |
| 4 | 1858 | Baldwin, Robert | 1871 | 1972 | McLaughlin, R. Sam | 1889 | 1963 | Morin, Paul |
| 0 | 1957 | Bennett, Richard B. | 1849 | 1919 | Osler, William | 1879 | 1941 | Nelligan, Emile |
| 3 | 1912 | Blake, Edward | 1891 | 1976 | Penfield, Wilder | 1862 | 1932 | Parker, Gilbert |
| 4 | 1937 | Borden, Robert | 1894 | 1976 | Thomson, Roy | 1883 | 1922 | Pickthall, Marjorie |
| 3 | 1917 | Bowell, Mackenzie | 1843 | 1915 | Van Horne, William | 1883 | 1964 | Pratt, Edwin J. |
| 8 | 1880 | Brown, George | | | | 1860 | 1943 | Roberts, Chas. G.D. |
| 4 | 1873 | Cartier, Georges | | | **Authors** | 1885 | 1961 | Roche, Mazo de la |
| 4 | 1873 | Howe, Joseph | 1888 | 1938 | Belaney, George S. | 1870 | 1943 | Routhier, Adolphe B. |
| 4 | 1950 | King, W. Mackenzie | | | (Grey Owl) | 1822 | 1893 | Roy, Camille |
| 1 | 1919 | Laurier, Wilfrid | 1868 | 1952 | Bourassa, Henri | 1862 | 1947 | Sangster, Charles |
| 4 | 1891 | Macdonald, John A. | 1875 | 1940 | Buchan, John | 1874 | 1958 | Scott, Duncan C. |
| 2 | 1892 | Mackenzie, Alexander | | | (Baron Tweedsmuir) | 1859 | 1931 | Service, Robert W. |
| 5 | 1861 | Mackenzie, Wm. Lyon | | | Campbell, W. Wilfred | 1860 | 1948 | Shortt, Adam |
| 7 | 1967 | Massey, Vincent | | | Carman, W. Bliss | | | Wrong, George M. |
| 5 | 1868 | McGee, Thomas D'Arcy | 1892 | 1977 | Clark, Gregory | | | |
| 4 | 1960 | Meighen, Arthur | 1827 | 1879 | Cremazie, Octave | | | **Anthropologists, Geologists, and** |
| 0 | 1903 | Mowat, Oliver | 1866 | 1944 | Dafoe, John Wesley | | | **Naturalists** |
| 6 | 1871 | Papineau, Louis-Joseph | 1895 | 1958 | Dawson, R. MacGregor | 1859 | 1942 | Adams, Frank D. |
| 7 | 1972 | Pearson, Lester B. | 1836 | 1880 | De Mille, James | 1876 | 1961 | Anderson, Rudolph M. |
| 4 | 1885 | Riel, Louis | 1860 | 1936 | Doughty, Arthur G. | 1820 | 1876 | Billings, Elkanah |
| 8 | 1896 | Tilley, Samuel Leonard | | | Duncan, Sara J. | 1846 | 1925 | Dionne, Charles Eusibe |
| 5 | 1927 | Tupper, Charles H. | 1862 | 1932 | Edwards, Robert (Bob) | 1817 | 1896 | Hale, Horatio |
| 4 | 1942 | Woodsworth, James S. | 1864 | 1922 | Frechette, Louis H. | 1859 | 1944 | Hill-Tout, Charles |
| | | | 1839 | 1908 | Gordon, Chas. W. | 1826 | 1892 | Hunt, Thomas Sterry |
| | | **Scientists, Industrialists** | | | (Ralph Connor) | 1886 | 1969 | Jenness, Diamond |
| 9 | 1964 | Aitken, William M. | 1860 | 1937 | Grove, Frederick | 1798 | 1875 | Logan, William E. |
| | | (Lord Beaverbrook) | 1796 | 1865 | Haliburton, Thos. C. | 1831 | 1920 | Macoun, John |
| 0 | 1882 | Allan, Hugh | | | Hemon, Louis | 1885 | 1944 | Marie-Victorin, Frere |
| 1 | 1941 | Banting, Fredk. G. | | | Innis, H.A. | 1865 | 1944 | Miner, John T. (Jack) |
| 7 | 1943 | Beatty, Edward W. | 1817 | 1906 | Kirby, William | 1820 | 1892 | Provancher, Leon, abbe |
| 0 | 1978 | Best, Charles H. | 1862 | 1913 | Johnson, Pauline | 1891 | 1957 | Rowan, William |
| 0 | 1939 | Bethune, Norman | 1861 | 1899 | Lampman, Archibald | 1836 | 1914 | Saunders, Charles E. |
| 4 | 1907 | Eaton, Timothy | 1869 | 1944 | Leacock, Stephen | 1875 | 1947 | Saunders, William |
| 7 | 1906 | Eddy, Ezra Butler | 1873 | 1951 | Lowry, Malcolm | 1802 | 1899 | Taverner, Percy A. |
| 7 | 1915 | Fleming, Sandford | 1872 | 1918 | McClung, Nellie | 1858 | 1957 | Traill, Catharine Parr |
| 9 | 1966 | Hilton, Hugh G. | | | McCrae, John | | | Tyrrell, Joseph Burr |

## Widely Known Canadians of the Present

Statesmen, authors, performers, artists, industrialists, and other prominent persons.

| me (Birthplace) | Birthdate | Name (Birthplace) | Birthdate |
|---|---|---|---|
| mand, Warren (Montreal, Que.) | 9/19/32 | Campbell, Alex (Summerside, P.E.I.) | 12/1/33 |
| dras, Robert (Lachine, Que.) | 2/20/21 | Carrier, Roch (Ste.-Justine-de-Dorchester, Que.) | 5/13/37 |
| wood, Margaret (Ottawa, Ont.) | 11/18/39 | Chuvalo, George (Toronto, Ont.) | 9/12/37 |
| gustyn, Frank (Hamilton, Ont.) | 1/27/53 | Charlebois, Robert (Montreal, Que.) | 6/25/44 |
| | | Chretien, Jean (Shawinigan, Que.) | 1/11/34 |
| chman, Randy (Winnipeg, Man.) | 9/27/43 | Clark, Joe (High River, Alta.) | 6/5/39 |
| sford, Ron (Winnipeg, Man.) | 4/22/32 | Cohen, Leonard (Montreal, Que.) | 9/21/34 |
| nnett, William (Kelowna, B.C.) | 4/14/32 | Colville, Alex (Toronto, Ont.) | 8/24/20 |
| rton, Pierre (Whitehorse, Yukon) | 7/12/20 | Connors, Stompin' Tom (Skinner's Pond, P.E.I.) | 2/9/36 |
| ney, Earle (Calgary, Alta.) | 5/13/04 | Cranston, Toller (Kirkland Lake, Ont.) | 4/20/49 |
| akeney, Allan (Bridgewater, N.S.) | 9/7/25 | Crombie, David (Toronto, Ont.) | 4/24/36 |
| ack, Conrad (Montreal, Que.) | 8/25/44 | Cummings, Burton (Winnipeg, Man.) | 12/31/47 |
| oadbent, Ed (Oshawa, Ont.) | 3/21/36 | | |
| onfman, Charles (Montreal, Que.) | 9/20/29 | Danby, Ken (Sault Ste. Marie, Ont.) | 3/16/40 |
| chanan, Judd (Edmonton, Alta.) | 7/25/29 | Danson, Barney (Toronto, Ont.) | 2/8/21 |
| illoch, John (Toronto, Ont.) | 8/24/33 | Davies, Robertson (Thamesville, Ont.) | 8/28/13 |
| | | Davey, Keith (Toronto, Ont.) | 4/21/26 |
| allaghan, Morley (Toronto, Ont.) | 2/22/03 | Davis, William (Brampton, Ont.) | 7/30/29 |
| amp, Dalton (Woodstock, N.B.) | 9/11/20 | Deschamps, Yvon (Montreal, Que.) | 7/31/35 |

Desmarais, Paul (Sudbury, Ont.)   1/4/27
Diefenbaker, John (Grey Co., Ont.)   9/18/95
Douglas, Tommy (Falkirk, Scotland)   10/20/04
Drapeau, Jean (Montreal, Que.)   2/18/16

Eagleson, Alan (St. Catharines, Ont.)   4/24/33
Evans, John (Toronto, Ont.)   10/1/29

Falls, Robert H. (Welland, Ont.)   4/29/24
Faulkner, Hugh (Montreal, Que.)   3/9/33
Forrester, Maureen (Montreal, Que.)   7/25/30
Frum, Barbara (Niagara Falls, Ont.)   9/8/38
Frye, Northrop (Sherbrooke, Que.)   7/14/12
Fulford, Robert (Ottawa, Ont.)   2/13/32

Gillespie, Alastair (Victoria, B.C.)   5/1/22
Gould, Glenn (Toronto, Ont.)   9/25/32
Goyer, Jean-Pierre (St. Larent, Que.)   1/17/32
Gzowski, Peter (Toronto, Ont.)   7/13/34

Harron, Don (Toronto, Ont.)   9/19/24
Hatfield, Richard (Hartland, N.B.)   4/9/31
Herzberg, Gerhard (Hamburg, Germany)   12/25/04
Hewitt, Foster (Toronto, Ont.)   11/21/03
Hill, Dan (Toronto, Ont.)   6/3/54
Horner, Jack (Blain Lake, Sask.)   7/20/27

Irving, K.C. (Buctouche, N.B.)   1899

Jamieson, Don (St. John's, Nfld.)   4/30/21

Kain, Karen (Hamilton, Ont.)   3/28/51
Karsh, Yousuf (Armenia–in-Turkey)   12/23/08
Kierans, Eric (Montreal, Que.)   2/2/14

Lalonde, Marc (Ile Perrot, Que.)   7/26/29
Lamarsh, Judy (Chatham, Ont.)   12/20/24
Lang, Otto (Handel, Sask.)   5/14/32
Laskin, Bora (Fort William, Ont.)   10/5/12
Laurence, Margaret (Neepawa, Man.)   7/18/26
Layton, Irving (Neamtz, Romania)   3/12/12
Leger, Jules (St. Anicet, Que.)   4/4/13
Levesque, Rene (New Carlisle, Que.)   8/24/22
Lewis, David (Swislocz, Poland)   6/23/09
Lightfoot, Gordon (Orillia, Ont.)   11/17/38
Lougheed, Peter (Calgary, Alta.)   7/26/28
Lyon, Sterling (Windsor, Ont.)   1/30/27

Macdonald, Flora (North Sydney, N.S.)   6/3/26
MacEachen, Allan (Inverness, N.S.)   7/6/21
Mackasey, Bryce (Quebec City, Que.)   8/25/27
Maloney, Arthur (Eganville, Ont.)   11/26/19
Marchand, Jean (Champlain, Que.)   12/20/18

McLauchlan, Murray (Paisley, Scotland)   6/30
McLuhan, Marshall (Edmonton, Alta.)   7/21
Mitchell, W.O. (Weyburn, Sask.)   3/13
Moores, Frank (Conception Bay, Nfld.)   2/18
Moriyama, Raymond (Vancouver, B.C.)   10/11
Mowat, Farley (Belleville, Ont.)   5/12
Mulroney, Brian (Baie Comeau, Que.)   3/20
Munro, John (Hamilton, Ont.)   3/13
Murray, Anne (Springhill, N.S.)   6/20

Newman, Peter (Vienna, Austria)   5/10

Parizeau, Jacques (Montreal, Que.)   8/9
Pepin, Jean Luc (Drummondville, Que.)   11/1
Pratt, Christopher (St. John's, Nfld.)   12/9

Regan, Gerald (Windsor, N.S.)   2/13
Reid, Kate (London, England)   11/4
Richardson, James (Winnipeg, Man.)   3/28
Richler, Mordecai (Montreal, Que.)   1/27
Robarts, John (Banff, Alta.)   1/11
Rohmer, Richard (Hamilton, Ont.)   1/24
Roman, Stephen (Slovakia)   4/17
Roy, Gabrielle (St. Boniface, Man.)   3/22
Ryan, Claude (Montreal, Que.)   1/26
Rubes, Jan (Volyne, Czechoslovakia)   6/6
Russell, Craig (Toronto, Ont.)   1/10

Sauve, Jeanne (Prud'Homme, Sask.)   4/26
Schreyer, Ed (Beausejour, Man.)   12/21
Selye, Hans (Vienna, Austria)   1/26
Sharp, Mitchell (Winnipeg, Man.)   5/11
Simard, Rene (Chicoutimi, Que.)   2/28
Simmonds, Robert H. (Hafford, Sask.)   4/6
Sinclair, Gordon (Toronto, Ont.)   6/3
Smallwood, Joey (Gambo, Nfld.)   11/24
Smythe, Conn (Toronto, Ont.)   2/1
Stanfield, Robert (Truro, N.S.)   4/11
Stevens, Sinclair (Esquesing Twp., Ont.)   2/11
Suzuki, David (Vancouver, B.C.)   3/24

Taylor, E.P. (Ottawa, Ont.)   1/29
Templeton, Charles (Toronto, Ont.)   10/7
Tennant, Vernonica (London, England)   1/15
Trudeau, Margaret (Vancouver, B.C.)   9/10
Trudeau, Pierre (Montreal, Que.)   10/18
Turner, John (Richmond, England)   6/7

Vigneault, Gilles (Natashquan, Que.)   11/27

Wagner, Claude (Shawinigan, Que.)   4/4
Whelan, Eugene (Amherstburg, Ont.)   7/11

---

# Canada's Largest Corporations

Source: The Financial Post 300; Toronto, Canada; Summer 1978
(Industrials, except M = Merchandiser)

| Company (Home office) | Sales or operating revenue C$000 | Foreign ownership % | Foreign owner(s) |
|---|---|---|---|
| General Motors of Canada Ltd. (Oshawa, Ont.) | 6,115,434[1] | 100 | General Motors Corp. Detroit |
| Ford Motor Company of Canada (Oakville, Ont.) | 5,725,000[1] | 88 | Ford Motor Co., Dearborn, Mich. |
| Imperial Oil Ltd. (Toronto) | 4,970,000[2] | 69.6 | Exxon Corp., New York |
| Canadian Pacific Ltd. (Montreal) | 4,700,136[3] | 29.2 | U.S. 14%; Britain 7.4%; other 7.8% |
| George Weston Ltd. (Toronto) M | 4,590,090 | | |
| Bell Canada (Montreal) | 3,559,887 | 6.1 | Wide distribution, U.S. and Europe |
| Alcan Aluminum Ltd. (Montreal) | 3,220,704[1] | 52.9 | U.S. 39.3%; other 13.6% |
| Chrysler Canada Ltd. (Windsor, Ont.) | 3,119,063[1] | 100 | Chrysler Corp., Detroit |
| Massey-Ferguson (Toronto) | 2,935,987[4] | 40 | Wide distribution, mostly U.S. |
| Canada Safeway Ltd. (Winnipeg) M | 2,581,893 | 100 | Safeway Stores Inc., Oakland, Cal. |
| Shell Canada Ltd. (Toronto) | 2,349,295[2] | 71 | Royal Dutch/Shell Group |
| Gulf Canada Ltd. (Toronto) | 2,322,100[2] | 68.3 | Gulf Oil Corp., Pittsburgh |
| Dominion Stores Ltd. (Toronto) M | 2,215,836 | — | |
| Simpson-Sears Ltd. (Toronto) M | 2,093,378 | 50 | Sears, Roebuck & Co., Chicago |
| Inco Ltd. (Toronto) | 2,077,364[4] | 35 | U.S. 33%; other 2% |
| Canada Packers Ltd. (Toronto) | 1,878,408 | — | |
| TransCanada PipeLines Ltd. (Toronto) | 1,870,325 | — | |
| MacMillan Bloedel Ltd. (Vancouver) | 1,707,260 | — | |
| Steinberg Inc. (Montreal) M | 1,767,687 | — | |
| Brascan Ltd. (Toronto) | 1,576,958[4] | 34 | Wide distribution, U.S. and Europe |

(1) Figures include sales to parent and affiliated companies: General Motors $2,753 million; Chrysler unstated; Ford $2,3 million. (Ford also consolidates $1,257 million sales of overseas subsidiaries.) (2) Excise taxes deducted. (3) After eliminati inter-company transactions. (4) In U.S. dollars.

## Canadian Government Budget

Source: Canadian Statistical Review (May 1978)
(millions of Canadian dollars)

### Expenditures

| Fiscal Year | National defense | Health and welfare | Agriculture | Post Office | Public works | Transport | Veterans affairs | Payments to provinces | Total expenditures |
|---|---|---|---|---|---|---|---|---|---|
| 1972-73 | 1,932.2 | 2,916.0 | 322.3 | 496.5 | 374.1 | 598.9 | 452.3 | 1,501.4 | 16,120.7 |
| 1973-74 | 2,232.0 | 3,775.0 | 426.0 | 591.0 | 470.0 | 827.0 | 538.0 | 1,874.0 | 20,056.0 |
| 1974-75 | 2,509.0 | 5,199.0 | 664.0 | 732.0 | 524.0 | 1,303.0 | 619.0 | 2,639.0 | 26,055.0 |
| 1975-76 | 2,973.0 | 9,731.0 | 651.0 | 913.0 | 624.0 | 1,185.0 | 684.0 | 2,460.0 | 33,977.0 |
| 1976-77 | 3,365.0 | 10,952.0 | 631.0 | 1,104.0 | 684.0 | 1,314.0 | 754.0 | 3,356.0 | 38,951.0 |
| 1977-78 | 3,556.0 | 11,091.0 | 828.0 | 1,181.0 | 739.0 | 1,380.0 | 834.0 | 3,651.0 | 41,380.0 |

### Revenues[1]

| Fiscal year | Personal income tax | Corporation income tax | Sales tax | Other excise tax[2] | Excise duties | Customs duties | Estate taxes | Post Office | Total budgetary revenues |
|---|---|---|---|---|---|---|---|---|---|
| 1972-73 | 7,172.8 | 2,653.5 | 2,288.7 | 400.4 | 638.0 | 1,181.8 | 61.4 | 470.1 | 16,601.6 |
| 1973-74 | 7,925.0 | 3,411.0 | 2,693.0 | 695.0 | 686.0 | 1,385.0 | 15.0 | 480.0 | 19,383.0 |
| 1974-75 | 10,069.0 | 4,285.0 | 2,900.0 | 2,083.0 | 748.0 | 1,809.0 | 7.0 | 485.0 | 24,909.0 |
| 1975-76 | 12,708.0 | 5,748.0 | 3,939.0 | 1,501.0 | 817.0 | 1,887.0 | 12.0 | 443.0 | 29,956.0 |
| 1976-77 | 14,620.0 | 5,377.0 | 4,529.0 | 1,146.0 | 865.0 | 2,097.0 | 70.0 | 615.0 | 32,650.0 |
| 1977-78 | 13,566.0 | 5,689.0 | 4,753.0 | 896.0 | 872.0 | 2,248.0 | 63.0 | 765.0 | 32,091.0 |

(1) This statement includes only receipts relating to revenue. Excluded are non-budgetary revenues such as Old Age Security Fund taxes, Prairie Farm Assistance Act levies, employer and employee contributions to government-held funds. (2) Beginning in Dec. 1973, this category includes oil export tax.

## Canadian Foreign Trade

Source: Canadian Statistical Review (May 1978)
(millions of Canadian dollars)

| | Exports including re-exports | | | | | Imports | | | | |
|---|---|---|---|---|---|---|---|---|---|---|
| Year | All countries | U.S. | Japan | UK | All other countries | All countries | U.S. | Japan | UK | All other countries |
| 1971 | 17,804 | 12,023 | 831 | 1,382 | 3,568 | 15,611 | 10,115 | 802 | 837 | 3,469 |
| 1972 | 19,977 | 13,922 | 881 | 1,328 | 3,846 | 18,654 | 12,870 | 1,103 | 949 | 3,320 |
| 1973 | 25,419.5 | 17,129 | 1,813.7 | 1,604.3 | 4,872.5 | 23,393.6 | 16,502 | 1,010.8 | 1,005.3 | 4,353 |
| 1974 | 32,176.7 | 21,325.1 | 2,229 | 1,902.9 | 6,719.7 | 31,639.3 | 21,305.9 | 1,428.1 | 1,126.5 | 6,488 |
| 1975 | 33,245.5 | 21,697.1 | 2,133.4 | 1,800.4 | 7,614.6 | 34,690.7 | 23,616.3 | 1,205.3 | 1,221.9 | 7,540.4 |
| 1976 | 38,146.3 | 25,795.9 | 2,389.3 | 1,867.7 | 8,093.4 | 37,468.8 | 25,736.6 | 1,525.4 | 1,152.4 | 7,757.7 |
| 1977 | 44,197.6 | 30,889.1 | 2,511.7 | 1,936.2 | 8,860.6 | 42,068.2 | 29,552 | 1,802.4 | 1,281.4 | 8,071.3 |

## Assets and Deposits of Chartered Banks in Canada

Source: Supplement to the Canada Gazette, July 8, 1978
(as of May 31, 1978 - thousands of Canadian dollars)

| Bank | Assets | Deposits | Bank | Assets | Deposits |
|---|---|---|---|---|---|
| Royal Bank of Canada | 37,692,800 | 34,231,181 | Banque Canadienne Nationale | 7,382,186 | 6,865,775 |
| Canadian Imperial Bank of Commerce | 34,431,346 | 31,488,931 | Banque Provinciale du Canada | 4,512,130 | 4,162,865 |
| | | | Mercantile Bank of Canada | 2,135,493 | 1,949,305 |
| Bank of Montreal | 28,468,809 | 25,867,340 | Bank of British Columbia | 1,317,251 | 1,219,238 |
| Bank of Nova Scotia | 24,556,061 | 22,177,402 | Commercial and Industrial Bank | 165,576 | 135,714 |
| Toronto-Dominion Bank | 21,648,797 | 19,453,347 | Northland Bank | 74,868 | 64,088 |

## Canadian Consumer Price Index

Source: Statistics Canada
(All items: 1971 = 100)

| Year | Avg. | Year | Avg. | Year | Avg. | Year | Avg. |
|---|---|---|---|---|---|---|---|
| 1963 | 77.2 | 1967 | 86.5 | 1971 | 100.0 | 1975 | 138.5 |
| 1964 | 78.6 | 1968 | 90.0 | 1972 | 104.8 | 1976 | 148.9 |
| 1965 | 80.5 | 1969 | 94.1 | 1973 | 112.7 | 1977 | 160.8 |
| 1966 | 83.5 | 1970 | 97.2 | 1974 | 125.0 | 1978 (Apr.) | 171.2 |

## Price Indexes By Item

Source: Canadian Statistical Review, May 1978 (1971 = 100)

| Year and month | All items | Food | Shelter | Clothing | Transportation | Health, personal | Recreation, education | Tobacco, alcohol | Total services |
|---|---|---|---|---|---|---|---|---|---|
| 1974 | 125.0 | 143.4 | 120.7 | 118.0 | 115.8 | 119.4 | 116.4 | 111.8 | 120.5 |
| 1975 | 138.5 | 161.9 | 130.9 | 125.1 | 129.4 | 133.0 | 128.5 | 125.3 | 133.4 |
| 1976 | 148.9 | 166.2 | 145.7 | 132.0 | 143.3 | 144.3 | 136.2 | 134.3 | 149.6 |
| 1977 | 160.8 | 180.1 | 159.3 | 141.0 | 153.3 | 155.0 | 142.7 | 143.8 | 163.2 |
| 1978 Jan. | 167.8 | 193.0 | 166.1 | 144.1 | 157.4 | 160.3 | 145.6 | 148.5 | 169.4 |
| Apr. | 171.2 | 200.4 | 168.1 | 143.2 | 159.8 | 163.3 | 145.8 | 154.0 | 172.0 |

## Personal Expenditure on Consumer Goods and Services in Current Dollars

Source: Statistics Canada
(millions of dollars)

| | 1969 | 1970 | 1971 | 1972 | 1973 | 1974 | 1975 | 197 |
|---|---|---|---|---|---|---|---|---|
| Food, beverage, and tobacco | 10,471 | 11,217 | 12,148 | 13,437 | 15,395 | 17,861 | 20,759 | 22,8 |
| Clothing and footwear | 3,908 | 4,034 | 4,143 | 4,550 | 5,120 | 5,944 | 6,782 | 7,7 |
| Gross rent, fuel and power | 8,742 | 9,861 | 10,581 | 11,412 | 12,506 | 14,209 | 16,399 | 19,0 |
| Furniture, furnishings, household equipment and operation | 4,658 | 4,785 | 5,295 | 6,135 | 7,304 | 8,868 | 10,251 | 11,4 |
| Medical care and health services | 1,912 | 1,758 | 1,618 | 1,804 | 2,054 | 2,404 | 2,790 | 3,2 |
| Transportation and communication | 6,863 | 6,946 | 8,014 | 9,030 | 10,551 | 12,167 | 14,196 | 16,4 |
| Recreation, entertainment, education and cultural services | 4,104 | 4,467 | 5,364 | 6,288 | 7,265 | 8,867 | 10,323 | 11,6 |
| Personal goods and services | 6,683 | 7,133 | 8,357 | 9,423 | 10,912 | 12,982 | 14,984 | 17,2 |
| Total | 47,492 | 50,327 | 55,616 | 62,208 | 71,278 | 83,441 | 97,016 | 110,5 |
| Durable goods | 6,975 | 6,799 | 7,883 | 9,440 | 11,481 | 13,650 | 16,026 | 17,8 |
| Semi-durable goods | 6,426 | 6,645 | 7,133 | 7,962 | 9,059 | 10,685 | 12,173 | 13,7 |
| Non-durable goods | 15,073 | 16,186 | 17,521 | 19,432 | 22,302 | 26,322 | 30,364 | 34,4 |
| Services | 19,018 | 20,697 | 23,079 | 25,374 | 28,436 | 32,784 | 38,453 | 44,5 |

## Canadian Shipping Traffic

Source: Canadian Statistical Review, May, 1978 (thousand short tons)
Total cargo handled includes cargo loaded and unloaded in foreign and coastwise shipping.

| Year and month | Halifax | Saint John | Quebec | Montreal | Toronto | Vancouver | All Ports | Coastw |
|---|---|---|---|---|---|---|---|---|
| 1972 | 11,355 | 10,263 | 14,901 | 20,431 | 4,534 | 29,894 | 298,076 | 122,4 |
| 1973 | 13,703 | 12,181 | 15,946 | 21,177 | 4,170 | 39,126 | 320,498 | 122,4 |
| 1974 | 13,290 | 9,998 | 12,943 | 19,654 | 4,605 | 36,761 | 302,138 | 118,2 |
| 1975 | 11,743 | 10,851 | 12,496 | 18,633 | 4,891 | 35,521 | 303,098 | 119,8 |
| 1976 | 11,828 | 10,740 | 13,082 | 17,063 | 5,185 | 35,364 | 306,482 | 118,7 |

## Canadian Sea Fish Catch and Exports

Source: Canadian Statistical Review, May 1978

| Year | Total Value | Landings of Sea Fish | | | | | | | Exports to[1] | | | Exports[1] | |
|---|---|---|---|---|---|---|---|---|---|---|---|---|---|
| | | Total | Nfld. | P.E.I. | N.S. | N.B. | Que. | B.C. | Total | U.S. | Other | Salmon | Lobste |
| | | (in metric tons) | | | | | | | (in millions of pounds) | | | | |
| 1972 | $219,829,000 | 1,004,763 | 294,520 | 27,170 | 296,652 | 178,944 | 82,600 | 152,726 | 642.0 | 443.6 | 169.3 | 77.6 | 19.8 |
| 1973 | 296,288,000 | 993,559 | 306,586 | 28,531 | 279,144 | 129,774 | 73,165 | 176,359 | 752.6 | 491.6 | 211.1 | 93.1 | 20.1 |
| 1974 | 259,108,000 | 834,165 | 234,510 | 16,329 | 283,045 | 160,120 | 53,524 | 132,904 | 551.4 | 394.6 | 155.0 | 78.5 | 18.2 |
| 1975 | 225,423,000 | 688,550 | 86,637 | 13,608 | 263,993 | 121,564 | 48,988 | 114,306 | 558.9 | 397.8 | 191.1 | 51.3 | 19.5 |
| 1976 | 364,754,000 | 1,063,071 | 340,241 | 17,123 | 368,456 | 117,937 | 41,948 | 177,366 | 652.9 | 427.2 | 225.7 | 47.2 | 19.3 |
| 1977 | 324,206,000 | 800,000 | 157,141 | 16,921 | 352,966 | 77,483 | 50,022 | 146,276 | 845.7 | 466.9 | 378.7 | 68.4 | 20.0 |

(1) Exports include sea and freshwater fish and shellfish products but exclude bait, meal, oils, offal, livers, fish roe, and fishery food and feeds.

## Value of Canadian Fishery Products and By-products

Source: Statistics Canada (thousands of Canadian dollars)
Final sales for the provinces by fish processors, handlers, and fishermen.

| Province | 1975 | 1976 | Province | 1975 | 197 |
|---|---|---|---|---|---|
| Newfoundland | 120,753 | 191,300 | Manitoba | | |
| Prince Edward Island | 27,760 | 30,409 | Saskatchewan | | |
| Nova Scotia | 208,754 | 251,705 | Alberta | 22,072 | 25,11 |
| New Brunswick | 116,274 | 144,881 | Northwest Territories | | |
| Quebec | 30,609 | 30,488 | British Columbia (2) | 167,018 | 297,62 |
| Ontario | 22,104 | 25,142 | Yukon | 81 | 9 |
| | | | Total(1) | 696,732 | 975,83 |

(1) The sum of the provincial totals differs from the Canada total as duplications (intershipments between provinces) have been removed from the Atlantic Coast totals. (2) Includes halibut landed in United States ports.

## Canadian Grain Deliveries at Western Grain Centers

Source: Canadian Grain Commission
(thousands of bushels)

Crop year 1975-76

| Province | Wheat | Oats | Barley | Rye | Flaxseed | Rapeseed | Total |
|---|---|---|---|---|---|---|---|
| Western Canada | 525,420 | 51,459 | 215,227 | 12,629 | 15,549 | 61,674 | 881,958 |
| Manitoba | 64,091 | 16,598 | 29,007 | 2,953 | 7,609 | 9,208 | 129,466 |
| Saskatchewan | 339,556 | 15,468 | 73,536 | 4,990 | 5,413 | 27,466 | 466,429 |
| Alberta & B.C. | 121,773 | 19,393 | 112,684 | 4,686 | 2,527 | 25,000 | 286,063 |

Crop year 1976-77

| Province | Wheat | Oats | Barley | Rye | Flaxseed | Rapeseed | Total |
|---|---|---|---|---|---|---|---|
| Western Canada | 549,030 | 54,864 | 267,039 | 11,863 | 9,688 | 45,417 | 937,901 |
| Manitoba | 70,494 | 16,843 | 44,738 | 2,589 | 4,814 | 5,647 | 145,125 |
| Saskatchewan | 351,786 | 13,608 | 82,428 | 5,454 | 3,568 | 19,279 | 476,123 |
| Alberta & B.C. | 126,750 | 24,413 | 139,873 | 3,820 | 1,306 | 20,491 | 316,653 |

# NATIONS OF THE WORLD

The nations of the world are listed in alphabetical order. Initials in the following articles include UN (United Nations), AS (Org. of American States), NATO (North Atlantic Treaty Org.), EC (European Communities or Common Market), AU (Org. of African Unity). Areas based primarily upon U.S. State Department figures.

*See special color section for maps and flags of all nations.*

## Afghanistan

### Republic of Afghanistan

**People: Population** (1977 est.): 20,340,000. **Pop. density:** 0.12 per sq. mi. **Ethnic groups:** Pushtuns (Pathans) nearly 50%; Tajiks nearly 30%; Uzbek over 5%; Hazara, others. **Languages:** Pushtun (Iranian), Dari Persian (spoken by Tajiks, Hazaras), Uzbek (Turkic). **Religions:** Moslem, mostly Sunni.

**Georgraphy: Area:** 253,861 sq. mi., slightly smaller than Texas. **Location:** Between Soviet Central Asia and the Indian subcontinent. **Neighbors:** Pakistan on E, S, Iran on W, USSR on (Turkmenistan, Uzbekistan, Tadzhikistan, Kirghizia); the NE tip touches China (Sinkiang). **Topography:** The country is landlocked and mountainous, much of it over 4,000 ft. above sea level. The Hindu Kush Mts. tower 16,000 ft. above Kabul and reach a height of 25,000 ft. to the E. Trade with Pakistan flows through the 35-mile long Khyber Pass. The climate is dry, with extreme temperatures, and large desert regions, though mountain rivers produce intermittent fertile valleys. **Capital:** Kabul. **Cities** (1976 est.): Kabul (met.) 587,643; Kandahar 149,361; Baghlan 118,269; Herat 116,003; Tagab 113,901.

**Government: Head of government:** Prime Min. Noor Mohammad Taraki; b. 1917; in office: Apr. 30, 1978. **Local divisions:** 28 provinces, each under a governor. **Armed forces:** regulars 110,000; reserves 162,000.

**Economy: Industries:** Textiles, carpets, cement, sheepskin, coats. **Chief crops:** Cotton, oilseeds, fruits. **Minerals:** Copper, lead, gas, coal, zinc, iron, silver, asbestos. **Crude oil reserves** (1978): 284 mln. bbls. **Other resources:** Wool, hides, karacul pelts. **Per capita arable land:** 1.0 acres. **Meat production** (1975): beef: 43,000 tons; lamb: 112,000 tons. **Electricity production** (1975): 748.00 mln. kwh. **Labor force:** 81% agriculture.

**Finance: Currency:** Afghani (May 1978: 45 = $1 US). **Gross domestic product** (1974 est.): $2 bln. **Per capita income** (1974): $100. **Imports** (1977): $308 mln.; partners (1974): USSR 50%, U.S., Jap., Ind., U.K., E. Ger. **Exports** (1977): $327 mln.; partners (1974): USSR 45%, U.S., U.K., Ind., Pak., Iran. **Tourists** (1975): 91,100; receipts (1975): $12 million. **International reserves** (May 1978): $323.71 mln. **Consumer prices** change in 1976): 0.04%

**Transport: Motor vehicles:** in use (1971): 38,400 passenger cars, 26,100 commercial vehicles.

**Communications: Radios:** 111,000 in use (1974), **Telephones in use** (1975): 25,000. **Daily newspaper circulation** (1974): 499,000; 27 per 1,000 pop.

**Health: Life expectancy at birth** (1975): 39.9 male; 40.7 female. **Births** (annual per 1,000 pop. 1972-75): 49.2. **Deaths** (annual per 1,000 pop. 1972-75): 23.8. **Natural increase** (annual 1970-75): 2.54%. **Pop. per hospital bed** (1975): 4,396. **Pop. per physician** (1975): 17,948. **Infant mortality** (per 1,000 live births 1975): 183.

**Education: Literacy (1975):** 8%. **Pop. 5-19:** in school (1975): 12%, per teacher (1975): 258.

Afghanistan, occupying a favored invasion route since antiquity, has been variously known as Ariana or Bactria (in ancient times) and Khorasan (in the Middle Ages). Foreign empires alternated rule with local emirs and kings until the 18th century, when unified kingdom was established. In 1973, a military coup ushered in a republic.

Afghanistan has received aid from the U.S., USSR, and China. Largest trade partner is the USSR, natural gas the chief export. Pro-Soviet leftists took power in a bloody 1978 coup.

In recent centuries, isolation has hampered modernization.

## Albania

### People's Republic of Albania

**People: Population** (1977 est.): 2,620,000. **Pop. density:** 36.04 per sq. mi. **Urban** (1971): 33.8%. **Ethnic groups:** Albanians (Gegs in N, Tosks in S) 95%, Greeks 2.5%. **Languages:**

Albanian (Tosk is official dialect), Greek. **Religions:** (historically) Moslems 70%, Orthodox 20%, Roman Catholic 10%. All public worship and religious institutions were outlawed in 1967.

**Geography: area:** 11,100 sq. mi., slightly larger than Maryland. **Location:** On SE coast of Adriatic Sea. **Neighbors:** Greece on S, Yugoslavia on N, E. **Topography:** Apart from a narrow coastal plain, Albania consists of hills and mountains covered with scrub forest, cut by small E-W rivers. **Capital:** Tirana. **Cities** (1976 est.): Tirana 192,300; Shkoder 62,500; Durres 61,000; Vlone 58,400.

**Government: Head of state:** Pres. Haxhi Lleshi; b. 1913; in office: Aug. 1953; **Head of government:** Chmn. Mehmet Shehu; b. 1913; in office: July 1954; **Head of Communist Party:** Enver Hoxha; b. 1908; in office: 1941. **Local divisions:** 26 administrative districts and one independent city. **Armed forces:** regulars 67,500; reserves 100,000.

**Economy: Industries:** Chem. fertilizers, textiles, electric cables. **Chief crops:** Grain, corn, sugar beets, cotton, tobacco, fruits. **Minerals:** Coal, chromium, copper, bitumen, iron, oil. **Other resources:** Forests. **Per capita arable land:** 0.5 acres. **Meat production** (1975): beef: 20,000 tons; pork: 11,000 tons; lamb: 22,000 tons. **Electricity production** (1975): 1.80 bln. kwh. **Labor force:** 62% agriculture.

**Finance: Currency:** Lek (1974: 10.25 = $1 US). **Gross domestic product** (1974 est.) $1.7 bln. **Per capita income** (1974): $650. **Imports** (1975): $250 mln.; partners (1975): P.R. China, E. Eur., It. **Exports** (1974): $200 mln.; partners (1975): P.R. China, E. Eur.

**Transport: Motor vehicles:** in use (1971): 38,400 passenger cars, 26,100 commercial vehicles. **Chief ports:** Durres, Vlone.

**Communications: Television sets:** 4,000 in use (1974), **Radios:** 173,000 in use (1974), **Telephones in use** (1963): 10,150. **Daily newspaper circulation** (1974): 115,000; 48 per 1,000 pop.

**Health: Life expectancy at birth** (1966): 64.9 male; 67.0 female. **Births** (per 1,000 pop. 1974): 33.4. **Deaths** (annual per 1,000 pop. 1972-75): 6.5. **Natural increase** (1971): 2.52%. **Pop. per hospital bed** (1975): 146. **Pop. per physician** (1975): 1,096. **Infant mortality** (per 1,000 live births 1965): 86.8.

**Education: Literacy** (1975): 75%. **Pop. 5-19:** in school (1975): 67%, per teacher (1975): 34.

Ancient Illyria was conquered by Romans, Slavs, and Turks (15th century); the latter Islamized the population. Independent Albania was proclaimed in 1912, republic was formed in 1920. Self-styled King Zog I ruled 1925-39, until Italy invaded.

Communist partisans took over in 1944, allied Albania with USSR, then broke with USSR in 1960 over de-Stalinization. Strong political alliance with China followed, leading to several billion dollars in aid, which was curtailed after 1974. China cut off aid in 1978 when Albania attacked its policies after the 1977 death of Chinese ruler Mao Tse-tung.

In 1971, after years of mistrust, Albania resumed relations with Greece and Yugoslavia, but ties with U.S. and USSR are still rejected.

Industrialization, pressed in 1960s, slowed in 1970s. Large-scale purges of officials occurred 1973-76.

## Algeria

### Democratic and Popular Republic of Algeria

**People: Population** (1977 est.); 17,910,000. **Age distrib.** (%): 0–14: 47.2; 15–59: 46.2; 60+: 6.6. **Pop. density:** 19.47 per sq. mi. **Urban** (1974): 52.0%. **Ethnic groups:** Arabs 75%, Berbers 25%. **Languages:** Arab, Berber (indigenous language), French (spoken by Arab elite). **Religions:** Sunni Moslem the state religion.

**Geography: Area:** 919,951 sq. mi., more than 3 times the size of Texas. **Location:** In NW Africa, from Mediterranean Sea into Sahara Desert. **Neighbors:** Morocco on W, Mauritania, Mali, Niger on S, Libya, Tunisia on E. **Topography:** The Tell, located on the coast, comprises fertile plains 50-100 miles wide, with a moderate climate and adequate rain. Two major chains of the Atlas Mts., running roughly E-W, and reaching 7,000 ft., enclose a dry plateau region. Below lies the Sahara, mostly desert with major mineral resources. **Capital:** Algiers. **Cities** (1973 est.): Algiers (met.) 1,200,000; (1966 cen.): Oran 327,493; Constantine 243,558; Annaba 152,006.

**Government: Head of state** and of government: Pres. Houari Boumedienne; b. 1925; in office: June 19, 1965. **Local divisions:** 31 wilayas (states); governors are responsible to the center. **Armed forces:** regulars 75,800; reserves 100,000.

**Economy: Industries:** Wine, cigarettes, oil products, iron, steel, textiles, fertilizer, plastics. **Chief crops:** Grains, corn, wine-grapes, potatoes, artichokes, flax, olives, tobacco, dates, figs, pomegranates. **Minerals:** Oil, iron, zinc, lead, mercury, coal, copper, natural gas, phosphates. **Crude oil reserves** (1978): 6.60 bln. bbls. **Other resources:** Cork trees. **Per capital arable land:** 1.0 acres. **Meat production** (1975): beef: 28,000 tons; lamb: 55,000 tons. **Fish catch** (1975): 37,700 metric tons. **Electricity production** (1976): 3.96 bln. kwh. **Labor force:** 50% agric.; 6% manuf.

**Finance: Currency:** Dinar (May 1978: 4.02 = $1 US). **Gross domestic product** (1976): $14.84 bln. **Per capita income** (1974): $660. **Imports** (1977): $7.09 bln.; partners (1977): France 33%, E. Ger. 11%, U.S. 11%, It. 8%. **Exports** (1977): $5.81 bln.; partners (1977): U.S. 22%, E. Ger. 18%, France 13%, It. 10%. **Tourists** (1975): 296,500; receipts (1975): $51 million. **Balance of payments** (1976): +$622,000,000. **National budget** (1974): $5.95 bln. revenues; $3.13 bln. expenditures. **International reserves** (May 1978): $1.50 bln. **Consumer prices** (change in 1976): 9.5%.

**Transport: Railway traffic** (1974): 657.02 mln. passenger-miles; 1.18 bln. net ton-miles. **Motor vehicles:** in use (1974); 180,000 passenger cars, 95,000 commercial vehicles; assembled (1976): 4,056 commercial vehicles. **Chief ports:** Algiers, Oran.

**Communications: Television sets:** 410,000 in use (1974), 32,000 manufactured (1973). **Radios:** 3,220,000 in use (1974), 19,000 manufactured (1973). **Telephones in use** (1977): 266,470. **Daily newspaper circulation** (1974): 275,000; 17 per 1,000 pop.

**Health: Life expectancy at birth** (1975): 51.7 male; 54.8 female. **Births** (annual per 1,000 pop. 1972-75): 47.8. **Deaths** (per annual 1,000 pop. 1972-75): 15.4. **Natural increase** (annual 1970-75); 3.33%. **Pop. per hospital bed.** (1975): 327. **Pop. per physician** (1975): 6,535. **Infant mortality** (per 1,000 live births 1965): 86.3.

**Education: Literacy** (1975): 26%. **Pop. 5-19:** in school (1975): 52%, per teacher (1975): 67.

Earliest known inhabitants were ancestors of Berbers, followed by Phoenicians, Romans, Vandals, and, finally, Arabs; but 25% still speak Berber dialects. Turkey ruled 1518 to 1830, when France took control.

Large-scale European immigration and French cultural inroads did not prevent an Arab nationalist movement from launching guerilla war. Peace, and French withdrawal, was negotiated with French Pres. Charles de Gaulle. One million Europeans left.

Ahmed Ben Bella was the victor of infighting, and ruled 1962-65, when an army coup installed Col. Houari Boumedienne as leader. Ben Bella and other opponents remain under house arrest.

In 1967, Algeria declared war with Israel, broke with U.S., and moved toward eventual military and political ties with the USSR. French oil interests were partly siezed in 1971, but relations with the West have since improved, based on oil and gas exports; U.S. ties were resumed 1974.

Algeria strongly backs Saharan guerrillas against Morocco, Mauritania and France.

The one-party Socialist regime faces endemic mass unemployment and poverty, despite land reform and industrialization attempts.

## Andorra

### Valleys of Andorra

**People: Population** (1977 est.): 20,000. **Age distrib. (%):** 0–14: 29.2; 14–59: 61.7; 60+: 9.1. **Pop. density:** 111.11 per sq. mi. **Ethnic groups:** Spanish over 60%, Andorran 30%, French 6%. **Languages:** Catalan (official), Spanish, French. **Religions:** Roman Catholic.

**Geography: Area:** 180 sq. mi., half the size of New York City.

**Location:** In Pyrenees Mtns. **Neighbors:** Spain on S, France on N. **Topography:** High mountains and narrow valleys over the country. **Capital:** Andorra la Vella.

**Government: Head of state:** Co-Princes are the president of France (Valery Giscard D'Estaing) and the bishop of Urgel in Spain. **Local divisions:** 6 parishes.

**Economy: Industries:** Tourism, sheep-raising.

**Finance: Currency:** Franc, Peseta.

**Communications: Radios:** 6,500 in use (1974).

**Health: Births** (per 1,000 pop. 1976): 16.5. **Deaths** (per 1,000 pop. 1976): 5.0. **Natural increase** (1976): 1.15%.

The present political status, with joint sovereignty by France and the bishop of Urgel, dates from 1278.

Tourism, especially skiing, is the economic mainstay. A new road from France is being built.

## Angola

### People's Republic of Angola

**People: Population** (1972 est.): 5,800,000. **Pop. density:** 12.05 per sq. mi. **Ethnic groups:** Ovimbundu 38%, Kimbundu 23%; Bacongo 13%, European 1%; Mesticos 2%. **Languages:** Portuguese (official), various Bantu languages. **Religions:** Roman Catholic 30%, Protestant 12%, others.

**Geography: Area:** 481,351 sq. mi., larger than Texas and California combined. **Location:** In SW Africa on Atlantic coast. **Neighbors:** Namibia (SW Africa) on S, Zambia on E, Zaire on N; Cabinda, an enclave separated from rest of country by short Atlantic coast of Zaire, borders Congo Republic. **Topography:** Most of Angola consists of a plateau elevated 3,000 to 5,000 feet above sea level, rising from a narrow coastal strip. There is also a temperate highland area in the west-central region, a desert in the S, and a tropical rain forest covering Cabinda. **Capital:** Luanda. **Cities** (1970 cen.): Luanda (met.) 475,328; Huambo 61,885; Lobito 59,528.

**Government: Head of state:** Pres. Agostinho Neto; b. 1922; in office: Nov. 11, 1975. **Head of government:** Prime Min. Lopo do Nascimento. **Local divisions:** 16 provinces. **Armed forces:** regulars 31,500.

**Economy: Industries:** Alcohol, cotton goods, fishmeal, paper, palm oil, footwear. **Chief crops:** Coffee (5% of world crop), corn, sugar, palm oil, cotton, wheat, tobacco, caeao, sisal, wax. **Minerals:** Iron, diamonds (over 2 min. carats a year), copper, manganese, sulphur, phosphates, oil. **Crude oil reserves** (1978): 1.16 bln. bbls. **Per capita arable land:** 0.3 acres. **Meat production** (1975): beef: 46,000 tons; pork: 12,000 tons. **Fish catch** (1975): 183,900 metric tons. **Electricity production** (1975): 1.31 bln. kwh. **Labor force:** 63% agriculture.

**Finance: Currency:** Escudo (1975: 28.89 = $1 US). **Per capita income** (1974): $510. **Imports** (1974): $625 mln.; partners (1973): Port. 26%, W. Ger. 13%, U.S. 10%, U.K. 8%. **Exports** (1974): $1.23 bln.; partners (1973): U.S. 28%, Port. 25%, Can. 10%, Jap. 9%. **Tourists** (1974): 995,100; receipts (1974) $109 bln.

**Transport: Railway traffic** (1974): 259.58 mln. passenger-miles; 3.39 bln. net ton-miles. **Motor vehicles:** in use (1973) 127,300 passenger cars, 35,700 commercial vehicles. **Chief ports:** Lobito, Luanda.

**Communications: Radios:** 116,000 licensed (1974), 26,000 manufactured (1973). **Telephones in use** (1977): 31,200. **Daily newspaper circulation** (1974): 78,000; 13 per 1,000 pop.

**Health: Life expectancy at birth** (1975): 37.0 male; 40.1 female. **Births** (annual per 1,000 pop. 1972-75): 47.2. **Deaths** (annual per 1,000 pop. 1972-75): 24.5. **Natural increase** (annual 1970-75): 2.27%. **Pop. per hospital bed** (1975): 538. **Pop. per physician** (1975): 15,744. **Infant mortality** (per 1,000 live births 1972): 24.1.

**Education: Literacy** (1975): 12%. **Pop. 5-19:** in school (1975): 30%, per teacher (1975): 111.

From the early centuries A.D. to 1500, Bantu tribes penetrated most of the region. Portuguese came in 1583, allied with the Bakongo kingdom in the north, and developed the slave trade. Large-scale colonization did not begin until the 20th century, when 400,000 Portuguese immigrated.

A guerrilla war begun in 1961 lasted until 1974, when Portugal offered independence. Violence between the National Front based in Zaire, the Soviet-backed Popular Movement, and the National Union, aided by the U.S. and S. Africa, killed thousands lacks, drove most whites to emigrate, and completed economic ruin. Some 15,000 Cuban troops and massive Soviet aid ed the Popular Movement win most of the country after independence Nov. 11, 1975. Some units of the National Union inued to resist in 1978. The regime, headed by whites or attos, crushed with Cuban help a revolt by black leaders n the Popular Movement in May, 1977.

ussian influence, backed by 20-25,000 Cubans, 1-2,000 East nans, and Portuguese Communists, is strong in the Marxist ne.

# Argentina

## Argentine Republic

**eople: Population** (1977 est.): 26,060,000. **Age distrib.** 0–14: 28.6; 15–59: 59.6; 60+: 11.7. **Pop. density:** 24.31 sq. mi. **Urban** (1970): 80.4%. **Ethnic groups:** Europeans (Spanish, Italian), Indians, Mestizos, Arabs. **Languages:** nish. **Religions:** Roman Catholic 94%, Protestant 2%, Jew-2%.

**eography: Area:** 1,072,067 sq. mi., 4 times the size of as, second largest in S. America. **Location:** Occupies most outhern S. America. **Neighbors:** Chile on W, Bolivia, Paray on N, Brazil, Uruguay on NE. **Topography:** The mountains Vest, are grouped into 4 systems: the Andean, Central, Miss, and Southern. Aconcagua is the highest peak in the Westhemisphere, altitude 22,834. East of the Andes are great ns, heavily wooded and called the Gran Chaco in the N, and fertile, treeless Pampas in the central region, given over to at and cattle raising. Patagonia, in the S, is bleak and arid; oleum and sheep are its main products. Rio de la Plata, 170 140 miles, is mostly fresh water, from 2,500-mi. Paranak and 00-mi. Uruguay. R. **Capital:** Buenos Aires. **Cities** (1975 est.): nos Aires (met.) 8,435,840; Rosario (met.) 806,942; Cordoba t.) 790,508; La Plata (met.) 478,666; Mendoza (met.) ,896.

**overnment: Head of state:** Pres. Jorge Rafael Videla; b. . 2, 1925; in office: Mar. 24, 1976. **Local divisions:** 22 provs, 1 natl. ter. and 1 federal dist., formerly with elected legisres and governors; now under military governors. **Armed ces:** regulars 129,900; reserves 250,000.

**conomy: Industries:** Meat processing, flour milling, chemis, textiles, machinery, autos. **Chief crops:** Cotton, grains, n, grapes, linseed, sugar, fruit, tobacco, peanuts. Grains are orted. **Minerals:** Oil, coal, lead, zinc, iron, sulphur, silver, per, gold. **Crude oil reserves** (1978): 2.53 bln. bbls. **Per ita arable land:** 2.2 acres. **Meat production** (1976): beef: 9 mln. tons; pork: 248,400 tons; lamb: 133,500 tons. **Fish ch** (1975): 224,400 metric tons. **Electricity production** 77): 27.34 bln. kwh. **Labor force:** 15% agric.; 20% manuf.

**inance: Currency:** Peso (May 1978: 776.50 = $1 US). **ss domestic product** (1975): $22.09 bln. **Per capita in** (1975): $1,876. **Imports** (1976): $3.03 bln.; partners 73): U.S. 22%, Jap. 11%, W. Ger. 11%, Braz. 9%. **Exports** 76): $3.92 bln.; partners (1973): It. 12%, Braz. 10%, W. Ger. , U.S. 8%. **Tourists** (1975): 1,200,000; receipts (1975): $154 ion. **Balance of payments** (1977): +$1,845,000,000. **Nanal budget** (1977): $2.13 bln. revenues; $3.56 bln. expendies. **International reserves** (Mar. 1978): $4.39 bln. **Con-ner prices** (change in 1977): 176.1%.

**Fransport: Railway traffic** (1975): 8.93 bln. passenger-miles; 3 bln. net ton-miles. **Motor vehicles:** in use (1974): 27,500 passenger cars, 879,800 commercial vehicles; manutured (1977): 168,000 passenger cars; (1976): 171,210 comrcial vehicles. **Civil aviation:** 2,981 mln. passenger-miles 77); 78,686 mln. freight ton-miles (1977). **Chief ports:** nos Aires, Bahia Blanca, La Plata.

**Communications: Television sets:** 4,500,000 in use (1974), ,000 manufactured (1975). **Radios:** 21,000,000 in use 73). **Telephones in use** (1977): 2,539,535. **Daily newspa-r circulation** (1974): 3,683,000; 154 per 1,000 pop.

**Health: Life expectancy at birth** (1975): 65.16 male; 71.38 nale. **Births** (per 1,000 pop. 1973): 22.7. **Deaths** (Annual per 00 pop. 1972-75): 8.8. **Natural increase** (1970): 1.35%. **Pop.** r **hospital bed** (1975): 186. **Pop. per physician** (1975): 494. ant mortality (per 1,000 live births 1970): 58.9.

**Education:** Literacy (1975): 93%. **Pop. 5-19:** in school 75): 58%, per teacher (1975): 27.

lomadic Indians roamed the Pampas when Spaniards arrived, 5-1516, led by Juan Diaz de Solis. Nearly all the Indians

were killed by the late 19th century. The colonists won independence, 1810-1819, and a long period of disorders ended in a strong centralized government.

Large-scale Italian, German, and Spanish immigraion in the decades after 1880 spurred modernization, making Argentina the most prosperous, educated, and industrialized of the major Latin American nations. Social reforms were enacted in the 1920s, but military coups prevailed 1930-46, until the election of Gen. Juan Peron as president.

Peron, with his wife Eva Duarte, effected labor reforms, but also suppressed speech and press freedoms, closed religious schools, and ran the country into debt. A 1955 coup exiled Peron, who was followed by a series of military and civilian regimes. Peron returned in 1973, and was once more elected president. He died ten months later, succeeded by his wife, Isabel, who had been elected vice president, and who became the first woman head of state in the Western hemisphere. Terrorist violence of right and left, long a problem, worsened in the 1970's, with 900 killed in 1975 alone; lucrative kidnappings netted tens of millions of dollars.

A military junta ousted Mrs. Peron in 1976 amid charges of corruption. Under a continuing state of siege, the army battled guerrillas and leftists, killed 2,000-5,000 people, and jailed and tortured others.

Gains in Argentina's productive agricultural sector did not prevent catastrophic inflation in the 1970s, and balance of payment problems.

# Australia

## Commonwealth of Australia

**People: Population** (1977 est): 14,070,000. **Age distrib.** (%): 0–14: 28.4; 15–59: 59.2; 60+: 12.4. **Pop. density:** 4.74 per sq. mi. **Urban** (1971): 85.6%. **Ethnic groups:** British 95%, other European 3%, aborigines (including mixed) 1.5%. **Languages:** English. **Religions:** Anglican 36%, other Protestant 20%, Roman Catholic 25%.

**Geography: Area:** 2,965,368 sq. mi., almost as large as the 48 conterminous U.S. states. **Location:** SE of Asia, Indian O. is W and S, Pacific O. (Coral, Tasman Seas) is E; they meet N of Australia in Timor and Arafura Seas: Tasmania lies 150 mi. S of Victoria-state, across Bass Strait. **Neighbors:** Nearest island neighbors are Indonesia, Papua New Guinea on N, Solomons, Fiji, and New Zealand on E. **Topography:** An island continent, Australia is bisected by the Tropic of Capricorn. The Great Dividing Range along the E coast has Mt. Kosciusko, 7,316 ft. The W plateau rises to 2,000 ft., with arid areas in the Great Sandy and Great Victoria Deserts. The NW part of Western Australia and Northern Terr. are arid and hot. The NE has heavy rainfall and Cape York Peninsula has jungles. The Murray R. rises in New South Wales and flows 1,600 mi. to the Indian O. **Capital:** Canberra. **Cities** (1974 est.): Sydney (met.) 2,898,330; Melbourne (met.) 2,620,400; Brisbane (met.) 940,800; Adelaide (met.) 885,400; Perth (met.) 760,000.

**Government: Head of state:** Queen Elizabeth II, represented by Gov.-Gen. Zelman Cowen; b. Oct. 7, 1919; in office: Dec. 8, 1977; **Head of government:** Prime Min. John Malcolm Fraser; b. May 21, 1930; in office: Dec. 22, 1975. **Local divisions:** 6 states, with elected governments and substantial powers; 2 territories. **Armed forces:** regulars 69,650; reserves 33,331.

**Economy: Industries:** Iron, steel, textiles, electrical equip., chemicals, autos, aircraft, ships, machinery. **Chief crops:** Wheat (a leading export), sugar, wine, fruit, vegetables. **Minerals:** Major uranium, iron, oil, gas producer, gold, coal, copper, silver, lead, nickel, tin, bauxite. **Crude oil reserves** (1978): 2.00 bln. bbls. **Other resources:** Wool (30% of world output). **Per capita arable land:** 8.1 acres. **Meat production** (1976): beef: 1.87 mln. tons; lamb: 594,000 tons. **Fish catch** (1975): 103,300 metric tons. **Electricity production** (1977): 82.46 bln. kwh. **Labor force:** 7% agric.; 25% manuf.

**Finance: Currency:** Dollar (May 1978: 1 = $1.13 US). **Gross domestic product** (1977): $88.08 bln. **Per capita income** (1975): $6,311. **Imports** (1976): $11.08 bln; partners (1976): U.S. 20%, Jap. 19.5%, U.K. 13%, W. Ger. 7%. **Exports** (1976): $12.87 bln.; partners (1976): Jap. 33%, U.S. 10%, U.K. 4%, USSR 4%. **Tourists** (1973): 472,100; receipts (1975): $303 million. **Balance of payments** (1977): −$1,150,000,000. **National budget** (1977): $26.58 bln. revenues; $29.45 bln. expenditures. **International reserves** (May 1978): $2.57 bln. **Consumer prices** (change in 1977): 12.3%.

**Transport: Railway traffic** (1975): 18.50 bln. net ton-miles.

**Motor vehicles:** in use (1975): 5,012,300 passenger cars, 1,200,300 commercial vehicles; manufactured (1977): 367,200 passenger cars; 85,200 commercial vehicles. **Civil aviation:** 11,946 mln. passenger-miles (1977); 256,587 mln. freight ton-miles (1977). **Chief ports:** Sydney, Melbourne, Newcastle, Port Kemble, Fremantle, Geelong.

**Communications: Television sets:** 3,013,000 licensed (1973), 465,000 manufactured (1975). **Radios:** 2,815,000 licensed (1973), 941,000 manufactured (1974). **Telephones in use** (1977): 5,501,508. **Daily newspaper circulation** (1973): 5,126,000; 386 per 1,000 pop.

**Health: Life expectancy at birth** (1967): 67.63 male; 74.15 female. **Births** (per 1,000 pop. 1975): 17.3. **Deaths** (per 1,000 pop. 1975): 8.1. **Natural increase** (1975): .92%. **Pop per hospital bed** (1975): 79.**Pop per physician** (1975): 731. **Infant mortality** (per 1,000 live births 1974): 16.1

**Education: Literacy** (1975): 98%. **Pop. 5-19:** in school (1975): 78%, per teacher (1975): 25.

Capt. James Cook explored the E coast in 1770, when the continent was inhabited by a variety of different tribes. Within decades, Britain had claimed the entire continent, which became a penal colony until immigration increased in the 1850s. The commonwealth was proclaimed Jan. 1, 1901, as a federation of six states and two territories. Northern Terr. is slated for 1979 statehood. Their capitals and Mar., 1977 pop.:

| | Area (sq. mi.) | Population |
|---|---|---|
| New South Wales, Sydney | 309,418 | 4,945,200 |
| Victoria, Melbourne | 87,854 | 3,773,700 |
| Queensland, Brisbane | 666,699 | 2,130,700 |
| South Aust., Adelaide | 379,824 | 1,273,700 |
| Western Aust., Perth | 974,843 | 1,190,300 |
| Tasmania, Hobart | 26,171 | 410,000 |
| Northern Terr., Darwin | 519,633 | 104,900 |
| Aust. Capital Terr., Canberra | 926 | 207,400 |

The U.S. succeeded Britain as the major ally following two world wars, with Japan as the leading trade and development partner in the 1970s.

Australia's racially discriminatory immigration policies were abandoned in 1973, after 3 million Europeans (half British) had entered since 1945. In 1975 there was a net emigration of 5,000. The 50,000 aborigines and 150,000 part-aborigines are mostly detribalized, but there are several preserves in the Northern Territory. They remain economically disadvantaged.

Australia's agricultural success makes it among the top exporters of beef, lamb, wool, and wheat. Major mineral deposits have been developed as well, largely for exports. Industrialization has been completed since 1945.

Australia harbors many plant and animal species not found elsewhere, including the kangaroo, koala bear, platypus, dingo (wild dog), Tasmanian devil (racoon-like marsupial), wombat (bear-like marsupial), and barking and frilled lizards.

## Australian External Territories

**Norfolk Island** was taken over by Australia, 1914. It has an area of 13.5 sq. mi. and a population (1974) of 1,894. The soil is very fertile and is suitable for citrus fruits, bananas, and coffee. Many of the inhabitants are descendants of the Bounty mutineers; some moved to Norfolk in 1856 from Pitcairn Is.

**Coral Sea Islands Territory,** 1 sq. mi., is administered from Norfolk Is.

**Territory of Ashmore and Cartier Islands,** area 2 sq. mi., in the Indian Ocean came under the authority of Australia May 1934 and are administered as part of Northern Territory. **Heard** and **McDonald Islands** are administered by the Department of Science.

**Cocos (Keeling) Islands,** 27 small coral islands in the Indian Ocean 1,300 miles NW of Australia. Pop. (1978) 600, area: 5 1/2 sq. mi.

**Christmas Island,** 52 sq. mi., pop 2,900 (1974), 230 mi. S of Java, was transferred by Britain in 1958. It has phosphate deposits.

**Australian Antarctic Territory** was claimed by Australia in 1933, including 2,472,000 sq. mi. of territory S of 60th parallel S Lat. and between 160th-45th meridians E Long.

## Austria

### Republic of Austria

**People: Population** (1977 est.): 7,520,000. **Age distrib.** (%): 0–14: 24.0; 15–59: 55.4; 60+: 20.6. **Pop. density:** 232.29 per sq. mi. **Urban** (1971): 51.9%. **Ethnic groups:** German 98%, Slovene, Croatian, Hungarian, Italian. **Languages:** German, Slovene. **Religions:** Roman Catholic 90%, Protestant 10%.

**Geography: Area:** 32,374 sq. mi., slightly smaller than Maine. **Location:** In S Central Europe. **Neighbors:** Switzerland, Liechtenstein on W, W. Germany, Czechoslovakia on N, Hungary on E, Yugoslavia, Italy on S. **Topography:** Austria is primarily mountainous, with the Alps and foothills covering the western and southern provinces. The eastern provinces and Vienna are located in the Danube River Basin. **Capital:** Vienna. **Cities** (1971 cen.): Vienna 1,614,841; Graz 248,500; Linz 202,874.

**Government: Head of State:** Pres. Rudolf Kirschschlager, b. Mar. 20, 1915; in office: Apr. 24, 1974; **Head of government:** Chancellor Bruno Kreisky; b. Jan. 22, 1911; in office: Mar. 1970. **Local divisions:** 9 lander (states), each with a legislature. **Armed forces:** regulars 62,300; reserves 112,700.

**Economy: Industries:** Steel, machinery, autos, electrical and optical equip., glassware, sport goods, paper, textiles, chemicals, cement. **Chief crops:** Grains, corn, potatoes, beets, grapes. **Minerals:** Iron ore, oil, magnesite, aluminum, coal, lignite, copper, graphite. **Crude oil reserves** (1977): 154.50 mln. bbls. **Other resources:** Forests, hydro power. **Per capita arable land:** 0.5 acres. **Meat production** (1976): beef: 184,000 tons; pork: 328,200 tons. **Electricity production** (1977): 37 bln. kwh. **Labor force:** 16% agric.; 29% manuf.

**Finance: Currency:** Schilling (May 1978: 15.11 = $1 U.S.). **Gross domestic product** (1976): $48.15 bln. **Per capita income** (1976): $4,823. **Imports** (1977): $14.25 bln.; partners (1974): W. Ger. 40%, It. 7%, Switz. 7%, U.K. 4%. **Exports** (1977): $9.81 bln.; partners (1974): W. Ger. 20%, Switz. 10%, It. 10%. **Tourists** (1975): 11,539,500; receipts (1975): $2.777 bln. **Balance of payments** (1977): −$349,000,000. **National budget** (1976): $8.23 bln. revenues; $10.24 bln. expenditures. **International reserves** (May 1978): $4.60 bln. **Consumer prices** (change in 1977): 5.5%.

**Transport: Railway traffic** (1975): 4.15 bln. passenger-miles; 5.90 bln. net ton-miles. **Motor vehicles:** in use (1977): 1,720,700 passenger cars, 445,600 commercial vehicles; manufactured (1977): 960 passenger cars; 7,920 commercial vehicles. **Civil aviation:** 572 mln. passenger-miles (1977); 6,9 mln. freight ton-miles (1977).

**Communications: Television sets:** 1,856,000 licensed (1974), 404,000 manufactured (1975). **Radios:** 2,170,000 licensed (1974), 82,000 manufactured (1972). **Telephones in use** (1977): 2,281,251. **Daily newspaper circulation** (1973): 2,316,000; 308 per 1,000 pop.

**Health: Life expectancy at birth** (1975): 67.7 male; 74.9 male. **Births** (per 1,000 pop. 1976): 11.6. **Deaths** (per 1,000 pop. 1975): 12.6. **Natural increase** (1976): −.10%. **Pop. per hospital bed** (1975): 146. **Pop. per physician** (1975): 1,010. **Infant mortality** (per 1,000 live births 1975): 20.6.

**Education: Literacy** (1975): 75%. **Pop. 5-19:** in school (1975): 67%, per teacher (1975): 34.

Rome conquered Austrian lands around 15 B.C. After centuries of invasions by Celts, Goths, Avars, and Magyars, Austria was incorporated into Charlemagne's empire in 788. By 1300 the House of Hapsburg had gained control; they added vast territories in all parts of Europe to their realm in the next few hundred years.

Austrian dominance of Germany was undermined in the 18 century and ended by Prussia by 1866. But the Congress of Vienna, 1815, confirmed Austrian control of a large empire in southeast Europe, conquered from the Turks over centuries of battle, and consisting of Germans, Hungarians, Slavs, Italians and others.

The dual Austro-Hungarian monarchy was established in 1867, giving autonomy to Hungary and 50 years of peace.

World War 1, started after the June 28, 1914 assassination of Archduke Ferdinand, the Hapsburg heir, by a Serbian nationalist destroyed the empire. By 1918 Austria was reduced to a small republic, almost entirely German-speaking, with the borders it has today.

Nazi Germany invaded Austria Mar. 13, 1938, after four years of control by right-wing dictators Dollfus and Schuschnigg. The republic was reestablished in 1948, under allied occupation. Its independence and neutrality were guaranteed by a 1955 treaty with the major powers.

Austria produces 85% of its food, as well as an array of industrial products. A large part of Austria's economy is controlled in state enterprises. Socialists have shared or alternated power with the conservative People's Party, and every president

...cted since 1945 has been a Socialist.

...Economic agreements with the Common Market give Austria ...cess to a free-trade area encompassing most of West Eu-...e.

# Bahamas
## Commonwealth of the Bahamas

**People: Population** (1977 est.): 220,000. **Age distrib.** (%): ...14: 43.6; 15–59: 50.9; 60+: 5.5. **Pop. density:** 49.95 per sq. ...Urban (1970): 57.9%. **Ethnic groups:** Negro 85%, Cauca-...n (British, Canadian, U.S.). **Languages:** English. **Religions:** ...ptist 29%, Anglican 23%, Roman Catholic 22%.

**Geography: Area:** 4,404 sq. mi., slightly smaller than Con-...cticut. **Location:** In Atlantic O., E of Florida. **Neighbors:** Near-...; are U.S. on W, Cuba on S. **Topography:** The Bahamas ...mprise nearly 700 islands (30 inhabited) and over 2,000 islets ...the western Atlantic. They extend 760 mi. NW to SE. **Capital:** ...ssau. **Cities** (1970 cen.): Nassau (met.) 101,503.

**Government: Head of state:** Queen Elizabeth II, represented ...Gov.-Gen. Milo Boughton Butler; in office: Aug. 1, 1973; **Head ...government:** Prime Min. Lynden Oscar Pindling; b. Mar. 22, ...30; in office: Jan. 10, 1967. **Local divisions:** 18 districts.

**Economy: Industries:** Tourism, intl. banking, rum, drugs. ...ief crops: Fruits, vegetables. **Minerals:** Salt. **Other re-...urces:** Lobsters. **Per capita arable land:** 0.025 acres. **Elec-...city production** (1975): 650.00 mln. kwh. **Labor force:** 7% ...ric.; 5% manuf.

**Finance: Currency:** Dollar (May 1978: 1 = $1 US). **Gross ...mestic product** (1974 est.): $250 mln. **Imports** (1976): ...56 bln.; partners (1976): U.S. 67%, U.K. 14%. **Exports** ...976): $2.88 bln.; partners (1976): U.S. 61%. **Tourists** (1975): ...3,000; receipts (1975): $317 million. **Balance of payments** ...977): +$19,200,000. **National budget** (1976): $134.21 mln. ...venues; $140.95 mln. expenditures. **International reserves** ...ay 1978): $90.9 mln. **Consumer prices** (change in 1977): ...3%

**Transport: Motor vehicles:** in use (1974): 40,100 passenger ...rs, 5,500 commercial vehicles. **Chief ports:** Nassau, Freeport.

**Communications: Radios:** 90,000 in use (1974). **Tele-...ones in use** (1977): 58,033. **Daily newspaper circulation** ...974): 31,000; 159 per 1,000 pop.

**Health: Life expectancy at birth** (1971): 64.0 male; 67.3 fe-...ale. **Births** (per 1,000 pop. 1975): 19.8. **Deaths** (per 1,000 ...op. 1975): 5.4. **Natural increase** (1975): 1.44%. **Infant mortal-...y** (per 1,000 live births 1975): 29.2.

...Christopher Columbus first set foot in the New World on San ...alvador (Watling I.) in 1492, when Arawak Indians inhabited the ...ands. British settlement began in 1647; the islands became a ...itish colony in 1783. Internal self-government was granted in ...64, with the election of the first black prime minister in 1967. ...ll independence within the Commonwealth was attained July ..., 1973.

...International banking and investment management has be-...ome a major industry alongside tourism, despite controversy ...er financial irregularities.

# Bahrain
## State of Bahrain

**People: Population** (1977 est.): 270,000. **Age distrib.** (%): ...14: 44.3; 15–59: 51.1; 60+: 4.6. **Pop. density:** 1,168.83 per ... mi. **Urban** (1972): 78.1%. **Ethnic groups:** Arabs 88%, Irani-...s 4%, Indians, Pakistanis 5%. **Languages:** Arabic, Persian. ...eligions: Sunni Moslem 50%, Shiite Moslem 50%.

**Geography: Area:** 231 sq. mi., smaller than New York City. ...ocation: In Persian Gulf. **Neighbors:** Nearest are Saudi Arabia ... W, Qatar on E. **Topography:** Bahrain Island, and several ad-...cent, smaller islands, are flat, hot and humid, with little rain. ...apital: Manama. **Cities** (1971 cen.): Manama 88,785; Muhar-...q 41,143.

**Government: Head of state:** Amir Shaikh Isa bin Salman ...Khalifa; b. July 3, 1933; in office: Dec. 16, 1961; **Head of gov-...nment:** Prime Nien Khalifa bin Salman al–Khalifa; b. 1935; in ...fice: Jan. 19, 1970. **Local divisions:** 6 towns and cities. ...rmed forces: regulars 2,300.

**Economy: Industries:** Oil Products, aluminum smelting, ship-...ng. **Chief crops:** Fruits, vegetables. **Minerals:** Oil, gas.**Crude ...l reserves** (1978): 270 mln. bbls. **Per capita arable land:** ...005 acres. **Electricity production** (1975): 400.00 mln. kwh. ...abor force: 7% agric.; 14% manuf.

**Finance: Currency:** Dinar (May 1978: 1 = $2.58 US). **Gross domestic product** (1974 est.): $1.1 bln. **Per capita income** (1974): $2,500. **Imports** (1977): $2.03 bln.; partners (1976): U.K., U.S., Jap. **Exports** (1977): $1.85 bln.; partners (1975): Dubai 42%, Jap. 28%, Saudi Arabia 5%. **International reserves** (May 1978): $568.1 mln. **Consumer prices** (change in 1977): 11.9%

**Transport: Motor vehicles:** in use (1975): 23,300 passenger cars, 9,500 commercial vehicles. **Chief ports:** Sitra.

**Communications: Television sets:** 30,000 in use (1974). **Radios:** 100,000 in use (1974). **Telephones in use** (1977): 30,803.

**Health: Births** (annual per 1,000 pop. 1972-75): 30.0. **Pop. per hospital bed** (1975): 240. **Pop. per physician** (1975): 1,279.

**Education: Literacy** (1975): 50%. **Pop. 5–19:** in school (1975): 68%, per teacher (1975): 29.

Long ruled by the Khalifa family, Bahrain was a British protec-torate from 1861 to Aug. 14, 1971, when it regained indepen-dence.

Pearls, shrimp, fruits, and vegetables were the mainstays of the economy until oil was discovered in 1932. By the 1970s, oil reserves were depleted; international banking thrived.

Bahrain took part in the 1973-74 Arab oil embargo against the U.S. and other nations. The government bought controling inter-est in the oil industry in 1975. U.S. Navy base rights were ended in a 1977 agreement.

# Bangladesh
## People's Republic of Bangladesh

**People: Population** (1977 est.): 80,560,000. **Pop. density:** 1,461.38 per sq. mi. **Urban** (1974): 8.8%. **Ethnic groups:** Ben-gali 98%, Bihari, tribesmen. **Languages:** Bengali, Urdu, English. **Religions:** Moslems 85%, Hindus 14%.

**Geography: Area:** 55,126 sq. mi. slightly smaller than Wis-consin. **Location:** In S Asia, on N bend of Bay of Bengal. **Neigh-bors:** India nearly surrounds country on W, N, E; Burma on SE. **Topography:** The country is mostly a low plain cut by the Gan-ges and Brahmaputra rivers and their delta. The land is alluvial and marshy along the coast, with hills only in the extreme SE and NE. A tropical monsoon climate prevails, among the rainiest in the world. **Capital:** Dacca. **Cities** (1974 cen.): Dacca (met.) 1,730,253; Chittagong (met.) 889,760; Khulna (met.) 437,304.

**Government: Head of state:** Pres. Ziaur Rahman; b. Jan. 19, 1936; in office: Apr. 21, 1977. **Local divisions:** 19 districts. **Armed forces:** regulars 71,000; para-military 48,000.

**Economy: Industries:** Cement, textiles, jute, fertilizers. **Chief crops:** Jute (most of world output), rice. **Minerals:** Natural gas, offshore oil. **Other resources:** Water. **Per capita arable land:** 0.3 acres. **Fish catch** (1975): 640,000 metric tons. **Electricity production** (1976): 1.38 bln. kwh. **Labor force:** 70% agricul-ture.

**Finance: Currency:** Taka (May 1978: 15.31 = $1 US). **Gross domestic product** (1977): $7.29 bln. **Per capita in-come** (1977): $70. **Imports** (1977): $308 mln.; partners (1974): U.S. 24% Austral. 9%, Jap. 7%, India 7%, W. Ger. 7%. **Exports** (1977): $327 mln.; partners (1974): U.S. 20%, U.K. 9%, India 8%, Austral. 5%. **Tourists** (1975): 63,800; receipts (1975): $3 million. **Balance of payments** (1977): −$20,100,000. **Interna-tional reserves** (May 1978): $269.8 mln. **Consumer prices** (change in 1976): −9.6%.

**Transport: Railway traffic** (1973): 2.07 bln. passenger-miles; 396.82 mln. net ton-miles. **Motor vehicles:** in use (1972): 31,700 passenger cars, 24,800 commercial vehicles. **Chief ports:** Chittagong, Chalna.

**Communications: Telephones in use** (1975): 80,000. **Daily newspaper circulation** (1974): 398,000; 193 per 1,000 pop.

**Health: Life expectancy at birth** (1975): 35.8 male; 35.8 fe-male. **Births** (annual per 1,000 pop. 1972-75): 49.5. **Deaths** (an-nual per 1,000 pop. 1972-75): 28.1. **Natural increase** (annual 1970-75): 2.14%. **Pop. per hospital bed** (1975): 7,132. **Pop. per physician** (1975): 9,896. **Infant mortality** per 1,000 live births 1973): 132.

**Education: Literacy** (1975): 25%. **Pop. 5–19:** in school (1975): 34%, per teacher (1975): 120.

Moslem invaders conquered the formerly Hindu area in the 12th century, British rule lasted from the 18th century to 1947, when East Bengal became part of Pakistan.

Charging West Pakistani domination, the Awami League, based in the East, won National Assembly control in 1971. Assembly sessions were postponed; riots broke out. Pakistani troops attacked Mar. 25; Bangladesh independence was proclaimed the next day. In the ensuing civil war, one million died amid charges of Pakistani atrocities. Ten million fled to India. Many of the 400,000 Bihari Moslems have sought to leave.

War between India and Pakistan broke out Dec. 3, 1971. Pakistan surrendered in the East Dec. 15. Sheik Mujibur Rahman became prime minister. The country moved into the Indian and Soviet orbits, in response to U.S. support of Pakistan, and much of the economy was nationalized.

In 1974, the government took emergency powers to curb widespread violence; Mujibur was assassinated and a series of coups followed.

Chronic destitution among the densely crowded population has been worsened by the decline of jute as a major world commodity. A 1970 cyclone killed 300,000, and 1974 floods, combined with the world oil price hike, caused famine deaths to soar.

A new regime in 1977 restored Islam to a central constitutional role. A Ganges waterpact with India was signed, 1977. About 150,000 Burmese Moslems fled to Bangladesh in 1978.

## Barbados

**People: Population** (1977 est.): 250,000. **Age distrib. (%):** 0–14: 36.3; 15–59: 52.5; 60+: 11.1. **Pop. density:** 1,506.02 per sq. mi. **Urban** (1970): 3.7%. **Ethnic groups:** Negro 90%, mixed 5%, Caucasian 5%. **Languages:** English. **Religions:** Anglican 70%, Methodist, Pentecostal, Roman Catholic.

**Geography: Area:** 166 sq. mi. **Location:** In Atlantic, farthest E of W. Indies. **Neighbors:** Nearest are Trinidad, Grenada on SW. **Topography:** The island lies alone in the Atlantic almost completely surrounded by coral reefs. Highest point is Mt. Hillaby, 1,115 ft. **Capital:** Bridgetown. **Cities** (1970 cen.): Bridgetown (met.) 85,000.

**Government: Head of state:** Queen Elizabeth II, represented by Gov.-Gen. Deighton L. Ward; **Head of government:** Prime Min. J.M.G. Adams; b. Sept. 24, 1931; in office: Sept. 2, 1976. **Local divisions:** 11 parishes, one city.

**Economy: Industries:** Rum, molasses, tourism. **Chief crops:** Sugar, cotton. **Minerals:** Lime. **Crude oil reserves** (1978): .001 mln. bbls. **Other resources:** Fish. **Per capita arable land:** 0.3 acres. **Electricity production** (1977): 252.00 mln. kwh. **Labor force:** 16% agric.; 15% manuf.

**Finance: Currency:** Dollar (May 1978: 2.01 = $1 US). **Gross domestic product** (1975): $349.34 bln. **Per capita income** (1974): $1,165. **Imports** (1977): $275 mln.; partners (1974): U.K. 21%, U.S. 19%, Trin. 12%, Venez. 10%. **Exports** (1977): $96 mln.; partners (1974): U.S. 26%, U.K. 16%, Windward Is. 7%, Trin. 6%. **Tourist receipts** (1975): $78 million. **Balance of payments** (1977): +$3,000,000. **National budget** (1973): $68.82 mln. revenues; $84.59 mln. expenditures. **International reserves** (May 1978): $54.67 mln. **Consumer prices** (change in 1977): 8.3%.

**Transport: Motor vehicles:** in use (1973): 20,500 passenger cars, 3,000 commercial vehicles. **Chief ports:** Bridgetown.

**Communications: Television sets:** 40,000 in use (1974). **Radios:** 116,000 in use (1973). **Telephones in use** (1977): 44,049. **Daily newspaper circulation** (1974): 24,000; 98 per 1,000 pop.

**Health: Life expectancy at birth** (1961): 62.74 male; 67.43 female. **Births** (per 1,000 pop. 1976): 18.6. **Deaths** (per 1,000 pop. 1976): 9.2. **Natural increase** (1976): .94%. **Pop. per hospital bed** (1975): 111. **Pop. per physician** (1975): 1,485. **Infant mortality** (per 1,000 live births 1973): 37.7

**Education: Literacy** (1975): 97%. **Pop. 5-19:** in school (1975): 74%, per teacher (1975): 44.

Barbados was probably named by Portuguese sailors in reference to bearded fig trees. An English ship visited in 1605, and British settlers arrived on the uninhabited island in 1627. Slaves worked the sugar plantations, but were freed in 1834.

Self-rule came gradually, with full independence proclaimed Nov. 30, 1966. British traditions have remained; literacy is almost universal.

## Belgium
### Kingdom of Belgium

**People: Population** (1977 est.): 9,830,000. **Age distrib. (%):** 0–14: 23.4; 15–59: 57.6; 60+: 19. **Pop. density:** 834.54 per sq.

mi. **Urban** (1974): 87.1%. **Ethnic groups:** Flemings 58%, Walloons 41%. **Languages:** Flemish (Dutch), French. **Religio**: Roman Catholic 90%, Protestant.

**Geography: Area:** 11,779 sq. mi., slightly larger than Ma land. **Location:** In NW Europe, on N. Sea. **Neighbors:** Frar on W, S, Luxembourg on SE, W. Germany on E, Netherlands N. **Topography:** Mostly flat, the country is trisected by Scheldt and Meuse, major commercial rivers. The land becom hilly and forested in the SE (Ardennes) region. **Capital:** Bruss **Cities** (1974 est.): Brussels (met.) 1,054,970; Antwerp (m 665,980; Liege (met.) 435,822; Ghent (met.) 220,259.

**Government: Head of state:** King Baudouin; b. Sept 1930; in office: July 17, 1951; **Head of government:** Prime N Leo Tindemans; b. Apr. 16, 1922; in office: Apr. 25, 1975. **Lo divisions:** 9 provinces, with elected governments & substar powers. **Armed forces:** regulars 112,500; reserves 55,500.

**Economy: Industries:** Steel, glassware, diamond cutting, tiles, chemicals. **Chief crops:** Grains, potatoes, sugar be **Minerals:** Coal. **Other resources:** Forests. **Per capita ara land:** 0.2 acres. **Meat production** (1976): beef: 294,900 tc pork: 611,400 tons. **Fish catch** (1975): 49,000 metric tons. **El tricity production** (1977): 47.10 bln. kwh. **Labor force:** agric.; 32% manuf.

**Finance: Currency:** Franc (May 1978: 32.88 = $1 U **Gross domestic product** (1976): $68.48 bln. **Per capita come** (1975): $5,851. **Imports** (1977): $40.14 bln.; partn (1975): W. Ger. 22%, France 17%, Neth. 16%, U.S. 6%. **ports** (1977): $37.46 bln.; partners (1975): W. Ger. 22%, Fran 19%, Neth. 17%, U.K. 6%. **Tourists** (1974): 7,477,400; recei (1974) (including Luxembourg): $719 million. **Balance of p ments** (1977): −$271,000,000. **National budget** (1977): 22 bln. revenues; $28.05 bln. expenditures. **International reser** (May 1978): $5.90 bln. **Consumer prices** (change in 197 7.1%.

**Transport: Railway traffic** (1975): 5.13 bln. passenger-mil 4.20 bln. net ton-miles. **Motor vehicles:** in use (197 2,613,900 passenger cars, 291,900 commercial vehicles; sembled (1976): 1,001,388 passenger cars; 70,620 commerce vehicles. **Civil aviation** (international only): 2,511 mln. pass ger-miles (1977); 247,310 mln. freight ton-miles (1977). **Ch ports:** Antwerp, Zeebrugge, Ghent.

**Communications: Television sets:** 2,464,000 licens (1974), 579,000 manufactured (1975). **Radios:** 3,769,000 censed (1974), 1,796,000 manufactured (1975). **Telephones use** (1977): 2,949,822. **Daily newspaper circulation** (197 2,416,000; 247 per 1,000 pop.

**Health: Life expectancy at birth** (1972): 67.79 male; 74 female. **Births** (per 1,000 pop. 1975): 12.2. **Deaths** (per 1,0 pop. 1975): 12.2. **Natural increase** (1975) .00%. **Pop. per ho pital bed** (1975): 111. **Pop. per physician** (1975): 563. **Infa mortality** (per 1,000 live births 1974): 17.4.

**Education: Literacy** (1975): 98%. **Pop. 5-19:** in sch (1975): 61%, per teacher (1975): 23.

Belgium derives its name from the Belgae, the first record inhabitants, probably Celts. The land was conquered by Jul Caesar, and was ruled for 1800 years by conquerors, includ Rome, the Franks, Burgundy, Spain, Austria, and France. Af 1815, Belgium was made a part of the Netherlands, but it b came an independent constitutional monarchy in 1830.

Belgian neutrality was violated by Germany in both wo wars. King Leopold III surrendered to Germany, May 28, 194 After the war, he was forced by political pressure to abdicate favor of his son, King Baudouin.

The Flemings of northern Belgium speak Dutch while Fren is the language of the Walloons in the south. The language ference has been a perennial source of controvery, particula as it affects education, with Flemish parents unwilling to ha their children taught in French.

Disagreement between the two groups became embittered 1968 elections. In 1970 and 1974 the government sought solve the problem through creation of decentralized administ tive and cultural communities and regional assemblies.

Belgium lives by its foreign trade; about 40% of its entire pr duction is sold abroad.

## Benin
### People's Republic of Benin

**People: Population** (1977 est.): 3,290,000. **Pop. densit** 75.66 per sq. mi. **Urban** (1976): 13.5%. **Ethnic groups:** For Adjas, Baribas, Yorubas. **Languages:** French is only comm language. **Religions:** Christian 15% (south), Moslem 13% (north), othes.

**Geography: Area:** 43,483 sq. mi., slightly smaller than Pennsylvania. **Location:** In W Africa on Gulf of Guinea. **Neighbors:** Togo on W, Upper Volta, Niger on N, Nigeria on E. **Topography:** most of Benin is flat and covered with dense vegetation. The coast is hot, humid, and rainy. **Capitals:** Porto–Novo, Cotonou. **Cities** (1975 est.): Cotonou 178,000; Porto-Novo 104,000.

**Government: Head of state:** Pres. Mathieu Kerekou; b. 1933; in office: Oct. 26, 1972. **Local divisions:** 6 departments. **Armed forces:** regulars 2,250; para-military 1,000.

**Economy: Chief crops:** Palm products, peanuts, cotton, kapok, coffee, tobacco. **Minerals:** Some oil. **Per capita arable land:** 1.2 acres. **Fish catch** (1975): 29,500 metric tons. **Electricity production** (1975): 57.00 mln. kwh. **Labor force:** 52% agriculture.

**Finance: Currency:** Franc (May 1978: 230.35 = $1 US). **Gross domestic product** (1976): $500.00 mln. **Per capita income** (1975): $174. **Imports** (1975): $150 mln.; partners (1975): U.S., France, E. Ger., U.K. **Exports** (1975): $46 mln.; partners (1975): U.S., France, E. Ger. **Tourists** (1975): 18,200; receipts (1975): $2 million. **Balance of payments** (1975): −$21,400,000. **International reserves** (Mar. 1978): $12.6 mln.

**Transport:** Railway traffic (1975): 60.23 mln. passenger-miles; 78.87 mln. net ton-miles. **Motor vehicles:** in use (1974): 14,000 passenger cars, 8,600 commercial vehicles. **Chief ports:** Cotonou.

**Communications: Radios:** 55,000 licensed (1974). **Telephones in use** (1974): 8,000. **Daily newspaper circulation** (1974): 1,000; 1 per 1,000 pop.

**Health: Life expectancy at birth** (1961): 37.3 male; 37.3 female. **Births** (annual per 1,000 pop. 1972-75): 49.9. **Deaths** (annual per 1,000 pop. 1972-75): 23.0. **Natural increase** (1970-75): 2.69%. **Pop. per hospital bed** (1975): 832. **Pop. per physician** (1975): 35,779. **Infant mortality** (per 1,000 live births 1961): 109.6.

**Education: Literacy** (1975): 20%. **Pop. 5-19:** in school (1975): 30%. **per teacher** (1975): 161.

The Kingdom of Abomey, rising to power in wars with neighboring kingdoms in the 17th century, came under French domination in the late 19th century, and was incorporated into French West Africa by 1904.

Under the name Dahomey, the country became independent Aug. 1, 1960. The name was changed to Benin in 1975. In the fifth coup since independence. Maj. Mathieu Kerekou took power in 1972; two years later he declared a socialist state with a "Marxist-Leninist" philosophy. The drought of 1972-73 damaged agriculture and slowed economic growth. A 3-yr. economic plan started in 1977.

## Bhutan
### Kingdom of Bhutan

**Ethnic groups:** Bhotia (Tibetan) 60%. Nepalese, Lepcha (indigenous), Indians **Languages:** Dzongkha Tibetan (official), Nepaleses. **Religions:** Buddhist 75%, Hindu 25%.

**Geography: Area:** 19,305 sq. mi., the size of Vermont and New Hampshire combined. **Location:** In eastern Himalayan Mts. **Neighbors:** India on W (Sikkim) and S, China on N. **Topography:** Bhutan is comprised of very high mountains in the North, fertile valleys in the center, and thick forests in the Duar Plain in the S. **Capital:** Thimphu. **City** (1971 est.): Thimphu 10,000.

**Government: Head of state:** King Jigme Singye Wangchuk; b. Nov. 11, 1955; in office: July 24, 1972. **Local divisions:** 4 regions comprised of 15 districts.

**Economy: Industries:** Cloth. **Chief crops:** Rice, corn, wheat, oranges, cardamon, yak butter, lac, wax. **Other resources:** Elephants, timber. **Per capita arable land:** 0.01 acres.

**Finance: Currency:** Ngultrum (Indian Rupee also used) (1974: 8.1 = $1 US). **Gross domestic product** (1974 est.): $80 mln. **Per capita income** (1974): $60. **Imports** (1974): $5 mln.; partners (1974): India 99%. **Exports** (1974): $1 mln.; partners (1974): India 99%.

**Transport:** Motor vehicles: in use (1974): 14,000 passenger cars, 8,600 commercial vehicles.

**Communications:** Telephones in use (1977): 1,082.

**Health: Life expectancy at birth** (1975): 42.2 male; 45.0 female. **Births** (annual per 1,000 pop. 1972-75): 43.6. **Deaths** (annual per 1,000 pop. 1972-75): 20.5. **Natural increase** (annual 1970-75): 2.31%. **Pop. per hospital bed** (1975): 1,616. **Pop. per physician** (1975): 4,264.

The region came under Tibetan rule in the 16th century. British influence grew in the 19th century. A monarchy, set up in 1907, became a British protectorate by a 1910 treaty. The country became independent in 1949, with India guiding foreign relations and supplying aid.

Links to India have been strengthened by airline service and a road network. Most of the population engages in subsistence agriculture.

## Bolivia
### Republic of Bolivia

**People: Population** (1977 est.): 5,950,000. **Age distrib.** (%): 0–14: 41.9; 15–59: 52.7; 60+: 5.4. **Pop. density:** 14.03 per sq. mi. **Ethnic groups:** Quechua 30%, Aymara 25%, Mestizo (cholo) 25-30%, European 5-15%. **Languages:** Spanish (official) 55%, Quechua, Aymara. **Religions:** Roman Catholic 95%.

**Geography: Area:** 424,162 sq. mi., the size of Texas and California combined. **Location:** In central Andes Mtns. **Neighbors:** Peru, Chile on W, Argentina, Paraguay on S, Brazil on E and N. **Topography:** The great central plateau, at an altitude of 12,000 ft., over 500 mi. long, lies between two great cordilleras having 3 of the highest peaks in S. America. Lake Titicaca, on Peruvian border, is highest lake in world on which steamboats ply (12,506 ft.). The E central region has semitropical forests; the llanos, or Amazon-Chaco lowlands are in E. **Capitals:** Sucre, La Paz. **Cities** (1976 cen.): La Paz 654,713; Santa Cruz 237,128; Cochabamba 194,156.

**Government: Head of state:** Pres. Juan Pereda Asbun; b. July 25, 1931; in office: July 21, 1978. **Local divisions:** 9 departments headed by prefects, 94 provinces. **Armed forces:** regulars 22,500.

**Economy: Chief crops:** Potatoes, sugar, coffee, barley, cocoa, rice, corn, bananas, citrus. **Minerals:** (chief industry) tin (12% of world output), silver, copper, lead, zinc, oil, gas, antimony, bismuth, wolfram, gold, iron, cadmium, borate of lime. **Crude oil reserves** (1978): 350 mln. bbls. **Other resources:** rubber, cinchona bark. **Per capita arable land:** 1.3 acres. **Meat production** (1975): beef: 72,000 tons; pork: 21,000 tons; lamb: 20,000 tons. **Electricity production** (1975): 1.00 bln. kwh. **Labor force:** 58% agriculture.

**Finance: Currency:** Peso (May 1978: 20.00 = $1 US). **Gross domestic product** (1976): $2.95 bln. **Per capita income** (1974): $299. **Imports** (1976): $3.03 bln.; partners (1974): U.S. 26%, Braz. 16%, Arg. 15%, Jap. 14%. **Exports** (1976): $3.92 bln.; partners (1974): U.S. 19%, Arg. 10%, Jap. 6%, Braz. 5%. **Tourist receipts** (1975): $15 million. **Balance of payments** (1977): +$43,900,000. **National budget** (1973): $123.93 mln. revenues; $168.48 mln. expenditures. **International reserves** (May 1978): $181.3 mln.

**Transport:** Railway traffic (1975): 192.51 mln. passenger-miles; 288.77 mln. net ton-miles. **Motor vehicles:** in use (1975): 9,100 passenger cars, 18,400 commercial vehicles. **Civil aviation:** 347 mln. passenger-miles (1977); 17,244 freight ton-miles (1977).

**Communications: Radios:** 425,000 in use (1974). **Telephones in use** (1973): 49,000. **Daily newspaper circulation** (1974): 135,000; 25 per 1,000 pop.

**Health: Life expectancy at birth** (1975): 45.7 male; 47.9 female. **Births** (annual per 1,000 pop. 1972-75): 43.7 **Deaths** (annual per 1,000 pop. 1972-75): 18.0. **Natural increase** (annual 1970-75): 2.49%. **Pop. per hospital bed** (1975): 460. **Pop. per physician** (1975): 1,900. **Infant mortality** (per 1,000 live births 1966): 77.3.

**Education: Literacy** (1975): 40%. **Pop. 5-19:** in school (1975): 48%. per teacher (1975): 45.

The Incas conquered the region from earlier Indian inhabitants in the 13th century. Spanish rule began in the 1530s, and lasted until Aug. 6, 1825. The country is named after Simon Bolivar, independence fighter.

In a series of wars, Bolivia lost its Pacific coast to Chile, the oilbearing Chaco to Paraguay, and rubber-growing areas to Brazil, 1879-1935.

Economic unrest, especially among the militant mine workers, has contributed to continuing political instability. A reformist government under Victor Paz Estenssoro, 1951-64, nationalized tin mines and attempted to improve conditions for the Indian majority, but was overthrown by a military junta. A series of coups and countercoups continued until 1971, when the present regime ousted the leftist regime of Gen. Juan Jose Torres.

In 1974, civilians were dismissed from the cabinet, and political parties and labor unions were banned. A new rightist coup followed a disputed 1978 election.

## Botswana
### Republic of Botswana

**People: Population** (1977 est.): 710,000. **Age distrib. (%):** 0–14: 47.5; 15–59: 44.9; 60+: 7.6. **Pop. density:** 3.23 per sq. mi. **Urban** (1974): 12.3%. **Ethnic groups:** Bantus (8 main tribes), Bushmen. **Languages:** English (official), Setswana. **Religions:** Christian 15%, others.

**Geography: Area:** 219,815 sq. mi., slightly smaller than Texas. **Location:** In southern Africa. **Neighbors:** Namibia (S.W. Africa) on N and W, S. Africa on S, Rhodesia on NE, Botswana claims border with Zambia on N. **Topography:** The Kalahari Desert, supporting nomadic Bushmen and wildlife, spreads over SW; there are swamplands and farming areas in N, and rolling plains in E where livestock are grazed. **Capital:** Gaborone. **Cities** (1971 cen.): Gaborone 17,718.

**Government: Head of State:** Pres. Seretse Khama; b. July 1, 1921; in office: 1965. **Local divisions:** 10 districts and 3 independent towns, all with local councils.

**Economy: Industries:** Tourism. **Chief crops:** Corn, sorghum, beans, peanuts. **Minerals:** Copper, coal, nickel, diamonds. **Other resources:** Big game. **Per capita arable land:** 2.1 acres. **Meat production** (1975): beef: 31,000 tons. **Electricity production** (1975): 274.00 mln. kwh. **Labor force:** 87% agriculture.

**Finance: Currency:** Pula (Nov. 1976: 1 = $1.15 US). **Gross domestic product** (1974): $99.76 mln. **Per capita income** (1974): $340. **Imports** (1974): $151 mln.; partners (1975): S. Africa, Rhod., U.K. **Exports** (1973): $91.9 mln.; partners (1975): U.K., S. Africa, Zambia, Rhod. **Consumer prices** (change in 1976): 11.9%.

**Transport: Motor vehicles:** in use (1974): 3,400 passenger cars, 6,800 commercial vehicles.

**Communications: Radios:** 55,000 in use (1974). **Telephones in use** (1975): 8,000. **Daily newspaper circulation** (1974): 13,000; 20 per 1,000 pop.

**Health: Life expectancy at birth** (1975): 41.9 male; 45.1 female. **Births** (annual per 1,000 pop. 1972-75): 48.0. **Deaths** (annual per 1,000 pop. 1972-75): 23.0. **Natural increase** (Annual 1970-75) 2.26%. **Pop. per hospital bed** (1975): 305. **Pop. per physician** (1975): 9,936. **Infant mortality** (per 1,000 live births 1973): 97.

**Education: Literacy** (1975): 20%. **Pop. 5-19:** in school (1975): 46%, per teacher (1975): 69.

First inhabited by bushmen, then by Bantus, the region became the British protectorate of Bechuanaland in 1886, halting encroachment by Boers and Germans from the south and southwest. The country became fully independent Sept. 30, 1966, changing its name to Botswana.

Cattle-raising, mining (diamonds, copper, nickel) are the chief economic activities. Many workers are migrants in S. Africa, and much of Botswana's exports go to that country.

## Brazil
### Federative Republic of Brazil

**People: Population** (1977 est.): 112,240,000. **Age distrib. (%):** 0–14: 41.7; 15–59: 53.2; 60+: 5.1. **Pop. density:** 34.15 per sq. mi. **Urban** (1976): 60.4%. **Ethnic groups:** Portuguese, Africans, and mulattoes make up the vast majority; Italians, Germans, Japanese, Indians, Jews, Arabs. **Languages:** Portuguese. **Religions:** Roman Catholic 89%, Protestant 10%.

**Geography: Area:** 3,286,470 sq. mi., larger than conterminous 48 U.S. states; largest country in S. America. **Location:** Occupies eastern half of S. America. **Neighbors:** French Guiana, Surinam, Guyana, Venezuela on N, Colombia, Peru, Bolivia, Paraguay, Argentina on W. Uruguay on S. **Topography:** Brazil's Atlantic coastline stretches 4,603 miles. In N is the heavily-wooded Amazon basin covering half the country. Its network of rivers navigable for 15,814 mi. The Amazon itself flows 2,093 miles in Brazil, all navigable. The NE region is semiarid scrubland, heavily settled and poor. The S central region, favored by climate and resources, has 45% of the population, produces 75% of farm goods and 80% of industrial output. The narrow coastal belt includes most of the major cities. Almost the entire country has a tropical or semitropical climate. **Capital:** Brasilia.

**Cities** (1970 cen.): San Paulo (met.) 5,869,966; Rio de Janeiro 4,252,009; Belo Horizonte (met.) 1,228,295; Recife 1,046,454 Salvador (met.) 1,005,216; Porto Alegre 869,795; Fortaleza (met.) 828,763; Belem (met.) 603,267; Curitiba (met.) 583,857 Brasilia 272,002.

**Government: Head of state:** Pres. Ernesto Geisel; b. Aug. 3 1908; in office: Mar. 15, 1974. **Local divisions:** 21 states, with individual constitutions and elected governments; the former autonomy has been curbed in recent years; 4 territories, 1 federal district. **Armed forces:** regulars 384,800; para-military 200,000.

**Economy: Industries:** Textiles, steel, autos, aluminum, chemicals, drugs, plastics, ships, appliances, shoes, paper, glass, machinery. **Chief crops:** Coffee (largest grower), cotton, soybeans, sugar, cocoa, rice, corn, fruits. **Minerals:** Iron (one third world reserve); leader in quartz crystals, beryl, sheet mica, manganese, columbium, titanium, diamonds, chrome; also thorium, gold, nickel, gem stones, coal, tin, tungsten, bauxite, oil. **Crude oil reserves** (1978): 880 mln. bbls. **Per capital arable land:** 0.6 acres. **Meat production** (1976): beef: 2.23 mln. tons; pork 784,500 tons; lamb: 52,400 tons. **Fish catch** (1975): 679,500 metric tons. **Electricity production** (1976): 88.38 bln. kwh. **Labor force:** 44% agric.; 11% manuf.

**Finance: Currency:** Cruzeiros (May 1978: 17.60 = $1 US). **Gross domestic product** (1977): $144.92 bln. **Per capita income** (1976): $1,239. **Imports** (1976): $554 mln.; partners (1976): U.S. 26%, Mid. East 19%, Jap. 7.9%, rest of Lat. Am. 5.6%. **Exports** (1976): $637 mln.; partners (1976): U.S. 17.5%, Japan 9.5%, rest of Lat. Am. 10.8%. **Tourists** (1975): 518,000; receipts (1975): $72 million. **Balance of payments** (1977) +$699,000,000. **National budget** (1977): $15.13 bln. revenues $15.07 bln. expenditures. **International reserves** (Feb. 1978) $6.73 bln. **Consumer prices** (change in 1977): 43.7%.

**Transport: Railway traffic** (1974): 6.61 bln. passenger-miles, 34.29 bln. net ton-miles. **Motor vehicles:** in use (1974): 3,679,300 passenger cars, 1,001,900 commercial vehicles; manufactured (1976): 555,600 passenger cars; 416,400 commercial vehicles. **Civil aviation:** 6,439 mln. passenger-miles (1976); 303,013 mln. freight ton-miles (1976). **Chief ports:** Santos, Rio de Janeiro, Vitoria, Salvador, Rio Grande, Recife.

**Communications: Television sets:** 8,650,000 in use (1974), 1,451,000 manufactured (1975). **Radios:** 6,275,000 in use (1974), 640,000 manufactured (1975). **Telephones in use** (1977): 3,987,072. **Daily newspaper circulation** (1973): 4,050,000; 39 per 1,000 pop.

**Health: Life expectancy at birth** (1970): 57.61 male; 61.10 female. **Births** (annual per 1,000 pop. 1972-75): 37.1. **Deaths** (annual per 1,000 pop. 1972-75): 8.8. **Natural increase** (annual 1970-75): 2.83%. **Pop. per hospital bed** (1975): 264. **Pop. per physician** (1975): 1,646. **Infant mortality** (per 1,000 live births 1973): 94.

**Education: Literacy** (1975): 68%. **Pop. 5-19:** in school (1975): 50%, per teacher (1975): 43.

Pedro Alvares Cabral, a Portuguese navigator, is generally credited as the first European to reach Brazil, in 1500. The country was thinly settled by various Indian tribes. Only a few have survived to the present, mostly in the Amazon basin, where they have been threatened by genocidal trends.

The first Portuguese governor-general was appointed in 1549. In the next centuries, colonists gradually pushed inland, bringing along large numbers of African slaves. Slavery was not abolished until 1888.

The King of Portugal, fleeing before Napoleon's army, moved the seat of government to Brazil in 1808. Brazil thereupon became a kingdom under Dom Joao VI. After his return to Portugal his son Pedro proclaimed the independence of Brazil, Sept. 7, 1822, and was acclaimed emperor. The second emperor, Dom Pedro II, was deposed in 1889, and a republic proclaimed, called the United States of Brazil. In 1967 the country was renamed the Federative Republic of Brazil.

A military junta took control in 1930, and dictatorial power was assumed by Getulio Vargas. He was elected president in 1933, ruled until a 1945 military coup, was reelected in 1950, but was forced out once more by the military in 1954. A democratic regime prevailed 1956-64, during which time the capital was moved from Rio de Janeiro to Brasilia in the interior.

In 1964, economic and social problems, including runaway inflation, led to political agitation. The elected government of Pres. Joao Goulart was overthrown in a military coup. The 1967 constitution strengthened presidential powers.

The next four presidents were all military leaders. Censorship was imposed, and much of the opposition was suppressed, amid charges of torture. In 1974 elections, the official opposition party made gains in the chamber of deputies, and some relaxation of censorship occurred, though church liberals, labor leaders, and intellectuals continued to report cases of arrest and torture. In 1977, a series of constitutional changes assured long-term control by the regime. Illegal strikes won industrial workers 1978 wage hikes.

Close ties with the U.S. were damaged in 1977, when the U.S. criticized the human rights situation in Brazil, and opposed construction of a nuclear fuel reprocessing plant. West Germany had agreed in 1975 to supply Brazil with the technology for a complete nuclear energy industry. Brazil cancelled a 25-year old U.S. military assistance agreement.

Since 1930, successive governments have pursued industrial and agricultural growth and the development of interior areas, with the state sector playing a larger role in recent years. Exploiting vast mineral resources, fertile soil in several regions, and a huge labor force, Brazil became the leading industrial power of Latin America by the 1970s, while agricultural output soared. Education was advanced and illiteracy reduced.

However, income maldistribution remained unaffected by economic growth, and a return of inflation (46% in 1976) aggravated malnutrition, which affected 40% of the population. A huge oil import bill increased the foreign debt.

# Bulgaria
## People's Republic of Bulgaria

**People: Population** (1977 est.): 8,800,000. **Age distrib.** (%): 0–14: 22.3; 15–59: 62.3; 60+: 15.5. **Pop. density:** 205.47 per sq. mi. **Urban** (1976): 58.4%. **Ethnic groups:** Bulgarians 85%, Turks 9%, Gypsies 2%. **Languages:** Bulgarian, Turkish, Greek. **Religions:** Orthodox 70%, Moslem 9%.

**Geography: Area:** 42,829 sq. mi., slightly larger than Tennessee. **Location:** In eastern Balkan Peninsula on Black Sea. **Neighbors:** Romania on N, Yugoslavia on W, Greece, Turkey on S. **Topography:** The Stara Planina (Balkan) Mts. stretch E-W across the center of the country, with the Danubian plain on N, the Rhodope Mts. on SW, and Thracian Plain on SE. **Capital:** Sofia. **Cities** (1974 est.): Sofia 962,500; Plovdiv 305,091; Varna 269,980.

**Government: Head of state:** Pres. Todor Zhivkov; b. Sept. 7, 1911; in office: July 7, 1971; **Head of government:** Prime Min. Stanko Todorov; b. 1920; in office: July 7, 1971; **Head of Communist Party:** First Sec. Todor Zhivkov; in office: 1954. **Local divisions:** 27 provinces, one city. **Armed forces:** regulars 241,500; reserves 235,000.

**Economy: Industries:** Chemicals, machinery, metals, textiles, fur, leather goods, vehicles, wine, processed food. **Chief crops:** Grains, fruit, corn, potatoes, tobacco. **Minerals:** Coal, oil, lead, zinc. **Per capita arable land:** 1.2 acres. **Meat production** (1976): beef: 98,100 tons; pork: 237,000 tons; lamb: 86,800 tons. **Fish catch** (1975): 158,100 metric tons. **Electricity production** (1977): 29.70 bln. kwh. **Labor force:** 42% agriculture.

**Finance: Currency:** Lev (Jul.-Sep. 1977: 7.39 = $1 US). **Gross domestic product** (1974 est.): $15 bln. **Per capita income** (1974): $1,650. **Imports** (1977): $6.33 bln.; partners (1974): USSR 44%, E. Ger. 9%, W. Ger. 7%, Pol. 5%, Czech. 4%. **Exports** (1977): $6.33 bln.; partners (1977): USSR 50%, E. Ger. 8%, Pol. 5%, Czech. 4%. **Tourists** (1975): 4,049,300; receipts (1975): $230 million.

**Transport: Railway traffic** (1975): 47.00 bln. passenger-miles; 10.73 bln. net ton-miles. **Motor vehicles:** in use (1970): 160,000 passenger cars. **Chief ports:** Burgas, Varna.

**Communications: Television sets:** 1,457,000 licensed (1974), 124,000 manufactured (1975). **Radios:** 2,273,000 licensed (1974), 228,000 manufactured (1975). **Telephones in use** (1977): 852,858. **Daily newspaper circulation** (1974): 1,971,000; 227 per 1,000 pop.

**Health: Life expectancy at birth** (1973): 68.58 male; 73.86 female. **Births** (per 1,000 pop. 1976): 16.5. **Deaths** (per 1,000 pop. 1976): 10.1. **Natural increase** (1976): .64%. **Pop. per hospital bed** (1975): 118. **Pop. per physician** (1975): 465. **Infant mortality** (per 1,000 live births 1975): 22.9.

**Education: Literacy** (1975): 95%. **Pop. 5-19:** in school (1975): 56%, per teacher (1975): 34.

Bulgaria was settled by Slavs in the 6th century. Turkic Bulgars arrived in the 7th century, merged with the Slavs, became Christians by the 9th century, and set up powerful empires in the

10th and 12th centuries. The Ottomans prevailed in 1396 and remained for 500 years.

A revolt in 1876 led to autonomy in 1878 and an independent kingdom in 1908. Bulgaria expanded after the first Balkan War but lost its Aegean coastline in World War I, when it sided with Germany. Bulgaria joined the Axis in World War II, but withdrew in 1944. Communists took power with Soviet aid, and the monarchy was abolished Sept. 8, 1946.

Industrialization has advanced. Most trade is with Comecon countries. Bulgaria is Moscow's most loyal supporter in international questions.

# Burma
## Socialist Republic of the Union of Burma

**People: Population** (1977 est.): 31,510,000. **Pop. density:** 120.36 per sq. mi. **Ethnic groups:** Burmans (related to Tibetans) 72%; Karen 7%, Shan 6%, Kachin 2%, Chinese 2%, Indians 3%, others. **Languages:** Burmese (official) 80%, English, others. **Religions:** Buddhist 85%; Hinduism, Islam, Christianity, others.

**Geography: Area:** 261,789 sq. mi., nearly as large as Texas. **Location:** Between S. and S.E. Asia, on Bay of Bengal. **Neighbors:** Bangladesh, India on W., China, Laos, Thailand on E. **Topography:** Mountains surround Burma on W, N, and E, and dense forests cover much of the nation. N-S rivers provide habitable valleys and communications, especially the Irrawaddy, navigable for 900 miles. The country has a tropical monsoon climate. **Capital:** Rangoon. **Cities** (1973 cen.): Rangoon 1,586,422; (1974 est.): Mandalay 417,000; Moulmein 202,000.

**Government: Head of state:** Pres. Ne Win; b. 1911; in office: Mar. 2, 1962; **Head of government:** Prime Min. Maung Kah, in office: Mar. 29, 1977. **Local divisions:** 7 states and 7 divisions. **Armed forces:** regulars 169,500; para-military 73,000.

**Economy: Chief crops:** Rice, cotton, maize, tobacco. **Minerals:** Oil, lead, silver, tin, tungsten, zinc, rubies, sapphires, jade. **Crude oil reserves** (1978): .055 mln. bbls. **Other resources:** Rubber, teakwood. **Per capita arable land:** 1.4 acres. **Fish catch** (1975): 485,100 metric tons. **Electricity production** (1977): 912.00 mln. kwh. **Labor force:** 64% agriculture.

**Finance: Currency:** Kyat (May 1978: 7.04 = $1 US). **Gross domestic product** (1976): $3.49 mln. **Per capita income** (1974): $100. **Imports** (1977): $185 mln.; partners (1975): Jap., U.K., W. Eur., India. **Exports** (1977): $177 mln.; partners (1975): India, Sri Lanka, Mauritius, W. Eur., Jap., U.K. **Tourist receipts** (1975): $3 million. **Balance of payments** (1977): –$25,800,000. **International reserves** (May 1978): $138.2 mln. **Consumer prices** (change in 1977): 25.7%.

**Transport: Railway traffic** (1975): 2.09 bln. passenger-miles; 252.75 mln. net ton-miles. **Motor vehicles:** in use (1974): 36,300 passenger cars, 39,300 commercial vehicles. **Civil aviation:** 101 mln. passenger-miles (1975); 745 mln. freight ton-miles (1975). **Chief ports:** Rangoon, Sittwe, Bassein, Moulmein, Tavoy.

**Communications: Radios:** 659,000 licensed (1974), 33,000 manufactured (1975). **Telephones in use** (1975): 31,456. **Daily newspaper circulation** (1974): 319,000; 11 per 1,000 pop.

**Health: Life expectancy at birth** (1975): 48.6 male; 51.5 female. **Births** (annual per 1,000 pop. 1972-75): 39.5. **Deaths** (annual per 1,000 pop. 1972-75): 10.3. **Natural increase** (annual 1970-75): 2.37%. **Pop. per hospital bed** (1975): 1,222. **Pop. per physician** (1975): 6,930. **Infant mortality** (per 1,000 live births 1967): 63.9.

**Education: Literacy** (1975): 76%. **Pop. 5-19:** in school (1975): 40%, per teacher (1975): 111.

The Burmese arrived from Tibet before the 9th century, displacing earlier cultures, and a Buddhist monarchy was established by the 11th. Burma was conquered by the Mongol dynasty of China in 1272, then ruled by Shans as a Chinese tributary, until the 16th century.

Britain subjugated Burma in three wars, 1824-84, and ruled the country as part of India until 1937, when it became self-governing. It was overrun by Japan in World War II. Burma became independent outside the Commonwealth, Jan. 4, 1948.

Gen. Ne Win has dominated politics since 1958. He led a Revolutionary Council set up in 1962, which drove Indians from the civil service and Chinese from commerce. Socialization of the economy was advanced, isolation from foreign countries enforced. Lagging production and export, and rebellions by communists and Karen and Shan ethnic groups plague the country.

Bangladesh charged in 1978 that religious persecution had driven 150,000 Moslems from Burma.

# Burundi
## Republic of Burundi

**People: Population** (1977 est.): 3,970,000. **Age distrib. (%):** 0–14: 46.9; 15–59: 47.3; 60+: 5.9. **Pop. density:** 369.68 per sq. mi. **Urban** (1970): 2.2%. **Ethnic groups:** Hutu 85%, Tutsi 14%, Twa (pygmy) 1%. **Languages:** French, Kirundi (official), Swahili. **Religions:** Roman Catholic 50%, Protestant 4%, others.

**Geography: Area:** 10,739 sq. mi., the size of Maryland. **Location:** In central Africa. **Neighbors:** Rwanda on N, Zaire on W, Tanzania on E. **Topography:** Much of the country is grassy highland, with mountains reaching 8,900 ft. The southernmost source of the White Nile is located in Burundi. Lake Tanganyika is the second deepest lake in the world. **Capital:** Bujumbura. **Cities** (1970 est.): Bujumbura (met.) 78,810.

**Government: Head of state:** Pres. Jean Baptiste Bagaza; b. Aug. 29, 1946; in office: Nov. 9, 1976; **Head of government:** Prime Min. Edouard Nzambimana; in office: Nov. 10, 1976. **Local divisions:** 8 provinces and capital city. **Armed forces:** regulars 7,000; para-military 2,000.

**Economy: Chief crops:** Coffee (chief export), cotton, tea. **Minerals:** Nickel. **Per capita arable land:** 0.6 acres. **Electricity production** (1975): 23.00 mln. kwh. **Labor force:** 86% agriculture.

**Finance: Currency:** Franc (May 1978: 90 = $1 US). **Gross domestic product** (1974 est.): $340 mln. **Per capita income** (1974): $90. **Imports** (1977): $74 mln.; partners (1974): Benelux 22.6%, W. Ger. 11.1%, France 8.8%, U.S. 5.2%, U.K. 4.7%. **Exports** (1977): $95 mln.; partners (1973): U.S. 54%, W. Ger. 12%, Belg. 6%, USSR 5%. **Tourists** (1975): 14,600; receipts (1975): $1 million. **National budget** (1976): $56.74 mln. revenues; $54.50 mln. expenditures. **International reserves** (May 1978): $77.03 mln. **Consumer prices** (change in 1976): 6.8%.

**Transport: Motor vehicles:** in use (1974): 4,200 passenger cars, 1,700 commercial vehicles.

**Communications: Radios:** 100,000 in use (1974). **Telephones in use** (1975): 4,000. **Daily newspaper circulation** (1974): 1,200; 0.3 per 1,000 pop.

**Health: Life expectancy at birth** (1971): 40 male; 43 female. **Births** (annual per 1,000 pop. 1972-75): 48.0. **Deaths** (annual per 1,000 pop. 1972-75): 24.7. **Natural increase** (annual 1970-71): 2.16%. **Pop. per hospital bed** (1975): 963. **Pop. per physician** (1975): 48,143. **Infant mortality** (per 1,000 live births 1965): 150.

**Education: Literacy** (1975): 10%. **Pop. 5-19:** in school (1975): 16%, per teacher (1975): 265.

The pygmy Twa were the first inhabitants, followed by Bantu Hutus, who were conquered in the 16th century by the tall Tutsi (Watusi), probably from Ethiopia. Under German control in 1899, the area fell to Belgium in 1916, which exercised successively a League of Nations mandate and UN trusteeship over Ruanda-Urundi (now two countries).

Independence came in 1962, and the monarchy was overthrown in 1966. An unsuccessful Hutu rebellion in 1972-73 left 10,000 Tutsi and 100,00 Hutu dead. Over 100,000 Hutu fled to Tanzania and Zaire. Michel Micombero, ruler for ten years, was overthrown in a military coup in 1976.

Burundi is one of the poorest and most densely populated countries in Africa.

# Cambodia
*See Kampuchea*

# Cameroon
## United Republic of Cameroon

**People: Population** (1977 est.): 6,670,000. **Pop. density:** 36.34 per sq. mi. **Urban** (1970): 20.3%. **Ethnic groups:** Some 200 tribes; largest are Bamileke 30%, Fulani 7%. **Languages:** English, French (both official), 24 others. **Religions:** Roman Catholic 20%, Protesant 15%, Islam (mostly in N) 12%, others.

**Geography: Area:** 183,568 sq. mi., somewhat larger than California. **Location:** Between W and central Africa. **Neighbors:** Nigeria on NW, Chad, Central African Empire on E, Congo, Gabon, Equatorial Guinea on S. **Topography:** A low coastal plain with rain forests is in S; plateaus in center lead to forested mountains in W, including Mt. Cameroon, 13,000 ft.; grasslands in N lead to marshes around Lake Chad. **Capital:** Yaounde. **Cities** (1974 est.): Douala (met.) 350,000; Yaounde (met.) 250,000.

**Government: Head of state:** Pres. Ahmadou Ahidjo; b. Aug. 24, 1924; in office: Feb., 1958. **Local divisions:** 7 provinces with appointed governors. **Armed forces:** regulars 6,000; para-military 7,000.

**Economy: Industries:** Aluminum processing, palm products. **Chief crops:** Cocoa, coffee, peanuts, tea, bananas, cotton, tobacco. **Crude oil reserves** (1978): .06 mln. bbls. **Other resources:** Timber, rubber. **Per capita arable land:** 2.5 acres. **Meat production** (1975): beef: 43,000 tons; lamb: 15,000 tons. **Fish catch** (1975): 71,600 metric tons. **Electricity production** (1976): 1.33 bln. kwh. **Labor force:** 82% agriculture.

**Finance: Currency:** Franc (May 1978: 230.35 = $1 US). **Gross domestic product** (1976): $2.18 bln. **Per capita income** (1974): $307. **Imports** (1977): $944 mln.; partners (1974): Fr. 47%, W. Ger. 9%, U.S. 6%, It. 6%. **Exports** (1977): $658 mln.; partners (1974): Fr. 29%, Neth. 24%, W. Ger. 10%, U.S. 7%. **Tourists** (1974): 96,100; receipts (1974): $17 million. **Balance of payments** (1976): −$7,700,000. **International reserves** (Feb. 1978): $34.72 mln. **Consumer prices** (change in 1976): 9.9%.

**Transport: Railway traffic** (1975): 172.02 mln. pasenger-miles; 257.09 mln. net ton-miles. **Motor vehicles:** in use (1972): 39,100 passenger cars, 37,300 commercial vehicles. **Chief ports:** Douala.

**Communications: Radios:** 603,000 licensed (1974), 60,000 manufactured (1971). **Telephones in use** (1973): 22,000. **Daily newspaper circulation** (1974): 20,000; 3 per 1,000 pop.

**Health: Life expectancy at birth** (1975): 39.4 male; 42.6 female. **Births** (annual per 1,000 pop. 1972-75): 40.4. **Deaths** (annual per 1,000 pop. 1972-75): 22.0. **Natural increase** (annual 1970-75): 1.84%. **Pop. per hospital bed** (1975): 360. **Pop. per physician** (1975): 22,359. **Infant mortality** (per 1,000 live births 1973): 137.

**Education: Literacy** (1975): 12%. **Pop. 5-19:** in school (1975): 52%, per teacher (1975): 90.

Portuguese sailors were the first Europeans to reach Cameroon, in the 15th century. The European and American slave trade was very active in the area. German control lasted from 1884 to 1916, when France and Britain divided the territory, later receiving League of Nations mandates and UN trusteeships. French Cameroon became independent Jan. 1, 1960; one part of British Cameroon joined Nigeria in 1961, the other part joined Cameroon. Stability has allowed for development of roads, railways, and agriculture.

# Canada
*See also Canada in index.*

**People: Population** (1977 est.): 23,320,000. **Pop. density:** 6.55 per sq. mi. **Urban** (1971): 76.1%. **Cities** (1974 est.): Montreal (met.) 2,798,000; Toronto (met.) 712,785; Ottawa (met.) 626,000; Winnipeg (met.) 570,000; Hamilton (met.) 520,000.

**Government: Head of state:** Queen Elizabeth II, represented by Gov.-Gen. Jules Leger; in office: Jan. 14, 1974; **Head of government:** Prime Min. Pierre Elliott Trudeau; b. Oct. 18, 1919; in office: Aug. 20, 1968. **Armed forces:** regulars 80,000; reserves 19,100.

**Economy: Crude oil reserves** (1978): 6.00 bln. bbls. **Per capita arable land:** 4.7 acres. **Meat production** (1976): beef: 1.14 mln. tons; pork 511,900 tons. **Fish catch** (1975): 1,023,800 metric tons. **Electricity production** (1977): 316.55 bln. kwh. **Labor force:** 5% agric.; 30% manuf.

**Finance: Currency:** Dollar (May 1978: 1.12 = $1 US). **Gross domestic product** (1977): $193.87 bln. **Per capita income** (1976): $7,340. **Imports** (1977): $39.56 bln.; partners (1975): U.S. 68%, U.K. 3.6%, Jap. 3.5%, Ven. 3.2%. **Exports** (1977): $41.45 bln.; partners (1975): U.S. 65%, Jap. 6.6%, U.K. 5.6%, Neth. 1.4%. **Tourists** (1975): 13,625,000; receipts (1975): $1.775 billion. **Balance of payments** (1977): −$1,349,000,000. **National budget** (1977): 37.02 bln. revenues; $42.67 bln. expenditures. **International reserves** (May 1978): $4.75 bln. **Consumer prices** (change in 1977): 8.0%.

**Transport: Railway traffic** (1975): 18.20 bln. passenger-miles; 122.47 bln. net ton-miles. **Motor vehicles:** in use (1974): 8,472,200 passenger cars, 2,027,600 commercial vehicles; manufactured (1977): 1,162,800 passenger cars; 613,200 commercial vehicles. **Civil aviation:** 15,470 mln. passenger-miles (1977); 385,037 mln. freight ton-miles (1977).

**Communications: Television sets:** 8,232,000 in use (1974), 510,000 manufactured (1975). **Radios:** 20,252,000 in use (1974), 1,009,000 manufactured (1975). **Telephones in use** (1977): 13,785,647. **Daily newspaper circulation** (1973): 5,207,000; 235 per 1,000 pop.

**Health: Life expectancy at birth** (1972): 69.34 male; 76.36 female. **Births** (per 1,000 pop. 1975): 15.7. **Deaths** (per 1,000 pop. 1975): 7.3. **Natural increase** (1975): .84%. **Pop. per hospital bed** (1975): 110. **Pop. per physician** (1975): 593. **Infant mortality** (per 1,000 live births 1974): 15.0.

**Education: Literacy** (1975): 95%. **Pop. 5-19:** in school (1975): 86%, per teacher (1975): 23.

## Cape Verde Islands
### Republic of Cape Verde

**People: Population** (1977 est.): 310,000. **Pop. density:** 199.10 per sq. mi. **Ethnic groups:** Creole (mulatto) 70%, African 28%, European 1%. **Languages:** Portuguese (official), Crioulo. **Religions:** Roman Catholicism prevails.

**Geography: Area:** 1,557 sq. mi., a bit larger than Rhode Island. **Location:** In Atlantic O., off western tip of Africa. **Neighbors:** Nearest are Mauritania, Senegal. **Topography:** Cape Verde Islands are 15 in number, volcanic in origin (active crater on Fogo). The landscape is eroded and stark, with vegetation mostly in interior valleys. **Capital:** Praia. **Cities** (1974 est.): Praia 11,000; Mindelo 8,000.

**Government: Head of state:** Pres. Aristides Pereiro; in office: July 5, 1975; **Head of government:** Premier Pedro Pires; in office: July 5, 1975. **Local divisions:** 14 concelhos (municipalities).

**Economy: Chief crops:** Coffee, fruit, grain. **Minerals:** Salt. **Other resources:** Fish. **Per capita arable land:** 0.3 acres. **Electricity production** (1975): 8.00 mln. kwh.

**Finance: Currency:** Escudo (1974: 25.4 = $1 US). **Gross domestic product** (1974 est.): $79 mln. **Per capita income** (1974): $250. **Imports** (1975): $31 mln.; partners (1973): Port. 53%, U.K. 13%, Ang. 11%, Moz. 4%. **Exports** (1975): $33 mln.; partners (1973): Port. 61%, U.S. 25%, Zaire 3%. **Consumer prices** (change in 1977): 4.8%.

**Transport: Motor vehicles:** in use (1974): 2,500 passenger cars, 700 commercial vehicles. **Chief ports:** Mindelo, Praia.

**Communications: Radios:** 5,200 licensed (1973). **Telephones in use** (1977): 1,579.

**Health: Life expectancy at birth** (1975): 48.3 male; 51.7 female. **Births** (per 1,000 pop. 1974): 29.2. **Deaths** (per 1,000 pop. 1974): 8.8. **Natural increase** (1974): 2.04%. **Infant mortality** (per 1,000 live births 1974): 78.9.

The uninhabited Cape Verdes were discovered by the Portuguese in 1456 or 1460. The first Portuguese colonists landed in 1462; African slaves were brought soon after, and most Cape Verdeans descend from both groups. Many of the relatively well-educated Cape Verdeans served as officials in Portuguese African countries. Others led the Guinea-Bissau independence movement. Cape Verde independence came July 5, 1975. The government backs eventual union with Guinea-Bissau.

## Central African Empire

**People: Population** (1974 est.): 2,610,000. **Age distrib. (%):** 0-14: 41.6; 15-59: 53.9; 60+: 4.5. **Pop. density:** 10.82 per sq. mi. **Ethnic groups:** Banda 47%, Baya 27%, 80 other groups. **Languages:** French (official), Sangho (national). **Religions:** Protestant, Roman Catholic 35-65%, Moslem 8%, others.

**Geography: Area:** 241,313 sq. mi., slightly smaller than Texas. **Location:** In central Africa. **Neighbors:** Chad on N, Cameroon on W, Congo, Zaire on S, Sudan on E. **Topography:** The country is mostly a rolling plateau, average altitude 2,000 ft., with rivers draining S to the Congo and N to Lake Chad. Open, well-watered savanna covers most of the area, with an arid area in NE, and tropical rainforest in SW. **Capital:** Bangui. **Cities** (1971 est.): Bangui 187,000.

**Government: Head of state:** Emp. Jean-Bedel Bokassa I; b. Feb. 22, 1920; in office: Jan. 1, 1966; **Head of government:** Prime Min. Henri Maldou; in office: July 14, 1978. **Local divisions:** 14 prefectures. **Armed forces:** regulars 1,200; paramilitary 1,400.

**Economy: Industries:** Textiles, radios. **Chief crops:** Cotton, coffee, peanuts, corn, sorghum. **Minerals:** Diamonds (chief export), uranium, iron, copper. **Other resources:** Timber. **Per cap-**

**ita arable land:** 8.0 acres. **Meat production** (1975): beef: 18,000 tons. **Electricity production** (1975): 52.00 mln. kwh. **Labor force:** 87% agriculture.

**Finance: Currency:** Franc (May-1978: 230.35 = $1 US). **Gross domestic product** (1974 est.): $310 mln. **Per capita income** (1974): $110. **Imports** (1976): $54 mln.; partners (1973): Fr. 57%, U.S. 9%, W. Ger. 7%, U.K. 4%. **Exports** (1976): $58 mln.; partners (1973): Fr. 41%, U.S. 15%, Isr. 11%, It. 6%. **Tourists** (1974): 4,100; receipts (1975): $3 million. **Balance of payments** (1976): +$15,400,000. **International reserves** (Feb. 1978): $30.25 mln. **Consumer prices** (change in 1977): 10.9%.

**Transport: Motor vehicles:** in use (1974): 9,100 passenger cars, 3,900 commercial vehicles.

**Communications: Radios:** 70,000 licensed (1974), 13,000 manufactured (1975). **Telephones in use** (1973): 5,000. **Daily newspaper circulation** (1972): 500; 0.3 per 1,000 pop.

**Health: Life expectancy at birth** (1960): 33 male; 36 female. **Births** (annual per 1,000 pop. 1972-75): 43.4. **Deaths** (annual per 1,000 pop. 1972-75): 22.5. **Natural increase** (annual 1970-75): 2.09%. **Pop. per hospital bed** (1975): 489. **Pop. per physician** (1975): 27,629. **Infant mortality** (per 1,000 live births 1959-60): 190.

**Education: Literacy** (1975): 12%. **Pop. 5-19:** in school (1975): 39%, per teacher (1975): 159.

Various Bantu tribes migrated through the region for centuries before French control was asserted in the late 19th century, when the region was named Ubangi-Shari. Complete independence was attained Aug. 13, 1960.

All political parties were dissolved in 1960, and the country became a center for Chinese political influence in Africa. Relations with China were severed after a 1965 coup. Elizabeth Domitien, premier 1975-76, was the first woman to hold that post in an African country. Pres. Jean-Bedel Bokassa, ruler since 1965, proclaimed himself constitutional emperor of the newly-named Central African Empire December 1976.

The landlocked nation has been unable to develop its large mineral resources.

## Chad
### Republic of Chad

**People: Population** (1977 est.): 4,200,000. **Age distrib. (%):** 0-14: 41.0; 15-59: 55.0; 60+: 4.0. **Pop. density:** 8.47 per sq. mi. **Urban** (1974): 13.9%. **Ethnic groups:** Sudanese Arab 30%, Sudanic tribes 25%, Nilotic, Saharan tribes. **Languages:** French (official), Arabic, others. **Religions:** Moslems 40%, Christians 30%, others.

**Geography: Area:** 495,752 sq. mi., four-fifths the size of Alaska. **Location:** In central N. Africa. **Neighbors:** Libya on N, Niger, Nigeria, Cameroon on W, Central African Empire on S, Sudan on E. **Topography:** Chad has a southern wooded savanna, a steppe, and a desert, part of the Sahara, in the N. Southern rivers flow N to Lake Chad, surrounded by marshland. **Capital:** N'Djamena. **Cities** (1972 est.): N'Djamena (met.) 179,000; Sarh 43,770; Mondon 39,600.

**Government: Head of state:** Pres. Felix Malloum N'Gakoutou Bey-NDi; b. Sept. 10, 1932; in office: Apr. 16, 1975; **Local divisions:** 14 prefectures with appointed governors. **Armed forces:** regulars 5,200; para-military 6,000.

**Economy: Chief crops:** Cotton. **Minerals:** Uranium. **Per capita arable land:** 4.0 acres. **Meat production** (1975): beef: 28,000 tons; lamb: 14,000 tons. **Fish catch** (1975): 115,000 metric tons. **Electricity production** (1976): 57.60 mln. kwh. **Labor force:** 91% agriculture.

**Finance: Currency:** Franc (May 1978: 230.35 = $1 US). **Gross domestic product** (1970): $.28 mln. **Per capita income** (1974): $94. **Imports** (1976): $115 mln.; partners (1973): Fr. 42%, Nigeria 12%, Congo 4%, Camer. 4%. **Exports** (1975): $70 mln.; partners (1973): Nigeria 6%, Congo 5%, Fr. 3%, Cent. Aft. Emp. 2%. **Tourists** (1973): 16,700; receipts (1975): $9 million. **Balance of payments** (1977): -$4,900,000. **International reserves** (Feb. 1978): $5.42 mln. **Consumer prices** (change in 1977): 31.0%.

**Transport: Motor vehicles:** in use (1973): 5,800 passenger cars, 6,300 commercial vehicles.

**Communications: Radios:** 70,000 in use (1974). **Telephones in use** (1975): 5,000. **Daily newspaper circulation** (1974): 1,500; 0.4 per 1,000 pop.

**Health: Life expectancy at birth** (1964): 29 male; 35 female.

**Births** (annual per 1,000 pop. 1972-75): 44.0. **Deaths** (annual per 1,000 pop. 1972-75): 24.0. **Natural increase** (annual 1970-75): 2.00%. **Pop. per hospital bed** (1975): 1,194. **Pop. per physician** (1975): 45,413. **Infant mortality** (per 1,000 live births 1963-64): 160.1.

**Education: Literacy** (1975): 7%. **Pop. 5-19:** in school (1975): 15%, per teacher (1975): 468.

Chad was the site of paleolithic and neolithic cultures before the Sahara Desert formed. A succession of kingdoms and Arab slave traders dominated Chad until France took control around 1900. Independence came Aug. 11, 1960.

Arab rebels, reportedly aided by Libya, fought government and French troops from 1966. French troops and jets fought rebels in 1978. French aid and influence is strong.

Libya, which reportedly switched some aid from rebels to the regime after it broke ties with Israel, annexed 37,000 sq. mi. of uranium and iron-rich land in northern Chad in 1976, stirring protests by Chad.

Chad was hardest hit among Sahel countries during the 1972-74 drought, whose effects have lingered.

# Chile

## Republic of Chile

**People: Population** (1977 est.): 10,660,000. **Age distrib.** (%): 0–14: 39.6; 15–59: 53.2; 60+: 7.2. **Pop. density:** 37.22 per sq. mi. **Urban** (1976): 78.7%. **Ethnic groups:** Mestizo 66%, Spanish 25%, Indian 5%. **Languages:** Spanish. **Religions:** Roman Catholic 90%, Protestants 6%.

**Geography: Area:** 286,396 sq. mi., larger than Texas. **Location:** Occupies western coast of southern S. America. **Neighbors:** Peru on N, Bolivia on NE, Argentina on E. **Topography:** Andes Mtns. are on E border including some of the world's highest peaks; on W is 2,650-mile Pacific Coast. Width varies between 100 and 250 miles. In N is Atacama Desert, in center are agricultural regions, in S are forests and grazing lands. **Capital:** Santiago. **Cities** (1975 est.) Santiago (met.) 3,262,990; Valparaiso (met.) 591,840; Concepcion (met.) 499,800.

**Government: Head of state:** Pres. Augusto Pinochet Ugarte; b. Nov. 25, 1915; in office: Sept. 11, 1973. **Local divisions:** 12 regions and Santiago region, comprised of 25 provinces, all headed by presidential appointees. **Armed forces:** regulars 106,600; reserves 160,000.

**Economy: Industries:** Steel, textiles, wood products. **Chief crops:** Grain, rice, beans, potatoes, peas, fruits, grapes. **Minerals:** Copper (10% world output), nitrates, iodine (half world output), iron, coal, oil, gas, gold, silver, molybdenum, cobalt, zinc, maganese, borate, mica, mercury, salt, sulphur, marble, onyx. **Crude oil reserves** (1978): 440 mln. bbls. **Other resources:** water, forests. **Per capita arable land:** 1.3 acres. **Meat production** (1976): beef: 198,100 tons; pork: 25,100 tons; lamb: 16,400 tons. **Fish catch** (1975): 1,128,300 metric tons. **Electricity production** (1977): 9.86 bln. kwh. **Labor force:** 21% agric.; 16% manuf.

**Finance: Currency:** Peso (May 1978: 31.60 = $1 US). **Gross domestic product** (1977): $11.49 bln. **Per capita income** (1976): $687. **Imports** (1976): $1.68 bln.; partners (1975): U.S. 21.9%, Iran 6%, W. Ger. 5.3%, Braz. 4.3%. **Exports** (1976): $2.08 bln.; partners (1975): W. Ger. 16%, Jap. 12.4%, Arg. 11.1%, U.K. 9.1%, Braz. 6.5%. **Tourists** (1975): 250,000; receipts (1973): $52 million. **Balance of payments** (1977): +$134,000,000 **National budget** (1975): $906.29 mln. revenues; $852.04 mln. expenditures. **International reserves** (May 1978): $937.5 mln. **Consumer prices** (change in 1977): 92.0%.

**Transport: Railway traffic** (1975): 1.30 bln. passenger-miles; 1.20 bln. net ton-miles. **Motor vehicles:** in use (1975): 236,800 passenger cars, 156,200 commercial vehicles; assembled (1976): 5,004 passenger cars; 6,540 commercial vehicles. **Civil aviation:** 731 mln. passenger-miles (1976); 43,043 mln. freight ton-miles (1976). **Chief ports:** Valparaiso, Arica, Antofagasta.

**Communications: Television sets:** 750,000 in use (1974), 223,000 manufactured (1974). **Radios:** 3,100,000 in use (1974), 139,000 manufactured (1974). **Telephones in use** (1977): 473,435. **Daily newspaper circulation** (1972): 907,000; 94 per 1,000 pop.

**Health: Life expectancy at birth** (1970): 60.48 male; 66.01 female. **Births** (per 1,000 pop. 1975): 25.0. **Deaths** (per 1,000 pop. 1975): 7.2. **Natural increase** (1975): 1.78%. **Pop. per hospital bed** (1975): 301. **Pop. per physician** (1975): 1,857.

**Infant mortality** (per 1,000 live births 1972): 76.5.

**Education: Literacy** (1975): 90%. **Pop. 5–19:** in school (1975): 73%, per teacher (1975): 42.

Northern Chile was under Inca rule before the Spanish conquest, 1536-40. The southern Araucanian Indians resisted until the late 19th century. Independence was gained 1810-18, under Jose de San Martin and Bernardo O'Higgins; the latter, as supreme director 1817-23, sought social and economic reforms until deposed. Chile defeated Peru and Bolivia in 1836-39 and 1879-84, gaining mineral-rich northern land.

After 30 years of intermittent reform attempts, Christian Democrats under Eduardo Frei Montalva came into office in 1964, and instituted social programs and gradual nationalization of foreign-owned mining companies. In 1970, Salvador Allende Gossens, a Marxist, became president with a third of the national vote, despite reported attempts by the U.S. Central Intelligence Agency and the International Telephone & Telegraph Corp. to foment a military coup.

The Allende government furthered nationalizations, and improved conditions for the poor. But illegal and violent actions by extremist supporters of the government, the regime's failure to attain majority support, and poorly planned socialist economic programs led to political and financial chaos and drastic declines in production. Protests by farmers and the urban middle class, some of them reportedly aided by U.S. government and business figures, helped provoke a crisis.

A military junta seized power Sept. 11, 1973, and said Allende killed himself. A few thousand were killed in street fighting and junta reprisals. The junta named a mostly-military cabinet, broke off relations with Cuba, which had been close under Allende, and announced plans to "exterminate Marxism."

Some 15,000 Allende supporters, mostly foreigners, were allowed to leave Chile. According to a 1977 statement of the Conference of Chilean Bishops, about 900 Chilean political prisoners had disappeared since the coup. Torture was still being used by the regime at that time, according to a UN report. Repression was eased in 1978.

The economy continued to deteriorate under the new regime, though inflation had been reduced by 1978.

**Tierra del Fuego** is the largest (18,800 sq. mi.) island in the archipelago of the same name at the southern tip of South America, an area of majestic mountains, torturous channels, and high winds. It was discovered 1520 by Magellan; he named the island Land of Fire because of its many Indian bonfires. Part of the island is in Chile, part in Argentina, Punta Arenas, on a mainland Peninsula in Chile, is a center of sheep-raising and the world's southernmost city (pop. 67,600); Puerto Williams, pop. 949, is the southernmost settlement.

# China

## People's Republic of China

**People: Population** (1977 est.): 865,680,000. **Pop. density:** 234.51 per sq. mi. **Ethnic groups:** Han Chinese 94%, Mongol, Korean, Turkic groups, Manchu, others. **Languages:** Mandarin Chinese (official), Shanghai, Canton, Fukien, Hakka dialects; Tibetan, Vigus (Turkic). **Religions:** Confucianism, Buddism, Taoism, are traditional; Moslems 5%.

**Geography: Area:** 3,691,502 sq. mi., slightly larger than the U.S. **Location:** Occupies most of the habitable mainland of E. Asia. **Neighbors:** Mongolia on N, USSR on NE and NW, Afghanistan, Pakistan on W, India, Nepal, Bhutan, Burma, Laos, Vietnam on S, N. Korea on NW. **Topography:** Two-thirds of the vast territory is mountainous or desert, and only one-tenth is cultivated. Rolling topography rises to high elevations in the N in the Khinghan Mtns. separating Manchuria and Mongolia; the Tarabagota Mtns. in Sinkiang; the Himalayan and Kunlun Mtns. in the SW and in Tibet. Length is 1,860 mi. from N to S, width E to W is more than 2000 mi. The eastern half of China is one of the best-watered lands in the world. Three great river systems, the Yangtze, the Hwang (Yellow) and the Xijiang (Si Kianj) provide water for vast farmlands. **Capital:** Peking. **Cities** (1970 est.): Shanghai 10,820,000; Peking 7,570,000; Tientsin 4,280,000; Canton 3,000,000; Shenyang 3,000,000; Wuhan 2,700,000; (1957 est.): Chunking 2,121,000; Harbin 1,552,000; Nanking 1,419,000; Sian 1,310,000; Tsinglao 1,121,000; Chengtu 1,107,000; Taiyuan 1,020,000.

**Government: Effective head of government:** First Dep. Prime Min. Teng Hsiao-ping; b. 1904; in office: July, 1977; **Communist Party Chmn.** Hua Kuo-fenj; b. 1921; in office: Feb. 1976.

**Local divisions:** 21 provinces, 5 ethnic autonomous regions, and 3 cities, local autonomy varies. **Armed forces:** regulars 3,950,000; para-military 11,000,000.

**Economy: Industries:** Textiles, steel, chemicals, cement, plastics, agriculture implements, trucks. **Chief crops:** Grain, corn, peas, soybeans in N; rice, sugar in S, abutilon, hemp, jute, ramie, flax, cotton, tea. **Minerals:** Coal (3d in world), iron, tin, antimony, tungsten, molybdenum, salt. **Other resources:** Silk. **Per capita arable land:** 0.3 acres. **Meat production** (1975): beef: 2.02 mln. tons; pork: 9.80 mln. tons; lamb: 607,000 tons. **Fish catch** (1975): 6,880,000 metric tons. **Labor force:** 67% agriculture.

**Finance: Currency:** Yuan (1974: 2 = $1 US). **Gross domestic product** (1974 est.): $170 bln. **Per capital income** (1974): $200. **Imports** (1974): $7.0 bln.; partners (1974): Jap. 32%, U.S. 13%, Can. 7%, W. Ger. 7%. **Exports** (1974): $5.6 bln.; partners (1974): Jap. 21%, Hong Kong 19% Sing. 5%. **Foreign currency reserves** (1978): $3 bln.

**Transport: Railway traffic** (1971): 186.92 bln. net ton-miles. **Motor vehicles:** in use (1973): 30,000 passenger cars, 650,000 commercial vehicles. **Chief ports:** Shanghai, Tientsin, Dairen.

**Communications: Television sets:** 500,000 in use (1973). **Radios:** 12,000,000 in use (1970). **Telephones in use** (1951): 255,000.

**Health: Life expectancy at birth** (1975): 59.9 male; 63.3 female. **Births** (annual per 1,000 pop. 1972-75): 26.9. **Deaths** (per 1,000 pop. 1976): 9.7. **Natural increase** (annual 1970-75): 1.66%. **Pop. per hospital bed** (1975): 1,000. **Pop. per physician** (1975): 8,000. **Infant mortality** (per 1,000 live births 1973): 55.

**Education: Literacy** (1975): 95%. **Pop. 5-19:** in school (1975): 62%, per teacher (1975): 46.

**History.** Remains of various man-like creatures who lived as early as several hundred thousand years ago have been found in many parts of China. Neolithic agricultural settlements dotted the Yellow River basin from about 5,000 B.C. Their language, religion, and art were the souces of later Chinese civilization.

A more developed culture, with the beginnings of literacy and metallurgy, emerged under the Shang Dynasty (c. 1500 B.C.-c. 1000B.C.) which ruled much of North China. Its relation to earlier Middle Eastern and Indian civilizations is unknown.

A succession of dynasties and interdynastic warring kingdoms ruled China for the next 3,000 years. They expanded Chinese political and cultural domination to the south and west, and developed a brilliant technologically and culturally advanced society. Rule by foreigners (Mongols in the Yuan Dynasty, 1271-1368, and Manchus in the Ch'ing Dynasty, 1644-1911) did not alter the underlying culture.

A period of relative stagnation left China vulnerable to internal and external pressures in the 19th century. Rebellions left tens of millions dead, and Russia, Japan, Britain, and other powers exercised political and economic control in large parts of the country. China became a republic Jan. 1, 1912, following the Wuchang Uprising inspired by Dr. Sun Yat-sen.

For a period of 50 years, 1894-1945, China was involved in conflicts with Japan. In 1895, China ceded Korea, Taiwan, and other areas. On Sept. 18, 1931, Japan seized the Northeastern Provinces (Manchuria) and set up a puppet state called Manchukuo. The border province of Jehol was cut off as a buffer state in 1933. Japan invaded China proper July 7, 1937. After its defeat in World War II, Japan gave up all seized land.

After the war with Japan ended, Aug. 15, 1945, internal disturbances arose involving the Kuomintang, communists, and other factions. Manchuria was lost by the Kuomintang regime in 1948, and China proper came under domination of Communist armies during 1949-1950. The Kuomintang government moved to Taiwan (Formosa), 90 mi. off the mainland, Dec. 8, 1949.

The People's Republic of China was proclaimed in Peking (Peiping) Sept. 21, 1949, by the Chinese People's Political Consultative Conference under Mao Tse-tung, communist leader. Chou En-lai was named premier and foreign minister Oct. 1, 1949.

The communist regime and the USSR signed a 30-year treaty of "friendship, alliance and mutual assistance," Feb. 15, 1950, repudiating the 1945 treaty between the Soviet Union and the Kuomintang government authorized by the Yalta Agreement. Great Britian recognized the People's Republic in 1950 and France did so in 1964. By 1975, over 100 nations had recognized the regime.

The U.S. refused recognition, and after its consular officers met with abuse, withdrew them. On Nov. 26, 1950, the People's Republic sent armies into Korea against U.S. troops and forced a stalemate.

By the 1960s, relations with the USSR deteriorated, with disagreements on borders, idealogy and leadership of world communism. The USSR cancelled aid accords, and China, with Albania, launched anti-Soviet propaganda drives.

On Mar. 2, 1969, Chinese and Russian soldiers fought one of a series of clashes on an island in the Ussuri River on the border between the two nations in the Far East. There were later clashes and reports of skirmishes to the west on the Sinkiang-USSR border. In 1970, ambassadors were exchanged for the first time since 1966. Border talks through 1975 were unsuccessful and minor skirmishes took place on both fronts in 1976 and 1978.

China sought to promote revolutionary movements in Africa, Asia and South America. The program suffered serious setbacks, 1965-66. In the 1970s, China was sending a few hundred million dollars a year in military and economic aid to several governments, two-thirds of them in Africa.

On Oct. 25, 1971, the UN General Assembly ousted the Taiwan governemnt from the UN and seated Communist China in its place. The U.S. had supported the mainland's admission but opposed Taiwan's expulsion.

In April 1971, after the U.S. relaxed restrictions on visits by its citizens, a U.S. table tennis team toured the People's Republic.

U.S. Pres. Nixon visited China Feb. 21-28, 1972, on invitation from Premier Chou En-lai, ending years of antipathy between the two nations. They agreed to continue progress toward normalization of relations. China and the U.S. moved close to formal diplomatic relations by opening liaison offices in each other's capitals, May-June 1973. Trade between the two countries neared $1 billion in 1974, largely U.S. grain exports, but declined in subsequent years.

**Internal developments.** After an initial period of consolidation, 1949-52, industry, agriculture, and social and economic institutions were forcibly molded according to Maoist ideals. However, frequent drastic changes in policy, and violent factionalism have, at times, interfered with economic development, and have prevented the return to stability and national unity lost a century ago.

In 1957, Mao Tse-tung admitted an estimated 800,000 people had been executed 1949-54; opponents claimed much higher figures. Some 110,000 political prisoners seized in 1957 were released in 1978.

The Great Leap Forward, 1958-60, tried to force the pace of economic development through intensive labor on the huge new rural communes, and through emphasis on ideological purity and enthusiasm. The program caused resistance and severe dislocations, and was largely abandoned; poor weather and suspension of Soviet aid were also blamed for the failure. Serious food shortages developed, and the government was forced to buy grain from Argentina, Mexico, Canada, and Australia, Light industries dependent on agriculture for raw materials were also affected.

Mao and his supporters within the Communist hierachy launched a movement in 1965 called the Great Proletarian Cultural Revolution, in an attempt to oppose pragmatism and bureaucratic power and instruct a new generation in revolutionary principles. Massive purges took place at the national and local levels. Red Guards, composed largely of students and other youths, helped leftists seize power in many areas, but factional fighting weakened their power. A program of forcibly relocating millions of urban teenagers into the countryside was launched.

By 1968 the movement had run its course. Revolutionary committees that had assumed control were largely dominated by the military. Many purged officials returned to office in subsequent years, and reforms in education and industry that had placed ideology above expertise were gradually weakened.

In the mid-1970s, factional and ideological fighting increased, and emerged into the open after the 1976 deaths of Mao and premier Chou En-lai. Chiang Ching, Mao's widow, and three other leading leftists were purged and placed under arrest, after reportedly trying to seize power. Their opponents said the "gang of four" had used severe repression and mass torture, had sparked local fighting and had disrupted production. The new ruling group modified Maoist policies in education, culture, and industry, and sought better ties with non-Communist countries. Relations with Vietnam deteriorated in 1978 as China charged persecution of ethnic Chinese. Aid to pro-Maoist Albania was severed in 1978.

About 800,000 people were killed in 1977 when an earthquake leveled the northern industrial city of Tangshan. Drought and transport disruptions reportedly caused food shortages.

Increased army influence was reflected by a series of nuclear test explosions in 1976, including the largest ever in China. The first Chinese atomic bomb was exploded in 1964; the first hydrogen bomb in 1967. There is a growing stockpile of nuclear weapons and intermediate range missiles. Long range missiles have been tested. The Chinese navy has been built into the world's third largest. The first orbiting space satellite was launched in 1970.

**Manchuria.** Home of the Manchus, rulers of China 1644-1911, Manchuria has accommodated millions of Chinese settlers in the 20th century. Under Japanese rule 1931-45, the area became industrialized. China no longer uses the name Manchuria for the region, which is divided into three provinces.

**Kwantung** is the southernmost part of Manchuria. Russia in 1898 forced China to lease it Kwantung, and built Port Arthur (Lushun) and the port of Dairen (Luda). Japan seized Port Arthur in 1905. It was turned over to the USSR by the 1945 Yalta agreement, but finally returned to China in 1950.

**Inner Mongolia** was organized by the People's Republic in 1947. Its boundaries have undergone frequent changes, allegedly in order to dilute the minority Mongol population. Only 20% of the 6.2 million inhabitants are Mongol. Capital: Huhehaote (Kweisui).

**Sinkiang Uigur Autonomous Region,** in Central Asia, comprising Chinese Turkestan, Kulia, and Kashgaria, is 633,802 sq. mi., pop. 7.3 million (75% Uigurs, a Turkic Moslem group, with a heavy Chinese increase in recent years). Capital: Urumchi. It is China's richest region in strategic minerals. Some Uigurs have fled to the USSR, claiming national oppression by China.

**Tibet,** 470,000 sq. mi., is a thinly populated region of high plateaus and massive mountains, the Himalayas on the S, the Kunluns on the N. High passes connect with India and Nepal; roads lead into China proper. Capital: Lhasa. Average altitude is 15,000 ft. Jiachan, 15,870 ft., is believed to be the highest inhabited town on earth. Agriculture is primitive. Pop. 1.7 million (of whom 500,000 are Chinese). Another four million Tibetans form the majority of the population of vast adjacent areas that have long been incorporated into China.

China ruled all of Tibet from the 18th century, but independence came in 1911. China reasserted control in 1951, and a communist goverment was installed in 1953, revising the theocratic Lamaist Buddhist rule. Serfdom was abolished, but all land remained collectivized.

A Tibetan uprising within China in 1956 spread to Tibet in 1959. The rebellion was crushed with Chinese troops, and Buddhism was almost totally suppressed. The Dalai Lama and 100,000 Tibetans fled to India. Chinese have taken nearly all major posts in the Tibet Autonomous Region set up in 1965. Revolts continued in 1965-66, and fighting was reported as late as 1976. The International Commission of Jurists charged the Chinese regime with genocide in Tibet in 1961.

## China (Taiwan)

### Republic of China

**People: Population** (1975): 16,050,000. **Pop. density:** 1,181 per sq. mi. **Ethnic groups:** Han Chinese 98% (18% from mainland), aborigines (of Indonesian origin) 2%. **Languages:** Mandarin Chinese (official), Taiwan, Hakka dialects, Japanese, English. **Religions:** Buddhism, Taoism, Confucianism prevail, Christians 2.5%.

**Geography: Area:** 13,592 sq. mi., the size of Maryland and Delaware combined. **Location:** Off SE coast of China, between E. and S. China Seas. **Neighbors:** Nearest is China. **Topography:** A range of mountains forms the backbone of the island, the eastern half is very steep and craggy, the western slope is flat, fertile, and well-cultivated. **Capital:** Taipei. **Cities** (1974 est.): Taipei (met.) 2,000,000; Kaohsiung 1,000,000; Tainau 500,000.

**Government: Head of state:** Chiang Ching-kuo; b. Mar. 18, 1910; in office: May 20, 1978; **Head of government:** Prime Min. Sun Yun-suan; b. Nov. 11, 1911; in office: May 30, 1978. **Local divisions:** Provincial Government is under a governor appointed by the national government; Provincial Assembly has limited powers. **Armed forces:** regulars 460,000; reserves 1,125,000.

**Economy: Industries:** Textiles, clothing, electrical and electronic equip., processed foods, chemicals, glass, machinery. **Chief crops:** Rice, bananas, pineapples, sugar cane, sweet potatoes, wheat, soybeans, peanuts, jute. **Minerals:** Coal, gold,

copper, sulphur, oil. **Crude oil reserves** (1978): 212 mln. bbls. **Per capita arable land:** 0.2 acres. **Meat production** (1976): beef: 9,000 tons; pork: 457,200 tons. **Labor force:** 37% agric.; 19% manuf.

**Finance: Currency:** Dollar (May 1978: 38.00 = $1 US). **Gross domestic product** (1977): $19.62 bln. **Per capita income** (1976): $800. **Imports** (1976): $7.59 bln.; partners (1974): Jap. 32%, U.S. 24%, W. Ger. 7%, Kuw. 6%. **Exports** (1976): $8.15 bln.; partners (1974): U.S. 37%, Jap. 15%, Hong Kong 6%, W. Ger. 6%. **Tourists** (1974): 362,900; receipts (1974): $102 million. **Balance of payments** (1977): −$244,000,000. **National budget** (1973): $2.27 bln. revenues; $2.01 bln. expenditures. **International reserves** (Apr. 1978): $1.43 bln. **Consumer prices** (change in 1977): 6.8%.

**Transport: Motor Vehicles:** in use (1973): 326,900 passenger cars, 107,000 commercial vehicles; assembled (1975): 23,000 passenger cars, 6,500 commercial vehicles. **Chief ports:** Kaohsiung, Keelung.

**Communications: Television sets:** 2,800,000 in use (1974). over 4,500,000 manufactured (1973). **Radios:** 3,500,000 in use (1974). **Telephones in use** (1977): 1,396,022. **Daily newspaper circulation** (1974): 1,300,000; 83 per 1,000 pop.

**Health: Life expectancy at birth** (1972): 66.8 male; 72.0 female. **Births** (per 1,000 pop. 1973): 23.8. **Deaths** (per 1,000 pop. 1973): 4.8. **Natural increase** (1973): 1.90%. **Pop. per hospital bed** (1975): 928. **Pop. per physician** (1975): 3,000. **Infant mortality** (per 1,000 live births 1973): 18.

**Education: Literacy** (1975): 88%. **Pop. 5-19:** in school (1975): 65%, per teacher (1975): 58.

Large-scale Chinese immigration began in the 17th century. The island came under mainland control after an interval of Dutch rule, 1620-62. Taiwan (also called Formosa) was ruled by Japan 1895-1945. Two million Kuomintang supporters fled to Taiwan in 1949. Both the Taipei and Peking governments consider Taiwan an integral part of China. The U.S., one of the few nations to maintain formal ties, keeps 1,100 troops on Taiwan.

Land reform, government planning, U.S. aid and investment, and free universal education have brought huge advances in industry, agriculture, and mass living standards. Native Taiwanese candidates gained in 1977 local elections.

**The Penghus** (Pescadores), 50 sq. mi., pop. 120,000, lie between Taiwan and the mainland. **Quemoy** and **Matsu,** civilian pop. 75,000, lie just off the mainland; the last U.S. advisers left in 1976.

## Colombia

### Republic of Colombia

**People: Population** (1977 est.) 25,050,000. **Pop. density:** 55.01 per sq. mi. **Urban** (1974): 64.3%. **Ethnic groups:** Mestizo 58%, Caucasian 20%, Mulatto 14%, Negro 4%, Indian 1%. **Languages:** Spanish. **Religions:** Roman Catholic 95%, Protestant under 1%.

**Geography: Area:** 455,355 sq. mi., larger than Texas and California combined. **Location:** At the NW corner of S. America. **Neighbors:** Panama on NW, Ecuador, Peru on S, Brazil, Venezuela on E. **Topography:** Three ranges of Andes, the Western, Central, and Eastern Cordilleras, run through the country from N to S. The eastern range consists mostly of high table lands, densely populated. The Magdalena R. rises in Andes, flows N to Carribean, through a rich alluvial plain. Sparsely-settled plains in E are drained by Orinoco and Amazon systems. **Capital:** Bogota. **Cities** (1973 cen.): Bogota 2,855,065; Medellin (met.) 1,417,384; Cali (met.) 923,264; Barranquilla (met.) 726,726.

**Government: Head of state:** Pres. Julio Cesar Turbay Ayala; b. June 8, 1916; in office: Aug. 7, 1978. **Local divisions:** 22 departments with elected legislatures and various special districts. **Armed forces:** regulars 56,500; reserves 250,000.

**Economy: Industries:** Textiles, rubber goods, hides, steel, paper, cement, chemicals. **Chief crops:** Coffee (2d in exports), rice, tobacco, cotton, cocoa, maize, potatoes, sugar, bananas. **Minerals:** Oil, gas, emeralds (95% world output), gold, silver, copper, lead, mercury, cinnabar, manganese, platinum, coal, iron, nickel, salt. **Crude oil reserves** (1960): 960 mln. bbls. **Other resources:** Rubber, balsam, dye-woods, copaiba, hydro power. **Per capita arable land:** 0.3 acres. **Meat production** (1976): beef: 541,800 tons; pork: 102,400 tons. **Fish catch** (1975): 66,600 metric tons. **Electricity production** (1976): 13.60 bln. kwh. **Labor force:** 45% agriculture.

**Finance: Currency:** Peso (Mar. 1978: 38.57 = $1 US). **Gross domestic product** (1975): $12.66 bln. **Per capita income** (1975): $513. **Imports** (1976): $1.57 bln.; partners (1974): U.S. 39.9%, W. Ger. 9.3%, Jap. 9%, Fr. 3.9%, Swed. 2.4%. **Exports** (1976): $1.69 bln.; partners (1974): U.S. 36.3%, W. Ger. 12.4%, Neth. 4.7%. **Tourists** (1975): 443,300; receipts (1975): $140 million. **Balance of payments** (1976): +$605,000,000. **National budget** (1977): $1.66 bln. revenues; $1.51 bln. expenditures. **International reserves** (May 1978): $2.05 bln. **Consumer prices** (change in 1977): 30.0%.

**Transport: Railway traffic** (1975): 324.78 mln. passenger-miles; 707.32 mln. net ton-miles. **Motor vehicles:** in use (1973): 326,900 passenger cars, 107,000 commercial vehicles; assembled (1976): 26,904 passenger cars; 9,504 commercial vehicles. **Civil aviation:** 2,072 mln. passenger-miles (1977); 109,381 mln. freight ton-miles (1977). **Chief ports:** Buena Ventura, Santa Marta, Barranquilla, Cartagena.

**Communications: Television sets:** 971,000 in use (1973), 71,000 manufactured (1973). **Radios:** 2,805,000 in use (1974), 7,000 manufactured (1973). **Telephones in use** (1977): 1,295,860. **Daily newspaper circulation** (1974): 1,449,000; 69 per 1,000 pop.

**Health: Life expectancy at birth** (1975): 59.2 male; 62.7 female. **Births** (annual per 1,000 pop. 1972-75): 40.6. **Deaths** (annual per 1,000 pop. 1972-75): 9.5. **Natural increase** (annual 1970-75): 3.18%. **Pop. per hospital bed** (1975): 574. **Pop. per physician** (1975): 2,264. **Infant mortality** (per 1,000 live births 1971): 62.8.

**Education: Literacy** (1975): 78%. **Pop. 5-19:** in school (1975): 47%, per teacher (1975): 62.

Spain subdued the local Indian kingdoms (Funza, Tunja) by the 1530s, and ruled Colombia and neighboring areas as New Granada for 300 years. Independence was won by 1819. Venezuela and Ecuador broke away in 1829-30, and Panama withdrew in 1903.

One of the few functioning Latin American democracies, Colombia is nevertheless plagued by rural and urban violence, though scaled down from "La Violencia" of 1948-58, which claimed 200,000 lives. Attempts at land and social reform, and progress in industrialization have not yet succeeded in reducing massive social problems aggravated by a very high birth rate.

## Comoros
### Republic of the Comoros

**People: Population** (1977 est.): 370,000. **Age distrib. (%):** 0–14: 45.6; 15–59: 49.6; 60+: 7.9. **Pop. density:** 533.91 per sq. mi. **Ethnic groups:** Arabs, Africans, East Indians. **Languages:** Arabic, French, Swahili. **Religions:** Islam prevails.

**Geography: Area:** 693 sq. mi., half the size of Rhode Island. **Location:** In the Mozambique Channel between NW Madagascar and SE Africa. **Neighbors:** Nearest are Mozambique on W, Madagascar on E.. **Topography:** The islands are of volcanic origin, with an active volcano on Grand Comoro. **Capital:** Moroni. **Cities** (1974 est.): Moroni (met.) 12,000.

**Government: Head of ruling council:** Ahmed Abdallah; in office: May 19, 1978. **Local divisions:** each of the 3 main islands is a prefecture.

**Economy: Industries:** Perfume. **Chief crops:** Vanilla, copra, perfume plants, fruits. **Per capita arable land:** 0.7 acres. **Electricity production** (1975): 3.00 mln. kwh.

**Finance: Currency:** Franc (Apr. 1977: 248 = $1 US). **Gross domestic product** (1974 est.): $50 mln. **Per capita income** (1974): $150. **Imports** (1973): $15 mln.; partners (1973): Fr. 50%, Madag. 15%, Ken. 5%. **Exports** (1973): $5 mln.; partners (1973): Fr. 75%, Madag. 19%, It. 7%.

**Transport: Chief ports:** Dzaoudzi.

**Communications: Radios:** 36,000 in use (1974). **Telephones in use** (1977): 1,035.

**Health: Life expectancy at birth** (1975): 40.9 male; 44.1 female. **Births** (annual per 1,000 pop. 1972-75): 46.6. **Deaths** (annual per 1,000 pop. 1972-75): 21.7. **Natural increase** (annual 1970-75): 2.49%. **Infant mortality** (per 1,000 live births 1952): 51.7.

The islands were controlled by Moslem sultans until the French acquired them 1841-1909. A 1974 referendum favored independence, with only the Christian island of Mayotte preferring association with France. The French National Assembly decided to allow each of the islands to decide its own fate. The Comoro Chamber of Deputies declared independence July 6,

1975. In a referendum in 1976, Mayotte voted to remain French. A leftist regime that seized power in 1975 was deposed in a pro-French 1978 coup.

## Congo
### People's Republic of the Congo

**People: Population** (1977 est.): 1,440,000. **Pop. density:** 10.91 per sq. mi. **Ethnic groups:** Bakongo 45%, Bateke 20%, others. **Languages:** French (official), others. **Religions:** Christians 50% (two-thirds Roman Catholic), others.

**Geography: Area:** 132,046 sq. mi., slightly smaller than Montana. **Location:** In western central Africa. **Neighbors:** Gabon, Cameroon on W, Central African Empire on N, Zaire on E, Angola (Cabinda) on SW. **Topography:** Much of the Congo is covered by thick forests. A coastal plain leads to the fertile Niari Valley. The center is a plateau; the Congo R. basin consists of flood plains in the lower and savanna in the upper portion. **Capital:** Brazzaville. **Cities** (1974 cen.): Brazzaville (met.) 289,700; Pointe-Noire 141,700.

**Government: Head of state:** Pres. Joachim Yombi Opango; b. 1939; in office: Apr. 3, 1977. **Head of government:** Prime Min. Louis Sylvain Ngoma; in office: Apr. 3, 1977. **Local divisions:** 9 regions and capital district. **Armed forces:** regulars 7,000; para-military 39,000.

**Economy: Chief crops:** Palm oil and kernals, cocoa, coffee, bananas, peanuts. **Minerals:** Oil, potash, lead, zinc. **Crude oil reserves** (1978): 360 mln. bbls. **Per capita arable land:** 1.1 acres. **Electricity production** (1976): 120.00 mln. kwh. **Labor force:** 45% agriculture.

**Finance: Currency:** Franc (May 1978: 230.35 = $1 US). **Gross domestic product** (1974 est.): $500 mln. **Per capita income** (1974): $350. **Imports** (1976): $177 mln.; partners (1972): Fr. 54%, W. Ger. 8%, U.S. 6%, P.R. China 5% **Exports** (1976): $182 mln.; partners (1972): Fr. 16%, W. Ger. 14%, So. Afr. 8%, Neth. 5%. **Tourist receipts** (1975): $3 million. **Balance of payments** (1976): —$4,500,000. **International reserves** (Feb. 1978): $7.66 mln. **Consumer prices** (change in 1976): 7.2%.

**Transport: Railway traffic** (1975): 133.52 mln. passenger-miles; 286.28 mln. net ton-miles. **Motor vehicles:** in use (1974): 19,000 passenger cars, 10,500 commercial vehicles. **Chief ports:** Pointe-Noire, Brazzaville.

**Communications: Radios:** 80,000 in use (1974). **Telephones in use** (1974): 10,000. **Daily newspaper circulation** (1973): 1,000; 1 per 1,000 pop.

**Health: Life expectancy at birth** (1975): 41.9 male; 45.1 female. **Births** (annual per 1,000 pop. 1972-75): 45.1. **Deaths** (annual per 1,000 pop. 1972-75): 20.8. **Natural increase** (annual 1970-75): 2.43%. **Pop. per hospital bed** (1975): 218. **Pop. per physician** (1975): 7,849. **Infant mortality** (per 1,000 live births 1960-61): 180.

**Education: Literacy** (1975): 20%. **Pop. 5-19:** in school (1975): 75%, per teacher (1975): 67.

The Loango Kingdom flourished in the 15th century, as did the Anzico Kingdom of the Batekes; by the late 17th century they had become weakened. France established control by 1885. Independence came Aug. 15, 1960.

After a 1963 coup sparked by trade unions, the country adopted a Marxist-Leninist stance, with the USSR and China vying for influence. Tribal divisions remain strong. Relations with the U.S. were broken in 1965; ties were restored in 1977. France remained the dominant trade partner and source of technical assistance, and French-owned private enterprise retained a major economic role. The 1973 constitution was suspended in 1977 following an unsuccessful coup, in which Pres. Marien Ngouabi was killed.

## Costa Rica
### Republic of Costa Rica

**People: Population** (1977 est.): 2,070,000. **Age distrib. (%):** 0–14: 44.1; 15–59: 50.4; 60+: 5.6. **Pop. density:** 105.33 per sq. mi. **Urban** (1973): 40.6%. **Ethnic groups:** Spanish (with Mestizo minority); Indians 0.4%, Jamaican Negroes 2%. **Languages:** Spanish (official), English. **Religions:** Roman Catholicism prevails.

**Geography: Area:** 19,653 sq. mi., smaller than W. Virginia. **Location:** In central America. **Neighbors:** Nicaragua on N, Panama on S. **Topography:** Lowlands by the Caribbean are tropical. The interior plateau, with an altitude of about 4,000 ft., is temperate. **Capital:** San Jose. **Cities** (1975 est.): San Jose (met.) 395,401.

**Government: Head of state:** Pres. Rodrigo Carazo Odio; b. 1927; in office May 8, 1978. **Local divisions:** 7 provinces, with presidentially-appointed governors.

**Economy: Industries:** Fiberglass, aluminum, textiles, fertilizers, roofing, cement. **Chief crops:** Coffee (chief export), bananas, sugar, cocoa, cotton, hemp. **Minerals:** Gold, salt, sulphur, iron. **Other resources:** Fish, forests. **Per capita arable land:** 0.3 acres. **Meat production** (1976): beef: 62,600 tons; pork: 6,000 tons. **Electricity production** (1976): 1.64 bln. kwh. **Labor force:** 37% agric.; 12% manuf.

**Finance: Currency:** Colones (May 1978: 8.57 = $1 US). **Gross domestic product** (1975): $2.35 bln. **Per capita income** (1976): $1,064. **Imports** (1976): $774 mln.; partners (1973): U.S. 35%, Jap. 9%, Guat. 7%, W. Ger. 7%. **Exports** (1976): $584 mln.; partners (1973): U.S. 33%, W. Ger. 13%, Nic. 8%, Guat. 6%. **Tourists** (1975): 297,200; receipts (1975): $53 million. **Balance of payments** (1977): +$87,900,000. **National budget** (1976): $279.99 mln. revenues; $333.75 mln. expenditures. **International reserves** (May 1978): $308.14 mln. **Consumer prices** (change in 1977): 4.1%.

**Transport: Railway traffic** (1974): 50.30 mln. passenger-miles; 8.69 mln. net ton-miles. **Motor vehicles:** in use (1974): 55,100 passenger cars, 37,200 commercial vehicles. **Civil aviation** (international only): 203 mln. passenger-miles (1976); 8,376 mln. freight ton-miles (1976). **Chief ports:** Limon, Puntarenas.

**Communications: Radios:** 3,500 in use (1974). **Telephones in use** (1977): 126,879. **Daily newspaper circulation** (1974): 186,000; 97 per 1,000 pop.

**Health: Life expectancy at birth** (1964): 61.87 male; 64.83 female. **Births** (per 1,000 pop. 1975): 29.3. **Deaths** (per 1,000 pop. 1975): 4.9. **Natural increase** (1975): 2.44%. **Pop. per hospital bed** (1975): 264. **Pop. per physician** (1975): 1,464. **Infant mortality** (per 1,000 live births 1974): 37.6.

**Education: Literacy** (1975): 89%. **Pop. 5-19:** in school (1975): 60%; per teacher (1975): 49.

Guamyi Indians inhabited Costa Rica when Spaniards arrived in 1502. Independence came in 1821. Costa Rica seceded from the Central American Federation in 1838. Since the civil war of 1948-49, there has been no violent social conflict, and free political institutions have been preserved.

Costa Rica, though still a largely agricultural country, has achieved a relatively high standard of living and social services, and land ownership is widespread.

The country has generally followed a pro-U.S. foreign policy.

# Cuba
## Republic of Cuba

**People: Population** (1976 est.): 9,460,000. **Age distrib.** (%): 0-14: 37.3; 15-59: 53.6; 60+: 9.1. **Pop. density:** 213.94 per sq. mi. **Urban** (1973): 60.3%. **Ethnic groups:** Spanish, Negro, and mixtures. **Languages:** Spanish. **Religions:** Roman Catholicism prevailed in past.

**Geography: Area:** 44,218 sq. mi., nearly as large as Pennsylvania. **Location:** Westernmost of West Indies. **Neighbors:** Nearest are Bahamas, U.S. on N, Mexico on W, Jamaica on S, Haiti on E. **Topography:** The coastline is about 2,500 miles. The N coast is steep and rocky, the S coast low and marshy. Low hills and fertile valleys cover more than half the country. The Sierra Maestra, in the east, is the highest of three mountain ranges. **Capital:** Havana. **Cities** (1975 est.): Havana (met.) 1,861,442; Santiago de Cuba 315,801; Camaguey 221,826.

**Government: Head of state:** Pres. Fidel Castro; b. Aug. 13, 1926; in office: Dec. 3, 1976 (formerly Prime Min. since Jan. 1, 1959). **Local divisions:** 14 provinces plus Isle of Pines, 169 municipal assemblies. **Armed forces:** regulars 189,000; reserves 90,000.

**Economy: Industries:** Texiles, wood products, cement, chemicals, cigars. **Chief crops:** Sugar cane (80% of exports), tobacco, coffee, pineapples, bananas, citrus fruit, coconuts. **Minerals:** Iron, copper, manganese, nickel, salt. **Other resources:** Forests. **Per capita arable land:** 0.9 acres. **Meat production** (1975): beef: 187,000 tons; pork: 38,000 tons. **Fish catch** (1975): 165,000 metric tons. **Electricity production** (1975): 6.15 bln. kwh. **Labor force:** 30% agriculture.

**Finance: Currency:** Peso (Oct.-Dec. 1976: 1 = $1.32 US). **Gross domestic product** (1974 est.): $5.8 bln. **Per capita income** (1974): $570. **Imports** (1976): $4.07 bln.; partners (1976): USSR, Spain, Jap., P.R. China, U.K., Arg. **Exports** (1976): $3.57 bln.; partners (1976): USSR, Spain, Jap., P.R. China, E. Ger.

**Transport: Railway traffic** (1975): 431.60 mln. passenger-miles; 1.13 bln. net ton-miles. **Motor vehicles:** in use (1973): 70,000 passenger cars, 33,000 commercial vehicles. **Chief ports:** Havana, Matanzas, Cienfuegos, Santiago de Cuba.

**Communications: Television sets:** 595,000 in use (1974). **Radios:** 1,805,000 in use (1974), 113,000 manufactured (1975). **Telephones in use** (1974): 289,000.

**Health: Life expectancy at birth:** (1970): 68.5 male; 71.8 female. **Births** (per 1,000 pop. 1975): 20.7. **Deaths** (per 1,000 pop. 1975): 5.4. **Natural increase** (1975): 1.53%. **Pop. per hospital bed** (1975): 230. **Pop. per physician** (1975): 941. **Infant mortality** (per 1,000 live births 1973): 28.9.

**Education: Literacy** (1975): 83%. **Pop. 5-19:** in school (1975): 70%, per teacher (1975): 28.

Some 50,000 Indians lived in Cuba when it was discovered by Columbus in 1492. Its name derives from the Indian Cubanacan. Except for British occupation of Havana, 1762-63, Cuba remained Spanish until 1898. A slave-based sugar plantation economy developed from the 18th century, aided by early mechanization of milling. Sugar remains the chief product and chief export despite government attempts to diversify.

Under Spanish governors Cubans were denied citizenship. A ten-year uprising ended in 1878 with guarantees of rights by Spain, which Spain failed to carry out. A full-scale movement under Jose Marti began Feb. 24, 1895.

The U.S. declared war on Spain in April, 1898, after the sinking of the U.S.S. Maine in Havana harbor, and defeated it in the short Spanish-American War. Spain gave up all claims to Cuba. U.S. troops withdrew in 1902, but under 1903 and 1934 agreements, the U.S. leased a site at Guantanamo Bay in the SE as a naval base. U.S. and other foreign investments acquired a dominant role in the economy.

In 1952, former president Fulgencio Batista seized control and established a dictatorship, which grew increasingly harsh and corrupt. Former student leader Fidel Castro assembled a rebel band in 1956; guerilla fighting intensified in 1958. Batista fled Jan. 1, 1959, and in the resulting political vacuum Castro took power, becoming premier Feb. 16.

The government, quickly dominated by extreme leftists, began a program of sweeping economic and social changes, without restoring promised liberties. Opponents were imprisoned, and some were executed. Many of Castro's former supporters joined some 700,000 Cubans who emigrated in the years after the Castro takeover, mostly to the U.S.

Cattle and tobacco lands were nationalized, while a system of cooperatives was instituted. By the end of 1960 all banks and industrial companies had been nationalized, including over $1 billion worth of U.S.-owned properties, mostly without compensation.

Soviet, Chinese, and Eastern European economic penetration was extended by trade and credit agreements, including preferential sugar purchases and credits for construction of factories. Cuba is a member of Comecon, the Soviet economic union.

Poor sugar crops resulted in collectivization of farms and stringent labor controls, and rationing despite continued aid from the USSR and other Communist countries (over $2.5 million a day by 1977). But health and education services were greatly improved, and social inequalities somewhat mitigated.

The U.S. cut back Cuba's sugar quota in 1960, and imposed a partial export embargo, which became total in 1962, severely damaging the economy. In 1961, some 1,400 Cubans, trained and backed by the U.S. Central Intelligence Agency, unsuccessfully tried to invade and overthrow the regime. It was revealed in 1975 that CIA agents had plotted to kill Castro in 1959 or 1960. Cuba complained of numerous raids by infiltrators, 1964-70.

In the fall of 1962, the U.S. learned that the USSR had brought nuclear missiles to Cuba. After an Oct. 22 warning from Pres. Kennedy, the missiles were removed.

The Organization of American States voted 15-4 in 1964 for mandatory sanctions against Cuba and for cooperation against Cuban revolutionary activities in Latin America. The sanctions were lifted in 1975, with the tacit concurrence of the U.S.

In 1973, Cuba and the U.S. signed an agreement providing for extradition or punishment of hijackers of planes or vessels, and for each nation to bar activity from its territory against the other. In 1977, the two countries signed agreements to exchange diplomats, without restoring full ties and to regulate offshore fishing.

But relations were strained by continued Cuban military involvement abroad. In 1975-78, Cuba sent over 20,000 troops to aid one faction in the Angola Civil War. Some 20,000 other Cuban troops or advisers were reported in the Congo, Ethiopia (where they fought Somali and Eritrean insurgents), Equatorial Guinea, Guinea, Guinea-Bissau, Somalia, and Mozambique. About 1,500 Cuban troops had died in African wars by 1978.

# Cyprus
## Republic of Cyprus

**People: Population** (1977 est.): 690,000. **Age distrib.** (%): 0–14: 28.9; 15–59: 57.6; 60+: 13.6. **Pop. density:** 193.17 per sq. mi. **Urban** (1974): 42.2%.**Ethnic groups:** Greeks 75%, Turks 20%, Armenians, Maronites. **Languages:** Greek, Turkish. **Religions:** Orthodox 76%, Moslems 20%.

**Geography: Area:** 3,572 sq. mi., smaller than Connecticut. **Location:** In eastern Mediterranean Sea, off Turkish coast. **Neighbors:** Nearest are Turkey on N, Syria, Lebanon on E. **Topography:** Two mountain ranges run E-W, separated by a wide, fertile plain. **Capital:** Nicosia. **Cities** (1973 cen.): Nicosia (met. 115,700.

**Government: Head of state:** Pres. Spyros Kyprianou; b. 1932; in office: Aug. 31, 1977. **Local divisions:** 6 districts.

**Economy: Industries:** Wine, clothing, shoes, tourism. **Chief crops:** Grains, grapes, carobs, citrus fruits, potatoes, olives. **Minerals:** Copper, iron, asbetos, gypsum, chrome, umber. **Per capita arable land:** 1.3 acres. **Meat production** (1975): pork: 13,000 tons. **Electricity production** (1977): 888.00 mln. kwh. **Labor force:** 34% agric.; 14% manuf.

**Finance: Currency:** Pound (May 1978: 1 = $2.58 US). **Gross domestic product** (1977): $1.04 bln. **Per capita income** (1976): $1,212. **Imports** (1977): $620 mln.; partners (1974): U.K. 21%, W. Ger. 9%, It. 8%, Gr. 7%. **Exports** (1977): $318 mln.; partners (1974): U.K. 38%, USSR 7%, W. Ger. 6%, Libya 5%. **Tourists** (1975): 47,100; receipts (1975): $15 million. **National budget** (1974): $138.48 mln. revenues; $207.15 mln. expenditures. **International reserves** (Apr. 1978): $298.9 mln. **Consumer prices** (change in 1976): 3.7%.

**Transport: Motor vehicles:** in use (1975): 66,200 passenger cars, 16,200 commercial vehicles. **Civil aviation:** 244 mln. passenger-miles (1977); 10,351 mln. freight ton-miles (1977). **Chief ports:** Famagusta, Limassol.

**Communications: Television sets:** 85,000 licensed (1974). **Radios:** 206,000 licensed (1974). **Telephones in use** (1977): 77,163. **Daily newspaper circulation** (1974): 78,000; 8 per 1,000 pop.

**Health: Life expectancy at birth** (1973): 70.0 male; 72.9 female. **Births** (annual per 1,000 pop. 1972-75): 22.2. **Deaths** (annual per 1,000 pop. 1972-75): 6.8. **Natural increase** (annual 1970-75): 1.54%. **Pop. per hospital bed** (1975): 200. **Pop. per physician** (1975): 1,183. **Infant mortality** (per 1,000 live births 1975): 29.2.

**Education: Literacy** (1975) 80%. **Pop. 5-19:** in school (1975): 53%, per teacher (1975): 50.

Agitation for enosis (union) with Greece increased after World War II, with the Turkish minority opposed, and broke into violence in 1955-56. In 1959, Britain, Greece, Turkey, and Cypriot leaders approved a plan for an independent republic, with constitutional guarantees for the Turkish minority and permanent division of offices on an ethnic basis. Greek and Turkish Communal Chambers dealth with religion, education, and other matters.

Archbishop Makarios, formerly the leader of the enosis movement, was elected president, and full independence became final Aug. 16, 1960.

Further communal strife led the United Nations to send a peace-keeping force in 1964; its mandate has been repeatedly renewed.

Makarios was re-elected in 1968 and 1973 with an overwhelming popular vote.

The Cypriot National Guard, led by officers from the army of Greece, seized the government July 15, 1974, and named Nikos Sampson, and advocate of union with Greece, president. Makarios fled the country. On July 20, Turkey invaded the island; Greece mobilized its forces but did not intervene. A cease-fire was arranged July 22. On the 23d, Sampson turned over the presidency to Glafkos Clerides (on the same day, Greece's military junta resigned). A peace conference collapsed Aug. 14; fighting resumed. Greek Cypriots and Turks charged each other with massacres and atrocities. By Aug. 16 Turkish forces had occupied the NE 40% of the island, despite the presence of UN peace forces. On Aug. 19 the U.S. ambassador to Cyprus was slain by a Greek Cypriot during a riot in Nicosia. Makarios resumed the presidency in December.

Turkish Cypriots voted overwhelmingly June 8, 1975 to form a separate Turkish Cypriot federated state. A president and assembly were elected in 1976. Some 200,000 Greeks had left the Turkish-controlled area, replaced by thousands of Turks, some from the mainland. Makarios died in 1978.

# Czechoslovakia
## Czechoslovak Socialist Republic

**People: Population** (1977 est.): 15,030,000. **Age distrib.** (%): 0–14: 22.8; 15–59: 59.9; 60+: 17.3. **Pop. density:** 304.43 per sq. mi. **Urban** (1974): 66.7%. **Ethnic groups:** Czechs 65%, Slovaks 30%, Hungarians 4%, Germans, Poles, Ukrainians. **Languages:** Czech, Slovak, Hungarian. **Religions:** Roman Catholics were majority, Lutherans, Orthodox.

**Geography: Area:** 49,371 sq. mi., the size of New York. **Location:** In E central Europe. **Neighbors:** Poland, E. Germany on N, W. Germany on W. Austria, Hungary on S, USSR on E. **Topography:** Bohemia, in W, is a plateau surrounded by mountains; Moravia is hilly, Slovakia, in E, has mountains (Carpathians) in N, fertile Danube plain in S. Vltava (Moldau) and Labe (Elbe) rivers flow N from Bohemia to G. **Capital:** Prague. **Cities** (1974 est.): Prague 1,095,615; Brno 343,860; Bratislava 328,765; Ostrava 292,404.

**Government: Head of state:** Pres. Gustav Husak; b. Jan 10, 1913; in office: May 1975; **Head of government:** Prime Min. Lubomir Strougal; b. Oct. 19, 1924; in office: Jan. 1970. **Head of Communist Party:** First Sec. Gustav Husak; in office: April 1969. **Local divisions:** Czech and Slovak republics each have an assembly. **Armed forces:** regulars 291,000; reserves 350,000.

**Economy: Industries:** Machinery, oil products, weapons, steel, glass, chemicals, aircraft, textiles, shoes. **Chief crops:** Wheat, sugar beets, potatoes, rye, hops. **Minerals:** Coal, iron. Jachymor has Europe's greatest pitchblend (for uranium and radium). **Per capita arable land:** 0.9 acres. **Meat production** (1976):. beef: 322,700 tons; pork: 481,800 tons. **Fish catch** (1975): 16,700 metric tons. **Electricity production** (1977): 66.30 bln. kwh. **Labor force:** 16% agric,; 38% manuf.

**Finance: Currency:** Koruna (Apr.-June 1977: 5.70 = $1 US). **Gross domestic product** (1974 est): $47 bln. **Per capia income** (1974): $3,000. **Imports** (1977): $11.15 bln.; partners (1973): USSR 30%, E. Ger. 13%, Pol. 8% Hung. 6%. **Exports** (1977): $10.82 bln.; partners (1973): USSR 32%, E. Ger. 11%, Pol. 10%, W. Ger. 6%. **Tourists** (1975): 14,078,500; receipts (1971): $61 million. **Consumer prices** (change in 1977): 1.2%.

**Transport: Railway traffic** (1975): 11.47 bln. passenger-miles 43.02 bln. net ton-miles. **Motor vehicles:** in use (1975): 1,505,100 passenger cars, 260,700 commercial vehicles; manufactured (1977): 158,400 passenger cars; 80,400 commercial vehicles. **Civil aviation:** 878 mln. passenger-miles (1977); 10,686 freight ton-miles (1977).

**Communications: Television sets:** 3,602,000 licensed (1974), 445,000 manufactured (1975). **Radios:** 3,910,000 licensed (1974), 183,000 manufactured (1975). **Telephones in use** (1977): 2,743,387. **Daily newspaper circulation** (1974): 4,231,000; 288 per 1,000 pop.

**Health: Life expectancy at birth** (1973): 66.53 male; 73.49 female. **Births** (per 1,000 pop. 1975): 19.5. **Deaths** (per 1,000 pop. 1975): 11.5. **Natural increase** (1975): .80%. **Pop. per hospital bed** (1975): 98. **Pop. per physician** (1975): 430. **Infant mortality** (per 1,000 live births 1975): 20.9.

**Education: Literacy** (1975): 99%. **Pop. 5–19:** in school (1975): 59%, per teacher (1975): 32.

Bohemia, Moravia and Slovakia were part of the Great Moravian Empire in the ninth century. Later, Slovakia was overrun by Magyars, while Bohemia and Moravia became part of the Holy Roman Empire. Under the kings of Bohemia, Prague in the 14th century was the cultural center of Central Europe. In 1526 Ferdinand, brother of Holy Roman Emperor Charles V, became king of Bohemia and Hungary. Later the lands became part of Austria-Hungary.

In 1914-1918 Thomas G. Masaryk and Eduard Benes formed a provisional government with the support of Slovak leaders including Milan Stefanik. They proclaimed the Republic of Czechoslovakia Oct. 30, 1918.

By 1938 Nazi Germany had worked up disaffection among German-speaking citizens in Sudetenland and demanded its cession.ª Prime Minister Neville Chamberlain of Britain, with the acquiescence of France, signed an agreement with Hitler at Munich, Sept. 30, 1938, agreeing to the cession, with a guarantee of peace by Hitler and Mussolini. Germany occupied Sudetenland Oct. 1-2.

Hitler on Mar. 15, 1939, dissolved Czechoslovakia, made protectorates of Bohemia and Moravia, and supported the autonomy of Slovkia, which was proclaimed independent Mar. 14, 1939, with Josef Tiso president.

Soviet troops won some Czechoslovak contingents entered eastern Czechoslovakia in 1944 and reached Prague in May 1945; Benes returned as president. In May 1946 elections, the Communist Party won 38% of the votes, and Benes accepted Klement Gottwald, a Communist, as prime minister. Tiso was executed in 1947.

Large numbers of Hungarians were moved out of Slovakia and many Slovaks were moved from Hungary to Slovakia in 1945-46. An estimated 3 million Sudeten Germans were transferred to Germany under the Potsdam Agreement.

In February, 1948, the Communists seized power in advance of scheduled elections. In May 1948 a new constitution was approved. Benes refused to sign it. On May 30 the voters were offered a one-slate ballot and the Communists won full control. Benes resigned June 7. Gottwald became president and Benes died Sept. 3. A harsh Stalinist period followed, with complete and violent suppression of all opposition. Communist Party head Rudolf Slansky and other leading officials were sentenced to death in 1952 on trumped-up charges of disloyalty.

In Jan. 1968 a liberalization movement spread explosively through Czechoslovakia. Antonin Novotny, long the Stalinist boss of the nation, was deposed as party leader and succeeded by Alexander Dubcek, a Slovak, who declared he intended to make communism democratic. On Mar. 22 Novotny resigned as president and was succeeded by Gen. Ludvik Svoboda. On Apr. 6, Premier Joseph Lenart resigned and was succeeded by Oldrich Cernik, whose new cabinet was pledged to carry out democratization and economic reforms.

In July 1968 the USSR and 4 hard-core Warsaw Pact nations demanded an end to liberalization. On Aug. 20, the Russian, Polish, East German, Hungarian and Bulgarian armies invaded Czechoslovakia.

Despite demonstrations and riots by students and workers, press censorship was imposed, liberal leaders were ousted from office and promises of loyalty to Soviet policies were made by some old-line Communist Party leaders.

On Apr. 17, 1969, Dubcek resigned as leader of the Communist Party and was succeeded by Gustav Husak. In Jan. 1970, Premier Cernick was ousted. Censorship was tightened and the Communist Party expelled a third of its members. In 1972, more than 40 liberals were jailed on subversion charges. In 1973, amnesty was offered to some of the 40,000 who fled the country after the 1968 invasion, but repressive policies remained in force through 1976.

More than 700 leading Czechoslovak intellectuals and former party leaders signed a human rights manifesto in 1977, called Charter 77, prompting a renewed crackdown by the regime.

Czechoslovakia has long been an industrial and technological leader of the eastern European countries, though its relative standing has declined in recent years.

# Denmark

## Kingdom of Denmark

**People: Population** (1977 est.): 5,090,000. **Age distrib.** (%): 0–14: 23.0; 15–59: 58.9; 60+: 18.1. **Pop. density:** 298.92 per sq. mi. **Urban** (1970): 66.9%. **Ethnic groups:** Almost all Scandinavian. **Languages:** Danish. **Religions:** Lutherans 97%.

**Geography: Area:** 17,028 sq. mi., the size of Massachusetts and New Hampshire combined. **Location:** In northern Europe, separating the North and Baltic Seas. **Neighbors:** W. Germany on S., Norway on NW (across Skagerrak), Sweden on NE (across Kattegat). **Topography:** Denmark consists of the Jutland Peninsula and about 500 islands, 100 inhabited. The land is flat or gently rolling, and is almost all in productive use. **Capital:** Copenhagen. **Cities** (1974 est.): Copenhagen (met.) 1,327,940; Arhus 245,941.

**Government: Head of state:** Queen Margrethe II; b. Apr. 16, 1940; in office: Jan. 14, 1972; **Head of government:** Prime Min.

Anker Joergensen; b. July 13, 1922; in office: Feb. 13, 1975. **Local divisions:** 14 counties, each with an elected council, and 2 urban communes. **Armed forces:** regulars 46,970; reserves 165,900.

**Economy: Industries:** Machinery, ships, textiles, furniture, steel. **Chief crops:** Dairy products, grains, potatoes. **Crude oil reserves** (1978): .05 mln. bbls. **Per capita arable land:** 1.3 acres. **Meat production** (1976): beef: 241,800 tons: pork: 715,700 tons. **Fish catch** (1975): 1,767,000 metric tons. **Electricity production** (1977): 22.49 bln. kwh. **Labor force:** 10% agric.; 24% manuf.

**Finance: Currency:** Kroner (May 1978: 5.66 = $1 US). **Gross domestic product** (1976): $40.24 bln. **Per capita income** (1976): $6,803. **Imports** (1977): $13.24 bln.; partners (1975): W. Ger. 19.7%; Swed. 14.2%, U.K. 10.2%, U.S. 6%. **Exports** (1977): $10.12 bln.; partners (1975): U.K. 18.8%, Swed. 15%, W. Ger. 13.3%, Nor. 6.5%. **Balance of payments** (1977): +$798,000,000. **National budget** (1972): $6.67 bln. revenues; $6.29 bln. expenditures. **International reverves** (May 1978): $2.42 bln. **Consumer prices** (change in 1977): 11.1%.

**Transport:** Railway traffic (1974): 2.14 bln. passenger-miles; 1.24 bln. net ton-miles. **Motor vehicles:** in use (1975): 1,300,000 passenger cars, 239,200 commercial vehicles; assembled (1975): 996 passenger cars; (1976): 696 commercial vehicles. **Civil aviation:** 1,595 mln. passenger-miles (1977); 77,076 mln. freight ton-miles (1977). **Chief ports:** Copenhagen, Alborg, Arhus, Odense.

**Communications: Television sets:** 1,556,000 licensed (1974), 64,000 manufactured (1975). **Radios:** 1,693,000 licensed (1974), 146,000 manufactured (1975). **Telephones in use** (1977): 2,528,585. **Daily newspaper circulation** (1974): 1,792,000; 355 per 1,000 pop.

**Health: Life expectancy at birth** (1973): 70.8 male; 76.3 female. **Births** (per 1,000 pop. 1975): 14.2. **Deaths** (per 1,000 pop. 1975): 10.0. **Natural increase** (1975): .42%. **Pop. per hospital bed** (1975): 117. **Pop. per physician** (1975): 522. **Infant mortality** (per 1,000 live births 1973): 11.5.

**Education: Literacy** (1975): 99%. **Pop. 5–19:** in school (1975): 71%, per teacher (1975): 20.

The origin of Copenhagen dates back to ancient times, when the fishing and trading place named Havn (port) grew up on a cluster of islets, but Bishop Absalon (1128-1201) is regarded as the actual founder of the city. On one of the islets he built a stronghold against the pirating Wends (a Slavic group).

Danes formed a large component of the Viking raiders in the early Middle Ages. The Danish kingdom was a major north European power until the 17th century, when it lost its land in southern Sweden. Norway was separated in 1815, and Schleswig-Holstein in 1864. Northern Schleswig was returned in 1920.

The **Faeroe Islands** in the North Atlantic, about 300 mi. NE of the Shetlands, and 850 mi. from Denmark proper, 18 inhabited, have an area of 540 sq. mi. and pop. (1976) of 41,211. They are self-governing in most matters.

## Greenland

Greenland, a huge island between the North Atlantic and the Polar Sea, is separated from the North American continent by Davis Strait and Baffin Bay. Its total area is 840,000 sq. mi., 705,234 of which are ice-capped. Most of the island is a lofty plateau 9,000 to 10,000 ft. in altitude. The average thickness of the ice cap is 1,000 ft. The population (1976) is 49,666. The capital is Godthaab. Under the 1953 Danish constitution the colony became an integral part of the realm with representatives in the Folketing. Fish and fur are exported.

## Djibouti

### Republic of Djibouti

**People: Population** (1977 est.) 300,000. Ethnic groups: Issa (Somali) 47%; Afar 37%; European 8%; Arab 6%. **Languages:** Somali, Afar, French, Arabic. **Religions:** Most are Moslems; Europeans are Roman Catholic.

**Geography: Area:** 8,800 sq. mi., about the size of Massachusetts. **Location:** On E coast of Africa, separated from Arabian Peninsula by the strategically vital strait of Bab el-Mandeb. **Neighbors:** Ethiopia on N (Eritera) and W, Somalia on S. **Topography:** The territory, divided into a low coastal plain, mountains behind, and an interior plateau, is arid, sandy, and desolate. The climate is generally hot and dry. **Capital:** Djibouti. **Cities**

(1970 est): Djibouti (met.) 62,000.

**Government: Head of state:** Pres. Hassan Gouled; b. 1916; in office: June 24, 1977; **Head of government:** Premier Abdallah Mohamed Kamil; in office: Feb. 5, 1978. **Local divisions:** 5 cercles (districts).

**Economy: Minerals:** Salt.

**Finance: Per capita income** (1974): $980. **Imports** (1974): $117 mln.; partners (1973): Fr. 49%, Eth. 12%, Jap. 6%. **Exports** (1974): $20 mln.; partners (1973): Fr. 84%, Eth. 4%, It. 2%.

**Transport: Motor vehicles:** in use (1969): 7,400 passenger cars, 1,500 commercial vehicles. **Chief ports:** Djibouti.

**Births** (per 1,000 pop. 1970): 42.0. **Deaths** (per 1,000 pop. 1970): 7.6.

France gained control of the territory in stages between 1862 and 1900.

Ethiopia and Somalia have renounced their claims to the area, but each has accused the other of trying to gain control. There were clashes between Afars (ethnically related to Ethiopians) and Issas (related to Somalis) in 1976. Immigrants from both countries continued to enter the country up to independence, which came June 27, 1977.

Unemployment is about 80%. French aid is the mainstay of the economy, and 4,000 French troops are present.

# Dominican Republic

**People: Population** (1977 est.): 5,000,000. **Age distrib.** (%): 0–14: 47.5; 15–59: 47.5; 60+: 4.9. **Pop. density:** 267.32 per sq. mi. **Urban** (1976): 46.8%. **Ethnic groups:** Caucasian 16%, mulatto 73%, Negro 11%. **Languages:** Spanish. **Religions:** Roman Catholic 95%, Protestant 2%.

**Geography: Area:** 18,704 sq. mi., the size of Vermont and New Hampshire combined. **Location:** In West Indies, sharing I. of Hispaniola with Haiti. **Neighbors:** Haiti on W. **Topography:** The Cordillera Central range crosses the center of the country, rising to over 10,000 ft., highest in the Caribbean. The Cibao valley to the N is major agricultural area. **Capital:** Santo Domingo. **Cities** (1970 cen.): Santo Domingo (met.) 817,645; Santiago de Los Caballeros (met.) 245,165.

**Government: Head of state:** Pres. Antonio Guzman; b. 1911; in office Aug. 16, 1978. **Local divisions:** 26 provinces and a national district; pres. appoints governors. **Armed forces:** regulars 18,500; para-military 10,000.

**Economy: Industries:** Molasses, rum, alcohol, cement, textiles, furniture, apparel. **Chief crops:** sugar, cocoa, coffee, tobacco, corn, peanuts, bananas. **Minerals:** Nickel, gold, copper, iron, salt, chalk, bauxite, marble, amber, kaolin. **Other resources:** Timber. **Per capita arable land:** 0.5 acres. **Meat production** (1976): beef: 42,000 tons; pork 21,000 tons. **Electricity production** (1975): 1.63 bln. kwh. **Labor force:** 44% agric.; 8% manuf.

**Finance: Currency:** Peso (May 1978: 1 = $1 US). **Gross domestic product** (1976): $3.91 bln. **Per capita income** (1976): $735. **Imports** (1977): $793 mln.; partners (1974): U.S. 68%, Jap. 8%, Can. 5%, W. Ger. 5%. **Exports** (1977): $794 mln.; partners (1974): U.S. 70%, Neth. 8%, Spain 3%, Algeria 2%. **Tourists** (1975): 232,900; receipts (1975): $61 million. **Balance of payments** (1976): −$14,800,000. **National budget** (1976): $634.60 mln. revenues; $621.00 mln. expenditures. **International reserves** (May 1978): $131.8 mln. **Consumer prices** (change in 1977): 12.9%.

**Transport: Motor vehicles:** in use (1975): 71,500 passenger cars, 35,600 commercial vehicles. **Chief ports:** Santo Domingo, San Pedro de Macoris, Puerto Plata.

**Communications: Television sets:** 156,000 in use (1974). **Radios:** 185,000 in use (1974). **Telephones in use** (1977): 127,332. **Daily newspaper circulation** (1974): 197,000; 43 per 1,000 pop.

**Health: Life expectancy at birth** (1961): 57.15 male; 58.59 female. **Births** (annual per 1,000 pop. 1972-75): 45.8. **Deaths** (annual per 1,000 pop. 1972-75): 11.0. **Natural increase** (annual 1970-75): 3.48%. **Pop. per hospital bed** (1975): 386. **Pop. per physician** (1975): 1,947. **Infant mortality** (per 1,000 live births 1974): 43.4.

**Education: Literacy** (1975): 68%. **Pop. 5–19:** in school (1975): 54%, per teacher (1975): 85.

Carib and Arawak Indians inhabited the island of Hispaniola when Columbus landed in 1492. The city of Santo Domingo, founded 1496, is the oldest settlement by Europeans in the hemisphere and has the supposed ashes of Columbus in an elaborate tomb in its ancient cathedral.

The western third of the island was ceded to France in 1697. Santo Domingo itself was ceded to France in 1795. Haitian leader Toussaint L'Ouverture seized it, 1801. Spain returned intermittently 1803-21, as several native republics came and went. Haiti ruled again, 1822-44, and Spanish occupation occurred 1861-63.

The country was occupied by U.S. Marines from 1916 to 1924, when a constitutionally elected government was installed.

In 1930, Gen. Rafael Leonidas Trujillo Molina was elected president. Trujillo remained in power, ruling brutally until his assassination in 1961.

Pres. Joaquin Balaguer, appointed by Trujillo in 1960, resigned under pressure in 1962, and Juan Bosch was elected president in the first free elections in 38 years. Bosch was overthrown in 1963.

On April 24, 1965, a revolt was launched by followers of Bosch and others, including a few communists. Four days later 405 U.S. Marines intervened against the pro-Bosch forces; their numbers grew to 21,000. Token units were later sent by 5 So. American countries as a peace-keeping force.

A provisional government, approved by all major local groups, supervised a June, 1966 election, in which Balaguer defeated Bosch by a 3-2 margin; there were some charges of election fraud. Balaguer's followers won control of Congress.

The Inter-American Peace Force completed its departure Sept. 20, 1966. Balaguer was reelected, 1970 and 1974; the latter time without real opposition. The moderate left opposition won 1978 elections.

In 1971, scores of leftists were reported killed by terrorists. Renewed violence occurred in 1975. A crash in world sugar prices since 1975, combined with the increased oil export bill, ended five years of economic growth.

# Ecuador
## Republic of Ecuador

**People: Population** (1977 est.): 7,560,000. **Age distrib.** (%): 0–14: 47.2; 15–59: 48.3; 60+: 4.5. **Pop. density:** 71.53 per sq. mi. **Urban** (1974): 41.4%. **Ethnic groups:** Indians 40%, Mestizos 40%, Caucasians 10%, Negroes 10%. **Languages:** Spanish 93%, Quechua dialects 7%. **Religions:** Roman Catholics 94%, Protestants 6%.

**Geography: Area:** 105,685 sq. mi., the size of Colorado. **Location:** In NW S. America, on Pacific coast, astride Equator. **Neighbors:** Colombia to N, Peru to E and S. **Topography:** Two ranges of Andes run N and S, splitting the country into 3 zones; hot, humid lowlands on the coast; temperate highlands between the ranges, and rainy, tropical lowlands to the E. **Capital:** Quito. **Cities** (1974 cen.): Guayaquil 823,219; Quito 599,828; Cuenca 104,470.

**Government: Head of state:** Pres. Alfredo Poveda Burbano; b. Jan. 24, 1926; in office: Jan. 11, 1976. **Local divisions:** 20 provinces, headed by presidentially-appointed governors. **Armed forces:** regulars 23,900; para-military 5,800.

**Economy: Industries:** Cement, edible oils, textiles, sugar, chemicals, oil products, paper. **Chief crops:** Bananas (largest exporter), rice, grains, potatoes, fruits, cocoa, kapok. **Minerals:** Oil, copper, iron, lead, coal, sulphur. **Crude oil reserves** (1978): 1.64 bln. bbls. **Other resources:** Rubber, bark. **Per capita arable land:** 1.0 acres. **Meat production** (1976): beef: 58,100 tons; pork: 13,400 tons. **Fish catch** (1975): 223,400 metric tons. **Electricity production** (1975): 1.29 bln kwh. **Labor force:** 54% agriculture.

**Finance: Currency:** Sucres (May 1978: 25.00 = $1 US). **Gross domestic product** (1977): $6.15 bln. **Per capita income** (1976): $620. **Imports** (1976): $993 mln.; partners (1973): U.S. 34%, Jap. 14%, W. Ger. 12%, Col. 6%. **Exports** (1976): $1.13 bln.; partners (1973): U.S. 32%, Trin. 12%, Pan. 9%, Peru 6%. **Tourists** (1975): 172,900; receipts (1975): $20 million. **Balance of payments** (1977): +$159,000,000. **National budget** (1976): $586.12 mln. revenues; $672.52 mln. expenditures. **International reserves** (May 1978): $623.4 mln. **Consumer prices** (change in 1977): 13.0%.

**Transport: Railway traffic** (1975): 40.37 mln. passengermiles; 28.57 mln. net ton-miles. **Motor vehicles:** in use (1974): 43,600 passenger cars, 68,400 commercial vehicles. **Chief ports:** Guayaquil, Manta, Esmeraldas.

**Communications: Television sets:** 250,000 in use (1974), 3,000 manufactured (1974). **Radios:** 1,700,000 in use (1970),

13,000 manufactured (1974). **Telephones in use** (1977): 174,046. **Daily newspaper circulation** (1974): 285,000; 41 per 1,000 pop.

**Health: Life expectancy at birth** (1963): 51.04 male; 53.67 female. **Births** (annual per 1,000 pop. 1972-75): 41.8. **Deaths** (annual per 1,000 pop. 1972-75): 9.5. **Natural increase** (annual 1970-75): 3.23%. **Pop. per hospital bed** (1975): 469. **Pop. per physician** (1975): 2,816. **Infant mortality** (per 1,000 live births 1974): 70.2.

**Education: Literacy** (1975): 75%. **Pop. 5–19:** in school (1975): 57%, per teacher (1975): 54.

Spain conquered the region, which was the northern Inca empire, in 1633. Liberation forces defeated the Spanish May 24, 1822, near Quito. Ecuador became part of the Great Colombia Republic but seceded, May 13, 1830.

Liberals became a dominant force in political life in 1895, but have been unable to end instability and a succession of military coups.

In June 1968 elections, Dr. Jose Maria Velasco Ibarra, who had been elected president 4 times but had been ousted 3 times by coups, was again chosen by the voters. In June 1970, he assumed dictatorial powers. On Feb. 15, 1972, he was ousted by a military junta. A new junta took over in 1976, after strikes, inflation, and other economic problems arose. Free elections were held in 1978.

Ecuador and Peru have long disputed their Amazon Valley boundary.

The **Galapagos Islands,** 600 mi. to the W, are the home of huge tortoises and other unusual animals.

# Egypt
## Arab Republic of Egypt

**People: Population** (1977 est.): 38,740,000. **Pop. density:** 100.14 per sq. mi. **Urban** (1975): 43.9%. **Ethnic groups:** Egyptians, Bedouins, Nubians. **Languages:** Arabic. **Religions:** Sunni Moslems (state religion) 92%, Christians 7% (mostly Copts).

**Geography: Area:** 386,872 sq. mi., the size of Texas and New Mexico combined. **Location:** NE corner of Africa. **Neighbors:** Libya on W, Sudan on S, Israel on E. **Topography:** Almost the entire country is desolate and barren, with hills and mountains in E and along Nile. The Nile Valley, where most of the people live, stretches 550 miles in Egypt. **Capital:** Cairo. **Cities** (1974 est.): Cairo 5,715,000; Alexandria 2,259,000; Giza 853,700; Suez 368,000; Subra-El Khema 346,000; Port Said 342,000; El Mahalla et Kubra 287,800.

**Government: Head of state:** Pres. Mohamed Anwar El-Sadat; b. Dec. 25, 1918; in office; Oct. 17, 1970. **Head of government:** Prime Min. Mamdouh Salem; b. Mar. 10, 1918; in office: Nov. 10, 1976. **Local divisions:** 25 governorates; pres. appoints governors. **Armed forces:** regulars 345,000; reserves 500,000.

**Economy: Industries:** Textiles, chemicals, steel, cement, fertilizers, motion pictures. **Chief crops:** Cotton (one of largest producers), grains, vegetables, sugar cane, fruits. **Minerals:** Oil, phosphates, salt, iron, manganese, cement, gold, gypsum, kaolin, titanium. **Crude oil reserves** (1978): 2.45 bln. bbls. **Per capita arable land:** 0.2 acres. **Meat production** (1975): beef: 236,000 tons; lamb: 47,000 tons. **Fish catch** (1975): 106,600 metric tons. **Electricity production** (1975): 10.42 bln. kwh. **Labor force:** 55% agriculture.

**Finance: Currency:** Pound (May 1978: 1 = $2.56 US). **Gross domestic product** (1977): $18.76 bln. **Per capita income** (1974): $263. **Imports** (1974): $4.82 bln.; partners (1973): U.S. 13%, Fr. 8%, W. Ger. 8%, USSR 7%. **Exports** (1977): $1.73 bln.; partners (1973): USSR 33%, Czech. 6%, Jap. 5%, It. 4%, E. Ger. 4%. **Tourists** (1975): 539,100. **Balance of payments** (1976): −$537,000,000. **International reserves** (Apr. 1978): $494 mln. **Consumer prices** (change in 1976): 10.3%.

**Transport: Railway traffic** (1974): 5.38 bln. passenger-miles; 1.12 bln. net ton-miles. **Motor vehicles:** in use (1975): 215,500 passenger cars, 46,300 commercial vehicles; assembled (1977): 14,436 passenger cars; 4,440 commercial vehicles. **Civil aviation:** 1,081 mln. passenger-miles (1976); 13,637 mln. freight ton-miles (1976). **Chief ports:** Alexandria, Port Said, Suez.

**Communications: Television sets:** 610,000 licensed (1974), 68,000 manufactured (1974). **Radios:** 5,115,000 licensed (1974), 157,000 manufactured (1974). **Telephones in use** (1977): 503,000. **Daily newspaper circulation** (1972): 773,000;

21 per 1,000 pop.

**Health: Life expectancy at birth** (1960): 51.6 male; 53.8 female. **Births** (per 1,000 pop. 1974): 35.5. **Deaths** (per 1,000 pop. 1974): 12.4. **Natural increase** (1974): 2.31%. **Pop. per hospital bed** (1975): 468. **Pop. per physician** (1975): 1,520. **Infant mortality** (per 1,000 live births 1974): 100.4.

**Education: Literacy** (1975): 40%. **Pop. 5-19:** in school (1975): 43%, per teacher (1975): 80.

Archeological records of ancient Egyptian civilization date back to 4000 B.C. A unified kingdom arose around 3200 B.C., and extended its way south into Nubia and north as far as Syria. A high culture of rulers and priests was built on an economic base of serfdom, fertile soil, and annual flooding of the Nile banks.

Imperial decline facilitated conquest by Asian invaders (Hyksos, Assyrians). The last native dynasty fell in 341 B.C. to the Persians, who were in turn replaced by Greeks (Alexander and the Ptolemies), Romans, Byzantines, and Arabs, who introduced Islam and the Arabic language. The ancient Egyptian language is preserved only in the liturgy of the Coptic Christians.

Egypt was ruled as part of larger Islamic empires for several centuries. The Mamluks, a military caste of Caucasian origin, ruled Egypt from 1250 until defeat by the Ottoman Turks in 1517.

Under Turkish sultans the khedive as hereditary viceroy had wide authority, but European influence grew along with the beginnings of modernization in the 19th century. Britain intervened in 1882 and took control of administration, though nominal allegiance to the Ottoman Empire continued until 1914.

The country was a British protectorate from 1914 to 1922. A 1936 treaty strengthened Egyptian autonomy, but Britian retained bases in Egypt and a condominium over the Sudan. Britain fought German and Italian armies from Egypt, 1940-42, but Egypt did not declare war against Germany until 1945. In 1951 Egypt abrogated the 1936 treaty. The Sudan became independent in 1956.

Delays in reforms, corruption in public office, and royal extravagance led to an uprising July 23, 1952, led by the Society of Free Officers which named Maj. Gen. Mohammed Naguib commander in chief and forced King Farouk to abdicate. When the republic was proclaimed June 18, 1953, Naguib became its first president and premier. Lt. Col. Gamal Abdel Nasser, the principal influence behind the revolt, removed Naguib and became premier in 1954. In 1956, he was voted president. Nasser died in 1970 and was replaced by Vice President Anwar Sadat.

A new constitution was approved Sept. 11, 1971. At the same time, Egypt adopted the name Arab Republic of Egypt, dropping the name United Arab Republic, which it has used since its brief union with Syria, 1958-1961.

A series of decrees in July, 1961, nationalized about 90% of industry and reduced land holdings to 52 acres per family. In 1974 an economic liberalization was begun, with more emphasis on private domestic and foreign investment. Riots over food price increases and severe poverty left scores dead in January, 1977.

In July, 1956, the United States and Great Britain withdrew support for loans to start the Aswan High Dam. President Nasser nationalized the Suez Canal and seized control of the assets of the canal company. Later he obtained credits and technicians from the USSR to build the dam.

The billion-dollar Aswan High Dam project, begun 1960, completed 1971, provided irrigation for more than a million acres of land and a potential of 10 billion kwh of electricity per year. Artesian wells, drilled in the Western Desert, reclaimed 43,000 acres. 1960-66.

When the state of Israel was proclaimed in 1948, Egypt joined other Arab nations invading Israel and was defeated. No peace treaties were made and Egypt later denied Israeli shipping the use of the Suez Canal.

After terrorist raids across its border, Israel invaded Egypt's Sinai Peninsuala, Oct. 29, 1956. Egypt rejected a cease-fire demand by Britain and France; on Oct. 31 the 2 nations dropped bombs and on Nov. 5-6 landed forces. Egypt and Israel accepted a UN cease-fire, followed by Britain and France; fighting ended Nov. 7.

A UN Emergency Force guarded the 117-mile long border between Egypt and Israel until May 19, 1967, when it was withdrawn at Nasser's demand. Egyptian troops entered the Gaza Strip and the heights of Sharm el Sheikh and 3 days later closed the Strait of Tiran to all Israeli shipping. Full-scale war broke out une 5 and before it ended under a UN cease-fire June 10, Israel had captured Gaza and the Sinai Peninsula, controlled the ast bank of the Suez Canal and reopened the gulf.

Sporadic fighting with Israel broke out late in 1968. In 1969-70 here were almost daily artillery duels across the Suez Canal, ground forays and air raids in which Israeli planes penetrated deep into Egypt. Military and economic aid was received from he USSR and it was est. in 1971 there were 19,000 or more Soviet military personnel in Egypt. Israel and Egypt agreed, Aug. ', 1970, to a cease-fire and peace negotiations proposed by the J.S. Negotiations, pressed by the UN and U.S., failed to achieve results, but the cease-fire continued into 1973.

In July 1972 Sadat ordered most of the 20,000 Soviet military advisers and personnel to leave Egypt. They complied, leaving behind bases and equipment they had installed for the Egypans. Some Soviet military shipments have continued, despite an Egyptian debt of several billion dollars.

In a surprise attack Oct. 6, 1973 Egyptian forces crossed the Suez Canal into the Sinai. (At the same time, Syrian forces attacked Israelis on the Golan Heights.) Egypt was supplied by a USSR military airlift; the U.S. responded with an airlift to Israel. Israel counter-attacked, crossed the canal, surrounded Suez City. A UN cease-fire took effect Oct. 24.

A disengagement agreement was signed Jan. 18, 1974. Under t, Israeli forces withdrew from the canal's W bank; limited numbers of Egyptian forces occupied a strip along the E bank. A second accord was signed in 1975, with Israel yielding Sinai oil fields. Pres. Sadat's suprise visit to Jerusalem, Nov. 1977, opened the prospect of peace with Israel, but worsened relaions with Libya (border clashes, July 1977).

The U.S. and Egypt resumed, in Feb. 1974, diplomatic relaions, severed by Egypt after the 1967 war.

Iran, Saudi Arabia, and Kuwait provided aid of several billion dollars and low interest loans between 1975 and 1978. The U.S. also has provided some $1 billion annually in loans and grants since 1975.

The **Suez Canal,** 103 mi. long, links the Mediterranean and Red Seas. It was built by a French corporation 1859-69, but Britain obtained controlling interest in 1875. The last British troops were removed June 13, 1956. On July 26, Egypt nationalized he canal. French and British stockholders eventually received some compensation.

Egypt has barred Israeli ships and cargoes destined for Israel since 1948, and closed the canal to all shipping after the 1967 Israeli-Arab War. The canal was reopened in 1975, after Israel agreed to withdraw its troops eastward, and Egypt agreed to allow passage to Israeli cargo in third party ships. By 1977, annual tolls, at $500 million, had once more become a major source of government revenue.

## El Salvador

### Republic of El Salvador

**People: Population** (1976 est.): 4,120,000. **Age distrib.** (%): 0–14: 46.2; 15–59: 48.4; 60+: 5.4. **Pop. density:** 498.79 per sq. mi. **Urban** (1974): 38.8%. **Ethnic groups:** Mestizos 89%, Indians 10%, Caucasians 1%. **Languages:** Spanish, Nahuatl (among some Indians). **Religions:** Roman Catholicism prevails.

**Geography: Area:** 8,260 sq. mi., the size of Massachusetts. **Location:** In Central America. **Neighbors:** Guatemala on W, Honduras on N. **Topography:** A hot Pacific coastal plain in the south rises to a cooler plateau and valley region, densely populated. The N is mountainous, including many volcanoes. **Capital:** San Salvador. **Cities** (1971 cen.): San Salvador 337,171; Santa Ana 172,300.

**Government: Head of state:** Pres. Carlos Humberto Romero, b. Feb. 29, 1929; in office: July 1, 1977. **Local divisions:** 14 departments; pres. appoints governors. **Armed forces:** regulars 7,130; para-military 3,000.

**Economy: Industries:** Cement, textiles, refined sugar. **Chief crops:** Coffee, cotton, rice, maize, cacao, tobacco, indigo, sugar. **Other resources:** Rubber, forests. **Per capita arable land:** 0.3 acres. **Meat production** (1976): beef: 30,200 tons; pork: 11,400 tons. **Electricity production** (1976): 120.00 mln. kwh. **Labor force:** 47% agriculture.

**Finance: Currency:** Colones (May 1978: 2.50 = $1 US). **Gross domestic product** (1976): $2.62 bln. **Per capita income** (1976): $503. **Imports** (1977): $950 mln. partners (1973): U.S. 29%, Guat. 16%, Jap. 10%, W. Ger. 8%. **Exports** (1977): $959 mln.; partners (1973): U.S. 33%, Guat. 18%, W. Ger. 13%,

Jap. 10%. **Tourists** (1975): 266,000; receipts (1975): $18 million. **Balance of payments** (1977): +$100,000. **National budget** (1977): $502.64 mln. revenues; $430.76 mln. expenditures. **International reserves** (May 1978): $175.4 mln. **Consumer prices** (change in 1977): 11.9%.

**Transport: Motor vehicles:** in use (1974): 41,000 passenger cars, 19,100 commercial vehicles. **Chief ports:** La Union, Acajutla.

**Communications: Television sets:** 111,000 in use (1974). **Radios:** 300,000 in use (1970). **Telephones in use** (1977): 54,156. **Daily newspaper circulation** (1974): 201,000; 51 per 1,000 pop.

**Health: Life expectancy at birth** (1961): 56.56 male; 60.42 female. **Births** (per 1,000 pop. 1975): 40.1. **Deaths** (per 1,000 pop. 1975): 8.0. **Natural increase** (1975): 3.21%. **Pop. per hospital bed** (1975): 558. **Pop. per physician** (1975): 4,081. **Infant mortality** (per 1,000 live births 1975): 58.3.

**Education: Literacy** (1975): 58%. **Pop. 5–19:** in school (1975): 49%, per teacher (1975) 86.

El Salvador became independent of Spain in 1821, and of the Central American Federation in 1839.

A fight with Honduras in 1969 over the presence of 300,000 Salvadorean workers left 2,000 dead. New clashes occurred in 1970 and 1974.

In 1977, the government faced protests charging election fraud, and an accusation by the national conference of Roman Catholic bishops that the government was "persecuting" priests working with landless peasants. Repression and executions continued in 1978.

## Equatorial Guinea

### Republic of Equatorial Guinea

**People: Population** (1977 est.): 320,000. **Age distrib.** (%): 0–14: 35.2; 15–59: 57.1; 60+: 7.7. **Pop. density:** 29.54 per sq. mi. **Ethnic groups:** Fangs 75%, several other groups. **Languages:** Spanish (official), Fang, English. **Religions:** Roman Catholics 60%, Protestants, others.

**Geography: Area:** 10,832 sq. mi., the size of Maryland. **Location:** Consists of Masie Nguema Biyogo Is. (area 780 sq. mi.) off W. Africa coast in Gulf of Guinea, and Rio Muni, enclave on Mainland. **Neighbors:** Gabon on S, Cameroon on E, N. **Topography:** Masie Nguema Biyogo Island consists of two volcanic mountains and a connecting valley. Rio Muni, with over 90% of the area, has a coastal plain and low hills beyond. **Capital:** Malabo. **Cities** (1973 est.): Bata 50,000; Malabo 23,000.

**Government: Head of state:** Pres. Masie Nguema Biyogo; b. Jan. 1924; in office: Oct. 12, 1968. **Local divisions:** 2 provinces. **Economy: Chief crops:** Cocoa, coffee, bananas, palm oil. **Other resources:** Timber. **Per capita arable land:** 1.8 acres. **Labor force:** 79% agriculture.

**Finance: Currency:** Ekpwele (1974: 57.7 = $1 US). **Gross domestic product** (1974 est.): $120 mln. **Per capita income** (1974): $350. **Imports** (1973): $36 mln.; partner (1974): Spain 41%. **Exports** (1973): $32 mln.; partner (1974): Spain 41%.

**Transport: Chief ports:** Malabo, Bata.

**Communications: Radios:** 7,500 in use (1970). **Daily newspaper circulation** (1967): 1,000; 4 per 1,000 pop.

**Health: Life expectancy at birth** (1975): 41.9 male; 45.1 female. **Births** (annual per 1,000 pop. 1972-75): 36.8. **Deaths** (annual per 1,000 pop. 1972-75): 19.7. **Natural increase** (annual 1970-75): 1.71%. **Pop. per hospital bed** (1975): 178. **Pop. per physician** (1975): 10,667. **Infant mortality** (per 1,000 live births 1966): 53.2.

**Education: Literacy** (1975): 20%. **Pop. 5–19:** in school (1975): 47%, per teacher (1975): 95.

Fernando Po Island was discovered by Portugal in the late 15th century and ceded to Spain in 1778. Independence came Oct. 12, 1968. Riots occurred in 1969 over disputes between the island and the more backward Rio Muni province on the mainland. Masie Nguema Biyogo, himself from the mainland, became president for life in 1972; he ended provincial autonomy in 1973.

Most of the nation's 7,000 Europeans have emigrated, and 45,000 Nigerian workers were evacuated amid charges of a reign of terror. According to reports, slavery has been revived. As many as 50,000 people have been murdered by government forces. The economy has deteriorated.

Relations with Cameroon and Gabon have cooled due to boundary disputes. The U.S. suspended relations in 1976. The

USSR, China, and North Korea maintain ties, and Cuba has a military advisory mission.

1970 secessionist guerrillas, aided by Arab states, have seiz[...] most of the area.

# Ethiopia

**People: Population** (1977 est.) 28,930,000. **Age distrib.** (%): 0–14: 45.5; 15–59: 42.7; 60+: 11.9. **Pop. density:** 63.28 per sq. mi. **Urban** (1976): 12.1%. **Ethnic groups:** Galla 33%, Amhara 25%, Tigre 12%, Somali, Afar, Sidama. **Languages:** Amharic, Tigre (Semitic languages); Galla (Hamitic), Arabic, others. **Religions:** Orthodox Christian 40%, Moslem 40%.

**Geography: Area:** 457,142 sq. mi., four-fifths the size of Alaska. **Location:** In E. Africa. **Neighbors:** Sudan on W, Kenya on S. Somalia, Djibouti on E. **Topography:** A high central plateau, between 6,000 and 10,000 ft. high, rises to higher mountains near the Great Rift Valley, cutting in from the SW. The Blue Nile and other rivers cross the plateau, which descends to plains on both W and SE. **Capital:** Addis Ababa. **Cities** (1976 est.): Addis Ababa 1,242,555; Asmara 340,206; (1977 est.): Dire Dawa 66,570.

**Government: Head of state:** Chmn. of military council Mengistu Haile Mariam; in office: Feb. 1977. **Local divisions:** 14 provinces. **Armed forces:** regulars 7,000; para-military 39,000.

**Economy: Industries:** Food processing, cement, shoes, textiles. **Chief crops:** Coffee (Ethiopia is reputed birthplace of coffee; yields 50% export earnings), grains, tobacco, sugar. **Minerals:** Coal, iron, platinum, gold, silver, manganese, tin, copper, asbestos, potash, sulphur, mica, cement, salt. **Other resources:** Hydro power potential. **Per capita arable land:** 1.1 acres. **Meat production** (1975): beef, 196,000 tons; lamb: 124,000 tons. **Fish catch** (1975): 26,800 metric tons. **Electricity production** (1976): 480 mln. kwh. **Labor force:** 85% agriculture.

**Finance: Currency:** Birr (May 1978: 2.09 = $1 US). **Gross domestic product** (1976): $2.89 bln. **Per capita income** (1975): $89. **Imports** (1976): $353 mln.; partners (1973): It. 15%, Jap. 12%, W. Ger. 12%, U.K. 9%. **Exports** (1976): $278 mln.; partners (1973): U.S. 30%, W. Ger. 9%, It. 8%, Djibouti 7%. **Tourists** (1975): 30,600; receipts (1975): $7 million. **National budget** (1974): $215.76 mln. revenues; $350.28 mln. expenditures. **International reserves** (May 1978) = $184.3 mln. **Consumer prices** (change in 1977): 16.6%.

**Transport: Railway traffic** (1975): 67.07 mln. passenger-miles; 151.52 mln. net ton-miles. **Motor vehicles:** in use (1972): 41,000 passenger cars, 12,700 commercial vehicles. **Civil aviation:** 325 mln. passenger-miles (1976); 12,467 mln. freight ton-miles (1976). **Chief ports:** Masewa, Aseb.

**Communications: Television sets:** 20,000 in use (1974). **Radios:** 200,000 in use (1974). **Telephones in use** (1977): 73,486. **Daily newspaper circulation** (1974): 51,000; 2 per 1,000 pop.

**Health: Life expectancy at birth** (1975): 36.5 male; 39.6 female. **Births** (annual per 1,000 pop. 1972-75): 49.4. **Deaths** (annual per 1,000 pop. 1972-75): 25.8. **Natural increase** (annual 1970-75): 2.36%. **Pop. per hospital bed** (1975): 3,414. **Pop. per physician** (1975): 75,715. **Infant mortality** (per 1,000 live births 1963): 84.2.

**Education: Literacy** (1975): 7%. **Pop 5-19:** in school (1975); 12%, per teacher (1975): 342.

Ethiopian culture was influenced by Egypt and Greece. The ancient monarchy was invaded by Italy in 1880, but maintained its independence until a second Italian invasion in 1936. British forces freed the country in 1941.

The last emperor, Haile Selassie I, established a parliament and judiciary system in 1931, but barred all political parties.

A 1973 famine killed 200,000 people. An army mutiny, strikes, and student demonstrations led to the dethronement of Selassie in 1974, and the execution of 60 former officials. The ruling junta pledged to form a one-party socialist state, and instituted a successful land reform; opposition was violently suppressed. The influence of the Coptic Church, embraced in 330 A.D., was curbed, and the monarchy was abolished in 1975. A new famine and a locust plague threatened 1.5 million people in 1978.

The regime, torn by bloody coups, faced uprisings by tribal and political groups in part aided by Sudan and Somalia. Ties with the U.S., once a major arms and aid source, deteriorated, while cooperation accords were signed with the USSR in 1977. In 1978, Soviet advisors and 20,000 Cuban troops helped defeat Somali rebels & Somalia forces.

**Eritrea,** an Italian colony since 1890, reverted to Ethiopia in 1952 in accordance with a UN General Assembly vote. Since

# Fiji

**People: Population** (1977 est.): 600,000. **Age distrib.** (%): 0–14: 40.4; 15–59: 55.3; 60+: 4.3. **Pop. density:** 85.05 per s[...] mi. **Ethnic groups:** Indian 50%, Fijians (Melanesian-Polynesia[...] 42%, Europeans 2%. **Languages:** English (official), Fijian, Hin[...] **Religions:** Most Fijians are Methodist, most Indians are Hindu.

**Geography: Area:** 7,055 sq. mi., the size of New Jersey. **L[...] cation:** In western S. Pacific O. **Neighbors:** Nearest are Sol[...] mons on NW, Tonga on E. **Topography:** There are 840 islan[...] (106 inhabited), many of them mountainous, with tropical fores[...] and large fertile areas. Viti Levu, the largest island, has over h[...] the total land area. **Capital:** Suva. **Cities** (1975 est.): Su[...] (met.) 96,000.

**Government: Head of state:** Queen Elizabeth II, represent[...] by Gov. Gen. George Cakobau; **Head of government:** Prin[...] Min. Kamisese Mara; b. May 13, 1920; in office. Oct. 10, 197[...] **Local divisions:** 4 administrative divisions. **Armed force[...]** 1,000 regulars.

**Economy: Industries:** Cement, shipyards, light industry, m[...] lasses, tourism. **Chief crops:** Sugar, coconut products, ginge[...] **Minerals:** Gold. **Other resources:** Timber. **Per capita arab[...] land:** 0.3 acres. **Electricity production** (1975): 241.00 ml[...] kwh. **Labor force:** 49% agriculture.

**Finance: Currency:** Dollar (May 1978: 1 = $1.14 US). **Gro[...] domestic product** (1976): $662.55 mln. **Per capita incom[...]** (1975): $1,133. **Imports** (1977): $306 mln.; partners (197[...] Austral. 30%, Jap. 16%, U.K., 14%, New Zea. 12%, Sing. 9[...] **Exports** (1977): $173 mln.; partners (1975): U.K. 56%, Austra[...] 9%, New Zea. 8%, Sing. 3%. **Tourists** (1971): 152,000; receip[...] (1975): $75 million. **Balance of payments** (197[...] +$13,100,000. **National budget** (1975): $134.36 mln. rev[...] nues; $160.69 mln. expenditures. **International reserves** (M[...] 1978): $126.66 mln. **Consumer prices** (change in 1977): 6.9%

**Transport: Motor Vehicles:** in use (1975): 21,500 passeng[...] cars, 10,800 commercial vehicles. **Chief ports:** Suva, Lautoka.

**Communications: Radios:** 300,000 in use (1974). **Tel[...] phones in use** (1977): 30,759. **Daily newspaper circulatio[...]** (1974): 20,000; 36 per 1,000 pop.

**Health: Life expectancy at birth** (1966): 66.99 male; 72.0[...] female. **Births** (per 1,000 pop. 1975): 29.0. **Deaths** (annual p[...] 1,000 pop. 1972-75): 4.3. **Natural increase** (annual 1970-75[...] 2.07%. **Pop. per hospital bed** (1975): 362. **Pop. per physicia[...]** (1975): 2,071. **Infant mortality** (per 1,000 live births 1974): 20.[...] **Education: Literacy** (1975): 64%. **Pop. 5-19:** in scho[...] (1975): 73%, per teacher (1975): 37.

A British colony since 1874, Fiji became an independent pa[...] liamentary democracy Oct. 10, 1970.

Cultural differences between the majority Indian communit[...] descendants of contract laborers brought to the islands in th[...] 19th century, and the less modernized native Fijians, who by la[...] own 83% of the land in communal villages, have led to politic[...] polarization.

# Finland

## Republic of Finland

**People: Population** (1977 est.): 4,740,000. **Age distrib.** (%[...] 0–14: 23.7; 15–59: 61.6; 60+: 14.7. **Pop. density:** 36.43 per s[...] mi. **Urban** (1975): 59.1%. **Ethnic groups:** Finns, Swedes. **La[...] guages:** Finnish 93.5%, Swedish 6.5% (both official). **Religion[...]** Lutheran 92%, Russian Orthodox 1.3%.

**Geography: Area:** 130,119 sq. mi., slightly smaller than Mo[...] tana. **Location:** In northern Baltic region of Europe. **Neighbo[...]** Norway on N, Sweden on W, USSR on E. **Topography:** Sout[...] and central Finland are mostly flat areas with low hills and man[...] lakes. The N has mountainous areas, 3,000-4,000 ft. **Capita[...]** Helsinki. **Cities** (1974 est.): Helsinki (met.) 852,955; Tampe[...] (met.) 234,806; Turku (met.) 231,129.

**Government: Head of state:** Pres. Urho K. Kekkonen; b[...] Sept. 3, 1900; in office: March 1, 1956. **Head of governmen[...]** Prime Min. Kalevi Sorsa; b. Dec. 21, 1930; in office: Mar. [...] 1978. **Local divisions:** 12 laanit (provinces). **Armed force[...]** regulars 71,000; reserves 690,000.

**Economy: Industries:** Machinery, metal, shipbuilding, textile[...] leather, chemicals, tourism. **Chief crops:** Grains, potatoes. **Min[...] erals:** Copper, iron, zinc, lead. **Other resources:** Forests (55[...]

exports). **Per capita arable land:** 1.4 acres. **Meat produc-**
n (1976): beef: 113,600 tons; pork: 136,000 tons. **Fish catch**
»75): 113,700 metric tons. **Electricity production** (1977):
87 bln. kwh. **Labor force:** 18% agric.; 26% manuf.

**Finance: Currency:** Markkaa (May 1978: 4.30 = $1 US).
**oss domestic product** (1977): $29.95 bln. **Per capita in-**
me (1976): $5,351. **Imports** (1977): $7.60 bln.; partners
»75): Swed. 18.2%, USSR 16.8%, W. Ger. 15.7%, U.K. 8.9%,
5. 7.4%. **Exports** (1977): $7.67 bln.; partners (1975): USSR
4%, Swed. 17.8%, U.K. 14.6%, W. Ger. 8.6%. **Balance of**
**yments** (1977): −$258,000,000. **National budget** (1977):
04 bln. revenues; $5.99 bln. expenditures. **International re-**
**rves** (May 1978): $1.07 bln. **Consumer prices** (change in
»77): 12.7%.

**Transport: Railway traffic** (1975): 1.94 bln. passenger-miles.
»9 bln. net ton-miles. **Motor vehicles:** in use (1975): 996,300
»ssenger cars, 137,100 commercial vehicles. **Civil aviation:** 7
7 mln. passenger-miles (1977); 24,033 mln. freight ton-miles
»77). **Chief ports:** Helsinki, Turku.

**Communications: Television sets:** 1,261,000 licensed
»74), 248,000 manufactured (1974). **Radios:** 1,997,000 li-
»nsed (1974), 174,000 manufactured (1974). **Telephones in**
»e (1977): 1,935,683. **Daily newspaper circulation** (1974):
»58,000; 440 per 1,000 pop.

**Health: Life expectancy at birth** (1974): 66.90 male; 75.41
»male. **Births** (per 1,000 pop. 1976): 14.1. **Deaths** (per 1,000
»p. 1976): 9.4. **Natural increase** (1976): .47%. **Pop. per hos-**
**tal bed** (1975): 86. **Pop. per physician** (1975): 702. **Infant**
**ortality** (per 1,000 live births 1974): 10.2.

**Education:** Literacy (1975): 99%. **Pop. 5–19:** in school
»75): 78%; per teacher (1975): 24.

The early Finns probably migrated from the Ural area at about
»e beginning of the Christian era. Swedish settlers brought the
»untry into Sweden, 1154 to 1809, when Finland became an
»tonomous grand duchy of the Russian Empire. Russian exac-
»ns created a strong national spirit; on Dec. 6, 1917, Finland
»clared its independence and in 1919 became a republic. On
»v. 30, 1939, the Soviet Union invaded, and the Finns were
»rced to cede 16,173 sq. mi., including the Karelian Isthmus,
»puri, and an area on Lake Ladoga. After World War II, in which
»nland tried to recover its lost territory, further cessions were
»acted. In 1948, Finland signed a treaty of mutual assistance
»th the USSR. In 1956 Russia returned Porkkala, which had
»en ceded as a military base.

Finland is oriented toward the West in trade and culture, but
»viet infuence is strong. The governing coalition usually in-
»des the Communist Party.

**Aland,** constituting an autonomous department, is a group of
»nall islands, 572 sq. mi., in the Gulf of Bothnia, 25 mi. from
»weden, 15 mi. from Finland. It is demilitarized. Mariehamn is
»e principal port.

# France
## French Republic

**People: Population** (1977 est.): 53,080,000. **Age distrib.**
%): 0–14: 23.7; 15–59: 57.6; 60+: 18.7. **Pop. density:** 251.56
»r sq. mi. **Urban** (1968): 70.0%. **Ethnic groups:** A mixture of
»rious European and Mediterranean groups. **Languages:**
»ench; minorities speak Breton, Alsatian German, Flemish, Ital-
»n, Basque, Catalan. **Religions:** Roman Catholic 90%, Protes-
»nt 1%, Jewish 1%, Moslems 1%.

**Geography: Area:** 211,000 sq. mi., four-fifths the size of
»xas. **Location:** In Western Europe, between Atlantic O. and
»editerranean Sea. **Neighbors:** Spain on S, Italy, Switzerland,
, Germany on E, Luxembourg, Belgium on N. **Topography:** A
»de plain covers more than half of the country, in N and W,
»ained to W by Seine, Loire, Garonne rivers. The Massif Cen-
»al, is a mountainous plateau in center. In E are Alps (Mt. Blanc
» tallest in W. Europe, 15,771 ft.), the lower Jura range, and the
»rested Vosges. The Rhone flows from Lake Geneva (Lac Le-
»an) to Mediterranean. Pyrenees are in SW, on border with
»pain. **Capital:** Paris. **Cities** (1975 cen.): Paris (met.) 9,863,000;
»968 cen.): Lyon (met.) 1,074,823; Marseilles (met.) 964,412;
»ile (met.) 881,439; Bordeaux (met.) 555,152; Toulouse (met.)
»9,764; Nantes (met.) 393,731; Nice (met.) 392,635; Rouen
»net.) 369,793.

**Government: Head of state:** Pres. Valery Giscard d'Estaing;
»b. 2, 1926; in office: May 24, 1974. **Head of government:**
»aymond Barre; b. Apr. 12, 1924; in office: Aug. 25, 1976. **Local**

**divisions:** 96 departments, grouped into 22 development regions. **Armed forces:** regulars 775,700; reserves 450,000.

**Economy: Industries:** Steel, chemicals, autos, textiles, wine,
perfume, aircraft, ships, instruments, plastics, electronic equipment. **Chief crops:** Grains, corn, rice, fruits, vegetables. France
is largest food producer, exporter, in W. Eur. **Minerals:** Iron,
bauxite, coal, asphalt, rock salt, potash. **Crude oil reserves**
(1978): .043 mln. bbls. **Other resources:** Forests. **Per capita**
**arable land:** 0.8 acres. **Meat production** (1976): beef: 1.40
mln. tons; pork: 1.50 mln. tons; lamb: 154,900 tons. **Fish catch**
(1975): 805,800 metric tons. **Electricity production** (1977):
210.35 bln. kwh. **Labor force:** 12% agric.; 27% manuf.

**Finance: Currency:** Franc (May 1978: 4.61 = $1 US). **Gross**
**domestic product** (1977): $397.51 bln. **Per capita income**
(1976): $5,860. **Imports** (1977): $70.50 bln.; partners (1975): W.
Ger. 18.8%, Belg. 9.4%, It. 8.7%, U.S. 7.5%. **Exports** (1977):
$63.56 bln.; partners (1975): W. Ger. 16.3%, Belg. 10%, It.
9.5%, U.K. 6.4%. **Tourists** (1975): 13,064,000; receipts (1975):
$3.475 billion. **Balance of payments** (1977): +$141,000,000.
**National budget** (1976): $70.57 bln. revenues; $73.12 bln. expenditures. **International reserves** (May 1978): $11.22 bln.
**Consumer prices** (change in 1977): 9.5%.

**Transport: Railway traffic** (1975): 31.66 bln. passenger-
miles; 39.76 bln. net ton-miles. **Motor vehicles:** in use (1975):
15,300,000 passenger cars, 2,134,000 commercial vehicles;
manufactured (1977): 3,564,000 passenger cars; 540,000 commercial vehicles. **Civil aviation:** 16,946 mln. passenger-miles
(1977); 1,036,640 freight ton-miles (1977). **Chief ports:** Marseilles, LeHavre, Nantes, Bordeaux, Rouen.

**Communications: Television sets:** 12,335,000 licensed
(1974), 1,606,000 manufactured (1975). **Radios:** 17,000,000
licensed (1974), 3,051,000 manufactured (1975). **Telephones**
**in use** (1977): 15,553,798. **Daily newspaper circulation**
(1973): 11,458,000; 220 per 1,000 pop.

**Health: Life expectancy at birth** (1972): 68.6 male; 76.4 female. **Births** (per 1,000 pop. 1976): 13.6. **Deaths** (per 1,000
pop. 1976): 10.5. **Natural increase** (1976): .31%. **Pop. per**
**hospital bed** (1975): 97. **Pop. per physician** (1975): 699. **In-**
**fant mortality** (per 1,000 live births 1973): 12.1.

**Education:** Literacy (1975): 99%. **Pop. 5-19:** in school
(1975): 69%; per teacher (1975): 24.

Celtic Gaul was conquered by Julius Caesar 58-51 B.C. Romans ruled for 500 years, bequeathing their language, which
survived Teutonic invasions. Under Charlemagne, Frankish rule
extended over much of Europe. After his death France emerged
as one of the successor kingdoms.

The monarchy was overthrown by the French Revolution
(1789-93) and succeeded by the First Republic; followed by the
First Empire under Napoleon (1804-15), a monarchy (1814-48),
the Second Republic (1848-52), the Second Empire (1852-70),
the Third Republic (1871-1946), the Fourth Republic (1946-58),
and the Fifth Republic (1958 to present).

France suffered severe losses in manpower and wealth in the
first World War, 1914-18, when it was invaded by Germany. By
the Treaty of Versailles, France exacted return of Alsace and
Lorraine, French provinces seized by Germany in 1871. Germany invaded France again in May, 1940, and signed an armistice with a government based in Vichy. After France was liberated by the allies Sept. 1944, Gen. Charles de Gaulle became
head of the provisional government, serving until 1946.

De Gaulle again became premier in 1958, during a crisis over
Algeria, and obtained voter approval for a new constitution, ush-
ering in the Fifth Republic. Using strong executive powers, he
promoted French economic and technological advances in the
context of the European Economic Community, and guarded
French foreign policy independence. France has become the
world's fifth greatest industrial power.

France had withdrawn from Indochina in 1954, and from Morocco and Tunisia in 1956. Most of its remaining African territories were freed 1958-62, but France retained strong economic
and political ties. French forces helped governments fight rebellions in Chad, Mauritania, and Zaire in 1978.

France tested atomic bombs in the Sahara beginning in 1960.
Land-based and submarine launched strategic missiles were
also developed. In 1966, France withdrew all its troops from the
integrated military command of NATO, though 60,000 remained
stationed in Germany. France continued to attend political meetings of NATO.

In May 1968 rebellious students in Paris and other centers
rioted, battled police, and were joined by workers who launched
nationwide strikes. The government awarded pay increases to

the strikers May 26. In elections to the Assembly in June, de Gaulle's backers won a landslide victory. Nevertheless, he resigned from office in April, 1969, after losing a nationwide referendum on constitutional reform.

De Gaulle's policies were largely continued after his death in 1970. Independent Republican Valery Giscard d'Estaing, president since 1974, has tried to resist electoral inroads by the Socialist-Communist alliance through moderate economic, social, and educational reforms. The fractious leftist alliance won a majority of local offices in 1976 and 1977 elections but failed to win 1978 parliamentary elections.

The island of **Corsica**, in the Mediterranean W of Italy and N of Sardinia, is an official region of France comprising 2 departments. Area: 3,369 sq. mi.; pop.: 220,000. The capital is Ajaccio, birthplace of Napoleon. A militant separatist movement led to violence after 1975.

## Overseas Departments

**French Guiana** is on the NE coast of South America with Surinam on the W and Brazil on the E and S. Its area is 37,740 sq. mi.; population (1975), 55,125. Guiana sends one senator and one deputy to the French Parliament. Guiana has a prefect and a Council General of 15 elected members; capital is Cayenne.

In 1944 France closed the famous penal colony, Devil's Island, and repatriated 2,800 inmates.

Immense forests of rich timber cover 90% of the land. The principal crops are rice, corn, manioc, cacao, bananas, and sugar cane. Placer gold mining is the most important industry. Exports are cocoa, bananas, wood, gold, fish glue, rum, rosewood essence, shrimp and hides.

**Guadeloupe**, in the West Indies' Leeward Islands, consists of 2 large islands, Basse-Terre and Grande-Terre, separated by the Salt River, plus Marie Galante and the Saintes group to the S and, to the N, Desirade, St. Barthelemy, and over half of St. Martin (the Netherlands portion is St. Maarten). A French possession since 1635, the department is represented in the French Parliament by 2 senators and 3 deputies; administration consists of a prefect (governor) and an elected General Council.

Area of the islands is 687 sq. mi.; population (1975) 334,900, mainly descendants of slaves; capital is Basse-Terre on Basse-Terre Is. The land is fertile; sugar, rum, and bananas are exported; tourism is an important industry.

**Martinique**, one of the Windward Islands, in the West Indies, has been a possession since 1635, and a Department since March, 1946. It is represented in the French Parliament by 2 senators and 3 deputies. Mt. Pelee, a volcano, erupted May 8, 1902, destroying the city of St. Pierre and 30,000 inhabitants. The island was the birthplace of Napoleon's Empress Josephine.

It has an area of 426 sq. mi. and population (1975) 324,832, mostly descendants of slaves. The capital is Fort-de-France. It is a popular tourist stop. The chief exports are sugar, rum, bananas, pineapples, and cocoa.

**Mayotte**, formerly part of Comoros, voted in 1976 to become an overseas department of France. An island NW of Madagascar, area is 144 sq. mi., pop. 36,000.

**Reunion** is an island in the Indian Ocean, about 420 miles east of Madagascar, and has belonged to France since 1665. The area is 969 sq. mi.; the population (1975) 476,675, is 30% of French extraction. Capital: Saint-Denis. The chief products are sugar, rum, corn, perfume essences, vanilla, and spices. It elects 3 deputies, 2 senators to the French Parliament.

**St. Pierre and Miquelon**, formerly an Overseas Territory, began the transition to department status in 1976. It consists of 2 groups of rocky islands near the SW coast of Newfoundland, inhabited by fishermen. The exports are chiefly fish products. The St. Pierre group has an area of 10 sq. mi.; Miquelon, 83 sq. mi. Total population (1974), 5,840. The capital is St. Pierre. A deputy and a senator are elected to the French Parliament.

## Overseas Territories

**French Polynesia.** Overseas Territory, comprises 130 islands widely scattered among 5 archipelagos in the South Pacific; administered by a governor. Territorial Assembly and a Council with headquarters at Papeete, Tahiti, one of the **Society Islands**. A deputy and a senator are elected to the French Parliament.

Other groups are the **Marquesas Islands**, the **Tuamotu Archipelago**, the **Gambier Islands** and the **Austral Islands**.

Total area of the islands administered from Tahiti is 1,544 sq. mi.; pop. (est. 1974), 130,000, more than half on Tahiti. Tahiti is picturesque and mountainous with a productive coastline bearing coconut, banana and orange trees, sugar cane and vanilla.

Tahiti was visited by Capt. James Cook in 1769 and by C Bligh in the Bounty, 1788-89. Its beauty impressed Herman M ville, Paul Gauguin, Charles Darwin and Robert Louis Stevens who called Tahitians "God's sweetest works."

**New Caledonia** and its dependencies, an Overseas Territo are a group of islands in the Pacific Ocean about 1,115 mi. E Australia and approx. the same distance NW of New Zeala Dependencies are the **Loyalty Islands**, the **Isle of Pines, Hu Islands** and the **Chesterfield Islands.**

New Caledonia, the largest, has 6,530 sq. mi. Total area the territory is 8,548 sq. mi.; population (est. 1975) 138,000, cluding 50,000 Europeans). The group was acquired by Fran in 1853.

The territory is administered by a governor and governm council. There is a popularly elected Territorial Assembly. A d uty and a senator are elected to the French parliament. Capi Noumea.

Mining is the chief industry. New Caledonia is the world's th largest nickel producer. Other minerals found are chrome, balt, manganese, antimony, mercury, cinnebar, silver, gold, le and copper. Agricultural products include coffee, copra, cott manioc (cassava), corn, tobacco, bananas and pineapples.

**Wallis and Futuna Islands**, 2 archipelagos raised to status Overseas Territory July 29, 1961, are in the SW Pacific S of Equator between Fiji and Samoa. The islands have a total a of 106 sq. mi. and population (est. 1974) of 9,000. **Alofi,** tached to Futuna, is uninhabited. Capital: Mata-Utu. Chief pro ucts are copra, yams, taro roots, bananas. A senator and a de uty are elected to the French parliament.

**French Southern and Antarctic Lands**, Overseas Territo comprises **Adelie Land,** on Antarctica, and 4 island groups the Indian Ocean. Adelie, discov. 1840, has 2 research bases coastline of 185 mi. and tapers 1,240 mi. inland to the So Pole. The US does not recognize national claims in Antarctic There are 2 huge glaciers, Ninnis, 22 mi. wide, 99 mi. long, a Mentz, 11 mi. wide, 140 mi. long. The Indian Ocean groups are

**Kerguelen Archipelago**, discovered 1772, 300 islands. T chief is 87 mi. long, 74 mi. wide, and has Mt. Ross, 6,429 ft. Principal research station is Port-aux-Francais. Seals oft weigh 2 tons; there are blue whales, coal, peat, semi-precio stones. **Crozet Archipelago** (discov. 1772), covers 195 sq. Eastern Island rises to 6,560 ft. **Saint Paul**, in southern Indi Ocean, has warm springs with earth at places heating to 120° 390° F. **Amsterdam** is nearby; both produce cod and rock lo ster.

The former **French Territory of the Afars and the Iss** became in 1977 the independent nation of Djibouti.

## New Hebrides

**New Hebrides**, a condominium administered since 1906 b France and Great Britain, is a group of 11 main islands ar about 69 islets 250 mi. NE of New Caledonia and 500 mi. W Fiji. It has 5,790 sq. mi. and population (est. 1975) of 95,00 mostly Melanesian. It has 2 administrations—French and Britis Chief products are copra, frozen fish, cocoa, and coffee.

# Gabon
## Gabonese Republic

**People: Population** (1977 est.): 530,000. **Age distrib.** (9 0–14: 25.2; 15–59: 64.9; 60+: 10.0. **Pop. density:** 5.18 per s mi. **Urban** (1970): 32.0%. **Ethnic groups:** Fangs 25%, Bapo non 10%, others. **Languages:** (French (official), Fang, Ban languages. **Religions:** Roman Catholics 25%, Protestants 10 others.

**Geography: Area:** 102,317 sq. mi., the size of Colorado. L cation: On Atlantic coast of central Africa. **Neighbors:** Equat rial Guinea, Cameroon on N, Congo on E, S. **Topography** Heavily forested, the country consists of coastal low-lands, pl teaus in N, E, and S, mountains in N, SE, and center. The Og oue R. system covers most of Gabon. **Capital:** Libreville. **Citie** (1970 est.): Libreville (met.) 75,000; Port-Gentil 30,000.

**Government: Head of state:** Pres. Albert-Bernard (Oma Bonjo; b. Dec. 30, 1935; in office: Dec. 2, 1967. **Local division** 9 provinces. **Armed forces:** regulars 1,250; para-military 1,600

**Economy: Industries:** Oil products. **Chief crops:** Cocoa, co fee, rice, peanuts, palm products, cassava, bananas. **Mineral** Manganese, oil, uranium, iron, gas. **Crude oil reserves** (1978 2.05 bln. bbls. **Other resources:** Timber. **Per capita arabl**

nd: 0.6 acres. **Electricity production** (1976): 228.00 mln.
rh. **Labor force:** 72% agriculture.

**Finance: Currency:** Franc (May 1978: 230.35 = $1 US).
ross domestic product (1975): 1.66 bln. **Per capita income**
975): $3,225. **Imports** (1976): $177 mln.; partners (1973): Fr.
%, W. Ger. 9%, U.S. 9%, U.K. 4%. **Exports** (1976): $186
n.; partners (1973): Fr. 37%, W. Ger. 10%, Neth. 7%, U.S.
%. **Tourists** (1973): 52,500; receipts (1975): $18 million. **Bal-
ce of payments** (1977): −$110,200,000. **International re-
rves** (Feb. 1978): $9.96 mln. **Consumer prices** (change in
75): 28.4%.

**Transport: Motor vehicles:** in use (1974): 10,100 passenger
rs, 7,300 commercial vehicles. **Chief ports:** Libreville, Port-
entil.

**Communications: Television sets:** 5,100 in use (1974). **Ra-
os:** 90,000 in use (1974). **Telephones in use** (1973): 11,000.
ally newspaper circulation (1974): 1,000; 5 per 1,000 pop.

**Health: Life expectancy at birth** (1961): 25 male; 45 female.
rths (annual per 1,000 pop. 1972-75): 32.2. **Deaths** (annual
r 1,000 pop. 1972-75): 22.2. **Natural increase** (annual
70-75): 1.00%. **Pop. per hospital bed** (1975): 115. **Pop. per
nysician** (1975): 4,718. **Infant mortality** (per 1,000 live births
60-61): 229.

**Education: Literacy** (1975): 12%. **Pop. 5-19:** in school
975): 75%, per teacher (1975): 34.

France established control over the region in the second half
' the nineteenth century. Gabon became independent Aug. 17,
960. It is one of the most prosperous black African countries,
anks to abundant natural resources, foreign private invest-
ent, and government development programs.

## Gambia
### Republic of the Gambia

**People: Population** (1977 est.): 550,000. **Age distrib.** (%):
-14: 41.4; 15–59: 55.2; 60+: 3.5. **Pop. density:** 137.40 per sq.
i. **Urban** (1973): 15.9%. **Ethnic groups:** Mandingo 40%, Fula
3%, Wolof 12%, others. **Languages:** English (official), others.
**eligions:** Moslems 85%, Christian 4%, others.

**Geography: Area:** 4,003 sq. mi., smaller than Connecticut.
**ocation:** On Atlantic coast near western tip of Africa. **Neigh-
ors:** Surrounded on three sides by Senegal. **Topography:** The
ountry consists of a narrow strip of land on each side of the
wer Gambia. **Capital:** Banjul. **Cities** (1976 est.): Banjul (met.)
9,333.

**Government: Head of state:** Pres. Dawda Kairaba Jawara;
May 16, 1924; in office: Apr. 24, 1970. **Local divisions:** 6 divi-
ons and Banjul.

**Economy: Industries:** Tourism. **Chief crops:** Peanuts (main
xport), rice. **Per capita arable land:** 1.0 acres. **Electricity pro-
uction** (1977): 31.20 mln. kwh. **Labor force:** 84% agriculture.

**Finance: Currency:** Dalasi (May 1978: 2.19 = $1 US).
ross domestic product (1976): 89.67 mln. **Per capita in-
ome** (1974): $120. **Imports** (1977): $72 mln.; partners (1973):
.K. 24%, P.R. China 10%, Neth. 6%. **Exports** (1977): $48
ln.; partners (1973): U.K. 37%, Fr. 23%, Neth. 17%, Port. 8%.
**ourist receipts** (1975): $6 million. **Balance of payments**
1977): +$1,200,000. **National budget** (1977): $30.77 mln. rev-
nues; $40.91 mln. expenditures. **International reserves** (May
978): $21.06 mln. **Consumer prices** (change in 1977): 12.4%.

**Transport: Motor vehicles:** in use (1972): 3,000 passenger
ars, 2,500 commercial vehicles. **Chief ports:** Banjul.

**Communications: Radios:** 60,000 in use (1974). **Tele-
hones in use** (1977): 2,752.

**Health: Life expectancy at birth** (1975): 38.5 male; 41.6 fe-
nale. **Births** (annual per 1,000 pop. 1972-75): 43.3. **Deaths** (an-
ual per 1,000 pop. 1972-75): 24.1. **Natural increase** (annual
970-75): 1.92%. **Pop. per hospital bed** (1975): 794. **Pop. per
hysician** (1975): 14,743. **Infant mortality** (per 1,000 live births
973): 165.

**Education: Literacy** (1975): 10%. **Pop. 5-19:** in school
1975): 18%, per teacher (1975): 173.

The tribes of Gambia were at one time associated with the
Vest African empires of Ghana, Mali, and Songhay. The area
ecame Britain's first African possession in 1588.

Independence came Feb. 18, 1965; republic status within the
Commonwealth was achieved in 1970. Gambia is one of the only
unctioning democracies in Africa. The country suffered from se-
ere famine in 1977-78.

## Germany

**Now comprises 2 nations: Federal Republic of Germany
(West Germany), German Democratic Republic (East Germany).**

Germany, prior to World War II, was a central European nation
composed of numerous states which had a common language
and traditions and which had been united in one country since
1871; since World War II it has been split in 2 parts (see below).

**History and Government.** Germanic tribes were defeated by
Julius Caesar, 55 and 53 B.C. but Roman expansion N of the
Rhine was stopped in 9 A.D. Charlemagne, ruler of the Franks,
consolidated Saxon, Bavarian, Rhenish, Frankish, and other
lands; after him the eastern part became the German Empire.
The Thirty Years' War, 1618-1648, split Germany into small prin-
cipalities and kingdoms. After Napoleon, Austria contended with
Prussia for dominance, but lost the Seven Weeks' War to Prus-
sia, 1866. Otto von Bismarck, Prussian chancellor, formed the
North German Confederation, 1867.

In 1870 Bismarck maneuvered Napoleon III into declaring war.
After the quick defeat of France, Bismarck formed the **German
Empire** and on Jan. 18, 1871, in Versailles, proclaimed King Wil-
helm I of Prussia German emperor (Deutscher kaiser).

The German Empire reached its peak before World War I in
1914, with 208,780 sq. mi., plus a colonial empire. After that war
Germany ceded Alsace-Lorraine to France; Eupen and Malmedy
to Belgium; parts of Silesia to Poland and Czechoslovakia; part
of Schleswig to Denmark; lost all of its colonies as well as the
ports of Memel and Danzig.

**Republic of Germany,** 1919-1933, adopted the Weimar constitution; met reparation payments and elected Friedrich Ebert
and Gen. Paul von Hindenburg presidents.

**Third Reich,** 1933-1945, Adolf Hitler, born in Austria, 1889,
led the National Socialist German Workers' (Nazi) party after
World War I. In 1923 he attempted to unseat the Bavarian government and was imprisoned. President von Hindenburg named
Hitler chancellor Jan. 30, 1933; on Aug. 3, 1934, the day after
Hindenburg's death, the cabinet joined the offices of president
and chancellor and made Hitler fuehrer (leader). Hitler abolished
freedom of speech and assembly, and began a long series of
persecutions climaxed by the murder of millions of Jews and
opponents.

Hitler repudiated the Versailles treaty and reparations agreements. He remilitarized the Rhineland 1936 and annexed Austria
(Anschluss, 1938). At Munich he made an agreement with
Neville Chamberlain, British prime minister, enabling him to annex Czechoslovakia. He signed a non-aggression treaty with the
Soviet Union, 1939. He declared war on Poland Sept. 1, 1939,
precipitating World War II.

With total defeat near, Hitler committed suicide in Berlin Apr.
1945. The victorious Allies voided all acts and annexations of
Hitler's Reich.

**Postwar changes.** The zones of occupation administered by
the Allied Powers and later relinquished gave the Soviet Union
Saxony, Saxony-Anhalt, Thuringia, and Mecklenburg, and the
former Prussian provinces of Saxony and Brandenburg.

The territory E of the Oder-Neisse line within 1937 boundaries
comprising the provinces of Silesia, Pomerania, West Prussia
and the southern part of East Prussia, totaling about 41,220 sq.
mi., population (1939) 9,600,000, was taken by Poland. Northern
East Prussia was taken by the Soviet Union. Several million Germans emigrated from these territories to W. Germany.

The Western Allies ended the state of war with Germany in
1951. The USSR did so in 1955.

There was also created the area of Greater Berlin, within but
not part of the Soviet zone, administered by the 4 occupying
powers under the Allied Command. In 1948 the Soviet Union
withdrew and established its single command in East Berlin. The
Communists cut off supplies, whereupon the Allies utilized a gi-
gantic airlift to bring food to West Berlin during 1948-1949. In
Aug. 1961 the East Germans built a wall dividing Berlin, after
over 3 million E. Germans had emigrated.

## East Germany

### German Democratic Republic

**People: Population** (1977 est.): 16,770,000. **Age distrib.**
(%): 0–14: 22.6; 15–59: 55.4; 60+: 22.0. **Pop. density:** 412.59
per sq. mi. **Urban** (1976): 75.5%. **Ethnic groups:** Germans,
Wends (0.7%). **Languages:** German. **Religions:** Protestant
80%, Roman Catholic 11%.

**Geography: Area:** 40,646 sq. mi., the size of Virginia. **Location:** In E. Central Europe. **Neighbors:** W. Germany on W, Czechoslovakia on S, Poland on E. **Topography:** East Germany lies mostly on the North German plains, with lakes in N, Harz Mtns., Elbe Valley, and sandy soil of Bradenburg in center, and highlands in S. **Capital:** East Berlin. **Cities** (1976 est.): Berlin 1,101,123; Leipzig 565,392; Dresden 509,253.

**Government: Head of state:** Chmn. Erich Honecker; b. Aug. 25, 1912; in office: Oct. 1976; **Head of government:** Prime Min. Willi Stoph; b. July 9, 1914; in office: 1964-73; Oct. 1976; **Head of Communist Party:** Sec.-Gen. Erich Honecker; in office: 1971. **Local divisions:** 15 administrative districts. **Armed forces:** regulars 149,000; reserves 255,000.

**Economy: Industries:** Steel, chemicals, cement, textiles, shoes, oil products, machinery. **Chief crops:** Grains, potatoes, sugar beets. **Minerals:** Lignite (largest producer), uranium, cobalt, bismuth, arsenic, antimony. **Per capita arable land:** 0.7 acres. **Meat production** (1976): beef: 355,200 tons; pork: 772,700 tons; lamb: 14,000 tons. **Fish catch** (1975): 374,500 metric tons. **Electricity production** (1977): 91.99 bln. kwh. **Labor force:** 12% agric.; 38% manuf.

**Finance: Currency:** Mark (Oct.-Dec. 1976: 3.48 = $1 US). **Gross domestic product** (1974 est.): $59 bln. **Per capita income** (1974): $3,300. **Imports** (1974): $13.20 bln.; partners (1974): USSR 30%, W. Ger. 9%, Czech. 7%, Pol. 7%. **Exports** (1976): $11.36 bln.; partners (1974): USSR 33%, Czech. 10%, W. Ger. 10%, Pol. 9%. **Tourists** (1975): 1,084,200.

**Transport: Railway traffic** (1975): 13.23 bln. passengermiles; 34.38 bln. net ton-miles. **Motor vehicles:** in use (1975): 1,880,500 passenger cars, 534,000 commercial vehicles; manufactured (1977): 166,800 passenger cars; 37,200 commercial vehicles. **Chief ports:** Rostock, Wismar, Stralsund.

**Communications: Television sets:** 5,096,000 licensed (1974), 509,000 manufactured (1975). **Radios:** 6,114,000 licensed (1974), 1,068,000 manufactured (1975). **Telephones in use** (1977): 21,161,787. **Daily newspaper circulation** (1974): 7,753,000; 452 per 1,000 pop.

**Health: Life expectancy at birth** (1970): 68.85 male; 74.19 female. **Births** (per 1,000 pop. 1975): 10.8. **Deaths** (per 1,000 pop. 1975): 14.3. **Natural increase** (1975): −.35%. **Pop. per hospital bed** (1975): 91. **Pop. per physician** (1975): 548. **Infant mortality** (per 1,000 live births 1975): 15.9.

**Education: Literacy** (1975): 99%. **Pop. 5-19: in school** (1975): 66%, per teacher (1975): 25.

The German Democratic Republic was proclaimed in the Soviet sector of Berlin Oct. 7, 1949. It was proclaimed fully sovereign in 1954, but 400,000 Soviet troops remain on grounds of security and the 4-power Potsdam agreement.

East Germany negotiated a treaty with Poland placing Poland's boundary at the line formed by the Oder and Neisse Rivers.

Coincident with the entrance of West Germany into the European Defense community in 1952, the East German government decreed a prohibited zone three miles deep along its 600-mile border with West Germany and cut Berlin's telephone system in two. Berlin was further divided by erection of a fortified wall in 1961, but the exodus of refugees to the West continued, though on a smaller scale. By 1978, over 50,000 had fled to the West since 1961, thousands of retired persons had been allowed to leave, and some 20,000 others held in East German jails were released upon West German payments totalling $250 million.

The government signed a 20-year friendship treaty with the USSR in 1964. The economy has been integrated with other communist nations.

East Germany suffered severe economic problems until the mid-1960s. A "new economic system" was introduced, easing the former central planning controls and allowing factories to make profits provided they were reinvested in operations or redistributed to workers as bonuses. By the early 1970s, the economy was highly industrialized. E. Germany was the world's ninth greatest industrial power. In May 1972 the few remaining private firms were ordered sold to the government. The nation was credited with the highest standard of living among communist countries. But growth slowed in the late 1970s, due to shortages of natural resources and labor, and a huge debt to lenders in the West.

Travel restrictions between the 2 Germanies were eased in their first formal treaty, in 1972, and millions of West Germans have since visited the GDR. The GDR gained admission to the UN in 1973. West Germany has spent over $3 bln. in GDR transport projects.

The U.S. and East Germany established diplomatic relations 1974. Several thousand military advisers were stationed in various African and Arab countries.

# West Germany
## Federal Republic of Germany

**People: Population** (1977 est.): 61,400,000. **Age distribution** (%): 0–14: 22.4; 15–59: 57.9; 60+: 19.7. **Pop. density:** 640.8 per sq. mi. **Ethnic groups:** Germans, immigrant workers from Spain, Italy, Yugoslavia, Turkey. **Languages:** German. **Religions:** Protestant 49%, Roman Catholic 45%.

**Geography: Area:** 95,815 sq. mi., the size of Oregon. **Location:** In central Europe. **Neighbors:** Denmark on N, Netherlands, Belgium, Luxembourg, France on W, Switzerland, Austria on S, Czechoslovakia, E. Germany on E. **Topography:** West Germany is flat in N, hilly in center and W, and mountainous in Bavaria (maximum altitude 9,719 ft.). Chief rivers are Elbe, Weser, Ems, Rhine, and Main, all flowing toward North Sea, and Danube, flowing toward Black Sea. **Capital:** Bonn. **Cities** (1977 est.): Berlin 2,984,837; Hamburg 1,717,383; Munich 1,336,576; Cologne 1,013,771; Essen 677,508; Dusseldorf 664,338; Frankfurt 636,197; Dortmund 630,309; Stuttgart 624,835.

**Government: Head of state:** Pres. Walter Scheel; b. July 8, 1919; in office: July 1, 1974; **Head of government:** Chancellor Helmut Schmidt; b. Dec. 23, 1918; in office: May 16, 1974. **Local divisions:** West Berlin and 10 laender (states) with substantial powers: Schleswig-Holstein, Hamburg, Lower Saxony, Bremen, North Rhine-Westphalia, Hessen, Rhineland-Palatinate, Baden-Wurttemberg, Bavaria, Saarland. **Armed forces:** regular 724,000; reserves 1,179,500.

**Economy: Industries:** Steel, ships, oil products, autos, machinery, textiles, electrical and electronic equip., wine. **Chief crops:** Grains, potatoes, sugar beets, fruits, tobacco, nuts. **Minerals:** Coal, lignite, iron, zinc, lead, copper, salt, potash, oil. **Crude oil reserves** (1978): 320 mln. bbls. **Per capita arable land:** 0.3 acres. **Meat production** (1976): beef: 1.40 mln. tons; pork: 2.48 mln. tons; lamb: 22,000 tons. **Fish catch** (1975): 441,700 metric tons. **Electricity production** (1977): 335.32 bln. kwh. **Labor force:** 7% agric.; 39% manuf.

**Finance: Currency:** Mark (May 1978: 2.10 = $1 US). **Gross domestic product** (1975): $398.70 mln. **Per capita income** (1976): $6,451. **Imports** (1977): $100.67 bln.; partners (1975): Neth. 13%, Fr. 11%, It. 8.5%, Belg. 7%. **Exports** (1977): $117.90 bln.; partners (1975): Fr. 20%, Neth. 17%, Belg. 13%, It. 12.5%. **Tourists** (1975): 7,403,300; receipts (1975): $2.84 billion. **Balance of payments** (1977): +$4,729,000,000. **National budget** (1977): $74.61 bln. revenues; $85.17 bln. expenditures. **International reserves** (May 1978): $40.04 bln. **Consumer prices** (change in 1977): 3.9%.

**Transport: Railway traffic** (1975): 23.43 bln. passenger miles; 34.21 bln. net ton-miles. **Motor vehicles:** in use (1975): 17,898,300 passenger cars, 1,340,800 commercial vehicles; manufactured (1977): 3,792,000 passenger cars; 312,000 commercial vehicles. **Civil aviation:** 9,874 mln. passenger-miles (1977); 787,893 mln. freight ton-miles (1977). **Chief ports:** Hamburg, Bremen, Lubeck.

**Communications: Television sets:** 18,920,000 licensed (1974), 3,356,000 manufactured (1975). **Radios:** 20,909,000 licensed (1974), 4,415,000 manufactured (1975). **Telephones in use** (1977): 2,750,597. **Daily newspaper circulation** (1974) 17,872,000; 289 per 1,000 pop.

**Health: Life expectancy at birth** (1975): 68.04 male; 74.54 female. **Births** (per 1,000 pop. 1976): 9.8. **Deaths** (per 1,000 pop. 1976): 11.9. **Natural increase** (1976): −.21%. **Pop. per hospital bed** (1975): 85. **Pop. per physician** (1975): 522. **Infant mortality** (per 1,000 live births 1975): 19.8.

**Education: Literacy** (1975): 99%. **Pop. 5-19:** in school (1975): 67%, per teacher (1975): 30.

The Federal Republic of Germany was proclaimed May 23, 1949, in Bonn, after a constitution had been drawn up by a consultative assembly formed by representatives of the 11 laender (states) in the French, British, and American zones. Later reorganized into 9 units, the laender numbered 10 with the addition of the Saar Jan. 1, 1957. Berlin also was granted land (state) status, but the 1945 occupation agreements placed restrictions on it.

The occupying powers, the U.S., Britain, and France, restored the civil status, Sept. 21, 1949. The U.S. resumed diplomatic relations July 2, 1951. The powers lifted controls and the republic became fully independent May 5, 1955.

r. Konrad Adenauer, Christian Democrat, was made chan-
or Sept. 15, 1949, re-elected 1953, 1957, 1961. Dr. Ludwig
ard, Christian Democrat, was elected 1963. Kurt Georg Kie-
er was elected chancellor Dec. 1, 1966, heading a coalition
ernment of Christian Democrats and Social Democrats. Willy
ndt, heading a coalition of Social Democrats and Free Demo-
ts, became chancellor Oct. 21, 1969.

In 1970 Brandt signed friendship treaties with the USSR and
and. In 1971, the U.S., Britain, France, and the USSR signed
agreement on Western access to West Berlin. In 1972 the
destag approved the USSR and Polish treaties and East and
st Germany signed their first formal treaty, implementing the
eement easing access to West Berlin. In 1973 a West Ger-
ny-Czechoslovakia pact normalized relations and nullified the
8 "Munich Agreement." In 1974 Bonn agreed to extend $350
ion yearly in long-term credits to East Germany until 1981.
er credits spurred trade with the East European countries.

In May 1974 Brandt resigned, saying he took full responsibility
"negligence" for allowing an East German spy to become a
mber of his staff. Helmut Schmidt, Brandt's finance minister,
cceeded him.

West Germany has experienced tremendous economic
wth since the 1950s. It is the world's fourth greatest eco-
mic power. Some of the 2.6 million foreigners working in West
rmany left during a 1974-75 industrial slowdown. The country
ds Europe in provisions for worker participation in the man-
ement of industry.

About 214,000 U.S., 55,000 British, and 50,000 French troops
stationed in West Germany.

**Helgoland,** an island of 130 acres in the North Sea, was
en from Denmark by a British Naval Force in 1807 and later
ded to Germany to become a part of Schleswig-Holstein prov-
e in return for rights in East Africa. The heavily fortified island
s surrendered to Great Britain, May 23, 1945, demilitarized in
47 and returned to West Germany, Mar 1, 1952. It is a free
rt.

**The Saar** (Fr. Sarre), 10th land (state) of the Federal Repub-
is an industrial and mining area N of Lorraine, originally 738
mi., now extended to about 991 and population (1973) of 1.1
lion. Capital: Saarbrucken. After World War II it had semi-
tonomy and economic links to France until it became a Ger-
an state again Jan. 1, 1957.

# Ghana
## Republic of Ghana

**People: Population** (1977 est): 10,480,000. **Age distrib.** (%):
4: 25.2; 15-59: 64.9; 60+: 10.0. **Pop. density:** 113.79 per
mi. **Urban** (1974): 31.4%. **Ethnic groups:** Akan 44%, Moshi-
gomba 16%, Ewe 13%, Ga 8%, others. **Languages:** English
icial), others. **Religions:** Protestant 29%, Roman Catholic
%, Moslem 12%, others.

**Geography: Area:** 92,100 sq. mi., slightly smaller than Ore-
n. **Location:** On southern coast of W. Africa. **Neighbors:**
ry Coast on W, Upper Volta on N, Togo on E. **Topography:**
st of Ghana consists of low fertile plains and scrubland, cut
rivers and by the artificial Lake Volta. **Capital:** Accra. **Cities**
970 cen.): Accra (met.) 738,498; Kumasi (met.) 345,117; Tako-
di 58,161.

**Government: Head of state:** Chmn. of Mil. Cncl. Fred W.K.
uffo; b. 1937; in office: July 6, 1978. **Local divisions:** 9 re-
ns. **Armed forces:** regulars 17,700; para-military 3,000.

**Economy: Industries:** Aluminum, light industry. **Chief crops:**
coa (largest producer), coffee, palm products, corn, rice, cas-
va, plantain, peanuts, yams, tobacco. **Minerals:** Industrial
amonds, manganese, gold, bauxite. **Other resources:** Timber,
re woods, rubber. **Per capita arable land:** 0.2 acres. **Meat
oduction** (1975): beef: 22,000 tons; lamb: 10,000 tons. **Fish
tch** (1975): 254,500 metric tons. **Electricity production**
975): 4.05 bln. kwh. **Labor force:** 55% agriculture.

**Finance: Currency:** New Cedi (May 1978): 1.15 = $1 US).
oss domestic product (1975): $5.26 bln. **Per capita in-
me** (1975): $394. **Imports** (1975): $805 mln.; partners (1974):
Ger. 16%, U.S. 9%, It. 9%, Fr. 7%. **Exports** (1975): $760
n.; partners (1974): W. Ger. 21%, It. 9%, U.S. 6%, Fr. 6%.
urists (1975): 42,800; receipts (1975): $2 million. **Balance of
yments** (1977): +$110,100,000. **National budget** (1975):
65.16 mln. revenues: $1.06 bln. expenditures. **International
serves** (May 1978): $276.0 mln. **Consumer prices** (change
1976): 52.7%.

**Transport: Railway traffic** (1972): 267.65 mln.. passenger-

miles; 189.41 mln. net ton-miles. **Motor vehicles:** in use (1974):
55,500 passenger cars, 43,900 commercial vehicles. **Civil aviation:** 137 mln. passenger-miles (1976); 2,295 mln. freight ton-
miles (1976). **Chief ports:** Tema, Sekondi-Takoradi.

**Communications: Television sets:** 33,000 in use (1974),
2,000 manufactured (1975). **Radios:** 1,060,000 in use (1974),
90,000 manufactured (1975). **Telephones in use** (1977):
66,287. **Daily newspaper circulation** (1973): 381,000; 41 per
1,000 pop.

**Health: Life expectancy at birth** (1960): 37.08 male. **Births**
(annual per 1,000 pop. 72-75): 48.8. **Deaths** (annual per 1,000
pop. 1972-75): 21.9. **Natural increase** (annual 1970-75): 2.69%.
**Pop. per hospital bed** (1975): 721. **Pop. per physician** (1975):
11,714. **Infant mortality** (per 1,000 live births 1960): 156.

**Education: Literacy** (1975): 25%. **Pop. 5-19:** in school
(1975): 42%, per teacher (1975): 63.

Named for an African empire along the Niger River, 400-1240
A.D., Ghana was ruled by Britain for 113 years as the Gold
Coast. The UN in 1956 approved merger with the British Togoland trust territory. Independence came March 6, 1957. Republic
status within the Commonwealth was attained in 1960.

President Kwame Nkrumah built hospitals and schools, and
promoted development projects like the Volta River hydroelectric and aluminum plants, but ran the country into debt, jailed
opponents, and was accused of corruption. In 1964 a referendum gave Nkrumah dictatorial powers and made Ghana a one-
party socialist state.

Nkrumah was overthrown in 1966 by a police-army coup,
which expelled Chinese and East German teachers and technicians. Elections were held in 1969, but two further bloodless
coups occurred in 1972 and 1978.

In 1972-73 the government pressed a program of agricultural
diversification to cut costly food imports.

# Greece
## Hellenic Republic

**People: Population** (1976 est.): 9,170,000. **Age distrib.** (%):
0-14: 24.4; 15-59: 58.7; 60+: 16.8. **Pop. density:** 181.42 per
sq. mi. **Urban** (1971): 64.8%. **Ethnic groups:** Greeks 98.5%,
Turks 0.9%, Bulgars 0.3%, Armenians 0.2%. **Languages:**
Greek, others. **Religions:** Greek Orthodox 97%, Moslem 1.2%.

**Geography: Area:** 50,547 sq. mi., the size of New York State.
**Location:** Occupies southern end of Balkan Peninsula in SE Eu-
rope. **Neighbors:** Albania, Yugoslavia, Bulgaria on N, Turkey on
E. **Topography:** About 75% of Greece is non-arable, with
mountains in all areas. Pindus Mts. run through the country N to
S. Total length of the heavily indented coastline is 9,385 mi. Of
hundreds of islands, 166 are inhabited, among them Crete,
Rhodes, Milos, Kerkira (Corfu), Chios, Lesbos, Samos. **Capital:**
Athens. **Cities** (1971 cen.): Athens (met.) 2,101,103; Saloniki
(met.) 557,360; Piraeus (met.) 439,138.

**Govenment: Head of state:** Pres. Constantine Tsatsos; b.
July 1, 1899; in office: June 20, 1975; **Head of government:**
Prime Min. Constantine Karamanlis; b. Feb. 23, 1907; in office:
July 24, 1974. **Local divisions:** 52 prefectures. **Armed forces:**
regulars 348,000; reserves 310,000.

**Economy: Industries:** Textiles, chemicals, aluminum, wine,
food processng, cement. **Chief crops:** Grains, corn, rice, cotton,
tobacco, olives, citrus fruits, raisins, figs. **Minerals:** Bauxite, iron,
emery, lignite, oil, silver, manganese, chromite, nickel, baryte.
**Crude oil reserves** (1978): .025 mln. bbls. **Per capita arable
land:** 0.8 acres. **Meat production** (1976): beef: 109,000 tons;
pork: 111,000 tons; lamb: 115,000 tons. **Fish catch** (1975):
70,700 metric tons. **Electricity production** (1977): 17.40 bln.
kwh. **Labor force:** 40% agric.; 16% manuf.

**Finance: Currency:** Drachmas (May 1978): 37.71 = $1 US).
**Gross domestic product** (1977): $26.81 bln. **Per capita in-
come** (1976): $2,324. **Imports** (1977): $6.85 bln.; partners
(1974): W. Ger. 16%, U.S. 9%, It. 9%, Fr. 7%. **Exports** (1977):
$2.76 bln.; partners (1974): W. Ger. 21%, It. 9%, U.S. 6%, Fr.
6%. **Tourists** (1974): 1,956,400; receipts (1974): $437 million.
**Balance of payments** (1977): +$129,000,000. **National bud-
get** (1977): $5.80 bln. revenues; $6.81 bln. expenditures. **International reserves** (Apr. 1978): $1.05 bln. **Consumer prices**
(change in 1977): 12.2%.

**Transport: Motor vehicles:** in use (1975): 439,100 passenger cars, 210,800 commercial vehicles. **Civil aviation:** 2,705
mln. passenger-miles (1977); 36,209 mln. freight ton-miles

(1977). **Chief ports:** Piraeus, Thessalonki, Patrai.

**Communications: Television sets:** 950,000 in use (1974), 196,000 manufactured (1974). **Radios:** 2,500,000 in use (1974). **Telephones in use** (1977): 2,180,243. **Daily newspaper circulation** (1974): 962,000; 107 per 1,000 pop.

**Health: Life expectancy at birth** (1962): 67.46 male; 70.70 female. **Births** (per 1,000 pop. 1975): 15.7. **Deaths** (per 1,000 pop. 1975): 8.9. **Natural increase** (1975): .68%. **Pop. per hospital bed** (1975): 158. **Pop. per physician** (1975): 499. **Infant mortality** (per 1,000 live births 1975): 24.0.

**Education: Literacy** (1975): 84%. **Pop. 5–19:** in school (1975): 67%, per teacher (1975): 43.

The achievements of Ancient Greece in art, architecture, science, mathematics, philosophy, drama, literature, and democracy became legacies for succeeding ages. Greece reached the height of its glory and power, particularly in the Athenian city-state, in the 5th century B.C.

Greece fell under Roman rule in the 2d and 1st centuries B.C. In the 4th century A.D. it became part of the Byzantine Empire and, after the fall of Constantinople to the Turks in 1453, part of the Ottoman Empire.

Greece won its war of independence from Turkey 1821-1829, and became a kingdom. A republic was established 1925; the monarchy was restored, 1935, and George II, King of the Hellenes, resumed the throne. In Oct., 1940, Greece rejected an ultimatum from Italy. Nazi support resulted in the defeat and occupation of Greece by Germans, Italians, and Bulgarians. By the end of 1944 the invaders withdrew. Communist resistance forces were defeated by Royalist and British troops.

A plebiscite recalled King George II. He died Apr. 1, 1947, and was succeeded by his brother, Paul I.

Communists waged guerrilla war 1947-49 against the government but were defeated with the aid of the U.S. (acting under the Truman Doctrine).

A period of reconstruction and rapid development followed, mainly with conservative governments under Premier Constantine Karamanlis. The Center Union led by George Papandreou won elections in 1963 and 1964. King Constantine, who acceded in 1964, forced Papandreou to resign. A period of political maneuvers ended in the military takeover of April 21, 1967, by Col. George Papadopoulos. King Constantine tried to reverse the consolidation of the harsh dictatorship Dec. 13, 1967, but failed and fled to Italy. Papadopoulos was ousted Nov. 25, 1973, in a coup led by rightist Brig. Demetrius Ioannides.

Greek army officers serving in the National Guard of Cyprus staged a coup on the island July 15, 1974. Turkey invaded Cyprus a week later, precipitating the collapse of the Greek junta, which was implicated in the Cyprus coup.

The military turned the government over to Karamanlis, who named a civilian cabinet, freed political prisoners, and sought to solve the Cyprus crisis. In Nov. 1974 elections his party won a large parliamentary majority, reduced by socialist gains in 1977. A Dec. 1974 referendum resulted in the proclamation of a republic.

The new government promoted educational and agricultural reforms, and sought to advance from associate to full membership in the EC.

The **Dodecanese** are a group of 13 islands in the southeastern Aegean Sea. They were seized from Turkey by Italy in 1912. Rhodes is the capital.

After World War II the islands were ceded to Greece at the Paris Conference of Foreign Ministers, June 27, 1946, and annexed Mar. 7, 1948.

**Crete,** largest Greek island and 5th largest in Mediterranean, original site of Minoan civilization, lies SE of the Peloponnesus peninsula and is 160 mi. long, 35 mi. wide, with area of 3,207 sq. mi. Principal towns: Heraklion (Candia) and Khania (Canea).

# Grenada
## State of Grenada

**People: Population** (1977 est.): 100,000. **Pop. density:** 751.88 per sq. mi. **Ethnic groups:** Negroes over 52%, whites 1%, mulattoes 43% (including some E. Indians), Carib. Indians. **Languages:** English, French-African patois. **Religions:** Roman Catholics, Anglicans.

**Geography: Area:** 133 sq. mi. **Location:** Southernmost of West Indies, 90 mi. N. of Venezuela. **Topography:** Main island is mountainous; country includes Carriacon and Petit Martinique islands, 13 sq. mi. together. **Capital:** St. George's. **Cities** (1975

est.): St. George's 30,000.

**Government: Head of state:** Queen Elizabeth II, represen… by Gov.-Gen. Leo V. de Gale; **Head of government:** Prime M… Eric M. Gairy; b. 1923; in office: Feb. 7, 1974. **Local divisions…** parishes.

**Economy: Industries:** Rum. **Chief crops:** Nutmegs, … nanas, cocoa, sugar, mace. **Electricity production** (197… 25.00 mln. kwh. **Labor force:** 26% agriculture.

**Finance: Currency:** Dollar (1974: 2.05 = $1 US). **Gross …mestic product** (1974 est.): $44 mln. **Per capita inco…** (1974): $390. **Imports** (1976): $26 mln.; partners (1974): U… 14.8%, Can. 5%, U.S. 4.5%. **Exports** (1976): $13 mln.; partn… (1974): U.K. 21.9%, U.S. 1.3%, Can. 1%. **Tourists** (197… 2,840,100; receipts (1975): $622 million.

**Transport: Motor Vehicles:** in use (1971): 3,800 passen… cars, 100 commercial vehicles. **Chief ports:** Saint George's.

**Communications: Radios:** 21,000 in use (1974). **Te… phones in use** (1977): 5,072.

**Health: Life expectancy at birth** (1961): 60.14 male; 65… female. **Births** (per 1,000 pop. 1975): 27.4. **Deaths** (per 1,0… pop. 1975): 5.9. **Natural increase** (annual 1970-75): 2.91%. … fant mortality (per 1,000 live births 1974): 31.5.

First European visitor was Columbus, 1498. First Europe… settlers were French, 1650. The island was held alternately… France and England until final British occupation, 1784. Grena… became fully independent Feb. 7, 1974 during a general strike… is the smallest independent nation in the Western Hemisphere…

# Guatemala
## Republic of Guatemala

**People: Population** (1977 est.): 6,440,000. **Age distrib.** (%… 0–14: 45.1; 15–59: 50.1; 60+: 4.7. **Pop. density:** 153.18 per … mi. **Urban** (1973): 36.4%. **Ethnic groups:** Indians 54%, Me… zos 42%, whites 4%. **Languages:** Spanish, 18 Maya-Quic… dialects. **Religions:** Roman Catholics over 90%; Mayan relig… practiced.

**Geography: Area:** 42,042 sq. mi., the size of Tennessee. L… cation: In Central America. **Neighbors:** Mexico N, W; El Sa… dor on S, Honduras, Belize on E. **Topography:** The central hig… land and mountain areas are bordered by the narrow Pac… coast and the lowlands and fertile river valleys on the Car… bean. There are numerous volcanoes in S, more than hal… dozen over 11,000 ft. **Capital:** Guatemala City. **Cities** (19… cen.): Guatemala City 706,920; (1973 est.) Escuintla 68,5… Quezaltenango 65,733.

**Government: Head of state:** Pres. Romeo Lucas Garcia;… 1925; in office: July 1, 1978. **Local divisions:** Guatemala C… and 22 departments; pres. appoints governors. **Armed force…** regulars 14,300; para-military 3,000.

**Economy: Industries:** Shoes, textiles. **Chief crops:** Cof… (one third of exports), sugar, bananas, cotton. **Minerals:** Zi… lead, antimony, tungsten, cadmium, silver, copper, nickel, g… **Crude oil reserves** (1978): .016 mln. bbls. **Other resourc…** Rare woods, fish, chicle. **Per capita arable land:** 0.5 acr… **Meat production** (1976): beef: 46,900 tons; pork: 8,900 to… **Electricity production** (1975): 1.30 bln. kwh. **Labor forc…** 57% agric.; 14% manuf.

**Finance: Currency:** Quetzale (May 1978: 1.00 = $1 U… **Gross domestic product** (1976): $4.29 bln. **Per capita i… come** (1975): $517. **Imports** (1976): $839 mln.; partners (197… U.S. 32%, Venez. 12%, El Salv. 10%, Jap. 9%. **Exports** (197… $760 mln.; partners (1974): U.S. 33%, El Salv. 11%, W. G… 11%, Nic. 7%. **Tourists** (1975): 454,400; receipts (1975): $… million. **Balance of payments** (1977): +$149,200,000. **Na… tional budget** (1977): $603.00 mln. revenues; $643.60 mln. e… penditures. **International reserves** (May 1978): $800.8 m… **Consumer prices** (change in 1977): 12.6%.

**Transport: Railway traffic** (1975): 18.88 mln. net ton-mile… **Motor vehicles:** in use (1975): 76,100 passenger cars, 40,1… commercial vehicles. **Civil aviation:** 88 mln. passenger-mil… (1977); 4,196 mln. freight ton-miles (1977). **Chief ports:** Pue… Barrios, San Jose.

**Communications: Television sets:** 106,000 in use (197… **Radios:** 261,000 in use (1974). **Telephones in use** (197… 53,000. **Daily newspaper circulation** (1974): 91,000; 68 p… 1,000 pop.

**Health: Life expectancy at birth** (1965): 48.29 male; 49.… female. **Births** (per 1,000 pop. 1974): 42.8. **Deaths** (per 1,0… pop. 1974): 11.8. **Natural increase** (1974): 3.10%. **Pop. p…**

spital bed (1975): 375. **Pop. per physician** (1975): 4,344. **fant mortality** (per 1,000 live births 1973): 81.2.
**Education: Literacy** (1975): 46%. **Pop. 5-19:** in school )75): 29%, per teacher (1975): 97.

The old Mayan Indian empire flourished in what is today Guaмala for over 1,000 years before the Spanish
Guatemala was a Spanish colony 1524-1821; briefly a part of exico and then of the U.S. of Central America, the republic as established in 1839.
Since 1945 when a liberal government was elected to replace e long-term dictatorship of Jorge Ubico, the country has seen swing toward socialism, an armed revolt, renewed attempts at cial reform and a military coup. Assassinations and political elence from left and right plagued the country. Some 20,000 uatemalans, mostly liberal or radical opponents of the regime, are killed in the decade up to 1976.
A 1976 earthquake killed 20,000 people and left over 1 million meless.

# Guinea
## Republic of Guinea

**People: Population** (1977 est.): 4,650,000. **Age distrib. (%):** -14: 43.7; 15-59: 47.0; 60+: 9.3. **Pop. density:** 48.99 per sq. . **Ethnic groups:** Fula 40%, Mandingo 25%, Soussous 10%, other tribes. **Languages:** French (official), tribal languages. **eligions:** Moslems 70%, Christians 1%, others.
**Geography: Area:** 94,925 sq. mi., slightly smaller than Ore-n. **Location:** On Atlantic coast of W. Africa. **Neighbors:** Gui-a-Bissau, Senegal, Mali on N, Ivory Coast on E, Liberia on S. **opography:** A narrow coastal belt leads to the mountainous iddle Guinea region, the source of the Gambia, Senegal, and ger rivers. Upper Guinea, farther inland, is a cooler upland re-on. The SE is forested. **Capital:** Conakry. **Cities** (1972 est.): onakry (met.) 525,671.
**Government: Head of State:** Pres. Ahmed Sekou Toure; b. an. 19, 1922; in office: Oct. 2, 1958; **Head of government:** ime Min. Lansana Beavogui; b. 1923; in office: Apr. 26, 1972. **ocal divisions:** 29 administrative regions. **Armed forces:** reg-ars 5,850; para-military 8,000.
**Economy: Chief crops:** Bananas, pineapples, rice, corn, alm nuts, coffee, honey. **Minerals:** Bauxite, iron, diamonds. **Per apita arable land:** 0.8 acres. **Electricity production** (1975): )0.00 mln. kwh. **Labor force:** 83% agriculture.
**Finance: Currency:** Sily (1974: 20.5 = $1 US). **Gross do-estic product** (1974 est.): $590 mln. **Per capita income** 974): $130. **Imports** (1973): $100 mln.; partners (1973): Fr. 3%, USSR 20%, U.S. 12%, P.R. China 10%. **Exports** (1973): 70 mln.; partners (1973): Nor. 15%, USSR 15%, Spain 14%, ameroon 10%.
**Transport: Motor vehicles:** in use (1972): 10,200 passenger ars, 10,800 commercial vehicles. **Chief ports:** Conakry.
**Communications: Radios:** 105,000 in use (1974). **Tele-hones in use** (1974): 10,000. **Daily newspaper circulation** 974): 5,000; 1 per 1,000 pop.
**Health: Life expectancy at birth** (1975): 39.4 male; 42.0 fe-ale. **Births** (annual per 1,000 pop. 1972-75): 46.6. **Deaths** (an-ual per 1,000 pop. 1972-75): 22.9. **Natural increase** (annual 970-75): 2.37%. **Pop. per hospital bed** (1975): 592. **Pop. per hysician** (1975): 20,852. **Infant mortality** (per 1,000 live births 955): 216.
**Education: Literacy** (1975): 10%. **Pop. 5-19:** in school 975): 18%, per teacher (1975): 112.

Part of the ancient West African empires, Guinea fell under French control 1849-98. Under Sekou Toure, it opted for full in-ependence in 1958, and France withdrew all aid.
Toure turned to Communist nations for support, and set up a ilitant one-party state. France and Guinea restored ties in 975, after a 10-year break. Western firms, as well as the Soviet overnment, have invested in Guinea's vast bauxite mines.
According to reports, thousands of opponents were jailed in he 1970s, in the aftermath of an unsuccessful Portuguese inva-ion. Many were tortured and killed.

# Guinea-Bissau
## Republic of Guinea-Bissau

**People: Population** (1977 est.): 540,000. **Pop. density:** 8.72 per sq. mi. **Ethnic groups:** Balanta 30%, Fula 20%, Man-

dyako 14%, other tribes. **Languages:** Portuguese (official), Cri-oulo, tribal languages. **Religions:** Moslems 30%, Christians 1%, others.
**Geography: Area:** 13,948 sq. mi. **Location:** On Atlantic coast of W. Africa. **Neighbors:** Senegal on N, Guinea on E, S. **Topog-raphy:** A swampy coastal plain covers most of the country; to the east is a low savanna region. **Capital:** Bissau. **Cities** (1973 est.): Bissau 60,000.
**Government: Head of state:** Pres. Luis de Almeida Cabral; b. 1931; in office: July 22, 1973; **Head of government:** Prime Min. Francisco Mendes; in office: Sept. 24, 1973. **Local divi-sions:** 12 regions.
**Economy: Chief crops:** Peanuts, palm oil. **Minerals:** Bauxite, oil. **Per capita arable land:** 1.2 acres. **Electricity production** (1975): 20.00 mln. kwh. **Labor force:** 86% agriculture.
**Finance: Currency:** Escudo (Jan.-Mar. 1977: 34.31 = $1 US). **Gross domestic product** (1974 est.): $160 mln. **Per cap-ita income** (1974): $300. **Imports** (1975): $38 mln.; partners (1973): Port. 56%, Spain 7%, U.K. 5%, Jap. 5%. **Exports** (1975): $12 mln.; partners (1973): Port. 90%, Neth. 3%, Cape Verde 2%.
**Communications: Radios:** 9,000 licensed (1974). **Tele-phones in use** (1973): 3,000. **Daily newspaper circulation** (1974): 6,000; 12 per 1,000 pop.
**Health: Life expectancy at birth** (1975): 37.0 male; 40.1 fe-male. **Births** (annual per 1,000 pop. 1972-75): 40.1. **Deaths** (an-nual per 1,000 pop. 1972-75): 25.1. **Natural increase** (annual 1970-75): 1.50%. **Infant mortality** (per 1,000 live births 1969): 47.1.

Portuguese mariners explored the area in the mid-15th cen-tury; the slave trade flourished in the 17t: and 18th centuries, and colonization began in the 19th.
Beginning in the 1960s, an independence movement waged a guerrilla war and formed a government in the interior that achieved international support. Full independence came Sept. 10, 1974, after the Portuguese regime was overthrown.
Union with Cape Verde was foreseen in a number of coopera-tion accords signed in 1975.

# Guyana
## Cooperative Republic of Guyana

**People: Population** (1977 est.): 810,000. **Age distrib. (%):** 0-14: 44.2; 5-59: 50.7; 60+: 5.0. **Pop. density:** 9.76 per sq. mi. **Urban** (1973): 40.0%. **Ethnic groups:** East Indians 55%, Ne-groes 36%, others (Amerindians, Chinese, Europeans) 10%. **Languages:** English (official), Hindi, Portuguese, Chinese, Negro patois. **Religions:** Christians 57%, Hindus 33%, Moslems 9%, others.
**Geography: Area:** 83,000 sq. mi., the size of Idaho. **Loca-tion:** On N coast of S. America. **Neighbors:** Venezuela on W, Brazil on S, Surinam on E. **Topography:** Dense tropical forests cover much of the land, although a flat coastal area up to 40 mi. wide, where 90% of the population lives, provides rich alluvial soil for agriculture. A grassy savanna divides the two zones. **Capital:** Georgetown. **Cities** (1970 cen.): Georgetown (met., 164,039.
**Government: Head of state:** Pres. Arthur Chung; b. Jan. 10, 1918; in office: Feb. 23, 1970; **Head of government:** Prime Min. Linden Forbes Sampson Burnham; b. Feb. 20, 1923; in office: Dec. 1964. **Local divisions:** 6 regions, with appointed regional ministers. **Armed forces:** regulars 2,000; para-military 2,250.
**Economy: Industries:** Cigarettes, rum, clothing, furniture, drugs. **Chief crops:** Sugar, rice, coconuts, coffee, cocoa, citrus and other fruits. **Minerals:** Bauxite (5th largest producer), gold, diamonds. **Other resources:** Timber, shrimp. **Per capita arable land:** 2.5 acres. **Fish catch** (1975): 20,100 metric tons. **Electric-ity production** (1976): 395.00 mln. kwh. **Labor force:** 32% ag-riculture.
**Finance: Currency:** Dollar (May 1978: 2.55 = $1 US). **Gross domestic product** (1975): $464.39 mln. **Per capita inccme** (1975): $588. **Imports** (1976): $363 mln.; partners (1975): U 29.3%, U.K. 21.4%, Can. 4.3%. **Exports** (1976): $269 m.., partners (1975): U.K. 28.4%, U.S. 21.9%, Can. 3.1%. **Tourist receipts** (1975): $3 million. **Balance of payments** (1977): -$30,900,000. **National budget** (1973): $70.61 mln: revenues; $133.43 mln. expenditures. **International reserves** (Apr. 1978): $36.41 mln. **Consumer prices** (change in 1977): 8.1%.
**Transport: Railway traffic** (1974): 3.73 mln. passenger-miles; 0.0 net ton-miles. **Motor vehicles:** in use (1975): 22,500

passenger cars, 12,200 commercial vehicles. **Chief ports:** Georgetown.

**Communications: Radios:** 268,000 in use (1974). **Telephones in use** (1977): 22,526. **Daily newspaper circulation** (1974): 120,000; 155 per 1,000 pop.

**Health: Life expectancy at birth** (1961): 59.03 male; 63.01 female. **Births** (per 1,000 pop. 1976): 26.7. **Deaths** (per 1,000 pop. 1976): 7.1. **Natural increase** (1976): 1.96%. **Pop. per hospital bed** (1975): 187. **Pop. per physician** (1975): 3,573. **Infant mortality** (per 1,000 live births 1971): 42.3.

**Education:** Literacy (1975): 85%. **Pop. 5-19:** in school (1975): 61%, per teacher (1975): 41.

Guyana became a Dutch possession in the 17th century, but sovereignty passed to Britain in 1815. Indentured servants from India soon outnumbered African slaves. Ethnic tension has affected political life.

Guyana became independent May 26, 1966. A Venezuelan claim to the western half of Guyana was suspended in 1970 for 12 years. The Surinam border is also disputed. The government has nationalized most of the economy in recent years.

## Haiti

### Republic of Haiti

**People: Population** (1977 est.): 4,750,000. **Age distrib. (%):** 4-14: 42.5; 15-59: 51.2; 60+: 6.3. **Pop. density:** 443.35 per sq. mi. **Urban** (1976): 23.1%. **Ethnic groups:** Negroes 95%, mulattoes 5%. **Languages:** French (official), Creole. **Religions:** Roman Catholics 80%, Protestants 10%; Voodoo widely practiced.

**Geography: Area:** 10,714 sq. mi., the size of Maryland. **Location:** in West Indies, occupies western third of I. of Hispaniola. **Neighbors:** Dominican Republic on E, Cuba on W (across Windward Passage). **Topography:** About two-thirds of Haiti is mountainous. Much of the rest is semiarid. The coastal areas are warm and moist. **Capital:** Port-au-Prince. **Cities** (1971 est.): Port-au-Prince (met.) 493,932.

**Government: Head of state:** Pres. Jean Claude Duvalier; b. July 3, 1951; in office: Apr. 22, 1971. **Local divisions:** 5 departments. **Armed forces:** regulars 6,550; para-military 14,900.

**Economy: Industries:** Rum, molasses, tourism. **Chief crops:** Coffee, sisal, cotton, sugar, bananas, cocoa, tobacco, rice. **Minerals:** Bauxite, copper, gold, silver, cement. **Other resources:** Timber. **Per capita arable land:** 0.2 acres. **Meat production** (1975): beef: 18,000 tons; pork: 24,000 tons. **Electricity production** (1975): 158.00 mln. kwh.

**Finance: Currency:** Gourdes (May 1978: 5.00 = $1 US). **Gross domestic product** (1974): $158. **Imports** (1975): $121 mln.; partners (1973): U.S. 43%, Jap. 9%, Can. 8%, Fr. 6%, W. Ger. 6%. **Exports** (1976): $126 mln.; partners (1973): U.S. 62%, Fr. 9%, Belg. 9%, It. 7%. **Tourists** (1974): 47,600; receipts (1975): $22 million. **Balance of payments** (1976): +$11,400,000. **National budget** (1976): $133.16 mln. revenues; $145.90 mln. expenditures. **International reserves** (Feb. 1978): $47.7 mln. **Consumer prices** (change in 1977): 6.8%.

**Transport: Motor vehicles:** in use (1973): 11,700 passenger cars, 1,300 commercial vehicles. **Chief ports:** Port-au-Prince, Les Cayes.

**Communications: Television sets:** 13,000 in use (1974). **Radios:** 91,000 in use (1974). **Telephones in use** (1977): 17,800. **Daily newspaper circulation** (1974): 93,000; 21 per 1,000 pop.

**Health: Life expectancy at birth** (1975): 49.0 male; 51.0 female. **Births** (annual per 1,000 pop. 1972-75): 35.8. **Deaths** (annual per 1,000 pop. 1972-75): 16.3. **Natural increase** (annual 1970-75): 1.95%. **Pop. per hospital bed** (1975): 1,366. **Pop. per physician** (1975): 9,359. **Infant mortality** (per 1,000 live births 1973): 150.

**Education:** Literacy (1975): 10%. **Pop. 5-19:** in school (1975): 24%, per teacher (1975): 186.

Haiti, visited by Columbus, 1492, and a French colony from 1677, attained its independence, 1804, following the rebellion led by former slave Toussaint L'Ouverture. Following a period of political violence, 1910-15, the U.S. occupied the country until 1934.

Dr. Francois Duvalier was voted president in 1957; in 1964 he was named president for life. Upon his death in 1971, he was succeeded by his son Jean-Claude. Under the latter's less violent rule, foreign investment and tourism revived. But drought 1975-77 brought famine, aggravated by erosion caused by destruction of most trees for charcoal.

## Honduras

### Republic of Honduras

**People: Population** (1976 est.): 2,830,000. **Age distrib.** (% 0-14: 46.8; 15-59: 49.3; 60+: 4.0. **Pop. density:** 65.39 per mi. **Urban** (1974): 31.1%. **Ethnic groups:** Mestizo 90%, Caucsian, Negroes, Indians. **Languages:** Spanish, English (on coast). **Religions:** Roman Catholics

**Geography: Area:** 43,277 sq. mi., slightly larger than Tenne see. **Location:** In Central America. **Neighbors:** Guatemala W, El Salvador, Nicaragua on S. **Topography:** The Caribbe coast is 500 mi. long. Pacific coast, on Gulf of Fonseca, is 40 long. Honduras is mountainous, with wide fertile valleys and r forests. **Capital:** Tegucigalpa. **Cities** (1973 est.): Tegucigal (met.) 302,483; San Pedro Sula (met.) 153,307.

**Government: Head of state:** Gens. Paz Garcia, Alvarez, C laya; in office: Aug. 8, 1978. **Local divisions:** 18 departmen pres. appoints governors. **Armed forces:** regulars 14,200; pa military 3,000.

**Economy: Industries:** Clothing, textiles, cement, chemica **Chief crops:** Bananas (chief export), coffee, cotton, sugar, bacco. **Minerals:** Gold, silver, copper, lead, zinc, iron, antimo coal. **Other resources:** Timber. **Per capita arable land:** ( acres. **Meat production** (1976): beef: 46,900 tons. **Electric production** (1975): 480.00 mln. kwh. **Labor force:** 67% agric ture.

**Finance: Currency:** Lempiras (May 1978): 2.00 = $1 U **Gross domestic product** (1977): $1.47 bln. **Per capita come** (1976): $392. **Imports** (1977): $410 mln.; partners (197 U.S. 41%, Jap. 10%, Venez. 8%, Guat. 6%. **Exports** (197 $392 mln.; partners (1974): U.S. 57%, W. Ger. 12%, Dom Rep. 4%, Jap. 3%. **Tourist receipts** (1975): $8 million. **Balan of payments** (1977): +$49,300,000. **National budget** (197 $228.55 mln. revenues; $160.00 mln. expenditures. **Intern tional reserves** (Apr. 1978): $217.53 mln. **Consumer price** (change in 1977): 8.4%.

**Transport: Motor vehicles:** in use (1974) 14,700 passeng cars, 22,900 commercial vehicles. **Civil aviation:** 159 mln. pas enger-miles (1976); 3,241 mln. freight ton-miles (1976). **Chi ports:** Puerto Cortes, La Ceiba.

**Communications:** Television sets: 46,000 in use (1974). **R dios:** 158,000 in use (1974). **Telephones in use** (1974): 19,22 **Daily newspaper circulation** (1974): 99,000; 34 per 1,000 pc

**Health: Live expectancy at birth** (1975): 52.1 male; 55 female. **Births** (annual per 1,000 pop. 1972-75): 49.3. **Death** (annual per 1,000 pop. 1972-75): 14.6. **Natural increase** (a nual 1970-75): 3.47%. **Pop. per hospital bed** (1975): 661. **Po per physician** (1975): 3,527. **Infant mortality** (per 1,000 liv births 1974): 34.1.

**Education:** Literacy (1975): 50%. **Pop. 5-19:** in scho (1975): 45%, per teacher (1975): 67.

Mayan civilization flourished in Honduras in the 1st milleniu A.D. Columbus arrived in 1502.

Honduras became independent after freeing itself from Spai 1821 and from the Fed. of Central America, 1838.

Gen. Oswaldo Lopez Arellano, president for most of the pe iod 1963-75 by virtue of 1 election and 2 coups, was ousted b the Army in 1975 over charges of pervasive bribery by Unite Brands Co. of the U.S.

Honduras and El Salvador fought a 5-day war in 1969 ove the presence in Honduras of 300,000 Salvadoreans. Furthe clashes occurred in 1970 and 1976.

## Hungary

### Hungarian People's Republic

**People: Population** (1977 est.): 10,650,000. **Age distril** (%): 0-14: 20.0; 15-59: 61.9; 60+: 18.1. **Pop. density:** 296.5 per sq. mi. **Urban** (1976): 50.1%. **Ethnic groups:** Magyar 98% German 0.5%, Slovak 0.3%, Gypsy 0.3%, Croatian 0.3%. **Lar guages:** Hungarian (Magyar). **Religions:** Roman Catholic 55%, Calvinist 20%, Lutherans 5%, Jews 1%.

**Geography: Area:** 35,919 sq. mi., slightly smaller than Ind na. **Location:** In East Central Europe. **Neighbors:** Czechoslo-akia on N, Austria on W, Yugoslavia on S, Romania, USSR on the W, then swings S to bisect the country. **Topography:** The Danube R. forms the Czech border on the W, then swings S to bisect the country. The eastern half of ungary is mainly a great fertile plain, the Alfold; the W and N re hilly. **Capital:** Budapest. **Cities** (1975 est.): Budapest .063,306; Mispolc 197,975; Debrecen 184,714.

**Government: Head of state:** Pres. Pal Losonczi; b. 1919; in ffice: Apr. 14, 1967; **Head of government:** Chmn. Gyorgy azar; b. 1924; in office: May 15, 1975; **Head of Communist arty:** Janos Kadar; b. May 26, 1912; in office: 1956. **Local divi-ions:** 19 counties, 5 cities with county status. **Armed forces:** gulars 163,000; reserves 143,000.

**Economy: Industries:** Iron and steel, machinery, chemicals, ehicles, communications equip., milling, distilling. **Chief crops:** rains, vegetables, fruits, grapes. **Minerals:** Bauxite, natural as. **Per capita arable land:** 1.2 acres. **Meat production** 976): beef: 141,200 tons; pork: 415,500 tons. **Fish catch** 975): 30,800 metric tons. **Electricity production** (1977): 3.39 bln. kwh. **Labor force:** 23% agric.; 36% manuf.

**Finance: Currency:** Forint (Oct.-Dec. 1977: 4.66 = $1 US). ross domestic product (1974 est.): $24.6 bln. **Per capita** come (1974): $2,200. **Imports** (1974): $6.52 bln.; partners 974): USSR 28%, W. Ger. 10%, E. Ger. 9%, Czech. 7%. **Ex-orts** (1977): $5.83 bln.; partners (1974): USSR 32%, E. Ger. 0%, Czech. 9%, W. Ger. 6%. **Tourists** (1975): 4,995,000; re-eipts (1975): $238 million. **Consumer prices** (change in 1977): 9%.

**Transport: Railway traffic** (1975): 8.49 bln. passenger-miles; 4.26 bln. net ton-miles. **Motor vehicles:** in use (1975): 579,900 assenger cars, 205,100 commercial vehicles; manufactured 977): 13,320 commercial vehicles.

**Communications:** Television sets: 2,296,000 licensed (1974), 00,000 manufactured (1975). **Radios:** 2,541,000 licensed 974), 255,000 manufactured (1975). **Telephones in use** 977): 1,076,064. **Daily newspaper circulation** (1974): ,431,000; 232 per 1,000 pop.

**Health: Life expectancy at birth** (1974): 66.54 male; 72.42 male. **Births** (per 1,000 pop. 1976): 17.5. **Deaths** (per 1,000 op: 1976): 12.5. **Natural increase** (1976): .50%. **Pop. per ospital bed** (1975): 120. **Pop. per physician** (1975): 458. In-ant mortality (per 1,000 live births 1975): 32.8.

**Education: Literacy** (1975): 98%. **Pop. 5-19:** in school 975): 53%, per teacher (1975): 29.

Earliest settlers, chiefly Slav and Germanic, were overrun by uns and Magyars from the east. Stephen I (997-1038) was ade king by Pope Sylvester II in 1001 A.D. The country suf-ered repeated Turkish invasions in the 15th-17th centuries. After e defeats of the Turks, 1686-1697, Austria dominated, but ungary obtained concessions until it regained internal indepen-ence in 1867, with the emperor of Austria as king of Hungary in dual monarchy with a single diplomatic service. Defeated with he Central Powers in 1918, Hungary lost Transylvania to Roma-ia, Croatia and Bacska to Yugoslavia, Slovakia and Carpatho-Ruthenia to Czechoslovakia, all of which had large Hungarian inorities. A republic under Michael Karolyi and a bolshevist re-olt under Bela Kun were followed by a vote for a monarchy in 920 with Admiral Nicholas Horthy as regent.

Hungary joined Germany in World War II, and was allowed to nnex most of its lost territories. Russian troops captured the ountry, 1944-1945. By terms of an armistice with the Allied owers Hungary agreed to give up territory acquired by the 938 dismemberment of Czechoslovakia and to return to its bor-ers of 1937.

Hungary declared for a republic Feb. 1, 1946, and elected oltan Tildy president. In 1947 the communists forced Tildy out.

Premier Imre Nagy, in office since mid-1953, was ousted for is moderate policy of favoring agriculture and consumer pro-uction, April 18, 1955.

In 1956, popular demands for the ousting of Erno Gero, Com-unist party secretary, and for formation of a government by agy, resulted in the latter's appointment Oct. 23; demonstra-ons against communist rule developed into open revolt. Gero alled in Soviet forces. On Nov. 4 Soviet forces launched a mas-ive attack against Budapest with 200,000 troops, 2,500 tanks nd armored cars.

Estimates varied from 6,500 to 32,000 dead, and thousands eported. About 200,000 persons fled the country. The U.S. re-eived 38,248 under a refugee emergency program. In the pring of 1963 the regime freed many anti-communists and cap-

tives from the revolution in a sweeping amnesty.

Nagy was executed by the Russians. Janos Kadar, sponsored by the USSR, became first secretary of the Hungarian Workers (Communist) party.

Some 40,000 Soviet troops are stationed in Hungary. Hungar-ian troops participated in the 1968 Warsaw Pact invasion of Czechoslovakia.

Major economic reforms were launched early in 1968, switch-ing from a central planning system to one in which market forces and profit control much of production. Productivity and living standards have improved. By the 1970s, Hungary led the com-munist states in comparative tolerance for cultural freedoms and small private enterprise. Some 60,000 of the 1956 emigres have returned.

In 1973 Hungary agreed to pay the U.S. $18,900,000 for na-tionalized U.S. properties in Hungary, and trade ties improved.

# Iceland

## Republic of Iceland

**People: Population** (1977 est.): 220,000. **Age distrib.** (%): 0-14: 31.0; 15-59: 56.4; 60+: 12.6. **Pop. density:** 5.54 per sq. mi. **Urban** (1975): 86.8%. **Ethnic groups:** Homogeneous, de-scendants of Norwegians, Celts. **Language:** Icelandic. **Religon:** Lutherans 98%.

**Geography: Area:** 39,702 sq. mi., the size of Virginia. **Loca-tion:** At N end of Atlantic O. **Neighbors:** Nearest is Greenland. **Topography:** Iceland is of recent volcanic origin. Three-quarters of the surface is wasteland: glaciers, lakes, a lava desert. There are geysers and hot springs, and the climate is moderated by the Gulf Stream. **Capital:** Reykjavik. **Cities** (1975 est.): Reykja-vik (met.) 99,990.

**Government: Head of state:** Pres. Kristjan Eldjorn; b. Dec. 6, 1916; in office: Aug. 1, 1968. **Local divisions:** 16 counties, each with a council; 14 urban municipalities.

**Economy: Industries:** Fish products, aluminum, cement, chemicals. **Chief crops:** Potatoes, turnips, hay. **Per capita ara-ble land:** 0.013 acres. **Meat production** (1975): lamb: 15,000 tons. **Fish catch** (1975): 994,800 metric tons. **Electricity pro-duction** (1977): 2.60 bln. kwh. **Labor force:** 16% agric.; 26% manuf.

**Finance: Currency:** Kronvr (May 1978: 259.80 = $1 US). **Gross domestic product** (1976): $1.40 bln. **Per capita in-come** (1976): $5,503. **Imports** (1977): $607 mln.; partners (1976): USSR 11.7%, W. Ger. 10.8%, U.S. 10.5%, U.K. 10%. **Exports** (1977): $513 mln.; partners (1976): U.S. 28.8%, U.K. 11.9%, Port. 10.4%, USSR 5.4%. **Tourists** (1972): 68,000; re-ceipts (1975): $12 million. **Balance of payments** (1977): +$29,400,000. **International reserves** (May 1978): $102.8 mln. **Consumer prices** (change in 1976): 32.1%.

**Transport: Motor vehicles:** in use (1975): 63,900 passenger cars, 7,600 commercial vehicles. **Civil aviation:** 1,155 mln. passenger-miles (1977); 17,743 mln. freight ton-miles (1977). **Chief ports:** Reykjavik.

**Communications: Television sets:** 50,000 in use (1974). **Radios:** 64,000 in use (1974). **Telephones in use** (1977): 93,678. **Daily newspaper circulation** (1974): 95,000; 436 per 1,000 pop.

**Health: Life expectancy at birth** (1975): 71.6 male; 77.5 fe-male. **Births** (per 1,000 pop. 1975): 20.1. **Deaths** (per 1,000 pop. 1975): 6.5. **Natural increase** (1975): 1.36%. **Pop. per hospital bed** (1975): 75. **Pop. per physician** (1975): 623. In-fant mortality (per 1,000 live births 1975): 11.1

**Education: Literacy** (1975): 99%. **Pop. 5-19:** in school (1975): 70%, per teacher (1975): 22.

Iceland was an independent republic from 930 to 1262, when it joined with Norway. Its language has maintained its purity, as in the Eddas, for 1,000 years. Danish rule lasted from 1380-1918; the last ties with the Danish crown were severed in 1941. The Althing, or assembly, is the world's oldest surviving parliament.

A four-year dispute with Britain ended in 1976 when the latter accepted Iceland's 200-mile territorial waters claim.

A conservative coalition won power in 1974 and stopped plans to oust U.S. NATO air and naval personnel, which totalled 2,900 in 1975. But the cabinet resigned, June 1978, after election losses.

# India

## Republic of India

**People: Population** (1977 est.): 625,820,000. **Age distrib.** (%): 0–14: 40.1; 15–59: 54.6; 60+: 5.3. **Pop. density:** 508.91 per sq. mi. **Urban** (1974): 20.6%. **Ethnic groups:** Indo-Aryan groups 72%, Dravidians 25%, Mongoloids 3%. **Languages:** 14 official languages, including English and Hindi. **Religions:** Hindus 84%, Moslems 10%, Christians 2.6%, Sikhs 1.9%, Buddhists 0.7%, Jains 0.5%, others.

**Geography: Area:** 1,229,737 sq. mi., one third the size of the U.S. **Location:** Occupies most of the Indian subcontinent in S. Asia. **Neighbors:** Pakistan on W, China, Nepal, Bhutan on N, Burma, Bangladesh on E. **Topography:** The Himalaya Mts., highest in world, stretch across India's northern borders. Below, the Ganges Plain is wide, fertile, and among the most densely populated regions of the world. The area below includes the Deccan Peninsula. Close to one quarter the area is forested. The climate varies from tropical heat in S to near-Arctic cold in N. Rajasthan Desert is in NW; NE Assam Hills get 400 in. of rain a year. **Capital:** New Delhi. **Cities** (1971 cen.): Calcutta (met.) 7,031,382; Bombay 5,970,575; Delhi (met.) 3,647,023; Madras (met.) 3,169,930; Hyderabad (met.) 1,796,339; Ahmedabad (met.) 1,741,522; Bangalore (met.) 1,653,779; Kanpur (met.) 1,275,242; Poona (met.) 1,135,034; Nagpur (met.) 930,459; Lucknow (met.) 813,982.

**Government: Head of state:** Pres. Neelam Sanjiva Reddy; b. May 13, 1913; in office: July 25, 1977; **Head of government:** Prime Min. Morarji Desai; b. Feb. 29, 1896; in office: Mar. 24, 1977. **Local divisions:** 22 states with elected governments and substantial powers, 9 union territories; largest state, Uttar Pradesh, had over 88 million people in 1971. **Armed forces:** regulars 1,096,000; reserves 240,000.

**Economy: Industries:** Textiles, steel, processed foods, cement, machinery, chemicals, fertilizers, consumer appliances, autos. **Chief crops:** Rice, grains, coffee, sugar cane, spices, tea, cashews, cotton, copra, coir, juta, linseed. **Minerals:** Coal, mica, manganese, salt, iron, bauxite, gypsum, oil. **Crude oil reserves** (1978): 3.00 bln. bbls. **Other resources:** Rubber, timber. **Per capita arable land:** 0.6 acres. **Meat production** (1975): beef: 189,000 tons; pork: 54,000 tons; lamb: 388,000 tons. **Fish catch** (1975): 2,328,000 metric tons. **Electricity production** (1977): 90.84 bln. kwh. **Labor force:** 72% agric.; 9% manuf.

**Finance: Currency:** Rupee (May 1978: 8.41 = $1 US). **Gross domestic product** (1975): $80.63 bln. **Per capita income** (1974): $136. **Imports** (1977): $5.64 bln. partners (1976): U.S. 24%, Iran 9.0%, W. Ger. 7.0%, Jap. 6.8%. **Exports** (1977): $5.29 bln.; partners (1976): U.S. 12.7%, Jap. 10.7%, USSR 10.4%, U.K. 10.1%, Iran 6.9%. **Tourists** (1975): 465,300; receipts (1975): $124 million. **Balance of payments** (1975): +$356,000,000. **National budget** (1977): $11.22 bln. revenues; $13.91 bln. expenditures. **International reserves** (Mar. 1978): $5.82 bln. **Consumer prices** (change in 1977): 8.5%.

**Transport: Railway traffic** (1975): 78.40 bln. passenger-miles; 75.37 bln. net ton-miles. **Motor vehicles:** in use (1975): 756,500 passenger cars, 434,400 commercial vehicles; manufactured (1977): 47,760 passenger cars, 39,000 commercial vehicles. **Civil aviation:** 4,561 mln. passenger-miles (1976): 171,359 freight ton-miles (1976). **Chief ports:** Calcutta, Bombay, Madras, Cochin, Vishalshapatnam.

**Communications: Television sets:** 275,000 licensed (1974). **Radios:** 14,848,000 licensed (1974), 1,542,000 manufactured (1975). **Telephones in use** (1977): 2,095,962. **Daily newspaper circulation** (1974): 9,222,000; 16 per 1,000 pop.

**Health: Life expectancy at birth** (1960): 41.89 male; 40.55 female. **Births** (per 1,000 pop. 1974): 34.5. **Deaths** (per 1,000 pop. 1974): 14.4. **Natural increase** (1974): 2.01%. **Pop. per hospital bed** (1975): 1,616. **Pop. per physician** (1975): 4,264. **Infant mortality** (per 1,000 live births 1971): 122.

**Education: Literacy** (1975): 36%. **Pop. 5-19:** in school (1975): 40%, per teacher (1975): 80.

India has one of the oldest civilizations in the world. Excavations trace the Indus Valley civilization back for at least 5,000 years. Paintings in the mountain caves of Ajanta, richly carved temples, the Taj Mahal in Agra and the Kutab Minar in Delhi are among relics of the past.

Aryan tribes, speaking Sanskrit (related to Persian and to European languages), invaded from the NW around 1500 B.C., and merged with the earlier inhabitants to create classical Indian civilization.

Asoka ruled most of the Indian subcontinent in the 3rd century B.C., and established Buddhism. But Hinduism revived and eventually predominated. During the Gupta kingdom, 4th-6th century A.D., science, literature, and the arts enjoyed a "golden age."

Arab invaders established a Moslem foothold in the W in the 8th century, and Turkish Moslems gained control of North India by 1200. The Mogul emperors ruled 1526-1707.

Vasco de Gama established Portuguese trading posts 1498-1503. The Dutch followed. The British East India Co. sent Capt. William Hawkins, 1609, to get concessions from the Mogul emperor for spices and textiles. Operating as the East India Co. the British gained control of most of India. The British parliament assumed political direction; under Lord Bentinck, 1828-35, rule by rajahs was curbed. After the Sepoy troops mutinied, 1857-58, the British supported the native rulers.

Nationalism grew rapidly after World War I. The Indian National Congress and the Moslem League demanded constitutional reform. A leader emerged in Mohandas K. Gandhi (called Mahatma, or Great Soul), born Oct. 2, 1869, assassinated Jan. 30, 1948. A Hindu, trained in law in England, he began advocating self-rule, non-violence, pursuit of native handicrafts, removal of untouchability (which forced millions of poor to remain menials by heredity) in 1919. In 1930 he launched "civil disobedience" including boycott of British goods and rejection of taxes without representation.

In 1935 Britain gave India a constitution providing a bicameral federal congress. Suffrage was granted about 30 million. Mohammed Ali Jinnah, head of the Moslem League, sought creation of a Moslem nation, Pakistan.

Following more than 40 years' active struggle for freedom by both Hindus and Moslems, the British government announced Feb. 20, 1947, its intention to partition India into 2 dominions and set June 3, 1948, for British withdrawal from India. Aug. 15, 1947 was designated Indian Independence Day. India became a self-governing member of the Commonwealth and a member of the UN. It became a democratic republic, Jan. 26, 1950.

It was estimated that more than 12 million refugees (Hindus and Moslems) crossed the India-Pakistan borders in a mass transferral of some of the two peoples during 1947; about 200,000 were killed in communal fighting.

After Pakistan troops began attacks on Bengali separatists in East Pakistan, Mar. 25, 1971, some 10 million refugees fled into India. On Aug. 9, India and the USSR signed a 20-year friendship pact while U.S.-India relations soured. India and Pakistan went to war Dec. 3, 1971, on both the East and West fronts. Pakistan troops in the East surrendered Dec. 16; Pakistan agreed to a cease-fire in the West Dec. 17.

India and Pakistan signed a pact agreeing to withdraw troops from their borders and seek peaceful solutions, July 3, 1972. Aug. 1973 India agreed to release 93,000 Pakistanis held prisoner since 1971; the return was completed in Apr. 1974. The two countries resumed full relations in 1976.

Prime Minister Mrs. Indira Gandhi, named Jan. 19, 1966, succeeded Lal Bahadur Shastri, who on June 2, 1964, succeeded India's first prime minister, Jawaharlal Nehru. Nehru, prime minister from the beginning of India's independence in 1947, died May 27, 1964.

Long the dominant power in India's politics, the Congress party lost some of its near monopoly by 1967. The party split into New and Old Congress parties in 1969. Mrs. Gandhi's New Congress party won control of the House.

Threatened with adverse court rulings in a voting law case, and opposition protest campaign and strikes, Gandhi invoked emergency provisions of the constitution June, 1975. Thousands of opponents were arrested and press censorship imposed. Measures to control prices, protect small farmers, and improve productivity were adopted.

The emergency, especially enforcement of coercive birth control measures in some areas, and the prominent extra-constitutional role of Indira Gandhi's son Sanjay, was widely resented. Opposition parties, united in the Janata coalition, scored massive victories in federal and state parliamentary elections 1977, turning the Congress Party from power.

Severe droughts in northern areas have repeatedly threatened mass starvation and brought large shipments of grain from the U.S. In July 1967 plentiful rains broke the drought; there were bumper crops, 1968-72; the drought and food shortage returned in 1972-75, but a bumper crop in 1976 assured self-sufficiency.

Indian agriculture has made progress with high-yield seeds, rtilizers, irrigation and limited mechanization.

For many years India has had large textile industries with a de variety of cotton, woolen, and silk products. In the 1960s, her industries, including steel, processed foods, cement, machinery, chemicals, and fertilizers came into prominence, along with many finished products such as sewing machines, typewriters, bicycles, telephones, and transportation equipment.

India's 1st nuclear power plant, built with U.S. help, was dedicated in 1970 near Bombay; Canada helped India build 2 reactors. In May 1974 India exploded a nuclear device underground, assertedly for peaceful development. Canada halted shipments of nuclear equipment and material to India. Restricted shipments from both the U.S. & Canada resumed in 1976. An Indian space satellite was launched by the USSR April 19, 1975.

There are 14 language groups, 12 originating from Sanskrit, and over 1,600 "mother tongues." Hindi is spoken by 30%, with Urdu, the principal Moslem language, spoken by 5%. Hindi became the official language in Jan. 1965 with English the associate official language. Much government work and instruction at universities is done in English. English-language dailies outsell those of any other language. Attempts to advance Hindi have met with resentment and violence in southern states.

**Sikkim**, bordered by Tibet, Bhutan, Nepal and India, formerly British protected, became a protectorate of India in 1950. Area, 2,818 sq. mi.; population 1974, 210,000; capital, Gangtok. In Sept. 1974 India's Parliament voted to make Sikkim an associate Indian state, absorbing it into India. The monarchy was abolished in an April, 1975 referendum.

**Kashmir**, a predominantly Moslem region in the northwest, has been in dispute between India and Pakistan since 1947 when British rule was ending and Indian and Pakistani troops entered the area. A cease-fire was negotiated by the U.N. Jan. 1, 1949; it gave Pakistan control of one-third of the area, in the west and northwest, and India the remaining two-thirds, the Indian state of Jammu and Kashmir, which enjoys internal autonomy. In late Aug. 1965, clashes broke out along the line.

A new truce line, slightly altering the old cease-fire line, was agreed on in Dec. 1972, accommodating changes made during the 1971 fighting.

There were also clashes in April 1965 along the Assam-East Pakistan border and in the **Rann** (swamp) of Cutch area along the West Pakistan-Gujarat border near the Arabian Sea. An international arbitration commission on Feb. 19, 1968, awarded 90% of the Rann to India, 10% to Pakistan.

France, 1952-54, peacefully yielded to India its 5 colonies on the Bay of Bengal, former French India, comprising Pondicherry, Karikal, Mahe, Yanaon, and Chandernagor, totalling 196 sq. mi. and 346,000 pop.

**Goa**, 1,426 sq. mi. pop., 1971, 857,771, which had been ruled by Portugal since 1505 A.D., was taken by India by military action Dec. 18, 1961, together with 2 other Portuguese enclaves, Daman and Diu, located near Bombay.

# Indonesia

## Republic of Indonesia

**People: Population** (1977 est.): 143,280,000. **Age distrib.** (%): 0–14: 44.1; 15–59: 51.5; 60+: 4.4. **Pop. density:** 194.87 per sq. mi. **Urban** (1974): 18.2%. **Ethnic groups:** Javanese 45%, Sundanese 13.6%, Chinese 2.3%, others. **Languages:** Bahasa Indonesian (Malay) (official), Javanese, other Austronesian languages. **Religions:** Moslems 90%, Christians 5%, Hindus 3%.

**Geography: Area:** 735,268 sq. mi. **Location:** Archipelago SE of Asia along the Equator. **Neighbors:** Malaysia on N, Papua New Guinea on E. **Topography:** Indonesia comprises 13,000 islands, including Java (one of the most densely populated areas in the world, with 1,500 persons to the sq. mi.), Sumatra, Kalimantan (most of Borneo), Sulawesi (Celebes), and West Irian or Irian Jaya, the west half of New Guinea. Among others are Bangka, Billiton, Madura, Bali, Timor. The mountains and plateaus on the major islands have a cooler climate than the tropical lowlands. **Capital:** Jakarta. **Cities** (1971 cen.): Jakarta 4,576,009; Surabaja 1,556,255; Bandung 1,201,730; Semarang 646,590; Medan 635,562.

**Government: Head of state:** Pres. Suharto; b. June 8, 1921; in office: May 27, 1968. **Local divisions:** 26 provinces with elected legislatures, appointed governors. **Armed forces:** regulars 247,000; para-military 112,000.

**Economy: Industries:** Food processing, textiles, light industry. **Chief crops:** Rice, maize, cassava, peanuts, soybeans, tobacco, coffee, pepper, kapok, coconuts, palm oil, tea, sugar, indigo. **Minerals:** Tin, oil, coal, bauxite, manganese, copper, nickel, gold, silver. **Crude oil reserves** (1978): 10.00 bln. bbls. **Other resources:** Rubber, cinchona. **Per capita arable land:** 0.3 acres. **Meat production** (1975): beef: 165,000 tons; pork: 94,000 tons, lamb: 39,000 tons. **Fish catch** (1975): 1,389,900 metric tons. **Electricity production** (1975): 3.35 bln. kwh. **Labor force:** 62% agric.; 7% manuf.

**Finance: Currency:** Rupiah (May 1978: 415.00 = $1 US). **Gross domestic product** (1976): $37.27 bln. **Per capita income** (1975): $195. **Imports** (1977): $6.23 bln.; partners (1974): Jap. 30%, U.S. 16%, W. Ger. 8%, Sing. 7%. **Exports** (1977): $10.85 bln.; partners (1974): Jap. 53%, U.S. 20%, Sing. 7%. **Tourists** (1974): 313,500; receipts (1975): $34 million. **Balance of payments** (1977): +$997,000,000. **National budget** (1976): $7.09 bln. revenues; $7.66 bln. expenditures. **International reserves** (May 1978): $2.28 bln. **Consumer prices** (change in 1977): 11.0%.

**Transport: Railway traffic** (1975): 2.19 bln. passenger-miles; 599.89 mln. net ton-miles. **Motor vehicles:** in use (1975): 383,100 passenger cars, 231,500 commercial vehicles. **Civil aviation:** 1,893 mln. passenger-miles (1976); 29,480 mln. freight ton-miles (1976). **Chief ports:** Jakarta, Surabaja, Medan, Palembang, Semarang.

**Communications: Television sets:** 90,000 in use (1970), 70,000 manufactured (1972). **Radios:** 5,000,000 licensed (1974), 900,000 manufactured (1973). **Telephones in use** (1977): 314,445. **Daily newspaper circulation** (1974): 2,035,000; 68 per 1,000 pop.

**Health:** Life expectancy at birth (1960): 47.5 male; 47.5 female. **Births** (annual per 1,000 pop. 1972-75): 42.9. **Deaths** (annual per 1,000 pop. 1972-75): 16.9. **Natural increase** (annual 1970-75): 2.60%. **Pop. per hospital bed** (1975): 1,549. **Pop. per physician** (1975): 19,364. **Infant mortality** (per 1,000 live births 1962): 125.

**Education:** Literacy (1975): 60%. **Pop. 5-19:** in school (1975): 32%, per teacher (1975): 91.

Hindu and Buddhist civilization from India reached the peoples of Indonesia nearly 2,000 years ago, taking root especially in Java. Islam spread along the maritime trade routes in the 15th century, and became predominant by the 16th century. The Dutch replaced the Portuguese as the most important European trade power in the area in the 17th century. They secured territorial control over Java by 1750. The outer islands were not finally subdued until the early 20th century, when the full area of present-day Indonesia was united under one rule for the first time in history.

Following Japanese occupation, 1942-45, nationalists led by Sukarno and Hatta proclaimed a republic. The Netherlands ceded sovereignty Dec. 27, 1949, after four years of intermittent fighting. West Irian, on New Guinea, remained under Dutch control.

After the Dutch in 1957 rejected proposals for new negotiations over West Irian, Indonesia stepped up the seizure of Dutch property. A U.S. mediator's plan was adopted in 1962. In 1963 the UN turned the area over to Indonesia, which promised a plebiscite. In 1969, voting by tribal chiefs favored staying with Indonesia, despite an uprising and widespread opposition.

Sukarno suspended Parliament in 1960, and was named president for life in 1963. Russian-armed Indonesian troops staged raids in 1964 and 1965 into Malaysia, whose formation Sukarno had opposed. Indonesia withdrew from the UN in 1965; anti-American demonstrations were staged.

Indonesia's popular, pro-Peking Communist party tried to seize control in 1965, killing 6 high generals. The army smashed the coup and later intimated that Sukarno had played a role in it. In parts of Java, Communists seized several districts before being defeated; over 300,000 Communists were executed. The last of those arrested then were to be released in 1979.

Gen. Suharto, head of the Army, was named president for 5 years in 1968, and elected to another term in 1973. A coalition of his supporters won a strong majority in House elections in 1971, the first national vote in 16 years. Moslem opposition parties made gains in 1977 elections. The military retains a predominant political role.

In 1966 Indonesia and Malaysia signed an agreement ending hostility, and Indonesia reentered the UN. After ties with Peking were cut in 1967, there were riots against the economically important ethnic Chinese minority. Riots against Chinese and Japanese also occurred in 1974.

The former Portuguese Timor became Indonesia's 27th province in 1976 during a local civil war. Thousands of civilians were reportedly killed by the Indonesians.

Oil export earnings, and a decline in the high birth rate, have given hope for future improvements in very low living conditions.

# Iran
## Imperial Government of Iran

**People: Population** (1976 est.): 33,590,000. **Age distrib.** (%): 0–14: 47.2; 15–59; 48.0; 60+: 4.9. **Pop. density:** 52.78 per sq. mi. **Urban** (1975): 44.0%. **Ethnic groups:** Iranian groups 66%, Turkish groups 25%, Kurds 5%, Arabs 4%. **Languages:** Persian, Turk, Kurdish, Arabic. **Religions:** Moslems 96% (mostly Shiites), Christians, Jews, Zoroastrians.

**Geography: Area:** 636,363 sq. mi. **Location:** Between the Middle East and S. Asia. **Neighbors:** Turkey, Iraq on W, USSR of N (Armenia, Azerbaijan, Turkmenistan), Afghanistan, Pakistan on E. **Topography:** Interior highlands and plains are surrounded by high mountains, up to 18,000 ft. Large salt deserts cover much of the area, but there are many oases and forest areas. Most of the population inhabits the N and NW. **Capital:** Teheran. **Cities** (1973 est.): Teheran 4,002,000; Isfahan 605,000; Mashhad 592,000; Tabriz 510,000.

**Government: Head of state:** Shah Mohammed Reza Pahlavi; b. Oct. 26, 1919; in office: Sept. 17, 1941; **Head of government:** Prime Min. Jamshid Amouzegar; b. 1920; in office: Aug. 7, 1977. **Local divisions:** 20 provinces, 2 governorates. **Armed forces:** regulars 342,000; reserves 300,000.

**Economy: Industries:** Steel, petrochemicals, cement, auto assembly, sugar refining, carpets. **Chief crops:** Grains, rice, fruits, sugar beets, cotton, grapes. **Minerals:** Oil, gas, chromite, copper, iron, lead, manganese, zinc, barite, sulphur, coal, emeralds, turquoise. **Crude oil reserves** (1978): 62.00 bln. bbls. **Other resources:** Gums, wool, silk, caviar. **Per capita arable land:** 1.1 acres. **Meat production** (1976): beef: 65,800 tons; lamb: 286,900 tons. **Electricity production** (1975): 15.00 bln. kwh. **Labor force:** 42% agric.; 17% manuf.

**Finance: Currency:** Rial (May 1978: 70.48 = $1 US). **Gross domestic product** (1976): $66.40 bln. **Per capita income** (1975): $1,529. **Imports** (1977): $14.07 bln.; partners (1975): U.S. 20%, W. Ger. 18%, Jap. 15%, U.K. 8%. **Exports** (1978): $24.25 bln.; partners (1975): Jap. 20%, Neth. 11%, U.S. 10%, W. Ger. 5%. **Tourists** 1975): 560,200; receipts (1975): $123 million. **Balance of payments** (1977): +$3,406,000,000. **National budget** (1977): $31.07 bln. revenues; $37.02 bln. expenditures. **International reserves** (May 1978): $12.49 bln. **Consumer prices** (change in 1977): 27.3%.

**Transport: Railway traffic** (1974): 1.32 bln. passenger-miles; 3.05 bln. net ton-miles. **Motor vehicles:** in use (1974): 589,200 passenger cars, 111,200 commercial vehicles; assembled (1976): 102,000,000 passenger cars; 66,000,000 commercial vehicles. **Chief ports:** Khorramshahr, Bushehr, Bandar-e Shahpur, Bendar Abbas.

**Communications: Television sets:** 1,500,000 in use (1974), 242,000 manufactured (1973). **Radios:** 8,000,000 in use (1974), 281,000 manufactured (1973). **Telephones in use** (1977): 781,537. **Daily newspaper circulation** (1974): 484,000; 15 per 1,000 pop.

**Health: Life expectancy at birth** (1975): 50.7 male; 51.3 female. **Births** (annual per 1,000 pop. 1972-75): 45.3. **Deaths** (annual per 1,000 pop. 1972-75): 15.6. **Natural increase** (1970-75): 2.97%. **Pop. per hospital bed** (1975): 728. **Pop. per physician** (1975): 2,649. **Infant mortality** (per 1,000 live births 1973): 139.

**Education: Literacy** (1975): 37%. **Pop. 5-19:** in school (1975): 45%, per teacher (1975): 56.

Iran is the official name of the country long known as Persia. The Iranians, who supplanted an earlier agricultural civilization, came from the E during the 2nd millenium B.C.; they were an Indo-European group related to the Aryans of India. The name Iran became widespread in the 1920s.

In 549 B.C. Cyrus the Great united the Medes and Persians in the Persian Empire, conquered Babylonia in 538 B.C. restored Jerusalem to the Jews. Alexander the Great conquered Persia in 333 B.C., but Persians regained their independence in the next century under the Parthians, themselves succeeded by Sassanian Persians in 226 A.D. Arabs brought Islam to Persia in the 7th century, replacing the indigenous Zoroastrian faith. After Per-

sian political and cultural autonomy was reasserted in the 9 century, the arts and sciences flourished for several centuries.

Turks and Mongols ruled Persia in turn from the 11th centur to 1502, when a native dynasty reasserted full independenc The British and Russian empires vied for influence in the 19 century, and Afghanistan was severed from Iran by Britain in 185

The current dynasty was founded by Reza Khan, a milita leader, in 1925. He abdicated as shah in 1941, and was suc ceeded by his son, Mohammed Reza Pahlavi.

British and Russian forces entered Iran Aug. 25, 1941, wit drawing later. Britian and the USSR signed an agreement Jar 29, 1942, to respect Iranian integrity and give economic aid. 1946 a Soviet attempt to take over the Azerbaijan region in th NW was defeated when a puppet regime was ousted by force.

Parliament, under Premier Mohammed Mossadegh, nationa ized the oil industry in 1951, leading to a British blockade. Mo sadegh was overthrown in 1953. The shah assumed control, ar has retained it ever since. Under his rule, Iran has undergor economic and social change, including land reform, the sprea of literacy, and gains in women's rights. However, political oppo sition is not tolerated. Thousands were arrested in the 1970 while hundreds of purported terrorists were executed. Conserva tive Moslem protests led to 1978 violence.

The shah in 1954 signed an agreement with a consortium British, U.S., Dutch and French companies. In 1973 a new agree ment gave the National Iranian Oil Co. control.

In 1969-74 Iran and Iraq were invlolved in a dispute ove Iran's right to use the Shatt al Arab, a border river estuary. Ira acceeded to Iran's border claims in a June 13, 1975 pact. In lat 1971, Iran occupied 3 islands at the mouth of the gulf, claime by states of the United Arab Emirates. Iran in the 1970s moderr ized its military forces, aided by multi-billion dollar purchase from the U.S. Economic aid to Egypt, and military aid agains leftist Oman rebels advanced Iran's regional status in the 1970s

In 1974 Iran invested some of its oil wealth in a multi-billio dollar trade pact with France including nuclear energy facilities a 25% interest in West Germany's Krupp enterprises, and a $1. billion loan to Britain. In 1975, Iran signed an 8-year agreemer to facilitate $25 billion in purchases in the U.S., to further Iran five-year development plan, including 8 large nuclear powe plants.

The first Iranian steel mill, near Isfahan, was built by the Sovie Union and paid for by natural gas piped to the USSR.

# Iraq
## Republic of Iraq

**People: Population** (1977 est.): 11,910,000. **Age distrib** (%): 0–14: 48.3; 15–59; 46.5; 60+: 5.3. **Pop. density:** 69.24 pe sq. mi. **Urban** (1976): 64.8%. **Ethnic groups:** Arabs 78%, Kurd 18%, Persians 1.2%, Turks 1.2%, Assyrians 0.5%. **Language** Arabic (official), Kurdish, others. **Religions:** Moslems 95 (Shiites two-thirds, Sunnis one-third), Christians 3%.

**Geography: Area:** 172,000 sq. mi., larger than California. **L** **cation:** In the Middle East, occupying most of historic Mesopota mia. **Neighbors:** Jordan, Syria on W, Turkey on N, Iran on E Kuwait, Saudi Arabia on S. **Topography:** Iraq is mostly an allu vial plain, including the Tigris and Euphrates rivers, descendin from mountains in N to SW of rivers is desert. Pesian Gulf regio is marshland. **Capital:** Baghdad. **Cities** (1974 est.): Baghda (met.) 2,760,000; Basra 620,000; Mosul 508,500.

**Government: Head of state:** Pres. Ahmed Hassan al-Bak b. 1912; in office: July 17, 1968. **Local divisions:** 16 province **Armed forces:** regulars 188,000; reserves 250,000.

**Economy: Industries:** Textiles, food processing, cigarette oil refining, cement. **Chief crops:** Grains, rice, dates, cotton, to bacco. **Minerals:** Oil, gas. **Crude oil reserves** (1977): 35.5 bln. bbls. **Other resources:** Wool, hides. **Per capita arabl land:** 1.1 acres. **Meat production** (1975): beef: 60,000 tons lamb: 95,000 tons. **Electricity production** (1975): 3.40 bln. kwh **Labor force:** 50% agriculture.

**Finance: Currency:** Dinar (May 1978: 1 = $3.39 US). **Gros domestic product** (1975): $13.62 bln. **Per capita incom** (1975): $1,155. **Imports** (1976): $3.47 bln.; partners (1973 USSR 9%, U.K. 9%, Fr. 8%, Jap. 7%. **Exports** (1977): $9.6 bln.; partners (1973): It. 25%, Fr. 23%, Braz. 10%, USSR 6% **Tourists** (1975): 482,100; receipts (1975): $78 million. **Balanc of payments** (1975): −$498,000,000. **International reserve** (Dec. 1977): $6.99 bln. **Consumer prices** (change in 1976 10.3%.

**Transport: Railway traffic** (1974): 400.54 mln. pasenge

iles; 1.16 bln. net ton-miles. **Motor vehicles:** in use (1974): 0,100 passenger cars, 48,600 commercial vehicles. **Civil aviation:** 759 mln. passenger-miles (1977); 20,038 mln. freight ton-miles (1977). **Chief ports:** Basra.

**Communications: Television sets:** 520,000 in use (1973), 000 manufactured (1969). **Radios:** 1,250,000 in use (1974). **elephones in use** (1977): 319,591. **Daily newspaper circulation** (1973): 226,000; 22 per 1,000 pop.

**Health: Life expectancy at birth** (1975): 51.2 male; 54.3 female. **Births** (annual per 1,000 pop. 1972-75): 45.3. **Deaths** (annual per 1,000 pop. 1972-75): 14.6. **Natural increase** (annual 970-75): 3.35%. **Pop. per hospital bed** (1975): 479. **Pop. Per** physician (1975): 2,257. **Infant mortality** (per 1,000 live births 973): 27.5.

**Education: Literacy** (1975): 26%. **Pop. 5-19:** in school 975): 48%, per teacher (1975): 49.

The Tigris-Euphrates valley, formerly called Mesopotamia, as the site of one of the earliest civilizations in the world. The sumerian city-states of 3,000 B.C. originated the culture later eveloped by the Semitic Akkadians, Babylonians, and Assyrians.

Mesopotamia ceased to be a separate political or cultural entity after the conquests of the Persians, Greeks, and Arabs. The atter founded Baghdad, from where the caliph ruled a vast empire and presided over a thriving culture in the 8th and 9th centuries. Mongol and Turkish conquests led to a decline in population, the economy, cultural life, and the irrigation system.

Britain secured a League of Nations mandate over Iraq after World War I. Independence under a king came in 1932. A leftist, an-Arab revolution established a republic in 1958, which oriented foreign policy toward the USSR. Most industry has been nationalized, and large land holdings broken up.

A local faction of the international Baath Arab Socialist party as ruled by decree since 1968. Russia and Iraq signed an aid act in 1972, and arms were sent along with several thousand dvisers. The 1978 execution of 21 Communists and a shift of ade to the West signalled a more neutral policy. In the 1973 rael-Arab war Iraq sent forces to aid Syria (some units had ought Israel in 1948), but disputes with Syria persisted over haring of river waters and other issues. Iraq has supported various terrorist groups within the Palestine Liberation Org. A war of assassination between Iraq and the PLO leadership raged in 978.

Several years of border clashes with Iran over navigation ghts were ended in a 1975 pact conceding Iranian claims. U.S. ade and diplomatic contracts increased in the 1970s, despite uspension of diplomatic relations in 1967.

Years of battling with the Kurdish minority resulted in total deat for the Kurds in 1975, when Iran withdrew support. Egyptian .rab immigrants have been settled in Kurdistan, and Iraq was ccused in 1977 of using executions and deportations to Arabize urdistan.

# Ireland
## Irish Republic

**People: Population** (1977 est.): 3,200,000. **Pop. density:** 20.30 per sq. mi. **Urban** (1971): 52.2%. **Ethnic groups:** Irish, nglo-Irish minority. **Languages:** English predominates, Irish 3aelic) spoken by minority. **Religions:** Roman Catholics 94%, piscopalians 5%.

**Geography: Area:** 26,600 sq. mi. **Location:** In the Atlantic O. st W of Great Britain. **Neighbors:** United Kingdom (Northern eland). **Topography:** Ireland consists of a central plateau surounded by isolated groups of hills and mountains. The coastline s heavily indented by the Atlantic O. **Capital:** Dublin. **Cities** 971 cen.): Dublin (met.) 650,153; Cork (met.) 125,283.

**Government: Head of State:** Pres. Patrick J. Hillery; b. May , 1923; in office: Dec. 3, 1976. **Head of government:** Prime lin. John Lynch; b. Aug. 15, 1917; in office: July 5, 1977. **Local** **ivisions:** 26 counties. **Armed forces:** regulars 14,650; reerves 18,665.

**Economy: Industries:** Tobacco, food processing, auto asembly, metals, textiles, chemicals, brewing, electrical and nonlectrical machinery, tourism. **Chief crops:** Potatoes, grain, ugar beets, fruits, vegetables. **Minerals:** Zinc, lead, silver, gas. **er capita arable land:** 0.9 acres. **Meat production** (1976): eef: 315,000 tons; pork: 120,000 tons; lamb: 39,000 tons. **Fish** atch (1975): 89,900 metric tons. **Electricity production** 1977): 9.31 bln. kwh. **Labor force:** 25% agric.; 20% manuf.

**Finance: Currency:** Pound (May 1978: 1 = $1.82 US). **Gross domestic product** (1977): $10.23 bln. **Per capita income** (1975): $2,378. **Imports** (1977): $5.38 bln.; partners (1975): U.K. 44.9%, U.S. 7.1%, W. Ger. 6.5%, Fr. 5.0%. **Exports** (1977): $4.40 bln.; partners (1975): U.K. 43%, W. Ger. 7.6%, Neth. 5.9%, Fr. 4.3%. **Tourists** (1975): 1,688,000; receipts (1975): $216 million. **Balance of payments** (1976): +$502,000,000. **National budget** (1977): $3.40 bln. revenues; $4.46 bln. expenditures. **International reserves** (May 1978): $2.13 bln. **Consumer prices** (change in 1977): 13.6%.

**Transport: Railway traffic** (1975): 432.84 mln. passengermiles; 294.35 mln. net ton-miles. **Motor vehicles:** in use (1975): 515,600 passenger cars, 57,600 commercial vehicles; assembled (1977): 49,932 passenger cars; 2,508 commercial vehicles. **Civil aviation:** 946 mln. passenger-miles (1976): 48,252 freight ton-miles. (1976). **Chief ports:** Dublin, Cork.

**Communications: Television sets:** 550,000 licensed (1974), 106,000 manufactured (1973). **Radios:** 886,000 licensed (1974), 72,000 manufactured (1973). **Telephones in use** (1977): 93,678. **Daily newspaper circulation** (1974): 729,000; 236 per 1,000 pop.

**Health: Life expectancy at birth** (1967): 68.58 male; 72.85 female. **Births** (per 1,000 pop. 1975): 21.6. **Deaths** (per 1,000 pop. 1975): 10.7. **Natural increase** (1975): 1.09%. **Pop. per hospital bed** (1975): 87. **Pop. per physician** (1975): 836. **Infant mortality** (per 1,000 live births 1974): 17.1.

**Education: Literacy** (1975): 99%. **Pop. 5-19:** in school (1975): 76%, per teacher (1975): 34.

Celtic tribes invaded the islands about the 4th century B.C.; their Gaelic culture and literature flourished and spread to Scotland and elsewhere in the 5th century A.D., the same century in which St. Patrick converted the Irish to Christianity. Invasions by Norsemen began in the 8th century, but were ended with defeat of the Danes by the Irish King Brian Boru in 1014. English invasions started in the 12th century; for over 700 years the Anglo-Irish struggle continued with bitter rebellions and savage repressions.

The Easter Monday Rebellion (1916) failed but was followed by guerrilla warfare and harsh reprisals by British troops, the "Black and Tans." The Dail Eireann, or Irish parliament, reaffirmed independence in Jan. 1919. The British offered dominion status to Ulster (6 counties) and southern Ireland (26 counties) Dec. 1921. The constitution of the Irish Free State, a British dominion, was adopted Dec. 11, 1922. Northern Ireland remained part of the United Kingdom.

A new constitution adopted by plebiscite came into operation Dec. 29, 1937. It declared the name of the state Eire in the Irish language and Ireland in the English and declared it a sovereign democratic state.

On Dec. 21, 1948, an Irish law declared the country a republic rather than a dominion and withdrew it from the Commonwealth. In 1949 the British Parliament recognized both actions, but reasserted its claim to incorporate the 6 northeastern counties in the United Kingdom. This claim has not been recognized by Ireland. *See United Kingdom — Northern Ireland.*

First president was William T. Cosgrave, 1922-32. Eamon de Valera, hero of the rebellion, was president 1932-38, 1959-66, 1966-73. He was prime minister 1937-48, 1951-54, 1957-59. He died in 1975.

Following Feb. 28, 1973, elections the Fianna Fail party was ousted from power after 16 years, but it returned to power in 1977 elections.

Irish governments have favored peaceful unification of all Ireland. Ireland cooperated with England against terrorist groups.

Emigration had been high and for years the population remained static. Since 1961, however, emigration has decreased and steady population growth has resumed. Industrialization increased after 1962, with over 750 new factories, many with foreign participation. Common Market membership has aided the economy since 1972. A mining boom has followed the discovery of zinc, lead, and silver deposits.

Although over 90% of the people profess Roman Catholicism, voters in 1972 repealed a constitutional provision giving the Church a "special position." The Irish language is a required study, but English is the native tongue of most.

# Israel
## State of Israel

**People: Population** (1977 est.): 3,610,000. **Age distrib. (%):** 0–14: 32.9; 15–59: 55.8; 60+: 11.4. **Pop. density:** 450.29 per sq. mi. **Urban** (1974): 81.9%. **Ethnic groups:** Jews (half Ashkenazi, half Sephardi), Arabs, Druzes. **Languages:** Hebrew and Arabic (official), Yiddish, various European and West Asian languages. **Religions:** Jews 85%, Moslems 11%, Christians 2.5%, Druzes 1.2%.

**Geography: Area:** 8,017 sq. mi. (the size of Massachusetts), within 1949 armistice lines, over 30,000 sq. mi. within 1973 cease-fire lines. **Location:** On eastern end of Mediterranean Sea. **Neighbors:** Lebanon on N, Syria, Jordan on E, Egypt on W. **Topography:** The Mediterranean coastal plain is fertile and well-watered. In the center is the Judean Plateau. A triangular-shaped semi-desert region, the Negev, extends from south of Beersheba to an apex at the head of the Gulf of Aqaba. The eastern border drops sharply into the Jordan Rift Valley, including Lake Tiberias (Sea of Galilee) and the Dead Sea, which is 1,296 ft. below sea level, lowest point on the earth's surface. **Capital:** Jerusalem. **Cities** (1975 est.): Tel Aviv-Yafo (met.) 1,180,700; Haifa (met.) 360,400; (1974 est.): Jerusalem 344,200.

**Government: Head of state:** Pres. Yitzhak Novon; b. 1921; in office: May 29, 1978; **Head of government:** Prime Min. Menachem Begin; b. July 31, 1913; in office: June 21, 1977. **Local divisions:** 6 administrative districts. **Armed forces:** regulars 287,000; reserves 460,000.

**Economy: Industries:** Diamond cutting, textiles, electronics, machinery, plastics, tires, drugs, aircraft, munitions, wine. **Chief crops:** Citrus fruit, grains, olives, fruits, grapes, figs, cotton, vegetables. **Minerals:** Limestone, gypsum, copper, iron, phosphates, magnesium, manganese, salt, sulphur, potash. **Crude oil reserves** (1978): .001 mln. bbls. **Per capita arable land:** 0.2 acres. **Meat production** (1976): beef: 22,300 tons. **Fish catch** (1975): 24,200 metric tons. **Electricity production** (1977): 11.16 bln. kwh. **Labor force:** 7% agric.; 24% manuf.

**Finance: Currency:** Pound (May 1978: 17.30 =$ 1 US). **Gross domestic product** (1977): $13.2 bln. **Per capita income** (1976): $3,355. **Imports** (1977): $4.66 bln.; partners (1974): U.S. 18%, W. Ger. 16%, U.K. 9%, Neth. 8%. **Exports** (1977): $2.96 bln.; partners (1974): U.S. 16%, U.K. 9%, Neth. 8%, W. Ger. 7%. **Tourists** (1975): 5,590,000; receipts (1975): $234 million. **Balance of payments** (1976): +$30,000,000. **National budget** (1974): $3.74 bln. revenues; $5.89 bln. expenditures. **International reserves** (Apr. 1978): $1.74 bln. **Consumer prices** (change in 1977): 34.6%.

**Transport: Railway traffic** (1974): 200.58 mln. passenger-miles; 288.14 mln. net ton-miles. **Motor vehicles** in use (1975): 284,000 passenger cars, 122,700 commercial vehicles. **Civil aviation:** 2,914 mln. passenger-miles (1977); 111,162 mln. freight ton-miles (1977). **Chief ports:** Haifa, Ashdod, Eilat.

**Communications: Television sets:** 441,000 licensed (1974), 61,000 manufactured (1975). **Radios:** 680,000 in use (1973), 11,000 manufactured (1975). **Telephones in use** (1977): 869,042. **Daily newspaper circulation** (1974): 1,330,000; 400 per 1,000 pop.

**Health: Life expectancy at birth** (1975): 70.3 male; 73.9 female. **Births** (per 1,000 pop. 1975): 28.2. **Deaths** (per 1,000 pop. 1975): 7.3. **Natural increase** (1975): 2.09%. **Pop. per hospital bed** (1975): 180. **Pop. per physician** (1975): 364. **Infant mortality** (per 1,000 live births 1975): 22.0.

**Education: Literacy** (1975): 88%. **Pop. 5-19:** in school (1975): 63%, per teacher (1975): 18.

Occupying the SW corner of the ancient Fertile Crescent, Israel contains some of the oldest known evidence of agriculture and of primitive town life. A more advanced civilization emerged in the 3d millenium B.C. The Hebrews, a people speaking a language similar to that of the earlier inhabitants, probably arrived early in the 2d millenium B.C. Under King David and his successors (c. 1000 B.C.-597 B.C.) Judaism was developed and secured. After conquest by Babylonians, Persians, and Greeks, an independent Jewish kingdom was revived, 168 B.C., but Rome took effective control in the next century, suppressed Jewish revolts in 70 A.D. and 135 A.D., and renamed Judea Palestine, after the earlier coastal inhabitants, the Philistines.

Arab invaders conquered Palestine in 636. The Arabic language and Islam prevailed within a few centuries, but a Jewish minority always remained. The land was ruled from the 11th century as a part of larger non-Arab empires by the Seljuks, the Mamluks, and the Ottomans (with a crusader interval, 1098-1291).

After 4 centuries of Ottoman rule, during which the population declined to a low of 250,000, the land was taken in 1917 by Britain, which in the Balfour Declaration that year pledged to support a Jewish national homeland there, as foreseen by the Zion-

ists. In 1920 a British Palestine Mandate was recognized; in 192(?) the land east of the Jordan was detached.

Jewish immigration, begun in the late 19th century, swelled the 1930s with refugees from the Nazis; heavy Arab immigration from Syria and Lebanon also occurred. Arab opposition to Jewish immigration turned violent in 1920, 1921, 1929, and 193(?). The UN General Assembly voted in 1947 to partition Palestine into an Arab and a Jewish state. Britain withdrew in May 1948.

Israel was declared an independent state May 14, 1948; the Arabs rejected partition. Egypt, Jordan, Syria, Lebanon, Iraq and Saudi Arabia invaded, but failed to destroy the Jewish state which gained territory. Separate armistices with the Arab nations were signed in 1949; Jordan occupied the West Bank, Egypt occupied Gaza, but neither granted Palestinian autonomy. No peace settlement was obtained, and the Arab nations continued policies of economic boycott, blockade in the Suez Canal, and support of guerrillas. Several hundred thousand Arabs left the area of Jewish control; an equal number of Jews left the Arab countries for Israel 1949-53, becoming a majority of the Jewish population.

After persistent terrorist raids, Israel invaded Egypt's Sinai Oct. 29, 1956, aided briefly by British and French forces. A UN cease-fire was arranged Nov. 6.

An uneasy truce between Israel and the Arab countries, supervised by a UN Emergency Force, prevailed until May 19(?) 1967, when the UN force withdrew at the demand of Egypt's President Gamal Abdel Nasser. Egyptian forces reoccupied the Gaza Strip and closed the Gulf of Aqaba to Israeli shipping. In a full-scale 6-day war that started June 5, the Israelis took the Gaza Strip, occupied the Sinai Peninsula to the Suez Canal, and captured Old Jerusalem, Syria's Golan Heights, and Jordan's West Bank. The fighting was halted June 10 by UN-arranged cease-fire agreements. The USSR and its satellites broke relations with Israel in 1967.

In 1969-70 there were almost daily Egyptian-Israeli artillery duels, ground forays and air raids with Israeli planes penetrating deep into Egypt. Palestinian guerrilla raids and Israeli reprisal continued across the Jordanian, Syrian, and Lebanese frontiers; there were also encounters with Syrian and Jordanian forces.

It was est. in 1970 there were 10,000 or more Soviet military men in Egypt and increasing supplies of Soviet planes and anti-aircraft missiles, some of which Israel charged were manned by Russians. In July 1972 most of the Russians, then est. at 20,000, were sent home by Egypt.

Egypt and Syria attacked Israel, Oct. 6, 1973 (Yom Kippur, most solemn day on the Jewish calendar). Egypt and Syria were supplied by massive USSR military airlifts; the U.S. responded with an airlift to Israel. Israel counter-attacked, driving the Syrians back, and crossing the Suez Canal.

A cease fire took effect Oct. 24; a UN peace-keeping force went to the area. A disengagement agreement was signed Jan. 18, 1974, following negotiations by U.S. Secretary of State Henry Kissinger. Israel withdrew from the canal's W bank. A second withdrawal was completed in 1976; Israel yielded additional territory including an oil field. Some 200 unarmed American technicians were stationed to monitor the cease-fire. The U.S. agreed to provide substantial arms aid to Israel.

Israel and Syria agreed to disengage June 1; Israel completed withdrawing from its salient (from a small part of the land taken in the 1967 war) June 25. Nearly all black African nations broke relations with Israel in 1972-74, reportedly at the urging of Libya despite Israel's technical aid programs.

In the wake of the war, Golda Meir, long Israel's premier, resigned; severe inflation gripped the nation. Palestinian guerrillas staged massacres, killing scores of civilians 1974-75. Israel conducted preventive attacks in Lebanon through 1975. Israel aided Christian forces in the 1975-76 Lebanese civil war. By mid-1976 the USSR had replenished arms and equipment lost by Syria in 1973.

Israeli forces raided Entebbe, Uganda, July 3, 1976, and rescued 103 hostages seized by Arab and German terrorists.

In 1977, the conservative opposition, led by Menachem Begin, was voted into office for the first time. Egypt Pres. Sadat's visit to Jerusalem Nov. 1977 raised peace hopes, but the issue of Arab Palestinian antonomy or independence complicated negotiations.

A massive Israeli invasion of S. Lebanon, March 1978, following a Lebanon-based terrorist attack in Israel, left over 1,000 Lebanese and Palestinians dead. Israel withdrew in favor of a 6,000-man UN force, but continued to aid Christian militiamen.

Israel's economy has grown rapidly, aided by German reparaons payments, U.S. aid (mostly since 1970), international loans, nd contributions. In 1975, Israel signed agreements with the .S. to facilitate investments in Israel, and with the Common Market allowing free trade.

Since 1955 total cultivated area has more than doubled, nostly through irrigation. A pipeline was completed in 1964 to arry water from Lake Kinneret (Galilee) to the Negev desert. Desalinization plants have been built.

Israël's first atomic reactor began operations in 1960. The nation launched its first successful solid-fuel rocket in 1961, Israel as denied reports that it has assembled 10-20 atom bombs.

Non-Jewish population (1974): Moslem 392,500; Christian 4,500; Druzes and other 41,600. The last remnant of martial aw for the Arab minority was ended in 1966. Druzes are subject o the military draft; Moslems and Christians may volunteer.

# Italy

## Italian Republic

**People: Population** (1977 est.): 56,450,000. **Age distrib. %):** 0–14: 24.3; 15–59: 59.6; 60+: 16.1. **Pop. density:** 485.37 er sq. mi. **Ethnic groups:** Italians, small minorities of Germans, Slovenes, Albanians, French, Latins, Greeks. **Languages:** Italian. **Religions:** Roman Catholics 99%.

**Geography: Area:** 116,303 sq. mi., slightly larger than Arizona. **Location:** In S Europe, jutting into Mediterranean Sea. **Neighbors:** France on W, Switzerland, Austria on N, Yugoslavia in E. **Topography:** Italy occupies a long boot-shaped peninsula, extending SE from the Alps into the Mediterranean, with the islands of Sicily and Sardinia offshore. The alluvial Poe Valley drains most of N. The rest of the country is rugged and mountainous, except for intermittent coastal plains, like the Campajna, 5 of Rome. Appenine Mts. run down through center of peninsula. **Capital:** Rome. **Cities** (1975 est.): Rome 2,868,248; Milan ,731,281; Naples 1,223,785; Turin 1,202,215; Genoa 805,855; Palermo 662,567; Bologna 491,330; Florence 465,823; Catania 498,642; Venice 365,208.

**Government: Head of state:** Pres. Sandro Pertini; b. Sept. *5, 1896; in office: July 8, 1978; **Head of government:** Prime Min. Giulio Andreotti; b. Jan. 14, 1919; in office: Mar. 16, 1978. Local divisions: 20 regions with some autonomy, 94 provinces. **Armed forces:** regulars 541,000; reserves 694,800.

**Economy: Industries:** Steel, machinery, autos, textiles, shoes, machine tools, chemicals, oil products, typewriters. **Chief crops:** Grapes, olives, citrus fruits, vegetables, wheat, rice. **Minerals:** Gas, marble, sulphur, mercury, coal. **Crude oil reserves** 1978): 600 mln. bbls. **Per capita arable land:** 0.4 acres. **Meat production** (1976): beef: 985,700 tons; pork: 781,000 tons; amb: 47,500 tons. **Fish catch** (1975): 405,700 metric tons. **Electricity production** (1977): 166.57 bln. kwh. **Labor force:** I 5% agric.; 31% manuf.

**Finance: Currency:** Lire (May 1978: 866.50 = 1 US). Gross domestic product (1976): $162.43 bln. **Per capita income** (1975): $2,758. **Imports** (1976): $43.43 bln.; partners 1975): W. Ger. 16%, Fr. 12%, U.S. 8%, Neth. 4%. **Exports** 1976): $36.97 bln.; partners (1975): W. Ger. 18%, Fr. 14%, U.S. 4.5%, U.K. 4.5%. **Tourists** (1975): 13,234,400; receipts (1975): $3.258 billion. **Balance of payments** (1976): −$317,000,000. **National budget** (1977): $49.45 bln. revenues; $63.39 bln. expenditures. **International reserves** (May 1978): $12.24 bln. **Consumer prices** (change in 1977): 6.4%.

**Transport: Railway traffic** (1975): 22.37 bln. passengermiles; 9.03 bln. net ton-miles. **Motor vehicles:** in use (1974): 14,295,000 passenger cars, 1,549,000 commercial vehicles; manufactured (1977): 1,452,000 passenger cars; 144,000 commercial vehicles. **Civil aviation:** 6,692 mln. passenger-miles 1976); 302,507 mln. freight ton-miles (1976). **Chief ports:** Genoa, Venice, Trieste, Taranto, Naples, La Spezia.

**Communications: Television sets:** 11,817,000 licensed (1974), 2,330,000 manufactured (1975). **Radios:** 12,641,000 licensed (1974), 1,800,000 manufactured (1974). **Telephones in use** (1977): 5,240,527. **Daily newspaper circulation** (1974): 6,963,000; 126 per 1,000 pop.

**Health: Life expectancy at birth** (1972): 68.97 male; 74.88 female. **Births** (per 1,000 pop. 1975): 14.8. **Deaths** (per 1,000 pop. 1975): 9.9. **Natural increase** (1975): .49%. **Pop. per hospital bed** (1975): 94. **Pop. per physician** (1975): 529. **Infant mortality** (per 1,000 live births 1974): 22.6.

**Education: Literacy** (1975): 94%. **Pop. 5-19:** in school (1975): 63%, per teacher (1975): 28.

Rome emerged as the major power in Italy after 500 B.C., dominating the more civilized Etruscans to the N and Greeks to the S. Under the Empire, which lasted until the 5th century A.D., Rome ruled most of Western Europe, the Balkans, the Near East, and North Africa.

After the Germanic invasions, lasting several centuries, a high civilization arose in the city-states of the N, culminating in the Renaissance. But German, French, Spanish, and Austrian intervention prevented the unification of the country. In 1859 Lombardy came under the crown of King Victor Emmanuel II of Sardinia. By plebiscite in 1860, Parma, Modena, Romagna, and Tuscany joined, followed by Sicily and Naples, and by the Marches and Umbria. The first Italian parliament declared Victor Emmanuel king of Italy Mar. 17, 1861. Mantua and Venetia were added in 1866 as an outcome of the Austro-Prussian war. The Papal States were taken by Italian troops Sept. 20, 1870, on the withdrawal of the French garrison. The states were annexed to the kingdom by plebiscite. Italy recognized the State of Vatican City as independent Feb. 11, 1929.

Fascism appeared in Italy Mar. 23, 1919, led by Benito Mussolini, who took over the government at the invitation of the king Oct. 28, 1922. Mussolini acquired dictatorial powers. He made war on Ethiopia and proclaimed Victor Emmanual III emperor, defied the sanctions of the League of Nations, joined the Berlin-Tokyo axis, sent troops to fight for Franco against the Republic of Spain and joined Germany in World War II.

After Fascism was overthrown in 1943, Italy declared war on Germany and Japan and contributed to the Allied victory. It surrendered conquered lands and lost its colonies. Mussolini was killed by partisans Apr. 28, 1945.

Victor Emmanuel III abdicated May 9, 1946; his son Humbert II was king until June 10, when Italy became a republic after a referendum, June 2-3.

Reorganization of the Fascist party is forbidden. The cabinet normally represents a coalition of the Christian Democrats, largest of Italy's many parties, and one or 2 other parties. After June 1976 elections, the Communists were given several important parliamentary posts, and entered into a formal cooperation with the Christian Democrats and other parties in parliament, without entering the government. They also controlled many local and regional governments, alone or in coalition with the Socialists.

The Vatican agreed in 1976 to revise its 1929 concordat with the state, depriving Roman Catholicism of its status as state religion. In 1974 Italians voted by a 3-to-2 margin to retain a 3-year-old law permitting divorce, which was opposed by the church.

Italy has enjoyed an extraordinary growth in industry and living standards since World War II, in part due to membership in the Common Market. But in 1973-74, a fourfold increase in international oil prices helped disrupt the economy. Taxes were boosted in 1974. Western aid helped ease the crisis in 1975, but inflation and decline in confidence continued through 1977. Trade unions agreed to some austerity measures. A wave of left-wing political violence worsened in 1977 with kidnappings and assassinations. Christian Dem. leader and former Prime Min. Moro was murdered May 1978 by Red Brigade terrorists.

**Sicily,** 9,927 sq. mi., pop. (1971) 4,680,715, is an island 180 by 120 mi., seat of a region that embraces the island of **Pantelleria,** 32 sq. mi., and the **Lipari** group, 44 sq. mi., pop. 14,000, including 2 active volcanoes. **Vulcano,** 1,637 ft. and **Stromboli,** 3,038 ft. From prehistoric times Sicily has been settled by various peoples; a Greek state had its capital at Syracuse. Rome took Sicily from Carthage 215 B.C. **Mt. Etna,** 10,705 ft. active volcano, is tallest peak.

**Sardinia,** 9,283 sq. mi., pop. (1971) 1,473,800, lies in the Mediterranean, 115 mi. W of Italy and 7-1/2 mi. S of Corsica. It is 160 mi. long, 68 mi. wide, and mountainous, with mining of coal, zinc, lead, copper. In 1720 Sardinia was added to the possessions of the Dukes of Savoy in Piedmont and Savoy to form the Kingdom of Sardinia. Giuseppe Garibaldi is buried on the nearby isle of Caprera. **Elba,** 87 sq. mi., pop. 30,000, lies 6 mi. west of Tuscany. Napoleon I lived in exile on Elba 1814-1815.

**Trieste,** An agreement was signed Oct. 5, 1954, by Italy and Yugoslavia which gave Italy provisional administration over the northern section and the seaport of Trieste, and Yugoslavia the part of Istrian peninsula it has occupied. A formal agreement signed Nov. 10, 1975, confirmed this division as permanent.

# Ivory Coast

## Republic of Ivory Coast

**People: Population** (1977 est.): 5,150,000. **Pop. density:** 41.36 per sq. mi. **Ethnic groups:** Baule 23%, Bete 18%, Senufo 15%, Malinke 11%, others. **Languages:** French (official), tribal languages. **Religions:** Moslems 25%, Christians 12%.

**Geography: Area:** 124,503 sq. mi., slightly larger than New Mexico. **Location:** On S. coast of W. Africa. **Neighbors:** Liberia, Guinea on W, Mali, Upper Volta on N, Ghana on E. **Topography:** Forests cover the W half of the country, and range from a coastal strip to halfway to the N on the E. A sparse inland plain leads to low mountains in NW. **Capital:** Abidjan. **Cities** (1974 est.): Abidjan (met.) 800,000; Bouaké (met.) 200,000.

**Government: Head of state:** Pres. Felix Houphouet-Boigny; b. Oct. 18, 1905; in office: Nov. 27, 1960. **Local divisions:** 24 departments. **Armed forces:** regulars 4,950; para-military 3,000.

**Economy: Chief crops:** Coffee, cocoa, bananas, cotton, pineapples, rice, oil palms. **Minerals:** Diamonds, manganese. **Other resources:** Tropical woods, rubber. **Fish catch** (1975): 63,500 metric tons. **Electricity production** (1976): 960.00 mln. kwh. **Labor force:** 81% agriculture.

**Finance: Currency:** Franc (May 1978: 230.35 = $1 US). **Gross domestic product** (1977): $6.32 bln. **Per capita income** (1974): $600. **Imports** (1976): $1.30 bln.; partners (1974): Fr. 39%, U.S. 7%, W. Ger. 6%, Iraq 6%. **Exports** (1976): $1.62 bln.; partners (1974): Fr. 26%, Neth. 15%, It. 9%, W. Ger. 9%. **Tourists** (1975): 108,900; receipts (1974): $23 million. **Balance of payments** (1976): −$33,000,000. **International reserves** (Mar. 1978): $476.4 mln. **Consumer prices** (changed in 1977): 27.5%.

**Transport: Railway traffic** (1974): 570.09 mln. passenger-miles; 328.51 mln. net ton-miles. **Motor vehicles:** in use (1972): 90,500 passenger cars, 57,400 commercial vehicles. **Chief ports:** Abidjan, Sassandra.

**Communications: Television sets:** 40,000 in use (1973). **Radios:** 70,000 in use (1970), 90,000 manufactured (1974). **Telephones in use** (1977): 58,796. **Daily newspaper circulation** (1973): 44,000; 10 per 1,000 pop.

**Health: Life expectancy at birth** (1975): 41.9 male; 45.1 female. **Births** (annual per 1,000 pop. 1972-75): 45.6. **Deaths** (annual per 1,000 pop. 1972-75): 20.6. **Natural increase** (annual 1970-75): 2.50%. **Pop. per hospital bed** (1975): 488. **Pop. per physician** (1975): 13,943. **Infant mortality** (per 1,000 live births 1957-58): 138.

**Education: Literacy** (1975): 20%. **Pop. 5-19:** in school (1975): 42%, per teacher (1975): 91.

A French protectorate from 1842, Ivory Coast became independent in 1960. It is the most prosperous of tropical African nations, due to diversification of agriculture for export, close ties to France (60,000 French people are present) and encouragement of foreign investment. About 20% of the population are workers from neighboring countries. Ivory Coast is a leader of the pro-Western bloc in Africa.

# Jamaica

**People: Population** (1977 est.): 2,090,000. **Age distrib.** (%): 0–14: 45.9; 15–59: 45.7; 60+: 8.4. **Pop. density:** 473.82 per sq. mi. **Urban** (1970): 37.1%. **Ethnic groups:** Negroes 85%, mixed 10%, Chinese, Caucasians, East Indians. **Languages:** English, Jamaican creole. **Religions:** Protestants 75%, Roman Catholics, 5%.

**Geography: Area:** 4,411 sq. mi., slightly smaller than Connecticut. **Location:** In West Indies. **Neighbors:** Nearest are Cuba on N, Haiti on E. **Topography:** The country is four-fifths covered by mountains. **Capital:** Kingston. **Cities** (1970 cen.): Kingston (met.) 475,548.

**Government: Head of state:** Queen Elizabeth II, represented by Gov.-Gen. Florizel A. Glasspole; **Head of government:** Prime Min. Michael Manley; b. Dec. 10, 1924; in office: Mar. 2, 1972. **Local divisions:** 12 parishes, Kingston and St. Andrew.

**Economy: Industries:** Aluminum, rum, molasses, cigars, oil products, tourism. **Chief crops:** Sugar cane, coffee, bananas, coconuts, ginger, cocoa, pimento, fruits. **Minerals:** Bauxite, marble, silica, gypsum. **Per capita arable land:** 0.3 acres. **Meat production** (1975): beef: 12,000 tons. **Fish catch** (1975): 10,100 metric tons. **Electricity production** (1976): 1.40 bln.

kwh. **Labor force:** 27% agriculture.

**Finance: Currency:** Dollar (May 1978: 1.05 = $1 US). **Gross domestic product** (1976): $3.04 bln. **Per capita income** (1976): $1,296. **Imports** (1976): $913 mln.; partners (197 U.S. 37%, Venez. 13.7%, U.K. 13.1%, Can. 4.8%, Jap. 3.7 **Exports** (1976): $633 mln.; partners (1975): U.S. 39%, U 23%, Nor. 11%, USSR 3.1%, Can. 2.9%. **Tourists** (1975 395,800; receipts (1975): $133 million. **Balance of paymen** (1977): −$21,600,000. **National budget** (1976): $677.93 ml revenues; $1.11 bln. expenditures. **International reserves** (Ma 1978): $79.1 mln. **Consumer prices** (change in 1977): 5.4%.

**Transport: Railway traffic** (1973): 39.74 mln. passenge miles; 96.88 mln. net ton-miles. **Motor vehicles:** in use (197: 86,400 passenger cars, 21,900 commercial vehicles. **Ch** ports: Kingston, Montego Bay.

**Communications: Television sets:** 97,000 in use (197 6,000 manufactured (1975). **Radios:** 633,000 in use (197: 7,000 manufactured (1975). **Telephones in use** (197 108,500. **Daily newspaper circulation** (1974): 180,000; 90 p 1,000 pop.

**Health: Life expectancy at birth** (1961): 62.65 male; 66.6 female. **Births** (per 1,000 pop. 1975): 30.3. **Deaths** (per 1,0( pop. 1975): 6.9. **Natural increase** (1975): 2.34%. **Pop. pe hospital bed** (1975): 257. **Pop. per physician** (1975): 3,63( **Infant mortality** (per 1,000 live births 1974): 26.3.

**Education: Literacy** (1975): 86%. **Pop. 5-19:** in scho (1975): 68%, per teacher (1975): 50.

Jamaica was visited by Columbus, 1494, and ruled by Spa (under whom Arawak Indians died out) until seized by Britai 1655, Jamaica won independence Aug. 6, 1962.

In 1974 Jamaica sought an increase in taxes paid by U.S. ar Canadian companies which mine bauxite on the island. The s cialist government acquired 50% ownership of the companie Jamaican interests in 1976, and was reelected that year. Ruc mentary welfare state measures have been passed, but unen ployment has increased. Political violence flared 1975-76. U.S relations improved in 1977.

# Japan

**People: Population** (1977 est.): 113,860,000. **Age distrib** (%): 0–14: 24.3; 15–59: 64.4; 60+: 11.3. **Pop. density:** 793.04 per sq. mi. **Urban** (1975): 75.9%. **Ethnic groups:** Japanese 99.4%, Korean 0.5%. **Religions:** Buddhism, Shintoism sharec by large majority, Christians 0.8%.

**Geography: Area:** 143,574 sq. mi., slightly smaller than Montana. **Location:** Archipelago off E. coast of Asia. **Neighbors** nearest are USSR on N, S. Korea on W. **Topography:** Japar consists of four main islands: Honshu ("mainland"), 88,952 sq mi.; Hokkaido, 30,304; Kyushu, 16,191; and Shikoku, 7,240. The coast is deeply indented, measuring 16,654 mi. The northern islands are a continuation of the Sakhalin Mts. The Kunlun range of China continues into southern islands, the ranges meeting in the Japanese Alps. In a vast transverse fissure crossing Honshu E-W rises a group of volcanoes, mostly extinct or inactive, including 12,388 ft. Fuji-San (Fujiyama) near Tokyo. **Capital:** Tokyo. **Cities** (1975 cen.): Tokyo 11,622,651; Osaka 2,780,000; Yokohama 2,620,000; Nagoya 2,080,000; Kyoto 1,460,000 Kobe 1,360,000; Sapporo 1,240,000; Kitakyushu 1,060,000; Kawasaki 1,020,000; Fukuoka 1,000,000; Hiroshima 761,240; Sakai 716,498; Chiba 613,787.

**Government: Head of state:** Emp. Hirohito; b. Apr. 29, 1901 in office: Dec. 25, 1926; **Head of government:** Prim Min. Takec Fukuda; b. Jan. 14, 1905; in office: Dec. 23, 1976. **Local divisions:** 46 prefectures, 1 territory. **Armed forces:** Regulars 238,000; reserves 45,000.

**Economy: Industries:** Steel, vehicles, machinery, ships, electronics, precision instruments, chemicals, textiles, ceramics, wood products. **Chief crops:** Rice, grains, potatoes, tobacco tea, beans, fruits. **Minerals:** Some gold, silver, copper, lead zinc, chromite, coal, sulphur, salt, oil, but most minerals are imported. **Crude oil reserves** (1978): .063 mln. bbls. **Per capita arable land:** 0.1 acres. **Meat production** (1975): beef: 297,900 tons; pork: 1.06 mln. tons. **Fish catch** (1975): 10,508,500 metric tons. **Electricity production** (1976): 511.78 bln. kwh. **Labor force:** 19% agric.; 26% manuf.

**Finance: Currency:** Yen (May 1978: 223.40 = $1 US). **Gross domestic product** (1976): $562.17 bln. **Per capita income** (1976): $ 4,478. **Imports** (1977): $70.66 bln.; partners

975): U.S. 20%, Austral. 7.1%, Can. 4.3%, P.R. China 2.6%. **xports** (1977): $80.47 bln.; partners (1975): U.S. 19.9%, P.R. **hina** 4%, Austral. 3.1%. **Tourists** (1975): 707,800; receipts (1975): $253 million. **Balance of payments** (1977): -$6,519,000,000. **National budget** (1977): $47.16 bln. reve- **ues**; $94.75 bln. expenditures. **International reserves** (May 978): $28.12 bln. **Consumer prices** (change in 1977): 8.1%.

**Transport: Railway traffic** (1975): 200.70 bln. passenger- **iles**; 29.43 bln. net ton-miles. **Motor vehicles:** in use (1975): 7,236,000 passenger cars, 10,315,000 commercial vehicles; **anufactured** (1977): 5,424,000 passenger cars; 3,072,000 **ommercial** vehicles. **Civil aviation:** 14,166 mln. passenger- **iles** (1977); 699,639 mln. freight ton-miles (1977). **Chief ports:** **okohama**, Tokyo, Kobe, Osaka, Nagoya, Chiba, Kawasaki, Ha- **odate.**

**Communications: Television sets:** 25,564,000 in use 974), 12,453,000 manufactured (1975). **Radios:** 70,794,000 in **se** (1973), 14,283,000 manufactured (1975). **Telephones in se** (1977): 48,431,414. **Daily newspaper circulation** (1975): 7,820,000; 526 per 1,000 pop.

**Health: Life expectancy at birth** (1974): 71.16 male; 76.31 **emale. Births** (per 1,000 pop. 1975): 17.2. **Deaths** (per 1,000 **op.** 1975): 6.4. **Natural increase** (1975): 1.08%. **Pop. per ospital bed** (1975): 96. **Pop. per physician** (1975): 867. **In- ant mortality** (per 1,000 live births 1975): 10.00.

**Education: Literacy** (1975): 99%. **Pop. 5–19:** in school 1975): 70%, per teacher (1975): 38.

According to Japanese legend, the empire was founded by **mperor** Jimmu, 660 B.C., but earliest records of a unified Ja- **an** date from 1,000 years later. Chinese influence was strong in **ne** formation of Japanese civilization. Buddhism was introduced **efore** the 6th century.

A feudal system, with locally powerful noble families and their **amurai** warrior retainers, dominated Japan from 1192. Central **ower** was held by successive families of shoguns (military dic- **ators**), 1192-1867, until recovered by the Emperor Meiji in 1868. **he** Portuguese and Dutch had minor trade with Japan in the **6th** and 17th centuries. U.S. Commodore Matthew C. Perry **pened** it to U.S. trade in a treaty ratified 1854, Japan fought **hina**, 1894-95, gaining Taiwan. After war with Russia, 1904-05, **ussia** ceded S half of Sakhalin and gave concessions in China. **apan** annexed Korea 1910. In World War I Japan ousted Ger- **any** from Shantung, took over German Pacific islands. Japan **ook** Manchuria 1931, started war with China 1932. Japan **aunched** war against the U.S. by attack on Pearl Harbor Dec. 7, **941.** Japan surrendered Aug. 14, 1945.

In a new constitution adopted May 3, 1947, Japan renounced **ne** right to wage war; the emperor gave up claims to divinity; the **iet** became the sole law-making authority.

The U.S. and 48 other non-communist nations signed a peace **eaty** and the U.S. a bilateral defense agreement with Japan, in **an** Francisco Sept. 8, 1951, restoring Japan's sovereignty as of **pril** 28, 1952. Japan signed separate treaties with Nationlist **hina**, 1952; India, 1952; a declaration with USSR ending a **echnical** state of war, 1956. In Dec. 1965 Japan and South Ko- **ea** agreed to resume diplomatic relations.

On June 26, 1968, the U.S. returned to Japanese control the **onin** Islands, the Volcano Islands (including Iwo Jima) and Mar- **us** Island. On May 15, 1972, Okinawa, the other Ryukyu Islands **nd** the Daito Islands were returned to Japan by the U.S., but it **vas** agreed the U.S. would continue to maintain large military **ases** on Okinawa. Japan and the USSR have failed to resolve **isputed** claims of sovereignty over four of the Kurile Is. and **ver** offshore fishing rights.

On Sept. 29, 1972, Japan and mainland China agreed to re- **ume** diplomatic relations; Japan and Taiwan severed diplomatic **elations.** A Japan-China friendship treaty was signed 1978.

Industrialization was begun in the late 19th century. After **Vorld** War II, Japan emerged as the third most powerful econ- **my** in the world, and as a leader in technology. Huge trade sur- **luses** caused the Yen to soar in value in the late 1970s.

The Liberal Democratic (conservative) party controlled almost **very** post-war government, but by declining margins. The oppo- **ition**, composed of Socialists, the Komeito (a Buddhist party), **'ommunists**, and independents, won nearly half the seats in 976 parliamentary elections.

During 1969 the U.S. began turning over 50 military installation **ites**, a third of its facilities in Japan, to the Japanese. By 1977, **.S.** forces had been reduced to 46,000 men and women.

# Jordan

## Hashemite Kingdom of Jordan

**People: Population** (1976 est.): 2,780,000. **Age distrib.** (%): 0–14: 47.5; 15–59: 47.5; 60+: 5.0. **Pop. density:** 74.54 per sq. mi. **Urban** (1974): 42.0%. **Ethnic groups:** Arabs, small minori- ties of Circassians, Armenians, Kurds. **Languages:** Arabic is uni- versal. **Religions:** Sunni Moslems 93.6%, Christians 6.4%.

**Geography: Area:** 37,297 sq. mi., slightly larger than Indiana. **Location:** In W Asia. **Neighbors:** Israel on W, Saudi Arabia on S, Iraq on E, Syria on N. **Topography:** About 88% of Jordan is arid. Fertile areas are in W. Only port is on short Aqaba Gulf coast. Country Shares Dead Sea (1,296 ft. below sea level) with Israel. **Capital:** Amman. **Cities** (1975 est.): Amman 634,000; Zarka 238,000; Irbid 125,000.

**Government: Head of state:** King Hussein I; b. Nov. 14, 1935; in office: May 2, 1952; **Head of government:** Prime Min. Mudhar Badran; in office: July 13, 1976. **Local divisions:** 8 gov- ernorates. **Armed forces:** regulars 67,810; reserves 30,000.

**Economy: Industries:** Textiles, plastics, cement, food pro- cessing. **Chief crops:** Grains, olives, vegetables, fruits. **Miner- als:** Potash, phosphates. **Electricity production** (1975): 443,000 mln. kwh. **Labor force:** 39% agriculture.

**Finance: Currency:** Dinar (May 1978: 1 = $3.19 US). **Gross domestic product** (1977): $1.49 bln. **Per capita income** (1975): $419. **Imports** (1977): $1.28 bln.; partners (1974): U.S. 11%, W. Ger. 9%, U.K. 8%, Leb. 5%. **Exports** (1977): $249 bln.; partners (1974): Fr. 26%, Neth. 15%, It. 9%, W. Ger. 9%. **Tourists** (1975): 707,600; receipts (1975): $101 million. **Bal- ance of payments** (1977): +$190,900,000. **National budget** (1977): $461.68 mln. revenues; $971.27 mln. expenditures. **In- ternational reserves** (May 1978): $787.5 mln. **Consumer prices** (change in 1977): 31.1%.

**Transport: Motor vehicles:** in use (1975): 33,100 passenger cars, 9,100 commercial vehicles. **Civil aviation:** 702 mln. pass- enger-miles (1977); 699,639 mln. freight ton-miles (1977). **Chief ports:** Aqaba.

**Communications: Television sets:** 85,000 in use (1974). **Radios:** 529,000 in use (1974). **Telephones in use** (1977): 43,720. **Daily newspaper circulation** (1974): 58,000; 22 per 1,000 pop.

**Health: Life expectancy at birth** (1963): 52.6 male; 52.0 fe- male. **Births** (per 1,000 pop. 1976): 42.5. **Deaths** (per 1,000 pop. 1976): 3.8. **Natural increase** (annual 1970-75): 3.29%. **Pop. per hospital bed** (1975): 1,264. **Pop. per physician** (1975): 3,318. **Infant mortality** (per 1,000 live births 1974): 21.9.

**Education: Literacy** (1975): 32%. **Pop. 5–19:** in school (1975): 52%, per teacher (1975): 51.

From ancient times to 1922 the lands to the E of the Jordan were culturally and politically united with the lands to the W. Arabs conquered the area in the 7th century; the Ottomans took control in the 16th. Britain's 1920 Palestine Mandate covered both sides of the Jordan. In 1921, Abdullah, son of the ruler of Hejaz in Arabia, was installed by Britain as amir of an autono- mous Transjordan, covering two-thirds of Palestine. An indepen- dent kingdom was proclaimed, 1946.

During the 1948 Arab-Israeli war the West Bank and old city of Jerusalem were added to the kingdom, which changed its name to Jordan. All these territories were lost to Israel in the 1967 war, which swelled the number of Arab refugees on the East Bank. A 1974 Arab summit conference designated the Pal- estine Liberation Organization as the sole representative of Arabs on the West Bank. Jordan accepted the move, and was granted an annual subsidy by Arab oil states. The U.S. has also provided substantial economic and military support.

In 1970 and 1971, Jordan dispersed all PLO commandos, who had raided Israel from bases in Jordan, 1968-70, and who threatened to seize power in Jordan, which they considered part of Palestine.

# Kampuchea

## Democratic Kampuchea

**People: Population** (1977 est.): 8,610,000. **Pop. density:** 123.18 per sq. mi. **Ethnic groups:** Khmers 90%, Vietnamese 4%, Chinese 3%. **Languages:** Cambodian (Khmer), French. **Religions:** Buddhism prevails.

**Geography: Area:** 69,898 sq. mi., the size of Missouri. **Loca-**

tion: In Indochina Peninsula. **Neighbors:** Thailand on W, N, Laos on NE, Vietnam on E. **Topography:** The central area, formed by the Mekong River basin and Tonle Sap lake, is level. Hills and mountains are in SE, a long escarpment separates the country from Thailand on NW. Three-fourths of the area is forested. **Capital:** Phnom Penh. **Cities** (1971 est.): Phnom Penh 393,995.

**Government: Head of state:** Pres. Khieu Samphan; in office: Apr. 14, 1976. **Head of government:** Prime Min. Pol Pot. in office: Apr. 1976. **Local divisions:** 5 regions and a special capital region. **Armed forces:** regulars 90,000.

**Economy: Industries:** Textiles, paper, plywood, oil products. **Chief crops:** Rice, corn, pepper, tobacco, cotton, oil seeds, beans, palm sugar. **Minerals:** Iron, copper, manganese, gold. **Other resources:** Forests, rubber, kapok. **Per capita arable land:** 0.5 acres. **Meat production** (1975): beef: 23,000 tons; pork: 31,000 tons. **Fish catch** (1975): 84,700 metric tons. **Electricity production** (1975): 150.00 mln. kwh.

**Finance: Currency:** Riel (1972: 120.05 = $1 US). **Per capita income** (1974): $100. **Imports** (1977): $185 mln. **Exports** (1972): $10 mln. **Tourists** (1973): 16,500; receipts (1973); $2 million.

**Transport: Railway traffic** (1973): 33.53 mln. passengermiles; 6.21 mln. net ton-miles. **Motor vehicles:** in use (1972): 27,200 passenger cars, 11,100 commercial vehicles. **Chief ports:** Kompong Som.

**Communications: Television sets:** 26,000 in use (1974). **Radios:** 112,000 in use (1974). **Telephones in use** (1977): 71,000. **Daily newspaper circulation** (1974): 17,000; 49 per 1,000 pop.

**Health: Life expectancy at birth** (1975): 44.0 male; 46.9 female. **Births** (annual per 1,000 pop. 1972-75): 46.7. **Deaths** (annual per 1,000 pop. 1972-75): 19.0. **Natural increase** (annual 1970-75): 2.77%. **Pop. per hospital bed** (1975): 1,057. **Pop. per physician** (1975): 16,920. **Infant mortality** (per 1,000 live births 1973): 127.

**Education: Literacy** (1975): 50%. **Pop. 5-19:** in school (1975): 40%, per teacher (1975): 124.

Early kingdoms dating from that of Funan in the 1st century A.D. (heavily influenced by Indian culture), culminated in the great Khmer empire which flourished from the 9th century to the 13th, encompassing present-day Thailand, Cambodia, Laos, and southern Vietnam. The peripheral areas were lost to invading Siamese and Vietnamese, and France established a protectorate in 1863. Independence came in 1953.

Prince Norodom Sihanouk, king 1941-1955 and head of state from 1960, tried to maintain neutrality. Relations with the U.S. were broken in 1965, after South Vietnam planes attacked Vietcong forces within Cambodia. Relations were restored in 1969, after Sihanouk charged Viet communists with arming Cambodian insurgents.

U.S. bombing raids on North Viet forces, 1969-70, were not revealed until 1973. In 1970, pro-U.S. premier Lon Nol seized power, demanding removal of 40,000 North Viet troops. The monarchy was abolished and the country's name changed to Khmer Republic. Sihanouk formed a government-in-exile in Peking, and open war began between the government and Khmer Rouge. The U.S. provided heavy military and economic aid. U.S. troops fought Vietcong forces within Cambodia for two months in 1970.

Khmer Rouge forces captured Phnom Penh April 17, 1975. Over 100,000 people had died in five years of fighting. The new government evacuated all cities and towns, and shuffled the rural population, sending virtually the entire population to clear jungle, forest, and scrub, which covered half the country.

The government guarded its international isolation, but repeated reports from refugees in Thailand and Vietnam indicated that over one million people were killed in executions and enforced hardships that continued unabated through 1978. Total enslavement of the populaton and bloody purges within the Communist leadership were also reported.

Relations with Thailand have been strained. China provides some assistance. Severe border fighting broke out with Vietnam in 1978.

# Kenya
## Republic of Kenya

**People: Population** (1977 est.): 14,340,000. **Age distrib.** (%): 0–14: 48.4; 15–59: 46.3; 60 +: 5.4. **Pop. density:** 63.74 per sq. mi. **Urban** (1969): 9.9%. **Ethnic groups:** Kikuyu 20%, Tuo

15%, Balhya 13%, Kamba 11%, others, including 280,0( Asians, Arabs, Europeans. **Languages:** Swahili, English bc official. **Religions:** Protestants 37%, Roman Catholics 22 Moslems 3%, others.

**Geography: Area:** 224,960 sq. mi., slightly smaller th Texas. **Location:** On Indian O. coast of E. Africa. **Neighbo** Uganda on W, Tanzania on S, Somalia on E, Ethopia, Sudan N. **Topography:** The northern three-fifths of Kenya is arid. M( economic production is centered in S, a low coastal area and plateau varying from 3,000 to 10,000 ft. The Great Rift Vall enters the country N-S, flanked by some high mountains. **Ca** tal: Nairobi. **Cities** (1976 est.): Nairobi (met.) 736,000; Momba (met.) 351,000.

**Government: Head of state:** Acting Pres. Daniel Arap Moi, office: Aug. 22, 1978. **Local divisions:** Nairobi and 7 province **Armed forces:** regulars 7,700; para-military 1,800.

**Economy: Industries:** Tourism, light industry. **Chief crop** Coffee, tea, cereals, cotton, sisal. **Minerals:** Gold, limestor diatomite, salt, barytes, magnesite, felspar, sapphires, fluospa garnets. **Other resources:** Timber, hides. **Per capita arab** land: 0.3 acres. **Meat production** (1975): beef: 113,000 tor lamb: 23,000 tons. **Fish catch** (1975): 27,300 metric tons. **Ele** tricity production (1976): 1.04 bln. kwh. **Labor force:** 80% a riculture.

**Finance: Currency:** Shilling (May 1978: 7.94 = $1 US **Gross domestic product** (1976): $3.43 bln. **Per capita i** come (1975): $209. **Imports** (1976): $941 mln.; partners (197! U.K. 13%, W. Ger. 8%, U.S. 7%. **Exports** (1976): $656 ml partners (1975): U.K. 13%, W. Ger: 12%, U.S. 5%, Jap. 3' **Tourists** (1975): 407,400; receipts (1975): $98 million. **Balan** of payments (1977): +$272,300,000. **National budget** (197 $737.75 mln. revenues; $866.10 mln. expenditures. **Intern** tional reserves (May 1978): $493.7 mln. **Consumer price** (change in 1977): 10.4%.

**Transport: Motor vehicles:** in use (1974): 130,900 passe ger cars, 23,800 commercial vehicles. **Chief ports:** Mombasa.

**Communications: Television sets:** 37,000 licensed (1974 **Radios:** 510,000 in use (1974). **Telephones in use** (197 131,843. **Daily newspaper circulation** (1974): 97,000; 8 p( 1,000 pop.

**Health: Life expectancy at birth** (1969): 46.9 male; 51.2 f male. **Births** (annual per 1,000 pop. 1972-75): 48.7. **Deaths** (a nual per 1,000 pop. 1972-75): 16.0. **Natural increase** (annu 1970-75): 3.27%. **Pop. per hospital bed** (1975): 777. **Pop. p( physician** (1975): 13,607. **Infant mortality** (per 1,000 live birt 1973): 51.4.

**Education: Literacy** (1975): 25%. **Pop. 5-19:** in scho (1975): 50%, per teacher (1975): 52.

Arab colonies exported spices and slaves from the Keny coast as early as the 8th century. Britain obtained control in th 19th century. Kenya won independence Dec. 12, 1963, fou years after the end of the violent Mau Mau uprising.

From 1968 on, thousands of Asians with British passport have been ordered to leave Kenya. But a sizeable minority c Asians and Europeans remain.

Kenya has shown steady growth in industry and agricultur under a modified private enterprise system, and has had a rela tively free political life. But stability was shaken in 1974-5, wi opposition charges of corruption and oppression.

In 1968 ties with Somalia were restored after 4 years of ski mishes. In 1976-77, relations with Uganda deteriorated. Tanza nia closed its Kenya border in 1977 in a dispute over the co lapse of the East African Community, an economic union of th 2 states and Uganda.

The U.S. agreed in 1976 to sell several jet fighters to Kenya.

# North Korea
## Democratic People's Republic of Korea

**People: Population** (1977 est.): 16,650,000. **Pop. densit** 356.01 per sq. mi. **Ethnic groups:** Korean. **Languages:** Korea **Religions:** Buddhism, Confucianism, Shamanism, Chondolsy prevailed before 1945, repressed since.

**Geography: Area:** 46,768 sq. mi., slightly smaller than Missi sippi. **Location:** In northern E. Asia. **Neighbors:** China (Manch ria), USSR on N, S. Korea on S. **Topography:** Mountains ar hills cover nearly all the country, with narrow valleys and sma plains in between. The N and the east coast are the most rugge areas. **Capital:** Pyongyang. **Cities** (1973 est.): Pyongyar

7,000; Hamhung 484,000; Chongjin 306,000.
**Government: Head of state:** Pres. Kim Il Sung; b. Apr. 15,
12; in office: Dec. 28, 1972; **Head of government:** Prime Min.
Jong Ok; in office: Dec., 1977; **Head of Communist Party:**
en. Sec. Kim Il Sung; in office: 1945. **Local divisions:** 9 prov-
es, 4 municipalities, 2 urban districts. **Armed forces:** regulars
0,000; para-military 1,040,000.
**Economy: Industries:** Textiles, fertilizers, cement. **Chief
ops:** Grain, rice. **Minerals:** Tungsten, graphite, magnesite,
al, lead, zinc, iron, copper, gold, phosphate, salt, fluorspar.
**er capita arable land:** 0.3 acres. **Meat production** (1975):
al beef: 24,000 tons; pork: 62,000 tons. **Fish catch** (1975):
0,000 metric tons. **Labor force:** 53% agriculture.
**Finance: Currency:** Won (1974): 1 = $1.02 US). **Gross do-**
**estic product** (1974 est.): $6.1 bln. **Per capita income**
974): $380. **Imports** (1973): $1.00 bln.; partners (1973): P.R.
ina 50%, USSR 30%, Jap. 10%. **Exports** (1973): $1.00 bln.;
rtners (1973); P.R. China 65%, USSR 18%, Jap. 7%, Fr. 2%.
**Transport: Chief ports:** Chonglin, Hamhung, Nampo.
**Health: Life expectancy at birth** (1975): 58.8 male; 62.5 fe-
ale. **Births** (annual per 1,000 pop. 1972-75): 35.7. **Deaths** (an-
al per 1,000 pop. 1972-75): 9.4. **Natural increase** (annual
70-75): 2.63%. **Pop. per hospital bed** (1975): 2,089. **Pop.**
**er physician** (1975): 3,000. **Infant mortality** (per 1,000 live
ths 1973): 110.
**Education: Literacy** (1975): 85%. **Pop. 5-19:** in school
975): 65%, per teacher (1975): 82.

The Democratic People's Republic of Korea was founded May
1948, in the zone occupied by Russian troops after World War
Its armies tried to conquer the south, 1950. After 3 years of
ghting with Chinese and U.S. intervention, a cease-fire was pro-
aimed. The U.S. has no diplomatic ties.
N. Korea has maintained ties with both China and Russia.
N. Korea's attempts to purchase western technology in the
70s foundered over $1 billion in defaulted loans. Industry, be-
un by the Japanese during their 1910-45 occupation, and na-
nalized in the 1940s, had grown substantially, using North Ko-
a's abundant mineral and hydroelectric resources. Political life
dominated by a cult of personality around Pres. Kim Il Sung.

# South Korea
## Republic of Korea

**People: Population** (1977 est.): 36,440,000. **Age distrib.**
%): 0–14: 39.9; 15–59: 54.5; 60+: 5.6. **Pop. density:** 958.17
r sq. mi. **Urban** (1975): 48.5%. **Ethnic groups:** Korean. **Lan-**
**uages:** Korean. **Religions:** Buddhism, Confucianism, Shaman-
m, Chondokyo widespread; Protestants 13%, Roman Catho-
s 3%.
**Geography: Area:** 38,031 sq. mi., slightly larger than Indiana.
**ocation:** In Northern E. Asia. **Neighbors:** N. Korea on N. **To-**
**ography:** The country is mountainous, with a rugged east
ast. The western and southern coast are deeply indented, with
any islands and harbors. **Capital:** Seoul. **Cities** (1977 est.):
eoul 7,525,629; Pusan 2,744,629; Taegu 1,415,759; Inchon
73,955; Kwangchu 657,455.
**Government: Head of state:** Pres. Park Chung Hee; b. Nov.
4, 1917; in office: Nov. 26, 1963; **Local divisions** 9 provinces,
special cities. **Armed forces:** regulars 635,000; reserves
125,000.
**Economy: Industries:** Electronics, ships, rubber, glass,
hemicals, oil products, steel. **Chief crops:** Rice, grain, tobacco,
eans. **Minerals:** Tungsten, coal, iron, bismuth, fluorspar, graph-
e. **Per capita arable land:** 0.1 acres. **Meat production** (1975):
eef: 56,000 tons; pork: 121,000 tons. **Fish catch:** (1975):
,133,400 metric tons. **Electricity production** (1977): 26.56 bln.
wh. **Labor force** 38% agric.; 14% manuf.
**Finance: Currency:** Won (Apr. 1977: 484 = $1 US). **Gross**
**omestic product** (1977): $31.63 bln. **Per capita income**
976): $642. **Imports** (1977): $10.80 bln.; partners (1974): Jap.
3%, U.S. 25%, Saudi Ar. 10%, Kuw. 4%. **Exports** (1977):
10.06 bln.; partners (1974): U.S. 33%, Jap. 31%, W. Ger. 5%,
an. 4%. **Tourists** (1977): 949,700; receipts (1975): $141 mil-
on. **Balance of payments** (1977): +$1,370,000,000. **National**
udget (1977): $6.94 bln. revenues; $6.81 bln. expenditures.
ternational reserves (Apr. 1978): $4.14 bln. **Consumer**
rices (change in 1977): 10.17%.
**Transport: Railway traffic** (1977): 10.7 bln. passenger-miles;
6 bln. net ton-miles. **Motor vehicles:** in use (1977): 125,000

passenger cars, 99,800 commercial vehicles; assembled (1977):
44,016 passenger cars; 42,132 commercial vehicles. **Chief**
**ports:** Pusan, Inchon.
**Communications: Television sets:** 1,619,000 in use (1974),
1,215,000 manufactured (1975). **Radios:** 4,812,000 in use
(1974), 4,280,000 manufactured (1975). **Telephones in use**
(1977): 1,681,254. **Daily newspaper circulation** (1974):
5,867,000; 175 per 1,000 pop.
**Health: Life expectancy at birth** (1975): 66 male; 70 female.
**Births** (per 1,000 pop. 1976): 24.3. **Deaths** (per 1,000 pop.
1976): 6.6. **Natural increase** (1976): 1.77%. **Pop. per hospital**
**bed** (1976): 796. **Pop. per physician** (1976): 1,732. **Infant**
**mortality** (per 1,000 live births 1975): 35.
**Education: Literacy** (1975): 88%. **Pop. 5-19:** in school
(1975): 66%, per teacher (1975): 71.

Korea, once called the Hermit Kingdom, has a recorded history since the 1st century B.C. It was united in a kingdom under
the Silla Dynasty, 668 A.D. It was at times associated with the
Chinese empire; the treaty that concluded the Sino-Japanese
war of 1894-95 recognized Korea's complete independence. In
1910 Japan forcibly annexed Korea as Chosun.
At the Potsdam conference, July, 1945, the 38th parallel was
designated as the line dividing the Soviet and the American occupation. Russian troops entered Korea Aug. 10, 1945, U.S.
troops entered Sept. 8, 1945. The Soviet military organized socialists and communists and blocked efforts to let the Koreans
unite their country. *(See Index for Korean War.)*
The South Koreans formed the Republic of Korea in May 1948
with Seoul as the capital. Dr. Syngman Rhee was chosen president July 20 and the republic was formally proclaimed Aug. 15,
1948. A movement spearheaded by college students forced his
resignation Apr. 26, 1960.
But in an army coup May 16, 1961, Gen. Park Chung Hee became chairman of the ruling junta. He was formally elected
president Oct. 15, 1963; a referendum Nov. 22, 1972, provided
more presidential powers and allowed him to be reelected for 6
year terms unlimited times. In 1974 scores of political dissidents
were jailed; eight were executed in 1975.
North Korean raids across the border tapered off in 1971, but
2 South Korean soldiers were killed in 1973; in 1974, 2 South
Korean boats were sunk and North Koreans fired on a U.S. helicopter south of the neutral zone. In July 1972 South and North
Korea agreed on a common goal of reunifying the 2 nations by
peaceful means. Red Cross delegates from both nations met to
find ways to save divided families.
The U.S. announced in 1977 that it would withdraw 33,000
ground troops by 1982. Some 12,000 Air Force and logistics
troops would remain. Alleged Korean agents were charged in
1976-77 with giving questionable gifts to U.S. congresspersons
to promote foreign aid.
Korea achieved major gains in the 1970s toward industrialization and higher living standards.

# Kuwait
## State of Kuwait

**People: Population** (1977 est.): 1,130,000. **Age distrib.** (%):
0–14: 43.2; 15–59: 54.0; 60+: 2.8. **Pop. density:** 145.24 per sq.
mi. **Ethnic groups:** Arabs 85%, Iranians, Indians, Pakistanis
13%. **Languages:** Arabic, others. **Religions:** Moslems (most
Sunni) predominate.
**Geography: Area:** 7,780 sq. mi., the size of Massachusetts.
**Location:** In Middle East, at N end of Persian Gulf. **Neighbors:**
Iraq on N, Saudi Arabia on S. **Topography:** The country is flat,
very dry, and extremely hot. **Capital:** Kuwait. **Cities** (1970 cen.):
Kuwait City (met.) 217,749; Hawalli 106,542.
**Government: Head of state:** Amir Shaikh Jaber Al-Ahmad
Al-Sabah; b. 1926; in office: Dec. 31, 1977; **Head of govern-**
**ment:** Prime Min. Shaikh Sa'ad Abdulla Al-Salem Al-Sabah; in
office: Feb. 8, 1978. **Local divisions:** 3 governorates. **Armed**
**forces:** regulars 10,000.
**Economy: Industries:** Oil products. **Minerals:** Oil, gas.
**Crude oil reserves** (1978): 67.00 bln. bbls. **Per capita arable**
**land:** 0.002 acres. **Electricity production** (1976): 5.21 bln. kwh.
**Labor force:** 2% agric.; 13% manuf.
**Finance: Currency:** Dinar (May 1978: 1 = $3.60 US). **Gross**
**domestic product** (1976): $12.80 bln. **Per capita income**
(1975): $11,431. **Imports** (1976): $3.32 bln.; partners (1974):
Jap. 17%, U.S. 14%, W. Ger. 11%, U.K. 8%. **Exports** (1977):

$9.77 bln.; partners (1974): Jap. 26%, U.K. 16%, Fr. 10%, Sing. 5%. **National budget** (1975): $8.77 bln. revenues; $2.96 bln. expenditures. **International reserves** (May 1978): $3.18 bln. **Consumer prices** (change in 1977): 8.2%.

**Transport: Motor vehicles:** in use (1975): 203,700 passenger cars, 68,500 commercial vehicles. **Chief ports:** Mina al-Ahmadi.

**Communications: Television sets:** 182,000 in use (1974). **Radios:** 215,000 in use (1974). **Telephones in use** (1977): 139,880. **Daily newspaper circulation** (1974): 80,000; 86 per 1,000 pop.

**Health: Life expectancy at birth** (1970): 66.14 male; 71.82 female. **Births** (annual per 1,000 pop. 1972-75): 47.1. **Deaths** (annual per 1,000 pop. 1972-75): 5.3. **Natural increase** (annual 1970-75): 4.18%. **Pop. per hospital bed** (1975): 209. **Pop. per physician** (1975): 1,006. **Infant mortality** (per 1,000 live births 1974): 44.30.

**Education: Literacy** (1975): 55%. **Pop. 5-19:** in school (1975): 55%, per teacher (1975): 25.

Kuwait is ruled by the Al-Sabah dynasty, founded 1759. Britain ran foreign relations and defense from 1899 until independence in 1961. The majority of the population is non-Kuwaiti, with many Palestinians, and can not vote.

Iraqi troops crossed the Kuwait border in 1973 but soon withdrew. Kuwait has ordered advanced weapons from France and the U.S.

Oil, first exported in 1946, is the fiscal mainstay. Reserves are 15% of the world total. Oil pays for free medical care, education, and social security. There are no taxes, except customs duties.

# Laos
## Lao People's Democratic Republic

**People: Population** (1977 est.): 3,460,000. **Pop. density:** 37.84 per sq. mi. **Urban** (1973): 14.7%. **Ethnic groups:** Lao 50%, Thai 20%, Meo and Yao 15%, others. **Languages:** Lao (official), others. **Religions:** Buddists 90%, animists, Christians 1.5%.

**Geography: Area:** 91,428 sq. mi., slightly larger than Utah. **Location:** In Indochina Peninsula in SE Asia. **Neighbors:** Burma, China on N, Vietnam on E, Cambodia on S, Thailand on W. **Topography:** Laos is a landlocked country dominated by jungle. High mountains along the eastern border are the source of the E-W rivers which slice across the country to the Mekong R., which defines most of the western border. **Capital:** Vientiane. **Cities** (1971 est.): Vientiane 160,000.

**Government: Head of state:** Pres. Souphanouvong; b. July 13, 1909; in office: Dec. 2, 1975; **Head of government:** Prime Min. Kaysone Phomvihane; b. Dec. 13, 1920; in office: Dec. 2, 1975; **Head of Communist Party:** Gen. Sec. Kaysone Phomvihane; in office: 1955. **Local divisions:** 20 provinces. **Armed forces:** regulars 48,550.

**Economy: Industries:** Wood products. **Chief crops:** Rice, corn, tobacco, cotton, opium, citrus fruits, coffee. **Minerals:** Tin. **Other resources:** Forests. **Per capita arable land:** 0.7 acres. **Electricity production:** (1975): 255.00 mln. kwh. **Labor force:** 78% agriculture.

**Finance: Currency:** Kip (1975: 598.80 = $1 US). **Gross domestic product** (1974 est.): $500 mln. **Per capita income** (1974): $150. **Imports** (1973): $65 mln.; partners (1973): Thai 47%, Jap. 13%, Fr. 10%, U.S. 7%. **Exports** (1973): $5 mln.; partners (1973): Thai 65%, Malaysia 29%, Hong Kong 2%, Jap. 2%. **Tourists** (1974): 23,100; receipts (1973): $3 million. **Consumer prices** (change in 1975): 84.3%.

**Transport: Motor vehicles:** in use (1974): 14,100 passenger cars, 2,500 commercial vehicles.

**Communications: Radios:** 125,000 licensed (1974). **Telephones in use** (1973): 5,000.

**Health: Life expectancy at birth** (1975): 39.1 male; 41.8 female. **Births** (annual per 1,000 pop. 1972-75): 44.6. **Deaths** (annual per 1,000 pop. 1972-75): 22.8. **Natural increase** (annual 1970-75): 2.18%. **Pop. per hospital bed** (1975): 1,031. **Pop. per physician** (1975): 13,608. **Infant mortality** (per 1,000 live births 1973): 123.

**Education: Literacy** (1975): 22%. **Pop. 5-19:** in school (1975): 25%, per teacher (1975): 130.

Laos became a French protectorate in 1893, but regained independence as a constitutional monarchy July 19, 1949.

Conflicts among neutralist, communist and conservative fac-

tions created a chaotic political situation. Armed conflict creased after 1960.

The 3 factions formed a coalition government in June 196 with neutralist Prince Souvanna Phouma as premier. A 14-nati conference in Geneva signed agreements, 1962, guaranteei neutrality and independence. By 1964 the Pathet Lao had wi drawn from the coalition, and, with aid from N. Vietname troops, renewed sporadic attacks. U.S. planes bombed the I Chi Minh trail, supply line from N. Vietnam to communist force in Laos and S. Vietnam. An estimated 2.75 million tons of bom were dropped on Laos during the fighting.

In 1970 the U.S. stepped up air support and military aid. The were an est. 67,000 North Vietnamese troops in Laos, and som 15,000 Thais financed by the U.S.

After Pathet Lao military gains, Souvanna Phouma in M 1975 ordered government troops to cease fighting, and the P thet Lao took effective control. The U.S. retained a reduced di lomatic presence. A Lao People's Democratic Republic was pr claimed Dec. 3, 1975; it is strongly influenced by Vietnar Armed resistance to the government has continued on a sm scale.

# Lebanon
## Republic of Lebanon

**People: Population** (1977 est.): 3,060,000. **Age distrib.** (% 0-14: 42.7; 15-59: 49.6; 60+: 7.7. **Pop. density:** 762.14 per s mi. **Urban** (1970): 60.1%. **Ethnic groups:** Arabs 93%, Arm nians 6%. **Languages:** Arabic, French, Armenian. **Religion** Moslems (Sunniad Shiite) 57%, Christians (Maronite, Orth dox) 40%, Druze 3%.

**Geography: Area:** 4,015 sq. mi., smaller than Connecticu **Location:** On Eastern end of Mediterranean Sea. **Neighbor** Syria on E. Israel on S. **Topography:** There is a narrow coasta strip, and two mountain ranges running N-S enclosing the fert Beqaa Valley. The Litani R. runs S through the valley, turning to empty into the Mediterranean. **Capital:** Beirut. **Cities** (197 est.): Beirut (met.) 938,940; (1971 est.): Tripoli 175,000.

**Government: Head of state:** Pres. Elias Sarkis; b. July 2 1924; in office: Sept. 23, 1976; **Head of government:** Prim Min. Salim al-Huss; b. Dec. 20, 1929; in office: Dec. 9, 1976. L cal divisions: 5 provinces.

**Economy: Industries:** Trade, food products, textiles, cemen oil products. **Chief crops:** Fruits, olives, tobacco, grapes, vege tables, grains. **Minerals:** Iron. **Per capita arable land:** 0.2 acres **Meat production** (1975): beef: 10,000 tons; lamb: 11,000 tons **Electricity production** (1976): 1.25 bln. kwh. **Labor force** 18% agric.; 17% manuf.

**Finance: Currency:** Pound (May 1978: 2.90 = $1 US **Gross domestic product** (1972): $2.11 bln. **Per capita in** come (1972): $786. **Imports** (1973): $1.22 bln.; partners (1973 U.S. 12%, W. Ger. 11%, Fr. 10%, It. 10%. **Exports** (1973 $497 mln.; partners (1973): Saudi Ar. 15%, Fr. 9%, U.K. 8% Libya 7%. **Tourists** (1974): 2,261,800; receipts (1974): $41 million. **International reserves** (May 1978): $2.11 bln. **Con** sumer prices (change in 1973): 11.1%.

**Transport: Railway traffic** (1974): 1.24 mln. passenge miles; 26.08 mln. net ton-miles. **Motor vehicles:** in use (1974 220,220 passenger cars, 23,400 commercial vehicles. **Civil av** ation: 1,101 mln. passenger-miles (1974); 26,306 mln. freigh ton-miles (1974). **Chief ports:** Beirut, Tripoli, Sidon.

**Communications: Television sets:** 375,000 in use (1974 **Radios:** 1,321,000 in use (1974). **Telephones in use** (1972 227,000. **Daily newspaper circulation** (1973): 280,000; 92 pe 1,000 pop.

**Health: Life expectancy at birth** (1975): 61.4 male; 65.1 fe male. **Births** (annual per 1,000 pop. 1972-75): 39.8. **Deaths** (an nual per 1,000 pop. 1972-75): 9.9. **Natural increase** (annu 1970-75): 2.99%. **Pop. per hospital bed** (1975): 231. **Pop. pe** physician (1975): 1,106. **Infant mortality** (per 1,000 live birth 1960): 13.6.

**Education: Literacy** (1975): 86%. **Pop. 5-19:** in schoo (1975): 72%, per teacher (1975): 24.

Lebanon was formed from 5 former Turkish Empire district and became an independent state Sept. 1, 1920, administere under French mandate 1920-41. French troops withdrew in 1946.

Under the 1943 National Covenant, all public positions wer divided among the various religious communities, with Christians the majority. By the 1970s, Moslems became the majority, nd demanded a larger political and economic role.

U.S. Marines intervened, May-Oct. 1958, during a Syrian-ided revolt. Lebanon's efforts to restrain Palestinian comman-os caused armed clashes in 1969. Continued raids against Is-aeli civilians, 1970-75, brought Israeli attacks against guerrilla amps and villages. Israeli troops occupied S. Lebanon, March 978, but were replaced by a UN force.

An estimated 60,000 were killed and billions of dollars in dam-ge inflicted in a 1975-76 civil war. Palestinian units and leftist Moslems fought against the Maronite militia, the Phalange, and ther Christians. Several Arab countries provided political and rms support to the various factions, while Israel aided Christian rces. Up to 15,000 Syrian troops intervened in 1976, and ught Palestinian groups. Arab League troops from several na-ons tried to impose a cease-fire. But sporadic fighting, among alestinian factions, among Christian factions, and between Pal-stinians and Christians near Israel continued in 1977.

Lebanon has a free enterprise economy. Literacy and life ex-ectancy are higher than in most Arab lands.

## Lesotho

### Kingdom of Lesotho

**People: Population** (1975 est.): 1,040,000. **Age distrib.** (%): 0–14: 39.5; 15–59: 53.9; 60+: 6.6. **Pop. density:** 88.77 per sq. mi. **Ethnic groups:** Sotho 85% Nguni 15%. **Languages:** English, Lesotho both official. **Religions:** Christians 70%, others.

**Geography: Area:** 11,716 sq. mi., slightly larger than Maryland. **Location:** In Southern Africa. **Neighbors:** Republic of South Africa completely surrounds Lesotho. **Topography:** Land-ocked Lesotho is mountainous, with altitudes ranging from 5,000 to 11,000 ft. Agriculture is pursued on the western lowlands. **Capital:** Maseru. **Cities** (1972 est.): Maseru (met.) 29,049.

**Government: Head of state:** King Moshoeshoe II, b. May 2, 1938; in office: Oct. 4, 1966; **Head of government:** Prime Min. Leabria Johnson; b. Oct. 31, 1914; in office: Oct. 4, 1966. **Local divisions:** 9 districts.

**Economy: Industries:** Diamond polishing. **Chief crops:** Corn, grains, peas, beans. **Other resources:** Wool, mohair. **Per cap-ita arable land:** 0.8 acres. **Electricity production** (1967): 5.00 mln. kwh. **Labor force:** 95% agriculture.

**Finance: Currency:** Rand (Apr. 1977: 1 = $1.15 US). **Gross domestic product** (1974 est.): $118 mln. **Per capita income** (1974): $140. **Imports** (1973): $87 mln.; partners (1973): Mostly So. Afr. **Exports** (1973): $13 mln.; partners (1973): Mostly So. Afr. **Consumer prices** (change in 1977): 17.7 %.

**Transport: Motor vehicles:** in use (1975): 4,600 passenger cars, 3,200 commercial vehicles.

**Communications: Radios:** 11,000 licensed (1974). **Tele-phones in use** (1974): 4,000.

**Health:** Life expectancy at birth (1975): 44.4 male; 47.6 fe-male. **Births** (annual per 1,000 pop. 1972-75): 39.0. **Deaths** (an-nual per 1,000 pop. 1972-75): 19.7. **Natural increase** (1970-75): 1.93%. **Pop. per hospital bed** (1975): 472. **Pop. per physician** (1975): 19,962. **Infant mortality** (per 1,000 live births 1956): 181.

**Education: Literacy** (1975): 50%. **Pop. 5-19:** in school (1975): 64%, per teacher (1975): 75.

Lesotho (once called Basutoland) became a British protector-ate in 1868 when Chief Mohesh sought protection against the Boers. Independence came Oct. 4, 1966. Elections were sus-pended in 1970. Up to 70% of males work abroad, most in So. Africa. Livestock raising is the chief industry; wool and mohair are the chief exports.

## Liberia

### Republic of Liberia

**People: Population** (1977 est.): 1,800,000. **Age distrib.** (%): 0–14: 41.6; 15–59: 53.1; 60+: 5.3. **Pop. density:** 41.86 per sq. mi. **Urban** (1971): 27.6%. **Ethnic groups:** Americo-Liberians 2.5%, 16 tribes 97.5%. **Languages:** English (official), 28 tribal languages. **Religions:** Moslems 10-20%, Christians 10%, oth-ers.

**Geography: Area:** 43,000 sq. mi., slightly smaller than Penn-sylvania. **Location:** On SW coast of W. Africa. **Neighbors:** Si-erra Leone on W, Guinea on N, Ivory Coast on E. **Topography:**

The marshy Atlantic coastline rises to low mountains and pla-teaus in the interior, which is largely forested. Six major rivers flow in parallel courses to the ocean. **Capital:** Monrovia. **Cities** (1970 est.): Monrovia 96,226.

**Government: Head of state:** Pres. William Richard Tolbert; b. May 13, 1913; in office: July 23, 1971. **Local divisions:** 9 counties. **Armed forces:** regulars 5,220; para-military 21,300.

**Economy: Industries:** Food processing and other light indus-try. **Chief crops:** Fibers, palm kernels, rice, cassava, coffee, cocoa, sugar. **Minerals:** Iron, diamonds, gold. **Other resources:** Rubber, timber. **Per capita arable land:** 0.2 acres. **Fish catch** (1975): 16,600 metric tons. **Electricity production** (1975): 870.00 mln. kwh. **Labor force:** 74% agriculture.

**Finance: Currency:** Dollar (May 1978: 1 = $1 US). **Gross domestic product** (1975): $855.00 mln. **Per capita income** (1976): $422. **Imports** (1975): $399 mln.; partners (1974): U.S. 18%, Saudi Ar. 9%, U.K. 9%, W. Ger. 5%. **Exports** (1976): $476 mln.; partners (1974): U.S. 20%, Belg. 18%, W. Ger. 17%, Neth. 13%. **National budget** (1975): $125.20 mln. revenues; $121.80 mln. expenditures. **International reserves** (May 1978): $25.94 mln. **Consumer prices** (change in 1977): 6.2%.

**Transport: Motor vehicles:** in use (1974): 12,100 passenger cars, 10,000 commercial vehicles. **Chief ports:** Monrovia, Bu-chanan.

**Communications: Television sets:** 8,500 in use (1973). **Ra-dios:** 261,000 in use (1974). **Telephones in use** (1974): 7,000. **Daily newspaper circulation** (1974): 11,000; 7 per 1,000 pop.

**Health:** Life expectancy at birth (1971): 45.8 male; 44.0 fe-male. **Births** (annual per 1,000 pop. 1972-75): 49.8. **Deaths** (an-nual per 1,000 pop. 1972-75): 20.7. **Natural increase** (1971): 2.89%. **Pop. per hospital bed** (1975): 603. **Pop. per physician** (1975): 11,193. **Infant mortality** (per 1,000 live births 1971): 159.2

**Education: Literacy** (1975): 10%. **Pop. 5-19:** in school (1975): 33%, per teacher (1975): 117.

Liberia was founded in 1822 by U.S. black freedmen who set-tled at Monrovia with the aid of colonization societies. It became a republic July 26, 1847, with a constitution modeled on that of the U.S. Descendants of freedmen dominate politics.

## Libya

### People's Socialist Libyan Arab Public

**People: Population** (1975 est.): 2,430,000. **Pop. density:** 3.58 per sq. mi. **Urban** (1974): 29.8%. **Ethnic groups:** Arab-Berber 97%, Italian 1.4%, others. **Languages:** Arabic. **Reli-gions:** Sunni Moslems 97%, Christians 2.5%.

**Geography: Area:** 679,536 sq. mi., larger than Alaska. **Loca-tion:** On Mediterranean coast of N. Africa. **Neighbors:** Tunisia, Algeria on W, Niger, Chad on S, Sudan, Egypt on E. **Topogra-phy:** Desert and semidesert regions cover 92% of the land, with some low mountains in N, and higher mountains in S. A narrow coastal zone and scattered oases contain most of the population and agriculture. **Capital:** Tripoli. **Cities** (1971 est.): Tripoli 247,000; Beghazi 137,000.

**Government: Head of state:** Sec.-Gen. Muammar el Qad-dafi; b. 1942; in office: Sept. 1, 1969; **Head of government:** Chmn. Abdulati al-Obeidi; b. 1933; in office: Mar. 2, 1977. **Local divisions:** 10 regions. **Armed forces:** regulars 29,000.

**Economy: Industries:** Carpets, textiles, shoes. **Chief crops:** Dates, olives, citrus and other fruits, grapes, tobacco. **Minerals:** Oil, gas. **Crude oil reserves** (1978): 25.00 bln. bbls. **Per capita arable land:** 2.3 acres. **Electricity production** (1976): 1.49 bln. kwh. **Labor force:** 43% agriculture.

**Finance: Currency:** Dinar (May 1978): 1 = $3.38 US). **Gross domestic product** (1975): $13.16 bln. **Per capita income** (1975): $4,618. **Imports** (1976): $3.21 bln.; partners (1975): It. 27%, W. Ger. 12%, Fr. 9%, U.K. 6%. **Exports** (1977): $10.11 bln.; partners (1975): U.S. 23%, It. 20%, W. Ger. 18%, Fr. 4%, U.K. 4%. **Tourists** (1975): 238,000; receipts (1975): $38 million. **Balance of payments** (1977): + $1,490,000,000. **International reserves** (May 1978): $4.29 bln. **Consumer prices** (change in 1977): 21.6%.

**Transport: Motor vehicles:** in use (1975): 263,100 passen-ger cars, 131,300 commercial vehicles. **Chief ports:** Tripoli, Bengazi.

**Communications: Television sets:** 6,000 licensed (1974). **Radios:** 105,000 licensed (1974). **Telephones in use** (1970):

41,000.

**Health: Life expectancy at birth** (1975): 51.4 male; 54.5 female. **Births** (annual per 1,000 pop. 1972-75): 45.0. **Deaths** (annual per 1,000 pop. 1972-75): 14.7. **Natural increase** (annual 1970-75): 3.03%. **Pop. per hospital bed** (1975): 244. **Pop. per physician** (1975): 1,060. **Infant mortality** (per 1,000 live births 1973): 130.

**Education: Literacy** (1975): 30%. **Pop. 5-19:** in school (1975): 80%, per teacher (1975): 24.

First settled by Berbers, Libya was ruled by Carthage, Rome, and Vandals, the Ottomans, Italy from 1912, and Britain and France after WW II. It became an independent constitutional monarchy Jan. 2, 1952. In 1969 a junta lead by Col. Muammar el-Qaddafi seized power, instituting socialist policies.

In 1972 Libya and Egypt agreed on a unification plan, which Egypt canceled in 1974, charging a Quaddafi role in the bombing of an Egyptian presidential palace.

In the mid-1970s, it was widely reported that Libya had armed violent revolutionary groups in Egypt and Sudan, and had aided terrorists of various nationalities including Moslem rebels in the Philippines. In 1970, Libya arranged to buy jets from France. The USSR sold several billion dollars worth of advanced arms after 1975, and established close political ties.

Libya and Egypt fought several air and land battles along their border in July, 1977. Chad charged Libya with military occupation of its uranium-rich northern region in 1977.

Over one third of all workers are foreigners, half of them Egyptians.

# Liechtenstein

## Principality of Liechtenstein

**People: Population** (1977 est.): 20,000. **Age distrib.** (%): 0–14: 27.9; 15–59: 60.2; 60+: 11.9. **Pop. density:** 327.87 per sq. mi. **Ethnic groups:** Germanic. **Languages:** German. **Religions:** Roman Catholics 90%, Protestants 10%.

**Geography: Area:** 61 sq. mi., the size of Washington, D.C. **Location:** In the Alps. **Neighbors:** Switzerland on W, Austria on E. **Topography:** The Rhine Valley occupies one-third of the country, the Alps cover the rest. **Capital:** Vaduz. **Cities** (1976 est.): Vaduz 4,620.

**Government: Head of state:** Prince Franz Josef II; b. Aug. 16, 1906; in office: July 26, 1938; **Head of government:** Hans Brunhart; b. Mar. 28, 1945; in office: Mar. 27, 1978. **Local divisions:** 11 communes.

**Economy: Industries:** Machines, textiles, precision instruments, false teeth, drugs, ceramics.

**Finance: Currency:** Franken, or Swiss Franc.

**Communications: Telephones in use** (1977): 16,247. **Daily newspaper circulation** (1974): 6,100; 277 per 1,000 pop.

**Health: Births** (per 1,000 pop. 1975): 12.6. **Deaths** (per 1,000 pop. 1975): 7.5. **Natural increase** (1975): .53%. **Infant mortality** (per 1,000 live births 1974): 9.2.

Liechtenstein became sovereign in 1866. Since 1923 Austria has run its posts, customs, and foreign affairs. Taxes are low; many international corporations have headquarters there. Foreign workers comprise a third of the population.

# Luxembourg

## Grand Duchy of Luxembourg

**People: Population:** (1977 est.): 360,000. **Age distrib.** (%): 0–14: 20.8; 15–59: 60.7; 60+: 18.5. **Pop. density:** 360.36 per sq. mi. **Urban** (1973): 68.9%. **Ethnic groups:** Mixture of French and Germans predominate, Italians 7%. **Languages:** French, German, Luxembourgish. **Religions:** Roman Catholics 94%, Protestants 1%.

**Geography: Area:** 999 sq. mi., smaller than Rhode Island. **Location:** In W. Europe. **Neighbors:** Belgium on W, France on S, W. Germany on E. **Topography:** Heavy forests (Ardennes) cover N, S is a low, open plateau. **Capital:** Luxembourg. **Cities** (1974 est.): Luxembourg 78,403.

**Government: Head of state:** Grand Duke Jean; b. Jan. 5, 1921; in office: Nov. 12, 1964; **Head of government:** Prime Min. Gaston Thorn; in office: June 18, 1974. **Local divisions:** 3 dis-

tricts, 12 cantons. **Armed forces:** regulars 625; para-military 430.

**Economy: Industries:** Steel, chemicals, beer, tires, tobacco, metal products, cement. **Chief crops:** Grain, potatoes, roses. **Minerals:** Iron. **Per capita arable land:** 0.4 acres. **Meat production** (1974): beef: 13,000 tons. **Electricity production** (1977): 1.31 bln. kwh. **Labor force:** 7% agric.; 34% manuf.

**Finance: Currency:** Franc (May 1978: 32.88 =$1 US). **Gross domestic product** (1975): $2.04 bln. **Per capita income** (1975): $5,435. **Consumer prices** (change in 1977): 6.7%.

**Transport: Railway traffic** (1975): 181.95 mln. passenger-miles; 409.86 mln. net ton-miles. **Motor vehicles:** in use (1975): 140,100 passenger cars, 12,000 commercial vehicles. **Civil aviation:** 84 mln. passenger-miles (1974); 142 mln. freight ton-miles (1974).

**Communications: Television sets:** 88,000 licensed (1974). **Radios:** 176,000 licensed (1974). **Telephones in use** (1977): 157,829. **Daily newspaper circulation** (1973): 161,000; 33 per 1,000 pop.

**Health: Life expectancy at birth** (1973): 67.0 male; 73.9 female. **Births** (per 1,000 pop. 1976): 10.9. **Deaths** (per 1,000 pop. 1976): 12.6. **Natural increase** (1976): −.17%. **Pop. per hospital bed** (1975): 91. **Pop. per physician** (1975): 965. **Infant mortality** (per 1,000 live births 1975): 14.8.

**Education: Literacy** (1975): 98%. **Pop. 5–19:** in school (1975): 56%, per teacher (1975): 25.

Luxembourg, founded about 963, was ruled by Burgundy, Spain, Austria, and France from 1448 to 1815. It left the Germanic Confederation in 1866. Overrun by Germany in two world wars, Luxembourg ended its neutrality in 1948, when a customs union with Belgium and Netherlands was adopted. Steel accounts for 65% of exports.

# Madagascar

## Democratic Republic of Madagascar

**People: Population** (1977 est.): 8,520,000. **Age distrib.** (%): 0–14: 46.5; 15–59: 47.7; 60+: 5.8. **Pop. density:** 37.59 per sq. mi. **Urban** (1970): 14.1%. **Ethnic groups:** 18 Malayan-Indonesian tribes (Merina 26%), with Arab and African presence. **Languages:** Malagasy spoken in various dialects by all tribes, Merina dialect official. **Religions:** Roman Catholics 20%, Protestant 18%, Moslems 9%, others.

**Geography: Area:** 226,657 sq. mi., slightly smaller than Texas. **Location:** In the Indian O., off the SE coast of Africa. **Neighbors:** Nearest are Comoro Is., Mozambique (across Mozambique Channel). **Topography:** Madagascar has a humid coastal strip in the E, fertile valleys in the mountainous center plateau region, and a wider coastal strip on the W. **Capital:** Tananarive. **Cities** (1972 est.): Tananarive 366,530; Majunga 67,450; Tamatave 59,503.

**Government: Head of state:** Pres. Didier Ratsiraka; b. Nov. 4, 1936; in office: Dec. 30, 1975; **Head of government:** Prime Min. Desire Rakotoarijaona; in office: Aug. 4, 1977. **Local divisions:** 6 provinces.

**Economy: Industries:** Light industry. **Chief crops:** Coffee, cloves, vanilla (80% world supply), rice, sugar, sisal, tobacco, peanuts. **Minerals:** Chromium, graphite. **Per capita arable land:** 0.9 acres. **Fish catch** (1975): 56,000 metric tons. **Electricity production** (1976): 252.00 mln. kwh. **Labor force:** 86% agriculture.

**Finance: Currency:** Franc (May 1978: 230.35 = $1 US). **Gross domestic product** (1976): $1.69 bln. **Per capita income** (1974): $175. **Imports** (1975): $363 mln.; partners (1973): Fr. 49%, W. Ger. 8%, U.S. 7%, Jap. 5%. **Exports** (1975): $292 mln.; partners (1973): Fr. 37%, U.S. 17%, Reunion 9%, Jap. 6%, Malaysia 6%. **Tourists** (1975): 50,200; receipts (1974): $2 million. **Balance of payments** (1975): −$23,000,000. **National budget** (1977): $262.11 mln. revenues; $284.31 mln. expenditures. **International reserves** (May 1978): $95.6 mln. **Consumer prices** (change in 1977): 3.0%.

**Transport: Railway traffic** (1975): 154.01 mln. passenger-miles; 128.55 mln. net ton-miles. **Motor vehicles:** in use (1974): 55,000 passenger cars, 51,000 commercial vehicles. **Civil aviation:** 171 mln. passenger-miles (1976); 4,866 mln. freight ton-miles (1976). **Chief ports:** Tamatave, Diego-Suarez, Majunga, Tulear.

**Communications: Television sets:** 7,500 in use (1974). **Radios:** 855,000 in use (1974). **Telephones in use** (1977): 27,660. **Daily newspaper circulation** (1974): 59,000; 9 per 1,000 pop.

**Health: Life expectancy at birth** (1966): 37.5 male; 38.3 female. **Births** (annual per 1,000 pop. 1972-75): 46.0. **Deaths** (annual per 1,000 pop. 1972-75): 25.9. **Natural increase** (1966): 1%. **Pop. per hospital bed** (1975): 367. **Pop. per physician** (1975): 10,740. **Infant mortality** (per 1,000 live births 1972): 3.2.

**Education: Literacy** (1975): 39%. **Pop. 5-19:** in school (1975): 41%, per teacher (1975): 121.

Madagascar was settled 2,000 years ago by Malayan-Indonesian people, whose descendants still predominate. A united kingdom ruled the 18th and 19th centuries. The island became a French protectorate, 1885, and a colony 1896. Independence came June 26, 1960.

Discontent with inflation and French domination led to a coup 1972. The new regime nationalized French-owned financial interests, closed French bases and a U.S. space tracking station, and obtained Chinese aid.

## Malawi
### Republic of Malawi

**People: Population** (1977 est.): 5,530,000. **Age distrib.** (%): 0-14: 43.9; 15–59: 50.4; 60+: 5.6. **Pop. density:** 120.88 per sq. mi. **Urban** (1972): 10.1%. **Ethnic groups:** Chewa, Nyanja, Tumbuka, other Bantu tribes. **Languages:** English (official), Chichewa, other Bantu languages. **Religions:** Christians 50% (half Roman Catholic, half Protestant), Moslems 30%.

**Geography: Area:** 45,747 sq. mi., the size of Pennsylvania. **Location:** in SE Africa. **Neighbors:** Zambia on W, Mozambique on S.E. Tanzania on N. **Topography:** Malawi stretches 560 mi. N-S along Lake Malawi (Lake Nyasa), most of which belongs to Malawi. High plateaus and mountains line the Rift Valley the length of the nation. **Capital:** Lilongwe. **Cities** (1972 est): Blantyre-Limbre (met.) 160,063; Lilongwe 20,000.

**Government: Head of state:** Pres. Hastings Kamuzu Banda 1906; in office: July 6, 1966. **Local divisions:** 3 regions, 24 districts, 3 sub-districts. **Armed forces:** regulars 2,400; paramilitary 460.

**Economy: Industries:** Textiles, sugar, farm implements. **Chief crops:** Tea, tobacco, peanuts, cotton, sugar, soybeans, coffee. **Other resources:** Rubber. **Per capita arable land:** 1.4 acres. **Fish catch** (1975): 71,000 metric tons. **Electricity production** (1977): 276.00 mln. kwh. **Labor force:** 87% agriculture.

**Finance: Currency:** Kwacha (May 1978: 1 = $1.15 US). **Gross domestic product** (1977): $875.31 mln. **Per capita income** (1975): $123. **Imports** (1977): $235 mln.; partners (1973): S. Afr. 23%, U.K. 23%, Rhod. 13%, Jap. 5%, W. Ger. 5%. **Exports** (1977): $195 mln.; partners (1973): U.K. 31%, U.S. 9%, Rhod. 7%, Neth. 7%. **Tourists** (1974): 28,400; receipts (1974): $4 million. **Balance of payments** (1977): +$51,000,000. **National budget** (1977): $116.24 mln. revenues; $151.38 mln. expenditures. **International reserves** (May 1978): $67.92 mln. **Consumer prices** (change in 1977): 4.2%.

**Transport: Railway traffic** (1975): 55.27 mln. passenger-miles; 170.78 mln. net ton-miles. **Motor vehicles:** in use (1974): 21,200 passenger cars, 9,500 commercial vehicles. **Civil aviation:** 76 mln. passenger-miles (1976); 2,906 mln. freight ton-miles (1976).

**Communications: Radios:** 125,000 in use (1974). **Telephones in use** (1977): 20,000. **Daily newspaper circulation** (1974): 12,000; 2 per 1,000 pop.

**Health: Life expectancy at birth** (1972): 40.9 male; 44.2 female. **Births** (per 1,000 pop. 1972): 50.5. **Deaths** (per 1,000 pop. 1972): 26.5. **Natural increase** (annual 1970-72): 2.40%. **Pop. per hospital bed** (1975): 590. **Pop. per physician** (1975): 73,156. **Infant mortality** (annual per 1,000 live births 1970-72): 142.1.

**Education: Literacy** (1975): 22%. **Pop. 5-19:** in school (1975): 35%, per teacher (1975): 163.

Bantus came in the 16th century, Arab slavers in the 19th. The area became a British protectorate Nyasaland, in 1891. It became independent July 6, 1964, and a republic in 1966. It has a pro-West foreign policy and cooperates economically with Rhodesia and S. Africa.

## Malaysia

**People: Population** (1977 est.): 12,600,000. **Age distrib.** (%): 0–14: 45.0; 15–59: 49.8; 60+: 5.2. **Pop. density:** 98.19 per sq. mi. **Urban** (1970): 28.8%. **Ethnic groups:** Malays 44%, Chinese 36%, Indians 10%, others. **Languages:** Malay (official), English, Chinese, Indian languages. **Religions:** Malays, some Indians are Moslem; Chinese, Indian, and local religions.

**Geography: Area:** 128,328 sq. mi., slightly larger than New Mexico. **Location:** Occupies the SE tip of Asia, plus the N. coast of the island of Borneo. **Neighbors:** Thailand on N, Indonesia on S. **Topography:** Most of West Malaysia is covered by tropical jungle, including the central mountain range that runs N-S through the peninsula. The western coast is marshy, the eastern coast sandy. East Malaysia has a wide, swampy coastal plain, with interior jungles and mountains. **Capital:** Kuala Lumpur. **Cities** (1970 cen.): Kuala Lumpur 451,977; George Town 269,003; Ipoh 247,953.

**Government: Head of state:** Paramount Ruler Tuanku Yahya Petra; b. Dec. 10, 1917; in office: Sept. 21, 1975; **Head of government:** Prime Min. Datuk Hussein Onn; b. Feb. 12, 1922; in office: Jan. 15, 1976. **Local divisions:** 13 states, each with legislature, chief minister, and titular ruler. **Armed forces:** regulars 64,000; reserves 27,000.

**Economy: Industries:** Rubber goods, pottery, fertilizers. **Chief crops:** Palm oil, copra, rice, tapioca, sugar, pepper. **Minerals:** Tin (35% world output), iron. **Crude oil reserves** (1978): 2.5 bln. bbls. **Other resources:** Rubber (35% world output). **Per capita arable land:** 0.2 acres. **Meat production** (1975): beef: 15,000 tons; pork: 54,000 tons. **Fish catch** (1975): 473,600 metric tons. **Electricity production** (1977): 3.58 bln. kwh. **Labor force:** 50% agric.; 8% manuf.

**Finance: Currency:** Ringgit (May 1978: 2.40 = $1 US). **Gross domestic product** (1976): $11.05 bln. **Per capita income** (1975): $718. **Imports** (1977): $4.02 bln.; partners (1974): Jap. 22%, U.S. 10%, U.K. 9%, Sing. 8%. **Exports** (1977): $4.57 bln.; partners (1974): Sing. 22%, Jap. 17%, U.S. 14%, U.K. 7%. **Tourists** (1975): 1,183,000; receipts (1975): $58 million. **Balance of payments** (1975): +$63,000,000. **National budget** (1976): $2.38 bln. revenues; $2.86 bln. expenditures. **International reserves** (Mar. 1978): $2.87 bln. **Consumer prices** (change in 1977): 4.8%.

**Transport: Railway traffic** (1975): 19.87 mln. passenger-miles; 4.35 mln. net ton-miles. **Motor vehicles:** in use (1975): 37,400 passenger cars, 15,100 commercial vehicles; assembled (1976): 44,172 passenger cars; 8,112 commercial vehicles. **Civil aviation:** 1,304 mln. passenger-miles (1977); 30,054 mln. freight ton-miles (1977). **Chief ports:** George Town, Kelang, Melaka, Kuching.

**Communications: Television sets:** 390,000 licensed (1974), 102,000 manufactured (1975). **Radios:** 365,000 licensed (1974). **Telephones in use** (1977): 329,644. **Daily newspaper circulation** (1974): 1,038,000; 89 per 1,000 pop.

**Health: Life expectancy at birth** (1974): 65.03 male; 70.30 female. **Births** (per 1,000 pop. 1975): 31.4. **Deaths** (per 1,000 pop. 1975): 6.4. **Natural increase** (1975): 2.50%. **Pop. per hospital bed** (1975): 337. **Pop. per physician** (1975): 4,858. **Infant mortality** (per 1,000 live births 1974): 35.4.

**Education: Literacy** (1975): 61%. **Pop. 5-19:** in school (1975): 50%, per teacher (1975): 52.

European traders appeared in the 16th century; Britain established control in 1867. Malaysia was created Sept. 16, 1963. It included Malaya (which had become independent in 1957 after the suppression of Communist rebels), plus the formerly-British Singapore, Sabah (N Borneo), and Sarawak (NW Borneo). Singapore was separated in 1965, in order to end tensions between Chinese, the majority in Singapore, and Malays in control of the Malaysian government. Chinese have charged economical and political discrimination.

Sabah and Sarawak have a pop. of 1,900,000 (1975).

A monarch is elected by a council of hereditary rulers of the Malayan states every 5 years. Free federal and state elections were held in 1978.

Abundant natural resources have assured prosperity, and foreign investment has aided industrialization.

## Maldives
### Republic of Maldives

**People: Population** (1977 est.): 140,000. **Age distrib.** (%):

0–14: 44.4; 15–59: 52.0; 60+: 3.6. **Pop. density:** 1,217.39 per sq. mi. **Urban** (1967): 11.3%. **Ethnic groups:** Sinhalese, Dravidian, Arab mixture. **Languages:** Divehi (Sinhalese dialect). **Religions:** Sunni Moslems.

**Geography: Area:** 115 sq. mi., twice the size of Washington, D.C. **Location:** In the Indian O. SW of India. **Neighbors:** Nearest is India on N. **Topography:** The Maldives comprise 19 atolls with 1,087 islands, 203 inhabited. None of the islands are over 5 sq. mi. in area, and all are nearly flat. **Capital:** Male. **Cities** (1967 cen.): Male 11,760.

**Government: Head of state:** Pres. Ibrahim Nasir; b. Sept. 2, 1926; in office: Nov. 11, 1968. **Local divisions:** 19 atolls, each with an elected committee with head man appointed by government.

**Economy: Industries:** Fish processing, tourism. **Chief crops:** Coconuts, fruit, millet. **Other resources:** Shells. **Fish catch** (1975): 27,900 metric tons.

**Finance: Currency:** Rupee (1974: 7.2 = $1 US). **Gross domestic product** (1974 est.): $12 mln. **Per capita income** (1974): $100. **Imports** (1974): $12 mln. **Exports** (1974): $3 mln. **Transport: Chief Ports:** Male Atoll.

**Communications: Radios:** 2,400 licensed (1974). **Telephones in use** (1977): 480.

**Health: Births** (per 1,000 pop. 1965): 50.1. **Deaths** (per 1,000 pop. 1965): 22.9. **Natural increase** (1965): 2.72%.

**Education: Literacy** (1975): 36%. **Pop. 5-19:** in school (1975): 40%, per teacher (1975): 80.

The islands had been a British protectorate since 1887. The country became independent July 26, 1965. Britain retained an air base until 1976. Long a sultanate, the Maldives became a republic in 1968. Tourism has increased.

# Mali

## Republic of Mali

**People: Population** (1977 est.): 5,990,000. **Age distrib. (%):** 0–14: 49.1; 15–59: 47.8; 60+: 3.1. **Pop. density:** 12.89 per sq. mi. **Ethnic groups:** Mande (Bambara, Malinke, Sarakolle) 50%, Peul 17%, Voltaic 12%, Songhai, Tuareg, Moors. **Languages:** French (official), Bambara, others. **Religions:** Moslems 90%, Christians 1%, others.

**Geography: Area:** 464,873 sq. mi., larger than Texas and California combined. **Location:** In the interior of W. Africa. **Neighbors:** Mauritania, Senegal on W, Guinea, Ivory Coast, Upper Volta on S, Niger on E, Algeria on N. **Topography:** Mali is a landlocked grassy plain in the upper basins of the Senegal and Niger rivers, extending N into the Sahara. **Capital:** Bamako. **Cities** (1972 est.): Bamako (met.) 196,800; (1971 est.): Mopti 32,000.

**Government: Head of state:** Pres. Moussa Traore; b. Sept. 25, 1936; in office: Nov. 19, 1968. **Local divisions:** 6 regions. **Armed forces:** regulars 4,200; para-military 5,700.

**Economy: Chief crops:** Millet, rice, peanuts, cotton. **Other resources:** Rubber. **Per capita arable land:** 4.9 acres. **Meat production** (1975): beef: 28,000 tons; lamb: 27,000 tons. **Fish catch** (1975): 100,000 metric tons. **Electricity production** (1975): 70.00 mln. kwh. **Labor force:** 91% agriculture.

**Finance: Currency:** Franc (May 1978: 460.70 = $1 US). **Gross domestic product** (1971): $.32 mln. **Per capita income** (1974): $73. **Imports** (1976): $150 mln.; partners (1973): Fr. 57%, Ivory Coast 15%, U.S. 7%, W. Ger. 6%. **Exports** (1976): $97 mln.; partners (1973): Fr. 34%, Ivory Coast 28%, Up. Volta 8%, Jap. 6%. **Tourist receipts** (1974): $1 million. **Balance of payments** (1977): +$13,100,000. **International reserves** (May 1978): $6.7 mln. **Consumer prices** (change in 1976): 8.0%.

**Transport: Railway traffic** (1975): 62.1 mln. passenger-miles; 96.88 mln. net ton-miles. **Motor vehicles:** in use (1970): 11,900 passenger cars, 8,400 commercial vehicles. **Civil aviation:** 61 mln. passenger-miles (1976); 581 mln. freight ton-miles (1976).

**Communications: Telephones in use** (1970): 5,000. **Daily newspaper circulation** (1972): 3,000; 0.5 per 1,000 pop.

**Health: Life expectancy at birth** (1973): 36.5 male; 39.6 female. **Births** (annual per 1,000 pop. 1972-75): 50.1. **Deaths** (annual per 1,000 pop. 1972-75): 25.9. **Natural increase** (annual 1970-75): 2.42%. **Pop. per hospital bed** (1975): 1,407. **Pop. per physician** (1975): 38,821. **Infant mortality** (per 1,000 live births 1960-61): 120.

**Education: Literacy** (1975): 10%. **Pop. 5-19:** in school (1975): 15%, per teacher (1975): 203.

Until the 15th century the area was part of the great Mali Empire. Timbuktu was a center of Islamic study. French rule was secured, 1898. The Sudanese Rep. and Senegal became independent as the Mali Federation June 20, 1960, but Senegal withdrew, and the Sudanese Rep. was renamed Mali.

Mali signed economic agreements with France and, in 1963 with Senegal. In 1968, a coup ended the socialist regime. Famine struck in 1973-74 killing as many as 100,000 people. Drought conditions returned 1977-78. Loss of livestock and dislocation of Tuareg nomads remained problems.

# Malta

**People: Population** (1977 est.): 330,000. **Age distrib. (%):** 0–14: 26.3; 15–59: 61.1; 60+: 12.6. **Pop. density:** 2,704.92 per sq. mi. **Urban** (1967): 94.3%. **Ethnic groups:** Italian, Arab, English, and Phoenician mixture. **Languages:** Maltese, English both official. **Religions:** Roman Catholics 98%.

**Geography: Area:** 122 sq. mi., twice the size of Washington D.C. **Location:** In center of Mediterranean Sea. **Neighbors:** Nearest is Italy on N. **Topography:** The Island of Malta is 95 sq. mi.; the other islands in the group are Gozo, 26 sq. mi., and Comino, 1 sq. mi. The coastline is heavily indented. Low hills cover the interior. **Capital:** Valletta. **Cities** (1974 est.): Sliema 22,000; Valletta 14,049.

**Government: Head of state:** Pres. Anton Buttigieg; b. Feb. 19, 1912; in office: Dec. 27, 1976; **Head of government:** Prime Min. Dom Mintoff; b. Aug. 6, 1916; in office: June 1971. **Local divisions:** 10 electoral districts.

**Economy: Industries:** Ship repair, textiles, tourism. **Chief crops:** Wheat, potatoes, onions, beans. **Per capita arable land** 0.1 acres. **Electricity production** (1977): 420.00 mln. kwh. **Labor force:** 29% manuf.

**Finance: Currency:** Pound (May 1978: 1 = $2.50 US). **Gross domestic product** (1977): $602.93 mln. **Per capita income** (1975): $1,417. **Imports** (1977): $513 mln.; partners (1973): U.K. 27%. **Exports** (1977): $289 mln.; partners (1973) U.K. 33%. **Tourists** (1975): 334,500; receipts (1975): $73 million. **Balance of payments** (1977): +$61,300,000. **National budget** (1976): $241.08 mln. revenues; $211.45 mln. expenditures. **International reserves** (May 1978): $773.1 mln. **Consumer prices** (change in 1977): 9.9%.

**Transport: Motor vehicles:** in use (1975): 54,000 passenger cars, 12,500 commercial vehicles. **Civil aviation:** 212 mln. passenger-miles (1976); 196 mln. freight ton-miles (1976). **Chief ports:** Valletta.

**Communications: Radios:** 129,000 licensed (1973). **Telephones in use** (1977): 62,324.

**Health: Life expectancy at birth** (1973): 68.10 male; 72.0 female. **Births** (per 1,000 pop. 1976): 19.1. **Deaths** (per 1,000 pop. 1976): 9.8. **Natural increase** (1976): .93%. **Pop. per hospital bed** (1975): 95. **Pop. per physician** (1975): 956. **Infant mortality** (per 1,000 live births 1975): 18.9.

**Education: Literacy** (1975): 80%. **Pop. 5-19:** in school (1975): 68%, per teacher (1975): 26.

Malta was ruled by Phoenicians, Romans, Arabs, Normans, the Knights of Malta, France, and Britain (since 1814). It became independent Sept. 21, 1964, with Britain retaining a naval base. Malta became a republic in 1974. In 1972 British base rights were extended for 7 years.

Maltese is a Semitic language, with Italian influences, written in the Latin alphabet. Malta is democratic but nonaligned, and receives aid from Libya and China.

# Mauritania

## Islamic Republic of Mauritania

**People: Population** (1975 est.): 1,320,000. **Age distrib. (%):** 0–14: 43.9; 15–59: 50.8; 60+: 5.3. **Pop. density:** 3.15 per sq. mi. **Urban** (1975): 23.1%. **Ethnic groups:** Arab-Berber 80%, Negroes 20%. **Languages:** French, Hassaniya Arabic, Niger-Congo languages. **Religions:** Moslems 95%, others.

**Geography: Area:** 419,229 sq. mi., the size of Texas and California combined. **Location:** In W. Africa. **Neighbors:** Morocco on N, Algeria, Mali on E, Senegal on S. **Topography:** The fertile

Senegal R. valley in the S gives way to a wide central region of sandy plains and scrub trees. The N is arid and extends into the Sahara. **Capital:** Nouakchott. **Cities** (1976 cen.): Nouakchott (met.) 134,986.

**Government: Head of state:** Mustapha Ould Salek, head of Military Committee; in office: July 10, 1978. **Local divisions:** 8 regions, one district. **Armed forces:** regulars 7,450; paramilitary 6,000.

**Economy: Chief crops:** Dates, grain. **Minerals:** Iron, copper. **Per capita arable land:** 0.5 acres. **Fish catch** (1975): 34,200 metric tons. **Electricity production** (1975): 95.00 mln. kwh. **Labor force:** 85% agriculture.

**Finance: Currency:** Ouguiya (May 1978: 46.29 = $1 US). **Gross domestic product** (1973): $277.04 mln. **Per capita income** (1974): $222. **Imports** (1976): $180 mln.; partners (1972): Fr. 41%, U.S. 11%, U.K. 7%, Senegal 7%. **Exports** (1976): $178 mln.; partners (1972): Fr. 20%, U.K. 18%, It. 14%, Belg. 12%. **Tourists** (1972): 10,300; receipts (1975): $6 million. **Balance of payments** (1977): −$50,600,000. **International reserves** (May 1978): $31.7 mln. **Consumer prices** (change in 1977): 10.3%.

**Transport: Railway traffic** (1973): 4.23 bln. net ton-miles. **Motor vehicles:** in use (1972): 4,400 passenger cars, 5,000 commercial vehicles. **Chief ports:** Nouakchott, Nouadhibou.

**Communications: Radios:** 82,000 in use (1974). **Telephones in use** (1969): 1,300. **Daily newspaper circulation** (1972): 300; 0.2 per 1,000 pop.

**Health: Life expectancy at birth** (1975): 37.0 male; 40.1 female. **Births** (annual per 1,000 pop. 1972-75): 44.8. **Deaths** (annual per 1,000 pop. 1972-75): 24.9. **Natural increase** (annual 1970-75): 1.99%. **Pop. per hospital bed** (1975): 2,480. **Pop. per physician** (1975): 16,986. **Infant mortality** (annual per 1,000 live births 1964-65): 187.

**Education: Literacy** (1975): 5%. **Pop. 5-19:** in school (1975): 12%, per teacher (1975): 151.

Mauritania became independent Nov. 28, 1960. It annexed the south of former Spanish Sahara in 1976. Saharan guerrillas stepped up attacks in 1977; 8,000 Moroccan troops and French bomber raids aided the government. A 1978 coup deposed Pres. Ould Daddah, who had ruled since independence. Famine struck in 1973-74 and again in 1977-78. France, China, and the U.S. have sent aid.

## Mauritius

**People: Population** (1977 est.): 880,000. **Age distrib.** (%): 0-14: 40.4; 15-59: 53.8; 60+: 5.8. **Pop. density:** 1,118.17 per sq. mi. **Urban** (1975): 43.7%. **Ethnic groups:** Indians 69%, mulattoes, whites 28%, Chinese 3%. **Languages:** English (official), French, Creole, Hindi, Urdu, Chinese. **Religions:** Hindu 49%, Roman Catholic 32%, Moslems 16%, Protestants 1%.

**Geography: Area:** 787 sq. mi., smaller than Rhode Island. **Location:** In the Indian O., 500 mi. E of Madagascar. **Neighbors:** Nearest is Madagascar on W. **Topography:** Mauritius is a volcanic island nearly surrounded by coral reefs. A central plateau is encircled by mountain peaks. **Capital:** Port Louis. **Cities** (1977 est.): Port Louis (met.) 141,100.

**Government: Head of state:** Queen Elizabeth II, represented by Gov.-Gen. Raman Osman; in office: Dec. 1972. **Local divisions:** 9 administrative divisions.

**Economy: Industries:** Tourism. **Chief crops:** Sugar cane, tea. **Per capita arable land:** 0.3 acres. **Electricity production** (1977): 312.00 mln. kwh. **Labor force:** 32% agriculture.

**Finance: Currency:** Rupee (May 1978: 6.34 = $1 US). **Gross domestic product** (1975): $518.42 mln. **Per capita income** (1975): $629. **Imports** (1977): $377 mln.; partners (1973): U.K. 14%, So.Afr. 9%, Taiwan 8%. **Exports** (1976): $265 mln.; partners (1974): Can. 36%, U.K. 35%, U.S. 8%, Iran 7%. **Tourists** (1974): 34,900; receipts (1975): $22 million. **Balance of payments** (1977): −$37,500,000. **National budget** (1976): $165.57 mln. revenues; $222.44 mln. expenditures. **International reserves** (May 1978): $94.1 mln. **Consumer prices** (change in 1977): 12.5%.

**Transport: Motor vehicles:** in use (1975): 17,800 passenger cars, 9,500 commercial vehicles. **Chief ports:** Port Louis.

**Communications: Television sets:** 38,000 licensed (1974). **Radios:** 107,000 licensed (1973). **Telephones in use** (1977): 26,505. **Daily newspaper circulation** (1974): 80,000; .92 per 1,000 pop.

**Health: Life expectancy at birth** (1973): 60.68 male; 65.31

female. **Births** (per 1,000 pop. 1976): 25.6. **Deaths** (annual per 1,000 pop. 1972-75): 6.8. **Natural increase** (1976): 1.78%. **Pop. per hospital bed** (1975): 260. **Pop. per physician** (1975): 3,800. **Infant mortality** (per 1,000 live births 1975): 48.6.

**Education: Literacy** (1975): 62%. **Pop. 5-19:** in school (1975): 64%, per teacher (1975): 42.

Mauritius was uninhabited when settled in 1638 by the Dutch, who introduced sugar cane. France took over in 1721, bringing African slaves. Britain ruled from 1810 to Mar. 12, 1968, bringing Indian workers for the sugar plantations. Mauritius has a free political life and high literacy and life expectancy. The 1970s brought declining birth rates and some economic growth. A nonethnic Marxist opposition emerged in 1976 elections.

## Mexico

### United Mexican States

**People: Population** (1977 est.): 64,590,000. **Age distrib.** (%): 0-14: 46.4; 15-59: 48.5; 60+: 5.0. **Pop. density:** 84.81 per sq. mi. **Urban** (1976): 63.6%. **Ethnic groups:** Mestizo 60%, Indian 30%, Caucasian 10%. **Languages:** Spanish, Indian languages 1.5%, bilingual 6.5%. **Religions:** Roman Catholics 96%, Protestants 2%.

**Geography: Area:** 761,601 sq. mi., three times the size of Texas. **Location:** In southern N. America. **Neighbors:** U.S. on N, Guatemala, Belize on S. **Topography:** The Sierra Madre Occidental Mts. run NW-SE near the west coast; the Sierra Madre Oriental Mts., run near the Gulf of Mexico. They join S of Mexico City. Between the two ranges lies the dry central plateau, altitude from 5,000 to 8,000 ft., generally rising toward the S, with temperate vegetation. The coastal lowlands are tropical. About 45% of land is arid. **Capital:** Mexico City. **Cities** (1976 est.): Mexico City (met.) 11,943,050; Guadalajara (met.) 2,075,773; Monterrey (met.) 1,725,013; Juarez 544,900; Tijuana (met.) 535,535; Leon 525,947; Puebla de Zaragoza 498,886.

**Government: Head of state:** Pres. Jose Lopez Portillo; b. June 16, 1920; in office: Dec. 1, 1976. **Local divisions:** Federal district and 31 states, each with governor, elected legislature, and substantial powers. **Armed forces:** regulars 345,000.

**Economy: Industries:** Steel, chemicals, electric goods, textiles, rubber, paper, cement, shoes, glass, handicrafts, tourism. **Chief crops:** Cotton, coffee, sugar cane, tomatoes, wheat, corn, rice, tobacco, beans, cocoa, sisal (50% world supply) bananas. **Minerals:** Silver, gold, copper, lead, zinc, antimony, mercury, arsenic, graphite, molybdenum, sulphur, coal, opal, oil, gas. **Crude oil reserves** (1978): at least 110 bln. bbls. according to unofficial estimates. **Per capita arable land:** 1.1 acres. **Meat production** (1976): beef: 986,000 tons; pork: 400,000 tons; lamb: 55,700. **Fish catch** (1975): 499,400 metric tons. **Electricity production** (1977): 50.05 bln. kwh. **Labor force:** 39% agric.; 17% manuf.

**Finance: Currency:** Peso (May 1978: 22.77 = $1 US). **Gross domestic product** (1976): $61.19 bln. **Per capita income** (1976): $1,130. **Imports** (1977): $5.49 bln.; partners (1975): U.S. 62.1%, W. Ger. 7.3%, Jap. 4.8%, U.K. 2.4%, Fr. 2.4%. **Exports** (1977): $4.12 bln.; partners (1975): U.S. 62.8%, Jap. 4.5%, W. Ger. 3.1%. **Tourists** (1975): 3,217,900; receipts (1975): $2.142 billion. **Balance of payments** (1976): −$906,000,000. **National budget** (1974): $7.39 bln. revenues; $9.86 bln. expenditures. **International reserves** (Feb. 1978): $1.74 bln. **Consumer prices** (change in 1977): 26.4%.

**Transport: Railway traffic** (1975): 2.61 bln. passenger-miles; 20.21 bln. net ton-miles. **Motor vehicles:** in use (1975): 2,400,900 passenger cars, 887,900 commercial vehicles; manufactured (1977): 193,200 passenger cars, 76,800 commercial vehicles. **Civil aviation:** 4,941 mln. passenger-miles (1976); 55,190 mln. freight ton-miles (1976). **Chief ports:** Veracruz, Tampico, Mazatlan, Coatzacoalcos.

**Communications: Television sets:** 4,885,000 in use (1974), 569,000 manufactured (1975). **Radios:** 17,514,000 in use (1974), 1,030,000 manufactured (1975). **Telephones in use** (1977): 3,308,832.

**Health: Life expectancy at birth** (1975): 62.76 male; 66.57 female. **Births** (annual per 1,000 pop. 1972-75): 42.0. **Deaths** (per 1,000 pop. 1975): 6.7. **Natural increase** (annual 1970-75): 3.34%. **Pop. per hospital bed** (1975): 604. **Pop. per physician** (1975): 1,410. **Infant mortality** (per 1,000 live births 1973): 51.9.

**Education: Literacy** (1975): 82%. **Pop. 5-19:** in school

(1975): 56%, per teacher (1975): 58.

Mexico was the site of advanced Indian civilizations before the Spanish conquest. The Mayas, an agricultural people, moved up from Yucatan and built immense stone pyramids and invented a calendar. The Toltecs were overcome by the Aztecs, who founded Tenochtitlan 1325 A.D., now Mexico City. Hernando Cortes, Spanish conquistador, destroyed the Aztec empire, 1519-1521.

After 3 centuries of Spanish rule the people rose, under Fr. Miguel Hidalgo y Costilla (a priest), 1810, Fr. Morelos y Payon (another priest), 1812, and Gen. Agustin Iturbide, who made independence effectual Sept. 27, 1821, but made himself emperor as Agustin I. A republic was declared in 1823.

Mexican territory extended into the present American Southwest and California until Texas revolted and established a republic in 1836; the Mexican legislature refused recognition but was unable to enforce its authority there. After numerous clashes, the U.S.-Mexican War, 1846-48, resulted in the loss by Mexico of the lands north of the Rio Grande.

French arms supported an Austrian archduke on the throne of Mexico as Maximilian I, 1864-67, but pressure from the U.S. forced France to withdraw. A dictatorial rule by Porfirio Diaz, president 1877-80, 1884-1911, led to fighting by rival forces until the new constitution of Feb. 5, 1917 provided social reform. Since then Mexico has developed large-scale programs of social security, labor protection and school improvement. A constitutional provision requires management to share profits with labor.

The Institutional Revolutionary party has been dominant in politics since 1929. Radical opposition, including some guerrilla activity, has been contained by strong measures. In 1970 the legal voting age was lowered from 21 to 18.

The presidency of Luis Echeverria, 1970-76, was marked by a more leftist foreign policy and domestic rhetoric. Some land redistribution begun in 1976 was reversed under the succeeding administration.

Gains in agriculture, industry, and social services have been achieved since 1940. The land is rich, but the rugged topography and lack of sufficient rainfall are major obstacles. 45% of the land is arid. Crops and farm prices are controlled, as are export and import. Large estates have been expropriated; since 1915 the government has distributed about 160 million acres to small farmers through landholding communities (ejidos). Four million peasants are still without land, and five million others hold minimal plots. Economic prospects brightened with the discovery of vast oil reserves, perhaps the world's greatest. But half the work force is jobless or underemployed.

## Monaco

### Principality of Monaco

**People: Population** (1977 est.): 30,000. **Age distrib. (%):** 0-14: 13.0; 15-59: 57.0; 60+: 30.1. **Ethnic groups;** French 58%, Italian 17%, Monegasque 15%. **Languages:** French (official), Monegasque, Italian, English. **Religions:** Roman Catholics 95%.

**Geography: Area:** 600 acres. **Location:** On the NW Mediterranean coast. **Neighbors:** France to W, N, E. **Topography:** Monaco-Ville sits atop a high promontory, the rest of the principality rises from the port up the hillside. **Capital:** Monaco.

**Government: Head of state:** Prince Rainier III; b. May 31, 1923; in office: May 9, 1949; **Head of government:** Min. of State Andre Saint-Mleux; in office: May 24, 1972.

**Economy: Industries:** Tourism, gambling.

**Finance: Tourists** (1975): 138,800.

**Transport: Chief ports:** La Condamine.

**Communications: Television sets:** 16,000 in use (1974). **Radios:** 7,500 in use (1974). **Telephones in use** (1977): 23,740.

**Health: Births** (per 1,000 pop. 1974): 8.2. **Deaths** (per 1,000 pop. 1974): 12.3. **Natural increase** (1974): −.41%. **Infant mortality** (per 1,000 live births 1970): 9.3.

An independent principality for over 300 years, Monaco has belonged to the House of Grimaldi since 1297 except during the French Revolution. It was placed under the protectorate of Sardinia in 1815, and under that of France, 1861. The Prince of Monaco was an absolute ruler until a constitution was promulgated in 1911.

Monaco's fame as a tourist resort and international conference city is widespread. It is noted for its mild climate and magnificent scenery. The area has been extended by land reclamation.

## Mongolia

### Mongolian People's Republic

**People: Population** (1977 est.): 1,530,000. **Pop. density** 2.53 per sq. mi. **Urban** (1973): 46.4%. **Ethnic groups:** Khalkh Mongols 76%, other Mongols 8%, Kazakhs 5%, other Turks Russians, Chinese. **Languages:** Khalkha Mongolian (official written in Cyrillic letters since 1941), Turkic 7%. **Religions:** Lama Buddhism prevailed, has been curbed.

**Geography: Area:** 604,247 sq. mi., more than twice the size of Texas. **Location:** In E Central Asia. **Neighbors:** USSR on N China on S. **Topography:** Much of Mongolia is a high plateau with mountains, salt lakes, and vast grasslands. Arid lands in the S are part of the Gobi Desert. **Capital:** Ulan Bator. **Cities** (1977 est.): Ulan Bator 326,000.

**Government: Head of state:** Chmn. Yumjaagiyn Tsedenbal b. Sept. 17, 1916; in office: June 11, 1974; **Head of government:** Chmn. Jambyn Batmunkh; b. May 10, 1926; in office June 1974; **Head of Communist Party:** First Sec. Yumjaagiy Tsedenbal; in office: 1958. **Local divisions:** Capital city and 1 provinces. **Armed forces:** Regulars 30,000; reserves 30,000.

**Economy: Industries:** Food processing, textiles, chemicals cement. **Chief crops:** Grain. **Minerals:** Coal, tungsten, coppe molybdenum, gold, tin. **Per capita arable land:** 1.3 acres. **Mea production** (1975): beef: 57,000 tons; lamb: 126,000 tons. **Elec tricity production** (1975): 818.00 mln. kwh. **Labor force:** 62% agric.; 10% manuf.

**Finance: Currency:** Togrog (1974: 3.33 = $1 US). **Gros domestic product** (1974 est.): $750 mln. **Per capita incom** (1974): $500. **Imports** (1973): $370 mln.; partners (1973 USSR 90%, Czech. 3%, E. Ger. 2%. **Exports** (1973): $16 mln.; partners (1973): USSR 76%, Czech. 7%, E. Ger. 5%, Po 4%.

**Transport: Railway traffic** (1975): 132.27 mln. passenger miles; 1.34 bln. net ton-miles.

**Communications: Television sets:** 3,000 in use (1974). **Ra dios:** 166,000 in use (1970). **Telephones in use** (1977): 37,792 **Daily newspaper circulation** (1974): 112,000; 80 per 1,00 pop.

**Health: Life expectancy at birth** (1975): 59.1 male; 62.3 fe male. **Births** (per 1,000 pop. 1972): 29.8. **Deaths** (annual pe 1,000 pop. 1972-75): 9.3. **Natural increase** (annual 1970-75 2.95%. **Pop. per hospital bed** (1975): 102. **Pop. per physician** (1975): 539. **Infant mortality** (per 1,000 live births 1973): 75.

**Education: Literacy** (1975): 95%. **Pop. 5-19:** in school (1975): 58%, per teacher (1975): 49.

One of the world's oldest countries, Mongolia reached the zel nith of its power in the 13th century when Genghis Khan and hi successors conquered all of China and extended their influenc as far W as Hungary and Poland. In later centuries, the empir dissolved and Mongolia came under the suzerainty of China.

With the advent of the 1911 Chinese revolution, Mongolia, with Russian backing, declared its independence. A Mongolian Com munist regime was established July 11, 1921.

In the early 1970s Mongolia was changing from a nomadi culture to one of settled agriculture and growing industries with aid from the USSR and East European nations.

Mongolia has sided with the Russians in the Sino-Soviet dis pute. A Mongolian-Soviet mutual assistance pact was signed Jan. 15, 1966, and thousands of Soviet troops are based in the country. Ties were expanded in a 1976 pact.

## Morocco

### Kingdom of Morocco

**People: Population** (1977 est.): 18,240,000. **Age distrib (%):** 0-14: 46.6; 15-59: 49.2; 60+: 4.2. **Pop. density:** 106.0 per sq. mi. **Urban** (1971): 37.9%. **Ethnic groups:** Arabs 65% Berbers 33%, Europeans 1%. **Languages:** Arabic, Berber French. **Religions:** Sunni Moslems 99%.

**Geography: Area:** 171,953 sq. mi., larger than California. **Lo cation:** on NW coast of Africa. **Neighbors:** Mauritania on S, Al geria on E. **Topography:** Morocco consists of five natural re gions: a series of mountain ranges (Riff in the N, Middle Atlas pper Atlas, and Anti-Atlas); a series of rich plains in the W; alluvial plains in SW; well-cultivated plateaus in the center; a pre-sahara arid zone extending from SE. **Capital:** Rabat. **Cities** (1973 est.): Casablanca (met.) 1,753,400; Rabat-Sale (met.) 96,600; Marrakech (met.) 436,300; Fez (met.) 426,000; Meknes (met.) 403,000.

**Government: Head of state:** King Hassan II; b. July 11, 1929; in office: Mar. 3, 1961; **Head of government:** Prime Min. Ahmed Osman; in office: Nov. 2, 1972. **Local divisions:** 2 urban prefectures, 22 provinces. **Armed forces:** regulars 84,650; para-military 30,000.

**Economy: Industries:** Carpets, clothing, leather goods, tourism. **Chief crops:** Grain, fruits, dates, grapes. **Minerals:** Phosphate (largest exporter), cobalt, antimony, manganese, zinc, lead, oil, coal. **Crude oil reserves** (1978): 150 mln. bbls. **Per capita arable land:** 1.0 acres. **Meat production** (1975): beef: 99,000 tons; lamb: 73,000 tons. **Fish catch** (1975): 210,500 metric tons. **Electricity production** (1977): 3.44 bln. kwh. **Labor force:** 61% agriculture.

**Finance: Currency:** Dirham (May 1978: 4.28 = $1 US). **Gross domestic product** (1976): $7.97 bln. **Per capita income** (1975): $440. **Imports** (1976): $2.62 bln.; partners (1973): Fr. 32%, U.S. 11%, W. Ger. 8%, Spain 5%. **Exports** (1976): $1.26 bln.; partners (1973): Fr. 34%, W. Ger. 10%, It. 7%, U.K. 5%. **Tourists** (1975): 1,244,800; receipts (1975): $296 million. **National budget** (1974): $1.76 bln. revenues; $2.11 bln. expenditures. **International reserves** (May 1978): $356 mln. **Consumer prices** (change in 1977): 12.5%.

**Transport: Railway traffic** (1975): 518.54 mln. passenger-miles; 1.79 bln. net ton-miles. **Motor vehicles:** in use (1975): 320,100 passenger cars, 127,200 commercial vehicles; assembled (1976): 20,460 passenger cars; 12,072 commercial vehicles. **Civil aviation:** 762 mln. passenger-miles (1976); 11,253 mln. freight ton-miles (1976). **Chief ports:** Tangier, Casablanca, Kenitra.

**Communications: Radios:** 157,000 manufactured (1975). **Telephones in use** (1977): 204,500. **Daily newspaper circulation** (1974): 235,000; 14 per 1,000 pop.

**Health: Life expectancy at birth** (1975): 51.4 male; 54.5 female. **Births** (annual per 1,000 pop. 1972-75): 46.2. **Deaths** (annual per 1,000 pop. 1972-75): 15.7. **Natural increase** (annual 1970-75): 3.05%. **Pop. per hospital bed** (1975): 729. **Pop. per physician** (1975): 12,503. **Infant mortality** (per 1,000 live births 1962): 149.

**Education: Literacy** (1975): 20%. **Pop. 5-19:** in school (1975): 28%, per teacher (1975): 115.

Berbers were the original inhabitants, followed by Carthaginians and Romans. Arabs conquered in 683. In the 11th and 12th centuries, a Berber empire ruled all NW Africa and most of Spain from Morocco.

Part of Morocco came under Spanish rule in the 19th century; in the early 20th France took control of the rest. Tribal uprisings lasted from 1911 to 1933. The country became independent Mar. 2, 1956. Tangier, an internationalized seaport, was turned over to Morocco in 1956. Ifni, a Spanish enclave, was ceded in 1969.

Morocco annexed over 70,000 sq. mi. of phosphate-rich land Apr. 14, 1976, two-thirds of former Spanish Sahara, with the remainder annexed by Mauritania. Spain had withdrawn in February. Polisario, a guerrilla movement, proclaimed the region independent Feb. 27, and launched attacks with Algerian support. Morocco accepted U.S. military and economic aid. It has agreements with France on economic cooperation. Conservative King Hassan II exercises considerable powers. Moroccan troops helped suppress an invasion of Zaire by Angola-based rebels, June 1978.

## Mozambique

### People's Republic of Mozambique

**People: Population** (1977 est.): 9,680,000. **Pop. density:** 31.91 per sq. mi. **Ethnic groups:** Bantu tribes. **Languages:** Portuguese (official), others. **Religions:** Christians 15%, Moslems 2.5%, others.

**Geography: Area:** 303,373 sq. mi., larger than Texas. **Location:** On SE coast of Africa. **Neighbors:** Tanzania on N, Malawi, Zambia, Rhodesia on W, South Africa, Swaziland on S. **Topography:** Coastal lowlands comprise nearly half the country with plateaus rising in steps to the mountains along the western bor-

der. **Capital:** Maputo. **Cities:** (1970 cen.): Maputo (met.) 383,775; Beira 115,000.

**Government: Head of state:** Pres. Samora Machel; b. Oct. 1933; in office: June 25, 1975; **Local divisions:** 10 provinces. **Armed forces:** regulars 19,000.

**Economy: Industries:** Cement, alcohol, textiles. **Chief crops:** Cashews, cotton, sugar, copra, sisal, tea. **Minerals:** Coal, tantalite, copper, iron, bauxite, gold. **Per capita arable land:** 0.7 acres. **Meat production** (1975): beef: 35,000 tons; pork: 12,000 tons. **Electricity production** (1976): 1.75 bln. kwh. **Labor force:** 74% agriculture.

**Finance: Currency:** Escudo (Jan.-Mar. 1977: 34.32 = $1 US). **Gross domestic product** (1974 est.): $3 bln. **Per capita income** (1974): $300. **Imports** (1976): $300 mln.; partners (1973): So. Afr. 20%, Port. 19%, W. Ger. 13%, Fr. 8%. **Exports** (1975): $202 mln.; partners (1973): Port. 36%, U.S. 14%, So. Afr. 9%, U.K. 6%. **Consumer prices** (change in 1976): 4.5%.

**Transport: Railway traffic** (1973): 245.92 mln. passenger-miles; 2.11 bln. net ton-miles. **Motor vehicles:** in use (1972): 89,300 passenger cars, 21,500 commercial vehicles. **Chief ports:** Maputo, Beira, Nacala.

**Communications: Television sets:** 1,000 licensed (1973). **Radios:** 176,000 licensed (1974), 24,000 manufactured (1975). **Telephones in use** (1974): 52,270. **Daily newspaper circulation** (1974): 47,000; 5 per 1,000 pop.

**Health: Life expectancy at birth** (1975): 41.9 male; 45.1 female. **Births** (annual per 1,000 pop. 1972-75): 43.1. **Deaths** (annual per 1,000 pop. 1972-75): 20.1. **Natural increase** (annual 1970-75): 2.30%. **Pop. per hospital bed** (1975): 781. **Pop. per physician** (1975): 16,473. **Infant mortality** (per 1,000 live births 1969): 92.5.

**Education: Literacy** (1975): 7%. **Pop. 5-19:** in school (1975): 20%, per teacher (1975): 272.

The first Portuguese post on the Mozambique coast was established in 1505, on the trade route to the East. Mozambique became independent June 25, 1975, after a ten-year war against Portuguese colonial domination. The 1974 revolution in Portugal paved the way for the orderly transfer of power to Frelimo (Front for the Liberation of Mozambique), which had earlier gained complete control of the independence movement. Frelimo took over local administration Sept. 20, 1974, over the opposition, in part violent, of some blacks and whites. The new government, led by Maoist Pres. Samora Machel, promised a gradual transition to a communist system, beginning with indoctrination to combat "individualism" and capitalist or traditionalist values. All private schools were closed. Rural collective farms were called for in a July 27, 1975, directive. All private homes were nationalized in 1976. Economic problems included the emigration of most of the country's 160,000 whites, a politically untenable economic dependence on white-ruled South Africa, and a large external debt.

Mozambique closed its border with Rhodesia in March 1976. Border clashes intensified, with Rhodesian troops attacking black Rhodesian guerrillas within Mozambique. Soviet arms were sent following a 1977 friendship treaty. But most aid comes from the West, with which most trade is conducted.

## Nauru

### Republic of Nauru

**People: Population** (1975 est.): 7,128. **Age distrib. (%):** 0-14: 40.0; 15-59: 57.8; 60+: 2.3. **Ethnic groups:** Polynesians, Chinese 15%, European 7%. **Languages:** Nauruan, English. **Religions:** Christianity nearly universal.

**Geography: Area:** 8 sq. mi. **Location:** In Western Pacific O. just S of Equator. **Neighbors:** Nearest are Solomon Is. **Topography:** The bulk of the island is a plateau bearing high grade phosphate deposits, surrounded by a coral cliff and a sandy shore in concentric rings. **Capital:** Yaren.

**Government: Head of state:** Pres. Hammer de Roburt; in office: May 15, 1978. **Local divisions:** 14 districts.

**Economy: Electricity production** (1975): 26.00 mln. kwh.

**Finance: Currency:** Dollar. **Gross domestic product** (1974 est.): $60 mln. **Per capita income** (1974): $7,000. **Imports** (1974): $14 mln.; partners (1974): Austral. 58%, Neth. 30%, U.K. 6%, Jap. 5%. **Exports** (1974): $50 mln.; partners (1974): Austral. 57%, Jap. 23%, New Zea. 18%.

**Communications: Radios:** 3,600 in use (1974). **Telephones**

**in use** (1977): 1,450.

**Health: Births** (per 1,000 pop. 1968): 32.2. **Deaths** (per 1,000 pop. 1968): 8.3. **Natural increase** (1968): 2.39%. **Infant mortality** (per 1,000 live births 1968): 51.8.

The island was discovered in 1798 by the British but was formally annexed to the German Empire in 1886. After World War I, Nauru became a league of Nations mandate administered by Australia. During World War II the Japanese occupied the island and shipped 1,200 Nauruans to the fortress island of Truk as slave laborers.

In 1947 Nauru was made a UN trust territory, administered by Australia on behalf of the 3 trust powers: Australia, Great Britain and New Zealand. Nauru became an independent republic Jan. 31, 1968.

Phosphate exports provide one of the world's highest per capita revenues for the 3,500 native Nauruans (883 Chinese, 627 Europeans and 1,787 Pacific Islanders also live in Nauru, many working in the phosphate industry). The deposits are expected to be nearly exhausted by 1990.

## Nepal

### Kingdom of Nepal

**People: Population** (1977 est.): 13,140,000. **Age distrib.** (%): 0–14: 40.6; 15–59: 53.9; 60+: 5.6. **Pop. density:** 241.71 per sq. mi. **Urban** (1971): 4.0%. **Ethnic groups:** The many tribes are descendants of Indian, Tibetan, and Central Asian migrants. **Languages:** Nepali (official) (an Indic language), Newari, 11 others. **Religions:** Hindus 90%, Buddhists 9%.

**Geography: Area:** 54,362 sq. mi., the size of North Carolina. **Location:** Astride the Himalaya Mts. **Neighbors:** China on N, India on S. **Topography:** The Himalayas stretch across the N, the hill country with its fertile valleys extends across the center, while the southern border region is part of the flat, subtropical Ganges Plain. **Capital:** Kathmandu. **Cities** (1971 cen.): Kathmandu (met.) 353,756.

**Government: Head of state:** King Birendra Bir Bikram; b. Dec. 28, 1945; in office: Jan. 31, 1972; **Head of government:** Prime Min. Kirtinidhi Bista; in office: Sept. 12, 1977. **Local divisions:** 14 zones; 75 districts. **Armed forces:** regulars 20,000; para-military 12,000.

**Economy: Industries:** Hides, drugs, tourism. **Chief crops:** Jute, rice, grain. **Minerals:** Quartz. **Other resources:** Forests. **Per capita arable land:** 0.4 acres. **Electricity production** (1975): 122.00 mln. kwh. **Labor force:** 94% agric.; 1% manuf.

**Finance: Currency:** Rupee (May 1978: 12.00 = $1 US). **Gross domestic product** (1975): $1.18 bln. **Per capita income** (1974): $98. **Imports** (1976): $166 mln.; partners (1974): India 80%, Jap. 10%, Hong Kong 3%. **Exports** (1976): $103 mln.; partners (1974): India 83%, Jap. 3%, Sing. 2%. **Tourists** (1974): 89,800; receipts (1974): $9 million. **National budget** (1977): $106.52 mln. revenues; $189.73 mln. expenditures. **International reserves** (Mar. 1978): $147.9 mln. **Consumer prices** (change in 1977): 8.5%.

**Transport: Motor vehicles:** in use (1968): 4,000 passenger cars, 3,000 commercial vehicles.

**Communications: Radios:** 76,000 in use (1974). **Telephones in use** (1973): 8,000.

**Health: Life expectancy at birth** (1975): 42.2 male; 45.0 female. **Births** (annual per 1,000 pop. 1972-75): 38.8. **Deaths** (annual per 1,000 pop. 1972-75): 20.3. **Natural increase** (annual 1970-75): 2.26%. **Pop. per hospital bed** (1975): 6,680. **Pop. per physician** (1975): 36,266. **Infant mortality** (per 1,000 live births 1973): 169.

**Education: Literacy** (1975): 36%. **Pop. 5-19:** in school (1975): 40%, per teacher (1975): 80.

Nepal was originally a group of petty principalities, the inhabitants of one of which, the Gurkhas, became dominant about 1769. In 1951 King Tribhubana Bir Bikram, member of the Shah family, ended the system of rule by hereditary premiers of the Ranas family, who had kept the kings virtual prisoners, and established a cabinet system of government.

Virtually closed to the outside world for centuries. Nepal is now linked to India and Pakistan by roads and air service and to Tibet by road. Polygamy, child marriage, and the caste system were officially abolished in 1963.

India has been the largest aid donor and is the chief trade partner, but Nepal has cultivated good relations with China as well.

Students and political opponents were arrested in 1974 following violent protests.

## Netherlands

### Kingdom of the Netherlands

**People: Population** (1977 est.) 13,850,000. **Age distrib. (%)** 0–14: 26.8; 15–59: 58.6; 60+: 14.7. **Pop. density:** 975.90 per sq. mi. **Urban** (1975): 76.3%. **Ethnic groups:** Dutch. **Languages:** Dutch. **Religions:** Roman Catholics 40%, Protestants 40%.

**Geography: Area:** 14,192 sq. mi., the size of Mass., Conn. and R.I. combined. **Location:** In NW Europe on North Sea. **Topography:** The land is flat, with average altitude of 37 ft. above sea level, with much land below sea level, reclaimed and protected by dikes, of which there are 1,500 miles. Since 1927 the government has been draining the IJsselmeer, formerly the Zuider Zee, converting the reclaimed land into farms. By 1972, 410,000 of a planned 550,000 acres had been drained. Work is also progressing on damming the SW estuaries, into which flow the Rhine, Meuse, and Scheldt rivers. **Capital:** Amsterdam. **Cities** (1975 est.): Rotterdam (met.) 1,031,778; Amsterdam (met.) 988,998; Hague (met.) 680,679; Utrecht (met.) 463,187.

**Government: Head of state:** Queen Juliana; b. Apr. 30, 1909; in office: Sept. 6, 1948; **Head of government:** Prime Min. Andries A.M. van Agt; b. Feb. 2, 1931; in office: Dec. 19, 1977. **Local divisions:** 11 provinces, with elected executives. **Armed forces:** regulars 158,800; reserves 176,500.

**Economy: Industries:** Metals, machinery, food products, chemicals, textiles, oil refinery, diamond cutting, pottery, electronics, tourism. **Chief crops:** Grains, potatoes, sugar beets, vegetables, fruits, flowers. **Minerals:** Natural gas, oil. **Per capita arable land:** 0.1 acres. **Meat production** (1976): beef: 362,000 tons; pork: 868,000 tons; lamb: 15,600. **Fish catch** (1975): 350,500 metric tons. **Electricity production** (1977): 58.29 bln. kwh. **Labor force:** 7% agric.; 25% manuf.

**Finance: Currency:** Guilder (May 1978: 2.25 = $1 US). **Gross domestic product** (1977): $113.18 bln. **Per capita income** (1976): $5,890. **Imports** (1977): $45.62 bln.; partners (1974): W. Ger. 26%, Belg. 14%, Iran 9%, U.S. 9%. **Exports** (1977): $43.70 bln.; partners (1974): W. Ger. 30%, Belg. 13%, Fr. 10%, U.K. 9%. **Tourists** (1975): 2,819,000; receipts (1975): $1.107 billion. **Balance of payments** (1977): +$299,000,000. **National budget** (1977): $38.25 bln. revenues; $37.44 bln. expenditures. **International reserves** (May 1978): $7.82 bln. **Consumer prices** (change in 1977): 6.4%.

**Transport: Railway traffic** (1975): 5.28 bln. passenger-miles; 1.69 bln. net ton-miles. **Motor vehicles:** in use (1975): 3,399,000 passenger cars, 345,000 commercial vehicles; manufactured (1977): 44,520 passenger cars; 12,720 commercial vehicles. **Civil aviation:** 7,094 mln. passenger-miles (1977); 46,731 mln. freight ton-miles (1977). **Chief ports:** Rotterdam, Amsterdam, IJmuiden.

**Communications: Television sets:** 3,510,000 licensed (1974). **Radios:** 3,846,000 licensed (1974). **Telephones in use** (1977): 5,411,617. **Daily newspaper circulation** (1973): 4,175,000; 311 per 1,000 pop.

**Health: Life expectancy at birth** (1975): 71.2 male; 77.2 female. **Births** (per 1,000 pop. 1976): 12.9. **Deaths** (per 1,000 pop. 1976): 8.3. **Natural increase** (1975): .46%. **Pop. per hospital bed** (1975): 85. **Pop. per physician** (1975): 624. **Infant mortality** (per 1,000 live births 1975): 10.6.

**Education: Literacy** (1975): 98%. **Pop. 5-19:** school (1975): 62%, per teacher (1975): 35.

Julius Caesar conquered the region in 55 B.C., when it was inhabited by Celtic and Germanic tribes.

After the empire of Charlemagne (d. 814) fell apart, the Netherlands (Holland, Belgium, Flanders) split among counts, dukes and bishops, passed to Burgundy and thence to Charles V of Spain. His son, Philip II, tried to check the Dutch drive toward political freedom and Protestantism (1568-1573). William the Silent, prince of Orange, led a confederation of the northern provinces, called Estates, in the Union of Utrecht, 1579. The Estates retained individual sovereignty, but were represented jointly in the States-General, a body that had control of foreign affairs and defense. In 1581 they repudiated allegiance to Spain. The rise of the Dutch republic to naval, economic and artistic minence came in the 17th Century.

The United Dutch Republic ended 1795 when the French formed the Batavian Republic. Napoleon made his brother Louis king of Holland, 1806; Louis abdicated 1810 when Napoleon annexed Holland. In 1813 the French were expelled. In 1815 the congress of Vienna formed a kingdom of the Netherlands, including Belgium, under William I. In 1830, the Belgians seceded and formed a separate kingdom.

The constitution, promulgated 1814, and subsequently revised, assures a hereditary constitutional monarchy. The reigning sovereign is Queen Juliana.

The Netherlands maintained its neutrality in World War I, but was invaded and brutally occupied by Germany from 1940 to 1945. After the war, neutrality was abandoned, and the country joined NATO, the Western European Union, the Benelux Union, and, in 1957, became a charter member of the Common Market.

In 1949, after several years of fighting, the Netherlands granted independence to Indonesia, where it had ruled since the 17th century. In 1963, West New Guinea was turned over to Indonesia, after five years of controversy and seizure of Dutch property in Indonesia.

Some 200,000 Indonesians emigrated to the Netherlands. Of them, 35,000 were from the South Moluccan islands. Terrorists demanding independence for South Molucca from Indonesia staged train hijackings and other incidents in the Netherlands in 1975 and 1977.

Surinam, a Dutch associated state on the northern coast of South America, became independent in 1975. About 160,000 Surinamers (most of them E. Indians), one third of the population, emigrated to the Netherlands, adding to problems of unemployment.

Though the Netherlands has been heavily industrialized, its productive small farms export large quantitites of pork and dairy bods.

Rotterdam, located along the principal mouth of the Rhine, handles the most cargo of any ocean port in the world. Canals, of which there are 3,478 miles, are important in transportation. The Rhine, Meuse, and Scheldt reach the sea through the Netherlands and carry enormous traffic.

## Netherlands Antilles

The **Netherland Antilles,** constitutionally on a level of equality with the Netherlands homeland within the Kingdom, consist of 2 groups of islands in the West Indies. **Curacao, Aruba** and **Bonaire** are near the South American coast; **St. Eustatius, Saba** and the southern part of **St. Maarten** are SE of Puerto Rico. Northern two-thirds of St. Maarten belong to French Guadeloupe; the French call the island St. Martin. Total area of the 2 groups is 395 sq. mi., including: Aruba 70, Bonaire 112, Curacao 180, St. Eustatius 12, Saba 5, St. Maarten (Dutch part) 16.

The Netherlands Antilles population (est. 1976) was 240,000. Willemstad is the capital. Chief products are corn, pulse, salt and phosphate; principal industry is the refining of crude oil from Venezuela. Tourism is an important industry, as are electronics and shipbuilding.

## New Zealand

### Dominion of New Zealand

**People: Population:** (1977 est.): 3,110,000. **Age distrib.** (%): 1–14: 30.8; 15–59: 56.5; 60+: 12.7. **Pop. density:** 29.98 per sq. mi. **Urban** (1971): 81.4%. **Ethnic groups:** European (mostly British) 90%, Polynesian (mostly Maori) 9%. **Languages:** English, Maori. **Religions:** Protestants 70%, Roman Catholics 16%.

**Geography: Area:** 103,736 sq. mi., the size of Colorado. **Location:** In SW Pacific O. **Neighbors:** Nearest are Australia on W, Fiji, Tonga on N. **Topography:** Each of the two main islands (North and South Is.) is mainly hilly and mountainous. The east coasts consist of fertile plains, especially the broad Canterbury Plains on South I. A volcanic plateau is in center of North I. South Island has glaciers and 15 peaks over 10,000 ft. **Capital:** Wellington. **Cities** (1976 est.): Auckland (met.) 742,786; Manukau (met.) 742,786; Wellington (met.) 327,414; Christchurch (met.) 295,296.

**Government: Head of state:** Queen Elizabeth II, represented by Gov.-Gen. Keith Jacka Holyoake; b. Feb. 1904; in office: Oct. 26, 1977; **Head of government:** Prime Min. Robert David Muldoon; b. Sept. 1921; in office: Nov. 1975. **Local divisions:** 105

counties, 136 boroughs, 12 town districts. **Armed forces:** regulars 12,466; reserves 12,065.

**Economy: Industries:** Food processing, paper, steel, aluminum, oil products. **Chief crops:** Grain. **Minerals:** Oil, gas, gold, iron, limestone, diatomite, coal, pumice. **Other resources:** Wool, timber. **Per capita arable land:** 0.6 acres. **Meat production** (1976): beef: 604,500 tons; pork: 34,600 tons; lamb: 510,900 tons. **Fish catch** (1975): 65,500 metric tons. **Electricity production** (1976): 20.90 bln. kwh. **Labor force:** 12% agric.; 25% manuf.

**Finance: Currency:** Dollar (May 1978: 1 = $1.01 US). **Gross domestic product** (1976): $12.53 bln. **Per capita income** (1975): $3,969. **Imports** (1977): $3.36 bln.; partners (1974): Austral. 20%, U.K. 18%, Jap. 15%, U.S. 13%. **Exports** (1977): $3.14 bln.; partners (1974): U.K. 20%, U.S. 14%, Jap. 13%, Austral. 11%. **Tourists** (1975): 377,500; receipts (1975): $159 million. **Balance of payments** (1977): −$118,000,000. **National budget** (1975): $3.30 bln. revenues; $4.24 bln. expenditures. **International reserves** (May 1978): $810 mln. **Consumer prices** (change in 1977): 14.4%.

**Transport: Railway traffic** (1975): 328.51 mln. passenger-miles; 2.24 bln. net ton-miles. **Motor vehicles:** in use (1975): 1,167,600 passenger cars, 205,700 commercial vehicles; assembled (1977): 63,468 passenger cars; 12,552 commercial vehicles. **Civil aviation:** 2,183 mln. passenger-miles (1977); 70,749 mln. freight ton-miles (1977). **Chief ports:** Aukland, Wellington, Lyttleton, Tauranga.

**Communications: Television sets:** 791,000 in use (1974), 147,000 manufactured (1975). **Radios:** 2,700,000 in use (1974), 164,000 manufactured (1975). **Telephones in use** (1977): 1,632,478.

**Health: Life expectancy at birth** (1972): 68.55 male; 74.60 female. **Births** (per 1,000 pop. 1975): 18.5. **Deaths** (per 1,000 pop. 1975): 8.2. **Natural increase** (1975): 1.03%. **Pop. per hospital bed** (1975): 140. **Pop. per physician** (1975): 739. **Infant mortality** (per 1,000 live births 1974): 13.8.

**Education: Literacy** (1975): 64%. **Pop. 5-19:** in school (1975): 73%, per teacher (1975): 37.

The Maoris, a Polynesian group from the eastern Pacific, reached New Zealand before and during the 14th century. The first European to sight New Zealand was the Dutch navigator Abel Janszoon Tasman, but Maoris refused to allow him to land. British Capt. James Cook explored the coasts, 1769-1770.

British sovereignty was proclaimed in 1840, with organized settlement beginning in the same year. Representative institutions were granted in 1853. Maori Wars ended in 1870 with British victory. The colony became a dominion in 1907, and is an independent member of the Commonwealth.

New Zealand fought on the side of the Allies in both world wars, and signed the ANZUS Treaty of Mutual Security with the U.S. and Australia in 1951. It sent 400 men to aid U.S. forces in South Vietnam. New Zealand joined with Australia and Britain in a pact to defend Singapore and Malaysia; New Zealand units are stationed in those two countries.

In 1973, to protest France's testing of nuclear devices above Mururoa Atoll, a New Zealand Navy frigate cruised just outside the French South Pacific island's 12-mile limit but within the test area. In 1974, New Zealand opposed U.S. plans for a military base on Diego Garcia island in the Indian Ocean.

A labor tradition in politics dates back to the 19th century. Private ownership is basic to the economy, but state ownership or regulation affects many industries. Transportation, broadcasting, mining, and forestry are largely state-owned.

The native Maoris numbered an estimated 200,000 in the early 19th century; violence and European diseases cut them to 40,000 by the end of the century. Recently they have increased at 3% annually and totaled over 250,000 in 1976. Four of 87 members of the House of Representatives are elected directly by the Maori people. Thousands of Samoans, Tongans, and other South Pacific islanders live and work in New Zealand.

New Zealand comprises **North Island,** 44,281 sq. mi.; **South Island,** 58,093 sq. mi.; **Stewart Island,** 670 sq. mi.; **Chatham Islands,** 372 sq. mi. Both the North and South Islands slightly exceed 500 mi. in length. Cook Strait, separating the two, is only 16 mi. wide at its narrowest.

In 1965, the **Cook Islands** (pop. 1976, 21,317; area 93 sq. mi.) became self-governing although New Zealand retains responsibility for defense and foreign affairs. **Niue** attained the same status in 1974; it lies 400 mi. to W (pop. 1974, 3,992; area 100 sq. mi.). **Tokelau Is.,** (pop. 1974, 1,574; area 4 sq. mi.) are

300 mi. N of Samoa.

**Ross Dependency**, administered by New Zealand since 1923, comprises 160,000 sq. mi. of Antarctic territory.

## Nicaragua
### Republic of Nicaragua

**People: Population** (1977 est.): 2,310,000. **Age distrib. (%):** 0–14: 48.1; 15–59: 47.2; 60+: 4.7. **Pop. density:** 40.42 per sq. mi. **Urban** (1972): 48.6%. **Ethnic groups:** Mestizo 70%, Caucasian 17%, Negro 9%, Indian 4%. **Languages:** Spanish, English (on Caribbean coast). **Religions:** Roman Catholics 95%.

**Geography: Area:** 57,143 sq. mi., slightly larger than Wisconsin. **Location:** In Central America. **Neighbors:** Honduras on N. Costa Rica on S. **Topography:** Both Atlantic and Pacific coasts are over 200 mi. long. The Cordillera mountains, including many volcanic peaks, runs NW-SE through the middle of the country. Between this range and a volcanic range to the E lie Lakes Managua and Nicaragua. **Capital:** Managua. **Cities** (1971 cen.): Managua 398,514; (1968 est.): Leon 79,939.

**Government: Head of state:** Pres. Anastasio Somoza-Debayle; b. 1925; in office: 1967-72; Dec. 1, 1974. **Local divisions:** 16 departments. **Armed forces:** regulars 7,100; para-military 4,000.

**Economy: Industries:** Oil refining, chemicals, textiles. **Chief crops:** Bananas, cotton, fruit, yucca, coffee, sugar, corn, beans, cocoa, rice, sesame, tobacco, wheat. **Minerals:** Gold, silver, copper, tungsten. **Other resources:** Forests, shrimp. **Per capita arable land:** 0.8 acres. **Meat production** (1976): beef: 66,100 tons; pork: 10,200 tons. **Electricity production** (1975): 835.00 mln. kwh. **Labor force:** 46% agriculture.

**Finance: Currency:** Cordoba (May 1978: 7.03 = $1 US). **Gross domestic product** (1977): $2.23 bln. **Per capita income** (1975): $676. **Imports** (1977): $721 mln.; partners (1974): U.S. 32%, Venez. 9%, Guat. 7%, Jap. 7%, Costa Rica 7%. **Exports** (1976): $542 mln.; partners (1974): U.S. 19%, W. Ger. 19%, Jap. 9%, Costa Rica 9%. **Tourists** (1972): 148,300; receipts (1975): $27 million. **Balance of payments** (1977): +$9,600,000. **National budget** (1976): $215.42 mln. revenues; $259.77 mln. expenditures. **International reserves** (Apr. 1978): $149.83 mln. **Consumer prices** (change in 1977): 11.4%.

**Transport: Railway traffic** (1972): 17.39 mln. passenger-miles; 8.69 mln. net ton-miles. **Motor vehicles:** in use (1973): 32,000 passenger cars, 20,000 commercial vehicles. **Chief ports:** Corinto, Puerto Somoza, San Juan del Sur.

**Communications: Television Sets:** 75,000 in use (1974), 2,000 manufactured (1970). **Radios:** 126,000 in use (1974), 6,000 manufactured (1969). **Telephones in use** (1977): 55,264. **Daily newspaper circulation** (1974): 53,000; 26 per 1,000 pop.

**Health: Life expectancy at birth** (1975): 51.2 male; 54.6 female. **Births** (annual per 1,000 pop. 1972-75): 48.3. **Deaths** (annual per 1,000 pop. 1972-75): 13.9. **Natural increase** (annual 1970-75): 3.44%. **Pop. per hospital bed** (1975): 426. **Pop. per physician** (1975): 1,559. **Infant mortality** (annual per 1,000 live births 1970-75): 46.0.

**Education: Literacy** (1975): 57%. **Pop. 5-19:** in school (1975): 44%, per teacher (1975): 84.

Nicaragua, inhabited by various Indian tribes, was conquered by Spain in 1552.

After gaining independence from Spain, 1821, Nicaragua was united for a short period with Mexico, then with the United Provinces of Central America, finally becoming an independent republic, 1838.

U.S. Marines occupied the country at times in the early 20th century, the last time from 1926 to 1933.

Gen. Anastasio Somoza-Debayle was elected president 1967. He resigned 1972 and was succeeded by a 3-man National Junta. He was elected president again Sept. 1, 1974. The Somozas, richest Nicaraguan family, have dominated politics for four decades. Martial law was imposed in Dec. 1974, after officials were kidnapped by the Marxist Sandinista guerrillas. The country's Roman Catholic bishops charged in 1977 that the government had tortured, raped, and executed civilians in its anti-guerrilla campaign. Violent and peaceful opposition spread to nearly all classes as U.S. support for Somoza weakened in 1978.

A severe earthquake, Dec. 23, 1972, destroyed much of Managua; about 6,000 died and 200,000 were left homeless. The nation was also hit by severe drought, lasting into 1973.

## Niger
### Republic of Niger

**People: Population** (1977 est.): 4,860,000. **Age distrib.** 0–14: 44.5; 15–59: 50.8; 60+: 4.7. **Pop. density:** 9.93 per mi. **Ethnic groups:** Hausas 50%, Djermas 23%, Fulanis 15 Tuaregs 12%. **Languages:** French (official), Hausa, Djerm others. **Religions:** Moslems 85%, others.

**Geography: Area:** 489,206 sq. mi., almost twice the size Texas. **Location:** In the interior of N. Africa. **Neighbors:** Liby Algeria on N, Mali, Upper Volta on W, Benin, Nigeria on S, Ch on E. **Topography:** Most of Niger consists of arid desert a mountains. A narrow savanna in the S and the Niger R. basin the SW contain most of the population. **Capital:** Niamey. **Citi** (1975 est.): Niamey 130,299.

**Government: Head of state:** Pres. Seyni Kountche; b. 193 in office: Apr. 17, 1974; **Local divisions:** 7 departments. **Arm** **forces:** regulars 2,050; para-military 1,800.

**Economy: Chief crops:** Peanuts, cotton are main ca crops. **Minerals:** Uranium (5th largest reserves in the worl **Per capita arable land:** 7.9 acres. **Meat production** (1975 beef: 22,000 tons; lamb: 16,000 tons. **Electricity productio** (1975): 70.00 mln. kwh. **Labor force:** 91% agriculture.

**Finance: Currency:** Franc (May 1978: 230.35 = $1 US **Gross domestic product** (1974 est.): $500 mln. **Per capi** **income** (1974): $100. **Imports** (1975): $100 mln.; partne (1973): Fr. 43%, W. Ger. 8%, U.S. 7%, Nigeria 6%. **Expor** (1975): $91 mln.; partners (1973): Fr. 51%, Nigeria 26%, It. 6° W. Ger. 5%. **Balance of payments** (1975): +$5,200,000. **I** **ternational reserves** (Mar. 1978): $82.6 mln. **Consum** **prices** (change in 1977): 23.3%.

**Transport: Motor vehicles:** in use (1974): 8,600 passeng cars, 9,100 commercial vehicles.

**Communications: Radios:** 145,000 in use (1970). **Tel** **phones in use** (1977): 8,147.

**Health: Life expectancy at birth** (1975): 37.0 male; 40.1 f male. **Births** (annual per 1,000 pop. 1972-75): 52.2. **Deaths** (a nual per 1,000 pop. 1972-75): 25.5. **Natural increase** (annu 1970-75): 2.67%. **Pop. per hospital bed** (1975): 1,685. **Po** **per physician** (1975): 40,634. **Infant mortality** (annual p 1,000 live births 1959-60): 200.

**Education: Literacy** (1975): 5%. **Pop. 5-19:** in school (1975 8%, per teacher (1975): 420.

Niger was part of ancient and medieval African empires. Euro pean explorers reached the area in the late 18th century. Th French colony of Niger was established 1900-22, after the de feat of Tuareg fighters, who had invaded the area from the N century before. The country became independent Aug. 3, 196 The next year it signed a bilateral agreement with France retai ing close economic and cultural ties, which have continue Hamani Diori, Niger's first president, was ousted in a 1974 cou Drought and famine struck in 1973-74, and again in 1975, an half the country's livestock died.

## Nigeria
### Federal Republic of Nigeria

**People: Population** (1977 est.): 66,630,000. **Pop. density** 186.81 per sq. mi. **Ethnic groups:** Yoruba 18%, Ibo 18% Hausa-Fulani 32%, 250 others. **Languages:** English (official Hausa, Yoruba, Ibo, others. **Religions:** Moslems 47% (in N Christians 34% (in S), others.

**Geography: Area:** 356,669 sq. mi., more than twice the siz of California. **Location:** On the S coast of W. Africa. **Neighbors** Benin on W, Niger on N, Chad, Cameroon on E. **Topography** Four E-W regions divide Nigeria: a coastal mangrove swam 10-60 mi. wide, a tropical rain forest 50-100 mi. wide, a platea of savanna and open woodland, and semidesert in the N. **Cap** **tal:** Lagos. **Cities** (1975 est.): Lagos (met.) 1,476,837; Ibada 847,000; Ogbomosho 432,000; Kano 399,000; Oshogb 282,000; Ilorin 282,000.

**Government: Head of state:** Head of military govt. Olusegu Obasanjo; b. Mar. 5, 1937; in office: Feb. 13, 1976. **Local divi** **sions:** 19 states, with military governors. **Armed forces:** regu lars 230,500; reserves 2,000.

**Economy: Industries:** Food processing, assembly of vehicles and other equipment. **Chief crops:** Cocoa (main export crop) tobacco, palm products, peanuts, cotton, soybeans. **Minerals**

il, gas, coal, iron, limestone, columbium, tin. **Crude oil reserves** (1978): 18.70 bln. bbls. **Other resources:** Timber, rubber, hides. **Per capita arable land:** 0.6 acres. **Meat production** 1975): beef: 193,000 tons; pork: 29,000 tons; lamb: 92,000 tons. **Fish catch** (1975): 506,800 metric tons. **Electricity production** 1976): 3.39 bln. kwh. **Labor force:** 67% agriculture.

**Finance: Currency:** Naira (May 1978: 1 = $1.57 US). **Gross omestic product** (1975): $246.52 bln. **Per capita income** 1973): $201. **Imports** (1976): $8.20 bln.; partners (1974): U.K. 3%, W. Ger. 15%, U.S. 12%, Jap. 9%. **Exports** (1976): $10.57 ln.; partners (1974): U.S. 27%, U.K. 17%, Neth. 14%, Fr. 10%. **Fourist receipts** (1975): $29 million. **Balance of payments** 1977): —$813,000,000. **National budget** (1976): $8.76 bln. evenues; $11.04 bln. expenditures. **International reserves** May 1978): $2.61 mln. **Consumer prices** (change in 1977): 1.6%.

**Transport: Railway traffic** (1974): 487.49 mln. passenger-miles; 6.04 bln. net ton-miles. **Motor vehicles:** in use (1973): 50,000 passenger cars, 82,000 commercial vehicles. **Civil aviation:** 394 mln. passenger-miles (1976); 2,415 mln. freight ton-miles (1976). **Chief ports:** Port Harcourt, Bonny, Lagos.

**Communications: Television sets:** 110,000 in use (1974), ,000 manufactured (1975). **Radios:** 5,000,000 in use (1974), 03,000 manufactured (1975). **Telephones in use** (1977): 21,032. **Daily newspaper circulation** (1974): 660,000; 9 per ,000 pop.

**Health: Life expectancy at birth** (1966): 37.2 male; 36.7 fe-nale. **Births** (annual per 1,000 pop. 1972-75): 49.3. **Deaths** (an-ual per 1,000 pop. 1972-75): 22.7. **Natural increase** (annual 970-75): 2.66%. **Pop. per hospital bed** (1975): 1,385. **Pop.** ber **physician** (1975): 23,341. **Infant mortality** (per 1,000 live virths 1962): 62.0.

**Education: Literacy** (1975): 25%. **Pop. 5-19:** in school 1975): 22%, per teacher (1975): 140.

Early cultures in Nigeria date back to at least 700 B.C. From he 12th to the 14th centuries, more advanced cultures devel-ped in the Yoruba area, at Ife, and in the north, where Moslem nfluence prevailed.

Portuguese and British slavers appeared from the 15th-16th centuries. Britain seized Lagos, 1861, during an anti-slave trade campaign, and gradually extended control inland until 1900. Ni-eria became independent Oct. 1, 1960, and a republic Oct. 1, 963. Its first constitution provided for 4 regions with local auton-my, and a democratic central government.

In 1966 there were 2 military coups and periods of political ssassination and inter-tribal strife, ending a long period of coali-ion governments of the majority Northern Region and other re-ions.

On May 30, 1967, the Eastern Region seceded, proclaiming self the Republic of Biafra. The move plunged the country into ivil war. Casualties in the war were estimated at over 1 million, ncluding many "Biafrans" (mostly Ibos) who died of starvation lespite international efforts to provide relief. The secessionists, fter steadily losing ground, capitulated Jan. 12, 1970. Within a ew years, the Ibos were reintegrated into national life, but mis-rust among the regions persists, putting all census figures in loubt. Nigeria has been redivided into 19 states.

A military coup in 1975, and a presidential assassination in 976, has prevented a full return to earlier free institutions.

Under "indigenization" programs, various categories of busi-nesses are to be run by Nigerians only by 1978, while others nust have local participation. Oil revenues have made possible a massive economic development program, largely using private enterprise, but agriculture has lagged.

Nigeria led in the formation of the West African Economic Community, linking 15 French, English, and Portuguese-speaking countries.

# Norway

## Kingdom of Norway

**People: Population** (1977 est.): 4,040,000. **Age distrib. (%):** −14: 24.1; 15–59: 57.1; 60+: 18.8. **Pop. density:** 32.27 per sq. ni. **Urban** (1975): 44.6% **Ethnic groups:** Only minority are apps 0.5%. **Languages:** Norwegian, Lapp. **Religions:** Luther-ns 95%.

**Geography: Area:** 125,181 sq. mi., slightly larger than New Mexico. **Location:** Occupies the W part of Scandinavian Penin-sula in NW Europe, and extends farther north than any Euro-pean land. **Neighbors:** Sweden, Finland, USSR on E. **Topography:** A highly indented coast is lined with tens of thousands of islands. Mountains and plateaus cover most of the country, which is only 25% forested. **Capital:** Oslo. **Cities** (1975 est.): Oslo (met.) 645,413; Bergen 213,807.

**Government: Head of state:** King Olav V; b. July 2, 1903; in office: Sept. 21, 1957; **Head of government:** Prime Min. Odvar Nordli; b. Nov. 3, 1927; in office: Jan. 15, 1976. **Local divisions:** Oslo and 19 fylkes (counties). **Armed forces:** regulars 64,000; reserves 160,000.

**Economy: Industries:** Paper, shipbuilding, engineering, met-als, chemicals, food processing shipping. **Chief crops:** Grains, potatoes, fruits. **Minerals:** Oil, copper, pyrites, nickel, iron, zinc, lead. **Crude oil reserves** (1978): 6.00 bln. bbls. **Other re-sources:** Forests. **Per capita arable land:** 0.5 acres. **Meat pro-duction** (1976): beef: 62,100 tons; pork: 76,300 tons; lamb: 16,400. **Fish catch** (1975): 2,550,400 metric tons. **Electricity production** (1977): 72.49 bln. kwh. **Labor force:** 10% agric.; 25% manuf.

**Finance: Currency:** Kroner (May 1978: 5.43 = $1 US). **Gross domestic product** (1977): $31.63 bln. **Per capita in-come** (1976): $6,511. **Imports** (1977): $12.88 bln.; partners (1975): Swed. 18%, W. Ger. 14%, U.K. 8%, U.S. 6%. **Exports** (1977): $8.65 bln.; partners (1975): U.K. 24%, Swed. 16.2%, W. Ger. 8.1%, Den. 7.3%. **Balance of payments** (1977): —$122,000,000. **National budget** (1976): $7.99 bln. revenues; 8.41 bln. expenditures. **International reserves** (May 1978): $3.00 bln. **Consumer prices** (change in 1977): 9.2%.

**Transport: Railway traffic** (1975): 1.21 bln. passenger-miles; 1.59 bln. net ton-miles. **Motor vehicles:** in use (1975): 953,700 passenger cars, 147,200 commercial vehicles. **Civil aviation:** 2,139 mln. passenger-miles (1977); 81,972 mln. freight ton-miles (1977). **Chief ports:** Bergen, Stavenjer, Oslo, Tonsberg.

**Communications: Television sets:** 1,021,000 licensed (1974), 108,000 manufactured (1974). **Radios:** 1,277,000 li-censed (1974), 111,000 manufactured (1973). **Telephones in use** (1977): 1,476,091. **Daily newspaper circulation** (1974): 1,567,000; 391 per 1,000 pop.

**Health: Life expectancy at birth** (1974): 71.50 male; 77.83 female. **Births** (per 1,000 pop. 1975): 14.1. **Deaths** (per 1,000 pop. 1975): 10.0. **Natural increase** (1975): .41%. **Pop. per hospital bed** (1975): 91. **Pop. per physician** (1975): 581. **In-fant mortality** (per 1,000 live births 1974): 10.5.

**Education: Literacy** (1975): 99%. **Pop. 5-19:** in school (1975): 69%, per teacher (1975): 20.

The first supreme ruler of Norway was Harald the Fairhaired who came to power in 872 A.D. Between 860 and 1000, Nor-way's Vikings raided and occupied widely dispersed parts of Eu-rope. Christianity was introduced in 1030.

The country was united with Denmark 1381-1814, and with Sweden, 1814-1905. In 1905, the country became independent with Prince Charles of Denmark as King.

Norway remained neutral during World War I. Germany at-tacked Norway Apr. 9, 1940, and held it until liberation May 8, 1945. The country abandoned its neutrality after the war, and joined the NATO alliance. Norway, a member of the European Free Trade Assoc., rejected membership in the Common Market in a 1972 referendum.

Abundant hydroelectric resources provided the base for Nor-way's industrialization, producing one of the highest living stan-dards in the world. Future exports from the huge North Sea oil fields may be limited by government production restrictions.

Despite an almost total lack of unemployment and an increas-ing labor shortage, Norway has refused to admit more than a small number of foreign workers.

Norway's merchant marine is the world's fourth largest.

Norway and the Soviet Union have disputed their territorial waters boundary in the Barents Sea, north of the two countries' common border. Oil and mineral deposits are believed to exist under the continental shelf.

## Svalbard

Svalbard is a group of mountainous islands in the Arctic Ocean, c. 23,957 sq. ml., pop. varying seasonally from 1,500 t0 3,500. The largest, West Spitsbergen, c. 15,000 sq. mi., seat of governor, is about 370 ml. N of Norway. By a treaty signed in Paris, 1920, major European powers recognized the sovereignty of Norway, which incorporated it in 1925. Both Norway and the USSR mine rich coal deposits. Mt. Newton (West Spitsbergen) is 5,633 ft. tall.

# Oman

## Sultanate of Oman

**People: Population** (1977 est.): 820,000. **Pop. density:** 10.0 per sq. mi. **Ethnic groups:** Arab 88%, Baluchi 4%, Persian 3%, Indian 2%, African 2%. **Languages:** Arabic, Persian, Urdu, others. **Religions:** Ibadi Moslems 50%, Sunni Moslems 25%, some Hindus.

**Geography: Area:** 82,000 sq. mi., the size of Kansas. **Location:** On SE coast of Arabian Peninsula. **Neighbors:** United Arab Emirates, Saudi Arabia, South Yemen on W. **Topography:** Oman has a narrow coastal plain up to 10 mi. wide, a range of barren mountains reaching 9,900 ft., and a wide, stony, mostly waterless plateau averaging 1,000 ft. in altitude. Oman also rules the tip of the Ruus-al-Jebal peninsula, controlling access to the Persian Gulf. **Capital:** Muscat. **Cities** (1975 est.): Matrah 20,000; Muscat 7,000.

**Government: Head of state:** Sultan Qabusbin Said; b. Nov. 18, 1940; in office: July 23, 1970. **Local divisions:** 1 province, 9 regions, and districts. **Armed forces:** regulars 13,000; paramilitary 3,000.

**Economy: Chief crops:** Dates, fruits vegetables, wheat, frankincense. **Minerals:** Oil. **Crude oil reserves** (1978): 5.65 bln. bbls. **Per capita arable land:** 0.5 acres. **Fish catch** (1975): 100,000 metric tons. **Electricity production** (1975): 310.0 mln. kwh. **Labor force:** 73% agriculture.

**Finance: Currency:** Rial (May 1978; 1 = $2.90 US). **Gross domestic product** (1977): $2.53 bln. **Per capita income** (1974): $1,600. **Imports** (1975): $668 mln.; partners (1973): U.A.E. 23%, U.K. 19%, Jap. 9%, Neth. 9%. **Exports** (1976): $1.58 bln.; partners (1973): Jap. 35%, Spain 18%, Fr. 12%, U.K. 9%. **National budget** (1974): $878.11 mln. revenues; $953.97 mln. expenditures. **International reserves** (Apr. 1978): $427.8 mln.

**Transport: Chief ports:** Matrah, Muscat.

**Communications: Telephones in use** (1977): 7,307. **Pop. per hospital bed** (1975): 598. **Pop. per physician** (1975): 2,364.

**Education: Literacy** (1975): 50%. **Pop. 5-19:** in school (1975): 20%, per teacher (1975): 138.

A long history of rule by other lands, including Portugal in the 16th century, ended with the ouster of the Persians in 1744. By the early 19th century, Muscat and Oman was one of the most important countries in the region, controlling much of the Persian and Pakistan coasts, and ruling far-away Zanzibar, which was separated in 1861 under British mediation.

British influence was confirmed in a 1951 treaty, and Britain helped supress an uprising by traditionally rebellious interior tribes against control by Muscat in the 1950s. Enclaves on the Pakistan coast were sold to that country in 1958.

On July 23, 1970, Sultan Said bin Taimur was overthrown by his son, who became Sultan Qabus bin Said. The new sultan changed the nation's name to Sultanate of Oman. He launched a domestic development program and battled leftist rebels in the southern Dhofar area. The government received arms aid and over 3,500 advisors from Iran, as well as British assistance; the guerrillas reportedly got arms from the USSR, Iraq, and Southern Yemen.

The government claimed it had defeated the rebels, Dec. 1975. The sole British base was closed down in 1977.

# Pakistan

## Islamic Republic of Pakistan

**People: Population** (1977 est.): 75,280,000. **Age distrib.** (%): 0–14: 43.4; 15–59: 49.9; 60+: 6.7. **Pop. density:** 219.64 per sq. mi. **Urban** (1972): 25.5%. **Ethnic groups:** Punjabi 66%, Sindhi 13%, Pushtun (Iranian) 8.5%, Urdu 7.6%, Baluchi 2.5%, others. **Languages:** Urdu, English are both official. **Religions:** Moslems 96%, Christians 1.4%, Hindus 1.5%.

**Geography: Area:** 342,750 sq. mi., larger than Texas. **Location:** In W part of South Asia. **Neighbors:** Iran on W, Afghanistan, China on N, India on E. **Topography:** The Indus R. rises in the Hindu Kush and Himalaya mtns. in the N (highest is K2, or Godwin Austen; 28,250 ft., 2d highest in world), then flows over 1,000 mi. through fertile valley, where most Pakistanis live, and empties into Arabian Sea. With its tributaries it supplies reservoirs, canals, and hydroelectric plants. Thar Desert, Eastern Plains flank Indus Valley. **Capital:** Islamabad. **Cities** (1972 cen): Karachi 3,498,634; Lahore 2,165,372; Lyallpur 822,263; Hyderabad 628,310; Rawalpindi 615,392.

**Government: Head of state:** Pres. Fazal Elahi Chaudry; Jan. 1, 1904; in office: Aug. 10, 1973; **Head of government:** Martial law admin. Mohammad Zia ul-Haq; b. 1924; in office: July 5, 1977. **Local divisions:** Federal capital and 4 provinces with elected legislatures: Punjab, Sind, Baluchistan, and NW Frontier. **Armed forces:** regulars 428,000; reserves 501,300.

**Economy: Industries:** Textiles, cement, paper, sugar, chemicals, fertilizers, surgical instruments. **Chief crops:** Rice, wheat, cotton, oilseeds, tobacco, sugar. **Minerals:** Sulphur, gypsum, salt, chromite, cement, oil, gas, asbestos, antimony, magnesite, silica. **Crude oil reserves** (1978): 280 mln. bbls. **Other resources:** Wool. **Per capita arable land:** 0.7 acres. **Meat production** (1975): beef: 188,000 tons; lamb: 89,000 tons. **Fish catch** (1975): 195,000 metric tons. **Electricity production** (1975): 8.80 bln. kwh. **Labor force:** 57% agric.; 12% manuf.

**Finance: Currency:** Rupee (May 1978: 9.93 = $1 US). **Gross domestic product** (1976): $13.22 bln. **Per capita income** (1975): $179. **Imports** (1977): $2.45 bln.; partners (1974): U.S., Jap., Ecuador, Venez. **Exports** (1977): $1.15 bln.; partners (1974): U.S., Braz., Neth. **Tourists** (1975): 172,000; receipts (1975): $33 million. **Balance of payments** (1977): −$13,000,000. **National budget** (1976): $1.79 bln. revenues; $2.25 bln. expenditures. **International reserves** (May 1978): $678 mln. **Consumer prices** (change in 1977): 10.1%.

**Transport: Railway traffic** (1973): 7.20 bln. passenger-miles; 4.56 bln. net ton-miles. **Motor vehicles:** in use (1973): 177,300 passenger cars, 79,100 commercial vehicles. **Civil aviation:** 2,116 mln. passenger-miles (1976); 92,092 mln. freight ton-miles (1976). **Chief ports:** Karachi.

**Communications: Television sets:** 125,000 in use (1974). **Radios:** 1,015,000 licensed (1974). **Telephones in use** (1975): 240,000.

**Health: Life expectancy at birth** (1962): 53.72 male; 48.8 female. **Births** (annual per 1,000 pop. 1972-75): 47.4. **Deaths** (annual per 1,000 pop. 1972-75): 16.5. **Natural increase** (1968): 2.4%. **Pop. per hospital bed** (1975): 1,873. **Pop. per physician** (1975): 3,894. **Infant mortality** (per 1,000 live births 1968): 124.3.

**Education: Literacy** (1975): 25%. **Pop. 5-19:** in school (1975): 26%, per teacher (1975): 115.

The land now called Pakistan shares the 5,000-year history of the India-Pakistan sub-continent. At the present day sites of Harappa and Mohenjo Daro, the Indus Valley Civilization, with large cities and elaborate irrigation systems, flourished c. 4,000-2,500 B.C.

Aryan invaders from the NW conquered the region around 1,500 B.C., forging a Hindu civilization that dominated Pakistan as well as India for 2,000 years, and bringing a language whose descendants are spoken by nearly all Pakistanis.

Beginning with the Persians in the 6th century B.C., and continuing with Alexander the Great and with the Sassanians, successive nations to the west ruled or influenced Pakistan, eventually separating the area from the Indian cultural sphere.

The first Arab invasion, 712 A.D., introduced Islam, which was adopted by the majority after a subsequent invasion two centuries later. Under the Mogul empire (1526-1867), Moslems ruled most of India, later yielding to British encroachment and resurgent Hindus.

After World War I the Moslems of British India began agitation for minority rights in elections.

Mohammad Ali Jinnah (1876-1948) was the principal architect of Pakistan. A lawyer who studied in England, he was a leader of the Moslem League from 1916, and worked for dominion status for India. From 1940 he advocated a separate Moslem state.

When the British withdrew Aug. 14, 1947, the Islamic majority areas of India acquired self-government as Pakistan, with dominion status in the Commonwealth.

Pakistan was divided into 2 sections, West Pakistan and East Pakistan. The 2 areas were nearly 1,000 mi. apart on opposite sides of India.

Pakistan became a republic in 1956. In Oct. 1958, Gen. Mohammad Ayub Khan took power in a coup. He was elected president in 1960 and reelected in 1965. Pakistan had a National Assembly (legislature) with equal membership from East and West Pakistan, and 2 Provincial Assemblies.

As a member of the Central Treaty Organization, along with neighboring Iran, Pakistan had been aligned with the West. For owing clashes between India and China in 1962, Pakistan made commercial and aid agreements with Communist China. U.S. aid to both Pakistan and India was suspended during the 1966 war over Kashmir but both economic aid and "nonlethal" military aid were resumed in 1966. The embargo was modified in 1973 and lifted in 1975.

Ayub resigned Mar. 25, 1969, after several months of violent rioting and unrest, most of it in East Pakistan. There were demands for a parliamentary form of government, for direct elections and economic reforms. In East Pakistan, which had about 56% of the population, there were demands for autonomy.

The government was turned over to Gen. Agha Mohammad Yahya Khan and martial law was declared; Yahya assumed the presidency.

The Awami League, which sought regional autonomy for East Pakistan, won a majority in Dec. 1970 elections to a National Assembly which was to write a new constitution. In March, 1971 Yahya postponed the Assembly. Rioting and strikes broke out in the East.

On Mar. 25, 1971, government troops launched attacks in the East. The Easterners, aided by India, proclaimed the independent nation of Bangladesh. In months of widespread fighting, countless thousands were killed. Some 10 million Easterners fled into India.

Full scale war between India and Pakistan had spread to both the East and West fronts by December 3. Pakistan troops in the East surrendered Dec. 16; Pakistan agreed to a cease-fire in the West Dec. 17.

Zulfikar Ali Bhutto, leader of the Pakistan People's party, which had won the most West Pakistan votes in the Dec. 1970 elections, became president Dec. 20. In 1972 he announced new and reforms and said the government would control management of major industries.

On July 3, 1972, Pakistan and India signed a pact agreeing to withdraw troops from their borders and seek peaceful solutions to all problems.

In Aug. 1973 India agreed to release 93,000 Pakistani prisoners held since 1971. The return was completed in April, 1974. Pakistan agreed to repatriate 200,000 Bengali nationals stranded in Pakistan, and agreed to accept some Biharis (non-Bengalis) unwanted in Bangladesh. India and Pakistan agreed in 1976 to resume full diplomatic relations.

A new constitution adopted Apr. 10, 1973, made Pakistan a federal Islamic republic. Bhutto became prime minister Aug. 14.

Bhutto was overthrown in a military coup July, 1977. Some 300 people had been killed in protests over alleged rigging of parliamentary elections earlier in the year. The new military rulers made concessions to Moslem conservatives.

# Panama

## Republic of Panama

**People: Population** (1977 est.): 1,770,000. **Age distrib. (%):** 0–14: 43.6; 15–59: 50.9; 60+: 5.7. **Pop. density:** 61.56 per sq. mi. **Urban** (1976): 50.0%. **Ethnic groups:** Mestizo 70%, Negro 13%, Caucasian 10%, Indian 6%. **Languages:** Spanish (official), English. **Religions:** Roman Catholics 93%, Protestants 6%.

**Geography: Area:** 28,753 sq. mi., slightly larger than West Virginia. **Location:** In Central America. **Neighbors:** Costa Rica on W., Colombia on E. **Topography:** Two mountain ranges run the length of the isthmus. Tropical rain forests cover the Caribbean coast and eastern Panama. **Capital:** Panama. **Cities** (1976 est.): Panama 415,790; San Miguelito 124,350.

**Government: Head of state:** Pres. Demetrio Lakas; b. Aug. 29, 1925; in office: Oct. 11, 1972. **Head of government:** Supreme Leader Gen. Omar Torrijos Herrera; b. Feb. 13, 1929; in office: Oct. 11, 1972. **Local divisions:** 9 provinces, 1 territory.

**Economy: Industries:** Oil refining, shipping, international banking. **Chief crops:** Bananas, pineapples, cocoa, coconuts, sugar. **Minerals:** Cement, clay, salt, copper. **Other resources:** Forests (Mahogany), shrimp. **Per capita arable land:** 0.6 acres. **Meat production** (1976): beef: 45,700 tons. **Fish catch** (1975): 80,200 metric tons. **Electricity production** (1977): 1.24 bln. kwh. **Labor force:** 38% agriculture.

**Finance: Currency:** Balboa (May 1978: 1.00 = $1 US). **Gross domestic product** (1976): $2.03 bln. **Per capita income** (1976): $1,055. **Imports** (1976): $3.67 bln.; partners (1976): U.S. 26%, Saudi Ar. 16%, Ecuador 16%, Venez. 9%. **Exports** (1976): $227 mln.; partners (1976): U.S. 44%, Canal

Zone 12%. **Tourists** (1975): 278,700; receipts (1975): $129 million. **Balance of payments** (1976): +$17,000,000. **National budget** (1976): $281.60 mln. revenues; $445.80 mln. expenditures. **International reserves** (May 1978): $153.5 mln. **Consumer prices** (change in 1977): 8.6%.

**Transport: Motor vehicles:** in use (1974): 62,600 passenger cars, 18,400 commercial vehicles. **Chief ports:** Balboa, Cristobal, Puerto Armuellas.

**Communications: Television sets:** 183,000 in use (1974). **Radios:** 260,000 in use (1974). **Telephones in use** (1977): 154,598. **Daily newspaper circulation** (1973): 145,000; 92 per 1,000 pop.

**Health: Life expectancy at birth** (1970): 64.26 male; 67.50 female. **Births** (per 1,000 pop. 1976): 32.2. **Deaths** (per 1,000 pop. 1975): 1.9. **Natural increase** (annual 1970-75): 2.91%. **Pop. per hospital bed** (1975): 283. **Pop. per physician** (1975): 1,238. **Infant mortality** (per 1,000 live births 1974): 32.9.

**Education: Literacy** (1975): 79%. **Pop. 5-19:** in school (1975): 67%, per teacher (1975): 37.

The coast of Panama was sighted by Rodrigo de Bastidas, sailing with Columbus for Spain in 1501, and was visited by Columbus in 1502. Vasco Nunez de Balboa crossed the isthmus and "discovered" the Pacific Ocean Sept. 13, 1513. Spanish colonies were ravaged by Francis Drake, 1572-95, and Henry Morgan, 1668-71. Morgan destroyed the old city of Panama which had been founded in 1519. Freed from Spain, Panama joined Colombia in 1821. Separatist forces in Panama sought to gain independence from Colombia several times.

Panama declared its independence from Colombia Nov. 3, 1903, with U.S. recognition. U.S. Naval forces deterred action by Colombia. On Nov. 18, 1903, Panama granted use, occupation and control of the Canal Zone to the U.S. by treaty, ratified Feb. 26, 1904. *(See also Canal Zone and Panama Canal.)*

Rioting began Jan. 9, 1964, in a dispute over the flying of the U.S. and Panamanian flags and terms of the 1903 treaty. At least 21 Panamanians and 3 U.S. soldiers died in the rioting.

In 1967 new treaties were proposed, but Panama rejected them in 1970. In Feb. 1974 the U.S. and Panama agreed to negotiate a new treaty which would give the U.S. the right to operate and protect the canal for a certain period, with Panama sharing in the revenues, and would also set a date for final transfer of jurisdiction to Panama. Opposition by U.S. Senators stalled the talks.

The U.S. and Panama initialed two treaties in 1977 that would provide for a gradual takeover by Panama of the canal, and withdrawal of U.S. troops, to be completed by 1999. U.S. payments would be substantially increased in the interim. The permanent neutrality of the canal would also be guaranteed. The treaties were ratified by the U.S. Senate in 1978.

Panama adopted its 4th constitution in 1972. The Assembly gave Gen. Omar Torrijos powers as head of government. He had been de facto ruler since 1969.

Due to easy Panama ship regulations and strictures in the U.S., merchant tonnage registered in Panama since World War II ranks high in size. Registered number of ships more than 1,000 gross tons each is about 1,700.

Similarly easy financial regulations have made Panama a center for international banking.

Inflation, unemployment, and uncertainty over the Canal have recently marred a record of economic growth and social improvement from 1950 to 1973.

# Papua New Guinea

**People: Population** (1977 est.): 2,910,000. **Age distrib. (%):** 0–14: 45.2; 15–59: 51.9; 60+: 2.9. **Pop. density:** 16.32 per sq. mi. **Urban** (1976): 12.9%. **Ethnic groups:** Papuans (in S and interior), Melanesian (N,E), pygmies, minorities of Chinese, Australians, Polynesians. **Languages:** Melanesian Pidgin, Police Motu, English, 750 local languages. **Religions:** Protestants 33%, Roman Catholic 18%, local religions.

**Geography: Area:** 178,260 sq. mi., slightly larger than California. **Location:** Occupies eastern half of island of New Guinea. **Neighbors:** Indonesia (West Irian) on W, Australia on S (across Torres Strait). **Topography:** Thickly forested mts. cover much of the center of the country, with lowlands along the coasts. Included are the nearby islands of Bismarck and Solomon groups, including Admiralty Is., New Ireland, New Britain, and Bougainville. **Capital:** Port Moresby. **Cities** (1976 cen.): Port Moresby (met.) 113,449.

**Government: Head of state:** Queen Elizabeth II, represented by Gov. Gen. Tore Lokoloko; in office: Feb. 18, 1977; **Head of government:** Prime Min. Michael Somare; b. 1936; in office: Sept. 16, 1975. **Local divisions:** National capital and 19 provinces with elected legislatures.

**Economy: Chief crops:** Coffee, coconuts, cocoa. **Minerals:** Copper, gold, silver, gas. **Per capita arable land:** 0.1 acres. **Fish catch** (1975): 42,700 metric tons. **Electricity production** (1975): 969.00 mln. kwh. **Labor force:** 82% agriculture.

**Finance: Currency:** Kina (July-Sep. 1977: 1 = $1.10 US). **Gross domestic product** (1974 est.): $1.57 mln. **Per capita income** (1974): $500. **Imports** (1976): $430 mln.; partners (1973): Austral. 54%, Jap. 16%, U.S. 9%, Sing. 4%. **Exports** (1976): $573 mln.; partners (1973): Jap. 35%, W. Ger. 23%, Austral. 20%, U.S. 5%. **Consumer prices** (change in 1977): 4.5%.

**Transport: Motor vehicles:** in use (1974): 17,300 passenger cars, 18,300 commercial vehicles. **Chief ports:** Port Moresby, Lae.

**Communications: Telephones in use** (1977): 37,531. **Daily newspaper circulation** (1974): 18,000; 7 per 1,000 pop.

**Health: Life expectancy at birth** (1975): 47.7 male; 47.6 female. **Births** (annual per 1,000 pop. 1972-75): 40.6 **Deaths** (annual per 1,000 pop. 1972-75): 17.1. **Natural increase** (annual 1970-75): 2.35%. **Pop. per hospital bed** (1975): 151. **Pop. per physician** (1975): 11,428.

**Education: Literacy** (1975): 29%. **Pop. 5-19:** in school (1975): 28%, per teacher (1975): 119.

Human remains have been found in the interior of New Guinea dating back at least 10,000 years and possibly much earlier. Successive waves of peoples probably entered the country from Asia through Indonesia. Europeans visited in the 15th century, but land claims did not begin until the 19th century, when the Dutch took control of the western half of the island.

The southern half of eastern New Guinea was first claimed by Britain in 1884, and transferred to Australia in 1905. The northern half was claimed by Germany in 1884, but captured in the first World War by Australia, which was granted a League of Nations mandate and then a UN trusteeship over the area. The two territories were administered jointly after 1949, were given self-government Dec. 1, 1973, and became independent Sept. 16, 1975. Australia promised $1 billion in aid for the 5 years starting 1976-77, and pledged assistance in defense and foreign affairs.

The indigenous population consists of a huge number of tribes, many living in almost complete isolation with mutually unintelligible languages.

A secession movement in copper-rich Bougainville led to violence in 1973 and 1976. Indonesian border incursions were reported in 1978.

# Paraguay

## Republic of Paraguay

**People: Population** (1977 est.): 2,800,000. **Age distrib.** (%): 0-14: 46.5; 15-59: 48.6; 60+: 4.9. **Pop. density:** 17.83 per sq. mi. **Urban** (1972): 37.4%. **Ethnic groups:** Mestizos 95%, small Caucasian, Indian, Negro minorities. **Languages:** Spanish, 75%, Guarani 90%. **Religions:** Roman Catholics 95%, Mennonites.

**Geography: Area:** 157,047 sq. mi., the size of California. **Location:** One of the two landlocked countries of S. America. **Neighbors:** Bolivia on N, Argentina on S, Brazil on E. **Topography:** Paraguay R. bisects the country. To E are fertile plains, wooded slopes, grasslands. To W is the Chaco plain, with marshes and scrub trees. Extreme W is arid. **Capital:** Asuncion. **Cities** (1974 est.): Asuncion (met.) 565,363.

**Government: Head of state:** Pres. Alfredo Stroessner; b. Nov. 3, 1912; in office: Aug. 15, 1954. **Local divisions:** 19 departments. **Armed forces:** regulars 17,000; para-military 4,000.

**Economy: Industries:** Food processing, wood products. **Chief crops:** Corn, wheat, cotton, beans, peanuts, tobacco, citrus fruits, yerba mate. **Minerals:** Iron, manganese, limestone. **Other resources:** Forests. **Per capita arable land:** 1.0 acres. **Meat production** (1975): beef: 85,000 tons; pork: 51,000 tons. **Electricity production** (1975): 510.00 mln. kwh. **Labor force:** 53% agriculture.

**Finance: Currency:** Guaranie (May 1978: 126.00 = $1 US). **Gross domestic product** (1976): $1.69 bln. **Per capita income** (1976): $574. **Imports** (1976): $301 mln.; partners (1974): Arg. 28%, Braz. 18%, U.S. 10%, W. Ger. 9%. **Exports** (1977):

$274 mln.; partners (1974): Arg. 23%, W. Ger. 13%, U.S. 11%, Neth. 9%. **Tourist receipts** (1975): $12 million. **Balance of payments** (1976): +$108,100,000. **National budget** (1976): $153.84 mln. revenues; $146.55 mln. expenditures. **International reserves** (May 1978): $386.81 mln. **Consumer prices** (change in 1977): 9.4%.

**Transport: Railway traffic** (1973): 16.15 mln. passenger-miles; 18.63 mln. net ton-miles. **Motor vehicles:** in use (1971): 16,000 passenger cars, 14,000 commercial vehicles. **Chief ports:** Asuncion.

**Communications: Television sets:** 53,000 in use (1974). **Radios:** 176,000 in use (1974). **Telephones in use** (1977): 41,644. **Daily newspaper circulation** (1973): 89,000; 30 per 1,000 pop.

**Health: Life expectancy at birth** (1975): 60.3 male; 63.6 female. **Births** (annual per 1,000 pop. 1972-75): 39.8 **Deaths** (annual per 1,000 pop. 1972-75): 8.9. **Natural increase** (annual 1970-75): 3.09%. **Pop. per hospital bed** (1975): 506. **Pop. per physician** (1975): 1,770. **Infant mortality** (per 1,000 live births 1971): 38.6.

**Education: Literacy** (1975): 74%. **Pop. 5-19:** in school (1975): 53%, per teacher (1975): 43.

The Guarani Indians were settled farmers speaking a common language before the arrival of Europeans.

Visited by Sebastian Cabot in 1527 and settled as a Spanish possession in 1535, Paraguay gained its independence from Spain in 1811. It lost much of its territory to Brazil, Uruguay, and Argentina in the War of the Triple Alliance, 1865-1870. Large areas were won from Bolivia in the Chaco War, 1932-35, but at great human and economic cost.

Gen. Alfredo Stroessner has ruled since 1954. Suppression of the opposition and decimation of small Indian groups has been charged by international rights groups.

The first stages of a large hydroelectric project were completed in 1968-70; a highway to Brazil was completed. In 1974 the two countries agreed to build a 10-million kilowatt hydroelectric plant, largest in the world, at Itaipu of the Parana River. Income from the project fueled an economic boom in 1977-78.

Organized international smuggling has been an important industry since the 1940s.

# Peru

## Republic of Peru

**People: Population** (1977 est.): 16,580,000. **Age distrib.** (%): 0-14: 44.5; 15-59: 50.6; 60+: 4.9. **Pop. density:** 33.41 per sq. mi. **Urban** (1974): 55.3%. **Ethnic groups:** Indians 46%, Mestizos 43%, Caucasians 11%. **Languages:** Spanish, Quechua both official, Aymara; 30% speak no Spanish. **Religions:** Roman Catholics over 90%.

**Geography: Area:** 496,222 sq. mi., five-sixths the size of Alaska. **Location:** On the Pacific coast of S. America. **Neighbors:** Ecuador, Colombia on N, Brazil, Bolivia on E, Chile on S. **Topography:** An arid coastal strip, 10 to 100 mi. wide, supports much of the population thanks to widespread irrigation. The Andes cover 27% of land area. The uplands are well-watered, as are the eastern slopes reaching the Amazon basin, which covers half the country with its forests and jungles. **Capital:** Lima. **Cities** (1972 cen.): Lima (met.) 3,302,523; Arequipa 303,316; Callao 296,721.

**Government: Head of state:** Pres. Francisco Morales Bermudez; b. 1922; in office: Aug. 29, 1975; **Head of government:** Prime Min. Oscar Molina Pallochia; in office: Jan. 31, 1978. **Local divisions:** 23 departments, 1 province. **Armed forces:** regulars 110,000; para-military 20,000.

**Economy: Industries:** Fish meal, steel. **Chief crops:** Cotton, sugar, coffee, rice, potatoes, beans, corn, barley, tobacco. **Minerals:** Copper, lead, zinc, iron, oil. **Crude oil reserves** (1978): 730 mln. bbls. **Other resources:** Wool, sardines. **Per capita arable land:** 0.4 acres. **Meat production** (1976): beef: 79,000 tons; pork: 52,900 tons; lamb: 32,500. **Fish catch** (1975): 3,447,500 metric tons. **Electricity production** (1975): 8.30 bln. kwh. **Labor force:** 47% agric.; 15% manuf.

**Finance: Currency:** Sol (May 1978: 150.90 = $1 US). **Gross domestic product** (1976): $11.08 bln. **Per capita income** (1975): $518. **Imports** (1976): $2.18 bln.; partners (1974): U.S. 31%, Jap. 12%, W. Ger. 10%, Ecuador 5%. **Exports** (1976): $1.37 bln.; partners (1974): U.S. 36%, Jap. 13%, W. Ger. 8%,

P.R. China 5%. **Tourists** (1975): 256,200; receipts (1975): $97 million. **Balance of payments** (1977): −$2,000,000. **National budget** (1973): $1.38 bln. revenues; $1.74 bln. expenditures. **International reserves** (Dec. 1977): $421.4 mln. **Consumer prices** (change in 1977): 38.1%.

**Transport: Railway traffic** (1973): 167.67 mln. passenger-miles; 456.44 mln. net ton-miles. **Motor vehicles:** in use (1974): 266,900 passenger cars, 139,900 commercial vehicles; manufactured (1975): 21,216,000 passenger cars; 12,852,000 commercial vehicles. **Chief ports:** Callao, Chimbate, Mollendo.

**Communications: Television sets:** 425,000 in use (1974), 35,000 manufactured (1970). **Radios:** 2,010,000 in use (1974), 88,000 manufactured (1970). **Telephones in use** (1977): 295,224. **Daily newspaper circulation** (1974): 1,436,000; 11 per 1,000 pop.

**Health: Life expectancy at birth** (1965): 52.59 male; 55.48 female. **Births** (annual per 1,000 pop. 1972-75): 41.0. **Deaths** (annual per 1,000 pop. 1972-75): 11.9. **Natural increase** (annual 1970-75): 2.91% **Pop. per hospital bed** (1975): 499. **Pop. per physician** (1975): 1,780. **Infant mortality** (per 1,000 live births 1970): 65.1.

**Education: Literacy** (1975): 72%. **Pop. 5-19:** in school (1975): 64%, per teacher (1975): 54.

The powerful Inca empire had its seat at Cuzco in the Andes (alt. 11,000 ft.), and covered most of Peru, Bolivia, and Ecuador, as well as parts of Colombia, Chile, and Argentina. Building on the achievements of 800 years of Andean civilization, the Incas had a high level of skill in architecture, engineering, textiles, and social organization.

A civil war had weakened the empire when Francisco Pizarro, Spanish conquistador, began raiding Peru for its wealth, 1532. In 1533 he had the ruling Inca, Atahualpa, fill a room with gold, then executed him and enslaved the natives.

Lima was the seat of Spanish viceroys until the Argentine liberator, Jose de San Martin, captured it in 1821, Spain was defeated by Simon Bolivar and Antonio J. de Sucre and recognized Peruvian independence, 1824. Chile defeated Peru and Bolivia, 1879-84, and took Tarapaca, Tacna, and Arica; returned Tacna, 1929.

On Oct. 3, 1968, a military coup ousted Pres. Fernando Belaunde Terry. In 1968-74, the military government converted large farmlands into cooperatives, expropriated several large U.S. companies with compensation, forced foreign mining companies to expand investments, and ordered local industries to turn over 50% of ownership to their workers.

Food shortages, escalating foreign debt, and strikes helped lead to another coup, Aug. 29, 1976, and to a slowdown of socialist programs. Labor protests culminated in a general strike in July, 1977. Moderate leftists led in free 1978 voting for a constituent assembly.

Peru is normally the world's top fishing nation; it takes about a sixth of total world tonnage, mostly anchovies from the plankton-rich waters of the coastal Peru current. Most of the take is ground into fish meal for poultry and livestock feed. But in 1972 the industry was crippled by a disappearance of anchovies from off-shore waters. In 1973 the government nationalized the crippled industry. In 1974 a shift in the ocean currents brought at least some of the anchovies back. Government increases in food prices caused widespread strikes and riots in 1978.

A severe earthquake hit northern Peru May 31, 1970, destroying many towns and killing 66,794.

# Philippines

## Republic of the Philippines

**People: Population** (1977 est.): 45,030,000. **Age distrib.** (%): 0–14: 43.2; 15–59: 51.4; 60+: 5.5. **Pop. density:** 389.17 per sq. mi. **Urban** (1970): 31.8%. **Ethnic groups:** Malays the large majority, Chinese, Americans, Spanish are minorities. **Languages:** Filipino (based on Tagalog), Spanish, English all official; 90 others spoken. **Religions:** Roman Catholics 83%, Protestants 9%, Moslems 5%.

**Geography: Area:** 115,707 sq. mi., slightly larger than Nevada. **Location:** An archipelago off the SE coast of Asia. **Neighbors:** Nearest are Malaysia, Indonesia on S, Taiwan on N. **Topography:** The country consists of some 7,100 islands stretching 1,100 mi. N-S. About 95% of area and population are on 11 largest islands. The largest islands are mountainous, ex-

cept for the heavily indented coastlines and for the central plain on Luzon. **Capital:** Quezon City (Manila is de facto capital). **Cities** (1975 est.): Manila 1,438,252; Quezon City 994,679; Davao 591,500.

**Government: Head of state:** Pres. Ferdinand E. Marcos; b. Sept. 11, 1917; in office: Dec. 30, 1965. **Local divisions:** 73 provinces, 61 chartered cities. **Armed forces:** regulars 99,000; reserves 45,000.

**Economy: Industries:** Food processing, clothing, drugs, paper, appliances. **Chief crops:** Hemp, copra, sugar, rice, corn, pineapple, tobacco. **Minerals:** Gold, silver, gypsum, sulphur, mercury, phosphates, zinc, nickel, copper, iron, coal, chromite, manganese. **Crude oil reserves** (1978): 100 mln. bbls. **Other resources:** Forests (42% of area). **Per capita arable land:** 0.5 acres. **Meat production** (1976): beef: 128,000 tons; pork: 372,600 tons. **Fish catch** (1975): 1,341,600 metric tons. **Electricity production** (1976): 14.74 bln. kwh. **Labor force:** 51% agric.; 11% manuf.

**Finance: Currency:** Peso (May 1978: 7.37 = $1 US). **Gross domestic product** (1977): $20.89 bln. **Per capita income** (1976): $364. **Imports** (1977): $4.22 bln.; partners (1974): Jap. 27%, U.S. 24%, Saudi Ar. 11%, Kuw. 5%. **Exports** (1977): $3.15 bln.; partners (1974): U.S. 42%, Jap. 35%, Neth. 6%, W. Ger. 3%. **Tourists** (1974): 400,100; receipts (1975): $109 million. **Balance of payments** (1977): −$26,000,000. **National budget** (1977): $3.36 bln. revenues; $3.73 bln. expenditures. **International reserves** (May 1978): $1.89 bln. **Consumer prices** (change in 1977): 7.9%.

**Transport: Railway traffic** (1975): 591.81 mln. passenger-miles; 40.99 mln. net ton-miles. **Motor vehicles:** in use (1974): 362,500 passenger cars, 247,300 commercial vehicles; assembled (1976): 33,816 passenger cars; 16,764 commercial vehicles. **Civil aviation:** 1,930 mln. passenger-miles (1976); 84,215 mln. freight ton-miles (1976). **Chief ports:** Cebu, Manila, Iloilo, Davalo.

**Communications: Television sets:** 711,000 in use (1974), 104,000 manufactured (1975). **Radios:** 1,825,000 in use (1974), 151,000 manufactured (1975). **Telephones in use** (1977): 541,681. **Daily newspaper circulation** (1974): 772,000; 18 per 1,000 pop.

**Health: Life expectancy at birth** (1975): 56.9 male; 60.0 female. **Births** (annual per 1,000 pop. 1972-75): 43.8. **Deaths** (annual per 1,000 pop. 1972-75): 10.5. **Natural increase** (annual 1970-75): 3.33%. **Pop. per hospital bed** (1975): 913. **Pop. per physician** (1975): 1,500. **Infant mortality** (per 1,000 live births 1974): 58.9.

**Education: Literacy** (1975): 80%. **Pop. 5-19:** in school (1975): 58%, per teacher (1975): 52.

The Malay peoples of the Philippine islands, whose ancestors probably migrated from Southeast Asia, were mostly hunters, fishers, and unsettled cultivators when first visited by Europeans. A few Moslem sultanates in the southern islands were the only direct link to other Asian civilizations.

The archipelago was visited by Magellan, 1521. The Spanish founded Manila, 1571. The islands, named for King Philip II of Spain, were ceded by Spain to the U.S. in the Treaty of Paris, Dec. 10, 1898, following the Spanish-American War. The U.S. paid Spain $20 million for the territory. U.S. troops suppressed a guerrilla uprising in a brutal 6-year war, 1899-1905.

Japan attacked the Philippines Dec. 8, 1941 (Far Eastern time). Japan conquered the islands in May, 1942. It was ousted by Sept. 1945.

On July 4, 1946, independence was proclaimed in accordance with an act passed by the U.S. Congress in 1934, providing for Philippine independence in 1946. A republic was established.

A rebellion by Communist-led Huk guerrillas was put down by 1954. But urban and rural political violence periodically reappears.

The Philippines and the U.S. have treaties for U.S. military and naval bases and a 1951 Mutual Defense Treaty.

President Ferdinand E. Marcos in 1966 concluded a pact reducing U.S. base leases from 99 to 25 years. There were riots by radical youth groups and terrorism by leftist guerrillas and outlaws, increasing from 1970. On Sept. 21, 1972, Marcos declared martial law. Ruling by decree, he ordered some land reform and stabilized prices. But opposition was suppressed, and a high population growth rate aggravated poverty and unemployment. Political corruption was believed to be widespread. On Jan. 17, 1973, Marcos proclaimed a new constitution with himself as president. His wife received wide powers in 1978 to supervise planning and development. Diplomatic and trade ties were set with China in 1975 and with the USSR in 1976.

Government troops battled Moslem (Moro) secessionists in 1973-76 in southern Mindanao. Fighting resumed in 1977 after a Libyan-mediated agreement on autonomy was rejected by the region's voters, a majority of whom are Christian. Casualties have been estimated at 50,000, half civilians (10,000 civilians dead).

The archipelago has a coastline of 10,850 mi. Manila Bay, with an area of 770 sq. mi., and a circumference of 120 mi., is the finest harbor in the Far East.

In the late 1960s self-sufficiency in rice production was achieved after introduction of "miracle" high-yield varieties.

In 1972 and 1974 severe floods destroyed crops in central Luzon. In 1974 the first in a series of flood-control dams, built with U.S. aid, was dedicated. Manufacturing has shown steady gains.

All natural resources of the Philippines belong to the state and their exploitation is limited to citizens of the Philippines or corporations and associations of which 60% of the capital is owned by citizens. In 1946 the right to develop natural resources and to own and operate public utilities until 1974 was extended to U.S. citizens.

# Poland

## Polish People's Republic

**People: Population** (1977 est.): 3,9(00,000. **Age distrib.** (%): 0–14: 25.5; 15–59: 61.2; 60+: 13.3. **Pop. density:** 288.30 per sq. mi. **Urban** (1975): 55.3%. **Ethnic groups:** Polish 98%, Germans, Ukrainians, Byelorussians. **Language:** Polish. **Religions:** Roman Catholics 90%, Protestants 1.5%.

**Geography: Area:** 120,359 sq. mi. **Location:** On the Baltic Sea in E Central Europe. **Neighbors:** E. Germany on W, Czechoslovakia on S, USSR (Lithuania, Byelorussia, Ukraine) on E. **Topography:** Most of the country consists of lowlands, forming part of the Northern European Plain. The Carpathian Mts. along the southern border rise to 8,200 ft. **Capital:** Warsaw. **Cities** (1976 est.): Warsaw 1,448,900; Lodz 804,300; Cracow 693,800; Wroclaw 579,660; Poznan 521,600.

**Government: Head of state:** Pres. Henryk Jablonski; b. Dec. 27, 1909; in office: Feb. 23, 1976; **Head of government:** Chmn. Piotr Jaroszewicz; b. Oct. 8, 1909; in office: Dec. 1970; **Head of Communist Party:** First Sec. Edward Gierek; b. Jan. 6, 1913; in office: Dec. 1970. **Local divisions:** 49 provinces. **Armed forces:** Regulars 497,000; reserves 605,000.

**Economy: Industries:** Shipbuilding, textiles, chemicals, wood products, metals, autos, aircraft, machinery, cement, aluminum, oil products. **Chief crops:** Grains, potatoes, sugar beets, tobacco, flax. **Minerals:** Coal, zinc, sulphur, salt, cadmium, iron, copper. **Per capita arable land:** 1.1 acres. **Meat production** (1976): beef: 802,700 tons; pork: 1.50 mln. tons; lamb: 21,800 tons. **Fish catch** (1975): 800,700 metric tons. **Electricity production** (1977): 109.37 bln. kwh. **Labor force:** 35% agric.; 30% manuf.

**Finance: Currency:** Zloty (July-Sep. 1977: 3.32 = $1 US). **Gross domestic product** (1974 est.): $71 bln. **Per capita income** (1974): $2,000. **Imports** (1977): $14.67 bln.; partners (1974): USSR 22%, W. Ger. 12%, E. Ger. 7%, Czech. 6%. **Exports** (1977): 12.34 bln.; partners (1974): USSR 29%, E. Ger. 9%, Czech. 7%, W. Ger. 6%. **Tourists** (1975): 9,320,000; receipts (1975): $163 million. **Consumer prices** (change in 1976): 4.2%.

**Transport: Railway traffic** (1975): 2.57 bln. passenger-miles; 90.25 bln. net ton-miles. **Motor vehicles:** in use (1975): 1,077,700 passenger cars, 425,000 commercial vehicles; manufactured (1977): 279,600 passenger cars; 70,800 commercial vehicles. **Civil aviation:** 1,036 mln. passenger-miles (1977); 9,762 mln. freight ton-miles (1977). **Chief ports:** Gdansk, Gdynia, Szczecin.

**Communications: Television sets:** 6,100,000 licensed (1974), 971,000 manufactured (1975). **Radios:** 7,988,000 licensed (1974), 1,651,000 manufactured (1975). **Telephones in use** (1977): 2,753,204. **Daily newspaper circulation** (1974): 7,994,000; 237 per 1,000 pop.

**Health: Life expectancy at birth** (1975): 67.02 male; 74.26 female. **Births** (per 1,000 pop. 1976): 19.5. **Deaths** (per 1,000 pop. 1976): 8.9. **Natural increase** (1976): 1.06%. **Pop. per hospital bed** (1975): 129. **Pop. per physician** (1975): 582. **In-**

**fant mortality** (per 1,000 live births 1975): 24.9.

**Education: Literacy** (1975): 98%. **Pop. 5-19:** in school (1975): 55%, per teacher (1975): 36.

Slavic tribes in the area were converted to Latin Christianity in the 10th century. Poland was a great power from the 14th to the 17th centuries. In 3 partitions (1772, 1793, 1795) it was apportioned among Prussia, Russia, and Austria. Overrun by the Austro-German armies in World War I, its independence, self-declared on Nov.11, 1918, was recognized by the Treaty of Versailles, June 28, 1919. Large territories to the east were taken in a war with Russia, 1921.

Nazi Germany and the Soviet Union invaded Poland Sept. 1-27, 1939, and divided the country. During the war, some 6 million Polish citizens were killed by the Nazis, half of them Jews. With Germany's defeat, a Polish government-in-exile in London was recognized by the U.S., but the Soviet Union pressed the claims of a rival group. The election of 1947 was completely dominated by the Communists.

In compensation for 69,860 sq. mi. ceded to the USSR, 1945, Poland received approx. 40,000 sq. mi. of German territory east of the Oder-Neisse line comprising Silesia, Pomerania, West Prussia, and part of East Prussia.

During 12 years of rule by Stalinists, large estates were abolished, industries nationalized, schools secularized, and some Roman Catholic prelates jailed. Farm production fell off. Harsh working conditions caused a riot by workmen in Poznan June 28-29, 1956.

A new Politburo, committed to development of a more independent Polish Communism, was named Oct. 1956, with Wladyslaw Gomulka as first secretary of the Communist Party. Collectivization of farms was ended and many collectives were abolished.

In 1968, Poland joined other Soviet bloc nations in invading Czechoslovakia. In 1970 Poland and West Germany signed a treaty to normalize relations.

In Dec. 1970 workers in port cities rioted because of price rises and new incentive wage rules. On Dec. 20 Gomulka resigned as party leader; he was succeeded by Edward Gierek; the incentive rules were dropped, price rises were revoked. In June 1971 a new 5-year plan was announced, placing more stress on housing and consumer goods production.

Poland was the first Communist state to get most-favored nation trade terms from the U.S. A 10-year W. Germany cooperation pact was signed in 1974.

A law promulgated Feb. 13, 1953, required government consent to high Roman Catholic church appointments. In 1956 Gomulka agreed to permit religious liberty and religious publications, provided the church kept out of politics. In 1961 religious studies in public schools were halted. Government relations with the Church improved in the 1970s. The number of priests and churches was greater in 1971 than in 1939, and 24 seminaries continued to function.

Key industries are state owned and operate under a planned economy. But about 85% of the farms and close to 200,000 small businesses are privately owned. Poland has become an important industrial power. Heavy indebtedness to Western lenders and rising import prices pose economic problems.

# Portugal

## Republic of Portugal

**People: Population** (1976 est.): 9,730,000. **Age distrib.** (%): 0–14: 28.3; 15–59: 57.1; 60+: 14.6. **Pop. density:** 275.33 per sq. mi. **Ethnic groups:** Homogeneous, with small African minority. **Languages:** Portuguese. **Religions:** Roman Catholics 98%.

**Geography: Area:** 35,340 sq. mi., slightly smaller than Indiana. **Location:** At SW extreme of Europe. **Neighbors:** Spain on N, E. **Topography:** Portugal N of Tajus R, which bisects the country NE-SW, is mountainous, cool and rainy. To the S there are drier, rolling plains, and a warm climate. **Capital:** Lisbon. **Cities** (1974 est.): Lisbon (met.) 1,611,887; Porto (met.) 1,314,794.

**Government: Head of state:** Pres. Antonio Ramalho Eanes; b. Jan. 25, 1935; in office: June 1976; **Head of government:** Prime Min. Alfredo Nobre da Costa; in office: Aug. 1978. **Local divisions:** 22 provinces, autonomous districts of Azores, Madeira. **Armed forces:** regulars 58,800; para-military 29,900.

**Economy: Industries:** Textiles, pottery, shipbuilding, oil products, paper, glassware, tourism. **Chief crops:** Grains, corn, rice, grapes, olives, fruits. **Minerals:** Coal, copper, tin, kaolin, gold, iron, manganese. **Other resources:** Forests (world leader in cork production). **Per capita arable land:** 10 acres. **Meat production** (1976): beef: 78,700 tons; pork: 127,500 tons; lamb: 22,300 tons. **Fish catch** (1975): 368,600 metric tons. **Electricity production** (1977): 13.87 bln. kwh. **Labor force:** 30% agric.; 22% manuf.

**Finance: Currency:** Escudos (May 1978: 45.72 = $1 US). **Gross domestic product** (1975): $13.71 bln. **Per capita income** (1975): $1,484. **Imports** (1977): $4.93 bln.; partners (1975): U.S. 12%, W. Ger. 11%, U.K. 8%, Fr. 7%, Spain 4%. **Exports** (1977): $2.02 bln.; partners (1975): U.K. 20%, W. Ger. 10%, U.S. 8%, Fr. 6%. **Tourists** (1975): 1,966,400; receipts (1975): $360 million. **Balance of payments** (1977): −$759,000,000. **National budget** (1973): $1.53 bln. revenues; $1.60 bln. expenditures. **International reserves** (Apr. 1978): $1.14 bln. **Consumer prices** (change in 1977): 24.3%.

**Transport: Railway traffic** (1975): 3.015 mln. passenger-miles; 468.23 mln. net ton-miles. **Motor vehicles:** in use (1975): 937,000 passenger cars, 259,000 commercial vehicles; assembled (1976): 39,432 passenger cars; 46,800 commercial vehicles. **Civil aviation:** 1,871 mln. passenger-miles (1977); 56,829 mln. freight ton-miles (1977). **Chief ports:** Lisbon, Setubal, Leixoes.

**Communications: Television sets:** 572,000 licensed (1974), 233,000 manufactured (1975). **Radios:** 1,516,000 licensed (1974), 610,000 manufactured (1975). **Telephones in use** (1977): 1,118,970. **Daily newspaper circulation** (1974): 799,000; 91 per 1,000 pop.

**Health: Life expectancy at birth** (1974): 65.29 male; 72.03 female. **Births** (per 1,000 pop. 1975): 19.0. **Deaths** (per 1,000 pop. 1974): 11.0. **Natural increase** (1974): .86% **Pop. per hospital bed** (1975): 154. **Pop. per physician** (1975): 854. **Infant mortality** (per 1,000 live births 1974): 37.9.

**Education: Literacy** (1975): 65%, **Pop. 5-19:** in school (1975): 60%, per teacher (1975): 34.

Portugal, an independent state since the 12th century, was a kingdom until a revolution in 1910 drove out King Manoel II and a republic was proclaimed.

From 1932 a strong, repressive government was headed by Premier Antonio de Oliveira Salazar. Illness forced his retirement in Sept. 1968; he was succeeded by Marcello Caetano. Portugal was the last European nation to hold an extensive empire in Africa, maintaining over 140,000 troops there to battle various independence movements.

On Apr. 25, 1974, the government was seized by a military junta led by Gen. Antonio de Spinola, who was named president.

The new government reached agreements providing independence for Guinea-Bissau, Mozambique, Cape Verde Islands, Angola, and Sao Tome and Principe. Up to 1 million refugees fled to Portugal. Spinola resigned Sept. 30, 1974, in face of increasing pressure from leftist officers. Despite a 64% victory for democratic parties in April 1975, the Soviet-supported Communist party increased its influence. Banks, insurance companies, transport, and other industries were nationalized. A countercoup in November halted this trend. Free elections under the new constitution were held in 1976, with the Socialist party gaining a parliamentary plurality. After three years of turmoil the economy and political life were in disarray, despite aid from the U.S. and West European countries.

Military forces, which totaled over 200,000 have been rapidly demobilized. A 1951 agreement gave the U.S. rights to use defense facilities in the Azores.

**Azores Islands,** in the Atlantic, 740 mi. W. of Portugal, have an area of 904 sq. mi. and a population (1970) of 291,028. The **Madeira Islands,** 360 mi. off the NW coast of Africa, have an area of 307 sq. mi. and a population (1976) of 270,000. Both groups were offered partial autonomy in 1974.

Portuguese Timor was annexed by Indonesia May 3, 1976, after 9 months of fighting between local factions. Portuguese troops had withdrawn in 1975.

**Macao,** with an area of 6 sq. mi., is an enclave, a peninsula and 2 small islands, at the mouth of the Canton River in China. Portugal granted broad autonomy in 1976. Population (UN est. 1977): 280,000.

# Qatar
## State of Qatar

**People: Population** (1977 est.): 100,000. **Pop. density:** 25.0

per sq. mi. **Ethnic groups:** Arabs 56%, Iranians 23%, Pakistani 7%, others. **Languages:** Arabic (official), Farsi (Persian). **Religions:** Moslems 98%.

**Geography: Area:** 4,000 sq. mi., smaller than Connecticut. **Location:** Occupies peninsula on W coast of Persian Gulf. **Neighbors:** Saudi Arabia on W, United Arab Emirates on S. **Topography:** Most of the country is a flat desert, with some limestone ridges, vegetation of any kind is scarce. **Capital:** Doha. **Cities** (1972 est.): Doha 100,000.

**Government: Head of state:** Emir Khalifa bin Hamad al-Thani; b. 1932; in office: Feb. 22, 1972. **Armed forces:** regulars 4,200. **Crude oil reserves** (1978): 5.60 bln. bbls.

**Finance: Currency:** Riyal (May 1978: 3.87 = $1 US). **Gross domestic product** (1974 est): $2.2 bln. **Per capita income** (1974): $12,500. **Imports** (1976): $817 mln.; partners (1974): Jap. 18%, U.K. 14%, U.S. 10%, Leb. 6%. **Exports** (1976): $2.19 bln.; partners (1974): U.K. 15%, Fr. 10%, U.A.E. 10%, It. 8%. **National budget** (1977): $2.06 bln. revenues: $2.89 bln. expenditures. **International reserves** (Dec. 1977): $162.2 mln.

**Transport: Chief ports:** Doha, Musayid.

**Communications: Telephones in use** (1977): 24,403.

**Health: Pop. per hospital bed** (1975): 282. **Pop. per physician** (1975): 1,739.

**Education: Literacy** (1975): 10%. **Pop. 5-19:** in school (1975): 95%, per teacher (1975): 20.

Qatar was under Bahrain's control until the 12th century. The Ottoman Turks took power, 1872 to 1915. In a treaty signed in 1916 Qatar gave Great Britain responsibility for its defense and foreign relations. After Britain announced it would remove its military forces from the Persian Gulf area by the end of 1971, Qatar sought a federation with other British protected States in the area; this failed and Qatar declared itself independent, Sept. 1 1971.

Qatar's first ruler under independence, Emir Ahmed bin Ali al-Thani, was replaced by his cousin, Khalifa bin Hamad al-Thani, Feb. 22, 1972, in a bloodless coup.

Oil revenues give Qatar a per capita income among the highest in the world, but lack of skilled labor hampers development plans.

# Rhodesia
## (Zimbabwe)

**People: Population** (1977 est.): 6,740,000. **Pop. density:** 44.83 per sq. mi. **Urban** (1976): 19.4%. **Ethnic groups:** Bantu tribes 96%, Caucasians 3%, Coloreds, Asians 1%. **Languages:** English (official), Shona, Ndebele. **Religions:** Christians and part Christians 75%, Moslems.

**Geography: Area:** 150,333 sq. mi., nearly as large as California. **Location:** In southern Africa. **Neighbors:** Zambia on N, Botswana on W, S. Africa on S, Mozambique on E. **Topography:** Rhodesia is high plateau country, rising to mountains on eastern border, sloping down on the other borders. **Capital:** Salisbury. **Cities** (1976 est.): Salisbury (met.) 568,000; Bulawayo (met.) 340,000.

**Government: Head of state:** John James Wrathall; b. Aug. 28, 1913; in office: Jan. 14, 1976; **Head of government:** Prime Min. Ian Douglas Smith; b. Apr. 8, 1919; in office: Apr. 14, 1964; since Mar. 21, 1978, Smith officially shares power with 3 Executive Cncl. members (see below). **Local divisions:** 7 provinces. **Armed forces:** regulars 9,550; reserves 58,000.

**Economy: Industries:** Clothing, chemicals, light industries. **Chief crops:** Tobacco, sugar, cotton, corn, tea. **Minerals:** Asbestos, copper, iron, coal, chrome. **Per capita arable land:** 0.7 acres. **Meat production** (1975): beef: 139,000 tons; pork: 11,000 tons; lamb: 10,000 tons. **Labor force:** 63% agriculture.

**Finance: Currency:** Dollar (1974: 1 = $1.76 US). **Gross domestic product** (1974 est.): $3.15 bln. **Per capita income** (1974): $502. **Imports** (1973): $541 mln.; partners (1965): U.K. 30%, So. Afr. 23%, U.S. 7%, Jap. 6%. **Exports** (1973): $650 mln.; partners (1965): Zamb. 25%, U.K. 22%, So. Afr. 10%, W. Ger, 9%. **Consumer prices** (change in 1977): 11.9%.

**Transport: Railway traffic** (1975): 3.81 bln. net ton-miles. **Motor vehicles:** in use (1974): 180,000 passenger cars, 70,000 commercial vehicles.

**Communications: Television sets:** 57,000 in use (1973). **Radios:** 225,000 in use (1974). **Telephones in use** (1977): 190,303. **Daily newspaper circulation** (1974): 100,000; 16 per 1,000 pop.

**Health: Life expectancy at birth** (1975): 49.8 male; 53.3 female. **Births** (annual per 1,000 pop. 1972-75): 47.9. **Deaths** (annual per 1,000 pop. 1972-75): 14.4. **Natural increase** (annual 1970-75): 3.35%. **Pop. per hospital bed** (1975): 342. **Pop. per physician** (1975): 6,918. **Infant mortality** (per 1,000 live births 1954): 33.5.

**Education: Literacy** (1975): 27%. **Pop. 5-19:** in school (1975): 37%, per teacher (1975): 98.

Britain took over the area as Southern Rhodesia in 1923 from the British South Africa Co. (which, under Cecil Rhodes, had conquered the area by 1897) and granted internal self-government. Under a 1961 constitution, voting was restricted to maintain whites in power. On Nov. 11, 1965, Prime Minister Ian D. Smith announced his country's unilateral declaration of independence. Britain termed the act illegal, and demanded Rhodesia broaden voting rights to provide for eventual rule by the majority Africans.

Urged by Britain, the UN imposed sanctions, including embargoes on oil shipments to Rhodesia. Some oil and gasoline reached Rhodesia, however, from South Africa and Mozambique, before the latter became independent in 1975. Some African nations denounced Britain for refusing to use force against the Rhodesian government. In May 1968, the UN Security Council ordered a trade embargo.

Rhodesia claimed the sanctions were ineffective. A new constitution came into effect, Mar. 2, 1970, providing for a republic with a president and prime minister. The election law effectively prevented full black representation through income tax requirements.

A proposed British-Rhodesian settlement was dropped in May 1972 when a British commission reported most Rhodesian blacks opposed it. In 1972-74 there were small clashes between black nationalist guerrillas and Rhodesian security forces. Intermittent negotiations between the government and various black groups failed to prevent increasing skirmishes. By mid-1978, over 6,000 soldiers and civilians had been killed. Rhodesian troops battled guerrillas within Mozambique and Zambia. An "internal settlement" signed Mar. 1978 in which Smith and 3 popular black leaders share control until transfer of power to the black majority in 1976, was rejected by guerrilla leaders.

In 1977, the U.S. congress repealed a law that had allowed U.S. import of Rhodesian chrome.

# Romania

## Socialist Republic of Romania

**People: Population** (1977 est.): 21,530,000. **Age distrib.** (%): 0–14: 25.2; 15–59; 60.8; 60+: 14.0. **Pop. density:** 234.79 per sq. mi. **Urban** (1975): 43.2%. **Ethnic groups:** Romanians 85%, Hungarians 9%, Germans 2%, Serbo-Croats, Ukrainians, Greeks, Turks. **Languages:** Romanian, Hungarian. **Religions:** Orthodox 80%, Roman Catholics 9%, Calvinists,, Jews, Lutherans.

**Geography: Area:** 91,699 sq. mi., slightly smaller than Oregon. **Location:** In SE Europe on the Black Sea. **Neighbors:** USSR on E (Moldavia) and N (Ukraine), Hungary, Yugoslavia on W, Bulgaria on S. **Topography:** The Carpathian Mts. encase the north-central Transylvanian plateau. There are wide plains S and E of the mountains, through which flow the lower reaches of the rivers of the Danube system. **Capital:** Bucharest. **Cities** (1974 est.): Bucharest 1,565,872; Cluj (met.) 222,491.

**Government: Head of state:** Pres. Nicolae Ceausescu; b. Jan. 26, 1918; in office; Dec. 7, 1967; **Head of government:** Prime Min. Manea Manescu; b. 1916; in office; Mar. 29, 1974; **Head of Communist Party:** Sec.-Gen. Nicolae Ceausescu; in office: 1965. **Local divisions:** Bucharest and 39 districts. **Armed forces:** regulars 290,000; reserves 345,500.

**Economy: Industries:** Steel, metals, machinery, oil products, chemicals, textiles, shoes, tourism. **Chief crops:** Corn, wheat, sugar beets, grapes, fruits. **Minerals:** Oil, gas, coal, salt, bauxite, manganese, lead, zinc, gold, silver. **Other resources:** Timber. **Per capita arable land:** 1.1 acres. **Meat Production** (1975): beef: 260,000 tons; pork: 760,000 tons; lamb: 68,000 tons. **Electricity production** (1976): 58.27 bln. kwh. **Labor force:** 40% agric.; 30% manuf.

**Finance: Currency:** Leu (1975: 4.97 = $1 US). **Gross domestic product** (1974 est.): $28 bln. **Per capita income** (1974): $1,200. **Imports** (1976): $6.10 bln.; partners (1974); W.

Ger. 15%, USSR 15%, U.S. 6%, E. Ger. 5%. **Exports** (1976): $6.14 bln.; partners (1974): USSR 17%, W. Ger. 10%, E. Ger. 6%, It. 5%. **Tourists** (1975): 3,205,900.

**Transport: Railway traffic** (1976): 13.89 bln. passenger-miles; 40.24 bln. net ton-miles. **Motor vehicles:** in use (1972): 125,000 passenger cars, 50,000 commercial vehicles; manufactured (1976): 71,160 passenger cars; 392,400 commercial vehicles. **Civil aviation:** 570 mln. passenger-miles (1977); 8,540 mln. freight ton-miles (1977). **Chief ports:** Constanta, Galati, Bealia.

**Communications: Television sets:** 2,405,000 licensed (1974), 512,000 manufactured (1975). **Radios:** 3,066,000 licensed (1974), 712,000 manufactured (1975). **Telephones in use** (1977): 1,076. **Daily newspaper circulation** (1974): 2,716,000; 129 per 1,000 pop.

**Health: Life expectancy at birth** (1975): 67.29 male; 71.82 female. **Births** (per 1,000 pop. 1975): 19.7. **Deaths** (per 1,000 pop. 1975): 9.3. **Natural increase** (1975): 1.04%. **Pop. per hospital bed** (1975): 112. **Pop. per physician** (1975): 793. **Infant mortality** (per 1,000 live births 1974): 35.0.

**Education: Literacy** (1975): 98%. **Pop. 5-19:** in school (1975): 59%, per teacher (1975): 33.

Romania's earliest known people were merged with invading Proto-Thracians, preceding by centuries the Dacians. The Dacian kingdom was occupied by Rome, 106 A.D.-271 A.D.; the people and language were Romanized. The principalities of Wallachia and Moldavia, dominated by Turkey, were united in 1859, became Romania in 1861. In 1877 Romania proclaimed independence from Turkey, became an independent state by the Treaty of Berlin, 1878, and kingdom, 1881, under Carol I. In 1886 Romania became a constitutional monarchy with a bicameral legislature.

Romania helped Russia in its war with Turkey, 1877-78. After World War I it acquired Bessarabia, Bukovina, Transylvania and Banat. In 1940 it ceded Bessarabia and Northern Bukovina to the USSR and part of Southern Dobrudja to Bulgaria.

Marshal Ion Antonescu, leader of a militarist movement, came to power and forced Romania to join Germany against the USSR in World War II in 1941. In 1944 Antonescu was overthrown by King Michael with Soviet help and Romania joined the Allies.

With occupation by Soviet troops the National Democratic Front headed by the Communist party, displaced the National Peasant party. A People's Republic was proclaimed, Dec. 30, 1947, and Michael was forced to abdicate. Land owners were dispossessed and most banks, factories and transportation units were nationalized.

On Aug. 22, 1965, a new constitution proclaimed Romania a Socialist, rather than a People's Republic. Since 1966, Romania has adopted an independent attitude toward the USSR, a stand pointed up by the visit of U.S. President Nixon in Aug. 1969 and Chinese Communist party chief Hua Kuo-feng in 1978. Romanian President Nicolae Ceausescu visited the U.S. in 1970 and 1973. The U.S. granted most-favored-nation tariff treatment in 1975, and a 10-year U.S. trade pact was signed in 1976. Since 1959, USSR troops have not been permitted to enter Romania. In 1974, Ceausescu declared Russia was Romania's top ally.

Romania has maintained friendly relations with China, and has refused to sever diplomatic and trade ties with Israel.

Internal policies remain oppressive. Ethnic Hungarians have protested cultural and job discrimination.

Romania has become industrialized, but lags in consumer goods and in personal freedoms. All industry is state owned, and state farms and cooperatives own over 90% of arable land. Romania is one of the few countries in Europe self-sufficient in oil, though reserves have been depleted.

A major earthquake struck Bucharest in March, 1977, killing over 1,300 people and causing extensive damage to housing and industry.

# Rwanda

## Republic of Rwanda

**People: Population** (1977 est.): 4,460,000. **Age distrib.** (%): 0–14: 43.8; 15–59: 51.0; 60+: 5.2. **Pop. density:** 438.59 per sq. mi. **Urban** (1975): 3.5%. **Ethnic groups:** Hutu 89%, Tutsi 10%, Twa (pygmies) 1%. **Languages:** French, Kinyarwandu (both official), Swahili. **Religions:** Roman Catholics 45%, Protestants

9%, Moslems 1%.

**Geography: Area:** 10,169 sq. mi., the size of Maryland. **Location:** In E central Africa. **Neighbors:** Uganda on N, Zaire on W, Burundi on S, Tanzania on E. **Topography:** Grassy uplands and hills cover most of the country, with a chain of volcanoes in the NW. The source of the Nile R. has been located in Rwanda. **Capital:** Kigali. **Cities** (1970 est.): Kigali (met.) 54,403.

**Government: Head of state:** Pres. Juvenal Habyarimana; b. Mar. 8, 1937; in office: July 5, 1973. **Local divisions:** 10 prefectures. **Armed forces:** regulars 3,750; para-military 1,200.

**Economy: Chief crops:** Coffee, cotton, tea, pyrethrum, tobacco. **Minerals:** Tin, gold, wolframite. **Per capita arable land:** 0.3 acres. **Electricity production** (1975): 140.00 mln. kwh. **Labor force:** 91% agriculture.

**Finance: Currency:** Franc (May 1978: 92.84 = $1 US). **Gross domestic product** (1974): $.31 mln. **Per capita income** (1974): $72. **Imports** (1976): $103 mln.; partners (1974): Belg. 16%, Kenya 10%, Jap. 9%, W. Ger. 9%. **Exports** (1976): $81 mln.; partners (1974): Belg. 13%, U.S. 3%, U.K. 3%, Zaire 1%. **Balance of payments** (1977): +$15,100,000. **National budget** (1972): $20.41 mln. revenues; $29.27 mln. expenditures. **International reserves** (May 1978): $98.25 mln. **Consumer prices** (change in 1974): 31.6%.

**Transport: Motor vehicles:** in use (1975): 6,500 passenger cars, 4,800 commercial vehicles.

**Communications: Radios:** 133,000 in use (1974), 12,000 manufactured (1975). **Telephones in use** (1977): 3,578. **Daily newspaper circulation** (1974): 200; 0.04 per 1,000 pop.

**Health: Life expectancy at birth** (1975): 39.4 male; 42.6 female. **Births** (annual per 1,000 pop. 1972-75): 50.0. **Deaths** (annual per 1,000 pop. 1972-75): 23.6. **Natural increase** (annual 1970-75): 2.64%. **Pop. per hospital bed** (1975): 572. **Pop. per physician** (1975): 53,012. **Infant mortality** (per 1,000 live births 1970): 132.8.

**Education: Literacy** (1975): 23%. **Pop. 5-19:** in school (1975): 27%, per teacher (1975): 168.

For centuries, the Tutsi (an extremely tall people) dominated the Hutus (90% of the population). A civil war broke out in 1959 and Tutsi power was ended. A referendum in 1961 abolished the monarchic system.

Rwanda, which had been part of the Belgian UN trusteeship of Rwanda-Urundi, became independent July 1, 1962. The government was overthrown in a 1973 military coup. Rwanda is one of the most densely populated countries in Africa. All available arable land is being used, and is being subject to erosion. The government has carried out economic and social improvement programs, using foreign aid and volunteer labor on public works projects.

The source of the Nile River, long sought by explorers and geographers, has been located in the headwaters of the Kagera (Akagera) River, SW of Kigali.

## Samoa

**People: Population** (1977 est.): 150,000. **Age distrib.** (%): 0–14: 51.3; 15–59: 44.5; 60+: 4.1. **Pop. density:** 132.39 per sq. mi. **Urban** (1974): 21.0%. **Ethnic groups:** Samoans (Polynesians) 88%, Euronesians (mixed) 10%, Europeans, other Pacific Islanders. **Languages:** Samoan, English both official. **Religions:** Protestants 75%, Roman Catholics 20%.

**Geography: Area:** 1,133 sq. mi., the size of Rhode Island. **Location:** In the S. Pacific O. **Neighbors:** Nearest are Fiji on W, Tonga on S. **Topography:** Comprises main islands, Savai'i (660 sq. mi.) and Upolu (430 sq. mi.), both ruggedly mountainous, and small islands Manono and Apolima. **Capital:** Apia. **Cities** (1974 est.): Apia (met.) 32,616.

**Government: Head of state:** King Malietoa Tanumafili II; b. Jan. 4, 1913; in office: Jan. 1, 1962; **Head of government:** Prime Min. Tupuola Efi; b. 1948; in office: Mar. 1976. **Local divisions:** 24 districts.

**Economy: Chief crops:** Cocoa, coconuts, bananas, taro, coffee, bark cloth. **Other resources:** Hardwoods, fish. **Electricity production** (1977): 25.20 mln. kwh. **Labor force:** 67% agric.; 2% manuf.

**Finance: Currency:** Tala (Oct.-Dec. 1977: 1 = $1.30 US). **Gross domestic product** (1974 est.): $45 mln. **Per capita income** (1974): $280. **Imports** (1977): $41 mln.; partners (1970): New Zea. 33%, Austral. 19%, Jap. 12%, U.S. 10%. **Exports** (1977): $13 mln.; partners (1970): New Zea. 47%, W. Ger. 15%,

Neth. 11%, U.S. 9%. **Tourist receipts** (1974): $5 million. **Consumer prices** (change in 1977): 14.7%.

**Transport: Motor vehicles:** in use (1975): 2,000 passenger cars, 2,000 commercial vehicles. **Chief ports:** Apia, Asau.

**Communications: Television sets:** 1,800 in use (1973). **Radio:** 10,000 in use (1974). **Telephones in use** (1977): 3,300.

**Health: Life expectancy at birth** (1966): 60.8 male; 65.2 female. **Births** (annual per 1,000 pop. 1972-75): 36.9. **Deaths** (per 1,000 pop. 1976): 6.7. **Natural increase** (1976): 3.02%. **Infant mortality** (per 1,000 live births 1974): 39.9.

Western Samoa was a German colony, 1899 to 1914, when New Zealand landed troops and took over. It became a New Zealand mandate under the League of Nations and, in 1945, a New Zealand UN trusteeship.

An elected local government took office in Oct. 1959 and the country became fully independent Jan. 1, 1962. New Zealand has continued economic aid and educational assistance.

The country's name was changed to Samoa in 1977.

## San Marino

### Most Serene Republic of San Marino

**People: Population** (1977 est.): 20,000. **Age distrib.** (%): 0–14: 25.7; 15–59: 60.0; 60+: 14.3. **Pop. density:** 851.06 per sq. mi. **Urban** (1970): 92.4%. **Ethnic groups:** Italian. **Languages:** Italian. **Religions:** Roman Catholics predominate.

**Geography: Area:** 23.5 sq. mi. **Location:** In N central Italy near Adriatic coast. **Neighbors:** Completely surrounded by Italy. **Topography:** The country lies on the slopes of Mt. Titano. **Capital:** San Marino.

**Government: Head of state:** Capitani Reggenti: Francesco Valli, Enrico Ghironzi; in office: Apr. 1, 1978 (6 mo. term). **Armed forces:** 180-man ceremonial army.

**Economy: Industries:** Postage stamps, tourism, woolen goods, paper, cement, ceramics.

**Finance: Currency:** Lira. **Tourists** (1975): 2,425,900.

**Communications: Television sets:** 3,300 licensed (1974). **Radios:** 3,400 licensed (1974). **Telephones in use** (1977): 5,696.

**Births** (per 1,000 pop. 1973): 17.4. **Deaths** (per 1,000 pop. 1973): 7.7. **Natural increase** (1973): .97%. **Infant mortality** (per 1,000 live births 1973): 9.2.

San Marino claims to be the oldest state in Europe and to have been founded in the 4th century. A communist-led coalition ruled 1947-57; a similar coalition took power in 1978. It has had a treaty of friendship with Italy since 1862.

## Sao Tome and Principe

### Democratic Republic of Sao Tome and Principe

**People: Population** (1977 est.): 80,000. **Pop. density:** 9.15 per sq. mi. **Ethnic groups:** Portuguese-African mixture, African minority (Angola, Mozambique immigrants). **Languages:** Portuguese. **Religions:** Christians 80%.

**Geography: Area:** 372 sq. mi., slightly larger than New York City. **Location:** In the Gulf of Guinea about 125 miles off W Central Africa. **Neighbors:** Nearest are Gabon, Equatorial Guinea on E. **Topography:** Sao Tome and Principe islands are both part of an extinct volcano chain. They are both covered by lush forests and croplands. **Capital:** Sao Tome. **Cities** (1960 cen.): Sao Tome 5,714.

**Government: Head of state:** Pres. Manuel Pinto da Costa; in office: July 12, 1975; **Head of government:** Prime Min. Miguel Trovoada; in office: July 12, 1975. **Local divisions:** 2 provinces, 12 counties.

**Economy: Chief crops:** Coffee, cocoa, coconut products, cinchona. **Electricity production** (1975): 8.00 mln. kwh.

**Finance: Currency:** Escudo (1974: 25.4 = $1 US). **Gross domestic product** (1974 est.): $35 mln. **Per capita income** (1974): $400. **Imports** (1973): 10 mln.; partners (1973): Port. 47%, Angola 23%, Neth. 6%, Fr. 5%. **Exports** (1973): $13 mln.; partners (1973): Port. 36%, Neth. 32%, W. Ger. 12%, U.S. 8%.

**Transport: Motor vehicles:** in use (1973): 1,600 passenger cars, 400 commercial vehicles. **Chief ports:** Sao Tome, Santo Antonio.

**Communications: Radios:** 7,500 in use (1974).

**Health: Births** (per 1,000 pop. 1972): 45.0. **Deaths** (per 1,000 pop. 1972): 11.2. **Natural increase** (1972): 3.38%. **Infant mortality** (per 1,000 live births 1972): 64.3.

The islands were uninhabited when discovered in 1471 by the Portuguese, who brought the first settlers — convicts and exiled Jews. Sugar planting was replaced by the slave trade as the chief economic activity until coffee and cocoa were introduced in the nineteenth century.

Portugal agreed in 1974 to turn the colony over to the Gabon-based Movement for the Liberation of Sao Tome and Principe, which proclaimed as the first president its East-German-trained leader Manuel Pinto da Costa. Independence came July 12, 1975.

Low cocoa prices, the emigration of most of the 1,000 whites, and the repatriation of Cape Verdean plantation foremen stymied the economy.

# Saudi Arabia

## Kingdom of Saudi Arabia

**People: Population** (1977 est.): 9,520,000. **Pop. density:** 10.90 per sq. mi. **Ethnic groups:** Arab tribes, immigrants from other Arab and Moslem countries. **Languages:** Arabic. **Religions:** Moslems 99%.

**Geography: Area:** 873,000 sq. mi., one-fourth the size of the U.S. **Location:** Occupies most of Arabian Peninsula in Middle East. **Neighbors:** Kuwait, Iraq, Jordan on N, Yemen, South Yemen, Oman on S, United Arab Emirates, Qatar on E. **Topography:** The highlands on W, up to 9,000 ft., slope as an arid, barren desert to the Persian Gulf. There are no permanent rivers. **Capital:** Riyadh. **Cities** (1974 cen.): Riyadh 666,840; Jeddah 561,104; Mecca 366,801.

**Government: Head of state:** King Khalid bin Abdul Aziz; b. 1913; in office: Mar. 28, 1975; **Head of government:** Dep. Prime Min. Fahd bin Abdul Aziz; Mar. 28, 1975. **Local divisions:** 6 major and 12 minor provinces. **Armed forces:** regulars 61,500; para-military 41,500.

**Economy: Industries:** Oil products. **Chief crops:** Dates, wheat, barley, fruit. **Minerals:** Oil, gas, gold, silver, iron. **Crude oil reserves** (1978): 150 bln. bbls. **Per capita arable land:** 0.2 acres. **Fish catch** (1975): 30,000 metric tons. **Electricity production** (1975): 1.99 bln. kwh. **Labor force:** 61% agric.; 2% manuf.

**Finance: Currency:** Riyal (May 1978: 3.45 = $1 US). **Gross domestic product** (1977): $55.10 bln. **Per capita income** (1976): $4,147. **Imports** (1976): $8.69 bln.; partners (1975): Jap. 30.3%, U.S. 29.9%, W. Ger. 12.2%, U.K. 10%. **Exports** (1977): $41.49 bln.; partners (1976): Jap. 15%, U.S. 13%, Fr. 10%, U.K. 8%. **Tourist receipts** (1975): $509 million. **Balance of payments** (1977): +$3,977,000. **International reserves** (Mar. 1978): $28.73 bln. **Consumer prices** (change in 1977): 11.3%.

**Transport: Railway traffic** (1974): 44.71 mln. passenger-miles; 40.99 mln. net ton-miles. **Motor vehicles:** in use (1970): 64,900 passenger cars, 50,400 commercial vehicles. **Chief ports:** Jidda, Ad-Dammam, Ras Tannurah.

**Communications: Television sets:** 122,000 in use (1974). **Radios:** 85,000 in use (1970). **Telephones in use** (1977): 160,000. **Daily newspaper circulation** (1974): 96,000; 11 per 1,000 pop.

**Health: Life expectancy at birth** (1975): 44.2 male; 46.5 female. **Births** (annual per 1,000 pop. 1972-76): 49.5. **Deaths** (annual per 1,000 pop. 1972-76): 20.2. **Natural increase** (annual 1970-75): 2.93%. **Pop. per hospital bed** (1975): 718. **Pop. per physician** (1975): 2,992. **Infant mortality** (per 1,000 live births 1973): 152.

**Education: Literacy** (1975): 15%. **Pop. 5-19:** in school (1975): 26%, per teacher (1975): 66.

Arabia was united for the first time by Mohammed, in the early 7th century. His successors conquered the entire Near East and North Africa, bringing Islam and the Arabic language. But Arabia itself soon returned to its former status as political and cultural backwater.

Nejd, long an independent state and center of the Wahhabi sect, fell under Turkish rule in the 18th century, but in 1913 Ibn Saud, founder of the Saudi dynasty, overthrew the Turks and captured the Turkish province of Hasa; took the Hejaz in 1925

and by 1926, most of Asir. The discovery of oil by an American oil company in the 1930s transformed the new country.

Crown Prince Khalid was proclaimed king on Mar. 25, 1975, after the assassination of King Faisal. There is no constitution and no parliament. The king exercises authority together with a Council of Ministers. The Islamic religious code is the law of the land. Alcohol and public entertainments are restricted, and women have an inferior legal status.

Saudi units fought against Israel in the 1948 and 1973 Arab-Israeli wars. Some 12,000 troops are deployed in Syria and Jordan. Many billions of dollars of advanced arms have been purchased from Britain, France, and the U.S., including jet fighters and missiles. Beginning with the 1967 Arab-Israeli war. Saudi Arabia provided large annual financial gifts to Egypt; aid was later extended to Syria, Jordan, and Palestinian guerrilla groups, as well as to other Moslem countries. The country has aided anti-radical forces in Yemen and Oman.

Faisal played a leading role in the 1973-74 Arab oil embargo against the U.S. and other nations in an attempt to force them to adopt an anti-Israel policy.

Between 1973 and 1976, Saudi Arabia acquired full ownership of Aramco (Arabian American Oil Co.). Oil had first been discovered by Western companies in the 1930s. A 5-year $140 billion development plan was approved in 1975, calling for importation of 500,000 workers. Some one million foreigners already lived in the country, whose native population may be less than 6 million. Plans were bogged down by lack of skilled labor and infrastructure.

The Hejaz contains the holy cities of Islam — Medina where the Mosque of the Prophet enshrines the tomb of Mohammed, who died in the city June.7, 632, and Mecca, his birthplace. More than 600,000 Moslems from 60 nations pilgrimage to Mecca annually.

# Senegal

## Republic of Senegal

**People: Population** (1976 est.): 5,090,000. **Pop. Density:** 66.86 per sq. mi. **Urban** (1971): 31.7%. **Ethnic groups:** Wolot 36%, Peuhl 17.5%, Serere 16.5%, Toucouleur 9%, others. **Languages:** French (official), tribal languages. **Religions:** Moslems 90%, Christians 6%.

**Geography: Area:** 76,124 sq. mi., the size of South Dakota. **Location:** At the western extreme of Africa. **Neighbors:** Mauritania on N, Mali on E, Guinea, Guinea-Bissau on S, Gambia surrounded on three sides. **Topography:** Low rolling plains cover most of Senegal, rising somewhat in the SE. Swamp and jungles are in SW. **Capital:** Dakar. **Cities** (1973 est.): Dakar (met.) 600,000; Kaolack 96,000; Thies 81,000.

**Government: Head of state:** Pres. Leopold Senghor; b. Oct. 9, 1906; in office: Sept. 5, 1960; **Head of government:** Prime Min. Abdou Diouf; b. 1935; in office: Feb. 1970. **Local divisions:** 8 regions. **Armed forces:** regulars 5,950; para-military 1,600.

**Economy: Industries:** Food processing, chemicals, cement. **Chief crops:** Peanuts are chief export; millet, corn, rice. **Minerals:** Phosphates. **Per capita arable land:** 3.1 acres. **Meat production** (1975): beef: 36,000 tons. **Fish catch** (1975): 361,700 metric tons. **Electricity production** (1976): 456.00 mln. kwh. **Labor force:** 76% agriculture.

**Finance: Currency:** Franc (May 1978: 230.35 = $1 US). **Gross domestic product** (1975): $1.57 bln. **Per capita income** (1974): $246. **Imports** (1975): $576 mln.; partners (1975): Fr. 50%, U.S. 7%, P.R. China 5%, W. Ger. 5%. **Exports** (1975): $461 mln.; partners (1975): Fr. 50%, Ivory Coast 8%, Mauritania 7%. **Tourists** (1975): 128,600; receipts (1975): $7 million. **Balance of payments** (1975); +$7,200,000. **International reserves** (Mar. 1978): $8.7 mln. **Consumer prices** (change in 1977): 9.6%.

**Transport: Railway traffic** (1974): 136.62 mln. passenger-miles; 243.43 mln. **Motor vehicles:** in use (1974): 44,800 passenger cars, 25,000 commercial vehicles. **Chief ports:** Dakar, Saint-Louis.

**Communications: Television sets:** 35,000 in use (1974). **Radios:** 286,000 in use (1974). **Telephones in use** (1977): 39,029. **Daily newspaper circulation** (1974): 30,000; 7 per 1,000 pop.

**Health: Life expectancy at birth** (1975): 38.5 male; 41.6 female. **Births** (annual per 1,000 pop. 1972-75): 47.6. **Deaths** (annual per 1,000 pop. 1972-75): 23.9. **Natural increase** (annual

1970-75): 2.37%. **Pop. per hospital bed** (1975): 730. **Pop. per physician** (1975): 15,114. **Infant mortality** (per 1,000 live births 1960-61): 92.9.

**Education: Literacy** (1975): 10%. **Pop. 5-19:** in school (1975): 23%, per teacher (1975): 196.

Portuguese settlers arrived in the 15th century, but French control grew from the 17th century. The last independent Moslem state was subdued in 1893. Dakar became the capital of French West Africa.

Independence as part, along with the Sudanese Rep., of the Mali Federation, came June 20, 1960. Senegal withdrew June 20 that year. French political and economic influence is strong.

A long drought brought famine, 1972-73, and again in 1978.

Two opposition parties were allowed to form in 1976, and free elections were held, 1978.

## Seychelles

**People: Population** (1977 est.): 60,000. **Age distrib.** (%): 0-14: 43.6; 15-59; 47.4; 60+: 9.1. **Pop. density:** 560.75 per sq. mi. **Urban** (1971): 26.1% **Ethnic groups:** Creoles (mixture of Asians, Africans, and French) predominate. **Languages:** English (official), Creole 94%, French 5%, others. **Religions:** Roman Catholics 90%, Protestants 8%, Hindus, Moslems.

**Geography: Area:** 107 sq. mi. **Location:** In the Indian O. 700 miles NE of Madagascar. **Neighbors:** Nearest are Madagascar on SW. Somalia on NW. **Topography:** The Seychelles are a group of 86 islands, about half of them composed of coral, the other half granite, the latter predominantly mountainous. **Capital:** Victoria. **Cities** (1971 cen.): Port Victoria (met.) 13,736.

**Government: Head of state:** Pres. France Albert Rene; in office: June 5, 1977. **Local divisions:** 8 districts.

**Economy: Industries:** Food processing, brewing. **Chief crops:** Coconut products, cinnamon, vanilla, tea, patchouli. **Other resources:** Guano, shark fins, tortoise shells, fish. **Electricity production** (1975): 25.00 mln. kwh.

**Finance: Currency:** Rupee (1974: 5.7 = $1 US). **Gross domestic product** (1974 est.): $28 mln. **Per capita income** (1974): $450. **Imports** (1974): $27 mln.; partners (1975): U.K. 27%, Kenya 19%, Austral. 8%, So. Afr. 7%, Sing. 4%. **Exports** (1974): $3 mln.; partners (1975): Pakistan 58%, Mauritius 25%, U.S. 12.5%. **Tourists** (1975): 37,300. **Consumer prices** (change in 1976): 14.9%.

**Transport: Motor vehicles:** in use (1975): 2,500 passenger cars, 600 commercial vehicles.

**Communications: Radios:** 9,000 in use (1973). **Telephones in use** (1977): 3,874. **Daily newspaper circulation** (1974): 2,400; 41 per 1,000 pop.

**Health: Life expectancy at birth** (1975): 38.5 male; 41.6 female. **Births** (annual per 1,000 pop. 1972-75): 27.7. **Deaths** (annual per 1,000 pop. 1972-75): 7.9. **Natural increase** (1976): 1.98%. **Infant mortality** (per 1,000 live births 1974): 39.3.

The islands were occupied by France in 1768, and seized by Britain in 1794. Ruled as part of Mauritius from 1814, the Seychelles became a separate colony in 1903. Several island groups were detached in 1965. The ruling party had opposed independence as impractical, but pressure from the OAU and the UN became irresistible, and independence was declared June 29, 1976. The first president was ousted in a coup a year later by a socialist leader.

## Sierra Leone
### Republic of Sierra Leone

**People: Population** (1977 est.): 3,470,000. **Pop. density:** 124.26 per sq. mi. **Ethnic groups:** Temne 30%, Mende 30%, other tribes. **Languages:** English (official), Krio (pidgin), tribal languages. **Religions:** Moslems 25%, Christians 5%, others.

**Geography: Area:** 27,925 sq. mi., slightly smaller than North Carolina. **Location:** On W coast of W. Africa. **Neighbors:** Guinea on N, E, Liberia on S. **Topography:** The heavily-indented, 210-mi. coastline has mangrove swamps to 60 mi. inland. Behind are wooded hills, rising to a plateau and mountains in the E. **Capital:** Freetown. **Cities** (1974 est.): Freetown 214,443.

**Government: triumvirate:** Pres. Siaka P. Stevens; b. Aug.

24, 1905; in office: Apr. 21, 1971 (prime min. since 1967); Vice Pres. Sorie Ibrahim Koroma; b. 1930; in office: Apr. 24, 1971; Prime Min. Christian Alusine Kamara-Taylor; b. 1917; in office: 1971. **Local divisions:** Freetown and 3 provinces. **Armed forces:** regulars 2,200; para-military 2,500.

**Economy: Industries:** Wood products. **Chief crops:** Cocoa, coffee, palm kernels, kola nuts, ginger. **Minerals:** Diamonds, iron ore, bauxite. **Per capita arable land:** 2.9 acres. **Fish catch** (1975): 67,800 metric tons. **Electricity production** (1975): 193.00 mln. kwh. **Labor force:** 73% agriculture.

**Finance: Currency:** Leone (May 1978: 1.10 = $1 US). **Gross domestic product** (1976): $522.04 mln. **Per capita income** (1975): $201. **Imports** (1976): $153 mln.; partners (1974): U.K. 21%, Jap. 10%, Nigeria 8%, W. Ger. 7%. **Exports** (1976): $112 mln.; partners (1974): U.K. 61%, Neth. 15%, U.S. 6%, Jap. 5%. **Tourists** (1974): 7,800; receipts (1974): $3 million. **Balance of payments** (1977): −$2,500,000. **International reserves** (May 1978): $52.6 mln. **Consumer prices** (change in 1977): 8.3%.

**Transport: Motor vehicles:** in use (1975): 14,800 passenger cars, 6,700 commercial vehicles. **Chief ports:** Freetown, Bonthe.

**Communications: Television sets:** 6,000 licensed (1974). **Radios:** 61,000 in use (1974). **Telephones in use** (1977): 15,060. **Daily newspaper circulation** (1974): 25,000; 9 per 1,000 pop.

**Health: Life expectancy at birth** (1975): 41.9 male; 45.1 female. **Births** (annual per 1,000 pop. 1972-75): 44.7. **Deaths** (annual per 1,000 pop. 1972-75): 20.7. **Natural increase** (annual 1970-75): 2.40%. **Pop. per hospital bed** (1975): 805. **Pop. per physician** (1975): 17,520. **Infant mortality** (per 1,000 live births 1973): 136.

**Education: Literacy** (1975): 15%. **Pop. 5-19:** in school (1975): 23%, per teacher (1975): 118.

Freetown was founded in 1787 by the British government as a home for destitute freed slaves. Their descendants, known as Creoles, number more than 80,000.

Successive steps toward independence followed introduction of a constitution in 1951. Full independence arrived Apr. 27, 1961. The People's Party was dominant until a military junta took over in March, 1967. Civilian rule was restored after another coup a year later. Sierra Leone became a republic Apr. 19, 1971.

## Singapore
### Republic of Singapore

**People: Population** (1977 est.): 2,310,000. **Age distrib.** (%): 0-14: 35.5; 15-59: 58.3; 60+: 6.3. **Pop. density:** 10,221.24 per sq. mi. **Ethnic groups:** Chinese 74%, Malays 14%, Indians, Pakistanis 8%. **Languages:** Chinese, Malay, Tamil, English all official. **Religions:** Buddhism, Taoism, Islam, Hinduism, Christianity.

**Geography: Area:** 226 sq. mi., smaller than New York City. **Location:** Off tip of Malayan Peninsula in S.E. Asia. **Neighbors:** Nearest are Malaysia on N, Indonesia on S. **Topography:** Singapore is a flat, formerly swampy island. The nation includes 40 nearby islets. **Capital:** Singapore. **Cities** (1975 est.): Singapore 2,249,900.

**Government: Head of state:** Pres. Benjamin H. Sheares; b. Aug. 12, 1907; in office: Jan. 1971; **Head of government:** Prime Min. Lee Kuan Yew; b. Sept. 16, 1923; in office: May 1959. **Armed forces:** regulars 36,000; reserves 45,000.

**Economy: Industries:** Shipbuilding, oil refining, electronics, banking, textiles, food, rubber, lumber processing, tourism. **Per capita arable land:** 0.003 acres. **Meat production** (1975): pork: 34,000 tons. **Fish catch** (1975): 17,600 metric tons. **Electricity production** (1977): 5.11 bln. kwh. **Labor force:** 3% agric.; 20% manuf.

**Finance: Currency:** Dollar (May 1978: 2.34 = $1 US). **Gross domestic product** (1977): $6.98 bln. **Per capita income** (1974): $2,200. **Imports** (1977): $10.47 bln.; partners (1974): Jap. 18%, U.S. 14%, Malaysia 13%, Kuw. 6%. **Exports** (1977): $8.24 bln.; partners (1974): Malaysia 17%, U.S. 15%, Jap. 11%, Hong Kong 6%. **Tourists** (1975): 1,324,300; receipts (1975): $335 million. **Balance of payments** (1977): +$293,000,000. **National budget** (1977): $1.66 bln. revenues; $1.32 bln. expenditures. **International reserves** (Feb. 1978): $3.99 bln. **Consumer prices** (change in 1977): 3.2%.

**Transport: Motor vehicles:** in use (1975): 149,000 passenger-cars, 46,300 commercial vehicles. **Civil aviation:** 4,881 mln. passenger-miles (1977); 161,045 mln. freight ton-miles (1977).

**Communications: Television sets:** 252,000 licensed (1974). **Radios:** 320,000 licensed (1974). **Telephones in use** (1977): 374,394.

**Health: Life expectancy at birth** (1970): 65.1 male; 70.0 female. **Births** (per 1,000 pop. 1976): 18.8. **Deaths** (per 1,000 pop. 1976): 5.1. **Natural increase** (1976): 1.37%. **Pop. per hospital bed** (1975): 271. **Pop. per physician** (1975): 1,399. **Infant mortality** (per 1,000 live births 1975): 13.9.

**Education: Literacy** (1975): 76%. **Pop. 5–19:** in school (1975): 61%, per teacher (1975): 47.

Founded in 1819 by Sir Thomas Stamford Raffles, Singapore was a British colony until 1959 when it became autonomous within the Commonwealth. On Sept. 16, 1963, it joined with Malaya, Sarawak and Sabah to form the Federation of Malaysia.

Tensions between Malayans, dominant in the federation, and ethnic Chinese, dominant in Singapore, led to an agreement under which Singapore became a separate nation. Aug. 9, 1965.

Singapore is the world's 4th largest port. Manufacturing has surpassed shipping, pushing per capita income to second place in Asia, following Japan. Standards in health, education, and housing are high. International banking has grown.

Formerly democratic, the government has suppressed opposition in recent years.

# Solomon Islands

**People: Population** (1977 est.): 200,000. **Pop. density:** 17.39 per sq. mi. **Urban** (1972): 8.8%. **Ethnic groups:** A variety of Melanesian groups and mixtures, some Polynesians. **Languages:** Pidgin English, Melanesian, and Papuan languages. **Religions:** Christianity, traditional religions.

**Geography: Area:** 11,500 sq. mi., slightly larger than Maryland. **Location:** A Melanesian archipelago in the western Pacific O. **Neighbors:** Nearest is Papua New Guinea on W. **Topography:** The Solomons include ten large islands and four groups of smaller ones. The larger islands are volcanic and rugged. **Capital:** Honiara. **Cities:** (1970 cen.): Honiara 11,191.

**Government: Head of state:** Queen Elizabeth II, represented by Gov.-Gen. Baddely Devesi; b. 1941; in office: July 7, 1978; **Head of government:** Prime Min. Peter Kenilorea; b. 1943; in office: July 7, 1978.

**Economy: Industries:** Fish canning. **Chief crops:** Coconuts, cocoa, rice, oil palm. **Other resources:** Forests, marine shell. **Electricity production** (1975): 16.00 mln. kwh.

**Finance: Currency:** Dollar (Oct.-Dec. 1976: 1 = $1.15 US). **Gross domestic products** (1974 est.): $58 mln. **Per capita income** (1974): $290. **Imports** (1973): $16 mln.; partners (1975): Austral. 44.5%, U.K. 15.8%. **Exports** (1973): $14 mln.; partners (1975): Jap. 52.8%, Austral. 13.9%, U.K. 2.2%. **Consumer prices** (change in 1976): 4.3%.

**Communications: Radios:** 7,700 in use (1974). **Telephones in use** (1977): 1,838.

**Health: Births** (per 1,000 pop. 1969): 36.1. **Deaths** (per 1,000 pop. 1969): 13.0. **Natural increase** (1969): 2.31%. **Infant mortality** (per 1,000 live births 1969): 52.4.

The Solomon Islands were sighted in 1568 by an expedition from Peru. Britain established a protectorate in the 1890s over most of the group, inhabited by Melanesians. The islands saw major World War II battles. Self-government came Jan. 2, 1976, and independence was formally attained July 7, 1978.

# Somalia

## Somali Democratic Republic

**People: Population** (1977 est.): 3,350,000. **Pop. density:** 13.61 per sq. mi. **Ethnic groups:** Somalis, related tribes 95%, Bantus 3.6%, Arabs 1.1%. **Languages:** Somali (official), Arabic, Italian, English. **Religions:** Sunni Moslems 99%.

**Geography: Area:** 246,155 sq. mi., slightly smaller than Texas. **Location:** Occupies the eastern horn of Africa. **Neighbors:** Afars and Issas, Ethiopia, Kenya on W. **Topography:** The coastline extends for 1,700 mi. Hills cover the N; the center and S are flat. **Capital:** Mogadishu. **Cities** (1972 est.): Mogadishu 230,000.

**Government: Head of state:** Pres. Mohammed Siad Barre; b. 1912; in office: Oct. 15, 1969. **Local divisions:** 16 regions. **Armed forces:** regulars 31,500; para-military 24,000.

**Economy: Chief crops:** Incense, sugar, bananas, sorghum, corn, kapole, gum. **Minerals:** Iron, tin, gypsum, uranium, bauxite, meerschaum, titanium, uranium. **Per capita arable land:** 0.7 acres. **Electricity production** (1975): 42.00 mln. kwh. **Labor force:** 82% agriculture.

**Finance: Currency:** Shilling (May 1978: 6.30 = $1 US). **Gross domestic product** (1974 est): $370 mln. **Per capita income** (1974): $110. **Imports** (1975): $162 mln.; partners (1972): It. 29%, USSR 10%, U.S. 6%, U.K. 6%. **Exports** (1976): $85 mln.; partners (1972): Saudi Ar. 53%, It. 18%, USSR 6%, Kuw. 6%. **Tourist receipts** (1975): $1 million. **Balance of payments** (1976): +$13,700,000. **International reserves** (Mar. 1978): $174.4 mln. **Consumer prices** (change in 1977): 10.6%.

**Transport: Motor Vehicles:** in use (1972): 8,000 passenger cars, 8,000 commercial vehicles. **Chief ports:** Mogadishu, Berbera.

**Communications: Radios:** 67,000 in use (1974). **Telephones in use** (1970): 5,000. **Daily newspaper circulation** (1973): 4,000; 1 per 1,000 pop.

**Health: Life expectancy at birth** (1975): 39.4 male; 42.6 female. **Births** (annual per 1,000 pop. 1972-75): 47.9 female. **Deaths** (annual per 1,000 pop. 1972-75): 21.7. **Natural increase** (annual 1970-75): 2.55%. **Pop. per hospital bed** (1975): 563. **Pop. per physician** (1975): 15,624. **Infant mortality** (per 1,000 live births 1973): 177.

**Education: Literacy** (1975): 5%. **Pop. 5-19:** in school (1975): 18%, per teacher (1975): 244.

Many of the Somali peoples are nomadic and include large numbers in Kenya and Ethiopia. Arab trading posts developed into coastal sultanates. The Italian Protectorate of Somalia, acquired from 1885 to 1927, extended along the Indian Ocean from the Gulf of Aden to the Juba River. The UN in 1949 approved eventual creation of Somalia as a sovereign state and in 1950 Italy took over the trusteeship held by Great Britain since World War II.

British Somaliland was formed in the 19th century in the northwest. Britain gave it independence June 26, 1960, and on July 1 it joined with the former Italian part to create the independent Somali Republic.

On Oct. 21, 1969, a Supreme Revolutionary Council seized power in a bloodless army and police coup, named a mainly civilian cabinet to aid it, and abolished the Assembly. It made Somali, a Hamitic language spoken by most of the population, the official language, and decreed a standardized spelling using Latin letters. In May, 1970, several foreign companies were nationalized.

A severe drought in 1975 killed tens of thousands, and spurred efforts to resettle nomads on collective farms. The U.S. charged in 1975 that Soviet naval facilities at Berbera included a missile storage site.

Somalia has laid claim to Ogaden, the huge eastern region of Ethiopia, peopled mostly by Somalis. Ethiopia battled Somali rebels and accused Somalia of sending troops and heavy arms in 1977. Russian forces were expelled in 1977 in retaliation for Soviet support of Ethiopia. Some 11,000 Cuban troops with Soviet arms defeated Somali army troops and ethnic Somali rebels in Ethiopia, 1978. As many as 500,000 refugees entered Somalia.

# South Africa

## Republic of South Africa

**People: Population** (1976 est.): 26,130,000. **Age distrib.** (%): 0–14: 14.8; 15–59: 52.9; 60+: 6.3. **Pop. density:** 55.38 per sq. mi. **Urban** (1972): 47.9%. **Ethnic groups:** Bantus 70% (of which Zulu 19%, Xhosa 18%, Tswana 8%), whites 17.5%. Colored 9.4%, Asiatic 2.9% **Religions:** Bantu Christian 14.5%, Dutch Reformed 14.3%, Methodist 10.7%, Anglican 8.8%, Roman Catholic 6.7%, other Christian 18.4%, Moslems, Hindus, and Jews 4%. **Languages:** Afrikaans, English, Bantu and Indian languages.

**Geography: Area:** 471,819 sq. mi., four-fifths the size of Alaska. **Location:** At the southern extreme of Africa. **Neighbors:** Namibia (SW Africa), Botswana, Rhodesia on N, Mozambique, Swaziland on E; surrounds Lesotho. **Topography:** The arge interior plateau reaches close to the country's 2,700-mi. coastline. There are few major rivers or lakes; rainfall is sparse n W. more plentiful in E. **Capitals:** Cape Town (legislative). Pretoria (administrative), and Bloemfontein (judicial). **Cities** (1970 est.): Johannesburg (met.) 1,432,643; Cape Town (met.) 1,096,597; Durban 843,327; Pretoria 561,703; Port Elizabeth 468,777.

**Government: Head of state:** Acting Pres. Marais Viljoen; in office: Aug. 14, 1978. **Head of government:** Prime Min. Balthazar Johannes Vorster; b. Doc. 13, 1915; in office: Sept. 13, 1966. **Local divisions:** 4 provinces with elected councils and some powers: Transvaal, Orange Free State, Cape of Good Hope, Natal. **Armed forces:** regulars 93,400; reserves 165,500.

**Economy: Industries:** Steel, tires, motors, textiles, plastics. **Chief crops:** Corn, grain, tobacco, sugar, fruit, peanuts, grapes. **Minerals:** Largest world production of gold, gem diamonds, antimony, platinum, chrome, copper, uranium, vanadium. **Other resources:** Wool. **Per capita arable land:** 1.2 acres. **Meat production** (1976): beef: 546,900 tons; pork: 86,600 tons; lamb: 184,300. **Fish catch** (1975): 1,314,700 metric tons. **Electricity production** (1977): 80.20 bln. kwh. **Labor force:** 28% agric.; 13% manuf.

**Finance: Currency:** Rand (May 1978: 1 = $1.15 US). **Gross domestic product** (1977): $38.89 bln. **Per capita income** (1976): $1,077. **Imports** (1976): $5.91 bln.; partners (1974): W. Ger. 19%, U.K. 17%, U.S. 16%, Jap. 12%. **Exports** (1977): $6.69 bln.; partners (1974): U.K. 29%, Jap. 11%, W. Ger. 9%, U.S. 7%. **Tourist receipts** (1975): $179 million. **Balance of payments** (1977): −$13,000,000. **National budget** (1977): $8.02 bln. revenues; $10.05 bln. expenditures. **International reserves** (May 1978): $845 mln. **Consumer prices** (change in 1977): 11.3%.

**Transport: Railway traffic** (1975): 40.40 bln. net ton-miles. **Motor vehicles:** in use (1975): 2,117,000 passenger cars, 800,300 commercial vehicles; assembled (1976): 168,648 passenger cars; 83,280 commercial vehicles. **Civil aviation:** 4,032 mln. passenger-miles (1977): 117,898 mln. freight ton-miles (1977). **Chief ports:** Durban, Cape Town, East London, Port Elizabeth.

**Communications: Radios:** 2,335,000 licensed (1974), 313,000 manufactured (1970). **Telephones in use** (1977): 2,191,404. **Daily newspaper circulation** (1974): 1,738,000; 14 per 1,000 pop.

**Health: Life expectancy at birth** (1975): 49.8 male; 53.3 female. **Births** (annual per 1,000 pop. 1972-75): 42.9. **Deaths** (annual per 1,000 pop. 1972-75): 15.5. **Natural increase** (annual 1970-75): 2.74%. **Pop. per hospital bed** (1975): 159. **Pop. per physician** (1975): 1,992. **Infant mortality** (per 1,000 live births 1973): 117.

**Education: Literacy** (1975): 35%. **Pop. 5-19:** in school (1975): 59%, per teacher (1975): 68.

Bushmen and Hottentots were the original inhabitants. Bantu tribes occupied lands in the N and E at about the time Europeans first arrived.

The Cape of Good Hope area was settled by Dutch, beginning in the 17th century. Britain seized the Cape in 1806. Many Dutch trekked north and founded 2 republics, the Transvaal and the Orange Free State. Diamonds were discovered, 1867, and gold, 1886. The Dutch (Boers) resented encroachments by the British and others; the Anglo-Boer War followed, 1899-1902. Britain won and, effective May 31, 1910, created the Union of South Africa, incorporating the British colonies of the Cape and Natal, the Transvaal and the Orange Free State.

After a referendum, the Union became the Republic of South Africa, May 31, 1961, and withdrew from the Commonwealth.

With the election victory of Daniel Malan's National party in 1948, the policy of separate development of the races, or apartheid, already existing unofficially, became official. This called for separate development, separate residential areas and ultimate political independence for the whites, Bantus, Asians, and Coloreds. In 1959 the government passed acts providing the eventual creation of several Bantu nations or Bantustans on 13% of the country's land area, though most black leaders have opposed the plan. In 1963, the Transkei, an area in the SE, became the first of these partially self-governing territories or "Homelands." By 1974 there were 10. Transkei became independent in Oct. 1976, and Bophuthatsvana followed in 1977; neither received international recognition.

Under apartheid, blacks are severely restricted to certain occupations, and are paid far lower wages than are whites for simi-

lar work. Only whites may vote or run for public office, and militant white opposition has been curbed. There is an advisory Indian Council, partly elected, partly appointed. In 1969, a Colored People's Representative Council was created. Minor liberalization measures were allowed in the 1970s.

At least 600 persons, mostly Bantus, were killed in 1976 riots protesting apartheid. Black protests continued partly fueled by rising unemployment.

## Namibia (South-West Africa)

South-West Africa is a sparsely populated land twice the size of California. Made a German protectorate in 1884, it was surrendered to South Africa in 1915 and was administered by that country under a League of Nations mandate. South Africa refused to accept UN authority under the trusteeship system.

Other African nations charged South Africa imposed apartheid, built military bases, and exploited S-W Africa; 36 African states called on the UN to take over the mandate. The UN General Assembly in May 1968 created an 11-nation council to take over administration of S-W Africa and lead it to independence. In April 1968 the council charged that South Africa had blocked its efforts to visit S-W Africa.

In 1968 the UN General Assembly gave the area the name Namibia. In Jan. 1970 the UN Security Council condemned South Africa for "illegal" control of the area. In an advisory opinion in June 1971 the International Court of Justice declared South Africa was occupying the area illegally.

In a 1977 referendum, white voters backed a plan for a multi-racial interim government to lead to independence. The Marxist South-West Africa People's Organization rejected the plan, and launched a guerrilla war. Both S. Africa and Namibian rebels agreed to a Western plan for independence by the end of 1978.

Most of S-W Africa is a plateau, 3,600 ft. high, with plains in the N. Kalahari Desert to the E. Orange River on the S, the Atlantic on the W. Area is 318,261 sq. mi.; population (Govt. est. 1975) 852,000 including about 100,000 whites; capital, Windhoek.

Products include cattle, sheep, diamonds, copper, lead, zinc, fish. People include Namas (Hottentots), Ovambos (Bantus), Bushmen, and others.

**Walvis Bay,** the only deepwater port in the country, was turned over to South African administration in 1922. South Africa said in 1978 it would discuss sovereignty only after Namibian independence.

## Spain
### Spanish State

**People: Population** (1977 est.): 36,350,000. **Age distrib.** (%): 0–14: 27.9; 15–59: 58.1; 60+: 14.1 **Pop. density:** 186.52 per sq. mi. **Ethnic groups:** Spanish (Castilian, Valencian, Andalusian) 72.8%, Catalan 16.4%, Galician 8.2%, Basque 2.3%. **Languages:** Spanish (official), Catalan, Galician, Valencian, Basque all legally recognized. **Religions:** Roman Catholicism nearly universal.

**Geography: Area:** 194,883 sq. mi., the size of Colorado and Wyoming combined. **Location:** In SW Europe. **Neighbors:** Portugal on W, France on N. **Topography:** The interior is a high, arid plateau broken by mountain ranges and river valleys. The NW is heavily watered, the south has lowlands and a Mediterranean climate. **Capital:** Madrid. **Cities** (1974 est.): Madrid (met.) 3,520,320; Barcelona (met.) 1,809,722; Valencia (met.) 713,026; Seville (met.) 588,784; Zaragoza (met.) 547,317; Bilbao (met.) 457,655; Malaga (met.) 402,978.

**Government: Head of state:** King Juan Carlos I de Borbon y Borbon, b. Jan. 5, 1938; in office: Nov. 22, 1975; **Head of government:** Prime Min. Adolfo Suarez; b. Sept. 25, 1932; in office: July 3, 1976. **Local divisions:** 50 provinces with appointed governors. **Armed forces:** regulars 526,000; para-military 103,000.

**Economy: Industries:** Machinery, textiles, shoes, paper, autos, ships, cement, tourism. **Chief crops:** Grains, olives, grapes, citrus fruits, onions, almonds, esparto, flax, hemp, pulse, tobacco, cotton, rice. **Minerals:** Lead, iron, copper, zinc, coal, cobalt, mercury, silver, sulphur, phosphates, oil. **Crude oil reserves** (1978): 265 mln. bbls. **Other resources:** Forests (cork). **Per capita arable land:** 1.1 acres. **Meat production** (1976): beef: 418,100 tons; pork: 648,800 tons; lamb: 145,800 tons. **Fish catch** (1975): 1,532,900 metric tons. **Electricity production** (1977): 93.71 bln. kwh. **Labor force:** 23% agric.; 26% manuf.

**Finance: Currency:** Pesata (May 1978: 80.35 = $1 US).

Gross domestic product (1976): $102.49 bln. Per capita income (1976): $2,663. Imports (1977): $17.85 bln.; partners (1974): U.S. 15%, Saudi Ar. 12%, W. Ger. 11%, Fr. 8%. Exports (1977): $10.23 bln.; partners (1974): Fr. 12%, U.S. 11%, W. Ger. 11%, U.K. 9%. Tourists (1975): 30,122,500; receipts (1975): $3,481 billion. Balance of payments (1977): +$1,520,000,000. National budget (1977): $14.38 bln. revenues; $13.98 bln. expenditures. International reserves (Apr. 1978): $7.57 bln. Consumer prices (change in 1977): 24.5%.

Transport: Railway traffic (1975): 10.03 bln. passenger-miles; 6.04 bln. net ton-miles. Motor vehicles: in use (1975): 4,806,800 passenger cars, 1,040,100 commercial vehicles; manufactured (1977): 1,021,200 passenger cars; 134,400 commercial vehicles. Civil aviation: 7,780 mln. passenger-miles (1977): 217,934 mln. freight ton-miles (1977). Chief ports: Barcelona, Bilbao, Valencia, Cartagena, Gijon.

Communications: Television sets: 6,125,000 in use (1974), 528,000 manufactured (1975). Radios: 8,050,000 in use (1974), 487,000 manufactured (1975). Telephones in use (1977): 8,597,781. Daily newspaper circulation (1974): 3,396,000; 96 per 1,000 pop.

Health: Life expectancy at birth (1970); 69.69 male; 74.96 female. Births (per 1,000 pop. 1976): 17.7. Deaths (per 1,000 pop. 1976): 8.0. Natural increase (1976): .97%. Pop. per hospital bed (1975): 194. Pop. per physician (1975): 726. Infant mortality (per 1,000 live births 1974): 13.8.

Education: Literacy (1975): 92%. Pop. 5-19: in school (1975): 66%, per teacher (1975): 35.

Spain was settled by Iberians, Basques, and Celts, partly overrun by Carthaginians, conquered by Rome c. 200 B.C. The Visigoths, in power by the 5th century A.D., adopted Christianity but by 711 A.D. lost to the Islamic invasion from Africa. Christian reconquest from the N led to a Spanish nationalism. In 1469 the kingdoms of Aragon and Castile were united by the marriage of Ferdinand II and Isabella I, and the last Moorish power was broken by the fall of the kingdom of Granada, 1492. Spain became a bulwark of Roman Catholicism.

Spain obtained a colonial empire with the discovery of America by Columbus, 1492, the conquest of Mexico by Cortes and Peru by Pizarro. It also controlled the Netherlands and parts of Italy and Germany. Spain lost its American colonies in the early 19th century: It lost Cuba, the Philippines, and Puerto Rico during the Spanish-American War, 1898.

Primo de Rivera became dictator in 1923. King Alfonso XIII revoked the dictatorship, 1930, but was forced to leave the country 1931. A republic was proclaimed which disestablished the church, curtailed its privileges, and secularized education. A conservative reaction occurred 1933 but was followed by a Popular Front (1936-1939) composed of socialists, communists, republicans, and anarchists.

Army officers headed a revolt against the government, 1936, under Francisco Franco. In a destructive 3-yr. war, in which one million were said to have died, Franco received massive help and troops from Italy and Germany, while the Soviet Union, France, and Mexico were active on behalf of the republic. War ended Mar. 28, 1939. Franco was named caudillo, or leader of the nation. Spain was neutral in World War II but its relations with fascist countries caused its exclusion from the UN in 1946. It was admitted in 1955.

In July 1969, Franco and the Cortes designated Prince Juan Carlos, then 31, as the future king and chief of state. After Franco's death, Nov. 20, 1975, Juan Carlos was sworn in as king. He presided over the formal dissolution of the institutions of the Franco regime. In free elections June 1976, moderates and democratic socialists emerged as the largest parties. Concessions were made to Basques and Catalans seeking autonomy, but violent Basque opposition continued.

Between 1960 and 1975 Spain changed from an agricultural nation to one of the world's important industrial powers.

The Balearic Islands in the western Mediterranean, 1,935 sq. mi., are a province of Spain; they include Majorca (Mallorca), with the capital, Palma; Minorca, Cabrera, Ibiza and Formentera. The Canary Islands, 2,807 sq. mi., in the Atlantic W of Morocco, form 2 provinces, including the islands of Tenerife, Palma, Gomera, Hierro, Grand Canary, Fuerteventura, and Lanzarote with Las Palmas and Santa Cruz thriving ports. Ceuta and Melilla, small enclaves on Morocco's Mediterranean coast, are part of Metropolitan Spain.

Spain has sought the return of Gibraltar, in British hands since 1704. (See Index.)

# Sri Lanka
## Republic of Sri Lanka

People: Population (1977 est.): 13,970,000. Pop. density: 551.48 per sq. mi. Urban (1971): 22.4%. Ethnic groups: Sinhalese 72%, Ceylon Tamil 11%, Indian Tamil 9.4%, Moor 6.7%. Languages: Sinhala (official), Tamil, English. Religions: Buddhists 67%, Hindus 18%, Christians 7.7%, Moslems 7.2%.

Geography: Area: 25,332 sq. mi. Location: In Indian O. off SE coast of India. Neighbors: Nearest is India on NW. Topography: The coastal area and the northern half are flat; the S-central area is hilly and mountainous. Capital: Colombo. Cities (1973 est.): Colombo 618,000; Dahiwala-Mount Lavina 136,000.

Government: Head of state: Pres. Junius Richard Jayewardene; b. Sept. 17, 1906; in office: Feb. 4, 1978. Local divisions: 22 districts. Armed forces: regulars 13,300; reserves 12,750.

Economy: Industries: Plywood, paper, glassware, ceramics, cement, chemicals, textiles. Chief crops: Tea, coconuts, rice, cacao, cinnamon, citronella, tobacco. Minerals: Graphite, limestone, iron, ilmenite, monazite, zircon, quartz, precious and semiprecious stones. Other resources: Forests, rubber. Per capita arable land: 0.2 acres. Meat production (1975): beef: 19,000 tons. Fish catch (1975): 129,100 metric tons. Electricity production (1975): 1.15 bln. kwh. Labor force: 41% agric.; 8% manuf.

Finance: Currency: Rupee (May 1978: 15.86 = $1 US). Gross domestic product (1976): $2.99 bln. Per capita income (1976): $214. Imports (1977): $701 mln.; partners (1975): P.R. China 12.5%, Saudi Ar. 12%, Jap. 8%, Austral. 8%, Fr. 8%. Exports (1977): $774 mln.; partners (1973): U.K. 11%, P.R. China 9%, Pakistan 8%, U.S. 7%. Tourists (1975): 103,200; receipts (1975): $18 million. Balance of payments (1976): +$55,400,000. National budget (1976): $650.09 mln. revenues; $980.18 bln. expenditures. International reserves (May 1978): $311 mln. Consumer prices (change in 1977): 1.2%.

Transport: Railway traffic (1975): 1.79 bln. passenger-miles; 183.82 mln. net ton-miles. Motor vehicles: in use (1975): 91,700 passenger cars, 48,600 commercial vehicles. Civil aviation: 189 mln. passenger-miles (1976), 1,654 mln. freight ton-miles (1976). Chief ports: Colombo, Trincomalee, Galle.

Communications: Radios: 505,000 in use (1974), 117,000 manufactured (1973). Telephones in use (1975): 72,000.

Health: Life expectancy at birth (1967): 64.8 male; 66.9 female. Births (per 1,000 pop. 1972): 29.5. Deaths (per 1,000 pop. 1972): 7.7. Natural increase (1972): 2.18%. Pop. per hospital bed (1975): 333. Pop. per physician (1975): 3,813. Infant mortality (per 1,000 live births 1972): 45.1.

Education: Literacy (1975): 84%. Pop. 5-19: in school (1975): 47%, per teacher (1975): 46.

The island was known to the ancient world as Taprobane (Greek for copper-colored) and later as Serendip (from Arabic). Colonists from northern Indian subdued the indigenous Veddahs about 543 B.C.; their descendants, the Buddhist Sinhalese, still form most of the population. Hindu descendants of Tamil immigrants from southern India account for one-fifth of the population; separatism has grown. Parts were occupied by the Portuguese in 1505 and by the Dutch in 1658. The British seized the island in 1796. As Ceylon it became an independent member of the Commonwealth in 1948. On May 22, 1972, Ceylon became the Republic of Sri Lanka. Prime Minister W. R. D. Bandaranaike was assassinated Sept. 25, 1959. In new elections, the Freedom Party was victorious under Mrs. Sirimavo Bandaranaike, widow of the former prime minister.

In April, 1962, the government expropriated service and terminal facilities of one British and 2 U.S. oil companies. In March 1965 elections, the conservative United National Party won the largest number of seats. The new government agreed to pay compensation for the seized oil companies. The U.S. in Feb. 1966, agreed to resume economic aid.

After May 1970 elections, Mrs. Bandaranaike became prime minister again. In 1971 the nation suffered economic problems and terrorist activities by ultra-leftists, thousands of whom were executed. Unemployment among graduates and food shortages plagued the nation from 1973 to 1976. Massive land reform and nationalization of foreign-owned plantations was undertaken in the mid-1970s. Mrs. Bandaranaike was ousted in 1977 elections by the more conservative United Nationals. A presidential form of government was installed in 1978 to restore stability; food subsidies were curbed. Sri Lanka enjoys a welfare state, high literacy, and declining birth rates.

# Sudan

## Democratic Republic of the Sudan

**People: Population** (1976 est.): 16,130,000. **Pop. density:** 16.67 per sq. mi. **Urban** (1976): 20.4%. **Ethnic groups:** North: Arabs, Nubians; South; Nilotic; Sudanic, Negro tribes. **Languages:** Arabic 51%, 32 other languages. **Religions:** Moslems 72%, Christians 5%, traditional 20%.

**Geography: Area:** 967,491 sq. mi., the largest country in Africa, over one-fourth the size of the U.S. **Location:** At the E end of Sahara desert zone. **Neighbors:** Egypt on N, Libya, Chad, Central African Empire on W, Zaire, Uganda, Kenya on S, Ethiopia on E. **Topography:** The N consists of the Libyan Desert in the W, and the mountainous Nubia desert in E, with narrow Nile valley between. The center contains large, fertile, rainy areas with fields, pasture, and forest. The S has rich soil, heavy rain. **Capital:** Khartoum. **Cities** (1971 est.): Khartoum 261,840; Omdurman 258,532; North Khartoum 127,672; Port Sudan 110,091.

**Government: Head of state:** Pres. Gaafar Mohammed Nimeiri; b. Jan. 1, 1930; in office: Sept. 1971 (prime min. since 1969); **Head of government:** Prime Min. Rashid el-Tahir Bakr; b. 1931; in office: Aug. 1976. **Local divisions:** 18 provinces; the southern 6 have a regional government. **Armed forces:** regulars 52,100; para-military 7,000.

**Economy: Industries:** Textiles, food processing. **Chief crops:** Gum arabic (principal world source), durra (sorghum), cotton (main export), sesame, peanuts, rice, coffee, sugar cane, tobacco, wheat, dates. **Minerals:** Chrome, gold, copper, white mica, vermiculite, asbestos. **Other resources:** Mahogany. **Per capita arable land:** 0.9 acres. **Meat production** (1975): beef: 118,000 tons; lamb: 100,000 tons. **Electricity production** (1975): 350.00 mln. kwh. **Labor force:** 80% agriculture.

**Finance: Currency:** Pound (May 1978: 2.87 = $1 US). **Gross domestic product** (1975): $4.34 bln. **Per capita income** (1974): $258. **Imports** (1976): $980 mln.; partners (1973): U.K. 17%, P.R. China 8%, U.S. 7%, India 7%. **Exports** (1976): $554 mln.; partners (1973): P.R. China 14%, It. 11%, Jap. 11%, W. Ger. 9%. **Tourists** (1975): 30,700; receipts (1975): $5 million. **Balance of payments** (1977): +$51,700,000. **International reserves** (May 1978): $28.1 mln. **Consumer prices** change in 1976): 1.7%.

**Transport: Railway traffic** (1973): 1.42 bln. net ton-miles. **Motor vehicles:** in use (1972): 29,200 passenger cars, 21,200 commercial vehicles. **Civil aviation:** 332 mln. passenger-miles 1976); 5,775 mln. freight ton-miles (1976). **Chief ports:** Port Sudan.

**Communications: Television sets:** 100,000 licensed (1974). **Radios:** 1,310,000 licensed (1973). **Telephones in use** (1977): 43,288. **Daily newspaper circulation** (1973): 140,000; 8 per 1,000 pop.

**Health: Life expectancy at birth** (1975): 47.3 male; 49.9 female. **Births** (annual per 1,000 pop. 1972-75): 47.8 **Deaths** (annual per 1,000 pop. 1972-75): 17.5. **Natural increase** (annual 1970-75): 3.03%. **Pop. per hospital bed** (1975): 1,184. **Pop. per physician** (1975): 12,231. **Infant mortality** (per 1,000 live births 1956): 93.6.

**Education: Literacy** (1975): 19%. **Pop. 5-19:** in school (1975): 23%, per teacher (1975): 155.

Northern Sudan, ancient Nubia, was settled by Egyptians in antiquity, and was converted to Coptic Christianity in the 6th century. Arab conquests brought Islam in the 15th century.

In the 1820s Egypt took over the Sudan, defeating the last of earlier empires, including the Fung. In the 1880s a revolution was led by Mohammed Ahmed who called himself the Mahdi (leader of the faithful) and his followers, the dervishes.

In 1898 an Anglo-Egyptian force which crushed the Mahdi's successors. In Oct. 1951 the Egyptian Parliament abrogated its 1899 and 1936 treaties with Great Britain, and amended the constitution, Oct. 16, to provide for a separate Sudanese constitution.

Sudan voted for complete independence effective Jan. 1, 1956. A parliamentary government was set up but in 1958 Gen. Ibrahim Abboud took power; he resigned under pressure in 1964.

In 1969, in a second military coup, a Revolutionary Council took power, but a civilian premier and cabinet were appointed; the government announced it would create a socialist state. It also announced plans to negotiate an end to guerrilla warfare, which had beset the southern third of the nation for years amid charges of government genocide. The northern 12 provinces are predominantly Arab-Moslem and have been dominant in the central government. The 3 southern provinces are Negro and predominantly pagan, with small Christian and Moslem minorities. A 1972 peace agreement gave the South regional autonomy. Renewed flare-ups occurred in 1975.

The government nationalized a number of businesses in May 1970. An attempted communist coup in July 1971 failed, leading to a temporary diplomatic break with the USSR. Soviet arms shipments were announced in 1975, but relations later deteriorated and U.S. ties improved.

Diplomatic relations with the U.S., broken by Sudan during the 1967 Arab-Israeli war, were restored in 1972; locally-owned firms were denationalized and foreign firms compensated.

On Mar. 2, 1973, the U.S. ambassador and the charge d'affaires and a Belgian diplomat were slain in Khartoum by 8 Palestinian terrorists. The 8 were freed and turned over to a Palestinian liberation group in Egypt. The U.S. agreed to sell advanced jet fighters.

Sudan charged Libya with aiding an unsuccessful coup in Sudan in 1976. Sudan has backed the Eritrean separatist movement in neighboring Ethiopia.

# Surinam

**People: Population** (1977 est.): 450,000. **Pop. density:** 7.11 per sq. mi. **Ethnic groups** (before independence): East Indians 35%, Creoles (racially mixed descendants of freed slaves) 30%, Javanese 15%, Bush Negroes (descendants of runaway slaves) 10%, Europeans, Chinese, Amerindians. **Languages:** Dutch (official), Sranan Tongo (Creole) universal, English, others. **Religions:** Hindus, Christians, Moslems.

**Geography: Area:** 63,251 sq. mi., slightly larger than Georgia. **Location:** On N shore of S. America. **Neighbors:** Guyana on W, Brazil on S, French Guiana on E. **Topography:** Most of the population inhabits the flat Atlantic coast, where dikes permit agriculture. Farther inland is a forest belt; to the S, largely unexplored hills cover three-fourths of the country. **Capital:** Paramaribo. **Cities** (1974 est.): Paramaribo 150,000.

**Government: Head of state:** Pres. Johan H.E. Ferrier; b. May 12, 1910; in office: Nov. 25, 1975; **Head of government:** Prime Min. Henck A.E. Arron; b. Apr. 25, 1936; in office: 1973. **Local divisions:** 9 districts.

**Economy: Industries:** Aluminum. **Chief crops:** Rice, sugar, fruits. **Minerals:** Bauxite. **Other resources:** Forests, shrimp. **Per capita arable land:** 0.2 acres. **Electricity production** (1975): 1.60 bln. kwh. **Labor force:** 27% agriculture.

**Finance: Currency:** Guilder (May 1978: 1.79 = $1 US). **Gross domestic product** (1975): $503.03 mln. **Per capita income** (1975): $1,038. **Imports** (1975): $262 mln.; partners (1972): U.S. 32%, Neth. 24%, Trin. 10%. **Exports** (1975): $277 mln.; partners (1972): U.S. 44%, Neth. 12%, W. Ger. 11%. **Tourist receipts** (1975): $6 million. **Balance of payments** (1976): −$906,000,000. **International reserves** (May 1978): $140.91 mln. **Consumer prices** (change in 1976): 10.1%.

**Transport: Motor vehicles:** in use (1973): 21,500 passenger cars, 5,600 commercial vehicles. **Chief ports:** Paramaribo, Nieuw-Nickerie.

**Communications: Telephones in use** (1977): 18,566. **Daily newspaper circulation** (1974): 24,000; 18 per 1,000 pop.

**Health: Life expectancy at birth** (1963): 62.5 male; 66.7 female. **Births** (per 1,000 pop. 1966): 40.9. **Deaths** (per 1,000 pop. 1966): 7.2. **Natural increase** (1966): 3.37%. **Infant mortality** (per 1,000 live births 1966): 30.4.

The Netherlands acquired Surinam in 1667 from Britain, in exchange for New Netherlands (New York). The 1954 Dutch constitution raised the colony to a level of equality with the Netherlands and the Netherlands Antilles. In the 1970s the Dutch government pressured for Surinam independence, which came Nov. 25, 1975, despite objections from East Indians and some Bush Negroes. Some 40% of the population (mostly East Indians) emigrated to the Netherlands in the months before independence. The Netherlands promised $1.5 billion in aid for the first decade of independence.

Both Guyana on the W and French Guiana on the E have disputed parts of their Surinam borders.

# Swaziland

## Kingdom of Swaziland

**People: Population** (1977 est.): 500,000. **Age distrib.** (%): 0–14: 48.2; 15–59: 47.5; 60+: 4.3. **Pop. density:** 74.57 per sq. mi. **Urban** (1973): 7.9%. **Ethnic groups:** Swazi 90%, Zulu 2.3%, European 2.1%, other African, non-African groups. **Languages:** siSwati (official). English. **Religions:** Christians 60%, others.

**Geography: Area:** 6,705 sq. mi., slightly smaller than New Jersey. **Location:** In southern Africa, near Indian O. coast. **Neighbors:** South Africa on N, W, S, Mozambique on E. **Topography:** The country descends from W-E in broad belts, becoming more arid in the lowveld region, then rising to a plateau in the E. **Capital:** Mbabane. **Cities** (1973 est.): Mbabane 20,800; Manzini 25,000.

**Government: Head of state:** King Sobhuza II; b. July 22, 1899; in office: 1921. **Head of government:** Prime Min. Makhosini Dlamini; b. 1922; in office: 1967. **Local divisions:** 4 districts, 2 municipalities.

**Economy: Industries:** Wood pulp. **Chief crops:** Corn, cotton, rice, pineapples, sugar, citrus fruits. **Minerals:** Asbestos, iron, coal. **Other resources:** Forests. **Per capita arable land:** 0.8 acres. **Meat production** (1975): beef: 14,000 tons. **Electricity production** (1975): 112.00 mln. kwh. **Labor force:** 83% agriculture.

**Finance: Currency:** Lilangeni (1974: 1 = $1.47 US). **Gross domestic product** (1974 est.) $200 mln. **Per capita income** (1973): $382. **Imports** (1973): $98 mln.; partners (1973): So. Afr., U.K. **Exports** (1973): $108 mln.; partners (1973): U.K. 25%, Jap. 24%, So. Afr. 21%. **Consumer prices** (change in 1977): 16.5%.

**Transport: Motor vehicles:** in use (1975): 7,100 passenger cars, 5,600 commercial vehicles.

**Communications: Radios:** 53,000 in use (1974). **Telephones in use** (1977): 8,207.

**Health: Life expectancy at birth** (1966): 44 male; 44 female. **Births** (annual per 1,000 pop. 1972-75): 49.0. **Deaths** (annual per 1,000 pop. 1972-75): 21.8. **Natural increase** (annual 1970-75): 2.72%. **Pop. per hospital bed** (1975): 274. **Pop. per physician** (1975): 9,130. **Infant mortality** (per 1,000 live births 1973): 149.

**Education: Literacy** (1975): 36%. **Pop. 5-19:** in school (1975): 57%, per teacher (1975): 60.

The royal house of Swaziland traces back 400 years, and is one of Africa's last ruling dynasties. The Swazis, a Bantu people, were driven to Swaziland from lands to the N by the Zulus in 1820. Their autonomy was later guaranteed by Britain and Transvaal, with Britain assuming control after 1903. Independence came Sept. 6, 1968. In 1973 the king repealed the constitution and assumed full powers.

Fertile lands and mineral resources have aided development. About 8,000 Swazis hold jobs in South Africa, which has a customs union with Swaziland. The population is homogeneous, except for 6,000 whites who dominate the economy.

# Sweden

## Kingdom of Sweden

**People: Population** (1977 est.): 8,260,000. **Age distrib.** (%): 0–14: 20.8; 15–59: 58.7; 60+: 20.5. **Pop. density:** 47.56 per sq. mi. **Urban** (1975): 82.7%. **Ethnic groups:** Swedish 93%, Finnish 3%, Lapps, European immigrants. **Languages:** Swedish, Finnish. **Religions:** Lutherans (official) 95%, other Protestants 5%.

**Geography: Area:** 173,665 sq. mi., larger than California. **Location:** On Scandinavian Peninsula in N. Europe. **Neighbors:** Norway on W, Denmark on S (across Kattegat), Finland on E. **Topography:** Mountains along NW border cover 25% of Sweden, flat or rolling terrain covers the central and southern areas, which includes several large lakes. **Capital:** Stockholm. **Cities** (1975 est.): Stockholm (met.) 1,357,558; Goteborg (met.) 691,098; Malmo (met.) 454,274.

**Government: Head of state:** King Carl XVI Gustaf; b. Apr. 30, 1946; in office: Sept. 19, 1973; **Head of government:** Prime Min. Thorbjorn Falldin; b. Apr. 24, 1926; in office: Oct. 7, 1976. **Local divisions:** 24 lan (counties). **Armed forces:** regulars, 107,850; reserves 500,000.

**Economy: Industries:** Steel, machinery, instruments, autos, shipbuilding, shipping, paper. **Chief crops:** Grains, potatoes, sugar beets. **Minerals:** Iron, lead, copper, zinc, gold, silver. **Other resources:** Forests (half the country); yield one fourth exports. **Per capita arable land:** 0.9 acres. **Meat production** (1976): beef: 149,000 tons; pork: 290,400 tons. **Fish catch** (1975): 215,300 metric tons. **Electricity production** (1977): 87.58 bln. kwh. **Labor force:** 7% agric.; 28% manuf.

**Finance: Currency:** Kronor (May 1978: 4.65 = $1 US) **Gross domestic product** (1977): $75.24 bln. **Per capita income** (1976): $8,044. **Imports** (1977): $19.57 bln.; partners (1975): W. Ger. 19%, U.K. 10.8%, Nor. 6.7%, Den. 5.4%. **Exports** (1977): $18.82 bln.; partners (1975): Nor. 11.1%, U.K. 10.8%, W. Ger. 9.8%, Den. 8.6%. **Balance of payments** (1977): +$1,046,000,000. **National budget** (1971): $13.67 bln. revenues; $11.66 bln. expenditures. **International reserves** (May 1978): $4.34 bln. **Consumer prices** (change in 1977): 11.4%.

**Transport: Railway traffic** (1975): 3.64 mln. passenger-miles; 9.97 mln. net ton-miles. **Motor vehicles:** in use (1975): 2,760,000 passenger cars, 171,000 commercial vehicles; manufactured (1976): 307,200 passenger cars; (1975): 49,200 commercial vehicles. **Civil aviation:** 2,318 mln. passenger-miles (1977); 114,515 mln. freight ton-miles (1977). **Chief ports:** Goteborg, Stockholm, Malmo.

**Communications: Television sets:** 2,841,000 licensed (1974). 370,000 manufactured (1974). **Radios:** 3,086,000 licensed (1974), 194,000 manufactured (1974). **Telephones in use** (1977): 5,673,427. **Daily newspaper circulation** (1974): 4,362,000; 536 per 1,000 pop.

**Health: Life expectancy at birth** (1975): 72.07 male; 77.65 female. **Births** (per 1,000 pop. 1976): 11.9. **Deaths** (per 1,000 pop. 1976): 11.0. **Natural increase** (1976): .09%. **Pop. per hospital bed** (1975): 71. **Pop. per physician** (1975): 616. **Infant mortality** (per 1,000 live births 1975): 8.3.

**Education: Literacy** (1975): 99%. **Pop. 5-19:** in school (1975): 76%, per teacher (1975): 17.

The Swedes have lived in present-day Sweden for at least 5,000 years, longer than nearly any other European people. Gothic tribes from Sweden played a major role in the disintegration of the Roman Empire. Other Swedes helped create the first Russian state in the 9th century.

The Swedes were Christianized from the 11th century, and a strong centralized monarchy developed. A parliament, the Riksdag, was first called in 1435, the earliest parliament on the European continent, with all classes of society represented.

Swedish independence from rule by Danish kings (dating from 1397) was secured by Gustavus I in a revolt, 1521-23; he built up the government and military and established the Lutheran Church. In the 17th century Sweden was a major European power, gaining most of the Baltic seacoast, but its international position subsequently declined.

The Napoleonic wars, in which Sweden acquired Norway (it became independent 1905), were the last in which Sweden participated. Armed neutrality was maintained in both world wars.

Over 4 decades of Social Democratic rule was ended in 1976 parliamentary elections. Although over 95% of the economy is in private hands, the government holds a large interest in water power production and the railroads are operated by a public agency. Worker participation in management is expanding.

Consumer cooperatives are in extensive operation, with 1,700,000 member households. Cooperatives also are important in agriculture and housing. Per capita GNP, 1976, was among the highest in the world.

The U.S. and Sweden in 1974 ended a 15-month diplomatic "freeze" and exchanged ambassadors.

Racial tensions between Swedes and the small number of foreign workers flared into prolonged violence in 1977. High wages have hurt exports, and the economy has slowed in recent years.

# Switzerland

## Swiss Confederation

**People: Population** (1977 est.): 6,330,000. **Age distrib.** (%): 0-14: 22.9; 15–59: 60.0; 60+: 17.1. **Pop. density:** 397.09 per sq. mi. **Urban** (1970): 54.6%. **Ethnic groups:** Defined by mother tongue. **Languages:** German 65%, French 18%, Italian 12%, omansch 0.8%. **Religions:** Protestant 48%, Roman Catholic 9%, Jews.

**Geography: Area:** 15,941 sq. mi., as large as Mass., Conn., nd R.I., combined. **Location:** In the Alps Mts. in Central Europe. **eighbors:** France on W, Italy on S, Austria on E, W. Germany n N. **Topography:** The Alps cover 60% of the land area, the ura, near France, 10%. Running between, from NE to SW, are idlands, 30%. **Capital:** Bern. **Cities** (1976 est.): Zurich (met.) 4,400; Basel (met.) 375,200; Geneva (met.) 323,200; Bern met.) 285,800.

**Government: Head of state:** Pres. Willi Ritschard; b. Sept. 3, 1918; in office: Jan. 1-Dec. 31, 1978. **Local divisions:** 19 full antons, 6 half cantons, all with elected legislatures and sub-antial powers. **Armed forces:** regulars 18,500; reserves 21,500.

**Economy: Industries:** Machinery, machine tools, steel, instru-ents, watches, textiles, foodstuffs (cheese, chocolate), chemi-als, drugs, banking, tourism. **Chief crops:** Grains, potatoes, gar beets, vegetables, tobacco. **Minerals:** Salt. **Other re-ources:** Hydro power potential. **Per capita arable land:** 0.1 cres. **Meat production** (1976): beef: 146,500 tons; pork: 38,200 tons. **Electricity production** (1977): 44.12 bln. kwh. **abor force:** 8% agric.; 38% manuf.

**Finance: Currency:** Franc (May 1978: 1.91 = $1 US). **Gross omestic product** (1977): $73.15 bln. **Per capita income** 1976): $8,248. **Imports** (1977): $17.98 bln.; partners (1975): W. er. 27.9%, Fr. 13.8%, It. 11.4%, U.K. 6.1%, Belg. 5%. **Exports** 1977): $17.68 bln.; partners (1975): W. Ger. 14.8%, Fr. 8.7%, It. 9%, U.K. 6.2%. **Tourists** (1975): 6,198,800; receipts (1975): 930 million. **Balance of payments** (1977): +$1,052,000,000. **ational budget** (1977): $6.48 bln. revenues; $7.11 bln. ex-enditures. **International reserves** (May 1978): $12.91 bln. **onsumer prices** (change in 1977): 1.3%.

**Transport: Railway traffic** (1975): 4.96 bln. passenger-miles; 19 bln. net ton-miles. **Motor vehicles:** in use (1974): ,723,000 passenger cars, 176,500 commercial vehicles. **Civil viation:** 5,760 mln. passenger-miles (1977); 234,649 mln. eight ton-miles (19   ).

**Communications: Television sets:** 1,714,000 licensed 974). **Radios:** 2,036,000 licensed (1974). **Telephones in use** (1977): 4,016,322. **Daily newspaper circulation** (1974): ,535,000; 391 per 1,000 pop.

**Health: Life expectancy at birth** (1973): 70.29 male; 76.22 emale. **Births** (per 1,000 pop. 1975): 12.3. **Deaths** (per 1,000 op. 1975): 8.7. **Natural increase** (1975): .36%. **Pop. per hos-ital bed** (1975): 89. **Pop. per physician** (1975): 569. **Infant ortality** (per 1,000 live births 1974): 12.5.

**Education:** Literacy (1975): 99%. **Pop. 5–19:** in school 1975): 60%, per teacher (1975): 23.

Switzerland, the Roman province of Helvetia, is a federation of 2 cantons (19 full cantons and 6 half cantons), 3 of which in 291 created a defensive league and later were joined by other istricts. (Voters in the French-speaking Jura approved a break-way canton in 1974.) In 1648 the Swiss Confederation obtained s independence from the Holy Roman Empire. The cantons vere joined under a federal constitution in 1848, with large pow-rs of local control retained by each canton.

Switzerland has maintained an armed neutrality since 1815, nd has not been involved in a foreign war since 1515. It is not a nember of the UN or NATO. It is, however, a member of several N agencies and of the European Free Trade Assoc. and has es with the EC. Switzerland is the seat of many UN and other nternational agencies.

Switzerland is a leading world banking center; stability of the urrency brings funds from many quarters. Some 20% of all vorkers are foreign residents.

# Syria

## Syrian Arab Republic

**People: Population** (1977 est.): 7,840,000. **Age distrib.** (%): –14: 49.3; 15–59: 44.3; 60+: 6.4. **Pop. density:** 109.65 per sq. i. **Urban** (1976): 46.6%. **Ethnic groups:** Arabs 88%, Kurds 3%, Armenians 2.8%, Turks, Circassians, Assyrians. **Lan-uages:** Arabic (official), French, Kurdish, Armenian. **Religions:** loslems (Sunni, Alawi, Druze) 88%, Christians 12%.

**Geography: Area:** 71,498 sq. mi., the size of North Dakota. **ocation:** At eastern end of Mediterranean Sea. **Neighbors:**

Lebanon, Israel on W, Jordan on S, Iraq on E, Turkey on N. **To-pography:** Syria has a short Mediterranean coastline, then stretches E and S with fertile lowlands and plains, alternating with mountains and large desert areas. **Capital:** Damascus. **Cit-ies** (1975 est.): Damascus 1,042,245; Aleppo 778,523; Homs 267,132.

**Government: Head of state:** Pres. Hafez al-Assad; b. Mar. 1930; in office: Mar. 12, 1971. **Head of government:** Prime Min. Mohammed Ali al-Halabi; in office: Mar. 27, 1978. **Local divi-sions:** Damascus and 13 provinces. **Armed forces:** regulars 227,500; para-military 41,500.

**Economy: Industries:** Oil products, textiles, cement, tobacco, glassware, sugar, brassware. **Chief crops:** Cotton, grain, olives, fruits, vegetables. **Minerals:** Oil, phosphate, gypsum. **Crude oil reserves** (1978): 2.15 bln. bbls. **Other resources:** Wool. **Per capita arable land:** 1.8 acres. **Meat production** (1975): beef: 13,000 tons; lamb: 55,000 tons. **Electricity production** (1976): 1.79 bln. kwh. **Labor force:** 54% agric.; 11% manuf.

**Finance: Currency:** Pound (May 1978: 3.95 = $1 US). **Gross domestic product** (1976): $5.81 bln. **Per capita in-come** (1974): $547. **Imports** (1976): $1.99 bln.; partners (1974): W. Ger. 12%, It. 9%, Fr. 9%, Leb. 8%. **Exports** (1976): $1.07 bln.; partners (1974): Gr. 18%, W. Ger. 15%, USSR 14%, U.K. 10%. **Tourists** (1975): 1,054,900; receipts (1975): $93 million. **Balance of payments** (1976): –$354,000,000. **International reserves** (Sept. 1977): $717 mln. **Consumer prices** (change in 1977): 12.6%.

**Transport: Railway traffic** (1975): 84.46 mln. passenger-miles; 77.63 mln. net ton-miles. **Motor vehicles:** in use (1975): 50,200 passenger cars, 34,400 commercial vehicles. **Chief ports:** Latakia, Tartus.

**Communications: Television sets:** 224,000 in use (1974), 39,000 manufactured (1975). **Radios:** 2,500,000 in use (1974). **Telephones in use** (1977): 176,930. **Daily newspaper circula-tion** (1974): 64,000; 118 per 1,000 pop.

**Health: Life expectancy at birth** (1970): 54.49 male; 58.73 female. **Births** (annual per 1,000 pop. 1972-75): 45.4. **Deaths** (annual per 1,000 1972-75): 15.4. **Natural increase** (annual 1970-75): 4.06%. **Pop. per hospital bed** (1975): 1,068. **Pop. per physician** (1975): 2,730. **Infant mortality** (per 1,000 live births 1972): 21.7.

**Education:** Literacy (1975): 40%. **Pop. 5–19:** in school (1975): 58%, per teacher (1975): 49.

Syria contains some of the most ancient remains of civiliza-tion. It was the center of the Seleucid empire, but later became absorbed in the Roman and Arab empires. Ottoman rule pre-vailed for 4 centuries, until the end of World War I.

The state of Syria was formed from former Turkish districts, made a separate entity by the Treaty of Sevres 1920 and di-vided into the states of Syria and Greater Lebanon. Both were administered under a French League of Nations mandate 1920-1941.

Syria was proclaimed a republic by the occupying French Sept. 16, 1941, and exercised full independence effective Jan. 1, 1944. French troops left in 1946. Syria joined in the Arab inva-sion of Israel in 1948.

Syria joined with Egypt in Feb. 1958 in the United Arab Re-public but seceded Sept. 30, 1961. The Socialist Baath party and military leaders seized power in Mar. 1963. The Baath, a pan-Arab organization, became the only legal party. The govern-ment has been dominated by members of the minority Alawite sect, many of whom were assassinated in 1977-78.

In the Israeli-Arab war of June 1967, Israel seized and occu-pied the Golan Heights area inside Syria, from which Israeli set-tlements had for years been shelled by Syria.

Syria aided Palestinian guerrillas fighting Jordanian forces in Sept. 1970 and, after a renewal of that fighting in July 1971, broke off relations with Jordan. But by 1975 the 2 countries had entered a military coordination pact.

Syria received large shipments of arms from the USSR in 1972-73 and on Oct. 6, 1973, Syria joined Egypt in an attack on Israel. (For details, see article on Israel.) Arab oil states agreed in 1974 to give Syria $1 billion a year to aid anti-Israel moves. Military supplies used or lost in the 1973 war were replaced by the USSR in 1974 and increased shipments of planes, tanks, and missiles were reported in 1978. U.S. economic aid has been extended. Some 30,000 Syrian troops entered Lebanon in 1976 to mediate in a civil war, and fought Palestinian guerrillas and, later, fought Christian militiamen. Syria has charged Iraqi com-plicity in a series of terrorist attacks (the 2 governments are con-trolled by rival Baathist factions).

# Tanzania

## United Republic of Tanzania

**People: Population** (1977 est.) 16,070,000. **Age distrib.** (%): 0–14: 44.4; 15–59: 53.0; 60+: 2.6. **Pop. density:** 44.18 per sq. mi. **Urban** (1973): 7.3%. **Ethnic groups:** Sukuma 12.6%, Maleonde 4%, 130 other tribes (most Bantu); Europeans, Arabs, Asians. **Languages:** Swahili, English are official. **Religions:** Moslems 30%, Christians 30%, Traditional 40%.

**Geography: Area:** 363,708 sq. mi., more than twice the size of California. **Location:** On coast of E. Africa. **Neighbors:** Kenya, Uganda on N, Rwanda, Burundi, Zaire on W, Zambia, Malawi, Mozambique on S. **Topography:** A hot, arid central plateau is surrounded by the lake region in the west, temperate highlands in N and S, and the coastal plains. Mt. Kilimanjaro, 19,340 ft., is highest in Africa. **Capital:** Dar-es-Salaam. **Cities** (1975 est.): Dar-es-Salaam 517,000.

**Government: Head of state:** Pres. Julius Kambarage Nyerere; b. 1922; in office: Oct. 1975. **Local divisions:** 24 regions (4 in Zanzibar). **Armed forces:** Regulars 18,600; para-military 36,400.

**Economy: Industries:** Food processing, clothing. **Chief crops:** Sisal, cotton, coffee, tea, tobacco. **Minerals:** Diamonds, gold, salt, tin, mica. **Other resources:** Hides. **Per capita arable land:** 2.3 acres. **Meat production** (1975): beef: 116,000 tons; lamb: 29,000 tons. **Fish catch** (1975): 180,700 metric tons. **Electricity production** (1976): 612.00 mln. kwh. **Labor force:** 86% agriculture.

**Finance: Currency:** Shilling (May 1978: 7.93 = $1 US). **Gross domestic product** (1975): $2.25 bln. **Per capita income** (1976): $168. **Imports** (1976): $566 mln.; partners (1974): P.R. China 11%, U.K. 10%, Jap. 9%, W. Ger. 8%. **Exports** (1976): $459 mln.; partners (1974): U.K. 13%, U.S. 7%, Kenya 6%, Hong Kong 6%. **Tourists** (1973): 120,000; receipts (1975): $11 million. **Balance of payments** (1977): +$160,500,000. **National budget** (1976): $488.08 mln. revenues; $759.88 mln. expenditures. **International reserves** (May 1978): $201.6 mln. **Consumer prices** (change in 1976): 6.9%.

**Transport: Motor vehicles:** in use (1974): 39,100 passenger cars, 42,300 commercial vehicles. **Chief ports:** Dar-es-Salaam, Tanga.

**Communications: Radios:** 231,000 in use (1974), 177,000 manufactured (1975). **Telephones in use** (1977): 68,413. **Daily newspaper circulation** (1973): 41,000; 380 per 1,000 pop.

**Health: Life expectancy at birth** (1967): 40.41 male; 40.41 female. **Births** (annual per 1,000 pop. 1972-75): 47.0. **Deaths** (annual per 1,000 pop. 1972-75): 20.1. **Natural increase** (1967): 2.5%. **Pop. per hospital bed** (1975): 566. **Pop. per physician** (1975): 22,151. **Infant mortality** (per 1,000 live births 1967): 160-165.

**Education: Literacy** (1975): 18%. **Pop. 5–19:** in school (1975): 27%, per teacher (1975): 182.

The Republic of Tanganyika in E. Africa and the Republic of Zanzibar, an island in the Indian Ocean off the coast of Tanganyika, joined into a single nation, the United Republic of Tanzania, Apr. 26, 1964. The central government was given jurisdiction over defense, foreign affairs, and public services. Zanzibar retains internal self-government. In 1973 Dodoma, in the country's center, was named the future capital.

**Tanganyika.** Arab colonization and slaving began in the 8th century A.D.; Portuguese sailors explored the coast by about 1500. Other Europeans followed.

In 1885 Germany established German East Africa of which Tanganyika formed the bulk. It became a League of Nations mandate and, after 1946, a UN trust territory, both under Britain. It became independent Dec. 9, 1961, and a republic within the Commonwealth a year later.

In 1967 the government set on a socialist course; it nationalized all banks and many industries; some of the latter were taken over completely, in others the government took a part interest. The government also ordered that Swahili, not English, be used in all official business. Nine million people have been moved into cooperative villages.

Relations with Kenya and Uganda, former partners in the East African Community, are strained.

**Zanzibar,** the Isle of Cloves, lies 23 mi. off the coast of Tanganyika; its area is 640 sq. mi. The island of **Pemba,** 25 mi. to the NE, area 380 sq. mi., is included in the administration. The total population (1976) is 450,000.

Chief industry is the production of cloves and clove oil of which Zanzibar and Pemba produce the bulk of the world's supply.

Zanzibar was for centuries the center for Arab slave-traders. Portugal ruled for 2 centuries until ousted by Arabs around 1700. The slave trade was suppressed under British influence, and Zanzibar became a British Protectorate in 1890. Independence came Dec. 10, 1963. Revolutionary forces overthrew the Sultan Jan. 12, 1964. The new government ousted American and British diplomats and newsmen, slaughtered thousands of Arabs, and nationalized farms. Union with Tanganyika followed 1964. The ruling parties of Tanganyika and Zanzibar were united in 1977 as political tension eased.

# Thailand

## Kingdom of Thailand

**People: Population** (1977 est.): 44,160,000. **Age distrib.** (%): 0–14: 45.1; 15–59: 50.0; 60+: 4.9. **Pop. density:** 222.52 per sq. mi. **Urban** (1970): 13.2%. **Ethnic groups:** Thais 75%, Chinese 14%, Malays 3%, Khmers, Soais, Karens, Indians. **Languages:** Thai, Chinese. **Religions:** Buddhists 94%, Moslems 4%, Christians 0.6%.

**Geography: Area:** 198,455 sq. mi., three-fourths the size of Texas. **Location:** On Indochinese and Malayan Peninsulas in S.E. Asia. **Neighbors:** Burma on W, Laos on N, Cambodia on E, Malaysia on S. **Topography:** A plateau dominates the NE third of Thailand, dropping to the fertile alluvial valley of the Chao Phraya R. in the center. Forested mountains are in N, with narrow fertile valleys. The southern peninsula region is covered by rain forests. **Capital:** Bangkok. **Cities** (1970 cen.): Bangkok 1,867,297; Thonburi 627,989.

**Government: Head of state:** King Bhumipol Adulyadej; b. Dec. 5, 1927; in office: Mar. 1935. **Head of government:** Prime Min. Kriangsak Chomanan; b. Dec. 17, 1917; in office: Oct. 1977. **Local divisions:** 72 provinces. **Armed forces:** regulars 211,000; reserves 500,000.

**Economy: Industries:** Auto assembly, drugs, textiles, electrical goods. **Chief crops:** Rice (a major export), corn tapioca, jute, sugar, coconuts, tobacco, pepper, peanuts, beans, cotton. **Minerals:** Tin (5th largest producer), iron, manganese, tungsten, antimony, gas. **Crude oil reserves** (1978): 270 bbls. **Other resources:** Forests (teak is exported), rubber. **Per capita arable land:** 0.7 acres. **Meat production** (1975): beef: 168,000 tons; pork: 240,000 tons. **Fish catch** (1975): 1,369,900 metric tons. **Electricity production** (1976): 10.30 bln. kwh. **Labor force** 78% agric.; 4% manuf.

**Finance: Currency:** Baht (May 1978: 20.40 = $1 US). **Gross domestic product** (1977): $18.16 bln. **Per capita income** (1976): $351. **Imports** (1976): $3.57 bln.; partners (1974): Jap. 31%, U.S. 13%, W. Ger. 7%, Qatar 6%. **Exports** (1976): $2.91 bln.; partners (1974): Jap. 26%, Neth. 9%, Sing. 8%, U.S. 8%. **Tourists** (1975): 1,180,100; receipts (1975): $220 million. **Balance of payments** (1977): +$10,000,000. **National budget** (1977): $2.64 bln. revenues; $3.24 bln. expenditures. **International reserves** (May 1978): $2.13 bln. **Consumer prices** (change in 1977): 8.4%.

**Transport: Railway traffic** (1974): 3.41 bln. passenger-miles, 1.43 bln. net ton-miles. **Motor vehicles:** in use (1974): 286,200 passenger cars, 264,300 commercial vehicles; assembled (1975): 15,504 passenger cars; (1974): 8,592 commercial vehicles. **Civil aviation:** 2,124 mln. passenger-miles (1977); 67,828 mln. freight ton-miles (1977). **Chief ports:** Bangkok, Sattahip.

**Communication: Television sets:** 715,000 in use (1974). **Radios:** 5,111,111 in use (1974). **Telephones in use** (1976): 333,761.

**Health: Life expectancy at birth** (1960): 53.6 male; 58.7 female. **Births** (annual per 1,000 pop. 1972-75): 43.4. **Deaths** (annual per 1,000 pop. 1972-75): 10.8. **Natural increase** (annual 1970-75): 3.26%. **Pop. per hospital bed** (1975): 797. **Pop. per physician** (1975): 7,819. **Infant mortality** (per 1,000 live births 1975): 26.3.

**Education: Literacy** (1975): 82%. **Pop. 5-19:** in school (1975): 47%, per teacher (1975): 64.

Thais began migrating from southern China in the 11th century. Thailand is the only country in SE Asia never taken over by a European power, thanks to King Mongkut and his son King Chulalongkorn who ruled from 1851 to 1910, modernized the untry, and signed trade treaties with both Britain and France.

Thailand underwent a bloodless revolution in 1932, which established a limited monarchy.

Japan occupied the country in 1941. After the war, Thailand llowed a pro-West foreign policy. Some 11,000 Thai troops ught in South Vietnam, but were withdrawn by 1972. About ,000 Thai troops, financed by the U.S., returned from Laos in 74. Some 100,000 Indo-chinese refugees have fled to Thaind.

Clashes with Loas and especially with Cambodia have contind to 1978. Tribal and political rebels have conducted guerrilla hting in the NE and extreme S, 1965-78.

A military-civilian junta, headed by Gen. Thanom Kittikachorn, ok over the government in Nov. 1971. Civilians, led by stunts, overwhelmed police, Oct. 1973, and forced Thanom to sign as premier. A civilian cabinet was named. After free elecns in January 1975, a coalition government was sworn in. The ilitary resumed control in a bloody 1976 coup.

The fertile land yields a rice surplus. Foreign investment has en encouraged.

# Togo

## Republic of Togo

**People: Population** (1977 est.): 2,350,000. **Pop. density:** 7.54 per sq. mi. **Urban** (1974): 15.2%. **Ethnic groups:** Ewe %, Mina 6%, Kabye 14%. **Languages:** French (official), oths. **Religions:** Roman Catholics 18%, Protestants 6.5%, Mosms 9%, others.

**Geography: Area:** 21,853 sq. mi., slightly smaller than West rginia. **Location:** On S coast of W. Africa. **Neighbors:** Ghana W, Upper Volta on N, Benin on E. **Topography:** A range of ls running SW-NE splits Togo into two savanna plains regions. apital: Lome. **Cities** (1970 cen.): Lome 148,443.

**Government: Head of state:** Pres. Gnassingbe Eyadema; b. 932; in office: Jan. 13, 1967. **Local divisions:** 21 circumscripns. **Armed forces:** regulars 2,500; para-military 1,400.

**Economy: Industries:** Textiles, shoes. **Chief crops:** Coffee, cocoa, palm kernals, copra, cotton, kapok, peanuts. **Minerals:** hosphates. **Per capita arable land:** 2.3 acres. **Electricity pro-uction** (1976): 75.60 mln. kwh. **Labor force:** 75% agriculture.

**Finance: Currency:** Franc (May 1978: 230.35 = $1 US). ross domestic product (1975): $.55 bln. **Per capita income** 972): $151. **Imports** (1975): $174 mln.; partners (1973): Fr. 3%, W. Ger. 10%, U.K. 7%, Neth. 7%. **Exports** (1975): $126 In.; partners (1973): Neth. 36%, Fr. 31%, W. Ger. 12%, Belg. %. **Balance of payments** (1975): +$7,600,000. **International eserves** (Mar. 1978): $39.5 mln. **Consumer prices** (change in 976): 11.6%.

**Transport: Railway traffic** (1974): 40.37 mln. passenger-iles; 13.66 mln. net ton-miles. **Motor vehicles:** in use (1974): 3,000 passenger cars, 7,000 commercial vehicles. **Chief ports:** ome.

**Communications: Radios:** 50,000 licensed (1974). **Tele-hones in use** (1974): 8,000. **Daily newspaper circulation** 973): 13,000; 6 per 1,000 pop.

**Health: Life expectancy at birth** (1961): 31.6 male; 38.5 fe-ale. **Births** (annual per 1,000 pop. 1972-75): 50.6. **Deaths** (an-ual per 1,000 pop. 1972-75): 23.3. **Natural increase** (annual 970-75): 2.73%. **Pop. per hospital bed** (1975): 656. **Pop. per hysician** (1975): 21,238. **Infant mortality** (per 1,000 live births 961): 127.

**Education:** Literacy (1975): 10%. **Pop. 5-19:** in school 975): 51%, per teacher (1975): 103.

The Ewe arrived in southern Togo several centuries ago. The ountry later became a major source of slaves. Germany took ontrol from 1884 on. France and Britain administered Togoland s UN trusteeships. The French sector became the republic of ogo Apr. 27, 1960.

The population is divided between Bantus in the S and Hamitic bes in the N. Togo has actively promoted regional integration, s a means of stimulating the backward economy.

# Tonga

## Kingdom of Tonga

**People: Population** (1977 est.): 90,000. **Age distrib.** (%):

0–14: 46.3; 15–59: 48.9; 60+: 4.9. **Pop. density:** 334.57 per sq. mi. **Ethnic groups:** Tongans (Polynesians). **Languages:** Tongan, English. **Religions:** Methodism.

**Geography: Area:** 269 sq. mi., smaller than New York City. **Location:** In western S. Pacific O. **Neighbors:** Nearest is Figi, on W, New Zealand, on S. **Topography:** Tonga comprises 150 volcanic and coral islands, 45 inhabited. **Capital** Nuku'alofa. **Cit-ies** (1972 est.): Nuku'alofa 22,000.

**Government: Head of state:** King Taufa'ahau Tupou IV; b. July 4, 1918; in office: July 4, 1967; **Head of government:** Prime Min. Fatafehi Tu'ipelehake; b. Jan. 7, 1922; in office: Dec. 16, 1965. **Local divisions:** 3 island districts.

**Economy: Industries:** Tourism. **Chief crops:** Coconut prod-ucts, bananas are exported. **Other resources:** Fish. **Electricity production** (1975): 5.00 mln. kwh.

**Finance: Currency:** Pa'anga (1974: 1 = $1.49 US). **Gross domestic product** (1974 est.): $25 mln. **Per capita income** (1974): $250. **Imports** (1974): $17 mln.; partners (1974): New Zea. 39%, Fiji 24%, Austral. 22%, U.K. 4%. **Exports** (1974): $7 mln.; partners (1974): Neth. 40%, Austral. 29%, New Zea. 22%, Fiji 6%. **Consumer prices** (change in 1976): 7.1%.

**Transport: Motor vehicles:** in use (1974): 1,000 passenger cars, 400 commercial vehicles. **Chief ports:** Nuku'alofa.

**Communications: Radios:** 10,000 in use (1974). **Tele-phones in use** (1977): 552.

**Health: Births** (per 1,000 pop. 1971): 28.3. **Deaths** (per 1,000 pop. 1971): 3.2. **Natural increase** (1976): 1.11%. **Infant mortal-ity** (per 1,000 live births 1971): 16.0.

The islands were first visited by the Dutch in the early 17th century. A series of civil wars ended in 1845 with establishment of the Tupou dynasty. In 1900 Tonga became a British protector-ate. On June 4, 1970. Tonga became completely independent and a member of the Commonwealth.

# Trinidad and Tobago

**People: Population** (1976 est.): 1,100,000. **Age distrib.** (%): 0–14: 39.7; 15–59: 53.9; 60+: 6.4. **Pop. density:** 555.84 per sq. mi. **Urban** (1970): 49.4%. **Ethnic groups:** Negroes 43%, East Indians 36%, white 2%, Chinese 1%, mixed 16%. **Languages:** English, Hindi. **Religions:** Roman Catholics 36%, Protestants 30%, Hindus 23%, Moslems 6%.

**Geography: Area:** 1,979 sq. mi., the size of Delaware. **Loca-tion:** Off eastern coast of Venezuela. **Neighbors:** Nearest is Venezuela on SW. **Topography:** Three low mountain ranges cross Trinidad E-W, with a well-watered plain between N and Central Ranges. Parts of E and W coasts are swamps. Tobago, 116 sq. mi., lies 20 mi. NE. **Capital:** Port-of-Spain. **Cities** (1975 est.): Port-of-Spain (met.) 250,000; San Fernando 50,000.

**Government: Head of state:** Pres. Ellis Emmanuel Innocent Clarke; b. Dec. 28, 1917; in office: July 31, 1976; **Head of gov-ernment:** Prime Min. Eric Eustace Williams; b. 1911; in office: Aug. 31, 1962. **Local divisions:** 8 counties, Ward of Tobago, 3 municipalities.

**Economy: Industries:** Oil products, rum, cement, tourism. **Chief crops:** Sugar, cocoa, coffee, citrus fruits, bananas. **Miner-als:** Asphalt, oil. **Per capita arable land:** 0.1 acres. **Electricity production** (1977): 1.43 bln. kwh. **Labor force:** 17% agricul-ture.

**Finance: Currency:** Dollar (May 1978: 2.40 = $1 US). **Gross domestic product** (1976): $2.72 bln. **Per capita income** (1974): $1,400. **Imports** (1977): $1.86 bln.; partners (1974): Saudi Ar. 38%, Indo. 18%, U.S. 11%. **Exports** (1977): $2.17 bln.; partners (1974): U.S. 61%, Puerto Rico 7%. **Tourists** (1975): 132,600; receipts (1975): $58 million. **Balance of pay-ments** (1977): +$500,600,000. **National budget** (1972): $258.73 mln. revenues; $277.91 mln. expenditures. **Interna-tional reserves** (May 1978): $1.59 bln. **Consumer prices** (change in 1977): 11.9%.

**Transport: Motor vehicles:** in use (1975): 101,300 passen-ger cars, 25,700 commercial vehicles; assembled (1976): 9,924 passenger cars; 1,632 commercial vehicles. **Civil aviation:** 646 mln. passenger-miles; 15,001 mln. freight ton-miles (1976). **Chief ports:** Port-of-Spain.

**Communications: Television sets:** 100,000 in use (1974). **Radios:** 250,000 licensed (1974), 16,000 manufactured (1975). **Telephones in use** (1977): 70,364. **Daily newspaper circula-tion** (1974): 98,000; 92 per 1,000 pop.

**Health: Life expectancy at birth** (1970): 64.08 male; 68.11 female. **Births** (per 1,000 pop. 1975): 23.0. **Deaths** (per 1,000 pop. 1975): 6.5. **Natural increase** (1975): 1.65%. **Pop. per hospital bed** (1975): 155. **Pop. per physician** (1975): 1,948. **Infant mortality** (per 1,000 pop. under 1 yr. 1974): 37.6.

**Education: Literacy** (1975): 90%. **Pop. 5-19:** in school (1975): 74%, per teacher (1975): 44.

Columbus sighted Trinidad in 1498. Second largest of the old British West Indies and a British possession since 1802, Trinidad and Tobago won independence Aug. 31, 1962. It became a republic in 1976. A leftist opposition party gained strength in 1976 elections.

The nation is one of the most prosperous in the Caribbean, but unemployment usually averages 13%. Oil production has increased with offshore finds. Middle Eastern oil is refined and exported, mostly to the U.S.

# Tunisia

## Republic of Tunisia

**People: Population** (1977 est.): 6,070,000. **Age distrib.** (%) 0-14: 44.6; 15-59: 48.7; 60+: 6.7. **Pop. density:** 95.77 per sq. mi. **Ethnic groups:** Arabs, small Berber minority; Europeans 1%. **Languages:** Arabic, French. **Religions:** Islam nearly universal.

**Geography: Area:** 63,378 sq. mi., slightly larger than Florida. **Location:** On N coast of Africa. **Neighbors:** Algeria on W, Libya on E. **Topography:** The N is wooded and fertile. The central coastal plains are given to grazing and orchards. The S is arid, approaching Sahara Desert. **Capital:** Tunis. **Cities** (1966 cen.): Tunis (met.) 647,640; Sfax (met.) 215,836.

**Government: Head of state:** Pres. Habib Bourguiba; b. Aug. 3, 1903; in office: July 25, 1957; **Head of government:** Prime Min. Hedi Nouira; b. Apr. 5, 1911; in office: Nov. 2, 1970. **Local divisions:** 18 governorates. **Armed forces:** regulars 35,200; para-military 18,000.

**Economy: Industries:** Food processing, textiles, clothing, leather, oil products, construction materials, tourism. **Chief crops:** Grains, dates, olives, citrus fruits, figs, vegetables, grapes. **Minerals:** Phosphates, iron, oil, lead, zinc. **Crude oil reserves** (1978): 2.67 bln. bbls. **Per capita arable land:** 1.9 acres. **Meat production** (1975): beef: 32,000 tons; lamb: 36,000 tons. **Fish catch** (1975): 42,700 metric tons. **Electricity production** (1977): 1.52 bln. kwh. **Labor force:** 46% agriculture.

**Finance: Currency:** Dinar (May 1978: 1 = $2.34 US). **Gross domestic product** (1977): $5.16 bln. **Per capita income** (1976): $712. **Imports** (1977): $1.77 bln.; partners (1974): Fr. 31%, It. 11%, U.S. 8%, W. Ger. 8%. **Exports** (1977): $910 mln.; partners (1974): It. 25%, Fr. 22%, Gr. 10%, Braz. 6%. **Tourists** (1975): 1,013,800; receipts (1974): $194 million. **Balance of payments** (1977): −$58,000,000. **International reserves** (May 1978): $303.6 mln. **Consumer prices** (change in 1977): 6.6%.

**Transport: Railway traffic** (1975): 365.15 mln. passenger-miles; 796.74 mln. net ton-miles. **Motor vehicles:** in use (1975): 102,600 passenger cars, 67,000 commercial vehicles; assembled (1977): 1,212 passenger cars; 4,176 commercial vehicles. **Civil aviation:** 613 mln. passenger-miles (1977); 5,626 mln. freight ton-miles (1977). **Chief ports:** Tunis, Sfax, Bizerte.

**Communications: Television sets:** 147,000 in licensed (1973), 35,000 manufactured (1975). **Radios:** 277,000 in use (1974), 91,000 manufactured (1975). **Telephones in use** (1977): 71,309. **Daily newspaper circulation** (1974): 156,000; 28 per 1,000 pop.

**Health: Life expectancy at birth** (1975): 52.5 male; 55.7 female. **Births** (per 1,000 pop. 1975): 39.4. **Deaths** (annual per 1,000 pop. 1972-75): 13.8. **Natural increase** (annual 1970-75): 2.62%. **Pop. per hospital bed** (1975): 437. **Pop. per physician** (1975): 5,251. **Infant mortality** (per 1,000 pop. under 1 yr. 1973): 62.6.

**Education: Literacy** (1975): 32%. **Pop. 5-19:** in school (1975): 47%, per teacher (1975): 72.

Site of ancient Carthage, and a former Barbary state under the suzerainty of Turkey, Tunisia became a protectorate of France under a treaty signed May 12, 1881. The nation became independent Mar. 20, 1956, and ended the monarchy the following year. Habib Bourguiba has headed the country since independence.

Although Tunisia is a member of the Arab League, Bourguib in the 1960s urged negotiations to end Arab-Israeli disputes an was denounced by other members. In 1966 he broke relation with Egypt but resumed them after the 1967 Israeli-Arab war. H again urged negotiations with Israel in June 1973.

Tunisia and Libya announced in Jan. 1974 that the 2 nation would merge, but Bourguiba soon dropped the plan.

Dozens were killed in rioting and labor violence in 1978, pro testing wage curbs.

# Turkey

## Republic of Turkey

**People: Population** (1977 est.): 42,130,000. **Age distrib** (%): 0-14: 41.8; 15-59: 51.0; 60+: 7.2. **Pop. density:** 139.4 per sq. mi. **Urban** (1976): 44.5%. **Ethnic groups:** Turks 90% Kurds 7%, Arabs 1.2%, Circassians, Greeks, Armenians, Geo gians, Jews. **Languages:** Turkish, Kurdish. **Religions:** Moslem over 99%.

**Geography: Area:** 301,380 sq. mi., twice the size of Califo nia. **Location:** Occupies Asia Minor, between Mediterranea and Black Seas. **Neighbors:** Bulgaria, Greece on W, USS (Georgia, Armenia) on N, Iran on E, Iraq, Syria on W. **Topogra phy:** Central Turkey has wide plateaus, with hot, dry summer and cold winters. High mountains ring the interior on all but V with more than 20 peaks over 10,000 ft. Rolling plains are in V mild, fertile coastal plains are in S, W. **Capital:** Ankara. **Citie** (1973 est.): Istanbul (met.) 3,135,354; Ankara (met.) 1,553,89 Izmir (met.) 819,276; Bursa (met.) 426,567.

**Government: Head of state:** Pres. Fahri Koruturk; b. 1903; i office: Apr. 6, 1973; **Head of government:** Prime Min. Bule Ecevit; b. 1925; in office: Jan. 1, 1978. **Local divisions:** 67 prov inces, with appointed governors. **Armed forces:** regular 775,000; reserves 700,000.

**Economy: Industries:** Silk, textiles, steel, shoes, furnitur cement, paper, glassware, appliances. **Chief crops:** Tobacc (6th largest producer), cereals, cotton, olives, figs, nuts, suga opium gums. **Minerals:** Antimony, borate, copper, chrome; als molybdenum, magnesite, asbestos. **Crude oil reserves** (1978 370 mln. bbls. **Other resources:** Wool, silk, forests. **Per capit arable land:** 1.5 acres. **Meat production** (1976): beef: 230,00 tons; lamb: 425,500 tons. **Fish catch** (1975): 259,400 metri tons. **Electricity production** (1976): 18.23 bln. kwh. **Labo force:** 69% agric.; 8% manuf.

**Finance: Currency:** Lira (May 1978: 25.25 = $1 US). **Gros domestic product** (1977): $41.51 bln. **Per capita incom** (1973): $533. **Imports** (1977): $5.69 bln.; partners (1974): U.S 12%, U.K. 11%, It. 11%. **Exports** (1977): $1.75 bln.; partner (1974): U.S. 12%, Switz. 9%, It. 6%. **Tourists** (1975 1,540,900; receipts (1975): $200 million. **Balance of payment** (1977): −$561,000,000. **National budget** (1975): $7.01 bln revenues; $7.81 bln. expenditures. **International reserves** (Ap 1978): $1.01 bln. **Consumer prices** (change in 1977): 27.2%.

**Transport: Railway traffic** (1975): 2.94 bln. passenger-mile 4.57 bln. net ton-miles. **Motor vehicles:** in use (1974): 303,80 passenger cars, 179,900 commercial vehicles; assemble (1975): 74,640 passenger cars; (1976): 22,392 commercial vehi cles. **Civil aviation:** 1,252 mln. passenger-miles (1976); 10,75. mln. freight ton-miles (1976). **Chief ports:** Istanbul, Izmir, Me sin, Samsun.

**Communications: Television sets:** 458,000 in use (1974 571,000 manufactured (1975). **Radios:** 4,096,000 in use (1975 272,000 manufactured (1974). **Telephones in use** (1977 1,130,978.

**Health: Life expectancy at birth** (1966): 53.7 male; 53.7 f male. **Births** (annual per 1,000 pop. 1972-75): 39.6. **Deaths** (an nual per 1,000 pop. 1972-75): 12.5. **Natural increase** (1967 2.50%. **Pop. per hospital bed** (1975): 469. **Pop. per physicia** (1975): 1,900. **Infant mortality** (per 1,000 pop. under 1 yr 1967): 153.

**Education: Literacy** (1975): 55%. **Pop. 5-19:** in schoo (1975): 47%, per teacher (1975): 68.

Ancient inhabitants of Turkey were among the worlds first ag riculturalists. Such civilizations as the Hittite, Phrygian, and Lyd ian flourished in Asiatic Turkey (Asia Minor), as did much o Greek civilization. After the fall of Rome in the 5th century, Con stantinople was the capital of the Byzantine Empire for 1,00 years. It fell in 1453 to Ottoman Turks, who ruled a vast empire or over 400 years.

Just before World War I, Turkey, or the Ottoman Empire, led what is now Syria, Lebanon, Iraq, Jordan, Israel, Arabia, Yemen, and islands in the Aegean Sea.

Turkey joined Germany and Austria in World War I and its defeat resulted in loss of much territory and fall of the sultanate. A republic was declared Oct. 29, 1923. The Caliphate (spiritual leadership of Islam) was renounced 1924. Martial law, imposed 1971, was ended in 1973 and political life is active and free.

Long embroiled with Greece over Cyprus, off Turkey's south coast, Turkey invaded the island July 20, 1974, after Greek officers seized the Cypriot government as a step toward unification with Greece. Turkey sought a new government for Cyprus, with Greek Cypriot and Turkish Cypriot zones. In reaction to Turkey's moves, the U.S. Congress cut off military aid in 1975. Turkey, in turn, suspended the use of most U.S. bases. A new base accord was tentatively reached in March, 1976 and aid was restored in 1978. Turkey and the USSR signed a nonaggression pact in 1978.

In June, 1971, Turkey agreed to stop all opium poppy production, in return for $37.5 million in economic aid from the U.S. In 1974 it announced it would resume opium production, with U.S. and U.N. controls, for medical use only.

Religious and ethnic tensions and active left and right extremists have caused endemic violence.

# Uganda

## Republic of Uganda

**People: Population** (1977 est.): 12,350,000. **Age distrib.** (%): 0–14: 46.2; 15–59: 48.0; 60+: 5.8. **Pop. density:** 135.51 per sq. mi. **Urban** (1972): 7.1%. **Ethnic groups:** Bantu, Nilotic, Nilo-Hamitic, Sudanic tribes. **Languages:** English (official), Swahili (national), Luganda, others. **Religions:** Christians 50%, Moslems 6%, others.

**Geography: Area:** 91,134 sq. mi., slightly smaller than Oregon. **Location:** In E. Central Africa. **Neighbors:** Sudan on N, Zaire on W, Rwanda, Tanzania on S, Kenya on E. **Topography:** Most of Uganda is a high plateau 3,000-6,000 ft. high, with high Ruwenzori range in W (Mt. Margherita 16,750 ft.), volcanoes in SW, NE is arid, W and SW rainy. Lakes Victoria, Edward, Albert form much of borders. **Capital:** Kampala. **Cities** (1969 cen.): Kampala (met.) 330,700.

**Government: Head of state:** Pres. Idi Amin Dada; b. 1925; in office: Jan. 25, 1971. **Local divisions:** 10 provinces. **Armed forces:** regulars 21,000.

**Economy: Chief Crops:** Coffee (68% of 1973 earnings), cotton, tea, corn, peanuts, sisal, oil seeds, tobacco, sugar. **Minerals:** Copper, tin. **Per capita arable land:** 0.8 acres. **Meat production** (1975): beef: 67,000 tons; lamb: 10,000 tons. **Fish catch** (1975): 169,700 metric tons. **Electricity production** 1976: 696.00 mln. kwh. **Labor force:** 86% agriculture.

**Finance: Currency:** Shilling (May 1978: 7.92 = $1 US). **Gross domestic product** (1976): $3.17 bln. **Per capita income** (1974): $151. **Imports** (1974): $80 mln. **Exports** (1974): $360 mln. **Tourists** (1974): 10,300; receipts (1975): $4 million. **Balance of payments** (1976): +$55,400,000. **National budget** 1972): $214.37 mln. revenues; $341.56 mln. expenditures. **Consumer prices** (change in 1976): 54.6%.

**Transport: Motor vehicles:** in use (1974): 27,000 passenger cars, 8,900 commercial vehicles.

**Communications: Television sets:** 15,000 in use (1973). **Radios:** 250,000 in use (1974). **Telephones in use** (1977): 46,344. **Daily newspaper circulation** (1974): 58,000; 5 per 1,000 pop.

**Health: Life expectancy at birth** (1975): 48.3 male; 51.7 female. **Births** (annual per 1,000 pop. 1972-75): 45.2. **Deaths** (annual per 1,000 pop. 1972-75): 15.9. **Natural increase** (annual 1970-75): 2.93%. **Pop. per hospital bed** (1975): 722. **Pop. per physician** (1975): 34,988. **Infant mortality** (per 1,000 live births 1959): 160.

**Education: Literacy** (1975): 20%. **Pop. 5-19:** in school (1975): 23%, per teacher (1975): 133.

Britain obtained a protectorate over Uganda in 1894. The country became independent Oct. 9, 1962, and a republic when the Commonwealth a year later. In 1967, the traditional kingdoms, including the powerful Buganda state, were abolished and the central government strengthened.

Milton Obote, then prime minister, seized full power in 1966. Gen. Idi Amin seized control in 1971. As many as 300,000 of his opponents were reported killed in subsequent years. Amin was named president for life in 1976.

A June 1977 Commonwealth conference condemned the Uganda government for its "disregard for the sanctity of human life."

In 1972 Amin expelled nearly all of Uganda's 45,000 Asians (Indians and Pakistanis), many of them business and professional men. In 1973 the U.S., Canada and Norway ended economic aid programs; and the U.S. withdrew all diplomatic personnel. Amin seized all British firms.

Several hundred Soviet and Cuban advisers have helped prop up the regime.

A state of economic chaos has been mitigated by the world rise in coffee prices.

Israeli forces raided Entebbe, Uganda, July 1976, and rescued 103 hostages seized by Arab and German terrorists.

# Union of Soviet Socialist Republics

**People: Population** (1977 est.): 258,700,000. **Age distrib.** (%): 0–19: 36.8; 20-59: 50.5; 60+: 12.7. **Pop. density:** 29.92 per sq. mi. **Urban** (1976): 61.6%. **Ethnic groups:** Russians 53%, Ukrainians 17%, Uzbeks 4%, Byelorussians 4%, 150 others. **Languages:** Slavic (Russian, Ukrainian, Byelorussian, Polish) 76%, Altaic (Turkish, etc.) 11%, other Indo-European 8%, Uralian 3%, Caucasian 2%. **Religions:** Russian Orthodox 18%, Moslems 9%, other Orthodox, Protestants, Jews, Buddhists.

**Geography: Area:** 8,647,250 sq. mi., the largest country in the world, nearly 2 1/2 times the size of the U.S. **Location:** Stretches from E. Europe across N Asia to the Pacific O. **Neighbors:** Finland, Poland, Czechoslovakia, Hungary, Romania on W, Turkey, Iran, Afghanistan, China, Mongolia, N. Korea on S. **Topography:** The USSR occupies the northern part of Asia and the eastern half of Europe. Cover N one-sixth of the earth's land area, the USSR contains every type of climate except the distinctly tropical, and has a varied topography.

The European portion is a low plain, grassy in S, wooded in N with Ural Mtns. on the E. Caucasus Mts. on the S. Urals stretch N-S for 2,500 mi. The Asiatic portion is also a vast plain, with mountains on the S and in the E; tundra covers extreme N, with forest belt below; plains, marshes are in W, desert in SW (Central Asia). **Capital:** Moscow. **Cities** (1976 est.): Moscow (met.) 7,734,000; Leningrad (met.) 4,372,000; Kiev 2,013,000; Tashkent 1,643,000; Baku (met.) 1,406,000; Kharkov 1,385,000; Gorky 1,305,000; Novosibirsk 1,286,000; Minsk (met.) 1,189,000; Kuibyshev 1,186,000; Sverdlovsk 1,171,000; Tbilisi 1,030,000; Odessa 1,023,000.

**Government: Head of state:** Pres. Leonid I. Brezhnev; b. Dec. 19, 1906; in office: June 16, 1977; **Head of government:** Alexei N. Kosygin; b. Feb. 1904; in office: Oct. 15, 1964; **Head of Communist Party:** Gen. Sec. Leonid Brezhnev; in office: Oct. 14, 1964. **Local divisions:** 15 union republics, within which are 20 autonomous republics, 6 krays, 120 oblasts (regions), 8 autonomous oblasts, 10 national areas. **Armed forces:** regulars 3,675,000 (army 1,825,000; navy 450,000; air force 475,000); reserves 4,200,000; para-military 450,000.

**Economy: Industries:** Steel, machinery, machine tools, vehicles, chemicals, cement, textiles, appliances, paper. **Chief crops:** Grain, cotton, sugar beets, potatoes, vegetables, sunflowers. **Minerals:** Coal (58% of world reserves), oil (59%), iron (41%), manganese (88%), potassium salts (54%), phosphates (30%), gold, and significant deposits of most commercial minerals. **Crude oil reserves** (1978): 75.00 bln. bbls. **Other resources:** Forests (25% of world reserves). **Per capita arable land:** 2.2 acres. **Fish catch** (1975): 9,876,000 metric tons. **Electricity production** (1977): 1,150 bln. kwh. **Labor force:** 26% agric.; 40% manuf. & constr.

**Finance: Currency:** Ruble (1974: 1 = $1.32 US). **Gross domestic product** (1974 est.): $560 bln. **Per capita income** (1974): $2,010. **Imports** (1977): $40.82 bln.; partners (1974): E. Ger. 11%, Pol. 9%, Czech. 8%, Bulg. 8%. **Exports** (1977): $45.16 bln.; partners (1974): E. Ger. 10%, Pol. 9%, Czech. 7%, Bulg. 7%. **Tourists** (1975): 3,690,800. **Consumer prices** (change in 1977): 0.0%.

**Transport: Railway traffic** (1975): 19.41 bln. passenger-miles; 200.99 bln. net ton-miles. **Motor vehicles:** in use (1974): 3,000,000 passenger cars, 4,000,000 commercial vehicles; manufactured (1975): 1,200,000 passenger cars; (1976): 789,600 commercial vehicles. **Civil aviation** (international only): 4,568 mln. passenger-miles (1977); 15,713 mln. freight ton-miles (1977). **Chief ports:** Leningrad, Odessa, Murmansk, Kaliningrad, Archangelsk, Riga, Vladivostock.

**Communications: Television sets:** 52,500,000 in use (1974), 6,960,000 manufactured (1975). **Radios:** 116,100,000 in use (1974), 8,376,000 manufactured (1975). **Telephones in use** (1977): 18,000,000. **Daily newspaper circulation** (1974): 97,664,000; 388 per 1,000 pop.

**Health:** Life expectancy at birth (1972): 64 male; 74 female. **Births** (annual per 1,000 pop. 1972-75): 18.1. **Deaths** (per 1,000 pop. 1975): 9.3. **Natural increase** (1975): .88%. **Pop. per hospital bed** (1975): 86. **Pop. per physician** (1975): 353. **Infant mortality** (per 1,000 live births 1974): 27.7.

**Education:** Literacy (1975): 99%. **Pop. 5-19:** in school (1975): 61%, per teacher (1975): 28.

The USSR is nominally a federation consisting of 15 union republics, within certain of which are further subdivisions. Four of the union republics contain 20 autonomous Soviet socialist republics and 8 autonomous regions; the largest union republic, the Russian Soviet Federated Socialist Republic, has also 10 national districts. Nationalist agitation has occasionally been reported in several of the republics. Important positions in the republics are filled by centrally chosen appointees, often ethnic Russians.

Beginning in 1939 the USSR by means of military action and negotiation overran contiguous territory and independent republics, including all or part of Lithuania, Latvia, Estonia, Poland, Czechoslovakia, Romania, Germany, Tannu-Tuva, and Japan. The union republics are:

| Republic | Area sq. mi. | Pop. (est. 1976) |
|---|---|---|
| Russian SFSR | 6,593,391 | 134,487,000 |
| Ukrainian SSR | 232,046 | 49,000,000 |
| Kazakh SSR | 1,064,092 | 14,672,000 |
| Uzbek SSR | 158,069 | 14,161,000 |
| Byelorussian SSR | 80,154 | 9,332,000 |
| Azerbaijan SSR | 33,436 | 5,700,000 |
| Georgian SSR | 26,911 | 4,962,000 |
| Moldavian SSR | 13,012 | 3,836,000 |
| Tadzhik SSR | 54,019 | 3,517,000 |
| Kirghiz SSR | 76,642 | 3,381,000 |
| Lithuanian SSR | 26,173 | 3,337,000 |
| Armenian SSR | 11,306 | 2,898,000 |
| Turkmen SSR. | 188,417 | 2,590,000 |
| Latvian SSR. | 24,695 | 2,506,000 |
| Estonian SSR | 17,413 | 1,440,000 |

The **Russian Soviet Federated Socialist Republic** contains over 50% of the population of the Soviet Union and includes 76% of its territory. Its territories stretch from the old Estonian, Latvian, and Finnish borders and the Byelorussian and Ukrainian lines on the W, to the shores of the Pacific, and from the Arctic on the N to the Black and Caspian Seas and the borders of Kazakh SSR, Mongolia, and Manchuria on the S. Siberia, divided into a number of administrative units, encompasses a large part of the RSFSR area. Capital: Moscow.

Parts of Eastern and Western Siberia have been transformed by steel mills, huge dams, oil and gas industries, electric railroads, and highways.

The **Ukraine** is the most densely populated of the major constituent republics. It borders on the Black Sea, with Poland, Czechoslovakia, Hungary, and Romania on the W and SW. The population is 75% Ukrainian. Capital: Kiev.

The Ukraine contains the arable black soil belt, the chief wheat-producing section of the Soviet Union. Sugar beets, potatoes, and livestock are important.

The Donets Basin has large deposits of coal, iron and other metals. There are chemical and machine industries and salt mines.

**Byelorussia** (White Russia). Capital: Minsk. Chief industries include machinery, tools, appliances, tractors, clocks, cameras, steel, cement, textiles, paper, leather, glass. Main crops are grain, flax, potatoes, sugar beets.

**Azerbaijan** boasts near Baku, the capital, important oil fields. Its natural wealth includes deposits of iron ore, cobalt, etc. Irrigation has boosted cotton production. A high-yield winter wheat also is grown, as are fruits. It produces iron, steel, cement, fertilizers, synthetic rubber, electrical and chemical equipment. It borders on Iran and Turkey.

**Georgia,** which lies in the western part of Transcaucasia, contains the largest manganese mines in the world. There are rich timber resources and coal mines. Basic industries are food, textiles, iron, steel. Grain, tea, tobacco, fruits, grapes are grown. Capital: Tbilisi (Tiflis). Despite massive party and government purges since 1972, illegal private enterprise and Georgian nationalist feelings persist; attempts to repress them have led to violence.

**Armenia** is mountainous, sub-tropical, extensively irrigated. Copper, zinc, aluminum, molybdenum, and marble are mined. Instrument making is important. Capital: Erevan.

**Uzbekistan,** most important economically of the Central Asian republics, produces 67% of USSR cotton, 50% of rice, 33% of silk, 34% of astrakhan, 85% of hemp. Industries include iron, steel, cars, tractors, TV and radio sets, textiles, food. Mineral wealth includes coal, sulphur, copper, and oil. Capital: Tashkent.

**Turkmenistan** in Central Asia, produces cotton, maize, carpets, chemicals. Minerals: oil, coal, sulphur, barite, lime, salt, gypsum. The Kara Kum desert occupies four-fifths of the area. Capital: Ashkhabad.

**Tadzhikistan** borders on China and Afghanistan. Over half the population are Tadzhiks, mostly Moslems, speaking an Iranian dialect. Chief occupations are farming and cattle breeding. Cotton, grain, rice, and a variety of fruits are grown. Heavy industry, based on rich mineral deposits, coal and hydroelectric power, has replaced handicrafts. Capital: Dushanbe.

**Kazakhstan** extends from the lower reaches of the Volga in Europe to the Altai Mtns. on the Chinese border. It has vast deposits of coal, oil, iron, tin, copper, lead, zinc, etc. Fish for the canning industry are caught in Lake Balkhash and the Caspian and Aral Seas. The capital is Alma-Ata. About 50% of the population is Russian or Ukrainian, working in the virgin-grain land opened up after 1954, and in the growing industries. Kazakhstan is third among industrial republics in the USSR.

**Kirghizia** is the eastern part of Soviet Central Asia, on the frontier of Sinkiang (western China). The people, once nomadic, breed cattle and horses and grow tobacco, cotton, rice, sugar beets. New industries include machine and instrument making, chemicals. Capital: Frunze.

**Moldavia** in the SW part of the USSR, is a fertile black earth plain bordering Romania, and includes Bessarabia. It is an agricultural region that grows grains, fruits, vegetables, and tobacco. Textiles, wine, food and electrical equipment industries have been developed. Capital: Kishinev. The region was taken from Romania in 1940; the people speak Romanian.

**Lithuania,** on the Baltic, produces cattle, hogs, electric motors, and appliances. The capital is Vilnius (Vilna). **Latvia** on the Baltic and the Gulf of Riga, has timber and peat resources estimated at 3 billion tons. In addition to agricultural products it produces rubber goods, dyes, fertilizers, glassware, telephone apparatus, TV and radio sets, railroad cars. The capital is Riga. **Estonia** also on the Baltic, has textiles, shipbuilding, timber, roadmaking and mining equipment industries and a shale oil refining industry. Tallinn is the capital. The 3 Baltic states were provinces of imperial Russia before World War I, were independent nations between World Wars I and II, but were conquered by Russia in 1940. The U.S. has never formally recognized the takeover. Russian immigration was encouraged after the war.

**Economy.** Almost all legal economic enterprises are state-owned. There were 29,600 collective farms in 1976, along with 18,064 larger state farms. Small private plots, from which farmers may sell produce, produced 61% of potatoes, a third of vegetables, meat, and milk, 43% of eggs, and 21% of wool in 1973. A huge illegal black market plays an important role in distribution; illegal private production and service firms are periodically exposed.

The USSR is incalculably rich in natural resources; distant Siberian reserves are being exploited with Japanese assistance. Its heavy industry is second only to the U.S. It leads the world in oil and steel production. Consumer industries have lagged comparatively. Agricultural output has expanded, but in poor crop years the USSR has been forced to make huge grain purchases from the West. Shortages and rationing of basic food products periodically occur.

In 1966 many major factories were put on an incentive profit-sharing system, while bonuses to farms and farm workers were introduced to spur food production. In 1973 steps were taken to group factories into "production associations" partly resembling large U.S. corporations. Most decisions remain centralized; strikes are outlawed.

In 1971 a proposed new 5-year plan stressed growth in consumer goods, but subsequent adjustments restored priority to eavy industry, and reduced overall goals. The 1976-80 plan alled for slower growth, emphasizing modernization of plants nd higher farm investment. Inefficiency prevented the targets om being met in 1977.

Exports include petroleum and its products, iron and steel, lled non-ferrous metals, industrial plant equipment, arms, lumer, cotton, asbestos, gold, manganese, and others. 55% of its ade is with Communist nations, 33% with the West, which upplies advanced technology. The USSR had a $4 billion trade eficit with the West in 1976, financed by gold sales, long-term ans, and a trade surplus with East Europe and underdeveloped ountries. Debt to the West reached $14.4 billion by 1977. Interational commercial shipping has advanced.

**History.** Slavic tribes began migrating into Russia from the W n the 5th century A.D. The first Russian state, founded by Scannavian chieftains, was established in the 9th century, centering Novgorod and Kiev.

In the 13th century the Mongols overran the country. It recovred under the grand dukes and princes of Muscovy, or Mosow, and by 1480 freed itself from the Mongols. Ivan the Terrible as the first to be formally proclaimed Tsar (1547). Peter the reat (1682-1725), extended the domain and in 1721 founded we Russian Empire.

Western ideas and the beginnings of modernization spread rough the huge Russian empire in the 19th and early 20th cenries. Industry, agriculture, transport, and education advanced, nd Russia attained leadership status in world literature, music nd art. But political evolution failed to keep pace.

Russian military reverses in the 1905 war with Japan and in Vorld War I led to the breakdown of the Tsarist regime. The 917 Revolution began in March with a series of sporadic strikes r higher wages by factory workers. A provisional democratic overnment under Prince Georgi Lvov was established but was uickly followed in May by the second provisional government, d by Alexander Kerensky. The Kerensky government and the eely-elected Constituent Assembly were overthrown in a Comunist coup led by Vladimir Ilyich Lenin Nov. 7.

Lenin's death Jan. 21, 1924, resulted in an internal power ruggle from which Joseph Stalin eventually emerged the absote ruler of Russia. Stalin secured his position at first by exiling pponents such as Leon Trotsky. But from the 1930s to 1953 he sorted to a series of "purge" trials, mass executions and mass ciles in work camps. These measures, along with forced collecization of agriculture, resulted in millions of deaths, according most estimates. In 1975 it was estimated there still were ),000 political prisoners, mostly in labor camps.

After Stalin died, Mar. 5, 1953, Nikita Khrushchev was elected st secretary of the Central Committee. In 1956 he condemned talin. Khrushchev lifted some restrictions, extended trade polis. The names of Stalin, Molotov, Malenkov, and other suporters of Stalin were eliminated from regions, cities, and other es in 1961-62 after Stalin's body was removed from the Leninkalin tomb in Moscow.

Under Khrushchev the open antagonism of Poles and Hungarns toward domination by Moscow was brutally suppressed in 956. He advocated peaceful co-existence with the capitalist ountries, but continued arming the USSR with nuclear weapns. He aided the Cuban revolution under Fidel Castro but withew Soviet missiles from Cuba during confrontation by U.S. esident Kennedy, Sept.-Oct. 1962.

The USSR, the U.S., and Great Britain initialed a joint treaty uly 25, 1963, banning above-ground nuclear tests.

The co-existence and economic reform policies; as well as rder disputes, alienated the leaders of Albania and Commust China.

Khrushchev was suddenly deposed, Oct. 14-15, 1964, and placed as party first secretary by Leonid I. Brezhnev, 57, and s premier by Aleksei N. Kosygin, 60. Brezhnev was named esident in 1977.

Communist China's Premier Chou En-lai visited the new SSR chiefs in Nov. 1964 but the visit failed to heal the growing t between the 2 Communist powers.

In 1968, the U.S. and USSR joined 59 other nations in signing treaty to bar spread of nuclear weapons.

In Aug. 1968 Russian, Polish, East German, Hungarian, and ulgarian military forces invaded Czechoslovakia to put a curb liberalization policies of the Czech government. The USSR clared it had a duty to intervene in nations where socialism as "imperiled" according to the "Brezhnev Doctrine."

In March 1969 troops of the USSR and Communist China ught the first of a series of clashes on a disputed island in the

Ussuri River on the border between the 2 nations in the Far East, north of Vladivostok. In 1970 ambassadors were exchanged, after a lapse; but both nations increased their border forces. Chinese officials actively tried to enlist Europe, the U.S., and nonaligned countries in an anti-Soviet political bloc in 1978.

The USSR in 1971 continued heavy arms shipments to Egypt. In July 1972 Egypt ordered most of the 20,000 Soviet military personnel in that country to leave. The USSR then increased arms shipments to Syria. When Egypt and Syria attacked Israel in Oct. 1973, the USSR launched huge arms airlifts to the 2 Arab nations. In 1974, the Soviet replenished the arms used or lost by the Syrians in the 1973 war, and continued some shipments to Egypt.

Massive Soviet military aid to North Vietnam in the late 1960s and early 1970s helped assure Communist victories throughout Indo-China in 1975. Similar aid helped leftist factions gain control of Angola in 1976. Soviet arms aid and advisers were sent to several African countries in the 1970s, including Algeria, Somalia, and Ethiopia. The Soviet navy expanded its deployment in foreign seas.

In 1972, the U.S. and USSR reached temporary agreements to freeze intercontinental missiles at their current levels, to limit defensive missiles to 200 each and to cooperate on health, environment, space, trade, and science.

Meanwhile, under Brezhnev, dissident intellectuals were repressed and purge-type trials resumed.

On Aug. 1, 1975, 35 countries of Europe and North America signed a European security pact tacitly approving current boundaries and urging freer movement of people and ideas. Most members of Russian groups set up to monitor the pact were jailed in a 1978 crackdown.

More than 130,000 Jews and over 40,000 ethnic Germans were allowed to emigrate from the USSR in the 1970s, following pressure from the West. Many leading figures in the arts also left the country.

**Government.** The Communist Party leadership dominates all areas of national life. A Politburo of 14 full members and 8 candidate members makes all major political, economic, and foreign policy decisions. Party membership in 1976 was reported to be 15,700,000.

## United Arab Emirates

**People: Population** (1977 est.): 240,000. **Age distrib. (%):** 0–14: 33.8; 15–59: 63.6; 60+: 2.6. **Pop. density:** 7.44 per sq. mi. **Ethnic groups:** Arabs 72%, Iranians, Pakistanis and Indians 26%. **Languages:** Arabic, (official), Persian, Hindi, Urdu. **Religions:** Moslems 96.7%, Christians 1.3%.

**Geography: Area:** 32,278 sq. mi., the size of Maine. **Location:** On the S shore of the Persian Gulf. **Neighbors:** Qatar on N, Saudi Ar. on W, S, Oman on E. **Topography:** A barren, flat coastal plain gives way to uninhabited sand dunes on the S. Hajar Mtns. are on E. **Capital:** Abu Dhabi. **Cities** (1975 est.): Dubai 66,000; Abu Dhabi 55,000.

**Government: Head of state:** Pres. Zayed bin Sultan al Nahayyan, b. 1923; in office: Dec. 2, 1972; **Head of government:** Prime Min. Maktoum bin Rashid al-Maktoum; in office: Dec. 12, 1972. **Local divisions:** 7 autonomous emirates: Abu Dhabi, Ajman, Dubai, Fujaira, Ras al-Khaimah, Sharjah, Umm al-Qaiwain. **Armed forces:** regulars 26,100.

**Economy: Chief crops:** Vegetables. **Minerals:** Oil. **Crude oil reserves** (1978): 31.30 bln. bbls. **Per capita arable land:** 0.2 acres. **Fish catch** (1975): 68,000 metric tons. **Electricity production** (1975): 500.00 mln. kwh.

**Finance: Currency:** Dirham (May 1978: 3.88 = $1 US). **Gross domestic product** (1974 est.): $6 bln. **Per capita income** (1974): $16,000. **Imports** (1976): $3.33 bln.; partners (1974): Jap. 18%, U.K. 16%, U.S. 13%, W. Ger. 5%. **Exports** (1976): $8.54 bln.; partners (1974): Jap. 33%, Fr. 21%, W. Ger. 15%, U.K. 10%. **International reserves** (May 1978): $744.0 mln.

**Transport: Chief ports:** Dubai, Abu Dhabi.

**Communications: Radios:** 51,000 in use (1974). **Telephones in use** (1977): 70,863.

**Health: Pop. per hospital bed** (1975): 326. **Pop. per physician** (1975): 1,306.

**Education: Literacy** (1975): 20%. **Pop. 5-19:** in school (1975): 95%, per teacher (1975): 18.

The 7 "Trucial Sheikdoms" gave Britain control of defense and foreign relations in the 19th century. They merged to become an independent state Dec. 2, 1971.

The Abu Dhabi Petroleum Co. was fully nationalized in 1975. Oil revenues have given the UAE the highest per capita GNP in the entire world. International banking has grown in recent years.

# United Kingdom of Great Britain and Northern Ireland

**People: Population** (1977 est.): 55,850,000. **Age distrib.** (%): 0–4: 23.9; 15–59: 56.8; 60+: 19.3. **Pop. density:** 592.83 per sq. mi. **Ethnic groups:** English 81.5%, Scottish 9.6%, Irish 2.4, Welsh 1.9%, Ulster 1.8%; West Indian, Indian, Pakistani over 2%; others. **Languages:** English nearly universal, Welsh spoken in western Wales. **Religions:** Church of England 55% (confirmed 20%), Roman Catholics 10%, Presbyterians 3%, Methodists 1%, Jews 1%, other Protestants, Hindus, Moslems.

**Geography: Area:** 94,209 sq. mi., slightly smaller than Oregon. **Location:** Off the NW coast of Europe, across English Channel, Strait of Dover, and North Sea. **Neighbors:** Ireland to W, France to SE. **Topography:** England is mostly rolling land, rising to Uplands of southern Scotland; Lowlands are in center of Scotland, granite Highlands are in N. Coast is heavily indented, especially on W. Northern Ireland is farming region. British isles have milder climate than N Europe, ample rainfall. Thames, 210 mi., and Severn are longest rivers. **Capital:** London. **Cities** (1974 est.): London (met.) 7,167,600; (1973 est.): Manchester (met.) 2,389,260; Birmingham 2,358,980; Leeds 1,735,700; Glasgow 1,727,625; Liverpool 1,226,310; Newcastle 788,130; Belfast 549,139; Sheffield 511,860; Bristol 421,800.

**Government: Head of state:** Queen Elizabeth II; b. Apr. 21, 1926; in office: Feb. 6, 1952; **Head of government:** Prime Min. James Callaghan; b. Mar. 27, 1912; in office: Apr. 5, 1976. **Local divisions:** England and Wales: 53 counties, 6 metro counties, London; Scotland: 9 regions, 3 island areas; N. Ireland: 26 districts. **Armed forces:** regulars 642,450; reserves 207,400.

**Economy: Industries:** Steel, metals, vehicles, shipbuilding, shipping, banking, insurance, appliances, textiles, chemicals, electronics, aircraft, machinery, scientific instruments, distilling. **Chief crops.** Grains, sugar beets, fruits, vegetables. **Minerals:** Oil, gas, coal, limestone, iron, salt, clay, chalk, gypsum, lead, tin, silica. **Crude oil reserves** (1978): 19.00 bln. bbls. **Per capita arable land:** 0.3 acres. **Meat Production** (1976): beef: 1.06 mln. tons; pork: 862,000 tons; lamb: 243,000 tons. **Fish catch** (1975): 979,800 metric tons. **Electricity production** (1977): 283.38 bln. kwh. **Labor force:** 3% agric.; 33% manuf.

**Finance: Currency:** Pound (May 1978: 1 = $1.82 US). **Gross domestic product** (1977): $266.52 bln. **Per capita income** (1976): $3,580. **Imports** (1977): $63.68 bln.; partners (1975): U.S. 10%, W. Ger. 8%, Neth. 8%, Fr. 7%. **Exports** (1977): $57.55 bln.; partners (1975): U.S. 9%, W. Ger. 6%, Fr. 6%, Neth. 6%. **Tourists** (1975): 8,880,000; receipts (1975): $2.443 billion. **Balance of payments** (1976): −$774,000,000. **National budget** (1977): $95.11 bln. revenues; $100.34 bln. expenditures. **International reserves** (May 1978): $17.28 bln. **Consumer prices** (change in 1977): 15.8%.

**Transport: Railway traffic** (1974): 22.44 bln. passenger-miles; 15.01 bln. net ton-miles. **Motor vehicles:** in use (1975): 13,263,000 passenger cars, 1,911,100 commercial vehicles; manufactured (1977): 1,332,000 passenger cars; 360,000 commercial vehicles. **Civil aviation:** 19,793 mln. passenger-miles (1977); 632,846 mln. freight ton-miles (1977). **Chief ports:** London, Liverpool, Glasgow, Southampton, Cardiff, Belfast.

**Communications: Television sets:** 17,641,000 in use (1974), 2,106,000 manufactured (1975). **Radios:** 42,000 in use (1974), 696,000 manufactured (1975). **Telephones in use** (1977): 22,012,304. **Daily newspaper circulation** (1974): 24,800,000; 443 per 1,000 pop.

**Health: Life expectancy at birth** (1972): 68.9 male; 75.1 female. **Births** United Kingdom (per 1,000 pop. 1976): 12.1; Northern Ireland (per 1,000 pop. 1976): 17.1. **Deaths** United Kingdom (per 1,000 pop. 1976): 12.2. Northern Ireland (per 1,000 pop. 1976): 11.1 **Natural increase** (1976): −.03% **Pop. per hospital bed** (1975): 106. **Pop. per physician** (1975): 728. **Infant mortality** (per 1,000 live births 1974): 16.3.

**Education: Literacy** (1975): 98%. **Pop. 5-19:** in school (1975): 84%, per teacher (1975): 23.

The United Kingdom of Great Britain and Northern Ireland comprises England, Wales, Scotland and Northern Ireland.

The climate of the British Isles is mild and somewhat warmer than that of the continent because of the Gulf Stream modifying the temperature, which has a mean of 48°. Rainfall averages 4 inches a year.

**Queen and Royal Family.** The ruling sovereign is Elizabeth of the House of Windsor, born Apr. 21, 1926, eldest daughter King George VI. She succeeded to the throne Feb. 6, 1952, an was crowned June 2, 1953. As Princess Elizabeth, she was ma ried Nov. 20, 1947 to Lt. Philip Mountbatten, born June 10, 192 former Prince of Greece. He was created Duke of Edinburg Nov. 19, 1947, H.R.H. Prince Philip Nov. 20, 1947, and given th title Prince of the United Kingdom Feb. 22, 1957. They have children. Prince Charles Philip Arthur George, born Nov. 1 1948, is the Prince of Wales and heir apparent.

**Parliament** is the legislative governing body for the Unite Kingdom, with certain powers over dependent units. It consists 2 Houses. The **House of Lords** includes heriditary and lif peers and peeresses, certain judges, 2 archbishops and 21 bish ops of the Church of England. Total membership is over 1,00 but daily attendance averages 270. Women became eligible t sit in the House of Lords for the first time in 1958. The **House c Commons** has 635 members, who are elected by direct ballo and divided as follows: England 516; Wales 36; Scotland 7 Northern Ireland 12.

Clergymen of the Church of England, ministers of the Churc in Scotland and Roman Catholic clergymen are disqualified fror sitting as members, as are certain government officers and she iffs. Women have had the right to vote since 1918.

A two-tier system of local government controls a large variet of social and economic activity. Reforms occurred in 1974-75.

**Resources and Industries.** Great Britain's major occupation are manufacturing and trade. Metals and metal-using industrie contribute more than 50% of the exports. Of about 60 millio acres of land in England, Wales and Scotland, 47 million ar farmed, of which 17.4 million are arable, the rest pastures.

Large oil and gas fields have been found in the North Sea Commercial oil production began in 1975; self-sufficiency is ex pected by the early 1980s with projected output of two millio barrels a day. There are large deposits of coal; 1975 output wa 127 million tons.

There are 150 civil and 50 service airports in Great Britair The railroads, nationalized since 1948, have been reduced ir total length, with a basic network of 11,326 mi. designated fo modernization and development. The merchant marine totaled 33,358,000 gross registered tons in June 1977, comprisin nearly 10% of active world shipping. About 2 million tons of ship ping were under construction in 1975.

The world's first power station using atomic energy to create electricity for civilian use began operation Oct. 17, 1956, at Cal der Hall in Cumbria.

The government in 1967 took ownership of 14 steel compa nies which comprised 90% of the nation's steel-making industry paying shareholders over $1.4 billion.

The Labor government raised taxes, 1966-69; devalued the pound to $2.40 in 1967 and took various measures to improve exports and cut imports. The Conservative government put a freeze on prices, wages and rents in 1972 to combat inflation. In 1973 it substituted "restraints." A Labor government elected in 1974, obtained trade union approval of wage curbs, confirmed in 1977. Yet inflation continued, and the pound dropped to recor lows in 1976. Unemployment rose to a postwar high in 1977 Inflation eased by 1978 but unemployment remained a problem.

Britons backed continued EC membership by a 67% vote in a referendum June 5, 1975.

On Feb. 15, 1971, Britain completed a changeover to decima currency. By 1975 it had in part converted to the metric system as well.

Britain imports all of its cotton, rubber, sulphur, four-fifths of its wool, half of its food and iron ore, also certain amounts of paper tobacco, chemicals. Manufactured goods made from these basic materials have been exported since the industrial age began.

Main exports are machinery, chemicals, woolen and synthetic textiles, clothing, autos and trucks, iron and steel, locomotives ships, jet aircraft, farm machinery, drugs, radio, TV, radar and navigation equipment, scientific instruments, arms, whisky.

**Religion and Education.** The Church of England is Protestan Episcopal. The queen is its temporal head, with rights of appoint ments to archbishoprics, bishoprics and other offices. There are 2 provinces, Canterbury and York, each headed by an arch bishop. About 50% of the population is baptized into the Church less than 20% is confirmed. Most famous church is Westminste Abbey (1050-1760), site of coronations, tombs of Elizabeth I Mary of Scots, kings, poets and of the Unknown Warrior.

Roman Catholic Church membership in the United Kingdom
as about 5,500,000 in 1975. There were about 14,000 Method-
churches and 650,000 full members in 1975.

Others: There are an est. 410,000 Jews in Great Britain, 80%
them are Orthodox; more than half live in the London area.
ere are 187,000 Baptists and 187,000 members of the United
formed Church (Congregational and Presbyterian). The Cal-
istic Methodist (Presbyterian) Church of Wales has 99,000
mmunicants. The Unitarians have 330 chapels. The Society of
ends has 20,000 members. There are 72,000 Mormons. The
urch of Christ Scientist has 302 branches in Great Britain and
land. The Presbyterian Church in Ireland has a membership in
rthern Ireland of about 140,000. The number of Hindus and
slems has been growing steadily with immigration.

The Church of Scotland is Presbyterian. It is presided over by
moderator, chosen annually. Members numbered 1,060,000 in
75.

Education is free and compulsory from 5 to 16. The most cele-
ated British universities are Oxford and Cambridge, each dat-
g to the 13th century. There are 40 other universities.

**History.** Britain was part of the continent of Europe until about
000 B.C., but migration of peoples across the English Channel
ntinued long afterward. Celts arrived 2,500 to 3,000 years
o. Their language survives in Welsh, Cornish, and Gaelic en-
aves. Religious and cultural ties with Celts in Gaul (France)
ere maintained.

England was added to the Roman Empire in 43 A.D. After the
thdrawal of Roman legions in 410, waves of Jutes, Angles and
axons arrived from German lands. They contended with Danish
ders for control of Great Britain from the 8th through 11th cenries.

The last successful invasion was by French-speaking Nor-
ans in 1066, who united the country with their dominions in
ance. Anglo-Norman nobles began the conquest of Ireland in
e next century.

Opposition by nobles to royal authority forced King John to
n the Magna Carta in 1215, a guarantee of rights and the rule
law. In the ensuing decades, the foundations of the parliamen-
ry system were laid.

Wales was subdued and added to the Kingdom of England by
82.

English dynastic claims to large parts of France led to the
undred Years War, 1338-1453, and the defeat of England. A
ng civil war, the War of the Roses, lasted 1455-85, and ended
th the establishment of the powerful Tudor monarchy. A dis-
ct English civilization flourished. The economy prospered over
ng periods of domestic peace unmatched in continental Eu-
pe. Religious independence was secured when the Church of
gland was separated from the authority of the Pope in 1534.

Under Queen Elizabeth I, Britain became a major naval
wer, leading to the founding of colonies in the new world and
e expansion of trade with Europe and the Orient. Scotland was
ited with England when James VI of Scotland was crowned
mes I of England in 1603.

A struggle between Parliament and the Stuart kings led to a
oody civil war, 1642-49, and the establishment of a republic
der the Puritan Oliver Cromwell. The monarchy was restored
1660, but the "Glorious Revolution" of 1688 confirmed the
vereignty of Parliament, and a Bill of Rights was granted the
llowing year.

In the 18th century, parliamentary rule was strengthened.
chnological and entrepreneurial innovations led to the Indus-
al Revolution. The 13 North American colonies were lost, but
placed by growing empires in Canada and India. Britain's role
the defeat of Napoleon, 1815, strengthened its position as the
ading world power.

The extension of the franchise in 1832 and 1867, the forma-
n of trade unions, and the development of universal public ed-
cation were among the drastic social changes which accompa-
ed the spread of industrialization and urbanization in the 19th
ntury. Large parts of Africa and Asia were added to the em-
re during the reign of Queen Victoria, 1837-1901.

Though victorious in World War I, Britain suffered huge casual-
es and economic dislocation. Ireland became independent in
21, and independence movements became active in India and
her colonies.

The first labor government took office in 1924, though some
bor reforms and social security measures had been enacted
y previous governments.

The country suffered major bombing damage in World War II,
ut held out against Germany singlehandedly for a year after the

fall of France in 1940.

Industrial growth continued in the postwar period, but Britain
lost its leadership position to other powers. Labor governments
passed socialist programs nationalizing some basic industries
and expanding social security. Nearly all of the empire was given
independence. Britain joined the NATO alliance and, in 1973, the
European Communities (Common Market).

## Wales

The Principality of Wales in western Britain has an area of
8,017 sq. mi. and a population (est. 1976) of 2,766,800.

England and Wales are administered as a unit. Less than one
fifth the population of Wales speak both English and Welsh;
about 32,000 speak Welsh solely. Welsh nationalism is advocated by a segment. The UK House of Commons in 1978 approved creation of an elected Welsh Assembly.

Early Anglo-Saxon invaders drove Celtic peoples into the
mountains of Wales, terming them Waelise (Welsh, or foreign).
There they developed a distinct nationality. Members of the ruling house of Gwynedd in the 13th century fought England but
were crushed, 1283. Edward of Caernarvon, son of Edward I of
England, was created Prince of Wales, 1301.

Cardiff is the capital, pop. (1974) 284,700.

## Scotland

Scotland, a kingdom now united with England and Wales in
Great Britain, occupies the northern 37% of the main British island, and the Hebrides, Orkney, Shetland and smaller islands.
Length, 275 mi., breadth approx. 150 mi., area, 30,411 sq. mi.,
population (est. 1975) 5,206,000.

The Lowlands, a belt of land approximately 60 miles wide
from the Firth of Clyde to the Firth of Forth, divide the farming
region of the Southern Uplands from the granite Highlands of the
North. Only one-tenth of the land area, the Lowlands contain
three-quarters of the population and most of the industry. The
Highlands, famous for hunting and fishing, have been opened to
industry by many hydroelectric power stations.

Edinburgh, pop. (est. 1975) 470,085, is the capital. It lies on
the Firth of Forth in the County of Lothian and has notable memorials of its royal and cultural history. Glasgow, pop. (est.
1975) 1,105,645, is the largest city, 3d largest in Britain (5th largest metro area), and Britain's greatest industrial center. It is a
shipbuilding complex on the Clyde and an ocean port. Aberdeen,
pop. (est. 1975) 210,362, NE of Edinburgh, is a major port, center of granite industry, fish processing, and North Sea oil exploitation. Dundee, pop. (1975) 194,732, NE of Edinburgh, is an industrial and fish processing center. About 90,000 persons speak
Gaelic as well as English.

**History.** Scotland was called Caledonia by the Romans who
battled early Pict and Celtic tribes and occupied southern areas
from the 1st to the 4th centuries. Missionaries from Britain introduced Christianity in the 4th century; St. Columba, an Irish
monk, converted most of Scotland in the 6th century.

The Kingdom of Scotland was founded in 1018. William
Wallace, patriot leader, defeated an English army, 1297, and
Robert Bruce defeated another, 1314. John Knox led the Scot-
tish Reformation in the 16th century.

In 1603 James VI of Scotland, son of Mary, Queen of Scots,
succeeded to the throne of England as James I, and effected the
Union of the Crowns. In 1707 Scotland received representation
in the British Parliament, resulting from the union of former separate Parliaments. Its executive in the British cabinet is the Secretary of State for Scotland. The growing Scottish National Party
urges independence. The UK House of Commons in 1978 approved creation of an elected Scotland Assembly.

There are 8 universities. Memorials of Robert Burns, Sir Walter Scott, John Knox, Mary, Queen of Scots draw many tourists,
as do the beauties of the Trossachs, Loch Katrine, Loch Lomond
and abbey ruins.

**Industries.** Engineering products are the most important industry, with growing emphasis on lighter products such as office
machinery, autos, electronics and other consumer goods and
less dependence on locomotives, ships, boilers, pumps, valves
and other industrial machinery. Oil has been discovered offshore
in the North Sea, stimulating on-shore support industries.

Scotland produces fine woolens, worsteds, tweeds, silks, fine
linens and jute. It is known for its special breeds of cattle and
sheep. Fisheries have large hauls of herring, cod, whiting.
Whisky is the biggest export.

Atomic projects produce plutonium and electrical energy at

Dounreay, Chapelcross, Hunterston.

The Hebrides are a group of c. 500 islands, 100 inhabited, off the W coast. The Inner Hebrides include **Skye, Mull,** and **Iona,** the last famous for the arrival of St. Columba, 563 A.D. The Outer Hebrides include **Lewis** and **Harris.** Industries include sheep raising and weaving. The **Orkney Islands,** c. 90, are to the NE. The capital is Kirkwall, on Pomona Is. Fish curing, sheep raising and weaving are occupations. NE of the Orkneys are the 200 **Shetland Islands,** 24 inhabited, home of Shetland pony. The Orkneys and Shetlands have become centers for the North Sea oil industry.

## Northern Ireland

Six of the 9 counties of Ulster, the NE corner of Ireland, constitute Northern Ireland, with the parliamentary boroughs of Belfast and Londonderry. The country has an area of 5,451 sq. mi. and a population (1975 est.) 1,537,000. Belfast is the capital and chief industrial center.

**Industries.** Shipbuilding, including large tankers, has long been an important industry, centered in Belfast, the largest port. Linen manufacture is also important, along with apparel, rope, and twine. Growing diversification has added engineering products, synthetic fibers, and electronics. They are large numbers of cattle, hogs, and sheep, potatoes, poultry, and dairy foods are also produced. There is an agricultural surplus, mostly shipped to England.

**Government.** An act of the British Parliament, 1920, divided Northern from Southern Ireland, each with a parliament and government. When Ireland became a dominion, 1921, and later a republic, Northern Ireland chose to remain a part of the United Kingdom. It elects 12 members to the British House of Commons.

During 1968-69, large demonstrations were conducted by Roman Catholics who charged they were discriminated against in voting rights, housing, and employment. The Catholics, a minority comprising about a third of the population, demanded abolition of property qualifications for voting in local elections. Violence and terrorism intensified, involving branches of the Irish Republican Army (outlawed in the Irish Republic). Protestant groups, police, and up to 15,000 British troops.

A succession of Northern Ireland prime ministers pressed reform programs but failed to satisfy extremists on both sides. Over 1,800 were killed in 9 years of bombings and shootings, some in England itself. Britain suspended the Northern Ireland parliament Mar. 30, 1972, and imposed direct British rule. A coalition government was formed in 1973 when moderates won election to a new one-house Assembly. But a Protestant general strike overthrew the government in 1974. Direct rule continued in 1978, after the failure of a constitutional convention to achieve a settlement.

**Education and Religion.** Northern Ireland is 2/3 Protestant, 1/3 Roman Catholic. Elementary education is compulsory through age 15. There are 2 universities and 24 technical colleges.

## Channel Islands

The Channel Islands, area 75 sq. mi., est. pop. 1974 130,000, off the NW coast of France, the only parts of the one-time Dukedom of Normandy belonging to England, are **Jersey, Guernsey** and the dependencies of Guernsey — **Alderney, Brechou, Great Sark, Little Sark, Herm, Jethou** and **Lihou.** Jersey and Guernsey have separate legal existences and lieutenant governors named by the Crown. The islands were the only British soil occupied by German troops in World War II.

## Isle of Man

The Isle of Man, area 227 sq. mi., 1976 census pop. 60,496, is in the Irish Sea, 20 mi. from Scotland, 30 mi. from Cumberland. It is rich in lead and iron. The island has its own laws and a lieutenant governor appointed by the Crown. The Tynwald (legislature) consists of the Legislative Council, partly elected, and House of Keys, elected. Capital: Douglas. Farming, tourism, fishing (kippers, scallops) are chief occupations. Man is famous for the Manx tailless cat.

## Gibraltar

Gibraltar, a dependency on the southern coast of Spain, guards the entrance to the Mediterranean. The width of the strait dividing Europe from Africa varies from 7.75 mi. at the narrowest part to 23.75 at the widest. The Rock has been in British possession since 1704. There is a large harbor and a naval base. The

Rock is 2.75 mi. long, 3/4 of a mi. wide and 1,396 ft. in height; narrow isthmus connects it with the mainland. Est. pop. 197 29,934.

In 1966 Spain called on Britain to give "substantial sove eignty" of Gibraltar to Spain and imposed a partial blockade. 1967, residents voted 12,138 for remaining under Britain, 44 f returning to Spain. A new constitution, May 30, 1969, gave a elected House of Assembly more control in domestic affairs. UN General Assembly resolution requested Britain to end Gibra tar's colonial status by Oct. 1, 1969. No settlement has bee reached.

## British West Indies

Swinging in a vast arc from the coast of Venezuela NE, then and NW toward Puerto Rico are the Windward and Leeward I lands, forming a coral and volcanic barrier sheltering the Cari bean from the open Atlantic. Many of the islands are se governing British possessions. Universal suffrage was institute 1951-54; ministerial systems were set up 1956-1960.

Moving northward from the southern end of the arc lie the Br ish **Windward Islands: St. Vincent,** (1975 pop. 100,000, are 150 sq. mi., capital Kingstown), **St. Lucia** (1975 pop. 114,00 area 238 sq. mi., capital Castries) and **Dominica** (1976 po 78,000, area 290 sq. mi., capital Roseau).

Further north, in the **Leeward Islands,** are **Montserrat** (197 pop. 12,300, area 33 sq. mi., capital Plymouth), **Antigua** (197 pop. 69,700, area 171 sq. mi., capital St. John's), and **St. Kitt (St. Christopher)-Nevis-Anguilla,** three islands (1974 po 70,000, area 138 sq. mi., capital Basseterre on St. Kitts. Nearb are the small **British Virgin Islands.**

Britain granted self-government to 5 of these islands and i land groups in 1967-1969; each became an Associated Stat with Britain controlling foreign affairs and defense. These wer Antigua, Dominica, St. Lucia, the St. Kitts-Nevis-Anguilla Federa tion, and St. Vincent. Dominica and St. Lucia are scheduled fo full independence in 1978.

Anguilla declared its independence from St. Kitts June 1967. A 1976 constitution provides for an autonomous elect government. Area is 35 sq. mi., pop. 6,500.

Sugar is the major crop of Antigua and St. Kitts; bananas ar the main product of the Windwards; Dominica produces cocoa Antigua, Montserrat, St. Kitts, and St. Vincent have Sea Islan cotton; St. Vincent has arrowroot; Dominica grows citrus fruit Imports include foods, clothing, machinery. Tourism is growing Dominica tried in 1975 to suppress leftist terrorists.

The three **Cayman Islands,** a dependency, lie S of Cuba, N of Jamaica. Population is 11,500 (1974), most of it on Gran Cayman. It is a free port; in the 1970s Grand Cayman became tax-free refuge for foreign funds and branches of many Wester banks were opened there. Total area: 93 sq. mi. Capita Georgetown.

The **Turks and Caicos Islands,** at the SE end of the Baham Islands, are a separate British possession. There are about 3 islands, only 6 inhabited; pop. est. 6,000, area 166 sq. mi., cap tal Grand Turk. Salt, crayfish and conch shells are the main ex ports.

## Bermuda

**Bermuda** is a British dependency governed by a royal gover nor and an Assembly, the oldest legislative body among Britis dependencies. Capital is Hamilton.

It is a group of 360 small islands of coral formation, 20 inhab ited, comprising 21 sq. mi. in the western Atlantic, 580 mi. E c North Carolina. Population, 1976, was 53,500 (about 60% c African descent). Density is high.

The Assembly dates from 1620. In elections May 22, 1968 the first on the basis of universal adult suffrage, the predomi nantly white United Bermuda party won 30 of the 40 Assembly seats (26 of 40 in 1976 elections); 16 of the 40 elected wer blacks. A black, Sir Edward Richards, became prime minister in 1971. The Assembly runs local affairs. Bermuda adopted a do lar-decimal currency in 1970.

Gov. Richard Sharples and an aide were slain by gunmen i 1973. The police commissioner was shot to death in 1972. Ra cial hostility increased with the 1977 execution of two black convicted of the killings.

The U.S. has air and naval bases under long-term lease, an a NASA tracking station.

Bermuda boasts many resort hotels, serving over 500,00 visitors a year. The government raises most revenue from impo

ies. Exports: lilies, drugs, cosmetics.

## Belize

Belize (formerly called British Honduras) is in Central America facing the Caribbean to the E, with Mexico on the N and Guatemala on the W. Population (UN est. 1977) 150,000, area 8,866 mi., capital Belmopan.

Internal self-government was granted by Britain in 1964.

The area has long been claimed by Guatemala, but also was promised independence by Britain. In Apr. 1968, a mediator proposed that British Honduras be made independent but have close association with Guatemala. The proposal was rejected by Belize. Britain moved several hundred troops to Belize in 1977 in counter Guatemalan "bellicosity."

Main export is sugar, along with citrus fruits, mahogany and other hardwoods, chicle, seafood.

## South Atlantic

Falkland Islands and Dependencies, a British dependency, is 300 mi. E of the Strait of Magellan at the southern end of South America.

The Falklands or Islas Malvinas include about 200 islands with area of 4,618 sq. mi. and pop. (1976) of 1,905. Sheep-grazing is the main industry; wool is the principal export. There are indications of large oil and gas deposits. The islands are also claimed by Argentina though 97% of inhabitants are of British origin. South Georgia, area 1,450 sq. mi., and the uninhabited South Sandwich Islands are dependencies of the Falklands.

British Antarctic Territory, south of 60° S lat., was made a separate colony in 1962 and comprises mainly the South Shetland Islands, the South Orkneys and Graham's Land. A chain meteorological stations is maintained.

St. Helena, an island 1,200 mi. off the W coast of Africa and 1000 E of South America, has 47 sq. mi. and est. pop., 1976 of 47. Flax, lace and rope making are the chief industries. After Napoleon Bonaparte was defeated at Waterloo the Allies exiled him to St. Helena, where he lived from Oct. 16, 1815, to his death, May 5, 1821. His remains were transferred to Paris in 1840. Capital is Jamestown.

Tristan da Cunha is the principal of a group of islands of volcanic origin, total area 40 sq. mi., half way between the Cape of Good Hope and South America. The other islands are inaccessible, Gough (or Diego Alvarez) and the 3 Nightingale Is. A volcanic peak 6,760 ft. high erupted in 1961. The 262 inhabitants were moved to England, but most returned in 1963. The islands are dependencies of St. Helena.

Ascension is an island of volcanic origin, 34 sq. mi. in area, 800 mi. NW of St. Helena, through which it is administered. It is a communications relay center for Britain, and has a U.S. satellite tracking center. Est. pop., 1971, was 1,232, half of them communications workers. The island is noted for sea turtles.

## Asia and Indian Ocean

Brunei was between 1888 and 1971 a protected sultanate. It is on the N side of the island of Borneo, between the Malaysian states of Sarawak and Sabah. Its area is 2,226 sq. mi., the size of Delaware, with population (1977 est.) 163,000, two-thirds Malay and indigenous races, one-third of Chinese descent.

A 1959 constitution was amended, 1965, to provide for general elections to the Legislative Council, some members of which are appointed. There is a sultan and a British high commissioner. A 1971 agreement gave Brunei full self-government, with Britain responsible for foreign affairs. Independence was set for 1983.

Brunei's rich Seria oilfield provides tax revenues well in excess of expenditures. Rubber is also exported. Some of the surplus has been spent on a growing program of schools and social services.

Hong Kong is a Crown Colony at the mouth of the Canton river in China, 90 mi. south of Canton. Its nucleus is Hong Kong Island, 35 1/2 sq. mi., acquired from China 1841, on which is located Victoria, the capital. Opposite is Kowloon Peninsula, 3 mi. and Stonecutters Island, 1/4 sq. mi., added, 1860. An additional 355 sq. mi. known as the New Territories, comprised of a mainland area and islands, were leased from China, 1898, for 99 years. Total area of the colony is 391 sq. mi., with a population, 1975 est., of 4,440,000 including fewer than 20,000 British. From 1949 to 1962 Hong Kong absorbed more than a million refugees from the mainland. The flow of refugees continued,

on a lesser scale, into the 1970's.

Hong Kong harbor was long an important British naval station and one of the world's great trans-shipment ports. Britain announced in 1975 a reduction of its garrison to 6,400 men.

Principal industries are textiles and apparel (52% of exports); also tourism, shipbuilding, iron and steel, fishing, cement, and small manufactures. Total exports exceeded $9 billion in 1977.

Spinning mills, among the best in the world, and low wages compete with textiles elsewhere and have resulted in the protective measures in some countries. Hong Kong also has a booming electronics industry. The U. S. is the largest market for Hong Kong products.

During 1967 Communist China launched a campaign against British authority in Hong Kong, including demonstrations, strikes, riots, bombings, border incidents and slowdowns in supplying food. The campaign later subsided.

British Indian Ocean Territory was formed Nov. 1965, embracing islands formerly dependencies of Mauritius or Seychelles: the Chagos Archipelago (including Diego Garcia), Aldabra, Farquhar and Des Roches. The latter three were transferred to Seychelles, which became independent in 1976. Population, 558. In 1973 the U. S. Navy established a communications station on Diego Garcia and in 1975 began constructing a naval base. The USSR and Asian nations opposed the step.

## Pacific Ocean

Pitcairn Island is in the Pacific, halfway between South America and Australia. The island was discovered in 1767 by Carteret but was not inhabited until 23 years later when the mutineers of the Bounty landed there. The area is 18 sq. mi. and population, 1976, was 74. It is a British colony and is administered by a British Representative in New Zealand and a local Council. The uninhabited islands of Henderson, Ducie and Oeno are in the Pitcairn group.

The British Solomon Islands, a protectorate, became independent in 1977. (See Index for Solomon Islands).

The Gilbert Islands were proclaimed a protectorate in 1892. Self-government was granted in 1971. The dependency includes the Gilbert Islands (16), Phoenix Islands, Ocean Islands, Line Islands, composed of Fanning, Washington and Christmas Islands, the largest atoll in the Pacific (also claimed by the U. S.). The total area is 264 sq. mi. and the population, 1973 census, 52,000. Exports: chiefly copra and phosphates.

Tuvalu, formerly called the Ellice Islands, was separated from Gilbert Islands administration, 1976; its 9 islands have an area of 10 sq. mi., pop. (1976) 7,000.

New Hebrides, a condominium jointly administered since 1906 by Great Britain and France, is a group of 11 main islands and about 69 islets lying 500 mi. W of Fiji, with an aggregate area of 5,790 sq. mi. Population, 1976, 100,000, mostly Melanesian. Chief products are copra, cotton, cocoa, fish and coffee. British and French resident commissioners are joint heads of the administration; representative bodies were elected in 1975. Banks (309 sq. mi.) and Torres (40 sq. mi.) Islands, with pop. of 2,640, are attached to the New Hebrides for administration.

# United States

People: Population (1977 est.): 216,820,000. Age distrib.(%): 0–14: 23.5; 15–59: 61.4; 60+: 15.1 Pop. density: 59.98 per sq. mi. Urban (1970): 73.5%. Cities (1975 est.): New York (met.) 11,571,899; Los Angeles (met.) 7,032,075; Chicago (met.) 6,978,947; Philadelphia (met.) 4,817,914; San Francisco (met.) 3,109,519.

Armed forces: regulars 2,088,000; reserves 870,500.

Economy: Crude oil reserves (1978): 29.50 bln. bbls. Per capita arable land: 2.1 acres. Meat production (1976): beef: 12.17 mln. tons; pork: 5.64 mln. tons; lamb: 168,700 tons. Fish catch (1975): 2,798,700 metric tons. Electricity production (1977): 2,210 bln. kwh.

Finance: Gross domestic product (1977): $1,872.50 bln. Per capita income (1976): $6,995. Imports (1977): $156.78 bln.; partners (1975): Can. 22%, Jap. 11.4%., W. Ger. 5.6%. Exports (1977): $119.01 bln.; partners (1975): Can. 19.6%, Jap. 8.4%, W. Ger. 4.7%. Tourists (1975): 15,698,000; receipts (1975): $4,875 billion. Balance of payments (1977): −$35,314,000,000. National budget (1977): $365.20 bln. revenues; (1973): $256.96 bln. expenditures. International reserves (May 1978): $19.10 bln. Consumer prices (change in 1977): 6.5%.

**Transport: Railway traffic** (1975): 9.76 bln. passenger-miles; 68.43 bln. net ton-miles. **Motor vehicles:** in use (1975): 106,712,500 passenger cars, 24,837,000 commercial vehicles; manufactured (1977): 11,040,000 passenger cars; 4,128,000 commercial vehicles. **Civil aviation:** 190,987 mln. passenger-miles (1977); 5,953,924 mln. freight ton-miles (1977).

**Communications: Television sets:** 121,100,000 in use (1974), 8,207,000 manufactured (1974). **Radios:** 401,600,000 in use (1974), 11,861,000 manufactured (1974). **Telephones in use** (1977): 155,000,000. **Daily newspaper circulation** (1974): 62,156,000; 293 per 1,000 pop.

**Health: Life expectancy at birth** (1975): 68.7 male; 76.5 female. **Births** (per 1,000 pop. 1976): 14.7. **Deaths** (per 1,000 pop. 1976): 8.9. **Natural increase** (1976): .58%. **Pop. per hospital bed** (1975): 152. **Pop. per physician** (1975): 583. **Infant mortality** (per 1,000 live births 1977): 14.5.

**Education: Literacy** (1975): 99%. **Pop. 5-19:** in school (1975): 85%, per teacher (1975): 24.

# Upper Volta

## Republic of Upper Volta

**People: Population (1977 est.): 6,320,000. Pop. density:** 581.47 per sq. mi. **Ethnic groups:** Voltaic groups (Mossi, Bobo), Mande. **Languages:** French (official), More, Sudanic tribal languages. **Religions:** Moslems 20%, Roman Catholics 5%, others.

**Geography: Area:** 105,869 sq. mi., the size of Colorado. **Location:** In W. Africa, S of the Sahara. **Neighbors:** Mali on NW, Niger on NE, Benin, Togo, Ghana, Ivory Coast on S. **Topography:** Landlocked Upper Volta is in the savannah region of W. Africa. The N is arid, hot, and thinly populated. **Capital:** Ouagadougou. **Cities** (1970 est.): Ouagadougou 110,000; Bobo-Dioulasso 78,478.

**Government: Head of state:** Pres. Sangoule Lamizana; b. 1916; in office: Jan. 3, 1966. **Head of government:** Premier Joseph Conombo; in office: July 7, 1978. **Local divisions:** 10 departments. **Armed forces:** regulars 8,070; para-military 1,850.

**Economy: Chief crops:** Cotton, rice, peanuts, karite, grain, corn. **Minerals:** Manganese, gold, diamonds. **Per capita arable land:** 2.2 acres. **Meat production** (1975): beef: 11,000 tons; lamb: 10,000 tons. **Electricity production** (1975): 53.00 mln. kwh. **Labor force:** 89% agriculture.

**Finance: Currency:** Franc (May 1978: 230.35 = $1 US). **Gross domestic product** (1974 est.): $420 mln. **Per capita income** (1974): $67. **Imports** (1976): $144 mln.; partners (1972): Fr. 54%, Ivory Coast 17%, W. Ger. 5%, Mali 4%. **Exports** (1976): $53 mln.; partners (1972): Ivory Coast 46%, Fr. 19%, It. 7%, Ghana 5%. **Tourists** (1973): 10,700; receipts (1973): $2 million. **Balance of payments** (1975): −$10,000,000. **International reserves** (Mar. 1978): $62.1 mln.

**Transport: Motor Vehicles:** in use (1975): 9,500 passenger cars, 10,100 commercial vehicles.

**Communications: Television sets:** 5,500 licensed (1970). **Radios:** 100,000 licensed (1974). **Telephones in use** (1975): 6,000. **Daily newspaper circulation** (1974): 2,000; 0.3 per 1,000 pop.

**Health: Life expectancy at birth** (1961): 32.1 male; 31.1 female. **Births** (annual per 1,000 pop. 1972-75): 48.5. **Death** (annual per 1,000 pop. 1972-75): 25.8. **Natural increase** (1970-75): 2.27%. **Pop. per hospital bed** (1975): 1,146. **Pop. per physician** (1975): 59,580. **Infant mortality** (per 1,000 live births 1960-61): 182.

**Education: Literacy** (1975): 7%. **Pop. 5-19:** in school (1975): 7%, per teacher (1975): 534.

The Mossi tribe entered the area in the 11th to 13th centuries. Their kingdoms ruled until defeated by the Mali and Songhai empires.

French control came by 1896, but Upper Volta was not finally established as a separate territory until 1947. Full independence came Aug. 5, 1960, and a pro-French government was elected. A 1966 coup established the current regime. Free multi-party presidential and parliamentary elections were held in 1978.

Several hundred thousand farm workers migrate each year to Ivory Coast and Ghana. A long drought brought famine in 1973-74; renewed drought occurred in 1977-78.

# Uruguay

## Oriental Republic of Uruguay

**People: Population** (1977 est.): 2,810,000. **Age distrib. (%** 0–14: 28.0; 15–59: 59.3; 60+: 12.7. **Pop. density:** 40.99 per s. mi. **Ethnic groups:** Caucasians (Iberians, Italians) 90%, mes zos 5-10%, mulatto and Negro 3-5%. **Languages:** Spanish. **R**. **ligions:** Roman Catholics 66%, Jews 2%, Protestants 2%. **G**. **ography: Area:** 68,548 sq. mi., the size of Washington Stat. **Location:** In southern S. America, on the Atlantic O. **Neighbor**. Argentina on W, Brazil on N. **Topography:** Uruguay is com posed of rolling, grassy plains and hills, well-watered by rive flowing W to Uruguay R. **Capital:** Montevideo. **Cities** (197 cen.): Montevideo 1,229,748.

**Government: Head of state:** Pres. Aparicio Mendez; 1904; in office: Sept. 1, 1976. **Local divisions:** 19 department **Armed forces:** regulars 27,000; para-military 2,200.

**Economy: Industries:** Meat-packing, metals, textiles, win cement, oil products. **Chief crops:** Corn, wheat, citrus frui rice, oats, linseed. **Per capita arable land:** 1.4 acres. **Meat pr** duction (1976): beef: 405,100 tons; pork: 26,000 tons; lam 60,200 tons. **Fish catch** (1975): 26,200 metric tons. **Electrici** production (1975): 2.60 bln. kwh. **Labor force:** 17% agricu ture.

**Finance: Currency:** New Peso (Mar. 1978: 5.41 = $1 US **Gross domestic product** (1976): $3.13 bln. **Per capita i**. come (1976): $1,237. **Imports** (1976): $587 mln.; partne (1976): Braz. 15%, Arg. 11%, U.S. 8%. **Exports** (1976): $5. mln.; partners (1976): Braz. 12%, U.S. 11%, Arg. 4.7%. **Tou**. ists (1973): 587,600; receipts (1975): $57 million. **Balance** payments (1977): +$124,800,000. **International reserve** (Mar. 1978): $486 mln. **Consumer prices** (change in 197 58.4%.

**Transport: Railway traffic** (1975): 2.22 bln. passenger-mile 174.50 mln. net ton-miles. **Motor vehicles:** in use (1974 151,600 passenger cars, 85,700 commercial vehicles. **Civil a**. ation: 51 mln. passenger-miles (1976); 104 mln. freight to. miles (1976). **Chief ports:** Montevideo.

**Communications: Television sets:** 350,000 in use (1974 **Radios:** 1,500,000 in use (1974). **Telephones in use** (197 257,624. **Daily newspaper circulation** (1973): 960,000; 3 p 1,000 pop.

**Health: Life expectancy at birth** (1964): 65.51 male; 71.5 female. **Births** (per 1,000 pop. 1974): 19.3. **Deaths** (per 1,00 pop. 1974): 9.2. **Natural increase** (1974): 1.01%. **Pop. p** hospital bed (1975): 181. **Pop. per physician** (1975): 900. I fant mortality (per 1,000 live births 1974): 48.1.

**Education: Literacy** (1975): 91%. **Pop. 5-19:** in scho (1975): 62%, per teacher (1975): 32.

Spanish settlers did not begin replacing the indigenous Cha rua Indians until 1624. Portuguese from Brazil arrived later, b Uruguay was attached to the Spanish Viceroyalty of Rio de Plata in the 18th century. Rebels fought against Spain beginnin in 1810. An independent republic was declared Aug. 25, 182 and recognized by Argentina and Brazil three years later.

Liberal governments adopted socialist measures as far bac as 1911. More than a third of the workers are employed by th state, which owns the power, telephone, railroad, cement, o refining and other industries. Social welfare programs a. among the most advanced in the world.

Uruguay's standard of living was one of the highest in Sou America, and political and labor conditions among the frees Economic stagnation, inflation, plus floods, drought and a co wave in 1967 and a general strike in 1968 brought attempts b the government to strengthen the economy through a series devaluations of the peso and wage and price controls. But infl. tion continued. The cost of living rose 1,200% between 1968 ar 1976.

Leftist guerrillas, drawn from the upper classes and calle Tupamaros, increased terrorist actions in 1970; a U.S. polic adviser was slain in Aug. In 1971 the guerrillas kidnaped an after 8 months, freed the British ambassador. Violence conti ued in Feb. 1973 President Juan Maria Bordaberry agree to military control of his administration. In June he abolishe Congress and set up a Council of State in its place. By 1974 th military had apparently defeated the Tupamaros, using seve repressive measures, including mass arrests and torture, a cording to many reports. The economic decline continued. Bo daberry was removed by the military in a 1976 coup.

# Vatican

## State of Vatican City

**People: Population** (1976 est.): 1,000. **Ethnic groups:** Italian, Swiss. **Languages:** Italian, Latin. **Religions:** Roman Catholicism.

**Geography: Area:** 108.7 acres. **Location:** In Rome, Italy. **Neighbors:** Completely surrounded by Italy.

**Currency:** Lira.

The popes for many centuries, with brief interruptions, held temporal sovereignty over mid-Italy (the so-called Papal States), comprising an area of some 16,000 sq. mi., with a population in the 19th century of more than 3 million. This territory was incorporated in the new Kingdom of Italy, the sovereignty of the pope being confined to the palaces of the Vatican and the Lateran in Rome and the villa of Castel Gandolfo, by an Italian law, May 13, 1871. This law also guaranteed to the pope and his successors a yearly indemnity of over $620,000. This allowance, however, remained unclaimed.

A Treaty of Conciliation, a concordat and a financial convention were signed Feb. 11, 1929, by Cardinal Gasparri and Premier Mussolini. The documents established the independent state of Vatican City, and gave the Catholic religion special status in Italy. The treaty (Lateran Agreement) was made part of the Constitution of Italy (Article 7) in 1947. Italy and the Vatican reached preliminary agreement in 1976 on revisions of the concordat, that would eliminate Roman Catholicism as the state religion and end required religious education in Italian schools.

Vatican City includes St. Peter's, the Vatican Palace and Museum covering over 13 acres, the Vatican gardens, and neighboring buildings between Viale Vaticano and the Church. Thirteen buildings in Rome, outside the boundaries, enjoy extraterritorial rights; these buildings house congregations or offices necessary for the administration of the Holy See.

The legal system is based on the code of canon law, the apostolic constitutions and the laws especially promulgated for the Vatican City by the pope. In cases not covered, the Italian law of Rome applies. The Secretariat of State represents the Holy See in its diplomatic relations. By the Treaty of Conciliation the pope pledged to a perpetual neutrality unless his mediation is specifically requested. This, however, does not prevent the defense of the Church whenever it is persecuted. A total of 84 nations maintain diplomatic representatives in Vatican City. The U.S. does not have an official ambassador.

The present sovereign of the State of Vatican City is the Supreme Pontiff John Paul I, Albino Luciani, born in Forno di Canale, Italy, Oct. 17, 1912, elected Aug. 26, 1978, in succession to Giovanni Battista Montini, Paul VI, who died Aug. 6, 1978.

# Venezuela

## Republic of Venezuela

**People: Population** (1977): 12,740,000. **Age distrib.** (%): 0-14: 44.6; 15-59: 50.6; 60+: 4.7. **Pop. density:** 36.18 per sq. mi. **Urban** (1976): 74.7%. **Ethnic groups:** Mestizo 70%, white (Spanish, Portuguese, Italian) 20%, Negro 8%, Indian 2%. **Languages:** Spanish, Indian languages 2%. **Religions:** Roman Catholics 96%, Protestants 2%.

**Geography: Area:** 352,143 sq. mi., more than twice the size of California. **Location:** On the Caribbean coast of S. America. **Neighbors:** Colombia on W, Brazil on S, Guyana on E. **Topography:** The flat coastal plain and Orinoco Delta are bordered by Andes Mtns. and hills. Plains, called llanos, extend between mountains and Orinoco. Guyana Highlands and plains are S of Orinoco, which stretches 1,700 mi. and drains 80% of Venezuela. **Capital:** Caracas. **Cities** (1971 cen.): Caracas (met.) 2,175,400; Maracaibo 651,574; Valencia 367,171.

**Government: Head of state:** Pres. Carlos Andres Perez; b. Oct. 27, 1922; in office: Mar. 12, 1974. **Local divisions:** 20 states, 2 federal territories, federal district, all with elected legislators. **Armed forces:** regulars 44,000; para-military 10,000.

**Economy: Industries:** Steel, oil products, textiles, containers, tobacco, paper, tires, shoes. **Chief crops:** Coffee, cocoa, fruits, sugar. **Minerals:** Oil (5th largest producer), iron (extensive reserves and production), gold, copper, salt, coal, nickel, manganese, asbestos, diamonds, mica. **Crude oil reserves** (1978): 8.20 bln. bbls. **Per capita arable land:** 0.9 acres. **Meat production** (1976): beef: 313,000 tons; pork: 67,800 tons. **Fish catch** (1975): 153,400 metric tons. **Electricity production**

(1975): 21.18 bln. kwh. **Labor force:** 20% agric.; 19% manuf.

**Finance: Currency:** Bolivare (May 1978: 4.29 = $1 US). **Gross domestic product** (1976): $31.00 bln. **Per capita income** (1976): $2,357. **Imports** (1976): $6.02 bln.; partners (1973): U.S. 42%, W. Ger. 13%, Jap. 8%. **Exports** (1976): $546 mln.; partners (1973): U.S. 57%, Can. 17%, U.K. 4%. **Tourists** (1975): 40,800; receipts (1975): $215 million. **Balance of payments** (1977): –$438,000,000. **National budget** (1974): $9.93 bln. revenues; $9.11 bln. expenditures. **International reserves** (May 1978): $7.47 bln. **Consumer prices** (change in 1977): 7.7%.

**Transport: Railway traffic** (1971): 26.08 mln. passenger-miles; 9.32 mln. net ton-miles. **Motor vehicles:** in use (1971): 601,100 passenger cars, 208,200 commercial vehicles. **Civil aviation:** 1,572 mln. passenger-miles (1976); 47,715 mln. freight ton-miles (1976). **Chief ports:** Maracaibo, La Guaira, Puerto Cabello.

**Communications: Television sets:** 1,200,000 in use (1974), 86,000 manufactured (1972). **Radios:** 1,709,000 in use (1974), 74,000 manufactured (1972). **Telephones in use** (1977): 742,050. **Daily newspaper circulation** (1974): 1,082,000; 11 per 1,000 pop.

**Health: Life expectancy at birth** (1961): 66.41 male; 68.75 female. **Births** (annual per 1,000 pop. 1972-75): 36.1. **Deaths** (annual per 1,000 pop. 1972-75): 7.0. **Natural increase** (annual 1970-75): 2.91%. **Pop. per hospital bed** (1975): 366. **Pop. per physician** (1975): 950. **Infant mortality** (per 1,000 live births 1974): 46.0.

**Education: Literacy** (1975): 82%. **Pop. 5-19:** in school (1975): 55%, per teacher (1975): 59.

Columbus first set foot on the South American continent on the peninsula of Paria, Aug. 1498. Alonso de Ojeda, 1499, found Lake Maracaibo, called the land Venezuela, or Little Venice, because natives had houses on stilts. Venezuela was under Spanish domination until 1821. The republic was formed after secession from the Colombian Federation in 1830.

Military governments ruled Venezuela for most of the 20th century. They promoted the oil industry; some social reforms were implemented. Since 1959, the country has enjoyed progressive, democratically-elected governments.

Venezuela helped found the Organization of Petroleum Exporting States (OPEC). On Jan. 1, 1976, the government nationalized the oil industry with compensation. Development has begun of the Orinoco tar belt, believed to contain the world's largest oil reserves; expensive refining techniques are necessary. Iron ore production was nationalized Jan. 1, 1975.

Construction is booming, including a new $3.8 billion city, Ciudad Guyana, 300 mi. SE of Caracas. Oil profits help finance the extensive industrial development. Government efforts at income redistribution were thwarted by inflation in 1974-5, but public works and welfare programs in slum areas have improved.

Several hundred thousand legal and illegal Columbian migrants work in Venezuela. European immigration has also been high.

# Vietnam

## Socialist Republic of Vietnam

**People: Population** (1977 est.): 47,870,000. **Pop. density:** 378.61 per sq. mi. **Ethnic groups:** Vietnamese 80%, Khmer, Tais, Montagnards, Tays, Muong, Nung. **Languages:** Vietnamese, others. **Religions:** Buddhism and Taoism most numerous, Roman Catholics 5%, Dao Dai, Hoa Hao.

**Geography: Area:** 126,436 sq. mi., the size of New Mexico. **Location:** On the E coast of the Indochinese Peninsula in SE Asia. **Neighbors:** China on N, Laos, Cambodia on W. **Topography:** Vietnam is long and narrow, with a 1,400-mi. coast. About 24% of country is readily arable, including the densely settled Red R. valley in the N, narrow coastal plains in center, and the wide, often marshy Mekong R Delta in the S. The rest consists of semi-arid plateaus and barren mountains, with some stretches of tropical rain forest. **Capital:** Hanoi. **Cities** (1973 est.): Saigon 1,825,297; Danang 492,194; (1960 cen.): Hanoi (met.) 643,576; Haiphong (met.) 369,248.

**Government: Head of state:** Pres. Ton Duc Thang; b. 1888; in office: Sept. 23, 1969; **Head of government:** Premier Pham Van Dong; b. 1906; in office: Sept. 20, 1955; **Head of Communist Party:** First Sec. Le Duan; b. 1907; in office: Sept. 1960. **Local divisions:** 38 provinces. **Armed forces:** regulars

615,000; para-military 1,570,000.

**Economy: Industries:** Food processing, textiles, paper. **Chief crops:** Rice, corn, sugar cane, sweet potatoes, coffee, tea, cotton, manioc, tobacco. **Minerals:** Coal, iron, manganese, bauxite, apatite, chromate, phosphates. **Other resources:** Forests. **Per capita arable land:** 0.3 acres. **Meat production** (1975): beef: 94,000 tons; pork: 428,000 tons. **Fish catch** (1975): 1,013,500 metric tons. **Electricity production** (1975): 1.32 bln. kwh. **Labor force:** 76% agriculture.

**Finance: Currency:** Dong (1974: 2.40 = $1 US). **Per capita income** (1974): $130. **Imports** (1973): $618 mln. **Exports** (1973): $59 mln. **Tourists** (1972): 79,200; receipts (1974): $16 million.

**Transport: Railway traffic** (1973): 105.57 mln. passenger-miles; 621,000 net ton-miles. **Motor vehicles:** in use (S. Vietnam only (1974): 70,000 passenger cars, 100,000 commercial vehicles. **Chief ports:** Saigon, Haiphong, Da Nang, Cam Raph.

**Communications: Radios:** 2,550,000 in use (1974), 87,000 manufactured (South only) (1973). **Telephones in use** (1973): (S. Vietnam only) 47,000. **Daily newspaper circulation** (1973): 588,000; 29 per 1,000 pop.

**Health: Life expectancy at birth** (1975): 43.2 male; 46.0 female. **Births** (annual per 1,000 pop. 1972-75): 41.5. **Deaths** (per 1,000 pop. 1975): 20.5. **Natural increase** (annual 1970-75): 2.10%. **Pop. per hospital bed** (1975): 563. **Pop. per physician** (1975): 15,022. **Infant mortality** (per 1,000 live births 1973): 150.

**Education: Literacy** (1975): 65%. **Pop. 5-19:** in school (1975): 55%, per teacher (1975): 54.

Vietnam's recorded history began in Tonkin before the Christian era. Settled by Viets from central China, Vietnam was held by China, 111 B.C.-939 A.D., and was a vassal state during subsequent periods. Vietnam defeated the armies of Kublai Khan, 1288. Conquest by France began in 1858 and ended in 1884 with protectorate status.

In 1940 Vietnam was occupied by Japan; nationalist aims gathered force. A number of groups formed the Vietminh (Independence) League, headed by Ho Chi Minh, communist guerrilla leader. In Aug. 1945 the Vietminh forced out Bao Dai, former emperor of Annam, head of a regime sponsored by Japan. France, seeking to reestablish colonial control, battled communist and nationalist forces, 1946-1954, and was finally defeated at Dienbienphu, May 8, 1954. Meanwhile, on July 1, 1949, Bao Dai had formed a State of Vietnam, with himself as chief of state, with French approval. Communist China backed Ho Chi Minh.

A cease-fire accord signed in Geneva July 21, 1954, divided Vietnam along the Ben Hai River. It provided for a buffer zone, withdrawal of French troops from the North and elections to determine the country's future. Under the agreement the communists gained control of territory north of the 17th parallel, 22 provinces with area of 62,000 sq. mi. and 13 million pop., with its capital at Hanoi and Ho Chi Minh as president. South Vietnam came to comprise the 39 southern provinces with approx. area of 65,000 sq. mi. and pop. of 12 million. Some 900,000 North Vietnamese fled to South Vietnam. Neither South Vietnam nor the U.S. signed the agreement.

On Oct. 26, 1955, Ngo Dinh Diem, premier of the interim government of South Vietnam, proclaimed the Republic of Vietnam and became its first president.

The Democratic Republic of Vietnam, established in the North, adopted a constitution Dec. 31, 1959, based on communist principles and calling for reunification of all Vietnam. President Ho Chi Minh, re-elected July 15, 1960, by unanimous vote of the National Assembly, had held office since 1945. He died Sept. 3, 1969.

North Vietnam sought to take over South Vietnam beginning in 1954. Fighting persisted from 1956, with the communist Vietcong, aided by North Vietnam, pressing war in the South and South Vietnam receiving U.S. aid. Northern aid to Vietcong guerrillas was intensified in 1959, and large-scale troop infiltration began in 1964, with Russian and Chinese arms assistance. Large Northern forces were stationed in border areas of Laos and Cambodia.

A serious political conflict arose in the South in 1963 when Buddhists denounced authoritarianism and brutality. This paved the way for a military coup Nov. 1-2, 1963, which overthrew Diem. Several military coups followed. In elections Sept. 3, 1967, Chief of State Nguyen Van Thieu was chosen president.

In 1964, the U.S. began air strikes against North Vietnam. Beginning in 1965, the raids were stepped up and U.S. troops be-

came combatants. U.S. troop strength in Vietnam, wh reached a high of 543,400 in Apr. 1969, was ordered reduced U.S. President Nixon in a series of withdrawals, beginning June 1969. U.S. bombings were resumed in 1972-73.

A ceasefire agreement was signed in Paris Jan. 27, 19 (EST), by the U.S., North and South Vietnam, and the Vietcor It was never implemented. U.S. aid was curbed in 1974 by t U.S. Congress. Heavy fighting continued for two years throug out Indochina.

Massive numbers of North Vietnamese troops, aided by tan launched attacks against remaining government outposts in t Central Highlands in the first months of 1975. Government r treats turned into a rout, and the Saigon regime surrender April 30. Conquest of the country was effectively complet within days.

A Provisional Revolutionary Government assumed cont aided by officials and technicians from Hanoi, and first ste were taken to transform society along communist lines. All bu nesses and farms were to be collectivized by 1979.

The U.S. accepted over 165,000 Vietnamese fleeing the ne regime, while scores of thousands more sought refuge in oth countries.

The war's toll included — Combat deaths: U.S. 46,079; Sou Vietnam over 200,000; other allied forces 5,225. Civilian casu ties were over a million. Displaced war refugees in South Vi nam totaled over 6.5 million.

After the fighting ended, eight Northern divisions remained s tioned in the South, while Southern forces of over 900,000 we demobilized, adding to severe economic problems. Over 1 m lion urban residents were resettled in the countryside by 197 the first of 10 million scheduled for forced resettlement, acco ing to the government (including 260,000 Montagnards); an u known number were sent to long-term re-education camps, cluding thousands of adherents of the Hoa Hao sect. Son military resistance against the new regime was periodically ported. A 1977 crop failure caused food shortages; the sou remained more prosperous than the north.

The first National Assembly of both parts of the country m June 24, 1976. The country was officially reunited July 2, 197 The Northern capital, flag, anthem, emblem, and currency we applied to the new state. Nearly all major government pos went to officials of the former Northern government, and tho sands of Northern officials were sent south.

The U.S. agreed in 1977 not to bar Vietnam's membership the UN.

Heavy fighting with Cambodia took place, 1977-78, amid m tual charges of aggression and atrocities against civilians. Son 40,000 Viet troops assure complete control of Laos.

Relations with China soured as 140,000 ethnic Chinese le Vietnam charging discrimination. China cut off economic a (over $3 bln. granted in 1976 alone). Soviet ties remaine strong: Vietnam joined Comecon (Soviet trade bloc) in 197 China said a Soviet guided missile base had been built in Vie nam.

# Yemen

## Yemen Arab Republic

**People: Population** (1977 est.): 7,080,000. **Pop. density** 94.04 per sq. mi. **Ethnic groups:** Arabs, some Negroids. **Lan guages:** Arabic. **Religions:** Sunni Moslems 50%, Shiite Mos lems 50%.

**Geography: Area:** 75,289 sq. mi., slightly smaller than Sou Dakota. **Location:** On the southern Red Sea coast of the Ara bian Peninsula. **Neighbors:** Saudi Arabia on NE, South Yeme on S. **Topography:** A sandy coastal strip leads to well-watere fertile mountains in interior. **Capital:** Sana. **Cities** (1970 est Sana 120,000.

**Government: Head of state:** Ali Abdullah Saleh; in offic July 17, 1978; **Head of government:** Prime Min. Abdul Aziz Ab dul-Ghani; in office: Jan. 15, 1975. **Local divisions:** 10 gove norates. **Armed forces:** regulars 39,850; para-military 20,000.

**Economy: Industries:** Textiles, cement. **Chief crops:** Coffe cotton; gat (narcotic shrub), grain, dates, cotton, sesame, herb fruits. **Minerals:** Salt. **Crude oil reserves** (1978): 370 mln. bbl **Per capita arable land:** 0.4 acres. **Fish catch** (1975): 127,30 metric tons. **Electricity production** (1975): 49.00 mln. kwh. **La bor force:** 73% agriculture.

**Finance: Currency:** Rial (May 1978: 4.56 = $1 US). **Gros domestic product** (1975): $1.14 bln. **Per capita incom**

4): $168. **Imports** (1976): $410 mln.; partners (1974): Jap. , P.R. China 7%, W. Ger. 6%, Saudi Ar. 5%. **Exports** 6): $8 mln.; partners (1974): Jap. 42%, P.R. China 20%, S. en 10%, Somalia 8%. **Tourist receipts** (1974): $4 million. nce of payments (1977): +$500,000,000. **International** rves (Mar. 1978): $1.29 bln. **Consumer prices** (change in ): 17.0%.

ansport: **Motor vehicles:** in use (1974): 10,600 passenger , 7,900 commercial vehicles. **Chief ports:** Al-Hudaydah, iukha.

ommunications: **Radios:** 86,000 in use (1974). **Tele-nes in use** (1970): 4,000. **Daily newspaper circulation** 0): 56,000; 10 per 1,000 pop.

ealth: **Life expectancy at birth** (1975): 43.7 male; 45.9 fe-e. **Births** (annual per 1,000 pop. 1972-75): 49.6. **Deaths** (an-per 1,000 pop. 1972-75): 20.6. **Natural increase** (annual )-75): 2.90%. **Pop. per hospital bed** (1975): 1,580. **Pop. physician** (1975): 26,031. **Infant mortality** (per 1,000 live s 1973): 152.

ducation: **Literacy** (1975): 10%. **Pop. 5-19:** in school '5): 12%, per teacher (1975): 135.

emen's territory once was part of the ancient kindgom of ba, or Saba, a prosperous link in trade between Africa and a. A Biblical reference speaks of its gold, spices and precious es as gifts borne by the Queen of Sheba to King Solomon. emen became independent in 1918, after years of Ottoman kish rule, but remained politically and economically back-d. Imam Ahmed ruled 1948-1962. The king was reported assinated Sept. 26, 1962, and a revolutionary group headed Brig. Gen. Abdullah al-Salal declared the country to be the nen Arab Republic.

he Imam Ahmed's heir, the Imam Mohamad al-Badr, fled to mountains where tribesmen joined royalist forces; internal fare between them and the republican forces continued. ptian president Nasser sent 70,000 troops to aid the republi-s; Saudi Arabia supported the royalists with military aid. ut 150,000 people were killed in the fighting.

fter Egypt's defeat in the June 1967 Israeli-Arab war, Egypt ounced it would withdraw its troops from Yemen; the last of n left Nov. 29, 1967, and Saudi Arabia said it would stop aid-the royalists.

his was accompanied by a bloodless coup Nov. 5, 1967. nting continued between the republican and royalist forces. udi Arabia announced in Feb. 1968 it was renewing its aid to royalists, charging that both Russia and Syria, as well as uthern Yemen, were aiding the republicans.

April 1970 hostilities ended with an agreement between Ye-n and Saudi Arabia and appointment of several royalists to Yemen government.

here were border skirmishes with forces of the People's mocratic Republic of Yemen in 1972-73. The U.S. and Yemen 1972 resumed diplomatic relations, broken by Yemen after 1967 Arab-Israeli war.

On June 13, 1974, an Army group, led by Col Ibrahim al-midi, seized the government. Hamidi pursued close Saudi and S. ties; he was killed in 1977 by unknown assassins. His suc-sor was murdered, reportedly by pro-South Yemen forces or the S. Yemen government.

here are periodic droughts. Per capita GNP is among the est in the world. A prolonged drought has forced imports of d. The remittances from 400,000 Yemens living in Arab oil untries provide most of foreign earnings.

## South Yemen

### People's Democratic Republic of Yemen

eople: **Population** (1977 est.): 1,800,000. **Age distrib. (%):** 4: 47.8; 15–59: 45.6; 60+: 6.6. **Pop. density:** 16.07 per sq. n. **Urban** (1973): 33.3%. **Ethnic groups:** Arabs, 75%, Indians %, Somalis 8%, others. **Languages:** Arabic. **Regligions:** slems (Sunni) 91%, Christians 4%, Hindus 3.5%.

Geography: **Area:** 112,000 sq. mi., the size of Nevada. **Loca-n:** On the southern coast of the Arabian Peninsula. **Neigh-rs:** Yemen on W, Saudi Arabia on N, Oman on E. **Topogra-y:** The entire country is very hot and very dry. A sandy coast es to mountains which give way to desert sands. **Capital:** en. **Cities** (1973 est.): Aden (met.) 285,373.

Government: **Head of state:** Pres. Ali Nasser Mohammed sani; in office: June, 1978; **Head of government:** Prime Min.

Ali Nasser Mohammed Hasani; in office: 1971; **Head of Communist Party:** Sec. Gen. Abdul Fattah Ismail. in office: 1971. **Local divisions:** 6 governorates. **Armed forces:** regulars 21,300; para-military, 1,500.

Economy: **Industries:** Transshipment. **Chief crops:** Cotton (main export), grains. **Per capita arable land:** 0.4 acres. **Electricity production** (1975): 180.00 mln. kwh. **Labor force:** 62% agriculture.

Finance: **Currency:** Dinar (May 1978: 1 = $2.90 US). **Gross domestic product** (1974 est.): $250 mln. **Per capita income** (1974): $140. **Imports** (1976): $414 mln.; partners (1972): Kuw. 18%, Iran 11%, U.K. 7%, Jap. 7%. **Exports** (1976): $249 mln.; partners (1972): Jap. 12%, U.K. 9%, Thai. 8%, U.A.E. 7%. **Balance of payments** (1974): −$24,400,000. **National budget** (1976): $71.68 mln. revenues; $113.35 mln. expenditures. **International reserves** (Mar. 1978): $136.10 mln.

Transport: **Motor vehicles:** in use (1973): 10,600 passenger cars, 7,900 commercial vehicles. **Chief ports:** Aden.

Communications: **Television sets:** 30,000 in use (1974). **Radios:** 600,000 in use (1974). **Telephones in use** (1973): 10,000. **Daily newspaper circulation** (1972): 2,000; 1 per 1,000 pop.

Health: **Life expectancy at birth** (1975): 43.7 male; 45.9 female. **Births** (annual per 1,000 pop. 1972-75): 49.6. **Deaths** (annual per 1,000 pop. 1972-75): 20.6. **Natural increase** (annual 1970-75): 2.90%. **Pop. per hospital bed** (1975): 705. **Pop. per physician** (1975): 11,280. **Infant mortality** (per 1,000 live births 1973): 152.

Education: **Literacy** (1975): 15%. **Pop. 5-19:** in school (1975): 38%, per teacher (1975): 76.

Aden, mentioned in the Bible, has been a port for trade in incense, spice and silk between the East and West for 2,000 years. British rule began in 1839. Aden provided Britain with a controlling position at the southern entrance to the Red Sea.

A war for independence began in 1963. The National Liberation Front (NLF) and the Egypt-supported Front for the Liberation of Occupied South Yemen, waged a guerrilla war against the British and local dynastic rulers. The 2 groups vied with each other for control. The NLF won out. Independence came Nov. 30, 1967. In 1969, the left wing of the NLF seized power and inaugurated a thorough nationalization of the economy and regimentation of daily life.

The new government broke off relations with the U.S. and nationalized some foreign firms. Aid has been furnished by the USSR and China, with the USSR supplying most military aid.

In 1972-73 there were border skirmishes with forces of the Yemen Arab Republic. South Yemen aided leftist guerrillas in neighboring Oman. Relations with Saudi Arabia later improved. S. Yemen troops fought in Ethiopia against Eritrean rebels in 1978; 500 Cuban troops and some Soviet facilities were reported in Yemen.

Pres. Salem Robaye Ali, who had tried to improve relations with Yemen, Saudi Arabia, Oman, and the U.S., was executed after a bloody coup June 1978. The new ruling faction was accused by N. Yemen of the murder of N. Yemen's president 2 days earlier. N. Yemen, Egypt, and Saudi Arabia froze ties with S. Yemen in July.

The Port of Aden is the country's most valuable resource, but with the closing of the Suez Canal after the Israeli-Arab War in June 1967, the port lost much of its business. Local products exported are cotton, fish, coffee, hides. The canal was reopened in 1975.

Socotra, the largest island in the Arabian Sea, Kamaran, an island in the Red Sea near the coast of North Yemen, and Perim, an island in the strait between the Gulf of Aden and the Red Sea, are controlled by South Yemen.

## Yugoslavia

### Socialist Federal Republic of Yugoslavia

People: **Population** (1977 est.): 21,720,000. **Age distrib. (%):** 0–14: 26.6; 15-59: 61.0; 60+: 12.5. **Pop. density:** 219.91 per sq. mi. **Urban** (1971): 38.6%. **Ethnic groups:** Serbs 40%, Croats 23%, Slovenes 8.6%, Macedonians 5.6%, Bosnian Moslems 5%, Albanians 5%, Montenegrin Serbs 2%, Hungarians 2%, Turks 1%. **Languages:** Serbo-Croatian, Macedonian, Slovene all official. **Religions:** Orthodox 50%, Róman Catholics 30%, Moslems 10%, Protestants 1%.

Geography: **Area:** 98,766 sq. mi., the size of Wyoming. **Location: On the Adriatic coast of the Balkan Peninsula in SE Europe. **Neighbors:** Italy on W, Austria, Hungary on N, Romania, Bulgaria on E, Greece, Albania on S. **Topography:** The Dinaric Alps run parallel to the Adriatic coast, which is lined by offshore islands. Plains stretch across N and E river basins. S and NW are mountainous. **Capital:** Belgrade. **Cities** (1971 cen.): Belgrade (met.) 774,744; Zagreb 566,224; Skoplje 312,980.

**Government: Head of state:** Pres. Josip Broz Tito; b. May 25, 1892; in office: Jan. 1953; **Head of government:** Premier Min. Veselin Djuranovic; b. May 17, 1925; in office: Mar. 15, 1977; **Head of Communist Party:** Josip Broz Tito; in office: 1937. **Local divisions:** 6 republics: Serbia, Croatia, Slovenia, Bosnia-Herzegovina, Macedonia, Montenegro; 2 autonomous provinces: Vojvodina, Kosovo. **Armed forces:** regulars 405,000; reserves 500,000.

**Economy: Industries:** Steel, chemicals, wood products, cement, textiles, tourism. **Chief crops:** Corn, grains, tobacco, hops, fruits, sugar beets, sunflowers. **Minerals:** Coal, iron, copper, chrome, manganese, lead, zinc, mercury, salt, bauxite. **Crude oil reserves** (1978): 325 mln. bbls. **Per capita arable land:** 0.8 acres. **Meat production** (1976): beef: 335,000 tons; pork: 450,000 tons; lamb: 56,000 tons. **Fish catch:** (1975): 56,600 metric tons. **Electricity production** (1977): 48.64 bln. kwh. **Labor force:** 45% agric.; 18% manuf.

**Finance: Currency:** Dinar (May 1978: 18.86 = $1 US). **Gross domestic product** (1975): $27.95 bln. **Imports** (1977): $9.63 bln.; partners (1974): W. Ger. 18%, It. 12%, USSR 10%, Austria 5%. **Exports** (1977): $5.25 bln.; partners (1974): USSR 18%, It. 11%, W. Ger. 10%, U.S. 8%. **Tourists** (1975): 5,835,300; receipts (1975): $776 million. **Balance of payments** (1977): +$60,000,000. **National budget** (1975): $6.02 bln. revenues; $6.58 bln. expenditures. **International reserves** (May 1978): $2.22 bln. **Consumer prices** (change in 1977): 14.6%.

**Transport: Railway traffic** (1975): 6.39 bln. passenger-miles; 13.48 bln. net ton-miles. **Motor vehicles:** in use (1975): 1,536,700 passenger cars, 178,900 commercial vehicles; manufactured (1977): 180,000 passenger cars; 48,000 commercial vehicles. **Civil aviation:** 1,334 mln. passenger-miles (1976); 12,817 mln. freight ton-miles (1970). **Chief ports:** Rijeka, Split, Dubrovnik.

**Communications: Television sets:** 2,784,000 licensed (1974), 425,000 manufactured (1975). **Radios:** 4,081,000 licensed (1974), 140,000 manufactured (1975). **Telephones in use** (1977): 1,430,575. **Daily newspaper circulation** (1974): 1,850,000; 87 per 1,000 pop.

**Health: Life expectancy at birth** (1972): 65.42 male; 70.22 female. **Births** (per 1,000 pop. 1976): 18.0. **Deaths** (per 1,000 pop. 1976): 8.2. **Natural increase** (1976): .98%. **Pop. per hospital bed** (1975): 168. **Pop. per physician** (1975): 837. **Infant mortality** (per 1,000 live births 1975): 40.5

**Education:** Literacy (1975): 86%. **Pop. 5–19:** in school (1975): 56%, per teacher (1975): 38.

Serbia, which had since 1389 been a vassal principality of Turkey, was established as an independent kingdom by the Treaty of Berlin, 1878. Montenegro, independent since 1389, also obtained international recognition in 1878. After the Balkan wars Serbia's boundaries were enlarged by the annexation of Old Serbia and Macedonia, 1913.

When the Austro-Hungarian empire collapsed after World War I, the Kingdom of the Serbs, Croats, and Slovenes was formed from the former provinces of Croatia, Dalmatia, Bosnia, Herzegovina, Slovenia, Voyvodina and the independent state of Montenegro. The name was later changed to Yugoslavia.

Nazi Germany invaded in 1941. Many Yugoslav partisan troops continued to operate. Among these were the Chetniks led by Draja Mikhailovich, who fought other partisans led by Josip Broz, known as Marshal Tito. Tito, backed by the USSR and Britain from 1943, was in control by the time the Germans had been driven from Yugoslavia in 1945. Mikhailovich was executed July 17, 1946, by the Tito regime.

A constituent assembly proclaimed Yugoslavia a republic Nov. 29, 1945. It became a federated republic Jan. 31, 1946, and Marshal Tito, a communist, became head of the government. By terms of a treaty with Italy, the greater part of Venezia-Giulia, Zara, Pelagosa, and adjacent islands were ceded to Yugoslavia.

The Stalin policy of dictating to all communist nations was rejected by Tito. He accepted economic aid and military equipment from the U.S. and received aid in foreign trade also from France and Great Britain.

Tito supported the liberal government of Czechoslovakia in 1968 before the Russian invasion, but he paid a friendship vis Moscow in 1972.

A separatist movement among Croatians, 2d to the Serb numbers, brought arrests and a change of leaders in the Cro Republic in Jan. 1972. Violence by extreme Croatian nationa and fears of Soviet political intervention have led to restrict on political and intellectual dissent, which had previously b freer than in other East European countries. Serbians, Mont grins, and Macedonians use Cyrillic, Croatians and Sloven use Latin letters. Croatia and Slovenia have been the most p perous republics.

Most industry is socialized and private enterprise is restric to small-scale production. Since 1952 workers are guarantee basic wage and a share in cooperative profits.

Management of industrial enterprises is handled by work councils. Farmland is 85% privately owned but farms are stricted to 25 acres.

Beginning in 1965, reforms designed to decentralize the ministration of economic development and to force industrie produce more efficiently in competition with foreign produc were introduced.

Yugoslavia has developed considerable trade with West Europe as well as with Eastern Europe. Money earned by Yu slavs working temporarily in Western Europe helps pay for ports. Unemployment and inflation became serious in 1975. U.S. agreed in 1977 to expand arms sales.

# Zaire

## Republic of Zaire

**People: Population** (1977 est.): 26,380,000. **Pop. dens** 29.15 per sq. mi. **Urban** (1976): 29.2%. **Ethnic groups:** Mo Bantus: Luba 18%, Mongo 17%, Kongo 12%, Ruanda 10%, ers. **Languages:** French (official), others. **Religions:** Ror Catholics, Protestants, syncretic sects 60%, Moslems 1%, ers.

**Geography: Area:** 905,063 sq. mi., one-fourth the size of U.S. **Location:** In central Africa. **Neighbors:** Congo on W, C tral African Empire, Sudan on N, Uganda, Rwanda, Buru Tanzania on E, Zambia, Angola on S. **Topography:** Zaire cludes the bulk of the Zaire (Congo) R. Basin. The vast cer region is a low-lying plateau covered by rain forest. Mountain terraces in the W, savannas in the S and SE, grasslands tow the N, and the high Ruwenzori Mtns. on the E surround the c tral region. A short strip of territory borders the Atlantic O. Zaire R. is 2,718 mi. long. **Capital:** Kinshasa. **Cities** (1974 e Kinshasa 2,008,352; Kananga 601,239; Lubumbashi 403,6 Mbuji-Mayi 336,654; Kisangani, 310,705.

**Government: Head of state:** Pres. Mobutu Sese Seko Oct. 14, 1930; in office: Nov. 24, 1965; **Local divisions:** 8 gions. **Armed forces:** regulars 33,400; para-military 30,000.

**Economy: Chief crops:** Coffee, cotton, rice, sugar cane, nanas, plantains, coconuts, manioc, mangoes, tea, cacao, p oil. **Minerals:** Cobalt (two-thirds of world output), copper, c mium, gold, silver, tin, germanium, zinc, iron, tungsten, man nese, uranium, radium. **Crude oil reserves** (1978): 150 r bbls. **Other resources:** Forests, rubber, ivory. **Per capita a ble land:** 0.7 acres. **Fish catch** (1975): 124,600 metric to **Electricity production** (1975): 3.44 bln. kwh. **Labor for** 78% agriculture.

**Finance: Currency:** Zaire (May 1978: 1.22 = $1 US). **Gro domestic product** (1976): $3.38 bln. **Per capita incon** (1975): $127. **Imports** (1976): $827 mln.; partners (1973): Be 20%, U.S. 17%, W. Ger. 14%, Fr. 11%. **Exports** (1976): $9 mln.; partners (1973): Belg. 48%, It. 13%, Jap. 7%, Fr. 7 **Tourists** (1975): 40,900; receipts (1975): $11 million. **Balar of payments** (1975): −$132,700,000. **National budget** (197 $863.80 mln. revenues; $1.42 bln. expenditures. **Internatio reserves** (May 1978): $279.46 mln. **Consumer prices** (char in 1977): 65.4%.

**Transport: Railway traffic** (1972): 2.78 bln. passenger-mil 1.87 bln. net ton-miles. **Motor vehicles:** in use (1974): 84,8 passenger cars, 76,400 commercial vehicles. **Civil aviation:** 4 mln. passenger-miles (1976); 41,463 mln. freight ton-mi (1976). **Chief ports:** Matadi, Boma.

**Communications: Television sets:** 7,000 in use (1974). R dios: 2,448,000 in use (1974), 35,000 manufactured (1969). 1 lephones in use (1977): 48,000. **Daily newspaper circulati** (1974): 45,000; 7 per 1,000 pop.

**Health: Life expectancy at birth** (1975): 41.9 male; 45.1

ale. **Births** (annual per 1,000 pop. 1972-75): 45.2. **Deaths** (annual per 1,000 1972-75): 20.5. **Natural increase** (annual 970-75): 2.47%. **Pop. per hospital bed** (1975): 332. **Pop. per hysician** (1975): 27,669. **Infant mortality** (per 1,000 live births 955-58): 104.

**Education: Literacy** (1975): 13%. **Pop. 5-19:** in school 975): 45%, per teacher (1975): 88.

The earliest inhabitants of Zaire may have been the pygmies, llowed by Bantus from the E and Nilotic tribes from the N. The rge Bantu Bakongo kingdom ruled much of Zaire and Angola hen Portuguese explorers visited in the 15th century.

Leopold II, king of the Belgians, formed an international group exploit the Congo in 1876. In 1877 Henry M. Stanley explored e Congo and in 1878 the king's group sent him back to orga- ze the region and win over the native chiefs. The Conference Berlin, 1884-85, organized the Congo Free State with Leopold s king and chief owner. Exploitation of native laborers on the bber plantations caused international criticism and led to grant- g of a colonial charter, 1908.

Belgian and Congolese leaders agreed Jan. 27, 1960, that the ngo would become independent June 30. In the first general ections, May 31, the National Congolese movement of Patrice mumba won 35 of 137 seats in the National Assembly, lower use of Parliament. He was appointed premier June 21, and rmed a coalition cabinet.

Widespread violence caused Europeans and others to flee. atanga, rich in minerals, seceded from the republic July 11, but ded the secession in 1963. The UN Security Council Aug. 9, 60, called on Belgium to withdraw its troops and sent a UN ntingent. President Kasavubu removed Lumumba as premier. mumba fought for control backed by Ghana, Guinea and India; e was murdered in 1961.

The last UN troops left the Congo June 30, 1964, and Moise shombe became president.

On Sept. 7, 1964, leftist rebels set up a "People's Republic" in anleyville. Tshombe hired foreign mercenaries and sought to uild the Congolese Army. In Nov. and Dec. 1964 rebels slew res of white hostages and thousands of Congolese; Belgian atroops, dropped from U.S. transport planes, rescued hun- ds. By July 1965 the rebels had lost their effectiveness.

n 1965 Gen. Joseph D. Mobutu was named president. He er changed his name to Mobutu Sese Seko. On July 1 he re- med Leopoldville, Kinshasa; Stanleyville, Kisangani; and sabethville, Lubumbashi.

The country changed its name to Republic of Zaire on Oct. 27, 71; in 1972 Zairians with Christian names were ordered to ange them to African names.

n 1969-74, political stability under Mobutu was reflected in proved economic conditions. In 1974 most foreign-owned busi- sses were ordered sold to Zaire citizens, but in 1977 the gov- ment asked the original owners to return. A fall in copper ces in 1975 brought a surge in foreign debt and economic dif- ilties, causing political unrest.

n 1977, a force of Zairians, apparently trained by Cubans, aded Shaba province (Katanga) from Angola, Zaire repelled attack, with the aid of 1,500 Moroccan troops flown in by nce and Egyptians pilots. The U.S. sent "nonlethal" supplies. many Belgian and other European mining experts failed to um after a second unsuccessful invasion from Angola in May 8, suppressed by French, Belgian, and Moroccan troops (the er ferried by the U.S.).

# Zambia
## Republic of Zambia

**People: Population** (1977 est.): 5,350,000. **Age distrib.** (%): 4: 46.3; 15–59: 50.1; 60+: 3.6. **Pop. density:** 18.40 per sq. **Urban** (1975): 36.3%. **Ethnic groups:** Africans 99%, mostly tu tribes, Europeans and Asians 1%. **Languages:** English

(official), 70 others. **Religions:** Christians 15%, traditional reli- gions.

**Geography: Area:** 290,724 sq. mi., larger than Texas. **Loca- tion:** In southern central Africa. **Neighbors:** Zaire on N, Tanza- nia, Malawi, Mozambique on E, Rhodesia Namibia on S, Angola on W. **Topography:** Zambia is mostly high plateau country cov- ered with thick forests, and drained by several important rivers, including the Zambezi. **Capital:** Lusaka. **Cities** (1972 est.): Lu- saka (met.) 448,000; Kitwe (met.) 331,000; Ndola (met.) 235,000.

**Government: Head of state:** Pres. Kenneth David Kaunda; b. Apr. 28, 1924; in office: Oct. 24, 1964; **Head of government:** Prime Min. Mainza Chona; in office: 1973-75; July 20, 1977. **Lo- cal divisions:** 9 provinces. **Armed forces:** regulars 8,500; para- military 700.

**Economy: Chief crops:** Corn, tobacco, peanuts, cotton, sugar. **Minerals:** Copper (most of exports), zinc, cobalt, gold, lead, vanadium, manganese, coal. **Other resources:** Rubber, ivory. **Per capita arable land:** 2.3 acres. **Meat production** (1975): beef: 35,000 tons. **Fish catch** (1975): 50,000 metric tons. **Electricity production** (1976): 70.44 bln. kwh. **Labor force:** 69% agriculture.

**Finance: Currency:** Kwacha (Apr. 1978: 1 = $1.16 US). **Gross domestic product** (1976): $2.02 bln. **Per capita in- come** (1975): $391. **Imports** (1976): $800 mln.; partners (1973): U.K. 22%, So. Afr. 12%, U.S. 9%, Jap. 9%. **Exports** (1976): $1.05 bln.; partners (1974): Jap. 25% U.K. 20%, It. 12%, W. Ger. 10%. **Tourists** (1975): 51,700; receipts (1975): $10 million. **Balance of payments** (1977): −$29,000,000. **National budget** (1977): $658.3 mln. revenues; $934.17 mln. expenditures. **Inter- national reserves** (Mar. 1978): $62.6 mln. **Consumer prices** (change in 1977): 18.7%.

**Transport: Motor vehicles:** in use (1974): 85,800 passenger cars, 62,000 commercial vehicles. **Civil aviation:** 233 mln. pass- enger-miles (1976); 11,618 mln. freight ton-miles (1976).

**Communications: Television sets:** 22,000 licensed (1974). **Radios:** 100,000 in use (1974), 40,000 manufactured (1973). **Telephones in use** (1977): 55,403. **Daily newspaper circula- tion** (1974): 105,000; 22 per 1,000 pop.

**Health: Life expectancy at birth** (1975): 42.9 male; 46.1 fe- male. **Births** (annual per 1,000 pop. 1972-75): 51.5. **Deaths** (an- nual per 1,000 pop. 1972-75): 20.3. **Natural increase** (annual 1970-75: 3.12%. **Pop. per hospital bed** (1975): 352. **Pop. per physician** (1975): 12,340. **Infant mortality** (per 1,000 live births 1950): 259.

**Education: Literacy** (1975): 40%. **Pop. 5-19:** in school (1975): 51%, per teacher (1975): 89.

As Northern Rhodesia, the country was under the administra- tion of the South Africa Company, 1889 until 1924, when the of- fice of governor was established, and, subsequently, a legisla- ture. The country became an independent republic within the Commonwealth Oct. 24, 1964.

After the white government of Rhodesia declared its indepen- dence from Britain Nov. 11, 1965, relations between Zambia and Rhodesia became strained and use of their jointly owned rail- road was disputed.

Britain gave Zambia an extra $12 million aid in 1966 after im- posing an oil embargo on Rhodesia, and Zambia set up a tem- porary airlift to carry copper out from its mines and gasoline in. In Aug. 1968 a 1,058-mi. pipeline was completed, bringing oil from Tanzania. In 1973 a truck road to carry copper to Tanza- nia's port of Dar es Salaam was completed with U.S. aid. A rail- road, built with Chinese aid across Tanzania, reached the Zam- bian border in 1974.

As part of a program of government participation in major in- dustries, a government corporation in 1970 took over 51% of the ownership of 2 foreign-owned copper mining companies, paying with bonds. Privately-held land and other enterprises were na- tionalized in 1975, as were all newspapers. Decline in copper prices hurt the economy in the late 1970s, but was partly offset by increased Western aid.

---

# United Nations

The 33d regular session of the United Nations General sembly was scheduled to open in September, 1978. See ronology for developments at UN sessions during 1978.
Proposals to establish an organization of nations for ntenance of world peace led to the United Nations Con- nce on International Organization at San Francisco,

Apr. 25-June 26, 1945, where the charter of the United Na- tions was drawn up. It was signed June 26 by 50 nations, and by Poland, one of the original 51, on Oct. 15, 1945. The charter came into effect Oct. 24, 1945, upon ratification by the permanent members of the Security Council, (China, France, Soviet Union, United Kingdom and United States) and a majority of other signatories.

UN headquarters are in New York, N.Y., between First Ave. and Roosevelt Drive and E. 42nd St. and E. 48th St. The General Assembly Bldg., Secretariat, Conference and Library bldgs. are interconnected. A new UN office building-hotel was opened in New York in 1976. The UN has a post office originating its own stamps. *See Postal Information.*

A European office at Geneva includes Secretariat and agency staff members. Other offices of UN bodies and related organizations are scattered throughout the world.

## Roster of the United Nations

### (As of Aug. 1978)

The 149 members of the United Nations, with the years in which they became members.

| Member | Year | Member | Year | Member | Year | Member | Yea |
|---|---|---|---|---|---|---|---|
| Afghanistan | 1946 | Ecuador | 1945 | Laos | 1955 | Samoa (Western) | 197 |
| Albania | 1955 | Egypt[2] | 1945 | Lebanon | 1945 | Soa Tome e Principe | 197 |
| Algeria | 1962 | El Salvador | 1945 | Lesotho | 1966 | Saudi Arabia | 194 |
| Angola | 1976 | Equatorial Guinea | 1968 | Liberia | 1945 | Senegal | 196 |
| Argentina | 1945 | Ethiopia | 1945 | Libya | 1955 | Seychelles | 197 |
| Australia | 1945 | Fiji | 1970 | Luxembourg | 1945 | Sierra Leone | 196 |
| Austria | 1955 | Finland | 1955 | Madagascar (Malagasy) | 1960 | Singapore[1] | 196 |
| Bahamas | 1973 | France | 1945 | Malawi | 1964 | Somalia | 196 |
| Bahrain | 1971 | Gabon | 1960 | Malaysia[1] | 1957 | South Africa[5] | 194 |
| Bangladesh | 1974 | Gambia | 1965 | Maldives | 1965 | Spain | 195 |
| Barbados | 1966 | Germany, East | 1973 | Mali | 1960 | Sri Lanka | 195 |
| Belgium | 1945 | Germany, West | 1973 | Malta | 1964 | Sudan | 195 |
| Benin | 1960 | Ghana | 1957 | Mauritania | 1961 | Surinam | 197 |
| Bhutan | 1971 | Greece | 1945 | Mauritius | 1968 | Swaziland | 196 |
| Bolivia | 1945 | Grenada | 1974 | Mexico | 1945 | Sweden | 194 |
| Botswana | 1966 | Guatemala | 1945 | Mongolia | 1961 | Syria[3] | 194 |
| Brazil | 1945 | Guinea | 1958 | Morocco | 1956 | Tanzania[3] | 196 |
| Bulgaria | 1955 | Guinea-Bissau | 1974 | Mozambique | 1975 | Thailand | 194 |
| Burma | 1948 | Guyana | 1966 | Nepal | 1955 | Togo | 196 |
| Burundi | 1962 | Haiti | 1945 | Netherlands | 1945 | Trinidad & Tobago | 196 |
| Byelorussia | 1945 | Honduras | 1945 | New Zealand | 1945 | Tunisia | 195 |
| Cameroon | 1960 | Hungary | 1955 | Nicaragua | 1945 | Turkey | 194 |
| Canada | 1945 | Iceland | 1946 | Niger | 1960 | Uganda | 196 |
| Cape Verde | 1975 | India | 1945 | Nigeria | 1960 | Ukraine | 19 |
| Central Afr. Emp. | 1960 | Indonesia | 1950 | Norway | 1945 | Union of Soviet Soc. | |
| Chad | 1960 | Iran | 1945 | Oman | 1971 |   Repubs. | 19 |
| Chile | 1945 | Iraq | 1945 | Pakistan | 1947 | United Arab Emirates | 19 |
| China[4] | 1945 | Ireland | 1955 | Panama | 1945 | United Kingdom | 19 |
| Colombia | 1945 | Israel | 1949 | Papua New Guinea | 1975 | United States | 19 |
| Comoros | 1975 | Italy | 1955 | Paraguay | 1945 | Upper Volta | 19 |
| Congo | 1960 | Ivory Coast | 1960 | Peru | 1945 | Uruguay | 19 |
| Costa Rica | 1945 | Jamaica | 1962 | Philippines | 1945 | Venezuela | 19 |
| Cuba | 1945 | Japan | 1956 | Poland | 1945 | Vietnam | 19 |
| Cyprus | 1960 | Jordan | 1955 | Portugal | 1955 | Yemen | 19 |
| Czechoslovakia | 1945 | Kampuchea (Cambodia) | 1955 | Qatar | 1971 | Yemen, South | 19 |
| Denmark | 1945 | Kenya | 1963 | Romania | 1955 | Yugoslavia | 19 |
| Djibouti | 1977 | Kuwait | 1963 | Rwanda | 1962 | Zaire | 19 |
| Dominican Rep. | 1945 | | | | | Zambia | 19 |

(1) Malaya joined the UN in 1957. In 1963, its name was changed to Malaysia following the accession of Singapore, Sabah, and Sarawak. Singapore became an independent UN member in 1965.

(2) Egypt and Syria were original members of the UN. In 1958, the United Arab Republic was established by a union of Egypt and Syria and continued as a single member of the UN. In 1961, Syria resumed its separate membership.

(3) Tanganyika was a member of the United Nations from 1961 and Zanzibar was a member from 1963. Following the ratification in 1964 of Articles Union between Tanganyika and Zanzibar, the United Republic of Tanganyika and Zanzibar continued as a single member of the United Nations, later changing its name to United Republic of Tanzania.

(4) The General Assembly voted in 1971 to expel the Chinese government on Taiwan and admit the Peking government in its place.

(5) The General Assembly rejected the credentials of the South African delegates in 1974, and suspended the country from the Assembly.

## Organization

*The text of the UN Charter may be obtained from the Office of Public Information, United Nations, N.Y.*

**General Assembly.** The General Assembly is composed of representatives of all the member nations. Each nation is entitled to one vote.

The General Assembly meets in regular annual sessions and in special session when necessary. Special sessions are convoked by the Secretary General at the request of the Security Council or of a majority of the members of the UN.

On important questions a two-thirds majority of members present and voting is required; on other questions a simple majority is sufficient.

The General Assembly must approve the budget and apportion expenses among members. A member in arrears will have no vote if the amount of arrears equals or exceeds the amount of the contributions due for the preceeding two years.

**Security Council.** The Security Council consists of members, 5 with permanent seats. The remaining 10 elected for 2-year terms by the General Assembly; they not eligible for immediate reelection.

Permanent members of the Council: China, France, USSR, United Kingdom, United States.

Non-permanent members were Canada, W. Germany, dia, Mauritius, Venezuela (until Dec. 31, 1978), and Bolivia, Czechoslovakia, Gabon, Kuwait, and Nigeria (until Dec. 1979).

The Security Council has the primary responsiblity with

UN for maintaining international peace and security. Council may investigate any dispute that threatens international peace and security.

ny member of the UN at UN headquarters may partici-e in its discussions and a nation not a member of UN appear if it is a party to a dispute.

ecisions on procedural questions are made by an affir-ive vote of 9 members. On all other matters the affirma-vote of 9 members must include the concurring votes of permanent members; it is this clause which gives rise to so-called "veto." A party to a dispute must refrain from ng.

he Security Council directs the various truce supervisory es deployed in the Middle East, India-Pakistan, and Cy-s.

conomic and Social Council. The Economic and Social ncil consists of 54 members elected by the General As-bly for 3-year terms of office. The council is responsible ler the General Assembly for carrying out the functions the United Nations with regard to international eco-nic, social, cultural, educational, health and related mat-. The council meets usually twice a year.

rusteeship Council. The administration of trust territo-is under UN supervision. The only remaining trust terri-y is the Pacific Islands, administered by the U.S.

ecretariat. The Secretary General is the chief administra-officer of the UN. He may bring to the attention of the urity Council any matter that threatens international ce. He reports to the General Assembly.

urt Waldheim (Austria), Secretary General, was relected second 5-year term beginning Jan. 1, 1977.

he 1976-77 program budget was $784,000,000 exclusive rust funds and special contributions. This does not in-le expenses for the Specialized or the Related Organiza-s.

he US contributes 25% of the regular budget, the Soviet on 11.33%, Japan 8.66%, W. Germany 7.74%, and nce, China, and Britain about 5% each.

or further information, consult the Public Inquiries Unit, ice of Public Information, United Nations, N. Y.

## International Court of Justice

The International Court of Justice is the principal judicial an of the United Nations. All members are *ipso facto* ties to the statute of the Court, as are three nonmembers Leichtenstein, San Marino, and Switzerland. Other states y become parties to the Court's statute.

The jurisdiction of the Court comprises cases which the ties submit to it and matters especially provided for in charter or in treaties. The Court gives advisory opinions d renders judgments. Its decisions are only binding be-en the parties concerned and in respect to a particular pute. If any party to a case fails to heed a judgment, the er party may have recourse to the Security Council.

The 15 judges are elected for 9-year terms by the General sembly and the Security Council. Retiring judges are eli-le for re-election. The Court remains permanently in ses-n, except during vacations. All questions are decided by jority. The Court sits in The Hague, Netherlands.

### Judges

Nine year term in office ending 1985: Taslim Olawala as, Nigeria. Hermann Mosier, W. Germany. Shigeru Oda, an. Salah El Dine Tarazi, Syria. Manfred Lachs, Poland.

Nine year term in office ending 1982: Isaac Forster, Sene-. Andre Gros, France. Jose Maria Ruda, Argentina. gendra Singh, India. Sir Humphrey Waldock, Britain.

Nine year term in office ending 1979: Hardy C. Dillard, S. Louis Ignacio-Pinto, Benin. Federico de Castro, Spain. ton D. Morozov, USSR. Eduardo Jimenez de Arechaga, uguay.

The president until 1979 is Eduardo Jimenez de Arechaga, the vice president is Nagendra Singh.

## Specialized and Related Agencies

These agencies are autonomous, with their own member-ships and organs which have a functional relationship or working agreements with the UN.

International Labor Org. (ILO) aims to promote social justice; improve labor conditions and living standards; and promote economic stability. (Geneva, 137 member nations)

Food & Agriculture Org. (FAO) aims to increase produc-tion from farms, forests, and fisheries; improve distribution, marketing, and nutrition; better conditions for rural people. (Rome, 144)

United Nations Educational, Scientific, & Cultural Org. (UNESCO) aims to promote collaboration among nations in the fields of education, science, and culture. (Paris, 144)

World Health Org. (WHO) aims to aid the attainment of the highest possible level of health. (Geneva, 151)

International Monetary Fund (IMF) aims to promote in-ternational monetary co-operation and currency stabiliza-tion. (Washington, D.C., 134)

International Civil Aviation Org. (ICAO) promotes inter-national civil aviation standards and regulations. (Montreal, 143)

Universal Postal Union (UPU) aims to perfect postal ser-vices and promote international collaboration. To this end, members agree to handle other members' mail by the best means used for their own mail. (Berne, 159)

International Telecommunication Union (ITU) sets up international regulations of radio, telegraph, telephone and space radio-communications. Allocates radio frequencies. (Geneva, 154)

World Meteorological Org. (WMO) aims to co-ordinate and improve world meteorological work, and promotes op-erational hydrology. (Geneva 148)

Intergovernmental Maritime Consultative Org. (IMCO) aims to promote co-operation on technical matters affecting international shipping. (London, 106)

World Intellectual Property Organization (WIPO) seeks to protect, through international cooperation, literary, in-dustrial, scientific, and artistic works, i.e. "intellectual prop-erty." (Geneva, 106)

International Atomic Energy Agency (IAEA) aims to pro-mote the safe, peaceful uses of atomic energy. (Vienna, 110)

General Agreement on Tariffs and Trade (GATT). In force since 1948, it is the only treaty setting rules for world trade. Provides a forum for settling trade disputes and nego-tiating trade liberalization. (Geneva, 84 members, 3 provi-sional members, 24 de facto members).

International Bank for Reconstruction and Development (World Bank) assists the economic development of its devel-oping member countries by providing loans and technical assistance for development projects. The Bank encourages cofinancing for projects from other public and private sources, both bilateral and multilateral, and in this way helps to mobilize additional capital for development projects. (Washington, D.C., 132)

International Development Association (IDA), an affiliate of the Bank, provides funds for development projects on concessionary terms to the poorer developing member countries. (Washington, D.C., 120)

International Finance Corporation (IFC) promotes the growth of the private sector in developing member countries by providing equity and loan capital for private enterprises; it encourages the development of local capital markets, and stimulates the international flow of private capital. (Wash-ington, D.C., 108)

## Major International Organizations

Association of Southeast Asian Nations (ASEAN), was med in 1967 to promote political and economic coopera-n among the non-Communist states of the region. Mem-rs are Indonesia, Malaysia, Philippines, Singapore, Thai-land. Annual ministerial meetings set policy; a Secretariat and 11 permanent committees work in trade, transportation, communications, agriculture, science, finance, and culture.

The Commonwealth, originally called the British Commonwealth of Nations, is an association of nations and dependencies loosely joined by a common interest based on having been parts of the old British Empire. The British monarch is the symbolic head of the Commonwealth.

There are 36 self-governing independent nations in the Commonwealth, plus various colonies and protectorates. As of June 1977, the members were the United Kingdom of Great Britian and Northern Ireland and ten other nations recognizing the British monarch, represented by a governor-general, as their head of state: Australia, Bahamas, Barbados, Canada, Fiji, Grenada, Jamaica, Mauritius, New Zealand, and Papua New Guinea; and 25 countries with their own heads of state: Bangladesh, Botswana, Cyprus, Gambia, Ghana, Guyana, India, Kenya, Lesotho, Malawi, Malaysia, Malta, Nauru (a special member), Nigeria, Samoa, Seychelles, Sierra Leone, Singapore, Sri Lanka (Ceylon), Swaziland, Tanzania, Tonga, Trinidad and Tobago, Uganda, Zambia. In addition various Caribbean dependencies take part in certain Commonwealth activities.

The Commonwealth facilitates consultation among member states through meetings of prime ministers and finance ministers, and through a permanent Secretariat established in 1949. Members consult on economic, scientific, educational, financial, legal, and military matters, and try to coordinate policies. Population (est. 1978) was about one billion in the member nations; total area, over ten million sq. mi.

**European Communities (EC)** is the collective designation of three organizations with common membership: the European Economic Community (Common Market), the European Coal and Steel Community, and the European Atomic Energy Community. The nine full members are: Belgium, Denmark, France, West Germany, Ireland, Italy, Luxembourg, Netherlands, United Kingdom. The Common Market also includes as associate members Greece, Turkey, Cyprus, Malta, Morocco, and Tunisia. Portugal and Spain applied in 1977 for membership. Another 49 nations in Africa, the Caribbean, and the Pacific are affiliated under the Lome Convention. the Common Market also has trade agreements with EFTA members, Israel, and several Arab nations.

A coordinated structure for the communities went into effect July 1, 1967, though the component organizations date back to 1951 and 1957. A Council of Ministers, an expert Commission, a European Parliament and a Court of Justice comprise the permanent structure. The communities aim to integrate their economies, coordinate social developments, and ultimately, bring about political union of the democratic states of Europe.

Direct elections for the European Parliament are scheduled in member countries for June 1979 and that a uniform Western Europe passport would be issued in that year.

**European Free Trade Association (EFTA),** consisting of Austria, Iceland, Norway, Portugal, Sweden, Switzerland and associated member Finland, was created by treaty Jan. 4, 1960, effective May 3, to gradually reduce customs duties and quantitative restrictions between members on industrial products, By Dec. 31, 1966, tariffs and restrictions had been eliminated. The United Kingdom and Denmark withdrew to become members of EC Jan. 1, 1973. Other EFTA members joined in an industrial tariff elimination pact with EC in 1972. All industrial customs barriers between the two blocs were removed July 1, 1976.

**League of Arab States (The Arab League)** was created March 22, 1945, by Egypt, Iraq, Jordan, Lebanon, Saudi Arabia, Syria, and Yemen. Joining later were Algeria, Bahrain, Djibouti, Kuwait, Libya, Mauritania, Morocco, Oman, Qatar, Somalia, Southern Yemen, Sudan, Tunisia, and United Arab Emirates. The Palestine Liberation Org. has been admitted as a full member. Cairo is headquarters for the secretary-general. The League mediates disputes between Arab states, represents Arab states in certain international negotiations, and coordinates a military, economic, and diplomatic offensive against Israel. The League fosters cultural, economic, and communications ties among the Arab states.

**North Atlantic Treaty Org. (NATO)** was created April 4, 1949, in a treaty signed in Washington, effective Aug. 24, by Belgium, Canada, Denmark, France, Iceland, Italy, Luxembourg, the Netherlands, Norway, Portugal, and the United

Kingdom, and the U.S. Greece, Turkey, and West Germa have joined since. The members agreed to settle disputes peaceful means; to develop their individual and collect capacity to resist armed attack; to regard an attack on as an attack on all, and to take necessary action to repel attack under Article 51 of the United Nations Charter.

Armed forces of NATO members include forces assig to NATO commands, forces earmarked for NATO cc mands, and forces under national command. The NA military command has five branches: Allied Command rope, Allied Command Atlantic, Allied Command Chann Canada-U.S. Regional Planning Group, and Allied Force, Central Europe.

Following announcement in 1966 of nearly total Frer withdrawal from the military affairs of NATO, the organi tion moved its headquarters in 1967 from Paris to Brusse In August, 1974, Greece announced a total withdrawal armed forces from NATO, in response to Turkish interv tion in Cyprus. Nevertheless, Greece has continued to p ticipate in NATO military planning activities.

**Organization of African Unity (OAU),** formed May 1963 by 30 African countries (49 by 1978) to coordinate c tural, political, scientific and economic policies; to end co nialism in Africa; to promote a common defense of me bers' independence. It holds annual conferences of heads state, has a council of foreign ministers meeting at le twice a year, a secretary-general and a mediation-arbitrati commission. Hq. is in Addis Ababa, Ethiopia. The OA has helped formulate common policies on problems of tra sea law, etc.

**Organization of American States (OAS)** was formed Bogota, Colombia, in 1948. Hq. are in Washington, D.C. has a Permanent Council, Inter-American Economic a Social Council, and Inter-American Council for Educatic Science and Culture, a Juridical Committee and a Comm sion on Human Rights. The Permanent Council can c meetings of foreign ministers to deal with urgent secur matters. A General Assembly meets annually. A secreta general and assistant are elected for 5-year terms. There a 26 members, each with one vote in the various organiz tions: Argentina, Barbados, Bolivia, Brazil, Chile, Colomb Costa Rica, Cuba, Dominican Republic, Ecuador, El Salv dor, Grenada, Guatemala, Haiti, Honduras, Jamaica, Me ico, Nicaragua, Panama, Paraguay, Peru, Surinam, Trinida Tobago, U.S., Uruguay, Venezuela. In 1962, the OAS e cluded Cuba from OAS activities but not from membership

**Organization for Economic Cooperation and Develo ment (OECD)** was established in 1960 to promote stab economic growth in member countries and the world large, and to help expand free trade. Nearly all the indust alized "free market" countries belong, with Yugoslavia as a associate member. OECD is active in collecting and dissem nating economic and environmental information, and channeling resources to developing countries. Members 1977 were: Australia, Austria, Belgium, Canada, Denmar Finland, France, West Germany, Greece, Iceland, Irelan Italy, Japan, Luxembourg, Netherlands, New Zealand, Nc way, Portugal, Spain, Sweden, Switzerland, Turkey, Unite Kingdom, United States.

**Organization of Petroleum Exporting Countries (OPE** was created in 1960 at Venezuelan initiative. The group ha successfully maintained high oil prices, and has tried to a vance members' interests in trade and development dealing with industrialized oil-consuming nations. Members in 197 were Algeria, Ecuador, Gabon, Indonesia, Iran, Iraq, K wait, Libya, Nigeria, Qatar, Saudi Arabia, United Ara Emirates, Venezuela.

**Warsaw Treaty Organization (Warsaw Pact)** was create May 14, 1955, as a mutual defense alliance by Albania, Bu garia, Czechoslovakia, East Germany, Hungary, Polan Romania and the USSR. It provides for a unified milita command with headquarters in Moscow; if one member attacked, the others will aid it with all necessary steps i cluding armed force; joint maneuvers are held; there is a P litical Consultative Committee and economic cooperation advanced. Albania was barred from meetings in 1962, wit drew in 1968.

# Ambassadors and Envoys

Envoys to U.S. as of May 1978; envoys from U.S. as of July 1978.
The address of foreign embassies to the United States is Washington, D.C. The address of U.S. embassies abroad is simply the appropriate foreign capital.

| Countries | Envoys from United States | Envoys to United States |
|---|---|---|
| Afghanistan | Adolph Dubs, Amb.. | Ghulam Farouk Turabaz, Chargé |
| Algeria | Ulric St. Clair Haynes Jr., Amb. | Abdelaziz Maoui, Amb. |
| Angola[10] | | |
| Argentina | Raul H. Castro, Amb. | Jorge A. Aja Espil, Amb. |
| Australia | Philip H. Alston Jr., Amb. | Alan Philip Renouf, Amb. |
| Austria | Milton A. Wolf, Amb. | Karl Herbert Schober, Amb. |
| Bahamas | William B. Schwartz Jr. Amb. | Livingston B. Johnson, Amb. |
| Bahrain | Wat Tyler Cluverius IV, Amb. | Abdulaziz Abdulrahman Buali, Amb. |
| Bangladesh | David T. Schneider, Amb. | Mustafizur Rahman Siddiqi, Amb. |
| Barbados | Frank V. Ortiz, Amb. | Oliver H. Jackman, Amb. |
| Belgium | Anne Cox Chambers, Amb. | Willy Van Cauwenberg, Amb. |
| Benin | *Vacant* | Thomas S. Boya, Amb. |
| Bolivia | Paul H. Boeker, Amb. | Carlos Iturralde, Amb. |
| Botswana | Donald R. Norland, Amb. | Bias Mookodi, Amb. |
| Brazil | Robert Marion Sayre, Amb. | Joao Baptista Pinheiro, Amb. |
| Bulgaria | Raymond L. Garthoff, Amb. | Konstantin N. Grigorov Amb. |
| Burma | Maurice D. Bean, Amb. | U Tin Lat, Amb. |
| Burundi | Thomas J. Corcoran, Amb. | Laurent Nzeyimana, Amb. |
| Cameroon | Mabel Murphy Smythe, Amb. | Benoit Bindzi, Amb. |
| Canada | Thomas O. Enders, Amb. | Peter M. Towe, Amb. |
| Cape Verde | Edward Marks, Amb. | Raul Querido Varela, Amb. |
| Centr. African Emp. | *Vacant* | Christophe Maidou, Amb. |
| Chad | William G. Bradford, Amb. | Pierre Toura Gaba, Amb. |
| Chile | George W. Landau, Amb. | Jose Miguel Barros, Amb. |
| China (Taiwan) | Leonard Unger, Amb. | James C.H. Shen, Amb. |
| China, People's Rep. | Leonard Woodcock, Head of Liason[2] | Chaitse-min[2] |
| Colombia | Diego C. Asencio, Amb. | Virgilio Barco, Amb. |
| Congo (Brazzaville)[3] | | |
| Costa Rica | Marvin Weissman, Amb. | Jose Rafael Echeverria, Amb. |
| Cuba[4] | | |
| Cyprus | Galen L. Stone, Amb. | Nicos G. Dimitriou, Amb. |
| Czechoslovakia | Thomas R. Byrne, Amb. | Jaromir Johanes, Amb. |
| Denmark | Warren Demian Manshel, Amb. | Otto R. Borch, Amb. |
| Dominican Republic | Robert L. Yost, Amb. | Horacio Vicioso-Soto, Amb. |
| Ecuador | Raymond E. González, Amb.[11] | Gustavo Ycaza Borja, Amb. |
| Egypt | Hermann F. Eilts, Amb. | Ashraf A. Ghorbal, Amb. |
| El Salvador | Frank J. Devine, Amb. | Roberto Quinonez Meza, Amb. |
| Equatorial Guinea[9] | | |
| Estonia[5] | | Ernst Jaakson, Consul General |
| Ethiopia | Frederic L. Chapin, Amb. | Tibabu Bekele, Chargé |
| Fiji | John P. Condon, Amb. | Berenado Vunibobo, Amb. |
| Finland | Rozanne L. Ridgway, Amb. | Jaakko Iloniemi, Amb. |
| France | Arthur A. Hartman, Amb. | Francois de Laboulaye, Amb. |
| Gabon | Arthur T. Tienken, Amb. | Jean-Daniel Mambouka, Amb. |
| Gambia | Herman J. Cohen, Amb. | *Vacant* |
| Germany, East | David B. Bolen, Amb. | Rolf Sieber, Amb. |
| Germany, West | Walter J. Stoessel Jr., Amb. | Berndt von Staden, Amb. |
| Ghana | Robert P. Smith, Amb. | Alex Quaison-Sackey, Amb. |
| Greece | Robert J. McCloskey, Amb. | Menelas D. Alexandrakis, Amb. |
| Grenada | Frank V. Ortiz, Amb. | Franklin O'Brien Dolland, Amb. |
| Guatemala | Davis E. Boster, Amb. | Jorge Lamport-Rodil, Amb. |
| Guinea | Oliver S. Crosby, Amb. | Ibrahima Camara, Amb. |
| Guinea-Bissau | Edward Marks, Amb. | Gil Vicente Vaz Fernandes, Amb. |
| Guyana | John Richard Burke, Amb. | Laurence E. Mann, Amb. |
| Haiti | William Bowdoin Jones, Amb. | Georges Salomon, Amb. |
| Honduras | Mari Luci Jaramillo, Amb. | Roberto Lazarus, Amb. |
| Hungary | Philip M. Kaiser, Amb. | Ferenc Esztergalyos, Amb. |
| Iceland | James J. Blake, Amb. | Hans G. Andersen, Amb. |
| India | Robert F. Goheen, Amb. | N.A. Palkhivala, Amb. |
| Indonesia | Edward E. Masters, Amb. | D. Ashari, Amb. |
| Iran | William H. Sullivan, Amb. | Ardeshir Zahedi, Amb. |
| Iraq[8] | | |
| Ireland | William V. Shannon, Amb. | John G. Molloy, Amb. |
| Israel | Samuel W. Lewis, Amb. | Simcha Dinitz, Amb. |
| Italy | Richard N. Gardner, Amb. | Paolo Pansa Cedronio, Amb. |
| Ivory Coast | Monteagle Stearns, Amb. | Timothee N'Guetta Ahoua, Amb. |
| Jamaica | Frederick Irving, Amb. | Alfred A. Rattray, Amb. |
| Japan | Michael J. Mansfield, Amb. | Fumihiko Togo, Amb. |
| Jordan | Thomas R. Pickering, Amb. | Abdullah Salah, Amb. |
| Kampuchea (Cambodia)[1] | | |
| Kenya | Wilbert John Le Melle, Amb. | John P. Mbogua, Amb. |
| Korea, South | William H. Gleysteen, Jr. Amb. | Yong Shik Kim, Amb. |
| Kuwait | Frank E. Maestrone, Amb. | Khalid M. Jaffar, Amb. |
| Laos | *Vacant* | Somphong Vanitsaveth, Chargé |
| Latvia[5] | | Anatol Dinbergs, Chargé |
| Lebanon | Richard B. Parker, Amb. | Najati Kabbani, Amb. |
| Lesotho | Donald R. Norland, Amb. | Thabo R. Makeka, Amb. |
| Liberia | W. Beverly Carter Jr., Amb. | Francis A. Dennis, Amb. |
| Libya | *Vacant* | Ahmed Dia Addin Madfai, Chargé |
| Lithuania[5] | | Stasys A. Backis, Chargé |
| Luxembourg | James G. Lowenstein, Amb. | Adrien Meisch, Amb. |
| Madagascar | *Vacant* | Norbert Rakotomalala, Chargé |

| Countries | Envoys from United States | Envoys to United States |
|---|---|---|
| Malawi | Robert A. Stevenson, Amb. | Jacob T. X. Muwamba, Amb. |
| Malaysia | Robert H. Miller, Amb. | Zain Azraai, Amb. |
| Maldives, Rep. | W. Howard Wriggins, Amb. | *Vacant* |
| Mali | Patricia M. Byrne, Amb. | Alpha Amadou Diaw, Chargé |
| Malta | L. Bruce Laingen, Amb. | Victor Gauci, Chargé |
| Mauritania | E. Gregory Kryza, Amb. | Mohamed Nassim Kochman, Amb. |
| Mauritius | Robert V. Keeley, Amb. | Pierre Guy Girald Balancy, Amb. |
| Mexico | Patrick J. Lucey, Amb. | Hugo B. Margain, Amb. |
| Morocco | Robert Anderson, Amb. | Ali Bengelloun, Amb. |
| Mozambique | William A. De Pree, Amb. | |
| Nauru | Philip H. Alston Jr., Amb.[11] | *Vacant* |
| Nepal | L. Douglas Heck, Amb. | Padma Bahadur Khatri, Amb. |
| Netherlands | Geri M. Joseph, Amb.[11] | Age R. Tammenoms Bakker, Amb. |
| New Zealand | Armistead I. Selden Jr., Amb. | Merwyn Norrish, Amb. |
| Nicaragua | Mauricio Solaun, Amb. | Guillermo Sevilla-Sacasa, Amb. |
| Niger | Charles A. James, Amb. | Andre Wright, Amb. |
| Nigeria | Donald B. Easum, Amb. | Olujimi Jolaoso, Amb. |
| Norway | Louis A. Lerner, Amb. | Soren Christian Sommerfelt, Amb. |
| Oman | William D. Wolle, Amb. | Farid Mbarak Ali Al-Hinai, Amb. |
| Pakistan | Arthur W. Hummel Jr., Amb. | Sahabzada Yaqub-Kahn, Amb. |
| Panama | William J. Jorden, Amb. | Gabriel Lewis, Amb. |
| Papua New Guinea | Mary S. Olmsted, Amb. | Paulias Nguna Matane, Amb. |
| Paraguay | Robert E. White, Amb. | Mario Lopez Escobar, Amb. |
| Peru | Harry W. Shlaudeman, Amb. | Carlos Garcia-Bedoya, Amb. |
| Philippines | Richard W. Murphy, Amb. | Eduarado Z. Romualdez, Amb. |
| Poland | William E. Schaufele Jr., Amb. | Romuald Spasowski, Amb. |
| Portugal | Richard J. Bloomfield, Amb. | Joao Hall Themido, Amb. |
| Qatar | Andrew I. Killgore, Amb. | Abdullah Saleh Al-Mana, Amb. |
| Romania | O. Rudolph Aggrey, Amb. | Nicolae M. Nicolae, Amb. |
| Rwanda | T. Frank Crigler, Amb. | Bonaventure Ubalijoro, Amb. |
| Samoa | Armistead I. Selden Jr., Amb. | Maiava Iulai Toma, Amb. |
| Sao Tome and Principe | Arthur T. Tienken, Amb. | |
| Saudi Arabia | John C. West, Amb. | Ali Abdallah Alireza, Amb. |
| Senegal | Herman J. Cohen, Amb. | Andre Coulbary, Amb. |
| Seychelles | Wilbert John Le Melle, Amb. | |
| Sierra Leone | John A. Linehan, Amb. | Philip J. Palmer, Amb. |
| Singapore | Richard F. Kneip, Amb. | Punch Coomaraswamy, Amb. |
| Solomon Islands | Mary S. Olmsted[11] | |
| Somali, Democratic Rep. | James L. Loughran, Amb. | Adbullahi Ahmed Addou, Amb. |
| South Africa | William B. Edmondson, Amb. | Donald B. Sole, Amb. |
| Spain | W. Howard Wriggins, Amb. | Juan Jose Rovira, Amb. |
| Sri Lanka (Ceylon) | W. Howard Wriggins, Amb. | W.S. Karunaratne, Amb. |
| Sudan | Donald Clayton Bergus, Amb. | Omer Salih Eissa, Amb. |
| Surinam | Nancy Ostrander, Amb. | Roel F. Karamat, Amb. |
| Swaziland | Donald R. Norland, Amb. | Simon M. Kunene, Amb. |
| Sweden | Rodney O. Kennedy-Minott Amb. | Wilhelm Wachtmeister, Amb. |
| Switzerland | Marvin L. Warner, Amb. | Raymond Probst, Amb. |
| Syrian Arab Rep. | *Vacant* | Sabah Kabbani, Amb. |
| Tanzania | James W. Spain, Amb. | Paul Bomani, Amb. |
| Thailand | Morton I. Abramowitz, Amb. | Sukho Suwansiri, Chargé |
| Togo | *Vacant* | Messani Kokou Kekeh, Amb. |
| Tonga | Armistead I. Selden Jr., Amb. | *Vacant* |
| Trinidad and Tobago | Richard K. Fox Jr., Amb. | Victor C. McIntyre, Amb. |
| Tunisia | Edward W. Mulcahy, Amb. | Ali Hedda, Amb. |
| Turkey[?] | Ronald I. Spiers, Amb. | Melih Esenbel, Amb. |
| Uganda[?] | | Mahmud Musa, Chargé |
| USSR | Malcolm Toon, Amb. | Anatoliy F. Dobrynin, Amb. |
| United Arab Emirates | Francois M. Dickman, Amb. | Hamad Abdul Rahman Al Madfa, Amb. |
| United Kingdom | Kingman Brewster, Amb. | Peter Jay, Amb. |
| Upper Volta | Thomas D. Boyatt[11] | Telesphore Yaguibou, Amb. |
| Uruguay | Lawrence A. Pezzullo, Amb. | Jose Perez Caldas, Amb. |
| Venezuela | *Vacant* | Ignacio Iribarren, Amb. |
| Vietnam[1] | | |
| Yemen, South[8] | | |
| Yemen, Arab Rep. | Thomas J. Scotes, Amb. | Yahya M. Al-Mutawakel, Amb. |
| Yugoslavia | Lawrence S. Eagleburger, Amb. | Dimce Belovski, Amb. |
| Zaire | Walter L. Cutler, Amb. | Kasongo Mutuale, Amb. |
| Zambia | Steven Low, Amb. | Putteho M. Ngonda, Amb. |

Ambassadors at Large: Elliott L. Richardson, Alfred L. Atherton Jr., Arthur J. Goldberg, Gerard C. Smith.

## Special Missions Headed by Ambassadors

U.S. Mission to North Atlantic Treaty Organization, Brussels—W. Tapley Bennett Jr.
U.S. Mission to the European Communities, Brussels—Deane R. Hinton
U.S. Mission to the International Atomic Energy Agency, Vienna—Gerard C. Smith
U.S. Mission to the United Nations, New York—Andrew Young
U.S. Mission to the European Office of the UN & Other Internatl. Orgs., Geneva, William J. vanden Heuvel.
U.S. Mission to the Organization for Economic Cooperation and Development—Herbert Salzman
U.S. Mission to the Organization of American States, Washington—Gale McGee.
United Nations Educational, Scientific, and Cultural Organization, Paris—Esteban Edward Torres
Council of the International Civic Aviation Organization, Montreal—John E. Downs

(1) U.S. embassy closed in 1975. (2) Liaison officers. (3) U.S. embassy closed in 1965; ties restored in 1977. (4) Relations severed in 196_ limited ties restored in 1977. (5) U.S. does not officially recognize 1940 annexation by USSR. (6) Relations severed in 1967, limited sta_ returned in 1972; Belgium protects U.S. interests. (7) U.S. embassy closed in 1973; West Germany protects U.S. interests. (8) U.S. embass_ closed in 1969; UK serves as protective power. (9) U.S. severed relations in 1976. (10) Post temporarily closed in 1975. (11) Nominated.

# U.S. Aid to Foreign Nations

Source: Bureau of Economic Analysis, U.S. Commerce Department

Figures are for calendar year 1977, and are in millions of dollars. (*Less than $500,000.)

Data shown by country includes the military supplies and services furnished under the Foreign Assistance Act and direct Defense Department appropriations. Data shown includes credits which have been extended to private entities in the country specified.

Grants are largely outright gifts for which no payment is expected or which at most involve an obligation on the part of the receiver to extend aid to the U.S. or other countries to achieve a common objective.    Net grants and credits take into account all known returns to the U.S. government, including reverse grants, returns of grants, and payments of principal. A minus sign (—) indicates that the total of these returns to the U.S. is greater than the total of grants or credits.

Other assistance represents the transfer of U.S. farm products in exchange for foreign currencies, less the government's disbursements of the currencies as grants, credits, or for purchases.

Amounts do not include investments in international financial institutions in 1977 as follows: Asian Development Bank, $31 million; Inter-American Development Bank, $307 million; International Development Assn., $521 million; African Development Fund, $10 million.

| | Total | Net grants | Net credits | Net other | | Total | Net grants | Net credits | Net other |
|---|---|---|---|---|---|---|---|---|---|
| TOTAL . . . . . . . . . . | 5853 | 3032 | 2860 | —39 | Botswana . . . . . . . . | 5 | 3 | 2 | — |
| Military grants . . . . . | 757 | 757 | — | — | Burundi . . . . . . . . . | 2 | 2 | — | — |
| Other grants, credits, ass't. | 5096 | 2275 | 2860 | —39 | Cameroon . . . . . . . . | 9 | 6 | 4 | — |
| Western Europe. . . . . . | —51 | 19 | —62 | —8 | Cape Verde . . . . . . . | 4 | 4 | — | — |
| Austria . . . . . . . . . . | —4 | — | —4 | — | Chad . . . . . . . . . . . | 11 | 11 | — | — |
| Belgium-Luxembourg. . . | —8 | — | —8 | — | Congo . . . . . . . . . . | 1 | 1 | — | — |
| Finland . . . . . . . . . . | —2 | — | —2 | * | Ethiopia. . . . . . . . . | 14 | 10 | 3 | * |
| France . . . . . . . . . . | —27 | — | —27 | — | Gabon . . . . . . . . . . | 7 | * | 7 | — |
| Germany, West . . . . . . | —14 | — | —14 | * | Gambia . . . . . . . . . | 2 | 2 | — | — |
| Iceland . . . . . . . . . . | —3 | — | —3 | * | Ghana . . . . . . . . . . | 19 | 13 | 6 | * |
| Ireland . . . . . . . . . . | —13 | — | —13 | — | Guinea . . . . . . . . . | 9 | 1 | 6 | 2 |
| Italy . . . . . . . . . . . | 1 | 1 | (y) | — | Guinea-Bissau . . . . . | 2 | 2 | — | — |
| Malta . . . . . . . . . . . | 11 | 11 | — | — | Ivory Coast. . . . . . . | 8 | 1 | 7 | — |
| Netherlands . . . . . . . | —10 | — | —10 | — | Kenya. . . . . . . . . . | 58 | 8 | 50 | — |
| Norway. . . . . . . . . . | —36 | — | —36 | — | Lesotho. . . . . . . . . | 6 | 6 | — | — |
| Portugal . . . . . . . . . | 166 | 6 | 160 | * | Liberia . . . . . . . . . | —1 | 7 | —8 | — |
| Spain . . . . . . . . . . . | 33 | 1 | 32 | * | Madagascar . . . . . . | 1 | 2 | * | — |
| Sweden . . . . . . . . . . | 4 | — | 4 | — | Malawi . . . . . . . . . | 5 | 1 | 4 | — |
| Switzerland . . . . . . . | 5 | — | 5 | * | Mali . . . . . . . . . . . | 6 | 6 | * | — |
| United Kingdom . . . . . | —152 | — | —152 | — | Mauritania . . . . . . . | 3 | 3 | * | — |
| Yugoslavia . . . . . . . . | 23 | — | 31 | —8 | Mauritius . . . . . . . . | 1 | 1 | — | — |
| Atomic EC . . . . . . . . | —5 | — | —5 | — | Morocco . . . . . . . . | 37 | 21 | 14 | 1 |
| Coal-Steel EC . . . . . . | —6 | — | —6 | — | Mozambique . . . . . . | 8 | 8 | * | — |
| Other & unspecified. . . | —13 | — | —13 | — | Niger . . . . . . . . . . | 8 | 8 | * | — |
| Eastern Europe . . . . . . | 214 | * | 246 | —33 | Nigeria . . . . . . . . . | —7 | 1 | —8 | — |
| Poland . . . . . . . . . . | 135 | — | 168 | —33 | Rwanda . . . . . . . . . | 4 | 3 | * | — |
| Romania . . . . . . . . . | —21 | * | —21 | — | Senegal . . . . . . . . | 14 | 11 | 2 | * |
| Soviet Union . . . . . . . | 99 | — | 99 | — | Sierra Leone . . . . . . | 10 | 3 | 7 | — |
| Near East & South Asia . . | 2661 | 1028 | 1642 | —9 | Somalia . . . . . . . . . | 3 | 3 | * | * |
| Afghanistan . . . . . . . | 13 | 10 | 3 | * | Sudan . . . . . . . . . . | 9 | 3 | 7 | —1 |
| Bangladesh . . . . . . . | 97 | 35 | 62 | * | Swaziland . . . . . . . | 1 | 1 | — | — |
| Cyprus . . . . . . . . . . | 47 | 44 | 3 | * | Tanzania . . . . . . . . | 30 | 17 | 13 | — |
| Egypt . . . . . . . . . . . | 417 | 53 | 382 | —17 | Togo . . . . . . . . . . | 4 | 4 | * | — |
| Greece . . . . . . . . . . | 172 | * | 172 | * | Tunisia . . . . . . . . . | 33 | 11 | 24 | —2 |
| India . . . . . . . . . . . | 46 | 121 | —74 | —1 | Upper Volta . . . . . . | 15 | 14 | 1 | — |
| Iran . . . . . . . . . . . | —105 | * | —105 | * | Zaire . . . . . . . . . . | 116 | 4 | 112 | * |
| Israel . . . . . . . . . . . | 1476 | 592 | 883 | * | Zambia . . . . . . . . . | 31 | * | 31 | — |
| Jordan . . . . . . . . . . | 139 | 51 | 88 | * | Other & unspecified. . . | 39 | 37 | 2 | — |
| Lebanon . . . . . . . . . | 32 | 17 | 15 | * | Western Hemisphere. . . . | 434 | 235 | 199 | * |
| Nepal . . . . . . . . . . . | 12 | 9 | * | 3 | Argentina . . . . . . . . | 6 | * | 6 | * |
| Pakistan . . . . . . . . . | 84 | 15 | 66 | 4 | Bahamas . . . . . . . . | —21 | — | —21 | — |
| Saudi Arabia. . . . . . . | —4 | — | —4 | — | Barbados . . . . . . . . | 1 | 1 | * | — |
| Sri Lanka (Ceylon) . . . | 38 | 6 | 32 | * | Bermuda . . . . . . . . | —6 | — | —6 | — |
| Syria . . . . . . . . . . . | 48 | 9 | 38 | * | Bolivia . . . . . . . . . | 32 | 14 | 18 | * |
| Turkey . . . . . . . . . . | 83 | 1 | 81 | 1 | Brazil . . . . . . . . . . | 41 | 6 | 35 | * |
| Yemen (Aden). . . . . . . | 1 | — | 1 | — | Canada. . . . . . . . . | —19 | — | —19 | — |
| Yemen (Sana) . . . . . . | 7 | 7 | — | — | Cayman Islands . . . . . | 1 | — | 1 | — |
| Other & unspecified. . . | 59 | 59 | —1 | 1 | Chile . . . . . . . . . . | 12 | 23 | —10 | —1 |
| East Asia & Pacific . . . . | 720 | 195 | 514 | 12 | Colombia . . . . . . . . | 1 | 13 | —12 | * |
| Australia . . . . . . . . . | —50 | — | —50 | — | Costa Rica . . . . . . . | 5 | 6 | —1 | — |
| Burma . . . . . . . . . . | 8 | 9 | —1 | * | Dominican Republic. . . | 1 | 11 | —9 | — |
| China-Taiwan . . . . . . | 69 | * | 69 | — | Ecuador . . . . . . . . | 5 | 5 | 1 | * |
| Fiji. . . . . . . . . . . . | 1 | 1 | — | — | El Salvador . . . . . . . | 14 | 5 | 8 | — |
| Hong Kong. . . . . . . . | —4 | * | —4 | — | Guatemala . . . . . . . | 24 | 19 | 5 | — |
| Indonesia. . . . . . . . . | 163 | 16 | 146 | 1 | Guyana . . . . . . . . . | 6 | 1 | 5 | — |
| Japan . . . . . . . . . . . | —48 | * | —48 | * | Haiti. . . . . . . . . . . | 28 | 17 | 11 | — |
| Korea (So.) . . . . . . . | 250 | 3 | 237 | 10 | Honduras . . . . . . . . | 18 | 7 | 11 | — |
| Malaysia . . . . . . . . . | 24 | 3 | 21 | — | Jamaica . . . . . . . . | 7 | 2 | 5 | — |
| New Zealand . . . . . . . | 3 | * | 3 | — | Mexico . . . . . . . . . | 75 | * | 75 | — |
| Papua New Guinea . . . . | —18 | * | —18 | — | Nicaragua . . . . . . . | 21 | 4 | 17 | — |
| Philippines . . . . . . . . | 151 | 56 | 96 | * | Panama . . . . . . . . . | 10 | 13 | —3 | — |
| Singapore . . . . . . . . | —3 | * | —3 | — | Paraguay. . . . . . . . | 4 | 4 | * | — |
| Thailand . . . . . . . . . | 72 | 6 | 67 | — | Peru . . . . . . . . . . | 96 | 11 | 86 | * |
| Trust Terr. Pacific . . . . | 91 | 91 | — | — | Trinidad-Tobago . . . . . | —1 | — | —1 | — |
| Western Samoa . . . . . | 1 | 1 | — | — | Uruguay . . . . . . . . | * | 1 | —1 | — |
| Other & unspecified. . . | 10 | 9 | 1 | 1 | Venezuela . . . . . . . | —19 | * | —19 | — |
| Africa . . . . . . . . . . . | 576 | 252 | 325 | * | Other & unspecified. . . | 92 | 72 | 17 | 1 |
| Algeria . . . . . . . . . . | 40 | 8 | 32 | — | International organizations & unspecified areas . . . . | 541 | 546 | —4 | —1 |
| Benin . . . . . . . . . . . | 9 | 2 | 7 | — | | | | | |

## Travel Costs Around the World

These 1978 figures, compiled by the staff of the *Financial Times* of London, reflect costs for business travelers or tourists traveling first class. The hotel figure covers one night in a first class/international category hotel plus breakfast. Dinner cost is for a meal at an average high quality restaurant. Wine covers a bottle of house wine in a restaurant. The index rates the relative price levels, with New York taken as 100. In other words, services purchased in New York for $100 would cost $129 in Frankfurt, but only $50 in Lagos. Economy class travelers can expect large savings in most cities.

| City | Index | Hotel | Dinner | Wine | City | Index | Hotel | Dinner | Wine |
|---|---|---|---|---|---|---|---|---|---|
| Frankfurt, W. Germany | 129 | $71.47 | $31.08 | $11.54 | Athens, Greece | 61 | $54.68 | $12.86 | $ 4.67 |
| Brussels, Belgium | 119 | 61.38 | 19.89 | 5.02 | Columbo, Sri Lanka | 61 | 47.95 | 4.91 | 19.26 |
| Paris, France | 117 | 96.07 | 31.06 | 7.25 | Sydney, Australia | 59 | 48.17 | 12.73 | 3.18 |
| Buenos Aires, Argentina | 104 | 72.28 | 18.57 | 12.53 | Cairo, Egypt | 58 | 47.77 | 8.37 | 3.79 |
| Dubai, United Arab Emirates | 100 | 76.54 | 25.83 | 11.21 | Hong Kong | 57 | 41.69 | 19.17 | 7.08 |
| New York, N.Y. | 100 | 84.00 | 28.12 | 14.33 | Ankara, Turkey | 57 | 45.96 | 5.48 | 4.33 |
| Kuwait, Kuwait | 94 | 95.97 | 21.23 | — | Seoul, S. Korea | 56 | 39.39 | 12.00 | 14.66 |
| Manama, Bahrain | 94 | 86.92 | 17.81 | 6.99 | Jakarta, Indonesia | 55 | 41.00 | 9.99 | 6.99 |
| Rio de Janeiro, Brazil | 85 | 79.14 | 14.76 | 2.24 | Singapore | 55 | 42.23 | 4.18 | 10.18 |
| Nassau, Bahamas | 84 | 76.29 | 16.10 | 7.29 | Nairobi, Kenya | 54 | 40.35 | 7.56 | 12.36 |
| Khartoum, Sudan | 84 | 57.62 | 15.00 | 25.01 | Warsaw, Poland | 53 | 46.99 | 6.24 | 8.83 |
| Amsterdam, Netherlands | 83 | 66.90 | 25.10 | 6.00 | Moscow, USSR | 53 | 54.70 | 7.19 | 3.88 |
| Algiers, Algeria | 82 | 63.99 | 14.48 | 10.87 | Karachi, Pakistan | 52 | 29.02 | 1.55 | 31.10 |
| London, England | 81 | 74.43 | 14.72 | 5.19 | Rome, Italy | 51 | 46.17 | 4.54 | 2.93 |
| Tokyo, Japan | 79 | 50.91 | 26.46 | 10.95 | Tunis, Tunisia | 50 | 41.77 | 7.73 | 1.47 |
| Oslo, Norway | 79 | 48.96 | 27.51 | 12.95 | Lagos, Nigeria | 50 | 38.44 | 8.81 | 10.67 |
| Copenhagen, Denmark | 78 | 62.32 | 17.42 | 5.78 | Damascus, Syria | 49 | 44.99 | 6.00 | 4.51 |
| Chicago, Ill. | 77 | 68.15 | 12.49 | 5.21 | Dublin, Ireland | 49 | 37.17 | 14.50 | 5.83 |
| Stockholm, Sweden | 75 | 57.24 | 18.18 | 5.92 | Port-of-Spain, Trinidad | 48 | 41.49 | 7.29 | 5.72 |
| Teheran, Iran | 72 | 60.19 | 11.41 | 5.23 | Amman, Jordan | 47 | 43.55 | 7.51 | 3.74 |
| Montreal, P.Q. | 71 | 52.81 | 15.35 | 7.53 | Madrid, Spain | 47 | 33.60 | 15.60 | 1.80 |
| Geneva, Switzerland | 71 | 58.20 | 13.41 | 3.28 | Johannesburg, S. Africa | 44 | 38.97 | 8.65 | 3.15 |
| Jeddah, Saudi Arabia | 70 | 66.17 | 20.04 | — | Rabat, Morocco | 41 | 31.96 | 7.89 | 2.34 |
| Beirut, Lebanon | 69 | 58.70 | 17.50 | 4.80 | Wellington, New Zealand | 41 | 31.13 | 12.95 | 4.97 |
| Vienna, Austria | 68 | 54.39 | 9.33 | 3.48 | Kuala Lumpur, Malaysia | 40 | 31.59 | 7.89 | 9.14 |
| New Delhi, India | 67 | 52.57 | 5.74 | 20.37 | Mexico City, Mexico | 39 | 34.37 | 8.68 | 1.62 |
| Lusaka, Zambia | 62 | 40.41 | 10.03 | 21.18 | Birmingham, England | 39 | 33.30 | 6.44 | 4.71 |
| Helsinki, Finland | 62 | 43.83 | 19.74 | 5.17 | Lisbon, Portugal | 35 | 27.20 | 6.13 | 2.28 |
| Tel Aviv, Israel | 62 | 52.90 | 9.77 | 4.05 | Belgrade, Yugoslavia | 32 | 21.53 | 6.81 | 2.45 |
| Caracas, Venezuela | 62 | 47.45 | 10.47 | 12.02 | Salisbury, Rhodesia | 31 | 21.95 | 9.09 | 3.46 |
| | | | | | Nicosia, Cyprus | 28 | 25.52 | 5.15 | 1.38 |

## Population of World's Largest Urban Areas

City populations often cannot be used to compare urban areas because city limits may fall short of or exceed the built-up or urban area. The problem of comparison is compounded by the difficulty in obtaining reliable population data for a common year. The ranking of urban areas below represents one attempt at comparing the world's largest urban areas, taking into account, where necessary and within the limits of available data, urban development extending outward from the principal city named in the table. Thus, the Tokyo area included Tokyo plus neighboring smaller cities, towns and villages. (Some computations include Yokohama as part of Tokyo's urban population.) New York's urban area in 1970 included part or all the population of 10 New Jersey and 5 New York counties in addition to the 5 boroughs of New York City.

| | | | |
|---|---|---|---|
| New York, N.Y. (census, 1970) | 16,206,841 | Istanbul, Turkey (est. 1973) | 3,135,354 |
| Mexico City, Mexico (est. 1976) | 11,943,050 | Washington, D.C.-Md.-Va. (est. 1974) | 3,015,300 |
| Tokyo, Japan (est. 1974) | 11,622,651 | Manila, Philippines (est. 1973) | 3,000,000 |
| Shanghai, China (est. 1970) | 10,820,000 | Sydney, Australia (est. 1974) | 2,898,330 |
| Paris, France (census, 1975) | 9,863,000 | Rome, Italy (est. 1975) | 2,868,248 |
| Buenos Aires, Argentina (est. 1974) | 8,925,000 | Bogota, Colombia (census, 1973) | 2,855,065 |
| Osaka, Japan (census, 1973) | 7,838,722 | Shenyang (Mukden), China (est. 1970) | 2,800,000 |
| Moscow, USSR (est. 1976) | 7,734,000 | Montreal, Quebec (est. 1974) | 2,798,000 |
| Sao Paulo, Brazil (est. 1973) | 7,693,000 | Pusan, S. Korea (est. 1977) | 2,744,629 |
| Peking, China (est. 1970) | 7,570,000 | Toronto, Ontario (est. 1974) | 2,741,000 |
| Seoul, S. Korea (est. 1977) | 7,525,629 | Melbourne, Australia (est. 1974) | 2,620,400 |
| Los Angeles-Long Beach, Cal. (est. 1975) | 7,367,677 | Yokohama, Japan (census, 1975) | 2,620,000 |
| London, England (est. 1973) | 7,281,000 | Wuhan, China (est. 1970) | 2,560,000 |
| Calcutta, India (census, 1971) | 7,031,382 | Athens, Greece (census, 1971) | 2,540,000 |
| Chicago, Ill. (est. 1975) | 6,978,947 | Dallas-Ft. Worth, Tex. (est. 1974) | 2,498,500 |
| Bombay, India (census, 1971) | 5,970,575 | Pittsburgh, Pa. (est. 1975) | 2,401,245 |
| Cairo, Egypt (est. 1974) | 5,715,000 | Manchester, England (est. 1973) | 2,389,260 |
| Essen (Ruhr-Gebiet), W. Germany (est. 1971) | 5,425,000 | St. Louis, Mo. (est. 1974) | 2,371,400 |
| Philadelphia, Pa. (est. 1975) | 4,372,000 | Birmingham, England (est. 1973) | 2,358,980 |
| Rio de Janeiro, Brazil (est. 1973) | 4,658,000 | Chungking, China (est. 1970) | 2,300,000 |
| Jakarta, Indonesia (census, 1971) | 4,576,009 | Alexandria, Egypt (est. 1974) | 2,259,000 |
| Detroit, Mich. (est. 1974) | 4,434,300 | Singapore (est. 1975) | 2,250,000 |
| Hong Kong (est. 1975) | 4,370,000 | Houston, Tex. (est. 1974) | 2,222,700 |
| Leningrad, USSR (1975) | 4,311,000 | Canton, China (est. 1970) | 2,200,000 |
| Tientsin, China (est. 1970) | 4,280,000 | Caracas, Venezuela (est. 1970) | 2,175,400 |
| Teheran, Iran (est. 1973) | 4,002,000 | Lahore, Pakistan (census, 1972) | 2,165,372 |
| Bangkok, Thailand (est. 1973) | 3,967,081 | Baltimore, Md. (est. 1974) | 2,140,400 |
| Boston, Mass. (est. 1974) | 3,918,400 | Nagoya, Japan (est. 1975) | 2,083,11 |
| Delhi-New Delhi, India (census, 1971) | 3,647,023 | Cleveland, Oh. (est. 1975) | 2,064,19 |
| Madrid, Spain (est. 1974) | 3,520,320 | Budapest, Hungary (est. 1975) | 2,063,30 |
| Karachi, Pakistan (census, 1972) | 3,498,634 | Rangoon, Burma (est. 1973) | 2,056,11 |
| San Francisco-Oakland, Cal. (est. 1975) | 3,440,170 | Newark, N.J. (est. 1974) | 2,019,20 |
| Lima, Peru (census, 1972) | 3,302,523 | Minneapolis-St. Paul, Minn. (est. 1974) | 2,010,80 |
| Santiago, Chile (est. 1975) | 3,262,990 | Kinshasa, Zaire (est. 1974) | 2,008,35 |
| Madras, India (census, 1971) | 3,169,930 | Taipei, China (est. 1974) | 2,000,40 |
| Berlin, E. and W. Germany (est. 1974, 1975) | 3,142,444 | | |

# U.S. Passport, Visa, and Health Requirements

Source: Passport Office, U.S. State Department and U.S. Public Health Service

Passports are issued by the United States Department of tate to citizens and nationals of the United States for the urpose of documenting them for their foreign travel and entifying them as Americans. Some countries require a sa, or stamp of approval, to be affixed to the passport by ie consulate of the country to be visited, while others waive is formality. Also some countries, which do not require sas, require tourist cards from visitors making a short stay.

## How to Obtain a Passport

An applicant for a passport who has never been previusly issued a passport in his own name, must execute an pplication in person before (1) a passport agent; (2) a clerk f any federal court or state court of record or a judge or erk of any probate court, accepting applications; (3) a ostal employee designated by the postmaster at a Post Ofce which has been selected to accept passport applications; r (4) a diplomatic or consular officer of the U.S. abroad. A ife/husband who is to be included in the passport must ppear with the applicant and execute the application.

A passport previously issued to the applicant, or one in hch he was included, will be accepted as proof of citizenhip in lieu of the following documents. A person born in ie United States shall present his birth certificate. To be cceptable, the certificate must show the given name and urname, the date and place of birth and that the birth reord was filed shortly after birth. A delayed birth certificate record filed more than one year after the date of birth) is cceptable provided that it shows that the report of birth as supported by acceptable secondary evidence of birth.

If such primary evidence is not obtainable, a notice from ie registrar shall be submitted stating that no birth record xists. The notice shall be accompanied by the best obtainble secondary evidence such as a baptismal certificate, a ertificate of circumcision, or a hospital birth record.

A person in the U.S. who has been issued a passport in is own name within the last eight years may obtain a new assport by filling out, signing and mailing a passport by iail application together with his previous passport, two lentical signed photographs taken within the last 6 months nd the established fee to the nearest Passport Agency or to ie Passport Office in Wash., D.C. If, however, an applicant applying for a passport for the first time, if his prior passort was issued before his 18th birthday, if he wishes to inlude a person other than himself in the passport, or if he is pplying for an official, diplomatic, or other no-fee passport, e must execute a passport application in person before a 'assport Agent; a clerk of any federal court or state court of ecord or a judge or clerk of any probate court accepting pplications; a postal employee designated by the postmaser at a Post Office which has been selected to accept passort applications; or a diplomatic or consular officer of the J.S. abroad.

A naturalized citizen should present his naturalization ertificate. A person born abroad claiming citizenship nrough either a native-born or naturalized citizen must subnit a certificate of citizenship issued by the Immigration and Naturalization Service; or a Consular Report of Birth or Certification of Birth issued by the Dept. of State. If one of he above documents has not been obtained, he must submit vidence of citizenship of the parent(s) through whom citienship is claimed and evidence which would establish the arent/child relationship. Additionally, if through birth to \merican parent(s), parents' marriage certificate plus an afidavit from parent(s) showing periods and places of resilence or physical presence in the United States and abroad, pecifying periods spent abroad in the employment of the J.S. government, including the armed forces, or with certain nternational organizations; if through naturalization of parnts, evidence of admission to the United States for permanent residence.

Under certain conditions, married women must present vidence of marriage. Special laws govern women married rior to Mar. 3, 1931 and should be discussed with the peron executing the application.

The applicant shall establish his identity to the satisfacion of the person executing the application. Proof of iden-tity may be established through a personal knowledge of the applicant by the Clerk or Agent or by an item which contains the signature and either a physical description or photograph of the applicant. The following items of identification are acceptable; previous United States Passport; certificate of naturalization; driver's license (not temporary or learner's license); a governmental (Federal State, Municipal) identification card or pass.

A person included in the passport of another may not use the passport for travel unless he is accompanied by the bearer.

**Aliens** — An alien leaving the U.S. must request passport facilities from his home government. He must have a permit from his local Collector of Internal Revenue, and if he wishes to return he should request a re-entry permit from the Immigration and Naturalization Service if it is required.

**Contract Employees** — Persons traveling because of a contract with the Government must submit with their applications letters from their employer stating position, destination and purpose of travel, armed forces contract number, and expiration date of contract when pertinent.

## Photographs and Fees

**Photographs** — Identical photographs taken within six months, both signed by the applicant and which are a good likeness, must accompany the passport application. An individual photograph of the passport bearer is required at all times. An additional photograph must be submitted showing other persons to be included in the passport.

**Fees** — The passport fee is $10. A fee of $3 shall be charged for execution of the application. No execution fee is payable where a passport is applied for by mail. All applicants must pay the passport fee and, where applicable, the execution fee unless specifically exempted by law. A passport is valid for five years unless otherwise limited.

The loss or theft of a valid passport is a serious matter and should be reported in writing immediately to the Passport Office, Dept., of State, Wash., D.C. 20524, or to the nearest passport agency, or to the nearest consular office of the U.S. when abroad.

## Foreign Regulations

A visa is an endorsement or a notation, usually rubber stamped in a passport by a representative of the country to be visited. It certifies that the bearer of the passport is to be permitted to enter that country for a certain purpose and length of time. With the exception of the Iron Curtain countries, no visas are required for brief tourist travel to Western European countries. Authoritative visa information can be obtained by writing directly to foreign consular officials.

## Health Information

**Smallpox** — Vaccination is required for travel to many countries. An International Certificate of Vaccination is not required for travel from the United States directly to Europe, Canada, Mexico, Australia, and New Zealand. For travel to more than one country in the Caribbean, a Certificate may be required.

**Yellow Fever** — A few African countries require a Vaccination Certificate of all travelers. A number of countries require vaccination if travelers arrive from infected or endemic areas. Vaccination is recommended for travel to infected areas, currently parts of Africa and South America. The United States has no vaccination requirement.

**Cholera** — A few countries require vaccination if travelers arrive from infected areas. The United States has no vaccination requirement.

**Plague** — Vaccination is not required by any country as a condition of entry. Selective immunization is advisable for travelers to Vietnam, Cambodia and Laos.

**Vaccination Information** — Yellow fever vaccine must be obtained at an officially designated Yellow Fever Vaccination Center, and the Certificate, valid for 10 years, must be stamped by the Center. Other vaccinations may be obtained from licensed physicians, and sometimes from local health departments.

Travelers are advised to contact their local health department 2 weeks prior to departure to obtain the most current information on countries to be visited.

## Passports Issued and Renewed

Source: Passport Office, U.S. State Department

Passports are actual count; other data based on sample.

| Item | 1960 | 1970⁵ | 1972 | 1973 | 1974 | 1975 | 1976 | 1977 |
|---|---|---|---|---|---|---|---|---|
| New and renewed passports... | 853,087 | 2,219,159 | 2,728,021 | 2,729,104 | 2,415,003 | 2,334,359 | 2,816,683 | 3,107,12 |
| **Object of Travel¹** | | | | | | | | |
| Government | 115,910 | 146,169 | 136,901 | 146,494 | 206,343 | 210,399 | 287,393 | 718,58 |
| Nongovernment | 737,177 | 2,072,990 | 2,591,120 | 2,582,610 | 2,208,660 | 2,123,960 | 2,529,290 | 2,388,54 |
| Personal reasons² | 321,590 | 1,791,330 | 2,042,560 | 1,245,780 | 384,930 | 376,400 | 602,980 | 1,005,63 |
| Pleasure³ | 350,897 | 216,700 | 441,010 | 1,077,240 | 1,382,100 | 1,315,600 | 1,511,060 | 1,102,25 |
| Business⁴ | 24,540 | 39,940 | 68,700 | 154,820 | 267,980 | 273,110 | 272,600 | 190,89 |
| Education | 31,240 | 20,230 | 33,290 | 95,240 | 153,210 | 132,490 | 125,590 | 78,55 |
| Religion | 6,780 | 3,350 | 3,980 | 7,930 | 16,510 | 22,450 | 13,690 | 9,16 |
| Health | 1,460 | 640 | 800 | 1,140 | 1,860 | 1,510 | 1,500 | 1,09 |
| Other | 670 | 800 | 780 | 460 | 2,070 | 2,400 | 1,870 | 97 |
| **First area destination:** | | | | | | | | |
| Africa | 8,440 | 18,790 | 29,750 | 26,420 | 32,110 | 32,930 | 35,390 | 33,98 |
| Australia and Oceania | 35,220 | 51,210 | 78,580 | 80,670 | 101,250 | 96,300 | 106,540 | 108,28 |
| Europe | 669,662 | 1,910,169 | 2,244,161 | 2,181,114 | 1,714,613 | 1,611,410 | 1,990,993 | 2,291,94 |
| Far East | 55,960 | 116,730 | 135,230 | 139,740 | 162,130 | 154,660 | 180,090 | 187,13 |
| North, Central, and South America | 58,935 | 72,410 | 135,720 | 189,280 | 287,260 | 317,980 | 347,020 | 316,59 |
| Middle-East | 24,670 | 48,890 | 103,870 | 111,000 | 117,110 | 121,010 | 156,530 | 169,06 |
| World Tour | 200 | 960 | 710 | 880 | 530 | 60 | 120 | 14 |
| **Sex of passport recipients:** | | | | | | | | |
| Male | 419,615 | 1,123,620 | 1,358,530 | 1,321,050 | 1,154,940 | 1,128,050 | 1,353,610 | 1,496,25 |
| Female | 433,472 | 1,095,539 | 1,369,491 | 1,408,054 | 1,260,063 | 1,206,309 | 1,463,073 | 1,610,87 |
| **Citizenship of passport recipients:** | | | | | | | | |
| Native | 710,172 | 2,072,560 | 2,553,750 | 2,511,266 | 2,154,920 | 2,039,690 | 2,458,050 | 2,853,29 |
| Naturalized | 142,915 | 146,599 | 174,271 | 217,838 | 260,083 | 294,669 | 358,633 | 253,83 |

(1) Data not entirely comparable because of changes in classifications in 1961. (2) Includes "Personal business," "Join hu band," "Accompany husband," "Business and pleasure," "Visit family." (3) Includes "Sightsee," "Vacation," "Visit," an "Tourist." (4) Includes applications formerly listed under "Employment" and "Commercial business." (5) Legislation effe tive Aug. 26, 1968 eliminated passport renewals. (6) Includes approximately 400,000 passports of applicants that did not in dicate the object of travel.

---

## Customs Exemptions and Advice to Travelers

United States residents returning after a stay abroad of at least 48 hours are, generally speaking, granted customs exemptions of $100 each. Each returning resident may bring home free of duty articles totaling $100 in fair retail value in the country of acquisition, subject to limitations on liquors and cigars. These articles must accompany the traveler at the time of his return, must be for his personal or household use, must have been acquired as an incident of his trip, and must be properly declared to Customs. Not more than one quart of alcoholic beverages may be included in the $100 exemption.

If a U.S. resident arrives directly or indirectly from American Samoa, Guam, or the Virgin Islands of the United States, his purchase may be valued up to $200 fair retail value, but not more than $100 of the exemption may be applied to the value of articles acquired elsewhere than in such insular possessions, and one gallon of alcoholic beverages may be included in his exemption, but not more than 1 quart of such beverages may have been acquired elsewhere than in the designated islands.

In either case, the exemption for alcoholic beverages is accorded only when the returning resident has attained 21 years of age at the time of his arrival. One hundred cigar may be included (except Cuban products) in either exemp tion.

The $100 or $200 exemption may be granted only if th exemption, or any part of it, has not been used within th preceding 30-day period and your stay abroad was for a least 48 hours. The 48-hour absence requirement does nc apply if you return from Mexico or the Virgin Islands of th United States.

Bona fide gifts costing no more than $10 fair retail valu or $20 from American Samoa, Guam, or Virgin Island may be mailed to friends at home duty-free; addressee can not receive in a single day gifts exceeding the $10 limit.

### Precautions for Travel

In some cases naturalized United States citizens desirin to visit the countries of their birth, and sometimes thei American-born children traveling to those countries, may b subject to military service and other regulations there. Th United States Department of State advises such travelers t get specific information from the consulates of the countrie concerned before departure.

## U.S. Immigration Law

Source: Immigration and Naturalization Service, U.S. Justice Department

The Immigration and Nationality Act as amended by the Act of October 3, 1965, and the Immigration and Nationality Amendments of 1976 (P.L. 94-571) "marked the final end of an immigration quota system based on nationality." The latter amendments eliminated inequities in the existing law regarding the admission of immigrants from countries in the Western Hemisphere. The seven-category preference system, the 20,000 per-country limit, and the provisions for adjustment of status, all of which were in effect for Eastern Hemisphere countries, were extended to the Western Hemisphere.

The Immigration and Nationality Act, as amended, provides for the numerical limitation of most immigration. Not subject to any numerical limitations are immigrants classified as immediate relatives who are spouses or children of U.S. citizens, or parents of citizens who are 21 years of age or older; returning residents; certain former U.S. citizens ministers of religion; and certain long-term U.S. governmen employees.

### Numerical Limitation of Immigrants

Immigration to the U.S. is numerically limited to 290,00 per year. This ceiling is subdivided into an annual limitatio of 170,000 for the Eastern and 120,000 for the Wester Hemisphere. Within each of these ceilings there is an annua limitation of 20,000 for each country. The colonies and de pendencies of foreign states are limited to 600 per yea chargeable to the hemisphere in which the area is locate and to the per-country limit of the mother country.

### Visa Categories

Applicants for immigration are classified as either prefer

ce or nonpreference. The preference visa categories are used on certain relationships to persons in the U.S., i.e., unmarried sons and daughters over 21 of U.S. citizens, spouses and unmarried sons and daughters of resident aliens, married sons and daughters of U.S. citizens, brothers and sisters of U.S. citizens 21 or over (first, 2d, 4th, and 5th reference, respectively); members of the professions or persons of exceptional ability in the sciences and arts whose services are sought by U.S. employers (3rd preference); and skilled and unskilled workers in short supply (6th preference); refugees (7th preference). Spouses and children of reference applicants are entitled to the same preference if accompanying or following to join such persons.

Except for refugee status, preference status is based upon approved petitions, filed with the Immigration and Naturalization Service, by the appropriate relative or employer (or in the 3rd preference by the alien himself). Visa numbers for qualified preference applicants are made available in the order of the filing dates of the petitions. Each preference is allotted a certain percentage of the hemisphere total.

Other immigrants not within one of the above-mentioned preference groups may qualify as nonpreference applicants and receive only those visa numbers not needed by preference applicants.

### Labor Certification

The Act of October 3, 1965, established new controls to protect the American labor market from an influx of skilled and unskilled foreign labor. Prior to the issuance of a visa, the would-be 3rd, 6th, and nonpreference immigrant must obtain the Secretary of Labor's certification, establishing that there are not sufficient workers in the U.S. at the alien's destination who are able, willing, and qualified to perform the job; and that the employment of the alien will not ad-

versely affect the wages and working conditions of workers in the U.S. similarly employed; or that there is satisfactory evidence that the provisions of that section do not apply to the alien's case.

### Extension of Adjustment of Status

The Act of October 3, 1965, excluded Western Hemisphere natives from adjusting their status to permanent residence under Section 245 of the Immigration and Nationality Act which allows a nonimmigrant alien to adjust to permanent resident without leaving the U.S. to secure a visa. The 1976 Amendments restored the adjustment of status provision to Western Hemisphere natives, and declared ineligible for adjustment of status aliens who are not defined as immediate relatives and who accept unauthorized employment prior to filing their adjustment application.

### Excludable Aliens

Aliens who are excludable on medical grounds are those who are mentally retarded, insane, psychopathic, mentally defective, sexual deviates, chronic alcoholics, narcotic addicts, and those who are afflicted with any dangerous contagious disease or who have a physical defect impairing the ability to earn a living. Also excludable are paupers, beggers, illiterates, stowaways, prostitutes, persons engaged in commercial vice, narcotics traffickers, persons convicted of crimes involving moral turpitude, persons who obtain or try to obtain a visa by fraud, or who left the U.S. to avoid military service. Those excludable on security grounds include persons who are anarchists, members or affiliates of certain proscribed organizations, and those who teach or advocate overthrow of the U.S. Government by force or violence.

For more detailed information consult the nearest office of the U.S. Immigration & Naturalization Service, or any U.S. Consul abroad.

## Immigrants Admitted from All Countries

Fiscal Year Ends June 30 through 1976, Sept. 30 thereafter

| Year | Number | Year | Number | Year | Number | Year | Number |
|------|--------|------|--------|------|--------|------|--------|
| 1820 . . . . . . | 8,385 | 1881-1890 . . . | 5,246,613 | 1941-1950 . . . | 1,035,039 | 1974 . . . . . . | 394,861 |
| 1821-1830 . . . | 143,439 | 1891-1900 . . . | 3,687,564 | 1951-1960 . . . | 2,515,479 | 1975 . . . . . . | 386,194 |
| 1831-1840 . . . | 599,125 | 1901-1910 . . . | 8,795,386 | 1961-1970 . . . | 3,321,777 | 1976 . . . . . . . | 398,613 |
| 1841-1850 . . . | 1,713,251 | 1911-1920 . . . | 5,735,811 | 1971 . . . . . . | 370,478 | 1976 July-Sept. | 103,676 |
| 1851-1860 . . . | 2,598,214 | 1921-1930 . . . | 4,107,209 | 1972 . . . . . . | 384,685 | 1977 . . . . . . | 462,315 |
| 1861-1870 . . . | 2,314,824 | 1931-1940 . . . | 528,431 | 1973 . . . . . . | 400,063 | **1820-1977 . . .** | **42,063,523** |
| 1871-1880 . . . | 2,812,191 | | | | | | |

## Naturalization: How to Become an American Citizen

### Source: The Federal Statutes

A person who desires to be naturalized as a citizen of the United States may obtain the necessary application form as well as detailed information from the nearest office of the Immigration and Naturalization Service or from the clerk of court handling naturalization cases.

There are no racial bars to naturalization. Women have the same right as men to become naturalized.

An applicant must be at least 18 years old. He must have been a lawful resident of the United States continuously for 5 years. For husbands and wives of U.S. citizens the period is 3 years in most instances. Special provisions apply to certain veterans of the Armed Forces.

An applicant must have been physically present in this country for at least half of the required 5 years' residence.

Every applicant for naturalization must:

(1) sign the petition in his own handwriting, if physically able to write.

(2) demonstrate an understanding of the English language, including an ability to read, write, and speak words in ordinary usage in the English language (persons physically unable to do so, and persons who were on December 24, 1952 over 50 years of age and had been residing in the United States for 20 years are excepted).

(3) have been a person of good moral character, attached to the principles of the Constitution, and well disposed to the good order and happiness of the United States for five years just before filing the petition or for whatever other period of residence is required in his case and continue to be such a person until admitted to citizenship; and

(4) demonstrate a knowledge and understanding of the fundamentals of the history, and the principles and form of government, of the U.S.

The petitioner also is obliged to have two credible citizen witnesses. These witnesses must have personal knowledge of the applicant.

A person not of good moral character includes a habitual drunkard, an adulterer, a polygamist, a violator of criminal law, a gambler, one who gave false testimony to obtain a benefit under the immigration law, one in prison for 180 days or more, one convicted of murder.

Naturalization is denied to any person who, within 10 years, has been subversive, including communists and others who favor totalitarian government, and who were members of a proscribed organization, unless the petitioner was under 16 or joined under duress.

When the applicant files his petition he pays the court clerk $25. At the preliminary hearing he may be represented by a lawyer or social service agency. There is a 30-day wait. If action is favorable, there is a final hearing before a judge, who administers the following oath of allegiance:

### Oath of Allegiance

I hereby declare, on oath, that I absolutely and entirely renounce and abjure all allegiance and fidelity to any foreign prince, potentate, state or sovereignty, to whom or which I have heretofore been a subject or citizen; that I will support and defend the Constitution and laws of the United States of America against all enemies, foreign and domestic; that I will bear true faith and allegiance to the same; that I will bear arms on behalf of the United States when required by the law; that I will perform noncombatant service in the armed forces of the United States when required by the law; that I will perform work of national importance under civilian direction when required by the law; and that I take this obligation freely without any mental reservation or purpose of evasion; so help me God.

# NORTH AMERICAN CITIES

### Their History, Business and Industry, Educational Facilities, Cultural Advantages, Tourist Attractions and Transportation

## Akron, Ohio

The World Almanac is sponsored in the Akron area by the Akron Beacon Journal, 44 E. Exchange Stree Akron, OH 44328; (216) 375-8111; a Knight-Ridder newspaper; founded 1809; circulation 167,040, daily 215,559, Sunday; John S. Knight, editor emeritus; Keith L. McGlade, vice president and general manage Paul Poorman, editor and vice president.

**Population:** 251,750 (city), 667,900 (metro) 5th in state; total employed 269,500; 1977 average metro median household effective household buying income $15,045.

**Area:** 56 sq. mi. (city), 413 sq. mi. (metro) on Ohio Canal 30 mi. south of Lake Erie; founded 1825; Summit County seat.

**Industry:** approx. $929.5 million value added by Akron area mfg. industry in 1977; home plants of Firestone, Goodyear, Goodrich, General and many smaller rubber firms employ 26,640, use 40% of entire world rubber supply; other products mfd. in area include auto bodies, salt, clay, matches, rubber toys, road building equipment, missile components.

**Transportation:** Akron-Canton Airport served by 3 major carriers; Akron Muni Airport; Conrail covers 9 former private rail and trunk lines; birthplace of trucking industry, served by 70 common and 50 contract carriers; metro transit system; Greyhound and Continental Trailways; 3 taxicab firms; city bisected east-west and north-south by interstate highway systems.

**Communications:** 5 TV, one cablevision, and 5 radio stations; 2 public broadcast TV outlets.

**New construction:** $13 million Northeastern Ohio Univ. College of Medicine; $16 million Ohio Edison Co. headquarters; $56 million downtown energy recycle plant; $10 million in additions to the Univ. of Akron; $6 million Akron Art Institute expansion program; $35 million in additions to 2 major hospitals; $125 million in new construction started in 1977.

**Federal facilities:** $17 million downtown federal office bldg Army Reserve Center; Navy-Marine Reserve Center.

**Medical facilities:** 7 major hospitals including specialize children's treatment center; State of Ohio Fallsview Psychi atric Hospital.

**Education:** University of Akron and School of Law; Ken State University; Firestone Conservatory of Music.

**Sports:** NBA Cleveland Cavaliers and WTT Nets play i nearby Richfield Township Coliseum; Firestone Countr Club, home of the World Series of Golf, American Go Classic; 35,000-seat Akron Rubber Bowl; Derby Downs home of the All-American Soap Box Derby; home of th annual PBA $100,000 Firestone Tournament of Champions

**Cultural attractions:** E. J. Thomas Performing Arts Center Blossom Music Center, summer home of the Cleveland Or chestra; Stan Hywet mansion; Akron Art Institute; Akron Symphony Orchestra.

**Other attractions:** Children's Zoo; John Brown Home; Si mon Perkins Mansion; Railway Museum.

**Accommodations:** Nearly 2,500 Class A hotel and mote rooms in the metro area.

**Further information:** Akron Regional Development Board Delaware Bldg., or Akron Convention Bureau, 1 Cascad Plaza, both Akron, OH 44308.

## Albuquerque, New Mexico

The World Almanac is sponsored in the Albuquerque area by the Albuquerque Tribune, 717 Silver Avenue SW, Albuquerque, NM 87101; (505) 842-2300; founded June 22, 1922 by Carl Magee; a Scripps-Howard Newspaper since Sept. 24, 1923; circulation 39,066; editor Ralph Looney; sponsors Tribune Annual Spelling Bee.

**Population:** 289,900 (city), 376,600 (county), 388,200 (metro area); first in state, 53d in nation; total employed 170,120 (1978).

**Area:** 87.1 sq. mi. on Rio Grande and Interstates 40, 25 and U.S. 66. Bernalillo County seat.

**Industry:** electronics with GTE-Lenkurt, Gulton, Sparton, Sandia Laboratories, General Electric, Digital Equipment Corp.; clothing with Levi Strauss, Pioneer Wear; movie production center.

**Commerce:** retail sales $1.57 billion; per capita income $5,801; bank resources $1.654 billion in 12 banks.

**Transportation:** Santa Fe Railway; Amtrak; Continental Trailways and Greyhound bus lines; Albuquerque Int'l Airport, hub for 7 airlines, average 646 air movements daily.

**Communications:** 5 TV and 20 radio stations.

**New construction:** value of building permits in 1977, $252 million, up from $140 million in 1976.

**Medical facilities:** 9 major hospitals.

**Cultural facilities:** symphony orchestra, 37 art galleries, museums, 8 library branches, 16 legitimate theaters.

**Educational facilities:** Univ. of New Mexico, Univ. of Albuquerque, 113 public schools.

**Recreational facilities:** Sandia Peak ski area with longes tramway in North America; 130 city parks, 17 swimming pools, 9 golf courses, 109 tennis courts; Cibola National Forest, Rio Grande Zoo.

**Convention facilities:** $9.2 million convention center with underground parking facility and 300-room hotel; 106 motels and hotels.

**Sports:** Dukes AAA baseball, Univ. of New Mexico athletic activities.

**History:** founded Feb. 7, 1706; named for Duke of Albur querque, viceroy of New Spain.

**Further information:** Chamber of Commerce, 401 2d NW, Albuquerque, NM 87102.

## Allentown, Pennsylvania

The World Almanac is sponsored in the Allentown-Bethlehem-Easton area by Call-Chronicle Newspapers 101 North 6th Street, Allentown, PA 18105; (215) 820-6500; Call founded 1883, daily circulation 103,000 Saturday Weekender 113,000; Sunday 158,000; Chronicle founded 1870, circulation 22,500; publisher Donald P. Miller, executive editor Edward D. Miller; sponsors Park & Shop, housing development, newspaper-in-the-classroom; newsprint recycling, mini-marathon.

**Population:** Allentown 109,871; Bethlehem 73,084; Easton 30,256; metro area 630,000, 3d in state; total employed

279,000.
**Area:** 1,490 sq. mi. (metro) in eastern Pa. at Lehigh and Delaware rivers; Lehigh County seat.
**Industry:** Bethlehem Steel Corp., 2d largest in U.S.; home offices for Mack Truck Inc., Air Products & Chemicals, Martin Guitar, Rodale Press, New Jersey Zinc Co., Allen Products (ALPO); area leads in textile production; transistor developed in Western Electric here. Other industries include Kraft Foods, F.&M. Schaefer Brewing Co., American Can Co. (Dixie), Durkee Foods.
**Commerce:** 3d largest Pa. market; metro retail sales $2 billion; average family buying power $16,674.
**Transportation:** 4 major rail lines, 5 bus lines; 9 federal and state highways intersect area; jet airport serves 575,000 passengers annually on 5 airlines.
**Communications:** 4 TV and 12 radio stations.
**Medical facilities:** 6 major hospitals.
**Cultural facilities:** Allentown Art Museum (including Kress Renaissance and Baroque collection), Bethlehem Bach Choir, Allentown Symphony, 8 theater groups (plus 4 sum-

mer); Allentown Band is oldest continuing concert band in U.S.; 10 colleges including Lehigh Univ., Muhlenberg, Cedar Crest, and Lafayette serve 12,000 students.
**Other attractions:** center of "Pennsylvania Dutch" area, covered bridges; 1,400-acre park system; 1,170-acre game preserve, pre-Cambrian mountain range, access to Appalachian Trail, many historic houses, Allentown Fair, Kutztown Folk Festival, Liberty Bell Shrine.
**Sports:** fishing, small game hunting, auto racing at Pocono Raceway, Allentown Jets basketball, Olympic bicycle velodrome at Trexlertown.
**History:** settled in 1600s by Germans seeking religious freedom; Allentown founded 1762; hiding place for Liberty Bell during Revolutionary War; GAR founded Flag Day here 1906; Allentown one of 5 First Defender Companies in Civil War.
**Further information:** Chambers of Commerce in Allentown: 462 Walnut Street, 18105; Bethlehem: 11 W. Market Street, 18018; Easton: 157 S. 4th Street, 18042.

---

## Amarillo, Texas

The World Almanac is sponsored in the Amarillo area by the Amarillo Globe-News, 900 S. Harrison, Amarillo, TX 79166, (806) 367-4488; a division of the Southwestern Newspapers Corp., and publisher of Daily News, Globe-Times and Sunday News-Globe; James L. Whyte, vice president and general manager; Jerry Huff, executive editor.

**Population:** 154,088 city; 175,162 metro area; 10th in state; total employed 85,270.
**Area:** 76.23 sq. mi. in central panhandle of Texas at junction of Interstate 40 and 27 in Potter and Randall counties; Potter County seat.
**Industry:** 3-state hub of $8.5 billion agribusiness market including wheat, beef, and produce, value $1.27 billion; ASARCO, Inc. copper refinery, Santa Fe Rail welding plant; Bell Helicopter, Levi Strauss, Iowa Beef Processors, Amarillo Gear, oil and gas, coal burning electricity plant, and Owens-Corning Fiberglas plant.
**Commerce:** wholesale-retail center for 5-state area; retail sales $590.52 million; bank resources $957.59 million, 5 savings and loan assns.; 104th in wholesale among 230 metro areas.
**Transportation:** served by 4 airlines (a 5th has made application to serve); 3 railroads, 4 bus lines, 18 truck lines, 2 interstate, 4 federal, and one state highway intersect Amarillo.
**Communications:** 4 TV, 12 radio stations.
**Medical facilities:** 5 hospitals (new one under construction)

including VA facilities in metro area; mental health centers, speech and hearing center.
**Culture, recreation:** Amarillo Symphony, fine arts complex, civic center complex and convention center, 2 dinner theaters, Amarillo Little Theatre (52d year of operation), Alibates National Monument, Lake Meredith, Wonderland Amusement Park and Storyland Zoo, Palo Duro Canyon State Park, Cal Farley's Boys Ranch, summer musical drama "Texas;" regional history museum, Discovery Center Planetarium, 46 parks, central library and 3 branches, 2 colleges, state vocational-technical school, National Helium Monument.
**Sports:** drag racing, stock car racing, college and high school football, basketball, baseball, wrestling, tennis, and track; Gold Sox baseball, rodeo, motorcycle racing.
**History:** Settled 1887 as railroad crew camp, incorporated 1892; named for yellow lake clay.
**Further information:** Amarillo Chamber of Commerce, Amarillo Bldg., 301 Polk, Amarillo, TX 79101.

---

## Anchorage, Alaska

The World Almanac is sponsored in the Anchorage area by The Anchorage Times, 820 W. 4th Avenue, Anchorage, AK 99510; (907) 279-5622; founded 1915; circulation 47,000; editor-publisher Robert B. Atwood; sponsors Spelling Bee, Kodak Photo Contest.

**Population:** city, borough unified in 1975; total population of new municipality is 200,000 (1976), almost half of state's population.
**Area:** 927 sq. mi. (census district), at head of Cook Inlet on south central coast.
**Industry and commerce:** business center for most of Alaska; aviation, oil companies, railroading, shipping, wholesaling, retailing, and national defense activities are largest elements in area's economy.
**Transportation:** Anchorage International Airport is major refueling stop on transpolar flights; thousands of small planes make city one of country's busiest air traffic centers with 5 airports and 25% of world's seaplanes in area; headquarters of Alaska Railroad; $10 million port.
**Communications:** 4 TV and 11 radio stations; 2 daily newspapers.
**Medical facilities:** 5 hospitals.

**Federal facilities:** Elmendorf AFB, Ft. Richardson.
**Cultural facilities:** annual Festival of Music; 4 theater groups; fine arts museum; community concert organization, opera company, civic symphony.
**Educational facilities:** 57 elementary and secondary schools enroll 42,000; Univ. of Alaska, Alaska Methodist Univ.
**Recreation:** 2 major ski areas; cross-country skiing and bicycling; annual Fur Rendezvous with dogsled races; Iditarod dogsled race to Nome; Chugach National Forest.
**Convention facilities:** 5 major hotels and motels offer facilities for over 3,000 persons.
**History:** founded 1915 as headquarters for Alaska Railroad; twice winner of All America city award, for coping with rapid growth, and for swift recovery from catastrophic 1964 earthquake.
**Further information:** Chamber of Commerce, 612 F Street, Anchorage, AK 99501.

## Atlanta, Georgia

**Population:** 440,300 (city), 1,849,300 (metro), first in state, 18th in nation; total employed, 790,100 (metro, 1977); state capital and Fulton County seat.

**Area:** 136 sq. mi. in north central Georgia, on Piedmont plateau of Blue Ridge foothills, 1,050 ft above sea level; 4,326 sq. mi. in 15-county metro area.

**Industry:** 2,200 manufacturers produce more than 3,500 commodities; 430 of Fortune 500 firms operate in Atlanta; Ford assembly plant, 2 GM assembly plants, Lockheed-Ga. Co.; home base for Coca-Cola, Fuqua, Ind., Delta Air Lines, Equifax, Scripto, Genuine Parts, Simmons Co., Gold Kist, Oxford Ind.

**Commerce:** financial, retail, wholesale center of Southeast; massive Merchandise Mart has 2d largest wholesale showroom in U.S. under one roof; 6th Federal Reserve District hdqtrs.; 75 banks, over 400 branches with resources of $8.8 billion (15-county metro); 22 savings and loan associations with 150 branches in metro area with assets of $3.4 billion (1977).

**Transportation:** founded as railroad center, now served by 7 lines of 2 systems; Greyhound and Trailways bus terminals used by 3 companies with 250 buses in and out daily; 10 domestic and international passenger airlines, 4 commuter carriers, 2 freight only carriers; more than 1200 scheduled flights daily; nonstop passenger service to 105 cities from Hartsfield International Airport, direct flights to 6 international cities including Brussels and London; 2d busiest airport in world, 30 million passengers (1977), and No. 1 commuting point in nation's domestic air route pattern. Metropolitan Atlanta rapid Transit Authority at $2.1 billion, most massive publicly financed project in Southeast since TVA; under construction is 52.9 mi. rapid rail, 8 mi. of rapid busways coordinated with street bus operations; Southeastern hub of 41,000 mi. interstate system with 6 legs of 3 interstate hwys. intersecting 100-acre downtown interchange; 63 mi. hwy. encircles city.

**Communications:** 8 TV stations; 36 radio stations; Protestant Radio and TV Center; largest Bell System toll-free dialing area; one of nation's 5 TV and radio network control centers; 10 daily newspapers.

**New construction:** $400 million expansion Hartsfield Int Airport, $70 million federal office bldg., $14 million downtown library, $2.1 billion MARTA rapid transit system; total value city building permits (1977) $332 million.

**Medical facilities:** 56 hospitals with 10,524 beds (metro), VA hospital; national Center for Disease Control of U.S. Pub. Health Dept., National Cancer Center at Emory Univ. Med. School.

**Federal facilities:** 29,500 federal, non-military employees (1977); Ft. McPherson, hdqtrs. U.S. Army Forces Command; Ft. Gillem; Dobbins AF Base; NAS Atlanta.

**Cultural facilities:** Memorial Arts Center with museum, symphony orchestra, ballet, School of Art; Civic Center with auditorium-theater-exhibition hall; Callanwolde, new multi-use arts center; 29 degree-granting colleges, including Ga. Tech, Ga. State Univ., Emory Univ.

**Sports:** NBA Hawks; NFL Falcons; NL Braves; NHL Flames; stadium seats 52,000; Omni arena, 16,500; World Championship Tennis, college football's Peach Bowl, PGA Atlanta Classic, Peachtree Road Race, road, sports car racing, motocross.

**Convention facilities:** 758,000 convention delegates in 1977; $35 million Ga. World Congress Center has largest single display room in U.S. equal to 8 football fields; simultaneous translation facilities; 28,000 hotel/motel rooms, most downtown or near.

**History:** named 1845; chartered 1847; burned by Union Gen. Sherman 1864.

**Further information:** Chamber of Commerce, 1300 N. Omni International, Atlanta, GA., 30302.

## Augusta, Georgia

The World Almanac is sponsored in the Augusta area by the Chronicle-Herald, 725 Broad Street, Augusta, GA 30903; (404) 724-0851; Chronicle established in 1785, circulation 55,531; Herald 19,270; Sunday, 79,490; William S. Morris III publisher, E.B. Skinner general manager, David L. Playford managing editor, Herald; W.H. Eanes managing editor, Chronicle.

**Population:** 57,100 (city), 281,100 (metro area); total employed, 107,824 (metro).

**Area:** 1,713 sq. mi. (metro: Richmond, Columbia counties, Ga.; Aiken County, S.C.) straddling Savannah River; Augusta County seat.

**Industry:** diversified; Continental Can, Du Pont, Procter & Gamble, Lily-Tulip, Olin, Dymo, Monsanto, Columbia Nitrogen, A.E.C., TRW Corp., Owens-Corning, Kendall, Textron, Kimberly-Clark.

**Commerce:** wholesale, retail center of 17 counties in 2 states; 1977 retail sales, $1,352 billion; per capita income, $4,007, per family income, $12,947; effective buying income, $2.166 billion; 7 banks, 5 savings-loan assns.; distribution center.

**Transportation:** 5 railroads, 26 truck lines, 3 airlines at modern airport and in-city field for executive planes; Interstate 20, other federal highways; river shipping.

**Communications:** 3 TV and 10 radio stations.

**Medical facilities:** 9 major hospitals, including Eisenhower Memorial at Ft. Gordon, Medical College of Georgia.

**Federal facilities:** Ft. Gordon and Savannah River (AEC) Plant.

**Cultural facilities:** Augusta College, Medical College of Ga., Paine College, Univ. of S.C. at Aiken; museum, art gallery, arts council with 25 affiliates; Augusta Symphony.

**Recreational facilities:** hunting, fishing, boating, camping; 7 golf courses; home of Masters Golf Tournament.

**History:** founded as fort 1717; named for wife of Prince of Wales 1735; capital of Georgia, 1778.

**Further information:** Chamber of Commerce of Greater Augusta, 600 Broad Street Plaza, Augusta, GA 30902.

## Bakersfield, California

The World Almanac is sponsored in the Bakersfield and Kern County area by The Bakersfield Californian (eves. and Sunday), 1707 Eye Street, Bakersfield, CA 93302; phone (805) 323-7631; founded 1866 as Havilah Courier, christened The Bakersfield Californian 1897; circulation: 62,584 daily, 70,593 Sunday; president Berenice Fritts Koerber, publisher Donald H. Fritts, executive director Alfred T. Fritts, managing editor James E. Griffith.

**Population:** 86,100 city, 210,000 metro, 359,281 Kern County.

**Area:** approximately 8,060 square miles in Kern County of which Bakersfield is county seat; in California's San Joaquin Valley.

**Industry:** oil, gas, agriculture, military; oil valuation $976 million; total agriculture production $799.4 million; Edwards AFB and China Lake Naval Test Station in eastern Kern County.

**Commerce:** retail sales in Kern $1.5 billion; total bank deposits $1.640 billion.

**Transportation:** 2 railroads, 3 airlines, 2 bus lines, Interstate 5, Highway 99.

**Communications:** 3 TV and 12 radio stations; cable TV from Los Angeles.

**Cultural facilities:** symphony orchestra, Cunningham Art Gallery; 4-year state college, city college; community thea-

ter.
**History:** Kern County organized April 2, 1866, from portions of Los Angeles and Tulare counties; discovery of gold on Kern River in 1851 brought influx of settlers; oil discovered in 1865, with major boom in 1909; gold mining town of Havilah first county seat, moved to Bakersfield in 1875.

## Baltimore, Maryland

The World Almanac is sponsored in the Baltimore area by The Baltimore News American, 301 E. Lombard Street, Baltimore, MD 21202; (301) 752-1212; founded in 1773 as the Maryland Journal and Baltimore Advertiser; Baltimore American founded 1799; Baltimore Evening News founded 1872; adopted present name 1964; daily circulation 169,332, Sunday 246,528; publisher, Mark F. Collins; general manager, Roy W. Anderson; executive editor, Thomas J. White; American Medical Association award, Howard W. Blakeslee and Albert Lasker awards.

**Population:** 807,800 (city) 1,334,800 (metro) first in state, 7th in U.S.; total employment 302,820 (city), 887,510 (metro).
**Area:** 91 sq. mi. (city), 2,225 sq. mi. (metro) on Patapsco River, a tributary of the Chesapeake Bay.
**Industry:** highly diversified, none dominating; most important are steel fabricating, shipbuilding and repairing; manufacture of electrical equipment and food containers; food processing, sugar, petroleum, chemicals, copper; added value of manufacturing in 1976 was $4.8 billion.
**Commerce:** metro area consists of city and 5 adjacent counties; estimated buying income $15,280 per average household; retail sales about $6 billion in 1976, area has 209 shopping centers with 3,591 stores; home ownership 57%.
**Transportation:** 3 railroads including Amtrak; Baltimore-Washington International Airport, served by 9 major and 7 commuter lines, served 3,160,074 passengers in 1977; 150 certified truck lines; the tunnel which carries motor traffic through the city under the harbor was aided by the 1977 opening of the Francis Scott Key Bridge over the harbor which averages 17,000 motor vehicles a day; buses operated by state authority carry 374,000 passengers daily.
**Port facilities:** World Trade Center, dedicated in 1977, is one of 22 focal points for maritime and international interests in the world; 120 steamship lines serve port, the nation's 4th largest and the farthest inland on the Atl Coast; 4,003 ships moved 30.8 million short tons of inte. .nal cargo in 1977; leading cargoes are petroleum products, ores, grain, coal, bananas, automobiles.
**Communications:** 3 daily newspapers in city, 2 more in metro area; 3 VHF TV stations, 2 UHF public broadcast stations; 25 radio stations.
**Cultural facilities:** Enoch Pratt Free Library with 33 agencies and 2.2 million volumes, metro county libraries have 28 branches; Baltimore Symphony Orchestra, Maryland Ballet Co., Baltimore Opera Co., Peale Museum, Carroll Mansion, Maryland Academy of Sciences, Morris A. Mechanic Theater and Center Stage.
**Educational facilities:** 14 (city) 29 (state) colleges and universities; 6 (city) 19 (state) junior colleges, including: Johns Hopkins Univ. and medical institutions, Univ. of Md. (downtown and county campuses) and medical institutions;

Loyola, Notre Dame, Goucher, Towson State Univ., Morgan State Univ., Peabody Conservatory of Johns Hopkins, Md. Inst. College of Art, St. Mary's Seminary and Univ., Ner Israel Rabbinical College.
**Medical facilities:** 26 general hospitals with 8,664 beds in metro area, including the renowned Johns Hopkins and the Univ. of Md. and its Institution for Emergency Medicine.
**Sports:** football and baseball at Memorial Stadium, home of the Colts and Orioles, lacrosse at Homewood Field, home Johns Hopkins, NCAA champions in 1978; horse racing at Pimlico, home of the Preakness, and at nearby Bowie, Laurel, and Timonium; steeplechase horse racing, featuring the Md. Hunt Cup in the countryside north of the metro area; Chesapeake Bay's 1,700 square miles of open water are noted for fishing, boating, and waterfowl hunting; ocean and ski resorts within a 3 hour drive.
**Convention facilities:** Civic Center, 45 meeting rooms, 87,160 sq. ft. of exhibition space; 7 hotels downtown and over 100 motels in or near the city.
**Other attractions:** Fort McHenry Historic Shrine where Francis Scott Key wrote "The Star Spangled Banner," U.S. Frigate Constellation; the Flag House; Baltimore and Ohio Transportation Museum; Edgar Allen Poe's home and grave; Babe Ruth's home; Mother Seton House; Baltimore City Fair in September, Preakness Festival Week in May, ethnic festival weekends throughout the summer; most of the central business district rebuilt in last 16 years, featuring Charles Center, Hopkins Plaza, the rebuilt Inner Harbor, and the restoration of early 19th century rowhouses.
**History:** founded 1729 by act of the Provincial Assembly of the Maryland Colony which was established by members of the Calvert family, the Lords of Baltimore; early economy based on shipment of tobacco, grain, flour, and on shipbuilding; privateering in the War of 1812 tempted British to try to capture the American "nest of pirates". When economic growth was threatened by completion of the Erie Canal, the city's business leaders countered by building the nation's first railroad, the Baltimore and Ohio.
**Further information:** Chamber of Commerce Metro Baltimore, 22 Light Street; Baltimore Promotion Council, 102 St. Paul Street, both Baltimore, MD 21202.

## Baton Rouge, Louisana

The World Almanac is sponsored in the Baton Rouge area by the Morning Advocate and State-Times, 525 Lafayette Street, Baton Rouge, LA 70821; (504) 383-1111; founded 1842; combined daily circ., 113,101; Sunday, 105,000; president, Charles P. Manship Jr.; publisher, Douglas L. Manship; vice president of news and production, Richard Palmer; vice president of business and advertising, Charles Garvey; executive editor, all newspapers, Jim Hughes; managing editors, Edwin Price Jr. (Morning Advocate), Jack Lord (State-Times).

**Population:** 165,963 (city), 392,400 (metro); total 1976 city-parish employment, 177,425.
**Area:** city, 42.83 sq. mi.; parish, 407.01 sq. mi.; on east bank of Mississippi River, 80 mi. northeast of New Orleans; state capital, East Baton Rouge Parish seat.
**Industry:** northern anchor of 100-mi. long petrochemical complex along Mississippi River.
**Commerce:** marketing center for major trade area of 400,000; bank resources, $1.9 billion; 6 banks, 7 savings and loan associations.
**Transportation:** major transfer point on southern federal interstate system; 2 airports with 4 airlines; 2 bus lines; 4 railroad trunk lines; Port of Baton Rouge, 4th largest in

U.S., handled over 62 million tons in 1977.
**Communications:** 4 TV and 9 radio stations: 2 daily newspapers, 2 weeklies.
**Cultural facilities:** 6 museums, 4 theaters, symphony, planetarium, 5 art galleries; new "Riverside Centroplex" civic center.
**Educational facilities:** Louisiana State Univ., founded 1860, center of 8-campus system; Southern Univ., largest Negro land-grant college in U.S., center of 3-college system.
**Sports:** LSU Tigers and Southern Jaguars home stadia, football, basketball, track.
**Other attractions:** state capitol; city-parish zoo and arboretum; 67 parks; major recreational lakes.

**History:** first noted by French explorer Iberville in 1699, Baton Rouge (French: red stick) was already occupied by the Istrouma (also translates red stick) Indians; Louisiana's capital since 1836; government structure is a city-parish combination with a mayor-president and city-parish council.

**Further information:** Chamber of Commerce, P.O. Box 1868, Baton Rouge, 70821; Louisiana Tourist Commission, P.O. Box 44291, Capitol Station, Baton Rouge, 70804; Baton Rouge Area Convention and Visitors Bureau, P.O. Box 3202, Baton Rouge, 70821.

## Billings, Montana

The World Almanac is sponsored in the Billings area by the Billings Gazette, 401 N. Broadway, Billings, MT, 59101; telephone (406) 245-3071; founded 1885; member of Lee Enterprises, Inc., since 1960; circulation; daily 57,812 Sunday 60,141; publisher George Remington, editor William N. Roesgen.

**Population:** 86,100 (city), 103,800 (metro area), first in state; total employed (non-agri) 45,900.
**Area:** south central Montana on Yellowstone River, 125 mi. from Yellowstone Park, Yellowstone County seat.
**Industry:** 3 oil refineries, beet sugar, refinery, 2 packing plants, 3d largest livestock auction yards in U.S., center for Northern Great Plains coal industry.
**Commerce:** wholesale-retail center for eastern Montana, northern Wyoming; retail sales $397 million; bank debits $6.5 billion; 8 banks, 2 savings and loan associations, 160 wholesale firms, 653 retail firms; average spendable family income $15,161.
**Transportation:** 4 airlines, 1 railroad, 2 bus lines, 98 motor carriers, Interstates 90 and 94.
**Communications:** 2 TV and 9 radio stations, one weekly, one daily newspaper.
**Medical facilities:** 2 hospitals, 434 beds, 11 clinics, 197 doctors, 72 dentists, 5 nursing homes, Northern Rockies Regional Cancer Treatment Ctr., Regional Mental Health Center.

**Cultural facilities:** 4 art galleries, symphony orchestra, 2 western museums, studio theater, liberal arts college, business college, private (church related) college, Metra Civic Center sports and concerts, 4 golf courses, 85 churches, 2 nursing schools, voc-tech program, 30 public schools, 10 parochial schools, Center for Handicapped Children, Migrant Children's Program.
**New construction:** $14 million Deaconess Hospital; $6 million hotel; 2 shopping centers; Oil and Gas Co. Bldg.
**Other attractions:** big game hunting, fishing, boating, skiing within hour's drive; snowmobiling, bicycling, saddle clubs; 22 city parks, 2,400 hotel-motel rooms, convention facilities 5,000; Metra capacity 10,000.
**History:** founded 1882 with arrival of Northern Pacific Railroad; named after Frederic Billings, then NP president; now largest city in 500-mile radius.
**Further information:** Tourist Information Bureau, Billings Chamber of Commerce, P.O. Box 2519, Billings, MT 59103.

## Binghamton, New York

The World Almanac is sponsored in the Binghamton area by The Evening Press and The Sun-Bulletin, Vestal Parkway East, Binghamton, NY 13902; 607-798-1234; circulation: evening 71,726; Sunday 80,421; morning 28,621; Saturday morning and Holidays 76,670; president and publisher Fred G. Eaton, Press editor George R. Venizelos; Sun-Bulletin editor Michael G. Doll.

**Population:** 57,900 (city), 304,700 (metro area), 7th among state metro areas; total employed 123,500.
**Area:** 10.98 sq. mi. at junction of Chenango and Susquehanna rivers; Broome County seat.
**Industry:** GAF; computers, IBM; electronics and simulators, Singer Co.; shoes, Endicott Johnson Corp.; a major railroad center.
**Commerce:** wholesale-retail center of area producing $628 million a year; 12 banks; national headquarters of Security Mutual Life Insurance Co. and Columbian Mutual Life Insurance Co.
**Transportation:** 5 airlines, major being Allegheny, out of Broome County Airport; intersection Interstates 81 & 88 and Route 17; Erie-Lackawanna and Delaware and Hudson freight rail carriers.
**Communications:** 3 TV and 4 radio stations.

**Medical facilities:** 4 major hospitals.
**Cultural facilities:** Roberson Center Arts & Sciences; State Univ. at Binghamton; Broome County College; Tri-Cities Opera Co.; symphony orchestra; public library; civic theater.
**Other attractions:** municipal parks zoo; major state park on outskirts; Veterans Memorial Arena, Oakdale Mall, Arena Art Open.
**Sports:** Dusters pro-hockey team; BC Open golf tournament.
**History:** Settled 1800; became rail center by 1848, with roads replacing old Chenango Canal that fed Erie Canal; named for Philadelphia patriot and multi-millionaire William Bingham.
**Further information:** Broome County Chamber of Commerce Tourist Information, 84 Court Street, Binghamton, NY 13902.

## Birmingham, Alabama

The World Almanac is sponsored in the Birmingham area by The Birmingham Post-Herald, 2200 Fourth Avenue N., Birmingham, AL 35202; telephone (205) 325-2222; Post founded 1921 by Scripps-Howard Newspapers; Herald founded 1887; circulation, 75,630; editor Angus McEachran, vice president W. H. Metz, managing editor George Cook; major public service projects include Goodfellow Christmas Fund, Alabama Favorite Teacher selection.

**Population:** 276,273 (city, 1975 est.), 644,688 (county, 1975 est.), 791,073 (metro, 1975 est.), employment 339,700 (metro, 1975).
**Area:** 89 sq. mi. in north central Alabama; state's largest city; Jefferson County seat.
**Industry:** heavy manufacturing in metals; U.S. Steel is area's largest employer; U.S. Pipe and Foundry and American Cast Iron Pipe Co. are in top 10 employers; South Central

Bell's 5-state headquarters located in city.
**Commerce:** wholesale-retail center for Alabama; retail sales, (1976) $4.15 billion; bank debits (1976) $70.7 billion; 14 banks (county); 6 bank holding companies; 7 savings and loan assns.
**Transportation:** 5 major rail freight lines, Amtrak; Greyhound and Continental Trailways bus lines; Eastern, Delta, United, and Southern air lines with modern airport terminal;

75 truck line terminals; 3 interstate highways, I-65, I-59 and I-20 all under construction.

**Communications:** 2 daily newspapers, 3 commercial TV stations, 16 commercial radio stations, one PBS TV and one PBS radio outlet.

**Medical facilities:** Univ. of Alabama in Birmingham Medical Center covers 60 sq. blocks; heart surgery team brings patients from all over the world; Veterans Administration hospital, in same complex, is the base of organ transplant program; Baptist Medical Centers have 2 major hospitals; 13 other hospitals.

**Cultural facilities:** symphony orchestra; Oscar Wells Museum of Art with more than $4 million in assets; Civic Opera; 4 resident civic theaters; 2 resident ballet companies.

**Education:** Samford Univ., Birmingham-Southern, Miles, and Daniel Payne colleges; Jefferson State and Lawson State junior colleges.

**Convention facilities:** civic center with exhibition hall, theater, music hall, and coliseum; several new convention hotels and motels in civic center area.

**Sports:** nicknamed "Football Capital of the South" for Univ. of Alabama and Auburn Univ. games played at municipal stadium, Legion Field.

**Other attractions:** world's 2d largest cast iron statue, Vulcan, mythical god of the forge, overlooks Birmingham from Red Mountain as a symbol of the steel industry; Arlington Shrine, antebellum home that housed federal troops during Civil War; Botanical Gardens complex with Japanese Garden; Jimmie Morgan Zoo; extensive city park system.

**History:** chartered 1871; soon became known as the "Magic City" because of its rapid growth brought on by the presence of the 3 ingredients in steelmaking — coal, iron ore, and lime; mining died out in recent years and most iron ore is now imported by ship and barge to Birmingport on Warrior River from South America; coal mining, in decline since the 1940s, is on the upswing.

**Further information:** Chamber of Commerce, 1914 Sixth Avenue N., Birmingham, AL 35203.

## Bismarck, North Dakota

The World Almanac is sponsored in western North Dakota by the Bismarck Tribune, 222 Fourth Street, Bismarck, ND 58501; (701) 223-2500; founded 1873 as weekly, became daily 1881; circ. 28,500; publisher A. G. Sorlie, editor John O. Hjelle, advertising manager James H. Hewitson; major awards include Pulitzer Prize Gold Medal, 1937.

**Population:** 43,000 (est. 1978), 3d in state; total employed 20,960.

**Area:** 14 sq. mi on Missouri River; state capital and Burleigh County seat.

**Industry:** agriculture, printing, trucking, farm machinery, state government, electric power, manufacturing, concrete products, railroad, insurance, livestock sales rings, lignite coal.

**Commerce:** retail trade area radius 100 miles, serving 150,000 people; retail sales (1977) $200 million; bank deposits (1977) $616 million; 6 banks, 4 building and loan associations.

**Transportation:** 2 rail lines, Amtrak; airport, hub for 3 airlines; 13 truck lines; 4 bus lines; U.S. Highways 18 and 83, I-94.

**Communications:** one daily newspaper; 3 AM, 3 FM radio stations, 2 TV stations.

**New construction:** 1977 building permits, $45.4 million (937 housing units).

**Medical facilities:** 2 hospitals, 453 bed capacity, served by 110 M.D.s.

**Federal facilities:** federal buildings house 20 offices; 14th Radar Bomb Scoring Detachment.

**Cultural facilities:** Bismarck Junior College, Mary College; 72,000-volume public library, state library, state museum; Elan Gallery; 45 churches.

**Recreation:** 20 parks with over 1,250 acres; indoor artificial ice arena; 3 golf courses, 5 swimming pools, playgrounds, tennis courts, YMCA; duck and goose hunting; fishing; nearby Fort Lincoln State Park.

**Convention facilities:** 8,000 seat Civic Center; 1,300 rooms; 5 banquet and meeting facilities for groups of 200-1,200.

**Other attractions:** Dakota Zoo; Garrison Dam; United Tribes of North Dakota Educational Technical Center; state capitol.

**History:** founded 1872 as Edwinton, a rail town; name changed to Bismarck in 1873 to encourage German investment capital.

**Further information:** Chamber of Commerce, 412 Sixth Street, Bismarck, ND 58501.

## Bloomington, Illinois

The World Almanac is sponsored in Bloomington-Normal and central Illinois by The Daily Pantagraph, 301 W. Washington Street, Bloomington, IL 61701; (309) 829-9411; founded 1837 by Jesse W. Fell; circulation 52,022; president and publisher Davis U. Merwin; editor Harold Liston; general manager William Diesel; managing editor Gene F. Smedley.

**Population:** 79,700 Bloomington-Normal, 120,000 (metro area) McLean County; mid-way between Chicago and St. Louis in central Illinois.

**Industry:** over 50 industries in county, ranks 9th in insurance cities in U.S., home offices of State Farm, Country Companies, Union Auto; uniform diversity of non-agricultural employment in all major work force areas; leads nation in corn and soybean production with 2,316 farms in county.

**Commerce:** 1977 metro retail sales $409.6 million; per household income $19,740; per household retail sales, $10,345.

**Transportation:** new terminal at B-N Airport, 3 bus lines, 6 federal and state highways, 4 railroads, Amtrak, 35 interstate and 23 intrastate motor carriers, Ozark Airlines and Britt Airways.

**Communications:** 6 radio stations.

**Medical facilities:** 3 hospitals; Watson-Gailey Foundation Eye Bank.

**Cultural facilities:** Illinois Wesleyan Univ., 1,550, in Bloomington; Illinois State Univ., 18,000, in Normal; 49 churches; home of American Passion Play; B-N Symphony, community players, amateur musical.

**History:** incorporated 1850; site of A. Lincoln's "Lost Speech" and David Davis mansion; state historical shrine; city's Stevenson family has produced 3 generations of leadership; vice president Adlai E.; governor, presidential candidate and UN Ambassador, Adlai E. II; and U.S. Senator Adlai E. III.

**Further information:** Association of Commerce and Industry of McLean County, 210 S. East Street, Bloomington, IL 61701.

## Boise, Idaho

The World Almanac is sponsored in the Boise area by the Idaho Statesman, 1200 N. Curtis Road, Boise, ID 83704; (208) 376-2121; founded 1864 as Tri-Weekly; daily circulation 60,282; Sunday 68,764; publisher Robert B. Miller Jr., managing editor Gary L. Watson; a Gannett newspaper.

**Population:** 115,000 (city) (Dec., 1977), 145,000 (metro area), first in state, 204th in nation; total employed 75,350.
**Area:** 1,054 sq. mi. on Boise River at foot of Salmon River Mountains; state capital and Ada County seat.
**Industry:** mobile home and recreational trailers produced $240 million in 1976; world headquarters Boise Cascade Corp., Morrison-Knudsen Co., and Albertson Food Stores.
**Commerce:** wholesale and retail center for southwest Idaho; retail sales $433.9 million (1976); bank resources $706.6 million in 6 banks with 27 branches; 4 savings and loan associations, and 7 insurance company offices.
**Transportation:** 2 major airlines, 2 feeder airlines, one rail freight line, 4 bus lines, 17 common carrier truck lines; Amtrak.
**Communications:** 4 TV and 9 radio stations.

**Medical facilities:** 3 major hospital complexes including a Veteran's Administration facility.
**Cultural facilities:** Boise Philharmonic Orchestra, art gallery, state museum, Boise Little Theatre, $1.4 million public library, Boise State Univ.
**Other attractions:** 33 parks, Southwestern Idaho Fairgrounds, 2 major recreational lakes, scenic mountain areas; Bogus Basin ski resort offers one of the world's longest illuminated ski runs.
**History:** founded 1863; named derived from "les bois" (the trees), a description for area used by French fur trappers in 1811.
**Further information:** Boise Chamber of Commerce, P. O. Box 2368, or Department of Commerce and Development, Idaho Statehouse, both Boise, ID 83701.

---

## Boston, Massachusetts

The World Almanac is sponsored in the Boston area by The Boston Herald American, 300 Harrison Avenue, Boston, MA 02106; (617) 426-3000. Herald American established 1972; daily circulation 293,004; Sunday 421,684. Publisher Robert Bergenheim, executive editor William McIlwain, general manager Dennis Mulligan. Pulitzer Prize, Sigma Delta Chi distinguished service awards, Heywood Broun award, AP & UPI first place awards.

**Population:** 636,960 (city), 2,899,000 (metro area of 92 cities and towns around Boston; 5th largest metropolitan area in nation.
**Area:** 46 sq. mi. on Massachusetts Bay; state capital and Suffolk County seat.
**Commerce:** northeast center for finance and insurance; home office for 50 insurance companies; banking center for New England with total commercial banking deposits of $14.778 billion (1976); accounts for 35% of the nation's mutual fund holdings; retail center for northern New England; major electronics industry and publishing center.
**Transportation:** terminating point for 2 railroads, Amtrak and Boston & Maine; MBTA (Massachusetts Bay Transportation Authority) provides surface and subway transportation for metropolitan Boston; Massachusetts Port Authority (operates Logan International Airport and the Port of Boston (shipping); 5 interstate highways.
**Communications:** 5 newspapers (3 daily, 2 weekly), 7 TV and 31 radio stations.
**New construction:** Federal Reserve Tower, Quincy Market area, West End residential-office complex, Waterfront building rehabilitation and the 60 State St. building.
**Medical facilities:** health care is Boston's largest industry in terms of dollars invested; major institutions: Mass. General, Children's, and New England medical centers; Boston City, Beth Israel, Deaconess hospitals; Harvard, Boston Univ., and Tufts medical schools; Lahey Clinic.
**Federal facilities:** 50 federal agencies employ 45,700 (military facilities not included).
**Cultural facilities:** the "Athens of America;" Boston Public Library includes capacity for 500,000 books on open shelf, plus large lecture hall; Boston Symphony Orchestra; Boston

Pops; opera company; Boston Ballet; Museum of Fine Art; Museum of Science and Hayden Planetarium; New England Aquarium; Isabella Stewart Gardner Museum; Museum of Transportation; Children's Museum.
**Educational facilities:** 16 degree-granting institutions in the city and 47 in the metro area, including Harvard, Boston College, Boston Univ., Tufts, M.I.T., Brandeis, Univ. of Mass., Suffolk, Emmanuel, Simmons, and Wentworth Inst.
**Recreation:** 2,327 acres of city recreation area, includes historic Boston Common and Public Garden; Metropolitan District Commission provides extensive facilities, including beaches and harbor islands.
**Convention facilities:** 49 hotels equipped to handle conventions; exhibition halls include Commonwealth Pier Exhibition Hall with 168,000 sq. ft. and John B. Hynes Veterans Auditorium in Prudential Center with 154,000 sq. ft. and auditorium seating 5,800.
**Sports:** professional teams include Red Sox (baseball), Celtics (basketball), New England Patriots (football), Bruins (hockey), Tea Men (soccer), and Lobsters (tennis).
**Other attractions:** Quincy Market (a reconstruction of the historic Boston marketplace), Faneuil Hall, the "Freedom Trail", a 1½ mile walk through historic Boston; Beacon Hill and Back Bay historical districts; U.S.S. Constitution - "Old Ironsides" - the oldest commissioned ship in the U.S. Navy.
**Nicknames:** The Hub (of the Universe), Bean Town.
**History:** capital city of commonwealth, founded 1630; from 1770, Boston was scene of many events leading to American Revolution, including Boston Tea Party on Dec. 16, 1773; incorporated Feb. 23, 1822.
**Further information:** Boston Chamber of Commerce, 125 High Street, Boston, MA 02110.

---

## Bridgeport, Connecticut

The World Almanac is sponsored in the Bridgeport area by The Bridgeport Post (evening), The Telegram (morning), and The Sunday Post, published by The Post Publishing Co., 410 State Street, Bridgeport, CT 06602; (203) 333-0161; circulation Post, 77,974, Telegram, 14,580, Sunday Post, 93,851; John E. Pfriem president and general manager, Leonard E. Gilbert managing editor.

**Population:** 153,200 (State Dept. of Health) largest in state; planning region, 407,100; 9-town district labor force, 308,800.
**Area:** 17.5 sq. mi. on north shore of Long Island Sound at mouth of the Pequonnock River in Fairfield County.
**Industry:** "Industrial Capital of Connecticut;" products include tools, metallic cartridges, wiring devices, brass goods, valves, corsets, electrical apparatus and appliances; nearby are Sikorsky Aircraft and Avco Lycoming; General Electric has its corporate headquarters in Fairfield, one mile from city line.

**Commerce:** retail sales, $417.9 million (1977); downtown renewal includes completed complex with Gimbels and Sears stores, mall, 2,000-car parking garage, U.S. courthouse; also 2 new bank buildings, major addition to another; new state courthouse; downtown townhouse residential project completed; construction begun on downtown $3 million 100-unit senior citizens apartment bldg.
**Transportation:** railroad station opened in 1975, to be connected with planned $7 million multi-transportation center with bus terminal, 1,500-car parking garage. City served by Conn. Turnpike (Interstate 95); historic U.S. 1 (Boston Post

Road); 2 airlines at municipal Sikorsky Memorial Airport; Conrail; 2 national bus lines; summer ferry to Port Jefferson, L.I.

**Medical facilities:** 3 general hospitals, state mental health center; municipal convalescent hospital; major Easter Seal rehabilitation center.

**Cultural facilities:** Univ. of Bridgeport, Fairfield Univ., Sacred Heart Univ., Housatonic Community College; Museum of Art, Science, Industry; P. T. Barnum museum; symphony orchestra; municipally-supported downtown cabaret theater; American Shakespeare theater in adjoining town of Stratford.

**Recreational facilities:** "The Park City" has 1,200 acres of parks, including Seaside with 2-mile shoreline; zoo; municipal indoor ice-skating rink; jai-alai fronton, one of the largest in world.

**Further information:** Bridgeport Area Chamber of Commerce, 180 Fairfield Avenue, Bridgeport, CT 06604.

## Buffalo, New York

The World Almanac is sponsored in the Buffalo area by The Courier-Express, 785 Main Street, Buffalo, NY 14240; (716) 847-5353; founded 1926 as merger of Courier and Express by William J. Conners Sr.; circulation mornings 125,252, Sunday 272,088; readership mornings 363,200, Sunday 653,000; publisher William J. Conners III, asst. to publisher William J. Conners IV; treasurer R. C. Lyons, gen. mgr. Donald J. Maul; sponsors miss the headpin tournament, learn to swim program, ski school, Goodfellows.

**Population:** 1,322,400 (metro area, 1976), 400,500 (city, 1976); 2d in state; employment 513,000 (metro, 1977); hub of broad 8 county area with population of 1,744,000.

**Area:** 49.6 sq. mi. city, 1,567 sq. mi. metro; at western end of N.Y. State on Lake Erie, Niagara River, and U.S.-Can. boundary; Erie County seat. Metro area includes cities of Niagara Falls, Lockport, Tonawanda, N. Tonawanda, Lackawanna.

**Industry:** 1,602 manufacturing establishments with $6.3 billion in shipments, highly diversified; headquarters for Rich Products, Buffalo Forge, Trico Products, Fisher-Price Toys; large plants for Republic Steel, Bethlehem Steel, Chevrolet, Ford, Westinghouse, Union Carbide.

**Commerce:** wholesale and financial center for western N.Y. area; retail sales $3.5 billion (metro); average income per household after taxes (metro) $14,222; distribution center for northeastern U.S. and Canada; $6.5 billion in trade between U.S. and Canada handled each year; 13 commercial banks, 7 savings banks, 3 savings and loans.

**Transportation:** Greater Buffalo Int. Airport served by 4 scheduled airlines with 3,079,000 passengers, 153,641 scheduled and non-scheduled flights in 1977; 6 major railroads, 10 freight terminals; about 150 motor carriers; highway system includes New York State Thruway. Direct highway and rail service to all parts of Canada; direct water service to entire Great Lakes-St. Lawrence Seaways system, overseas, and Atlantic seaboard.

**Communications:** 2 Buffalo newspapers, 3 additional dailies and one Sunday in surrounding cities; 5 TV and 19 AM and FM radio stations; 3 cable systems.

**Cultural facilities:** Buffalo Philharmonic in Kleinhans Music Hall; Albright-Knox Art Gallery; Studio Arena theater; Museum of Science; Historical Museum; Zoological Gardens (23 acres); Shaw Festival at Niagara-on-the-Lake, Ontario; performing arts center (Artpark) in Lewiston.

**Educational facilities:** State Univ. at Buffalo (now building $650 million new campus); State College at Buffalo, Niagara Univ., Canisius College; 5 other colleges; several 2-year institutions.

**Convention facilities:** Memorial Auditorium seats up to 17,000; new Buffalo convention center; Niagara Falls Convention Center seats up to 12,000; additional facilities available at several hotels and motels.

**Sports:** Bills football (NFL), Sabres hockey (NHL), Braves basketball (NBA); Rich Stadium; Bisons pro women's softball, Blazers pro soccer.

**Recreation:** abundant facilities for all year around sports and activities; near both U.S. and Canada vacationlands.

**Other attractions:** Niagara Falls and river areas from Buffalo to Lake Ontario; Robert Moses and Adam Beck hydro stations; St. Lawrence Seaway, Welland Canal locks, aquarium (Niag. Falls), Our Lady of Victory Basilica (Lackawanna); Old Fort Niagara; Letchworth and Allegany state parks.

**Further information:** Chamber of Commerce, 238 Main, Buffalo, NY 14202.

## Calgary, Alberta, Canada

The World Almanac is sponsored in the Calgary and southern Alberta area by The Calgary Albertan, 830 10th Avenue SW, Calgary, Alta. T2R 0B1; (403) 263-7730; founded 1902; circulation 49,180; publisher John A. Hamilton; managing editor Les Buhasz; business manager Al Vogt.

**Population:** 505,637.

**Area:** 235 sq. mi.; elevation 3,440 feet; in foothills of Rocky Mountains, 150 miles north of the Alberta-Montana border.

**Industry:** 594 firms directly connected with the oil industry have headquarters in Calgary; also chemical, fertilizer and supply industries, and older agricultural industries; number of industrial plants (1977) 978; manufacturing value (1977) $1.8 billion; manufacturing payroll (1977) $324 million; trading area population (1978 est.) 950,000; assistance in locating industrial information provided by Bruce McDonald, Director, Business Development, PO Box 2100, Calgary.

**Commerce:** retail sales volume (1977) $1.686 billion, per capita expenditure $3,430; gross income of market area population $5.230 billion; disposable income (1977) $3.502 billion; no sales or gasoline tax.

**Transportation:** 2 railways, Greyhound bus lines, new International Airport served by 6 airlines.

**Communications:** 4 TV and 7 radio stations; 4 local, 4 U.S. cable stations; 2 daily, 3 weekly newspapers.

**Medical facilities:** 6 major hospital complexes.

**New construction:** building permits in 1977 totalled $820.4 million.

**Cultural facilities:** 2,700-seat auditorium; Glenbow Museum, QR Arts Centre; centennial planetarium; symphony orchestra, live theater, ballet troupe, opera company.

**Federal facilities:** Gov't of Canada building, armed forces base.

**Education:** public schools enroll more than 100,000; separate (Catholic) schools enroll 20,000; one French school; 2 alternative schools; Univ. of Calgary enrolls 15,000; Mount Royal Junior College, Southern Alberta Institute of Technology, Strathcona-Tweedsmuir co-ed private school.

**Recreation:** 5 public, 6 private golf courses; 11 indoor, 12 outdoor swimming pools; 13 ice arenas; 11 athletic parks; Olympic-size swimming pool at univ.; Glencoe Club, private recreational facility; skiing nearby.

**Sports:** facilities for hockey, football, and curling; Stampeders of Canadian Football League; Calgary Cardinal baseball team; Calgary Canucks, Western Canada Hockey League.

**Other attractions:** Calgary Stampede in July; Heritage Park reconstructs pioneer life; Calgary Zoo and Dinosaur Park; 626 ft. rotating Calgary Tower gives panoramic view of city, seats 200 for dining and 300 in observation area; more than 100 specialty restaurants.

**History:** began as mounted police outpost; in 1885, when

railway arrived, had population of 1,800; discovery of oil in 1914 at Turner Valley contributed to Calgary's present prominence.

**Further information:** Chamber of Commerce, 273-One Palliser Square; Tourist and Convention Bureau, Mewata Park, 1300 6th Avenue SW, both Calgary, Alta.

## Charleston, West Virginia

The World Almanac is sponsored in the Charleston area by The Charleston Gazette, 1001 Virginia Street, East, Charleston, WV 25330; (304) 348-5140; circulation (morn) 56,248, (Sun.) 105,715; founded 1873 as the Kanawha Chronicle, became The Charleston Gazette 1898; W. E. Chilton III publisher; Don Marsh editor; Dallas C. Higbee executive editor.

**Population:** 75,100 (city), 221,200 (Kanawha County), most populous county in state; county labor force, 111,000.

**Area:** 29.3 sq. mi. at meeting place of the Elk and Kanawha rivers; state capital.

**Industry:** diversified industrial complex, with coal and chemicals dominating; center for production of limestone, lumber, salt brines, vitreous clays and natural gas; also glass, petroleum products, alloys.

**Commerce:** wholesale, retail center for central and southern West Virginia; county retail sales, $910.8 million; average family income, $16,955.

**Transportation:** 2 rail freight lines, Amtrak, bus lines, state's busiest airport; barge lines, 3 interstate highways.

**Communications:** 3 TV and 7 radio stations.

**Medical facilities:** 6 hospitals, 2 of them major complexes.

**Cultural facilities:** modern civic center and auditorium, Sunrise Cultural and Art Center, symphony orchestra, Community Music Assn., Light Opera Guild, Kanawha Players, State Museum, Morris Harvey College, W. Va. Univ. Graduate Center.

**Other attractions:** Coonskin Park, Kanawha State Forest, 6 golf courses, public tennis, International League baseball.

**History:** first settlement, Fort Lee, 1788; Virginia Assembly established Charles Town 1794; names Charleston 1818.

**Further information:** Charleston Area Chamber of Commerce, 818 Virginia Street, East, Charleston, WV 25301.

## Charlotte, North Carolina

The World Almanac is sponsored in the Charlotte area by The Charlotte Observer, 600 S. Tryon Street, Charlotte, NC 28233; (704) 374-7070; founded 1886 as Charlotte Chronicle; changed to Charlotte Daily Observer, March 1892; sold to Knight Newspapers Inc. 1955; circulation 171,478 daily, 238,250 Sunday; president and publisher Rolfe Neill; editor David Lawrence.

**Population:** 325,000 (city), 400,000 (Mecklenburg County), 626,000 (Charlotte-Gastonia metro area), 65th in nation; labor force 323,500.

**Area:** 123.4 sq. mi. in Piedmont section of N.C., a plateau extending from the Appalachians to the Coastal Plains.

**Industry:** over 670 manufacturing companies, industrial chemicals, textiles, food products, machinery, printing and publishing.

**Commerce:** major trucking center, photographic and data processing center, 1,400 wholesale firms with $6.7 billion sales; retail sales $3.06 billion (Mecklenburg County) EBI per household $15,607; 16 banks, 11 mortgage banks, 6 building and loan associations.

**Transportation:** 115 trucking firms; 2 major railway lines; 4 bus lines; 5 airlines with 184 air movements per day.

**Communications:** 5 TV and 12 radio stations.

**Medical facilities:** an outstanding center in Southeast, 7 hospitals including 3 large general.

**Cultural facilities:** Opera Assn.; Charlotte Symphony Orchestra; Oratorio Society; Mint Museum (art); Nature Museum; Spirit Square (facility for all art activities under one

roof); over 400 churches; Discovery Place (new museum).

**Education:** Univ. of N.C.-Charlotte; Davidson College; Johnson C. Smith Univ.; Queens College; Central Piedmont Community College; Kings College; Hamilton College.

**Convention facilities:** Charlotte Coliseum-Auditorium; Civic Center; Trade Mart; Merchandise Mart; many private convention facilities.

**Sports:** Charlotte Motor Speedway (NASCAR) with World 600 and National 500 races; Kemper Open golf tournament; NCNB Tennis Classic; Charlotte Orioles (professional baseball).

**Other attractions:** 2 major recreational lakes; Carowinds (family theme park); climate — four distinct seasons, avg. daily max. temp. 71.3, yearly avg. temp. 60.5; Festival in the Park; Southern Living Show.

**History:** incorporated 1768, named for Queen Charlotte of England; played major role in American Revolution; was gold mining capital of country before 1849; U.S. Mint built in 1836 to serve gold mining industry.

**Further information:** Chamber of Commerce, P.O. Box 1867, Charlotte, NC 28233. 704/377-6911

## Chattanooga, Tennessee

The World Almanac is sponsored in the Chattanooga area by the Chattanooga News-Free Press, 400 E. 11th Street, Chattanooga, TN 37401, (615) 756-6900; circulation 65,065 daily and 77,501 Sunday; publisher Roy McDonald, president Frank McDonald, senior vice president Everett Allen, vice president and editor Lee Anderson, secretary J. W. Hoback, treasurer Clifford Welch.

**Population:** 170,046 (city), 391,300 (metro area); 4th in state, 89th in nation; 174,100 employed in labor force.

**Area:** 2,109.8 sq. mi. metropolitan shopping area at juncture of Tennessee River and North Georgia boundary line; Hamilton County seat.

**Industry:** over 600 manufacturers employ 57,300; receipts added by manufacture in 1973, $989 million; producing more than 1,500 classified products including principal products of textile, fabricated metals, chemicals, primary metals, food products, machinery, apparel, paper products, and leather goods.

**Commerce:** Wholesale and retail center; wholesale sales (1975) $752 million; bank assets (1976), $1.2 billion; 9 banks, 2 mortgage banks, 4 savings and loan associations, 3 major life insurance companies.

**Transportation:** 2 major freight lines, 2 bus lines, 13 federal and state highways; modern municipal airport serves 4 airlines.

**New construction:** 3 savings and loan associations building new headquarters; development of 11-story Krystal office building; facility for various business-oriented organizations; Tennessee Valley Authority Credit Union structure.

**Communications:** 1 cable TV, 5 TV, 20 radio stations; 2 newspapers.

**Medical facilities:** speech and hearing rehabilitation center; children and adults rehabilitation and education center; 11 major hospital complexes including psychiatric hospital.

**Cultural facilities:** Univ. of Tenn. at Chattanooga; 3 liberal arts colleges; state tech community college; state vocational-tech school; symphony orchestra; opera association, civic chorus, community concert association, Boys Choir, conservatory of music, Little Theatre, programs and performances at the Tivoli Theater, Memorial Auditorium, and Miller Park.

**Other attractions:** multi-million dollar vacation complex; Chattanooga Choo-Choo, in one of the world's largest restaurants, in restored railroad terminal; recreational lakes, mountains, and museums.

**History:** explored by DeSoto 1540, settled 1828 at Ross's Landing, incorporated 1839.

**Further information:** Chattanooga Convention and Visitors Bureau, Memorial Auditorium, Chattanooga, TN.

## Chicago, Illinois

The World Almanac is sponsored in the Chicago area by the Chicago Tribune, 435 N. Michigan Avenue, Chicago, IL 60611; (312) 222-3232; founded 1847; circulation daily 757,117, Sunday 1,155,572; publisher Stanton R. Cook; editor Clayton Kirkpatrick; major awards include 8 Pulitzer prizes won by staff members.

**Population:** est. 3.5 million (city), 2d largest in nation; est. 7.6 million (8-county metro area in Illinois and Indiana); est. resident labor force 3,519,500; est. 3.8 million suburban residents; est. 19% of U.S. pop dwells within a 300 mile radius.

**Area:** 228.124 sq. miles; 4,657 sq. miles (metro area).

**Industry:** est. 53 million tons of manufactures transported out of Chicago yearly; metro area is first in production of steel, metal products, sausages, cookies, candy, metal furniture, mattresses, envelopes, boxes, inorganic chemicals, soap, paint, gaskets, cans, saws, screws, bolts, barrels, machine tools, blowers, switchgear, radios, TV's, communications equipment, railroad equipment, and surgical appliances; Chicago produces a gross metro product of $83 billion, 5% of GNP.

**Commerce:** 14,400 manufacturers in Chicago with sales over $69 billion; 57,000 retailers in metro area with sales over $28 billion in 1977; 13,000 wholesalers in metro area with sales over $43 billion; 56,000 service establishments in the area do a $6.4 billion business; effective buying income per household $19,253. Midwest Stock Exchange markets stocks and bonds; 7th Federal Reserve District Bank; world's leading grain futures market; Chicago Board of Trade; Mercantile Exchange.

**Transportation:** 3 major airports with 29 commercial airlines handle over 43 million passengers, 642,000 aircraft a year; 231 destinations are served by direct flights from Chicago; O'Hare is world's busiest and largest airport handling 404,000 tons of freight and mail and processing 41% of all U.S. International passengers; 314,000 trucks registered in Chicago; 38 million tons of manufactured goods shipped yearly; Chicago trucks service more than 54,000 communities; over 12 major highways, expressways, tollways; 3d largest Interstate Highway system in nation. Railways ship 23 million tons; 37,000 freight cars, 137,000 passengers handled daily; Amtrak headquarters. Ships carry 72 million tons of cargo in and out of metro area; barges carry 23 million tons; 318 overseas ships handled yearly; 14 overseas steamship lines carry freight to 47 ports in 24 countries.

**Construction:** $7.1 billion in industrial construction since 1965; $10.8 billion in residential construction; $8 billion in commercial construction; site of 3 of the 5 tallest man-made structures — the John Hancock, the Standard Oil, and Sears Tower buildings.

**Convention facilities:** (1977) 1004 conventions, 176 trade shows, 17,676 corporate meetings, est. 2,314,000 total attendance; est. $509 million income generated.

**Educational facilities:** 95 institutions of higher learning, including Univ. of Chicago, Illinois Institute of Technology, Loyola Univ., Univ. of Illinois - Circle Campus; 6 medical schools, 3 dental colleges, and a college of pharmacy and osteopathy.

**Recreation:** 131 forest preserves; 79 city parks; 147 golf courses; 15 athletic parks and race tracks; 35 museums, zoos, and permanent exhibitions; 73 swimming pools; athletic clubs, tennis courts.

**Cultural facilities:** Art Institute, Museum of Contemporary Art, Museum of Science and Industry; Shedd Aquarium is largest in world; Adler Planetarium; Lincoln Park and Brookfield zoos; museums of Academy of Science and Historical Society.

**Sports:** NFL Bears, American League White Sox, National League Cubs, NHL Black Hawks, NBA Bulls, NA Soccer League Sting.

**History:** Indians named the area Checagou after area's strong-smelling wild onions; incorporated 1837 with population of 4,170.

**Further information:** Visitors Bureau and Information Center, Association of Commerce and Industry, 130 S. Michigan Ave., Chicago, IL 60603.

## Cincinnati, Ohio

The World Almanac is sponsored in the Cincinnati area by The Cincinnati Post, a Scripps-Howard Newspaper, 800 Broadway, Cincinnati, OH 45202; (513) 352-2000; founded in 1881 by Alfred and Walter Wellman; evening circulation 187,096; editor William R. Burleigh, business manager John L. Feldmann.

**Population:** 412,564 (city), 1,381,196 (metro area), 2d in state, 26th in nation; total employment 583,300.

**Area:** 2,149 sq. mi. (metro) in SW Ohio, SE Ind. and 3 north central counties in Ky.; Hamilton County seat.

**Industry:** home of Procter & Gamble, Federated Department Stores, Kroger Foods, Armco Steel, U.S. Shoe, Western Southern Life Insurance, Baldwin Piano and Organ, Cincinnati Milacron; also home of GM, Ford, and GE plants; production of jet engines, playing cards, cosmetics, chemicals, machine tools, printing and publishing.

**Commerce:** retail sales $4.2 billion; bank assets $5 billion; bank deposits $4.1 billion with 41 banks with 207 branches; 66 savings and loan associations in metro area.

**Transportation:** 7 major railroads and Amtrak; 85 common motor carriers; Greater Cincinnati Airport with 7 trunk line air carriers with 270 daily commercial flights serving 7 airlines; Lunken Airport with 4 hard surface runways and FAA control tower; Blue Ash Airport serving private aircraft; port of Cincinnati; Ohio River navigable entire year links Cincinnati with Mississippi River; 9 public water terminals; 23 private and 2 major transcontinental bus lines; city-owned local bus lines; metro freeway.

**Communications:** 5 TV, 12 AM and 25 FM radio stations; 2 daily newspapers.

**New construction:** Fountain Square South redevelopment underway, new U.C. law school in planning, Yeatman's Cove and Sawyer Point Park planning underway. Skywalk 4th St. bridge from Pogue's to McAlpin's completed late 1978, and Skywalk enclosure from Stouffer's to Race St. in planning stages; modifications in bus-taxi ramp going to Riverfront Stadium in planning stages. Block D (Emery Development) under construction early 1979, Government Square canopy seating benches completion late 1980, Central Trust Tower & Federated Office Tower completion 1979.

**Medical facilities:** 27 hospitals with 8,692 beds; 135.8 physicians per 100,000 population; UC Medical Center where Sabin oral vaccine was discovered; Burn Institute and VA Hospital.

**Cultural facilities:** art museum; historical society, symphony orchestra, Krohn Conservatory, Lloyd Library, May Festival, Taft Museum, Cincinnati Opera, arts consortium, Cincinnati Ballet, Museum of Natural History, Contemporary Arts Center, Playhouse in the Park, UC Observatory.

**Educational facilities:** Cincinnati, Xavier, Northern Kentucky univs.; Cincinnati Bible, Mt. St. Joseph, Edgecliff, Hebrew Union, St. Gregory, Thomas More colleges; 8 technical and 2-year colleges; 47 vocational schools.

**Convention facilities:** numerous hotels, motels, and restaurants; Convention and Exposition Center, Music Hall, Cincinnati Gardens, Emery and Taft auditoriums, Riverfront Coliseum.

**Other attractions:** zoo, Reds, '76 baseball world champions, Bengals football, Stingers ice hockey, Cincinnati Suds softball, Fountain Square Plaza, River Downs and Latonia race tracks, Kings Island Amusement Park, Delta Queen and New Mississippi Queen travel riverboats.

**Further information:** Chamber of Commerce, 120 W. Fifth Street, Cincinnati, OH 45202.

## Cleveland, Ohio

The World Almanac is sponsored in the Cleveland area by The Cleveland Press, 901 Lakeside Avenue, Cleveland, OH 44114; (216) 623-1111; founded 1878 by E.W. Scripps; circulation 322,265; editor Thomas L. Boardman; managing editor Robert Sullivan; business manager William Holcombe; major awards include Pulitzer Prize, Lasker Award.

**Population:** 625,000 (city), 1,960,200 (metro area), first in state, total employed 879,000 (non-agricultural).

**Area:** 1,519 sq. mi., SMSA 4 county area; along southern shore of Lake Erie, east and west of Cuyahoga River.

**Industry:** city has been described as "an industrial powerhouse;" bills itself "The Best Location in the Nation." Within 600 miles are: more than 56% of U.S. population, more than 67% of U.S. manufacturing plants, more than 50% of retail sales in the U.S. and more than 60% of U.S. product value. No single industry dominates economy — steel and metal products are mainstays; manufacturing complex occupied essentially with primary metals, fabricated metal products, machinery, tools, automotive products. Important industries include making of electric motors, products of petroleum, rubber, plastic, stone, clay and glass, chemicals, paints, wearing apparel, measuring instruments, electronic components, food products, and publishing-printing. Value of products is $15 billion a year. Retail sales are more than $6 billion; median income of families is $15,832.

**Transportation:** Hopkins Airport with more than 6 million passengers each year; Burke Lakefront Airport, 5 minutes from Public Square and capable of handling intermediate jets; Port of Cleveland visited by more than 23 overseas steamship lines and Great Lakes fleet; largest city on Lake Erie and 3d largest on Great Lakes. Cleveland is only U.S. city with airport-to-downtown rail service; ride takes 20 minutes and costs about $10 less than a cab ride; Amtrak train service.

**Communications:** Cleveland Press, evening daily; Cleveland Plain Dealer, morning daily plus Sunday; numerous foreign language newspapers; 5 TV stations; 15 AM and 20 FM radio stations.

**New construction:** $50 million Medical Mutual Bldg., $50 million office complex, $26 million State of Ohio Bldg.

**Cultural facilities:** Cleveland Orchestra; Play House, nation's oldest and largest resident professional theater; Museum of Art; Karamu House for interracial arts; Western Reserve Historical Society; Health Museum; Natural Science Museum; Cultural Gardens; zoo; Blossom Music Center; Salvador Dali Museum; Garden Center; Sea World; aquarium.

**Educational facilities:** Case Western Reserve Univ., Baldwin-Wallace College, Cleveland State Univ., Cuyahoga Community College, John Carroll Univ.; Notre Dame and Ursuline colleges.

**Sports:** NFL Browns, American League Indians, NBA Cavaliers, and World Team Tennis Nets; also golfing, horse and car racing, boating.

**Other attractions:** downtown Convention Center is largest city-owned convention facility in U.S.; public library is 5th in size of book collection in U.S.; Public Square, hub of city, marked by 52-story Terminal Tower. "The Forest City" is encircled by "Emerald Necklace," 18,000 acres of metropolitan parks. Cleveland Clinic, known for medical research, attracts patients from throughout the world. Many nationality restaurants, due to large ethnic population (close to 4,000 immigrants each year).

**History:** settlement established in summer, 1796 by Gen. Moses Cleaveland, was capital of the Western Reserve, became a city in 1836.

**Further information:** Greater Cleveland Growth Assn., 690 Union Commerce Bldg., Cleveland, OH 44115.

## Columbia, South Carolina

The World Almanac is sponsored in the Columbia area by Columbia Newspapers, Inc., P.O. Box 1333, Columbia, SC 29202; phone (803) 771-6161; circulation, The State (am) 104,631; The Columbia Record (pm) 33,694; The State (Sun.) 120,776 (ABC 3/31/78); Ambrose G. Hampton, publisher; Ben R. Morris, co-publisher; Arthur D. Cooper, associate publisher, president and general manager; James W. Holton Jr., assistant general manager and advertising director; William E. Rone, editorial page editor (The State); Thomas N. McLean, editor, The Columbia Record.

**Population:** 113,542 (1970 census), city corporate limits; 2-county metro area (Richland and Lexington) estimated 384,500 (Fed-State Co-op '78).

**Area:** 105 sq. mi. (Richland County); 1,525 sq. mi. (metro); center of South Carolina, at confluence of Broad and Saluda rivers (at Columbia).

**Government:** state capital with about 100 agencies (state); 19 (federal) agencies; government employees total more than 25,000; Fort Jackson Military Post numbers over 25,000 personnel.

**Industry:** more than 50 national firms such as General Electric, Allied Chemical, Continental Can, Burlington, Litton, Bendix, M. Lowenstein, Rockwell Int., Square D, Westinghouse, Colite Ind., Tamper, Shakespeare, Allis-Chalmers, fibres, heavy equipment, electronics, textiles, fertilizer, and cement products. Columbia (SMSA) industrial wages for 1976 exceeded $210 million; industrial capital invested is estimated to exceed $475 million.

**Commerce:** retail sales (metro) over $1.2 billion ('78); consumer spendable income $1.7 billion; median household income (metro) $15,750; 11 commercial (main) banking institutions.

**Transportation:** Metropolitan Airport with 4 major airlines and freight service; 3 rail freight lines, Amtrak; 44 major freight companies; 3 interstate, 6 federal, and 5 state highways.

**Communications:** 4 TV and 12 radio stations.

**Medical facilities:** 6 general hospitals, including modern Richland Memorial; William S. Hall Psychiatric Institute; 2 state mental hospitals.

**Cultural facilities:** Town Theatre, the oldest continuous community theater in nation; 3 other theaters; Museum of Art and Sciences; Gibbes Planetarium; Township Auditorium, home of Artist Series; Dreher Auditorium with Philharmonic Orchestra, City Ballet, Lyric Theatre and Choral Society; Fraser Hall; Columbia Coliseum with seating capacity of 13,000.

**Recreation facilities:** 13 golf courses; city park system; 2 municipal pools; wide range of hunting activities; Riverbanks Zoological Park, part of 135-acre complex; Lake Murray, water sports.

**Sports:** Williams-Brice Stadium, home of Univ. of South Carolina Fighting Gamecock football team; Carolina Coliseum for basketball, conventions.

**Educational facilities:** 25,000-student Univ. of South Carolina; 4 private colleges; Technical Education Center; Lutheran Seminary.

**History:** established 1786 as state capital; burned in 1865 by Union General Sherman.

**Further information:** Chamber of Commerce, 1308 Laurel Street, Columbia, SC 29202.

## Columbus, Georgia — Phenix City, Alabama

The World Almanac is sponsored in the Columbus, Ga. - Phenix City, Ala., area by the Columbus Enquirer and the Columbus Ledger, 17 W. 12th Street, Columbus, GA 31902; phone (404) 322-8831; combined daily circulation 66,352; Sunday 68,717. Enquirer founded 1828, awarded Pulitzer Prize 1926; Ledger founded 1886, awarded Pulitzer Prize 1955. Published by the R. W. Page Corporation; Glenn Vaughn, president and general manager; J. Carrol Dadisman, vice-president and executive editor. Owned by Knight-Ridder Newspapers, Inc.

**Population:** 172,000 (Columbus); 26,000 (Phenix City); 250,000 (metro); 81,700 employed (metro).

**Area:** 1,100 sq. miles (metro: Muscogee and Chattahoochee counties, Ga.; Russell County, Ala.) straddling the Chattahoochee River.

**Industry:** major textile production center: Swift, Fieldcrest, Gomibo U.S.A., Cartersville, Columbus Mills, Bibb Mfg., Reeves Bros., West Point Pepperell, Union Carbide TRW, International hqs. Tom's Foods Ltd. and Burnham Van Lines; lumber products, beverages, concrete, bakery goods, and paper.

**Commerce:** center of west Georgia—east Alabama finance, agriculture, textiles, hydroelectric power; metro retail sales $684.9 million; avg. household buying income $13,984; 9 banks, 6 savings and loan associations.

**Federal facilities:** Ft. Benning, world's largest infantry school, $321.5 million annual disbursements.

**Transportation:** 2 rail lines, 2 bus lines; Delta, Eastern, Southern airlines; 33 truck lines; Chattahoochee is navigable river.

**Communications:** 3 TV and 10 radio stations.

**New construction:** 70,000 sq. ft. convention and trade center, TRW, Westvaco, metro airport expansion; Ft. Benning expansion for One Station Training; Bradley Office Park, Union Carbide, Georgia Power, I-185, Oscar Mayer.

**Medical facilities:** 5 hospitals.

**Cultural facilities:** Museum of Arts and Sciences, Springer Theater (state theater of Georgia), Three Arts Theater, Bradley Memorial Library; Columbus College, Chattahoochee Valley Community College.

**Sports:** Astros, Southern baseball league.

**History:** Columbus founded 1828; gained early prominence as shipping center for cotton, fish; birthplace of Coca-Cola formula. Phenix City founded 1883, growing from a Creek Indian trading post.

**Further information:** Columbus Chamber of Commerce, P.O. Box 1200, Columbus, GA 31902, or Phenix City-Russell County Chamber of Commerce, P.O. Box 1326, Phenix City, AL 36867.

## Columbus, Ohio

The World Almanac is sponsored in the Columbus area by the Columbus Citizen-Journal, 34 S. Third Street, Columbus, OH 43216; (614) 461-5000; Citizen founded 1899, Journal 1811; circ. 113,500 a.m. daily except Sun.; owned by E. W. Scripps Co.; editor Richard R. Campbell, business manager Gregory A. Dembski, managing editor Seymour Raiz.

**Population:** 605,200 (city), 19th in nation, 1,114,800 (metro area), 1977 ests.; 2d in state, total employed 480,000.

**Area:** 174.5 sq. mi. central Ohio; state capital and Franklin County seat.

**Industry:** diversified; 1,019 manufacturers including General Motors, Rockwell International, Western Electric, Columbus Products Co., Borden (natl. hqs.); planes, missiles, refrigerators, mining machinery, telephones, glass products, auto parts; est. 1975 production-workers payroll $989 million; home office of Battelle Memorial Institute with worldwide research laboratories.

**Commerce:** wholesale, retail center for central, southern Ohio, parts of W. Va., Ky. Retail sales, $3.9 billion; financial assets $9.9 billion; 8 banks, 20 savings and loan assns.; 52 insurance co. home offices, assets $5.4 billion. Per capita income $5,321. Defense Construction Supply Center, world's largest; 21% of employment is government.

**Transportation:** 125 truck lines, 3 intercity bus lines, 5 railroads, 10 airlines using Port Columbus International with 750 air movements daily; 8 major highways.

**Communications:** 5 TV stations, 12 radio stations.

**Medical facilities:** 18 hospitals, medical centers; Children's Hospital leads nation in children admitted; Ohio State Univ. School of Medicine.

**Cultural facilities:** Ohio Theatre, symphony orchestra, new Cultural Arts Center facing Bicentennial Park; art museums including new open-air sculpture garden about Columbus Museum of Art; Players Theatre, public library with 22 branches; Center for Science and Industry, Ohio Historical Society with 19th century village.

**Other attractions:** Ohio Expositions Center with its coliseum and Ohio State Fair; German Village (restored South Side, urban); Lynn Street Mall, Park of Roses, world's largest; Ohio Railway Museum, 252 parks, zoo, boating, floating amphitheater.

**Educational facilities:** Ohio State, Capital, Franklin univs., Ohio Dominican College, Columbus College of Art & Design, Columbus Technical Institute.

**New construction:** Ohio Center (for conventions), linked hotel, access boulevards, $90 million; Capitol South redevelopment, high rises with sunken skating rink, $209 million; Municipal Courts high-rise; Shrine mosque (completed); Port Columbus expansion and renovation; 2 existing hospitals to be replaced; 10 Arlington Place (condominiums).

**Federal facilities:** Rickenbacker AFB.

**Sports:** Ohio Stadium and Franklin County Stadium; Clippers (baseball), Beulah Park (thoroughbreds), Scioto Downs (harness); Muirfield Memorial golf tournament.

**History:** founded 1812 as state capital, named for Christopher Columbus.

**Further information:** Chamber of Commerce, P. O. Box 1527, Columbus, OH 43216.

## Corpus Christi, Texas

The World Almanac is sponsored in the Corpus Christi area by The Caller and The Times, P.O. Box 9136, Corpus Christi, TX 78408; Caller (a.m.) founded 1883; Times (p.m.) founded 1911; merged 1929; Caller circ. 62,606, Times 27,120, Sunday 84,978; publisher Edward H. Harte; president Allan P. Johnson III; executive editor Robert E. Rhodes; Caller managing editor John B. Anderson; Times managing editor Bill Duncan.

**Population:** 221,000 (est.); labor force 107,200.
**Area:** 328 sq. mi. (226 water), 210 miles SW of Houston on Corpus Christi Bay; Nueces County seat.
**Industry:** oil refineries; offshore oil rig fabrication; chemical, petrochemical, synthetics, aluminum, and zinc plants.
**Commerce:** Port of Corpus Christi handled 60.7 million tons in 1977; economic hub of south Texas; farming, ranching, oil and gas production, commercial fishing, tourist trade; 13 banks have deposits in excess of $879 million.
**Transportation:** 5 airlines, 2 bus lines, 3 railroads but no rail passenger service.
**Communications:** 2 daily newspapers, 5 TV stations (one public service, one Spanish), 12 radio stations.
**New construction:** permits issued for $82.7 million in new construction in 1977.
**Medical facilities:** 9 hospitals, including a children's center, with 1,537 beds.
**Federal facilities:** Corpus Christi Naval Air Station is headquarters for Naval Air Training Command; Corpus Christi

Army Depot is army's only complete helicopter overhaul plant; combined payroll more than $100 million.
**Cultural facilities:** Corpus Christi Museum, Art Museum of South Texas, Japanese Art Museum; symphony, little theatre, Del Mar College, Corpus Christi State Univ.
**Recreation:** public beaches and fishing piers on the bay and along Gulf of Mexico on Mustang Island and in 88-mile-long Padre Island National Seashore; surf and charter boat fishing; sailing, city marina with public launching ramps; large public tennis center, 3 private tennis clubs, 5 golf courses.
**History:** Spanish explorer Alonzo de Pineda discovered Corpus Christi Bay in 1519; Blas Maria de la Garza Falcon established San Petronilla Ranch on Petronilla Creek about 1765; city grew from a frontier trading post est. in 1839; city incorporated Feb. 16, 1852.
**Further information:** Corpus Christi Chamber of Commerce, P.O. Box 640, Corpus Christi, TX 78403.

## Dallas, Texas

The World Almanac is sponsored in Dallas by The Dallas Morning News, Communications Center, Dallas, TX 75265; telephone (214) 745-8222; published by the oldest business in Texas, the News was founded in 1842 by Samuel Bangs; circulation, 352,257 Sunday, 282,751 daily; president Joe M. Dealey, executive editor Tom J. Simmons. Winner of numerous national awards including Freedoms Foundation and National Headliner. Sponsors Teen-age Citizenship Tribute, Fly-the-Flag program, Spelling Bee, Sports Show, Involved Citizen Award, etc.

**Population:** city, 826,000 (8th in nation); county 1,430,000; Dallas-Fort Worth metro area, 2,630,400 (10th in nation); total employed, 1,316,100 with 3.7% unemployment.
**Area:** 900 sq. mi. astride Trinity River in north Texas about 75 miles south of Oklahoma border; elevation from 450 to 750 feet. Dallas County seat.
**Industry:** banking and insurance capital of the Southwest, Dallas ranks 4th among U.S. cities in the number of million-dollar-net-worth companies with 657 such firms. Half of area wage and salary jobs are in the trades (27%) and manufacturing (22%), including food products, apparel, and printing-publishing.
**Commerce:** a $5 billion wholesale market ($10 billion retail), Dallas ranks first nationally in giftware, home furnishing and floor covering wholesaling, 2d in apparel and toys. Metro retail sales totaled $8.8 billion in 1977, while estimated buying income reached $15.8 billion and bank deposits $19.4 billion.
**Transportation:** Dallas-Fort Worth Airport is the nation's largest. In 1977, it was 3d in the world in air carrier operations with 365,634; 8.7 million passengers enplaned there. City is served by 12 major commercial and 4 commuter air lines, 8 railroads, 2 trans-continental bus lines, 87 motor freight lines, 3 taxicab companies with 525 cabs. Dallas Transit System serves 110,000 people daily on 110 lines, 544 route miles.
**Communications:** 2 metropolitan daily newspapers, numerous suburban dailies, 4 commercial VHF TV stations, public television, 1 UHF station, 17 AM and 21 FM radio stations, 2 city magazines.
**New construction:** $1.2 billion in building permits in 1977 ($466 million nonresidential); projects include sports center, 300-acre, $300 million office park, and $210 million Union Terminal area redevelopment.
**Medical facilities:** 59 hospitals with 9,735 beds, 500 bassinets. Baylor University Medical Center consistently ranks in the top 10 among the country's "super hospitals."
**Culture:** symphony orchestra, civic opera, summer musicals, civic ballet, Sunday concert series — among others — offer

varied programs; drama at Dallas Theater Center, Theater Three, National Children's Theater, Repertory Theater, and 4 dinner theaters; 7 museums; SMU's Owens Fine Arts Center with a collection of paintings and sculpture; numerous art galleries.
**Education:** 155,000 students attend 28 colleges and universities within 50 miles of Dallas; Southern Methodist Univ., the Univ. of Texas at Dallas, Univ. of Dallas, North Texas State, Univ. of Texas at Arlington, Baylor Univ. College of Dentistry, Southwestern Medical School; the Dallas Community College system with 65,000 students on 7 campuses.
**Convention facilities:** 3 major convention centers, including expanded Dallas Convention Center with more combined meeting-exhibit space (611,000 sq. ft.) than any other in U.S.; 25,000 air-conditioned hotel rooms. Dallas always among nation's top 3 convention cities. In 1977, 1.5 million people attended 1,048 conventions.
**Sports:** professional sports include football, baseball, tennis, golf, hockey, soccer, and rodeo. Cotton Bowl is site of annual New Year's Day football game and SMU home games.
**Other attractions:** Six Flags Over Texas, Dallas Zoo, Texas Safari; Fair Park is home of State Fair of Texas 16 days each October; museums of fine arts, health and science, natural history; Hall of State; Garden Center and Music Hall; excellent lakes, golf courses, parks, luxury hotels, and restaurants.
**History:** first settler was Tennessee frontiersman John Neely Bryan who established a trading post and plotted the townsite in 1844; incorporated 1856; named for Vice-President George Mifflin Dallas. Since 1931, the city has had council-manager form of government. Spectacular population growth began after World War II, when aircraft manufacturing augmented an economy that had been built first on cotton, then on oil, banking, and insurance. Diversified economic expansion fed the growth of the 1960s.
**Further information:** Dallas Chamber of Commerce, Fidelity Union Tower, Dallas, TX 75201.

## Dayton, Ohio

The World Almanac is sponsored in the Dayton area by The Journal Herald, 37 S. Ludlow Street, Dayton, H, 45402; 225-2421; founded as Dayton Repertory; circulation 100,851; editor Dennis Shere, managing edi-r William Worth; editorial page editor William Wild, "Day" section editor Mickey Davis.

**opulation:** 197,100 (city), 835,200 (metro), 4th in state, ith in nation; total employed 353,700.

**rea:** 43.7 sq. mi. (1977) at junction Mad, Miami, and Still-ater rivers; Montgomery County seat.

**dustry:** NCR Corp., Dayton Press, Inc., General Motors orp. (Delco Moraine, Delco Products, Delco Air, Inland Ifg., and Frigidaire), Standard Register, Monarch Market-g Systems, Mead Corporation, Dayton Tire and Rubber o., Duriron Co., Inc., Monsanto Research Corp., Ohio ell, Dayton Newspapers, Inc., Dayton Power and Light; ore than 800 other manufacturing facilities.

**ommerce:** retail sales $2.8 billion, average effective buying ousehold income, $18,982.

**ransportation:** 2 airports, 6 airlines, 3 trunk rail systems, 4 is lines, Dayton Regional Transit Auth.

**ommunications:** 4 TV, 8 radio stations.

**ledical facilities:** 10 hospitals, including Wright Patterson FB Hosp. and a VA facility.

**ederal facilities:** Wright Patterson AFB headquarters for ir Force Logistics Command and Aeronautical System iv.; Defense Electronics Supply Center, Federal Bldg.

**onvention facilities:** modern downtown convention and xhibition center.

**ew or recent construction:** downtown arcade, Gem City avings Assoc. headquarters, Great Miami River Low Dam, ayton Career Academy, Courthouse Square Plaza, which includes dept. store, bank bldg., utilities bldg., Mead Tower World Headquarters, and 2 restaurants; Univ. of Dayton Law School, Wright State Med. School, and expansion of Sinclair Community College.

**Educational facilities:** Univ. of Dayton (new Law School), Wright State Univ. (new Med. School); 2 jr. colleges: Sinclair (downtown campus), Miami Jacobs (business); United Theological Seminary, Central State Univ., Wilberforce Univ., Antioch College.

**Cultural facilities:** Dayton Art Institute, Philharmonic Orchestra, opera, ballet, 4 amateur theatrical groups, 2 professional companies; Diehl band shell, Deed's Carillon, dinner theater.

**Sports:** Amateur Trapshoot Headquarters, college sports, Bogie Busters Tourn., Dayton Hydroglobe; 5 amateur soccer teams.

**Other attractions:** Air Force Museum, Carillon Park, Aviation Hall of Fame, Dayton Air Fair, Old Courthouse Museum, A World A'Fair, Dayton River Corridor Festival, Paul Lawrence Dunbar Home, Wright Bros. Memorial, Oregon Historic District.

**History:** "Birthplace of Aviation".

**Further information:** Dayton Area Chamber of Commerce, Suite 1980, Winters Bank Tower, 40 N. Main Street, Dayton, OH 45402

## Denver, Colorado

The World Almanac is sponsored in the Denver area by the Rocky Mountain News, 400 W. Colfax Avenue, enver, CO 80201, (303) 892-5000; founded 1859 by William N. Byers; circulation daily 255,270, Sunday 75,487; editor Michael Balfe Howard, business manager William W. Fletcher; sponsors Colorado-Wyoming pelling bee, Golden Wedding party, Huck Finn Day, Showagon.

**opulation:** 530,600 (city), 1,574,000 (metro area), first in ate, 26th in nation; total employed 700,000.

**rea:** 116.4 sq. mi. on S. Platte River at edge of Great ains near Rocky Mountains. State capital and Denver ounty seat.

**dustry:** Gates Rubber Co. is world's largest maker of v-elts and hose, 6th largest U.S. rubber company; Samsonite orp. is world's largest luggage manufacturer, also makes arniture; Adolph Coors Co. is nation's 4th largest brewer of eer; center for smokeless industry with 1,600 manufactur-g firms.

**ommerce:** largest distribution center in region embracing ne-third of U.S. geographical area; retail sales $10.9 billion 1977), bank deposits $5.6 billion, 94 banks, 16 savings and an associations, and 45 insurance company home offices; er capita income, $5,950.

**ransportation:** 6 major rail freight lines, Amtrak; Conti-ental and Greyhound bus lines; 3 interstate highways inter-ct city; Stapleton International Airport is nation's 8th argest, with 720 daily flights, hub for 8 trunk airlines; Fron-er Air Lines; United Air Lines Flight Training Center.

**ommunications:** 5 TV and 33 radio stations.

**ledical facilities:** largest medical center between Kansas ity and San Francisco; one of 17 regional comprehensive ancer centers; Univ. of Colorado Medical Center. National ewish Hospital, Children's Asthma Research Institute and ospital (CARIH); 22 major hospitals.

**ederal facilities:** largest complex of federal offices outside Washington, D.C., with 37,700 federal employes; site of Energy Research and Development Administration's Rocky Flats plant, U.S. Mint, Lowry AFB, Air Force Accounting and Finance Center, Fitzsimons Army Medical Center, Army's Rocky Mountain Arsenal.

**Cutural facilities:** symphony orchestra, 3 nonprofessional orchestras, 3 choral groups, Denver Art Museum. 12 theater companies; 3-sq.-block convention center; 12,000-seat Red Rocks outdoor theater; new Performing Arts Center.

**Educational facilities:** Univ. of Colorado, Univ. of Denver, Colorado School of Mines; Colorado Women's, Metropolitan State, Loretto Heights, and Regis colleges; Univ. of Colorado School of Medicine, Iliff School of Theology.

**Recreational facilities:** 150 parks, 8,030 acres of mountain parks, 40 golf courses in metro area. City Park Zoo, 2 amusement parks; many ski areas.

**Sports:** pro teams include Broncos, NFL; Bears, baseball, American Assn.; Nuggets, NBA; Rockies, NHL; Caribous, professional soccer; Comets professional volleyball.

**Other attractions:** Museum of Natural History, Botanic Gardens, State Historical Museum.

**History:** founded 1858 with discovery of gold, fast became supply center for mountain mining camps; named for territorial governor.

**Further information:** Denver Chamber of Commerce, 1301 Welton Street, Denver, CO 80204; Hospitality Center, 280 14th Street, Denver, CO 80202.

## Des Moines, Iowa

The World Almanac is sponsored in Iowa by the Des Moines Register and Tribune, 715 Locust Street, Des Moines, IA 50304; (515) 284-8000; founded 1849; circulation evening Tribune 96,043, morning Register 34,648, Sunday Register 439,222; board chairman and publisher David Kruidenier, president and editor Mi-

chael Gartner, business manager Louis Norris; sales director J. Robert Hudson. Major awards include 12 Pul
litzer prizes.

**Population:** 201,404 (city, 1970), 333,400 (1977 est. metro area).
**Area:** 66 sq. mi., at juncture of Raccoon and Des Moines rivers, south central Iowa. State capital and Polk County seat.
**Industry:** considered to be 2d largest insurance center in nation (56 home companies) and 2d largest tire center with Firestone, Armstrong plants; publishing center — Meredith Co., Better Homes and Gardens, Wallace-Homestead, others; farm implements — North American headquarters and plant of Massey-Ferguson, John Deere; lawn and garden equipment, sporting goods, food products, cosmetics, dental equipment, automotive accessories, concrete forms, nozzles, tools; 700 wholesale and jobbing firms; Standard Oil credit card center, bulk mail center.
**Commerce:** retail sales in metro area, $1.165 billion (1976); per capita income, $6,201 (1976); average household income, $17,697.
**Transportation:** newly enlarged in-city airport, 4 major airlines; 4 bus lines; 6 railroads; 69 truck lines, Interstate Highways 80 and 35.
**New construction:** civic theater and park, major hospital

additions, botanical center, hotel, office bldgs., insurance co
addition.
**Communications:** 13 radio, 4 TV, cablevision.
**Medical facilities:** 11 hospitals with 2,700 beds.
**Cultural facilities:** art center, Center of Science and Indus
try, community playhouse, drama workshop, Drake Univer
sity, symphony orchestra, Grand View Junior, Area Com
munity, and 2 bible colleges; College of Osteopathi
Medicine and Surgery, ballet.
**Recreation:** 1,400 acres of parks, 9 public golf courses, 1
public pools, tennis, YWCA, YMCA; new $96 million reser
voir at north edge of city.
**Other attractions:** AAA baseball, Drake Relays, Missou
Valley and Big Eight (Iowa State U.) conferences; 15,000
seat auditorium; boys and girls state basketball tourna
ments, State Fair, Living History Farm, Children's Zoo, 36
story Ruan Center, tallest in Iowa, Terrace Hill (Governor
Mansion), state capitol and state historical bldg.
**History:** founded 1843 as a fort to protect rights of Indian
incorporated 1853, became Iowa capital 1857.
**Further information:** Chamber of Commerce, 8th and Hig
Streets, Des Moines, IA 50309.

## Detroit, Michigan

The World Almanac is sponsored in the Detroit area by The Detroit News, 615 Lafayette, Detroit, MI 48231
(313) 222-2000; founded 1873 by James E. Scripps; circulation (D) 633,708 (S) 826,111; president and pub
lisher Peter B. Clark, sr. v.p. R. M. Spitzley, exec. v.p. J. T. Dorris, v.p. and editor W. E. Giles; major award
won include Pulitzer Prize, Nat'l Headliners; over 70 community projects include NCAA Indoor Track Champi
onships, Science Fair, Scholastic Writing Awards, Spelling Bee.

**Population:** 1,335,085 (city, 1975) first in state, 6th in U.S.; 4,420,300 (metro area).
**Area:** 139.6 sq. mi. on the Detroit River, a Great Lakes connecting link and the world's busiest inland waterway; Wayne County seat.
**Industry:** "The Motor City"; area plants produce 25% of the nation's cars and trucks, employing more than 231,000. Nonautomotive manufacturing and nonmanufacturing firms employ more than 1.4 million; other products are machine tools, iron products, metal stampings, hardware, industrial chemicals, drugs, paint, wire products.
**Commerce:** metro median income per household $16,618 (1976); area retail sales $15.2 billion (1977).
**Transportation:** served by 5 railroads, over 200 intercity truck lines, 19 airlines, and 31 scheduled steamship lines serving more than 40 countries.
**Communications:** 8 TV and 18 radio stations.
**New construction:** $350 million riverfront development, Renaissance Center, located on east side riverfront area, incorporating business offices, and the Plaza Hotel opened in 1977; other projects include 72 acre, $23.5 million Detroit Riverfront Arena; 22 acre, $38 million Detroit Free Press printing plant, and a 235 acre, $500 million midtown medical center.
**Cultural facilities:** symphony orchestra, International Institute, Meadow Brook music and drama programs, Institute of Arts, concert band, and the annual Freedom Festival, celebrating Canada's Dominion Day, July 1, and U.S. Independence Day, July 4.
**Educational facilities:** 11 colleges and universities are located in the metro area including Wayne State Univ., Univ. of Detroit, and branches of the Univ. of Michigan and

Michigan State.
**Convention facilities:** 75 acre, $100 million Civic Center
including Cobo Hall and Convention Arena with 400,000
sq. ft. of exhibit space, more than 25,000 rooms in 250 ho
tels and motels.
**Sports:** Tigers baseball (American League), Express (Nort
American Soccer League), NFL Lions, NHL Red Wing
NBA Pistons; 6 winter skiing areas within short driving dis
tance.
**Other attractions:** Chrysler, Ford, and General Motors aut
plants; Henry Ford Museum and Greenfield Village histor
cal displays, Cranbrook Institute (science museum and arts
Belle Isle (1,000 acre park), zoo, public library, historica
museum, and Fort Wayne Military Museum.
**History:** founded 1701 by the Frenchman Cadillac as a stra
tegic frontier fort and trading post, ceded to the British i
1763 and turned over to the U.S. in 1796 as a village of
2,500; reoccupied by the British for a year in the War of
1812. Completion of the Erie Canal in 1825 opened a chea
water transport route from New York to the Northwest an
made Detroit an important commercial center. R. E. Old
built Detroit's first auto factory in 1899; and Henry For
who handbuilt his first car in 1896, formed his first com
pany in 1899, and the present Ford Motor Co. in 1903. Th
area's industries made it the "Arsenal of Democracy" i
World War II.
**Further information:** Greater Detroit Chamber of Com
merce, 150 Michigan Avenue; and Detroit Public Informa
tion Dept., City-County Bldg., both Detroit, MI 48226; an
Detroit Convention Bureau, 100 Renaissance Center, De
troit, MI 48243.

## Edmonton, Alberta, Canada

The World Almanac is sponsored in central and northern Alberta by the Edmonton Journal, 10006 - 10
Street, Edmonton, Alberta, T5J 2S6; telephone (403) 425-9120; founded November 11, 1903. A division o
Southam Press Limited; circulation 185,000; publisher J. Patrick O'Callaghan; editor Andrew Snaddon. Spon
sor Learn to Ski, curl, play golf, tennis, and Shape Up Fitness programs; Literary Awards, Newspaper in Edu
cation.

**Population:** (est.) 479,000 (city), 598,000 (metro); capital of Alberta, largest Alberta city, 5th in Canada; total metro employed 419,726 (June 30, 1978).

**Area:** 123.34 sq. mi. on North Saskatchewan River.
**Industry:** 2d largest refining center in Canada, 7,000 pro
ducing wells; petrochemical industries include plastics, ferti

zers, man made fibers, steel tube mills, 2d largest meat processing center in Canada; prosperous mixed farming.

**Commerce:** major supply center for Northwest Territories, Yukon, northeastern B.C., and Canadian Arctic; originating terminus of 5 oil and natural gas pipelines east and west from Alberta, Alaska, and the Canadian north; retail sales (est. '78) $3.08 billion, mfg. shipments (est. '78) $3.04 billion; trading area population (est.) 1,100,000.

**Transportation:** Alaska and Mackenzie highways; Canadian National, Canadian Pacific; Northern Alberta, Great Slave, and Alberta Resources railroads; 4 airports, 6 airlines, 245,828 itinerant movements in 1978; new Light Rapid Transit System opened in 1978.

**Communications:** 8 radio stations including one French station, 4 TV including one French station, 3 cable TV.

**Medical facilities:** 5 general and 5 auxiliary hospitals, 2 rehabilitation centers, 9 nursing homes.

**Cultural facilities:** Edmonton Symphony Orchestra, Edmonton Art Gallery, Centennial Library, Provincial Museum and Archives, Univ. of Alberta (Canada's 3d largest), Northern Alberta Institute of Technology (Canada's largest technical college), Grant McEwan Community College, Alberta and Edmonton ballet companies. Canada's most active professional theater, housed in the new $6 million Citadel Theatre complex; Edmonton Opera, Northern Alberta Jubilee Auditorium, Queen Elizabeth Planetarium, Muttart Conservatory.

**Other attractions:** Klondike Days, annual celebration of the 1898 Yukon gold rush is held in mid-July; Valley Zoo, Fort Edmonton, Capital City Recreation Park, Hawrelak Park; Alberta Game Farm, Elk Island Park, and many lakes nearby.

**Sports:** CFL Edmonton Eskimos, WHA Edmonton Oilers, Western Major Fastball League Monarchs; 16,000 seat Coliseum opened in 1974; 45,000 seat sport complex and $8.5 million aquatic center built for the 1978 Commonwealth Games; Kinsmen Field House indoor track seats 4,000.

**History:** Fort Edmonton built in 1795, named after town now a borough of London, England; oil discovered at Leduc (20 miles south) in 1947 rocketed the city into prominence as one of the world's leading petrochemical centers.

## El Paso, Texas

The World Almanac is sponsored in the El Paso area by the El Paso Herald-Post, 401 Mills Avenue, El Paso, TX 79999, phone (915) 747-6700; Herald founded 1881, Post 1922, merged (under Scripps-Howard) 1931; circulation 36,135, Robert W. Lee, editor; Robert McBrinn, managing editor.

**Population:** 382,754 (Chamber of Commerce city estimate) with twin city Juarez, Mex., 518,726; 5th in state, 33d in nation; total employed 143,200.

**Area:** 174 sq. mi., western tip of Texas where Rio Grande cuts boundaries of Texas, New Mexico, and Mexico at foot of the Rockies (including Franklin Mtns.); El Paso County seat.

**Industry:** manufacturing payroll, $232.9 million in 1977; manufacturing employment, 29,650; clothing largest employer, including Farah, Levi Straus, Mann, Hicks-Ponder, Billy the Kid; Juarez-El Paso border in-bond industries at 75 and 27,545 employed, including electronic and other, such as RCA, GTE, Sylvania, General Instruments, American Hospital Supply, and Allen Bradley; home of El Paso Natural Gas, ASARCO, Inc., Peyton Packing, Tony Lama Boots, Phelps Dodge, Standard and Texaco refineries, Old El Paso (pet foods) and Ashley's of Texas canned Mexican foods; nut processing, cattle, pecans, cotton and other agriculture.

**Commerce:** wholesale-retail center for west Texas, New Mexico, northern Mexico; retail sales in 1977 $1.5 billion; 1977 bank deposits $1.4 billion; bank clearings, $9.6 billion; 20 banks, 6 savings and loan associations. Value added in 1977 $517.7 million including $229.9 million in labor; exports in 1977, $448.3 million, with $783.9 million in imports.

**Transportation:** 5 major rail lines, Amtrak; 8 bus lines, 18 truck lines, 5 major highways; gateway to Mexico, busiest crossing point on the U.S. border with 62.2 million crossings in 1977; International Airport, 4 airlines with 223,866 flights in 1977 and 1,442,056 passengers, 15,608 tons of freight.

**Communications:** 5 TV and 18 radio stations.

**New construction:** 1977 building permits totaled $214.8 million.

**Medical facilities:** 16 hospitals with 2,994 beds; area cancer treatment center; Univ. of Texas System School of Nursing, Texas Tech Univ. School of Medicine.

**Federal facilities:** Ft. Bliss (U.S. Army Air Defense center, Allied Students Missile Center, Sgts. Major Academy), William Beaumont Army Medical Center, and nearby McGregor Range, White Sands Missile Range, and Holloman AFB in New Mexico.

**Cultural facilities:** Univ. of Texas at El Paso, El Paso Community College, El Paso Symphony, Museum of Art with Kress Collection, Ballet El Paso, opera companies, theater groups, Chamizal National Memorial theater, and McKelligon Canyon Pavilion; $20 million civic-convention center; public libraries.

**Other attractions:** annual Sun Carnival and Sun Bowl football game; Tigua Indian community arts and crafts center, missions that pre-date those of the Californias, horse racing in nearby New Mexico, horse and dog racing in Juarez, zoo, Cavalry Museum, Wilderness Park Museum, Guadalupe Mountains and Big Bend National Parks within 300 miles; skiing in Ruidoso, N.M. and Carlsbad Caverns within 200 miles; exotic Juarez, Mexico and Pancho Villa country.

**Further information:** Convention and Visitors Bureau, Five Civic Center Plaza, El Paso, TX 79901.

## Erie, Pennsylvania

The World Almanac is sponsored in the Erie area by The Erie Daily Times, 205 W. 12th Street, Erie, PA 16501; (814) 456-8531; founded in 1888; circulation 74,000 daily, 92,000 Sunday; Edward M. Mead, Michael Mead, co-publishers; executive editor Joseph Meagher, managing editor Len Kholos.

**Population:** 127,895 (city), 265,618 (metro area), 3d in state; total employed, 55,971.

**Area:** 19.53 sq. mi. at tip of northwestern Pa.; Erie County seat.

**Commerce:** Erie County, pop. 275,000, produces $133 million in exports, highest per capita export in U.S.; tourism — 5 miles of beaches, good fishing, boating, winter sports; seaport — 60 or more oceangoing vessels each year; over 506 industrial plants producing machinery and parts; iron and steel forgings; hardware, meters, plastics, paper (Hammermill), furniture, and toys; General Electric producing Amtrak passenger trains.

**New construction:** addition to Erie Marine Terminal of a 300 ton heavy-lift derrick crane, the largest on the American shores of the Great Lakes; $4 million, 30 acre diked disposal area for dredgings from the Erie harbor; 300,000 sq. ft. terminal shed for storage of specialty ores and materials; conversion of St. Joseph Orphanage into home for elderly and handicapped, addition to Erie Insurance Exchange office headquarters, alterations to Hamot Medical Center, renovation of Erie stadium, conversion of Richford Hotel to apartments for elderly, renovation of Erie firehouses.

**Special awards:** Freedom Foundation Award for 1977 "We Love Erie By Day" celebration.

**Transportation:** 4 railroads, Boston-Chicago Amtrak line; airport; 35 trucking companies, 4 bus lines.

**Cultural facilities:** Penn State Univ. extension, Gannon,

Mercyhurst, and Villa Maria colleges; Philharmonic Society, Council of the Arts, theater groups; new field house for plays, entertainment, sports.
**History:** Named after Eriez Indians; site of building of ship

Niagara with which Oliver Hazard Perry defeated British in 1813 in Lake Erie battle.
**Further information:** Chamber of Commerce, 1006 State, Erie, PA 16501.

## Evansville, Indiana

The World Almanac is sponsored in southwestern Indiana, western Kentucky, and southeastern Illinois by the Evansville Press, 201 N.W. Second Street, Evansville, IN 47701; (812) 464-7600; founded July 2, 1906, by E.W. Scripps and J.C. Harper; circulation, 45,600; editor, William W. Sorrels; managing editor, Paul Knue.

**Population:** 133,566 (city), 286,700 (metro area), 4th in state.
**Area:** 47 sq. mi. at bend of Ohio River in southwest corner of state; Vanderburgh County seat.
**Industry:** Whirlpool Corp. plants (refrigeration and air conditioning); Mead Johnson & Co. (pharmaceutical division of Bristol-Myers Co.); Alcoa Warrick Operations (aluminum) just east of city; 283 manufacturing firms.
**Commerce:** retail sales, $1.029 billion (1977); effective buying income per household, $15,582 (1977); home offices of CrediThrift of America, Inc.; 4 banks, 6 savings and loan associations.
**Transportation:** world headquarters of Atlas Van Lines; 4 railroads; 5 commercial barge lines; 4 interstate bus lines;

Allegheny, Delta, Eastern air lines.
**Communications:** 2 daily newspapers; 4 TV and 6 radio stations.
**Medical facilities:** 4 general and mental hospitals; branch of Indiana University Medical School.
**Cultural facilities:** Philharmonic Orchestra, Museum of Arts and Science, Mesker Zoo, Univ. of Evansville, Indiana State Univ., Evansville; national headquarters of Phi Mu Alpha music fraternity. Abraham Lincoln boyhood home nearby.
**Sports:** Evansville Triplets baseball of American Assn. (AAA), farm team of Detroit Tigers.
**Further information:** Chamber of Commerce, Southern Securities Building, Evansville, IN 47708.

## Fort Wayne, Indiana

The World Almanac is sponsored in the Fort Wayne area by the Journal-Gazette, 600 W. Main Street, Fort Wayne, IN 46802 (219) 461-8333; established June 14, 1899 by consolidation of The Journal and The Daily Gazette; circulation daily 61,743, Sundays 102,384; president-publisher Richard G. Inskeep; secretary-treasurer Naomi Erb; editor Larry W. Allen.

**Population:** 189,100 (city), 372,800 (metro area); total employed 171,100.
**Area:** 51.96 sq. mi. at confluence of St. Joseph, St. Mary's, and Maumee rivers in NE Ind.; Allen County seat. Allen County is largest of Indiana's 92 counties (671 sq. mi.), and has greatest number of farms in state, 2,011.
**Industry:** General Electric and International Harvester largest employers; Magnavox, Essex International, and Central Soya home offices; several firms manufacture about 85% of world's diamond wire dies.
**Commerce:** wholesale and retail center for northeastern Indiana, southeastern Michigan, northwestern Ohio; retail sales (metro) over $1.065 billion; bank deposits $1,878 billion; 5 banks, 4 savings-and-loan assns.; E. B. I. per household (metro) $19,040; 6 life insurance companies, including Lincoln National Life, based here.
**Transportation:** 2 major rail freight lines; Amtrak; 56 motor freight lines including home-based North American Van, Elway Express, Scott, and Transport Motor; I-69 connects

city with Indianapolis and Indiana Toll Road; U.S. 30 dual lane to Chicago; municipal airport; hq. for 122D Tactical Fighter Wing, Indiana Air National Guard; United, Delta, Air Wisconsin airlines.
**Communications:** 10 radio, 3 TV stations.
**Medical facilities:** 4 hospitals including VA.
**Cultural facilities:** Philharmonic Orchestra; Fine Arts and Performing Arts complex; 9 universities and colleges; 3 museums; Foellinger outdoor theater.
**Sports:** Komet hockey team (IHL) plays at Allen Co. War Memorial Coliseum; annual Mad Anthony celebrities golf tournament.
**Other attractions:** replica of 3d Fort Wayne (1815); children's zoo; 88 parks and playgrounds; 19 golf courses; 37 shopping centers.
**History:** first white settlement in Indiana (circa 1692).
**Further information:** Chamber of Commerce, 826 Ewing Street, Ft. Wayne, IN 46802.

## Fort Worth, Texas

The World Almanac is sponsored in the Fort Worth area by the Fort Worth Star-Telegram, 400 West Seventh, Fort Worth, TX 76101; phone (817) 336-9271; circulation (morn.) 87,989, (eve.) 142,355, (Sat.) 207,403, (Sun.) 233,464. Established in 1906, Publisher Amon G. Carter Jr.; executive editor Jack Tinsley; vice-president and general manager Phil J. Meek.

**Population:** 414,950 (city, 1978 est.); Ft. Worth/Dallas metro area 2.7 million (1978 est.); 4th largest Texas city; work force of 367,330 (1978 avg.), unemployment average 4.9%.
**Area:** 233 sq. mi. on the Trinity River in north central Texas; Tarrant County seat.
**Commerce:** all types of manufacturing; wholesale and retail center for large area including west Texas; retail sales $2.6 billion (1978 est.); effective buying income $4.3 billion (1978 est.); bank deposits $3.8 billion (48 Tarrant County banks); over 60 mortgage institutions, insurance companies, and savings and loan associations.
**Transportation:** Dallas-Fort Worth Regional Airport, 17 miles from downtown; Meacham Field, general aviation airport, many smaller airports; 9 railroads; Amtrak, 38 motor carriers, and 5 bus companies.

**Communications:** 2 TV and 18 area radio stations; 1 daily newspaper; weekly and monthly publications.
**Medical facilities:** over 20 hospitals.
**Federal facilities:** 14 federal agencies and Carswell AFB; reserve training centers.
**Cultural facilities:** Casa Manana, America's first permanent musical arena theater; symphony, opera; Van Cliburn Piano Competition; museums include Kimball Art Museum, Amon Carter Museum of Western Art, Fort Worth Museum of Science & History, and Fort Worth Art Center.
**Educational facilities:** 3 campuses of Tarrant County Junior College; Texas Christian Univ., Univ. of Texas at Arlington, Texas Wesleyan College, Southwestern Baptist Seminary, Texas Woman's Univ., and other technical and vocational schools.
**Recreation:** 6 Flags Over Texas, Forest Park and Fort

Worth Zoological Park; several other parks.
**Convention facilities:** Tarrant County Convention Center, Will Rogers Memorial Center.
**Sports attractions:** Texas Rangers baseball; Fort Worth Texans in hockey; Colonial National Golf Tournament; TCU football, other college and semi-pro teams.

**Other attractions:** Fat Stock Show and Rodeo; Miss Texas Pageant.
**History:** founded 1849 as a frontier Army post on the Chisholm Trial; became major railhead.
**Further information:** Chamber of Commerce, 700 Throckmorton Street, Fort Worth, TX 76102.

## Fresno, California

The World Almanac is sponsored in the Fresno area by The Fresno Bee, 1626 E Street, Fresno, CA 93721; phone (209) 268-5221; founded 1922; circulation daily 125,548, Sunday 144,999; president Eleanor McClatchy, editor C. K. McClatchy, managing editor George Gruner.

**Population:** 194,800 (city), 475,000 (county); total employed 202,200.
**Area:** one of largest counties in the state, 3,819,456 acres; located in geographical center of the state; Fresno County seat.
**Agriculture:** leading county in U.S. in farm production, number of farms, and annual value of agriculture production; state's leading county in production of field and seed crops, grapes, cantaloupes, barley, tomatoes, turkeys, peaches, boysenberries, figs, nectarines, potatoes, cotton seed, alfalfa seed, fruit and nuts.
**Industry:** 475 diversified manufacturing establishments; food processing is major industry; 2d in importance is production of beverages, primarily wine, brandy and spirits; metro retail sales (1977) over $1.7 billion.
**Transportation:** airports, daily service by 5 airlines; freeways connect to all major metropolitan areas in California; served by 23 common truck carriers, 2 interstate bus lines and 2 mainline railroads with freight handling facilities.

**Communications:** 5 TV and 16 radio stations.
**Medical facilities:** 6 general hospitals, including a Veterans' Administration installation.
**Cultural facilities:** Community and Convention Center; community philharmonic, opera, ballet, and theater; California State Univ.-Fresno, Pacific College, 3 community colleges.
**Recreation:** golf courses; tennis courts; swimming pools; 3 national parks; Yosemite, Sequoia, and Kings Canyon with groves of giant Sequoia trees plus facilities for boating, sailing, hunting, fishing, skiing, hiking, pack trips and camping.
**Other attractions:** city zoo, nationally famous rodeo, county fair, underground gardens, Kearney Museum; downtown malls with one of the best outdoor art displays in the West.
**History:** area explored by the Spaniards in the early 1800s and visited by fur trappers before 1840; settlement began when gold miners came in the 1850s; county created Apr. 19, 1856, from parts of Mariposa, Merced, and Tulare counties.

## Halifax, Nova Scotia, Canada

The World Almanac is sponsored in Nova Scotia by The Chronicle-Herald and The Mail-Star, 1650 Argyle Street, Halifax; phone (902) 426-2811; circulation Chronicle (morning) 70,627, Mail-Star (aft.) 54,675; publisher Graham W. Dennis, president Fred G. Mounce, chairman of the board L. F. Daley, general manager Frank Huelin, acting managing editor Ken Foran, treasurer W.D. Coleman.

**Population:** 117,882 (1976); labor force 57,305, employed 53,170.
**Area:** 24.19 sq. mi. of land, on the southeast coast of the province, capital city.
**Industry:** leading industrial area in Atlantic provinces; establishments include oil refineries, electronic equipment manufacturers, ship yards, car assembly plants, plastic fabricators, metal works, breweries, and fish processing; 3d largest and one of Canada's most diversified scientific research centers.
**Commerce:** financial center of region, regional head offices for all major banks and investment houses; retail sales over $379.5 million annually in Halifax County; average family income $16,203 (1976); all 3 levels of government constitute employment for 18,000; armed forces have over 14,000 stationed in city.
**Transportation:** 2 major passenger-freight lines; 8 container lines call regularly at easternmost commercial port on mainland North America; container port with 3 sea-shore cranes handled 200,000 20-foot equivalent containers (1977); over

700,000 tons break bulk cargo and 12 million tons bulk cargo; international airport.
**Communications:** 5 radio, 2 TV stations; 2 daily and 1 weekly newspapers.
**New construction:** building permits issued for $80 million worth of construction in 1977; new container port being built.
**Education:** 6 degree-granting universities; 48 common and 3 private schools, one technical institute.
**Medical facilities:** 9 hospitals (3 teaching).
**Cultural facilities:** Atlantic Symphony Orchestra; one professional live theater and 2 amateur; 2 public libraries.
**Parks:** 3 major parks (403 acres).
**Sports:** home of Halifax Voyageurs of the AHL.
**History:** founded in 1749; meeting place of first legislative assembly in Canada (1758).
**Further information:** Halifax Visitors and Convention Bureau, suite 508, Market Mall, Scotia Square; phone (902) 426-8736.

## Hamilton, Ontario, Canada

The World Almanac is sponsored in Hamilton and the Niagara Peninsula by the Spectator (a division of Southam Press Ltd.) 44 Frid Street, Hamilton, Ontario; (416) 526-3333; founded in 1846; circulation 140,000; publisher John D. Muir; assistant to the publisher Thomas J. McCarthy; executive editor John Doherty, managing editor Alex Beer.

**Population:** 311,907 (city), 411,358 (Hamilton-Wentworth region); 7th in Canada, 2d in province.
**Area:** 54.4 sq. mi. (city), 426 sq. mi. (region) at west end of Lake Ontario.
**Industry:** 62 per cent of Canada's steel is produced at the

Steel Company of Canada Ltd., Dominion Foundries and Steel Ltd., and Slater Steel Ltd.; 678 plants in the metro area manufacturing iron and steel products, electrical appliances, agricultural equipment, tires, wire, food products, heavy machinery, chemicals, and textiles.

**Commerce:** retail sales (1977) $1.457 billion or 2.38 per cent of Canadian total sales; average weekly wage $257.83; disposable income per capita $6,930.

**Transportation:** Hamilton Street Railway, Canadian National and Canadian Pacific railways as well as Toronto, Hamilton, and Buffalo line; western terminus for GO transit (provincial rapid transit system); provincial highways to Toronto, Windsor, and Buffalo pass through region; city airport 9 miles south at Mount Hope.

**Communications:** TV station, community programming cable station, 4 radio stations.

**New construction:** $11 million library-market complex under construction, scheduled for completion in early 1979; $16 million convention center slated to begin construction.

**Medical facilities:** 5 major hospitals, including medical center at McMaster University; Hamilton Psychiatric Hospital; St. Peter's Center for chronically ill and geriatric patients.

**Educational facilities:** McMaster Univ., Mohawk College of Applied Arts and Technology.

**Cultural facilities:** Hamilton Place theater-auditorium; new $5.5 million art gallery; Hamilton Philharmonic Orchestra; Hamilton Players' Guild; Theatre Aquarius; Multicultural Centre.

**Convention facilities:** proposed convention center will have 17 meeting rooms, banquet space for up to 2,300 people in one room, topped by a 15-story office tower.

**Other attractions:** Dundurn Castle, restored prime minister's residence circa 1850; Whitehearn, restored Victorian home; Canadian Football Hall of Fame; Royal Botanical Gardens, one of the largest park systems per capita in Canada; Hess Village boutiques and restaurants in old restored homes; hiking on Bruce Trail, winding through region along Niagara Escarpment.

**Sports:** Hamilton Tiger-Cats football club, 2 municipal golf courses, Royal Hamilton Yacht Club.

**History:** explorer Sieur de la Salle discovered Hamilton area in 1669; city takes name from George Hamilton, who laid out streets on part of the farm he bought in 1813.

**Further information:** Chamber of Commerce, 155 James Street South.

---

## Hartford, Connecticut

**Population:** city, 147,000 (1977 est.); county, 826,200 (1976 est.); total employed in greater Hartford, 345,000 (1976 est.)

**Area:** 17.2 sq. mi. in central Connecticut; state capital.

**Industry:** "Insurance City," headquarters for 38 insurance firms employing 35,000; headquarters of United Technologies Corp., manufacturers of Pratt & Whitney jet engines, employing 46,000 in state.

**Commerce:** total retail sales (county, 1975) $2.59 billion; per household spendable income (1975) $15,529.

**Transportation:** intersection of interstates 84 and 91; Amtrak, Conrail; Bradley International Airport with 8 scheduled airlines and freight service; Brainard Airport in city with charter service.

**Communications:** one daily newspaper, 4 AM, 8 FM radio stations, 3 commercial TV stations, one educational station.

**Educational facilities:** Trinity College, Univ. of Hartford, Graduate Center of Rensselaer Polytechnic Institute, St. Joseph College, Greater Hartford Community College, Univ. of Connecticut Law School, School of Social Work, and Hartford branch.

**Cultural facilities:** Wadsworth Atheneum, the oldest public museum in America, Hartford Symphony, Connecticut Opera Assn., Hartford Stage Co., Hartford Ballet, Mark Twain Masquers.

**Convention facilities:** Hartford Civic Center complex including retail arcade, 20-story hotel, exhibition and assembly halls and coliseum being rebuilt and expanded for late-1979 re-opening.

**Sports:** Greater Hartford Open (golf), Aetna World Cup Tennis, New England Whalers (hockey), Travelers Criterium (bicycle racing).

**Other attractions:** Mark Twain House, Elizabeth Park Rose Gardens, New England Fiddle Contest in spring.

**History:** founded by Dutch in 1633; settled by Thomas Hooker and company from Newtown (now Cambridge), Mass. in 1636; named sole state capital, a distinction formerly shared with New Haven, in 1875.

**Further information:** Chamber of Commerce, 250 Constitution Plaza, Hartford, CT 06103.

---

## Honolulu, Hawaii

The World Almanac is sponsored in Hawaii by The Honolulu Advertiser, P.O. Box 3110, Honolulu, HI 96802; (808) 537-2977; founded July 2, 1856, as Pacific Commercial Advertiser by Henry M. Whitney; circulation 76,196 mornings, 184,528 Sunday; president and publisher Thurston Twigg-Smith, editor-in-chief George Chaplin, executive editor Buck Buchwach, managing editor Mike Middlesworth; awards from American Political Science Assn., American Assn. for the Advancement of Science, others.

**Population:** 724,100 (metro), 81% of state population; total employed, 297,000.

**Area:** 595 sq. mi., encompassing Oahu Island; state capital.

**Commerce:** major destination for U.S., Japanese tourists; persons staying a night or more, 3.4 million in 1977, up from 1.1 million a decade earlier; average daily visitor census, 87,000 in 1977, up from 28,000 a decade earlier; tourist spending, $1.6 billion in 1977, up from $380 million in 1967; visitor dollars top military spending, $1.0 billion in 1977; sugarcane and pineapple major agriculture export crops; retail sales (statewide) $4.3 billion (est.); total personal income $6.4 billion (est.); per capita personal income $7,445 (est.); Pacific basin business and financial center.

**Transportation:** dependent on ships, planes for most goods; passengers arrive mostly by air; 15 airlines serve airport; 5 domestic carriers, 8 foreign, 2 inter-island.

**Communications:** 5 TV, 33 radio stations; 2 major daily newspapers.

**Medical facilities:** 20 general hospitals, 7 special hospitals, including Tripler Army Medical Center, Univ. of Hawaii School of Medicine.

**Federal facilities:** 7 major military bases, including Pearl Harbor Naval Base.

**Cultural facilities:** statewide public school system, 223 schools with 172,181 students in 1977, 127 private schools with 35,822 students in 1977; 10-campus Univ. of Hawaii with 43,888 students; main campus at Manoa in Honolulu, 21,106 students in 1977; university stresses oceanography, tropical environment problems and resources, tsunami research, volcanology, interrace relations; East-West Center, Inc., at Manoa is public education corp. funded by federal government, attracts international students and researchers; Bernice Pauahi Bishop Museum is center for studies of Pacific cultures, houses artifacts, maintains floating square rigger Falls of Clyde plus branch museum in Waikiki; Polynesian Cultural Center showcases native dances, music, arts; Honolulu Academy of Arts.

**Recreation:** surfing, swimming, sailing, fishing, football, basketball, baseball.

**Other attractions:** Waikiki Beach, extinct volcano Diamond Head, Arizona Memorial, balmy weather, tradewinds, multi-racial population, cultural diversity, Polynesian heritage.

**History:** Honolulu ("sheltered bay" in Hawaiian) was a small village when first Westerners called aboard 2 British ships in 1786, 8 years after Capt. James Cook became first known European to discover Hawaiian Islands.

**Further information:** Hawaii Visitors Bureau, 2270 Kalakaua Avenue, Honolulu, HI 96815.

# Houston, Texas

The World Almanac is sponsored in the Southwest by The Houston Post, 4747 Southwest Freeway, Houston, TX 77001; phone (713) 621-7000; founded 1836; Oveta Culp Hobby, chairman of the board and editor; William P. Hobby, president; circulation daily 303,436, Saturday 335,465, Sunday 360,602; awards include Pulitzer Prize, Grand Prix, Editor & Publisher; community events sponsored: Educational Services, Science Engineering Fair; Scholastic Art Awards, travel shows, Houston Post Family Night at the Shrine Circus, the Rodeo, the Ice Capades.

**Population:** (city) 1,623,000, 5th in nation; (SMSA) 2,661,000; total employed (SMSA) 1,271,900; total wages and salaries (SMSA) $19.4 billion.

**Area:** 541 sq. mi. (city) on upper center Gulf Coast prairies, 49 ft. above sea level; Harris County seat; connected to Gulf of Mexico by 50-mile inland waterway, the Ship Channel.

**Industry:** nation's leading manufacturer in petroleum refining and petrochemicals, 5th in machinery manufacturing and 6th in fabricated metals; supplies nation with over 50% petrochemicals, 80% synthetic rubber, 25% natural gas; 9 refineries, 200 chemical plants, 3500 mfg. plants; produces $2 billion annually in steel, $50.7 million in agriculture, $10.8 million in rice; 300 firms in underwater, offshore, and oceanographic markets; exports chemicals, oilfield equip. machinery, food supplies.

**Commerce:** Houston-Galveston SCSA leads south and southwest in retail sales volume; average spendable family income $15,488; 197 metro banks with resources of $20 billion and deposits of $16.8 billion; 30 foreign banks.

**Transportation:** Port of Houston (nation's 3d in tonnage) connects with 250 world ports by 120 steamship lines, hosts 4500 ships yearly; 16 major airlines, 2 airports; 6 major rail systems; 32 common carrier truck lines; 207-mile freeway system; 800-mile bus transit system and expanding minibus fleet in downtown area.

**Communications:** 2 daily newspapers; 29 radio stations; 5 commercial, one educational TV station.

**New construction:** non-residential contracts awarded in 1977 $1.7 billion, residential units completed value $1.4 billion (1977).

**Medical facilities:** Texas Medical Center includes 35 buildings on 230 acres, 11 hospitals plus medical, dental, nursing schools employ 21,430 with annual budget of $458 million; Harris County has 59 hospitals (including VA) with 15,900 beds.

**Federal facilities:** Lyndon B. Johnson Space Center, $202 million manned-spacecraft center; Ellington AFB.

**Cultural facilities:** 11 theatrical organizations perform at $3 million Alley Theatre & Miller Outdoor Theatre; Houston Symphony Orchestra, Grand Opera Assn.; Houston Ballet Foundation perform in $7.5 million Jones Hall for Performing Arts; 30 major art galleries including Museum of Fine Arts (permanent collection valued at $14 million) and Contemporary Arts Museum; Houston Public Library, 26 branches; Harris County Public Library, 18 branches.

**Education:** 28 major universities including Rice, Univ. of Houston, Texas Southern; 2 major medical schools including Baylor College of Medicine and Univ. of Texas Health Science Center (8 branches). Houston Independent School District, 7th largest in nation; total enrollment 206,998; 22 school districts in Harris County, total enrollment 468,341; private and parochial school enrollment 30,000.

**Recreational facilities:** 265 parks, 5 municipal golf courses, 38 municipal swimming pools, 3 tennis centers with 54 courts and 85 neighborhood courts; Astroworld 60-acre amusement park; botanical garden arboretum, Herman Park and Zoo; 52 community centers, 45 county parks, 70 miles of Gulf beaches in one hour's drive.

**Convention facilities:** 319 major conventions held in Houston in 1977 with 580,785 delegates attending; hotels and motels have 26,000 rooms; the Astrodome can seat 60,000 for conventions; Astrohall has 795,000 sq. ft.; downtown locations include Albert Thomas Convention Center, 300,000 sq. ft.; Sam Houston Coliseum, 50,000 sq. ft.; Music Hall seats 3,036; Exposition Hall, 83,000 sq. ft. exhibit area.

**Sports:** Astros baseball, Oilers football, Rockets basketball, Hurricanes soccer; sports events centers are Astrodome and Summit.

**Climate:** temperature moderated by winds from Gulf of Mexico, abundant rainfall; average daily temp. 67.5, total precip. 34.94 inches (1977).

**Scientific facilities:** one of the top 10 science centers in the nation; 84 research firms maintain facilities for study in petroleum, chemicals, medicine, earth sciences, aerospace, oceanography.

**History:** founded 1836 by J. K. and A. C. Allen; city eventually encompassed Old Harrisburg which was an 1826 townsite laid out by John Harris; named for Gen. Sam Houston, commander of the Texas Army, which won independence from Mexico for the Republic of Texas Apr. 21, 1836. Houston was first president of the Republic, later governor of the state of Texas; both Houston and Harrisburg were for brief periods capitals of the republic.

**Further information:** Houston Convention and Visitor Council, 10006 Main; Houston Chamber of Commerce, 1100 Milam, both Houston, TX 77002.

---

# Huntington, West Virginia

The World Almanac is sponsored in the Huntington-Ashland-Ironton area by The Herald-Dispatch (morn.) and The Huntington Advertiser (aft.), Huntington Publishing Company, 946 Fifth Avenue, Huntington, WV 25720, member of the Gannett Group; circulation 55,810, Sunday 50,435. Publisher and president Harold E. Burdick, controller Ed Burns, managing editors, C. Donald Hatfield (Advertiser), and Bill Southerland (Herald-Dispatch).

**Population:** 74,315 (city); 297,200 (5-county metro area); largest city in the state.

**Area:** 15.86 sq. mi., on Ohio River near where West Virginia, Ohio, and Kentucky meet; Cabell County seat.

**Industry:** center for coal transport and for hand-crafted glass; leading industries are Ashland Oil, Armco Steel Co., Huntington Alloys, Inc., division of International Nickel Co.

**Commerce:** largest port for inland vessels in U.S. handles nearly 20 million tons of materials per year, moved by 5 freight companies; 1975 total retail sales in metro area, $750.1 million.

**Transportation:** Tri-State Airport, with the longest runway in the state, is served by 2 airlines, 500 air movements a month; Amtrak; 18 truck lines; urban bus transport system; 2 interstate bus lines.

**Communications:** 4 TV and 11 radio stations.

**Cultural facilities:** Marshall University; Ashland Community College (University of Kentucky); The Huntington Galleries of Art.

**Medical facilities:** 5 general hospitals with 1,076 total beds; 3 specialty hospitals including a VA hospital.

**New construction:** $32 million renewal program includes completion of downtown pedestrian shopping plaza and civic center; new city-county library under construction; riverfront marina and parkland development being planned.

**Further information:** Chamber of Commerce, 522 Ninth Street, Huntington, WV 25701.

## Indianapolis, Indiana

The World Almanac is sponsored in the Indianapolis area by The Indianapolis Star, The Indianapolis News, 307 N. Pennsylvania Street, Indianapolis, IN 46206; phone (317) 633-1240. News founded 1869; Star 1903; circulation daily Star, 214,979; daily News, 154,648; Sunday Star, 354,602; publisher-Eugene S. Pulliam; president-William A. Dyer Jr; Star editor-Frank Crane; News editor-Dr. Harvey Jacobs; Pulitzer prizes-News, Star; Nat'l. Headliners first prize-Star.

**Population:** 745,739 (consolidated city 1970), nation's 11th largest; 1,111,173 (metro 1970); total employed 518,000.
**Area:** 379.4 sq. mi.; geographic center of state; state capital and Marion County seat.
**Industry:** over 1,400 diversified manufacturers including plane and auto engines and parts, electronics, pharmaceuticals, machinery; 1977 manufacturing payroll over $1.8 billion.
**Commerce:** commercial center for Indiana; retail sales $4.1 billion; per capita personal income $6,175; 6 banks with resources over $6.5 billion; home offices of over 60 insurance companies.
**Transportation;** 6 airlines; Indianapolis International Airport; 5 rail freight lines; Amtrak; 3 interstate bus lines; 65 truck lines; 7 interstate freeway routes.
**New construction:** projects totalling over $189.3 million under construction in 1978.
**Communications:** 6 TV stations and 18 radio stations.
**Medical facilities:** 17 hospitals, over 6,800 beds.
**Federal facilities:** Fort Harrison incl. Army Finance and Accounting Center, U.S.A. Admin. Center.
**Cultural facilities:** Museum of Art and Oldfields Museum of Decorative Arts; Indiana State Museum; Indianapolis Zoo;

Children's Museum; Conner Prairie Pioneer Settlement and Museum of Indiana Heritage; Clowes Hall, home of symphony orch.; Civic Theatre, oldest U.S. amateur theatrical group; repertory theater.
**Education facilities:** Butler Univ., Indiana Central Univ. Marian College, Christian Theological and St. Mauer's seminaries, Purdue Univ. at Indianapolis, and Indiana Univ. with nation's largest medical center.
**Convention facilities:** Indiana Convention-Exposition Center, Indiana State Fairgrounds.
**Recreational facilities:** 13,000 park acres, 16 municipal swimming pools, 12 golf courses; pro basketball and hockey in 18,000-seat domed sports arena, home of the Pacers NBA; Racers WHA; Loves WTA; minor league baseball.
**Other attractions:** Indianapolis 500; Yankee 300; annual National Drag Racing championships.
**History:** sesquicentennial in 1971; important before Civil War, with nation's first union railway station (1853); home of James Whitcomb Riley, Booth Tarkington, and President Benjamin Harrison.
**Additional information:** Indianapolis Chamber of Commerce, 320 N. Meridian Street, Indianapolis, IN 46204; (317) 635-4747.

## Jacksonville, Florida

The World Almanac is sponsored in the Jacksonville area by The Florida Times-Union and the Jacksonville Journal, One Riverside Avenue, Jacksonville, FL 32202; phone (904) 791-4111; circulation, Times-Union 146,844, Journal 52,976, combined Sunday 181,340; publisher J.J. Daniel, president John A. Tucker, executive editor John S. Walters; Journal won Pultizer Prize for photography in 1967.

**Population:** 590,000 (1978); total employment 224,900 (1977).
**Area:** 840 sq. mi., includes nearly all of Duval Co. in northeast Florida; under one consolidated government.
**Industry:** 592 industries, added value total $505 million annually; Offshore Power Systems investing $250 million in floating nuclear power plant production facility to employ 10,000 when completed.
**Commerce:** emphasis on finance distribution; home or regional headquarters for 34 insurance companies; 1976 retail sales $2.0 billion; effective buying income per household in 1976 $13,731.
**Transportation:** 3 major railroads and Amtrak; over 40 truck lines; 5 airlines averaging 101 air movements daily; 2 interstate bus lines; port handled 15 million tons in 1977.
**Communications:** 4 TV and 25 radio stations.
**New construction:** $198.7 million in building permits issued in 1977.
**Medical facilities:** 11 general hospitals and one naval hospital with total of 3,358 beds.

**Federal facilities:** 2 naval air stations, one naval station add $435 million yearly to the economy.
**Cultural facilities:** Cummer Art Gallery, Jacksonville Art Museum, Jacksonville Museum of Arts and Sciences, Jacksonville Symphony, Ballet Guild, 4 community theaters.
**Education:** Univ. of North Florida, Jacksonville Univ., Edward Waters College, Florida Junior College, Jones College
**Sports:** Gator Bowl, Tournament Players Championships golf tournament, $400,000 purse; professional baseball, intercollegiate sports.
**Other attractions:** civic auditorium, coliseum, Jacksonville Zoo, Fort Caroline, Kingsley Plantation, 8 miles of public beaches.
**History.** founded in 1822 by Isiah Hart, named for Andrew Jackson; fire in 1901 destroyed 2,368 buildings, left 10,000 homeless; city and county governments merged in 1968 after referendum.
**Further information:** Chamber of Commerce, 815 South Main Street, Suite 100, P.O. Drawer 329, Jacksonville, FL 32201.

## Kalamazoo, Michigan

The World Almanac is sponsored in the Kalamazoo area by The Kalamazoo Gazette, 401 S. Burdick, Kalamazoo, MI 49003; telephone (616) 345-3511, founded 1833; circulation daily 58,959, Sunday 65,586, owned and operated by Booth Newspapers Inc.; president James E. Sauter, editor Daniel M. Ryan, manager Ralph H. Bastien Jr.

**Population:** 85,800 (city), 207,700 (county); total employed (Kalamazoo-Portage SMSA) 124,000.
**Area:** located equidistant to the 3d and 5th largest metro areas in nation — Chicago and Detroit, 140 miles away.
**Industry:** paper-making is the traditional industry, with 5 large plants. Checker Motors Corp. manufactures cars; large Fisher Body Division body stamping plant; Upjohn Company, pharmaceuticals.
**Commerce:** shopping center for large part of southwestern Michigan. In 1959, city became first in country to close

downtown streets and create a pedestrian mall; now known as "Mall City." Retail sales (1977) $736 million; 4 banks had combined assets in 1977 of $854 million, 2 savings and loan associations have assets of over $200 million.
**Transportation:** 2 railroads provide freight service, Amtrak passenger service; 34 general carriers provide trucking services; airport with freight and passenger service; 3 bus lines.
**Cultural facilities:** 5 auditoriums offering music and theatrical performances, 6 live arts theaters, an art center, sym

phony orchestra, Kalamazoo Civic Players.
**Educational facilities:** 3 colleges and one university with combined student enrollment over 30,000.
**Other attractions:** Kalamazoo Nature Center, 83 lakes (county), National Junior Tennis Championships, 2 major

hospitals, Kalamazoo Hilton Convention Center, IHL Kalamazoo Wings (hockey).
**Further information:** Kalamazoo County Chamber of Commerce, 500 W. Crosstown, Kalamazoo, MI 49008, telephone (616) 381-4000.

## Kansas City, Missouri

**Population:** 460,700 (city); 1,290,300 (metro area), 28th in nation; total employed, 655,900.
**Area:** 3,341 sq. mi., SMSA, at confluence of Missouri and Kansas rivers in Jackson, Clay, and Platte counties.
**Industry:** 2d in nation in automotive assembly; first in production of envelopes and greeting cards, farm equipment distribution, frozen food storage and distribution, foreign trade zone space, underground storage space, and hard winter wheat marketing. Top employers: U.S. government, General Motors, TWA, Bendix, Western Electric, Ford. Presently Kansas City is a leading hard wheat center, stocker and feeder market, and is among the top 5 cities in flour production and grain elevator capacity.
**Commerce:** total retail sales in 1976, $4.624 billion; the center of a 7-county metro area: Jackson, Clay, Platte, Cass, and Ray counties in Missouri; Johnson and Wyandotte counties in Kansas.
**Transportation:** 10 airlines with 420 scheduled arrivals and departures daily at Kansas City International Airport; 169 truck lines and 4 barge companies; city is one of the nation's major rail centers.
**New construction:** $350 million Crown Center business and apartment complex covers 25 square blocks; new medical center of University of Missouri and Univ. of Kansas; American Royal Arena; Mercantile Bank Building; United Missouri Bank headquarters; City Center Square, a 32-story office and retail building downtown; 27-story Mutual Benefit Life bldg. on IBM Plaza; H. Roe Bartle exposition hall; Worlds of Fun recreation center. More than 6 large hotels

and extensive hospital additions.
**Cultural facilities:** Starlight Theater, nation's 2d largest outdoor theater; William Rockhill Nelson Gallery of Art, among the 10 top American museums with the 3d largest Oriental collection outside China; Performing Arts Foundation formed in 1965 to present festival events; University of Missouri at Kansas City; Rockhurst College; Kansas City Art Institute; University of Kansas Medical Center. Within commuting distance are University of Kansas, Park College, William Jewell College, Truman Library in Independence. Linda Hall Library of Science and Technology is one of the largest privately endowed technical reference libraries in the nation.
**Recreational facilities:** more than 100 parks cover 5,345 acres, including Swope Park, 2d largest in nation, with fine zoo.
**Sports:** The American Royal Livestock and Horse Show each fall attracts entries from throughout the country; home of the Chiefs of the NFL, Royals, American League baseball, Kings, NBA.
**History:** Kansas City's beginnings can be traced to a trading post of French fur trappers about 1826. It became an important trade and transportation center as the overland routes of the Oregon and Santa Fe trails spread westward. As agricultural production boomed, it became an important market and distribution center for crops from throughout the middle west.
**Further information:** Chamber of Commerce of Greater Kansas City, 920 Main, Kansas City, MO 64105.

## Kitchener-Waterloo, Ontario, Canada

The World Almanac is sponsored in the Kitchener-Waterloo area by the Kitchener-Waterloo Record, 225 Fairway Road, Kitchener, Ont.; phone (519) 579-2231; founded 1878; circulation 68,391, president and publisher K. A. Baird.

**Population:** 133,815 (Kitchener) and 51,473 (Waterloo), 296,113 (region); total employed 138,300.
**Area:** 51.74 sq. mi. (Kitchener) and 25.47 sq. mi. (Waterloo), 65 miles west of Toronto.
**Industry:** highly diversified industry (487 companies), rubber, plastics, electronics, metal fabrication, brewing, distilling, meat packing, footwear, furniture, food processing, automotive components; Budd Automotive Co., largest autoframe manufacturer in Canada; Deilcraft furniture plant is the largest under one roof in North America. Annual gross product exceeds $1 billion.
**Agricultural:** hog and dairy area; Waterloo Region's 1,976 farms accounted for $100 million production in 1976.
**Commerce:** wholesale and retail center for area; metro retail sales (1978) $840 million; 8 banks, 64 branches; 12 trust companies, 25 branches; 41 life insurance offices, 29 other insurance offices; Waterloo, "The Hartford of Canada," head office for 6 insurance companies.
**Transportation:** 2 major rail lines, 34 truck lines, on Ontar-

io's key highway 401; Waterloo-Wellington Airport; 45 mi. from Toronto International.
**Communications:** one TV and 4 radio stations; one daily, one weekly newspaper.
**Medical facilities:** 2 major hospitals.
**Cultural facilities:** symphony orchestra, Kitchener-Waterloo Art Gallery, Doon Pioneer Village; 28 mi. from famed Stratford Festival Theatre.
**Educational facilities:** Univ. of Waterloo, Wilfrid Laurier Univ., Conestoga College.
**Other attractions:** nationally-known farmers market; Canada's largest annual Oktoberfest celebration; Woodside, national historic park, boyhood home of W. L. Mackenzie King, Canadian prime minister 22 years.
**History:** founded 1807 by German settlers; retains strong Germanic flavor.
**Further information:** Kitchener Chamber of Commerce, 67 King East; Waterloo Chamber of Commerce, 5 Bridgeport Road W.

## Knoxville, Tennessee

The World Almanac is sponsored in the Knoxville area by The Knoxville News-Sentinel, 204 West Church Avenue, Knoxville, TN 37901. Sentinel founded in 1886; News in 1921 by Scripps-Howard Newspapers; Sentinel purchased by Scripps-Howard in 1926 and combined with News. Circulation 104,948 daily; 160,922 Sunday; president and general manager Roger A. Daley; editor Ralph L. Millett Jr.; managing editor Harold E. Harlow.

**Population:** 181,150 (city), 322,530 (county); 461,880 (metro area), 3d in state; 188,000 total employed in metro area.
**Area:** city 77.6 sq. mi., county 528 sq. mi., located almost in exact center of that portion of United States lying east of the

Mississippi River and south of Great Lakes; Knox County seat.
**Industry:** major manufacturing industries are chemicals and primary metals; nearly 500 plants representing 51 diversified

major industries (coal and zinc mining, marble quarrying, meat packing, electronics, steel fabrication, industrial controls eqpt., furniture, auto safety eqpt., refuse eqpt., apparel), with Aluminum Co. of America, Union Carbide Corp. Nuclear Div. at Oak Ridge, included in area market.

**Commerce:** wholesale and retail trade center of a multicounty area in east Tennessee, Virginia, Kentucky, and N. Carolina; county retail sales (1976) $1.2 billion.

**Transportation:** 2 rail lines, 5 airlines, 2 interstate bus lines, 25 motor freight carriers; Interstate Highways I-40 and I-75 intersect in heart of city, Tennessee River barges.

**New construction:** continuance in immediate downtown redevelopment program, over $139 million expended since 1972; in progress 30-story bank bldg. and new City-County bldg.; Univ. of Tennessee main campus recently completed or under construction; Neyland Stadium (football) enlarged to seat 81,000.

**Cultural facilities:** Univ. of Tennessee, Knoxville College,

Knoxville Symphony Orchestra, 13 museums, art gallery, auditorium-coliseum, city-county library (612,684 volume), Zoological Park, university community theater, choral society, opera workshop, Lamar House-Bijou Theater.

**Sports:** Univ. of Tennessee (all major collegiate sports); Knoxville Sox, Chicago White Sox farm club.

**Other attractions:** Great Smoky Mountains National Park, 39 miles from Knoxville, offers year-round scenic beauty, skiing in season; within 30 miles of Knoxville, with 9 million visitations annually, 6 TVA lakes, 2,320 miles of shoreline providing fishing, boating, swimming. Oak Ridge, known for its nuclear developments, 22 miles from Knoxville; American Museum of Atomic Energy and Oak Ridge National Lab; Dogwood Arts Festival held each April.

**Further information:** Chamber of Commerce, 301 E. Church Avenue, or Tourist Bureau, 811 Henley Street, both Knoxville, TN 37902.

## Las Vegas, Nevada

The World Almanac is sponsored in the Las Vegas area by the Las Vegas Review-Journal, P.O. Box 70, 1111 W. Bonanza, Las Vegas, NV 89101; phone (702) 385-4241; founded as a weekly in 1909; purchased 1956 by Donald W. Reynolds, present publisher; member Donrey Media Group; circulation 72,246 weekdays, 78,960 Sundays; general manager William Wright; editor Don Digilio.

**Population:** 417,414 (1977, county/SMSA est.); 423,200 (1978, primary market - ABC est.); total employment 165,200.

**Area:** southern Nevada, Clark County seat; 7,927 sq. miles; 53 people per sq. mile; 283 miles NW of Phoenix, 289 miles NE of Los Angeles; home of Nellis Air Force Base.

**Industry:** 24 hour tourism, hotel/gaming/recreation; no. of wage earners: gaming/tourist 49,700, Nellis Air Force Base 9,100, wholesale, retail, eat and drink 40,800, construction mining, and manufacturing 13,100.

**Commerce:** 6 commercial banks (deposits $1.1 billion), 6 Savings and Loan (deposits $655 million); retail sales $222 million; average spendable family income $16,334.

**Transportation:** McCarran Int'l Airport, total passengers (1977) 7,964,687; 7 major airlines (Air West, Western, United, TWA, National, Delta, Frontier) plus foreign carriers, charters, commuter, and 3d level carriers; 3 bus lines; daily auto traffic entering area 20,525.

**Communications:** 5 TV stations, 16 radio stations, 3 newspapers.

**Medical facilities:** 8 major hospitals, 25 clinics, 19 convalescent homes, acupuncture clinics.

**Federal facilities:** Nellis AFB: 8000 military, 1,100 civilian personnel; $77 million annual payroll.

**Education:** Univ. of Nevada, Las Vegas; Clark County Community College; 8 libraries; 74 elementary schools, 16

junior high schools, 10 high schools.

**Cultural facilities:** Las Vegas Art League and Museum; Reed Whipple Cultural Arts Center; Judy Bayley Theatre; Artemus W. Ham Concert Hall; Las Vegas Civic Symphony; Nevada Dance Theatre; City Museum of Archeology; Southern Nevada Museum and Cultural Center; Las Vegas Valley Zoo.

**Recreation:** Lake Mead, Lake Mojave, Hoover Dam, Tule Springs, Valley of Fire, Red Rock Canyon area, Toiyabe National Forest (Mt. Charleston), Rogers Springs, Colorado River, skiing, boating, fishing, swimming, hiking, camping.

**Sports:** amateur and professional competition in tennis, golf, auto racing, bowling, basketball, boccie ball, boxing; UNLV sports competitions; Mint 400 Off Road race, Sahara Invitational golf tournament, Alan King tennis classic, WCT Challenge Cup, Pizza Hut basketball invitational, racquet ball.

**History:** first recorded group to enter the Las Vegas Valley was Antonio Armijo's party in early 1839. Las Vegas, Spanish for "The Meadows," first settled by Europeans in June of 1855 by a 30-man Mormon group under William Bringhurst; city of Las Vegas founded May 15, 1905, as a result of public land auction by the railroad.

**Further information:** Las Vegas Chamber of Commerce, 2301 E. Sahara Avenue, Las Vegas, NV 89104; telephone (702) 457-4664.

## Lethbridge, Alberta, Canada

The World Almanac is sponsored in the Lethbridge area by The Lethbridge Herald, 504 7th Street S., Lethbridge, Alberta, phone (403) 328-4411; founded as a daily in 1907; circulation, weekdays 26,940; Saturdays 28,200; editor Cleo W. Mowers; general manager Donald Doram; managing editor Don H. Pilling.

**Population:** 49,350

**Area:** 23 square miles; located on Oldman River, 60 miles north of Montana border, 130 miles south of Calgary.

**Industry:** heavily dependent on agriculture; 3 federally inspected packing plants slaughtered 35% of cattle slaughtered in Alberta in 1977; large dryland grain growing, ranching area, and extensive irrigation district; brewery, distillery, flour mill, food processing plant, foundry, oilseed processing, mobile home construction.

**Commerce:** 1977 retail sales of $299 million, 5% more than 1976; 5 banks, 4 trust companies, 11 finance companies.

**Transportation:** CP Rail, 2 bus lines, depots for 52 trucking firms; regional airline flies out of Lethbridge to all major Alberta cities.

**Communications:** one newspaper, 2 TV, 3 radio stations.

**New construction:** building permits valued at $57.2 million in 1977, compared with $60.8 million in 1976.

**Medical facilities:** 2 general hospitals, one long-term care

hospital, 4 nursing homes for the aged.

**Cultural facilities:** Canada agriculture research station, Univ. of Lethbridge, Lethbridge Community College, Alexander Galt Museum, Nikka Yuko Centennial Japanese Garden, symphony orchestra and chorus, local theater groups, Bowman Arts Centre, Yates Memorial Centre.

**Other attractions:** 4 major parks, 5 artificial ice arenas, 3 golf courses, 2 indoor and one outdoor pools.

**Sports:** Dodgers, Los Angeles Dodgers farm team in Pioneer League; Broncos, Western Canada Hockey League.

**History:** early coal-mining town, named Lethbridge Oct. 16, 1885, after a coal executive. A whiskey traders' depot, Fort Whoop-Up, was booming, 5 miles southwest of what is now Lethbridge, in the 1860's; first settlers in area came 15 years later, many from the United States.

**Further information:** Lethbridge Chamber of Commerce, 817 4th Avenue South; Southern Alberta Tourist and Convention Association, 122 5th Avenue South.

## Little Rock, Arkansas

The World Almanac is sponsored by the Arkansas Gazette, 112 West Third Street, Little Rock, AR 72203, phone (501) 371-3700; founded 1819 at Arkansas Post, A.T., by Wm. E. Woodruff, moved to Little Rock 1821; circulation 129,725 daily, 153,790 Sunday; Hugh B. Patterson Jr., publisher and president; Carrick H. Patterson, executive editor; J. O. Powell, editorial director; Robert R. Douglas, managing editor; J. R. Williamson, executive vice president-general manager.

**Population:** 146,000 (city), 376,600 (metro); 152,600 employed (metro).

**Area:** Little Rock, 51 sq. mi.; Pulaski County, 781.0 sq. mi.; State capital and Pulaski County seat.

**Industry:** (metro) 350 manufacturing plants, employing 30,000 persons, including Allis-Chalmers, Armstrong Rubber Co., Timex, AMF Cycle Div., Remington Arms, Jacuzzi Bros., Teletype, Westinghouse, CPC, International, and General Electric.

**Commerce:** Retail sales (est. 1977) $1.4 billion; bank resources (Jan. 1978) $1.9 billion; building permits (1977) $28 million; 11 banks, 6 building & loan associations, 4 old line insurance companies.

**Transportation:** 3 railroads, 6 federally certified airlines, 3 interstate bus lines, 1 inter-city line, 34 truck lines, 12 common carrier barge lines.

**Communications:** 3 commercial TV, one ETV, 14 radio stations; 2 daily, one weekly newspaper.

**Medical facilities:** 10 hospitals including UA Medical Sciences campus, 2 VA hospitals, and Ark. State Hospital for Nervous Diseases.

**Federal facilities:** Little Rock AFB, Tactical Airlift Wing; Camp Joseph T. Robinson, Arkansas National Guard headquarters and training center; U.S. National Guard Bureau's Non-Commissioned Officers Institute.

**Education:** Univ. of Arkansas at Little Rock with Schools of Law, Medicine, Nursing, and Pharmacy; UA Graduate Institute of Technology; Philander Smith, Shorter and Arkansas Baptist colleges; 104 public schools; 18 private and special schools.

**Cultural facilities:** Arkansas Symphony, Arkansas Arts Center, 3 major public libraries, convention center-auditorium-hotel; Arkansas Repertory Theatre; Arkansas Territorial Restoration and Museum of Science & Natural History.

**History:** French explorer Bernard de la Harpe noted "le petit roche" on his map of the Arkansas River Valley in 1722.

**Further information:** Metropolitan Chamber of Commerce, One Spring Street; Arkansas Parks & Tourist Dept., State Capitol; both Little Rock, AR 72201.

## Los Angeles, California

The World Almanac is sponsored in Los Angeles by the Los Angeles Herald Examiner, 1111 S. Broadway, Los Angeles, CA 90015, phone (213) 748-1212; Los Angeles Examiner founded 1903 by Wm. R Hearst, merged Los Angeles Herald Express 1962; circulation 322,143 daily, 325,426 Sunday; Francis L. Dale, publisher; James G. Bellows, editor; Theodore P. Grassi, general manager; David W. Feldman, director of sales.

**Population:** 2.7 million (city), 6.9 million (county), (Jan. '76); 5-county urban area 11.3 million (Jan. '77); first in state, 2d county in nation, 3d urban area; total civilians employed 3.1 million (county, June '77); labor force 3.3 million (county, Mar. '77).

**Area:** 463.7 sq. mi. on Pacific, 418 mi. south of San Francisco, 145 mi. north of Mexico; Los Angeles County seat; one of 79 cities in county.

**Industry:** leading aerospace industry with 7 of the top 10 defense contractors in the nation located in the area; center of entertainment industry with more than 600 firms in movie and television entertainment work. Women's clothing, sportswear, electronics, rubber tires, printing, furniture, paper, autos, auto parts, chemicals, manufacturing. Work force (county, June '77) 825,100; agriculture 18,900; oil and mining 11,600; construction 105,600; transport, utilities, and communication 178,100; trade 747,300 (237,900 wholesale, 509,400 retail.); finance, insurance, and real estate 196,800; services and misc. 680,800; government 497,200. Among top 20 counties in U.S. in agricultural production; farm income $174.1 million (county '76); livestock (dairy, eggs, meat) production $47.2 million; sea fish harvested 589.6 million pounds (county '76).

**Commerce:** total taxable retail sales $27.4 billion (county '76), $10.2 billion (city '76); median family income $13,205; personal income $43.9 billion (county '76); 79 banks, 1,088 branches, more than 65 savings and loans with 565 branches; bank deposits $27.5 billion (June '76); S&L savings $25.9 billion (Mar. '77).

**Transportation:** Sante Fe, Union Pacific, Southern Pacific railroads; Amtrak; Continental, Greyhound bus lines; Southern California Rapid Transit District serving 4,150 mi. with 2,064 buses plus other local and intercity bus lines; Airport Transit Bus and Grey Line tours; 4.3 million vehicles (county, June '77), one of largest concentrations in nation — 3.5 million autos, 638,841 trucks, 165,563 motorcycles, 217,343 trailers; 156.6 mi. freeway (city) 491.2 (county) June '77); airlines (36 scheduled, 13 charter, 4 commuter) serving Los Angeles International airport, 482,587 takeoffs and landings, 25.9 million passengers, 1.5 billion pounds

cargo ('76); 9 other airports; more than 46 miles of commercial waterfront in Los Angeles-Long Beach Harbor, 5,407 ships, 61.7 million tons cargo (Los Angeles 30.3 million, Long Beach 31.4 million) in '76.

**Communications:** 13 TV stations (7 UHF, 6 VHF), approx. 75 radio stations, 60 commercial; more than 45 newspapers in English and foreign languages, more than 25 publishing daily (county).

**New construction:** building permits $845.5 million, including $324.4 million for 3,816 residential units (city, fiscal '76), plus $425.6 million in county building permits.

**Medical facilities:** 813 hospitals and clinics with 76,086 beds, including 178 general care hospitals, 34,654 beds, 24 psychiatric, 2,497 beds, 410 nursing homes, 38,570 beds (county, June '77).

**Educational facilities:** 1,208 elementary, 208 jr. high, 168 sr. high, 89 continuation, 80 adult, 36 special; approx. 800 private all levels (county '77); 62 libraries (city) plus 177 others in the county; UCLA, Univ. Southern Cal., California Institute of Technology; Loyola, Marymount, Pepperdine universities; Claremont, Woodbury, Occidental, Whittier, Mt. St. Mary colleges; 21 community colleges; campuses of California State University-Los Angeles, Long Beach, Northridge, Dominguez Hills.

**Cultural facilities:** 1,838 churches, Huntington Art Gallery and Library, Hollywood Bowl, Greek Theater, Music Center, Mark Taper Forum, Ahmanson Theater, Huntington Hartford Theater, Griffith Park Planetarium, Mt. Wilson and Mt. Palomar observatories; Los Angeles Museum, County Art Museum, UCLA Botanical Gardens, La Brea Tar Pits and natural history museum, Southwest Museum.

**Recreational facilities:** 273 city parks and playgrounds, plus 122 county parks; 5 public golf courses, 15 public beaches within 35 miles of city center; ocean, mountains, desert, lakes, forests: Disneyland, Marineland, Knott's Berry Farm, Lion County Safari, Universal Movie Studio tour.

**Convention facilities:** approx. 20,000 hotel rooms (city), 50,000 (county); large convention center.

**Sports:** collegiate sports, including Rose Bowl; pro teams in baseball (Dodgers), basketball (Lakers), tennis (Strings),

hockey (Kings), Soccer (Aztecs, Skyhawks).
**History:** discovered 1542 by Portuguese navigator Juan Rodriguez Cabrillo; Mission San Gabriel founded Sept., 1771; city formally founded Sept. 4, 1781 by Spanish colonial governor as El Pueblo de Nuestra Senora la Reina de los Angeles de Porciuncula; inc. April 4, 1850.
**Further information:** Chamber of Commerce, P.O. Box 3696, Terminal Annex, Los Angeles, CA 90051.

## Louisville, Kentucky

The World Almanac is sponsored in Kentucky and southern Indiana by The Courier-Journal and The Louisville Times, 525 West Broadway, Louisville, KY 40202, (502) 582-4011; Courier-Journal founded 1868; Times 1884; Courier circulation 205,430, Times 160,637, Sunday 348,667, chairman of the board Barry Bingham Sr., editor and publisher Barry Bingham Jr.; major awards include 7 Pulitzer prizes.

**Population:** 326,400 (city), 932,000 (metro area); first in state; total employed 392,700.
**Area:** 65.2 sq. mi. (city), 1,392 sq. mi. (metro); on southern bank of Ohio River.
**Industry and Commerce:** 10th in total industrial shipments; famous for baseball bats, cigarettes, railroad repair shops, electrical appliances, farm machinery, motor vehicles, plumbing fixtures, and whiskey; 1,011 manufacturing firms in area; estimated retail sales (Jefferson County, 1977) $2.810 billion.
**Transportation:** 6 trunk-line railroads, 1 terminal railroad, 100 inter-city truck lines; 5 barge lines; 3 bus lines; 7 airlines, and 2 municipal airports.
**Communications:** 20 radio and 4 TV stations, 2 educational.
**Medical facilities:** 21 hospitals, 6,000 total beds.
**Cultural facilities:** Louisville Orchestra, Kentucky Opera Association, Art Center Association, J.B. Speed Art Museum; 20 private art galleries, Macauley Theatre, Actors Theatre, The Children's Theatre, Louisville Civic Ballet, Louisville-Jefferson County Youth Orchestra, The Louisville Free Public Library (23 branches); 700 churches, 40 denominations.
**Education:** 10 colleges and universities, 3 business colleges and technical schools in area.
**Recreation:** 158 public parks, covering more than 7,000 acres.
**Convention facilities:** Kentucky Fair & Exposition Center, largest ground-level exhibit hall and auditorium complex in North America with 650,000 sq. ft., 20,000-plus seating, parking for 27,000 cars; new 100,000 sq. ft. Commonwealth Convention Center in downtown Louisville; Louisville Gardens, downtown, handles up to 7,000.
**Sports:** Kentucky Derby, held annually at Churchill Downs since 1875; Louisville Downs harness racing.
**Other:** Belle of Louisville excursion steamboat; Churchill Downs Museum; Louisville Zoo, American Printing House for the Blind; Kentucky Railway Museum; Museum of Natural History and Science.
**History:** founded by explorer George Rogers Clark, in 1778; named after King Louis XVI of France.
**Further information:** Louisville Area Chamber of Commerce, 300 West Liberty, Louisville, KY 40202.

## Lubbock, Texas

The World Almanac is sponsored in the Lubbock area by the Lubbock Avalanche-Journal, 8th Street and Avenue J, Lubbock, TX 79408: (806) 762-8844; founded 1900 as Leader, became Avalanche 1908, daily 1921; Plains Journal weekly founded 1923; consolidated 1926: circulation (morn) 56,932, (eve) 15,055, (Sat) 65,817, (Sun) 78,327; member Southwestern Newspaper Corp.; general manager Robert Norris; editor Jay Harris.

**Population:** 175,250 (city), 195,250 (metro area), 8th in state; total employed 96,790.
**Area:** 82.2 sq. mi.; center of South Plains territory of northwest Texas; Lubbock County seat.
**Industry:** vegetable oils, cotton seed flour, grain sorghum, livestock, petroleum, sand and gravel; 250 manufacturing companies.
**Commerce:** wholesale and retail center for west Texas and eastern New Mexico; retail sales $629.8 million; bank resources $1.131 billion; 8 banks.
**Transportation:** 12 motor freight carriers; 2 major railroads, bus line; Lubbock Regional Airport, 4 major airlines averaging 62 flights per day; 2 intrastate airlines; 6 major federal and state highways.
**Communications:** 4 TV and 12 radio stations.
**Medical facilities:** 8 hospitals, Lubbock State School for Mentally Retarded; Texas Tech Medical School.
**Federal facilities:** Reese AFB, federal building, Federal Aviation Admin., and National Weather Service, U.S. Customs port of entry.
**Cultural facilities:** symphony orchestra, Theatre Centre Museum of Texas Tech Univ., Moody Planetarium; Ranching Heritage Center (authentic ranch houses dating to 1835), Lubbock Christian College; Texas Tech Univ., Lubbock Cultural Affairs Council, Lubbock Garden & Arts Center.
**Recreational facilities:** 55 city parks, 3,000 acres, Mackenzie State Park, state's largest, with Prairie Dog Town; Buffalo Lakes, Canyon Lakes-Parks; Municipal Auditorium, 3,200 seats, Municipal Coliseum, 10,000 capacity; annual Panhandle South Plains Fair; Lubbock Memorial Civic Center modern convention facility with 200,000 sq. ft. including 44,000 sq. ft. exhibit hall with banquet facilities for 1,500 auditorium seating 1,400.
**Sports:** Texas Tech, and Lubbock Christian college sports Tech Jones Stadium, indoor rodeos.
**Further information:** Chamber of Commerce, P.O. Box 561 Lubbock, TX 79408.

## Macon, Georgia

The World Almanac is sponsored in the Macon area by the Macon Telegraph & News, 120 Broadway, Macon, GA 31201; phone (912) 743-2621; acquired by Knight-Ridder Newspapers, Inc., 1969; circulation Telegraph (morn.) 54,586, News (eve.) 25,941, Sat. 69,388, Sun. 90,397; publisher and president Bert Struby, Telegraph and executive editor Billy Watson, News editor Joe Parham.

**Population:** 126,100 (city), 265,200 (metro). 3d in state; labor force 103,740.
**Area:** 52 sq. mi., 6 miles northwest of geographical center of Georgia; Bibb County seat.
**Industry:** textiles; Bibb Company, longtime industry leader and largest employer, headquartered in area; textile-related are YKK Zipper Co. of Japan and Texprint; Armstrong Cork Co. acoustical tile plant is one of area's largest; Ga. Kraft container board manufacturer; Brown & Williamson Tobacco Corp.; Keebler Co. cracker manufacturing plant.

Kaolin deposits are mined in area and processed in numerous ways; Government Employees Insurance Co. regional office.

**Federal facilities:** Warner Robins Air Logistics Center and Robins AFB, 16 miles from Macon, are area's largest employers.

**Educational facilities:** Wesleyan College, nation's oldest college for women, and Mercer Univ. with law school; Macon Jr. College.

**Other attractions:** Ocmulgee National Monument displays archeological remains of 3 prehistoric Indian civilization; $4.5 million coliseum seats 10,000

**History:** Settled when U. S. established Fort Hawkins in 1806; chartered in 1823, named for Nathaniel Macon of North Carolina.

**Further information:** Macon Chamber of Commerce, 305 Coliseum Drive, Macon, GA 31201.

## Madison, Wisconsin

The World Almanac is sponsored in Madison by Madison Newspapers, Inc., publisher of The Capital Times and the Wisconsin State Journal, 1901 Fish Hatchery Road, Madison, WI 53713; (608) 252-6100; circulation, Wisconsin State Journal (m) 74,270, The Capital Times (eve) 37,680, combined daily 111,950, Sunday Wisconsin State Journal 120,950.

**Population:** 172,300 (city), 314,800 (county), 2d in state; metro work force 174,500.
**Area:** 52 sq. mi. (city), 1,194 sq. mi. (county), in south central Wisconsin, state capital and Dane County seat.
**Commerce:** home office of 29 insurance firms; 375 industrial firms, 26 banks, 7 savings and loans, retail sales $1.1 billion; average effective buying income $17,700.
**Transportation:** Dane County regional airport, 3 airlines, 3 railroads, Amtrak (within county), major Interstate highway system, 3 bus lines, 30 common carriers, city owned bus system.
**Communications:** 4 TV, 2 cable; 6 AM and 10 FM radio stations.
**Medical facilities:** 9 hospitals, including U.W. and VA; 20 major clinics; approx. 600 physicians.
**Federal facilities:** Forest Products Laboratory.
**Cultural facilities:** Dane County Coliseum; Madison Civic Center, 2 art centers, ballet company, dinner playhouse, 11

drama groups, 8 music organizations, 15 Catholic, 150 Protestant, and one Greek Orthodox Church, 2 synagogues.
**Education:** Univ. of Wisconsin, (39,100 enrolled), 35 elementary, 10 middle, 5 high schools; 15 parochial, one vocational-technical; Madison Area Technical College, Madison Business College, and Edgewood College, and 7 city and 32 university libraries.
**Recreation:** 5 lakes with total of 18,000 acres of water surface, and 4,676 acres of parks.
**Convention facilities:** Dane County coliseum, 5 major convention-size hotels, 55 supper clubs.
**Sports:** Univ. of Wisconsin in Big Ten. Football, basketball, and other major sports; national 1977 hockey champions.
**Other attractions:** U. of W. Arboretum, Vilas Zoo, numerous political organizations, weekly Farmer's Market (May-Sept.), World Dairy Exposition headquarters.
**Further information:** Greater Madison Chamber of Commerce, 615 E. Washington Avenue, Madison, WI 53701.

## Memphis, Tennessee

The World Almanac is sponsored in the Memphis area by The Memphis Press-Scimitar, 495 Union Avenue, Memphis, TN 38101; phone (901) 526-2141; Scimitar founded 1880 by G. P. M. Turner; Press 1906 by Scripps-McRae League, predecessor of Scripps-Howard Newspapers; circulation 111,957; editor Milton R. Britten, managing editor Van Pritchartt Jr.

**Population:** 670,600 (city), 880,500 (metro area); first in state, 17th in nation; 347,000 employed.
**Area:** 290 sq. mi., Shelby County seat, on east bank of the Mississippi River.
**Industry:** extensive cotton marketing-warehousing and processing of cotton seed into vegetable oil products; headquarters of Holiday Inns Inc., and Conwood Corp. (tobacco and food products). Other large industries include Schering-Plough (drugs), International Harvester (cotton pickers, hay balers), and Firestone (tires).
**Commerce:** wholesale-retail center for large parts of Tennessee, Arkansas, and Mississippi; retail sales (1976) $2.9 billion; bank deposits $2.3 billion; 12 banks, 6 savings-loan assns. Per capita personal income $5,456 (1975).
**Transportation:** 11 airlines; 7 trunk line railroads, 87 motor freight lines, 7 barge lines; river port handled 12.2 million tons of freight in 1976.
**Communications:** 4 TV and 19 radio stations.
**Medical facilities:** Univ. of Tennessee Center for Health Sciences and a VA hospital in complex with public hospital; 3 private hospitals and St. Jude Hospital, research center for childhood illnesses particularly leukemia.
**Federal facilities:** Naval Air Station, Naval Air Technical Training Center, Defense Depot Memphis, and Air Force's 164th Air Transport Group.
**Cultural facilities:** Memphis Symphony Orchestra, opera theater, Theatre Memphis, Brooks Art Gallery, Chucalissa

Indian Village & Museum, Memphis Museum; annual performances of Metropolitan Opera.
**Educational facilities:** Memphis State Univ., Southwestern College, LeMoyne-Owen College, Christian Brothers College, U-T Center for Health Sciences, Shelby State Community College, State Technical Institute, Southern College of Optometry, Mid-South Bible College,
**Recreational facilities:** Meeman-Shelby Forest state park, 12,500 acres; 137 other parks.
**Convention facilities:** $27 million Cook Convention Center, 1.3 million sq. ft., seating 16,500.
**Sports:** Liberty Bowl, home of Memphis State University football, site of Liberty Bowl game; Mid-South Coliseum, home of MSU basketball team; Memphis Chicks, Southern League baseball (AA); Danny Thomas Memphis Classic golf tournament.
**Other attractions:** Cotton Carnival each May; Mid-South Fair each September; Beale Street, home of the blues, where composer W. C. Handy lived; Mid-America Mall; Libertyland; Graceland, home of Elvis Presley.
**History:** DeSoto, exploring Mississippi River, stopped here in 1541; Ft. Adams established in 1797; Memphis incorporated in 1826; Yellow fever in 1878 nearly depopulated city, but its population grew back to 64,589 in 1890.
**Further information:** Memphis Area Chamber of Commerce, 950 Commerce Square, Memphis, TN 38103.

## Mexico City (Ciudad de Mexico), Mexico

**Population:** 8,299,209 (UN est. 1974).
**Area:** about 53 sq. mi. within the 573 sq. mi. Federal District (Distrito Federal; population, 1976 est. 11 million); in central Mexico at an altitude of 7,349 ft.

**Industry and commerce:** capital of Mexico; the political and economic hub of the nation; manufactures include steel, automobiles, appliances, textiles, rubber goods, furniture, and electrical equipment; marketing center of Mexico.

**Transportation:** center of modern highway and rail system; 25-mi. subway system is being extended and will eventually extend 40 to 50 miles; served by most international air lines, Mexico City is 4 hrs. by jet from New York and 3 hrs. from Los Angeles.

**Communications:** major media center for Mexico and parts of Latin America; major film center.

**Cultural facilities:** Palace of Fine Arts and Ballet Folklorico; National Palace (Diego Rivera murals); National University with over 90,000 students; National Museum of Anthropology; Polyforum Cultural Siqueiros, containing world's largest mural; city itself is an architectural exhibit of Aztec ruins, baroque cathedrals, and ultra-modern buildings.

**Other attractions:** Xochimilco with the "floating gardens" and gondolas; Chapultepec Castle, palace of the French-supported Emperor and Empress of Mexico, Maximilian and Carlota; 22-ton Aztec Calendar Stone; 2 volcanoes, Popocatepetl (17,887 ft.) and Iztaccihuatl (17,343 ft.); sports centers.

**History:** traditionally founded 1321 by Aztecs, city was called Tenochtitlan; captured by Spanish under Cortez in 1519 and again in 1521; occupied by the U.S. in 1847 and by the French from 1863 to 1867.

**Further information:** Mexican National Tourist Council, Mariano Escobedo 726, Mexico, D.F., or 405 Park Avenue, NY 10022; or 9701 Wilshire Boulevard, Beverly Hills, CA 90212.

## Miami, Florida

The World Almanac is sponsored in the Miami area by The Miami Herald, 1 Herald Plaza, Miami, FL 33101; phone (305) 350-2111; founded Dec. 1, 1910, by Frank B. Shutts; circulation (1977) 412,177 daily, 508,318 Sunday; chairman James L. Knight, executive editor John McMullan, editor Jim Hampton, managing editor Bob Ingle; newspaper or staff writers have won or shared in 5 Pulitzer prizes, the latest in 1976, and numerous other honors.

**Population:** 354,000 (city), 1,468,000 (metro); first in state, 24th in nation; total employed in metro area, 621,100 (1977 average).

**Area:** 53.8 sq. mi. land and water, on Biscayne Bay at mouth of Miami River in southeast Florida; largest of 28 municipalities in Dade County; Dade County seat.

**Industry:** 5,000 light manufacturing plants; tourism and aviation are mainstays of economy; 851 hotels and motels with 64,000 rooms handle 13 million visitors a year; aviation hub with Eastern (largest industrial employer) and National headquarter bases; winter agriculture center.

**Commerce:** center of Pan-American finance and commerce with more than 100 banks, 16 savings and loan associations, new Federal Reserve branch to be built; annual retail sales total nearly $5 billion; Port of Miami busy in waterborne commerce and largest cruise center in world with 20 liners and 978,000 passengers (1977).

**Transportation:** Miami International, served by 109 air carriers, handled more than 13 million travelers in 1977; Seaboard Coast Line, Amtrak, and all-freight Fla. East Coast Railroads operate in Miami, as do Greyhound and Trailways buses; 65 truck lines.

**Communications:** 6 commercial and 5 educational or closed-circuit TV stations; 31 radio stations.

**New construction:** $75 million Omni International Hotel with restaurants, shops, and theaters; $50 million restoration of Miami Beach beachfront under way; new $5.7 million Amtrak station.

**Medical facilities:** 39 hospitals, 11,894 beds; 5,362 beds at 39 nursing homes in metro area; 2,975 members of Dade County Medical Association; VA hospital, Jackson Memorial Hospital one of area's leading research facilities.

**Federal facilities:** Homestead AFB south of Miami with 8,379 Air Force, Army, and Navy personnel; Federal Aviation Administration; Coast Guard bases; 2 federal hospitals; oceanographic center; 13,700 U.S. employees.

**Cultural facilities:** Philharmonic, Opera Guild, and other musical groups perform regularly; 18 auditoriums, resident and touring theatrical productions, 6 major art museums; 29 public libraries; 12 playhouses and 60 night clubs and theater restaurants, some in major hotels.

**Educational facilities:** 6 colleges and universities, plus 3 campuses of Miami-Dade Community College; total enrollment, 86,000; Univ. of Miami is largest independent institution of higher learning in southeast; Florida International Univ.; public school system has 229,858 students and is 5th largest in nation.

**Recreational facilities:** 14 miles of public beach on ocean and bay; 365 parks and playgrounds, 11 stadiums and grandstands, 45 golf courses, 57 marinas with 37,000 boats registered; 105 movie houses, 100 miles of bikeways, 28 bowling alleys.

**Convention facilities:** newly expanded Miami Beach convention hall can handle largest conventions; 202 conventions brought 86,150 delegates to Miami in 1977; 570 conventions brought 290,000 delegates to Miami Beach in same year.

**Sports:** pro football Miami Dolphins and Univ. of Miami play in Orange Bowl, which seats 75,000; stadium also hosts Orange Bowl game, Orange Blossom Classic; Miami Stadium is spring home of Baltimore Orioles; parimutuel wagering at 5 horse and greyhound tracks, jai-alai frontons.

**Other attractions:** balmy subtropical climate with mean annual temperature of 75.3 degrees; 600 Protestant churches; 53 Catholic churches, 55 synagogues; city is bilingual with 524,000 Latin American residents; one of nation's largest Jewish communities; marine stadium features powerboat and regatta racing; Everglades National Park, 40 miles south of Miami, is virgin wilderness.

**History:** America's newest big city, Miami had only 3 houses in 1895 in a community called Fort Dallas. Julia Tuttle persuaded Henry Flagler to extend his railroad south from West Palm Beach to stimulate Miami development; city was incorporated in 1896, when railroad arrived.

**Further information:** Miami-Metro Department of Publicity and Tourism, 499 Biscayne Boulevard, Miami, FL 33132.

## Milwaukee, Wisconsin

The World Almanac is sponsored in the Milwaukee area by The Milwaukee Journal, Journal Square, Milwaukee, WI 53201; telephone (414) 224-2000; founded 1882 by Lucius W. Nieman; circulation 334,167 daily, 532,692 Sunday; chairman of the board Donald B. Abert; publisher Warren J. Heyse; president of The Journal Co. Thomas J. McCollow; editor Richard H. Leonard; major awards include 2 Pulitzer prizes to the newspaper and 3 to staff members.

**Population:** 653,100 (city), 1,442,600 (SMSA); city 13th and metro area 25th in U.S.; total employment 655,000 (metro area).

**Area:** 95.8 sq. mi. on shore of Lake Michigan, Milwaukee County seat.

**Industry:** largest U.S. producer of diesel and gasoline engines, outboard motors, motorcycles, tractors, padlocks, beer; 4th largest U.S. automaking center; graphic arts and food processing are largest nondurable goods employers; location for 11 "Fortune 500" industries.

**Commerce:** wholesale and retail trade center for Wisconsin, upper Michigan; total retail sales $4.8 billion (SMSA); wholesale trade $8.2 billion (SMSA). Average household spendable income $17,255 (SMSA); 79 banks with $5.2 billion deposits; 49 savings and loan associations home offices in the (SMSA), with deposits of over $3.3 billion.

**Transportation:** 5 major rail lines; Amtrak, 8 airlines provide direct service to East and West coasts, south, southeast, southwest, and Florida for 2 million users of Gen. Mitchell field which has International air arrivals facility; 30 U.S. and foreign-flag ship lines use Milwaukee's St. Lawrence Seaway port, handling nearly 3.6 million tons annually including 553,000 tons overseas cargo; port of Milwaukee gateway for 350 cities in 31 states and overseas ports. Wisconsin ranks 11th in foreign trade-exports and imports; Milwaukee SMSA 4th largest U.S. machinery exporter and 14th largest exporter all products; 4 inter-city bus lines, 70 motor freight carriers; I-94, 5 federal and 14 state highways intersect Milwaukee.

**Communications:** morning, evening, and Sunday metropolitan newspaper; 4 commercial, 2 educational TV stations; 28 AM and FM radio stations.

**Medical facilities:** 21 major hospitals and medical centers, including 600 bed VA hospital.

**Cultural facilities:** Milwaukee Symphony, Repertory Theater, opera and operetta companies; Mid-America Ballet; Milwaukee Art Center, $5 million addition opened 1977; Milwaukee museum, 4th largest in U.S.; University of Wisconsin-Milwaukee, Marquette University, Medical College of Wisconsin, 8 other colleges and vocational schools enroll over 45,000 annually; 3-theater Performing Arts Center; $15.9 million exhibition addition to convention arena-auditorium complex; Mitchell Park Conservatory; Milwaukee County Stadium, and Milwaukee County Zoo are parts of 13,000 acre county park system.

**Sports:** baseball, Brewers (American League); basketball, Bucks (NBA), Marquette Univ., Univ. Wisconsin-Milwaukee; football, Green Bay Packers (NFL) play 5 of 11 home games in Milwaukee.

**History:** founded by Solomon Juneau, (1818), one of many French trappers in area in early 1800s; incorporated as town 1837; as city 1846.

**Further information:** Metropolitan Milwaukee Association of Commerce, 828 N. Broadway, Milwaukee, WI 53202.

## Minneapolis, Minnesota

**Population:** 361,000 (city), 1,236,500 (metro); first in state, 31st in nation; total employed (city, 1977) 276,724.

**Area:** 59 sq. mi. (city), 4,000 sq. mi. (10-county metro area) around St. Anthony Falls near junction of Minnesota and Mississippi rivers; Hennepin County seat.

**Industry:** diverse; major electronics-computer manufacturing center, including Honeywell, Control Data, Medtronics; headquarters for nation's 4 largest grain millers, including General Mills, Pillsbury, and International Multifoods.

**Commerce:** $14,654 median household income; $4.1 billion total retail sales metro area (1977); 24 commercial banks, 6 savings and loan assns.; headquarters for Ninth Federal Reserve District; world trade center, 12th among U.S. metro areas in exports.

**Transportation:** Amtrak regional terminal, 5 trunk railroads; 150 trucking firms; 5 major barge lines headquartered in city; Mpls.-St. Paul International Airport, averaging 350 flights daily.

**Communications:** 4 commercial, 2 educational TV stations; 39 radio stations.

**Medical facilities:** 21 hospitals, including a leading heart hospital at Univ. of Minn.

**Federal facilities:** Farm Credit Administration regional office; FBI regional office; EPA district office, area headquarters HUD.

**Cultural facilities:** Minnesota Orchestra, 7 art galleries-museums, Tyrone Guthrie Theatre, Walker Art Center, Univ. of Minnesota.

**Sports:** Minnesota Twins (American League), Minnesota Vikings (NFL), Minnesota North Stars (NHL), Minnesota Kicks (NASL).

**Other attractions:** 153 parks, 22 lakes; 57-story IDS Tower; Mpls. Aquatennial celebration in July; average yearly snowfall, 41 inches.

**History:** first visited in 1680s by Fr. Louis Hennepin who discovered and named St. Anthony Falls on the Mississippi River; French fur traders used the area in 18th century; incorp. 1871. Falls became power source for lumber and milling operations in 19th century.

**Further information:** Greater Minneapolis Chamber of Commerce Information, 15 S. 5th Street, Minneapolis, MN 55402.

## Mobile, Alabama

The World Almanac is sponsored in the Mobile area by The Mobile Press Register, 304 Government Street, 36630; phone (205) 433-1551; circulation, Register (morn.) 48,812, Press (eve.) 56,123, Sunday, 98,514. Register founded 1813; Press 1928. William J. Hearin publisher and president. Fallon Trotter executive editor, John Fay associate executive editor.

**Population:** 196,600 (city), 416,600 (metro), 2d city in state, 65th in nation; total employed (metro) 163,900.

**Area:** 142 sq. mi. at head of Mobile Bay; Mobile County seat.

**Industry:** home of Alabama State Docks, a $300 million complex where 33 ocean-going ships can be docked at one time; over $2 billion is invested in diversified industry, including paper and paper products, forest products, ship-building, chemicals, roofing, paints, alumina, oil, aircraft engines, and metals.

**Commerce:** wholesale-retail center for large portion of southwest Alabama and southeast Mississippi; Mobile County retail sales over $1 billion (1977).

**Transportation:** served by 4 major railroads, one of the great river systems, 3 major airlines, 55 truck lines, and about 100 steamship lines.

**Communications:** 2 TV and 15 radio stations.

**Medical facilities:** Univ. of South Alabama Medical College and 5 modern hospitals.

**Cultural facilities:** Municipal Auditorium-Theater complex seats 16,000; art gallery, museum, amateur dramatic theater, public library and branches; Univ. of South Alabama; Spring Hill and Mobile colleges, and Bishop State Junior College.

**Military facilities:** Coast Guard base and Coast Guard aviation training center.

**Annual attractions:** America's Junior Miss Pageant, Senior Bowl football game, and Mardi Gras.

**History:** founded in 1702 by Jean Baptiste Le Moyne; 6 flags have flown over city since then.

**Further information:** Chamber of Commerce, Commercial Guaranty Bank Bldg., Mobile, AL.

## Montgomery, Alabama

The World Almanac is sponsored in the Montgomery area by the Advertiser-Journal, 200 Washington Street, Montgomery, AL 36102; phone: (205) 262-1611; Advertiser founded 1828, Journal 1881; circulation Advertiser (morn) 51,184; Journal (eve) 25,959; combined Sunday 75,446; publisher Harold Martin.

**Population:** 154,700 (city), 267,000 (metro); 147th in nation; total employed, 102,300.

**Area:** 50.94 sq. mi. (city), 442 sq. mi. (county).

**Industry:** machinery manufacture, glass products, textiles, refrigeration equipment, axles, furniture, food products, paper, and fertilizers; over 250 industries.

**Commerce:** wholesale-retail center for 13 counties in central Alabama: retail trade area sales (1974), $1 billion; 7 banks, 3 savings & loans associations, 6 insurance company home offices; state capital.
**Transportation:** 5 railroads, 4 airlines, 2 national bus lines, one city bus line; Interstates 65 and 85 intersect in the city; Alabama River navigable to the Gulf of Mexico.
**Medical facilities:** 5 general hospitals, Air Force hospital, area mental health hospital, and a VA hospital; over 1,529 beds.
**Military:** home of Maxwell AFB, The Air University, and Gunther Field.
**Cultural facilities:** art guild, civic ballet, little theater, and a community concert series; Museum of Fine Arts; 5 major

colleges and universities; $14 million civic center opened in 1976.
**Sports:** Rebels, farm team of Detroit Tigers; Blue-Gray Football Classic; Southeastern Championship Rodeo; George Lindsey Celebrity Golf Tournament.
**Other attractions:** a riverboat, accommodating 300 passengers, makes regular-scheduled excursions on the now navigable Alabama River; state capitol housed Confederate offices. White House of Confederacy, home of Jefferson Davis, open to public. Nearby Lownesboro — antebellum town with many colonial mansions and churches.
**History:** incorporated 1819; Jefferson Davis inaugurated president of the Confederate States of America, Feb. 18, 1861, in Montgomery.

## Montreal, Quebec, Canada

The World Almanac is sponsored in Montreal area by The Gazette, a Southam newspaper, 1000 St. Antoine Street, Montreal H3C 3R7, Quebec, Canada; phone (514) 861-1111; founded 1778 by Fleury Mesplet; circulation 115,000 daily; publisher Ross Munro, general manager Robert McConnell, editor Mark Harrison, managing editor Geoff Stevenson, editorial page editor Joan Fraser; sponsors Christmas fund; 12 National Newspaper awards in last 6 years.

**Population:** 1,214,300 (city), 2,761,000 (metro); after Paris, the 2d largest French-speaking city in the world, 67% French origin, 12% Anglo-Saxon, 21% other origins; Canada's largest urban center.
**Area:** 68 sq. mi. on an island of 190 sq. mi. in the St. Lawrence River where the Ottawa and Richelieu rivers flow into it at the head of the St. Lawrence Seaway; metro area extends over 1,000 sq. mi.; the 769 ft. Mount Royal dominates the Island which averages 100 ft. above sea level.
**Industry:** Canada's industrial hub ($7 billion, value of shipments of goods of own manufacturer).
**Commerce:** retail sales of $5 billion, headquarters of many of Canada's largest financial institutions, home of the Montreal and Canadian stock exchanges, about 75% of countries have consulates or representatives in Montreal.
**Transportation:** $1 billion St. Lawrence Seaway, Port of Montreal; 14 miles long, 42 miles of harbour with 140 berths; $500 million Mirabel jetport opened in 1975 with multi-million electric train link to downtown planned for early 1980's; existing 14 mile Metro to expand to 46 miles by 1981; world headquarters of International Civil Aviation Organization and International Air Transport Association serving 2 major airports; headquarters of Canadian National and Canadian Pacific railways.
**Communications:** 4 TV stations, 19 radio stations, 6 daily newspapers; headquarters for Bell Canada, CN-CP Telecommunications.
**Educational facilities:** Concordia University, McGill University, Universite de Montreal, Universite de Quebec; enrollment 78,000; faculty 5,500.
**Cultural facilities:** Place des Arts with 3,000 seat hall and 2

theaters, attracting the finest forms of artistic, cultural, and musical entertainment; the Montreal Museum of Fine Arts, the Musee de l'Art Contemporain; some of the world's most beautiful churches, including the Mary Queen of The World Basilica, a half-size replica of St. Peter's in Rome.
**Sports:** $1 billion Olympic complex; including a 56,000 permanent seat stadium, home of the National Baseball League Expos and the Canadian Football League Alouettes; 7,200 seat Velodrome, 2 50-meter pools, 25-meter diving pool, and a scuba diving pool — 15-meter depth; the Montreal Forum, home of the National Hockey League Canadiens.
**Recreational facilities:** within an hour of the Laurentien and Eastern townships skiing, hunting, and fishing resort areas; over 5,000 restaurants of all lands; over 100 cinemas, 19 museums, 13 city libraries, the Montreal Botanical Gardens, St. Helen's Island Park, Dow Planetarium, Montreal Municipal Golf Course.
**Convention facilities:** over 15,000 hotel and motel rooms; full facilities for conventions.
**Medical facilities:** over 80 hospitals with 26,000 beds, including the renowned Montreal Neurological Institute, and the Montreal Children's Hospital.
**History:** Montreal was first visited by Jacques Cartier in 1535; founded under the name of Ville Marie in 1642; Old Montreal, some 1,000 acres in all, is the largest such restoration in North America and retains the general atmosphere of the 18th century.
**Further information:** Convention and Visitor's Bureau of Greater Montreal, 1270 Sherbrooke Street W., H3G 1H7; The Montreal Tourist Bureau, 85 Notre Dame Street East, Montreal, Quebec.

## Nashville, Tennessee

The World Almanac is sponsored in Nashville by The Tennessean, 1100 Broadway, Nashville, TN 37202; phone (615) 255-1221; founded as The Tennessean in 1907 but incorporated publications date to 1812; circulation daily 134,700, Sunday 234,600; president Amon Carter Evans, publisher John Seigenthaler; 3 Pulitzer prizes, 8 Headliner awards, 3 Sigma Delta Chi awards.

**Population:** 486,000 ('77 est.) in unified metro government, 2d in state; labor force 326,900.
**Area:** 533 sq. mi., straddling Cumberland River, in north central part of state.
**Industry:** music (52% of U.S. singles are recorded in 40 studio complexes); clothing, headquarters of Genesco, world's largest and most diversified clothing and footwear manufacturer; insurance, 2 of largest U.S. companies located here; world's largest glass plant; chemicals, printing (especially religious materials), aerostructures, tires, air conditioning, heating equipment.
**Commerce:** retail center for middle Tennessee, south Kentucky; retail sales (1977) $2.2 billion; bank resources, over

$3.9 billion in 8 banks, 109 branches.
**Transportation:** 9 U.S. highways and 6 branches of the interstate system radiate from Nashville; 10 commercial airlines with 204 daily flights; 2 railroads, Amtrak; bus service, 73 motor freight lines.
**Communications:** 5 TV stations (one public), and 22 AM and FM radio stations.
**Medical facilities:** 18 hospitals (6,310 beds), 2 medical schools, VA hospital, speech-hearing center.
**Cultural:** symphony orchestra; replica of Parthenon with art gallery; public and state libraries; botanic garden and fine arts center, 3 community theaters.
**Educational facilities:** 17 colleges and universities; 137 pub-

lic schools, 39 private schools.
**Convention facilities:** 10,000-seat auditorium; Opryland convention center.
**Other attractions:** Grand Ole Opry, Opryland U.S.A. ($32 million theme park featuring music); Country Music Hall of Fame; Hermitage (home of Andrew Jackson); Belle Meade antebellum mansion.

**Recreation facilities:** water sports, outdoor activity on Old Hickory and Percy Priest lakes.
**History:** settled in 1780 as a fort in then western North Carolina; incorporated, 1784, with first written charter west of Alleghenies.
**Further information:** Chamber of Commerce, 161 4th Avenue N., Nashville, TN 37219.

## New Haven, Connecticut

The World Almanac is sponsored in the greater New Haven area by the New Haven Register (founded 1812) and the New Haven Journal-Courier (founded 1755); circulation Register (eve.) 101,911; Sunday 139,428; Journal-Courier (morn.) 32,018; president, publisher, editor-in-chief Lionel S. Jackson; assistant publisher Lionel S. Jackson Jr.; vp and general manager, Donald A. Spargo; vp and editor, Robert J. Leeney.

**Population:** 137,700 (city), 365,300 metro, 3d in state.
**Area:** 21.1 sq. mi. southern coast of Conn. on north shore of Long Island Sound; county seat.
**Industry:** 1,000 firms in immediate area; principal products are guns, hardware, rubber goods, paper products, machinery, and tools.
**Commerce:** wholesale-retail center for southern Conn., total retail sales (1977) $2.5 billion; serves 850,000 people within a radius of 25 miles; busy harbor, particularly oil tankers.
**Transportation:** Conrail, Amtrak Cosmopolitan turbotrain; 25 major truck lines; 14 federal and state highways; Tweed-New Haven Airport served by 2 airlines, limo service to N. Y. airports, bus line.
**Communications:** VHF, 2 UHF TV stations, and 6 radio stations.
**Medical facilities:** Yale Medical Center, Yale-New Haven Hospital; Hospital of St. Raphael.
**Cultural facilities:** Yale Univ. Library with over 6 million books, one of the world's largest collections; Yale's Peabody Museum of Natural History, art gallery, and Beinecke Rare Book Library; The Yale Center for British Art (Paul Mellon

$10 million gallery opened in 1977), New Haven Colony Historical Society, cultural center, 3 legitimate theaters; New Haven Symphony, Woolsey Hall.
**Educational facilities:** Yale Univ. and graduate schools; Albertus Magnus, Southern Conn. State, South Central Community, Quinnipiac, Greater New Haven Technical colleges; Univ. of New Haven.
**Recreational facilities:** Yale Bowl, Payne-Whitney Gym, Ingalls Rink, The Coliseum, 15 parks including Frederick Brewster's estate, West and East Rock scenic drives; West Rock Nature Center; 7 golf courses, 6 skating rinks.
**Convention facilities:** coliseum-convention center with 19-story hotel nearby.
**Sports:** AHL Nighthawks (hockey), West Haven Yankees (baseball).
**History:** founded 1638 by Puritans; named after Newhaven in England; incorporated 1638, became a part of Conn. 1662; first mayor was Roger Sherman, signer of Declaration of Independence.
**Further information:** Greater New Haven Chamber of Commerce, 195 Church Street, New Haven, CT. 06510.

## New Orleans, Louisiana

The World Almanac is sponsored in New Orleans by The States-Item, 3800 Howard Avenue, New Orleans, LA 70140; phone (504) 586-3560; founded June 11, 1877, circulation 116,575 daily, 106,591 Saturday; editor Walter G. Cowan, associate editor Charles A. Ferguson, city editor William U. Madden; sponsors Football Fund for Underprivileged.

**Population:** 568,000 (city), 1,117,000 (metro area); first in state; total employed, 439,600 (metro area as of Apr. 1978).
**Area:** 363.5 sq. mi. of which 199.4 are land.
**Industry:** Port of New Orleans, 2d largest in nation handled 98.3 million tons domestic cargo and 57.7 million tons foreign in 1977; foreign trade valued at $9.9 billion; tourist business is 2d largest, with $1,146,000 spent in metro area in 1976.
**Commerce:** trade center for lower Mississippi Valley; metro area bank assets, $5.4 billion in 1976, deposits $4.3 billion; savings and loan associations, assets of $2.3 billion in 1976; average household income 1976, $14,995; retail sales, $3.5 billion in 1976; per capita effective buying income. $5,476.
**Transportation:** rail hub with direct lines north, east and west; Amtrak passenger service to Chicago, Los Angeles; Southern railway to New York. New Orleans International Airport serves airlines, Lakefront Airport commercial aviation; cruise ships to Mexico and Caribbean.
**New construction:** $500 million Canal Place and $50 million, 59-story Sheraton Hotel.
**Communications:** 4 commercial TV stations and educational channel; 20 radio stations.
**Medical facilities:** major medical center with 2 schools of medicine; Charity Hospital 2d largest in nation; Ochsner Medical Institutions.
**Federal facilities:** hdqtrs. 5th U. S. Circuit Court of Appeals and 8th Naval District; regional office U. S. Census Bureau and field office U. S. Dept. Agriculture Marketing Service.
**Recreation:** City Park, 1500 acres with golf, tennis, boating;

Audubon Park, 250 acres with golf, tennis and zoo; Pontchartrain Beach Amusement Park, large lakeside amusement center.
**Convention facilities:** 20,000 rooms in major hotels; 160,000 sq. ft. exhibition space in Superdome, 134,000 sq. ft. in Rivergate, and 32,500 sq. ft. Municipal Auditorium.
**Cultural facilities:** Theater for the Performing Arts seats 2,317 for operas, concerts; Municipal Auditorium seats up to 8,000 for special events; museums include New Orleans Museum of Art, Louisiana State Museum, Historic New Orleans Collection, and many small galleries.
**Educational facilities:** Tulane Univ., Univ. of New Orleans, Loyola Univ., Dillard, Southern Univ. in New Orleans, Xavier, St. Mary's Dominican.
**Other attractions:** Lousiana Superdome seats 75,000; French Quarter is historic tourist attraction.
**Sports:** Saints (NFL), Jazz (NBA), Sugar Bowl game on New Year's day.
**History:** named after the Duke of Orleans, founded in swamp within crescent of the Mississippi River 100 miles from Gulf of Mexico by Jean Baptiste Le Moyne, Sieur de Bienville, in 1718; became capital of Louisiana Territory in 1722, when Adrien de Pauger laid out what is now the French Quarter; became part of U.S. with Louisiana Purchase in 1803.
**Further information:** Chamber of Commerce of New Orleans Area, 301 Camp Street; Greater New Orleans Tourist and Convention Commission, 334 Royal Street, both New Orleans, LA 70130.

## New York City, New York

The World Almanac is sponsored in the greater New York City metropolitan area by the New York Daily News, 220 E. 42d Street, New York, N.Y. 10017, phone (212) 949-1234. New York News Inc. founded June 26, 1919 by Joseph Medill Patterson; circulation daily 1,824,836; Sunday 2,656,981; president and publisher W. H. James; vice president and editor Michael J. O'Neill; vice president and managing editor William J. Brink; vice president and general manager Joseph F. Barletta; secretary and treasurer Robert C. Schneider. Pulitzer Prizes for editorial writing, news photography, cartoon, international and local investigative reporting; sponsors Golden Gloves, National Spelling Bee championships for New York City, Long Island, Westchester, and other major school athletic, cultural, and educational events as community service programs.

**Population:** 7,477,563 (city), 10,927,837 (consolidated area, N.Y. City, Westchester, Nassau, Suffolk counties); first in state and nation; total employed 3,159,500 (1977); per capita personal income $6,696.

**Area:** 300 sq. mi. at mouth of Hudson River; embraces 5 boroughs — Manhattan, Bronx, Brooklyn, Queens, and Staten Island.

**Industry:** nation's leader in manufacturing and service industries; produces 25.2% of America's apparel, 15.7% of printing and publishing; 20,600 manufacturing establishments (June 1977).

**Commerce:** nation's richest port, handling annual 179.5 million tons of maritime cargo; Wall Street, world's largest financial center, with New York and American Stock exchanges; wholesale-retail center for New York, New Jersey and southwestern Connecticut, retail sales $16.1 billion (1977); 40 commercial banks, resources $164.4 billion (1978); 42 savings banks, resources $59.6 billion (1978); World Trade Center, twin 110-story towers, cost $850 million.

**Transportation:** Kennedy International Airport handles 40.8% of nation's overseas air travel and 56.4% of export-import air tonnage, served by 56 scheduled air carriers; LaGuardia Airport served by 15 domestic airlines; 5 heliports. Penn Central Railroad, Amtrak; 2 major rail terminals, Pennsylvania and Grand Central stations; 40 interstate bus lines; subway network covers every borough except Staten Island; ferry and the 4,260-ft. Verrazano-Narrows Bridge (world's longest suspension span) link Staten Island to Manhattan and Brooklyn; 18 bridges connect Manhattan with other boroughs, George Washington Bridge over the Hudson connects New Jersey; 5 tunnels under the Hudson and East rivers.

**Communications:** 17 TV stations (6 commercial, 4 educational, 1 municipal, 2 Spanish, 4 CATV); 38 AM and FM radio stations; WPIX-TV and WPIX-FM are broadcast affiliates of The News.

**Medical facilities:** 104 hospitals, (15 municipal, 28 private, 59 voluntary non-profit); 5 major medical research centers specialize in cancer, heart diseases, sickle cell anemia, and other research; Sloan-Kettering Institute for Cancer Research; 4 VA hospitals.

**Federal facilities:** Fort Wadsworth, Staten Island; Governors Island, many federal agencies represented in buildings at Federal Plaza and 90 Church St.

**Educational facilities:** 6 universities, 23 colleges, including 5 medical colleges, 4 law schools, 3 colleges of pharmacy, 2 colleges of dentistry, 2 institutes of art and architecture; 994 schools in the public school system; more than 1,000 private schools; public libraries total 189.

**Cultural facilities:** Lincoln Center for the Performing Arts (Philharmonic, Ballet Company, Metropolitan Opera, and other theatrical arts), Carnegie Hall, Brooklyn Academy of Music. Broadway and Off-Broadway alliance for varied theatrical productions; outdoor Delacorte Theatre in Central Park; 65 museums including American Museum of Natural History, Metropolitan Museum of Art, Museum of the Performing Arts, Museum of Modern Art, Whitney Museum, and South Street Seaport Museum.

**Other attractions:** United Nations; botanic gardens in the Bronx and Brooklyn; Central Park and Prospect Park; Bronx Zoo and 4 other zoos; 13 municipal golf courses, 535 tennis courts, 37 outdoor swimming pools.

**Sports:** NBA Knicks, NHL Rangers, Islanders: NL Mets and NFL Jets play in Shea Stadium; AL Yankees play in Yankee Stadium; NFL Giants and NASL Cosmos play in Giants Stadium in nearby E. Rutherford, N.J.; tennis WTT Apples. Thoroughbred racing at Belmont and Aqueduct; harness racing at Roosevelt, Yonkers, and the Meadowlands; area has off-track betting.

**History:** discovered by Giovanni da Verrazano in 1524; in 1626 Peter Minuit bought the island from the Manhattan Indians for about $24 in goods and trinkets; settlement named New Amsterdam. In 1664, British troops occupied city without resistance and named it New York in honor of the Duke of York, brother of the King. On Jan. 1, 1898, Manhattan and large areas to the NE, E, and S were consolidated into one city of New York.

**Further information:** Department of Commerce and Industry, 225 Broadway; Convention and Vistors Bureau, 90 East 42d Street, both New York, NY.

---

## Newark, New Jersey

**Population:** 378,670; first in state, swells on weekdays with non-residents working and attending school; 2,011,800 (metro area) including Essex, Morris, Somerset, and Union counties; 136,042 employed (city).

**Area:** 24.14 sq. mi. (city), 8 miles W of New York City; Essex County seat.

**Industry:** wide diversity of manufacturers, fine craftsmanship; major beer, chemicals, and plastics industries; more than 10,000 businesses, major banking and insurance center; headquarters for several national firms.

**Transportation:** international airport; major port; 4 railroads; world's largest privately owned bus system; one of world's largest truck terminals; world's largest containerized shipping center.

**Communications:** 5 radio stations, one VHF public TV station and 2 UHF TV stations.

**Medical facilities:** 6 major hospitals with new home of the College of Medicine and Dentistry completed in 1978; Beth Israel Medical Center.

**Federal facilities:** federal building; old federal courthouse.

**Cultural facilities:** museum, library, New Jersey Historical Society, New Jersey Symphony Orchestra, New Jersey Opera, Garden State Ballet, Newark Community Center of the Arts, Symphony Hall, and Newark Boys Chorus.

**Educational facilities:** New Jersey College of Medicine and Dentistry; Rutgers Univ.; Seton Hall Univ. Law School; New Jersey Institute of Technology; Essex County College.

**Recreational facilities:** parks cover 870 acres; 7 pools, 74 playgrounds, one ice rink, 2 lakes.

**Convention facilities:** large hotel and 3 motor inns.

**Other attractions:** annual Cherry Blossom Festival; 7 famous works of sculpture, including "John F. Kennedy" by Jacques Lipchitz and a seated Abraham Lincoln by Gutzon Borglum; Sacred Heart, one of the largest Gothic cathedrals in the world, the historic Plume House, built in 1710, and Ballantine House, built in 1885.

**History:** founded in 1666, incorporated 1836; British troops ravaged the town during the Revolution.

**Further information:** Greater Newark Chamber of Commerce, 50 Park Place, Newark, NJ 07102; and Newark Public Library, 5 Washington Street, Newark, NJ 07101.

## Norfolk, Virginia

The World Almanac is sponsored in the Norfolk metro area by The Virginian-Pilot and The Ledger-Star, 150 W. Brambleton Avenue, Norfolk, VA 23501; phone (804) 446-2000; Va. founded 1865, Ledger, 1876; circulation: LS (eve.) 99,588; VP (morn.) 128,201; VP/LS (Sun.) 199,361; Perry Morgan publisher, Robert D. Benson resident & general manager, J. Harvie Wilkinson III VP editor, George J. Hebert LS editor.

**Population:** 278,000 (city), 790,300 (metro); first in state; civilian employed, 286,700; military pop., 85,000.

**Area:** 915 sq. mi. in SE Virginia.

**Industry:** General Electric, Ford Motor Co., Norfolk Shipbuilding & Drydock Corp., Royster Co., Smith-Douglas Div. of Borden Co.

**Commerce:** retail sales (1977) $2.3 billion; aver. household income, $16,797 (1977 effective buying income).

**Transportation:** Port of Hampton Roads, world's finest natural harbor, ranks first in export tonnage (39,980,500 tons handled in 1976) among Atlantic ports; biggest coal port in world; International Airport, 4 major airlines; Chesapeake Bay Bridge-Tunnel supplies direct north highway route; 7 trunk line railroads, 50 trucking companies, 2 bus companies.

**Communications:** 5 TV, 13 AM, 12 FM radio stations.

**Medical facilities:** 12 hospitals including oldest and 2d largest naval hospital in U.S.

**Federal facilities:** greatest concentration of naval installations in world; approx. 36 major commands include Atlantic Fleet, Second Fleet, NATO Supreme Allied Command Atlantic (SACLANT), Armed Forces Staff College, and Commandant 5th Naval Dist.

**Cultural facilities:** symphony orchestra, Feldman Chamber Quartet, repertory theater, dinner and little theaters, civic and univ. ballet; Chrysler Museum collection; Va. Opera Assoc.

**Educational facilities:** Old Dominion Univ., Norfolk State, Virginia Wesleyan, Tidewater Community colleges; Eastern Va. Medical School.

**Recreational facilities:** General Douglas MacArthur Memorial, Adam Thoroughgood House (1636), Gardens-by-the-sea; Dismal Swamp located in Chesapeake; resort city of Virginia Beach offers 38 mi. of swimming, fishing, and surfing; camping at Seashore State Park; Hermitage Foundation Museum.

**Convention facilities:** Scope, $30 million cultural and convention center.

**Sports:** Tidewater Tides, International League baseball.

**Other attractions:** Azalea Festival, Norfolk Harbor Fest, Va. Beach boardwalk art show, Portsmouth Sewall art show.

**Climate:** Average temp. 70° to 52°.

**Further information:** Chamber of Commerce, 475 St. Paul Boulevard, Norfolk, VA 23501.

## Oakland, California

**Population:** 328,188; employed in Oakland, 180,000.

**Area:** 53.4 sq. mi.; Alameda County seat.

**Industry:** food processing, fabricated metal products, transportation equipment, chemicals and paint; Port of Oakland 2d in containerized cargo; home base for Kaiser Industries.

**Commerce:** 8,449 retail outlets with taxable sales (1977) of $1.4 billion; median income for family, $11,997 per annum.

**Transportation:** western terminus for Southern Pacific, Santa Fe, and Western Pacific railroads; International Airport is major airfreight terminal and center for supplemental air carriers; headquarters for Bay Area Rapid Transit, underground, underwater 75-mile subway connecting 15 communities.

**Medical facilities:** 9 hospitals include Children's Hospital Medical Center, Kaiser Foundation, and the Veterans Administration.

**New construction:** Pacific Telephone Bldg., Wells Fargo Bldg., Clorox Bldg.; 16 square block city center project, and major downtown garage under construction.

**Cultural facilities:** museum, half garden, half gallery design, has divisions of natural science, history, and art; symphony, Chinese Community Cultural Center.

**Educational facilities:** Univ. of California at Berkeley, Mills College, College of Holy Names, Cal. State, Hayward, Chabot, California College of Arts and Crafts, Peralta Community College.

**Recreational facilities:** 26,000 acre regional park system serving the East Bay; zoo in 100-acre Knowland State Park has large collection of gibbons and aerial tram; Lake Merritt Park includes botanical garden, wildfowl refuge, natural science center, and Children's Fairyland.

**Sports:** Raiders (football), Athletics (baseball), Golden State Warriors (basketball).

**Other attractions:** Oakland Coliseum, over 50,000 capacity, for theatrical entertainment, exhibits, conventions, and circus; Jack London Square.

**History:** area explored in 1772, settled in 1850; incorporated as town in 1852, as city in 1854.

**Further information:** Chamber of Commerce, 1320 Webster Street, Oakland, CA 94612.

## Oklahoma City, Oklahoma

The World Almanac is sponsored in the Oklahoma City area by The Daily Oklahoman and Oklahoma City Times, Oklahoma City, OK 73125; phone (405) 232-3311; The Oklahoman founded in 1894; Times in 1888; Oklahoma Publishing Co. acquired The Oklahoman 1903 and the Times 1916; circulation Oklahoman 182,232; Times 95,413; Sunday, 291,002; editor and publisher E. L. Gaylord, managing editor Jim Standard.

**Population:** (1978 est.) 382,400 (city), 555,400 (Oklahoma County), 783,000 (metro); largest in state; labor force 387,200.

**Area:** city area, among nation's largest, is 649 sq. mi.; metro area, 3,491 sq. mi.; located in state's center on Canadian River in Oklahoma, Cleveland, Canadian, McClain, and Pottawatomie counties.

**Industry:** oil, with about 1,500 producing wells in metro area, employs about 13,000; Tinker AFB, one of world's largest air depots, employs 17,200 civilians and 3,500 military on $100 million installation; FAA and other aviation employ some 30,000, with annual payroll of $300 million; agricultural and ranching area; manufactured goods include aircraft, telecommunications equipment, computers, oil field machinery, oil and greases, building materials, feed, flour, meat, and tires.

**Commerce:** regional, national, and international marketing center; median house E.B.I., $12,972 (metro), consumer sales near $2.8 billion (metro).

**Transportation:** 5 passenger airlines; 4 primary federal and 3 major state highways, with I-40 and I-35 intersecting the city; fully planned urban expressway system, major bus, truck, and rail lines.

**Medical facilities:** Oklahoma Univ. Health Sciences Center and 25 hospitals and clinics.

**Cultural facilities:** symphony and junior symphony; Oklahoma Art Ctr.; Lyric Theater at Oklahoma City Univ.; Oklahoma Theater Ctr.; Southwest Repertory Theater, Univ. of Oklahoma.

**Education:** Univ. of Oklahoma, Oklahoma City Univ., Central State Univ., Oklahoma State Univ.

**Convention facilities:** $23 million Myriad Convention Center, seating 15,000 in the center of a downtown redevelopment project, hosts 350 conventions yearly with more than

325,000 delegates.
**Other attractions:** National Cowboy Hall of Fame; 130 municipal parks; major college sports; pro sports; Oklahoma City 89ers, American Assn. baseball; International Softball headquarters.
**History:** founded by land run, Apr. 22, 1889.
**Further information:** Chamber of Commerce, 1 Santa Fe Plaza, Oklahoma City, OK 73102.

---

## Omaha, Nebraska

The World Almanac is sponsored in Nebraska by The Omaha World-Herald, World-Herald Square, Omaha, NE 68102; phone (402) 444-1000; Evening World, founded 1885 by G. M. Hitchcock, acquired Daily Herald founded 1865; adopted present name 1889; circulation 236,545 daily, 280,663 Sunday; president Harold W. Andersen, executive editor Louis G. Gerdes; 3 Pulitzer Prizes; sponsors Midwest Spelling Bee, Newspaper in Education, Music in the Parks; Show Wagon, Good Fellows charities, college scholarships, Consumer Preference Studies.

**Population:** (1978 est.) 382,000, city, 590,000 metro; first in state, 68th in U.S.; 260,000 work force.
**Area:** eastern Nebraska, 83 sq. mi. of rolling hills on west bank of Missouri River; Douglas County seat.
**Industry:** manufacturing shipments $3.8 billion annually; 600 plants employ 35,000; food processing center; 4th largest livestock market in nation receipts.
**Commerce:** major trade center, $2.1 billion retail sales; 3,000 retail, 1,200 wholesale firms; $16,422 median household income; 46 banks, $2 billion deposits; 14 savings and loans, $2 billion assets; 4th largest insurance center in U.S. (35 home offices, including Mutual of Omaha). Also headquarters Union Pacific, Northern Natural Gas, Northwestern Bell, ConAgra.
**Transportation:** 7 major airlines; 4th largest rail center, served by 8 major railroads, 122 truck lines, Interstate highways 80 and 29, 2 intercity bus, 3 barge lines; 3.3 million tons carried on Missouri River annually; port of entry, foreign trade zone.
**Communications:** served by Nebraska's largest daily newspaper, 6 TV channels, 7 radio stations.
**Medical facilities:** 15 hospitals, 4,500 beds; 2 medical schools (Nebraska U., Creighton U.), 7 nursing schools,

Eppley Institute for Cancer Research.
**Federal facilities:** Strategic Air Command's global headquarters, U.S. Army Corps of Engineers.
**Cultural facilities:** Orpheum performing arts center, symphony orchestra, opera company, ballet society; 10 live theater groups, 22 art galleries, 16 museums, Joslyn Art Museum's $20 million collection.
**Educational facilities:** 3 universities, 5 colleges educate 30,000 students; 30 adult education schools.
**Recreation:** 6,000 acres of public parks include 150 tennis courts, 30 pools, 17 golf courses, ice rinks.
**Sports:** Omaha Royals AAA baseball, Ak-Sar-Ben horse racing, NCAA College World Series.
**Other attractions:** 1,300-acre Fontenelle Forest, Henry Doorly Zoo, Boys Town, President Ford birthsite, General Dodge House, Aerospace Museum. Ranked 10th among 50 largest U.S. cities in quality of life.
**History:** Lewis and Clark, 1804; Indian trading post, 1825; Mormon settlement, 1846; Omaha (named after Indian tribe) laid out when Nebraska Territory opened, 1854; chartered as city, 1867.
**Further information:** Greater Omaha Chamber of Commerce, 1620 Dodge Street, Omaha, NE 68102.

---

## Orange County, California

The World Almanac is sponsored in Orange County by The Register, 625 N. Grand Avenue, Santa Ana, CA 92711; telephone (714) 835-1234; circulation combined daily morning and evening 211,364; Sunday 240,890 founded 1905, purchased in 1935 by the late R.C. Hoiles, founder of Freedom Newspapers Inc., a 28-daily newspaper group; son Clarence H. Hoiles, chairman of the board of Freedom Newspapers and co-publisher of The Register; son Harry Hoiles, Register co-publisher and president of Freedom Newspapers; Richard Wallace, general manager; Jim Dean, executive editor; Mike Maloney, managing editor; Jim Lyons Sr., research and promotion director.

**Population:** 1,844,000 (July 1978 est.) 2d most populous county in the state, compares with 212,364 in 1950, 2.5 million projected for 1990; county encompasses 26 cities.
**Area:** 511,040 acres in S. California from Pacific Ocean inland 25 miles to Cleveland National Forest; 42-mile coastline stretches from Long Beach past Huntington Beach surfing, Newport Beach yacht harbor, Laguna Beach art colony, Dana Point small-craft harbor, to San Clemente and Camp Pendleton.
**Commerce and Industry:** median income (1978) $22,350 (United California Bank forecast) compared with (1976) $17,780; total personal income 1978 forecast $17.3 billion; taxable retail sales (1977) $8.66 billion, 1978 forecast $9.70 billion; total automotive purchases led the retail sales category with $1.9 billion in taxable sales during 1977; general merchandise was 2d with $1.02 billion in sales, followed by eating and drinking places with $515 million. The unemployment rate average about 4 percent during 1977. Fluor Corp. moved its facilities to Irvine during 1977 with about 5,000 employees housed in the $100 million complex. Rockwell International's Autonetics was the largest employer in the county. Hughes Aircraft, Beckman Instruments, Hunt-Wesson Foods, Philco-Ford Aeronutronics, AMF-Voit are a few of the large employers. Santa Fe International, Baker International, and Smith International are a few of the oil and oil related firms with corporate headquarters located in the county.
**New construction:** 27,504 permits were issued for single and multiple family construction during 1977; the median price

of a single family home was $68,000 in 1977 and jumped to $74,000 during the first half of 1978; the median price of new homes was $102,000 during 1977; vacancy factor was below 4 percent during the year.
**Transportation:** 8 major freeways, including main Los Angeles-San Diego artery; transit district with countywide routes including freeway commuter buses and Dial-A-Ride in some areas; nation's 2d busiest airport with 639,624 tower operations in 1977.
**Communications:** local UHF-TV station, 7 VHF-TV stations regionally, over 40 radio stations.
**Federal facilities:** Marine Corps Air Station at El Toro, Los Alamitos Naval Air Station, Seal Beach Naval Weapons Station, Santa Ana Marine Corps Lighter-Than-Air Station (now used for helicopters, once for dirigibles), federal building in Santa Ana, general services administration building, national archives center in Laguna Niguel, Cleveland National Forest, Marine Corps Camp Pendleton in nearby San Diego County.
**Medical facilities:** Univ. of Cal. medical school at Irvine, 6 hospitals and convalescent hospitals.
**Recreation:** 781 acres of beaches, more than 13,000 acres for regional parks, 141 scenic sea cliffs, 3 yacht basins, 3 fishing lakes, wilderness campgrounds, 35 golf courses, 21-mile equestrian and bicycle trail along Santa Ana River.
**Other attractions:** Disneyland, Knott's Berry Farm amusement park, Lion Country Safari, Movieland Wax Museum, Los Alamitos Racetrack; motorcycle park, auto raceway

mid-summer Laguna Beach Art Festival-Pageant of Masters, Santa Ana Zoo, air and car museums, Anaheim Stadium.

**Convention facilities:** Anaheim Convention Center, Disneyland Convention Center, hotels in Anaheim, Buena Park, Costa Mesa, Irvine, Newport Beach, Santa Ana.

**Sports:** AL Angels, Anaheim Oranges (tennis), school sports.

**Cultural-Educational facilities:** 2 major tax-supported universities, 4 private liberal arts colleges, 7 community colleges, multiple trade and special interest schools, 607 tax-supported K-12 schools; 71 private and church K-12 schools; city and county libraries, symphony orchestra society; 2 master chorales, 6 ballet companies, 32 community

theater groups, repertory theater, 4 art museums.

**History:** first Spanish expedition 1769 by Capt. Gaspar de Portola, who recorded first reported earthquake in the state; county formed March 11, 1889 from Los Angeles County; Glen Martin tested his first plane near Santa Ana; Madame Modjeska resided in local forest hideaway; Toastmasters International founded in Santa Ana 1924; Howard Hughes set world's speed record in Santa Ana in 1935 with 351 mph airplane flight. Swallows traditionally return each year to Mission San Juan Capistrano on March 19.

**Further information:** Anaheim Visitor and Convention Center Bureau, 800 W. Katella Avenue, Anaheim, CA, Orange County Chamber of Commerce, One City Boulevard W., Orange, CA.

## Orlando, Florida

The World Almanac is sponsored in the Orlando area by the Sentinel Star, 633 N. Orange Avenue, Orlando, FL 32802; phone (305) 420-5000; Sentinel and Evening Star founded as dailies in 1913; merged in 1931; acquired by Tribune Company of Chicago in 1965; combined to create "all day" newspaper in 1973; circulation (ABC Newspaper Publisher's Statement 6 months ending March 31, 1978), 192,868 weekdays, 186,487 Saturday, 219,438 Sunday; president and chief executive officer Charles T. Brumback, editor James Squires.

**Population:** 122,090 (city, July '77), 645,000 (metro, '78); 253,100 employed (metro) average for year of '77.

**Area:** 30.1 sq. mi. (city), 2528 sq. mi. (metro) in east central Florida; 52 lakes inside city limits; avg. temperature 72.5; Orange County seat.

**Industry:** center of citrus belt; heart of foliage industry; 6 regional and 9 national home insurance company offices; 5 largest employers in manufacturing (metro)—Martin Marietta Co. aerospace division, Green Thumb, Scott Electronics, Stromberg Carlson, General Electric; manufacturers opening or expanding (metro)—Mogul Corp., Control Laser, Stokely Van Camp, DeSoto Paint, R.F. Systems, Applied Devices, A.T. & T., Quip Systems; 27 (metro) industrial parks; naval training center, $102 million payroll (military and civilian), 28 commands and activities.

**Commerce:** 24 main commercial banks (excluding branches) in metro area; total metro deposits (year end '77) over $1.4 billion; 6 savings and loan assns. based in metro area with 55 branches; 30 major shopping centers with 4 regional malls; retail sales (metro) $2.4 billion in 1976; estimated buying income per household $14,719 in 1976.

**Transportation:** 4 major commercial airlines serving Orlando International Airport, 1977 passenger total (in and out) 4.2 million; Seaboard Coastline Railroad, Amtrak; 2 intercity bus lines; 23 common carrier truck lines; 8 freight forwarding companies (3 air, 4 surface, 1 export); Port Canaveral and Jacksonville, nearest ports of entry.

**Communications:** 16 radio and 4 TV stations.

**New construction:** $150 million international airport terminal to open early in '80s; $100 million Sea World expansion to continue over 10 year period; $4 million Martin Marietta expansion; $150 million Lake Buena Vista office complex, $4 million first phase; $300 million Walt Disney World EPCOT Center, first phase of experimental prototype of city of to-

morrow, to begin in '79; money earmarked for $25 million convention center; residential permits (metro) for '77, 5,755; 7,000 permits projected for '78.

**Medical facilities:** 14 hospitals (metro) including Orlando Regional Medical Center, 2d largest nonprofit private hospital in Southeast.

**Cultural facilities:** Florida Symphony Orchestra, Loch Haven Art Center, John Young Museum and Planetarium, Central Florida Civic Theater, Central Florida Zoological Park, Orlando Public Library with 12 community libraries, 700,000 volumes; Rollins College, Florida Tech. Univ.; Valencia (3 campuses) and Seminole community colleges; Maitland Art Center.

**Other attractions:** Walt Disney World, destination resort 18 miles from downtown Orlando, annual attendance 13 million; Sea World, entertainment, education, and research facilities, annual attendance 2.4 million; Ringling Bros. and Barnum & Bailey Circus World; Church Street Station, renovated area in downtown Orlando; Stars Hall of Fame, wax museum; Wet and Wild, $3.5 million attraction.

**Convention facilities:** 31,000 rooms; 1,761 conventions attended by 380,923 in 1977.

**Sports:** Minnesota Twins spring training site; Tangerine Sports Holiday (football, basketball, swimming, soccer meets) each December; Golden South Classic, annual AAU sanctioned post season track and field meet; 3 PGA tournaments, National PGA Team Championship at Walt Disney World, $250,000 Bay Hill Classic, March 1-4, $100,000 LPGA Tournament of Champions, April 16-19; Ben White Harness Raceway; Sanford-Orlando Kennel Club; Jai Alai Fronton.

**Additional information:** Orlando Area Chamber of Commerce, P. O. Box 1913, Orlando, FL 32802.

## Ottawa, Ontario, Canada

**Population:** 309,000 (city), 693,288 (metro region including greater Ottawa 521,341 and Hull, Que. 171,470); Canada's 8th largest city, linked with neighboring city of Hull (pop. 71,000) by 5 bridges. Labor force of 234,000.

**Area:** 30,481 acres (city), 1,100 sq. mi. (region) on Ontario-Quebec border at the Chaudiere Falls on the Ottawa River. National capital.

**National Capital Region:** Ottawa and Hull, occupying 1,800 square miles of eastern Ontario and western Quebec, form the National Capital Region of Canada, administered by the National Capital Commission (NCC), created by Parliament in 1959, which deals directly with 2 provincial governments, 2 regional governments, and 57 municipal jurisdictions, all of which exercise their own proper authority.

**Industry:** major employer (87,400) is the federal government; tourism provides 9,700 jobs; E.B. Eddy Co. largest

private employer.

**Commerce:** 1977 retail sales total of $2.3 billion; per capita spendable income $2,830; 3d largest convention site in Canada with capacity for 5,000; 3,300 hotel rooms (motels not included), exhibit space: 60,000 sq. ft. in 3 major hotels, 120,000 sq. ft. in the Civic Centre and 75,700 sq. ft. in the Nepean Sportsplex.

**Transportation:** Ottawa International Airport, 15 minutes from downtown, ranks as the nation's 10th busiest, more than 85 scheduled flights daily by 7 airlines; surface transportation provided by VIA Rail and intercity bus service.

**Communications:** 3 daily (one in French), 4 weekly newspapers; 5 TV and 10 radio stations.

**Education facilities:** Carleton Univ., the bi-lingual Univ. of Ottawa, and Algonquin community college.

**Medical facilities:** 11 hospitals, many include a public psychiatric unit; bed capacity over 4,000.
**Cultural facilities:** $45 million National Arts Centre with 2,300-seat opera house-concert hall, and an 800-seat theatre; Ottawa Little Theatre.
**National museums:** National Gallery of Canada, Museum of Man, Museum of Natural Sciences, Museum of Science and Technology, Canadian War Museum, National Aeronautical Collection.
**Sports:** Ottawa Rough Riders, CFL; Ottawa 67's hockey.
**Other attractions:** gothic-style Parliament buildings, housing Canada's House of Commons and Senate; during the summer, Changing of the Guard ceremony 2 militia regiments; Peace Tower, memorial to Canada's war dead; Cen-

tral Canada Exhibition; Ottawa's oldest building, the Bytown Museum; Royal Mint; Rideau Canal provides boating facilities in summer, the longest skating rink in the world; 5 miles of the Rideau Canal from downtown Ottawa to Carleton Univ.; the Experimental Farm, 1,200 working acres in the heart of Ottawa; Winter Fair; 80 camping and trailer parks, 7 regional beaches; mountain lake recreation facilities; Gatineau Park (88,218 acres).
**History:** founded 1827 as Bytown, inc. as Ottawa 1855; named after Outaouac (or Outaouais Indian tribe); chosen as Canada's capital in 1857 by Queen Victoria.
**Further information:** Canada's Capital Visitors and Convention Bureau, 7th Floor, 222 Queen Street, Ottawa, Ont. K1P 5V9.

## Pensacola, Florida

The World Almanac is sponsored in the Pensacola area by the Pensacola News-Journal, One News Journal Plaza, Pensacola FL 32501; (904) 433-0041; predecessor The Floridian founded in 1821, first daily News 1899, Journal 1898, merged 1924; combined circulation daily 74,027, Sunday 68,593; member Gannett Group; publisher Clifford W. Barnhart, editor J. Earle Bowden.

**Population:** 66,800 (city), 230,800 (county), 281,400 (Metro area).
**Area:** Southern end of 759 sq. mi. Escambia County at westernmost edge of Florida panhandle.
**Industry:** Monsanto Corporation, St. Regis Pulp & Paper Co., Vanity Fair, American Cyanamid, Armstrong Cork, Westinghouse, Air Products, Reichhold Chemicals.
**Labor force:** civilian labor force 110,200, military labor force 13,000.
**Commerce:** retail sales $1.1 billion; average family income $11,731; effective buying income over $1.3 billion.
**Transportation:** 3 airlines, 2 railroads, 2 bus lines, 16 truck lines, intercoastal waterway, interstate 10, 3 U.S. highways.
**Communications:** 2 TV, 10 radio stations.
**New construction:** Interstate 110 spur, Regional Sewage Plant, West Campus of Pensacola Junior College, addition to Mutual Federal Savings & Loan Assoc., Bayfront Parkway.

**Medical facilities:** Baptist Hospital, University Hospital, West Florida Hospital, U.S. Naval Hospital, Sacred Heart Hospital.
**Federal facilities:** Naval Air Station, Corry Field, Saufley Field, Whiting Field, Ellyson Field.
**Cultural facilities:** public library, Historical Museum, T.T. Wentworth Museum, Hispanic Museum, Transportation Museum, Museum of Naval Aviation, Saenger Theater, Art Association, Arts Council, Inc., Oratorio Society.
**Educational facilities:** Univ. of West Florida, Pensacola Junior College.
**Recreation facilities:** Pensacola Beach, 5 golf courses.
**Sports:** The Pensacola Open, American Amateur Golf Classic, Virginia Slims tennis, International Bill Fishing Tournament, Biggs Shark Rodeo; intercollegiate sports.
**Further information:** Pensacola Area Chamber of Commerce, 117 West Garden Street, Pensacola, FL 32593; phone (904) 438-4081.

## Philadelphia, Pennsylvania

The World Almanac is sponsored in the Philadelphia area by the Philadelphia Inquirer, 400 N. Broad Street, Philadelphia, PA 19101; phone (215) 854-2000; established 1829, lineage traced to Pennsylvania Packet, founded 1771; circulation 414,556 daily, 853,952 Sunday; Pulitzer prizes 1975, 1976, 1977, 1978; published by Philadelphia Newspaper, Inc.; president Sam S. McKeel; vice president and general manager David Gelsanliter; executive editor Eugene L. Roberts Jr.; editor Edwin Guthman; managing editor Gene Foreman; sponsors Delaware Valley Science Fair, Book & Author Luncheons, Old Newsboys Day. PNI also publishes the Philadelphia Daily News, an afternoon tabloid, at same address; founded 1925; circulation 232,660; editor F. Gilman Spencer; managing editor Zachary Stalberg; sponsors Secret Witness rewards, sports clinic.

**Population:** 1.8 million (city/co.); 4.8 million (8-co. metro); 6.0 million (14-co. RTA); 7.0 million (20-co. ADI); employment: 1.9 million (metro).
**Area:** 130 sq. mi. (city), 3,553 sq. mi. (metro); city located in southeastern Pa. on Delaware and Schuylkill rivers; 90 mi. from N.Y.C., 136 mi. from Wash., D.C., 60 mi. from Atlantic City; Philadelphia is county seat (city and co. coextensive).
**Industry:** diversified, with over 90% of all U.S. basic industries represented: major center for textiles and apparel, food processing, petroleum (largest oil refining region on East Coast), printing and publishing, instruments, chemicals and pharmaceuticals, finance and insurance; companies headquartered in metro area include Sun Co., Campbell Soup, Scott Paper, Rohm & Haas, Crown Cork & Seal, Pennwalt, Certain-teed, SmithKline, Thiokol, Penn Mutual Life, INA, Food Fair, ARA Services.
**Commerce:** 62 comm. banks (metro) $19.6 billion deposits, 4 mutual savings banks $9.1 billion; retail sales (metro) $16.0 billion; average household income (metro) $19,559.
**Transportation:** biggest fresh-water port in world (50 mi. waterfront) received foreign trade zone certification in 1978; leader in intl. cargo among N. Atl. American ports (76.8

million tons in 1977); 2 modern marine terminals for containerized cargo; rail service by Conrail (Penn Central, Reading), Chessie Syst. (B & O), and Amtrak; over 250 truck lines, vast highway network, 6 bridges in metro area between Pa. and N.J.; Intl. Airport terminal, expanded at cost of $200 million, handled 8.5 million passengers in 1977; freight handled by airport and its $50 million Cargo City facility totaled 131,221 tons; area transit (SEPTA) conveyed 235.6 million passengers on subway, el, rail commuter, bus, and streetcar lines in 1977.
**Communications:** 4 daily newspapers: Inquirer, Bulletin, Daily News, and Journal; 33 AM, 15 FM, 6 comm. TV stations; cable TV.
**New construction:** $1.1 billion of new construction under way in 1978, incl. $308 million center-city RR commuter tunnel (largest public bldg. project in city's history); Intl. Airport highspeed line, Franklin Town development (30-story, 800-rm. Franklin Plaza Hotel; 24-story SmithKline hdqtrs. bldg.).
**Medical facilities:** 96 hospitals, 22,000 beds.
**Federal facilities:** Phila. Naval Base; Defense Industrial Supply Ctr.; Defense Personnel Support Ctr.; U.S. Navy Aviation Supply Office Compound; U.S. Mint; Ft. Dix and

cGuire AFB (metro).

**ultural facilities:** Phila. Orchestra; Pa. Ballet; Opera Co. of nila.; Acad. of Music; Museum of Art; Franklin Inst.; Pa. cad. of the Fine Arts; Rodin Museum; University Museum; Acad. of Natural Sciences; Barnes Fdtn.; Robin Hood ells (East and new West); Walnut St. Theater (oldest in merica); Shubert, Forrest, and New Locust theaters; community and summer theaters.

**ducational facilities:** 54 colleges and universities within 25 i. of City Hall; 6 medical schools in city; University City ience Center.

**onvention facilities:** Civic Ctr. with 382,000 sq. ft. of air nd. exhibit space, 11,500-seat Convention Hall; over 500 otels/hotels (metro) with 18,350 first-class rooms.

**ecreational facilities:** over 8,000 acres of parks incl. 4,079-re Fairmount Park; hundreds of playgrounds, swimming ools, golf courses, tennis courts, ice-skating rinks; close to ashore, mountains.

**orts:** NL Phillies, NFL Eagles and NASL Fury (Veterans tadium); NBA 76ers and NHL Flyers (Spectrum); NAHL irebirds (Civic Ctr.); Penn Relays (Franklin Fld.); Army-avy football (J.F. Kennedy Stadium); sculling races

(Schuylkill R.); area horse racing (Keystone, Liberty Bell, Atlantic City, Brandywine, Delaware Park).

**Other attractions:** old city district* and Benjamin Franklin Parkway centers of interest; many historic bldgs. preserved, restored or reconstructed; Penn's Landing waterfront dev.; Afro-American Historical and Cultural Museum; City Hall; Elfreth's Alley; Franklin Ct.; Society Hill; Fairmount Park mansions; zoo (America's first); Mummers Parade (Jan. 1); Freedom Week (climaxed by July 4th celebration); Super Sunday festival (early Oct.); nearby attractions incl. Valley Forge, Longwood Gardens, Great Adventure.

**History:** Wm. Penn founded his "Greene Countrie Towne" as Quaker colony in 1682; gave it name that means "City of Brotherly Love"; national capital 1790-1800; historical shrines incl. Independence Hall, Liberty Bell (in new pavilion), Carpenters' Hall, Franklin's grave, Betsy Ross House, Gloria Dei Church, Christ Church, USS Olympia, Fort Mifflin.

**Further information:** Victor Kendrick, Office of City Representative, 1660 Municipal Services Bldg., Phila., PA 19107; Phila. Tourist Bureau, 1525 J.F. Kennedy Boulevard, Phila., PA 19102.

---

## Phoenix, Arizona

The World Almanac is sponsored in the Phoenix area by The Phoenix Gazette, 120 East Van Buren Street, Phoenix, AZ 85004; phone (602) 271-8000; founded Oct. 28, 1880, as Arizona Gazette by Charles H. McNeil; irculation 104,273; publisher Mason Walsh, general manager and associate publisher Darrow Tully, managg editor Alan D. Moyer; sponsors Christmas Fund Drive, Music Memory Programs, Family Symphony Concerts, Phoenix Giants' Bat Boy contest, Tennis Clinic, Cactus Show, and other events.

**opulation:** 704,000 (city); 1,410,000 (metro); capital and argest city in state, 14th (city) in nation; total employed 50,500.

**Area:** 278 sq. mi. (city), 9,226 sq. mi. (metro), in south central Arizona.

**ndustry:** electronic equipment manufacturers, Honeywell nformation Systems, and Motorola, Inc. each employ more han 2,500; aircraft and parts manufacturers, AiResearch, a ivision of The Garrett Corp., and Sperry Flight Systems ach employ more than 2,500; other major employers are E. . Gruber (apparel), Goodyear Aerospace, General Electric, Vestern Electric Cable, Reynolds Metals, Marathon Steel, Arizona Public Service, Salt River Project, Mountain Bell, Courier Terminal Systems, Spring City Knitting Co., Siemens Corp., Amerco, Greyhound, American Express, and Phoenix Newspapers.

**ommerce:** wholesale-retail center for state; retail sales 1977) $5.6 billion; effective household buying income, 16,944; bank and S&L assets $12.2 billion; 14 banks with 61 area offices, 7 S&Ls with 103 offices in metro area.

**ransportation:** transportation center of the Southwest; Sky Harbor International Airport served by 9 airlines, 5 million assengers (1977); 2 railroads; 2 transcontinental bus lines; 0 transcontinental truck lines; 25 transcontinental heavy quipment haulers; 34 interstate and 39 intrastate truck nes.

**ommunications:** 6 TV and 32 radio stations.

**New construction:** In 1977, 27,748 new residential building nits were permitted; total value all types of building permits, $1.1 billion.

**Medical facilities:** Barrow Neurological Institute; 21 general care hospitals, Veterans' Hospital; other special service facilities.

**Cultural facilities:** art museum, public library, symphony orchestra, Indian museums, zoo, botanical gardens, community and professional theaters; Civic Plaza convention center; Gammage Auditorium.

**Federal facilities:** Luke AFB, Williams AFB.

**Educational facilities:** Arizona State Univ., American Graduate School of International Management; 4 community colleges; Maricopa Technical College (vocational); 76 public and parochial high schools.

**Sports:** 50 golf courses and $200,000 Phoenix Open; inland surfing beach; ice skating rinks; amusement park; pro basketball, baseball teams; auto, greyhound, and horse racing; annual Fiesta Bowl (holiday football game).

**Other attractions:** Frank Lloyd Wright's Taliesin West; Paolo Soleri's Arcosanti; Firebird Festival of the Arts; Dons' Club guided tours of Arizona; full calendar of events including state and county fairs and rodeos, horse shows, regattas, polo tournaments.

**History:** founded 1870, on site of ancient Indian settlement; the Hohokam tribe, which flourished ca. 500-1200 A.D., developed an intricate system of irrigation canals which form the base of the canal system in use today.

**Further information:** Phoenix and Valley of the Sun Convention and Visitors Bureau, 2701 E. Camelback Road, Phoenix, AZ 85016.

---

## Pittsburgh, Pennsylvania

The World Almanac is sponsored in the Pittsburgh area by The Pittsburgh Press, 34 Boulevard of the Allies, Pittsburgh, PA 15230; phone (412) 263-1100; founded June 23, 1884, as Evening Penny Press by Thomas J. Keenan; circulation 265,114 daily, 667,297 Sunday; editor John Troan, president and business manager Robert Hartmann, executive editor Leo Koeberlein, managing editor Ralph Brem; sponsors Press Old Newsboys Fund for Children's Hospital which raised $1,730,350 in 1977.

**opulation:** 458,651 (city), 2,322,274 (4-county metro area), d in state and 28th in nation; metro area labor force of 15,800 is 6th in nation.

**Area:** 55.5 sq. mi at juncture of Allegheny and Monongaela rivers which form Ohio River; Allegheny County seat;

altitude, 702 feet.

**Industry:** one-fifth of nation's steelmaking capacity concentrated in metro area; western Pennsylvania mines produce 44 million tons of bituminous coal annually; 6,000 different products made in area; home of world's first full-scale nuclear power plant, world's largest manufacturers of aluminum, steel rolls, rolling mill machinery, air brakes, plate and window glass, and safety equipment; 3d largest headquarters city in nation.

**Commerce:** retail sales (Allegheny County, 1976) $4.6 billion; exports abroad of products manufactured here totaled $842,768,000 (1976); average household effective buying income (Allegheny County) $15,123.

**Transportation:** 7 scheduled airlines handled 8,739,491 passengers on 319,845 flights at International Airport (1977); 7 railroads; Continental Trailways and Greyhound bus lines; over 400 common carriers; Port Authority Transit vehicles carried 101.3 million passengers (1977) over 165 routes, 5 trolley lines; 9 major highways serve the city; a 4.5 mile busway opened in 1977, and another 6.8 mile busway and 2.5 mile light rail trolley system are under construction.

**Communications:** 2 daily newspapers; 5 TV (including country's first educational station) and 27 radio stations.

**New construction:** $32 million, 140,000 sq. ft. convention center set for completion in 1979.

**Medical facilities:** 21 hospitals include Univ. of Pittsburgh Health and Medical complex where Dr. Jonas Salk developed polio vaccine; VA installation.

**Federal facilities:** Federal Building contains scores of U.S. government offices (information center: 412/644-3456); Army base at Oakdale; Air Force base.

**Cultural facilities:** Heinz Hall is home of the opera co., ballet, civic light opera, youth symphony and symphony orchestra; 5 community theaters, one legitimate theater; Frick Art Museum; Carnegie Museum and Art Gallery, home of the new Pittsburgh International series, a biennial one-man art show offering a $55,000 prize; American Wind Symphony.

**Educational facilities:** Univ. of Pittsburgh, Duquesne Univ., Point Park, Chatham, Carlow, Robert Morris, and La Roche colleges; Carnegie-Mellon Univ., Community College of Allegheny Co.; 18 Carnegie public libraries, 3 bookmobile community libraries.

**Sports:** NL Pirates, NFL Steelers, NHL Penguins.

**Other attractions:** Highland Park Zoo, children's zoo, Twilight Zoo, aquarium, aviary, Buhl Planetarium, Allegheny Observatory, Phipps Conservatory, Fort Pitt Museum; amusement parks; 2 operating passenger inclines; folk festival; Three Rivers Art Festival every June; harness racing; river cruises; Civic Arena; Three Rivers Stadium.

**History:** first hunters and trappers came through in 1714; city dates from Nov. 25, 1758, when English forces under Brig. Gen. John Forbes occupied the ruins of Fort Duquesne, which French soldiers had burned and abandoned, and built a new and bigger fortress called Fort Pitt. When incorporated in 1816, it already had a reputation as a "Smoky City" from factories and coal-burning homes. Massive "Renaissance Plan" has cleared the skies and rebuilt the heart of the city during the past 25 years.

**Further information:** Chamber of Commerce, 411 Seventh Avenue, Pittsburgh, PA 15219; Convention and Visitors Bureau, 200 Roosevelt Boulevard, Pittsburgh, PA 15222.

## Portland, Maine

The World Almanac is sponsored in the Portland area by the Maine Sunday Telegram, 390 Congress, Portland, ME 04104; phone (207) 775-5811; published by Guy Gannett Publishing Co., founded 1921; circulation 111,616, publisher Jean Gannett Hawley; editor John K. Murphy; also publishes morning Press Herald, circulation 52,858, and Evening Express, 30,038.

**Population:** 66,500 (city), 210,000 (metro area), first in state; total employed 30,000.

**Area:** 21.6 sq. mi.; peninsula on Casco Bay; Cumberland County seat.

**Industry:** Atlantic Coast's 2d busiest oil shipping center, east terminus Montreal pipeline; fishing fleet base, seafood shipping center; landbased products: printed materials, clothing, metal, processed food, electronic parts, wooden goods.

**Commerce:** tourist center, regional retail-wholesale hub, large shopping complex, 1,000 retail, 350 wholesale, 600 service enterprises; retail sales (1977) $368 million; median family income (1977) $13,570.

**Transportation:** municipal jetport, Delta airline; 3 rail freight lines, integrated bus system, Greyhound, Continental bus terminals, 25 truck lines; Maine Turnpike, Interstate 95 and 295 highways connect to all New England; deep water anchorage, auto cruise ferries year round to Yarmouth, Nova Scotia.

**Communications:** 3 TV, 5 AM, 4 FM stations.

**New construction:** housing for elderly, public library, sewage treatment system.

**Medical facilities:** medical center, 2 hospitals.

**Cultural facilities:** symphony orch., Kotzschmar organ, one of world's largest; public, historical libraries; Victorian, art museums; Henry Longfellow home (1785); branch Univ. of Maine, Westbrook College, art, vocational, and business schools; Portland Headlight, oldest lighthouse in country.

**Recreation:** 18-hole municipal golf course, 9 others in area; scenic cruises; swimming, tennis, fishing within easy travel; scenic parks.

**Conventional facilities:** civic center, 3 large assembly halls, meeting rooms in modern hotels and motels.

**Further information:** Tourist Bureau, 142 Free Street, Portland, ME.

## Portland, Oregon

The World Almanac is sponsored in the Portland area by The Oregon Journal, 1320 SW Broadway, Portland, OR 97201; phone (503) 221-8275; founded Mar. 1902; circulation 106,773; editor Donald J. Sterling Jr.; managing editor Edward F. O'Meara.

**Population:** 384,500 (city), 1,322,200 (metro), first in state; 34th in nation; total employed, 490,300.

**Area:** 80 sq. mi., at juncture of Columbia and Willamette rivers.

**Industry:** electrical and electronic industries along with lumber and wood products, food, and paper; ranks first in manufacture of logging, lumbering equipment; home of Georgia-Pacific, Louisiana-Pacific (forest products), Tektronix (oscilloscopes), Omark (saw cutting chain), Hyster (lifts, hoists, lumber handling), White Stag, Pendleton, Jantzen (clothing).

**Commerce:** wholesale-retail center for large part of Oregon, SW Washington; retail sales metro area (1976), $3.6 billion. There are 11 banks, 11 savings and loan associations.

**Transportation:** 4 major rail freight lines, Amtrak; Greyhound, Trailways buses; 10th largest freshwater port in U.S., with 27-mile frontage, 29 marine berths; 18 million tons of cargo pass over docks annually; more than 2,100 ships visit annually, most active harbor in U.S.; hub for airlines, flights to all parts of world.

**Communications:** 5 TV and 22 radio stations.

**Medical facilities:** 17 major hospitals, Univ. of Oregon Medical School, VA hospital.

**Cultural facilities:** art museum, Oregon Symphony Orchestra, Opera Association, Oregon Historical Society, Portland State Univ., Univ. of Portland, and Lewis & Clark, Reed and Concordia colleges.

**Other attractions:** annual Rose Festival, Rose Show; park system includes Washington Park, Hoyt Arboretum International Rose Test Garden, Portland Zoo, Oregon Museum of Science and Industry; Forest Park is largest forest area in

U.S. city's limits. Analysis of 243 population centers by Midwest Research Institute in mid-1970s named Portland as America's Most Liveable City", based on "economic, political, environmental, health and education, and social components."

**Sports:** Trail Blazers of the NBA play at the Memorial Coliseum.

**History:** charterd 1851 with population of 821; named after Portland, Me., rather than Boston, Mass., on flip of coin by 2 early citizens.

**Further information:** Chamber of Commerce, 824 SW 5th, Portland, OR 97204.

## Providence, Rhode Island

The World Almanac is sponsored in the Providence area by The Providence Journal-Bulletin, 75 Fountain Street, Providence, RI 02902; phone (401) 277-7000; Journal founded 1829, Bulletin 1863, Sunday Journal 1883; circulation, Journal (morn) 66,234, Bulletin (eve) 142,680, Sunday Journal 210,551; publisher John C. A. Watkins, president Michael P. Metcalf, v.p.-admin. Charles P. O'Donnell, v.p. and exec. editor Charles McC. Hauser.

**Population:** 166,000 (city), 875,100 (metro); total employed 409,219.

**Area:** 18.91 sq. mi., at the head of Narragansett Bay in Providence County; state capital.

**Industry:** jewelry, silverware, plated ware, costume jewelry are largest industries; Textron is based in Providence, 950 manufacturing companies in the city.

**Commerce:** wholesale-retail center for entire state; retail sales $2.6 billion (metro); consumer spendable income per household $17,123 (metro); Allendale Insurance, world's largest mutual insurer of industrial firms, is based outside of city in Johnston; home of Narragansett Capital, largest small business investment company in nation; 2 savings and loan assns., 2 mutual savings banks, one cooperative bank, 6 commercial banks.

**Transportation:** Amtrak, passenger service between Boston, Providence, New York, and Washington; 5 bus lines; 45 locally-based common carriers and contract truckers; 9 major highways link Providence to every corner of R.I.; 6 major airlines out of T. F. Green Airport in Warwick (15 min. away); port is 3d largest in New England with 25 wharves and docks, 10.5 miles of commercial waterfront on the bay.

**Communications:** 3 TV and 8 radio stations.

**Medical facilities:** 7 hospitals; one VA hospital.

**Cultural facilities:** Trinity Square Repertory Co., R. I. Philharmonic, R. I. School of Design Museum; R. I. Historical Society.

**Education:** Brown University, founded 1764, is 7th oldest college in nation; 7-year M.D. program inaugurated 1973; Providence and R. I. colleges, and R. I. School of Design.

**Recreation:** one of America's most attractive recreational areas centers around Providence; 69 salt water beaches, 26 fresh water beaches, 50 golf and country clubs, 4 ski areas, 29 yacht clubs, 28 parks, all within 45 minutes of city.

**Convention facilities:** R.I. Civic Center (seats 12,000).

**Sports:** America's Cup races since 1930; Newport-Bermuda race starts at Newport every other year; Reds (hockey), Oceaneers (soccer).

**Other attractions:** largest collection of original early American homes of any city; located along Benefit St., they have been preserved by the Providence Preservation Society.

**History:** founded 1636 by Roger Williams; incorporated 1832; official state name is "Rhode Island and Providence Plantations."

**Further information:** Chamber of Commerce, 10 Dorrance Street, Providence, RI 02903.

## Quebec City, Quebec, Canada

**Population:** 186,088 (city), 480,500 (metro); oldest city in Canada (1608) and the capital city of the province of Quebec.

**Area:** 30 sq. mi.; natural citadel on north shore of St. Lawrence River at confluence with St. Charles River; 400 miles from Gulf of St. Lawrence; 167 miles east of Montreal; older part is built on a cliff 360 ft. above the St. Lawrence.

**Industry:** some 300 industrial firms, ranging from primary industry products to a variety of consumer products, employ over 16,000 people; food and beverage, leather footwear and leather products, textiles, apparel, wood products, pulp and paper, printing and publishing, iron and steel products, non-ferrous metal and chemical products.

**Commerce:** Quebec harbor, one of the busiest seaports of Canada, accommodates the largest ocean-going vessels with year-round facilities, an important container terminal on the North Atlantic coast; Provincial Government, with more than 15,000 employees, is the largest single employer and consumer in the city.

**Transportation:** Canadian Pacific and Canadian National railroads; Air Canada, Quebecair, Nordair; major bus center.

**Communications:** 3 TV stations (2 French, 1 bilingual); 6 radio stations (French), 2 newspapers (French).

**Medical facilities:** 5 large general hospitals, many smaller ones.

**Cultural facilities:** historic character, cultural appeal and natural beauty make tourism important area of economic activity; annual "Carnaval" in Feb. is internationally known; annual summer festival (July) changes the city into an open theater for numerous artistic events; Expo-Quebec, an annual provincial exhibition (industrial, commercial, and agricultural), draws over 500,000 people a year.

**Educational facilities:** Laval University, the first in North America; Quebec University; 3 colleges for general and vocational training, numerous private schools.

**Sports:** home of WHA Nordiques.

**Other attractions:** only walled city in North America with fortifications standing today as they were 125 years ago; the Citadel, built from 1823-1832, contains within its walls 25 buildings, including the summer residence of Governor-General of Canada, Parliament buildings (1886), Quebec Museum, Battlefield Park, Ursulines Museum, Seminary (1663), Talon cellars, Notre Dame des Victoires Church, and Tresor Street.

**History:** founded 1608 by French explorer Samuel de Champlain; cradle of French civilization in America; once the key to the interior of the North American continent.

## Raleigh, North Carolina

The World Almanac is sponsored in eastern North Carolina by The News and Observer and The Raleigh Times, 215 S. McDowell Street, Raleigh, NC 27602, (919) 821-1234; circulation N&O (morn) 128,147; Times (eve) 32,646; N&O Sunday 159,798; publisher Frank Daniels Jr., editorial director Claude Sitton, editor Times A.C. Snow, managing editor N&O Bob Brooks, Times Mike Yopp.

**Population:** 160,000 (city), 280,000 (county), 500,000 (metro); 3d in state; 261,400 employed (metro).

**Area:** 49 square miles in the geographical center of the state where piedmont joins coastal plains; alt. 363 ft., temperate

climate; state capital and Wake County seat.
**Industry:** major industry is government, employing 25% of work force.
**Commerce:** retail center of eastern N.C., retail sales $1.28 billion (1977); 16 banks and 6 savings and loans; average annual income per household $19,500.
**Education:** 11 colleges, N.C. State Univ. (Raleigh) Univ. of N.C. (Chapel Hill), and Duke Univ. (Durham) form Research Triangle; Triangle Park employs 12,500 in drug, fiber, biomedical, environmental, engineering, and humanities research; metro area has more Ph.Ds per capita than anywhere in world.
**Transportation:** 3 rail and 4 bus lines, Amtrak, 39 motor freight companies; airport has 4 airlines carrying 711,000 passengers per year; one interstate, 4 U.S., and 2 state highways into city; city mass transit bus system.
**Communications:** 4 TV and 16 radio stations; 2 daily newspapers, 9 weeklies.

**New construction:** $87 million (1977).
**Medical facilities:** 3 hospitals (1,000 beds); major state mental hospital; 350 doctors, 150 dentists.
**Convention facilities:** 33 motels, 4,000 rooms; new Civic Center seats 10,000; Dorton Arena, 9,111; Memorial Auditorium, 3,000; Reynolds Coliseum, 12,000.
**Cultural facilities:** 3 museums, state fairgrounds, state symphony; community, college, and professional theater groups.
**Recreation:** 4,200-acre Umstead State Park, Carter Stadium, 100 city parks; first Green Survival City on U.S.
**Sports:** pro golf, pro tennis; annual powerboat regatta; college sports.
**History:** founded 1792; Andrew Johnson birthplace; Oakwood Historic District preserves large Victorian neighborhood.
**Further information:** Raleigh-Wake County Chamber of Commerce, 411 S. Salisbury Street, Raleigh, NC 27602 (919) 833-3005.

## Regina, Saskatchewan, Canada

The World Almanac is sponsored in southern Saskatchewan by The Leader-Post, 1964 Park Street, Regina, Sask., S4P 3GA, phone (306) 527-8511; founded 1883 by Nicholas Flood Davin; circulation 67,239; president Michael Sifton, Toronto; executive vice-president Max Macdonald; editor W. Ivor Williams; associate editor C.E.W. Bell; managing editor J.R. Guay; business manager William Duffus; advertising manager George Crawford; MacLaren Trophy for editorial page reproduction excellence.

**Population:** 157,059, first in province, 17th in nation; labor force, 79,570.
**Area:** 37.5 sq. mi., 100 miles north of Canada-U.S. border; provincial capital.
**Industry:** over 270 manufacturing industries; gross production value (1977) $360 million, 32% of Saskatchewan total.
**Commerce:** service center for oil, potash; grain production area; retail sales (1977) $630.1 million, 24.5% of province.
**Transportation:** 2 rail lines, 2 airlines, 3 bus lines, and 125 trucking companies; main Trans-Canada highway bisects; city-run transit system, including Telebus, hybrid system with demand/response taxi service and mass transit, provides to-and-from service to user's home.
**Communications:** 3 TV, 6 radio stations, conventional and closed circuit cable television.
**Medical facilities:** 4 major hospitals, 1,391 beds.
**Cultural facilities:** Saskatchewan Centre of Arts, multipurpose theater-convention center with: Jubilee theater (seats 450) stage, ballroom, reception hall and dining room;

Centennial theater (seats 2,029); Hanbidge Hall convention area, 12,200 square feet, 9 meeting rooms, seats 1,600; Regina Symphony; Globe Repertory; Museum Natural History; Norman Mackenzie Art Gallery; RCMP Museum.
**Educational facilities:** Regina University; 13 collegiates; 9 elementary, 7 specialized schools; Wascana Institute of Applied Arts and Sciences.
**Recreation facilities:** Saskatchewan Roughriders (Canadian pro football); 137 parks and playgrounds; 8 golf courses; swimming pools; 8 indoor ice rinks.
**Other attractions:** Wascana Centre, 2,500-acre development with man-made lake, public buildings, parks, recreation in heart of city; home of Canadian Western Agribition, Canada's major international livestock show.
**History:** founded 1882, and since that time headquarters for RCMP training depot. Marked 75th anniversary of incorporation as a city in 1978.
**Further information:** Regina Chamber of Commerce, 2145 Albert Street, Regina, Sask.

## Reno, Nevada

The World Almanac is sponsored in the northern Nevada area by the Nevada State Journal and Reno Evening Gazette, 401 West Second Street, Post Office Box 280, Reno, NV 89520; phone 702/786-8989. Journal founded 1870, Gazette founded 1876, combined daily circulation, 51,055, Sunday 42,429; publisher, Warren L. Lerude.

**Population:** est. 1977 pop. 94,380 (city), 168,581 (county), including Sparks; 2d largest in the state, 1977 labor force 89,000.
**Area:** 36.8 square miles (including Stead annexation) in northwestern part of the state at the eastern foot of the Sierra Nevada; Washoe County seat.
**Industry:** gross gaming revenue for county, $280.3 million (1977) netted state taxes of $20.3 million; 108,679 delegates attended 261 conventions. Warehousing continued to grow because of Nevada's liberal free port law with est. 15 million square feet in the county; marriages 34,556) outnumbered divorces (2,970).
**Commerce:** taxable sales in metro area (including Sparks) for 1977, $1.2 billion, assessed valuation (city) $596.9 million; median household income $18,200; bank resources $2.3 billion.
**Transportation:** 13 motor freight lines, 3 freight railroads, Amtrak, 3 commercial bus lines; airport handled (1977) 1.4 million passengers as U.S. port of entry; U.S. 395 and Interstate 80.
**Communications:** 3 TV, 12 radio, one CATV.
**New construction:** 161 commercial, 4,493 residential units totaling $205.3 million, new assessed valuation (1976 includes county).

**Medical facilities:** 3 hospitals, including VA.
**Educational facilities:** Univ. of Nevada, Reno, 9,181 enrollment (1977); community college 4,497; public school 31,855; private/parochial schools 1,615.
**Cultural facilities:** 1,428 seat Pioneer Theater Auditorium, Atmospherium Planetarium, and 280,000 volume library; national air races; Nevada Historical Society; Nevada Opera Guild, Reno Philharmonic Orchestra; Nevada Art Gallery.
**Recreation:** 24-hour gambling; world's largest gambling casino; 21 ski resorts within a 2-hour drive; Lake Tahoe and Pyramid Lake offering fishing, boating, swimming, sun bathing, medium game-hunting, camping; historic Virginia City mining town and tourist attraction within 1/2 hour drive.
**Sports:** Silver Sox minor league baseball.
**History:** established 1868 with public auction of land by Central Pacific Railroad Company, known prior as Lake's Crossing; named after Civil War hero General Jesse L. Reno.
**Further information:** Chamber of Commerce, P.O. Box 3499, Reno, NV 89505; Marketing Department, Reno Newspapers, Inc., P.O. Box 280, Reno, NV 89520.

## Richmond, Virginia

The World Almanac is sponsored in the Richmond area by the Richmond Times-Dispatch and News Leader, 333 E. Grace Street, Richmond, VA 23213; (804) 649-6000; Times-Dispatch founded 1850 by James Cowardin, circulation 136,266 daily, 214,092 Sunday; News Leader founded 1896 by Joseph Bryan, circulation 116,234; chairman, D. Tennant Bryan; publisher, J. Stewart Bryan III; president, Alan S. Donnahoe, executive editor John E. Leard, Times-Dispatch managing editor Alf Goodykoontz, News Leader managing editor J.A. Finch.

**Population:** 226,400 (city), 556,400 (metro area), total employed (non-agricultural) 292,700.

**Area:** 62.5 sq. mi. (city), located at fall line of James River, 0 miles from Atlantic Ocean; independent city.

**Industry:** tobacco, with 10,600 workers, and chemicals, with 9,200 are leaders in employment; Philip Morris cigarette plant which began production in 1974 is world's largest and most modern; printing, publishing, manufacture of paper and allied products, and food.

**Commerce:** wholesale-retail center for central Virginia; retail sales $2 billion in 1977, per capita income $6,748, $14,956 median family effective buying income, total income $3.4 billion.

**Transportation:** 4 major railroads, 5 intercity bus lines, 3 commercial air lines, one commuter air line, 50 motor truck lines; 3 interstate, 6 U.S., and 9 state highways; deepwater terminal accessible to ocean-going ships.

**Communications:** 4 TV, 16 radio stations.

**Medical facilities:** Medical College of Virginia known worldwide for heart and kidney transplants, medical research; 21 other hospitals, including McGuire VA Hospital.

**Federal facilities:** Defense General Supply Center, Fifth Federal Reserve Bank, U. S. Fourth Circuit Court, Ft. Lee Quartermaster Corps).

**Cultural facilities:** Va. Museum and Theater with professional artists make city a center for dramatic, other performing arts; variety of other drama groups; symphony orchestra.

**Educational facilities:** Virginia Commonwealth Univ. has state's largest enrollment; Univ. of Richmond, Virginia Union Univ., Union Theological Seminary (Presbyterian), Randolph-Macon College.

**Recreational facilities:** Coliseum for athletic, entertainment events; city-owned Mosque auditorium, Parker Field, City Stadium, numerous parks.

**Convention facilities:** large downtown hotels near Mosque and Coliseum.

**Sports:** Braves (IL baseball), national ranked track and tennis events.

**Other attractions:** St. John's Church, scene of Patrick Henry's "Liberty or Death" speech; Virginia Capitol, designed by Thomas Jefferson; White House of the Confederacy; Civil War battlefields.

**History:** exploration here in 1607 by Capt. John Smith, first settlement 1609, incorporated as town 1742, made Va. capital 1779, Confederate Capital 1861-65; burned 1781 by Benedict Arnold, and 1865 when cotton, tobacco stockpiles fire set by fleeing Confederates spread to city; damaged by floods 1771, 1969, 1972.

**Further information:** Chamber of Commerce, 201 E. Franklin Street, Richmond, VA 23219.

## Roanoke, Virginia

The World Almanac is sponsored in the Roanoke area by the Roanoke Times & World-News, 201-203 Campbell Avenue, Roanoke, VA 24010, telephone (703) 981-3000; Times founded 1886, World-News founded 1889; Barton W. Morris Jr., president and publisher; circulation combined daily, 114,435; Sunday 114,600.

**Population:** 109,500 (city, 1977), 217,000 (metro area); labor force 110,740.

**Area:** 43.25 sq. mi.; Metro SMSA includes Roanoke City, Salem City; Roanoke, Craig, Botetourt counties; located at southern extremity of Shenandoah Valley midway between Maryland and Tennessee.

**Industry:** 14% of work force in manufacturing. Leading firms are General Electric, Eaton Corp., ITT, Singer, Burlington Industries, Mohawk Rubber, Ingersoll Rand.

**Commerce:** headquarters Shenandoah Life Ins. Co., Estate Life Ins. Co., Appalachian Power Co., Advance Stores, Mick or Mack Groceries; Regional Allstate Ins. Co. offices; Kroger (central warehouse); retail sales metro area (1977) $754 million; average spendable family income, $14,851 (metro area); retail center for 20 counties and parts of W. Va. and N.C.

**Transportation:** Norfolk & Western Railway Co. headquarters; 2 airlines; Trailways and Greyhound buses; Amtrak north-south Washington, D.C.-West Va.; 30 interstate trucking firms with terminals; Highways Interstate 81, Spur 581, US 11, US 460, US 220, US 221, Blue Ridge Parkway.

**Communications:** 3 TV and 13 radio stations.

**Medical facilities:** 4 general, 4 specialty hospitals, VA facility; state hospital.

**Cultural facilities:** 2 civic centers with auditorium, coliseums and exhibit halls, symphony orchestra, art center, theaters, Roanoke College, Hollins College, Virginia Western Community College, National Business College; commuting distance from Va. Polytechnic Inst. and State Univ.; concert and lecture series.

**Other attractions:** Mill Mt. Park rising 1,000 ft. in center of city; children's zoo; Transportation and Historical Museum; Smith Mt.; Fairy Stone and Claytor Lakes state parks; Natural Bridge, Dixie Caverns, Peaks of Otter.

**Sports:** baseball; schools sports, winter skiing nearby; public recreation and parks programs.

**History:** formerly named Big Lick, Roanoke, an Indian word for shell money, became a city in 1884 with the linking of the Shenandoah Valley Railroad with Norfolk and Western Railroad.

**Further information:** Roanoke Valley Chamber of Commerce, 14 West Kirk Avenue, P.O. Box 20, Roanoke, VA 24001.

## Rochester, New York

The World Almanac is sponsored in the Rochester area by Gannett Rochester Newspapers, 55 Exchange Street, Rochester, NY 14614; phone (716) 232-7100; circulation, Democrat and Chronicle (morn.) 127,503; Times-Union (eve.) 129,285; Democrat and Chronicle (Sun.) 226,395; publisher Eugene C. Dorsey, executive editor Robert Giles, director of advertising Peter Stegner. Times-Union reporters awarded a 1972 Pulitzer Prize.

**Population:** 5 county metro area 978,700 (est.); 415,500 employed; unemployment 6.6%.

**Area:** 675 sq. mi. (Monroe County), straddling Genesee River, on Lake Ontario, 2,966 sq. mi. (metro); Monroe

County seat.

**Industry:** world leader in production of photographic, optical, and scientific instruments, with Eastman Kodak (45,000 employees), Xerox (14,000), and Bausch & Lomb (5,000), all founded in Rochester, the most prominent; other fields include machinery, food products, apparel, printing and publishing; industrial wage increase, 41% since 1969.

**Commerce:** retail sales 1976 (est.) $2.7 billion; 20 commercial and savings banks; 1976 average household effective buying income $17,598 (metro area).

**Transportation:** Monroe County Airport, with 3 major airlines and several freight companies; rail freight service by 4 lines, Amtrak, port of Rochester; over 75 motor freight firms.

**Communications:** 4 TV and 15 radio stations.

**New construction:** First Federal Bldg., 22 story office tower.

**Medical facilities:** one of the nation's most advanced health care centers; 8 general hospitals, including Strong Memorial Hospital.

**Cultural facilities:** Eastman Theater, part of Univ. of East-man School of Music, and home of the Philharmonic Orchestra; Memorial Art Gallery; Museum and Science Center including Strasenburgh Planetarium; George Eastman House of Photography; 3 resident theater companies.

**Educational facilities:** 8 private and 2 public 4-year colleges; 3 community colleges.

**Recreational facilities:** Finger Lakes area, with 13 parks, summer and winter sports, golf, tennis, bowling; 16-park Monroe County System, including Seneca Park Zoo, Highland Park, Lilac Festival.

**Convention facilities:** 2d largest used site in NY; War Memorial, 7,500 cap.; Dome Arena, 5,000 cap.; 4,600 rm available.

**Sports:** International League Red Wings, top Baltimore Orioles farm team; AHL Amerks, North American Soccer League Lancers, thoroughbred racing and Finger Lake race track (Canandaigua).

**Further information:** Chamber of Commerce, 55 St. Paul Street, 14604 or Covention and Publicity Bureau, 100 Exchange Street, 14614.

---

## Rockford, Illinois

The World Almanac is sponsored in the Rockford area by the Rockford Newspapers, Inc., 97 E. State Street, Rockford, IL 61105, phone (815) 987-1200, publisher of the Morning Star, Register-Republic and Sunday Register-Star, combined daily circulation 80,000. Publisher and Vice President Gannett Central Maurice Hickey, general manager Jerry Bean; member of the Gannett Group and Gannett Central Headquarters.

**Population:** 141,300 (city); 243,400 (county); 129,547 work force (county).

**Area:** 36.4 sq. mi. (city) on Rock River in extreme north central Illinois; Winnebago County seat; 519 sq. mi. (county).

**Industry:** 575 manufacturing establishments; products include machine tools (Sundstrand, Ingersoll Milling Machine, Barber-Colman, Greenlee Bros.), screws and bolts (Rockford Products, Elco, Camcar, National Lock), pharmaceuticals (Warner-Lambert, American Chicle), and paints (Valspar). Chrysler Corp. assembly plant is in nearby Belvidere (Dodge Omni and Plymouth Horizon).

**Commerce:** retail "magnet" for northern Illinois and southern Wisconsin; 15 shopping centers of 12 stores or more, including Mall at CherryVale (95 stores); retail sales (1977) $650.8 million (city); 16 commercial banks, resources (1977) $887.8 million; 4 savings and loan associations, resources (1977) $444.6 million.

**Transportation:** Amtrack Chicago connection; 4 rail freight lines; 3 bus lines; 50 truck lines; Ozark Air Lines (Denver, Detroit connections); Coleman Air Transport Co. (Detroit, Minneapolis-St. Paul, St. Louis connections); U.S. 51, U.S. 20, and Interstate 90.

**Communications:** 4 TV, 8 radio stations; 2 cable TV operations; 7 weekly newspapers; 2 daily newspapers.

**Medical facilities:** 3 hospitals; 2 public supported extended care facilities.

**Cultural facilities:** symphony orchestra; concert band, civic theater, 2 male and one mixed choral organizations.

**Education:** (1977-78 school year) 73 public schools (K-12); 24 parochial and private schools (K-12); Rockford College (4 years, liberal arts), Rock Valley College (2 years, liberal arts), UI-Rockford School of Medicine, Rockford Business College (2 years).

**Recreation:** 20 forest preserves, over 100 parks totaling 3,000 acres; 1 state park, 4 public golf courses, 4 country club courses, 61 public tennis courts, 7 private tennis courts, 2 indoor tennis facilities, 2 private platform tennis facilities, 3 public swimming pools, 7 private swim clubs, 76 baseball diamonds; Riverview Ice House (indoor skating); 3 roller skating rinks.

**Agriculture:** 242,944 acres tilled farmland (est. value $242 million); 4,000 persons on 975 commercial farms in county.

**Other attractions:** Children's Farm, Time Museum, Tinker Swiss Cottage, Rockford Museum, John Erlander Home, Burpee Natural History Museum, Burpee Art Museum.

**New construction:** Machesney Park Mall (95 stores); Luther Center, high-rise for the elderly (16 stories); Jefferson High School.

**History:** founded in 1834 by Germanicus Kent and Thatcher Blake beside fording place across Rock River; incorporated in 1852.

**Further information:** Rockford Area Chamber of Commerce: 815 E. State Street, Rockford, IL 61101.

---

## Sacramento, California

The World Almanac is sponsored in the Sacramento area by The Sacramento Bee, 21st & Q, Sacramento, CA 95816; telephone (916) 446-9211; founded 1857; circulation daily 186,300, Sunday 216,048; president Eleanor McClatchy, editor C. K. McClatchy, managing editor Frank McCulloch.

**Population:** 261,500 (city), 725,000 (county), 993,000 (metro); total employed (metro) 373,300.

**Area:** 94 sq. mi. (city), 997 sq. mi. (county) in Sacramento Valley, 85 mi. northeast of San Francisco; state capital and Sacramento County seat.

**Industry:** 475 manufacturing plants including Campbell Soup, Procter and Gamble, Libby McNeil and Libby, California Almond Growers Exchange, Del Monte, Teichert Construction, and Aerojet-General.

**Commerce:** wholesale-retail center for large area of Sacramento Valley; retail sales (metro), over $3 billion (1977).

**Transportation:** 3 county operated airports, including metropolitan airport, plus numerous private airports; $55-million

Port of Sacramento gives access to the Pacific; 2 mainline transcontinental rail carriers; junction 4 major highways.

**Communications:** 6 TV and 21 radio stations.

**New construction:** downtown Mall; Old Sacramento being restored as state and federal historical project; Rancho Seco Atomic Power Plant; regional sewage treatment plant; major hotel, 2 department stores.

**Medical facilities:** 10 major hospitals, Univ. of California Medical School in nearby Davis.

**Federal facilities:** 2 large Air Force bases, Army depot, many regional federal offices.

**Cultural facilities:** Sacramento Earl Warren Community

enter complex; Eagle Theater; symphony orchestra; ballet; ivic Theater; Crocker Art Gallery; California State Univ., acramento; McGeorge College of Law; Lincoln Univ. Law chool, and 3 community colleges.

**ther attractions:** zoo, 95 public parks; 74 playgrounds; 8 ublic and 4 private golf courses, Sutter's Fort, State Capi-l, Stanford Home, Pony Express Terminal, Fairytale own, and Governor's Mansion; fishing, hunting, boating,

camping, hiking, and skiing in nearby high Sierras; annual State Fair at Cal Expo.

**History:** first permanent settlement founded by John Augustus Sutter Sr. in 1839; James Marshall discovered gold at Sutter's Mill, in 1848, 35 miles northeast, gateway to Mother Lode Country; Pony Express and Central Pacific Railroad which crossed the Sierra Nevada were part of early history.

## St. Louis, Missouri

The World Almanac is sponsored in the St. Louis area by the Post-Dispatch, 900 N. 12th Boulevard, St. ouis, MO 63101; telephone (314) 621-1111; founded Dec. 12, 1878 by Joseph Pulitzer; circulation 256,905 aily, 448,681 Sunday; editor and publisher Joseph Pulitzer Jr., associate editor Michael E. Pulitzer, managing ditor Evarts A. Graham Jr., sr. vice president Alex T. Primm, general manager of newspaper operations ilenn Christopher; major awards include 5 Pulitzer Prizes to the newspaper and 11 to staff members.

**opulation:** 515,000 (city), 993,000 (county), 2,420,000 netro), 12th in nation in payroll employment (938,500 in pril 1978).

**rea:** 4,935 sq. mi. (metro) just south of confluence of Mis->uri and Mississippi rivers.

**ndustry:** 2d to Detroit in auto and truck assembly with ord, GM, and Chrysler plants; McDonnell Douglas head-uarters, aerospace manufacturer; other headquarters in-ude nation's largest shoe company, Interco; Anheuser-usch, world's largest brewer; Monsanto, General Dynam-s, Ralston-Purina, Pet, Inc., Chromalloy American, Con-olidated Aluminum, Emerson Electric, Brown Group; grain narket with 65.8 million bushel annual yield; 3,290 manu-cturing concerns employing 251,600 persons.

**ommerce:** $6.9 billion retail sales (1977 metro); $18,572 nedian family income; 197 banking institutions, total depos-s $10.6 billion (1977).

**ransportation:** 10 major airlines with 7.2 million passenger novements (1977); 2d largest rail center in nation, 17 trunk ne railroads; largest inland river port in nation; 9 major ighways; 14 motor-bus lines; 350 motor freight lines.

**communications:** 6 TV and 28 radio stations.

**Vew construction:** industrial and commercial contracts to-aled $301 million (1977); residential $484 million; Mercan-ile Center, $150 million office, store and hotel complex; 3M, Equitable, First National Bank, $40 million; rail-to-arge coal terminal $20 million.

**Medical facilities:** 48 acute care hospitals with 14,754 beds; Vashington Univ. and St. Louis Univ. medical schools and ffiliated hospitals provide specialized treatment in many reas.

**ederal facilities:** Military Personnel Records Center, De-ense Mapping Agency Aerospace Center, Army Troop Sup-ort and Aviation Material Readiness Command, Army Aviation Research & Development Command, Army Logis-ics Management Systems Agency, Postal Service Data Pro-essing Center, Scott AFB.

**Cultural facilities:** Art Museum; Museum of Science and Natural History; restored historic homes; symphony orches-ra; Mississippi River Festival near Edwardsville in summer; Loretto Hilton Repertory Theatre; St. Louis Opera Theater 3-week summer season, 1978 production filmed by PBS/BBC TV); American Theater; 4 dinner theaters; Laumeier Sculpture Garden; Municipal Theatre (Muny

Opera) offers Broadway shows in big outdoor theater in Forest Park.

**Educational facilities:** 4 major universities: Washington, St. Louis, Univ. of Missouri at St. Louis, and Southern Illinois Univ. at Edwardsville; 5 private colleges; 3-branch junior college system.

**Recreational facilities:** Jefferson National Expansion Memorial with 630-foot Gateway Arch on riverfront; 1,326-acre Forest Park with 3 golf courses, ball fields, floral displays, zoo, McDonnell Planetarium, Steinberg skating arena, and Jefferson Memorial displaying Lindbergh trophies; National Museum of Transport; Six Flags Over Mid-America with world's fastest roller coaster; Grant's Farm with President Grant's cabin and animal displays; Missouri Botanical Garden with floral displays, Japanese garden, and advanced research display greenhouse, the Climatron; excursion boats, show boat, minesweeper, Army Corps of Engineers museum on riverfront; Dental Health Theater with world's largest model teeth.

**Convention facilities:** 14,000 hotel rooms; 90,000 sq. ft. exhibit space in Kiel Auditorium; 240,000 sq. ft. exhibit space in new Gateway Convention Center.

**Sports:** Busch Stadium home of the Cardinal baseball and football teams; St. Louis Blues (NHL); St. Louis Hummers, women's pro softball; horse racing at Cahokia Downs and Fairmont Park.

**Other attractions:** climate has 4 distinct seasons; spring and autumn warm, winters mild, summers hot with 90-degree temperatures; average temperature 55.9 degrees; average precipitation 35.9 inches; downtown area contains significant architecture including Eads Bridge, Old Post Office, Union Station, Old Courthouse, Old Cathedral, Spanish International Pavilion which now contains a hotel tower; Louis Sullivan's Wainwright Building that is being refurbished, and restoration of Laclede's Landing area on riverfront adjoining Gateway Arch.

**History:** named for French King Louis IX by fur trapper Pierre Laclede whose trading post became major fur market and gateway to the West; starting point of Lewis and Clark expedition and other explorations.

**Further information:** Convention and Visitors Bureau, 500 N. Broadway, or Regional Commerce and Growth Assn., 10 S. Broadway, both St. Louis, Mo.

## St. Paul, Minnesota

The World Almanac is sponsored in the St. Paul area by the St. Paul Dispatch and Pioneer Press, 55 E. 4th Street, St. Paul, MN 55101; phone (612) 222-5011; founded 1849 as Minnesota Pioneer by James Goodhue; circulation, Pioneer Press (morn M-F) 100,439; Dispatch (eve M-F) 117,985; Pioneer Press/Dispatch (morn Sat.) 174,810; Sunday Pioneer Press, 240,696; Bernard H. Ridder Jr., president, Ridder Pub., Inc. and vice-chairman Knight-Ridder Newspapers, Inc.; publisher Thomas L. Carlin, executive editor John R. Finnegan, edi-or William G. Sumner. First newspaper published in Minnesota.

**Population:** 270,700 (city); 805,800 (metro), 2d in state, 47th n nation; total employed (city, 1977), 182,029.

**Area:** 55 sq. mi. in eastern Minnesota on banks of Missis-sippi River close to Minnesota and Wisconsin vacationlands; state capital and Ramsey County seat.

**Industry:** West Publishing, world's largest law book publisher; international center for electronics and computer technology; Union Stockyards is largest livestock center in nation (2.7 million head in 1977). Headquarters 3M Co., Am. Hoist & Derrick Co., Burlington Northern RR, Univac, Brown & Bigelow, Whirlpool, Economics Laboratory,

Hoerner-Waldorf Corp., St. Paul Companies (insurance).
**Commerce:** retail sales (1977) $2.3 billion; median household income, $17,018; 25 banks and 6 savings and loan associations.
**Transportation:** 5 major and 2 regional rail lines, Amtrak; 21 intercity truck firms, 37 terminals; 3 interstate bus lines; 730-mile public transit system; metropolitan airport, hub of 8 commercial airlines, headquarters for Northwest and North Central airlines, averages 350 air movements per day; Downtown Airport; 60 firms operate barges on Mississippi River, using a 9-foot channel downtown.
**Communications:** 4 commercial and 2 educational TV stations; 29 radio stations.
**Medical facilities:** 12 private hospitals; a 611 bed community hospital and research center: St. Paul-Ramsey Hospital.
**Federal facilities:** Ft. Snelling; area headquarters for HEW; district headquarters for IRS, FCC, Immigration and Naturalization Service; U.S. District Court.
**Cultural facilities:** Minnesota Symphony Orchestra; Univ. of Minnesota Institute of Agriculture, Hamline Univ., St. Thomas, St. Catherine, Bethel, Concordia, and Macalester colleges, and William Mitchell College of Law; $66 milli city school system with 80 public schools and 61 priva schools.
**Recreational facilities:** more than 900 lakes in metro are 438 tennis courts, 148 swimming beaches, 513 parks, 50 gc courses, 27 ski centers; 52 neighborhood recreation center 35 miles of parkways, 100 miles of hiking and biking trails.
**Convention facilities:** Civic Center with 101,000 sq. ft. e hibit space, seating for 35,00 in 4 main buildings, 15 meetin halls; 50 hotels and motels.
**Other attractions:** Winter Carnival in Jan., Minnesota Sta Fair, Como Park Zoo and Conservatory; onyx statue Indian God of Peace in City Hall, Minnesota Historical S ciety Museums, Arts & Science Center, Fort Snelling Sta Park.
**History:** once called "Pig's Eye" for first settler, Pier "Pig's Eye" Parrant; changed to St. Paul when Fath Lucien Galtier built St. Paul's Chapel 1841; became tow 1847, city 1854.
**Further information:** St. Paul Area Chamber of Commerc Osborn Bldg., St. Paul, MN 55102.

## St. Petersburg, Florida

The World Almanac is sponsored in Florida's Suncoast Area by The St. Petersburg Times and Evening I dependent, 490 1st Avenue S., St. Petersburg, FL 33701; phone (813) 893-8111. Times founded 1884; Inde pendent 1906; circulation, Times (morn) 195,960; Independent (evening) 37,269; Sunday Times 243,152. E gene C. Patterson, editor of The Times and president of The Times.Publishing Co.; Robert Stiff, editor, Th Independent; John B. Lake, executive vice president and publisher, The Times Publishing Co.

**Population:** 238,750 (city), 727,228 (Pinellas County), 1,472,000 (metro); Pinellas County April 1978 employment 222,300, unemployment 5.9%.
**Industry and Commerce:** tourism, just under 3 million visited county in 1977, spending about $1.0 billion; industries include General Electric, Honeywell, Sperry, Milton Roy Co., Eckerd Drugs, Jim Walter Research, All-State Insurance regional office, U.S. Homes headquarters, Morgan Yacht; county 1977 retail sales $2.8 billion.
**Transportation:** U.S. 19, 41, and 98 link city to rest of Gulf Coast Florida; Interstates 275, 75, and 4 link St. Petersburg with Tampa, Orlando, and east coast; Tampa International Airport 25 minutes from downtown St. Petersburg; other airports are St. Petersburg-Clearwater International and Albert Whitted; Amtrak, Seaboard Coast Line railroads; Greyhound and Trailways bus lines.
**Communications:** 6 TV and 46 radio stations.
**Convention and Tourist facilities:** over 52,000 units can house 160,000 visitors; Bayfront Center seats 8,250 in arena, 2,250 in auditorium; Pinellas restaurants can serve 112,244 people at one time; Disney World 2 hours away.

**Medical facilities:** 13 major hospitals; Bay Pines veteran complex to be greatly expanded adding 1,150 new beds; A Children's Hospital.
**Cultural facilities:** Museum of Fine Arts, Gulf Coast Syr phony, Historical Museum, community theaters, Ecke College Free Institutions Forums, varied musical, theatric and dance events at Bayfront Center Complex.
**Educational facilities:** Univ. of South Florida's downtow Bayboro Campus to expand enrollment from 1,700 to 7,50 first building phase of $5 million is underway; Stetson Cc lege of Law, Eckerd College, St. Petersburg Junior College.
**Recreational facilities:** 76 parks on 1,800 acres, many wi recreational buildings, pools, tennis courts, boat ramps, ar picnic areas; municipal and private marinas; deep sea fisl ing, golf courses, baseball fields.
**Sports:** St. Louis Cardinals and New York Mets sprin training; spectator sports include greyhound racing, bas ball, jai alai, horse racing, NFL football, basketball, pro te nis, boat racing, NASL soccer.
**Additional Information:** St. Petersburg Chamber of Cor merce 225 4th Street S., St. Petersburg, FL 33701.

## Salem, Oregon

The World Almanac is sponsored in the Salem area by the Statesman Journal Newspapers, 280 Churc Street NE, P.O. Box 13009, Salem, OR 97309, (503) 399-6611; publisher of the morning Oregon Statesma and the evening Capital Journal; combined daily circulation 64,271; Sunday 54,372. N.S. Hayden, publishe John H. McMillan, executive editor.

**Population:** 84,900 (city), 217,200 (metro).
**Area:** 32 sq. mi. on the Willamette River in the center of the bountiful Willamette Valley 50 miles south of Portland; 61 miles from Pacific Ocean; state capital and Marion County seat.
**Industry:** government (over 15,000 state employees), agriculture (over 100 crops), food processing — 2d in nation for fruit, berries, and vegetables; over 16 canneries produced over 16 million cases of canned goods and 260 million pounds of frozen foods; lumber and lumber products; manufacturing (batteries, radios, metal products, feeds, paints, textiles, food processing cans); pulp and paper mill.
**Commerce:** retail sales (1976) $593 million; med. household income (1976) $12,201; 7 commercial banks, deposits (1977) $416 million; 6 savings & loan associations, deposits (1977) $380 million.
**Transportation:** 2 rail freight lines, Amtrak; Greyhound,

Trailways bus lines, 11 truck lines, United Airlines.
**Communications:** one public TV, 6 radio stations, 2 dai newspapers, 1 farm weekly newspaper.
**Medical facilities:** hospital with 2 units, General and M morial.
**Cultural facilities:** symphony orchestra, art association, l tle theater, Bush House museum, Deepwood, Mission M museum, Northwest History collection, Willamette Univ $10.5 million Civic Center.
**Education:** metro area includes 108 public schools — 87 el mentary, 12 junior highs, 19 high schools, and 15 parochia schools; State Schools for the Blind and Deaf, Chemeke Community College, Willamette Univ., Western Baptist B ble College, and Oregon College of Education.
**Recreation:** back-packing, fishing, golf, snow and water sk ing, camping, 44 parks in 5 mile radius; hunting for dee elk, and fowl; Bush Pasture Park; within one hour drive M Hood, Detroit Lake, Oregon Coast, Mt. Jefferson; 9 gc

urses in 15 mile radius; 70 tennis courts in area.
orts: Salem Senators baseball, Northwest League.
istory: founded in 1842 by Methodist missionary, Jason Lee.

**Further information:** Chamber of Commerce, P.O. Box 231, Salem, OR 97308.

## Salt Lake City, Utah

The World Almanac is sponsored in the Salt Lake City area by The Salt Lake Tribune, 143 S. Main Street, alt Lake City, UT 84111; phone (801) 237-2001; founded Apr. 15, 1871; circulation, 110,945 daily, 181,110 unday; publisher, John W. Gallivan; executive editor, Arthur C. Deck; 1957 Pulitzer Prize; civic projects, tatewide civic beautification awards; Sub for Santa program; Community Christmas Tree Plantings; Spring arden Festival; Ski Race; No Champs Tennis Tournament.

opulation: (1976 est.) 180,538 (city), 563,551 (county), 49,100 (metro); first in state, 46th in nation; 52% of state op. lives within 30 miles; state capital and Salt Lake ounty seat.

rea: nestled in a vast valley (elev. 4,327 ft.) surrounded by Vasatch and Oquirrh mountains.

ndustry: labor force 253,120; effective buying income $3.9 illion (1976); per family income $14,402; total construction alue $464.4 million; employers are Hill AFB (30 miles orth), local defense industries, and Kennecott Copper orp., Utah Mining Division; metro area becoming major enter for electronics; apparel manufacturing, mining, smelt-g, refining, distribution, warehousing center of Mountain Vest.

ransportation: 6 air lines, customs office, free-trade zone, nternational Airport; geographic center of 11 western tates; hub of central transcontinental highway system; 3 ailroads, all major western truck, bus lines.

ommunications: 2 daily newspapers, 3 commercial, 3 cable V, one public TV, and 18 radio stations.

ew construction: Bicentennial Center for the Cultural Arts; heraton Hotel, Empire State Bank; high-rise addition to ittle America Motel; 2 major office buildings, small park.

**Medical facilities:** 10 hospitals, including Univ. of Utah Medial Center, major research in transplant surgery.

**Educational facilities:** Univ. of Utah, Westminster College, Utah Technical College.

**Cultural facilities:** Utah Symphony Orchestra among 12 best in U.S.; Mormon Tabernacle Choir, Ballet West, Utah Opera Co., Ririe-Woodbury Co., Repertory Dance Theatre, 2 cultural arts halls.

**Other attractions:** Temple Square, home of 3.5 million-member Church of Jesus Christ of Latter-Day Saints (Mormons); Salt Palace Civic Auditorium; 700 acres in 22 parks, 25 playgrounds, 10 golf courses, 85 tennis courts; near Great Salt Lake (7 times more salty than ocean); Hogle Zoological Gardens, Kennecott Copper's Bingham mine; 4 well-defined seasons, mean annual temperature 51.0 degrees F.

**Sports:** 9 major ski resorts; Golden Eagles (Central Hockey League), Salt Lake Gulls, Triple A baseball; Bonneville Salt Flats.

**History:** founded July 24, 1847 by Brigham Young and contingent of pioneers.

**Further information:** Chamber of Commerce, 19 E. 2d So.; Utah Travel Council, Council Hall; Salt Lake Valley Visitors and Convention Bureau, West Temple at First South, all Salt Lake City, UT.

## San Antonio, Texas

The World Almanac is sponsored in the San Antonio area by the S. A. Express (morning) and S. A. News evening), P.O. Box 2171, San Antonio, TX 78297; tel. (512) 225-7411; circulation daily, Express 82,511, Jews 75,971, Sunday Express-News 176,057; chairman K. Rupert Murdoch, publisher and editor Charles O. Kilpatrick; Express-News Corp. is a division of News America, Inc.

opulation: 802,092 city, 922,904 Bexar County, total em-ployed 377,904.

rea: Bexar County, 1,247 sq. mi., 2 1/2 hours from Gulf Coast and Mexican border.

ndustry: 5 military bases include Kelly AFB, largest em-loyer; fast-growing medical industry; diverse manufactur-g, tourism, construction, trade, and service industries.

ommerce: center for 100 mile radius retail trade area, truck rops, livestock production; retail sales (1977) $3.6 billion.

ederal facilities: Kelly AFB, hq. AF Air Security Service; Randolph AFB, hq. AF Air Training Command & AF Per-onnel Center; Brooks AFB, hq. AF Aerospace Medical Di-ision; Lackland AFB with Wilford Hall USAF Medical Center; Fort Sam Houston, hq. Fifth Army, & Army Health Services Command, Brooke Army Medical Center.

Medical facilities: University of Texas Medical, Dental, Nursing schools; Audie Murphy VA Hospital; Southwest Research Institute; Southwest Foundation of Research and Education.

ransportation: International Airport, 9 major airlines; 3 ail freight, Amtrak.

**Educational facilities:** Univ. of Texas at San Antonio; Trinity, St. Mary's, and Our Lady of the Lake universities; Incarnate Word College; 2 jr. colleges, San Antonio College, St. Philip's College; permanent extension of National University of Mexico.

**Convention facilities:** Convention Center with large arena, theater, exhibit, meeting space.

**Cultural facilities:** symphony orchestra; Institute of Texan Cultures, Mexican Cultural Institute, Witte Museum, McNay Art Institute.

**Other attractions:** historic Alamo, old Spanish missions of San Jose, Concepcion, Capistrano, Espada; Hemis Fair Plaza with 622-foot observation tower-restaurant; downtown River Walk; zoo; annual events: Fiesta San Antonio, Livestock Show & Rodeo, Folklife Festival, Texas Open PGA tournament; pro sports: Spurs (NBA); Dodgers, minor league baseball, Rowels, pro rodeo team.

**Further information:** Greater San Antonio Chamber of Commerce, 602 E. Commerce, P. O. Box 1628, San Antonio, TX 78296.

## San Bernardino, California

The World Almanac is sponsored in the San Bernardino area by the Sun-Telegram, 399 North D Street, San Bernardino, CA 92401, phone (714) 889-9666; Telegram founded 1873, Sun 1894; daily circulation 75,835, Sunday 82,280; member Gannett chain; publisher William Honeysett, advertising director William Ridenour, editor Wayne C. Sargent.

opulation: 105,384 (city), 1,262,900 (2-county metro area); 3d in state, 148th in nation; total employed 42,700.

**Area:** 47.22 sq. mi. at base of Cajon Pass, 58 miles east of Los Angeles; San Bernardino County seat.

**Industry:** 173 business and industrial firms including Culligan, Edginton Oil, Fleetwood Enterprises, Hanford Foundry, Knudsen Dairy, Lifetime Foam, Mode O'Day, Pepsi Cola and Seven-Up bottling plants, Santa Fe Railway, TRW Systems, Monier Tile and Terry Industries.

**Commerce:** trading center for 20,189 sq. mi. San Bernardino county, largest in the nation; retail sales (1977) $751 million; 7 banks, 22 branches; 12 savings and loan assns.; 2 major shopping center complexes, each parking over 5,000 cars.

**Transportation:** Santa Fe, Southern Pacific, and Union Pacific rail lines, Amtrak; Greyhound and Continental bus lines; major interstate highways leading from Mexico to Canada and West to East Coast; municipal airport and nearby Ontario International Airport, over 1.6 million passengers (1977).

**Communications:** 15 radio and one VHF educational TV station; access to 5 Los Angeles channels.

**Medical facilities:** 3 major hospitals with 995 beds; maj research and training center for heart surgery and hip ar knee replacement surgery.

**Federal facilities:** Norton Air Force Base.

**Cultural facilities:** symphony orchestra, Civic Light Oper nearby Redlands Bowl (summer concerts); National Oran Show with orange festival every spring; Convention Cente Exhibit Hall complex.

**Educational facilities:** California State College, junior cc lege, 3 major universities nearby.

**New construction:** 8 redevelopment project areas with cor mercial and industrial development sites.

**Sports:** Little League Western Regional Headquarters.

**History:** founded 1852 by Mormons who purchased lar from Spanish grant holders.

**Further information:** Chamber of Commerce, 546 West 6 Street, San Bernardino, CA 92401.

---

## San Diego, California

The World Almanac is sponsored in San Diego by The San Diego Union and The Evening Tribune (Cople Newspapers), P.O. Box 191, San Diego, CA 92112; (714) 299-3131; Union founded 1868 (pioneer daily Southwest); circulation, Union (morn) 198,351, Tribune (eve) 131,374, Sunday Union 325,055; publish Helen K. Copley, general manager Al De Bakcsy, Union editor Gerald L. Warren, Tribune editor Fred Kinne.

**Population:** 797,384 (1978 city); 1,694,814 (county); 11th in U.S. (official state estimate); total civilian employment, 590,200.

**Area:** (county) 4,255 sq. mi.; 70 mi. Pacific Coast, San Clemente to Mexican border.

**Industry:** tourism, manufacturing, military and agriculture; manufactured products earn $3.2 billion a year; non-military payroll $4.1 billion, military $908.8 million; tourist spending over $794 million; corporations with bases or divisions include Bendix, Burroughs, Control Data, Cubic, General Dynamics, Gulf, Honeywell, International Harvester's Solar division, NCR Corp., Pacific Southwest Airlines, Rohr, Sea World, Teledyne Ryan, TraveLodge, Wickes, Van Camp sea food, Foodmaker (Jack-in-the-Box); aerospace, rapid transit design and manufacture, oceanography, nuclear energy, medicine important; also shipbuilding, tuna fishing, clothing, ocean shippping; among top 20 counties in farm products (avocados, cut flowers, eggs); Marine Corps Recruit Depot, Naval Training Center, North Island and Miramar Naval Air Stations, Naval Electronics Lab and Undersea Center, Marine Corps base at Camp Pendleton.

**Transportation:** Freeway system, state's 2d largest; urban transit service 35-cent fare, Mexican border to 35 miles north; Amtrak, 9 airlines, bus lines; primary airport Lindbergh Field.

**Communications:** Some 30 TV and radio stations.

**Medical facilities:** Salk Institute for Biological Studies, Scripps Clinic & Research Foundation; Naval Hospital; many hospitals.

**Education and Cultural facilities:** San Diego State Uni U.S. International Univ., Univ. of San Diego, Univ. of Ca fornia, San Diego (3 colleges and Scripps Institution Oceanography), Point Loma College; symphony; Old Glo Theatre (functioning reproduction of Shakespeare's Glo Theatre); opera; ballet; Fine Arts and Timken Galleries; Jolla Museum of Contemporary Art.

**Other attractions:** world famous zoo and wild animal par Balboa Park, central 1,400 acres containing museums, zc Fleet Space Theatre (computerized planetarium), man other attractions; Mission Bay Park includes Sea Worl "Old San Diego" State Historical Park; "Star of Indi ship-museum; visits to neighboring Mexico (Tijuana); miles of beaches.

**Sports:** NFL Chargers, NL Padres; hockey, tennis, socce volleyball teams; racing at Del Mar, Caliente.

**Other attractions:** climiate sunny; summer and winter sort; average temp. 68° in summer, 57° in winter, rainfa mainly December to March; famous "place names" inclu La Jolla (part of city of San Diego); 70 golf courses, inclu ing Torrey Pines; large convention facilities; off-sho "whale watching."

**History:** area discovered 1542 by Cabrillo, founded in 17 by Father Junipero Serra.

**Further information:** San Diego Chamber of Commerce, 2 A Street, San Diego, CA 92101.

---

## San Francisco, California

The World Almanac is sponsored in the San Francisco-Oakland area by The San Francisco Examiner, P.C Box 3100, Rincon Annex, San Francisco, CA 94119; (415) 777-2424; founded June 12, 1865; circulation dai Examiner, 156,083; Sunday Examiner & Chronicle, 668,550; president, R. A. Hearst; editor and publisher, Re Murphy; major awards: Pulitzer Prize, Freedoms Foundation; Examiner sponsors Examiner Games, Golde Gloves, Bay to Breakers Race, Opera in the Park.

**Population:** 654,400, 3d in state, 13th in nation; total employed 490,100.

**Area:** 44.6 sq. mi. on the northern tip of a peninsula. San Francisco County seat.

**Industry:** food products, printing, publishing, fabricated metal products; west's financial capital and administrative center for many of the nation's leading corporations; West Coast operations' headquarters for a majority of the federal agencies; finance, insurance, and real estate; chief port of the Pacific Coast.

**Commerce:** wholesale-retail trade employment, 96,800; services 120,200; manufacturing 46,700; total retail outlets 22,575, taxable sales $3.5 billion; 40 banks with 157 branches; 25 savings and loans with 39 branches; total deposits in banks $19.2 billion.

**Transportation:** 27 major airlines serve the Bay Area; Inte national Airport processed 20.2 million passengers, 371,6 tons of freight (1977); Municipal Railway (intra-city); A( Transit and Bay Area Rapid Transit System (BART) East Bay cities; Greyhound bus and Southern Pacific Ra road to Peninsula areas; Golden Gate Bridge District b and ferry service to Marin County; Port of San Francisc services available: LASH, BULK, general cargo, containe ization and barge service.

**Communications:** 2 major newspapers; 118 others servin the Bay Area; 45 radio stations, 7 TV channels received d rectly, one TV cable system.

**Medical facilities:** 24 general hospitals with over 7,406 tot ds; and 5 specialty hospitals with over 1,935 beds; 3,033 ysicians/surgeons and 772 dentists; Univ. of Cal. Medical nter, with 42 buildings, is a general teaching and research stitute and is the largest kidney transplant center in the rld.

ltural facilities: San Francisco Opera, Spring Opera, estern Opera Theater, symphony, ballet, Civic Light era, American Conservatory Theater, Japanese Cultural nter, Chinese Cultural Center, International Film Festi- l, 3 museums, 29 libraries, and 540 churches.

ucational facilities: 97 public elementary schools with a al enrollment of 31,419 and 17 junior high and 11 high ools with a combined enrollment of 32,466 students; iv. of California, San Francisco; California State Univ., iv. of San Francisco, and City College of San Francisco.

creational facilities: 120 parks and many miniparks, 78 ygrounds, 6 golf courses, numerous tennis courts, 10 swimming pools, 5½ miles of ocean beach, one lake, one fishing pier, Marina small craft harbor and 3 yacht clubs.

Convention facilities: 102 hotels and motels with over 20,000 rooms.

Sports: Candlestick Park, home of the NL Giants and NFL 49ers.

Other attractions: zoo and 1,013-acre Golden Gate Park containing the California Academy of Sciences, De Young Museum, Japanese Tea Garden, and Arboretum; cable cars, Fisherman's Wharf, Chinatown, the Ferry Building, Coit Tower, the Palace of Fine Arts, and Grace Cathedral.

History: San Francisco Bay discovered 1769 by Sgt. Jose Ortega; pueblo of Yerba Buena established 1834, renamed San Francisco on January 3, 1847; incorporated April 15, 1850.

Further information: Chamber of Commerce, 465 California Street, San Francisco, CA 94104.

## San Jose, California

The World Almanac is sponsored in the San Jose area by The Mercury and News, 750 Ridder Park Drive, an Jose, CA 95190; (408) 289-5000; Mercury founded June 20, 1851; News July 23, 1883; combined daily rculation 202,590: Sunday Mercury News; 231,446; publisher P. Anthony Ridder; editor Larry Jinks; presi- nt Joseph B. Ridder.

pulation: 587,700 (city), 1,222,800 (metro area coexten- ve with Santa Clara County); total employed 610,800 etro, Mar. '78).

rea: broad alluvial 832,256-acre valley at south end of San ancisco Bay.

dustry: largest county in northern Cal. for manufacturing ployment and total wages; called "Silicone Valley" due to gh technology semi-conductor and other electronics firms; M, Fairchild Semi-conductor, Hewlett-Packard, Varian ssociates, Intel Corp., National Semi-conductor; diversity own by Ford Motor Co., Lockheed Missiles & Space, MC Corp., Syntex Laboratories; county a major producer cut flowers.

mmerce: leading retail trade center of northern Cal., .90 billion in sales; 137 shopping centers; 4th nationally in edian household income among U.S. metro areas with one llion and over population, 76% of households earn 0,000 and over annually, 58% earn $15,000 and over an- ally (metro).

ansportation: Municipal Airport served by 13 airlines; ghway system interconnected with interstate in north- uth, east-west directions; Southern Pacific and Western Pacific railroads.

Education: San Jose State, Santa Clara, and Stanford univer- sities, plus community colleges have total enrollments of 128,027; 37% of adult pop. is college educated (metro).

Cultural facilities: symphony, First State Capital Museum, Rosicrucian Egyptian Temple, Science Museum and Plane- tarium, De Saisset Gallery and Museum, Villa Montalvo estate and arboretum, City Gallery, Triton Museum of Art, New Almaden Museum.

Sports: Earthquakes (soccer); Missions, farm club for Seattle Mariners; Sunbirds, women's professional softball; 8 reser- voirs with boat ramps, 2 with camping; outlet to S.F. Bay for ocean sports.

Other attractions: Japanese Tea Gardens, Lick Observatory, Winchester Mystery House.

History: founded 1777, first civil settlement in Cal.; county is one of the original 27 in Cal.; first public school in state, San Jose Granary, 1795; first state capitol, Dec. 15, 1849.

Further information: Chamber of Commerce Metro-San Jose, One Paseo de San Antonio, San Jose, CA 95113, (408) 998-7000.

## San Juan, Puerto Rico

The World Almanac is sponsored in Puerto Rico by the San Juan Star, GPO Box 4187, San Juan, PR 0936; telephone (809) 782-4200; founded Nov. 2, 1959; circulation 42,000 daily; 43,000 Sunday; president d general manager John A. Zerbe Jr.; vice president and editor Andrew T. Viglucci; major awards include 061 Pulitzer Prize for editorial writing; APME citations 1960, 1965; staff awards include 1970 LAPA Mergen- aler Award, 1972 Overseas Press Club Award; National Spelling Bee 1975 champion.

pulation: 512,300 (city), 1,027,222 (metro area) first in mmonwealth.

rea: 47 sq. mi. in Caribbean, capital city.

dustry: seat of Puerto Rico's tourism industry with 19 lux- y hotels and several dozen high rise condominiums. City is o the commercial and shipping hub of the island and is a ajor stop for cruise ships plying the Caribbean. Major in- stries are electronics, pharmaceuticals, and an expanding trochemical industry serviced by 3 major refineries. Petro- emical industry represents $1.5 billion in investments. enter of island's rum industry with the Bacardi distillery San Juan Bay, the largest in the world. More than 75 per nt of all rum sold in U.S. is Puerto Rican rum.

ansportation: San Juan International Airport handles ore than 500,000 passengers monthly with 3 major U.S. rlines and 10 foreign lines. Isla Grande Airport handles all aircraft traffic.

ucation: seat of the Rio Piedras campus of the University Puerto Rico, the public university system, InterAmerican niversity, College of the Sacred Heart, UPR Medical Sci- ces campus and UPR Law School, World University, and several junior and regional colleges.

Federal facilities: Ft. Buchanan army base with 9-hole golf course on grounds.

Cultural facilities and events: The Casals Festival, guided for 18 years by the late Maestro Casals, is an annual June event bringing together some of the world's finest musicians; annual San Juan Carnival, last week in June; the Puerto Rico Institute of Culture is housed in a restored Dominican convent; El Morro, the Spanish-built fortress that guards the entrance to San Juan Harbor; numerous art museums in Old San Juan; the Puerto Rico Symphony Orchestra in con- certs spread over the year; the capitol building and gover- nor's mansion.

Convention facilities: new Condado Convention Center built by state government seats 5,000 for meetings, 3,000 for meals.

New construction: Old City restoration program, Ponce Art Museum; banking district located in Hato Rey; expansion of Plaza las Americas shopping center to house Sears Roebuck, Inc.; new Banco de San Juan multi-story office bldg.; new

Carolina Plaza shopping mall 3 miles east of San Juan; expanded Condado Holiday Inn, up from 328 rooms to 578.
**Sports:** Hiram Bithorn Stadium, winter baseball, track, and outdoor events; Roberto Clemente Coliseum, basketball, boxing, and indoor events; soccer, cockfighting arenas (legal); 1979 PanAm Games.
**History:** discovered by Columbus on his 2d voyage to the

New World in 1493, colonized by Juan Ponce de Leo Puerto Rico's first Spanish governor; since 1952 a commo wealth freely associated with the United States. Free mark with U.S. and same currency, common citizenship.
**Further information:** Chamber of Commerce, 100 Tetua Street, Old San Juan; Dept. of Tourism, Banco de Pon Bldg., Hato Rey, PR.

---

## Santa Ana, California

*See Orange County, California*

---

## Saskatoon, Saskatchewan, Canada

The World Almanac is sponsored in northern Saskatchewan by the Saskatoon Star-Phoenix, 204 Fifth Ave nue North, Saskatoon, Sask., S7K 2P1; (306) 652-9200; Daily Star and Phoenix, founded in 1906 and 190 respectively, merged in 1928 into the Star-Phoenix; circulation daily, 53,655; publisher Michael C. Sifton, e ecutive vice president James K. Struthers.

**Population:** 145,000, 2d in prov., 12th in nation.
**Area:** 39.4 sq. mi. land, 1.5 sq. mi. water, on S. Sask. River, center of agricultural province.
**Commerce:** retail, wholesale, service, distribution hub for 400,000 in north central trading area; North America's potash capital; meat packing, grain handling dominant; electronics and research newest; base for billion dollar uranium mining, refining companies, retail sales (1977) $512 million.
**Transportation:** 2 railways, 2 airlines, new air terminal, direct flight to U.K.; 2 bus lines, 55 transport firms; Yellowhead Highway, easiest access through Rockies from Prairies to Pacific.
**Communications:** One daily; 2 TV, stations, cable, and 5 radio stations; one farm weekly, one community weekly.
**Medical facilities:** 3 major hospitals, 6 nursing homes; Univ. Hospital known for kidney transplants, open-heart surgery.

**Cultural facilities:** $7 million, 2,000-seat Centennial Audit rium, convention facilities for over 1,800; Mendel Art Ga lery/Civic Conservatory; Western Development Museu houses N. America's largest display of antique cars, far implements, and 1910 Pioneer Village; theme pavilion f summer fair.
**Education:** Univ. of Sask. (17,500 students), famed for ag culture, space, Arctic, physics, medicine, veterinary colleg Kelsey Institute for Applied Arts and Science (4,700 st dents); School for Deaf.
**Recreation:** 1,456 acres parkland; wild animal farm; ma made ski mountain; camping, fishing.
**History:** founded 1883 as temperance colony; incorporat 1906; battle sites of 1885 Riel Rebellion.
**Further information:** Board of Trade, Bessborough Hote Saskatoon, Sask. S7K 3GB.

---

## Savannah, Georgia

The World Almanac is sponsored in the Savannah area by the Savannah News-Press, 111 West Ba Street, Savannah GA 31402, phone (912) 236-9511. Publisher of the Savannah Morning News and Evenin Press; combined circulation 78,698 daily, Sunday 72,499. Donald E. Harwood, general manager; Wallace N Davis, Jr., executive editor, Michael Boisclair, advertising director.

**Population:** 155,000 (city) 223,000 (metro).
**Area:** 50 sq. mi. on Savannah River, 18 mi. from Atlantic Ocean; Chatham Co. seat.
**Industry:** world's largest pulp-to-paper container plant owned by Union Camp Corp.; Savannah Sugar Refining Corp., nation's 3d largest seller; jet aircraft manufacturer (Grumman American Aviation); tea packaging (Tetley), fertilizer materials, ship repair, titanium dioxide production (American Cyanamid).
**Commerce:** hub of "Coastal Empire" economic center of 8 Ga. and 3 S. Carolina counties; The city is Georgia's gate to world trade; the Southeast's leading foreign trade port between Baltimore and New Orleans and a major container port; served by 100 steamship lines, 43 deep water terminals; retail sales (1977) over one billion dollars; 7 commercial banks, 3 savings and loan assns.
**Transportation:** 2 rail freight lines, Seaboard Coastline and Southern; Amtrak; Greyhound, Trailways bus lines, 74 truck lines; Delta, National airlines; Intercoastal Waterway.
**Communications:** Savannah News-Press, Inc. (daily and Sunday), 4 weekly papers: The Herald, The Tribune, The Journal-Record, The Georgia Gazette; 5 TV and 14 radio stations; 151,422 telephones in area (1977).
**New construction:** Chatham Co. Courthouse complex, Riverfront restoration, Ga. Port Authority's port expansion program, Hyatt Hotel on River Street, motel complex on Abercorn, shopping mall at Georgetown, EM Labs. industrial chemical plant.
**Medical facilities:** 8 hospitals, Medical Arts Center.
**Federal facilities:** U. S. Customs House. Ft. Stewart/Hunter assigned the 24th Infantry Division, 16,000 troops; Ft. Stewart is located on one of the largest military reservations east of the Mississippi, 280,000 acres, 35 mi. so. of Savan-

nah.
**Cultural facilities:** Savannah Art Assn., Savannah Sym phony, Ballet Guild, little theatre, Telfair Academy of Ar and Sciences, Kennedy Fine Arts Center, SSC; Fine Ar Building, ASC; maritime museum, Fort Pulaski Nation Monument and military museum, civic center.
**Education:** Armstrong State College and Savannah Sta College, both units of the Univ. System of Ga., 4-year inst tutions; 60 public, 3 vocational-tech, 18 parochial, 10 p vate, 3 business schools; Skidaway Inst. of Oceanograph and Aquarium.
**Recreation:** 14 theatres; 6 golf courses; 33 public tenn courts; 32 squares, parks, and playgrounds; 3 sports fields; recreation centers; 2 stadiums.
**Convention facilities:** 8,000 seat auditorium at the civic ce ter.
**Sports:** Savannah Braves baseball, Southern League; Sava nah Speedway, SSC Tigers, ASC Pirates.
**Annual events:** St. Patrick's Day Parade, Oktober Festiva Blessing of the Fleet, Night in Olde Savannah, tour homes, arts festival, farmer's market, Christmas Parade, ga den club show.
**Other attractions:** antique car museum, Davenport Hous Owens-Thomas House, river cruises, tour of downtown S vannah's historic section, River Street, Fort Jackson, B thesda, first orphanage in U.S.
**History:** mother city of Georgia, Gen. James Oglethor and a band of 120 followers settled last of 13 original col nies here; site of Revolutionary War battle, end of Ge Sherman's Civil War "March to the Sea"; Much of the o city is a national historic landmark, largest in the country.
**Further information:** Chamber of Commerce, P.O.B. 53 Savannah, GA 31402.

## Seattle, Washington

The World Almanac is sponsored in the Seattle area by The Seattle Times, Fairview Avenue N. & John treet, P.O. Box 70, Seattle, WA 98111; phone (206) 464-2111; founded 1896 by Alden J. Blethen; circulation 45,614 daily, 327,818 Sunday; publisher John A. Blethen; president W.J. Pennington; vice president and gen-al manager Harold G. Fuhrman.

**opulation:** 500,000 (city), 1,445,600 (metro); first in state, d in nation; total employed (metro) 704,000.

**rea:** 91.6 sq. mi. between Puget Sound and Lake Washing-n; King County seat.

**ndustry:** headquarters for Boeing, 57,000 employes, world's rgest manufacturer of commercial jet aircraft; Port of Seat-has $800 million current value of properties and facilities cluding Seattle-Tacoma airport; nation's 4th largest con-nerized-shipping seaport; area has 36,098 employer units; ajor industries are transportation products, retail trade, ipbuilding, wood products, and food products.

**ommerce:** business center for western Wash. and Alaska; ajor import-export center for Far East; total retail sales 977) $5.876 billion; per capita income (1977) $7,011; 29 mmercial banks and branches.

**ransportation:** 3 transcontinental railroads, Amtrak; Inter-tional Airport served by 12 scheduled airlines, 6 com-uter airlines, handled 7 million passengers (1977); ferries rve Puget Sound, Canada, and Alaska.

**ommunications:** 4 daily newspapers in metro area; 6 TV, AM and 20 FM stations.

**ew construction:** $242.8 million (city).

**Medical facilities:** 26 hospitals, including Univ. of Wash. ealth Sciences Center and Fred Hutchinson Cancer Re-arch Center.

**ducational facilities:** Four 4-year colleges: Univ. of Wash., attle Univ., Cornish Institute, and Seattle Pacific Univ.; 7 ommunity colleges.

**Federal facilities:** 13th Naval Dist. Hdqts.; Pacific Marine center, National Oceanic & Atmospheric Admin.; 13th Coast Guard Dist. Hdqts.; many regional offices, 37-story federal office bldg.

**Cultural facilities:** symphony orchestra, opera association, art museum and 10 other museums, 2 professional theater companies.

**Recreation:** major boating center; salmon and trout fishing; several nearby ski areas; Mt. Rainier, North Cascades, and Olympic National parks within 2-hour drive.

**Sports:** NBA SuperSonics; IVA Smashers (volleyball); WTT Sea-Port Cascades (tennis); Kingdome, concrete-dome stadium, home of NFL Seahawks, American League Mariners, and North American Soccer League Sounders.

**Other attractions:** $50 million Seattle Center, site of 1962 world's fair, has 14,000-seat coliseum, opera house, playhouse, arena, Space Needle, and Pacific Science Center, Seattle Aquarium; Woodland Park Zoo.

**History:** settled 1851, named for an Indian chief who befriended the settlers; virtually destroyed by fire in 1889, quickly rebuilt; Alaska Gold Rush of 1897 spurred growth and propelled Seattle toward its status as the Northwest's principal city.

**Further information:** Chamber of Commerce, 215 Columbia Street, Seattle, WA 98104, or Convention and Visitors Bureau, 1815 7th Avenue, 98101.

## Sioux Falls, South Dakota

The World Almanac is sponsored in the Sioux Falls area by the Sioux Falls Argus-Leader, 200 S. Minne-ota Avenue, Sioux Falls, SD 57102; tel. (605) 336-1130; a Gannett newspaper, founded in 1885; circulation, 7,333 daily, 55,583 Sunday; publisher Dean C. Smith, executive editor Larry Fuller.

**opulation:** 85,000 (city); 112,000 (metro area), largest in ate.

**rea:** 37 square miles in southeastern South Dakota, located junction of interstates 29 and 90; Minnehaha County at.

**ederal facilities:** Earth Resources Observation Systems ata Center of the U.S. Dept. of Interior.

**ndustry and Commerce:** located in the nation's breadbas-et; Sioux Falls Stockyards is the 3d largest public market in e U.S.; John Morrell & Co. is the largest of 170 manufac-arers; there are 28 banks and 7 savings and loan associa-ons; wholesale and retail center for South Dakota, parts of innesota and Iowa; yearly retail sales over $502 million; fective buying family income in 1977 was $16,569.

**ransportation:** served by 5 major highways, 2 bus lines, nd 3 major rail lines; Joe Foss Field with modern terminal

is within 2 miles of business district, has 3 major airlines offering 34 daily flights.

**Medical facilities:** 4 hospitals, including Royal C. Johnson VA hospital and Crippled Children's Hospital and School.

**Communications:** 1 daily newspaper, 3 TV and 12 radio stations; state headquarters for Northwestern Bell Telephone Co.

**Culture and Education:** public library; convention center, Civic Fine Arts Center, Sioux Falls Symphony, Community Playhouse; Augustana College, Sioux Falls College, North American Baptist Seminary, the SD School for the Deaf, a vocational school, 2 business schools, 2 nurses training schools, 3 high schools, 29 public and 9 parochial schools, 91 churches.

**Further information:** Chamber of Commerce, 101 W. 9th Street, Sioux Falls, SD 57101.

## Springfield, Illinois

The World Almanac is sponsored in the Springfield area by the State Journal-Register (morning and eve-ing), oldest newspaper in Illinois, 313 S. Sixth Street, P.O. Box 219, Springfield, IL 62705; (217) 544-5711; irculation, 72,208; John P. Clarke, publisher; Edward H. Armstrong, editor; Patrick Coburn, managing editor.

**opulation:** 98,000 (city), 186,000 (metro), 4th in state; total mployed, 96,350.

**rea:** 43.3 square miles on Sangamon River in center of ate; state capital and Sangamon County seat.

**ommerce:** state and federal offices; 11 banks, 8 savings and an associations, 8 insurance company home offices; 125 ational, regional, and state associations; 27 civic clubs; 80 cial service organizations; 65 women's organizations; an-ual retail sales, estimated $695 million.

**ransportation:** 7 railroads, 41 truck carriers; one airport;

nearby barge facilities.

**Communications:** one TV station and 7 radio stations.

**Medical facilities:** 3 hospitals with 1,620 beds; 256 doctors; 353 doctors, including dentists and chiropractors; 35 clinics, 20 licensed nursing homes, the Springfield Regional Trauma Center.

**Cultural facilities:** Municipal band, opera, symphony, chorus; Theatre Guild; state museum, Lincoln historical sites; New Salem State Park, Old State Capitol, art associations, summer theater, Growth Stock Company Theater of the Unemployed, Illinois Country Opry, Clayville renovated stagecoach stop; arts and crafts festivals; Oliver Parks Telephone Museum; Saddle Tramp Gap Western Ranch, new Lincoln Library, Lincoln Memorial Garden, Nelson Recreation Center, Henson Robinson Children's Zoo, civic convention center under construction.

**Education:** Sangamon State Univ., Lincoln Land Community College, Springfield College in Illinois, Southern Illinois Univ. School of Medicine; new Capital Area Vocational

School.

**Recreation:** 33 parks; swimming, boating, skiing at 5 park on Lake Springfield; 4 public golf courses, tennis courts.

**Special events:** Illinois State Fair, Old Capitol Art Fai NCAA college division world series, International Carillo Festival, Midwest Charity Horse Show, LPGA Rail Go Classic; Springfield Redbirds AAA American Associatio baseball team.

---

## Springfield, Massachusetts

The World Almanac is sponsored in the Springfield area by The Springfield Union, Sunday Republican, an Daily News, 1860 Main Street, Springfield, MA 01101; phone (413) 787-2411. Union founded 1864; Republi can 1824; Daily News 1880; circulation, Union, 76,003; Republican 142,350; Daily News, 79,865; presiden Sidney R. Cook; publisher, David Starr; Union-Republican editor Arnold S. Friedman; Daily News editor Rich ard C. Garvey.

**Population:** 168,785 (city), 536,898 (metro); 3d in state (city), 4th in New England, 84th in U.S.; 76,081 employed in city.

**Area:** 33.1 sq. mi. in SW part of state; I-91 skirts city; Hampden County seat.

**Industry:** 231 manufacturing plants produce boxes, children's games, wallets, auto tires, handguns, plastics, envelopes, hair shampoo, chemicals, paper; among major employers Monsanto, Milton Bradley, Smith & Wesson, Breck.

**Commerce:** metro retail sales $1.74 billion; avg. household spendable income $14,482; Mass Mutual Life Ins. Co., number 10 in U.S.; Baystate West, a combined highrise shopping mall, office-hotel complex.

**Transportation:** Amtrak, 2 rail lines, 5 bus lines, Bradley International Airport (Hartford-Springfield) 18 miles south; major truck depot.

**Communications:** 3 TV, 9 radio stations.

**Medical facilities:** 6 major hospital complexes.

**Educational facilities:** college belt of N.E.; North Adam State, Williams, Smith, Hampshire, Amherst, Univ. of Ma sachusetts at Amherst, Mount Holyoke, Our Lady of th Elms, American International, Springfield, Western Ne England and Law School; Westfield State, Greenfield, an Holyoke community colleges, Springfield Technical Com munity College.

**Cultural facilities:** Stage West Theater; quadrangle comple 2 museums of art; library, natural history museum includin planetarium; 145 churches and 7 synagogues; Tanglewoo Festival, 155 parks; civic center.

**Sports:** Indians (AHL) hockey; Basketball Hall of Fame.

**History:** founded 1636 by William Pynchon; first U.S. mu ket developed at city's armory (now a U.S. landmark) 179 Springfield rifle developed in 1903 and produced here as w the Garand M-1 rifle.

**Further information:** Chamber of Commerce, 1500 Ma Street, Springfield, MA 01103.

---

## Syracuse, New York

The World Almanac is sponsored in the Syracuse area by the Herald-Journal, Clinton Square, P.O. Bo 4915, Syracuse, NY, 13221; telephone (315) 473-7700; founded Jan. 15, 1877, by Arthur Jenkins; circulatio 121,876 daily, 236,465 Sunday Herald-American Post Standard; publisher, Stephen Rogers; editor, William [ Cotter; sponsors camp scholarships and Christmas toy fund.

**Population:** 197,297 (city), 636,507 (metro), 5th in state, 66th in nation; 273,700 employed.

**Area:** 25.82 sq. mi. near center of state; interstate routes 90 and 81 intersect at Syracuse.

**Industry:** some 500 manufacturing plants produce electrical and non-electrical machinery, primary metals, food, transportation equipment, chemicals, pharmaceuticals, paper, candles, china; new $100 million Schlitz brewery, world's largest ever built at one time, opened in 1975 in suburban Lysander as did major Miller brewery north of city; major employers: General Electric, Carrier Corp., Crucible Steel, Crouse-Hinds, Allied Chemical.

**Commerce:** retail sales (1978 est.) $1.8 billion; average household spendable income (1978 est.) $17,939.

**Transportation:** 2 rail freight lines, Amtrak; 3 bus lines, 152 truck lines; 3 airlines.

**Communications:** 4 TV, 17 radio stations.

**Medical facilities:** 4 major hospital complexes.

**Cultural facilities:** Syracuse Univ., State Univ. College Environmental Science and Forestry, and Le Moyne, Mar Regina, and Onondaga community colleges; Everson M seum of Art; symphony; $22 million county office-cultur center.

**Sports:** Syracuse Univ. football; Chiefs (baseball).

**History:** first explored 1615 by French; salt deposits led area development, known as "Salt City;" "crossroads" sin Indian days; became city 1847.

**Further information:** Chamber of Commerce, One MON Plaza, Syracuse, NY 13202.

---

## Tallahassee, Florida

The World Almanac is sponsored in the north Florida-south Georgia Panhandle area by The Tallahasse Democrat, 227 N. Magnolia Drive, Tallahassee, FL 32302; (904) 599-2100, founded 1905; circulation 43,55 (morn), 49,654 Sunday; member Knight-Ridder Newspapers, Inc., W. H. Harwell Jr. president and gener manager; Richard Oppel, vice president and executive editor.

**Population:** 85,300 (city) 142,700 (metro); total employment 65,400.

**Area:** 26.14 sq. mi. between Gulf of Mexico and Georgia line; state capital and Leon County seat.

**Commerce:** 44% of economic base is state and local government; small manufacturers; agriculture only 1.1% of economic base; retail-wholesale center serving 17 county area; 3 shopping malls and 17 shopping centers containing 358 out-

lets; retail sales (1977) $571 million; effective buying incom per household is $17,152, 3d highest in state; 15 commerci banks (resources, $376 million) and 5 savings & loan (n sources $302 million).

**Transportation:** 3 major airlines, 2 commuter flight service one railroad, 5 motor carriers.

**Communications:** 11 radio, 10 TV stations by cable.

Medical facilities: major hospital, retardation hospital, university hospital.

Recreational facilities: 5 recreation centers, 10 playgrounds, 5 ball fields, 21 tennis courts; salt water fishing in Gulf of Mexico, bass fishing in Lake Jackson; deer, dove, quail, duck, geese hunting; 4 golf courses, PGA Tallahassee Open Invitational.

Other attractions: college athletic events at Florida State Univ., and Florida A&M; symphony, ballet, repertory theater, opera, touring plays, and art exhibits; 1845 historic capitol and 22-story capitol tower; Apalachicola National Forest; Junior Museum; Wakulla Springs, Maclay Gardens State Park, LeMoyne Art Gallery, Natural Bridge State Historic Memorial, Florida State Univ. "Flying High" Circus.

History: established as state capital 1823; Tallahassee means "old town" or "deserted fields" in Creek; area prospered with large plantations and antebellum mansions, many still standing.

Further information: Chamber of Commerce, P.O. Box 1639, Tallahassee, FL 32302. (904) 224-8116.

## Tampa, Florida

The World Almanac is sponsored in the Tampa Bay area by The Tampa Tribune and The Tampa Times, 202 S. Parker Street, Tampa, FL 33606; (813) 272-7711; Times founded 1893, Tribune 1894; combined circulation 200,568. D. T. Bryan, Chairman of the Board; A. S. Donnahoe, President; R. F. Pittman Jr., Publisher; J. Urbanski, Vice President/General Manager; J. Clendinen, Chairman of Editorial Board; P. Hogan, Tribune Managing Editor; B. Witwer, Times Managing Editor.

Population: 273,162 (city), 602,667 (county); total employed county 231,700 (civilian, non-agricultural employment).

Area: 84.45 sq. mi. (city), 1,062.0 sq. mi. (county) on Gulf of Mexico, halfway between the northern edge and southern tip of Florida; Hillsborough County seat.

Industry: Port of Tampa is the closest U. S. deepwater port to the Panama Canal and the 8th largest in the nation; total tonnage for 1977 reached 46.3 million (both imports and exports); principal export cargo, phosphate; Bone Valley formation - 30% of world's phosphate production, 75% of the U. S. output; Ybor City section well known for cigar manufacturing, Cuesta-Rey, Fuenta Arturo, Hav-A-Tampa, standard; strong shrimp industry, Singleton; beer breweries, Anheuser-Busch and Joseph Schlitz; only steel industry in Florida, Florida Steel Corp.; other industries here include Jim Walter Corp., General Telephone, Florida Mining & Materials, and Lykes Bros.

Commerce: retail sales for the county (1976) $1.947 billion; 11 banks with total assets (1977) of $2.280 billion; 8 savings and loans.

Transportation: 22 freight lines, Amtrak train service, Seaboard Coast Line Railroad Co.; 5 bus lines, Greyhound, Trailways; city-owned bus system expanding into county; 50 trucking lines; junction of I-75 and I-4; Tampa International airport, 5.8 million passengers in 1977, 9 major airlines and direct flights to Europe; Port of Tampa.

Communications: 6 TV and 21 radio stations; 2 daily newspapers.

Convention facilities: Curtis Hixon Hall, capacity Main Hall, 8,000 plus 10 other rooms; Tampa hotels and motels have over 10,000 guest rooms and over 125 meeting/banquet rooms with seating from 25 to 1,000.

New construction: Univ. of So. Fla. continuing expansion; continuing expansion of Busch Gardens ($10.0 million for 1978); Tampa's State Regional Office Bldg.; U.S. Homes support div.; phosphate mining and processing operation; visual arts facility; downtown redevelopment; home office for Shriners, Walden Lake complex; waterfront revitalization, City Hall expansion (quad block), Ybor Square in Ybor City expansion, Florida State fairgrounds expansion; county expressway expansion.

Medical facilities: 6 major hospitals.

Federal facilities: MacDill AFB, Federal Bldg.

Cultural facilities: Florida Gulf Coast Symphony, Tampa Bay Art Center, 3 museums, Tampa Theatre, Tampa Ballet Co.; $2.4 million library; community theatre and theatre companies, Gasparilla Art Fair.

Education: Univ. of So. Fla., Univ. of Tampa, Florida College, and Hillsborough Community College with 2 campuses.

Other attractions: Busch Gardens (#2 attraction in attendance in Florida), Lowry Park Zoo, Ybor City (Latin Quarter); 62 parks, 31 recreation areas, annual Gasparilla Pirate Invasion, site for Florida State Fair.

Sports: pro-football Tampa Bay Buccaneers with 71,500 capacity stadium, NASL (Soccer) Tampa Bay Rowdies, Tampa Tarpons (baseball farm team for the Cincinnati Reds), Cincinnati Reds spring training headquarters; greyhound racing, jai-alai.

History: Fort Brooke est. 1824 on site of present Tampa; incorporated 1885.

Further information: Greater Tampa Chamber of Commerce, 801 E. Kennedy Boulevard, Tampa, FL 33602; (813) 228-7777.

## Toledo, Ohio

The World Almanac is sponsored in the Toledo area by The Blade, 541 Superior Street, Toledo, OH 43660; phone (419) 259-6000; founded 1835; circulation, 170,650 daily, 208,174 Sunday; publishers Paul Block Jr. and William Block; associate publisher John D. Willey; editor Bernard Judy; executive editor Joseph O'Connor; managing editor William Rosenberg.

Population: 365,400 (city), 782,100 (metro), 5th in state, 40th in nation; total employed 300,000.

Area: 85.3 sq. mi. at juncture of Maumee River and Lake Erie, in northwestern Ohio; Lucas County seat.

Industry: glass, headquarters for Owens-Illinois, Owens Corning & Libbey-Owens-Ford; automotive parts, largest producer in nation, home of American Motors Jeep, Toledo Scale, and Haughton Elevator; largest petroleum refining center between Chicago and the East Coast.

Commerce: Port of Toledo is one of the prime bulk shipping ports on the Great Lakes, handling vast quantities of grain, coal, iron ore, and petroleum products; ranks 4th on Great Lakes and 23d in U.S.; total retail sales $2.44 billion; spendable income per household: $16,231.

Transportation: 9 railroads, 4 major airlines, 120 motor freight lines, 2 interstate bus lines; 13 major highways converge here, permitting the rapid flow of goods to almost 60% of the nation's consumers.

Communications: 4 TV, 12 radio stations and one cablevision company.

Medical facilities: 10 major hospital complexes, including the Medical College of Ohio Hospital.

Cultural facilities: Museum of Art with largest display of antique glass in the world; Peristyle used for the performing arts; symphony, opera company.

Education: Univ. of Toledo and its Community and Technical College; Michael J. Owens Technical College; Bowling Green State Univ.; Monroe Community College.

Other attractions: Municipal Zoo among top 10 in the nation; modern 2,500 seat Masonic Auditorium with a Great Hall annex.

Sports: Mud Hens, farm club of the Minnesota Twins, at the Lucas County Recreation Center.

History: founded in 1836; took its name from sister city, Toledo, Spain.

Further information: Convention and Vistors Bureau, 218 Huron, Toledo, OH 43604.

## Toronto, Ontario, Canada

The World Almanac is sponsored in the metropolitan Toronto area by The Toronto Star, One Yonge Stree Toronto, Ontario, M5E 1E6. (416) 367-2000; established 1892, Joseph E. Atkinson, publisher, 1899-1948; c culation daily 491,454; Saturday, 784,258, Sunday (est. Oct. 16, 1977), 275,923; chairman and publisher, B land H. Honderich; president, William A. Dimma; editor-in-chief, Martin Goodman. Canada's largest newspa per in circulation, display, and classified advertising lineage; winner of 38 national newspaper awards ar sponsor of the Santa Claus Fund and Fresh Air Fund.

**Population:** 663,822 (city), 2,145,243 (metro); largest city in Canada, 12th in North America; labor force 1.5 million.

**Area:** 241 sq. mi. on northwest shore of Lake Ontario; provincial capital.

**Industry:** Canada's leading commercial and industrial center; 6004 manufacturing establishments; value of 1977 factory shipments $17 billion; principal industries: slaughtering and meat packing, clothing, printing and publishing, machinery, electrical goods, furniture, food products, rubber goods, sheet metal products.

**Commerce:** retail sales (1977) $8.1 billion; headquarters for Eaton's and Simpson's, Canada's largest department stores; head offices of 10 trust companies and 3 of 9 federally chartered banks; Toronto Stock Exchange, 4th in North America, traded shares worth $6 billion in 1977; per capita disposable income $7,260.

**Transportation:** 10 railway lines carry 350 freight and passenger trains daily; 11,400 trucks use 12 major highways; Transit Commission carries 348 million passengers annually on 722 miles of routes including 32 miles of subway; 2.9 million tons of cargo from 26 nations unloaded (1977) at this major Great Lakes port; 46 airlines handle 11.2 million passengers annually at International Airport.

**Communications:** 6 TV stations including educational and French-language channels; 10 AM and 5 FM radio stations; 3 daily newspapers, 42 foreign language newspapers.

**New construction:** value of building permits (1977) $991.2 million; $250-million Eaton Centre with 300 shops to be completed 1979; $7 million community center for the deaf; $80 million downtown housing-commercial development will include concert hall.

**Medical facilities:** 26 active-treatment hospitals including renowned Hospital for Sick Children; special treatment centers: Clark Institute for Psychiatry, Addiction Research Centre, Ontario Crippled Children's Centre.

**Cultural facilities:** 37 alternate and cabaret theater groups, including Canada's largest children's theater; National Ballet of Canada and Canadian Opera Company perform in 3,200-seat O'Keefe Centre; symphony orchestra and Me delssohn Choir at Massey Hall; touring shows at Roy Alexandra Theatre; 82 public libraries, Royal Ontario M seum; Henry Moore collection of sculptures and drawings Art Gallery of Ontario.

**Education:** 2 universities, York and Toronto, Canada's la est (1977-78 enrollment: 44,740); Ryerson Polytechnical I stitute, 4 colleges of applied arts and technology, 2 teache colleges, Royal Conservatory of Music, Ontario College Art, Osgoode Hall Law School.

**Recreation:** Canadian National Exhibition, world's bigge annual fair; Ontario Place, 100 acres of offshore islands wi restaurants, marina, and 1,000-seat Cinesphere for fil showings; Toronto Islands have 3 yacht clubs, 560 acres beaches and picnic grounds; Harborfront, 86-acre spor arts, and entertainment park.

**Convention facilities:** Canada's top convention cent 221,407 visitors attended 490 conventions in 1977 and spe $66.5 million; total rooms 19,000.

**Sports:** 9 public golf courses; thoroughbred and harness ra ing; NHL Maple Leafs play in 16,435-seat Gardens; T onto Blue Jays play AL baseball and Argonauts play Can dian Football League games in 54,000-seat Exhibiti Stadium.

**Other attractions:** Ontario Science Centre, designed for pa ticipation and involvement; Black Creek Pioneer Villag living displays of Upper Canada; McMichael Conservatio collection of works by Canada's famed Group of Se painters; Metro Zoo has 500 species roaming 5 continer areas covering 700 acres; CN Tower, world's tallest fre standing structure, has revolving restaurant, sightseein decks.

**History:** town of York founded 1793 on site of French fo as capital of British Colony of Upper Canada; incorporate as city 1834 and named Toronto from Indian word for mee ing place.

**Further information:** Convention and Tourist Bureau, Tc onto Eaton Centre, Toronto, Ontario, M5B 2H1.

## Tucson, Arizona

The World Almanac is sponsored in the Tucson area by The Arizona Daily Star, 4850 S. Park Avenue, Tu son, AZ 85726; (602) 294-4433; founded 1877 as a weekly, Michael E. Pulitzer, editor and publisher; Willia J. Woestendiek, executive editor; Frank E. Johnson, managing editor; Stephen E. Auslander, editorial pag editor; Frank Delehanty, business manager; William Waters, public affairs editor; sponsors Sportsmen's Fur for less-chance youngsters.

**Population:** 475,000 est. for Greater Tucson; 305,525 within city limits, 453,900 in Pima County (as of latest count, July, 1976, by Arizona Dept. of Economic Security;) 175,400 employed in county, out of total civilian labor force of 186,500.

**Area:** Sonoran Desert of southern Arizona, elev. 2,500 ft.; Santa Catalina Mts. immediately N and E reach 9,000 ft.; Pima County seat.

**Industry:** Hughes Aircraft, IBM, Gates Learjet, Davis-Monthan AFB, and various aircraft reclamation plants handling surplus craft from Davis-Monthan; electronics, light manufacturing, and tourism; center of the "copper circle" — hundreds of millions of dollars have been invested in the area by Anaconda, Duval, American Smelting and Refining, Kennecott, Magma, Pima and other mining operations.

**Transportation:** International Airport served by AeroMexico and Hughes AirWest (to and from Mexico), most major airlines nationally and Cochise Airlines within Arizona; 3 smaller airports; 2 national, one local bus line; Southern Pacific Railroad; trucks.

**Communications:** 2 newspapers; 5 TV and 18 radio stations.

**Medical facilities:** 10 hospitals, including Arizona Medical Center, which has teaching hospital.

**Climate:** mild, dry; rare freezing temperatures in winte summer brings some rain, mostly after July 1, and temper tures of about 100° F.

**Culture:** Univ. of Arizona; Tucson Museum of Art; Tucs Symphony; Arizona Civic Theater; Tucson Civic Balle many musical, drama, and dance groups; Tucson Bo Chorus, Los Changuitos Feos mariachi group provide loc flavor.

**Convention facilities:** convention center accommodat 10,000 theater-style in arena; sit-down functions 5,00 meeting-rooms 1,000 theater-style; music hall, 2,300; conti uous exhibit space 64,000 sq. ft.

**Sports:** Toros, Pacific Coast League farm team of Tex Rangers; Cleveland Indians spring training site; Tucs Open golf tournament; various pro tennis tournament PAC-10 collegiate athletics.

**History:** Presidio of Tucson est. 1775; Mission San Xavi del Bac founded nearby by Rev. Eusebio Francisco Kin S.J., who first visited area in 1692.

**Further information:** Tucson Chamber of Commerce, P. Box 991, Tucson, AZ 85702.

## Tulsa, Oklahoma

The World Almanac is sponsored in the Tulsa area by The Tulsa Tribune, 315 So. Boulder, Tulsa, OK 102; phone (918) 582-1101; founded 1904 as The Tulsa Democrat, renamed the Tulsa Tribune in 1920; circulation, 88,210; editor Jenkin Lloyd Jones; managing editor Gordon Fallis; executive editor Jenkin Lloyd Jones Jr.

**Population:** 352,000 (city), 422,000 (metro); 275,000 employed.

**Area:** 181.26 sq. mi. on Arkansas River at 96th meridian in Tulsa, Osage, and Rogers counties.

**Industry:** manufacturing, which includes aerospace, metal fabrication, and oil, provides jobs for 21% of the SMSA work force; in 1976, there were 48,000 mfg. employees including 32,100 production workers; total payroll was almost $97 million; of these totals, 34,200 mfg. employees worked in the city, earning $458 million; retail trade employs 17% of Tulsa SMSA workers, and 19% are in the service industry. Top employers are American Airlines, Cities Service, Sun McDonnell Douglas, Rockwell International, The Williams Companies, and C-E Natco. These top 7 provide round 16,650 jobs to Tulsans.

**Commerce:** retail sales (1976) $1.527 billion; 17 banks (reserves $1.914 billion), 10 savings and loan assns.; per capita income, $4,565.

**Transportation:** Tulsa Port of Catoosa, nation's most inland port, head of Arkansas-Verdigris navigation channel, total '76 barge tonnage, 745,600; 4 rail freight lines; 3 bus lines; 4 truck lines; 6 airlines with 1,516,543 passenger move-

ments (1976).

**Communications:** 2 daily newspapers, 3 TV and 15 radio stations.

**New construction:** building permits valued at $241 million (1977).

**Medical facilities:** 5 hospitals, 2,250 beds; Osteopathic College, Univ. of Oklahoma medical school branch.

**Federal facilities:** District Corps of Engineers, 1,200 employees; hq. Southwestern Power Administration.

**Cultural facilities:** Univ. of Tulsa, Oral Roberts Univ., Tulsa junior college, Philharmonic, opera, civic ballet, 2 art museums, including Thomas Gilcrease Institute of American History and Art.

**Convention facilities:** Assembly Center seats 10,000; 370 conventions with 145,525 attendance (1976).

**Sports:** Tulsa Roughnecks, pro soccer; Tulsa Ice Oilers, pro hockey in the Central Hockey League; Tulsa Dillers, farm team for the Texas Rangers; intercollegiate athletics; 4 public and 7 country club golf courses.

**Further information:** Metropolitan Tulsa Chamber of Commerce, 616 S. Boston Avenue, Tulsa, OK 74119.

## Vancouver, British Columbia, Canada

The World Almanac is sponsored in the Vancouver area by The Vancouver Sun, 2250 Granville Street, Vancouver, B.C., V6H 3G2; phone (604) 732-2111; founded 1886; circulation 240,453; publisher Stu Keate, editorial director Bruce Hutchison; sponsors world's largest free Salmon Derby, Sun Family Pops Concerts; Sun Match Play Golf, Sun Tournament of Soccer Champions, and many other community services.

**Population:** 410,188 (city) 1,805,242 (metro area), first in province, 3d in Canada.

**Area:** 44 sq. mi. on the Pacific coast at the mouth of the north arm of the Fraser River; scenic beauty of the city accented by the towering, snowcapped Coast Mountains to the north and rich greenery of agricultural land to the east and south.

**Industry:** 98 miles of waterfront, stretching up Burrard Inlet the largest cargo port on the Pacific and Canada's 2d busiest, with 47.1 million tons handled in 1977; major cargos: grain, lumber, coal, mineral ore, chemicals, and manufactured goods; tourism a major industry with an estimated 6.9 million visitors bringing in $600 million in 1977.

**Commerce:** retail sales; 3.5 billion in 1977; value of shares traded on the Vancouver stock exchange $544.4 million in '77.

**Transportation:** western terminus of Canada's 2 national railways, Canadian National Railway and Canadian Pacific; headquarters of provincially operated British Columbia railway, which is linked to the U.S. by Amtrak along the Burlington Northern Railway right-of-way; 3 major long-distance bus carriers, Provincial Stage Lines, Trailways, and Greyhound; International Airport served by 7 major airlines handled more than 7.8 million passengers in 1977.

**Communications:** 11 AM, 5 FM radio stations; 4 local TV stations; also 5 U.S. network TV outlets.

**Medical facilities:** General and St. Paul's are largest hospitals; also Shaughnessy in Vancouver, Royal Columbian in New Westminster, Burnaby General, Lion's Gate in North Vancouver and Riverview Psychiatric Hospital.

**Cultural facilities:** symphony orchestra, opera association, several professional theater groups, Centennial and Maritime Museums and Art Gallery; Queen Elizabeth Theatre and The Orpheum are the major art facilities.

**Other attractions:** Pacific National Exhibition, Gastown, Chinatown, the H.R. MacMillan Planetarium, Bloedel Conservatory, aquarium, 1,000 acre Stanley Park, zoo, Capilano Suspension Bridge, VanDusen Botanical Garden, Park & Tilford Garden, Lynn Canyon Ecology Centre, Heritage Village, 18 golf courses, Grouse Mountain, Cypress Bowl and Mount Seymour ski areas; Univ. of British Columbia, Simon Fraser Univ.; 18 beaches, fresh and salt water fishing.

**Sports:** professional teams; B.C. Lions (CFL football); Canucks (NHL hockey); Whitecaps (NASL soccer); Vancouver Canadians (PCL baseball); Exhibition Park racetrack (thoroughbreds); Cloverdale Raceway (harness racing), and several amateur teams and sports activities.

**History:** discovered by Spaniards, first mapped 1791; taken possession by Capt. George Vancouver for British 1792; Hudson's Bay Company post established early 1800s; city incorporated 1886.

## Washington, District of Columbia

The World Almanac is sponsored in the Washington, D.C., area by the Washington Star (a subsidiary of Time Inc.), 225 Virginia Avenue SE, Washington, DC 20061; phone (202) 484-5000; founded Dec. 16, 1852; chairman of the board James R. Shepley; publisher George W. Hoyt; editor Murray J. Gart; executive editor Sidney Epstein; awards received by newspaper and staff include 8 Pulitzer Prizes.

**Population:** (1977) 693,200 (city), 3,072,100 (metro area including D.C. and parts of Md. and Va.).

**Area:** 67 sq. mi. (city), 2,812 (metro) at head of tidewater of Potomac R., 30 miles from Chesapeake Bay, 130 miles from Atlantic O., 240 miles from NYC.

**Industry:** U.S. Capital, federal government employs 411,000 civilian and military personnel (1977), total labor force 1,541,939 (1977); government related activity, law, journalism, professional and trade associations, unions, lobbying groups, and scientists provide another large portion of employment base; tourism a major industry.

**Commerce:** metro area average household spendable income, $22,991 (1977); metro area retail sales for 1977, $11.1 billion.

**Transportation:** circumferential highway; 100-mile rapid rail transit system to be completed 1982 with 23 miles in city and nearby suburbs now open; Metroliner to New York; long distance rail and bus service; National, Dulles, and Baltimore-Washington International airports; National Visitors Center at Union Station; Concorde service at Dulles.

**Communications:** several national magazines; news bureaus of major newspapers, wire services, and TV networks; 21 FM, 23 AM radio stations; 7 TV stations; 2 daily metropolitan newspapers, over 40 weekly newspapers.

**Educational facilities:** American, Catholic, District of Columbia, Georgetown, George Washington, and Howard universities, and Gallaudet College; nearby Univ. of Maryland and George Mason Univ.

**Medical facilities:** major medical research center; National

Institutes of Health, Walter Reed Hospital, Bethesda Na-Medical Center; about 40 general hospitals and 3 teachi hospitals.

**Cultural facilities:** Kennedy Center with 3 performa halls and Wolf Trap Farm Park in nearby Vienna, Va., pr ent major concerts, ballet, opera; Arena Stage, Ford's Th tre, National Theater, many community theater grou Smithsonian Institution; Corcoran Gallery of Art, Libr of Congress; D.C. Public Library with 23 branches.

**Sports:** pro sports include football (Redskins), basketb (Bullets), hockey (Capitals), soccer (Diplomats).

**History:** named for George Washington and Christoph Columbus; Georgetown in the District of Columbia first s tled 1665, then annexed by the city when D.C. created seat of federal government by Act of Congress 1790; g erned by elected mayor and city council with budget c trolled by Congress.

**Further information:** Convention and Visitors Bureau, 1 20th Street NW, Washington, DC 20036.

---

### West Palm Beach, Florida

The World Almanac is sponsored in Palm Beach County, Florida, by Palm Beach Newspapers, Inc., 2751 Dixie Highway, West Palm Beach, FL 33405; phone (305) 833-7411; publisher of The Palm Beach Post a Times; combined daily circulation 117,459; Sunday, The Palm Beach Post-Times, 129,123.

P lation: (1977) 64,934 (city), 587,095 (metro); total la-t force 196,400.

**Area:** 43.5 sq. mi. (city), 2,023 sq. mi. (metro); southeast Fla., 8th largest county east of the Mississippi; 2d largest county in Fla., Palm Beach County seat, on top of Fla.'s "Gold Coast."

**Industry:** Pratt & Whitney Aircraft, IBM, U.S. Sugar Corp., Atlantic Sugar Assn., Osceola Farms Co., Sugar Cane Growers Coop. of Fla., Gulf & Western Food Products Co., American Foods Inc. farms, Duda & Sons Coop. Assoc. farms, Rinker Materials Corp., Solitron Devices Inc., NCI Inc., Perry Oceanographics Inc., Rel Reeves Inc., and tourism.

**Commerce:** 48 general service banks, 14 savings and loans, total assets $4 billion (1977); retail sales $2.49 billion (1977); per capita EBI $6,642 (1977).

**Transportation:** Palm Beach Intl. Airport; 2 rail freight lines; Amtrak; Greyhound, Trailways bus lines; Palm Beach County Transportation Authority (bus); 15 truck lines; Port of Palm Beach for freight shipping.

**Communications:** 2 TV, 13 radio stations, cable TV, 3 daily newspapers, 1 winter-season daily, 6 weeklies, society journal magazine, 7 special publications.

**Medical facilities:** 12 hospitals, 2,108 beds.

**Cultural facilities:** Society of Four Arts, Henry Morris Flagler Museum; Morikami Museum and Park, 4 comm nity theaters, 2 legitimate theaters, 3 college theaters, W Palm Beach Auditorium, and Lion Country Safari.

**Education:** Florida Atlantic Univ. (Jr. & Sr.), Palm Bea Jr. College, North & South Tech. Ed. centers, and Pa Beach Atlantic College.

**Sports:** West Palm Beach Expos minor league baseball, lanta Braves spring training; greyhound racing, jai-alai fr ton, Gold Coast Barracudas semi-pro football team, 74 g courses, 2 polo fields, county fairgrounds, auto race tra tennis, water sports, and hunting.

**History:** founded late 1800s by workers and business peo associated with the construction of the famed Royal Poin ana Hotel in Palm Beach by Henry Morrison Flagler w set aside 48 homesites on the western shore of Lake Wor Inc. 1894.

**Further information:** Area Planning Board of Palm Bea County, 2300 Palm Beach Lakes Boulevard, WPB, 33407; Chamber of Commerce, 501 N. Flagler Drive, WF FL 33401.

---

### Wichita, Kansas

The World Almanac is sponsored in the Wichita area by the Wichita Eagle and Beacon Publishing Co., In 825 East Douglas, Wichita, KS 67202; phone (316) 268-6000; founded 1872 as weeklies; became daili 1884; consolidated 1961; circulation: Eagle (morn) 126,980, Beacon (eve) 43,971, Sunday Eagle and Beac 183,884; Britt Brown, chairman; Eugene Lambert, president and publisher; W. Davis Merritt Jr., executive e tor; Joe Harper, managing editor.

**Population:** Jan., 1977, (city) 263,499, first in state; (SMSA) 383,800, first in state; SMSA employment 204,150.

**Area:** (city) 95.98 sq. mi. in Sedgwick County at juncture of Big and Little Arkansas rivers; Sedgwick County seat. Elevation 1,280 feet, average rainfall 30.06; Mean temp.; Jan.—31.5, July—80.3.

**Industry:** 60% of free world aviation aircraft is manufactured in Wichita. Aircraft employment: Beech (city) 7,200 (total) 9,524; Cessna 12,200; Gates Learjet 2,300; Boeing 8,600; other fields: meat processing, flour milling, grain storage, petroleum refining, natural gas, chemicals; largest non-aero manufacturer Coleman Co.

**Commerce:** wholesale-retail center for large part of Kansas and northern Oklahoma; metro (SMSA) retail sales (1977) $1.8 billion; bank resources (18 city banks) $1.6 billion; median household income $12,650.

**Transportation:** 4 major rail freight lines, Amtrak; Continental bus lines; 54 truck lines; 8 major highways; Mid-

Continent Airport, 5 airlines, averages 622 air movemen per day; National Flying Farmers headquarters.

**Communications:** 4 TV, 7 AM and 6 FM radio stations.

**Medical facilities:** world's largest speech and hearing reh bilitation center (Institute of Logopedics); 5 hospital co plexes including VA installation.

**Federal facility:** McConnell Air Force Base.

**Educational facilities:** Wichita State University and WS Medical Branch; Friends University; Kansas Newman C lege.

**Cultural facilities:** Wichita Symphony Orchestra; Omn phere (Planetarium); Wichita Art Museum; Wichita Art A sociation (museum) and Children's Theater; Century II a ditorium and convention complex; community theater; c library; 443 churches. Mid-America All Indian Center.

**Other attractions:** city-county zoo; 67 parks; recreati lakes; Cow Town (restoration of 1872 Wichita); Histori Museum; National Junior Livestock Show.

**Sports:** Aeros, Chicago Cubs farm team. National Baseb

ngress (semi-pro) headquarters and tournaments.
story: founded 1870, became railhead (shipping point) for
tle herds driven up Chisholm Trail; named after Wichita

Indians.
**Further information:** Chamber of Commerce, 350 West Douglas, Wichita, KS 67202.

## Wilmington, Delaware

The World Almanac is sponsored in Delaware by The News-Journal Company, 831 Orange Street, Wilmington, DE 19899, (302) 573-2000, publisher of The Morning News, Evening Journal, and Saturday News urnal, circulation 136,221; The Sunday News Journal circulation 96,000; member Gannett Group; president d publisher, Brian Donnelly; executive vice president and general manager, Frederick Walter; vice president d executive editor, Frederick W. Hartmann; editor of the editorial page, James E. O'Brien.

pulation: 73,000 (Wilmington), 418,000 (New Castle unty), 537,000 (metro); Wilmington is largest city in te.

ea: 15.1 sq. mi. at the confluence of the Brandywine, ristina, and Delaware rivers.

dustry: one of the largest chemical and petrochemical cens in the U.S.; autos, utilities, steel; about 400 manufacturg firms, offices for many insurance firms and holding comnies.

mmerce: port is major auto importing center; retail sales MSA, 1978) $2.1 billion, est. 1978 income in SMSA $3.4 lion, est. 1978 per capita median income in SMSA, $2.1 lion; state has 12 state-chartered commercial banks, 19 te-chartered savings and loans, 5 national banks, 2 mual savings banks, 2 federally chartered savings and loans.

ansportation: 2 major railway lines, 3 bus lines, 35 motor ight carriers, airport.

mmunications: one public TV station; 6 radio stations.

edical facilities: Wilmington Medical Center (4 divisions); private hospitals; Alfred I. duPont Institute.

**Cultural attractions:** Grand Opera House, Winterthur Museum, Hagley Museum, Old Brandywine Village, Fort Christina Park; Wilmington Symphony Orchestra, Wilmington Opera Society, Wilmington Drama League, Museum of Natural History; Univ. of Delaware (Newark), Delaware State College (Dover), Delaware Technical and Community College.

**Sports:** Delaware Park, Brandywine Raceway, Dover Downs (Dover), Harrington Raceway (Harrington), Univ. of Delaware football.

**Other attractions:** Rehoboth Beach; Longwood Gardens and Brandywine River Museum (both in nearby Pa.); several state parks and recreational areas; historic old New Castle; Hillendale Museum.

**History:** Founded as Fort Christina in 1638; named for Queen of Sweden; name changed to Willington in 1731 and then to Wilmington in 1739 in honor of the Earl of Wilmington; it is the first city in the first state of the union.

**Further information:** Delaware State Chamber of Commerce, 1102 West Street, Wilmington, DE 19801.

## Windsor, Ontario, Canada

The World Almanac is sponsored in Windsor and a large part of southwestern Ontario including Essex, ent, and Lambton counties, by The Windsor Star (cir. 88,362), 167 Ferry Street, Windsor, Ontario, N9A 4M5; division of Southam Press Limited; published daily since 1890 (present name since 1957); publisher R.M. earson; general manager A.H. Fast; editor G.C. Morgan.

pulation: 195,800 (city), 271,200 (metro), 540,000 (triunty); 11th largest in Canada; 4th largest in Ontario; total ployed 111,000.

ea: 50 sq. mi., one-half mile across Detroit River from troit, Mich.; largest Canadian city on U.S.-Canada borr.

dustry: autos and feeder plants, more than 25% national oduction (Chrysler, Ford, GM); tool and die shops; alcolic beverages (home office Hiram Walker and Sons); food ocessing (H.J. Heinz, Green Giant); pharmaceutical pplies (Wyeth Ltd., G.E. Jamieson Ltd.); salt mining; zinc d plastic die-casting; agriculture (rich producer early vegebles) tomatoes, corn, soybeans, peaches, tobacco; tourism argest port of entry in nation for U.S. vistors).

mmerce: retail sales $686.2 million; personal disposable come $1,823.7 million; average weekly income $287.90; 6 anks, 74 branches; 10 trust companies; 11 loan companies.

ransportation: 6 rail lines, 2 airlines; linked to Detroit by spension bridge and underwater tunnel; western terminus

Highway 401; major harbor terminal (deep water port); private marinas, yacht club, municipal bus line.

**Communications:** one daily newspaper; 6 radio, 1 TV outlet; access to Detroit's 50 radio and 6 TV outlets; one monthly magazine.

**New construction:** $105. million in 1978.

**Cultural facilities:** Univ. of Windsor, enrollment 6,755; St. Clair Community College, enrollment 4,500; Light Opera Association; Art Gallery of Windsor; Windsor Symphony Orchestra; Hiram Walker Museum; Fort Malden National Historic Park and Museum, Amherstburg; public libraries; Cleary Auditorium and Convention Centre.

**Other attractions:** 96 parks and playgrounds, sunken gardens; close access to Great Lakes resort areas; site of International Freedom Festival; access to Detroit Ethnic Festival.

**Further information:** Chamber of Commerce, 500 Riverside Drive West; Tourist Information, 135 Ouellette Avenue, both Windsor, Ontario.

## Winnipeg, Manitoba, Canada

The World Almanac is sponsored in the Winnipeg area by the Winnipeg Free Press, 300 Carlton Street, innipeg, Man., Canada; phone (204) 943-9331; founded 1872; daily circulation 140,000; publisher Richard . Malone; general manager R.H. Shelford; editor Peter McLintock; managing editor Don Nicol; the newspaer and its staff have received numerous journalism awards.

pulation: 560,874.

ea: 224 sq. mi. surrounding junction of Red and Assiniine rivers, near center of North America; capital of the ovince of Manitoba.

dustry: manufacturing and agriculture are the largest urce of jobs; 850 establishments, 40,700 employees; value

of factory shipments $2.09 billion.

**Commerce:** retail sales over $1.6 billion in 1977; Winnipeg Commodity Exchange only gold futures market in Canada; headquarters Canada Grains Council, Canadian Grain Commission, Canadian Wheat Board.

**Transportation:** International Airport served by 8 airlines, 2 national railways, Via-Rail passenger service, one rail line to U.S.; 5 national and regional bus lines; major trucking hub.

**Communications:** 9 TV channels, 4 stations; 12 radio stations.

**New construction:** valued $645.3 million in 1977, compared with $547.5 million in 1976.

**Medical facilities:** one of Canada's largest medical teaching centers; research in immunology, transplant-tissue rejection, cancer, blood diseases, respiratory diseases, endocrinology, neo-natal, pre-natal medicine; of Manitoba's 85 active treatment hospitals, 13 are in Winnipeg, including 2 major teaching centers plus University of Manitoba Rh Inst.; new 300-plus bed Seven Oaks Hospital to be completed in 1980.

**Federal facilities:** passport office, Canada Mint.

**Cultural facilities:** art gallery, Royal Winnipeg Ballet, contemporary dancers, Winnipeg Symphony Orchestra, Manitoba Chamber Orchestra, Manitoba Opera Association, Manitoba Theatre Centre, Cercle Moliere, Museum of Man and Nature, summer Rainbow Stage, Manitoba theater workshop, over 18 amateur theater groups.

**Educational facilities:** Univ. of Manitoba with 4 affiliat colleges, Univ. of Winnipeg, and Red River Commun College.

**Sports:** Blue Bombers (Canadian Football League), Win peg Jets (WHA), Assiniboia Downs race track.

**Convention facilities:** Winnipeg Convention Centre in dow town handles up to 5,000 delegates.

**Other attractions:** major zoo at Assiniboine Park; R River exhibition, multi-cultural Folklorama festival ea summer; French Canadian winter carnival in St. Bonifa planetarium.

**History:** first colony, Lord Selkirk Settlers, 1812; Incorp rated Nov. 8, 1873; on Jan. 1, 1972 amalgamation of government replacing 7 cities, 4 urban municipalities, town, and a metropolitan government.

**Additional information:** Chamber of Commerce, 700 — Lombard Ave; Tourist Information, 101 Legislative Bld and Tourist and Convention Association of Manitoba, 2 — 375 York Avenue.

## Winston-Salem, North Carolina

The World Almanac is sponsored in the Piedmont Triad area by the Winston-Salem Journal and The Ser nel, 416-420 N. Marshall Street, Winston-Salem, NC 27102, phone 919-727-7211; Sentinel founded 185 Journal 1897; brought under one ownership in 1926; now an affiliate of Media General Inc.; general manage Thomas E. Waldrop; publisher, Joe Doster.

**Population:** 144,000 (city); 230,000 (Forsyth County); 1978 est.

**Area:** 61.34 square miles (city); 419 square miles (county); in north central North Carolina; Forsyth County seat.

**Industry:** R. J. Reynolds Industries with diversified interests in tobacco, food, shipping, oil, packaging; Western Electric Co.; Jos. Schlitz Brewery; Westinghouse; Hanes Corp., Hanes Dye and Finishing Co.; Brenner Industries, Bahnson, Graveley Corp, Dennis Inc., Wachovia Corp.

**Commerce:** total retail sales county (1977) $1.3 billion; part of the Piedmont Triad which, with Greensboro and High Point, comprise a rapidly growing industrial and business area.

**Transportation:** headquarters for Piedmont Airlines at Smith Reynolds Airport; city also served by regional airport with 4 airlines, 2 bus lines and 54 motor freight carriers.

**Communications:** 4 TV, 10 radio stations.

**Medical facilities:** Bowman Gray School of Medicine of Wake Forest Univ., Baptist, Forsyth Memorial, Medical Park and other treatment centers and clinics.

**Cultural facilities:** one of the nation's first arts counc formed in 1949; N.C. School of the Arts, Wake Fore Univ., Salem College, Winston-Salem State Univ.; Old S lem, restoration of colonial town as it was between 1766 a 1830.

**Convention facilities:** Hyatt House hotel complex sits acro from the Benton Convention Center; hotels and motels o about 2,400 rooms.

**Recreation:** more than 50 public parks, 10 community ce ters, 10 swimming centers, fishing and boating in Winst and Salem lakes; 17 golf courses including Tanglewood.

**Sports:** Red Sox, Carolina League farm club of Boston R Sox; stock car racing; Wake Forest football at Groves st dium; Atlantic Coast Conference basketball at Memor Coliseum.

**History:** Salem founded 1766 by members of the Moravi Church; Winston, 1849; merged in 1913.

**Further information:** Chamber of Commerce, 2640 N. Ma shall Street, Winston-Salem, NC 27102

## Yakima, Washington

The World Almanac is sponsored in the Yakima area by the Yakima Herald-Republic (morning and evenin Mon.-Fri.) (mornings Sat.-Sun.), 114 North Fourth Street, Yakima, WA 98909; phone (509) 248-1251; founde in 1903 as the Yakima Republic, given present name in 1970; circulation 39,176 daily and 43,434 Sunda publisher James E. Tonkin, editorial page editor J. M. (Tom) Thomas, managing editor Stephen M. Kent.

**Population:** 51,100 (1977 est.); average monthly work force 73,460 (county).

**Area:** Yakima County seat, latitude 46° 34′ north, longitude 120° 32′ west, altitude 1,052 feet; located in southcentral Washington, an area of rich volcanic soil, 11.78 sq. mi. in area; 142 miles southeast of Seattle, 146 miles south of Canadian border.

**Industry:** agriculture, timber, first in the nation in production of apples, hops, mints; first in number of fruit trees.

**Commerce:** (1977) retail sales $558 million, EBI per household $12,689, postal receipts $3.3 million, $487 million Yakima Clearing House bank deposits.

**Transportation:** Hughes Airwest and Cascade Airways, Burlington Northern, Union Pacific railroads; Amtrak, Greyhound; Interstate 82, Highways 12 and 97.

**Communications:** one daily, one weekly newspaper, 4 TV, 8 radio stations.

**New construction:** 1,037 building permits totalling over $22 million issued in 1977.

**Medical facilities:** 3 hospitals with 460 beds, 150 physicians, 11 osteopaths, 64 dentists, 13 optometrists.

**Federal facilities:** U.S. Army Firing Center, 409 permanent personnel trains active and reserve units on 263,131 acre U.S. Army, Marine, and Navy reserve facilities, U.S. Pos Service regional center.

**Cultural facilities:** Yakima Valley Museum, Yakima Vall Regional Library, Allied Arts Council, Yakima Sympho and Chorus, Little Theater, Capitol Theater; over churches.

**Education:** Yakima Valley College, J.M. Perry Institu Yakima Business College; 7 public school districts in ar around city; 5 parochial schools; St. Elizabeth Health Sc ences Library.

**Sports and Recreation:** 6 theaters; 6 drive-ins, 2 histor trolleys, hunting and fishing, skiing in Cascade Mountai 45 minutes from city, golf, 30 tennis courts, 9 swimmi pools, 31 parks, auto racing, horse racing, youth baseba softball, Central Washington Fair.

**Convention facilities:** Yakima Center, over 1,400 mot units.

**History:** Founded Jan. 27, 1886 as North Yakima on rou of Northern Pacific Railroad.

**Further information:** Greater Yakima Chamber of Con merce, P.O. Box 1490, Yakima, WA 98907.

## Youngstown, Ohio

The World Almanac is sponsored in the Youngstown area by The Vindicator, Vindicator Square, Youngs-wn, OH 44501; phone (216) 747-1471; founded 1863 by J. H. Odell; Wm. F. Maag began daily Sept. 25, ᴽ89; daily circulation 100,324, Sunday 156,657; president, publisher, general manager William J. Brown; ad-ᵣtising manager William Mittler; managing editor Ann N. Przelomski.

**ᵖulation:** 140,909 (city) Ohio's 7th largest; 536,836 ᴬetro) 63d largest in U.S.; Mahoning County seat.

**ᵉa:** 35 sq. mi. in northeastern Ohio at juncture of Ohio ᵣnpike, I-80, and Ohio Rt. 11.

**ᵈustry:** historically a strong iron and steel center, still im-ᵣtant producer with Youngstown Sheet & Tube, Republic ᵉel, and U.S. Steel; local steel supplied to big nearby ᵃnts of General Motors Packard Electric Div. in Warren ᵈ GMAD plant in Lordstown, where Chevrolet Monzas, ᵃs, and other GM models are assembled; GF Business ᵠuipment sells office furnishings world wide; Commercial ᵉaring does world-wide tunnel frame and hydraulics busi-ᵉs; other fabricators use local steel, rubber.

**ᵒmmerce:** wholesale-retail center for large area of northeast ᵃio, western Penna.; retail sales of metro area (est.) over .7 billion; (est.) value added by manufacturing $2.4 bil-ᵅn; average spendable family income $16,773.

**ᵉw construction:** $88 million in 1977.

**ᵣansportation:** truck transport center with 95 motor freight ᵣminals; rail lines; airport served by 2 major airlines, head-ᵠarters for Beckett Aviation, largest fleet of executive air-ᵃft in U.S.

**Communications:** 4 TV stations, all major networks and PBS; 9 radio stations.

**Medical facilities:** Northeastern Ohio Universities College of Medicine, 6 large hospitals in area.

**Federal facilities:** U.S. Air Force Reserve base flying tactical fighters at airport; regional post office; army and navy reserve centers.

**Cultural facilities:** symphony orchestra with downtown bldg., ballet guild, Youngstown Playhouse in own modern bldg., Butler Institute of American Art.

**Educational facilities:** Youngstown State Univ. with over 15,500 students and graduate program; Penn-Ohio Junior College; Youngstown College of Business and Professional Drafting; 55 public and parochial schools; branches of Kent State Univ. in nearby Warren, Salem, and East Liverpool.

**Recreational facilities:** in city, 10 parks, 44 playgrounds, golf course, 6 swimming pools; Mill Creek Park with 2,383 acres; 4 large reservoirs in area for recreation, many golf courses.

**Further information:** Youngstown Area Chamber of Commerce, 200 Wick Bldg., Youngstown, OH 44503.

---

# Washington, Capital of the U.S.

## The Capitol

The United States Capitol has presented an entirely new east ᵗral front since 1961. That portion was extended 32 ft. 6 in. and ᵖroduced in Georgia marble. The extension added 100 rooms and ᵃst $11.4 million. The original wall of Virginia sandstone became ᵃ inner wall.

Dr. William Thornton, an amateur architect, submitted a plan ᵣ the Capitol in the spring of 1793 that won him $500 and a city ᵗ. The design consisted of a center section topped with a low ᵊme and on either side were wings to accomodate the House and ᵃnate that measured about 126 ft. by 120 ft. George Washington ᵈ the cornerstone Sept. 18, 1793 with Masonic ceremonies and in ᵥv. 1800 Congress met in that north or Senate wing. Also housed ᵗ that small wing were the Supreme Court, other local courts, and ᵉ Library of Congress.

The south, or House wing, was completed in 1807 under the di-ᶜtion of Benjamin H. Latrobe. At the time the Capitol was ᵣned by the British in 1814 the Capitol consisted of these 2 ᵣngs joined by a wooden walkway. The interiors were gutted by ᵉ fire and nearly 5 laborious years were needed to rebuild the ᵃpitol. It was occupied again in 1819 and the central portion with ᵊ low copper-covered wooden dome was completed in 1829 by the ᵉ architect of the Capitol, Charles Bulfinch.

The present Senate and House wings and the iron dome were ᵈsigned and constructed by Thomas U. Walter, the 4th architect ᵗ the Capitol, between 1851-1863. The House moved into its ᵃmber Dec. 16, 1857 and the Senate Jan. 4, 1859. These moves ᵃabled the Supreme Court to occupy the Old Senate Chamber ᵒm 1860-1935 when it moved into its own building. The Old Hall ᵗ the House became Statuary Hall.

Recently those original chambers have been restored and are ᵖen to the public.

The present cast iron dome at its greatest exterior measures 135 .5 in., and it is topped by the bronze Statue of Freedom that ᵃnds 19½ ft. and weighs 14,985 pounds. On its base are the ᵒrds "E Pluribus Unum (Out of Many One). The sculptor was ᵗhomas Crawford and the cost, including casting, $23,796. The ᵒtunda, covered by the hugh dome, measures 96 ft. in diameter. ᵒoking upward 180 ft. into the "eye" of the dome one sees the ᵘgh fresco, "Apotheosis of Washington," by Constantino ᵣumidi. Encircling the rotunda 58 ft. up is a frescoed frieze depict-ᵍ scenes from the landing of Columbus in 1492 to Kitty Hawk in ᵃ03. It measures 300 ft.

Inaugurations of presidents and vice presidents are usually held ᵃ a platform erected over the great steps on the east front. The

oath of office of the president is usually given by the Chief Justice of the United States.

### Prayer Room

A nondenominational room where members of Congress may pray and meditate is located off the rotunda. Dominating the room is a stained glass window of George Washington kneeling in prayer at Valley Forge. Beneath it is an altar of white oak on which stands an open Bible. Flanking either side is a floor candelabra, each with the traditional seven lights. The prayer room is not open to the public.

### National Statuary Hall

Statuary Hall was created in 1864 and occupies the former Old Hall of the House. States were invited to contribute not more than 2 statues of distinguished deceased persons to the collection. Statues now number 92 and it has become necessary to display them throughout the Capitol. There remain only 8 states to contribute a 2d statue. The statues in Statuary Hall are:

**Alabama**—Gen. Jos. Wheeler, U.S.A., C.S.A.
**Arizona**—John C. Greenway, U.S.A.
**Arkansas**—Uriah M. Rose, jurist.
**California**—Junipero Serra, mission founder.
**Colorado**—Dr. Florence Rena Sabin, scientist.
**Florida**—Dr. John Gorrie, inventor.
**Georgia**—Alex H. Stephens, statesman.
**Hawaii**—King Kamehameha I, uniter of islands.
**Idaho**—Geo. L. Shoup, first governor.
**Illinois**—Frances E. Willard, WCTU head.
**Indiana**—Lew Wallace, U.S.A., author.
**Iowa**—Saml. J. Kirkwood, governor.
**Kansas**—John J. Ingalls, senator.
**Kentucky**—Henry Clay, statesman.
**Louisiana**—Huey P. Long, senator.
**Maine**—Hannibal Hamlin, vice president.
**Michigan**—Lewis Cass, statesman.
**Minnesota**—Henry M. Rice, senator.
**Mississippi**—Jefferson Davis, statesman.
**Missouri**—Thos. H. Benton, senator.
**Montana**—Charles Marion Russell, artist.
**Nebraska**—Wm. Jennings Bryan, statesman.
**Nevada**—Patrick A. McCarran, senator.
**New Hampshire**—Daniel Webster, statesman.
**North Carolina**—Zebulon B. Vance, governor.
**North Dakota**—John Burke, U.S. treasurer.
**Ohio**—William Allen, senator, governor.

**Oklahoma**—Sequoya, Cherokee leader.
**Oregon**—Rev. Jason Lee, pioneer.
**Pennsylvania**—Robert Fulton, inventor.
**South Dakota**—Gen. W.H.H. Beadle, educator.
**Tennessee**—John Sevier, first governor.
**Texas**—Sam Houston, pioneer leader.
**Utah**—Brigham Young, Mormon leader.
**Vermont**—Ethan Allen, revolutionary leader.
**Virginia**—Robt. E. Lee, U.S.A., C.S.A.
**Washington**—Dr. Marcus Whitman, pioneer.
**West Virginia**—Francis H. Pierpont, statesman.
**Wisconsin**—Robt. M. La Follette Sr., statesman.
**Wyoming**—Esther Hobart Morris, suffragette.

Under the dome in the **Great Rotunda** are statues of Washington (Va.), Andrew Jackson (Tenn.), James A. Garfield (Ohio).

Adjoining it, the **South Small Rotunda** has statues of George Clinton (N.Y.), Stephen A. Austin (Tex.), and John Peter Muhlenberg (Pa.). The corridor leading from Statuary Hall to the House has statues of Jonathan Trumbull (Conn.), Wm. King (Me.), Father Jacques Marquette (Wis.), Wade Hampton (S.C.), Will Rogers (Okla.), E. L. "Bob" Bartlett (Alaska), and Dr. John McLoughlin (Ore.).

In the foyer of the old Senate Chamber are statues of John Stark (N.H.), Dennis Chavez (N.M.), and in the corridor leading to the Senate wing are statues of Dr. Ephraim McDowell (Ky.), eminent physician and surgeon, John Hanson (Md.), 9th president of the Continental Congress, and John M. Clayton (Del.), secretary of state, Wm. E. Borah (Ida.), Edward D. White (La.), and Maria L. Sanford (Minn.).

In the **Hall of Columns** on the first floor, House wing, are statues of E. Kirby Smith (Fla.), Zachariah Chandler (Mich.), Jas. Harlan (Ia.), Francis P. Bair Jr. (Mo.), Gen. Philip Kearny (N.J.), Gen. Jas. Shields (Ill.), John Winthrop (Mass.), Oliver P. Morton (Ind.), J. Sterling Morton (Neb.), Rev. Thos. Starr King (Cal.), J. L. M. Curry (Ala.), J. P. Clarke (Ark.), Geo. W. Glick (Kan.), Jas. Z. George (Miss.), Roger Williams (R.I.), Jacob Collamer (Vt.), John E. Kenna (W. Va.), Joseph Ward (S.D.), Eusebio F. Kino, S. J. (Ariz.), and Father Damien (Ha.), and Ernest Gruening (Alask.).

In the **Main Hall** on the first floor are statues of Roger Sherman (Conn.), Caesar Rodney (Del.), Dr. Crawford W. Long (Ga.), Samuel Adams (Mass.), Charles Carroll of Carrollton (Md.), Richard Stockton (N.J.), Robert R. Livingston (N.Y.), Charles B. Aycock (N.C.), Nathanael Greene (R.I.), and John C. Calhoun (S.C.).

### Office Buildings for Members

Members of Congress meet constituents and transact other business in five office buildings on Capitol Hill, two for the Senate and three for the House.

The original Senate building, the Richard Brevard Russell Office Building, was completed in 1909, enlarged in 1933; the second Senate building, the Everett McKinley Dirksen Office Building, was constructed in 1958. A subway connects both with the Capitol.

The original House building (1908) was named for former Speaker Joseph G. Cannon (R. Ill.), the second (1933) for former Speaker Nicholas Longworth (R. Oh.), and the third (1964) for former Speaker Sam Rayburn (D. Tex.). The Rayburn Building has underground transportation to the Capitol.

Also on Capitol Hill is the bell tower and statue memorial to Sen. Robert A. Taft of Ohio (1889-1953). It was erected by popular subscription and dedicated Apr. 14, 1959, by President Eisenhower.

### Hours for Visiting

The Capitol is normally open from 9 a.m. to 4:30 p.m. daily. The Capitol is closed Christmas, New Year's Day, and Thanksgiving Day. Should either the House or the Senate remain in session beyond closing time, the wing of the Capitol in use stays open until the session closes.

Tours through the Capitol, including the House and Senate Galleries, are conducted from 9 a.m. to 4 p.m. without charge. It is not necessary to take a tour to see the Capitol. Visitors desiring to hear debate in either chamber for a longer period than the tour allows must obtain a visitor's card from their Senator or Representative.

### The White House

The White House, the president's residence, stands on 18 acres on the south side of Pennsylvania Avenue, between the Treasury and the Executive Office Building. The main building 168 by 85-1/2 ft., has 6 floors, with the East Terrace, 135 by 35 ft., leading to the East Wing, a 3-story building, 139 by 82 ft., used for offices and as an entrance for official functions. The West Terrace,

174 by 35 ft., contains offices and press facilities, and leads to the Executive Office, 3 stories high, 148 by 98 ft., erected in 1902 and enlarged several times since.

The White House was designed by James Hoban, an Irish-born architect, in a competition that paid $500. The main facade resembles the Duke of Leinster's house in Dublin. President Washington chose the site, which was included on the plan of the Federal City prepared by the French engineer, Major Pierre L'Enfant. The cornerstone was laid Oct. 13, 1792. President Washington never lived in the house. President John Adams entered in Nov. 1800, and Mrs. Adams hung her washing in the uncompleted East Room.

The walls were of sandstone, quarried at Aquia Creek, Va. The exterior walls were painted during the course of construction, causing the building to be termed the "White House." For many years, however, it was generally referred to as the "President's House" or the "President's Palace." Thomas Jefferson developed the east and west terraces and built one-story offices, woodsheds, and a wine cellar. On Aug. 24, 1814, during Madison's administration, the house was burned by the British. James Hoban completed rebuilding by Dec. 1817, and President Monroe moved in.

The south portico was added in 1824 and the north portico in 1829. In 1948 President Truman had a second-floor balcony built into the south portico. In 1948 he had Congress authorize complete rebuilding because the White House was unsafe. During its reconstruction he lived in Blair House, 1651 Pennsylvania Ave. Reconstruction cost $5,761,000. The interior was completely removed, new underpinning 24 ft. deep was placed under the outside walls, and a steel frame was built to support the interior.

The **Green Room** is a Federal-style drawing room with most of the furniture made in New York about 1815-1825 by Duncan Phyfe or his contemporaries. The walls are covered with green silk moiré.

The **Blue Room**, an oval drawing room, is the main reception room. The parquet floor is covered by an oval Chinese rug; the walls are covered with wallpaper reproduced from a French document of 1800. Portraits of Washington, Adams, Jefferson, Jackson, Monroe, and Tyler decorate the walls. Seven chairs and a French clock from Monroe's original 1817 furnishings are used in the room.

The **Red Room**, used as a parlor, is furnished in the American Empire style, hung in red twill satin with gold scroll borders. The room has a Savonnerie carpet of the period and a marble-topped gueridon labeled by Charles Honore Lannuier. There are portraits of Pierce, Polk, Van Buren, Dolley Madison, Angelica Van Buren, Audubon, and Alexander Hamilton in the room. There is also a marble bust of Martin Van Buren by Hiram Powers.

The **State Dining Room** has a large ornamental table on which is displayed a French bronze-doré plateau purchased by Monroe in 1817. For large dinners, small circular tables are brought in. The neo-classically carved oak wall paneling is painted ivory.

The **Family Dining Room**, used for breakfasts and luncheons, has a portrait of Mrs. Theodore Roosevelt by Theobold Chartran.

The **President's Dining Room**, on the second floor, is furnished with American Federal furniture, an 18th century chandelier, and blue silk window hangings. There is a mahogany sideboard once owned by Daniel Webster. It is used for private dining by the first family.

The **Diplomatic Reception Room**, an oval room on the ground floor, is used as the south entrance to the mansion at state functions. It has scenic wallpaper based on 1820 engravings, and an Aubusson style rug with seals of the 50 states.

The **Library**, on the ground floor, has the painted decor of an early 19th century American room. In Aug. 1963, 2,780 titles were selected by a distinguished committee to be placed in the library. All but a few are by American authors.

The **Map Room**, on the ground floor, a top-secret war room during World War II, was redecorated in 1970 in American Chippendale style. A portrait of Benjamin Franklin which was taken from Franklin's Philadelphia home by a British officer quartered there during the American Revolution hangs there.

The **Lincoln Bedroom** which contains an ornately carved bed and furniture of his period, is at the east end of the second floor. It served as Lincoln's cabinet room and in it he signed the Emancipation Proclamation of Jan. 1, 1863. A portrait of Jackson, admired by Lincoln, hangs there today. Seven pieces of furniture have Lincoln associations. The bed was used in the State Bedroom during the Lincoln administration. In the room is a copy of the **Gettysburg Address**, written out by Lincoln.

The **Treaty Room** was used as the cabinet room by Andrew Johnson and his successors until 1902. Here in 1899 was signed the peace protocol, a forerunner to the final treaty of peace with Spain. It is now a waiting or meeting room for the President and contains some of the original Victorian furniture. There are portraits of Presidents Andrew Johnson, Grant, and Taylor and paintings of McKinley observing the signing of the protocol, and of Lincoln and Grant in conference during the Civil War.

The **Queen's Bedroom** is assigned to distinguished women guests, and has sheltered five queens — Queen Mother Elizabeth and Queen Elizabeth II of Britain, Wilhelmina and Juliana of the Netherlands, Queen Mother Frederika of Greece. The English overmantel mirror was presented by Princess Elizabeth in 1951.

The **Yellow Oval Room**, directly above the Blue Room is used as a private sitting room by the president and first lady.

The **President's Office**, oval in form, is in the West Wing and looks out on the rose garden. The office was added in 1909 to the West Wing, which had been built 7 years earlier by Theodore Roosevelt. The West Wing also contains the Roosevelt Room and the Cabinet Room.

### Visiting Hours

The White House is open from 10 a.m. to 12 noon, Tuesday through Friday, except on holidays. Also Saturdays, 10 a.m. to 2 p.m. Jun. 1 through Labor Day, and 10 a.m. to noon Labor Day through May 31. Only the public rooms on the ground floor and state floor may be visited.

### President's Guest House

**Blair House, the President's Guest House,** fronts on Pennsylvania Ave., northwest of the White House grounds. It is supervised by the Dept. of State and is the official residence of heads of state who visit Washington. Built 1824, it was the home of Francis Preston Blair (1791-1876), political leader and Lincoln advisor. President Truman lived there 1948-1952 during rebuilding of the White House, and 2 Puerto Rican fanatics tried to shoot their way in Nov. 1, 1950, killing one guard and wounding 2 others.

Restoration and refurnishing began in 1963 and the house was reopened Jan. 14, 1964, on the occasion of the visit of President Antonio Segni of the Italian Republic. The Blair House Fine Arts Committee continues to provide for the house.

### Other Centers of Interest
## Arlington National Cemetery

**Arlington National Cemetery,** on the former Custis estate in Virginia, is the site of the **Tomb of the Unknown Soldier** and the final resting place of John Fitzgerald Kennedy, president of the United States, who was buried here Nov. 25, 1963. A torch burns day and night over his grave. The remains of his brother Sen. Robert F. Kennedy (N.Y.) were interred on June 8, 1968, in an area adjacent. Many other famous Americans are also buried at Arlington, as well as American soldiers from every major war.

Arlington National Cemetery, administered by the Department of the Army, was established June 15, 1864, on land originally the estate of George Washington Parke Custis. The land was part of the District of Columbia from 1791 until 1847, when Arlington County was returned to Virginia.

The Unknown Soldier of World War I was entombed on the east front of the Arlington Memorial Amphitheater Nov. 11, 1921, in the presence of President Warren G. Harding. The tomb is inscribed: *Here rests in honored glory an American solider known but to God.* The body had been chosen at Chalons-sur-Marne from unidentified dead in Europe. On Memorial Day, May 30, 1958, 2 unidentified servicemen, one of whom died in World War II and one in the Korean War, were placed in crypts beside the first, in ceremonies led by President Eisenhower and Vice President Nixon.

As of May 31, 1978, a total of 173,186 interments had been made in Arlington National Cemetery. Among the unknown dead are 2,111 who died on the battlefields of Virginia in the Civil War and 167 who lost their lives when the battleship Maine was blown up in Havana Harbor Feb. 15, 1898. The total of unknown dead interred in Arlington National Cemetery is 4,724.

### Arlington House, The Robert E. Lee Memorial

On a hilltop above the cemetery, stands Arlington House, the Robert E. Lee Memorial, which from 1955 to 1972 was officially called the Custis-Lee Mansion. The house has a portico 60 ft. wide, with 8 Doric columns, and faces the Potomac. With its 2 wings the house extends 140 ft. It was built by George Washington Parke Custis, grandson of Martha Washington and father of Mary Ann

Randolph Custis, who married Lee in this house in 1831. Here Lee wrote his resignation from the U.S. Army, Apr. 20, 1861. The house became a military headquarters and was confiscated by the government. The U.S. Supreme Court restored it to the legal heir, George Washington Custis Lee, grandson of the builder, who sold the entire estate (including the mansion) to the Government in 1883 for $150,000.

The mansion and grounds are administered by the National Park Service of the Dept. of the Interior.

### U.S. Marine Corps War Memorial

North of the National Cemetery, approximately 350 yards, stands the bronze statue of the raising of the United States flag on Iwo Jima, executed by Felix de Weldon from the photograph by Joe Rosenthal, and presented to the nation by members and friends of the U.S. Marine Corps, at a cost of $850,000. It was dedicated Nov. 10, 1954, and is under the administration of the Dept. of the Interior, National Park Service.

## Folger Shakespeare Library

The **Folger Shakespeare Library** on Capitol Hill, Washington, D. C., is a research institution devoted to the advancement of learning in the background of Anglo-American civilization in the 16th and 17th centuries and in most aspects of the continental Renaissance. It has the largest collection of Shakespeareana in the world with 79 copies of the First Folio. Its collection of English books printed before 1640 is the largest in the Western Hemisphere. It also has extensive source materials for the history of theater and drama from the Middle Ages to the end of the 18th century, both English and American. The library owns approximately 250,000 books and manuscripts, about half of them rare.

The library was founded and endowed by Henry Clay Folger, a former president of the Standard Oil Co. of New York, and his wife, Emily Jordan Folger. He left its administration to the trustees of his alma mater, Amherst College. The exhibition gallery and replica Elizabethan Theatre are open free 10 a.m. to 4:30 p.m. daily; closed federal holidays and on Sundays after Labor Day to April 15.

## Library of Congress

Established by and for Congress in 1800, the Library of Congress has extended its services over the years to other Government agencies and other libraries, to scholars, and to the general public, and it now serves as the national library. Two buildings, an ornate Italian Renaissance structure, the Library of Congress Building, (1897) and a modern annex, the Thomas Jefferson Building, (1939), cover 6 acres of the 15⅓-acre library site and contain 35 acres of floor space. In addition the library occupies 10 other buildings dispersed through the Metropolitan area. In Oct. 1965 Congress passed a law authorizing construction of a third library building, the James Madison Memorial Building; completion is expected in 1980.

Dr. Daniel J. Boorstin became the 12th Librarian of Congress on November 12, 1975.

The library had over 3,000 volumes when it was destroyed in the burning of the Capitol, Aug. 24-25, 1814. In Jan. 1815 Congress bought Thomas Jefferson's library of some 6,000 volumes. In 1851 fire destroyed about half the collections. In 1866 the science library of the Smithsonian Institution was transferred to the library, and in 1870 the library became the repository for materials deposited for copyright. Today the library's collections contain more than 73 million items, including more than 18 million volumes and pamphlets.

In addition to providing a variety of reference and bibliographic services to other government agencies, the Library of Congress serves as a cataloging and bibliographic center for libraries throughout the country. Its cataloging data is available on printed cards (a service offered since 1901), on magnetic tapes for libraries using computers, and in book catalogs. A program called Cataloging in Publication makes cataloging information available in books themselves so that they can be processed and put into circulation almost immediately after their delivery to libraries.

The library's exhibit halls are open to the public. Guided tours are given every hour from 9 a.m. through 8 p.m. Monday through Friday; and at 9 a.m. through 5 p.m. Saturday, Sunday and holidays. Arrangements for groups should be made in advance with the Tour Coordinator. Many of the library's treasures are on permanent exhibit and changing exhibits feature interesting selections from the library's collections of photographs, rare books, music, maps, and manuscipts. The library's resources are also made available to the public through publication of guides, bibliographies, catalogs, and facsimiles. An annual list of **Publications in Print** is available free of charge from Central Services Division, Library of Congress, Washington, DC 20540. A monthly **Calendar of Events** listing current exhibits and programs is also available from the same address. Information about the Library of Congress, publications, posters, color slides, and greeting and postal cards are available at the Information Counter, in the west entrance ground floor lobby of the Library of Congress Building.

## Thomas Jefferson Memorial

The **Thomas Jefferson Memorial** stands on the south shore of the Tidal Basin in West Potomac park. It is a circular stone structure, with Vermont marble on the exterior and Georgia white marble inside and combines architectural elements of the dome of the Pantheon in Rome and the rotunda designed by Jefferson for the University of Virginia. The central circular chamber, 86¼ ft. in diameter, is dominated by a 19-ft. tall full-length figure of Thomas Jefferson by the American sculptor Rudulph Evans. The architects were John Russell Pope and his associates Otto R. Eggers and Daniel P. Higgins. The Memorial was dedicated by President F. D. Roosevelt Apr. 13, 1943, the 200th anniversary of Jefferson's birth.

On the pediment over the portico is a sculptured group by Adolph A. Weinman showing Jefferson standing before the committee appointed by the Continental Congress to draft the Declaration of Independence. On the interior walls are four panels with inscriptions from Jefferson's writings. On the frieze of the main entablature are Jefferson's lines: "I have sworn upon the altar of God eternal hostility against every form of tyranny over the mind of man."

The memorial is open daily from 8 a.m. to midnight, except Christmas Day. An elevator and curb ramps for the handicapped are in service.

## John F. Kennedy Center

**John F. Kennedy Center for the Performing Arts,** designated by Congress as the National Cultural Center and the official memorial in Washington to President Kennedy, was opened September 8, 1971. The white marble building, designed by Edward Durell Stone, houses a 2,300-seat Opera House, a 2,750-seat Concert Hall, the 1,150-seat Eisenhower Theater, the 224-seat American Film Institute Theater, and 3 restaurants. A 500-seat Studio Theater/Recital Hall will open in 1979. All facilities are in full operation throughout the year. Tours are available daily, free of charge, between 10:00 a.m. and 1:15 p.m.

## Lincoln Memorial

The **Lincoln Memorial** in West Potomac Park, on the axis of the Capitol and the Washington Monument, consists of a large marble hall enclosing a heroic statue of Abraham Lincoln in meditation sitting on a large armchair. It was dedicated on Memorial Day, May 30, 1922. The Memorial was designed by Henry Bacon. The statue was made by Daniel Chester French. Murals and ornamentation on the bronze ceiling beams are by Jules Guerin.

The memorial, built on bedrock, is of white Colorado-Yule marble. There are 2 Doric columns at the entrance and 36 others in the colonnade. The frieze above the 36 columns bears the names of the 36 states existing at the time of Lincoln's death. On the attic parapet are recorded names of the 48 states existing in 1922.

Inside are 3 memorials to Lincoln. The seated figure of Lincoln is 19 ft. from head to foot and the classic armchair is 12½ ft. tall. Over the back of the chair a flag is draped in marble. The statue was fashioned out of 28 blocks of Georgia white marble. On the north wall is inscribed the Second Inaugural Address. On the south wall is the Gettysburg Address.

The walls of the interior are Indiana limestone. The panels between the overhead girders are of Alabama marble saturated with melted beeswax to produce translucency. The interior floor and the wall base are of pink Tennessee marble. The cost of the Memorial was $2,957,000 and of the statue $88,400.

The memorial is open daily from 8 a.m. to midnight, except Christmas Day. A new elevator for the handicapped is in service.

## Mount Vernon

**Mount Vernon** on the south bank of the Potomac, 16 miles below Washington, D. C., is part of a large tract of land in northern Virginia which was originally included in a royal grant made to Lord Culpepper, who in 1674 granted 5,000 acres to Nicholas

Spencer and John Washington. The division between Spencer and Washington put John Washington's son Lawrence in possession of the Washington half in 1690. Later it became the property of Lawrence Washington's son Augustine, the father of George Washington.

The present house is an enlargement of one apparently built on the site of an earlier one by Augustine Washington, who lived there 1735-1738. His son Lawrence came there in 1743, when he renamed the plantation Mount Vernon in honor of Admiral Vernon under whom he had served in the West Indies. Lawrence Washington died in 1752 and was succeeded as proprietor of Mount Vernon by his half-brother, George Washington.

Washington brought his wife, Martha Dandridge Custis, to Mount Vernon in 1759, having previously enlarged the house from 1-½ to 2-½ stories. Just before the Revolution he planned additions, and when he was called away to war his kinsman Lund Washington supervised the work, which was completed after Washington returned in 1783. During the Revolution Washington visited Mount Vernon only twice, on the way to and from Yorktown in 1781. In 1789 he left to become president and lived in New York and Philadelphia, with brief visits to the plantation. He came back in 1797 and died in Mount Vernon Dec. 14, 1799. He was buried in the old family vault. He had made plans for a new burial vault and this was built in 1831. Both his remains and those of Martha, who died in 1802, were transferred there.

Mount Vernon was left to Washington's nephew, U.S. Supreme Court Justice Bushrod Washington, and by him to his nephew, John Augustine Washington, whose son, John A. Washington Jr., was the last private owner. In 1853 Miss Ann Pamela Cunningham of South Carolina organized the Mount Vernon Ladies' Assn., which bought the mansion and 200 acres, since extended to just under 500 acres. The Association reassembled original Washington furniture and repaired the buildings. It restored the kitchen garden, flower garden, and experimental botanical garden, reconstructed the greenhouse, and built a museum. Several trees planted by Washington still exist, and the boxwood dates from 1798.

The Association preserves house and tomb with the visitor's fee. The regent of the Mount Vernon Ladies' Association is Mrs. John H. Guy Jr. About 30 states are represented by vice regents. The Resident Director is Harrison M. Symmes.

## National Arboretum

The **National Arboretum** is one of Washington's great showplaces, occupying 444 acres in the northeastern section of the city. Collections of azaleas, magnolias, hollies, cherries, crabapples, conifers, and ferns and wildflowers are prime attractions. The National Herb Garden and National Bonsai Collection are special attractions in the nation's only federally-supported gardens.

The Arboretum is open every day of the year except Christmas. The visiting hours are 8 a.m. to 5 p.m. Monday through Friday and 10 a.m. to 5 p.m. on Saturday and Sunday.

## National Archives

The Declaration of Independence, the Constitution of the United States, and the Bill of Rights are on permanent display in the National Archives Exhibition Hall. They are sealed in glass-and-bronze cases and can be lowered 20 feet at a moment's notice into a large shockproof and fireproof safe.

The National Archives holds the permanently valuable federal records of the United States government, 1774 to the present. As a research institution, it is designed to preserve these records and make them available to government agencies, scholars, students, writers, and the general public.

The National Archives and Records Service is a part of the General Services Administration. Through the Presidential Libraries Office it administers the Franklin D. Roosevelt Library at Hyde Park, N. Y., the Harry S. Truman Library at Independence, Mo., the Dwight D. Eisenhower Library at Abilene, Kan., the Herbert Hoover Library at West Branch, Iowa, the Lyndon Baines Johnson Library at Austin, Tex., and the John Fitzgerald Kennedy Library, temporarily at Waltham, Mass., and the Gerald Ford Library to be built in Ann Arbor, Mich., and museum to stand in Grand Rapids.

The National Archives and Records Service is headed by Dr. James B. Rhoads, archivist of the United States, Pennsylvania Ave. and 8th St. N.W. For research information, call 202-523-3218. For visitor information, call 202-523-3000.

## National Gallery of Art

The **National Gallery of Art**, situated in an area bounded by Constitution Avenue and the Mall, between Third and Seventh

Streets, was established by Joint Resolution of Congress Mar. 24, 1937, and opened Mar. 17, 1941. Although technically a bureau of the Smithsonian Institution, the gallery is an autonomous organization governed by its own board of trustees. The chairman of the board is the chief justice of the United States. Other members are the secretaries of state and of the treasury, the secretary of the Smithsonian Institution, and 5 distinguished private citizens.

The collections comprise gifts of over 300 donors (none of the works were acquired with Government funds) and cover the American and various European schools of art from the 13th century to the present.

The building was erected with funds given by Andrew W. Mellon, who also gave his collection of 126 paintings and 26 pieces of sculpture, which included such masterpieces as Raphael's Alba Madonna, the Niccolini-Cowper Madonna, and St. George and the Dragon. van Eyck's Annunciation, Botticelli's Adoration of the Magi, and 9 Rembrandts. Twenty-nine paintings came from the Hermitage in Leningrad. Also in this collection are the Vaughan Portrait of George Washington, by Gilbert Stuart, and The Washington Family, by Edward Savage.

The Samuel H. Kress Collection includes the great tondo of the Adoration of the Magi by Fra Angelico and Fra Filippo Lippi, the Laocoon by El Greco, and fine examples by Giorgione, Titian, Grunewald, Durer, Memling, Bosch, Juan de Flandes, Francois Clouet, Poussin, Watteau, Chardin, Boucher, Fragonard, David, and Ingres. Also included are a number of masterpieces of sculpture, especially of the Italian and French schools.

The Widener Collection of over 100 paintings includes 14 Rembrandts, 8 Van Dycks, 2 Vermeers, and examples of Italian, Spanish, English, and French painting, and Italian and French sculpture and decorative arts.

The Chester Dale collection includes masterpieces by Manet, Cézanne, Renoir, Toulouse-Lautrec, Monet, Modigliani, Pissarro, Degas, van Gogh, Gauguin, Matisse, Picasso, Braque, and such American artists as Gilbert Stuart, Childe Hassam, and George Bellows.

Several major works of art by some of the most important artists of the last hundred years, including Picasso, Cézanne, Gauguin, and the American painter Walt Kuhn, have been given to the gallery by the W. Averell Harriman Foundation in memory of Marie N. Harriman.

The Collection of Edgar William and Bernice Chrysler Garbisch includes more than 300 American naive paintings and watercolors covering the 18th and 19th centuries. Among them are Edward Hicks' Cornell Farm, Winthrop Chandler's portraits of Captain Samuel Chandler and Mrs. Samuel Chandler, and Linton Park's Flax Scutching Bee.

Pictures to round out the collection have been bought with funds provided by the late Ailsa Mellon Bruce, daughter of Andrew W. Mellon. Preeminent among them is the portrait of Ginevra de' Benci, the only generally acknowledged painting by Leonardo da Vinci outside Europe; Georges de la Tour's Repentant Magdalen, one of the rarest paintings of the 17th century; and Pablo Picasso's Nude Woman, the key work of the artist's analytical cubist period. Among others are: Rubens' Daniel in the Lions' Den; Claude Lorrain's Judgment of Paris; Saint George and the Dragon, attributed to van der Weyden; and a number of American paintings, including Cole's second set of The Voyage of Life.

Cézanne's great early portrait of his father and 351 paintings by George Catlin, mostly of North and South American Indians, are among recent acquisitions given by Paul Mellon, president of the gallery and son of Andrew Mellon. A fine collection of French impressionist pictures are on loan to the gallery from Mr. and Mrs. Mellon.

Among other works donated to the gallery's collection are Vermeer's A Lady Writing, given by Harry Waldron Havemeyer and Horace Havemeyer Jr., in memory of their father, Horace Havemeyer; Copley's Watson and the Shark, given by Ferdinand Lammot Belin; Goya's Victor Guye, given by William Nelson Cromwell; and Mondrian's Lozenge in Red, Yellow and Blue, given by Herbert and Nannette Rothschild.

The National Gallery's rapidly expanding graphic arts holdings number about 62,000 items and date from the 12th century to the present. Almost half of these works were the gift of Lessing J. Rosenwald, who had gathered one of the world's great collections of prints and drawings.

The Index of American Design contains over 17,000 watercolor renderings and 500 photographs of American crafts and folk arts from before 1700 until 1900.

The gallery's Education Department gives daily talks on the gallery's collection. The Extension Service lends films and slide programs to schools, colleges, and civic groups in more than 4,000 communities in the United States and Canada. Nearly all of the gallery's services are available to the public free of charge.

The National Gallery is in the process of moving into its new East Building, which adjoins the original West Building. Funds for the new construction have come from Mr. Paul Mellon, the late Ailsa Mellon Bruce, and The Andrew W. Mellon Foundation. The architect is I. M. Pei. The gallery segment of the East Building, which opened in 1978, provides space for temporary exhibitions and the gallery's growing collection. Alongside the gallery segment is the administrative and research segment, which will open in 1979 and will house the Center for Advanced Study in the Visual Arts together with a greatly expanded library, photographic archive, and office facilities. Already open to the public is an underground concourse connecting the East and West Buildings and containing a major new restaurant complex, the Cafe/Buffet.

Open daily except Christmas and New Year's, from 10 a.m. to 5 p.m. Monday through Saturday and noon to 9 p.m. Sunday. During the summer open Monday through Saturday 10 a.m. to 9 p.m., noon to 9 p.m. on Sunday.

## National Geographic Society

The National Geographic Society, founded in 1888 "for the increase and diffusion of geographic knowledge," is the world's largest nonprofit scientific and educational institution. The Society produces the illustrated monthlies, National Geographic and National Geographic World, books, maps, globes, atlases, other educational materials, and television programs. Its activities are supported by the dues of 10,000,000 members.

The society's 10-story headquarters building in Washington, D.C., was dedicated by President Lyndon B. Johnson in 1964. It attracts many thousands of visitors, including members of the society from all over the world. Explorers Hall offers exhibits, artifacts, and mementos depicting the organization's research and exploration activities.

Executive officers are: Robert E. Doyle, president; Owen R. Anderson, vice president and secretary; Gilbert M. Grosvenor, vice president and editor; Melvin M. Payne, chairman of the board; Melville Bell Grosvenor, chairman emeritus and editor emeritus; Thomas W. McKnew, advisory chairman of the board; Hilleary F. Hoskinson, vice president and treasurer.

## The Pentagon

The Pentagon, headquarters of the Department of Defense, is the world's largest office building, with 3 times the floor space of the Empire State Building in New York. Situated in Arlington, Va., it houses 22,000 employees in offices that occupy 3,707,745 square feet.

The Pentagon was completed Jan. 15, 1943, at a cost of about $83 million. It covers 34 acres, is 5 stories high and consists of 5 rings of buildings connected by 10 corridors, with a 5-acre pentagonal court in the center. Each of the outermost sides of the building is 921 ft. long and the perimeter is 7/8's of a mile. Total length of the corridors is 17 1/2 miles.

Tours are available Monday through Friday (excluding federal holidays), and start every 30 minutes at the Concourse. The first tour begins at 9 a.m. and the last at 3:30 p.m. Walk-ins are welcome. During the summer tourist season, tours are conducted every 15 minutes.

## Smithsonian Institution

The Smithsonian Institution is one of the world's great historical, scientific, educational, and cultural establishments. It comprises numerous facilities, mostly in the metropolitan Wash., D.C., area. It was founded by an Act of Congress in 1846, pursuant to a bequest of James Smithson, a British scholar-scientist, to the United States to found at Washington "an establishment for the increase and diffusion of knowledge among men." The Smithsonian, ever since its founding, has been a center for basic scientific research; it engages in programs of education and it is also the largest museum-gallery complex in the world. More than 20 million persons visit its halls annually. S. Dillon Ripley became the 8th secretary of the Smithsonian Feb. 1, 1964.

The Anacostia Neighborhood Museum, the first of its kind in the nation, opened in 1967 in a low-income urban community. The museum develops and presents exhibits on topics of interest to the residents of the community as well as the greater Washington area. The staff also conducts independent research in the areas of Afro-American history, minority and ethnic studies, and the history of the Anacostia community and Washington, D.C. Independent programs and activities, such as teacher workshops, seminars, and a circulating library of children's books on African and Afro-American history serve the local school community.

The **Arts and Industries Building** reopened in May 1976 with an exhibit entitled "1876: A Centennial Exhibition" which displays actual items from the Centennial exhibition in Philadelphia as well as others of the same era. The 4 halls are devoted to various subjects including machinery, with a large number of the machines in operation; items from the military, U.S. Treasury and the Patent Office; manufactured articles; and displays from many of the 37 states in existence in 1876 and from the foreign countries represented in the Philadelphia exhibition.

The **Freer Gallery of Art**, the gift of Detroit industrialist Charles Lang Freer, is an outstanding museum and research center in art of the Far and Near East. The gallery also houses the Whistler Peacock Room and a fine collection of works by James A. McNeill Whistler.

The **Hirshhorn Museum and Sculpture Garden**, opened in 1974, houses works in the Joseph H. Hirshhorn collection which were donated in 1966 to the people of the United States. Primary emphasis is on art of the 20th century although the sculpture section ranges from antiquity to works of the most significant European and American contemporaries.

The **National Museum of History and Technology** has exhibits illustrating American culture, civil and military history, and the history of science and technology. In the rotunda the visitor will find the original Star-Spangled Banner and a Foucault pendulum demonstrating the earth's rotation. "A Nation of Nations" is a museum within a museum tracing the peopling of America through 6,000 objects. Other major exhibits feature gowns of the first ladies, the Petroleum Hall, the history of transportation, American political and military history, numismatics, philately, ceramics and glass, musical instruments, timekeeping, physical and medical sciences, graphic arts, electricity, photography, and news reporting. National treasures on display include the desk on which Thomas Jefferson drafted the Declaration of Independence and Samuel Morse's first telegraph. A popular attraction is an authentic 19th century country store-post office where mail is hand-stamped with a "Smithsonian Station" postmark.

The **National Museum of Natural History** serves as a national and international center for the natural sciences. It maintains the largest reference collection in the nation and conducts a broad program of basic research on man, plants, animals, fossil organisms, rocks, minerals, and materials from outer space. Exhibits show aspects of life and cultures in Asia, Africa, the Pacific, and North and South America. Other exhibits include fossil plants and invertebrate animals, mammals, fishes, amphibians, dinosaurs, and primitive reptiles. There are halls of North American archeology, osteology, and physical anthropology. Also on view are geology exhibits on the earth, the moon, and meteorites as well as a Hall of Minerals and Gems which includes the 45$^1$/$_2$-carat blue Hope diamond and the largest gem emerald on public exhibit, the 858-carat Gachala emerald. The World of Mammals, the Hall of Birds, the Fenykovi Elephant, and the Insect Zoo are additional major exhibits.

The **National Air and Space Museum**, which opened in a newly constructed building July 1, 1976, houses exhibits on space exploration, air travel and related scientific and technical topics. Its Milestones of Flight Gallery exhibits 'famous firsts' of air and space development such as the Wright Flyer, Lindbergh's "Spirit of St. Louis," John Glenn's Mercury capsule, the Friendship 7 craft, the Apollo 11 command module Columbia, and a moon rock. Aspects of space exploration and air travel are displayed in some galleries with others focusing on balloons and airships, flight technology, sea-air operations, and various kinds of military aviation. There is a giant screen theater with presentations related to air and space travel and the Albert Einstein Spacearium presents programs of sky and space simulation.

The **National Collection of Fine Arts** presents a panorama of American painting, sculpture, and graphic art from the 18th century to today with 18,000 works in its collections and approximately 25 special exhibitions each year. It is housed in the historic Old Patent Office Building; its Lincoln Gallery was the site of Abraham Lincoln's second inaugural reception. The **Renwick Gallery**, a curatorial department of the National Collection of Fine

Arts, is a national showcase for American creativity in design, crafts, and the decorative arts. In addition to special temporary exhibitions, 2 rooms refurnished in the late 19th century period can be seen.

The **National Portrait Gallery**, also located in the Old Patent Office Bldg., exhibits the likenesses of persons who have made significant contributions to the history, development, and culture of the people of the United States. The gallery's temporary exhibitions are based on a variety of historical themes.

The **National Zoological Park** is noted for its outstanding collections including 2 giant pandas from China. Its research includes investigation in animal behavior, ecology, nutrition and reproduction physiology, pathology, and clinical medicine. Conservation-oriented studies cover maintenance of wild population and long-term captive breeding and care of endangered species.

The **Smithsonian Associates** was founded to stimulate interest and active participation in the Smithsonian's work. Its membership programs for adults and young people include seminars, lectures, workshops, demonstrations, concerts, theater, exhibition previews, dramas, films, tours, and field and camping trips. *Smithsonian*, a monthly magazine of the arts, sciences, and history, is available to members of the Associates.

The **Smithsonian Institution Traveling Exhibition Service (SITES)** organizes and circulates exhibitions for art and science museums, colleges, and other educational institutions around the United States and Canada. More than 200 exhibitions are on continuous tour, with 75 or 80 openings of these shows occurring monthly across the country.

## Washington Monument

The **Washington Monument** is a tapering shaft or obelisk of white marble, 555 ft., 5-$^1$/$_8$ inches in height and 55 ft., 1-$^1$/$_2$ inches square at base. Eight small windows, 2 on each side, are located at the 500-ft. level, where Washington points of interest are indicated.

The capstone weighs 3,300 lbs. and was placed Dec. 6, 1884. The monument was dedicated Feb. 21, 1885, and opened Oct. 9, 1888. It weighs 81,120 tons. It is dressed with white Maryland marble in 2-ft. courses. The first 150 ft. are backed by rubble masonry. From that point to 452 ft. Maine granite was used as backing, and above 452 ft. marble was used. The face of the monument is primarily marble from Maryland. Set into the interior wall are 190 memorial stones from states, foreign countries, and organizations. An iron stairway has 50 landings and 898 steps. A modern elevator takes sightseers to the 500-ft. level in one minute, compared with 12 "precarious minutes" in 1888.

The erection of the monument by the Washington National Monument society with funds obtained by popular subscription was authorized by Congress in 1848. The conerstone was laid July 4 of the same year. Work progressed slowly until 1854 when $300,000 had been subscribed and 152 ft. of the shaft erected. In that year the enterprise became controversial and contributions ceased. Work was resumed in 1880 at government expense by the Corps of Engineers.

The Monument is open 7 days a week, 9 a.m. to 5 p.m. Extended summer hours are 8 a.m. to 12 midnight. It is closed Christmas Day.

## Famous Churches

The **National Shrine of the Immaculate Conception**, at Fourth St. and Michigan Ave. NE, Washington, D. C. is the largest Catholic church in the United States and one of the largest in the world. Built by all the bishops and Catholics of the U.S., it honors the Blessed Virgin Mary as Patroness of the United States. The Shrine is impressive not only in size but also in beauty, its blue and gold dome and soaring bell-tower having become Washington landmarks. Open daily from 7 a.m. to 8 p.m., Sunday masses, 7:30, 9:00, 10:30 a.m., 12 noon, 1:30 and 4 p.m. (5:15 p.m. Sat. eve.). Free guided tours 9 a.m. to 5 p.m. daily; Sunday tours 2 p.m. to 4 p.m. Carillon concerts on Sundays and preceding organ and choral concerts. Organ recitals every Sun. at 7:00 p.m. (June through August) and 4th Friday organ recitals (Sept. through May).

**Washington Cathedral**, Massachusetts and Wisconsin Aves. NW, is atop Mt. Saint Alban. It is the seat of the Presiding Bishop of the Episcopal Church and of the Bishop of Washington. Started in 1907, the cathedral is nearly complete. The nave was finished and opened in 1976, with a festive dedicatory ceremony July 8, marking the visit of Queen Elizabeth to the nation's capital. It is the 6th largest cathedral in the world. Notables buried in the cathedral include Woodrow Wilson, Adm. George Dewey, Cordell Hull, and Frank B. Kellogg. The cathedral is considered one of the finest examples of Gothic architecture in the country.

Several Protestant churches commemorate the association of presidents with their congregations. **St. John's Episcopal Church**, across Lafayette Sq. from the White House, designed by Benj. Latrobe in 1815, has been attended by every president since Madison. **New York Ave. Presbyterian Church**, 1313 New York Ave. NW, established in 1803, retains the pew in which Lincoln sat, also an original manuscript of his first proposal to abolish slavery. The church was rebuilt on same site in 1950-51.

**The National Presbyterian Church**, on a 13-acre tract, at Nebraska Ave. and Van Ness St. NW, was dedicated on May 10, 1970. The Church traces its origin to a group of stonemasons who met in a carpenter's shop in the grounds of the White House in 1795, later becoming the First Presbyterian Church in the District of Columbia. The Church of the Covenant, founded in 1883, united with the original Presbyterian body in 1930 to become the congregation of the National Presbyterian Church. President Eisenhower was baptized by the pastor, Dr. Edward L. R. Elson, and became a member of the Church on Feb. 1, 1953. He laid the cornerstone of the new Church on his 77th birthday, Oct. 14, 1967, and the Chapel of Presidents is dedicated to him. The Chapel of the Presidents contains the Eisenhower pew, and pews representing 16 additional presidents who worshipped with the congregation. The oldest president's pew, occupied by Jackson, Polk, Pierce, Buchanan, and Cleveland, is on view together with much historic memorabilia.

**The Islamic Center**, 2551 Massachusetts Ave. NW, a magnificent Islamic monument, institution for Islamic culture, and an outstanding landmark for visitors.

## Cherry Blossom Time

Cherry blossom time in Washington is looked upon as the opening of spring. The famous cherry trees encircle the Tidal Basin in West Potomac Park and for 2 miles line the roadside in East Potomac Park. A gift by the Mayor of Tokyo to the city of Washington, the original 3,000 tress were propagated from the trees on the Arawaka River in a suburb of Tokyo. The first trees were planted by Mrs. William Howard Taft, wife of the president, and by Viscountess Chinda, wife of the Japanese Ambassador, Mar. 27, 1912. Today many of the 650 trees around the Tidal Basin have white blossoms, while some have pink; deep pink blossoms are in East Potomac Park. The trees usually are in full blossom the first week in April, but no precise date can be given earlier than 10 days prior to full blossom, which lasts about one week.

## Other Points of Interest

**Organization of American States Building**, 17th St. and Constitution Ave., NW, houses the General Secretariat of the OAS, the oldest major international organization in the world, representing 26 countries of the western hemisphere. Of traditional Spanish architecture with a tropical garden courtyard, the building is one of the more gracious sights in Washington. It contains the Hall of the Americas assembly room, art exhibitions, the Columbus Memorial Library, and behind the building, the Aztec Gardens, and the Museum of Modern Art of Latin America.

**National Society, Daughters of the American Revolution**, established in 1890, stands on a block bounded by 17th and 18th Sts., and C and D Sts. NW.

**American Red Cross**, 17th and D Sts. NW, occupies 3 white marble buildings of neoclassic design, embellished with a Corinthian portico, colonnades, and bronze doors. The Red Cross Museum is in the east building.

**Federal Reserve Building**, Constitution Ave., between 20th and 21st Sts. NW, is a 4-story white marble building of Georgian design, with formal gardens and fountains, and tasteful but relatively simple interiors, built 1937. An annex, the William McChesney Martin Building, was occupied in 1974.

**The Corcoran Gallery of Art**, 17th St. between New York Ave. and E St., NW. Permanent collections: 18th through 20th century American painting, sculpture; European painting, decorative arts. Contemporary exhibitions of painting, sculpture, photography. Open 11 a.m. to 5 p.m. Tuesday to Sunday; closed Monday, major holidays. Admission: $1.50; free on Tues. and Wed., at all times to members, senior citizens, children under 12 accompanied by an adult.

---

# N.Y. City Places of Interest

## Museums, Zoos, Libraries, Churches, Historic Sites, Buildings, Other Attractions

*See Index for Statue of Liberty*

**The New York Aquarium**, in Coney Island, exhibits marine life from all climes, with over 3,000 live specimens including whales, sharks, seals, and sea lions.

**The New York Botanical Garden**, covering 250 acres in the Bronx, features specialized gardens, a botanical library, and a plant and book shop.

**The Frick Collection**, 1 E. 70th St., was founded by Henry Clay Frick (1849-1919). The principal part of the collection consists of 14th-19th century paintings as well as sculpture and Chinese and French enamels.

**The Solomon R. Guggenheim Museum**, 5th Ave. and 89th St.; permanent collection contains over 3,000 paintings, drawings, sculptures, and graphic works by 19th and 20th century artists. The museum's spiral building was designed by Frank Lloyd Wright.

**The Hayden Planetarium**, facing 81st St. near Central Park W., presents changing sky shows with a Zeiss projector under the world's largest planetarium dome; "Astronomia," an exhibit of astronomy fact and fantasy throughout history; Guggenheim Space Theater shows, and a "Hall of the Sun."

**The Jewish Museum**, 5th Ave. at 92d St., offers exhibitions of Jewish art and ceremonial objects and exhibits of Jewish interest. The permanent collection of Judaica is considered the most comprehensive in the world.

**The Metropolitan Museum of Art**, 5th Ave. at 82d St. With over 1 million works of art, the museum's collection is the largest of its kind in the Western Hemisphere. Great masters of all the ages of art are included in the collections; Egyptian, Greek, Roman, Ancient Near Eastern, Islamic, Far Eastern, Medieval, Arms and Armor, European, Pre-Columbian, American, Contemporary Arts, Musical Instruments, Costume Institute.

**The Cloisters**, in Manhattan's Fort Tryon Park, is a branch of the Metropolitan devoted to Medieval art and architecture in 5 cloisters and other early European structures.

**The Museum of the American Indian**, Heye Foundation, Broadway at 155th St., maintains the world's largest collection of American Indian materials, extensive archeological and ethnological displays from North, Central, and South America.

**The Museum of Modern Art**, 11 W. 53d St., presents 20th century painting, sculpture, drawings, prints, architectural and industrial design, photography, and film.

**The American Museum of Natural History**, Central Park W. between 77th and 81st Sts., has large exhibits of man and beast from the most primitive times to the present, with extensive reconstruction of fossilized remains, dinosaurs, birds, Indians, and Eskimos. The collections of gems, mollusks, meteorites, and ocean life are famous.

**The Museum of the City of New York** on 5th Ave. at 103d St., illustrates the history and life of the city with dioramas, paintings, prints, maps, photographs, portraits, ship models, silver, furniture, toys, and rare books.

**The New-York Historical Society**, founded 1804, is at 170 Central Park W. between 76th and 77th Sts. The society maintains a museum devoted to Americana; American portrait, landscape, and genre paintings; a reference library; manuscripts; maps, prints, broadsides, and photographs. Of special interest are the original watercolor drawings by John James Audubon for his *Birds of America*.

**The New York Public Library:** In 1977, its resources were placed at more than 34.5 million items of which over 9 million were books, over 10 million manuscripts, over 6 million pictures, 3.5 million posters, photographs, and broadsides, 6 million pamphlets, scrapbooks, and clippings. Of this total, 6 million books and the pictures are in the collections of the 82 Branch Libraries which are maintained by N.Y. City. The Research Libraries, based at 5th Ave. and 42d St., includes the Performing Arts Research Center, in Lincoln Center, and the Schomburg Center for Research in Black Culture, 103 W. 135th St.

**South Street Seaport Museum,** on the East River waterfront in lower Manhattan, is a growing restoration of earlier eras of New York's port. At piers off South St. at Fulton, the museum has 8 ships, including an iron-hulled windjammer, one of the world's longest square-riggers, and the original Ambrose Lightship. Ashore on Fulton St. are museum galleries, a printing museum, and a bookshop.

**Whitney Museum of American Art,** Madison Ave. at 75th St., holds exhibitions of group and individual artists, historical and contemporary. Comprehensive permanent collection of American art. Has downtown branch at 55 Water St.

**The New York Zoological Society Park (The Bronx Zoo),** Pelham Parkway and Southern Boulevard, the Bronx, is one of the world's largest zoos. About 3,000 mammals, birds, reptiles are displayed in its 252 acres.

## Brooklyn Centers

**Brooklyn Academy of Music,** 30 Lafayette Ave., presents a Sept.-through-June program of music, dance, theater, and film.

**Brooklyn Botanic Garden,** Eastern Parkway, Washington and Flatbush Aves., has 50 acres of gardens, including rose, rock, bonsai, herb, wild flower, Japanese, a fragrance garden for the blind, and conservatory.

**The Brooklyn Museum,** Eastern Parkway and Washington Ave., estab. 1825, has comprehensive exhibitions in all major fields of art. An Outdoor Sculpture Garden contains ornaments from razed N.Y. area buildings.

## Houses of Worship

**Central Synagogue** (Reform), Lexington Ave. at 55th St., is the oldest Jewish house of worship in N.Y. City (1872), and combines 2 earlier congregations founded in 1839 and 1846.

**John Street United Methodist Church,** 44 John St., erected 1841, on site of Wesley Chapel of 1768, "first Methodist preaching-house in America," houses oldest Methodist Society, formed 1766.

**Marble Collegiate Church** (Collegiate Reformed Protestant Dutch), 5th Ave. and W. 29th St., erected 1854, is headquarters for Dr. Norman Vincent Peale.

**Plymouth Church of the Pilgrims** (Congregational), Orange and Hicks Sts., Brooklyn, is a Nat'l. Historic Site, built 1847, present structure 1849. Has windows illustrating Puritan influence on America and pew where Lincoln sat to hear Henry Ward Beecher, the first minister.

**Riverside Church** (Interdenominational), Riverside Drive and W. 122d St. The chief donor was John D. Rockefeller Jr. The tower, reminiscent of Chartres, is 100 ft. square, rises 392 ft.; it has the world's largest carillon, with 74 bells, and is open to public from 11 to 3.

**Cathedral of St. John the Divine** on Morningside Heights, Amsterdam Ave. and W. 112th St. (Episcopal), is the world's largest cathedral. It was begun 1892 as a Romanesque building; the design was changed to Gothic. The church is 603 ft. long, 146 ft. wide at nave, and will be 330 ft. wide at transept. Plans calls for two front towers which will rise to nearly 300 ft.

**St. Mark's-in-the-Bowery** (Episcopal), 2d Ave. and E. 10th St., originally a chapel built on the farm of Director General Peter Stuyvesant in 1660, rebuilt in 1799. A statue of Stuyvesant in the churchyard was presented by Netherlands Queen Wilhelmina in 1915.

**St. Patrick's Cathedral** (Roman Catholic), 5th Ave. between E. 50th and E. 51st Sts., opposite Rockefeller Center, was begun in 1858 in granite and marble in a Gothic revival style designed by James Renwick. It was opened in part in 1877 and dedicated May 25, 1879. It has 2 spires, 330 ft. tall, and a 26-ft. rose window. St. Patrick's is the cathedral church of the Archdiocese of N.Y.

**St. Paul's Chapel of Trinity Parish** (Episcopal), Broadway and Vesey St., is the oldest public building in continuous use in Manhattan. It was opened Oct. 30, 1766. Much of the interior decoration was by L'Enfant, who laid the plans for Washington, D.C.

**St. Thomas Church** (Episcopal), 5th Ave. at 53d St., is the 4th church building, consecrated 1916, of a parish founded in 1823. The limestone Gothic edifice was designed by architects Bertram G. Goodhue and Ralph Adams Cram.

**Temple Emanu-El,** 5th Ave. and 65th St., was erected 1929 by Congregation Emanu-El (Reform), which dates from 1845. It was built of limestone in early Romanesque style, its auditorium 77 ft. wide by 150 ft. long and 103 ft. high, one of the largest temples in the world. Noteworthy are the high arch at the entrance, the rose window, mosaics, and 6 bronze doors.

**Trinity Church** (Episcopal) faces Broadway at the head of Wall St. It was built 1841-46 of brown sandstone in perpendicular Gothic, designed by Richard Upjohn, is 78 ft. wide by 202 ft. long. The first church was completed in 1697. Alexander Hamilton and Robert Fulton are buried in the churchyard.

## Historic Sites

**Castle Clinton,** Battery Park, lower Manhattan is an 1811 fort, restored 1975; historical exhibits.

**Edgar Allan Poe Cottage,** Grand Concourse and Kingsbridge Rd., Bronx, is a wood frame cottage, built 1812, was the final home of Poe from 1846-49 and where his wife, Virginia Clem, died in 1847.

**Federal Hall National Memorial,** Wall and Nassau Sts., is a Greek Revival structure of 1842, originally the Custom House, later the U.S. Sub-Treasury. The site was first occupied by the Colonial City Hall and next by Federal Hall, where the Stamp Act Congress, Continental, and U.S. Congresses met, and George Washington took the oath of office as president.

**Fraunces Tavern,** Broad and Pearl Sts., was erected 1719 as the DeLancey mansion, acquired 1762 by Samuel Fraunces and operated as the Queen's Head Tavern. The Long Room was the scene of Washington's Farewell to his officers, Dec. 4, 1783.

**General Grant National Memorial (Grant's Tomb),** Riverside Dr. and W. 122d St., is a formal Roman-style mausoleum, 165 ft. tall, where Gen. U.S. Grant, 18th president, and Mrs. Grant are buried.

**The Morris-Jumel Mansion and Museum,** W. 160th St. and Edgecombe Ave., is a 3-story Georgian mansion with 4-pillared portico built in 1765 by retired Bristish Lt. Col. Roger Morris. From Sept. 14-Oct. 18, 1776, it was the headquarters of Gen. George Washington. In 1810 Stephen Jumel bought 36 of the original 100 acres of the property. In 1833, the widowed Eliza Jumel married Aaron Burr in the mansion's front parlor.

**Washington Square,** at the foot of 5th Ave., is the best known landmark of **Greenwich Village,** a colorful community and tourist attraction. Facing the lower end of 5th Ave. is the marble **Washington Arch,** designed by Stanford White to mark the centennial of the first inauguration and completed in 1895.

## Important Buildings

**City Hall,** headquarters of the mayor, the City Council, and the Board of Estimate of the City of New York, is in City Hall Park (the original Common), bounded by Broadway, Park Row, and Chambers St. Erected 1803-1812, it is an adaptation of French Renaissance with clock cupola surmounted by a figure of Justice.

**The Coliseum,** facing Columbus Circle between W. 58th and W. 60th Sts., is New York's principal center for national and international exhibitions. Opened in 1956, it cost about $35 million. The Coliseum has over 320,000 sq. ft. of exhibition space.

**Empire State Building,** 5th Ave., between W. 33d and 34th Sts., is one of the world's tallest buildings (see also World Trade Center, below), 1,250 ft. high plus a 222-ft. television and FM radio transmitting tower. The building was opened May 1, 1931. Nearly 2 million persons annually visit the 86th and 102d floor observatories.

**Lincoln Center for the Performing Arts** opened 1962 with a concert in Philharmonic (later renamed Avery Fisher) Hall. The center lies between W. 62d and 66th Sts., Amsterdam and Columbus Aves. It is a private, nonprofit, tax-exempt corporation of 8 constituent organizations. The New York State Theater opened in 1964; the Vivian Beaumont

| City | Hgt. ft. | Stories |
|---|---|---|
| Diamond Shamrock Bldg. | 300 | 23 |
| CEI Bldg. | 300 | 22 |
| Union Commerce Bldg. | 289 | 21 |
| Standard Bldg. | 282 | 21 |
| East Ohio Bldg. | 275 | 21 |

### Columbus, Oh.

| City | Hgt. ft. | Stories |
|---|---|---|
| State Office Tower, 30 E. Broad | 624 | 41 |
| LeVeque-Lincoln Tower, 50 W. Broad. | 555 | 47 |
| OneNationwide Plaza | 485 | 40 |
| Borden Bldg., 180 E. Broad | 438 | 34 |
| Franklin Cty. Municipal Courts Bldg. | 357 | 19 |
| Columbus Center, 100 E. Broad | 357 | 20 |
| Ohio Bell Bldg., 150 E. Gay St. | 348 | 26 |
| 88 E. Broad St. | 324 | 20 |
| BancOhio Plaza, 155 E. Broad | 317 | 25 |
| Motorists Bldg., 471 E. Broad | 297 | 21 |
| Midland Bldg., 250 E. Broad | 278 | 21 |

### Dallas, Tex.

| City | Hgt. ft. | Stories |
|---|---|---|
| First International Bldg. | 710 | 56 |
| First National Bank | 625 | 52 |
| Republic Bank Tower | 598 | 50 |
| Reunion Tower | 560 | 50 |
| Southland Life Tower | 550 | 42 |
| 2001 Bryan St. | 512 | 40 |
| Republic Bank Bldg., not incl. 150-ft. ornamental tower | 452 | 36 |
| One Main Place | 445 | 34 |
| Ling-Tempco-Vought Tower | 434 | 31 |
| Mercantile Natl. Bank Bldg., not incl. 115-ft. weather beacon | 430 | 31 |
| Mobil Bldg. | 430 | 31 |
| Fidelity Union Tower | 400 | 33 |
| Southwestern Bell Toll Bldg. | 372 | 22 |
| Court House & Fedl. Office Bldg. | 362 | 16 |
| Mercantile Dallas Bldg. | 360 | 22 |
| Sheraton Hotel. | 352 | 38 |
| Hyatt Hotel, 303 Reunion Blvd. | 343 | 30 |
| Elm Place, 1005-09 Elm St. | 341 | 22 |
| Main Tower. | 336 | 26 |
| Park Central No. 3. | 327 | 20 |
| Adolphus Tower | 327 | 27 |
| Bell Telephone Bldg. | 326 | 23 |
| Davis Bldg. | 323 | 21 |
| Manor House, Bank of Service & Trust | 319 | 26 |
| Preston Tower | 316 | 29 |
| Tower Petroleum Bldg. | 315 | 23 |
| Adolphus Hotel | 312 | 25 |
| Fairmont Hotel. | 308 | 24 |
| Baptist Annuity Center | 303 | 17 |
| Life Bldg. | 302 | 22 |
| Santa Fe Bldg. (1st unit) | 300 | 23 |

### Dayton, Oh.

| City | Hgt. ft. | Stories |
|---|---|---|
| Winters Bank Bldg. | 404 | 30 |
| Mead Tower, 10 W. 2d St. | 365 | 28 |
| Centre City Office Bldg. | 297 | 21 |
| Hulman Bldg.. | 295 | 23 |
| Grant-Deneau Bldg. | 290 | 22 |

### Denver, Col.

| City | Hgt. ft. | Stories |
|---|---|---|
| Anaconda Bldg. | 580 | 40 |
| Brooks Towers, 1020 15th St. | 420 | 42 |
| First of Denver Plaza | 415 | 32 |
| Energy Center 1 | 405 | 29 |
| Colorado Nat'l. Bank, 17th & Curtis | 389 | 26 |
| First National Bank | 385 | 28 |
| Security Life Bldg. | 384 | 33 |
| Lincoln Center | 367 | 30 |
| Western Fed. Savings. | 354 | 27 |
| Colorado State Bank | 352 | 27 |
| Brooks Tower Annex | 350 | 30 |
| 410 Building | 335 | 24 |
| Mountain Bell, 17th & Curtis | 330 | 21 |
| D&F Tower. | 330 | 20 |
| Prudential Tower Plaza | 322 | 26 |

### Des Moines, Ia.

| City | Hgt. ft. | Stories |
|---|---|---|
| Ruan Center | 457 | 36 |
| Financial Center, 7th & Walnut. | 345 | 25 |
| Equitable Bldg.. | 318 | 19 |
| State Capitol. | 275 | 4 |

### Detroit, Mich.

| City | Hgt. ft. | Stories |
|---|---|---|
| Detroit Plaza Hotel | 720 | 71 |
| City Natl. Bank Bldg., 637 Griswold | 557 | 47 |
| Guardian, 500 Griswold. | 485 | 40 |
| Renaissance Center (4 bldgs.). | 479 | 39 |
| Book Tower, 1227 Wash. Blvd. | 472 | 35 |
| Cadillac Tower, 51 Cadillac Sq. | 437 | 40 |
| David Stott, 1150 Griswold. | 436 | 38 |
| Mich. Cons. Gas Co. Bldg. | 430 | 32 |
| Fisher, W. Grand Blvd. & 2d St. | 420 | 28 |
| J. L. Hudson Bldg. | 397 | 28 |
| McNamara Federal Office Bldg. | 393 | 28 |
| Detroit Bank & Trust Bldg. | 370 | 25 |
| Edison Plaza | 365 | 28 |
| Woodward Tower | 358 | 34 |
| Buhl, 535 Griswold | 350 | 28 |
| Michigan Bell Telephone | 340 | 19 |
| 1st Federal Savings & Loan | 338 | 23 |
| Pontchartrain Motor Hotel | 336 | 23 |
| Commonwealth Bldg. | 325 | 25 |
| 1300 Lafayette East. | 325 | 30 |

### Edmonton, Alta.

| City | Hgt. ft. | Stories |
|---|---|---|
| AGT Tower, 10020-100 St.. | 441 | 34 |
| CN Tower, 1004-104 Ave. | 365 | 26 |
| Toronto Dominion Tower. | 325 | 27 |
| Oxford Tower | 325 | 29 |
| Sun Life Bldg. | 320 | 25 |
| Edmonton House | 315 | 34 |
| Royal Trust Tower. | 289 | 25 |

### Fort Wayne, Ind.

| City | Hgt. ft. | Stories |
|---|---|---|
| Ft. Wayne Natl. Bank | 339 | 26 |
| Lincoln Natl. Bank | 312 | 23 |

### Fort Worth, Tex.

| City | Hgt. ft. | Stories |
|---|---|---|
| Ft. Worth Natl. Bank. | 454 | 37 |
| Continental Natl. Bank Bldg. | 380 | 30 |
| First National Bank, 500 W. 7th | 300 | 21 |
| Continental Life Ins. Bldg. | 282 | 23 |

### Harrisburg, Pa.

| City | Hgt. ft. | Stories |
|---|---|---|
| *State Office Tower #2 | 334 | 21 |
| City Towers | 291 | 25 |
| State Capitol | 272 | 6 |

### Hartford, Conn.

| City | Hgt. ft. | Stories |
|---|---|---|
| Travelers Ins. Co. Bldg. | 527 | 34 |
| Hartford Plaza | 420 | 22 |
| Hartford Natl. Bank & Trust | 360 | 26 |
| One Financial Plaza, 755 Main | 335 | 26 |

### Honolulu, Ha.

| City | Hgt. ft. | Stories |
|---|---|---|
| Ala Moana Hotel. | 390 | 38 |
| Pacific Trade Center | 360 | 30 |
| Discovery Bay | 350 | 42 |
| Hyatt Regency Waikiki | 350 | 39 |
| Hemmeter Center | 350 | 39 |
| Mehelani Waikiki Lodge | 350 | 43 |
| Regency Tower, 2525 Date St. | 350 | 42 |
| *Regency Tower #2 | 350 | 43 |
| Yacht Harbor Towers | 350 | 40 |
| Canterbury Place | 350 | 40 |
| Iolani Towers. | 350 | 38 |
| Diamond Head Tower. | 350 | 38 |
| Ala Wai Sunset | 350 | 44 |
| Century Center | 350 | 41 |
| Pacific Beach Hotel | 350 | 43 |
| Waikiki Ala Wai Waterfront. | 350 | 43 |
| Waikiki Lodge II | 350 | 43 |
| Chateau Waikiki | 349 | 39 |
| Rainbow Plaza | 348 | 37 |
| Waikiki Beach Tower | 347 | 39 |
| 2121 Ala Wai Blvd. | 347 | 41 |
| Royal Kuhio | 346 | 39 |
| Waipuna | 343 | 38 |
| *Ioloni Court Tower | 341 | 40 |
| Waikiki Banyon. | 341 | 36 |
| Waikiki Sunset Makai. | 341 | 37 |
| The Villa on Eaton Square | 335 | 37 |
| Kukui Plaza. | 333 | 33 |
| The Skyrise | 333 | 38 |
| *Grosvenor Center | 330 | 30 |
| Ke Aloha at Waikiki | 330 | 35 |

### Houston, Tex.

| City | Hgt. ft. | Stories |
|---|---|---|
| *Texas Commerce Plaza. | 800 | 60 |

| City | Hgt. ft. | Stories |
|---|---|---|
| *First International Plaza | 748 | 55 |
| One Shell Plaza (not incl. 285 ft. TV tower) | 714 | 50 |
| One Houston Center | 678 | 47 |
| 1100 Milam Bldg. | 651 | 47 |
| *3 Allen Center | 650 | 50 |
| Exxon Bldg. | 606 | 44 |
| 2 Houston Center | 570 | 40 |
| Dresser Tower | 550 | 40 |
| Pennzoil, 700 Milam. | 523 | 36 |
| Two Allen Center | 521 | 36 |
| Entex Bldg. | 518 | 35 |
| Tenneco Bldg. | 502 | 33 |
| Conoco Bldg. | 465 | 32 |
| One Allen Center | 452 | 34 |
| *Summit Tower West | 441 | 32 |
| Summit Tower East | 441 | 32 |
| Gulf Bldg. | 428 | 37 |
| First City Natl. Bank. | 410 | 32 |
| Houston Lighting & Power | 410 | 27 |
| Neils Esperson Bldg. | 409 | 31 |
| Hyatt Regency Houston | 401 | 34 |
| Houston Natural Gas Bldg. | 386 | 28 |
| Bank of the Southwest | 369 | 24 |
| Sheraton-Lincoln Hotel | 352 | 28 |
| Two Shell Plaza | 341 | 26 |
| American General Life | 337 | 25 |
| Transco. | 333 | 25 |
| Allied Chemical Bldg. | 328 | 25 |
| 609 Fannin Bldg.. | 325 | 22 |
| Holiday Inn | 325 | 30 |
| *Post Oak Central 2 | 321 | 24 |
| Capital Natl. Bank | 320 | 21 |
| Post Oak Central | 318 | 25 |
| St. Luke's Hospital | 316 | 26 |
| 500 Jefferson Bldg. | 316 | 21 |
| Marathon Manufacturing Co. Bldg. | 313 | 21 |
| Sterling Bldg. | 312 | 22 |
| Melrose Bldg. | 308 | 21 |
| Chamber of Commerce Bldg. | 306 | 22 |
| Control Data Center. | 303 | 22 |
| First National Life Bldg. | 302 | 22 |
| Prudential Bldg. | 300 | 21 |
| Kellogg Bldg.. | 300 | 22 |

### Indianapolis, Ind.

| City | Hgt. ft. | Stories |
|---|---|---|
| Indiana Natl. Bank Tower | 504 | 37 |
| City-County Bldg. | 377 | 26 |
| Indiana Bell Telephone | 320 | 20 |
| Blue Cross-Blue Shield Bldg.. | 302 | 18 |
| Riley Towers (2 bldgs.) | 294 | 30 |
| Indiana Bell "220" Bldg. | 284 | 20 |
| Monument Circle | 284 | ... |
| Market Square Office Bldg. | 283 | 20 |

### Jacksonville, Fla.

| City | Hgt. ft. | Stories |
|---|---|---|
| Independent Life & Accident Ins. Co.. | 535 | 37 |
| Gulf Life Ins. Co. Bldg. | 432 | 28 |
| Prudential Ins. Co. of America | 295 | 22 |
| Blue Cross-Blue Shield | 287 | 20 |
| Atlantic National Bank. | 278 | 19 |

### Jersey City, N.J.

Medical Center (5 bldgs.; 332 ft., 294 ft., 274 ft., (2) 273 ft.)

### Kansas City, Mo.

| City | Hgt. ft. | Stories |
|---|---|---|
| Kansas City Power and Light Bldg. | 476 | 32 |
| City Hall | 443 | 29 |
| Federal Office Bldg.. | 413 | 35 |
| Commerce Tower | 402 | 32 |
| Southwest Bell Telephone Bldg.. | 394 | 27 |
| Pershing Road Associates | 352 | 28 |
| A. T. & T. Long Line Bldg. | 331 | 20 |
| Bryant Bldg. | 319 | 26 |
| Federal Reserve Bldg. | 311 | 21 |
| City Center Square, 1100 Main | 302 | 30 |
| Holiday Inn. | 300 | 28 |

### Las Vegas, Nev.

| City | Hgt. ft. | Stories |
|---|---|---|
| Las Vegas Hilton | 375 | 30 |
| MGM Grand | 362 | 26 |
| Landmark Hotel | 356 | 31 |
| Sahara Hotel. | 294 | 24 |
| Dunes Hotel | 277 | 24 |
| Mint Hotel | 275 | 26 |

### Little Rock, Ark.

| City | Hgt. ft. | Stories |
|---|---|---|
| First National Bank | 454 | 33 |
| Worthen Bank & Trust | 375 | 28 |
| Union National Bank. | 331 | 24 |
| Tower Bldg. | 300 | 18 |

### Los Angeles, Cal.

| City | Hgt. ft. | Stories |
|---|---|---|
| United Cal. Bank. | 858 | 62 |
| Security Pacific Natl. Bank | 738 | 55 |
| Atlantic Richfield Plaza (2 bldgs.) | 699 | 52 |
| Crocker-Citizen Plaza | 620 | 42 |
| Century Plaza Towers (2 bldgs.). | 571 | 44 |
| Union Bank Square | 516 | 41 |
| City Hall | 454 | 28 |
| Equitable Life Bldg. | 454 | 34 |
| Occidental Life Bldg. | 452 | 32 |
| Mutual Benefit Life Ins. Bldg. | 435 | 31 |
| Broadway Plaza | 414 | 33 |
| 1900 Ave. of Stars | 398 | 27 |
| 1 Wilshire Bldg. | 395 | 28 |
| Bonaventure Hotel, 404 S. Figueroa | 367 | 34 |
| Cal. Fed. Savings & Loan Bldg. | 363 | 28 |
| Century City Office Bldg. | 363 | 24 |
| Bunker Hill Towers | 349 | 32 |
| International Industries Plaza. | 347 | 24 |
| City Natl. Bank Bldg. | 344 | 24 |
| Wilshire West Plaza | 327 | 24 |

### Louisville, Ky.

| City | Hgt. ft. | Stories |
|---|---|---|
| First Natl. Bank | 512 | 40 |
| Citizen's Plaza | 420 | 30 |
| *Kincaid Tower | 333 | 22 |
| Galt House | 325 | 25 |
| Louisville Trust Bldg. | 312 | 24 |
| 800 Apartments Bldg. | 290 | 29 |

### Memphis, Tenn.

| City | Hgt. ft. | Stories |
|---|---|---|
| 100 N. Main Bldg. | 430 | 37 |
| Commerce Square | 396 | 31 |
| Sterick Bldg. | 365 | 31 |
| Clark, 5100 Poplar | 365 | 32 |
| First Natl. Bank Bldg. | 332 | 25 |
| Hyatt Regency. | 329 | 28 |
| Lowenstein's Towers | 296 | 25 |
| Lincoln American Life Tower | 290 | 22 |
| White Station Tower. | 280 | 24 |

### Miami, Fla.

| City | Hgt. ft. | Stories |
|---|---|---|
| One Biscayne Corp.. | 456 | 40 |
| First Federal Savings & Loan | 375 | 32 |
| Dade County Court House | 357 | 28 |
| Ferre Bldg. | 340 | 30 |
| *Plaza Venetia. | 332 | 33 |
| Flagler Center Bldg.. | 318 | 25 |
| Omni International Hotel | 296 | 29 |
| Brickell Bay Club | 286 | 29 |
| Palm Bay Club. | 279 | 24 |

### Milwaukee, Wis.

| City | Hgt. ft. | Stories |
|---|---|---|
| First Wis. Center & Office Tower | 625 | 42 |
| City Hall | 350 | 9 |
| Wisconsin Telephone Co.. | 313 | 19 |
| Marine Plaza Bldg. | 288 | 22 |
| Allen-Bradley Co. | 280 | 17 |
| Marshall & Ilsley Bank | 277 | 21 |

### Minneapolis, Minn.

| City | Hgt. ft. | Stories |
|---|---|---|
| IDS Center | 772 | 57 |
| *Allsbury Center. | 493 | 36 |
| Foshay Tower, not including 163-ft. antenna tower. | 447 | 32 |
| Hennepin County Government Center | 403 | 24 |
| First Natl. Bank Bldg. | 366 | 28 |
| Municipal Building | 355 | 14 |
| North Western Bell Telephone | 350 | 26 |
| Cedar-Riverside | 337 | 39 |
| Dain Tower | 311 | 26 |
| Midwest Federal Savings & Loan | 276 | 20 |

### Montreal, Que.

| City | Hgt. ft. | Stories |
|---|---|---|
| Place Victoria | 624 | 47 |
| Place Ville Marie. | 616 | 42 |
| Canadian Imperial Bank of Commerce | 604 | 43 |
| Le Complexe Desjardins La Tour du Sud | 498 | 40 |

| City | Hgt. ft. | Stories |
|---|---|---|
| La Tour du L'Est | 428 | 32 |
| La Tour du Nord | 355 | 27 |
| La Tour Laurier | 425 | 36 |
| C.I.L. House | 429 | 32 |
| Chateau Champlain Hotel | 420 | 38 |
| Port Royal Apts. | 400 | 33 |
| Royal Bank Tower | 397 | 22 |
| Sun Life Bldg. | 390 | 26 |
| Banque Canadienne National | 390 | 32 |
| Place du Canada | 372 | 33 |
| Hydro Quebec | 360 | 27 |
| Alexis Nihon Plaza. | 331 | 33 |
| Bell Telephone | 324 | 22 |
| Le Cartier Apts. | 320 | 32 |

### Nashville, Tenn.

| City | Hgt. ft. | Stories |
|---|---|---|
| Natl. Life & Acc. Ins. Co. | 452 | 31 |
| Nashville Life & Casualty Tower | 409 | 30 |
| First American Natl. Bank | 354 | 28 |
| Hyatt Regency | 300 | 28 |
| Third Natl. Bank Bldg. | 292 | 20 |
| Andrew Jackson State Office Bldg. | 286 | 17 |

### Newark, N.J.

| City | Hgt. ft. | Stories |
|---|---|---|
| National Newark & Essex Bank | 465 | 36 |
| Raymond-Commerce | 448 | 36 |
| Prudential Corporate Bldg. | 369 | 27 |
| Prudential Ins. Co., 753 Broad St. | 360 | 26 |
| Western Electric Bldg. | 359 | 31 |
| Gateway 1 | 359 | 31 |
| American Insurance Company | 326 | 21 |
| Prudential Ins. Co., 213 Washington St. | 300 | 15 |
| N.J. Bell Telephone Co. | 275 | 21 |

### New Haven, Conn.

| City | Hgt. ft. | Stories |
|---|---|---|
| Knights of Columbus Hqs. | 319 | 23 |

### New Orleans, La.

| City | Hgt. ft. | Stories |
|---|---|---|
| One Shell Square | 697 | 51 |
| Plaza Tower | 531 | 45 |
| Marriott Hotel | 450 | 42 |
| Bank of New Orleans | 438 | 31 |
| Int'l. Trade Mart Bldg. | 407 | 33 |
| 225 Baronne St. | 362 | 28 |
| Hyatt-Regency Hotel, Poydras Plaza | 360 | 25 |
| Hibernia Bank Bldg. | 355 | 23 |
| New Orleans Hilton, Intl. River Center | 340 | 29 |
| American Bank Bldg. | 330 | 24 |
| Canal LaSalle Bldg. | 288 | 24 |
| Charity Hospital of Louisiana | 279 | 19 |
| Lykes Center, 300 Poydras | 276 | 22 |

### New York, N.Y.

| City | Hgt. ft. | Stories |
|---|---|---|
| World Trade Center (2 towers) | 1,350 | 110 |
| Empire State, 34th St. & 5th Ave. | 1,250 | 102 |
| TV tower, 222 ft., makes total | 1,472 | ... |
| Chrysler, Lexington Ave. & 43d St. | 1,046 | 77 |
| American International Bldg., 70 Pine St. | 950 | 67 |
| 40 Wall Tower | 927 | 71 |
| Citicorp Center | 914 | 45 |
| RCA, Rockefeller Center | 850 | 70 |
| 1 Chase Manhattan Plaza | 813 | 60 |
| Pan Am Bldg., 200 Park Ave. | 808 | 59 |
| Woolworth, 233 Broadway | 792 | 60 |
| 1 Penn Plaza | 764 | 57 |
| Exxon, 1251 Ave. of Americas | 750 | 54 |
| 1 Liberty Plaza | 743 | 50 |
| Citibank | 741 | 57 |
| One Astor Plaza | 730 | 54 |
| Union Carbide Bldg., 270 Park Ave. | 707 | 52 |
| General Motors Bldg. | 705 | 50 |
| Metropolitan Life, 1 Madison Ave. | 700 | 50 |
| 500 5th Ave. | 697 | 60 |
| 9 W. 57th St. | 688 | 50 |
| Chem. Bank, N.Y. Trust Bldg. | 687 | 50 |
| 55 Water St. | 687 | 53 |
| Chanin, Lexington Ave. & 42d St. | 680 | 56 |
| Gulf & Western Bldg., 15 Columbus Circle. | 679 | 44 |
| Marine Midland Bldg., 140 Bway. | 677 | 52 |
| McGraw Hill, 1221 Ave. of Am. | 674 | 51 |
| Lincoln, 60 E. 52d Street | 673 | 53 |
| 1633 Broadway | 670 | 48 |
| American Brands, 245 Park Ave. | 648 | 47 |
| *A. T. & T. Tower | 645 | 37 |

| City | Hgt. ft. | Stories |
|---|---|---|
| General Electric, 570 Lexington | 640 | 50 |
| Irving Trust, 1 Wall St. | 640 | 50 |
| 345 Park Ave. | 634 | 44 |
| Grace Plaza, 1114 Ave. of Am. | 630 | 50 |
| 1 New York Plaza | 630 | 50 |
| Home Insurance Co. Bldg. | 630 | 44 |
| N.Y. Telephone, 1095 Ave. of Am. | 630 | 40 |
| 888 7th Ave. | 628 | 42 |
| 1 Hammarskjold Plaza | 628 | 50 |
| Waldorf-Astoria, 301 Park Ave. | 625 | 47 |
| Burlington House, 1345 Ave. of Am. | 625 | 50 |
| Olympic Tower, 645 5th Ave. | 620 | 51 |
| 10 E. 40th St. | 620 | 48 |
| New York Life, 51 Madison Ave. | 615 | 40 |
| Penney Bldg., 1301 Ave. of Am. | 609 | 46 |
| 560 Lexington Ave. | 600 | 46 |
| Celanese Bldg., 1211 Ave. of Am. | 592 | 45 |
| U.S. Court House, 505 Pearl St. | 590 | 37 |
| Federal Bldg., Foley Square | 587 | 41 |
| Time & Life, 1271 Ave. of Am. | 587 | 47 |
| Cooper Bregstein Bldg., 1250 Bway. | 580 | 40 |
| 1185 Ave. of Americas | 580 | 42 |
| Municipal, Park Row & Centre St. | 580 | 34 |
| 1 Madison Square Plaza | 576 | 42 |
| Westvaco Bldg. 299 Park Ave. | 574 | 42 |
| Socony Mobil Bldg., East 42d St. | 572 | 45 |
| Sperry Rand Bldg., 1290 Ave. of Am. | 570 | 43 |
| 600 3d Ave. | 570 | 42 |
| N.Y. General, 230 Park Ave. | 565 | 35 |
| 1 Bankers Trust Plaza | 565 | 40 |
| 30 Broad St. | 562 | 48 |
| Sherry-Netherland, 5th Ave. & 59th St. | 560 | 40 |
| Continental Can, 633 3d Ave. | 557 | 39 |
| Sperry & Hutchinson, 330 Madison | 555 | 39 |
| Galleria, 117 E. 57th St. | 552 | 57 |
| Interchem Bldg., 1133 Ave. of Am. | 552 | 45 |
| N.Y. Telephone, 323 Bway. | 550 | 45 |
| 919 3d Ave. | 550 | 47 |
| Burroughs Bldg., 605 3d Ave. | 550 | 44 |
| Bankers Trust, 33 E. 48 St. | 547 | 41 |
| Transportation Bldg., 225 Bway. | 546 | 45 |
| Equitable Life, 1285 Ave. of Am. | 540 | 42 |
| Ritz Tower, Park Ave. & 57th St. | 540 | 41 |
| Bankers Trust, 6 Wall St. | 540 | 39 |
| 1166 Ave. of Americas | 540 | 44 |
| Equitable, 120 Broadway | 538 | 40 |
| 1700 Broadway | 533 | 41 |
| Downtown Athletic Club, 19 West St. | 530 | 45 |
| Nelson Towers, 7th Ave. & 34th St. | 525 | 45 |
| Hotel Pierre, 5th Ave. & 61st St. | 525 | 44 |
| House of Seagram, 375 Park Ave. | 525 | 38 |
| Random House, 825 3d Ave. | 522 | 40 |
| 3 Park Ave. | 522 | 42 |
| North American Plywood, 800 3d Ave. | 520 | 41 |
| Du Mont Bldg., 515 Madison Ave. | 520 | 42 |
| 26 Broadway | 520 | 31 |
| Newsweek Bldg., 444 Madison Ave. | 518 | 43 |
| Sterling Drug. Bldg., 90 Park Ave. | 515 | 41 |
| First National City Bank. | 515 | 41 |
| Bank of New York, 48 Wall St. | 513 | 32 |
| Navarre, 512 7th Ave. | 513 | 43 |
| Williamsburg Savings Bank, Bklyn. | 512 | 42 |
| ITT—American, 437 Madison Ave. | 512 | 40 |
| International, Rockefeller Center | 512 | 41 |
| 1407 Broadway Realty Corp. | 512 | 44 |
| United Nations, 405 E. 42 St. | 505 | 39 |
| Park Vendome Tower. | 505 | 48 |
| 2 New York Plaza | 504 | 40 |
| 22 E. 40th St. | 503 | 43 |
| 60 Broad St. | 503 | 39 |
| Americana Hotel. | 501 | 51 |
| World Apparel Center, 1411 Bway. | 501 | 41 |

### Oakland, Cal.

| City | Hgt. ft. | Stories |
|---|---|---|
| Ordway Bldg., 2150 Valdez St. | 404 | 28 |
| Kaiser Bldg. | 390 | 28 |
| Clorox Bldg. | 330 | 24 |
| City Hall | 319 | 15 |
| Tribune Tower | 305 | 21 |
| United Cal. Bank Bldg. | 297 | 18 |
| Blue Cross Bldg. | 296 | 21 |
| Telephone Bldg. | 289 | 15 |

### Oklahoma City, Okla.

| City | Hgt. ft. | Stories |
|---|---|---|
| Liberty Tower | 500 | 36 |
| First National Bank | 493 | 33 |
| City National Bank Tower | 440 | 32 |

| City | Hgt. ft. | Stories |
|---|---|---|
| Kerr-McGee Center | 393 | 30 |
| Fidelity Plaza | 310 | 15 |
| Southwestern Bell Telephone | 303 | 15 |
| The Regency Tower | 288 | 25 |

### Omaha, Neb.

| City | Hgt. ft. | Stories |
|---|---|---|
| Woodmen Tower | 469 | 30 |
| Northwestern Bell Telephone Hdqrs. | 334 | 16 |
| Masonic Manor | 320 | 22 |
| First Natl. Bank | 295 | 22 |

### Ottawa, Ont.

| City | Hgt. ft. | Stories |
|---|---|---|
| Place de Ville, tower C | 368 | 29 |
| Place Bell Canada | 318 | 26 |
| DBS Tower | 308 | 26 |
| Holiday Inn | 308 | 28 |
| Parliament Bldgs., Peace Tower | 291 | ... |
| Skyline Hotel | 286 | 25 |
| L'Esplanade Laurier (2 towers) | 285 | 22 |

### Philadelphia, Pa.

| City | Hgt. ft. | Stories |
|---|---|---|
| City Hall Tower, incl. 37-ft. statue of Wm. Penn. | 548 | 7 |
| 1818 Market St. | 500 | 40 |
| Fidelity Mutual Life Ins. Bldg. | 490 | 38 |
| Phila. Saving Fund Society | 490 | 39 |
| Central Penn Natl. Bank | 490 | 36 |
| Centre Square | 490 | 40 |
| Industrial Valley Bank Bldg. | 482 | 32 |
| Philadelphia National Bank | 475 | 25 |
| 2000 Market St. Bldg. | 435 | 29 |
| Atlantic Richfield Tower, Centre Square | 412 | 33 |
| Fidelity Bank Bldg. | 410 | 30 |
| Two Girard Plaza | 404 | 30 |
| Lewis Tower, 15th & Locust | 397 | 33 |
| Fifteen Hundred Locust | 390 | 44 |
| Philadelphia Electric Co. | 384 | 27 |
| INA Annex, 1600 Arch St. | 383 | 27 |
| Academy House, 1420 Locust St. | 377 | 37 |
| Penn Mutual Life | 375 | 20 |
| The Drake, 15th & Spruce | 375 | 33 |
| Medical Tower, 255 So. 17th. | 364 | 33 |
| State Bldg., 1400 Spring Garden | 351 | 18 |
| United Engineers, 17th & Ludlow | 344 | 20 |
| Packard, 15th & Chestnut | 340 | 25 |
| Inquirer Building | 340 | 18 |
| Dorchester | 339 | 32 |
| Transportation Centre | 336 | 18 |
| Land Title, Broad & Chestnut | 331 | 22 |
| Suburban Station Bldg. | 330 | 21 |

### Phoenix, Ariz.

| City | Hgt. ft. | Stories |
|---|---|---|
| Valley National Bank | 483 | 40 |
| Arizona Bank Downtown | 407 | 31 |
| First National Bank | 372 | 27 |
| First Federal Savings Bldg. | 341 | 26 |
| Regency Apts. | 297 | 21 |
| Hyatt-Regency Hotel | 281 | 21 |
| Del Webb TowneHouse | 280 | 23 |

### Pittsburgh, Pa.

| City | Hgt. ft. | Stories |
|---|---|---|
| U.S. Steel Bldg. | 841 | 64 |
| Gulf, 7th Ave. and Grant St. | 582 | 44 |
| University of Pittsburgh | 535 | 42 |
| Mellon Bank Bldg. | 520 | 41 |
| 1 Oliver Plaza | 511 | 39 |
| Grant, Grant St. at 3rd Ave. | 485 | 40 |
| Koppers, 7th Ave. and Grant | 475 | 34 |
| Equibank Bldg. | 445 | 34 |
| Pittsburgh National Bldg. | 424 | 30 |
| Alcoa Bldg., 425 Sixth Ave. | 410 | 30 |
| Westinghouse Bldg. | 355 | 23 |
| Oliver, 535 Smithfield St. | 347 | 25 |
| Gateway Bldg. No. 3 | 344 | 24 |
| Centre City Tower | 341 | 26 |
| Federal Bldg., 1000 Liberty Ave. | 340 | 23 |
| Bell Telephone, 416 7th Ave. | 339 | 21 |
| Hilton Hotel | 333 | 22 |
| Frick, 437 Grant St. | 330 | 20 |
| 301 Fifth Ave. | 322 | 24 |
| Washington Plaza Apts. | 300 | 23 |
| Commonwealth, 316 Fourth Ave. | 300 | 21 |

### Portland, Ore.

| City | Hgt. ft. | Stories |
|---|---|---|
| First Natl. Bank of Oregon | 538 | 41 |
| Georgia Pacific Bldg. | 367 | 27 |

### Providence, R.I.

| City | Hgt. ft. | Stories |
|---|---|---|
| Industrial National Bank | 420 | 26 |
| Rhode Island Hospital Trust Tower | 410 | 30 |
| 40 Westminster Bldg. | 301 | 24 |

### Richmond, Va.

| City | Hgt. ft. | Stories |
|---|---|---|
| Federal Reserve Bank | 393 | 21 |
| First & Merchants Natl. Bank | 313 | 26 |
| City Hall | 310 | 18 |
| One James River Plaza | 302 | 21 |
| Central National Bank Bldg. | 282 | 24 |

### Rochester, N.Y.

| City | Hgt. ft. | Stories |
|---|---|---|
| Xerox Tower | 443 | 30 |
| Lincoln First Tower | 390 | 26 |
| Eastman Kodak Bldg. | 360 | 19 |
| First Federal Bank Plaza | 305 | 22 |
| Marine Midland Bank Bldg. | 280 | 22 |

### St. Louis, Mo.

| City | Hgt. ft. | Stories |
|---|---|---|
| Gateway Arch | 630 | ... |
| *1st National Bank/IBM | 560 | 40 |
| Mercantile Trust Bldg. | 485 | 35 |
| Laclede Gas. Bldg., 8th & Olive | 400 | 30 |
| S.W. Bell Telephone Bldg. | 398 | 31 |
| Civil Courts | 387 | 13 |
| Queeny Tower | 321 | 24 |
| Counsil House Plaza | 320 | 30 |
| Park Plaza Hotel | 310 | 30 |
| Pierre Laclede Tower | 309 | 24 |
| Stauffer's Riverfront Inn, 3rd St. | 301 | 22 |
| Riverfront Holiday Inn | 290 | 22 |
| Mansion House | 285 | 22 |
| 7777 Bonhomme Bldg. | 285 | 22 |
| 500 Broadway | 282 | 22 |
| Inn of the Spanish Pavilion | 280 | 22 |
| Equitable Bldg. | 280 | 21 |

### St. Paul, Minn.

| City | Hgt. ft. | Stories |
|---|---|---|
| First Natl. Bank Bldg., incl. 100-ft. sign | 517 | 32 |
| Osborn Bldg. | 368 | 20 |
| Kellogg Square Apts. | 366 | 32 |
| Northwestern Bell Telephone Bldg. | 340 | 15 |
| American National Bank Bldg. | 335 | 25 |
| St. Paul Cathedral | 307 | ... |
| U.S. Post Office Bldg. | 274 | 12 |
| St. Paul Radisson Hotel | 273 | 24 |

### Salt Lake City, Ut.

| City | Hgt. ft. | Stories |
|---|---|---|
| L.D.S. Church Office Bldg. | 420 | 30 |
| Beneficial Life Tower | 351 | 27 |
| City & County Bldg. | 290 | ... |
| State Capitol | 285 | ... |
| Univ. Club Bldg. | 277 | 24 |

### San Antonio, Tex.

| City | Hgt. ft. | Stories |
|---|---|---|
| Tower of the Americas | 622 | ... |
| Tower Life | 404 | 30 |
| Nix Professional Bldg. | 375 | 23 |
| Natl. Bank of Commerce | 310 | 24 |
| First Natl. Bank Tower | 302 | 20 |
| Frost Bank Tower | 300 | 21 |
| Alamo National Bldg. | 288 | 23 |
| Milam Bldg. | 280 | 20 |

### San Diego, Cal.

| City | Hgt. ft. | Stories |
|---|---|---|
| California First Bank | 388 | 27 |
| Crocker Natl. Bank Bldg. | 340 | 25 |
| Financial Square | 339 | 24 |
| Central Federal | 320 | 22 |
| Union Bank | 320 | 22 |
| Little America Westgate Hotel | 303 | 19 |
| San Diego Gas & Electric Bldg. | 293 | 21 |
| Charter Oil Bldg. | 281 | 23 |
| Security Pacific Natl. Bank Bldg. | 278 | 18 |
| Home Tower | 278 | 18 |

### San Francisco, Cal.

| City | Hgt. ft. | Stories |
|---|---|---|
| Transamerica Pyramid | 853 | 48 |
| Bank of America | 778 | 52 |
| Security Pacific Bank | 569 | 45 |
| One Market Plaza, Spear St. | 565 | 43 |
| Wells Fargo Bldg. | 561 | 43 |

bought Alaska from Russia for $7.2 million, a bargain which some called "Seward's Folly." In 1896, gold was discovered and the famed Gold Rush was on.

**Tourist attractions:** Glacier Bay National Monument, Mt. McKinley National Park, one of North America's great wildlife sanctuaries, Pribilof Islands for seal rookeries, restored St. Michael's Russian Orthodox Cathedral, Sitka.

**Famous Alaskans** include Carl Eielson, Ernest Gruening, Joe Juneau, Sydney Laurence, James Wickersham.

**Chamber of Commerce:** 310 2d St. Juneau, AK 99801.

# Arizona

## Grand Canyon State

**People. Population** (1977): 2,296,000; **rank:** 32. **Pop. density:** 20.2 per sq. mi. **Urban** (1970): 79.6%. **Racial distrib.** (1975): 90.7% White; 3.0% Black; 6.2% Other (includes American Indians); Hispanic (1970): 333,349. **Major ethnic groups:** Mexican, German, English, Italian. **Net migration** (1970-76): +356,000.

**Geography. Total area:** 113,909 sq. mi.; **rank:** 6. **Land area:** 113,417 sq. mi. **Acres forested land:** 18,583,000. **Location:** in the southwestern U.S. **Climate:** clear and dry in the southern regions and northern plateau; high central areas have heavy winter snows. **Topography:** Colorado plateau in the N, containing the Grand Canyon; Mexican Highlands running diagonally NW to SE; Sonoran Desert in the SW. **Capital:** Phoenix.

**Economy. Principal industries:** manufacturing, mining and construction. **Principal manufactured goods:** electronics, printing and publishing, foods, primary and fabricated metals, aircraft and missiles, apparel. **Value added by manufacture:** $2.1 million/yr. **Agriculture:** Chief crops: cotton, sorghum, barley, corn, wheat, sugar beets, citrus fruits. **Livestock:** 1,135,000 cattle; 99,000 hogs/pigs; 490,000 sheep; 565,000 poultry. **Minerals** (1977): copper (prod. valued at $1.2 billion, 75% of total mineral production), gold, silver, molybdenum, sand and gravel, lime. **International airports at:** Phoenix, Tucson. **Value of construction** (1977): $3,834,413,000. **Employment distribution:** 2.6% agriculture; 12.8% manufacturing; 11.0% services. **Per capita income** (1976): $5,817. **Unemployment** (1976): 9.8%. **Tourism** (1976): out-of-state visitors spent $1.87 billion.

**Finance. No. banks:** 18; **No. savings and loan assns.:** 16.

**Federal government. No. federal employees** (1976): 36,100. **Federal payroll** (1976): $83.5 million. **Notable federal facilities:** Williams, Luke, Davis-Montham AF bases; Ft. Huachuca Army Base; Yuma Proving Grounds.

**Energy. Electricity production** (1977, mwh, by source): Hydroelectric: 6.5 million; Mineral: 23.3 million; Nuclear: —.

**Education. No. schools:** 737 elementary; 242 secondary; 22 higher education. **Avg. salary, public school teachers** (1977): $13,743.

**State data. Motto:** Ditat Deus (God enriches). **Flower:** Blossom of the Seguaro cactus. **Bird:** Cactus wren. **Tree:** Paloverde. **Song:** Arizona. **Entered union** Feb. 14, 1912; rank, 48th. **State fair** at: Phoenix; late Oct.–early Nov.

**History.** Marcos de Niza, a Franciscan, and Estevan, a black slave, explored the area in 1539. Eusebio Francisco Kino, Jesuit missionary, taught Indians Christianity and farming, 1690-1711, and left a chain of missions. Spain ceded Arizona to Mexico, 1821. The U. S. took over at the end of the Mexican War, 1848. The area below the Gila River was obtained from Mexico in the Gadsden Purchase, 1854. Long Apache wars did not end until 1886, with Geronimo's surrender.

**Tourist attractions.** The Grand Canyon of the Colorado, an immense, vari-colored fissure 217 mi. long, 4 to 13 mi. wide at the brim, 4,000 to 5,500 ft. deep; the Painted Desert, extending for 30 mi. along U.S. 66; the Petrified Forest; Canyon Diablo, 225 ft. deep and 500 ft. wide; Meteor Crater, 4,150 ft. across, 570 ft. deep, made by a prehistoric meteor. Also, London Bridge at Lake Havasu City.

**Famous Arizonans** include Cochise, Geronimo, Barry Goldwater, Zane Gray, George W. P. Hunt, Helen Jacobs, Percival Lowell, William H. Pickering, Morris Udall, Stewart Udall, Frank Lloyd Wright.

**Chamber of Commerce:** 2701 E. Camelback Rd. Phoenix, AZ 85016.

# Arkansas

## Land of Opportunity

**People. Population** (1977): 2,144,000; **rank:** 33. **Pop. density:** 41.2 per sq. mi. **Urban** (1970): 50%. **Racial distrib.** (1975): 81.6% White; 16.9% Black; Hispanic (1970): 9,333. **Major ethnic groups:** German, English, Italian, Polish. **Net migration** (1970-76): +106,000.

**Geography. Total area:** 53,104 sq. mi.; **rank:** 3. **Land area:** 51,945 sq. mi. **Acres forested land:** 18,277,000. **Location:** in the west south-central U.S. **Climate:** long, hot summers, mild winters; generally abundant rainfall. **Topography:** eastern delta and prairie, southern lowland forests, and the northwestern highlands, which include the Ozark Plateaus. **Capital:** Little Rock.

**Economy. Principal industries:** manufacturing, agriculture, tourism. **Principal manufactured goods:** poultry products, forestry products, aluminum, electric motors, transformers, garments, shoes, bricks, fertilizer, petroleum products. **Value added by manufacture:** $2,805,500/yr. **Gross Domestic Product** (1975): $10.1 billion. **Agriculture:** Chief crops: soybeans, rice, cotton, hay, wheat, sorghum, tomatoes, strawberries. **Livestock:** 2,120,000 cattle; 395,000 hogs/pigs; 5,100 sheep; 35,882,000 poultry. **Timber/lumber:** oak, hickory, gum, cypress, pine. **Minerals** (1977): bauxite, bromine, and vanadium prod. 1st in U.S. Also natural gas, crude petroleum. Total mineral production valued at $567.7 million. **Commercial fishing:** $1,999,000. **Chief ports:** Little Rock, Pine Bluff, Osceola, Helena. **Value of construction** (1977): $1,236,816. **Employment distribution:** 8.9% argiculture; 26.9% manufacturing; 13.0% services; 19.5% trade. **Per capita income** (1976): $5,073. Unemployment (1977): 6.6% **Tourism** (1976): out-of state visitors spent $1 billion.

**Finance. No. banks:** 359; **No. savings and loan assns.:** 73.

**Federal government. No. federal employees** (June, 1977): 19,570. **Federal payroll** (1977): $279 million. **Notable federal facilities:** Nat'l. Center for Toxicological Research, Jefferson; Pine Bluff Arsenal.

**Energy. Electricity production** (1977, mwh, by source): Hydroelectric: 1.8 million; Mineral: 8.7 million; Nuclear: 5 million.

**Education. No. schools:** 783 elementary; 474 secondary; 29 higher education. **Avg. salary, public school teachers** (1977): $9,733.

**State data. Motto:** Regnat Populus (The people rule). **Flower:** Apple Blossom. **Bird:** Mockingbird. **Tree:** Pine. **Song:** Arkansas. **Entered union:** June 15, 1836; rank, 25th. **State fair at:** Little Rock; late Sept.- early Oct.

**History.** First European explorers were de Soto, 1541, Jolliet, 1673; La Salle, 1682. First settlement was by the French under Henri de Tonty, 1686, at Arkansas Post. In 1762 the area was ceded by France to Spain, then back again in 1800, and was part of the Louisiana Purchase by the U.S. in 1803. Arkansas seceded from the Union in 1861, only after the Civil War began, and many Arkansans (over 10,000) fought on the Union side.

**Tourist Attractions.** Hot Springs National Park, water ranging from 95° to 147°F; Blanchard Caverns, near Mountain View, are among the nation's largest; Crater of Diamonds, near Murfreesboro.

**Famous Arkansans** include Hattie Caraway, "Dizzy" Dean, Orval Faubus, James W. Fulbright, Douglas MacArthur, John L. McClellan, Winthrop Rockefeller, Edward Durell Stone, Archibald Yell.

**Chamber of Commerce:** 911 Wallace Bldg., Little Rock, AR 72201.

# California

## Golden State

**People. Population** (1977): 21,896,000; **rank: 1. Pop. density:** 140.0 per sq. mi. **Urban** (1970): 90.9%. **Racial distrib: (1975):** 88.0% White; 7.6% Black; 4.4% Other (includes American Indians, Asian Americans, and Pacific Islanders); Hispanic (1970): 3,101,589. **Major ethnic groups:** English, German, Italian, Russian. **Net migration** (1970-76): +623,000.

**Geography. Total area** 158,693 sq. mi.; **rank: 3. Land area:** 156,361 sq. mi. **Acres forested land:** 42,408,000. **Location:** on western coast of the U.S. **Climate:** moderate temperatures and rainfall along the coast; extremes in the interior. **Topography:** long mountainous coastline; central valley; Sierra Nevada on the east; desert basins of the southern interior; rugged mountains of the north. **Capital:** Sacramento.

**Economy. Principal industries:** agriculture, aerospace, manufacturing, recreation, and mining. **Principal manufactured goods:** foods, primary and fabricated metals, machinery, electric and electronic equipment, chemicals and allied products. **Value added by manufacture:** $31.1 billion/yr. **Agriculture:** Chief crops: cotton, grapes, dairy products, lettuce, eggs, tomatoes, nursery products, nuts, apricots, avocados, citrus fruits, barley, rice, olives. **Livestock:** 4,430,000 cattle; 133,000 hogs/pigs; 1,113,000 sheep; 62,840,000 poultry. **Timber/lumber:** fur, pine, redwood, oak. **Minerals** (1977): crude petroleum, natural gas, and natural gas liquids 69% of total value mineral production, $572 million. Also sand and gravel, boron materials, cement. **Commercial fishing:** $194,957,000. **Chief ports:** Long Beach, San Diego, Oakland, San Francisco, Sacramento, Stockton. **International airports at:** Los Angeles, San Francisco. **Value of construction** (1977): $14,447,422,000. **Employment distribution:** 3.6% agriculture; 19.3% manufacturing; 19.7 services; 22% trade; 19.6% government. **Per capita income** (1977): $7,933. **Unemployment** (1977): 8.2% **Tourism** (1976): out-of-state visitors spent $12.4 billion.

**Finance. Notable industries:** banking, insurance, real estate, investment. **No. banks:** 210; **No. savings and loan assns.:** 164.

**Federal government. No. federal employees** (1977): 312,900. **Federal payroll** (1977): $7.9 million. **Notable federal facilities:** Vandenberg, Beale, Travis, McClellan AF bases, San Francisco Mint.

**Energy. Electricity production** (1977, mwh, by source): Hydroelectric: 14.2 million; Mineral: 112.9 million; Nuclear: 8.1 million.

**Education. No. schools:** 6,748 elementary; 1,862 secondary; 247 higher education. **Avg. salary, public school teachers** (1977): $16,500.

**State Data. Motto:** Eureka (I have found it). **Flower:** Golden poppy. **Bird:** California valley quail. **Tree:** California redwood. **Song:** I Love You, California. **Entered Union** Sept. 9, 1850; rank, 31st. **State fair** at: Sacramento; late Aug.—early Sept.

**History.** First European explorers were Cabrillo, 1542, and Drake, 1579. First settlement was the Spanish Alta California mission at San Diego, 1769, first in a string founded by Franciscan Father Junipero Serra. U. S. traders and settlers arrived in the 19th century and staged the abortive Bear Flag Revolt, 1846; the Mexican War began later in 1846 and U.S. forces occupied California; Mexico ceded the province to the U.S. in 1848, the same year the Gold Rush began.

**Tourist attractions.** Scenic regions are Yosemite Valley; Lassen and Sequoia-Kings Canyon national parks; Lake Tahoe; the Mojave and Colorado deserts; San Francisco Bay; and Monterey Peninsula. Oldest living things on earth are believed to be a stand of Bristlecone pines in the Inyo National Forest, est. to be 4,600 years old. The world's tallest tree, the Howard Libbey redwood, 362 ft. with a girth of 44 ft., stands on Redwood Creek, Humboldt County.

Also, Palomar Observatory; Disneyland; J. Paul Getty Museum, Malibu; Tournament of Roses and Rose Bowl.

**Famous Californians** include Luther Burbank, John C. Fremont, Bret Harte, Wm. R. Hearst, Jack London, Aimee Semple McPherson, John Muir, William Saroyan, Junipero Serra, Leland Stanford, John Steinbeck, Earl Warren.

**Chamber of Commerce:** 455 Capitol Mall, Sacramento, CA 95814.

# Colorado

## Centennial State

**People. Population** (1977): 2,619,000; **rank: 28. Pop. density:** 25.2 per sq. mi. **Urban** (1970): 78.5%. **Racial distrib.** (1975): 95.3% White; 3.4% Black; Hispanic (1970): 286,467. **Major ethnic groups:** German, Russian, English, Italian. **Net migration** (1970-76): +237,000.

**Geography. Total area:** 104,247 sq. mi.; **rank: 8. Land area:** 103,766 sq. mi. **Acres forested land:** 22,534,000. **Location:** in west central U.S. **Climate:** low relative humidity, abundant sunshine, wide daily, seasonal temperatures ranges; alpine conditions in the high mountains. **Topography:** eastern dry high plains; hilly to mountainous central plateau; western Rocky Mountains of high ranges alternating with broad valleys and deep, narrow canyons. **Capital:** Denver.

**Economy. Principal industries:** manufacturing, government, mining, tourism, agriculture, aerospace. **Principal manufactured goods:** computer equipment, instruments, foods, machinery, aerospace products, rubber, steel. **Value added by manufacture:** $3.39 billion/yr. **Agriculture:** Chief crops: corn, wheat, hay, sugar beets, barley, potatoes, apples, peaches, pears. **Livestock:** 3,180,000 cattle; 280,000 hogs/pigs; 830,000 sheep; 6,350,000 poultry. **Timber/lumber:** oak, ponderosa pine, Douglas fir. **Minerals** (1977): molybdenum, uranium, coal, natural gas, petroleum. Total mineral production valued at $1.3 billion. **International airports at:** Denver. **Value of construction** (1977): $2,027,298,000. **Employment distribution:** 3.9% agriculture; 12.6% manufacturing; 17.3% services; 19% government; 21% trade. **Per capita income** (1976): $6,503. **Unemployment** (1977): 5.6% **Tourism** (1976): out-of-state visitors spent $2.2 billion.

**Finance. No. banks:** 284; **No. savings and loan assns.:** 47.

**Federal government. No. federal employees** (1977) 51,700. **Federal payroll** (1976): $1.25 billion. **Notable federal facilities:** U.S. Air Force Academy; U.S. Mint; Ft Carson, Lowry AFB; Solar Energy Research Institute.

**Energy. Electricity production** (1977, mwh, by source) Hydroelectric: 1 million; Mineral: 19.2 million; Nuclear: 224,844.

**Education. No. schools:** 971 elementary; 464 secondary; 39 higher education. **Avg. salary, public school teachers** (1977): $13,117.

**State data. Motto:** Nil Sine Numine (Nothing without Providence). **Flower:** Rocky Mountain columbine. **Bird:** Lark bunting. **Tree:** Colorado blue spruce. **Song:** Where the Columbines Grow. **Entered union** Aug. 1, 1876; rank 38th. **State fair** at: Pueblo; last week in Aug.

**History.** Early civilization centered around Mesa Verde 2,000 years ago. The U.S. acquired eastern Colorado in the Louisiana Purchase, 1803; Lt. Zebulon M. Pike explored the area, 1806, discovering the peak that bears his name. After the Mexican War, 1846-48, U.S. immigrants settled in the east, former Mexicans in the south.

**Tourist attractions.** Rocky Mountain National Park Garden of the Gods; Great Sand Dunes and Dinosaur national monuments; Pikes Peak and Mt. Evans highways Mesa Verde National Park (pre-historic cliff dwellings); 35 major ski areas. The Grand Mesa tableland comprises Grand Mesa Forest, 659,584 acres, with 200 lakes stocked with trout.

**Famous Coloradans** include Frederick Bonfils, William N. Byers, M. Scott Carpenter, Jack Dempsey, Douglas Fairbanks, Lowell Thomas, Byron R. White, Paul Whiteman.

**Chamber of Commerce:** 1390 Logan St., Suite 308 Denver, CO 80203.

# Connecticut

*Constitution State, Nutmeg State*

**People. Population** (1977): 3,108,000; **rank:** 24. **Pop. density:** 639.2 per sq. mi. **Urban** (1970): 77.4%. **Racial distrib.** (1975): 93.4% White; 6.1% Black; Hispanic (1970): 73,357. **Major ethnic groups:** Italian, Polish, English, Irish. **Net migration** (1970-76): −2,000.
**Geography. Total area:** 5,009 sq. mi.; **rank:** 48. **Land area:** 4,862 sq. mi. **Acres forested land:** 2,186,000. **Location:** New England state in the northeastern corner of the U.S. **Climate:** moderate; winters avg. slightly below freezing, warm, humid summers. **Topography:** western upland, the Berkshires, in the NW, highest elevations; narrow central lowland N-S; hilly eastern upland drained by rivers. **Capital:** Hartford.
**Economy. Principal industries:** manufacturing, retail trade, government, services. **Principal manufactured goods:** aircraft engines and parts, submarines, copper wire and tubing, silverware, helicopters, bearings, cutlery, machine tools. **Value added by manufacture:** $8.76 billion/yr. **Gross Domestic Product** (1977): $24.1 billion. **Agriculture. Chief crops:** tobacco, hay, apples, potatoes, nursery stock. **Livestock:** 108,000 cattle; 9,000 hogs/pigs; 5,400 sheep; 5,313,000 poultry. **Timber/lumber:** oak, birch, beech, maple. **Minerals** (1977): stone, sand and gravel. Total mineral production valued at $34.5 million. **Commercial fishing:** $2,379,000. **Chief ports:** New Haven, Bridgeport, New London. **International airports at:** Windsor Locks. **Value of construction** (1977): $1,169,346,000. **Employment distribution:** — % agriculture; 32% manufacturing; 18% services; 50% other. **Per capita income** (1976): $7,373. **Unemployment** (1977): 7.1% **Tourism** (1976): out-of-state visitors spent $1 billion.
**Finance. Notable industries:** insurance, finance, banking. **No. banks:** 139; **No. savings and loan assns.:** 17.
**Federal Government. No. federal employees** (1976): 21,000. **Notable federal facilities:** U.S. Coast Guard Academy.
**Energy. Electricity production** (1977, mwh, by source): Hydroelectric: 424,523; Mineral: 11.1 million; Nuclear: 13.1 million.
**Education. No. schools:** 1,130 elementary; 324 secondary; 46 higher education. **Avg. salary, public school teachers** (1977): $13,651.
**State data. Motto:** Qui Transtulit Sustinet (He who transplanted still sustains). **Flower:** Mountain laurel. **Bird:** American robin. **Tree:** White oak. **Song:** Yankee Doodle Dandy. **Fifth** of the 13 original states to ratify the Constitution, Jan. 9, 1788.

**History.** Adriaen Block, Dutch explorer, was the first European visitor, 1614. By 1633, settlers from Plymouth Bay started colonies along the Connecticut River and in 1637 defeated the Pequot Indians. In the Revolution, Connecticut men fought in most major campaigns and turned back British raids on Danbury and other towns, while Connecticut privateers captured British merchant ships.
**Tourist attractions.** Winchester Gun Museum, Yale University's Art Gallery, Peabody Museum, all in New Haven; Mystic Seaport, Mystic, a recreated 19th century seaport village; P.T. Barnum Museum, Bridgeport.
**Famous "Nutmeggers"** include Ethan Allen, Phineas T. Barnum, Samuel Colt, Jonathan Edwards, Nathan Hale, Katharine Hepburn, Isaac Hull, J. Pierpont Morgan, Israel Putnam, Harriet Beecher Stowe, Mark Twain, Noah Webster, Eli Whitney.
**Chamber of Commerce:** Suite 1202, 60 Washington St., Hartford, CT 06106.

# Delaware

*First State, Diamond State*

**People. Population** (1977): 582,000; **rank:** 47. **Pop. density:** 293.6 per sq. mi. **Urban** (1970): 72.2%. **Racial distrib.** (1975): 84.8% White; 14.7% Black; Hispanic (1970): 6,267. **Major ethnic groups:** Italian, English, Polish, German. **Net migration** (1970-76): +9,000.
**Geography. Total area:** 2,057 sq. mi.; **rank:** 49. **Land**

area: 1,982 sq. mi. **Acres forested land:** 391,000. **Location:** occupies the Delmarva Peninsula on the Atlantic coastal plain. **Climate:** moderate. **Topography:** Piedmont plateau to the N, sloping to a near sea-level plain. **Capital:** Dover.
**Economy. Principal industries:** chemistry, agriculture, poultry, shellfish, tourism. **Principal manufactured goods:** nylon, apparel, luggage, foods, cash registers. **Value added by manufacture:** $1.5 billion/yr. **Agriculture. Chief crops:** corn, soybeans, dairy products, vegetables, peaches, fruit, grain, hay. **Livestock:** 31,000 cattle; 50,000 hogs/pigs; 1,900 sheep; 950,000 poultry. **Minerals** (1977): Sand and gravel. Total mineral production valued at $1.8 million. **Commercial fishing:** $778,000. **Chief ports:** Wilmington. **International airports at:** Philadelphia/Wilmington. **Value of construction** (1977): $283,427,000. **Employment distribution:** 1.6% agriculture; 28.3% manufacturing; 70.1% services. **Per capita income** (1976): $7,290. **Unemployment** (1976): 8.9%. **Tourism** (1976): out-of-state visitors spent $328.5 million.
**Finance. No. banks:** 188; **No. savings and loan assns.:** 19.
**Federal government. No. federal employees** (1976): 5,000. **Federal payroll** (1974): $15.5 million. **Notable federal facilities:** Dover Air Force Base, Federal Wildlife Refuge, Bombay Hook.
**Energy. Electricity production** (1977, mwh, by source): Hydroelectric: —; Mineral: 6.5 million; Nuclear: —.
**Education. No. schools:** 180 elementary; 67 secondary; 10 higher education. **Avg. salary, public school teachers** (1977): $13,170.
**State data. Motto:** Liberty and independence. **Flower:** Peach blossom. **Bird:** Blue hen chicken. **Tree:** American holly. **Song:** Our Delaware. **First** of original 13 states to ratify the Constitution, Dec. 7, 1787. **State fair** at: Harrington; end of July.

**History.** The Dutch first settled in Delaware near present Lewes, 1631, but were wiped out by Indians. Swedes settled at present Wilmington, 1638; Dutch settled anew, 1651, near New Castle and seized the Swedish settlement, 1655, only to lose all Delaware and New Netherland to the British, 1664.
**Tourist attractions.** Ft. Christina Monument, the site of founding of New Sweden; John Dickinson "Penman of the Revolution" home, Dover; Henry Francis du Pont Winterthur Museum; Hagley Museum, Wilmington; Old Swedes (Trinity Parish) Church, erected 1698, is the oldest Protestant church in the U.S. still in use.
**Famous Delawareans** include Thomas F. Bayard, Henry Seidel Canby, E. I. du Pont, John P. Marquand, Howard Pyle, Caesar Rodney.
**Chamber of Commerce:** 1102 West St., Wilmington, DE 19081.

# Florida

*Sunshine State*

**People. Population** (1977): 8,452,000; **rank:** 8. **Pop. density:** 156.2 per sq. mi. **Urban** (1970): 80.5%. **Racial distrib.** 1975: 85.1% White; 14.2% Black; Hispanic (1970): 451,382. **Major ethnic groups:** German, English, Italian, Russian. **Net migration** (1970-76): +1,464,000.
**Geography. Total area:** 58,560 sq. mi.; **rank:** 22. **Land area:** 54,090 sq. mi. **Acres forested land:** 17,932,000. **Location:** peninsula jutting southward 500 mi. bet. the Atlantic and the Gulf of Mexico. **Climate:** subtropical N of Bradenton-Lake Okeechobee-Vero Beach line; tropical S of line. **Topography:** land is flat or rolling; highest point is 345 ft. in the NW. **Capital:** Tallahassee.
**Economy. Principal industries:** agriculture, tourism, manufacturing, aerospace, food processing, chemical. **Principal manufactured goods:** metal products, paper, electrical and transportation equipment. **Value added by manufacture:** $4 billion/yr. **Agriculture. Chief crops:** citrus fruits, vegetables, sugarcane, avocados, watermelons, peanuts, cotton, tobacco, strawberries. **Livestock:** 2,350,000 cattle; 320,000 hogs/pigs; 4,500 sheep; 17,042,000 poultry. **Timber/lumber:** pine, oak, cypress,

palm. **Minerals** (1977): natural gas, petroleum, stone, Portland cement. Total mineral production valued at $1.6 billion. **Commercial fishing:** $95,485,000. **Chief ports:** Pensacola. **International airports at:** Miami, Tampa. **Value of construction** (1977): $6,945,511. **Per capita income** (1976): $6,108. **Unemployment** (1976): 9.0%. **Tourism** (1976): out-of-state visitors spent $9.3 billion.

**Finance. No. banks:** 753; **No. savings and loan assns.:** 125.

**Federal government. No. federal employees** (1976): 78,000. **Notable federal facilities:** John F. Kennedy Space Center, Cape Canaveral.

**Energy. Electricity production** (1977, mwh, by source): Hydroelectric: 243,128; Mineral: 69 million; Nuclear: 17.5 million.

**Education. No. schools:** 1,785 elementary; 574 secondary; 74 higher education. **Avg. salary, public school teachers** (1977): $10,811.

**State data. Motto:** In God we trust. **Flower:** Orange blossom. **Bird:** Mockingbird. **Tree:** Sabal palmetto palm. **Song:** Swanee River. **Entered union** Mar. 3, 1845; rank, 27th.

**History.** First European to see Florida was Ponce de Leon, 1513. France established a colony, Fort Caroline, on the St. Johns River, 1564; Spain settled St. Augustine, 1565, and Spanish troops massacred most of the French. Britain's Francis Drake burned St. Augustine, 1586. Britain held the area briefly, 1763-83, returning it to Spain. After Andrew Jackson led a U.S. invasion, 1818, Spain ceded Florida to the U.S., 1819. The Seminole War, 1835-42, resulted in removal of most Indians to Oklahoma. Florida seceded from the Union, 1861, was readmitted, 1868.

**Tourist attractions.** Miami, with the nation's greatest concentration of luxury hotels at Miami Beach; St. Augustine, oldest city in U.S.; Walt Disney World, an entertainment and vacation development near Orlando.

Everglades National Park, 3d largest of U.S. national parks, preserves the beauty of the vast Everglades swamp. Castillo de San Marcos, St. Augustine, is a national monument. Also, the Ringling Museum of Art, the Ringling Museum of the Circus, and the Circus Hall of Fame, all in Sarasota.

**Famous Floridians** include Henry M. Flagler, James Weldon Johnson, MacKinlay Kantor, Henry B. Plant, Marjorie Kinnan Rawlings, Joseph W. Stilwell, Charles P. Summerall.

**Chamber of Commerce:** P.O. Box 5497, Tallahassee, FL 32301.

# Georgia

### Empire State of the South, Peach State

**People. Population** (1977): 5,048,000; **rank:** 14. **Pop. density:** 86.9 per sq. mi. **Urban** (1970): 60.3%. **Racial distrib.** (1975): 73.5% White; 26.1% Black; Hispanic (1970): 29,824. **Major ethnic groups:** German, English, Russian, Italian. **Net migration** (1970-76): +105,000.

**Geography. Total area:** 58,876 sq. mi.; **rank:** 21. **Land area:** 58,073 sq. mi. **Acres forested land:** 25,545,000. **Location:** South Atlantic state. **Climate:** maritime tropical air masses dominate in summer; continental polar air masses in winter; east central area drier. **Topography:** most southerly of the Blue Ridge Mtns. cover NE and N central; central Piedmont extends to the fall line of rivers; coastal plain levels to the coast flatlands. **Capital:** Atlanta.

**Economy. Principal industries:** manufacturing, forestry, agriculture, chemicals. **Principal manufactured goods:** textiles, transportation equipment, foods, clothing, paper and wood products, chemical products, cigarettes. **Value added by manufacture:** $9.78 billion/yr. **Gross Domestic Product** (1975): $30.8 billion. **Agriculture:** Chief **crops:** cotton, peanuts, tobacco, pecans, peaches, rye, corn, soybeans. **Livestock:** 1,975,000 cattle; 1,600,000 hogs/pigs; 3,700 sheep; 38,556,000 poultry. **Timber/lumber:** pine, hardwood. **Minerals** (1977): clay and crushed stone accounted for 85% of the total mineral production (valued at $471 million). Also Portland cement. **Commercial fishing:** $9,096,000. **Chief ports:** Savannah, Brunswick. **International airports at:** Atlanta. **Value of con-**struction (1977): $5,208,849,000. **Employment distribution:** 5% agriculture; 25% manufacturing; 19% services; 22% trade. **Per capita income** (1976): $5,571. **Unemployment** (1977): 6.9% **Tourism** (1976): out-of-state visitors spent $2.3 billion.

**Finance. No. banks:** 441; **No. savings and loan assns:** 97.

**Federal government. No. federal employees** (1976): 75,700. **Federal payroll** (1976): $1.2 billion. **Notable federal facilities:** Robins AFB; Fts. Benning, Gordon, McPherson; Nat'l. Law Enforcement Training Ctr., Glynco.

**Energy. Electricity production** (1977, mwh, by source): Hydroelectric: 3.9 million; Mineral: 43.8 million; Nuclear 3.7 million.

**Education. No. schools:** 1,384 elementary; 483 secondary; 66 higher education. **Avg. salary, public school teachers** (1977): $9,911.

**State data. Motto:** Wisdom, justice and moderation. **Flower:** Cherokee rose. **Bird:** Brown thrasher. **Tree:** Live oak. **Song:** Georgia. **Fourth** of the 13 original states to ratify the Constitution, Jan. 2, 1788. **State fair at:** Atlanta Sept.—Oct.

**History.** Gen. James Oglethorpe established the first settlements, 1733, for poor and religiously-persecuted Englishmen. Oglethorpe defeated a Spanish army from Florida at Bloody Marsh, 1742. In the Revolution, Georgians seized the Savannah armory, 1775, and sent the munitions to the Continental Army; they fought seesaw campaigns with Cornwallis' British troops, twice liberating Augusta and forcing final evacuation by the British from Savannah, 1782.

**Tourist attractions.** The Little White House in Warm Springs where Pres. Franklin D. Roosevelt died Apr. 12, 1945, 2,500-acre Callaway Gardens, Jekyll Island State Park, the restored 1850s farming community of Westville, Dahlonega, site of America's first gold rush; Stone Mountain, and Six Flags Over Georgia.

Okefenokee in the SE is one of the largest swamps in the U.S., a wetland wilderness and peat bog covering 660 sq. mi. A large part of it is a National Wildlife Refuge, home for wild birds, alligators, bear, deer.

**Famous Georgians** include James Bowie, Erskine Caldwell, Lucius D. Clay, Ty Cobb, John C. Fremont, Joel Chandler Harris, Martin Luther King Jr., Sidney Lanier, Margaret Mitchell, Joseph Wheeler.

**Chamber of Commerce:** 1200 Commerce Bldg., Atlanta, GA 30303.

# Hawaii

### Aloha State

**People. Population** (1977): 895,000; **rank:** 40. **Pop. density:** 139.2 per sq. mi. **Urban** (1970): 83.1%. **Racial distrib.** (1975): 36.5% White; —% Black; 62.2% Other (includes Asian Americans and Pacific Islanders); Hispanic (1970): 23,276. **Major ethnic groups:** Japanese, Chinese. **Net migration.** (1970-76): +45,000.

**Geography. Total area:** 6,450 sq. mi.; **rank:** 47. **Land area:** 6,425 sq. mi. **Acres forested land:** 1,974,000. **Location:** Hawaiian Islands lie in the North Pacific, 2,397 mi. SW from San Francisco. **Climate:** temperate, mountain regions cooler; Mt. Waialeale, on Kauai, wettest spot in the world, annual rainfall 486.1 in. **Topography:** islands are tops of a chain of submerged volcanic mountains; active volcanoes: Mauna Loa, Kilauea. **Capital:** Honolulu.

**Economy. Principal industries:** tourism, government, sugar refining, agriculture, aquaculture, fishing, motion pictures, manufacturing. **Principal manufactured goods:** sugar, canned pineapple, clothing, foods. **Value added by manufacture:** $700,300,000/yr. **Gross Domestic Product** (1975): $6.6 million. **Agriculture:** Chief **crops:** sugar, pineapples, macadamia nuts, coffee, vegetables and melons. **Livestock:** 234,000 cattle; 60,000 hogs/pigs; 1,301,000 poultry. **Minerals** (1977): Portland cement, stone. Total mineral production valued at $44 million. **Commercial fishing:** $9,412,000. **Chief ports:** Honolulu, Port Allen, Kahului, Hilo. **International airports at:** Honolulu. **Value of construction** (1977): $610,041,000. **Employment distribution:** 3.7% agriculture; 5.9% manufacuring; 21.4% services; 69.0% among government, onstruction, trade. **Per capita income** (1976): $6,969. **Unemployment** (1977): 7.4%. **Tourism** (1976): out-of-state visitors spent $1.2 billion.

**Finance. No. banks:** 8; **No. savings and loan assns.:** 1.

**Federal government. No. federal employees** (1977): 9,300. **Federal payroll** (1976): $459 million. **Notable federal facilities:** Pearl Harbor Naval Base Shipyard; Hickham AFB; Schofield Barracks.

**Energy. Electricity production** (1977, mwh, by source): Hydroelectric: 20,025; Mineral: 6 million; Nuclear: —.

**Education. No. schools:** 221 elementary; 65 secondary; 12 higher education. **Avg. salary, public school teachers** (1977): $17,192.

**State data. Motto:** The life of the land is perpetuated in righteousness. **Flower:** Hibiscus. **Bird:** Hawaiian goose. **Tree:** Candlenut. **Song:** Hawaii Ponoi. **Entered union** Aug. 21, 1959; rank, 50th. **State fair** at: Honolulu; 2d week of July.

**History.** Polynesians from islands 2,000 mi. to the south settled the Hawaiian Islands, probably about 700 A.D. First European visitor was British Capt. James Cook, 1778. Missionaries arrived, 1820, taught religion, reading and writing. King Kamehameha III and his chiefs created the first Constitution and a Legislature which set up a public school system. Sugar production began in 1835; it became the dominant industry. In 1893, Queen Liliuokalani was deposed, followed, 1894, by a republic headed by Sanford B. Dole. Annexation by the U.S. came in 1898.

**Tourist attractions.** USS Arizona Memorial, Pearl Harbor; Hawaii Volcanoes, Haleakala national parks, Kilauea; Diamond Head, Waikiki Beach, Oahu.

**Famous Hawaiians** include Father Joseph Damien, Sanford Dole, Hiram L. Fong, Daniel K. Inouye, Duke Kahanamoku, Bette Midler, Patsy Mink.

**Chamber of Commerce:** Dillingham Bldg., 735 Bishop St., Honolulu, HI 96813.

# Idaho
## Gem State

**People. Population** (1977): 857,000; **rank:** 41. **Pop. density:** 10.3 per sq. mi. **Urban** (1970): 54.1%. **Racial distrib.** (1975): 98.2% White; —% Black; Hispanic (1970); 8,476. **Major ethnic groups:** English, German, Swedish, Norwegian. **Net migration** (1970-76): +64,000.

**Geography. Total area:** 83,557 sq. mi.; **rank:** 13. **Land area:** 82,677 sq. mi. **Acres forested land:** 21,591,000. **Location:** Pacific Northwest-Mountain state bordering on British Columbia. **Climate:** tempered by Pacific westerly winds; drier, colder, continental clime in SE; altitude an important factor. **Topography:** Snake R. plains in the S; central region of mountains, canyons, gorges (Hells Canyon, 7,000 ft., deepest in N.A.); subalpine northern region. **Capital:** Boise.

**Economy. Principal industries:** agriculture, manufacturing, tourism, lumber, mining. **Principal manufactured goods:** processed foods, lumber and wood products, chemical products, primary metals, fabricated metal products, machinery. **Value added by manufacture:** $815,406,000/yr. **Gross Domestic Product** (1975): $6.12 billion. **Agriculture:** Chief crops: potatoes, peas, sugar beets, alfalfa seed, wheat, hops, barley, plums and prunes, mint, onions, corn, cherries, apples, trout. **Livestock:** 1,870,000 cattle; 45,000 hogs/pigs; 503,000 sheep; 1,187,000 poultry. **Timber/lumber:** yellow, white pine; Douglas fir; white spruce. **Minerals** (1977): silver, phosphate rock, lead, zinc, sand and gravel. Total mineral production valued at $218 million. **Commercial fishing:** $38,000. **Chief ports:** Lewiston. **International airports at:** Boise. **Value of construction** (1977): $701,087,000. **Employment distribution:** 11.2% agriculture; 15.6% manufacturing; 15.1% services; 22% trade; 19.5% government; 5.6% construction. **Per capita income** (1976): $5,726. **Unemployment** (1977): 6.3%. **Tourism** (1976): out-of-state visitors spent $540 million.

**Finance. No. banks:** 25; **No. savings and loan assns.:** 32.

**Federal government. No. federal employees** (1977):

11,700. **Notable federal facilities:** Ida. Nat'l. Engineering Lab, Idaho Falls; Nat'l. Reactor Testing Sta., Upper Snake River Plains.

**Energy. Electricity production** (1977, mwh, by source): Hydroelectric: 6.7 million; Mineral: 58,401; Nuclear —.

**Education: No. schools:** 393 elementary; 201 secondary; 9 higher education. **Avg. salary, public school teachers** (1977): $10,987.

**State data. Motto:** Esto Perpetua (It is perpetual). **Flower:** Syringa. **Bird:** Mountain bluebird. **Tree:** White pine. **Song:** Here We Have Idaho. **Entered union** July 3, 1890; rank, 43d. **State fair** at: Boise and Blackfoot; late Aug.—early Sept.

**History.** Exploration of the Idaho area began with Lewis and Clark, 1805-06. Next came fur traders, setting up posts, 1809-34, and missionaries, establishing missions, 1830s-1850s. Mormons made their first permanent settlement at Franklin, 1860. Idaho's Gold Rush began that same year, and brought thousands of permanent settlers. Strangest of the Indian Wars was the 1,300-mi. trek in 1877 of Chief Joseph and the Nez Perce tribe, pursued by troops that caught them a few miles short of the Canadian border. By 1890, Idaho adopted a progressive Constitution and became a state that year.

**Tourist attractions.** Hells Canyon, deepest gorge in N.A.; Craters of the Moon; Sun Valley, year-round resort in the Sawtooth Mtns.; Crystal Falls Cave; Shoshone Falls; Lava Hot Springs; Lake Pend Oreille; Lake Coeur d'Alene.

**Famous Idahoans** include William E. Borah, Fred T. Dubois, Chief Joseph, Sacagawea.

**Chamber of Commerce:** P.O. Box 389, Boise, ID 83701.

# Illinois
## The Inland Empire

**People. Population** (1977): 11,245,000; **rank:** 5. **Pop. density:** 201.7 per sq. mi. **Urban** (1970): 83%. **Racial distrib.** (1975): 85.3% White; 13.7% Black; Hispanic (1970): 364,397. **Major ethnic groups:** German, Polish, Italian, English, Russian. **Net migration** (1970-76): —324,000.

**Geography. Total area:** 56,400 sq. mi.; **rank:** 24. **Land area:** 55,748 sq. mi. **Acres forested land:** 3,789,000. **Location:** east-north central state; western, southern, and eastern boundaries formed by Mississippi, Ohio, and Wabash Rivers, respectively. **Climate:** temperate; typically cold, snowy winters, hot summers. **Topography:** prairie and fertile plains throughout; open hills in the southern region. **Capital:** Springfield.

**Economy. Principal industries:** manufacturing, wholesale and retail trade, agriculture, finance, insurance, real estate, publishing. **Principal manufactured goods:** machinery, electric and electronic equipment, foods, primary and fabricated metals, chemical products, precision instruments. **Value added by manufacture:** $32.1 billion/yr. **Gross Domestic Product** (1975): $88.2 billion. **Agriculture:** Chief crops: corn, soybeans, wheat, oats, hay. **Livestock:** 2,950,000 cattle; 6,400,000 hogs/pigs; 180,000 sheep; 8,139,000 poultry. **Timber/lumber:** cottonwood, gum, walnut. **Minerals** (1977): mineral fuels (coal, natural gas, petroleum) accounted for 75% of the total $1.7 billion mineral production. Also stone, sand and gravel, cement. **Commercial fishing:** $931,000. **Chief ports:** Chicago. **International airports at:** Chicago. **Value of construction** (1977): $5,801,767,000. **Employment distribution:** 3% agriculture; 24% manufacturing; 16% services; 57% other. **Per capita income** (1976): $7,432. **Unemployment** (1976) 6.5%. **Tourism** (1975): out-of-state visitors spent $3.7 billion.

**Finance. Notable industries:** insurance, real estate. **No. banks:** 1,225; **No. savings and loan assns.:** 443.

**Federal government. No. federal employees** (1975): 108,300. **Federal payroll** (1975): $2 billion. **Notable federal facilities:** Fermi Nat'l. Accelerator Lab; Argonne Nat'l. Lab; Ft. Sheridan; Rock Island, Scott Field military installations.

**Energy. Electricity production** (1977, mwh, by source):

Hydroelectric: 108,691; Mineral: 72 million; Nuclear: 28.5 million.

**Education. No. schools:** 4,285 elementary; 1,446 secondary; 147 higher education. **Avg. salary, public school teachers** (1977): $14,656.

**State data. Motto:** State sovereignty—national union. **Flower:** Native violet. **Bird:** Cardinal. **Tree:** White oak. **Song:** Illinois. **Entered union** Dec. 3, 1818; rank, 21st. **State fair** at: Springfield; mid-Aug.

**History.** Fur traders were the first Europeans in Illinois, followed shortly, 1673, by Jolliet and Marquette, and, 1680, La Salle, who built a fort near present Peoria. First settlements were French, at Fort St. Louis on the Illinois River, 1692, and Kaskaskia, 1700. France ceded the area to Britian, 1763; Amer. Gen. George Rogers Clark, 1778, took Kaskaskia from the British without a shot. Defeat of Indian tribes in Black Hawk War, 1832, and railroads in 1850s, inspired immigration.

**Tourist attractions:** Lincoln shrines at Springfield, New Salem, Sangamon; Cahokia Mounds, E. St. Louis; Starved Rock State Park; Crab Orchard Wildlife Refuge; Mormon settlement at Nauvoo; Fts. Kaskaskia, Chartres, Massac (parks).

**Famous Illinoisans** include Jane Addams, William Jennings Bryan, Stephen A. Douglas, James T. Farrell, Ernest Hemingway, Edgar Lee Masters, Carl Sandburg, Adlai Stevenson, Frank Lloyd Wright.

**Chamber of Commerce:** 20 N. Wacker Dr., Chicago, IL 60606.

# Indiana
## Hoosier State

**People. Population** (1977): 5,330,000; **rank:** 12. **Pop. density:** 147.6 per sq. mi. **Urban** (1970): 64.9%. **Racial distrib.** (1975): 92.4% White; 7.3% Black; Hispanic (1970): 67,188. **Major ethnic groups:** German, Polish, English, Mexican. **Net migration** (1970-76): —138,000.

**Geography. Total area:** 36,291 sq. mi.; **rank:** 38. **Land area:** 36,097 sq. mi. **Acres forested land:** 3,908,000. **Location:** east north-central state; Lake Michigan on northern border. **Climate:** 4 distinct seasons with a temperate climate. **Topography:** hilly southern region; fertile rolling plains of central region; flat, heavily glaciated north; dunes along Lake Michigan shore. **Capital:** Indianapolis.

**Economy. Principal industries:** manufacturing, wholesale and retail trade, agriculture, government, services. **Principal manufactured goods:** primary and fabricated metals, transportation equipment, electrical and electronic equipment, non-electrical machinery, chemical products, foods. **Value added by manufacture:** $16 billion/yr. **Agriculture: Chief crops:** corn, sorghum, oats, barley, wheat, rye, soybeans, hay. **Livestock:** 2,025,000 cattle; 4,100,000 hogs/pigs; 187,000 sheep; 23,196,000 poultry. **Timber/lumber:** oak, tulip, beech, sycamore. **Minerals** (1977): mineral fuels, esp. coal, accounted for 58% of the total $616.9 million mineral production. Also sand and gravel, stone. **Commercial fishing:** $118,000. **Chief ports:** Lake Michigan facility, east of Gary. **International airports at:** Indianapolis. **Value of construction** (1977): $4,280,256,000. **Employment distribution:** 0.13% agriculture; 34.17% manufacturing; 13.1% services. **Per capita income** (1976): $7,432. **Unemployment** (1977): 5.7%. **Tourism** (1976): out-of-state visitors spent $1.6 billion.

**Finance. No. banks:** 411; **No. savings and loan assns.:** 153.

**Federal government. No. federal employees** (1975): 41,893. **Federal payroll** (1975): $515.5 million. **Notable federal facilities:** Naval Avionics Ctr.; Ft. Benjamin Harrison; Griffith AFB; Navy Weapons Support Ctr., Crane.

**Energy. Electricity production** (1977, mwh, by source): Hydroelectric: 373,596; Mineral: 62.8 million; Nuclear: — .

**Education. No. schools:** 1,920 elementary; 561 secondary; 64 higher education. **Avg. salary, public school teachers** (1977): $11,967.

**State data. Motto:** Crossroads of America. **Flower:** Peony. **Bird:** Cardinal. **Tree:** Tulip poplar. **Song:** On the Banks of the Wabash, Far Away. **Entered union** Dec. 11,

1816; rank, 19th. **State fair** at: Indianapolis; mid-Aug.

**History:** Pre-historic Indian Mound Builders of 1,00 years ago were the earliest known inhabitants. A Frenc trading post was built, 1731-32, at Vincennes and La Sal visited the present South Bend area, 1679 and 168 France ceded the area to Britain, 1763. During the Revc lution, American Gen. George Rogers Clark captured Vir cennes, 1778, and defeated British forces 1779; at war' end Britain ceded the area to the U.S. Miami Indians de feated U.S. troops twice, 1790, but were beaten, 1794, a Fallen Timbers by Gen. Anthony Wayne. At Tippecanoe 1811, Gen. William H. Harrison defeated Tecumseh' Indian confederation.

**Tourist attractions.** Lincoln, George Rogers Clark me morials; Wyandotte Cave; Vincennes, Tippecanoe sites Indiana Dunes; Hoosier Nat'l. Forest; Benjamin Harriso Home.

**Famous "Hoosiers"** include Ambrose Burnside Hoagy Carmichael, Eugene V. Debs, Theodore Dreise Paul Dresser, Cole Porter, Gene Stratton Porter, Ern Pyle, James Whitcomb Riley, Booth Tarkington, Le Wallace, Wendell L. Wilkie, Wilbur Wright.

**Chamber of Commerce:** 320 N. Meridian St., Indian apolis, IN 46204.

# Iowa
## Hawkeye State

**People. Population** (1977): 2,879,000; **rank:** 25. **Pop density:** 51.4 per sq. mi. **Urban** (1970): 57.2%. **Racia distrib.** (1975): 98.4% White; 1.4% Black; Hispan (1970): 17,448. **Major ethnic groups:** German, Scandina vian, English, Dutch. **Net migration** (1970-76): —37,000.

**Geography. Total area:** 56,290 sq. mi.; **rank:** 25. **Lan area:** 55,941 sq. mi. **Acres forested land:** 2,455,000. **L cation:** Midwest state bordered by Mississippi R. on th and Missouri R. on the W. **Climate:** humid, continenta **Topography:** Watershed from NW to SE; soil especiall rich and land level in the N central counties. **Capital:** De Moines.

**Economy. Principal industries:** manufacturing, agricu ture. **Principal manufactured goods:** tires, farm machin ery, electronic products, appliances, office furnitur chemicals, fertilizers, auto accessories. **Value added b manufacture:** $7 billion/yr. **Gross Domestic Produc** (1976): $23.3 billion. **Agriculture: Chief crops:** silage an grain corn, soybeans, oats, hay. **Livestock:** 7,800,00 cattle; 14,200,000 hogs/pigs; 388,000 sheep; 17,079,00 poultry. **Timber/lumber:** red cedar. **Minerals** (1977 cement, stone, and sand and gravel accounted fc 90% of the total $231 million production. **Commerci fishing:** $891,000. **Value of construction** (1977 $1,509,082,000. **Employment distribution** (numbers agriculture: 224,000; industry: 231,000. **Per capita in come** (1976): $6,439. **Unemployment** (1976): 4.0% **Tourism** (1976): out-of-state visitors spent $943 million.

**Finance. No. banks:** 654; **No. savings and loan assns** 84.

**Federal government. No. federal employees** (1976 19,000.

**Energy. Electricity production** (1977, mwh, by source Hydroelectric: 778,745; Mineral: 14.5 million; Nuclear: 2. million.

**Education. No. schools:** 1,420 elementary; 755 second ary; 63 higher education. **Avg. salary, public schoo teachers** (1977): $12,533.

**State data. Motto:** Our liberties we prize and our right we will maintain. **Flower:** Wild rose. **Bird:** Eastern golc finch. **Tree:** Oak. **Song:** The Song of Iowa. **Entered ur ion** Dec. 28, 1846; rank, 29th. **State fair** at: Des Moines mid-Aug.

**History.** A thousand years ago several groups of pre historic Indian Mound Builders dwelt on Iowa's fertil plains. Marquette and Jolliet gave France its claim to th area, 1673. It became U.S. territory through the 1803 Lou isiana Purchase. Indian tribes were moved into the are from states further east, but by mid-19th century wer forced to move on to Kansas. Before and during the Civ War, Iowans strongly supported Abraham Lincoln and be came traditional Republicans.

**Tourist attractions.** Herbert Hoover birthplace and library, West Branch; Effigy Mounds Nat'l. Monument, Marette, a pre-historic Indian burial site; Davenport Municial Art Gallery's collection of Grant Wood's paintings and emorabilia.

**Famous Iowans** include James A. Van Allen, Marquis hilds, Buffalo Bill Cody, Susan Glaspell, James Norman all, Harry Hansen, Billy Sunday, Carl Van Vechten, enry Wallace, Meredith Willson, Grant Wood.

**Chamber of Commerce:** None.

# Kansas
## Sunflower State

**eople. Population** (1977): 2,326,000; **rank:** 31. **Pop. ensity:** 28.4 per sq. mi. **Urban** (1970): 66.1%. **Racial istrib.** (1975): 94.4% White; 4.7% Black; Hispanic 970): 46,706. **Major ethnic groups:** German, Russian, nglish, Mexican. **Net migration** (1970-76): —13,000.

**eography. Total area:** 82,264 sq. mi.; **rank:** 14. **Land rea:** 81,787 sq. mi. **Acres forested land:** 1,344,000. **Lo-ation:** West North Central state, with Missouri R. on E. **limate:** temperate but continental, with great extremes et. summer and winter. **Topography:** hilly Osage Plains the E; central region level prairie and hills; high plains in e W. **Capital:** Topeka.

**conomy. Principal industries:** agriculture, mining, aero-pace, chemical. **Principal manufactured goods:** pro-essed foods, aircraft, petroleum products, farm machin-ry, camping gear, heating, air conditioning equipment. **alue added by manufacture:** $4.4 billion/yr. **Gross Do-estic Product** (1977): $19.1 billion. **Agriculture: Chief rops:** wheat, sorghum, corn, hay. **Livestock:** 6,000,000 attle; 1,850,000 hogs/pigs; 173,000 sheep; 2,563,000 oultry. **Timber/lumber:** oak, walnut. **Minerals** (1977): ement, high-purity helium, natural gas liquids, petroleum, alt, sand and gravel. Total mineral production exceeded 1.3 billion. **Commercial fishing:** $8,000. **Chief ports:** ansas City. **International airports at:** Wichita. **Value of onstruction** (1977): $3,100,041,000. **Employment dis-ibution:** 7.0% agriculture; 15.8% manufacturing; 13.9% ervices; 19.6% trade; 16.4% government. **Per capita come** (1976): $6,495. **Unemployment** (1977): 4%. **ourism** (1976): out-of-state visitors spent $975 million. **inance. No. banks:** 615; **No. savings and loan assns.:** 3.

**ederal government. No. federal employees** (1976): 5,600. **Federal payroll** (1975): $328.4 million. **Notable ederal facilities:** McConnell AFB; Fts. Riley, Leaven-orth.

**nergy. Electricity production** (1977, mwh, by source): ydroelectric: 2,488; Mineral: 20.9 million; Nuclear: — .

**ducation. No. schools:** 1,292 elementary; 546 second-ry; 52 higher education. **Avg. salary, public school eachers** (1977): $11,769.

**tate data. Motto:** Ad Astra per Aspera (To the stars rough difficulties). **Flower:** Native sunflower. **Bird:** West-rn meadowlark. **Tree:** Cottonwood. **Song:** Home on the ange. **Entered union** Jan. 29, 1861; rank, 34th. **State air at:** Hutchinson; 2d week of Sept.

**History.** Coronado marched through the Kansas area, 541; French explorers came next. The U.S. took over in e Louisiana Purchase, 1803. In the pre-war North-South truggle over slavery, so much violence swept the area it as called Bleeding Kansas. Railroad construction after e war made Abilene and Dodge City terminals of large attle drives from Texas.

**Tourist attractions.** Eisenhower Center and "Place of leditation," Abilene; Agricultural Hall of Fame and Na-onal Ctr., Bonner Springs, displays farm equipment; odge City; Ft. Scott.

**Famous Kansans** include Thomas Hart Benton, John rown, Walter P. Chrysler, Amelia Earhart, Cyrus Holli-ay, Gen. Hugh Johnson, Walter Johnson, Alf Landon,

Brock Pemberton, Robert Stroud.

**Chamber of Commerce:** 500 First National Tower, One Townsite Plaza, Topeka, KS 66603.

# Kentucky
## Blue Grass State

**People. Population** (1977): 3,458,000; **rank:** 23. **Pop. density:** 87.2 per sq. mi. **Urban** (1970): 52.3%. **Racial Distrib.** (1975): 92.5% White; 7.2% Black; Hispanic (1970): 11,112. **Major ethnic groups:** German, English, Italian, Irish. **Net migration** (1970-76): +67,000.

**Geography. Total area:** 40,395 sq. mi.; **rank:** 37. **Land area:** 39,650 sq. mi. **Acres forested land:** 11,968,000. **Location:** east south central state, bordered on N by Illinois, Indiana, Ohio; on E by West Virginia and Virginia; in S by Tennessee; on W by Missouri. **Climate:** moderate, with plentiful rainfall. **Topography:** mountainous in E; rounded hills of the Knobs in the N; Bluegrass, heart of state; wooded rocky hillsides of the Pennyrile; Western Coal Field; the fertile Purchase the SW. **Capital:** Frankfort.

**Economy. Principal industries:** tourism, agriculture, tobacco, manufacturing, mining, horse breeding. **Principal manufactured goods:** whiskey, textiles, cigarettes, steel products, trucks. **Value added by manufacture:** $6.5 billion/yr. **Agriculture: Chief crops:** tobacco, corn, hay, soybeans, wheat, fruit. **Livestock:** 3,120,000 cattle; 1,080,000 hogs/pigs; 30,000 sheep; 3,500,000 poultry. **Timber/lumber:** hardwoods, pines. **Minerals** (1977): fossil fuels accounted for 95% of the total $3.1 billion mineral production. **Commercial fishing:** $820,000. **Chief ports:** Paducah, Louisville, Covington, Owensboro, Ashland. **International airports at:** Lexington, Louisville, Covington. **Value of construction** (1977): $2,264,536,000. **Per capita income** (1976): $5,423. **Unemployment** (1977): 4.6% **Tourism** (1976): out-of-state visitors spent $1.5 billion.

**Finance. No. banks:** 263; **No. savings and loan assns.:** 12.

**Federal government. No. federal employees** (1976): 36,000. **Notable federal facilities:** U.S. Gold Bullion Depository; Fts. Campbell, Knox; U.S. Gov't. Hospital for Narcotics Addicts, Lexington.

**Energy. Electricity production** (1977, mwh, by source): Hydroelectric: 3.3 million; Mineral: 53.2 million; Nuclear: —.

**Education. No. schools:** 1,275 elementary; 390 secondary; 38 higher education. **Avg. salary, public school teachers** (1977): $10,950.

**State data. Motto:** United we stand, divided we fall. **Flower:** Goldenrod. **Bird:** Cardinal. **Tree:** Kentucky coffee tree. **Song:** My Old Kentucky Home. **Entered union** June 1, 1792; rank, 15th. **State fair at:** Louisville.

**History.** Kentucky was the first area west of the Alleghenies settled by American pioneers; first permanent settlement, Harrodsburg, 1774. Daniel Boone blazed the Wilderness Trail through the Cumberland Gap and founded Boonesboro, 1775. Indian attacks, spurred by the British, were unceasing until, during the Revolution, Gen. George Rogers Clark captured British forts in Indiana and Illinois, 1778. In 1792, after Virginia dropped its claims to the region, Kentucky became the 15th state.

**Tourist attractions.** Kentucky Derby and accompanying festivities, Louisville; Land Between the Lakes Nat'l. Recreation Area encompassing Kentucky Lake and Lake Barkley; Mammoth Cave with 150 mi. of passageways, 200-ft. high rooms, blind fish, and Echo River, 360 ft. below ground; Old Ft. Harrod State Park; Lincoln birthplace, Hodgenville; My Old Kentucky Home, Bardstown.

**Famous Kentuckians** include Alben Barkley, Daniel Boone, Louis D. Brandeis, Kit Carson, Henry Clay, Jefferson Davis, John Fox Jr., Thomas Hunt Morgan, Elizabeth Madox Roberts, Robert Penn Warren.

**Chamber of Commerce:** Versailles Rd., P.O. Box 817, Frankfort, KY 40601.

# Louisiana

## Pelican State

**People. Population** (1977): 3,921,000; **rank:** 20. **Pop. density:** 87.2 per sq. mi. **Urban** (1970): 66.1%. **Racial distrib.** (1975): 69.8% White; 29.8% Black; Hispanic (1970): 69,678. **Major ethnic groups:** Italian, German, English, French. **Net migration** (1970-76): −23,000.

**Geography. Total area:** 48,523 sq. mi.; **rank:** 31. **Land area:** 44,930 sq. mi. **Acres forested land:** 15,380,000. **Location:** south central Gulf Coast state. **Climate:** subtropical, affected by continental weather patterns. **Topography:** lowlands of marshes and Mississippi R. flood plain; Red R. Valley lowlands; upland hills in the Florida Parishes; average elevation, 100 ft. **Capital:** Baton Rouge.

**Economy. Principal industries:** wholesale and retail trade, government, manufacturing, construction, transportation, mining. **Principal manufactured goods:** chemical products, foods, transportation equipment, electronic equipment, apparel, petroleum products. **Value added by manufacture:** $4.28 billion/yr. **Gross Domestic Product** (1974): $20 billion. **Agriculture. Chief crops:** soybean, cotton, hay, grass, silage, sweet potatoes, corn, vegetables, sugar cane, melons, rice. **Livestock:** 1,425,000 cattle; 150,000 hogs/pigs; 13,000 sheep; 3,791,000 poultry. **Timber/lumber:** pines, hardwoods, oak. **Minerals** (1977): mineral fuels (natural gas, liquified petroleum gases, crude petroleum, natural gasoline and cycle products, salt, sand and gravel. Total mineral production valued at $10.5 billion. **Commercial fishing:** $137,936,000. **Chief ports:** New Orleans, Baton Rouge, Lake Charles. **International airports at:** New Orleans. **Value of construction** (1977): $3,593,490,000. **Employment distribution:** 15% manufacturing; 17% services; 22% trade. **Per capita income** (1976): $5,386. **Unemployment** (1977): 7.0% **Tourism** (1976): out-of-state visitors spent $1.8 billion.

**Finance. Notable industries:** finance, insurance, real estate. **No. banks:** 254; **No. savings and loan assn.:** 121.

**Federal government. No. federal employees** (Feb. 1978): 33,400. **Notable federal facilities:** Barksdale, England, Ft. Polk military bases; Strategic Petroleum Reserve, New Orleans.

**Energy. Electricity production** (1977, mwh, by source): Hydroelectric: —; Mineral: 8.7 million; Nuclear: —.

**Education. No. schools:** 1,208 elementary; 484 secondary; 30 higher education. **Avg. salary, public school teachers** (1977): $11,092.

**State data. Motto:** Union, justice and confidence. **Flower:** Magnolia. **Bird:** Eastern brown pelican. **Tree:** Cypress. **Song:** Give Me Louisiana. **Entered union** Apr. 30, 1812; **rank,** 18th. **State fair** at: Shreveport; Oct.

**History.** The area was first visited, 1530, by Cabeza de Vaca and Panfilo de Narvaez. The region was claimed for France by LaSalle, 1682. First permanent settlement was by French at Fort St. Jean Baptiste (now Natchitoches), 1717. France ceded the region to Spain, 1762, took it back, 1800, and sold it to the U.S., 1803, in the Louisiana Purchase. During the Revolution, Spanish Louisiana aided the Americans. Admitted to statehood, 1812, Louisiana was the scene of the Battle of New Orleans, 1815.

Louisiana Creoles are descendants of early French and/or Spanish settlers. About 4,000 Acadians, French settlers in Nova Scotia, Canada, were forcibly transported by the British to Louisiana in 1755 (an event commemorated in Longfellow's *Evangeline*) and settled near Bayou Teche; their descendants became known as Cajuns. Another group, the Islenos, were descendants of Canary Islanders brought to Louisiana by a Spanish governor in 1770. Traces of Spanish and French survive in local dialects.

**Tourist attractions.** Mardi Gras, French Quarter, Superdome, Dixieland Jazz, all New Orleans; Battle of New Orleans site; Longfellow-Evangeline Memorial Park.

**Famous Louisianians** include Louis Armstrong, Pierre Beauregard, Judah P. Benjamin, Braxton Bragg, Grace King, Huey Long, Leonidas K. Polk, Henry Miller Shreve, Edward D. White Jr..

**Chamber of Commerce:** P.O. Box 3988, Baton Rouge, LA 70821.

# Maine

## Pine Tree State

**People. Population** (1977): 1,085,000; **rank:** 38. **Pop. density:** 35.0 per sq. mi. **Urban** (1970): 50.8%. **Racial distrib.** (1975): 99.3% White; — % Black; Hispanic (1970): 3,730. **Major ethnic groups:** English, Irish, Italian, German. **Net migration** (1970-76): +42,000.

**Geography. Total area:** 33,215 sq. mi.; **rank:** 39. **Land area:** 30,920 sq. mi. **Acres forested land:** 17,748,000. **Location:** New England state at northeastern tip of U.S. **Climate:** Southern interior and coastal, influenced by air masses from the S and W; northern clime harsher, avg. +100 in. snow in winter. **Topography:** Appalachian Mtns. extend through state; western borders have rugged terrain; long sand beaches on southern coast; northern coast mainly rocky promontories, peninsulas, fjords. **Capital:** Augusta.

**Economy. Principal industries:** manufacturing, agriculture, forestry. **Principal manufactured goods:** paper and wood products, textiles, leather, processed foods. **Value added by manufacture:** $1.6 billion/yr. **Agriculture. Chief crops:** potatoes (80% of total farm income, $17 million), apples, blueberries, sweet corn, peas, beans. **Livestock:** 132,000 cattle; 7,100 hogs/pigs; 11,000 sheep; 10,089,000 poultry. **Timber/lumber:** pine, spruce, fir. **Minerals** (1977): sand and gravel, cement, zinc, stone, copper. Total mineral production valued at $42.1 million. **Commercial fishing:** $61,997,000. **Chief ports:** Searsport, Portland. **International airports at:** Portland, Bangor. **Value of construction** (1977): $399,239,000. **Employment distribution:** 0.4% agriculture; 27.5% manufacturing; 16.7% services; 21% trade; 20.1% government. **Per capita income** (1976): $5,385. **Unemployment** (1976): 8.9% **Tourism** (1976): out-of-state visitors spent $895 million.

**Finance. No. banks:** 74; **No. savings and loan assns.:** 15.

**Federal government. No. federal employees** (1976): 16,400. **Federal payroll** (1975): $323,745. **Notable federal facilities:** Kittery Naval Shipyard; Brunswick Naval Air Sta.; Loring AFB.

**Energy. Electricity production** (1977, mwh, by source): Hydroelectric: 2 million; Mineral: 737,194; Nuclear: 5.1 million.

**Education. No. schools:** 754 elementary; 178 secondary; 25 higher education. **Avg. salary, public school teachers** (1977): $10,724.

**State data. Motto:** Dirigo (I direct). **Flower:** White pine cone and tassel. **Bird:** Chickadee. **Tree:** Eastern white pine. **Song:** State of Maine Song. **Entered union** Mar. 15, 1820; **rank,** 23d.

**History.** Maine's rocky coast was explored by the Cabots, 1498-99. French settlers arrived, 1604, at the St. Croix River; English, 1607, on the Kennebec. In 1691 Maine was made part of Massachusetts. In the Revolution, a Maine regiment fought at Bunker Hill; a British fleet destroyed Falmouth (now Portland), 1775, but the British ship Margaretta was captured near Machiasport. In 1820 Maine broke off from Massachusetts, became a separate state.

**Tourist attractions.** Acadia Nat'l. Park, Bar Harbor, on Mt. Desert Is.; Bath Iron Works and Marine Museum; Boothbay (Harbor) Railway Museum; Sugarloaf/USA Ski Area; Oganquit, Portland, York.

**Famous "Down Easters"** include James G. Blaine, Cyrus H.K. Curtis, Hannibal Hamlin, Longfellow, Sir Hiram and Hudson Maxim, Edna St. Vincent Millay, Kate Douglas Wiggin, Ben Ames Williams.

**Chamber of Commerce:** 477 Congress St., Portland, ME 04111.

# Maryland

## Old Line State, Free State

**People. Population** (1977): 4,139,000; **rank:** 18. **Pop. density:** 418.4 per sq. mi. **Urban** (1970): 76.6%. **Racial distrib.** (1975): 78.9% White; 20.1% Black; Hispanic

70): 52,974. **Major ethnic groups:** German, Italian, ssian, English, Polish. **Net migration** (1970-76): 5,000.

ography. Total area: 10,577 sq. mi.; **rank:** 42. Land a: 9,891 sq. mi. **Acres forested land:** 2,960,000. Lo-ion: Middle Atlantic state stretching from the Ocean to Alleghany Mtns. **Climate:** continental in the west; hu-subtropical in the east. **Topography:** Eastern Shore :oastal plain and Maryland Main of coastal plain, pied-nt plateau, and the Blue Ridge, separated by the Ches-ake Bay. **Capital:** Annapolis.

**onomy. Principal industries:** government, manufac-ng, fishing, service publishing. **Principal manufac-ed goods:** metals, foods, transportation equipment, arel, electric machinery. **Value added by manufac-er:** $4.7 billion/yr. **Agriculture: Chief crops:** tobacco, n, soybeans, apples, tomatoes, oysters, soft-shelled ns. **Livestock:** 390,000 cattle; 190,000 hogs/pigs; 000 sheep; 1,866,000 poultry. **Timber/lumber:** hard-ods. **Minerals** (1977): coal, stone, sand and gravel. To-value of mineral production, $196 million. **Commercial ling:** $30,787,000. **Chief ports:** Baltimore. **Interna-nal airports at:** Baltimore. **Value of construction** 77): $2,203,028,000. **Per capita income** (1976): 036. **Unemployment** (1976): 6.8% **Tourism** (1976): -of-state visitors spent $1.7 billion.

ance. **No. banks:** 113; **No. savings and loan assns.:**

deral government. No. federal employees (1976): ,000. **Notable federal facilities:** U.S. Naval Acad-y, Annapolis.

ergy. Electricity production (1977, mwh, by source): droelectric: 2 million; Mineral: 20.7 million; Nuclear: 9 million.

ucation. No. schools: 1,257 elementary; 412 second-; 52 higher education. **Avg. salary, public school ichers** (1977): $14,689.

ite data. Motto. Fatti Maschii, Parole Femine (Manly eds, womanly words). **Flower:** Black-eyed susan. **Bird:** timore oriole. **Tree:** White oak. **Song:** Maryland, My ryland. **Seventh** of the original 13 states to ratify Con-ution, Apr. 28, 1788. **State fair** at: Baltimore; end-Aug. nid-Sept.

listory. Capt. John Smith first explored Maryland, 08. William Claiborne set up a trading post on Kent Is. Chesapeake Bay, 1631. Britain granted land to Cecilius 'vert, Lord Baltimore, 1632; his brother led 200 settlers St. Marys River, 1634. The bravery of Maryland troops he Revolution, as at the Battle of Long Island, won the ie its nickname, The Old Line State. In the War of 2, when a British fleet tried to take Fort McHenry, rylander Francis Scott Key, 1814, wrote *The Star-angled Banner*.

Tourist Attractions. Racing events include the Preak-ss, at Pimlico track, Baltimore; the International at Lau-Race Course; the John B. Campbell Handicap at wie. Also Annapolis yacht races; Ocean City summer ort; restored Ft. McHenry, Baltimore, near which Fran-Scott Key wrote *The Star-Spangled Banner;*Antietam ttlefield, 1862, near Hagerstown; South Mountain Bat-ield, 1862; Edgar Allan Poe house, Baltimore; The ite House, Annapolis, 1772, the oldest still in use in the s.

'amous Marylanders include Benjamin Banneker, incis Scott Key, H.L. Mencken, William Pinkney, Upton clair, Roger B. Taney, Charles Willson Peale. Chamber of Commerce: 60 West St., Annapolis, MD 401.

# Massachusetts

## Bay State, Old Colony

**ople. Population** (1977): 5,782,000; **rank:** 10. **Pop. nsity:** 738.8 per sq. mi. **Urban** (1970): 84.6%. **Racial trib.** (1975): 95.7% White; 3.6% Black; Hispanic 70): .64,860. **Major ethnic groups:** Italian, Irish, En-h, Polish, Russian. **Net migration** (1970-76): —7,000. ography. Total area: 8,257 sq. mi.; **rank:** 45. Land a: 7,826 sq. mi. **Acres forested land:** 3,520,000. Lo-tion: New England state along Atlantic seaboard. Cli-

mate: temperate, with colder and drier clime in western region. **Topography:** jagged indented coast from Rhode Island around Cape Cod; flat land yields to stony upland pastures near central region and gentle hilly country in west; except in west, land is rocky, sandy, and not fertile. **Capital:** Boston.

Economy. Principal industries: manufacturing, services, wholesale-retail trade, construction, publishing, tourism. **Principal manufactured goods:** fabricated metal prod-ucts, apparel and finished goods, transportation equip-ment. **Value added by manufacture:** $14.4 billion/yr. **Gross Domestic Product** (1976): $4.36 billion. **Agricul-ture: Chief crops:** corn, hay, cranberries, apples, to-bacco, potatoes, peaches, maple syrup. **Livestock:** 99,000 cattle; 50,000 hogs/pigs; 6,700 sheep; 2,045,000 poultry. **Timber/lumber:** white pine, oak, spruce. **Minerals** (1977): sand and gravel, stone. Total value of mineral production $73.5 million. **Commercial fishing:** $114,017,000. **Chief ports:** Boston, Salem, Plymouth, Gloucester, Kingston. **International airports at:** Boston. **Value of construction** (1977): $1,830,839,000. **Employ-ment distribution:** 1.0% agriculture; 24.1% manufactur-ing; 20.8% services; 20.7% trade. **Per capita income** (1976): $6,585. **Unemployment** (1976): 9.5%. **Tourism** (1976): out-of-state visitors spent $2.6 billion.

Finance. No. banks: 836; No. savings and loan assns.: 30.

Federal government. No. federal employees (Mar. 1977): 51,721. **Federal payroll** (1977): $807.3 million. **Notable federal facilities:** Ft. Devens; U.S. Custom House, Boston.

Energy. Electricity production (1977, mwh, by source): Hydroelectric: 374,647; Mineral: 29.3 million; Nuclear: 3.7 million.

Education. No. schools: 2,376 elementary; 711 second-ary; 119 higher education.

State data. Motto: Ense Petit Placidam Sub Libertate Quietem (By the sword we seek peace, but peace only under liberty). **Flower:** Mayflower. **Bird:** Chickadee. **Tree:** American elm. **Song:** All Hail to Massachusetts. **Sixth** of the original 13 states to ratify Constitution, Feb. 6, 1788.

History. The Pilgrims, seeking religious freedom, made their first settlement at Plymouth, 1620; the following year they gave thanks for their survival with the first Thanksgiv-ing Day. Indian opposition reached a high point in King Philip's War, 1675-76, won by the colonists. Demonstra-tions against British restrictions set off the "Boston Mas-sacre," 1770, and Boston "tea party," 1773. First blood-shed of the Revolution was at Lexington, 1775.

Tourist attractions. Cape Code with Provincetown art-ists' colony; Berkshire Music Festival, Tanglewood; Bos-ton "Pops" concerts; Museum of Fine Arts, Arnold Arbo-retum, both Boston; Jacob's Pillow Dance Festival, West Becket; historical Shaker Village, Old Sturbridge, Lexing-ton, Concord, Salem, Plymouth Rock.

Famous "Bay Staters" include Samuel Adams, Louisa May Alcott, Horatio Alger, Clara Barton, Emily Dickinson, Emerson, Hancock, Hawthorne, Oliver W. Holmes, Wins-low Homer, Elias Howe, Samuel F.B. Morse, Poe, Revere, Sargent, Thoreau, Whistler, Whittier.

Chamber of Commerce: None.

# Michigan

## Great Lake State, Wolverine State

**People. Population** (1977): 9,129,000; **rank:** 7. **Pop. density:** 160.6 per sq. mi. **Urban** (1970): 73.8%. **Racial distrib.** (1975): 87.5% White; 11.9% Black; Hispanic (1970): 120,687. **Major ethnic groups:** Polish, German, English, Italian. **Net migration** (1970-76): —214,000. Geography. Total area: 58,216 sq. mi.; **rank:** 23. Land area: 56,817 sq. mi. **Acres forested land:** 19,273,000. **Location:** east north central state bordering on 4 of the 5 Great Lakes, divided into an Upper and Lower Peninsula by the Straits of Mackinac, which link lakes Michigan and Huron. **Climate:** well-defined seasons tempered by the Great Lakes. **Topography:** low rolling hills give way to northern tableland of hilly belts in Lower Peninsula; Upper

Peninsula is level in the east, with swampy areas; western region is higher and more rugged. **Capital:** Lansing.
**Economy. Principal industries:** manufacturing, mining, agriculture, food processing, tourism, fishing. **Principal manufactured goods:** automobiles, machine tools, chemicals, foods, primary metals and metal products, plastics. **Value added by manufacture:** $32 billion/yr. **Gross Domestic Product** (1976): $75.5 billion. **Agriculture: Chief crops:** corn, winter wheat, soybeans, dry beans, oats, hay, sugar beets, honey, asparagus, sweet corn, apples, cherries, grapes, peaches, blueberries, flowers. **Livestock:** 1,470,000 cattle; 720,000 hogs/pigs; 149,000 sheep; 9,169,000 poultry. **Timber/lumber:** hickory, ash, oak, hemlock. **Minerals** (1977): crude petroleum, iron ore, cement, natural gas, stone, sand and gravel. Total mineral production valued at $1.51 billion. **Commercial fishing:** $3,275,000. **Chief ports:** Detroit, Muskegon, Sault Ste. Marie. **International airports at:** Detroit. **Value of construction** (1977): $4,292,314,000. **Employment distribution:** 32% manufacturing; 17% services. **Per capita income** (1976): $6,994. **Unemployment** (1977): 8.2%. **Tourism** (1976): out-of-state visitors spent $3.8 billion.
**Finance. No. banks:** 362; **No. savings and loan assns.:** 66.
**Federal government. No. federal employees** (1976): 55,000. **Federal payroll** (1975): $721 million. **Notable federal facilities:** Isle Royal, Sleeping Bear Dunes national parks.
**Energy. Electricity production** (1977, mwh, by source): Hydroelectric: 804,383; Mineral: 57.7 million; Nuclear: 10.2 million.
**Education. No. schools:** 3,560 elementary; 1,270 secondary; 93 higher education. **Avg. salary, public school teachers** (1977): $16,269.
**State data. Motto:** Si Quaeris Peninsulam Amoenam Circumspice (If you seek a pleasant peninsula, look about you). **Flower:** Apple blossom. **Bird:** Robin. **Tree:** White pine. **Song:** Michigan, My Michigan. **Entered union** Jan. 26, 1837; rank, 26th. **State fair** at: Detroit; Aug.–early Sept.

**History.** French fur traders and missionaries visited the region, 1616, set up a mission at Sault Ste. Marie, 1641, and a settlement there, 1668. The whole region went to Britain, 1763. During the Revolution, the British led attacks from the area on American settlements to the south until Anthony Wayne defeated their Indian allies at Fallen Timbers, Ohio, 1794. The British returned, 1812, seized Ft. Mackinac and Detroit. Oliver H. Perry's Lake Erie victory and William H. Harrison's troops, who carried the war to the Thames River in Canada, 1813, freed Michigan once more.

**Tourist attractions.** Henry Ford Museum, Greenfield Village, reconstruction of a typical 19th cent. American village, both in Dearborn; Michigan Space Ctr., Jackson; Tahquamenon *(Hiawatha)* Falls; DeZwaan windmill and Tulip Festival, Holland; "Soo Locks," St. Marys Falls Ship Canal, Sault Ste. Marie.

**Famous Michiganders** include George Custer, Paul de Kruif, Thomas Dewey, Edna Ferber, Henry Ford, Edgar Guest, Betty Hutton, Robert Ingersoll, Will Kellogg, Danny Thomas, Stewart Edward White.

**Chamber of Commerce:** 501 S. Capitol Ave., Suite 500, Lansing, MI 48933.

# Minnesota

*North Star State, Gopher State*

**People. Population** (1977): 3,975,000; **rank:** 19. **Pop. density:** 50.1 per sq. mi. **Urban** (1970): 66.4%. **Racial distrib.** (1975): 98.0% White; 1.0% Black; Hispanic (1970): 23,198. **Major ethnic groups:** German, Swedish, Norwegian. **Net migration** (1970-76): +5,000.
**Geography. Total area:** 84,068 sq. mi.; **rank:** 12. **Land area:** 79,289 sq. mi. **Acres forested land:** 18,984,000. **Location:** north central state bounded on the E by Wisconsin and Lake Superior, on the N by Canada, on the W by the Dakotas, and on the S by Iowa. **Climate:** northern part of state lies in the moist Great Lakes storm belt; the

western border lies at the edge of the semi-arid Gr  Plains. **Topography:** central hill and lake region cover approx. half the state; to the NE, rocky ridges and de  lakes; to the NW, flat plain; to the S, rolling plains a  deep river valleys. **Capital:** St. Paul.
**Economy. Principal industries:** dairy, lumber, mini  manufacturing, tourism. **Principal manufactured goo  food processing, non-electrical machinery, chemicals,  per, stone-clay-glass products, apparel, lumber, fal  cated metal products. **Value added by manufactu  $6.7 billion/yr. **Agriculture: Chief crops:** oats, whe  corn, rye, alfalfa, sugar beets. **Livestock:** 3,700,000 c  tle; 3,600,000 hogs/pigs; 275,000 sheep; 35,149,0  poultry. **Timber/lumber:** needle-leaves and hardwoo  **Minerals** (1977): iron ore (91% of the total $873.7 mill  of mineral production), sand and gravel, stone. **Comm  cial fishing:** $1,283,000. **Chief ports:** Duluth, St. Pa  Minneapolis. **International airports at:** Minneapolis-  Paul. **Value of construction** (1977): $2,567,772,000. **P  capita income** (1976): $6,153. **Unemployment** (197  5.9%. **Tourism** (1976): out-of-state visitors spent $2.9 m  lion.
**Finance. No. banks:** 750; **No. savings and loan assn  68.
**Federal government. No. federal employees** (197  30,000.
**Energy. Electricity production** (1977, mwh, by sourc  Hydroelectric: 536,513; Mineral: 21.5 million; Nucle  11.1 million.
**Education. No. schools:** 1,524 elementary; 681 secon  ary; 66 higher education. **Avg. salary, public scho  teachers** (1977): $13,944.
**State data. Motto:** L'Etoile du Nord (The star of  north). **Flower:** Pink and white lady's-slipper. **Bird:** Co  mon loon. **Tree:** Red pine. **Song:** Hail! Minnesota. **E  tered union** May 11, 1858; rank, 32d. **State fair** at: Sa  Paul; end-Aug. to early Sept.

**History.** Fur traders and missionaries from Fren  Canada opened the region in the 17th century. Brita  took the area east of the Mississippi, 1763. The U.S. to  over that portion after the Revolution and in 1803 bou  the western area as part of the Louisiana Purchase. T  U.S. built present Ft. Snelling, 1820, bought lands fr  the Indians, 1837. Sioux Indians staged a bloody uprisi  1862, and were driven from the state.

**Tourist attractions.** Minnehaha Falls, Minneapolis,  spiration for Longfellow's *Hiawatha;* Voyageurs Na  Park, a water wilderness along the Canadian bord  Mayo Clinic, Rochester; St. Paul Winter Carnival; t  "land of 10,000 lakes" actually has 12,034 lakes over  acres in size; many water and winter sports and activit  throughout the state.

**Famous Minnesotans** include F. Scott Fitzgera  Cass Gilbert, Hubert Humphrey, Sinclair Lewis, Paul Ma  ship, E. G. Marshall, William and Charles Mayo, Walter  Mondale, Harold Stassen, Thorstein Veblen.

**Chamber of Commerce:** 200 Hanover Bldg., 480 C  dar St., St. Paul, MN 55101.

# Mississippi

*Magnolia State*

**People. Population** (1977): 2,389,000; **rank:** 29. **P  density:** 50.5 per sq. mi. **Urban** (1970): 44.5%. **Rac  distrib.** (1975): 63.6% White; 35.9% Black; Hispa  (1970): 8,182. **Major ethnic groups:** German, Italian, E  glish. **Net migration** (1970-76): −1,000.
**Geography. Total area:** 47,716 sq. mi.; **rank:** 32. **La  area:** 47,296 sq. mi. **Acres forested land:** 16,913,0  **Location:** south central state bordered on the W by t  Mississippi R. and on the S by the Gulf of Mexico. C  mate: semi-tropical, with abundant rainfall, long growi  season, and extreme temperatures unusual. **Topog  phy:** low, fertile delta bet. the Yazoo and Mississippi riv  ers; loess bluffs stretching around delta border; san  Gulf coastal terraces followed by piney woods and prair  rugged, high sandy hills in extreme NE followed by blac  prairie belt. Pontotoc Ridge, and flatwoods into the no  central highlands. **Capital:** Jackson.

conomy. **Principal industries:** manufacturing, seafood, ⸱deral government, wholesale and retail trade, agricul- ⸱re. **Principal manufactured goods:** apparel, transpor- ⸱tion equipment, lumber and wood products, foods, cot- ⸱n. **Value added by manufacture:** $4.9 billion/yr. **Gross** **omestic Product** (1976): $13 billion. **Agriculture: Chief rops:** soybeans, cotton, rice, pecans, sweet potatoes. **ivestock:** 2,130,000 cattle; 405,000 hogs/pigs; 5,400 ⸱eep; 11,541,000 poultry. **Timber/lumber:** oak, hard- ⸱oods. **Minerals** (1977): crude petroleum and natural gas ⸱5% of total $499 million value of mineral production), ⸱nd and gravel. **Commercial fishing:** $26,341,000. ⸱hief ports: Pascagoula, Greenville, Vicksburg, Biloxi, ⸱ulfport, Natchez. **Value of construction** (1977): ⸱,415,043,000. **Employment distribution:** 4% agricul- ⸱re; 25.8% manufacturing; 12% services; 17.9% govern- ⸱ent. **Per capita income** (1976): $4,575. **Unemploy-** ⸱ent (1977): 7.4%. **Tourism** (1976): out-of-state visitors ⸱ent $850.5 million.

⸱inance. **No. banks:** 185; **No. savings and loan assns.:** ⸱0.

⸱ederal government. **No. federal employees** (1976): ⸱4,000. **Federal payroll** (1976): $347.2 million. **Notable** ⸱ederal facilities: Columbus, Fairchild, Kessler AF bases; ⸱ASA/NOAA International Earth Sciences Center.

⸱nergy. **Electricity production** (1977, mwh, by source): ⸱ydroelectric: —; Mineral 16.5 million; Nuclear: —.

⸱ducation. **No. schools:** 805 elementary; 553 second- ⸱ry; 45 higher education. **Avg. salary, public school** ⸱eachers (1977): $9,397.

⸱tate data. **Motto:** Virtute et Armis (By valor and arms). ⸱ower: Magnolia. **Bird:** Mockingbird. **Tree:** Magnolia. ⸱ong: Go, Mississippi! **Entered union** Dec. 10, 1817; ⸱nk, 20th. **State fair** at: Jackson; Spring.

**History.** De Soto explored the area, 1540, discovered ⸱e Mississippi River, 1541. La Salle traced the river from ⸱inois to its mouth and claimed the entire valley for ⸱rance, 1682. First settlement was the French Ft. Maure- ⸱as, near Ocean Springs, 1699. The area was ceded to ⸱ritain, 1763; American settlers followed. During the Rev- ⸱lution, Spain seized part of the area and refused to leave ⸱ven after the U.S. acquired title at the end of the Revolu- ⸱on, finally moving out, 1798. Mississippi seceded 1861. ⸱nion forces captured Corinth and Vicksburg and de- ⸱troyed Jackson and much of Meridian.

**Tourist attractions.** Vicksburg National Military Park ⸱nd Cemetery, other Civil War sites; Natchez Trace; ⸱dian mounds; estate pilgrimage at Natchez; Mardi Gras ⸱nd blessing of the shrimp fleet, Aug., both in Biloxi.

**Famous Mississippians** include Dana Andrews, Wil- ⸱am Faulkner, Lucius O.C. Lamar, Elvis Presley, Leontyne ⸱rice, Hiram Revels, Eudora Welty.

**Chamber of Commerce:** P.O. Box 1849, Jackson, MS ⸱9205.

## Missouri

### Show Me State

⸱eople. **Population** (1977): 4,801,000; **rank:** 15. **Pop.** ⸱ensity: 69.5 per sq. mi. **Urban** (1970): 70.1%. **Racial** ⸱istrib. (1975): 88.8% White; 10.6% Black; Hispanic ⸱1970): 40,640. **Major ethnic groups:** German, Italian, ⸱nglish, Russian. **Net migration** (1970-76): −32,000

⸱eography. **Total area:** 69,686 sq. mi.; **rank:** 19. **Land** ⸱rea: 68,995 sq. mi. **Acres forested land:** 14,919,000. ⸱ocation: West North central state near the geographic ⸱enter of the conterminous U.S.; bordered on the E by the ⸱lississippi R., on the NW by the Missouri R. **Climate:** con- ⸱nental, susceptible to cold Canadian air, moist, warm ⸱ulf air, and drier SW air. **Topography:** Rolling hills, ⸱pen, fertile plains, and well-watered prairie N of the Mis- ⸱ouri R.; south of the river land is rough and hilly with ⸱eep, narrow valleys; alluvial plain in the SE; low elevation ⸱ the west. **Capital:** Jefferson City.

⸱conomy. **Principal industries:** manufacturing, aero- ⸱pace, agriculture, tourism. **Principal manufactured** ⸱oods: transportation equipment, esp. space capsules, ⸱ocket engines, aircraft; food processing, esp. meat pack- ⸱ng, beer; chemicals; metal products; shoes. **Value added**

by manufacture: $9.1 billion/yr. **Agriculture: Chief crops:** soybeans, cotton, melons, corn, clover, winter wheat, tobacco, apples, peaches, alfalfa, popcorn. **Live-stock:** 6,000,000 cattle; 3,750,000 hogs/pigs; 134,000 sheep; 17,096,000 poultry. **Timber/lumber:** oak, hickory. **Minerals** (1977): lead, cement, stone, lime, zinc. Total value of mineral production $886 million. **Commercial fishing:** $149,000. **Chief ports:** St. Louis, Kansas City. **International airports at:** St. Louis, Kansas City. **Value of construction** (1977): $2,450,869,000. **Per capita in-come** (1976): $6,005. **Unemployment** (1976): 6.2%. **Tourism** (1976): out-of-state visitors spent $2.5 billion.

Finance. **Notable industries:** banking. **No. banks:** 706; **No. savings and loan assns.:** 121.

Federal government. **No. federal employees** (1976): 66,000. **Notable federal facilities:** Federal Reserve banks, St. Louis, Kansas City; Ft. Leonard Wood, Rolla.

Energy. **Electricity production** (1977, mwh, by source): Hydroelectric: 454,129; Mineral: 45.5 million; Nuclear: —.

Education. **No. schools:** 1,971 elementary; 838 second-ary; 81 higher education. **Avg. salary, public school teachers** (1977): $11,592.

State data. **Motto:** Salus Populi Suprema Lex Esto (The welfare of the people shall be the supreme law). **Flower:** Hawthorn. **Bird:** Bluebird. **Tree:** Dogwood. **Song:** Missouri Waltz. **Entered union** Aug. 10, 1821; rank, 24th. **State fair** at: Sedalia; 3d week in Aug.

**History.** DeSoto visited the area, 1541. French hunters and lead miners made the first settlement, c. 1735, at Ste. Genevieve. The U.S. acquired Missouri as part of the Lou-isiana Purchase, 1803. The fur trade and the Santa Fe Trail provided prosperity; St. Louis became the "jump-off" point for pioneers on their way West. Pro- and anti-slavery forces battled each other there during the Civil War.

**Tourist attractions.** Mark Twain State Park, Florida; Tom Sawyer and Huckleberry Finn statues, Hannibal; Jesse James birthplace, Excelsior Springs; Pony Express Museum, St. Joseph. The Harry S. Truman Library, near Independence, contains presidential papers and memora-bilia. Mr. Truman is buried in the library courtyard.

**Famous Missourians** include Zoe Akins, Thomas Hart Benton, Omar Bradley, George Washington Carver, Thomas Dooley, T. S. Eliot, Bernarr Macfadden, J. C. Penney; John J. Pershing, Joseph Pulitzer, Sara Teas-dale, Mark Twain.

**Chamber of Commerce:** 400 E. High St., P.O. Box 149, Jefferson City, MO 65101.

## Montana

### Treasure State

People. **Population** (1977): 761,000; **rank:** 43. **Pop. den-sity:** 5.2 per sq. mi. **Urban** (1970): 53.4%. **Racial distrib.** (1975): 95.2% White; —% Black; 4.5% Other. (includes American Indians); Hispanic (1970): 7,771. **Major ethnic groups:** German, Norwegian, Russian, English. **Net mi-gration** (1970-76): +25,000.

Geography. **Total area:** 147,138 sq. mi.; **rank:** 4. **Land area:** 145,587 sq. mi. **Acres forested land:** 22,777,000. **Location:** Mountain state bounded on the E by the Dako-tas, on the S by Wyoming, on the S/SW by Idaho, and on the N by Canada. **Climate:** colder, continental climate with low humidity. **Topography:** Rocky Mtns. in western third of the state; eastern two-thirds gently rolling northern Great Plains. **Capital:** Helena.

Economy. **Principal industries:** agriculture, mining, man-ufacturing, tourism. **Principal manufactured goods:** pe-troleum products, primary metals and minerals, lumber and wood products, farm machinery, processed foods. **Value added by manufacture:** $771 million/yr. **Gross Domestic Product** (1976): $4.5 billion. **Agriculture: Chief crops:** wheat, cattle, barley, sheep, sugar beets, hay, flax, oats. **Livestock:** 2,570,000 cattle; 186,000 hogs/pigs; 570,000 sheep; 985,000 poultry. **Timber/lum-ber:** Douglas fir, pines, larch. **Minerals** (1977): mineral fuels (69% of the total $686 million mineral production), copper, silver. **International airports at:** Great Falls. **Value of construction** (1977): $443,174,000. **Employ-**

ment distribution: 10.5% agriculture; 7.3% manufacturing; 46% services; 21.4% government. Per capita income (1976): $5,600. Unemployment (1977): 6.2%. Tourism (1976): out-of-state visitors spent $618.6 million.
Finance. No. banks: 160; No. savings and loan assns.: 16.
Federal government. No. federal employees (1977): 14,000. Notable federal facilities: Malmstrom AFB; Ft. Peck, Hungry Horse, Yellowtail dams.
Energy. Electricity production (1977, mwh, by source): Hydroelectric: 8.4 million; Mineral: 5.0 million; Nuclear: —.
Education. No. schools: 669 elementary; 210 secondary; 12 higher education. Avg. salary, public school teachers (1977): $11,746.
State data. Motto: Oro y Plata (Gold and silver). Flower: Bitterroot. Bird: Western meadowlark. Tree: Ponderosa pine. Song: Montana. Entered union Nov. 8, 1889; rank, 41st. State fair at: Great Falls; 1st week in Aug.

History. French explorers visited the region, 1742. The U.S. acquired the area partly through the Louisiana Purchase, 1803, and partly through the explorations of Lewis and Clark, 1805-06. Fur traders and missionaries established posts in the early 19th century. Indian uprisings reached their peak with the Battle of the Little Big Horn, 1876. The coming of the Northern Pacific Railway, 1883, brought population growth.
Tourist attractions. Glacier National Park, on the Continental Divide, is a scenic and recreational wonderland, with 60 glaciers, 200 lakes, and many trout streams.
Also, Museum of the Plains Indian, Blackfeet Reservation near Browning; Custer Battlefield National Cemetery; Flathead Lake, in the NW, Lewis and Clark Cavern, Morrison Cave State Park, near Whitehall.
There are 7 Indian reservations, covering over 5 million acres; tribes are Blackfeet, Crow, Confederated Salish & Kootenai, Assiniboine, Gros Ventre, Sioux, Northern Cheyenne, Chippewa, Cree. Population of the reservations is approximately 25,500.
Famous Montanans include Gary Cooper, Marcus Daly, Chet Huntley, Will James, Myrna Loy, Mike Mansfield, Jeannette Rankin, Charles M. Russell.
Chamber of Commerce: 110 Neil Ave., P.O. Box 1730, Helena, MT 59601.

## Nebraska

### Cornhusker State

People. Population (1977): 1,561,000; rank: 35. Pop. density: 20.4 per sq. mi. Urban (1970): 61.5%. Racial distrib. (1975): 96.2% White; 3.0% Black; Hispanic (1970): 21,067. Major ethnic groups: German, Czechoslovakian, Swedish, Russian. Net migration (1970-76): +11,000.
Geography. Total area: 77,227 sq. mi.; rank: 15. Land area: 76,483 sq. mi. Acres forested land: 1,045,000. Location: West North Central state with the Missouri R. for a N/NE border. Climate: continental semi-arid. Topography: till plains of the central lowland in the eastern third rising to the Great Plains and hill country of the north central and NW. Capital: Lincoln.
Economy. Principal industries: agriculture, food processing, manufacturing. Principal manufactured goods: foods, machinery, electric and electronic equipment, chemicals, primary and fabricated metal products. Value added by manufacture: $2.6 billion/yr. Gross Domestic Product (1976): $11.8 billion. Agriculture: Chief crops: corn, wheat, sorghum, hay, oats, beans, sugar beets, popcorn, barley, potatoes. Livestock: 6,500,000 cattle; 3,100,000 hogs/pigs; 190,000 sheep; 4,561,000 poultry. Minerals (1977): cement, sand and gravel, natural gas liquids, petroleum. Total mineral production valued at $125.1 million. Commercial fishing: $21,000. Chief ports: Omaha, Sioux City, Brownsville, Blair, Plattsmouth. Value of construction (1977): $1,197,195,000. Employment distribution: 12.1% agriculture; 12.9% manufacturing; 15.4% services; 17.8% government; 22.3% trade. Per capita income (1976): $6,240. Unemployment (1976): 5.0%. Tourism (1976): out-of-state visitors spent $720.7 million.

Finance. No. banks: 450; No. savings and loan assns. 43.
Federal government. No. federal employees (1976): 16,500. Federal payroll (1976): $423 million. Notable federal facilities: Strategic Air Command Base, Omaha.
Energy. Electricity production (1977, mwh, by source): Hydroelectric: 1.2 million; Mineral: 6.2 million; Nuclear: 7. million.
Education. No. schools: 1,588 elementary; 442 secondary; 30 higher education. Avg. salary, public school teachers (1977): $11,172.
State data. Motto: Equality before the law. Flower: Goldenrod. Bird: Western meadowlark. Tree: Cottonwood. Song: Beautiful Nebraska. Entered union Mar. 1, 1867 rank, 37th. State fair at: Lincoln; first week of Sept.

History. Spanish and French explorers and fur trader visited the area prior to the Louisiana Purchase, 1803 Lewis and Clark passed through, 1804-06. First permanent settlement was Bellevue, near Omaha, 1823. Many Civil War veterans settled under free land terms of the 1862 Homestead Act; struggles followed between home steaders and ranchers.
Tourist attractions. Boys Town, founded by Fr. Flanagan, west of Omaha, is a self-contained community of underprivileged and homeless boys. Arbor Lodge State Park, Nebraska City, is a memorial to J. Sterling Morton founder of Arbor Day. Buffalo Bill Ranch State Historical Park, North Platte, contains Cody's home and memorabilia of his Wild West Show.
Also, Pioneer Village, Minden; Oregon Trail, landmarks Scotts Bluff National Mountain and Chimney Rock Historic Site.
Famous Nebraskans include Fred Astaire, Charles W and William Jennings Bryan, Willa Cather, Michael and Edward A. Cudahy, Loren Eiseley, Rev. Edward J. Flanagan, Henry Fonda, Rollin Kirby, Harold Lloyd, Malcolm X Roscoe Pound.
Chamber of Commerce: 424 Terminal Bldg., Lincoln NE 68508.

## Nevada

### Sagebrush State, Battle Born State

People. Population (1977): 633,000; rank: 46. Pop. density: 5.7 per sq. mi. Urban (1970): 80.9%. Racial distrib. (1975): 91.7 White; 6.0% Black; Hispanic (1970): 27,142 Major ethnic groups: Italian, German, English, Mexican. Net migration (1970-76): +91,000.
Geography. Total area: 110,540 sq. mi.; rank: 7. Land area: 109,889 sq. mi. Acres forested land: 7,660,000. Location: Mountain state borderd on N by Oregon and Idaho, on E by Utah and Arizona, on SE by Arizona, and on SW/W by California. Climate: semi-arid. Topography rugged N-S mountain ranges; southern area is within the Mojave Desert; lowest elevation, Colorado R. Canyon 470 ft. Capital: Carson City.
Economy. Principal industries: tourism, mining, manufacturing, lumber, government, agriculture, warehousing trucking. Principal manufactured goods: gaming devices, electronics, chemicals, forest products, stone-clay glass products. Agriculture: Chief crops: alfalfa, barley wheat, oats, cotton. Livestock: 570,000 cattle; 8,000 hogs/pigs; 133,000 sheep; 14,000 poultry. Timber/lumber: pine, fir, spruce. Minerals (1977): gold (2d largest in U.S. with 26% of total output), copper, sand and gravel Total mineral production valued at $251.2 million. International airports at Las Vegas, Reno. Value of construction (1977): $926,347,000. Per capita income (1976) $7,337. Unemployment (1976): 9.0%. Tourism (1976) out-of-state visitors spent $1.3 billion.
Finance. No banks: 8; No. savings and loan assns.: 7. Federal government. No. federal employees (1976) 9,000. Notable federal facilities: Nevada Test Site.
Energy. Electricity production (1977, mwh, by source) Hydroelectric: 1.6 million; Mineral: 14.2 million; Nuclear —.
Education. No. schools: 174 elementary; 83 secondary 6 higher education. Avg. salary, public school teachers (1977): $13,415.

tate data. Motto: All for our country. Flower: Sage-
ush. Bird: Mountain bluebird. Tree: Single-leaf pinon.
ong: Home Means Nevada. Entered union Oct. 31,
464; rank, 36th. State fair at Reno; early Sept.

History. Nevada was first explored by Spaniards in
776. Hudson's Bay Co. trappers explored the north and
entral region, 1825; trader Jedediah Smith crossed the
ate, 1826 and 1827. The area was acquired by the U.S.,
1848, at the end of the Mexican War. First settlement,
ormon Station, now Genoa, was est. 1849. In the early
0th century, Nevada adopted progressive measures
uch as the initiative, referendum, recall, and woman suf-
age.

Tourist attractions. Legalized gambling provided the
npetus for the development of resort areas Lake Tahoe,
eno, and Las Vegas. Ghost towns, rodeos, trout fishing,
ater sports and hunting important.
Notable are Helldorado Week in May, Las Vegas;
asque Festival, Elko; Reno Rodeo, 4th of July; Valley of
re State Park, Overton; Death Valley, on the California
order; Lehman Caves National Monument.

Famous Nevadans include Walter Van Tilburg Clark,
arah Winnemucca Hopkins, Dr. Robert C. Lynch, Pat
cCarran, William Morris Stewart.
Chamber of Commerce: P.O. Box 3499, Reno, NV
9505.

## New Hampshire
### Granite State

eople. Population (1977): 849,000; rank: 42. Pop. den-
ty: 94.0 per sq. mi. Urban (1970): 56.4%. Racial dis-
ib. (1975): 99.3% White; — % Black; Hispanic (1970):
681. Major ethnic groups: English, Irish, Polish, Italian,
erman. Net migration (1970-76): +56,000.
eography. Total area: 9,304 sq. mi.; rank: 44. Land
ea: 9,027 sq. mi. Acres forested land: 5,131,000. Lo-
ation: New England state bounded on S by Massa-
usetts, on W by Vermont, on N/NW by Canada, on E
Maine and the Atlantic O. Climate: highly varied, due
its nearness to high mountains and ocean. Topogra-
hy: low, curving coast followed by countless hills and
ountains rising out of a central plateau. Capital: Con-
ord.

conomy. Principal industries: manufacturing, commu-
cations, trade, agriculture, mining. Principal manufac-
ured goods: leather products, wood and paper products,
ectrical equipment, machinery, minerals. Gross Do-
estic Product (1975): $4.58 billion. Agriculture: Chief
rops: maple syrup, apples, peaches, vegetables. Live-
ock: 74,000 cattle; 8,500 hogs/pigs; 6,500 sheep;
425,000 poultry. Timber/lumber: white pine. Minerals
977): sand and gravel. Total mineral production valued
$16.9 million. Commercial fishing: $1,473,000. Chief
orts: Portsmouth. Value of construction (1977):
,651,357,000. Per capita income (1976): $5,973. Un-
mployment (1976): 6.4%. Tourism (1976): out-of-state
sitors spent $690.6 million.
nance. Notable industries: insurance, banking. No.
anks: 77; No. savings and loan assns.: 18.
ederal government. No. federal employees (1976):
,000.
nergy. Electricity production (1977, mwh, by source):
ydroelectric: 1.2 million; Mineral: 4.0 million; Nuclear: —.
ducation: No. schools: 460 elementary; 128 second-
y; 24 higher education. Avg. salary, public school
achers (1977): $10,250.
tate data. Motto: Live free or die. Flower: Purple lilac.
rd: Purple finch. Tree: White birch. Song: Old New
ampshire. Ninth of the original 13 states to ratify the
onstitution, June 21, 1788.

History. First explorers to visit the New Hampshire
ea were England's Martin Pring, 1603, and Champlain,
05. First settlement was Little Harbor, near Rye, 1623.
dian raids were halted, 1759, by Robert Rogers' Rang-
s. Before the Revolution, New Hampshire men seized a
itish fort at Portsmouth, 1774, and drove the royal gov-
nor out, 1775. Three regiments served in the Continen-
l Army and scores of privateers raided British shipping.

Tourist attractions. Crawford, Franconia, Pinkham
notches in the White Mtn. region. Franconia is famous for
the Old Man of the Mountains, described by Hawthorne
as the Great Stone Face; the Flume, a spectacular gorge,
the aerial tramway on Cannon Mtn. Also, numerous skiing
resorts and facilities.
The MacDowell Colony at Peterborough, est. 1908 in
honor of composer Edward MacDowell, is a summer haven for writers, composers, artists.
Famous New Hampshirites include Salmon P. Chase,
Ralph Adams Cram, Mary Baker Eddy, Daniel Chester
French, Robert Frost, Horace Greeley, Sarah Buell Hale,
Augustus Saint-Gaudens, Daniel Webster.
Chamber of Commerce: 540 Chestnut St., Manches-
ter, NH 03101.

## New Jersey
### Garden State

People. Population (1977): 7,329,000; rank: 9. Pop.
density: 974.4 per sq. mi. Urban (1970): 88.9%. Racial
distrib. (1975): 87.2% White; 11.9% Black; Hispanic
(1970): 135,677. Major ethnic groups: Italian, German,
Polish. Net migration (1970-76): —38,000.
Geography. Total area: 7,836 sq. mi.; rank: 46. Land
area: 7,521 sq. mi. Acres forested land: 2,463,000. Location: Middle Atlantic state bounded on the N and E by
New York and the Atlantic O., on the S and W by Delaware and Pennsylvania. Climate: moderate, with marked
difference bet. NW and SE extremities. Topography: Appalachian Valley in the NW also has highest elevation,
High Pt., 1,801 ft.; Appalachian Highlands, flat-topped NE-
SW mountain ranges; Piedmont Plateau, low plains broken by high ridges (Palisades) rising 400-500 ft.; Coastal
Plain, covering three-fifths of state in SE, gradually rises
from sea level to gentle slopes. Capital: Trenton.
Economy. Principal industries: chemical production,
manufacturing, agriculture, printing and publishing, tourism. Principal manufactured goods: pharmaceuticals,
textiles, clothing, plastics, petroleum products, electronic
equipment, glassware, processed foods. Value added by
manufacture: $20.2 billion/yr. Gross Domestic Product
(1976): $60 billion. Agriculture: Chief crops: tomatoes,
cranberries, blueberries, corn, peaches, soybeans, asparagus, potatoes, onions, strawberries, cabbage, apples,
wheat, barley. Livestock: 114,000 cattle; 75,000 hogs/-
pigs; 8,300 sheep; 2,116,000 poultry. Timber/lumber:
pine, white cedar, oak, elm. Minerals (1977): sand and
gravel, stone, zinc. Total value of mineral production,
$127 million. Commercial fishing: $38,480,000. Chief
ports: Newark, Elizabeth, Hoboken, Ameri-Port (Delaware R.). International airports at: Newark. Value of
construction (1977): $4,773,416,000. Employment dis-
tribution: 1.0% agriculture; 25.4% manufacturing; 17.8%
services; 16.7% government; 22.6% trade. Per capita
income (1977): $7,269. Unemployment (1977): 9.4%
Tourism (1976): out-of-state visitors spent $3.1 billion.
Finance. Notable industries: banking, insurance. No.
banks: 218; No. savings and loan assns.: 220.
Federal government. No. federal employees (1976):
71,017. Federal payroll (1977): $994 million. Notable
federal facilities: Ft. Dix; McGuire AFB; Picatinny Arsenal; Lakewood Naval Air Station.
Energy. Electricity production (1977, mwh, by source):
Hydroelectric: —; Mineral: 23.7 million; Nuclear: 7 million.
Education. No. schools: 2,577 elementary; 599 secondary; 64 higher education. Avg. salary, public school
teachers (1977): $14,500.
State Data. Motto: Liberty and prosperity. Flower: Purple violet. Bird: Eastern goldfinch. Tree: Red oak. Third
of the original 13 states to ratify the Constitution, Dec. 18,
1787. State fair at: Hamilton Twp., Mercer Co.; 2d week
of Sept.

History. The Lenni Lenape (Delaware) Indians had
mostly peaceful relations with European colonists who arrived after the explorers Verrazano, 1524, and Hudson,
1609. The Dutch were first; when the British took New
Netherland, 1664, the area between the Delaware and
Hudson Rivers was given to Lord John Berkeley and Sir

George Carteret. New Jersey was the scene of nearly 100 battles, large and small, during the Revolution, including Trenton, 1776, Princeton, 1777, Monmouth, 1778.

**Tourist attractions.** Grover Cleveland birthplace, Caldwell; Walt Whitman Poetry Center, Camden; Edison Lab National Monument, West Orange; numerous Revolutionary historic sites; Great Adventure amusement park; 127 miles of Atlantic Ocean beaches; Miss America Pageant, Atlantic City; legalized casino gambling, inaugurated 1978, in Atlantic City.

**Famous New Jerseyites** include Aaron Burr, James Fenimore Cooper, Stephen Crane, Thomas Edison, Alexander Hamilton, Joyce Kilmer, Gen. George McClellan, Thomas Paine, Molly Pitcher, Paul Robeson, Walt Whitman, Alexander Woolcott.

**Chamber of Commerce:** 5 Commerce St., Newark, NJ 07102.

# New Mexico
## Land of Enchantment

**People. Population** (1977): 1,190,000; **rank: 37. Pop. density:** 9.8 per sq. mi. **Urban** (1970): 69.8%. **Racial distrib. (1975):** 90.2% White; —% Black; 8.0% Other (includes American Indians); Hispanic (1970): 407,286. **Major ethnic groups:** Mexican, German, English. **Net migration** (1970-76): +67,000.

**Geography. Total area:** 121,666 sq. mi.; **rank: 5. Land area:** 121,412 sq. mi. **Acres forested land:** 18,313,000. **Location:** southwestern state bounded by Colorado on the N, Oklahoma, Texas, and Mexico on the E and S, and Arizona on the W. **Climate:** dry, with temperatures rising or falling 5°F with every 1,000 ft. elevation. **Topography:** eastern third, Great Plains; central third Rocky Mtns. (85% of the state is over 4,000 ft. elevation); western third high plateau. **Capital:** Santa Fe.

**Economy. Principal industries:** government, retail and wholesale trade, manufacturing. **Principal manufactured goods:** Lumber, foods, machinery, electrical equipment. **Value added by manufacture:** $364 million/yr. **Gross Domestic Product** (1976): $6.2 billion. **Agriculture: Chief crops:** wheat, hay, sorghum, cotton, vegetables, fruits and nuts. **Livestock:** 1,550,000 cattle; 73,000 hogs/pigs; 560,000 sheep; 1,970,000 poultry. **Timber/lumber:** Ponderosa pine, Douglas fir. **Minerals** (1977): perlite, potassium salts, uranium each ranked first in U.S. production. Also copper, molybdenum, natural gas, natural gasliquids, pumice, crude petroleum. Total value of mineral production, $2.9 billion. **International airports at:** Alburquerque. **Value of construction** (1977): $951,843,000. **Employment distribution:** 18.0% agriculture; 10.0% manufacturing; 23.0% services; 8.9% government. **Per capita income** (1976): $5,213. **Unemployment** (1977): 7.8% **Tourism** (1976): out-of-state visitors spent $881.8 million.

**Finance. No. banks:** 85; **No. savings and loan assns.:** 34.

**Federal government. No. federal employees** (1977): 38,000. **Federal payroll** (1975): $62.6 million. **Notable federal facilities:** Kirkland, Cannon, Hollomon AF bases; Los Alamos Scientific Laboratory; White Sands Missile Range.

**Energy. Electricity production** (1977, mwh, by source): Hydroelectric: 27,928; Mineral: 21.5 million; Nuclear: —.

**Education. No. schools:** 483 elementary; 204 secondary; 17 higher education. **Avg. salary, public school teachers** (1977): $12,032.

**State data. Motto:** Crescit Eundo (It grows as it does). **Flower:** Yucca. **Bird:** Roadrunner. **Tree:** Pinon. **Song:** O, Fair New Mexico, Asi Es Nuevo Mexico. **Entered union** Jan. 6, 1912; rank, 47th. **State fair** at: Albuquerque; mid-Sept.

**History.** Franciscan Marcos de Niza and a black slave Estevan explored the area, 1539, seeking gold. First settlements were at San Juan Pueblo, 1598, and Santa Fe, 1610. Settlers alternately traded and fought with the Apaches, Comanches, and Navajos. Trade on the Santa Fe Trail to Missouri started 1821. Before the Mexican War, Gen. Stephen Kearney took Santa Fe, 1846. In the

1870s, cattlemen staged the famed Lincoln County War in which Billy (the Kid) Bonney played a leading role. Pancho Villa raided Columbus, 1916.

**Tourist Attractions.** Carlsbad Caverns, a national park, has caverns on 3 levels and the largest natural cave "room" in the world, 1,500 by 300 ft., 300 ft. high.

Pueblo ruin from 100 AD, Chaco Canyon; Acoma, the "sky city," built atop a 357-ft. mesa; 19 Pueblo, 4 Navajo and 2 Apache reservations. Also, ghost towns, dude ranches, skiing, hunting, and fishing.

**Famous New Mexicans** include Billy (the Kid) Bonney, Kit Carson, Peter Hurd, Archbishop John Lamy, Bill Mauldin, Georgia O'Keeffe, Kim Stanley, Lew Wallace.

**Chamber of Commerce:** P.O. Box 1395, Gallup, NM 87301.

# New York
## Empire State

**People. Population** (1977): 17,924,000; **rank: 2. Pop. density:** 374.7 per sq. mi. **Urban** (1970): 88.9%. **Racial distrib. (1975):** 85.4% White; 13.2% Black; Hispanic (1970): 872,471. **Major ethnic groups:** Italian, Russian, Polish, German. **Net migration** (1970-76): −640,000.

**Geography. Total area:** 49,576 sq. mi.; **rank: 30. Land area:** 47,831 sq. mi. **Acres forested land:** 17,377,000. **Location:** Middle Atlantic state, bordered by the New England states, Atlantic Ocean, New Jersey and Pennsylvania, Lakes Ontario and Erie, and Canada. **Climate:** variable; the SE region moderated by the ocean. **Topography:** highest and most rugged mountains in the NE Adirondack upland; St. Lawrence-Champlain lowlands extend from Lake Ontario NE along the Canadian border; Hudson-Mohawk lowland follows the flows of the rivers N and W, 10-30 mi. wide; Atlantic coastal plain in the SE; Appalachian Highlands, covering half the state westward from the Hudson Valley, include the Catskill Mtns., Finger Lakes; plateau of Erie-Ontario lowlands. **Capital:** Albany.

**Economy. Principal industries:** printing and publishing, manufacturing, finance, communications, tourism, transportation. **Principal manufactured goods:** books and periodicals, clothing, pharmaceuticals, machinery, apparel, electronic equipment, automotive and aircraft components. **Value added by manufacture:** $35 billion/yr. **Agriculture: Chief crops:** potatoes, apples, corn, grapes, onions, hay. **Products:** milk, eggs, nursery products, poultry, wines. **Livestock:** 1,760,000 cattle; 120,000 hogs/pigs; 69,000 sheep; 10,538,000 poultry. **Timber/lumber:** evergreens, maples, red cedar. **Minerals** (1977): natural gas, sand and gravel, stone, peat, clay. First in garnet, talc, ilmenite production. Total value mineral production $439.5 million. **Commercial fishing:** $30,790,000. **Chief ports:** New York, Buffalo, Albany. **International airports at:** New York, Buffalo, Syracuse. **Value of construction** (1977): $4,328,890,000. **Employment distribution:** 1.3% agriculture; 24% manufacturing; 29% services; 15% trade. **Per capita income** (1976): $7,100. **Unemployment** (1977): 9.1%. **Tourism** (1976): out-of-state visitors spent $6.4 billion.

**Finance. Notable industries:** banking, trade, security and commodity brokerage and exchange, insurance, real estate. **No. banks:** 357; **No. savings and loan assns.:** 138.

**Federal government. No. federal employees** (1976): 165,500. **Federal payroll** (1976): $2.4 billion. **Notable federal facilities:** West Point Military Academy; Merchant Marine Academy; Ft. Drum; Griffiss, Plattsburgh AF bases; Watervliet Arsenal.

**Energy. Electricity production** (1977, mwh, by source): Hydroelectric: 25.4 million; Mineral: 66.5 million; Nuclear: 20.6 million.

**Education. No. schools:** 4,538 elementary; 1,581 secondary; 285 higher education. **Avg. salary, public school teachers** (1977): $17,100.

**State data. Motto:** Excelsior (Ever upward). **Flower:** Rose. **Bird:** Bluebird. **Tree:** Sugar maple. **Eleventh** of the original 13 states to ratify the Constitution, July 26, 1788. **State fair** at: Syracuse, mid-Aug.

**History.** In 1609 Henry Hudson discovered the river at bears his name and Champlain explored the lake, far ostate, which was named for him. Dutch built posts near bany 1614 and 1624; in 1626 they settled Manhattan. A ritish fleet seized New Netherland, 1664. Ninety-two of e 300 or more engagements of the Revolution were ught in New York, including the Battle of Bemis Heights-aratoga, a turning point of the war.

**Tourist attractions.** New York City; Adirondack and atskill mtns.; Finger Lakes, Great Lakes; Thousand Is-nds; Niagara Falls; Saratoga Springs racing and spas; nilipsburg Manor, Sunnyside, the restored home of /ashington Irving, The Dutch Church of Sleepy Hollow, l in North Tarrytown; Corning Glass Center and Steuben ctory, Corning; Fenimore House, National Baseball Hall f Fame and Museum, both in Cooperstown; Ft. Ticon-eroga overlooking lakes George and Champlain.

The Franklin D. Roosevelt National Historic Site, Hyde ark, includes the graves of Pres. and Mrs. Roosevelt, the mily home since 1867, the Roosevelt Library. Sagamore ill, Oyster Bay, the Theodore Roosevelt estate, includes s home.

**Famous New Yorkers** include Peter Cooper, George astman, Julia Ward Howe, Charles Evans Hughes, enry and William James, Herman Melville, Alfred E. mith, Elizabeth Cady Stanton, Walt Whitman.

**Chamber of Commerce:** 150 State St., Albany, NY 2207.

# North Carolina

*Tar Heel State, Old North State*

**eople. Population** (1977): 5,525,000; **rank:** 11. **Pop. ensity:** 113.2 per sq. mi. **Urban** (1970): 45%. **Racial istrib.** (1975): 76.9% White; 21.9% Black; Hispanic 970): 22,611. **Major ethnic groups:** German, English. **et migration** (1970-76): +124,000.

**eography. Total area:** 52,586 sq. mi.; **rank:** 28. **Land rea:** 48,798 sq. mi. **Acres forested land:** 20,613,000. **ocation:** South Atlantic state bounded by Virginia, South arolina, Georgia, Tennessee, and the Atlantic O. **Cli-ate:** sub-tropical in SE, medium-continental in mountain egion; tempered by the Gulf Stream and the mountains in V. **Topography:** coastal plain and tidewater, two-fifths of tate, extending to the fall line of the rivers; piedmont pla-au, another two-fifths, 200 mi. wide of gentle to rugged lls; southern Applachian Mtns. contains the Blue Ridge nd Great Smoky mtns. **Capital:** Raleigh.

**conomy. Principal industries:** manufacturing, agricul-re, tobacco. **Principal manufactured goods:** furniture, ood and paper products, tobacco products, textiles, ap-arel. **Value added by manufacture:** $15.8 billion/yr. **ross Domestic Product** (1977): $20 billion. **Agricul-re:** Chief crops: tobacco, peanuts, corn, soybeans, weet potatoes, cotton, grains, peaches, apples. **Live-tock:** 1,100,000 cattle; 1,940,000 hogs/pigs; 9,000 heep; 37,900,000 poultry. **Timber/lumber:** spruce, fir, almetto. **Minerals** (1977): stone, phosphate rock, sand nd gravel, cement, lithium compounds. Total mineral pro-uction valued at $218 million. **Commercial fishing:** 28,855,000. **Chief ports:** Morehead City, Wilmington. **alue of construction** (1977): $2,995,272,000. **Employ-ent distribution:** .05% agriculture; 29.6% manufactur-g; 11.2% services; 15.5% trade; 12.7% government. **er capita income** (1976): $5,409. **Unemployment** 976): 6.2%. **Tourism** (1976): out-of-state visitors spent 2.2 billion.

**inance. No. banks:** 127; **No. savings and loan assns.:** 42.

**ederal government. No. federal employees** (1976): 6,732. **Federal payroll** (1976): $611.7 million. **Notable ederal facilities:** Ft. Bragg; Camp LeJeune Marine Base; J.S. EPA Research and Development Labs.

**nergy. Electricity production** (1977, mwh, by source): ydroelectric: 5.3 million; Mineral: 52.6 million; Nuclear: .7 million.

**ducation. No. schools:** 1,587 elementary; 618 second-ry; 114 higher education. **Avg. salary, public school** eachers (1977): $12,034.

**State data. Motto:** Esse Quam Videri (To be rather than to seem). **Flower:** Dogwood. **Bird:** Cardinal. **Tree:** Pine. **Song:** The Old North State. **Twelfth** of the original 13 states to ratify the Constitution, Nov. 21, 1789. **State fair** at: Raleigh; mid-Oct.

**History.** The first English colony in America was the first of 2 established by Sir Walter Raleigh on Roanoke Is., 1585 and 1587. The first group returned to England; the second, the "Lost Colony," disappeared without trace. Permanent settlers came from Virginia, c. 1660. Roused by British repressions, the colonists drove out the royal governor, 1775; the province's congress was the first to vote for independence; ten regiments were furnished to the Continental Army. Cornwallis' forces were defeated at Kings Mountain, 1780, and forced out after Guilford Court-house, 1781.

**Tourist attractions.** Cape Hatteras and Cape Lookout national seashores; Great Smoky Mtns. (half in Tennes-see); Guilford Courthouse and Moore's Creek parks, Rev-olutionary battle sites; Bennett Place, NW of Durham, where Gen. Joseph Johnston surrendered the last Con-federate army to Gen. Wm. Sherman; Ft. Raleigh, Roa-noke Is., where Virginia Dare, first child of English parents in the New World, was born Aug. 18, 1587; Wright Broth-ers National Memorial, Kitty Hawk.

**Famous North Carolinians** include Richard J. Gatling, Billy Graham, Wm. Rufus King, Dolley Madison, Edward R. Murrow, Enos Slaughter, Moses Waddel.

**Chamber of Commerce:** None.

# North Dakota

*Sioux State, Flickertail State*

**People. Population** (1977): 653,000; **rank:** 45. **Pop. den-sity:** 9.4 per sq. mi. **Urban** (1970): 44.3%. **Racial distrib.** (1975): 96.7% White; —% Black; Hispanic (1970): 2,007. **Major ethnic groups** Norwegian, Russian, German. **Net migration** (1970-76): −4,000.

**Geography. Total area:** 70,665 sq. mi.; **rank:** 17. **Land area:** 69,273 sq. mi. **Acres forested land:** 421,000. **Lo-cation:** West North Central state, situated exactly in the middle of North America, bounded on the N by Canada, on the E by Minnesota, on the S by South Dakota, on the W by Montana. **Climate:** continental, with a wide range of temperature and moderate rainfall. **Topography:** Central Lowland in the E comprises the flat Red River Valley and the Rolling Drift Prairie; Missouri Plateau of the Great Plains on the W. **Capital:** Bismarck.

**Economy. Principal industries:** agriculture, manufactur-ing. **Principal manufactured goods:** farm equipment, processed foods. **Value added by manufacture:** $387 million/yr. **Gross Domestic Product** (1976): $4.9 billion. **Agriculture:** Chief crops: spring wheat, durum, barley, rye, flaxseed, oats, potatoes, soybeans, sugarbeets, sun-flowers, hay. **Livestock:** 2,050,000 cattle; 330,000 hogs/-pigs; 236,000 sheep; 1,215,000 poultry. **Minerals** (1977): petroleum (70% of the total $277.3 million output value), natural gas, natural gas liquids, salt, lime. **Commercial fishing:** $79,000. **International airports at:** Fargo, Grand Forks, Bismarck, Minot. **Value of construction** (1977): $726,656,000. **Employment distribution:** 19.4% agricul-ture; 5.4% manufacturing; 13.9% services. **Per capita income** (1976): $5,400. **Unemployment** (1977): 5.5% **Tourism** (1976): out-of-state visitors spent $385 million.

**Finance. No. banks:** 169; **No. savings and loan assns.:** 13.

**Federal government. No. federal employees** (1976): 9,000. **Notable federal facilities:** Strategic Air Command bases at Minot, Grand Forks.

**Energy. Electricity production** (1977, mwh, by source): Hydroelectric: 2 million; Mineral: 8.3 million; Nuclear: —.

**Education. No. schools:** 504 elementary; 319 second-ary; 15 higher education. **Avg. salary, public school teachers** (1977): $10,063.

**State data. Motto:** Liberty and union, now and forever, one and inseparable. **Flower:** Wild prairie rose. **Bird:**

Western Meadowlark. **Tree:** American elm. **Song:** North Dakota Hymn. **Entered union** Nov. 2, 1889; rank, 39th. **State fair** at: Minot; 3d week in July.

**History.** Pierre La Verendrye was the first French fur trader in the area, 1738, followed later by the English. The U.S. acquired half the territory in the Louisiana Purchase, 1803. Lewis and Clark built Ft. Mandan, spent the winter of 1804-05 there. In 1818, American ownership of the other half was confirmed by agreement with Britain. First permanent settlement was at Pembina, 1812. Missouri River steamboats reached the area, 1832; the first railroad, 1873, bringing many homesteaders. The state was first to hold a presidential primary, 1912.

**Tourist attractions.** International Peace Garden, a 2,200-acre tract extending across the border into Manitoba, commemorates the friendly relations between the U.S. and Canada; 65,000-acre Theodore Roosevelt National Memorial Park, Badlands, contains the president's Elkhorn Ranch; Ft. Abraham Lincoln State Park and Museum, S of Mandan.

**Famous North Dakotans** include Maxwell Anderson, Angie Dickinson, John Bernard Flannagan; Louis L'Amour, Peggy Lee, Eric Sevareid, Vilhjalmur Stefansson, Lawrence Welk.

**Chamber of Commerce:** P.O. Box 2467, Fargo, ND 58102.

**Song:** Beautiful Ohio. **Entered union** Mar. 1, 1803; rank 17th. **State fair** at: Columbus; late Aug.

**History.** LaSalle visited the Ohio area, 1669. America fur-traders arrived, beginning 1685; the French an Indians sought to drive them out. During the Revolution Virginians defeated the Indians, 1774, but hostilities we renewed, 1777. The region became U.S. territory after th Revolution. First organized settlement was at Marietta 1788. Indian warfare ended with Anthony Wayne's victor at Fallen Timbers, 1794. In the War of 1812, Oliver H Perry's victory on Lake Erie and William H. Harrison's in vasion of Canada, 1813, ended British incursions.

**Tourist attractions.** Memorial City Group Nationa Monuments, a group of 24 prehistoric Indian buria mounds; Neil Armstrong Air and Space Museum Wapakoneta; Air Force Museum, Dayton; Pro Footba Hall of Fame, Canton; birthplaces, homes, and memoria to Ohio's 6 U.S. presidents: Wm. Henry Harrison, U.S Grant, Garfield, Hayes, McKinley, Harding.

**Famous Ohioans** include Sherwood Anderson, Georg Bellows, Ambrose Bierce, Paul Laurence Dunbar, Thoma Edison, John Glenn, Bob Hope, Eddie Rickenbacker, Joh S. Rockefeller Sr. and Jr., Gen. Wm. Sherman, Orvill Wright.

**Chamber of Commerce:** 17 S. High St., 8th Fl., Co lumbus, OH 43215.

# Ohio

## Buckeye State

**People. Population** (1977): 10,701,000; **rank:** 6. **Pop. density:** 261.1 per sq. mi. **Urban** (1970): 75.3%. **Racial distrib.** (1975): 89.9% White; 9.6% Black; Hispanic (1970): 95,128. **Major ethnic groups:** German, Italian, Polish, English. **Net migration** (1970-76): −411,000.

**Geography. Total area:** 41,222 sq. mi.; **rank:** 35. **Land area:** 40,975 sq. mi. **Acres forested land:** 6,498,000. **Location:** East North Central state bounded on the N by Michigan and Lake Erie; on the E and S by Pennsylvania, West Virginia; and Kentucky; on the W by Indiana. **Climate:** temperate but variable; weather subject to much precipitation. **Topography:** generally rolling plain; Allegheny plateau in E; Lake [Erie] plains extend southward; central plains in the W. **Capital:** Columbus.

**Economy. Principal industries:** manufacturing, tourism, government, trade. **Principal manufactured goods:** machinery, transportation equipment, primary and fabricated metal products. **Value added by manufacture:** $32.4 billion/yr. **Gross Domestic Product** (1976): $85.4 billion. **Agriculture: Chief crops:** corn, hay, winter wheat, oats, soybeans. **Livestock:** 2,025,000 cattle; 1,900,000 hogs/pigs; 445,000 sheep; 14,050,000 poultry. **Timber/lumber:** oak, ash, maple, walnut, beech. **Minerals** (1977): mineral, fuels (69% of the total $1.49 billion value of mineral production), clays, sand and gravel, stone, gypsum. **Commercial fishing:** $1,978,000. **Chief ports:** Cleveland, Toledo,Cincinnati, Ashtabula. **International airports at:** Cleveland, Columbus, Dayton. **Value of construction** (1977): $7,266,589,000. **Employment distribution:** 10.9% agriculture; 27.7% manufacturing; 16.1% services; 14.5% government. **Per capita income** (1976): $6,432. **Unemployment** (1976): 7.8% **Tourism** (1976): out-of-state visitors spent $3.18 billion.

**Finance. Notable industries:** banking, insurance. **No. banks:** 491; **No. savings and loan assns.:** 404.

**Federal government. No. federal employees** (1977): 91,065. **Federal payroll** (1977): $1.5 billion. **Notable federal facilities:** Wright Paterson, Rickenbacker AF bases; Lewis Research Ctr.; Portsmouth Gaseous Diffusion Plant; Mound Laboratory.

**Energy. Electricity production** (1977, mwh, by source): Hydroelectric: 5,230; Mineral: 109.7 million; Nuclear: 467,923.

**Education. No. schools:** 3,837 elementary: 1,175 secondary; 129 higher education. **Avg. salary, public school teachers** (1977): $12,500.

**State data. Motto:** With God, all things are possible. **Flower:** Scarlet carnation. **Bird:** Cardinal. **Tree:** Buckeye.

# Oklahoma

## Sooner State

**People. Population** (1977): 2,811,000; **rank:** 27. **Pop density:** 40.8 per sq. mi. **Urban** (1970): 68%. **Racial dis trib.** (1975): 88.7% White; 7.1% Black; Hispanic (1970 36,007. **Major ethnic groups:** German, English, Mexican **Net migration** (1970-76): +107,000.

**Geography. Total area:** 69,919 sq. mi.; **rank:** 18. **Lan area:** 68,782 sq. mi. **Acres forested land:** 9,340,000. **Location:** West South Central state bounded on the N b Colorado and Kansas; on the E by Missouri and Arkansas on the S and W by Texas and New Mexico. **Climate:** tem perate; southern humid belt merging with colder norther continental; humid eastern and dry western zones. **To pography:** high plains predominate the W, hills and sma mountains in the E; the east central region is dominate by the Arkansas R. Basin, and the Red R. Plains, in the S **Capital:** Oklahoma City.

**Economy. Principal industries:** agriculture, mining, man ufacturing. **Principal manufactured goods:** machinery foods, fabricated metal products, mineral products. **Value added by manufacture:** $3.4 billion/yr. **Gross domestic Product** (1975): $16.7 billion. **Agriculture: Chief crops** wheat, cotton lint, sorghum grain, peanuts, hay, soybeans cotton seed, barley, oats, pecans. **Livestock:** 5,900,00 cattle; 330,000 hogs/pigs; 72,000 sheep; 5,550,000 poul try. **Timber/lumber:** pine, oaks, hickory. **Minerals** (1977) mineral fuels (96% of the total $3.5 billion mineral produc tion), gypsum, sand and gravel, stone, feldspar, pumice **Commercial fishing:** $503,000. **Chief ports:** Catoosa Muskogee. **International airports at:** Oklahoma City Tulsa. **Value of construction** (1977): $2,425,381,000 **Employment distribution:** 5.9% agriculture; 16.6% man ufacturing; 16.3% services; 21.9% government; 23.6% trade. **Per capita income** (1976): $5,657. **Unemploy ment** (1977): 5.0%. **Tourism** (1976): out-of-state visitors spent $1.3 billion.

**Finance. No. banks:** 479; **No. savings and loan assns.** 58.

**Federal government. No. federal employees** (1976) 49,500. **Federal payroll** (1976): $1.06 billion. **Notable federal facilities:** Tinker AFB, Oklahoma City; Ft. Sill Lawton.

**Energy. Electricity production** (1977, mwh, by source) Hydroelectric: 1.7 million; Mineral: 34.7 million; Nuclear —.

**Education. No. schools:** 1,218 elementary; 726 second ary; 44 higher education. **Avg. salary, public school teachers** (1977): $10,480.

**State data. Motto:** Labor Omnia Vincit (Labor conquers

all things). **Flower:** Mistletoe. **Bird:** Scissortailed fly-catcher. **Tree:** Redbud. **Song:** Oklahoma! **Entered union** Nov. 16, 1907; rank, 46th. **State fair** at: Oklahoma City; last week of Sept.

**History.** First permanent white settlement was made, 1796, by Maj. Jean Pierre Chouteau, at present-day Sali-na. Part of the Louisiana Purchase, 1803, Oklahoma was known as Indian Territory (but was not given territorial government) after it became the home of the "Five Civi-ized Tribes"—Cherokee, Choctaw, Chickasaw, Creek, and Seminole—1828-1846. The land was also used by Comanche, Osage, and other Plains Indians. As white set-lers pressed west, land was opened for homesteading by runs and lottery, the first run taking place Apr. 22, 1889. The most famous run was to the Cherokee Outlet, 1893.

**Tourist attraction.** Will Rogers Memorial, Claremore, contains his collections of saddles, ropes, trophies; his tomb is there. Also, National Cowboy Hall of Fame, Okla-homa City; restored Ft. Gibson Stockade, near Muskogee, the Army's largest outpost in Indian lands; Indian pow-wows; rodeos; fishing; hunting; Ouachita National Forest.

**Famous Oklahomans** include Carl Albert, Woody Guthrie, Gen. Patrick J. Hurley, Karl Jansky, Mickey Man-le, Wiley Post, Oral Roberts, Will Rogers, Maria Tallchief, Jim Thorpe.

**Chamber of Commerce:** 4020 N. Lincoln Blvd., Okla-homa City, OK 73105.

# Oregon

### Beaver State

**People. Population** (1977): 2,376,000; **rank:** 30. **Pop. density:** 24.7 per sq. mi. **Urban** (1970): 67.1%. **Racial distrib. (1975):** 97.0% White; 1.3% Black; Hispanic 1970): 34,577. **Major ethnic groups:** German, Scandina-rian, English, Russian. **Net migration** (1970-76): +159,000.

**Geography. Total area:** 96,981 sq. mi.; **rank:** 10. **Land area:** 96,184 sq. mi. **Acres forested land:** 30,404,000. **Location:** Pacific state, bounded on N by Washington; on E by Idaho; on S by Nevada and California; on W by the Pacific. **Climate:** coastal mild and humid climate; conti-ental dryness and extreme temperatures in the interior. **Topography:** Coast Range of rugged mountains; fertile Willamette R. Valley to E and S; Cascade Mtn. Range of olcanic peaks E of the valley; plateau E of Cascades, remaining two-thirds of state. **Capital:** Salem.

**Economy. Principal industries:** manufacturing, mining, orestry, food processing, tourism, agriculture. **Principal manufactured goods:** furniture, lumber, paper, foods, ransportation equipment, fabricated metal. **Value added y manufacture:** $4.3 billion/yr. **Agriculture: Chief rops:** wheat, oats, potatoes, berries, pears, cherries, fil-erts, walnuts, vegetables. **Livestock:** 1,490,000 cattle; 5,000 hogs/pigs; 395,000 sheep; 4,100,000 poultry. **Tim-er/lumber:** Douglas fir, hemlock, ponderosa pine. **Min-rals** (1977): nickel, stone, sand and gravel, cement, lays, diatomite, lime, pumice, talc. Total mineral produc-on valued at $116.6 million. **Commercial fishing:** 48,532,000. **Chief ports:** Portland, Astoria, Newport, Coos Bay. **International Airports at:** Portland. **Value of onstruction** (1977): $1,928,590,000. **Per capita in-ome** (1976): $6,331. **Unemployment** (1976): 9.5%. ourism (1976): out-of-state visitors spent $1.5 billion.

**inance. No. banks:** 46; **No. savings and loan assns.:** 43.

**ederal government. No. federal employees** (1976): 6,000. **Notable federal facilities:** Bonneville Power Ad-inistration.

**nergy: Electricity production** (1977, mwh, by source): Hydroelectric: 24.3 million; Mineral: 123,640; Nuclear: 6.5 illion.

**ducation. No. schools:** 1,069 elementary; 366 second-ry; 43 higher education. **Avg. salary, public school eachers** (1977): $13,500.

**tate data. Motto:** The union. **Flower:** Oregon grape. **Bird:** Western meadowlark. **Tree:** Douglas fir. **Song:** Ore-on, My Oregon. **Entered union** Feb. 14, 1859; rank, 33d. **State fair** at: Salem; end-Aug. to early Sept.

**History.** American Capt. Robert Gray discovered and sailed into the Columbia River, 1792; Lewis and Clark, traveling overland, wintered at its mouth 1805-06; fur trad-ers followed. Settlers arrived in the Willamette Valley, 1834. In 1843 the first large wave of settlers arrived via the Oregon Trail. Early in the 20th century, the "Oregon System," reforms which included the initiative, referen-dum, recall, direct primary, and woman suffrage, was adopted.

**Tourist attractions.** Crater Lake National Park, deep-est lake in the U.S. (1,932 ft.) in a former volcano, 6 mi. in diameter; Oregon Dunes National Recreation Area; Ft. Clatsop National Memorial includes a replica of the fort in which Lewis and Clark spent the winter of 1805-06. Ore-gon Caves National Monument contains stone waterfalls. Also skiing, annual Pendleton Round-Up.

**Famous Oregonians** include Ernest Bloch, Childe Has-sam, Ernest Haycox, Chief Joseph, Edwin Markham, Dr. John McLoughlin, Joaquin Miller, Linus Pauling, John Reed, William Simon U'Ren.

**Chamber of Commerce:** 1149 Court St., N.E., P.O. Box 12519, Salem, OR 97309.

# Pennsylvania

### Keystone State

**People. Population** (1977): 11,785,000; **rank:** 4. **Pop. density:** 262.0 per sq. mi. **Urban** (1970): 71.5%. **Racial distrib.** (1975): 90.6% White; 8.8% Black; Hispanic (1970): 44,535. **Major ethnic groups:** Italian, Polish, Ger-man, English. **Net migration** (1970-76): −173,000.

**Geography. Total area:** 45,333 sq. mi.; **rank:** 33. **Land area:** 44,966 sq. mi. **Acres forested land:** 17,832,000. **Location:** Middle Atlantic state, bordered on the E by the Delaware R., on the S by the Mason-Dixon Line; on the W by West Virginia and Ohio; on the N/NE by Lake Erie and New York. **Climate:** continental with wide fluctuations in seasonal temperatures. **Topography:** Allegheny Mtns. run SW to NE, with Piedmont and Coast Plain in the SE triangle; Allegheny Front a diagonal spine across the state's center; N and W rugged plateau falls to Lake Erie Lowland. **Capital:** Harrisburg.

**Economy. Principal industries:** manufacturing, electron-ics, steel, coal, agriculture. **Prinipcal manufactured goods:** steel, foods, industrial machinery, fabricated metal products, apparel, mineral products, chemicals, leather and rubber goods, lumber. **Value added by man-ufacture:** $32 million/yr. **Gross Domestic Product** (1977): $98.3 billion. **Agriculture:** Chief crops: corn, hay, mushrooms, wheat, tobacco, Christmas trees, apples, sour cherries, grapes, maple syrup. **Livestock:** 1,900,000 cattle; 700,000 hogs/pigs; 100,000 sheep, 20,087,000 poultry. **Timber/lumber:** hickory, locust, maple. **Minerals** (1977): mineral fuels (83% of the total $3.2 billion value of mineral production), esp. bituminous coal, stone, cement, lime. **Commercial fishing:** $246,000. **Chief ports:** Phila-delphia, Pittsburgh, Erie. **International airports at:** Phila-delphia, Pittsburgh, Erie, Harrisburg. **Value of construc-tion** (1977): $3,796,779,000. **Employment distribution:** 0.7% agriculture; 37% manufacturing; 20% services; 24% trade; 6.1% finance/real estate. **Per capita income** (1976): $6,466. **Unemployment** (1976): 7.9% **Tourism** (1976): out-of-state visitors spent $4.69 billion.

**Finance. No. banks:** 383; **No. savings and loan assns.:** 482.

**Federal government. No. federal employees** (1976): 132,000. **Federal payroll** (1975): $418 million. **Notable federal facilities:** Army War College, Carlisle; Ships Con-trol Ctr., Mechanicsburg; New Cumberland Army Depot.

**Energy. Electricity production** (1977, mwh, by source): Hydroelectric: 1.2 million; Mineral: 97.8 million; Nuclear: 17.8 million.

**Education. No. schools:** 4,174 elementary; 1,283 sec-ondary; 175 higher education. **Avg. salary, public school teachers** (1977): $13,600.

**State data. Motto:** Virtue, liberty and independence. **Flower:** Mountain laurel. **Bird:** Ruffed grouse. **Tree:** Hem-lock. **Second** of the original 13 states to ratify the Constitution, Dec. 12, 1787. **State fair** at: Harrisburg; 2d week in Jan.

**History.** First settlers were Swedish, 1643, on Tinicum Is. In 1655 the Dutch seized the settlement but lost it to the British, 1664. The region was given by Charles II to William Penn, 1681, Philadelphia (brotherly love) was the capital of the colonies during most of the Revolution, and of the U.S., 1790-1800. Philadelphia was taken by the British, 1777; Washington's troops encamped at Valley Forge in the bitter winter of 1777-78. The Declaration of Independence, 1776, and the Constitution, 1787, were signed in Philadelphia.

**Tourist attractions.** Independence Hall, Liberty Bell, Carpenters Hall, all in Philadelphia; Valley Forge; Gettysburg battlefield; Amish festivals, Lancaster Cty., Hershey Chocolate World; Pocono Mtns.; Delaware Water Gap; Longwood Gardens, near Kennett Square; Pine Creek Gorge; hunting, fishing, winter sports.

**Famous Pennsylvanians** include Marian Anderson, Maxwell Anderson, Andrew Carnegie, Stephen Foster, Benjamin Franklin, George C. Marshall, Andrew W. Mellon; Robert E. Peary, Mary Roberts Rinehart, Betsy Ross.

**Chamber of Commerce:** 222 N. 3d St., Harrisburg, PA 17101.

# Rhode Island

## *Little Rhody, Ocean State*

**People. Population** (1977): 935,000; **rank:** 39. **Pop. density:** 891.3 per sq. mi. **Urban** (1970): 87.1% **Racial distrib. (1975):** 96.3% White; 3.0% Black; Hispanic (1975): 6,961. **Major ethnic groups:** Italian, English, Irish. **Net migration** (1970-76): −45,000.

**Geography. Total area:** 1,214 sq. mi.; **rank:** 50. **Land area:** 1,049 sq. mi. **Acres forested land:** 433,000. **Location:** New England state. **Climate:** invigorating and changeable. **Topography:** eastern lowlands of Narragansett Basin; western uplands of flat and rolling hills. **Capital:** Providence.

**Economy. Prinicipal industries:** manufacturing, services. **Principal manufactured goods:** costume jewelry, machinery, textiles, electronics, silverware. **Value added by manufacture:** $2.02 billion/yr. **Gross Domestic Product** (1975): $5.72 billion. **Agriculture:** Chief crops: potatoes, apples, corn. **Livestock:** 10,000 cattle; 8,700 hogs/pigs; 2,100 sheep; 260,000 poultry. **Timber/lumber:** oak, chestnut. **Minerals** (1977): gem stones, sand and gravel, stone. Total value mineral production, $5.5 million. **Commercial fishing:** $22,920,000. **Chief ports:** Providence, Newport, Tiverton. **Value of construction** (1977): $308,417,000. **Employment distribution:** 0.1% agriculture; 34.0% manufacturing, 19.0% services; 20% trade. **Per capita income** (1976): $6,498. **Unemployment** (1977): 8.6% **Tourism** (1977): out-of-state visitors spent $248 million.

**Finance. Notable industries:** banking, insurance. **No. banks:** 24; **No. savings and loan assns.:** 12.

**Federal government. No. federal employees** (1976): 9,800. **Federal payroll** (1976): $148.7 million. **Notable federal facilities:** Naval War College.

**Energy. Electricity production** (1977, mwh, by source): Hydroelectric: 3,548; Mineral: 561,274; Nuclear: —.

**Education. No. schools:** 387 elementary; 94 secondary; 13 higher education. **Avg. salary, public school teachers** (1977): $14,420.

**State data. Motto:** Hope. **Flower:** Violet. **Bird:** Rhode Island red. **Tree:** Red maple. **Song:** Rhode Island. **Thirteenth** of original 13 states to ratify the Constitution, May 29 1790. **State fair** at: E. Greenwich; mid-Aug.

**History.** Rhode Island is distinguished for its battle for freedom of conscience and action, begun by Roger Williams, founder of Providence, who was exiled from Massachusetts Bay Colony in 1636, and Anne Hutchinson, exiled in 1638. Rhode Island gave protection to Quakers in 1657 and to Jews from Holland in 1658.

The colonists broke the power of the Narragansett Indians in the Great Swamp Fight, 1675, the decisive bat-

tle in King Philip's War. British trade restrictions angered the colonists and they burned the British revenue cutter Gaspee, 1772. The colony declared its independence May 4, 1776. Gen. John Sullivan and Lafayette won a partial victory, 1778, but failed to oust the British.

**Tourist attractions.** Newport mansions; summer resorts and water sports; Touro Synagogue, Newport, 1763; first Baptist Church in America, Providence, 1638; Gilbert Stuart birthplace, Saunderstown; Narragansett Indian Fall Festival.

**Famous Rhode Islanders** include Ambrose Burnside, George M. Cohan, Nelson Eddy, Jabez Gorham, Nathaneal Greene, Christopher and Oliver La Farge, Matthew C. and Oliver Perry, Gilbert Stuart.

**Chamber of Commerce:** 206 Smith St., Providence, RI 02908.

# South Carolina

## *Palmetto State*

**People. Population** (1977): 2,876,000; **rank:** 26. **Pop. density:** 95.1 per sq. mi. **Urban** (1970): 47.6%. **Racial distrib. (1975):** 68.8% White; 30.8% Black; Hispanic (1970): 10,999. **Major ethnic groups:** German, English. **Net migration** (1970-76): +97,000.

**Geography. Total area:** 31,055 sq. mi.; **rank:** 40. **Land area:** 30,225 sq. mi. **Acres forested land:** 12,493,000. **Location:** south Atlantic coast state, bordering North Carolina on the N; Georgia on the SW and W; the Atlantic O. on the E, SE and S. **Climate:** humid sub-tropical. **Topography:** Blue Ridge province in NW has highest peaks; piedmont lies between the mountains and the fall line; coastal plain covers two-thirds of the state. **Capital:** Columbia.

**Economy. Principal industries:** tourism, textiles, apparel, chemical, agriculture, manufacturing. **Principal manufactured goods:** textiles, chemicals and allied products, non-electrical machinery. **Value added by manufacture:** $4.9 billion/yr. **Agriculture:** Chief crops: tobacco, soybeans, corn, cotton, peaches, hay, vegetables. **Livestock:** 690,000 cattle; 470,000 hogs/pigs; 1,300 sheep; 10,010,000 poultry. **Timber/lumber:** pine, oak. **Minerals** (1977):cement, stone, sand and gravel, clays; vermiculite, kaolin, both 2d in U.S. production. Total mineral production valued at $146.6 million. **Commercial fishing:** $9,497,000. **Chief ports:** Charleston, Georgetown. **International airports at:** Charleston, Greenburg-Spartanburg **Value of construction** (1977): $1,555,870,000. **Employment distribution:** 4% agriculture; 30% manufacturing; 11% services; 16% government. **Per capita income** (1976): $5,126. **Unemployment** (1977): 5.0%. **Tourism** (1976): out-of-state visitors spent $1.7 billion.

**Finance. No. banks:** 88; **No. savings and loan assns.:** 74.

**Federal government: No. federal employees** (1978): 36,100. **Notable federal facilities:** Polaris Submarine Base; Barnwell Nuclear Power Plant; Ft. Jackson.

**Energy. Electricity production** (1977, mwh, by source): Hydroelectric: 3 million; Mineral: 19.1 million; Nuclear: 17.2 million.

**Education. No. schools:** 922 elementary; 372 secondary; 55 higher education. **Avg. salary, public school teachers** (1977): $10,391.

**State data. Motto:** Dum Spiro Spero (While I breathe, I hope). **Flower:** Carolina jessamine. **Bird:** Carolina wren. **Tree:** Palmetto. **Song:** Carolina. **Eighth** of the original 13 states to ratify the Constitution, May 23, 1788. **State fair** at: Columbia; 3d week in Oct.

**History.** The first English colonists settled, 1670, on the Ashley River, moved to the site of Charleston, 1680. The colonists seized the government, 1775, and the royal governor fled. The British took Charleston, 1780, but were defeated at Kings Mountain that year, and at Cowpens and Eutaw Springs, 1781. In the 1830s, South Carolinians, angered by federal protective tariffs, holding the Nullification Doctrine, holding a state can void an act of Congress. The state was the first to secede and, in 1861, Confederate troops fired on and forced the surrender of U. S.

troops at Ft. Sumter, in Charleston Harbor, launching the Civil War.

**Tourist attractions.** Restored historic Charleston harbor area and Charleston gardens: Middleton Place, Magnolia, Cypress; other gardens at Brookgreen, Edisto, Glencairn; state parks; coastal islands; shore resorts such as Myrtle Beach; fishing and quail hunting; Ft. Sumter National Monument, in Charleston Harbor; Charleston Museum, est. 1773, is the oldest museum in the U.S..

**Famous South Carolinians** include James F. Byrnes, John C. Calhoun, DuBose Heyward, James Longstreet, Francis Marion, Charles Pinckney, John Rutledge, Thomas Sumter.

**Chamber of Commerce:** 1002 Calhoun St., Columbia, SC 29201.

# South Dakota

*Coyote State, Sunshine State*

**People. Population** (1977): 689,000; **rank:** 44. **Pop. density:** 9.0 per sq. mi. **Urban** (1970): 44.6%. **Racial distrib.** (1975): 93.9% White; —% Black; 5.8% Other (includes American Indians); Hispanic (1970): 2,954. **Major ethnic groups:** German, Norwegian, Russian. **Net migration** (1970-76): —9,000.

**Geography. Total area:** 77,047 sq. mi.; **rank:** 16. **Land area:** 75,955 sq. mi. **Acres forested land:** 334,000. **Location:** West North Central state bounded on the N by North Dakota; on the E by Minnesota and Iowa; on the S by Nebraska; on the W by Wyoming and Montana. **Climate:** characterized by extremes of temperature, persistent winds, low precipitation and humidity. **Topography:** Prairie Plains in the E; rolling hills of the Great Plains in the W; the Black Hills, rising 3,500 ft. in the SW corner. **Capital:** Pierre.

**Economy. Principal industries:** mining, manufacturing, agriculture. **Principal manufactured goods:** processed meats, electrical appliances, occupational health and safety products, computer sub-assemblies. **Value added by manufacture:** $423.8 million/yr. **Agriculture:** Chief **crops:** rye, flaxseed, oats, durum and spring wheat, honey, alfalfa. **Livestock:** 3,925,000 cattle; 1,500,000 hogs/pigs; 659,000 sheep; 4,312,000 poultry. **Timber/lumber:** ponderosa pine. **Minerals** (1977): gold (1st in U.S.), crude oil, stone, sand and gravel. Total value mineral production, $108 million. **Commercial fishing:** $288,000. **Value of construction** (1977): $466,514,000. **Employment distribution:** 18.6% agriculture; 6.6% manufacturing; 15% services; 60% other. **Per capita income** (1976): $4,796. **Unemployment** (1976): 3.6%. **Tourism** (1976): out-of-state visitors spent $414 million.

**Finance. No. banks:** 324; **No. savings and loan assns.:** 18.

**Federal government. No. federal employees** (1976): 11,000. **Federal payroll** (1976): $144.9 million. **Notable federal facilities:** Bureau of Indian Affairs.

**Energy. Electricity production** (1977, mwh, by source): Hydroelectric: 5.3 million; Mineral: 2.7 million; Nuclear: —.

**Education. No. schools:** 675 elementary; 243 secondary; 17 higher education. **Avg. salary, public school teachers** (1977): $10,183.

**State data. Motto:** Under God, the people rule. **Flower:** Pasque flower. **Bird:** Ringnecked pheasant. **Tree:** Black Hills spruce. **Song:** Hail, South Dakota. **Entered union** Nov. 2, 1889; **rank,** 40th. **State fair** at: Huron; late Aug.-early Sept.

**History.** La Verendrye explored the region, 1742-43. Lewis and Clark passed through the area, 1804 and 1806. First American settlement was at Sioux Falls, 1857. Gold was discovered, 1874, on the Sioux Reservation; miners rushed in. The U.S. first tried to stop them, then relaxed its opposition. Custer's defeat by the Sioux followed; the Sioux relinquished the land, 1877 and the "great Dakota Boom" began. A new Indian uprising came in 1890, climaxed by the massacre of Indian families at Wounded Knee.

**Tourist attractions.** Needles Highway through the Black Hills; Badlands National Monument "moonscape"; Custer State Park's bison and burro heads; Ft. Sisson, a

restored army frontier post of 1864; the "Great Lakes of South Dakota," reservoirs created behind Oahe, Big Bend, Ft. Randall, and Gavins Point dams on the Missouri R.

Mount Rushmore, in the Black Hills, has an altitude of 6,200 ft. Sculptured on its granite face are the heads of Washington, Jefferson, Lincoln, and Theodore Roosevelt. These busts by Gutzon Borglum are proportionate to men 465 ft. tall. Rushmore is visited by about 2 million persons annually.

**Famous South Dakotans** include Crazy Horse, Alvin H. Hansen, Dr. Ernest O. Lawrence, Sacagawea, Sitting Bull.

**Chamber of Commerce:** P.O. Box 190, Pierre, SD 57501.

# Tennessee

*Volunteer State*

**People. Population** (1977): 4,299,000; **rank:** 17. **Pop. density:** 104.0 per sq. mi. **Urban** (1970): 58.7%. **Racial distrib.** (1975): 84.1% White; 15.6% Black; Hispanic (1970): 13,873. **Major ethnic groups:** German, English, Italian. **Net migration** (1970-76): +119,000.

**Geography. Total area:** 42,244 sq. mi.; **rank:** 34. **Land area:** 41,328 sq. mi. **Acres forested land:** 13,136,000. **Location:** East South Central state bounded on the N by Kentucky and Virginia; on the E by North Carolina; on the S by Georgia, Alabama, and Mississippi; on the W by Arkansas and Missouri. **Climate:** humid continental to the N; humid sub-tropical to the S. **Topography:** rugged country in the E; the Great Smoky Mtns. of the Unakas; low ridges of the Appalachian Valley; the flat Cumberland Plateau; slightly rolling terrain and knobs of the Interior Low Plateau, the largest region; Eastern Gulf Coastal Plain to the W, is laced with meandering streams; Mississippi Alluvial Plain, a narrow strip of swamp and flood plain in the extreme W. **Capital:** Nashville.

**Economy. Principal industries:** manufacturing, agriculture, publishing, music. **Principal manufactured goods:** primary and fabricated metals, foods, electrical and electronic machinery, transportation equipment, apparel. **Value added by manufacture:** $10.7 billion/yr. **Agriculture:** Chief **crops:** soybeans, tobacco, cotton, corn, nursery stock, hay. **Livestock:** 2,700,000 cattle; 1,010,000 hogs/pigs; 17,000 sheep; 5,603,000 poultry. **Timber/lumber:** locust, poplar, maple, oak. **Minerals** (1977): bituminous coal, stone, zinc, cement. Total value mineral production, $446.4 million. **Commercial fishing:** $1,249,000. **Chief ports:** Memphis, Nashville, Knoxville, Chattanooga. **International airports at:** Memphis, Nashville, Knoxville, Chattanooga. **Value of construction** (1977): $6,232,661,000. **Employment distribution:** 3% agriculture; 35% manufacturing; 15% services. **Per capita income** (1976): $5,432. **Unemployment** (1976): 6%. **Tourism** (1976): out-of-state visitors spent $1.8 billion.

**Finance. Notable industries:** insurance. **No. banks:** 347; **No. savings and loan assns.:** 24.

**Federal government. No. federal employees** (1976): 57,491 civilians. **Federal payroll** (1977): $863.2 million. **Notable federal facilities:** Tennessee Valley Authority; Oak Ridge Nat'l. Laboratories.

**Energy. Electricity production** (1977, mwh, by source): Hydroelectric: 10.4 million; Mineral: 49.2 million; Nuclear: —.

**Education. No. schools:** 1,379 elementary; 345 secondary; 67 higher education. **Avg. salary, public school teachers** (1977): $11,120.

**State data. Motto:** Agriculture and commerce. **Flower:** Iris. **Bird:** Mockingbird. **Tree:** Tulip poplar. **Song:** The Tennessee Waltz. **Entered union** June 1, 1796; **rank,** 16th. **State fair** at: Nashville; 3d week of Sept.

**History.** Spanish explorers first visited the area, 1541. English traders crossed the Great Smokies from the east while France's Marquette and Jolliet sailed down the Mississippi on the west, 1673. First permanent settlement was by Virginians on the Watauga River, 1769. During the Revolution, the colonists helped win the Battle of Kings Mountain, N.C., 1780, and joined other eastern campaigns. The state seceded from the Union 1861, and saw many engagements of the Civil War, but 30,000 soldiers fought for the Union.

**Tourist attractions.** Natural wonders include Reelfoot Lake, the reservoir basin of the Mississippi R. formed by the 1811 earthquake; Lookout Mountain, Chattanooga; Fall Creek Falls, 256 ft. high; Great Smoky Mountains National Park.

Also, the Hermitage, 13 mi. E of Nashville, home of Andrew Jackson; the homes of presidents Polk and Andrew Johnson; the Parthenon, Nashville, a replica of the Parthenon of Athens; the Grand Old Opry, Nashville.

**Famous Tennesseans** include Davy Crockett, David Farragut, William C. Handy, Sam Houston, Cordell Hull, Grace Moore, Dinah Shore, Alvin York.

**Chamber of Commerce:** 505 Fesslers La., Nashville, TN 37210.

# Texas

*Lone Star State*

**People. Population** (1977): 12,830,000; **rank:** 3. **Pop. density:** 48.9 per sq. mi. **Urban** (1970): 79.7%. **Racial distrib. (1975):** 86.9% White; 12.5% Black; Hispanic (1970): 2,059,671. **Major ethnic groups:** Mexican, German. **Net migration** (1970-76): +543,000.

**Geography: Total area:** 267,338 sq. mi.; **rank:** 2. **Land area:** 262,134 sq. mi. **Acres forested land:** 24,091,000. **Location:** Southwestern state, bounded on the SE by the Gulf of Mexico; on the SW by Mexico, separated by the Rio Grande; surrounding states are Louisiana, Arkansas, Oklahoma, New Mexico. **Climate:** extremely varied; driest region is the Trans-Pecos; wettest is the NE. **Topography:** Gulf Coast Plain in the S and SE; North Central Plains slope upward with some hills; the Great Plains extend over the Panhandle, are broken by low mountains; the Trans-Pecos is the southern extension of the Rockies. **Capital:** Austin.

**Economy. Principal industries:** agriculture, petroleum, manufacturing. **Principal manufactured goods:** machinery, transportation equipment, foods, refined petroleum, apparel. **Value added by manufacture:** $17.68 billion/yr. **Agriculture: Chief crops:** cotton, maize, citrus fruits, sorghum, rice, peanuts, watermelons, pecans, sweet potatoes. **Livestock:** 14,500,000 cattle; 850,000 hogs/pigs; 2,520,000 sheep; 22,300,000 poultry. **Timber/lumber:** pine, cypress. **Minerals** (1977): petroleum, natural gas, natural gas liquids (94.4% of the total $19.9 billion value of mineral production), cement, sulfur, stone, sand and gravel, lime, salt. **Commercial fishing:** $134,237,000. **Chief ports:** Houston, Galveston, Brownsville, Beaumont, Port Arthur, Corpus Christi. **International airports at:** Houston, Dallas/Ft. Worth, San Antonio. **Value of construction** (1977): $10,414,311,000. **Employment distribution:** 3% agriculture; 15% manufacturing; 7% services; 8% transportation. **Per capita income** (1976): $6,243. **Unemployment** (1976): 5.7%. **Tourism** (1977): out-of-state visitors spent $6 billion.

**Finance. No. banks:** 596; **No. savings and loan assns.:** 316.

**Federal government. No. federal employees** (1976): 160,232. **Federal payroll** (1976): $2.1 billion. **Notable federal facilities:** LBJ Manned Spacecraft Ctr., (NASA).

**Energy. Electricity production** (1977, mwh, by source): Hydroelectric: 1.2 million; Mineral: 170.2 million; Nuclear: —.

**Education. No. schools:** 3,688 elementary; 2,196 secondary; 145 higher education. **Avg. salary, public school teachers** (1977): $11,542.

**State data. Motto:** Friendship. **Flower:** Bluebonnet. **Bird:** Mockingbird. **Tree:** Pecan. **Song:** Texas, Our Texas. **Entered union** Dec. 29, 1845; **rank,** 28th. **State fair at:** Dallas; mid-Oct.

**History.** Pineda sailed along the Texas coast, 1519; Cabeza de Vaca and Coronado visited the interior, 1541. Spaniards made the first settlement at Ysleta, near El Paso, 1682. Americans moved into the land early in the

19th century. Mexico, of which Texas was a part, won independence from Spain, 1821; Santa Anna became dictator, 1835. Texans rebelled; Santa Anna wiped out defenders of the Alamo, 1836. Sam Houston's Texans defeated Santa Anna at San Jacinto and independence was proclaimed the same year. In 1845, Texas was admitted to the Union.

**Tourist attractions.** Padre Island National Seashore; Big Bend, Guadalupe Mtns. national parks; The Alamo; Ft. Davis; Six Flags Amusement Park. Named for Pres. Lyndon B. Johnson are a national historic site, a national park, and a state park, marking his birthplace, boyhood home, and ranch, all near Johnson City, and a library in Austin.

**Famous Texans** include Stephen Austin, James Bowie, J. Frank Dobie, Sam Houston, Howard Hughes, Mary Martin, Chester Nimitz, Katharine Ann Porter, Sam Rayburn.

**Chamber of Commerce:** 1004 International Life Bldg., Austin, TX 78701.

# Utah

*Beehive State*

**People. Population** (1977): 1,268,000; **rank:** 36. **Pop. density:** 15.4 per sq. mi. **Urban** (1970): 80.4%. **Racial distrib. (1975):** 97.5% White; —% Black; Hispanic (1970): 43,550. **Major ethnic groups:** English, German, Danish. **Net migration** (1970-76): +35,000.

**Geography. Total area:** 84,916,000 sq. mi.; **rank:** 11. **Land area:** 82,096 sq. mi. **Acres forested land:** 15,288. **Location:** Middle Rocky Mountain state; its southeastern corner touches Colorado, New Mexico, and Arizona, and is the only spot in the U.S. where 4 states join. **Climate:** arid; with the SW having a semitropical climate. **Topography:** high Colorado plateau is cut by brilliantly-colored canyons; broad, flat, desert-like Basin of the W; the Great Salt Lake and Bonneville Salt Flats to the SW; Middle Rockies in the NE run E-W; valleys and plateaus of the Wasatch Front. **Capital:** Salt Lake City.

**Economy. Principal industries:** mining, manufacturing, tourism, trade. **Principal manufactured goods:** aircraft and parts, electronic components, apparel, lumber and wood products, primary metals. **Agriculture: Chief crops:** wheat, hay, sugar beets, barley, potatoes. **Livestock:** 864,000 cattle; 51,000 hogs/pigs; 580,000 sheep; 4,758,000 poultry. **Timber/lumber:** scrub oak, aspen, spruce, pine. **Minerals** (1977): iron ore, tungsten, beryllium, uranium, gold, copper, cement; sand and gravel, potassium salts, mineral fuels. Total value of mineral production valued at $1.14 billion. **International airports at:** Salt Lake City. **Value of construction** (1977): $1,047,577,000. **Employment distribution:** 2% agriculture; 15.4% manufacturing; 16.7% services; 24.4% trade. **Per capita income** (1976): $5,482. **Unemployment** (1977): 5.3% **Tourism** (1976): out-of-state visitors spent $919 million.

**Finance. No. banks:** 69; **No. savings and loan assns.:** 14.

**Federal government. No. federal employees** (1977): 36,400. **Notable federal facilities:** Hill AFB; Tooele Army Depot.

**Energy. Electricity production** (1977, mwh, by source): Hydroelectric: 755,850; Mineral: 6.1 million; Nuclear: —.

**Education. No. schools:** 399 elementary; 164 secondary; 14 higher education. **Avg. salary, public school teachers** (1977): $12,170.

**State data. Motto:** Industry. **Flower:** Sego lily. **Bird:** Seagull. **Tree:** Blue spruce. **Song:** Utah, We Love Thee. **Entered union** Jan. 4, 1896; **rank,** 45th. **State fair at:** Salt Lake City; Sept.

**History.** Spanish Franciscans visited the area, 1776, the first 2 white men to do so. American fur traders followed. Permanent settlement began with the arrival of the Mormons, 1847. They made the arid land bloom and created a prosperous economy, organized the State of Deseret, 1849, and asked admission to the Union. This was not achieved until 1896, after a long period of controversy over the Mormon Church's doctrine of polygamy, which it discontinued in 1890.

**Tourist attractions.** Temple Square, Mormon Church hdqtrs., Salt Lake City; Great Salt Lake; fishing streams; lakes and reservoirs, numerous winter sports; campgrounds. Natural Wonders may be seen at Zion, Canyonlands, Bryce Canyon, Arches, and Capitol Reef national parks; Dinosaur, Rainbow Bridge, Timpanogas Cave, and Natural Bridges national monuments. Also Lake Powell and Flaming Gorge Dam.

**Famous Utahans** include Maude Adams, John Moses Browning, Philo Farnsworth, Ivy Baker Priest, George Romney, Brigham Young, Loretta Young.

**Chamber of Commerce:** None.

# Vermont

## Green Mountain State

**People. Population** (1977): 483,000; **rank:** 48. **Pop. density:** 52.1 per sq. mi. **Urban** (1970): 32.2%. **Racial distrib.** (1975): 99.2% White; —% Black; Hispanic (1970): 2,469. **Major ethnic groups:** English, Italian, German. **Net migration** (1970-76): +14,000.

**Geography. Total area:** 9,609 sq. mi.; **rank:** 43. **Land area:** 9,267 sq. mi. **Acres forested land:** 4,391,000. **Location:** northern New England state. **Climate:** temperate, with considerable temperature extremes; heavy snowfall in mountains. **Topography:** Green Mtns. N-S backbone 20-36 mi. wide; avg. altitude 1,000 ft. **Capital:** Montpelier.

**Economy. Principal industries:** manufacturing, tourism, agriculture, mining, government, printing. **Principal manufactured goods:** machine tools, furniture, scales, books, computer components, skis, fishing rods. **Value added by manufacture:** $952.3 million/yr. **Gross Domestic Product** (1976): $2.8 billion. **Agriculture:** Chief crops: apples, maple syrup, hay; also, dairy products. **Livestock:** 336,000 cattle; 6,000 hogs/pigs; 7,100 sheep; 658,000 poultry. **Timber/lumber:** pine, spruce, fir, hemlock. **Minerals** (1977): stone; asbestos (2d in U.S.); talc (1st in U.S.); sand and gravel; gemstones; dimension granite, marble, and slate (2d in U.S.). Total value mineral production, $38.3 million. **International airports at:** Burlington. **Value of construction** (1977): $235,782,000. **Employment distribution:** 6% agriculture; 21% manufacturing; 20% services; 15% retail trade. **Per capita income** (1976): $5,480. **Unemployment** (1977): 8% **Tourism** (1976): out-of-state visitors spent $501 million.

**Finance. No. banks:** 35; **No. savings and loan assns.:** 5.

**Federal government. No. federal employees** (1976): 4,333.

**Energy. Electricity production** (1977, mwh, by source): Hydroelectric: 886,582; Mineral: 63,005; Nuclear: 3.5 million.

**Education. No. schools:** 365 elementary; 80 secondary; 23 higher education. **Avg. salary, public school teachers** (1977): $12,170.

**State data. Motto:** Freedom and unity. **Flower:** Red clover. **Bird:** Hermit thrush. **Tree:** Sugar maple. **Song:** Hail, Vermont. **Entered union** Mar. 4, 1791; rank, 14th. **State fair** at: Rutland; early Sept.

**History.** Champlain explored the lake that bears his name, 1609. First American settlement was Ft. Dummer, 1724, near Brattleboro. Ethan Allen and the Green Mountain Boys captured Ft. Ticonderoga, 1775; John Stark defeated part of Burgoyne's forces near Bennington, 1777. In the War of 1812, Thomas MacDonough defeated a British fleet on Champlain off Plattsburgh, 1814.

**Tourist attractions.** Year-round outdoor sports, esp. hiking, camping and skiing; there are over 56 ski areas in the state. Popular are the Shelburne Museum; Rock of Ages Tourist Center, Graniteville; Vermont Marble Exhibit, Proctor; Bennington Battleground; Pres. Coolidge homestead, Plymouth.

**Famous Vermonters** include Ethan Allen, Adm. George Dewey, John Dewey, Stephen A. Douglas, Dorothy Canfield Fisher, James Fisk.

**Chamber of Commerce:** P.O. Box 37, Montpelier, VT 05602.

# Virginia

## Old Dominion

**People. Population** (1977): 5,135,000; **rank:** 13. **Pop. density:** 129.0 per sq. mi. **Urban** (1970): 63.1%. **Racial distrib.** (1975): 80.5% White; 18.7% Black; Hispanic (1970): 48,742. **Major ethnic groups:** English, German, Italian. **Net migration** (1970-76): +162,000.

**Geography. Total area:** 40,817 sq. mi.; **rank:** 36. **Land area:** 39,780 sq. mi. **Acres forested land:** 16,389,000. **Location:** South Atlantic state bounded by the Atlantic O. on the E and surrounded by North Carolina, Tennessee, Kentucky, West Virginia, and Maryland. **Climate:** mild and equable. **Topography:** mountain and valley region in the W, including the Blue Ridge Mtns.; rolling piedmont plateau; tidewater, or coastal plain, including the eastern shore. **Capital:** Richmond.

**Economy. Principal industries:** federal government, manufacturing, agriculture, tourism, trade. **Principal manufactured goods:** textiles, foods, chemicals and allied products, transportation equipment, tobacco products. **Value added by manufacture:** $9.36 billion/yr. **Gross Domestic Product** (1976): $26.3 billion. **Agriculture:** Chief crops: tobacco, corn, peanuts, soybeans. **Livestock:** 1,620,000 cattle; 650,000 hogs/pigs; 164,000 sheep; 14,216,000 poultry. **Timber/lumber:** pine and hardwoods. **Minerals** (1977): bituminous coal, stone, cement, lime, sand and gravel, zinc. Total value mineral production, $1.1 billion. **Commercial fishing:** $55,351,000. **Chief ports:** Hampton Roads, Chesapeake Bay. **International airports at:** Norfolk, Dulles, Richmond, Newport News. **Value of construction** (1977): $3,503,401,000. **Employment distribution:** 30% agriculture; 20.9% manufacturing; 17% services. **Per capita income** (1976): $6,276. **Unemployment** (1977): 5.6% **Tourism** (1976): out-of-state visitors spent $2.2 billion.

**Finance. No. banks:** 283; **No. savings and loan assns.:** 82.

**Federal government. No. federal employees** (1977): 152,100. **Federal payroll** (1976): $2.5 billion. **Notable federal facilities:** Pentagon; Naval Sta., Norfolk; Naval Air Stas., Norfolk, Virginia Beach; Naval Shipyard, Portsmouth; Marine Corps Base, Quantico; Langley AFB; NASA at Langley.

**Energy. Electricity production** (1977, mwh, by source): Hydroelectric: 687,081; Mineral: 28 million; Nuclear: 9.5 million.

**Education. No. schools:** 1,451 elementary; 538 secondary; 73 higher education. **Avg. salary, public school teachers** (1977): $11,970.

**State data. Motto:** Sic Semper Tyrannis (Thus always to tyrants). **Flower:** Dogwood. **Bird:** Cardinal. **Tree:** Dogwood. **Song:** Carry Me Back to Old Virginia. **Tenth** of the original 13 states to ratify the Constitution, June 25, 1788. **State fair** at: Richmond; late Sept.-early Oct.

**History.** English settlers founded Jamestown, 1607. Virginians took over much of the government from royal Gov. Dunmore in 1775, forcing him to flee. Virginians under George Rogers Clark freed the Ohio-Indiana-Illinois area of British forces. Benedict Arnold burned Richmond and Petersburg for the British, 1781. That same year, Britain's Cornwallis was trapped at Yorktown and surrendered.

**Tourist attractions.** Colonial Williamsburg; Busch Gardens; Wolf Trap Farm, near Falls Church; Arlington National Cemetery; Mt. Vernon, home of George Washington; Jamestown Festival Park; Yorktown; Jefferson's Monticello, Charlottesville; Robert E. Lee's birthplace, Stratford Hall, and grave, at Lexington; Appomattox; Shenandoah National Park; Blue Ridge Parkway; Virginia Beach.

**Famous Virginians** include Richard E. Byrd, James B. Cabell, Patrick Henry, Joseph E. Johnston, Robert E. Lee, Meriwether Lewis and William Clark, John Marshall, Edgar Allan Poe, Walter Reed, Booker T. Washington.

**Chamber of Commerce:** 611 E. Franklin St., Richmond, VA 23219.

# Washington

*Evergreen State*

**People. Population** (1977): 3,658,000; **rank:** 22. **Pop. density:** 54.9 per sq. mi. **Urban** (1970): 72.6%. **Racial distrib.** (1970): 94.9% White; 2.3% Black; Hispanic (1970): 70,734. **Major ethnic groups:** German, English, Norwegian. **Net migration** (1970-76): +64,000.

**Geography. Total area:** 68,192 sq. mi.; **rank:** 20. **Land area:** 66,570 sq. mi. **Acres forested land:** 23,098,000.

**Location:** northwestern coastal state bordered by Canada on the N; Idaho on the E; Oregon on the S; and the Pacific O. on the W. **Climate:** mild, dominated by the Pacific O. and protected by the Rockies. **Topography:** Olympic Mtns. on NW peninsula; open land along coast to Columbia R.; flat terrain of Puget Sound Lowland; Cascade Mtn. region's high peaks to the E; Columbia Basin in central portion; highlands to the NE; mountains to the SE. **Capital:** Olympia.

**Economy. Principal industries:** aerospace, agriculture, aluminum, lumber, trade. **Principal manufactured goods:** transportation equipment, electronics, machinery, fabricated metals, foods. **Value added by manufacture:** $4.68 billion/yr. **Gross Domestic Product** (1972): $19.17 billion. **Agriculture: Chief crops:** Wheat, apples, hay, potatoes, barley, sugar beets, hops, peas, pears, corn, mint, asparagus, sweet cherries. **Livestock:** 1,275,000 cattle; 62,000 hogs/pigs; 74,000 sheep; 5,716,000 poultry. **Timber/lumber:** Douglas fir, cedar, Sitka spruce. **Minerals** (1977): sand and gravel, stone, coal, cement. Total value mineral production, $194.7 million. **Commercial fishing:** $80,785,000. **Chief ports:** Seattle, Tacoma, Vancouver, Kelso-Longview. **International airports at:** Seattle/Tacoma, Spokane, Yakima, Pasco. **Value of construction** (1977): $2,916,341,000. **Employment distribution:** 2.76% agriculture; 16.05% manufacturing; 16.12% services; 18.76% trade; 22.11% government. **Per capita income** (1976): $6,772. **Unemployment** (1977): 8.8% **Tourism** (1976): out-of-state visitors spent $2.1 billion.

**Finance. No. banks:** 89; **No. savings and loan assns.:** 53.

**Federal government. No. federal employees** (1976): 60,996. **Federal payroll** (1976): $913 million. **Notable federal facilities:** Bonneville Power Admin.; Ft. Lewis; McChord AFB; Hanford Nuclear Reservation; Bremerton Naval Shipyards.

**Energy. Electricity production** (1977, mwh, by source): Hydroelectric: 66.5 million; Mineral: 8.1 million; Nuclear: 4.3 million.

**Education. No. schools:** 1,281 elementary; 582 secondary; 47 higher education. **Avg. salary, public school teachers** (1977): $15,361.

**State data. Motto.** Alki (By and by). **Flower:** Western rhododendron. **Bird:** Willow goldfinch. **Tree:** Western hemlock. **Song:** Washington, My Home. **Entered union** Nov. 11, 1889; **rank:** 42d.

**History.** Spain's Bruno Hezeta sailed the coast, 1775. American Capt. Robert Gray sailed up the Columbia River, 1792. Canadian fur traders set up Spokane House, 1810; Americans under John Jacob Astor established a post at Fort Okanogan, 1811. Missionary Marcus Whitman settled near Walla Walla, 1836. Final agreement on the border of Washington and Canada was made with Britain, 1846, and gold was discovered in the state's northeast, 1855, bringing new settlers.

**Tourist attractions.** Mt. Rainier, Olympic, North Cascades national parks; Pacific beaches; outdoor year-round sports; rodeos; Indian reservations.

**Famous Washingtonians** include Chester Carlson, Bing Crosby, Mary McCarthy, Marcus Whitman, Minoru Yamasaki.

**Chamber of Commerce:** P.O. Box 658, Olympia, WA 98507.

# West Virginia

*Mountain State*

**People. Population** (1977): 1,859,000; **rank:** 34. **Pop. density:** 77.2 per sq. mi. **Urban** (1970): 39%. **Racial distrib.** (1975): 96.1% White; 3.6% Black; Hispanic (1970): 6,261. **Major ethnic groups:** Italian, English, German. **Net migration** (1970-76): -21,000.

**Geography. Total area:** 24,181 sq. mi.; **rank:** 41. **Land area:** 24,070 sq. mi. **Acres forested land:** 12,172,000. **Location:** South Atlantic state bounded on the N by Ohio, Pennsylvania, Maryland; on the S and W by Virginia, Kentucky, Ohio; on the E by Maryland and Virginia. **Climate:** humid continental climate except for marine modification in the lower panhandle. **Topography:** rugged, ranging from hilly to mountainous; Allegheny Plateau in the W covers two-thirds of the state; mountains here are the highest in the state, over 4,000 ft. **Capital:** Charleston.

**Economy. Principal industries:** mining, mineral and chemical production, agriculture. **Principal manufactured goods:** synthetic fibers, plastics. **Value added by manufacture:** $7.3 billion/yr. **Agriculture: Chief crops:** apples, peaches. **Chief products:** dairy products. **Livestock:** 550,000 cattle; 55,000 hogs/pigs; 125,000 sheep; 3,045,000 poultry. **Timber/lumber:** oak, yellow poplar, maple, pines. **Minerals** (1977): bituminous coal, natural gas, crude petroleum, clay, cement, lime. Total value mineral production $3.7 billion. **Commercial fishing:** $7,000. **Chief port:** Huntington. **Value of construction** (1977): $653,372,000. **Per capita income** (1976): $5,394. **Unemployment** (1976): 7.5% **Tourism** (1976): out-of-state visitors spent $771 million.

**Finance. No. banks:** 222; **No. savings and loan assns.** 37.

**Federal government. No. federal employees** (1976): 16,000. **Notable federal facilities:** National Radio Astronomy Observatory, Green Bank.

**Energy. Electricity production** (1977, mwh, by source): Hydroelectric: 416,663; Mineral: 65.9 million; Nuclear: —.

**Education. No. schools:** 950 elementary; 362 secondary; 28 higher education. **Avg. salary, public school teachers** (1977): $11,436.

**State Data. Motto:** Montani Semper Liberi (Mountaineers are always free) **Flower:** Big rhododendron. **Bird:** Cardinal. **Tree:** Sugar maple. **Songs:** The West Virginia Hills; This Is My West Virginia; West Virginia, My Home, Sweet Home. **Entered union** June 20, 1863; **rank:** 35th. **State fair** at: Lewisburg; 3d week in Aug.

**History.** Early explorers included George Washington, 1753, and Daniel Boone. The area became part of Virginia and often objected to rule by the eastern part of the state. When Virginia seceded, 1861, the Wheeling Conventions repudiated the act and created a new state, Kanawha, subsequently changed to West Virginia. It was admitted to the Union as such, 1863.

**Tourist attractions.** Harpers Ferry National Historic Park has been restored to its condition in 1859, when John Brown seized the U.S. Armory. Still standing is the fire-engine house in which Brown and a score of followers were besieged and captured by a force of U.S. Marines under Col. Robert E. Lee.

Also Science and Cultural Center, Charleston; White Sulphur and Berkeley Springs mineral water resorts; state parks and forests; trout fishing; turkey, deer, and bear hunting.

**Famous West Virginians** include Newton D. Baker, Pearl Buck, John W. Davis, Thomas "Stonewall" Jackson, Dwight Whitney Morrow, Michael Owens.

**Chamber of Commerce:** P.O. Box 2789, Charleston, WV 25330.

# Wisconsin

*Badger State*

**People. Population** (1977): 4,651,000; **rank:** 16. **Pop. density:** 85.3 per sq. mi. **Urban** (1970): 65.9%. **Racial distrib.** (1975): 96.1% White; 3.1% Black; Hispanic (1970): 41,402. **Major ethnic groups:** German, Norwean, Italian. **Net migration** (1970-76): +27,000.

**eography. Total area:** 56,154 sq. mi.; **rank:** 26. **Land rea:** 54,464 sq. mi. **Acres forested land:** 14,945,000. **ocation:** North central state, bounded on the N by Lake uperior and Upper Michigan; on the E by Lake Michigan; n the S by Illinois; on the W by the St. Croix and Missisppi rivers. **Climate:** long, cold winters and short, warm ummers tempered by the Great Lakes. **Topography:** arrow Lake Superior Lowland plain met by Northern ighland which slopes gently to the sandy cresent Central lain; Western Upland in the SW; 3 broad parallel limeone ridges running N-S are separated by wide and shalw lowlands in the SE. **Capital:** Madison.

**conomy. Principal industries:** manufacturing, trade, ervices, government, transportation, communications, griculture. **Principal manufactured goods:** machinery, ods, fabricated metals, transportation equipment, paper nd wood products. **Value added by manufacture:** 13.011 million/yr. **Agriculture: Chief crops:** corn, eans, beets, peas, hay, oats, cabbage, cranberries. **hief products:** milk, cheese. **Livestock:** 4,100,000 cate; 1,250,000 hogs/pigs; 80,000 sheep; 11,285,000 pouly. **Timber/lumber:** maple, birch, oak, evergreens. **Minals** (1977): sand and gravel and crushed stone, 66% of e total $140.6 million value of mineral production, lime. **ommercial fishing:** $3,623,000. **Chief ports:** Superior, ilwaukee, Green Bay, La Crosse. **International airports t:** Milwaukee. **Value of construction** (1977): 2,619,745,000. **Employment distribution:** 5.6% agricul- re; 25.9% manufacturing; 15.1% services; 19.9% trade, 4.5% government. **Per capita income** (1976): $6,293. **nemployment** (1977): 4.5%. **Tourism** (1976): out-of- ate visitors spent $2.4 billion.

**inance. Notable industries:** insurance. **No. banks:** 503; **o. savings and loan assns.:** 118.

**ederal government. No. federal employees** (1976): 7,000 civilians. **Federal payroll** (1976): $397 million. **No- ble federal facilities:** Ft. McCoy.

**nergy. Electricity production** (1977, mwh, by source): ydroelectric: 1.5 million; Mineral: 23.7 million; Nuclear: 0.9 million.

**ducation. No. schools:** 2,318 elementary; 702 second- ry; 58 higher education. **Avg. salary, public school achers** (1977): $14,980.

**tate data. Motto:** Forward. **Flower:** Wood violet. **Bird:** obin. **Tree:** Sugar maple. **Song:** On, Wisconsin! **En- ered union** May 29, 1848; rank, 30th. **State fair** at: West llis; mid-Aug.

**History.** Jean Nicolet was the first European to see the Visconsin area, arriving in Green Bay, 1634; French mis- onaries and fur traders followed. The British took over, 763. The U.S. won the land after the Revolution but the ritish were not ousted until after the War of 1812. Lead iners came next and then farmers. Railroads were tarted in 1851, serving growing wheat harvests and iron ines.

**Tourist attractions.** Old Wade House and Carriage useum, Greenbush; Villa Louis, Prairie du Chien; Circus Vorld Museum, Baraboo; Wisconsin Dells; Door County eninsula; Chequamegon and Nicolet national forests; ake Winnebago; numerous lakes for water sports, ice oating and fishing; skiing and hunting.

**Famous Wisconsinites** include Edna Ferber, King amp Gillette, Harry Houdini, Robert LaFollette, Alfred unt, Joseph R. McCarthy, Spencer Tracey, Thorstein eblen, Orson Wells, Thorton Wilder, Frank Lloyd Wright.

**Chamber of Commerce:** 111 E. Wisconsin Ave., Mil- aukee, WI 53202.

# Wyoming

*Equality State*

**eople. Population** (1977): 406,000; **rank:** 50. **Pop. den- ity:** 4.1 per sq. mi. **Urban** (1970): 60.5%. **Racial distrib. 975):** 96.9% White; —% Black; Hispanic (1970): 8,551. **Major ethnic groups:** German, English, Russian. **et migration** (1970-76): +37,000.

**eography. Total area:** 97,914 sq. mi.; **rank:** 9. **Land rea:** 97,203 sq. mi. **Acres forested land:** 10,085,000.

**Location:** Mountain state lying in the high western pla- teaus of the Great Plains. **Climate:** semi-desert conditions throughout; true desert in the Big Horn and Great Divide basins. **Topography:** the eastern Great Plains rise to the foothills of the Rocky Mtns.; the Continental Divide crossed the state from the NW to the SE. **Capital:** Chey- enne

**Economy. Principal industries:** mining, agriculture, for- estry, tourism. **Principal manufactured goods:** refined petroleum products, foods, wood products. **Value added by manufacture:** $266.8 million/yr. **Gross Domestic Product** (1975): $3.169 billion. **Agriculture: Chief crops:** wheat, barley, oats, sugar beets. **Livestock:** 1,280,000 cattle; 32,000 hogs/pigs; 1,206,000 sheep; 105,000 poul- try. **Timber/lumber:** aspen, yellow pine. **Minerals** (1977): petroleum, sodium carbonate, coal, uranium, natural gas. Energy minerals accounted for 79% of the total $2.18 bil- lion value of mineral production. **International airports at:** Casper. **Value of construction** (1977): $437,860,000. **Employment distribution:** 10% agriculture; 5% manu- facturing; 13% services; 12% mining. **Per capita income** (1976): $6,723. **Unemployment** (1977): 3.6%. **Tourism** (1976): out-of-state visitors spent $421 million.

**Finance. No. banks:** 83; **No. savings and loan assns.:** 14.

**Federal government. No. federal employees** (1975): 6,677 civilians. **Federal payroll** (1975): $89.6 million. **No- table federal facilities:** Warren AFB; Laramie Energy Research Ctr.

**Energy. Electricity production** (1977, mwh, by source): Hydroelectric: 761,936; Mineral: 19 million; Nuclear: —.

**Education. No. schools:** 258 elementary; 86 secondary; 8 higher education. **Avg. salary, public school teachers** (1977): $12,190.

**State data. Motto:** Equal Rights. **Flower:** Indian paint- brush. **Bird:** Meadowlark. **Tree:** Cottonwood. **Song:** Wyo- ming. **Entered union** July 10, 1890; rank, 44th. **State fair** at: Douglas; last week of Aug.

**History.** Francés Francois and Louis Verendrye were the first Europeans, 1743. John Colter, American, was first to traverse Yellowstone Park, 1807-08. Trappers and fur traders followed in the 1820s. Forts Laramie and Bridger became important stops on the pioneer trial to the West Coast. Indian wars followed massacres of army de- tachments in 1854 and 1866. Population grew after the Union Pacific crossed the state, 1869. Women won the vote, for the first time in the U.S., from the Territorial Leg- islature, 1869.

**Tourist attractions.** Yellowstone National Park, 3,472 sq. mi. in the NW corner of Wyoming and the adjoining edges of Montana and Idaho, the oldest U.S. national park, est. 1872, has some 10,000 geysers, hot springs, mud volcanoes, fossil forests, a volcanic glass (obsidian) mountain, the 1,000-ft.-deep canyon and 308-ft.-high wa- terfall of the Yellowstone River, and a wide variety of ani- mals living free in their natural habitat.

Grand Teton National Park, with mountains 13,000 ft. high, comprises 299,326 acres; the National Elk Refuge covers 25,000 acres; Devils Tower, a cluster of rock col- umns 865 ft. high; Fort Laramie and surrounding areas of pioneer trails; Buffalo Bill Museum, Cody; Cheyenne Fron- tier Days Celebration, last full week in July, is the state's largest rodeo.

**Famous Wyomingites** include James Bridger, Buffalo Bill Cody, Nellie Tayloe Ross.

**Chamber of Commerce:** none.

# District of Columbia

**Area:** 67 sq. mi. **Population:** (U.S. est. 1977): 690,000. **Motto:** Justitia omnibus, Justice for all. **Flower:** American beauty rose. **Tree:** Scarlet oak. **Bird:** Wood thrush. The city of Washington is coextensive with the District of Co- lumbia.

The District of Columbia is the seat of the federal gov- ernment of the United States. It lies on the west central edge of Maryland on the Potomac River, opposite Virginia. Its area was originally 100 sq. mi. taken from the sover- eignty of Maryland and Virginia. Virginia's portion south of the Potomac was given back to that state in 1846.

The 23d Amendment, ratified in 1961, granted residents of the District the right to vote for president and vice president for the first time and gave them 3 members in the Electoral College. Residents cast the first such votes in Nov. 1964.

Congress, which has legislative authority over the District under the Constitution, experimented with various forms of municipal government until 1878 when it established a government of 3 commissioners appointed by the president. The Reorganization Plan of 1967 substituted a single commissioner (also called mayor) and assistant, and a 9-member City Council; funds were still appropriated by Congress; residents had no vote in local government (except to elect school board members).

In Sept. 1970, Congress approved legislation giving the District one delegate to the House of Representatives. The delegate could vote in committee but not on the House floor. The first was elected 1971.

In May 1974 voters approved a charter giving them the right to elect their own mayor and a 13-member city council in Nov. 1974. The first mayor and council took office Jan. 2, 1975. The district won the right to levy its own taxes but Congress retained power to kill council actions.

Proposals for a "federal town" for the deliberations of the Continental Congress were made in 1783, 4 years before the adoption of the Constitution that gave the Confederation a national government. Rivalry between northern and southern delegates over the site appeared in the First Congress, meeting in New York in 1789. John Adams, presiding officer of the Senate, cast the deciding vote of that body for Germantown, Pa. In 1790 Congress compromised by making Philadelphia the temporary capital for 10 years. The Virginia members of the House wanted a capital on the eastern bank of the Potomac; they were defeated by the Northerners, while the Southerners defeated the Northern attempt to have the nation assume the war debts of the 13 original states, the Assumption Bill fathered by Alexander Hamilton. Hamilton and Jefferson arranged a compromise: the Virginia men voted for the Assumption Bill, and the Northerners conceded the capital to the Potomac. President Washington chose the site in Oct. 1790 and persuaded landowners to sell their holdings to the government at £25, then about $66, an acre. The capital was named Washington.

Washington appointed Pierre Charles L'Enfant, a French engineer who had come over with Lafayette, to plan the capital on an area not over 10 mi. square. The L'Enfant plan was considered grandiose, for streets 100 to 110 feet wide and one avenue 400 feet wide and a mile long on the Potomac pastures seemed foolhardy. But Washington endorsed his plans. When L'Enfant ordered a wealthy landowner to remove his new manor house because it obstructed a vista, and demolished it when the owner refused, Washington stepped in and dismissed L'Enfant. The official map was completed by Andrew Ellicott and Benjamin Banneker.

On Sept. 18, 1793, Pres. Washington laid the cornerstone of the north wing of the Capitol. The occasion was expected to drum up sales of city lots, but there were few purchasers. Washington bought several lots. In the next few years Robert Morris and others invested. By 1799 the Senate wing of the Capitol had been roofed, the walls of the president's house were up and the Treasury building was ordered. On June 3, 1800, Pres. John Adams moved to Washington and on June 10, Philadelphia ceased to be the temporary capital. The City of Washington was incorporated in 1802; the District of Columbia was created as a municipal corporation in 1871, embracing Washington, Georgetown, and Washington County.

# Outlying U.S. Areas

# Commonwealth of Puerto Rico

### *(Estado Libre Asociado de Puerto Rico)*

**People. Population** (1977): 3,337,000. **Pop. density:** 976.6 per sq. mi. **Urban** (1975): 61.8%. **Racial distribution:** 99% Hispanic. **Net migration** (1977): +46,812.

**Geography. Total area:** 3,435 sq. mi. **Land area:** 3,4 sq. mi. **Location:** island lying between the Atlantic to t N and the Caribbean to the S; it is easternmost of t West Indies group called the Greater Antilles, of whi Cuba, Hispaniola, and Jamaica are the larger units. C **mate:** mild, with a mean temperature of 76°. **Topog phy:** mountainous throughout three-fourths of its recta gular area, surrounded by a broken coastal plain; highe peak is Cerro de Punta, 4,389 ft. **Capital:** San Juan.

**Principal industries:** manufacturing. **Principal manufa tured goods:** apparel; electronics; petrochemicals; pha maceuticals; scientific instruments; medical supplies; ru food products, especially canned tuna fish. **Value adde by manufacture:** $3.3 billion/yr. **Gross Domestic Pro uct** (1977): $9.7 billion. **Agriculture: Chief crops:** sug plantains; coffee; bananas; yams; taniers; pineapples; p geon peas; peppers; tomatoes; pumpkins; coriander; le tuce; tobacco. **Livestock** (1976): 563,000 cattle; 269,0 pigs; 5,544,000 poultry. **Minerals:** undeveloped depos of copper and nickel; petroleum exploration is planne **Commercial fishing:** $6.4 million. **Chief ports/riv shipping:** San Juan, Ponce, Mayaguez, Guayanilla, Yat coa, Aguirre. **International airports at:** San Juan; Agu dilla. **Value of construction** (1977): $903 million. E ployment distribution: 5.5% agriculture; 19.5 manufacturing; 17.2% services; 22.7% government; 5.8 construction; 29.3% other. **Per capita income** (197 $2,472. **Unemployement (1976-7):** 20.1%. **Touris** (1977): No. out-of-area visitors: 1,376,000; $424 milli spent.

**Finance. Notable industries:** life insurance, mortga banks, credit unions, retirement fund systems. **Financi institutions:** No. banks: 143; No. savings and loan assn 12; No. other (specify): 4 retirement fund systems; ov 100 credit unions.

**Federal government. No. federal employees** (Mar. 3 1977): 8,558 full-time. **Federal payroll** (197 $117,512,249 (civilians). **Notable federal facilities:** U. Naval Station at Roosevelt Roads; U.S. Army Salin Training Area and Ft. Allen; Sabana SECA Communic tions Center (U.S. Navy).

**Energy. Production** (1977): Hydroelectric: 125,000 Kw **Education. Number schools:** 1,767 elementary; 1 secondary; 13 higher education. **Avg. salary, publ school teachers** (1978): $5,600.

**Misc. Data. Motto.** Joannes Est Nomen Ejus (John is h name). **Flower:** Maga. **Bird:** Reinita. **Tree:** Ceiba. **Son** La Borinquena.

**History:** Puerto Rico (or Borinquen, after the origin Arawak Indian name Boriquen), was discovered by C lumbus, Nov. 19, 1493. Ponce de Leon conquered it f Spain, 1509, and established the first settlement Caparra, across the bay from San Juan.

Sugar cane was introduced, 1515, and slaves were in ported 3 years later. Gold mining petered out, 157 Spaniards fought off a series of British and Dutch attack slavery was abolished, 1873. The U.S. took the island du ing the Spanish-American War, 1898, without any maj battle.

**General tourist attractions:** Ponce Museum of A forts El Morro and San Cristobal; Old Walled City of Sa Juan; Arecibo Observatory; Cordillera Central and stat parks; El Yungue Rain Forest; San Juan Cathedral; Por Coeli Chapel and Museum of Religious Art, San Germa Condado Convention Center; Casa Blanca, Ponce d Leon family home, now the Puerto Rican Family Museu of 16th and 17 centuries.

**Cultural facilities, festivals, etc.:** Festival Casals clas sical music concerts, mid-June; San Juan Bautista, patro saint fiesta, June 24th, Puerto Rico Symphony Orchestr at Music Conservatory; Botanical Garden and Museum Anthropology, Art, and History at the University of Puer Rico; Institute of Puerto Rican Culture, at the Dominic Convent.

The Commonwealth of Puerto Rico is a self-governin part of the U.S. with a primary Hispanic culture. Puer Ricans are U.S. citizens and about 1.5 million now live the continental U.S., although since 1974, a reverse m gration flow has resulted in net immigration to the island.

The current commonwealth political status of Puerto
ico gives the island's citizens virtually the same control
ver their internal affairs as the fifty states of the U.S.
owever, they do not vote in national elections, although
ey do vote in national primary elections.

Puerto Rico is represented in Congress solely by a resi-
ent commissioner who has a voice but no vote, except in
mmittees of which he is a member.

Most federal taxes are not levied in Puerto Rico, except
ose, such as Social Security, which are imposed by mu-
al consent. No federal income tax is collected from resi-
ents on income earned from local sources in Puerto
ico.

The 2 major political parties are the New Progressive
arty (NPP) and the Popular Democratic Party (PDP)
hich respectively favor eventual statehood for Puerto
ico and continuance of the present commonwealth sta-
us. Together these 2 parties (and their factions) account
or well over 90% of the popular vote.

Puerto Rico's famous "Operation Bootstrap" begun in
e late 1940s succeeded in changing the island from
The Poorhouse of the Caribbean" to an area with the
ghest per capita income in Latin America. This pioneer-
g program encouraged manufacturing and the develop-
ent of the tourist trade by selective tax exemption, low-
terest loans, and other incentives. Despite the marked
uccess of Puerto Rico's development efforts over an ex-
ended period of time, per capita income in Puerto Rico is
w in comparison to that of the U.S. In calendar year
977, net transfer payments from the U.S. government to
dividuals and governments in Puerto Rico totalled
2.183 billion, or 22.5% of the Gross Domestic Product of
9.717 billion.

amous Puerto Ricans include: Pablo Casals, Orlando
epeda, Roberto Clemente, Jose Feliciano, Jose Ferrer,
ona Felisa, Rincon de Gantier, Luis Munoz Marin, Rita
loreno, Adm. Horatio Rivero.

hamber of Commerce: 100 Tetuan P.O.B. S3789, San
uan, PR 00904.

## Guam

### Pearl of the Pacific

The World Almanac is sponsored on Guam by the Pacific
Daily News, 90 O'Hara St., Agana, GU 96910; phone
77-9711; successor in 1970 to Guam Daily News; circula-
on throughout Micronesia, 18,344; a Gannett newspaper;
resident and publisher, Robert E. Udick; editor Joseph
lurphy, managing editor, John Teare.

**eople. Population** (1975): 105,400. **Pop. density:**
04.3 per sq. mi. **Urban** (1970): 25.5%. Native Guamani-
ns, ethnically called chamorros, are basically of Indone-
ian stock, with a mixture of Spanish and Filipino. In addi-
on to the offical language, they speak the native
hamorros.

**eography. Total area:** 209 sq. mi. land, 30 mi. long and
to 8.5 mi. wide. **Location:** largest and southernmost of
e Mariana Islands in the West Pacific, 3,000 mi. W of
lawaii. **Climate:** tropical, with temperatures from 70° to
0°F; avg. annual rainfall, about 70 in. **Topography:** coral-
e limestone plateau in the N; southern chain of low vol-
anic mountains sloping gently to the W, more steeply to
oastal cliffs on the E; general elevation, 500 ft.; highest
t., Mt. Lamlam, 1,334 ft. **Capital:** Agana.

.conomy. Principal industries: contruction, manufactur-
g, tourism, petroleum refining, watch assembly. **Princi-
al manufactured goods:** textiles, foods. **Value added
y manufacture:** $151.8 million/yr. **Agriculture:** Chief
rops: cabbages, eggplants, cucumber, taro, bananas,
oconuts, watermelon, yams, avocados, papayas, maize,
weet potatoes, sugar cane. **Livestock:** 1,829 cattle;
,442 hogs/pigs; 91,360 poultry. **Commercial fishing:**
187,000. **Chief ports:** Apra Harbor. **International air-
orts at:** Tamuning. **Value of construction** (1976):
64,035,622. **Employment distribution:** 11% agricultur-
5% manufacturing; 3% services; 16% trade. **Per capita
ncome** (1974): $3,333. **Unemployment** (1976): 13.3%
ourism (1976): No. out-of-area visitors: 201,344.

**Finance. Notable industries:** insurance, real estate, finance. **No. banks:** 16; **No. savings and loan assns.:** 2.
**Federal government. No. federal employees** (1976):
6,014. **Notable federal facilities:** Andersen AFB; other
naval and air bases, including a nuclear submarine installation and a large ship-repair yard.
**Education. No. public schools:** 27 elementary; 9 secondary; 1 higher education. **Avg. salary, public school
teachers** (1977): $12,488.
**Misc. Data. Flower:** Puti Tai Nobio (Bougainvillea). **Bird:**
Toto (Fruit dove). **Tree:** Ifit (Intsiabijuga). **Song:** Stand Ye
Guamanians.

**History.** Magellan arrived in the Marianas Mar. 6, 1521,
and called them the Ladrones (thieves). They were colonized in 1668 by Spanish missionaries who renamed them
the Mariana Islands in honor of Maria Anna, queen of
Spain. When Spain ceded Guam to the U.S., it sold the
other Marianas to Germany. Japan obtained a League of
Nations mandate over the German islands in 1919; in Dec.
1941 it seized Guam; the island was retaken by the U.S.
in July 1944.

Guam is under the jurisdiction of the Interior Department. It is administered under the Organic Act of 1950,
which provides for a governor and a 21-member unicameral legislature, elected biennially by the residents who
are American citizens but do not vote for president.

Beginning in Nov., 1970, Guamanians elected their own
governor, previously appointed by the U.S. president. He
took office in Jan. 1971. In 1972 a U.S. law gave Guam
one delegate to the U.S. House of Representatives; the
delegate may vote in committee but not on the House
floor.

**General tourist attractions.** annual mid-Aug. Merizo
Water Festival; Tarzan Falls; beaches; water sports, duty-
free port shopping.

## Virgin Islands

### St. John, St. Croix, St. Thomas

**People. Population** (1978): 100,000. **Pop. density:**
757.6 per sq. mi. **Urban** (1970): 25%. **Racial distribution:** 15% White; 85% Black. **Major ethnic groups:** West
Indian, Chachas. **Net migration** (1977): +9,000.
**Geography. Total area:** 133 sq. mi.; **Land area:** 132 sq.
mi. **Location:** 3 larger and 50 smaller islands and cays in
the S and W of the V.I. group (British V.I. colony to the N
and E) which is situated 70 mi. E of Puerto Rico, located
W of the Anegada Passage, a major channel connecting
the Atlantic O. and the Caribbean Sea. **Climate:** subtropical; the sun tempered by gentle trade winds; humidity is
low; average temperature, 78° F. **Topography:** St.
Thomas is mainly a ridge of hills running E and W, and
has little tillable land; St. Croix rises abruptly in the N but
slopes to the S to flatlands and lagoons; St. John has
steep, lofty hills and valleys with little level tillable land.
**Capital:** Charlotte Amalie, St. Thomas.
**Economy. Principal industries:** tourism, rum, petroleum
refining, bauxite processing, watch assembly, textiles.
**Principal manufactured goods:** rum, textiles, pharmaceuticals, perfumes. **Gross Domestic Product** (1977):
$500 million. **Agriculture: Chief crops:** truck garden pro-
duce. **Minerals:** sand, gravel. **Chief ports:** Cruz Bay, St.
John; Frederiksted, St. Croix; Charlotte Amalie, St.
Thomas. **International airports on:** St. Thomas, St.
Croix. **Value of construction** (1976): $42,303,000. **Per
capita income** (1977): $5,000. **Unemployment** (1977):
7.9%. **Tourism** (1977): No. out-of-area visitors:
1,119,726; $152.2 million spent. **No. banks:** 8.
**Education. No. public schools:** 26 elementary; 5 secondary; 1 higher education. **Avg. salary, public school
teachers** (1977): $10,738.
**Misc. data. Flower:** Yellow elder or yellow cedar. **Bird:**
Yellow breast. **Song:** Virgin Islands March.

**History.** The islands were discovered by Columbus in
1493, who named them for the virgins of St. Ursula, the
sailor's patron saint. Spanish forces, 1555, defeated the
Caribes and claimed the territory; by 1596 the native pop-

ulation was annihilated. First permanent settlement in the U.S. territory, 1672, by the Danes; U.S. purchased the islands, 1917, for defense purposes.

The inhabitants have been citizens of the U.S. since 1927. Legislation originates in a unicameral house of 15 senators, elected for 2 years. The governor, formerly appointed by the U.S. president, was popularly elected for the first time in Nov. 1970. In 1972 a U.S. law gave the Virgin Islands one delegate to the U.S. House of Representatives; the delegate may vote in committee but not in the House.

**General tourist attractions.** Megen Bay, St. Thomas; duty-free shopping; Virgin Islands National Park, 14,488 acres on St. John of lush growth, beaches, Indian relics, and evidence of colonial Danes.

**Chamber of Commerce:** for St. Thomas and St. John: P.O. Box 324, St. Thomas, VI 00801; for St. Croix: 17 Church St., Christiansted, St. Croix, VI 00820.

## American Samoa

**Capital:** Fagotogo, Island of Tutuila. **Area:** 76 sq. mi. **Population:** (1977 est.) 30,600. **Motto:** Samoa Muamua Le Atua (In Samoa, God Is First). **Song:** Amerika Samoa. **Flower:** Paogo (Ula-fala). **Plant:** Ava.

Blessed with spectacular scenery and delightful South Seas climate, American Samoa is the most southerly of all lands under U. S. ownership. It is an unincorporated territory consisting of 6 small islands of the Samoan group: **Tutila, Aunuu, Manua islands (Tau, Olosega and Ofu),** and **Rose.** Also administered as part of American Samoa is **Swain's Island,** 210 mi. to the NW, acquired by the U.S. in 1925. The islands are 2,600 mi. SW of Honolulu.

American Samoa became U. S. territory by a treaty with the United Kingdom and Germany in 1899. The islands were ceded by local chiefs in 1900 and 1904. Pago Pago had been a U.S. navy coaling station under an 1872 commercial treaty.

Samoa (Western), comprising the larger islands of the Samoan group, was a New Zealand mandate and UN Trusteeship until it became an independent nation Jan. 1, 1962 *(see Index.)*

Tutuila has an area of 52 sq. mi. Tau has an area of 17 sq. mi., and the islets of Ofu and Olosega, 5 sq. mi. with a population of a few thousand. Swain's Island has nearly 2 sq. mi. and a population of about 100.

About 70% of the land is forest. Chief products and exports are fish products, copra, and handicrafts. Taro, bread-fruit, yams, coconuts, pineapples, oranges, and bananas are also produced.

Formerly under jurisdiction of the Navy, since July 1, 1951, it has been under the Interior Dept. On Jan. 3, 1978, the first popularly elected Samoan governor and lieutenant governor were inaugurated. Previously, the governor was appointed by the Secretary of the Interior. American Samoa has a bicameral legislature and an elected delegate to appear before U.S. agencies in Washington.

The American Samoans are of Polynesian origin. They are nationals of the U.S.; there are some 15,000 in Hawaii and 75,000 on the U.S. west coast.

## Minor Caribbean Islands

**Quita Suena Bank, Roncador Cay, and Serrana Bank** lie in the Caribbean between Nicaragua and Jamaica. They are uninhabited. They were to be turned over to Colombia under a 1972 agreement, but this still awaits U.S. Senate action.

**Navassa** lies between Jamaica and Haiti, covers about 2 sq. mi., is reserved by the U.S. for a lighthouse and is uninhabited.

## Wake, Midway, Other Islands

**Wake Island,** and its sister islands, **Wilkes** and **Peale,** lie in the Pacific Ocean on the direct route from Hawaii to

Hong Kong, about 2,000 mi. W of Hawaii and 1,290 mi. of Guam. The group is 4.5 mi. long, 1.5 mi. wide, and te tals less than 3 sq. mi. Population (1970 census) wa 1,647.

The U.S. flag was hoisted over Wake Island, July 1898. Formal possession was taken Jan. 17, 1899; Wak has been administered by the U.S. Air Force since 197: Population (1978) was 200.

The **Midway Islands,** acquired in 1867, consist of **Sand** and **Eastern,** in the North Pacific 1,150 mi. NW Hawaii, with area of about 2 sq. mi., administered by th Navy Dept. Population (1975 est.) was 2,256.

**Johnston Atoll,** SW of Hawaii, area 1 sq. mi., pop. 3C (1978), is under Air Force control, and **Kingman Reef,** of Hawaii, is under Navy control.

**Howland, Jarvis,** and **Baker Islands** south of the Ha waiian group, uninhabited since World War II, are unde the Interior Dept.

**Palmyra** is an atoll SW of Hawaii, 4 sq. mi. Private owned, it is under the Interior Dept.

## Islands Under Trusteeship

The U. S Trust Territory of the Pacific Islands, als called Micronesia, includes 3 major archipelagoes: th **Caroline Islands, Marshall Islands,** and **Mariana Is lands** (except **Guam:** see above). There are 2,141 is lands, 98 of them inhabited: total land area 687 sq. m but the islands are scattered over 3 million sq. mi. in th western Pacific N of the equator and E of the Philippine Population (1977) at 126,440.

### The Marianas

In process of becoming a U.S. commonwealth in 197 were the Northern Mariana Islands, which since 1947 ha been part of the Trust Territory of the Pacific Islands, as signed to U.S. administration by the United Nations. Th Northern Marianas comprise all the Marianas excep Guam, stretching N-S in a 500-mi. arc of tropical island east of the Philippines and southeast of Japan.

Residents of the islands on June 17, 1975, voted 78% in favor of becoming a commonwealth of the U.S. rathe than continuing with the Carolines and Marshalls in th U S.-UN Trusteeship. On Mar. 24, 1976, U.S. Pres. For signed a congressionally-approved commonwealth cove nant giving the Marianas control of domestic affairs an giving the U.S. control of foreign relations and defense and the right to maintain military bases on the islands.

Pres. Carter, on Oct. 24, 1977, approved the Constitu tion of the Northern Mariana Islands with the effectiv date of Jan. 9, 1978. In December 1977, the voters of th Northern Marianas elected a governor, lieutenant gover nor, and members of a bicameral legislature for the nev government.

Ferdinand Magellan was the first European to visit th Marianas, 1521. Spain, Germany, and Japan held the is lands in turn until World War II when the U.S. seized then in bitter battles on 2 of the main islands, Saipan and Ti nian.

Population in 1977 was estimated at 16,260, mostly o Saipan. English is the official language; Roman Catholi cism is the major religion. The people are descendants o the early Chamorros, Spanish, Japanese, Filipinos, an Mexicans. Land area is 181.9 sq. mi.

Tourism is an important industry; vistors are mostl from Japan. Crops include sugar, cotton, coconuts, maize rice, tobacco, coffee, and breadfruit.

### The Carolines and Marshalls

In 1885, many of the Carolines, Marshalls, and Maria nas were claimed by Germany. Others, held by Spain were sold to Germany at the time of the Spanish American War, 1898. After the outbreak of World War I Japan took over the 3 archipelagoes and, following tha war, League of Nations mandates over them were warded to Japan.

After World War II, the United Nations assigned them, 1947, as a Trust Territory to be administered by the U.S. They were placed, 1951, under administration of the U.S. Interior Dept.

There is a high commissioner, appointed by the U.S. president. Saipan is the headquarters of the administration. The Congress of Micronesia, an elected legislature with limited powers, held its first meeting in 1965. It has a senate of 12 members and a house of representatives of 21.

In 1969, a commission of the Congress of Micronesia recommended that Micronesia be given internal self-government in free association with the U.S.

A U.S. offer of commonwealth status was rejected by Micronesian leaders in 1970.

In May of 1977, Pres. Carter announced the intention of this administration to take steps to terminate the trusteeship by 1981. The U.S. and three Trust Territory negotiating commissions representing, respectively, the Marshall Islands, Palau, and the central districts of Truk, Yap, Ponape and Kosrae, are negotiating a free association arrangement whereby the three Micronesian areas would enjoy full self-government while the U.S. would retain responsibility for defense.

Among the noted islands are the former Japanese strongholds of **Palau, Peleliu, Truk,** and **Yap** in the Carolines; **Bikini** and **Eniwetok,** where U.S. nuclear tests were staged, and **Kwajalein,** another World War II battle scene, all in the Marshalls.

Many of the islands are volcanic with luxuriant vegetation; others are of coral formation. Only a few are self-sustaining. Principal exports are copra, trochus shells, fish products, handicrafts, and vegetables.

## Disputed Pacific Islands

In the central Pacific, S and SW of Hawaii, lie 25 islands claimed by the U.S.; 18 of them are also claimed by the United Kingdom and 7 by New Zealand. All are S of the Equator except Christmas Is.

Those claimed by the UK are:

The **Line Islands,** S of Hawaii, including Christmas, Flint, Malden, Starbuck, Vostok, and Caroline; only Christmas is inhabited. All administered by the UK as part of the Gilbert Islands colony.

Also, the **Phoenix Islands,** SW of Hawaii, including Canton and Enderbury; and Birnie, Gardner, Hull, McKean, Sydney, and Phoenix. All are inhabited and administered by the UK as part of the Gilbert Islands colony except for Canton and Enderbury which are under joint U.S. and UK administration.

Also, the **Tuvalu (Ellice) Islands,** further to the SW, including Funafuti, Nukufetau, Nukulailai, and Nurakita; all are inhabited and administered by the UK.

Those claimed by New Zealand are:

The **Tokelau (Union) Islands,** S of the Phoenix group, including Nukunono, Atafu, and Fakaofu. All are inhabited and administered by New Zealand as part of a dependency.

Also, the **Cook Islands,** E of the Tokelaus, including Danger, Manahiki, Rakahanga, and Penrhyn (Tongareva). All are inhabited and administered as part of a New Zealand self-governing territory.

## Panama Canal

*For Panama Canal cargo traffic see Index.*

The Canal Zone has been, in effect, a U.S. government reservation. It is a strip of land extending 5 mi. on each side of the axis of the Canal, under jurisdiction of the U.S. by treaty with the Republic of Panama in 1903.

Two new treaties governing the future operation and defense of the Panama Canal were signed by the United States and Panama in a ceremony at OAS headquarters in Washington on Sept. 7, 1977. They were approved by Panama in a plebiscite on Oct. 23d of that year and the U.S. Senate gave its advice and consent to their ratification in Mar. and Apr., 1978. The 2 countries exchanged the instruments of ratification on June 16, 1978. The exchange becomes effective Mar. 31, 1979. Six months later, Oct. 1, 1979, the Canal Zone will cease to exist; Panama will have full sovereignty over the area, except for limited U.S. police and legal authority during a 30-month transition period.

The canal connects the Caribbean with the Bay of Panama on the Pacific. Because of the geographic loop made by the Isthmus of Panama, the Caribbean end of the canal, which could be called the eastern end, is actually further west than the Pacific end.

The zone has an area of 647 sq. mi. of which 372 are land. Population (1978 est.) was 39,000. About 9,100 U.S. army, air force, and navy personnel are normally stationed in the zone. Government headquarters is Balboa Heights.

The Canal Zone government and the Panama Canal Co. are the 2 operating agencies, both headed by an individual who acts as governor of the Canal Zone and president of the company. The governor is appointed by the president of the U.S. As governor he reports directly to the secretary of the army; as president of the company he reports to its board of directors, appointed by the secretary of the army. The Canal Zone government maintains civil government. The company operates the canal, the Panama Railroad, terminals, employee services, and utilities.

A French company under Ferdinand de Lesseps failed to complete a canal, 1880-89, and a second French company failed in 1899. The U.S. bought their rights for $40 million, paid private owners $4 million, and offered Colombia compensation for a canal zone, but Colombia failed to ratify the treaty, Oct. 1903. Panama declared itself independent of Colombia Nov. 3, 1903, and was recognized by Pres. Theodore Roosevelt Nov. 6. American naval forces discouraged action by Colombia. On Nov. 18 Panama granted the canal strip to the U.S. by treaty, ratified Feb. 26, 1904, compensation $10 million, with annual payments of $250,000 after 9 years, and a guarantee of Panama's independence.

Under terms of the 1903 treaty, Panama granted the U.S. perpetual sovereignty over the Canal Zone.

The canal was opened to traffic Aug. 15, 1914. In 1922, Colombia accepted $25 million from the U.S. plus special land transportation privileges, and agreed to recognize Panama. The U.S. increased its annual payment to Panama to $430,000 and withdrew its guarantee of independence.

A further treaty regulating relations between the U.S. and Panama was signed Jan. 25, 1955, increasing the annuity paid Panama to $1.9 million (actually increasing it to $2.3 million because of devaluation of the U.S. dollar.) In addition, the U.S. gave Panama $28 million worth of real estate and buildings. U.S. citizen and non-citizen employees were guaranteed equality of pay and opportunity. In addition, the U.S. agreed to build a high level bridge over the Pacific entrance to the canal. The bridge was opened Oct. 12, 1962, as a link in the Inter-American Highway.

Negotiations for a new treaty began after Panamanian riots protesting the 1903 and 1955 treaties caused the death of 20 Panamanians and 4 U.S. soldiers, Jan. 9, 1964. Preliminary agreement was reached in 1967, but in 1970, after a change of governement, Panama rejected the proposal.

Under the new Panama Canal Treaty, the U.S. will retain primary responsibility for defense and administration of the canal until the year 2000, but with Panama assuming an increasing role in both until the final turnover date, Dec. 31, 1999. The Panama Canal Co. will be replaced with a new U.S. agency with a board of 9, composed of 5 Americans and 4 Panamanians. Until 1990 the chief administrator will be American and his deputy Panamanian; in 1990 the positions will be reversed.

On Oct. 1, 1979, the U.S. will turn over some 65% of the zone to Panamanian jurisdiction. Times for withdrawal of U.S. troops and disposal of bases will be up to the U.S. The U.S. will pay Panama $50 to $70 million a year from canal revenues.

# HISTORY

## Memorable Dates in U.S. History

**1492**
Christopher Columbus and crew sighted land Oct. 12 in the Caribbean.

**1497**
John Cabot explored northeast coast to Delaware.

**1513**
Juan Ponce de Leon explored Florida coast.

**1524**
Giovanni da Verrazano led French expedition along coast from Carolina north to Nova Scotia; entered New York harbor.

**1539**
Hernando de Soto landed in Florida May 28; crossed Mississippi River, 1541.

**1540**
Francisco Vazquez de Coronado explored Southwest north of Rio Grande. Hernando de Alarcon reached Colorado River, Don Garcia Lopez de Cardenas reached Grand Canyon. Others explored California coast.

**1565**
St. Augustine, Fla. founded by Pedro Menendez. Razed by Francis Drake 1586.

**1579**
Francis Drake claimed California for Britain. Left metal plate found in Marin Co. 1936.

**1607**
Capt. John Smith and 105 cavaliers in 3 ships landed on Virginia coast, started first permanent English settlement in New World at Jamestown, May 13.

**1609**
Henry Hudson, English explorer of Northwest Passage, employed by Dutch, sailed into New York harbor in Sept., and up Hudson to Albany. The same year, Samuel de Champlain explored Lake Champlain just to the north.
Spaniards settled Santa Fe, N.M.

**1619**
House of Burgesses, first representative assembly in New World, elected July 30 at Jamestown, Va.
First Negro laborers — indentured servants — in English N. American colonies, landed by Dutch at Jamestown in Aug. Chattel slavery legally recognized, 1650.

**1620**
Plymouth Pilgrims, Puritan separatists from Church of England, some living in Holland, left Plymouth, England Sept. 15 on Mayflower. Original destination Virginia, they reached Cape Cod Nov. 19, explored coast; 103 passengers landed Dec. 21 (Dec. 11 Old Style) at Plymouth. Mayflower Compact, signed shipboard, was agreement to form a local government and abide by its laws. Half of colony died during harsh winter.

**1624**
Dutch left 8 men from ship New Netherland on Manhattan Island in May. Rest sailed to Albany.

**1626**
Peter Minuit bought Manhattan for Dutch from Man-a-hat-a Indians May 6 for trinkets valued at $24.

**1634**
Maryland founded as Catholic colony with religious tolerance.

**1636**
Harvard College founded Oct. 28, now oldest in U.S., Grammar school, compulsory education established at Boston.
Roger Williams founded Providence, R.I., June, as a democratically ruled colony with separation of church and state. Charter was granted, 1644.

**1654**
First Jews arrived in New Amsterdam.

**1660**
British Parliament passed Navigation Act, regulating colonial commerce to suit English needs.

**1664**
Three hundred British troops Sept. 8 seized New Nethe land from Dutch, who yield peacefully. Charles II grant province of New Netherland and city of New Amsterdam brother, Duke of York; both renamed New York. T Dutch recaptured the colony Aug. 9, 1673, but ceded it Britain Nov. 10, 1674.

**1676**
Nathaniel Bacon led planters against autocratic Briti Gov. Berkeley, burned Jamestown, Va. Bacon died, 23 fo lowers executed.
Bloody Indian war in New England ended Aug. 12. Ki Philip, Wampanoag chief, and many Narragansett Indiar killed.

**1682**
Robert Cavelier, Sieur de La Salle, claimed lower Missi sippi River country for France, called it Louisiana Apr. Had French outposts built in Illinois and Texas, 168 Killed during mutiny Mar. 19, 1687.

**1683**
William Penn signed treaty with Delaware Indians ar made payment for Pennsylvania lands.

**1692**
Witchcraft delusion at Salem (now Danvers) Mass. i spired by preaching; 19 persons executed.

**1696**
Capt. William Kidd, American hired by British to fig pirates and take booty, becomes pirate. Arrested and sent England, where he was hanged 1701.

**1699**
French settlements made in Mississippi, Louisiana.

**1704**
Indians attacked Deerfield, Mass. Feb. 28-29, killed carried off 100.
Boston News Letter, first regular newspaper, started b John Campbell, postmaster. (Publick Occurences was sup pressed after one issue 1690.)

**1709**
British-Colonial troops captured French fort, Port Roya Nova Scotia, in Queen Anne's War 1701-13. France yielde Nova Scotia by treaty 1713.

**1712**
Slaves revolted in New York Apr. 6. Six committed su cide, 21 were executed. Second rising, 1741; 13 slave hanged, 13 burned, 71 deported.

**1716**
First theater in colonies opened in Williamsburg, Va.

**1728**
Pennsylvania Gazette founded by Samuel Keimer in Phila delphia. Benjamin Franklin bought interest 1729.

**1732**
Benjamin Franklin published first Poor Richard's Alme nac; published annually to 1757.

**1735**
Freedom of the press recognized in New York by acqui tal of John Peter Zenger, editor of Weekly Journal, or charge of libeling British Gov. Cosby by criticizing his con duct in office.

**1740-41**
Capt. Vitus Bering, Dane employed by Russians, reache Alaska.

**1744**
King George's War pitted British and colonials vs French. Colonials captured Louisburg, Cape Breton Is. Jun 17, 1745. Returned to France 1748 by Treaty of Aix-la Chapelle.

**1752**
Benjamin Franklin, flying kite in thunderstorm, prove

ghtning is electricity **June 15**; invented lightning rod.

## 1754

**French and Indian War** (in Europe called 7 Years War, :arted 1756) began when French occupied Ft. Duquesne Pittsburgh). British moved Acadian French from Nova Sco- a to Louisiana **Oct. 1755**. British captured Quebec **Sept. 8, 1759** in battles in which French Gen. Montcalm and ritish Gen. Wolfe were killed. Peace signed **Feb. 10 1763**. rench lost Canada and American Midwest. British tight- ned colonial administration in North America.

## 1764

**Sugar Act** placed duties on lumber, foodstuffs, molasses nd rum in colonies.

## 1765

**Stamp Act** required revenue stamps to help defray cost of oyal troops. Nine colonies, led by New York and Massa- husetts at Stamp Act Congress in New York **Oct. 7-25, 765**, adopted Declaration of Rights opposing taxation ithout representation in Parliament and trial without jury y admiralty courts. Stamp Act **repealed Mar. 17, 1766.**

## 1767

**Townshend Acts** levied taxes on glass, painter's lead, pa- er, and tea. In 1770 all duties except on tea were repealed.

## 1770

British troops fired **Mar. 5** into Boston mob, killed 5 in- luding **Crispus Attucks**, a Negro, reportedly leader of roup; later called **Boston Massacre.**

## 1773

**East India Co.** tea ships turned back at Boston, New ork, Philadelphia in **May**. Cargo ship burned at Annapolis )ct. 14, cargo thrown overboard at **Boston Tea Party Dec. 6.**

## 1774

**"Intolerable Acts"** of Parliament curtailed Massachusetts elf-rule; barred use of Boston harbor till tea was paid for.

**First Continental Congress** held in Philadelphia **Sept. i-Oct. 26**; protested British measures, called for civil disobe- lience.

**Rhode Island** abolished slavery.

## 1775

**Patrick Henry** addressed Virginia convention, **Mar. 23** aid "Give me liberty or give me death."

**Paul Revere** and William Dawes on night of **Apr. 18** rode o alert patriots that British were on way to Concord to de- troy arms. At Lexington, Mass. **Apr. 19** Minutemen lost 8 illed. On return from Concord British took 273 casualties.

Col. Ethan Allen (joined by Col. Benedict Arnold) cap- ured Ft. **Ticonderoga, N.Y. May 10**; also Crown Point. Co- onials headed for **Bunker Hill**, fortified Breed's Hill, :harlestown, Mass., repulsed British under Gen. William Howe twice before retreating **June 17**; British casualties ,000; called Battle of Bunker Hill. Continental Congress une 15 named **George Washington** commander-in-chief.

## 1776

**France and Spain** each agreed **May 2** to provide one mil- ion livres in arms to Americans.

In Continental Congress **June 7**, Richard Henry Lee (Va.) noved "that these united colonies are and of right ought to e free and independent states." Resolution adopted July 2. **Declaration of Independence** approved **July 4.**

Col. Moultrie's batteries at **Charleston, S.C.** repulsed British sea attack **June 28.**

Washington, with 10,000 men, lost **Battle of Long Island** Aug. 27, evacuated New York.

**Nathan Hale** executed as spy by British **Sept. 22.**

Brig. Gen. Arnold's **Lake Champlain** fleet was defeated at Valcour Oct. 11, but British returned to Canada. Howe ailed to destroy Washington's army at **White Plains Oct. 18**. Hessians captured Ft. Washington, Manhattan, and ,000 men **Nov. 16**; Ft. Lee, N.J. **Nov. 18.**

Washington in Pennsylvania, recrossed **Delaware River** Dec. 25-26, defeated 1,400 Hessians at Trenton, N.J. **Dec. 26.**

## 1777

Washington defeated Lord Cornwallis at **Princeton Jan.**

**3.** Continental Congress adopted Stars and Stripes. *See Flag article.*

Maj. Gen. John Burgoyne with 8,000 from Canada cap- tured **Ft. Ticonderoga July 6.** Americans beat back Bur- goyne at Bemis Heights **Oct. 7** and cut off British escape route. Burgoyne surrendered 5,000 men at **Saratoga N.Y. Oct. 17.**

**Marquis de Lafayette**, aged 20, made major general.

**Articles of Confederation** and Perpetual Union adopted by Continental Congress **Nov. 15**

**France** recognized independence of 13 colonies **Dec. 17.**

## 1778

**France signed treaty** of aid with U.S. **Feb. 6.** Sent fleet; British evacuated Philadelphia in consequence **June 18.**

## 1779

**John Paul Jones** on the Bonhomme Richard defeated Se- rapis in British North Sea waters **Sept. 23.**

## 1780

**Charleston, S.C.** fell to the British **May 12**, but a British force was defeated near **Kings Mountain, N.C. Oct. 7** by mi- litiamen.

**Benedict Arnold** found to be a traitor **Sept. 23.** Arnold escaped, made brigadier general in British army.

## 1781

**Bank of North America** incorporated in Philadelphia **May 26.**

Cornwallis, harrassed by U.S. troops, retired to **York- town, Va.** Adm. De Grasse landed 3,000 French and stopped British fleet in Hampton Roads. Washington and Rochambeau joined forces, arrived near Williamsburg **Sept. 26.** When siege of Cornwallis began **Oct. 6**, British had 6,000, Americans 8,846, French 7,800. **Cornwallis surren- dered Oct. 19.**

## 1782

New **British** cabinet agreed **in March** to **recognize U.S.** independence. Preliminary agreement signed in Paris **Nov. 30.**

## 1783

Massachusetts Supreme Court **outlawed slavery** in that state, noting the words in the state Bill of Rights "all men are born free and equal."

Britain, U.S. signed **peace treaty Sept. 3** (Congress rati- fied it **Jan. 14, 1784**).

**Washington ordered army disbanded Nov. 3**, bade fare- well to his officers at Fraunces Tavern, N.Y. City **Dec. 4.**

Noah Webster published *American Spelling Book*, great bestseller.

## 1784

First successful daily newspaper, **Pennsylvania Packet & General Advertiser**, published **Sept. 21.**

## 1786

Delegates from 5 states at **Annapolis, Md. Sept. 11-14** asked Congress to call convention in Philadelphia to write practical constitution for the 13 states.

## 1787

**Shays rebellion**, of debt-ridden farmers in Massachusetts, failed **Jan. 25.**

**Northwest Ordinance** adopted **July 13** by Continental Congress. Determined government of Northwest Territory north of Ohio River, west of New York; 60,000 inhabitants could get statehood. Guaranteed freedom of religion, sup- port for schools, no slavery.

**Constitutional convention** opened at Philadelphia **May 25** with George Washington presiding. Constitution adopted by delegates **Sept. 17**; ratification by 9th state, New Hamp- shire, **June 21, 1788**, meant adoption; declared in effect **Mar. 4, 1789.**

## 1789

**George Washington chosen president** by all electors vot- ing (73 eligible, 69 voting, 4 absent); John Adams, vice pres- ident, 34 votes. **Feb. 4.** First Congress met at Federal Hall, N.Y. City; regular sessions began **Apr. 6.** Washington inau- gurated there **Apr. 30.** Supreme Court created by Federal Judiciary Act **Sept. 24.**

## 1790

**Congress met** in Philadelphia **Dec. 6**, new temporary Capital.

### 1791
Bill of Rights went into effect Dec. 15.

### 1792
Gen. "Mad" Anthony Wayne made commander in Ohio-Indiana area, trained "American Legion"; established string of forts. Routed Indians at Fallen Timbers on Maumee River Aug. 20, 1794, checked British at Fort Miami, Ohio.

### 1793
Eli Whitney invented cotton gin, reviving southern slavery.

### 1794
Whiskey Rebellion, west Pennsylvania farmers protesting liquor tax of 1791, was suppressed by 15,000 militiamen Sept. 1794. Alexander Hamilton used incident to establish authority of the new federal government in enforcing its laws.

### 1795
U.S. bought peace from Algiers and Tunis by paying $800,000, supplying a frigate and annual tribute of $25,000 Nov. 28.

Gen. Wayne signed peace with Indians at Fort Greenville.

Univ. of North Carolina became first operating state university.

### 1796
Washington's Farewell Address as president delivered Sept. 19. Gave strong warnings against permanent alliances with foreign powers, big public debt, large military establishment and devices of "small, artful, enterprising minority" to control or change government.

### 1797
U.S. frigate United States launched at Philadelphia July 10; Constellation at Baltimore Sept. 7; Constitution (Old Ironsides) at Boston Sept. 20.

### 1798
War with France threatened over French raids on U.S. shipping and rejection of U.S. diplomats. Congress voided all treaties with France, ordered Navy to capture French armed ships. Navy (45 ships) and 365 privateers captured 84 French ships. USS Constellation took French warship Insurgente 1799. Napoleon stopped French raids after becoming First Consul.

### 1801
Tripoli declared war June 10 against U.S., which refused added tribute to commerce-raiding Arab corsairs. Land and naval campaigns forced Tripoli to conclude peace June 4, 1805.

### 1803
Supreme Court, in Marbury v. Madison case, for the first time overturned a U.S. law Feb. 24.

Napoleon, who had recovered Louisiana from Spain by secret treaty, sold all of Louisiana, stretching to Canadian border, to U.S., for $11,250,000 in bonds, plus $3,750,000 indemnities to American citizens with claims against France. U.S. took title Dec. 20. Purchases doubled U.S. area.

### 1804
Lewis and Clark expedition ordered by Pres. Jefferson to explore what is now northwest U.S. Started from St. Louis May 14; ended Sept. 23, 1806. Sacajawea, an Indian woman, served as guide.

Vice Pres. Aaron Burr, after long political rivalry, shot Alexander Hamilton in a duel July 11 in Weehawken, N.J.; Hamilton died the next day.

### 1807
Robert Fulton made first practical steamboat trip; left N.Y. City Aug. 17, reached Albany, 150 mi., in 32 hrs.

### 1808
Slave importation outlawed. Some 250,000 slaves were illegally imported 1808-1860.

### 1811
William Henry Harrison, governor of Indiana, defeated Indians under the Prophet, in battle of Tippecanoe Nov. 7.

Cumberland Road begun at Cumberland, Md.; became important route to West.

### 1812
War of 1812 had 3 main causes: Britain seized U.S. ships trading with France; Britain seized 4,000 naturalized U.S. sailors by 1810; Britain armed Indians who raided western border. U.S. stopped trade with Europe 1807 and 1809. Trade with Britain only was stopped, 1810.

Unaware that Britain had raised the blockade 2 days before, Congress declared war June 18 by a small majority. The West favored war, New England opposed it. The British were handicapped by war with France.

U.S. naval victories in 1812 included: USS Essex captured Alert Aug. 13; USS Constitution destroyed Guerriere Aug. 19; USS Wasp took Frolic Oct. 18; USS United States defeated Macedonian off Azores Oct. 25; Constitution beat Java Dec. 29. British captured Detroit Aug. 16.

### 1813
Commodore Oliver H. Perry defeated British fleet at Battle of Lake Erie, Sept. 10. U.S. victory at Battle of the Thames, Ont., Oct. 5, broke Indian allies of Britain, and made Detroit frontier safe for U.S. But Americans failed in Canadian invasion attempts. York (Toronto) and Buffalo were burned.

### 1814
British landed in Maryland in August, defeated U.S. force Aug. 24, burned Capitol and White House. Maryland militia stopped British advance Sept. 12. Bombardment of Ft. McHenry, Baltimore, for 25 hours, Sept. 13-14, by British fleet failed; Francis Scott Key wrote words to Star Spangled Banner.

U.S. won naval Battle of Lake Champlain Sept. 11. Peace treaty signed at Ghent Dec. 24.

### 1815
Some 5,300 British, unaware of peace treaty, attacked U.S. entrenchments near New Orleans, Jan. 1. British had over 2,000 casualties, Americans lost 71.

U.S. flotilla finally ended piracy by Algiers, Tunis, Tripoli by Aug. 6.

### 1816
Second Bank of the U.S. chartered.

### 1817
Rush-Bagot treaty signed Apr. 28-29; limited U.S., British armaments on the Great Lakes.

### 1819
Spain cedes Florida to U.S. Feb. 22.

American steamship Savannah made first part steampowered, part sail-powered crossing of Atlantic, Savannah, Ga. to Liverpool, Eng., 29 days.

### 1820
Henry Clay's Missouri Compromise bill passed by Congress May 3. Slavery was allowed in Missouri, but not elsewhere west of the Mississippi River north of 36° 30′ latitude (the southern line of Missouri). Repealed 1854.

### 1821
Emma Willard founded Troy Female Seminary, first U.S. women's college.

### 1823
Monroe Doctrine enunciated Dec. 2, opposing European intervention in the Americas.

### 1824
Pawtucket, R.I. weavers strike in first such action by women.

### 1825
Erie Canal opened; first boat left Buffalo Oct. 26, reached N.Y. City Nov. 4. Canal cost $7 million but cut travel time one-third, shipping costs nine-tenths; opened Great Lakes area, made N.Y. City chief Atlantic port.

John Stevens, of Hoboken, N.J., built and operated first experimental steam locomotive in U.S.

### 1828
South Carolina Dec. 19 declared the right of state nullification of federal laws, opposing the "Tariff of Abominations."

Noah Webster published his American Dictionary of the English Language.

Baltimore & Ohio first U.S. passenger railroad, was begun July 4.

## 1830
Mormon church organized by Joseph Smith in Fayette, N.Y. Apr. 6.

## 1831
Nat Turner, Negro slave in Virginia, led local slave rebellion, killed 57 whites in Aug. Army called in, Turner captured, tried, and hanged.

## 1832
Black Hawk War (Ill.-Wis.) Apr.-Sept. pushed Sauk and Fox Indians west across Mississippi.

South Carolina convention passed Ordinance of Nullification in Nov. against permanent tariff, threatening to withdraw from the Union. Congress Feb. 1833 passed a compromise tariff act, whereupon South Carolina repealed its act.

## 1833
Oberlin College, first in U.S. to adopt coeducation; refused to bar students on account of race, 1835.

## 1835
Texas proclaimed independence from Mexico in convention Nov. 1, provisional government formed. Stephen Austin and Sam Houston leaders.

Gold discovered on Cherokee land in Georgia. Indians forced to cede lands Dec. 20 and to cross Mississippi.

## 1836
Texans besieged in Alamo in San Antonio by Mexicans under Santa Ana Feb. 23-Mar. 6; entire garrison killed. At San Jacinto Apr. 21 Sam Houston and Texans defeated Mexicans.

Marcus Whitman, H.H. Spaulding and wives reached Fort Walla Walla on Columbia River, Oregon. First white women to cross plains.

Seminole Indians in Florida under Osceola began attacks Nov. 1, protesting forced removal. The unpopular 8-year war ended Aug. 14, 1842; Indians were sent to Oklahoma. War cost the U.S. 1,500 soldiers.

## 1841
First emigrant wagon train for California, 47 persons, left Independence, Mo. May 1, reached Cal. Nov. 4.

Brook Farm commune set up by New England transcendentalist intellectuals. Lasts to 1846.

## 1842
Webster-Ashburton Treaty signed Aug. 9, fixing the U.S.-Canada border in Maine and Minnesota.

First use of anesthetic (sulphuric ether gas).

Settlement of Oregon begins via Oregon Trail.

## 1844
First message over first telegraph line sent May 24 by inventor Samuel F.B. Morse from Washington to Baltimore: "What hath God wrought!"

## 1845
Texas Congress voted for annexation to U.S. July 4. U.S. Congress admits Texas to Union Dec. 29.

## 1846
Mexican War. Pres. James K. Polk ordered Gen. Zachary Taylor to seize disputed Texan land settled by Mexicans. After border clash, U.S. declared war May 13; Mexico May 23. Northern Whigs opposed war, southerners backed it.

Bear flag of Republic of California raised by American settlers at Sonoma June 14.

About 12,000 U.S troops took Vera Cruz May 27, Mexico City Sept. 14. By treaty, Feb. 1848, Mexico ceded claims to Texas, California, Arizona, New Mexico, Nevada, Utah, part of Colorado. U.S. assumed $3 million American claims and paid Mexico $15 million.

Treaty with Great Britain June 15 set boundary in Oregon territory at 49th parallel (extension of existing line). Expansionists had used slogan "54° 40' or fight."

Mormons, after violent clashes with settlers over polygamy, left Nauvoo, Ill. for West under Brigham Young, settled July 1847 at Salt Lake City, Utah.

Elias Howe invented sewing machine.

## 1847
First adhesive U.S. postage stamps on sale July 1; Benjamin Franklin 5¢, Washington 10¢.

Ralph Waldo Emerson published first book of poems; Henry Wadsworth Longfellow published Evangeline.

## 1848
Gold discovered Jan. 24 in California; 80,000 prospectors emigrate in 1849.

Lucretia Mott and Elizabeth Cady Stanton lead Seneca Falls, N.Y. Women's Rights Convention July 19-20.

## 1850
Sen. Henry Clay's Compromise of 1850 admitted California as 31st state Sept. 9, slavery forbidden; made Utah and New Mexico territories without decision on slavery; made Fugitive Slave Law more harsh; ended District of Columbia slave trade.

## 1851
Herman Melville's Moby Dick, Nathaniel Hawthorne's House of the Seven Gables published.

## 1852
Uncle Tom's Cabin, by Harriet Beecher Stowe, published.

## 1853
Commodore Matthew C. Perry, U.S.N., received by Lord of Toda, Japan July 14; negotiated treaty to open Japan to U.S. ships.

## 1854
Republican party formed at Ripon, Wis. Feb. 28. Opposed Kansas-Nebraska Act (became law May 30) which left issue of slavery to vote of settlers.

Henry David Thoreau published Walden.

## 1855
Walt Whitman published Leaves of Grass.

First railroad train crossed Mississippi on the river's first bridge, Rock Island, Ill.-Davenport, Ia. Apr. 21.

Republican party's first nominee for president, John C. Fremont, defeated. Abraham Lincoln made 50 speeches for him.

Lawrence, Kan. sacked May 21 by slavery party; abolitionist John Brown led anti-slavery men against Missourians at Osawatomie, Kan. Aug. 30

## 1857
Dred Scott decision by U.S. Supreme Court Mar. 6 held, 6-3, that a Negro slave did not become free when taken into a free state, Congress could not bar slavery from a territory, and Negroes could not be citizens.

## 1858
First Atlantic cable completed by Cyrus W. Field Aug. 5; cable failed Sept. 1. Field tried again in 1865, succeeded in 1866.

Lincoln-Douglas debates in Ilinois Aug. 21-Oct. 15.

## 1859
First commercially productive oil well, drilled near Titusville, Pa., by Edwin L. Drake Aug. 27.

Abolitionist John Brown with 21 men seized U.S. Armory at Harpers Ferry (then Va.) Oct. 16. U.S. Marines captured raiders, killing several. Brown was hanged for treason by Virginia Dec. 2.

## 1860
New England shoe-workers, 20,000, strike, win higher wages.

Abraham Lincoln, Republican, elected president in 4-way race.

First Pony Express between Sacramento, Cal. and St. Joseph, Mo. started Apr. 3; service ended Oct. 24, 1861 when first transcontinental telegraph line was completed.

## 1861
Seven southern states set up Confederate States of America Feb. 8, with Jefferson Davis as president. Confederates fired on Ft. Sumter in Charleston, S.C. Apr. 12, captured it Apr. 14.

President Lincoln called for 75,000 volunteers Apr. 15. By May, 11 states had seceded. Lincoln blockaded southern ports Apr. 19, cutting off vital exports, aid.

Confederates repelled Union forces at first Battle of Bull Run July 21.

First transcontinental telegraph was put in operation.

## 1862
Homestead Act was approved May 20; it granted free

family farms to settlers.

**Land Grant Act** approved **July 7**, providing for public land sale to benefit agricultural education; eventually led to establishment of state university systems.

Union forces were victorious in western campaigns, took **New Orleans.** Battles in East were inconclusive.

### 1863

Lincoln issues **Emancipation Proclamation** Jan. 1, freeing "all slaves in areas still in rebellion."

The entire **Mississippi River** was in Union hands by **July 4.** Union forces won a major victory at **Gettysburg, Pa. July 1-July 4.** Lincoln read his **Gettysburg Address Nov. 19.**

**Draft riots** in N.Y. City killed about 1,000, including Negroes who were hung by mobs **July 13-16.** Rioters protested provision allowing money payment in place of service. Such payments were ended 1864.

### 1864

**Gen. Sherman marched through Georgia,** taking Atlanta **Sept. 1,** Savannah **Dec. 22.**

**Sand Creek massacre** of Cheyenne and Arapaho Indians **Nov. 29** in a raid by 900 cavalrymen who killed 150-500 men, women, and children; 9 soldiers died. The tribes were awaiting surrender terms when attacked.

### 1865

**Robert E. Lee surrendered** 27,800 Confederate troops to Grant at Appomattox Court House, Va. **Apr. 9.** J.E. Johnston surrendered 31,200 to Sherman at Durham Station, N.C. **Apr. 18.** Last rebel troops surrendered **May 26.**

President **Lincoln was shot Apr. 14** by John Wilkes Booth in Ford's Theater, Washington; died the following morning. Booth was reported dead **Apr. 26.** Four assassins were hung **July 7.**

**Thirteenth Amendment,** abolishing slavery, took effect **Dec. 18.**

### 1866

First post of the **Grand Army of the Republic** formed **Apr. 6;** was a major national political force for years. Last encampment, **Aug. 31, 1949,** attended by 6 of the 16 surviving veterans.

**Ku Klux Klan** formed secretly in South to terrorize Negros who voted. Disbanded **1869-71.** A second Klan was organized **1915.**

Congress took control of southern Reconstruction, backed freedmen's rights.

### 1867

**Alaska** sold to U.S. by Russia for $7.2 million **Mar. 30** through efforts of Sec. of St. William H. Seward.

**Horatio Alger** published first book, *Ragged Dick.*

The **Grange** was organized **Dec 4,** to protect farmer interests.

### 1868

The **World Almanac,** a publication of the *New York World,* appeared for the first time.

Pres. **Andrew Johnson** tried to remove Edwin M. Stanton, secretary of war; was impeached for violation of Tenure of Office Act by House **Feb. 24;** acquitted by Senate **March-May.** Stanton resigned.

### 1869

Financial **"Black Friday"** in New York **Sept. 24;** caused by attempt to "corner" gold.

**Transcontinental railroad** completed; golden spike driven at Promontory, Utah **May 10** marking the junction of Central Pacific and Union Pacific.

**Knights of Labor** formed in Philadelphia. By **1886,** it had 700,000 members nationally.

**Woman suffrage** law passed in Territory of Wyoming **Dec. 10.**

### 1871

**Great fire destroyed** Chicago **Oct. 8-11;** loss est. at $196 million.

### 1872

**Amnesty Act** restored civil rights to citizens of the South **May 22** except for 500 Confederate leaders.

Congress founded first national park — **Yellowstone** in Wyoming.

### 1873

First U.S. **postal card** issued **May 1.**

**Banks failed,** panic began in **Sept.** Depression lasted 5 years.

**"Boss" William Tweed** of N.Y. City convicted of stealing Public funds. He died in jail in **1878.**

Bellevue Hospital in N.Y. City started the first **school of nursing.**

### 1875

Congress passed **Civil Rights Act Mar. 1** giving equal rights to Negroes in public accomodations and jury duty. Act invalidated in **1883** by Supreme Court.

First **Kentucky Derby** held **May 17** at Churchill Downs Louisville, Ky.

### 1876

**Samuel J. Tilden,** Democrat, received majority of popular votes for president over **Rutherford B. Hayes,** Republican, but 22 electoral votes were in dispute; issue left to Congress. Hayes given presidency **in Feb., 1877** after Republicans agree to end Reconstruction of South.

Col. **George A. Custer** and 264 soldiers of the 7th Cavalry killed **June 25** in "last stand," Battle of the Little Big Horn, Mont., in Sioux Indian War.

**Mark Twain** published *Tom Sawyer.*

### 1877

**Molly Maguires,** Irish society in Scranton, Pa. mining areas, broken up by hanging of 11 leaders for murders of mine officials and police.

Pres. Hayes sent troops in violent national **railroad strike.**

### 1878

First commercial **telephone** exchange opened, New Haven, Conn. **Jan. 28.**

### 1879

**F.W. Woolworth** opened his first five-and-ten store in Utica, N.Y. **Feb. 22.**

**Henry George** published *Progress & Poverty,* advocating single tax on land.

### 1881

Pres. **James A. Garfield shot** in Washington, D.C. **July 2;** died **Sept. 19.**

**Booker T. Washington** founded Tuskegee Institute for Negroes.

**Helen Hunt Jackson** published *A Century of Dishonor* about mistreatment of Indians.

### 1883

**Pendleton Act,** passed **Jan. 16,** reformed federal civil service.

**Brooklyn Bridge** opened **May 24.**

### 1886

**Haymarket riot** and bombing, evening of **May 4,** followed bitter labor battles for 8-hour day in Chicago; 7 police and 4 workers died, 66 wounded. Eight anarchists found guilty. Gov. John P. Altgeld denounced trial as unfair.

**Geronimo,** Apache Indian, finally surrendered **Sept. 4.**

**American Federation of Labor** (AFL) formed **Dec. 8** by 25 craft unions.

### 1888

**Great blizzard** in eastern U.S. **Mar. 11-14;** 400 deaths.

### 1889

**Johnstown, Pa. flood May 31;** 2,200 lives lost.

### 1890

First execution by **electrocution;** William Kemmler **Aug. 6** at Auburn Prison, Auburn, N.Y., for murder.

Battle of **Wounded Knee, S.D. Dec. 29,** the last major conflict between Indians and U.S. troops. About 200 Indian men, women, and children, and 29 soldiers were killed.

Castle Garden closed as N.Y. immigration depot; **Ellis Island** opened **Dec. 31,** closed **1954.**

**Sherman Antitrust Act** begins federal effort to curb monopolies.

**Jacob Riis** published *How the Other Half Lives,* about city slums.

### 1892

**Homestead, Pa.,** strike at Carnegie steel mills; 7 guards and 11 strikers and spectators shot to death **July 6;** unions set back.

**1893**

Financial panic began, led to 4-year depression.

**1894**

Thomas A. Edison's kinetoscope (motion pictures) (invented 1887) given first public showing Apr. 14 in N.Y. City.

Jacob S. Coxey led 500 unemployed from the Midwest into Washington, D.C. Apr. 29. Coxey was arrested for trespassing on Capitol grounds.

**1896**

William Jennings Bryan delivered "Cross of Gold" speech at Democratic National Convention in Chicago July 8.

Supreme Court, in Plessy v. Ferguson, approved racial segregation under the "separate but equal" doctrine.

**1898**

U.S. battleship Maine blown up Feb. 15 at Havana, 260 killed

U.S. blockaded Cuba Apr. 22 in aid of independence forces. Spain declared war Apr. 24. U.S. destroyed Spanish fleet in Philippines May 1, took Guam June 20.

Puerto Rico taken by U.S. July 25-Aug. 12. Spain agreed Dec. 10 to cede Philippines, Puerto Rico, and Guam, and approved independence for Cuba.

U.S. annexed independent republic of Hawaii.

**1899**

Filipino insurgents, unable to get recognition of independence from U.S., started guerrilla war Feb. 4. Crushed with capture May 23, 1901 of leader, Emilio Aguinaldo.

U.S. declared Open Door Policy to make China an open international market and to preserve its integrity as a nation.

John Dewey published School and Society, backing progressive education.

**1900**

Carry Nation, Kansas anti-saloon agitator, began raiding with hatchet.

U.S. helped suppress "Boxers" in Peking.

**1901**

Pres. William McKinley was shot Sept. 6 by an anarchist, Leon Czolgosz; died Sept. 14.

**1903**

Treaty between U.S. and Colombia to have U.S. dig Panama Canal signed Jan. 22, rejected by Colombia. Panama declared independence with U.S. support Nov. 3; recognized by Pres. Theodore Roosevelt Nov. 6. U.S., Panama signed canal treaty Nov. 18.

Wisconsin set first direct primary voting system May 23.

First automobile trip across U.S. from San Francisco to New York May 23-Aug. 1.

First successful flight in heavier-than-air mechanically propelled airplane by Orville Wright Dec. 17 near Kitty Hawk, N.C., 120 ft. in 12 seconds. Fourth flight same day by Wilbur Wright, 852 ft. in 59 seconds. Improved plane patented May 22, 1906.

Jack London published Call of the Wild.

Great Train Robbery, pioneering film, produced.

**1904**

Ida Tarbel published muckraking History of Standard Oil.

**1905**

First Rotary Club of local businessmen founded in Chicago.

**1906**

San Francisco earthquake and fire Apr. 18-19 left 452 dead, $350 million damages.

Pure Food and Drug Act and Meat Inspection Act both passed June 30.

**1907**

Financial panic and depression started Mar. 13.

First round-world cruise of U.S. "Great White Fleet"; 16 battleships, 12,000 men.

**1909**

Adm. Robert E. Peary reached North Pole Apr. 6 on 6th attempt, accompanied by Matthew Henson, a black, and 4 Eskimos.

National Conference on the Negro convened May 30, leading to founding of the National Association for the Advancement of Colored People.

**1910**

Boy Scouts of America founded Feb. 8.

**1911**

Supreme Court dissolved Standard Oil Co.

First transcontinental airplane flight (with numerous stops) by C.P. Rodgers, New York to Pasadena, Sept. 17-Nov. 5; time in air 82 hrs., 4 min.

**1912**

U.S. sent marines Aug. 14 to Nicaragua, which was in default of loans to U.S. and Europe.

**1913**

N.Y. Armory Show introduced modern art to U.S. public Feb. 17.

U.S. blockaded Mexico in support of revolutionaries.

Charles Beard published his Economic Interpretation of the Constitution.

Federal Reserve System was authorized Dec. 23, in a major reform of U.S. banking and finance.

**1914**

Ford Motor Co. raised basic wage rates from $2.40 for 9-hr. day to $5 for 8-hr. day Jan. 5.

When U.S. sailors were arrested at Tampico Apr. 9, Atlantic fleet was sent to Veracruz, occupied city.

Pres. Wilson proclaimed U.S. neutrality in the European war Aug. 4.

The Clayton Antitrust Act was passed Oct. 15, strengthening federal anti-monopoly powers.

**1915**

First telephone talk, New York to San Francisco, Jan. 25 by Alexander Graham Bell and Thomas A. Watson.

British ship Lusitania sunk May 7 by German submarine; 128 American passengers lost (Germany had warned passengers in advance). As a result of U.S. campaign, Germany issued apology and promise of payments Oct. 5. Pres. Wilson asked for a military fund increase Dec. 7.

U.S. troops landed in Haiti July 28. Haiti became a virtual U.S. protectorate under Sept. 16 treaty.

**1916**

Gen. John J. Pershing entered Mexico to pursue Francisco (Pancho) Villa, who had raided U.S. border areas. Forces withdrawn Feb. 5, 1917.

Rural Credits Act passed July 17, followed by Warehouse Act. Aug. 11; both provided financial aid to farmers.

Bomb exploded during San Francisco Preparedness Day parade July 22, killed 10. Thomas J. Mooney, labor organizer, and Warren K. Billings, shoe worker, were convicted; both pardoned in 1939.

U.S. bought Virgin Islands from Denmark Aug. 4.

U.S. established military government in the Dominican Republic Nov. 29.

Trade and loans to European Allies soared during the year.

John Dewey published Democracy in Education.

Carl Sandburg published Chicago Poems.

**1917**

Germany, suffering from British blockade, declared almost unrestricted submarine warfare Jan. 31. U.S. cut diplomatic ties with Germany Feb. 3, and formally declared war Apr. 6.

Conscription law was passed May 18. First U.S. troops arrived in Europe June 26.

The 18th (Prohibition) Amendment to the Constitution was submitted to the states by Congress Dec. 18. On Jan. 16, 1919, the 36th state (Nebraska) ratified it. Franklin D. Roosevelt, as 1932 presidential candidate, endorsed repeal; 21st Amendment repealed 18th; ratification completed Dec. 5, 1933.

## 1918

Over one million **American troops** were in Europe by **July.** War ended **Nov. 11.**

**Influenza** epidemic killed an estimated 20 million worldwide, 548,000 in U.S.

## 1919

First **transatlantic flight,** by U.S. Navy seaplane, left Rockaway, N.Y. **May 8,** stopped at Newfoundland, Azores, Lisbon **May 27.**

**Boston police strike** Sept. 9; National Guard breaks strike.

**Sherwood Anderson** published *Winesburg, Ohio.*

About 250 **alien radicals** are deported **Dec. 22.**

## 1920

In national **Red Scare,** some 2,700 Communists, anarchists, and other radicals were arrested **Jan.-May.**

Senate refused **Mar. 19** to ratify the **League of Nations** Covenant.

**Nicola Sacco,** 29, shoe factory employee and radical agitator, and **Bartolomeo Vanzetti,** 32, fish peddler and anarchist, accused of killing 2 men in Mass. payroll holdup **Apr. 15.** Found guilty 1921. A 6-year worldwide campaign for release on grounds of want of conclusive evidence and prejudice failed. Both were executed **Aug. 23, 1927.**

First regular licensed **radio broadcasting** begun **Aug. 20.**

**Wall St.,** N.Y. City, bomb explosion killed 30, injured 100, did $2 million damage **Sept. 16.**

**Sinclair Lewis'** *Main Street,* **F. Scott Fitzgerald's** *This side of Paradise* published.

## 1921

Congress sharply curbed **immigration,** set national quota system **May 19.**

Joint Congressional resolution declaring **peace with Germany, Austria, and Hungary** signed **July 2** by Pres. Harding; treaties were signed in **Aug.**

**Limitation of Armaments** Conference met in Washington **Nov. 12 to Feb. 6, 1922.** Major powers agreed to curtail naval construction, outlaw poison gas, restrict submarine attack on merchantmen, respect integrity of China. Ratified **Aug. 5, 1925.**

**Ku Klux Klan** began revival with violence against blacks in North, South, and Midwest.

## 1922

Violence during **coal-mine strike** at Herrin, Ill., **June 22-23** cost 36 lives, 21 of them non-union miners.

**Reader's Digest** founded.

## 1923

First **sound-on-film motion picture,** "Phonofilm" was shown by Lee de Forest at Rivoli Theater, N.Y. City, beginning in **April.**

## 1924

Law approved by Congress **June 15** making all **Indians citizens.**

**Nellie Tayloe Ross** elected governor of Wyoming **Nov. 9** after death of her husband **Oct. 2;** installed **Jan. 5, 1925,** first woman governor. **Miriam (Ma) Ferguson** was elected governor of Texas **Nov. 9;** installed **Jan. 20, 1925.**

**George Gershwin** wrote *Rhapsody in Blue.*

## 1925

**John T. Scopes** found guilty of having taught evolution in Dayton, Tenn. high school, fined $100 and costs **July 24.**

## 1926

Dr. **Robert H. Goddard** demonstrated practicality of **rockets Mar. 16** at Auburn, Mass. with first liquid fuel rocket; rocket traveled 184 ft. in 2.5 secs.

**Air Commerce Act** passed, providing federal aid for airlines and airports.

## 1927

About 1,000 **marines landed in China Mar. 5** to protect property in civil war. U.S. and British consulates looted by nationalists **Mar. 24.**

Capt. **Charles A. Lindberg** left Roosevelt Field, N.Y. **May 20** alone in plane Spirit of St. Louis on first New York-Paris nonstop flight. Reached Le Bourget airfield **May 21,** 3,610 miles in 33 ½ hours.

*The Jazz Singer,* with **Al Jolson,** demonstrated part-talking pictures in N.Y. City **Oct. 6.**

*Show Boat* opened in New York **Dec. 27.**

**Edvart Rolvaag** published *Giants in the Earth.*

## 1929

**"St. Valentine's Day massacre"** in Chicago **Feb. 14;** gangsters killed 7 rivals.

Farm price stability aided by **Agricultural Marketing Act,** passed **June 15.**

**Albert B. Fall,** former sec. of the interior, was convicted of accepting a bribe of $100,000 in the leasing of the **Elk Hills (Teapot Dome)** naval oil reserve; sentenced **Nov. 1** to $100,000 fine and year in prison.

**Stock Market crash Oct. 29** marked end of postwar prosperity as stock prices plummeted. Stock losses for 1929-31 estimated at $50 billion; worst American depression began.

**Thomas Wolfe** published *Look Homeward, Angel.* **William Faulkner** published *The Sound and the Fury.*

## 1930

London **Naval Reduction Treaty** signed by U.S., Britain, Italy, France, and Japan **Apr. 22;** in effect **Jan. 1, 1931;** expired **Dec. 31, 1936.**

**Hawley-Smoot Tariff** signed; rate hikes slash world trade.

## 1931

**Empire State Building** opened in N.Y. City **May 1.**

**Pearl Buck** published *The Good Earth.*

## 1932

**Reconstruction Finance Corp.** established **Jan. 22** to stimulate banking and business. Unemployment stood at 12 million.

**Charles Lindbergh Jr. kidnaped Mar. 1,** found dead **May 12.**

**Bonus March** on Washington **May 29** by World War I veterans demanding Congress pay their bonus in full. Army, under Gen. Douglas MacArthur, disbanded the marchers on Pres. Hoover's orders.

## 1933

All **banks in the U.S. were ordered closed** by Pres. Roosevelt **Mar. 6.**

In the "100 days" special session, **Mar. 9—June 16,** Congress passed **New Deal** social and economic measures.

**Gold standard dropped** by U.S.; announced by Pres. Roosevelt **Apr. 19,** ratified by Congress **June 5.**

**Prohibition ended** in the U.S. as 36th state ratified 21st Amendment **Dec. 5.**

U.S. foreswore armed intervention in **Western Hemisphere** nations **Dec. 26.**

## 1934

U.S. troops pull out of **Haiti Aug. 6.**

## 1935

Comedian **Will Rogers** and aviator Wiley Post **killed Aug. 15** in Alaska plane crash.

**Social Security Act** passed by Congress **Aug. 14.**

**Huey Long,** Senator from Louisiana and national political leader, was **assassinated Sept. 8.**

*Porgy and Bess,* **George Gershwin** opera on American Negro theme, opened **Oct. 10** in N.Y. City.

**Committee for Industrial Organization** (CIO) formed to expand industrial unionism **Nov. 9.**

## 1936

**Boulder Dam** completed.

**Margaret Mitchell** published *Gone With the Wind.*

## 1937

**Amelia Earhart Putnam,** aviator, and co-pilot Fred Noonan lost **July 2** near Howland Is. in the Pacific.

Pres. Roosevelt asks for 6 additional Supreme Court justices; "**packing**" plan defeated.

**Auto, steel labor unions** win first big contracts.

## 1938

**Naval Expansion Act** passed **May 17.**

**National minimum wage** enacted **June 28.**

**Orson Welles** radio dramatization of *War of the Worlds* caused nationwide scare **Oct. 30.**

## 1939

Pres. Roosevelt asked **defense budget hike Jan. 5, 12.**

**N.Y. World's Fair** opened **Apr. 30,** closed **Oct. 31;** reopened **May 11, 1940,** and finally closed **Oct. 21.**

Einstein alerts FDR to **A-bomb** opportunity in **Aug. 2** letter.

**U.S. declares its neutrality** in European war **Sept. 5.**

Roosevelt proclaimed a limited **national emergency Sept. 8,** an unlimited emergency **May 27, 1941.** Both ended by Pres. Truman **Apr. 28, 1952.**

**John Steinbeck** published *Grapes of Wrath.*

## 1940

U.S. authorized sale of **surplus war material** to Britain **June 3;** announced transfer of 50 overaged destroyers **Sept.3.**

First **peacetime draft** approved **Sept. 14.**

**Richard Wright** published *Native Son.*

## 1941

The **Four Freedoms** termed essential by Pres. Roosevelt in speech to Congress **Jan. 6;** freedom of speech and religion, freedom from want and fear.

**Lend-Lease Act** signed **Mar. 11,** providing $7 billion in military credits for Britain. Lend-Lease for USSR approved in **Nov.**

U.S. occupied **Iceland July 7.**

The **Atlantic Charter,** 8-point declaration of principles, issued by Roosevelt and Winston Churchill **Aug. 14.**

Japan attacked **Pearl Harbor,** Hawaii, 7:55 a.m. **Dec. 7,** 19 ships sunk or damaged, 2,300 dead. U.S. declared war on Japan **Dec. 8,** on Germany and Italy **Dec. 11** after those countries declared war.

## 1942

Federal government forcibly moved 110,000 **Japanese-Americans** (including 75,000 U.S. citizens) from West Coast to detention camps. Exclusion lasted 3 years.

Battle of **Midway June 3-6** was Japan's first major defeat.

Marines landed on **Guadalcanal Aug. 7;** last Japanese not expelled until **Feb. 9, 1943.**

U.S., Britain invaded North Africa **Nov. 8.**

First **nuclear chain reaction** (fission of uranium isotope U-235) produced at Univ. of Chicago, under physicists Arthur Compton, Enrico Fermi, others **Dec. 2.**

## 1943

All war contractors barred from **radical discrimination May 27.**

Pres. Roosevelt signed **June 10** the pay-as-you-go income tax bill. Starting **July 1** wage and salary earners were subject to a **paycheck withholding** tax.

**Race riot in Detroit June 21;** 34 dead, 700 injured. Riot in Harlem section of N.Y. City; 6 killed.

U.S. troops invaded Italy **Sept. 9.**

Marines advanced in **Gilbert Is. in Nov.**

## 1944

U.S., Allied forces invaded Europe at **Normandy June 6.**

**G.I. Bill of Rights** signed **June 22,** providing veterans benefits.

U.S. forces landed on **Leyte,** Philippines **Oct. 20.**

## 1945

**Yalta Conference** met in the Crimea, USSR, **Feb. 3-11.** Roosevelt, Churchill, and Stalin agreed Russia would enter war against Japan.

Marines landed on **Iwo Jima Feb. 19;** U.S. forces invaded **Okinawa Apr. 1.**

**Pres. Roosevelt,** 63, **died** of cerebral hemorrhage in Warm Springs, Ga. **Apr. 12.**

**Germany surrendered May 7.**

First **atomic bomb,** produced at Los Alamos, N.M., exploded at Alamogordo, N.M. **July 16.** Bomb dropped on **Hiroshima Aug. 6,** on **Nagasaki Aug. 9.** Japan surrendered **Aug. 15.**

U.S. forces entered **Korea** south of 38th parallel to displace Japanese **Sept. 8.**

**Gen. Douglas MacArthur** took over supervision of Japan **Sept. 9.**

## 1946

Strike by 400,000 **mine workers** began **Apr. 1;** other industries followed.

**Philippines** given independence by U.S. **July 4.**

## 1947

**Truman Doctrine:** Pres. Truman asked Congress to aid Greece and Turkey to combat Communist terrorism **Mar. 12.** Approved **May 15.**

United Nations Security Council voted unanimously **Apr. 2** to place under U.S. **trusteeship** the Pacific islands formerly mandated to Japan.

**Jackie Robinson** on Brooklyn Dodgers **Apr. 11,** the first black to play in major league baseball.

**Taft-Hartley** Labor Act curbing strikes was vetoed by Truman **June 20;** Congress overrode the veto.

Proposals later known as the **Marshall Plan,** under which the U.S. would extend aid to European countries, were made by Sec. of State George C. Marshall **June 5.** Congress authorized some $12 billion in next 4 years.

## 1948

USSR began a land **blockade of Berlin's** Allied sectors **Apr. 1.** This blockade and Western counter-blockade were lifted **Sept. 30, 1949,** after British and U.S. planes had lifted 2,343,315 tons of food and coal into the city.

**Organization of American States** founded **Apr. 30.**

**Alger Hiss,** former State Dept. official, indicted Dec. 15 for perjury, after denying he had passed secret documents to Whittaker Chambers for transmission to a communist spy ring. His second trial ended in conviction **Jan. 21, 1950,** and a sentence of 5 years in prison.

**Kinsey Report** on Sexuality in the Human Male published.

## 1949

North Atlantic Treaty Organization **(NATO)** established **Mar. 18** by U.S., Canada, and 10 West European nations, agreeing that "an armed attack against one or more of them in Europe and North America shall be considered an attack against all."

U.S. troops withdrawn from **Korea June 29.**

Mrs. I. Toguri D'Aquino **(Tokyo Rose** of Japanese wartime broadcasts) was sentenced **Oct. 7** to 10 years in prison for treason. Paroled **1956,** pardoned **1977.**

Eleven leaders of U.S. **Communist party** convicted **Oct. 14,** after 9-month trial in N.Y. City, of advocating violent overthrow of U.S. government. Ten defendants sentenced to 5 years in prison each and the 11th, to 3 years. Supreme Court upheld the convictions **June 4, 1951.**

## 1950

U.S. **Jan 14** recalled all consular officials from **China** after the latter seized the American consulate general in Peking.

Masked bandits robbed **Brink's Inc.,** Boston express office, **Jan. 17** of $2.8 million, of which $1.2 million was in cash. Case solved **1956,** 8 sentenced to life.

United Nations asked for troops to restore Korea peace **June 25.**

Pres. Truman authorized **hydrogen bomb Jan. 31.**

Truman ordered Air Force and Navy to Korea **June 27** after North Korea invaded South. Truman approved ground forces, air strikes against North **June 30.**

U.S. sent 35 military advisers to **South Vietnam June 27,** and agreed to provide military and economic aid to anti-Communist government.

**Army seized all railroads Aug. 27** on Truman's order to prevent a general strike; roads returned to owners in **1952.**

**U.S. forces landed at Inchon Sept. 15;** UN force took Pyongyang **Oct. 20,** reached China border **Nov. 20,** China sent troops across border **Nov. 26.**

Two members of a **Puerto Rican nationalist** movement tried to kill Pres. Truman Nov. 1. (See Assassinations)

U.S. **Dec. 8** banned shipments to **Communist China** and to Asiatic ports trading with it.

### 1951

Sen. **Estes Kefauver** led Senate investigation into organized crime. Preliminary report **Feb. 28** said gambling take was over $20 billion a year.

**Julius Rosenberg,** his wife, Ethel, and Morton Sobell, all U.S. citizens, were found guilty **Mar. 29** of conspiracy to commit wartime espionage. Rosenbergs sentenced to death, Sobell to 30 years. Rosenbergs **executed June 19, 1953.** Sobell released **Jan. 14, 1969.**

Gen. **Douglas MacArthur** was removed from his Korea command **Apr. 11** for making unauthorized policy statements.

Korea cease-fire talks began in July; lasted 2 years. Fighting ended July 27, 1953.

**Tariff** concessions by the U.S. to the Soviet Union, Communist China, and all communist-dominated lands were suspended **Aug. 1.**

The U.S., **Australia,** and **New Zealand** signed a mutual security pact **Sept. 1.**

**Transcontinental television** inaugurated **Sept. 4** with Pres. Truman's address at the Japanese Peace Treaty Conference in San Francisco.

**Japanese Peace Treaty** signed in San Francisco **Sept. 8** by U.S., Japan, and 47 other nations.

**J.D. Salinger** published *Catcher in the Rye.*

### 1952

U.S. **seizure of nation's steel mills** was ordered by Pres. Truman **Apr. 8** to avert a strike. Ruled illegal by Supreme Court **June 2.**

**Peace contract** between West Germany, U.S., Great Britain, and France was signed **May 26.**

**Puerto Rico** became an "associated free state" or commonwealth of the U.S. **July 25** after Truman gave approval to a new constitution.

First **hydrogen device** explosion **Nov. 1** at Eniwetok Atoll in Pacific.

### 1953

Pres. Eisenhower announced **May 8** that U.S. had given France $60 million for **Indochina War.** More aid was announced in Sept. In 1954 it was reported that three fourths of the war's costs were met by U.S.

### 1954

**Nautilus,** first atomic-powered submarine, was launched at Groton, Conn. **Jan. 21.**

Five members of Congress were wounded in the House **Mar. 1** by 4 **Puerto Rican independence supporters** who fired at random from a spectators' gallery.

Sen. **Joseph McCarthy** led televised hearings **Apr. 22-June 17** into alleged Communist influence in the Army.

**Racial segregation** in public schools was unanimously ruled unconstitutional by the Supreme Court **May 17,** as a violation of the 14th Amendment clause guaranteeing equal protection of the laws.

**Southeast Asia Treaty Organization (SEATO)** formed by collective defense pact signed in Manila **Sept. 8** by the U.S., Britain, France, Australia, New Zealand, Philippines, Pakistan, and Thailand.

Condemnation of Sen. **Joseph R. McCarthy** (R. Wis.) voted by Senate, 67-22 **Dec. 2** for contempt of a Senate elections subcommittee, for abuse of its members, and for insults to the Senate during his Army investigation hearings.

### 1955

U.S. agreed **Feb. 12** to help train **South Vietnamese** army.

Supreme Court ordered **"all deliberate speed"** in integration of public schools **May 31.**

A **summit meeting** of leaders of U.S., Britain, France, and USSR took place **July 18-23** in Geneva, Switzerland.

**Rosa Parks** refused **Dec. 1** to give her seat to a white man on a bus in Montgomery, Ala. Bus segregation ordinance

declared unconstitutional by a federal court following boycott and NAACP protest.

**Merger** of America's 2 largest labor organizations was effected **Dec. 5** under the name American Federation of Labor and Congress of Industrial Organizations. The merged **AFL-CIO** had a membership estimated at 15 million.

### 1956

**Massive resistance** to Supreme Court desegregation rulings was called for **Mar. 12** by 101 Southern congressmen.

**Federal-Aid Highway Act** signed **June 29,** inaugurating interstate highway system.

First transatlantic **telephone cable** went into operation **Sept. 25.**

### 1957

Congress approved first **civil rights bill** for Negroes since Reconstruction **Apr. 29,** to protect voting rights.

National Guardsmen, called out by Arkansas Gov. Orval Faubus **Sept. 4,** barred 9 Negro students from entering previously all-white Central High School in **Little Rock.** Faubus complied **Sept. 21** with a federal court order to remove the National Guardsmen. The Negroes entered school **Sept. 23** but were ordered to withdraw by local authorities because of fear of mob violence. Pres. Eisenhower sent federal troops **Sept. 24** to enforce the court's order.

**Jack Kerouac** published *On the Road,* beatnik journal.

### 1958

First U.S. earth satellite to go into orbit, **Explorer I,** launched by Army **Jan. 31** at Cape Canaveral, Fla.; discovered Van Allen radiation belt.

Five thousand U.S. Marines sent to **Lebanon** to protect elected government from threatened overthrow **July-Oct.**

First domestic **jet airline** passenger service in U.S. opened by National Airlines **Dec. 10** between New York and Miami.

### 1959

**Alaska** admitted as 49th state **Jan. 3; Hawaii** admitted **Aug. 21.**

**St. Lawrence Seaway** opened **Apr. 25.**

**The George Washington,** first U.S. ballistic-missile submarine, launched at Groton, Conn. **June 9.**

**N.S. Savannah,** world's first atomic-powered merchant ship, launched **July 21** at Camden, N.J.

Soviet Premier **Khrushchev** paid unprecedented visit to U.S. **Sept. 15-27,** made transcontinental tour.

### 1960

A wave of **sit-ins** began **Feb. 1** when 4 Negro college students in Greensboro, N.C. refused to move from a Woolworth lunch counter when they were denied service. By **Sept. 1961** more than 70,000 students, whites and blacks, had participated in sit-ins.

U.S. launched first **weather satellite,** Tiros I, **Apr. 1.**

Congress approved a strong **voting rights act Apr. 21.**

A **U-2 reconnaisance plane** of the U.S. was shot down in the Soviet Union **May 1.** The incident led to cancellation of an imminent Paris summit conference.

Mobs attacked U.S. embassy in **Panama Sept. 17** in dispute over flying of U.S. and Panamanian flags.

U.S. announced **Dec. 15** it backed rightist group in **Laos,** which took power the next day.

### 1961

The U.S. severed diplomatic and consular relations with **Cuba Jan. 3,** after disputes over nationalizations of U.S. firms, U.S. military presence at Guantanamo base, etc.

Invasion of Cuba's "Bay of Pigs" **Apr. 17** by Cuban exiles trained, armed, and directed by the U.S., attempting to overthrow the regime of Premier Fidel Castro, was repulsed.

**Commander Alan B. Shepard Jr.** was rocketed from Cape Canaveral, Fla., 116.5 mi. above the earth in a Mercury capsule **May 5** in the first U.S. manned sub-orbital space flight.

### 1962

**Lt. Col. John H. Glenn Jr.** became the first American in orbit **Feb. 20** when he circled the earth 3 times in the Mercury capsule **Friendship 7.**

Pres. Kennedy said **Feb. 14** U.S. military advisers in Vietnam would fire if fired upon.

Supreme Court **Mar. 26** backed **one-man one-vote** apportionment of seats in state legislatures.

First U.S. **communications satellite** launched in **July.**

The **largest cash robbery** to date in U.S. history occurred **Aug. 14** when a gang held up a U.S. mail truck near Plymouth, Mass., and stole $1,551,277.

**James Meredith** became first black student at Univ. of Mississippi **Oct. 1** after 3,000 troops put down riots.

A Soviet **offensive missile buildup in Cuba** was revealed **Oct. 22** by Pres. Kennedy, who ordered a naval and air quarantine on shipment of offensive military equipment to the island. Kennedy and Soviet Premier Khrushchev reached agreement **Oct. 28** on a formula to end the crisis. Kennedy announced **Nov. 2** that Soviet missile bases in Cuba were being dismantled.

**Rachel Carson's** *Silent Spring* launched environmentalist movement.

### 1963

Supreme Court ruled **Mar. 18** that all **criminal defendants** must have counsel and that illegally acquired evidence was not admissible in state as well as federal courts.

Supreme Court ruled, 8-1, **June 17** that laws requiring **recitation of the Lord's Prayer** or Bible verses in public schools were unconstitutional.

A limited **nuclear test-ban treaty** was agreed upon **July 25** by the U.S., Soviet Union and Britain, barring all nuclear tests except underground.

Washington demonstration by 200,000 persons **Aug. 28** in support of **Negro demands** for equal rights. Highlight was speech in which Dr. Martin Luther King said: "I have a dream that this nation will rise up and live out the true meaning of its creed, 'We hold these truths to be self-evident: that all men are created equal.' "

South Vietnam Pres. **Ngo Dinh Diem assassinated Nov. 2**; U.S. had earlier withdrawn support.

Pres. **John F. Kennedy was shot** and fatally wounded by an assassin **Nov. 22** as he rode in a motorcade through downtown Dallas, Tex. Vice Pres. Lyndon B. Johnson was inaugurated president shortly after in Dallas. Lee Harvey Oswald was arrested and charged with the murder. Oswald was shot and fatally wounded **Nov. 24** by Jack Ruby, 52, a Dallas nightclub owner, who was convicted of murder **Mar. 14, 1964** and sentenced to death. Ruby died of natural causes **Jan. 3, 1967** while awaiting retrial.

U.S. troops in **Vietnam** totalled over 15,000 by year-end; aid to South Vietnam was over $500 million in **1963.**

### 1964

**Panama** suspended relations with U.S. **Jan. 9** after riots. U.S. offered **Dec. 18** to negotiate a new canal treaty.

Supreme Court ordered **Feb. 17** that **congressional districts** have equal populations.

U.S. reported **May 27** it was sending military planes to **Laos.**

Omnibus **civil rights bill** passed **June 29** banning discrimination in voting, jobs, public accomodations, etc.

Three **civil rights workers** were reported missing in Mississippi **June 22**; found buried **Aug. 4.** Twenty-one white men were arrested. On **Oct. 20, 1967**, an all-white federal jury convicted 7 of conspiracy in the slayings.

U.S. Congress **Aug. 7** passed **Tonkin Resolution**, authorizing presidential action in Vietnam, after North Vietnam boats reportedly attacked 2 U.S. destroyers **Aug. 2.**

Congress approved War on Poverty bill **Aug. 11.**

The **Warren Commission** released **Sept. 27** a report concluding that Lee Harvey Oswald was solely responsible for the Kennedy assassination.

### 1965

Pres. Johnson in **Feb.** ordered continuous **bombing of North Vietnam** below 20th parallel.

Some 14,000 U.S. troops sent to **Dominican Republic** during civil war **Apr. 28.** All troops withdrawn by following year.

New **Voting Rights Act** signed **Aug. 6.**

Los Angeles riot by blacks living in **Watts** area resulted in death of 35 persons and property damage est. at $200 million **Aug. 11-16.**

**Water Quality Act** passed **Sept. 21** to meet pollution, shortage problems.

National origins quota system of **immigration** abolished **Oct. 3.**

Massive **electric power failure** blacked out most of northeasten U.S, parts of 2 Canadian provinces the night of **Nov. 9-10.**

U.S. forces in **South Vietnam** reached 184,300 by year-end.

### 1966

U.S. forces began firing into **Cambodia May 1.**

**Bombing of Hanoi** area of North Vietnam by U.S. planes began **June 29.** By **Dec. 31**, 385,300 U.S. troops were stationed in South Vietnam, plus 60,000 offshore and 33,000 in Thailand.

**Medicare,** government program to pay part of the medical expenses of citizens over 65, began **July 1.**

**Edward Brooke** (R, Mass.) elected **Nov. 8** as first Negro U.S. senator in 85 years.

### 1967

Black representative **Adam Clayton Powell** (D, N.Y.) was denied **Mar. 1** his seat in Congress because of charges he misused government funds. Reelected in 1968, he was seated, but fined $25,000 and stripped of his 22 years' seniority.

Massive **tariff cuts** were approved **May 15** by 53 countries.

Pres. Johnson and Soviet Premier Aleksei Kosygin met **June 23 and 25** at **Glassboro State College** in N.J.; agreed not to let any crisis push them into war.

Black riots in **Newark, N.J. July 12-17** killed some 26, injured 1,500; over 1,000 arrested. In Detroit, Mich., **July 23-30** at least 40 died; 2,000 injured, and 5,000 left homeless by rioting, looting, burning in city's black ghetto. Quelled by 4,700 federal paratroopers and 8,000 National Guardsmen.

**Thurgood Marshall** sworn in **Oct. 2** as first black U.S. Supreme Court Justice. Carl B. Stokes (D, Cleveland) and Richard G. Hatcher (D, Gary, Ind.) were elected first black mayors of major U.S. cities **Nov. 7.**

By December 475,000 U.S. troops were in **South Vietnam**, all North Vietnam was subject to bombing. Protests against the war mounted in U.S. during year.

### 1968

USS Pueblo and 83-man crew seized in Sea of Japan **Jan. 23** by North Koreans; 82 men released **Dec. 22.**

**"Tet offensive":** Communist troops attacked Saigon, 30 province capitals **Jan. 30,** suffer heavy casualties.

Pres. Johnson **curbed bombing** of North Vietnam **Mar. 31.** Peace talks began in Paris **May 10.** All bombing of North is halted **Oct. 31.**

**Martin Luther King Jr., 39, assassinated Apr. 4** in Memphis, Tenn. James Earl Ray, an escaped convict, pleaded guilty to the slaying, was sentenced to 99 years.

**Sen. Robert F. Kennedy** (D, N.Y.) 42, **shot June 5** in Hotel Ambassador, Los Angeles, after celebrating presidential primary victories. Died **June 6.** Sirhan Bishara Sirhan, Jordanian, convicted of murder.

### 1969

Expanded four-party **Vietnam peace talks** began **Jan. 18.** U.S. force peaked at 543,400 in April. Withdrawal started **July 8.** Pres. Nixon set Vietnamization policy **Nov. 3.**

Unarmed **U.S. reconnaissance plane,** with 31 aboard, shot down by North Korean jets **Apr. 15** in the Sea of Japan about 100 mi. from the mainland. No survivors found.

A car driven by Sen. **Edward M. Kennedy** (D, Mass.) plunged off a bridge into a tidal pool on Chappaquiddick Is., Martha's Vineyard, Mass. **July 18.** The body of Mary Jo Kopechne, a 28-year-old secretary, was found drowned in the car.

U.S. astronaut Neil A. Armstrong, 38, commander of the Apollo 11 mission, became the first man to set foot on the moon July 20. Air Force Col. Edwin E. Aldrin Jr. accompanied Armstrong.

Anti-Vietnam War demonstrations reached peak in U.S.; some 250,000 marched in Washington, D.C. Nov. 15.

Massacre of hundreds of civilians at Mylai, South Vietnam, in 1968 incident is reported Nov. 16.

## 1970

United Mine Workers official Joseph A. Yablonski, his wife, and their daughter were found shot Jan. 5 in their Clarksville, Pa. home. UMW chief W. A. (Tony) Boyle was later convicted of the killing.

A federal jury Feb. 18 found the defendants in the "Chicago 7" trial innocent of conspiring to incite riots during the 1968 Democratic National Convention. However, 5 were convicted of crossing state lines with intent to incite riots.

Millions of Americans participated in anti-pollution demonstrations Apr. 22 to mark the first Earth Day.

U.S. and South Vietnamese forces crossed Cambodian borders Apr. 30 to get at enemy bases. Four students were killed May 4 at Kent St. Univ. in Ohio by National Guardsmen during a protest against the war.

Two women generals, the first in U.S. history, were named by Pres. Nixon May 15.

A postal reform measure was signed Aug. 12, creating an independent U.S. Postal Service, thus relinquishing governmental control of the U.S. mails after almost 2 centuries.

## 1971

Charles Manson, 36, and 3 of his followers were found guilty Jan. 26 of first-degree murder in the 1969 slaying of actress Sharon Tate and 6 others.

U.S. air and artillery forces aided a 44-day incursion by South Vietnam forces into Laos starting Feb. 8.

A treaty prohibiting installation of nuclear weapons on the seabed beyond any nation's 12-mi. coastal zone was signed by 63 nations Feb. 11.

A Constitutional Amendment lowering the voting age to 18 in all elections was approved in the Senate by a vote of 94-0 Mar. 10. The proposed 26th Amendment got House approval by a 400-19 vote Mar. 23. Thirty-eighth state ratified June 30.

A court-martial jury of 6 officers Mar. 29, after 13 days deliberation, convicted Lt. William L. Calley Jr. of premeditated murder of 22 South Vietnamese at Mylai on Mar. 16, 1968. He was sentenced to life imprisonment Mar. 31. Sentence was reduced to 20 years Aug. 20, 1971.

Amtrak, the nation's new rail passenger system, went into operation May 1 with the goal to "get people back on trains."

Publication of classified Pentagon papers on the U.S. involvement in Vietnam was begun June 13 by the New York Times. In a 6-3 vote, the U.S. Supreme Court June 30 upheld the right of the Times and the Washington Post to publish the documents under the protection of the First Amendment.

U.S., Japan signed treaty June 17 for return of Okinawa I., seized during World War II.

Pres. Nixon began a sweeping new economic program Aug. 15 imposing a 90-day wage, price, and rent freeze. He also devalued the dollar by cutting its tie with gold.

More than 1,000 N.Y. State troopers and police stormed the Attica State Correctional Facility where 1,200 inmates held 38 guards hostage Sept. 13, ending a 4-day rebellion in the maximum-security prison; 9 hostages, 28 convicts killed in the assault.

U.S. bombers struck massively in North Vietnam for 5 days starting Dec. 26, in retaliation for alleged violations of agreements reached prior to the 1968 bombing halt. U.S. forces at year-end were down to 140,000.

## 1972

Pres. Nixon arrived in Peking Feb. 21 for an 8-day visit to China, which he called a "journey for peace." The unprece-

dented visit ended with a joint communique pledging that both powers would work for "a normalization of relations."

By a vote of 84 to 8, the Senate approved Mar. 22 a Constitutional Amendment banning discrimination against women because of their sex and sent the measure to the states for ratification.

North Vietnamese forces launched the biggest attacks in 4 years across the demilitarized zone Mar. 30. The U.S. responded Apr. 15 by resumption of bombing of Hanoi and Haiphong after a 4-year lull.

Nixon announced May 8 the mining of North Vietnam ports. Last U.S. combat troops left Aug. 11.

Alabama Gov. George C. Wallace, campaigning at a Laurel, Md. shopping center May 15, was shot and seriously wounded as he greeted a large crowd. Arthur H. Bremer, 21, was sentenced Aug. 4 to 63 years for shooting Wallace and 3 bystanders.

In the first visit of a U.S. president to Moscow, Nixon arrived May 22 for a week of summit talks with Kremlin leaders which culminated in a landmark strategic arms pact.

The Environmental Protection Agency announced June 14 a near-total ban on agricultural and other uses of the pesticide DDT, to be effective Dec. 31.

Five men were arrested June 17 for breaking into the offices of the Democratic National Committee in the Watergate office complex in Washington, D.C.

The White House announced July 8 that the U.S. would sell to the USSR at least $750 million of American wheat, corn, and other grains over a period of 3 years. But the USSR bought most of it in 1st year.

Less than 2 weeks after Sen. Thomas F. Eagleton received the Democratic vice-presidential nomination, he confirmed July 25 reports that he had undergone electroshock therapy on 2 occasions years before. He withdrew as the nominee July 31.

By a vote of 88-2, the Senate Aug. 3 ratified the strategic arms treaty limiting the U.S. and Russia to 2 antiballistic missile sites each and curbing land and submarine missile forces.

Life ended publication with its Dec. 29 issue after 36 years as the leading weekly pictorial magazine.

## 1973

Five of seven defendants in the Watergate break-in trial pleaded guilty Jan. 11 and 15, and the other 2 were convicted Jan. 30.

All state laws that limited a woman's right to an abortion during the first 3 months of pregnancy were overturned Jan. 22 by the U.S. Supreme Court 7-2.

Four-party Vietnam peace pacts were signed in Paris Jan. 27, and North Vietnam released some 590 U.S. prisoners by Apr. 1. Last U.S. troops left Mar. 29.

The end of the military draft was announced Jan. 27 by Defense Sec. Melvin R. Laird.

China and the U.S. agreed Feb. 22 to set up permanent liaison offices in each other's country.

Some 200-300 members of the militant American Indian Movement Feb. 27 seized the trading post and church at historic Wounded Knee on the Oglala Sioux Reservation in South Dakota. The insurgents demanded that the U.S. Senate Foreign Relations Committee hold hearings on treaties made with Indians, and that the Senate start a "full-scale investigation" of government treatment of Indians. The hamlet was evacuated May 8.

Top Nixon aides H.R. Haldeman, John D. Ehrlichman, and John W. Dean, and Attorney General Richard Kleindienst resigned Apr. 30 amid charges of White House efforts to obstruct justice in the Watergate case.

Soviet leader Leonid Brezhnev visited the U.S. June 16-25, and signed 9 cooperation agreements with the U.S.

The Federal Trade Commission July 9 charged 8 of the largest U.S. oil companies with conspiracy to monopolize the refining of petroleum products. The commission said the conspiracy had led to shortages of gasoline and higher prices, and caused some independent marketers to close down.

The Senate Armed Services Committee **July 16** began a probe into allegations that the U.S. Air Force had made 3,500 secret **B-52 raids into Cambodia** in 1969 and 1970.

**John Dean,** former Nixon counsel, told Senate hearings **June 25** that Nixon, his staff and campaign aides, and the Justice Department all had conspired to cover up Watergate facts. Nixon refused July 23 to release **tapes** of relevant White House conversations. Some tapes were turned over to the court **Nov. 26.**

The U.S. officially ceased bombing in **Cambodia** at midnight **Aug. 14** in accord with a June Congressional action.

Pres. Nixon's 1972 **campaign finance** aides revealed **Sept. 28** that campaign fund raisers had collected a record $60.2 million.

Vice Pres. **Spiro T. Agnew Oct. 10 resigned** and pleaded "nolo contendere" (no contest) to charges of tax evasion on payments made to him by Maryland contractors. Agnew was sentenced to 3 years probation and fined $10,000. Gerald Ford Dec. 6 became the first appointed vice president under the 25th Amendment.

A total ban on **oil exports** to the U.S. was imposed by Arab oil-producing nations **Oct. 19-21** after the outbreak of an Arab-Israeli war. The ban was lifted **Mar. 18, 1974.**

Atty. Gen. **Elliot Richardson** resigned, and his deputy William D. Ruckelshaus and Watergate Special Prosecutor Archibald Cox were fired by Pres. Nixon **Oct. 20** when Cox threatened to secure a judicial ruling that Nixon was violating a court order to turn tapes over to Watergate case Judge John Sirica.

The U.S. **Oct. 25** placed its military forces on a worldwide "precautionary alert" because of reported USSR plans to send a Russian force to the Middle East. A 7,000-man UN peace-keeping force was approved **Oct. 27.**

**Leon Jaworski,** conservative Texas Democrat, was named **Nov. 1** by the Nixon administration to be special prosecutor to succeed Archibald Cox.

Congress overrode **Nov. 7** Nixon's veto of the **war powers** bill which curbed the president's power to commit armed forces to hostilities abroad without Congressional approval.

**Alaska pipeline** bill, permitting construction of 789-mi. pipe from Alaska's North Shore oilfield to port of Valdez, signed **Nov. 16.**

**Gerald Rudolph Ford** was sworn in **Dec. 6** as 40th vice president, the first who was not elected, under 25th Amendment.

### 1974

U.S. **oil companies reported huge profits** for the 4th quarter of 1973, during the Arab oil embargo, in their **Jan. 1974** reports. Exxon profits were up 59% over the same period in 1972; Mobil, 68%; Texaco, 70%; Ashland, 52%.

**Herbert W. Kalmbach,** Pres. Nixon's personal lawyer and fundraiser, pleaded guilty **Feb. 25** to promising a contributor an ambassadorship for a $100,000 contribution.

Arab nations ended their **oil embargo** against the U.S. **Mar. 18.**

Nixon said **Apr. 3** he would pay $432,787.13 **in back taxes** plus interest for 1969 through 1972, after a Joint Congressional Committee, acting on his request, found him liable.

**Impeachment** hearings were opened **May 9** against Nixon by the House Judiciary Committee.

Ex-Atty. Gen. **Richard G. Kleindienst** pleaded guilty May 16 to a misdemeaner charge that he did not testify accurately and fully before a Congressional committee probing handling of an ITT anti-trust settlement.

John D. Ehrlichman and 3 **White House "plumbers"** were found guilty **July 12** of conspiring to violate the civil rights of Dr. Lewis Feilding, formerly psychiatrist to Pentagon Papers leaker Daniel Ellsberg, by breaking into his Beverly Hills, Cal. office.

The U.S. Supreme Court ruled, 8-0, **July 24** that Nixon had to turn over **64 tapes** of White House conversations sought by Watergate Special Prosecutor Leon Jaworski.

The House Judiciary Committee, in televised hearings **July 24-30,** recommended 3 **articles of impeachment** against Nixon. The first, voted 27-11 **July 27,** charged Nixon with taking part in a criminal conspiracy to obstruct justice in the Watergate cover-up. The second, voted 28-10 **July 29,** charged he "repeatedly" failed to carry out his constitutional oath in a series of alleged abuses of power. The third, voted 27-17 **July 30,** accused him of unconstitutional defiance of committee subpoenas. The House of Representatives voted without debate **Aug. 20,** by 412-3, to accept the committee report, which included the recommended impeachment articles.

Ex-presidential counsel **John W. Dean 3d** was sentenced **Aug. 2** to 1-3 years, on his plea of guilty of conspiring to obstruct justice.

**Nixon resigned Aug. 9** His support began eroding **Aug. 5** when he released 3 tapes, admitting he originated plans to have the FBI stop its probe of the Watergate break-in for political as well as national security reasons.

An **unconditional pardon** to ex-Pres. Nixon for all federal crimes that he "committed or may have committed" while president was issued by Pres. Gerald Ford **Sept. 8.**

A **Boston school busing** plan for racial integration was met with violent protest by whites starting **Sept. 12.** The court-ordered plan was rejected by the Boston School Committee **Dec. 16,** 3-2; 3 members were fined for contempt.

Charges that the Central Intelligence Agency **(CIA)** abused its powers by massive domestic operations were published **Dec. 21.**

### 1975

Found guilty of **Watergate** cover-up charges **Jan. 1** were ex-Atty. Gen. John N. Mitchell, ex-presidential advisers H.R. Haldeman and John D. Ehrlichman.

U.S. civilians were evacuated from **Saigon Apr. 29** as communist forces completed takeover of South Vietnam.

U.S. merchant ship **Mayaguez** and crew of 39 seized by Cambodian forces in Gulf of Siam **May 12.** In rescue operation, U.S. Marines attacked Tang Is., planes bombed air base; Cambodia surrendered ship and crew; U.S. losses were 15 killed in battle and 23 dead in a helicopter crash.

Congress voted $405 million for South **Vietnam refugees May 16;** 140,000 were flown to the U.S.

Gulf Oil Corp. admitted **May 16** it had paid $5 million in **illegal gifts** to foreign politicians; many other large U.S. corporations admitted making gifts and bribes to do business in foreign countries.

U.S. **unemployment** reached 9.2%, the Labor Dept. reported **June 6.**

Illegal **CIA operations,** including records on 300,000 persons and groups, infiltration of agents into black, anti-war and political movements, monitoring of overseas phone calls, mail surveillance, and drug-testing, were described by a "blue-ribbon" panel headed by Vice Pres. Rockefeller **June 10.** Information on assassination plots against foreign leaders was ordered withheld by Pres. Ford.

**N.Y. City default** on notes was avoided **June 10** by creation of a state Municipal Assistance Corp. to refinance $3 billion in loans.

A U.S. **Apollo** and a USSR **Soyuz** linked together 140 mi. above the Atlantic **July 17.** The crews exchanged visits and shared meals in the 2 crafts.

**James R. Hoffa,** Teamsters Union ex-president, disappeared **July 30.** The FBI entered the search **Aug. 3.**

Two **assassination attempts** against Pres. Ford, by women in California, failed **Sept. 5** and **22.**

**William L. Calley's** court-martial conviction for the murder of 22 Vietnamese, overturned in lower courts, was reinstated by the U.S. Court of Appeals in New Orleans **Sept. 10.**

Mother Elizabeth Bayley Seton was canonized as the Catholic Church's first U.S.-born saint, by Pope Paul VI **Sept. 10.**

FBI agents captured **Patricia (Patty) Hearst,** kidnaped **Feb. 4, 1974,** in San Francisco **Sept. 18** with others. She was indicated for bank robbery; a San Francisco jury convicted her **Mar. 20, 1976.**

The Senate Committee on Intelligence reported **Nov. 20** that the **CIA had instigated death plots** against Cuba's Fidel Castro, Patrice Lumumba of the Congo (now Zaire), South Vietnam's Ngo Dinh Diem, the Dominican Republic's Rafael Trujillo, and Gen. Rene Schneider, Chile's chief of staff. All but Castro were killed but the committee said there was no evidence the deaths resulted from the CIA plots.

An end of covert military aid to factions in the **Angolan civil war** backed by the U.S. was voted **Dec. 19** by the U.S. Senate after revelations that the U.S. had sent $25 million in arms aid to the groups. The Soviet-backed faction claimed victory in the war **Feb. 12, 1976.**

**1976**

**Payments abroad** of $22 million in bribes by Lockheed Aircraft Corp. to sell its planes were revealed **Feb. 4** by a Senate subcommittee. Lockheed admitted payments in Japan, Turkey, Italy, and Holland.

A mechanical respirator that had been keeping **Karen Anne Quinlan,** 22, alive for 11 months could be turned off, the New Jersey Supreme Court ruled **Mar. 31;** her parents had asked the ruling so that Karen might die "with grace and dignity." The respirator was disconnected but Karen did not die.

Multi-millionaire **Howard Hughes,** 70, died **Apr. 5** en route by plane to a hospital. An autopsy blamed kidney failure.

**Cadet cheating** on exams at West Point was more widespread than previously reported, the U.S. Military Academy admitted **May 23;** the scandal involved possibly 70 to 90 cadets in addition to the 50 convicted **Apr. 22.**

The U.S. celebrated its **Bicentennial July 4,** marking the 200th anniversary of its independence with festivals, parades, and N.Y. City's Operation Sail, a gathering of tall ships from around the world viewed by 6 million persons.

A mystery ailment **"legionnaire's disease"** killed 29 prsons who attended an American Legion convention **July 21-24** in Philadelphia. The cause was found to be a bacterium, it was reported **June 18, 1977.**

The **Viking II** lander set down on **Mars'** Utopia Plains **Sept. 3,** following the successful landing by Viking I July

**20.** Photographs and other reports sent to earth by the unmanned craft showed rocks, reddish soil, light blue skies; there was evidence of possibly biological activity, and it appeared that Mars' north polar cap was frozen water.

A nationwide program of **swine flu** vaccinations was halted **Oct. 12** following the deaths of several persons after receiving the shots. The program had been launched **Mar. 24** by Pres. Ford after government scientists warned of a possible recurrence of the flu pandemic of **1918-19.**

**1977**

Pres. Jimmy Carter **Jan. 27** pardoned most Vietnam War **draft evaders,** who numbered some 10,000.

A **natural gas shortage** caused by severe winter weather led Congress **Feb. 2** to approve an emergency federal allocation program.

Convicted murderer **Gary Gilmore** was executed by a Utah firing squad **Jan. 17,** in the first exercise of capital punishment anywhere in the U.S. since **1967.** Gilmore had opposed all attempts to delay the execution.

The Food and Drug Administration **Mar. 9** said it would seek to ban the artificial sweetener **saccharin.** The FDA proposed a more limited curb **Apr. 14,** bowing to public complaints.

The Teamsters and **Farm Workers** unions signed a California jurisdictional pact ending ten years of disputes **Mar. 11.**

Pres. Carter announced **June 30** that he was dropping the **B-1 strategic bomber** program as costly and unnecessary.

A 25-hour **blackout hit N.Y. City** and some suburbs July 13-14; looting and vandalism resulted in losses of millions of dollars.

Carter signed an act **Aug. 4** creating a new Cabinet-level **Energy Department.**

David Berkowitz, suspected of being the **"Son of Sam"** who murdered 6 young people in a year-long series of random attacks in N.Y. City, was arrested **Aug. 10** in Yonkers, N.Y.

Carter announced **Sept. 21** that budget director **Bert Lance,** a personal friend, had resigned due to pressure over his disputed private financial practices.

For events of 1978 and late 1977,
see Chronology

## Paleontology: The History of Life

All dates are approximate, and are subject to change based on new fossil finds or new dating techniques; but the sequence of events is generally accepted. Dates are in years before the present.

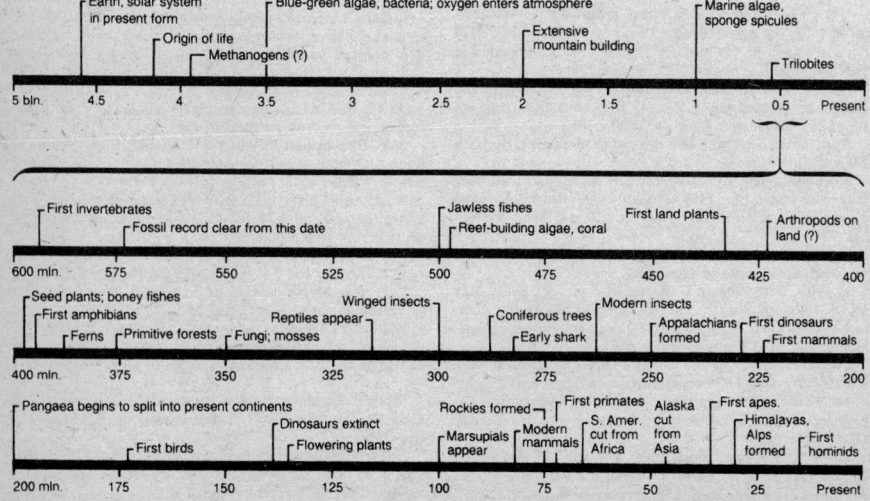

## Prehistory: Our Ancestors Take Over

*Homo sapiens.* The precise origins of *homo sapiens,* the species to which all humans belong, are subject to broad speculation based on a small number of fossils, genetic and anatomical studies, and the geological record. But nearly all scientists agree that we evolved from ape-like primate ancestors in a process that began millions of years ago.

Current theories say the first hominid (human-like primate) was *Ramapithecus,* who emerged 12 million years ago. Its remains have been found in Asia, Europe, and Africa. Further development was apparently limited to Africa, where 2 lines of hominids appeared some 5 or 6 million years ago. One was *Australopithecus,* a tool-maker and social animal, who lived from at least 3 to 2 million years ago, and then apparently became extinct.

The 2nd was a human line, *Homo habillus,* a large-brained specimen that walked upright and had a dextrous hand. *Homo habillus* lived in semi-permanent camps and had a food-gathering and sharing economy.

*Homo erectus,* our nearest ancestor, appeared in Africa perhaps 1.75 million years ago, and began spreading into Asia and Europe soon after. It had a fairly large brain and a skeletal structure similar to ours. *Homo erectus* learned to control fire, and probably had primitive language skills. The final brain development to *Homo sapiens* and then to our sub-species *Homo sapiens sapiens* occurred between 500,000 and 50,000 years ago, over a wide geographic area and in many different steps and recombinations. All humans of all races belong to this sub-species.

The spread of mankind into the remaining habitable continents probably took place during the last ice age up to 100,000 years ago: to the Americas across a land bridge from Asia, and to Australia across the then-narrow Timor Straits.

**Earliest cultures.** A variety of cultural modes — in tool-making, diet, shelter, and possibly social arrangements and spiritual expression, arose as early mankind adapted to different geographic and climatic zones.

Three basic tool-making traditions are recognized by archeologists as arising and often coexisting from one million years ago to the near past: the *chopper tradition,* found largely in E. Asia, with crude chopping tools and simple flake tools; the *flake tradition,* found in Africa and W. Europe, with a variety of small cutting and flaking tools, and the *biface tradition,* found in all of Africa, W. and S. Europe, and S. Asia, producing pointed hand axes chipped on both faces. Later biface sites yield more refined axes and a variety of other tools, weapons, and ornaments using bone, antler, and wood as well as stone.

Only sketchy evidence remains for the different stages in man's increasing control over the environment. Traces of 400,000-year-old covered wood shelters have been found at Nice, France. Scraping tools at Neanderthal sites (200,000-30,000 BC in Europe, N. Africa, the Middle East and Central Asia) suggest the treatment of skins for clothing. Sites from all parts of the world show seasonal migration patterns and exploitation of a wide range of plant and animal food sources.

Painting and decoration, for which there is evidence at the Nice site, flourished along with stone and ivory sculpture after 30,000 years ago; 60 caves in France and 30 in Spain show remarkable examples of wall painting. Other examples have been found in both N. and S. Africa. Proto-religious rites are suggested by these art works, and by evidence of ritual cannibalism by Peking Man, 500,000 BC, and of ritual burial with medicinal plants and flowers by Neanderthals at Shanidar in Iraq.

**The Neolithic Revolution.** Sometime after 10,000 BC, among widely separated human communities, a series of dramatic technological and social changes occurred that are summed up as the Neolithic Revolution. The cultivation of previously wild plants encouraged the growth of permanent settlements. Animals were domesticated as a work force and food source. The manufacture of pottery and cloth began. These techniques permitted a huge increase in world population and in human control over the earth.

No one region can safely claim priority as the "inventor" of these techniques. Dispersed sites in Cen. and S. America, S.E. Europe, and the Middle East show roughly contemporaneous (10-8,000 BC) evidence of one or another "neolithic" trait. Dates near 6-3,000 BC have been given for E. and S. Asian, W. European, and sub-Saharan African neolithic remains. The variety of crops — field grains, rice, maize, and roots, and the varying mix of other traits suggest that the revolution occurred independently in whole or in part in all these regions.

## History Begins: 4000 - 1000 BC

**Near Eastern cradle.** If history began with writing, the first chapter opened in Mesopotamia, the Tigris-Euphrates river valley. Clay tablets with pictographs were used by the Sumerians to keep records after 4000 BC. A **cuneiform** (wedge shaped) script evolved by 3000 BC as a full syllabic alphabet. Neighboring peoples adapted the script to their own language.

**Sumerian** life centered, from 4000 BC, on large cities (Eridu, Ur, Uruk, Nippur, Kish, Lagash) organized around temples and priestly bureaucracies, with the surrounding plains watered by vast irrigation works and worked with traction plows. Sailboats, wheeled vehicles, potters wheels, and kilns were used. Copper was smelted and tempered in Sumeria from c4000 BC and bronze was produced not long after. Ores, as well as precious stones and metals were obtained through long-distance ship and caravan trade. Iron was used from c2000 BC. Improved ironworking, developed partly by the **Hittites,** became widespread by 1200 BC.

Sumerian political primacy passed among cities and their kingly dynasties. Semitic-speaking peoples, with cultures derived from the Sumerian, founded a succession of dynasties that ruled in Mesopotamia and neighboring areas for most of 1800 years; among them the **Akkadians** (first under Sargon c2350 BC), the Amorites (whose laws, codified by **Hammurabi,** c1792-1750 BC, have Biblical parallels), and the Assyrians, with interludes of rule by the Hittites, Kassites, and Mitanni, all possibly Indo-Europeans. The political and cultural center of gravity shifted northwest with each successive empire.

Mesopotamian learning, maintained by scribes and preserved by successive rulers in vast libraries, was not abstract or theoretical. Algebraic and geometric problems could be solved on a practical basis in construction, commerce, or administration. Systematic lists of astronomical phenomena, plants, animals and stones were kept; medical texts listed ailments and their herbal cures.

The Sumerians worshipped anthropomorphic gods representing natural forces — Anu, god of heaven; Enlil (Ea), god of water. Epic poetry related these and other gods in a hierarchy. Sacrifices and votive offerings were made at **ziggurats** — huge stepped temples. Gods were thought to control all events, which could be foretold using elaborate oracular materials. The basic religious pattern persisted in the region into the first millenium BC.

The Syria-Palestine area, site of some of the earliest urban remains (Jericho, 7000 BC), and of the recently uncovered **Ebla** civilization (fl. 2500 BC), experienced Egyptian cultural and political influence along with Mesopotamian. The **Phoenician** coast was an active commerical center. A phonetic alphabet was invented here before 1600 BC. It became the ancestor of all European, Middle Eastern, Indian, S.E.

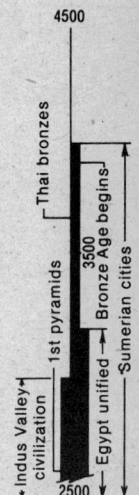

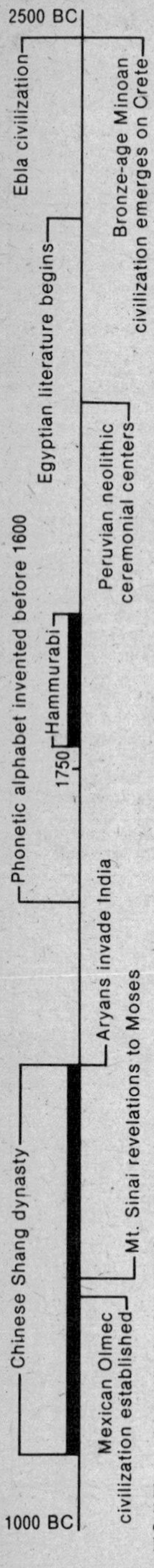
2500 BC
Ebla civilization
Bronze-age Minoan civilization emerges on Crete
Egyptian literature begins
Peruvian neolithic ceremonial centers
Phonetic alphabet invented before 1600
Hammurabi
1750
Aryans invade India
Mt. Sinai revelations to Moses
Chinese Shang dynasty
Mexican Olmec civilization established
1000 BC

Asian, Ethiopian, and Korean alphabets.

Regional commerce and diplomacy were aided by the use of Akkadian as a *lingua franca*, later replaced by Aramaic.

**Egypt.** Agricultural villages along the Nile were united by 3300 BC into two kingdoms, Upper and Lower Egypt, unified under the Pharoah Menes c3100 BC; Nubia to the south was added 2600 BC. A national bureaucracy supervised construction of canals and monuments (**pyramids** starting 2700 BC). Brilliant First Dynasty achievements in architecture, sculpture and painting, set the standards and forms for all subsequent Egyptian civilization and are still admired. **Hieroglyphic writing** appeared by 3400 BC, recording a sophisticated literature including romantic and philosophical modes after 2300 BC.

An ordered hierarchy of gods, including totemistic animal elements, was served by a powerful priesthood in Memphis. The pharaoh was identified with the falcon god Horus. Later trends were the belief in an afterlife, and the quasi-monotheistic reforms of **Akhenaton** (c1379-1362 BC).

After a period of conquest by Semitic Hyksos from Asia (c1700-1500 BC), the New Kingdom established an empire in Syria. Egypt became increasingly embroiled in Asiatic wars and diplomacy. Eventually it was conquered by Persia in 525 BC, and it faded away as an independent culture.

**India.** An urban civilization with a so-far-undeciphered writing system stretched across the Indus Valley and along the Arabian Sea c3000-1500 BC. Major sites are Harappa and **Mohenjo-Daro** in Pakistan, well-planned geometric cities with underground sewers and vast granaries. The entire region (600,000 sq. mi.) may have been ruled as a single state. Bronze was used, and arts and crafts were highly developed. Religious life apparently took the form of fertility cults.

Indus civilization was probably in decline when it was destroyed by **Aryan invaders** from the northwest, speaking an Indo-European language from which all the languages of Pakistan, north India and Bangladesh descend. Led by a warrior aristocracy whose legendary deeds are recorded in the **Rig Veda**, the Aryans spread east and south, bringing their pantheon of sky gods, elaborate priestly (Brahmin) ritual, and the beginnings of the caste system; local customs and beliefs were assimilated by the conquerors.

**Europe.** On Crete, the bronze-age **Minoan civilization** emerged c2500 BC. A prosperous economy and richly decorative art (e.g. at Knossos palace) was supported by seaborne commerce. Mycenae and other cities in Greece and Asia Minor (e.g. **Troy**) preserved elements of the culture to c1100 BC. Cretan Linear A script, c2000-1700 BC, is undeciphered; Linear B, c1300-1200 BC, records a Greek dialect.

Possible connection between Minoan-Mycenaen monumental stonework, and the great megalithic monuments and tombs of W. Europe, Iberia, and Malta (c4000-1500 BC) is unclear.

**China.** Proto-Chinese neolithic cultures had long covered northern and southeast China when the first large political state was organized in the north by the **Shang dynasty** c1500 BC. Shang kings called themselves Sons of Heaven, and presided over a cult of human and animal sacrifice to ancestors and nature gods. The Chou dynasty, starting c1100 BC, expanded the area of the Son of Heaven's dominion, but feudal states exercised most temporal power.

A writing system with 2,000 different characters was already in use under the Shang, with **pictographs** later supplemented by phonetic characters. The system, with modifications, is still in use, despite changes in spoken Chinese.

Technical advances allowed urban specialists to create fine ceramic and jade products, and bronze casting after 1500 BC was the most advanced in the world.

Bronze artifacts have recently been discovered in northern Thailand dating to 3600 BC, hundreds of years before similar Middle Eastern finds.

**Americas. Olmecs** settled on the Gulf coast of Mexico, 1500 BC, and soon developed the first civilization in the Western Hemisphere. Temple cities and huge stone sculpture date to 1200 BC. A rudimentary calendar and writing system existed. Olmec religion, centering on a jaguar god, and art forms influenced all later Meso-American cultures.

Neolithic ceremonial centers were built on the Peruvian desert coast, c2000 BC.

## Classical Era of Old World Civilizations

**Greece.** After a period of decline during the Dorian Greek invasions (1200-1000 BC), Greece and the Aegean area developed a unique civilization. Drawing upon Mycenaean traditions, Mesopotamian learning (weights and measures, lunisolar calendar, astronomy, musical scales), the Phoenician alphabet (modified for Greek), and Egyptian art, the revived **Greek city-states** saw a rich elaboration of intellectual life. Long-range commerce was aided by metal coinage (introduced by the Lydians in Asia Minor before 700 BC); colonies were founded around the Mediterranean and Black Sea shores (Cumae in Italy 760 BC, Massalia in France c600 BC).

**Philosophy,** starting with Ionian speculation on the nature of matter and the universe (Thales c634-546), and including mathematical speculation (Pythagoras c580-c500), culminated in Athens in the rationalist idealism of **Plato** (c428-347) and **Socrates** (c470-399); the latter was executed for alleged impiety. Aristotle (384-322) united all fields of study in his system. The arts were highly valued. Architecture culminated in the **Parthenon** in Athens (438, sculpture by Phidias); poetry and drama (Aeschylus 525-456) thrived. Male beauty and strength, a chief artistic theme, were enhanced at the gymnasium and the national games at Olympia.

Ruled by local tyrants or oligarchies, the Greeks were never politically united, but managed to resist inclusion in the Persian Empire (Darius defeated at Marathon 490 BC, Xerxes at Salamis, Platae 479 BC). Local warfare was common; the **Peloponnesian Wars,** 431-404 BC, ended in Sparta's victory over Athens. Greek political power waned, but classical Greek cultural forms spread thoughout the ancient world from the Atlantic to India.

**Hebrews.** Nomadic Hebrew tribes entered Canaan before 1200 BC, settling among other Semitic peoples speaking the same language. They brought from the desert a **monotheistic faith** said to have been revealed to Abraham in Canaan c1800 BC and to Moses at Mt. Sinai c1250 BC, after the Hebrews' escape from bondage in Egypt. David (ruled 1000-961 BC) and Solomon (ruled 961-922 BC) united the Hebrews in a kingdom that briefly dominated the area. Phoenicians to the north established colonies

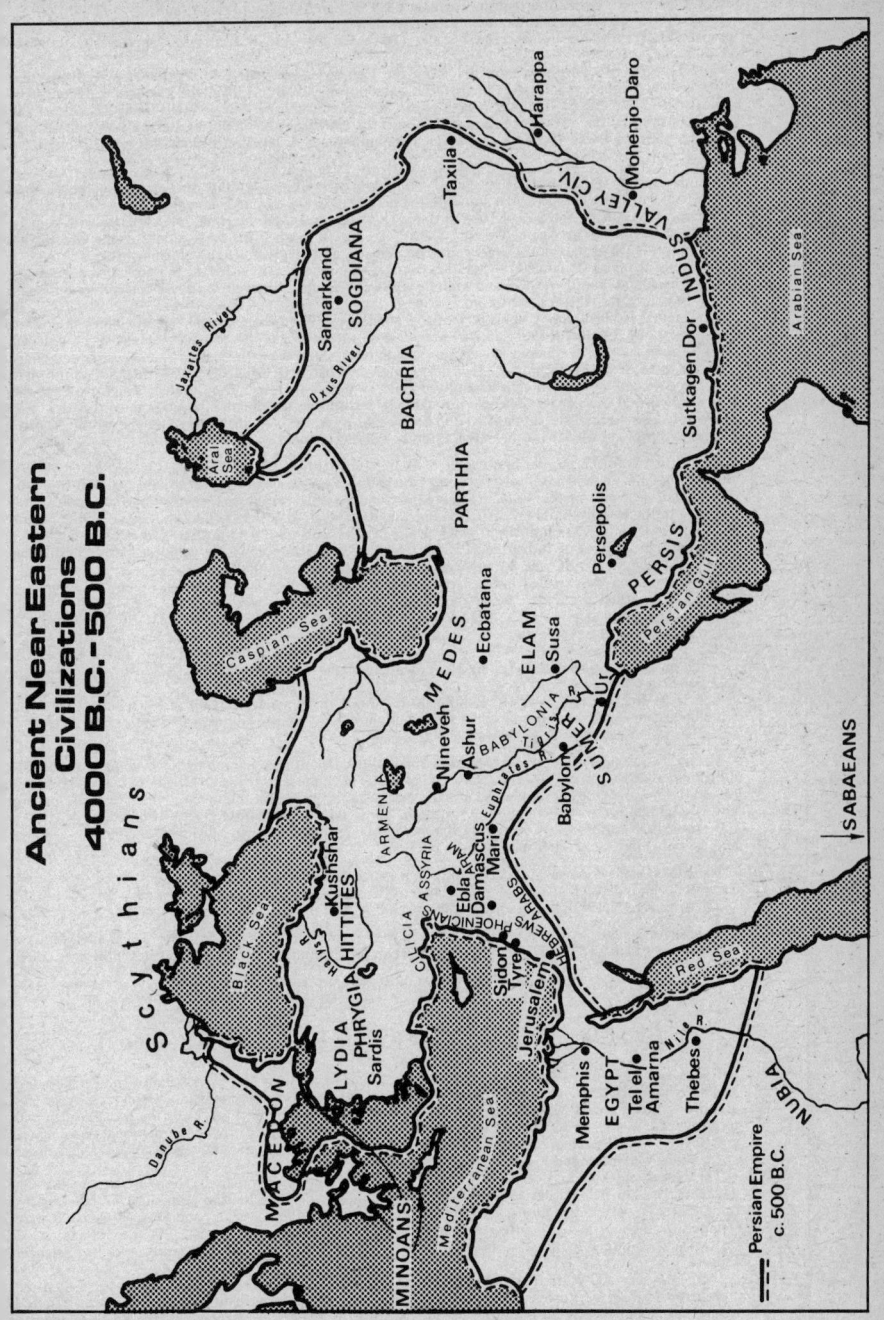

Ancient Near Eastern
Civilizations
4000 B.C.-500 B.C.

*Timeline labels (left margin):*
- Chavin dynasty begins in Peru
- Hebrew kingdom divided
- Carthage established
- Chou dynasty begins in China
- 800
- Metal coins in Asia Minor
- Isaiah d.
- Nubia begins rule of Egypt
- Zoroaster b.
- Pythagoras b.
- Indian Buddhism, Jainism begin
- Confucius b., 600
- Siddarta b.
- Aeschylus b.
- Socrates b.
- Plato b.
- Parthenon
- Peloponnesian Wars
- 400 BC

around the E. and W. Mediterranean (**Carthage** c814 BC) and sailed into the Atlantic.

A temple in Jerusalem became the national religious center, with sacrifices performed by a hereditary priesthood. Polytheistic influences, especially of the fertility cult of Baal, were opposed by **prophets** (Elijah, Amos, Isaiah).

Divided into **two kingdoms** after Solomon, the Hebrews were unable to resist the revived Assyrian empire, which conquered Israel, the northern kingdom in 722 BC. Judah, the southern kingdom, was conquered in 586 BC by the Babylonians under Nebuchadnezzar II. But with the fixing of most of the Biblical canon by the mid-fourth century BC, and the emergence of rabbis, arbiters of law and custom, Judaism successfully survived the loss of Hebrew autonomy. A Jewish kingdom was revived under the Hasmoneans (168-42 BC).

**China.** During the **Eastern Chou** dynasty (770-256 BC), Chinese culture spread east to the sea and south to the Yangtze. Large feudal states on the periphery of the empire contended for pre-eminence, but continued to recognize the Son of Heaven (king), who retained a purely ritual role enriched with courtly music and dance. In the Age of Warring States (403-221 BC), when the first sections of the **Great Wall** were built, the Ch'in state in the West gained supremacy, and finally united all of China.

Iron tools entered China c500 BC, and casting techniques were advanced, aiding agriculture. Peasants owned their land, and owed civil and military service to nobles. Cities grew in number and size, though barter remained the chief trade medium.

Intellectual ferment among noble scribes and officials produced the Classical Age of Chinese literature and philosophy. **Confucius** (551-479 BC) urged a restoration of a supposedly harmonious social order of the past through proper conduct in accordance with one's station and through filial and ceremonial piety. The *Analects*, attributed to him, are revered throughout East Asia. **Mencius** (d. 289 BC) added the view that the Mandate of Heaven can be removed from an unjust dynasty. The Legalists sought to curb the supposed natural wickedness of people through new institutions and harsh laws; they aided the Ch'in rise to power. The Naturalists emphasized the balance of opposites — yin, yang — in the world. **Taoists** sought mystical knowledge through meditation and disengagement.

**India.** The political and cultural center of India shifted from the Indus to the Ganges River Valley. Buddhism, Jainism, and mystical revisions of orthodox Vedism all developed around 500-300 BC. The *Upanishads*, last part of the *Veda*, urged escape from the illusory physical world. Vedism remained the preserve of the priestly Brahmin caste. In contrast, **Buddhism**, founded by Siddarta Guatama (c563-c483 BC), appealed to merchants in the growing urban centers, and took hold at first (and most lastingly) on the geographic fringes of Indian civilization. The classic Indian epics were composed in this era: The *Ramayana* around 300 BC, the *Mahabharata* over a period starting 400 BC.

Northern India was divided into a large number of monarchies and aristocratic republics, probably derived from tribal groupings, when the Magadha kingdom was formed in Bihar c542 BC. It soon became the dominant power. The **Maurya dynasty,** founded by Chandragupta c321 BC, expanded the kingdom, uniting most of N. India in a centralized bureaucratic empire. The third Mauryan king, **Asoka** (ruled c274-236) conquered most of the subcontinent: he converted to Buddhism, and inscribed its tenents on pillars throughout India. He downplayed the caste system and tried to end expensive sacrificial rites.

Before its final decline in India, Buddhism developed the popular worship of heavenly Bodhisatvas (enlightened beings), and produced a refined architecture (stupa—shrine—at Sanchi 100 AD) and sculpture (Gandhara reliefs 1-400 AD).

**Persia.** Aryan peoples (Pesians, Medes) dominated the area of present Iran by the beginning of the first millenium BC. The prophet **Zoroaster** (born c628 BC) introduced a dualistic religion in which the forces of good (Ahura Mazda, Lord of Wisdom) and evil (Ahiram) battle for dominance; individuals are judged by their actions and earn damnation or salvation. Zoroaster's hymns (*Gathas* ) are included in the *Avesta*, the Zoroastrian scriptures. A version of this faith became the established religion of the Persian Empire, and probably influenced later monotheistic religions.

**Africa.** Nubia, periodically occupied by Egypt since the third millenium, ruled Egypt c750-661, and survived as an independent Egyptianized kingdom (**Kush;** capital Meroe) for 1,000 years.

The Iron Age Nok culture flourished c500 BC-200 AD on the Benue Plateau of **Nigeria.**

**Americas.** The Chavin culture controlled north Peru from 900-200 BC. Its ceremonial centers, featuring the jaguar god, survived long after. Chavin architecture, ceramics, and textiles influenced other Peruvian cultures.

**Mayan civilization** began to develop in Central America in the 5th century BC.

# Great Empires Unite the Civilized World: 400 BC - 400 AD

**Persia and Alexander. Cyrus,** ruler of a small kingdom in Persia from 559 BC, united the Persians and Medes within 10 years, conquered Asia Minor and Babylonia in another 10. His son Cambyses and grandson **Darius** (ruled 522-486) added vast lands to the east and north as far as the Indus Valley and Central Asia, as well as Egypt and Thrace. The whole empire was ruled by an international bureaucracy and army, with Persians holding the chief positions. The resources and styles of all the subject civilizations were exploited to create a rich syncretic art.

The Hellenized kingdom of Macedon, which under Phillip II dominated Greece, passed to his son **Alexander** in 336 BC. Within 13 years, Alexander conquered all the Persian dominions. Imbued by his tutor Aristotle with Greek ideals, Alexander encouraged Greek colonization, and Greek-style cities were founded throughout the empire (e.g. Alexandria, Egypt). After his death in 323 BC, wars of succession divided the empire into three parts — **Macedon,** Egypt (ruled by the **Ptolemies**), and the **Seleucid** Empire.

In the ensuing 300 years (the **Hellenistic Era**), a cosmopolitan Greek-oriented culture permeated the ancient world from W. Europe to the borders of India, absorbing native elites everywhere.

Hellenistic philosophy stressed the private individual's search for happiness. The Cynics followed Diogenes (c372-287), who stressed satisfaction of animal needs and contempt for social convention. Zeno (c335-c263) and the Stoics exalted reason, identified it with virtue, and counseled an ascetic disregard for misfortune. The Epicureans tried to build lives of moderate pleasure without political or emotional

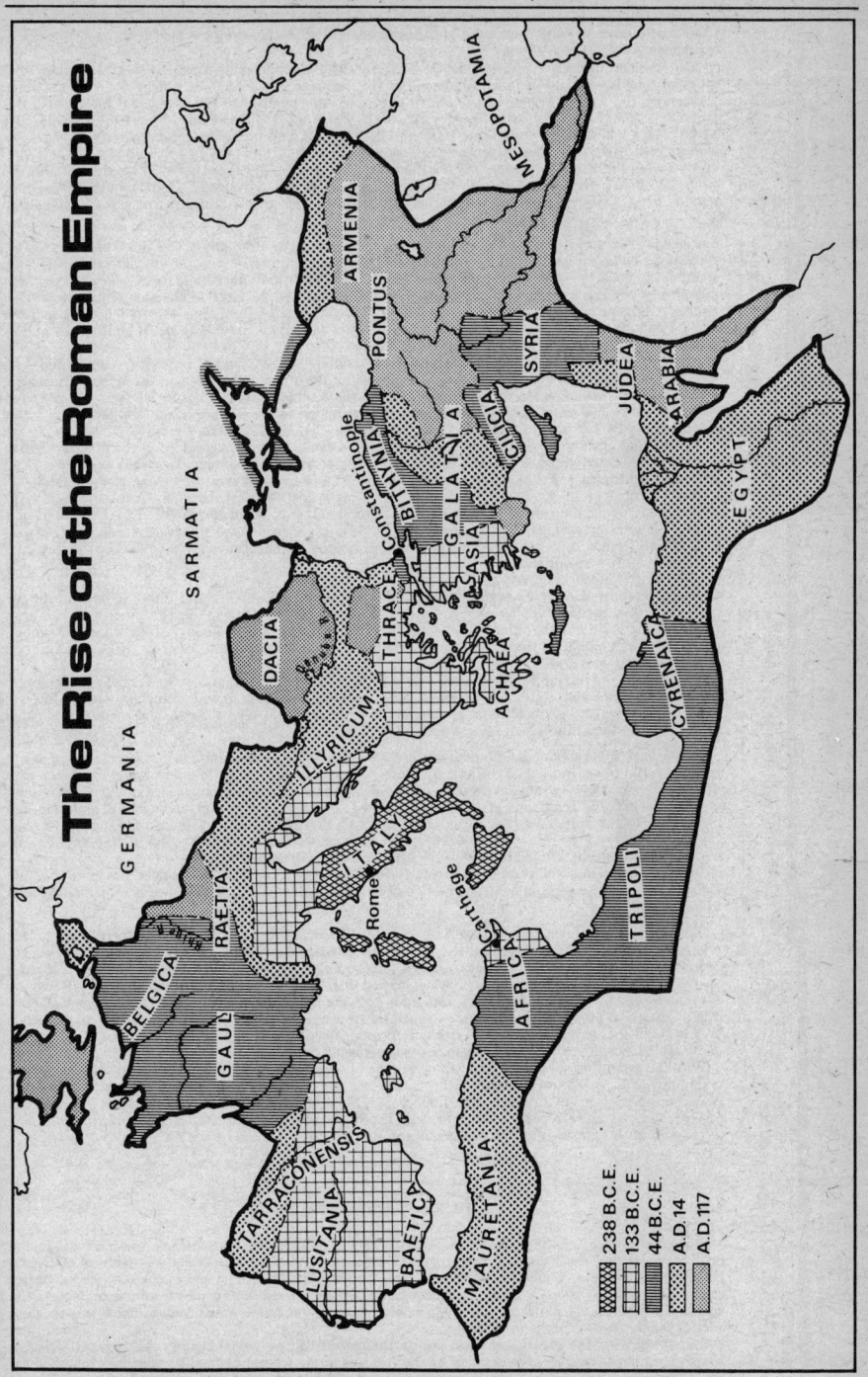

The Rise of the Roman Empire

238 B.C.E.
133 B.C.E.
44 B.C.E.
A.D. 14
A.D. 117

400 BC

Alexander becomes king

Aristotle b.

Mahabarata begun

Chinese Age of Warring States

Euclid's geometry

200 BC

Great Wall of China begun

1st Roman slave revolt

Hellenistic Era

Hannibal invades Italy

Julius Caesar b.

Punic Wars end

Anthony, Cleopatra defeated

Mayan civilization begins in Guatemala

Julian calendar

Roman Empire

1 AD

Jesus d.

Nero's persecution

200 AD

involvement. Hellenistic arts imitated life realistically, especially in sculpture and literature (comedies of Menander, 342-292).

The sciences thrived, especially at Alexandria, where the Ptolemies financed a great library and museum. Fields of study included mathematics (**Euclid's** geometry, c300 BC; Menelaus' non-Euclidian geometry, c100 AD); astronomy (heliocentric theory of Aristarchus, 310-230 BC; Julian calendar 45 BC; Ptolemy's *Almagest*, c150 AD); geography (world map of Eratosthenes, 276-194 BC); hydraulics (**Archimedes**, 287-212 BC); medicine (Galen, 130-200 AD), and chemistry. Inventors refined uses for siphons, valves, gears, springs, screws, levers, cams, and pulleys.

A restored Persian empire under the **Parthians** (N. Iranian tribesmen) controlled the eastern Hellenistic world 250 BC-229 AD. The Parthians and the succeeding Sassanian dynasty (229-651) fought with Rome periodically. The **Sassanians** revived Zoroastrianism as a state religion, and patronized a nationalistic artistic and scholarly renaissance.

**Rome.** The city of Rome was founded, according to legend, by Romulus in 753 BC. Through military expansion and colonization, and by granting citizenship to conquered tribes, the city annexed all of Italy south of the Po in the 100-year period before 268 BC. The Latin and other Italic tribes were annexed first, followed by the Etruscans (a civilized people north of Rome) and the Greek colonies in the south. With a large standing army and reserve forces of several hundred thousand, Rome was able to defeat Carthage in the 3 **Punic Wars**, 264-241, 218-201, 149-146 (despite the invasion of Italy by Hannibal, 218), thus gaining Sicily and territory in Spain and North Africa.

New provinces were added in the East, as Rome exploited local disputes to conquer Greece and Asia Minor in the 2d century BC, and Egypt in the first (after the defeat and suicide of **Antony and Cleopatra**, 30 BC). All the Mediterranean civilized world up to the disputed Parthian border was now Roman, and remained so for 500 years. Less civilized regions were added to the Empire: Gaul (conquered by Julius Caesar, 56-49 BC), Britain (43 AD) and Dacia NE of the Danube (117 AD).

The original aristocratic republican government, with democratic features added in the fifth and fourth centuries BC, deteriorated under the pressures of empire and class conflict (**Gracchus** brothers, social reformers, murdered 133, 121; slave revolts 135, 73). After a series of civil wars (Marius vs. Sulla 88-82, Caesar vs. Pompey 49-45, triumverate vs. Caesar's assassins 44-43, Antony vs. Octavian 32-30), the empire came under the rule of a deified monarch (first emperor, **Augustus**, 27 BC-14 AD). Provincials (nearly all granted citizenship by Caracalla, 212 AD) came to dominate the army and civil service. Traditional Roman law, systematized and interpreted by independent jurists, and local self-rule in provincial cities were supplanted by a vast tax-collecting bureaucracy in the 3d and 4th centuries. The legal rights of women, children and slaves were strengthened.

Roman innovations in civil engineering included water mills, windmills, and rotary mills, and the use of cement that hardened under water. Monumental architecture (baths, theaters, apartment houses), relied on the arch and the dome. The network of roads (some still standing) stretched 53,000 miles, passing through mountain tunnels as long as 3.5 miles. Aqueducts brought water to cities, underground sewers removed waste.

Roman art and literature were derivative of Greek models. Innovations were made in sculpture (naturalistic busts and equestrian statues), decorative wall painting (as at Pompeii), satire (Juvenal, 60-127), history (Tactus, 56-120), prose romance (Petronius, d. 66 AD). Violence and torture dominated mass public amusements, which were supported by the state.

**India.** The **Gupta** monarchs reunited N. India c320 AD. Their peaceful and prosperous reign saw a revival of Hindu religious thought and Brahmin power. The old Vedic traditions were combined with devotion to a plethora of indigenous deities (who were seen as manifestations of Vedic gods). **Caste** lines were reinforced, and Buddhism gradually disappeared. The art (often erotic), architecture, and literature of the period, patronized by the Gupta court, are considered to be among India's finest achievements (Kalidasa, poet and dramatist, fl. c400). Mathematical innovations included the use of zero and decimal numbers. Invasions by White Huns from the NW destroyed the empire c550.

Rich cultures also developed in S. India in this era. Emotional Tamil religious poetry aided the Hindu revival. The Pallava kingdom controlled much of S. India c350-880, and helped spread Indian civilization to S.E. Asia.

**China.** The Ch'in ruler Shih Huang Ti (ruled 221-210 BC), known as the First Emperor, centralized political authority in China, standardized the written language, laws, weights, measures, and coinage, and conducted a census, but tried to destroy most philosophical texts. The **Han dynasty** (206 BC-220 AD) instituted the mandarin bureaucracy, which lasted for 2,000 years. Local officials were selected by examination in the Confucian classics and trained at the imperial university and at provincial schools. The invention of **paper** facilitated this bureaucratic system. Agriculture was promoted, but the peasants bore most of the tax burden. Irrigation was improved; water clocks and sundials were used; astronomy and mathematics thrived; landscape painting was perfected.

With the expansion south and west (to nearly the present borders of today's China), trade was opened with India, S.E. Asia, and the Middle East, over sea and caravan routes. Indian missionaries brought Mahayana Buddhism to China by the first century AD, and spawned a variety of sects. Taoism was revived, and merged with popular superstitions. Taoist and Buddhist monasteries and convents multiplied in the turbulent centuries after the collapse of the Han dynasty.

# The One God Triumphs: 1-750 AD

**Christianity.** Religions indigenous to particular Middle Eastern nations became international in the first 3 centuries of the Roman Empire. Roman citizens worshipped **Isis** of Egypt, **Mithras** of Persia, **Demeter** of Greece, and the great mother **Cybele** of Phrygia. Their cults centered on mysteries (secret ceremonies) and the promise of an afterlife, symbolized by the death and rebirth of the god. Judaism, which had begun as the national cult of Judea, also spread by emigration and conversion. It was the only ancient religion west of India to survive.

Christians, who emerged as a distinct sect in the second half of the 1st century AD, revered **Jesus**, a Jewish preacher said to have been killed by the Romans at the request of Jewish authorities in Jerusalem c30 AD. They considered him the Savior (Messiah, or Christ) who rose from the dead and could grant

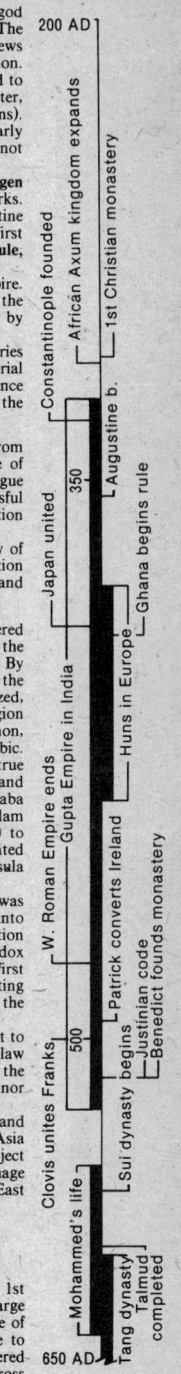

eternal life to the faithful, despite their sinfulness. They believed he was an incarnation of the one god worshipped by the Jews, and that he would return soon to pass final judgment on the world. The missionary activities of such early leaders as **Paul of Tarsus** spread the faith, at first mostly among Jews or among quasi-Jews attracted by the Pauline rejection of such difficult Jewish laws as circumcision. Intermittent persecution, as in Rome under Nero in 64 AD, on grounds of suspected disloyalty, failed to disrupt the New Christian communities. Each congregation, generally urban and of plebian character, was tightly organized under a leader (bishop) elders (presbyters or priests), and assistants (deacons). Stories about Jesus (the Gospels) and the early church (Acts) were written down in the late first and early 2d centuries, and circulated along with letters of Paul. An authoritative canon of these writings was not fixed until the 4th century.

A school for priests was established at Alexandria in the second century. Its teachers (**Origen** c182-251) helped define Christian doctrine and promote the faith in Greek-style philosophical works. Pagan Neoplatonism was given Christian coloration in the works of Church Fathers such as Augustine (354-430). Christian hermits, often drawn from the lower classes, began to associate in monasteries, first in Egypt (St. Pachomius c290-345), then in other eastern lands, then in the West (**St. Benedict's rule,** 529). Popular adoration of saints, especially Mary, mother of Jesus, spread.

Under **Constantine** (ruled 306-337), Christianity became in effect the established religion of the Empire. Pagan temples were expropriated, state funds were used to build huge churches and support the hierarchy, and laws were adjusted in accordance with Christian notions. Pagan worship was banned by the end of the fourth century, and severe restrictions were placed on Judaism.

The newly established church was rocked by doctrinal disputes, often exacerbated by regional rivalries both within and outside the Empire. Chief heresies (as defined by church councils backed by imperial authority) were **Arianism,** which denied the divinity of Jesus; **Donatism,** which rejected the convergence of church and state and denied the validity of sacraments performed by sinful clergy; and the **Monophysite** position denying the dual nature of Christ.

**Judaism.** First century Judaism embraced several sects, including: the **Sadducees,** mostly drawn from the Temple priesthood, who were culturally Hellenized; the **Pharisees,** who upheld the full range of traditional customs and practices as of equal weight to literal scriptural law, and elaborated synagogue worship; and the **Essenes,** an ascetic, millenarian sect. Messianic fervor led to repeated, unsuccessful rebellions against Rome (66-70, 135). As a result, the Temple was destroyed, and the population decimated.

To avoid the dissolution of the faith, a program of codification of law was begun at the academy of Yavneh. The work continued for some 500 years in Palestine and Babylonia, ending in the final redaction of the Talmud (c600), a huge collection of legal and moral debates, rulings, liturgy, Biblical exegesis, and legendary materials.

**Islam.** The earliest Arab civilization emerged by the end of the 2d millenium BC in the watered highlands of Yemen. Seaborne and caravan trade in frankincense and myrrh connected the area with the Nile and Fertile Crescent. The Minaean, Sabean (Sheba), and Himyarite states successively held sway. By Mohammed's time (7th century AD), the region was a province of Sassanian Persia. In the North, the **Nabataean kingdom** at Petra and the kingdom of Palmyra were first Aramaicized and then Romanized, and finally absorbed like neighboring Judea into the Roman Empire. Nomads shared the central region with a few trading towns and oases. Wars between tribes and raids on settled communities were common, and were celebrated in a poetic tradition that by the 6th century helped establish a classic literary Arabic.

In 611 **Mohammed,** a wealthy 40-year-old Arab of Mecca, had a revelation from Allah, the one true god, calling on him to repudiate pagan idolatry. Drawing on elements of Judaism and Christianity, and eventually incorporating some Arab pagan traditions (such as reverence for the black stone at the kaaba shrine in Mecca), Mohammed's teachings, recorded in the **Koran,** forged a new religion, Islam (submission to Allah). Opposed by the leaders of Mecca, Mohammed made a *hejira* (migration) to Medina to the north in 622, the beginning of the Moslem lunar calendar. He and his followers defeated the Meccans in 624 in the first *jihad* (holy war), and by his death (632), nearly all the Arabian peninsula accepted his religious and secular leadership.

Under the first two **caliphs** (successors) Abu Bakr (632-34) and Oman (634-44), Moslem rule was confirmed over Arabia. Raiding parties into Byzantine and Persian border areas developed into campaigns of conquest against the two empires, which had been weakened by wars and by disaffection among subject peoples (including Coptic and Syriac Christians opposed to the Byzantine orthodox church). Syria, Palestine, Egypt, Iraq, and Persia all fell to the inspired Arab armies. The Arabs at first remained a distinct minority, using non-Moslems in the new administrative system, and tolerating Christians, Jews, and Zoroastrians as self-governing "Peoples of the Book," whose taxes supported the empire.

Disputes over the succession, and puritan reaction to the wealth and refinement that empire brought to the ruling strata, led to the growth of schismatic movements. The followers of Mohammed's son-in-law Ali (assassinated 661) and his descendants became the founders of the more mystical **Shi'ite** sect, still the largest non-orthodox Moslem sect. The **Karijites,** puritanical, militant, and egalitarian, persist as a minor sect to the present.

Under the **Ummayad** caliphs (661-750), the boundaries of Islam were extended across N. Africa and into Spain. Arab armies in the West were stopped at Tours in 732 by the Frank **Charles Martel.** Asia Minor, the Indus Valley, and Transoxiana were conquered in the East. The vast majority of the subject population gradually converted to Islam, encouraged by tax and career privileges. The Arab language supplanted the local tongues in the central and western areas, but Arab soldiers and rulers in the East eventually became assimilated to the indigenous languages.

## New Peoples Enter History: 400-900

**Barbarian invasions. Germanic tribes** infiltrated S and E from their Baltic homeland during the 1st millenium BC, reaching S. Germany by 100 BC and the Black Sea by 214 AD. Organized into large federated tribes under elected kings, most resisted Roman domination and raided the empire in time of civil war (Goths took Dacia 214, raided Thrace 251-269). German troops and commanders came to dominate the Roman armies by the end of the 4th century. **Huns,** Mongol invaders from Asia, entered Europe 372, driving more Germans into the western empire. Emperor Valens allowed Visigoths to cross

Left margin timeline labels:

- 650
- Greek replaces Latin in Byzantium
- Slav-Turk Bulgarian Empire begins
- Chinese poet Li Po b.
- Nara period begins, Japan
- 750
- Baghdad founded
- Charlemagne rules
- Byzantine Empire
- Justinian
- Arab-Moslem golden age
- Viking explorations, raids
- 850
- Vietnam independent
- 950

the Danube 376. Huns under Attila (d. 453) raided Gaul, Italy, Balkans. The western empire, weakened by overtaxation and social stagnation, was overrun in the 5th century. Gaul was effectively lost 406-Spain 409, Britain 410, Africa 429-39. Rome itself was sacked 410 by Visigoths under Alaric, 455 b Vandals. The last western emperor, Romulus Augustulus, was deposed 476 by the Germanic chi Odoacer.

**Celts.** Celtic cultures, which in pre-Roman times covered most of W. Europe, were confined almos entirely to the British Isles after the Germanic invasions. **St. Patrick** completed the conversion of Irelan (c457-92). A strong monastic tradition took hold. Irish monastic missionaries in Scotland, England, an the continent (Columba c521-597; Columban c543-615) helped restore Christianity after the German invasions. The monasteries became reknowned centers of classic and Christian learning, and preside over the recording of a Christianized Celtic mythology, elaborated by secular writers and bards. A intricate decorative art style developed, especially in book illumination (Lindisfarne Gospels, c700, Boo of Kells, 8th century).

**Successor states.** The Visigoth kingdom in Spain (from 419) and much of France (to 507) saw continuation of much Roman administration, language, and law (Breviary of Alaric 506), until i destruction by the Moslems, 711. The Vandal kingdom in Africa, from 429, was conquered by th Byzantines, 533. Italy was ruled in succession by an Ostrogothic kingdom under Byzantine suzeraint 489-554, direct Byzantine government, and the German Lombards (568-774). The latter divided th peninsula with the Byzantines and the papacy under the dynamic reformer Pope Gregory the Grea (590-604) and his successors.

King Clovis (ruled 481-511) united the Franks on both sides of the Rhine, and after his conversion t orthodox Christianity, defeated the Arian Burgundians (after 500) and Visigoths (507) with the suppor of the native clergy and the papacy. Under the **Merovingian** kings a feudal system emerged: power wa fragmented among hierarchies of military landowners. Social stratification, which in late Roman time had acquired legal, hereditary sanction, was reinforced. The Carolingians (747-987) expanded th kingdom and restored central power. **Charlemagne** (ruled 768-814) conquered nearly all the Germani lands, including Lombard Italy, and was crowned Emperor by Pope Leo III in Rome in 800. H centuries-long decline in commerce and the arts was reversed under Charlemagne's patronage. H welcomed Jews to his kingdom, which became a center of Jewish learning (Rashi 1040-1105). H sponsored the "Carolingian Renaissance" of learning under the Anglo-Latin scholar Alcuin (c732-804 who reformed church liturgy.

**Byzantine Empire.** Under Diocletian (ruled 284-305) the empire had been divided into 2 parts t facilitate administration and defense. Constantine founded **Constantinople**, 330, (at old Byzantium) as fully Christian city. Commerce and taxation financed a sumptuous, orientalized court, a class o hereditary bureaucratic families, and magnificent urban construction (Hagia Sophia, 532-37). The city' fortifications and naval innovations (Greek fire) repelled assaults by Goths, Huns, Slavs, Avars Arabs, and Scandinavians. Greek replaced Latin as the official language by c700. Byzantine art, a solemn sacral, and stylized variation of late classical styles (mosaics at S. Vitale, Ravenna, 526-48) was a startin point for medieval art in E. and W. Europe.

**Justinian** (ruled 527-65) reconquered parts of Spain, N. Africa, and Italy, codified Roman law (code Justinianus, 529, was medieval Europe's chief legal text), closed the Platonic Academy at Athens an ordered all pagans to convert. Lombards in Italy, Arabs in Africa retook most of his conquests. The Isaurian dynasty from Anatolia (from 717) and the Macedonian dynasty (867-1054) restored military an commercial power. The Iconoclast controversy (726-843) over the permissibility of images, helpe alienate the Eastern Church from the papacy.

**Arab Empire. Baghdad,** founded 762, became the seat of the **Abbasid** Caliphate (founded 750), whil Ummayads continued to rule in Spain. A brilliant cosmopolitan civilization emerged, inaugurating ar Arab-Moslem golden age. Arab lyric poetry revived; Greek, Syriac, Persian, and Sanskrit books wer translated into Arabic, often by Syriac Christians and Jews, whose theology and Talmudic law respectively, influenced Islam. The arts and music flourished at the court of **Harun al-Rashid** (786-809 celebrated in *The Arabian Nights*. The sciences, medicine, and mathematics were pursued at Baghdad Cordova, and Cairo (founded 969). Science and Aristotelian philosophy culminated in the systems o Avicenna (980-1037), Averroes (1126-98), and Maimonides (1135-1204); all influenced later Christia scholarship and theology. The Islamic ban on images encouraged a sinuous, geometric decorativ tradition, applied to architecture and illumination. A gradual loss of Arab control in Persia (from 874 led to the capture of Baghdad by Persians, 945. By the next century, Spain and N. Africa were ruled b Berbers, while Turks prevailed in Asia Minor and the Levant. The loss of political power by the caliph allowed for the growth of non-orthodox trends, especially the mystical **Sufi** tradition (theologian Ghazali 1058-1111).

**Africa.** Immigrants from Saba in S. Arabia helped set up the **Axum** kingdom in Ethiopia in the 2d century (their language, Ge'ez, is preserved by the Ethiopian Church). In the 4th century, when the kingdom became Christianized, it defeated Kushite Meroe and expanded into Yemen. Axum was the center of a vast ivory trade; it controlled the Red Sea coast until c1100. Arab conquest in Egypt cu Axum's political and economic ties with Byzantium.

The Iron Age entered W. Africa by the end of the 1st millenium BC. **Ghana**, the first know sub-Saharan state, ruled in the upper Senegal-Niger region c400-1240, controlling the trade of gold from mines in the S to trans-Sahara caravan routes to the N. The **Bantu** peoples, probably of W. African origin, began to spread E and S perhaps 2000 years ago, displacing the Pygmies and Bushmen of central and southern Africa over a 1,500-year period.

**Japan.** The advanced Neolithic Yayoi period, when irrigation, rice farming, and iron and bronze casting techniques were introduced from China or Korea, persisted to c400 AD. The myriad Japanese states were then united by the **Yamato** clan, under an emperor who acted as the chief priest of the animistic **Shinto** cult. Japanese political and military intervention in Korea by the 6th century quickened a Chinese cultural invasion, bringing Buddhism, the Chinese language (which long remained a literary and governmental medium), Chinese ideographs and Buddhist styles in painting, sculpture, literature, and architecture (7th c. Horyu-ji temple at Nara). The Taika Reforms, 646, tried to centralize Japan according to Chinese bureaucratic and Buddhist philosophical values, but failed to curb traditional Japanese decentralization. A nativist reaction against the Buddhist **Nara period** (710-94) ushered in the

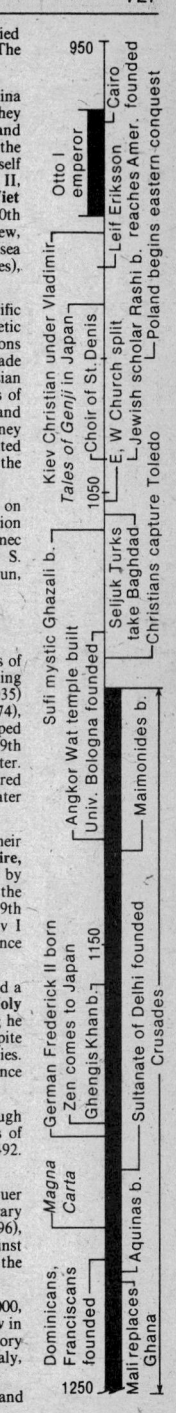

...eian period (794-1185) centered at the new capital, Kyoto. Japanese elegance and simplicity modified Chinese styles in architecture, scroll painting, and literature; the writing system was also simplified. The courtly novel *Tale of Genji* (1010-20) testifies to the enhanced role of women.

**Southeast Asia.** The historic peoples of southeast Asia began arriving some 2500 years ago from China and Tibet, displacing scattered aborigines. Their agriculture relied on rice and tubers (yams), which they may have introduced to Africa. Indian cultural influences were strongest; literacy and Hindu and Buddhist ideas followed the southern India-China trade route. From the southern tip of Indochina, the kingdom of **Funan** (1st-7th centuries) traded as far west as Persia. It was absorbed by Chenla, itself conquered by the **Khmer Empire** (600-1300). The Khmers, under Hindu god-kings (Suryavarman II, 1113-c1150), built the monumental Angkor Wat temple center for the royal phallic cult. The **Nam-Viet** kingdom in Annam, dominated by China and Chinese culture for 1,000 years, emerged in the 10th century, growing at the expense of the Khmers, who also lost ground in the NW to the new, highly-organized **Thai** kingdom. On Sumatra, the **Srivijaya** Empire at Palembang controlled vital sea lanes (7th to 10th centuries). A Buddhist dynasty, the Sailendras, ruled central **Java** (8th-9th centuries), building at Borobudur one of the largest stupas in the world.

**China.** The short-lived Sui dynasty (581-618) ushered in a period of commercial, artistic, and scientific achievement in China, continuing under the T'ang dynasty (618-906). Such inventions as the magnetic compass, gunpowder, the abacus, and printing were introduced or perfected. Medical innovations included cataract surgery. The state, from the cosmopolitan capital, Ch'ang-an, supervised foreign trade which exchanged Chinese silks, procelains, and art works for spices, ivory, etc., over Central Asian caravan routes and sea routes reaching Africa. A golden age of poetry bequeathed tens of thousands of works to later generations (Tu Fu 712-70, Li Po 701-62). Landscape painting flourished. Commercial and industrial expansion continued under the **Northern Sung** dynasty (960-1126), facilitated by paper money and credit notes. But commerce never achieved respectability; government monopolies expropriated successful merchants. The population, long stable at 50 million, doubled in 200 years with the introduction of early-ripening rice and the double harvest. In art, native Chinese styles were revived.

**Americas.** An Indian empire stretched from the Valley of Mexico to Guatemala, 300-600, centering on the huge city **Teotihuacan** (founded 100 BC). To the S, in Guatemala, a high **Mayan** civilization developed, 150-900, around hundreds of rural ceremonial centers. The Mayans improved on Olmec writing and the calendar, and pursued astronomy and mathematics (using the idea of zero). In S. America, a widespread pre-Inca culture grew from **Tiahuanaco** near Lake Titicaca (Gateway of the Sun, 700).

## Christian Europe Regroups and Expands: 900-1300

**Scandinavians.** Pagan Danish and Norse **(Viking)** adventurers, traders, and pirates raided the coasts of the British Isles (Dublin founded c831), France, and even the Mediterranean for over 200 years beginning in the late 8th century. Inland settlement in the W was limited to Great Britain (King Canute, 994-1035) and Normandy, settled under Rollo, 911, as a fief of France. Other Vikings reached Iceland (874), Greenland (c986), and probably N. America (Leif Eriksson c1000). Norse traders **(Varangians)** developed Russian river commerce from the 8th-11th centuries, and helped set up a state at Kiev in the late 9th century. Conversion to Christianity occurred during the 10th century, reaching Sweden 100 years later. Eleventh century Norman bands conquered S. Italy and Sicily. Duke **William of Normandy** conquered England, 1066, bringing continental feudalism and the French language, essential elements in later English civilization.

**East Europe.** Slavs inhabited areas of E. Central Europe in prehistoric times, and reached most of their present limits by c850. The first Slavic states were in the Balkans (Slav-Turk **Bulgarian Empire,** 680-1018) and Moravia (628). Missions of St. Cyril (whose Greek-based Cyrillic alphabet is still used by S. and E. Slavs) converted Moravia, 863. The Eastern Slavs, part-civilized under the overlordship of the Turkish-Jewish **Khazar** trading empire (7th-10th centuries), gravitated toward Constantinople by the 9th century. The **Kievan state** adopted Eastern Christianity under Prince Vladimir, 989. King Boleslav I (992-1025) began **Poland's** long history of eastern conquest. The Magyars **(Hungarians)** in Europe since 896, accepted Latin Christianity, 1001.

**Germany.** The German kingdom that emerged after the breakup of Charlemagne's Empire remained a confederation of largely autonomous states. The Saxon Otto I, king from 936, established the **Holy Roman Empire** of Germany and Italy in alliance with Pope John XII, who crowned him emperor, 962; he defeated the Magyars, 955. Imperial power was greatest under the **Hohenstaufens** (1138-1254), despite the growing opposition of the papacy, which ruled central Italy, and the Lombard League cities. Frederick II (1194-1250) improved administration, patronized the arts; after his death German influence was removed from Italy.

**Christian Spain.** From its northern mountain redoubts, Christian rule slowly migrated south through the 11th century, when Moslem unity collapsed. After the capture of **Toledo** (1085), the kingdoms of Portugal, Castile, and Aragon undertook repeated crusades of reconquest, finally completed in 1492. Elements of Islamic civilization persisted in recaptured areas, influencing all W. Europe.

**Crusades.** Pope Urban II called, 1095, for a crusade to restore Asia Minor to Byzantium and conquer the Holy Land from the Turks. Some 10 crusades (to 1291) succeeded only in founding 4 temporary Frankish states in the Levant. The 4th crusade sacked Constantinople, 1204. In Rhineland (1096), England (1290), France (1306), Jews were massacred or expelled, and wars were launched against Christian heretics (**Albigensian** crusade in France, 1229). Trade in eastern luxuries expanded, led by the Venetian naval empire.

**Economy.** The agricultural base of European life benefitted from improvements in **plow design** c1000, and by draining of lowlands and clearing of forests, leading to a rural population increase. Towns grew in N. Italy, Flanders, and N. Germany (Hanseatic League). Improvements in **loom design** permitted factory textile production. **Guilds** dominated urban trades from the 12th century. Banking (centered in Italy, 12th-15th century) facilitated long-distance trade.

**The Church.** The split between the Eastern and Western churches was formalized in 1054. W. and

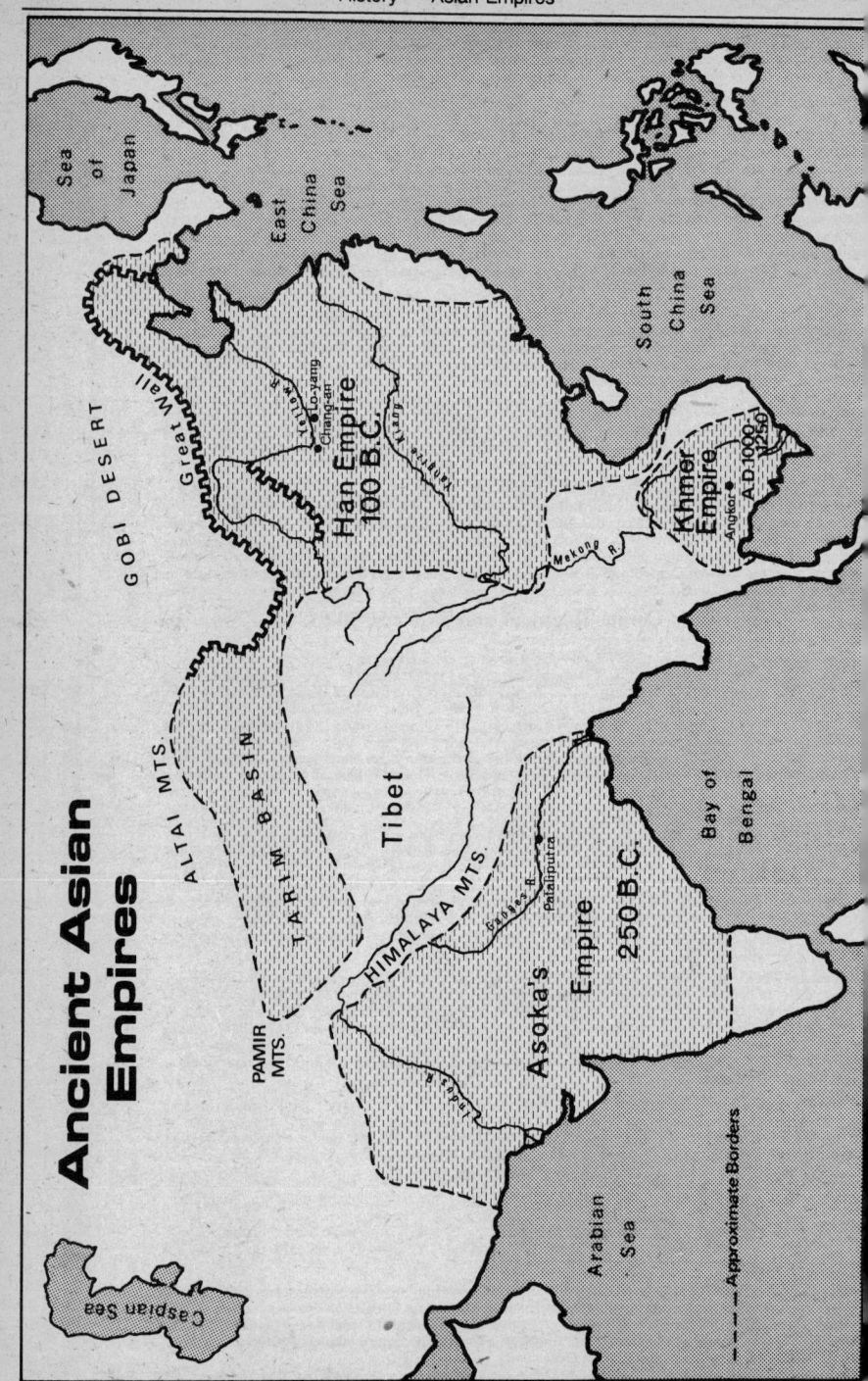

Ancient Asian Empires

Caspian Sea

Sea of Japan

East China Sea

South China Sea

GOBI DESERT

Great Wall

Yellow R.

Lo-yang
Chang-an

Han Empire 100 B.C.

Yangtze R.

Mekong R.

Khmer Empire A.D. 1000-1250

Angkor

ALTAI MTS.

TARIM BASIN

PAMIR MTS.

Tibet

HIMALAYA MTS.

Ganges R.

Pataliputra

Asoka's Empire 250 B.C.

Indus R.

Bay of Bengal

Arabian Sea

------ Approximate Borders

Central Europe was divided into 500 bishoprics under one united hierarchy, but conflicts between secular and church authorities were frequent (German **Investiture Controversy**, 1075-1122). Clerical power was first strengthened through the international monastic reform begun at Cluny, 910. Popular religious enthusiasm often expressed itself in heretical movements (Waldensians from 1173), but was channelled by the **Dominican** (1215) and **Franciscan** (1223) friars into the religious mainstream.

**Arts.** **Romanesque** architecture (11th-12th centuries) expanded on late Roman models, using the rounded arch and massed stone to support enlarged basilicas. Painting and sculpture followed Byzantine models. The literature of **chivalry** was exemplified by the epic (Chanson de Roland, c1100) and by courtly love poems of the troubadours of Provence and minnesingers of Germany. **Gothic architecture** emerged in France (choir of St. Denis, c1040) and spread as French cultural influence predominated in Europe. Rib vaulting and pointed arches were used to combine soaring heights with delicacy, and freed walls for display of stained glass. Exteriors were covered with painted relief sculpture and elaborate architectural detail.

**Learning.** Law, medicine, and philosophy were advanced at independent **universities** (Bologna, late 11th century), originally corporations of students and masters. Twelfth century translations of Greek classics, especially Aristotle, encouraged an analytic approach. Scholastic philosophy, from Anselm (1033-1109) to Aquinas (1225-74) attempted to reconcile reason and revelation.

## Apogee of Central Asian Power; Islam Grows: 1250-1500

**Turks.** Turkic peoples, of Central Asian ancestry, were a military threat to the Byzantine and Persian Empires from the 6th century. After several waves of invasions, during which most of the Turks adopted Islam, the **Seljuk Turks** took Baghdad, 1055. They ruled Persia, Iraq, and, after 1071, Asia Minor, where massive numbers of Turks settled. The empire was divided in the 12th century into smaller states ruled by Seljuks, Kurds (**Saladin** c1137-93), and Mamelukes (a military caste of former Turk, Kurd, and Circassian slaves), which governed Egypt and the Middle East until the Ottoman era (c1290-1922).

Osman I (ruled c1290-1326) and succeeding sultans united Anatolian Turkish warriors in a militaristic state that waged holy war against Byzantium and Balkan Christians. Most of the Balkans had been subdued, and Anatolia united, when **Constantinople fell**, 1453. By the mid-16th century, Hungary, the Middle East, and North Africa had been conquered. The Turkish advance was stopped at Vienna, 1529, and at the naval battle of Lepanto, 1571, by Spain, Venice, and the papacy.

**The Ottoman state** was governed in accordance with orthodox Moslem law. Greek, Armenian, and Jewish communities were segregated, and ruled by religious leaders responsible for taxation; they dominated trade. State offices and most army ranks were filled by slaves through a system of child conscription among Christians.

**India.** Mahmud of Ghazni (971-1030) led repeated Turkish raids into N. India. Turkish power was consolidated in 1206 with the start of the **Sultanate at Delhi.** Centralization of state power under the early Delhi sultans went far beyond traditional Indian practice. Moslem rule of most of the subcontinent lasted until the British conquest some 600 years later.

**Mongols.** Genghis Khan (c1162-1227) first united the feuding Mongol tribes, and built their armies into an effective offensive force around a core of highly mobile cavalry. He and his immediate successors created the largest land empire in history; by 1279 it stretched from the east coast of Asia to the Danube, from the Siberian steppes to the Arabian Sea. East-West trade and contacts were facilitated (Marco Polo c1254-1324). The western Mongols were Islamized by 1295; successor states soon lost their Mongol character by assimilation. They were briefly reunited under the Turk Tamerlane (1336-1405).

**Kublai Khan** ruled China from his new capital Peking (founded 1264). Naval campaigns against Japan (1274, 1281) and Java (1293) were defeated, the latter by the Hindu-Buddhist maritime kingdom of Majapahit. The **Yuan** dynasty made use of Mongols and other foreigners (including Europeans) in official posts, and tolerated the return of Nestorian Christianity (suppressed 841-45) and the spread of Islam in the South and West. A native reaction expelled the Mongols, 1367-68.

**Russia.** The Kievan state in Russia, weakened by the decline of Byzantium and the rise of the Catholic Polish-Lithuanian state, was overrun by the Mongols, 1238-40. Only the northern trading republic of Novgorod remained independent. The grand dukes of Moscow emerged as leaders of a coalition of princes that eventually defeated the Mongols, by 1481. With the fall of Constantinople, the **Tsars** (Caesars) at Moscow (from Ivan III, ruled 1462-1505) set up an independent Russian Orthodox Church. Commerce failed to revive. The isolated Russian state remained agrarian, with the peasant class falling into serfdom.

**Persia.** A revival of Persian literature, using the Arab alphabet and literary forms, began in the 10th century (epic of Firdausi, 935-1020). An art revival, influenced by Chinese styles, began in the 12th century. Persian cultural and political forms, and often the Persian language, were used for centuries by Turkish and Mongol elites from the Balkans to India. Persian mystics from Rumi (1207-73) to Jami (1414-92) promoted **Sufism** in their poetry.

**Africa.** Two Berber dynasties, imbued with Islamic militance, emerged from the Sahara to carve out empires from the Sahel to central Spain — the **Almoravids**, c1050-1140, and the fanatical **Almohads**, 1125-1269. The Ghanaian empire was replaced in the upper Niger by Mali, c1230-c1340, whose Moslem rulers imported Egyptians to help make **Timbuktu** a center of commerce (in gold, leather, slaves) and learning. The Songhay empire (to 1590) replaced Mali. To the S, forest kingdoms produced refined art works (Ife terra cotta, **Benin** bronzes). Other Moslem states in Nigeria (Hausas) and Chad originated in the 11th century, and continued in some form until the 19th century European conquest. Less developed Bantu kingdoms existed across central Africa.

Some 40 Moslem Arab-Persian trading colonies and city-states were established all along the E. African coast from the 10th century (Kilwa, Mogadishu). The interchange with Bantu peoples produced the **Swahili** language and culture. Gold, palm oil, and slaves were brought from the interior, stimulating the growth of the Monamatapa kingdom of the Zambezi (15th century). The Christian Ethiopian empire (from 13th century) continued the traditions of Axum.

**Southeast Asia.** Islam was introduced into Malaya and the Indonesian islands by Arab, Persian, and

---

Timeline (1250–1500):

- 1250
- Dante b.
- Giotto b.
- Marco Polo's journeys
- Peking founded
- Hapsburgs in Austria
- Philip IV rules France
- Petrarch b.
- Western Mongols Islamized
- Ciompi revolt, Florence
- Mongols expelled from China
- Chaucer b.
- Tamerlane b.
- Wycliffe b.
- Bubonic plague in Europe
- Jacquerie in Fr.
- Van Eyck b.
- Gutenberg b.
- 1375
- Medicis begin rule
- Masaccio b.
- Persian poet Jami b.
- Joan of Arc executed
- Hundred Years War
- Leonardo b.
- Portugese explorations begin
- Constantinople falls
- Michelangelo b.
- Russia
- Copernicus b.
- Columbus in Amer.
- Inca empire begins
- Ivan III rules Russia
- Rifle invented
- 1500

**Timeline (left margin, top to bottom):**

- 1500
- Brazil discovered
- Calvin b.
- Watch invented
- Persian Safavids rule
- Vesalius b.
- St. Theresa of Avila b.
- Luther's 95 Theses
- Cortes conquers Aztecs
- Mughal empire starts
- So. Ger. peasants rise
- Pizarro conquers Incas
- Jesuits founded
- Council of Trent
- 1550
- Dutch republic founded
- Japan persecutes Christians
- Civil War in France
- Velasquez b.
- Descartes b.
- 1600

---

Indian traders. Coastal Moslem cities and states (starting before 1300), enriched by trade, soon dominated the interior. Chief among these was the **Malacca** state, on the Malay peninsula, c1400-1511.

# Arts and Statecraft Thrive in Europe: 1350-1600

**Italian Renaissance & humanism.** Distinctive Italian achievements in the arts in the late Middle Ages (Dante, 1265-1321, Giotto, 1276-1337) led to the vigorous new styles of the Renaissance (14th-16th centuries). Patronized by the rulers of the quarreling petty states of Italy (Medicis in Florence and the papacy, c1400-1737), the plastic arts perfected realistic techniques, including **perspective** (Masaccio, 1401-28, Leonardo 1452-1519). Classical motifs were used in architecture and increased talent and expense were put into secular buildings. The Florentine dialect was refined as a national literary language (Petrarch, 1304-74). Greek refugees from the E strengthened the respect of humanist scholars for the classic sources (Bruni 1370-1444). Soon an international movement aided by the spread of **printing** (Gutenberg c1400-1468), **humanism** was optimistic about the power of human reason (Erasmus of Rotterdam, 1466-1536, Thomas More's *Utopia*, 1516) and valued individual effort in the arts and in politics (Machiavelli, 1469-1527).

**France.** The French monarchy, strengthened in its repeated struggles with powerful nobles (Burgundy, Flanders, Aquitaine) by alliances with the growing commercial towns, consolidated bureaucratic control under Philip IV (ruled 1285-1314) and extended French influence into Germany and Italy (popes at Avignon, France, 1309-1417). The **Hundred Years War**, 1338-1453, ended English dynastic claims in France (battles of Crécy, 1346, Poitiers, 1356; Joan of Arc executed, 1431). A French Renaissance, dating from royal invasions of Italy, 1494, 1499, was encouraged at the court of Francis I (ruled 1515-47), who centralized taxation and law. French vernacular literature consciously asserted its independence (La Pleiade, 1549).

**England.** The evolution of England's unique political institutions began with the Magna Carta, 1215, by which King John guaranteed the privileges of nobles and church against the monarchy and assured jury trial. After the Wars of the Roses (1455-85), the **Tudor dynasty** reasserted royal prerogatives (Henry VIII, ruled 1509-47), but the trend toward independent departments and ministerial government also continued. English trade (wool exports from c1340) was protected by the nation's growing maritime power (**Spanish Armada** destroyed, 1588).

English replaced French and Latin in the late 14th century in law and literature (Chaucer, 1340-1400) and English translation of the Bible began (Wycliffe, 1380s). Elizabeth I (ruled 1558-1603) presided over a confident flowering of poetry (Spencer, 1552-99), drama (**Shakespeare**, 1552-1616), and music.

**German Empire.** From among a welter of minor feudal states, church lands, and independent cities, the **Hapsburgs** assembled a far-flung territorial domain, based in Austria from 1276. The family held the title Holy Roman Emperor from 1452 to the Empire's dissolution in 1806, but failed to centralize its domains, leaving Germany disunited for centuries. Resistance to Turkish expansion brought Hungary under Austrian control from the 16th century, curbing French expansion. The Netherlands, Luxembourg, and Burgundy were added in 1477, curbing French expansion.

The Flemish painting tradition of naturalism, technical proficiency, and bourgeois subject matter began in the 15th century (Jan Van Eyck, 1366-1440), the earliest northern manifestation of the Renaissance. **Durer** (1471-1528) typified the merging of late Gothic and Italian trends in 16th century German art. Imposing civic architecture flourished in the prosperous commercial cities.

**Spain.** Despite the unification of Castille and Aragon in 1479, the 2 countries retained separate governments, and the nobility, especially in Aragon and Catalonia, retained many privileges. Spanish lands in Italy (Naples, Sicily) and the Netherlands entangled the country in European wars through the mid-17th century, while explorers, traders, and conquerors built up a Spanish empire in the Americas and the Philippines.

From the late 15th century, a **golden age** of literature and art produced works of social satire (plays of Lope de Vega, 1562-1635; Cervantes, 1547-1616), as well as spiritual intensity (El Greco, 1541-1614; Velazquez, 1599-1660).

**Black Death.** The bubonic plague reached Europe from the E in 1348, killing as much as half the population by 1350. Labor scarcity forced a rise in wages and brought greater freedom to the peasantry, making possible **peasant uprisings** (Jacquerie in France, 1358, Wat Tyler's rebellion in England, 1381). In the ciompi revolt, 1378, Florentine wage earners demanded a say in economic and political power.

**Explorations.** Organized European maritime exploration began, seeking to evade the Venice-Ottoman monopoly of eastern trade and to promote Christianity. Expeditions from Portugal beginning 1418 explored the west coast of Africa, until **Vasco da Gama** rounded the Cape of Good Hope in 1497 and reached India. A Portuguese trading empire was consolidated by the seizure of Goa, 1510, and Malacca, 1551. Japan was reached in 1542. Spanish voyages (**Columbus**, 1492-1504) uncovered a new world, which Spain hastened to subdue. Navigation schools in Spain and Portugal, the development of large sailing ships (carracks), and the invention of the rifle, c1475, aided European penetration.

**Mughals and Safavids.** East of the Ottoman empire, two Moslem dynasties ruled unchallenged in the 16th and 17th centuries. The Mughal empire in India, founded by Persianized Turkish invaders from the NW under Babur, dates from their 1526 conquest of Delhi. The dynasty ruled most of India for over 200 years, surviving nominally until 1857. **Akbar** (ruled 1556-1605) consolidated administration at his glorious court, where Urdu (Persian-influenced Hindi) developed. Trade relations with Europe increased. Under Shah Jahan (1629-58), a secularized art fusing Hindu and Moslem elements flourished in miniature painting and architecture (**Taj Mahal**). Sikhism, founded c1519, combined elements of both faiths. Suppression of Hindus and Shi'ite Moslems in S India in the late 17th century weakened the empire.

Fanatical devotion to the Shi'ite sect characterized the Safavids of Persia, 1502-1736, and led to hostilities with the Sunni Ottomans for over a century. The prosperity and strength of the empire are evidenced by the mosques at its capital, **Isfahan**. The dynasty enhanced Iranian national consciousness.

**China.** The Ming emperors, 1368-1644, the last native dynasty in China, wielded unprecedented personal power, while the Confucian bureaucracy began to suffer from inertia. European trade (Portugese onopoly through **Macao** from 1557) was strictly controlled. Jesuit scholars and scientists (Matteo Ricci, 552-1610) introduced some Western science; their writings familiarized the West with China. Chinese echnological inventiveness declined from this era, but the arts thrived, especially painting and ceramics.

**Japan.** After the decline of the first hereditary shogunate (chief generalship) at **Kamakura** (1185-1333), agmentation of power accelerated, as did the consequent social mobility. Under Kamakura and the shikaga shogunate, 1338-1573, the daimyos (lords) and samurai (warriors) grew more powerful and romoted a martial ideology. Japanese pirates and traders plied the China coast. Popular Buddhist ovements included the nationalist Nichiren sect (from c1250) and **Zen** (brought from China, 1191), hich stressed meditation and a disciplined esthetic (tea ceremony, landscape gardening, judo, No rama).

# Reformed Europe Expands Overseas: 1500-1700

**Reformation begun.** Theological debate and protests against real and perceived clerical corruption xisted in the medieval Christian world, expressed by such dissenters as Wycliffe (c1320-84) and his ollowers, the Lollards, in England, and **Huss** (burned as a heretic, 1415) in Bohemia.
**Luther** (1483-1546) preached that only faith could lead to salvation, without the mediation of clergy or ood works. He attacked the authority of the Pope, rejected priestly celibacy, and recommended dividual study of the Bible (which he translated, c1525). His 95 Theses (1517) led to his xcommunication (1520). **Calvin** (1506-64) said God's elect were predestined for salvation; good conduct nd success were signs of election. Calvin in Geneva and Knox (1505-72) in Scotland erected theocratic ates.
Henry VIII asserted English national authority and secular power by breaking away from the Catholic hurch, 1534. Monastic property was confiscated, and some Protestant doctrines given official sanction.

**Religious wars.** A century and a half of religious wars began with a South German peasant uprising, 524, repressed with Luther's support. Radical sects—democratic, pacifist, milennarian—arose Anabaptists ruled Muenster, 1534-35), and were suppressed violently. Civil war in France from 1562 etween **Huguenots** (Protestant nobles and merchants) and Catholics ended with the 1598 Edict of Jantes tolerating Protestants (revoked 1685). Hapsburg attempts to restore Catholicism in Germany ere resisted in 25 years of fighting; the 1555 Peace of Augsburg guarantee of religious independence to cal princes and cities was confirmed only after the **Thirty Years War**, 1618-48, when much of Germany as devastated by local and foreign armies (Sweden, France).
A Catholic Reformation, or **counter-reformation**, met the Protestant challenge, clearly defining an fficial theology at the Council of Trent, 1545-63. The **Jesuit** order, founded 1534 by Loyola (1491-1556), elped reconvert large areas of Poland, Hungary, and S. Germany and sent missionaries to the New Vorld, India, and China, while the Inquisition helped suppress heresy in Catholic countries. A revival of iety appeared in the devotional literature (Theresa of Avila, 1515-82) and the grandiose Baroque art Bernini, 1598-1680) of Roman Catholic countries.

**Scientific Revolution.** The late nominalist thinkers (Ockham, c1300-49) of Paris and Oxford challenged ristotelian orthodoxy, allowing for a freer scientific approach. But metaphysical values, such as the leoplatonic faith in an orderly, mathematical cosmos, still motivated and directed subsequent inquiry. opernicus (1473-1543) promoted the heliocentric theory, which was confirmed when Kepler (1571-1630) iscovered the mathematical laws describing the orbits of the planets. The Christian-Aristotelian belief nat heavens and earth were fundamentally different collapsed when Galileo (1564-1642) discovered noving sunspots, irregular moon topography, and moons around Jupiter. He and Newton (1642-1727) eveloped a mechanics that unified cosmic and earthly phenomena. To meet the needs of the new physics, Iewton and Leibnitz (1646-1716) invented calculus, Descartes (1596-1650) invented analytic geometry.
An explosion of observational science included the discovery of blood circulation (Harvey, 1378-1657) nd microscopic life (Leeuwenhoek, 1632-1723), and advances in anatomy (Vesalius, 1514-64, dissected orpses) and chemistry (Boyle, 1627-91). Scientific research institutes were founded: Florence, 1657, ondon (**Royal Society**), 1660, Paris, 1666. Inventions proliferated (Savery's steam engine, 1696).

**Arts.** Mannerist painters of the high Renaissance (**Michelangelo**, 1475-1564) exploited virtuosity, grace, ovelty, and exotic subjects and poses. The notion of artistic genius was promoted, in contrast to the nonymous medieval artisan. Private connoisseurs entered the art market. These trends were elaborated n the 17th century **Baroque** era, on a grander scale. Dynamic movement in painting and sculpture was mphasized by sharp lighting effects, use of rich materials (colored marble, gilt), realistic details. Curved acades, broken lines, rich, deep-cut detail, and ceiling decoration characterized Baroque architecture, specially in Germany. Monarchs, princes, and prelates, usually Catholic, used Baroque art to enhance nd embellish their authority, as in royal portraits by Velazquez (1599-1660) and Van Dyck (1599-1641).
National styles emerged. In France, a taste for rectilinear order and serenity (Poussin, 1594-1665), nked to the new rational philosophy, was expressed in classical forms. The influence of **classical values** n French literature (tragedies of Racine, 1639-99) gave rise to the "battle of the Ancients and Moderns." lew forms included the essay (Montaigne, 1533-92) and novel (*Princesse de Cleves*, La Fayette, 1678).
Dutch painting of the 17th century was unique in its wide social distribution. The Flemish tradition of ndemonstrative realism reached its peak in **Rembrandt** (1606-69) and Vermeer (1632-75).

**Economy.** European economic expansion was stimulated by the new trade with the East, New World old and silver, and a doubling of population (50 mln. in 1450, 100 mln. in 1600). New business and nancial techniques were developed and refined, such as joint-stock companies, insurance, and letters of redit and exchange. The Bank of Amsterdam, 1609, and the Bank of England, 1694, broke the old nonopoly of private banking families. The rise of a business mentality was typified by the spread of clock owers in cities in the 14th century. By the mid-15th century, portable clocks were available; the first vatch was invented in 1502.
By 1650, most governments had adopted the **mercantile system,** in which they sought to amass netallic wealth by protecting their merchants' foreign and colonial trade monopolies. The rise in prices nd the new coin-based economy undermined the craft guild and feudal manorial systems. Expanding ndustries, such as clothweaving and mining, benefitted from technical advances. Coal replaced isappearing wood as the chief fuel; it was used to fuel new 16th century blast furnaces making cast iron.

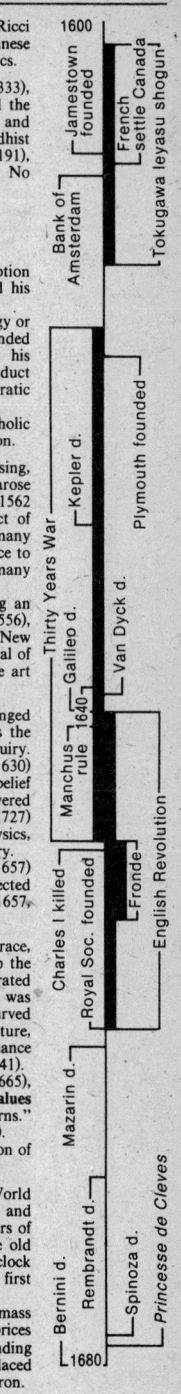

1600
Jamestown founded
French settle Canada
Tokugawa Ieyasu shogun
Bank of Amsterdam
Plymouth founded
Kepler d.
Van Dyck d.
Galileo d.
Thirty Years War
1640
Manchus rule
Charles I killed
Royal Soc. founded
English Revolution
Fronde
Mazarin d.
Bernini d.
Rembrandt d.
Spinoza d.
Princesse de Cleves
1680

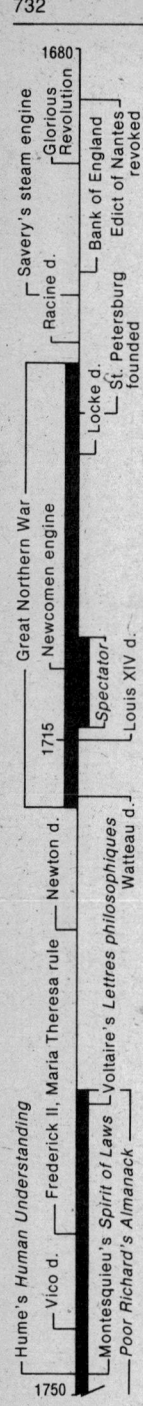

**New World.** The **Aztecs** united much of the Mesoamerican culture area in a militarist empire by 151? from their capital, Tenochtitlan (pop. 300,000), which was the center of a cult requiring enormous level of ritual human sacrifice. Most of the civilized areas of S. America were ruled by the centralized **Inc Empire** (1476-1534), stretching 2,000 miles from Ecuador to N.W. Argentina. Lavish and sophisticate traditions in pottery, weaving, sculpture, and architecture were maintained in both regions.

These empires, beset by revolts, fell in 2 short campaigns to gold-seeking Spanish forces based in th' Antilles and Panama. **Cortes** took Mexico, 1519-21; **Pizarro** Peru, 1531-35. From these centers, land an sea expeditions claimed most of N. and S. America for Spain. The Indian high cultures did not surviv the impact of Christian missionaries and the new upper class of whites and mestizos. In turn, New Worl silver, and such Indian products as potatoes, tobacco, corn, peanuts, chocolate, and rubber exercized major economic influence on Europe. While the Spanish administration intermittently concerned itse with the welfare of Indians, the population remained impoverished at most levels, despite the growth of distinct South American civilization. European diseases reduced the native population.

Brazil, which the Portuguese discovered in 1500 and settled after 1530, and the Caribbean colonies o several European nations developed a plantation economy where sugar cane, tobacco, cotton, coffee, rice indigo, and lumber were grown commercially by slaves. From the early 16th to the late 19th centuries some 10 million Africans were transported to **slavery** in the New World.

**Netherlands.** The urban, Calvinist northern provinces of the Netherlands rebelled against Hapsbu: Spain, 1568, and founded an oligarchic mercantile republic. Their strategic control of the Baltic grai market enabled them to exploit Mediterranean food shortages. Religious refugees — French and Belgia Protestants, Iberian Jews — added to the cosmopolitan commercial talent pool. After Spain absorbe Portugal in 1580, the Dutch seized Portuguese possessions and created a vast, though generall short-lived commercial empire in Brazil, the Antilles, Africa, India, Ceylon, Malacca, Indonesia, an Taiwan, and challenged or supplanted Portuguese traders in China and Japan.

**England.** Anglicanism became firmly established under Elizabeth I after a brief Catholic interlud under "Bloody Mary," 1553-58. But religious and political conflicts led to a rebellion by Parliamen 1642. Roundheads (Puritans) defeated Cavaliers (Royalists); Charles I was beheaded, 1649. The nev **Commonwealth** was ruled as a military dictatorship by Cromwell, who also brutally crushed an Iris! rebellion, 1649-51. Conflicts within the Puritan camp (democratic Levelers defeated 1649) aided th Stuart restoration, 1660, but Parliament was permanently strengthened and the peaceful **"Gloriou Revolution"**, 1688, it advanced political and religious liberties (writings of Locke, 1632-1704). Britisl privateers (Drake, 1540-96) challenged Spanish control of the New World, and penetrated Asian trad routes (Madras taken, 1639). N. American colonies (Jamestown, 1607, Plymouth, 1620) provided a outlet for religious dissenters.

**France.** Emerging from the religious civil wars in 1628, France regained military and commercial grea power status under the ministries of **Richelieu** (1624-42), Mazarin (1643-61), and Colbert (1662-83) Under Louis XIV (ruled 1643-1715) royal absolutism triumphed over nobles and local *parlements*(defea of Fronde, 1648-53). Permanent colonies were founded in Canada (1608), the Caribbean (1626), an India (1674).

**Sweden.** Sweden seceded from the Scandinavian Union in 1523. The thinly-populated agrarian stat (with copper, iron, and timber exports) was united by the Vasa kings, whose conquests by the mid-17t! century made Sweden the dominant Baltic power. The empire collapsed in the Great Northern Wa (1700-21).

**Poland.** After the union with Lithuania in 1447, Poland ruled vast territories from the Baltic to th Black Sea, resisting German and Turkish incursions. Catholic nobles failed to gain the loyalty of the Orthodox Christian peasantry in the East; commerce and trades were practiced by German and Jewisl immigrants. The bloody 1648-49 cossack uprising began the kingdom's dismemberment.

**China.** A new dynasty, the **Manchus**, invaded the NE and seized power in 1644, and expande Chinese control to its greatest extent in Central and Southeast Asia. Trade and diplomatic contact wit! Europe grew, carefully controlled by China. New crops (sweet potato, maize, peanut) allowed ar economic and population growth (300 million pop. in 1800). Traditional arts and literature were pursue with increased sophistication (*Dream of the Red Chamber*, novel, mid-18th century).

**Japan.** Tokugawa Ieyasu, shogun from 1603, finally unified and pacified feudal Japan. Hereditary daimyos and samurai monopolized government office and the professions. An urban merchant class grew literacy spread, and a cultural renaissance occurred (haiku of Basho, 1644-94). Fear of Europear domination led to persecution of Christian converts from 1597, and stringent isolation from outside contact from 1640.

## Philosophy, Industry, and Revolution: 1700-1800

**Science and Reason.** Faith in human reason and science as the source of truth and a means to improve the physical and social environment, espoused since the Renaissance (Francis Bacon, 1561-1626), was bolstered by scientific discoveries in spite of theological opposition (**Galileo's forced retraction**, 1633) Descartes applied the logical method of mathematics to discover "self-evident" scientific and philosophical truths, while Newton emphasized induction from experimental observation.

The challenge of reason to traditional religious and political values and institutions began with Spinoza (1632-77), who interpreted the Bible historically and called for political and intellectual freedom.

French philosophes assumed leadership of the **"Enlightenment"** in the 18th century. Montesquieu (1689-1755) used British history to support his notions of limited government. Voltaire's (1694-1778) diaries and novels of exotic travel illustrated the intellectual trends toward secular ethics and relativism. Rousseau's (1712-1778) radical concepts of the **social contract** and of the inherent goodness of the common man gave impetus to anti-monarchical republicanism. The *Encyclopedia*, 1751-72, edited by Diderot and d'Alembert, designed as a monument to reason, was largely devoted to practical technology.

In England, ideals of political and religious liberty were connected with empiricist philosophy and science in the followers of Locke. But the extreme **empiricism of Hume** (1711-76) and Berkeley

685-1753) posed limits to the identification of reason with absolute truth, as did the evolutionary approach to law and politics of Burke (1729-97) and the utilitarianism of Bentham (1748-1832). Adam Smith (1723-90) and other **physiocrats** called for a rationalization of economic activity by removing artificial barriers to a supposedly natural free exchange of goods.

Despite the political disunity and backwardness of most of Germany, German writers participated in the new philosophical trends popularized by Wolff (1679-1754). **Kant's** (1724-1804) **idealism**, unifying an empirical epistemology with *a priori* moral and logical concepts, directed German thought away from skepticism. Italian contributions included work on electricity by Galvani (1737-98) and Volta 1745-1827), the pioneer **historiography of Vico** (1668-1744), and writings on penal reform by Beccaria 1738-94). The American Franklin (1706-90) was celebrated in Europe for his varied achievements.

The growth of the **press** (*Spectator*, 1711-14) and the wide distribution of realistic but sentimental novels attested to the increase of a large bourgeois public.

**Arts.** Rococo art, characterized by extravagant decorative effects, asymmetries copied from organic models, and artificial pastoral subjects, was favored by the continental aristocracy for most of the century Watteau, 1684-1721), and had musical analogies in the ornamentalized polyphony of late Baroque. The Neoclassical art after 1750, associated with the new scientific archeology, was more streamlined, and infused with the supposed moral and geometric rectitude of the Roman Republic (David, 1748-1825). In England, **town planning** on a grand scale began (Edinburgh, 1767).

**Industrial Revolution in England.** Agricultural improvements, such as the sowing drill (1701) and livestock breeding, were implemented on the large fields provided by enclosure of common lands by private owners. Profits from agriculture and from colonial and foreign trade (1800 volume, £ 54 million) were channelled through hundreds of banks and the **Stock Exchange** (founded 1773) into new industrial processes.

The Newcomen steam pump (1712) aided coal mining. Coal fueled the new efficient steam engines patented by Watt in 1769, and coke-smelting produced cheap, sturdy iron for machinery by the 1730s. The **flying shuttle** (1733) and **spinning jenny** (1764) were used in the large new cotton textile factories, where women and children were much of the work force. Goods were transported cheaply over **canals** 2,000 miles built 1760-1800).

**Central and East Europe.** The monarchs of the three states that dominated eastern Europe — Austria, Prussia, and Russia — accepted the advice and legitimation of philosophes in creating more modern, centralized institutions in their kingdoms, enlarged by the division of Poland (1772-95).

Under **Frederick II** (ruled 1740-86) Prussia, with its efficient modern army, doubled in size. State monopolies and tariff protection fostered industry, and some legal reforms were introduced. Austria's heterogeneous realms were legally unified under **Maria Theresa** (ruled 1740-80) and **Joseph II** (1780-90). Reforms in education, law, and religion were enacted, and the Austrian serfs were freed (1781). With its defeat in the Seven Years War in 1763, Austria lost Silesia and ceased its active role in Germany, but was compensated by expansion to the E and S (Hungary, Croatia, 1699, Galicia, 1772).

Russia, whose borders continued to expand in all directions, adopted some Western bureaucratic and economic policies under **Peter I** (ruled 1682-1725) and **Catherine II** (ruled 1729-96). Trade and cultural contacts with the West multiplied from the new Baltic Sea capital, **St. Petersburg** (founded 1703).

**American Revolution.** The British colonies in N. America attracted a mass immigration of religious dissenters and poor people throughout the 17th and 18th centuries, coming from all parts of the British isles, Germany, the Netherlands, and other countries. The population reached 3 million whites and blacks by the 1770s. The small native population was decimated by European diseases and wars with and between the various colonies. British attempts to control colonial trade, and to tax the colonists to pay for the costs of colonial administration and defense clashed with traditions of local self government, and eventually provoked the colonies to rebellion. (*See American Revolution in Index*.)

**French Revolution.** The growing French middle class lacked political power, and resented aristocratic tax privileges, especially in light of liberal political ideals popularized by the American Revolution. Peasants lacked adequate land and were burdened with feudal obligations to nobles. Wars with Britain drained the treasury, finally forcing the king to call the **Estates-General** in 1789 (first time since 1614), in an atmosphere of food riots (poor crop in 1788).

Aristocratic resistance to absolutism was soon overshadowed by the reformist Third Estate (middle class), which proclaimed itself the **National Constituent Assembly** June 17 and took the "Tennis Court Oath" on June 20 to secure a constitution. The storming of the Bastille July 14 by Parisian artisans was followed by looting and seizure of aristocratic property throughout France. Assembly reforms included abolition of class and regional privileges, a Declaration of Rights, suffrage by taxpayers (75% of males), and the **Civil Constitution of the Clergy** providing for election and loyalty oaths for priests. A republic was declared Sept. 22, 1792, in spite of royalist pressure from Austria and Prussia, which had declared war in April (joined by Britain the next year). Louis XVI was beheaded Jan. 21, 1793, Queen Marie Antoinette was beheaded Oct. 16, 1793.

Royalist uprisings in La Vendee and the S and military reverses led to a **reign of terror** in which tens of thousands of opponents of the Revolution and criminals were executed. Radical reforms in the Convention period (Sept. 1793-Oct. 1795) included the abolition of colonial slavery, economic measures to aid the poor, support of public education, and a short-lived de-Christianization.

Division among radicals (execution of Hebert, March 1794, Danton, April, and Robespierre, July) aided the ascendance of a moderate **Directory**, which consolidated military victories. **Napoleon Bonaparte** (1769-1821), a popular young general, exploited political divisions and participated in a coup Nov. 9, 1799, making himself first consul (dictator).

**India.** Sikh and Hindu rebels (Rajputs, Marathas) and Afghans destroyed the power of the Mughals during the 18th century. After France's defeat in the Seven Years War, 1763, Britain was the chief European trade power in India. Its control of inland **Bengal and Bihar** was recognized by the Mughal shah in 1765, who granted the **British East India Co.** (under Clive, 1727-74) the right to collect land revenue there. Despite objections from Parliament (1784 India Act) the company's involvement in local wars and politics led to repeated acquisitions of new territory. The company exported Indian textiles, sugar, and indigo.

<!-- Right-margin timeline, 1750 to 1800 -->
1750

Watt's engine
Brit. rules Bengal
Spinning jenny
Rosseau's Social Contract
Encyclopedia
Edinburgh plan
Kant's Critique of Pure Reason
American Revolution
Austria serfs free

1775

Bastille stormed
Fr. Repub. declared
Adam Smith d.
Divisions of Poland
Burke d.
China bans opium
China pop. at 300 mln.

1800

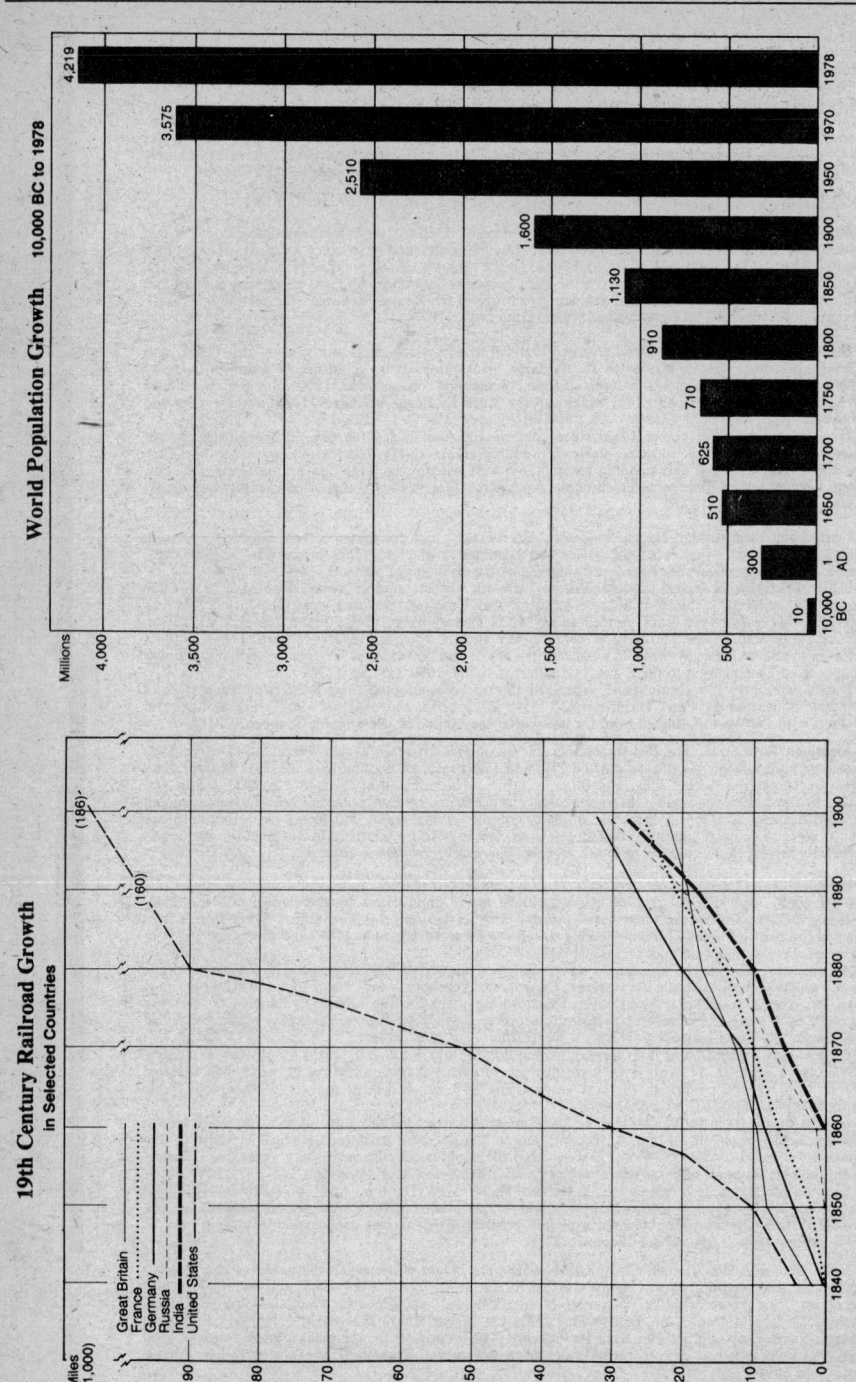

## World Population Growth  10,000 BC to 1978

| Year | Millions |
|---|---|
| 10,000 BC | 10 |
| 1 AD | 300 |
| 1650 | 510 |
| 1700 | 625 |
| 1750 | 710 |
| 1800 | 910 |
| 1850 | 1,130 |
| 1900 | 1,600 |
| 1950 | 2,510 |
| 1970 | 3,575 |
| 1978 | 4,219 |

## 19th Century Railroad Growth in Selected Countries

Miles (1,000)

Great Britain
France
Germany
Russia
India
United States

# Change Gathers Steam: 1800-1840

**French ideals and empire spread.** Inspired by the ideals of the French Revolution, and supported by the expanding French armies, new republican regimes arose near France: the **Batavian** Republic in the Netherlands (1795-1806), the **Helvetic** Republic in Switzerland (1798-1803), the **Cisalpine** Republic in N. Italy (1797-1805), the **Ligurian** Republic in Genoa (1797-1805), and the **Parthenopean** Republic in S. Italy (1799). A Roman Republic existed briefly in 1798 after Pope Pius VI was arrested by French troops. In Italy and Germany, new nationalist sentiments were stimulated both in imitation of and in reaction to France (anti-French and anti-Jacobin peasant uprisings in Italy, 1796-9).

From 1804, when Napoleon declared himself emperor, to 1812, a succession of military victories (Austerlitz, 1805, Jena, 1806) extended his control over most of Europe, through puppet states (Confederation of the Rhine united W. German states for the first time and Grand Duchy of Warsaw revived Polish national hopes), expansion of the empire, and alliances.

Among the lasting reforms initiated under Napoleon's absolutist reign were: establishment of the Bank of France, centralization of tax collection, codification of law along Roman models (*Code Napoleon*), and reform and extension of secondary and university education. In an 1801 concordat, the papacy recognized the effective autonomy of the French Catholic Church. Some 400,000 French soldiers were killed in the Napoleonic Wars, along with 600,000 foreign troops.

**Last gasp of old regime.** France's coastal blockade of Europe (**Continental System**) failed to neutralize Britain. The disastrous 1812 invasion of Russia exposed Napoleon's overextension. After an 1814 exile at Elba, Napoleon's armies were defeated at **Waterloo**, 1815, by British and Prussian troops.

At the **Congress of Vienna**, the monarchs and princes of Europe redrew their boundaries, to the advantage of Prussia (in Saxony and the Ruhr), Austria (in Illyria and Venetia), and Russia (in Poland and Finland). British conquest of Dutch and French colonies (S. Africa, Ceylon, Mauritius) was recognized, and France, under the restored Bourbons, retained its expanded 1792 borders. The settlement brought 50 years of international peace to Europe.

But the Congress was unable to check the advance of liberal ideals and of nationalism among the smaller European nations. The 1825 **Decembrist uprising** by liberal officers in Russia was easily suppressed. But an independence movement in **Greece**, stirred by commercial prosperity and a cultural revival, succeeded in expelling Ottoman rule by 1831, with the aid of Britain, France, and Russia.

A constitutional monarchy was secured in France by an **1830 revolution**; Louis Philippe became king. The revolutionary contagion spread to **Belgium**, which gained its independence from the Dutch monarchy, 1830; to **Poland**, whose rebellion was defeated by Russia, 1830-31; and to Germany.

**Romanticism.** A new style in intellectual and artistic life began to replace Neo-classicism and rococo after the mid-18th century. By the early 19th, this style, Romanticism, had prevailed in the European world.

**Rousseau** had begun the reaction against excessive rationalism and skepticism; in education (*Emile*, 1762) he stressed subjective spontaneity over regularized instruction. In Germany, Lessing (1729-81) and Herder (1744-1803) favorably compared the German folk song to classical forms, and began a cult of Shakespeare, whose passion and "natural" wisdom was a model for the Romantic *Sturm und Drang* (storm and stress) movement. **Goethe's** *Sorrows of Young Werther* (1774) set the model for the tragic, passionate genius.

A new interest in **Gothic architecture** in England after 1760 (Walpole, 1717-97) spread through Europe, associated with an aesthetic Christian and mystic revival (Blake, 1757-1827). Celtic, Norse, and German mythology and folk tales were revived or imitated (Macpherson's Ossian translation, 1762, Grimm's *Fairy Tales*, 1812-22). The medieval revival (Scott's *Ivanhoe*, 1819) led to a new interest in history, stressing national differences and organic growth (Carlyle, 1795-1881; Michelet, 1798-1874), corresponding to theories of natural evolution (Lamarck's *Philosophie zoologique*, 1809, Lyell's *Geology*, 1830-33).

Revolution and war fed an obsession with freedom and conflict, expressed by poets (Byron, 1788-1824, Hugo, 1802-85) and philosophers (Hegel, 1770-1831).

Wild gardens replaced the formal French variety, and painters favored rural, stormy, and mountainous landscapes (Turner, 1775-1851; Constable, 1776-1837). Clothing became freer, with wigs, hoops, and ruffles discarded. Originality and genius were expected in the life as well as the work of inspired artists (Murger's *Scenes from Bohemian Life*, 1847-49). Exotic locales and themes (as in "Gothic" horror stories) were used in art and literature (Delacroix, 1798-1863, Poe, 1809-49).

Music exhibited the new dramatic style and a breakdown of classical forms (Beethoven, 1770-1827). The use of folk melodies and modes aided the growth of distinct national traditions (Glinka in Russia, 1804-57).

**Latin America.** Haiti, under the former slave **Toussaint L'Ouverture**, was the first Latin American independent state, 1800. All the mainland Spanish colonies won their independence 1810-24, under such leaders as **Bolivar** (1783-1830). Brazil became an independent empire under the Portuguese prince regent, 1822. A new strata of military officers divided power with large landholders and the church.

**United States.** Heavy immigration and exploitation of ample natural resources fueled rapid economic growth. The spread of the franchise, public education, and antislavery sentiment were signs of a widespread democratic ethic.

**China.** Failure to keep pace with Western arms technology exposed China to greater European influence, and hampered efforts to bar imports of opium, which had damaged Chinese society and drained wealth overseas. In the **Opium War**, 1839-42, Britain forced China to expand trade opportunities and to cede Hong Kong.

---

Timeline (1800–1845):

- 1800
- Haiti indep.
- Hugo b.
- Dix b.
- Mill b.
- Lamarck's *Philosophie Zoologique*
- Napoleon emperor
- Congress of Vienna
- 1815
- Scott's *Ivanhoe*
- S. Amer. colonies win indep.
- Grimm's *Fairy Tales*
- Brazil indep.
- Greek indep. movement
- Byron d.
- Decembrist uprising
- 1830
- Blake d.
- Volta d.
- Beethoven d.
- Belgian indep.
- 1st Eng. reform bill
- 1st Brit. Factory Act
- Brit. Emp. slavery banned
- Opium War
- Brook Farm, Mass.
- Telegraph perfected by Morse
- 1845

# Triumph of Progress: 1840-80

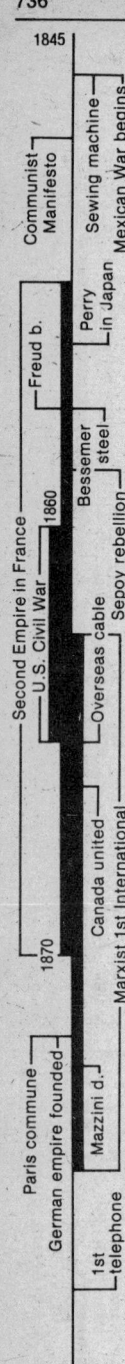

**Idea of Progress.** As a result of the cumulative scientific, economic, and political changes of th preceding eras, the idea took hold among literate people in the West that continuing growth an improvement was the usual state of human and natural life.

Darwin's statement of the **theory of evolution** and survival of the fittest (*Origin of Species*, 185✦ defended by intellectuals and scientists against theological objections, was taken as confirmation th progress was the natural direction of life. The controversy helped define popular ideas of the dedicate scientist and ever-expanding human knowledge of and control over the world (Foucault's demonstratio of earth's rotation, 1851, Pasteur's germ theory, 1861).

Liberals following Ricardo (1772-1823) in their faith that unrestrained competition would bri continuous economic expansion sought to adjust political life to the new social realities, and believed th unregulated competition of ideas would yield truth (Mill, 1806-73). In England, successive reform bil (1832, 1867, 1884) gave representation to the new industrial towns, and extended the franchise to th middle and lower classes and to Catholics, Dissenters, and Jews. On both sides of the Atlantic, reformis tried to improve conditions for the mentally ill (Dix, 1802-87), women (Anthony, 1820-1906), an prisoners. Slavery was barred in the British Empire, 1833; the United States, 1865; and Brazil, 1888.

Socialist theories based on ideas of human perfectibility or historical progress were wide disseminated. Utopian socialists like Saint-Simon (1760-1825) envisaged an orderly, just society directe by a technocratic elite. A model factory town, New Lanark, Scotland, was set up by utopian Robe Owen (1771-1858), and utopian communal experiments were tried in the U.S. (Brook Farm, Mass 1841-7). Bakunin's (1814-76) anarchism represented the opposite utopian extreme of total freedom. Mar (1818-83) posited the inevitable triumph of socialism in the industrial countries through a historic process of class conflict.

**Spread of industry.** The technical processes and managerial innovations of the English industri revolution spread to Europe (especially Germany) and the U.S., causing an explosion of industri production, demand for raw materials, and competition for markets. Inventors, both trained an self-educated, provided the means for larger-scale production (Bessemer steel, 1856, sewing machin 1846). Many inventions were shown at the 1851 London Great Exhibition at the Crystal Palace, who theme was universal prosperity.

Local specialization and long-distance trade were aided by a revolution in transportation an communication. Railroads were first introduced in the 1820s in England and the U.S. Over 150,000 mile of track had been laid worldwide by 1880, with another 100,000 miles laid in the next decad Steamships were improved (*Savannah* crossed Atlantic, 1819). The telegraph, perfected by 184 (Morse), connected the Old and New Worlds by cable in 1866, and quickened the pace of internation commerce and politics. The first commercial telephone exchange went into operation in the U.S. in 1878.

The new class of industrial workers, uprooted from their rural homes, lacked job security, and suffere from dangerous overcrowded conditions at work and at home. Many responded by organizing trad unions (legalized in England, 1824; France, 1884). The U.S. Knights of Labor had 700,000 members b 1886. The First International, 1864-76, tried to unite workers internationally around a Marxist progran The quasi-Socialist Paris Commune uprising, 1871, was violently suppressed. Factory Acts to reduc child labor and regulate conditions were passed (1833-50 in England). Social security measures wer introduced by the Bismarck regime in Germany, 1883-89.

**Revolutions of 1848.** Among the causes of the continent-wide revolutions were an internation collapse of credit and resulting unemployment, bad harvests in 1845-7, and a cholera epidemic. The ne urban proletariat and expanding bourgeoisie demanded a greater political role. Republics wer proclaimed in France, Rome, and Venice. Nationalist feelings reached fever pitch in the Hapsbur empire, as Hungary declared independence under Kossuth, a Slav Congress demanded equality, an Piedmont tried to drive Austria from Lombardy. A national liberal assembly at Frankfurt called fo German unification.

But riots fueled bourgeois fears of socialism (Marx and Engels' 1848 *Communist Manifesto*) an peasants remained conservative. The old establishment — The Papacy, the Hapsburgs (using Croats an Romanians against Hungary), the Prussian army — was able to rout the revolutionaries by 1849. Th French Republic succumbed to a renewed monarchy by 1852 (Emperor Napoleon III).

**Great nations unified.** Using the "blood and iron" tactics of Bismarck from 1862, Prussia controlle N. Germany by 1867 (war with Denmark, 1864, Austria, 1866). After defeating France in 1870 (loss o Alsace-Lorraine), it won the allegiance of S. German states. A new **German Empire** was proclaime 1871. **Italy**, inspired by Mazzini (1805-72) and Garibaldi (1807-82), was unified by the reforme Piedmont kingdom through uprisings, plebiscites, and war.

The U.S., its area expanded after the 1846-47 Mexican War, defeated a secession attempt by slav states, 1861-65. The Canadian provinces were united in an autonomous **Dominion of Canada,** 186✦ Control in **India** was removed from the East India Co. and centralized under British administration afte the 1857-58 Sepoy rebellion, laying the groundwork for the modern Indian State. Queen Victoria wa named Empress of India, 1876.

**Europe dominates Asia.** The Ottoman Empire began to collapse in the face of Balkan nationalisms an European imperial incursions in N. Africa (Suez Canal, 1869). The Turks had lost control of most of bot regions by 1882. Russia completed its expansion south by 1884 (despite the temporary setback of th Crimean War with Turkey, Britain, and France, 1853-56) taking Turkestan, all the Caucasus, an Chinese areas in the East and sponsoring Balkan Slavs against the Turks. A succession of reformist an reactionary regimes presided over a slow modernization (serfs freed, 1861). Persian independence suffere as Russia and British India competed for influence.

China was forced to sign a series of unequal treaties with European powers and Japan. Overpopulatio and an inefficient dynasty brought misery and caused rebellions (Taiping, Moslems) leaving tens o millions dead. Japan was forced by the U.S. (Commodore Perry's visits, 1853-54) and Europe to end i isolation. The Meiji restoration, 1868, gave power to a Westernizing oligarchy. Intensifie empire-building gave Burma to Britain, 1824-86, and Indo-China to France, 1862-95. Christia missionary activity followed imperial and trade expansion in Asia.

**Respectability.** The fine arts were expected to reflect and encourage the progress of morals an

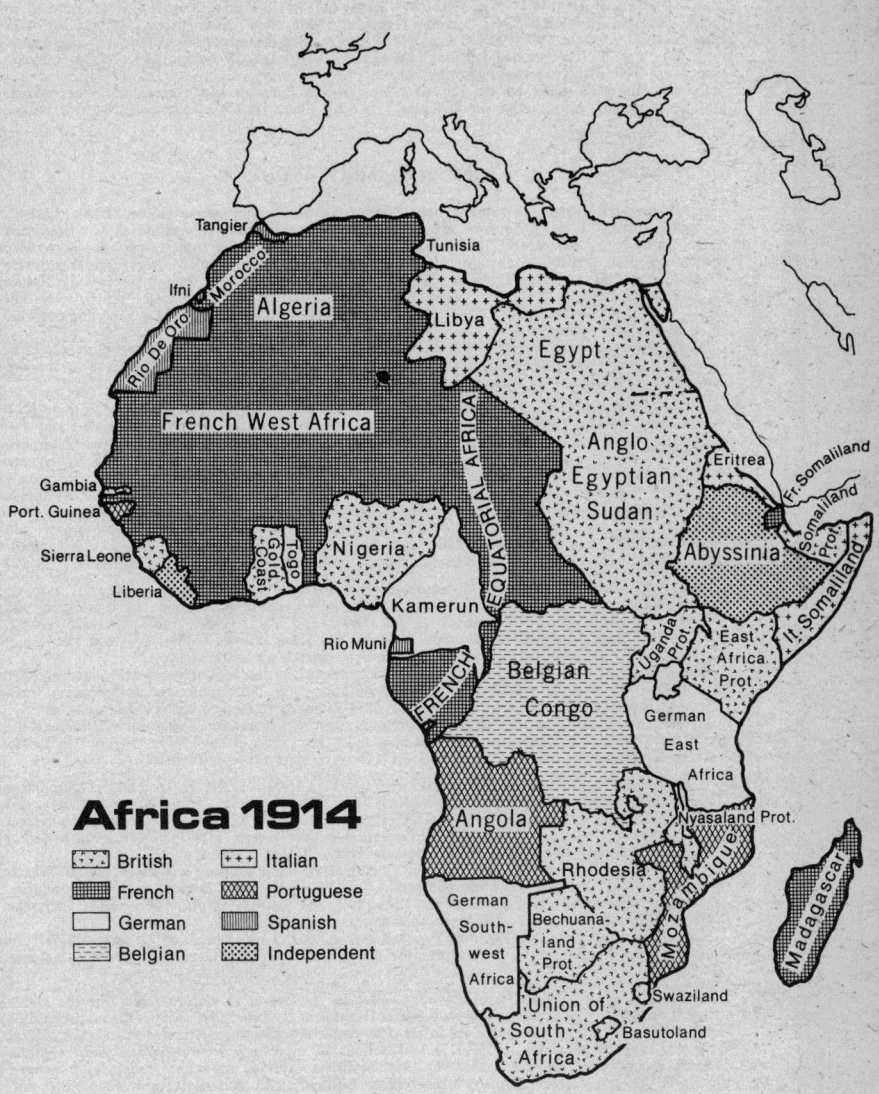

Tangier
Tunisia
Ifni
Morocco
Algeria
Libya
Rio De Oro
Egypt
French West Africa
EQUATORIAL AFRICA
Anglo Egyptian Sudan
Eritrea
Fr. Somaliland
Gambia
Port. Guinea
Sierra Leone
Togo
Gold Coast
Nigeria
Liberia
Kamerun
Rio Muni
FRENCH
Belgian Congo
Abyssinia
It. Somaliland
Somaliland Prot.
Uganda Prot.
East Africa Prot.
German East Africa
Angola
Rhodesia
Nyasaland Prot.
Mozambique
Madagascar
German South-west Africa
Bechuana-land Prot.
Swaziland
Union of South Africa
Basutoland

# Africa 1914

- [.·.·] British
- [▦] French
- [☐] German
- [▥] Belgian
- [+++] Italian
- [▨] Portuguese
- [▥] Spanish
- [▒] Independent

manners among the different classes. "Victorian" prudery, exaggerated delicacy, and familial piety were heralded by **Bowdler's** expurgated edition of Shakespeare (1818). Government-supported mass education inculcated a work ethic as a means to escape poverty (Horatio Alger, 1832-99).

The official **Beaux Arts** school in Paris set an international style of imposing public buildings (Paris Opera, 1861-74, Vienna Opera, 1861-69) and uplifting statues (Bartholdi's *Statue of Liberty*, 1885). Realist painting, influenced by photography (Daguerre, 1837), appealed to a new mass audience with social or historical narrative (Wilkie, 1785-1841, Poynter, 1836-1919) or with serious religious, moral, or social messages (pre-Raphaelites, Millet's Angelus, 1858) often drawn from ordinary life. The **Impressionists** (Pissarro, 1830-1903, Renoir, 1841-1919) rejected the central role of serious subject matter in favor of a colorful and sensual depiction of a moment, but their sunny, placid depictions of bourgeois scenes kept them within the respectable consensus.

Realistic **novelists** presented the full panorama of social classes and personalities, but retained sentimentality and moral judgment (Dickens, 1812-70, Eliot, 1819-80, Tolstoy, 1828-1910, Balzac, 1799-1850).

## Veneer of Stability: 1880-1900

**Imperialism triumphant.** The vast **African** interior, visited by European explorers (Barth, 1821-65, Livingstone, 1813-73) was conquered by the European powers in rapid, competitive thrusts from their coastal bases after 1880, mostly for domestic political and international strategic reasons. W. African Moslem kingdoms (Fulani), Arab slave traders (Zanzibar), and Bantu military confederations (Zulu) were alike subdued. Only Christian Ethiopia (defeat of Italy, 1896) and Liberia resisted successfully. France (W. Africa) and Britain ("Cape to Cairo," Boer War, 1899-1902) were the major beneficiaries. The ideology of "the white man's burden" (Kipling, *Barrack Room Ballads*, 1892) or of a "civilizing mission" (France) justified the conquests.

West European foreign capital investments soared to nearly $40 billion by 1914, but most was in E. Europe (France, Germany) the Americas (Britain) and the white colonies. The foundation of the modern interdependent world economy was laid, with cartels dominating raw material trade.

**An industrious world.** Industrial and technological proficiency characterized the 2 new great powers — Germany and the U.S. Coal and iron deposits enabled Germany to reach second or third place status in iron, steel, and shipbuilding by the 1900s. German electrical and chemical industries were world leaders. The U.S. post-civil war boom (interrupted by "panics," 1884, 1893, 1896) was shaped by massive immigration from S. and E. Europe from 1880, government subsidy of railroads, and huge private monopolies (Standard Oil, 1870, U.S. Steel, 1901). The **Spanish-American War**, 1898 (Phillipine rebellion, 1899-1901) and the Open Door policy in China (1899) made the U.S. a world power.

England led in **urbanization** (72% by 1890), with **London** the world capital of finance, insurance, and shipping. Electric subways (London, 1890), sewer systems (Paris, 1850s), parks, and bargain department stores helped improve living standards for most of the urban population of the industrial world.

**Asians assimilate.** Asian reaction to European economic, military, and religious incursions took the form of imitation of Western techniques and adoption of Western ideas of progress and freedom. The Chinese "self-strengthening" movement of the 1860s and 70s included rail, port, and arsenal improvements and metal and textile mills. Reforms like K'ang Yu-wei (1858-1927) won liberalizing reforms in 1898, right after the European and Japanese "scramble for concessions."

A universal education system in Japan and importation of foreign industrial, scientific, and military experts aided Japan's unprecedented rapid modernization after 1868, under the authoritarian Meiji regime. Japan's victory in the **Sino-Japanese War**, 1894-95, put Formosa and Korea in its power.

In India, the British alliance with the remaining princely states masked reform sentiment among the Westernized urban elite; higher education had been conducted largely in English for 50 years. The **Indian National Congress**, founded in 1885, demanded a larger government role for Indians.

**"Fin-de-siecle" sophistication.** **Naturalist** writers pushed realism to its extreme limits, adopting a quasi-scientific attitude and writing about formerly taboo subjects like sex, crime, extreme poverty, and corruption (Flaubert, 1821-80, Zola, 1840-1902, Hardy, 1840-1928). Unseen or repressed psychological motivations were explored in the clinical and theoretical works of **Freud** (1856-1939) and in the fiction of Dostoevsky (1821-81), James (1843-1916), Schnitzler (1862-1931) and others.

A contempt for bourgeois life or a desire to shock a complacent audience was shared by the French **symbolist** poets (Verlaine, 1844-96, Rimbaud, 1854-91), neo-pagan English writers (Swinburne, 1837-1909), continental dramatists (Ibsen, 1828-1906) and satirists (Wilde, 1854-1900). **Nietzsche** (1844-1900) was influential in his elitism and pessimism.

Post-impressionist art neglected long-cherished conventions of representation (Cezanne, 1839-1906) and showed a willingness to learn from primitive and non-European art (Gauguin, 1848-1903, Japanese prints).

**Racism.** Gobineau (1816-82) gave a pseudo-biological foundation to modern racist theories, which spread in the latter 19th century along with **Social Darwinism**, the belief that societies are and should be organized as a struggle for survival of the fittest. The Medieval period was interpreted as an era of natural Germanic rule (Chamberlain, 1855-1927) and notions of superiority were associated with German national aspirations (Treitschke, 1834-96). **Anti-Semitism**, with a new racist rationale, became a significant political force in Germany (Anti-Semitic Petition, 1880), Austria (Lueger, 1844-1910), and France (Dreyfus case, 1894-1906).

## Last Respite: 1900-1909

**Alliances.** While the peace of Europe (and its dependencies) continued to hold (1907 **Hague Conference** extended the rules of war and international arbitration procedures), imperial rivalries, protectionist trade practices (in Germany and France), and the escalating arms race (British *Dreadnought* battleship launched, Germany widens Kiel canal, 1906) exacerbated minor disputes (German-French Moroccan "crises", 1905, 1911).

Security was sought through alliances: **Triple Alliance** (Germany, Austria-Hungary, Italy) renewed

---

**Left margin timeline (1880–1904):**

- 1880
- Dostoyevsky d.
- Marx d.
- Indian Natl. Cong.
- 1885
- Brazil bans slavery
- Kipling's *Barrack Room Ballads*
- Europe conquers Africa
- Rimbaud d.
- radio
- Sino-Jap. War
- Span.-Am. War
- 1895
- Russ. Soc. Dem. Party
- Dreyfus case
- Gorky's *Lower Depths*
- Wilde d.
- Boxer rebellion
- Ford Motor Co.
- Panama Canal
- Australia united
- 1904

1902, 1907; Anglo-Japanese Alliance, 1902; Franco-Russian Alliance, 1899; **Entente Cordiale** (Britain, France) 1904; Anglo-Russian Treaty, 1907; German-Ottoman friendship.

**Ottomans decline.** The inefficient, corrupt Ottoman government was unable to resist further loss of territory. Nearly all European lands were lost in 1912 to Serbia, Greece, Montenegro, and Bulgaria. Italy took Libya and the Dodecanese islands the same year, and Britain took Kuwait, 1899, and the Sinai, 1906. The **Young Turk** revolution in 1908 forced the sultan to restore a constitution, introduced some social reform, industrialization, and secularization.

**British Empire.** British trade and cultural influence remained dominant in the empire, but constitutional reforms presaged its eventual dissolution: the colonies of **Australia** were united in 1901 under a self-governing commonwealth. **New Zealand** acquired dominion status in 1907. The old Boer republics joined Cape Colony and Natal in the self-governing **Union of South Africa** in 1910.
The 1909 Indian Councils Act enhanced the role of elected province legislatures in **India.** The Moslem League, founded 1906, sought separate communal representation.

**East Asia.** Japan exploited its growing industrial power to expand its empire. Victory in the 1904-05 war against Russia (naval battle of Tsushima, 1905) assured Japan's domination of **Korea** (annexed 1910) and Manchuria (took Port Arthur 1905).
In China, central authority began to crumble (empress died, 1908). Reforms (Confucian exam system ended 1905, modernization of the army, building of railroads) were inadequate and secret societies of reformers and nationalists, inspired by the Westernized **Sun Yat-sen** (1866-1925) fomented periodic uprisings in the south.
**Siam,** whose independence had been guaranteed by Britain and France in 1896, was split into spheres of influence by those countries in 1907.

**Russia.** The population of the Russian Empire approached 150 million in 1900. Reforms in education, law, and local institutions (*zemstvos*), and an industrial boom starting in the 1880s (oil, railroads) created the beginnings of a modern state, despite the autocratic tsarist regime. Liberals (1903 Union of Liberation), Socialists (Social Democrats founded 1898, Bolsheviks split off 1903), and populists (Social Revolutionaries founded 1901) were periodically repressed, and national minorities persecuted (anti-Jewish pogroms, 1903, 1905-6).
An industrial crisis after 1900 and harvest failures aggravated poverty in the urban proletariat, and the 1905-6 defeat by Japan (which checked Russia's Asian expansion) sparked the revolution of 1905-06. A **Duma** (parliament) was created, and an agricultural reform (under Stolypin, prime minister 1906-11) created a large class of landowning peasants (kulaks).

**The world shrinks.** Developments in transportation and communication and mass population movements helped create an awareness of an interdependent world. Early **automobiles** (Daimler, Benz, 1885) were experimental, or designed as luxuries. Assembly-line mass production (Ford Motor Co., 1903) made the invention practicable, and by 1910 nearly 500,000 motor vehicles were registered in the U.S. alone. **Heavier-than-air flights** began in 1903 in the U.S. (Wright brothers), preceded by glider, balloon, and model plane advances in several countries. Trade was advanced by improvements in ship design (gyrocompass, 1907), speed (Lusitania crossed Atlantic in 5 days, 1907), and reach (Panama Canal begun, 1904).
The first transatlantic **radio** telegraphic transmission occurred in 1901, 6 years after Marconi discovered radio. Radio transmission of human speech had been made in 1900. Telegraphic transmission of photos was achieved in 1904, lending immediacy to news reports. **Phonographs,** popularized by Caruso's recordings (starting 1902) made for quick international spread of musical styles (ragtime). **Motion pictures,** perfected in the 1890s (Dickson, Lumiere brothers), became a popular and artistic medium after 1900; newsreels appeared in 1909.

**Emigration** from crowded European centers soared in the decade: 9 million migrated to the U.S., and millions more went to Siberia, Canada, Argentina, Australia, South Africa, and Algeria. Some 70 million Europeans emigrated in the century before 1914. Several million Chinese, Indians, and Japanese migrated to Southeast Asia, where their urban skills often enabled them to take a predominant economic role.

**Social reform.** The social and economic problems of the poor were kept in the public eye by realist fiction writers (Dreiser's *Sister Carrie,* 1900; Gorky's *Lower Depths,* 1902; Sinclair's *Jungle,* 1906), journalists (U.S. muckrakers — Steffens, Tarbell) and artists (Ashcan school). Frequent labor strikes and occasional assassinations by anarchists or radicals (Austrian Empress, 1898; U.S. Pres. McKinley, 1901; King Umberto I of Italy, 1900; Russian Interior Minister Plehve, 1904; Portugal's King Carlos, 1908) added to social tension and fear of revolution.
But democratic reformism prevailed. In Germany, Bernstein's (1850-1932) **revisionist Marxism,** downgrading revolution, was accepted by the powerful Social Democrats and trade unions. The British Fabian Society (the Webbs, Shaw) and the Labour Party (founded 1906) worked for reforms such as social security and union rights (1906), while women's suffragists grew more militant. U.S. **progressives** fought big business (Pure Food and Drug Act, 1906). In France, the 10-hour work day (1904) and separation of church and state (1905) were reform victories, as was universal suffrage in Austria (1907).

**Arts.** An unprecedented period of experimentation, centered in France, produced several new **painting** styles: fauvism exploited bold color areas (Matisse, *Woman with Hat,* 1905); expressionism reflected powerful inner emotions (the Brücke group, 1905); cubism combined several views of an object on one flat surface (Picasso's *Demoiselles,* 1906-07); futurism tried to depict speed and motion (Italian Futurist Manifesto, 1910). **Architects** explored new uses of steel structures, with facades either neo-classical (Adler and Sullivan in U.S.); curvilinear Art Nouveau (Gaudi's Casa Mila, 1905-10); or functionally streamlined (Wright's Robie House, 1909).

**Music** and **Dance** shared the experimental spirit. Ruth St. Denis (1877-1968) and Isadora Duncan (1878-1927) pioneered modern dance, while Diaghilev in Paris revitalized classic ballet from 1909. Composers explored atonal music (Debussy, 1862-1918) and dissonance (Schönberg, 1874-1951), or revolutionized classical forms (Stravinsky, 1882-71), often showing jazz or folk music influences.

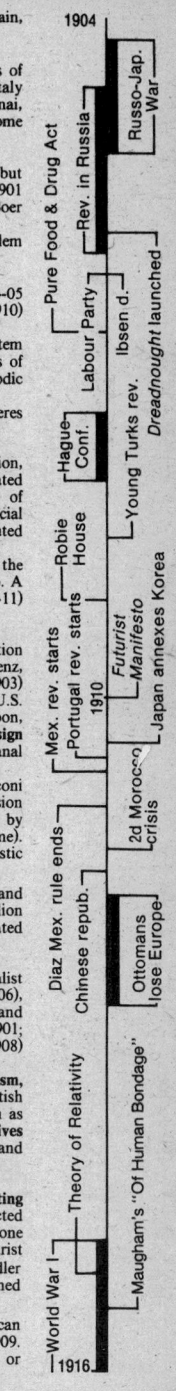

1904

Russo-Jap. War
Rev. in Russia
Pure Food & Drug Act
Labour Party
Ibsen d.
Dreadnought launched
Hague Conf.
Young Turks rev.
Robie House
Futurist Manifesto
Japan annexes Korea
Mex. rev. starts
Portugal rev. starts
1910
2d Morocco crisis
Diaz Mex. rule ends
Chinese repub.
Ottomans lose Europe
Theory of Relativity
Maugham's "Of Human Bondage"
World War I
1916

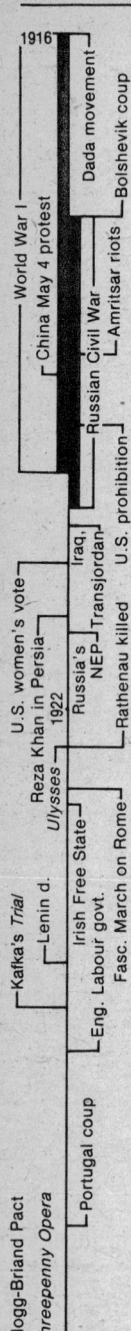

1916 —
World War I
China May 4 protest
Dada movement
Bolshevik coup
Russian Civil War
Amritsar riots
U.S. prohibition
Iraq,
Transjordan
Rathenau killed
Russia's
NEP
Reza Khan in Persia
1922
U.S. women's vote
Ulysses
Kafka's *Trial*
Lenin d.
Irish Free State
Fasc. March on Rome
Eng. Labour govt.
Portugal coup
Kellogg-Briand Pact
*Threepenny Opera*
1928 —

# War and Revolution: 1910-1919

**War threatens.** Germany under Wilhelm II sought a political and imperial role consonant with its industrial strength, challenging Britain's world supremacy and threatening France, still resenting the loss of Alsace-Lorraine. Austria wanted to curb an expanded Serbia (after 1912) and the threat it posed to its own Slav lands. Russia feared Austrian and German political and economic aims in the Balkans and Turkey. An accelerated arms race resulted: the German standing army rose to over 2 million men by 1914. Russia and France had over a million each, Austria and the British Empire nearly a million each. Dozens of enormous battleships were built by the powers after 1906.

The **assassination of Austrian Archduke Ferdinand** by a Serbian, June 28, 1914, was the pretext for war. The system of alliances made the conflict Europe-wide; Germany's invasion of Belgium to outflank France forced Britain to enter the war. Patriotic fervor was nearly unanimous among all classes in most countries.

**World War I.** German forces were stopped in France in one month. The rival armies dug **trench networks.** Artillery and improved machine guns prevented either side from any lasting advance despite repeated assaults (600,000 dead at Verdun, Feb.-July 1916). Poison gas, used by Germany in 1915, proved ineffective. Over one million U.S. troops tipped the balance after mid-1917, forcing Germany to sue for peace.

In the East, the Russian armies were thrown back (battle of **Tannenberg,** Aug. 20, 1914) and the war grew unpopular. An allied attempt to relieve Russia through Turkey failed (**Gallipoli** 1916). The new Bolshevik regime signed the capitulatory Brest-Litovsk peace in March, 1918. Italy entered the war on the allied side, Apr. 1915, but was pushed back by Oct. 1917. A renewed offensive with Allied aid in Oct.-Nov. 1918 forced Austria to surrender.

The British Navy successfully blockaded Germany, which responded with submarine U-boat attacks; **unrestricted submarine warfare** against neutrals after Jan. 1917 helped bring the U.S. into the war. Other battlefields included Palestine and Mesopotamia, both of which Britain wrested from the Turks in 1917, and the African and Pacific colonies of Germany, most of which fell to Britain, France, Australia, Japan, and South Africa.

From 1916, the civilian population and economy of both sides were mobilized to an unprecedented degree. Over 10 million soldiers died (May 1917 French mutiny crushed). *For further details, see 1978 and earlier editions of The World Almanac.*

**Settlement.** At the **Versailles conference** (Jan.-June 1919) and in subsequent negotiations and local wars (Russian-Polish War 1920), the map of Europe was redrawn with a nod to U.S. Pres. Wilson's principle of self-determination. Austria and Hungary were separated and much of their land was given to Yugoslavia (formerly Serbia), Romania, Italy, and the newly independent Poland and Czechoslovakia. Germany lost territory in the West, North, and East, while Finland and the Baltic states were detached from Russia. Turkey lost nearly all its Arab lands to British-sponsored Arab states or to direct French and British rule.

A huge **reparations** burden and partial demilitarization were imposed on Germany. Wilson obtained approval for a League of Nations, but the U.S. Senate refused to allow the U.S. to join.

**Russian revolution.** Military defeats and high casualties caused a contagious lack of confidence in Tsar Nicholas, who was forced to abdicate, Mar. 1917. A liberal provisional government failed to end the war, and massive desertions, riots, and fighting between factions followed. A moderate socialist government under Kerensky was overthrown in a violent **coup by the Bolsheviks** in Petrograd under Lenin, who disbanded the elected Constituent Assembly, Nov. 1917.

The Bolsheviks brutally suppressed all opposition and ended the war with Germany, Mar. 1918. **Civil war** broke out in the summer between the Red Army, including the Bolsheviks and their supporters, and monarchists, anarchists, nationalities (Ukrainians, Georgians, Poles) and others. Small U.S., British, French and Japanese units also opposed the Bolsheviks, 1918-19 (Japan in Vladivostok to 1922). The civil war, anarchy, and pogroms devastated the country until the 1920 Red Army victory. The wartime total monopoly of political, economic, and police power by the Communist Party leadership was retained.

**Other European revolutions.** An unpopular monarchy in **Portugal** was overthrown in 1910. The new republic took severe anti-clerical measures, 1911.

After a century of Home Rule agitation, during which **Ireland** was devastated by famine (one million dead, 1846-47) and emigration, republican militants staged an unsuccessful uprising in Dublin, Easter 1916. The execution of the leaders and mass arrests by the British won popular support for the rebels. The Irish Free State, comprising all but the 6 northern counties, achieved dominion status in 1922.

In the aftermath of the world war, radical revolutions were attempted in Germany (**Spartacist** uprising Jan. 1919), **Hungary** (Kun regime 1919), and elsewhere. All were suppressed or failed for lack of support.

**Chinese revolution.** The Manchu Dynasty was overthrown and a republic proclaimed, Oct. 1911. First president Sun Yat-sen resigned in favor of strongman Yuan Shih-k'ai. Sun organized the parliamentarian **Kuomintang** party.

Students launched protests May 4, 1919 against League of Nations concessions in China to Japan. Nationalist, liberal, and socialist ideas and political groups spread. The **Communist Party** was founded 1921. A communist regime took power in Mongolia with Soviet support in 1921.

**India restive.** Indian objections to British rule erupted in nationalist riots as well as in the non-violent tactics of Gandhi (1869-1948). Nearly 400 unarmed demonstrators were shot at **Amritsar,** Apr. 1919. Britain approved limited self-rule that year.

**Mexican revolution.** Under the long Diaz dictatorship (1876-1911) the economy advanced, but Indian and mestizo lands were confiscated, and concessions to foreigners (mostly U.S.) damaged the middle class. A **revolution in 1910** led to civil wars and U.S. intervention (1914, 1916-17). Land reform and a more democratic constitution (1917) were achieved.

# The Aftermath of War: 1920-29

**U.S.** Easy credit, technological ingenuity, and war-related industrial decline in Europe caused a long economic boom, in which ownership of the new products — autos, phones, radios — became democratized. Prosperity, an increase in women workers, women's suffrage (1920) and drastic change in fashion (flappers, mannish bob for women, clean-shaven men), created a wide perception of social change, despite prohibition of alcoholic beverages (1919-33). Union membership and strikes increased. Fear of radicals led to Palmer raids (1919-20) and Sacco/Vanzetti case (1921-27).

**Europe sorts itself out.** Germany's liberal **Weimar constitution** (1919) could not guarantee a stable government in the face of rightist violence (Rathenau assassinated 1922) and Communist refusal to cooperate with Socialists. Reparations and allied occupation of the Rhineland caused staggering inflation which destroyed middle class savings, but economic expansion resumed after mid-decade, aided by U.S. loans. A sophisticated, innovative culture developed in architecture and design (Bauhaus, 1919-28), film (Lang, *M*, 1931), painting (Grosz), music (Weill, *Threepenny Opera*, 1928), theater (Brecht, *A Man's a Man*, 1926), criticism (Benjamin), philosophy (Jung), and fashion. This culture was considered decadent and socially disruptive by rightists.

**England** elected its first labor governments (Jan. 1924, June 1929). A 10-day general strike in support of coal miners failed, May 1926. In **Italy**, strikes, political chaos and violence by small Fascist bands culminated in the Oct. 1922 Fascist March on Rome, which established Mussolini's dictatorship. Strikes were outlawed (1926), and Italian influence was pressed in the Balkans (Albania a protectorate 1926). A conservative dictatorship was also established in **Portugal** in a 1926 military coup.

**Czechoslovakia,** the only stable democracy to emerge from the war in Central or East Europe, faced opposition from Germans (in the Sudetenland), Ruthenians, and some Slovaks. As the industrial heartland of the old Hapsburg empire, it remained fairly prosperous. With French backing, it formed the Little Entente with Yugoslavia (1920) and **Romania** (1921) to block Austrian or Hungarian irridentism. **Hungary** remained dominated by the landholding classes and expansionist feeling. Croats and Slovenes in **Yugoslavia** demanded a federal state until King Alexander proclaimed a dictatorship (1929). Poland faced nationality problems as well (Germans, Ukrainians, Jews); Pilsudski ruled as dictator from 1926. The Baltic states were threatened by traditionally dominant ethnic Germans and by Soviet-supported communists.

An economic collapse and famine in **Russia,** 1921-22, claimed 5 million lives. The New Economic Policy (1921) allowed land ownership by peasants and some private commerce and industry. Stalin was absolute ruler within 4 years of Lenin's 1924 death. He inaugurated a brutal collectivization program 1929-32, and used foreign communist parties for Soviet state advantage.

**Internationalism.** Revulsion against World War I led to pacifist agitation, the Kellogg-Briand Pact renouncing aggressive war (1928), and **naval disarmament** pacts (Washington, 1922, London, 1930). But the League of Nations was able to arbitrate only minor disputes (Greece-Bulgaria, 1925).

**Middle East.** Mustafa Kemal (Ataturk) led **Turkish** nationalists in resisting Italian, French, and Greek military advances, 1919-23. The sultanate was abolished 1922, and elaborate reforms passed, including secularization of law and adoption of the Latin alphabet. Ethnic conflict led to persecution of **Armenians** (over 1 million dead in 1915, 1 million expelled), Greeks (forced Greek-Turk population exchange, 1923), and Kurds (1925 uprising).

With evacuation of the Turks from **Arab** lands, the puritanical Wahabi dynasty of eastern Arabia conquered present Saudi Arabia, 1919-25. British, French, and Arab dynastic and nationalist maneuvering resulted in the creation of two more Arab monarchies in 1921: Iraq and Transjordan (both under British control), and two French mandates: Syria and Lebanon. Jewish immigration into British-mandated **Palestine,** inspired by the Zionist movement, was resisted by Arabs, at times violently (1921, 1929 massacres).

Reza Khan ruled **Persia** after his 1921 coup (shah from 1925), centralized control, and created the trappings of a modern state.

**China.** The Kuomintang under **Chiang Kai-shek** (1887-1975) subdued the warlords by 1928. The Communists were brutally suppressed after their alliance with the Kuomintang was broken in 1927. Relative peace thereafter allowed for industrial and financial improvements, with some Russian, British, and U.S. cooperation.

**Arts.** Nearly all bounds of subject matter, style, and attitude were broken in the arts of the period. **Abstract** art first took inspiration from natural forms or narrative themes (Kandinsky from 1911), then worked free of any representational aims (Malevich's suprematism, 1915-19, Mondrian's geometric style from 1917). The **Dada** movement from 1916 mocked artistic pretension with absurd collages and constructions (Arp, Tzara, from 1916). Paradox, illusion, and psychological taboos were exploited by **surrealists** by the latter 1920s (Dali, Magritte). Architectural schools celebrated industrial values, whether vigorous abstract constructivism (Tatlin, *Monument to 3rd International*, 1919) or the machined, streamlined **Bauhaus** style, which was extended to many design fields (Helvetica type face).

Prose writers explored revolutionary narrative modes related to dreams (Kafka's *Trial*, 1925), internal monologue (Joyce's *Ulysses*, 1922), and word play (Stein's *Making of Americans*, 1925). Poets and novelists wrote of modern alienation (Eliot's *Waste Land*, 1922) and aimlessness (Lost Generation).

**Sciences.** Scientific specialization prevailed by the 20th century. Advances in knowledge and technological aptitude increased with the geometric increase in the number of practitioners. Physicists challenged common-sense views of causality, observation, and a mechanistic universe, putting science further beyond popular grasp (Einstein's general theory of relativity, 1915; Bohr's quantum mechanics, 1913; Heisinger's uncertainty principle, 1927).

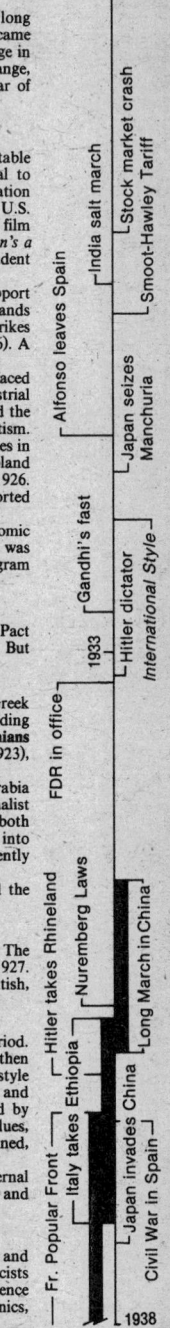

1928 · Stock market crash · Smoot-Hawley Tariff · India salt march · Alfonso leaves Spain · Japan seizes Manchuria · Gandhi's fast · Hitler dictator · *International Style* · 1933 · FDR in office · Nuremberg Laws · Hitler takes Rhineland · Long March in China · Japan invades China · Italy takes Ethiopia · Fr. Popular Front · Civil War in Spain · 1938

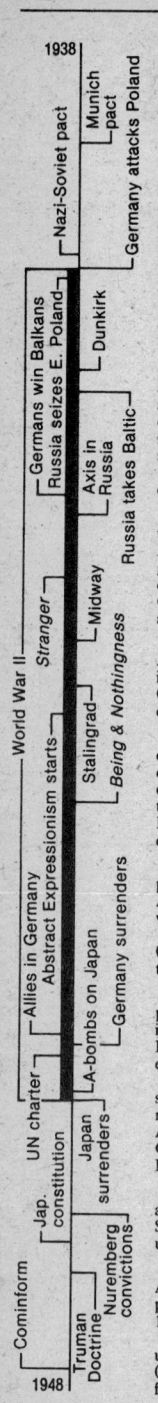

# Rise of the Totalitarians: 1930-39

**Depression.** A worldwide financial panic and economic depression began with the Oct. 1929 U.S. stock market crash and the May 1931 failure of the Austrian Credit-Anstalt. A credit crunch caused international bankruptcies and **unemployment:** 12 million jobless by 1932 in the U.S., 5.6 million in Germany, 2.7 million in England. Governments responded with **tariff restrictions** (Smoot-Hawley Act 1930; Ottawa Imperial Conference, 1932) which dried up world trade. Government public works programs were vitiated by deflationary budget balancing.

**Germany.** Years of agitation by violent extremists was brought to a head by the Depression. Nazi leader **Hitler** was named chancellor by Pres. Hindenburg Jan. 1933, and given dictatorial power by the Reichstag in Mar. Opposition parties were disbanded, strikes banned, and all aspects of economic, cultural, and religious life brought under central government and Nazi party control and manipulated by sophisticated propaganda. Severe persecution of Jews began (**Nuremburg Laws** Sept. 1935). Many Jews, political opponents and others were sent to concentration camps (Dachau, 1933) where thousands died or were killed. Public works, renewed conscription (1935), arms production, and a 4-year plan (1936) ended unemployment.

Hitler's expansionism started with reincorporation of the Saar (1935), occupation of the **Rhineland** (Mar. 1936), and annexation of Austria (Mar. 1938). At **Munich,** Sept. 1938, an indecisive Britain and France sanctioned German dismemberment of Czechoslovakia.

**Russia.** Urbanization and education advanced. Rapid industrialization was achieved through successive **5-year-plans** starting 1928, using severe labor discipline and mass forced labor. Industry was financed by a decline in living standards and exploitation of agriculture, which was almost totally collectivized by the early 1930s (*kolkhoz*, collective farm; *sovkhoz*, state farm, often in newly-worked lands). Successive **purges** increased the role of professionals and management at the expense of workers. Millions perished in a series of man-made disasters: elimination of kulaks (peasant land-owners), 1929-34; severe famine, 1932-33; party purges (Great Purge, 1936-38); suppression of nationalities; and poor conditions in labor camps.

**Spain.** An industrial revolution during World War I created an urban proletariat, which was attracted to socialism and anarchism; Catalan nationalists challenged central authority. The 5 years after King Alfonso left Spain, Apr. 1931, were dominated by tension between intermittent leftist and anti-clerical governments and clericals, monarchists and other rightists. Anarchist and communist rebellions were crushed, but a July, 1936, extreme right rebellion led by Gen. Francisco Franco and aided by Nazi Germany and Fascist Italy succeeded, after a 3-year **civil war** (over 1 million dead in battles and atrocities). The war polarized international public opinion.

**Italy.** Despite propaganda for the ideal of the Corporate State, few domestic reforms were attempted. An entente with Hungary and Austria, Mar. 1934, a pact with Germany and Japan, Nov. 1937, and intervention by 50-75,000 troops in Spain, 1936-39, sealed Italy's identification with the fascist bloc (anti-Semitic laws after Mar. 1938). Ethiopia was conquered, 1935-37, and **Albania** annexed, Jan. 1939, in conscious imitation of ancient Rome.

**East Europe.** Repressive regimes fought for power against an active opposition (liberals, socialists, communists, peasants, Nazis). Minority groups and Jews were restricted within national boundaries that did not coincide with ethnic population patterns. In the destruction of **Czechoslovakia, Hungary** occupied southern Slovakia (Mar. 1938) and Ruthenia (Mar. 1939), and a pro-Nazi regime took power in the rest of Slovakia. Other boundary disputes (e.g. Poland-Lithuania, Yugoslavia-Bulgaria, Romania-Hungary) doomed attempts to build joint fronts against Germany or Russia. Economic depression was severe.

**East Asia.** After a period of liberalism in **Japan,** nativist militarists dominated the government with peasant support. Manchuria was seized, Sept. 1931-Feb. 1932, and a puppet state set up (Manchukuo). Adjacent Jehol (inner Mongolia) was occupied in 1933. China proper was invaded July 1937; large areas were conquered by Oct. 1938.

In **China** Communist forces left Kuomintang-besieged strongholds in the South in a Long March (1934-35) to the North. The Kuomintang-Communist civil war was suspended Jan. 1937 in the face of threatening Japan.

**The democracies.** The Roosevelt Administration, in office Mar. 1933, embarked on an extensive program of social reform and economic stimulation, including protection for labor unions (heavy industries organized), social security, public works, wages and hours laws, assistance to farmers. Isolationist sentiment (1937 Neutrality Act) prevented U.S. intervention in Europe, but military expenditures were increased in 1939.

French political instability and polarization prevented resolution of economic and international security questions. The **Popular Front** government under Blum (June 1936-Apr. 1938) passed social reforms (40-hour week) and raised arms spending. National coalition governments ruled Britain from Aug. 1931, brought some economic recovery, but failed to define a consistent foreign policy until Chamberlain's government (from May 1937), which practiced deliberate **appeasement** of Germany and Italy.

**India.** Twenty years of agitation for autonomy and then for independence (Gandhi's **salt march,** 1930) achieved some constitutional reform (extended provincial powers, 1935) despite Moslem-Hindu strife. Social issues assumed prominence with peasant uprisings (1921), strikes (1928), Gandhi's efforts for untouchables (1932 "fast unto death"), and social and agrarian reform by the provinces after 1937.

**Arts.** The streamlined, geometric design motifs of Art Deco (from 1925) prevailed through the 1930s. Abstract art flourished (Moore sculptures from 1931) alongside a new realism related to social and political concerns (**Socialist Realism** the official Soviet style from 1934; Mexican muralists Rivera, 1886-1957, and Orozco, 1883-1949), which was also expressed in fiction and poetry (Steinbeck's *Grapes of Wrath,* 1939; Sandburg's *The People, Yes,* 1936). Modern architecture (*International Style,* 1932) was unchallenged in its use of man-made materials (concrete, glass), lack of decoration, and monumentality (Rockefeller Center, 1929-40). U.S.-made films captured a world-wide audience with their larger-than-life fantasies (*Gone with the Wind,* 1939).

# War, Hot and Cold: 1940-49

**War in Europe.** The Nazi-Soviet non-agression pact (Aug. '39) freed Germany to attack Poland (Sept.). Britain and France, who had guaranteed Polish independence, declared war on Germany. Russia seized East Poland (Sept.), attacked Finland (Nov.) and took the Baltic states (July '40). Mobile German forces staged **"blitzkrieg"** attacks Apr.-June, '40, conquering neutral Denmark, Norway, and the low countries and defeating France; 350,000 British and French troops were evacuated at **Dunkirk** (May). The Battle of Britain, June-Dec. '40, denied Germany air superiority, German-Italian campaigns won the Balkans by Apr. '41. Three million Axis troops **invaded Russia** June '41, marching through the Ukraine to the Caucasus, and through White Russia and the Baltic republics to Moscow and Leningrad.

Russian winter counterthrusts, '41-'42 and '42-'43 stopped the German advance (Stalingrad Sept. '42-Feb. '43). With British and U.S. Lend-Lease aid and sustaining great casualties, the Russians drove the Axis from all E. Europe and the Balkans in the next 2 years. Invasions of N. Africa (Nov. '42), Italy (Sept. '43), and Normandy (June '44) brought U.S., British, Free French and allied troops to Germany by spring '45. Germany surrendered May 7, 1945.

**War in Asia-Pacific.** Japan occupied Indochina Sept. '40, dominated Thailand Dec. '41, attacked Hawaii, the Philippines, Hong Kong, Malaya Dec. 7, 1941. Indonesia was attacked Jan. '42, Burma conquered Mar. 42. Battle of **Midway** (June '42) turned back the Japanese advance. "Island-hopping" battles (Guadalcanal Aug. '42-Jan. '43, **Leyte Gulf** Oct. '44, Iwo Jima Feb.-Mar. '45, Okinawa Apr. '45) and massive bombing raids on Japan from June '44 wore out Japanese defenses. Two U.S. atom bombs, dropped Aug. 6 and 9, forced Japan to surrender Aug. 14, 1945. *For further details, see 1978 and earlier editions of The World Almanac.*

**Atrocities.** The war brought 20th-century cruelty to its peak. Nazi murder camps (Auschwitz) systematically killed 6 million Jews. Gypsies, political opponents, sick and retarded people, and others deemed undesirable were murdered by the Nazis, as were vast numbers of Slavs, especially leaders. German bombs killed 70,000 English civilians. Some 100,000 Chinese civilians were killed by Japanese forces in the capture of Nanking. Severe retaliation by the Soviet army, E. European partisans, Free French and others took a heavy toll. U.S. and British bombing of Germany killed hundreds of thousands, as did U.S. bombing of Japan (80-200,000 at Hiroshima alone). Some 45 million people lost their lives in the war.

**Home front.** All industries were reoriented to war production and support, and rationing was universal. Science was harnessed for the war effort, yielding such innovations as radar, jet planes, and synthetic materials. Unscathed U.S. industry, partly staffed by women, helped decide the war.

**Settlement.** The United Nations charter was signed in San Francisco June 26, 1945 by 50 nations. The International Tribunal at Nuremberg convicted 22 German leaders for war crimes Sept. '46, 23 Japanese leaders were convicted Nov. '48. Postwar border changes included large gains in territory for the USSR, losses for Germany, a shift westward in Polish borders, and minor losses for Italy. Communist regimes, supported by Soviet troops, took power in most of E. Europe, including Soviet-occupied Germany (GDR proclaimed Oct. '49). Japan lost all overseas lands.

**Recovery.** Basic political and social changes were imposed on Japan and W. Germany by the western allies (Japan constitution Nov. '46, W. German basic law May '49). U.S. Marshall Plan aid ($12 billion '47-'51) spurred W. European economic recovery after a period of severe inflation and strikes in Europe and the U.S. The British Labour Party introduced a national health service and nationalized basic industries in 1946.

**Cold War.** Western fears of further Soviet advances (Cominform formed Oct. '47, Czechoslovakia coup, Feb. '48, Berlin blockade Apr.'48-Sept. '49) led to formation of NATO. Civil War in Greece and Soviet pressure on Turkey led to U.S. aid under the Truman Doctrine (Mar. '47). Other anti-communist security pacts were the Org. of American States (Apr. '48) and Southeast Asia Treaty Org. (Sept. '54). A new wave of Soviet purges and repression intensified in the last years of Stalin's rule, extending to E. Europe (Slansky trial in Czechoslovakia, 1951). Only Yugoslavia resisted Soviet control (expelled by Cominform, June '48; U.S. aid, June '49).

**China, Korea.** Communist forces emerged from World War II strengthened by the Soviet takeover of industrial Manchuria. In 4 years of fighting, the Kuomintang was driven from the mainland; the People's Republic was proclaimed Oct. 1, 1949. Korea was divided by Russian and U.S. occupation forces. Separate republics were proclaimed in the 2 zones Aug.-Sept. '48.

**India.** India and Pakistan became independent dominions Aug. 15, 1947. Millions of Hindu and Moslem refugees were created by the partition; riots, 1946-47, took hundreds of thousands of lives; Gandhi himself was assassinated Jan. '48. Burma became completely independent Jan. '48; Ceylon took dominion status in Feb.

**Middle East.** The UN approved partition of Palestine into Jewish and Arab states. Israel was proclaimed May 14, 1948. Arabs rejected partition, but failed to defeat Israel in war, May '48-July '49. Immigration from Europe and the Middle East swelled Israel's Jewish population. British and French forces left Lebanon and Syria, 1946. Transjordan occupied most of Arab Palestine.

**Southeast Asia.** Communists and others fought against restoration of French rule in Indochina from 1946; a non-communist government was recognized by France Mar. '49, but fighting continued. Both Indonesia and the Philippines became independent, the former in 1949 after 4 years of war with Netherlands, the latter in 1946. Philippine economic and military ties with the U.S. remained strong; a communist-led peasant rising was checked in '48.

**Arts.** New York became the center of the world art market; abstract expressionism was the chief mode (Pollock from '43, de Kooning from '47). Literature and philosophy explored existentialism (Camus' *Stranger*, 1942, Sartre's *Being and Nothingness*, 1943). Non-western attempts to revive or create regional styles (Senghor's Negritude, Mishima's novels) only confirmed the emergence of a universal culture. Radio and phonograph records spread American popular music (swing, bebop) around the world.

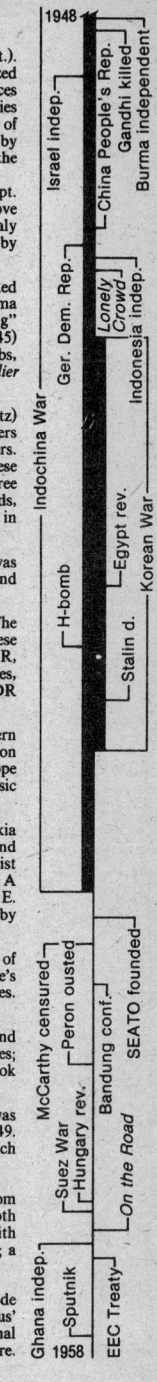

# The American Decade: 1950-59

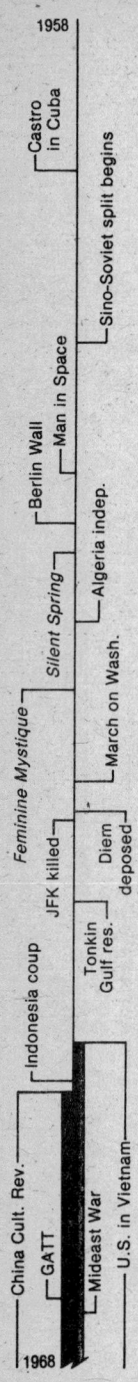

1958

Castro in Cuba

Sino-Soviet split begins

Man in Space

Berlin Wall

Algeria indep.

Silent Spring

March on Wash.

Feminine Mystique

JFK killed

Diem deposed

Tonkin Gulf res.

Indonesia coup

China Cult. Rev.

GATT

Mideast War

U.S. in Vietnam

1968

**Polite decolonization.** The peaceful decline of European political and military power in Asia and Africa accelerated in the 1950s. Nearly all of N. Africa was freed by 1956, but France fought a bitter war to retain Algeria, with its large European minority, until 1962. **Ghana,** independent 1957, led a parade of new black African nations (over 2 dozen by 1962) which altered the political character of the UN. Ethnic disputes often exploded in the new nations after decolonization (UN troops in Cyprus 1964; **Nigeria** civil war 1967-70). Leaders of the new states, mostly sharing socialist ideologies, tried to create an Afro-Asian bloc (Bandung Conf. 1955), but Western economic influence and U.S. political ties remained strong (Baghdad Pact, 1955).

**Trade.** World trade volume soared, in an atmosphere of monetary stability assured by international accords (**Bretton Woods** 1944). In Europe, economic integration advanced (**European Economic Community** 1957, European Free Trade Association 1960). Comecon (1949) coordinated the economies of Soviet-bloc countries.

**U.S.** Economic growth produced an abundance of consumer goods (9.3 million motor vehicles sold 1955). Suburban housing tracts changed life patterns for middle and working classes (Levittown 1946-51). **Eisenhower's** landside election victories (1952, 1956) reflected consensus politics. Censure of McCarthy (Dec. '54) curbed the political abuse of anti-communism. A system of alliances and military bases bolstered U.S. influence on all continents. Trade and payments surpluses were balanced by overseas investments and foreign aid ($50 billion, 1950-59).

**USSR.** In the "thaw" after Stalin's death in 1953, relations with the West improved (evacuation of Vienna, Geneva summit conf., both 1955). Repression of scientific and cultural life eased, and many prisoners were freed or rehabilitated culminating in **de-Stalinization** (1956). Khrushchev's leadership aimed at consumer sector growth, but farm production lagged, despite the virgin lands program (from 1954). The 1956 Hungarian revolution, the 1960 U-2 spy plane episode, and other incidents renewed East-West tension and domestic curbs.

**East Europe.** Resentment of Russian domination and Stalinist repression combined with nationalist, economic and religious factors to produce periodic violence. East Berlin workers rioted in 1953, Polish workers rioted in Poznan, June 1956, and a broad-based revolution broke out in Hungary, Oct. 1956. All were suppressed by Soviet force or threats (at least 7,000 dead in Hungary). But Poland was allowed to restore private ownership of farms, and a degree of personal and economic freedom returned to Hungary. Yugoslavia experimented with worker self-management and a market economy.

**Korea.** The 1945 division of Korea left industry in the North, which was organized into a military regime and armed by Russia. The South was politically disunited. Over 60,000 North Korean troops invaded the South June 25, 1950. The U.S., backed by the UN Security Council, sent troops. UN troops reached the Chinese border in Nov. Some 200,000 Chinese troops crossed the Yalu River and drove back UN forces. Cease-fire in July 1951 found the opposing forces near the original 38th parallel border. After 2 years of sporadic fighting, an armistice was signed July 27, 1953. U.S. troops remained in the South and U.S. economic and military aid continued. The war stimulated rapid economic recovery in Japan. For details, see 1978 and earlier editions of The World Almanac.

**China.** Starting in 1952, industry, agriculture, and social institutions were forcibly collectivized. As many as several million people were executed as Kuomintang supporters or as class and political enemies. The Great Leap Forward, 1958-60, unsuccessfully tried to force the pace of development by substituting labor for investment.

**Indochina.** Ho's forces, aided by Russia and the new Chinese Communist government, fought French and pro-French Vietnamese forces to a standstill, and captured the strategic Dienbienphu camp in May 1954. The Geneva Agreements divided Vietnam in half pending elections (never held), and recognized Laos and Cambodia as independent. The U.S. aided the anti-Communist Republic of Vietnam in the South.

**Middle East.** Arab revolutions placed leftist, militantly nationalist regimes in power in Egypt (1952) and Iraq (1958). But Arab unity attempts failed (United Arab Republic joined Egypt, Syria, Yemen, 1958-61). Arab refusal to recognize Israel (Arab League economic blockade began Sept. 1951) led to a permanent state of war, with repeated incidents (Gaza, 1955). Israel occupied Sinai, Britain and France took the Suez Canal, Oct. 1956, but were replaced by the UN Emergency Force. The Mossadegh government in Iran nationalized the British-owned oil industry May 1951, but was overthrown in a U.S.-aided coup Aug. 1953.

**Latin America.** Dictator Juan Peron, in office 1946, enforced land reform, some nationalization, welfare state measures, and curbs on the Roman Catholic Church, but crushed opposition. A Sept. 1955 coup deposed Peron. The 1952 revolution in Bolivia brought land reform, nationalization of tin mines, and improvement in the status of Indians, who nevertheless remained poor. The Batista regime in Cuba was overthrown, Jan. 1959, by Fidel Castro, who imposed a communist dictatorship, aligned Cuba with Russia, improved education and health care. A U.S.-aided anti-Castro invasion (Bay of Pigs, Apr. 1961) was crushed. Self-government advanced in the British Caribbean.

**Technology.** Large outlays on research and development in the U.S. and USSR focussed on military applications (H-bomb in U.S. 1952, USSR 1953, Britain 1957, intercontinental missiles late 1950s). Soviet launching of the Sputnik satellite, Oct. 1957, spurred increases in U.S. science education funds (National Defense Education Act).

**Literature and letters.** Alienation from social and literary conventions reached an extreme in the theater of the absurd (Beckett's *Waiting for Godot* 1952), the "new novel" (Robbe-Grillet's *Voyeur* 1955), and avant-garde film (Antonioni's *L'Avventura* 1960). U.S. Beatniks (Kerouac's *On the Road* 1957) and others rejected the supposed conformism of Americans (Riesman's *Lonely Crowd* 1950).

## Rising Expectations: 1960-69

**Economic boom.** The longest sustained economic boom on record spanned almost the entire decade in the capitalist world; the closely-watched GNP figure doubled in the U.S. 1960-70, fueled by Vietnam War-related budget deficits. The **General Agreement on Tariffs and Trade,** 1967, stimulated West European prosperity, which spread to peripheral areas (Spain, Italy, E. Germany). Japan became a top economic power ($20 billion exports 1970). Foreign investment aided the industrialization of Brazil. Soviet 1965 economic reform attempts (decentralization, material incentives) were limited; but growth continued.

**Reform and radicalization.** A series of political and social reform movements took root in the U.S., later spreading to other countries with the help of ubiquitous U.S. film and television programs and heavy overseas travel (2.2 million U.S. passports issued 1970). Blacks agitated peaceably and with partial success against segregation and poverty (1963 March on Washington, 1964 **Civil Rights Act**); but some urban ghettos erupted in extensive riots (Watts, 1965; Detroit, 1967; King assassination, Apr. 4, 1968). New concern for the poor (Harrington's *Other America,* 1963) led to Pres. Johnson's **"Great Society"** programs (Medicare, Water Quality Act, Higher Education Act, all 1965). Concern with the **environment** surged (Carson's *Silent Spring,* 1962). **Feminism** revived as a cultural and political movement (Friedan's *Feminine Mystique,* 1963, National Organization for Women founded 1966) and a movement for homosexual rights emerged (Stonewall riot, in NYC, 1969).

Opposition to U.S. involvement in Vietnam, especially among university students (**Moratorium** protest Nov. '69) turned violent (Weatherman Chicago riots Oct. '69). New Left and Marxist theories became popular, and membership in radical groups swelled (Students for a Democratic Society, Black Panthers). Maoist groups, especially in Europe, called for total transformation of society. In France, students sparked a nationwide strike affecting 10 million workers May-June '68, but an electoral reaction barred revolutionary change.

**Arts and styles.** The boundary between fine and popular arts were blurred by Pop Art (Warhol) and rock musicals (Hair, 1968). Informality and exaggeration prevailed in fashion (beards, miniskirts). A non-political "counterculture" developed, rejecting traditional bourgeois life goals and personal habits, and use of marijuana and hallucinogens spread (Woodstock festival Aug. '68). Indian influence was felt in music (Beatles), religion (Ram Dass), and fashion.

**Science.** Achievements in space (men on moon July '69) and electronics (lasers, integrated circuits) encouraged a faith in scientific solutions to problems in agriculture ("green revolution"), medicine (heart transplants 1967) and other areas. The harmful effects of science, it was believed, could be controlled (1963 nuclear weapon test ban treaty, 1968 non-proliferation treaty).

**China.** Mao's revolutionary militance caused disputes with Russia under "revisionist" Khrushchev, starting 1960. The two powers exchanged fire in 1969 border disputes. China used force to capture areas disputed with India, 1962. The "Great Proletarian Cultural Revolution" tried to impose a utopian egalitarian program in China and spread revolution abroad; political struggle, often violent, convulsed China 1965-68.

**Indochina.** Communist-led guerrillas aided by N. Vietnam fought from 1960 against the S. Vietnam government of Ngo Dinh Diem (killed 1963). The U.S. military role increased after the 1964 Tonkin Gulf incident. U.S. forces peaked at 543,400, Apr. '69. Massive numbers of N. Viet troops also fought. Laotian and Cambodian neutrality were threatened by communist insurgencies and U.S. intrigues. *For details, see 1978 and earlier editions of The World Almanac.*

**Third World.** A bloc of authoritarian leftist regimes among the newly independent nations emerged in political opposition to the U.S.-led Western alliance, and came to dominate the conference of nonaligned nations (Belgrade 1961, Cairo 1964, Lusaka 1970). Soviet political ties and military bases were established in Cuba, Egypt, Algeria, Guinea, and other countries, whose leaders were regarded as revolutionary heros by opposition groups in pro-Western or colonial countries. Some leaders were ousted in coups by pro-Western groups—Zaire's Lumumba (killed 1961), Ghana's Nkrumah (exiled 1966), and Indonesia's Sukarno (effectively ousted 1965 after a Communist coup failed).

**Middle East.** Arab-Israeli tension erupted into a brief war June 1967. Israel emerged as a major regional power. Military shipments before and after the war brought much of the Arab world into the Soviet political sphere. Most Arab states broke U.S. diplomatic ties, while Communist countries cut their ties to Israel. Intra-Arab disputes continued: Egypt and Saudi Arabia supported rival factions in a bloody Yemen civil war 1962-70; Lebanese troops fought Palestinian commandos in 1969.

**East Europe.** To stop the large-scale exodus of citizens, E. German authorities built a fortified wall across Berlin Aug. '61. Soviet sway in the Balkans was weakened by Albania's support of China (USSR broke ties Dec. '61) and Romania's assertion of industrial and foreign policy autonomy in 1964. Liberalization in Czechoslovakia, spring 1968, was crushed by troops of 5 Warsaw Pact countries. West German treaties with Russia and Poland, 1970, facilitated the transfer of German technology and confirmed post-war boundaries.

## Disillusionment: 1970-78

**U.S.: Caution and neoconservatism.** A relatively sluggish economy, energy and resource shortages (natural gas crunch 1975), and environmental problems contributed to a **"limits of growth"** philosophy that affected politics (Cal. Gov. Brown). Suspicion of science and technology killed or delayed major projects (supersonic transport dropped 1971, DNA recombination curbed 1976, Seabrook A-plant protests 1977-78).

Mistrust of big government weakened support for government reform plans among liberals. School busing and racial quotas were opposed (**Bakke decision** June '78); the Equal Rights Amendment for women languished; civil rights for homosexuals were opposed (Dade County referendum June '77).

U.S. defeat in **Indochina** (evacuation Apr. '75), revelations of Central Intelligence Agency misdeeds (Rockefeller Commission report June '75), and the **Watergate scandals** (Nixon quit Aug. '74) reduced

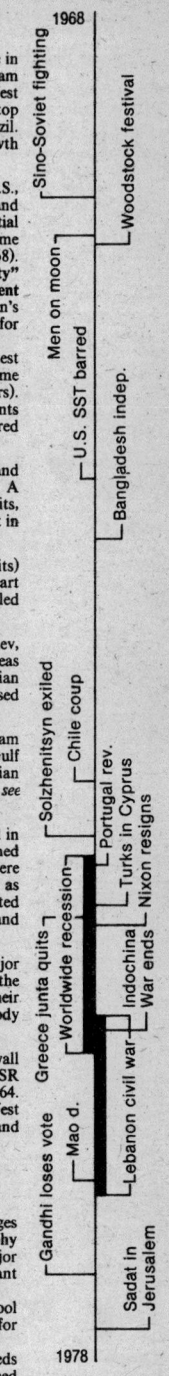

1968

Sino-Soviet fighting

Woodstock festival

Men on moon

U.S. SST barred

Bangladesh indep.

Solzhenitsyn exiled

Chile coup

Portugal rev.

Turks in Cyprus

Nixon resigns

Worldwide recession

Indochina War ends

Greece junta quits

Mao d.

Lebanese civil war

Gandhi loses vote

Sadat in Jerusalem

1978

faith in U.S. moral and material capacity to influence world affairs. Revelations of Soviet crimes (Solzhenitsyn's *Gulag Archipelago* from 1974) and Russian intervention in Africa aided a revival of anti-Communist sentiment.

**Economy sluggish.** The 1960s boom faltered in the 1970s; a severe recession in the U.S. and Europe 1974-75 followed a huge oil price hike Dec. '73. Monetary instability (U.S. cut ties to gold Aug. '71), the decline of the dollar, and **protectionist** moves by industrial countries (1977-78) threatened trade. Business investment and spending for research declined. Severe inflation plagued many countries (25% in Britain, 1975).

**China picks up pieces.** After the 1976 deaths of Mao and Chou, a power struggle for the leadership succession was won by pragmatists. A nationwide purge of orthodox Maoists was carried out, and the **"Gang of Four"**, led by Mao's widow Chiang Ching, was arrested.
The new leaders freed over 100,000 political prisoners, and reduced public adulation of Mao. Political and trade ties were expanded with Japan, Europe, and the U.S., as relations with Russia, Cuba, and Vietnam worsened. Ideological guidelines in industry, science, education, and the armed forces, which the ruling faction said had caused chaos and decline, were reversed (bonuses to workers, Dec. '77; exams for college entrance, Oct. '77). Severe restrictions on cultural expression were eased (Beethoven ban lifted Mar. '77).

**Europe.** European unity moves (EEC-EFTA trade accord 1972) faltered as economic problems appeared (Britain floated pound 1972; France floated franc 1974). Germany and Switzerland curbed guest workers from S. Europe. Greece and Turkey quarreled over Cyprus (Turks intervened 1974) and Aegean oil rights.
All of non-Communist Europe was under democratic rule after free elections were held in **Spain** June '76, 7 months after the death of Franco. The conservative, colonialist regime in **Portugal** was overthrown Apr. '74. In **Greece**, the 7-year-old military dictatorship yielded power in 1974. Northern Europe, though ruled mostly by Socialists (**Swedish** Socialists unseated 1976, after 44 years in power), turned conservative. The **British** Labour government imposed wage curbs 1975, and suspended nationalization schemes. Terrorism in **Germany** (1972 Munich Olympics killings) led to laws curbing some civil liberties. **French** "new philosophers" rejected leftist ideologies, and the shaky Socialist-Communist coalition lost a 1978 election bid.

**Religion back in politics.** The improvement in Moslem countries' political fortunes by the 1950s (with the exception of Central Asia under Soviet and Chinese rule), and the growth of Arab oil wealth, was followed by a resurgence of traditional piety. **Libyan** dictator Qaddafi mixed strict Islamic laws with socialism in his militant ideology and called for an eventual Moslem return to Spain and Sicily. The illegal Moslem Brotherhood in **Egypt** was accused of violence, while extreme Moslem groups bombed theaters, 1977, to protest secular values.
In **Turkey**, the National Salvation Party was the first Islamic group to share power (1974) since secularization in the 1920s. Conservative Moslems participated in violent opposition to **Iran's** modernization programs (e.g. women in universities), 1978, while Moslem puritan opposition to **Pakistan** Pres. Bhutto helped lead to his overthrow July '77. However, Moslem solidarity could not prevent Pakistan's eastern province (**Bangladesh**) from declaring independence, Dec. '71, after a bloody civil war.
Moslem and Hindu resentment against coerced sterilization in **India** helped defeat the Gandhi government, which was replaced Mar. '77 by a coalition including religious Hindu parties and led by devout Hindu Desai. Moslems in the southern **Philippines**, aided by Libya, conducted a long rebellion against central rule from 1973.
Evangelical Protestant groups grew in numbers and prosperity in the U.S. ("born again" Pres. Carter elected 1976), and the Catholic charismatic movement obtained respectability. A revival of interest in Orthodox Christianity occurred among **Russian** intellectuals (Solzhenitsyn). The secularist **Israeli** Labor party, after decades of rule, was ousted in 1977 by conservatives led by Begin, an observant Jew; religious militants founded settlements on the disputed West Bank, part of Biblically-promised Israel. U.S. Reform Judaism revived many previously discarded traditional practices.
The Buddhist Soka Gakkai movement launched the Komeito party in Japan, 1964, which became a major opposition party in 1972 and 1976 elections.
Old-fashioned religious wars raged intermittently in **N. Ireland** (Catholic vs. Protestant, 1969-   ) and **Lebanon** (Christian vs. Moslem, 1975-   ), while religious militancy complicated the Israel-Arab dispute (1973 Israel-Arab war; Arab opposition to Egypt Pres. **Sadat's** Nov. '77 Jerusalem visit).

**South America.** Repressive conservative regimes strengthened their hold on most of the continent, with the violent coup against the elected Allende government in **Chile**, Sept. '73, the 1976 military coup in **Argentina**, and coups against reformist regimes in **Bolivia**, 1971, and **Peru**, 1976.

**Indochina.** Communist victory in Vietnam, Cambodia, and Laos by May '75 did not bring peace. In 1978 battles were fought at the Cambodia-Viet border, and China disputed Vietnam's treatment of ethnic Chinese. Over one million **Cambodians** were reportedly killed by the new regime, 1975-78.

**Russian expansion.** Soviet influence, checked in some countries (troops ousted by Egypt 1972) was projected further afield, often with the use of Cuban troops (Angola 1975-   , Ethiopia 1977-   ), and aided by a growing navy, merchant fleet, and international banking ability. Detente with the West — 1972 Berlin pact, 1970 strategic arms pact (**SALT**) — gave way to a more antagonistic relationship in the late 1970s.

**Africa.** The last remaining European colonies were granted independence (**Spanish Sahara** 1976, **Djibouti** 1977) but white domination remained in **S. Africa** and **Rhodesia** (Rhodesia guerrilla war intensified 1976-   ). Great power involvement in local wars (Russia in **Angola, Ethiopia;** France in **Chad, Zaire, Mauritania**) and the use of tens of thousands of Cuban troops was denounced by some African leaders as neocolonialism. Ethnic or tribal clashes made Africa the chief world locus of sustained warfare in the late 1970s.

**Arts.** Traditional modes in painting, architecture, and music, pursued in relative obscurity for much of the 20th century, returned to popular and critical attention in the 1970s. The pictorial emphasis in neorealist and photorealist painting, the return of many architects to detail, decoration, and traditional natural materials, and the concern with ordered structure in musical composition were, ironically, novel experiences for artistic consumers after the exhaustion of experimental possibilities. However, these more conservative styles coexisted with modernist works in an atmosphere of variety and tolerance.

## The Most Significant Battles in History

Name, date. . .Winner vs. Loser. . .Consequences

**Salamis, 480 BC.** . .Greek vs. Persian fleets. . .ended greatest Persian threat to Greece

**Plataea, 479 BC.** . . .Greeks, mostly Spartans, vs. Persian army. . .end of any Persian threat to Greece

**Arbela, 331 BC.** . .Greeks under Alexander the Great vs. Persians. . .end of ancient Persian empire

**Cannae, near Rome, 216 BC.** . .Carthaginians under Hannibal vs. Romans. . .height of Carthage's threat to Rome

**Zama, in no. Africa, 202 BC.** . .Romans under Scipio Africanus vs. Carthage. . .end of Carthage as a major power

**Pharsalia**, in Greece, 48 BC. . .Julius Caesar vs. Pompey in Roman civil war. . .secured Caesar's absolute power

**Actium**, in Greece, 31 BC. . .Romans under Octavian vs. Romans and Egyptians under Mark Anthony. . .beginning of Roman Empire under Octavian (Augustus Caesar)

**Chalons**, near Troyes, France, 451 AD. . .Romans and Visigoths vs. Huns under Attila. . .ended westward advance of Huns

**Yarmuk**, in Syria, 636. . .Moslem Arabs vs. Byzantines. . .secured Near East for Islam

**Tours** (Poitiers), in so. France, 732. . .Franks under Charles Martel vs. Saracens. . .ended further advance of Islam in W. Europe

**Hastings**, so. of London, Oct. 14, 1066. . .Normans under William vs. Saxons. . .beginning of modern British monarchy

**Manzikert**, no. of Lake Van, Turkey, 1071. . .Seljuk Turks vs. Byzantines. . .virtual end of Byzantine power in Asia

**Las Navas de Tolosa**, July 16, 1212. . .Christian Spaniards vs. Moslem Moors. . .end of Moslem power in Spain

**Liegnitz**, in Silesia, E. Germany, 1241. . .Mongols vs. Poles and Germans. . .farthest westward movement of Mongols

**Bannockburn**, June 24, 1324. . .Scots under Robert Bruce vs. English. . .secured Scottish independence for another 300 years

**Kulikovo**, Sept. 8, 1380. . .Russians vs. Tatars. . .beginning of decline of Tatar power

**Kossovo**, 1389 (traditionally June 15). . .Ottoman Turks vs. Serbs, Bosnians. . .established Turks in the Balkans

**Agincourt**, in no. France, Oct. 25, 1415. . .English and Burgundians vs. French. . .height of English power in France

**Orleans**, siege of, 1428-29. . .French vs. British; relief column led by Jeanne d'Arc. . .beginning of restoration of French power and of the story of the Maid of Orleans

**Constantinople**, siege of, Apr. 26-May 29, 1453. . .Ottoman Turks vs. Byzantines. . .end of Byzantine state

**Nancy**, Jan. 5, 1477. . .French, Swiss vs. Burgundians. . .end of Burgundian power, beginning of modern French state

**Bosworth Field**, Aug. 22, 1485. . .English vs. English in dynastic war. . .secured English throne for the Tudors

**Vienna**, siege of, Sept. 26, 1529. . .Holy Roman Empire vs. Ottoman Turks. . .height of Turkish threat to central Europe

**Lepanto**, in Greece, Oct. 7, 1571. . .Spanish, Venetian and Papal fleets vs. Ottoman Turks; greatest naval battle since Actium. . .ended threat of Turkish Mediterranean hegemony

**Armada**, defeat of, July 31-Aug. 8, 1588. . .30 English navy and additional private ships vs. 130 Spanish ships. . .beginning of decline of Spanish power

**Ivry**, Mar. 14, 1590. . .French vs. French in religious and dynastic war. . .secured French throne for the Bourbons

**Sekigahara**, in Japan, 1600. . .Tokugawa vs. other nobles. . .established Tokugawa shogunate, beginning of modern Japanese state

**La Rochelle**, siege of, 1627-1628. . .French Army under Richelieu vs. Protestant Huguenots. . .end of Huguenot power in France

**Breitenfeld/Leipzig**, Sept. 17, 1631. . .Protestant Saxons and Swedes under Gustavus Adolphus vs. Holy Roman Empire. . .height of Protestant power in central Europe

**Lutzen**, Nov. 16, 1632. . .Protestant Germans and Swedes vs. Holy Roman Empire. . .secured Protestant power in no. Germany

**Nordlingen**, Aug. 27, 1634. . .Holy Roman Empire vs. Swedes. . .secured Roman Catholic power in so. Germany

**Rocroi**, May 19, 1643. . .French vs. Spaniards. . .end of Spanish military supremacy in no. Europe.

**Naseby**, June 14, 1645. . .Cromwell's Puritan republicans vs. English royalists and religious conservatives. . .secured Cromwell's power

**Mohacs** (second battle), Aug. 12, 1687. . .Holy Roman Empire vs. Turks. . .secured Hungary for Austrian empire

**Boyne**, July 1, 1690. . .British under William of Orange vs. Irish. . .end of effective Irish resistance to British rule

**Poltava**, July 8, 1709. . .Russians under Peter the Great vs. Swedes. . .end of Swedish power so. of Baltic, emergence of Russia as European power

**Culloden**, Apr. 16, 1746. . .British vs. Scottish Highlanders. . .end of Scottish resistance to British rule

**Plassey**, June 23, 1757. . .British forces under Clive vs. Bengalis and Indians. . .secured British commitment to the development of an empire in India

**Plains of Abraham**, near Quebec City, Sept. 13, 1759. . .British vs. French. . .end of French power in New World

**Yorktown**, siege of, Sept. 30-Oct. 19, 1781. . .Americans and French vs. British. . .secured American independence

**Hohenlinden**, Dec. 3, 1800. . .French vs. Holy Roman Empire. . .dismemberment of Holy Roman Empire

**Trafalgar**, near Gibraltar, Oct. 21, 1805. . .British vs. French, Spanish fleets. . .secured British worldwide naval supremacy for 100 years

**Austerlitz**, Dec. 2, 1805. . .French under Napoleon vs. Austrians, Russians. . .secured Italy and most of west Germany for Napoleon, end of Holy Roman Empire

**Friedland**, June 14, 1807. . .Napoleon vs. Russians. . .height of Napoleonic power in north and central Europe

**Wagram**, July 5-6, 1809. . .French vs. Austrians. . .height of Napoleonic power in south-central Europe

**Beresina**, Nov. 26-28, 1812. . .Russians vs. French. . .destruction of Napoleon's 500,000-man Grand Army

**Leipzig (Battle of Nations)**, Oct. 16-19, 1813. . .Russia, Prussia, and Austria vs. Napoleon. . .end of Napoleonic power in Europe

**Waterloo**, June 18, 1815. . .British and Prussians vs. Napoleon. . .end of Napoleonic power in France

**Navarino**, Oct. 20, 1827. . .British, French, Russian ships vs. Egyptian-Turk fleet. . .secured independence of Greece

**Solferino**, June 24, 1859. . .Piedmontese (Italians) and French vs. Austrians. . .secured Italian independence

**Gettysburg**, July 1-3, 1863. . .Union vs. Confederacy in American civil war. . .put Confederacy on defensive

**Sadowa (Königgrätz)**, July 3, 1866. . .Prussians vs. Austrians. . .secured unity of Germany under Prussia

**Sedan**, Sept. 1, 1870. . .Germans vs. French. . .secured allegiance of south Germany to new German Empire.

**Plevna**, siege of, July 20-Dec. 10, 1877. . .Russians vs. Turks. . .secured independence of Serbia and Romania.

**Manila**, May 1, 1898. . .U.S. vs. Spanish fleets. . .beginning of direct U.S. involvement in Asia

**Sea of Japan (Tsushima Straits)**, May 27-29, 1905. . .Japanese vs. Russian fleets. . .emergence of Japan as a major Asian-Pacific power

**Marne**, Sept. 5-12, 1914. . .French and British vs. Germans. . .stopped German advance on Paris

**Verdun and Somme**, Feb. 21-Dec. 18, 1916. . .2 indecisive battles, French and British vs. Germans. . .about 2 million casualties brought a slow end to 19th century European optimism

**Vittorio Veneto**, Oct. 24-Nov. 4, 1918. . .Italians vs. Austrians. . .end of Austrian empire and Hapsburg dynasty

**Britain, Battle of**, Aug. 8-Nov. 10, 1940. . .British vs. German air forces. . .ended westward advance of Germany, crippled German bomber force

**Coral Sea**, no. of Australia, May 7, 1942. . .U.S., British, Australian vs. Japanese fleets. . .stopped southward advance of Japan

**Midway**, west of Hawaii, June 4-7, 1942. . .U.S. vs. Japanese fleets. . .stopped eastward advance of Japan

**Stalingrad**, Sept. 21, 1942-Feb. 2, 1943. . .Russians vs. Germans. . .beginning of German retreat from Russia

**El Alemein**, Oct. 23, 1942. . .British, others vs. Germans. . .beginning of German retreat from Africa

**Normandy**, June 6-July 9, 1944. . .U.S., British, others vs. Germans. . .greatest concentration of men and materiel in history, beginning of German retreat from France

**Philippine Sea**, Oct. 21-22, 1944. . .U.S. vs. Japanese navies. . .end of Japanese naval power

**Dienbienphu**, siege of, Mar. 13-May 7, 1954. . .Vietnamese vs. French. . .secured independence of North Vietnam

**Six Day War**, June 5-10, 1967. . .Israel vs. Egypt, Syria, Jordan. . .Israel occupied area of ancient kingdom plus Sinai

**Tet**, Jan. 30-Feb. 24, 1968. . .U.S. and So. Vietnamese vs. No. Vietnamese. . .tactical victory, but decisive psychological defeat for U.S.

## Some Notable Marine Disasters Since 1865
(Figures indicate estimated lives lost)

**1865, Apr. 27—Sultana;** a Mississippi River steamer blew up near Memphis, Tenn., 1,400.

**1869, Oct. 27—Stonewall;** steamer burned on Mississippi River below Cairo, Ill.; 200.

**1870, Jan. 28—City of Boston;** American steamer of Inman Line vanished between New York and Liverpool; 191.

**1872, Nov. 7—Mary Celeste;** American half-brig sailed from New York for Genoa; found abandoned in Atlantic 4 weeks later in mystery of sea; crew never heard from; loss of life unknown.

**1873, Jan. 22—Northfleet;** British steamer foundered off Dungeness, England; 300.

**1873, Apr. 1—Atlantic;** British (White Star) steamer wrecked off Nova Scotia; 547.

**1873, Nov. 23—Ville de Havre;** French steamer, New York to Havre, sank after collision with Loch Earn; 230.

**1875, May 7—Schiller;** German mail steamer wrecked off Scilly Islands; 200.

**1875, Nov. 4—Pacific;** American Steamer sank after collision off Cape Flattery; 236.

**1878, Sept. 3—Princess Alice;** British steamer sank after collision in Thames; 700.

**1878, Dec. 18—Byzantin;** French steamer sank after Dardanelles collision; 210.

**1880, Nov. 24—Uncle Joseph;** French steamer sank in collision off Spezzia, Greece; 250.

**1881, May 24—Victoria;** steamer capsized in Thames River, Canada; 200.

**1883, Jan. 19—Cambria;** German steamer hit iceberg in North Sea; 389.

**1887, Nov. 15—Wah Yeung;** British steamer burned at sea; 400.

**1890, Feb. 17—Duburg;** British steamer wrecked, China Sea; 400.

**1890, Sept. 19—Ertogrul;** Turkish frigate foundered off Japan; 540.

**1891, Mar. 17—Utopia;** British steamer sank in collision off Gibraltar; 574.

**1895, Jan. 30—Elbe;** German steamer sank in collision with British steamer Crathie in North Sea; 335.

**1895, Mar. 11—Reina Regenta;** Spanish cruiser foundered near Gibraltar; 400.

**1898, Feb. 15—Maine;** U.S. battleship blown up in Havana Harbor; 266.

**1898, July 4—La Bourgogne, Cromartyshire;** French steamer and British sailing ship collided off Nova Scotia; 560.

**1904, June 15—General Slocum;** excursion steamer burned in East River, New York City; 1,030.

**1904, June 28—Norge;** steamer wrecked on Rockall Reef off Scotland; 590.

**1906, Aug. 4—Sirio;** Italian steamer wrecked off Cape Palos, Spain; 350.

**1908, Mar. 23—Matsu Maru;** Japanese steamer sank in collision near Hakodate, Japan; 300.

**1909, Aug. 1—Waratah;** British steamer, Sydney to London, vanished; 300.

**1910, Feb. 9—General Chanzy;** French steamer wrecked off Minorca, Spain; 200.

**1911, Sept. 25—Liberté;** French battleship exploded at Toulon; 285.

**1912, Mar. 5—Principe de Asturias;** Spanish steamer wrecked off Spanish coast; 500.

**1912, Apr. 14-15—Titanic;** British (White Star) liner hit iceberg in North Atlantic; 1,517.

**1912, Sept. 28—Kichemaru;** Japanese steamer sank off Japanese coast; 1,000.

**1914, May 29—Empress of Ireland;** Canadian steamer sank after collision with collier in St. Lawrence River; 1,024.

**1915, May 7—Lusitania;** British (Cunard Line) steamer torpedoed by German submarine, sank off Ireland; 1,198.

**1915, July 24—Eastland;** excursion steamer capsized in Chicago River; 812.

**1916, Feb. 26—Provence;** French cruiser sank in Mediterranean; 3,100.

**1916, Aug. 29—Hsin Yu;** Chinese steamer sank off Chinese coast; 1,000.

**1917, Dec. 6—Mont Blanc, Imo;** French ammunition ship and Belgian steamer collided in Halifax Harbor; 1,600.

**1918, Apr. 25—Kiang-Kwan** Chinese steamer sank in collision off Hankow; 500.

**1918, July 12—Kawachi;** Japanese battleship blew up in Tokayama Bay; 500.

**1918, Oct. 25—Princess Sophia;** Canadian steamer sank off Alaskan coast; 398.

**1919, Jan. 17—Chaonia;** French steamer lost in Straits of Messina, Italy; 460.

**1919, Sept. 9—Valbanera;** Spanish steamer lost off Florida coast; 500.

**1921, Mar. 18—Hong Kong;** steamer wrecked in South China Sea; 1,000.

**1922, Aug. 26—Niitaka;** Japanese cruiser sank in storm off Kamchatka, USSR; 300.

**1923, Apr. 23—Mossamedes;** Portuguese mail steamer went aground at Cape Frio, Africa; 220.

**1924, Jan. 10—L-24;** British submarine in collision off Portland, England; 48.

**1924, Mar. 19—No. 43;** Japanese submarine in collision off Sasebo, Japan; 49.

**1925, Sept. 25—S-51;** American submarine in collision with steamer City of Rome off Block Island, R.I.; 34.

**1925, Nov. 11—M-1;** British submarine in English Channel collision; 69.

**1927, Oct. 25—Principessa Mafalda;** Italian steamer blew up, sank off Porto Seguro, Brazil; 314.

**1927, Dec. 17—S-4;** American submarine in collision off Provincetown, Mass.; 40.

**1934, Sept. 8—Morro Castle;** American steamer, Havana to New York, burned off Asbury Park, N.J.; 125.

**1939, May 23—Squalus;** American submarine sank off Portsmouth, N.H.; 26.

**1939, June 1—Thetis;** British submarine, sank in Liverpool Bay; 99.

**1941, June 16—O-9;** American submarine lost in test dive off Maine; 33.

**1942, Feb. 18—Truxton and Pollux;** American destroyer and cargo ship ran aground, sank off Newfoundland; 204.

**1942, Oct. 2—Curacao;** British cruiser sank after collision with liner Queen Mary; 335.

**1947, Jan. 19—Himera;** Greek steamer hit a mine off Athens; 392.

**1947, Apr. 16—Grandcamp;** French freighter exploded in Texas City, Tex., Harbor, starting fires; 510.

**1950, Jan. 12—Truculent;** British submarine in Thames collision; 65.

**1951, Apr. 16—Affray;** British submarine lost in English Channel; 75.

**1952, Apr. 26—Hobson and Wasp;** American destroyer and aircraft carrier collided in Atlantic; 176.

**1952, Sept. 24—La Sibylle;** French submarine lost off Toulon; 48.

**1953, Jan. 31—Princess Victoria;** British ferry foundered off northern Irish coast; 134.

**1954, Sept. 26—Toya Maru;** Japanese ferry sank in Tsugaru Strait, Japan; 1,172.

**1956, July 26—Andrea Doria and Stockholm;** Italian liner and Swedish liner collided off Nantucket; 51.

**1957, July 14—Eshghabad;** Soviet ship ran aground in Caspian Sea; 270.

**1961, Apr. 8—Dara;** British liner burned in Persian Gulf; 212.

**1961, July 8—Save;** Portuguese ship ran aground off Mozambique; 259.

**1963, Apr. 10—Thresher;** U.S. Navy atomic submarine sank in North Atlantic; 129.

**1964, Feb. 10—Voyager, Melbourne;** Australian destroyer sank after collision with Australian aircraft carrier Melbourne off New South Wales; 82.

**1968, Jan. 25—Dakar;** Israeli submarine vanished in Mediterranean; 69.

**1968, Jan. 27—Minerve;** French submarine vanished in Mediterranean; 52.

**1968, May 21—Scorpion;** U.S. nuclear submarine sank in Atlantic near Azores; 99.

**1969, June 2—Evans;** U.S. destroyer cut in half by Australian carrier Melbourne, S. China Sea; 74.

**1970, Mar. 4—Eurydice;** French submarine sank in Mediterranean near Toulon; 57.

**1970, Dec. 15—Namyong-Ho;** South Korean ferry sank in Korea Strait; 308.

**1973, May 5—** Three river boats collided near Dacca, Bangladesh; c. 250.

**1973, Dec. 24—** Ferry capsized off coast of Ecuador; nearly 200.

**1974, May 1—** Motor launch capsized off Bangladesh; 250.

**1974, Sept. 26—** Soviet destroyer burned and sank in Black Sea; est. 200.

**1975, Aug. 9—** Two Chinese riverboats collided and sank near Canton; c. 500.

**1976, Oct. 20—George Prince and Frosta;** ferryboat and Norwegian tanker collided on Mississippi R. at Luling, La.; c. 100.

**1976, Dec. 25—Patria;** Egyptian liner caught fire and sank in the Red Sea; c. 100.

**1977, Jan. 11—Grand Zenith;** Panamanian-registered tanker sank off Cape Cod, Mass.; 38.

**1977, Jan. 17—** Spanish freighter collided with launch in Barcelona, Spain harbor; 46.

## Major Earthquakes

**Sources:** National Earthquake Information Service, U.S. Geological Survey, and historical records

Magnitude of earthquakes (Mag.), distinct from deaths or damage caused, is measured on the Richter scale, on which each higher number represents a tenfold increase in energy measured in ground motion. Adopted in 1935, the scale has been applied in the following table to earthquakes as far back as reliable seismograms are available.

| Date | Place | Deaths | Mag. | Date | Place | Deaths | Mag. |
|---|---|---|---|---|---|---|---|
| 526 May 20 | Syria, Antioch | 250,000 | N.A. | 1948 June 28 | Japan, Fukui | 5,131 | 7.3 |
| 856 .... | Greece, Corinth | 45,000 | " | 1949 Aug. 5 | Ecuador, Pelileo | 6,000 | 6.8 |
| 1057 .... | China, Chihli | 25,000 | " | 1950 Aug. 15 | India, Assam | 1,530 | 8.7 |
| 1268 .... | Asia Minor, Cilicia | 60,000 | " | 1953 Mar. 18 | NW Turkey | 1,200 | 7.2 |
| 1290 Sept. 27 | China, Chihli | 100,000 | " | 1954 Sept. 9-12 | Northern Algeria | 1,250 | 6.8 |
| 1293 May 20 | Japan, Kamakura | 30,000 | " | 1956 June 10-17 | " Afghanistan | 2,000 | 7.7 |
| 1531 Jan. 26 | Portugal, Lisbon | 30,000 | " | 1957 July 2 | Northern Iran | 2,500 | 7.4 |
| 1556 Jan. 24 | China, Shensi | 830,000 | " | 1957 Dec. 13 | Western Iran | 2,000 | 7.1 |
| 1667 Nov. | Caucasia, Shemaka | 80,000 | " | 1960 Feb. 29 | Morocco, Agadir | 12,000 | 5.8 |
| 1693 Jan. 11 | Italy, Catania | 60,000 | " | 1960 May 21-30 | Southern Chile | 5,000 | 8.3 |
| 1730 Dec. 30 | Japan, Hokkaido | 137,000 | " | 1962 Sept. 1 | Northwestern Iran | 12,230 | 7.1 |
| 1737 Oct. 11 | India, Calcutta | 300,000 | " | 1963 July 26 | Yugoslavia, Skopje | 1,100 | 6.0 |
| 1755 June 7 | Northern Persia | 40,000 | " | 1964 Mar. 27 | Alaska | 114 | 8.5 |
| 1755 Nov. 1 | Portugal, Lisbon | 60,000 | 8.75* | 1966 Aug. 19 | Eastern Turkey | 2,520 | 6.9 |
| 1783 Feb. 4 | Italy, Calabria | 30,000 | N.A. | 1968 Aug. 31 | Northeastern Iran | 12,000 | 7.4 |
| 1797 Feb. 4 | Ecuador, Quito | 41,000 | N.A. | 1970 Mar. 28 | Western Turkey | 1,086 | 7.4 |
| 1822 Sept. 5 | Asia Minor, Aleppo | 22,000 | N.A. | 1970 May 31 | Northern Peru | 66,794 | 7.7 |
| 1828 Dec. 28 | Japan, Echigo | 30,000 | " | 1972 Apr. 10 | Southern Iran | 5,057 | 6.9 |
| 1868 Aug. 13-15 | Peru and Ecuador | 40,000 | " | 1972 Dec. 23 | Nicaragua | 5,000 | 6.2 |
| 1875 May 16 | Venezuela, Colombia | 16,000 | " | 1974 Dec. 28 | Pakistan (9 towns) | 5,200 | 6.3 |
| 1896 June 15 | Japan, sea wave | 27,120 | " | 1975 Sept. 6 | Turkey (Lice, etc.) | 2,312 | 6.8 |
| 1906 Apr. 18-19 | Cal., San Francisco | 452 | 8.3 | 1976 Feb. 4 | Guatemala | 22,778 | 7.5 |
| 1906 Aug. 16 | Chile, Valparaiso | 20,000 | 8.6 | 1976 May 6 | Northeast Italy | 946 | 6.5 |
| 1908 Dec. 28 | Italy, Messina | 83,000 | 7.5 | 1976 June 26 | New Guinea, Irian Jaya | 443 | 7.1 |
| 1915 Jan. 13 | Italy, Avezzano | 29,980 | 7.5 | 1976 July 14 | Indonesia, N. Bali | 500 | 5.6 |
| 1920 Dec. 16 | China, Kansu | 100,000 | 8.6 | 1976 July 28 | China, Tangshan | 655,235 | 8.2 |
| 1923 Sept. 1 | Japan, Tokyo | 99,330 | 8.3 | 1976 Aug. 17 | Philippines, Mindanao | 8,000 | 7.8 |
| 1927 May 22 | China, Nan-Shan | 200,000 | 8.3 | 1976 Nov. 24 | Eastern Turkey | 4,000 | 7.9 |
| 1932 Dec. 26 | China, Kansu | 70,000 | 7.6 | 1977 Mar. 4 | Romania, Bucharest, etc. | 1,541 | 7.5 |
| 1933 Mar. 2 | Japan | 2,990 | 8.9 | 1977 Mar. 22-23 | Southeastern Iran | 167 | 7.0 |
| 1934 Jan. 15 | India, Bihar-Nepal | 10,700 | 8.4 | 1977 Aug. 19 | Indian Ocean, SE Indonesia | 200 | 8.3 |
| 1935 May 31 | India, Quetta | 30,000 | 7.5 | 1977 Nov. 23 | Northwestern Argentina | 100 | 8.2 |
| 1939 Jan. 24 | Chile, Chillan | 28,000 | 8.3 | | (*) estimated from earthquake intensity. (N.A.) not available. | | |
| 1939 Dec. 26 | Turkey, Erzincan | 30,000 | 7.9 | | | | |
| 1946 Dec. 21 | Japan, Honshu | 2,000 | 8.4 | | | | |

## Floods, Tidal Waves

| Date | Location | Deaths | Date | Location | Deaths |
|---|---|---|---|---|---|
| 1887 .... | Hwang-ho River, China | 900,000 | 1962 Sept. 27 | Barcelona, Spain | 445 |
| 1889 May 31 | Johnstown, Pa. | 2,200 | 1963 Oct. 9 | Dam collapse, Vaiont, Italy | 1,800 |
| 1900 Sept. 8 | Galveston, Tex. | 5,000 | 1966 Nov. 4-6 | Florence, Venice, Italy | 113 |
| 1903 June 15 | Heppner, Ore. | 325 | 1967 Jan. 18-24 | Eastern Brazil | 894 |
| 1911 .... | Yangtze River, China | 100,000 | 1967 Mar. 19 | Rio de Janeiro, Brazil | 436 |
| 1913 Mar. 25-27 | Ohio, Indiana | 732 | 1968 Aug. 7-14 | Gujarat State, India | 1,000 |
| 1915 Aug. 17 | Galveston, Tex. | 275 | 1968 Oct. 7 | Northeastern India | 780 |
| 1928 Mar. 13 | Collapse of St. Francis Dam, Santa Paula, Cal. | 450 | 1969 Mar. 17 | Mundau Valley, Alagoas, Brazil | 218 |
| 1928 Sept. 13 | Lake Okeechobee, Fla. | 2,000 | 1969 Aug. 25 | Western Virginia | 189 |
| 1931 Aug. | Hwang-ho River, China | 3,700,000 | 1969 Sept. 15 | South Korea | 250 |
| 1937 Jan. 22 | Ohio, Miss. Valleys | 250 | 1969 Oct. 1-8 | Tunisia | 500 |
| 1939 .... | Northern China | 200,000 | 1970 May 20 | Central Romania | 160 |
| 1947 .... | Honshu Island, Japan | 1,900 | 1970 July 22 | Himalayas, India | 500 |
| 1951 Aug. | Manchuria | 1,800 | 1971 Feb. 26 | Rio de Janeiro, Brazil | 130 |
| 1953 Jan. 31 | Western Europe | 2,000 | 1972 June 9 | Rapid City, S.D. | 236 |
| 1954 Aug. 17 | Farahzad, Iran | 2,000 | 1972 Aug. 7 | Luzon Is., Philippines | 454 |
| 1955 Oct. 7-12 | India, Pakistan | 1,700 | 1974 Mar. 29 | Tubaro, Brazil | 1,000 |
| 1959 Nov. 1 | Western Mexico | 2,000 | 1974 Aug. 12 | Monty-Long, Bangladesh | 2,500 |
| 1959 Dec. 2 | Frejus, France | 412 | 1975 Jan. 11 | Southern Thailand | 131 |
| 1960 Oct. 10 | Bangladesh | 6,000 | 1976 June 5 | Teton Dam collapse, Ida. | 11 |
| 1960 Oct. 31 | Bangladesh | 4,000 | 1976 July 31 | Big Thompson Canyon, Col. | 130 |
| 1962 Feb. 17 | German North Sea coast | 343 | 1976 Nov. 17 | East Java, Indonesia | 136 |
| | | | 1977 July 19-20 | Johnstown, Pa. | 68 |

## Some Major Tornadoes Since 1925

**Source:** National Climatic Center, NOAA, U.S. Commerce Department

| Date | Place | Deaths | Date | Place | Deaths |
|---|---|---|---|---|---|
| 1925 Mar. 18 | Mo., Ill. Ind. | 689 | 1930 May 6 | Hill & Ellis Co., Tex. | 41 |
| 1926 Nov. 25 | Belleville to Portland, Ark. | 53 | 1932 Mar. 21 | Ala. (series of tornadoes) | 268 |
| 1927 Apr. 12 | Rock Springs, Tex. | 74 | 1936 Apr. 5 | Tupelo, Miss. | 216 |
| 1927 May 9 | Arkansas, Poplar Bluff, Mo. | 92 | 1936 Apr. 6 | Gainesville, Ga. | 203 |
| 1927 Sept. 29 | St. Louis, Mo. | 72 | 1938 Sept. 29 | Charleston, S.C. | 32 |
| 1929 Apr. 25 | SE-Central Ga. | 40 | 1942 Mar. 16 | Central to NE Miss. | 75 |

| Date | | | Place | Deaths | Date | | | Place | Deaths |
|---|---|---|---|---|---|---|---|---|---|
| 1942 | Apr. | 27 | Rogers & Mayes Co., Okla. | 52 | 1958 | June | 4 | Northwestern Wisconsin | 30 |
| 1944 | June | 23 | Oh., Pa., W. Va., Md. | 150 | 1959 | Feb. | 10 | St. Louis, Mo. | 21 |
| 1945 | Apr. | 12 | Okla.-Ark. | 102 | 1960 | May | 5, 6 | SE Oklahoma, Arkansas | 30 |
| 1947 | Apr. | 9 | Tex., Okla. & Kan. | 169 | 1965 | Apr. | 11 | Ind., Ill., Mich., Wis. | 271 |
| 1948 | Mar. | 19 | Bunker Hill & Gillespie, Ill. | 33 | 1966 | Mar. | 3 | Jackson, Miss. | 57 |
| 1949 | Jan. | 3 | La. & Ark. | 58 | 1966 | Mar. | 3 | Mississippi, Alabama | 61 |
| 1952 | Mar. | 21 | Ark., Mo., Tenn. (series) | 208 | 1967 | Apr. | 21 | Illinois | 33 |
| 1953 | May | 11 | Waco, Tex. | 114 | 1968 | May | 15 | Arkansas | 34 |
| 1953 | June | 8 | Flint to Lakeport, Mich. | 116 | 1969 | Jan. | 23 | Mississippi | 32 |
| 1953 | June | 9 | Worcester and vicinity, Mass. | 90 | 1971 | Feb. | 21 | Mississippi delta | 110 |
| 1953 | Dec. | 5 | Vicksburg, Miss. | 38 | 1973 | May | 26-7 | South, Midwest (series) | 47 |
| 1955 | May | 25 | Udall, Kan. | 80 | 1974 | Apr. | 3-4 | Ala., Ga., Tenn., Ky., Oh. | 350 |
| 1957 | May | 20 | Williamsburg, Kan., to Ruskin Heights, Mo. | 48 | 1977 | Apr. | 1 | Southeast Bangladesh | 600 |
| | | | | | 1977 | Apr. | 4 | Ala., Miss., Ga. | 22 |

## Number of U. S. Tornadoes Since 1935, Deaths

| Year | No. | Deaths | Year | No. | Deaths | Year | No. | Deaths | Year | No. | Deaths |
|---|---|---|---|---|---|---|---|---|---|---|---|
| 1935 | 180 | 70 | 1946 | 106 | 78 | 1957 | 856 | 191 | 1968 | 660 | 131 |
| 1936 | 151 | 552 | 1947 | 165 | 313 | 1958 | 563 | 66 | 1969 | 608 | 66 |
| 1937 | 147 | 29 | 1948 | 183 | 140 | 1959 | 604 | 58 | 1970 | 652 | 72 |
| 1938 | 213 | 183 | 1949 | 249 | 212 | 1960 | 616 | 47 | 1971 | 889 | 156 |
| 1939 | 152 | 87 | 1950 | 199 | 70 | 1961 | 698 | 51 | 1972 | 741 | *27 |
| 1940 | 124 | 65 | 1951 | 264 | 34 | 1962 | 658 | 28 | 1973 | †1109 | 87 |
| 1941 | 118 | 53 | 1952 | 240 | 230 | 1963 | 461 | 31 | 1974 | 945 | 361 |
| 1942 | 167 | 384 | 1953 | 422 | 515 | 1964 | 703 | 73 | 1975 | 920 | 60 |
| 1943 | 152 | 58 | 1954 | 550 | 36 | 1965 | 901 | 296 | 1976 | 835 | 44 |
| 1944 | 169 | 275 | 1955 | 595 | 126 | 1966 | 585 | 99 | 1977 | 852 | 43 |
| 1945 | 121 | 210 | 1956 | 503 | 83 | 1967 | 929 | 114 | *Record low, †Record high. | | |

## Hurricanes, Typhoons, Blizzards, Other Storms

Names of hurricanes and typhoons in italics—H.—hurricane; T.—typhoon

| Date | Location | Deaths | Date | Location | Deaths |
|---|---|---|---|---|---|
| 1888 Mar. 11-14 | Blizzard, Eastern U.S. | 400 | 1964 Nov. 12 | Flooding, S. Vietnam | 7,000 |
| 1900 Sept. 8 | H., Galveston, Tex. | 6,000 | 1965 May 11-12 | Windstorm, Bangladesh | 17,000 |
| 1926 Sept. 16-22 | H., Fla., Ala. | 372 | 1965 June 1-2 | Windstorm, Bangladesh | 30,000 |
| 1926 Oct. 20 | H., Cuba | 600 | 1965 Sept. 7-10 | H. Betsy, Fla., Miss., La. | 74 |
| 1928 Sept. 12-17 | H., W. Indies, Fla. | 4,000 | 1965 Dec. 15 | Windstorm, Bangladesh | 10,000 |
| 1930 Sept. 3 | H., San Domingo | 2,000 | 1966 June 4-10 | H. Alma, Honduras, SE U.S. | 51 |
| 1938 Sept. 21 | H., New England | 600 | 1966 Sept. 24-30 | H. Inez, Carib., Fla., Mex. | 293 |
| 1942 Oct. 15-16 | H., Bengal, India | 11,000 | 1967 July 9 | T. Billie, Japan | 347 |
| 1944 Sept. 12-16 | H., N.C. to New Eng. | 389 | 1967 Sept. 5-23 | H. Beulah, Carib., Mex., Tex. | 54 |
| 1953 Sept. 25-27 | T., Vietnam, Japan | 1,300 | 1967 Dec. 12-20 | Blizzard, Southwest, U.S. | 51 |
| 1954 Aug. 30 | H. Carol, Northeast U.S. | 68 | 1968 Nov. 18-28 | T. Nina, Philippines | 63 |
| 1954 Oct. 12-13 | H. Hazel, Eastern, U.S., Haiti | 347 | 1969 Aug. 17-18 | H. Camille, Miss., La. | 258 |
| 1955 Aug. 12-13 | H. Connie, Carolinas, Va., Md. | 43 | 1970 July 30- | | |
| 1955 Aug. 18-19 | H. Diane, Eastern U.S. | 400 | Aug. 5 | H. Celia, Cuba, Fla., Tex. | 31 |
| 1955 Sept. 19 | H. Hilda, Mexico | 200 | 1970 Aug. 20-21 | H. Dorothy, Martinique | 42 |
| 1955 Sept. 22-28 | H. Janet, Caribbean | 500 | 1970 Sept. 15 | T. Georgia, Philippines | 300 |
| 1956 Feb. 1-29 | Blizzard, Western Europe | 1,000 | 1970 Oct. 14 | T. Sening, Philippines | 583 |
| 1957 June 27-30 | H. Audrey, La., Tex. | 430 | 1970 Oct. 15 | T. Titang, Philippines | 526 |
| 1958 Feb. 15-16 | Blizzard, NE U.S. | 171 | 1970 Nov. 13 | Cyclone, Bangladesh (est.) | 300,000 |
| 1959 Sept. 17-19 | T. Sarah, Far East. | 2,000 | 1971 Aug. 1 | T. Rose, Hong Kong | 130 |
| 1959 Sept. 26-27 | T. Vera, Honshu, Japan. | 4,466 | 1972 June 19-29 | H. Agnes, Fla. to N.Y. | 118 |
| 1960 Sept. 4-12 | H. Donna, Caribbean, E. U.S. | 148 | 1972 Dec. 3 | T. Theresa, Philippines | 169 |
| 1961 Oct. 31 | H. Hattie, Br. Honduras | 400 | 1973 June-Aug. | Monsoon rains in India | 1,217 |
| 1962 Feb. 17 | Flooding, German Coast. | 343 | 1974 June 11 | Storm Dinah, Luzon Is., Philip. | 71 |
| 1962 Sept. 27 | Flooding, Barcelona, Spain | 445 | 1974 July 11 | T. Gilda, Japan, S. Korea | 108 |
| 1963 May 28-29 | Windstorm, Bangladesh | 22,000 | 1974 Sept. 19-20 | T. Fifi, Honduras | 2,000 |
| 1963 Oct. 4-8 | H. Flora, Cuba, Haiti | 6,000 | 1974 Dec. 25 | Cyclone leveled Darwin, Aus. | 50 |
| 1964 Oct. 4-7 | H. Hilda, La., Miss., Ga. | 38 | 1975 Sept. 13-27 | H. Eloise, Caribbean–NE U.S. | 71 |
| 1964 June 30 | T. Winnie, N. Philippines | 107 | 1976 May 20 | T. Olga, floods, Philippines | 215 |
| 1964 Sept. 5 | T. Ruby, Hong Kong and China | 735 | 1977 July 25, 31 | T. Thelma, T. Vera, Taiwan | 39 |
| 1964 Sept. 14 | Flooding, central S. Korea | 563 | | | |

## Record Oil Spills, 1967-1977

Source: Conservation Division, U.S. Geological Survey, U.S. Interior Department

| Date | Name and Place | Cause of Spill | Gallons |
|---|---|---|---|
| 1967 Mar. 18 | Tanker Torrey Canyon; off England | Grounding | 29,400,000 |
| 1967 Sept. 6 | Tanker R.C. Stoner, Wake Is. | Grounding | 6,006,000 |
| 1967 Oct. 15 | Pipeline; West Delta, La. | Dragging anchor | 6,720,000 |
| 1968 May 5 | Tanker Andron; off W. Africa | Sinking | 4,914,000 |
| 1968 June 13 | Tanker World Glory; off S. Africa | Hull failure | 13,524,000 |
| 1969 Jan. 3 | Offshore oil rig, Santa Barbara, Cal. | Leakage | 235,000 |
| 1969 Nov. 4 | Storage tank; Sewaren, N.J. | Tank rupture | 8,400,000 |
| 1969 Nov. 5 | Tanker Keo; off Massachusetts | Hull failure | 8,820,000 |
| 1971 Nov. 30 | Tanker; off Japan | Ship broke in half | 6,258,000 |
| 1976 May 12 | Tanker Urquiola; LaCoruna, Spain | Grounding, explosion | 21,941,000 |
| 1976 June 23 | Barge; St. Lawrence Seaway, N.Y. | Grounding | 300,000 |
| 1976 Oct. 14 | Tanker Boehlen; Brest, France | Sunk in storm | 3,134,460 |
| 1976 Dec. 15 | Tanker Argo Merchant; Nantucket Is., Mass. | Grounding | 7,700,000 |

| Date | Name and Place | Cause of Spill | Gallons |
|---|---|---|---|
| 1976 Dec. 30 | Tanker Olympic Games; Delaware River | Grounding | 133,500 |
| 1977 Jan. 9 | Barge; off Tampa Bay, Fla. | Crash | 79,000 |
| 1977 Jan. 17 | Tanker Irenes Challenger; near Midway Is. | Broke in half | 3,150,000 |
| 1977 Feb. 4 | Barge; Hudson River, Bear Mtn., N.Y. | Hit rock | 420,000 |
| 1977 Feb. 24 | Tanker Hawaiian Patriot; W. of Hawaii | Explosion | 30,000,000 |
| 1977 Mar. 3 | Tanker Borag; off Taiwan | Hit reef | 3,134,460 |
| 1977 Mar. 20 | Tanker Claude Conway; off N. Carolina | Explosion | 536,000 |
| 1977 Apr. 22 | Ekofisk oil field; North Sea | Oil well blowout | 8,200,000 |
| 1978 Mar. 17 | Tanker Amoco Cadiz, Brittany, France | Broke in half | 54,600,000 |

---

# Explosions

| Date | Location | Deaths | Date | Location | Deaths |
|---|---|---|---|---|---|
| 1910 Oct. 1 | Los Angeles Times Bldg., | 21 | 1960 Mar. 4 | Belgian munitions ship, Havana | 100 |
| 1913 Mar. 7 | Dynamite, Baltimore harbor | 55 | 1960 Oct. 25 | Gas, Windsor, Ont., store | 11 |
| 1915 Sept. 27 | Gasoline tank car, Ardmore, Okla. | 47 | 1962 Jan. 16 | Gas pipeline, Alberta, Canada | 19 |
| 1917 Apr. 10 | Munitions plant, Eddystone, Pa. | 133 | 1962 Mar. 3 | Gasoline truck, Syria | 31 |
| 1917 Dec. 6 | Halifax Harbor, Canada | 1,654 | 1962 Oct. | Telephone Co. office, N. Y. City | 23 |
| 1918 July 2 | Explosives, Split Rock, N.Y. | 50 | 1963 Jan. 2 | Packing plant, Terre Haute, Ind. | 16 |
| 1918 Oct. 4 | Shell plant, Morgan Station, N.J. | 64 | 1963 Mar. 9 | Dynamite plant, S. Africa | 45 |
| 1919 May 22 | Food plant, Cedar Rapids, Ia. | 44 | 1963 Mar. 9 | Steel plant, Belecke, W. Germany | 19 |
| 1920 Sept. 16 | Wall Street, New York, bomb | 30 | 1963 Aug. 15 | Explosives dump, Gauhiti, India | 32 |
| 1924 Jan. 3 | Food plant, Pekin, Ill. | 42 | 1963 Oct. 31 | State Fair Coliseum, Indianapolis | 73 |
| 1928 April 13 | Dance hall, West Plains, Mo. | 40 | 1964 July 23 | Bone, Algeria, harbor munitions | 100 |
| 1937 Mar. 18 | New London, Tex., school | 294 | 1965 Mar. 4 | Gas pipeline, Natchitoches, La. | 17 |
| 1940 Sept. 11 | Hercules Powder, Kenvil, N.J. | 51 | 1965 Aug. 9 | Missile silo, Searcy, Ark. | 53 |
| 1942 June 5 | Ordnance plant, Elwood, Ill. | 49 | 1965 Oct. 21 | Bridge, Tila Bund, Pakistan | 80 |
| 1944 Apr. 14 | Bombay, India, harbor | 700 | 1965 Oct. 30 | Cartagena, Colombia | 48 |
| 1944 July 17 | Port Chicago, Cal., pier | 322 | 1965 Nov. 24 | Armory, Keokuk, Ia. | 20 |
| 1944 Oct. 21 | Liquid gas tank, Cleveland | 135 | 1966 Oct. 13 | Chemical plant, La Salle, Que. | 11 |
| 1947 Apr. 16 | Texas City, Tex., pier. | 561 | 1967 Feb. 17 | Chemical plant, Hawthorne, N.J. | 11 |
| 1948 July 28 | Farben works, Ludwigshafen, Ger. | 184 | 1967 Dec. 25 | Apartment bldg., Moscow | 20 |
| 1950 May 19 | Munitions barges, S. Amboy, N. J. | 30 | 1968 Apr. 6 | Sports store, Richmond, Ind. | 43 |
| 1956 Aug. 7 | Dynamite trucks, Cal., Colombia | 1,100 | 1970 Apr. 8 | Subway construction, Oska, Japan. | 73 |
| 1958 Apr. 18 | Sunken munitions ship, Okinawa | 40 | 1971 June 24 | Tunnel, Sylmar, Cal. | 17 |
| 1958 May 22 | Nike missiles, Leonardo, N.J. | 10 | 1971 June 28 | School, fireworks, Pueblo, Mex. | 13 |
| 1959 Apr. 10 | World War II bomb, Philippines | 38 | 1971 Oct. 21 | Shopping center, Glasgow, Scot. | 20 |
| 1959 June 2 | Gas truck, Pa. Turnpike | 10 | 1973 Feb. 10 | Liquified gas tank, Staten Is., N.Y. | 40 |
| 1959 June 28 | Rail tank cars, Meldrin, Ga. | 25 | 1975 Dec. 27 | Chasnala, India, mine | 431 |
| 1959 Aug. 7 | Dynamite truck, Roseburg, Ore. | 13 | 1976 Apr. 13 | Lapua, Finland, munitions works | 45 |
| 1959 Nov. 2 | Jamuri Bazar, India, explosives | 46 | 1977 Nov. 11 | Freight train, Iri, S. Korea | 57 |
| 1959 Dec. 13 | Dortmund, Ger., 2 apt. bldgs. | 26 | 1977 Dec. 22 | Grain elevator, Westwego, La. | 35 |

---

# Fires

| Date | Location | Deaths | Date | Location | Deaths |
|---|---|---|---|---|---|
| 1845 May | Theater, Canton, China | 1,670 | 1949 Apr. 5 | Hospital, Effingham, Ill. | 77 |
| 1871 Oct. 8 | Chicago, $196 million loss | 250 | 1950 Jan. 7 | Davenport, Ia., Mercy Hospital | 41 |
| 1871 Oct. 9 | Peshtigo, Wis., forest fire | 1,182 | 1953 Mar. 29 | Largo, Fla., nursing home | 35 |
| 1876 Dec. 5 | Brooklyn (N.Y.), theater | 295 | 1953 Apr. 16 | Chicago, metalworking plant | 35 |
| 1877 June 20 | St. John, N. B., Canada | 100 | 1957 Feb. 17 | Home for aged, Warrenton, Mo. | 72 |
| 1881 Dec. 8 | Ring Theater, Vienna. | 850 | 1958 Mar. 19 | New York City loft building | 24 |
| 1887 May 25 | Opera Comique, Paris | 200 | 1958 Dec. 1 | Parochial school, Chicago. | 95 |
| 1887 Sept. 4 | Exeter, England, theater | 200 | 1958 Dec. 16 | Store, Bogota, Colombia | 83 |
| 1894 Sept. 1 | Hinckley, Minn., forest fire | 413 | 1959 June 23 | Resort hotel, Stalheim, Norway. | 34 |
| 1897 May 4 | Charity bazaar, Paris. | 150 | 1960 Mar. 12 | Pusan, Korea, chemical plant | 68 |
| 1900 June 30 | Hoboken, N. J., docks | 326 | 1960 July 14 | Mental hospital, Guatemala City | 225 |
| 1902 Sept. 20 | Church, Birmingham, Ala. | 115 | 1960 Nov. 13 | Movie theater, Amude, Syria | 152 |
| 1903 Dec. 30 | Iroquois Theater, Chicago | 602 | 1961 Jan. | Thomas Hotel, San Francisco. | 20 |
| 1908 Jan. 13 | Rhoads Thea., Boyertown, Pa. | 170 | 1961 May 15 | Tenement, Hong Kong | 25 |
| 1908 Mar. 4 | School, Collinwood, Oh. | 176 | 1961 Dec. 8 | Hospital, Hartford, Conn. | 16 |
| 1911 Mar. 25 | Triangle factory, N. Y. City | 145 | 1961 Dec. 17 | Circus, Niteroi, Brazil. | 323 |
| 1913 Oct. 14 | Colliery, Mid Glamorgan, Wales | 439 | 1963 May 7 | Theater, Diourbel, Senegal | 64 |
| 1918 Apr. 13 | Norman Okla., state hospital | 38 | 1963 Nov. 13 | Surfside Hotel, Atlantic City, N.J. | 25 |
| 1918 Oct. 12 | Cloquet, Minn., forest fire | 400 | 1963 Nov. 23 | Rest home, Fitchville, Oh. | 63 |
| 1919 June 20 | Mayaguez Theater, San Juan. | 150 | 1963 Dec. 29 | Roosevelt hotel, Jacksonville, Fla. | 22 |
| 1923 May 17 | School, Camden, S. C. | 76 | 1964 May 8 | Apartment building, Manila | 30 |
| 1924 Dec. 24 | School, Hobart, Okla. | 35 | 1964 Dec. 18 | Nursing home, Fountaintown, Ind. | 20 |
| 1929 May 15 | Clinic, Cleveland, Oh. | 125 | 1965 Mar. 1 | Apartment, LaSalle, Canada | 28 |
| 1930 Apr. 21 | Penitentiary, Columbus, Oh. | 320 | 1966 Mar. 1 | Numata, Japan, 2 ski resorts | 31 |
| 1931 July 24 | Pittsburgh, Pa., home for aged | 48 | 1966 Aug. 13 | Melbourne, Australia, hotel | 29 |
| 1938 May 16 | Atlanta, Ga., Terminal Hotel. | 35 | 1966 Sept. 1 | Anchorage, Alaska, hotel | 14 |
| 1940 Apr. 23 | Dance hall, Natchez, Miss. | 198 | 1966 Oct. 17 | N. Y. City bldg. (firemen) | 12 |
| 1942 Nov. 28 | Cocoanut Grove, Boston | 491 | 1966 Dec. 7 | Erzurum, Turkey, barracks | 68 |
| 1942 | Hostel, St. John's, Newfoundland | 100 | 1967 Feb. 7 | Restaurant, Montgomery, Ala. | 25 |
| 1943 Sept. 7 | Gulf Hotel, Houston | 55 | 1967 May 22 | Store, Brussels, Belgium | 322 |
| 1944 July 6 | Ringling Circus, Hartford. | 168 | 1967 July 16 | State prison, Jay, Fla. | 37 |
| 1946 June 5 | LaSalle Hotel, Chicago | 61 | 1968 Jan. 9 | Brooklyn, N. Y., tenement | 13 |
| 1946 Dec. 7 | Winecoff Hotel, Atlanta | 119 | 1968 Feb. 26 | Shrewsbury, England, hospital | 22 |
| 1946 Dec. 12 | New York, ice plant, tenement | 37 | 1968 May 11 | Vijayawada, India, wedding hall. | 58 |

| Date | | Location | Deaths | Date | | Location | Deaths |
|---|---|---|---|---|---|---|---|
| 1968 | Nov. 18 | Glasgow, Scotland, factory | 24 | 1973 | Feb. 6 | Paris, France, school | 21 |
| 1969 | Jan. 26 | Victoria Hotel, Dunnville, Ont. | 13 | 1973 | Nov. 6 | Fukui, Japan, train | 28 |
| 1969 | Dec. 2 | Nursing home, Notre Dame, Can. | 54 | 1973 | Nov. 29 | Kumamoto, Japan, department store | 107 |
| 1970 | Jan. 9 | Nursing home, Marietta, Oh. | 27 | 1973 | Dec. 2 | Seoul, Korea, theater | 50 |
| 1970 | Mar. 20 | Hotel, Seattle, Wash. | 19 | 1974 | Feb. 1 | Sao Paulo, Brazil, bank building | 189 |
| 1970 | Nov. 1 | Dance hall, Grenoble, France | 145 | 1974 | June 30 | Port Chester, N. Y., discotheque | 24 |
| 1970 | Nov. 5 | Nursing home, Pointe-aux-Trembles, Que. | 17 | 1974 | Nov. 3 | Seoul, So. Korea, hotel discotheque | 88 |
| 1970 | Dec. 20 | Hotel, Tucson, Arizona | 28 | 1975 | Dec. 12 | Mina, Saudi Arabia, Tent City | 138 |
| 1971 | Mar. 6 | Psychiatric clinic, Burghoezli, Switzerland | 28 | 1976 | Oct. 24 | Bronx, N.Y., social club | 25 |
| 1971 | Apr. 20 | Hotel, Bangkok, Thailand | 24 | 1977 | Feb. 25 | Rossiya Hotel, Moscow | 45 |
| 1971 | Oct. 19 | Nursing home, Honesdale, Pa. | 15 | 1977 | May 28 | Southgate, Ky., nightclub | 164 |
| 1971 | Dec. 25 | Hotel, Seoul, So. Korea | 162 | 1977 | June 9 | Abidjan, Ivory Coast nightclub | 41 |
| 1972 | May 13 | Osaka, Japan, nightclub | 116 | 1977 | June 26 | Columbia, Tenn., jail | 42 |
| 1972 | July 5 | Sherborne, England, hospital | 30 | 1977 | Nov. 14 | Manila, PI, hotel | 47 |

## Major U.S. Railroad Wrecks

Source: Office of Safety, Federal Railroad Administration

| Date | | Location | Deaths | Date | | Location | Deaths |
|---|---|---|---|---|---|---|---|
| 1876 | Dec. 29 | Ashtabula, Oh. | 92 | 1922 | Dec. 13 | Humble, Tex. | 22 |
| 1880 | Aug. 11 | Mays Landing, N. J. | 40 | 1923 | Sept. 27 | Lockett, Wy. | 31 |
| 1887 | Aug. 10 | Chatsworth, Ill. | 81 | 1925 | June 16 | Hackettstown, N. J. | 50 |
| 1888 | Oct. 10 | Mud Run, Pa. | 55 | 1925 | Oct. 27 | Victoria, Miss. | 21 |
| 1896 | July 30 | Atlantic City, N. J. | 60 | 1926 | Sept. 5 | Waco, Col. | 30 |
| 1903 | Dec. 23 | Laurel Run, Pa. | 53 | 1928 | Aug. 24 | I.R.T. subway, Times Sq., N. Y. | 18 |
| 1904 | Aug. 7 | Eden, Col. | 96 | 1938 | June 19 | Saugus, Mont. | 47 |
| 1904 | Sept. 24 | New Market Tenn. | 56 | 1939 | Aug. 12 | Harney, Nev. | 24 |
| 1906 | Mar. 16 | Florence, Col. | 35 | 1940 | Aug. 19 | Little Falls, N. Y. | 31 |
| 1906 | Oct. 28 | Atlantic City, N. J. | 40 | 1940 | July 31 | Cuyahoga Falls, Oh. | 43 |
| 1906 | Dec. 30 | Washington, D. C. | 53 | 1943 | Aug. 29 | Wayland, N. Y. | 27 |
| 1907 | Jan. 2 | Volland, Kan. | 33 | 1943 | Sept. 6 | Frankford Junction, Philadelphia, Pa. | 79 |
| 1907 | Jan. 19 | Fowler, Ind. | 29 | 1943 | Dec. 16 | Between Rennert and Buie, N. C. | 72 |
| 1907 | Feb. 16 | New York City | 22 | 1944 | July 6 | High Bluff, Tenn. | 35 |
| 1907 | Feb. 23 | Colton, Cal. | 26 | 1944 | Aug. 4 | Near Stockton, Ga. | 47 |
| 1907 | July 20 | Salem, Mich. | 33 | 1944 | Sept. 14 | Dewey, Ind. | 29 |
| 1907 | Sept. 15 | Canaan, N. H. | 24 | 1944 | Dec. 31 | Bagley, Utah | 50 |
| 1910 | Mar. 1 | Wellington, Wash. | 96 | 1945 | Aug. 9 | Michigan, N. D. | 34 |
| 1910 | Mar. 21 | Green Mountain, Ia. | 55 | 1946 | Apr. 25 | Naperville, Ill. | 45 |
| 1911 | Aug. 25 | Manchester, N. Y. | 29 | 1947 | Feb. 18 | Gallitzin, Pa. | 24 |
| 1912 | July 4 | East Corning, N. Y. | 39 | 1950 | Feb. 17 | Rockville Centre, N. Y. | 31 |
| 1912 | July 5 | Ligonier, Pa. | 23 | 1950 | Sept. 11 | Coshocton, Oh. | 33 |
| 1913 | Sept. 2 | North Haven, Conn. | 21 | 1950 | Nov. 22 | Richmond Hill, N. Y. | 79 |
| 1914 | Aug. 5 | Tipton Ford, Mo. | 43 | 1951 | Feb. 6 | Woodbridge, N. J. | 84 |
| 1914 | Sept. 15 | Lebanon, Mo. | 28 | 1951 | Nov. 12 | Wyuta, Wyo. | 17 |
| 1916 | Mar. 29 | Amherst, Oh. | 27 | 1951 | Nov. 25 | Woodstock, Ala. | 17 |
| 1917 | Feb. 27 | Mount Union, Pa. | 20 | 1953 | Mar. 27 | Conneaut, Oh. | 21 |
| 1917 | Sept. 28 | Kellyville, Okla. | 23 | 1956 | Jan. 22 | Los Angeles, Cal. | 30 |
| 1917 | Dec. 20 | Shepherdsville, Ky. | 46 | 1956 | Feb. 28 | Swampscott, Mass. | 13 |
| 1918 | June 22 | Ivanhoe, Ind. | 68 | 1956 | Sept. 5 | Springer, N. M. | 20 |
| 1918 | July 9 | Nashville, Tenn. | 101 | 1957 | June 11 | Vroman, Col. | 12 |
| 1918 | Nov. 2 | Brooklyn, N. Y., Malbone St. Tunnel | 97 | 1958 | Sept. 15 | Elizabethport, N. J. | 48 |
| 1919 | Jan. 12 | South Byron, N. Y. | 22 | 1960 | Mar. 14 | Bakersfield, Cal. | 14 |
| 1919 | July 1 | Dunkirk, N. Y. | 12 | 1962 | July 28 | Steelton, Pa. | 19 |
| 1919 | Dec. 20 | Onawa, Maine | 23 | 1966 | Dec. 28 | Everett, Mass. | 13 |
| 1921 | Feb. 27 | Porter, Ind. | 37 | 1971 | June 10 | Salem, Ill. | 11 |
| 1921 | Dec. 5 | Woodmont, Pa. | 27 | 1972 | Oct. 30 | Chicago, Ill. | 45 |
| 1922 | Aug. 5 | Sulphur Spring, Mo. | 34 | 1977 | Jan. 4 | Chicago, Ill., elevated train | 11 |

World's worst train wreck occurred Dec. 12, 1917, Modane, France, passenger train derailed, 543 killed.

## Some Notable Aircraft Disasters Since 1937

| Date | | Aircraft | Site of accident | Deaths |
|---|---|---|---|---|
| 1937 | May 6 | German zeppelin Hindenburg | Burned at mooring, Lakehurst, N.J. | 36 |
| 1944 | Aug. 23 | U.S. Air Force B-24 | Hit school, Freckelton, England | 76[1] |
| 1945 | July 28 | U.S. Army B-25 | Hit Empire State bldg., N.Y.C. | 14[1] |
| 1952 | Dec. 20 | U.S. Air Force C-124 | Fell, burned, Moses Lake, Wash. | 87 |
| 1953 | Mar. 3 | Canadian Pacific Comet Jet | Karachi, Pakistan | 11[2] |
| 1953 | June 18 | U.S. Air Force C-124 | Crashed, burned near Tokyo | 129 |
| 1955 | Nov. 1 | United Air Lines DC-6B | Exploded, crashed near Longmont, Col. | 44[3] |
| 1956 | June 20 | Venezuelan Super-Constellation | Crashed in Atlantic off Asbury Park, N.J. | 74 |
| 1956 | June 30 | TWA Super-Const., United DC-7 | Collided over Grand Canyon, Arizona | 128 |
| 1960 | Dec. 16 | United DC-8 jet, TWA Super-Const. | Collided over N.Y. City | 134[4] |
| 1962 | Mar. 4 | Br. Caledonian Airlines DC-7C | Crashed near Douala, Cameroon | 111 |
| 1962 | Mar. 16 | Flying Tiger Super-Const. | Vanished in Western Pacific | 107 |
| 1962 | June 3 | Air France Boeing 707 jet | Crashed on takeoff from Paris | 130 |
| 1962 | June 22 | Air France Boeing 707 jet | Crashed in storm, Guadeloupe, W.I. | 113 |
| 1963 | June 3 | Chartered Northw. Airlines DC-7 | Crashed in Pacific off British Columbia | 101 |
| 1963 | Nov. 29 | Trans-Canada Airlines DC-8F | Crashed after takeoff from Montreal | 118 |
| 1965 | May 20 | Pakistani Boeing 720-B | Crashed at Cairo, Egypt, airport | 121 |
| 1966 | Jan. 24 | Air India Boeing 707 jetliner | Crashed on Mont Blanc, France-Italy | 117 |
| 1966 | Feb. 4 | All-Nippon Boeing 727 | Plunged into Tokyo Bay | 133 |
| 1966 | Mar. 5 | BOAC Boeing 707 jetliner | Crashed on Mount Fuji, Japan | 124 |
| 1966 | Dec. 24 | U.S. military-chartered CL-44 | Crashed into village in So. Vietnam | 129 |
| 1967 | Apr. 20 | Swiss Britannia turboprop | Crashed at Nicosia, Cyprus | 126 |

| Date | | Aircraft | Site of accident | Deaths |
|---|---|---|---|---|
| 1967 | July 19 | Piedmont Boeing 727, Cessna 310 | Collided in air, Hendersonville, N.C. | 82 |
| 1968 | Apr. 20 | S. African Airways Boeing 707 | Crashed on takeoff, Windhoek, SW Africa | 122 |
| 1968 | May 3 | Braniff International Electra | Crashed in storm near Dawson, Tex. | 85 |
| 1969 | Mar. 16 | Venezuelan DC-9 | Crashed after takeoff from Maracaibo, Venezuela | 155[5] |
| 1969 | Mar. 20 | United Arab Ilyushin-18 | Crashed at Aswan airport, Egypt | 87 |
| 1969 | June 4 | Mexican Boeing 727 | Rammed into mountain near Monterrey, Mexico | 79 |
| 1969 | Nov. 20 | Nigerian VC-10 | Crashed near Iju, Nigeria | 87 |
| 1969 | Dec. 8 | Olympia Airways DC-6B | Crashed near Athens in storm | 93 |
| 1970 | Feb. 15 | Dominican DC-9 | Crashed into sea on takeoff from Santo Domingo | 102 |
| 1970 | July 3 | British chartered jetliner | Crashed near Barcelona, Spain | 112 |
| 1970 | July 5 | Air Canada DC-8 | Crashed near Toronto International Airport | 108 |
| 1970 | Aug. 9 | Peruvian turbojet | Crashed after takeoff from Cuzco, Peru | 101[1] |
| 1970 | Nov. 14 | Southern Airways DC-9 | Crashed in mountains near Huntington, W. Va. | 75[6] |
| 1970 | Dec. 31 | Soviet Aeroflot Ilyushin-18 | Crashed on takeoff, Leningrad | 90 |
| 1971 | July 30 | All-Nippon Boeing 727 and Japanese Air Force F-86 | Collided over Morioka, Japan | 162[7] |
| 1971 | Aug. 11 | Soviet Aeroflot Tupolev-104 | Crashed at Irkutsk airport, USSR | 97 |
| 1971 | Sept. 4 | Alaska Airlines Boeing 727 | Crashed into mountain near Juneau, Alaska | 111 |
| 1972 | Mar. 14 | Danish Airliner | Crashed near Dubai, United Arab Emirates | 112 |
| 1972 | Aug. 14 | E. German Ilyushin-62 | Crashed on take-off East Berlin | 156 |
| 1972 | Oct. 13 | Aeroflot Ilyushin-62 | E. German airline crashed near Moscow | 176 |
| 1972 | Dec. 4 | Chartered Spanish airliner | Crashed on take-off, Canary Islands | 155 |
| 1972 | Dec. 29 | Eastern Airlines Lockheed Tristar | Crashed on approach to Miami Int'l. Airport | 100 |
| 1973 | Jan. 22 | Chartered Boeing 707 | Burst into flames during landing, Kano Airport, Nigeria | 176 |
| 1973 | Apr. 10 | British Vanguard turboprop | Crashed during snowstorm at Basel, Switzerland | 104 |
| 1973 | June 3 | Soviet Supersonic TU-144 | Exploded in air near Goussainville, France | 14[8] |
| 1973 | July 11 | Brazilian Boeing 707 | Crashed on approach to Orly Airport, Paris | 122 |
| 1973 | July 31 | Delta Airlines jetliner | Crashed, landing in fog at Logan Airport, Boston | 89 |
| 1973 | Aug. 13 | Spanish Caravelle jet | Exploded and crashed near La Coruna, Spain | 85 |
| 1973 | Dec. 23 | French Caravelle jet | Crashed in Morocco | 106 |
| 1974 | Jan. 31 | Pan American Boeing 707 jet | Crashed in Pago Pago, American Samoa | 96 |
| 1974 | Mar. 3 | Turkish DC-10 jet | Crashed at Ermenonville near Paris | 346 |
| 1974 | Apr. 23 | Pan American 707 jet | Crashed in Bali, Indonesia | 107 |
| 1974 | Sept. 8 | TWA 707 jet | Crashed in Ionian Sea off Greece, after bomb explosion Arab guerrilla group claimed responsibility | 80 |
| 1974 | Dec. 1 | TWA-727 | Crashed in storm, Upperville, Va. | 92[1] |
| 1974 | Dec. 4 | Dutch-chartered DC-8 | Crashed in storm near Colombo, Sri Lanka | 191 |
| 1975 | Apr. 4 | Air Force Galaxy C-58 | Crashed near Saigon, So. Vietnam, after takeoff with load of orphans | 172 |
| 1975 | June 24 | Eastern Airlines 727 jet | Crashed in storm, JFK Airport, N.Y. City | 113 |
| 1975 | Aug. 3 | Chartered 707 | Hit mountainside, Agadir, Morocco | 188 |
| 1976 | Sept. 10 | British Airways Trident, Yugoslav DC-9 | Collided near Zagreb, Yugoslavia | 176 |
| 1976 | Sept. 19 | Turkish 727 | Hit mountain, southern Turkey | 155 |
| 1976 | Oct. 6 | Cuban DC-8 | Crashed near Barbados after bomb explosion | 73 |
| 1976 | Oct. 12 | Indian Caravelle jet | Crashed after takeoff, Bombay airport | 95 |
| 1976 | Oct. 13 | Bolivian 707 cargo jet | Crashed in Santa Cruz, Bolivia | 100[9] |
| 1976 | Dec. 25 | Egyptian 707 | Exploded and crashed at Bangkok, Thailand airport | 81[1] |
| 1976 | Dec. 28 | Aeroflot TU-104 | Crashed at Moscow's Sheremetyevo airport | 72 |
| 1977 | Jan. 13 | Aeroflot TU-104 | Exploded and crashed at Alama-Ata, Central Asia | 90 |
| 1977 | Mar. 27 | KLM 747, Pan American 747 | Collided on runway, Tenerife, Canary Islands | 581 |
| 1977 | Nov. 19 | TAP Boeing 727 | Crashed on Madeira | 124 |
| 1977 | Dec. 4 | Malaysian Boeing 737 | Hijacked, then exploded in mid-air and crashed in Straits of Johore | 100 |
| 1978 | Mar. 16 | Bulgarian TU-134 | Crashed at Vratsa, Bulgaria | 73 |

(1) Including those on the ground and in buildings. (2) First fatal crash of commercial jet plane. (3) Caused by bomb planted by John G. Graham in insurance plot to kill his mother, a passenger. (4) Including all 128 aboard the planes and 6 on ground. (5) Killed 84 on plane and 71 on ground. (6) Including 43 Marshall U. football players and coaches. (7) Airliner-fighter crash, pilot of fighter parachuted to safety, was arrested for negligence. (8) First supersonic plane crash killed 6 crewmen and 8 on the ground; there were no passengers. (9) Crew of 3 killed; 97, mostly children, killed on ground.

## Principal U.S. Mine Disasters

Source: Bureau of Mines, U.S. Interior Department

**Note:** Prior to 1968, only disasters with losses of 50 or more lives are listed; for 1968-72, all disasters in which 5 or more men are killed are listed. Only fatalities to mining company employees are included. All Bituminous-coal mines unless otherwise noted.

| Date | Location | Deaths | Date | Location | Deaths |
|---|---|---|---|---|---|
| 1855 Mar. | Coalfield, Va. | 55 | 1908 Mar. 28 | Hanna, Wy. | 59 |
| 1867 Apr. 3 | Winterpock, Va. | 69 | 1908 Nov. 28 | Marianna, Pa. | 154 |
| 1869[1] Sept. 6 | Plymouth, Pa. | 110 | 1908 Dec. 29 | Switchback, W. Va. | 50 |
| 1883 Feb. 16 | Braidwood, Ill. | 69 | 1909 Jan. 12 | Switchback, W. Va. | 67 |
| 1884 Jan. 24 | Crested Butte, Col. | 59 | 1909 Nov. 13 | Cherry, Ill. | 259 |
| 1884 Mar. 13 | Pocahontas, Va. | 112 | 1910 Jan. 31 | Primero, Col. | 75 |
| 1891 Jan. 27 | Mount Pleasant, Pa. | 109 | 1910 May 5 | Palos, Ala. | 90 |
| 1892 Jan. 7 | Krebs, Okla. | 100 | 1910 Oct. 8 | Starkville, Col. | 56 |
| 1895 Mar. 20 | Red Canyon, Wy. | 60 | 1910 Nov. 8 | Delagua, Col. | 79 |
| 1896[1] June 28 | Pittston, Pa. | 58 | 1911 Apr. 7 | Throop, Pa. | 72 |
| 1900 Jan. 1 | Scofield, Ut. | 200 | 1911 Apr. 8 | Littleton, Ala. | 128 |
| 1902 May 19 | Coal Creek, Tenn. | 184 | 1911 Dec. 9 | Briceville, Tenn. | 84 |
| 1902 July 10 | Johnstown, Pa. | 112 | 1912 Mar. 20 | McCurtain, Okla. | 73 |
| 1903 June 30 | Hanna, Wy. | 169 | 1912 Mar. 26 | Jed, W. Va. | 83 |
| 1904 Jan. 25 | Cheswick, Pa. | 179 | 1913 Apr. 23 | Finleyville, Pa. | 96 |
| 1905 Feb. 20 | Virginia City, Ala. | 112 | 1913 Oct. 22 | Dawson, N.M. | 263 |
| 1907 Jan. 29 | Stuart W. Va. | 84 | 1914 Apr. 28 | Eccles, W. Va. | 181 |
| 1907 Dec. 6 | Monongah, W. Va. | 361 | 1914 Oct. 27 | Royalton, Ill. | 52 |
| 1907 Dec. 16 | Yolande, Ala. | 57 | 1915 Mar. 2 | Layland, W. Va. | 112 |
| 1907 Dec. 19 | Jacobs Creek, Pa. | 239 | 1917 Apr. 27 | Hastings, Col. | 121 |

| Date | Location | Deaths | Date | Location | Deaths |
|---|---|---|---|---|---|
| 1917[2] June 8 | Butte, Mon. | 163 | 1929 Dec. 17 | McAlester, Okla. | 61 |
| 1917 Aug. 4 | Clay, Ky. | 62 | 1930 Nov. 5 | Millfield, Oh. | 79 |
| 1919[1] June 5 | Wilkes-Barre, Pa. | 92 | 1932 Dec. 23 | Moweaqua, Ill. | 54 |
| 1922 Nov. 6 | Spangler, Pa. | 77 | 1940 Jan. 10 | Bartley, W. Va. | 91 |
| 1922 Nov. 22 | Dolomite, Ala. | 90 | 1940 Mar. 16 | St. Clairsville, Oh. | 72 |
| 1923 Feb. 8 | Dawson, N.M. | 120 | 1940 July 15 | Portage, Pa. | 63 |
| 1923 Aug. 14 | Kemmerer, Wy. | 99 | 1942 May 12 | Osage, W. Va. | 56 |
| 1924 Mar. 8 | Castle Gate, Ut. | 171 | 1943 Feb. 27 | Washoe, Mon. | 74 |
| 1924 Apr. 28 | Benwood, W. Va. | 119 | 1944 July 5 | Belmont, Oh. | 66 |
| 1925 Feb. 20 | Sullivan, Ind. | 52 | 1947 Mar. 25 | Centralia, Ill. | 111 |
| 1925 May 27 | Coal Glen, N.C. | 53 | 1951 Dec. 21 | West Frankfort, Ill. | 119 |
| 1925 Dec. 10 | Acmar, Ala. | 53 | 1968[3] Mar. 6 | Calumet, La. | 21 |
| 1926 Jan. 13 | Wilburton, Okla. | 91 | 1968 Nov. 20 | Farmington, W. Va. | 78 |
| 1926[2] Nov. 3 | Ishpeming, Mich. | 51 | 1970 Dec. 30 | Hyden, Ky. | 38 |
| 1927 Apr. 30 | Everettville, W. Va. | 97 | 1972[2] May 2 | Kellogg, Ida | 91 |
| 1928 May 19 | Mather, Pa. | 195 | 1976 Mar. 9, 11 | Oven Fork, Ky. | 26 |

(1) Anthracite mine. (2) Metal mine. (3) Nonmetal mine.
World's worst mine disaster killed 1,549 workers in Honkeiko Colliery in Manchuria Apr. 25, 1942.

---

# Historic Assassinations Since 1865

**1865**—Apr. 14. U. S. Pres. Abraham Lincoln, shot in Washington, D. C.; died Apr. 15.

**1881**—Mar. 13. Alexander II, of Russia—July 2. U. S. Pres. James A. Garfield, Washington; died Sept. 19.

**1900**—July 29. Umberto I, king of Italy.

**1901**—Sept. 6. U. S. Pres. William McKinley in Buffalo, N. Y., died Sept. 14. Leon Czolgosz executed for the crime Oct. 29.

**1913**—Feb. 23. Mexican Pres. Francisco, I, Madero and Vice Pres. Jose Pino Suarez.—Mar. 18. George, king of Greece.

**1914**—June 28. Archduke Francis Ferdinand of Austria-Hungary and his wife in Sarajevo, Bosnia (later part of Yugoslavia), by Gavrillo Princip.

**1916**—Dec. 30. Grigori Rasputin, politically powerful Russian monk.

**1918**—July 12. Grand Duke Michael of Russia, at Perm.—July 16. Nicholas II, abdicated as czar of Russia; his wife, the Czarina Alexandra, their son, Czarevitch Alexis, and their daughters, Grand Duchesses Olga, Tatiana, Marie, Anastasia, and 4 members of their household were executed by Bolsheviks at Ekaterinburg.

**1920**—May 20. Mexican Pres. Gen. Venustiano Carranza in Tlaxcalantongo.

**1922**—Aug. 22. Michael Collins, Irish revolutionary.

**1923**—July 20. Gen. Francisco "Pancho" Villa, ex-rebel leader, in Parral, Mexico.

**1928**—July 17. Gen. Alvaro Obregon, president-elect of Mexico, in San Angel, Mexico.

**1933**—Feb. 15. In Miami, Fla. Joseph Zangara, anarchist, shot at Pres.-elect Franklin D. Roosevelt, but a woman seized his arm, and the bullet fatally wounded Mayor Anton J. Cermak, of Chicago, who died Mar. 6. Zangara was electrocuted on Mar. 20, 1933.

**1934**—July 25. In Vienna, Austrian Chancellor Engelbert Dollfuss by Nazis, in the chancellery. Otto Planetta convicted and hanged.

**1935**—Sept. 8. U. S. Sen. Huey P. Long, shot in Baton Rouge, La., by Dr. Carl Austin Weiss, who was slain by Long's bodyguards.

**1940**—Aug. 20. Leon Trotsky (Lev Bronstein), 63, exiled Russian war minister, near Mexico City. Killer identified as Ramon Mercador del Rio, a Spaniard, served 20 years in Mexican prison.

**1948**—Jan. 30. Mohandas K. Gandhi, 78, shot in New Delhi, India, by Nathuran Vinayak Godse, 36—Sept. 17. Count Folke Bernadotte, UN mediator for Palestine, ambushed in Jerusalem.

**1951**—July 20. King Abdul ibn Hussein of Jordan.

**1956**—Sept. 21. Pres. Anastasio Somoza of Nicaragua, in Leon; died Sept. 29.

**1957**—July 26. Pres. Carlos Castillo Armas of Guatemala, in Guatemala City by one of his own guards, who then committed suicide.

**1958**—July 14. King Faisal of Iraq; his uncle, Crown Prince Abdul Illah, and July 15, Premier Nuri as-Said, by rebels in Baghdad.

**1959**—Sept. 25. Prime Minister S.W.R.D. Bandaranaike of Ceylon, by Buddhist monk in Colombo.

**1961**—Jan. 17. Ex-Premier Patrice Lumumba of the Congo, in Katanga Province—May 30. Dominican dictator Rafael Leonidas Trujillo Molina shot to death by assassins near Ciudad Trujillo.

**1963**—Jan. 13. Pres. Sylvanus Olympio of Togo, by ex-soldiers at Lome.—June 12. Medgar W. Evers, NAACP's Mississippi field secretary, in Jackson, Miss.—Nov. 12. Pres. Ngo Dinh Diem of the Republic of Vietnam and his brother, Ngo Dinh Nhu, in a military coup.—Nov. 22. U. S. Pres. John F. Kennedy fatally shot in Dallas, Tex.; accused Lee Harvey Oswald murdered while awaiting trial.

**1965**—Jan. 21. Iranian premier Hassan Ali Mansour fatally wounded by assassin in Teheran; 4 executed.—Feb. 21. Malcolm X, Negro nationalist, fatally shot in N. Y. City; 3 sentenced to life.

**1966**—Sept. 6. Prime Minister Hendrik F. Verwoerd of South Africa stabbed to death in parliament at Capetown by drifter later ruled insane.

**1968**—Apr. 4. Rev. Dr. Martin Luther King Jr. fatally shot in Memphis, Tenn.; James Earl Ray sentenced to 99 years.—June 5. Sen. Robert F. Kennedy (D-N. Y.) fatally shot in Los Angeles; Sirhan Sirhan, resident alien, convicted of murder.

**1969**—July 5. Tom Mboya, Kenya's minister of economic planning and development, in Nairobi.—Oct. 17. Pres. A. A. Shermarke of Somalia, at Las Anos, Somalia.

**1971**—Nov. 28. Jordan Prime Minister Wasfi Tal, in Cairo, by Palestinian guerrillas.

**1973**—Mar. 2. U. S. Ambassador Cleo A. Noel Jr., U. S. Charge d'Affaires George C. Moore and Belgian Charge d'Affaires Guy Eid tortured and killed by Palestinian guerrillas in Khartoum, Sudan.

**1974**—Aug. 15. Mrs. Park Chung Hee, wife of president of So. Korea, hit by bullet meant for her husband. Police said plot was organized in No. Korea.—Aug. 19. U. S. Ambassador to Cyprus, Rodger P. Davies, killed by sniper's bullet in Nicosia.

**1975**—Feb. 11. Pres. Richard Ratsimandrava, 43, of Madagascar, machine-gunned in Tananarive.—Mar. 25. King Faisal of Saudi Arabia shot by nephew Prince Musad Abdel Aziz, 31, in royal palace, Riyadh.

**1975**—May 21. U. S. Col. Paul R. Shaffer Jr. and U. S. Lt. Col. John H. Turner slain by 3 Iranian terrorists in Teheran.

**1975**—Aug. 15. Bangladesh Pres. Sheik Mujibur Rahman and wife and son killed in army coup.

**1976**—Feb. 13. Nigerian head of state, Gen. Murtala Ramat Mohammed, slain by self-styled "young revolutionaries." Several arrests were made.

**1977**—Mar. 16. Kamal Jumblat, Lebanese Druse chieftain, was shot and killed on a mountain road near Beirut, along with his driver and bodyguard.

**1977**—Mar. 18. Congo Pres. Marien Ngouabi shot in Brazzaville.

---

## Assassination Attempts

**1910**—Aug. 6. N. Y. City Mayor Wm. J. Gaynor shot and seriously wounded by discharged city employee.

**1912**—Oct. 14. Former U. S. President Theodore Roosevelt shot and seriously wounded by demented man in Milwaukee.

**1950**—Nov. 1. In an attempt to assassinate President Truman, 2 men identified as members of a Puerto Rican nationalist movement—Griselio Torresola and Oscar Collazo—tried to shoot their way into Blair House. Torresola was killed, and a guard, Pvt. Leslie Coffelt was fatally shot. Collazo, wounded, recovered and was tried and convicted Mar. 7, 1951 for the murder of Coffelt. His death sentence was commuted to life imprisonment by President Truman.

**1970**—Nov. 27. Pope Paul VI unharmed by knife-wielding assailant dressed as priest who attempted to attack him in Manila airport. Benjamin Mendoza, Bolivian, charged with attempted murder.

**1972**—May 15. Alabama Gov. George Wallace shot in Laurel, Md.; seriously crippled.

1972—Dec. 7. Mrs. Ferdinand E. Marcos, wife of the Philippine president, was stabbed and seriously injured in Pasay City, Philippines.

1975—Sept. 5. Pres. Gerald R. Ford was unharmed when a Secret Service agent grabbed a pistol aimed at him by Lynette

(Squeaky) Fromme, a Charles Manson follower, in Sacramento, Cal.

1975—Sept. 22. Pres. Gerald R. Ford escaped unharmed when Sara Jane Moore, a political activist, fired a revolver at him, but it was deflected by bystander Oliver Sipple.

# Major Kidnapings

**Edward A. Cudahy Jr.,** 16, in Omaha, Neb., **Dec. 18, 1900.** Returned Dec. 20 after $25,000 paid. Pat Crowe confessed.

**Robert Franks,** 13, in Chicago, **May 22, 1924,** by 2 youths, Richard Loeb and Nathan Leopold, who killed boy. Demand for $10,000 ignored. Loeb died in prison, Leopold paroled 1958, freed 1963.

**Charles A. Lindbergh Jr.,** 20 mos. old, in Hopewell, N.J., **Mar. 1, 1932;** found dead May 12. Ransom of $50,000 was paid to man identified as Bruno Richard Hauptmann, 35, paroled German convict who entered U.S. illegally. Hauptmann passed ransom bill and $14,000 marked money was found in his garage. He was convicted after spectacular trial at Flemington, and electrocuted in Trenton, N.J., prison, Apr. 3. 1936.

**William A. Hamm Jr.,** 39, in St. Paul, **June 15, 1933.** $100,000 paid. Alvin Karpis given life, paroled in 1969.

**Charles F. Urschel,** in Oklahoma City, **July 22, 1933.** Released July 31 after $200,000 paid. George (Machine Gun) Kelly and 5 others given life.

**George Weyerhaeuser,** 9, in Tacoma, Wash., **May 24, 1935.** Returned home June 1 after $200,000 paid. Kidnappers given 20 to 60 years.

**Charles Mattson,** 10, in Tacoma, Wash., **Dec. 27, 1936.** Found dead Jan. 11, 1937. Kidnaper asked $28,000, failed to contact.

**Arthur Fried,** in White Plains, N.Y., **Dec. 4, 1937.** Body not found. Two kidnapers executed.

**Robert C. Greenlease,** 6, son of a Kansas City, Mo. motor car dealer, taken from school **Sept. 28, 1953,** and held for $600,000. Body found Oct. 7, when Mrs. Bonnie Brown Heady and Carl A. Hall were arrested. They pleaded guilty and were executed Dec. 18.

**Peter Weinberger,** 32 days old, Westbury, N.Y., **July 4, 1956,** for $2,000 ransom, not paid. Child found dead. Angelo John LaMarca, 31, convicted, executed.

**Cynthia Ruotolo,** 6 wks old, taken from carriage in front of Hamden, Conn. store **Sept. 1, 1956.** Body found in lake.

**Lee Crary,** 8 in Everett, Wash., **Sept. 22, 1957,** $10,000 ransom, not paid. He escaped after 3 days, led police to George E. Collins, who was convicted.

**Eric Peugeot,** 4, taken from playground at St. Cloud golf course, Paris, **Apr. 12, 1960.** Released unharmed 3 days later after payment of undisclosed sum to kidnaper who had demanded $100,000. Two sentenced to prison.

**Frank Sinatra Jr.,** 19, from hotel room in Lake Tahoe, Cal., **Dec. 8, 1963.** Released **Dec. 11** after his father paid $240,000 ransom. John W. Irwin, Barry W. Keenan and Joseph C. Amsler sentenced to prison; most of ransom recovered.

**Barbara Jane Mackle,** 20, abducted **Dec. 17, 1968,** from Atlanta, Ga., motel, was found unharmed 3 days later, buried in a coffin-like wooden box 18 inches underground, after her father had paid $500,000 ransom; Gary Steven Krist sentenced to life, Ruth Eisenmann-Schier to 7 years; most of ransom recovered.

**Anne Katherine Jenkins,** 22, abducted **May 10, 1969,** from her Baltimore apartment, freed 3 days later after her father paid $10,000 ransom; Edward Lee Dull and Marie Calvert charged with crime.

**Mrs. Roy Fuchs,** 35, and 3 children held hostage 2 hours, **May 14, 1969,** in Long Island, N. Y., released after her husband, a bank manager, paid kidnapers $129,000 in bank funds; 4 men arrested, ransom recovered.

**C. Burke Elbrick,** U.S. ambassador to Brazil, kidnaped by revolutionaries in Rio de Janeiro **Sept. 4, 1969;** released 3 days later after Brazil yielded to kidnaper's demands to publish manifesto and release 15 political prisoners.

**Patrick Dolan,** 18, found shot to death near Sao Paulo, Brazil, **Nov. 5, 1969,** after he was kidnaped and $12,500 paid.

**Sean M. Holly,** U.S. diplomat, in Guatemala **Mar. 6, 1970;** freed 2 days later upon release of 3 terrorists from prison.

**Lt. Col. Donald J. Crowley,** U.S. air attache, in Dominican Republic **Mar. 24, 1970;** released after government allowed 20 prisoners to leave the country.

**Count Karl von Spreti,** W. German ambassador to Guatemala, **Mar. 31, 1970;** slain after Guatemala refused demands for $700,000 and release of 22 prisoners.

**Pedro Eugenio Aramburu,** former Argentine president, by terrorists **May 29, 1970;** body found July 17.

**Rudy W. Martinez,** Guatemalan coffee exporter, by terrorists **Apr. 23, 1970;** released on payment of large ransom.

**Ehrenfried von Holleben,** W. German ambassador to Brazil, by terrorists **June 11, 1970;** freed after release of 40 prisoners.

**Daniel A. Mitrione,** U.S. diplomat, **July 31, 1970,** by terrorists

in Montevideo, Uruguay; body found Aug. 10 after government rejected demands for release of all political prisoners.

**Aloysio Dias Gomide,** Brazilian vice counsul, in Montevideo, **July 31, 1970;** released Feb. 1, 1971, after wife paid ransom estimated at over $250,000.

**James R. Cross,** British trade commissioner, **Oct. 5, 1970,** by French Canadian separatists in Quebec; freed Dec. 3 after 3 kidnapers and relatives flown to Cuba by government.

**Pierre Laporte,** Quebec Labor Minister, by separatists **Oct. 10, 1970;** body found Oct. 18.

**Eugen Beihl,** W. German businessman, by Basque separatists, in San Sebastian, Spain, **Dec. 1, 1970;** released Dec. 25 unharmed.

**Giovanni E. Bucher,** Swiss ambassador **Dec. 7, 1970,** by revolutionaries in Rio de Janeiro; freed Jan. 16, 1971, after Brazil released 70 political prisoners.

**Geoffrey Jackson,** British ambassador, in Montevideo, **Jan. 8, 1971,** by Tupamaro terrorists. Held as ransom for release of imprisoned terrorists, he was released Sept. 9, after the prisoners escaped.

**Four U.S. airmen,** in Ankara, by Turkish leftist terrorists on **Mar. 4, 1971.** $400,000 ransom was not paid, but the 4 were released unharmed Mar. 8.

**Ephraim Elrom,** Israel consul general in Istanbul, **May 17, 1971.** Held as ransom for imprisoned terrorists, he was found dead May 23.

**Mrs. Virginia Piper,** 49 abducted **July 27, 1972,** from her home in suburban Minneapolis; found unharmed near Duluth 2 days later after her husband paid $1 million ransom to the kidnapers.

**Victor E. Samuelson,** Exxon executive, **Dec. 6, 1973,** in Campana, Argentina, by Marxist guerrillas, freed Apr. 29, 1974, after payment of record $14.2 million ransom.

**J. Paul Getty 3d,** 17, grandson of the U.S. Oil mogul, released by kidnapers **Dec. 15, 1973,** in southern Italy after family paid $2.8 million ransom. Kidnapers had severed his right ear, sent it with ransom demand.

**Patricia (Patty) Hearst,** 19, taken from her Berkeley, Cal., apartment **Feb. 4, 1974.** Symbionese Liberation Army demanded her father, Randolph A. Hearst, publisher, give millions to poor. Hearst offered $2 million in food; the Hearst Corp. offered $4 million worth. Kidnapers objected to way food was distributed. Patricia, in message, said she had joined SLA; she was identified by FBI as taking part in a San Francisco bank holdup, **Apr. 15;** she claimed, in message, she had been coerced. Again identified by FBI in a store holdup, **May 16,** she was classified by FBI as "an armed, dangerous fugitive." FBI, **Sept. 18, 1975,** captured Patricia and others in San Francisco; they were indicted on various charges. Patricia for bank robbery. A San Francisco jury convicted her, **Mar. 20, 1976.** William and Emily Harris were indicted, 1976, for the Hearst kidnaping.

**J. Reginald Murphy,** 40, an editor of *Atlanta* (Ga.) *Constitution,* kidnaped **Feb. 20, 1974,** freed Feb. 22 after payment of $700,000 ransom by the newspaper. Police arrested William A. H. Williams, a contractor; most of the money was recovered.

**J. Guadalupe Zuno Hernandez,** 83, father-in-law of Mexican President Luis Echeverria Alvarez, seized by 4 terrorists **Aug. 28, 1974;** government refused to negotiate; he was released **Sept. 8.**

**E. B. Reville,** Hepzibah, Ga., banker, and wife Jean, kidnaped **Sept. 30, 1974.** Ransom of $30,000 paid. He was found alive; Mrs. Reville was found dead of carbon monoxide fumes in car trunk Oct. 2.

**Jack Teich,** Kings Point, N.Y., steel executive, seized **Nov. 12, 1974;** released Nov. 19 after payment of $750,000.

**Samuel Bronfman,** 21, heir to Seagram liquor fortune, abducted **Aug. 9, 1975,** in Purchase, N.Y.; $2.3 million ransom paid by father, Edgar. FBI and N.Y.C. police rescued Samuel **Aug. 17** in Brooklyn, N.Y., apartment, recovered ransom, and arrested Mel Patrick Lynch, a city fireman, and Dominic Byrne, a limousine operator. Two found not guilty of kidnap, but convicted of extortion after they claimed young Bronfman masterminded ransom plot.

**Richard O. Hall,** seized **Feb. 8, 1977,** shotgun wired to his neck, by Anthony Kiritsis in Indianapolis in dispute with Hall's mortgage company. After negotiations with officials, Kiritsis surrendered; Hall was unharmed.

**Hanns-Martin Schleyer,** a West German industrialist, was kidnaped in Cologne, **Sept. 5, 1977** by armed terrorists. His driver and 3 of his police guards were killed in the terrorist action. Schleyer was found dead, **Oct. 19,** in an abandoned car shortly after 3 jailed terrorist leaders of the Baader-Meinhof gang were found dead in their prison cells nears Stuttgart, West Germany.

# ASTRONOMY AND CALENDAR

**Edited by Dr. Kenneth L. Franklin, Astronomer**
American Museum-Hayden Planetarium

## Celestial Events Highlights, 1979
(All times are Greenwich Mean Time)

The main astronomical event for North America is the total eclipse of the sun on Feb. 26. It begins at dawn off the mouth of the Columbia River. The shadow passes over Portland, Oregon; Walla Walla, Washington; Helena, Montana; Brandon, Manitoba, and on to Hudson's Bay and Greenland, where it will end at sunset. Greatest duration will be just over 3 minutes. This is the last total solar eclipse visible in continental United States until 2017. In 1991, a total eclipse will be visible from the state of Hawaii, but the path may miss the islands.

The series of lunar occultations of Aldebaran continues. Although several of these will be visible from North America, mention of them in the following pages indicates certainly a *close* approach of the moon to that star as seen from your location. It also means that watching the moon with a telescope before such an occultation may reward you with the observation of a fainter star being occulted. The moon must pass through the "face of the bull", the cluster called the Hyades, before it gets to Aldebaran. It will surely touch a few on the way. The alpha star in Leo, Regulus, is also beginning a series of occultations in November. As with Aldebaran, this will repeat for many months.

Conjunctions between planets are fairly common, but they usually occur close to the sun, hence are not easily observed. December 13, 1979, however, is the data of the first of 3 conjunctions between Mars and Jupiter which will be easier to see. (Although the actual moment of conjunction may not be visible from your location, mention of the event is an indication of a close encounter the night before and after.) Mars in its rapid eastward motion passes slower moving Jupiter. Then the two planets will reverse their motions to conjoin again on Mar. 2, 1980. After resuming direct motion, they will pass each other (0°.8) a third time, on May 4, 1980, for a rare triple conjunction.

The Perseid meteor shower around August 12 of each year is regarded as the "Old Faithful" of showers. It is almost always good for a display of up to about 50 meteors an hour as seen by one observer. The comet discovered by Swift and Tuttle in 1862 was noted to have an orbit similar to the path followed by the Perseid meteoroids. This was interpreted then (and later verified) that the comet itself was the origin of the Perseid meteoroids. Indeed, all shower particles must have come from known or unknown comets. Comet Swift/Tuttle has a period of about 120 years and may reappear in 1982. The Perseid shower is not known for fire balls — exceptionally bright meteors — but some were observed in 1977. These may be precursors of the comet, being fragments of the 1862 comet broken off at that time. These did not have the energy to go as far away as the main body; so they are returning early having made a shorter trip. If this is correct, the Perseid meteor shower should be an exciting event for the next several years.

### January

**Mercury** is too close to the sun for observation this month.

**Venus** is in the morning sky, 8° north of Antares in Scorpius on the 15th; it is 2° south of the moon on the 24th and 1°.9 north of Neptune on the 26th. Neptune is magnitude 7.7, easily visible in steady binoculars.

**Mars** is in conjunction with the sun on the 20th, thus out of sight.

**Jupiter** is 4° north of the moon on the 14th and at opposition on the 24th, in Cancer, 399 million miles away; magnitude −2.2.

**Saturn** is 2° north of the moon in Leo on the 17th.

**Moon** is at apogee on the 15th, 252,400 miles away, and at perigee on the 28th, 221,700 miles away. It occults Juno on the 1st and Aldebaran on the 9th, and passes Jupiter on the 14th, Saturn on the 17th, Uranus on the 22nd, Venus on the 24th, and Neptune on the 25th. It occults Juno again on the 30th.

**Jan. 3** — Quadrantid meteor shower tonight and tomorrow morning.

**Jan. 4** — Earth at perihelion, 91.41 million miles away from the sun.

**Jan. 9** — Moon occults Aldebaran.

**Jan. 18** — Venus at greatest western elongation, 47° from the sun.

**Jan. 19** — Sun enters Capricornus.

**Jan. 20** — Mars, 222 million miles from the earth, in conjunction with the sun.

**Jan. 24** — Jupiter, 399 million miles from earth, in opposition to the sun.

### February

**Mercury** is in superior conjunction beyond the sun on the 9th, and will be occulted by the moon 25 hours after new moon.

**Venus** is 3° south of the moon on the 23rd.

**Mars** is still too close to the sun to be seen.

**Jupiter** is 4° north of the moon on the 10th.

**Saturn** is 3° north of the moon on the 13th.

**Moon** is at apogee on the 11th, 252,500 miles away, and at perigee on the 25th, 222,400 miles away. It occults Aldebaran on the 6th, and passes Jupiter on the 10th, Saturn on the 13th, and Venus on the 23rd. It totally eclipses the sun on the 26th, and occults Juno and Mercury on the 27th.

**Feb. 6** — Moon occults Aldebaran.

**Feb. 9** — Mercury in superior conjunction, 130 million miles away.

**Feb. 16** — Sun enters Aquarius.

**Feb. 26** — Total solar eclipse.

**Feb. 27** — Moon occults Juno and Mercury.

### March

**Mercury** is at greatest eastern elongation on the 8th, 18° from the sun. This is not an especially favorable distance, but it should be nearly vertically up from the setting sun, looking like a zero magnitude star low in the bright twilight of the 7th. It is stationary on the 14th, beginning retrograde motion.

**Venus** is 2° south of the moon in Capricornus on the 25th.

**Mars** is 0°.7 south of the moon on the 27th, the moon just 25 hours from new moon.

**Jupiter** is 5° north of the moon on the 9th, and is stationary on the 20th, resuming its direct eastward motion in Cancer.

**Saturn** is in opposition on the 1st, and 3° north of the moon on the 12th. Saturn appears as a +0.5 magnitude star in Leo.

**Moon** is at apogee on the 10th, 252,200 miles away, and at perigee on the 26th, 225,000 miles away. It occults Aldebaran on the 5th, and passes Jupiter on the 9th and Saturn on the 12th. It is partially eclipsed on the 13th, and passes Venus on the 2nd and Mars on the 27th.

**Mar. 1** — Saturn is in opposition, 775 million miles away.

**Mar. 5** — Moon occults Aldebaran.

**Mar. 8** — Mercury at greatest eastern elongation, 18° from the sun.

**Mar. 11** — Sun enters Pisces.

**Mar. 13** — Partial eclipse of the moon.

**Mar. 14** — Mercury stationary.

**Mar. 21** — Vernal equinox; Spring beginning at 5:22 AM n Greenwich.

**Mar. 24** — Mercury in inferior conjunction, 55.5 million miles away.

**Mar. 26** — Jupiter stationary.

### April

**Mercury** is 3° north of Mars on the 1st. It is stationary on the 6th, resuming its direct eastward motion, and is occulted by the moon on the 24th.

**Venus** is occulted by the moon on the 24th, the moon being two days before new.

**Mars** is in conjunction with Mercury on the 1st, 5° south, and is occulted by the moon on the 24th.

**Jupiter** is 5° north of the moon on the 5th, in Cancer.

**Saturn** is 3° north of the moon on the 9th, in Leo.

**Moon** is at apogee on the 7th, 251,000 miles away, and at perigee on the 22nd, 228,200 miles away. It occults Aldebaran on the 1st, and passes Jupiter on the 5th, Saturn on the 9th. It occults Venus and Mercury and passes Mars on the 24th, before it occults Juno on the 25th and Aldebaran again on the 29th.

**Apr. 1** — Moon occults Aldebaran. Mercury in conjunction with Mars.

**Apr. 6** — Mercury stationary.

**Apr. 8** — Pluto in opposition in Virgo, 2.725 billion miles away.

**Apr. 18** — The sun enters Aries.

**Apr. 21** — Mercury at greatest western elongation, 27° from the sun.

**Apr. 22** — The Lyrid meteor shower, although weak, may be visible without interference from the waning crescent moon.

**Apr. 24** — The moon occults Venus and Mercury.

**Apr. 25** — The moon occults Juno.

**Apr. 29** — The moon occults Aldebaran.

### May

**Mercury** is in conjunction with Mars on the 5th, 2° south, and in superior conjunction on the 23rd.

**Venus** is in conjunction with Mars on the 20th, 1°.1 south; it is 3° north of the moon on the 30th.

**Mars** is in conjunction with Mercury on the 5th, 2° north, and with Venus on the 20th, 1°.1 north; it is 3° north of the moon on the 23rd. Its magnitude is +1.5.

**Jupiter** is 4° south of the moon on the 3rd, and again on the 30th.

**Saturn** is 3° north of the moon on the 6th, and stationary near Regulus in Leo on the 10th, resuming its direct eastward motion.

**Moon** is at apogee on the 4th, 251,100 miles away, and at perigee on the 18th, 229,700 miles away. It passes Jupiter on the 3rd, Saturn on the 6th, and Mars on the 23rd, 3 hours before occulting Juno and passing Venus. It passes Jupiter again on the 30th.

**May 5** — Mercury and Mars in conjunction, 2° apart; Eta Aquarids may not be cancelled by the first quarter moon.

**May 10** — Saturn stationary; Uranus in opposition in Libra, 1.643 billion miles away.

**May 13** — Sun enters Taurus.

**May 20** — Venus and Mars in conjunction, 1°.1 apart.

**May 29** — Mercury in superior conjunction, 123 million miles away.

### June

**Mercury** is 5° south of Pollux on the 22nd, and 5° north of the moon on the 26th.

**Venus** is too near the sun for convenient viewing.

**Mars** is 5° north of the moon on the 21st.

**Jupiter** is 3° north of the moon on the 27th.

**Saturn** is 2° north of the moon on the 2nd and on the 30th.

**Moon** is at apogee on the 1st, 251,200 miles away, at perigee on the 13th, 227,300 miles away, and at apogee again on the 29th, 251,700 miles away. It passes Saturn on the 2nd and Mars on the 21st, occults Aldebaran on the 22nd, and passes Venus on the 23rd, Mercury on the 26th, Jupiter on the 27th, and Saturn again on the 30th.

**June 10** — Neptune in opposition, 2.721 billion miles away, in Scorpius.

**June 20** — Sun enters Gemini; Venus 5° north at Aldebaran.

**June 21** — Summer solstice; Summer begins at 23:56 GMT.

**June 22** — Moon occults Aldebaran; Mercury 5° south of Pollux.

### July

**Mercury** is stationary on the 17th and in inferior conjunction on the 31st.

**Venus** is too close to the sun for observation.

**Mars** is 5° north of Aldebaran on the 10th and 5° north of the moon on the 20th.

**Jupiter** is too close to the sun for observation.

**Saturn** is 2° north of the crescent moon on the 27th.

**Moon** is at perigee on the 11th, 224,300 miles away, and at apogee on the 27th, 252,300 miles away. It occults Aldebaran on the 19th, and passes Mars on the 20th and Saturn on the 27th.

**July 3** — Earth at aphelion, 94.51 million miles from the sun; Mercury at greatest elongation, 26° east of the sun.

**July 10** — Mars is 5° north of Aldebaran.

**July 17** — Mercury is stationary, beginning its retrograde motion.

**July 19** — The moon occults Aldebaran.

**July 20** — Mars is 5° north of the moon; sun enters Cancer.

**July 27** — Saturn is 2° north of the moon.

**July 29** — The weak Delta Aquarid meteor shower may show a display for a few nights before and after this date.

**July 31** — Mercury in inferior conjunction, 54.6 million miles away.

### August

**Mercury** is stationary on the 10th, resuming its eastward motion, and is 0°.7 north of Jupiter on the 30th.

**Venus** is in superior conjunction on the 25th.

**Mars** is a faint (+1.5 magnitude) object in Gemini, 5° north of the moon on the 18th.

**Jupiter** is in conjunction on the 13th.

**Saturn** is too close to the sun to be observed.

**Moon** is at perigee on the 8th, 222,300 miles away, and at apogee on the 23rd, 252,600 miles away. It occults Aldebaran on the 16th, and passes Mars on the 10th and Mercury on the 21st. It eclipses the sun annullarly on the 22nd.

**Aug. 10** — Mercury is stationary; sun enters Leo.

**Aug. 12** — Perseid meteor shower. Make every effort to watch.

**Aug. 13** — Jupiter in conjunction, 591 million miles away from earth.

**Aug. 16** — Moon occults Aldebaran.

**Aug. 17** — Pallas in opposition, 227 million miles away, in Aquarius.

**Aug. 19** — Mercury at greatest elongation, 19° west of the sun.

**Aug. 22** — Annular eclipse of the sun.

**Aug. 25** — Venus in superior conjunction, 160.8 million miles away.

**Aug. 30** — Mercury and Jupiter in conjunction, 0°.7 apart.

### September

**Mercury** is 1°.2 north of Regulus on the 2nd, and in superior conjunction on the 13th.

**Venus** is still too close to the sun for observation.

**Mars** is 6° south of Pollux on the 14th, and 5° north of the moon on the 10th.

**Jupiter** is 2° north of the moon on the 18th, and 0°.3 north of Regulus on the 26th.

**Saturn** is in conjunction on the 10th.

**Moon** is at perigee on the 6th, 221,900 miles away, and at apogee on the 19th, 252,427 miles away. It is in total eclipse on the 6th, 6 hours after perigee (watch for extreme tides). It occults Aldebaran on the 12th, and passes Mars on the 16th and Jupiter on the 18th.

**Sept. 2** — Mercury is 1°.2 north of Regulus.

**Sept. 6** — Total lunar eclipse.

**Sept. 10** — Saturn is in conjunction, 966 million miles away.

**Sept. 12** — Moon occults Aldebaran.

**Sept. 13** — Mercury in superior conjunction, 128 million miles away.

**Sept. 14** — Mars 6° south of Pollux.

**Sept. 16** — Sun enters Virgo.

**Sept. 23** — Autumnal equinox; Fall begins at 15:17 GMT.

**Sept. 26** — Jupiter 0°.3 north of Regulus.

### October

**Mercury** is 1°.9 north of Spica on the 2nd, and 8° south of the moon on the 22nd.

**Venus** is 3° north of Spica on the 5th, 5° south of the moon on the 22nd, and 0°.2 south of Uranus on the 27th. Uranus, in Libra, looks like a +5.7 magnitude star through steady binoculars.

**Mars** is 4° north of the moon on the 14th. It is beginning to brighten slowly as it approaches the earth before its opposition next year.

**Jupiter** is 1° north of the moon on the 16th.

**Saturn** is occulted by the moon on the 18th.

**Moon** is at perigee on the 4th, 223,200 miles away, and at apogee on the 16th, 251,900 miles away. It occults Aldebaran on the 9th and passes Mars on the 14th and Jupiter on the 16th. It occults Saturn on the 18th and passes Venus and Mercury on the 22nd.

**Oct. 2** — Mercury is 1°.9 north of Spica.

**Oct. 5** — Venus is 3° north of Spica.

**Oct. 6** — Ceres in opposition, 181 million miles away, in Cetus.

**Oct. 9** — The moon occults Aldebaran.

**Oct. 13** — Pluto in conjunction, 2.897 billion miles away.

**Oct. 18** — The moon occults Saturn.

**Oct. 21** — Orionid meteor shower, although weak, will have freedom from moonlight.

**Oct. 29** — Mercury is at greatest elongation, 24° east of the sun.

**Oct. 30** — Sun enters Libra.

### November

**Mercury** is 2° south of Venus on the 8th and stationary on the 9th, beginning its retrograde motion. It is in inferior conjunction on the 20th and stationary again on the 29th, resuming its direct motion.

**Venus** is 4° north of Antares on the 11th, 2° south of Neptune (which resembles a star of +7.7 magnitude) on the 20th, and is 6° south of the crescent moon on the 21st.

**Mars** is 3° north of the moon on the 12th, appearing as a first magnitude star a little northwest of Regulus, being 1°.6 north of that star on the 17th.

**Jupiter** is occulted by the moon on the 13th.

**Saturn** is occulted by the moon on the 14th.

**Moon** is at perigee on the 1st, 226,200 miles away, at apogee on the 13th, 251,400 miles away, and at perigee again on the 29th, 229,400 miles away. It occults Aldebaran on the 6th, passes Mars and occults Regulus on the 12th, passes Jupiter on the 13th, occults Saturn on the 14th, and passes Venus on the 21st.

**Nov. 6** — The moon occults Aldebaran.

**Nov. 8** — Mercury and Venus in conjunction, 2° apart.

**Nov. 11** — Venus 4° north of Antares.

**Nov. 12** — The moon occults Regulus.

**Nov. 13** — The moon occults Jupiter.

**Nov. 14** — Uranus is in conjunction, 1.832 billion miles away; the moon occults Saturn.

**Nov. 17** — Mars is 1°.6 north of Regulus; the unpredictable Leonid meteor shower is free from moonlight.

**Nov. 20** — Mercury is in inferior conjunction, 63 million miles away. Venus is 2° south of Neptune (+7.7 magnitude).

**Nov. 22** — Sun enters Scorpius.

**Nov. 29** — Mercury stationary; sun enters Ophiuchus.

### December

**Mercury** is 4° south of the moon on the 17th, and 6° north of Antares on the 18th.

**Venus** is 5° south of the crescent moon on the 21st.

**Mars** is 2° north of the moon on the 10th, and 1°.7 north of Jupiter on the 13th in the first of three conjunctions, two more coming next year. Mars is now magnitude +0.6.

**Jupiter** is occulted by the moon on the 10th, at magnitude −1.7. It is 1°.7 south of Mars on the 13th (see above), and is stationary on the 27th.

**Saturn** is occulted by the moon on the 12th.

**Moon** is at apogee on the 11th, 251,200 miles away, and at perigee on the 23rd, 229,200 miles away. It occults Aldebaran on the 3rd and Regulus on the 9th, and passes Mars on the 10th. It occults Jupiter on the 10th and Saturn on the 12th, and passes Mercury on the 17th and Venus on the 21st. It occults Aldebaran again on the 31st.

**Dec. 3** — The moon occults Aldebaran.

**Dec. 7** — Mercury is at greatest elongation, 21° west of the sun.

**Dec. 9** — The moon occults Regulus.

**Dec. 10** — The moon occults Jupiter.

**Dec. 12** — The moon occults Saturn; Neptune is in conjunction, 2.906 billion miles away.

**Dec. 13** — Mars and Jupiter in conjunction, 1°.7 apart.

**Dec. 14** — The Geminid meteor shower is usually good for a few fireballs, and the moon is faint.

**Dec. 16** — Sun enters Sagittarius.

**Dec. 18** — Mercury is 6° north of Antares.

**Dec. 22** — Winter solstice; Winter begins at 11:10 AM GMT; the Ursid meteor shower, rather weak, will not be disturbed by moonlight.

**Dec. 27** — Jupiter stationary, beginning its retrograde motion.

**Dec. 31** — The moon occults Aldebaran.

---

## Astronomical Signs and Symbols

| | | | |
|---|---|---|---|
| ☉ The Sun | ⊕ The Earth | ♅ Uranus | ⃞ Quadrature |
| ☽ The Moon | ♂ Mars | ♆ Neptune | ☍ Opposition |
| ☿ Mercury | ♃ Jupiter | ♇ Pluto | ☊ Ascending Node |
| ♀ Venus | ♄ Saturn | ☌ Conjunction | ☋ Descending Node |

Two heavenly bodies are in "conjunction" ( ☌ ) when they are due north and south of each other, either in Right Ascension (with respect to the north celestial pole) or in Celestial Longitude (with respect to the north ecliptic pole). If the bodies are seen near each other, they will rise and set at nearly the same time. They are in "opposition" ( ☍ ) when their Right Ascensions differ by exactly 12 hours, or their Celestial Longitudes differ by 180°. One of the two objects in opposition will rise while the other is setting. "Quadrature" ( ⃞ ) refers to the arrangement when the coordinates of two bodies differ by exactly 90°. These terms may refer to the relative positions of any two bodies as seen from the earth, but one of the bodies is so frequently the sun that

mention of the sun is omitted; otherwise both bodies are named. The geocentric angular separation between sun and object is termed "elongation." Elongation is limited only for Mercury and Venus; the "greatest elongation" for each of these bodies is noted in the appropriate tables and is approximately the time for longest observation. When a planet is in its "ascending" ( ☊ ) or "descending" ( ☋ ) node, it is passing northward or southward, respectively, through the plane of the earth's orbit, across the celestial circle called the ecliptic. The term "perihelion" means nearest to the sun, and "aphelion," farthest from the sun. An "occultation" of a planet or star is an eclipse of it by some other body, usually the moon.

# Planets and the Sun

The planets of the solar system, in order of their distance from the sun, are Mercury, Venus, Earth, Mars, Jupiter, Saturn, Uranus, Neptune and Pluto. Uranus, Neptune and Pluto are not included in the celestial list because they are too faint to be seen without optical aid. Both Uranus and Neptune are visible through good field glasses, but Pluto is so distant and so small that only large telescopes or long exposure photographs can make it visible.

Since Mercury and Venus are nearer to the sun than is the earth, their motions about the sun are seen from the earth as wide swings first to one side of the sun and then to the other, although they are both passing continuously around the sun in orbits that are almost circular. When their passage takes them either between the earth and the sun, or beyond the sun as seen from the earth, they are invisible to us. Because of the laws which govern the motions of planets about the sun, both Mercury and Venus require much less time to pass between the earth and the sun than around the far side of the sun, so their periods of visibility and invisibility are unequal.

The planets that lie farther from the sun than does the earth may be seen for longer periods of time and are invisible only when they are so located in our sky that they rise and set about the same time as the sun when, of course, they are overwhelmed by the sun's great brilliance. None of the planets has any light or radiant heat of its own but each shines only by reflecting sunlight from its surface. Mercury and Venus, because they are between the earth and the sun, show phases very much as the moon does. The planets farther from the sun are always seen as full, although Mars does occasionally present a slightly gibbous phase — like the moon when not quite full.

The planets move rapidly among the stars because they are very much nearer to us. The stars are also in motion, some of them at tremendous speeds, but they are so far away that their motion does not change their apparent positions in the heavens sufficiently for anyone to perceive that change in a single lifetime. The very nearest star is about 7,000 times as far away as the most distant planet.

# Visible Planets of the Solar System

## Mercury, Venus, Mars, Jupiter and Saturn

### Mercury

Mercury, nearest planet to the sun, is also the smallest of the nine planets known to be orbiting the sun. Its diameter is 3,100 miles and its mean distance from the sun is 36,000,000 miles.

Mercury moves with great speed in its journey about the sun, averaging about 30 miles a second to complete its circuit in 88 of our days. Mercury rotates upon its axis over a period of nearly 59 days, thus exposing all of its surface periodically to the sun. It is believed that the surface passing before the sun may have a temperature of about 800° F., while the temperature on the side turned temporarily away from the sun does not fall as low as might be expected. This night temperature has been described by Russian astronomers as "room temperature" — possibly about 70°. This would contradict the former belief that Mercury did not possess an atmosphere, for some sort of atmosphere would be needed to retain the fierce solar radiation that strikes Mercury. A shallow but dense layer of carbon dioxide would produce the "greenhouse" effect, in which heat accumulated during exposure to the sun would not completely escape at night. The actual presence of a carbon dioxide atmosphere is in dispute.

This uncertainty about conditions upon Mercury and its motion arise from its shorter angular distance from the sun as seen from the earth, for Mercury is always too much in line with the sun to be observed against a dark sky, but is always seen during either morning or evening twilight.

Mariner 10 made three passes by Mercury in 1974 and 1975. A large fraction of the surface was photographed from varying distances, revealing a degree of cratering similar to that of the moon. An atmosphere of hydrogen and helium may be made up of gases of the solar wind temporarily concentrated by the presence of Mercury. The discovery of a weak but permanent magnetic field was a surprise. It has been held that both a fluid core and rapid rotation were necessary for the generation of a planetary magnetic field. Mercury may demonstrate these conditions to be unnecessary, or the field may reveal something about the history of Mercury.

### Venus

Venus is slightly smaller than the earth. Its diameter is about 200 miles less than the earth's diameter. Venus moves about the sun at a mean distance of 67,000,000 miles in 225 of our days. Its synodical revolution — its return to the same relationship with the earth and the sun, which is a result of the combination of its own motion and that of the earth — is 584 days. Every 19 months, then, Venus will be nearer to the earth than any other planet of the solar system. The planet is covered with a dense, white, cloudy atmosphere that conceals whatever is below it. This same cloud reflects sunlight efficiently so that when Venus is favorably situated, it is the third brightest object in the sky, exceeded only by the sun and the moon.

Spectral analysis of sunlight reflected from Venus' cloud tops has shown features that can best be explained by identifying the material of the clouds as sulphuric acid (oil of vitriol). Infrared spectroscopy from a ballon-borne telescope nearly 20 miles above the earth's surface gave indications of a small amount of water vapor present in the same region of the atmosphere of Venus. In 1956, a breakthrough in our knowledge came from radio astronomers at the Naval Research Laboratories in Washington, D. C. Their observations indicated a temperature for Venus of about 600° F., in marked contrast to minus 125° F., previously found at the cloud tops. Subsequent radio work confirmed a high temperature and produced evidence for this temperature to be associated with the solid body of Venus. With this peculiarity in mind, space scientists devised experiments for the U.S. space probe Mariner 2 to perform when it flew by in 1962. Mariner 2 confirmed the high temperature and the fact that it pertained to the ground rather than to some special activity of the atmosphere. In addition, Mariner 2 was unable to detect any radiation belts similar to the earth's so-called Van Allen belts. Nor was it able to detect the existence of a magnetic field even as weak as 1/100,000 of that of the earth.

An international scientific drama occurred in 1967 when a Russian space probe, Venera 4, and the American Mariner 5 arrived at Venus within a few hours of each other. Venera 4 was unique in that it was designed to allow an instrument package to land gently on the planet's surface via parachute. It ceased transmission of information about 75 minutes when the temperature it read went above 500° F. After considerable controversy, it was agreed that it still had 20 miles to go to reach the surface. The U.S. probe, Mariner 5, went around the dark side of Venus at a distance of about 6,000 miles. Again, it detected no significant magnetic field but its radio signals passed to earth through Venus' atmosphere twice — once on the night side and once on the day side.

The results are startling. Venus' atmosphere is nearly all carbon dioxide and must exert a pressure at the planet's surface of up to 100 times the earth's normal sea-level pressure of one atmosphere. Since the earth and Venus are about the same size, and were presumably formed at the same time by the same general process from the same mixture of chemical elements, one is faced with the question: which is the planet with the unusual history — earth or Venus?

In the last several years, astronomers using powerful transmitters as well as sensitive receivers and computers have succeeded in determining the rotation period of Venus. It turns out to be 243 days clockwise — in other words, contrary to the spin of most of the other planets and to its own motion around the sun. If it were exactly 243.16 days, Venus would always present the same face toward the earth at every inferior conjunction. This rate and sense of rotation allows a "day" on Venus of 117.4 earth days. Any part of Venus will receive sunlight on its clouds for over 58 days and will be in darkness for 58 days.

Mariner 10 passed Venus before traveling on to Mercury. The carbon dioxide molecule found in such abundance in the atmosphere is rather opaque to certain ultraviolet wavelengths, enabling sensitive television cameras to take pictures of the Venusian cloud cover. Photos radioed to earth show a spiral pattern in the clouds from equator to the poles. Long-lived features in the clouds have been detected moving at speeds of the order of a hundred miles per hour or more. If this is a typical wind speed, it can account for the transfer of heat to the night side in spite of the low rotation rate of the planet.

Recent radar observations have shown surface features below the clouds. Large craters have been identified. We should soon have radar-derived pictures of Venus that are as revealing as ordinary telescopic views of our moon taken by earth-based telescopes.

## Mars

Mars is the first planet beyond the earth, away from the sun. Mars' diameter is about 4,200 miles, although a determination of the radius and mass of Mars by the space-probe, Mariner 4, which flew by Mars on July 14, 1965 at a distance of less than 6,000 miles, indicated that these dimensions were slightly larger than had been previously estimated. While Mars' orbit is also nearly circular, it is somewhat more eccentric than the orbits of many of the other planets, and Mars is more than 30 million miles farther from the sun in some parts of its year than it is at others. Mars takes 687 of our days to make one circuit of the sun, traveling at about 15 miles a second. Mars rotates upon its axis in almost the same period of time that the earth does — 24 hours and 37 minutes. Mars' mean distance from the sun is 141 million miles, so that the temperature on Mars would be lower than that on the earth even if Mars' atmosphere were about the same as ours. The atmosphere is not, however, for Mariner 4 reported that atmospheric pressure on Mars is between 1% and 2% of the earth's atmospheric pressure. This thin atmosphere appears to be largely carbon dioxide. No evidence of free water was found.

There appears to be no magnetic field about Mars. This would eliminate the previous conception of a dangerous radiation belt around Mars. The same lack of a magnetic field would expose the surface of Mars to an influx of cosmic radiation about 100 times as intense as that on earth.

Deductions from years of telescopic observation indicate that 5/8ths of the surface of Mars is a desert of reddish rock, sand, and soil. The rest of Mars is covered by irregular patches that appear generally green in hues that change through the Martian year. These were formerly held to be some sort of primitive vegetation, but with the findings of Mariner 4 of a complete lack of water and oxygen, such growth does not appear possible. The nature of the green areas is now unknown. They may be regions covered with volcanic salts whose color changes with changing temperatures and atmospheric conditions, or they may be gray, rather than green. When large gray areas are placed beside large red areas, the gray areas will appear green to the eye.

Mars' axis of rotation is inclined from a vertical to the plane of its orbit about the sun by about 25° and therefore has seasons as does the earth, except that the Martian seasons are longer because Mars' year is longer. White caps form about the winter pole of Mars, growing through the winter and shrinking in summer. These polar caps are now believed to be both water ice and carbon dioxide ice. It is the carbon dioxide that is seen to come and go with the seasons. The water ice is apparently in many layers with dust between them, indicating climatic cycles.

The canals of Mars have become more of a mystery than they were before the voyage of Mariner 4. Markings forming a network of fine lines crossing much of the surface of Mars have been seen there by men who have devoted much time to the study of the planet, but no canals have shown clearly enough upon previous photographs to be universally accepted. A few of the 21 photographs sent back to earth by Mariner 4 covered areas crossed by canals. The pictures show faint, ill-defined, broad, dark markings, but no positive identification of the nature of the markings.

Mariners 6 & 7 in 1969 sent back many more photographs of higher quality than those of the pioneering Mariner 4. These pictures showed cratering similar to the earlier views, but in addition showed two other types of terrain. Some regions seemed featureless for many square miles, but others were chaotic, showing high relief without apparent organization into mountain chains or craters.

Mariner 9, the first artificial body to be placed in an orbit about Mars, has transmitted over 10,000 photographs covering 100% of the planet's surface. Preliminary study of these photos and other data shows that Mars resembles no other planet we know. Using terrestrial terms, however, scientists describe features that seem to be clearly of volcanic origin. One of these features is Nix Olympica, apparently a caldera whose outer slopes are over 300 miles in diameter. Some features may have been produced by cracking (faulting) of the surface and the sliding of one region over or past another. Many craters seem to have been produced by impacting bodies such as may have come from the nearby asteroid belt. Features near the south pole may have been produced by glaciers that are no longer present. Flowing water, nonexistent on Mars at the present time, probably carved canyons, one 10 times longer and 3 times deeper than the Grand Canyon.

Although the Russians landed a probe on Martian surface, it transmitted for only 20 seconds. In 1976, the U.S. landed 2 Viking spacecraft on the Martian surface. The landers had devices aboard to perform chemical analyses of the soil in search of evidence of life. So far, the results have been inconclusive. The 2 Viking orbiters have returned the best pictures yet of Martian topographic features. Many features can be explained only if Mars once had large quantities of flowing water.

Mars' position in its orbit and its speed around that orbit in relation to the earth's position and speed bring Mars fairly close to the earth on occasions about two years apart and then move Mars and the earth too far apart for accurate observation and photography. Every 15-17 years, the close approaches are especially favorable to close observation.

Mars has 2 satellites, discovered in 1877 by Asaph Hall. The outer satellite, Deimos, revolves around Mars in about 31 hours. The inner satellite, Phobos, whips around Mars in a little more than 7 hours, making 3 trips around the planet each Martian day. Mariner and Viking photos show these bodies to be irregularly shaped and pitted with numerous craters. Phobos also shows a system of linear grooves, each about 1/3-mile across and roughly parallel. Phobos measures about 8 by 12 miles and Deimos about 5 by 7.5 miles in size.

## Jupiter

Jupiter is the largest of the planets. Its equatorial diameter is 88,000 miles, 11 times the diameter of the earth. Its polar diameter is about 6,000 miles shorter. This is an equilibrium condition resulting from the liquidity of the planet and its extremely rapid rate of rotation: a Jupiter day is only 10 earth hours long. For a planet this size, this rotational speed is amazing, and it moves a point on Jupiter's equator at a speed of 22,000 miles an hour, as compared with 1,000 miles an hour for a point on the earth's equator. Jupiter is at an average distance of 480 million miles from the sun and takes almost 12 of our years to make one complete circuit of the sun.

The only directly observable chemical constituents of Jupiter's atmosphere are methane ($CH_4$) and ammonia ($NH_3$), but it is reasonable to assume the same mixture of elements available to make Jupiter as to make the sun. This would mean a large fraction of hydrogen and helium must be present also, as well as water ($H_2O$). The temperature at the tops of the clouds may be about minus 260° F. The clouds are probably ammonia ice crystals, becoming ammonia droplets lower down. There may be a space before water ice crystals show up as clouds: in turn, these become water droplets near the bottom of the entire cloud layer. The total atmosphere may be only a few hundred miles in depth, pulled down by the surface gravity (= 2.64 times earth's) to a relatively thin layer. Of course, the gases become denser with depth until they may turn into a slush or a slurry. Perhaps there is no surface — no real interface between the gaseous atmosphere and the body of Jupiter. Pioneers 10 and 11 provided evidence for considering Jupiter to be almost entirely liquid hydrogen. Long before a rocky core about the size of the earth is reached, hydrogen mixed with helium becomes a liquid metal at very high temperature. Jupiter's cloudy atmosphere is a fairly good reflector of sunlight and makes it far brighter than any of the stars.

Jupiter has 14 known satellites, although the last one discovered by Kowal at the Hale Observatory is so faint that it has been lost. Four of the moons are large and bright, rivaling our own moon and the planet Mercury in diameter, and may be seen through a field glass. They move rapidly around Jupiter and their change of position from night to night is extremely interesting to watch. The other satellites are much smaller and in all but one instance much farther from Jupiter and cannot be seen except through powerful telescopes. The 4 outermost satellites are revolving around Jupiter clockwise as seen from the north, contrary to the motions of the great majority of the satellites in the solar system and to the direction of revolution of the planets around the sun. The reason for this retrograde motion is not known, but one theory is that Jupiter's tremendous gravitational power may have captured 4 of the minor planets or asteroids that move about the sun between Mars and Jupiter, and that these would necessarily revolve backward. At the great distance of these bodies from Jupiter — some 14 million miles — direct motion would result in decay of the orbits, while retrograde orbits would be stable. Jupiter's mass is more than twice the mass of all the other planets put together, and accounts for Jupiter's tremendous gravitational field and so, probably, for its numerous satellites and its dense atmosphere.

In December, 1973, Pioneer 10 passed about 80,000 miles from the equator of Jupiter and was whipped into a path taking it out of our solar system in about 50 years. In December, 1974, Pioneer 11 passed within 30,000 miles of Jupiter, moving roughly from south to north, over the poles. Photographs from both encounters reveal much detail in the clouds, including what appear to be cyclonic storms. The Great Red Spot shows a spiral nature suggesting it is a long lived hurricane-like feature. The magnetic field is eccentric and tilted. It is stronger than was thought and of the opposite sign to that of the earth. The action of the trapped particles — the Jovian Van Allen Belts — is too violent to let man pass through in present spacecraft without serious radiation injury.

Both Pioneers contain a pictorial message for extra-solar system finders of the derelicts.

## Saturn

Saturn, last of the planets visible to the unaided eye, is almost twice as far from the sun as Jupiter, almost 900 million miles. It is second in size to Jupiter but its mass is much smaller. Saturn's specific gravity is less than that of water. Its diameter is about 71,000 miles at the equator; its rotational speed spins it completely around in a little more than 10 hours, and its atmosphere is much like that of Jupiter, except that its temperature at the top of its cloud layer is at least 100° colder. At about 300° F. below zero, the ammonia would be frozen out of Saturn's clouds. The theoretical construction of Saturn resembles that of Jupiter; it is either all gas, or it has a small dense center surrounded by a layer of liquid and a deep atmosphere.

Saturn has 10 satellites, the 10th having been discovered by the French astronomer Audouin Dollfus in December, 1966. The newly found satellite is a few thousand miles outside Saturn's ring system.

Because of Saturn's inclination, as stated above, there are two periods during Saturn's journey around the sun when the rings are presented to us edge-on. At these times, the rings disappear. Nothing that is only 10 miles wide can be seen from a distance of nearly 900 million miles. The rings are receding from a favorable position to be seen. They were edge-on in 1966, reached maximum visibility in 1973, and will be edge-on again in 1981.

Saturn's ring system begins about 7,000 miles above the visible disk of Saturn, lying above its equator and extending about 35,000 miles into space. The diameter of the ring system, including Saturn itself, is about 170,000 miles; the rings are estimated to be no thicker than 10 miles. In 1973, radar observation showed the ring particles to be large chunks of material averaging a meter on a side.

Pioneer 11 was guided to pass Jupiter in such a way that Jupiter will swing Pioneer 11 into an orbit that will bring it near Saturn in 1979. If the space craft is functioning adequately at that time, it will send us the photos and physical data possible only from a close fly-by. This will complete man's initial on-site inspection of the classical planets.

---

## Greenwich Sidereal Time for 0ʰ GMT, 1979

(Add 12 hours to obtain Right Ascension of Mean Sun)

| Date | | h | m | Date | | h | m | Date | | h | m | Date | | h | m |
|---|---|---|---|---|---|---|---|---|---|---|---|---|---|---|---|
| Jan. | 1 | 6 | 40.2 | Apr. | 1 | 12 | 35.0 | July | 10 | 19 | 9.3 | Oct. | 8 | 1 | 04.1 |
| | 11 | 7 | 19.6 | | 11 | 13 | 14.5 | | 20 | 19 | 48.7 | | 18 | 1 | 43.6 |
| | 21 | 7 | 59.1 | | 21 | 13 | 53.9 | | 30 | 20 | 28.1 | | 28 | 2 | 23.0 |
| | 31 | 8 | 38.5 | May | 1 | 14 | 33.3 | Aug. | 9 | 21 | 07.6 | Nov. | 7 | 3 | 02.4 |
| Feb. | 10 | 9 | 17.9 | | 11 | 15 | 12.7 | | 19 | 21 | 47.0 | | 17 | 3 | 41.8 |
| | 20 | 9 | 57.3 | | 21 | 15 | 52.2 | | 29 | 22 | 26.4 | | 27 | 4 | 21.3 |
| Mar | 2 | 10 | 36.8 | | 31 | 16 | 31.6 | Sept. | 8 | 23 | 05.9 | Dec. | 7 | 5 | 00.7 |
| | 12 | 11 | 16.2 | June | 10 | 17 | 11.0 | | 18 | 23 | 45.3 | | 17 | 5 | 40.1 |
| | 22 | 11 | 55.6 | | 20 | 17 | 50.4 | | 28 | 0 | 24.7 | | 27 | 6 | 19.5 |
| | | | | | 30 | 18 | 29.9 | | | | | | | | |

## Planetary Configurations, 1979

Greenwich Mean Time (0 designates midnight; 12 designates noon)

| Date | h. m. | | |
|---|---|---|---|
| Jan. 4 | 22 | - | ⊕ at perihelion |
| 9 | 18 | - ☌ * ☽ | Aldebaran 0°.5 S; occultation |
| 14 | 11 | - ☌ ♃ ☽ | ♃ 4° N |
| 15 | 18 | - ☌ * ♀ | ♀ 8° N of Antares |
| 17 | 16 | - ☌ ♄ ☽ | ♄ 2° N |
| 18 | 06 | - | ♀ gr. elong. W (47°) |
| 20 | 12 | - ☌ ♂ ☉ | |
| 24 | 15 | - ☍ ♃ ☉ | |
| 24 | 22 | - ☌ ♀ ☽ | ♀ 2° S |
| Feb. 6 | 00 | - ☌ * ☽ | Aldebaran 0°.3 S; occultation |
| 9 | 06 | - ☌ ☿ ☉ | superior |
| 10 | 10 | - ☌ ♃ ☽ | ♃ 4° N |
| 13 | 19 | - ☌ ♄ ☽ | ♄ 3° N |
| 23 | 15 | - ☌ ♀ ☽ | ♀ 3° S |
| 26 | 17 | - ☌ ☽ ☉ | Total solar eclipse |
| 27 | 18 | - ☌ ☿ ☽ | ☿ 0°.6 N; occultation |
| Mar. 1 | 18 | - ☍ ♄ ☉ | |
| 5 | 07 | - ☌ * ☽ | Aldebaran 0°.2 S; occultation |
| 8 | 01 | - | ☿ gr. elong. E (18°) |
| 9 | 12 | - ☌ ♃ ☽ | ♃ 5° N |
| 12 | 21 | - ☌ ♄ ☽ | ♄ 3° N |
| 13 | 21 | - ☍ ☽ ☉ | Partial lunar eclipse |
| 14 | 15 | - | ☿ stationary |
| 21 | 05 22 | | **Vernal Equinox; Spring begins** |
| 24 | 14 | - ☌ ☿ ☉ | inferior |
| 25 | 09 | - ☌ ♀ ☽ | ♀ 2° S |
| 26 | 01 | - | ♃ stationary |
| 27 | 02 | - ☌ ♂ ☽ | ♂ 0°.7 S |
| Apr. 1 | 16 | - ☌ * ☽ | Aldebaran 0°.3 S; occultation |
| 1 | 22 | - ☌ ☿ ♂ | ☿ 3° N |
| 5 | 18 | - ☌ ♃ ☽ | ♃ 5° N |
| 6 | 01 | - | ☿ stationary |
| 9 | 01 | - ☌ ♄ ☽ | ♄ 3° N |
| 21 | 13 | - | ☿ gr. elong. W (27°) |
| 24 | 03 | - ☌ ♀ ☽ | ♀ 0°.3 S; occultation |
| 24 | 13 | - ☌ ☿ ☽ | ☿ 1° S; occultation |
| 24 | 23 | - ☌ ♂ ☽ | ♂ 2° N |
| 29 | 01 | - ☌ * ☽ | Aldebaran 0°.4 S; occultation |
| May 3 | 06 | - ☌ ♃ ☽ | ♃ 4° N |
| 5 | 08 | - ☌ ☿ ♂ | ☿ 2° S |
| 6 | 07 | - ☌ ♄ ☽ | ♄ 3° N |
| 10 | 04 | - | ♄ stationary |
| 20 | 06 | - ☌ ♀ ♂ | ♀ 1°.1 S |
| 23 | 19 | - ☌ ♂ ☽ | ♂ 3° N |
| 23 | 22 | - ☌ ♀ ☽ | ♀ 3° N |
| 29 | 23 | - ☌ ☿ ☉ | superior |
| 30 | 22 | - ☌ ♃ ☽ | ♃ 4° N |
| June 2 | 16 | - ☌ ♄ ☽ | ♄ 2° N |
| 20 | 03 | - ☌ * ♀ | ♀ 5° N of Aldebaran |
| 21 | 16 | - ☌ ♂ ☽ | ♂ 5° N |
| 21 | 23 56 | | **Summer Solstice; Summer begins** |
| 22 | 17 | - ☌ * ☽ | Aldebaran 0°.4 S; occultation |
| 22 | 22 | - ☌ * ☿ | ☿ 5° S of Pollux |
| 23 | 00 | - ☌ ♀ ☽ | ♀ 4° N |
| 26 | 18 | - ☌ ☿ ☽ | ☿ 5° N |
| 27 | 16 | - ☌ ♃ ☽ | ♃ 3° N |
| 30 | 03 | - ☌ ♄ ☽ | ♄ 2° N |
| July 3 | 22 | - | ⊕ at aphelion |
| 3 | 22 | - | ☿ gr. elong. E (26°) |
| 10 | 16 | - ☌ * ♂ | ♂ 5° N of Aldebaran |
| 17 | 02 | - | ☿ stationary |
| 19 | 23 | - ☌ * ☽ | Aldebaran 0°.3 S; occultation |
| 20 | 12 | - ☌ ♂ ☽ | ♂ 5° N |
| 27 | 14 | - ☌ ♄ ☽ | ♄ 2° N |
| 31 | 17 | - ☌ ☿ ☉ | inferior |
| Aug. 10 | 12 | - | ☿ stationary |
| 13 | 09 | - ☌ ♃ ☉ | |
| 16 | 04 | - ☌ * ☽ | Aldebaran 0°.2 S; occultation |
| 18 | 08 | - ☌ ♂ ☽ | ♂ 5° N |
| 19 | 04 | - | ☿ gr. elong. W (19°) |
| 21 | 02 | - ☌ ☿ ☽ | ☿ 2° N |
| 22 | 17 | - ☌ ☽ ☉ | Partial solar eclipse |
| 25 | 12 | - ☌ ♀ ☉ | superior |
| 30 | 11 | - ☌ ☿ ♃ | ☿ 0°.7 N |
| Sept. 2 | 11 | - ☌ * ☿ | ☿ 1°.2 N of Regulus |
| 6 | 11 | - ☍ ☽ ☉ | Total lunar eclipse |
| 10 | 11 | - ☌ ♄ ☉ | |
| 12 | 11 | - ☌ * ☽ | Aldebaran 0°.2 S; occultation |
| 13 | 05 | - ☌ ☿ ☉ | superior |
| 14 | 23 | - ☌ * ♂ | ♂ 6° S of Pollux |
| 16 | 03 | - ☌ ♂ ☽ | ♂ 5° N |
| 18 | 22 | - ☌ ♃ ☽ | ♃ 2° N |
| 23 | 15 17 | | **Autumnal Equinox; Autumn begins** |
| 26 | 13 | - ☌ * ♃ | ♃ 0°.3 N of Regulus |
| Oct 2 | 12 | - ☌ * ☿ | ☿ 1°.9 N of Spica |
| 5 | 07 | - ☌ * ♀ | ♀ 3° N of Spica |
| 9 | 20 | - ☌ * ☽ | Aldebaran 0°.3 S; occultation |
| 14 | 20 | - ☌ ♂ ☽ | ♂ 4° N |
| 16 | 15 | - ☌ ♃ ☽ | ♃ 1° N |
| 18 | 05 | - ☌ ♄ ☽ | ♄ 0°.7 N; occultation |
| 22 | 08 | - ☌ ♀ ☽ | ♀ 5°S |
| 22 | 22 | - ☌ ☿ ☽ | ☿ 8° S |
| 29 | 16 | - | ☿ gr. elong. E (24°) |
| Nov. 6 | 06 | - ☌ * ☽ | Aldebaran 0°.4 S; occultation |
| 8 | 20 | - ☌ ☿ ♀ | ☿ 2° S |
| 9 | 18 | - | ☿ stationary |
| 11 | 14 | - ☌ * ♀ | ♀ 4° N of Antares |
| 12 | 10 | - ☌ ♂ ☽ | ♂ 3° N |
| 12 | 15 | - ☌ * ☽ | Regulus 10° N; occultation |
| 13 | 07 | - ☌ ♃ ☽ | ♃ 0°.8 N; occultation |
| 14 | 18 | - ☌ ♄ ☽ | ♄ 0°.3 N; occultation |
| 17 | 17 | - ☌ * ♂ | ♂ 1°.6 N of Regulus |
| 20 | 04 | - ☌ ☿ ☉ | inferior |
| 21 | 14 | - ☌ ♀ ☽ | ♀ 6° S |
| 29 | 10 | - | ☿ stationary |
| Dec. 3 | 16 | - ☌ * ☽ | Aldebaran 0°.5 S; occultation |
| 7 | 16 | - | ☿ gr. elong. W (21°) |
| 9 | 23 | - ☌ * ☽ | Regulus 0°.8 N; occultation |
| 10 | 18 | - ☌ ♂ ☽ | ♂ 2° N |
| 10 | 20 | - ☌ ♃ ☽ | ♃ 0°.4 N; occultation |
| 12 | 05 | - ☌ ♄ ☽ | ♄ 0°.01 S; occultation |
| 13 | 17 | - ☌ ♂ ♃ | ♂ 1°.7 N |
| 17 | 20 | - ☌ ☿ ☽ | ☿ 4° S |
| 18 | 20 | - ☌ * ☿ | ☿ 6° N of Antares |
| 21 | 17 | - ☌ ♀ ☽ | ♀ 5° S |
| 22 | 11 10 | | **Winter Solstice; Winter begins** |
| 27 | 05 | - | ♃ stationary |
| 31 | 00 | - ☌ * ☽ | Aldebaran 0°.4 S; occultation |

## Planetary Configurations 1980

| Date | h. m. | | |
|---|---|---|---|
| Jan. 3 | 15 | - | ⊕ at perihelion |
| 8 | 01 | - | ♄ stationary |
| 17 | 08 | - | ♂ stationary |
| 21 | 09 | - ☌ ☿ ☉ | superior |
| Feb. 12 | | | ☿ gr. elong. E (18°) |
| 24 | 18 | - ☍ ♃ ☉ | |
| 25 | 06 | - ☍ ♂ ☉ | |
| 25 | 11 | - | ☿ stationary |
| Mar. 2 | 19 | - ☌ ♂ ♃ | ♂ 3° N |
| 14 | 02 | - ☍ ♄ ☉ | |
| 18 | 15 | - | ☿ stationary |
| 20 | 11 10 | | Vernal Equinox; Spring begins |
| Apr. 2 | 17 | - | ☿ gr. elong. W (28°) |
| 5 | 15 | - | ♀ gr. elong. E (46°) |
| 7 | 14 | - | ♂ stationary |
| 26 | 17 | - | ♃ stationary |
| May 4 | 06 | - ☌ ♂ ♃ | ♂ 0°.8 N |
| 9 | 03 | - | ♀ gr. brilliancy |
| 13 | 09 | - ☌ ☿ ☉ | superior |
| 23 | 07 | - | ♄ stationary |
| 24 | 19 | - | ♀ stationary |

# Rising and Setting of Planets, 1979

**Greenwich Mean Time (0 designates midnight)**

| 1979 | 20° N. Latitude Rise | Set | 30° N. Latitude Rise | Set | 40° N. Latitude Rise | Set | 50° N. Latitude Rise | Set | 60° N. Latitude Rise | Set |
|---|---|---|---|---|---|---|---|---|---|---|
| | | | | | **Venus, 1979** | | | | | |
| Jan. 1 | 3:12 | 14:31 | 3:25 | 14:18 | 3:41 | 14:02 | 4:04 | 13:40 | 4:39 | 13:04 |
| 15 | 3:14 | 14:25 | 3:30 | 14:09 | 3:50 | 13:50 | 4:17 | 13:23 | 5:01 | 12:39 |
| Feb. 1 | 3:26 | 14:29 | 3:44 | 14:11 | 4:07 | 13:48 | 4:38 | 13:17 | 5:31 | 12:24 |
| 15 | 3:38 | 14:40 | 3:57 | 14:21 | 4:20 | 13:58 | 4:53 | 13:25 | 5:47 | 12:30 |
| Mar. 1 | 3:49 | 14:55 | 4:07 | 14:37 | 4:28 | 14:16 | 4:58 | 13:46 | 5:48 | 12:56 |
| 15 | 3:57 | 15:13 | 4:11 | 14:58 | 4:29 | 14:40 | 4:54 | 14:16 | 5:33 | 13:37 |
| Apr. 1 | 3:48 | 15:21 | 3:57 | 15:12 | 4:09 | 15:01 | 4:23 | 14:46 | 4:47 | 14:23 |
| 15 | 4:01 | 15:51 | 4:05 | 15:47 | 4:09 | 15:42 | 4:16 | 15:36 | 4:26 | 15:26 |
| May 1 | 3:58 | 16:10 | 3:56 | 16:12 | 3:53 | 16:15 | 3:49 | 16:19 | 3:43 | 16:25 |
| 15 | 3:57 | 16:27 | 3:49 | 16:35 | 3:39 | 16:45 | 3:26 | 16:58 | 3:05 | 17:19 |
| June 1 | 3:58 | 16:50 | 3:44 | 17:04 | 3:27 | 17:22 | 3:02 | 17:47 | 2:23 | 18:26 |
| 15 | 4:05 | 17:11 | 3:47 | 17:30 | 3:24 | 17:53 | 2:51 | 18:26 | 1:55 | 19:22 |
| July 1 | 4:20 | 17:36 | 3:59 | 17:58 | 3:32 | 18:25 | 2:53 | 19:04 | 1:42 | 20:14 |
| 15 | 4:39 | 17:56 | 4:17 | 18:18 | 3:50 | 18:45 | 3:10 | 19:25 | 1:59 | 20:37 |
| Aug. 1 | 5:06 | 18:14 | 4:47 | 18:33 | 4:23 | 18:57 | 3:50 | 19:30 | 2:52 | 20:28 |
| 15 | 5:29 | 18:22 | 5:14 | 18:37 | 4:56 | 18:55 | 4:30 | 19:20 | 3:49 | 20:01 |
| Sept. 1 | 5:39 | 18:12 | 5:31 | 18:20 | 5:20 | 18:30 | 5:06 | 18:45 | 4:43 | 19:07 |
| 15 | 5:50 | 18:01 | 5:48 | 18:03 | 5:45 | 18:05 | 5:42 | 18:09 | 5:36 | 18:15 |
| Oct. 1 | 6:35 | 18:22 | 6:39 | 18:17 | 6:45 | 18:11 | 6:53 | 18:03 | 7:05 | 17:51 |
| 15 | 6:55 | 18:22 | 7:05 | 18:11 | 7:19 | 17:58 | 7:37 | 17:40 | 8:05 | 17:12 |
| Nov. 1 | 7:22 | 18:28 | 7:39 | 18:11 | 8:01 | 17:49 | 8:30 | 17:20 | 9:20 | 16:30 |
| 15 | 7:46 | 18:40 | 8:07 | 18:19 | 8:34 | 17:52 | 9:11 | 17:15 | 10:17 | 16:09 |
| Dec. 1 | 8:13 | 19:01 | 8:36 | 18:38 | 9:04 | 18:10 | 9:45 | 17:29 | 11:00 | 16:14 |
| 15 | 8:31 | 19:24 | 8:53 | 19:03 | 9:20 | 18:36 | 9:58 | 17:58 | 11:05 | 16:51 |
| | | | | | **Mars, 1979** | | | | | |
| Jan. 1 | 6:58 | 17:50 | 7:19 | 17:29 | 7:46 | 17:02 | 8:24 | 16:23 | 9:32 | 15:16 |
| 15 | 6:46 | 17:44 | 7:06 | 17:24 | 7:31 | 16:59 | 8:06 | 16:24 | 9:06 | 15:24 |
| Feb. 1 | 6:30 | 17:37 | 6:47 | 17:20 | 7:08 | 16:59 | 7:37 | 16:30 | 8:25 | 15:42 |
| 15 | 6:14 | 17:31 | 6:14 | 17:31 | 6:45 | 17:00 | 7:08 | 16:37 | 7:45 | 16:00 |
| Mar. 1 | 5:56 | 17:25 | 6:06 | 17:14 | 6:19 | 17:02 | 6:36 | 16:44 | 7:03 | 16:18 |
| 15 | 5:36 | 17:17 | 5:43 | 17:10 | 5:51 | 17:02 | 6:02 | 16:51 | 6:19 | 16:34 |
| Apr. 1 | 5:10 | 17:07 | 5:13 | 17:05 | 5:15 | 17:02 | 5:18 | 16:59 | 5:23 | 16:54 |
| 15 | 4:49 | 16:58 | 4:47 | 17:00 | 4:45 | 17:02 | 4:42 | 17:05 | 4:38 | 17:09 |
| May 1 | 4:41 | 17:05 | 4:36 | 17:11 | 4:28 | 17:18 | 4:19 | 17:28 | 4:03 | 17:44 |
| 15 | 4:35 | 17:11 | 4:26 | 17:21 | 4:15 | 17:32 | 3:59 | 17:48 | 3:34 | 18:13 |
| June 1 | 3:37 | 16:27 | 3:24 | 16:40 | 3:07 | 16:57 | 2:44 | 17:20 | 2:07 | 17:57 |
| 15 | 3:18 | 16:17 | 3:02 | 16:34 | 2:44 | 16:51 | 2:13 | 17:22 | 1:26 | 18:10 |
| July 1 | 2:58 | 16:06 | 2:39 | 16:25 | 2:15 | 16:49 | 1:41 | 17:23 | 0:42 | 18:21 |
| 15 | 2:41 | 15:55 | 2:20 | 16:16 | 1:54 | 16:42 | 1:16 | 17:20 | 0:09 | 18:27 |
| Aug. 1 | 2:39 | 15:57 | 2:17 | 16:19 | 1:49 | 16:47 | 1:09 | 17:28 | 23:55 | 18:42 |
| 15 | 2:07 | 15:26 | 1:45 | 15:49 | 1:17 | 16:17 | 0:36 | 16:58 | 23:21 | 18:13 |
| Sept.1 | 1:49 | 15:06 | 1:28 | 15:28 | 1:00 | 15:55 | 0:21 | 16:35 | 23:09 | 17:47 |
| 15 | 1:34 | 14:47 | 1:13 | 15:07 | 0:47 | 15:33 | 0:10 | 16:10 | 23:04 | 17:16 |
| Oct. 1 | 1:14 | 14:21 | 0:55 | 14:40 | 0:32 | 15:04 | 23:59 | 15:37 | 23:01 | 16:34 |
| 15 | 0:55 | 13:56 | 0:38 | 14:13 | 0:17 | 14:34 | 23:48 | 15:04 | 22:58 | 15:54 |
| Nov. 1 | 0:29 | 13:22 | 0:15 | 13:37 | 23:57 | 14:55 | 23:31 | 14:20 | 22:50 | 15:01 |
| 15 | 0:05 | 12:51 | 23:52 | 13:04 | 23:36 | 13:19 | 23:15 | 13:41 | 22:40 | 14:16 |
| Dec. 1 | 23:32 | 12:12 | 23:21 | 12:23 | 23:08 | 12:36 | 22:50 | 12:54 | 22:22 | 13:22 |
| 15 | 22:59 | 11:34 | 22:50 | 11:43 | 22:38 | 11:55 | 22:23 | 12:10 | 21:58 | 12:35 |
| | | | | | **Jupiter, 1979** | | | | | |
| Jan. 1 | 19:26 | 8:29 | 19:09 | 8:47 | 18:47 | 9:08 | 18:16 | 9:39 | 17:29 | 10:27 |
| 15 | 18:23 | 7:28 | 18:06 | 7:46 | 17:43 | 8:08 | 17:11 | 8:40 | 16:18 | 9:34 |
| Feb. 1 | 17:02 | 6:08 | 16:44 | 6:27 | 16:20 | 6:50 | 15:48 | 7:26 | 14:51 | 8:19 |
| 15 | 15:59 | 5:07 | 15:40 | 5:26 | 15:17 | 5:50 | 14:43 | 6:23 | 13:45 | 7:21 |
| Mar. 1 | 14:58 | 4:07 | 14:39 | 4:26 | 14:15 | 4:50 | 13:41 | 5:25 | 12:41 | 6:24 |
| 15 | 14:00 | 3:09 | 13:40 | 3:29 | 13:16 | 3:53 | 12:41 | 4:28 | 11:41 | 5:28 |
| Apr. 1 | 12:52 | 2:02 | 12:33 | 2:21 | 12:09 | 2:46 | 11:34 | 3:21 | 10:34 | 4:21 |
| 15 | 12:00 | 1:09 | 11:41 | 1:29 | 11:17 | 1:53 | 10:42 | 2:27 | 9:43 | 3:27 |
| May 1 | 11:03 | 0:12 | 10:44 | 0:30 | 10:21 | 0:54 | 9:47 | 1:28 | 8:49 | 2:26 |
| 15 | 10:16 | 23:23 | 9:58 | 23:41 | 9:34 | 0:05 | 9:01 | 0:38 | 8:05 | 1:34 |
| June 1 | 9:21 | 22:26 | 9:03 | 22:44 | 8:41 | 23:05 | 8:09 | 23:38 | 7:15 | 0:32 |
| 15 | 8:37 | 21:40 | 8:20 | 21:57 | 7:58 | 22:19 | 7:27 | 22:49 | 6:36 | 23:41 |
| July 1 | 7:48 | 20:48 | 7:31 | 21:05 | 7:11 | 21:25 | 6:42 | 21:54 | 5:54 | 22:42 |
| 15 | 7:06 | 20:03 | 6:50 | 20:19 | 6:30 | 20:39 | 6:03 | 21:06 | 5:18 | 21:51 |
| Aug. 1 | 6:15 | 19:09 | 6:01 | 19:24 | 5:42 | 19:42 | 5:17 | 20:08 | 4:35 | 20:50 |
| 15 | 5:34 | 18:25 | 5:20 | 18:39 | 5:03 | 18:56 | 4:39 | 19:20 | 4:00 | 19:58 |
| Sept.1 | 4:43 | 17:31 | 4:31 | 17:43 | 4:15 | 17:59 | 3:53 | 18:21 | 3:18 | 18:56 |
| 15 | 4:01 | 16:45 | 3:50 | 16:57 | 3:35 | 17:12 | 3:15 | 17:32 | 2:42 | 18:04 |
| Oct. 1 | 3:12 | 15:53 | 3:02 | 16:04 | 2:48 | 16:17 | 2:30 | 16:36 | 2:01 | 17:05 |
| 15 | 2:29 | 15:07 | 2:19 | 15:17 | 2:06 | 15:29 | 1:49 | 15:46 | 1:23 | 16:13 |
| Nov. 1 | 1:34 | 14:09 | 1:25 | 14:18 | 1:14 | 14:29 | 0:58 | 14:45 | 0:34 | 15:09 |
| 15 | 0:47 | 13:20 | 0:39 | 13:29 | 0:28 | 13:39 | 0:14 | 13:54 | 23:51 | 14:16 |
| Dec. 1 | 23:51 | 12:22 | 23:43 | 12:30 | 23:33 | 12:40 | 23:19 | 12:54 | 22:58 | 13:15 |
| 15 | 22:59 | 11:30 | 22:52 | 11:38 | 22:42 | 11:48 | 22:29 | 12:01 | 22:08 | 12:22 |

| | 20° N. Latitude | | 30° N. Latitude | | 40° N. Latitude | | 50° N. Latitude | | 60° N. Latitude | |
|---|---|---|---|---|---|---|---|---|---|---|
| | Rise | Set | Rise | Set | Rise | Set | Rise | Set | Rise | Set |
| | | | | | Saturn, 1979 | | | | | |
| Jan. 1 | 22:12 | 10:41 | 22:05 | 10:48 | 21:56 | 10:57 | 21:44 | 11:09 | 21:25 | 11:28 |
| 15 | 21:12 | 9:41 | 21:04 | 9:48 | 20:55 | 9:57 | 20:43 | 10:10 | 20:23 | 10:29 |
| Feb. 1 | 20:01 | 8:31 | 19:54 | 8:39 | 19:44 | 8:49 | 19:31 | 9:02 | 19:11 | 9:22 |
| 15 | 19:02 | 7:33 | 18:54 | 7:41 | 18:44 | 7:51 | 18:30 | 8:05 | 8:09 | 8:26 |
| Mar. 1 | 18:02 | 6:35 | 17:54 | 6:43 | 17:43 | 6:54 | 17:29 | 7:08 | 17:07 | 7:31 |
| 15 | 16:58 | 5:32 | 16:49 | 5:41 | 16:39 | 5:52 | 16:24 | 6:07 | 16:00 | 6:31 |
| Apr. 1 | 15:46 | 4:22 | 15:37 | 4:31 | 15:26 | 4:42 | 15:10 | 4:58 | 14:45 | 5:23 |
| 15 | 14:48 | 3:24 | 14:39 | 3:34 | 14:27 | 3:46 | 14:11 | 4:02 | 13:46 | 4:27 |
| May 1 | 13:43 | 2:20 | 13:34 | 2:30 | 13:22 | 2:41 | 13:06 | 2:58 | 12:40 | 3:23 |
| 15 | 12:48 | 1:25 | 12:39 | 1:34 | 12:27 | 1:46 | 12:11 | 2:02 | 11:45 | 2:28 |
| June 1 | 11:43 | 0:19 | 11:34 | 0:29 | 11:22 | 0:40 | 11:06 | 0:56 | 10:41 | 1:21 |
| 15 | 10:51 | 23:26 | 10:42 | 23:35 | 10:31 | 23:47 | 10:15 | 0:02 | 9:51 | 0:57 |
| July 1 | 9:53 | 22:27 | 9:45 | 22:36 | 9:34 | 22:47 | 9:19 | 23:01 | 8:56 | 23:25 |
| 15 | 9:04 | 21:36 | 8:55 | 21:44 | 8:45 | 21:54 | 8:31 | 22:08 | 8:09 | 22:30 |
| Aug. 1 | 8:05 | 20:35 | 7:57 | 20:42 | 7:47 | 20:52 | 7:34 | 21:05 | 7:14 | 21:25 |
| 15 | 7:16 | 19:45 | 7:09 | 19:52 | 7:01 | 20:01 | 6:49 | 20:13 | 6:30 | 20:31 |
| Sept.1 | 6:18 | 18:44 | 6:12 | 18:51 | 6:04 | 18:59 | 5:53 | 19:09 | 5:36 | 19:26 |
| 15 | 5:31 | 17:55 | 5:25 | 18:01 | 5:18 | 18:08 | 5:08 | 18:18 | 4:53 | 18:33 |
| Oct. 1 | 4:36 | 16:58 | 4:31 | 17:03 | 4:25 | 17:10 | 4:16 | 17:18 | 4:03 | 17:32 |
| 15 | 3:48 | 16:08 | 3:44 | 16:13 | 3:38 | 16:19 | 3:30 | 16:26 | 3:18 | 16:39 |
| Nov. 1 | 2:49 | 15:07 | 2:45 | 15:11 | 2:40 | 15:16 | 2:34 | 15:23 | 2:23 | 15:34 |
| 15 | 2:00 | 14:16 | 1:56 | 14:20 | 1:52 | 14:24 | 1:46 | 14:30 | 1:36 | 14:40 |
| Dec. 1 | 1:02 | 13:17 | 0:59 | 13:20 | 0:55 | 13:24 | 0:49 | 13:30 | 0:41 | 13:39 |
| 15 | 0:10 | 12:25 | 0:07 | 12:28 | 0:03 | 12:31 | 23:58 | 12:37 | 23:50 | 12:45 |

# The Planets and the Solar System

| Planet | Mean daily motion " | Orbital velocity miles per sec. | Sidereal revolution days | Synodical revolution days | Dist. from sun in millions of mi. Max. | Min. | Dist. from Earth in millions of mi. Max. | Min. | Light at perihelion | aphelion |
|---|---|---|---|---|---|---|---|---|---|---|
| Mercury | 14732.420 | 29.75 | 87.9693 | 115.9 | 43.403 | 28.597 | 136 | 50 | 10.58 | 4.59 |
| Venus | 5767.668 | 21.76 | 224.7009 | 583.9 | 67.726 | 66.813 | 161 | 25 | 1.94 | 1.89 |
| Earth | 3548.192 | 18.51 | 365.2564 | — | 94.555 | 91.445 | — | — | 1.03 | 0.97 |
| Mars | 1886.519 | 14.99 | 686.9796 | 779.9 | 154.936 | 128.471 | 248 | 35 | 0.524 | 0.360 |
| Jupiter | 299.160 | 8.12 | 4332.1248 | 398.9 | 507.046 | 460.595 | 600 | 368 | 0.0408 | 0.0336 |
| Saturn | 119.713 | 5.99 | 10825.863 | 378.1 | 937.541 | 838.425 | 1031 | 745 | 0.01230 | 0.00984 |
| Uranus | 42.248 | 4.23 | 30676.15 | 369.7 | 1859.748 | 1699.331 | 1953 | 1606 | 0.00300 | 0.00250 |
| Neptune | 21.632 | 3.38 | 59911.13 | 367.5 | 2821.686 | 2760.386 | 2915 | 2667 | 0.00114 | 0.00109 |
| Pluto | 14.269 | 2.95 | 90824.2 | 366.7 | 4551.386 | 2756.427 | 4644 | 2663 | 0.00114 | 0.00042 |

Light at perihelion and aphelion is solar illumination in units of mean illumination at Earth.

| Planet | Mean longitude of:* ascending node ° ' " | perihelion ° ' " | Inclination* of orbit to ecliptic ° ' " | Mean distance** | Eccentricity of orbit | Mean longitude at the epoch* ° ' " |
|---|---|---|---|---|---|---|
| Mercury | 48 05 11 | 77 08 03 | 7 00 15 | 0.387099 | 0.205630 | 337 18 42 |
| Venus | 76 29 38 | 131 16 49 | 3 23 40 | 0.723332 | 0.006783 | 334 25 03 |
| Earth | | 102 35 07 | | 1.000000 | 0.016718 | 224 14 58 |
| Mars | 49 23 53 | 335 40 44 | 1 50 59 | 1.523691 | 0.093386 | 1 35 32 |
| Jupiter | 100 13 33 | 14 17 59 | 1 18 20 | 5.203210 | 0.0479014 | 127 19 30 |
| Saturn | 113 30 07 | 95 13 35 | 2 29 11 | 9.581006 | 0.0568997 | 156 57 20 |
| Uranus | 74 00 31 | 170 44 02 | 0 46 17 | 19.21970 | 0.0494552 | 224 13 11 |
| Neptune | 131 31 42 | 61 53 56 | 1 46 22 | 30.01922 | 0.0091507 | 259 12 43 |
| Pluto | 109 54 40 | 222 58 14 | 17 08 14 | 39.70237 | 0.2522630 | 208 26 04 |

*Consistent for the standard Epoch: 1979 May 7.0 Ephemeris Time　**Astronomical units

| Sun and planets | Semi-diameter at unit distance | at mean least dist. | in miles mean s.d. | Volume ⊕=1. | Mass. ⊕=1. | Density ⊕=1. | Axial rotation d | h | m | s | Gravity at surface ⊕=1. | Reflecting power Pct. | Probable temperature °F. |
|---|---|---|---|---|---|---|---|---|---|---|---|---|---|
| Sun | 15 59.62 | | 432560 | 1303730 | 332830 | 0.26 | 24 | 16 | 48 | | 27.9 | | + 10,000 |
| Mercury | 3.37 | 5.45 | 1505 | 0.054 | 0.0554 | 0.98 | 59 | | | | 0.37 | 0.06 | + 620 |
| Venus | 8.46 | 30.50 | 3762 | 0.880 | 0.8150 | 0.94 | 244.3 (R) | | | | 0.88 | 0.72 | + 900 |
| Earth | — | | 3960 | 1.000 | 1.000 | 1.00 | | 23 | 56 | 4 | 1.00 | 0.39 | + 72 |
| Moon | 2.40 | 16 43.00 | 1080 | 0.020 | 0.0123 | 0.61 | 27 | 7 | 43 | 12 | 0.17 | 0.07 | + 10 / — 10 |
| Mars | 4.68 | 8.94 | 2107 | 0.149 | 0.1075 | 0.72 | | 24 | 37 | 23 | 0.38 | 0.16 | — 10 |
| Jupiter | 98.37 | 23.43 | 44270 | 1316. | 317.84 | 0.24 | | 9 | 50 | 30 | 2.64 | 0.70 | — 240 |
| Saturn | 82.80 | 9.76 | 37300 | 755. | 95.147 | 0.13 | | 10 | 14 | | 1.15 | 0.75 | — 300 |
| Uranus | 32.90 | 1.80 | 15000 | 52. | 14.54 | 0.29 | | 10 | 49 (R) | | 1.15 | 0.90 | — 340 |
| Neptune | 31.10 | 1.06 | 15600 | 57. | 17.23 | 0.30 | | 15 | 48 | | 1.12 | 0.82 | — 370 |
| Pluto* | 1.80 | 0.06 | 800 | 0.008 | 0.0016 | 0.19 | 6 | 9 | | | 0.04 | 0.14 | ? / ? |

*Much of this information is too new to be verified, but observers at the U.S. Naval Observatory have derived values similar to these after having discovered that Pluto has a satellite. It apparently revolves about Pluto in a period equal to Pluto's rotation period.

(R) retrograde of Venus and Uranus.

# Four Eclipses in 1979

Greenwich Mean Time

## First Eclipse

A total eclipse of the sun, February 26. The eclipse begins in the eastern Pacific Ocean; contacts land about Portland, Oregon; moves east, turning northeast about Winnipeg, Manitoba; passes over Hudson's Bay; and ends in middle Greenland. (This is the last total solar eclipse in continental United States until August 21, 2017. A total solar eclipse may be seen near Honolulu July 11, 1991.) Partial phases visible throughout North America, except western Alaska, and Central America, except Panama.

### Circumstances of the Eclipse

| | |
|---|---|
| Eclipse begins . . . . . . . . | Feb. 26, 14:45.2 |
| Central eclipse begins . . . . | 26, 16:09.2 |
| Central eclipse at local apparent noon . . . | 26, 17:21.4 |
| Central eclipse ends . . . . . | 26, 17:39.0 |
| Eclipse ends . . . . . . . . | 26, 19:03.1 |
| Maximum duration of totality . . . . . . . . . . | 2m 49s |

## Second Eclipse

A partial eclipse of the moon, March 13. The beginning is generally visible in the western Pacific Ocean, Australia, Asia, the Indian Ocean, Africa, Europe, part of Antarctica, the extreme eastern part of the Atlantic Ocean, and the arctic region. The end is generally visible in western Asia, the Indian Ocean, Africa, Europe, the Atlantic Ocean, eastern South America, northeastern North America, Greenland, and part of Antarctica.

### Circumstances of the Eclipse

| | |
|---|---|
| Moon enters penumbra . . . | March 13, 18:10.9 |
| Moon enters umbra . . . . . | 13, 19:28.9 |
| Middle of eclipse . . . . . . | 13, 21:08.0 |
| Moon leaves umbra . . . . . | 13, 22:47.3 |
| Moon leaves penumbra . . . | 14, 00:05.1 |
| Magnitude of the eclipse . . | 0.858 |

## Third Eclipse

An annular eclipse of the sun, August 22. The short path of central eclipse swings over the extreme southern Pacific Ocean and part of Antarctica. Partial phases visible over southern South America.

### Circumstances of the Eclipse

| | |
|---|---|
| Eclipse begins . . . . . . . . | Aug. 22, 14:55.1 |
| Central eclipse begins . . . . | 22, 16:51.0 |
| Central eclipse at local apparent noon . . . | 22, 17:51.9 |
| Central eclipse ends . . . . . | 22, 17:52.2 |
| Eclipse ends . . . . . . . . | 22, 19:48.3 |
| Maximum duration of annularity . . . . . . . . . | 5m 58.9s |

## Fourth Eclipse

A total eclipse of the moon, September 6. The beginning is generally visible in North America (except the Northeastern part), South America (except the extreme eastern part), the Pacific Ocean, the eastern half of Australia, New Zealand, the extreme northeast part of Asia, and part of Antarctica. The end is generally visible in the western half of North America, the Pacific Ocean, Australia, New Zealand, the eastern part of Asia, part of Antarctica, and the eastern Indian Ocean.

### Circumstances of the Eclipse

| | |
|---|---|
| Moon enters penumbra . . . | September 6, 08:20.2 |
| Moon enters umbra . . . . . | 6, 09:17.9 |
| Total eclipse begins . . . . | 6, 10:31.3 |
| Middle of eclipse . . . . . . | 6, 10:54.2 |
| Total eclipse ends . . . . . . | 6, 11:17.1 |
| Moon leaves umbra . . . . . | 6, 12:30.5 |
| Moon leaves penumbra . . . | 6, 13:28.3 |
| Magnitude of the eclipse . . | 1.099 |

# Morning and Evening Stars

Greenwich Mean Time

| | Morning | Evening | | Morning | Evening |
|---|---|---|---|---|---|
| Jan. | Mercury<br>Venus<br>Mars (from Jan. 20)<br>Jupiter (to Jan. 24)<br>Saturn | Mars (to Jan. 20)<br>Jupiter (from Jan. 24) | July | Mercury (from July 31)<br>Venus<br>Mars<br>Jupiter | Mercury (to July 31)<br>Saturn |
| Feb. | Mercury (to Feb. 9)<br>Venus<br>Mars<br>Saturn | Mercury (from Feb. 9)<br>Jupiter | Aug. | Mercury<br>Venus (to Aug. 25)<br>Mars<br>Jupiter (to Aug. 13) | Venus (from Aug. 25)<br>Jupiter (from Aug. 13)<br>Saturn |
| Mar. | Mercury (from Mar. 24)<br>Venus<br>Mars | Mercury (to Mar. 24)<br>Jupiter<br>Saturn (from Mar. 1) | Sept. | Mercury (to Sept. 13)<br>Mars<br>Saturn (from Sept. 10) | Mercury (from Sept. 13)<br>Venus<br>Jupiter<br>Saturn (to Sept. 10) |
| Apr. | Mercury<br>Venus<br>Mars<br>Jupiter | Saturn | Oct. | Mars<br>Saturn | Mercury<br>Venus<br>Jupiter |
| May | Mercury (to May 29)<br>Venus<br>Mars<br>Jupiter | Mercury (from May 29)<br>Saturn | Nov. | Mercury (from Nov. 20)<br>Mars<br>Saturn | Mercury (to Nov. 20)<br>Venus<br>Jupiter |
| June | Venus<br>Mars<br>Jupiter | Mercury<br>Saturn | Dec. | Mercury<br>Mars<br>Saturn | Venus<br>Jupiter |

# Astronomical Constants; Speed of Light

The following astronomical constants were adopted in 1968, in accordance with the resolutions and recommendations of the International Astronomical Union (Hamburg 1964): Velocity of light, 299,792.5 kilometers per second, or about 186,282.3976 statute miles per second: solar parallax, 8'.794: constant of nutation, 9'.210; and constant of aberration, 20'.496.

## Star Tables, 1979

These tables include stars of visual magnitude 2.5 and brighter. Co-ordinates are for the epoch Jan. 0.705, 1979. Where n parallax figures are given, the trigonometric parallax figure is smaller than the margin for error and the distance given is ob tained by indirect methods. Stars of variable magnitude designated by v.

To find the time when the star is on meridian, subtract R.A.M.S. of the sun table on page 761 from the star's right ascen sion, first adding 24h to the latter, if necessary. Mark this result P.M., if less than 12h; but if greater than 12, subtract 12 and mark the remainder A.M.

| Star | Magnitude | Parallax " | Light yrs. | Right ascen. h. m. | Declination ° ' |
|---|---|---|---|---|---|
| α Andromedae (Alpheratz) | 2.06 | 0.02 | 90 | 0 07.3 | +28 58 |
| β Cassiopeiae | 2.26v | 0.07 | 45 | 0 08.1 | +59 02 |
| α Phoenicis | 2.39 | 0.04 | 93 | 0 25.2 | −42 25 |
| α Cassiopeiae (Schedir) | 2.22 | 0.01 | 150 | 0 39.3 | +56 25 |
| β Ceti | 2.02 | 0.06 | 57 | 0 42.5 | −18 06 |
| γ Cassiopeiae | 2.13v | 0.03 | 96 | 0 55.4 | +60 36 |
| β Andromedae | 2.02 | 0.04 | 76 | 1 08.5 | +35 31 |
| α Eridani (Achernar) | 0.51 | 0.02 | 118 | 1 36.9 | −57 21 |
| γ Andromedae | 2.14 | | 260 | 2 02.6 | +42 14 |
| α Arietis | 2.00 | 0.04 | 76 | 2 06.0 | +23 22 |
| α Ursae Min. (Pole Star) | 1.99v | | 680 | 2 10.9 | +89 10 |
| o Ceti | 2.00v | 0.01 | 103 | 2 18.3 | −3 04 |
| β Persei (Algol) | 2.06v | 0.03 | 105 | 3 06.8 | +40 53 |
| α Persei | 1.80 | 0.03 | 570 | 3 22.8 | +49 47 |
| α Tauri (Aldebaran) | 0.86v | 0.05 | 68 | 4 34.7 | +16 28 |
| β Orionis (Rigel) | 0.14v | | 900 | 5 13.5 | −8 14 |
| α Aurigae (Capella) | 0.05 | 0.07 | 45 | 5 15.1 | +45 59 |
| γ Orionis (Bellatrix) | 1.64 | 0.03 | 470 | 5 24.0 | +6 20 |
| β Tauri (El Nath) | 1.65 | 0.02 | 300 | 5 25.0 | +28 35 |
| δ Orionis | 2.20v | | 1500 | 5 30.9 | −0 19 |
| ε Orionis | 1.70 | | 1600 | 5 35.1 | −1 13 |
| ξ Orionis | 1.79 | 0.02 | 1600 | 5 39.7 | −1 57 |
| κ Orionis | 2.06 | 0.01 | 2100 | 5 46.7 | −9 41 |
| α Orionis (Betelgeuse) | 0.41v | | 520 | 5 54.0 | +7 24 |
| β Aurigae | 1.86 | 0.04 | 88 | 5 58.0 | +44 57 |
| β Canis Majoris | 1.96 | 0.01 | 750 | 6 21.8 | −17 57 |
| α Carinae (Canopus) | −0.72 | 0.02 | 98 | 6 23.5 | −52 41 |
| γ Geminorum | 1.93 | 0.03 | 105 | 6 36.5 | +16 25 |
| α Canis Majoris (Sirius) | −1.47 | 0.38 | 8.7 | 6 44.2 | −16 41 |
| ε Canis Majoris | 1.48 | | 680 | 6 57.8 | −28 57 |
| δ Canis Majoris | 1.85 | | 2100 | 7 07.5 | −26 22 |
| η Canis Majoris | 2.46 | | 2700 | 7 23.2 | −29 16 |
| α Geminorum (Castor) | 1.97 | 0.07 | 45 | 7 33.3 | +31 56 |
| α Canis Minoris (Procyon) | 0.37 | 0.29 | 11.3 | 7 38.2 | +5 17 |
| β Geminorum (Pollux) | 1.16 | 0.09 | 35 | 7 44.0 | +28 05 |
| ξ Puppis | 2.23 | | 2400 | 8 02.8 | −39 57 |
| λ Velorum | 1.88 | | 520 | 8 08.9 | −47 16 |
| ε Carinae | 1.90 | | 340 | 8 22.1 | −59 26 |
| δ Velorum | 1.95 | 0.04 | 76 | 8 44.1 | −54 38 |
| γ Velorum | 2.24 | 0.02 | 750 | 9 07.2 | −43 21 |
| β Carinae | 1.67 | 0.04 | 86 | 9 13.0 | −69 38 |
| ι Carinae | 2.25 | | 750 | 9 16.5 | −59 11 |
| κ Velorum | 2.49 | 0.01 | 470 | 9 21.5 | −54 55 |
| α Hydrae | 1.98 | 0.02 | 94 | 9 26.6 | −8 34 |
| α Leonis (Regulus) | 1.36 | 0.04 | 84 | 10 07.3 | +12 04 |
| γ Leonis | 1.99 | 0.02 | 90 | 10 18.8 | +19 57 |

| Star | Magnitude | Parallax " | Light yrs. | Right ascen. h. m. | Declination ° ' |
|---|---|---|---|---|---|
| β Ursae Majoris (Merak) | 2.37 | 0.04 | 78 | 11 00.6 | +56 30 |
| α Ursae Majoris (Dubhe) | 1.81 | 0.03 | 105 | 11 02.4 | +61 52 |
| β Leonis (Denebola) | 2.14 | 0.08 | 43 | 11 48.0 | +14 41 |
| γ Ursae Majoris (Phecda) | 2.44 | 0.02 | 90 | 11 52.7 | +53 49 |
| α Crucis | 1.39 | | 370 | 12 25.4 | −62 59 |
| γ Crucis | 1.69 | | 220 | 12 30.0 | −57 06 |
| γ Centauri | 2.17 | | 160 | 12 40.3 | −48 57 |
| β Crucis | 1.28v | | 490 | 12 46.4 | −59 34 |
| ε Ursae Majoris (Alioth) | 1.79v | 0.01 | 68 | 12 53.1 | +56 04 |
| ξ Ursae Majoris (Mizar) | 2.26 | 0.04 | 88 | 13 23.1 | +55 02 |
| α Virginis (Spica) | 0.91v | 0.02 | 220 | 13 24.1 | −11 03 |
| ε Centauri | 2.33v | | 570 | 13 38.5 | −53 22 |
| η Ursae Majoris (Alkaid) | 1.87 | | 210 | 13 46.7 | +49 25 |
| β Centauri | 0.63v | 0.02 | 490 | 14 02.3 | −60 16 |
| θ Centauri | 2.04 | 0.06 | 55 | 14 05.4 | −36 16 |
| α Bootis (Arcturus) | −0.06 | 0.09 | 36 | 14 14.7 | +19 17 |
| η Centauri | 2.39v | | 390 | 14 34.2 | −42 04 |
| α Centauri | 0.01 | 0.75 | 4.3 | 14 38.2 | −60 45 |
| α Lupi | 2.32v | | 430 | 14 40.5 | −47 18 |
| ε Bootis | 2.37 | 0.01 | 103 | 14 44.1 | +27 10 |
| β Ursae Minoris | 2.07 | 0.03 | 105 | 14 50.8 | +74 14 |
| α Coronae Borealis | 2.23v | 0.04 | 76 | 15 33.8 | +26 47 |
| δ Scorpii | 2.34 | | 590 | 15 59.1 | −22 34 |
| α Scorpii (Antares) | 0.92v | 0.02 | 520 | 16 28.1 | −26 23 |
| α Trianguli Australis | 1.93 | 0.02 | 82 | 16 46.3 | −68 59 |
| ε Scorpii | 2.28 | 0.05 | 66 | 16 48.8 | −34 15 |
| η Ophiuchi | 2.43 | 0.05 | 69 | 17 09.2 | −15 42 |
| λ Scorpii | 1.60v | | 310 | 17 32.2 | −37 05 |
| α Ophiuchi | 2.09 | 0.06 | 58 | 17 34.0 | +12 34 |
| θ Scorpii | 1.86 | 0.02 | 650 | 17 35.8 | −42 59 |
| κ Scorpii | 2.39v | | 470 | 17 41.0 | −39 01 |
| γ Draconis | 2.21 | 0.02 | 108 | 17 56.1 | +51 29 |
| ε Sagittarii | 1.81 | 0.02 | 124 | 18 22.8 | −34 24 |
| α Lyrae (Vega) | 0.04 | 0.12 | 26.5 | 18 36.2 | +38 46 |
| σ Sagittarii | 2.12 | | 300 | 18 54.0 | −26 20 |
| α Aquilae (Altair) | 0.77 | 0.20 | 16.5 | 19 49.8 | +8 49 |
| γ Cygni | 2.22 | | 750 | 20 21.5 | +40 11 |
| α Pavonis | 1.95 | | 310 | 20 24.0 | −56 48 |
| α Cygni (Deneb) | 1.26 | | 1600 | 20 40.7 | +45 12 |
| ε Cygni | 2.46 | 0.04 | 74 | 20 45.4 | +33 53 |
| α Cephei | 2.44 | 0.06 | 52 | 21 18.1 | +62 30 |
| ε Pegasi | 2.38 | | 780 | 21 43.2 | +9 47 |
| α Gruis | 1.76 | 0.05 | 64 | 22 06.9 | −47 04 |
| β Gruis | 2.17v | | 280 | 22 41.4 | −47 00 |
| α Piscis Austrinis (Fomalhaut) | 1.15 | 0.14 | 22.6 | 22 56.5 | −29 44 |
| β Pegasi | 2.50v | 0.02 | 210 | 23 02.8 | +27 58 |
| α Pegasi | 2.50 | 0.03 | 109 | 23 03.7 | +15 06 |

## Aurora Borealis and Aurora Australis

The Aurora Borealis, also called the Northern Lights, is a broad display of rather faint light in the northern skies at night. The Aurora Australis, a similar phenomenon, appears at the same time in southern skies. The aurora appears in a wide variety of forms. Sometimes it is seen as a quiet glow, almost foglike in character; sometimes as vertical streamers in which there may be considerable motion; sometimes as a series of luminous expanding arcs. There are many colors, with white, yellow, and red predominating.

The auroras are most vivid and most frequently seen at about 20 degrees from the magnetic poles, along the northern coast of the North American continent and the eastern part of the northern coast of Europe. They have been seen as far south as Key West and as far north as Australia and New Zealand, but such occasions are rare.

While the cause of the auroras is not known beyond question, there does seem to be a definite correlation between auroral displays and sun-spot activity. It is thought that atomic particles ex-

pelled from the sun by the forces that cause solar flares speed through space at velocities of 400 to 600 miles per second. These particles are entrapped by the earth's magnetic field, forming what are termed the Van Allen belts. The encounter of these clouds of the solar wind with the earth's magnetic field weakens the field so that previously trapped particles are allowed to impact the upper atmosphere. The collisions between solar and terrestrial atoms result in the glow in the upper atmosphere called the aurora. The glow may be vivid where the lines of magnetic force converge near the magnetic poles.

The auroral displays appear at heights ranging from 50 to about 600 miles and have given us a means of estimating the extent of the earth's atmosphere.

The auroras are often accompanied by magnetic storms whose forces, also guided by the lines of force of the earth's magnetic field, disrupt electrical communication.

## Comet Table 1979-1986

| Name | Year of first known perihelion | Due to return | Period in years | Perihelion dist. | Aphelion dist. | Inclination to ecliptic degree | Long. of ascend. node degree | From asc. node to perihelion degree |
|---|---|---|---|---|---|---|---|---|
| hajn-Schaldach | 1949 | Jan. 1979 | 7.27 | 2.23 | 5.27 | 6 | 167 | 215 |
| iacobini-Zinner | 1900 | Feb. 1979 | 6.52 | 0.99 | 5.98 | 32 | 195 | 172 |
| olmes | 1892 | Feb. 1979 | 7.05 | 2.16 | 5.20 | 19 | 328 | 23 |
| onda-Mrkos-Pajdusakova | 1969 | Apr. 1980 | 5.28 | 0.58 | 5.48 | 13 | 233 | 185 |
| Virtanen | 1947 | May 1980 | 5.84 | 1.26 | 5.25 | 12 | 84 | 35 |
| ohoutek* | 1975 | Aug. 1980 | 5.67 | 1.56 | 4.80 | 5 | 274 | 169 |
| orbes | 1929 | Oct. 1980 | 6.40 | 1.53 | 5.36 | 5 | 25 | 260 |
| rooks II | 1889 | Nov. 1980 | 6.88 | 1.84 | 5.39 | 6 | 176 | 198 |
| arrington | 1953 | Nov. 1980 | 6.80 | 1.58 | 5.59 | 9 | 119 | 233 |
| einmuth I | 1928 | Nov. 1980 | 7.63 | 2.00 | 5.75 | 8 | 121 | 9 |
| ncke | 1786 | Dec. 1980 | 3.30 | 0.34 | 4.02 | 12 | 334 | 186 |
| uttle | 1790 | Jan. 1981 | 13.77 | 1.02 | 10.47 | 54 | 270 | 207 |
| einmuth II | 1947 | Feb. 1981 | 6.74 | 1.94 | 5.20 | 7 | 296 | 45 |
| orrelly | 1905 | Feb. 1981 | 6.76 | 1.32 | 5.84 | 30 | 75 | 353 |
| chwassmann-Wachmann II | 1929 | Feb. 1981 | 6.51 | 2.14 | 4.83 | 4 | 126 | 357 |
| eujmin II | 1916 | May 1981 | 5.43 | 1.34 | 4.84 | 11 | 328 | 194 |
| inlay | 1886 | June 1981 | 6.95 | 1.10 | 6.19 | 4 | 42 | 322 |
| tephan-Oterma | 1867 | Oct. 1981 | 38.84 | 1.60 | 21.34 | 18 | 79 | 358 |
| wift-Gehrels | 1889 | Nov. 1981 | 9.23 | 1.35 | 7.44 | 9 | 314 | 84 |
| laughter-Burnham | 1958 | Nov. 1981 | 11.62 | 2.54 | 7.72 | 8 | 346 | 44 |
| ehrels II* | 1973 | Nov. 1981 | 7.94 | 2.35 | 5.61 | 7 | 216 | 183 |
| earns-Kwee | 1963 | Dec. 1981 | 9.01 | 2.23 | 6.43 | 9 | 315 | 131 |
| terma | 1942 | Jan. 1982 | 7.88 | 3.39 | 4.53 | 4 | 155 | 355 |
| errine-Mrkos | 1896 | Apr. 1982 | 6.72 | 1.27 | 5.85 | 18 | 240 | 166 |
| ale | 1927 | June 1982 | 10.99 | 1.18 | 8.70 | 12 | 67 | 209 |
| wift-Tuttle* | 1862 | Aug. 1982 | 119.98 | 0.96 | 47.69 | 114 | 139 | 153 |
| unn | 1969 | Nov. 1982 | 6.80 | 2.45 | 4.74 | 10 | 68 | 198 |
| alley | 240 B.C. | May 1986 | 76.1 | 0.59 | 35.3 | 162 | 58 | 112 |

*One appearance only.

Most of the comets in the table will not be seen except by rofessional astronomers or by well-equipped amateurs. At ny given time, these observers may be able to follow about half dozen comets of which the public is unaware. An easy seen comet is rare, one or two every ten to fifteen years.

Comets are named for their discoverers, up to three independent observers being so honored. If a comet becomes unsual, it may be well-known by these names. Usually, however, a preliminary designation is used: the year followed by a letter of the alphabet assigned in the order of discovery during that year. About two years later after any likely late discoveries, comets are given their permanent designation which states the year of their perihelion passage and a Roman numeral giving the order of passage during that year. Well-known periodic comets receive these designations at each appearance, but the literature and the Comet Table will continue to identify them by their discoverers' names.

## Moon's Perigee and Apogee, 1979

| | Perigee | | | | | | Apogee | | | | | |
|---|---|---|---|---|---|---|---|---|---|---|---|---|
| Day | Hour GMT | EST | Day | Hour GMT | EST | Day | Hour GMT | EST | Day | Hour GMT | EST | |
| an. 28 | 10 | 05 | Aug. 8 | 19 | 14 | Jan. 15 | 03 | 22* | July 27 | 00 | 19* | |
| Feb. 25 | 22 | 17 | Sept. 6 | 05 | 00 | Feb. 11 | 03 | 22* | Aug. 3 | 07 | 02 | |
| Mar. 26 | 06 | 01 | Oct. 4 | 15 | 10 | Mar. 10 | 10 | 05 | Sept. 19 | 10 | 05 | |
| Apr. 22 | 22 | 17 | Nov. 1 | 20 | 15 | Apr. 7 | 03 | 22* | Oct. 16 | 20 | 15 | |
| May 18 | 09 | 04 | Nov. 29 | 00 | 19* | May 4 | 22 | 17 | Nov. 13 | 14 | 09 | |
| une 13 | 16 | 11 | Dec. 23 | 16 | 11 | June 1 | 17 | 12 | Dec. 11 | 11 | 06 | |
| uly 11 | 12 | 07 | | | | June 29 | 11 | 06 | | | | |

Previous date.

## Largest Telescopes Are in Northern Hemisphere

Most of the world's major astronomical installations are n the northern hemisphere, while many of astronomy's major problems are found in the southern sky. This imbalance as long been recognized and is being remedied.

In the northern hemisphere the largest reflector is the 236-nch mirror at the Special Astrophysical Observatory in the Caucasus in the Soviet Union. The largest reflectors in the U.S. include 3 in California: at Palomar Mtn., 200 inches; at Lick Observatory, Mt. Hamilton, 120 inches; and at Mt. Wilson Observatory, 100 inches. Also in the U.S. are a 158 inch reflector at Kitt Peak, Arizona, dedicated in June 1973, and a 107-inch telescope at the McDonald Observatory on Mt. Locke in Texas. A telescope at the Crimean Astrophysical Observatory in the Soviet Union has a 104-inch mirror.

Placed in service in 1975 were three large reflectors for the southern hemisphere. Associated Universities for Research in Astronomy (AURA), the operating organization of Kitt Peak National Observatory, dedicated the 158-inch reflector (twin of the telescope on Kitt Peak) at Cerro Tololo International Observatory, Chile; the European Southern Observatory has a 141-inch reflector at La Silla, Chile; and the Anglo-Australian telescope, 152 inches in diameter, is at Siding Spring Observatory in Australia.

### Optical Telescopes

Optical astronomical telescopes are of two kinds, refracting and reflecting. In the first, light passes through a lens which brings the light rays into focus, where the image may be examined after being magnified by a second lens, the eyepiece, or directly photographed.

The reflector consists of a concave parabolic mirror, generally of Pyrex or now of a relatively heat insensitive material, cervit, coated with silver or aluminum, which reflects the light rays back toward the upper end of the telescope, where they are either magnified and observed by the eyepiece or, as in the case of the refractors, photographed. In most reflecting telescopes, the light is reflected again by a secondary mirror and comes to a focus after passing through a hole in the side of the telescope, where the eye-piece or camera is located, or after passing through a hole in the center of the primary mirror.

## World's Largest Refractors

Location and diameter in inches

| | |
|---|---:|
| Yerkes Obs., Williams Bay, Wis. | 40 |
| Lick Obs., Mt. Hamilton, Cal. | 36 |
| Astrophys. Obs., Potsdam, E. Germany | 32 |
| Paris Observatory, Meudon, France | 32 |
| Allegheny Obs., Pittsburgh, Pa. | 30 |
| Univ. of Paris, Nice, France | 30 |
| Royal Greenwich Obs., Herstmonceux, England | 28 |
| Union Obs., Johannesburg, South Africa | 26.5 |
| Universitats-Sternwarte, Vienna, Austria | 26.5 |
| University of Virginia | 26 |
| Obs., Academy of Sciences, Pulkova, USSR | 26 |
| Astronomical Obs., Belgrade, Yugoslavia | 26 |
| Leander McCormick Obs., Charlottesville, Va. | 26 |
| Obs. Mitaka, Tokyo-to, Japan | 26 |
| US Naval Obs., Washington, D.C. | 26 |
| Mt. Stromlo Obs., Canberra, Australia | 26 |

## World's Largest Reflectors

| | |
|---|---:|
| Special Astrophysical Obs., Zelenchukskaya, USSR | 236 |
| Hale Obs., Palomar Mtn., Cal. | 200, 100, 60 |
| Kitt Peak National Obs., Tucson, Ariz. | 158, 84, 60 |
| Cerro Tololo, Chile | 158, 60 |
| Siding Spring, Australia | 153 |
| La Silla, Chile | 141, 60 |
| Lick Obs., Mt. Hamilton, Cal. | 120 |
| McDonald Obs., Fort Davis, Tex. | 107, 82 |
| Crimean Astrophys. Obs., Nauchny, USSR | 104 |

| | |
|---|---:|
| Byurakan Obs., Armenia S.S.R. | 102 |
| Royal Greenwich Obs., Herstmonceux, England | 98 |
| Steward Obs., Tucson, Ariz. | 90 |
| Mauna Kea Obs., Univ. of Hawaii, Ha. | 88, 84 |
| Shemakha Astroph. Obs., Azerbaijan S.S.R. | 79 |
| Saint Michel l'Observatoire, (Basses Alpes), Fr. | 77 |
| Haute Provence, France | 76, 60 |
| Tokyo Obs., Japan | 74 |
| Mt. Stromlo, Australia | 74 |
| David Dunlap Obs., Ont., Canada | 74 |
| Helwan Obs., Helwan, Egypt | 74 |
| Astrophys. Obs., Kamogata, Okayama-ken, Japan | 74 |
| Sutherland, South Africa | 74 |
| Dominion Astrophys. Obs., Victoria, B.C. | 73 |
| Perkins Obs., Flagstaff, Ariz. | 72 |
| Obs., Padua Univ., Asiago, Italy | 72 |
| Agassiz Station Harvard Obs., Cambridge, Mass. | 61 |
| National Obs., Bosque Alegre Sta., Argentina | 61 |
| U.S. Naval Obs., Flagstaff, Ariz. | 61 |
| Catalina Mtn., Ariz. | 61 |
| Arizona Univ. Obs., Tucson, Ariz. | 60 |
| Boyden Obs., Bloemfontein, South Africa | 60 |
| Mt. Haleakala, Ha. | 60 |
| Mt. Hopkins (SAO), Ariz. | 60 |
| Figl Astroph. Obs., Vienna, Austria | 60 |
| Mt. Wilson Obs., Pasadena, Cal. | 60 |

## Major U.S. Planetariums

Academy Planetarium, U.S. Air Force Academy
Adler Planetarium, Chicago, Ill.
American Museum-Hayden Planetarium, N.Y.C.
Buhl Planetarium, Pittsburgh, Pa.
Charles Hayden Planetarium, Boston, Mass.
Einstein Spacearium, Washington, D.C.
Fels Planetarium, Philadelphia, Pa.
Fernbank Science Center Planetarium, Altanta, Ga.
Griffith Planetarium, Los Angeles, Cal.
La. Arts and Science Planetarium, Baton Rouge, La.
McDonnell Planetarium, St. Louis, Mo.
Morehead Planetarium, Chapel Hill, N.C.
Morrison Planetarium, San Francisco, Cal.
Robert T. Longway Planetarium, Flint, Mich.
Strassenburgh Planetarium, Rochester, N.Y.

# The Sun

The sun, the controlling body of our solar system, is a star whose dimensions cause it to be classified among stars as average in size, temperature, and brightness. Its proximity to the earth makes it appear to us as tremendously large and bright. A series of thermo-nuclear reactions involving the atoms of the elements of which it is composed produces the heat and light that make life possible on earth.

The sun has a diameter of 864,000 miles and is distant, on the average, 92,900,000 miles from the earth. It is 1.41 times as dense as water. The light of the sun reaches the earth in 499.012 seconds or slightly more than 8 minutes. The average solar surface temperature has been measured by several indirect methods which agree closely on a value of 6,000° Kelvin or about 10,000° F. The interior temperature of the sun is about 35,000,000 F.°.

When sunlight is analyzed with a spectroscope, it is found to consist of a continuous spectrum composed of all the colors of the rainbow in order, crossed by many dark lines. The "absorption lines" are produced by gaseous materials in the atmosphere of the sun. More than 60 of the natural terrestrial elements have been identified in the sun, all in gaseous form because of the intense heat of the sun.

## Spheres and Corona

The radiating surface of the sun is called the **photosphere**, and just above it is the **chromosphere**. The chromosphere is visible to the naked eye only at times of total solar eclipses, appearing then to be a pinkish-violet layer with occasional great prominences projecting above its general level. With proper instruments the chromosphere can be seen or photographed whenever the sun is visible without waiting for a total eclipse. Above the chromosphere is the **corona**, also visible to the naked eye only at times of total eclipse. Instruments also permit the brighter portions of the corona to be studied whenever conditions are favorable. The pearly light of the corona surges millions of miles from the sun. Iron, nickel, and calcium are believed to be principal contributors to the composition of the corona, all in a state of extreme attenuation and high ionization that indicates temperatures on the order of a million degrees Fahrenheit.

## Sunspots

There is an intimate connection between sunspots and the corona. At times of low sunspot activity, the fine streamers of the corona will be much longer above the sun's equator than over the polar regions of the sun, while during high sunspot activity, the corona extends fairly evenly outward from all regions of the sun, but to a much greater distance in space. Sunspots are dark, irregularly-shaped regions whose diameters may reach tens of thousands of miles. The average life of a sunspot group is from two to three weeks, but there have been groups that have lasted for more than a year, being carried repeatedly around as the sun rotated upon its xis. The record for the duration of a sunspot is 18 months. unspots reach a low point every 11.3 years, with a peak of ctivity occurring irregularly between two successive min- na.

The sun is 400,000 times as bright as the full moon and gives the earth 6 million times as much light as do all the other stars put together. Actually, most of the stars that can be easily seen on any clear night are brighter than the sun.

# The Moon

The moon completes a circuit around the earth in a period vhose mean or average duration is 27 days 7 hours 43.2 minutes. This is the moon's sidereal period. The motion of the moon in common with the earth around the un, the mean duration of the lunar month — the period rom one new moon to the next new moon — is 29 days 12 hours 44.05 minutes. This is the moon's synodical period.

The mean distance of the moon from the earth according to the American Ephemeris is 238,857 miles. Because the orbit of the moon about the earth is not circular but ellipti- al, however, the maximum distance from the earth that the moon may reach is 252,710 miles and the least distance is 221,463 miles. All distances are from the center of one ob- ect to the center of the other.

The moon's diameter is 2,160 miles. If we deduct the ra- dius of the moon, 1,080 miles, and the radius of the earth, 3,963 miles from the minimum distance or perigee, given above, we shall have for the nearest approach of the bodies' surfaces 216,420 miles.

The moon rotates on its axis in a period of time exactly equal to its sidereal revolution about the earth — 27.321666 days. The moon's revolution about the earth is irregular be- cause of its elliptical orbit. The moon's rotation, however, is regular and this, together with the irregular revolution, pro- duces what is called "libration in longitude" which permits us to see first farther around the east side and then farther

around the west side of the moon. The moon's variation north or south of the ecliptic permits us to see farther over first one pole and then the other of the moon and this is "li- bration in latitude." These two libration effects permit us to see a total of about 60% of the moon's surface over a period of time. The hidden side of the moon was photographed in 1959 by the Soviet space vehicle Lunik III. Since then many excellent pictures have been transmitted to earth by Lunar Orbiters launched by the U.S.

The tides are caused mainly by the moon, because of its proximity to the earth. The ratio of the tide-raising power of the moon to that of the sun is 11 to 5.

## Harvest Moon and Hunter's Moon

The Harvest Moon, the full moon nearest the Autumnal Equinox, ushers in a period of several successive days when the moon rises soon after sunset. This phenomenon gives farmers in temperate latitudes extra hours of light in which to harvest their crops before frost and winter come. The 1979 Harvest Moon falls on Oct. 5. Harvest moon in the south temperate latitudes falls on Mar. 13.

The next full moon after Harvest Moon is called the Hun- ter's Moon, accompanied by a similar phenomenon but less marked; — Nov. 4, northern hemisphere; Apr. 12, southern hemisphere.

# The Zodiac

The sun's apparent yearly path among the stars is known as the **ecliptic**. The zone 16° wide, 8° on each side of the ecliptic, is known as the **zodiac**. Inside of this zone are the apparent paths of the sun, moon, earth, and major planets. Beginning at the point on the ecliptic which marks the posi- tion of the sun at the vernal equinox, and thence proceeding eastward, the zodiac is divided into twelve signs of 30° each, as shown herewith.

These signs are named from the twelve constellations of the zodiac with which the signs coincided in the time of the astronomer Hipparchus, about 2,000 years ago. Owing to the precession of the equinoxes, that is to say, to the retro- grade motion of the equinoxes along the ecliptic, each sign in the zodiac has, in the course of 2,000 years, moved back- ward 30° into the constellation west of it; so that the sign Aries is now in the constellation Pisces, and so on. The ver-

nal equinox will move from Pisces into Aquarius about the middle of the 26th century. The signs of the zodiac with their Latin and English names are as follows:

| Spring | 1. | ♈ Aries. | The Ram. |
|--------|-----|----------|----------|
|        | 2. | ♉ Taurus. | The Bull. |
|        | 3. | ♊ Gemini. | The Twins. |
| Summer | 4. | ♋ Cancer. | The Crab. |
|        | 5. | ♌ Leo. | The Lion. |
|        | 6. | ♍ Virgo. | The Virgin. |
| Autumn | 7. | ♎ Libra. | The Balance. |
|        | 8. | ♏ Scorpio. | The Scorpion. |
|        | 9. | ♐ Sagittarius. | The Archer. |
| Winter | 10. | ♑ Capricorn. | The Goat. |
|        | 11. | ♒ Aquarius. | The Water Bearer. |
|        | 12. | ♓ Pisces. | The Fishes. |

# The Earth: Size, Computation of Time, Seasons

## Size and Dimensions

The earth is the fifth largest planet and the third from the sun. Its mass is 6 sextillion, 588 quintillion short tons. Using the parameters of an ellipsoid adopted by the International Astronomical Union in 1964 and recognized by the Interna- tional Union of Geodesy and Geophysics in 1967, the length of the equator is 24,901.55 miles, the length of a meridian is 24,859.82 miles, the equatorial diameter is 7,926.41 miles, and the area of this reference ellipsoid is approximately 196,938,800 square miles.

The earth is considered a solid, rigid mass with a dense core of magnetic, probably metallic material. The outer part of the core is probably liquid. Around the core is a thick shell or mantle of heavy crystalline rock which in turn is covered by a thin crust forming the solid granite and basalt base of the continents and ocean basins. Over broad areas of

the earth's surface the crust has a thin cover of sedimentary rock such as sandstone, shale, and limestone formed by weathering of the earth's surface and deposition of sands, clays, and plant and animal remains.

The temperature in the earth increases about 1°F. with every 100 to 200 feet in depth, in the upper 100 kilometers of the earth, and the temperature near the core is believed to be near the melting point of the core materials under the conditions at that depth. The heat of the earth is believed to be derived from radioactivity in the rocks, pressures devel- oped within the earth, and original heat (if the earth in fact was formed at high temperatures).

## Atmosphere of the Earth

The earth's atmosphere is a blanket composed of nitrogen, oxygen, and argon, in amounts of about 78, 21, and 1% by volume. Also present in minute quantities are carbon dioxide, hydrogen, neon, helium, krypton, and xenon.

Water vapor displaces other gases and varies from nearly zero to about 4% by volume. The height of the ozone layer varies from approximately 12 to 21 miles above the earth. Traces exist as low as 6 miles and as high as 35 miles. Traces of methane have been found.

The atmosphere rests on the earth's surface with the weight equivalent to a layer of water 34 ft. deep. For about 300,000 ft. upward the gases remain in the proportions stated. Gravity holds the gases to the earth. The weight of the air compresses it at the bottom, so that the greatest density is at the earth's surface. Pressure, as well as density, decreases as height increases because the weight pressing upon any layer is always less than that pressing upon the layers below.

The temperature of the air drops with increased height until the **tropopause** is reached. This may vary from 25,000 to 60,000 ft. The atmosphere below the tropopause is the **troposphere**; the atmosphere for about twenty miles above the tropopause is the **stratosphere**, where the temperature generally increases with height except at high latitudes in winter. A temperature maximum near the 30-mile level is called the **stratopause**. Above this boundary is the **mesosphere** where the temperature decreases with height to a minimum, the **mesopause**, at a height of 50 miles. Extending above the mesosphere to the outer fringes of the atmosphere is the **thermosphere**, a region where temperature increases with height to a value measured in thousands of degrees Fahrenheit. The lower portion of this region, extending from 50 to about 400 miles in altitude, is characterized by a high ion density, and is thus called the **ionosphere**. The outer region is called **exosphere**; this is the region where gas molecules traveling at high speed may escape into outer space, above 600 miles.

## Latitude, Longitude

Position on the globe is measured by means of meridians and parallels. Meridians, which are imaginary lines drawn around the earth through the poles, determine **longitude**. The meridian running through Greenwich, England, is the **prime meridian of longitude**, and all others are either east or west. Parallels, which are imaginary circles parallel with the equator, determine **latitude**. The length of a degree of longitude varies as the cosine of the latitude. At the equator a degree is 69.171 statute miles; this is gradually reduced toward the poles. Value of a longitude degree at the poles is zero.

**Latitude** is reckoned by the number of degrees north or south of the equator, an imaginary circle on the earth's surface everywhere equidistant between the two poles. According to the IAU Ellipsoid of 1964, the length of a degree of latitude is 68.708 statute miles at the equator and varies slightly north and south because of the oblate form of the globe; at the poles it is 69.403 statute miles.

## Computation of Time

The earth rotates on its axis and follows an elliptical orbit around the sun. The rotation makes the sun appear to move across the sky from East to West. It determines day and night and the complete rotation, in relation to the sun, is called the **apparent** or **true solar day.** This varies but an average determines the **mean solar day** of 24 hours.

The mean solar day is in universal use for civil purposes. It may be obtained from apparent solar time by correcting observations of the sun for the equation of time, but when high precision is required, the mean solar time is calculated from its relation to sidereal time. These relations are extremely complicated, but for most practical uses, they may be considered as follows:

**Sidereal time** is the measure of time defined by the diurnal motion of the vernal equinox, and is determined from observation of the meridian transits of stars. One complete rotation of the earth relative to the equinox is called the **sidereal day**. The **mean sidereal day** is 23 hours, 56 minutes, 4,091 seconds of mean solar time.

The **Calendar Year** begins at 12 o'clock precisely local clock time, on the night of Dec. 31-Jan. 1. The day and the calendar month also begin at midnight by the clock. The interval required for the earth to make one absolute revolution around the sun is a **sidereal year;** it consisted of 36 days, 6 hours, 9 minutes, and 9.5 seconds of mean solar time (approximately 24 hours per day) in 1900, and is increasing at the rate of 0.0001-second annually.

The **Tropical Year**, on which the return of the seasons depends, is the interval between two consecutive returns of the sun to the vernal equinox. The tropical year consists of 36. days, 5 hours, 48 minutes, and 46 seconds in 1900. It is decreasing at the rate of 0.530 seconds per century.

In 1956 the unit of time interval was defined to be identical with the second of **Ephemeris Time**, 1/31,556,925.974 of the tropical year for 1900 January 0d 12th hour E.T. A physical definition of the second based on a quantum transition of cesium (atomic second) was adopted in 1964. The atomic second is equal to 9,192,631,770 cycles of the emitted radiation. In 1967 this atomic second was adopted as the unit of time interval for the Intern'l System of Units.

## The Zones and Seasons

The five zones of the earth's surface are Torrid, lying between the Tropics of Cancer and Capricorn; North Temperate, between Cancer and the Arctic Circle; South Temperate between Capricorn and the Antarctic Circle; The Frigid Zones, between the polar Circles and the Poles.

The inclination or tilt of the earth's axis with respect to the sun determines the seasons. These are commonly marked in the North Temperate Zone, where spring begins at the vernal equinox, summer at the summer solstice, autumn at the autumnal equinox and winter at the winter solstice.

In the South Temperate Zone, the seasons are reversed Spring begins at the autumnal equinox, summer at the winter solstice, etc.

If the earth's axis were perpendicular to the plane of the earth's orbit around the sun there would be no change of seasons. Day and night would be of nearly constant length and there would be equable conditions of temperature. But the axis is tilted 23° 27′ away from a perpendicular to the orbit and only in March and September is the axis at right angles to the sun.

The points at which the sun crosses the equator are the equinoxes, when day and night are most nearly equal. The points at which the sun is at a maximum distance from the equator are the solstices. Days and nights are then most unequal.

In June the North Pole is tilted 23° 27′ toward the sun and the days in the northern hemisphere are longer than the nights, while the days in the southern hemisphere are shorter than the nights. In December the North Pole is tilted 23° 27′ away from the sun and the situation is reversed.

### The Seasons in 1979

In 1979 the 4 seasons will begin as follows: add one hour to EST for Atlantic Time; subtract one hour for Central two hours for Mountain, 3 hours for Pacific, 4 hours for Yukon, 5 hours for Alaska-Hawaii and six hours for Bering Time. Also shown in Greenwich Mean Time.

| | Date | GMT | EST |
|---|---|---|---|
| Vernal Equinox | **Spring** Mar. 21 | 05:22 | 00:22 |
| Summer Solstice | **Summer** June 21 | 23:56 | 18:56 |
| Autumnal Equinox | **Autumn** Sept. 23 | 15:17 | 10:17 |
| Winter Solstice | **Winter** Dec. 22 | 11:10 | 06:10 |

## Poles of The Earth

The geographic (rotation) poles, or points where the earth's axis of rotation cuts the surface, are not absolutely fixed in the body of the earth. The pole of rotation describes an irregular curve about its mean position.

Two periods have been detected in this motion: (1) an annual period due to seasonal changes in barometric pressure load of ice and snow on the surface and to other phenomena of seasonal character; (2) a period of about 14 months due to the shape and constitution of the earth.

In addition there are small but as yet unpredictable irregularities. The whole motion is so small that the actual pole at any time remains within a circle of 30 or 40 feet in radius centered at the mean position of the pole.

The pole of rotation for the time being is of course the pole having a latitude of 90° and an indeterminate longitude.

## Magnetic Poles

The **north magnetic pole** of the earth is that region where the magnetic force is vertically downward and the **south magnetic pole** that region where the magnetic force is vertically upward. A compass placed at the magnetic poles experiences no directive force.

There are slow changes in the distribution of the earth's magnetic field. These changes were at one time attributed in part to a periodic movement of the magnetic poles around the geographical poles, but later evidence refutes this theory and points, rather, to a slow migration of "disturbance" foci over the earth.

There appear shifts in position of the magnetic poles due to the changes in the earth's magnetic field. The center of the area designated as the north magnetic pole was estimated to be in about latitude 70.5° N and longitude 96° W in 1905; from recent nearby measurements and studies of the secular changes, the position in 1970 is estimated as latitude 75.2° N and longitude 101° W. Improved data rather than actual motion account for at least part of the change.

The position of the south magnetic pole in 1912 was near 71° S and longitude 150° E; the position in 1970 is estimated at latitude 66° S and longitude 139.1° E.

The direction of the horizontal components of the magnetic field at any point is known as magnetic north at that point, and the angle by which it deviates east or west of true north is known as the magnetic declination, or in the mariner's terminology, the **variation of the compass.**

A compass without error points in the direction of magnetic north. (In general this is *not* the direction of the magnetic north pole.) If one follows the direction indicated by the north end of the compass, he will travel along a rather irregular curve which eventually reaches the north magnetic pole (though not usually by a great-circle route). However,

the action of the compass should not be thought of as due to any influence of the distant pole, but simply as an indication of the distribution of the earth's magnetism at the place of observation.

## Rotation of The Earth

The **speed of** rotation of the earth about its axis has been found to be slightly variable. The variations may be classified as:

(A) **Secular.** Tidal friction acts as a brake on the rotation and causes a slow secular increase in the length of the day, about 1 millisecond per century.

(B) **Irregular.** The speed of rotation may increase for a number of years, about 5 to 10, and then start decreasing. The maximum difference from the mean in the length of the day during a century is about 5 milliseconds. The accumulated difference in time has amounted to approximately 44 seconds since 1900. The cause is probably motion in the interior of the earth.

(C) **Periodic.** Seasonal variations exist with periods of one year and six months. The cumulative effect is such that each year the earth is late about 30 milliseconds near June 1 and is ahead about 30 milliseconds near Oct. 1. The maximum seasonal variation in the length of the day is about 0.5 millisecond. It is believed that the principal cause of the annual variation is the seasonal change in the wind patterns of the Northern and Southern Hemispheres. The semiannual variation is due chiefly to tidal action of the sun, which distorts the shape of the earth slightly.

The secular and irregular variations were discovered by comparing time based on the rotation of the earth with time based on the orbital motion of the moon about the earth and of the planets about the sun. The periodic variation was determined, largely with the aid of quartz-crystal clocks. The introduction of the cesium-beam atomic clock in 1955 made it possible to determine in greater detail than before the nature of the irregular and periodic variations.

## Astronomical Twilight—Meridian of Greenwich

| Date 1979 | 20° Begin h m | 20° End h m | 30° Begin h m | 30° End h m | 40° Begin h m | 40° End h m | 50° Begin h m | 50° End h m | 60° Begin h m | 60° End h m |
|---|---|---|---|---|---|---|---|---|---|---|
| Jan. 1 | 5 16 | 6 50 | 5 30 | 6 35 | 5 45 | 6 21 | 6 00 | 6 07 | 6 18 | 5 49 |
| 11 | 5 19 | 6 56 | 5 33 | 6 43 | 5 46 | 6 30 | 6 00 | 6 17 | 6 15 | 6 01 |
| 21 | 5 21 | 7 01 | 5 32 | 6 51 | 5 43 | 6 40 | 5 55 | 6 30 | 6 06 | 6 18 |
| Feb. 1 | 5 21 | 7 07 | 5 29 | 6 58 | 5 38 | 6 51 | 5 45 | 6 44 | 5 51 | 6 38 |
| 11 | 5 18 | 7 11 | 5 24 | 7 05 | 5 29 | 7 01 | 5 32 | 6 59 | 5 32 | 7 01 |
| 21 | 5 13 | 7 15 | 5 17 | 7 12 | 5 17 | 7 12 | 5 16 | 7 14 | 5 09 | 7 23 |
| Mar. 1 | 5 08 | 7 18 | 5 08 | 7 19 | 5 06 | 7 21 | 4 59 | 7 29 | 4 44 | 7 45 |
| 11 | 5 00 | 7 21 | 4 58 | 7 24 | 4 50 | 7 32 | 4 38 | 7 46 | 4 12 | 8 12 |
| 21 | 4 52 | 7 24 | 4 45 | 7 32 | 4 33 | 7 44 | 4 14 | 8 04 | 3 37 | 8 43 |
| Apr. 1 | 4 42 | 7 28 | 4 31 | 7 39 | 4 14 | 7 57 | 3 47 | 8 25 | 2 53 | 9 21 |
| 11 | 4 32 | 7 32 | 4 18 | 7 47 | 3 56 | 8 09 | 3 20 | 8 47 | 2 03 | 10 10 |
| 21 | 4 23 | 7 36 | 4 04 | 7 54 | 3 37 | 8 23 | 2 52 | 9 11 | 0 37 | 11 47 |
| May 1 | 4 14 | 7 41 | 3 52 | 8 04 | 3 19 | 8 37 | 2 22 | 9 39 | | |
| 11 | 4 08 | 7 46 | 3 41 | 8 13 | 3 03 | 8 53 | 1 49 | 10 09 | | |
| 21 | 4 02 | 7 52 | 3 32 | 8 22 | 2 48 | 9 07 | 1 13 | 10 46 | | |
| June 1 | 3 58 | 7 58 | 3 26 | 8 30 | 2 36 | 9 20 | 0 21 | 11 52 | | |
| 11 | 3 56 | 8 03 | 3 22 | 8 36 | 2 29 | 9 30 | | | | |
| 21 | 3 57 | 8 06 | 3 22 | 8 40 | 2 28 | 9 35 | | | | |
| July 1 | 3 59 | 8 07 | 3 25 | 8 41 | 2 30 | 9 35 | | | | |
| 11 | 4 03 | 8 06 | 3 30 | 8 39 | 2 40 | 9 30 | | | | |
| 21 | 4 08 | 8 03 | 3 39 | 8 33 | 2 52 | 9 18 | 1 12 | 11 23 | | |
| Aug. 1 | 4 15 | 7 56 | 3 48 | 8 23 | 3 09 | 9 01 | 1 49 | 10 20 | | |
| 11 | 4 20 | 7 50 | 3 56 | 8 13 | 3 22 | 8 46 | 2 21 | 9 46 | | |
| 21 | 4 24 | 7 41 | 4 05 | 8 01 | 3 34 | 8 27 | 2 47 | 9 15 | | |
| Sept. 1 | 4 29 | 7 31 | 4 14 | 7 46 | 3 51 | 8 08 | 3 13 | 8 43 | 1 40 | 10 02 |
| 11 | 4 32 | 7 20 | 4 20 | 7 33 | 4 02 | 7 50 | 3 33 | 8 16 | 2 36 | 9 12 |
| 21 | 4 35 | 7 11 | 4 26 | 7 19 | 4 14 | 7 31 | 3 52 | 7 52 | 3 11 | 8 31 |
| Oct. 1 | 4 38 | 7 02 | 4 33 | 7 05 | 4 25 | 7 13 | 4 10 | 7 28 | 3 41 | 7 54 |
| 11 | 4 40 | 6 53 | 4 40 | 6 53 | 4 35 | 6 58 | 4 26 | 7 05 | 4 07 | 7 23 |
| 21 | 4 43 | 6 47 | 4 45 | 6 44 | 4 45 | 6 43 | 4 41 | 6 46 | 4 32 | 6 55 |
| Nov. 1 | 4 46 | 6 41 | 4 52 | 6 34 | 4 56 | 6 30 | 4 58 | 6 27 | 4 56 | 6 27 |
| 11 | 4 50 | 6 38 | 4 59 | 6 28 | 5 06 | 6 21 | 5 13 | 6 14 | 5 17 | 6 08 |
| 21 | 4 55 | 6 36 | 5 06 | 6 25 | 5 16 | 6 15 | 5 26 | 6 04 | 5 37 | 5 52 |
| Dec. 1 | 5 00 | 6 37 | 5 13 | 6 24 | 5 25 | 6 11 | 5 38 | 5 58 | 5 53 | 5 42 |
| 11 | 5 06 | 6 40 | 5 20 | 6 26 | 5 34 | 6 12 | 5 48 | 5 57 | 6 06 | 5 38 |
| 21 | 5 11 | 6 45 | 5 25 | 6 30 | 5 39 | 6 16 | 5 55 | 6 00 | 6 15 | 5 40 |
| 31 | 5 15 | 6 50 | 5 30 | 6 35 | 5 44 | 6 21 | 6 00 | 6 06 | 6 18 | 5 48 |

# Latitude, Longitude, and Altitude of North American Cities

Source: National Oceanic and Atmospheric Administration, U.S. Commerce Department for geographic positions.
Source for Canadian cities: Geodetic Survey of Canada, Dept. of Energy, Mines, and Resources.
Altitudes U.S. Geological Survey and various sources. *Approx. altitude at downtown business area U.S.; in Canada at tower of major airport.

| City | Lat. N ° | ' | " | Long. W ° | ' | " | Alt. feet |
|---|---|---|---|---|---|---|---|
| Abilene, Tex. | 32 | 27 | 05 | 99 | 43 | 51 | 1710 |
| Akron, Oh. | 41 | 05 | 00 | 81 | 30 | 44 | 874 |
| Albany, N.Y. | 42 | 39 | 01 | 73 | 45 | 01 | 20 |
| Albuquerque, N.M. | 35 | 05 | 01 | 106 | 39 | 05 | 4,945 |
| Allentown, Pa. | 40 | 36 | 11 | 75 | 28 | 06 | 255 |
| Altoona, Pa. | 40 | 30 | 55 | 78 | 24 | 03 | 1,180 |
| Amarillo, Tex. | 35 | 12 | 27 | 101 | 50 | 04 | 3,685 |
| Anchorage, Alas. | 61 | 10 | 00 | 149 | 59 | 00 | 118 |
| Ann Arbor, Mich. | 42 | 16 | 59 | 83 | 44 | 52 | 880 |
| Asheville, N.C. | 35 | 35 | 42 | 82 | 33 | 26 | 1,985 |
| Ashland, Ky. | 38 | 28 | 36 | 82 | 38 | 23 | 536 |
| Atlanta, Ga. | 33 | 45 | 10 | 84 | 23 | 37 | 1,050 |
| Atlantic City, N.J. | 39 | 21 | 32 | 74 | 25 | 53 | 10 |
| Augusta, Ga. | 33 | 28 | 20 | 81 | 58 | 00 | 143 |
| Augusta, Me. | 44 | 18 | 53 | 69 | 46 | 29 | 45 |
| Austin, Tex. | 30 | 16 | 09 | 97 | 44 | 37 | 505 |
| Bakersfield, Cal. | 35 | 22 | 31 | 119 | 01 | 18 | 400 |
| Baltimore, Md. | 39 | 17 | 26 | 76 | 36 | 45 | 20 |
| Bangor, Me. | 44 | 48 | 13 | 68 | 46 | 18 | 20 |
| Baton Rouge, La. | 30 | 26 | 58 | 91 | 11 | 00 | 57 |
| Battle Creek, Mich. | 42 | 18 | 58 | 85 | 10 | 48 | 820 |
| Bay City, Mich. | 43 | 36 | 04 | 83 | 53 | 15 | 595 |
| Beaumont, Tex. | 30 | 05 | 20 | 94 | 06 | 09 | 20 |
| Belleville, Ont. | 44 | 09 | 30 | 77 | 22 | 30 | 280 |
| Bellingham, Wash. | 48 | 45 | 34 | 122 | 28 | 36 | 60 |
| Berkeley, Cal. | 37 | 52 | 10 | 122 | 16 | 17 | 40 |
| Bethlehem, Pa. | 40 | 37 | 16 | 75 | 22 | 34 | 235 |
| Billings, Mon. | 45 | 47 | 00 | 108 | 30 | 04 | 3,120 |
| Biloxi, Miss. | 30 | 23 | 48 | 88 | 53 | 00 | 20 |
| Binghamton, N.Y. | 42 | 06 | 03 | 75 | 54 | 47 | 865 |
| Birmingham, Ala. | 33 | 31 | 01 | 86 | 48 | 36 | 600 |
| Bismarck, N.D. | 46 | 48 | 23 | 100 | 47 | 17 | 1,674 |
| Bloomington, | 40 | 28 | 58 | 88 | 59 | 36 | 800 |
| Boise, Ida. | 43 | 37 | 07 | 116 | 11 | 58 | 2,704 |
| Boston, Mass. | 42 | 21 | 24 | 71 | 03 | 25 | 21 |
| Bowling Green, Ky. | 36 | 59 | 41 | 86 | 26 | 33 | 510 |
| Brattleboro, Vt. | 42 | 51 | 06 | 72 | 33 | 48 | 300 |
| Brandon, Man. | 49 | 51 | 00 | 99 | 57 | 00 | 1,265 |
| Brantford, Ont. | 43 | 07 | 30 | 80 | 15 | 30 | 705 |
| Bridgeport, Conn. | 41 | 10 | 49 | 73 | 11 | 22 | 10 |
| Brockton, Mass. | 42 | 05 | 02 | 71 | 01 | 25 | 130 |
| Brownsville, Tex. | 25 | 54 | 07 | 97 | 29 | 58 | 35 |
| Buffalo, N.Y. | 42 | 52 | 52 | 78 | 52 | 21 | 585 |
| Burlington, Ont. | 43 | 18 | 30 | 79 | 46 | 30 | 875 |
| Burlington, Vt. | 44 | 28 | 34 | 73 | 12 | 46 | 110 |
| Butte, Mon. | 46 | 01 | 06 | 112 | 32 | 11 | 5,765 |
| Calgary, Alta. | 51 | 02 | 46 | 114 | 03 | 24 | 3,557 |
| Cambridge, Mass. | 42 | 22 | 01 | 71 | 06 | 22 | 20 |
| Camden, N.J. | 39 | 56 | 41 | 75 | 07 | 14 | 30 |
| Canton, Oh. | 40 | 47 | 50 | 81 | 22 | 37 | 1,030 |
| Carson City, Nev. | 39 | 10 | 00 | 119 | 46 | 00 | 4,680 |
| Cedar Rapids, Ia. | 41 | 58 | 01 | 91 | 39 | 53 | 730 |
| Central Islip, N.Y. | 40 | 47 | 24 | 73 | 12 | 00 | 80 |
| Champaign, Ill. | 40 | 07 | 05 | 88 | 14 | 48 | 740 |
| Charleston, S.C. | 32 | 46 | 35 | 79 | 55 | 53 | 9 |
| Charleston, W.Va. | 38 | 21 | 01 | 81 | 37 | 52 | 601 |
| Charlotte, N.C. | 35 | 13 | 44 | 80 | 50 | 45 | 720 |
| Charlottetown, P.E.I. | 46 | 14 | 00 | 63 | 07 | 45 | 181 |
| Chattanooga, Tenn. | 35 | 02 | 41 | 85 | 18 | 32 | 675 |
| Cheyenne, Wy. | 41 | 08 | 09 | 104 | 49 | 07 | 6,100 |
| Chicago, Ill. | 41 | 52 | 28 | 87 | 38 | 22 | 595 |
| Churchill, Man. | 58 | 45 | 15 | 94 | 10 | 00 | 94 |
| Cincinnati, Oh. | 39 | 06 | 07 | 84 | 30 | 35 | 550 |
| Cleveland, Oh. | 41 | 29 | 51 | 81 | 41 | 50 | 660 |
| Colorado Springs | 38 | 50 | 07 | 104 | 49 | 16 | 5,980 |
| Columbia, Mo. | 38 | 57 | 03 | 92 | 19 | 46 | 730 |
| Columbia, S.C. | 34 | 00 | 02 | 81 | 02 | 00 | 190 |
| Columbus, Ga. | 32 | 28 | 07 | 84 | 59 | 24 | 265 |
| Columbus, Oh. | 39 | 57 | 47 | 83 | 00 | 17 | 780 |
| Concord, N.H. | 43 | 12 | 22 | 71 | 32 | 25 | 290 |
| Corpus Christi, Tex. | 27 | 47 | 51 | 97 | 23 | 45 | 35 |
| Dallas, Tex. | 32 | 47 | 09 | 96 | 47 | 37 | 435 |
| Dartmouth, N.S. | 44 | 38 | 39 | 63 | 34 | 34 | 476 |
| Davenport, Ia. | 41 | 31 | 19 | 90 | 34 | 33 | 590 |
| Dawson, Yukon | 64 | 03 | 30 | 139 | 26 | 00 | 1,211 |
| Dayton, Oh. | 39 | 45 | 32 | 84 | 11 | 43 | 574 |
| Daytona Beach, Fla. | 29 | 12 | 44 | 81 | 01 | 10 | 7 |
| Decatur, Ill. | 39 | 50 | 42 | 88 | 56 | 47 | 682 |
| Denver, Col. | 39 | 44 | 58 | 104 | 59 | 22 | 5,280 |
| Des Moines, Ia. | 41 | 35 | 14 | 93 | 37 | 00 | 805 |
| Detroit, Mich. | 42 | 19 | 48 | 83 | 02 | 57 | 585 |
| Dodge City, Kan. | 37 | 45 | 17 | 100 | 01 | 09 | 2,480 |
| Dubuque, Ia. | 42 | 29 | 55 | 90 | 40 | 08 | 620 |
| Duluth, Minn. | 46 | 46 | 56 | 92 | 06 | 24 | 610 |
| Durham, N.C. | 36 | 00 | 00 | 78 | 54 | 45 | 405 |
| Eau Claire, Wis. | 44 | 48 | 31 | 91 | 29 | 49 | 790 |

| City | Lat. N ° | ' | " | Long. W ° | ' | " | Alt. feet |
|---|---|---|---|---|---|---|---|
| Edmonton, Alta. | 53 | 32 | 45 | 113 | 29 | 15 | 2,37 |
| El Paso, Tex. | 31 | 45 | 36 | 106 | 29 | 11 | 3,69 |
| Elizabeth, N.J. | 40 | 39 | 43 | 74 | 12 | 59 | 2 |
| Enid, Okla. | 36 | 23 | 40 | 97 | 52 | 35 | 1,24 |
| Erie, Pa. | 42 | 07 | 15 | 80 | 04 | 57 | 68 |
| Eugene, Ore. | 44 | 03 | 16 | 123 | 05 | 30 | 42 |
| Eureka, Cal. | 40 | 48 | 08 | 124 | 09 | 46 | 4 |
| Evansville, Ind. | 37 | 58 | 20 | 87 | 34 | 21 | 38 |
| Fairbanks, Alas. | 64 | 48 | 00 | 147 | 51 | 00 | 44 |
| Fall River, Mass. | 41 | 42 | 06 | 71 | 09 | 18 | 4 |
| Fargo, N.D. | 46 | 52 | 30 | 96 | 47 | 18 | 90 |
| Flagstaff, Ariz. | 35 | 11 | 36 | 111 | 39 | 06 | 6,90 |
| Flint, Mich. | 43 | 00 | 50 | 83 | 41 | 33 | 75 |
| Ft. Smith, Ark. | 35 | 23 | 10 | 94 | 25 | 36 | 44 |
| Fort Wayne, Ind. | 41 | 04 | 21 | 85 | 08 | 26 | 79 |
| Fort Worth, Tex. | 32 | 44 | 55 | 97 | 19 | 44 | 67 |
| Fredericton, N.B. | 45 | 57 | 40 | 66 | 38 | 30 | 6 |
| Fresno, Cal. | 36 | 44 | 12 | 119 | 47 | 11 | 28 |
| Gadsden, Ala. | 34 | 00 | 57 | 86 | 00 | 41 | 55 |
| Gainesville, Fla. | 29 | 38 | 56 | 82 | 19 | 19 | 17 |
| Gallup, N.M. | 35 | 31 | 30 | 108 | 44 | 30 | 6,54 |
| Galveston, Tex. | 29 | 18 | 10 | 94 | 47 | 43 | 5 |
| Gary, Ind. | 41 | 36 | 12 | 87 | 20 | 19 | 59 |
| Grand Junction, Col. | 39 | 04 | 06 | 108 | 33 | 54 | 4,59 |
| Grand Rapids, Mich. | 42 | 58 | 03 | 85 | 40 | 13 | 61 |
| Great Falls, Mon. | 47 | 29 | 33 | 111 | 18 | 23 | 3,34 |
| Green Bay, Wis. | 44 | 30 | 48 | 88 | 00 | 50 | 59 |
| Greensboro, N.C. | 36 | 04 | 17 | 79 | 47 | 25 | 83 |
| Greenville, S.C. | 34 | 50 | 50 | 82 | 24 | 01 | 96 |
| Guelph, Ont. | 43 | 32 | 30 | 80 | 15 | 30 | 1,07 |
| Gulfport, Miss. | 30 | 22 | 04 | 89 | 05 | 36 | 2 |
| Halifax, N.S. | 44 | 38 | 39 | 63 | 34 | | 47 |
| Hamilton, Ont. | 43 | 15 | 17 | 79 | 52 | 28 | 77 |
| Hamilton, Oh. | 39 | 23 | 59 | 84 | 33 | 47 | 60 |
| Harrisburg, Pa. | 40 | 15 | 43 | 76 | 52 | 59 | 365 |
| Hartford, Conn. | 41 | 46 | 12 | 72 | 40 | 49 | 40 |
| Helena, Mon. | 46 | 35 | 33 | 112 | 02 | 24 | 4,15 |
| Hilo, Hawaii | 19 | 43 | 30 | 155 | 05 | 24 | 40 |
| Holyoke, Mass. | 42 | 12 | 29 | 72 | 36 | 36 | 11 |
| Honolulu, Ha. | 21 | 18 | 22 | 157 | 51 | 35 | 2 |
| Houston, Tex. | 29 | 45 | 26 | 95 | 21 | 37 | 4 |
| Hull, Que. | 45 | 26 | 00 | 75 | 44 | 00 | 22 |
| Huntington, W.Va. | 38 | 25 | 12 | 82 | 26 | 33 | 56 |
| Huntsville, Ala. | 34 | 44 | 18 | 86 | 35 | 19 | 64 |
| Indianapolis, Ind. | 39 | 46 | 07 | 86 | 09 | 46 | 71 |
| Iowa City, Ia. | 41 | 39 | 37 | 91 | 31 | 53 | 68 |
| Jackson, Mich. | 42 | 14 | 43 | 84 | 24 | 22 | 94 |
| Jackson, Miss. | 32 | 17 | 56 | 90 | 11 | 06 | 29 |
| Jacksonville, Fla. | 30 | 19 | 44 | 81 | 39 | 42 | 2 |
| Jersey City, N.J. | 40 | 43 | 50 | 74 | 03 | 56 | 2 |
| Johnstown, Pa. | 40 | 19 | 35 | 78 | 55 | 03 | 1,18 |
| Joplin, Mo. | 37 | 05 | 26 | 94 | 42 | 11 | 99 |
| Juneau, Alas. | 58 | 18 | 12 | 134 | 24 | 30 | 5 |
| Kalamazoo, Mich. | 42 | 17 | 29 | 85 | 35 | 14 | 75 |
| Kansas City, Kan. | 39 | 07 | 04 | 94 | 38 | 24 | 75 |
| Kansas City, Mo. | 39 | 04 | 56 | 94 | 35 | 20 | 75 |
| Kenosha, Wis. | 42 | 35 | 43 | 87 | 50 | 11 | 61 |
| Key West, Fla. | 24 | 33 | 30 | 81 | 48 | 12 | 4 |
| Kingston, Ont. | 44 | 13 | 30 | 76 | 30 | 00 | 31 |
| Kitchener, Ont. | 43 | 26 | 59 | 80 | 29 | 17 | 1,03 |
| Knoxville, Tenn. | 35 | 57 | 39 | 83 | 55 | 07 | 89 |
| Lafayette, Ind. | 40 | 25 | 11 | 86 | 53 | 39 | 55 |
| Lancaster, Pa. | 40 | 02 | 25 | 76 | 18 | 29 | 35 |
| Lansing, Mich. | 42 | 44 | 01 | 84 | 33 | 15 | 83 |
| Laredo, Tex. | 27 | 30 | 22 | 99 | 30 | 30 | 44 |
| La Salle, Que. | 45 | 25 | 30 | 73 | 38 | 00 | 10 |
| Las Vegas, Nev. | 36 | 10 | 20 | 115 | 08 | 37 | 2,03 |
| Laval, Que. | 45 | 35 | 30 | 73 | 45 | 30 | 10 |
| Lawrence, Mass. | 42 | 42 | 16 | 71 | 10 | 08 | 6 |
| Lethbridge, Alta. | 49 | 41 | 30 | 112 | 49 | 00 | 2,99 |
| Lexington, Ky. | 38 | 02 | 50 | 84 | 29 | 46 | 95 |
| Lihue, Ha. | 21 | 58 | 48 | 159 | 22 | 30 | 21 |
| Lima, Oh. | 40 | 44 | 35 | 84 | 06 | 20 | 86 |
| Lincoln, Neb. | 40 | 48 | 59 | 96 | 42 | 15 | 1,15 |
| Little Rock, Ark. | 34 | 44 | 42 | 92 | 16 | 37 | 28 |
| London, Ont. | 42 | 59 | 00 | 81 | 15 | 00 | 91 |
| Long Beach, Cal. | 33 | 46 | 14 | 118 | 11 | 18 | 33 |
| Lorain, Oh. | 41 | 28 | 05 | 82 | 10 | 49 | 61 |
| Los Angeles, Cal. | 34 | 03 | 15 | 118 | 14 | 28 | 34 |
| Louisville, Ky. | 38 | 14 | 47 | 85 | 45 | 49 | 45 |
| Lowell, Mass. | 42 | 38 | 25 | 71 | 19 | 14 | 10 |
| Lubbock, Tex. | 33 | 35 | 05 | 101 | 50 | 33 | 3,19 |
| Macon, Ga. | 32 | 50 | 12 | 83 | 37 | 36 | 33 |
| Madison, Wis. | 43 | 04 | 23 | 89 | 22 | 55 | 86 |

| City | Lat. N ° | ′ | ″ | Long. W ° | ′ | ″ | Alt.* Feet |
|---|---|---|---|---|---|---|---|
| Manchester, N.H. | 42 | 59 | 28 | 71 | 27 | 41 | 175 |
| Marshall, Tex. | 32 | 33 | 00 | 94 | 23 | 00 | 410 |
| Memphis, Tenn. | 35 | 08 | 46 | 90 | 03 | 13 | 275 |
| Meriden, Conn. | 41 | 32 | 06 | 72 | 47 | 30 | 190 |
| Mexico City, Mexico | 19 | 25 | 45 | 99 | 07 | 00 | 7,347 |
| Miami, Fla. | 25 | 46 | 37 | 80 | 11 | 32 | 10 |
| Milwaukee, Wis. | 43 | 02 | 19 | 87 | 54 | 15 | 635 |
| Minneapolis, Minn. | 44 | 58 | 57 | 93 | 15 | 43 | 815 |
| Minot, N.D. | 48 | 14 | 09 | 101 | 17 | 38 | 1,550 |
| Mississauga, Ont. | 43 | 33 | 00 | 79 | 35 | 00 | 260 |
| Mobile, Ala. | 30 | 41 | 36 | 88 | 02 | 33 | 5 |
| Moline, Ill. | 41 | 30 | 31 | 90 | 30 | 49 | 585 |
| Moncton, N.B. | 46 | 05 | 30 | 64 | 47 | 30 | 75 |
| Montgomery, Ala. | 32 | 22 | 33 | 86 | 18 | 31 | 160 |
| Montpelier, Vt. | 44 | 15 | 36 | 72 | 34 | 41 | 485 |
| Montreal, Que. | 45 | 30 | 30 | 73 | 33 | 20 | 117 |
| Moose Jaw, Sask. | 50 | 23 | 30 | 105 - | 32 | 30 | 1,810 |
| Muncie, Ind. | 40 | 11 | 28 | 85 | 23 | 16 | 950 |
| Nashville, Tenn. | 36 | 09 | 33 | 86 | 46 | 55 | 450 |
| Natchez, Miss. | 31 | 33 | 48 | 91 | 23 | 30 | 210 |
| Newark, N.J. | 40 | 44 | 14 | 74 | 10 | 19 | 55 |
| New Bedford, Mass. | 41 | 38 | 13 | 70 | 55 | 41 | 15 |
| New Britain, Conn. | 41 | 40 | 08 | 72 | 46 | 59 | 200 |
| New Haven, Conn. | 41 | 18 | 25 | 72 | 55 | 30 | 40 |
| New Orleans, La. | 29 | 56 | 53 | 90 | 04 | 10 | 5 |
| New York, N.Y. | 40 | 45 | 06 | 73 | 59 | 39 | 55 |
| Niagara Falls, N.Y. | 43 | 05 | 34 | 79 | 03 | 26 | 570 |
| Niagara Falls, Ont. | 43 | 05 | 30 | 79 | 03 | 30 | 585 |
| Nome, Alas. | 64 | 30 | 00 | 165 | 25 | 00 | 25 |
| Norfolk, Va. | 36 | 51 | 10 | 76 | 17 | 21 | 10 |
| North Bay, Ont. | 46 | 18 | 30 | 79 | 27 | 30 | 925 |
| Oakland, Cal. | 37 | 48 | 03 | 122 | 15 | 54 | 25 |
| Ogden, Ut. | 41 | 13 | 31 | 111 | 58 | 21 | 4,295 |
| Oklahoma City. | 35 | 28 | 26 | 97 | 31 | 04 | 1,195 |
| Omaha, Neb. | 41 | 15 | 42 | 95 | 56 | 14 | 1,040 |
| Orlando, Fla. | 28 | 32 | 42 | 81 | 22 | 38 | 70 |
| Oshawa, Ont. | 43 | 54 | 00 | 78 | 52 | 00 | 350 |
| Ottawa, Ont. | 45 | 25 | 40 | 75 | 42 | 45 | 374 |
| Paducah, Ky. | 37 | 05 | 13 | 88 | 35 | 56 | 345 |
| Pasadena, Cal. | 34 | 08 | 44 | 118 | 08 | 41 | 830 |
| Paterson, N.J. | 40 | 55 | 01 | 74 | 10 | 21 | 100 |
| Pensacola, Fla. | 30 | 24 | 51 | 87 | 12 | 56 | 15 |
| Peoria, Ill. | 40 | 41 | 42 | 89 | 35 | 33 | 470 |
| Peterborough, Ont. | 44 | 18 | 00 | 78 | 19 | 30 | 685 |
| Philadelphia, Pa. | 39 | 56 | 58 | 75 | 09 | 21 | 100 |
| Phoenix, Ariz. | 33 | 27 | 12 | 112 | 04 | 28 | 1,090 |
| Pierre, S.D. | 44 | 22 | 18 | 100 | 20 | 54 | 1,480 |
| Pittsburgh, Pa. | 40 | 26 | 19 | 80 | 00 | 00 | 745 |
| Pittsfield, Mass. | 42 | 26 | 53 | 73 | 15 | 14 | 1,015 |
| Pocatello, Ida. | 42 | 51 | 38 | 112 | 27 | 01 | 4,460 |
| Port Arthur, Tex. | 29 | 52 | 30 | 93 | 56 | 15 | 10 |
| Portland, Me. | 43 | 39 | 33 | 70 | 15 | 19 | 25 |
| Portland, Ore. | 45 | 31 | 06 | 122 | 40 | 35 | 77 |
| Portsmouth, N.H. | 43 | 04 | 30 | 70 | 45 | 24 | 20 |
| Portsmouth, Va. | 36 | 50 | 07 | 76 | 18 | 14 | 10 |
| Prince Rupert, B.C. | 54 | 19 | 00 | 130 | 19 | 00 | 125 |
| Providence, R.I. | 41 | 49 | 32 | 71 | 24 | 41 | 80 |
| Provo, Ut. | 40 | 14 | 06 | 111 | 39 | 24 | 4,550 |
| Pueblo, Col. | 38 | 16 | 17 | 104 | 36 | 33 | 4,690 |
| Quebec City, Que. | 46 | 48 | 46 | 71 | 12 | 20 | 239 |
| Racine, Wis. | 42 | 43 | 49 | 87 | 47 | 12 | 630 |
| Rapid City, S.D. | 44 | 04 | 52 | 103 | 13 | 11 | 3,230 |
| Raleigh, N.C. | 35 | 46 | 38 | 78 | 38 | 21 | 365 |
| Reading, Pa. | 40 | 20 | 09 | 75 | 55 | 40 | 265 |
| Regina, Sask. | 50 | 27 | 02 | 104 | 36 | 30 | 1,894 |
| Reno, Nev. | 39 | 31 | 27 | 119 | 48 | 40 | 4,490 |
| Richmond, Va. | 37 | 32 | 15 | 77 | 26 | 09 | 160 |
| Roanoke, Va. | 37 | 16 | 13 | 79 | 56 | 44 | 905 |
| Rochester, Minn. | 44 | 01 | 21 | 92 | 28 | 03 | 990 |
| Rochester, N.Y. | 43 | 09 | 41 | 77 | 36 | 21 | 515 |
| Rockford, Ill. | 42 | 16 | 07 | 89 | 05 | 48 | 715 |
| Sacramento, Cal. | 38 | 34 | 57 | 121 | 29 | 41 | 30 |
| Saginaw, Mich. | 43 | 25 | 52 | 83 | 56 | 05 | 595 |
| St. Catharines, Ont. | 43 | 09 | 30 | 79 | 14 | 30 | 362 |
| Saint John, N.B. | 45 | 16 | 00 | 66 | 04 | 30 | 80 |
| St. Cloud, Minn. | 45 | 34 | 00 | 94 | 10 | 24 | 1,040 |
| St. John's, Nfld. | 47 | 34 | 00 | 52 | 43 | 30 | 200 |
| St. Joseph, Mo. | 39 | 45 | 57 | 94 | 51 | 02 | 850 |
| St. Louis, Mo. | 38 | 37 | 45 | 90 | 12 | 22 | 455 |
| St. Paul, Minn. | 44 | 57 | 19 | 93 | 06 | 07 | 780 |
| St. Petersburg, Fla. | 27 | 46 | 18 | 82 | 38 | 19 | 20 |
| Salem, Ore. | 44 | 56 | 24 | 123 | 01 | 59 | 155 |

| City | Lat. N ° | ′ | ″ | Long. W ° | ′ | ″ | Alt.* Feet |
|---|---|---|---|---|---|---|---|
| Salina, Kan. | 38 | 50 | 36 | 97 | 36 | 46 | 1,229 |
| Salt Lake City, Ut. | 40 | 45 | 23 | 111 | 53 | 26 | 4,390 |
| San Angelo, Tex. | 31 | 27 | 39 | 100 | 26 | 03 | 1,845 |
| San Antonio, Tex. | 29 | 25 | 37 | 98 | 29 | 06 | 650 |
| San Bernardino, Cal. | 34 | 06 | 30 | 117 | 17 | 28 | 1,080 |
| San Diego, Cal. | 32 | 42 | 53 | 117 | 09 | 21 | 20 |
| San Francisco, Cal. | 37 | 46 | 39 | 122 | 24 | 40 | 65 |
| San Jose, Cal. | 37 | 20 | 16 | 121 | 53 | 24 | 90 |
| San Juan, P.R. | 18 | 27 | 00 | 66 | 04 | 15 | 35 |
| Santa Barbara, Cal. | 34 | 25 | 18 | 119 | 41 | 55 | 100 |
| Santa Cruz, Cal. | 36 | 58 | 18 | 122 | 01 | 18 | 20 |
| Santa Fe, N.M. | 35 | 41 | 11 | 105 | 56 | 10 | 6,950 |
| Sarasota, Fla. | 27 | 20 | 05 | 82 | 32 | 30 | 20 |
| Saskatoon, Sask. | 52 | 07 | 50 | 106 | 39 | 41 | 1,653 |
| Sault Ste. Marie, Ont. | 46 | 31 | 30 | 84 | 20 | 00 | 650 |
| Savannah, Ga. | 32 | 04 | 42 | 81 | 05 | 37 | 20 |
| Schenectady, N.Y. | 42 | 48 | 42 | 73 | 55 | 42 | 245 |
| Scranton, Pa. | 41 | 24 | 32 | 75 | 39 | 46 | 725 |
| Seattle, Wash. | 47 | 36 | 32 | 122 | 20 | 12 | 10 |
| Sheboygan, Wis. | 43 | 45 | 03 | 87 | 42 | 52 | 630 |
| Sherbrooke, Que. | 45 | 24 | 00 | 71 | 53 | 30 | 625 |
| Sheridan, Wy. | 44 | 47 | 55 | 106 | 57 | 10 | 3,740 |
| Shreveport, La. | 32 | 30 | 46 | 93 | 44 | 58 | 204 |
| Sioux City, Ia. | 42 | 29 | 46 | 96 | 24 | 30 | 1,110 |
| Sioux Falls, S.D. | 43 | 32 | 35 | 96 | 43 | 35 | 1,395 |
| Somerville, Mass. | 42 | 23 | 15 | 71 | 06 | 07 | 13 |
| South Bend, Ind. | 41 | 40 | 33 | 86 | 15 | 01 | 710 |
| Spartanburg, S.C. | 34 | 57 | 03 | 81 | 56 | 06 | 875 |
| Spokane, Wash. | 47 | 39 | 32 | 117 | 25 | 33 | 1,890 |
| Springfield, Ill. | 39 | 47 | 58 | 89 | 38 | 51 | 610 |
| Springfield, Mass. | 42 | 06 | 21 | 72 | 35 | 32 | 85 |
| Springfield, Mo. | 37 | 13 | 03 | 93 | 17 | 32 | 1,300 |
| Springfield, Oh. | 39 | 55 | 38 | 83 | 48 | 29 | 980 |
| Stamford, Conn. | 41 | 03 | 09 | 73 | 32 | 24 | 35 |
| Steubenville, Oh. | 40 | 21 | 42 | 80 | 36 | 53 | 660 |
| Stockton, Cal. | 37 | 57 | 30 | 121 | 17 | 16 | 20 |
| Sudbury, Ont. | 46 | 28 | 30 | 80 | 58 | 30 | 917 |
| Superior, Wis. | 46 | 43 | 14 | 92 | 06 | 07 | 630 |
| Sydney, N.S. | 46 | 08 | 30 | 60 | 11 | 00 | 50 |
| Syracuse, N.Y. | 43 | 03 | 04 | 76 | 09 | 14 | 400 |
| Tacoma, Wash. | 47 | 14 | 59 | 122 | 26 | 15 | 110 |
| Tallahassee, Fla. | 30 | 26 | 30 | 84 | 16 | 56 | 150 |
| Tampa, Fla. | 27 | 56 | 58 | 82 | 27 | 25 | 15 |
| Terre Haute, Ind. | 39 | 28 | 03 | 87 | 24 | 26 | 496 |
| Texarkana, Tex. | 33 | 25 | 48 | 94 | 02 | 30 | 324 |
| Thunder Bay, Ont. | 48 | 25 | 00 | 89 | 14 | 00 | 650 |
| Toledo, Oh. | 41 | 39 | 14 | 83 | 32 | 39 | 585 |
| Topeka, Kan. | 39 | 03 | 16 | 95 | 40 | 23 | 930 |
| Toronto, Ont. | 43 | 39 | 12 | 79 | 23 | 00 | 532 |
| Trenton, N.J. | 40 | 13 | 14 | 74 | 46 | 13 | 35 |
| Trois-Rivieres, Que. | 46 | 21 | 00 | 72 | 33 | 00 | 115 |
| Troy, N.Y. | 42 | 43 | 45 | 73 | 40 | 58 | 35 |
| Tucson, Ariz. | 32 | 13 | 15 | 110 | 58 | 08 | 2,390 |
| Tulsa, Okla. | 36 | 09 | 12 | 95 | 59 | 34 | 804 |
| Urbana, Ill. | 40 | 06 | 42 | 88 | 12 | 06 | ... |
| Utica, N.Y. | 43 | 06 | 12 | 75 | 13 | 33 | 415 |
| Vancouver, B.C. | 49 | 16 | 30 | 123 | 07 | 30 | 388 |
| Victoria, B.C. | 48 | 25 | 40 | 123 | 21 | 45 | ... |
| Waco, Tex. | 31 | 33 | 12 | 97 | 08 | 00 | 405 |
| Walla Walla, Wash. | 46 | 04 | 08 | 118 | 20 | 24 | 936 |
| Washington, D.C. | 38 | 53 | 51 | 77 | 00 | 33 | 25 |
| Waterbury, Conn. | 41 | 33 | 13 | 73 | 02 | 31 | 260 |
| Waterloo, Ia. | 42 | 29 | 40 | 92 | 20 | 20 | 850 |
| West Palm Beach, Fla. | 26 | 42 | 36 | 80 | 03 | 07 | 15 |
| Wheeling, W. Va. | 40 | 04 | 00 | 80 | 43 | 20 | 650 |
| Whitehorse, Yukon | 60 | 43 | 15 | 135 | 03 | 15 | 2,305 |
| White Plains, N.Y. | 41 | 02 | 00 | 73 | 45 | 48 | 220 |
| Wichita, Kan. | 37 | 41 | 30 | 97 | 20 | 16 | 1,290 |
| Wichita Falls, Tex. | 33 | 54 | 34 | 98 | 29 | 28 | 945 |
| Wilkes-Barre, Pa. | 41 | 14 | 32 | 75 | 53 | 17 | 640 |
| Wilmington, Del. | 39 | 44 | 46 | 75 | 32 | 51 | 135 |
| Wilmington, N.C. | 34 | 14 | 14 | 77 | 56 | 58 | 35 |
| Windsor, Ont. | 42 | 19 | 50 | 83 | 03 | 00 | 590 |
| Winnipeg, Man. | 49 | 53 | -56 | 97 | 08 | 20 | 765 |
| Winston-Salem, N.C. | 36 | 05 | 52 | 80 | 14 | 42 | 860 |
| Worcester, Mass. | 42 | 15 | 37 | 71 | 48 | 17 | 475 |
| Yakima, Wash. | 46 | 36 | 09 | 120 | 30 | 39 | 1,060 |
| Yellowknife, N.W.T. | 62 | 28 | 15 | 114 | 22 | 00 | 674 |
| Yonkers, N.Y. | 40 | 55 | 55 | 73 | 53 | 54 | 10 |
| York, Pa. | 39 | 57 | 35 | 76 | 43 | 36 | 370 |
| Youngstown, Oh. | 41 | 05 | 57 | 80 | 39 | 02 | 840 |
| Yuma, Ariz. | 32 | 42 | 54 | 114 | 37 | 24 | 160 |
| Zanesville, Oh. | 39 | 56 | 18 | 82 | 00 | 30 | 720 |

## World Cities

| City | Lat. N ° | ′ | ″ | Long. W ° | ′ | ″ | Alt.* Feet |
|---|---|---|---|---|---|---|---|
| London, UK (Greenwich) | 51 | 30 | 00N | 0 | 0 | 0 | 245 |
| Paris, France | 48 | 50 | 14N | 2 | 20 | 14E | 300 |
| Berlin, Germany | 52 | 32 | 00N | 13 | 25 | 00E | 110 |
| Rome, Italy | 41 | 53 | 00N | 12 | 30 | 00E | 95 |
| Warsaw, Poland | 52 | 15 | 00N | 21 | 00 | 00E | 360 |
| Moscow, USSR | 55 | 45 | 00N | 37 | 42 | 00E | 394 |
| Athens, Greece | 37 | 58 | 00N | 23 | 44 | 00E | 300 |
| Jerusalem, Israel | 31 | 47 | 00N | 35 | 13 | 00E | 2,500 |
| Johannesburg, So. Afr. | 26 | 10 | 00S | 28 | 02 | 00E | 5,740 |
| New Delhi, India | 28 | 38 | 00N | 77 | 12 | 00E | 770 |
| Peking, China | 39 | 54 | 00N | 116 | 28 | 00E | 600 |
| Rio de Janeiro, Brazil | 22 | 53 | 43S | 43 | 13 | 22W | 30 |
| Tokyo, Japan | 35 | 45 | 00N | 139 | 45 | 00E | 30 |
| Sydney, Australia | 33 | 52 | 00S | 151 | 12 | 00E | 25 |

## Calendar Adjustment Tables

The tables below will allow you to determine the approximate time of the rise or set of the sun and moon at your specific location. It will be necessary to consider only the latitude adjustment for the sun, but rise and set times of the moon for your location can be more than one-half hour later than the times given on the following pages.

A. Find your latitude and longitude or that of a nearby city in the tables on pages 772-773. Mark the appropriate rows in tables A and B. Now, find the times of the event in the calendar table in the columns for the latitude to your south and to your north. Subtract the southern time from the northern time. Find the nearest tens of minutes to your answer in a column head in Table A. Run down the column to the latitude row you have marked. Add (or subtract, if your answer is negative) to the southern time the number you find there.

B. Find the time of the event for the next day at the southern latitude. Subtract the time for the present day from the time for the next day. In Table B, find the column headed by the nearest tens of minutes to your answer. Run down the column to the longitude row you have marked. Add this number to your previous answer.

C. To determine the clock time, subtract the nearest time zone meridian used in your state from your longitude. (These are: Atlantic, 60°; Eastern, 75°; Central, 90°; Mountain, 105°; Pacific, 120°; Alaska-Hawaii, 150°.) Change this to degrees and decimals of a degree (divide the minutes by 60) and multiply by 4. Write this number on this page for future use and add it (or subtract, if minus) to your answer from Table B. Watch out for Daylight Time.

Example: Find the approximate time of moonset for April 1 in San Francisco, latitude: 37°46'; longitude: 122°25', or 122°.4 A resident there should mark rows 7°40' in Table A and 120° in Table B.

| A | Calendar time for 40°— | 23:12 | |
|---|---|---|---|
| | Calendar time for 30°— | 22:53 | 22:5 |
| | Difference: North minus South— | +19 min. | + |
| | Table A: 20 min. and 7°40'— | 15 | 23:0 |
| B. | Calendar time for Apr. 2, 30°— | 23:46 | |
| | Calendar time for Apr. 1, 30°— | 22:53 | 23:0 |
| | Difference: Apr. 2 minus Apr. 1 = | 53 min. | +1 |
| | Table B: 50 min. and 120°— | 17 | 23:2 |
| C. | SF longitude— | 122.4 | |
| | PST longitude— | −120.0 | 23:2 |
| | 2°.4x4 min. per degree= | 9.6 min. | +1 |
| | PST of moon set Apr. 1 in SF | | 23:3 |

## Table A: Latitude Adjustment

| Diff. in Min. Lat. | 10 | 20 | 30 | 40 | 50 | 60 | 70 | 80 | 90 | 100 | 110 | 120 |
|---|---|---|---|---|---|---|---|---|---|---|---|---|
| 0° 20 | 0 | 1 | 1 | 1 | 2 | 2 | 2 | 3 | 3 | 3 | 4 | 4 |
| 40 | 1 | 1 | 2 | 3 | 3 | 4 | 5 | 5 | 6 | 7 | 7 | 8 |
| 1 00 | 1 | 2 | 3 | 4 | 5 | 6 | 7 | 8 | 9 | 10 | 11 | 12 |
| 20 | 1 | 3 | 4 | 5 | 7 | 8 | 9 | 11 | 12 | 13 | 15 | 16 |
| 40 | 2 | 3 | 5 | 7 | 8 | 10 | 12 | 13 | 15 | 17 | 18 | 20 |
| 2 00 | 2 | 4 | 6 | 8 | 10 | 12 | 14 | 16 | 18 | 20 | 22 | 24 |
| 20 | 2 | 5 | 7 | 9 | 12 | 14 | 16 | 19 | 21 | 23 | 26 | 28 |
| 40 | 3 | 5 | 8 | 11 | 13 | 16 | 19 | 21 | 24 | 27 | 29 | 32 |
| 3 00 | 3 | 6 | 9 | 12 | 15 | 18 | 21 | 24 | 27 | 30 | 33 | 36 |
| 20 | 3 | 7 | 10 | 13 | 17 | 20 | 23 | 27 | 30 | 33 | 37 | 40 |
| 40 | 4 | 7 | 11 | 15 | 18 | 22 | 26 | 29 | 33 | 37 | 40 | 44 |
| 4 00 | 4 | 8 | 12 | 16 | 20 | 24 | 28 | 32 | 36 | 40 | 44 | 48 |
| 20 | 4 | 9 | 13 | 17 | 22 | 26 | 30 | 35 | 39 | 43 | 48 | 52 |
| 40 | 5 | 9 | 14 | 19 | 23 | 28 | 33 | 37 | 42 | 47 | 51 | 56 |
| 5 00 | 5 | 10 | 15 | 20 | 25 | 30 | 35 | 40 | 45 | 50 | 55 | 60 |
| 20 | 5 | 11 | 16 | 21 | 27 | 32 | 37 | 43 | 48 | 53 | 59 | 64 |
| 40 | 6 | 11 | 17 | 23 | 28 | 34 | 40 | 45 | 51 | 57 | 62 | 68 |
| 6 00 | 6 | 12 | 18 | 24 | 30 | 36 | 42 | 48 | 54 | 60 | 66 | 72 |
| 20 | 6 | 13 | 19 | 25 | 32 | 38 | 44 | 51 | 57 | 63 | 70 | 76 |
| 40 | 7 | 13 | 20 | 27 | 33 | 40 | 47 | 53 | 60 | 67 | 73 | 80 |
| 7 00 | 7 | 14 | 21 | 28 | 35 | 42 | 49 | 56 | 63 | 70 | 77 | 84 |
| 20 | 7 | 15 | 22 | 29 | 37 | 44 | 51 | 59 | 66 | 73 | 81 | 88 |
| 40 | 8 | 15 | 23 | 31 | 38 | 46 | 54 | 61 | 69 | 77 | 84 | 92 |
| 8 00 | 8 | 16 | 24 | 32 | 40 | 48 | 56 | 64 | 72 | 80 | 88 | 96 |
| 20 | 8 | 17 | 25 | 33 | 42 | 50 | 58 | 67 | 75 | 83 | 92 | 100 |
| 40 | 9 | 17 | 26 | 35 | 43 | 52 | 61 | 69 | 78 | 87 | 95 | 104 |
| 9 00 | 9 | 18 | 27 | 36 | 45 | 54 | 63 | 72 | 81 | 90 | 99 | 108 |
| 20 | 9 | 19 | 28 | 37 | 47 | 56 | 65 | 75 | 84 | 93 | 103 | 112 |
| 40 | 10 | 19 | 29 | 39 | 48 | 58 | 68 | 77 | 87 | 97 | 106 | 116 |

## Table B: Longitude Adjustment

| Diff. in Min. Long. | 10 | 20 | 30 | 40 | 50 | 60 | 70 | 80 | 90 | 100 | 110 | 120 |
|---|---|---|---|---|---|---|---|---|---|---|---|---|
| 50° | 1 | 3 | 4 | 6 | 7 | 8 | 10 | 11 | 12 | 14 | 15 | 17 |
| 55 | 2 | 3 | 5 | 6 | 8 | 9 | 11 | 12 | 14 | 15 | 17 | 18 |
| 60 | 2 | 3 | 5 | 7 | 8 | 10 | 12 | 13 | 15 | 17 | 18 | 20 |
| 65 | 2 | 4 | 5 | 7 | 9 | 11 | 13 | 14 | 16 | 18 | 20 | 22 |
| 70 | 2 | 4 | 6 | 8 | 10 | 12 | 14 | 16 | 18 | 19 | 21 | 23 |
| 75 | 2 | 4 | 6 | 8 | 10 | 12 | 15 | 17 | 19 | 21 | 23 | 25 |
| 80 | 2 | 4 | 7 | 9 | 11 | 13 | 16 | 18 | 20 | 22 | 24 | 27 |
| 85 | 2 | 5 | 7 | 9 | 12 | 14 | 16 | 19 | 21 | 24 | 26 | 28 |
| 90 | 2 | 5 | 8 | 10 | 12 | 15 | 18 | 20 | 22 | 25 | 28 | 30 |
| 95 | 3 | 5 | 8 | 11 | 13 | 16 | 18 | 21 | 24 | 26 | 29 | 32 |
| 100 | 3 | 6 | 8 | 11 | 14 | 17 | 19 | 22 | 25 | 28 | 31 | 33 |
| 105 | 3 | 6 | 9 | 12 | 15 | 18 | 20 | 23 | 26 | 29 | 32 | 35 |
| 110 | 3 | 6 | 9 | 12 | 15 | 18 | 21 | 24 | 28 | 31 | 34 | 37 |
| 115 | 3 | 6 | 10 | 13 | 16 | 19 | 22 | 26 | 29 | 32 | 35 | 38 |
| 120 | 3 | 7 | 10 | 13 | 17 | 20 | 23 | 27 | 30 | 33 | 37 | 40 |
| 125 | 4 | 7 | 10 | 14 | 17 | 21 | 24 | 28 | 31 | 35 | 38 | 42 |
| 130 | 4 | 7 | 11 | 14 | 18 | 22 | 25 | 29 | 32 | 36 | 40 | 43 |
| 135 | 4 | 8 | 11 | 15 | 19 | 22 | 26 | 30 | 34 | 38 | 41 | 45 |
| 140 | 4 | 8 | 12 | 16 | 19 | 23 | 27 | 31 | 35 | 39 | 43 | 47 |
| 145 | 4 | 8 | 12 | 16 | 20 | 24 | 28 | 32 | 36 | 40 | 44 | 48 |
| 150 | 4 | 8 | 12 | 17 | 21 | 25 | 29 | 33 | 38 | 42 | 46 | 50 |
| 155 | 4 | 9 | 13 | 17 | 22 | 26 | 30 | 34 | 39 | 43 | 47 | 52 |
| 160 | 4 | 9 | 13 | 18 | 22 | 27 | 31 | 36 | 40 | 44 | 49 | 53 |
| 165 | 5 | 9 | 14 | 18 | 23 | 28 | 32 | 37 | 41 | 46 | 50 | 55 |
| 170 | 5 | 9 | 14 | 19 | 24 | 28 | 33 | 38 | 42 | 47 | 52 | 57 |

**st Month**　　　# January, 1979　　　**31 days**

Greenwich Mean Time

**NOTE:** Light figures indicate Sun. **Dark** figures indicate **Moon.** *Degrees are North Latitude.*

**CAUTION:** Must be converted to local time. For instruction see page 774.

| Day of month / week / year | Sun on meridian / Moon phase (h m s) | 20° Rise Sun/Moon | 20° Set Sun/Moon | 30° Rise | 30° Set | 40° Rise | 40° Set | 50° Rise | 50° Set | 60° Rise | 60° Set |
|---|---|---|---|---|---|---|---|---|---|---|---|
| Mo 1 | 12 03 24 | 6 35 | 17 32 | 6 56 | 17 11 | 7 22 | 16 45 | 7 59 | 16 08 | 9 02 | 15 04 |
| (Moon) | | 8 50 | 20 39 | 9 02 | 20 29 | 9 17 | 20 16 | 9 37 | 19 57 | 10 09 | 19 29 |
| Tu 2 | 12 23 52 | 6 35 | 17 32 | 6 56 | 17 12 | 7 22 | 16 46 | 7 59 | 16 09 | 9 02 | 15 06 |
| (Moon) | | 9 41 | 21 41 | 9 49 | 21 34 | 10 00 | 21 26 | 10 14 | 21 15 | 10 35 | 20 57 |
| We 3 | 12 04 20 | 6 35 | 17 33 | 6 57 | 17 12 | 7 22 | 16 46 | 7 58 | 16 11 | 9 01 | 15 07 |
| (Moon) | | 10 28 | 22 40 | 10 32 | 22 38 | 10 38 | 22 35 | 10 45 | 22 30 | 10 57 | 22 23 |
| Th 4 | 12 04 48 | 6 36 | 17 33 | 6 57 | 17 13 | 7 22 | 16 47 | 7 58 | 16 12 | 9 01 | 15 09 |
| (Moon) | | 11 12 | 23 38 | 11 13 | 23 39 | 11 13 | 23 41 | 11 14 | 23 43 | 11 16 | 23 47 |
| Fr 5 | 12 05 15 / 11 15 ☽ | 6 36 | 17 34 | 6 57 | 17 14 | 7 22 | 16 48 | 7 58 | 16 13 | 9 00 | 15 10 |
| (Moon) | | 11 55 | | 11 52 | | 11 48 | | 11 42 | | 11 34 | |
| Sa 6 | 12 05 41 | 6 36 | 17 35 | 6 57 | 17 15 | 7 22 | 16 49 | 7 58 | 16 14 | 8 59 | 15 12 |
| (Moon) | | 12 37 | 0 33 | 12 30 | 0 39 | 12 22 | 0 45 | 12 10 | 0 54 | 11 53 | 1 08 |
| Su 7 | 12 06 08 | 6 36 | 17 36 | 6 57 | 17 16 | 7 22 | 16 50 | 7 57 | 16 15 | 8 58 | 15 14 |
| (Moon) | | 13 20 | 1 28 | 13 10 | 1 37 | 12 57 | 1 48 | 12 40 | 2 03 | 12 14 | 2 26 |
| Mo 8 | 12 06 33 | 6 37 | 17 36 | 6 57 | 17 16 | 7 22 | 16 51 | 7 57 | 16 17 | 8 57 | 15 16 |
| (Moon) | | 14 04 | 2 21 | 13 51 | 2 33 | 13 34 | 2 48 | 13 12 | 3 08 | 12 38 | 3 41 |
| Tu 9 | 12 06 59 | 6 37 | 17 37 | 6 57 | 17 20 | 7 22 | 16 52 | 7 56 | 16 18 | 8 56 | 15 18 |
| (Moon) | | 14 49 | 3 14 | 14 33 | 3 28 | 14 15 | 3 46 | 13 49 | 4 11 | 13 07 | 4 51 |
| We 10 | 12 07 23 | 6 37 | 17 38 | 6 57 | 17 18 | 7 22 | 16 53 | 7 56 | 16 19 | 8 55 | 15 20 |
| (Moon) | | 15 35 | 4 05 | 15 19 | 4 22 | 14 58 | 4 42 | 14 29 | 5 10 | 13 43 | 5 56 |
| Th 11 | 12 07 47 | 6 37 | 17 39 | 6 57 | 17 19 | 7 22 | 16 54 | 7 55 | 16 20 | 8 54 | 15 22 |
| (Moon) | | 16 23 | 4 56 | 16 06 | 5 13 | 15 45 | 5 34 | 15 15 | 6 03 | 14 26 | 6 52 |
| Fr 12 | 12 08 11 | 6 37 | 17 39 | 6 57 | 17 20 | 7 21 | 16 55 | 7 55 | 16 22 | 8 53 | 15 24 |
| (Moon) | | 17 12 | 5 44 | 16 55 | 6 01 | 16 35 | 6 22 | 16 06 | 6 51 | 15 18 | 7 39 |
| Sa 13 | 12 08 34 / 07 09 ○ | 6 38 | 17 40 | 6 57 | 17 20 | 7 21 | 16 57 | 7 54 | 16 23 | 8 51 | 15 27 |
| (Moon) | | 18 02 | 6 30 | 17 46 | 6 46 | 17 27 | 7 06 | 17 01 | 7 33 | 16 17 | 8 18 |
| Su 14 | 12 08 56 | 6 38 | 17 40 | 6 57 | 17 21 | 7 20 | 16 58 | 7 54 | 16 25 | 8 50 | 15 29 |
| (Moon) | | 18 51 | 7 14 | 18 38 | 7 28 | 18 21 | 7 46 | 17 58 | 8 10 | 17 22 | 8 48 |
| Mo 15 | 12 09 18 | 6 38 | 17 41 | 6 57 | 17 22 | 7 20 | 16 59 | 7 53 | 16 26 | 8 49 | 15 31 |
| (Moon) | | 19 40 | 7 55 | 19 29 | 8 07 | 19 16 | 8 22 | 18 58 | 8 42 | 18 29 | 9 13 |
| Tu 16 | 12 09 39 | 6 38 | 17 42 | 6 57 | 17 23 | 7 20 | 17 00 | 7 52 | 16 27 | 8 47 | 15 33 |
| (Moon) | | 20 29 | 8 35 | 20 21 | 8 44 | 20 12 | 8 55 | 19 59 | 9 10 | 19 38 | 9 34 |
| We 17 | 12 09 57 | 6 38 | 17 42 | 6 57 | 17 24 | 7 19 | 17 01 | 7 51 | 16 29 | 8 45 | 15 35 |
| (Moon) | | 21 18 | 9 13 | 21 13 | 9 19 | 21 08 | 9 26 | 21 00 | 9 36 | 20 49 | 9 51 |
| Th 18 | 12 10 19 | 6 38 | 17 43 | 6 56 | 17 24 | 7 19 | 17 02 | 7 51 | 16 30 | 8 44 | 15 38 |
| (Moon) | | 22 06 | 9 51 | 22 05 | 9 53 | 22 04 | 9 56 | 22 03 | 10 01 | 22 00 | 10 07 |
| Fr 19 | 12 10 38 | 6 38 | 17 43 | 6 56 | 17 25 | 7 18 | 17 03 | 7 50 | 16 32 | 8 42 | 15 40 |
| (Moon) | | 22 56 | 10 28 | 22 59 | 10 27 | 23 02 | 10 26 | 23 06 | 10 25 | 23 13 | 10 23 |
| Sa 20 | 12 10 56 | 6 38 | 17 44 | 6 56 | 17 26 | 7 18 | 17 04 | 7 49 | 16 33 | 8 40 | 15 42 |
| (Moon) | | 23 47 | 11 06 | 23 53 | 11 02 | | 10 57 | | 10 50 | | 10 39 |
| Su 21 | 12 11 13 / 11 23 ☾ | 6 38 | 17 45 | 6 56 | 17 27 | 7 18 | 17 05 | 7 48 | 16 35 | 8 38 | 15 45 |
| (Moon) | | | 11 46 | | 11 39 | 0 01 | 11 29 | 0 11 | 11 17 | 0 27 | 10 57 |
| Mo 22 | 12 11 30 | 6 38 | 17 45 | 6 55 | 17 28 | 7 17 | 17 06 | 7 47 | 16 36 | 8 36 | 15 47 |
| (Moon) | | 0 40 | 12 30 | 0 50 | 12 19 | 1 02 | 12 05 | 1 18 | 11 47 | 1 43 | 11 19 |
| Tu 23 | 12 11 46 | 6 37 | 17 46 | 6 55 | 17 29 | 7 16 | 17 08 | 7 46 | 16 38 | 8 35 | 15 50 |
| (Moon) | | 1 36 | 13 17 | 1 49 | 13 03 | 2 04 | 12 46 | 2 26 | 12 23 | 3 01 | 11 45 |
| We 24 | 12 12 01 | 6 37 | 17 46 | 6 54 | 17 30 | 7 16 | 17 09 | 7 45 | 16 39 | 8 33 | 15 52 |
| (Moon) | | 2 34 | 14 09 | 2 49 | 13 53 | 3 08 | 13 33 | 3 35 | 13 05 | 4 18 | 12 21 |
| Th 25 | 12 12 16 | 6 37 | 17 47 | 6 54 | 17 31 | 7 15 | 17 10 | 7 44 | 16 41 | 8 31 | 15 55 |
| (Moon) | | 3 34 | 15 06 | 3 51 | 14 48 | 4 12 | 14 27 | 4 42 | 13 57 | 5 30 | 13 08 |
| Fr 26 | 12 12 29 | 6 37 | 17 48 | 6 54 | 17 32 | 7 14 | 17 11 | 7 43 | 16 43 | 8 29 | 15 57 |
| (Moon) | | 4 35 | 16 07 | 4 53 | 15 50 | 5 14 | 15 29 | 5 44 | 14 59 | 6 34 | 14 10 |
| Sa 27 | 12 12 42 | 6 37 | 17 48 | 6 53 | 17 33 | 7 13 | 17 12 | 7 41 | 16 45 | 8 27 | 16 00 |
| (Moon) | | 5 36 | 17 12 | 5 52 | 16 56 | 6 12 | 16 37 | 6 40 | 16 10 | 7 25 | 15 26 |
| Su 28 | 12 12 54 / 06 20 ● | 6 36 | 17 49 | 6 53 | 17 33 | 7 13 | 17 14 | 7 40 | 16 46 | 8 24 | 16 02 |
| (Moon) | | 6 33 | 18 17 | 6 47 | 18 05 | 7 04 | 17 49 | 7 28 | 17 28 | 8 05 | 16 53 |
| Mo 29 | 12 13 06 | 6 36 | 17 49 | 6 52 | 17 34 | 7 12 | 17 15 | 7 38 | 16 48 | 8 22 | 16 05 |
| (Moon) | | 7 27 | 19 22 | 7 38 | 19 13 | 7 51 | 19 02 | 8 08 | 18 47 | 8 36 | 18 24 |
| Tu 30 | 12 13 16 | 6 36 | 17 50 | 6 52 | 17 35 | 7 11 | 17 16 | 7 37 | 16 50 | 8 20 | 16 07 |
| (Moon) | | 8 18 | 20 25 | 8 25 | 20 21 | 8 38 | 20 15 | 8 44 | 20 07 | 9 00 | 19 55 |
| We 31 | 12 13 26 | 6 36 | 17 51 | 6 51 | 17 36 | 7 10 | 17 17 | 7 36 | 16 52 | 8 18 | 16 10 |
| (Moon) | | 9 06 | 21 26 | 9 08 | 21 25 | 9 11 | 21 25 | 9 15 | 21 24 | 9 21 | 21 23 |

# 2nd Month     February, 1979     28 Days

Greenwich Mean Time

**NOTE:** Light figures indicate Sun. **Dark** figures indicate **Moon**. *Degrees are North Latitude.*

**CAUTION:** Must be converted to local time. For instruction see page 774.

| Day of month / week / year | Sun on meridian Moon phase h m s | 20° Rise Sun/Moon | 20° Set Sun/Moon | 30° Rise Sun/Moon | 30° Set Sun/Moon | 40° Rise Sun/Moon | 40° Set Sun/Moon | 50° Rise Sun/Moon | 50° Set Sun/Moon | 60° Rise Sun/Moon | 60° Set Sun/Moon |
|---|---|---|---|---|---|---|---|---|---|---|---|
| 1 Th | 12 13 34 | 6 36 | 17 51 | 6 51 | 17 37 | 7 09 | 17 18 | 7 34 | 16 53 | 8 15 | 16 13 |
| 32 | | 9 51 | 22 24 | 9 49 | 22 28 | 9 47 | 22 33 | 9 45 | 22 39 | 9 41 | 22 48 |
| 2 Fr | 12 13 42 | 6 35 | 17 52 | 6 50 | 17 37 | 7 08 | 17 20 | 7 33 | 16 55 | 8 13 | 16 15 |
| 33 | | 10 35 | 23 21 | 10 29 | 23 28 | 10 23 | 23 38 | 10 14 | 23 50 | 10 00 | |
| 3 Sa | 12 13 50 | 6 35 | 17 52 | 6 50 | 17 38 | 7 07 | 17 21 | 7 31 | 16 56 | 8 10 | 16 18 |
| 34 | | 11 19 | | 11 10 | | 10 58 | | 10 44 | | 10 21 | 0 10 |
| 4 Su | 12 13 56  00 36 ☽ | 6 35 | 17 53 | 6 49 | 17 39 | 7 06 | 17 22 | 7 30 | 16 58 | 8 08 | 16 21 |
| 35 | | 12 03 | 0 16 | 11 50 | 0 27 | 11 36 | 0 40 | 11 15 | 0 59 | 10 44 | 1 28 |
| 5 Mo | 12 14 01 | 6 35 | 17 54 | 6 48 | 17 40 | 7 05 | 17 23 | 7 28 | 17 00 | 8 06 | 16 24 |
| 36 | | 12 47 | 1 10 | 12 33 | 1 23 | 12 15 | 1 40 | 11 50 | 2 03 | 11 11 | 2 41 |
| 6 Tu | 12 14 06 | 6 34 | 17 54 | 6 47 | 17 41 | 7 04 | 17 24 | 7 27 | 17 02 | 8 03 | 16 26 |
| 37 | | 13 33 | 2 02 | 13 17 | 2 17 | 12 57 | 2 37 | 12 30 | 3 03 | 11 45 | 3 47 |
| 7 We | 12 14 10 | 6 34 | 17 54 | 6 47 | 17 41 | 7 03 | 17 26 | 7 25 | 17 03 | 8 01 | 16 29 |
| 38 | | 14 21 | 2 52 | 14 04 | 3 09 | 13 43 | 3 30 | 13 13 | 3 59 | 12 25 | 4 47 |
| 8 Th | 12 14 13 | 6 33 | 17 55 | 6 46 | 17 42 | 7 02 | 17 27 | 7 24 | 17 05 | 7 58 | 16 31 |
| 39 | | 15 09 | 3 41 | 14 52 | 3 58 | 14 31 | 4 19 | 14 02 | 4 48 | 13 14 | 5 37 |
| 9 Fr | 12 14 15 | 6 33 | 17 56 | 6 45 | 17 43 | 7 01 | 17 28 | 7 22 | 17 07 | 7 56 | 16 34 |
| 40 | | 15 58 | 4 28 | 15 42 | 4 44 | 15 22 | 5 04 | 14 55 | 5 32 | 14 10 | 6 18 |
| 10 Sa | 12 14 16 | 6 32 | 17 57 | 6 44 | 17 44 | 7 00 | 17 29 | 7 20 | 17 09 | 7 53 | 16 37 |
| 41 | | 16 47 | 5 12 | 16 33 | 5 27 | 16 16 | 5 45 | 15 52 | 6 11 | 15 13 | 6 51 |
| 11 Su | 12 14 17 | 6 32 | 17 57 | 6 43 | 17 45 | 6 59 | 17 30 | 7 19 | 17 11 | 7 51 | 16 39 |
| 42 | | 17 36 | 5 54 | 17 25 | 6 07 | 17 10 | 6 23 | 16 50 | 6 44 | 16 19 | 7 18 |
| 12 Mo | 12 14 17  02 39 ○ | 6 31 | 17 58 | 6 43 | 17 45 | 6 57 | 17 32 | 7 17 | 17 12 | 7 48 | 16 42 |
| 43 | | 18 25 | 6 35 | 18 17 | 6 45 | 18 06 | 6 57 | 17 51 | 7 14 | 17 28 | 7 40 |
| 13 Tu | 12 14 16 | 6 31 | 17 58 | 6 42 | 17 46 | 6 56 | 17 33 | 7 16 | 17 14 | 7 46 | 16 44 |
| 44 | | 19 14 | 7 14 | 19 09 | 7 21 | 19 02 | 7 29 | 18 52 | 7 41 | 18 38 | 7 59 |
| 14 We | 12 14 14 | 6 30 | 17 59 | 6 41 | 17 47 | 6 55 | 17 34 | 7 14 | 17 16 | 7 43 | 16 47 |
| 45 | | 20 03 | 7 51 | 20 01 | 7 55 | 19 58 | 8 00 | 19 55 | 8 06 | 19 49 | 8 16 |
| 15 Th | 12 14 12 | 6 29 | 17 59 | 6 40 | 17 48 | 6 54 | 17 35 | 7 12 | 17 18 | 7 40 | 16 50 |
| 46 | | 20 53 | 8 29 | 20 54 | 8 29 | 20 55 | 8 30 | 20 58 | 8 31 | 21 01 | 8 32 |
| 16 Fr | 12 14 09 | 6 29 | 18 00 | 6 39 | 17 49 | 6 53 | 17 36 | 7 10 | 17 19 | 7 37 | 16 52 |
| 47 | | 21 43 | 9 07 | 21 48 | 9 04 | 21 53 | 9 00 | 22 01 | 8 55 | 22 14 | 8 48 |
| 17 Sa | 12 14 05 | 6 28 | 18 00 | 6 39 | 17 49 | 6 51 | 17 38 | 7 08 | 17 21 | 7 35 | 16 55 |
| 48 | | 22 34 | 9 46 | 22 48 | 9 39 | 22 53 | 9 31 | 23 06 | 9 21 | 23 28 | 9 05 |
| 18 Su | 12 14 00 | 6 28 | 18 01 | 6 38 | 17 50 | 6 50 | 17 39 | 7 06 | 17 22 | 7 32 | 16 57 |
| 49 | | 23 28 | 10 27 | 23 39 | 10 17 | 23 53 | 10 05 | | 9 49 | | 9 24 |
| 19 Mo | 12 13 55 | 6 27 | 18 01 | 6 37 | 17 51 | 6 49 | 17 40 | 7 04 | 17 24 | 7 29 | 17 00 |
| 50 | | | 11 11 | | 10 58 | | 10 43 | 0 12 | 10 22 | 0 43 | 9 48 |
| 20 Tu | 12 13 49  01 17 ☾ | 6 26 | 18 01 | 6 36 | 17 52 | 6 48 | 17 41 | 7 02 | 17 26 | 7 26 | 17 03 |
| 51 | | 0 23 | 11 59 | 0 37 | 11 44 | 0 55 | 11 25 | 1 19 | 11 00 | 1 58 | 10 19 |
| 21 We | 12 13 43 | 6 26 | 18 02 | 6 35 | 17 53 | 6 46 | 17 42 | 7 00 | 17 28 | 7 23 | 17 05 |
| 52 | | 1 20 | 12 52 | 1 36 | 12 35 | 1 56 | 12 14 | 2 24 | 11 46 | 3 10 | 10 58 |
| 22 Th | 12 13 36 | 6 25 | 18 02 | 6 34 | 17 53 | 6 45 | 17 44 | 6 59 | 17 29 | 7 21 | 17 08 |
| 53 | | 2 18 | 13 49 | 2 36 | 13 32 | 2 57 | 13 10 | 3 27 | 12 40 | 4 16 | 11 51 |
| 23 Fr | 12 13 28 | 6 25 | 18 03 | 6 33 | 17 54 | 6 43 | 17 45 | 6 57 | 17 31 | 7 18 | 17 10 |
| 54 | | 3 17 | 14 50 | 3 34 | 14 33 | 3 55 | 14 13 | 4 24 | 13 45 | 5 12 | 12 58 |
| 24 Sa | 12 13 20 | 6 24 | 18 03 | 6 32 | 17 55 | 6 42 | 17 45 | 6 55 | 17 33 | 7 15 | 17 13 |
| 55 | | 4 14 | 15 53 | 4 30 | 15 39 | 4 48 | 15 22 | 5 14 | 14 57 | 5 56 | 14 17 |
| 25 Su | 12 13 11 | 6 23 | 18 03 | 6 31 | 17 56 | 6 40 | 17 47 | 6 53 | 17 35 | 7 12 | 17 16 |
| 56 | | 5 10 | 16 58 | 5 22 | 16 47 | 5 37 | 16 34 | 5 58 | 16 15 | 6 31 | 15 45 |
| 26 Mo | 12 13 01  16 45 ● | 6 22 | 18 04 | 6 30 | 17 57 | 6 39 | 17 48 | 6 51 | 17 36 | 7 09 | 17 18 |
| 57 | | 6 02 | 18 03 | 6 11 | 17 56 | 6 22 | 17 47 | 6 36 | 17 35 | 6 59 | 17 16 |
| 27 Tu | 12 12 51 | 6 22 | 18 04 | 6 29 | 17 57 | 6 37 | 17 50 | 6 48 | 17 38 | 7 06 | 17 21 |
| 58 | | 6 52 | 19 06 | 6 57 | 19 03 | 7 03 | 19 00 | 7 10 | 18 55 | 7 22 | 18 48 |
| 28 We | 12 12 40 | 6 21 | 18 05 | 6 28 | 17 58 | 6 36 | 17 51 | 6 47 | 17 39 | 7 03 | 17 23 |
| 59 | | 7 40 | 20 07 | 7 40 | 20 09 | 7 41 | 20 11 | 7 42 | 20 13 | 7 43 | 20 17 |

# 3rd Month

## March, 1979

**31 Days**

Greenwich Mean Time

**NOTE:** Light figures indicate Sun. **Dark** figures indicate **Moon**. *Degrees are North Latitude.*

**CAUTION:** Must be converted to local time. For instruction see page 774.

*In each day the upper line gives Sun values; the lower line gives Moon values. Rise/Set headings apply to both Sun and Moon.*

| Day of month / week / year | Sun on meridian / Moon phase (h m s) | 20° Rise | 20° Set | 30° Rise | 30° Set | 40° Rise | 40° Set | 50° Rise | 50° Set | 60° Rise | 60° Set |
|---|---|---|---|---|---|---|---|---|---|---|---|
| 1 Th | 12 12 29 | 6 20 | 18 05 | 6 27 | 17 59 | 6 34 | 17 51 | 6 45 | 17 41 | 7 00 | 17 26 |
| 60 | | 8 26 | 21 07 | 8 22 | 21 12 | 8 18 | 21 19 | 8 12 | 21 29 | 8 03 | 21 44 |
| 2 Fr | 12 12 18 | 6 19 | 18 05 | 6 26 | 18 00 | 6 33 | 17 52 | 6 43 | 17 43 | 6 57 | 17 28 |
| 61 | | 9 11 | 22 04 | 9 04 | 22 14 | 8 55 | 22 25 | 8 43 | 22 41 | 8 24 | 23 06 |
| 3 Sa | 12 12 05 | 6 19 | 18 06 | 6 25 | 18 00 | 6 31 | 17 53 | 6 41 | 17 44 | 6 54 | 17 31 |
| 62 | | 9 57 | 23 00 | 9 46 | 23 13 | 9 33 | 23 28 | 9 15 | 23 50 | 8 47 | |
| 4 Su | 12 11 53 | 6 18 | 18 06 | 6 23 | 18 01 | 6 30 | 17 55 | 6 38 | 17 46 | 6 52 | 17 33 |
| 63 | | 10 43 | 23 55 | 10 29 | | 10 12 | | 9 49 | | 9 13 | 0 24 |
| 5 Mo | 12 11 40 | 6 18 | 18 07 | 6 22 | 18 01 | 6 28 | 17 56 | 6 36 | 17 47 | 6 49 | 17 36 |
| 64 | 16 23 ☽ | 11 29 | | 11 14 | 0 10 | 10 54 | 0 28 | 10 28 | 0 53 | 9 45 | 1 35 |
| 6 Tu | 12 11 26 | 6 17 | 18 07 | 6 21 | 18 02 | 6 27 | 17 57 | 6 34 | 17 49 | 6 46 | 17 38 |
| 65 | | 12 17 | 0 47 | 12 00 | 1 03 | 11 39 | 1 24 | 11 11 | 1 52 | 10 24 | 2 38 |
| 7 We | 12 11 12 | 6 16 | 18 07 | 6 20 | 18 03 | 6 25 | 17 58 | 6 32 | 17 51 | 6 43 | 17 41 |
| 66 | | 13 05 | 1 37 | 12 48 | 1 54 | 12 27 | 2 15 | 11 58 | 2 44 | 11 10 | 3 32 |
| 8 Th | 12 10 57 | 6 15 | 18 07 | 6 19 | 18 03 | 6 24 | 17 59 | 6 30 | 17 52 | 6 40 | 17 43 |
| 67 | | 13 54 | 2 25 | 13 38 | 2 41 | 13 17 | 3 02 | 12 50 | 3 30 | 12 04 | 4 17 |
| 9 Fr | 12 10 43 | 6 14 | 18 08 | 6 17 | 18 04 | 6 22 | 18 00 | 6 28 | 17 54 | 6 37 | 17 46 |
| 68 | | 14 43 | 3 10 | 14 28 | 3 25 | 14 10 | 3 44 | 13 45 | 4 10 | 13 04 | 4 53 |
| 10 Sa | 12 10 27 | 6 13 | 18 08 | 6 16 | 18 04 | 6 21 | 18 01 | 6 26 | 17 55 | 6 34 | 17 48 |
| 69 | | 15 32 | 3 53 | 15 20 | 4 06 | 15 04 | 4 23 | 14 43 | 4 45 | 14 09 | 5 22 |
| 11 Su | 12 10 12 | 6 12 | 18 08 | 6 15 | 18 05 | 6 19 | 18 02 | 6 24 | 17 57 | 6 31 | 17 51 |
| 70 | | 16 21 | 4 34 | 16 11 | 4 45 | 15 59 | 4 58 | 15 43 | 5 16 | 15 17 | 5 45 |
| 12 Mo | 12 09 56 | 6 11 | 18 08 | 6 14 | 18 06 | 6 17 | 18 03 | 6 22 | 17 59 | 6 28 | 17 53 |
| 71 | | 17 10 | 5 13 | 17 03 | 5 21 | 16 55 | 5 31 | 16 44 | 5 44 | 16 26 | 6 05 |
| 13 Tu | 12 09 40 | 6 10 | 18 09 | 6 13 | 18 07 | 6 16 | 18 04 | 6 20 | 18 01 | 6 25 | 17 56 |
| 72 | 21 14 ○ | 17 59 | 5 51 | 17 56 | 5 56 | 17 52 | 6 02 | 17 46 | 6 10 | 17 38 | 6 23 |
| 14 We | 12 09 23 | 6 10 | 18 09 | 6 12 | 18 07 | 6 14 | 18 05 | 6 17 | 18 02 | 6 22 | 17 58 |
| 73 | | 18 49 | 6 29 | 18 49 | 6 31 | 18 49 | 6 33 | 18 50 | 6 35 | 18 50 | 6 39 |
| 15 Th | 12 09 06 | 6 09 | 18 10 | 6 11 | 18 08 | 6 13 | 18 06 | 6 15 | 18 04 | 6 19 | 18 01 |
| 74 | | 19 39 | 7 07 | 19 43 | 7 05 | 19 48 | 7 03 | 19 54 | 7 00 | 20 03 | 6 55 |
| 16 Fr | 12 08 49 | 6 08 | 18 10 | 6 10 | 18 09 | 6 11 | 18 07 | 6 13 | 18 06 | 6 16 | 18 03 |
| 75 | | 20 31 | 7 46 | 20 38 | 7 41 | 20 47 | 7 34 | 20 59 | 7 25 | 21 18 | 7 12 |
| 17 Sa | 12 08 32 | 6 07 | 18 10 | 6 09 | 18 10 | 6 09 | 18 08 | 6 11 | 18 07 | 6 13 | 18 05 |
| 76 | | 21 24 | 8 27 | 21 34 | 8 18 | 21 47 | 8 07 | 22 05 | 7 53 | 22 33 | 7 31 |
| 18 Su | 12 08 15 | 6 06 | 18 10 | 6 08 | 18 10 | 6 08 | 18 09 | 6 09 | 18 09 | 6 10 | 18 08 |
| 77 | | 22 18 | 9 10 | 22 31 | 8 58 | 22 48 | 8 44 | 23 11 | 8 24 | 23 48 | 7 53 |
| 19 Mo | 12 07 57 | 6 06 | 18 11 | 6 06 | 18 11 | 6 06 | 18 11 | 6 06 | 18 11 | 6 07 | 18 10 |
| 78 | | 23 14 | 9 56 | 23 29 | 9 42 | 23 49 | 9 24 | | 9 00 | | 8 21 |
| 20 Tu | 12 07 40 | 6 05 | 18 11 | 6 05 | 18 11 | 6 05 | 18 11 | 6 04 | 18 12 | 6 04 | 18 13 |
| 79 | | | 10 46 | | 10 30 | | 10 10 | | 9 42 | | 8 56 |
| 21 We | 12 07 22 | 6 04 | 18 11 | 6 04 | 18 12 | 6 03 | 18 12 | 6 02 | 18 13 | 6 01 | 18 15 |
| 80 | 11 22 ☾ | 0 10 | 11 40 | 0 27 | 11 23 | 0 48 | 11 02 | 1 18 | 10 32 | 2 06 | 9 43 |
| 22 Th | 12 07 04 | 6 03 | 18 11 | 6 03 | 18 13 | 6 01 | 18 13 | 6 00 | 18 15 | 5 58 | 18 18 |
| 81 | | 1 07 | 12 37 | 1 24 | 12 21 | 1 45 | 12 00 | 2 15 | 11 30 | 3 04 | 10 42 |
| 23 Fr | 12 06 46 | 6 02 | 18 12 | 6 02 | 18 13 | 6 00 | 18 14 | 5 58 | 18 16 | 5 55 | 18 20 |
| 82 | | 2 03 | 13 38 | 2 19 | 13 22 | 2 39 | 13 03 | 3 06 | 12 37 | 3 51 | 11 54 |
| 24 Sa | 12 06 28 | 6 02 | 18 12 | 6 00 | 18 14 | 5 58 | 18 15 | 5 55 | 18 18 | 5 53 | 18 23 |
| 83 | | 2 57 | 14 40 | 3 11 | 14 27 | 3 28 | 14 12 | 3 51 | 13 50 | 4 28 | 13 15 |
| 25 Su | 12 06 10 | 6 01 | 18 13 | 5 59 | 18 14 | 5 57 | 18 16 | 5 53 | 18 19 | 5 49 | 18 25 |
| 84 | | 3 49 | 15 42 | 3 59 | 15 33 | 4 13 | 15 22 | 4 30 | 15 07 | 4 58 | 14 42 |
| 26 Mo | 12 05 52 | 6 00 | 18 13 | 5 58 | 18 15 | 5 55 | 18 17 | 5 51 | 18 21 | 5 46 | 18 28 |
| 85 | | 4 39 | 16 45 | 4 45 | 16 40 | 4 54 | 16 34 | 5 05 | 16 25 | 5 23 | 16 12 |
| 27 Tu | 12 05 33 | 5 59 | 18 13 | 5 57 | 18 16 | 5 53 | 18 18 | 5 49 | 18 23 | 5 43 | 18 30 |
| 86 | | 5 27 | 17 47 | 5 29 | 17 46 | 5 33 | 17 45 | 5 37 | 17 44 | 5 44 | 17 42 |
| 28 We | 12 05 15 | 5 58 | 18 13 | 5 55 | 18 16 | 5 52 | 18 19 | 5 47 | 18 24 | 5 40 | 18 33 |
| 87 | 02 59 ● | 6 13 | 18 47 | 6 12 | 18 51 | 6 10 | 18 55 | 6 08 | 19 01 | 6 04 | 19 11 |
| 29 Th | 12 04 57 | 5 57 | 18 14 | 5 54 | 18 17 | 5 50 | 18 21 | 5 44 | 18 26 | 5 36 | 18 35 |
| 88 | | 7 00 | 19 47 | 6 54 | 19 55 | 6 47 | 20 04 | 6 38 | 20 17 | 6 25 | 20 37 |
| 30 Fr | 12 04 39 | 5 56 | 18 14 | 5 52 | 18 17 | 5 49 | 18 22 | 5 42 | 18 27 | 5 33 | 18 38 |
| 89 | | 7 46 | 20 45 | 7 37 | 20 57 | 7 25 | 21 10 | 7 10 | 21 29 | 6 47 | 21 59 |
| 31 Sa | 12 04 21 | 5 55 | 18 14 | 5 51 | 18 18 | 5 47 | 18 23 | 5 40 | 18 29 | 5 30 | 18 40 |
| 90 | | 8 33 | 21 42 | 8 20 | 21 56 | 8 05 | 22 13 | 7 44 | 22 37 | 7 12 | 23 16 |

# 4th Month      April, 1979      30 Day

### Greenwich Mean Time

**NOTE:** Light figures indicate Sun. **Dark** figures indicate **Moon**. *Degrees are North Latitude.*

**CAUTION:** Must be converted to local time. For instruction see page 774.

| Day/week year | Sun on meridian / Moon phase | Body | 20° Rise | 20° Set | 30° Rise | 30° Set | 40° Rise | 40° Set | 50° Rise | 50° Set | 60° Rise | 60° Set |
|---|---|---|---|---|---|---|---|---|---|---|---|---|
| 1 Su 91 | 12 04 03 | Sun | 5 54 | 18 14 | 5 50 | 18 19 | 5 45 | 18 24 | 5 38 | 18 31 | 5 27 | 18 4 |
| | | Moon | 9 20 | 22 37 | 9 06 | 22 53 | 8 47 | 23 12 | 8 22 | 23 40 | 7 42 | |
| 2 Mo 92 | 12 03 45 | Sun | 5 53 | 18 14 | 5 49 | 18 19 | 5 44 | 18 25 | 5 36 | 18 32 | 5 24 | 18 4 |
| | | Moon | 10 09 | 23 29 | 9 52 | 23 46 | 9 32 | | 9 04 | | 8 18 | 0 2 |
| 3 Tu 93 | 12 03 28 | Sun | 5 53 | 18 15 | 5 48 | 18 20 | 5 42 | 18 26 | 5 34 | 18 34 | 5 21 | 18 4 |
| | | Moon | 10 58 | | 10 41 | | 10 20 | 0 07 | 9 51 | 0 36 | 9 22 | 1 2 |
| 4 We 94 | 12 03 10  09 57 ☽ | Sun | 5 52 | 18 15 | 5 47 | 18 20 | 5 41 | 18 27 | 5 32 | 18 35 | 5 18 | 18 5 |
| | | Moon | 11 47 | 0 19 | 11 31 | 0 36 | 11 10 | 0 57 | 10 41 | 1 26 | 9 54 | 2 1 |
| 5 Th 95 | 12 02 53 | Sun | 5 51 | 18 15 | 5 46 | 18 21 | 5 39 | 18 28 | 5 30 | 18 37 | 5 15 | 18 5 |
| | | Moon | 12 37 | 1 05 | 12 21 | 1 21 | 12 02 | 1 41 | 11 36 | 2 09 | 10 52 | 2 5 |
| 6 Fr 96 | 12 02 35 | Sun | 5 50 | 18 15 | 5 45 | 18 22 | 5 37 | 18 29 | 5 28 | 18 39 | 5 12 | 18 5 |
| | | Moon | 13 26 | 1 49 | 13 13 | 2 04 | 12 56 | 2 21 | 12 33 | 2 46 | 11 56 | 3 2 |
| 7 Sa 97 | 12 02 18 | Sun | 5 49 | 18 16 | 5 44 | 18 22 | 5 36 | 18 30 | 5 26 | 18 40 | 5 09 | 18 5 |
| | | Moon | 14 15 | 2 31 | 14 04 | 2 43 | 13 51 | 2 58 | 13 32 | 3 18 | 13 03 | 3 5 |
| 8 Su 98 | 12 02 01 | Sun | 5 49 | 18 16 | 5 42 | 18 23 | 5 34 | 18 31 | 5 23 | 18 42 | 5 06 | 18 5 |
| | | Moon | 15 04 | 3 11 | 14 56 | 3 20 | 14 47 | 3 32 | 14 33 | 3 47 | 14 12 | 4 1 |
| 9 Mo 99 | 12 01 44 | Sun | 5 48 | 18 17 | 5 41 | 18 23 | 5 33 | 18 32 | 5 21 | 18 43 | 5 03 | 19 0 |
| | | Moon | 15 53 | 3 49 | 15 49 | 3 56 | 15 43 | 4 03 | 15 35 | 4 13 | 15 23 | 4 2 |
| 10 Tu 100 | 12 01 28 | Sun | 5 47 | 18 17 | 5 40 | 18 24 | 5 31 | 18 33 | 5 19 | 18 45 | 5 00 | 19 0 |
| | | Moon | 16 43 | 4 27 | 16 42 | 4 30 | 16 40 | 4 34 | 16 38 | 4 38 | 16 35 | 4 4 |
| 11 We 101 | 12 01 12 | Sun | 5 46 | 18 17 | 5 39 | 18 25 | 5 29 | 18 34 | 5 17 | 18 47 | 4 57 | 19 0 |
| | | Moon | 17 34 | 5 05 | 17 36 | 5 05 | 17 39 | 5 04 | 17 43 | 5 03 | 17 49 | 5 0 |
| 12 Th 102 | 12 00 56  13 15 ○ | Sun | 5 45 | 18 17 | 5 38 | 18 25 | 5 28 | 18 35 | 5 15 | 18 48 | 4 54 | 19 0 |
| | | Moon | 18 25 | 5 44 | 18 31 | 5 40 | 18 39 | 5 35 | 18 49 | 5 28 | 19 04 | 5 1 |
| 13 Fr 103 | 12 00 40 | Sun | 5 45 | 18 18 | 5 36 | 18 26 | 5 26 | 18 36 | 5 13 | 18 50 | 4 51 | 19 1 |
| | | Moon | 19 18 | 6 25 | 19 28 | 6 17 | 19 39 | 6 08 | 19 55 | 5 55 | 20 21 | 5 3 |
| 14 Sa 104 | 12 00 25 | Sun | 5 44 | 18 18 | 5 35 | 18 26 | 5 25 | 18 37 | 5 11 | 18 51 | 4 48 | 19 1 |
| | | Moon | 20 13 | 7 08 | 20 26 | 6 57 | 20 41 | 6 44 | 21 03 | 6 25 | 21 37 | 5 5 |
| 15 Su 105 | 12 00 10 | Sun | 5 43 | 18 18 | 5 34 | 18 27 | 5 23 | 18 38 | 5 09 | 18 53 | 4 45 | 19 1 |
| | | Moon | 21 09 | 7 54 | 21 24 | 7 40 | 21 43 | 7 23 | 22 09 | 7 00 | 22 52 | 6 2 |
| 16 Mo 106 | 11 59 55 | Sun | 5 42 | 18 18 | 5 33 | 18 28 | 5 22 | 18 39 | 5 07 | 18 54 | 4 42 | 19 1 |
| | | Moon | 22 06 | 8 43 | 22 23 | 8 27 | 22 44 | 8 07 | 23 13 | 7 40 | | 6 5 |
| 17 Tu 107 | 11 59 41 | Sun | 5 41 | 18 19 | 5 32 | 18 28 | 5 20 | 18 40 | 5 05 | 18 56 | 4 39 | 19 2 |
| | | Moon | 23 03 | 9 36 | 23 20 | 9 19 | 23 41 | 8 57 | | 8 28 | 0 01 | 7 3 |
| 18 We 108 | 11 59 27 | Sun | 5 41 | 18 19 | 5 31 | 18 29 | 5 19 | 18 41 | 5 02 | 18 58 | 4 37 | 19 2 |
| | | Moon | 23 58 | 10 32 | | 10 15 | | 9 53 | 0 11 | 9 24 | 1 01 | 8 3 |
| 19 Th 109 | 11 59 14  18 30 ☾ | Sun | 5 40 | 18 20 | 5 30 | 18 29 | 5 17 | 18 42 | 5 00 | 18 59 | 4 34 | 19 2 |
| | | Moon | | 11 30 | 0 15 | 11 14 | 0 35 | 10 54 | 1 04 | 10 27 | 1 51 | 9 3 |
| 20 Fr 110 | 11 59 01 | Sun | 5 39 | 18 20 | 5 29 | 18 30 | 5 16 | 18 43 | 4 58 | 19 01 | 4 31 | 19 2 |
| | | Moon | 0 52 | 12 30 | 1 06 | 12 17 | 1 25 | 12 00 | 1 50 | 11 36 | 2 30 | 10 5 |
| 21 Sa 111 | 11 58 48 | Sun | 5 38 | 18 20 | 5 28 | 18 31 | 5 15 | 18 44 | 4 56 | 19 02 | 4 28 | 19 3 |
| | | Moon | 1 43 | 13 31 | 1 55 | 13 20 | 2 09 | 13 07 | 2 30 | 12 49 | 3 01 | 12 2 |
| 22 Su 112 | 11 58 36 | Sun | 5 37 | 18 20 | 5 27 | 18 31 | 5 13 | 18 45 | 4 54 | 19 04 | 4 25 | 19 3 |
| | | Moon | 2 32 | 14 31 | 2 40 | 14 25 | 2 50 | 14 16 | 3 05 | 14 05 | 3 26 | 13 4 |
| 23 Mo 113 | 11 58 24 | Sun | 5 37 | 18 21 | 5 25 | 18 32 | 5 12 | 18 46 | 4 53 | 19 05 | 4 22 | 19 3 |
| | | Moon | 3 18 | 15 31 | 3 23 | 15 29 | 3 29 | 15 26 | 3 36 | 15 21 | 3 48 | 15 1 |
| 24 Tu 114 | 11 58 13 | Sun | 5 36 | 18 21 | 5 24 | 18 32 | 5 10 | 18 47 | 4 51 | 19 07 | 4 19 | 19 3 |
| | | Moon | 4 04 | 16 31 | 4 05 | 16 33 | 4 05 | 16 35 | 4 06 | 16 37 | 4 07 | 16 4 |
| 25 We 115 | 11 58 02 | Sun | 5 35 | 18 21 | 5 23 | 18 33 | 5 09 | 18 48 | 4 49 | 19 08 | 4 16 | 19 4 |
| | | Moon | 4 50 | 17 30 | 4 46 | 17 36 | 4 42 | 17 43 | 4 36 | 17 53 | 4 27 | 18 0 |
| 26 Th 116 | 11 57 52  13 15 ● | Sun | 5 34 | 18 21 | 5 22 | 18 34 | 5 08 | 18 49 | 4 47 | 19 10 | 4 13 | 19 4 |
| | | Moon | 5 35 | 18 29 | 5 28 | 18 39 | 5 18 | 18 50 | 5 06 | 19 06 | 4 47 | 19 3 |
| 27 Fr 117 | 11 57 42 | Sun | 5 34 | 18 22 | 5 21 | 18 34 | 5 06 | 18 50 | 4 45 | 19 11 | 4 11 | 19 4 |
| | | Moon | 6 22 | 19 27 | 6 11 | 19 40 | 5 57 | 19 55 | 5 39 | 20 17 | 5 10 | 20 5 |
| 28 Sa 118 | 11 57 33 | Sun | 5 33 | 18 22 | 5 21 | 18 35 | 5 05 | 18 51 | 4 43 | 19 13 | 4 08 | 19 4 |
| | | Moon | 7 09 | 20 23 | 6 55 | 20 39 | 6 38 | 20 58 | 6 15 | 21 24 | 5 38 | 22 0 |
| 29 Su 119 | 11 57 24 | Sun | 5 33 | 18 23 | 5 20 | 18 35 | 5 03 | 18 52 | 4 41 | 19 14 | 4 06 | 19 5 |
| | | Moon | 7 58 | 21 18 | 7 42 | 21 35 | 7 22 | 21 55 | 6 55 | 22 24 | 6 11 | 23 1 |
| 30 Mo 120 | 11 57 16 | Sun | 5 32 | 18 23 | 5 19 | 18 36 | 5 02 | 18 53 | 4 39 | 19 16 | 4 03 | 19 5 |
| | | Moon | 8 48 | 22 10 | 8 31 | 22 27 | 8 10 | 22 48 | 7 40 | 23 18 | 6 52 | |

# th Month　　　　　May, 1979　　　　　31 days

### Greenwich Mean Time

**NOTE:** Light figures indicate Sun. **Dark** figures indicate **Moon**. *Degrees are North Latitude.*

**CAUTION:** Must be converted to local time. For instruction see page 774.

In the table below, for each day the first (light) row gives **Sun** data and the second (dark) row gives **Moon** data. Times are h m.

| Day (week) | Day of year | Sun on meridian (h m s) / Moon phase | 20° Rise | 20° Set | 30° Rise | 30° Set | 40° Rise | 40° Set | 50° Rise | 50° Set | 60° Rise | 60° Set |
|---|---|---|---|---|---|---|---|---|---|---|---|---|
| 1 Tu | 121 | 11 57 08 | 5 31 | 18 23 | 5 18 | 18 37 | 5 01 | 18 54 | 4 37 | 19 18 | 4 00 | 19 56 |
| | | | 9 38 | 22 59 | 9 21 | 23 15 | 9 00 | 23 36 | 8 30 | | 7 41 | 0 07 |
| 2 We | 122 | 11 57 01 | 5 31 | 18 24 | 5 17 | 18 37 | 5 00 | 18 55 | 4 36 | 19 19 | 3 57 | 19 59 |
| | | | 10 28 | 23 44 | 10 12 | | 9 52 | | 9 24 | 0 05 | 8 38 | 0 51 |
| 3 Th | 123 | 11 56 54 | 5 30 | 18 24 | 5 16 | 18 38 | 4 58 | 18 56 | 4 34 | 19 21 | 3 55 | 20 01 |
| | | | 11 18 | | 11 04 | 0 00 | 10 46 | 0 19 | 10 21 | 0 45 | 9 41 | 1 26 |
| 4 Fr | 124 | 11 56 48 / 04 25 ) | 5 30 | 18 25 | 5 15 | 18 38 | 4 57 | 18 57 | 4 33 | 19 22 | 3 52 | 20 04 |
| | | | 12 08 | 0 27 | 11 56 | 0 41 | 11 41 | 0 57 | 11 20 | 1 19 | 10 47 | 1 54 |
| 5 Sa | 125 | 11 56 43 | 5 29 | 18 25 | 5 14 | 18 39 | 4 56 | 18 58 | 4 31 | 19 24 | 3 49 | 20 06 |
| | | | 12 57 | 1 08 | 12 48 | 1 19 | 12 36 | 1 31 | 12 20 | 1 49 | 11 56 | 2 16 |
| 6 Su | 126 | 11 56 38 | 5 28 | 18 25 | 5 13 | 18 40 | 4 55 | 18 59 | 4 29 | 19 25 | 3 46 | 20 08 |
| | | | 13 46 | 1 47 | 13 40 | 1 54 | 13 32 | 2 04 | 13 22 | 2 16 | 13 06 | 2 35 |
| 7 Mo | 127 | 11 56 33 | 5 28 | 18 26 | 5 12 | 18 41 | 4 54 | 19 00 | 4 27 | 19 27 | 3 44 | 20 11 |
| | | | 14 35 | 2 25 | 14 32 | 2 29 | 14 29 | 2 34 | 14 24 | 2 41 | 14 17 | 2 52 |
| 8 Tu | 128 | 11 56 29 | 5 27 | 18 26 | 5 12 | 18 41 | 4 52 | 19 01 | 4 26 | 19 28 | 3 41 | 20 13 |
| | | | 15 25 | 3 02 | 15 26 | 3 03 | 15 27 | 3 03 | 15 28 | 3 01 | 15 31 | 2 54 |
| 9 We | 129 | 11 56 26 | 5 27 | 18 27 | 5 11 | 18 42 | 4 51 | 19 02 | 4 24 | 19 30 | 3 39 | 20 16 |
| | | | 16 16 | 3 41 | 16 21 | 3 38 | 16 26 | 3 34 | 16 34 | 3 26 | 16 45 | 3 13 |
| 10 Th | 130 | 11 56 23 | 5 26 | 18 27 | 5 10 | 18 43 | 4 50 | 19 03 | 4 22 | 19 31 | 3 36 | 20 18 |
| | | | 17 09 | 4 20 | 17 17 | 4 14 | 17 27 | 4 07 | 17 41 | 3 57 | 18 02 | 3 41 |
| 11 Fr | 131 | 11 56 20 | 5 26 | 18 27 | 5 09 | 18 44 | 4 49 | 19 04 | 4 21 | 19 32 | 3 34 | 20 20 |
| | | | 18 04 | 5 03 | 18 15 | 4 53 | 18 30 | 4 41 | 18 49 | 4 25 | 19 20 | 4 01 |
| 12 Sa | 132 | 11 56 19 / 02 01 ○ | 5 25 | 18 28 | 5 09 | 18 44 | 4 48 | 19 05 | 4 19 | 19 34 | 3 31 | 20 23 |
| | | | 19 01 | 5 48 | 19 15 | 5 35 | 19 33 | 5 19 | 19 58 | 4 58 | 20 38 | 4 24 |
| 13 Su | 133 | 11 56 17 | 5 25 | 18 28 | 5 08 | 18 45 | 4 47 | 19 06 | 4 18 | 19 35 | 3 29 | 20 25 |
| | | | 19 59 | 6 37 | 20 15 | 6 22 | 20 36 | 6 03 | 21 04 | 5 37 | 21 51 | 4 55 |
| 14 Mo | 134 | 11 56 17 | 5 24 | 18 29 | 5 08 | 18 45 | 4 46 | 19 07 | 4 16 | 19 37 | 3 26 | 20 28 |
| | | | 20 57 | 7 30 | 21 15 | 7 13 | 21 36 | 6 52 | 22 06 | 6 22 | 22 57 | 5 34 |
| 15 Tu | 135 | 11 56 17 | 5 24 | 18 29 | 5 07 | 18 46 | 4 45 | 19 08 | 4 15 | 19 38 | 3 24 | 20 30 |
| | | | 21 54 | 8 26 | 22 11 | 8 09 | 22 33 | 7 47 | 23 02 | 7 16 | 23 51 | 6 26 |
| 16 We | 136 | 11 56 18 | 5 24 | 18 29 | 5 06 | 18 47 | 4 44 | 19 09 | 4 14 | 19 39 | 3 22 | 20 32 |
| | | | 22 49 | 9 25 | 23 05 | 9 08 | 23 24 | 8 47 | 23 51 | 8 18 | | 7 30 |
| 17 Th | 137 | 11 56 19 | 5 23 | 18 30 | 5 06 | 18 47 | 4 43 | 19 10 | 4 12 | 19 41 | 3 20 | 20 35 |
| | | | 23 41 | 10 25 | 23 54 | 10 10 | | 9 52 | | 9 27 | 0 34 | 8 45 |
| 18 Fr | 138 | 11 56 20 / 23 57 ( | 5 23 | 18 30 | 5 05 | 18 48 | 4 43 | 19 10 | 4 11 | 19 42 | 3 17 | 20 37 |
| | | | | 11 25 | | 11 14 | 0 10 | 10 59 | 0 32 | 10 39 | 1 07 | 10 07 |
| 19 Sa | 139 | 11 56 23 | 5 22 | 18 31 | 5 05 | 18 48 | 4 42 | 19 11 | 4 09 | 19 44 | 3 15 | 20 40 |
| | | | 0 30 | 12 25 | 0 40 | 12 17 | 0 52 | 12 07 | 1 08 | 11 53 | 1 33 | 11 31 |
| 20 Su | 140 | 11 56 26 | 5 22 | 18 31 | 5 04 | 18 49 | 4 41 | 19 12 | 4 08 | 19 45 | 3 13 | 20 42 |
| | | | 1 17 | 13 24 | 1 23 | 13 20 | 1 30 | 13 15 | 1 40 | 13 08 | 1 55 | 12 57 |
| 21 Mo | 141 | 11 56 29 | 5 22 | 18 31 | 5 04 | 18 50 | 4 40 | 19 13 | 4 07 | 19 46 | 3 11 | 20 44 |
| | | | 2 01 | 14 22 | 2 03 | 14 22 | 2 06 | 14 22 | 2 09 | 14 22 | 2 15 | 14 22 |
| 22 Tu | 142 | 11 56 33 | 5 22 | 18 32 | 5 03 | 18 50 | 4 39 | 19 14 | 4 06 | 19 48 | 3 09 | 20 46 |
| | | | 2 45 | 15 20 | 2 43 | 15 24 | 2 41 | 15 29 | 2 38 | 15 36 | 2 33 | 15 46 |
| 23 We | 143 | 11 56 38 | 5 21 | 18 32 | 5 03 | 18 51 | 4 39 | 19 15 | 4 05 | 19 49 | 3 06 | 20 49 |
| | | | 3 29 | 16 17 | 3 20 | 16 25 | 3 16 | 16 35 | 3 07 | 16 49 | 2 52 | 17 10 |
| 24 Th | 144 | 11 56 43 | 5 21 | 18 32 | 5 02 | 18 51 | 4 38 | 19 16 | 4 04 | 19 51 | 3 04 | 20 51 |
| | | | 4 14 | 17 15 | 4 05 | 17 26 | 3 53 | 17 40 | 3 37 | 18 00 | 3 13 | 18 31 |
| 25 Fr | 145 | 11 56 48 | 5 21 | 18 33 | 5 02 | 18 52 | 4 37 | 19 17 | 4 03 | 19 52 | 3 02 | 20 53 |
| | | | 5 01 | 18 11 | 4 41 | 18 25 | 4 32 | 18 43 | 4 11 | 19 08 | 3 37 | 19 47 |
| 26 Sa | 146 | 11 56 54 / 00 00 ● | 5 21 | 18 33 | 5 02 | 18 53 | 4 36 | 19 18 | 4 02 | 19 53 | 3 00 | 20 55 |
| | | | 5 48 | 19 07 | 5 33 | 19 23 | 5 14 | 19 43 | 4 49 | 20 11 | 4 07 | 20 57 |
| 27 Su | 147 | 11 57 01 | 5 21 | 18 34 | 5 01 | 18 53 | 4 36 | 19 19 | 4 01 | 19 54 | 2 58 | 20 57 |
| | | | 6 38 | 20 00 | 6 21 | 20 17 | 6 00 | 20 39 | 5 31 | 21 08 | 4 44 | 21 58 |
| 28 Mo | 148 | 11 57 08 | 5 20 | 18 34 | 5 01 | 18 54 | 4 35 | 19 19 | 4 00 | 19 56 | 2 57 | 20 59 |
| | | | 7 28 | 20 51 | 7 01 | 21 08 | 6 49 | 21 29 | 6 19 | 21 59 | 5 30 | 22 48 |
| 29 Tu | 149 | 11 57 16 | 5 20 | 18 35 | 5 00 | 18 54 | 4 35 | 19 20 | 3 59 | 19 57 | 2 55 | 21 01 |
| | | | 8 19 | 21 38 | 8 02 | 21 54 | 7 41 | 22 14 | 7 12 | 22 42 | 6 24 | 23 27 |
| 30 We | 150 | 11 57 24 | 5 20 | 18 35 | 5 00 | 18 55 | 4 34 | 19 21 | 3 58 | 19 58 | 2 53 | 21 03 |
| | | | 9 10 | 22 23 | 8 54 | 22 37 | 8 35 | 22 55 | 8 08 | 23 19 | 7 24 | 23 58 |
| 31 Th | 151 | 11 57 32 | 5 20 | 18 35 | 5 00 | 18 55 | 4 34 | 19 22 | 3 57 | 19 59 | 2 51 | 21 05 |
| | | | 10 00 | 23 05 | 9 46 | 23 16 | 9 30 | 23 31 | 9 07 | 23 51 | 8 30 | |

## 6th Month     June, 1979     30 da

### Greenwich Mean Time

**NOTE:** Light figures indicate Sun. **Dark** figures indicate **Moon**. *Degrees are North Latitude.*

**CAUTION:** Must be converted to local time. For instruction see page 774.

| Day of month / week / year | Sun on meridian · Moon phase (h m s) | 20° Rise Sun/Moon | 20° Set Sun/Moon | 30° Rise Sun/Moon | 30° Set Sun/Moon | 40° Rise Sun/Moon | 40° Set Sun/Moon | 50° Rise Sun/Moon | 50° Set Sun/Moon | 60° Rise Sun/Moon | 60° Set |
|---|---|---|---|---|---|---|---|---|---|---|---|
| 1 Fr | 11 57 41 | 5 20 | 18 36 | 5 00 | 18 56 | 4 33 | 19 22 | 3 56 | 20 00 | 2 50 | 21 |
| 152 | | 10 49 | 23 44 | 10 38 | 23 53 | 10 25 | | 10 07 | | 9 38 | 0 |
| 2 Sa | 11 57 50 | 5 20 | 18 36 | 4 59 | 18 57 | 4 33 | 19 23 | 3 56 | 20 01 | 2 49 | 21 |
| 153 | 22 37 )) | 11 38 | | 11 30 | | 11 21 | 0 04 | 11 08 | 0 19 | 10 48 | 0 |
| 3 Su | 11 57 59 | 5 20 | 18 37 | 4 59 | 18 57 | 4 32 | 19 23 | 3 55 | 20 02 | 2 47 | 21 |
| 154 | | 12 27 | 0 22 | 12 22 | 0 28 | 12 17 | 0 35 | 12 10 | 0 45 | 11 58 | 1 |
| 4 Mo | 11 58 09 | 5 20 | 18 37 | 4 59 | 18 58 | 4 32 | 19 24 | 3 54 | 20 03 | 2 46 | 21 |
| 155 | | 13 16 | 0 59 | 13 15 | 1 02 | 13 14 | 1 05 | 13 12 | 1 09 | 13 10 | 1 |
| 5 Tu | 11 58 19 | 5 20 | 18 37 | 4 59 | 18 59 | 4 32 | 19 25 | 3 54 | 20 04 | 2 45 | 21 |
| 156 | | 14 06 | 1 37 | 14 08 | 1 36 | 14 17 | 1 35 | 14 16 | 1 33 | 14 24 | 1 |
| 6 We | 11 58 30 | 5 20 | 18 37 | 4 59 | 18 59 | 4 32 | 19 25 | 3 53 | 20 05 | 2 44 | 21 |
| 157 | | 14 57 | 2 15 | 15 04 | 2 11 | 15 12 | 2 05 | 15 22 | 1 58 | 15 39 | 1 |
| 7 Th | 11 58 41 | 5 20 | 18 38 | 4 58 | 19 00 | 4 31 | 19 26 | 3 53 | 20 05 | 2 42 | 21 |
| 158 | | 15 51 | 2 56 | 16 01 | 2 48 | 16 13 | 2 38 | 16 30 | 2 25 | 16 57 | 2 |
| 8 Fr | 11 58 52 | 5 20 | 18 38 | 4 58 | 19 00 | 4 31 | 19 26 | 3 52 | 20 06 | 2 41 | 21 |
| 159 | | 16 47 | 3 39 | 17 00 | 3 28 | 17 17 | 3 14 | 17 39 | 2 55 | 18 15 | 2 |
| 9 Sa | 11 59 03 | 5 20 | 18 38 | 4 58 | 19 00 | 4 31 | 19 27 | 3 52 | 20 07 | 2 40 | 21 |
| 160 | | 17 46 | 4 27 | 18 01 | 4 13 | 18 21 | 3 55 | 18 48 | 3 31 | 19 32 | 2 |
| 10 Su | 11 59 15 | 5 20 | 18 38 | 4 58 | 19 00 | 4 31 | 19 28 | 3 52 | 20 08 | 2 39 | 21 |
| 161 | 11 55 O | 18 45 | 5 19 | 19 02 | 5 02 | 19 24 | 4 42 | 19 54 | 4 14 | 20 44 | 3 |
| 11 Mo | 11 59 27 | 5 20 | 18 39 | 4 58 | 19 01 | 4 31 | 19 28 | 3 51 | 20 08 | 2 39 | 21 |
| 162 | | 19 45 | 6 15 | 20 02 | 5 57 | 20 24 | 5 35 | 20 54 | 5 05 | 21 45 | 4 |
| 12 Tu | 11 59 39 | 5 20 | 18 39 | 4 58 | 19 01 | 4 30 | 19 29 | 3 51 | 20 09 | 2 38 | 21 |
| 163 | | 20 42 | 7 14 | 20 59 | 6 57 | 21 19 | 6 35 | 21 48 | 6 05 | 22 34 | 5 |
| 13 We | 11 59 51 | 5 20 | 18 40 | 4 58 | 19 02 | 4 30 | 19 29 | 3 50 | 20 09 | 2 38 | 21 |
| 164 | | 21 37 | 8 16 | 21 51 | 8 00 | 22 09 | 7 41 | 22 33 | 7 13 | 23 12 | 6 |
| 14 Th | 12 00 04 | 5 20 | 18 40 | 4 58 | 19 02 | 4 30 | 19 30 | 3 50 | 20 10 | 2 37 | 21 |
| 165 | | 22 28 | 9 18 | 22 39 | 9 05 | 22 53 | 8 49 | 23 11 | 8 26 | 23 41 | 7 |
| 15 Fr | 12 00 16 | 5 20 | 18 40 | 4 58 | 19 02 | 4 30 | 19 30 | 3 50 | 20 10 | 2 37 | |
| 166 | | 23 16 | 10 19 | 23 24 | 10 10 | 23 33 | 9 58 | 23 45 | 9 42 | | 9 |
| 16 Sa | 12 00 29 | 5 20 | 18 40 | 4 58 | 19 02 | 4 30 | 19 31 | 3 50 | 20 11 | 2 36 | 21 |
| 167 | | | 11 19 | | 11 14 | | 11 07 | | 10 57 | 0 04 | 10 |
| 17 Su | 12 00 42 | 5 21 | 18 41 | 4 59 | 19 03 | 4 31 | 19 31 | 3 50 | 20 11 | 2 36 | 21 |
| 168 | 05 01 (( | 0 02 | 12 18 | 0 05 | 12 16 | 0 09 | 12 14 | 0 15 | 12 12 | 0 24 | 12 |
| 18 Mo | 12 00 55 | 5 21 | 18 41 | 4 59 | 19 03 | 4 31 | 19 32 | 3 50 | 20 12 | 2 35 | 21 |
| 169 | | 0 46 | 13 15 | 0 45 | 13 18 | 0 44 | 13 21 | 0 43 | 13 25 | 0 42 | 13 |
| 19 Tu | 12 01 08 | 5 21 | 18 41 | 4 59 | 19 03 | 4 31 | 19 32 | 3 50 | 20 12 | 2 35 | 21 |
| 170 | | 1 29 | 14 12 | 1 24 | 14 18 | 1 19 | 14 26 | 1 11 | 14 37 | 1 00 | 14 |
| 20 We | 12 01 21 | 5 21 | 18 41 | 4 59 | 19 03 | 4 31 | 19 32 | 3 50 | 20 12 | 2 35 | 21 |
| 171 | | 2 12 | 15 08 | 2 04 | 15 18 | 1 54 | 15 31 | 1 40 | 15 48 | 1 20 | 16 |
| 21 Th | 12 01 34 | 5 21 | 18 41 | 4 59 | 19 04 | 4 31 | 19 32 | 3 50 | 20 12 | 2 35 | 21 |
| 172 | | 2 57 | 16 04 | 2 45 | 16 17 | 2 31 | 16 33 | 2 12 | 16 56 | 1 42 | 17 |
| 22 Fr | 12 01 47 | 5 22 | 18 42 | 5 00 | 19 04 | 4 32 | 19 33 | 3 51 | 20 13 | 2 36 | 21 |
| 173 | | 3 43 | 16 58 | 3 29 | 17 14 | 3 11 | 17 33 | 2 47 | 18 00 | 2 09 | 18 |
| 23 Sa | 12 02 00 | 5 22 | 18 42 | 5 00 | 19 05 | 4 32 | 19 33 | 3 51 | 20 13 | 2 36 | 21 |
| 174 | | 4 31 | 17 52 | 4 15 | 18 09 | 3 55 | 18 30 | 3 27 | 19 00 | 2 42 | 19 |
| 24 Su | 12 02 13 | 5 22 | 18 42 | 5 00 | 19 05 | 4 32 | 19 33 | 3 51 | 20 13 | 2 36 | 21 |
| 175 | 11 58 ● | 5 21 | 18 44 | 5 03 | 19 01 | 4 42 | 19 22 | 4 12 | 19 53 | 3 23 | 20 |
| 25 Mo | 12 02 26 | 5 22 | 18 42 | 5 00 | 19 05 | 4 32 | 19 33 | 3 51 | 20 13 | 2 37 | 21 |
| 176 | | 6 11 | 19 32 | 5 54 | 19 49 | 5 32 | 20 10 | 5 02 | 20 39 | 4 13 | 21 |
| 26 Tu | 12 02 39 | 5 22 | 18 42 | 5 00 | 19 05 | 4 33 | 19 33 | 3 52 | 20 13 | 2 37 | 21 |
| 177 | | 7 02 | 20 18 | 6 46 | 20 34 | 6 25 | 20 53 | 5 57 | 21 19 | 5 11 | 22 |
| 27 We | 12 02 52 | 5 23 | 18 43 | 5 01 | 19 05 | 4 33 | 19 33 | 3 52 | 20 13 | 2 38 | 21 |
| 178 | | 7 52 | 21 01 | 7 38 | 21 14 | 7 20 | 21 31 | 6 55 | 21 53 | 6 15 | 22 |
| 28 Th | 12 03 04 | 5 23 | 18 43 | 5 01 | 19 05 | 4 34 | 19 33 | 3 53 | 20 13 | 2 38 | 21 |
| 179 | | 8 42 | 21 42 | 8 30 | 21 52 | 8 15 | 22 05 | 7 55 | 22 22 | 7 22 | 22 |
| 29 Fr | 12 03 17 | 5 23 | 18 43 | 5 01 | 19 05 | 4 34 | 19 33 | 3 53 | 20 13 | 2 39 | 21 |
| 180 | | 9 31 | 22 20 | 9 22 | 22 28 | 9 11 | 22 37 | 8 56 | 22 49 | 8 31 | 23 |
| 30 Sa | 12 03 28 | 5 23 | 18 43 | 5 01 | 19 05 | 4 34 | 19 33 | 3 53 | 20 13 | 2 40 | 21 |
| 181 | | 10 20 | 22 58 | 10 14 | 23 02 | 10 07 | 23 07 | 9 57 | 23 13 | 9 42 | 23 |

# 7th Month — July, 1979 — 31 Days

Greenwich Mean Time

**NOTE:** Light figures indicate Sun. **Dark** figures indicate **Moon.** *Degrees are North Latitude.*

**CAUTION:** Must be converted to local time. For instruction see page 774.

| Day of month / week / year | Sun on meridian / Moon phase (h m s) | 20° Rise | 20° Set | 30° Rise | 30° Set | 40° Rise | 40° Set | 50° Rise | 50° Set | 60° Rise | 60° Set |
|---|---|---|---|---|---|---|---|---|---|---|---|
| 1 Su 182 | 12 03 41 | 5 23 | 18 43 | 5 02 | 19 05 | 4 35 | 19 33 | 3 54 | 20 13 | 2 41 | 21 25 |
|  |  | 11 08 | 23 34 | 11 06 | 23 35 | 11 03 | 23 36 | 10 59 | 23 37 | 10 52 | 23 39 |
| 2 Mo 183 | 12 03 52  15 24 ☽ | 5 24 | 18 44 | 5 02 | 19 05 | 4 35 | 19 32 | 3 55 | 20 12 | 2 43 | 21 25 |
|  |  | 11 57 |  | 11 58 |  | 11 59 |  | 12 01 |  | 12 04 | 23 54 |
| 3 Tu 184 | 12 04 03 | 5 25 | 18 44 | 5 03 | 19 05 | 4 36 | 19 32 | 3 55 | 20 12 | 2 44 | 21 24 |
|  |  | 12 43 | 0 12 | 12 52 | 0 09 | 12 57 | 0 05 | 13 05 | 0 01 | 13 17 |  |
| 4 We 185 | 12 04 14 | 5 25 | 18 44 | 5 03 | 19 05 | 4 36 | 19 32 | 3 56 | 20 12 | 2 45 | 21 23 |
|  |  | 13 39 | 0 50 | 13 47 | 0 44 | 13 57 | 0 36 | 14 11 | 0 26 | 14 32 | 0 10 |
| 5 Th 186 | 12 04 25 | 5 25 | 18 44 | 5 04 | 19 05 | 4 37 | 19 32 | 3 57 | 20 11 | 2 46 | 21 22 |
|  |  | 14 33 | 1 32 | 14 44 | 1 22 | 14 58 | 1 10 | 15 18 | 0 54 | 15 49 | 0 29 |
| 6 Fr 187 | 12 04 35 | 5 26 | 18 44 | 5 04 | 19 05 | 4 37 | 19 32 | 3 58 | 20 11 | 2 48 | 21 21 |
|  |  | 15 29 | 2 16 | 15 44 | 2 03 | 16 01 | 1 48 | 16 26 | 1 26 | 17 07 | 0 52 |
| 7 Sa 188 | 12 04 45 | 5 26 | 18 43 | 5 05 | 19 04 | 4 38 | 19 31 | 3 59 | 20 10 | 2 49 | 21 19 |
|  |  | 16 28 | 3 05 | 16 45 | 2 50 | 17 05 | 2 31 | 17 34 | 2 05 | 18 21 | 1 22 |
| 8 Su 189 | 12 04 55 | 5 27 | 18 43 | 5 05 | 19 04 | 4 38 | 19 31 | 4 00 | 20 10 | 2 51 | 21 18 |
|  |  | 17 28 | 3 59 | 17 46 | 3 42 | 18 08 | 3 21 | 18 38 | 2 51 | 18 29 | 2 03 |
| 9 Mo 190 | 12 05 04  19 59 ○ | 5 27 | 18 43 | 5 06 | 19 04 | 4 39 | 19 31 | 4 01 | 20 09 | 2 52 | 21 17 |
|  |  | 18 28 | 4 58 | 18 45 | 4 40 | 19 06 | 4 18 | 19 36 | 3 47 | 20 25 | 2 56 |
| 10 Tu 191 | 12 05 13 | 5 27 | 18 43 | 5 06 | 19 04 | 4 40 | 19 31 | 4 02 | 20 08 | 2 54 | 21 16 |
|  |  | 19 26 | 6 00 | 19 41 | 5 43 | 20 00 | 5 22 | 20 27 | 4 53 | 21 10 | 4 05 |
| 11 We 192 | 12 05 21 | 5 27 | 18 43 | 5 07 | 19 04 | 4 40 | 19 30 | 4 03 | 20 07 | 2 55 | 21 14 |
|  |  | 20 20 | 7 03 | 20 33 | 6 49 | 20 48 | 6 31 | 21 10 | 6 06 | 21 43 | 5 25 |
| 12 Th 193 | 12 05 29 | 5 28 | 18 43 | 5 07 | 19 04 | 4 41 | 19 30 | 4 04 | 20 07 | 2 57 | 21 13 |
|  |  | 21 11 | 8 07 | 21 20 | 7 56 | 21 31 | 7 42 | 21 46 | 7 23 | 22 09 | 6 53 |
| 13 Fr 194 | 12 05 36 | 5 28 | 18 43 | 5 08 | 19 03 | 4 41 | 19 29 | 4 05 | 20 06 | 2 58 | 21 11 |
|  |  | 21 59 | 9 10 | 22 04 | 9 03 | 22 10 | 8 54 | 22 19 | 8 41 | 22 31 | 8 22 |
| 14 Sa 195 | 12 05 43 | 5 28 | 18 43 | 5 08 | 19 03 | 4 42 | 19 29 | 4 06 | 20 05 | 3 00 | 21 10 |
|  |  | 22 45 | 10 11 | 22 46 | 10 08 | 22 47 | 10 04 | 22 48 | 9 59 | 22 50 | 9 51 |
| 15 Su 196 | 12 05 50 | 5 28 | 18 43 | 5 09 | 19 03 | 4 43 | 19 28 | 4 07 | 20 04 | 3 02 | 21 08 |
|  |  | 23 29 | 11 10 | 23 26 | 11 11 | 23 22 | 11 12 | 23 17 | 11 14 | 23 09 | 11 17 |
| 16 Mo 197 | 12 05 56  10 59 ☾ | 5 29 | 18 43 | 5 09 | 19 02 | 4 44 | 19 28 | 4 08 | 20 03 | 3 04 | 21 06 |
|  |  |  | 12 07 |  | 12 13 | 23 57 | 12 17 | 23 45 | 12 28 | 23 28 | 12 41 |
| 17 Tu 198 | 12 06 02 | 5 29 | 18 42 | 5 10 | 19 02 | 4 44 | 19 27 | 4 09 | 20 02 | 3 06 | 21 05 |
|  |  | 0 13 | 13 04 | 0 05 | 13 13 |  | 13 24 |  | 13 39 | 23 49 | 14 03 |
| 18 We 199 | 12 06 07 | 5 30 | 18 42 | 5 10 | 19 01 | 4 45 | 19 27 | 4 10 | 20 01 | 3 08 | 21 03 |
|  |  | 0 57 | 13 59 | 0 46 | 14 11 | 0 33 | 14 27 | 0 16 | 14 47 |  | 15 21 |
| 19 Th 200 | 12 06 11 | 5 30 | 18 42 | 5 11 | 19 01 | 4 46 | 19 26 | 4 11 | 20 00 | 3 10 | 21 01 |
|  |  | 1 42 | 14 54 | 1 28 | 15 09 | 1 12 | 15 27 | 0 49 | 15 52 | 0 14 | 16 34 |
| 20 Fr 201 | 12 06 15 | 5 30 | 18 42 | 5 12 | 19 01 | 4 47 | 19 25 | 4 12 | 19 59 | 3 12 | 20 59 |
|  |  | 2 29 | 15 47 | 2 13 | 16 04 | 1 54 | 16 24 | 1 27 | 16 53 | 0 44 | 17 40 |
| 21 Sa 202 | 12 06 19 | 5 31 | 18 41 | 5 12 | 19 00 | 4 48 | 19 24 | 4 13 | 19 58 | 3 14 | 20 57 |
|  |  | 3 17 | 16 39 | 3 00 | 16 56 | 2 39 | 17 18 | 2 10 | 17 48 | 1 22 | 18 37 |
| 22 Su 203 | 12 06 22 | 5 31 | 18 41 | 5 13 | 19 00 | 4 48 | 19 24 | 4 15 | 19 57 | 3 17 | 20 55 |
|  |  | 4 06 | 17 28 | 3 49 | 17 45 | 3 27 | 18 07 | 2 57 | 18 36 | 2 08 | 19 24 |
| 23 Mo 204 | 12 06 24 | 5 32 | 18 40 | 5 13 | 18 59 | 4 49 | 19 23 | 4 16 | 19 56 | 3 19 | 20 53 |
|  |  | 4 57 | 18 15 | 4 40 | 18 31 | 4 19 | 18 51 | 3 50 | 19 18 | 3 02 | 20 02 |
| 24 Tu 205 | 12 06 26  01 41 ● | 5 32 | 18 40 | 5 14 | 18 59 | 4 50 | 19 22 | 4 17 | 19 55 | 3 21 | 20 51 |
|  |  | 5 47 | 18 59 | 5 32 | 19 13 | 5 13 | 19 30 | 4 47 | 19 54 | 4 04 | 20 32 |
| 25 We 206 | 12 06 27 | 5 32 | 18 40 | 5 15 | 18 58 | 4 51 | 19 21 | 4 18 | 19 54 | 3 23 | 20 49 |
|  |  | 6 37 | 19 40 | 6 24 | 19 52 | 6 08 | 20 06 | 5 46 | 20 25 | 5 10 | 20 55 |
| 26 Th 207 | 12 06 28 | 5 33 | 18 40 | 5 15 | 18 58 | 4 52 | 19 20 | 4 20 | 19 52 | 3 25 | 20 46 |
|  |  | 7 26 | 20 20 | 7 16 | 20 28 | 7 03 | 20 39 | 6 46 | 20 53 | 6 18 | 21 15 |
| 27 Fr 208 | 12 06 28 | 5 33 | 18 39 | 5 16 | 18 57 | 4 53 | 19 19 | 4 21 | 19 51 | 3 28 | 20 44 |
|  |  | 8 15 | 20 57 | 8 08 | 21 03 | 7 59 | 21 09 | 7 47 | 21 18 | 7 28 | 21 32 |
| 28 Sa 209 | 12 06 27 | 5 34 | 18 39 | 5 16 | 18 56 | 4 54 | 19 18 | 4 23 | 19 49 | 3 30 | 20 41 |
|  |  | 9 03 | 21 34 | 8 59 | 21 36 | 8 55 | 21 39 | 8 48 | 21 42 | 8 38 | 21 47 |
| 29 Su 210 | 12 06 26 | 5 34 | 18 39 | 5 17 | 18 56 | 4 55 | 19 17 | 4 24 | 19 48 | 3 32 | 20 39 |
|  |  | 9 51 | 22 11 | 9 51 | 22 09 | 9 51 | 22 08 | 9 50 | 22 05 | 9 49 | 22 02 |
| 30 Mo 211 | 12 06 24 | 5 34 | 18 38 | 5 18 | 18 55 | 4 56 | 19 16 | 4 25 | 19 46 | 3 34 | 20 37 |
|  |  | 10 40 | 22 48 | 10 43 | 22 43 | 10 47 | 22 37 | 10 52 | 22 30 | 11 00 | 22 18 |
| 31 Tu 212 | 12 06 21 | 5 35 | 18 38 | 5 18 | 18 54 | 4 57 | 19 15 | 4 27 | 19 45 | 3 37 | 20 34 |
|  |  | 11 30 | 23 27 | 11 37 | 23 19 | 11 45 | 23 09 | 11 56 | 22 56 | 12 13 | 22 35 |

# 8th Month     August, 1979     31 Days

Greenwich Mean Time

**NOTE:** Light figures indicate Sun. **Dark** figures indicate **Moon.** *Degrees are North Latitude.*

**CAUTION:** Must be converted to local time. For instruction see page 774.

| Day of month/week/year | Sun on meridian / Moon phase | 20° Rise Sun/Moon | 20° Set Sun/Moon | 30° Rise | 30° Set | 40° Rise | 40° Set | 50° Rise | 50° Set | 60° Rise | 60° Set |
|---|---|---|---|---|---|---|---|---|---|---|---|
| 1 We | 12 06 18 | 5 35 | 18 37 | 5 19 | 18 54 | 4 57 | 19 14 | 4 28 | 19 43 | 3 39 | 20 32 |
| 213 | 05 57 ) | 12 22 | | 12 32 | 23 58 | 12 44 | 23 44 | 13 01 | 23 25 | 13 28 | 22 55 |
| 2 Th | 12 06 15 | 5 36 | 18 37 | 5 19 | 18 53 | 4 58 | 19 13 | 4 30 | 19 42 | 3 42 | 20 28 |
| 214 | | 13 16 | 0 09 | 13 29 | | 13 45 | | 14 07 | 23 59 | 14 43 | 23 21 |
| 3 Fr | 12 06 10 | 5 36 | 18 36 | 5 20 | 18 52 | 4 59 | 19 12 | 4 31 | 19 40 | 3 44 | 20 27 |
| 215 | | 14 12 | 0 55 | 14 27 | 0 40 | 14 47 | 0 23 | 15 13 | | 15 57 | 23 55 |
| 4 Sa | 12 06 05 | 5 36 | 18 35 | 5 21 | 18 51 | 5 00 | 19 11 | 4 32 | 19 38 | 3 46 | 20 24 |
| 216 | | 15 10 | 1 45 | 15 27 | 1 28 | 15 48 | 1 08 | 16 18 | 0 40 | 17 08 | |
| 5 Su | 12 06 00 | 5 37 | 18 35 | 5 21 | 18 50 | 5 01 | 19 10 | 4 34 | 19 37 | 3 49 | 20 22 |
| 217 | | 16 09 | 2 40 | 16 27 | 2 22 | 16 49 | 2 01 | 17 19 | 1 30 | 18 09 | 0 44 |
| 6 Mo | 12 05 53 | 5 37 | 18 34 | 5 22 | 18 50 | 5 02 | 19 09 | 4 35 | 19 35 | 3 51 | 20 19 |
| 218 | | 17 08 | 3 39 | 17 24 | 3 22 | 17 45 | 3 01 | 18 13 | 2 30 | 19 00 | 1 40 |
| 7 Tu | 12 05 47 | 5 38 | 18 34 | 5 22 | 18 49 | 5 03 | 19 08 | 4 37 | 19 34 | 3 54 | 20 17 |
| 219 | | 18 05 | 4 43 | 18 19 | 4 27 | 18 37 | 4 07 | 19 01 | 3 40 | 19 39 | 2 58 |
| 8 We | 12 05 39 | 5 38 | 18 33 | 5 23 | 18 48 | 5 04 | 19 07 | 4 38 | 19 32 | 3 56 | 20 14 |
| 220 | 03 21 ○ | 18 59 | 5 47 | 19 10 | 5 34 | 19 23 | 5 18 | 19 41 | 4 56 | 20 10 | 4 20 |
| 9 Th | 12 05 31 | 5 38 | 18 32 | 5 24 | 18 47 | 5 05 | 19 06 | 4 40 | 19 30 | 3 58 | 20 11 |
| 221 | | 19 50 | 6 52 | 19 57 | 6 43 | 20 05 | 6 32 | 20 17 | 6 16 | 20 35 | 5 51 |
| 10 Fr | 12 05 23 | 5 38 | 18 32 | 5 24 | 18 46 | 5 06 | 19 04 | 4 41 | 19 28 | 4 01 | 20 08 |
| 222 | | 20 38 | 7 56 | 20 41 | 7 51 | 20 44 | 7 45 | 20 49 | 7 36 | 20 56 | 7 22 |
| 11 Sa | 12 05 14 | 5 39 | 18 31 | 5 25 | 18 46 | 5 07 | 19 03 | 4 43 | 19 27 | 4 03 | 20 00 |
| 223 | | 21 24 | 8 58 | 21 23 | 8 57 | 21 21 | 8 57 | 21 19 | 8 55 | 21 15 | 8 53 |
| 12 Su | 12 05 04 | 5 39 | 18 31 | 5 25 | 18 45 | 5 08 | 19 01 | 4 44 | 19 25 | 4 06 | 20 03 |
| 224 | | 22 10 | 9 58 | 22 04 | 10 02 | 21 57 | 10 06 | 21 48 | 10 12 | 21 35 | 10 23 |
| 13 Mo | 12 04 54 | 5 39 | 18 30 | 5 26 | 18 44 | 5 09 | 19 00 | 4 46 | 19 23 | 4 08 | 20 00 |
| 225 | | 22 55 | 10 57 | 22 46 | 11 04 | 22 34 | 11 14 | 22 19 | 11 27 | 21 55 | 11 44 |
| 14 Tu | 12 04 43 | 5 39 | 18 29 | 5 27 | 18 43 | 5 10 | 18 59 | 4 48 | 19 21 | 4 10 | 19 55 |
| 226 | 19 02 ( | 23 40 | 11 54 | 23 28 | 12 05 | 23 13 | 12 19 | 22 52 | 12 38 | 22 19 | 13 0 |
| 15 We | 12 04 32 | 5 40 | 18 29 | 5 27 | 18 42 | 5 11 | 18 58 | 4 49 | 19 19 | 4 13 | 19 5 |
| 227 | | | 12 49 | | 13 03 | 23 54 | 13 21 | 23 28 | 13 45 | 22 48 | 14 2 |
| 16 Th | 12 04 20 | 5 40 | 18 28 | 5 28 | 18 41 | 5 12 | 18 56 | 4 51 | | 4 15 | 19 5 |
| 228 | | 0 27 | 13 44 | 0 12 | 14 00 | | 14 19 | | 14 47 | 23 23 | 15 3 |
| 17 Fr | 12 04 08 | 5 41 | 18 28 | 5 28 | 18 40 | 5 13 | 18 55 | 4 52 | 19 16 | 4 18 | 19 4 |
| 229 | | 1 15 | 14 36 | 0 58 | 14 53 | 0 38 | 15 14 | 0 09 | 15 44 | | 16 3 |
| 18 Sa | 12 03 55 | 5 41 | 18 27 | 5 29 | 18 39 | 5 14 | 18 54 | 4 53 | 19 14 | 4 20 | 19 4 |
| 230 | | 2 04 | 15 26 | 1 46 | 15 43 | 1 25 | 16 04 | 0 55 | 16 34 | 0 06 | 17 2 |
| 19 Su | 12 03 41 | 5 41 | 18 26 | 5 30 | 18 38 | 5 15 | 18 52 | 4 54 | 19 12 | 4 22 | 19 4 |
| 231 | | 2 53 | 16 13 | 2 36 | 16 29 | 2 15 | 16 49 | 1 46 | 17 17 | 0 57 | 18 0 |
| 20 Mo | 12 03 28 | 5 41 | 18 25 | 5 30 | 18 37 | 5 16 | 18 51 | 4 56 | 19 10 | 4 25 | 19 4 |
| 232 | | 3 43 | 16 57 | 3 28 | 17 12 | 3 08 | 17 30 | 2 41 | 17 55 | 1 56 | 18 3 |
| 21 Tu | 12 03 13 | 5 42 | 18 25 | 5 31 | 18 36 | 5 16 | 18 49 | 4 57 | 19 08 | 4 27 | 19 3 |
| 233 | | 4 33 | 17 40 | 4 19 | 17 52 | 4 02 | 18 07 | 3 39 | 18 28 | 3 00 | 19 0 |
| 22 We | 12 02 59 | 5 42 | 18 24 | 5 31 | 18 35 | 5 17 | 18 48 | 4 59 | 19 06 | 4 30 | 19 2 |
| 234 | 17 10 ● | 5 23 | 18 19 | 5 11 | 18 29 | 4 57 | 18 41 | 4 38 | 18 57 | 4 08 | 19 2 |
| 23 Th | 12 02 44 | 5 42 | 18 23 | 5 32 | 18 34 | 5 18 | 18 46 | 5 00 | 19 04 | 4 32 | 19 3 |
| 235 | | 6 11 | 18 57 | 6 03 | 19 04 | 5 53 | 19 12 | 5 39 | 19 23 | 5 17 | 19 3 |
| 24 Fr | 12 02 28 | 5 42 | 18 22 | 5 32 | 18 33 | 5 19 | 18 45 | 5 02 | 19 02 | 4 34 | 19 |
| 236 | | 7 00 | 19 35 | 6 55 | 19 38 | 6 49 | 19 42 | 6 40 | 19 47 | 6 27 | 19 |
| 25 Sa | 12 02 12 | 5 42 | 18 21 | 5 33 | 18 32 | 5 20 | 18 43 | 5 03 | 19 00 | 4 37 | 19 |
| 237 | | 7 48 | 20 11 | 7 46 | 20 11 | 7 44 | 20 11 | 7 42 | 20 11 | 7 38 | 20 1 |
| 26 Su | 12 01 56 | 5 43 | 18 21 | 5 33 | 18 30 | 5 21 | 18 42 | 5 05 | 18 58 | 4 39 | 19 2 |
| 238 | | 8 36 | 20 48 | 8 38 | 20 44 | 8 41 | 20 40 | 8 44 | 20 34 | 8 49 | 20 2 |
| 27 Mo | 12 01 39 | 5 43 | 18 20 | 5 34 | 18 29 | 5 22 | 18 40 | 5 06 | 18 56 | 4 42 | 19 |
| 239 | | 9 26 | 21 26 | 9 31 | 21 19 | 9 37 | 21 11 | 9 46 | 20 59 | 10 00 | 20 |
| 28 Tu | 12 01 21 | 5 43 | 18 19 | 5 34 | 18 28 | 5 23 | 18 39 | 5 08 | 18 54 | 4 44 | 19 |
| 240 | | 10 16 | 22 06 | 10 24 | 21 56 | 10 35 | 21 44 | 10 50 | 21 27 | 11 13 | 21 |
| 29 We | 12 01 04 | 5 43 | 18 18 | 5 35 | 18 27 | 5 24 | 18 37 | 5 09 | 18 52 | 4 46 | 19 |
| 241 | | 11 08 | 22 49 | 11 19 | 22 36 | 11 34 | 22 20 | 11 54 | 21 58 | 12 27 | 21 |
| 30 Th | 12 00 46 | 5 43 | 18 17 | 5 35 | 18 26 | 5 25 | 18 36 | 5 11 | 18 50 | 4 49 | 19 |
| 242 | 18 09 ) | 12 01 | 23 36 | 12 16 | 23 21 | 12 34 | 23 02 | 12 59 | 22 35 | 13 39 | 21 |
| 31 Fr | 12 00 27 | 5 44 | 18 17 | 5 36 | 18 24 | 5 26 | 18 34 | 5 12 | 18 49 | 4 51 | 19 |
| 243 | | 12 57 | | 13 13 | | 13 34 | 23 49 | 14 02 | 23 20 | 14 50 | 22 |

**th Month**            September, 1979            **30 Days**

Greenwich Mean Time

**NOTE:** Light figures indicate Sun. **Dark** figures indicate **Moon**. *Degrees are North Latitude.*

**CAUTION:** Must be converted to local time. For instruction see page 774.

| Day of month / week / year | Sun on meridian / Moon phase (h m s) | 20° Rise Sun / Moon | 20° Set Sun / Moon | 30° Rise Sun / Moon | 30° Set Sun / Moon | 40° Rise Sun / Moon | 40° Set Sun / Moon | 50° Rise Sun / Moon | 50° Set Sun / Moon | 60° Rise Sun / Moon | 60° Set Sun / Moon |
|---|---|---|---|---|---|---|---|---|---|---|---|
| Sa | 12 00 09 | 5 44 | 18 16 | 5 36 | 18 23 | 5 27 | 18 33 | 5 14 | 18 45 | 4 54 | 19 06 |
| 244 | | 13 54 | 0 27 | 14 11 | 0 10 | 14 33 | | 15 03 | | 15 54 | 23 23 |
| Su | 11 59 50 | 5 44 | 18 15 | 5 37 | 18 22 | 5 28 | 18 31 | 5 15 | 18 43 | 4 56 | 19 03 |
| 245 | | 14 51 | 1 23 | 15 08 | 1 05 | 15 29 | 0 43 | 15 59 | 0 13 | 16 48 | |
| Mo | 11 59 30 | 5 44 | 18 14 | 5 38 | 18 21 | 5 29 | 18 29 | 5 17 | 18 41 | 4 58 | 19 00 |
| 246 | | 15 48 | 2 22 | 16 03 | 2 06 | 16 22 | 1 45 | 16 49 | 1 16 | 17 32 | 0 28 |
| Tu | 11 59 11 | 5 44 | 18 13 | 5 38 | 18 20 | 5 30 | 18 28 | 5 18 | 18 39 | 5 00 | 18 57 |
| 247 | | 16 42 | 3 25 | 16 55 | 3 11 | 17 11 | 2 53 | 17 32 | 2 27 | 18 06 | 1 46 |
| We | 11 58 51 | 5 45 | 18 13 | 5 39 | 18 18 | 5 31 | 18 26 | 5 20 | 18 37 | 5 03 | 18 53 |
| 248 | | 17 35 | 4 30 | 17 44 | 4 18 | 17 55 | 4 04 | 18 10 | 3 45 | 18 34 | 3 14 |
| Th | 11 58 31 | 5 45 | 18 12 | 5 39 | 18 17 | 5 32 | 18 25 | 5 21 | 18 35 | 5 05 | 18 50 |
| 249 | 10 59 ○ | 18 25 | 5 34 | 18 30 | 5 27 | 18 36 | 5 18 | 18 44 | 5 06 | 18 57 | 4 46 |
| Fr | 11 58 10 | 5 45 | 18 11 | 5 40 | 18 16 | 5 33 | 18 23 | 5 23 | 18 33 | 5 07 | 18 47 |
| 250 | | 19 13 | 6 38 | 19 14 | 6 35 | 19 15 | 6 32 | 19 16 | 6 27 | 19 18 | 6 19 |
| Sa | 11 57 50 | 5 45 | 18 10 | 5 40 | 18 15 | 5 34 | 18 21 | 5 24 | 18 31 | 5 09 | 18 44 |
| 251 | | 20 01 | 7 41 | 19 57 | 7 43 | 19 52 | 7 45 | 19 47 | 7 47 | 19 38 | 7 51 |
| Su | 11 57 29 | 5 46 | 18 09 | 5 41 | 18 14 | 5 35 | 18 20 | 5 26 | 18 29 | 5 12 | 18 41 |
| 253 | | 20 47 | 8 43 | 20 40 | 8 48 | 20 30 | 8 56 | 20 18 | 9 05 | 19 58 | 9 21 |
| Mo | 11 57 08 | 5 46 | 18 08 | 5 41 | 18 12 | 5 35 | 18 18 | 5 27 | 18 26 | 5 14 | 18 38 |
| 253 | | 21 34 | 9 42 | 21 23 | 9 52 | 21 09 | 10 04 | 20 51 | 10 21 | 20 22 | 10 47 |
| Tu | 11 56 47 | 5 47 | 18 07 | 5 42 | 18 11 | 5 36 | 18 17 | 5 29 | 18 24 | 5 17 | 18 35 |
| 254 | | 22 22 | 10 41 | 22 08 | 10 54 | 21 51 | 11 10 | 21 27 | 11 32 | 20 49 | 12 07 |
| We | 11 56 26 | 5 47 | 18 06 | 5 42 | 18 10 | 5 37 | 18 15 | 5 30 | 18 22 | 5 19 | 18 32 |
| 255 | | 23 11 | 11 37 | 22 54 | 11 52 | 22 35 | 12 11 | 22 07 | 12 38 | 21 22 | 13 21 |
| Th | 11 56 05 | 5 47 | 18 05 | 5 43 | 18 09 | 5 38 | 18 13 | 5 32 | 18 20 | 5 21 | 18 29 |
| 256 | 06 15 ☾ | | 12 31 | 23 43 | 12 48 | 23 22 | 13 08 | 22 52 | 13 38 | 22 03 | 14 26 |
| Fr | 11 55 44 | 5 47 | 18 04 | 5 43 | 18 08 | 5 39 | 18 12 | 5 33 | 18 18 | 5 24 | 18 26 |
| 257 | | 0 00 | 13 22 | | 13 39 | | 14 01 | 23 42 | 14 31 | 22 52 | 15 20 |
| Sa | 11 55 23 | 5 48 | 18 03 | 5 44 | 18 06 | 5 40 | 18 10 | 5 35 | 18 15 | 5 26 | 18 23 |
| 258 | | 0 50 | 14 10 | 0 33 | 14 27 | 0 11 | 14 48 | | 15 17 | 23 49 | 16 04 |
| Su | 11 55 01 | 5 48 | 18 02 | 5 44 | 18 05 | 5 41 | 18 09 | 5 36 | 18 13 | 5 29 | 18 20 |
| 259 | | 1 40 | 14 56 | 1 24 | 15 11 | 1 03 | 15 30 | 0 35 | 15 56 | | 16 38 |
| Mo | 11 54 40 | 5 48 | 18 01 | 5 45 | 18 04 | 5 42 | 18 07 | 5 38 | 18 11 | 5 31 | 18 17 |
| 260 | | 2 30 | 15 39 | 2 15 | 15 52 | 1 57 | 16 08 | 1 32 | 16 30 | 0 52 | 17 05 |
| Tu | 11 54 19 | 5 48 | 18 00 | 5 46 | 18 03 | 5 43 | 18 05 | 5 39 | 18 09 | 5 33 | 18 14 |
| 261 | | 3 19 | 16 19 | 3 07 | 16 30 | 2 52 | 16 43 | 2 31 | 17 00 | 1 58 | 17 27 |
| We | 11 53 57 | 5 48 | 17 59 | 5 46 | 18 01 | 5 44 | 18 05 | 5 41 | 18 07 | 5 36 | 18 11 |
| 262 | | 4 08 | 16 58 | 3 59 | 17 05 | 3 47 | 17 15 | 3 32 | 17 27 | 3 07 | 17 46 |
| Th | 11 53 36 | 5 49 | 17 59 | 5 47 | 18 00 | 5 45 | 18 02 | 5 42 | 18 04 | 5 38 | 18 08 |
| 263 | | 4 57 | 17 35 | 4 51 | 17 39 | 4 43 | 17 45 | 4 33 | 17 52 | 4 17 | 18 02 |
| Fr | 11 53 15 | 5 49 | 17 58 | 5 47 | 17 58 | 5 46 | 18 00 | 5 44 | 18 02 | 5 41 | 18 05 |
| 264 | 09 47 ● | 5 45 | 18 12 | 5 42 | 18 13 | 5 39 | 18 14 | 5 34 | 18 15 | 5 27 | 18 18 |
| Sa | 11 52 54 | 5 49 | 17 57 | 5 48 | 17 57 | 5 47 | 17 58 | 5 45 | 18 00 | 5 43 | 18 02 |
| 265 | | 6 34 | 18 49 | 6 34 | 18 46 | 6 35 | 18 43 | 6 37 | 18 39 | 6 39 | 18 33 |
| Su | 11 52 33 | 5 49 | 17 56 | 5 49 | 17 57 | 5 48 | 17 56 | 5 47 | 17 58 | 5 45 | 17 59 |
| 266 | | 7 23 | 19 27 | 7 27 | 19 21 | 7 32 | 19 13 | 7 39 | 19 04 | 7 51 | 18 49 |
| Mo | 11 52 12 | 5 49 | 17 55 | 5 49 | 17 55 | 5 49 | 17 55 | 5 48 | 17 56 | 5 47 | 17 56 |
| 267 | | 8 13 | 20 06 | 8 20 | 19 57 | 8 30 | 19 46 | 8 43 | 19 30 | 9 03 | 19 07 |
| Tu | 11 51 51 | 5 50 | 17 54 | 5 50 | 17 53 | 5 50 | 17 53 | 5 50 | 17 53 | 5 50 | 17 53 |
| 268 | | 9 04 | 20 48 | 9 15 | 20 36 | 9 28 | 20 21 | 9 47 | 20 00 | 10 16 | 19 28 |
| We | 11 51 31 | 5 50 | 17 53 | 5 50 | 17 52 | 5 51 | 17 52 | 5 51 | 17 51 | 5 52 | 17 50 |
| 269 | | 9 57 | 21 33 | 10 10 | 21 18 | 10 27 | 21 00 | 10 51 | 20 35 | 11 29 | 19 55 |
| Th | 11 51 10 | 5 50 | 17 52 | 5 51 | 17 51 | 5 52 | 17 50 | 5 53 | 17 49 | 5 54 | 17 47 |
| 270 | | 10 51 | 22 21 | 11 06 | 22 05 | 11 26 | 21 44 | 11 54 | 21 15 | 12 39 | 20 29 |
| Fr | 11 50 50 | 5 50 | 17 51 | 5 51 | 17 50 | 5 53 | 17 48 | 5 54 | 17 47 | 5 56 | 17 44 |
| 271 | | 11 46 | 23 13 | 12 03 | 22 56 | 12 24 | 22 34 | 12 54 | 22 04 | 13 44 | 21 14 |
| Sa | 11 50 30 | 5 50 | 17 50 | 5 52 | 17 49 | 5 54 | 17 47 | 5 56 | 17 45 | 5 59 | 17 41 |
| 272 | 04 20 ☽ | 12 41 | | 12 58 | 23 52 | 13 20 | 23 31 | 13 50 | 23 01 | 14 40 | 22 11 |
| Su | 11 50 10 | 5 51 | 17 50 | 5 52 | 17 47 | 5 55 | 17 45 | 5 57 | 17 42 | 6 01 | 17 38 |
| 273 | | 13 36 | 0 10 | 13 52 | | 14 12 | | 14 41 | | 15 27 | 23 22 |

# 10th Month      October, 1979      31 Days

Greenwich Mean Time

**NOTE:** Light figures indicate Sun. **Dark** figures indicate **Moon**. *Degrees are North Latitude.*

**CAUTION:** Must be converted to local time. For instruction see page 774.

| Day of month / week / year | Sun on meridian / Moon phase (h m s) | 20° Rise Sun/Moon (h m) | 20° Set Sun/Moon (h m) | 30° Rise (h m) | 30° Set (h m) | 40° Rise (h m) | 40° Set (h m) | 50° Rise (h m) | 50° Set (h m) | 60° Rise (h m) | 60° Set (h m) |
|---|---|---|---|---|---|---|---|---|---|---|---|
| 1 Mo 274 | 11 49 50 | 5 51 | 17 49 | 5 53 | 17 48 | 5 56 | 17 44 | 5 59 | 17 40 | 6 04 | ·17 |
|  |  | 14 29 | 1 09 | 14 43 | 0 53 | 15 01 | 0 34 | 15 25 | 0 07 | 16 04 |  |
| 2 Tu 275 | 11 49 31 | 5 51 | 17 48 | 5 53 | 17 45 | 5 57 | 17 42 | 6 00 | 17 38 | 6 06 | 17 |
|  |  | 15 21 | 2 11 | 15 32 | 1 58 | 15 46 | 1 41 | 16 04 | 1 19 | 16 33 | 0 |
| 3 We 276 | 11 49 12 | 5 51 | 17 47 | 5 54 | 17 44 | 5 58 | 17 40 | 6 02 | 17 36 | 6 08 | 17 |
|  |  | 16 11 | 3 13 | 16 18 | 3 04 | 16 27 | 2 52 | 16 39 | 2 36 | 16 57 | 2 |
| 4 Th 277 | 11 48 53 | 5 51 | 17 46 | 5 54 | 17 43 | 5 59 | 17 39 | 6 03 | 17 34 | 6 11 | 17 |
|  |  | 17 00 | 4 17 | 17 03 | 4 11 | 17 06 | 4 05 | 17 11 | 3 56 | 17 18 | 3 |
| 5 Fr 278 | 11 48 35 | 5 52 | 17 45 | 5 55 | 17 41 | 5 59 | 17 37 | 6 05 | 17 31 | 6 13 | 17 |
|  | 19 35 ○ | 17 47 | 5 20 | 17 46 | 5 19 | 17 44 | 5 18 | 17 42 | 5 16 | 17 39 | 5 |
| 6 Sa 279 | 11 48 17 | 5 52 | 17 44 | 5 55 | 17 40 | 6 00 | 17 36 | 6 06 | 17 29 | 6 16 | 17 |
|  |  | 18 35 | 6 22 | 18 29 | 6 26 | 18 22 | 6 30 | 18 13 | 6 36 | 17 59 | 6 |
| 7 Su 280 | 11 47 59 | 5 52 | 17 43 | 5 56 | 17 39 | 6 01 | 17 34 | 6 08 | 17 27 | 6 18 | 17 |
|  |  | 19 23 | 7 24 | 19 13 | 7 32 | 19 01 | 7 42 | 18 46 | 7 55 | 18 21 | 8 |
| 8 Mo 281 | 11 47 42 | 5 52 | 17 42 | 5 57 | 17 38 | 6 02 | 17 32 | 6 10 | 17 25 | 6 20 | 17 |
|  |  | 20 11 | 8 25 | 19 59 | 8 36 | 19 43 | 8 51 | 19 21 | 9 10 | 18 47 | 9 |
| 9 Tu 282 | 11 47 25 | 5 53 | 17 41 | 5 57 | 17 37 | 6 03 | 17 31 | 6 11 | 17 23 | 6 23 | 17 |
|  |  | 21 01 | 9 24 | 20 46 | 9 38 | 20 27 | 9 56 | 20 01 | 10 21 | 19 18 | 11 |
| 10 We 283 | 11 47 09 | 5 53 | 17 41 | 5 58 | 17 35 | 6 05 | 17 29 | 6 13 | 17 20 | 6 25 | 17 |
|  |  | 21 52 | 10 21 | 21 35 | 10 37 | 21 14 | 10 58 | 20 45 | 11 26 | 19 57 | 12 |
| 11 Th 284 | 11 46 53 | 5 54 | 17 40 | 5 58 | 17 34 | 6 06 | 17 28 | 6 14 | 17 18 | 6 28 | 17 |
|  |  | 22 43 | 11 15 | 22 25 | 11 32 | 22 04 | 11 53 | 21 34 | 12 24 | 20 44 | 13 |
| 12 Fr 285 | 11 46 38 | 5 54 | 17 39 | 5 59 | 17 33 | 6 07 | 17 26 | 6 16 | 17 16 | 6 30 | 17 |
|  | 21 24 ◁ | 23 34 | 12 05 | 23 17 | 12 22 | 22 56 | 12 44 | 22 27 | 13 13 | 21 39 | 14 |
| 13 Sa 286 | 11 46 23 | 5 54 | 17 38 | 6 00 | 17 32 | 6 08 | 17 25 | 6 18 | 17 14 | 6 33 | 16 |
|  |  |  | 12 53 |  | 13 09 | 23 50 | 13 28 | 23 24 | 13 56 | 22 40 | 14 |
| 14 Su 287 | 11 46 08 | 5 54 | 17 37 | 6 01 | 17 31 | 6 09 | 17 23 | 6 19 | 17 12 | 6 35 | 16 |
|  |  | 0 24 | 13 37 | 0 09 | 13 51 |  | 14 08 |  | 14 32 | 23 46 | 15 |
| 15 Mo 288 | 11 45 54 | 5 55 | 17 37 | 6 01 | 17 30 | 6 10 | 17 22 | 6 21 | 17 10 | 6 38 | 16 |
|  |  | 1 14 | 14 18 | 1 01 | 14 30 | 0 45 | 14 44 | 0 22 | 15 03 |  | 15 |
| 16 Tu 289 | 11 45 41 | 5 55 | 17 36 | 6 02 | 17 29 | 6 11 | 17 20 | 6 22 | 17 08 | 6 40 | 16 |
|  |  | 2 03 | 14 57 | 1 53 | 15 06 | 1 40 | 15 16 | 1 23 | 15 31 | 0 55 | 15 |
| 17 We 290 | 11 45 29 | 5 55 | 17 35 | 6 03 | 17 28 | 6 12 | 17 19 | 6 24 | 17 06 | 6 43 | 16 |
|  |  | 2 52 | 15 35 | 2 45 | 15 40 | 2 36 | 15 47 | 2 24 | 15 56 | 2 04 | 16 |
| 18 Th 291 | 11 45 17 | 5 55 | 17 34 | 6 04 | 17 27 | 6 13 | 17 17 | 6 26 | 17 04 | 6 45 | 16 |
|  |  | 3 41 | 16 12 | 3 37 | 16 14 | 3 32 | 16 16 | 3 25 | 16 20 | 3 15 | 16 |
| 19 Fr 292 | 11 45 05 | 5 56 | 17 34 | 6 04 | 17 26 | 6 14 | 17 16 | 6 27 | 17 02 | 6 48 | 16 |
|  |  | 4 29 | 16 48 | 4 29 | 16 47 | 4 28 | 16 46 | 4 27 | 16 43 | 4 26 | 16 |
| 20 Sa 293 | 11 44 54 | 5 56 | 17 33 | 6 05 | 17 25 | 6 15 | 17 14 | 6 29 | 17 00 | 6 50 | 16 |
|  |  | 5 18 | 17 26 | 5 21 | 17 21 | 5 25 | 17 15 | 5 31 | 17 08 | 5 39 | 16 |
| 21 Su 294 | 11 44 44 | 5 57 | 17 33 | 6 05 | 17 24 | 6 16 | 17 13 | 6 30 | 16 58 | 6 53 | 16 |
|  | 02 23 ● | 6 08 | 18 05 | 6 15 | 17 57 | 6 23 | 17 47 | 6 35 | 17 34 | 6 52 | 17 |
| 22 Mo 295 | 11 44 35 | 5 57 | 17 32 | 6 06 | 17 23 | 6 17 | 17 11 | 6 32 | 16 56 | 6 55 | 16 |
|  |  | 7 00 | 18 47 | 7 10 | 18 35 | 7 22 | 18 21 | 7 39 | 18 02 | 8 06 | 17 |
| 23 Tu 296 | 11 44 26 | 5 57 | 17 31 | 6 07 | 17 22 | 6 18 | 17 10 | 6 34 | 16 54 | 6 57 | 16 |
|  |  | 7 53 | 19 31 | 8 06 | 19 17 | 8 22 | 18 59 | 8 44 | 18 35 | 9 20 | 17 |
| 24 We 297 | 11 44 18 | 5 58 | 17 31 | 6 08 | 17 21 | 6 19 | 17 09 | 6 35 | 16 52 | 7 00 | 16 |
|  |  | 8 47 | 20 18 | 9 02 | 20 02 | 9 22 | 19 42 | 9 48 | 19 14 | 10 32 | 18 |
| 25 Th 298 | 11 44 10 | 5 58 | 17 30 | 6 08 | 17 20 | 6 21 | 17 07 | 6 37 | 16 50 | 7 03 | 16 |
|  |  | 9 42 | 21 09 | 9 59 | 20 52 | 10 20 | 20 30 | 10 50 | 20 00 | 11 40 | 19 |
| 26 Fr 299 | 11 44 03 | 5 59 | 17 30 | 6 09 | 17 19 | 6 22 | 17 06 | 6 38 | 16 49 | 7 05 | 16 |
|  |  | 10 37 | 22 04 | 10 54 | 21 46 | 11 16 | 21 24 | 11 55 | 20 54 | 12 38 | 20 |
| 27 Sa 300 | 11 43 57 | 5 59 | 17 29 | 6 10 | 17 18 | 6 23 | 17 05 | 6 40 | 16 47 | 7 08 | 16 |
|  |  | 11 31 | 23 01 | 11 48 | 22 45 | 12 09 | 22 24 | 12 39 | 21 55 | 13 27 | 21 |
| 28 Su 301 | 11 43 52 | 5 59 | 17 28 | 6 11 | 17 17 | 6 24 | 17 04 | 6 42 | 16 45 | 7 11 | 16 |
|  | 13 06 )) | 12 23 |  | 12 39 | 23 46 | 12 58 | 23 28 | 13 24 | 23 04 | 14 06 | 22 |
| 29 Mo 302 | 11 43 49 | 6 00 | 17 28 | 6 11 | 17 16 | 6 25 | 17 02 | 6 44 | 16 43 | 7 13 | 16 |
|  |  | 13 14 | 0 00 | 13 27 |  | 13 42 |  | 14 03 |  | 14 36 | 23 |
| 30 Tu 303 | 11 43 43 | 6 00 | 17 27 | 6 12 | 17 16 | 6 26 | 17 01 | 6 45 | 16 42 | 7 16 | 16 |
|  |  | 14 03 | 1 00 | 14 12 | 0 49 | 14 23 | 0 36 | 14 38 | 0 17 | 15 01 |  |
| 31 We 304 | 11 43 40 | 6 01 | 17 27 | 6 12 | 17 15 | 6 27 | 16 59 | 6 47 | 16 40 | 7 18 | 16 |
|  |  | 14 50 | 2 01 | 14 55 | 1 54 | 15 01 | 1 45 | 15 09 | 1 33 | 15 22 | 1 |

# 11th Month                    November, 1979                    30 Days

Greenwich Mean Time

**NOTE:** Light figures indicate Sun. **Dark** figures indicate **Moon.** *Degrees are North Latitude.*

**CAUTION:** Must be converted to local time. For instruction see page 774.

| Day of month / week / year | Sun on meridian / Moon phase (h m s) | 20° Rise Sun/Moon | 20° Set Sun/Moon | 30° Rise Sun/Moon | 30° Set Sun/Moon | 40° Rise Sun/Moon | 40° Set Sun/Moon | 50° Rise Sun/Moon | 50° Set Sun/Moon | 60° Rise Sun/Moon | 60° Set Sun/Moon |
|---|---|---|---|---|---|---|---|---|---|---|---|
| 1 Th — 305 | 11 43 34 | 6 01 | 17 26 | 6 13 | 17 14 | 6 28 | 16 58 | 6 49 | 16 38 | 7 21 | 16 06 |
|  |  | 15 36 | 3 02 | 15 37 | 2 59 | 15 38 | 2 55 | 15 39 | 2 50 | 15 41 | 2 42 |
| 2 Fr — 306 | 11 43 36 | 6 02 | 17 25 | 6 14 | 17 13 | 6 29 | 16 57 | 6 51 | 16 36 | 7 23 | 16 03 |
|  |  | 16 23 | 4 03 | 16 19 | 4 05 | 16 15 | 4 06 | 16 09 | 4 09 | 16 00 | 4 12 |
| 3 Sa — 307 | 11 43 36 | 6 02 | 17 25 | 6 15 | 17 12 | 6 30 | 16 56 | 6 52 | 16 35 | 7 26 | 16 01 |
|  |  | 17 10 | 5 04 | 17 02 | 5 10 | 16 53 | 5 17 | 16 40 | 5 27 | 16 21 | 5 42 |
| 4 Su — 308 | 11 43 36 — 05 47 ○ | 6 03 | 17 24 | 6 15 | 17 12 | 6 32 | 16 55 | 6 54 | 16 33 | 7 28 | 15 58 |
|  |  | 17 58 | 6 05 | 17 47 | 6 15 | 17 33 | 6 27 | 17 14 | 6 44 | 16 44 | 7 10 |
| 5 Mo — 309 | 11 43 36 | 6 03 | 17 24 | 6 16 | 17 11 | 6 33 | 16 54 | 6 55 | 16 32 | 7 31 | 15 56 |
|  |  | 18 48 | 7 06 | 18 33 | 7 19 | 18 16 | 7 36 | 17 51 | 7 58 | 17 12 | 8 35 |
| 6 Tu — 310 | 11 43 38 | 6 04 | 17 23 | 6 17 | 17 10 | 6 34 | 16 53 | 6 57 | 16 30 | 7 33 | 15 53 |
|  |  | 19 39 | 8 05 | 19 22 | 8 21 | 19 02 | 8 40 | 18 34 | 9 08 | 17 48 | 9 53 |
| 7 We — 311 | 11 43 41 | 6 04 | 17 23 | 6 18 | 17 09 | 6 35 | 16 52 | 6 59 | 16 28 | 7 36 | 15 51 |
|  |  | 20 31 | 9 02 | 20 14 | 9 19 | 19 52 | 9 41 | 19 22 | 10 11 | 18 31 | 11 00 |
| 8 Th — 312 | 11 43 44 | 6 05 | 17 22 | 6 19 | 17 08 | 6 36 | 16 51 | 7 00 | 16 27 | 7 38 | 15 48 |
|  |  | 21 24 | 9 56 | 21 06 | 10 13 | 20 44 | 10 35 | 20 14 | 11 06 | 19 24 | 11 56 |
| 9 Fr — 313 | 11 43 48 | 6 05 | 17 22 | 6 19 | 17 08 | 6 38 | 16 50 | 7 02 | 16 25 | 7 41 | 15 46 |
|  |  | 22 16 | 10 46 | 21 59 | 11 02 | 21 39 | 11 23 | 21 11 | 11 52 | 20 25 | 12 40 |
| 10 Sa — 314 | 11 43 53 | 6 06 | 17 21 | 6 20 | 17 07 | 6 39 | 16 49 | 7 03 | 16 24 | 7 43 | 15 43 |
|  |  | 23 07 | 11 32 | 22 52 | 11 47 | 22 35 | 12 06 | 22 10 | 12 32 | 21 30 | 13 13 |
| 11 Su — 315 | 11 43 59 — 16 24 ☽ | 6 06 | 17 21 | 6 21 | 17 06 | 6 40 | 16 48 | 7 05 | 16 22 | 7 46 | 15 41 |
|  |  | 23 57 | 12 15 | 23 45 | 12 28 | 23 30 | 12 44 | 23 11 | 13 05 | 22 39 | 13 39 |
| 12 Mo — 316 | 11 44 06 | 6 07 | 17 21 | 6 22 | 17 06 | 6 41 | 16 47 | 7 07 | 16 21 | 7 49 | 15 39 |
|  |  |  | 12 55 |  | 13 05 |  | 13 17 |  | 13 34 | 23 49 | 14 00 |
| 13 Tu — 317 | 11 44 14 | 6 07 | 17 21 | 6 23 | 17 05 | 6 42 | 16 46 | 7 08 | 16 20 | 7 51 | 15 37 |
|  |  | 0 46 | 13 33 | 0 37 | 13 40 | 0 26 | 13 49 | 0 12 | 13 54 |  | 14 18 |
| 14 We — 318 | 11 44 22 | 6 08 | 17 20 | 6 23 | 17 05 | 6 44 | 16 46 | 7 10 | 16 18 | 7 54 | 15 34 |
|  |  | 1 34 | 14 10 | 1 29 | 14 14 | 1 22 | 14 18 | 1 13 | 14 24 | 0 59 | 14 38 |
| 15 Th — 319 | 11 44 32 | 6 08 | 17 20 | 6 24 | 17 04 | 6 45 | 16 45 | 7 11 | 16 17 | 7 56 | 15 33 |
|  |  | 2 23 | 14 47 | 2 21 | 14 47 | 2 18 | 14 47 | 2 15 | 14 47 | 2 10 | 14 48 |
| 16 Fr — 320 | 11 44 42 | 6 09 | 17 20 | 6 25 | 17 04 | 6 46 | 16 44 | 7 13 | 16 16 | 7 59 | 15 30 |
|  |  | 3 11 | 15 24 | 3 13 | 15 21 | 3 15 | 15 16 | 3 18 | 15 11 | 3 22 | 15 02 |
| 17 Sa — 321 | 11 44 53 | 6 10 | 17 20 | 6 26 | 17 04 | 6 47 | 16 43 | 7 15 | 16 15 | 8 01 | 15 28 |
|  |  | 4 01 | 16 02 | 4 06 | 15 56 | 4 13 | 15 47 | 4 22 | 15 36 | 4 35 | 15 19 |
| 18 Su — 322 | 11 45 05 | 6 10 | 17 20 | 6 27 | 17 03 | 6 48 | 16 42 | 7 16 | 16 14 | 8 04 | 15 26 |
|  |  | 4 53 | 16 43 | 5 01 | 16 33 | 5 12 | 16 20 | 5 27 | 16 03 | 5 50 | 15 37 |
| 19 Mo — 323 | 11 45 18 — 18 04 ● | 6 11 | 17 19 | 6 28 | 17 03 | 6 49 | 16 42 | 7 18 | 16 12 | 8 06 | 15 24 |
|  |  | 5 46 | 17 27 | 5 58 | 17 13 | 6 12 | 16 57 | 6 33 | 16 35 | 7 06 | 15 59 |
| 20 Tu — 324 | 11 45 32 | 6 11 | 17 19 | 6 29 | 17 02 | 6 50 | 16 41 | 7 19 | 16 11 | 8 09 | 15 22 |
|  |  | 6 40 | 18 14 | 6 55 | 17 58 | 7 13 | 17 39 | 7 39 | 17 12 | 8 21 | 16 28 |
| 21 We — 325 | 11 45 46 | 6 12 | 17 19 | 6 30 | 17 02 | 6 51 | 16 40 | 7 21 | 16 10 | 8 11 | 15 20 |
|  |  | 7 36 | 19 05 | 7 53 | 18 47 | 8 14 | 18 26 | 8 43 | 17 56 | 9 32 | 17 06 |
| 22 Th — 326 | 11 46 01 | 6 13 | 17 19 | 6 31 | 17 02 | 6 52 | 16 39 | 7 23 | 16 09 | 8 13 | 15 18 |
|  |  | 8 32 | 19 59 | 8 50 | 19 41 | 9 12 | 19 19 | 9 44 | 18 48 | 10 36 | 17 56 |
| 23 Fr — 327 | 11 46 17 | 6 13 | 17 19 | 6 32 | 17 01 | 6 53 | 16 39 | 7 24 | 16 08 | 8 16 | 15 16 |
|  |  | 9 28 | 20 56 | 9 45 | 20 39 | 10 07 | 20 18 | 10 38 | 19 48 | 11 29 | 18 58 |
| 24 Sa — 328 | 11 46 34 | 6 14 | 17 19 | 6 32 | 17 01 | 6 55 | 16 38 | 7 26 | 16 07 | 8 18 | 15 15 |
|  |  | 10 21 | 21 55 | 10 37 | 21 40 | 10 58 | 21 21 | 11 25 | 20 54 | 12 10 | 20 11 |
| 25 Su — 329 | 11 46 52 | 6 14 | 17 19 | 6 33 | 17 00 | 6 56 | 16 38 | 7 27 | 16 06 | 8 21 | 15 13 |
|  |  | 11 12 | 22 54 | 11 26 | 22 42 | 11 43 | 22 27 | 12 06 | 22 06 | 12 43 | 21 31 |
| 26 Mo — 330 | 11 47 10 — 21 09 ☾ | 6 15 | 17 19 | 6 34 | 17 00 | 6 57 | 16 37 | 7 29 | 16 05 | 8 23 | 15 11 |
|  |  | 12 01 | 23 54 | 12 11 | 23 45 | 12 24 | 23 34 | 12 41 | 23 20 | 13 08 | 22 56 |
| 27 Tu — 331 | 11 47 29 | 6 16 | 17 19 | 6 35 | 17 00 | 6 58 | 16 37 | 7 30 | 16 04 | 8 25 | 15 10 |
|  |  | 12 47 |  | 12 54 |  | 13 02 |  | 13 13 |  | 13 30 |  |
| 28 We — 332 | 11 47 49 | 6 16 | 17 19 | 6 36 | 17 00 | 6 59 | 16 37 | 7 32 | 16 04 | 8 27 | 15 08 |
|  |  | 13 32 | 0 53 | 13 35 | 0 48 | 13 38 | 0 43 | 13 42 | 0 35 | 13 48 | 0 22 |
| 29 Th — 333 | 11 48 09 | 6 17 | 17 19 | 6 36 | 17 00 | 7 00 | 16 36 | 7 33 | 16 03 | 8 30 | 15 07 |
|  |  | 14 17 | 1 52 | 14 15 | 1 52 | 14 13 | 1 51 | 14 10 | 1 51 | 14 06 | 1 49 |
| 30 Fr — 334 | 11 48 30 | 6 17 | 17 19 | 6 37 | 17 00 | 7 01 | 16 36 | 7 35 | 16 03 | 8 32 | 15 05 |
|  |  | 15 02 | 2 51 | 14 56 | 2 55 | 14 49 | 3 00 | 14 39 | 3 06 | 14 25 | 3 16 |

## 12th Month       December, 1979        31 day

Greenwich Mean Time

**NOTE:** Light figures indicate Sun. **Dark** figures indicate **Moon**. *Degrees are North Latitude.*

**CAUTION:** Must be converted to local time. For instruction see page 774.

| Day of month / week / year | Sun on meridian / Moon phase (h m s) | 20° Rise Sun/Moon | 20° Set Sun/Moon | 30° Rise Sun/Moon | 30° Set Sun/Moon | 40° Rise Sun/Moon | 40° Set Sun/Moon | 50° Rise Sun/Moon | 50° Set Sun/Moon | 60° Rise Sun/Moon | 60° Set Sun/Moon |
|---|---|---|---|---|---|---|---|---|---|---|---|
| 1 Sa 335 | 11 48 52 | 6 18 | 17 19 | 6 38 | 17 00 | 7 02 | 16 36 | 7 36 | 16 02 | 8 34 | 15 0 |
|  |  | **14 58** | **3 50** | **15 38** | **3 58** | **15 26** | **4 08** | **15 10** | **4 22** | **14 46** | **4 4** |
| 2 Su 336 | 11 49 14 | 6 19 | 17 19 | 6 39 | 17 00 | 7 03 | 16 36 | 7 37 | 16 01 | 8 36 | 15 0 |
|  |  | **16 36** | **4 50** | **16 23** | **5 02** | **16 07** | **5 16** | **15 45** | **5 36** | **15 10** | **6 0** |
| 3 Mo 337 | 11 49 37   18 08 ○ | 6 19 | 17 19 | 6 40 | 17 00 | 7 04 | 16 36 | 7 38 | 16 01 | 8 38 | 15 0 |
|  |  | **17 26** | **5 49** | **17 10** | **6 04** | **16 51** | **6 22** | **16 24** | **6 47** | **15 41** | **7 2** |
| 4 Tu 338 | 11 50 01 | 6 20 | 17 20 | 6 40 | 17 00 | 7 05 | 16 35 | 7 40 | 16 00 | 8 39 | 15 0 |
|  |  | **18 18** | **6 47** | **18 00** | **7 04** | **17 39** | **7 25** | **17 09** | **7 54** | **16 20** | **8 4** |
| 5 We 339 | 11 50 25 | 6 20 | 17 20 | 6 41 | 17 00 | 7 06 | 16 35 | 7 41 | 16 00 | 8 41 | 14 5 |
|  |  | **19 11** | **7 43** | **18 53** | **8 01** | **18 31** | **8 23** | **18 00** | **8 53** | **17 08** | **9 4** |
| 6 Th 340 | 11 50 50 | 6 21 | 17 20 | 6 42 | 17 00 | 7 07 | 16 35 | 7 42 | 15 59 | 8 43 | 14 5 |
|  |  | **20 04** | **8 35** | **19 47** | **8 53** | **19 25** | **9 15** | **18 56** | **9 45** | **18 06** | **10 3** |
| 7 Fr 341 | 11 51 15 | 6 22 | 17 20 | 6 43 | 17 00 | 7 08 | 16 35 | 7 43 | 15 59 | 8 45 | 14 5 |
|  |  | **20 56** | **9 24** | **20 41** | **9 41** | **20 21** | **10 01** | **19 55** | **10 28** | **19 11** | **11 1** |
| 8 Sa 342 | 11 51 41 | 6 22 | 17 20 | 6 43 | 17 00 | 7 09 | 16 35 | 7 44 | 15 59 | 8 46 | 14 5 |
|  |  | **21 48** | **10 10** | **21 27** | **10 24** | **21 18** | **10 41** | **20 56** | **11 05** | **20 20** | **11 4** |
| 9 Su 343 | 11 52 08 | 6 23 | 17 21 | 6 44 | 17 01 | 7 09 | 16 35 | 7 46 | 15 58 | 8 48 | 14 5 |
|  |  | **22 38** | **10 51** | **22 27** | **11 03** | **22 15** | **11 17** | **21 57** | **11 36** | **21 30** | **12 0** |
| 10 Mo 344 | 11 52 34 | 6 23 | 17 21 | 6 44 | 17 01 | 7 10 | 16 35 | 7 47 | 15 58 | 8 49 | 14 5 |
|  |  | **23 26** | **11 31** | **23 19** | **11 39** | **23 11** | **11 50** | **22 59** | **12 04** | **22 41** | **12 2** |
| 11 Tu 345 | 11 53 02   13 59 ☽ | 6 24 | 17 21 | 6 45 | 17 01 | 7 11 | 16 35 | 7 48 | 15 58 | 8 51 | 14 5 |
|  |  |  | **12 08** |  | **12 13** |  | **12 20** |  | **12 28** | **23 51** | **12 4** |
| 12 We 346 | 11 53 29 | 6 25 | 17 21 | 6 46 | 17 01 | 7 12 | 16 35 | 7 49 | 15 58 | 8 52 | 14 5 |
|  |  | **0 15** | **12 44** | **0 11** | **12 46** | **0 07** | **12 48** | **0 01** | **12 51** |  | **12 5** |
| 13 Th 347 | 11 53 57 | 6 25 | 17 22 | 6 47 | 17 01 | 7 13 | 16 35 | 7 50 | 15 58 | 5 54 | 14 5 |
|  |  | **1 03** | **13 21** | **1 03** | **13 19** | **1 03** | **13 17** | **1 03** | **13 14** | **1 03** | **13 1** |
| 14 Fr 348 | 11 54 26 | 6 26 | 17 22 | 6 47 | 17 02 | 7 13 | 16 36 | 7 50 | 15 58 | 8 55 | 14 5 |
|  |  | **1 52** | **13 58** | **1 55** | **13 53** | **2 00** | **13 47** | **2 06** | **13 38** | **2 15** | **13 2** |
| 15 Sa 349 | 11 54 55 | 6 26 | 17 23 | 6 48 | 17 02 | 7 14 | 16 36 | 7 51 | 15 58 | 8 57 | 14 5 |
|  |  | **2 42** | **14 37** | **2 49** | **14 29** | **2 58** | **14 18** | **3 10** | **14 04** | **3 29** | **13 4** |
| 16 Su 350 | 11 55 24 | 6 27 | 17 23 | 6 49 | 17 02 | 7 15 | 16 36 | 7 52 | 15 58 | 8 58 | 14 5 |
|  |  | **3 34** | **15 19** | **3 45** | **15 08** | **3 58** | **14 53** | **4 15** | **14 33** | **4 44** | **14 0** |
| 17 Mo 351 | 11 55 53 | 6 28 | 17 24 | 6 49 | 17 02 | 7 16 | 16 36 | 7 53 | 15 58 | 8 59 | 14 5 |
|  |  | **4 28** | **16 05** | **4 42** | **15 50** | **4 59** | **15 32** | **5 22** | **15 07** | **6 00** | **14 2** |
| 18 Tu 352 | 11 56 22 | 6 28 | 17 24 | 6 50 | 17 03 | 7 16 | 16 37 | 7 54 | 15 59 | 9 00 | 14 5 |
|  |  | **5 24** | **16 55** | **5 40** | **16 38** | **6 00** | **16 17** | **6 28** | **15 48** | **7 14** | **15 0** |
| 19 We 353 | 11 56 52   08 23 ● | 6 29 | 17 25 | 6 50 | 17 03 | 7 17 | 16 37 | 7 54 | 15 59 | 9 00 | 14 5 |
|  |  | **6 22** | **17 49** | **6 39** | **17 31** | **7 01** | **17 09** | **7 32** | **16 38** | **8 24** | **15 4** |
| 20 Th 354 | 11 57 22 | 6 29 | 17 25 | 6 51 | 17 04 | 7 17 | 16 38 | 7 55 | 16 00 | 9 01 | 14 5 |
|  |  | **7 19** | **18 47** | **7 37** | **18 29** | **8 00** | **18 07** | **8 31** | **17 36** | **9 23** | **16 4** |
| 21 Fr 355 | 11 57 52 | 6 30 | 17 26 | 6 51 | 17 04 | 7 18 | 16 38 | 7 56 | 16 00 | 9 02 | 14 5 |
|  |  | **8 15** | **19 47** | **8 32** | **19 31** | **8 53** | **19 10** | **9 23** | **18 42** | **10 11** | **17 5** |
| 22 Sa 356 | 11 58 22 | 6 31 | 17 26 | 6 52 | 17 05 | 7 18 | 16 38 | 7 56 | 16 01 | 9 02 | 14 5 |
|  |  | **9 09** | **20 48** | **9 24** | **20 34** | **9 42** | **20 17** | **10 07** | **19 54** | **10 48** | **19 1** |
| 23 Su 357 | 11 58 52 | 6 31 | 17 27 | 6 52 | 17 05 | 7 19 | 16 39 | 7 57 | 16 01 | 9 03 | 14 5 |
|  |  | **9 59** | **21 48** | **10 11** | **21 38** | **10 26** | **21 26** | **10 45** | **21 09** | **11 16** | **20 4** |
| 24 Mo 358 | 11 59 21 | 6 32 | 17 27 | 6 53 | 17 06 | 7 19 | 16 39 | 7 57 | 16 02 | 9 03 | 14 5 |
|  |  | **10 47** | **22 48** | **10 55** | **22 42** | **11 05** | **22 35** | **11 18** | **22 24** | **11 38** | **22 0** |
| 25 Tu 359 | 11 59 51 | 6 32 | 17 28 | 6 53 | 17 06 | 7 20 | 16 40 | 7 58 | 16 02 | 9 04 | 14 5 |
|  |  | **11 33** | **23 47** | **11 37** | **23 45** | **11 41** | **23 43** | **11 48** | **23 40** | **11 58** | **23 3** |
| 26 We 360 | 12 00 21   05 11 ● | 6 33 | 17 28 | 6 54 | 17 07 | 7 20 | 16 40 | 7 58 | 16 03 | 9 04 | 14 5 |
|  |  | **12 17** |  | **12 16** |  | **12 16** |  | **12 16** |  | **12 15** |  |
| 27 Th 361 | 12 00 51 | 6 33 | 17 29 | 6 54 | 17 08 | 7 20 | 16 41 | 7 58 | 16 04 | 9 04 | 14 5 |
|  |  | **13 00** | **0 45** | **12 56** | **0 48** | **12 51** | **0 51** | **12 44** | **0 55** | **12 33** | **1 0** |
| 28 Fr 362 | 12 01 20 | 6 34 | 17 29 | 6 55 | 17 08 | 7 21 | 16 42 | 7 58 | 16 05 | 9 04 | 14 5 |
|  |  | **13 45** | **1 43** | **13 37** | **1 50** | **13 27** | **1 58** | **13 13** | **2 09** | **12 52** | **2 26** |
| 29 Sa 363 | 12 01 50 | 6 34 | 17 30 | 6 55 | 17 09 | 7 21 | 16 42 | 7 59 | 16 05 | 9 03 | 15 0 |
|  |  | **14 31** | **2 41** | **14 19** | **2 51** | **14 04** | **3 04** | **13 45** | **3 21** | **13 14** | **3 49** |
| 30 Su 364 | 12 02 19 | 6 35 | 17 30 | 6 56 | 17 09 | 7 22 | 16 43 | 7 59 | 16 06 | 9 03 | 15 02 |
|  |  | **15 18** | **3 39** | **15 04** | **3 52** | **14 46** | **4 09** | **14 21** | **4 32** | **13 41** | **5 10** |
| 31 Mo 365 | 12 02 48 | 6 35 | 17 31 | 6 56 | 17 10 | 7 22 | 16 44 | 7 59 | 16 07 | 9 03 | 15 03 |
|  |  | **16 08** | **4 36** | **15 52** | **4 52** | **15 31** | **5 12** | **15 02** | **5 39** | **14 15** | **6 25** |

# Julian and Gregorian Calendars; Leap Year

Calendars based on the movements of sun and moon have been used since ancient times, but none has been perfect. The Julian calendar, under which western nations measured time until 1582 A.D., was authorized by Julius Caesar in 46 B.C., the year 709 of Rome. His expert was a Greek, Sosigenes. The Julian calendar, on the assumption that the true year was 365 1/4 days long, gave every fourth year 366 days. The Venerable Bede, an Anglo-Saxon monk, announced in 730 A.D. that the 365-day Julian year was 11 min., 14 sec. too long, making a cumulative error of about a day every 128 years, but nothing was done about it for over 800 years.

By 1582 the accumulated error was estimated to have amounted to 10 days. In that year Pope Gregory XIII decreed that the day following Oct. 4, 1582, should be called Oct. 15, thus dropping 10 days.

However, with common years 365 days and a 366-day leap year every fourth year, the error in the length of the year would have recurred at the rate of a little more than 3 days every 400 years. So 3 of every 4 centesimal years (ending in 00) were made common years, not leap years. Thus 1600 was a leap year, 1700, 1800 and 1900 were not, but 2000 will be. Leap years are those divisible by 4 except centesimal years, which are common unless divisible by 400.

The Gregorian calendar was adopted at once by France, Italy, Spain, Portugal and Luxembourg. Within 2 years most German Catholic states, Belgium and parts of Switzerland and the Netherlands were brought under the new calendar, and Hungary followed in 1587. The rest of the Netherlands, along with Denmark and the German Protestant states made the change in 1699-1700 (German Protestants retained the old reckoning of Easter until 1776).

The British Government imposed the Gregorian calendar on all its possessions, including the American colonies, in 1752. The British decreed that the day following Sept. 2, 1752, should be called Sept. 14, a loss of 11 days. All dates preceding were marked O.S., for Old Style. In addition New Year's Day was moved to Jan. 1 from Mar. 25. (e.g., under the old reckoning, Mar. 24, 1700 had been followed by Mar. 25, 1701.) George Washington's birth date, which was Feb. 11, 1731, O.S., became Feb. 22, 1732, N.S. In 1753 Sweden too went Gregorian, retaining the old Easter rules until 1844.

In 1793 the French Revolutionary Government adopted a calendar of 12 months of 30 days each with 5 extra days in September of each common year and a 6th extra day every 4th year. Napoleon reinstated the Gregorian calendar in 1806.

The Gregorian system later spread to non-European regions, first in the European colonies, then in the independent countries, replacing traditional calendars at least for official purposes. Japan in 1873, Egypt in 1875, China in 1912 and Turkey in 1917 made the change, usually in conjunction with political upheavals. In China, the republican government began reckoning years from its 1911 founding — e.g., 1948 was designated the year 37. After 1949, the Communists adopted the Common, or Christian Era year count, even for the traditional lunar calendar.

In 1918 the revolutionary government in Russia decreed that the day after Jan. 31, 1918, Old Style, would become Feb. 13, 1918, New Style. Greece followed in 1923. (In Russia the Orthodox Church has retained the Julian calendar, as have various Middle Eastern Christian sects.) For the first time in history, all major cultures have been brought under one calendar.

To change from the Julian to the Gregorian calendar, add 10 days to dates Oct. 5, 1582, through Feb. 28, 1700; after that date add 11 days through Feb. 28, 1800; 12 days through Feb. 28, 1900; and 13 days through Feb. 28, 2100.

## Julian Calendar

To find which of the 14 calendars printed on pages 788-789 applies to any year under the Julian system, find the century for the desired year in the three left-hand columns below; read across. Then find the year in the four top rows; read down. The number in the intersection is the calendar designation for that year.

**Year** (last two figures of desired year)

| | | 01 02 03 04 | 05 06 07 08 | 09 10 11 12 | 13 14 15 16 | 17 18 19 20 | 21 22 23 24 | 25 26 27 28 |
|---|---|---|---|---|---|---|---|---|
| | | 29 30 31 32 | 33 34 35 36 | 37 38 39 40 | 41 42 43 44 | 45 46 47 48 | 49 50 51 52 | 53 54 55 56 |
| | | 57 58 59 60 | 61 62 63 64 | 65 66 67 68 | 69 70 71 72 | 73 74 75 76 | 77 78 79 80 | 81 82 83 84 |
| Century | 00 | 85 86 87 88 | 89 90 91 92 | 93 94 95 96 | 97 98 99 | | | |
| 0 | 700 1400 | 12  7  1  2 | 10   5  6  7 | 8   3  4  5 | 13     1  2 | 3 11     6  7 | 1  9     4  5 | 6 14     2  3  4 12 |
| 100 | 800 1500 | 11  6  7  1 | 9   4  5  6 | 14   2  3  4 | 12     7  1 | 2 10     5  6 | 7  8     3  4 | 5 13     1  2  3 11 |
| 200 | 900 1600 | 10  5  6  7 | 8   3  4  5 | 13   1  2  3 | 11     6  7 | 1  9     4  5 | 6 14     2  3 | 4 12     7  1  2 10 |
| 300 | 1000 1700 | 9  4  5  6 | 14   2  3  4 | 12   7  1  2 | 10     5  6 | 7  8     3  4 | 5 13     1  2 | 3 11     6  7  1  9 |
| 400 | 1100 1800 | 8  3  4  5 | 13   1  2  3 | 11   6  7  1 | 9     4  5 | 6 14     2  3 | 4 12     7  1 | 2 10     5  6  7  8 |
| 500 | 1200 1900 | 14  2  3  4 | 12   7  1  2 | 10   5  6  7 | 8     3  4 | 5 13     1  2 | 3 11     6  7 | 1  9     4  5  6 14 |
| 600 | 1300 2000 | 13  1  2  3 | 11   6  7  1 | 9   4  5  6 | 14     2  3 | 4 12     7  1 | 2 10     5  6 | 7  8     3  4  5 13 |

## Gregorian Calendar

Pick desired year from table below or on page 788 (for years 1800 to 2059). The number shown with each year shows which calendar to use for that year, as shown on pages 788-789 (The Gregorian calendar was inaugurated Oct. 15, 1582. From that date to Dec. 31, 1582, use calendar 6.)

### 1583-1799

| | | | | | | | | | | | |
|---|---|---|---|---|---|---|---|---|---|---|---|
| 1583 . . 7 | 1603 . . 4 | 1623 . . 1 | 1643 . . 5 | 1663 . . 5 | 1683 . . 6 | 1703 . . 2 | 1723 . . 6 | 1743 . . 3 | 1763 . . 7 | 1783 . . 4 |
| 1584 . . 8 | 1604 . 12 | 1624 . . 9 | 1644 . 13 | 1664 . 10 | 1684 . 14 | 1704 . 10 | 1724 . 14 | 1744 . 11 | 1764 . . 8 | 1784 . 12 |
| 1585 . . 3 | 1605 . . 7 | 1625 . . 4 | 1645 . . 1 | 1665 . . 5 | 1685 . . 2 | 1705 . . 5 | 1725 . . 2 | 1745 . . 5 | 1765 . . 3 | 1785 . . 7 |
| 1586 . . 4 | 1606 . . 1 | 1626 . . 5 | 1646 . . 2 | 1666 . . 6 | 1686 . . 3 | 1706 . . 6 | 1726 . . 3 | 1746 . . 7 | 1766 . . 4 | 1786 . . 1 |
| 1587 . . 5 | 1607 . . 2 | 1627 . . 6 | 1647 . . 3 | 1667 . . 7 | 1687 . . 4 | 1707 . . 7 | 1727 . . 4 | 1747 . . 1 | 1767 . . 5 | 1787 . . 2 |
| 1588 . 13 | 1608 . 10 | 1628 . 14 | 1648 . 11 | 1668 . . 8 | 1688 . 12 | 1708 . . 8 | 1728 . 12 | 1748 . . 9 | 1768 . 13 | 1788 . 10 |
| 1589 . . 1 | 1609 . . 5 | 1629 . . 2 | 1649 . . 6 | 1669 . . 3 | 1689 . . 7 | 1709 . . 3 | 1729 . . 7 | 1749 . . 4 | 1769 . . 1 | 1789 . . 5 |
| 1590 . . 2 | 1610 . . 6 | 1630 . . 3 | 1650 . . 7 | 1670 . . 4 | 1690 . . 1 | 1710 . . 4 | 1730 . . 1 | 1750 . . 5 | 1770 . . 2 | 1790 . . 6 |
| 1591 . . 3 | 1611 . . 7 | 1631 . . 4 | 1651 . . 1 | 1671 . . 5 | 1691 . . 2 | 1711 . . 5 | 1731 . . 2 | 1751 . . 6 | 1771 . . 3 | 1791 . . 7 |
| 1592 . 11 | 1612 . . 8 | 1632 . 12 | 1652 . . 9 | 1672 . 13 | 1692 . 10 | 1712 . 13 | 1732 . 10 | 1752 . 14 | 1772 . 11 | 1792 . . 8 |
| 1593 . . 6 | 1613 . . 3 | 1633 . . 7 | 1653 . . 4 | 1673 . . 1 | 1693 . . 5 | 1713 . . 1 | 1733 . . 5 | 1753 . . 2 | 1773 . . 6 | 1793 . . 3 |
| 1594 . . 7 | 1614 . . 4 | 1634 . . 1 | 1654 . . 5 | 1674 . . 2 | 1694 . . 6 | 1714 . . 2 | 1734 . . 6 | 1754 . . 3 | 1774 . . 7 | 1794 . . 4 |
| 1595 . . 1 | 1615 . . 5 | 1635 . . 2 | 1655 . . 6 | 1675 . . 3 | 1695 . . 7 | 1715 . . 3 | 1735 . . 7 | 1755 . . 4 | 1775 . . 1 | 1795 . . 5 |
| 1596 . . 9 | 1616 . 13 | 1636 . 10 | 1656 . 14 | 1676 . 11 | 1696 . . 8 | 1716 . 11 | 1736 . . 8 | 1756 . 12 | 1776 . . 9 | 1796 . 13 |
| 1597 . . 4 | 1617 . . 1 | 1637 . . 5 | 1657 . . 2 | 1677 . . 6 | 1697 . . 3 | 1717 . . 6 | 1737 . . 3 | 1757 . . 7 | 1777 . . 4 | 1797 . . 1 |
| 1598 . . 5 | 1618 . . 2 | 1638 . . 6 | 1658 . . 3 | 1678 . . 7 | 1698 . . 4 | 1718 . . 7 | 1738 . . 4 | 1758 . . 1 | 1778 . . 5 | 1798 . . 2 |
| 1599 . . 6 | 1619 . . 3 | 1639 . . 7 | 1659 . . 4 | 1679 . . 1 | 1699 . . 5 | 1719 . . 1 | 1739 . . 5 | 1759 . . 2 | 1779 . . 6 | 1799 . . 3 |
| 1600 . 14 | 1620 . 11 | 1640 . . 8 | 1660 . 12 | 1680 . . 9 | 1700 . . 6 | 1720 . . 9 | 1740 . 13 | 1760 . 10 | 1780 . 14 | . . . . . . |
| 1601 . . 2 | 1621 . . 6 | 1641 . . 3 | 1661 . . 7 | 1681 . . 4 | 1701 . . 7 | 1721 . . 4 | 1741 . . 1 | 1761 . . 5 | 1781 . . 2 | . . . . . . |
| 1602 . . 3 | 1622 . . 7 | 1642 . . 4 | 1662 . . 1 | 1682 . . 5 | 1702 . . 1 | 1722 . . 5 | 1742 . . 2 | 1762 . . 6 | 1782 . . 3 | . . . . . . |

## Perpetual Calendar

The number shown for each year indicates which Gregorian calendar to use. For 1583-1799, or for Julian calendar, see page 788.

# The Julian Period

How many days have you lived? To determine this, you must multiply your age by 365, add the number of days since your last birthday until today, and account for all leap years. Chances are your answer would be wrong. Astronomers, however, find it convenient to express dates and long time intervals in days rather than in years, months and days. This is done by placing events within the Julian period.

The Julian period was devised in 1582 by Joseph Scaliger and named after his father Julius (not after the Julian calendar). Scaliger had Julian Day (JD) #1 begin at noon, Jan. 1, 4713 B. C., the most recent time that three major chronological cycles began on the same day — 1) the 28-year solar cycle, after which dates in the Julian calendar (e.g., Feb. 11)

return to the same days of the week (e.g., Monday); 2) the 19-year lunar cycle, after which the phases of the moon return to the same dates of the year; and 3) the 15-year indiction cycle, used in ancient Rome to regulate taxes. It will take 7980 years to complete the period, the product of 28, 19, and 15.

Noon of Dec. 31, 1978, marks the beginning of JD 2,443,874; that many days will have passed since the start of the Julian period. The JD at noon of any date in 1979 may be found by adding to this figure the day of the year for that date, which is given in the left hand column in the chart below. Simple JD conversion tables are used by astronomers.

# Days Between Two Dates

Table covers period of two ordinary years. Example—Days between Feb. 10, 1978 and Dec. 15, 1979; subtract 41 from 714; answer is 673 days. For leap year, such as 1976, one day must be added after Feb. 28.

| Date | Jan. | Feb. | Mar. | April | May | June | July | Aug. | Sept. | Oct. | Nov. | Dec. | Date | Jan. | Feb. | Mar. | April | May | June | July | Aug. | Sept. | Oct. | Nov. | Dec. |
|---|---|---|---|---|---|---|---|---|---|---|---|---|---|---|---|---|---|---|---|---|---|---|---|---|---|
| 1 | 1 | 32 | 60 | 91 | 121 | 152 | 182 | 213 | 244 | 274 | 305 | 335 | 1 | 366 | 397 | 425 | 456 | 486 | 517 | 547 | 578 | 609 | 639 | 670 | 700 |
| 2 | 2 | 33 | 61 | 92 | 122 | 153 | 183 | 214 | 245 | 275 | 306 | 336 | 2 | 367 | 398 | 426 | 457 | 487 | 518 | 548 | 579 | 610 | 640 | 671 | 701 |
| 3 | 3 | 34 | 62 | 93 | 123 | 154 | 184 | 215 | 246 | 276 | 307 | 337 | 3 | 368 | 399 | 427 | 458 | 488 | 519 | 549 | 580 | 611 | 641 | 672 | 702 |
| 4 | 4 | 35 | 63 | 94 | 124 | 155 | 185 | 216 | 247 | 277 | 308 | 338 | 4 | 369 | 400 | 428 | 459 | 489 | 520 | 550 | 581 | 612 | 642 | 673 | 703 |
| 5 | 5 | 36 | 64 | 95 | 125 | 156 | 186 | 217 | 248 | 278 | 309 | 339 | 5 | 370 | 401 | 429 | 460 | 490 | 521 | 551 | 582 | 613 | 643 | 674 | 704 |
| 6 | 6 | 37 | 65 | 96 | 126 | 157 | 187 | 218 | 249 | 279 | 310 | 340 | 6 | 371 | 402 | 430 | 461 | 491 | 522 | 552 | 583 | 614 | 644 | 675 | 705 |
| 7 | 7 | 38 | 66 | 97 | 127 | 158 | 188 | 219 | 250 | 280 | 311 | 341 | 7 | 372 | 403 | 431 | 462 | 492 | 523 | 553 | 584 | 615 | 645 | 676 | 706 |
| 8 | 8 | 39 | 67 | 98 | 128 | 159 | 189 | 220 | 251 | 281 | 312 | 342 | 8 | 373 | 404 | 432 | 463 | 493 | 524 | 554 | 585 | 616 | 646 | 677 | 707 |
| 9 | 9 | 40 | 68 | 99 | 129 | 160 | 190 | 221 | 252 | 282 | 313 | 343 | 9 | 374 | 405 | 433 | 464 | 494 | 525 | 555 | 586 | 617 | 647 | 678 | 708 |
| 10 | 10 | 41 | 69 | 100 | 130 | 161 | 191 | 222 | 253 | 283 | 314 | 344 | 10 | 375 | 406 | 434 | 465 | 495 | 526 | 556 | 587 | 618 | 648 | 679 | 709 |
| 11 | 11 | 42 | 70 | 101 | 131 | 162 | 192 | 223 | 254 | 284 | 315 | 345 | 11 | 376 | 407 | 435 | 466 | 496 | 527 | 557 | 588 | 619 | 649 | 680 | 710 |
| 12 | 12 | 43 | 71 | 102 | 132 | 163 | 193 | 224 | 255 | 285 | 316 | 346 | 12 | 377 | 408 | 436 | 467 | 497 | 528 | 558 | 589 | 620 | 650 | 681 | 711 |
| 13 | 13 | 44 | 72 | 103 | 133 | 164 | 194 | 225 | 256 | 286 | 317 | 347 | 13 | 378 | 409 | 437 | 468 | 498 | 529 | 559 | 590 | 621 | 651 | 682 | 712 |
| 14 | 14 | 45 | 73 | 104 | 134 | 165 | 195 | 226 | 257 | 287 | 318 | 348 | 14 | 379 | 410 | 438 | 469 | 499 | 530 | 560 | 591 | 622 | 652 | 683 | 713 |
| 15 | 15 | 46 | 74 | 105 | 135 | 166 | 196 | 227 | 258 | 288 | 319 | 349 | 15 | 380 | 411 | 439 | 470 | 500 | 531 | 561 | 592 | 623 | 653 | 684 | 714 |
| 16 | 16 | 47 | 75 | 106 | 136 | 167 | 197 | 228 | 259 | 289 | 320 | 350 | 16 | 381 | 412 | 440 | 471 | 501 | 532 | 562 | 593 | 624 | 654 | 685 | 715 |
| 17 | 17 | 48 | 76 | 107 | 137 | 168 | 198 | 229 | 260 | 290 | 321 | 351 | 17 | 382 | 413 | 441 | 472 | 502 | 533 | 563 | 594 | 625 | 655 | 686 | 716 |
| 18 | 18 | 49 | 77 | 108 | 138 | 169 | 199 | 230 | 261 | 291 | 322 | 352 | 18 | 383 | 414 | 442 | 473 | 503 | 534 | 564 | 595 | 626 | 656 | 687 | 717 |
| 19 | 19 | 50 | 78 | 109 | 139 | 170 | 200 | 231 | 262 | 292 | 323 | 353 | 19 | 384 | 415 | 443 | 474 | 504 | 535 | 565 | 596 | 627 | 657 | 688 | 718 |
| 20 | 20 | 51 | 79 | 110 | 140 | 171 | 201 | 232 | 263 | 293 | 324 | 354 | 20 | 385 | 416 | 444 | 475 | 505 | 536 | 566 | 597 | 628 | 658 | 689 | 719 |
| 21 | 21 | 52 | 80 | 111 | 141 | 172 | 202 | 233 | 264 | 294 | 325 | 355 | 21 | 386 | 417 | 445 | 476 | 506 | 537 | 567 | 598 | 629 | 659 | 690 | 720 |
| 22 | 22 | 53 | 81 | 112 | 142 | 173 | 203 | 234 | 265 | 295 | 326 | 356 | 22 | 387 | 418 | 446 | 477 | 507 | 538 | 568 | 599 | 630 | 660 | 691 | 721 |
| 23 | 23 | 54 | 82 | 113 | 143 | 174 | 204 | 235 | 266 | 296 | 327 | 357 | 23 | 388 | 419 | 447 | 478 | 508 | 539 | 569 | 600 | 631 | 661 | 692 | 722 |
| 24 | 24 | 55 | 83 | 114 | 144 | 175 | 205 | 236 | 267 | 297 | 328 | 358 | 24 | 389 | 420 | 448 | 479 | 509 | 540 | 570 | 601 | 632 | 662 | 693 | 723 |
| 25 | 25 | 56 | 84 | 115 | 145 | 176 | 206 | 237 | 268 | 298 | 329 | 359 | 25 | 390 | 421 | 449 | 480 | 510 | 541 | 571 | 602 | 633 | 663 | 694 | 724 |
| 26 | 26 | 57 | 85 | 116 | 146 | 177 | 207 | 238 | 269 | 299 | 330 | 360 | 26 | 391 | 422 | 450 | 481 | 511 | 542 | 572 | 603 | 634 | 664 | 695 | 725 |
| 27 | 27 | 58 | 86 | 117 | 147 | 178 | 208 | 239 | 270 | 300 | 331 | 361 | 27 | 392 | 423 | 451 | 482 | 512 | 543 | 573 | 604 | 635 | 665 | 696 | 726 |
| 28 | 28 | 59 | 87 | 118 | 148 | 179 | 209 | 240 | 271 | 301 | 332 | 362 | 28 | 393 | 424 | 452 | 483 | 513 | 544 | 574 | 605 | 636 | 666 | 697 | 727 |
| 29 | 29 | — | 88 | 119 | 149 | 180 | 210 | 241 | 272 | 302 | 333 | 363 | 29 | 394 | — | 453 | 484 | 514 | 545 | 575 | 606 | 637 | 667 | 698 | 728 |
| 30 | 30 | — | 89 | 120 | 150 | 181 | 211 | 242 | 273 | 303 | 334 | 364 | 30 | 395 | — | 454 | 485 | 515 | 546 | 576 | 607 | 638 | 668 | 699 | 729 |
| 31 | 31 | — | 90 | — | 151 | — | 212 | 243 | — | 304 | — | 365 | 31 | 396 | — | 455 | — | 516 | — | 577 | 608 | — | 669 | — | 730 |

# Lunar Calendar, Chinese New Year, Vietnamese Tet

The ancient Chinese lunar calendar is divided into 12 months of either 29 or 30 days (compensating for the fact that the mean duration of the lunar month is 29 days, 12 hours, 44.05 minutes). The calendar is synchronized with the solar year by the addition of extra months at fixed intervals.

The Chinese calendar runs on a sexagenary cycle, i.e., 60 years. The cycles 1864-1923 and 1924-1983, with the years grouped under their twelve animal designations, are printed below. The Year 1979 is found in the eighth column, under Sheep, and is known as a "Year of the Sheep." Readers can find the animal name for the year of their birth, marriage, etc., in the same chart. (Note: the first 3-7 weeks of each of the western years belong to the previous Chinese year and animal designation.)

Both the western (Gregorian) and traditional lunar calendars are used publicly in China, and two New Year's celebrations are held. On Taiwan, in overseas Chinese communities, and in Vietnam, the lunar calendar has been used only to set the dates for traditional festivals, with the Gregorian system in general use.

The four-day Chinese New Year, Hsin Nien, and the three-day Vietnamese New Year festival, Tet, begin at the first new moon after the sun enters Aquarius. The day may fall, therefore, between Jan. 21 and Feb. 19 of the Gregorian calendar. Jan. 28, 1979 marks the start of the new Chinese year. The date is fixed according to the date of the new moon in the Far East. Since this is west of the International Date Line the date may be one day later than that of the new moon in the United States.

| Rat | Ox | Tiger | Hare (Rabbit) | Dragon | Snake | Horse | Sheep (Goat) | Monkey | Rooster | Dog | Pig |
|---|---|---|---|---|---|---|---|---|---|---|---|
| 1864 | 1865 | 1866 | 1867 | 1868 | 1869 | 1870 | 1871 | 1872 | 1873 | 1874 | 1875 |
| 1876 | 1877 | 1878 | 1879 | 1880 | 1881 | 1882 | 1883 | 1884 | 1885 | 1886 | 1887 |
| 1888 | 1889 | 1890 | 1891 | 1892 | 1893 | 1894 | 1895 | 1896 | 1897 | 1898 | 1899 |
| 1900 | 1901 | 1902 | 1903 | 1904 | 1905 | 1906 | 1907 | 1908 | 1909 | 1910 | 1911 |
| 1912 | 1913 | 1914 | 1915 | 1916 | 1917 | 1918 | 1919 | 1920 | 1921 | 1922 | 1923 |
| 1924 | 1925 | 1926 | 1927 | 1928 | 1929 | 1930 | 1931 | 1932 | 1933 | 1934 | 1935 |
| 1936 | 1937 | 1938 | 1939 | 1940 | 1941 | 1942 | 1943 | 1944 | 1945 | 1946 | 1947 |
| 1948 | 1949 | 1950 | 1951 | 1952 | 1953 | 1954 | 1955 | 1956 | 1957 | 1958 | 1959 |
| 1960 | 1961 | 1962 | 1963 | 1964 | 1965 | 1966 | 1967 | 1968 | 1969 | 1970 | 1971 |
| 1972 | 1973 | 1974 | 1975 | 1976 | 1977 | 1978 | 1979 | 1980 | 1981 | 1982 | 1983 |

## Chronological Eras, 1979

e year 1979 of the Christian Era comprises the latter part of the 203d and the beginning of the 204th year of the inde-
ence of the United States of America.

| Era | Year | Begins in 1979 | | Era | Year | Begins in 1979 |
|---|---|---|---|---|---|---|
| ntine | 7488 | Sept. 14 | | Japanese | 2639 | Jan. 1 |
| h | 5740 | Sept. 22 (sunset) | | Grecian (Seleucidae) | 2291 | Sept. or Oct. *14 |
| piads | 2755 | July 1 | | Diocletian | 1696 | Sept. 12 |
| ird year of Olympiad 689) | | | | Indian (Saka) | 1901 | Mar. 22 |
| an (Ab Urbe Condita) | 2732 | Jan. 14 | | Mohammedan (Hegira) | 1400 | Nov. 21 |
| nassar (Babylonian) | 2728 | Apr. 29 | | | | |

## Chronological Cycles, 1979

| | | | | |
|---|---|---|---|---|
| nical Letter | G | Golden Number (Lunar Cycle) | IV | Roman Indiction | 2 |
| t | 2 | Solar Cycle | 28 | Julian Period (year of) | 6692 |

## Standard Time Differences — North American Cities

At 12 o'clock noon, Eastern Standard Time, the standard time in N.A. cities is as follows:

| City | Time | | City | Time | | City | Time |
|---|---|---|---|---|---|---|---|
| ron, Oh. | 12.00 Noon | | Fort Worth, Tex. | 11.00 A.M. | | Philadelphia, Pa. | 12.00 Noon |
| uquerque, N.M. | 10.00 A.M. | | Frankfort, Ky. | 12.00 Noon | | *Phoenix, Ariz. | 10.00 A.M. |
| anta, Ga. | 12.00 Noon | | Galveston, Tex. | 11.00 A.M. | | Pierre, S.D. | 11.00 A.M. |
| stin, Tex. | 11.00 A.M. | | Grand Rapids, Mich. | 12.00 Noon | | Pittsburgh, Pa. | 12.00 Noon |
| timore, Md. | 12.00 Noon | | Halifax, N.S. | 1.00 P.M. | | Portland, Me. | 12.00 Noon |
| mingham, Ala. | 11.00 A.M. | | Hartford, Conn. | 12.00 Noon | | Portland, Ore. | 9.00 A.M. |
| marck, N.D. | 11.00 A.M. | | Helena, Mon. | 10.00 A.M. | | Providence, R.I. | 12.00 Noon |
| se, Ida. | 10.00 A.M. | | *Honolulu, Ha. | 7.00 A.M. | | *Regina, Sask. | 11.00 A.M. |
| ston, Mass. | 12.00 Noon | | Houston, Tex. | 11.00 A.M. | | Reno, Nev. | 9.00 A.M. |
| falo, N.Y. | 12.00 Noon | | *Indianapolis, Ind. | 12.00 Noon | | Richmond, Va. | 12.00 Noon |
| te, Mon. | 10.00 A.M. | | Jacksonville, Fla. | 12.00 Noon | | Rochester, N.Y. | 12.00 Noon |
| gary, Alta. | 10.00 A.M. | | Juneau, Alas. | 9.00 A.M. | | Sacramento, Cal. | 9.00 A.M. |
| arleston, S.C. | 12.00 Noon | | Kansas City, Mo. | 11.00 A.M. | | St. John's, Nfld. | 1.30 P.M. |
| arleston, W.Va. | 12.00 Noon | | Knoxville, Tenn. | 12.00 Noon | | St. Louis, Mo. | 11.00 A.M. |
| arlotte, N.C. | 12.00 Noon | | Lexington, Ky. | 12.00 Noon | | St. Paul, Minn. | 11.00 A.M. |
| arlottetown, P.E.I. | 1.00 P.M. | | Lincoln, Neb. | 11.00 A.M. | | Salt Lake City, Ut. | 10.00 A.M. |
| attanooga, Tenn. | 12.00 Noon | | Little Rock, Ark. | 11.00 A.M. | | San Antonio, Tex. | 11.00 A.M. |
| eyenne, Wy. | 10.00 A.M. | | Los Angeles, Cal. | 9.00 A.M. | | San Diego, Cal. | 9.00 A.M. |
| icago, Ill. | 11.00 A.M. | | Louisville, Ky. | 12.00 Noon | | San Francisco, Cal. | 9.00 A.M. |
| eveland, Oh. | 12.00 Noon | | *Mexico City | 11.00 A.M. | | Santa Fe, N.M. | 10.00 A.M. |
| lorado Spr., Col. | 10.00 A.M. | | Memphis, Tenn. | 11.00 A.M. | | Savannah, Ga. | 12.00 Noon |
| lumbus, Oh. | 12.00 Noon | | Miami, Fla. | 12.00 Noon | | Seattle, Wash. | 9.00 A.M. |
| llas, Tex. | 11.00 A.M. | | Milwaukee, Wis. | 11.00 A.M. | | Shreveport, La. | 11.00 A.M. |
| wson, Yuk. | 8.00 A.M. | | Minneapolis, Minn. | 11.00 A.M. | | Sioux Falls, S.D. | 11.00 A.M. |
| yton, Oh. | 12.00 Noon | | Mobile, Ala. | 11.00 A.M. | | Spokane, Wash. | 9.00 A.M. |
| nver, Col. | 10.00 A.M. | | Montreal, Que. | 12.00 Noon | | Tampa, Fla. | 12.00 Noon |
| s Moines, Ia. | 11.00 A.M. | | Nashville, Tenn. | 11.00 A.M. | | Toledo, Oh. | 12.00 Noon |
| troit, Mich. | 12.00 Noon | | New Haven, Conn. | 12.00 Noon | | Topeka, Kan. | 11.00 A.M. |
| luth, Minn. | 11.00 A.M. | | New Orleans, La. | 11.00 A.M. | | Toronto, Ont. | 12.00 Noon |
| Paso, Tex. | 10.00 A.M. | | New York, N.Y. | 12.00 Noon | | *Tuscon, Ariz. | 10.00 A.M. |
| e, Pa. | 12.00 Noon | | Nome, Alas. | 6.00 A.M. | | Tulsa, Okla. | 11.00 A.M. |
| ansville, Ind. | 11.00 A.M. | | Norfolk, Va. | 12.00 Noon | | Vancouver, B.C. | 9.00 A.M. |
| irbanks, Alas. | 7.00 A.M. | | Okla. City, Okla. | 11.00 A.M. | | Washington, D.C. | 12.00 Noon |
| nt, Mich. | 12.00 Noon | | Omaha, Neb. | 11.00 A.M. | | Wichita, Kan. | 11.00 A.M. |
| rt Wayne, Ind. | 12.00 Noon | | Peoria, Ill. | 11.00 A.M. | | Wilmington, Del. | 12.00 Noon |
| | | | | | | Winnipeg, Man. | 11.00 A.M. |

ities with an asterisk do not observe daylight savings time. During much of the year, it is necessary to add one hour to
ities which do observe daylight savings time to get the proper time relation.

## Standard Time Differences—World Cities

e time indicated in the table is fixed by law and is called the legal time, or, more generally, Standard Time. Use of Day-
Saving time varies widely. *Indicates morning of the following day. At 12.00, Eastern Standard Time, the standard
(in 24-hour time) in foreign cities is as follows:

| City | Time | | City | Time | | City | Time |
|---|---|---|---|---|---|---|---|
| andria | 19 00 | | Caracas | 13 00 | | Lima | 12 00 | Saigon | 1 00* |
| terdam | 18 00 | | Copenhagen | 18 00 | | Lisbon | 18 00 | Santiago (Chile) | 13 00 |
| ns | 19 00 | | Dacca | 23 00 | | Liverpool | 17 00 | Seoul | 2 00* |
| land | 5 00* | | Delhi | 22 30 | | London | 17 00 | Shanghai | 1 00* |
| dad | 20 00 | | Djakarta | 0 00 | | Madrid | 18 00 | Singapore | 12 30* |
| kok | 0 00 | | Dublin | 17 00 | | Manila | 1 00* | Stockholm | 18 00 |
| st | 17 00 | | Gdansk | 18 00 | | Melbourne | 3 00* | Sydney (Austrialia) | 3 00* |
| | 18 00 | | Geneva | 18 00 | | Montevideo | 14 00 | Tashkent | 23 00 |
| ta | 12 00 | | Havana | 12 00 | | Moscow | 20 00 | Teheran | 20 30 |
| bay | 22 30 | | Helsinki | 19 00 | | Nagasaki | 2 00* | Tel Aviv | 19 00 |
| en | 18 00 | | Hong Kong | 1 00* | | Oslo | 18 00 | Tokyo | 2 00* |
| sels | 18 00 | | Istanbul | 19 00 | | Paris | 18 00 | Valparaiso | 13 00 |
| arest | 19 00 | | Jerusalem | 19 00 | | Peking | 1 00* | Vladivostok | 3 00* |
| pest | 18 00 | | Johannesburg | 19 00 | | Prague | 18 00 | Vienna | 18 00 |
| os Aires | 14 00 | | Karachi | 22 00 | | Rangoon | 23 30 | Warsaw | 18 00 |
| utta | 22 30 | | Le Havre | 18 00 | | Rio De Janeiro | 14 00 | Wellington (N.Z.) | 5 00* |
| Town | 19 00 | | Leningrad | 20 00 | | Rome | 18 00 | Yokohama | 2 00* |
| | | | | | | | Zurich | 18 00 |

## Standard Time, Daylight Saving Time, and Others

**Source:** Defense Mapping Agency Hydrographic Center; Department of Transportation; National Bureau of Standards; U.S. Naval Observatory

### Standard Time

Standard time is reckoned from Greenwich, England, recognized as the Prime Meridian of Longitude. The world is divided into 24 zones, each 15° of arc, or one hour in time apart. The Greenwich meridian (0°) extends through the center of the initial zone, and the zones to the east are numbered from 1 to 12 with the prefix "minus" indicating the number of hours to be subtracted to obtain Greenwich Time.

Westward zones are similarly numbered, but prefixed "plus" showing the number of hours that must be added to get Greenwich Time. While these zones apply generally to sea areas, it should be noted that the Standard Time maintained in many countries does not coincide with zone time. A graphical representation of the zones is shown on the Standard Time Zone Chart of the World published by the Defense Mapping Agency Hydrographic Center, Washington, DC 20390.

The United States and possessions are divided into eight Standard Time zones, as set forth by the Uniform Time Act of 1966, which also provides for the use of Daylight Saving Time therein. Each zone is approximately 15° of longitude in width. All places in each zone use, instead of their own local time, the time counted from the transit of the "mean sun" across the Standard Time meridian which passes near the middle of that zone.

These time zones are designated as Atlantic, Eastern, Central, Mountain, Pacific, Yukon, Alaska-Hawaii, and Bering, and the time in these zones is basically reckoned from the 60th, 75th, 90th, 105th, 120th, 135th, 150th, 165th meridians west of Greenwich. The line wanders to conform to local geographical regions. The time in the various zones is earlier than Greenwich Time by 4, 5, 6, 7, 8, 9, 10, and 11 hours respectively.

### 24-Hour Time

24-hour time is widely used in scientific work throughout the world. In the United States it is used also in operat of the Armed Forces. In Europe it is used in preferenc the 12-hour a.m. and p.m. system. With the 24-hour sys the day begins at midnight and hours are numbere through 23.

### International Date Line

The Date Line is a zig-zag line that approximately c cides with the 180th meridian, and it is where each caler day begins. The date must be advanced one day when cr ing in a westerly direction and set back one day when cr ing in an easterly direction.

The line is deflected between north latitude 48° and 75 that all Asia lies to the west of it.

### Daylight Saving Time

Daylight Saving Time is achieved by advancing the c one hour. Under the Uniform Time Act, which became fective in 1967, all states, the District of Columbia, and possessions were to observe Daylight Saving Time begin at 2 a.m. on the last Sunday in April and ending at 2 on the last Sunday in October. Any state could, by law empt itself; a 1972 amendment to the act authorized st split by time zones to take that into consideration in empting themselves. Arizona, Hawaii, Puerto Rico, the gin Islands, American Samoa, and part of Indiana are exempt. Some local zone boundaries in Kansas, Texas, F ida, and Michigan have been modified in the last sev years by the Dept. of Transportation, which oversees act. To conserve energy Congress put most of the natio year-round Daylight Saving Time for two years effec Jan. 6, 1974 through Oct. 26, 1975; but a further bill, sig in October, 1974, restored Standard Time from the last S day in that month to the last Sunday in February, 1975.

---

# Legal or Public Holidays, 1979

Technically there are no national holidays in the United States; each state has jurisdiction over its holidays, which are ignated by leglislative enactment or executive proclamation. In practice, however, most states observe the federal legal pu holidays, even though the President and Congress can legally designate holidays only for the District of Columbia and federal employees.

Federal legal public holidays are: New Year's Day, Washington's Birthday, Memorial Day, Independence Day, La Day, Columbus Day, Veterans Day, Thanksgiving, and Christmas.

## Chief Legal or Public Holidays

When a holiday falls on a Sunday or a Saturday it is usually observed on the following Monday or preceding Friday. For some holidays, government and business closing practices vary. In most states, the office of the Secretary of State can provide details of holiday closings.

**Jan. 1 (Monday) — New Year's Day.** All the states.

**Feb. 12 (Monday) — Lincoln's Birthday.** Ariz., Cal., Col., Conn., Ill., Ind., Ia., Kan., Md., Mich., Mo., Mont., Neb., N.H., N.J., N.Y., Pa., Tenn., Ut., Vt., Wash., W.Va., In Del. and Ore., celebrated Feb. 5 in 1979.

**Feb. 19 (3d Monday in Feb.) — Washington's Birthday.** All the states except N.C. In several states, the holiday is called Presidents' Day or Washington-Lincoln Day.

**Apr. 13 — Good Friday.** Observed in all the states. A legal or public holiday in Conn., Del., Fla., Ha., Ind., Ky., La., Md., Mich., N.J., N.D., Tenn. W.Va. Partial holiday in N.M. and Wis.

**May 28 (last Monday in May) — Memorial Day.** All the states except Ala., Miss., S.C., (Confederate Memorial Day in Va.). Observed May 30 in Del., Ill., Md., N.H., N.M., N.Y., Vt. W.Va.

**July 4 (Wednesday) — Independence Day.** All the sta (July 3 in Nev.)

**Sept. 3 (1st Monday in Sept.) — Labor Day.** All states.

**Oct. 8 (2d Monday in Oct.) — Columbus Day.** A Ariz., Cal., Col., Conn., Del., Fla., Ga., Ida., Ill., Ind., Ka Ky., Me., Mass., Mich., Minn., Mo., Mont., Neb., N. N.J., N.M., N.Y., Oh., Okla., Pa., R.I., Tenn., Tex., Vt., Va., W.Va., Wis. Wy. Observed Oct. 12 in Md. (Disc erer's Day in Hawaii; Pioneer's Day in S.D.).

**Nov. 6 (1st Tuesday after 1st Monday in Nov.) — G eral Election Day.** Ind., N.J., N.Y., Va., W.Va. (Obser usually only when presidential or general elections are he Primary election days are observed as holidays or part h days in some states.)

**Nov. 11 (Sunday observed Nov. 12) — Armistice** (Veterans Day). All the states.

**Nov. 22 (4th Thursday in Nov.) — Thanksgiving Day.** the states. The day after Thanksgiving is observed as a or partial holiday in several states.

**Dec. 25 (Tuesday) — Christmas.** All the states.

## Other Legal or Public Holidays

Dates are for 1979 observance, when known.

**Jan. 8** — Battle of New Orleans. In La.

**Jan. 15** — Martin Luther King Birthday. Conn., Fla., Ill., Ky., La. (some years), Md., Mass., Mich., N.J., N.Y., Oh. Many schools and black groups in other states also observe the day.

**Jan. 15** (3d Monday in Jan.) — Robert E. Lee's Birthday. Ala., Miss.; Lee-Jackson Day in Va.

**Jan. 19** — Robert E. Lee's Birthday, Ark., Fla., Ga., Ky., La., N.C., S.C., Tenn. (special observance); Confederate Heroes' Day in Tex.

**Jan. 20** — Inauguration Day. In the District of Columbia; observed every fourth year.

**Jan. 30** — Franklin D. Roosevelt's Birthday. In Ky.

**Feb. 2** — Arbor Day. In Ariz. (most counties).

**Feb. 14** — Admission Day. In Ariz.

**Feb. 27** — Mardi Gras (Shrove Tuesday). Ala., La.

**Mar. 2** — Texas Independence Day. In that state.

**Mar. 6** — Town Meeting Day (1st Tuesday in Mar.). In Vt.

**Mar. 15** — Andrew Jackson Day. In Tenn. (special observance).

**Mar. 17** — Evacuation Day. In Boston and Suffolk County, Mass.

**Mar. 25** — Maryland Day. In that state.

**Mar. 26** — Kuhio Day. In Ha.

**Mar. 28** — Seward's Day. In Alas.

**Apr. 2** — Pascua Florida Day. In Fla.

**Apr. 6** — Arbor Day. In Ariz. (5 counties).

**Apr. 12** — Halifax Independence Day. In N.C.

**Apr. 13** — Thomas Jefferson's Birthday. In Ala.

**Apr. 16** — Easter Monday. In. N.C.

**Apr. 17** — Patriot's Day (3d Monday in Apr.). Me., Mass.

**Apr. 21** — San Jacinto Day. In Tex.

**Apr. 22** — Arbor Day in Neb.

**Apr. 23** — Fast Day (4th Monday in Apr.). In N.H.

**Apr. 23** — Confederate Memorial Day (4th Monday in Apr.). In Ala.

**Apr. 26** — Confederate Memorial Day. Fla., Ga.

**Apr. 27** — Arbor Day (last Friday in Apr.) In Ut.

**Apr. 30** (last Monday in Apr.) — Confederate Memorial Day. In Miss.

**May 8** — Harry Truman's Birthday. In Mo.

**May 10** — Confederate Memorial Day. In N.C., S.C.

**May 20** — Mecklenburg Day. In N.C.

**May 28** (last Monday in May) — Confederate Memorial Day. In Va.

**June 3** — Confederate Memorial Day. In Ky., La. (some years), Tenn. (special observance).

**June 4** (first Monday in June) — Birthday of Jefferson Davis. Ala., Fla., Ga., Ky., Miss.

**June 11** — Kamehameha Day. In Ha.

**June 14** — Flag Day. Observed in all states; a legal holiday in Pa. Observed June 10 in N.Y.

**June 18** — Bunker Hill Day. In Boston and Suffolk County, Mass.

**June 20** — West Virginia Day. In W.Va.

**July 24** — Pioneer Day. In Ut.

**Aug. 6** — Colorado Day (1st Monday in Aug.). In that state.

**Aug. 13** — Victory Day (2d Monday in Aug.). In R.I.

**Aug. 16** — Bennington Battle Day. In Vt.

**Aug. 17** — Admission Day (3d Friday in Aug.). In Ha.

**Aug. 27** — Lyndon Johnson's Birthday. In Tex.

**Aug. 30** — Huey Long's Birthday. In La. (some years).

**Sept. 9** — Admission Day. In Cal.

**Sept. 12** — Defenders' Day. In Md.

**Oct. 8** — Alaska Day. In that state.

**Oct. 31** — Nevada Day. In that state.

**Dec. 10** — Wyoming Day. Commemorates woman's suffrage in that state.

**Dec. 24** — Christmas Eve. In Ark.

**Dec. 26** — Day after Christmas. In S.C.

## Days Usually Observed

**All Saints' Day, Nov. 1.** A public holiday in Louisiana.

**American Indian Day (Sept. 28 in 1979).** Always fourth Friday in September.

**Arbor Day.** Tree-planting day. First observed April 10, 1872, in Nebraska. Now observed in every state in the Union except Alaska (often on the last Friday in April). A legal holiday in Utah (always last Friday in April), and in Nebraska (April 22).

**Armed Forces Day (May 19 in 1979).** Always third Saturday in that month, by presidential proclamation. Replaced Army, Navy, and Air Force Days.

**Bill of Rights Day, Dec. 15.** By Act of Congress. Bill of Rights took effect Dec. 15, 1791.

**Bird Day.** Often observed with Arbor Day.

**Child Health Day (Oct. 1 in 1979).** Always first Monday October, by presidential proclamation.

**Citizenship Day, Sept. 17.** President Truman, Feb. 29, '52, signed bill designating Sept. 17 as annual Citizenship Day. It replaced I Am An American Day, formerly 3rd Sunday in May and Constitution Day, formerly Sept. 17.

**Easter Monday (Apr. 16 in 1979).** A statutory day in Canada.

**Easter Sunday (Apr. 15 in 1979).**

**Elizabeth Cady Stanton Day, Nov. 12.** Birthday of pioneer leader for equal rights for women.

**Farmers's Day (Oct. 8 in 1979).** In Florida.

**Father's Day (June 17, in 1979).** Always third Sunday in that month.

**Flag Day, June 14.** By presidential proclamation. It is a legal holiday in Pennsylvania. Observed June 10 in N.Y. in '79.

**Forefathers' Day, Dec. 21.** Landing on Plymouth Rock, 1620. Is celebrated with dinners by New England societies — especially "Down East."

**Nathan Bedford Forrest's Birthday, July 13.** Observed in Tennessee to honor the Civil War general.

**Four Chaplains Memorial Day, Feb. 3.**

**Gen. Douglas MacArthur Day, Jan. 26.** A memorial day in Arkansas.

**Gen. Pulaski Memorial Day, Oct. 11.** Native of Poland and Revolutionary War hero; died (Oct. 11, 1779) from wounds received at the seige of Savannah, Ga. Observed officially in Indiana.

**Gen. von Steuben Memorial Day, Sept. 17.** By presidential proclamation.

**Georgia Day, Feb. 12.** Observed in that state. Commemorates landing of first colonists in 1733.

**Groundhog Day, Feb. 2.** A popular belief is that if the groundhog sees his shadow this day, he returns to his burrow and winter continues 6 weeks longer.

**Halloween, Oct. 31.** The evening before All Saints or All-Hallows Day. Informally observed in the U.S. with masquerading and pumpkin-decorations. Traditionally an occasion for children to play pranks.

**Leif Ericsson Day, Oct. 9.** Observed in Minnesota, Wisconsin.

**Loyalty Day, May 1.** By act of Congress.

**May Day.** Name popularly given to May 1st. Celebrated as Labor Day in most of the world, and by some groups in the U.S. Observed in many schools as a Spring Festival.

**Minnesota Day, May 11.** In that state.

**Mother's Day (May 13 in 1979).** Always second Sunday in that month. First celebrated in Philadelphia in 1908. Mother's Day has become an international holiday.

**National Aviation Day, Aug. 19.** By presidential proclamation.

**National Day of Prayer.** By presidential proclamation each year on a day other than a Sunday.

**National Freedom Day, Feb. 1.** To commemorate the signing of the Thirteenth amendment, abolishing slavery, Feb. 1, 1865. By presidential proclamation.

**National Maritime Day, May 22.** First proclaimed 1935 in commemoration of the departure of the SS Savannah, from Savannah, Ga., on May 22, 1819, on the first successful transatlantic voyage under steam propulsion. By presidential proclamation.

**Pan American Day, Apr. 14.** In 1890 the First International Conference of American States, meeting in Washington, was held on that date. A resolution was adopted which resulted in the creation of the organization known today as the Pan American Union. By presidential proclamation.

**Primary Election Day.** Observed usually only when presidential or general elections are held.

**Reformation Day, Oct. 31.** Observed by Protestant groups.

**Sadie Hawkins Day (Nov. 17 in 1979).** First Saturday after November 11.

**St. Patrick's Day, Mar. 17.** Observed by Irish Societies, especially with parades.

**St. Valentine's Day, Feb. 14.** Festival of a martyr beheaded at Rome under Emperor Claudius. Association of this day with lovers has no connection with the saint a probably had its origin in an old belief that on this day bi begin to choose their mates.

**Senior Citizens' Day (Sept. 23 in 1979).** Celebrated in diana on the fourth Sunday in September.

**Susan B. Anthony Day, Feb. 15.** Birthday of a pione crusader for equal rights for women.

**United Nations Day, Oct. 24.** By presidential proclam tion, to commemorate founding of United Nations.

**Verrazano Day, Apr. 7.** Observed by New York State, commemorate the probable discovery of New York harb by Giovanni da Verrazano in April, 1524.

**Victoria Day (May 21 in 1979).** Birthday of Queen V toria, a statutory day in Canada, celebrated the first Mo day before May 25.

**Francis Willard Day, Sept. 28.** Observed in Minnesota honor the educator and temperance leader.

**Will Rogers Day, Nov. 4.** In Oklahoma.

**World Poetry Day, Oct. 15.**

**Wright Brothers Day, Dec. 17.** By presidential design tion, to commemorate first successful flight by Orville a Wilbur Wright, Dec. 17, 1903.

**Youth Honor Day, Oct. 31.** Iowa day of observance.

## Other Holidays, Anniversaries, Events — 1979

| | | | |
|---|---|---|---|
| Jan. 5, 1779 | — Zebulon Pike born. | | Jean Day in Quebec. |
| Jan. 15, 1929 | — Martin Luther King born. | July 1 (Sun.) | — Dominion Day, or Canada Day. |
| Jan. 21 (Sun.) | — Superbowl game. | July 14 (Sat.) | — Bastille Day in France. |
| Feb. 1 (Thurs.) | — Robinson Crusoe Day. | July 20, 1969 | — U.S. astronauts land on moon. |
| Feb. 14 (Wed.) | — St. Valentine's Day. | Aug. 1, 1779 | — Francis Scott Key born. |
| Mar. 14, 1629 | — Massachusetts Bay Co. chartered. | Aug. 14, 1879 | — Ethel Barrymore born. |
| Mar. 14, 1879 | — Albert Einstein born. | Sept. 16 (Sat.) | — Mexican Independence Day. |
| Mar. 21 (Wed.) | — Spring begins, 12:22 A.M. EST. | Sept. 23 (Sun.) | — Autumn begins, 10:17 A.M., EST. |
| Mar. 27, 1879 | — Edward Steichen born. | Sept. 28, 1779 | — John Paul Jones captures *Serapis*. |
| Apr. 1 (Sun.) | — April Fool's Day. | Oct. 15 (Mon.) | — World Poetry Day. |
| Apr. 16 (Mon.) | — Boston Marathon. | Oct. 23 (Tues.) | — Swallows return to Capistrano. |
| May 1 (Tues.) | — Law Day. | Oct. 29, 1929 | — Stock Market crashes. |
| May 5 (Sat.) | — Kentucky Derby. | Nov. 2, 1879 | — Wallace Stevens born. |
| May 17, 1954 | — Supreme Court outlaws school segregation. | Nov. 4, 1879 | — Will Rogers born. |
| | | Nov. 5 (Mon.) | — Guy Fawkes Day in England. |
| May 24, 1879 | — William Lloyd Garrison dies. | Nov. 10, 1879 | — Vachel Lindsay born. |
| May 27, 1679 | — Parliament passes Habeas Corpus Act. | Dec. 7 (Fri.) | — Pearl Harbor Day. |
| May 27 (Sun.) | — Indianapolis 500 auto race. | Dec. 18, 1879 | — Paul Klee born. |
| June 21 (Thurs.) | — Summer begins, 6:56 P.M. EST. | Dec. 22 (Sun.) | — Winter begins, 6:10 A.M., EST. |
| June 24 (Sun.) | — San Juan Day in Puerto Rico, St. | Dec. 29, 1879 | — Billy Mitchell born. |

---

### The Meaning of "One Inch of Rain"

An acre of ground contains 43,560 square feet. Consequently, a rainfall of 1 inch over 1 acre of ground would mean a to of 6,272,640 cubic inches of water. This is equivalent of 3,630 cubic feet.

As a cubic foot of pure water weighs about 62.4 pounds, the exact amount varying with the density, it follows that weight of a uniform coating of 1 inch of rain over 1 acre of surface would be 226,512 pounds, or about 113 short tons. T weight of 1 U.S. gallon of pure water is about 8.345 pounds. Consequently a rainfall of 1 inch over 1 acre of ground wou mean 27,143 gallons of water.

---

### Temperature-Humidity (Discomfort) Index

The temperature-humidity index, THI, is a measure of summertime human discomfort resulting from the combined effe of temperature and humidity. (The THI may be calculated by adding wet-bulb and dry-bulb temperatures, multiplying sum by 0.4 and adding 15.)

The following chart shows the combinations of temperature degrees and humidity percentages which produce discomf for most persons (the equivalent of a THI value of 75) and those which produce acute discomfort for almost everyone (equ alent to a THI of 80).

| Discomfort temp.-humid. | Acute discomfort temp.-humid. | Discomfort temp.-humid. | Acute discomfort temp.-humid. | Discomfort temp.-humid. | Acute discomfort temp.-humic |
|---|---|---|---|---|---|
| 75°—100% | 81°—100% | 82°—49% | 88°—54% | 90°—14% | 96°—20% |
| 76°— 91% | 82°—93% | 83°—43% | 89°—49% | 91°—10% | 97°—16% |
| 77°— 82% | 83°—86% | 84°—38% | 90°—43% | 92°— 7% | 98°—13% |
| 78°— 75% | 84°—78% | 85°—33% | 91°—38% | 93°— 5% | 99°—11% |
| 79°— 68% | 85°—71% | 86°—29% | 92°—34% | 94°— 3% | 100°— 8% |
| 80°— 61% | 86°—65% | 87°—25% | 93°—30% | 95°— 1% | 101°— 6% |
| 81°— 55% | 87°—59% | 88°—20% | 94°—26% | 96°— 1% | 102°— 3% |
| | | 89°—17% | 95°—23% | 97°— 1% | 103°— 1% |

From 95 degrees up there is discomfort at any humidity. When the temperature is over 102 degrees there is acute disco fort at any humidity.

## Tides and Their Causes

Source: National Oceanic and Atmospheric Administration. U.S. Commerce Department

ιe tides are a natural phenomenon involving the alter-
ιg rise and fall in the large fluid bodies of the earth
ιed by the combined gravitational attraction of the sun
moon. The combination of these two variable force in-
ιces produce the complex recurrent cycle of the tides.
ς may occur in both oceans and seas, to a limited extent
ιrge lakes, the atmosphere, and, to a very minute degree,
ιe earth itself. The period between succeeding tides var-
ς the result of many factors and force influences.

ιe tide-generating force represents the difference be-
ιn (1) the centrifugal force produced by the revolution of
ιarth around the common center-of-gravity of the earth-
ιn system and (2) the gravitational attraction of the
ιn acting upon the earth's overlying waters. Since, on the
ιage, the moon is only 238,857 miles from the earth com-
ιd with the sun's much greater distance of 93,000,000
ς, this closer distance outranks the much smaller mass
ιe moon compared with that of the sun, and the moon's
ιraising force is, accordingly, 2½ times that of the sun.

ιe effect of the tide-generating forces of the moon and
ιacting tangentially to the earth's surface (the so-called
ιctive force") tends to cause a maximum accumulation
ιe waters of the oceans at two diametrically opposite po-
ιns on the surface of the earth and to withdraw compen-
ιg amounts of water from all points 90° removed from
ιpositions of these tidal bulges. As the earth ςotates be-
ιh the maxima and minima of these tide-generating
ιes, a sequence of two high tides, separated by two low
ς, ideally is produced each day.

ιwice in each lunar month, when the sun, moon, and
ιn are directly aligned, with the moon between the earth
ιthe sun (at new moon) or on the opposite side of the

earth from the sun (at full moon), the sun and the moon exert their gravitational force in a mutual or additive fashion.
Higher high tides and lower low tides are produced. These
are called *spring* tides. At two positions 90° in between, the
gravitational forces of the moon and sun — imposed at right
angles—tend to counteract each other to the greatest extent,
and the range between high and low tides is reduced. These
are called *neap* tides. This semi-monthly variation between
the spring and neap tides is called the *phase inequality.*

The inclination of the moon's orbit to the equator also
produces a difference in the height of succeeding high tides
and in the extent of depression of succeeding low tides
which is known as the *diurnal inequality.* In extreme cases,
this phenomenon can result in only one high tide and one
low tide each day.

The actual amount of the uplift of the waters in the deep
ocean may amount to only one or two feet. However, as this
tide approaches shoal waters and its effects are augmented
the tidal range may be greatly increased. In Nova Scotia
along the narrow channel of the Bay of Fundy, the range of
tides or difference between high and low waters, may reach
43 1/2 feet or more (under spring tide conditions) due to
resonant amplification.

At New Orleans, the periodic rise and fall of the tide varies with the state of the Mississippi, being about 10 inches at
low stage and zero at high. The Canadian Tide Tables for
1972 gave a maximum range of nearly 50 feet at Leaf Basin,
Ungava Bay.

In every case, actual high or low tide can vary considerably from the average due to weather conditions such as
strong winds, abrupt barometric pressure changes, or prolonged periods of extreme high or low pressure.

### The Average Rise and Fall of Tides

| ιes | Ft. | In. | Places | Ft. | In. | Places | Ft. | In. |
|---|---|---|---|---|---|---|---|---|
| ιmore, Md. | 1 | 6 | Mobile, Ala. | 1 | 6 | San Diego, Cal. | 4 | 1 |
| ιon, Mass. | 9 | 6 | New London, Conn. | 2 | 7 | Sandy Hook, N.J. | 4 | 7 |
| ιrleston, S.C. | 5 | 2 | Newport, R.I. | 3 | 6 | San Francisco, Cal. | 4 | 0 |
| ιn, Panama | 1 | 1 | New York, N.Y. | 4 | 6 | Savannah, Ga. | 7 | 5 |
| ιport, Me. | 18 | 2 | Old Pt. Comfort, Va. | 2 | 6 | Seattle, Wash. | 7 | 7 |
| ιveston, Tex. | 1 | 5 | Philadelphia, Pa. | 5 | 11 | Tampa, Fla. | 2 | 10 |
| ιax, N.S. | 4 | 5 | Portland, Me. | 9 | 0 | Vancouver, B.C. | 10 | 6 |
| ι West, Fla. | 1 | 4 | St. John's, Nfld. | 2 | 7 | Washington, D.C. | 2 | 11 |

### Speed of Winds in the U.S.

Source: National Oceanic and Atmospheric Administration. U.S. Commerce Department
Miles per hour — average through 1977. High through 1977. Wind velocities in true values.

| Station | Avg. | High | Station | Avg. | High | Station | Avg. | High |
|---|---|---|---|---|---|---|---|---|
| ιquerque, N.M. | 9.0 | 90 | Helena, Mont. | 7.9 | 73 | New York, N.Y.(c) | 9.4 | 70 |
| ιhorage, Alas. | 6.7 | 61 | Honolulu, Ha. | 11.9 | 67 | Omaha, Neb. | 10.8 | 109 |
| ιnta, Ga. | 9.1 | 70 | Jacksonville, Fla. | 8.5 | 82 | Pensacola, Fla. | 8.3 | (b)37 |
| ιnarck, N.D. | 10.5 | 72 | Key West, Fla. | 11.2 | 122 | Philadelphia, Pa. | 9.6 | 73 |
| ιton, Mass. | 12.6 | 61 | Knoxville, Tenn. | 7.3 | 73 | Pittsburgh, Pa. | 9.4 | 58 |
| ιalo, N.Y. | 12.3 | 91 | Little Rock, Ark. | 8.1 | 65 | Portland, Ore. | 7.8 | 88 |
| ιe Hatteras, N.C. | 11.6 | (b)110 | Louisville, Ky. | 8.4 | 61 | Rochester, N.Y. | 9.7 | 73 |
| ιttanooga, Tenn. | 6.3 | 82 | Memphis, Tenn. | 9.1 | 40 | St. Louis, Mo. | 9.5 | (b)60 |
| ιago, Ill. | 10.4 | 60 | Miami, Fla. | 9.1 | (a)74 | Salt Lake City, Ut. | 8.7 | 71 |
| ιcinnati, Oh. | 7.1 | 49 | Minneapolis, Minn. | 10.5 | 92 | San Diego, Cal. | 6.7 | 51 |
| ιveland, Oh. | 10.8 | 74 | Mobile, Ala. | 9.2 | (b)63 | San Francisco, Cal. | 10.5 | 58 |
| ιver, Col. | 9.1 | 56 | Montgomery, Ala. | 6.8 | 72 | Savannah, Ga. | 8.1 | 66 |
| ιroit, Mich. | 10.2 | 46 | Mt. Washington, N.H. | 35.2 | 231 | Spokane, Wash. | 8.7 | 59 |
| ι Smith, Ark. | 7.6 | 58 | Nashville, Tenn. | 8.0 | 73 | Toledo, Oh. | 9.5 | 72 |
| ιveston, Tex. | 11.0 | (d)100 | New Orleans, La. | 8.3 | (b)98 | Washington, D.C. | 9.3 | 78 |

ιHighest velocity ever recorded in Miami area was 132 mph, at former station in Miami Beach in September, 1926.
ι Previous location. (c) Data for Central Park, Battery Place data through 1960, avg. 14.5, high 113. (d) Recorded before anemometer
ιw away. Estimated high 120.

### Men's Names Added to Hurricane List

J.S. government agencies responsible for weather and re-
ιd communications have used girls' names to identify ma-
ιtropical storms since 1953. A U.S. proposal that both
ιle and female names be adopted for Atlantic hurricanes,
ιting in 1979, has been accepted by a committee of the
ιrld Meterological Organization. Final approval by WMO
ιxpected before the 1979 season, June 1 through Nov. 30.
ιlames proposed for 1979 — Ana, Bob, Claudette, David,

Elena, Frederic, Gloria, Henri, Isabel, Juan, Kate, Larry,
Mindy, Nicolas, Odette, Peter, Rose, Sam, Teresa, Victor,
Wanda.

Names assigned to Eastern Pacific hurricanes, 1979 —
Andres, Blanca, Carlos, Dolores, Enrique, Fefa, Guillermo,
Hilda, Ignacio, Jimena, Kevin, Linda, Marty, Nora, Olaf,
Pauline, Rick, Sandra, Terry, Vivian, Waldo.

## National Weather Service Watches and Warnings

Source: National Weather Service, NOAA, U.S. Commerce Department

National Weather Service forecasters issue a Tornado Watch for a specific area where it is reasonably possible that tornadoes may occur during the valid time of the watch. A Watch is to alert people to watch for tornado activity and listen for a Tornado Warning. A Tornado Warning means that a tornado has been sighted or indicated by radar, and that safety precautions should be taken at once. A Hurricane Watch means that an existing hurricane poses a threat to coastal and inland communities in the area specified by the Watch. A Hurricane Warning means hurricane force winds and/or dangerously high water and exceptionally high waves are expected in a specified coastal area within 24 hours.

**Tornado**—A violent rotating column of air pendant from a thundercloud, usually recognized as a funnel-shaped vortex accompanied by a loud roar. With rotating winds est. up to 300 mph., it is the most destructive storm. Tornado paths have varied in length from a few feet to nearly 300 miles (avg. 5 mi.); diameter from a few feet to over a mile (average 220 yards); average forward speed, 25-40 mph.

**Cyclone**—An atmospheric circulation of winds rotating counterclockwise in the northern hemisphere and clockwise in the southern hemisphere. Tornadoes, hurricanes, and the lows shown on weather maps are all examples of cyclones having various sizes and intensities. Cyclones are usually accompanied by precipitation or stormy weather.

**Hurricane**—A severe cyclone originating over tropical ocean waters and having winds 74 miles an hour or higher (In the western Pacific, such storms are known as ty phoons.) The area of strong winds takes the form of a circle or an oval, sometimes as much as 500 miles in diameter. I the lower latitudes hurricanes usually move toward the wes or northwest at 10 to 15 mph. When the center approache 25° to 30° North Latitude, direction of motion often change to northeast, with increased forward speed.

**Blizzard**—A severe weather condition characterized b low temperatures and by strong winds bearing a grea amount of snow (mostly fine, dry snow picked up from th ground). The National Weather Service specifies, for bliz zard, a wind of 35 miles an hour or higher, temperature 20°F. or lower, and sufficient falling and/or blowing snow t reduce visibility to less than ¼ of a mile. For "severe bliz zard" wind speeds of 45 mph or more, temperature near below 10°F., and visibility reduced by snow to near zero.

**Monsoon**—A name for seasonal winds (derived from Ara bic "mausim," a season). It was first applied to the wind over the Arabian Sea, which blow for six months fro northeast and six months from southwest, but it has bee extended to similar winds in other parts of the world. Th monsoons are strongest on the southern and eastern sides Asia.

**Flood**—The condition that occurs when water overflow the natural or artificial confines of a stream or other body water, or accumulates by drainage over low-lying areas.

---

## National Weather Service Marine Warnings and Advisories

**Small Craft Advisory:** A Small Craft Advisory alerts mariners to sustained (exceeding two hours) weather and/or sea conditions either present or forecast, potentially hazardous to small boats. Hazardous conditions may include winds of 18 to 33 knots and/or dangerous wave or inlet conditions. It is the responsibility of the mariner, based on his experience and size or type of boat, to determine if the conditions are hazardous. When a mariner becomes aware of a Small Craft Advisory, he should immediately obtain the latest marine forecast to determine the reason for the Advisory.

**Gale Warning** indicates that winds within the range 34 to 47 knots are forecast for the area.

**Storm Warning** indicates that winds 48 knots and above, no matter how high the speed, are forecast for the area.

However, if the winds are associated with a tropical cyclo (hurricane), the storm warning indicates that winds with the range 48 to 63 knots are forecast.

**Hurricane Warning** indicates that winds 64 knots a above are forecast for the area.

Primary sources of dissemination are commercial rad TV, U.S. Coast Guard Radio stations, and NOAA VH FM broadcasts. These broadcasts on 162.40 and 162. MHz can usually be received 20-40 miles from the transm ting antenna site, depending on terrain and quality of receiver used. Where transmitting antennas are on hi ground, the range is somewhat greater, reaching 60 miles more.

---

## Wind Chill Table

Source: National Oceanic and Atmospheric Administration, U.S. Commerce Department

Both temperature and wind cause heat loss from body surfaces. A combination of cold and wind makes a body feel col than the actual temperature. The table shows, for example, that a temperature of 20 degrees Fahrenheit, plus a wind of miles per hour, causes a body heat loss equal to that in minus 10 degrees with no wind. In other words, the wind makes degrees feel like minus 10.

Top line of figures shows actual temperatures in degrees Fahrenheit. Column at left shows wind speeds.

| MPH | 35 | 30 | 25 | 20 | 15 | 10 | 5 | 0 | −5 | −10 | −15 | −20 | −25 | −30 | −35 | −40 |
|---|---|---|---|---|---|---|---|---|---|---|---|---|---|---|---|---|
| 5 | 33 | 27 | 21 | 19 | 12 | 7 | 0 | −5 | −10 | −15 | −21 | −26 | −31 | −36 | −42 | −47 |
| 10 | 22 | 16 | 10 | 3 | −3 | −9 | −15 | −22 | −27 | −34 | −40 | −46 | −52 | −58 | −64 | −71 |
| 15 | 16 | 9 | 2 | −5 | −11 | −18 | −25 | −31 | −38 | −45 | −51 | −58 | −65 | −72 | −78 | −85 |
| 20 | 12 | 4 | −3 | −10 | −17 | −24 | −31 | −39 | −46 | −53 | −60 | −67 | −74 | −81 | −88 | −95 |
| 25 | 8 | 1 | −7 | −15 | −22 | −29 | −36 | −44 | −51 | −59 | −66 | −74 | −81 | −88 | −96 | −103 |
| 30 | 6 | −2 | −10 | −18 | −25 | −33 | −41 | −49 | −56 | −64 | −71 | −79 | −86 | −93 | −101 | −109 |
| 35 | 4 | −4 | −12 | −20 | −27 | −35 | −43 | −52 | −58 | −67 | −74 | −82 | −89 | −97 | −105 | −113 |
| 40 | 3 | −5 | −13 | −21 | −29 | −37 | −45 | −53 | −60 | −69 | −76 | −84 | −92 | −100 | −107 | −115 |
| 45 | 2 | −6 | −14 | −22 | −30 | −38 | −46 | −54 | −62 | −70 | −78 | −85 | −93 | −102 | −109 | −117 |

*(Wind speeds greater than 45 mph have little additional chilling effect.)*

---

## Explanation of Normal Temperatures

Normal temperatures listed in the tables on pages 797 and 799 are based on records of the National Weather Service the 30-year period from 1941-1970 inclusive. To obtain the average maximum or minimum temperature for any month, daily temperatures are added; the total is then divided by the number of days in that month.

The normal maximum temperature for January, for example, is obtained by adding the average maximums for Jan., 19 Jan., 1942, etc., through Jan., 1970. The total is then divided by 30. The normal minimum temperature is obtained in a si lar manner by adding the average minimums for each January in the 30-year period and dividing by 30. The normal temp ture for January is one half of the sum for the normal maximum and minimum temperatures for that month. The mean t perature for any one day is one-half the total of the maximum and minimum temperatures for that day.

# Monthly Normal Temperature and Precipitation

Source: National Oceanic and Atmospheric Administration, U.S. Commerce Department

These normals are based on records for the 30-year period 1941 to 1970 inclusive. See explanation on page 796. For stations that did not have continuous records from the same instrument site for the entire 30 years, the means have been adjusted to the record at the present site.

Airport station; *city office stations. T, temperature in Fahrenheit; P, precipitation in inches; L, less than .05 inch.

| Station | Jan. T. | Jan. P. | Feb. T. | Feb. P. | Mar. T. | Mar. P. | Apr. T. | Apr. P. | May T. | May P. | June T. | June P. | July T. | July P. | Aug. T. | Aug. P. | Sept. T. | Sept. P. | Oct. T. | Oct. P. | Nov. T. | Nov. P. | Dec. T. | Dec. P. |
|---|---|---|---|---|---|---|---|---|---|---|---|---|---|---|---|---|---|---|---|---|---|---|---|---|
| Albany, N.Y. | 22 | 2.2 | 24 | 2.1 | 33 | 2.6 | 47 | 2.7 | 58 | 3.3 | 68 | 3.0 | 72 | 3.1 | 70 | 2.9 | 62 | 3.1 | 51 | 2.6 | 40 | 2.8 | 26 | 2.9 |
| Albuquerque, N.M. | 35 | 0.3 | 40 | 0.4 | 46 | 0.5 | 56 | 0.5 | 65 | 0.5 | 75 | 0.5 | 79 | 1.4 | 77 | 1.3 | 70 | 0.8 | 58 | 0.8 | 45 | 0.3 | 36 | 0.5 |
| Anchorage, Alas. | 12 | 0.8 | 18 | 0.8 | 24 | 0.6 | 35 | 0.6 | 46 | 0.6 | 55 | 1.1 | 58 | 2.1 | 56 | 2.3 | 48 | 2.4 | 35 | 1.4 | 21 | 1.0 | 13 | 1.1 |
| Asheville, N.C. | 38 | 3.4 | 39 | 3.6 | 46 | 4.7 | 56 | 3.5 | 64 | 3.3 | 71 | 4.0 | 74 | 4.9 | 73 | 4.5 | 67 | 3.6 | 57 | 3.3 | 46 | 2.9 | 39 | 3.6 |
| Atlanta, Ga. | 42 | 4.3 | 45 | 4.4 | 51 | 5.8 | 61 | 4.6 | 69 | 3.7 | 76 | 3.7 | 78 | 4.9 | 78 | 3.5 | 72 | 3.2 | 62 | 2.5 | 51 | 3.4 | 44 | 4.2 |
| Baltimore, Md. | 42 | 2.9 | 44 | 2.8 | 53 | 3.7 | 65 | 3.1 | 75 | 3.6 | 83 | 3.8 | 87 | 4.1 | 85 | 4.2 | 79 | 3.1 | 68 | 2.8 | 56 | 3.1 | 44 | 3.3 |
| Barrow, Ala. | -15 | 0.2 | -19 | 0.2 | -15 | 0.2 | -1 | 0.2 | 19 | 0.2 | 33 | 0.4 | 39 | 0.9 | 38 | 1.0 | 30 | 0.6 | 15 | 0.6 | -1 | 0.3 | -12 | 0.2 |
| Birmingham, Ala. | 44 | 4.8 | 47 | 5.3 | 53 | 6.2 | 63 | 4.6 | 71 | 3.6 | 77 | 4.0 | 80 | 5.2 | 79 | 4.3 | 74 | 3.6 | 63 | 2.6 | 52 | 3.7 | 45 | 5.2 |
| Bismarck, N.D. | 8 | 0.5 | 14 | 0.4 | 25 | 0.7 | 43 | 1.4 | 54 | 2.2 | 64 | 3.6 | 71 | 2.2 | 69 | 2.0 | 58 | 1.3 | 47 | 0.8 | 29 | 0.6 | 16 | 0.5 |
| Boise, Ida. | 29 | 1.5 | 36 | 1.2 | 41 | 1.0 | 49 | 1.1 | 57 | 1.3 | 65 | 1.1 | 75 | 0.2 | 72 | 0.3 | 63 | 0.4 | 52 | 0.8 | 40 | 1.3 | 32 | 1.4 |
| Boston, Mass. | 29 | 3.7 | 30 | 3.5 | 38 | 4.0 | 49 | 3.5 | 59 | 3.5 | 68 | 3.2 | 73 | 2.7 | 71 | 3.5 | 65 | 3.2 | 55 | 3.0 | 45 | 4.5 | 33 | 4.2 |
| Buffalo, N.Y. | 24 | 2.9 | 24 | 2.6 | 32 | 2.9 | 45 | 3.2 | 55 | 3.0 | 66 | 2.2 | 70 | 2.9 | 68 | 3.5 | 62 | 3.3 | 52 | 3.0 | 40 | 3.7 | 28 | 3.0 |
| Burlington, Vt. | 17 | 1.7 | 19 | 1.7 | 29 | 1.9 | 43 | 2.6 | 55 | 3.0 | 65 | 3.5 | 70 | 3.5 | 67 | 3.7 | 59 | 3.1 | 49 | 2.7 | 37 | 2.9 | 23 | 2.2 |
| Caribou, Me. | 11 | 2.0 | 13 | 2.1 | 24 | 2.2 | 37 | 2.4 | 50 | 3.0 | 60 | 3.4 | 65 | 4.0 | 62 | 3.8 | 54 | 3.5 | 44 | 3.3 | 31 | 3.5 | 16 | 2.6 |
| Charleston, S.C. | 49 | 2.9 | 51 | 3.3 | 57 | 4.8 | 65 | 3.0 | 72 | 3.8 | 78 | 6.3 | 80 | 8.2 | 80 | 6.4 | 75 | 5.2 | 66 | 3.1 | 56 | 2.1 | 49 | 3.1 |
| Chicago, Ill. | 24 | 1.9 | 27 | 1.6 | 37 | 2.7 | 50 | 3.8 | 60 | 3.4 | 71 | 4.0 | 75 | 4.1 | 74 | 3.1 | 66 | 3.0 | 55 | 2.6 | 40 | 2.2 | 29 | 2.1 |
| Cincinnati, Oh.* | 32 | 3.4 | 34 | 3.0 | 43 | 4.1 | 55 | 3.9 | 64 | 4.0 | 73 | 3.9 | 76 | 4.0 | 75 | 3.0 | 68 | 2.7 | 58 | 2.2 | 45 | 3.1 | 34 | 2.9 |
| Cleveland, Oh. | 27 | 2.6 | 28 | 2.2 | 36 | 3.1 | 48 | 3.5 | 58 | 3.5 | 68 | 3.3 | 71 | 3.5 | 70 | 3.0 | 64 | 2.8 | 54 | 2.6 | 42 | 2.8 | 30 | 2.4 |
| Columbus, Oh. | 28 | 2.9 | 30 | 2.3 | 39 | 3.4 | 51 | 3.7 | 61 | 4.1 | 70 | 4.1 | 74 | 4.2 | 72 | 2.9 | 65 | 2.4 | 54 | 1.9 | 42 | 2.7 | 31 | 2.4 |
| Dallas, Tex. | 45 | 2.0 | 49 | 2.6 | 56 | 3.0 | 66 | 4.7 | 74 | 4.9 | 82 | 3.3 | 86 | 1.8 | 86 | 2.4 | 78 | 3.3 | 68 | 3.2 | 56 | 2.6 | 48 | 2.3 |
| Denver, Col. | 30 | 0.6 | 33 | 0.7 | 37 | 1.2 | 48 | 1.9 | 57 | 2.6 | 66 | 1.9 | 73 | 1.8 | 72 | 1.3 | 63 | 1.1 | 52 | 1.1 | 39 | 0.8 | 33 | 0.4 |
| Des Moines, Ia. | 19 | 1.1 | 24 | 1.1 | 34 | 2.3 | 50 | 2.9 | 61 | 4.2 | 71 | 4.9 | 75 | 3.3 | 73 | 3.3 | 64 | 3.1 | 54 | 2.1 | 38 | 1.4 | 25 | 1.1 |
| Detroit, Mich. | 26 | 1.9 | 27 | 1.8 | 35 | 2.3 | 48 | 3.1 | 58 | 3.4 | 69 | 3.0 | 73 | 3.0 | 72 | 3.0 | 75 | 2.3 | 54 | 2.5 | 41 | 2.3 | 30 | 2.2 |
| Dodge City, Kan. | 31 | 0.5 | 35 | 0.6 | 41 | 1.1 | 54 | 1.7 | 64 | 3.1 | 74 | 3.3 | 79 | 3.1 | 78 | 2.6 | 69 | 1.7 | 58 | 1.7 | 43 | 0.6 | 33 | 8.5 |
| Duluth, Minn. | 9 | 1.2 | 12 | 0.9 | 24 | 1.8 | 39 | 2.6 | 49 | 3.4 | 59 | 4.4 | 66 | 3.7 | 64 | 3.8 | 54 | 3.1 | 45 | 2.3 | 28 | 1.7 | 14 | 1.4 |
| Eureka, Cal.* | 47 | 7.4 | 48 | 5.2 | 48 | 4.8 | 50 | 3.0 | 53 | 2.1 | 55 | 0.7 | 56 | 0.1 | 57 | 0.3 | 57 | 0.7 | 54 | 3.2 | 52 | 5.8 | 49 | 6.6 |
| Fairbanks, Alas. | -12 | 0.6 | -3 | 0.5 | 10 | 0.5 | 29 | 0.3 | 47 | 0.7 | 59 | 1.4 | 61 | 1.9 | 55 | 2.2 | 44 | 1.1 | 25 | 0.7 | 3 | 0.7 | -10 | 0.7 |
| Ft. Worth, Tex. | 45 | 1.8 | 49 | 2.4 | 55 | 2.5 | 65 | 4.3 | 73 | 4.5 | 81 | 3.1 | 85 | 1.8 | 85 | 2.3 | 78 | 3.2 | 68 | 2.7 | 56 | 2.0 | 48 | 1.8 |
| Fresno, Cal. | 45 | 1.8 | 50 | 1.7 | 54 | 1.6 | 60 | 1.2 | 67 | 0.3 | 74 | 0.1 | 81 | L | 78 | L | 74 | 0.1 | 64 | 0.4 | 54 | 1.2 | 46 | 1.7 |
| Galveston, Tex.* | 54 | 3.0 | 56 | 2.7 | 61 | 2.6 | 69 | 2.6 | 76 | 3.2 | 81 | 4.1 | 83 | 4.4 | 83 | 4.4 | 80 | 5.6 | 73 | 2.8 | 64 | 3.2 | 57 | 3.7 |
| Grand Junction, Col. | 27 | 0.6 | 34 | 0.6 | 41 | 0.8 | 52 | 0.8 | 62 | 0.6 | 71 | 0.6 | 79 | 0.5 | 75 | 1.1 | 67 | 0.8 | 55 | 0.9 | 40 | 0.6 | 30 | 0.6 |
| Gr. Rapids, Mich. | 23 | 1.9 | 25 | 1.5 | 33 | 2.5 | 47 | 3.4 | 57 | 3.2 | 67 | 3.4 | 72 | 3.1 | 70 | 2.5 | 62 | 3.3 | 52 | 2.6 | 39 | 2.8 | 27 | 2.2 |
| Helena, Mon. | 18 | 0.6 | 25 | 0.4 | 31 | 0.7 | 43 | 0.9 | 52 | 1.8 | 59 | 2.4 | 68 | 1.0 | 66 | 1.0 | 56 | 1.0 | 45 | 0.6 | 32 | 0.6 | 23 | 0.6 |
| Honolulu, Ha. | 72 | 4.4 | 72 | 2.5 | 73 | 3.2 | 75 | 1.4 | 77 | 1.0 | 79 | 0.3 | 80 | 0.6 | 81 | 0.8 | 80 | 0.7 | 79 | 1.5 | 77 | 3.0 | 74 | 3.7 |
| Houston, Tex. | 52 | 3.6 | 55 | 3.5 | 61 | 2.7 | 69 | 3.5 | 76 | 5.1 | 81 | 4.5 | 83 | 4.1 | 83 | 4.4 | 79 | 4.7 | 71 | 4.1 | 61 | 4.0 | 55 | 4.0 |
| Huron, S.D. | 13 | 0.4 | 18 | 0.8 | 29 | 1.1 | 46 | 2.0 | 57 | 2.8 | 67 | 3.8 | 74 | 2.2 | 72 | 2.0 | 61 | 1.8 | 50 | 1.5 | 32 | 0.7 | 19 | 0.5 |
| Indianapolis, Ind. | 28 | 2.9 | 31 | 2.4 | 40 | 3.8 | 52 | 3.9 | 62 | 4.1 | 72 | 4.2 | 75 | 3.7 | 73 | 2.8 | 66 | 2.9 | 56 | 2.5 | 42 | 3.1 | 31 | 2.7 |
| Jacksonville, Fla. | 55 | 2.8 | 56 | 3.6 | 61 | 3.6 | 68 | 3.1 | 74 | 3.2 | 79 | 6.3 | 81 | 7.4 | 81 | 7.9 | 78 | 7.8 | 71 | 4.5 | 61 | 1.8 | 55 | 2.6 |
| Juneau, Ala. | 24 | 3.9 | 28 | 3.4 | 32 | 3.6 | 39 | 3.8 | 47 | 3.3 | 53 | 2.9 | 56 | 4.7 | 54 | 5.0 | 49 | 6.9 | 42 | 7.9 | 33 | 5.5 | 27 | 4.5 |
| Kansas City, Mo. | 28 | 1.3 | 33 | 1.3 | 41 | 2.6 | 55 | 3.5 | 65 | 4.3 | 74 | 5.6 | 79 | 4.4 | 77 | 3.8 | 69 | 4.2 | 59 | 3.2 | 44 | 1.5 | 32 | 1.5 |
| Knoxville, Tenn. | 41 | 4.7 | 43 | 4.7 | 50 | 4.9 | 60 | 3.6 | 68 | 3.3 | 76 | 3.6 | 78 | 4.7 | 77 | 3.2 | 72 | 2.8 | 61 | 2.7 | 49 | 3.6 | 42 | 4.5 |
| Lander, Wyo. | 20 | 0.5 | 26 | 0.7 | 31 | 1.2 | 43 | 2.4 | 53 | 2.6 | 61 | 1.9 | 71 | 0.6 | 69 | 0.4 | 58 | 1.1 | 47 | 1.2 | 32 | 0.9 | 23 | 0.5 |
| Little Rock, Ark. | 40 | 4.2 | 43 | 4.4 | 50 | 4.9 | 62 | 5.3 | 70 | 5.3 | 78 | 3.5 | 81 | 3.4 | 81 | 3.0 | 73 | 3.6 | 62 | 3.0 | 50 | 3.9 | 42 | 4.1 |
| Los Angeles, Cal.* | 57 | 3.0 | 48 | 2.8 | 59 | 2.2 | 62 | 1.3 | 65 | 0.1 | 68 | L | 73 | L | 74 | L | 73 | 0.2 | 68 | 0.3 | 63 | 2.0 | 58 | 2.2 |
| Louisville, Ky. | 33 | 3.5 | 36 | 3.5 | 44 | 5.1 | 56 | 4.1 | 65 | 4.2 | 73 | 4.1 | 77 | 3.8 | 76 | 3.0 | 69 | 2.9 | 58 | 2.4 | 45 | 3.3 | 36 | 3.3 |
| Marquette, Mich.* | 18 | 1.5 | 20 | 1.5 | 27 | 1.9 | 40 | 2.6 | 50 | 2.9 | 60 | 3.4 | 66 | 3.1 | 66 | 3.0 | 57 | 3.5 | 49 | 2.4 | 34 | 3.0 | 24 | 2.0 |
| Memphis, Tenn. | 41 | 4.9 | 44 | 4.7 | 51 | 5.1 | 63 | 5.4 | 71 | 4.4 | 79 | 3.5 | 82 | 3.5 | 80 | 3.3 | 74 | 3.0 | 63 | 2.6 | 51 | 3.9 | 43 | 4.7 |
| Miami, Fla. | 67 | 2.2 | 68 | 2.0 | 71 | 2.1 | 75 | 3.6 | 78 | 6.1 | 81 | 9.0 | 82 | 6.9 | 83 | 6.7 | 82 | 8.7 | 78 | 8.2 | 72 | 2.7 | 68 | 1.6 |
| Milwaukee, Wis. | 19 | 1.6 | 23 | 1.1 | 31 | 2.2 | 45 | 2.8 | 54 | 2.9 | 65 | 3.6 | 70 | 3.4 | 69 | 2.7 | 61 | 3.0 | 51 | 2.0 | 37 | 2.0 | 24 | 1.8 |
| Minneapolis, Minn. | 12 | 0.7 | 17 | 0.8 | 28 | 1.7 | 45 | 2.0 | 57 | 3.4 | 67 | 3.9 | 72 | 3.7 | 70 | 3.1 | 60 | 2.7 | 50 | 1.8 | 32 | 1.2 | 19 | 0.9 |
| Mobile, Ala. | 51 | 4.7 | 54 | 4.8 | 59 | 7.1 | 68 | 5.6 | 75 | 4.5 | 80 | 6.1 | 82 | 8.9 | 82 | 6.9 | 78 | 6.6 | 69 | 2.6 | 59 | 3.4 | 53 | 5.9 |
| Moline, Ill. | 22 | 1.7 | 26 | 1.3 | 36 | 2.6 | 51 | 3.8 | 61 | 3.9 | 71 | 4.4 | 75 | 4.6 | 73 | 3.4 | 65 | 3.8 | 54 | 2.7 | 39 | 1.9 | 27 | 1.8 |
| Nashville, Tenn. | 38 | 4.8 | 41 | 4.4 | 49 | 5.0 | 60 | 4.1 | 69 | 4.1 | 77 | 3.4 | 80 | 3.8 | 79 | 3.2 | 72 | 3.1 | 61 | 2.2 | 48 | 3.5 | 40 | 4.5 |
| Newark, N.J. | 31 | 2.9 | 33 | 3.0 | 41 | 3.9 | 52 | 3.4 | 62 | 3.6 | 71 | 3.0 | 76 | 4.0 | 75 | 4.3 | 68 | 3.4 | 58 | 2.8 | 46 | 3.6 | 35 | 3.5 |
| New Haven, Conn. | 29 | 3.2 | 30 | 3.1 | 37 | 4.0 | 48 | 3.7 | 57 | 3.7 | 67 | 2.7 | 72 | 3.1 | 71 | 3.8 | 65 | 3.1 | 55 | 3.1 | 44 | 4.3 | 32 | 4.1 |
| New Orleans, La. | 53 | 4.5 | 56 | 4.8 | 61 | 5.5 | 69 | 4.2 | 75 | 4.2 | 80 | 4.7 | 82 | 6.7 | 82 | 5.3 | 78 | 5.6 | 70 | 2.3 | 60 | 3.9 | 55 | 5.1 |
| New York, N.Y.* | 32 | 2.9 | 33 | 3.1 | 41 | 4.0 | 52 | 3.6 | 62 | 3.4 | 72 | 2.9 | 77 | 3.9 | 75 | 4.5 | 68 | 3.2 | 58 | 3.0 | 47 | 3.8 | 35 | 3.6 |
| Nome, Alas. | 6 | 0.9 | 5 | 0.8 | 7 | 0.8 | 19 | 0.7 | 35 | 0.7 | 46 | 1.0 | 50 | 2.4 | 49 | 3.6 | 42 | 2.4 | 29 | 1.4 | 16 | 1.0 | 4 | 0.7 |
| Norfolk, Va. | 41 | 3.4 | 41 | 3.3 | 48 | 3.4 | 58 | 2.7 | 67 | 3.3 | 75 | 3.6 | 78 | 5.7 | 77 | 5.9 | 72 | 4.2 | 62 | 3.1 | 52 | 2.9 | 42 | 3.1 |
| Okla. City, Okla. | 37 | 1.1 | 41 | 1.3 | 48 | 2.1 | 60 | 3.5 | 68 | 5.2 | 77 | 4.2 | 82 | 2.7 | 81 | 2.6 | 73 | 3.6 | 62 | 2.6 | 49 | 1.4 | 40 | 1.3 |
| Omaha, Neb. | 23 | 0.8 | 28 | 1.0 | 37 | 1.6 | 52 | 3.0 | 63 | 4.1 | 72 | 4.9 | 77 | 3.7 | 76 | 4.0 | 66 | 3.3 | 56 | 1.9 | 40 | 1.1 | 28 | 0.8 |
| Parkersburg, W.Va.* | 33 | 3.1 | 35 | 2.8 | 43 | 3.8 | 55 | 3.5 | 64 | 3.6 | 72 | 4.0 | 75 | 4.3 | 74 | 3.3 | 67 | 2.8 | 57 | 2.1 | 45 | 2.5 | 35 | 2.8 |
| Philadelphia, Pa. | 34 | 3.9 | 34 | 3.0 | 47 | 3.5 | 53 | 6.7 | 60 | 4.1 | 75 | 7.9 | 78 | 2.4 | 79 | 2.0 | 71 | 3.4 | 59 | 2.2 | 48 | 0.6 | 39 | 6.3 |
| Phoenix, Ariz. | 51 | 0.1 | 58 | 1.4 | 57 | 1.7 | 67 | 0.1 | 81 | 0.1 | 88 | L | 94 | 1.3 | 93 | L | 85 | L | 74 | L | 61 | 1.4 | 55 | L |
| Pittsburgh, Pa. | 30 | 2.0 | 29 | 1.8 | 48 | 3.9 | 49 | 4.7 | 56 | 5.9 | 71 | 3.1 | 73 | 2.2 | 73 | 3.4 | 67 | 3.6 | 56 | 4.5 | 44 | 2.7 | 33 | 2.2 |
| Portland, Me. | 23 | 2.6 | 23 | 2.6 | 38 | 2.6 | 46 | 9.9 | 51 | 6.3 | 64 | 4.9 | 71 | 1.7 | 71 | 3.5 | 58 | 2.2 | 49 | 3.4 | 38 | 2.4 | 34 | 9.6 |
| Portland, Ore. | 39 | 3.7 | 45 | 1.9 | 48 | 2.5 | 52 | 1.3 | 59 | 1.4 | 64 | 1.5 | 70 | 0.1 | 66 | 1.4 | 64 | 3.3 | 54 | 3.1 | 44 | 11.6 | 45 | 10.0 |
| Providence, R.I. | 28 | 3.5 | 29 | 3.5 | 37 | 4.0 | 47 | 3.7 | 57 | 3.5 | 66 | 2.7 | 72 | 2.9 | 70 | 3.9 | 63 | 3.3 | 54 | 3.3 | 43 | 4.5 | 32 | 4.1 |
| Raleigh, N.C. | 41 | 3.2 | 42 | 3.3 | 49 | 3.4 | 60 | 3.1 | 67 | 3.3 | 74 | 3.7 | 78 | 5.1 | 77 | 4.9 | 71 | 3.8 | 60 | 2.8 | 50 | 2.8 | 41 | 3.1 |
| Rapid City, S.D. | 22 | 0.5 | 26 | 0.6 | 31 | 1.0 | 45 | 2.1 | 55 | 2.8 | 64 | 3.7 | 73 | 2.1 | 72 | 1.5 | 61 | 1.2 | 50 | 0.9 | 35 | 0.5 | 27 | 0.4 |
| Reno, Nev. | 32 | 1.2 | 37 | 0.9 | 40 | 0.7 | 47 | 0.5 | 55 | 0.7 | 62 | 0.4 | 69 | 0.3 | 67 | 0.2 | 60 | 0.2 | 50 | 0.4 | 40 | 0.7 | 33 | 1.1 |
| Richmond, Va. | 38 | 2.9 | 39 | 3.0 | 47 | 3.4 | 58 | 2.8 | 67 | 3.4 | 74 | 3.5 | 78 | 5.6 | 76 | 5.1 | 70 | 3.6 | 59 | 2.9 | 49 | 3.2 | 39 | 3.2 |
| St. Louis, Mo. | 31 | 1.9 | 35 | 2.1 | 43 | 3.0 | 57 | 3.9 | 66 | 3.9 | 75 | 4.4 | 79 | 3.7 | 77 | 2.9 | 70 | 2.9 | 59 | 2.8 | 45 | 2.5 | 35 | 2.0 |
| Salt Lake City, Ut. | 20 | 1.5 | 32 | 0.9 | 42 | 2.7 | 48 | 1.6 | 62 | 1.7 | 70 | 0.2 | 77 | 1.1 | 77 | 1.2 | 62 | 4.1 | 54 | 0.7 | 41 | 2.5 | 33 | 2.3 |
| San Antonio, Tex. | 51 | 1.7 | 55 | 2.1 | 61 | 1.5 | 70 | 2.5 | 76 | 3.1 | 82 | 2.8 | 84 | 1.7 | 85 | 2.4 | 79 | 3.7 | 71 | 2.8 | 60 | 1.8 | 53 | 1.5 |
| San Diego, Cal. | 56 | 1.7 | 60 | 1.6 | 58 | 2.3 | 62 | 0.1 | 63 | L | 68 | L | 69 | L | 71 | L | 69 | L | 67 | L | 61 | 1.6 | 58 | 0.2 |
| San Francisco, Cal. | 48 | 4.4 | 51 | 3.0 | 53 | 2.5 | 55 | 1.6 | 58 | 0.4 | 62 | 0.1 | 63 | L | 63 | 0.0 | 64 | 0.2 | 61 | 1.0 | 55 | 2.3 | 50 | 4.0 |
| San Juan, P.R. | 75 | 3.7 | 75 | 2.5 | 76 | 2.0 | 78 | 3.4 | 79 | 6.5 | 81 | 5.6 | 81 | 6.4 | 81 | 7.0 | 81 | 6.1 | 81 | 5.6 | 79 | 5.5 | 77 | 4.7 |
| Sault Ste. Marie, Mich.* | 14 | 1.9 | 15 | 1.5 | 24 | 1.7 | 38 | 2.2 | 49 | 3.0 | 59 | 3.3 | 64 | 2.6 | 63 | 3.1 | 55 | 3.9 | 46 | 2.9 | 33 | 3.3 | 20 | 2.4 |
| Savannah, Ga. | 50 | 2.9 | 52 | 2.9 | 58 | 4.4 | 66 | 2.9 | 73 | 4.2 | 79 | 5.9 | 81 | 7.9 | 81 | 6.5 | 76 | 5.6 | 67 | 2.8 | 57 | 1.9 | 50 | 3.3 |
| Sea.-Tac., Wash. | 38 | 5.8 | 42 | 4.2 | 44 | 3.6 | 49 | 2.5 | 55 | 1.7 | 60 | 1.5 | 65 | 0.7 | 64 | 1.1 | 60 | 2.0 | 52 | 3.9 | 45 | 5.9 | 41 | 5.9 |
| Spokane, Wash. | 25 | 2.5 | 32 | 1.7 | 38 | 1.5 | 46 | 1.1 | 55 | 1.5 | 62 | 1.4 | 70 | 0.4 | 68 | 0.6 | 60 | 0.8 | 48 | 1.4 | 36 | 2.2 | 29 | 2.4 |
| Springfield, Mo. | 33 | 1.7 | 37 | 2.2 | 44 | 3.0 | 57 | 4.3 | 65 | 4.9 | 74 | 4.7 | 78 | 3.6 | 77 | 2.9 | 69 | 4.1 | 59 | 3.4 | 46 | 2.3 | 36 | 2.5 |
| Syracuse, N.Y. | 24 | 2.7 | 25 | 2.8 | 33 | 3.0 | 47 | 3.1 | 57 | 3.0 | 67 | 3.1 | 72 | 3.1 | 70 | 3.5 | 63 | 2.7 | 53 | 3.1 | 41 | 3.3 | 28 | 3.1 |
| Tampa, Fla. | 60 | 2.3 | 62 | 2.9 | 66 | 3.9 | 72 | 2.1 | 77 | 2.4 | 81 | 6.5 | 82 | 8.4 | 82 | 8.0 | 81 | 6.4 | 75 | 2.5 | 67 | 1.8 | 62 | 2.2 |
| Trenton, N.J.* | 32 | 2.8 | 33 | 2.7 | 41 | 3.8 | 52 | 3.2 | 62 | 3.4 | 71 | 3.2 | 76 | 4.7 | 74 | 4.2 | 67 | 3.2 | 57 | 2.5 | 46 | 3.3 | 35 | 3.3 |
| Vicksburg, Miss.* | 48 | 4.9 | 51 | 5.3 | 57 | 0.5 | 66 | 5.4 | 73 | 4.2 | 79 | 3.3 | 82 | 3.6 | 81 | 3.0 | 76 | 2.8 | 67 | 2.3 | 56 | 4.1 | 50 | 5.5 |
| Washington, D.C. | 36 | 2.6 | 37 | 2.5 | 45 | 3.3 | 56 | 2.9 | 66 | 3.7 | 75 | 3.5 | 79 | 4.1 | 77 | 4.7 | 71 | 3.1 | 60 | 2.7 | 48 | 2.9 | 37 | 3.0 |
| Wilmington, Del. | 32 | 2.9 | 34 | 2.8 | 42 | 3.7 | 52 | 3.2 | 62 | 3.4 | 71 | 3.2 | 76 | 4.3 | 74 | 4.0 | 68 | 3.4 | 57 | 2.6 | 46 | 3.5 | 35 | 3.3 |

# Annual Climatological Data

Source: National Oceanic and Atmospheric Administration, U.S. Commerce Department

## 1977

| Station | Elev. ft. | Temp Highest | Date | Lowest | Date | Precip Total (in.) | Greatest in 24 hrs. | Date | Sleet/snow Total (in.) | Greatest in 24 hrs. | Date | Wind MPH | Date | Clear* | Cloudy* | Prec. .01 in. or more | Snow, sleet 1 in. or more |
|---|---|---|---|---|---|---|---|---|---|---|---|---|---|---|---|---|---|
| Albany, N.Y. | 275 | 96 | 7/21 | -15 | 1/28 | 44.30 | 2.11 | 3/13-14 | 85.3 | 11.6 | 2/20-21 | 44 | 4/8 | 64 | 190 | 146 | 25 |
| Albuquerque, N.M. | 5311 | 99 | 8/6 | -4 | 1/10 | 7.91 | 0.75 | 10/6 | 14.7 | 4.1 | 1/8-9 | 49 | 2/22 | 165 | 90 | 49 | 6 |
| Anchorage, Alas. | 114 | 82 | 8/21 | -16 | 12/9 | 15.51 | 0.87 | 9/28-29 | 69.1 | 8.0 | 4/1 | 29 | 1/4 | 43 | 257 | 112 | 23 |
| Asheville, N.C. | 2140 | 94 | 7/20 | -5 | 1/17 | 50.45 | 4.03 | 11/5-6 | 14.1 | 6.0 | 1/9 | 40 | 6/6 | 106 | 136 | 126 | 4 |
| Atlanta, Ga. | 1010 | 98 | 7/8 | 1 | 1/19 | 46.68 | 3.90 | 11/4-5 | 1.0 | 1.0 | 1/31 | 40 | 1/30 | 125 | 145 | 118 | 1 |
| Baltimore, Md. | 148 | 99 | 7/17 | -2 | 1/17 | 36.39 | 3.39 | 12/18-19 | 9.6 | 4.0 | 1/6-7 | 46 | 12/30 | 65 | 187 | 96 | 2 |
| Barrow, Alas. | 31 | 69 | 8/4 | -42 | 2/2 | 3.27 | 0.37 | 8/18-19 | 20.0 | 1.8 | 10/27-28 | 49 | 4/4 | 102 | 150 | 114 | 1 |
| Birmingham, Ala. | 620 | 105 | 7/7 | 3 | 1/19 | 60.04 | 5.03 | 9/6-7 | 1.4 | 1.0 | 1/18 | 45 | 7/30 | 94 | 161 | 106 | 17 |
| Bismarck, N.D. | 1647 | 103 | 7/17 | -41 | 1/19 | 18.54 | 3.02 | 9/23-24 | 52.6 | 8.3 | 11/19-20 | 42 | 3/27 | 89 | 176 | 92 | 7 |
| Boise, Ida. | 2838 | 102 | 8/1 | -14 | 1/8 | 12.20 | 1.15 | 6/9-10 | 22.7 | 5.1 | 1/2-3 | 60 | 3/22 | 115 | 155 | 131 | 11 |
| Boston, Mass. | 15 | 102 | 7/21 | 3 | 1/18 | 44.17 | 3.09 | 5/9-10 | 46.2 | 13.8 | 1/7 | 50 | 1/28 | 45 | 222 | 197 | 55 |
| Buffalo, N.Y. | 705 | 91 | 7/18 | -7 | 1/29 | 53.55 | 2.35 | 8/6-7 | 175.6 | 14.0 | 12/8-9 | 41 | 4/11 | 33 | 228 | 163 | 25 |
| Burlington, Vt. | 332 | 99 | 7/20 | -20 | 1/18 | 40.44 | 2.94 | 8/16-17 | 90.6 | 9.8 | 1/31 | 32 | 3/22 | 112 | 136 | 105 | 0 |
| Charleston, S.C. | 40 | 101 | 7/22 | 17 | 2/8 | 41.24 | 2.36 | 3/4-5 | 1.3 | 0.6 | 1/31 | 33 | 4/5 | 73 | 180 | 150 | 22 |
| Charleston, W. Va. | 939 | 96 | 7/20 | -10 | 1/17 | 39.62 | 2.48 | 4/3-4 | 64.3 | 9.9 | 1/9-10 | 47 | 3/29 | 91 | 171 | 134 | 21 |
| Chicago, Ill. | 607 | 99 | 7/15 | -19 | 1/16 | 41.29 | 4.16 | 8/31-9/1 | 53.9 | 8.0 | 1/9-10 | 44 | 3/4 | 75 | 189 | 140 | 14 |
| Cincinnati, Oh. | 869 | 94 | 7/20 | -25 | 1/18 | 41.55 | 1.92 | 4/1-2 | 69.6 | 7.8 | 12/6 | 35 | 12/1 | 63 | 217 | 168 | 25 |
| Cleveland, Oh. | 777 | 94 | 7/15 | -17 | 1/17 | 36.09 | 1.90 | 6/30 | 34.9 | 4.5 | 1/14 | 47 | 3/4 | 74 | 192 | 154 | 14 |
| Columbus, Oh. | 812 | 96 | 7/6 | -19 | 1/17 | 36.12 | 2.32 | 8/7 | 93.3 | 15.5 | 1/7 | 33 | 12/10 | 92 | 167 | 129 | 21 |
| Concord, N.H. | 342 | 101 | 7/17 | -16 | 1/18 | 41.64 | 2.19 | 9/20-21 | 5.4 | 4.0 | 1/30 | 36 | 2/22 | 135 | 121 | 68 | 2 |
| Dallas, Tex. | 551 | 108 | 7/24 | 10 | 1/31 | 27.19 | 4.39 | 3/26-27 | 27.9 | 8.0 | 3/10-11 | 47 | 3/11 | 117 | 115 | 81 | 10 |
| Denver, Col. | 5283 | 98 | 7/17 | -4 | 1/17 | 10.34 | 1.10 | 3/10-11 | 39.4 | 7.7 | 12/31 | 43 | 3/29 | 96 | 171 | 111 | 13 |
| Des Moines, Ia. | 938 | 103 | 7/13 | -18 | 1/16 | 37.15 | 4.68 | 8/25-26 |  |  |  | 37 | 9/26 |  |  |  |  |
| Detroit, Mich. | 633 | 100 | 7/15 | -6 | 1/28 | 25.11 | 2.55 | 8/18-19 | 9.2 | 2.7 | 4/3 | 29 | 2/23 | 127 | 133 | 80 | 5 |
| Dodge City, Kan. | 2582 | 106 | 7/3 | -3 | 1/10 | 34.02 | 3.39 | 9/23-24 | 59.0 | 8.7 | 3/3-4 | 45 | 9/9 | 62 | 204 | 139 | 15 |
| Duluth, Minn. | 1428 | 89 | 7/19 | -35 | 1/9 | 12.98 | 0.99 | 9/24-25 | 75.8 | 12.6 | 2/1-2 | 28 | 6/22 | 53 | 208 | 115 | 23 |
| Fairbanks, Alas. | 436 | 90 | 7/30 | -52 | 12/13 | 6.56 | 1.10 | 12/17 | 0.0 | 0.0 | ... | 29 | 3/12 | 175 | 107 | 34 | 0 |
| Fresno, Cal. | 328 | 107 | 7/7 | 27 | 11/20 | 42.07 | 5.09 | 4/19-20 | 0.0 | 0.0 | ... | 34 | 12/9 |  |  | 94 | 0 |
| Galveston, Tex. | 7 | 92 | 9/3 | 21 | 1/10 | 37.78 | 2.05 | 7/3-4 | 76.4 | 6.0 | 1/28 | 41 | 10/11 | 67 | 205 | 161 | 21 |
| Grand Rapids, Mich. | 784 | 94 | 7/15 | -14 | 1/19 | 11.33 | 1.10 | 5/14-15 | 56.9 | 7.1 | 12/4-5 | 41 | 11/26 | 64 | 191 | 103 | 16 |
| Helena, Mont. | 3828 | 93 | 8/19 | -20 | 12/31 | 12.36 | 1.50 | 5/14 | 0.0 | 0.0 | 5/14 | 33 | 7/15 | 78 | 72 | 81 | 0 |
| Honolulu, Ha. | 7 | 92 | 8/13 | 59 | 1/22 | 34.94 | 2.92 | 4/19-20 | 0.0 | 0.0 | ... | 37 | 7/15 | 110 | 141 | 96 | 0 |
| Houston, Tex. | 96 | 100 | 8/3 | 18 | 1/19 | 23.14 | 2.60 | 3/11-12 | 37.0 | 8.1 | 2/23-24 | 48 | 9/8 | 97 | 173 | 131 | 14 |
| Huron, S.D. | 1281 | 105 | 7/18 | -25 | 1/16 | 38.05 | 3.05 | 9/30-10/1 | 44.5 | 8.0 | 1/9-10 | 44 | 1/26 | 113 | 142 | 113 | 2 |
| Indianapolis, Ind. | 792 | 95 | 7/19 | -20 | 1/17 | 53.58 | 3.88 | 11/29-30 | 5.8 | 3.2 | 1/30-31 | 32 | 7/8 | 110 | 137 | 102 | 12 |
| Jackson, Miss. | 310 | 98 | 7/8 | 6 | 1/19 | 39.56 | 2.96 | 8/20-21 | T | T | 2/16 | 33 | 9/8 | 110 | 137 | 102 | 0 |
| Jacksonville, Fla. | 26 | 100 | 7/22 | 19 | 1/19 | 47.18 | 1.49 | 9/21-22 | 61.7 | 10.9 | 11/10-11 | 36 | 2/19 | 47 | 279 | 230 | 20 |
| Juneau, Alas. | 12 | 83 | 8/20 | -7 | 12/8 | 47.11 | 8.82 | 9/12 | 16.3 | 3.2 | 1/4-5 | 36 | 4/10 | 108 | 159 | 120 | 6 |
| Kansas City, Mo. | 1014 | 97 | 7/17 | -10 | 1/16 | 12.22 | 2.13 | 7/24-25 | 105.6 | 15.4 | 3/25 | 50 | 3/8 | 121 | 113 | 63 | 24 |
| Lander, Wyo. | 5563 | 95 | 7/17 | -16 | 1/9 | 17.66 | 2.58 | 11/16 | 3.8 | 2.0 | 1/18 | 35 | 3/28 | 107 | 136 | 91 | 2 |
| Little Rock, Ark. | 257 | 101 | 7/6 | 4 | 3/15 | 47.66 | 2.58 | 8/16-17 | 0.0 | 0.0 | ... | 41 | 11/27 | 143 | 102 | 32 | 0 |
| Los Angeles, Cal. | 97 | 91 | 11/25 | 40 | 3/15 | 13.68 | 2.40 | 8/16-17 | 0.0 | 0.0 | ... | 39 | 12/23 | 76 | 180 | 148 | 8 |
| Louisville, Ky. | 477 | 97 | 7/15 | -13 | 1/17 | 49.10 | 3.25 | 9/30-10/1 | 28.3 | 7.8 | 1/9-10 | 36 | 11/21 |  |  |  | 172 |
| Marquette, Mich. | 677 | 104 | 7/19 | 8 | 1/9 | 36.02 | 2.66 | 9/18-19 | 114.9 | 10.3 | 3/3-4 | 36 | 6/6 | 126 | 153 | 96 | 1 |
| Memphis, Tenn. | 258 | 92 | 7/1 | 31 | 1/20 | 64.95 | 11.59 | 5/4-5 | 3.5 | 1.5 | 1/6 | 32 | 12/21 | 64 | 148 | 118 | 0 |
| Miami, Fla. | 7 | 92 | 10/3 | 31 | 1/20 | 7.32 | 1.13 | 5/13-14 | 0.0 | 0.0 | ... | 49 | 5/6 | 155 | 99 | 64 | 7 |
| Milford, Ut. | 5028 | 99 | 8/2 | -12 | 11/20 | 36.59 | 2.81 | 7/17-18 | 21.6 | 7.3 | 3/24-25 | 45 | 3/29 | 80 | 172 | 149 | 20 |
| Milwaukee, Wis. | 672 | 96 | 7/14 | -18 | 1/16 | 34.88 | 7.36 | 7/17-18 | 72.5 | 6.0 | 11/24-25 | 41 | 11/20 | 76 | 177 | 145 | 18 |
| Minneapolis, Minn. | 834 | 100 | 7/19 | -32 | 1/19 | 64.57 | 4.82 | 8/30-31 | 60.5 | 8.0 | 2/2-3 | 32 | 5/22 | 97 | 147 | 138 | 1 |
| Mobile, Ala. | 211 | 97 | 7/2 | 12 | 1/19 | 41.96 | 3.03 | 11/21-22 | 1.9 | 1.4 | 1/30-31 | 47 | 7/10 | 95 | 168 | 124 | 20 |
| Moline, Ill. | 582 | 98 | 7/15 | -22 | 1/17 | 50.71 | 3.03 | 6/30 | 52.2 | 5.8 | 3/21 | 35 | 6/24 | 103 | 150 | 116 | 5 |
| Nashville, Tenn. | 590 | 99 | 7/17 | -5 | 1/17 | 72.80 | 5.18 | 3/3-4 | 18.6 | 5.3 | 1/24 | 30 | 1/9 | 96 | 153 | 132 | 0 |
| New Orleans, La. | 4 | 97 | 7/1 | 19 | 1/19 | 54.73 | 8.09 | 4/20-21 | T | T | 1/14-15 | 30 | 11/26 |  |  | 114 | 7 |
| New York, N.Y. | 132 | 104 | 7/21 | -2 | 1/17 | 13.63 | 1.06 | 11/7-8 | 20.0 | 5.2 | 12/27-28 | 52 | 12/29 | 119 | 189 | 125 | 23 |
| Nome, Alas. | 13 | 86 | 7/31 | -42 | 3/5 | 43.77 | 3.32 | 9/5-6 | 69.8 | 8.0 | 1/16 | 46 | 6/6 | 125 | 136 | 112 | 4 |
| Norfolk, Va. | 24 | 102 | 8/7 | 5 | 1/17 | 28.59 | 2.32 | 11/6-7 | 3.2 | 2.6 | 1/8-9 | 53 | 3/10 | 129 | 128 | 82 | 1 |
| Oklahoma City, Okla. | 1285 | 106 | 7/25 | -3 | 1/17 | 41.52 | 3.72 | 5/19 | 30.4 | 4.4 | 1/14-15 |  |  | 106 | 151 | 116 | 12 |
| Omaha, Neb. | 977 | 100 | 7/6 | -21 | 1/16 | 49.42 | 3.99 | 7/16-17 | 16.3 | 4.4 | 1/14 | 49 | 8/8 | 92 | 158 | 119 | 6 |
| Philadelphia, Pa. | 5 | 100 | 7/21 | -4 | 1/17 | 3.16 | 0.50 | 11/7 | 0.0 | 0.0 | ... | 64 | 9/8 | 210 | 73 | 28 | 0 |
| Phoenix, Ariz. | 1112 | 114 | 6/29 | 31 | 1/11 | 33.20 | 1.49 | 9/27 | 47.5 | 5.6 | 12/8-9 | 36 | 2/25 | 56 | 193 | 168 | 17 |
| Pittsburgh, Pa. | 1137 | 91 | 7/20 | -17 | 1/17 | 57.63 | 3.56 | 4/2 | 88.8 | 13.0 | 1/7-8 | 38 | 2/25 | 99 | 172 | 133 | 23 |
| Portland, Me. | 43 | 99 | 7/21 | -15 | 12/12 | 37.03 | 2.59 | 1/10-11 | 7.6 | 7.4 | 11/21-22 | 43 | 12/15 | 57 | 229 | 160 | 1 |
| Portland, Ore. | 21 | 105 | 8/17 | 17 | 1/8 | 48.84 | 2.20 | 12/10-11 | 42.0 | 8.0 | 1/7 | 33 | 11/27 | 110 | 160 | 129 | 10 |
| Providence, R.I. | 51 | 100 | 7/21 | -2 | 1/18 | 37.10 | 2.93 | 9/7-8 | 3.6 | 1.8 | 1/24 | 39 | 6/6 | 125 | 128 | 98 | 7 |
| Raleigh, N.C. | 434 | 103 | 7/8 | -1 | 1/17 | 19.40 | 2.12 | 9/22-23 | 61.9 | 10.8 | 3/29-30 | 63 | 1/7 | 92 | 134 | 111 | 19 |
| Rapid City, S.D. | 3162 | 105 | 7/18 | -17 | 1/16 | 44.08 | 4.36 | 9/22-23 | 12.3 | 2.0 | 2/18 | 48 | 12/15 | 135 | 131 | 45 | 6 |
| Reno, Nev. | 4404 | 100 | 8/1 | 6 | 1/9 | 6.84 | 0.77 | 12/16-17 | 11.3 | 3.8 | 1/6-7 | 38 | 11/17 | 103 | 144 | 108 | 5 |
| Richmond, Va. | 164 | 105 | 7/6 | -1 | 1/17 | 35.10 | 1.64 | 10/26 | 108.5 | 11.3 | 12/5-6 | 49 | 12/25 | 50 | 213 | 173 | 32 |
| Rochester, N.Y. | 547 | 95 | 7/7 | -14 | 1/16 | 43.41 | 2.95 | 3/27-28 | 49.2 | 6.6 | 12/5 | 42 | 5/4 | 100 | 169 | 123 | 12 |
| St. Louis, Mo. | 535 | 98 | 7/7 | -14 | 1/16 | 17.67 | 1.04 | 8/26-27 | 76.0 | 11.1 | 3/1-2 | 42 | 3/27 | 107 | 157 | 96 | 21 |
| Salt Lake City, Ut. | 4220 | 101 | 8/2 | -2 | 1/9 | 29.64 | 4.88 | 4/19-20 | 0.0 | 0.0 | ... | 42 | 9/13 | 101 | 132 | 77 | 0 |
| San Antonio, Tex. | 788 | 99 | 9/5 | 20 | 2/2 | 9.21 | 2.13 | 8/16-17 | 0.0 | 0.0 | ... | 33 | 3/1 | 137 | 106 | 44 | 0 |
| San Diego, Cal. | 13 | 87 | 7/26 | 44 | 3/15 | 12.54 | 1.51 | 11/21 | 0.0 | 0.0 | ... | 39 | 12/21 | 132 | 116 | 50 | 0 |
| San Francisco, Cal. | 8 | 97 | 7/30 | 35 | 1/19 | 38.89 | 1.66 | 7/5-6 | 160.1 | 12.0 | 1/30-31 | 38 | 9/24 | 104 | 155 | 119 | 48 |
| Sault Ste. Marie, Mich. | 721 | 91 | 7/20 | -30 | 1/19 | 41.84 | 2.92 | 8/24 | 2.0 | 1.3 | 1/31 | 38 | 9/10 | 104 | 155 | 119 | 1 |
| Savannah, Ga. | 46 | 103 | 7/22 | 16 | 1/19 | 32.84 | 1.56 | 12/9-10 | 5.4 | 1.9 | 11/22-23 | 39 | 11/11 | 103 | 162 | 108 | 1 |
| Seattle, Wash. | 400 | 98 | 8/17 | 21 | 11/21 | 35.03 | 3.65 | 7/20-21 | 25.5 | 7.3 | 3/2 | 56 | 11/9 | 65 | 206 | 106 | 13 |
| Sioux City, Ia. | 1095 | 98 | 8/18 | -9 | 12/31 | 15.57 | 1.13 | 6/7-8 | 53.5 | 7.8 | 12/29 | 42 | 12/3 | 113 | 155 | 119 | 7 |
| Spokane, Wash. | 2356 | 100 | 8/18 | -11 | 1/16 | 38.94 | 2.05 | 6/21-22 | 20.0 | 7.2 | 1/9 | 37 | 5/30 | 43 | 216 | 186 | 47 |
| Springfield, Mo. | 1268 | 99 | 8/10 | -11 | 1/16 | 44.64 | 1.80 | 10/16-17 | 144.5 | 9.4 | 12/5-6 | 44 | 1/11 | 82 | 146 | 109 | 0 |
| Syracuse, N.Y. | 410 | 96 | 8/12 | 26 | 1/20 | 31.47 | 1.90 | 8/21-22 | 0.2 | 0.2 | 1/19 | 32 | 2/24 | 97 | 154 | 123 | 5 |
| Tampa, Fla. | 19 | 98 | 6/12 | 26 | 1/20 | 51.18 | 2.90 | 11/7-8 | 17.0 | 6.0 | 1/14-15 | 43 | 1/9 | 108 | 154 | 123 | 5 |
| Trenton, N.J. | 56 | 99 | 7/21 | -4 | 1/17 | 36.14 | 2.86 | 12/17-18 | 10.0 | 5.0 | 1/6-7 | 50 | 9/8 | 69 | 175 | 106 | 12 |
| Washington, D.C. | 10 | 100 | 7/7 | 0 | 1/17 | 13.43 | 1.09 | 5/17 | 34.6 | 5.8 | 1/6-7 | 47 | 3/29 | 69 | 175 | 106 | 12 |
| Williston, N.D. | 1899 | 99 | 7/17 | -37 | 12/9 | 10.23 | ... | 3/22 | 15.8 | 5.0 | 1/7 | 40 | 1/28 | 99 | 159 | 124 | 4 |
| Wilmington, Del. | 74 | 97 | 7/21 | -1 | 1/17 | 40.13 | 2.22 | 3/22 |  |  |  |  |  |  |  |  |  |

*To get partly cloudy days deduct the total of clear and cloudy days from 365 (1 yr.). T—trace. (1) Date shown is the starting date of the storm (in some cases it lasted more than one day).

# Normal Temperatures, Highs, Lows, Precipitation

Source: National Oceanic and Atmospheric Administration, U.S. Commerce Department

These normals are based on records for the thirty-year period 1941-1970. (See explanation on page 796.) The extreme temperatures (through 1977) are listed for the stations shown and may not agree with the states records shown on page 800. Airport stations; * designates city office stations. The minus (−) sign indicates temperatures below zero. Fahrenheit thermometer registration.

| State | Station | Normal temperature January Max. | January Min. | July Max. | July Min. | Extreme temperature Highest | Lowest | Normal annual precipitation (inches) |
|---|---|---|---|---|---|---|---|---|
| Alabama | Mobile | 61 | 41 | 91 | 73 | 102 | 8 | 66.98 |
| Alabama | Montgomery | 59 | 38 | 92 | 72 | 102 | 5 | 50.69 |
| Alaska | Juneau | 29 | 18 | 64 | 48 | 86 | −22 | 54.67 |
| Arizona | Phoenix | 65 | 38 | 105 | 78 | 116 | 19 | 7.05 |
| Arkansas | Little Rock | 50 | 29 | 93 | 70 | 108 | −4 | 48.52 |
| California | Los Angeles* | 67 | 47 | 83 | 64 | 110 | 28 | 14.05 |
| California | San Francisco | 55 | 41 | 71 | 54 | 106 | 24 | 19.53 |
| Colorado | Denver | 44 | 16 | 87 | 59 | 103 | −25 | 15.51 |
| Connecticut | New Haven (1) | 37 | 22 | 81 | 63 | 100 | −8 | 46.02 |
| Delaware | Wilmington | 40 | 24 | 86 | 66 | 102 | −4 | 40.25 |
| Dist. of Col. | Washington | 44 | 28 | 88 | 69 | 101 | 3 | 38.89 |
| Florida | Jacksonville | 65 | 45 | 90 | 72 | 105 | 12 | 54.47 |
| Florida | Key West | 74 | 65 | 87 | 79 | 95 | 46 | 39.99 |
| Florida | Miami | 76 | 59 | 89 | 76 | 96 | 34 | 59.80 |
| Georgia | Atlanta | 51 | 33 | 87 | 69 | 98 | −3 | 48.34 |
| Hawaii | Honolulu | 79 | 65 | 87 | 73 | 92 | 53 | 22.90 |
| Idaho | Boise | 36 | 21 | 91 | 59 | 111 | −23 | 11.50 |
| Illinois | Chicago-Midway | 32 | 17 | 84 | 65 | 101 | −16 | 34.44 |
| Indiana | Indianapolis | 36 | 20 | 85 | 65 | 99 | −20 | 38.74 |
| Iowa | Des Moines | 28 | 11 | 85 | 65 | 104 | −24 | 30.85 |
| Iowa | Dubuque | 27 | 11 | 84 | 62 | 97 | −28 | 35.71 |
| Kansas | Wichita | 42 | 22 | 92 | 69 | 113 | −12 | 28.41 |
| Kentucky | Louisville | 42 | 25 | 87 | 66 | 101 | −20 | 43.11 |
| Louisiana | New Orleans | 62 | 44 | 90 | 73 | 100 | 14 | 56.77 |
| Maine | Portland | 31 | 12 | 79 | 57 | 100 | −39 | 40.80 |
| Maryland | Baltimore | 42 | 25 | 87 | 66 | 102 | −7 | 40.46 |
| Massachusetts | Boston | 36 | 23 | 81 | 65 | 99 | −4 | 42.52 |
| Michigan | Detroit-City | 32 | 19 | 83 | 63 | 105 | −16 | 30.96 |
| Michigan | Sault Ste. Marie* | 22 | 6 | 75 | 53 | 98 | −28 | 31.70 |
| Minnesota | Minn.-St. Paul | 21 | 3 | 82 | 61 | 101 | −34 | 25.94 |
| Mississippi | Vicksburg (2) | 57 | 41 | 90 | 73 | 101 | 2 | 49.50 |
| Missouri | St. Louis | 40 | 23 | 88 | 69 | 106 | −11 | 35.89 |
| Montana | Helena | 28 | 8 | 84 | 52 | 105 | −38 | 11.38 |
| Nebraska | Omaha | 33 | 12 | 89 | 66 | 110 | −22 | 30.18 |
| Nevada | Winnemucca | 40 | 15 | 92 | 50 | 106 | −34 | 8.63 |
| New Hampshire | Concord | 31 | 10 | 83 | 57 | 102 | −29 | 36.17 |
| New Jersey | Atlantic City | 43 | 27 | 84 | 66 | 106 | −8 | 42.36 |
| New Mexico | Albuquerque | 47 | 24 | 92 | 65 | 105 | −17 | 7.77 |
| New Mexico | Roswell | 55 | 21 | 95 | 62 | 110 | −8 | 11.62 |
| New York | Albany | 30 | 13 | 84 | 60 | 98 | −28 | 33.36 |
| New York | New York-La Guardia | 38 | 26 | 84 | 69 | 107 | −2 | 41.61 |
| No. Carolina | Charlotte | 51 | 34 | 89 | 70 | 100 | 2 | 43.38 |
| No. Carolina | Raleigh | 51 | 30 | 88 | 67 | 98 | 0 | 42.54 |
| No. Dakota | Bismarck | 19 | −3 | 84 | 57 | 109 | −43 | 16.16 |
| Ohio | Cincinnati-Abbe | 40 | 24 | 87 | 66 | 109 | −17 | 40.03 |
| Ohio | Cleveland | 33 | 20 | 82 | 61 | 98 | −19 | 34.99 |
| Oklahoma | Oklahoma City | 48 | 26 | 93 | 70 | 108 | −1 | 31.37 |
| Oregon | Portland* | 44 | 33 | 79 | 55 | 107 | −3 | 37.61 |
| Pennsylvania | Harrisburg | 39 | 24 | 87 | 65 | 107 | −8 | 37.65 |
| Pennsylvania | Philadelphia | 40 | 24 | 87 | 67 | 104 | −5 | 39.93 |
| Rhode Island | Block Island | 38 | 26 | 76 | 63 | 91 | −4 | 40.45 |
| So. Carolina | Charleston | 60 | 37 | 89 | 71 | 103 | 8 | 52.12 |
| So. Dakota | Huron | 23 | 2 | 87 | 61 | 112 | −39 | 19.44 |
| So. Dakota | Rapid City | 34 | 10 | 86 | 59 | 110 | −27 | 17.12 |
| Tennessee | Nashville | 48 | 29 | 90 | 69 | 103 | −6 | 46.00 |
| Texas | Amarillo | 50 | 24 | 94 | 67 | 104 | −9 | 19.67 |
| Texas | Galveston* | 59 | 48 | 87 | 79 | 101 | 8 | 42.20 |
| Texas | Houston | 63 | 42 | 94 | 73 | 101 | 19 | 48.19 |
| Utah | Salt Lake City | 37 | 18 | 93 | 61 | 107 | −18 | 15.17 |
| Vermont | Burlington | 26 | 8 | 81 | 59 | 98 | −27 | 32.54 |
| Virginia | Norfolk | 49 | 32 | 87 | 70 | 103 | 8 | 44.68 |
| Washington | Seattle-Tacoma | 43 | 33 | 75 | 54 | 99 | 6 | 38.79 |
| Washington | Spokane | 31 | 20 | 84 | 55 | 108 | −25 | 17.42 |
| West Virginia | Parkersburg* | 41 | 24 | 86 | 65 | 106 | −27 | 38.44 |
| Wisconsin | Madison | 26 | 9 | 82 | 60 | 98 | −30 | 30.16 |
| Wisconsin | Milwaukee | 27 | 11 | 80 | 59 | 99 | −24 | 29.07 |
| Wyoming | Cheyenne | 37 | 14 | 85 | 55 | 98 | −27 | 15.06 |
| Puerto Rico | San Juan | 81 | 67 | 87 | 74 | 96 | 60 | 64.21 |

(1) Closed June 14, 1969. (2) Closed December 1966.

**Mean Annual Snowfall** (inches) based on record through 1972: Boston, Mass. 42.8; Sault Ste. Marie, Mich., 108.2; Albany, N.Y. 67.3; Rochester, N.Y. 86.3; Burlington, Vt., 79; Cheyenne, Wyo., 51.7; Juneau, Alas. 106.3.

**Wettest Spot:** Mount Waialeale, Ha., on the island of Kauai, is the rainiest place in the world, according to the National Geographic Society, with an average annual rainfall of 460 inches.

**Highest Temperature:** A temperature of 136° F. observed at Azizia, Tripolitania in Northern Africa on Sept. 13, 1922, is generally accepted as the world's highest temperature recorded under standard conditions.
The record high in the United States was 134° in Death Valley, Cal., July 10, 1913.

**Lowest Temperature:** A record low temperature of −126.9° F. (−88.3° C.) was recorded at the Soviet Antarctic station Vostok on Aug. 24, 1960.
The record low in the United States was −80° at Prospect Creek, Alas., Jan. 23, 1971.
The lowest official temperature on the North American continent was recorded at 81 degrees below zero in February, 1947, at a lonely airport in the Yukon called Snag.
These are the meteorological champions—the official temperature extremes—but there are plenty of other claimants to thermometer fame. However, sun readings are unofficial records, since meteorological data to qualify officially must be taken on instruments in a sheltered and ventilated location.

## Record Temperatures by States Through 1977

**Source:** National Oceanic and Atmospheric Administration, U.S. Commerce Department

| State | Lowest °F | Highest | Latest date | Station | Approximate elevation in feet |
|---|---|---|---|---|---|
| Alabama | −27 | | Jan. 30, 1966 | New Market | 725 |
| | | 112 | Sept. 5, 1925 | Centerville | 345 |
| Alaska | −79.8 | | Jan. 23, 1971 | Prospect Creek Camp | 1,100 |
| | | 100 | June 27, 1915 | Fort Yukon | *419 |
| Arizona | −40 | | Jan. 7, 1971 | Hawley Lake | 8,180 |
| | | 127 | July 7, 1905 | Parker | 345 |
| Arkansas | −29 | | Feb. 13, 1905 | Pond | 1,250 |
| | | 120 | Aug. 10, 1936 | Ozark | 396 |
| California | −45 | | Jan. 20, 1937 | Boca | 5,532 |
| | | 134 | July 10, 1913 | Greenland Ranch | −178 |
| Colorado | −60 | | Feb. 1, 1951 | Taylor Park | 9,206 |
| | | 118 | July 11, 1888 | Bennett | 5,484 |
| Connecticut | −32 | | Feb. 16, 1943 | Falls Village | 585 |
| | | 105 | July 22, 1926 | Waterbury | 409 |
| Delaware | −17 | | Jan. 17, 1893 | Millsboro | 20 |
| | | 110 | July 21, 1930 | Millsboro | 20 |
| Dist. of Col. | −15 | | Feb. 11, 1899 | Washington | 112 |
| | | 106 | July 20, 1930 | Washington | 112 |
| Florida | −2 | | Feb. 13, 1899 | Tallahassee | 193 |
| | | 109 | June 29, 1931 | Monticello | 207 |
| Georgia | −17 | | Jan. 27, 1940 | CCC Camp F-16 | 1,000 |
| | | 112 | July 24, 1952 | Louisville | 337 |
| Hawaii | 14 | | Jan. 2, 1961 | Haleakala, Maui | 9,750 |
| | | 100 | Apr. 27, 1931 | Pahala | 850 |
| Idaho | −60 | | Jan. 16, 1943 | Island Park Dam | 6,285 |
| | | 118 | July 28, 1934 | Orofino | 1,027 |
| Illinois | −35 | | Jan. 22, 1930 | Mount Carroll | 817 |
| | | 117 | July 14, 1954 | E. St. Louis | 410 |
| Indiana | −35 | | Feb. 2, 1951 | Greensburg | 954 |
| | | 116 | July 14, 1936 | Collegeville | 672 |
| Iowa | −47 | | Jan. 12, 1912 | Washta | 1,157 |
| | | 118 | July 20, 1934 | Keokuk | 614 |
| Kansas | −40 | | Feb. 13, 1905 | Lebanon | 1,812 |
| | | 121 | July 24, 1936 | Alton (near) | 1,651 |
| Kentucky | −34 | | Jan. 28, 1963 | Cynthiana | 719 |
| | | 114 | July 28, 1930 | Greensburg | 581 |
| Louisiana | −16 | | Feb. 13, 1899 | Minden | 194 |
| | | 114 | Aug. 10, 1936 | Plain Dealing | 268 |
| Maine | −48 | | Jan. 19, 1925 | Van Buren | 510 |
| | | 105 | July 10, 1911 | North Bridgton | 450 |
| Maryland | −40 | | Jan. 13, 1912 | Oakland | 2,461 |
| | | 109 | July 10, 1936 | Cumberland and Frederick | 623-325 |
| Massachusetts | −34 | | Jan. 18, 1957 | Birch Hill Dam | 840 |
| | | 107 | Aug. 2, 1975 | Chester and New Bedford | 120-640 |
| Michigan | −51 | | Feb. 9, 1934 | Vanderbilt | 785 |
| | | 112 | July 13, 1936 | Mio | 963 |
| Minnesota | −59 | | Feb. 16, 1903 | Pokegama Dam | 1,280 |
| | | 114 | July 6, 1936 | Moorhead | 904 |
| Mississippi | −19 | | Jan. 30, 1966 | Corinth | 420 |
| | | 115 | July 29, 1930 | Holly Springs | 600 |
| Missouri | −40 | | Feb. 13, 1905 | Warsaw | 700 |
| | | 118 | July 14, 1954 | Warsaw and Union | 687-560 |
| Montana | −70 | | Jan. 20, 1954 | Rogers Pass | 5,470 |
| | | 117 | July 5, 1937 | Medicine Lake | 1,950 |
| Nebraska | −47 | | Feb. 12, 1899 | Camp Clarke | 3,700 |
| | | 118 | July 24, 1936 | Minden | 2,169 |
| Nevada | −50 | | Jan. 8, 1937 | San Jacinto | 5,200 |
| | | 122 | June 23, 1954 | Overton | 1,240 |
| New Hampshire | −46 | | Jan. 28, 1925 | Pittsburg | 1,575 |
| | | 106 | July 4, 1911 | Nashua | 125 |
| New Jersey | −34 | | Jan. 5, 1904 | River Vale | 70 |
| | | 110 | July 10, 1936 | Runyon | 18 |
| New Mexico | −50 | | Feb. 1, 1951 | Gavilan | 7,350 |
| | | 116 | July 14, 1934 | Orogrande | 4,171 |
| New York | −52 | | Feb. 9, 1934 | Stillwater Reservoir | 1,670 |
| | | 108 | July 22, 1926 | Troy | 35 |
| North Carolina | −29 | | Jan. 30, 1966 | Mt. Mitchell | 6,525 |
| | | 109 | Sept. 7, 1954 | Weldon | 81 |
| North Dakota | −60 | | Feb. 15, 1936 | Parshall | 1,929 |
| | | 121 | July 6, 1936 | Steele | 1,857 |
| Ohio | −39 | | Feb. 10, 1899 | Milligan | 800 |
| | | 113 | July 21, 1934 | Gallipolis (near) | 673 |
| Oklahoma | −27 | | Jan. 18, 1930 | Watts | 958 |
| | | 120 | July 26, 1943 | Tishmoningo | 670 |
| Oregon | −54 | | Feb. 10, 1933 | Seneca | 4,700 |
| | | 119 | Aug. 10, 1938 | Pendleton | 1,074 |
| Pennsylvania | −42 | | Jan. 5, 1904 | Smethport | 1,469 |
| | | 111 | July 10, 1936 | Phoenixville | 100 |
| Rhode Island | −23 | | Jan. 11, 1942 | Kingston | 100 |
| | | 104 | Aug. 2, 1975 | Providence | 51 |
| South Carolina | −20 | | Jan. 18, 1977 | Longcreek (near) | 1,631 |
| | | 111 | June 28, 1954 | Camden | 170 |
| South Dakota | −58 | | Feb. 17, 1936 | McIntosh | 2,277 |
| | | 120 | July 5, 1936 | Gannvalley | 1,750 |

| State | Lowest °F | Highest | Latest date | Station | Approximate elevation in feet |
|---|---|---|---|---|---|
| Tennessee | -32 | | Dec. 30, 1917 | Mountain City | 2,471 |
| | | 113 | Aug. 9, 1930 | Perryville | 377 |
| Texas | -23 | | Feb. 8, 1933 | Seminole | 3,275 |
| | | 120 | Aug. 12, 1936 | Seymour | 1,291 |
| Utah | -50 | | Jan. 5, 1913 | Strawberry Tunnel | 7,650 |
| | | 116 | June 28, 1892 | Saint George | 2,880 |
| Vermont | -50 | | Dec. 30, 1933 | Bloomfield | 915 |
| | | 105 | July 4, 1911 | Vernon | 310 |
| Virginia | -29 | | Feb. 10, 1899 | Monterey | 3,008 |
| | | 110 | July 15, 1954 | Balcony Falls | 725 |
| Washington | -48 | | Dec. 30, 1968 | Mazama | 2,120 |
| | -48 | | Dec. 30, 1968 | Winthrop | 1,755 |
| | | 118 | Aug. 5, 1961 | Ice Harbor Dam | 475 |
| West Virginia | -37 | | Dec. 30, 1917 | Lewisburg | 2,200 |
| | | 112 | July 10, 1936 | Martinsburg | 435 |
| Wisconsin | -54 | | Jan. 24, 1922 | Danbury | 908 |
| | | 114 | July 13, 1936 | Wisconsin Dells | 900 |
| Wyoming | -63 | | Feb. 9, 1933 | Moran | 6,770 |
| | | 114 | July 12, 1900 | Basin | 3,500 |

## Canadian Normal Temperatures, Highs, Lows, Precipitation

Source: Atmospheric Environment Service, Department of Fisheries and the Environment

These normals are based on varying periods of record over the thirty-year period 1941 to 1970 inclusive. Extreme temperatures are based on varying periods of record for each station through 1977. Airport station; * designates city office stations. The minus (−) sign indicates temperatures below zero. Celsius thermometer registration.

| Province | Station | Normal January Max. | Normal January Min. | Normal July Max. | Normal July Min. | Extreme Highest | Extreme Lowest | Precipitation normal annual (millimeters) |
|---|---|---|---|---|---|---|---|---|
| Alberta | Calgary | -5 | -17 | 24 | 10 | 36 | -45 | 437 |
| Alberta | Edmonton (Industrial Airport) | -10 | -19 | 23 | 12 | 34 | -48 | 446 |
| British Columbia | Prince George | -7 | -16 | 22 | 8 | 34 | -50 | 621 |
| British Columbia | Victoria | 6 | 2 | 20 | 11 | 35 | -16 | 657 |
| British Columbia | Vancouver | 5 | 0 | 22 | 13 | 33 | -18 | 1068 |
| Manitoba | Churchill | -24 | -31 | 17 | 7 | 33 | -45 | 397 |
| Manitoba | Winnipeg | -13 | -23 | 26 | 14 | 41 | -45 | 535 |
| Newfoundland | Gander | -2 | -10 | 22 | 11 | 36 | -27 | 1078 |
| Newfoundland | St. John's | -1 | -7 | 20 | 10 | 31 | -23 | 1511 |
| New Brunswick | Fredericton | -4 | -14 | 26 | 13 | 37 | -37 | 1060 |
| New Brunswick | Moncton | -3 | -13 | 25 | 13 | 37 | -32 | 1099 |
| New Brunswick | Saint John | -2 | -13 | 22 | 11 | 34 | -37 | 1400 |
| Nova Scotia | Halifax | -2 | -10 | 23 | 13 | 34 | -26 | 1396 |
| Nova Scotia | Sydney | -1 | -8 | 23 | 13 | 35 | -25 | 1341 |
| Ontario | Ottawa | -6 | -16 | 26 | 15 | 38 | -36 | 851 |
| Ontario | Sudbury | -8 | -18 | 25 | 13 | 36 | -38 | 835 |
| Ontario | Toronto | -1 | -8 | 27 | 17 | 41 | -33 | 790 |
| Ontario | Windsor | -1 | -8 | 28 | 17 | 38 | -26 | 836 |
| Prince Edward Island | Charlottetown | -3 | -11 | 23 | 14 | 34 | -28 | 1128 |
| Quebec | Montreal | -5 | -14 | 26 | 16 | 36 | -38 | 941 |
| Quebec | Quebec City | -7 | -16 | 25 | 13 | 36 | -36 | 1089 |
| Quebec | Val-d'Or | -11 | -23 | 23 | 11 | 34 | -44 | 902 |
| Saskatchewan | Prince Albert | -15 | -27 | 25 | 11 | 38 | -50 | 389 |
| Saskatchewan | Regina | -12 | -23 | 26 | 12 | 43 | -50 | 398 |
| Northwest Territories | Alert* | -28 | -36 | 7 | 1 | 20 | -49 | 156 |
| Northwest Territories | Yellowknife | -24 | -33 | 21 | 11 | 32 | -51 | 250 |
| Yukon Territory | Dawson* | -25 | -32 | 22 | 9 | 35 | -58 | 325 |
| Yukon Territory | Whitehorse* | -15 | -23 | 20 | 8 | 34 | -52 | 260 |

## Low and High Temperature Records Through 1977

Source: Atmospheric Environment Service, Department of Fisheries and the Environment

| Province | Lowest °C | Highest | Latest date | Station | Approximate elevation in meters |
|---|---|---|---|---|---|
| Alberta | -61 | | Jan. 11, 1911 | Fort Vermillion | 278 |
| | | 42 | July 12, 1886 | Medicine Hat | 721 |
| British Columbia | -59 | | Jan. 31, 1947 | Smith River | 673 |
| | | 44 | July 17, 1941 | Chinook Cove | 404 |
| | | 44 | July 17, 1941 | Lillooet | 290 |
| | | 44 | July 17, 1941 | Lytton | 183 |
| Manitoba | -53 | | Jan. 9, 1899 | Norway House | 219 |
| | | 44 | July 12, 1936 | Emerson | 241 |
| Newfoundland | -49 | | Mar. 7, 1968 | Twin Falls | 457 |
| | | 42 | Aug. 11, 1914 | Northwest River | 61 |
| New Brunswick | -47 | | Feb. 1, 1955 | Sisson Dam | 278 |
| | | 39 | Aug. 19, 1935 | Rexton | 6 |
| Nova Scotia | -41 | | Jan. 31, 1920 | Upper Stewiacke | 23 |
| | | 38 | Aug. 19, 1935 | Collegeville | 76 |
| Ontario | -58 | | Jan. 23, 1935 | Iroquois Falls | 244 |
| | | 42 | July 13, 1936 | Fort Frances | 354 |
| Prince Edward Island | -37 | | Jan. 26, 1884 | Kilmahumaig | 6 |
| | | 37 | Aug. 19, 1935 | Charlottetown | 22 |
| Quebec | -54 | | Feb. 5, 1923 | Doucet | 376 |
| | | 40 | Aug. 15, 1928 | Bark Lake | 365 |
| Saskatchewan | -57 | | Feb. 1, 1893 | Prince Albert | 436 |
| | | 45 | July 5, 1937 | Midale | 582 |
| | | 45 | July 5, 1937 | Yellow Grass | 579 |
| North West Territories | -57 | | Dec. 26, 1917 | Fort Smith | 202 |
| | | 39 | July 18, 1941 | Fort Smith | 207 |
| Yukon Territory | -63 | | Feb. 3, 1947 | Snag | 586 |
| | | 35 | June 18, 1950 | Mayo | 495 |

# Canadian Normal Temperature and Precipitation

**Source:** Atmospheric Environment Service, Department of Fisheries and the Environment

Normal refers to the mean daily temperature and total monthly precipitation based on varying periods of record over the thirty-year period 1941 to 1970 inclusive. In most cases no adjustment factor was used.

Airport station; *designates city office stations. T. temperature in Celsius; P, precipitation in millimeters.

| Station | Jan. T. | Jan. P. | Feb. T. | Feb. P. | Mar. T. | Mar. P. | Apr. T. | Apr. P. | May T. | May P. | June T. | June P. | July T. | July P. | Aug. T. | Aug. P. | Sept. T. | Sept. P. | Oct. T. | Oct. P. | Nov. T. | Nov. P. | Dec. T. | Dec. P. |
|---|---|---|---|---|---|---|---|---|---|---|---|---|---|---|---|---|---|---|---|---|---|---|---|---|
| Calgary, Alta. | -11 | 17 | -7 | 20 | -4 | 20 | 3 | 30 | 9 | 50 | 13 | 92 | 17 | 68 | 15 | 56 | 11 | 35 | 6 | 19 | -3 | 16 | -8 | 15 |
| Charlottetown, P.E.I. | -7 | 111 | -7 | 95 | -3 | 85 | 2 | 82 | 9 | 82 | 14 | 83 | 18 | 73 | 18 | 93 | 14 | 86 | 9 | 97 | 3 | 126 | -4 | 116 |
| Churchill, Man. | -28 | 14 | -27 | 13 | -20 | 18 | -11 | 24 | -2 | 28 | 6 | 40 | 12 | 49 | 12 | 58 | 6 | 52 | -1 | 40 | -12 | 40 | -22 | 20 |
| Dawson, Yukon* | -29 | 19 | -23 | 16 | -14 | 13 | -2 | 9 | 8 | 22 | 14 | 37 | 16 | 53 | 13 | 51 | 6 | 28 | -3 | 27 | -17 | 25 | -25 | 26 |
| Edmonton, Alta. | -15 | 25 | -11 | 20 | -5 | 17 | 4 | 23 | 11 | 37 | 15 | 75 | 18 | 83 | 16 | 72 | 11 | 36 | 5 | 19 | -4 | 19 | -11 | 21 |
| Fredericton, N.B. | -9 | 95 | -8 | 93 | -2 | 69 | 4 | 74 | 11 | 81 | 16 | 79 | 19 | 88 | 18 | 88 | 13 | 82 | 8 | 88 | 2 | 109 | -6 | 114 |
| Frobisher Bay, N.W.T. | -26 | 24 | -25 | 28 | -22 | 21 | -14 | 22 | -3 | 23 | 4 | 38 | 8 | 53 | 7 | 58 | 2 | 43 | -5 | 42 | -12 | 37 | -20 | 26 |
| Halifax, N.S. | -6 | 137 | -7 | 128 | -2 | 104 | 3 | 108 | 9 | 99 | 15 | 79 | 18 | 92 | 18 | 108 | 14 | 95 | 9 | 118 | 4 | 163 | -3 | 179 |
| Hamilton, Ont.* | -5 | 66 | -4 | 60 | 0 | 66 | 7 | 78 | 13 | 72 | 19 | 71 | 22 | 72 | 21 | 77 | 17 | 71 | 11 | 69 | 5 | 67 | -2 | 67 |
| Kitchener, Ont.* | -7 | 61 | -6 | 56 | -1 | 71 | 7 | 71 | 13 | 83 | 18 | 81 | 21 | 80 | 20 | 73 | 16 | 73 | 10 | 71 | 3 | 78 | -4 | 74 |
| London, Ont. | -6 | 76 | -6 | 65 | -1 | 72 | 7 | 78 | 12 | 75 | 18 | 81 | 21 | 81 | 20 | 73 | 16 | 79 | 10 | 74 | 3 | 83 | -4 | 87 |
| Moncton, N.B. | -8 | 107 | -8 | 100 | -3 | 93 | 3 | 84 | 10 | 80 | 15 | 91 | 19 | 80 | 18 | 80 | 14 | 73 | 8 | 91 | 2 | 113 | -5 | 109 |
| Montreal, Que. | -10 | 76 | -9 | 71 | -2 | 71 | 6 | 74 | 13 | 67 | 19 | 83 | 21 | 85 | 20 | 87 | 15 | 80 | 9 | 75 | 2 | 87 | -7 | 86 |
| Ottawa, Ont. | -11 | 60 | -10 | 57 | -3 | 61 | 6 | 68 | 12 | 70 | 18 | 73 | 21 | 81 | 19 | 82 | 15 | 79 | 9 | 66 | 1 | 79 | -8 | 77 |
| Quebec City, Que. | -12 | 86 | -11 | 77 | -4 | 69 | 3 | 75 | 11 | 81 | 16 | 102 | 19 | 108 | 18 | 103 | 13 | 106 | 7 | 82 | 0 | 100 | -9 | 101 |
| Regina, Sask. | -17 | 18 | -14 | 17 | -8 | 18 | 3 | 23 | 11 | 41 | 15 | 83 | 19 | 58 | 18 | 50 | 12 | 36 | 5 | 19 | -5 | 18 | -13 | 16 |
| Saint John, N.B. | -7 | 145 | -8 | 131 | -3 | 105 | 3 | 112 | 9 | 102 | 14 | 95 | 17 | 89 | 16 | 99 | 13 | 103 | 8 | 110 | 3 | 154 | -5 | 157 |
| St. John's, Nfld. | -4 | 145 | -4 | 156 | -2 | 133 | 1 | 114 | 6 | 99 | 10 | 89 | 15 | 83 | 15 | 113 | 12 | 112 | 7 | 139 | 4 | 161 | -1 | 167 |
| Saskatoon, Sask. | -19 | 18 | -15 | 18 | -9 | 17 | 3 | 21 | 11 | 34 | 15 | 57 | 19 | 53 | 17 | 45 | 11 | 33 | 5 | 19 | -6 | 19 | -14 | 18 |
| Sault Ste. Marie, Ont. | -11 | 81 | -11 | 55 | -5 | 57 | 3 | 56 | 9 | 85 | 15 | 88 | 18 | 72 | 18 | 67 | 13 | 95 | 8 | 79 | 1 | 106 | -6 | 94 |
| Toronto, Ont. | -4 | 63 | -4 | 57 | 1 | 66 | 8 | 67 | 13 | 73 | 19 | 63 | 22 | 81 | 21 | 67 | 17 | 61 | 11 | 62 | 5 | 67 | -2 | 64 |
| Vancouver, B.C. | 2 | 147 | 4 | 117 | 6 | 94 | 9 | 61 | 12 | 48 | 15 | 45 | 17 | 30 | 17 | 37 | 14 | 61 | 10 | 122 | 6 | 141 | 4 | 165 |
| Victoria, B.C. | 4 | 107 | 6 | 76 | 7 | 49 | 9 | 34 | 12 | 21 | 14 | 21 | 16 | 12 | 16 | 20 | 14 | 33 | 11 | 74 | 7 | 95 | 5 | 115 |
| Whitehorse, Yukon | -19 | 19 | -13 | 14 | -8 | 15 | 0 | 11 | 7 | 14 | 12 | 29 | 14 | 33 | 12 | 36 | 8 | 29 | 1 | 20 | -9 | 22 | -16 | 20 |
| Windsor, Ont. | -4 | 55 | -3 | 52 | 1 | 66 | 8 | 81 | 14 | 83 | 20 | 84 | 22 | 83 | 21 | 82 | 17 | 61 | 12 | 63 | 4 | 62 | -2 | 64 |
| Winnipeg, Man. | -18 | 24 | -16 | 19 | -8 | 26 | 3 | 37 | 11 | 57 | 17 | 80 | 20 | 80 | 19 | 74 | 13 | 53 | 7 | 35 | -4 | 27 | -14 | 23 |
| Yellowknife, N.W.T. | -29 | 14 | -26 | 12 | -19 | 12 | -8 | 10 | 4 | 14 | 12 | 17 | 16 | 33 | 14 | 36 | 7 | 28 | -1 | 31 | -14 | 24 | -24 | 19 |

# Canadian Annual Climatological Data

**Source:** Atmospheric Environment Service, Department of Fisheries and the Environment

| Station 1977 | Elev. meters | Temperature (Celsius) Highest | Date D./Mo. | Lowest | Date D./Mo. | Precipitation Total (mm) | Greatest in 24 hrs. | Date D./Mo. | Snowfall Total (cm) | Greatest in 24 hrs. | Date D./Mo. | Fastest Wind Km/h | Date D./Mo. | No. of Days Precip. measurable | Snow, sleet |
|---|---|---|---|---|---|---|---|---|---|---|---|---|---|---|---|
| Calgary, Alta. | 1084 | 33 | 7/7 | -37 | 8/12 | 421 | 27 | 12/7 | 78 | 5 | 6/12 | 63 | sev. | 118 | 45 |
| Charlottetown, P.E.I. | 55 | 26 | 23/5 | -22 | 15/1 | 1346 | 52 | 31/7 | 332 | 28 | 19/3 | 72 | 4/4 | 192 | 77 |
| Churchill, Man. | 29 | 26 | 21/6 | -40 | 11/1 | 347 | 26 | 19/7 | 175 | 23 | 14/3 | 65 | 28/1 | 139 | 79 |
| Dawson, Yukon | 369 | 33 | 5/8 | -51 | 5/12 | 246 | 9 | 22/9 | 120 | 7 | 23/2 | 37 | 18/5 | 129 | 74 |
| Edmonton, Alta. | 671 | 33 | 7/6 | -36 | 9/12 | 438 | 32 | 6/7 | 86 | 9 | 27/1 | 56 | 16/10 | 141 | 51 |
| Fredericton, N.B. | 20 | 35 | 23/5 | -30 | 20/1 | 1261 | 41 | 17/8 | 329 | 40 | 6/12 | 52 | 3/4 | 158 | 56 |
| Frobisher Bay, N.W. | 21 | 19 | 27/7 | -38 | 20/2 | 469 | 27 | 15/7 | 320 | 25 | 9/1 | 83 | 27/1 | 178 | 139 |
| Halifax, N.S. | 145 | 32 | 23/5 | -19 | 14/1 | 1364 | 50 | 30/7 | 165 | 18 | 6/12 | 70 | 11/1 | 157 | 50 |
| Hamilton, Ont. | 102 | 35 | 20/7 | -25 | 18/1 | 1072 | 59 | 24/9 | 154 | 24 | 5/12 | 45 | 18/3 | 156 | 53 |
| London, Ont. | 278 | 34 | 6/6 | -27 | 11/12 | 998 | 37 | 8/10 | 268 | 57 | 7/12 | 63 | 5/12 | 178 | 69 |
| Moncton, N.B. | 71 | 34 | 23/5 | -26 | 20/1 | 1449 | 58 | 3/6 | 398 | 36 | 17/1 | 63 | 4/4 | 191 | 55 |
| Montreal, Que. | 36 | 33 | 22/5 | -26 | 17/1 | 966 | 26 | 1/9 | 237 | 24 | 25/2 | 70 | 3/4 | 175 | 69 |
| Ottawa, Ont. | 114 | 34 | 20/7 | -28 | 17/1 | 1010 | 40 | 1/9 | 267 | 31 | 21/12 | 59 | 3/4 | 173 | 66 |
| Quebec City, Que. | 73 | 33 | 22/5 | -29 | 12/12 | 1174 | 54 | 9/10 | 325 | 30 | 10/1 | 59 | 10/1 | 180 | 76 |
| Regina, Sask. | 577 | 32 | 22/7 | -41 | 9/12 | 345 | 30 | 10/7 | 59 | 9 | 26/11 | 69 | 28/3 | 93 | 28 |
| Saint John, N.B. | 109 | 31 | 21/7 | -29 | 20/1 | 1673 | 63 | 2/10 | 282 | 31 | 6/12 | 70 | 10/1 | 174 | 59 |
| Saint John's, Nfld. | 140 | 29 | 30/8 | -20 | 13/2 | 1383 | 40 | 31/7 | 327 | 22 | 6/12 | 120 | 20/1 | 163 | 89 |
| Saskatoon, Sask. | 504 | 34 | 24/6 | -39 | 17/1 | 345 | 32 | 5/5 | 66 | 7 | 17/12 | 59 | 8/3 | 116 | 46 |
| Sault Ste. Marie, On. | 192 | 35 | 20/7 | -35 | 9/1 | 966 | 30 | 27/8 | 296 | 20 | 31/12 | 74 | 24/12 | 193 | 89 |
| Thunder Bay, Ont. | 199 | 34 | 23/7 | -38 | 9/1 | 1046 | 131 | 8/9 | 202 | 42 | 8/12 | 50 | 24/2 | 142 | 45 |
| Toronto, Ont. | 107 | 37 | 20/7 | -23 | 18/1 | 1111 | 60 | 7/11 | 175 | 25 | 8/12 | 70 | 28/12 | 144 | 41 |
| Vancouver, B.C. | 2 | 31 | 17/8 | -8 | 22/11 | 1033 | 40 | 25/11 | 31 | 7 | 9/12 | 48 | 27/3 | 155 | 9 |
| Victoria, B.C. | 70 | 29 | 11/8 | -4 | 21/11 | 515 | 28 | 1/11 | 9 | 5 | 23/11 | 85 | 6/12 | 122 | 6 |
| Waterloo-Wellington | 314 | 33 | 20/7 | -30 | 18/1 | 1048 | 42 | 24/9 | 155 | 15 | 10/1 | 56 | 28/1 | 164 | 68 |
| Whitehorse, Yukon | 703 | 30 | 18/8 | -46 | 11/12 | 316 | 16 | 31/7 | 118 | 8 | 18/3 | 66 | 28/11 | 113 | 72 |
| Windsor, Ont. | 190 | 36 | 6/7 | -24 | 17/1 | 996 | 43 | 25/4 | 114 | 19 | 8/12 | 67 | 26/1 | 153 | 45 |
| Winnipeg, Man. | 239 | 32 | 13/5 | -38 | 17/1 | 715 | 53 | 8/9 | 89 | 17 | 20/11 | 70 | 20/11 | 136 | 50 |
| Yellowknife, N.W.T. | 205 | 26 | 20/6 | -45 | 8/12 | 220 | 16 | 24/10 | 123 | 12 | 10/11 | 56 | 7/1 | 122 | 78 |

# Speed of Winds in Canada

**Source:** Atmospheric Environment Service, Department of Fisheries and the Environment

Kilometers-per-hour average in most cases is for the period of record 1955 to 1972. High is based on varying periods of record dependent on the origin of the station through 1977.

| Station | Avg. | High | Station | Avg. | High | Station | Avg. | High |
|---|---|---|---|---|---|---|---|---|
| Calgary, Alta. | 21.4 | 105 | London, Ont. | 16.4 | 101 | Sault Ste. Marie, Ont. | 15.3 | 89 |
| Charlottetown, P.E.I. | 19.3 | 103 | Moncton, N.B. | 18.7 | 100 | Thunder Bay, Ont. | 14.2 | 81 |
| Churchill, Man. | 25.2 | 126 | Montreal, Que. | 15.8 | 82 | Toronto, Ont. | 17.2 | 90 |
| Dawson, Yukon. | 6.7 | 52 | Ottawa, Ont. | 15.1 | 87 | Vancouver, B.C. | 12.1 | 89 |
| Edmonton, Alta. | 14.9 | 71 | Quebec City, Que. | 16.7 | 109 | Victoria, B.C. | 17.7 | 109 |
| Fredericton, N.B. | 14.2 | 81 | Regina, Sask. | 21.5 | 97 | Whitehorse, Yukon | 15.1 | 81 |
| Frobisher Bay, N.W.T. | 16.6 | 129 | Saint John, N.B. | 19.0 | 97 | Windsor, Ont. | 17.1 | 92 |
| Halifax, N.S. | 18.3 | 97 | Saint John's, Nfld. | 24.3 | 137 | Winnipeg, Man. | 19.3 | 90 |
| Hamilton, Ont. | 12.8 | 66 | Saskatoon, Sask. | 17.9 | 105 | Yellowknife, N.W.T. | 16.1 | 72 |

# WEIGHTS AND MEASURES

Source: National Bureau of Standards, U.S. Commerce Department

## U.S. Moving, Inch by 25.4 mm, to Metric System

The U.S. is the only industrial country in the world which is not on the metric system and is not yet involved in an official changeover program.

On July 2, 1971, following the report of a metric conversion study committee, Commerce Secy. Maurice H. Stans recommended a gradual U.S. changeover during a 10-year period at the end of which the U.S. would be predominantly, but not exclusively, on the metric system. The Metric Conversion Act of 1975, signed Dec. 23, 1975, declared a national policy of coordinating the increased use of the Metric System and established a U. S. Metric Board to coordinate voluntary conversion.

## The International System of Units

Two systems of weights and measures exist side by side in the United States today, with roughly equal but separate legislative sanction: the U.S. Customary System and the International (Metric) System. Throughout U.S. history, the Customary System (inherited from, but now different from, the British Imperial System) has been, as its name implies, customarily used; a plethora of federal and state legislation has given it, through implication, standing as our primary weights and measures system. However, the Metric System (incorporated in the scientists' new SI or Systeme International d'Unites) is the only system that has ever received specific legislative sanction by Congress. The "Law of 1866" reads:

It shall be lawful throughout the United States of America to employ the weights and measures of the metric system; and no contract or dealing, or pleading in any court, shall be deemed invalid or liable to objection because the weights or measures expressed or referred to therein are weights or measures of the metric system.

Over the last 100 years, the Metric System has seen slow, steadily increasing use in the United States and, today, is of importance nearly equal to the Customary System.

On Feb. 10, 1964, the National Bureau of Standards issued the following bulletin:

Henceforth it shall be the policy of the National Bureau of Standards to use the units of the International System (SI), as adopted by the 11th General Conference on Weights and Measures (October 1960), except when the use of these units would obviously impair communication or reduce the usefulness of a report.

What had been the Metric System became the International System (SI), a more complete scientific system.

Seven units have been adopted to serve as the base for the International System as follows: **Length**—meter; **Mass**—kilogram; **Time**—second; **Electric Current**—ampere; **Thermodynamic Temperature**—kelvin; **Amount of Substance**—Mole; and **Light Intensity**—Candela.

## Prefixes

The following prefixes, in combination with the basic unit names, provide the multiples and submultiples in the International System. For example, the unit name "meter," with the prefix "kilo" added, produces "kilometer," meaning "1,000 meters."

| Prefix | Symbol | Multiples and submultiples | Equivalent | Prefix | Symbol | Multiples and submultiples | Equivalent |
|---|---|---|---|---|---|---|---|
| tera | T | $10^{12}$ | trillionfold | centi | c | $10^{-2}$ | hundredth part |
| giga | G | $10^{9}$ | billionfold | milli | m | $10^{-3}$ | thousandth part |
| mega | M | $10^{6}$ | millionfold | micro | mu | $10^{-6}$ | millionth part |
| kilo | k | $10^{3}$ | thousandfold | nano | n | $10^{-9}$ | billionth part |
| hecto | h | $10^{2}$ | hundredfold | pico | p | $10^{-12}$ | trillionth part |
| deka | da | 10 | tenfold | femto | f | $10^{-15}$ | quadrillionth part |
| deci | d | $10^{-1}$ | tenth part | atto | a | $10^{-18}$ | quintillionth part |

## Tables of Metric Weights and Measures

### Linear Measure

| 10 millimeters (mm) | = 1 centimeter (cm) |
| 10 centimeters | = 1 decimeter (dm) = 100 millimeters |
| 10 decimeters | = 1 meter (m) = 1,000 millimeters |
| 10 meters | = 1 dekameter (dam) |
| 10 dekameters | = 1 hectometer (hm) = 100 meters |
| 10 hectometers | = 1 kilometer (km) = 1,000 meters |

### Area Measure

| 100 square millimeters (mm²) | = 1 square centimeter (cm²) |
| 10,000 square centimeters | = 1 square meter (m²) = 1,000,000 square millimeters |
| 100 square meters | = 1 are (a) |
| 100 ares | = 1 hectare (ha) = 10,000 square meters |
| 100 hectares | = 1 square kilometer (km²) = 1,000,000 square meters |

### Volume Measure

| 10 milliliters (mL) | = 1 centiliter (cL) |
| 10 centiliters | = 1 deciliter (dL) = 100 milliliters |

| 10 deciliters | = 1 liter (L) = 1,000 milliliters |
| 10 liters | = 1 dekaliter (daL) |
| 10 dekaliters | = 1 hectoliter (hL) = 100 liters |
| 10 hectoliters | = 1 kiloliter (kL) = 1,000 liters |

### Cubic Measure

| 1,000 cubic millimeters (mm³) | = 1 cubic centimeter (cm³) |
| 1,000 cubic centimeters | = 1 cubic decimeter (dm³) = 1,000,000 cubic millimeters |
| 1,000 cubic decimeters | = 1 cubic meter (m³) = 1 stere = 1,000,000 cubic centimeters = 1,000,000,000 cubic millimeters |

### Weight

| 10 milligrams (mg) | = 1 centigram (cg) |
| 10 centigrams | = 1 decigram (dg) = 100 milligrams |
| 10 decigrams | = 1 gram (g) = 1,000 milligrams |
| 10 grams | = 1 dekagram (dag) |
| 10 dekagrams | = 1 hectogram (hg) = 100 grams |
| 10 hectograms | = 1 kilogram (kg) = 1,000 grams |
| 1,000 kilograms | = 1 metric ton (t) |

## Table of U.S. Customary Weights and Measures

### Linear Measure

| 12 inches (in) | = 1 foot (ft) |
| 3 feet | = 1 yard (yd) |
| 5 ½ yards | = 1 rod (rd), pole, or perch (16 ½ feet) |
| 40 rods | = 1 furlong (fur) = 220 yards = 660 feet |
| 8 furlongs | = 1 statute mile (mi) = 1,760 yards = 5,280 feet |
| 3 miles | = 1 league = 5,280 yards = 15,840 feet |
| 6076.11549 feet | = 1 International Nautical Mile |

### Liquid Measure

When necessary to distinguish the liquid pint or quart from the dry pint or quart, the word "liquid" or the abbreviation "liq" should be used in combination with the name or abbreviation of the liquid unit.

| | |
|---|---|
| 4 gills | = 1 pint (pt) = 28.875 cubic inches |
| 2 pints | = 1 quart (qt) = 57.75 cubic inches |
| 4 quarts | = 1 gallon (gal) = 231 cubic inches = 8 pints = 32 gills |

### Area Measure

Squares and cubes of units are sometimes abbreviated by using "superior" figures. For example, ft$^2$ means square foot, and ft$^3$ means cubic foot.

| | |
|---|---|
| 144 square inches | = 1 square foot (ft$^2$) |
| 9 square feet | = 1 square yard (yd$^2$) = 1,296 square inches |
| 30 1/4 square yards | = 1 square rod (rd$^2$) = 272 1/4 square feet |
| 160 square rods | = 1 acre = 4,840 square yards = 43,560 square feet |
| 640 acres | = 1 square mile (mi$^2$) |
| 1 mile square | = 1 section (of land) |
| 6 miles square | = 1 township = 36 sections = 36 square miles |

### Cubic Measure

| | |
|---|---|
| 30 1/4 square yards | = 1 square rod (rd$^2$) = 262 1/4 (in$^3$) |
| 1 cubic foot (ft$^3$) | = 1,728 cubic inches (in$^3$) |
| 27 cubic feet | = 1 cubic yard (yd$^3$) |

### Gunter's or Surveyors' Chain Measure

| | |
|---|---|
| 7.92 inches (in) | = 1 link |
| 100 links | = 1 chain (ch) = 4 rods = 66 feet |
| 80 chains | = 1 statute mile (mi) = 320 rods = 5,280 feet |

### Troy Weight

| | |
|---|---|
| 24 grains | = 1 pennyweight (dwt) |
| 20 pennyweights | = 1 ounce troy (oz t) = 480 grains |
| 12 ounces troy | = 1 pound troy (lb t) = 240 pennyweights = 5,760 grains |

### Dry Measure

When necessary to distinguish the dry pint or quart from the liquid pint or quart, the word "dry" should be used in combination with the name or abbreviation of the dry unit.

| | |
|---|---|
| 2 pints (pt) | = 1 quart (qt) = (67.2006 cubic inches) |
| 8 quarts | = 1 peck (pk) = (537.605 cubic inches) = 16 pints |
| 4 pecks | = 1 bushel (bu) = (2,150.42 cubic inches) = 32 quarts |

### Avoirdupois Weight

When necessary to distinguish the avoirdupois ounce or pound from the troy ounce or pound, the word "avoirdupois" or the abbreviation "avdp" should be used in combination with the name or abbreviation of the avoirdupois unit.

(The "grain" is the same in avoirdupois and troy weight.)

| | |
|---|---|
| 27 11/32 grains | = 1 dram (dr) |
| 16 drams | = 1 ounce (oz) = 437 1/2 grains |
| 16 ounces | = 1 pound (lb) = 256 drams = 7,000 grains |
| 100 pounds | = 1 hundredweight (cwt)* |
| 20 hundredweights | = 1 ton = 2,000 pounds* |

In "gross" or "long" measure, the following values are recognized.

| | |
|---|---|
| 112 pounds | = 1 gross or long hundredweight* |
| 20 gross or long hundredweights | = 1 gross or long ton = 2,240 pounds* |

*When the terms "hundredweight" and "ton" are used unmodified, they are commonly understood to mean the 100-pound hundredweight and the 2,000-pound ton, respectively; these units may be designated "net" or "short" when necessary to distinguish them from the corresponding units in gross or long measure.

# Tables of Equivalents

When the name of a unit is enclosed in brackets thus, [1 hand], this indicates (1) that the unit is not in general current use in the United States, or (2) that the unit is believed to be based on "custom and usage" rather than on formal definition.

Equivalents involving decimals are, in most instances, rounded off to the third decimal place except where they are exact, in which case these exact equivalents are so designated.

### Lengths

| | |
|---|---|
| Angstrom (A) | 0.1 nanometer (exactly) 0.000 1 micron (exactly) 0.000 000 1 millimeter (exactly) 0.000 000 004 inch |
| 1 cable's length | 120 fathoms 720 feet 219.456 meters (exactly) |
| 1 centimeter (cm) | 0.3937 inch |
| 1 chain (ch) (Gunter's or surveyors) | 66 feet 20.1168 meters (exactly) |
| 1 chain (engineers) | 100 feet 30.48 meters (exactly) |
| 1 decimeter (dm) | 3.937 inches |
| 1 degree (geographical) | 364,566.929 feet 69.047 miles (avg.) 111.123 kilometers (avg.) |
| -of latitude | 68.078 miles at equator 69.043 miles at poles |
| -of longtitude | 69.171 miles |
| 1 dekameter (dam) | 32.808 feet |
| 1 fathom | 6 feet 1.8288 meters (exactly) |
| 1 foot (ft) | 0.3048 meters (exactly) |
| 1 furlong (fur) | 10 chains (surveyors) 660 feet 220 yards 1/8 statute mile 201.168 meters |
| [1 hand] (height measure for horses from ground to top of shoulders) | 4 inches |
| 1 inch (in) | 2.54 centimeters (exactly) |
| 1 kilometer (km) | 0.621 mile 3,280.8 feet |

| | |
|---|---|
| 1 league (land) | 3 statute miles 4.828 kilometers |
| 1 link (Gunter's or surveyors) | 7.92 inches 0.201 meter |
| 1 link engineers | 1 foot 0.305 meter |
| 1 meter (m) | 39.37 inches 1.904 yards |
| 1 micron (u) [the Greek letter mu] | 0.001 millimeter (exactly) 0.000 039 37 inch |
| 1 mil | 0.001 inch (exactly) 0.025 4 millimeter (exactly) |
| 1 mile (mi) (statute or land) | 5,280 feet 1.609 kilometers |
| 1 international nautical mile (INM) | 1,852 kilometers (exactly) 1.150779 statute miles 6,076.11549 feet |
| 1 millimeter (mm) | 0.039 37 inch |
| 1 nanometer (nm) | 0.001 micron (exactly) 0.000 000 039 37 inch (exactly) |
| 1 pica (typography) | 0.013 837 inch (exactly) 12 points |
| 1 point (typography) | 0.351 millimeter |
| 1 rod (rd), pole, or perch | 16 1/2 feet 5 1/2 yards 5.029 meters |
| 1 yard (yd) | 0.9144 meter (exact) |

### Areas or Surfaces

| | |
|---|---|
| 1 acre | 43,560 square feet 4,840 square yards 0.405 hectare |
| 1 are (a) | 119.599 square yards 0.025 acre |

*continued*)
bolt (cloth measure):
length . . . . . . . . . . . . 100 yards (on modern looms)
width . . . . . . . . . . . . {42 inches (usually, for cotton)
{60 inches (usually, for wool)
hectare (ha) . . . . . . . . . . . . . . . . . . . 2.471 acres
square (building)] . . . . . . . . . . . . . . 100 square feet
square centimeter (cm²) . . . . . . . . . . 0.155 square inch
square decimeter (dm²). . . . . . . . . . 15.500 square inches
square foot (ft²) . . . . . . . . . . . 929.030 square centimeters
square inch (in²) . . . . . . . . . . . . 6.452 square centimeters
square kilometer (km²) . . . . . {247.105 acres
{0.386 square mile
{1.196 square yards
square meter (m²) . . . . . . . . . . . 10.764 square feet
square mile (mi²) . . . . . . . . . . . . 258.999 hectares
square millimeter (mm²) . . . . . . . . . 0.002 square inch
square rod (rd²) sq. pole, or
sq. perch . . . . . . . . . . . . . . 25.293 square meters
square yard (yd²) . . . . . . . . . . . . 0.836 square meter

### Capacities or Volumes

barrel (bbl) liquid . . . . . . . . . . . . . . . 31 to 42 gallons*
"There are a variety of "barrels," established by law or usage.
For example: federal taxes on fermented liquors are based on a barrel of 31 gallons: many state laws fix the "barrel for liquids" as 31½ gallons; one state fixes a 36-gallon barrel for cistern measurement; federal law recognizes a 40-gallon barrel for "proof spirits"; by custom, 42 gallons comprise a barrel of crude oil or petroleum products for statistical purposes, and this equivalent is recognized for liquids" by 4 states.

barrel (bbl), standard, {7,056 cubic inches
for fruits, vegetables, {105 dry quarts
and other dry com-
modities except dry {3.281 bushels, struck
cranberries . . . . . . . . measure

barrel (bbl), standard, {5,826 cubic inches
cranberry {86⁴⁵/₆₄ dry quarts
{2.709 bushels, struck
measure
board foot (lumber measure) . . a foot-square board 1 inch thick
bushel (bu) (U.S.) {2,150.42 cubic inches
(struck measure) {(exactly)
{35.238 liters
bushel, heaped (U.S.)] {2,747.715 cubic inches
{1.278 bushels, struck
measure*
Frequently recognized as 1¼ bushels, struck measure.
bushel (bu) (British {1.032 U.S. bushels
Imperial) (struck {struck measure
measure)] {2,219.36 cubic inches
cord (cd) firewood . . . . . . . . . . . . . . 128 cubic feet
cubic centimeter (cm³). . . . . . . . . . 0.061 cubic inch
cubic decimeter (dm³) . . . . . . . . . . 61.024 cubic inches
cubic inch (in³) . . . . . . . {0.554 fluid ounce
{4.433 fluid drams
{16.387 cubic centimeters
cubic foot (ft³) . . . . . . . {7.481 gallons
{28.317 cubic decimeters
cubic meter (m³) . . . . . . . . . . . 1.308 cubic yards
cubic yard (yd³) . . . . . . . . . . . . 0.765 cubic meter
cup, measuring . . . . . . . . {8 fluid ounces
{½ liquid pint
dram, fluid (fl dr) {0.961 U.S. fluid dram
(British)] . . . . . . . {0.217 cubic inch
{3.552 milliliters
dekaliter (dal). . . . . . . . {2.642 gallons
{1.135 pecks
{231 cubic inches
gallon (gal) (U.S.) . . . . . {3.785 liters
{0.833 British gallon
{128 U.S. fluid-ounces
gallon (gal) {277.42 cubic inches
British Imperial] . . . . . {1.201 U.S. gallons
{4.546 liters
{160 British fluid ounces
gill. . . . . . . . . . . . . {7.219 cubic inches
{4 fluid ounces
{0.118 liter
hectoliter (hl) . . . . . . . . {26.417 gallons
{2.838 bushels
liter (l). . . . . . . . . . . . {1.057 liquid quarts
{0.908 dry quart
{61.024 cubic inches

1 milliliter (ml) (1 cu cm exactly) . . . . . {0.271 fluid dram
{16.231 minims
{0.061 cubic inch
1 ounce, liquid {1.805 cubic inches
(U.S.) . . . . . . . . . . . {29.573 milliliters
{1.041 British fluid ounces
[1 ounce, fluid (fl oz) (British)] {0.961 U.S. fluid ounce
{1.734 cubic inches
{28.412 milliliters
1 peck (pk). . . . . . . . . . . . . . . . . . . 8.810 liters
1 pint (pt), dry . . . . . . . {33.600 cubic inches
{0.551 liter
1 pint (pt), liquid . . . . . . . {28.875 cubic inches (exactly)
{0.473 liter
1 quart (qt) dry (U.S.) . . . . {67.201 cubic inches
{1.101 liters
{0.969 British quart
1 quart (qt) liquid (U.S.) . . . {57.75 cubic in (exactly)
{0.946 liter
{0.833 British quart
[1 quart (qt) (British)] . . . . {69.354 cubic inches
{1.032 U.S. dry quarts
{1.201 U.S. liquid quarts
1 tablespoon {3 teaspoons*
{4 fluid drams
{½ fluid ounce
1 teaspoon {⅓ tablespoon*
{1⅓ fluid drams*
*The equivalent "1 teaspoon—1⅓ fluid drams" has been found by the bureau to correspond more closely with the actual capacities of "measuring" and silver teaspoons than the equivalent "1 teaspoon—1 fluid dram" which is given by many dictionaries.

### Weights or Masses

1 assay ton* (AT) . . . . . . . . . . . . . . . . 29.167 grams
*Used in assaying. The assay ton bears the same relation to the milligram that a ton of 2,000 pounds avoirdupois bears to the ounce troy; hence the weight in milligrams of precious metal obtained from one assay ton of ore gives directly the number of troy ounces to the net ton.

1 bale (cotton measure). . . . {500 pounds in U.S.
{750 pounds in Egypt
1 carat (c). . . . . . . . . . . {200 milligrams
{3.086 grains
1 dram avoirdupois (dr avdp) {27¹¹/₃₂ (=27.344) grains
gamma, see microgram {1.722 grams
1 grain . . . . . . . . . . . . . . . . . 64.799 milligrams
1 gram . . . . . . . . {15.432 grains
1 gram . . . . . . . . {0.035 ounce, avoirdupois
1 hundredweight, gross or {112 pounds
long* (gross cwt) . . . . . {50.802 kilograms
1 hundredweight, net or short {100 pounds
(cwt. or net cwt.). . . . . . {45.359 kilograms
1 kilogram (kg) . . . . . . . . . 2.205 pounds
1 microgram (γ [the Greek
letter gamma]) . . . . . . . . . . . . 0.000001 gram (exactly)
1 milligram (mg) . . . . . . . . . . . . . . 0.015 grain
1 ounce, avoirdupois {437.5 grains (exactly)
(oz avdp) . . . . . . . {0.911 troy ounce
{28.350 grams
{480 grains
1 ounce, troy (oz t) . . . . . {1.097 avoirdupois ounces
{31.103 grams
1 pennyweight (dwt) . . . . . . 1.555 grams
1 pound, avoirdupois {7,000 grains
(lb avdp) . . . . . . . {1.215 troy pounds
{453.592 37 grams (exactly)
{5,760 grains
1 pound, troy (lb t) . . . . . {0.823 avoirdupois pound
{373.242 grams
1 ton, gross or long* {2,240 pounds
(gross ton) . . . . . . . {1.12 net tons (exactly)
{1.016 metric tons
*The gross or long ton and hundredweight are used commercially in the United States to only a limited extent, usually in restricted industrial fields. These units are the same as British "ton" and "hundredweight."

1 ton, metric (t) . . . . . . . {2,204.623 pounds
{0.984 gross ton
{1.102 net tons
1 ton, net or short (sh ton) . . {2,000 pounds
{0.893 gross ton
{0.907 metric ton

## Tables of Interrelation of Units of Measurement

Bold face type indicates exact values

### Units of Length

| Units | Inches | Links | Feet | Yards | Rods | Chains | Miles | cm | Meters |
|---|---|---|---|---|---|---|---|---|---|
| 1 inch= | 1 | 0.126 263 | 0.083 333 | 0.027 778 | 0.005 051 | 0.001 263 | 0.000 016 | 2.54 | 0.025 4 |
| 1 link= | 7.92 | 1 | 0.66 | 0.22 | 0.04 | 0.01 | 0.000 125 | 20.117 | 0.201 168 |
| 1 foot= | 12 | 1.515 152 | 1 | 0.333 333 | 0.060 606 | 0.015 152 | 0.000 189 | 30.48 | 0.304 8 |
| 1 yard= | 36 | 4.545 45 | 3 | 1 | 0.181 818 | 0.045 455 | 0.000 568 | 91.44 | 0.914 4 |
| 1 rod= | 198 | 25 | 16.5 | 5.5 | 1 | 0.25 | 0.003 125 | 502.92 | 5.029 2 |
| 1 chain= | 792 | 100 | 66 | 22 | 4 | 1 | 0.012 5 | 2011.68 | 20.116 8 |
| 1 mile= | 63 360 | 8000 | 5280 | 1760 | 320 | 80 | 1 | 160 934.4 | 1609.344 |
| 1 cm= | 0.3937 | 0.049 710 | 0.032 808 | 0.010 936 | 0.001 988 | 0.000 497 | 0.000 006 | 100 | 0.01 |
| 1 meter= | 39.37 | 4.970 970 | 3.280 840 | 1.093 613 | 0.198 839 | 0.049 710 | 0.000 621 | 100 | 1 |

### Units of Area

| Units | Sq. inches | Sq. links | Sq. feet | Sq. yards | Sq. rods | Sq. chains |
|---|---|---|---|---|---|---|
| 1 sq. inch= | 1 | .015 942 3 | 0.006 944 | 0.000 771 605 | 0.000 025 5 | 0.000 001 594 |
| 1 sq. link= | 62.726 4 | 1 | 0.435 6 | 0.0484 | 0.0016 | 0.000 1 |
| 1 sq. foot= | 144 | 2.295 684 | 1 | 0.111 111 1 | 0.003 673 09 | 0.000 229 568 |
| 1 sq. yard= | 1296 | 20.661 16 | 9 | 1 | 0.033 057 85 | 0.002 066 12 |
| 1 sq. rod= | 39 204 | 625 | 272.25 | 30.25 | 1 | 0.062 5 |
| 1 sq. chain= | 627 264 | 10 000 | 4 356 | 484 | 16 | 1 |
| 1 acre= | 6 272 640 | 100 000 | 43 560 | 4 840 | 160 | 10 |
| 1 sq. mile= | 4 014 489 600 | 64 000 000 | 27 878 400 | 3 097 600 | 102 400 | 6400 |
| 1 sq. cm= | 0.155 000 3 | 0.002 471 05 | 0.001 076 | 0.000 119 599 | 0.000 003 954 | 0.000 000 247 |
| 1 sq. meter= | 1550.003 | 24.710 54 | 10.763 91 | 1.195 990 | 0.039 536 86 | 0.002 471 054 |
| 1 hectare= | 15 500 031 | 247.105 4 | 107 639.1 | 11 959.90 | 395.368 6 | 24.710 54 |

| Units | Acres | Sq. miles | Sq. cm | Sq. meters | Hectares |
|---|---|---|---|---|---|
| 1 sq. inch= | 0.000 000 159 423 | 0.000 000 000 249 10 | 6.451 6 | 0.000 645 16 | 0.000 000 065 |
| 1 sq. link= | 0.000 01 | 0.000 000 015 625 | 404.685 642 24 | 0.040 468 56 | 0.000 004 047 |
| 1 sq. foot= | 0.000 022 956 84 | 0.000 000 035 870 06 | 929.034 1 | 0.092 903 41 | 0.000 009 290 |
| 1 sq. yard= | 0.000 206 611 6 | 0.000 000 322 830 6 | 8 361.273 6 | 25.292 852 64 | 0.000 083 613 |
| 1 sq. rod= | 0.006 25 | 0.000 009 765 625 | 252 928.526 4 | 25.292 852 64 | 0.002 529 285 |
| 1 sq. chain= | 0.1 | 0.000 156 25 | 4 046 856 | 404.685 642 24 | 0.040 468 564 |
| 1 acre= | 1 | 0.001 562 5 | 40 468 564 | 4046.856 422 4 | 0.404 685 642 |
| 1 sq. mile= | 640 | 1 | 25 899 881 103 | 2 589 988.11 | 258.998 811 034 |
| 1 sq. cm= | 0.000 000 024 711 | 0.000 000 000 038 610 | 1 | 0.000 1 | 0.000 000 01 |
| 1 sq. meter= | 0.000 247 105 4 | 0.000 000 386 102 2 | 10 000 | 1 | 0.0001 |
| 1 hectare= | 2.471 054 | 0.003 861 022 | 100 000 000 | 10 000 | 1 |

### Units of Mass Not Greater than Pounds and Kilograms

| Units | Grains | Pennyweights | Avdp drams | Avdp ounces |
|---|---|---|---|---|
| 1 grain= | 1 | 0.041 666 67 | 0.036 571 43 | 0.002 285 71 |
| 1 pennyweight= | 24 | 1 | 0.877 714 3 | 0.054 857 14 |
| 1 dram avdp= | 27.343 75 | 1.139 323 | 1 | 0.062 5 |
| 1 ounce avdp= | 437.5 | 18.229 17 | 16 | 1 |
| 1 ounce troy= | 480 | 20 | 17.554 29 | 1.097 143 |
| 1 pound troy= | 5760 | 240 | 210.651 4 | 13.165 71 |
| 1 pound avdp= | 7000 | 291.666 7 | 256 | 16 |
| 1 milligram= | 0.015 432 | 0.000 643 015 | 0.000 564 383 | 0.000 035 274 |
| 1 gram= | 15.432 36 | 0.643 014 9 | 0.564 383 4 | 0.035 273 96 |
| 1 kilogram= | 15 432.36 | 643.014 9 | 564.383 4 | 35.273 96 |

| Units | Troy ounces | Troy pounds | Avdp pounds | Milligrams | Grams | Kilograms |
|---|---|---|---|---|---|---|
| 1 grain= | 0.002 083 33 | 0.000 173 611 | 0.000 142 857 | 64.798 91 | 0.064 798 91 | 0.000 064 799 |
| 1 pennyw't.= | 0.05 | 0.004 166 667 | 0.003 428 571 | 1555.173 84 | 1.555 173 84 | 0.001 555 174 |
| 1 dram avdp= | 0.056 966 15 | 0.004 747 179 | 0.003 906 25 | 1771.845 195 | 1.771 845 195 | 0.001 771 845 |
| 1 oz avdp= | 0.911 458 3 | 0.075 954 86 | 0.062 5 | 28 349.523 125 | 28.349 523 125 | 0.028 349 52 |
| 1 oz troy= | 1 | 0.083 333 333 | 0.068 571 43 | 31 103.476 8 | 31.103 476 8 | 0.031 103 48 |
| 1 lb troy= | 12 | 1 | 0.822 857 1 | 373 241.721 6 | 373.241 721 6 | 0.373 241 722 |
| 1 lb avdp= | 14.583 33 | 1.215 278 | 1 | 453 592.37 | 453.592 37 | 0.453 592 37 |
| 1 milligram= | 0.000 032 151 | 0.000 002 679 | 0.000 002 205 | 1 | 0.001 | 0.000 001 |
| 1 gram= | 0.032 150 75 | 0.002 679 229 | 0.002 204 623 | 1000 | 1 | 0.001 |
| 1 kilogram= | 32.150 75 | 2.679 229 | 2.204 623 | 1 000 000 | 1000 | 1 |

### Units of Mass Not Less than Avoirdupois Ounces

| Units | Avdp oz | Avdp lb | Short cwt | Short tons | Long tons | Kilograms | Metric tons |
|---|---|---|---|---|---|---|---|
| 1 oz av= | 1 | 0.0625 | 0.000 625 | 0.000 031 25 | 0.000 027 902 | 0.028 349 523 | 0.000 028 35 |
| 1 lb av= | 16 | 1 | 0.01 | 0.000 5 | 0.000 446 429 | 0.453 592 37 | 0.000 453 59 |
| 1 sh cwt= | 1 600 | 100 | 1 | 0.05 | 0.044 642 86 | 45.359 237 | 0.045 359 23 |
| 1 sh ton= | 32 000 | 2000 | 20 | 1 | 0.892 857 1 | 907.184 74 | 0.907 184 74 |
| 1 long ton= | 35 840 | 2240 | 22.4 | 1.12 | 1 | 1016.046 908 8 | 1.016 046 90 |
| 1 kg= | 35.273 96 | 2.204 623 | 0.022 046 23 | 0.001 102 311 | 0.000 984 207 | 1 | 0.001 |
| 1 metric ton= | 35 273.96 | 2 204.623 | 22.046 23 | 1.102 311 | 0.984 206 5 | 1000 | 1 |

*(continued)*

## Units of Volume

| Units | Cubic inches | Cubic feet | Cubic yards | Cubic cm | Cubic dm | Cubic meters |
|---|---|---|---|---|---|---|
| 1 cubic inch= | 1 | 0.000 578 704 | 0.000 021 433 | 16.387 064 | 0.016 387 | 0.000 016 387 |
| 1 cubic foot= | 1728 | 1 | 0.037 037 04 | 28 316.846 592 | 28.316 847 | 0.028 316 847 |
| 1 cubic yard= | 46 656 | 27 | 1 | 764 554.857 984 | 764.554 858 | 0.764 554 858 |
| 1 cubic cm= | 0.061 023 74 | 0.000 035 315 | 0.000 001 308 | 1 | 0.001 | 0.000 001 |
| 1 cubic dm= | 61.023 74 | 0.035 314 67 | 0.001 307 951 | 1 000 | 1 | 0.001 |
| 1 cubic meter | 61 023.74 | 35.314 67 | 1.307 951 | 1 000 000 | 1000 | 1 |

## Units of Capacity (Liquid Measure)

| Units | Minims | Fluid drams | Fluid ounces | Gills | Liquid pt |
|---|---|---|---|---|---|
| 1 minim= | 1 | 0.016 666 7 | 0.002 083 33 | 0.000 520 833 | 0.000 130 208 |
| 1 liquid dram= | 60 | 1 | 0.125 | 0.031 25 | 0.007 812 5 |
| 1 liquid ounce= | 480 | 8 | 1 | 0.25 | 0.062 5 |
| 1 gill= | 1920 | 32 | 4 | 1 | 0.25 |
| 1 liquid pint= | 7680 | 128 | 16 | 4 | 1 |
| 1 liquid quart= | 15 360 | 256 | 32 | 8 | 2 |
| 1 gallon= | 61 440 | 1024 | 128 | 32 | 8 |
| 1 cubic inch= | 265.974 | 4.432 900 | 0.554 112 6 | 0.138 528 1 | 0.034 632 03 |
| 1 cubic foot= | 459 603.1 | 7 660.052 | 957.506 5 | 239.376 6 | 59.844 16 |
| 1 milliliter= | 16.230 73 | 0.270 512 18 | 0.033 814 02 | 0.008 435 506 | .002 113 376 |
| 1 liter= | 16 230.73 | 270.512 18 | 33.814 02 | 8.453 506 | 2.113 376 |

| Units | Liquid quarts | Gallons | Cubic inches | Cubic feet | Liters |
|---|---|---|---|---|---|
| 1 minim= | 0.000 065 104 17 | 0.000 016 276 04 | 0.003 759 766 | 0.000 002 175 790 | 0.000 061 611 52 |
| 1 liq. dram= | 0.003 906 25 | 0.000 976 562 5 | 0.225 585 9 | 0.000 130 547 4 | 0.003 696 691 |
| 1 liquid oz= | 0.031 25 | 0.007 812 5 | 1.804 687 5 | 0.001 044 379 | 0.029 573 53 |
| 1 gill= | 0.125 | 0.031 25 | 7.218 75 | 0.004 177 517 | 0.118 294 118 25 |
| 1 liquid pt= | 0.5 | 0.125 | 28.875 | 0.016 710 07 | 0.473 176 473 |
| 1 liquid qt= | 1 | 0.25 | 57.75 | 0.033 420 14 | 0.946 352 946 |
| 1 gallon= | 4 | 1 | 231 | 0.133 680 6 | 3.785 411 784 |
| 1 cubic in.= | 0.017 316 02 | 0.004 329 004 | 1 | 0.000 578 703 7 | 0.016 387 064 |
| 1 cubic foot= | 29.922 08 | 7.480 519 | 1728 | 1 | 28.316 846 592 |
| 1 liter= | 1.056 688 | 0.264 172 05 | 61.023 74 | 0.035 314 67 | 1 |

## Units of Capacity (Dry Measure)

| Units | Dry pints | Dry quarts | Pecks | Bushels | Cubic in. | Liters |
|---|---|---|---|---|---|---|
| 1 dry pint= | 1 | 0.5 | 0.062 5 | 0.015 625 | 33.600 312 5 | 0.550 610 47 |
| 1 dry quart= | 2 | 1 | 0.125 | 0.031 25 | 67.200 625 | 1.101 220 9 |
| 1 peck= | 16 | 8 | 1 | 0.25 | 537.605 | 8.809 767 5 |
| 1 bushel= | 64 | 32 | 4 | 1 | 2150.42 | 35.239 07 |
| 1 cubic inch= | 0.029 761 6 | 0.014 880 9 | 0.001 860 10 | 0.000 465 025 | 1 | 0.016 387 064 |
| 1 liter= | 1.816 166 | 0.908 083 | 0.113 510 37 | 0.028 377 59 | 61.023 74 | 1 |

## Measures of Force and Pressure

**Dyne** = force necessary to accelerate a 1-gram mass 1 centimeter per second per second = 0.000072 poundals

**Poundal** = force necessary to accelerate a 1-pound mass 1 foot per second per second = 13,825.5 dynes = 0.138255 newtons

**Newton** = force which, applied for 1 second, will give a velocity of 1 meter per second to a 1-kilogram mass = 100 dynes per square centimeter = 100 microbars = 7.233 poundals

**Pascal** (pressure) = 1 newton per square meter = 0.020885 pound per square foot.

**Atmosphere** (air pressure at sea level) = 2,116.102 pounds per square foot = 14.6952 pounds per square inch = 1.0332 kilograms per square centimeter = 10,132.3066 newtons

## Miscellaneous Measures

**Caliber**—the diameter of a gun bore. In the U.S., caliber is traditionally expressed in hundredths of inches, eg. .22 or .30. In Britain, caliber is often expressed in thousandths of inches, eg. .270 or .465. Now, it is commonly expressed in millimeters, eg. the 7.62 mm. M14 rifle and the 5.56 mm. M16 rifle. Heavier weapons' caliber has long been expressed in millimeters, eg. the 81 mm. mortar, the 105 mm. howitzer (light), the 155 mm. howitzer (medium or heavy).

Naval guns' caliber refers to the barrel length as a multiple of the bore diameter. A 5-inch, 50-caliber naval gun has a 5-inch bore and a barrel length of 250 inches.

**Carat**, **karat**—a measure of the amount of alloy per 24 parts in gold. Thus 24-carat gold is pure; 18-carat gold is one-fourth alloy.

**Decibel (db)**—a measure of the relative loudness or intensity of sound. A 20-decibel sound is 10 times louder than a 10-decibel sound; 30 decibels is 100 times louder; 40 decibels is 1,000 times louder, etc. One decibel is the smallest difference between sounds detectable by the human ear. A 140-decibel sound is painful.

| 10 decibels | – a light whisper |
|---|---|
| 20 | – quiet conversation |
| 30 | – normal conversation |
| 40 | – light traffic |
| 50 | – typewriter, loud conversation |
| 60 | – noisy office |
| 70 | – normal traffic, quiet train |
| 80 | – rock music, subway |
| 90 | – heavy traffic, thunder |
| 100 | – jet plane at takeoff |

**Em**—a printer's measure designating the square width of any given type size. Thus, an em of 10-point type is 10 points. An en is half an em.

**Gauge**—a measure of shotgun bore diameter. Gauge numbers originally referred to the number of lead balls of the gun barrel diameter in a pound. Thus, a 16 gauge shotgun's bore was smaller than a 12-gauge shotgun's. Today, an international agreement assigns millimeter measures to each gauge, eg:

| Gauge | Bore diameter in mm. |
|---|---|
| 6 | 23.34 |
| 10 | 19.67 |
| 12 | 18.52 |
| 14 | 17.60 |
| 16 | 16.81 |
| 20 | 15.90 |

**Horsepower**—the energy needed to lift 550 pounds one foot in one second, or to lift 33,000 pounds one foot in one minute. Equivalent to 746 watts or 2,546.0756 btu.

**Quire**—25 sheets of paper

**Ream**—500 sheets of paper

## Spirits Measures

| Pony | 0.5 jigger |
|---|---|
| Shot | { 0.666 jigger<br>{ 1.0 ounce |
| Jigger | 1.5 shot |
| Pint | { 16 shots<br>{ 0.625 fifth |
| Fifth | { 25.6 shots<br>{ 1.6 pints<br>{ 0.8 quart<br>{ 0.75706 liter |

| Quart | { 32 shots<br>{ 1.25 fifth |
|---|---|
| Magnum | { 2 quarts<br>{ 2.49797 bottles<br>(wine) |

For champagne and brandy only:

| Jeroboam | { 6.4 pints<br>{ 1.6 magnum<br>{ 0.8 gallon |
|---|---|

For champagne only:

| Rehoboam | 3 magnums |
|---|---|
| Methuselah | 4 magnums |
| Salmanazar | 6 magnums |
| Balthazar | 8 magnums |
| Nebuchadnezzar | 10 magnums |

| Wine bottle (standard): | { 0.800633 quart<br>{ 0.7576778 liter |
|---|---|

## Ancient Measures

**Biblical**
| Cubit | = | 21.8 inches |
|---|---|---|
| Omer | = | 0.45 peck |
| | | 3.964 liters |
| Epaph | = | 10 omers |
| Shekel | = | 0.497 ounce |
| | | 14.1 grams |

**Greek**
| Cubit | = | 18.3 inches |
|---|---|---|
| Stadion | = | 607.2 or 622 feet |
| Obolos | = | 715.38 milligrams |
| Drachma | = | 4.2923 grams |
| Mina | = | 0.9463 pounds |
| Talent | = | 60 mina |

**Roman**
| Cubit | = | 17.5 inches |
|---|---|---|
| Stadium | = | 202 yards |
| As, libra,<br>pondus | = | 325.971 grams<br>.71864 pounds |

## Electrical Units

The **watt** is the unit of power (electrical, mechanical, thermal, etc.). Electrical power is given by the product of the voltage and the current.

Energy is sold by the **joule**, but in common practice the billing of electrical energy is expressed in terms of the **kilowatt-hour**, which is 3,600,000 joules or 3.6 megajoules.

The **horsepower** is a non-metric unit sometimes used in mechanics. It is equal to 746 watts.

The **ohm** is the unit of electrical resistance and represents the physical property of a conductor which offers a resistance to the flow of electricity, permitting just 1 ampere to flow at 1 volt of pressure.

## Weight of Water

| 1 | cubic inch | .0360 | pound |
|---|---|---|---|
| 12 | cubic inches | .433 | pound |
| 1 | cubic foot | 62.4 | pounds |
| 1 | cubic foot | 7.48052 | U.S. gal |
| 1.8 | cubic feet | 112.0 | pounds |
| 35.96 | cubic feet | 2240.0 | pounds |

| 1 | imperial gallon | 10.0 | pounds |
|---|---|---|---|
| 11.2 | imperial gallons | 112.0 | pounds |
| 224 | imperial gallons | 2240.0 | pounds |
| 1 | U.S. gallon | 8.33 | pounds |
| 13.45 | U.S. gallons | 112.0 | pounds |
| 269.0 | U.S. gallons | 2240.0 | pounds |

## Density of Gases and Vapors

Source: National Bureau of Standards (kilograms per cubic meter)

| Gas | Wgt. | Gas | Wgt. | Gas | Wgt. |
|---|---|---|---|---|---|
| Acetylene | 1.171 | Ethylene | 1.260 | Methyl fluoride | 1.545 |
| Air | 1.293 | Fluorine | 1.696 | Mono methylamine | 1.38 |
| Ammonia | .759 | Helium | .178 | Neon | .900 |
| Argon | 1.784 | Hydrogen | .090 | Nitric oxide | 1.341 |
| Arsene | 3.48 | Hydrogen bromide | 3.50 | Nitrogen | 1.250 |
| Butane-iso | 2.60 | Hydrogen chloride | 1.639 | Nitrosyl chloride | 2.99 |
| Butane-n | 2.519 | Hydrogen iodide | 5.724 | Nitrous oxide | 1.997 |
| Carbon dioxide | 1.977 | Hydrogen selenide | 3.66 | Oxygen | 1.429 |
| Carbon monoxide | 1.250 | Hydrogen sulfide | 1.539 | Phosphine | 1.48 |
| Carbon oxysulfide | 2.72 | Krypton | 3.745 | Propane | 2.020 |
| Chlorine | 3.214 | Methane | .717 | Silicon tetrafluoride | 4.67 |
| Chlorine monoxide | 3.89 | Methyl chloride | 2.25 | Sulfur dioxide | 2.927 |
| Ethane | 1.356 | Methyl ether | 2.091 | Xenon | 5.897 |

## Temperature Conversion Table

The numbers in **bold face type** refer to the temperature either in degrees Celsius or Fahrenheit which are to be converted. If converting from degrees Fahrenheit to Celsius, the equivalent will be found in the column on the left, while if converting from degrees Celsius to Fahrenheit the answer will be found in the column on the right.

**For temperatures not shown.** To convert Fahrenheit to Celsius subtract 32 degrees and multiply by 5, divide by 9; to convert Celsius to Fahrenheit, multiply by 9, divide by 5 and add 32 degrees.

| Celsius | | Fahrenheit | Celsius | | Fahrenheit | Celsius | | Fahrenheit |
|---|---|---|---|---|---|---|---|---|
| − 273.2 | **− 459.7** | | − 17.8 | **0** | 32 | 35.0 | **95** | 203 |
| − 184 | **− 300** | | − 12.2 | **10** | 50 | 36.7 | **98** | 208.4 |
| − 169 | **− 273** | − 459.4 | − 6.67 | **20** | 68 | 37.8 | **100** | 212 |
| − 157 | **− 250** | − 418 | − 1.11 | **30** | 86 | 43 | **110** | 230 |
| − 129 | **− 200** | − 328 | 4.44 | **40** | 104 | 49 | **120** | 248 |
| − 101 | **− 150** | − 238 | 10.0 | **50** | 122 | 54 | **130** | 266 |
| − 73.3 | **− 100** | − 148 | 15.6 | **60** | 140 | 60 | **140** | 284 |
| − 45.6 | **− 50** | − 58 | 21.1 | **70** | 158 | 66 | **150** | 302 |
| − 40.0 | **− 40** | − 40 | 23.9 | **75** | 167 | 93 | **200** | 392 |
| − 34.4 | **− 30** | − 22 | 26.7 | **80** | 176 | 121 | **250** | 482 |
| − 28.9 | **− 20** | − 4 | 29.4 | **85** | 185 | 149 | **300** | 572 |
| − 23.3 | **− 10** | 14 | 32.2 | **90** | 194 | | | |

Water boils at 212° Fahrenheit at sea level. For every 550 feet above sea level, boiling point of water is lower by about 1° Fahrenheit. Methyl alcohol boils at 148° Fahrenheit. Average human oral temperature, 98.6° Fahrenheit. Water freezes at 32° Fahrenheit. Although "Centigrade" is still frequently used, the International Committee on Weights and Measures and the National Bureau of Standards have recommended since 1948 that this scale be called "Celsius."

# World Weights and Measures

**Source:** National Bureau of Standards, U.S. Commerce Department

Most of the measures listed below have been legally superseded by the metric system. However, many of these measures continue to be used informally.

| Unit | Where used | U.S. equiv. |
|---|---|---|
| Almude | Portugal | 4.423 gal |
| Ardeb | Egypt | 5.6189 bu |
| Arratel (Libra) | Portugal | 1.012 lb |
| Arroba | Argentina | 25.32 lb |
| " | Brazil | 32.38 lb |
| " | Cuba | 25.36 lb |
| " | Paraguay | 25.32 lb |
| " | Venezuela | 25.40 lb |
| " (liquid) | Cuba, Spain, and Venezuela | 4.263 gal |
| Arshine | USSR | 28 in |
| " (sq) | " | 5.44 sq ft |
| Artel | Morocco | 1.12 lb |
| Baril | Argentina | 20.077 gal |
| " | Mexico | 20.0787 gal |
| Barile (wine) | Malta | 11.2 gal |
| Berkovets | USSR | 361.128 lb |
| Bongkal | Malaysia | 832 grains |
| Bouw | Sumatra | 1.75 acres |
| Bu | Japan | 0.12 inch |
| Bushel (Brit.) | various | 1.03205 U.S. bu |
| Caballeria | Cuba | 33.162 acres |
| Caban (cavan) | Philippines | 2.13 bu |
| " | | 19.8 gal |
| Caffiso | Malta | 5.40 gal |
| Candy | Bombay | 560 lb |
| " | India (Madras) | 500 lb |
| Cantaro | Malta | 175 lb |
| Carat | World | 3.086 grains |
| Catty | China | 1.333⅓ lb |
| " | Japan (see Kin) | |
| " | Java, Malacca | 1.36 lb |
| " | Thailand | 2⅔ lb |
| " (stand) | Thailand | 1.32 lb |
| " | Sumatra | 2.12 lb |
| Centaro | Central America | 4.2631 gal |
| Centne | Brunswick | 117.5 lb |
| " | Bremen | 127.5 lb |
| " | Denmark, Norway | 110.23 lb |
| " | Germany | 113.44 lb |
| " | Sweden | 93.7 lb |
| Chetvert | USSR | 5.957 bu |
| Ch'ih | China | 12.60 in |
| " (metric) | China | 39.37 in = 1 meter |
| Cho | Japan | 2.451 acres |
| Coomb | England | 4.1282 bu |
| Coyan | Thailand | 2,645.5 lb |
| Cuadra | Argentina | 4.2 acres |
| " | Paraguay | 94.71 yd |
| " (sq) | Paraguay | 1.85 acres |
| " | Uruguay | 1.82 acres |
| Cwt. (Brit.) | various | 112 lb |
| Dessiatine | USSR | 2.6997 acres |
| Drachma | Greece | 49.38 grains |
| Dunam | Israel | 0.22239 acre |
| Fanega (dry) | Ecuador, El Salv. | 1.5745 bu |
| " (dry) | Chile | 2.75268 bu |
| " (dry) | Guatemala, Spain | 1.57744 bu |
| " | Mexico | 2.57716 bu |
| " (dry) | Spain | 1.57501 bu |
| " (liquid) | Spain | 16 gal |
| " (dry) | Trinidad & Tobago | 110 lb |
| " (double) | Uruguay | 7.776 bu |
| " (single) | Uruguay | 3.888 bu |
| " | Venezuela | 3.334 bu |
| Feddan | Egypt | 1.04 acres |
| Frail (raisins) | Spain | 50 lb |
| Frasco | Argentina | 2.51 liq qt |
| Frasila | Zanzibar | 35 lb |
| Fuder | Luxembourg | 264.18 gal |
| Funt | USSR | 0.9028 lb |
| Gallon (Brit.) | various | 1.20094 U.S. gal |
| Garniec | Poland | 1.0567 gal |
| Jerib | Iran | 2.471 acres |
| Joch | Austria | 1.422 acres |
| " | Hungary | 1.067 acres |
| Kantar | Egypt | 99.05 lb |
| " | Morocco | 112 lb |
| " | Turkey | 124.45 lb |
| Ken | Japan | 5.97 feet |
| Kin | Japan | 1.32 lb |

| Unit | Where used | U.S. equiv. |
|---|---|---|
| Klafter | Austria | 2.074 yd |
| Klafter | Germany | 1.90 yd |
| Koku | Japan | 5.119 bu |
| Kwan | Japan | 8.2673 lb |
| Last | Belgium, Holland | 85.134 bu |
| " | England | 82.56 bu |
| " | Germany | 2 metric tons |
| " | Prussia | 112.29 bu |
| League (land) | Paraguay | 4.633 acres |
| Li | China | 1890 ft |
| " | China | 0.01260 in = (1/1000 ch'ih) |
| Libra (lb) | Argentina | 1.0128 lb |
| " | Cent. Amer., Chile | 1.014 lb |
| " | Cuba | 1.0143 lb |
| " | Mexico | 1.01467 lb |
| " | Peru, Venezuela | 1.0143 lb |
| " | Uruguay | 1.0127 lb |
| Load, timber | England | 50 cu ft |
| Manzana | Nicaragua | 1.742 acres |
| " | Costa Rica, El Salv. | 1.727 acres |
| Marco | Bolivia | 0.507 lb |
| Maund | Bengal | 82²/₇ lb |
| Mil | Denmark | 4.68 miles |
| Milla | Nicaragua | 1.1594 miles |
| " | Honduras | 1.1493 miles |
| Mina | Greece | 0.95 lb |
| Morgen | Germany | 0.63 acre |
| Oka (Oke) | Greece | 2.82 lb |
| Oke | Egypt | 2.7514 lb |
| " | Turkey | 2.826 lb |
| Pic | Egypt | 22.83 inches |
| Picul | Borneo, Celebes | 135.64 lb |
| " | China | 133⅓ lb |
| " | Java | 136.16 lb |
| " | Philippines | 139.44 lb |
| Pie | Argentina | 0.9471 ft |
| " | Spain | 0.91416 ft |
| Pik | Turkey | 27.9 inches |
| Pood | USSR | 36.113 lb |
| Pund (lb) | Denmark | 1.102 lb |
| Quart (Brit.) | various | 1.20094 liq qt |
| " | " | 1.03205 dry qt |
| Quarter | | 8.256 bu |
| Quintal | Argentina | 101.3 lb |
| " | Brazil | 129.54 lb |
| " | Castile, Peru, Chile | 101.43 lb |
| " | Mexico | 101.47 lb |
| Rotl | Israel | 6.35 lb |
| Sagene | USSR | 7 feet |
| Salm | Malta | 8.26 bu |
| Se | Japan | 0.02451 acre |
| Seer | India | 2²/₃₅ lb |
| Shaku | Japan | 11.9303 in |
| Sho | " | 1.91 liq qt |
| Skalpund | Sweden | 0.937 lb |
| Stone (Brit.) | various | 14 lb |
| Sun | Japan | 1.193 inches |
| Tael (Kuping) | China | 575.64 grs (troy) |
| Tan | Japan | 0.25 acre |
| To | Japan | 2.05 pecks |
| Tonde (cereal) | Denmark | 3.9480 bu |
| Tonde (land) | Denmark | 1.36 acres |
| Tonne | France | 2,204.62 lb |
| Tsubo | Japan | 35.58 sq ft |
| Ts'un | China | 1.26 inches |
| Tunna (wheat) | Sweden | 4.16 bu |
| Tunnland | " | 1.22 acres |
| Vara | Argentina | 34.0944 inches |
| " | Costa Rica, El Salv. | 32.913 inches |
| " | Guatemala | 32.909 inches |
| " | Honduras | 32.874 inches |
| " | Nicaragua | 33.057 inches |
| " | Chile, Peru | 32.913 inches |
| " | Cuba | 33.386 inches |
| " | Mexico | 32.992 inches |
| Vedro | USSR | 3.249 gal |
| Verst | " | 0.663 mile |
| Vloka | Poland | 41.50 acres |
| Wey | Scotland, Ireland | 40 bu |

The metric carat of 200 milligrams is now very generally in use.

## Breaking the Sound Barrier; Speed of Sound

The prefix Mach is used to describe supersonic speed. It derives from Ernst Mach, a Czech-born German physicist, who contributed to the study of sound. When a plane moves at the speed of sound it is Mach 1. When twice the speed of sound it is Mach 2. When it is near but below the speed of sound its speed can be designated at less than Mach 1, for example, Mach .90. Mach is defined as "in jet propulsion, the ratio of the velocity of a rocket or a jet to the velocity of sound in the medium being considered."

When a plane passes the sound barrier—flying faster than sound travels—listeners in the area hear thunderclaps, but pilots do not hear them.

Sound is produced by vibrations of an object and is transmitted by alternate increase and decrease in pressures that radiate outward through a material media of molecules —somewhat like waves spreading out on a pond after a rock has been tossed into it.

The frequency of sound is determined by the number of times the vibrating waves undulate per second, and is measured in cycles per second. The slower the cycle of waves, the lower the sound. As frequencies increase, the sound is higher.

Sound is audible to human beings only if the frequency falls within a certain range. The human ear is usually not sensitive to frequencies of less than 20 vibrations per second, or more than about 20,000 vibrations per second—although this range varies among individuals. Anything at a pitch higher than the human ear can hear is termed ultrasonic.

Intensity or loudness is the strength of the pressure of these radiating waves, and is measured in decibles. The human ear responds to intensity in a range from zero to 120 decibles. Any sound with pressure over 120 decibles is painful.

The speed of sound is generally placed at 1,088 ft. per second at sea level at 32°F. It varies in other temperatures and in different media. Sound travels faster in water than in air, and even faster in iron and steel. If in air it travels a mile in 5 seconds, it does a mile under water in 1 second, and through iron in 1/3 of a second. It travels through ice cold vapor at approximately 4,708 ft. per sec., ice-cold water, 4,938; granite, 12,960; hardwood, 12,620; brick, 11,960; glass, 16,410 to 19,690; silver, 8,658; gold, 5,717.

## Colors of the Spectrum

Color, an electromagnetic wave phenomenon, is a sensation produced through the excitation of the retina of the eye by rays of light. The colors of the spectrum may be produced by viewing a light beam refracted by passage through a prism, which breaks the light into its wave lenghts.

Customarily, the primary colors of the spectrum are thought of as those 6 monochromatic colors which occupy relatively large areas of the spectrum: red, orange, yellow, green, blue, and violet. However, Sir Isaac Newton named a 7th, indigo, situated between blue and violet on the spectrum. Aubert estimated (1865) the solar spectrum to contain approximately 1,000 distinguishable hues of which according to Rood (1881) 2 million tints and shades can be distinguished; Luckiesh stated (1915) that 55 distinctly different hues have been seen in a single spectrum.

By many physicists only 3 primary colors are recognized: red, yellow, and blue (Mayer, 1775); red, green, and violet (Thomas Young, 1801); red, green, and blue (Clerk Maxwell, 1860).

The color sensation of black is due to complete lack of stimulation of the retina, that of white to complete stimulation. The infra-red and ultra-violet rays, below the red (long) end of the spectrum and above the violet (short) end respectively, are invisible to the naked eye. Heat is the principal effect of the infra-red rays and chemical action that of the ultra-violet rays.

## Common Fractions Reduced to Decimals

| 8ths | 16ths | 32ds | 64ths | | 8ths | 16ths | 32ds | 64ths | | 8ths | 16ths | 32ds | 64ths | |
|------|-------|------|-------|------|------|-------|------|-------|------|------|-------|------|-------|------|
| | | | 1 | .015625 | | | | 23 | .359375 | | | | 45 | .703125 |
| | | 1 | 2 | .03125 | 3 | 6 | 12 | 24 | .375 | | | 23 | 46 | .71875 |
| | | | 3 | .046875 | | | | 25 | .390625 | | | | 47 | .734375 |
| | 1 | 2 | 4 | .0625 | | | | 13 26 | .40625 | 6 | 12 | 24 | 48 | .75 |
| | | | 5 | .078125 | | | | 27 | .421875 | | | | 49 | .765625 |
| | | 3 | 6 | .09375 | | 7 | 14 | 28 | .4375 | | | 25 | 50 | .78125 |
| | | | 7 | .109375 | | | | 29 | .453125 | | | | 51 | .796875 |
| 1 | 2 | 4 | 8 | .125 | | | 15 | 30 | .46875 | | 13 | 26 | 52 | .8125 |
| | | | 9 | .140625 | | | | 31 | .484375 | | | | 53 | .828125 |
| | | 5 | 10 | .15625 | 4 | 8 | 16 | 32 | .5 | | | 27 | 54 | .84375 |
| | | | 11 | .171875 | | | | 33 | .515625 | | | | 55 | .859375 |
| | 3 | 6 | 12 | .1875 | | | 17 | 34 | .53125 | 7 | 14 | 28 | 56 | .875 |
| | | | 13 | .203125 | | | | 35 | .546875 | | | | 57 | .890625 |
| | | 7 | 14 | .21875 | | 9 | 18 | 36 | .5625 | | | 29 | 58 | .90625 |
| | | | 15 | .234375 | | | | 37 | .578125 | | | | 59 | .921875 |
| 2 | 4 | 8 | 16 | .25 | | | 19 | 38 | .59375 | | 15 | 30 | 60 | .9375 |
| | | | 17 | .265625 | | | | 39 | .609375 | | | | 61 | .953125 |
| | | 9 | 18 | .28125 | 5 | 10 | 20 | 40 | .625 | | | 31 | 62 | .96875 |
| | | | 19 | .296875 | | | | 41 | .640625 | | | | 63 | .984375 |
| | 5 | 10 | 20 | .3125 | | | 21 | 42 | .65625 | 8 | 16 | 32 | 64 | 1. |
| | | | 21 | .328125 | | | | 43 | .671875 | | | | | |
| | | 11 | 22 | .34375 | | | 11 22 | 44 | .6875 | | | | | |

## Simple Interest Table

| | Time | 4% | 5% | 6% | 7% | 8% | | Time | 4% | 5% | 6% | 7% | 8% |
|------|------|------|------|------|------|------|------|------|------|------|------|------|------|
| $1.00 | 1 month | $.003 | $.004 | $.005 | $.005 | $.006 | $100.00 | 4 days | $.045 | $.053 | $.066 | $.077 | $.889 |
| " | 2 months | .007 | .008 | .010 | .011 | .013 | " | 5 | .056 | .069 | .082 | .097 | .111 |
| " | 3 | .010 | .013 | .015 | .017 | .020 | " | 6 | .067 | .083 | .100 | .116 | .133 |
| " | 6 | .020 | .025 | .030 | .035 | .040 | " | 1 month | .334 | .416 | .500 | .583 | .667 |
| " | 12 | .040 | .050 | .060 | .070 | .080 | " | 2 months | .667 | .832 | 1.000 | 1.166 | 1.333 |
| $100.00 | 1 day | .011 | .013 | .016 | .019 | .022 | " | 3 | 1.000 | 1.250 | 1.500 | 1.750 | 2.000 |
| " | 2 days | .022 | .027 | .032 | .038 | .044 | " | 6 | 2.000 | 2.500 | 3.000 | 3.500 | 4.000 |
| " | 3 | .033 | .041 | .050 | .058 | .067 | " | 12 | 4.000 | 5.000 | 6.000 | 7.000 | 8.000 |

# Mathematical Formulas

### To find the CIRCUMFERENCE of a:

Circle — Multiply the diameter by 3.14159265 (usually 3.1416).

### To find the AREA of a:

Circle — Multiply the square of the diameter by .785398 (usually .7854).
Rectangle — Multiply the length of the base by the height.
Sphere (surface) — Multiply the square of the radius by 3.1416 and multiply by 4.

Square — Square the length of one side.
Trapezoid — Add the two parallel sides, multiply by the height and divide by 2.
Triangle — Multiply the base by the height and divide by 2.

### To find the VOLUME of a:

Cone — Multiply the square of the radius of the base by 3.1416, multiply by the height, and divide by 3.
Cube — Cube the length of one edge.
Cylinder — Multiply the square of the radius of the base by 3.1416 and multiply by the height.
Pyramid — Multiply the area of the base by the height and

divide by 3.
Rectangular Prism — Multiply the length by the width by the height.
Sphere — Multiply the cube of the radius by 3.1416, multiply by 4 and divide by 3.

# Playing Cards and Dice Chances

## Poker Hands

| Hand | Number possible | Odds against |
|---|---|---|
| Royal flush | 4 | 649,739 to 1 |
| Other straight flush | 36 | 72,192 to 1 |
| Four of a kind | 624 | 4,164 to 1 |
| Full house | 3,744 | 693 to 1 |
| Flush | 5,108 | 508 to 1 |
| Straight | 10,200 | 254 to 1 |
| Three of a kind | 54,912 | 46 to 1 |
| Two pairs | 123,552 | 20 to 1 |
| One pair | 1,098,240 | 4 to 3 (1.37 to 1) |
| Nothing | 1,302,540 | 1 to 1 |
| **Total** | **2,598,960** | |

## Dice
### (Probabilities of consecutive winning plays)

| No. consecutive wins | By 7, 11, or point | No. consecutive wins | By 7, 11 or point |
|---|---|---|---|
| 1 | 244 in 495 | 6 | 1 in 70 |
| 2 | 6 in 25 | 7 | 1 in 141 |
| 3 | 3 in 25 | 8 | 1 in 287 |
| 4 | 1 in 17 | 9 | 1 in 582 |
| 5 | 1 in 34 | | |

## Dice
### (probabilities on 2 dice)

| Total | Odds against (Single toss) | Total | Odds against (Single toss) |
|---|---|---|---|
| 2 | 35 to 1 | 8 | 31 to 5 |
| 3 | 17 to 1 | 9 | 8 to 1 |
| 4 | 11 to 1 | 10 | 11 to 1 |
| 5 | 8 to 1 | 11 | 17 to 1 |
| 6 | 31 to 5 | 12 | 35 to 1 |
| 7 | 5 to 1 | | |

## Pinochle Auction
### (Odds against finding in "widow" of 3 cards)

| Open places | Odds against | Open places | Odds against |
|---|---|---|---|
| 1 | 5 to 1 | 4 | 3 to 2 for |
| 2 | 2 to 1 | 5 | 2 to 1 for |
| 3 | Even | | |

## Bridge

The odds—against suit distribution in a hand of 4-4-3-2 are about 4 to 1, against 5-4-2-2 about 8 to 1, against 6-4-2-1 about 20 to 1, against 7-4-1-1 about 254 to 1, against 8-4-1-0 about 2,211 to 1, and against 13-0-0-0 about 158,753,389,899 to 1.

# Medical Signs and Abbreviations

**Source:** American Medical Association

| | | |
|---|---|---|
| ℞ (Lat. Recipe) | take | |
| ʒ | drachm | |
| f ʒ | fluid drachm | |
| ℥ | ounce | |
| f ℥ | fluid ounce | |
| ℥ ss | half an ounce | |
| ℥ i | one ounce | |
| ℥ iss | one ounce and a half | |
| ℥ii | 2 ounces | |
| m. | minim, or drop | |
| o | pint | |
| aa | of each | |
| a.c. | before meals | |
| ad | to, up to | |
| ad libitum | at pleasure | |
| agit | shake | |
| aqua | water | |

| | |
|---|---|
| b.i.d. | twice daily |
| cap | capsule |
| cum, or c | with |
| e.m.p. | as directed |
| fiant(ft) | make |
| gargarisma | a gargle |
| Gm | gram |
| gr. | grain |
| gtt | drops |
| h.s. | at bedtime |
| inject | injection |
| lb. | pound |
| m. | mix |
| mg | milligram |
| ml | milliliter |

| | |
|---|---|
| non. rep. or n.r. | do not repeat |
| p.c. | after meals |
| p.r.n. | as circumstances may require |
| pulvis | powder |
| q. 3 h. | every 3 hours |
| q.i.d. | 4 times daily |
| q.s. | as much as is sufficient |
| sig. | sign, write |
| solutio. | a solution |
| ss | one-half |
| stat | at once |
| tab | tablet |
| t.i.d. | 3 times daily |
| ung | ointment |
| ut dict | as directed |

# Large Numbers

| U.S., French | Number of zeros | British, German | U.S., French | Number of zeros | British, German |
|---|---|---|---|---|---|
| million | 6 | million | sextillion | 21 | 1,000 trillion |
| billion | 9 | milliard | septillion | 24 | quadrillion |
| trillion | 12 | billion | octillion | 27 | 1,000 quadrillion |
| quadrillion | 15 | 1,000 billion | nonillion | 30 | quintillion |
| quintillion | 18 | trillion | decillion | 33 | 1,000 quintillion |

## Squares, Square Roots, Cubes and Cube Roots of Nos. 1 to 100

Square and cube roots are approximate

| No. | Sq. | Cube | Sq. root | Cube root | No. | Sq. | Cube | Sq. root | Cube root | No. | Sq. | Cube | Sq. root | Cube root |
|---|---|---|---|---|---|---|---|---|---|---|---|---|---|---|
| 1 | 1.000 | 1.000 | 1.000 | 1.000 | 35 | 1225 | 42875 | 5.916 | 3.271 | 68 | 4624 | 314432 | 8.246 | 4.081 |
| 2 | 4 | 8 | 1.414 | 1.259 | 36 | 1296 | 46656 | 6.000 | 3.301 | 69 | 4761 | 328509 | 8.306 | 4.101 |
| 3 | 9 | 27 | 1.732 | 1.442 | 37 | 1369 | 50653 | 6.082 | 3.332 | 70 | 4900 | 343000 | 8.366 | 4.121 |
| 4 | 16 | 64 | 2.000 | 1.587 | 38 | 1444 | 54872 | 6.164 | 3.362 | 71 | 5041 | 357911 | 8.426 | 4.140 |
| 5 | 25 | 125 | 2.236 | 1.710 | 39 | 1521 | 59319 | 6.244 | 3.391 | 72 | 5184 | 373248 | 8.485 | 4.160 |
| 6 | 36 | 216 | 2.449 | 1.817 | 40 | 1600 | 64000 | 6.324 | 3.420 | 73 | 5329 | 389017 | 8.544 | 4.179 |
| 7 | 49 | 343 | 2.645 | 1.913 | 41 | 1681 | 68921 | 6.403 | 3.448 | 74 | 5476 | 405224 | 8.602 | 4.198 |
| 8 | 64 | 512 | 2.828 | 2.000 | 42 | 1764 | 74088 | 6.480 | 3.476 | 75 | 5625 | 421875 | 8.660 | 4.217 |
| 9 | 81 | 729 | 3.000 | 2.080 | 43 | 1849 | 79507 | 6.557 | 3.503 | 76 | 5776 | 438976 | 8.717 | 4.235 |
| 10 | 100 | 1000 | 3.162 | 2.154 | 44 | 1936 | 85184 | 6.633 | 3.530 | 77 | 5929 | 456533 | 8.775 | 4.254 |
| 11 | 121 | 1331 | 3.316 | 2.224 | 45 | 2025 | 91125 | 6.708 | 3.556 | 78 | 6084 | 474552 | 8.831 | 4.272 |
| 12 | 144 | 1728 | 3.464 | 2.289 | 46 | 2116 | 97336 | 6.782 | 3.583 | 79 | 6241 | 493039 | 8.888 | 4.290 |
| 13 | 169 | 2197 | 3.605 | 2.351 | 47 | 2209 | 103823 | 6.855 | 3.608 | 80 | 6400 | 512000 | 8.944 | 4.308 |
| 14 | 196 | 2744 | 3.741 | 2.410 | 48 | 2304 | 110592 | 6.928 | 3.634 | 81 | 6561 | 531441 | 9.000 | 4.326 |
| 15 | 225 | 3375 | 3.873 | 2.466 | 49 | 2401 | 117649 | 7.000 | 3.659 | 82 | 6724 | 551368 | 9.055 | 4.344 |
| 16 | 256 | 4096 | 4.000 | 2.519 | 50 | 2500 | 125000 | 7.071 | 3.684 | 83 | 6889 | 571787 | 9.110 | 4.362 |
| 17 | 289 | 4913 | 4.123 | 2.571 | 51 | 2601 | 132651 | 7.141 | 3.708 | 84 | 7056 | 592704 | 9.165 | 4.379 |
| 18 | 324 | 5832 | 4.242 | 2.620 | 52 | 2704 | 140608 | 7.211 | 3.732 | 85 | 7225 | 614125 | 9.219 | 4.396 |
| 19 | 361 | 6859 | 4.358 | 2.668 | 53 | 2809 | 148877 | 7.280 | 3.756 | 86 | 7396 | 636056 | 9.273 | 4.414 |
| 20 | 400 | 8000 | 4.472 | 2.714 | 54 | 2916 | 157464 | 7.348 | 3.779 | 87 | 7569 | 658503 | 9.327 | 4.431 |
| 21 | 441 | 9261 | 4.582 | 2.758 | 55 | 3025 | 166375 | 7.416 | 3.803 | 88 | 7744 | 681472 | 9.380 | 4.448 |
| 22 | 484 | 10648 | 4.690 | 2.802 | 56 | 3136 | 175616 | 7.483 | 3.825 | 89 | 7921 | 704969 | 9.434 | 4.464 |
| 23 | 529 | 12167 | 4.795 | 2.843 | 57 | 3249 | 185193 | 7.549 | 3.848 | 90 | 8100 | 729000 | 9.486 | 4.481 |
| 24 | 576 | 13824 | 4.899 | 2.884 | 58 | 3364 | 195112 | 7.615 | 3.870 | 91 | 8281 | 753571 | 9.539 | 4.497 |
| 25 | 625 | 15625 | 5.000 | 2.924 | 59 | 3481 | 205379 | 7.681 | 3.893 | 92 | 8464 | 778688 | 9.591 | 4.514 |
| 26 | 676 | 17576 | 5.099 | 2.962 | 60 | 3600 | 216000 | 7.746 | 3.914 | 93 | 8649 | 804357 | 9.643 | 4.530 |
| 27 | 729 | 19683 | 5.196 | 3.000 | 61 | 3721 | 226981 | 7.810 | 3.936 | 94 | 8836 | 830584 | 9.695 | 4.546 |
| 28 | 784 | 21952 | 5.291 | 3.036 | 62 | 3844 | 238328 | 7.874 | 3.957 | 95 | 9025 | 857375 | 9.746 | 4.562 |
| 29 | 841 | 24389 | 5.385 | 3.072 | 63 | 3969 | 250047 | 7.937 | 3.979 | 96 | 9216 | 884736 | 9.798 | 4.578 |
| 30 | 900 | 27000 | 5.477 | 3.107 | 64 | 4096 | 262144 | 8.000 | 4.000 | 97 | 9409 | 912673 | 9.848 | 4.594 |
| 31 | 961 | 29791 | 5.567 | 3.141 | 65 | 4225 | 274625 | 8.062 | 4.020 | 98 | 9604 | 941192 | 9.899 | 4.610 |
| 32 | 1024 | 32768 | 5.656 | 3.174 | 66 | 4356 | 287496 | 8.124 | 4.041 | 99 | 9801 | 970299 | 9.949 | 4.626 |
| 33 | 1089 | 25937 | 5.744 | 3.207 | 67 | 4489 | 300763 | 8.185 | 4.061 | 100 | 10000 | 1000000 | 10.000 | 4.641 |
| 34 | 1156 | 39304 | 5.831 | 3.239 | | | | | | | | | | |

## Square Roots and Cube Roots, 1000 to 2000

| No. | Square root | Cube root | No. | Square root | Cube root | No. | Square root | Cube root | No. | Square root | Cube root |
|---|---|---|---|---|---|---|---|---|---|---|---|
| 1000 | 31.62 | 10.00 | 1255 | 35.43 | 10.79 | 1510 | 38.86 | 11.47 | 1765 | 42.01 | 12.09 |
| 1005 | 31.70 | 10.02 | 1260 | 35.50 | 10.80 | 1515 | 38.92 | 11.49 | 1770 | 42.07 | 12.10 |
| 1010 | 31.78 | 10.03 | 1265 | 35.57 | 10.82 | 1520 | 38.99 | 11.50 | 1775 | 42.13 | 12.11 |
| 1020 | 31.94 | 10.07 | 1275 | 35.71 | 10.84 | 1530 | 39.12 | 11.52 | 1785 | 42.25 | 12.13 |
| 1025 | 32.02 | 10.08 | 1280 | 35.78 | 10.86 | 1535 | 39.18 | 11.54 | 1790 | 42.31 | 12.14 |
| 1030 | 32.09 | 10.10 | 1285 | 35.85 | 10.87 | 1540 | 39.24 | 11.55 | 1795 | 42.37 | 12.15 |
| 1035 | 32.17 | 10.12 | 1290 | 35.92 | 10.89 | 1545 | 39.31 | 11.56 | 1800 | 42.43 | 12.16 |
| 1045 | 32.33 | 10.15 | 1300 | 36.06 | 10.91 | 1555 | 39.43 | 11.59 | 1810 | 42.54 | 12.19 |
| 1050 | 32.40 | 10.16 | 1305 | 36.12 | 10.93 | 1560 | 39.50 | 11.60 | 1815 | 42.60 | 12.20 |
| 1060 | 32.56 | 10.20 | 1315 | 36.26 | 10.96 | 1570 | 39.62 | 11.62 | 1825 | 42.72 | 12.22 |
| 1065 | 32.63 | 10.21 | 1320 | 36.33 | 10.97 | 1575 | 39.69 | 11.63 | 1830 | 42.78 | 12.23 |
| 1075 | 32.79 | 10.24 | 1330 | 36.47 | 11.00 | 1585 | 39.81 | 11.66 | 1840 | 42.90 | 12.25 |
| 1080 | 32.86 | 10.26 | 1335 | 36.54 | 11.01 | 1590 | 39.87 | 11.67 | 1845 | 42.95 | 12.26 |
| 1085 | 32.94 | 10.28 | 1340 | 36.61 | 11.02 | 1595 | 39.94 | 11.68 | 1850 | 43.01 | 12.28 |
| 1090 | 33.02 | 10.29 | 1345 | 36.67 | 11.04 | 1600 | 40.00 | 11.70 | 1855 | 43.07 | 12.29 |
| 1095 | 33.09 | 10.31 | 1350 | 36.74 | 11.05 | 1605 | 40.06 | 11.71 | 1860 | 43.13 | 12.30 |
| 1100 | 33.17 | 10.32 | 1355 | 36.81 | 11.07 | 1610 | 40.12 | 11.72 | 1865 | 43.19 | 12.31 |
| 1105 | 33.24 | 10.34 | 1360 | 36.88 | 11.08 | 1615 | 40.19 | 11.73 | 1870 | 43.24 | 12.32 |
| 1110 | 33.32 | 10.35 | 1365 | 36.95 | 11.09 | 1620 | 40.25 | 11.74 | 1875 | 43.30 | 12.33 |
| 1115 | 33.39 | 10.37 | 1370 | 37.01 | 11.11 | 1625 | 40.31 | 11.76 | 1880 | 43.36 | 12.34 |
| 1120 | 33.47 | 10.38 | 1375 | 37.08 | 11.12 | 1630 | 40.37 | 11.77 | 1885 | 43.42 | 12.35 |
| 1125 | 33.54 | 10.40 | 1380 | 37.15 | 11.13 | 1635 | 40.44 | 11.78 | 1890 | 43.47 | 12.36 |
| 1130 | 33.62 | 10.42 | 1385 | 37.22 | 11.15 | 1640 | 40.50 | 11.79 | 1895 | 43.53 | 12.37 |
| 1135 | 33.69 | 10.43 | 1390 | 37.28 | 11.16 | 1645 | 40.56 | 11.80 | 1900 | 43.59 | 12.39 |
| 1140 | 33.76 | 10.45 | 1395 | 37.35 | 11.17 | 1650 | 40.62 | 11.82 | 1905 | 43.65 | 12.40 |
| 1145 | 33.84 | 10.46 | 1400 | 37.42 | 11.19 | 1655 | 40.68 | 11.83 | 1910 | 43.70 | 12.41 |
| 1150 | 33.91 | 10.48 | 1405 | 37.48 | 11.20 | 1660 | 40.74 | 11.84 | 1915 | 43.76 | 12.42 |
| 1155 | 33.99 | 10.49 | 1410 | 37.55 | 11.21 | 1665 | 40.80 | 11.85 | 1920 | 43.82 | 12.43 |
| 1160 | 34.06 | 10.51 | 1415 | 37.62 | 11.23 | 1670 | 40.87 | 11.86 | 1925 | 43.87 | 12.44 |
| 1165 | 34.13 | 10.52 | 1420 | 37.68 | 11.24 | 1675 | 40.93 | 11.88 | 1930 | 43.93 | 12.45 |
| 1170 | 34.21 | 10.54 | 1425 | 37.75 | 11.25 | 1680 | 40.99 | 11.89 | 1935 | 43.99 | 12.46 |
| 1175 | 34.28 | 10.55 | 1430 | 37.82 | 11.27 | 1685 | 41.05 | 11.90 | 1940 | 44.05 | 12.47 |
| 1180 | 34.35 | 10.57 | 1435 | 37.88 | 11.28 | 1690 | 41.11 | 11.91 | 1945 | 44.10 | 12.48 |
| 1185 | 34.42 | 10.58 | 1440 | 37.95 | 11.29 | 1695 | 41.17 | 11.92 | 1950 | 44.16 | 12.49 |
| 1190 | 34.50 | 10.60 | 1445 | 38.01 | 11.31 | 1700 | 41.23 | 11.93 | 1955 | 44.22 | 12.50 |
| 1195 | 34.57 | 10.61 | 1450 | 38.08 | 11.32 | 1705 | 41.29 | 11.95 | 1960 | 44.27 | 12.51 |
| 1200 | 34.64 | 10.63 | 1455 | 38.14 | 11.33 | 1710 | 41.35 | 11.96 | 1965 | 44.33 | 12.53 |
| 1205 | 34.71 | 10.64 | 1460 | 38.21 | 11.34 | 1715 | 41.41 | 11.97 | 1970 | 44.38 | 12.54 |
| 1210 | 34.79 | 10.66 | 1465 | 32.28 | 11.36 | 1720 | 41.47 | 11.98 | 1975 | 44.44 | 12.55 |
| 1215 | 34.86 | 10.67 | 1470 | 38.34 | 11.37 | 1725 | 41.53 | 11.99 | 1980 | 44.50 | 12.56 |
| 1220 | 34.93 | 10.69 | 1475 | 38.41 | 11.38 | 1730 | 41.59 | 12.00 | 1985 | 44.55 | 12.57 |
| 1225 | 35.00 | 10.70 | 1480 | 38.47 | 11.40 | 1735 | 41.65 | 12.02 | 1990 | 44.61 | 12.58 |
| 1235 | 35.14 | 10.73 | 1490 | 38.60 | 11.42 | 1745 | 41.77 | 12.04 | 1995 | 44.67 | 12.59 |
| 1245 | 35.28 | 10.76 | 1500 | 38.73 | 11.45 | 1755 | 41.89 | 12.06 | 2000 | 44.72 | 12.60 |

## Roman Numerals

| | | | | | | | | | | | |
|---|---|---|---|---|---|---|---|---|---|---|---|
| I | – 1 | VI | – 6 | XI | – 11 | L | – 50 | CD | – 400 | X̄ | – 10,000 |
| II | – 2 | VII | – 7 | XIX | – 19 | LX | – 60 | D | – 500 | L̄ | – 50,000 |
| III | – 3 | VIII | – 8 | XX | – 20 | XC | – 90 | CM | – 900 | C̄ | – 100,000 |
| IV | – 4 | IX | – 9 | XXX | – 30 | C | – 100 | M | – 1,000 | D̄ | – 500,000 |
| V | – 5 | X | – 10 | XL | – 40 | CC | – 200 | V̄ | – 5,000 | M̄ | – 1,000,000 |

# Chemical Elements, Discoverers, Atomic Weights

Atomic weights, based on the exact number 12 as the assigned atomic mass of the principal isotope of carbon, carbon 12, are provided through the courtesy of the International Union of Pure and Applied Chemistry and Butterworth Scientific Publications.

For the radioactive elements, with the exception of uranium and thorium, the mass number of either the isotope of longest half-life (*) or the better known isotope (**) is given.

| Chemical element | Symbol | Atomic number | Atomic weight | Year discov. | Discoverer |
|---|---|---|---|---|---|
| Actinium | Ac | 89 | 227* | 1899 | Debierne |
| Aluminum | Al | 13 | 26.9815 | 1825 | Oersted |
| Americium | Am | 95 | 243* | 1944 | Seaborg, et al. |
| Antimony | Sb | 51 | 121.75 | 1450 | Valentine |
| Argon | Ar | 18 | 39.948 | 1894 | Rayleigh, Ramsay |
| Arsenic | As | 33 | 74.9216 | 13th c. | Albertus Magnus |
| Astatine | At | 85 | 210* | 1940 | Corson, et al. |
| Barium | Ba | 56 | 137.34 | 1808 | Davy |
| Berkelium | Bk | 97 | 249** | 1949 | Thompson, Ghiorso, Seaborg |
| Beryllium | Be | 4 | 9.0122 | 1798 | Vanquelin |
| Bismuth | Bi | 83 | 208.980 | 15th c. | Valentine |
| Boron | B | 5 | 10.811a | 1808 | Davy |
| Bromine | Br | 35 | 79.904b | 1826 | Balard |
| Cadmium | Cd | 48 | 112.40 | 1817 | Stromeyer |
| Calcium | Ca | 20 | 40.08 | 1808 | Davy |
| Californium | Cf | 98 | 249** | 1950 | Thompson, et al. |
| Carbon | C | 6 | 12.01115a | B.C. | |
| Cerium | Ce | 58 | 140.12 | 1803 | Klaproth |
| Cesium | Cs | 55 | 132.905 | 1861 | Bunsen Kirchhoff |
| Chlorine | Cl | 17 | 35.453b | 1774 | Scheele |
| Chromium | Cr | 24 | 51.996b | 1797 | Vanquelin |
| Cobalt | Co | 27 | 58.9332 | 1735 | Brandt |
| Copper | Cu | 29 | 63.546b | B.C. | |
| Curium | Cm | 96 | 247* | 1944 | Seaborg, et al. |
| Dysprosium | Dy | 66 | 162.50 | 1886 | Boisbaudran |
| Einsteinium | Es | 99 | 254* | 1952 | Ghiorso, et al. |
| Erbium | Er | 68 | 167.26 | 1843 | Mosander |
| Europium | Eu | 63 | 151.96 | 1901 | Demarcay |
| Fermium | Fm | 100 | 257* | 1953 | Ghiorso, et al. |
| Fluorine | F | 9 | 18.9984 | 1771 | Scheele |
| Francium | Fr | 87 | 223* | 1939 | Perey |
| Gadolinium | Gd | 64 | 157.25 | 1886 | Marignac |
| Gallium | Ga | 31 | 69.72 | 1875 | Boisbaudran |
| Germanium | Ge | 32 | 72.59 | 1886 | Winkler |
| Gold | Au | 79 | 196.967 | B.C. | |
| Hafnium | Hf | 72 | 178.49 | 1923 | Coster, Hevesy |
| Hahnium | Ha | 105 | 262* | 1970 | Ghiorso, et al. |
| Helium | He | 2 | 4.0026 | 1895 | Ramsay |
| Holmium | Ho | 67 | 164.930 | 1879 | Cleve |
| Hydrogen | H | 1 | 1.00797a | 1766 | Cavendish |
| Indium | In | 49 | 114.82 | 1863 | Reich, Richter |
| Iodine | I | 53 | 126.9044 | 1811 | Courtois |
| Iridium | Ir | 77 | 192.2 | 1804 | Tennant |
| Iron | Fe | 26 | 55.847b | B.C. | |
| Krypton | Kr | 36 | 83.80 | 1898 | Ramsay, Travers |
| Lanthanum | La | 57 | 138.91 | 1839 | Mosander |
| Lawrencium | Lr | 103 | 260* | 1961 | Ghiorso, T. Sikkeland, A.E. Larsh, and R.M. Latimer |
| Lead | Pb | 82 | 207.19 | B.C. | |
| Lithium | Li | 3 | 6.939 | 1817 | Arfvedson |
| Lutetium | Lu | 71 | 174.97 | 1907 | Welsbach, Urbain |
| Magnesium | Mg | 12 | 24.312 | 1830 | Liebig, Bussy |
| Manganese | Mn | 25 | 54.9380 | 1774 | Gahn |
| Mendelevium | Md | 101 | 258* | 1955 | Ghiorso, et al. |
| Mercury | Hg | 80 | 200.59 | B.C. | |
| Molybdenum | Mo | 42 | 95.94 | 1782 | Hjelm |
| Neodymium | Nd | 60 | 144.24 | 1885 | Welsbach |
| Neon | Ne | 10 | 20.183 | 1898 | Ramsay, Travers |
| Neptunium | Np | 93 | 237* | 1940 | McMillan, Abelson |
| Nickel | Ni | 28 | 58.71 | 1751 | Cronstedt |
| Niobium[1] | Nb | 41 | 92.906 | 1801 | Hatchett |
| Nitrogen | N | 7 | 14.0067 | 1772 | Rutherford |
| Nobelium | No | 102 | 259* | 1958 | Ghiorso, et al. |
| Osmium | Os | 76 | 190.2 | 1804 | Tennant |
| Oxygen | O | 8 | 15.9994a | 1774 | Priestley, Scheele |
| Palladium | Pd | 46 | 106.4 | 1803 | Wollaston |
| Phosphorus | P | 15 | 30.9738 | 1669 | Brandt |
| Platinum | Pt | 78 | 195.09 | 1735 | Ulloa |
| Plutonium | Pu | 94 | 242** | 1940 | Seaborg, et al. |
| Polonium | Po | 84 | 210** | 1898 | P. and M. Curie |
| Potassium | K | 19 | 39.102 | 1807 | Davy |
| Praseodymium | Pr | 59 | 140.907 | 1885 | Welsbach |
| Promethium | Pm | 61 | 147** | 1945 | Glendenin, Marinsky |
| Protactinium | Pa | 91 | 231* | 1917 | Hahn, Meitner |
| Radium | Ra | 88 | 226* | 1898 | P. & M. Curie, Bemont |
| Radon | Rn | 86 | 222* | 1900 | Dorn |
| Rhenium | Re | 75 | 186.2 | 1925 | Noddack, Tacke |
| Rhodium | Rh | 45 | 102.905 | 1803 | Wollaston |
| Rubidium | Rb | 37 | 85.47 | 1861 | Bunsen, Kirchhoff |
| Ruthenium | Ru | 44 | 101.07 | 1845 | Claus |
| Rutherfordium | Rf | 104 | 261* | 1969 | Ghiorso, et al. |

| Chemical element | Symbol | Atomic number | Atomic weight | Year discov. | Discoverer |
|---|---|---|---|---|---|
| Samarium | Sm. | 62 | 150.35 | 1879 | Boisbaudran |
| Scandium | Sc | 21 | 44.956 | 1879 | Nilson |
| Silicon | Si | 14 | 28.086a | 1823 | Berzelius |
| Silver | Ag | 47 | 107.868b | B.C. | |
| Sodium | Na | 11 | 22.9898 | 1807 | Davy |
| Strontium | Sr | 38 | 87.62 | 1790 | Crawford |
| Sulfur | S. | 16 | 32.064a | B.C. | |
| Tantalum | Ta | 73 | 180.948 | 1802 | Eckeberg |
| Technetium | Tc | 43 | 99** | 1937 | Perrier and Segre |
| Tellurium | Te | 52 | 127.60 | 1782 | Von Reichenstein |
| Terbium | Tb | 65 | 158.924 | 1843 | Mosander |
| Thallium | Tl | 81 | 204.37 | 1861 | Crookes |
| Thorium | Th | 90 | 232.038 | 1828 | Berzelius |
| Thulium | Tm. | 69 | 168.934 | 1879 | Cleve |
| Tin | Sn | 50 | 118.69 | B.C. | |
| Titanium | Ti | 22 | 47.90 | 1789 | Gregor |
| Tungsten (Wolfram) | W | 74 | 183.85 | 1783 | d'Elhujar |
| Uranium | U. | 92 | 238.03 | 1789 | Klaproth |
| Vanadium | V. | 23 | 50.942 | 1830 | Sefstrom |
| Xenon | Xe | 54 | 131.30 | 1898 | Ramsay, Travers |
| Ytterbium | Yb | 70 | 173.04 | 1878 | Marignac |
| Yttrium | Y. | 39 | 88.905 | 1794 | Gadolin |
| Zinc | Zn | 30 | 65.37 | B.C. | |
| Zirconium | Zr | 40 | 91.22 | 1789 | Klaproth |

(1) Formerly Columbium. (a) Atomic weights so designated are known to be variable because of natural variations in isotopic composition. The observed ranges are: hydrogen±0.0001; boron±0.003; carbon±0.005; oxygen±0.0001; silicon±0.001; sulfur±0.003. (b) Atomic weights so designated are believed to have the following experimental uncertainties: chlorine±0.001; chromium±0.001; iron±0.003; bromine±0.001; silver±0.001; copper±0.001.

## Inventions and Scientific Discoveries

| Invention | Date | Inventor | Nation. |
|---|---|---|---|
| Adding machine | 1642 | Pascal. | French |
| Adding machine | 1885 | Burroughs | U.S. |
| Addressograph | 1892 | Duncan | U.S. |
| Aerosol spray | 1941 | Goodhue | U.S. |
| Air brake | 1868 | Westinghouse | U.S. |
| Air conditioning | 1911 | Carrier | U.S. |
| Air pump | 1650 | Guericke | German |
| Airplane, automatic pilot | 1929 | Green | U.S. |
| Airplane, experimental | 1896 | Langley | U.S. |
| Airplane jet engine | 1939 | Ohain | German |
| Airplane with motor | 1903 | Wright bros. | U.S. |
| Airplane, hydro | 1911 | Curtiss | U.S. |
| Airship | 1852 | Giffard | French |
| Airship, rigid dirigible | 1900 | Zeppelin | German |
| Arc tube | 1923 | Alexanderson | U.S.. |
| Autogyro | 1920 | de la Cierva | Spanish |
| Automobile, differential gear | 1885 | Benz. | German |
| Automobile, electric | 1892 | Morrison | U.S. |
| Automobile, exp'mtl | 1875 | Marcus | Austrian |
| Automobile, gasoline | 1887 | Daimler | German |
| Automobile, gasoline | 1892 | Duryea | U.S. |
| Automobile, magneto | 1897 | Bosch | German |
| Automobile muffler | ... | Maxim, H.P. | U.S. |
| Automobile self-starter | 1911 | Kettering | U.S. |
| Automobile, steam | 1889 | Roper | U.S. |
| Babbitt metal | 1839 | Babbit | U.S. |
| Bakelite | 1907 | Baekeland | Belg., U.S. |
| Balloon | 1783 | Montgolfier | French |
| Barometer | 1643 | Torricelli | Italian |
| Bicycle, modern | 1884 | Starley | English |
| Bifocal lens | 1780 | Franklin | U.S. |
| Block signals, railway | 1867 | Hall | U.S. |
| Bomb, depth | 1916 | Tait | U.S. |
| Bottle machine | 1903 | Owens | U.S. |
| Braille printing | 1829 | Braille | French |
| Burner, gas | 1855 | Bunsen | German |
| Calculating machine | 1823 | Babbage | English |
| Camera—see also Photography | | | |
| Camera, Kodak | 1888 | Eastman, Walker | U.S. |
| Camera, Polaroid Land | 1948 | Land | U.S. |
| Car coupler | 1873 | Janney | U.S. |
| Carburetor, gasoline | 1876 | Daimler | German |
| Card time recorder | 1894 | Cooper | U.S. |
| Carding machine | 1797 | Whittemore | U.S. |
| Carpet sweeper | 1876 | Bissell | U.S. |
| Cash register | 1879 | Ritty | U.S. |
| Cathode ray tube | 1878 | Crookes | English |
| Cellophane | 1911 | Brandenberger | Swiss |
| Celluloid | 1870 | Hyatt | U.S. |

| Invention | Date | Inventor | Nation. |
|---|---|---|---|
| Cement, Portland | 1845 | Aspdin. | English |
| Chronometer | 1735 | Harrison. | English |
| Circuit breaker | 1925 | Hilliard | U.S. |
| Clock, pendulum | 1657 | Huygens | Dutch |
| Coaxial cable system | 1929 | Affel, Espensched | U.S. |
| Coke oven | 1893 | Hoffman | Austrian |
| Compressed air rock drill | 1871 | Ingersoll. | U.S. |
| Comptometer | 1887 | Felt | U.S. |
| Computer, automatic sequence | 1939 | Aiken et al. | U.S. |
| Condenser microphone (telephone) | 1920 | Wente | U.S. |
| Corn, hybrid | 1917 | Jones | U.S. |
| Cotton gin | 1793 | Whitney | U.S. |
| Cream separator | 1880 | DeLaval | Swedish |
| Cultivator, disc | 1878 | Mallon | U.S. |
| Cystoscope | 1877 | Nitze | German |
| Dental plate, rubber | 1855 | Goodyear | U.S. |
| Diesel engine | 1895 | Diesel | German |
| Dynamite | 1866 | Nobel | Swedish |
| Dynamo, continuous current | 1860 | Picinotti | Italian |
| Dynamo, hydrogen cooled | 1915 | Schuler | U.S. |
| Electric battery | 1800 | Volta | Italian |
| Electric fan | 1882 | Wheeler | U.S. |
| Electrocardiograph | 1903 | Einthoven | Dutch |
| Electroencephalograph | 1929 | Berger | German |
| Electromagnet | 1824 | Sturgeon | English |
| Electron spectrometer | 1944 | Deutsch, Elliott, Evans | U.S. |
| Electron tube multigrid | 1913 | Langmuir | U.S. |
| Electroplating | 1805 | Brugnatelli | Italian |
| Electrostatic generator | 1929 | Van de Graaff | U.S. |
| Elevator brake | 1852 | Otis | U.S. |
| Elevator, push button | 1922 | Larson | U.S. |
| Engine, automobile | 1879 | Benz | German |
| Engine, coal-gas 4-cycle | 1877 | Otto | German |
| Engine, compression ignition | 1883 | Daimler | German |
| Engine, electric ignition | 1880 | Benz | German |
| Engine, gas, compound | 1926 | Eickemeyer | U.S. |
| Engine, gasoline | 1872 | Brayton, Geo. | U.S. |
| Engine, gasoline | 1886 | Daimler | German |
| Engine, steam, piston | 1705 | Newcomen | English |
| Engine, steam, piston | 1769 | Watt | Scottish |
| Engraving, half-tone | 1893 | Ives | U.S. |

| Invention | Date | Inventor | Nation. |
|---|---|---|---|
| ament, tungsten | 1915 | Langmuir | U.S. |
| anged rail | 1831 | Stevens | U.S. |
| atiron, electric | 1882 | Seeley | U.S. |
| nace (for steel) | 1861 | Siemens | German |
| lvanometer | 1820 | Sweigger | German |
| s discharge tube | 1922 | Hull | U.S. |
| s lighting | 1792 | Murdoch | Scottish |
| s mantle | 1885 | Welsbach | Austrian |
| soline (lead ethyl) | 1922 | Midgely | U.S. |
| soline, cracked | 1913 | Burton | U.S. |
| soline, high octane | 1930 | Ipatieff | Russian |
| iger counter | 1913 | Geiger | German |
| ass, laminated safety | 1909 | Benedictus | French |
| der | 1853 | Cayley | English |
| n, breechloader | 1811 | Thornton | U.S. |
| n, Browning | 1916 | Browning | U.S. |
| n, magazine | 1875 | Hotchkiss | U.S. |
| n, silencer | 1909 | Maxim, H.P. | U.S. |
| ncotton | 1846 | Schoenbein | German |
| rocompass | 1911 | Sperry | U.S. |
| roscope | 1852 | Foucault | French |
| rvester-thresher | 1888 | Matteson | U.S. |
| licopter | 1939 | Sikorsky | U.S. |
| drometer | 1768 | Baume | French |
| -making machine | 1851 | Gorrie | U.S. |
| n lung | 1928 | Drinker, Slaw | U.S. |
| leidoscope | 1817 | Brewster | English |
| etoscope | 1887 | Edison | U.S. |
| cquer, nitrocellulose | 1921 | Flaherty | U.S. |
| mp, arc | 1879 | Brush | U.S. |
| mp, incandescent | 1879 | Edison | U.S. |
| mp, incand, frosted | 1924 | Pipkin | U.S. |
| mp, incand, gas | 1916 | Langmuir | U.S. |
| mp, Klieg | 1911 | Kliegl, A.&J. | U.S. |
| mp, mercury vapor | 1912 | Hewitt | U.S. |
| mp, miner's safety | 1816 | Davy | English |
| mp, neon | 1915 | Claude | French |
| he, turret | 1845 | Fitch | U.S. |
| underette | 1934 | Cantrell | U.S. |
| ns, achromatic | 1758 | Dollond | English |
| ns, fused bifocal | 1908 | Borsch | U.S. |
| ydenjar (condenser) | 1745 | von Kleist | German |
| oleum | 1860 | Walton | English |
| htning rod | 1752 | Franklin | U.S. |
| otype | 1885 | Mergenthaler | U.S. |
| ck, cylinder | 1865 | Yale | U.S. |
| comotive, electric | 1851 | Vail | U.S. |
| comotive, exp'mtl | 1801 | Trevithick | English |
| comotive, exp'mtl | 1812 | Fenton et al | English |
| comotive, exp'mtl | 1813 | Hedley | English |
| comotive, exp'mtl | 1814 | Stephenson | English |
| comotive practical | 1829 | Stephenson | English |
| comotive, 1st U.S. | 1830 | Cooper, P. | U.S. |
| om, power | 1785 | Cartwright | English |
| udspeaker, dynamic | 1924 | Rice, Kellogg | U.S. |
| achine gun | 1861 | Gatling | U.S. |
| achine gun, improved | 1872 | Hotchkiss | U.S. |
| chine gun (Maxim) | 1883 | Maxim, H.S. | U.S., Eng. |
| gnet, electro | 1828 | Henry | U.S. |
| ntle, gas | 1885 | Welsbach | Austrian |
| ason jar | 1858 | Mason, J. | U.S. |
| tch, friction | 1827 | John Walker | English |
| rcerized textiles | 1843 | Mercer, J. | English |
| ter, induction | 1888 | Shallenberger | U.S. |
| tronome | 1816 | Malzel | Austrian |
| crometer | 1636 | Gascoigne | English |
| crophone | 1877 | Berliner | U.S. |
| croscope, compound | 1590 | Janssen | Dutch |
| croscope, electronic | 1931 | Knoll, Ruska | German |
| croscope, field ion | 1951 | Mueller | Germany |
| onitor, warship | 1861 | Ericsson | U.S. |
| notype | 1887 | Lanston | U.S. |
| tor, AC | 1892 | Tesla | U.S. |
| tor, induction | 1887 | Tesla | U.S. |
| torcycle | 1885 | Daimler | German |
| vie machine | 1894 | Jenkins | U.S. |
| vie, panoramic | 1952 | Waller | U.S. |
| vie, talking | 1927 | Warner Bros. | U.S. |
| wer, lawn | 1868 | Hills | U.S. |
| wing machine | 1831 | Manning | U.S. |
| oprene | 1930 | Carothers | U.S. |
| on synthetic | 1930 | Carothers | U.S. |

| Invention | Date | Inventor | Nation. |
|---|---|---|---|
| Nylon | 1937 | Du Pont lab. | U.S. |
| Oil cracking furnace | 1891 | Gavrilov | Russian |
| Oil filled power cable | 1921 | Emanueli | Italian |
| Oleomargarine | 1868 | Mege-Mouries | French |
| Ophthalmoscope | 1851 | Helmholtz | German |
| Paper machine | 1809 | Dickinson | U.S. |
| Parachute | 1785 | Blanchard | French |
| Pen, ballpoint | 1888 | Loud | U.S. |
| Pen, fountain | 1884 | Waterman | U.S. |
| Pen, steel | 1780 | Harrison | English |
| Pendulum | 1581 | Galileo | Italian |
| Percussion cap | 1814 | Shaw | U.S. |
| Phonograph | 1877 | Edison | U.S. |
| Photo, color | 1892 | Ives | U.S. |
| Photo film, celluloid | 1887 | Goodwin | U.S. |
| Photo film, transparent | 1878 | Eastman, Goodwin | U.S. |
| Photoelectric cell | 1895 | Elster | German |
| Photographic paper | 1898 | Baekeland | U.S. |
| Photography | 1835 | Talbot | English |
| Photography | 1837 | Daguerre | French |
| Photography | 1839 | Niepce | French |
| Photophone | 1880 | Bell | U.S. |
| Phototelegraphy | 1925 | Bell Labs | U.S. |
| Piano | 1709 | Cristofori | Italian |
| Piano, player | 1863 | Fourneaux | French |
| Pin, safety | 1849 | Hunt | U.S. |
| Pistol (revolver) | 1835 | Colt | U.S. |
| Plow, cast iron | 1797 | Newbold | U.S. |
| Plow, disc | 1896 | Hardy | U.S. |
| Pneumatic hammer | 1890 | King | U.S. |
| Powder, smokeless | 1863 | Schultze | German |
| Printing press, rotary | 1846 | Hoe | U.S. |
| Printing press, web | 1865 | Bullock | U.S. |
| Propeller, screw | 1804 | Stevens | U.S. |
| Propeller, screw | 1837 | Ericsson | Swedish |
| Punch card accounting | 1884 | Hollerith | U.S. |
| Radar | 1922 | Taylor, Young | U.S. |
| Radio amplifier | 1907 | De Forest | U.S. |
| Radio beacon | 1928 | Donovan | U.S. |
| Radio crystal oscillator | 1918 | Nicolson | U.S. |
| Radio receiver, cascade tuning | 1913 | Alexanderson | U.S. |
| Radio receiver, heterodyne | 1913 | Fessenden | U.S. |
| Radio transmitter triode modulation | 1914 | Alexanderson | U.S. |
| Radio tube-diode | 1905 | Fleming | English |
| Radio tube oscillator | 1915 | De Forest | U.S. |
| Radio tube triode | 1907 | De Forest | U.S. |
| Radio, signals | 1895 | Marconi | Italian |
| Radio, magnetic detector | 1902 | Marconi | Italian |
| Radio FM 2-path | 1929 | Armstrong | U.S. |
| Rayon | 1883 | Swan | English |
| Razor, electric | 1931 | Schick | U.S. |
| Razor, safety | 1895 | Gillette | U.S. |
| Reaper | 1834 | McCormick | U.S. |
| Record, cylinder | 1887 | Bell, Tainter | U.S. |
| Record, disc | 1887 | Berliner | U.S. |
| Record, long playing | 1948 | Goldmark | U.S. |
| Record, wax cylinder | 1888 | Edison | U.S. |
| Refrigerants, low-boiling fluorine compound | 1930 | Midgely and co-workers | U.S. |
| Refrigerator car | 1868 | David | U.S. |
| Resin, synthetic | 1931 | Hill | English |
| Rifle, repeating | 1860 | Spencer | U.S. |
| Rocket engine | 1929 | Goddard | U.S. |
| Rubber, vulcanized | 1839 | Goodyear | U.S. |
| Saw, band | 1808 | Newberry | English |
| Saw, circular | 1777 | Miller | English |
| Searchlight, arc | 1915 | Sperry | U.S. |
| Sewing machine | 1846 | Howe | U.S. |
| Shoe-sewing machine | 1860 | McKay | U.S. |
| Shrapnel shell | 1784 | Shrapnel | English |
| Shuttle, flying | 1733 | Kay | English |
| Sleeping-car | 1858 | Pullman | U.S. |
| Slide rule | 1620 | Oughtred | English |
| Soap, hardwater | 1928 | Bertsch | German |
| Spectroscope | 1859 | Kirchoff, Bunsen | German |
| Spectroscope (mass) | 1918 | Dempster | U.S. |
| Spinning jenny | 1767 | Hargreaves | English |
| Spinning mule | 1779 | Crompton | English |
| Steamboat, exp'mtl | 1783 | Jouffroy | French |

| Invention | Date | Inventor | Nation |
|---|---|---|---|
| Steamboat, exp'mtl | 1785 | Fitch | U.S. |
| Steamboat, exp'mtl | 1787 | Rumsey | U.S. |
| Steamboat, exp'mtl | 1788 | Miller | Scottish |
| Steamboat, exp'mtl | 1803 | Fulton | U.S. |
| Steamboat, exp'mtl | 1804 | Stevens | U.S. |
| Steamboat, practical | 1802 | Symington | Scottish |
| Steamboat, practical | 1807 | Fulton | U.S. |
| Steam car | 1770 | Cugnot | French |
| Steam turbine | 1884 | Parsons | English |
| Steel | 1856 | Bessemer | English |
| Steel alloy | 1891 | Harvey | U.S. |
| Steel alloy, high-speed | 1901 | Taylor, White | U.S. |
| Steel, electric | 1900 | Heroult | French |
| Steel, manganese | 1884 | Hadfield | English |
| Steel, stainless | 1916 | Brearley | English |
| Stereoscope | 1838 | Wheatstone | English |
| Stethoscope | 1819 | Laennec | French |
| Stethoscope, binaural | 1840 | Cammann | U.S. |
| Stock ticker | 1870 | Edison | U.S. |
| Storage battery, electric | 1812 | Ritter | German |
| Stove, electric | 1896 | Hadaway | U.S. |
| Submarine | 1891 | Holland | U.S. |
| Submarine, even keel | 1894 | Lake | U.S. |
| Submarine, torpedo | 1776 | Bushnell | U.S. |
| Tank, military | 1914 | Swinton | English |
| Tape recorder, magnetic | 1899 | Poulsen | Danish |
| Telegraph, magnetic | 1837 | Morse | U.S. |
| Telegraph, quadruplex | 1874 | Edison | U.S. |
| Telegraph, railroad | ... | Woods | U.S. |
| Telegraph, wireless high frequency | 1896 | Marconi | Italian |
| Telephone | 1876 | Bell | U.S.-Can. |
| Telephone amplifier | 1912 | De Forest | U.S. |
| Telephone, automatic | 1891 | Stowger | U.S. |
| Telephone, radio | 1902 | Poulsen, Fessenden | U.S. |
| Telephone, radio | 1906 | De Forest | U.S. |
| Telephone, radio, l. d | 1915 | AT&T | U.S. |
| Telephone, recording | 1898 | Poulson | Danish |
| Telephone, wireless | 1899 | Collins | U.S. |
| Telescope | 1608 | Lippershey | Neth. |
| Telescope | 1609 | Galileo | Italian |

| Invention | Date | Inventor | Nation |
|---|---|---|---|
| Telescope, astronomical | 1611 | Kepler | German |
| Teletype | 1928 | Morkrum, Kleinschmidt | U.S. |
| Television, iconoscope | 1923 | Zworykin | U.S. |
| Television, electronic | 1927 | Farnsworth | U.S. |
| Television, (mech. scanner) | 1926 | Baird | Scottish |
| Thermometer | 1593 | Galileo | Italian |
| Thermometer | 1710 | Reaumur | French |
| Thermometer, mercury | 1714 | Fahrenheit | German |
| Time recorder | 1890 | Bundy | U.S. |
| Time, self-regulator | 1918 | Bryce | U.S. |
| Tire, double-tube | 1845 | Thompson | English |
| Tire, pneumatic | 1888 | Dunlop | Irish |
| Toaster, automatic | 1918 | Strite | U.S. |
| Tool, pneumatic | 1865 | Law | English |
| Torpedo, marine | 1804 | Fulton | U.S. |
| Tractor, crawler | 1900 | Holt | U.S. |
| Transformer A.C. | 1885 | Stanley | U.S. |
| Transistor | 1947 | Shockley, Brattain, Bardeen | U.S. |
| Trolley car, electric | 1884 | Van Depoel, | |
| | -87 | Sprague | U.S. |
| Tungsten, ductile | 1912 | Coolidge | U.S. |
| Turbine, gas | 1899 | Curtis, C.G. | U.S. |
| Turbine, hydraulic | 1849 | Francis | U.S. |
| Turbine, steam | 1896 | Curtis, C.G. | U.S. |
| Type, movable | 1450 | Gutenberg | German |
| Typewriter | 1868 | Soule, Glidden | U.S. |
| Vacuum cleaner, electric | 1907 | Spangler | U.S. |
| Washer, electric | 1907 | Hurley Co. | U.S. |
| Welding, atomic hydrogen | 1924 | Langmuir, Palmer | U.S. |
| Welding, electric | 1877 | Thomson | U.S. |
| Wind tunnel | 1923 | Munk | U.S. |
| Wire, barbed | 1874 | Glidden | U.S. |
| Wire, barbed | 1875 | Haisn | U.S. |
| X-ray tube | 1913 | Coolidge | U.S. |
| Zipper | 1891 | Judson | U.S. |

## Discoveries and Innovations: Chemistry, Physics, Biology, Medicine

| | Date | Discoverer | Nation |
|---|---|---|---|
| Acetylene gas | 1892 | Wilson | U.S. |
| ACTH | 1949 | Armour & Co. | U.S. |
| Adrenalin | 1901 | Takamine | Japan |
| Aluminum, electrolytic process | 1886 | Hall | U.S. |
| Aluminum, isolated | 1825 | Oersted | Danish |
| Analine dye | 1856 | Perkin | English |
| Anesthesia, ether | 1842 | Long | U.S. |
| Anesthesia, local | 1885 | Koller | Austria |
| Anesthesia, spinal | 1898 | Bier | German |
| Anti-rabies | 1885 | Pasteur | French |
| Antiseptic surgery | 1867 | Lister | English |
| Antitoxin, diphtheria | 1891 | Von Behring | German |
| | | Barnes | U.S. |
| Argyro | 1910 | Ehrlich | German |
| Arsphenamine | 1889 | Dresser | German |
| Aspirin | ... | Mietzsch, et al. | German |
| Atabrine | | | |
| Atomic numbers | 1913 | Moseley | English |
| Atomic theory | 1803 | Dalton | English |
| Atomic time clock | 1947 | Libby | U.S. |
| Atom-smashing theory | 1919 | Rutherford | English |
| Aureomycin | 1948 | Duggar | U.S. |
| Bacitracin | 1945 | Johnson, et al. | U.S. |
| Bacteria (described) | 1676 | Leeuwenhoek | Dutch |
| Barbital | 1903 | Fischer | German |
| Bleaching powder | 1798 | Tennant | English |
| Blood, circulation | 1628 | Harvey | English |
| Bordeaux mixture | 1885 | Millardet | French |
| Bromine from sea | 1924 | Edgar Kramer | U.S. |
| Calcium carbide | 1888 | Wilson | U.S. |
| Calculus | 1670 | Newton | English |
| Camphor synthetic | 1896 | Haller | French |
| Canning (food) | 1804 | Appert | French |
| Carbomycin | 1952 | Tanner | U.S. |
| Carbon oxides | 1925 | Fisher | German |
| Chlorine | 1810 | Davy | English |

| | Date | Discoverer | Nation |
|---|---|---|---|
| Chloroform | 1831 | Guthrie, S. | U.S. |
| Chloromycetin | 1947 | Burkholder | U.S. |
| Classification of plants and animals | 1735 | Linnaeus | Swedish |
| Cocaine | 1860 | Niermann | German |
| Combustion explained | 1777 | Lavoisier | French |
| Conditioned reflex | 1914 | Pavlov | Russian |
| Conteben | 1950 | Belmisch, Mietzsch, Dornagk | German |
| Cortisone | 1936 | Kendall | U.S. |
| Cortisone, synthesis | 1946 | Sarett | U.S. |
| Cosmic rays | 1910 | Gockel | Swiss |
| Cyanimide | 1905 | Frank, Caro | German |
| Cyclotron | 1930 | Lawrence | U.S. |
| DDT (not applied as insecticide until 1939) | 1874 | Zeidler | German |
| Deuterium | 1932 | Urey, Brickwedde, Murphy | U.S. |
| DNA (structure) | 1951 | Crick | English |
| | | Watson | U.S. |
| | | Wilkins | English |
| Electric resistance (law) | 1827 | Ohm | German |
| Electric waves | 1888 | Hertz | German |
| Electrolysis | 1852 | Faraday | English |
| Electromagnetism | 1819 | Oersted | Danish |
| Electron | 1897 | Thomson, J. | English |
| Electron diffraction | 1936 | Thomson, G. | English |
| | | Davisson | U.S. |
| Electroshock treatment | 1938 | Cerletti, Bini | Italy |
| Erythromycin | 1952 | McGuire | U.S. |
| Evolution, natural selection | 1858 | Darwin | English |
| Falling bodies, law | 1590 | Galileo | Italian |

| | Date | Discoverer | Nation. | | Date | Discoverer | Nation. |
|---|---|---|---|---|---|---|---|
| ...ses, law of combining volumes | 1808 | Gay-Lussac | French | Polymixin | 1947 | Ainsworth | English |
| ...ometry, analytic | 1619 | Descartes | French | Positron | 1932 | Anderson | U.S. |
| ...ild (cyanide process for extraction) | 1887 | MacArthur, Forest | British | Proton | 1919 | Rutherford | English |
| ...avitation, law | 1687 | Newton | English | Psychoanalysis | 1900 | Freud | Austrian |
| ...olograph | 1948 | Gabor | British | Quantum theory | 1900 | Planck | German |
| ...man heart transplant | 1967 | Barnard | S. Africa | Quasars | 1963 | Matthews, Sandage | U.S. |
| ...ligo, synthesis of | 1880 | Baeyer | German | Quinine synthetic | 1918 | Rabe | German |
| ...duction, electric | 1830 | Henry | U.S. | Radioactivity | 1896 | Becquerel | French |
| ...sulin | 1922 | Banting, Best, MacLeod | Canada | Radium | 1898 | Curie, Pierre | French |
| ...elligence testing | 1905 | Binet, Simon | French | | | Curie, Marie | Pol.-Fr. |
| ...iazid | 1952 | Hoffman-La-Roche | U.S. | Relativity theory | 1905 | Einstein | German |
| | | Domagk | German | Reserpine | 1949 | Jal Vaikl | Indian |
| ...otopes, theory | 1912 | Soddy | English | Salvarsan (606) | 1910 | Ehrlich | German |
| ...ser (light amplification by stimulated emission of radiation) | 1958 | Townes, Schaw-low | U.S. | Schick test | 1913 | Schick | U.S. |
| ...ght, velocity | 1675 | Roemer | Danish | Silicon | 1823 | Berzelius | Swedish |
| ...ght, wave theory | 1690 | Huygens | Dutch | Streptomycin | 1945 | Waksman | U.S. |
| ...hography | 1796 | Senefelder | Bohemia | Sulfadiazine | 1940 | Roblin | U.S. |
| ...obotomy | 1935 | Egas Moniz | Portugal | Sulfanilamide | 1934 | Domagk | German |
| ...D-25 | 1943 | Hoffman | Swiss | Sulfanilamide theory | 1908 | Gelmo | German |
| ...ndelian laws | 1866 | Mendel | Austrian | Sulfapyridine | 1938 | Ewins, Phelps | English |
| ...ercator projection (map) | 1568 | Mercator (Kremer) | Flemish | Sulfathiazole | ... | Fosbinder, Walter | U.S. |
| ...ethanol | 1925 | Patard | French | Sulfuric acid | 1831 | Phillips | English |
| ...k condensation | 1853 | Borden | U.S. | Sulfuric acid, lead | 1746 | Roebuck | English |
| ...olecular hypothesis | 1811 | Avogadro | Italian | Terramycin | 1950 | Finlay, et al. | U.S. |
| ...tion, laws of | 1687 | Newton | English | Tuberculin | 1890 | Koch | German |
| ...omycin | 1949 | Waksman, Lechevalier | U.S. | Uranium fission (theory) | 1939 | Hahn, Meitner, Strassmann | German |
| ...utron | 1932 | Chadwick | English | | | Bohr | Danish |
| ...ric acid | 1648 | Glauber | German | | | Fermi | Italian |
| ...ric oxide | 1772 | Priestley | English | | | Einstein, Pegran, Wheeler | U.S. |
| ...roglycerin | 1846 | Sobrero | Italian | Uranium fission, atomic reactor | 1942 | Fermi, Szilard | U.S. |
| ...l cracking process | 1891 | Dewar | U.S. | Vaccine, measles | 1954 | Enders, Peebles | U.S. |
| ...xygen | 1774 | Priestley | English | Vaccine, polio | 1953 | Salk | U.S. |
| ...zone | 1840 | Schonbein | German | Vaccine, polio, oral | 1955 | Sabin | U.S. |
| ...per, sulfite process | 1867 | Tilghman | U.S. | Vaccine, rabies | 1885 | Pasteur | French |
| ...per, wood pulp, sulfate process | 1884 | Dahl | German | Vaccine, smallpox | 1796 | Jenner | English |
| ...nicillin | 1929 | Fleming | English | Vaccine, typhus | 1909 | Nicolle | French |
| ...practical use | 1941 | Florey, Chain | English | Van Allen belts, radiation | 1958 | Van Allen | U.S. |
| ...riodic law and table of elements | 1869 | Mendeleyev | Russian | Vitamin A | 1913 | McCollum, Davis | U.S. |
| ...anetary motion, laws | 1609 | Kepler | German | Vitamin B | 1916 | McCollum | U.S. |
| ...utonium fission | 1940 | Kennedy, Wahl, Seaborg, Segre | U.S. | Vitamin C | 1912 | Holst, Froelich | Norway |
| | | | | Vitamin D | 1922 | McCollum | U.S. |
| | | | | Wassermann test | 1906 | Wassermann | German |
| | | | | Xerography | 1938 | Carlson | U.S. |
| | | | | X-ray | 1895 | Roentgen | German |

# Copyright Law of The United States

Source: Copyright Office, Library of Congress

Original works of authorship fixed in any tangible medium of expression are entitled to protection under the copyright law (Title 17 of the United States Code) in accordance with a complete revision of the statute which was signed by President Gerald R. Ford on Oct. 19, 1976 (Public Law 94-553, 90 Stat. 2541). The new law came into effect on Jan. 1, 1978; it supersedes the copyright act of 1909, as amended. Prior to the 1976 Act, there had been only three general revisions of the original copyright law of 1790, namely those of 1831, 1870, and 1909.

## Categories of Works

Copyright protection under the new law extends to original works of authorship fixed in any tangible medium of expression, now known or later developed, from which they can be perceived, reproduced, or otherwise communicated, either directly or with the aid of a machine or device. Works of authorship include books, periodicals and other literary works, musical compositions with accompanying lyrics, dramas and dramatico-musical compositions, pantomimes and choreographic works, motion pictures and other audiovisual works, and sound recordings.

The owner of a copyright is given the exclusive right to reproduce the copyrighted work in copies or phonorecords and distribute them to the public by sale, rental, lease, or lending. The owner of a copyright also enjoys the exclusive right to make derivative works based upon the copyrighted work, to perform the work publicly if it be a literary, musical, dramatic, or choreographic work, a pantomime, motion picture, or other audiovisual work, and in the case of literary, musical, dramatic, and choreographic works, pantomimes, and pictorial, graphic, or sculptural works, including the individual images of a motion picture or other audiovisual work, to display the copyrighted work publicly. All of these rights are subject to certain specified exceptions, including the so-called judicial doctrine of "fair use," which is included in the law for the first time.

The new act also provides special provisions permitting compulsory licensing for the recording and distribution of phonorecords of nondramatic musical compositions, noncommercial transmissions by public broadcasters of published musical and graphic works, performances of copyrighted nondramatic music by means of jukeboxes, and the secondary transmission of copyrighted works on cable television systems.

## Single National System

The new law establishes a single national system of statutory protection for all copyrightable works fixed in tangible form, whether published or unpublished. Prior to Jan. 1, 1978 unpublished works were entitled to protection under the common law of the various states while published works came under the Federal statute.

Registration of a claim to copyright in any work, whether published or unpublished, may be made voluntarily at any time during the copyright term by the owner of the copyright or of any exclusive right in the work. Registration will not be a condition of copyright protection, but will be a prerequisite to an infringement suit. Subject to certain exceptions, the remedies of statutory damages and attorney's fees will not be available for those infringements occurring before registration. Even if registration is not made, copies or phonorecords of works published in the U.S. with notice of copyrights are required to be deposited for the collections of the Library of Congress. This deposit requirement is not a condition of protection, but does render the copyright owner subject to penalties for failure to deposit after a demand by the Register of Copyrights.

## Duration of Copyright

For works created on or after Jan. 1, 1978, copyright subsists from their creation for a term consisting of the life of the author and 50 years after the author's death. For works made for hire, and for anonymous and pseudonymous works (unless the author's identity is revealed in Copyright Office records), the term is 100 years from creation or 75 years from first publication, whichever is shorter.

The new law retains for works already under statutory protection, the present term of copyright of 28 years from first publication (or from registration in some cases), renewable by certain persons for a second term of protection, but it increases the length of the second or renewal period to 47 years. Copyrights in their first 28-year term on Jan. 1, 1978, will still have to be renewed in order to be protected for the full new maximum term of 75 years. Copyrights in their second term on Jan. 1, 1978 were automatically extended to last for a total term of 75 years.

For works that had been created before the new law came into effect but had neither been published nor registered for copyright before Jan. 1, 1978, the term of copyright will generally be computed in the same way as for new works: the life-plus-50 or 75/100-year terms will apply. However, all works in this category are guaranteed at least 25 years of statutory protection. The law specifies that copyright in a work of this kind will not expire before Dec. 31, 2002, and if the work is published before that date the term is extended by another 25 years, through the end of the year 2027.

## Notice of Copyright

Under the 1909 copyright law the copyright notice was the most important requirement for obtaining copyright protection for a published work. For published works, all copies had to bear the prescribed notice from the time of first publication. If a work was published before Jan. 1, 1978 without the required notice, copyright protection was lost permanently and cannot be regained.

The new copyright law requires a notice on copies or phonorecords of sound recordings that are distributed to the public. Errors and omissions, however, will not immediately result in forfeiture of the copyright and can be corrected within prescribed time limits. Innocent infringers misled by an omission or error in the notice will generally be shielded from liability.

The notice of copyright required on all visually perceptible copies published in the U.S. or elsewhere under the 1976 Act consists of the symbol © (the letter C in a circle), the word "Copyright," or the abbreviation "Copr.," and the year of first publication of the work, and the name of the owner of copyright in the work. Example:

© 1979 JOHN DOE

The notice must be affixed in such manner and location as to give reasonable notice of the claim of copyright.

The notice of copyright prescribed for all published phonorecords of sound recordings consists of the symbol ℗ (the letter P in a circle), the year of first publication of the sound recording, and the name of the owner of copyright in the sound recording, placed on the surface of the phonorecord or on the phonorecord label or container in such manner and location as to give reasonable notice of the claim of copyright. Example:

℗ 1979 DOE RECORDS, INC.

## Manufacturing Requirements

Under the 1909 Act certain works had to be manufactured in the U.S. to receive copyright protection. The new law does not make manufacture in the U.S. a condition of protection; additionally, it narrows the coverage of the manufacturing provisions, permits the importation of 2,000 copies manufactured abroad instead of the previous limit of 1,500 copies, and equates manufacture in Canada with manufacture in the U.S. Even the narrower requirement is scheduled to terminate on July 1, 1982.

The manufacturing requirements of the new law apply as a general rule only to the copies of a work that consist "preponderantly of a nondramatic literary material that is in the English language." They do not extend to dramatic, musical, pictorial, or graphic works; foreign language, bilingual or multilingual works; public domain material; or work consisting preponderantly of material not subject to the manufacturing provision.

Under the new statute, compliance with the manufacturing requirements will no longer constitute a condition of copyright, but, in cases where the requirements are not satisfied, the rights with respect to reproduction and the distribution of copies are limited as against certain infringers. Even if copies are imported or distributed in violation of the new law, there would be no effect on the copyright owner's right to make and distribute phonorecords of the work, to make derivative works including dramatizations and motion pictures, and to perform or display the work publicly.

## International Protection

The U.S. has copyright relations with more than 70 countries, under which works of American authors are protected in those countries, and the works of their authors are protected in the U.S. The basic feature of this protection is "national treatment," under which the alien author is treated by a country in the same manner that it treats its own authors. Relations exist by virtue of bilateral agreements or through the Buenos Aires Convention or the Universal Copyright Convention. U.S. legislation implementing the latter convention, which became effective Sept. 16, 1955 gives the works of foreign authors the benefit of exemption from the manufacturing requirements of the U.S. copyright law, provided the works are first published abroad with a copyright notice including the symbol © , the name of the copyright owner and the year date of first publication, and that the work either is by an "author" who is a citizen or subject of a foreign country which belongs to the Convention or is first published in a foreign member country. Conversely, works of U.S. authors are exempt from certain burdensome requirements in particular foreign member countries.

Works published on or after Jan. 1, 1978, are subject to protection under the new copyrights statute if, on the date of first publication, one or more of the authors is a national or domiciliary of the U.S., or is a national, domiciliary, or sovereign authority of a foreign nation that is a party to a copyright treaty to which the United States is also a party, or is a stateless person, regardless of domicile, or if the work is first published either in the U.S. or in a foreign nation that, on the date of first publication is a party to the Universal Copyright Convention.

A U.S. citizen may obtain copyright protection in all countries that are members of the Universal Copyright Convention (UCC), provided the copyright notice appears on all copies from the date of first publication includes the symbol © , together with the name of the copyright owner and the year date of publication. Example:

© JOHN DOE 1979

Further information and application forms may be obtained free of charge by writing to the Copyright Office, The Library of Congress, Washington, D.C. 20559.

# SPORTS OF 1978

## Olympic Games Records

The modern Olympic Games, first held in Athens, Greece, in 1896, were the result of efforts by Baron Pierre de Coubertin, French educator, to promote interest in education and culture, also to foster better international understanding through the universal medium of youth's love of athletics.

His source of inspiration for the Olympic Games was the ancient Greek Olympic Games, most notable of the four Panhellenic celebrations. The games were combined patriotic, religious, and athletic festivals held every four years. The first such recorded festival was that held in 776 B.C., the date from which the Greeks began to keep their calendar by "Olympiads," or four-year spans between the games.

The first Olympiad is said to have consisted merely of a 200-yard foot race near the small city of Olympia, but the games gained in scope and became demonstrations of national pride. Only Greek citizens — amateurs — were permitted to participate. Winners received laurel, wild olive, and palm wreaths and were accorded many special privileges. Under the Roman emperors, the games deteriorated into professional carnivals and circuses. Emperor Theodosius banned them in 394 A.D.

Baron de Coubertin enlisted 9 nations to send athletes to the first modern Olympics in 1896; now more than 100 nations compete. Winter Olympic Games were started in 1924.

### Sites and Unofficial Winners of Games

| | | | |
|---|---|---|---|
| 96 Athens (U.S.) | 1912 Stockholm (U.S.) | 1936 Berlin (Germany) | 1964 Tokyo (U.S.) |
| 00 Paris (U.S.) | 1920 Antwerp (U.S.) | 1948 London (U.S.) | 1968 Mexico City (U.S.) |
| 04 St. Louis (U.S.) | 1924 Paris (U.S.) | 1952 Helsinki (U.S.) | 1972 Munich (USSR) |
| 06 Athens (U.S.)* | 1928 Amsterdam (U.S.) | 1956 Melbourne (USSR) | 1976 Montreal (USSR) |
| 08 London (U.S.) | 1932 Los Angeles (U.S.) | 1960 Rome (USSR) | 1980 Moscow (scheduled) |

*Games not recognized by International Olympic Committee. Games 6 (1916), 12 (1940), and 13 (1944) were not celebrated. East and West Germany began competing separately in 1968.

## Olympic Games Champions, 1896—1976

### (*Indicates Olympic Records)

### Track and Field — Men

#### 60-Meter Run

| | | |
|---|---|---|
| 00 | Alvin Kraenzlein, United States | 7s* |
| 04 | Archie Hahn, United States | 7s* |

#### 100-Meter Run

| | | |
|---|---|---|
| 96 | Thomas Burke, United States | 12s |
| 00 | Francis W. Jarvis, United States | 10.8s |
| 04 | Archie Hahn, United States | 11s |
| 08 | Reginald Walker, South Africa | 10.8s |
| 12 | Ralph Craig, United States | 10.8s |
| 20 | Charles Paddock, United States | 10.8s |
| 24 | Harold Abrahams, Great Britain | 10.6s |
| 28 | Percy Williams, Canada | 10.8s |
| 32 | Eddie Tolan, United States | 10.3s |
| 36 | Jesse Owens, United States | 10.3s |
| 48 | Harrison Dillard, United States | 10.3s |
| 52 | Lindy Remigino, United States | 10.4s |
| 56 | Bobby Morrow, United States | 10.5s |
| 60 | Armin Hary, Germany | 10.2s |
| 64 | Bob Hayes, United States | 10.0s |
| 68 | Jim Hines, United States | 9.9s* |
| 72 | Valeri Borzov, USSR | 10.14s |
| 76 | Hasely Crawford, Trinidad | 10.06s |

#### 200-Meter Run

| | | |
|---|---|---|
| 00 | Walter Tewksbury, United States | 22.2s |
| 04 | Archie Hahn, United States | 21.6s |
| 08 | Robert Kerr, Canada | 22.4s |
| 12 | Ralph Craig, United States | 21.7s |
| 20 | Allan Woodring, United States | 22s |
| 24 | Jackson Scholz, United States | 21.6s |
| 28 | Percy Williams, Canada | 21.8s |
| 32 | Eddie Tolan, United States | 21.2s |
| 36 | Jesse Owens, United States | 20.7s |
| 48 | Mel Patton, United States | 21.1s |
| 52 | Andrew Stanfield, United States | 20.7s |
| 56 | Bobby Morrow, United States | 20.6s |
| 60 | Livio Berruti, Italy | 20.5s |
| 64 | Henry Carr, United States | 20.3s |
| 68 | Tommie Smith, United States | 19.8s* |
| 72 | Valeri Borzov, USSR | 20.00s |
| 76 | Donald Quarrie, Jamaica | 20.23s |

#### 400-Meter Run

| | | |
|---|---|---|
| 96 | Thomas Burke, United States | 54.2s |
| 00 | Maxey Long, United States | 49.4s |
| 04 | Harry Hillman, United States | 49.2s |
| 08 | Wyndham Halswelle, Great Britain, walkover | 50s |
| 12 | Charles Reidpath, United States | 48.2s |
| 20 | Bevil Rudd, South Africa | 49.6s |
| 24 | Eric Liddell, Great Britain | 47.6s |
| 28 | Ray Barbuti, United States | 47.8s |
| 32 | William Carr, United States | 46.2s |
| 1936 | Archie Williams, United States | 46.5s |
| 1948 | Arthur Wint, Jamaica, B W I | 46.2s |
| 1952 | George Rhoden, Jamaica, B W I | 45.9s |
| 1956 | Charles Jenkins, United States | 46.7s |
| 1960 | Otis Davis, United States | 44.9s |
| 1964 | Michael Larrabee, United States | 45.1s |
| 1968 | Lee Evans, United States | 43.8s* |
| 1972 | Vincent Matthews, United States | 44.66s |
| 1976 | Alberto Juantorena, Cuba | 44.26s |

#### 800-Meter Run

| | | |
|---|---|---|
| 1896 | Edwin Flack, Great Britain | 2m. 11s |
| 1900 | Alfred Tysoe, Great Britain | 2m. 1.4s |
| 1904 | James Lightbody, United States | 1m. 56s |
| 1908 | Mel Sheppard, United States | 1m. 52.8s |
| 1912 | James Meredith, United States | 1m. 51.9s |
| 1920 | Albert Hill, Great Britain | 1m. 53.4s |
| 1924 | Douglas Lowe, Great Britain | 1m. 52.4s |
| 1928 | Douglas Lowe, Great Britain | 1m. 51.8s |
| 1932 | Thomas, Hampson, Great Britain | 1m. 49.8s |
| 1936 | John Woodruff, United States | 1m. 52.9s |
| 1948 | Mal Whitfield, United States | 1m. 49.2s |
| 1952 | Mal Whitfield, United States | 1m. 49.2s |
| 1956 | Thomas Courtney, United States | 1m. 47.7s |
| 1960 | Peter Snell, New Zealand | 1m. 46.3s |
| 1964 | Peter Snell, New Zealand | 1m. 45.1s |
| 1968 | Ralph Doubell, Australia | 1m. 44.3s |
| 1972 | Dave Wottle, United States | 1m. 45.9s |
| 1976 | Alberto Juantorena, Cuba | 1m. 43.50s* |

#### 1,500-Meter Run

| | | |
|---|---|---|
| 1896 | Edwin Flack, Great Britain | 4m. 33.2s |
| 1900 | Charles Bennett, Great Britain | 4m. 6s |
| 1904 | James Lightbody, United States | 4m. 5.4s |
| 1908 | Mel Sheppard, United States | 4m. 3.4s |
| 1912 | Arnold Jackson, Great Britain | 3m. 56.8s |
| 1920 | Albert Hill, Great Britain | 4m. 1.8s |
| 1924 | Paavo Nurmi, Finland | 3m. 53.6s |
| 1928 | Harry Larva, Finland | 3m. 53.2s |
| 1932 | Luigi Beccali, Italy | 3m. 51.2s |
| 1936 | Jack Lovelock, New Zealand | 3m. 47.8s |
| 1948 | Henri Eriksson, Sweden | 3m. 49.8s |
| 1952 | Joseph Barthel, Luxemburg | 3m. 45.2s |
| 1956 | Ron Delany, Ireland | 3m. 41.2s |
| 1960 | Herb Elliott, Australia | 3m. 35.6s |
| 1964 | Peter Snell, New Zealand | 3m. 38.1s |
| 1968 | Kipchoge Keino, Kenya | 3m. 34.9s* |
| 1972 | Pekka Vasala, Finland | 3m. 36.3s |
| 1976 | John Walker, New Zealand | 3m. 39.17s |

#### 3,000-Meter Steeplechase

| | | |
|---|---|---|
| 1920 | Percy Hodge, Great Britain | 10m. 2.4s |
| 1924 | Willie Ritola, Finland | 9m. 33.6s |

| 1928 | Toivo Loukola, Finland | 9m. 21.8s |
|---|---|---|
| 1932 | Volnari Iso-Hollo, Finland | 10m. 33.4s |
| | (About 3450 mtrs. extra lap by error) | |
| 1936 | Volnari Iso-Hollo, Finland | 9m. 3.8s |
| 1948 | Thure Sjoestrand, Sweden | 9m. 4.6s |
| 1952 | Horace Ashenfelter, United States | 8m. 45.4s |
| 1956 | Chris Brasher, Great Britain | 8m. 42.2s |
| 1960 | Zdzislaw Krzyszkowiak, Poland | 8m. 34.2s |
| 1964 | Gaston Roelants, Belgium | 8m. 30.8s |
| 1968 | Amos Biwott, Kenya | 8m. 51s |
| 1972 | Kipchoge Keino, Kenya | 8m. 23.6s |
| 1976 | Anders Garderud, Sweden | 8m. 08.2s* |

### 5,000-Meter Run

| 1912 | Hannes Kolehmainen, Finland | 14m. 36.6s |
|---|---|---|
| 1920 | Joseph Guillemot, France | 14m. 55.6s |
| 1924 | Paavo Nurmi, Finland | 14m. 31.2s |
| 1928 | Willie Ritola, Finland | 14m. 38s |
| 1932 | Lauri Lehtinen, Finland | 14m. 30s |
| 1936 | Gunnar Hockert, Finland | 14m. 22.2s |
| 1948 | Gaston Reiff, Belgium | 14m. 17.6s |
| 1952 | Emil Zatopek, Czechoslovakia | 14m. 6.0s |
| 1956 | Vladimir Kuts, USSR | 13m. 39.6s |
| 1960 | Murray Halberg, New Zealand | 13m. 43.4s |
| 1964 | Bob Schul, United States | 13m. 48.8s |
| 1968 | Mohamed Gammoudi, Tunisia | 14m. 05.0s |
| 1972 | Lasse Viren, Finland | 13m. 26.4s |
| 1976 | Lasse Viren, Finland | 13m. 24.76s* |

### Cross-Country

| 1912 | Hannes Kolehmainen, Finland | 45m. 11.6s |
|---|---|---|

### 5-Mile Run

| 1908 | Emil Voigt, Great Britain | 25m. 11.2s* |
|---|---|---|

### 10,000-Meter Run

| 1912 | Hannes Kolehmainen, Finland | 31m. 20.8s |
|---|---|---|
| 1920 | Paavo Nurmi, Finland | 31m. 45.8s |
| 1924 | Willie Ritola, Finland | 30m. 23.2s |
| 1928 | Paavo Nurmi, Finland | 30m. 18.8s |
| 1932 | Janusz Kusocinski, Poland | 30m. 11.4s |
| 1936 | Ilmari Salminen, Finland | 30m. 15.4s |
| 1948 | Emil Zatopek, Czechoslovakia | 29m. 59.6s |
| 1952 | Emil Zatopek, Czechoslovakia | 29m. 17.0s |
| 1956 | Vladimir Kuts, USSR | 28m. 45.6s |
| 1960 | Pytor Bolotnikov, USSR | 28m. 32.2s |
| 1964 | Billy Mills, United States | 28m. 24.4s |
| 1968 | Naftali Temu, Kenya | 29m. 27.4s |
| 1972 | Lasse Viren, Finland | 27m. 38.4s* |
| 1976 | Lasse Viren, Finland | 27m. 40.38s |

### Marathon

| 1896 | Spyros Loues, Greece | 2h. 55m. 20s |
|---|---|---|
| 1900 | Michael Teato, France | 2h. 59m. 45s |
| 1904 | Thomas Hicks, United States | 3h. 28m. 53s |
| 1908 | John J. Hayes, United States | 2h. 55m. 18.4s |
| 1912 | Kenneth McArthur, South Africa | 2h. 36m. 54.8s |
| 1920 | Hannes Kolehmainen, Finland | 2h. 32m. 35.8s |
| 1924 | Albin Stenroos, Finland | 2h. 41m. 22.6s |
| 1928 | El Ouafl, France | 2h. 32m. 57s |
| 1932 | Juan Zabala, Argentina | 2h. 31m. 36s |
| 1936 | Kitei Son, Japan | 2h. 29m. 19.2s |
| 1948 | Delfo Cabera, Argentina | 2h. 34m. 51.6s |
| 1952 | Emil Zatopek, Czechoslovakia | 2h. 23m. 03.2s |
| 1956 | Alain Mimoun, France | 2h. 25m. |
| 1960 | Abebe Bikila, Ethiopia | 2h. 15m. 15.2s |
| 1964 | Abebe Bikila, Ethiopia | 2h. 12m. 11.2s |
| 1968 | Mamo Wolde, Ethiopia | 2h. 20m. 26.4s |
| 1972 | Frank Shorter, United States | 2h. 12m. 19.8s |
| 1976 | Waldemer Cierpinski, E. Germany | 2h. 09m. 55s* |

### 10,000-Meter Cross-Country

| 1920 | Paavo Nurmi, Finland | 27m. 15s* |
|---|---|---|
| 1924 | Paavo Nurmi, Finland | 32m. 54.8s |

### 10,000-Meter Walk

| 1912 | George Goulding, Canada | 46m. 28.4s |
|---|---|---|
| 1920 | Ugo Frigerio, Italy | 48m. 6.2s |
| 1924 | Ugo Frigerio, Italy | 47m. 49s |
| 1948 | John Mikaelsson, Sweden | 45m. 13.2s |
| 1952 | John Mikaelsson, Sweden | 45m. 02.8s* |

### 20,000-Meter Walk

| 1956 | Leonid Spirine, USSR | 1h. 31m. 27.4s |
|---|---|---|
| 1960 | Vladimir Golubnichy, USSR | 1h. 34m. 7.2s |
| 1964 | Kenneth Mathews, Great Britain | 1h. 29m. 34.0s |
| 1968 | Vladimir Golubnichy, USSR | 1h. 33m. 58.4s |
| 1972 | Peter Frenkel, E. Germany | 1h. 26m. 42.4s |
| 1976 | Daniel Bautista, Mexico | 1h. 24m. 40.6s* |

### 50,000-Meter Walk

| 1932 | Thomas W. Green, Great Britain | 4h. 50m. 1 |
|---|---|---|
| 1936 | Harold Whitlock, Great Britain | 4h. 30m. 41. |
| 1948 | John Lundgren, Sweden | 4h. 41m. 5. |
| 1952 | Giuseppe Bordoni, Italy | 4h. 28m. 07. |
| 1956 | Norman Read, New Zealand | 4h. 30m. 42. |
| 1960 | Donald Thompson, Great Britain | 4h. 25m. 3 |
| 1964 | Abdon Pamich, Italy | 4h. 11m. 11. |
| 1968 | Christoph Hohne, E. Germany | 4h. 20m. 13. |
| 1972 | Bern Kannenberg, W. Germany | 3h. 56m. 11.6 |

### 110-Meter Hurdles

| 1896 | Thomas Curtis, United States | 17. |
|---|---|---|
| 1900 | Alvin Kraenzlein, United States | 15. |
| 1904 | Frederick Schule, United States | 1 |
| 1908 | Forrest Smithson, United States | 1s |
| 1912 | Frederick Kelly, United States | 15. |
| 1920 | Earl Thomson, Canada | 14. |
| 1924 | Daniel Kinsey, United States | 1 |
| 1928 | Sydney Atkinson, South Africa | 14. |
| 1932 | George Saling, United States | 14. |
| 1936 | Forrest Towns, United States | 14. |
| 1948 | William Porter, United States | 13. |
| 1952 | Harrison Dillard, United States | 13. |
| 1956 | Lee Calhoun, United States | 13. |
| 1960 | Lee Calhoun, United States | 13. |
| 1964 | Hayes Jones, United States | 13. |
| 1968 | Willie Davenport, United States | 13. |
| 1972 | Rod Milburn, United States | 13.24 |
| 1976 | Guy Drut, France | 13.3 |

### 200-Meter Hurdles

| 1900 | Alvin Kraenzlein, United States | 25. |
|---|---|---|
| 1904 | Harry Hillman, United States | 24.6 |

### 400-Meter Hurdles

| 1900 | J.W.B. Tewksbury, United States | 57. |
|---|---|---|
| 1904 | Harry Hillman, United States | 5 |
| 1908 | Charles Bacon, United States | 5 |
| 1920 | Frank Loomis, United States | 5 |
| 1924 | F. Morgan Taylor, United States | 52. |
| 1928 | Lord Burghley, Great Britain | 53. |
| 1932 | Robert Tisdall, Ireland | 51. |
| 1936 | Glenn Hardin, United States | 51. |
| 1948 | Roy Cochran, United States | 51. |
| 1952 | Charles Moore, United States | 50. |
| 1956 | Glenn Davis, United States | 50. |
| 1960 | Glenn Davis, United States | 49. |
| 1964 | Rex Cawley, United States | 49. |
| 1968 | Dave Hemery, Great Britain | 48. |
| 1972 | John Akii-Bua, Uganda | 47.8 |
| 1976 | Edwin Moses, United States | 47.64 |

### Standing High Jump

| 1900 | Ray Ewry, United States | 5ft. 5 |
|---|---|---|
| 1904 | Ray Ewry, United States | 4ft. 11 |
| 1908 | Ray Ewry, United States | 5ft. 2 |
| 1912 | Platt Adams, United States | 5ft. 4 1-4 in |

### Running High Jump

| 1896 | Ellery Clark, United States | 5ft. 11 1-4 |
|---|---|---|
| 1900 | Irving Baxter, United States | 6ft. 2 4-5 |
| 1904 | Samuel Jones, United States | 5ft. 11 |
| 1908 | Harry Porter, United States | 6ft. 3 |
| 1912 | Almer W. Richards, United States | 6ft. 4 |
| 1920 | Richard Landon, United States | 6ft. 4 3-8 |
| 1924 | Harold Osborn, United States | 6ft. 6 |
| 1928 | Robert W. King, United States | 6ft. 4 3-8 |
| 1932 | Duncan McNaughton, Canada | 6ft. 5 5-8 |
| 1936 | Cornelius Johnson, United States | 6ft. 7 15-16 |
| 1948 | John L. Winter, Australia | 6ft. 6 |
| 1952 | Walter Davis, United States | 6ft. 8.32 |
| 1956 | Charles Dumas, United States | 6ft. 11 1-4 |
| 1960 | Robert Shavlakadze, USSR | 7ft. 1 |
| 1964 | Valery Brumel, USSR | 7ft. 1 7-8 |
| 1968 | Dick Fosbury, United States | 7ft. 4 1-4 |
| 1972 | Yuri Tarmak, USSR | 7ft. 3 3-4 |
| 1976 | Jacek Wszola, Poland | 7ft. 4 1-2 in |

### Standing Broad Jump

| 1900 | Ray Ewry, United States | 10ft. 6 2-5 |
|---|---|---|
| 1904 | Ray Ewry, United States | 11ft. 4 7-8 in |
| 1908 | Ray Ewry, United States | 10ft. 11 1-4 |
| 1912 | Constantin Tsicilitras, Greece | 11ft. 3-4 |

### Long Jump

| 1896 | Ellery Clark, United States | 20ft. 9 3-4 |
|---|---|---|
| 1900 | Alvin Kraenzlein, United States | 23ft. 6 7-8 |
| 1904 | Myer Prinstein, United States | 24ft. 1 |

| 1908 | Frank Irons, United States | 24ft. 6 1-2 in. |
|---|---|---|
| 1912 | Albert Gutterson, United States | 24ft. 11 1-4 in. |
| 1920 | Wm. Petterrson, Sweden | 23ft. 5 1-2 in. |
| 1924 | DeHart Hubbard, United States | 24ft. 5 1-8 in. |
| 1928 | Edward B. Hamm, United States | 25ft. 4 3-4 in. |
| 1932 | Edward Gordon, United States | 25ft. 3-4 in. |
| 1936 | Jesse Owens, United States | 26ft. 5 5-16 in. |
| 1948 | William Steele, United States | 25ft. 8 in. |
| 1952 | Jerome Biffle, United States | 24ft. 10.03 in. |
| 1956 | Gregory Bell, United States | 25ft. 8 1-4 in. |
| 1960 | Ralph Boston, United States | 26ft. 7 3-4 in. |
| 1964 | Lynn Davies, Great Britain | 26ft. 5 3-4 in. |
| 1968 | Bob Beamon, United States | 29ft. 2 1-2 in.* |
| 1972 | Randy Williams, United States | 27ft. 1-2 in. |
| 1976 | Arnie Robinson, United States | 27ft. 4 1-2 in. |

## 400-Meter Relay

| 1912 | Great Britain | 42.4s |
|---|---|---|
| 1920 | United States | 42.2s |
| 1924 | United States | 41s |
| 1928 | United States | 41s |
| 1932 | United States | 40s |
| 1936 | United States | 39.8s |
| 1948 | United States | 40.3s |
| 1952 | United States | 40.1s |
| 1956 | United States | 39.5s |
| 1960 | Germany (U.S. disqualified) | 39.5s |
| 1964 | United States | 39.0s |
| 1968 | United States | 38.2s |
| 1972 | United States | 38.19s* |
| 1976 | United States | 38.33s |

## 1,600-Meter Relay

| 1908 | United States | 3m. 27.2s |
|---|---|---|
| 1912 | United States | 3m. 16.6s |
| 1920 | Great Britain | 3m. 22.2s |
| 1924 | United States | 3m. 16s |
| 1928 | United States | 3m. 14.2s |
| 1932 | United States | 3m. 8.2s |
| 1936 | Great Britain | 3m. 9s |
| 1948 | United States | 3m. 10.4s |
| 1952 | Jamaica, B.W.I. | 3m. 03.9s |
| 1956 | United States | 3m. 04.8s |
| 1960 | United States | 3m. 02.2s |
| 1964 | United States | 3m. 00.7s |
| 1968 | United States | 2m. 56.1s* |
| 1972 | Kenya | 2m. 59.8s |
| 1976 | United States | 2m. 58.65s |

## Pole Vault

| 1896 | William Hoyt, United States | 10ft. 9 3-4 in. |
|---|---|---|
| 1900 | Irving Baxter, United States | 10ft. 9.9in. |
| 1904 | Charles Dvorak, United States | 11ft. 6 in. |
| 1908 | A. C. Gilbert, United States | |
| | Edward Cook Jr., United States | 12ft. 2 in. |
| 1912 | Harry Babcock, United States | 12ft. 11 1-2 in. |
| 1920 | Frank Foss, United States | 13ft. 5 in. |
| 1924 | Lee Barnes, United States | 12ft. 11 1-2 in. |
| 1928 | Sabin W. Carr, United States | 13ft. 9 1-2 in. |
| 1932 | William Miller, United States | 14ft. 1 7-8 in. |
| 1936 | Earle Meadows, United States | 14ft. 3 1-4 in. |
| 1948 | Guinn Smith, United States | 14ft. 1 1-4 in. |
| 1952 | Robert Richards, United States | 14ft. 11 1-4 in. |
| 1956 | Robert Richards, United States | 14ft. 11 1-2 in. |
| 1960 | Don Bragg, United States | 15ft. 5 1-8 in. |
| 1964 | Fred Hansen, United States | 16ft. 8 1-2 in. |
| 1968 | Bob Seagren, United States | 17ft. 8 1-2 in. |
| 1972 | Wolfgang Nordwig, E. Germany | 18ft. 1-2 in.* |
| 1976 | Tadeusz Slusarski, Poland | 18ft. 1-2 in.* |

## 16-lb. Hammer Throw

| 1900 | John Flannagan, United States | 167ft. 4 in. |
|---|---|---|
| 1904 | John Flannagan, United States | 168ft. 1 in. |
| 1908 | John Flannagan, United States | 170ft. 4 1-4 in. |
| 1912 | Matt McGrath, United States | 179ft. 7 1-8 in. |
| 1920 | Pat Ryan, United States | 172ft. 5 5-8 in. |
| 1924 | Fred Tootell, United States | 174ft. 10 1-8 in. |
| 1928 | Patrick O'Callaghan, Ireland | 168ft. 7 3-8 in. |
| 1932 | Patrick O'Callaghan, Ireland | 176ft. 11 1-8 in. |
| 1936 | Karl Hein, Germany | 185ft. 4 3-16 in. |
| 1948 | Imre Nemeth, Hungary | 183ft. 11 1-2 in. |
| 1952 | Jozsef Csermak, Hungary | 197ft. 11.67 in. |
| 1956 | Harold Connolly, United States | 207ft. 3 1-2 in. |
| 1960 | Vasily Rudenkov, USSR | 220ft. 2 in. |
| 1964 | Romuald Klim, USSR | 228ft. 9 1-2 in. |
| 1968 | Gyula Zsivotsky, Hungary | 240ft. 8 in. |
| 1972 | Anatoli Bondarchuk, USSR | 248ft. 8 in. |
| 1976 | Yuri Sedyh, USSR | 254ft. 3 3-4 in.* |

## Discus Throw

| 1896 | Robert Garrett, United States | 95ft. 7 1-2 in. |
|---|---|---|
| 1900 | Rudolf Bauer, Hungary | 118ft. 2.9-10 in. |
| 1904 | Martin Sheridan, United States | 128ft. 10 1-2 in. |
| 1908 | Martin Sheridan, United States | 134ft. 2 in. |
| 1912 | Armas Taipale, Finland | 148ft. 4 in. |
| | Both hands—Armas Taipale, Finland | 271ft. 10 1-4 in. |
| 1920 | Elmer Niklander, Finland | 146ft. 7 1-4 in. |
| 1924 | Clarence Houser, United States | 151ft. 5 1-8 in. |
| 1928 | Clarence Houser, United States | 155ft. 3 in. |
| 1932 | John Anderson, United States | 162ft. 4 7-8 in. |
| 1936 | Ken Carpenter, United States | 165ft. 7 3-8 in. |
| 1948 | Adolfo Consolini, Italy | 173ft. 2 in. |
| 1952 | Sim Iness, United States | 180ft. 6.85 in. |
| 1956 | Al Oerter, United States | 184ft. 11 in. |
| 1960 | Al Oerter, United States | 194ft. 2 in. |
| 1964 | Al Oerter, United States | 200ft. 1 1-2 in. |
| 1968 | Al Oerter, United States | 212ft. 6 1-2 in. |
| 1972 | Ludik Danek, Czechoslovakia | 211ft. 3 in. |
| 1976 | Mac Wilkins, United States | 221ft. 5.4 in.* |

## Standing Hop, Step, and Jump

| 1900 | Ray Ewry, United States | 34ft. 8 1-2 in.* |
|---|---|---|
| 1904 | Ray Ewry, United States | 34ft. 7 1-4 in. |

## Triple Jump

| 1896 | James Connolly, United States | 45ft. |
|---|---|---|
| 1900 | Myer Prinstein, United States | 47ft. 4 1-4 in. |
| 1904 | Myer Prinstein, United States | 47 ft. |
| 1908 | Timothy Aheame, Great Britain | 48ft. 11 1-4 in. |
| 1912 | Gustaf Lindblom, Sweden | 48ft. 5 1-8 in. |
| 1920 | Vilho Tuulos, Finland | 47ft. 7 in. |
| 1924 | Archie Winter, Australia | 50ft. 11 1-4 in. |
| 1928 | Mikio Oda, Japan | 49ft. 11 in. |
| 1932 | Chuhei Nambu, Japan | 51ft. 7 in. |
| 1936 | Naoto Tajima, Japan | 52ft. 5 7-8 in. |
| 1948 | Arne Ahman, Sweden | 50ft. 6 1-4 in. |
| 1952 | Adhemar de Silva, Brazil | 53ft. 2.59 in. |
| 1956 | Adhemar de Silva, Brazil | 53ft. 7 1-2 in. |
| 1960 | Jozef Schmidt, Poland | 55ft. 1 3-4 in. |
| 1964 | Jozef Schmidt, Poland | 55ft. 3 1-2 in. |
| 1968 | Viktor Saneev, USSR | 57ft. 3-4 in.* |
| 1972 | Viktor Saneev, USSR | 56ft. 11 in. |
| 1976 | Viktor Saneev, USSR | 56ft. 8 3-4 in. |

## 16-lb. Shot Put

| 1896 | Robert Garrett, United States | 36ft. 2 in. |
|---|---|---|
| 1900 | Robert Sheldon, United States | 46ft. 3 1-8 in. |
| 1904 | Ralph Rose, United States | 48ft. 7 in. |
| 1908 | Ralph Rose, United States | 46ft. 7 1-2 in. |
| 1912 | Pat McDonald, United States | 50ft. 4 in. |
| | Both hands—Ralph Rose, United States | 90ft. 5 1-2 in. |
| 1920 | Ville Porhola, Finland | 48ft. 7 1-8 in. |
| 1924 | Clarence Houser, United States | 49ft. 2 3-8 in. |
| 1928 | John Kuck, United States | 52ft. 3-4 in. |
| 1932 | Leo Sexton, United States | 52ft. 6 3-16 in. |
| 1936 | Hans Woelke, Germany | 53ft. 1 13-16 in. |
| 1948 | Wilbur Thompson, United States | 56ft. 2 in. |
| 1952 | Parry O'Brien, United States | 57ft. 1.43 in. |
| 1956 | Parry O'Brien, United States | 60ft. 11 in. |
| 1960 | William Nieder, United States | 64ft. 6 3-4 in. |
| 1964 | Dallas Long, United States | 66ft. 8 1-2 in. |
| 1968 | Randy Matson, United States | 67ft. 4 3-4 in. |
| 1972 | Wladyslaw Komar, Poland | 69ft. 6 in. |
| 1976 | Udo Beyer, E. Germany | 69ft. 6.7 in.* |

## Discus Throw—Greek Style

| 1908 | Martin Sheridan, United States | 124ft. 8 in.* |
|---|---|---|

## Javelin Throw

| 1908 | Erik Lemming, Sweden | 178ft. 7 1-2 in. |
|---|---|---|
| | Held in middle—Erik Lemming, Sweden | 179ft. 10 1-2 in. |
| 1912 | Erik Lemming, Sweden | 198ft. 11 1-4 in. |
| | Both hands, Julius Saaristo, Finland | 358ft. 11 7-8 in. |
| 1920 | Jonni Myrra, Finland | 215ft. 9 3-4 in. |
| 1924 | Jonni Myrra, Finland | 206ft. 6 3-4 in. |
| 1928 | Eric Lundquist, Sweden | 218ft. 6 1-8 in. |
| 1932 | Matti Jarvinen, Finland | 238ft. 7 in. |
| 1936 | Gerhard Stoeck, Germany | 235ft. 8 5-16 in. |
| 1948 | Kaj T. Rautavaara, Finland | 228ft. 10 1-2 in. |
| 1952 | Cy Young, United States | 242ft. 0.79 in. |
| 1956 | Egil Danielsen, Norway | 281ft. 2 1-4 in. |
| 1960 | Viktor Tsibulenko, USSR | 277ft. 8 3-8 in. |
| 1964 | Pauli Nevala, Finland | 271ft. 2 1-2 in. |
| 1968 | Yanis Lusis, USSR | 295ft. 7 1-4 in. |
| 1972 | Klaus Wolferman, W. Germany | 296ft. 10 in. |
| 1976 | Miklos Nemeth, Hungary | 310ft. 4 1-2 in.* |

### Decathlon

| | | |
|---|---|---|
| 1912 | Hugo Wieslander, Sweden | 7,724.49 pts. |
| 1920 | Helge Loveland, Norway | 6,804.35 pts. |
| 1924 | Harold Osborn, United States | 7,710.775 pts. |
| 1928 | Paavo Yrjola, Finland | 8,056.20 pts. |
| 1932 | James Bausch, United States | 8,462.23 pts. |
| 1936 | Glenn Morris, United States | 7,900 pts. |
| 1948 | Robert Mathias, United States | 7,139 pts. |
| 1952 | Robert Mathias, United States | 7,887 pts. |
| 1956 | Milton Campbell, United States | 7,937 pts. |
| 1960 | Rafer Johnson, United States | 8,392 pts. |
| 1964 | Willi Holdorf, Germany | 7,887 pts. |
| 1968 | Bill Toomey, United States | 8,193 pts. |
| 1972 | Nikola Avilov, USSR | 8,454 pts. |
| 1976 | Bruce Jenner, United States | 8,618 pts.* |

Former point systems used prior to 1964.

## Track and Field—Women

### 100-Meter Run

| | | |
|---|---|---|
| 1928 | Elizabeth Robinson, United States | 12.2s |
| 1932 | Stella Walsh, Poland | 11.9s |
| 1936 | Helen Stephens, United States | 11.5s |
| 1948 | Francina Blankers-Koen, Netherlands | 11.9s |
| 1952 | Marjorie Jackson, Australia | 11.5s |
| 1956 | Betty Cuthbert, Australia | 11.5s |
| 1960 | Wilma Rudolph, United States | 11.0s* |
| 1964 | Wyomia Tyus, United States | 11.4s |
| 1968 | Wyomia Tyus, United States | 11.0s* |
| 1972 | Renate Stecher, E. Germany | 11.07s |
| 1976 | Annegret Richter, W. Germany | 11.01s* |

### 200-Meter Run

| | | |
|---|---|---|
| 1948 | Francina Blankers-Koen, Netherlands | 24.4s |
| 1952 | Marjorie Jackson, Australia | 23.7s |
| 1956 | Betty Cuthbert, Australia | 23.4s |
| 1960 | Wilma Rudolph, United States | 24.0s |
| 1964 | Edith McGuire, United States | 23.0s |
| 1968 | Irene Szewinska, Poland | 22.5s |
| 1972 | Renate Stecher, E. Germany | 22.40s |
| 1976 | Baerbel Eckert, E. Germany | 22.37s* |

### 400-Meter Run

| | | |
|---|---|---|
| 1964 | Betty Cuthbert, Australia | 52s |
| 1968 | Colette Besson, France | 52s |
| 1972 | Monika Zehrt, E. Germany | 51.08s |
| 1976 | Irena Szewinska, Poland | 49.29s* |

### 800-Meter Run

| | | |
|---|---|---|
| 1928 | Linda Radke, Germany | 2m. 16.8s |
| 1960 | Ludmila Shevcova, USSR | 2m. 4.3s |
| 1964 | Ann Packer, Great Britain | 2m. 1.1s |
| 1968 | Madeline Manning, United States | 2m. 0.9s |
| 1972 | Hildegard Flack, W. Germany | 1m. 58.6s |
| 1976 | Tatyana Kazankina, USSR | 1m. 54.94* |

### 1,500-Meter Run

| | | |
|---|---|---|
| 1972 | Ludmila Bragina, USSR | 4m. 01.4s* |
| 1976 | Tatyana Kazankina, USSR | 4m. 05.48s |

### 400-Meter Relay

| | | |
|---|---|---|
| 1928 | Canada | 48.4s |
| 1932 | United States | 47.0s |
| 1936 | United States | 46.9s |
| 1948 | Netherlands | 47.5s |
| 1952 | United States | 45.9s |
| 1956 | Australia | 44.5s |
| 1960 | United States | 44.5s |
| 1964 | Poland | 43.6s |
| 1968 | United States | 42.8s |
| 1972 | West Germany | 42.81s |
| 1976 | East Germany | 42.55s* |

### 1,600-Meter Relay

| | | |
|---|---|---|
| 1972 | East Germany | 3m. 23s |
| 1976 | East Germany | 3m. 19.23s* |

### 80-Meter Hurdles

| | | |
|---|---|---|
| 1932 | Mildred Didrikson, United States | 11.7s |
| 1936 | Trebisonda Villa, Italy | 11.7s |
| 1948 | Francina Blankers-Koen, Netherlands | 11.2s |
| 1952 | Shirley Strickland de la Hunty, Australia | 10.9s |
| 1956 | Shirley Strickland de la Hunty, Australia | 10.7s |
| 1960 | Irina Press, USSR | 10.8s |
| 1964 | Karen Balzer, Germany | 10.5s |
| 1968 | Maureen Caird, Australia | 10.3s* |

### 100-Meter Hurdles

| | | |
|---|---|---|
| 1972 | Annelie Ehrhardt, E. Germany | 12.59* |
| 1976 | Johanna Schaller, E. Germany | 12.77s |

### High Jump

| | | |
|---|---|---|
| 1928 | Ethel Catherwood, Canada | 5ft. 3 in. |
| 1932 | Jean Shiley, United States | 5ft. 5 1-4 in. |
| 1936 | Ibolya Csak, Hungary | 5ft. 3 in. |
| 1948 | Alice Coachman, United States | 5ft. 6 1-8 in. |
| 1952 | Esther Brand, South Africa | 5ft. 5 3-4 in. |
| 1956 | Mildred L. McDaniel, United States | 5ft. 9 1-4 in. |
| 1960 | Iolanda Balas, Romania | 6ft. 1-4 in. |
| 1964 | Iolanda Balas, Romania | 6ft. 2 7-8 in. |
| 1968 | Miloslava Reskova, Czechoslovakia | 5ft. 11 3-4 in. |
| 1972 | Ulrike Meyfarth, W. Germany | 6ft. 3 1-4 in. |
| 1976 | Rosemarie Ackermann, E. Germany | 6ft. 3 3-4 in.* |

### Discus Throw

| | | |
|---|---|---|
| 1928 | Helena Konopacka, Poland | 129ft. 11 7-8 in. |
| 1932 | Lillian Copeland, United States | 133ft. 2 in. |
| 1936 | Gisela Mauermayer, Germany | 156ft. 3 3-16 in. |
| 1948 | Micheline Ostermeyer, France | 137ft. 6 1-2 in. |
| 1952 | Nina Romaschkova, USSR | 168ft. 8 1-2 in. |
| 1956 | Olga Fikotova, Czechoslovakia | 176ft. 1 1-2 in. |
| 1960 | Nina Ponomareva, USSR | 180ft. 8 1-4 in. |
| 1964 | Tamara Press, USSR | 187ft. 10 1-2 in. |
| 1968 | Lia Manolin, Romania | 191ft. 2 1-2 in. |
| 1972 | Faina Melnik, USSR | 218ft. 7 in. |
| 1976 | Evelin Schlaak, E. Germany | 226ft. 4 1-2 in.* |

### Javelin Throw

| | | |
|---|---|---|
| 1932 | Mildred Didrikson, United States | 143ft. 4 in. |
| 1936 | Tilly Fleischer, Germany | 148ft. 2 3-4 in. |
| 1948 | Herma Bauma, Austria | 149ft. 6 in. |
| 1952 | Dana Zatopekova, Czechoslovakia | 165ft. 7 in. |
| 1956 | Inessa Janzeme, USSR | 176ft. 8 in. |
| 1960 | Elvira Ozolina, USSR | 183ft. 8 in. |
| 1964 | Mihaela Penes, Romania | 198ft. 7 1-2 in. |
| 1968 | Angela Nemeth, Hungary | 198ft. 1-2 in. |
| 1972 | Ruth Fuchs, E. Germany | 209ft. 7 in. |
| 1976 | Ruth Fuchs, E. Germany | 216ft. 4 in.* |

### Shot Put

| | | |
|---|---|---|
| 1948 | Micheline Ostermeyer, France | 45ft. 1 1-2 in. |
| 1952 | Galina Zybina, USSR | 50ft. 1 1-2 in. |
| 1956 | Tamara Tishkyevich, USSR | 54ft. 5 in. |
| 1960 | Tamara Press, USSR | 56ft. 9 7-8 in. |
| 1964 | Tamara Press, USSR | 59ft. 6 1-4 in. |
| 1968 | Margitta Gummel, E. Germany | 64ft. 4 in. |
| 1972 | Nadezwda Chizova, USSR | 69ft. |
| 1976 | Ivanka Christova, Bulgaria | 69ft. 5 in.* |

### Long Jump

| | | |
|---|---|---|
| 1948 | Olga Gyarmati, Hungary | 18ft. 8 1-4 in. |
| 1952 | Yvette Williams, New Zealand | 20ft. 5 3-4 in. |
| 1956 | E. Krzeskinska, Poland | 20ft. 9 3-4 in. |
| 1960 | Vyera Krepina, USSR | 20ft. 10 3-4 in. |
| 1964 | Mary Rand, Great Britain | 22ft. 2 1-4 in. |
| 1968 | V. Viscopoleanu, Romania | 22ft. 4 1-2 in.* |
| 1972 | Heidemarie Rosendahl, W. Germany | 22ft. 3 in. |
| 1976 | Angela Voigt, E. Germany | 22ft. 2 1-2 in. |

### Pentathlon

| | | |
|---|---|---|
| 1964 | Irina Press, USSR | 5,246 pts. |
| 1968 | Ingred Becker, W. Germany | 5,098 pts. |
| 1972 | Mary Peters, England | 4,801 pts.* |
| 1976 | Sigrun Siegl, E. Germany | 4,745 pts. |

Former point system, 1964–1968

## Value of Olympic Medals

An Olympic gold medal is basically silver coated with about six grams of fine gold. It is worth $125. The silver medal is pure silver, and its actual value is about $75. The bronze, which is pure bronze, is worth $32.

## Swimming—Men

### 100-Meter Freestyle

| | | |
|---|---|---|
| 1896 | Alfred Hajos, Hungary. | 1:22.2 |
| 1904 | Zoltan de Halmay, Hungary (100 yards) | 1:02.8 |
| 1908 | Charles Daniels, U.S. | 1:05.6 |
| 1912 | Duke P. Kahanamoku, U.S. | 1:03.4 |
| 1920 | Duke P. Kahanamoku, U.S. | 1:01.4 |
| 1924 | John Weissmuller, U.S. | 59.0 |
| 1928 | John Weissmuller, U.S. | 58.6 |
| 1932 | Yasuji Miyazaki, Japan | 58.2 |
| 1936 | Ferenc Csik, Hungary | 57.6 |
| 1948 | Wally Ris, U.S. | 57.3 |
| 1952 | Clark Scholes, U.S. | 57.4 |
| 1956 | Jon Henricks, Australia | 55.4 |
| 1960 | John Devitt, Australia | 55.2 |
| 1964 | Don Schollander, U.S. | 53.4 |
| 1968 | Mike Wenden, Australia | 52.2 |
| 1972 | Mark Spitz, U.S. | 51.22 |
| 1976 | Jim Montgomery, U.S. | 49.99* |

### 200-Meter Freestyle

| | | |
|---|---|---|
| 1968 | Mike Wenden, Australia | 1:55.2 |
| 1972 | Mark Spitz, U.S. | 1:52.78 |
| 1976 | Bruce Furniss, U.S. | 1:50.29* |

### 400-Meter Freestyle

| | | |
|---|---|---|
| 1904 | C. M. Daniels, U.S. (440 yards) | 6:16.2 |
| 1908 | Henry Taylor, Great Britain | 5:36.8 |
| 1912 | George Hodgson, Canada | 5:24.4 |
| 1920 | Norman Ross, U.S. | 5:26.8 |
| 1924 | John Weissmuller, U.S. | 5:04.2 |
| 1928 | Albert Zorilla, Argentina | 5:01.6 |
| 1932 | Clarence Crabbe, U.S. | 4:48.4 |
| 1936 | Jack Medica, U.S. | 4:44.5 |
| 1948 | William Smith, U.S. | 4:41.0 |
| 1952 | Jean Boiteux, France | 4:30.7 |
| 1956 | Murray Rose, Australia | 4:27.3 |
| 1960 | Murray Rose, Australia | 4:18.3 |
| 1964 | Don Schollander, U.S. | 4:12.2 |
| 1968 | Mike Burton, U.S. | 4:09.0 |
| 1972 | Brad Cooper, Australia | 4:00.27 |
| 1976 | Brian Goodell, U.S. | 3:51.93* |

### 1,500-Meter Freestyle

| | | |
|---|---|---|
| 1908 | Henry Taylor, Great Britain | 22:48.4 |
| 1912 | George Hodgson, Canada | 22:00.0 |
| 1920 | Norman Ross, U.S. | 23:23.2 |
| 1924 | Andrew Charlton, Australia | 20:06.6 |
| 1928 | Arne Borg, Sweden | 19:51.8 |
| 1932 | Kasuo Kitamura, Japan | 19:12.4 |
| 1936 | Noboru Terada, Japan | 19:13.7 |
| 1948 | James P. McClane, U.S. | 19:18.5 |
| 1952 | Ford Konno, U.S. | 18:30.0 |
| 1956 | Murray Rose, Australia | 17:58.9 |
| 1960 | Jon Konrads, Australia | 17:19.6 |
| 1964 | Robert Windle, Australia | 17:01.7 |
| 1968 | Mike Burton, U.S. | 16:38.9 |
| 1972 | Mike Burton, U.S. | 15:52.58 |
| 1976 | Brian Goodell, U.S. | 15:02.40* |

### 400-Meter Medley Relay

| | | |
|---|---|---|
| 1960 | United States | 4:05.4 |
| 1964 | United States | 3:58.4 |
| 1968 | United States | 3:54.9 |
| 1972 | United States | 3:48.16 |
| 1976 | United States | 3:42.22* |

### 400-Meter Freestyle Relay

| | | |
|---|---|---|
| 1964 | United States | 3:33.2 |
| 1968 | United States | 3:31.7 |
| 1972 | United States | 3:26.4* |

### 800-Meter Freestyle Relay

| | | |
|---|---|---|
| 1908 | Great Britain | 10:55.6 |
| 1912 | Australia | 10:11.6 |
| 1920 | United States | 10:04.4 |
| 1924 | United States | 9:53.4 |
| 1928 | United States | 9:36.2 |
| 1932 | Japan | 8:58.4 |
| 1936 | Japan | 8:51.5 |
| 1948 | United States | 8:46.0 |
| 1952 | United States | 8:31.1 |
| 1956 | Australia | 8:23.6 |
| 1960 | United States | 8:10.2 |
| 1964 | United States | 7:52.1 |

| | | |
|---|---|---|
| 1968 | United States | 7:52.3 |
| 1972 | United States | 7:35.78 |
| 1976 | United States | 7:23.22* |

### 100-Meter Backstroke

| | | |
|---|---|---|
| 1904 | Walter Brack, Germany (100 yds.) | 1:16.8 |
| 1908 | Arno Bieberstein, Germany | 1:24.6 |
| 1912 | Harry Hebner, U.S. | 1:21.2 |
| 1920 | Warren Kealoha, U.S. | 1:15.2 |
| 1924 | Warren Kealoha, U.S. | 1:13.2 |
| 1928 | George Kojac, U.S. | 1:08.2 |
| 1932 | Masaji Kiyokawa, Japan | 1:08.6 |
| 1936 | Adolph Kiefer, U.S. | 1:05.9 |
| 1948 | Allen Stack, U.S. | 1:06.4 |
| 1952 | Yoshi Oyokawa, U.S. | 1:05.4 |
| 1956 | David Thiele, Australia. | 1:02.2 |
| 1960 | David Thiele, Australia. | 1:01.9 |
| 1968 | Roland Matthes, E. Germany | 58.7 |
| 1972 | Roland Matthes, E. Germany | 56.58 |
| 1976 | John Naber, U.S. | 55.49* |

### 200-Meter Backstroke

| | | |
|---|---|---|
| 1964 | Jed Graef, U.S. | 2:10.3 |
| 1968 | Roland Matthes, E. Germany | 2:09.6 |
| 1972 | Roland Matthes, E. Germany | 2:02.82 |
| 1976 | John Naber, U.S. | 1:59.19* |

### 100-Meter Breaststroke

| | | |
|---|---|---|
| 1968 | Don McKenzie, U.S. | 1:07.7 |
| 1972 | Nobutaka Taguchi, Japan | 1:04.94 |
| 1976 | John Hencken, U.S. | 1:03.11* |

### 200-Meter Breaststroke

| | | |
|---|---|---|
| 1908 | Frederick Holman, Great Britain | 3:09.2 |
| 1912 | Walter Bathe, Germany | 3:01.8 |
| 1920 | Haken Malmroth, Sweden | 3:04.4 |
| 1924 | Robert Skelton, U.S. | 2:56.6 |
| 1928 | Yoshiyuki Tsuruta, Japan | 2:48.8 |
| 1932 | Yoshiyuki Tsuruta, Japan | 2:45.4 |
| 1936 | Tetsuo Hamuro, Japan | 2:42.5 |
| 1948 | Joseph Verdeur, U.S. | 2:39.3 |
| 1952 | John Davies, Australia. | 2:34.4 |
| 1956 | Masura Furukawa, Japan | 2:34.7 |
| 1960 | William Mulliken, U.S. | 2:37.4 |
| 1964 | Ian O'Brien, Australia | 2:27.8 |
| 1968 | Felipe Munoz, Mexico | 2:28.7 |
| 1972 | John Hencken, U.S. | 2:21.55 |
| 1976 | David Wilkie, Great Britain | 2:15.11* |

### 100-Meter Butterfly

| | | |
|---|---|---|
| 1968 | Doug Russell, U.S. | 55.9 |
| 1972 | Mark Spitz, U.S. | 54.27* |
| 1976 | Matt Vogel, U.S. | 54.35 |

### 200-Meter Butterfly

| | | |
|---|---|---|
| 1956 | William Yorzyk, U.S. | 2:18.6 |
| 1960 | Michael Troy, U.S. | 2:12.8 |
| 1964 | Kevin J. Berry, Australia. | 2:06.6 |
| 1968 | Carl Robie, U.S. | 2:08.7 |
| 1972 | Mark Spitz, U.S. | 2:00.70 |
| 1976 | Mike Bruner, U.S. | 1:59.23* |

### 200-Meter Individual Medley

| | | |
|---|---|---|
| 1968 | Charles Hickcox, U.S. | 2:12.0 |
| 1972 | Gunnar Larsson, Sweden | 2:07.2* |

### 400-Meter Individual Medley

| | | |
|---|---|---|
| 1964 | Dick Roth, U.S. | 4:45.4 |
| 1968 | Charles Hickcox, U.S. | 4:48.4 |
| 1972 | Gunnar Larsson, Sweden | 4:31.98 |
| 1976 | Rod Strachan, U.S. | 4:23.68* |

### Springboard Diving — Points

| | | |
|---|---|---|
| 1904 | Dr. G. E. Sheldon, U.S. | 12 2-3 |
| 1908 | Albert Zuerner, Germany | 85.5 |
| 1912 | Paul Guenther, Germany. | 6 |
| 1920 | Louis Kuehn, U.S. | 6 |
| 1924 | Albert White, U.S. | 7 |
| 1928 | Pete Desjardins, U.S. | 185.04 |
| 1932 | Michael Gallitzen, U.S. | 161.38 |
| 1936 | Richard Degener, U.S. | 161.57 |
| 1948 | Bruce Harlan, U.S. | 163.64 |
| 1952 | David Browning, U.S. | 205.29 |

| | | |
|---|---|---|
| **1956** | Robert Clothworthy, U.S. | 159.56 |
| **1960** | Gary Tobian, U.S. | 170.00 |
| **1964** | Kenneth Sitzberger, U.S. | 159.90 |
| **1968** | Bernie Wrightson, U.S. | 170.15 |
| **1972** | Vladimir Vasin, USSR | 594.09 |
| **1976** | Phil Boggs, U.S. | 619.52 |

| | **Platform Diving** | **Points** |
|---|---|---|
| **1928** | Pete Desjardins, U.S. | 98.74 |

| | | |
|---|---|---|
| **1932** | Harold Smith, U.S. | 124.80 |
| **1936** | Marshall Wayne, U.S. | 113.58 |
| **1948** | Sammy Lee, U.S. | 130.05 |
| **1952** | Sammy Lee, U.S. | 156.28 |
| **1956** | Joaquin Capilla, Mexico | 152.44 |
| **1960** | Robert Webster, U.S. | 165.56 |
| **1964** | Robert Webster, U.S. | 148.58 |
| **1968** | Klaus Dibiasi, Italy | 164.18 |
| **1972** | Klaus Dibiasi, Italy | 504.12 |
| **1976** | Klaus Dibiasi, Italy | 600.51 |

# Swimming—Women

## 100-Meter Freestyle

| | | |
|---|---|---|
| **1912** | Fanny Durack, Australia | 1:22.2 |
| **1920** | Ethelda Bleibtrey, U.S. | 1:13.6 |
| **1924** | Ethel Lackie, U.S. | 1:12.4 |
| **1928** | Albina Osipowich, U.S. | 1:11.0 |
| **1932** | Helene Madison, U.S. | 1:06.8 |
| **1936** | Hendrika Mastenbroek, Holland | 1:05.9 |
| **1948** | Greta Anderson, Denmark | 1:06.3 |
| **1952** | Katalin Szoke, Hungary | 1:06.3 |
| **1956** | Dawn Fraser, Australia | 1:02.0 |
| **1960** | Dawn Fraser, Australia | 1:01.2 |
| **1964** | Dawn Fraser, Australia | 59.5 |
| **1968** | Jan Henne, U.S. | 1:00.0 |
| **1972** | Sandra Neilson, U.S. | 58.59 |
| **1976** | Kornelia Ender, E. Germany | 55.65* |

## 200-Meter Freestyle

| | | |
|---|---|---|
| **1968** | Debbie Meyer, U.S. | 2:10.5 |
| **1972** | Shane Gould, Australia | 2:03.56 |
| **1976** | Kornelia Ender, E. Germany | 1:59.26* |

## 400-Meter Freestyle

| | | |
|---|---|---|
| **1924** | Martha Norelius, U.S. | 6:02.2 |
| **1928** | Martha Norelius, U.S. | 5:42.8 |
| **1932** | Helene Madison, U.S. | 5:28.5 |
| **1936** | Hendrika Mastenbroek, Netherlands | 5:26.4 |
| **1948** | Ann Curtis, U.S. | 5:17.8 |
| **1952** | Valerie Gyenge, Hungary | 5:12.1 |
| **1956** | Lorraine Crapp, Australia | 4:54.6 |
| **1960** | Susan Chris von Saltza, U.S. | 4:50.6 |
| **1964** | Virginia Duenkel, U.S. | 4:43.3 |
| **1968** | Debbie Meyer, U.S. | 4:31.8 |
| **1972** | Shane Gould, Australia | 4:19.04 |
| **1976** | Petra Thumer, E. Germany | 4:09.89* |

## 800-Meter Freestyle

| | | |
|---|---|---|
| **1968** | Debbie Meyer, U.S. | 9:24.0 |
| **1972** | Keena Rothhammer, U.S. | 8:53.68 |
| **1976** | Petra Thumer, E. Germany | 8:37.14* |

## 100-Meter Backstroke

| | | |
|---|---|---|
| **1924** | Sybil Bauer, U.S. | 1:23.3 |
| **1928** | Marie Braun, Netherlands | 1:22.0 |
| **1932** | Eleanor Holm, U.S. | 1:19.4 |
| **1936** | Dina Senff, Netherlands | 1:18.9 |
| **1948** | Karen Harup, Denmark | 1:14.4 |
| **1952** | Joan Harrison, South Africa | 1:14.3 |
| **1956** | Judy Grinham, Great Britain | 1:12.9 |
| **1960** | Lynn Burke, U.S. | 1:09.3 |
| **1964** | Cathy Ferguson, U.S. | 1:07.7 |
| **1968** | Kaye Hall, U.S. | 1:06.2 |
| **1972** | Melissa Belote, U.S. | 1:05.78 |
| **1976** | Ulrike Richter, E. Germany | 1:01.83* |

## 200-Meter Backstroke

| | | |
|---|---|---|
| **1968** | Pokey Watson, U.S. | 2:24.8 |
| **1972** | Melissa Belote, U.S. | 2:19.19 |
| **1976** | Ulrike Richter, E. Germany | 2:13.43* |

## 100-Meter Breaststroke

| | | |
|---|---|---|
| **1968** | Djurdjica Bjedov, Yugoslavia | 1:15.8 |
| **1972** | Cathy Carr, U.S. | 1:13.58 |
| **1976** | Hannelore Anke, E. Germany | 1:11.16* |

## 200-Meter Breaststroke

| | | |
|---|---|---|
| **1924** | Lucy Morton, Great Britain | 3:32.2 |
| **1928** | Hilde Schrader, Germany | 3:12.6 |
| **1932** | Clare Dennis, Australia | 3:06.3 |
| **1936** | Hideko Maehata, Japan | 3:03.6 |
| **1948** | Nelly Van Vliet, Netherlands | 2:57.2 |
| **1952** | Eva Szekely, Hungary | 2:51.7 |
| **1956** | Ursula Happe, Germany | 2:53.1 |
| **1960** | Anita Lonsbrough, Great Britain | 2:49.5 |
| **1964** | Galina Prozumenschikova, USSR | 2:46.4 |
| **1968** | Sharon Wichman, U.S. | 2:44.4 |
| **1972** | Beverly Whitfield, Australia | 2:41.71 |
| **1976** | Marina Koshevala, USSR | 2:33.35* |

## 200-Meter Individual Medley

| | | |
|---|---|---|
| **1968** | Claudia Kolb, U.S. | 2:24.7 |
| **1972** | Shane Gould, Australia | 2:23.1* |

## 400-Meter Individual Medley

| | | |
|---|---|---|
| **1964** | Donna de Varona, U.S. | 5:18.7 |
| **1968** | Claudia Kolb, U.S. | 5:08.5 |
| **1972** | Gail Neall, Australia | 5:02.97 |
| **1976** | Ulrike Tauber, E. Germany | 4:42.77* |

## 100-Meter Butterfly

| | | |
|---|---|---|
| **1956** | Shelley Mann, U.S. | 1:11.0 |
| **1960** | Carolyn Schuler, U.S. | 1:09.5 |
| **1964** | Sharon Stouder, U.S. | 1:04.7 |
| **1968** | Lynn McClements, Australia | 1:05.5 |
| **1972** | Mayumi Aoki, Japan | 1:03.34 |
| **1976** | Kornelia Ender, E. Germany | 1:00.13* |

## 200-Meter Butterfly

| | | |
|---|---|---|
| **1968** | Ada Kok, Netherlands | 2:24.7 |
| **1972** | Karen Moe, U.S. | 2:15.57 |
| **1976** | Andrea Pollack, E. Germany | 2:11.41* |

## 400-Meter Medley Relay

| | | |
|---|---|---|
| **1960** | United States | 4:41.1 |
| **1960** | United States | 4:33.9 |
| **1968** | United States | 4:28.3 |
| **1972** | United States | 4:20.7 |
| **1976** | East Germany | 4:07.95* |

## 400-Meter Freestyle Relay

| | | |
|---|---|---|
| **1912** | Great Britain | 5:52.8 |
| **1920** | United States | 5:11.6 |
| **1924** | United States | 4:58.8 |
| **1928** | United States | 4:47.6 |
| **1932** | United States | 4:38.0 |
| **1936** | Netherlands | 4:36.0 |
| **1948** | Netherlands | 4:29.2 |
| **1952** | Hungary | 4:24.4 |
| **1956** | Australia | 4:17.1 |
| **1960** | United States | 4:08.9 |
| **1964** | United States | 4:03.8 |
| **1968** | United States | 4:02.5 |
| **1972** | United States | 3:55.19 |
| **1976** | United States | 3:44.82* |

| | **Springboard Diving** | **Points** |
|---|---|---|
| **1920** | Aileen Riggin, U.S. | 9 |
| **1924** | Elizabeth Becker, U.S. | 8 |
| **1928** | Helen Meany, U.S. | 78.62 |
| **1932** | Georgia Coleman, U.S. | 87.52 |
| **1936** | Marjorie Gestring, U.S. | 89.27 |
| **1948** | Victoria M. Draves, U.S. | 108.74 |
| **1952** | Patricia McCormick, U.S. | 147.30 |
| **1956** | Patricia McCormick, U.S. | 142.36 |
| **1960** | Ingrid Kramer, Germany | 155.81 |
| **1964** | Ingrid Engel-Kramer, Germany | 145.00 |
| **1968** | Sue Gossick, U.S. | 150.77 |
| **1972** | Micki King, U.S. | 450.03 |
| **1976** | Jenni Chandler, U.S. | 506.19 |

| | **Platform Diving** | **Points** |
|---|---|---|
| **1928** | Elizabeth B. Pinkston, U.S. | 31.60 |
| **1932** | Dorothy Poynton, U.S. | 40.26 |
| **1936** | Dorothy Poynton Hill, U.S. | 33.93 |
| **1948** | Victoria M. Draves, U.S. | 68.87 |
| **1952** | Patricia McCormick, U.S. | 79.37 |
| **1956** | Patricia McCormick, U.S. | 84.85 |
| **1960** | Ingrid Kramer, Germany | 91.28 |
| **1964** | Lesley Bush, U.S. | 99.80 |
| **1968** | Milena Duchkova, Czech. | 109.59 |
| **1972** | Ulrika Knape, Sweden | 390.00 |
| **1976** | Elena Vaytsekhouskaya, USSR | 406.59 |

# 21st Summer Olympics

Montreal, Quebec, July 17-Aug. 1, 1976

## Final Medal Standings

(nations in alphabetical order)

| | Gold | Silver | Bronze | Total | | Gold | Silver | Bronze | Total |
|---|---|---|---|---|---|---|---|---|---|
| Australia | 0 | 1 | 4 | 5 | Korea, North | 1 | 1 | 0 | 2 |
| Austria | 0 | 0 | 1 | 1 | Korea, South | 1 | 1 | 4 | 6 |
| Belgium | 0 | 3 | 3 | 6 | Mexico | 1 | 0 | 1 | 2 |
| Bermuda | 0 | 0 | 1 | 1 | Mongolia | 0 | 1 | 0 | 1 |
| Brazil | 0 | 0 | 2 | 2 | New Zealand | 2 | 1 | 1 | 4 |
| Britain | 3 | 5 | 5 | 13 | Norway | 1 | 1 | 0 | 2 |
| Bulgaria | 7 | 8 | 9 | 24 | Pakistan | 0 | 0 | 1 | 1 |
| Canada | 0 | 5 | 6 | 11 | Poland | 8 | 6 | 11 | 25 |
| Cuba | 6 | 4 | 3 | 13 | Portugal | 0 | 2 | 0 | 2 |
| Czechoslovakia | 2 | 2 | 4 | 8 | Puerto Rico | 0 | 0 | 1 | 1 |
| Denmark | 1 | 0 | 2 | 3 | Romania | 4 | 9 | 14 | 27 |
| Germany, East | 40 | 25 | 25 | 90 | Spain | 0 | 2 | 0 | 2 |
| Germany, West | 10 | 12 | 17 | 39 | Sweden | 4 | 1 | 0 | 5 |
| Finland | 4 | 2 | 0 | 6 | Switzerland | 1 | 1 | 2 | 4 |
| France | 2 | 2 | 5 | 9 | Thailand | 0 | 0 | 1 | 1 |
| Holland | 0 | 2 | 3 | 5 | Trinidad | 1 | 0 | 0 | 1 |
| Hungary | 4 | 5 | 12 | 21 | USSR | 47 | 43 | 35 | 125 |
| Iran | 0 | 1 | 1 | 2 | United States | 34 | 35 | 25 | 94 |
| Italy | 2 | 7 | 4 | 13 | Venezuela | 0 | 1 | 0 | 1 |
| Jamaica | 1 | 1 | 0 | 2 | Yugoslavia | 2 | 3 | 3 | 8 |
| Japan | 9 | 6 | 10 | 25 | Duplicate medals awarded in some events | | | |

## Olympic Gold Medal Winners

### Track and Field — Men

**100 Meters** — Hasely Crawford, Trinidad. **Time — 0:10.06.**
**200 Meters** — Donald Quarrie, Jamaica. **Time — 0:20.23.**
**400 Meters** — Alberto Juantorena, Cuba. **Time — 0:44.26.**
**800 Meters** — Alberto Juantorena, Cuba. **Time — 1:43.50.**
**1,500 Meters**—John Walker, New Zealand.**Time —3:39.17.**
**5,000 Meters** — Lasse Viren, Finland. **Time — 13:27.76.**
**10,000 Meters** — Lasse Viren, Finland. **Time — 27:40.38.**
**110 - Meter Hurdles** — Guy Drut, France. **Time — 0:13.30.**
**400 - Meter Hurdles** — Edwin Moses, U.S. **Time — 0:47.64.**
**400 - Meter Relay** — U.S. (Glance, Jones, Hampton, Riddick). **Time — 0:38.33.**
**1,600 - Meter Relay** — U.S. (Frazier, Brown, Newhouse, Parks). **Time — 2:58.65.**
**3,000 - Meter Steeplechase** — Anders Garderud, Sweden. **Time — 8:08.2.**
**20 - Km. Walk** — Daniel Bautista, Mexico. **Time — 1:24:40.6.**
**Marathon** — Waldemer Cierpinski, E. Germany. **Time — 2:09:55.**
**Long Jump** — Arnie Robinson, U.S. 27 ft. 1/2 in.
**Triple Jump** — Viktor Saneev, USSR. 56 ft. 8.7 in.
**High Jump** — Jacek Wszola, Poland. 7 ft. 4½ in.
**Discus** — Mac Wilkins, U.S. 221 ft. 5.4 in.
**Hammer** — Yuri Sedykh, USSR. 254 ft. 3¾ in.
**Javelin** — Miklos Nemeth, Hungary. 310 ft. 3¾ in.
**Shot Put** — Udo Beyer, E. Germany. 69 ft. ¾ in.
**Pole Vault** — Tadeusz Slusraski, Poland. 18 ft. ½ in.
**Decathlon** — Bruce Jenner, U.S. 8,618 pts.

### Track and Field — Women

**100 Meters** — Annegret Richter, W. Germany. **Time — 0:11.01.**
**200 Meters** — Baerbel Eckert, E. Germany. **Time — 0:22.37.**
**400 Meters** — Irena Szewinska, Poland. **Time — 0:49.29.**
**800 Meters** — Tatyana Kazankina, USSR. **Time — 1:54.94.**
**1,500 Meters** — Tatyana Kazankina, USSR. **Time — 4:05.48.**
**100 - Meter Hurdles** — Johanna Schaller, E. Germany. **Time — 0:12.77.**
**400 - Meter Relay** — E. Germany. **Time — 0:42.55.**
**1,600 - Meter Relay** — E. Germany. **Time — 3:19.23.**
**Long Jump** — Angela Voigt, E. Germany. 22 ft. 2½ in.
**High Jump** — Rosemarie Ackermann, E. Germany, 6 ft. 3¾ in.
**Javelin** — Ruth Fuchs, E. Germany. 216 ft. 4 in.
**Discus** — Evelin Schlaak, E. Germany. 226 ft. 4½ in.
**Shot Put** — Ivanka Khristova, Bulgaria. 69 ft. 5 in.
**Pentathlon** — Sigrun Siegl, E. Germany. 4,745 pts.

### Swimming — Men

**100 - Meter Freestyle** — Jim Montgomery, U.S. **Time — 0:49.99.**
**200 - Meter Freestyle** — Bruce Furniss, U.S. **Time — 1:50.29.**
**400 - Meter Freestyle** — Brian Goodell, U.S. **Time — 3:51.93.**
**1,500 - Meter Freestyle** — Brian Goodell, U.S. **Time — 15:02.40.**
**100 - Meter Breaststroke** — John Hencken, U.S. **Time — 1:03.11.**
**200 - Meter Breaststroke** — David Wilkie, Gr. Britain. **Time — 2:15.11.**
**100 - Meter Butterfly** — Matt Vogel, U.S. **Time — 0:54.35.**
**200 - Meter Butterfly** — Mike Bruner, U.S. **Time — 1:59.23.**
**100 - Meter Backstroke** — John Naber, U.S. **Time — 0:55.49.**
**200 - Meter Backstroke** — John Naber, U.S., **Time — 1:59.19.**
**400 - Meter Individual Medley** — Rod Strachan, U.S. **Time — 4:23.68.**
**400 - Meter Medley Relay** — U.S. (Hencken, Naber, Montgomery, Vogel). **Time — 3:42.22.**
**800 - Meter Freestyle Relay** — U.S. (Bruner, Furniss, Naber, Montgomery). **Time — 7:23.22.**

### Swimming — Women

**100 - Meter Freestyle** — Kornelia Ender, E. Germany. **Time — 0:55.65.**
**200 - Meter Freestyle** — Kornelia Ender, E. Germany. **Time — 1:59.26.**
**400 - Meter Freestyle** — Petra Thumer, E. Germany. **Time — 4:09.89.**
**800 - Meter Freestyle** — Petra Thumer, E. Germany. **Time — 8:37.14.**
**100 - Meter Breaststroke** — Hannelore Anke, E. Germany. **Time — 1:11.16.**
**200 - Meter Breaststroke** — Marina Koshevaia, USSR. **Time — 2:33.35.**
**100 - Meter Butterfly** — Kornelia Ender, E. Germany. **Time — 1:10.13.**
**200 - Meter Butterfly** — Andrea Pollack, E. Germany. **Time — 2:11.41.**
**100 - Meter Backstroke** — Ulrike Richter, E. Germany. **Time — 1:01.83.**
**200 - Meter Backstroke** — Ulrike Richter, E. Germany. **Time — 2:13.43.**
**400 - Meter Individual Medley** — Ulrike Tauber, E. Germany. **Time — 4:42.77.**
**400 - Meter Freestyle Relay** — U.S. (Peyton, Boglioli, Sterkel, Babashoff). **Time — 3:44.82.**
**400 - Meter Medley Relay** — E. Germany (Richter, Anke, Pollack, Ender). **Time — 4:07.95.**

### Archery

**Men's Individual** — Darrell Pace, U.S.
**Women's Individual** — Luann Ryon, U.S.

### Basketball

**Men** — U.S.
**Women** — USSR.

## Boxing

**Light Flyweight** — Jorge Hernandez, Cuba.
**Flyweight** — Leo Randolph, U.S.
**Bantamweight** — Yong Jo Gu, No. Korea.
**Featherweight** — Angel Herrera, Cuba.
**Lightweight** — Howard Davis, U.S.
**Light Welterweight** — Ray Leonard, U.S.
**Welterweight** — Jochen Bachfeld, E. Germany.
**Light Middleweight** — Jerzy Rybicki, Poland.
**Middleweight** — Mike Spinks, U.S.
**Light Heavyweight** — Leon Spinks, U.S.
**Heavyweight** — Teofilo Stevenson, Cuba.

## Canoeing — Men

**500 - Meter Kayak Singles** — Vasile Diba, Romania.
**1,000 - Meter Kayak Singles** — Rudiger Helm, E. Germany.
**500 - Meter Kayak Doubles** — E. Germany.
**1,000 - Meter Kayak Doubles** — USSR.
**1,000 - Meter Kayak Fours** — USSR.
**500 - Meter Canadian Singles** — Aleksandr Rogov, USSR.
**1,000 - Meter Canadian Singles** — Matija Lujbek, Yugoslavia.
**500 - Meter Canadian Doubles** — USSR.
**1,000 - Meter Canadian Doubles** — USSR.

## Canoeing — Women

**500 - Meter Kayak Singles** — Carola Zirzow, E. Germany.
**500 - Meter Kayak Doubles** — USSR.

## Cycling

**Individual Road Race** — Bernt Johansson, Sweden.
**1,000 - Meter Time Trial** — Klaus-Jurgen Grunke, E. Germany.
**4,000 - Meter Individual Pursuit** — Gregor Braun, W. Germany.
**4,000 - Meter Team Pursuit** — W. Germany.
**Match Sprint** — Anton Tkac, Czech.
**100-Km. Team** — USSR.

## Diving — Men

**Springboard** — Phil Boggs, U.S.
**Platform** — Klaus Dibiasi, Italy.

## Diving — Women

**Springboard** — Jenni Chandler, U.S.
**Platform** — Elena Vaytsekhovskaya, USSR.

## Equestrian

**3 - Day Individual** — Tad Coffin, U.S.
**3 - Day Team** — U.S.
**Individual Grand Prix Dressage** — Christine Stueckelberger, Switzerland.
**Individual Grand Prix Jumping** — Alwin Schockemoehle, W. Germany.
**Team Dressage** — W. Germany.
**Team Jumping** — France.

## Fencing — Men

**Individual Foil** — Fabio Dal Zotto, Italy.
**Team Foil** — W. Germany.
**Individual Epee** — Alexander Pusch, W. Germany.
**Team Epee** — Sweden.
**Individual Saber** — Viktor Krovopouskov, USSR.
**Team Saber** — USSR.

## Fencing — Women

**Individual Foil** — Ildiko Schwarczenberger, Hungary.
**Team Foil** — USSR.

## Field Hockey

**Team Championship** — New Zealand.

## Gymnastics — Men

**All - Around** — Nikolai Andrianov, USSR.
**Floor Exercise** — Nikolai Andrianov, USSR.
**Pommeled Horse** — Zoltan Magyar, Hungary.
**Rings** — Nikolai Andrianov, USSR.
**Vault** — Nikolai Andrianov, USSR.
**Parallel Bars** — Sawao Kato, Japan.
**Horizontal Bar** — Mitsuo Tsukahara, Japan.
**Team Championship** — Japan.

## Gymnastics — Women

**All - Around** — Nadia Comaneci, Romania.
**Floor Exercise** — Nelli Kim, USSR.
**Vault** — Nelli Kim, USSR.
**Uneven Parallel Bars** — Nadia Comaneci, Romania.
**Balance Beam** — Nadia Comaneci, Romania.
**Team Championship** — Romania.

## Team Handball

**Men** — USSR. **Women** — USSR.

## Judo

**Lightweight** — Hector Rodriguez, Cuba.
**Light Middleweight** — Vladimir Nevzorov, USSR.
**Middleweight** — Isamu Sonoda, Japan.
**Light Heavyweight** — Kazuhiro Nimomiya, Japan.
**Heavyweight** — Sergei Novikov, USSR.
**Open** — Haruki Uemura, Japan.

## Modern Pentathlon

**Individual** — Janusz Pyciak-Peciak, Poland.
**Team** — Gt. Britain.

## Rowing — Men

**Single Sculls** — Pertti Karppinen, Finland.
**Double Sculls** — Norway.
**Quadruple Sculls** — E. Germany.
**Pairs with Coxswain** — E. Germany.
**Pairs without Coxswain** — E. Germany.
**Fours with Coxswain** — USSR.
**Fours without Coxswain** — E. Germany.
**Eights with Coxswain** — E. Germany.

## Rowing — Women

**Single Sculls** — Christine Scheiblich, E. Germany.
**Double Sculls** — Bulgaria.
**Quadruple Sculls** — E. Germany.
**Pairs without Coxswain** — Bulgaria.
**Fours with Coxswain** — E. Germany.
**Eights with Coxswain** — E. Germany.

## Shooting

**Small-bore Rifle Prone** — Karlheinz Smieszek, W. Germany.
**Small-bore Rifle (3-positions)** — Lanny Bassham, U.S.
**Rapid Fire Pistol** — Norbert Klaar, E. Germany.
**Free Pistol** — Uwe Potteck, E. Germany.
**Moving Target** — Alexandr Gaxov, USSR.
**Trapshooting** — Don Haldeman, U.S.
**Skeetshooting** — Josef Panacek, Czechoslovakia.

## Soccer

**Team Championship** — E. Germany.

## Volleyball

**Men** — Poland. **Women** — Japan.

## Water Polo

**Team Championship** — Hungary.

## Weight Lifting

**Flyweight** — Alexandr Voronin, USSR.
**Bantamweight** — Norair Nourikian, Bulgaria.
**Featherweight** — Nikolai Kolesnikov, USSR.
**Lightweight** — Zbigniew Kaczmarek, Poland.
**Middleweight** — Yordan Mitkov, Bulgaria.
**Light Heavyweight** — Valery Shary, USSR.
**Middle Heavyweight** — David Rigert, USSR.
**Heavyweight** — Valentin Khristov, Bulgaria.
**Super Heavyweight** — Vasily Alexeev, USSR.

## Wrestling — Freestyle

**Paperweight** — Khassan Issaev, Bulgaria.
**Flyweight** — Yuji Takada, Japan.
**Bantamweight** — Vladimir Yumin, USSR.
**Featherweight** — Jung-Mo Yang, S. Korea.
**Lightweight** — Pavel Pinigin, USSR.
**Welterweight** — Date Jiichiro, Japan.
**Middleweight** — John Peterson, U.S.
**Light Heavyweight** — Levan Tediashvily, USSR.
**Heavyweight** — Ivan Yarygin, USSR.
**Super Heavyweight** — Soslan Andiev, USSR.

## Wrestling — Greco-Roman

**Paperweight** — Alexey Shumakov, USSR.
**Flyweight** — Vitaly Konstantinov, USSR.
**Bantamweight** — Pertti Ukkola, Finland.
**Featherweight** — Kazimer Lipien, Poland.
**Lightweight** — Suren Nalbandyan, USSR.
**Welterweight** — Antoly Bykov, USSR.
**Middleweight** — Momir Petkovic, Yugoslavia.
**Light Heavyweight** — Valery Rezantsev, USSR.
**Heavyweight** — Nikolai Balboshin, USSR.
**Super Heavyweight** — Alexandr Kolchinsky, USSR.

## Yachting

**Soling** — Denmark.
**Tempest** — Sweden.
**Flying Dutchman** — W. Germany.
**470 Class** — W. Germany.
**Tornado** — Gt. Britain.
**Finn** — E. Germany.

# Winter Olympic Games Champions, 1924-1976

## Sites and Unofficial Winners of Games

| | | |
|---|---|---|
| 1924 Chamonix, France (Norway) | 1948 St. Moritz (Sweden) | 1968 Grenoble, France (Norway) |
| 1928 St. Moritz, Switzerland (Norway) | 1952 Oslo, Norway (Norway) | 1972 Sapporo, Japan (USSR) |
| 1932 Lake Placid, N.Y. (U.S.) | 1956 Cortina d'Ampezzo, Italy (USSR) | 1976 Innsbruck, Austria, (USSR) |
| 1936 Garmisch-Partenkirchen (Norway) | 1960 Squaw Valley, Cal. (USSR) | 1980 Lake Placid, N.Y. (scheduled) |
| | 1964 Innsbruck, Austria (USSR) | |

### Biathlon (20 km)

| | Time |
|---|---|
| 1960 Klas Lestander, Sweden | 1:33:21.6 |
| 1964 Vladimir Melanin, USSR | 1:20:26.8 |
| 1968 Magnar Solberg, Norway | 1:13:45.9 |
| 1972 Magnar Solberg, Norway | 1:15:55.50 |
| 1976 Nikolai Kruglov, USSR | 1:14:12.26 |

### Biathlon Relay (40 km)

| | Time |
|---|---|
| 1968 USSR, Norway, Sweden | 2:13.02 |
| 1972 USSR, Finland, E. Germany | 1:51.44 |
| 1976 USSR, Finland, E. Germany | 1:57.55.64 |

## Bobsledding
### 4-Man Bob

| (Driver in parentheses) | Time |
|---|---|
| 1924 Switzerland (Edward Scherrer) | 5:45.54 |
| 1928 *United States (William Fiske) (A) | 3:20.5 |
| 1932 United States (William Fiske) | 7:53.68 |
| 1936 Switzerland (Pierre Musy) | 5:19.85 |
| 1948 United States (Edward Rimkus) | 5:20.1 |
| 1952 Germany (Andreas Ostler) | 5:07.84 |
| 1956 Switzerland (Frank Kapus) | 5:10.44 |
| 1964 Canada (Victor Emery) | 4:14.46 |
| 1968 Italy (Eugenio Monti) (A) | 2:17.39 |
| 1972 Switzerland (Jean Wicki) | 4:43.07 |
| 1976 E. Germany (Meinhard Nehmer) | 3:40.43 |

*Five-man Bobsled (A) 2 races

### 2-Man Bob

| | Time |
|---|---|
| 1932 United States (Hubert Stevens) | 8:14.74 |
| 1936 United States (Ivan Brown) | 5:29.29 |
| 1948 Switzerland (F. Enrich) | 5:29.2 |
| 1952 Germany (Andreas Ostler) | 5:24.54 |
| 1956 Italy (Dalla Costa) | 5:30.14 |
| 1964 Great Britain (Antony Nash) | 4:21.90 |
| 1968 Italy (Eugenio Monti) | 4:41.54 |
| 1972 W. Germany (Wolfgang Zimmerer) | 4:47.07 |
| 1976 E. Germany (Meinhard Nehmer) | 3:40.43 |

## Figure Skating
### Men's Singles

| | |
|---|---|
| 1908 Ulrich Sachow, Sweden | |
| 1920 Gillis Grafstrom, Sweden | |
| 1924 Gillis Grafstrom, Sweden | |
| 1928 Gillis Grafstrom, Sweden | |
| 1932 Karl Schaefer, Austria | |
| 1936 Karl Schaefer, Austria | |
| 1948 Richard T. Button, U.S. | |
| 1952 Richard T. Button, U.S. | |
| 1956 Hayes Alan Jenkins, U.S. | |
| 1960 David W. Jenkins, U.S. | |
| 1964 Manfred Schnelldorfer, Germany | |
| 1968 Wolfgang Schwartz, Austria | |
| 1972 Ondrej Nepela, Czechoslovakia | |
| 1976 John Curry, Great Britain | |

### Women's Singles

| | |
|---|---|
| 1908 Madge Syers, Great Britain | |
| 1920 Magda Julin-Mauroy, Sweden | |
| 1924 Mrs. Heima von Szabo-Planck, Austria | |
| 1928 Sonja Henie, Norway | |
| 1932 Sonja Henie, Norway | |
| 1936 Sonja Henie, Norway | |
| 1948 Barbara Ann Scott, Canada | |
| 1952 Jeanette Altwegg, Great Britain | |
| 1956 Tenley Albright, U.S. | |
| 1960 Carol Heiss, U.S. | |
| 1964 Sjoukje Dijkstra, Netherlands | |
| 1968 Peggy Fleming, U.S. | |
| 1972 Beatrix Schuba, Austria | |
| 1976 Dorothy Hamill, U.S. | |

### Pairs

| | |
|---|---|
| 1908 Anna Hubler & Heinrich Burger, Germany | |
| 1920 Ludovika & Walter Jakobsson, Finland | |
| 1924 Helene Engelman & Alfred Berger, Austria | |
| 1928 Andree Joly & Pierre Brunet, France | |
| 1932 Andree Joly & Pierre Brunet, France | |
| 1936 Maxie Herber & Ernest Baier, Germany | |

| | |
|---|---|
| 1948 Micheline Lannoy & Pierre Baugniet, Belgium | |
| 1952 Ria and Paul Falk, Germany | |
| 1956 Elisabeth Schwarz & Kurt Oppelt, Austria | |
| 1960 Barbara Wagner & Robert Paul, Canada | |
| 1964 Ludmila Beloussova & Oleg Protopopov, USSR | |
| 1968 Ludmila Beloussova & Oleg Protopopov, USSR | |
| 1972 Irina Rodina & Alexei Ulanov, USSR | |
| 1976 Irina Rodina & Aleksandr Zaitsev, USSR | |

### Ice Dancing

1976 Ludmila Pakhomova & Aleksandr Gorschkov, USSR

## Alpine Skiing
### Men's Downhill

| | Time |
|---|---|
| 1948 Henri Oreiller, France | 2:55.0 |
| 1952 Zeno Colo, Italy | 2:30.8 |
| 1956 Anton Sailer, Austria | 2:52.2 |
| 1960 Jean Vuarnet, France | 2:06.0 |
| 1964 Egon Zimmermann, Austria | 2:18.16 |
| 1968 Jean Claude Killy, France | 1:59.85 |
| 1972 Bernhard Russi, Switzerland | 1:51.43 |
| 1976 Franz Klammer, Austria | 1:45.73 |

### Men's Giant Slalom

| | Time |
|---|---|
| 1952 Stein Eriksen, Norway | 2:25.0 |
| 1956 Anton Sailer, Austria | 3:00.1 |
| 1960 Roger Staub, Switzerland | 1:48.3 |
| 1964 Francois Bonlieu, France | 1:46.7 |
| 1968 Jean Claude Killy, France | 3:29.28 |
| 1972 Gustavo Thoeni, Italy | 3:09.62 |
| 1976 Heini Hemmi, Switzerland | 3:26.97 |

### Men's Slalom

| | Time |
|---|---|
| 1948 Edi Reinalter, Switzerland | 2:10.3 |
| 1952 Othmar Schneider, Austria | 2:00.0 |
| 1956 Anton Sailer, Austria | 194.7 pts. |
| 1960 Ernst Hinterseer, Austria | 2:08.9 |
| 1964 Josef Stiegler, Austria | 2:11.13 |
| 1968 Jean Claude Killy, France | 1:39.73 |
| 1972 Francesco Fernandez Ochoa, Spain | 1:49.27 |
| 1976 Piero Gros, Italy | 2:03.29 |

### Women's Downhill

| | Time |
|---|---|
| 1948 Heidi Schlunegger, Switzerland | 2:28.3 |
| 1952 Trude Jochum-Beiser, Austria | 1:47.1 |
| 1956 Madeline Bethod, Switzerland | 1:40.7 |
| 1960 Heidi Biebl, Germany | 1:37.6 |
| 1964 Christi Haas, Austria | 1:55.3 |
| 1968 Olga Pall, Austria | 1:40.87 |
| 1972 Marie Therese Nadig, Switzerland | 1:36.68 |
| 1976 Rosi Mittermaier, W. Germany | 1:46.16 |

### Women's Giant Slalom

| | Time |
|---|---|
| 1952 Andrea Mead Lawrence, U.S. | 2:06.8 |
| 1956 Ossi Reichert, Germany | 1:56.5 |
| 1960 Yvonne Ruegg, Switzerland | 1:39.9 |
| 1964 Marielle Goitschel, France | 1:52.2 |
| 1968 Nancy Greene, Canada | 1:51.97 |
| 1972 Marie Therese Nadig, Switzerland | 1:29.90 |
| 1976 Kathy Kreiner, Canada | 1:29.13 |

### Women's Slalom

| | Time |
|---|---|
| 1948 Gretchen Fraser, U.S. | 1:57.2 |
| 1952 Andrea Mead Lawrence, U.S. | 2:10.6 |
| 1956 Renee Colliard, Switzerland | 112.3 pts. |
| 1960 Anne Heggtveigt, Canada | 1:49.6 |
| 1964 Christine Goitschel, France | 1:35.11 |
| 1968 Marielle Goitschel, France | 1:25.86 |
| 1972 Barbara Cochran, U.S. | 1:31.24 |
| 1976 Rosi Mittermaier, W. Germany | 1:30.54 |

## Nordic Skiing
### Men's Cross-Country Events
#### 15 kilometers (9.3 miles) or equivalent

| | Time |
|---|---|
| 1924 Thorleif Haug, Norway | 1:14:31 |
| 1928 Johan Grottumsbraaten, Norway | 1:37:01 |
| 1932 Sven Utterstrom, Sweden | 1:23:07 |
| 1936 Erik-August Larsson, Sweden | 1:14:38 |

| | | |
|---|---|---|
| **1948** Martin Lundstrom, Sweden | 1:13:50 |
| **1952** Hallgeir Brenden, Norway | 1:01:34 |
| **1956** Hallgeir Brenden, Norway | 49:39.0 |
| **1960** Haakon Brusveen, Norway | 51:55.0 |
| **1964** Eero Mantyranta, Finland | 50:54.1 |
| **1968** Harald Groenningen, Norway | 47:54.2 |
| **1972** Sven-Ake Lundback, Sweden | 45:28.24 |
| **1976** Nikolai Bajukov, USSR | 43:58.47 |
| (Note: approx. 18-kilometer course 1924-1952) | |

| **30 kilometers (18.6 miles)** | **Time** |
|---|---|
| **1956** Veikko Hakulinen, Finland | 1:44:06.0 |
| **1960** Sixten Jernberg, Sweden | 1:51:03.9 |
| **1964** Eero Mantyranta, Finland | 1:30:50.7 |
| **1968** Franco Nones, Italy | 1:35:39.2 |
| **1972** Vyacheslav Vedenin, USSR | 1:36:31.1 |
| **1976** Sergei Savaliev, USSR | 1:30:29.38 |

| **50 kilometers (31 miles)** | **Time** |
|---|---|
| **1924** Thorleif Haug, Norway | 3:44:32.0 |
| **1928** Per Erik Hedlund, Sweden | 4:52:03.0 |
| **1932** Veli Saarinen, Finland | 4:28:00.0 |
| **1936** Elis Viklund, Sweden | 3:30:11.0 |
| **1948** Nils Karlsson, Sweden | 3:47:48.0 |
| **1952** Veikko Hakulinen, Finland | 3:33:33.0 |
| **1956** Sixten Jernberg, Sweden | 2:50:27.0 |
| **1960** Kalevi Hamalainen, Finland | 2:59:06.3 |
| **1964** Sixten Jernberg, Sweden | 2:43:52.6 |
| **1968** Ole Ellefsaeter, Norway | 2:28:45.8 |
| **1972** Paal Tyldum, Norway | 2:43:14.7 |
| **1976** Ivar Formo, Norway | 2:37:30.05 |

| **40-km. Cross-Country Relay** | **Time** |
|---|---|
| **1936** Finland, Norway, Sweden | 2:41:33.0 |
| **1948** Sweden, Finland, Norway | 2:32:08.0 |
| **1952** Finland, Norway, Sweden | 2:20:16.0 |
| **1956** USSR, Finland, Sweden | 2:15:30.0 |
| **1960** Finland, Norway, USSR | 2:18:45.6 |
| **1964** Sweden, Finland, USSR | 2:18:34.6 |
| **1968** Norway, Sweden, Finland | 2:08:33.5 |
| **1972** USSR, Norway, Switzerland | 2:04:47.94 |
| **1976** Finland, Norway, USSR | 2:07:59.72 |

| **15-km. Cross-Country & Jumping** | **Points** |
|---|---|
| **1924** Thorleif Haug, Norway | 453.800 |
| **1928** Johan Grottumsbraaten, Norway | 427.800 |
| **1932** Johan Grottumsbraaten, Norway | 446.200 |
| **1936** Oddbjorn Hagen, Norway | 430.300 |
| **1948** Heikki Hasu, Finland | 448.800 |
| **1952** Simon Slattvik, Norway | 451.621 |
| **1956** Sverre Stenersen, Norway | 455.000 |
| **1960** Georg Thoma, Germany | 457.952 |
| **1964** Tormod Knutsen, Norway | 469.280 |
| **1968** Franz Keller, W. Germany | 449.040 |
| **1972** Ulrich Wehling, E. Germany | 413.340 |
| **1976** Ulrich Wehling, E. Germany | 423.390 |

| **Ski Jumping (90 meters)** | **Points** |
|---|---|
| **1924** Jacob T. Thams, Norway | 227.5 |
| **1928** Alfred Andersen, Norway | 230.5 |
| **1932** Birger Ruud, Norway | 228.0 |
| **1936** Birger Ruud, Norway | 232.0 |
| **1948** Petter Hugsted, Norway | 228.1 |
| **1952** A. Bergmann, Norway | 226.0 |
| **1956** Antti Hyvarinen, Finland | 227.0 |
| **1960** Helmut Recknagel, Germany | 227.2 |
| **1964** Toralf Engan, Norway | 230.7 |
| **1968** Vladimir Beloussov, USSR | 231.3 |
| **1972** Wojiech Fortuna, Poland | 219.9 |
| **1976** Karl Schnabl, Austria | 234.8 |

| **Ski Jumping (70 meters)** | **Points** |
|---|---|
| **1964** Veikko Kankkonen, Finland | 229.9 |
| **1968** Jiri Raska, Czechoslovakia | 216.5 |
| **1972** Yukio Kasaya, Japan | 244.2 |
| **1976** Hans Aschenbach, E. Germany | 252.0 |

### Women's Events

| **5 kilometers (approx. 3.1 miles)** | **Time** |
|---|---|
| **1964** Claudia Boyarskikh, USSR | 17:50.5 |
| **1968** Toini Gustafsson, Sweden | 16:45.2 |
| **1972** Galina Koulacova, USSR | 17:00.5 |
| **1976** Helena Takalo, Finland | 15:48.69 |

| **10 kilometers (6.2 miles)** | **Time** |
|---|---|
| **1952** Lydia Wideman, Finland | 41:40.0 |
| **1956** Lyubov Kosyreva, USSR | 38:11.0 |
| **1960** Maria Gusakova, USSR | 39:46.6 |
| **1964** Claudia Boyarskikh, USSR | 40:24.3 |
| **1968** Toini Gustafsson, Sweden | 36:46.5 |

| | | |
|---|---|---|
| **1972** Galina Koulacova, USSR | 34:17.82 |
| **1976** Raisa Smetanina, USSR | 30:13.41 |

| **15-km. Cross-Country Relay** | **Time** |
|---|---|
| **1956** Finland, USSR, Sweden | 1:09:01.0 |
| **1960** Sweden, USSR, Finland | 1:04:21.4 |
| **1964** USSR, Sweden, Finland | 59:20.2 |
| **1968** Norway, Sweden, USSR | 57:30.0 |
| **1972** USSR, Finland, Norway | 48:46.1 |
| **1976** USSR, Finland, E. Germany | 1:07:49.75 |
| (20 km. in 1976) | |

## Ice Hockey

| | |
|---|---|
| **1920** Canada, U.S., Czechoslovakia |
| **1924** Canada, U.S., Great Britain |
| **1928** Canada, Sweden, Switzerland |
| **1932** Canada, U.S., Germany |
| **1936** Great Britain, Canada, U.S. |
| **1948** Canada, Czechoslovakia, Switzerland |
| **1952** Canada, U.S., Sweden |
| **1956** USSR, U.S., Canada |
| **1960** U.S., Canada, USSR |
| **1964** USSR, Sweden, Czechoslovakia |
| **1968** USSR, Czechoslovakia, Canada |
| **1972** USSR, U.S., Czechoslovakia |
| **1976** USSR, Czechoslovakia, W. Germany |

## Luge

| **Men's Singles** | **Time** |
|---|---|
| **1964** Thomas Kohler, Germany | 3:26.77 |
| **1968** Manfred Schmid, Austria | 2:52.48 |
| **1972** Wolfgang Scheidel, E. Germany | 3:27.58 |
| **1976** Detlef Guenther, E. Germany | 3:27.688 |

| **Men's Doubles** | **Time** |
|---|---|
| **1964** Austria | 1:41.62 |
| **1968** East Germany | 1:35.85 |
| **1972** Italy, E. Germany (tie) | 1:28.35 |
| **1976** E. Germany | 1:25.604 |

| **Women's Singles** | **Time** |
|---|---|
| **1964** Ortun Enderlein, Germany | 3:24.67 |
| **1968** Erica Lechner, Italy | 2:28.66 |
| **1972** Anna M. Muller, E. Germany | 2:59.18 |
| **1976** Margit Schumann, E. Germany | 2:50.621 |

## Speed Skating

### Men's Events

| **500 meters (approx. 547 yds.)** | **Time** |
|---|---|
| **1924** Charles Jewtraw, U.S. | 0:44.0 |
| **1928** Clas Thunberg, Finland & Bernt Evensen, Norway (tie) | 0:43.4 |
| **1932** John A. Shea, U.S. | 0:43.4 |
| **1936** Ivar Ballangrud, Norway | 0:43.4 |
| **1948** Finn Helgesen, Norway | 0:43.1 |
| **1952** Kenneth Henry, U.S. | 0:43.2 |
| **1956** Evgeniy Grishin, USSR | 0:40.2 |
| **1960** Evgeniy Grishin, USSR | 0:40.2 |
| **1964** Terry McDermott, U.S. | 0:40.1 |
| **1968** Erhard Keller, W. Germany | 0:40.3 |
| **1972** Erhard Keller, W. Germany | 0:39.44 |
| **1976** Evgeny Kulikov, USSR | 0:39.17 |

| **1,000 meters** | **Time** |
|---|---|
| **1976** Peter Mueller, U.S. | 1:19.32 |

| **1,500 meters** | **Time** |
|---|---|
| **1924** Clas Thunberg, Finland | 2:20.8 |
| **1928** Clas Thunberg, Finland | 2:21.1 |
| **1932** John A. Shea, U.S. | 2:57.2 |
| **1936** Charles Mathiesen, Norway | 2:19.2 |
| **1948** Sverre Farstad, Norway | 2:17.6 |
| **1952** Hjalmar Anderson, Norway | 2:20.4 |
| **1956** Evgeniy Grishin, USSR | 2:08.6 |
| **1960** Roald Edgar Aas, Norway & Evgeniy Grishin, USSR (tie) | 2:10.4 |
| **1964** Ants Anston, USSR | 2:10.3 |
| **1968** Cornelis Verkerk, Netherlands | 2:03.4 |
| **1972** Ard Schenk, Netherlands | 2:02.96 |
| **1976** Jan Egil Storholt, Norway | 1:59.38 |

| **5,000 meters** | **Time** |
|---|---|
| **1924** Clas Thunberg, Finland | 8:39.0 |
| **1928** Ivar Ballangrud, Norway | 8:50.5 |
| **1932** Irving Jaffee, U.S. | 9:40.8 |
| **1936** Ivar Ballangrud, Norway | 8:19.6 |
| **1948** Reidar Liakleb, Norway | 8:29.4 |
| **1952** Hjalmar Anderson, Norway | 8:10.6 |

| 956 Boris Shilkov, USSR | 7:48.7 |
| 960 Viktor Kosichkin, USSR | 7:51.3 |
| 964 Knut Johannesen, Norway | 7:38.4 |
| 968 F. Anton Maier, Norway | 7:22.4 |
| 972 Ard Schenk, Netherlands | 7:23.61 |
| 976 Sten Stensen, Norway | 7:24.48 |

### 10,000 meters

| | Time |
| --- | --- |
| 924 Julius Skutnabb, Finland | 18:04.8 |
| 928 Event not held, thawing of ice | |
| 932 Irving Jaffee, U.S. | 19:13.6 |
| 936 Ivar Ballangrud, Norway | 17:24.3 |
| 948 Ake Seyffarth, Norway | 17:26.3 |
| 952 Hjalmar Anderson, Norway | 16:45.8 |
| 956 Sigvard Ericsson, Sweden | 16:35.9 |
| 960 Knut Johannesen, Norway | 15:46.6 |
| 964 Jonny Nilsson, Sweden | 15:50.1 |
| 968 Jonny Hoeglin, Sweden | 15:23.6 |
| 972 Ard Schenk, Netherlands | 15:01.3 |
| 976 Piet Kleine, Netherlands | 14:50.59 |

### Women's Events
### 500 meters

| | Time |
| --- | --- |
| 960 Helga Haase, Germany | 0:45.9 |
| 964 Lydia Skoblikova, USSR | 0:45.0 |

| 1968 Ludmila Titova, USSR | 0:46.1 |
| 1972 Anne Henning, U.S. | 0:43.44 |
| 1976 Sheila Young, U.S. | 0:42.76 |

### 1,000 meters

| | Time |
| --- | --- |
| 1960 Klara Guseva, USSR | 1:34.1 |
| 1964 Lydia Skoblikova, USSR | 1:33.2 |
| 1968 Carolina Geijssen, Netherlands | 1:32.6 |
| 1972 Monika Pflug, W. Germany | 1:31.40 |
| 1976 Tatiana Averina, USSR | 1:28.43 |

### 1,500 meters

| | Time |
| --- | --- |
| 1960 Lydia Skoblikova, USSR | 2:52.2 |
| 1964 Lydia Skoblikova, USSR | 2:22.6 |
| 1968 Kaija Mustonen, Finland | 2:22.4 |
| 1972 Dianne Holum, U.S. | 2:20.85 |
| 1976 Galina Stepanskaya, USSR | 2:16.58 |

### 3,000 meters

| | Time |
| --- | --- |
| 1960 Lydia Skoblikova, USSR | 5:14.3 |
| 1964 Lydia Skoblikova, USSR | 5:14.9 |
| 1968 Johanna Schut, Netherlands | 4:56.2 |
| 1972 Stien Baas-Kaiser, Netherlands | 4:52.14 |
| 1976 Tatiana Averina, USSR | 4:45.19 |

## 1976 Final Medal Standing

Innsbruck, Austria, Feb. 4-15

| | Gold | Silver | Bronze | Total | | Gold | Silver | Bronze | Total |
| --- | --- | --- | --- | --- | --- | --- | --- | --- | --- |
| Austria | 2 | 2 | 2 | 6 | Italy | 1 | 2 | 1 | 4 |
| Canada | 1 | 1 | 1 | 3 | Liechtenstein | 0 | 0 | 2 | 2 |
| Czechoslovakia | 0 | 1 | 0 | 1 | Netherlands | 1 | 2 | 3 | 6 |
| Finland | 2 | 4 | 1 | 7 | Norway | 3 | 3 | 1 | 7 |
| France | 0 | 0 | 1 | 1 | Sweden | 0 | 0 | 2 | 2 |
| Germany, East | 7 | 5 | 7 | 19 | Switzerland | 1 | 3 | 1 | 5 |
| Germany, West | 2 | 5 | 3 | 10 | USSR | 13 | 6 | 8 | 27 |
| Great Britain | 1 | 0 | 0 | 1 | United States | 3 | 3 | 4 | 10 |

## Olympic Information

**Symbol:** Five rings or circles, linked together to represent the sporting friendship of all peoples. The rings also symbolize the 5 continents—Europe, Asia, Africa, Australia, and America. Each ring is a different color—blue, yellow, black, green, and red.

**Flag:** The symbol of the 5 rings on a plain white background.

**Motto:** "Citius, Altius, Fortius." Latin meaning "faster, higher, braver," or the modern interpretation "swifter, higher, stronger". The motto was coined by Father Didon, a French educator, in 1895.

**Creed:** "The most important thing in the Olympic Games is not to win but to take part, just as the most important thing in life is not the triumph but the struggle. The essential thing is not to have conquered but to have fought well."

**Oath:** An athlete of the host country recites the following at the opening ceremony. "In the name of all competitors I promise that we will take part in these Olympic Games, respecting and abiding by the rules which govern them, in the true spirit of sportsmanship for the glory of sport and the honor of our teams." Both the oath and the creed were composed by Pierre de Coubertin, the founder of the modern Games.

**Flame:** Symbolizes the continuity between the ancient and modern Games. The modern version of the flame was adopted in 1936. The torch used to kindle the flame is first lit by the sun's rays at Olympia, Greece, and then carried to the site of the Games by relays of runners. Ships and planes are used when necessary.

## James E. Sullivan Memorial Trophy Winners

The James E. Sullivan Memorial Trophy, named after the former president of the AAU and inaugurated in 1930, is awarded annually by the AAU to the athlete who "by his or her performance, example and influence as an amateur, has done the most during the year to advance the cause of sportmanship."

| Year | Winner | Sport | Year | Winner | Sport | Year | Winner | Sport |
| --- | --- | --- | --- | --- | --- | --- | --- | --- |
| 930 | Bobby Jones | Golf | 1946 | Arnold Tucker | Football | 1962 | James Beatty | Track |
| 931 | Barney Berlinger | Track | 1947 | John Kelly Jr. | Rowing | 1963 | John Pennel | Track |
| 932 | Jim Bausch | Track | 1948 | Robert Mathias | Track | 1964 | Don Schollander | Swimming |
| 933 | Glen Cunningham | Track | 1949 | Dick Button | Skating | 1965 | Bill Bradley | Basketball |
| 934 | Bill Bonthron | Track | 1950 | Fred Wilt | Track | 1966 | Jim Ryun | Track |
| 935 | Lawson Little | Golf | 1951 | Rev. Robert Richards | Track | 1967 | Randy Matson | Track |
| 936 | Glenn Morris | Track | 1952 | Horace Ashenfelter | Track | 1968 | Debbie Meyer | Swimming |
| 937 | Don Budge | Tennis | 1953 | Dr. Sammy Lee | Diving | 1969 | Bill Toomey | Track |
| 938 | Don Lash | Track | 1954 | Mal Whitfield | Track | 1970 | John Kinsella | Swimming |
| 939 | Joe Burk | Rowing | 1955 | Harrison Dillard | Track | 1971 | Mark Spitz | Swimming |
| 940 | Greg Rice | Track | 1956 | Patricia McCormick | Diving | 1972 | Frank Shorter | Track |
| 941 | Leslie MacMitchell | Track | 1957 | Bobby Joe Morrow | Track | 1973 | Bill Walton | Basketball |
| 942 | Cornelius Warmerdam | Track | 1958 | Glen Davis | Track | 1974 | Rick Wohlhuter | Track |
| 943 | Gilbert Dodds | Track | 1959 | Parry O'Brien | Track | 1975 | Tim Shaw | Swimming |
| 944 | Ann Curtis | Swimming | 1960 | Rafer Johnson | Track | 1976 | Bruce Jenner | Track |
| 945 | Doc Blanchard | Football | 1961 | Wilma Rudolph Ward | Track | 1977 | John Naber | Swimming |

# National Basketball Association, 1977-78

Final Standings

## Eastern Conference

### Atlantic Division

| Club | W | L | Pct | GB |
|------|---|---|-----|----|
| Philadelphia | 55 | 27 | .671 | ..... |
| New York | 43 | 39 | .524 | 12 |
| Boston | 32 | 50 | .390 | 23 |
| Buffalo | 27 | 55 | .329 | 28 |
| New Jersey | 24 | 58 | .293 | 31 |

### Central Division

| Club | W | L | Pct | GB |
|------|---|---|-----|----|
| San Antonio | 52 | 30 | .634 | ..... |
| Washington | 44 | 38 | .537 | 8 |
| Cleveland | 43 | 39 | .524 | 9 |
| Atlanta | 41 | 41 | .500 | 11 |
| New Orleans | 39 | 43 | .476 | 13 |
| Houston | 28 | 54 | .341 | 24 |

## Western Conference

### Midwest Division

| Club | W | L | Pct | GB |
|------|---|---|-----|----|
| Denver | 48 | 34 | .585 | ..... |
| Milwaukee | 44 | 38 | .537 | 4 |
| Chicago | 40 | 42 | .488 | 8 |
| Detroit | 38 | 44 | .463 | 10 |
| Kansas City | 31 | 51 | .378 | 17 |
| Indiana | 31 | 51 | .378 | 17 |

### Pacific Division

| Club | W | L | Pct | GB |
|------|---|---|-----|----|
| Portland | 58 | 24 | .707 | ..... |
| Phoenix | 49 | 33 | .598 | 9 |
| Seattle | 47 | 35 | .573 | 11 |
| Los Angeles | 45 | 37 | .549 | 13 |
| Golden State | 43 | 39 | .524 | 15 |

## NBA Playoff Results

Milwaukee defeated Phoenix 2 games to 0.
Washington defeated Atlanta 2 games to 0.
New York defeated Cleveland 2 games to 0.
Seattle defeated Los Angeles 2 games to 1.
Philadelphia defeated New York 4 games to 0.
Washington defeated San Antonio 4 games to 2.

Denver defeated Milwaukee 4 games to 3.
Seattle defeated Portland 4 games to 2.
Seattle defeated Denver 4 games to 2.
Washington defeated Philadelphia 4 games to 2.
Washington defeated Seattle 4 games to 3.

## Final Statistics

### Individual Scoring Leaders

(Minimum: 70 games played or 1400 points)

| | G | FG | FT | Pts | Avg |
|---|---|----|----|----|-----|
| Gervin, San Antonio | 82 | 864 | 504 | 2232 | 27.2 |
| Thompson, Denver | 80 | 826 | 520 | 2172 | 27.2 |
| McAdoo, New York | 79 | 814 | 469 | 2097 | 26.5 |
| Abdul-Jabbar Los Angeles | 62 | 663 | 274 | 1600 | 25.8 |
| Murphy, Houston | 76 | 852 | 245 | 1949 | 25.6 |
| Westphal, Phoenix | 80 | 809 | 396 | 2014 | 25.2 |
| R. Smith, Buffalo | 82 | 789 | 443 | 2021 | 24.6 |
| Lanier, Detroit | 63 | 622 | 298 | 1542 | 24.5 |
| W. Davis, Phoenix | 81 | 786 | 387 | 1959 | 24.2 |
| King, New Jersey | 79 | 798 | 313 | 1909 | 24.2 |
| Williamson, New Jersey | 75 | 723 | 331 | 1777 | 23.7 |
| Drew, Atlanta | 70 | 593 | 437 | 1623 | 23.2 |
| Barry, Golden State | 82 | 760 | 378 | 1898 | 23.1 |
| Gilmore, Chicago | 82 | 704 | 471 | 1879 | 22.9 |
| Robinson, New Orleans | 82 | 748 | 366 | 1862 | 22.7 |
| Dantley, Los Angeles | 79 | 578 | 541 | 1697 | 21.5 |
| Issel, Denver | 82 | 659 | 428 | 1746 | 21.3 |
| Erving, Philadelphia | 74 | 611 | 306 | 1528 | 20.6 |
| Kenon, San Antonio | 81 | 698 | 276 | 1672 | 20.6 |
| McGinnis, Philadelphia | 78 | 588 | 411 | 1587 | 20.3 |

### Field Goal Leaders

(Minimum: 300 FG made)

| | FGM | FGA | Pct |
|---|-----|-----|-----|
| B. Jones, Denver | 440 | 761 | .578 |
| Dawkins, Philadelphia | 332 | 577 | .575 |
| Gilmore, Chicago | 704 | 1260 | .559 |
| Abdul-Jabbar, Los Angeles | 663 | 1205 | .550 |
| English, Milwaukee | 343 | 633 | .542 |
| Lanier, Detroit | 622 | 1159 | .537 |
| Gervin, San Antonio | 864 | 1611 | .536 |
| Gross, Portland | 381 | 720 | .529 |
| Paultz, San Antonio | 518 | 979 | .529 |
| W. Davis, Phoenix | 786 | 1494 | .526 |

### Free Throw Leaders

(Minimum: 125 FT made)

| | FTM | FTA | Pct |
|---|-----|-----|-----|
| Barry, Golden State | 378 | 409 | .924 |
| Murphy, Houston | 245 | 267 | .918 |
| E. Brown, Seattle | 176 | 196 | .898 |
| Newlin, Houston | 152 | 174 | .874 |
| Wedman, Kansas City | 221 | 254 | .870 |
| Maravich, New Orleans | 240 | 276 | .870 |
| Havlicek, Boston | 230 | 269 | .855 |
| Kenon, San Antonio | 276 | 323 | .854 |
| Boone, Kansas City | 322 | 377 | .854 |
| Frazier, Cleveland | 153 | 180 | .850 |

### Assists Leaders

(Minimum: 70 games or 400 assists)

| | G | No | Avg |
|---|---|----|-----|
| K. Porter, New Jersey | 82 | 837 | 10.2 |
| J. Lucas, Houston | 82 | 768 | 9.4 |
| Sobers, Indiana | 79 | 584 | 7.4 |
| Nixon, Los Angeles | 81 | 553 | 6.8 |
| Van Lier, Chicago | 78 | 531 | 6.8 |
| Bibby, Philadelphia | 82 | 464 | 5.7 |
| F. Walker, Cleveland | 81 | 453 | 5.6 |
| R. Smith, Buffalo | 82 | 458 | 5.6 |
| Buckner, Milwaukee | 82 | 456 | 5.6 |
| Westphal, Phoenix | 80 | 437 | 5.5 |

### Rebound Leaders

(Minimum: 70 games or 800 rebounds)

| | G | Off | Def | Tot | Av |
|---|---|-----|-----|-----|----|
| Robinson New Orleans | 82 | 298 | 990 | 1288 | 15 |
| Malone, Houston | 59 | 380 | 506 | 886 | 15 |
| Cowens, Boston | 77 | 248 | 830 | 1078 | 14 |
| Hayes, Washington | 81 | 335 | 740 | 1075 | 13 |
| Nater, Buffalo | 78 | 278 | 751 | 1029 | 13 |
| Gilmore, Chicago | 82 | 318 | 753 | 1071 | 13 |
| Abdul-Jabbar, Los Angeles | 62 | 186 | 615 | 801 | 12 |
| McAdoo, New York | 79 | 236 | 774 | 1010 | 12 |
| Webster, Seattle | 82 | 361 | 674 | 1035 | 12 |
| Unseld, Washington | 80 | 286 | 669 | 955 | 11 |

### Steals Leaders

(Minimum: 70 games or 125 steals)

| | G | No | Avg |
|---|---|----|-----|
| Lee, Phoenix | 82 | 225 | 2.74 |
| G. Williams, Seattle | 79 | 185 | 2.34 |
| Buckner, Milwaukee | 82 | 188 | 2.29 |
| Gale, San Antonio | 70 | 159 | 2.27 |
| Buse, Phoenix | 82 | 185 | 2.26 |
| F. Walker, Cleveland | 81 | 176 | 2.17 |
| Sobers, Indiana | 79 | 170 | 2.15 |
| R. Smith, Buffalo | 82 | 172 | 2.10 |
| C. Ford, Detroit | 82 | 166 | 2.02 |

### Blocked Shots Leaders

(Minimum: 70 games or 100 blocked shots)

| | G | No | Avg |
|---|---|----|-----|
| G. Johnson, New Jersey | 81 | 274 | 3.38 |
| Abdul-Jabbar, Los Angeles | 62 | 185 | 2.98 |
| Rollins, Atlanta | 80 | 218 | 2.73 |
| B. Walton, Portland | 58 | 146 | 2.52 |
| Paultz, San Antonio | 80 | 194 | 2.42 |
| Gilmore, Chicago | 82 | 181 | 2.21 |
| Meriweather, New Orleans | 54 | 118 | 2.19 |
| E. Smith, Cleveland | 81 | 176 | 2.17 |

## NBA Champions 1947-1978

| Year | Regular season | | Playoffs | |
|---|---|---|---|---|
| | Eastern Conference | Western Conference | Winner | Runner-up |
| '47 | Washington | Chicago | Philadelphia | Chicago |
| '48 | Philadelphia | St. Louis | Baltimore | Philadelphia |
| '49 | Washington | Rochester | Minneapolis | Washington |
| '50 | Syracuse | Minneapolis | Minneapolis | Syracuse |
| '51 | Philadelphia | Minneapolis | Rochester | New York |
| '52 | Syracuse | Rochester | Minneapolis | New York |
| '53 | New York | Minneapolis | Minneapolis | New York |
| '54 | New York | Minneapolis | Minneapolis | Syracuse |
| '55 | Syracuse | Ft. Wayne | Syracuse | Ft. Wayne |
| '56 | Philadelphia | Ft. Wayne | Philadelphia | Ft. Wayne |
| '57 | Boston | St. Louis | Boston | St. Louis |
| '58 | Boston | St. Louis | St. Louis | Boston |
| '59 | Boston | St. Louis | Boston | Minneapolis |
| '60 | Boston | St. Louis | Boston | St. Louis |
| '61 | Boston | St. Louis | Boston | St. Louis |
| '62 | Boston | Los Angeles | Boston | Los Angeles |
| '63 | Boston | Los Angeles | Boston | Los Angeles |
| '64 | Boston | San Francisco | Boston | San Francisco |
| '65 | Boston | Los Angeles | Boston | Los Angeles |
| '66 | Philadelphia | Los Angeles | Boston | Los Angeles |
| '67 | Philadelphia | San Francisco | Philadelphia | San Francisco |
| '68 | Philadelphia | St. Louis | Boston | Los Angeles |
| '69 | Baltimore | Los Angeles | Boston | Los Angeles |
| '70 | New York | Atlanta | New York | Los Angeles |

| Year | Atlantic | Central | Midwest | Pacific | Winner | Runner-up |
|---|---|---|---|---|---|---|
| '71 | New York | Baltimore | Milwaukee | Los Angeles | Milwaukee | Baltimore |
| '72 | Boston | Baltimore | Milwaukee | Los Angeles | Los Angeles | New York |
| '73 | Boston | Baltimore | Milwaukee | Los Angeles | New York | Los Angeles |
| '74 | Boston | Capital | Milwaukee | Los Angeles | Boston | Milwaukee |
| '75 | Boston | Washington | Chicago | Golden State | Golden State | Washington |
| '76 | Boston | Cleveland | Milwaukee | Golden State | Boston | Phoenix |
| '77 | Philadelphia | Houston | Denver | Los Angeles | Portland | Philadelphia |
| '78 | Philadelphia | San Antonio | Denver | Portland | Washington | Seattle |

## NBA Scoring Leaders

| Year | Scoring champion | Pts | Avg | Year | Scoring champion | Pts | Avg |
|---|---|---|---|---|---|---|---|
| '47 | Joe Fulks, Philadelphia | 1,389 | 23.2 | 1964 | Wilt Chamberlain, San Francisco | 2,948 | 36.5 |
| '48 | Max Zaslofsky, Chicago | 1,007 | 21.0 | 1965 | Wilt Chamberlain, San Fran., Phila. | 2,534 | 34.7 |
| '49 | George Mikan, Minneapolis | 1,698 | 28.3 | 1966 | Wilt Chamberlain, Philadelphia | 2,649 | 33.5 |
| '50 | George Mikan, Minneapolis | 1,865 | 27.4 | 1967 | Rick Barry, San Francisco | 2,775 | 35.6 |
| '51 | George Mikan, Minneapolis | 1,932 | 28.4 | 1968 | Dave Bing, Detroit | 2,142 | 27.1 |
| '52 | Paul Arizin, Philadelphia | 1,674 | 25.4 | 1969 | Elvin Hayes, San Diego | 2,327 | 28.4 |
| '53 | Neil Johnston, Philadelphia | 1,564 | 22.3 | 1970 | Jerry West, Los Angeles | 2,309 | 31.2 |
| '54 | Neil Johnston, Philadelphia | 1,759 | 24.4 | 1971 | Lew Alcindor, Milwaukee | 2,596 | 31.7 |
| '55 | Neil Johnston, Philadelphia | 1,631 | 22.7 | 1972 | Kareem Abdul-Jabar (Alcindor), Milwaukee | 2,822 | 34.8 |
| '56 | Bob Pettit, St. Louis | 1,849 | 25.7 | | | | |
| '57 | Paul Arizin, Philadelphia | 1,817 | 25.6 | 1973 | Nate Archibald, Kansas City-Omaha | 2,719 | 34.0 |
| '58 | George Yardley, Detroit | 2,001 | 27.8 | 1974 | Bob McAdoo, Buffalo | 2,261 | 30.6 |
| '59 | Bob Pettit, St. Louis | 2,105 | 29.2 | 1975 | Bob McAdoo, Buffalo | 2,831 | 34.5 |
| '60 | Wilt Chamberlain, Philadelphia | 2,707 | 37.9 | 1976 | Bob McAdoo, Buffalo | 2,427 | 31.1 |
| '61 | Wilt Chamberlain | 3,033 | 38.4 | 1977 | Pete Maravich, New Orleans | 2,273 | 31.1 |
| '62 | Wilt Chamberlain, Philadelphia | 4,029 | 50.4 | 1978 | George Gervin, San Antonio | 2,232 | 27.2 |
| '63 | Wilt Chamberlain, San Francisco | 3,586 | 44.8 | | | | |

## Basketball Hall of Fame

Springfield, Mass.

**Players**

Arizin, Paul
Baylor, Elgin
Beckman, John
Borgmann, Bennie
Brennan, Joseph
Cooper, Charles
Cousy, Bob
Davies, Bob
DeBernardi, Forrest
Dehnert, Dutch
Endacott, Paul
Foster, Bud
Friedman, Max
Fulks, Joe
Gale, Lauren
Gola, Tom
Gruenig, Ace
Hagan, Cliff
Hanson, Victor
Holman, Nat
Hyatt, Chuck
Johnson, William
Krause, Moose
Kurland, Bob

Lapchick, Joe
Luisetti, Hank
McCracken, Branch
McCracken, Jack
Macauley, Ed
Mikan, George
Murphy, Stretch
Page, Pat
Pettit, Bob
Phillip, Andy
Pollard, Jim
Roosma, John S.
Russell, Honey
Russell, Bill
Schayes, Adolph
Schmidt, Ernest
Schommer, John
Sedran, Barney
Sharman, Bill
Steinmetz, Christian
Thompson, Cat
Vandivier, Fuzzy
Wachter, Edward
Wooden, John

**Coaches**

Auerbach, Red
Blood, Ernest
Cann, Howard
Carlson, Dr. H. C.
Carnevale, Ben
Dean, Everett
Diddle, Edgar
Drake, Bruce
Gill, Slats
Hobson, Howard
Iba, Hank
Julian, Alvin
Keaney, Frank
Keogan, George
Lambert, Ward
Litwack, Harry
Loeffler, Kenneth
Lonborg, Dutch
McGuire, Frank
Meanwell, Dr. W. E.
Rupp, Adolph
Sachs, Leonard
Wooden, John

**Referees**

Hepbron, George
Hoyt, George
Kennedy, Matthew
Nucatola, John
Quigley, Ernest
Tobey, David
Walsh, David

**Contributors**

Allen, Phog
Bee, Clair
Brown, Walter
Bunn, John
Douglas, Bob
Fisher, Harry
Gottlieb, Edward
Gulick, Dr. L. H.
Hickox, Edward
Hinkle, Tony
Irish, Ned
Jones, R. W.
Liston, Emil
Mokray, Bill

Morgan, Ralph
Morgenweck, Frank
Naismith, Dr. James
O'Brien, John
Olsen, Harold
Podoloff, Maurice
Porter, H. V.
Reid, William
Ripley, Elmer
St. John, Lynn
Saperstein, Abe
Schabinger, Arthur
Stagg, Amos Alonzo
Taylor, Chuck
Tower, Oswald
Trester, Arthur
Wells, Clifford

**Teams**

First Team
Original Celtics
Buffalo Germans
Renaissance

## NBA Team Statistics in 1977-78

### Offense

| Team | Field Goals | | | Free Throws | | | Rebounds | | | Scoring | |
|---|---|---|---|---|---|---|---|---|---|---|---|
| | Made | Att | Pct | Made | Att | Pct | Off | Def | Tot | Pts | Avg |
| Philadelphia . . . . | 3628 | 7471 | .486 | 2153 | 2863 | .752 | 1299 | 2694 | 3993 | 9409 | 114.7 |
| San Antonio . . . . | 3794 | 7594 | .500 | 1797 | 2234 | .804 | 1030 | 2594 | 3624 | 9385 | 114.5 |
| New York. . . . . . | 3815 | 7822 | .488 | 1670 | 2225 | .751 | 1180 | 2689 | 3869 | 9300 | 113.4 |
| Milwaukee . . . . . | 3801 | 7883 | .482 | 1612 | 2220 | .726 | 1239 | 2480 | 3719 | 9214 | 112.4 |
| Phoenix . . . . . . | 3731 | 7836 | .476 | 1749 | 2329 | .751 | 1166 | 2579 | 3745 | 9211 | 112.3 |
| Denver . . . . . . . | 3548 | 7441 | .477 | 2068 | 2705 | .765 | 1177 | 2736 | 3913 | 9164 | 111.8 |
| Washington. . . . . | 3580 | 7772 | .461 | 1887 | 2655 | .711 | 1349 | 2815 | 4164 | 9047 | 110.3 |
| Los Angeles . . . * | 3734 | 7672 | .487 | 1576 | 2095 | .752 | 1136 | 2647 | 3783 | 9044 | 110.3 |
| Kansas City . . . . | 3601 | 7731 | .466 | 1775 | 2262 | .785 | 1208 | 2632 | 3840 | 8977 | 109.5 |
| Detroit . . . . . . . | 3552 | 7424 | .478 | 1832 | 2490 | .736 | 1229 | 2601 | 3830 | 8936 | 109.0 |
| Indiana . . . . . . . | 3500 | 7783 | .450 | 1904 | 2564 | .743 | 1386 | 2624 | 4010 | 8904 | 108.6 |
| Portland . . . . . . | 3556 | 7367 | .483 | 1717 | 2259 | .760 | 1187 | 2686 | 3873 | 8829 | 107.7 |
| New Orleans . . . . | 3568 | 7717 | .462 | 1690 | 2331 | .725 | 1309 | 2907 | 4216 | 8826 | 107.6 |
| New Jersey . . . . | 3547 | 8004 | .443 | 1652 | 2304 | .717 | 1306 | 2595 | 3901 | 8746 | 106.7 |
| Golden State. . . . | 3574 | 7654 | .467 | 1550 | 2081 | .745 | 1183 | 2629 | 3812 | 8698 | 106.1 |
| Boston . . . . . . . | 3494 | 7635 | .458 | 1682 | 2159 | .779 | 1235 | 2850 | 4085 | 8670 | 105.7 |
| Buffalo . . . . . . . | 3413 | 7323 | .466 | 1808 | 2314 | .781 | 1083 | 2538 | 3621 | 8634 | 105.3 |
| Seattle . . . . . . . | 3445 | 7715 | .447 | 1675 | 2352 | .712 | 1456 | 2601 | 4057 | 8565 | 104.5 |
| Cleveland. . . . . | 3496 | 7707 | .454 | 1569 | 2116 | .741 | 1187 | 2676 | 3863 | 8561 | 104.4 |
| Chicago. . . . . . . | 3330 | 7041 | .473 | 1863 | 2471 | .754 | 1248 | 2577 | 3825 | 8523 | 103.9 |
| Houston . . . . . . | 3523 | 7691 | .458 | 1467 | 1896 | .774 | 1301 | 2421 | 3722 | 8513 | 103.8 |
| Atlanta . . . . . . . | 3335 | 7253 | .460 | 1836 | 2316 | .793 | 1160 | 2359 | 3519 | 8506 | 103.7 |

### Defense

| Allowed by | Field Goals | | | Free Throws | | | Rebounds | | | Scoring | | |
|---|---|---|---|---|---|---|---|---|---|---|---|---|
| | Made | Att | Pct | Made | Att | Pct | Off | Def | Tot | Pts | Avg | Dif |
| Portland . . . . . . | 3289 | 7318 | .449 | 1747 | 2282 | .766 | 1187 | 2523 | 3710 | 8325 | 101.5 | +6 |
| Seattle. . . . . . . | 3384 | 7377 | .459 | 1670 | 2203 | .758 | 1121 | 2600 | 3721 | 8438 | 102.9 | +1 |
| Atlanta. . . . . . . | 3162 | 6671 | .474 | 2193 | 2930 | .748 | 1160 | 2606 | 3766 | 8517 | 103.9 | −0 |
| Cleveland . . . . . | 3474 | 7620 | .456 | 1574 | 2113 | .745 | 1214 | 2779 | 3993 | 8522 | 103.9 | +0 |
| Chicago . . . . . . | 3565 | 7273 | .490 | 1466 | 1980 | .740 | 1065 | 2367 | 3432 | 8596 | 104.8 | −0 |
| Golden State . . . | 3425 | 7368 | .465 | 1820 | 2408 | .756 | 1185 | 2794 | 3979 | 8670 | 105.7 | −0 |
| Los Angeles. . . . | 3648 | 7880 | .463 | 1529 | 2050 | .746 | 1365 | 2599 | 3964 | 8825 | 107.6 | +2 |
| Boston . . . . . . . | 3539 | 7761 | .456 | 1752 | 2278 | .769 | 1142 | 2575 | 3717 | 8830 | 107.7 | −2 |
| Houston . . . . . . | 3571 | 7404 | .482 | 1699 | 2238 | .759 | 1195 | 2525 | 3720 | 8841 | 107.8 | −4 |
| Phoenix . . . . . . | 3578 | 7622 | .469 | 1749 | 2319 | .754 | 1202 | 2743 | 3945 | 8905 | 108.6 | +3 |
| Buffalo . . . . . . . | 3623 | 7609 | .476 | 1695 | 2250 | .753 | 1178 | 2587 | 3765 | 8941 | 109.0 | −3 |
| Washington . . . . | 3767 | 8065 | .467 | 1437 | 1895 | .758 | 1166 | 2683 | 3849 | 8971 | 109.4 | +0 |
| New Orleans . . . . | 3659 | 7938 | .461 | 1661 | 2213 | .751 | 1273 | 2747 | 4020 | 8979 | 109.5 | −1 |
| Philadelphia . . . . | 3592 | 7788 | .461 | 1803 | 2435 | .740 | 1363 | 2473 | 3836 | 8987 | 109.6 | +5 |
| Detroit . . . . . . . | 3688 | 7706 | .479 | 1662 | 2177 | .763 | 1244 | 2494 | 3738 | 9038 | 110.2 | −1 |
| Denver. . . . . . . | 3678 | 7799 | .472 | 1740 | 2365 | .736 | 1267 | 2546 | 3813 | 9096 | 110.9 | +0 |
| Indiana. . . . . . . | 3634 | 7663 | .474 | 1841 | 2455 | .750 | 1350 | 2793 | 4143 | 9109 | 111.1 | −2 |
| San Antonio . . . . | 3808 | 8063 | .472 | 1494 | 1996 | .748 | 1345 | 2576 | 3921 | 9110 | 111.1 | +3 |
| Kansas City . . . . | 3564 | 7521 | .474 | 2004 | 2635 | .761 | 1232 | 2684 | 3916 | 9132 | 111.4 | −1 |
| New Jersey . . . . | 3544 | 7620 | .465 | 2135 | 2830 | .754 | 1312 | 2996 | 4308 | 9223 | 112.5 | −5 |
| Milwaukee. . . . . | 3715 | 7728 | .481 | 1832 | 2404 | .762 | 1234 | 2617 | 3851 | 9262 | 113.0 | −0 |
| New York . . . . . . | 3658 | 7742 | .472 | 2029 | 2785 | .729 | 1254 | 2623 | 3877 | 9345 | 114.0 | −0 |

### Podoloff Cup Winners

Bill Walton of the Portland Trail Blazers was selected as the winner of the Maurice Podoloff Cup (named after the former league commissioner) for Most Valuable Player in the NBA for the 1977-78 season.

| | | | |
|---|---|---|---|
| 1956 | Bob Pettit, St. Louis | 1968 | Wilt Chamberlain, Philadelphia |
| 1957 | Bob Cousy, Boston | 1969 | Wes Unseld, Baltimore |
| 1958 | Bill Russell, Boston | 1970 | Willis Reed, New York |
| 1959 | Bob Pettit, St. Louis | 1971 | Lew Alcindor, Milwaukee |
| 1960 | Wilt Chamberlain, Philadelphia | 1972 | Kareem Abdul-Jabbar (Alcindor), Milwaukee |
| 1961 | Bill Russell, Boston | 1973 | Dave Cowens, Boston |
| 1962 | Bill Russell, Boston | 1974 | Kareem Abdul-Jabbar, Milwaukee |
| 1963 | Bill Russell, Boston | 1975 | Bob McAdoo, Buffalo |
| 1964 | Oscar Robertson, Cincinnati | 1976 | Kareem Abdul-Jabbar, Los Angeles |
| 1965 | Bill Russell, Boston | 1977 | Kareem Abdul-Jabbar, Los Angeles |
| 1966 | Wilt Chamberlain, Philadelphia | 1978 | Bill Walton, Portland |
| 1967 | Wilt Chamberlain, Philadelphia | | |

### NBA Rookie of the Year Awards

| | | | |
|---|---|---|---|
| 1954 | Don Meineke, Ft. Wayne | 1967 | Dave Bing, Detroit |
| 1955 | Ray Felix, Baltimore | 1968 | Earl Monroe, Baltimore |
| 1956 | Maurice Stokes, Rochester | 1969 | Wes Unseld, Baltimore |
| 1957 | Tom Heinsohn, Boston | 1970 | Lew Alcindor, Milwaukee |
| 1958 | Woody Sauldsberry, Philadelphia | 1971 | Dave Cowens, Boston; |
| 1959 | Elgin Baylor, Minnesota | | Geoff Petrie, Portland (tie) |
| 1960 | Wilt Chamberlain, Philadelphia | 1972 | Sidney Wicks, Portland |
| 1961 | Oscar Robertson, Cincinnati | 1973 | Bob McAdoo, Buffalo |
| 1962 | Walt Bellamy, Chicago | 1974 | Ernie DiGregorio, Buffalo |
| 1963 | Terry Dischinger, Chicago | 1975 | Keith Wilkes, Golden State |
| 1964 | Jerry Lucas, Cincinnati | 1976 | Alvan Adams, Phoenix |
| 1965 | Willis Reed, New York | 1977 | Adrian Dantley, Buffalo |
| 1966 | Rick Barry, San Francisco | 1978 | Walter Davis, Phoenix |

## NBA All Star Team in 1978

| First team | Position | Second team |
|---|---|---|
| Julius Erving, Philadelphia | Foward | Walter Davis, Phoenix |
| Truck Robinson, New Orleans | Forward | Maurice Lucas, Portland |
| Bill Walton, Portland | Center | Kareem Abdul-Jabbar, Los Angeles |
| David Thompson, Denver | Guard | Pete Maravich, New Orleans |
| George Gervin, San Antonio | Guard | Paul Westphal, Phoenix |

## NBA All-Defensive Team in 1978

| First team | Position | Second team |
|---|---|---|
| Bobby Jones, Denver | Forward | E.C. Coleman, Golden State |
| Maurice Lucas, Portland | Forward | Bob Gross, Portland |
| Bill Walton, Portland | Center | (Tie) Artis Gilmore, Chicago |
| | | Kareem Abdul-Jabbar, Los Angeles |
| Don Buse, Phoenix | Guard | Norm Van Lier, Chicago |
| Lionel Hollins, Portland | Guard | Quinn Buckner, Milwaukee |

## 1978 NBA Player Draft

The following are the first round picks of the National Basketball Association.

Portland—Mychal Thompson, Minnesota
Kansas City—Phil Ford, North Carolina
Indiana—Rick Robey, Kentucky
New York—Mike Richardson, Montana
Golden State—Pervis Short, Jackson State
Boston—Larry Bird, Indiana State
Portland—Ron Brewer, Arkansas
Boston—Freeman Williams, Portland State
Chicago—Reggie Theus, Nevada, Las Vegas
Atlanta—Butch Lee, Marquette
New Orleans—James Hardy, San Francisco

Milwaukee—George Johnson, St. John's, N.Y.
New Jersey—Wilfred Boynes, San Francisco
Washington—Roger Phegley, Bradley
Cleveland—Mike Mitchell, Auburn
Atlanta—Jack Givens, Kentucky
Denver—Rod Griffin, Wake Forest
Washington—Dave Corzine, DePaul
Phoenix—Marty Byrnes, Syracuse
San Antonio—Frankie Sanders, Southern
Denver—Mike Evans, Kansas State
Golden State—Ray Townsend, UCLA

# American Basketball Association, 1968-1976

## Champions

| | Regular season | | Playoffs | |
|---|---|---|---|---|
| Year | Eastern division | Western division | Winner | Runner-up |
| 1968 | Pittsburgh | New Orleans | Pittsburgh | New Orleans |
| 1969 | Indiana | Oakland | Oakland | Indiana |
| 1970 | Indiana | Denver | Indiana | Los Angeles |
| 1971 | Virginia | Indiana | Utah | Kentucky |
| 1972 | Kentucky | Utah | Indiana | New York |
| 1973 | Carolina | Utah | Indiana | Kentucky |
| 1974 | New York | Utah | New York | Utah |
| 1975 | Kentucky | Denver | Kentucky | Indiana |
| 1976 | | Denver | New York | Denver |

## Scoring Leaders

| Year | Leader | Pts | Avg | Year | Leader | Pts | Avg |
|---|---|---|---|---|---|---|---|
| 1968 | Connie Hawkins, Pittsburgh | 1,875 | 26.7 | 1973 | Julius Erving, Virginia | 2,268 | 31.9 |
| 1969 | Rick Barry, Oakland | 1,190 | 34.0 | 1974 | Julius Erving, New York | 2,299 | 27.3 |
| 1970 | Spencer Haywood, Denver | 2,519 | 29.9 | 1975 | George McGinnis, Indiana | 2,353 | 29.7 |
| 1971 | Dan Issel, Kentucky | 2,480 | 29.8 | 1976 | Julius Erving, New York | 2,462 | 29.3 |
| 1972 | Charlie Scott, Virginia | 2,524 | 34.5 | | | | |

## Most Valuable Player & Rookie of Year

| Year | MVP | Rookie |
|---|---|---|
| 1968 | Connie Hawkins, Pittsburgh | Mel Daniels, Indiana |
| 1969 | Mel Daniels, Indiana | Warren Armstrong, Oakland |
| 1970 | Spencer Haywood, Denver | Spencer Haywood, Denver |
| 1971 | Mel Daniels, Indiana | Dan Issel, Kentucky; Charlie Scott, Virginia (tie) |
| 1972 | Artis Gilmore, Kentucky | Artis Gilmore, Kentucky |
| 1973 | Billy Cunningham, Carolina | Brian Taylor, New York |
| 1974 | Julius Erving, New York | Swen Nater, San Antonio |
| 1975 | Julius Erving, New York; George McGinnis, Indiana (tie) | Marvin Barnes, St. Louis |
| 1976 | Julius Erving, New York | David Thompson, Denver |

# National AAU Elite Gymnastics Championships in 1978

Houston, Tex., May 18-20, 1978

## Men

**Still Rings**—(tie) Larry Gerard, Nebraska Gym Club and Mike Silverstein, Owl Gym Club, Philadelphia.
**Vault**—Carl Antonelli, New York AC.
**Parallel Bars**—John Corritore, Univ. of Michigan.
**Horizontal Bar**—Melvin Cooley, Univ. of Michigan.
**Floor Exercise**—Mike Silverstein.
**Pommel Horse**—Joel Ulloa, Cal. State Fullerton.
**All Around**—Phil Cahoy, Nebraska Gym Club.
**Team champion**—New York AC.

## Women

**Floor Exercise**—Karen Lemond, Reno, Nev., Flips.
**Balance Beam**—Karen Lemond.
**Uneven Balance Beam**—(tie) Karen Lemond and Jackie Chagnovich, Utah Academy.
**Vault**—(tie) Jackie Chagnovich and Pam Lee, El Paso Supernovas.
**All Around**—Karen Lemond.
**Team champion**—Utah Academy.

# Figure Skating Champions

## National Champions

## World Champions

| Men | Women | Year | Men | Women |
|---|---|---|---|---|
| Richard Button | Tenley Albright | 1952 | Richard Button, U.S. | Jacqueline du Bief, France |
| Hayes Jenkins | Tenley Albright | 1953 | Hayes Jenkins, U.S. | Tenley Albright, U.S. |
| Hayes Jenkins | Tenley Albright | 1954 | Hayes Jenkins, U.S. | Gundi Busch, W. Germany |
| Hayes Jenkins | Tenley Albright | 1955 | Hayes Jenkins, U.S. | Tenley Albright, U.S. |
| Hayes Jenkins | Tenley Albright | 1956 | Hayes Jenkins, U.S. | Carol Heiss, U.S. |
| Dave Jenkins | Carol Heiss | 1957 | Dave Jenkins, U.S. | Carol Heiss, U.S. |
| Dave Jenkins | Carol Heiss | 1958 | Dave Jenkins, U.S. | Carol Heiss, U.S. |
| Dave Jenkins | Carol Heiss | 1959 | Dave Jenkins, U.S. | Carol Heiss, U.S. |
| Dave Jenkins | Carol Heiss | 1960 | Alain Giletti, France | Carol Heiss, U.S. |
| Bradley Lord | Laurence Owen | 1961 | none | none |
| Monty Hoyt | Barbara Roles Pursley | 1962 | Don Jackson, Canada | Sjoukie Dijkstra, Neth. |
| Tommy Litz | Lorraine Hanlon | 1963 | Don McPherson, Canada | Sjoukie Dijkstra, Neth. |
| Scott Allen | Peggy Fleming | 1964 | Manfred Schnelldorfer, W. Germany | Sjoukie Dijkstra, Neth. |
| Gary Visconti | Peggy Fleming | 1965 | Alain Calmat, France | Petra Burka, Canada |
| Scott Allen | Peggy Fleming | 1966 | Emmerich Danzer, Austria | Peggy Fleming, U.S. |
| Gary Visconti | Peggy Fleming | 1967 | Emmerich Danzer, Austria | Peggy Fleming, U.S. |
| Tim Wood | Peggy Fleming | 1968 | Emmerich Danzer, Austria | Peggy Fleming, U.S. |
| Tim Wood | Janet Lynn | 1969 | Tim Wood, U.S. | Gabriele Seyfert, E. Germany |
| Tim Wood | Janet Lynn | 1970 | Tim Wood, U.S. | Gabriele Seyfert, E. Germany |
| John Misha Petkevich | Janet Lynn | 1971 | Ondrej Nepela, Czech. | Beatrix Schuba, Austria |
| Ken Shelley | Janet Lynn | 1972 | Ondrej Nepela, Czech. | Beatrix Schuba, Austria |
| Gordon McKellen Jr. | Janet Lynn | 1973 | Ondrej Nepela, Czech. | Karen Magnussen, Canada |
| Gordon McKellen Jr. | Dorothy Hamill | 1974 | Jan Hoffman, E. Germany | Christine Errath, E. Germany |
| Gordon McKellen Jr. | Dorothy Hamill | 1975 | Sergei Volkov, USSR | Dianne de Leeuw, Neth.-U.S. |
| Terry Kubicka | Dorothy Hamill | 1976 | John Curry, Gt. Britain | Dorothy Hamill, U.S. |
| Charles Tickner | Linda Fratianne | 1977 | Vladimir Kovalev, USSR | Linda Fratianne, U.S. |
| Charles Tickner | Linda Fratianne | 1978 | Charles Tickner, U.S. | Anett Potzsch, E. Germany |

## Canadian National Figure Skating Champions

| Year | Men | Women | Year | Men | Women |
|---|---|---|---|---|---|
| 1961 | Donald Jackson | Wendy Griner | 1970 | David McGillivray | Karen Magnussen |
| 1962 | Donald Jackson | Wendy Griner | 1971 | Toller Cranston | Karen Magnussen |
| 1963 | Donald McPherson | Wendy Griner | 1972 | Toller Cranston | Karen Magnussen |
| 1964 | Charles Snelling | Petra Burka | 1973 | Toller Cranston | Karen Magnussen |
| 1965 | Donald Knight | Petra Burka | 1974 | Toller Cranston | Lynn Nightingale |
| 1966 | Donald Knight | Petra Burka | 1975 | Toller Cranston | Lynn Nightingale |
| 1967 | Donald Knight | Valerie Jones | 1976 | Toller Cranston | Lynn Nightingale |
| 1968 | Jay Humphrey | Karen Magnussen | 1977 | Ron Shaver | Lynn Nightingale |
| 1969 | Jay Humphrey | Linda Carbonetto | 1978 | Brian Pockar | Heather Kemkaran |

# Skiing in 1978

## U.S. National Alpine Championships

Lake Placid, N.Y., Feb. 23-28

**Men's Downhill**—Karl Anderson. **Time—1:55.36.**
**Men's Slalom**—Phil Mahre. **Time—1:34.17.**
**Men's Giant Slalom**—Phil Mahre. **Time—2:40.86.**
**Combined**—Billy Taylor.

**Women's Downhill**—Cindy Nelson. **Time—1:47.14.**
**Women's Slalom**—Becky Dorsey. **Time—1:13.56.**
**Women's Giant Slalom**—Becky Dorsey. **Time—2:34.18.**
**Combined**—Cindy Nelson.

## North American Cross-Country Championships

Lake Placid, N.Y., Mar. 9-12

**Jr. Men's 10 km.**—Scott Taylor, U.S. **Time—32:18.28.**
**Jr. Men's 15 km.**—Robert Vellend, Canada. **Time—46:39.88.**
**Men's 15 km.**—John Kreuzer, Switzerland. **Time—42:44.71.**
**Men's 30 km.**—Craig Ward, U.S. **Time—1:30:58.34.**

**Men's 3 × 10 km. Relays**—Switzerland. **Time—1:29:56.93.**
**Women's 10 km.**—Joanne Groothuysen, Canada. **Time—35:10.59.**
**Women's 3 × 5 Relays**—Canada. **Time—54:17.70.**

## The World Cup Winners

| | Men | | Women | | Nation's Cup |
|---|---|---|---|---|---|
| 1967 | Jean Claude Killy, France | 1967 | Nancy Greene, Canada | 1967 | France |
| 1968 | Jean Claude Killy, France | 1968 | Nancy Greene, Canada | 1968 | France |
| 1969 | Karl Schranz, Austria | 1969 | Gertrud Gabl, Austria | 1969 | Austria |
| 1970 | Karl Schranz, Austria | 1970 | Michele Jacot, France | 1970 | France |
| 1971 | Gustavo Thoeni, Italy | 1971 | Annemarie Proell, Austria | 1971 | France |
| 1972 | Gustavo Thoeni, Italy | 1972 | Annemarie Proell, Austria | 1972 | France |
| 1973 | Gustavo Thoeni, Italy | 1973 | Annemarie Proell, Austria | 1973 | Austria |
| 1974 | Piero Gros, Italy | 1974 | Annemarie Proell, Austria | 1974 | Austria |
| 1975 | Gustavo Thoeni, Italy | 1975 | Annemarie Proell, Austria | 1975 | Austria |
| 1976 | Ingemar Stenmark, Sweden | 1976 | Rose Mittermaier, W. Germany | 1976 | Italy |
| 1977 | Ingemar Stenmark, Sweden | 1977 | Lise-Marie Morerod, Austria | 1977 | Austria |
| 1978 | Ingemar Stenmark, Sweden | 1978 | Hanni Wenzel, Leichtenstein | 1978 | Austria |

# Boston Marathon in 1978

Bill Rodgers of Melrose, Mass. covered the traditional distance of 26 miles 385 yards in 2 hours 10 minutes 13 seconds to win the 82d annual Boston Marathon on April 17, 1978. A record 4,212 runners competed in the event. Jeff Wells of Dallas finished second.

## Badminton Championships in 1978

### World Championships

en's Singles—Liem Swie King, Indonesia def. D. Dartika, Indonesia, 15-9, 15-5.
omen's Singles—S. Ng, Malaysia def. Serawaty Wiharyo, Indonesia, 4-11, 11-4, 11-5.
en's Doubles—Tjun Tjun and Johan Wahjudi, Indonesia def. P. Soparajee and P. Kongsirithavorn, Thailand, 15-9, 15-3.
Women's Doubles—Regina Masli and T. Widiastuti, Indonesia def. S. Ng and Rosalind Ang, Malaysia, 15-2, 15-4.
Mixed Doubles—Christian and Regina Masli, Indonesia def. Dominic Soong and Yap Hei Lin, Malaysia, 15-10, 15-6.

### U.S. Championships

#### Austin, Texas

en's Singles—Mike Walker, Man. Beach, Cal. def. Chris Kinhard, Pasadena, Cal., 15-12, 15-10.
omen's Singles—Cheryl Carton, San Diego, Cal. def. Pam Bristol, Flint, Mich., 8-11, 11-5, 11-2.
en's Doubles—John Britton and Charles Coakley, Pasadena, Cal. def. Bob Dickey, and Gary Higgins, Man. Beach, Cal., 15-12, 14-17, 15-8.
omen's Doubles—Diana Osterhues and Janet Wilts, Pasadena, Cal. def. Pam Bristol, Flint, Mich. and Judianne Kelly, Man. Beach, Cal., 17-14, 17-15.
xed Doubles—Bruce Pontow, Chicago, Ill. and Pam Bristol, Flint, Mich. def. Charles Coakley and Janet Wilts, Pasadena, Cal., 15-11, 15-11.

Senior Men's Singles—Jim Poole, Man. Beach, Cal. def. Rod Starkey, San Diego, Cal., 15-6, 15-7.
Senior Men's Doubles—Bill Goodman, Wellesley, Mass. and Tom Heden, Millwood, N.Y. def. Dale Miller and Kang Yang, 15-3, 15-8.
Senior Women's Doubles—Rosine Lemon, N.Y. and Carlene Starkey, San Diego, Cal. def. Sandra Fogarty, Mass. and Gloria Ollech, Chicago, Ill., 15-4, 15-4.
Senior Mixed Doubles—Carlene & Rod Starkey def. Francis and Bill Goodman, Wellesley, Mass., 15-8, 15-4.
Master Men's Singles—Waldo Foy, Chicago, Cal. def. Amrit Dewan, Oh. 6-15, 15-11, 15-1.

### U.S. National Junior Championships

#### Austin, Texas

oy's Singles—Geoff Stensland, Seattle, Wash. def. Tony Alston, Pasadena, Cal., 15-0, 15-17, 15-5
rl's Singles—Lisa DeRousie, Wash. def. Barb Bidermann, N.Y., 11-6, 11-9.
oy's Doubles—David Collis and Gary Shelstad, Man. Beach, Cal. def. Chris Black and Danny Rubin, Man. Beach, Cal., 15-3, 15-2.
Girl's Doubles—Lisa DeRousie, and Ann French, Chicago, Ill. def. Lori Ball and Tracy McDonald, Man. Beach, Cal., 15-7, 15-9.

## Westminster Kennel Club

| ar | Best-in-show | Breed | Owner |
|---|---|---|---|
| 67 | Ch. Bardene Bingo | Scottish terrier | E. H. Stuart |
| 68 | Ch. Stingray of Derryabah | Lakeland terrier | Mr. and Mrs. James A. Farrell Jr. |
| 69 | Ch. Glamoor Good News | Skye terrier | Walter & Mrs. Adele F. Goodman |
| 70 | Ch. Arriba's Prima Donna | Boxer | Dr. & Mrs. P. J. Pagano & Dr. Theodore S. Fickles |
| 71 | Ch. Chinoe's Adamant James | English springer spaniel | Dr. Milton Prickett |
| 72 | Ch. Chinoe's Adamant James | English springer spaniel | Dr. Milton Prickett |
| 73 | Ch. Acadia Command Performance | Poodle | Mrs. Jo Ann Sering & Edward B. Jenner |
| 74 | Ch. Gretchenhof Columbia River | German pointer | Dr. Richard Smith |
| 75 | Ch. Sir Lancelot of Barvan | Old English sheepdog | Mr. & Mrs. Ronald Vanword |
| 76 | Ch. Jo-Ni's Red Baron of Crofton | Lakeland terrier | Virginia Dickson |
| 77 | Ch. Dersade Bobby's Girl | Sealyham | Dorothy Wymer |
| 78 | Ch. Cede Higgens | Yorkshire terrier | Barbara & Charles Switzer |

### Leonard Brumby Sr. Memorial Trophy

#### Junior Winner at Westminster Kennel Club

67 David L. Brumbaugh, Perry, Ga. **Breed**—Min. Schnauzer.
68 Cheryl Baker, Kennesaw, Ga. **Breed**—Beagle.
69 Charles Garvin, Columbus, Oh. **Breed**—Dalmatian.
70 Pat Hardy, Cincinnati, Oh. **Breed**—Golden Retriever.
71 Heidi Shellenbarger, Costa Mesa, Cal. **Breed**—Whippet.
72 Deborah Dagny Von Aherns, Edison Township, N. J.

**Breed**—Afghan.
1973 Teresa Nail, Ft. Worth, Tex. **Breed**—Doberman Pinscher.
1974 Leslie Church, St. Louis, Mo. **Breed**—Min. Schnauzer.
1975 Virginia Westfield, Huntington, N.Y. **Breed**—Bulldog.
1976 Cathy Hritzo, Hubbard, Oh. **Breed**—Samoyed.
1977 Randy McAteer, Ocala, Fla. **Breed**—Irish Setter.
1978 Sonna Peterson, San Diego, Cal. **Breed**—Boxer

## Canadian Intercollegiate Athletic Union Champions

| | Basketball | Football | Hockey | Soccer | Swimming, Diving | Volleyball | Wrestling |
|---|---|---|---|---|---|---|---|
| 65 | Acadia | Toronto | Manitoba | — | British Columbia | — | — |
| 66 | Windsor | St. Francis Xavier | Toronto | — | Toronto | — | — |
| 67 | Windsor | Alberta | Toronto | — | Toronto | British Columbia | — |
| 68 | Waterloo Lutheran | Queen's | Alberta | — | Toronto | Ottawa | — |
| 69 | Windsor | Manitoba | Toronto | — | Toronto | Winnipeg | — |
| 70 | British Columbia | Manitoba | Toronto | — | Toronto | Montreal | Alberta |
| 71 | Acadia | Western Ontario | Toronto | — | Toronto | Winnipeg | Alberta |
| 72 | Bristish Columbia | Alberta | Toronto | Alberta | McGill | Winnipeg | Alberta |
| 73 | St. Mary's | St. Mary's | Toronto | Loyola | Toronto | Winnipeg | O.U.A.A. |
| 74 | Guelph | Western Ontario | Waterloo | British Columbia | Toronto | Winnipeg | O.U.A.A. |
| 75 | Waterloo | Ottawa | Alberta | Victoria | Toronto | Sherbrooke | O.U.A.A. |
| 76 | Manitoba | Western Ontario | Toronto | Concordia | Toronto | British Columbia | O.U.A.A. |
| 77 | Acadia | Western Ontario | Toronto | York | Waterloo | Winnipeg | O.U.A.A. |
| 78 | St. Mary's | | Alberta | | Waterloo | Manitoba | O.U.A.A. |

# National Hockey League, 1977-78

### Final Standings

## Clarence Campbell Conference

### Lester Patrick Division

| Club | W | L | T | Pts | GF | GA |
|------|---|---|---|-----|----|----|
| N.Y. Islanders | 48 | 17 | 15 | 111 | 334 | 210 |
| Philadelphia | 45 | 20 | 15 | 105 | 296 | 200 |
| Atlanta | 34 | 27 | 19 | 87 | 273 | 252 |
| N.Y. Rangers | 30 | 37 | 13 | 73 | 279 | 280 |

### Conn Smythe Division

| Club | W | L | T | Pts | GF | GA |
|------|---|---|---|-----|----|----|
| Chicago | 32 | 29 | 19 | 83 | 230 | 220 |
| Colorado | 19 | 40 | 21 | 59 | 257 | 305 |
| Vancouver | 20 | 43 | 17 | 57 | 241 | 315 |
| St. Louis | 20 | 47 | 13 | 53 | 195 | 304 |
| Minnesota | 18 | 53 | 9 | 45 | 218 | 325 |

## Prince of Wales Conference

### Charles F. Adams Division

| Club | W | L | T | Pts | GF | GA |
|------|---|---|---|-----|----|----|
| Boston | 51 | 18 | 11 | 113 | 333 | 218 |
| Buffalo | 44 | 19 | 17 | 105 | 288 | 215 |
| Toronto | 41 | 29 | 10 | 92 | 271 | 237 |
| Cleveland | 22 | 45 | 13 | 57 | 230 | 325 |

### James Norris Division

| Club | W | L | T | Pts | GF | GA |
|------|---|---|---|-----|----|----|
| Montreal | 59 | 10 | 11 | 129 | 359 | 183 |
| Detroit | 32 | 34 | 14 | 78 | 252 | 266 |
| Los Angeles | 31 | 34 | 15 | 77 | 243 | 245 |
| Pittsburgh | 25 | 37 | 18 | 68 | 254 | 321 |
| Washington | 17 | 49 | 14 | 48 | 195 | 321 |

### Stanley Cup Playoff Results

Detroit defeated Atlanta 2 games to 0.
Philadelphia defeated Colorado 2 games to 0.
Buffalo defeated N.Y. Rangers 2 games to 1.
Toronto defeated Los Angeles 2 games to 0.
Boston defeated Chicago 4 games to 0.
Montreal defeated Detroit 4 games to 1.

Philadelphia defeated Buffalo 4 games to 1.
Toronto defeated N.Y. Islanders 4 games to 3.
Montreal defeated Toronto 4 games to 0.
Boston defeated Philadelphia 4 games to 1.
Montreal defeated Boston 4 games to 2.

### Leading Scorers

| Player, club | GP | G | A | Pts | Player, club | GP | G | A | P |
|--------------|----|---|---|-----|--------------|----|---|---|---|
| Lafleur, Montreal | 78 | 60 | 72 | 132 | Paiement, Colorado | 80 | 31 | 56 | 8 |
| Trottier, Islanders | 77 | 46 | 77 | 123 | Shutt, Montreal | 80 | 49 | 37 | 8 |
| Sittler, Toronto | 80 | 45 | 72 | 117 | Gilles, Islanders | 80 | 35 | 50 | 8 |
| Lemaire, Montreal | 76 | 36 | 61 | 97 | Ratelle, Boston | 80 | 25 | 59 | 8 |
| Potvin, Islanders | 80 | 30 | 64 | 94 | Esposito, Rangers | 79 | 38 | 43 | 8 |
| Bossy, Islanders | 73 | 53 | 38 | 91 | McNab, Boston | 79 | 41 | 39 | 8 |
| O'Reilly, Boston | 77 | 29 | 61 | 90 | Boldirev, Chicago | 80 | 35 | 45 | 8 |
| Perreault, Buffalo | 79 | 41 | 48 | 89 | Dionne, Los Angeles | 70 | 36 | 43 | 7 |
| Clarke, Philadelphia | 71 | 21 | 68 | 89 | Park, Boston | 80 | 22 | 57 | 7 |
| McDonald, Toronto | 74 | 47 | 40 | 87 | Gare, Buffalo | 69 | 39 | 38 | 7 |

### Leading Goalies

#### (25 or more games)

| Goalie, club | G | GA | ShO | Avg | Goalie, club | G | GA | ShO | Av |
|--------------|---|----|-----|-----|--------------|---|----|-----|----|
| Ken Dryden, Montreal | 52 | 105 | 5 | 2.05 | Mike Palmateer, Toronto | 63 | 172 | 5 | 2.7 |
| Bernie Parent, Phila. | 49 | 108 | 7 | 2.22 | Dan Bouchard, Atlanta | 58 | 153 | 2 | 2.7 |
| Gilles Gilbert, Boston | 25 | 56 | 2 | 2.53 | Wayne Stephenson, Phila. | 26 | 68 | 3 | 2.7 |
| Glenn Resch, Islanders | 45 | 112 | 3 | 2.55 | Ron Grahame, Boston | 40 | 107 | 3 | 2.7 |
| Tony Esposito, Chicago | 64 | 168 | 5 | 2.63 | Rogie Vachon, Los Angeles | 70 | 196 | 4 | 2.8 |
| Don Edwards, Buffalo | 72 | 185 | 5 | 2.64 | John Davidson, Rangers | 34 | 98 | 1 | 3.1 |
| Billy Smith, Islanders | 38 | 95 | 2 | 2.65 | Jim Rutherford, Detroit | 43 | 134 | 1 | 3.2 |
| Michael Larocque, Montreal | 30 | 77 | 1 | 2.67 | | | | | |

### NHL Attendance

| Club | 1977 | 1978 | Increase decrease | Club | 1977 | 1978 | Increase decrease |
|------|------|------|-------------------|------|------|------|-------------------|
| Atlanta | 490,343 | 420,841 | − 69,502 | N.Y. Islanders | 598,551 | 604,031 | + 5,48 |
| Boston | 470,444 | 494,744 | + 24,300 | N.Y. Rangers | 700,000 | 695,164 | − 4,83 |
| Buffalo | 657,288 | 647,390 | − 9,898 | Philadelphia | 683,010 | 671,151 | − 11,85 |
| Chicago | 450,600 | 443,512 | − 7,088 | Pittsburgh | 401,581 | 421,924 | + 20,34 |
| Cleveland | 238,543 | 227,029 | − 11,514 | St. Louis | 587,135 | 425,323 | − 161,81 |
| Colorado | 341,985 | 355,930 | + 13,945 | Toronto | 658,455 | 659,162 | + 70 |
| Detroit | 385,008 | 547,272 | + 162,264 | Vancouver | 599,722 | 568,841 | − 30,88 |
| Los Angeles | 497,714 | 471,923 | − 25,791 | Washington | 437,081 | 434,864 | − 2,21 |
| Minnesota | 363,389 | 347,279 | − 16,110 | Totals | 9,229,063 | 9,101,023 | − 128,04 |
| Montreal | 668,214 | 664,643 | − 3,571 | | | | |

### NHL All Star Team, 1978

| First team | Position | Second team |
|------------|----------|-------------|
| Ken Dryden, Montreal | Goalie | Don Edwards, Buffalo |
| Denis Potvin, N.Y. Islanders | Defense | Larry Robinson, Montreal |
| Brad Park, Boston | Defense | Borje Salming, Toronto |
| Bryan Trottier, N.Y. Islanders | Center | Darryl Sittler, Toronto |
| Guy Lafleur, Montreal | Right Wing | Mike Bossy, N.Y. Islanders |
| Clark Gillies, N.Y. Islanders | Left Wing | Steve Shutt, Montreal |

# Team Scoring Leaders

| Atlanta | GP | G | A | Pts |
|---|---|---|---|---|
| Bob MacMillan | 80 | 38 | 33 | 71 |
| Tom Lysiak | 80 | 27 | 42 | 69 |
| Guy Chouinard | 73 | 28 | 30 | 58 |
| Eric Vail | 79 | 22 | 36 | 58 |
| Harold Phillipoff | 67 | 17 | 36 | 53 |

| Boston | GP | G | A | Pts |
|---|---|---|---|---|
| Terry O'Reilly | 77 | 29 | 61 | 90 |
| Jean Ratelle | 80 | 25 | 59 | 84 |
| Peter McNab | 79 | 41 | 39 | 80 |
| Brad Park | 80 | 22 | 57 | 79 |
| Wayne Cashman | 76 | 24 | 38 | 62 |

| Buffalo | GP | G | A | Pts |
|---|---|---|---|---|
| Gil Pereault | 79 | 41 | 48 | 89 |
| Danny Gare | 69 | 39 | 38 | 77 |
| Rene Robert | 67 | 25 | 48 | 73 |
| Craig Ramsay | 80 | 28 | 43 | 71 |
| Rick Martin | 65 | 28 | 34 | 62 |

| Chicago | GP | G | A | Pts |
|---|---|---|---|---|
| Ivan Boldirev | 80 | 35 | 45 | 80 |
| Stan Mikita | 77 | 18 | 41 | 59 |
| Ted Bulley | 79 | 23 | 28 | 51 |
| J. P. Bordeleau | 76 | 15 | 25 | 40 |
| Grant Mulvey | 78 | 14 | 24 | 38 |

| Cleveland | GP | G | A | Pts |
|---|---|---|---|---|
| Dennis Maruk | 76 | 36 | 35 | 71 |
| Mike Fidler | 78 | 23 | 28 | 51 |
| J. P. Parise | 79 | 21 | 29 | 50 |
| Kris Manery | 78 | 22 | 27 | 49 |
| Al MacAdam | 80 | 16 | 32 | 48 |

| Colorado | GP | G | A | Pts |
|---|---|---|---|---|
| Wilf Paiement | 80 | 31 | 56 | 87 |
| Barry Beck | 75 | 22 | 38 | 60 |
| John Van Boxmeer | 80 | 12 | 42 | 54 |
| Paul Gardner | 46 | 30 | 22 | 52 |
| Dennis Owchar | 82 | 10 | 31 | 41 |

| Detroit | GP | G | A | Pts |
|---|---|---|---|---|
| Dale McCourt | 76 | 33 | 39 | 72 |
| Andre St. Laurent | 79 | 31 | 39 | 70 |
| Reed Larson | 75 | 19 | 41 | 60 |
| Dennis Hextall | 78 | 16 | 33 | 49 |
| Nick Libett | 80 | 23 | 22 | 45 |

| Los Angeles | GP | G | A | Pts |
|---|---|---|---|---|
| Marcel Dionne | 70 | 36 | 43 | 79 |
| Butch Goring | 80 | 37 | 36 | 73 |
| Mike Murphy | 72 | 20 | 36 | 56 |
| Syl Apps | 79 | 19 | 33 | 52 |
| Dave Taylor | 64 | 22 | 21 | 43 |

| Minnesota | GP | G | A | Pts |
|---|---|---|---|---|
| Roland Eriksson | 78 | 21 | 39 | 60 |
| Tim Young | 78 | 23 | 35 | 58 |
| Per-Olov Brasar | 77 | 20 | 37 | 57 |
| Glen Sharpley | 79 | 22 | 33 | 55 |
| Brad Maxwell | 75 | 18 | 29 | 47 |

| Montreal | GP | G | A | Pts |
|---|---|---|---|---|
| Guy Lafleur | 78 | 60 | 72 | 132 |
| Jacques Lemaire | 76 | 36 | 61 | 97 |
| Steve Shutt | 80 | 49 | 37 | 86 |
| Larry Robinson | 80 | 13 | 52 | 65 |
| Pierre Larouche | 67 | 23 | 37 | 60 |

| N.Y. Islanders | GP | G | A | Pts |
|---|---|---|---|---|
| Bryan Trottier | 77 | 46 | 77 | 123 |
| Denis Potvin | 80 | 30 | 64 | 94 |
| Mike Bossy | 73 | 53 | 38 | 91 |
| Clark Gillies | 80 | 35 | 50 | 85 |
| Bob Bourne | 80 | 30 | 33 | 63 |

| N.Y. Rangers | GP | G | A | Pts |
|---|---|---|---|---|
| Phil Esposito | 79 | 38 | 43 | 81 |
| Pat Hickey | 80 | 40 | 33 | 73 |
| Ron Greschner | 78 | 24 | 48 | 72 |
| Walt Tkaczuk | 80 | 26 | 40 | 66 |
| Steve Vickers | 79 | 19 | 44 | 63 |

| Philadelphia | GP | G | A | Pts |
|---|---|---|---|---|
| Bobby Clarke | 71 | 21 | 68 | 89 |
| Bill Barber | 80 | 41 | 31 | 72 |
| Rick MacLeish | 75 | 31 | 39 | 70 |
| Orest Kindrachuk | 74 | 17 | 45 | 62 |
| Bob Dailey | 77 | 21 | 36 | 57 |

| Pittsburgh | GP | G | A | Pts |
|---|---|---|---|---|
| Pete Mahovlich | 74 | 28 | 41 | 69 |
| Jean Pronovost | 79 | 40 | 25 | 65 |
| Greg Malone | 80 | 18 | 43 | 61 |
| Gene Carr | 75 | 19 | 37 | 56 |
| Tom Edur | 78 | 10 | 45 | 55 |

| St. Louis | GP | G | A | Pts |
|---|---|---|---|---|
| Garry Unger | 80 | 32 | 20 | 52 |
| Bernie Federko | 72 | 17 | 24 | 41 |
| Inge Hammarstrom | 73 | 20 | 20 | 40 |
| Red Berenson | 80 | 13 | 25 | 38 |
| Larry Patey | 80 | 17 | 17 | 34 |

| Toronto | GP | G | A | Pts |
|---|---|---|---|---|
| Darryl Sittler | 80 | 45 | 72 | 117 |
| Lanny McDonald | 74 | 47 | 40 | 87 |
| Borje Salming | 80 | 16 | 60 | 76 |
| Ian Turnbull | 77 | 14 | 47 | 61 |
| Dan Maloney | 79 | 19 | 33 | 52 |

| Vancouver | GP | G | A | Pts |
|---|---|---|---|---|
| Mike Walton | 65 | 29 | 37 | 66 |
| Rick Blight | 80 | 25 | 38 | 63 |
| Dennis Ververgaert | 80 | 21 | 33 | 54 |
| Don Lever | 75 | 17 | 32 | 49 |
| Pit Martin | 74 | 16 | 32 | 48 |

| Washington | GP | G | A | Pts |
|---|---|---|---|---|
| Guy Charron | 80 | 38 | 35 | 73 |
| Bob Sirois | 72 | 24 | 37 | 61 |
| Gerry Meehan | 78 | 19 | 24 | 43 |
| Robert Picard | 75 | 10 | 27 | 37 |
| Bob Girard | 77 | 9 | 18 | 27 |

## Stanley Cup Champions

| | | | | | | | | | |
|---|---|---|---|---|---|---|---|---|---|
| 1928 | New York | 1939 | Boston | 1949 | Toronto | 1959 | Montreal | 1969 | Montreal |
| 1929 | Boston | 1940 | New York | 1950 | Detroit | 1960 | Montreal | 1970 | Boston |
| 1930 | Montreal | 1941 | Boston | 1951 | Toronto | 1961 | Chicago | 1971 | Montreal |
| 1931 | Montreal | 1942 | Toronto | 1952 | Detroit | 1962 | Toronto | 1972 | Boston |
| 1932 | Toronto | 1943 | Detroit | 1953 | Montreal | 1963 | Toronto | 1973 | Montreal |
| 1933 | New York | 1944 | Montreal | 1954 | Detroit | 1964 | Toronto | 1974 | Philadelphia |
| 1934 | Chicago | 1945 | Toronto | 1955 | Detroit | 1965 | Montreal | 1975 | Philadelphia |
| 1935 | Montreal Maroons | 1946 | Montreal | 1956 | Montreal | 1966 | Montreal | 1976 | Montreal |
| 1936 | Detroit | 1947 | Toronto | 1957 | Montreal | 1967 | Toronto | 1977 | Montreal |
| 1937 | Detroit | 1948 | Toronto | 1958 | Montreal | 1968 | Montreal | 1978 | Montreal |
| 1938 | Chicago | | | | | | | | |

## Conn Smythe Trophy (MVP in Playoffs)

| | | | |
|---|---|---|---|
| 1965 | Jean Beliveau, Montreal | 1970 | Bobby Orr, Boston |
| 1966 | Roger Crozier, Detroit | 1971 | Ken Dryden, Montreal |
| 1967 | Dave Keon, Toronto | 1972 | Bobby Orr, Boston |
| 1968 | Glenn Hall, St. Louis | 1973 | Yvan Cournoyer, Montreal |
| 1969 | Serge Savard, Montreal | 1974 | Bernie Parent, Philadelphia |
| 1975 | Bernie Parent, Philadelphia | | |
| 1976 | Reg Leach, Philadelphia | | |
| 1977 | Guy Lafleur, Montreal | | |
| 1978 | Larry Robinson, Montreal | | |

## NHL Trophy Winners

| Ross Trophy Leading scorer | Norris Trophy Best defenseman | Calder Trophy Best rookie |
|---|---|---|
| 1978 Guy Lafleur, Montreal | 1978 Denis Potvin, N.Y. Islanders | 1978 Mike Bossy, N.Y. Islanders |
| 1977 Guy Lafleur, Montreal | 1977 Larry Robinson, Montreal | 1977 Willi Plett, Atlanta |
| 1976 Guy Lafleur, Montreal | 1976 Denis Potvin, N.Y. Islanders | 1976 Bryan Trottier N.Y. Islanders |
| 1975 Bobby Orr, Boston | 1975 Bobby Orr, Boston | 1975 Eric Vail, Atlanta |
| 1974 Phil Esposito, Boston | 1974 Bobby Orr, Boston | 1974 Denis Potvin, N.Y. Islanders |
| 1973 Phil Esposito, Boston | 1973 Bobby Orr, Boston | 1973 Steve Vickers, N.Y. Rangers |
| 1972 Phil Esposito, Boston | 1972 Bobby Orr, Boston | 1972 Ken Dryden, Montreal |
| 1971 Phil Esposito, Boston | 1971 Bobby Orr, Boston | 1971 Gil Perreault, Buffalo |
| 1970 Bobby Orr, Boston | 1970 Bobby Orr, Boston | 1970 Tony Esposito, Chicago |
| 1969 Phil Esposito, Boston | 1969 Bobby Orr, Boston | 1969 Danny Grant, Minnesota |
| 1968 Stan Mikita, Chicago | 1968 Bobby Orr, Boston | 1968 Derek Sanderson, Boston |
| 1967 Stan Mikita, Chicago | 1967 Harry Howell, N.Y. Rangers | 1967 Bobby Orr, Boston |
| 1966 Bobby Hull, Chicago | 1966 Jacques Laperriere, Montreal | 1966 Brit Selby, Toronto |
| 1965 Stan Mikita, Chicago | 1965 Pierre Pilote, Chicago | 1965 Roger Crozier, Detroit |
| 1964 Stan Mikita, Chicago | 1964 Pierre Pilote, Chicago | 1964 Jacques Laperriere, Montreal |

| Hart Trophy MVP | Vezina Trophy Leading goalie | Lady Byng Trophy Sportsmanship |
|---|---|---|
| 1978 Guy Lafleur, Montreal | 1978 Dryden, Larocque, Montreal | 1978 Butch Goring, Los Angeles |
| 1977 Guy Lafleur, Montreal | 1977 Dryden, Larocque, Montreal | 1977 Marcel Dionne, Los Angeles |
| 1976 Bobby Clarke, Philadelphia | 1976 Ken Dryden, Montreal | 1976 Jean Ratelle, Boston |
| 1975 Bobby Clarke, Philadelphia | 1975 Bernie Parent, Philadelphia | 1975 Marcel Dionne, Detroit |
| 1974 Phil Esposito, Boston | 1974 Tony Esposito, Chicago | 1974 John Bucyk, Boston |
| 1973 Bobby Clarke, Philadelphia |      Bernie Parent, Philadelphia | 1973 Gilbert Perreault, Buffalo |
| 1972 Bobby Orr, Boston | 1973 Ken Dryden, Montreal | 1972 Jean Ratelle, N.Y. Rangers |
| 1971 Bobby Orr, Boston | 1972 Esposito, Smith, Chicago | 1971 John Bucyk, Boston |
| 1970 Bobby Orr, Boston | 1971 Giacomin, Villemure, | 1970 Phil Goyette, St. Louis |
| 1969 Phil Esposito, Boston |      N.Y. Rangers | 1969 Alex Devecchio, Detroit |
| 1968 Stan Mikita, Chicago | 1970 Tony Esposito, Chicago | 1968 Stan Mikita, Chicago |
| 1967 Stan Mikita, Chicago | 1969 Hall, Plante, St. Louis | 1967 Stan Mikita, Chicago |
| 1966 Bobby Hull, Chicago | 1968 Worsley, Vachon, Montreal | 1966 Alex Devecchio, Detroit |
| 1965 Bobby Hull, Chicago | 1967 Hall, De Jordy, Chicago | 1965 Bobby Hull, Chicago |
| 1964 Jean Beliveau, Montreal | 1966 Hodge, Worsley, Montreal | 1964 Ken Wharram, Chicago |
| | 1965 Sawchuck, Bower, Toronto | |
| | 1964 Charlie Hodge, Montreal | |

**Frank Selke Trophy** (best defensive forward)—Bob Gainey, Montreal.

## Players in the Hockey Hall of Fame

Canadian National Exhibition Park, Toronto, Ont.

| | | | |
|---|---|---|---|
| Abel, Sid | Denney, Cy | Johnson, Moose | Rayner, Chuck |
| Adams, Jack | Drillon, Gordon | Johnson, Ching | Reardon, Ken |
| Apps, Syl | Drinkwater, Charles | Johnson, Tom | Richard, Maurice (Rocket) |
| Armstrong, George | Dunderdale, Tommy | Joliat, Aurel | Richardson, George |
| Bailey, Ace | Durnan, Bill | Keats, Gordon | Roberts, Gordon |
| Bain, Donald | Dutton, Red | Kelly, Red | Ross, Arthur |
| Baker, Hobey | Dye, Babe | Kennedy, Ted | Russell, Blair |
| Barry, Marty | Farrell, Arthur | Lach, Elmer | Russell, Ernie |
| Bathgate, Andy | Foyston, Frank | Lalonde, Newsy | Ruttan, Jack |
| Beliveau, Jean | Fredrickson, Frank | Laviolette, Jack | Sawchuck, Terry |
| Benedict, Clint (Benny) | Gadsby, Bill | Lehman, Hugh | Scanlan, Fred |
| Bentley, Doug | Gardiner, Chuck | LeSuer, Percy | Schmidt, Milt |
| Bentley, Max | Gardiner, Herb | Lindsay, Ted | Schriner, Sweeney |
| Blake, Toe | Gardner, Jimmy | Mackay, Duncan | Seibert, Earl |
| Boon, Dickie | Geoffrion, Bernie (Boom Boom) | Mantha, Sylvio | Seibert, Oliver |
| Bouchard, Emile (Butch) | Gerard, Eddie | Malone, Joe | Shore, Eddie |
| Boucher, Frank | Gilmour, Billy | Marshall, Jack | Siebert, Babe |
| Boucher, George (Buck) | Goodfellow, Ebbie | Maxwell, Fred | Simpson, H.J. (Bullet Joe) |
| Bower, John | Goheen, Moose | McGee, Frank | Smith, Alf |
| Bowie, Russell | Grant, Mike | McGimsie Billy | Smith, Hooley |
| Brimsek, Frank | Green, Shorty | McNamara, George | Smith, Tommy |
| Broadbent, Punch | Griffis, Silas | Moore, Dickie | Stanley, Barney |
| Broda, Turk | Hainsworth, George | Moran, Patrick | Stewart, John (Black Jack) |
| Burch, Billy | Hall, Glenn | Morenz, Howie | Stewart, Nels |
| Cameron, Harry | Hall, Joe | Mosienko, Bill | Stuart, Bruce |
| Clancy, King | Harvey, Doug | Nighbor, Frank | Stuart, Hod |
| Clapper, Dit | Hay, George | Noble, Reginald | Taylor, Fred (Cyclone) |
| Cleghorn, Sprague | Hern, Riley | Oliver, Harry | Trihey, Harry |
| Colville, Neil | Hextall, Bryan | Patrick, Lester | Thompson, Tiny |
| Conacher, Charlie | Holmes, Hap | Phillips, Tom | Vezina, Georges |
| Connell, Alex | Hooper, Tom | Pilote, Pierre | Walsh, Martin |
| Cook, Bill | Horner, Red | Pitre, Pit | Walker, Jack |
| Coulter, Art | Horton, Tim | Plante, Jacques | Watson, Harry |
| Cowley, Bill | Howe, Gordie | Pratt, Babe | Westwick, Harry |
| Crawford, Samuel (Rusty) | Howe, Syd | Primeau, Joe | Weiland, Cooney |
| Darragh, Jack | Hutton, John | Pronovost, Marcel | Whitcroft, Fred |
| Davidson, Allen (Scotty) | Hyland, Harry | Pulford, Harvey | Wilson Phat |
| Day, Hap | Irvin, James | Quakenbush, Bill | Worters, Roy |
| Delvecchio, Alex | Jackson, Busher | Rankin, Frank | |

## NHL Amateur Draft, 1978

First-round selections

| Team | Player | Pos | 1977-78 team | Team | Player | Pos. | 1977-78 team |
|------|--------|-----|--------------|------|--------|------|--------------|
| Minnesota | Bob Smith | C | Ottawa | Chicago | Tim Higgins | RW | Ottawa |
| Washington | Ryan Walter | C | Seattle | Atlanta | Brad Marsh | D | London |
| St. Louis | Wayne Babych | RW | Portland | Detroit | Brent Peterson | C | Portland |
| Vancouver | Bill Derlago | C | Brandon | Buffalo | Larry Playfair | D | Portland |
| Colorado | Mike Gillis | LW | Kingston | Philadelphia | Dan Lucas | LW | Sault Ste. Marie |
| Philadelphia | Behn Wilson | D | Kingston | N.Y. Islanders | Steve Tambellini | C | Lethbridge |
| Philadelphia | Ken Linseman | C | Birmingham (WHA) | Boston | Al Secord | LW | Hamilton |
| Montreal | Danny Geoffrion | RW | Cornwall | Montreal | Dave Hunter | LW | Sudbury |
| Detroit | Willie Huber | D | Hamilton | | | | |

## World Hockey Association, 1977-78

Final Standings

| Club | W | L | T | Pts | GF | GA | Club | W | L | T | Pts | GF | GA |
|------|---|---|---|-----|----|----|------|---|---|---|-----|----|----|
| Winnipeg | 50 | 28 | 2 | 102 | 381 | 270 | Birmingham | 36 | 41 | 3 | 75 | 287 | 314 |
| New England | 44 | 31 | 5 | 93 | 335 | 269 | Cincinnati | 35 | 42 | 3 | 73 | 298 | 332 |
| Houston | 42 | 34 | 4 | 88 | 296 | 302 | Indianapolis | 24 | 51 | 5 | 53 | 267 | 353 |
| Quebec | 40 | 37 | 3 | 83 | 349 | 347 | Russians-Czechs | 4 | 10 | 2 | 10 | 48 | 76 |
| Edmonton | 38 | 39 | 3 | 79 | 309 | 307 | | | | | | | |

### Avco World Trophy Playoffs

Winnipeg defeated Birmingham 4 games to 1.
New England defeated Edmonton 4 games to 1.
Quebec defeated Houston 4 games to 2.

New England defeated Quebec 4 games to 1.
Winnipeg defeated New England 4 games to 0.

### Leading Scorers

| Player, club | GP | G | A | Pts | Player, club | GP | G | A | Pts |
|--------------|----|----|----|-----|--------------|----|----|----|-----|
| Tardif, Quebec | 78 | 65 | 89 | 154 | S. Bernier, Quebec | 58 | 26 | 52 | 78 |
| Cloutier, Quebec | 73 | 56 | 73 | 129 | Linseman, Birmingham | 71 | 38 | 38 | 76 |
| U. Nilsson, Winnipeg | 73 | 37 | 89 | 126 | Lukowich, Houston | 80 | 40 | 35 | 75 |
| Hedberg, Winnipeg | 77 | 63 | 59 | 122 | Ruskowski, Houston | 78 | 15 | 57 | 72 |
| Hull, Winnipeg | 77 | 46 | 71 | 117 | Dudley, Cincinnati | 72 | 30 | 41 | 71 |
| Lacroix, Houston | 78 | 36 | 77 | 113 | Rogers, New England | 80 | 28 | 43 | 71 |
| Ftorek, Cincinnati | 80 | 59 | 50 | 109 | Marrin, Birmingham | 80 | 28 | 43 | 71 |
| K. Nilsson, Winnipeg | 80 | 42 | 65 | 107 | Flett, Edmonton | 74 | 41 | 28 | 69 |
| G. Howe, New England | 76 | 34 | 62 | 96 | MacDonald, Edmonton | 80 | 34 | 34 | 68 |
| Mark Howe, New England | 70 | 30 | 61 | 91 | Antonovich, New England | 75 | 32 | 35 | 67 |
| Chipperfield, Edmonton | 80 | 33 | 52 | 85 | Hislop, Cincinnati | 80 | 24 | 43 | 67 |
| Leduc, Indianapolis | 82 | 37 | 46 | 83 | Henderson, Birmingham | 80 | 37 | 29 | 66 |
| St. Sauveur, Indianapolis | 72 | 36 | 42 | 78 | | | | | |

### Leading Goalies

| Goalie, club | G | GA | ShO | Avg | Goalie, club | G | GA | ShO | Avg |
|--------------|---|----|----|-----|--------------|---|----|----|-----|
| Al Smith, New England | 55 | 174 | 2 | 3.22 | Dave Dryden, Edmonton | 48 | 150 | 2 | 3.49 |
| Joe Daley, Winnipeg | 37 | 114 | 1 | 3.30 | Michel Dion, Cincinnati | 45 | 140 | 4 | 3.57 |
| Louie Levasseur, New England | 27 | 91 | 3 | 3.30 | Don McLeod, Edmonton | 40 | 130 | 2 | 3.67 |
| Gary Bromley, Winnipeg | 39 | 124 | 1 | 3.30 | Richard Brodeur, Quebec | 36 | 122 | 0 | 3.73 |
| Ernie Wakely, Houston | 57 | 192 | 2 | 3.42 | John Garrett, Birmingham | 58 | 210 | 2 | 3.81 |

### Team Scoring Leaders

| Birmingham | GP | G | A | Pts | Indianapolis | GP | G | A | Pts |
|------------|----|----|----|-----|--------------|----|----|----|-----|
| Ken Linseman | 71 | 38 | 38 | 76 | Richie Leduc | 82 | 37 | 46 | 83 |
| Peter Marrin | 80 | 28 | 43 | 71 | Claude St. Sauveur | 72 | 36 | 42 | 78 |
| Paul Henderson | 80 | 37 | 29 | 66 | Claude Larose | 79 | 25 | 36 | 61 |
| Mark Napier | 79 | 33 | 32 | 65 | Kevin Morrison | 75 | 17 | 40 | 57 |
| Brent Hughes | 80 | 9 | 35 | 44 | Peter Driscoll | 77 | 28 | 28 | 56 |
| **Cincinnati** | GP | G | A | Pts | **New England** | GP | G | A | Pts |
| Robbie Ftorek | 80 | 59 | 50 | 109 | Gordie Howe | 76 | 34 | 62 | 96 |
| Rick Dudley | 72 | 30 | 41 | 71 | Mark Howe | 70 | 30 | 61 | 91 |
| Jamie Hislop | 80 | 24 | 43 | 67 | Mike Rogers | 80 | 28 | 43 | 71 |
| Peter Marsh | 74 | 25 | 25 | 50 | Mike Antonovich | 75 | 32 | 35 | 67 |
| Pat Stapleton | 65 | 4 | 45 | 49 | Dave Keon | 77 | 24 | 38 | 62 |
| **Edmonton** | GP | G | A | Pts | **Quebec** | GP | G | A | Pts |
| Ron Chipperfield | 80 | 33 | 52 | 85 | Marc Tardif | 78 | 65 | 89 | 154 |
| Bill Flett | 74 | 41 | 28 | 69 | Real Cloutier | 73 | 56 | 73 | 129 |
| Blair MacDonald | 80 | 34 | 34 | 68 | Serge Bernier | 58 | 26 | 52 | 78 |
| Mike Zuke | 71 | 23 | 34 | 57 | Paul Bordeleau | 77 | 42 | 23 | 65 |
| Al Hamilton | 59 | 11 | 43 | 54 | Matti Hagman | 53 | 25 | 31 | 56 |
| **Houston** | GP | G | A | Pts | **Winnipeg** | GP | G | A | Pts |
| Andre Lacroix | 78 | 36 | 77 | 113 | Ulf Nilsson | 73 | 37 | 89 | 126 |
| Morris Lukowich | 80 | 40 | 35 | 75 | Anders Hedberg | 77 | 63 | 59 | 122 |
| Terry Ruskowski | 78 | 15 | 57 | 72 | Bobby Hull | 77 | 46 | 71 | 117 |
| John Tonelli | 65 | 23 | 41 | 64 | Kent Nilsson | 80 | 42 | 65 | 107 |
| Don Larway | 69 | 24 | 35 | 59 | Willy Lindstrom | 77 | 30 | 30 | 60 |

## WHA Champions and Trophy Winners

| | Avco World Trophy Playoff winner | | Gordie Howe Trophy MVP | | Hunter Trophy Leading scorer |
|---|---|---|---|---|---|
| 1973 | New England Whalers | 1973 | Bobby Hull, Winnipeg | 1973 | Andre Lacroix, Philadelphia |
| 1974 | Houston Aeros | 1974 | Gordie Howe, Houston | 1974 | Mike Walton, Minnesota |
| 1975 | Houston Aeros | 1975 | Bobby Hull, Winnipeg | 1975 | Andre Lacroix, San Diego |
| 1976 | Winnipeg Jets | 1976 | Marc Tardif, Quebec | 1976 | Marc Tardif, Quebec |
| 1977 | Quebec Nordiques | 1977 | Robbie Ftorek, Phoenix | 1977 | Real Cloutier, Quebec |
| 1978 | Winnipeg Jets | 1978 | Marc Tardif, Quebec | 1978 | Marc Tardif, Quebec |

## NCAA Hockey Champions

| | | | | | | | |
|---|---|---|---|---|---|---|---|
| 1951 | Michigan | 1958 | Denver | 1965 | Michigan Tech | 1972 | Boston Univ |
| 1952 | Michigan | 1959 | North Dakota | 1966 | Michigan State | 1973 | Wisconsin |
| 1953 | Michigan | 1960 | Denver | 1967 | Cornell | 1974 | Minnesota |
| 1954 | Rensselaer Poly | 1961 | Denver | 1968 | Denver | 1975 | Michigan Tech |
| 1955 | Michigan | 1962 | Michigan Tech | 1969 | Denver | 1976 | Minnesota |
| 1956 | Michigan | 1963 | North Dakota | 1970 | Cornell | 1977 | Wisconsin |
| 1957 | Colorado College | 1964 | Michigan | 1971 | Boston Univ. | 1978 | Boston Univ. |

## National AAU Judo Championships in 1978

### Men

**132 lbs.**—Keith Nakasone, San Jose, Cal.
**143 lbs.**—James Martin, Sacramento, Cal.
**156 lbs.**—Steven Seck, Los Angeles, Cal.
**172 lbs.**—Teimoc Jonston-Ono, New York, N.Y.
**189 lbs.**—Clyde Worthen, New Milford, N.J.
**Under 209 lbs.**—Irwin Cohen, Wheeling, Ill.
**Over 209 lbs.**—John Saylor, Columbus, Oh.
**Open Division**—Michinori Ishibashi, Ft. Worth, Tex.

### Women

**106 lbs.**—Ann Marie Waddell, Hopkins, Minn.
**114 lbs.**—Lynn Lewis, Revere, Mass.
**123 lbs.**—Darlene Hill, Memphis, Tenn.
**134 lbs.**—Pamela Adams, Beverly, Mass.
**145 lbs.**—Dolores Brodie, San Jose, Cal.
**Under 158 lbs.**—Amy Kublin, Sharon, Mass.
**Over 158 lbs.**—Margaret Castro, New York, N.Y.
**Open Division**—Barbara Fest, Salem, Mass.

## Sports Arenas

The seating capacity of sports arenas can vary depending on the event being presented. The figures below are the normal seating capacity for basketball. (*) indicates hockey seating capacity.

| Name, location | Capacity |
|---|---|
| Allen County Memorial, Ft. Wayne | *8,032 |
| Astrohall, Houston | 10,000 |
| Atlantic City Audit, Atlantic City, N.J. | 40,000 |
| Baltimore Civic Center | 13,043-*11,329 |
| Bismarck Coliseum, N.D. | 7,000 |
| Boston Garden | 15,040-*14,597 |
| Buffalo Memorial Auditorium | 17,900-*16,433(a) |
| Calgary Corral | *7,000 |
| Capital Centre, Landover, Md. | 19,035-*18,130 |
| Charlotte Coliseum | 11,666-*9,575 |
| Checkerdome, St. Louis | *18,006 |
| Chicago Stadium | 17,374-*18,000 |
| Cincinnati Gardens | 11,650-*10,606 |
| Cobo Hall, Detroit | 11,147 |
| The Coliseum, Richfield Township, Oh. | 19,548-*18,544 |
| Convention Center, San Antonio | 10,146 |
| Convention Hall, Philadelphia | 9,200-*9,500 |
| Cow Palace, San Francisco | 14,500 |
| Dallas State Fair Coliseum | *7,513 |
| Denver Coliseum | *9,038 |
| Dorton Arena, Raleigh, N.C. | 8,058 |
| Edmonton Coliseum | *15,273 |
| Fairgrounds Coliseum, Indianapolis | 9,479 |
| Freedom Hall, Louisville, Ky. | 16,613 |
| Greensboro Coliseum | 15,500-*13,280 |
| Halifax Metro Centre | *9,631 |
| Hampton Coliseum, Va. | 10,000-*7,648 |
| HemisFair Arena, San Antonio | 10,446 |
| Hersheypark Arena, Pa. | *7,286 |
| Hofheinz Pavilion, Houston | 10,218 |
| International Amphitheatre, Chicago | 9,000 |
| Jacksonville Coliseum | *7,900 |
| Jefferson County Civic Center, Birmingham, Ala. | 16,753 |
| Kemper Memorial Arena, Kansas City | 16,320-15,998 |
| Kiel Auditorium, St. Louis | 10,574 |
| Las Vegas Convention Center | 9,000 |
| Long Beach Arena, Cal. | 11,168 |
| Los Angeles Forum | 17,505-*16,005 |
| Los Angeles Sports Arena | 15,333-*11,325 |
| Louisiana Superdome | 26,318 |
| Lubbock Municipal Coliseum, Tex. | 10,400 |
| Macon Coliseum | *8,000 |
| Madison Square Garden, New York | 19,694-*17,500 |
| Maple Leaf Gardens, Toronto | 17,000-*16,485(a) |
| Market Square Arena, Indianapolis | 16,926-*16,040 |
| McNichols Sports Arena, Denver | 17,297-*16,401 |

| Name, location | Capacity |
|---|---|
| Met. Sports Center, Bloomington, Minn. | *15,184 |
| Mid-South Coliseum, Memphis | 11,065 |
| Milwaukee Arena | 10,938-*8,000 |
| Mobile Municipal Auditorium | 13,100 |
| Montreal Forum | *18,350 |
| Moody Coliseum, Dallas | 9,500 |
| Municipal Auditorium, Kansas City | 9,929 |
| Myriad, Oklahoma City | *13,494 |
| Nashville Municipal Auditorium | 8,000 |
| Nassau Coliseum, Uniondale, N.Y. | 15,527-*14,865 |
| New Orleans Municipal Auditorium | 9,100 |
| Norfolk Scope, Va. | 10,600-*9,364 |
| Oakland Coliseum Arena | 13,155 |
| Olympia Stadium, Detroit | *16,200(a) |
| Olympic Auditorium, Los Angeles | 10,500 |
| Omaha Civic Auditorium | 9,144 |
| The Omni, Atlanta | 15,389-*15,191 |
| Ottawa Civic Center | *9,355 |
| Pacific Coliseum, Vancouver, B.C. | *15,569 |
| Penn Palestra, Philadelphia | 9,200 |
| Philadelphia Civic Center | *8,055 |
| Pittsburgh Civic Arena | *16,033 |
| Providence Civic Center | 11,619-*10,730 |
| Portland Memorial Coliseum | 12,411-*10,500 |
| Quebec Coliseum | *10,000 |
| Reynolds Coliseum, Raleigh, N.C. | 12,400 |
| Richmond Coliseum, Va. | 10,700-*9,674 |
| Riverfront Coliseum, Cincinnati | *15,820 |
| Roanoke Civic Center, Va. | 10,000-*8,372 |
| St. Paul Civic Center, Minn. | *15,594 |
| Salt Palace, Salt Lake City | 12,201-*10,640 |
| Sam Houston Coliseum, Houston | 8,925-*9,300 |
| San Diego Intl. Sports Arena | 14,000-*13,039 |
| Seattle Center Coliseum | 14,098 |
| Spectrum, Philadelphia | 18,276-*17,077 |
| Springfield Civic Center, Mass. | *7,466 |
| The Summit, Houston | 15,676-*15,256 |
| Tarrant County Convention Center, Ft. Worth | 13,500 |
| Tingley Coliseum, Albuquerque | *12,000 |
| Uline Arena, Washington, D. C. | 11,000 |
| Veterans Memorial Audit., Des Moines | 15,000 |
| Veterans Memorial Coliseum, New Haven | *8,765 |
| Veterans Memorial Coliseum, Phoenix | 13,214-*12,474 |
| Winnipeg Arena | *10,390 |
| Winston-Salem Memorial Coliseum | 9,020 |
| (a) includes standees | |

# Notable Sports Personalities

**Henry Aaron**, b. 1934: Milwaukee-Atlanta outfielder hit record 755 home runs; led NL 4 times.

**Kareem Abdul-Jabbar**, b. 1947: Milwaukee, L.A. Lakers center; MVP 5 times; leading scorer twice.

**Grover Cleveland Alexander**, (1887-1950): pitcher won 374 NL games; pitched 16 shutouts, 1916.

**Muhammad Ali**, b. 1942: twice heavyweight champion.

**Mario Andretti**, b. 1940: U.S. Auto Club national champ 3 times; won Indy 500, 1969.

**Earl Anthony**, b. 1938: bowler won record $110,833, 1976.

**Eddie Arcaro**, b. 1916: jockey rode 4,779 winners including the Kentucky Derby 5 times; the Preakness and Belmont Stakes 6 times each.

**Henry Armstrong**, b. 1912: boxer held feather-, bantam-, light-weight titles simultaneously, 1937-38.

**Arthur Ashe**, b. 1943: U.S. singles champ, 1968, Wimbledon champ, 1975.

**Red Auerbach**, b. 1917: coached Boston Celtics to 9 NBA championships.

**Ernie Banks**, b. 1931: Chicago Cubs slugger hit 512 NL homers; twice MVP.

**Roger Bannister**, b. 1929: Briton ran first sub 4-minute mile, May 6, 1954.

**Rick Barry**, b. 1944: NBA scoring leader, 1967; ABA, 1969.

**Sammy Baugh**, b. 1914: Washington Redskins quarterback held numerous records upon retirement after 16 pro seasons.

**Elgin Baylor**, b. 1934: L.A. Lakers forward; 1st team all-star 10 times.

**Bob Beamon**, b. 1946: long jumper won 1968 Olympic gold medal with record 29 ft. 2½ in.

**Jean Beliveau**, b. 1931: Montreal Canadiens center scored 507 goals; twice MVP.

**Johnny Bench**, b. 1947: Cincinnati Reds catcher; MVP twice; led league in home runs twice, RBIs 3 times.

**Patty Berg**, b. 1918: won over 80 golf tournaments; AP Woman Athlete-of-the-Year 3 times.

**Yogi Berra**, b. 1925: N.Y. Yankees catcher; MVP 3 times; played in 14 World Series.

**Raymond Berry**, b. 1933: Baltimore Colts receiver caught 631 passes.

**George Blanda**, b. 1927: quarterback, kicker; 26 years as active player, scoring record 2,002 points.

**Fanny Blankers-Koen**, b. 1918: Dutch track star won 4 1948 Olympic gold medals.

**Bjorn Borg**, b. 1956: led Sweden to first Davis Cup, 1975; Wimbledon champion, 3 times.

**Julius Boros**, b. 1920: won U.S. Open, 1952, 1963; PGA champ, 1968.

**Jack Brabham**, b. 1926: Grand Prix champ 3 times.

**Lou Brock**, b. 1939: St. Louis Cardinals outfielder stole record 118 bases, 1974; led NL 8 times.

**Jimmy Brown**, b. 1936: Cleveland Browns fullback ran for record 12,312 career yards; MVP 3 times.

**Valery Brumel**, b. 1942: Soviet high jumper won 1964 Olympic gold metal; world record holder until 1973.

**Don Budge**, b. 1915: won numerous amateur and pro tennis titles, "grand slam," 1938.

**Maria Bueno**, b. 1939: U.S. singles champ 4 times; Wimbledon champ 3 times.

**Mike Burton**, b. 1947: swimmer won 1968, 1972 Olympic 1,500 meter freestyle.

**Dick Butkus**, b. 1942: Chicago Bears linebacker twice chosen best NFL defensive player.

**Dick Button**, b. 1929: figure skater won 1948, 1952 Olympic gold medals; world titlist, 1948-52.

**Walter Camp**, (1859-1925): Yale football player, coach, athletic director; established many rules; promoted All-America designations.

**Roy Campanella**, b. 1921: Brooklyn Dodgers catcher; MVP 3 times.

**Rod Carew**, b. 1945: Minnesota Twins infielder won 6 batting titles; MVP, 1977.

**Steve Carlton**, b. 1944: NL pitcher won 20 games 4 times, Cy Young award twice.

**Don Carter**, b. 1930: bowler-of-the-Year 6 times.

**Billy Casper**, b. 1931: PGA Player-of-the-Year 3 times; U.S. Open champ twice.

**Steve Cauthen**, b. 1960: jockey whose mounts won record $6,151,750, 1977; rode triple crown winner Affirmed, 1978.

**Wilt Chamberlain**, b. 1936: center scored NBA career record 31,419 points; MVP 4 times.

**Jim Clark**, (1936-1968): world driving champ twice; won Indy 500, 1965.

**Bobby Clarke**, b. 1949: Philadelphia Flyers center led team to 2 Stanley Cup championships; MVP 3 times.

**Roberto Clemente**, (1934-1972): Pittsburgh Pirates outfielder won 4 batting titles; MVP, 1966.

**Ty Cobb**, (1886-1961): Detroit Tigers outfielder had record .367 lifetime batting average, 4,191 hits, 12 batting titles.

**Nadia Comaneci**, b. 1961: Romanian gymnast won 3 gold medals, achieved 7 perfect scores, 1976 Olympics.

**Maureen Connolly**, (1934-1969): won tennis "grand slam," 1953; AP Woman-Athlete-of-the-Year 3 times.

**Jimmy Connors**, b. 1952: U.S. singles champ twice; won record $922,657, 1977.

**James J. Corbett**, (1866-1933): heavyweight champion, 1892-97; credited with being the first "scientific" boxer.

**Margaret Smith Court**, b. 1942: Australian won U.S. singles championship 5 times; Wimbledon champ 3 times.

**Bob Cousy**, b. 1928: Boston Celtics guard led team to 6 NBA championships; MVP, 1957.

**Dave Cowens**, b. 1948: Boston Celtics center chosen MVP, 1973.

**Stanley Dancer**, b. 1927: harness racing driver drove Hambletonian winner 3 times, Little Brown Jug winner 4 times.

**Dizzy Dean**, (1911-1974): colorful pitcher for St. Louis Cardinals "Gashouse Gang" in the 30s; MVP, 1934.

**Jack Dempsey**, b. 1895: heavyweight champion, 1919-26.

**Joe DiMaggio**, b. 1914: N.Y. Yankees outfielder hit safely in record 56 consecutive games, 1941; MVP twice.

**Leo Durocher**, b. 1906: colorful manager of Dodgers, Giants, and Cubs; won 3 NL pennants.

**Gertrude Ederle**, b. 1906: first woman to swim English Channel, broke existing men's record, 1926.

**Kornelia Ender**, b. 1958: E. German swimmer broke 23 world records; won 4 1976 Olympic gold medals.

**Julius Erving**, b. 1950: MVP and leading scorer in ABA 3 times.

**Phil Esposito**, b. 1942: scored record 76 goals and 152 points in 1970-71; NHL scoring leader 5 times.

**Chris Evert**, b. 1954: U.S. singles champ 3 times, Wimbledon champ twice.

**Ray Ewry**, (1873-1937): track and field star won 8 gold medals, 1900, 1904, and 1908 Olympics.

**Juan Fangio**, b. 1911: Argentine World Grand Prix champion 5 times.

**Bob Feller**, b. 1918: Cleveland Indians pitcher won 266 games; pitched 3 no-hitters, 12 one-hitters.

**Peggy Fleming**, b. 1948: world figure skating champion, 1966-68; gold medalist 1968 Olympics.

**Whitey Ford**, b. 1928: N.Y. Yankees pitcher won record 10 world series games.

**Chuck Foreman**, b. 1950: Minnesota Vikings back rushed for 1,155 yds., caught 55 passes, 1976.

**Dick Fosbury**, b. 1947: high jumper won 1968 Olympic gold medal; developed the "Fosbury Flop."

**George Foster**, b. 1951: Cincinnati Reds outfielder hit 52 home runs, selected MVP, 1977.

**Jimmy Foxx**, (1907-1967): Red Sox, Athletics slugger; MVP 3 times; triple crown, 1933.

**A.J. Foyt**, b. 1935: won Indy 500 4 times; U.S. Auto Club champ 6 times.

**Dawn Fraser**, b. 1937: Australian swimmer won Olympics 100-meter freestyle 3 times.

**Joe Frazier**, b. 1944: heavyweight champion, 1970-73.

**Walt Frazier**, b. 1945: New York-Cleveland guard; first team all-star 4 times.

**Lou Gehrig**, (1903-1941): N.Y. Yankees 1st baseman played record 2,130 consecutive games, MVP, 1936.

**Althea Gibson**, b. 1927: twice U.S. and Wimbledon singles champ.

**Bob Gibson**, b. 1935: St. Louis Cardinals pitcher won Cy Young award twice; struck out NL record 3,117 batters.

**Frank Gifford**, b. 1930: N.Y. Giants back; MVP 1956.

**Pancho Gonzalez**, b. 1928: World professional tennis champ, 8 years.

**Otto Graham**, b. 1921: Cleveland Browns quarterback; all-pro 4 times.

**Red Grange**, b. 1903: All-America at Univ. of Illinois; played for Chicago Bears, 1925-35.

**Joe Greene**, b. 1946: Pittsburgh Steelers lineman; twice NFL outstanding defensive player.

**Lefty Grove**, (1900-1975): pitcher won 300 AL games; 20-game winner 8 times.

**Walter Hagen**, (1892-1969): won PGA championship 5 times. British Open 4 times.

**George Halas**, b. 1895: founder-coach of Chicago Bears; won 5 NFL championships.

**Bill Hartack**, b. 1932: jockey rode 5 Kentucky Derby winners.

**Doug Harvey**, b. 1930: Montreal Canadiens defenseman; Norris Trophy 7 times.

**Bill Haughton**, b. 1923: harness racing driver won Little Brown Jug 4 times, Hambletonian 3 times.

**John Havlicek**, b. 1940: Boston Celtics forward scored over 25,000 NBA points.

**Carol Heiss,** b. 1940: world champion figure skater 5 consecutive years, 1956-60; won 1960 Olympic gold medal.

**Sonja Henie,** (1912-1969): world champion figure skater, 1927-36; Olympic gold medalist, 1928, 1932, 1936.

**Graham Hill,** (1929-1975): Twice World Grand Prix champ.

**Ben Hogan,** b. 1912: won 4 U.S. Open championships, 2 PGA, 2 Masters.

**Willie Hoppe,** (1887-1959): won some 50 world billiard titles.

**Rogers Hornsby,** (1896-1963): NL 2d baseman batted record .424 in 1924; twice won triple crown; batting leader 6 consecutive years, 1920-25.

**Paul Hornung,** b. 1935: Green Bay Packers runner-placekicker scored record 176 points, 1960.

**Gordie Howe,** b. 1928: Detroit Red Wings forward holds NHL career records in goals, assists, and points; NHL MVP 6 times, leading scorer 6 times.

**Carl Hubbell,** b. 1903: N.Y. Giants pitcher; 20-game winner 5 consecutive years, 1933-37.

**Bobby Hull,** b. 1939: scored 604 NHL goals; NHL all-star 10 times, WHA all-star 4 times.

**Catfish Hunter,** b. 1946: pitched perfect game, 1968; 20-game winner 5 times.

**Don Hutson,** b. 1913: Green Bay Packers receiver caught NFL record 99 touchdown passes.

**Reggie Jackson,** b. 1946; slugger twice led AL in home runs; MVP, 1973; hit 5 world series home runs, 1977.

**Bruce Jenner,** b. 1949: decathlon gold medalist, 1976.

**Jack Johnson,** (1878-1946): heavyweight champion, 1910-15.

**Rafer Johnson,** b. 1935: decathlon gold medalist, 1960.

**Walter Johnson,** (1887-1946): Washington Senators pitcher won 414 games.

**Bert Jones,** b. 1951: Baltimore Colts quarterback; MVP, 1976.

**Bobby Jones,** (1902-1971): won "grand slam of golf" 1930; U.S. Amateur champ 5 times, U.S. Open champ 4 times.

**Deacon Jones,** b. 1938: L.A. Rams lineman; twice NFL outstanding defensive player.

**Sonny Jurgensen,** b. 1934: quarterback named all-pro 5 times; completed record 288 passes, 1967.

**Duke Kahanamoku,** (1890-1968): swimmer won 1912, 1920 Olympic gold medals in 100-meter freestyle.

**Kipchoge Keino,** b. 1940: Kenyan distance runner won 1968, 1972 Olympic gold medals.

**Harmon Killebrew,** b. 1936: Minnesota Twins slugger led AL in home runs 6 times.

**Jean Claude Killy,** b. 1943: French skier won 3 1968 Olympic gold medals.

**Ralph Kiner,** b. 1922: Pittsburgh Pirates slugger led NL in home runs 7 consecutive years, 1946-52.

**Billie Jean King,** b. 1943: U.S. singles champ 4 times; Wimbledon champ 6 times.

**Olga Korbut,** b. 1956: Soviet gymnast won 3 1972 Olympic gold medals.

**Sandy Koufax,** b. 1935: Dodgers pitcher won Cy Young award 3 times; lowest ERA in NL, 1962-66; pitched 4 no-hitters, one a perfect game.

**Jack Kramer,** b. 1921: twice U.S. singles champ.

**Guy Lafleur,** b. 1951: Montreal Canadiens forward led NHL in scoring 3 times; MVP, 1977, 1978.

**Tom Landry,** b. 1924: Dallas Cowboys head coach since 1960.

**Rod Laver,** b. 1938: Australian won tennis "grand slam," 1962, 1969; Wimbledon champ 4 times.

**Vince Lombardi,** (1913-1970): Green Bay Packers coach led team to 5 NFL championships and 2 Super Bowl victories.

**Johnny Longden,** b. 1970: jockey rode 6,032 winners.

**Joe Louis,** b. 1914: heavyweight champion, 1937-49.

**Sid Luckman,** b. 1916: Chicago Bears quarterback led team to 4 NFL championships; MVP, 1943.

**Connie Mack,** (1892-1956): Philadelphia Athletics manager, 1901-50; won 9 pennants, 5 championships.

**Bill Madlock,** b. 1951: NL batting leader, 1975 and 1976.

**Mickey Mantle,** b. 1931: N.Y. Yankees outfielder; triple crown, 1956; 18 World Series home runs.

**Pete Maravich,** b. 1948: averaged 44.2 ppg at LSU; led NBA in scoring, 1977.

**Alice Marble,** b. 1913: U.S. singles champ 4 times.

**Rocky Marciano,** (1923-1969): heavyweight champion, 1952-56; retired undefeated.

**Roger Maris,** b. 1934: N.Y. Yankees outfielder hit record 61 home runs, 1961; MVP, 1960 and 1961.

**Christy Mathewson,** (1880-1925): N.Y. Giants pitcher won 373 games.

**Bob Mathias,** b. 1930: decathlon gold medalist, 1948, 1952.

**Willie Mays,** b. 1931: N.Y.-S.F. Giants center fielder hit 660 home runs; twice MVP.

**Bob McAdoo,** b. 1951: leading NBA scorer, 1974-76; MVP, 1975.

**John McGraw,** (1873-1934): N.Y. Giants manager led team to 10 pennants, 3 championships.

**Debbie Meyer,** b. 1952: swimmer won 200-, 400-, and 800- meter freestyle events, 1968 Olympics.

**George Mikan,** b. 1924: Minneapolis Lakers center selected in a 1950 AP poll as the greatest basketball player of the first half of the 20th century.

**Stan Mikita,** b. 1940: Chicago Black Hawks center led NHL in scoring 4 times; MVP twice.

**Archie Moore,** b. 1913: world light-heavyweight champion, 1952-62.

**Howie Morenz,** (1902-1937): Montreal Canadiens forward chosen in a 1950 Canadian press poll as the outstanding hockey player of the first half of the 20th century; MVP 3 times.

**Joe Morgan,** b. 1943: Cincinnati Reds 2d baseman; MVP, 1975, 1976.

**Thurman Munson,** b. 1947: N.Y. Yankees catcher; MVP, 1976.

**Isaac Murphy,** (1856-1896): jockey rode 3 Kentucky Derby winners.

**Stan Musial,** b. 1920: St. Louis Cardinals star won 7 NL batting titles; MVP 3 times; NL record 3,630 hits.

**Bronco Nagurski,** b. 1908: Chicago Bears fullback and tackle; gained over 4,000 yds. rushing.

**Joe Namath,** b. 1943: quarterback passed for record 4,007 yds., 1967.

**Ilie Nastase,** b. 1946: temperamental Romanian won U.S. singles title, 1972.

**Byron Nelson,** b. 1912: won 11 consecutive golf tournaments in 1945, ending the year with record 19 victories; twice Masters and PGA titlist.

**Ernie Nevers,** (1903-1976): Stanford star selected the best college fullback to play between 1919-1969, in a poll of the Football Writers Assn.; played pro football and baseball.

**John Newcombe,** b. 1943: Australian twice U.S. singles champ; Wimbledon titlist 3 times.

**Jack Nicklaus,** b. 1940: PGA Player-of-the-Year, 1967, 1972; leading money winner 7 times.

**Paavo Nurmi,** (1897-1973): Finnish distance runner won 6 Olympic gold medals, 1920, 1924, 1928.

**Al Oerter,** b. 1936: discus thrower won gold medal at 4 consecutive Olympics, 1956-68.

**Barney Oldfield,** (1878-1946): turn-of-the-century auto racer.

**Bobby Orr,** b. 1948: Boston Bruins defenseman; Norris Trophy 8 times; led NHL in scoring twice, assists 5 times.

**Mel Ott,** (1909-1958): N.Y. Giants outfielder hit 511 home runs; led NL 6 times.

**Jesse Owens,** b. 1913: track and field star won 4 1936 Olympic gold medals.

**Satchel Paige,** b. 1906: pitcher starred in Negro leagues, 1924-48; entered major leagues at age 42.

**Arnold Palmer,** b. 1929: golf's first $1 million winner; won 4 Masters, 2 British Opens.

**Jim Palmer,** b. 1945: Baltimore Orioles pitcher; Cy Young award 3 times; 20-game winner 7 times.

**Floyd Patterson,** b. 1935: twice heavyweight champion.

**Walter Payton,** 1954: Chicago Bears running back ran for game record 275 yards, 1977.

**Pele,** b. 1940: Brazilian soccer star scored 1,281 goals during 22-year career.

**Bob Pettit,** b. 1932: Milwaukee-St. Louis Hawks forward was first NBA player to score 20,000 points; twice NBA scoring leader.

**Richard Petty,** b. 1937: NASCAR national champ 6 times; 5-times Daytona 500 winner.

**Laffit Pincay Jr.,** b. 1946: leading money-winning jockey, 1970-74.

**Jacques Plante,** b. 1929: goalie, 7 Vezina trophies; first goalie to wear a mask in a game.

**Gary Player,** b. 1935: South African won the Masters, U.S. Open, PGA, and twice the British Open.

**Annemarie Proell,** b. 1953: Austrian skier won the World Cup championship 5 times.

**Willis Reed,** b. 1942: N.Y. Knicks center; MVP, 1970; playoff MVP, 1970, 1973.

**Maurice Richard,** b. 1924: Montreal Canadiens forward scored 544 regular season goals, 82 playoff goals.

**Branch Rickey,** (1881-1965): executive instrumental in breaking baseball's color barrier, 1947; initiated farm system, 1919.

**Oscar Robertson,** b. 1938: guard averaged career 25.7 points per game; record 9,887 career assist; MVP, 1964.

**Brooks Robinson,** b. 1937: Baltimore Orioles 3d baseman played in 4 World Series; MVP, 1964.

**Frank Robinson,** b. 1935: slugger MVP in both NL and AL; triple crown winner, 1966; first black manager in majors.

**Jackie Robinson,** (1919-1972): broke baseball's color barrier with Brooklyn Dodgers, 1947; MVP, 1949.

**Sugar Ray Robinson,** b. 1920: middleweight champion 4 times, welterweight champion.

**Knute Rockne,** (1883-1931): Notre Dame football coach, 1918-31; revolutionized game by stressing forward pass.

**Pete Rose,** b. 1942: Cincinnati Reds star won 3 batting titles; led NL in hits 5 times; has over 3,000 hits.

**Ken Rosewall,** b. 1934: Australian twice U.S. singles champ.

**lma Rudolph,** b. 1940: sprinter won 3 1960 Olympic gold medals.

**. Russell,** b. 1934: Boston Celtics center led team to 11 NBA titles; MVP 5 times; first black coach of major pro sports team.

**be Ruth,** (1895-1948): N.Y. Yankees outfielder hit 60 home runs, 1927; 714 lifetime; led AL 11 times.

**lan Ryan,** b. 1947: Cal. Angels pitcher struck out record 383 batters, 1973; pitched 4 no-hitters.

**n Ryun,** b. 1947: runner set records for the mile and 1,500 meters, 1967.

**ene Sarazen,** b. 1902: won PGA championship 3 times, U.S. Open twice; developer of sand wedge.

**le Sayers,** b. 1943: Chicago Bears back twice led NFC in rushing.

**ke Schmidt,** b. 1949: Phillies 3d baseman led NL in home runs, 1974-76.

**m Seaver,** b. 1944: NL pitcher won Cy Young award 3 times.

**llie Shoemaker,** b. 1931: jockey rode 3 Kentucky Derby and 5 Belmont Stakes winners; leading career money winner.

**die Shore,** b. 1902: Boston Bruins defenseman; MVP 4 times, first-team all-star 7 times.

**Simmons,** (1902-1956): AL outfielder had lifetime .334 batting average.

**J. Simpson,** b. 1947: Buffalo Bills back rushed for record 2,003 yds., 1973; AFC leading rusher 4 times.

**orge Sisler,** (1893-1973): St. Louis Browns 1st baseman had record 257 hits, 1920; batted .340 lifetime.

**m Snead,** b. 1912: PGA and Masters champ 3 times each.

**ter Snell,** b. 1938: New Zealand runner won 800-meter race, 1960, 1964 Olympics.

**arren Spahn,** b. 1921: Boston-Milwaukee Braves pitcher won 363 games; 20-game winner 13 times; Cy Young award, 1957.

**is Speaker,** (1885-1958): AL outfielder batted .344 over 22 seasons; hit record 793 career doubles.

**ark Spitz,** b. 1950: swimmer won 7 1972 Olympic gold medals.

**nos Alonzo Stagg,** (1862-1965): coached Univ. of Chicago football team for 41 years, including 5 undefeated seasons; introduced huddle, man-in-motion, and end-around play.

**art Starr,** b. 1934: Green Bay Packers quarterback led team to 5 NFL titles and 2 Super Bowl victories.

**oger Staubach,** b. 1942: Navy-Dallas Cowboys quarterback; Heisman Trophy, 1963.

**asey Stengel,** (1890-1975): managed Yankees to 10 pennants, 7 championships, 1949-60.

**ckie Stewart,** b. 1939: Scot auto racer retired with record 27 Grand Prix victories.

**uis Suggs,** b. 1923: U.S. Women's Open champ, 1949, 1952; LPGA titlist, 1957.

**hn L. Sullivan,** (1858-1918): last bareknuckle heavyweight champion, 1882-1892.

**an Tarkenton,** b. 1940: quarterback holds career passing records for touchdowns, completions, yardage.

**Gustave Thoeni,** b. 1951: Italian 4-time world alpine ski champ.

**Jim Thorpe,** (1888-1953): football All-America, 1911, 1912; won pentathlon and decathlon, 1912 Olympics; played major league baseball for 6 seasons.

**Bill Tilden,** (1893-1953): U.S. singles champ 7 times; played on 11 Davis Cup teams.

**Y.A. Tittle,** b. 1926: N.Y. Giants quarterback; MVP, 1961, 1963.

**Lee Trevino,** b. 1939: won the U.S. and British Open championships twice.

**Gene Tunney,** b. 1897: heavyweight champion, 1926-28.

**Wyomia Tyus,** b. 1945: sprinter won 1964, 1968 Olympic 100-meter dash.

**Johnny Unitas,** b. 1933: Baltimore Colts quarterback passed for over 40,000 yds.; MVP, 1957, 1967.

**Al Unser,** b. 1939: Indy 500 winner, 3 times.

**Bobby Unser,** b. 1934: Indy 500 winner, 1968, twice U.S. Auto Club national champ.

**Norm Van Brocklin,** b. 1926: quarterback passed for game record 554 yds., 1951; MVP, 1960.

**Honus Wagner,** (1874-1955): Pittsburgh Pirates shortstop won 8 NL batting titles.

**Joe Walcott,** b. 1914: heavyweight champion, 1951-52.

**John Walker,** b. 1952: New Zealander ran record mile, 3:49.4, Aug. 12, 1975.

**Mickey Walker,** b. 1901: colorful welter- and middleweight champion of the 20s and 30s.

**Bill Walton,** b. 1952: led Portland Trail Blazers to NBA championship, 1977; MVP, 1978.

**Johnny Weissmuller,** b. 1903: swimmer won 52 national championships, 3 Olympic gold medals; set 67 world records.

**Jerry West,** b. 1938: L.A. Lakers guard had career average 27 points per game; first team all-star 10 times.

**Kathy Whitworth,** b. 1939: women's golf leading money winner 4 times; first woman to earn over $300,000.

**Ted Williams,** b. 1918: Boston Red Sox outfielder won 6 batting titles; last major leaguer to hit over .400: .406 in 1941: .344 lifetime batting average.

**Helen Wills,** b. 1906: winner of 7 U.S., 8 British, 4 French women's singles titles.

**John Wooden,** b. 1910: coached UCLA basketball team to 8 national championships.

**Mickey Wright,** b. 1935: won LPGA championship 4 times, Vare Trophy 5 times; twice AP Woman-Athlete-of-the-Year.

**Carl Yastrzemski,** b. 1939: Boston Red Sox slugger won 3 batting titles, triple crown, 1967.

**Cy Young,** (1867-1955): pitcher won record 511 major league games.

**Babe Didrikson Zaharias,** (1914-1956): track star won 2 1932 Olympic gold medals; won numerous golf tournaments.

**Emil Zatopek,** b. 1922: Czech distance runner won 5,000- and 10,000-meter and marathon, 1952 Olympics.

## Rodeo Championship Standings in 1977

| Event | Winner | Money won | Event | Winner | Money won |
|---|---|---|---|---|---|
| . Around | Tom Ferguson, Miami, Oklahoma | $100,080 | Calf Roping | Roy Cooper, Durant, Oklahoma | $47,713 |
| addle Bronc | Bobby Berger, Norman, Okla. | 25,436 | Steer Wrestling | Larry Ferguson, Miami, Oklahoma | 27,437 |
| areback Bronc | Joe Alexander, Cora, Wyoming | 41,555 | Team Roping | Jerold Camarillo, Oakdale, California | 18,454 |
| ull Riding | Don Gay, Mesquite, Texas | 35,053 | | | |

## Rodeo Cowboy All Around Champions

| ear | Winner | Money won | Year | Winner | Money won |
|---|---|---|---|---|---|
| 60 | Harry Tompkins, Dublin, Texas | $32,522 | 1969 | Larry Mahan, Brooks, Oregon | $57,726 |
| 61 | Benny Reynolds, Melrose, Montana | 31,309 | 1970 | Larry Mahan, Brooks, Oregon | 41,493 |
| 62 | Tom Nesmith, Bethel, Oklahoma | 32,611 | 1971 | Phil Lyne, George West, Texas | 49,245 |
| 63 | Dean Oliver, Boise, Idaho | 31,329 | 1972 | Phil Lyne, George West, Texas | 60,852 |
| 64 | Dean Oliver, Boise, Idaho | 31,150 | 1973 | Larry Mahan, Dallas, Texas | 64,447 |
| 65 | Dean Oliver, Boise, Idaho | 33,163 | 1974 | Tom Ferguson, Miami, Oklahoma | 66,929 |
| 66 | Larry Mahan, Brooks, Oregon | 40,358 | 1975 | Leo Camarillo, Oakdale, California | 50,830 |
| 67 | Larry Mahan, Brooks, Oregon | 51,996 | 1976 | Tom Ferguson, Miami, Oklahoma | 87,908 |
| 68 | Larry Mahan, Salem, Oregon | 49,129 | 1977 | Tom Ferguson, Miami, Oklahoma | 100,080 |

## National AAU Trampoline and Tumbling Championships in 1978

New Brunswick, N.J., Apr. 27-28, 1978

**Men**

Trampoline—Stuart Ransom, Memphis, Tenn.
umbling—Steve Elliott, Amarillo, Tex.
ouble Mini-tramp—Ron Merriott, Rockford, Ill.
ynchronized Trampoline—Chris Eilertsen & Jim Cartledge, Memphis, Tenn.

**Women**

Trampoline—Leigh Hennessey, Lafayette, La.
Tumbling—Nancy Quattrocki, Chicago, Ill.
Double Mini-tramp—Leigh Hennessey.
Synchronized Trampoline—Shelly Grant, Springfield, Oh. & Leigh Hennessey.

# World Record Fish Caught by Rod and Reel

**Source:** International Game Fish Association.
Records confirmed to June, 1978

## Saltwater Fish

The International Game Fish Assn. revised its standards for world records, effective July 1, 1970. Line samples and lir tests are now required in order for a world record application to be recognized. Records listed below are based on the ne standards.

| Species | Weight | Where Caught | Date | Angler |
|---|---|---|---|---|
| Albacore | 88 lbs. 2 oz. | Pt. Mogan, Canary Islands | Nov. 11, 1977 | Siegried Dickemann |
| Amberjack | 149 lbs. | Bermuda | June 21, 1964 | Peter Simons |
| Barracuda, great | 83 lbs. | Lagos, Nigeria | Jan. 13, 1952 | K.J.W. Hackett |
| Bass, black sea | 8 lbs. | Nantucket Sound, Mass. | May 13, 1951 | H.R. Rider |
| Bass, giant sea | 563 lbs. 8 oz. | Anacaba Island, Cal. | Aug. 20, 1968 | James D. McAdam Jr. |
| Bass, Striped | 72 lbs. | Cuttyhunk, Mass. | Oct. 10, 1969 | Edward J. Kirker |
| Bluefish | 31 lbs. 12 oz. | Hatteras Inlet, N.C. | Jan. 30, 1972 | James M. Hussey |
| Bonefish | 19 lbs. | Zululand, S. Africa | May 26, 1962 | Brian W. Batchelor |
| Bonito, Atlantic | 8 lbs. 8 oz. | Woods Hole, Mass. | Sept. 7, 1976 | Dennis Kowal |
| Bonito, Pacific | 23 lbs. 8 oz. | Victoria, Mahe Seychelles | Feb. 2, 1975 | Anne Cochain |
| Cobia | 110 lbs. 5 oz. | Mombasa, Kenya | Sept. 8, 1964 | Eric Tinworth |
| Cod | 98 lbs. 12 oz. | Isle of Shoals, N.H. | June 8, 1969 | Alphonse Bielevich |
| Dolphin | 87 lbs. | Papagallo Gulf, Costa Rica | Sept. 5, 1976 | Manual Salazar |
| Drum, black | 113 lbs. 1 oz. | Lewes, Del. | Sept. 15, 1975 | Gerald Townsend |
| Drum, red | 90 lbs. | Rodanthe, N.C. | Nov. 7, 1973 | Elvin Hooper |
| Flounder, summer | 22 lb. 7 oz. | Montauk, N.Y. | Sept. 15, 1975 | Charles Nappi |
| Jewfish | 680 lbs. | Fernandina Beach, Fla. | May 20, 1961 | Lynn Joyner |
| Kawakawa | 21 lbs. | Kauai, Ha. | Aug. 21, 1975 | E. John O'Dell |
| Mackerel, king | 90 lbs. | Key West, Fla. | Feb. 16, 1976 | Norton Thomton |
| Marlin, Atlantic blue | 1,282 lbs. | St. Thomas, Virgin Islands | Aug. 6, 1977 | Larry Martin |
| Marlin, black | 1,560 lbs. | Cabo Blanco, Peru | Aug. 4, 1953 | A. C. Glassell Jr. |
| Marlin, Pacific blue | 1,153 lbs. | Guam | Aug. 21, 1969 | Greg Perez |
| Marlin, striped | 417 lb. 8 oz. | Cavalli Islands, N.Z. | Jan. 14, 1977 | Phillip Bryers |
| Marlin, white | 174 lbs. 3 oz. | Vitoria, Brazil | Nov. 1, 1975 | Otavio Cunha Reboucas |
| Permit | 50 lbs. 8 oz. | Key West, Fla. | Mar. 15, 1971 | Marshall Earnest |
| Pollock | 46 lbs. 7 oz. | Brielle, N.J. | May 26, 1975 | John Tomes Holton |
| Roosterfish | 114 lbs. | La Paz, Mex. | June 1, 1960 | Abe Sackheim |
| Runner, rainbow | 33 lbs. 10 oz. | Clarion Is., Mexico | Mar. 14, 1976 | Ralph A. Mikkelsen |
| Sailfish, Atlantic | 128 lbs. 1 oz. | Luanda, Angola | Mar. 27, 1974 | Harm Steyn |
| Sailfish, Pacific | 221 lbs. | Santa Cruz Is., Ecuador | Feb. 12, 1947 | C. W. Stewart |
| Seabass, white | 83 lbs. 12 oz. | San Felipe, Mex. | Mar. 31, 1953 | L.C. Baumgardner |
| Seatrout, spotted | 16 lbs. | Mason's Beach, Va. | May 28, 1977 | William Katko |
| Shark, blue | 437 lbs. | Catherine Bay, N.S.W. Australia | Oct. 2, 1976 | Peter Hyde |
| Shark, hammerhead | 703 lbs. | Jacksonville Beach, Fla. | July 5, 1975 | H.B. Reasor |
| Shark, man-eater or white | 2,664 lbs. | Ceduna, Australia | Apr. 21, 1959 | Alfred Dean |
| Shark, porbeagle | 465 lbs. | Cornwall, Eng. | July 23, 1976 | Jorge Potier |
| Shark, shortfin mako | 1,061 lbs. | Mayor Island, N.Z. | Feb. 17, 1970 | James Penwarden |
| Shark, thresher | 739 lbs. | Tutukaka, N.Z. | Feb. 17, 1975 | Brian Galvin |
| Shark, tiger | 1,780 lbs. | Cherry Grove, S.C. | June 14, 1964 | Walter Maxwell |
| Snook | 43 lbs. 8 oz. | Parasmina, Costa Rica | Oct. 11, 1976 | James Snyder |
| Swordfish | 1,182 lbs. | Iquique, Chile | May 7, 1953 | L. Marron |
| Tanguigue | 81 lbs. | Karachi, Pakistan | Aug. 27, 1960 | George E. Rusinak |
| Tarpon | 283 lbs. | L. Maracaibo, Venezuela | Mar. 19, 1956 | M. Salazar |
| Tautog | 21 lbs. 6 oz. | Cape May, N.J. | June 12, 1954 | R.N. Sheafer |
| Tuna, Atlantic bigeye | 375 lbs. 8 oz. | Ocean City Md. | Aug. 26, 1977 | Cecil Browne |
| Tuna, blackfin | 39 lbs. 8 oz. | Commissioner's Pt., Bermuda | Nov. 18, 1977 | Carlston H. Spencer |
| Tuna, bluefin | 1,200 lbs. | Chaleur Bay, N.B., Can. | Sept. 22, 1976 | Leslie Vibert |
| Tuna, dog-tooth | 153 lbs. 8 oz. | Cooktown, Aust. | Sept. 25, 1975 | William Chapman |
| Tuna, longtail | 60 lbs. | Bermagui, Australia | Mar. 17, 1975 | N. Noel Webster |
| Tuna, Pacific bigeye | 435 lbs. | Cabo Blanco, Peru | Apr. 17, 1957 | Dr. Russel Lee |
| Tuna, skipjack | 39 lbs. 15 oz. | Walker Cay, Bahamas | Jan. 21, 1952 | F. Dowley |
| | 40 lbs. | Mauritius | Apr. 19, 1971 | Joseph Caboche Jr. |
| Tuna, South bluefin | 213 lb. 3 oz. | Tasmania, Australia | May 31, 1977 | Gerald Harvey |
| Tuna, Yellowfin | 388 lbs. 12 oz. | San Benedicto Island, Mexico | Apr. 1, 1977 | Curt Wiesenhutter |
| Tunny, little | 27 lbs. | Key Largo, Fla. | Apr. 20, 1976 | William E. Allison |
| Wahoo | 149 lbs. | Cat Cay, Bahamas | June 15, 1962 | John Pirovano |
| Weakfish | 19 lbs. 8 oz. | Trinidad, W. Indies | Apr. 13, 1962 | Dennis Hall |
| Yellowtail, southern | 111 lbs. | Bay of Islands, N.Z. | June 11, 1961 | A.F. Plim |

## Freshwater Fish

| Species | Weight | Where caught | Date | Angler |
|---|---|---|---|---|
| Bass, largemouth | 22 lbs. 4 oz. | Montgomery Lake, Ga. | June 2, 1932 | George W. Perry |
| Bass, redeye | 8 lbs. 3 oz. | Flint River, Ga. | Oct. 23, 1977 | David A. Hubbard |
| Bass rock | 3 lbs. | York River, Ont. | Aug. 1, 1974 | Peter Gulgin |
| Bass, smallmouth | 11 lbs. 15 oz. | Dale Hollow Lake, Ky. | July 9, 1955 | David L. Hayes |
| Bass, spotted | 8 lbs. 10½ oz. | Smith Lake, Ala. | Feb. 25, 1972 | Billy Henderson |
| Bass, white | 5 lbs. 5 oz. | Ferguson Lake, Cal. | Mar. 8, 1972 | Norman W. Mize |
| Bass, whiterock | 20 lbs. | Savannah River, Ga. | May 5, 1977 | Don Raley |
| Bass, yellow | 2 lbs. 4 oz. | L. Monroe, Ind. | Mar. 27, 1977 | Donald L. Stalker |
| Black bullhead | 8 lbs. | Lake Waccabuc, N.Y. | Aug. 1, 1951 | Kani Evans |
| Bluegill | 4 lbs. 12 oz. | Ketona Lake, Ala. | Apr. 9, 1950 | T.S. Hudson |

| Species | Weight | Where caught | Date | Angler |
|---|---|---|---|---|
| Bowfin | 19 lbs. 12 oz. | Lake Marion, S.C. | Nov. 5, 1972 | M.R. Webster |
| Buffalo, bigmouth | 56 lbs. | Lock Loma L., Mo. | Aug. 19, 1976 | W. J. Long |
| Buffalo, smallmouth | 32 lbs. 8 oz. | Sardis Res., Miss. | Oct. 22, 1977 | Eddie O'Daniel |
| Carp | 55 lbs. 5 oz. | Clearwater Lake, Minn. | July 10, 1952 | Frank J. Ledwein |
| Catfish, blue | 97 lbs. | Missouri River, S.D. | Sept. 16, 1959 | E.B. Elliott |
| Catfish, channel | 58 lbs. | Santee-Cooper Res., S.C. | July 7, 1964 | W.B. Whaley |
| Catfish, flathead | 79 lbs. 8 oz. | White River, Ind. | Aug. 13, 1955 | Glenn T. Simpson |
| Catfish, white | 10 lbs. 5 oz. | Raritan R., N.J. | June 23, 1976 | Lewis W. Lomerson |
| Char, Arctic | 29 lbs. 11 oz. | Arctic River, N.W.T. | Aug. 21, 1968 | Jeanne P. Branson |
| Crappie, black | 5 lbs. | Santee-Cooper Res., S.C. | Mar. 15, 1957 | Paul E. Foust |
| Crappie, white | 5 lbs. 3 oz. | Enid Dam, Miss. | July 31, 1957 | Fred L. Bright |
| Dolly Varden | 32 lbs. | L. Pend Oreille, Ida. | Oct. 27, 1949 | N.L. Higgins |
| Drum, freshwater | 54 lbs. 8 oz. | Nickajack Lake, Tenn. | Apr. 20, 1972 | Benny E. Hull |
| Gar, alligator | 279 lbs. | Rio Grande R., Tex. | Dec. 2, 1951 | Bill Valverde |
| Gar, longnose | 50 lbs. 5 oz. | Trinity River, Tex. | July 30, 1954 | Townsend Miller |
| Grayling, American | 5 lbs. 15 oz. | Katseyedie R., N.W.T. | Aug. 16, 1967 | Jeanne P. Branson |
| Kokanee | 6 lbs. 9¾ oz. | Priest Lake, Ida. | June 9, 1975 | Jerry Verge |
| Muskellunge | 69 lbs. 15 oz. | St. Lawrence R., N.Y. | Sept. 22, 1957 | Arthur Lawton |
| Perch, white | 4 lbs. 12 oz. | Messalonskee Lake, Me. | June 4, 1949 | Mrs. Earl Small |
| Perch, yellow | 4 lbs. 3½ oz. | Bordentown, N.J. | May, 1865 | Dr. C.C. Abbot |
| Pickerel, chain | 9 lbs. 6 oz. | Homerville, Ga. | Feb. 17, 1961 | Baxley McQuaig Jr. |
| Pike, northern | 46 lbs. 2 oz. | Sacandaga Res., N.Y. | Sept. 15, 1940 | Peter Dubuc |
| Redhorse, silver | 4 lbs. 2 oz. | Gasconade River, Mo. | Oct. 5, 1974 | C. Larry McKinney |
| Salmon, Atlantic | 79 lbs. 2 oz. | Tana R., Norway | 1928 | Henrik Henriksen |
| Salmon, chinook | 93 lbs. | Kelp Bay, Alas. | June 24, 1977 | Howard C. Rider |
| Salmon, chum | 27 lbs. 3 oz. | Raymond Cove, Alas. | June 11, 1977 | Robert A. Jahnke |
| Salmon, landlocked | 22 lbs. 8 oz. | Sebago Lake, Me. | Aug. 1, 1907 | Edward Blakely |
| Salmon, silver | 31 lbs. | Cowichan Bay, B.C. | Oct. 11, 1947 | Mrs. Lee Hallberg |
| Sauger | 8 lbs. 12 oz. | Lake Sakakawea, N.D. | Oct. 6, 1971 | Mike Fischer |
| Shad, American | 9 lbs. 2 oz. | Enfield, Conn. | Apr. 28, 1973 | Edward P. Nelson |
| Sturgeon, white | 360 lbs. | Snake River, Ida. | Apr. 24, 1956 | Willard Cravens |
| Sunfish, green | 2 lbs. 2 oz. | Stockton Lake, Mo. | June 18, 1971 | Paul M. Dilley |
| Sunfish, redbreast | 1 lb. 8½ oz. | Suwannee River, Fla. | Apr. 30, 1977 | Tommy D. Cason Jr. |
| Sunfish, redear | 4 lbs. 8 oz. | Chase City, Va. | June 19, 1970 | Maurice E. Ball |
| Trout, brook | 14½ lbs. | Nipigon R., Ont. | July, 1916 | Dr. W.J. Cook |
| Trout, brown (record being reviewed.) | | | | |
| Trout, cutthroat | 41 lbs. | Pyramid Lake, Nev. | Dec., 1925 | J. Skimmerhorn |
| Trout, golden | 11 lbs. | Cook's Lake, Wyo. | Aug. 5, 1948 | Charles S. Reed |
| Trout, lake | 65 lbs. | Great Bear Lake, N.W.T. | Aug. 8, 1970 | Larry Daunis |
| Trout, rainbow Stind. or Kamloopa | 42 lbs. 2 oz. | Bell Island, Alas. | June 22, 1970 | David Robert White |
| Trout sunapee | 11 lbs. 8 oz. | Lake Sunapee, N.H. | Aug. 1, 1954 | Ernest Theoharis |
| Trout, tiger | 17 lbs. | Lake Michigan, Wis. | Aug. 2, 1977 | Edward Rudnicki |
| Walleye | 25 lbs. | Old Hickory Lake, Tenn. | Aug. 1, 1960 | Mabry Harper |
| Warmouth | 2 lbs. | Sylvania, Ga. | May 4, 1974 | Carlton Robbins |
| Whitefish, lake | 13 lbs. | Great Bear Lake, N.W.T. | July 14, 1974 | Robert L. Stintsman |
| Whitefish, mountain | 5 lbs. | Athabasca R., Alta. | June 3, 1963 | Orville Welch |

## The America's Cup

Competition for the America's Cup grew out of the first contest to establish a world yachting championship, one of the carnival features of the London Exposition of 1851. The race, open to all classes of yachts from all over the world, covered a 60-mile course around the Isle of Wight; the prize was a cup worth about $500, donated by the Royal Yacht Squadron of England, known as the "America's Cup" because it was first won by the United States yacht America. Successive efforts of British and Australian yachtsmen have failed to win the famous trophy, which remains in the United States.

On Sept. 18, 1977, the 66-foot 12-meter yacht Courageous won a fourth straight victory over the Australian challenger, Australia, to keep the symbol of world sailing supremacy in the United States. In four races, Australia lost to Courageous by a total of 7 minutes, 48 seconds. The U.S. yacht was designed by Olin Stephens and skippered by Ted Turner.

### Winners of the America's Cup

| | | | |
|---|---|---|---|
| 1851 | America | 1903 | Reliance defeated Shamrock III, England, (3-0) |
| 1870 | Magic defeated Cambria, England, (1-0) | 1920 | Resolute defeated Shamrock IV, England, (3-2) |
| 1871 | Columbia (first three races) and Sappho (last two races) defeated Livonia, England, (4-1) | 1930 | Enterprise defeated Shamrock V, England, (4-0) |
| 1876 | Madeline defeated Countess of Dufferin, Canada, (2-0) | 1934 | Rainbow defeated Endeavour, England, (4-2) |
| 1881 | Mischief defeated Atalanta, Canada, (2-0) | 1937 | Ranger defeated Endeavour II, England, (4-0) |
| 1885 | Puritan defeated Genesta, England, (2-0) | 1958 | Columbia defeated Sceptre, England, (4-0) |
| 1886 | Mayflower defeated Galatea, England, (2-0) | 1962 | Weatherly defeated Gretel, Australia, (4-1) |
| 1887 | Volunteer defeated Thistle, Scotland, (2-0) | 1964 | Constellation defeated Sovereign, England, (4-0) |
| 1893 | Vigilant defeated Valkyrie II, England, (3-0) | 1967 | Intrepid defeated Dame Pattie, Australia, (4-0) |
| 1895 | Defender defeated Valkyrie III, England, (3-0) | 1970 | Intrepid defeated Gretel II, Australia, (4-1) |
| 1899 | Columbia defeated Shamrock, England, (3-0) | 1974 | Courageous defeated Southern Cross, Australia, (4-0) |
| 1901 | Columbia defeated Shamrock II, England, (3-0) | 1977 | Courageous defeated Australia, Australia, (4-0) |

## National AAU Weightlifting Championships in 1978

Erie, Pa., June 10-11, 1978
(Note: weights are in kilograms; one kilogram = 2.2 lbs.)

52 kg.—Ronald Crawley, Crushers Unlimited. **175 kg.**
56 kg.—Stewart Thornburg, Charleston-Oakland WLC. **220 kg.**
60 kg.—Don Warner, York BBC. **247.5 kg.**
67.5 kg.—Don Abrahamson, Catharsis WLC. **260 kg.**
75 kg.—David Jones, Eastman, Ga. **295 kg.**
82.5 kg.—Michael Karchut, Sayre Park WLC. **337.5 kg.**

90 kg.—Lee James, York BBC. **355 kg.**
100 kg.—Kurt Setterberg, F.O.P. 34. **345 kg.**
110 kg.—Mark Cameron, York BBC. **370 kg.**
Over 110 kg.—Tom Stock, Belleville WLC. **377.5 kg.**
Best lifter—Lee James.
Team champion—York (Pa.) Barbell Club.

## Kentucky Derby

### Churchill Downs, Louisville, Ky.

Inaugurated 1875, Distance 1-1/4 miles; 1-1/2 miles until 1896. 3-yr. olds. Times—seconds in fifths.

| Year | Winner | Jockey | Trainer | Wt. | Second | Winner's share | Time |
|---|---|---|---|---|---|---|---|
| 1905 | Agile | J. Martin | R. Tucker | 122 | Ram's Horn | $4,850 | 2:10.3 |
| 1906 | Sir Huon | R. Troxer | P. Coyle | 117 | Lady Navarre | 4,850 | 2:08.4 |
| 1907 | Pink Star | A. Minder | W. H. Fizer | 117 | Zal | 4,850 | 2:12.3 |
| 1908 | Stone Street | A. Pickens | J. W. Hall | 117 | Sir Cleges | 4,850 | 2:15.1 |
| 1909 | Wintergreen | V. Powers | C. Mack | 117 | Miami | 4,850 | 2:08.1 |
| 1910 | Donau | F. Herbert | G. Ham | 117 | Joe Morris | 4,850 | 2:06.2 |
| 1911 | Meridian | G. Archibald | A. Ewing | 117 | Governor Gray | 4,850 | 2:05. |
| 1912 | Worth | C. H. Shilling | F. M. Taylor | 117 | Duval | 4,850 | 2:09.2 |
| 1913 | Donerail | R. Goose | T. P. Hayes | 117 | Ten Point | 5,475 | 2:04.4 |
| 1914 | Old Rosebud | J. McCabe | F. D. Weir | 117 | Hodge | 9,125 | 2:03.2 |
| 1915 | Regret* | J. Notter | J. Rowe Sr. | 112 | Pebbles | 11,450 | 2:05.2 |
| 1916 | George Smith | J. Loftus | H. Hughes | 117 | Star Hawk | 16,600 | 2:04.3 |
| 1917 | Omar Khayyam | C. Borel | C. T. Patterson | 117 | Ticket | 9,750 | 2:04. |
| 1918 | Exterminator | W. Knapp | H. McDaniel | 114 | Escoba | 14,700 | 2:10.4 |
| 1919 | Sir Barton | J. Loftus | H. G. Bedwell | 112 | Billy Kelly | 20,825 | 2:09.4 |
| 1920 | Paul Jones | T. Rice | W. Garth | 126 | Upset | 30,375 | 2:09. |
| 1921 | Behave Yourself | C. Thompson | H. J. Thompson | 126 | Black Servant | 38,450 | 2:04.1 |
| 1922 | Morvich | A. Johnson | F. Burlew | 126 | Bet Mosie | 46,775 | 2:04.3 |
| 1923 | Zev | E. Sande | D. J. Leary | 126 | Martingale | 53,600 | 2:05.2 |
| 1924 | Black Gold | J. D. Mooney | H. Webb | 126 | Chilhowee | 52,775 | 2:05.1 |
| 1925 | Flying Ebony | E. Sande | W. B. Duke | 126 | Captain Hal | 52,950 | 2:07.3 |
| 1926 | Bubbling Over | A. Johnson | H. J. Thompson | 126 | Bagenbagggage | 50,075 | 2:03.4 |
| 1927 | Whiskery | L. McAtee | F. Hopkins | 126 | Osmand | 51,000 | 2:06. |
| 1928 | Reigh Count | C. Lang | B. S. Michell | 126 | Misstep | 55,375 | 2:10.2 |
| 1929 | Clyde Van Dusen | L. McAtee | C. Van Dusen | 126 | Naishapur | 53,950 | 2:10.4 |
| 1930 | Gallant Fox | E. Sande | J. Fitzsimmons | 126 | Gallant Knight | 50,725 | 2:07.3 |
| 1931 | Twenty Grand | C. Kurtsinger | J. Rowe Jr. | 126 | Sweep All | 48,725 | 2:01.4 |
| 1932 | Burgoo King | E. James | H. J. Thompson | 126 | Economic | 52,350 | 2:05.1 |
| 1933 | Brokers Tip | D. Meade | H. J. Thompson | 126 | Head Play | 48,925 | 2:06.4 |
| 1934 | Cavalcade | M. Garner | R. A. Smith | 126 | Discovery | 28,175 | 2:04. |
| 1935 | Omaha | W. Saunders | J. Fitzsimmons | 126 | Roman Soldier | 39,525 | 2:05. |
| 1936 | Bold Venture | I. Hanford | M. Hirsch | 126 | Brevity | 37,725 | 2:03.3 |
| 1937 | War Admiral | C. Kurtsinger | G. Conway | 126 | Pompoon | 52,050 | 2:03.1 |
| 1938 | Lawrin | E. Arcaro | B. A. Jones | 126 | Dauber | 47,050 | 2:04.4 |
| 1939 | Johnstown | J. Stout | J. Fitzsimmons | 126 | Challedon | 46,350 | 2:03.2 |
| 1940 | Gallahadion | C. Bierman | R. Waldron | 126 | Bimelech | 60,150 | 2:05. |
| 1941 | Whirlaway | E. Arcaro | B. A. Jones | 126 | Staretor | 61,275 | 2:01.2 |
| 1942 | Shut Out | W. D. Wright | J. M. Gaver | 126 | Alsab | 64,225 | 2:04.2 |
| 1943 | Count Fleet | J. Longden | G. D. Cameron | 126 | Blue Swords | 60,275 | 2:04. |
| 1944 | Pensive | C. McCreary | B. A. Jones | 126 | Broadcloth | 64,675 | 2:04.1 |
| 1945 | Hoop, Jr. | E. Arcaro | I. H. Parke | 126 | Pot o'Luck | 64,850 | 2:07. |
| 1946 | Assault | W. Mehrtens | M. Hirsch | 126 | Spy Song | 96,400 | 2:06.3 |
| 1947 | Jet Pilot | E. Guerin | T. Smith | 126 | Phalanx | 92,160 | 2:06.3 |
| 1948 | Citation | E. Arcaro | B. A. Jones | 126 | Coaltown | 83,400 | 2:05.2 |
| 1949 | Ponder | S. Brooks | B. A. Jones | 126 | Capot | 91,600 | 2:04.1 |
| 1950 | Middleground | W. Boland | M. Hirsch | 126 | Hill Prince | 92,650 | 2:01.3 |
| 1951 | Count Turf | C. McCreary | S. Rutchick | 126 | Royal Mustang | 98,050 | 2:02.3 |
| 1952 | Hill Gail | E. Arcaro | B. A. Jones | 126 | Sub Fleet | 96,300 | 2:01.3 |
| 1953 | Dark Star | H. Moreno | E. Hayward | 126 | Native Dancer | 90,050 | 2:02. |
| 1954 | Determine | R. York | W. Molter | 126 | Hasty Road | 102,050 | 2:03. |
| 1955 | Swaps | W. Shoemaker | M. A. Tenney | 126 | Nashua | 108,400 | 2:01.4 |
| 1956 | Needles | D. Erb | H. L. Fontaine | 126 | Fabius | 123,450 | 2:03.2 |
| 1957 | Iron Liege | W. Hartack | H. A. Jones | 126 | Gallant Man | 107,950 | 2:02.1 |
| 1958 | Tim Tam | I. Valenzuela | H. A. Jones | 126 | Lincoln Road | 116,400 | 2:05. |
| 1959 | Tomy Lee | W. Shoemaker | F. Childs | 126 | Sword Dancer | 119,650 | 2:02.1 |
| 1960 | Venetian Way | W. Hartack | V. Sovinski | 126 | Bally Ache | 114,850 | 2:02.2 |
| 1961 | Carry Back | J. Sellers | J. A. Price | 126 | Crozier | 120,500 | 2:04. |
| 1962 | Decidedly | W. Hartack | H. Luro | 126 | Roman Line | 119,650 | 2:00.2 |
| 1963 | Chateaugay | B. Baeza | J. Conway | 126 | Never Bend | 108,900 | 2:01.4 |
| 1964 | Northern Dancer | W. Hartack | H. Luro | 126 | Hill Rise | 114,300 | 2:00. |
| 1965 | Lucky Debonair | W. Shoemaker | F. Catrone | 126 | Dapper Dan | 112,000 | 2:01.1 |
| 1966 | Kauai King | D. Brumfield | H. Forrest | 126 | Advocator | 120,500 | 2:02. |
| 1967 | Proud Clarion | R. Ussery | L. Gentry | 126 | Barbs Delight | 119,700 | 2:00.3 |
| 1968 | Dancer's Image (a) | R. Ussery | H. Forrest | 126 | Forward Pass | 122,600 | 2:02.1 |
| 1969 | Majestic Prince | W. Hartack | J. Longden | 126 | Arts and Letters | 113,200 | 2:01.4 |
| 1970 | Dust Commander | M. Manganello | D. Combs | 126 | My Dad George | 127,800 | 2:03.2 |
| 1971 | Canonero II | G. Avila | J. Arias | 126 | Jim French | 145,500 | 2:03.1 |
| 1972 | Riva Ridge | R. Turcotte | L. Laurin | 126 | No Le Hace | 140,300 | 2:01.4 |
| 1973 | Secretariat | R. Turcotte | L. Laurin | 126 | Sham | 155,050 | 1:59.2 |
| 1974 | Cannonade | A. Cordero | W. C. Stephens | 126 | Hudson County | 274,000 | 2:04. |
| 1975 | Foolish Pleasure | J. Vasquez | L. Jolley | 126 | Avatar | 209,611 | 2:02. |
| 1976 | Bold Forbes | A. Cordero | L. Barrea | 126 | Honest Pleasure | 165,200 | 2:01.3 |
| 1977 | Seattle Slew | J. Cruquet | W. H. Turner Jr. | 126 | Run Dusty Run | 214,700 | 2:02.1 |
| 1978 | Affirmed | S. Cauthen | L. Barrera | 126 | Alydar | 186,900 | 2:01.1 |

(a) Dancer's Image was disqualified from purse money by order of the Churchill Downs stewards after tests disclosed that he had run with a pain-killing drug, phenylbutazone, in his system. All wagers were paid on Dancer's Image. Forward Pass was awarded first place money.

The Kentucky Derby has been won five times by two jockeys, Eddie Arcaro, 1938, 1941, 1945, 1948 and 1952; and Bill Hartack, 1957, 1960, 1962, 1964 and 1969; and three times by each of three jockeys, Isaac Murphy, 1884, 1890, and 1891; Earle Sande, 1923, 1925 and 1930, and Willie Shoemaker, 1955, 1959, 1965, *Regret was only filly ever to win the Derby.

## Belmont Stakes

Elmont, N.Y.; inaugurated 1867; 1 ½ miles, 3 yr. olds, Time—seconds in fifths.

| Year | Winner | Jockey | Trainer | Wt. | Second | Winner's share | Time |
|------|--------|--------|---------|-----|--------|----------------|------|
| 1939 | Johnstown | J. Stout | J. Fitzsimmons | 126 | Belay | $37,020 | 2:29.3 |
| 1940 | Bimelech | F.A. Smith | W.J. Hurley | 126 | Your Chance | 35,030 | 2:29.3 |
| 1941 | Whirlaway | E. Arcaro | B.A. Jones | 126 | Robert Morris | 39,770 | 2:31 |
| 1942 | Shut Out | J.M. Garver | G.D. Cameron | 126 | Alsab | 44,520 | 2:29.1 |
| 1943 | Count Fleet | J. Longden | G.D. Cameron | 126 | Fairy Manhurst | 35,340 | 2:28.1 |
| 1944 | Bounding Home | G.L. Smith | M. Brady | 126 | Pensive | 55,000 | 2:32.1 |
| 1945 | Pavot | E. Arcaro | O. White | 126 | Wildlife | 52,675 | 2:30.1 |
| 1946 | Assault | W. Mehrtens | M. Hirsch | 126 | Natchez | 75,040 | 2:30.4 |
| 1947 | Phalanx | R. Donoso | S. Veitch | 126 | Tide Rips | 78,900 | 2:29.2 |
| 1948 | Citation | E. Arcaro | H.A. Jones | 126 | Better Self | 77,700 | 2:28.1 |
| 1949 | Capot | T. Atkinson | J.M. Gaver | 126 | Ponder | 60,900 | 2:30.1 |
| 1950 | Middleground | W. Boland | M. Hirsch | 126 | Lights Up | 61,350 | 2:28.3 |
| 1951 | Counterpoint | D. Gorman | S. Veitch | 125 | Battlefield | 82,000 | 2:29 |
| 1952 | One Count | E. Arcaro | O. White | 126 | Blue Man | 82,400 | 2:30.1 |
| 1953 | Native Dancer | E. Guerin | W.C. Winfrey | 126 | Jamie K. | 82,500 | 2:28.3 |
| 1954 | High Gun | E. Guerin | M. Hirsch | 126 | Fisherman | 89,000 | 2:30.4 |
| 1955 | Nashua | E. Arcaro | J. Fitzsimmons | 126 | Blazing Count | 83,700 | 2:29 |
| 1956 | Needles | D. Erb | H. Fontaine | 126 | Career Boy | 83,600 | 2:29.4 |
| 1957 | Gallant Man | W. Shoemaker | J. Nerud | 126 | Inside Tract | 77,300 | 2:26.3 |
| 1958 | Cavan | P. Anderson | T.J. Barry | 126 | Tim Tam | 73,440 | 2:30.1 |
| 1959 | Sword Dancer | W. Shoemaker | J.E. Burch | 126 | Bagdad | 93,525 | 2:28.2 |
| 1960 | Celtic Ash | W. Hartack | T.J. Barry | 126 | Venetian Way | 96,785 | 2:29.3 |
| 1961 | Sherluck | B. Baeza | H. Young | 126 | Globemaster | 104,900 | 2:29.1 |
| 1962 | Jaipur | W. Shoemaker | W.F. Mulholland | 126 | Admiral's Voyage | 109,550 | 2:28.4 |
| 1963 | Chateaugay | B. Baeza | J.P. Conway | 126 | Candy Spots | 101,700 | 2:30.1 |
| 1964 | Quadrangle | M. Ycaza | J.E. Burch | 126 | Roman Brother | 110,850 | 2:28.2 |
| 1965 | Hail to All | J. Sellers | E. Yowell | 126 | Tom Rolfe | 104,150 | 2:28.2 |
| 1966 | Amberoid | W. Boland | L. Laurin | 126 | Buffle | 117,700 | 2:29.3 |
| 1967 | Damascus | W. Shoemaker | F.Y. Whiteley Jr. | 126 | Cool Reception | 104,950 | 2:28.4 |
| 1968 | Stage Door Johnny | H. Gustines | J.M. Gaver | 126 | Forward Pass | 117,700 | 2:27.1 |
| 1969 | Arts and Letters | B. Baeza | J.E. Burch | 126 | Majestic Prince | 104,050 | 2:28.4 |
| 1970 | High Echelon | J.L. Rotz | J.W. Jacobs | 126 | Needles N Pens | 115,000 | 2:34 |
| 1971 | Pass Catcher | W. Blum | E. Yowell | 126 | Jim French | 97,710 | 2:30.2 |
| 1972 | Riva Ridge | R. Turcotte | L. Laurin | 126 | Ruritania | 93,950 | 2:28 |
| 1973 | Secretariat | R. Turcotte | L. Laurin | 126 | Twice A Prince | 90,120 | 2:24 |
| 1974 | Little Current | M. Rivera | L. Rondinello | 126 | Jolly Johu | 101,970 | 2:29.1 |
| 1975 | Avatar | W. Shoemaker | A.T. Doyle | 126 | Foolish Pleasure | 116,160 | 2:28.1 |
| 1976 | Bold Forbes | A. Cordero | L.S. Barrera | 126 | McKenzie Bridge | 116,850 | 2:29 |
| 1977 | Seattle Slew | J. Cruquet | W.H. Turner Jr. | 126 | Run Dusty Run | 109,080 | 2:29.3 |
| 1978 | Affirmed | S. Cauthen | L.S. Barrera | 126 | Alydar | 110,580 | 2:26.4 |

## Preakness

Pimlico, Baltimore, Md.; inaugurated 1873; 1 3-16 miles, 3 yr. olds. Time—seconds in fifths.

| Year | Winner | Jockey | Trainer | Wt. | Second | Winner's share | Time |
|------|--------|--------|---------|-----|--------|----------------|------|
| 1939 | Challedon | G. Seabo | L.J. Schaefer | 126 | Gilded Knight | $53,710 | 1:59.4 |
| 1940 | Bimelech | F.A. Smith | W.J. Hurley | 126 | Mioland | 53,230 | 1:58.3 |
| 1941 | Whirlaway | E. Arcaro | B.A. Jones | 126 | King Cole | 49,365 | 1:58.4 |
| 1942 | Alsab | B. James | A. Swenke | 126 | Requested, Sun Again (tie). | 58,175 | 1:57 |
| 1943 | Count Fleet | J. Longden | G.D. Cameron | 126 | Blue Swords | 43,190 | 1:57.2 |
| 1944 | Pensive | C. McCreary | B.A. Jones | 126 | Platter | 60,075 | 1:59.1 |
| 1945 | Polynesian | W.D. Wright | M. Dixon | 126 | Hoop Jr. | 66,170 | 1:58.4 |
| 1946 | Assault | W. Mehrtens | M. Hirsch | 126 | Lord Boswell | 96,620 | 2:01.2 |
| 1947 | Faultless | D. Dodson | H.A. Jones | 126 | On Trust | 98,005 | 1:59 |
| 1948 | Citation | E. Arcaro | H.A. Jones | 126 | Vulcan's Forge | 91,870 | 2:02.2 |
| 1949 | Capot | T. Atkinson | J.M. Gaver | 126 | Palestinian | 79,985 | 1:56 |
| 1950 | Hill Prince | E. Arcaro | J.H. Hayes | 126 | Middleground | 56,115 | 1:59.1 |
| 1951 | Bold | E. Arcaro | P.M. Burch | 126 | Counterpoint | 83,110 | 1:56.2 |
| 1952 | Blue Man | C. McCreary | W.C. Stephens | 126 | Jampol | 86,135 | 1:57.2 |
| 1953 | Native Dancer | E. Guerin | W.C. Winfrey | 126 | Jamie K | 65,200 | 1:57.4 |
| 1954 | Hasty Road | J. Adams | H. Trotsek | 126 | Correlation | 91,600 | 1:57.2 |
| 1955 | Nashua | E. Arcaro | J. Fitzsimmons | 126 | Saratoga | 67,550 | 1:54.3 |
| 1956 | Fabius | W. Hartack | H.A. Jones | 126 | Needles | 84,250 | 1:58.2 |
| 1957 | Bold Ruler | E. Arcaro | J. Fitzsimmons | 126 | Iron Liege | 65,250 | 1:56.1 |
| 1958 | Tim Tam | I. Valenzuela | H.A. Jones | 126 | Lincoln Road | 97,900 | 1:57.1 |
| 1959 | Royal Orbit | W. Harmatz | R. Cornell | 126 | Sword Dancer | 136,200 | 1:57 |
| 1960 | Bally Ache | R. Ussery | H.J. Pitt | 126 | Victoria Park | 121,000 | 1:57.3 |
| 1961 | Carry Back | J. Sellers | J.A. Price | 126 | Globemaster | 126,200 | 1:57.3 |
| 1962 | Greek Money | J.L. Rotz | V.W. Raines | 126 | Ridan | 135,800 | 1:56.1 |
| 1963 | Candy Spots | W. Shoemaker | M.A. Tenney | 126 | Chateaugay | 127,500 | 1:56.1 |
| 1964 | Northern Dancer | W. Hartack | H. Luro | 126 | The Scoundrel | 124,200 | 1:56.4 |
| 1965 | Tom Rolfe | R. Turcotte | F.Y. Whiteley Jr. | 126 | Dapper Dan | 128,100 | 1:56.1 |
| 1966 | Kauai King | D. Brumfield | H. Forrest | 126 | Stupendous | 129,000 | 1:55.2 |
| 1967 | Damascus | W. Shoemaker | F.Y. Whiteley Jr. | 126 | In Reality | 141,500 | 1:55.1 |
| 1968 | Forward Pass | I. Valenzuela | H. Forrest | 126 | Out of the Way | 142,700 | 1:56.4 |
| 1969 | Majestic Prince | W. Hartack | J. Longden | 126 | Arts and Letters | 129,500 | 1:55.3 |
| 1970 | Personality | E. Belmonte | J.W. Jacobs | 126 | My Dad George | 151,300 | 1:56.1 |
| 1971 | Canonero II | G. Avila | J. Arias | 126 | Eastern Fleet | 137,400 | 1:54 |
| 1972 | Bee Bee Bee | E. Nelson | D.W. Carroll | 126 | No Le Hace | 135,300 | 1:55.3 |
| 1973 | Secretariat | R. Turcotte | L. Laurin | 126 | Sham | 129,900 | 1:54.2 |
| 1974 | Little Current | M. Rivera | L. Rondinello | 126 | Neopolitan Way | 156,000 | 1:56.3 |
| 1975 | Master Derby | D. McHargue | W.E. Adams | 126 | Foolish Pleasure | 158,100 | 1:56.2 |
| 1976 | Elocutionist | J. Lively | P.T. Adwell | 126 | Play The Red | 129,700 | 1:55 |
| 1977 | Seattle Slew | J. Cruquet | W.H. Turner Jr. | 126 | Iron Constitution | 138,600 | 1:54.2 |
| 1978 | Affirmed | S. Cauthen | L. Barrera | 126 | Alydar | 136,200 | 1:54.2 |

## Triple Crown Turf Winners, Jockeys, and Trainers

### (Kentucky Derby, Preakness, and Belmont Stakes)

| Year | Horse | Jockey | Trainer | Year | Horse | Jockey | Trainer |
|------|-------|--------|---------|------|-------|--------|---------|
| 1919 | Sir Barton | J. Loftus | H. G. Bedwell | 1946 | Assault | Mehrtens | M. Hirsch |
| 1930 | Gallant Fox | E. Sande | J. Fitzsimmons | 1948 | Citation | E. Arcaro | H.A. Jones |
| 1935 | Omaha | W. Sanders | J. Fitzsimmons | 1973 | Secretariat | R. Turcotte | L. Laurin |
| 1937 | War Admiral | C. Kurtsinger | G. Conway | 1977 | Seattle Slew | J. Cruguet | W.H. Turner J |
| 1941 | Whirlaway | E. Arcaro | B.A. Jones | 1978 | Affirmed | S. Cauthen | L.S. Barrera |
| 1943 | Count Fleet | J. Longden | G.D. Cameron | | | | |

## American Thoroughbred Records

### Dirt Course. Time—seconds in fifths.

| Furlongs | Horse, age, weight | Track, state | Date | Time |
|----------|--------------------|--------------|------|------|
| 3 | El Macho | Gulfstream, Fla. | Feb. 26, 1974 | 0:32.1 |
| 3½ | Deep Sun, 7, 120 | Shenandoah Downs, W. Va. | July 11, 1959 | 0:39 |
| | Crying For More, 7, 128 | Shenandoah Downs, W. Va. | Mar. 18, 1972 | 0:39 |
| 4 (½ mile) | Norgor, 9, 118 | Ruidoso Downs, N.M. | Aug. 14, 1976 | 0:44.3 |
| 4½ | Kathryn's Doll, 2, 111 | Turf Paradise, Ariz. | Apr. 9, 1967 | 0:50.2 |
| | Dear Ethel, 2, 114 | Miles Park, Ky. | July 4, 1967 | 0:50.2 |
| | Bold Liz, 2, 118 | Sunland Park, N.M. | Mar. 19, 1972 | 0:50.2 |
| | Scott's Poppy, 2, 118 | Turf Paradise, Ariz. | Feb. 22, 1975 | 0:50.2 |
| 5 | Zip Pocket, 3, 122 | Turf Paradise, Ariz. | Apr. 22, 1967 | 0:55.2 |
| 5½ | Zip Pocket, 3, 129 | Turf Paradise, Ariz. | Nov. 19, 1967 | 1:01.2 |
| 6 (¾ mile) | Grey Papa, 6, 116 | Longacres, Wash. | Sept. 4, 1972 | 1:07.1 |
| 6½ | Best Hitter, 4, 114 | Longacres, Wash. | Aug. 24, 1973 | 1:13.4 |
| 7 | Triple Bend, 4, 123 | Hollywood, Cal. | May 6, 1972 | 1:19.4 |
| 7½ | Aurecolt, 3, 122 | Churchill Downs, Ky. | Nov. 12, 1957 | 1:29 |
| 8 (1 mile) | Dr. Fager, 4, 134 | Arlington, Ill. | Aug. 24, 1968 | 1:32.1 |
| 8½ | Swaps, 4, 130 | Hollywood, Cal. | June 23, 1956 | 1:39 |
| 9 | Secretariat, 3, 124 | Belmont, N.Y. | Sept. 15, 1973 | 1:45.2 |
| 9½ | Riva Ridge, 4, 127 | Aqueduct, N.Y. | July 4, 1973 | 1:52.2 |
| 10 | Noor, 5, 127 | Golden Gate, Cal. | June 24, 1950 | 1:58.1 |
| | Quack, 3, 115 | Hollywood, Cal. | July 15, 1972 | 1:58.1 |
| 10½ | Tempted, 4, 128 | Aqueduct, N.Y. | Oct. 12, 1959 | 2:09 |
| 11 | Man o' War, 3, 126 | Belmont, N.Y. | June 12, 1920 | 2:14.1 |
| 11½ | Theoretic, 6, 111 | Sportsman Park, Ill. | Oct. 15, 1973 | 2:24.1 |
| 12 (1½ miles) | Secretariat, 3, 126 | Belmont, N.Y. | June 9, 1973 | 2:24 |
| 13 | Swaps, 4, 130 | Hollywood, Cal. | July 25, 1956 | 2:38.1 |
| 14 | Noor, 5, 117 | Santa Anita, Cal. | Mar. 4, 1950 | 2:52.4 |
| 15 | Pharawell, 5, 119 | Gulfstream, Fla. | Apr. 8, 1947 | 3:13.4 |
| 16 (2 miles) | Kelso, 7, 124 | Aqueduct, N.Y. | Oct. 31, 1964 | 3:19.1 |
| 18 | Fenelon, 4, 119 | Belmont, N.Y. | Oct. 4, 1941 | 3:47 |
| 20 | Miss Grillo, 6, 118 | Pimlico, Md. | Nov. 12, 1948 | 4:14.3 |

## Annual Leading Money-Winning Horses

| Year | Horse | Dollars | Year | Horse | Dollars | Year | Horse | Dollars |
|------|-------|---------|------|-------|---------|------|-------|---------|
| 1942 | Shut Out | 238,872 | 1954 | Determine | 328,700 | 1966 | Buckpasser | 669,0 |
| 1943 | Count Fleet | 174,055 | 1955 | Nashua | 752,550 | 1967 | Damascus | 817,9 |
| 1944 | Pavot | 179,040 | 1956 | Needles | 440,850 | 1968 | Forward Pass | 546,6 |
| 1945 | Busher | 273,735 | 1957 | Round Table | 600,383 | 1969 | Arts and Letters | 555,6 |
| 1946 | Assault | 424,195 | 1958 | Round Table | 662,780 | 1970 | Personality | 444,0 |
| 1947 | Armed | 376,325 | 1959 | Sword Dancer | 537,004 | 1971 | Riva Ridge | 503,2 |
| 1948 | Citation | 709,470 | 1960 | Bally Ache | 455,045 | 1972 | Droll Roll | 471,6 |
| 1949 | Ponder | 321,825 | 1961 | Carry Back | 565,349 | 1973 | Secretariat | 860,4 |
| 1950 | Noor | 346,940 | 1962 | Never Bend | 402,969 | 1974 | Chris Evert | 551,0 |
| 1951 | Counterpoint | 250,525 | 1963 | Candy Spots | 604,481 | 1975 | Foolish Pleasure | 716,2 |
| 1952 | Crafty Admiral | 277,255 | 1964 | Gun Bow | 580,100 | 1976 | Forego | 491,7 |
| 1953 | Native Dancer | 513,425 | 1965 | Buckpasser | 568,096 | 1977 | Seattle Slew | 641,3 |

## Annual Leading Jockey—Money Won

| Year | Jockey | Dollars | Year | Jockey | Dollars | Year | Jockey | Dollars |
|------|--------|---------|------|--------|---------|------|--------|---------|
| 1950 | Eddie Arcaro | 1,410,160 | 1960 | Willie Shoemaker | 2,123,961 | 1969 | Jorge Velasquez | 2,542,3 |
| 1951 | Willie Shoemaker | 1,329,890 | 1961 | Willie Shoemaker | 2,690,819 | 1970 | Laffit Pincay Jr. | 2,626,5 |
| 1952 | Eddie Arcaro | 1,859,591 | 1962 | Willie Shoemaker | 2,916,844 | 1971 | Laffit Pincay Jr. | 3,784,3 |
| 1953 | Willie Shoemaker | 1,784,187 | 1963 | Willie Shoemaker | 2,526,925 | 1972 | Laffit Pincay Jr. | 3,225,8 |
| 1954 | Willie Shoemaker | 1,876,760 | 1964 | Willie Shoemaker | 2,649,553 | 1973 | Laffit Pincay Jr. | 4,093,4 |
| 1955 | Eddie Arcaro | 1,864,796 | 1965 | Braulio Baeza | 2,582,702 | 1974 | Laffit Pincay Jr. | 4,251,0 |
| 1956 | Bill Hartack | 2,343,955 | 1966 | Braulio Baeza | 2,951,022 | 1975 | Braulio Baeza | 3,695,1 |
| 1957 | Bill Hartack | 3,060,501 | 1967 | Braulio Baeza | 3,088,888 | 1976 | Angel Cordero Jr. | 4,709,5 |
| 1958 | Willie Shoemaker | 2,961,693 | 1968 | Braulio Baeza | 2,835,108 | 1977 | Steve Cauthen | 6,151,7 |
| 1959 | Willie Shoemaker | 2,843,133 | | | | | | |

## All-time Winning Jockeys

| Jockey | Wins | Jockey | Wins | Jockey | Wins | Jockey | Wins |
|--------|------|--------|------|--------|------|--------|------|
| Willie Shoemaker | 7,331 | Walter Blum | 4,383 | Ralph Neves | 3,771 | Sandy Hawley | 3,2 |
| Johnny Longden | 6,026 | Bill Hartack | 4,272 | Robert Lee Baird | 3,647 | Johnny Adams | 3,2 |
| Eddie Arcaro | 4,779 | Avelino Gomez | 3,896 | Bobby Ussery | 3,611 | Jorge Velasquez | 3,2 |
| Steve Brooks | 4,447 | Ted Atkinson | 3,795 | Angel Cordero Jr. | 3,307 | | |

## Eclipse Awards in 1977

Sponsored by the Thoroughbred Racing Assns., Daily Racing Form, and the National Turf Writers Assn.

orse of the Year—Seattle Slew
est 2-year-old colt—Affirmed
est 2-year-old filly—Lakeville Miss
est 3-year-old colt—Seattle Slew
est 3-year-old filly—Our Mims
est colt, horse, or gelding (4-year-olds & up)—Forego
est filly or mare (4-year-olds & up)—Cascapedia

Best turf horse—Johnny D.
Best sprinter—What a Summer
Best steeplechase horse—Cafe Prince
Outstanding trainer—Laz Barrera
Outstanding jockey—Steve Cauthen
Outstanding apprentice jockey—Steve Cauthen
Leading breeder—E.P. Taylor

## Leading Money-Winning Horses

As of Jan. 1, 1978

| orse, year foaled | Sts. | 1st | 2d | 3d | Dollars | Horse, year foaled | Sts. | 1st | 2d | 3d | Dollars |
|---|---|---|---|---|---|---|---|---|---|---|---|
| elso, 1957 . . . . . . . | 63 | 39 | 12 | 2 | 1,977,896 | Secretariat, 1970 . . . . . | 21 | 16 | 3 | 1 | 1,316,808 |
| orego (A), 1970 . . . . | 57 | 34 | 9 | 7 | 1,938,957 | Nashua, 1952 . . . . . . . | 30 | 22 | 4 | 1 | 1,288,565 |
| ound Table, 1954 . . . | 66 | 43 | 8 | 5 | 1,749,869 | Susan's Girl, 1969 . . . | 63 | 29 | 14 | 11 | 1,251,667 |
| ahlia, 1970. . . . . . . | 48 | 15 | 3 | 7 | 1,543,139 | Carry Back, 1958. . . . . | 62 | 21 | 11 | 11 | 1,241,165 |
| uckpasser, 1963 . . . . | 31 | 25 | 4 | 1 | 1,462,014 | (a) as of July, 1978 when he was retired. | | | | | |
| lez France, 1970 . . . . | 21 | 13 | 3 | 1 | 1,386,146 | | | | | | |

## Lacrosse Champions in 1978

Source: Jack Kelly, U.S. Lacrosse Information

CAA University Champions—Johns Hopkins Univ.
CAA College Champions—Roanoke College.
.S. Club Lacrosse Champions—Long Island LC.
.S. Intercollegiate Lacrosse Association Champions—Johns Hopkins Univ.
tlantic Coast Conference Champions—Univ. of Maryland.
ry League Champion—Cornell Univ.
ndependent College Athletic Conference—Hobart College.
ew England Intercollegiate Champions—Univ. of Massachusetts.
ortheast Division Champions—Univ. of Massachusetts.
liddle Atlantic League Champions—Western Maryland College.
lason-Dixon League Champions—UMBC.
ast Coast League Champions—Bucknell, Delaware, Drexel (3 way tie).
lidwest League Champions—Ohio State.
olonial League (New England) Champions—Boston State.
nickerbocker League Champions—Montclair (N.J.) State College.
pstate New York League Champions—SUNY Cortland.
ri State League Champions—St. Mary's (Md.).
.S. National Jr. College Champions—Nassau (N.Y.).

### NCAA University Championship

At New Brunswick, N.J., May 27—Johns Hopkins 13, Cornell 8.

### Semi-finals

Johns Hopkins 17, Maryland 11; Cornell 13, Navy 7.

### Quarter-finals

Johns Hopkins 20, Hofstra 8; Maryland 15, Virginia 10; Cornell 2, W & L 2; Navy 16, Army 13.

### NCAA College Championship

At Geneva, N.Y., May 21—Roanoke College 14, Hobart 13.
12 college teams were selected to play in the NCAA College Division II tournament—Adelphi (N.Y.), Baltimore, Cortland, Hobart, Ithaca, New Haven, Ohio Wesleyan, Roanoke, Salisbury (Md.), Towson (Md.), UMBC, and Washington (Md.).

### All—Star College Game

At Ithaca, N.Y., June 10—North 19, South 6.

### United States Junior College Championship

At Farmingdale, N.Y., May 14—Nassau CC, N.Y. 14, Farmingdale 6.

### United States Lacrosse Club Championship

At Baltimore, Md., June 17—Long Island LC 16, Maryland LC 12.

### Coach-of-the-Year

University—Dick Edell, U.S. Military Academy.
College—Paul S. Griffin, Roanoke College.

### USILA University All-America Team in 1978

Goalie—Mike Federico, Hopkins.
Defense—Don DelGiorno, Penn; Willie Hazelhurst, Hopkins; Chris Kane, Cornell.
Midfield—Bob DeSimone, Navy; Scott Baugher, Hopkins; Bob Henrickson, Cornell; Craig Jaeger, Cornell.
Attack—Mike O'Neill, Hopkins; Tom Marino, Cornell; Brendan Schneck, Navy.
Note—4 midfield players selected for the 3 midfield positions.

### USILA College All America Team in 1978

Goalie—Rick Blick, Hobart.
Defense—Jim Burke, Cortland; Robert Rotanz, Roanoke; Tom Schardt, Hobart.
Midfield—Rick Wey, UMBC; G.P. Lindsay, Washington; Steve Kopf, Baltimore.
Attack—Mike Hoppey, Cortland; Richard Graham, Roanoke; Terry Corcoran, Hobart.

### International Lacrosse World Championship

Stockport, England—Championship: Canada 17, United States 16 (o.t.). Third place: Australia 19, England 9. First Round: United States 22, Australia 17; Canada 21, England 15.

## National Rowing Championships in 1978

Cooper River, Collingswood, N.J., July 23, 1978

enior Fours with Coxswain—Vesper BC.
enior Pairs without Coxswain—Vesper BC.
enior Singles—Tom Hazeltine, Undine BC.
enior Eights—Vesper BC.
enior Doubles—Detroit BC.
lite Quarter-Mile Singles—Jim Dietz, New York AC.
lite Doubles—Harvard Univ.

Elite Pairs with Coxswain—Pennsylvania.
Elite Lightweight Doubles—New York AC.
Elite Lightweight Fours without Coxswain—New York AC.
Elite Lightweight Pairs—New York AC.
Elite Quads—New York AC.
Team champion—New York AC.

# World Track and Field Records

### As of July 12, 1978

*Indicates pending record; a number of new records await confirmation. The International Amateur Athletic Federation, the world body of track and field, announced July 27, 1976, a plan to overhaul the track and field record book. Eliminated are all records in yards except for the mile. Also eliminated are all hand-timed records for distances up to and including 400 meters. The records below meet the new standards except where noted. Records in yards and miles are included although they are no longer officially considered world records.

## Men's Records

### Running

| Event | Record | Holder | Country | Date | Where made |
|---|---|---|---|---|---|
| 100 yds. | 9.0 s. | Ivory Crockett | U.S. | May 11, 1974 | Knoxville, Tenn. |
|  |  | Houston McTear | U.S. | May 9, 1975 | Winter Park, Fla. |
| 220 yds. | 19.5 s. | Tommie Smith | U.S. | May 7, 1966 | San Jose, Cal. |
| 220 yds. | 19.9 s(turn). | Don Quarrie | Jamaica | June 7, 1975 | Eugene, Ore. |
|  |  | Steve Williams | U.S. | June 7, 1975 | Eugene, Ore. |
| 440 yds. | 44.5 s. | John Smith | U.S. | June 26, 1972 | Eugene, Ore. |
| 880 yds. | 1 m., 44.1 s. | Rick Wohlhuter | U.S. | June 8, 1974 | Eugene, Ore. |
| 1 mile | 3m., 49.4 s. | John Walker | New Zealand. | Aug. 12, 1975 | Goteborg, Sweden |
| 2 miles | 8 m., 13.8 s. | Brendon Foster | Gr. Britain | Aug. 27, 1973 | London |
| 3 miles | 12 m., 47.8 s. | Emiel Puttemans | Belgium | Sept. 20, 1972 | Brussels |
| 6 miles | 26 m., 47.0 s. | Ron Clarke | Australia. | July 14, 1965 | Oslo |
| 10 miles | 45 m., 57.2 s. | Jos Hermens | Netherlands | Sept. 14, 1975 | Netherlands |
| 15 miles | 1 hr., 11 min., 52.6 s. | Pekka Paivarinta. | Finland | May 15, 1975 | Oulu, Finland |

### Running — Metric Distances

| Event | Record | Holder | Country | Date | Where made |
|---|---|---|---|---|---|
| 100 meters | 9.95 s. | Jim Hines | U.S. | Oct. 14, 1968 | Mexico City |
| 200 meters | 19.8 s(turn). | Donald Quarrie | Jamaica | Aug. 3, 1971 | Cali, Colombia |
| 400 meters | 43.89 s. | Lee Evans | U.S. | Oct. 18, 1968 | Mexico City |
| 800 meters | 1 m., 43.43 s. | Alberto Juantorena | Cuba | Aug. 21, 1977 | Bulgaria |
| 1,000 meters | 2 m., 13.9 s. | Rick Wohlhuter | U.S. | July 30, 1974 | Oslo |
| 1,500 meters | 3 m., 32.2 s. | Filbert Bayi | Tanzania | Feb. 2, 1974 | Christchurch, N.Z. |
| 2,000 meters | 4 m., 51.4 s. | John Walker | New Zealand. | June 30, 1976 | Oslo |
| 3,000 meters | *7 m., 32.1 s. | Henry Rono | Kenya | June, 1978 | Oslo |
| 5,000 meters | *13 m., 08.4 s. | Henry Rono | Kenya. | Apr. 8, 1978 | Berkeley, Cal. |
| 10,000 meters | *27 m., 22.47 s. | Henry Rono | Kenya. | June 11, 1978 | Vienna |
| 20,000 meters | 57 m., 24.2 s. | Jos Hermens | Netherlands | May 1, 1976 | Netherlands |
| 25,000 meters | 1 hr., 14 m., 16.8 s. | Pekka Paivarinta. | Finland | May 15, 1975 | Oulu, Finland |
| 30,000 meters | 1 hr., 31 m., 30.4 s. | Jim Adler | Gr. Britain | Sept. 5, 1970 | London |
| 3,000 meter stpl | 8 m., 08 s. | Anders Garderud | Sweden | July 28, 1976 | Montreal |

### Hurdles

| Event | Record | Holder | Country | Date | Where made |
|---|---|---|---|---|---|
| 120 yards | 13.0 s. | Rod Milburn | U.S. | June 25, 1971 | Eugene, Ore. |
|  |  | Rod Milburn | U.S. | June 20, 1973 | Eugene, Ore. |
|  |  | Guy Drut | France | Aug. 22, 1975 | Berlin, W. Ger. |
| 220 yards | 21.9 s. | Don Styron. | U.S. | Apr. 2, 1960 | Baton Rouge |
| 440 yards | 48.7 s. | Jim Bolding | U.S. | July 24, 1974 | Turin, Italy |
| 110 meters | 13.21 s. | Alejandro Casanas | Cuba | Aug. 21, 1977 | Bulgaria |
| 200 meters | 21.9 s. (not ET) | Don Styron | U.S. | Apr. 2, 1960 | Baton Rouge |
| 200 meters | 22.5 s. (not ET) (turn) | Martin Lauer | W. Germany | July 7, 1959 | Zurich |
|  | (not ET) | Glen Davis | U.S. | Aug. 20, 1960 | Bern |
| 400 meters | 47.45 s. | Edwin Moses. | U.S. | June 11, 1977 | Los Angeles |

### Relay Races

| Event | Record | Holder | Country | Date | Where made |
|---|---|---|---|---|---|
| 440 yds. (4×110) (2 turns) | 38.6 s. | USC (McCullough, Kuller, Simpson, Miller) | U.S. | June 17, 1967 | Provo, Utah |
| 830 yds. (4×220) | 1 m., 21.7 s. | Texas A&M (Rogers, Woods, M. Mills, C. Mills) | U.S. | Apr. 24, 1970 | Des Moines |
| 1 mile (4×440) | 3 m., 02.4 s. | National team (Ray, Taylor, Peoples, Vinson) | U.S. | July 18, 1975 | Durham, N.C. |
| 2 miles (4×880) | 7 m., 10.4 s. | Chicago TC (Bach, Sparks, Paul, Wohlhuter) | U.S. | May 12, 1973 | Durham, N.C. |
| 4 miles (4×1) (mile) | 16 m., 02.8 s. | National team (Ross, Polhill, Tayler, Quax) | New Zealand | Feb. 3, 1972 | Auckland, N.Z. |

### Relay Races — Metric Distances

| Event | Record | Holder | Country | Date | Where made |
|---|---|---|---|---|---|
| 400 mtrs. | 38.03 s. | National team (Collins, Riddick, Wiley, Williams) | U.S. | Sept. 3, 1977 | Dusseldorf |
| 800 mtrs. (4×200) | 1 m., 21.4 s. | Arizona State | U.S. | Apr. 30, 1977 | Philadelphia |
| 1,600 mtrs. (4×400) | 2 m., 56.1 s. | National team (Matthews, Freeman, James, Evans) | U.S. | Oct. 20, 1968 | Mexico City |
| 3,200 mtrs. (4×800) | 7 m., 08.6 s. | National team (Kinder, Adams, Bogatzki, Kemper) | W. Germany | Aug. 13, 1966 | Wiesbaden |

### Field Events

| Event | Record | Holder | Country | Date | Where made |
|---|---|---|---|---|---|
| High jump | *7 ft., 8 in. | Vladimir Yashchenko | USSR | June, 1978 | Tbilsi |
| Long jump | 29 ft., 2½ in. | Bob Beamon | U.S. | Oct. 18, 1968 | Mexico City |
| Triple jump | 58 ft., 8¼ in. | Joao de Oliveira | Brazil | Oct. 15, 1975 | Mexico City |
| Pole vault | *18 ft., 8¾ in. | Mike Tully | U.S. | May 19, 1978 | Corvallis, Ore. |
| 16 lb. shot put | *72 ft., 8 in. | Udo Beyer | E. Germany | July 6, 1978 | Sweden |
| Discus throw | 232 ft., 6 in. | Mac Wilkins | U.S. | May 1, 1976 | San Jose, Cal. |
| Javelin throw | 310 ft., 4 in. | Miklos Nemeth | Hungary | July 26, 1976 | Montreal |
| 16 lb. hammer throw | 260 ft., 2 in. | Walter Schmidt | W. Germany | Aug. 14, 1975 | Frankfurt |
| Decathlon | 8,618 pts. | Bruce Jenner | U.S. | July 29-30, 1976 | Montreal |

### Walking

| | | | | | |
|---|---|---|---|---|---|
| 20 miles | 2 h., 27 m., 38.0 s. | Vittorio Visini | Italy | Nov. 1, 1975 | Vicenza, Italy |
| 30 miles | 3 h., 48 m., 23.4 s. | Bernd Kannenberg | W. Germany | Nov. 16, 1975 | Milan |
| 2 hours | 16 mi., 1,270 yds. | Bernd Kannenberg | W. Germany | May 11, 1974 | Kassel, W. Germany |
| 20 km. | 2 h., 12 m., 58.0 s. | Bernd Kannenberg | W. Germany | May 11, 1974 | Kassel, W. Germany |
| 50 km. | 3 hr., 56 m., 39 s. | Enrique Vera | Mexico | May 16, 1977 | Norway |

## Women's Records

### Running

| | | | | | |
|---|---|---|---|---|---|
| 100 yards | 10.0 s. | Chi Cheng | Taiwan | June 13, 1970 | Portland, Ore. |
| 220 yards | 22.6 s. | Chi Cheng | Taiwan | July 3, 1970 | Los Angeles |
| 440 yards | 52.2 s. | Kathy Hammond | U.S. | Aug. 12, 1972 | Urbana, Ill. |
| | | Debra Sapenter | U.S. | June 29, 1974 | Bakersfield, Cal. |
| 880 yards | 2 m., 02.0 s. | Judy Pollock | Australia | July 5, 1967 | Sweden |
| | | Dixie Willis | Australia | Mar. 3, 1962 | Perth, Australia |
| mile | 4 m., 23.8 s. | Natalia Maracescu | Romania | May 21, 1977 | Romania |
| 100 meters | 10.88 s. | Marlies Oelsner | E. Germany | July 1, 1977 | Dresden |
| 200 meters | 22.2 s. | Irena Szewinska | Poland | June 13, 1974 | Potsdam |
| 400 meters | *49.19 s. | Marita Koch | E. Germany | July 3, 1978 | E. Berlin |
| 800 meters | 1 m., 54.9 s. | Tatyana Kazankina | USSR | July 26, 1976 | Montreal |
| 1,500 meters | 3 m., 56 s. | Tatyana Kazankina | USSR | June 28, 1976 | USSR |

### Hurdles

| | | | | | |
|---|---|---|---|---|---|
| 100 meters | *12.48 s. | Grazyna Rabsztyn | Poland | June, 1978 | W. Germany |
| 400 meters | 56.63 s. | Karin Rossley | E. Germany | Aug. 14, 1977 | Helsinki |

### Field Events

| | | | | | |
|---|---|---|---|---|---|
| High jump | 6 ft., 6¾ in. | Rosemarie Ackermann | E. Germany | Aug. 26, 1977 | W. Berlin |
| Shot put | 73 ft., 2¾ in. | Helena Fibigerova | Czech. | Aug. 20, 1977 | Czech. |
| Long jump | 22 ft., 11¼ in. | Sigrun Siegl | E. Germany | May 19, 1976 | Dresden |
| Discus throw | 231 ft., 3 in. | Faina Meinik | USSR | Apr. 24, 1976 | USSR |
| Javelin | 227 ft., 5 in. | Kate Schmidt | U.S. | Sept. 11, 1977 | W. Germany |
| Pentathlon | 4,839 pts. | Nadyezhda Tkachenko | USSR | Sept. 17-18, 1977 | W. Germany |

### Relay Races

| | | | | | |
|---|---|---|---|---|---|
| 400 mtrs. (4×100) | 42.50 s. | National team | E. Germany | May 29, 1976 | E. Germany |
| 800 mtrs. (4×200) | 1 m., 20.3 s. | National team | U.S. | May, 1978 | Tempe, Ariz. |
| 880 yds. (4×220) | 1 m., 35.8 s. | (Hoffman, Boyle, Kilborn, Lamy) | Australia | Nov. 9, 1969 | Brisbane, Australia |
| 1,600 mtrs. (4×400) | 3 m., 19.2 s. | National team | E. Germany | July 31, 1976 | Montreal |
| mile (4×440) | 3 m., 30.3 s. | National team (Krause, Jost, Weinstein, Barth) | W. Germany | July 19, 1975 | Durham, N.C. |

## Evolution of the World Record for the One-Mile Run

The table below shows how the world record for the one-mile has been lowered in the past 114 years.

| Year | Individual, country | Time | Year | Individual, country | Time |
|---|---|---|---|---|---|
| 1864 | Charles Lawes, Britain | 4:56 | 1934 | Glenn Cunningham, U.S. | 4:06.8 |
| 1865 | Richard Webster, Britain | 4:36.5 | 1937 | Sydney Wooderson, Britain | 4:06.4 |
| 1868 | William Chinnery, Britain | 4:29 | 1942 | Gunder Haegg, Sweden | 4:06.2 |
| 1868 | W. C. Gibbs, Britain | 4:28.8 | 1942 | Arne Andersson, Sweden | 4:06.2 |
| 1874 | Walter Slade, Britain | 4:26 | 1942 | Gunder Haegg, Sweden | 4:04.6 |
| 1875 | Walter Slade, Britain | 4:24.5 | 1943 | Arne Andersson, Sweden | 4:02.6 |
| 1880 | Walter George, Britain | 4:23.2 | 1944 | Arne Andersson, Sweden | 4:01.6 |
| 1882 | Walter George, Britain | 4:21.4 | 1945 | Gunder Haegg, Sweden | 4:01.4 |
| 1882 | Walter George, Britain | 4:19.4 | 1954 | Roger Bannister, Britain | 3:59.4 |
| 1884 | Walter George, Britain | 4:18.4 | 1954 | John Landy, Australia | 3:58 |
| 1894 | Fred Bacon, Scotland | 4:18.2 | 1957 | Derek Ibbotson, Britain | 3:57.2 |
| 1895 | Fred Bacon, Scotland | 4:17 | 1958 | Herb Elliott, Australia | 3:54.5 |
| 1895 | Thomas Conneff, U.S. | 4:15.6 | 1962 | Peter Snell, New Zealand | 3:54.4 |
| 1911 | John Paul Jones, U.S. | 4:15.4 | 1964 | Peter Snell, New Zealand | 3:54.1 |
| 1913 | John Paul Jones, U.S. | 4:14.6 | 1965 | Michel Jazy, France | 3:53.6 |
| 1915 | Norman Taber, U.S. | 4:12.6 | 1966 | Jim Ryun, U.S. | 3:51.3 |
| 1923 | Paavo Nurmi, Finland | 4:10.4 | 1967 | Jim Ryun, U.S. | 3:51.1 |
| 1931 | Jules Ladoumegue, France | 4:09.2 | 1975 | Filbert Bayi, Tanzania | 3:51 |
| 1933 | Jack Lovelock, New Zealand | 4:07.6 | 1975 | John Walker, New Zealand | 3:49.4 |

# Track and Field Events in 1978

## 71st Annual Millrose Games

New York, N.Y., Jan. 27, 1978

### Men

**60 Yds.**—Houston McTear, Cerritos College. **Time—0:06.11.**
**60-Yd. High Hurdles**—Renaldo Nehamiah, Maryland. **Time—0:07.07.**
**500 Yds.**—Glenn Bogue, Villanova. **Time—0:56.5.**
**600 Yds.**—Fred Sowerby, D.C. Striders. **Time—1:11.3.**
**880 Yds.**—Tom McLean, Philadelphia Pioneer Club. **Time—1:52.7.**
**1,000 Yds.**—Don Paige, Villanova. **Time—2:09.**
**One Mile**—Dick Buerkle, New York AC. **Time—3:58.4.**
**2 Miles**—Nick Rose, Mason Dixon AC. **Time—8:31.7.**
**One-Mile Walk**—Todd Scully, Shore AC. **Time—6:34.3.**

**Pole Vault**—Mike Tully, UCLA. **18 ft. 1 in.**
**High Jump**—Franklin Jacobs, Fairleigh Dickinson. **7 ft. 7 ¼ in.**

### Women

**60 Yds.**—Andres Lynch, Muhammad Ali TC. **Time—0:06.8.**
**60-Yd. High Hurdles**—Patty Van Wolvelaere, Los Angeles Naturite TC. **Time—0:07.7.**
**440 Yds.**—Lorna Forde, Atoms TC. **Time—0:54.7.**
**880 Yds.**—Jan Merrill, Age Group AA. **Time—2:10.1.**
**1,500 Meters**—Jan Merrill. **Time—4:19.7.**
**High Jump**—Joni Huntley, Pacific Coast TC. **6 ft. 3 in.**

## 10th Annual U.S. Olympic Invitational

New York, N.Y., Feb. 4, 1978

### Men

**55 Meters**—Harvey Glance, Auburn. **Time—0:06.2.**
**55-Meter Hurdles**—Renaldo Nehemiah, Maryland. **Time—0:07.2.**
**400 Meters**—Willie Smith, Auburn. **Time—0:47.6.**
**500 Meters**—Stan Vinson, Chicago TC. **Time—1:02.8.**
**800 Meters**—Mark Belger, Villanova. **Time—1:48.7.**
**1,000 Meters**—Don Paige, Villanova. **Time—2:21.6.**
**1,500 Meters**—Niell O'Shaugnessy, Arkansas. **Time—3:39.8.**
**3,000 Meters**—Marty Liquori, Athletic Attic. **Time—7:52.9.**
**1,500-Meter Walk**—Todd Scully, Shore AA. **Time—5:47.9.**
**Pole Vault**—Mike Tully, UCLA. **17 ft. 8 ½ in.**

**High Jump**—Franklin Jacobs, Fairleigh Dickinson. **7 ft. 4 ½ in.**

### Women

**55 Meters**—Chandra Cheeseborough, Tennessee St. **Time—0:06.8.**
**55-Meter High Hurdles**—Johanna Schaller Klier, E. Germany. **Time—0:07.4.**
**400 Meters**—Lorna Forde, Atoms TC. **Time—0:54.6.**
**800 Meters**—Jan Merrill, Age Group AA. **Time—2:09.7.**
**1,500 Meters**—Francie Larrieu, Pacific Coast Club. **Time—4:14.7.**

## Toronto Star — Maple Leaf Indoor Games

Toronto, Ont., Feb. 10, 1978

### Men

**50 Yds.**—Houston McTear, California. **Time—0:05.25.**
**50-Yd. Hurdles**—James Owen, UCLA. **Time—0:06.07.**
**600 Yds.**—Stan Vinson, Univ. of Chicago TC. **Time—1:11.2.**
**1,000 Yds.**—Mike Boit, Kenya. **Time—2:08.8.**
**One Mile**—Eamonn Coghlan, Ireland. **Time—4:00.4.**
**3 Miles**—Nick Rose, Britain. **Time—13:03.**
**High Jump**—Greg Joy, Vancouver, B.C. **7 ft. 4¼ in.**

**Pole Vault**—Dan Ripley, Pacific Coast Club. **18 ft. ¼ in.**

### Women

**50 Yds.**—Deandre Carney, Los Angeles, Cal. **Time—0:05.86.**
**50-Yd. Hurdles**—Johanna Klier, E. Germany. **Time—0:06.2.**
**600 Meters**—Lorna Forde, New York, N.Y. **Time—1:30.8.**
**1,500 Meters**—Mary Decker, Univ. of Colorado. **Time—4:13.4.**

## National AAU Indoor Track and Field Championships

New York, N.Y., Feb. 24, 1978

### Men

**60 Yds.**—Houston McTear, Muhammad Ali TC. **Time—0:06.04.**
**60-Yd. Hurdles**—Charles Foster, Philadelphia Pioneer Club. **Time—0:07.11.**
**600 Yds.**—Stan Vinson, Chicago TC. **Time—1:10.**
**1,000 Yds.**—Gideon Terer, Fairleigh Dickinson. **Time—2:09.3.**
**One Mile**—Eamonn Coghlan, New York AC. **Time—4:01.6.**
**3 Miles**—Suleiman Nyambui, Tanzania. **Time—13:09.8.**
**2-Mile Walk**—Todd Scully, Shore AC. **Time—13:07.6.**
**One-Mile Relay**—Philadelphia Pioneer Club. **Time—3:14.3.**
**2-Mile Relay**—Adelphi. **Time—7:40.1.**
**High Jump**—Dwight Stones, Desert Oasis TC. **7 ft. 4½ in.**
**Pole Vault**—Larry Jessee, El Paso, Tex. **17 ft. 8½ in.**
**Long Jump**—Charlton Ehizuelen, Maccabi Union TC. **25 ft. 4¾ in.**
**Triple Jump**—Ron Livers, San Jose State. **55 ft. 3½ in.**
**Shot Put**—Al Feuerbach, San Jose, Cal. **67 ft. 9 in.**
**35-Lb. Weight Throw**—Ed Kania, Dartmouth. **64 ft. 9 in.**
**Team champion**—Philadelphia Pioneer Club.

### Women

**60 Yds.**—Brenda Morehead, Tennessee St. **Time—0:06.73.**
**60-Yd. Hurdles**—Deby La Plante, Englewood, N.J. **Time—0:07.53.**
**220 Yds.**—Freida Nichols, D.C. Striders. **Time—0:24.23.**
**440 Yds.**—Kim Thomas, St. John's Univ. **Time—0:55.53.**
**880 Yds.**—Debbie Vetter, Iowa State. **Time—2:08.8.**
**One Mile**—Francie Larrieu, Sunnyvale, Cal. **Time—4.37**
**2 Miles**—Brenda Webb, Knoxville TC. **Time—9:55.8.**
**One-Mile Walk**—Susan Brodock, Rialto Roadrunners. **Time—7:01.7.**
**High Jump**—Debbie Brill, Canada. **6 ft. 2 in.**
**Long Jump**—Modupe Oshikoya, Maccabi Union TC. **20 ft. 6¼ in.**
**Shot Put**—Maren Seidler, San Jose Stars. **61 ft.**
**640-Yd. Relay**—Tennessee St. **Time—1:09.7**
**880-Yd. Medley Relay**—Atoms TC. **Time—1:44.3.**
**One-Mile Relay**—Los Angeles Mercurettes. **Time—3:51.7.**
**Team champion**—Tennessee St.

## NCAA Outdoor Track and Field Championships

Eugene, Ore., June 1-3, 1978

**200 Meters**—Clancy Edwards, Southern Cal. **Time—0:20.16.**
**400 Meters**—Billy Mullens, Southern Cal. **Time—0:45.33.**
**800 Meters**—Peter Lamasbon, Texas, El Paso. **Time—1:45.68.**
**1,500 Meters**—Steve Scott, California at Irving. **Time—3:37.58.**
**5,000 Meters**—Rudy Chapa, Oregon. **Time—13:35.29.**
**400-Meter Intermediate Hurdles**—James Walker, Auburn. **Time—0:48.92.**
**3,000-Meter Steeplechase**—Henry Rono, Washington St. **Time—8:12.39.**

**400-Meter Relay**—Southern Cal. **Time—0:39.31.**
**One-Mile Relay**—Southern Cal. **Time—3:05.09.**
**Javelin**—Bob Roggy, So. Illinois. **283 ft. 9 in.**
**Pole Vault**—Mike Tully, UCLA. **18 ft. 1 ¾ in.**
**High Jump**—Franklin Jacobs, Fairleigh Dickinson. **7 ft. 3 in.**
**Triple Jump**—Ron Livers, San Jose St. **56 ft. 3 ¼ in.**
**Discus**—Keith Gardenkrans, Brigham Young. **210 ft.**
**Decathlon**—Maurleo Bardeles, California at Irving. **8,007 pts.**
**Team champion**—Southern Cal.

# National AAU Outdoor Track and Field Championships

Westwood, Cal., June 8-10, 1978

## Men

**100 Meters**—Clancy Edwards, Tobias Striders. **Time—0:10.14.**
**200 Meters**—Clancy Edwards. **Time—0:20.25.**
**400 Meters**—Maxie Parks, Athletes in Action. **Time—0:45.15.**
**800 Meters**—James Robinson, Inner City AC. **Time—1:45.5.**
**1,500 Meters**—Steve Scott, Irvine TC. **Time—3:38.8.**
**3,000 Meter Steeplechase**—Henry Marsh, Athletics West. **Time—8:27.3.**
**5,000 Meters**—Marty Liquori, Florida Athletic Attic. **Time—13:40.2.**
**10,000 Meters**—Craig Virgin, Athletics West. **Time—28:15.0.**
**5-Km. Walk**—Joseph Berendt, U.S. Army. **Time—22:31.6.**
**20-Km. Walk**—Todd Scully, Shore AC. **Time—1:34:46.**
**110-Meter Hurdles**—Renaldo Nehemiah, New Jersey Flyers. **Time—0:13.28.**
**400-Meter Hurdles**—James Walker, Athletes in Action. **Time—0:49.03.**
**High Jump**—Dwight Stones, unattached. **7 ft. 6½ in.**
**Pole Vault**—Dan Ripley, unattached. **18 ft. 3 in.**
**Long Jump**—Arnie Robinson, San Diego Southeast Ghetto Striders. **27 ft. 4 in.**
**Triple Jump**—James Butts, Athletes in Action. **55 ft. 5½ in.**
**Shot Put**—Al Feuerbach, Athletics West. **67 ft. 11½ in.**
**Discus**—Mac Wilkins, Athletics West. **219 ft. 9 in.**
**Hammer**—Doris Djerassi, New York AC. **224 ft. 3 in.**
**Javelin**—Bill Schmidt, Knoxville TC. **276 ft. 9 in.**
**Outstanding performer**—Clancy Edwards.

**Team champion**—Tobias Striders.

## Women

**100 Meters**—Leleith Hodges, Texas Women's Univ. **Time—0:11.23.**
**200 Meters**—Evelyn Ashford, Maccabi TC. **Time—0:22.66.**
**400 Meters**—Lorna Forde, Atoms TC. **Time—0:51.04.**
**800 Meters**—Ruth Caldwell, Citrus College. **Time—2:02.0.**
**1,500 Meters**—Jan Merrill, Age Group AA. **Time—4:09.4.**
**3,000 Meters**—Jan Merrill. **Time—8:56.4.**
**10,000 Meters**—Ellison Goodall, Duke Univ. **Time—33:40.2.**
**100-Meter Hurdles**—Deby LaPlante, unattached. **Time—0:13.19.**
**400-Meter Hurdles**—Debbie Esser, Iowa State. **Time—0:57.85.**
**5,000-Meter Walk**—Susan Liers, Island TC. **Time—25:46.8.**
**10,000-Meter Walk**—Sue Brodock, Southern California Roadrunners. **Time—52:18.2.**
**440-Yd. Relay**—Texas Women's Univ. **Time—0:44.61.**
**High Jump**—Louise Ritter, Texas Women's Univ. **6 ft. 1¼ in.**
**Long Jump**—Jodi Anderson, Los Angeles Naturite TC. **22 ft. 7½ in.**
**Shot Put**—Maren Seidler, San Jose Stars. **59 ft. 8 in.**
**Discus**—Lynne Winbigler, Oregon TC. **178 ft. 6 in.**
**Javelin**—Sherry Calvert, Lakewood International. **203 ft. 7 in.**
**Outstanding performer**—Jodi Anderson.
**Team champion**—Tennessee State.

# Table Tennis Championships in 1978

## 48th U.S. National Open

Oklahoma City, Okla., June 29-July 2, 1978

**Men's Singles** — Norio Takashima, Japan.
**Women's Singles** — Hong Ja Park, South Korea.
**Mixed Doubles** — Errol Caetano & Mariann Domonkos, Canada.
**Women's Doubles** — Seong Heui Kim & Hong Ja Park, South Korea.
**Men's Doubles** — Masami Ohshima & Norio Takashima, Japan.
**Senior Women over 40** — Yvonne Kronlage, Ellicott City, Md.
**Senior Men over 40** — Jack Howard, Hermosa Beach, Cal.

**Youth under 21** — Ricky Seemiller, Pittsburgh, Pa.
**Youth under 21 doubles** — Eric Boggan & Roger Sverdlik, Merrick, Rockville Center, N.Y.
**Boys under 17** — Eric Boggan, Merrick, N.Y.
**Girls under 17** — Kasia Dawidowicz, Aurora, Col.
**Girls under 17 doubles** — Kasia Dawidowicz & Debbie Payotelis, Aurora, Southfield, Mich.
**Men's team** — Japan.
**Women's team** — South Korea "A".

# Salaries of Athletes

The actual amount of money paid by a club to an athlete is known only to the club, the athlete, his agent, and the IRS. The following salary and earnings figures have been taken from published sources, reliable, but not official. The figures do not include outside income, such as fees for personal appearances and commercial endorsements.

## Estimated Earnings of Athletes

| Athlete | Dollars |
|---|---|
| Muhammad Ali (boxing) | 5.75 million (1977) |
| | 3.5 million (Spinks fight) |
| (about ⅓ of Ali's earnings go for taxes, about ⅓ goes to his manager, leaving Ali with about ⅓, before expenses.) | |
| Ken Norton (boxing) | 2.2 million (1977) |
| (Norton gets about ⅓, before expenses.) | |
| Jimmy Connors (tennis) (1977) | 922,000 |
| Guillermo Vilas, tennis (1977) | 800,000 |
| David Thompson, basketball | 650,000-750,000 |
| O. J. Simpson, football | 733,000 |
| Julius Erving, basketball | 500,000-700,000 |
| Pete Maravich, basketball | 600,000-650,000 |
| Kareem Abdul-Jabbar, basketball | 600,000-625,000 |
| Steve Cauthen, horse racing 1977 | 615,000 |
| Bobby Orr, hockey | 600,000 |
| Reggie Jackson, baseball | 580,000 |
| Catfish Hunter, baseball | 560,000-578,000 |
| Mike Schmidt, baseball | 560,000 |
| Larry Hisle, baseball | 530,000 |
| Angel Cordero, horse racing (1977) | 521,000 |
| Chris Evert, tennis (1977) | 503,000 |
| Anders Hedberg, hockey | 500,000 |
| Ulf Nilsson, hockey | 500,000 |
| Bob McAdoo, basketball | 500,000 |
| Bjorn Borg, tennis (1977) | 480,000 |
| Cale Yarborough, auto racing (1977) | 477,000 |
| Oscar Gamble, baseball | 475,000 |
| Bob Lanier, basketball | 450,000 |

| Athlete | Dollars |
|---|---|
| Rick Barry, basketball | 450,000 |
| Lyman Bostock, baseball | 450,000 |
| George McGinnis, basketball | 450,000 |
| Ernie DiGregorio, basketball | 450,000 |
| Rich Gossage, baseball | 450,000 |
| Joe Rudi, baseball | 440,000 |
| Laffit Pincay, horse racing (1977) | 438,000 |
| Bill Walton, basketball | 400,000 |

### Other noteworthy earnings

| | |
|---|---|
| Bill Shoemaker, horse racing (1977) | 363,000 |
| A.J. Foyt, auto racing (1977) | 356,000 |
| Fran Tarkenton, football | 300,000-350,000 |
| Tom Watson, golf (1977) | 310,000 |
| Bobby Hull, hockey | 300,000 |
| Jack Nicklaus, golf (1977) | 284,000 |
| Giorgio Chinaglia, soccer | 283,000 |
| Herve Filion, harness racing (1977) | 255,000 |
| Franz Beckenbauer, soccer | 250,000 |
| Judy Rankin, golf (1977) | 122,000 |
| Mike Roth, bowling (1977) | 105,000 |
| Andre Arnold, pro (1977) | 92,000 |

### Comparatively underpaid

| | |
|---|---|
| Rod Carew, baseball | 200,000 |
| Chuck Foreman, football | 190,000 |
| Guy Lafleur, hockey | 180,000 |

# National Football League

### Final 1977 Standings

## National Conference

### Eastern Division

|  | W | L | T | Pct. | PF | PA |
|---|---|---|---|---|---|---|
| Dallas | 12 | 2 | 0 | .857 | 345 | 212 |
| Washington | 9 | 5 | 0 | .643 | 196 | 189 |
| St. Louis | 7 | 7 | 0 | .500 | 272 | 287 |
| Giants | 5 | 9 | 0 | .357 | 181 | 265 |
| Philadelphia | 5 | 9 | 0 | .357 | 220 | 207 |

### Central Division

| Minnesota | 9 | 5 | 0 | .643 | 231 | 227 |
|---|---|---|---|---|---|---|
| Chicago | 9 | 5 | 0 | .643 | 255 | 253 |
| Detroit | 6 | 8 | 0 | .429 | 183 | 252 |
| Green Bay | 4 | 10 | 0 | .286 | 134 | 219 |
| Tampa Bay | 2 | 12 | 0 | .143 | 103 | 223 |

### Western Division

| Los Angeles | 10 | 4 | 0 | .714 | 302 | 146 |
|---|---|---|---|---|---|---|
| Atlanta | 7 | 7 | 0 | .500 | 179 | 129 |
| San Francisco | 5 | 9 | 0 | .357 | 220 | 260 |
| New Orleans | 3 | 11 | 0 | .214 | 232 | 336 |

## American Conference

### Eastern Division

|  | W | L | T | Pct. | PF | P |
|---|---|---|---|---|---|---|
| Baltimore | 10 | 4 | 0 | .714 | 295 | 22 |
| Miami | 10 | 4 | 0 | .714 | 313 | 19 |
| New England | 9 | 5 | 0 | .643 | 278 | 2 |
| N.Y. Jets | 3 | 11 | 0 | .214 | 191 | 30 |
| Buffalo | 3 | 11 | 0 | .214 | 160 | 3 |

### Central Division

| Pittsburgh | 9 | 5 | 0 | .643 | 283 | 24 |
|---|---|---|---|---|---|---|
| Cincinnati | 8 | 6 | 0 | .571 | 238 | 23 |
| Houston | 8 | 6 | 0 | .571 | 299 | 23 |
| Cleveland | 6 | 8 | 0 | .429 | 269 | 26 |

### Western Division

| Denver | 12 | 2 | 0 | .857 | 274 | 14 |
|---|---|---|---|---|---|---|
| Oakland | 11 | 3 | 0 | .786 | 351 | 23 |
| San Diego | 7 | 7 | 0 | .500 | 222 | 20 |
| Seattle | 5 | 9 | 0 | .357 | 282 | 37 |
| Kansas City | 2 | 12 | 0 | .143 | 225 | 34 |

NFC Playoffs—Dallas 37, Chicago 7; Minnesota 14, Los Angeles 7; Dallas 23, Minnesota 6.
AFC Playoffs—Oakland 37, Baltimore 31; Denver 34, Pittsburgh 21; Denver 20, Oakland 17.
Championship Game—Dallas 27, Denver 10.

## Dallas Defeats Denver in Super Bowl

The Dallas Cowboys won their second Super Bowl championship by defeating the Denver Broncos 27-10 on Jan. 15, 1978 at the Louisiana Superdome in New Orleans.

### Score by Periods

| | | | | |
|---|---|---|---|---|
| Dallas | 10 | 3 | 7 | 7—27 |
| Denver | 0 | 0 | 10 | 0—10 |

### Scoring

Dallas—Dorsett 3 run (Herrera kick).
Dallas—Field goal Herrera 35.
Dallas—Field goal Herrera 43.
Denver—Field goal Turner 47.
Dallas—Johnson 45 pass from Staubach (Herrera kick).
Denver—Lytle 1 run (Turner kick).
Dallas—Richards 29 pass from Newhouse (Herrera kick).

### Individual Statistics

Dallas rushing—Johnson, 1 for minus 9 yards; Dorsett, 15 for 66; Newhouse, 14 for 55; P. Pearson, 3 for 11; Staubach, 3 for 6; D. White, 1 for 13; Laidlaw, 1 for 1.

Denver rushing—Keyworth, 5 for 9 yards; Armstrong, 7 for 27; Lytle, 10 for 35; Perrin, 3 for 8; Jensen, 1 for 16; Weese, 3 for 26.

Dallas passing—Staubach, 17 of 25 for 183 yards; D. White, 1 of 2 for 5; Newhouse, 1 of 1 for 29.

Denver passing—Morton, 4 of 15 for 39 yards (four intercepted); Weese, 4 of 10 for 22.

Dallas pass receiving—P. Pearson, 5 for 37 yards; Dorsett, 2 for 11; DuPree, 4 for 66; Newhouse, 3 for minus 1; Johnson, 2 for 53; Richards, 1 for 29; D. Pearson, 1 for 13.

Denver pass receiving—Moses, 1 for 21 yards; Perrin, 1 for minus 7; Dolbin, 2 for 24; Odoms, 2 for 9; Jensen, 1 for 5; Upchurch, 1 for 9.

Dallas interceptions—Hughes, 1 for 0 yards; Kyle, 1 for 19; Barnes, 1 for 0; Henderson, 1 for 27.

Denver interceptions—None.

Dallas punting—D. White, 5 for 208 yards (41.6 average).

Denver punting—Dilts, 4 for 153 yards (38.2 average).

Dallas punt returns—Hill, 1 for 0 yards.

Denver punt returns—Upchurch, 3 for 22 yards; Schultz, 1 for 0.

Dallas kickoff returns—Johnson, 2 for 29 yards; Brinson, 1 for 22.

Denver kickoff returns—Schultz, 2 for 62 yards; Upchurch, 1 for 94; Jensen, 1 for 17.

Dallas opposition fumble recoveries—Hughes, 2 for 21 yards; Huther, 1 for 0; Kyle, 1 for 0.

Denver opposition fumble recoveries—None.

### Team Statistics

|  | Dallas | Denver |
|---|---|---|
| Total First Downs | 17 | 11 |
| First downs rushing | 8 | 8 |
| First downs passing | 8 | 1 |
| First downs by penalty | 1 | 2 |
| Third Down Efficiency | 6-17 | 3-14 |
| Total Offensive Yards | 325 | 156 |
| Total offensive plays | 71 | 58 |
| Average gain per play | 4.6 | 2.7 |
| Net Rushing Yardage | 143 | 121 |
| Total rushing plays | 38 | 29 |
| Average gain per rush | 3.8 | 4.2 |
| Net Passing Yardage | 182 | 35 |
| Gross yards passing | 217 | 61 |
| Yards lost attempting pass | 5-35 | 4-26 |
| Passes | 19-28-0 | 8-25-4 |
| Average gain per pass | 6.6 | 2.1 |
| Punts | 5-41.6 | 4-38.2 |
| Blocked | 0 | 0 |
| Fumbles/Lost | 6-2 | 4-4 |
| Penalties/Yards | 12-94 | 8-60 |
| Total Return Yardage | 97 | 195 |
| Punts | 0 | 22 |
| Kickoffs | 51 | 173 |
| Interception | 46 | 9 |
| Time of Possession | 38:34 | 21:26 |

Attendance—76,400.

## Super Bowl

| Year | Winner | Loser | Site |
|---|---|---|---|
| 1967 | Green Bay Packers, 35 | Kansas City Chiefs, 10 | Los Angeles Coliseum |
| 1968 | Green Bay Packers, 33 | Oakland Raiders, 14 | Orange Bowl, Miami |
| 1969 | New York Jets, 16 | Baltimore Colts, 7 | Orange Bowl, Miami |
| 1970 | Kansas City Chiefs, 23 | Minnesota Vikings, 7 | Tulane Stadium, New Orleans |
| 1971 | Baltimore Colts, 16 | Dallas Cowboys, 13 | Orange Bowl, Miami |
| 1972 | Dallas Cowboys, 24 | Miami Dolphins, 3 | Tulane Stadium, New Orleans |
| 1973 | Miami Dolphins, 14 | Washington Redskins, 7 | Los Angeles Coliseum |
| 1974 | Miami Dolphins, 24 | Minnesota Vikings, 7 | Rice Stadium, Houston |
| 1975 | Pittsburgh Steelers, 16 | Minnesota Vikings, 6 | Tulane Stadium, New Orleans |
| 1976 | Pittsburgh Steelers, 21 | Dallas Cowboys, 17 | Orange Bowl, Miami |
| 1977 | Oakland Raiders, 32 | Minnesota Vikings, 14 | Rose Bowl, Pasadena |
| 1978 | Dallas Cowboys, 27 | Denver Broncos, 10 | Louisiana Superdome, New Orleans |

## National Football League Champions

| Year | East Winner (W.L.T.) | West Winner (W.L.T.) | Playoff |
|------|----------------------|----------------------|---------|
| 1933 | New York Giants (11-3-0) | Chicago Bears (10-2-1) | Chicago Bears 23, New York 21 |
| 1934 | New York Giants (8-5-0) | Chicago Bears (13-0-0) | New York 30, Chicago Bears 13 |
| 1935 | New York Giants (9-3-0) | Detroit Lions (7-3-2) | Detroit 26, New York 7 |
| 1936 | Boston Redskins (7-5-0) | Green Bay Packers (10-1-1) | Green Bay 21, Boston 6 |
| 1937 | Washington Redskins (8-3-0) | Chicago Bears (9-1-1) | Washington 28, Chicago Bears 21 |
| 1938 | New York Giants (8-2-1) | Green Bay Packers (8-3-0) | New York 23, Green Bay 17 |
| 1939 | New York Giants (9-1-1) | Green Bay Packers (9-2-0) | Green Bay 27, New York 0 |
| 1940 | Washington Redskins (9-2-0) | Chicago Bears (8-3-0) | Chicago Bears 73, Washington 0 |
| 1941 | New York Giants (8-3-0) | Chicago Bears (10-1-1)(a) | Chicago Bears 37, New York 9 |
| 1942 | Wash. Redskins (10-1-1) | Chicago Bears (11-0-0) | Washington 14, Chicago Bears 6 |
| 1943 | Wash. Redskins (6-3-1)(a) | Chicago Bears (8-1-1) | Chicago Bears, 41, Washington 21 |
| 1944 | New York Giants (8-1-1) | Green Bay Packers (8-2-0) | Green Bay 14, New York 7 |
| 1945 | Wash. Redskins (8-2-0) | Cleveland Rams (9-1-0) | Cleveland 15, Washington 14 |
| 1946 | New York Giants (7-3-1) | Chicago Bears (8-2-1) | Chicago Bears 24, New York 14 |
| 1947 | Philadelphia Eagles (8-4-0)(a) | Chicago Cardinals (9-3-0) | Chicago Cardinals 28, Philadelphia 21 |
| 1948 | Philadelphia Eagles (9-2-1) | Chicago Cardinals (11-1-0) | Philadelphia 7, Chicago Cardinals 0 |
| 1949 | Philadelphia Eagles (11-1-0) | Los Angeles Rams (8-2-2) | Philadelphia 14, Los Angeles 0 |
| 1950 | Cleveland Browns (10-2-0)(a) | Los Angeles Rams (9-3-0)(a) | Cleveland 30, Los Angeles 28 |
| 1951 | Cleveland Browns (11-1-0) | Los Angeles Rams (8-4-0) | Los Angeles 24, Cleveland 17 |
| 1952 | Cleveland Browns (8-4-0) | Detroit Lions (9-3-0)(a) | Detroit 17, Cleveland 7 |
| 1953 | Cleveland Browns (11-1-0) | Detroit Lions (10-2-0) | Detroit 17, Cleveland 16 |
| 1954 | Cleveland Browns (9-3-0) | Detroit Lions (9-2-1) | Cleveland 56, Detroit 10 |
| 1955 | Cleveland Browns (9-2-1) | Los Angeles Rams (8-3-1) | Cleveland 38, Los Angeles 14 |
| 1956 | New York Giants (8-3-1) | Chicago Bears (9-2-1) | New York 47, Chicago Bears 7 |
| 1957 | Cleveland Browns (9-2-1) | Detroit Lions (8-4-0)(a) | Detroit 59, Cleveland 14 |
| 1958 | New York Giants (9-3-0)(a) | Baltimore Colts (9-3-0) | Baltimore 23, New York 17(b) |
| 1959 | New York Giants (10-2-0) | Baltimore Colts (9-3-0) | Baltimore 31, New York 16 |
| 1960 | Philadelphia Eagles (10-2-0) | Green Bay Packers (8-4-0) | Philadelphia 17, Green Bay 13 |
| 1961 | New York Giants (10-3-1) | Green Bay Packers (11-3-0) | Green Bay 37, New York 0 |
| 1962 | New York Giants (12-2-0) | Green Bay Packers (13-1-0) | Green Bay 16, New York 7 |
| 1963 | New York Giants (11-3-0) | Chicago Bears (11-1-2) | Chicago 14, New York 10 |
| 1964 | Cleveland Browns (10-3-1) | Baltimore Colts (12-2-0) | Cleveland 27, Baltimore 0 |
| 1965 | Cleveland Browns (11-3-0) | Green Bay Packers (10-3-1)(a) | Green Bay 23, Cleveland 12 |
| 1966 | Dallas Cowboys (10-3-1) | Green Bay Packers (12-2-0) | Green Bay 34, Dallas 27 |

(a) Won divisional playoff. (b) Won at 8:15 sudden death overtime period.

| Year | Conference | Division | Winner (W-L-T) | Playoff |
|------|-----------|----------|----------------|---------|
| 1967 | East | Century | Cleveland (9-5-0) | Dallas 52, Cleveland 14 |
| | | Capitol | Dallas (9-5-0) | |
| | West | Central | Green Bay (9-4-1) | Green Bay 28, Los Angeles 7 |
| | | Coastal | Los Angeles (11-1-2)(a) | Green Bay 21, Dallas 17 |
| 1968 | East | Century | Cleveland (10-4-0) | Cleveland 31, Dallas 20 |
| | | Capitol | Dallas (12-2-0) | |
| | West | Central | Minnesota (8-6-0) | Baltimore 24, Minnesota 14 |
| | | Coastal | Baltimore (13-1-0) | Baltimore 34, Cleveland 0 |
| 1969 | East | Century | Cleveland (10-3-1) | Cleveland 38, Dallas 14 |
| | | Capitol | Dallas (11-2-1) | |
| | West | Central | Minnesota (12-2-0) | Minnesota 23, Los Angeles 20 |
| | | Coastal | Los Angeles (11-3-0) | Minnesota 27, Cleveland 7 |
| 1970 | American | Eastern | Baltimore (11-2-1) | Baltimore 17, Cincinnati 0 |
| | | Central | Cincinnati (8-6-0) | Oakland 21, Miami 14 |
| | | Western | Oakland (8-4-2) | Baltimore 27, Oakland 17 |
| | National | Eastern | Dallas (10-4-0) | Dallas 5, Detroit 0 |
| | | Central | Minnesota (12-2-0) | San Francisco 17, Minnesota 14 |
| | | Western | San Francisco (10-3-1) | Dallas 17, San Francisco 10 |
| 1971 | American | Eastern | Miami (10-3-1) | Miami 27, Kansas City 24 |
| | | Central | Cleveland (9-5-0) | Baltimore 20, Cleveland 3 |
| | | Western | Kansas City (10-3-1) | Miami 21, Baltimore 0 |
| | National | Eastern | Dallas (11-3-0) | Dallas 20, Minnesota 12 |
| | | Central | Minnesota (11-3-0) | San Francisco 24, Washington 20 |
| | | Western | San Francisco (9-5-0) | Dallas 14, San Francisco 3 |
| 1972 | American | Eastern | Miami (14-0-0) | Miami 20, Cleveland 14 |
| | | Central | Pittsburgh (11-3-0) | Pittsburgh 13, Oakland 7 |
| | | Western | Oakland (10-3-1) | Miami 21, Pittsburgh 17 |
| | National | Eastern | Washington (11-3-0) | Washington 16, Green Bay 3 |
| | | Central | Green Bay (10-4-0) | Dallas 30, San Francisco 28 |
| | | Western | San Francisco (8-5-1) | Washington 26, Dallas 3 |
| 1973 | American | Eastern | Miami (12-2-0) | Miami 34, Cincinnati 16 |
| | | Central | Cincinnati (10-4-0) | Oakland 33, Pittsburgh 14 |
| | | Western | Oakland (9-4-1) | Miami 27, Oakland 10 |
| | National | Eastern | Dallas (10-4-0) | Dallas 27, Los Angeles 16 |
| | | Central | Minnesota (12-2-0) | Minnesota 27, Washington 20 |
| | | Western | Los Angeles (12-2-0) | Minnesota 27, Dallas 10 |
| 1974 | American | Eastern | Miami (11-3-0) | Oakland 28, Miami 26 |
| | | Central | Pittsburgh (10-3-1) | Pittsburgh 32, Buffalo 14 |
| | | Western | Oakland (12-2-0) | Pittsburgh 24, Oakland 13 |
| | National | Eastern | St. Louis (10-4-0) | Minnesota 30, St. Louis 14 |
| | | Central | Minnesota (10-4-0) | Los Angeles 19, Washington 10 |
| | | Western | Los Angeles (10-4-0) | Minnesota 14, Los Angeles 10 |
| 1975 | American | Eastern | Baltimore (10-4-0) | Pittsburgh 28, Baltimore 10 |
| | | Central | Pittsburgh (12-2-0) | Oakland 31, Cincinnati 28 |
| | | Western | Oakland (11-3-0) | Pittsburgh 16, Oakland 10 |
| | National | Eastern | St. Louis (11-3-0) | Dallas 17, Minnesota 14 |

(continued)

*(continued)*

| Year | Conference | Division | Winner (W-L-T) | Playoff |
|------|-----------|----------|----------------|---------|
| | | Central | Minnesota (12-2-0) | Los Angeles 35, St. Louis 23 |
| | | Western | Los Angeles (12-2-0) | Dallas 37, Los Angeles 7 |
| 1976 | American | Eastern | Baltimore (11-3-0) | Pittsburgh 40, Baltimore 14 |
| | | Central | Pittsburgh (10-4-0) | Oakland 24, New England 21 |
| | | Western | Oakland (13-1-0) | Oakland 24, Pittsburgh 12 |
| | National | Eastern | Dallas (11-3-0) | Minnesota 35, Washington 20 |
| | | Central | Minnesota (11-2-1) | Los Angeles 14, Dallas 12 |
| | | Western | Los Angeles (10-3-1) | Minnesota 24, Los Angeles 13 |
| 1977 | American | Eastern | Baltimore (10-4-0) | Oakland 37, Baltimore 31 |
| | | Central | Pittsburgh (9-5-0) | Denver 34, Pittsburgh 21 |
| | | Western | Denver (12-2-0) | Dallas 37, Chicago 7 |
| | National | Eastern | Dallas (12-2-0) | Minnesota 14, Los Angeles 7 |
| | | Central | Minnesota (9-5-0) | Denver 20, Oakland 17 |
| | | Western | Los Angeles (10-4-0) | Dallas 23, Minnesota 6 |

# 1977 NFL Individual Leaders

## National Football Conference

### Passing[1]

| | Att | Cmp | Pct Cmp | Yds | Avg Gain | TD | Int | Rating Pts |
|---|-----|-----|---------|-----|----------|-----|-----|------------|
| Staubach, Dallas | 361 | 210 | 58.2 | 2620 | 7.26 | 18 | 9 | 87.1 |
| Haden, Los Angeles | 216 | 122 | 56.5 | 1551 | 7.18 | 11 | 6 | 84.4 |
| Tarkenton, Minnesota | 258 | 155 | 60.1 | 1734 | 6.72 | 9 | 14 | 69.3 |
| Landry, Detroit | 240 | 135 | 56.3 | 1359 | 5.66 | 6 | 7 | 68.8 |
| Manning, New Orleans | 205 | 113 | 55.1 | 1284 | 6.26 | 8 | 9 | 68.8 |
| Kilmer, Washington | 201 | 99 | 49.3 | 1187 | 5.91 | 8 | 7 | 66.6 |
| Hart, St. Louis | 355 | 186 | 52.4 | 2542 | 7.16 | 13 | 20 | 64.6 |
| Plunkett, S.F. | 248 | 128 | 51.6 | 1693 | 6.83 | 9 | 14 | 62.2 |
| Avellini, Chicago | 293 | 154 | 52.6 | 2004 | 6.84 | 11 | 18 | 61.7 |
| Jaworski, Philadelphia | 346 | 166 | 48.0 | 2183 | 6.31 | 18 | 21 | 60.3 |
| Theismann, Washington | 182 | 84 | 46.2 | 1097 | 6.03 | 7 | 9 | 58.0 |
| Dickey, Green Bay | 220 | 113 | 51.4 | 1346 | 6.12 | 5 | 14 | 51.4 |
| Pisarcik, N.Y. Giants | 241 | 103 | 42.7 | 1346 | 5.59 | 4 | 14 | 42.5 |

### Rushing

| | Att | Yds | Avg | TDs |
|---|-----|-----|-----|-----|
| Payton, Chicago | 339 | 1852 | 5.5 | 14 |
| McCutcheon, Los Angeles | 294 | 1238 | 4.2 | 7 |
| Foreman, Minnesota | 270 | 1112 | 4.1 | 6 |
| Dorsett, Dallas | 208 | 1007 | 4.8 | 12 |
| Williams, San Francisco | 268 | 931 | 3.5 | 7 |
| Stanback, Atlanta | 247 | 873 | 3.5 | 6 |
| Muncie, New Orleans | 201 | 811 | 4.0 | 6 |
| Thomas, Washington | 228 | 806 | 3.5 | 3 |
| Jackson, San Francisco | 179 | 780 | 4.4 | 7 |
| Metcalf, St. Louis | 149 | 739 | 5.0 | 4 |

### Punt Returns

| | No | Yds | Avg | TDs |
|---|-----|-----|-----|-----|
| Marshall, Philadelphia | 46 | 489 | 10.6 | 0 |
| Hammond, N.Y. Giants | 32 | 334 | 10.4 | 0 |
| Payton, Clev.-Det. | 30 | 290 | 9.7 | 1 |
| Schubert, Chicago | 31 | 291 | 9.4 | 1 |
| Harrell, Green Bay | 28 | 253 | 9.0 | 1 |
| Reece, Tampa Bay | 31 | 274 | 8.8 | 0 |
| Johnson, Dallas | 50 | 423 | 8.5 | 0 |
| Brown, Washington | 57 | 452 | 7.9 | 0 |
| Metcalf, St. Louis | 14 | 108 | 7.7 | 0 |
| Mauti, New Orleans | 37 | 281 | 7.6 | 0 |

### Pass Receiving

| | No | Yds | Avg | TDs |
|---|-----|-----|-----|-----|
| Rashad, Minnesota | 51 | 681 | 13.4 | 2 |
| Scott, Chicago | 50 | 809 | 16.2 | 3 |
| Pearson, D., Dallas | 48 | 870 | 18.1 | 2 |
| Jackson, Los Angeles | 48 | 666 | 13.9 | 6 |
| Carmichael, Philadelphia | 46 | 665 | 14.5 | 7 |
| Pearson, P., Dallas | 46 | 535 | 11.6 | 4 |
| White, Minnesota | 41 | 760 | 18.5 | 9 |
| Galbreath, New Orleans | 41 | 265 | 6.5 | 0 |
| Harris, St. Louis | 40 | 547 | 13.7 | 3 |
| King, Detroit | 40 | 238 | 6.0 | 0 |

### Kickoff Returns

| | No | Yds | Avg | TDs |
|---|-----|-----|-----|-----|
| Montgomery, Philadelphia | 23 | 619 | 26.9 | 0 |
| Chapman, New Orleans | 15 | 385 | 25.7 | 1 |
| Brown, Washington | 34 | 852 | 25.1 | 0 |
| Payton, Clev.-Det. | 22 | 548 | 24.9 | 1 |
| Johnson, Dallas | 22 | 536 | 24.4 | 0 |
| Baschnagel, Chicago | 23 | 557 | 24.2 | 1 |
| Hofer, San Francisco | 36 | 871 | 24.2 | 0 |
| Metcalf, St. Louis | 32 | 772 | 24.1 | 0 |
| Brinson, Dallas | 17 | 409 | 24.1 | 0 |
| Kane, Detroit | 16 | 376 | 23.5 | 0 |

### Interceptions

| | No | Yds | Avg | TDs |
|---|-----|-----|-----|-----|
| Lawrence, Atlanta | 7 | 138 | 19.7 | 0 |
| Simpson, Los Angeles | 6 | 157 | 26.2 | 0 |
| Sanders, Philadelphia | 6 | 122 | 20.3 | 0 |
| Hunter, Detroit | 6 | 104 | 17.3 | 0 |
| Ellis, Chicago | 6 | 23 | 3.8 | 0 |
| Edwards, Philadelphia | 6 | 9 | 1.5 | 0 |
| Logan, Philadelphia | 5 | 124 | 24.8 | 0 |
| Thomas, Los Angeles | 5 | 97 | 19.4 | 0 |
| Jackson, Los Angeles | 5 | 73 | 14.6 | 0 |
| Washington, Tampa Bay | 5 | 71 | 14.2 | 1 |

### Scoring

| | TDs | XP | XPA | FG | FGA | Pts |
|---|-----|-----|-----|-----|-----|-----|
| Payton, Chicago | 16 | 0 | 0 | 0 | 0 | 96 |
| Herrera, Dallas | 0 | 39 | 41 | 18 | 29 | 93 |
| Septien, Los Angeles | 0 | 32 | 35 | 18 | 30 | 86 |
| Moseley, Washington | 0 | 19 | 19 | 21 | 37 | 82 |
| Dorsett, Dallas | 13 | 0 | 0 | 0 | 0 | 78 |
| Thomas, Chicago | 0 | 27 | 30 | 14 | 27 | 69 |
| Danelo N.Y. Giants | 0 | 19 | 20 | 14 | 23 | 61 |
| Bakken, St. Louis | 0 | 35 | 36 | 7 | 16 | 56 |
| Childs, New Orleans | 9 | 0 | 0 | 0 | 0 | 54 |
| Foreman, Minnesota | 9 | 0 | 0 | 0 | 0 | 54 |

### Punting

| | No | Yds | Avg | | No | Yds | Avg |
|---|-----|-----|-----|---|-----|-----|-----|
| Blanchard, New Orleans | 82 | 3474 | 42.4 | Beverly, Green Bay | 85 | 3391 | 39.9 |
| James, Atlanta | 105 | 4349 | 41.4 | Clabo, Minnesota | 83 | 3302 | 39.8 |
| Parsons, Chicago | 80 | 3232 | 40.4 | White, Dallas | 80 | 3171 | 39.6 |
| Green, Tampa Bay | 98 | 3948 | 40.3 | Bragg, Washington | 91 | 3502 | 38.5 |
| Jennings, N.Y. Giants | 100 | 3993 | 39.9 | Jones, Philadelphia | 93 | 3463 | 37.2 |

## American Conference

### Passing[1]

| | Att | Cmp | Pct Cmp | Yds | Avg Gain | TD | Int | Rating Pts |
|---|---|---|---|---|---|---|---|---|
| Griese, Miami | 307 | 180 | 58.6 | 2252 | 7.34 | 22 | 13 | 88.0 |
| Morton, Denver | 254 | 131 | 51.6 | 1929 | 7.59 | 14 | 8 | 82.1 |
| Jones, Baltimore | 393 | 224 | 57.0 | 2686 | 6.83 | 17 | 11 | 80.7 |
| Stabler, Oakland | 294 | 169 | 57.5 | 2176 | 7.40 | 20 | 20 | 75.2 |
| Bradshaw, Pittsburgh | 314 | 162 | 51.6 | 2523 | 8.04 | 17 | 19 | 71.2 |
| Anderson, Cincinnati | 323 | 166 | 51.4 | 2145 | 6.64 | 11 | 11 | 69.8 |
| Grogan, New England | 305 | 160 | 52.5 | 2162 | 7.09 | 17 | 21 | 65.3 |
| Pastorini, Houston | 319 | 169 | 53.0 | 1987 | 6.23 | 13 | 18 | 62.6 |
| Sipe, Cleveland | 195 | 112 | 57.4 | 1233 | 6.32 | 9 | 14 | 61.6 |
| Todd, N.Y. Jets | 265 | 133 | 50.2 | 1863 | 7.03 | 11 | 17 | 60.6 |
| Livingston, Kansas City | 282 | 143 | 50.7 | 1823 | 6.46 | 9 | 15 | 59.8 |
| Harris, San Diego | 211 | 109 | 51.7 | 1240 | 5.88 | 5 | 11 | 56.0 |
| Ferguson, Buffalo | 457 | 221 | 48.4 | 2803 | 6.13 | 12 | 24 | 54.6 |
| Zorn, Seattle | 251 | 104 | 41.4 | 1687 | 6.72 | 16 | 19 | 54.3 |

(1) At least 150 passes needed to qualify. Leader based on percentage of completions—touchdown passes—interceptions——and average yards.

### Rushing

| | Att | Yds | Avg | TDs |
|---|---|---|---|---|
| Van Eeghen, Oakland | 324 | 1273 | 3.9 | 7 |
| Harris, Pittsburgh | 300 | 1162 | 3.9 | 11 |
| Mitchell, Baltimore | 301 | 1159 | 3.9 | 3 |
| Pruitt, Cleveland | 236 | 1086 | 4.6 | 3 |
| Cunningham, New England | 270 | 1015 | 3.8 | 4 |
| Davis, Oakland | 194 | 787 | 4.1 | 5 |
| Smith, Seattle | 163 | 763 | 4.7 | 4 |
| Miller, Cleveland | 163 | 756 | 4.6 | 4 |
| Calhoun, New England | 198 | 727 | 3.7 | 4 |
| Coleman, Houston | 185 | 660 | 3.6 | 5 |

### Punt Returns

| | No | Yds | Avg | TDs |
|---|---|---|---|---|
| Johnston, Houston | 35 | 539 | 15.4 | 2 |
| Morgan, New England | 16 | 220 | 13.8 | 0 |
| Moody, Buffalo | 15 | 196 | 13.1 | 1 |
| Fuller, San Diego | 28 | 360 | 12.9 | 1 |
| Upchurch, Denver | 51 | 653 | 12.8 | 1 |
| Harper, N.Y. Jets | 34 | 425 | 12.5 | 0 |
| Davis, Cincinnati | 19 | 220 | 11.6 | 0 |
| Kimbrough, Buffalo | 16 | 184 | 11.5 | 1 |
| Rodgers, San Diego | 15 | 158 | 10.5 | 0 |
| Colzie, Oakland | 32 | 334 | 10.4 | 0 |

### Pass Receiving

| | No | Yds | Avg | TDs |
|---|---|---|---|---|
| Mitchell, Baltimore | 71 | 620 | 8.7 | 4 |
| Chandler, Buffalo | 60 | 745 | 12.4 | 4 |
| Gaines, N.Y. Jets | 55 | 469 | 8.5 | 1 |
| Moore, Miami | 52 | 765 | 14.7 | 12 |
| McCauley, Baltimore | 51 | 495 | 9.7 | 2 |
| Swann, Pittsburgh | 50 | 789 | 15.8 | 7 |
| White, Kansas City | 48 | 674 | 14.0 | 5 |
| Casper, Oakland | 48 | 584 | 12.2 | 6 |
| Young, San Diego | 48 | 423 | 8.8 | 0 |
| Stallworth, Pittsburgh | 44 | 784 | 17.8 | 7 |

### Kickoff Returns

| | No | Yds | Avg | TDs |
|---|---|---|---|---|
| Clayborn, New England | 28 | 869 | 31.0 | 3 |
| Davis, Miami | 14 | 414 | 29.6 | 0 |
| Johnson, Houston | 25 | 630 | 25.2 | 1 |
| Harper, N.Y. Jets | 42 | 1035 | 24.6 | 0 |
| J. Smith, Pittsburgh | 16 | 381 | 23.8 | 0 |
| Kimbrough, Buffalo | 15 | 346 | 23.1 | 0 |
| L. Smith, Pittsburgh | 16 | 365 | 22.8 | 0 |
| Upchurch, Denver | 20 | 456 | 22.8 | 0 |
| Hunter, Seattle | 36 | 820 | 22.8 | 0 |
| Laird, Baltimore | 24 | 541 | 22.5 | 0 |

### Interceptions

| | No | Yds | Avg | TDs |
|---|---|---|---|---|
| Blackwood, Baltimore | 10 | 163 | 16.3 | 0 |
| Greene, Buffalo | 9 | 144 | 16.0 | 0 |
| Barbaro, Kansas City | 8 | 165 | 20.6 | 1 |
| Clark, Buffalo | 7 | 151 | 21.6 | 0 |
| White, Baltimore | 7 | 84 | 12.0 | 0 |
| Tatum, Oakland | 6 | 146 | 24.3 | 0 |
| Darden, Cleveland | 6 | 107 | 17.8 | 1 |
| Blount, Pittsburgh | 6 | 65 | 10.8 | 0 |
| Beamon, Seattle | 6 | 36 | 6.0 | 0 |
| Thompson, Denver | 5 | 122 | 24.4 | 0 |

### Scoring

| | TDs | XP | XPA | FG | FGA | Pts |
|---|---|---|---|---|---|---|
| Mann, Oakland | 0 | 39 | 42 | 20 | 28 | 99 |
| Linhart, Baltimore | 0 | 32 | 35 | 17 | 26 | 83 |
| Bahr, Cincinnati | 0 | 25 | 26 | 19 | 27 | 82 |
| Cockroft, Cleveland | 0 | 30 | 31 | 17 | 23 | 81 |
| Moore, Miami | 13 | 0 | 0 | 0 | 0 | 78 |
| Smith, New England | 0 | 33 | 33 | 15 | 21 | 78 |
| Turner, Denver | 1 | 31 | 34 | 13 | 19 | 76 |
| Benirschke, San Diego | 0 | 21 | 24 | 17 | 23 | 72 |
| Yepremian, Miami | 0 | 37 | 40 | 10 | 22 | 67 |
| Harris, Pittsburgh | 11 | 0 | 0 | 0 | 0 | 66 |

### Punting

| | No | Yds | Avg | | | No | Yds | Avg |
|---|---|---|---|---|---|---|---|---|
| Guy, Oakland | 59 | 2552 | 43.3 | | Parsley, Houston | 77 | 3030 | 39.4 |
| McInally, Cincinnati | 67 | 2802 | 41.8 | | Dilts, Denver | 90 | 3525 | 39.2 |
| Wilson, Kansas City | 88 | 3510 | 39.9 | | Coleman, Cleveland | 61 | 2389 | 39.2 |
| Bateman, Buffalo | 81 | 3229 | 39.9 | | Lee, Baltimore | 82 | 3142 | 38.3 |
| Weaver, Seattle | 58 | 2293 | 39.5 | | Michel, Miami | 35 | 1338 | 38.2 |

## Bert Bell Memorial Trophy

The Bert Bell Memorial Trophy, named after the former NFL commissioner, is awarded annually to the outstanding rookies in a poll conducted by Murray Olderman of Newspaper Enterprise Assn.

| | |
|---|---|
| 1964 | Charlie Taylor, Washington, WR |
| 1965 | Gale Sayers, Chicago, RB |
| 1966 | Tommy Nobis, Atlanta, LB |
| 1967 | Mel Farr, Detroit, RB |
| 1968 | Earl McCullouch, Detroit, WR |
| 1969 | Calvin Hill, Dallas, RB |
| 1970 | Raymond Chester, Oakland, TE |
| 1971 | AFC: Jim Plunkett, New England, QB |
| | NFC: John Brockington, Green Bay, RB |
| 1972 | AFC: Franco Harris, Pittsburgh, RB |
| | NFC: Willie Buchanon, Green Bay, DB |
| 1973 | AFC: Boobie Clark, Cincinnati, RB |
| | NFC: Chuck Foreman, Minnesota, RB |
| 1974 | Don Woods, San Diego, RB |
| 1975 | AFC: Robert Brazile, Houston, LB |
| | NFC: Steve Bartkowski, Atlanta, QB |
| 1976 | AFC: Mike Haynes, New England, CB |
| | NFC: Sammy White, Minnesota, WR |
| 1977 | Tony Dorsett, Dallas, RB |

## National Football Conference Leaders

### (National Football League prior to 1970)

#### Passing

| Player, team | Atts | Com | YG | TD | Year |
|---|---|---|---|---|---|
| Y.A. Tittle, N.Y. Giants | 367 | 221 | 3,145 | 14 | 1963 |
| Bart Starr, Green Bay | 272 | 163 | 2,144 | 4 | 1964 |
| Rudy Bukich, Chicago | 312 | 176 | 2,641 | 9 | 1965 |
| Bart Starr, Green Bay | 251 | 156 | 2,257 | 3 | 1966 |
| Sonny Jurgensen, Washington | 508 | 288 | 3,747 | 16 | 1967 |
| Earl Morrall, Baltimore | 317 | 182 | 2,909 | 17 | 1968 |
| Sonny Jurgensen, Washington | 422 | 274 | 3,102 | 15 | 1969 |
| John Brodie, San Francisco | 378 | 223 | 2,941 | 24 | 1970 |
| Roger Staubach, Dallas | 211 | 126 | 1,882 | 15 | 1971 |
| Norm Snead, N.Y. Giants | 325 | 196 | 2,307 | 17 | 1972 |
| Roger Staubach, Dallas | 286 | 179 | 2,428 | 23 | 1973 |
| Sonny Jurgensen, Washington | 167 | 107 | 1,185 | 11 | 1974 |
| Fran Tarkenton, Minnesota | 425 | 273 | 2,294 | 25 | 1975 |
| James Harris, Los Angeles | 158 | 91 | 1,460 | 8 | 1976 |
| Roger Staubach, Dallas | 361 | 210 | 2,620 | 18 | 1977 |

#### Pass-Receiving

| Year | Player, team | Ct | YG | TD |
|---|---|---|---|---|
| 1963 | Bobby Conrad, Cards, St. Louis | 73 | 967 | 10 |
| 1964 | Johnny Morris, Chicago | 93 | 1,200 | 10 |
| 1965 | Dave Parks, San Francisco | 80 | 1,344 | 12 |
| 1966 | Charlie Taylor, Washington | 72 | 1,119 | 12 |
| 1967 | Charlie Taylor, Washington | 70 | 990 | 9 |
| 1968 | Clifton McNeil, San Francisco | 71 | 944 | 7 |
| 1969 | Dan Abramowicz, New Orleans | 73 | 1,015 | 7 |
| 1970 | Dick Gordon, Chicago | 71 | 1,026 | 13 |
| 1971 | Bob Tucker, Giants | 59 | 791 | 4 |
| 1972 | Harold Jackson, Philadelphia | 62 | 1,048 | 4 |
| 1973 | Harold Carmichael, Philadelphia | 67 | 1,116 | 9 |
| 1974 | Charles Young, Philadelphia | 63 | 696 | 3 |
| 1975 | Chuck Foreman, Minnesota | 73 | 691 | 9 |
| 1976 | Drew Pearson, Dallas | 58 | 806 | 6 |
| 1977 | Ahmad Rashad, Minnesota | 51 | 681 | 2 |

#### Scoring

| Player, team | TD | PAT | FG | Pts | Year |
|---|---|---|---|---|---|
| Don Chandler, New York | 0 | 52 | 18 | 106 | 1963 |
| Lenny Moore, Baltimore | 20 | 0 | 0 | 120 | 1964 |
| Gale Sayers, Chicago | 22 | 0 | 0 | 132 | 1965 |
| Bruce Gossett, Los Angeles | 0 | 29 | 28 | 113 | 1966 |
| Jim Bakken, St. Louis | 0 | 36 | 27 | 117 | 1967 |
| Leroy Kelly, Cleveland | 20 | 0 | 0 | 120 | 1968 |
| Fred Cox, Minnesota | 0 | 43 | 26 | 121 | 1969 |
| Fred Cox, Minnesota | 0 | 35 | 30 | 125 | 1970 |
| Curt Knight, Washington | 0 | 27 | 29 | 114 | 1971 |
| Chester Marcol, Green Bay | 0 | 29 | 33 | 128 | 1972 |
| David Ray, Los Angeles | 0 | 40 | 30 | 130 | 1973 |
| Chester Marcol, Green Bay | 0 | 19 | 25 | 94 | 1974 |
| Chuck Foreman, Minnesota | 22 | 0 | 0 | 132 | 1975 |
| Mark Moseley, Washington | 0 | 31 | 22 | 97 | 1976 |
| Walter Payton, Chicago | 16 | 0 | 0 | 96 | 1977 |

#### Rushing

| Year | Player, team | Yds | Atts | TD |
|---|---|---|---|---|
| 1963 | Jimmy Brown, Cleveland | 1,863 | 291 | 12 |
| 1964 | Jimmy Brown, Cleveland | 1,446 | 280 | 7 |
| 1965 | Jimmy Brown, Cleveland | 1,544 | 289 | 17 |
| 1966 | Gale Sayers, Chicago | 1,231 | 229 | 8 |
| 1967 | Leroy Kelly, Cleveland | 1,205 | 235 | 11 |
| 1968 | Leroy Kelly, Cleveland | 1,239 | 248 | 16 |
| 1969 | Gayle Sayers, Chicago | 1,032 | 236 | 8 |
| 1970 | Larry Brown, Washington | 1,125 | 237 | 5 |
| 1971 | John Brockington, Green Bay | 1,105 | 216 | 4 |
| 1972 | Larry Brown, Washington | 1,216 | 285 | 8 |
| 1973 | John Brockington, Green Bay | 1,144 | 265 | 3 |
| 1974 | Larry McCutcheon, Los Angeles | 1,109 | 236 | 3 |
| 1975 | Jim Otis, St. Louis | 1,076 | 269 | 5 |
| 1976 | Walter Payton, Chicago | 1,390 | 311 | 13 |
| 1977 | Walter Payton, Chicago | 1,852 | 339 | 14 |

## American Football Conference Leaders

### (American Football League prior to 1970)

#### Passing

| Player, team | Atts | Com | YG | TD | Year |
|---|---|---|---|---|---|
| Tobin Rote, San Diego | 287 | 170 | 2,510 | 17 | 1963 |
| Len Dawson, Kansas City | 354 | 199 | 2,879 | 18 | 1964 |
| Jack Hadl, San Diego | 348 | 174 | 2,798 | 21 | 1965 |
| Len Dawson, Kansas City | 284 | 159 | 2,527 | 10 | 1966 |
| Daryle Lamonica, Oakland | 425 | 220 | 3,228 | 20 | 1967 |
| Len Dawson, Kansas City | 224 | 131 | 2,109 | 9 | 1968 |
| Greg Cook, Cincinnati | 197 | 106 | 1,845 | 11 | 1969 |
| Daryle Lamonica, Oakland | 356 | 179 | 2,516 | 22 | 1970 |
| Bob Griese, Miami | 263 | 145 | 2,089 | 19 | 1971 |
| Earl Morrall, Miami | 150 | 83 | 1,360 | 11 | 1972 |
| Ken Stabler, Oakland | 260 | 163 | 1,997 | 14 | 1973 |
| Ken Anderson, Cincinnati | 328 | 213 | 2,667 | 18 | 1974 |
| Ken Anderson, Cincinnati | 377 | 228 | 3,169 | 21 | 1975 |
| Ken Stabler, Oakland | 291 | 194 | 2,737 | 27 | 1976 |
| Bob Griese, Miami | 307 | 180 | 2,252 | 22 | 1977 |

#### Pass-Receiving

| Year | Player, team | Ct | YG | TD |
|---|---|---|---|---|
| 1963 | Lionel Taylor, Denver | 78 | 1,101 | 10 |
| 1964 | Charlie Hennigan, Houston | 101 | 1,561 | 8 |
| 1965 | Lionel Taylor, Denver | 85 | 1,131 | 6 |
| 1966 | Lance Alworth, San Diego | 73 | 1,383 | 13 |
| 1967 | George Sauer, N.Y. Jets | 75 | 1,189 | 6 |
| 1968 | Lance Alworth, San Diego | 68 | 1,312 | 10 |
| 1969 | Lance Alworth, San Diego | 64 | 1,003 | 4 |
| 1970 | Marlin Briscoe, Buffalo | 57 | 1,036 | 8 |
| 1971 | Fred Biletnikoff, Oakland | 61 | 929 | 9 |
| 1972 | Fred Biletnikoff, Oakland | 58 | 802 | 7 |
| 1973 | Fred Willis, Houston | 57 | 371 | 1 |
| 1974 | Lydell Mitchell, Baltimore | 72 | 544 | 2 |
| 1975 | Reggie Rucker, Cleveland | 60 | 770 | 3 |
|  | Lydell Mitchell, Baltimore | 60 | 554 | 4 |
| 1976 | MacArthur Lane, Kansas City | 66 | 686 | 1 |
| 1977 | Lydell Mitchell, Baltimore | 71 | 620 | 4 |

#### Scoring

| Player, team | TD | PAT | FG | Pts | Year |
|---|---|---|---|---|---|
| Gino Cappelletti, Boston | 2 | 35 | 22 | 113 | 1963 |
| Gino Cappelletti, Boston | 7 | 36 | 25 | 155 | 1964 |
| Gino Cappelletti, Boston | 9 | 27 | 17 | 132 | 1965 |
| Gino Cappelletti, Boston | 6 | 35 | 16 | 119 | 1966 |
| George Blanda, Oakland | 0 | 56 | 20 | 116 | 1967 |
| Jim Turner, N.Y. Jets | 0 | 43 | 34 | 145 | 1968 |
| Jim Turner, N.Y. Jets | 0 | 33 | 32 | 129 | 1969 |
| Jan Stenerud, Kansas City | 0 | 26 | 30 | 116 | 1970 |
| Garo Yepremian, Miami | 0 | 33 | 28 | 117 | 1971 |
| Bobby Howfield, N.Y. Jets | 0 | 40 | 27 | 121 | 1972 |
| Roy Gerela, Pittsburgh | 0 | 36 | 29 | 123 | 1973 |
| Roy Gerela, Pittsburgh | 0 | 33 | 20 | 93 | 1974 |
| O.J. Simpson, Buffalo | 23 | 0 | 0 | 138 | 1975 |
| Toni Linhart, Baltimore | 0 | 49 | 20 | 109 | 1976 |
| Errol Mann, Oakland | 0 | 39 | 20 | 99 | 1977 |

#### Rushing

| Year | Player, team | Yds | Atts | TD |
|---|---|---|---|---|
| 1963 | Clem Daniels, Oakland | 1,098 | 214 | 3 |
| 1964 | Cookie Gilchrist, Buffalo | 981 | 230 | 6 |
| 1965 | Paul Lowe, San Diego | 1,121 | 222 | 7 |
| 1966 | Jim Nance, Boston | 1,458 | 299 | 11 |
| 1967 | Jim Nance, Boston | 1,216 | 269 | 7 |
| 1968 | Paul Robinson, Cincinnati | 1,023 | 238 | 8 |
| 1969 | Dickie Post, San Diego | 873 | 182 | 6 |
| 1970 | Floyd Little, Denver | 901 | 209 | 3 |
| 1971 | Floyd Little, Denver | 1,133 | 284 | 6 |
| 1972 | O.J. Simpson, Buffalo | 1,251 | 292 | 6 |
| 1973 | O.J. Simpson, Buffalo | 2,003 | 332 | 12 |
| 1974 | Otis Armstrong, Denver | 1,407 | 263 | 9 |
| 1975 | O.J. Simpson, Buffalo | 1,817 | 329 | 16 |
| 1976 | O.J. Simpson, Buffalo | 1,503 | 290 | 8 |
| 1977 | Mark van Eeghen, Oakland | 1,273 | 324 | 7 |

## George Halas Trophy Winners

The Halas Trophy, named after football coach George Halas, is awarded annually to the outstanding defensive player in football in a poll conducted by Murray Olderman of Newspaper Enterprise Assn.

| 1966 | Larry Wilson, St. Louis | 1970 | Dick Butkus, Chicago | 1974 | Joe Greene, Pittsburgh |
|---|---|---|---|---|---|
| 1967 | Deacon Jones, Los Angeles | 1971 | Carl Eller, Minnesota | 1975 | Curley Culp, Houston |
| 1968 | Deacon Jones, Los Angeles | 1972 | Joe Greene, Pittsburgh | 1976 | Jerry Sherk, Cleveland |
| 1969 | Dick Butkus, Chicago | 1973 | Alan Page, Minnesota | 1977 | Harvey Martin, Dallas |

## NEA All-NFL Team in 1977

Chosen by team captains, team representatives, and coaches of the 28 NFL teams in a poll conducted by Newspaper Enterprise Assn.

| First team | Offense | Second team |
|---|---|---|
| Cliff Branch, Oakland | Wide receiver | Harold Jackson, Los Angeles |
| Drew Pearson, Dallas | Wide receiver | Ken Burrough, Houston |
| Dave Casper, Oakland | Tight end | Russ Francis, New England |
| Dan Dierdorf, St. Louis | Tackle | George Kunz, Baltimore |
| Art Shell, Oakland | Tackle | Ron Yary, Minnesota |
| John Hannah, New England | Guard | Gene Upshaw, Oakland |
| Joe DeLameilleure, Buffalo | Guard | Bob Kuechenberg, Miami |
| Jim Langer, Miami | Center | Tom Banks, St. Louis |
| Bob Griese, Miami | Quarterback | Bert Jones, Baltimore |
| Walter Payton, Chicago | Running back | Gregg Pruitt, Cleveland |
| Franco Harris, Pittsburgh | Running back | Chuck Foreman, Minnesota |
| Efren Herrera, Dallas | Placekicker | Errol Mann, Oakland |

| First team | Defense | Second team |
|---|---|---|
| Harvey Martin, Dallas | End | Lyle Alzado, Denver |
| Claude Humphrey, Atlanta | End | Jack Youngblood, Los Angeles |
| Cleveland Elam, San Francisco | Tackle | Curley Culp, Houston |
| Louis Kelcher, San Diego | Tackle | Joe Greene, Pittsburgh |
| Bill Bergey, Philadelphia | Middle linebacker | Randy Gradishar, Denver |
| Jack Ham, Pittsburgh | Linebacker | Isiah Robertson, Los Angeles |
| Robert Brazile, Houston | Linebacker | Ted Hendricks, Oakland |
| Mel Blount, Pittsburgh | Corner back | Rolland Lawrence, Atlanta |
| Roger Wehrli, St. Louis | Corner back | Louis Wright, Denver |
| Ken Houston, Washington | Strong safety | Charlie Waters, Dallas |
| Cliff Harris, Dallas | Free safety | Jack Tatum, Oakland |
| Ray Guy, Oakland | Punter | John James, Atlanta |

## 1978 NFL Player Draft

The following are the first round picks of the National Football League

| Team | Player | Pos. | College | Team | Player | Pos. | College |
|---|---|---|---|---|---|---|---|
| 1—Houston | Earl Campbell | RB | Texas | 15—St. Louis | Steve Little | K | Arkansas |
| 2—Kansas City | Art Still | DE | Kentucky | 16—Cincinnati | Blair Bush | C | Washington |
| 3—New Orleans | Wes Chandler | WR | Florida | 17—Tampa Bay | Doug Williams | QB | Grambling |
| 4—N.Y. Jets | Chris Ward | OT | Ohio State | 18—New England | Bob Cryder | G | Alabama |
| 5—Buffalo | Terry Miller | RB | Oklahoma State | 19—St. Louis | Ken Greene | DB | Washington State |
| 6—Green Bay | James Lofton | WR | Stanford | 20—Los Angeles | Elvis Peacock | RB | Oklahoma |
| 7—San Francisco | Ken MacAfee | TE | Notre Dame | 21—Minnesota | Randy Holloway | DE | Pittsburgh |
| 8—Cincinnati | Ross Browner | DE | Notre Dame | 22—Pittsburgh | Ron Johnson | DB | Eastern Michigan |
| 9—Seattle | Keith Simpson | DB | Memphis State | 23—Cleveland | Ozzie Newsome | WR | Alabama |
| 10—N.Y. Giants | Gordon King | OT | Stanford | 24—San Francisco | Dan Bunz | LB | Long Beach State |
| 11—Detroit | Luther Bradley | DB | Notre Dame | 25—Baltimore | Reese McCall | TE | Auburn |
| 12—Cleveland | Clay Matthews | LB | So. Cal. | 26—Green Bay | John Anderson | LB | Michigan |
| 13—Atlanta | Mike Kenn | OT | Michigan | 27—Denver | Don Latimer | DT | Miami |
| 14—San Diego | John Jefferson | WR | Arizona State | 28—Dallas | Larry Bethea | DE | Michigan State |

## Jim Thorpe Trophy Winners

The winner of the Jim Thorpe Trophy, named after the athletic great, is picked by Murray Olderman of Newspaper Enterprise Assn. in a poll of players from the 28 NFL teams. It goes to the most valuable NFL player and is the oldest and highest professional football award.

| Year | Player, team | Year | Player, team |
|---|---|---|---|
| 1955 | Harlon Hill, Chicago Bears | 1966 | Bart Starr, Green Bay Packers |
| 1956 | Frank Gifford, N.Y. Giants | 1967 | John Unitas, Baltimore Colts |
| 1957 | John Unitas, Baltimore Colts | 1968 | Earl Morrall, Baltimore Colts |
| 1958 | Jim Brown, Cleveland Browns | 1969 | Roman Gabriel, Los Angeles Rams |
| 1959 | Charley Conerly, N.Y. Giants | 1970 | John Brodie, San Francisco 49ers |
| 1960 | Norm Van Brocklin, Philadelphia Eagles | 1971 | Bob Griese, Miami Dolphins |
| 1961 | Y.A. Tittle, N.Y. Giants | 1972 | Larry Brown, Washington Redskins |
| 1962 | Jim Taylor, Green Bay Packers | 1973 | O.J. Simpson, Buffalo Bills |
| 1963 | (tie) Jim Brown, Cleveland Browns, | 1974 | Ken Stabler, Oakland Raiders |
|  | and Y.A. Tittle, N.Y. Giants | 1975 | Fran Tarkenton, Minnesota Vikings |
| 1964 | Lenny Moore, Baltimore Colts | 1976 | Bert Jones, Baltimore Colts |
| 1965 | Jim Brown, Cleveland Browns | 1977 | Walter Payton, Chicago Bears |

## American Football League

| Year | Eastern Division | Western Division | Playoff |
|---|---|---|---|
| 1960 | Houston Oilers (10-4-0) | L. A. Chargers (10-4-0) | Houston 24, Los Angeles 16 |
| 1961 | Houston Oilers (10-3-1) | San Diego Chargers (12-2-0) | Houston 10, San Diego 3 |
| 1962 | Houston Oilers (11-3-0) | Dallas Texans (11-3-0) | Dallas 20, Houston 17(b) |
| 1963 | Boston Patriots (8-6-1)(a) | San Diego Chargers (11-3-0) | San Diego 51, Boston 10 |
| 1964 | Buffalo Bills (12-2-0) | San Diego Chargers (8-5-1) | Buffalo 20, San Diego 7 |
| 1965 | Buffalo Bills (10-3-1) | San Diego Chargers (9-2-3) | Buffalo 23, San Diego 0 |
| 1966 | Buffalo Bills (9-4-1) | Kansas City Chiefs (11-2-1) | Kansas City 31, Buffalo 7 |
| 1967 | Houston Oilers (9-4-1) | Oakland Raiders (13-1-0) | Oakland 40, Houston 7 |
| 1968 | New York Jets (11-3-0) | Oakland Raiders (12-2-0)(a) | New York 27, Oakland 23 |
| 1969 | New York Jets (10-4-0) | Oakland Raiders (12-1-1) | Kansas City 17, Oakland 7(c) |

(a) won divisional playoff (b) won at 2:45 of second overtime. (c) Kansas City defeated Jets to make playoffs.

## Pro Football Hall of Fame

Canton, Ohio

| | | | | |
|---|---|---|---|---|
| Lance Alworth | Turk Edwards | Elroy Hirsch | John (Blood) McNally | Gale Sayers |
| Cliff Battles | Weeb Ewbank | Cal Hubbard | Mike Michalske | Joe Schmidt |
| Sammy Baugh | Tom Fears | Lamar Hunt | Wayne Millner | Bart Starr |
| Chuck Bednarik | Ray Flaherty | Don Hutson | Lenny Moore | Ernie Stautner |
| Bert Bell | Len Ford | Walt Kiesling | Marion Motley | Ken Strong |
| Raymond Berry | Dr. Daniel Fortmann | Frank (Bruiser) Kinard | Bronco Nagurski | Joe Stydahar |
| Charles Bidwell | Bill George | Curly Lambeau | Greasy Neale | Jim Taylor |
| Jim Brown | Frank Gifford | Dick (Night Train) Lane | Ernie Nevers | Jim Thorpe |
| Paul Brown | Otto Graham | Dante Lavelli | Ray Nitschke | Y. A. Tittle |
| Roosevelt Brown | Red Grange | Bobby Layne | Leo Nomellini | George Trafton |
| Tony Canadeo | Forrest Gregg | Tuffy Leemans | Steve Owen | Charlie Trippi |
| Joe Carr | Lou Groza | Vince Lombardi | Clarence (Ace) Parker | Emlen Tunnell |
| Guy Chamberlin | Joe Guyon | Sid Luckman | Jim Parker | Clyde (Bulldog) Turner |
| Jack Christiansen | George Halas | Link Lyman | Joe Perry | Norm Van Brocklin |
| Dutch Clark | Ed Healey | Tim Mara | Pete Pihos | Steve Van Buren |
| George Connor | Mel Hein | Gino Marchetti | Hugh (Shorty) Ray | Bob Waterfield |
| Jim Conzelman | Pete Henry | George Marshall | Dan Reeves | Bill Willis |
| Art Donovan | Arnold Herber | Ollie Matson | Andy Robustelli | Larry Wilson |
| Paddy Driscoll | Bill Hewitt | George McAfee | Art Rooney | Alex Wojciechowicz |
| Bill Dudley | Clarke Hinkle | Hugh McElhenny | | |

## Football Stadiums

See index for major league baseball seating capacity, and college stadiums.

| Name, location | Capacity | Name, location | Capacity |
|---|---|---|---|
| Arrowhead Stadium, Kansas City, Mo. | 78,097 | Los Angeles Memorial Coliseum | 90,000 |
| Atlanta-Fulton County Stadium | 60,489 | Louisiana Superdome, New Orleans | 74,726 |
| Astrodome, Houston, Tex. | 50,000 | Metropolitan Stadium, Bloomington, Minn. | 48,446 |
| Balboa Stadium, San Diego, Cal. | 34,500 | Mile High Stadium, Denver, Col. | 75,100 |
| Baltimore Memorial Stadium | 60,002 | Milwaukee County Stadium | 55,958 |
| Buffalo War Memorial Stadium | 46,206 | Mississippi Memorial Stadium, Jackson | 46,000 |
| Busch Memorial Stadium, St. Louis | 51,392 | Oakland-Alameda County Coliseum | 54,615 |
| Candlestick Park, San Francisco, Cal. | 61,115 | Orange Bowl, Miami, Fla. | 80,045 |
| Cleveland Stadium | 80,233 | Pontiac Silverdome, Mich. | 80,638 |
| Columbus (Ga.) Memorial Stadium | 35,000 | Rich Stadium, Buffalo, N.Y. | 80,020 |
| Cotton Bowl, Dallas, Tex. | 72,000 | Riverfront Stadium, Cincinnati, Oh. | 56,200 |
| Exhibition Stadium, Toronto, Ontario | 39,485 | Rose Bowl, Pasadena, Cal. | 106,721 |
| Franklin Field, Philadelphia, Pa. | 60,658 | Rubber Bowl, Akron, Oh. | 35,007 |
| Gator Bowl, Jacksonville, Fla. | 70,000 | San Diego Stadium | 52,568 |
| Giants Stadium, E. Rutherford, N.J. | 76,500 | Schaefer Stadium, Foxboro, Mass. | 61,279 |
| John F. Kennedy Stadium, Philadelphia, Pa. | 105,000 | Shea Stadium, New York, N.Y. | 60,000 |
| Robert F. Kennedy Memorial Stadium, Wash., D.C. | 55,004 | Soldier Field, Chicago, Ill. | 57,359 |
| Kezar Stadium, San Francisco, Cal. | 59,636 | Sugar Bowl, New Orleans, La. | 80,982 |
| Kingdome, Seattle, Wash. | 64,752 | Tampa Stadium, Tampa, Fla. | 71,600 |
| Ladd Memorial Stadium, Mobile, Ala. | 40,605 | Texas Stadium, Dallas, Tex. | 65,101 |
| Lambeau Field, Green Bay, Wis. | 56,267 | Three Rivers Stadium, Pittsburgh, Pa. | 50,350 |
| Legion Field, Birmingham, Ala. | 72,000 | Veterans Stadium, Philadelphia, Pa. | 66,052 |
| Liberty Bowl, Memphis, Tenn. | 50,164 | | |

## Canadian Football League

1977 Final Standings

| Eastern Conference | W | L | T | PF | PA | Pts | Western Conference | W | L | T | PF | PA | Pts |
|---|---|---|---|---|---|---|---|---|---|---|---|---|---|
| Montreal | 11 | 5 | 0 | 311 | 245 | 22 | *Edmonton | 10 | 6 | 0 | 412 | 320 | 20 |
| Ottawa | 8 | 8 | 0 | 368 | 344 | 16 | British Columbia | 10 | 6 | 0 | 369 | 326 | 20 |
| Toronto | 6 | 10 | 0 | 251 | 266 | 12 | Winnipeg | 10 | 6 | 0 | 382 | 336 | 20 |
| Hamilton | 5 | 11 | 0 | 283 | 394 | 10 | Saskatchewan | 8 | 8 | 0 | 330 | 389 | 16 |
| | | | | | | | Calgary | 4 | 12 | 0 | 241 | 327 | 8 |

*Placed first with better record in games against British Columbia and Winnipeg.

**East semifinal**—Ottawa 21, Toronto 16     **West final**—Edmonton 38, British Columbia 1
**West semifinal**—British Columbia 33, Winnipeg 32     **Championship (Grey Cup)**—Montreal 41, Edmonton 6
**East final**—Montreal 21, Ottawa 18

## Canadian Football League (Grey Cup)

Winners of Eastern and Western divisions meet in championship game for Grey Cup (donated by Governor-General Earl Grey in 1909). Canadian football features 3 downs, 110-yard field, and each team can have 12 players on field at one time.

| | | | |
|---|---|---|---|
| 1948 | Calgary Stampeders 12, Ottawa Rough Riders 7 | 1963 | Hamilton Tiger-Cats 21, British Columbia Lions 10 |
| 1949 | Montreal Alouettes 28, Calgary Stampeders 15 | 1964 | British Columbia Lions 34, Hamilton Tiger-Cats 24 |
| 1950 | Toronto Argonauts 13, Winnipeg Blue Bombers 0 | 1965 | Hamilton Tiger-Cats 22, Winnipeg Blue Bombers 16 |
| 1951 | Ottawa Rough Riders 21, Saskatchewan Roughriders 14 | 1966 | Saskatchewan Roughriders 29, Ottawa Rough Riders 14 |
| 1952 | Toronto Argonauts 21, Edmonton Eskimos 11 | 1967 | Hamilton Tiger-Cats 24, Saskatchewan Roughriders 1 |
| 1953 | Hamilton Tiger-Cats 12, Winnipeg Blue Bombers 6 | 1968 | Ottawa Rough Riders 24, Calgary Stampeders 21 |
| 1954 | Edmonton Eskimos 26, Montreal Alouettes 25 | 1969 | Ottawa Rough Riders 29, Saskatchewan Roughriders 11 |
| 1955 | Edmonton Eskimos 34, Montreal Alouettes 19 | 1970 | Montreal Alouettes 23, Calgary Stampeders 10 |
| 1956 | Edmonton Eskimos 50, Montreal Alouettes 27 | 1971 | Calgary Stampeders 14, Toronto Argonauts 11 |
| 1957 | Hamilton Tiger-Cats 32, Winnipeg Blue Bombers 7 | 1972 | Hamilton Tiger-Cats 13, Saskatchewan Roughriders 10 |
| 1958 | Winnipeg Blue Bombers 35, Hamilton Tiger-Cats 28 | 1973 | Ottawa Rough Riders 22, Edmonton Eskimos 18 |
| 1959 | Winnipeg Blue Bombers 21, Hamilton Tiger-Cats 7 | 1974 | Montreal Alouettes 20, Edmonton Eskimos 7 |
| 1960 | Ottawa Rough Riders 16, Edmonton Eskimos 6 | 1975 | Edmonton Eskimos 9, Montreal Alouettes 8 |
| 1961 | Winnipeg Blue Bombers 21, Hamilton Tiger-Cats 14 | 1976 | Ottawa Rough Riders 23, Saskatchewan Roughriders 20 |
| 1962 | Winnipeg Blue Bombers 28, Hamilton Tiger-Cats 27 | 1977 | Montreal Alouettes 41, Edmonton Eskimos 6 |

# All-Time Pro Football Records

## NFL, AFL, and All-American Football Conference

(as of Sept. 1, 1978)

### Leading Lifetime Rushers

| Player | League | Yrs | Att | Yards | Avg | Player | League | Yrs | Att | Yards | Avg |
|---|---|---|---|---|---|---|---|---|---|---|---|
| Jim Brown | NFL | 9 | 2,359 | 12,312 | 5.2 | Ken Willard | NFL | 10 | 1,622 | 6,105 | 3.8 |
| O.J. Simpson | AFL-NFL | 9 | 2,123 | 10,183 | 4.8 | Larry Brown | NFL | 8 | 1,530 | 5,875 | 3.8 |
| Joe Perry | AAFC-NFL | 16 | 1,929 | 9,723 | 5.0 | Steve Van Buren | NFL | 8 | 1,320 | 5,860 | 4.3 |
| Jim Taylor | NFL | 10 | 1,941 | 8,597 | 4.4 | Bill Brown | NFL | 14 | 1,649 | 5,838 | 3.4 |
| Leroy Kelly | NFL | 10 | 1,727 | 7,274 | 4.2 | Rick Casares | NFL-AFL | 12 | 1,431 | 5,797 | 4.1 |
| Larry Csonka | AFL-NFL | 9 | 1,580 | 6,933 | 4.4 | Calvin Hill | NFL | 8 | 1,314 | 5,567 | 4.2 |
| John Henry Johnson | NFL-AFL | 13 | 1,571 | 6,803 | 4.3 | Lawrence McCutcheon | NFL | 6 | 1,244 | 5,523 | 4.4 |
| Floyd Little | AFL-NFL | 9 | 1,641 | 6,323 | 3.8 | Lydell Mitchell | NFL | 6 | 1,391 | 5,487 | 3.9 |
| Franco Harris | NFL | 6 | 1,435 | 6,295 | 4.4 | Mike Garrett | AFL-NFL | 9 | 1,308 | 5,481 | 4.2 |
| Don Perkins | NFL | 8 | 1,500 | 6,217 | 4.1 | Dick Bass | NFL | 10 | 1,218 | 5,417 | 4.4 |

**Most Yards Gained, Season** — 2,003, O.J. Simpson, Buffalo Bills, 1973.
**Most Yards Gained, Game** — 275, Walter Payton, Chicago Bears vs. Minnesota Vikings, Nov. 20, 1977.
**Most Games, 100 Yards or more, Season** — 11, O.J. Simpson, Buffalo Bills, 1973.
**Most Games, 100 Yards or more, Career** — 58, Jim Brown, Cleveland Browns, 1957-1965.
**Most Games, 200 Yards or more, Career** — 6, O.J. Simpson, Buffalo Bills, 1969-1977.
**Most Touchdowns Rushing,, Career** — 106, Jim Brown, Cleveland Browns, 1957-1965.
**Most Touchdowns Rushing, Season** — 19, Jim Taylor, Green Bay Packers, 1962.
**Most Touchdowns Rushing, Game** — 6, Ernie Nevers, Chicago Cardinals vs. Chicago Bears, Nov. 8, 1929.
**Most Rushing Attempts, Season** — 339, Walter Payton, Chicago Bears, 1977.
**Most Rushing Attempts, Game** — 41, Franco Harris, Pittsburgh vs. Cincinnati, Oct. 17, 1976.
**Longest run from Scrimmage** — 97 yds., Andy Uram, Green Bay vs. Chicago Cardinals, Oct. 8, 1939; Bob Gage, Pittsburgh vs. Chicago Bears, Dec. 4, 1949. (Both scored touchdown)

### Leading Lifetime Passers

(Minimum 1,500 attempts)

| Player | League | Yrs | Att | Comp | Yds | Pts* | Player | League | Yrs | Att | Comp | Yds | Pts* |
|---|---|---|---|---|---|---|---|---|---|---|---|---|---|
| Otto Graham | AAFC-NFL | 10 | 2,626 | 1,464 | 23,584 | 86.8 | Bob Griese | AFL-NFL | 11 | 2,784 | 1,541 | 20,351 | 76.8 |
| Ken Stabler | AFL-NFL | 8 | 1,577 | 945 | 12,519 | 83.6 | Norm Van Brocklin | NFL | 12 | 2,895 | 1,553 | 23,611 | 75.3 |
| Sonny Jurgensen | NFL | 18 | 4,262 | 2,433 | 32,224 | 82.8 | Sid Luckman | NFL | 12 | 1,744 | 904 | 14,686 | 75.0 |
| Len Dawson | NFL-AFL | 19 | 3,741 | 2,136 | 28,711 | 82.6 | Don Meredith | NFL | 9 | 2,308 | 1,170 | 17,199 | 74.7 |
| Ken Anderson | NFL | 7 | 2,127 | 1,208 | 15,471 | 82.1 | Roman Gabriel | NFL | 15 | 4,495 | 2,365 | 29,429 | 74.5 |
| Fran Tarkenton | NFL | 17 | 5,895 | 3,341 | 43,535 | 81.5 | Y.A. Tittle | AAFC-NFL | 17 | 4,395 | 2,427 | 33,070 | 74.4 |
| Roger Staubach | NFL | 9 | 2,084 | 1,187 | 15,924 | 81.2 | Earl Morrall | NFL | 21 | 2,689 | 1,379 | 20,809 | 74.2 |
| Bart Starr | NFL | 16 | 3,149 | 1,808 | 24,718 | 80.3 | Frank Albert | AAFC-NFL | 7 | 1,564 | 831 | 10,795 | 73.5 |
| Johnny Unitas | NFL | 18 | 5,186 | 2,830 | 40,239 | 78.2 | Greg Landry | NFL | 10 | 1,670 | 909 | 11,999 | 73.1 |
| Frank Ryan | NFL | 13 | 2,133 | 1,090 | 16,042 | 77.7 | Daryle Lamonica | AFL-NFL | 12 | 2,601 | 1,288 | 19,154 | 72.9 |

*Rating points based on performances in the following categories: Percentage of completions, percentage of touchdown passes, percentage of interceptions, and average gain per pass attempt.

**Most Yards Gained, Season** — 4,007, Joe Namath, New York Jets, 1967.
**Most Yards Gained, Game** — 554, Norm Van Brocklin, Los Angeles Rams vs. New York Yankees, Sept. 18, 1951 (27 completions in 41 attempts).
**Most Touchdowns Passing, Career** — 317, Fran Tarkenton, Minnesota Vikings, 1961-65; N.Y. Giants, 1967-71; Minnesota Vikings, 1972-77.
**Most Touchdown Passing, Season** — 36, George Blanda, Houston Oilers, 1961 and Y.A. Tittle, N.Y. Giants, 1963.
**Most Touchdown Passing, Game** — 7, Sid Luckman, Chicago Bears vs. New York Giants, Nov. 14, 1943; Adrian Burk, Philadelphia Eagles vs. Washington Redskins, Oct. 17, 1954; George Blanda, Houston Oilers vs. New York Titans, Nov. 19, 1961; Y.A. Tittle, New York Giants vs. Washington Redskins, Oct. 28, 1962; Joe Kapp, Minnesota Vikings vs. Baltimore Colts, Sept. 28, 1969.
**Most Passing Attempts, Season** — 508, Sonny Jurgensen, Washington Redskins, 1967 (288 completions).
**Most Passing Attempts, Game** — 68, George Blanda, Houston Oilers vs. Buffalo Bills, Nov. 1, 1964 (37 completions).
**Most Passes Completed, Season** — 288, Sonny Jurgensen, Washington Redskins, 1967 (508 attempts).
**Most Passes Completed, Game** — 37, George Blanda, Houston Oilers vs. Buffalo Bills, Nov. 1, 1964 (68 attempts).
**Most Consecutive Passes Completed** — 17, Bert Jones, Baltimore Colts vs. N.Y. Jets, Dec. 15, 1974.

### Leading Lifetime Receivers

| Player | League | Yrs | No | Yds | Avg | Player | League | Yrs | No | Yds | Avg |
|---|---|---|---|---|---|---|---|---|---|---|---|
| Charley Taylor | NFL | 13 | 649 | 9,110 | 14.0 | Jackie Smith | NFL | 15 | 480 | 7,918 | 16.5 |
| Don Maynard | AFL-NFL | 15 | 633 | 11,834 | 18.7 | Art Powell | AFL-NFL | 10 | 479 | 8,046 | 16.8 |
| Ray Berry | NFL | 13 | 631 | 9,275 | 14.7 | Boyd Dowler | NFL | 12 | 474 | 7,270 | 15.4 |
| Fred Biletnikoff | AFL-NFL | 13 | 569 | 8,689 | 15.3 | Pete Retzlaff | NFL | 11 | 452 | 7,412 | 16.4 |
| Lionel Taylor | AFL | 10 | 567 | 7,195 | 12.7 | Roy Jefferson | NFL | 12 | 451 | 7,539 | 16.7 |
| Lance Alworth | AFL-NFL | 11 | 542 | 10,266 | 18.9 | Carroll Dale | NFL | 14 | 438 | 8,271 | 18.9 |
| Bobby Mitchell | NFL | 11 | 521 | 7,954 | 15.3 | Paul Warfield | NFL | 13 | 427 | 8,565 | 20.1 |
| Billy Howton | NFL | 12 | 503 | 8,459 | 16.8 | Mike Ditka | NFL | 12 | 427 | 5,812 | 13.6 |
| Tommy McDonald | NFL | 12 | 495 | 8,410 | 17.0 | Bobby Joe Conrad | NFL | 12 | 422 | 5,902 | 14.0 |
| Don Hutson | NFL | 11 | 488 | 7,991 | 16.4 | Jerry Smith | NFL | 12 | 420 | 5,490 | 13.1 |

**Most Yards Gained, Season** — 1,746, Charley Hennigan, Houston Oilers, 1961.
**Most Yards Gained, Game** — 303, Jim Benton, Cleveland Rams vs. Detroit Lions, Nov. 22, 1945 (10 receptions).
**Most Pass Receptions, Season** — 101, Charley Hennigan, Houston Oilers, 1964.
**Most Pass Receptions, Game** — 18, Tom Fears, Los Angeles Rams vs. Green Bay Packers, Dec. 3, 1950 (189 yards).
**Most Consecutive Games, Pass Receptions** — 105, Dan Abramowicz, New Orleans Saints, 1967-1973; San Francisco 49ers, 1973-1974.
**Most Touchdown Passes, Career** — 99, Don Hutson, Green Bay Packers, 1935-1945.
**Most Touchdown Passes, Season** — 17, Don Hutson, Green Bay Packers, 1942; Elroy Hirsch, Los Angeles Rams, 1951; Bill Groman, Houston Oilers, 1961.
**Most Touchdown Passes, Game** — 5, Bob Shaw, Chicago Cardinals vs. Baltimore Colts, Oct. 2, 1950.
**Most Consecutive Games, Touchdown Passes** — 11, Elroy Hirsch, Los Angeles Rams, 1950-1951; Buddy Dial, Pittsburgh, 1959-1960.

## Leading Lifetime Scorers

| Player | League | Yrs | TD | PAT | FG | Total | Player | League | Yrs | TD | PAT | FG | Total |
|---|---|---|---|---|---|---|---|---|---|---|---|---|---|
| George Blanda | NFL-AFL | 26 | 9 | 943 | 335 | 2,002 | Bobby Walston | NFL | 12 | 46 | 365 | 80 | 881 |
| Lou Groza | AAFC-NFL | 21 | 1 | 810 | 264 | 1,608 | Pete Gogolak | AFL-NFL | 10 | 0 | 344 | 173 | 863 |
| Fred Cox | NFL | 15 | 0 | 519 | 282 | 1,365 | Don Hutson | NFL | 11 | 105 | 172 | 7 | 823 |
| Jim Bakken | NFL | 16 | 0 | 507 | 271 | 1,320 | Roy Gerela | AFL-NFL | 9 | 0 | 301 | 171 | 814 |
| Jim Turner | AFL-NFL | 14 | 1 | 458 | 280 | 1,304 | Garo Yepremian | AFL-NFL | 10 | 0 | 327 | 161 | 810 |
| Gino Cappelletti | AFL | 11 | 42 | 350 | 176 | 1,130 | Don Cockroft | NFL | 10 | 0 | 318 | 164 | 810 |
| Jan Stenerud | AFL-NFL | 11 | 0 | 341 | 247 | 1,082 | Errol Mann | NFL | 10 | 0 | 282 | 165 | 777 |
| Bruce Gossett | NFL | 11 | 0 | 374 | 219 | 1,031 | Paul Hornung | NFL | 9 | 62 | 190 | 66 | 760 |
| Sam Baker | NFL | 15 | 2 | 428 | 179 | 977 | Jim Brown | NFL | 9 | 126 | 0 | 0 | 756 |
| Lou Michaels | NFL | 13 | 1 | 386 | 187 | 955* | Tom Davis | NFL | 11 | 0 | 348 | 130 | 738 |

*Includes safety.

**Most Points, Season** — 176, Paul Hornung, Green Bay Packers, 1960 (15 TD's, 41 PAT's, 15 FG's).
**Most Points, Game** — 40, Ernie Nevers, Chicago Cardinals vs. Chicago Bears, Nov. 28, 1929 (6 TD's, 4 PAT's).
**Most Touchdowns, Season** — 23, O.J. Simpson, Buffalo Bills, 1975 (16 rushing, 9 pass receptions).
**Most Touchdowns, Game** — 6, Ernie Nevers, Chicago Cardinals vs. Chicago Bears, Nov. 28, 1929 (6 rushing); Dub Jones, Cleveland Browns vs. Chicago Bears, Nov. 25, 1951 (4 rushing, 2 pass receptions); Gale Sayers, Chicago Bears vs. San Francisco 49ers, Dec. 12, 1965 (4 rushing, 1 pass reception, 1 punt return).
**Most Points After Touchdown, Season** — 64, George Blanda, Houston Oilers, 1961 (65 attempts).
**Most Consecutive Points After Touchdown** — 234, Tommy Davis, San Francisco 49ers, 1959-1965.
**Most Field Goals, Game** — 7, Jim Bakken, St. Louis Cardinals vs. Pittsburgh Steelers, Sept. 24, 1967.
**Most Field Goals, Season** — 34, Jim Turner, New York Jets, 1968 and 1969.
**Most Field Goals Attempted, Season** — 49, Bruce Gossett, Los Angeles Rams, 1966; Curt Knight, Washington Redskins, 1971.
**Most Field Goals Attempted, Game** — 9, Jim Bakken, St. Louis Cardinals vs. Pittsburgh Steelers, Sept. 24, 1967 (7 successful).
**Most Consecutive Field Goals** — 16, Jan Stenerud, Kansas City Chiefs, 1969; Don Cockroft, Cleveland Browns, 1974-75.
**Most Consecutive Games, Field Goal** — 31, Fred Cox, Minnesota Vikings, 1968-1970.
**Longest Field Goal** — 63 yds., Tom Dempsey, New Orleans Saints vs. Detroit Lions, Nov. 8, 1970.
**Highest Field Goal Completion Percentage, Season (20 attempts)** — 88.5, Lou Groza, Cleveland Browns, 1953 (23 FG's in 26 attempts).

## Pass Interceptions

**Most Passes Had Intercepted, Game** — 8, Jim Hardy, Chicago Cardinals vs. Philadelphia Eagles, Sept. 24, 1950 (39 attempts).
**Most Passes Had Intercepted, Season** — 42, George Blanda, Houston Oilers, 1962 (418 attempts).
**Most Passes Had Intercepted, Career** — 277, George Blanda, Chicago Bears, 1949-1958; Houston Oilers, 1960-1966; Oakland Raiders, 1967-1975 (4,000 attempts).
**Most Consecutive Passes Attempted Without Interception** — 294, Bart Starr, Green Bay Packers, 1964-1965.
**Most Interceptions By, Season** — 14, Dick Lane, Los Angeles Rams, 1952.
**Most Interceptions By, Career** — 79, Emlen Tunnell, New York Giants, 1948-1958; Green Bay Packers, 1959-1961.
**Most Consecutive Games, Passes Intercepted By** — 8, Tom Morrow, Oakland Raiders, 1962 (4), 1963 (4).
**Most Touchdowns Scored via Pass Interceptions, Lifetime** — 9, Ken Houston, Houston Oilers, 1967 (2); 1968 (2); 1969; 71 (4).

## Punting

**Highest Punting Average, Career (300 punts)** — 45.10, Sam Baugh, Washington Redskins, 1937-1952 (338 punts).
**Highest Punting Average, Season (20 punts)** — 51.3, Sam Baugh, Washington Redskins, 1940 (35 punts).
**Highest Punting Average, Game (4 punts)** — 59.4, Sam Baugh, Washington Redskins vs. Detroit Lions, Oct. 27, 1940 (5 punts).
**Longest Punt** — 98 yds., Steve O'Neal, New York Jets vs. Denver Broncos, Sept. 21, 1969.

## Kickoff Returns

**Most Yardage Returning Kickoffs, Career** — 6,922, Ron Smith, Chicago Bears, 1965; Atlanta Falcons, 1966-67; Los Angeles Rams, 1968-69; Chicago Bears, 1970-72; San Diego Chargers, 1973; Oakland Raiders, 1974.
**Most Yardage Returning Kickoffs, Season** — 1,317, Bobby Jancik, Houston Oilers, 1963.
**Most Yardage Returning Kickoffs, Game** — 294, Wally Triplett, Detroit Lions vs. Los Angeles Rams, Oct. 29, 1950 (4 returns).
**Most Touchdowns Scored via Kickoff Returns, Career** — 6, Ollie Matson, Chicago Cardinals, 1952 (2), 1954, 1956, 1958 (2); Gale Sayers, Chicago Bears, 1965, 1966 (2), 1967 (3); Travis Williams, Green Bay Packers, 1967 (4), 1969; Los Angeles Rams, 1971.
**Most Touchdowns Scored via Kickoff Returns, Season** — 4, Travis Williams, Green Bay Packers, 1967; Cecil Turner, Chicago Bears, 1970.
**Most Touchdowns Scored via Kickoff Returns, Game** — 2, Tim Brown, Philadelphia Eagles vs. Dallas Cowboys, Nov. 6, 1966; Travis Williams, Green Bay Packers vs. Cleveland Browns, Nov. 12, 1967.
**Most Kickoff Returns, Career** — 275, Ron Smith, Chicago Bears, 1965; Atlanta Falcons, 1966-67; Los Angeles Rams, 1968-69; Chicago Bears, 1970-72; San Diego Chargers, 1973; Oakland Raiders, 1974.
**Most Kickoff Returns, Season** — 47, Odell Barry, Denver Broncos, 1964; Larry Jones, Washington Redskins, 1975.
**Longest Kickoff Return** — 106 yds., Al Carmichael, Green Bay Packers vs. Chicago Bears, October 7, 1956 (scored touchdown); Noland Smith, Kansas City vs. Denver, Dec. 17, 1967 (scored touchdown).

## Punt Returns

**Most Yardage Returning Punts, Career** — 2,209, Emlen Tunnell, New York Giants, 1948-1958; Green Bay Packers, 1959-1961.
**Most Yardage Returning Punts, Season** — 655, Neal Colzie, Oakland Raiders, 1975.
**Most Yardage Returning Punts, Game** — 205, George Atkinson, Oakland Raiders vs. Buffalo Bills, Sept. 15, 1968.
**Most Touchdowns Scored via Punt Returns, Career** — 8, Jack Christiansen, Detroit Lions, 1951 (4), 1952 (2), 1954, 1956.
**Most Punt Returns, Career** — 258, Emlen Tunnell, New York Giants, 1948-1958; Green Bay Packers, 1959-1961.
**Most Punt Returns, Season** — 57, Eddie Brown, Washington Redskins, 1977.
**Longest Punt Return** — 98, Gil LeFebvre, Cincinnati Reds vs. Brooklyn Dodgers, Dec. 3, 1933 (scored touchdown); Charles West, Minnesota Vikings vs. Washington Redskins, Nov. 3, 1968 (scored touchdown).

## Miscellaneous Records

**Most Fumbles, Season** — 17, Dan Pastorini, Houston Oilers, 1973.
**Most Fumbles, Game** — 7, Len Dawson, Kansas City Chiefs vs. San Diego Chargers, Nov. 15, 1964.
**Longest Run with Recovered Fumble** — 104 yds., Jack Tatum, Oakland Raiders vs. Green Bay Packers, Sept. 24, 1972.
**Longest Winning Streak (regular season)** — 17 games, Chicago Bears, 1933-1934.
**Longest Undefeated Streak (includes tie games)** — 29 games, Cleveland Browns, 1947-1949 (won 27, tied 2).
**Most Seasons, Active Player** — 26, George Blanda, Chicago Bears, 1949-1958; Houston Oilers, 1960-1966 and Oakland, 67-75.

## NFL Attendance

The National Football League drew 11,018,632 fans for the 196 regular season games in 1977, a decrease of 51,911 from the previous year.

# Contract Bridge Championships in 1977-78

Source: American Contract Bridge League, Memphis, Tenn.

## Fall Championships

Atlanta, Ga., Nov. 18-27, 1977; attendance, 10,702 tables.

**Open Teams (Board-A-Match) (Reisinger Trophy)** — Alan Greenberg, James Cayne, New York City; Kyle Larsen, Walnut Creek, Cal.; Jim Jacoby, Dallas; Michael Lawrence, Berkeley, Cal.

**Blue Ribbon Pairs** — Thomas Sanders, Nashville; Lou Bluhm, Atlanta.

**Life Master Men's Pairs** — David Schroeder, Atlanta; David Hoffner, Knoxville, Tenn.

**Life Master Women's Pairs** — Edith Kemp, Miami Beach; Barbara Rappaport, New York City.

**Mixed Pairs** — Nancy Gruver, Ellicott City, Md.; Joel Friedberg, New York City.

**Most Master Points for the Tournament** — John Mohan, Leucadia, Cal.

## Spring Championships

Houston, Tex., March 10-19, 1978; attendance, 9,388 tables.

**Open Teams (Vanderbilt Trophy)** — Malcolm Brachman, Bobby Goldman, Mike Passell, Dallas; Eddie Kantar, Billy Eisenberg, Paul Soloway, Los Angeles.

**Men's Teams** — Steve Robinson, Kit Woolsey, Arlington, Va.; John Schermer, Neil Chambers, Seattle; Peter Nagy, Eric Kokish, Montreal.

**Women's Knockout Teams** — Nancy Gruver, Ellicott City, Md.; Carol Sanders, Nashville; Betty Kennedy, Shreveport, La.; Evelyn Levitt, Wilmington, Del.; Nancy Alpaugh, New Orleans;

Kerry Shuman, Los Angeles.

**Men's Pairs** — Larry Kozlove, Louisville; John Sheridan, Indianapolis.

**Women's Pairs** — Flo Rotman, Skokie, Ill.; Babs Charney, Milwaukee.

**Open Pairs** — Mike Passell, Dallas; Robert Levin, Miami.

**Most Master Points for the Tournament** — Mike Passell, Dallas.

## Summer Championships

Toronto, Ont., July 21-31, 1978; attendance, 18,408 tables.

**Masters Teams (Spingold Trophy)** — Malcolm Brachman, Mike Passell, Bobby Goldman, Dallas; Paul Soloway, Eddie Kantar, Los Angeles.

**Grand National Teams (Morehead Trophy)** — Dan Rotman, Skokie, Ill.; Gerald Caravelli, Des Plaines, Ill.; William Rosen, Highland Park, Ill.; Charles Peres, Chicago; Milton Rosenberg, Lombard, Ill. (Zone V.)

**Master Mixed Teams** — Sidney Lazard, Nancy Alpaugh, New Orleans; Mark Lair, Canyon, Tex.; Joan Dewitt, Chicago.

**Life Master Pairs** — Marilyn Johnson, Houston; Mary Jane Farell, Beverly Hills, Cal.

**Most Master Points for Tournament** — Mike Passell, Dallas.

## World Bridge Federation Pair Olympiad

New Orleans, La., June 17-30, 1978

**Open Pairs** — Brazil, Marcelo Branco and Gabino Cintra.

**Women's Pairs** — U.S., Katherine Wei and Judi Radin, New York City.

**Mixed Pairs** — U.S., Barry Crane and Kerri Shuman, Los Angeles.

**Venice Cup (Women's World Team Championship)** — Jacqui Mitchell, Gail Moss, Dorothy Hayden Truscott, New York

City; Emma Jean Hawes, Ft. Worth; Mary Jane Farell, Beverly Hills, Cal.; Marilyn Johnson, Houston; Ruth McConnell, Columbia City, Ind., non-playing captain.

**Open Teams (Rosenblum Trophy)** — Poland; Marian Frenkiel, Andrzej Macieszczak, Andrzej Wilkosz, Janusz Polec.

**Solomon Trophy (Nation with best overall performance)** — U.S.

# Power Boat Racing Champions

## APBA Gold Cup Race

| Year | Boat | Owner | Driver | Winner's fastest heat MPH | Site |
|------|------|-------|--------|---------------------------|------|
| 1965 | Miss Bardahl | Ole Bardahl | Ron Musson | 110.655 | Seattle, Wash. |
| 1966 | Tahoe Miss | Harrah's | Mira Slovak | 97.861 | Detroit, Mich. |
| 1967 | Miss Bardahl | Ole Bardahl | Bill Schumacher | 104.691 | Seattle, Wash. |
| 1968 | Miss Bardahl | Ole Bardahl | Bill Schumacher | 111.248 | Detroit, Mich. |
| 1969 | Miss Budweiser | Bernard Little & Tom Friedkin | Bill Sterett | 103.587 | San Diego, Cal. |
| 1970 | Miss Budweiser | Hydroplanes, Inc. | Dean Chenoweth | 101.848 | San Diego, Cal. |
| 1971 | Miss Madison | Miss Madison, Inc. | Jim McCormick | 101.522 | Madison, Ind. |
| 1972 | Atlas Van Lines | Atlas Van Lines | Bill Muncey | 103.547 | Detroit, Mich. |
| 1973 | Miss Budweiser | Hydroplanes, Inc. | Dean Chenoweth | 104.046 | Tri-Cities, Wash. |
| 1974 | Pay'N Pak | David J. Heerensperger | George Henley | 112.056 | Seattle, Wash. |
| 1975 | Pay 'N Pak | David J. Heerensperger | George Henley | 113.350 | Tri-Cities, Wash. |
| 1976 | Miss U.S. | U.S. Racing Team, Inc. | Tom D'Eath | 108.021 | Detroit, Mich. |
| 1977 | Atlas Van Lines | Bill Muncey Industries, Inc. | Bill Muncey | 114.869 | Tri-Cities, Wash. |
| 1978 | Atlas Van Lines | Bill Muncey Industries, Inc. | Bill Muncey | 104.448 | Owensboro, Ky. |

# World Bobsled Championships in 1978

The Swiss team of Erich Scharer and Josef Benz won the world 2-man bobsled championship at Lake Placid, N.Y. on Feb. 5, 1978. The combined time for the 2 runs was 4 minutes, 22.89 seconds. The East German team finished second.

The East German team of Horst Schonau, Harold Seifert, Horst Bernhard, and Bogdan Musiol won the world 4-man championship on Feb. 12. Their combined time was 4 minutes, 17.50 seconds. The Swiss team finished second.

# American Bowling Congress Championships in 1978

75th Tournament, St. Louis, Mo.

## Regular Division

### Individual

1. Rich Mersek, Cleveland, Oh. 239, 256, 244 — 739.
2. Russell Goodrich, Pontiac, Mich. 216, 248, 267 — 731.
3. Fran Eighme, Waterloo, Ia. 231, 254, 244 — 729.

Runners-up — Mike Cirrincione, Indanapolis, Ind. 726; Earl Gray Jr., Decatur, Ill. 725; Kevin Krout, Seattle, Wash. 720; Ralph Quay, Toledo, Oh. 718; Bill Stewart, Litchfield, Ill. 718; Loren Kaiser, Albert Lea, Minn. 717; Jerry Ward, Cleveland, Oh. 714.

### All Events

1. Chris Cobus, Milwaukee, Wis. 646, 663, 685 — 1,994.
2. Gary Bower, Mechanicsburg, Pa. 580, 686, 707 — 1,973.
3. John (Ted) Carter, Tavernier, Fla. 666, 649, 649 — 1,964.

Runners-up — Jim Ewald, Louisville, Ky. 1,956; Darwin Skrzynicki, Chicago, Ill. 1,956; Rick Davis, Kent, Oh. 1,944; Gary Mills, Lincoln, Neb. 1,943; Charlie Hart, Dexter, Mo. 1,935; Terry Kulibert, Oshkosh, Wis. 1,931; Tony Eder, N. Vernon, Ind. 1,925; Duane Carlson, Minneapolis, Minn. 1,925.

### Doubles

1. Bob Kulaszewicz, Milwaukee, Wis. 203, 184, 257 — 644; Don Gazzana, Milwaukee, Wis. 214, 237, 257 — 708. Aggregate — 1,352.
2. Dan Anthony, Dayton, Oh. 217, 226, 205 —648; Ed Hounshell, Dayton, Oh. 211, 199, 266 — 676. Aggregate — 1,324.
3. Pat Quinn, Ft. Wayne, Ind. 191, 235, 237 — 663; Herb Mulmahn, Ft. Wayne, Ind. 245, 191, 220 — 656. Aggregate — 1,319.

### Team

1. Berlin's Pro Shop, Muscatine, Ia. — Tim Taylor 213, 207, 227 — 647; Dave Capshaw 207, 265, 290 — 762; Harold Hetzler Jr. 215, 180, 169 — 564; Larry Roberson 194, 190, 182 — 566; Butch Ballenger 175, 203, 160 — 538. Aggregate — 3,077.
2. Micky (Sic) Mouse Tavern, Beloit, Wis. — Wayne LaVelle 255, 212, 178 — 645; Jim Redler 171, 204, 220 — 595; Dave Pollentier 206, 256, 198 —660; Mike Truitt 180, 203, 193 — 576; Larry Hesker 188, 204, 204 — 596. Aggregate — 3,072.

## Classic Division

### Individual

1. Bill Beach, Sharon, Pa. 245, 237, 219 — 701.
2. Willie Wells, St. Louis, Mo. 193, 258, 247 — 698.
3. Skip Tucker, Tampa, Fla. 266, 215, 215 — 696.

Runners-up — Paul Moser, Somerset, Mass. 695; Wendell Thomasson, Aurora, Col. 681; Bus Oswalt, Muncie, Ind. 679; Jimmy Certain, Huntsville, Ala. 677; Fred Jaskie, Milwaukee, Wis. 674; George Pappas, Charlotte, N.C. 668; Earl Bauman Jr., Aurora, Col. 667.

### All Events

1. Bill Beach, Sharon, Pa. 666, 574, 701 — 1,941.
2. Skip Tucker, Tampa, Fla. 546, 695, 696 — 1,937.
3. Frankie May Jr., Reading, Pa. 685, 611, 638 — 1,934.

Runners-up — Don Findlay, Springfield, Mo. 1,918; Stan Marchut, River Edge, N.J. 1,908; Fred Jaskie, Milwaukee, Wis. 1,899; Paul Moser, Somerset, Mass. 1,895; Tommy Hudson, Cuyahoga Falls, Oh. 1,889; Dave Danielson, St. Louis, Mo. 1,882; Larry Brott, Denver, Col. 1,881.

### Doubles

1. Steve Fehr, Cincinnati, Oh. 207, 187, 220 — 614; Dave Newrath, Cincinnati, Oh. 216, 223, 247 — 686. Aggregate 1,300.
2. Ron Landry, Lafayette, La. 209, 203, 216 — 628; Joe Signorelli, Lafayette, La. 230, 235, 199 — 664. Aggregate — 1,292.
3. Harold Eder Jr., N. Vernon, Ind. 194, 223, 213 — 630; Tom Eder, N. Vernon, Ind. 181, 216, 254 — 651. Aggregate 1,281.

### Team

1. The Untouchable Lounge, Kirksville, Mo. — Tom Wright 158, 228, 233 — 619; Ken Fernandez 190, 201, 190 — 581; Dave Wheeler 192, 199, 222 — 613; Tim Harahan 172, 166, 189 — 527; Gary Patterson 234, 157, 180 — 571. Aggregate 2,911.
2. King Louie International, Kansas City, Mo. — Gil Sliker 179, 269, 223 — 671; Craig Cutsor 163, 190, 169 — 522; Warren Nelson 189, 191, 135 — 515; Peter McCordic 211, 171, 161 — 543; Dale Glenn 229, 169, 164 — 562. Aggregate — 2,813.

## Other Bowling Championships in 1978

8th U.S. Open — Men — Greensboro, N.C. March 7-11. Nelson Burton Jr., St. Louis, Mo., average 225, prize $10,000. Women — Miami, Fla. May 16-20. Donna Adamek, Monrovia, Cal., average 212, prize $7,000.

National Intercollegiate Championships — St. Louis, Mo. April 4-5; doubles, Bob Weeks, Cornell U. and Dan Eberl, Erie C.C., Buffalo, N.Y.; singles, Jeffrey Bellinger, South Carolina; all events, Jeffrey Bellinger, South Carolina.

Invitational Tournament of the Americas — Miami, Fla. July 9-15; men's doubles, Xavier Issa and Alfonso Rodriguez, Mexico; singles, Alfonso Rodriguez, Mexico; all events, Alfonso Rodriguez, Mexico. Women's doubles, Annese Kelly and Faydra Austin, U.S.; singles, Annese Kelly, U.S.; all events, Annese Kelly, U.S.

## Masters Bowling Tournament Champions

| Year | Winner | Runner-up | W-L | Avg |
|---|---|---|---|---|
| 1966 | Bob Strampe, Detroit | Al Thompson, Cleveland | 7-0 | 219-8 |
| 1967 | Lou Scalia, Miami | Bill Johnson, New Orleans | 7-0 | 216-9 |
| 1968 | Pete Tountas, Tucson | Buzz Fazio, Detroit | 9-1 | 220-15 |
| 1969 | Jim Chestney, Denver | Barry Asher, Costa Mesa, Cal. | 10-1 | 223-2 |
| 1970 | Don Glover, Bakersfield, Cal. | Bob Strampe, Detroit | 9-1 | 215-10 |
| 1971 | Jim Godman, Lorain, Oh. | Don Johnson, Akron. | 9-1 | 229-8 |
| 1972 | Bill Beach, Sharon, Pa. | Jim Godman, Lorain, Oh. | 8-1 | 220-27 |
| 1973 | Dave Soutar, Gilroy, Cal. | Dick Ritger, Hartford, Wis. | 7-0 | 218-61 |
| 1974 | Paul Colwell, Tucson | Steve Neff, Sarasota, Fla. | 7-0 | 234-17 |
| 1975 | Ed Ressler Jr., Allentown, Pa. | Sam Flanagan, Parkersburg, W. Va. | 9-1 | 213-57 |
| 1976 | Nelson Burton Jr., St. Louis | Steve Carson, Oklahoma City | 7-0 | 220-79 |
| 1977 | Earl Anthony, Tacoma, Wash. | Jim Godman, Lorain, Oh. | 7-0 | 218-21 |
| 1978 | Frank Ellenburg, Mesa, Ariz. | Earl Anthony, Tacoma, Wash. | 8-1 | 200-11 |

## All-Time Records for League and Tournament Play

| Type of record | Holder of record | Year | Score | Competition |
|---|---|---|---|---|
| High team total | Budweiser Beer, St. Louis | 1958 | 3,858 | League |
| High team game | Hook Grip Five, Lodi, N.J. | 1950 | 1,342 | League |
| High doubles total | Nelson Burton Jr., Billy Walden, St. Louis | 1970 | 1,614 | Tournament |
| High doubles game | Jesse Foley and Wendell Cromer, Shreveport, La. | 1976 | 598* | League |
| High individual total | Albert Brandt, Lockport, N.Y. | 1939 | 886 | League |
| High all events score | Denny Campbell, Chicago | 1976 | 2,314 | Tournament |

* In 4-person league.

## Record Averages for Consecutive Tournaments

| No. in row | Holder of record | Span | Games | Average |
|---|---|---|---|---|
| Two | Jim Godman, Lorain, Oh. | 1974-75. | 18 | 228.78 |
| Three | Jim Godman, Lorain, Oh. | 1974-76. | 27 | 223.96 |
| Four | Jim Godman, Lorain, Oh. | 1974-77. | 36 | 219.44 |
| Five | Jim Godman, Lorain, Oh. | 1973-77. | 45 | 216.33 |
| Ten | Bob Strampe, Detroit. | 1961-70. | 111 | 211.10 |

## Official Records of Annual ABC Tournaments

| Type of record | Holder of record | Year | Score |
|---|---|---|---|
| High team total | Ace Mitchell Shur-Hooks, Akron | 1966 | 3,357 |
| High team game | Falstaff Beer, San Antonio | 1958 | 1,226 |
| High doubles score | John Klares-Steve Nagy, Cleveland | 1952 | 1,453 |
| High doubles game | Tommy Hudson, Akron, Ohio-Les Zikes, Chicago | 1976 | 558 |
| High singles total | Mickey Higham, Kansas City, Mo. | 1977 | 801 |
| High all events score | Jim Godman, Lorain, Oh. | 1974 | 2,184 |
| High team all events | Falstaff Beer, St. Louis | 1958 | 9,608 |
| High life-time pin total | Bill Doehrman, Ft. Wayne | 1908-1978 | 108,334 |

## Bowlers with 6 or More Sanctioned 300 Games

| | | |
|---|---|---|
| Elvin Mesger, Sullivan, Mo. 27 | Lou Foxie, Paterson, N.J. 9 | Don Glover, Rosenberg, Tex. 7 |
| George Billick, Old Forge, Pa. 17 | Jerry Woji, Stockton, Cal. 9 | Don Dubro, St. Louis 7 |
| Dick Weber, St. Louis 17 | Tom Hennessey, St. Louis 9 | Mark Sutter, St. Louis. 7 |
| Dave Soutar, Gilroy, Cal. 15 | Howard Holmes, Los Angeles 8 | Salvatore Bivona, Paterson, N.J. 6 |
| Ron Graham, Louisville 15 | Russell Field, San Jose, Cal. 8 | Lou Campi, Dumont, N.J. 6 |
| Don Johnson, Las Vegas 15 | Roger Fink, Lodi, Cal. 8 | Ed Davis, Milford, N.J. 6 |
| Al Faragalli, Wayne, N.J. 14 | Dennis Wright, Milwaukee 8 | *Bill Flynn, Cleveland. 6 |
| Don Carter, Miami, Fla. 13 | Ray Eklund, Milwaukee. 8 | Sam Garofalo, St. Louis 6 |
| Ray Bluth, St. Louis 12 | Walter King, Detroit 8 | Joe Joseph, Lansing, Mich. 6 |
| Walter Ward, Cleveland 12 | Junie McMahon, Lodi, N.J. 8 | Pete Kozloski, Plains, Pa. 6 |
| Casey Jones, Plymouth, Wis. 12 | Bud Horn, Los Angeles 8 | Vince Lucci, Trenton, N.J. 6 |
| *Hank Marino, Milwaukee 11 | Joe Donato, Schenectady, N.Y. 7 | Steve Nagy, Cleveland. 6 |
| Frank Clause, Old Forge, Pa. 11 | Eddie Botten, Union City, N.J. 7 | Frank Pollak, Pittsburgh 6 |
| Ed Lubanski, Detroit 11 | Dick Hoover, Akron. 7 | Robert Pinkalla, Milwaukee 6 |
| Pat Patterson, St. Louis 11 | Ken McKenzie, Dallas 7 | Harold Schaeffer, St. Louis 6 |
| Dennis Soper, Tustin, Cal. 11 | Ray Schanen, Milwaukee 7 | Harry Smith, Rochester, N.Y. 6 |
| Dave Williams, Sebastopol, Cal. 11 | Wayne Pinkalla, Milwaukee 7 | Bob Strampe, Detroit 6 |
| Mike Durbin, Lorain, Oh. 10 | Bob Ramirez, Los Angeles 7 | Jerry Tharp, St. Louis. 6 |
| Norm Meyers, St. Louis 10 | Don McCune, Munster, Ind. 7 | George Tomek, Plymouth, Pa. 6 |
| George Pappas, Charlotte, N.C. 10 | Mickey Higham, Kansas City, Mo. 7 | Stephen Tomek, Plymouth, Pa. 6 |
| Boss Bosco, Akron 9 | Jim Godman, Lorain, Oh. 7 | William Capleton, Prospect Park, N.J. 6 |
| Al Savas, Milwaukee 9 | | |

*Bowled two 300 games in official 3-game series.

## PBA Winter Tour, 1978

| Date | Event | Winner | Winner's share |
|---|---|---|---|
| Jan. 4-7 | Lite Classic, Torrance, Cal. | Mark Roth | $15,000 |
| Jan. 10-14 | Ford Open, Alameda, Cal. | Marshall Holman | 12,000 |
| Jan. 15-21 | Showboat Invitational, Las Vegas | Bill Coleman | 21,000 |
| Jan. 24-28 | Quaker State Open, Grand Prairie, Tex. | Mark Roth | 15,000 |
| Jan. 31-Feb. 4 | King Louie Open, Overland Park, Kan. | Mark Roth | 9,000 |
| Feb. 7-11 | Dutch Masters Open, Cleveland | Dick Ritger | 10,000 |
| Feb. 14-18 | Midas Golden Challenge, New Orleans | Pete Couture | 15,000 |
| Feb. 21-25 | MagicScore Open, Kissimmee, Fla. | Earl Anthony | 15,000 |
| Mar. 1-4 | Burger King Open, Miami | Randy Lightfoot | 30,000 |
| Mar. 5-11 | BPAA U. S. Open, Greensboro, N.C. | Nelson Burton Jr. | 10,000 |
| Mar. 14-18 | Rolaids Open, St. Louis | Dave Davis | 15,000 |
| Mar. 21-25 | Miller High Life Open, Milwaukee | Fred Jaskie | 15,000 |
| Mar. 28-Apr. 1 | Long Island Open, Garden City, N.Y. | Johnny Petraglia | 8,000 |
| Apr. 4-8 | Greater Hartford Open, Windsor Locks, Conn. | Mark Roth | 8,000 |
| Apr. 11-15 | Fair Lanes Open, Towson, Md. | Butch Soper | 9,000 |
| Apr. 17-22 | Firestone Tournament of Champions, Akron | Earl Anthony | 30,000 |

## Leading Averages in 1977

(16 or More Tournaments)

| Pos. | Name, City | Tournaments | Games | Pinfall | Average |
|---|---|---|---|---|---|
| 1. | Mark Roth, Staten Island, N.Y. | 28 | 1,130 | 246,537 | 218.174 |
| 2. | Earl Anthony, Tacoma, Wash. | 24 | 867 | 188,206 | 217.077 |
| 3. | Tommy Hudson, Akron, Oh. | 35 | 1,200 | 259,486 | 216.238 |
| 4. | Marshall Holman, Medford, Ore. | 29 | 1,018 | 219,711 | 215.826 |
| 5. | Wayne Zahn, Tempe, Ariz. | 16 | 470 | 100,515 | 213.862 |
| 6. | Steve Neff, Sarasota, Fla. | 26 | 734 | 156,956 | 213.837 |
| 7. | Dennis Lane, Kingsport, Tenn. | 34 | 1,095 | 233,254 | 213.017 |
| 8. | Pete Couture, Windsor, Conn. | 30 | 966 | 205,484 | 212.716 |
| 9. | Dale Glenn, Glendale, Cal. | 33 | 950 | 201,835 | 212.458 |
| 10. | Cliff McNealy, San Lorenzo, Cal. | 26 | 673 | 142,928 | 212.374 |
| 11. | Mike Berlin, Muscatine, Ia. | 20 | 620 | 131,205 | 211.621 |
| 12. | Steve Jones, Independence, Mo. | 28 | 719 | 152,027 | 211.442 |
| 13. | George Pappas, Charlotte, N.C. | 32 | 933 | 197,166 | 211.325 |
| 14. | Rick Minier, Portland, Ore. | 31 | 914 | 193,105 | 211.275 |
| 15. | Mike Durbin, Chagrin Falls, Oh. | 31 | 916 | 193,471 | 211.213 |

## Firestone Tournament of Champions

This is professional bowling's richest tournament and has been held each year since its inception in 1965, in Akron, Oh., the home of the Professional Bowlers Association. First prize is $25,000.

| Year | Winner | Year | Winner | Year | Winner | Year | Winner |
|---|---|---|---|---|---|---|---|
| 1965 | Billy Hardwick | 1969 | Jim Godman | 1973 | Jim Godman | 1976 | Marshall Holman |
| 1966 | Wayne Zahn | 1970 | Don Johnson | 1974 | Earl Anthony | 1977 | Mike Berlin |
| 1967 | Jim Stefanich | 1971 | Johnny Petraglia | 1975 | Dave Davis | 1978 | Earl Anthony |
| 1968 | Dave Davis | 1972 | Mike Durbin | | | | |

## Leading PBA Averages by Year

| Year | Bowler | Tournaments | Average | Year | Bowler | Tournaments | Average |
|------|--------|-------------|---------|------|--------|-------------|---------|
| 1962 | Don Carter, St. Louis, Mo. | 25 | 212.844 | 1970 | Nelson Burton Jr., St. Louis, Mo. | 32 | 214.908 |
| 1963 | Billy Hardwick, Louisville, Ky. | 26 | 210.346 | 1971 | Don Johnson, Akron, Oh. | 31 | 213.977 |
| 1964 | Ray Bluth, St. Louis, Mo. | 27 | 210.512 | 1972 | Don Johnson, Akron, Oh. | 30 | 215.290 |
| 1965 | Dick Weber, St. Louis, Mo. | 19 | 211.895 | 1973 | Earl Anthony, Tacoma, Wash. | 29 | 215.799 |
| 1966 | Wayne Zahn, Atlanta, Ga. | 27 | 208.663 | 1974 | Earl Anthony, Tacoma, Wash. | 28 | 219.394 |
| 1967 | Wayne Zahn, Atlanta, Ga. | 29 | 212.342 | 1975 | Earl Anthony, Tacoma, Wash. | 30 | 219.060 |
| 1968 | Jim Stefanich, Joliet, Ill. | 33 | 211.895 | 1976 | Mark Roth, New York, N.Y. | 28 | 215.970 |
| 1969 | Bill Hardwick, Louisville, Ky. | 33 | 212.957 | 1977 | Mark Roth, New York, N.Y. | 28 | 218.174 |

## PBA Leading Money Winners

Total winnings are from PBA, ABC Masters, and BPAA All-Star tournaments only, and do not include numerous other tournaments or earnings from special television shows and matches.

| Year | Bowler | Total | Year | Bowler | Total | Year | Bowler | Total |
|------|--------|-------|------|--------|-------|------|--------|-------|
| 1960 | Don Carter | $22,525 | 1966 | Wayne Zahn | $54,720 | 1972 | Don Johnson | $56,648 |
| 1961 | Dick Weber | 26,280 | 1967 | Dave Davis | 54,165 | 1973 | Don McCune | 69,000 |
| 1962 | Don Carter | 49,972 | 1968 | Jim Stefanich | 67,377 | 1974 | Earl Anthony | 99,585 |
| 1963 | Dick Weber | 46,333 | 1969 | Billy Hardwick | 64,160 | 1975 | Earl Anthony | 107,585 |
| 1964 | Bob Strampe | 33,592 | 1970 | Mike McGrath | 52,049 | 1976 | Earl Anthony | 110,833 |
| 1965 | Dick Weber | 47,674 | 1971 | Johnny Petraglia | 85,065 | 1977 | Mark Roth | 105,583 |

# Women's International Bowling Congress Champions

| Individual | All events | Year | 2-woman teams | 5-woman teams |
|------------|-----------|------|---------------|---------------|
| D.D. Jacobson, Playa Del Rey, Cal. 737 | Mildred Martorella, Rochester, N.Y. 1,877 | 1972 | Judy Roberts-Betty Remmick, Denver, Lakewood, Col. 1,247 | Angeltown Creations, Placentia, Cal. 2,838 |
| Bobbie Buffaloe, Costa Messa, Cal. 706 | Toni Starin, Midwest City, Okla. 1,910 | 1973 | Dorothy Fothergill, N. Attleboro, Mass.-Mildred Martorella Rochester, N.Y. 1,238 | Fitzpatrick Chevrolet, Concord, Cal. 2,897 |
| Shirley Garms, Lake Island, Ill. 702 | Judy Soutar, Kansas City, Mo. 1,944 | 1974 | Jane Leszczynski, Milwaukee-Carol Miller, Waukesha, Wis. 1,313 | Kalicak International Construction, Kansas City, Mo. 2,973 |
| Barbara Leicht, Albany, N.Y. 689 | Virginia Norton Whittier, Cal. 1,821 | 1975 | Jennette James, Oyster Bay, Dawn Raddatz, Northport, N.Y. 1,234 | Atlanta Bowling Center (Ga.) Buffalo, N.Y. 2,836 |
| Beverly Shonk, Canton, Oh. 686 | Betty Morris, Stockton, Cal. 1,866 | 1976 | Georgene Cordes-Shirley Stostrom, Bloomington, Minn.; Eloise Vacco-Debbie Rainone, Cleveland Hts., Oh. (tie). 1,232 | PWBA 1, Oklahoma City, Okla. 2,839 |
| Akiko Yamaga, Tokyo. 714 | Akiko Yamaga 1,895 | 1977 | Ozella Houston-Dorothy Jackson, Detroit, Mich. 1,234 | Allgauer's Restaurant Chicago, Ill. 2,818 |
| Mae Bolt, Berwyn, Ill. 709 | Annese Kelly, Brooklyn, N.Y. 1,896 | 1978 | Barbara Shelton, Annese Kelly, New York, N.Y. 1,211 | Cook County Vending, Chicago, Ill. 2,956 |

## Sanctioned 300 Games During 1977-78 Season

Lyn Ables, Plano, Tex.; Pat Aliberti, Glassboro, N.J.; Kathie Berger, Sheboygan, Wis.; Barbara Birkhead, Winfield, Mo.; Luci Bonneau, Missouri City, Tex.; Jan Busby, San Jose, Cal.; Marjorie Caruso, Hayward, Cal. (2); Joyce Casella, LaGrange Park, Ill.; Janice Cochran, Plant City, Fla.; Lorraine Delgado, Espanola, N.M.; Carolyn Durkin, Louisville, Oh.; Alice Felsinger, Sheboygan, Wis.; Toni Gillard, Beverly, Oh.; Bonnie Hannestad, St. Paul Park, Minn.; Jackie Harris, Utica, N.Y.; Susan Holcomb, Mansfield, Tex.; Linda Hudson, Dayton, Oh.; Regi Jonak, St. Louis, Mo.; JoAnn LaBarbera, St. Louis, Mo.; Beverly Logan, Canton, Oh.; Judy MacMaster, Sacramento, Cal.; Peggy Mantke, Niles, Mich.; Carol Miller, Waukesha, Wis.; Betty Morris, Stockton, Cal.; Edie Jo Neal, Miami, Fla.; Cheri Nelson, Independence, Mo.; Virginia Norton, South Gate, Cal. (2); Joli Pollard, Lee's Summit, Mo.; Diane Ponza, Santa Cruz, Cal.; Gerry Ritter, Clawson, Mich.; Janet Rohrbaugh, Santa Barbara, Cal.; Margie Rountree, Houston, Tex.; Janet Scarr, Pompano Beach, Fla.; Marie Sherbinsky, Willoughby, Oh.; Marjorie Siemer, Columbus, Oh.; Dana Stewart, Mountain View, Cal.; Marion Strouse, Central Point, Ore.; Amy Takehara, Los Angeles, Cal.; Ruby Thomas, Abilene, Tex.; Karen Thompson, Park Forest, Ill.; Dorothy Tsal, Astoria, N.Y.; Debra VanNuland, Kimberly, Wis.; Margaret Wasilchuk, South Lake Tahoe, Cal.; Darlene Weekly, Tempe, Ariz.; Kathy Wodka, Groton, Conn.; Charlene Wright, Breckenridge, Mich.

## Most Sanctioned 300 Games

| Bowler | | Bowler | | Bowler | |
|--------|--|--------|--|--------|--|
| Betty Morris, Stockton, Cal. | 5 | Betty Mivalez, Tujunga, Cal. | 2 | Marjorie Caruso, Hayward, Cal. | 2 |
| Beverly Ortner, Tuscon, Ariz. | 4 | Norma Rittelmeyer, Dallas, Tex. | 2 | Virginia Norton, South Gate, Cal. | 2 |
| Sylvia Wene Martin, Philadelphia. | 3 | Patricia Robinette, Louisville, Ky. | 2 | Janet Rohrbaugh, Santa Barbara, Cal. | 2 |
| Mary Altmeyer, St. Louis, Mo. | 2 | Jean Worthy, Norwalk, Cal. | 2 | Velda Gooden, Richmond, Cal. | 2 |
| Joan McRae, Northridge, Cal. | 2 | | | | |

# National Duckpin Bowling Champions in 1978

**Men's Singles**—Jim Simmons, Baltimore, Md. 599.
**Women's Singles**—Doris Graveling, Jewett City, Conn., 493.
**Men's Doubles**—Dan Lopardo and Nick Tronsky, Torrington, Conn., 993.
**Women's Doubles**—Chickey Balesano and Cathy Dyak, Manchester, Conn., 838.
**Mixed Doubles**—Patricia Price, W. Hartford, Conn. and Herb Steadman, Southington, Conn., 940.
**Men's team**—Troc Pleasure Palace, Baltimore, Md., 2,271.
**Women's team**—IBEW #42, Glastonbury, Conn., 2,129.

# Boxing Champions by Classes

As of Sept. 16, 1978, the only universally accepted title holders were in the middleweight and lightweight divisions. The following are the recognized champions of the World Boxing Association and the World Boxing Council.

| | WBA | WBC |
|---|---|---|
| Heavyweight | Muhammad Ali, Chicago, Ill. | Larry Holmes, Easton, Pa. |
| Light Heavyweight | Mike Rossman, Turnersville, N.J. | Mate Parlov, Yugoslavia |
| Middleweights | Hugo Corro, Argentina | Hugo Corro |
| Jr. Middleweight | Masashi Kudo, Japan | Rocky Mattioli, Australia |
| Welterweight | Jose Cuevas, Mexico | Carlos Palomino, Mexico |
| Jr. Welterweight | Antonio Cervantes, Colombia | Shengsak Muangsurin, Thailand |
| Lightweight | Roberto Duran, Panama | Roberto Duran |
| Jr. Lightweight | Sammy Serrano, Puerto Rico | Alexis Arguello, Nicaragua |
| Featherweight | Eusebio Pedroza, Panama | Danny Lopez, Los Angeles, Cal. |
| Bantamweight | Jorge Lujan, Panama | Carlos Zarate, Mexico |
| Flyweight | Betulio Gonzalez, Venezuela | Miguel Canto, Mexico |

# Ring Champions by Years

*Abandoned title

## Heavyweights

| | |
|---|---|
| 1882-1892 | John L. Sullivan (a) |
| 1892-1897 | James J. Corbett (b) |
| 1897-1899 | Robert Fitzsimmons |
| 1899-1905 | James J. Jeffries (c) |
| 1905-1906 | Marvin Hart |
| 1906-1908 | Tommy Burns |
| 1908-1915 | Jack Johnson |
| 1915-1919 | Jess Willard |
| 1919-1926 | Jack Dempsey |
| 1926-1928 | Gene Tunney* |
| 1928-1930 | vacant |
| 1930-1932 | Max Schmeling |
| 1932-1933 | Jack Sharkey |
| 1933-1934 | Primo Carnera |
| 1934-1935 | Max Baer |
| 1935-1937 | James J. Braddock |
| 1937-1949 | Joe Louis* |
| 1949-1951 | Ezzard Charles |
| 1951-1952 | Joe Walcott |
| 1952-1956 | Rocky Marciano* |
| 1956-1959 | Floyd Patterson |
| 1959-1960 | Ingemar Johansson |
| 1960-1962 | Floyd Patterson |
| 1962-1964 | Sonny Liston |
| 1964-1967 | Cassius Clay* (Muhammad Ali) (d) |
| 1970-1973 | Joe Frazier |
| 1973-1974 | George Foreman |
| 1974-1978 | Muhammad Ali |
| 1978 | Leon Spinks (e), Muhammad Ali |

(a) London Prize Ring (bare knuckle champion).
(b) First Marquis of Queensberry champion.
(c) Jeffries abandoned the title (1905) and designated Marvin Hart and Jack Root as logical contenders and agreed to referee a fight between them, the winner to be declared champion. Hart defeated Root in 12 rounds (1905) and in turn was defeated by Tommy Burns (1906) who immediately laid claim to the title. Jack Johnson defeated Burns (1908) and was recognized as champion. He clinched the title by defeating Jeffries in an attempted comeback (1910).
(d) Title declared vacant by the World Boxing Assn. and other groups in 1967 after Clay's refusal to fulfill his military obligation.
(e) After Spinks defeated Ali, the WBC recognized Ken Norton as champion. Norton subsequently lost his title to Larry Holmes.

## Light Heavyweights

| | |
|---|---|
| 1903 | Jack Root, George Gardner |
| 1903-1905 | Bob Fitzsimmons |
| 1905-1912 | Philadelphia Jack O'Brien* |
| 1912-1916 | Jack Dillon |
| 1916-1920 | Battling Levinsky |
| 1920-1922 | George Carpentier |
| 1922-1923 | Battling Siki |
| 1923-1925 | Mike McTigue |
| 1925-1926 | Paul Berlenbach |
| 1926-1927 | Jack Delaney* |
| 1927-1929 | Tommy Loughran* |
| 1930-1934 | Maxey Rosenbloom |
| 1934-1935 | Bob Olin |
| 1935-1939 | John Henry Lewis* |
| 1939 | Melio Bettina |
| 1939-1941 | Billy Conn* |

| | |
|---|---|
| 1941 | Anton Christoforidis (won NBA title) |
| 1941-1948 | Gus Lesnevich, Freddie Mills |
| 1948-1950 | Freddie Mills |
| 1950-1952 | Joey Maxim |
| 1952-1960 | Archie Moore |
| 1961-1962 | vacant |
| 1962-1963 | Harold Johnson |
| 1963-1965 | Willie Pastrano |
| 1965-1966 | Jose Torres |
| 1966-1968 | Dick Tiger |
| 1968-1974 | Bob Foster* |

## Middleweights

| | |
|---|---|
| 1884-1891 | Jack "Nonpareil" Dempsey |
| 1891-1897 | Bob Fitzsimmons* |
| 1897-1907 | Tommy Ryan* |
| 1907-1908 | Stanley Ketchel, Billy Papke |
| 1908-1910 | Stanley Ketchel |
| 1911-1913 | vacant |
| 1913 | Frank Klaus, George Chip |
| 1914-1917 | Al McCoy |
| 1917-1920 | Mike O'Dowd |
| 1920-1923 | Johnny Wilson |
| 1923-1926 | Harry Greb |
| 1926-1931 | Tiger Flowers, Mickey Walker |
| 1931-1932 | Gorilla Jones (NBA) |
| 1932-1937 | Marcel Thil |
| 1938 | Al Hostak (NBA), Solly Krieger (NBA) |
| 1939-1940 | Al Hostak (NBA) |
| 1941-1947 | Tony Zale |
| 1947-1948 | Rocky Graziano |
| 1948 | Tony Zale, Marcel Cerdan |
| 1949-1951 | Jake LaMotta |
| 1951 | Ray Robinson, Randy Turpin, Ray Robinson* |
| 1953-1955 | Carl (Bobo) Olson |
| 1955-1957 | Ray Robinson |
| 1957 | Gene Fullmer, Ray Robinson, Carmen Basilio |
| 1958 | Ray Robinson |
| 1959 | Gene Fullmer (NBA); Ray Robinson (N.Y.) |
| 1960 | Gene Fullmer (NBA); Paul Pender (New York and Mass.) |
| 1961 | Gene Fullmer (NBA); Terry Downes (New York, Mass., Europe) |
| 1962 | Gene Fullmer, Dick Tiger (NBA); Paul Pender (New York and Mass.)* |
| 1963 | Dick Tiger (universal). |
| 1963-1965 | Joey Giardello |
| 1965-1966 | Dick Tiger |
| 1966-1967 | Emile Griffith |
| 1967 | Nino Benvenuti |
| 1967-1968 | Emile Griffith |
| 1968-1970 | Nino Benvenuti |
| 1970-1978 | Carlos Monzon* |
| 1978 | Hugh Corro |

## Welterweights

| | |
|---|---|
| 1892-1894 | Mysterious Billy Smith |
| 1894-1896 | Tommy Ryan |
| 1896 | Kid McCoy (outgrew class) |
| 1900 | Rube Ferns, Matty Matthews |

| | |
|---|---|
| 1901 | Rube Ferns |
| 1901-1904 | Joe Walcott |
| 1904-1906 | Dixie Kid, Joe Walcott, Honey Mellody |
| 1907-1911 | Mike Sullivan |
| 1911-1915 | vacant |
| 1915-1919 | Ted Lewis |
| 1919-1922 | Jack Britton |
| 1922-1926 | Mickey Walker |
| 1926 | Pete Latzo |
| 1927-1929 | Joe Dundee |
| 1929 | Jackie Fields |
| 1930 | Jack Thompson, Tommy Freeman |
| 1931 | Freeman, Thompson, Lou Brouillard |
| 1932 | Jackie Fields |
| 1933 | Young Corbett, Jimmy McLarnin |
| 1934 | Barney Ross, Jimmy McLarnin |
| 1935-1938 | Barney Ross |
| 1938-1940 | Henry Armstrong |
| 1940-1941 | Fritzie Zivic |
| 1941-1946 | Fred Cochrane |
| 1946-1946 | Marty Servo*; Ray Robinson (a) |
| 1946-1950 | Ray Robinson* |
| 1951 | Johnny Bratton (NBA) |
| 1951-1954 | Kid Gavilan |
| 1954-1955 | Johnny Saxton |
| 1955 | Tony De Marco, Carmen Basilio |
| 1956 | Carmen Basilio, Johnny Saxton, Carmen Basilio |
| 1957 | Carmen Basilio* |
| 1958-1960 | Virgil Akins, Don Jordan |
| 1960 | Benny Paret |
| 1961 | Emile Griffith, Benny Paret |
| 1962 | Emile Griffith |
| 1963 | Luis Rodriguez, Emile Griffith |
| 1964-1966 | Emile Griffith* |
| 1966-1969 | Curtis Cokes |
| 1969-1970 | Jose Napoles, Billy Backus |
| 1971-1975 | Jose Napoles |
| 1975-1976 | John Stracey |
| 1976 | Carlos Palomino (WBC) |

(a) Robinson gained the title by defeating Tommy Bell in an elimination agreed to by the NY Commission and the NBA. Both claimed Robinson waived his title when he won the middleweight crown from LaMotta in 1951, Gavilan defeated Bratton in an elimination to find a successor.

### Lightweights

| | |
|---|---|
| 1896-1899 | Kid Lavigne |
| 1899-1902 | Frank Erne |
| 1902-1908 | Joe Gans |
| 1908-1910 | Battling Nelson |
| 1910-1912 | Ad Wolgast |
| 1912-1914 | Willie Ritchie |
| 1914-1917 | Freddie Welsh |
| 1917-1925 | Benny Leonard* |
| 1925 | Jimmy Goodrich, Rocky Kansas |
| 1926-1930 | Sammy Mandell |
| 1930 | Al Singer, Tony Canzoneri |
| 1930-1933 | Tony Canzoneri |
| 1933-1935 | Barney Ross* |

| | |
|---|---|
| 1935-1936 | Tony Canzoneri |
| 1936-1938 | Lou Ambers |
| 1938 | Henry Armstrong |
| 1939 | Lou Ambers |
| 1940 | Lew Jenkins |
| 1941-1943 | Sammy Angott |
| 1944 | S. Angott (NBA), J. Zurita (NBA) |
| 1945-1951 | Ike Williams (NBA: later universal) |
| 1951-1952 | James Carter |
| 1952 | Lauro Salas, James Carter |
| 1953-1954 | James Carter |
| 1954 | Paddy De Marco; James Carter |
| 1955 | James Carter; Bud Smith |
| 1956 | Bud Smith, Joe Brown |
| 1956-1962 | Joe Brown |
| 1962-1965 | Carlos Ortiz |
| 1965 | Ismael Laguna |
| 1965-1968 | Carlos Ortiz |
| 1968-1969 | Teo Cruz |
| 1969-1970 | Mando Ramos |
| 1970 | Ismael Laguna |
| 1970-1972 | Ken Buchanan |
| 1972 | Roberto Duran |

### Featherweights

| | |
|---|---|
| 1892-1900 | George Dixon (disputed) |
| 1900-1901 | Terry McGovern, Young Corbett* |
| 1901-1912 | Abe Attell |
| 1912-1923 | Johnny Kilbane |
| 1923 | Eugene Criqui, Johnny Dundee |
| 1923-1925 | Johnny Dundee* |
| 1925-1927 | Kid Kaplan* |
| 1927-1928 | Benny Bass, Tony Canzoneri |
| 1928-1929 | Andre Routis |
| 1929-1932 | Battling Battalino* |
| 1932-1934 | Tommy Paul (NBA) |
| 1933-1936 | Freddie Miller |
| 1936-1937 | Petey Sarron |
| 1937-1938 | Henry Armstrong* |
| 1938-1940 | Joey Archibald (b) |
| 1942-1948 | Willie Pep |
| 1948-1949 | Sandy Saddler |
| 1949-1950 | Willie Pep |
| 1950-1957 | Sandy Saddler* |
| 1957-1959 | Hogan (Kid) Bassey |
| 1959-1963 | Davey Moore |
| 1963-1964 | Sugar Ramos |
| 1964-1969 | Vicente Saldivar* |
| 1969 | John Famechon |
| 1969-1970 | Vicente Saldivar |
| 1970-1971 | Kuniaki Shibata |
| 1971-1972 | Clemente Sanchez* |
| 1972-1974 | Ernesto Marcell (WBA) |
| 1975-1977 | Alexis Arguello (WBA) |

(b) After Petey Scalzo knocked out Archibald (Dec. 5, 1938) in an overweight match and was refused a title bout, the NBA named Scalzo champion. The NBA title succession was: Petey Scalzo, 1938-1941: Richard Lemos, 1941: Jackie Wilson, 1941-1943: Jackie Callura, 1943: Phil Terranova, 1943-1944: Sal Bartolo, 1944-1946.

## History of Heavyweight Championship Bouts

*Title Changed Hands

**1889**—July 8—John L. Sullivan def. Jake Kilrain, 75, Richburg, Miss. Last championship bare knuckles bout.

**\*1892**—Sept. 7—James J. Corbett def. John L. Sullivan, 21, New Orleans. Big gloves used for first time.

**1894**—Jan. 25—James J. Corbett KOd Charley Mitchell, 3, Jacksonville, Fla.

**\*1897**—Bob Fitzsimmons def. James J. Corbett, 14, Carson City, Nev.

**\*1899**—June 9—James J. Jeffries def. Bob Fitzsimmons, 11, Coney Island, N.Y.

**1899**—Nov. 3—James J. Jeffries def. Tom Sharkey, 25, Coney Island, N.Y.

**1900**—May 11—James J. Jeffries KOd James J. Corbett, 23, Coney Island, N.Y.

**1901**—Nov. 15—James J. Jeffries KOd Gus Ruhlin, 5, San Francisco.

**1902**—July 25—James J. Jeffries KOd Bob Fitzsimmons, 8, San Francisco.

**1903**—Aug. 14—James J. Jeffries KOd James J. Corbett, 10, San Francisco.

**1904**—Aug. 26—James J. Jeffries KOd Jack Monroe, 2, San Francisco.

**\*1905**—James J. Jeffries retired, July 3—Marvin Hart KOd Jack Root, 12, Reno. Jeffries refereed and presented the title to the victor. Jack O'Brien also claimed the title.

**\*1906**—Feb. 23—Tommy Burns def. Marvin Hart, 20, Los Angeles.

**1906**—Nov. 28—Philadelphia Jack O'Brien and Tommy Burns, 20, draw, Los Angeles.

**1907**—May 8—Tommy Burns def. Jack O'Brien, 20, Los Angeles.

**1907**—July 4—Tommy Burns KOd Bill Squires, 1, Colma, Cal.

**1907**—Dec. 2—Tommy Burns KOd Gunner Moir, 10, London.

**1908**—Feb. 10—Tommy Burns KOd Jack Palmer, 4, London.

**1908**—March 17—Tommy Burns KOd Jem Roche, 1, Dublin.

**1908**—April 18—Tommy Burns KOd Jewey Smith, 5, Paris.

**1908**—June 13—Tommy Burns KOd Bill Squires, 8, Paris.

**1908**—Aug. 24—Tommy Burns KOd Bill Squires, 13, Sydney, New South Wales.

**1908**—Sept. 2—Tommy Burns KOd Bill Lang, 2, Melbourne, Australia.

**\*1908**—Dec. 26—Jack Johnson KOd Tommy Burns, 14, Sidney, Australia. Police halted contest.

**1909**—May 19—Jack Johnson and Jack O'Brien, 6, draw,

Philadelphia.

1909—June 30—Jack Johnson and Tony Ross, 6, draw, Pittsburgh.

1909—Sept. 9—Jack Johnson and Al Kaufman, 10, draw, San Francisco.

1909—Oct. 16—Jack Johnson KOd Stanley Ketchel, 12, Colma, Cal.

1910—July 4—Jack Johnson KOd Jim Jeffries, 15, Reno, Nev. Jeffries came back from retirement.

1912—July 4—Jack Johnson def. Jim Flynn, 9, Las Vegas, N.M. Contest stopped by police.

1913—Nov. 28—Jack Johnson KOd Andre Spaul, 2, Paris.

1913—Dec. 9—Jack Johnson and Jim Johnson, 10, draw, Paris. Bout called a draw when Jack Johnson declared he had broken his arm.

1914—June 27—Jack Johnson def. Frank Moran, 20, Paris.

*1915—April 5—Jess Willard KOd Jack Johnson, 26, Havana, Cuba.

1916—March 25—Jess Willard and Frank Moran, 10, draw, New York.

*1919—July 4—Jack Dempsey KOd Jess Willard, Toledo, Oh. Willard failed to answer bell for 4th round.

1920—Sept. 6—Jack Dempsey KOd Billy Miske, 3, Benton Harbor, Mich.

1920—Dec. 14—Jack Dempsey KOd Bill Brennan, 12, New York.

1921—July 2—Jack Dempsey KOd George Carpentier, 4, Boyle's Thirty Acres, Jersey City, N.J. Carpentier had held the so-called white heavyweight title since July 16, 1914, in a series established in 1913, after Jack Johnson's exile in Europe late in 1912.

1923—July 4—Jack Dempsey def. Tom Gibbons, 15, Shelby, Mont.

1923—Sept. 14—Jack Dempsey KOd Luis Firpo, 2, New York.

*1926—Sept. 23—Gene Tunney def. Jack Dempsey, 10, Philadelphia.

1927—Sept. 22—Gene Tunney def. Jack Dempsey, 10, Chicago.

1928—July 26—Gene Tunney KOd Tom Heeney, 11, New York; soon afterward he announced his retirement.

*1930—June 12—Max Schmeling def. Jack Sharkey, 4, New York. Sharkey fouled Schmeling in a bout which was generally considered to have resulted in the election of a successor to Gene Tunney, New York.

1931—July 3—Max Schmeling KOd Young Stribling, 15, Cleveland.

*1932—June 21—Jack Sharkey def. Max Schmeling, 15, New York.

*1933—June 29—Primo Carnera def. Jack Sharkey, 6, New York.

1933—Oct. 22—Primo Carnera def. Paulino Uzcudun, 15, Rome.

1934—March 1—Primo Carnera def. Tommy Loughran, 15, Miami.

*1934—June 14—Max Baer KOd Primo Carnera, 11, New York.

*1935—June 13—James J. Braddock def. Max Baer, 15, New York.

*1937—June 22—Joe Louis KOd James J. Braddock, 8, Chicago.

1937—Aug. 30—Joe Louis def. Tommy Farr, 15, New York.

1938—Feb. 23—Joe Louis KOd Nathan Mann, 3, New York.

1938—April 1—Joe Louis KOd Harry Thomas, 5, New York.

1938—June 22—Joe Louis KOd Max Schmeling, 1, New York.

1939—Jan. 25—Joe Louis KOd John H. Lewis, 1, New York.

1939—April 17—Joe Louis KOd Jack Roper, 1, Los Angeles.

1939—June 28—Joe Louis KOd Tony Galento, 4, New York.

1939—Sept. 20—Joe Louis KOd Bob Pastor, 11, Detroit.

1940—February 9—Joe Louis def. Arturo Godoy, 15, New York.

1940—March 29—Joe Louis KOd Johnny Paycheck, 2, New York.

1940—June 20—Joe Louis KOd Arturo Godoy, 8, New York.

1940—Dec. 16—Joe Louis KOd Al McCoy, 6, Boston.

1941—Jan. 31—Joe Louis KOd Red Burman, 5, New York.

1941—Feb. 17—Joe Louis KOd Gus Dorazio, 2, Philadelphia.

1941—March 21—Joe Louis KOd Abe Simon, 13, Detroit.

1941—April 8—Joe Louis KOd Tony Musto, 9, St. Louis.

1941—May 23—Joe Louis def. Buddy Baer, 7, Washington, D.C., on a disqualification.

1941—June 18—Joe Louis KOd Billy Conn, 13, New York.

1941—Sept. 29—Joe Louis KOd Lou Nova, 6, New York.

1942—Jan. 9—Joe Louis KOd Buddy Baer, 1, New York.

1942—March 27—Joe Louis KOd Abe Simon, 6, New York.

1946—June 19—Joe Louis KOd Billy Conn, 8, New York.

1946—Sept. 18—Joe Louis KOd Tami Mauriello, 1, New York.

1947—Dec. 5—Joe Louis def. Joe Walcott, 15, New York.

1948—June 25—Joe Louis KOd Joe Walcott, 11, New York.

*1949—June 22—Following Joe Louis' retirement Ezzard Charles def. Joe Walcott, 15, Chicago, NBA recognition only.

1949—Aug. 10—Ezzard Charles KOd Gus Lesnevich, 7, New York.

1949—Oct. 14—Ezzard Charles KOd Pat Valentino, 8, San Francisco; clinched American title.

1950—Aug. 15—Ezzard Charles KOd Freddy Beshore, 14, Buffalo.

1950—Sept. 27—Ezzard Charles def. Joe Louis in latter's attempted comeback, 15, New York; universal recognition.

1950—Dec. 5—Ezzard Charles KOd Nick Barone, 11, Cincinnati.

1951—Jan. 12—Ezzard Charles KOd Lee Oma, 10, New York.

1951—March 7—Ezzard Charles def. Joe Walcott, 15, Detroit.

1951—May 30—Ezzard Charles def. Joey Maxim, light heavyweight champion, 15, Chicago.

*1951—July 18—Joe Walcott KOd Ezzard Charles, 7, Pittsburgh.

1952—June 5—Joe Walcott def. Ezzard Charles, 15, Philadelphia.

*1952—Sept. 23—Rocky Marciano KOd Joe Walcott, 13, Philadelphia.

1953—May 15—Rocky Marciano KOd Joe Walcott, 1, Chicago.

1953—Sept. 24—Rocky Marciano KOd Roland LaStarza, 11, New York.

1954—June 17—Rocky Marciano def. Ezzard Charles, 15, New York.

1954—Sept. 17—Rocky Marciano KOd Ezzard Charles, 8, New York.

1955—May 16—Rocky Marciano KOd Don Cockell, 9, San Francisco.

1955—Sept. 21—Rocky Marciano KOd Archie Moore, 9, New York. Marciano retired undefeated, Apr. 27, 1956.

*1956—Nov. 30—Floyd Patterson KOd Archie Moore, 5, Chicago.

1957—July 29—Floyd Patterson KOd Hurricane Jackson, 10, New York.

1957—Aug. 22—Floyd Patterson KOd Pete Rademacher, 6, Seattle.

1958—Aug. 18—Floyd Patterson KOd Roy Harris, 12, Los Angeles.

1959—May 1—Floyd Patterson KOd Brian London, 11, Indianapolis.

*1959—June 26—Ingemar Johansson KOd Floyd Patterson, 3, New York.

*1960—June 20—Floyd Patterson KOd Ingemar Johansson, 5, New York. First heavyweight in boxing history to regain title.

1961—Mar. 13—Floyd Patterson KOd Ingemar Johansson, 6, Miami Beach.

1961—Dec. 4—Floyd Patterson KOd Tom McNeeley, 4, Toronto.

*1962—Sept. 25—Sonny Liston KOd Floyd Patterson, 1, Chicago.

1963—July 22—Sonny Liston KOd Floyd Patterson, 1, Las Vegas.

*1964—Feb. 25—Cassius Clay KOd Sonny Liston, 7, Miami Beach.

1965—May 25—Cassius Clay KOd Sonny Liston, 1, Lewiston, Maine.

1965—Nov. 11—Cassius Clay KOd Floyd Patterson, 12, Las Vegas.

1966—Mar. 29—Cassius Clay def. George Chuvalo, 15, Toronto.

1966—May 21—Cassius Clay KOd Henry Cooper, 6, London.

1966—Aug. 6—Cassius Clay KOd Brian London, 3, London.

1966—Sept. 10—Cassius Clay KOd Karl Mildenberger, 12, Frankfurt, Germany.

1966—Nov. 14—Cassius Clay KOd Cleveland Williams, 3, Houston.

1967—Feb. 6—Cassius Clay def. Ernie Terrell, 15, Houston.

1967—Mar. 22—Cassius Clay KOd Zora Folley, 7, New York. Clay was stripped of his title by the WBA and others for refusing military service.

1970—Feb. 16—Joe Frazier KOd Jimmy Ellis, 5, New York.

1970—Nov. 18—Joe Frazier KOd Bob Foster, 2, Detroit.

1971—Mar. 8—Joe Frazier def. Cassius Clay (Muhammad Ali), 15, New York.

1972—Jan. 15—Joe Frazier KOd Terry Daniels, 4, New Orleans.

1972—May 25—Joe Frazier KOd Ron Stander, 5, Omaha.

*1973—Jan. 22—George Foreman KOd Joe Frazier, 2, Kingston, Jamaica.

1973—Sept. 1—George Foreman KOd Joe Roman, 1, Tokyo.

1974—Mar. 3—George Foreman KOd Ken Norton, 2, Caracas.

*1974—Oct. 30—Muhammad Ali KOd George Foreman, 8,

Zaire.

**1975**—Mar. 24—Muhammad Ali KOd Chuck Wepner, 15, Cleveland.
**1975**—May 16—Muhammad Ali KOd Ron Lyle, 11, Las Vegas.
**1975**—June 30—Muhammad Ali def. Joe Bugner, 15, Malaysia.
**1975**—Oct. 1—Muhammad Ali KOd Joe Frazier, 14, Manila.
**1976**—Feb. 20—Muhammad Ali KOd Jean-Pierre Coopman, 5, San Juan.
**1976**—Apr. 30—Muhammad Ali def. Jimmy Young, 15, Landover, Md.
**1976**—May 25—Muhammad Ali KOd Richard Dunn, 5, Munich.
**1976**—Sept. 28—Muhammad Ali def. Ken Norton, 15, New York.
**1977**—May 16—Muhammad Ali def. Alfredo Evangelista, 15, Landover, Md.
**1977**—Sept. 29—Muhammad Ali def. Earnie Shavers, 15, New York.
***1978**—Feb. 15—Leon Spinks def. Muhammad Ali, 15, Las Vegas.
***1978**—Sept. 15—Muhammad Ali def. Leon Spinks, 15, New Orleans.

## National AAU Boxing Championships in 1978

Biloxi, Miss., Apr. 18-22, 1978

**106 lbs.**—James Cullins, Bladensburg, Md.
**112 lbs.**—Mike Felde, Missoula, Mont.
**119 lbs.**—Jackie Beard, Jackson, Tenn.
**125 lbs.**—Eiichi Jamawan, Wahiawa, Ha.
**132 lbs.**—Melvin Paul, New Orleans, La.
**139 lbs.**—Donald Curry, Ft. Worth, Tex.

**147 lbs.**—Roger Leonard, U.S. Air Force.
**156 lbs.**—J. B. Williamson, U.S Marines.
**165 lbs.**—Jeff McCracken, U.S. Marines.
**178 lbs.**—Elmer Martin, U.S. Navy.
**Heavyweight**—Greg Page, Louisville, Ky.
**Team champion**—U.S. Marines.

# Rifle and Pistol Individual Championships in 1978

Source: National Rifle Association of America

## National Outdoor Rifle and Pistol Championships

**Pistol** — SFC Charles E. McCowan, USA, Fort Benning, Ga., 2635-126X.
**Civilian pistol** — Raymond J. Tourigny Jr., Glendale, R.I., 2628-122X.
**Woman pistol** — SP5 Kimberly S. Dyer, USA, Ft. Benning, Ga., 2565-97X.
**Senior pistol** — Gil Hebard, Knoxville, Ill., 2531-61X.
**Police pistol** — John L. Farley, Americus, Ga., 2596-96X.
**National Guard pistol** — SSG James R. Lenardson, ARNG, Toledo, Oh., 2630-111X.
**Collegiate pistol** — John A. Miller, USMA, West Point, N.Y., 2505-61X.
**Smallbore rifle prone** — SP5 Mary E. Stidworthy, ARNG, Prescott, Ariz., 6392-520X.
**Service smallbore rifle prone** — Mary E. Stidworthy, 6392-520X.
**Civilian smallbore rifle prone** — Douglas A. Knoop, Louisville, Ky., 6391-485X.
**Woman smallbore rifle prone** — Mary E. Stidworthy, 6391-485X.
**Collegiate smallbore rifle prone** — Marsha A. Beasley, Wilmington, Del., 6389-492X.
**Senior smallbore rifle prone** — Richard F. Hanson, Punta Gorda, Fla., 6382-494X.
**Junior smallbore rifle prone** — John A. Rost, Cincinnati, Oh., 6386-457X.
**Smallbore rifle position** — LTC Lones W. Wigger Jr., USA, Ft. Benning, Ga., 2258.
**Service smallbore rifle position** — Lones W. Wigger Jr., 2258.
**Civilian smallbore rifle position** — Gloria K. Parmentier, Ft.

Benning, Ga., 2219.
**Woman smallbore rifle position** — Gloria K. Parmentier, 2219.
**Junior smallbore rifle position** — John A. Rost, Cincinnati, Oh., 2127.
**Senior smallbore rifle position** — Kenneth B. Atkinson, Mishawaka, Ind., 2057.
**Collegiate smallbore rifle position** — Gloria K. Parmentier, 2219.
**High power rifle** — Carl R. Bernosky, Gordon, Pa., 2375-111X.
**High power civilian** — Carl R. Bernosky, 2375-111X.
**Match rifle senior** — Frederick J. Willing, Long Island City, N.Y., 2336-58X.
**Match rifle woman** — Noma J. McCullough, Los Angeles, Cal., 2293-56X.
**Match rifle junior** — Nancy H. Clark, Phoenix, Ariz., 2289-61X.
**Match rifle collegiate** — Carl R. Bernosky, 2375-111X.
**Service rifle champion** — LTC Tommy G. Pool, USAR, Ft. Benning, Ga., 2368-99X.
**Service rifle civilian** — Gerritt H. Stekeur, Latham, N.Y., 2340-83X.
**Service rifle woman** — SP5 Diane L. Klimas, USA, Ft. Benning, Ga., 2313-68X.
**Service rifle junior** — Mark DelCotto, Chicago Heights, Ill., 2278-33X.
**Service rifle senior** — Gerritt H. Stekeur, Latham, N.Y., 2340-83X.
**Service rifle regular service** — MSG William R. Lee, USA, Ft. Benning, Ga., 2367-108X.
**Service rifle collegiate** — Mark DelCotto 2278-33X.

## U.S. NRA International Shooting Championships

**English Match** — Lanny Bassham, San Antonio, Tex., 1787.
**Smallbore 3-position** — Lanny Bassham, 3465.
**Air rifle** — John Akemon, Johnson City, Tenn., 1166.
**Jr. air rifle** — Kurt Fitz-Randolph, El Paso, Tex., 1154.
**Ladies air rifle** — Sue Ann Sandusky, Ft. Benning, Ga., 1167.
**Ladies standard rifle prone** — Sue Ann Sandusky, 1759.
**Jr. standard rifle prone** — Kurt Fitz-Randolph, 1755.
**Ladies standard rifle 3-position** — Karen Monez, Ft. Benning, Ga., 1717.
**Free rifle, 300 meter** — Lones Wigger Jr., Ft. Benning, Ga., 3454.
**Big bore standard rifle** — Lones Wigger Jr., 1152.
**Free pistol** — Steve Reiter, Daly City, Cal., 1642.
**Air pistol** — Jan Brundin, Quakertown, Pa., 1139.
**Ladies air pistol** — Kim Dyer, Ft. Benning, Ga., 1123.

**Jr. air pistol** — Ashleigh Liston, Los Altos, Cal., 1094.
**Center fire pistol** — Jerry Wilder, Remington, Ind., 1761.
**Rapid fire pistol** — Melvin Makin, Aumsville, Ore., 1763.
**Standard pistol** — Jerry Wilder, 1714.
**Ladies smallbore pistol** — Kim Dyer, 1758.
**Running boar slow & fast** — Charles Davis, Ft. Benning, Ga., 1691.
**Running boar mixed** — Louis Theimer, Wichita Falls, Tex., 380.
**Clay pigeon** — Daniel Carlisle, Conroe, Tex., 395.
**Ladies clay pigeon** — Audrey Grosch, Minneapolis, Minn., 368.
**Jr. clay pigeon** — Michael Coleman, Ackerly, Tex., 389.
**International skeet** — Matt Dryke, Ft. Benning, Ga., 393.
**Ladies int'l skeet** — Ila Hill, Birmingham, Mich., 364.
**Jr. int'l skeet** — Jeff Sizemore, Corpus Christi, Tex., 388.

## National Indoor Rifle and Pistol Championships

**Conventional rifle** — Lance C. Peters, North St. Paul, Minn., 799.
**Conventional rifle woman** — Karen E. Monez, Ft. Benning, Ga., 798.
**International rifle** — Lones W. Wigger Jr., Ft. Benning, Ga., 1176.
**International rifle woman** — Karen E. Monez, Ft. Benning, Ga.,

1171.
**Conventional pistol** — Donald L. Hamilton, Kingston, Mass., 882.
**Conventional pistol woman** — Kim Dyer, Ft. Benning, Ga., 868.
**International pistol** — Steve F. Reiter, Daly City, Cal., 570.
**International pistol woman** — Kim Dyer, 550.

## World Swimming Records

As of Aug. 31, 1978

Effective June 1, 1969, FINA recognizes only records made over a 50-meter course.

### Men's Records

#### Freestyle

| Distance | Time | Holder | Country | Where made | Date |
|---|---|---|---|---|---|
| 0 Meters | 0:49.44 | Jonty Skinner | So. Africa | Philadelphia | Aug. 14, 1976 |
| 0 Meters | 1:50.29 | Bruce Furniss | U.S. | Montreal | July 19, 1976 |
| 0 Meters | 3:51.56 | Brian Goodell | U.S. | E. Berlin | Aug. 27, 1977 |
| 0 Meters | 8:01.54 | Bobby Hackett | U.S. | Long Beach, Cal. | June 21, 1976 |
| 500 Meters | 15:02.40 | Brian Goodell | U.S. | Montreal | July 20, 1976 |

#### Breaststroke

| | | | | | |
|---|---|---|---|---|---|
| 0 Meters | 1:02.86 | Gerald Morken | W. Germany | Jonkoping, Sweden | Aug. 17, 1977 |
| 0 Meters | 2:15.11 | David Wilkie | Gt. Britain | Montreal | July 24, 1976 |

#### Butterfly

| | | | | | |
|---|---|---|---|---|---|
| 0 Meters | 0:54.18 | Joe Bottom | U.S. | E. Berlin | Aug., 1977 |
| 0 Meters | 1:59.23 | Mike Bruner | U.S. | Montreal | July 18, 1976 |

#### Backstroke

| | | | | | |
|---|---|---|---|---|---|
| 0 Meters | 0:55.49 | John Naber | U.S. | Montreal | July 19, 1976 |
| 0 Meters | 1:59.19 | John Naber | U.S. | Montreal | July 24, 1976 |

#### Individual Medley

| | | | | | |
|---|---|---|---|---|---|
| 0 Meters | 2:03.65 | Graham Smith | Canada | W. Berlin | Aug., 1978 |
| 0 Meters | 4:20.05 | Jessee Vassallo | U.S. | W. Berlin | Aug. 22, 1978 |

#### Freestyle Relays

| | | | | | |
|---|---|---|---|---|---|
| 00 M. (4×100) | 3:19.74 | Babashoff, Gaines, McCag, Montgomery | U.S. | W. Berlin | Aug. 22, 1978 |
| 00 M. (4×200) | 7:20.83 | Forrester, Furniss, Gaines, Hackett | U.S. | W. Berlin | Aug., 1978 |

#### Medley Relays

| | | | | | |
|---|---|---|---|---|---|
| 00 M. (4×100) | 3:42.22 | Hencken, Naber, Montgomery, Vogel | U.S. | Montreal | July 22, 1976 |

### Women's Records

#### Freestyle

| | | | | | |
|---|---|---|---|---|---|
| 00 Meters | 0:55.41 | Barbara Krause | E. Germany | E. Berlin | July, 1978 |
| 00 Meters | 1:58.53 | Cynthia Woodhead | U.S. | W. Berlin | Aug., 1978 |
| 00 Meters | 4:06.28 | Tracey Wickham | Australia | Aug., 1978 |
| 00 Meters | 8:24.62 | Tracey Wickham | Australia | Edmonton | Aug. 5, 1978 |
| 500 Meters | 16:24.60 | Alice Browne | U.S. | Mission Viejo, Cal. | Aug. 21, 1977 |

#### Breaststroke

| | | | | | |
|---|---|---|---|---|---|
| 00 Meters | 1:10.31 | Iulia Bogbanova | USSR | W. Berlin | Aug., 1978 |
| 00 Meters | 2:31.42 | Lina Kachushite | USSR | W. Berlin | Aug., 1978 |

#### Butterfly

| | | | | | |
|---|---|---|---|---|---|
| 00 Meters | 0:59.46 | Andrea Pollack | E. Germany | E. Berlin | July, 1978 |
| 00 Meters | 2:11.22 | Rosemarie Gabriel | E. Germany | E. Berlin | June 5, 1976 |

#### Backstroke

| | | | | | |
|---|---|---|---|---|---|
| 00 Meters | 1:01.51 | Ulrike Richter | E. Germany | E. Berlin | June 5, 1976 |
| 00 Meters | 2:11.93 | Linda Jezek | U.S. | W. Berlin | Aug., 1978 |

#### Individual Medley

| | | | | | |
|---|---|---|---|---|---|
| 00 Meters | 2:14.07 | Tracy Caulkins | U.S. | W. Berlin | Aug., 1978 |
| 00 Meters | 4:40.83 | Tracy Caulkins | U.S. | W. Berlin | Aug., 1978 |

#### Freestyle Relays

| | | | | | |
|---|---|---|---|---|---|
| 00 M. (4×100) | 3:44.82 | Boglioli, Sterkel, Peyton, Babashoff | U.S. | Montreal | July 25, 1976 |

#### Medley Relays

| | | | | | |
|---|---|---|---|---|---|
| 00 M. (4×100) | 4:07.95 | Richter, Anke, Pollack, Ender | E. Germany | Montreal | July 18, 1976 |

## National AAU Outdoor Synchronized Swimming Championships

Purchase, N.Y., July 20-22

olo—Linda Shelley, Santa Clara Aquamaids.
uet—Michele Barone & Pam Tryon, Santa Clara Aquamaids.
eam—Santa Clara Aquamaids:

Allen, Michele Barone, Erin Barr, Gerri Brandly, Jane Goeppinger, Michele Beaulieu, Linda Shelley, Pam Tryon.

# Swimming Events in 1978

## National AAU Short Course Championships

Austin, Tex., Apr. 5-8, 1978

### Men

100-Yd. Freestyle—Jonty Skinner, N. River YC. Time—0:43.64.
200-Yd. Freestyle—Andy Veris, Mustang. Time—1:36.84.
500-Yd. Freestyle—Brian Goodell, Mission Viejo. Time—4:16.40.
1,650-Yd. Freestyle—Brian Goodell. Time—14:54.54.
100-Yd. Backstroke—Peter Rocca, Concord SC. Time—0:49.83.
200-Yd. Backstroke—Peter Rocca. Time—1:47.02.
100-Yd. Breaststroke—John Hencken, Santa Clara SC. Time—0:55.27.
200-Yd. Breaststroke—Nick Nevid, Nashville SC. Time—2:00.53.
100-Yd. Butterfly—Scott Spann, Florida Aquatic. Time—0:48.08.
200-Yd. Butterfly—Greg Jagenburg, Foxcatcher. Time—1:45.55.
200-Yd. Individual Medley—Scott Spann. Time—1:48.43.
400-Yd. Individual Medley—Jesse Vassallo, Mission Viejo. Time—3:51.69.
400-Yd. Medley Relay—Florida 'A'. Time—3:18.14.
400-Yd. Freestyle Relay—Gatorade 'A'. Time—2:55.27.
800-Yd. Freestyle Relay—Florida 'A'. Time—6:29.81.
Team champion—Florida Aquatic.

### Women

100-Yd. Freestyle—Stephanie Elkins, Amberjax. Time—0:49.66.
200-Yd. Freestyle—Stephanie Elkins. Time—1:45.91.
500-Yd. Freestyle—Cynthia Woodhead, Riverside AA. Time—4:39.94.
1,650-Yd. Freestyle—Cynthia Woodhead. Time—15:55.15.
100-Yd. Backstroke—Linda Jezek, Santa Clara SC. Time—0:55.08.
200-Yd. Backstroke—Linda Jezek. Time—1:57.79.
100-Yd. Breaststoke—Tracy Caukins, Nashville AC. Time—1:02.20.
200-Yd. Breaststroke—Tracy Caukins. Time—2:14.07.
100-Yd. Butterfly—Diane Johannigman, Cin Pepsi Marli Time—0:54.11.
200-Yd. Butterfly—Nancy Hogshead, Amberjax. Time—1:55.74.
200-Yd. Individual Medley—Tracy Caukins. Time—1:59.33.
400-Yd. Individual Medley—Tracy Caukins. Time—4:11.38.
400-Yd. Medley Relay—Nashville 'A'. Time—3:42.54.
400-Yd. Freestyle Relay—Nashville 'A'. Time—3:20.69.
800-Yd. Freestyle Relay—Nashville 'A'. Time—7:17.62.
Team champion—Nashville AC.

## National AAU Long Course Swimming Championships

The Woodlands, Tex., Aug. 2-6, 1978

### Men

100-Meter Freestyle—David McCagg, Florida Aquatics. Time—0:50.79.
200-Meter Freestyle—Bill Forrester, Florida Aquatics. Time—1:51.67.
400-Meter Freestyle—Jeff Float, Arden Hills SC. Time—3:54.32.
1,500-Meter Freestyle—Ed Ryder, Mission Viejo. Time—15:24.84.
100-Meter Backstroke—Bob Jackson, Camden SC. Time—0:57.22.
200-Meter Backstroke—Jesse Vassallo, Mission Viejo. Time—2:03.57.
100-Meter Breaststroke—Steve Lundquist, Tallman Polls ST. Time—1:04.44.
200-Meter Breaststroke—Jeff Freeman, Santa Clara SC. Time—2:21.78.
100-Meter Butterfly—Joe Bottom, Dutch Boy SC. Time—0:54.93.
200-Meter Butterfly—Steve Gregg, Beach SC. Time—2:00.84.
200-Meter Individual Medley—Jesse Vassallo. Time—2:05.90.
400-Meter Individual Medley—Jesse Vassallo. Time—4:23.39.
400-Meter Medley Relay—Cummins Engine SC. Time—3:47.84.
400-Meter Freestyle Relay—Florida Aquatics. Time—3:23.85.
800-Meter Freestyle Relay—Florida Aquatics. Time—7:30.23
Team Champion—Florida Aquatics.

### Women

100-Meter Freestyle—Cynthia Woodhead, Riverside AA. Time—0:56.73.
200-Meter Freestyle—Cynthia Woodhead. Time—1:59.49.
400-Meter Freestyle—Kim Linehan, Sarasota YMCA Sharks. Time—4:07.66.
800-Meter Freestyle—Kim Linehan. Time—8:31.99.
100-Meter Backstroke—Linda Jezek. Santa Clara SC. Time—1:03.50.
200-Meter Backstroke—Linda Jezek. Time—2:14.39.
100-Meter Breaststroke—Tracy Caulkins, Nashville AC. Time—1:10.97.
200-Meter Breaststroke—Tracy Caulkins. Time—2:35.23.
100-Meter Butterfly—Joan Pennington, Nashville AC. Time—1:00.58.
200-Meter Butterfly—Tracy Caulkins. Time—2:10.09.
200-Meter Individual Medley—Tracy Caulkins. Time—2:15.09.
400-Meter Individual Medley—Tracy Caulkins. Time—4:47.06.
400-Meter Medley Relay—Nashville AC. Time—4:15.15.
400-Meter Freestyle Relay—Nashville AC. Time 3:51.60.
800-Meter Freestyle Relay—Mission Viejo. Time—8:21.19.
Team champion—Nashville AC.

## NCAA Championships

Long Beach, Cal., Mar. 23-25, 1978

50-Yd. Freestyle—Andy Coan, Tennessee. Time—0:19.29.
100-Yd. Freestyle—Andy Coan. Time—0:44.10.
200-Yd. Freestyle—Bruce Furniss, So. Cal. Time—1:37.02.
500-Yd. Freestyle—Brian Goodell, California. Time—4:18.05.
1,650-Yd. Freestyle—Brian Goodell. Time—14:55.53.
100-Yd. Backstroke—Bob Jackson, Long Beach St. Time—0:49.88.
200-Yd. Backstroke—Peter Rocca, California. Time—1:47.48.
100-Yd. Breaststroke—Scott Spann, Auburn. Time—0:56.62.
200-Yd. Breaststroke—Graham Smith, California. Time—2:02.24.
100-Yd. Butterfly—Greg Jagenburg, Long Beach St. Time—0:48.77.
200-Yd. Butterfly—Greg Jagenburg. Time—1:46.01.
400-Yd. Individual Medley—Brian Goodell. Time—3:53.61.
One-Meter Dive—Wayne Chester, Alabama. 485.10 pts.
3-Meter Dive—Chris Snodo, Florida. 543.18 pts.
Team champion—Tennessee.

## National AAU Indoor Diving Championships

Cleveland, Oh., Apr. 12-15, 1978

### Men

One-Meter Springboard—Greg Louganis, Mission Viejo Nadadores. 811.56 pts.
3-Meter Springboard—Jim Kennedy, Gatorade/Tennessee. 822.72 pts.
Platform—Greg Louganis. 576.18 pts.

### Women

One-Meter Springboard—Julie Bachman, Kimball Divers 632.61 pts.
3-Meter Springboard—Jenni Chandler, Ron O'Brien Diving School. 657.90 pts.
Platform—Melissa Briley, Hurricane Divers. 350.28 pts.

# Annual Results of Major Bowl Games

## Rose Bowl, Pasadena

1902 Michigan 49, Stanford 0
1916 Wash. State 14, Brown 0
1917 Oregon 14, Pennsylvania 0
1918-19 Service teams
1920 Harvard 7, Oregon 6
1921 California 28, Ohio State 0
1922 Wash. & Jeff. 0, California 0
1923 So. California 14, Penn State 3
1924 Navy 14, Washington 14
1925 Notre Dame 27, Stanford 10
1926 Alabama 20, Washington 19
1927 Alabama 7, Stanford 7
1928 Stanford 7, Pittsburgh 6
1929 Georgia Tech 8, California 7
1930 So. California 47, Pittsburgh 14
1931 Alabama 24, Wash. State 0
1932 So. California 21, Tulane 12
1933 So. California 35, Pittsburgh 0
1934 Columbia 7, Stanford 0
1935 Alabama 29, Stanford 13
1936 Stanford 7, So. Methodist 0
1937 Pittsburgh 21, Washington 0

1938 California 13, Alabama 0
1939 So. California 7, Duke 3
1940 So. California 14, Tennessee 0
1941 Stanford 21, Nebraska 13
1942 Oregon St. 20, Duke 16
　(at Durham)
1943 Georgia 9, UCLA 0
1944 So. California 29, Washington 0
1945 So. California 25, Tennessee 0
1946 Alabama 34, So. California 14
1947 Illinois 45, UCLA 14
1948 Michigan 49, So. California 0
1949 Northwestern 20, California 14
1950 Ohio State 17, California 14
1951 Michigan 14, California 6
1952 Illinois 40, Stanford 7
1953 So. California 7, Wisconsin 0
1954 Mich. State 28, UCLA 20
1955 Ohio State 20, So. California 7
1956 Mich. State 17, UCLA 14
1957 Iowa 35, Oregon St. 19

1958 Ohio State 10, Oregon 7
1959 Iowa 38, California 12
1960 Washington 44, Wisconsin 8
1961 Washington 17, Minnesota 7
1962 Minnesota 21, UCLA 3
1963 So. California 42, Wisconsin 37
1964 Illinois 17, Washington 7
1965 Michigan 34, Oregon St. 7
1966 UCLA 14, Mich. State 12
1967 Purdue 14, So. California 13
1968 Southern Cal. 14, Indiana 3
1969 Ohio State 27, Southern Cal 16
1970 Southern Cal 10, Michigan 3
1971 Stanford 27, Ohio State 17
1972 Stanford 13, Michigan 12
1973 So. California 42, Ohio State 17
1974 Ohio State 42, So. California 21
1975 So. California 18, Ohio State 17
1976 UCLA 23, Ohio State 10
1977 So. California 14, Michigan 6
1978 Washington 27, Michigan 20

## Orange Bowl, Miami

1933 Miami (Fla.) 7, Manhattan 0
1934 Duquesne 33, Miami (Fla.) 7
1935 Bucknell 26, Miami (Fla.) 0
1936 Catholic U. 20, Mississippi 19
1937 Duquesne 13, Miss. State 12
1938 Auburn 6, Mich. State 0
1939 Tennessee 17, Oklahoma 0
1940 Georgia Tech 21, Missouri 7
1941 Miss. State 14, Georgetown 7
1942 Georgia 40, TCU 26
1943 Alabama 37, Boston Col. 21
1944 LSU 19, Texas A&M 14
1945 Tulsa 26, Georgia Tech 12
1946 Miami (Fla.) 13, Holy Cross 6
1947 Rice 8, Tennessee 0
1948 Georgia Tech 20, Kansas 14

1949 Texas 41, Georgia 28
1950 Santa Clara 21, Kentucky 13
1951 Clemson 15, Miami (Fla.) 14
1952 Georgia Tech 17, Baylor 14
1953 Alabama 61, Syracuse 6
1954 Oklahoma 7, Maryland 0
1955 Duke 34, Nebraska 7
1956 Oklahoma 20, Maryland 6
1957 Colorado 27, Clemson 21
1958 Oklahoma 48, Duke 21
1959 Oklahoma 21, Syracuse 6
1960 Georgia 14, Missouri 0
1961 Missouri 21, Navy 14
1962 LSU 25, Colorado 7
1963 Alabama 17, Oklahoma 0

1964 Nebraska 13, Auburn 7
1965 Texas 21, Alabama 17
1966 Alabama 39, Nebraska 28
1967 Florida 27, Georgia Tech 12
1968 Oklahoma 26, Tennessee 24
1969 Penn State 15, Kansas 14
1970 Penn State 10, Missouri 3
1971 Nebraska 17, Louisiana St. 12
1972 Nebraska 38, Alabama 6
1973 Nebraska 40, Notre Dame 6
1974 Penn State 16, Louisiana St. 9
1975 Notre Dame 13, Alabama 11
1976 Oklahoma 14, Michigan 6
1977 Ohio State 27, Colorado 10
1978 Arkansas 31, Oklahoma 6

## Sugar Bowl, New Orleans

1935 Tulane 20, Temple 14
1936 TCU 3, LSU 2
1937 Santa Clara 21, LSU 14
1938 Santa Clara 6, LSU 0
1939 TCU 15, Carnegie Tech 7
1940 Texas A&M 14, Tulane 13
1941 Boston Col. 19, Tennessee 13
1942 Fordham 2, Missouri 0
1943 Tennessee 14, Tulsa 7
1944 Georgia Tech 20, Tulsa 18
1945 Duke 29, Alabama 26
1946 Oklahoma A&M 33, St. Mary's 13
1947 Georgia 20, No. Carolina 10
1948 Texas 27, Alabama 7
1949 Oklahoma 14, No. Carolina 6

1950 Oklahoma 35, LSU 0
1951 Kentucky 13, Oklahoma 7
1952 Maryland 28, Tennessee 13
1953 Georgia Tech. 24, Mississippi 7
1954 Georgia Tech 42, West Virginia 19
1955 Navy 21, Mississippi 0
1956 Georgia Tech 7, Pittsburgh 0
1957 Baylor 13, Tennessee 7
1958 Mississippi 39, Texas 7
1959 LSU 7, Clemson 0
1960 Mississippi 21, LSU 0
1961 Mississippi 14, Rice 6
1962 Alabama 10, Arkansas 3
1963 Mississippi 17, Arkansas 13
1964 Alabama 12, Mississippi 7

1965 LSU 13, Syracuse 10
1966 Missouri 20, Florida 18
1967 Alabama 34, Nebraska 7
1968 LSU 20, Wyoming 13
1969 Arkansas 16, Georgia 2
1970 Mississippi 27, Arkansas 22
1971 Tennessee 34, Air Force 13
1972 Oklahoma 40, Auburn 22
*1972 (Dec.) Oklahoma 14, Penn State 0
1973 Notre Dame 24, Alabama 23
1974 Nebraska 13, Florida 10
1975 Alabama 13, Penn State 6
1977 (Jan.) Pittsburgh 27, Georgia 3
1978 Alabama 35, Ohio State 6
*Penn St. awarded game by forfeit

## Cotton Bowl, Dallas

1937 TCU 16, Marquette 6
1938 Rice 28, Colorado 14
1939 St. Mary's 20, Texas Tech 13
1940 Clemson 6, Boston Col. 3
1941 Texas A&M 13, Fordham 12
1942 Alabama 29, Texas A&M 21
1943 Texas 14, Georgia Tech 7
1944 Randolph Field 7, Texas 7
1945 Oklahoma A&M 34, TCU 0
1946 Texas 40, Missouri 27
1947 Arkansas 0, LSU 0
1948 So. Methodist 13, Penn State 13
1949 So. Methodist 21, Oregon 13
1950 Rice 27, No. Carolina 13

1951 Tennessee 20, Texas 14
1952 Kentucky 20, TCU 7
1953 Texas 16, Tennessee 0
1954 Rice 28; Alabama 6
1955 Georgia Tech 14, Arkansas 6
1956 Mississippi 14, TCU 13
1957 TCU 28, Syracuse 27
1958 Navy 20, Rice 7
1959 TCU 0, Air Force 0
1960 Syracuse 23, Texas 14
1961 Duke 7, Arkansas 6
1962 Texas 12, Mississippi 7
1963 LSU 13, Texas 0
1964 Texas 28, Navy 6

1965 Arkansas 10, Nebraska 7
1966 LSU 14, Arkansas 7
1967 Georgia 24, So. Methodist 9
1968 Texas A&M 20, Alabama 16
1969 Texas 36, Tennessee 13
1970 Texas 21, Notre Dame 7
1971 Notre Dame 24, Texas 11
1972 Penn State 30, Texas 6
1973 Texas 17, Alabama 13
1974 Nebraska 19, Texas 3
1975 Penn State 41, Baylor 20
1976 Arkansas 31, Georgia 10
1977 Houston 30, Maryland 21
1978 Notre Dame 38, Texas 10

## Fiesta Bowl, Phoenix

1971 Arizona St. 45, Flordia St. 38
1972 Arizona St. 49, Missouri 35
1973 Arizona St. 28, Pittsburgh 7

1974 Okla. St. 16, Brigham Young 6
1975 Arizona St. 17, Nebraska 14

1976 Oklahoma 41, Wyoming 7
1977 Penn St. 42, Arizona St. 30

## Liberty Bowl, Memphis

| | | |
|---|---|---|
| 1959 Penn State 7, Alabama 0 | 1966 Miami (Fla.) 14, Va. Tech 7 | 1972 Georgia Tech 31, Iowa State 30 |
| 1960 Penn State 41, Oregon 12 | 1967 N.C. State 14, Georgia 7 | 1973 No. Carolina St. 31, Kansas 18 |
| 1961 Syracuse 15, Miami 14 | 1968 Mississippi 34, Va. Tech 17 | 1974 Tennessee 7, Maryland 3 |
| 1962 Oregon 6, Villanova 0 | 1969 Colorado 47, Alabama 33 | 1975 USC 20, Texas A&M 0 |
| 1963 Miss. State 16, N.C. State 12 | 1970 Tulane 17, Colorado 3 | 1976 Alabama 36, UCLA 6 |
| 1964 Utah 32, West Virginia 6 | 1971 Tennessee 14, Arkansas 13 | 1977 Nebraska 27, N. Carolina 17 |
| 1965 Mississippi 13, Auburn 7 | | |

## Sun Bowl, El Paso

| | | |
|---|---|---|
| 1936 Hardin Simmons 14, New Mex. St. 14 | 1950 Texas Western 33, Georgetown 20 | 1964 Oregon 21, So. Methodist 14 |
| 1937 Hardin-Simmons 34, Texas Mines 6 | 1951 West Texas St. 14, Cincinnati 13 | 1965 Georgia 7, Texas Tech 0 |
| 1938 West Virginia 7, Texas Tech 6 | 1952 Texas Tech 25, Col. Pacific 14 | 1966 Texas Western 13, TCU 12 |
| 1939 Utah 26, New Mexico 0 | 1953 Col. Pacific 26, Miss. Southern 7 | 1967 Wyoming 28, Florida St. 20 |
| 1940 Catholic U. 0, Arizona St. 0 | 1954 Texas Western 37, Miss. Southern 14 | 1968 UTex El Paso 14, Mississippi 7 |
| 1941 Western Reserve 26, Arizona St. 13 | 1955 Texas Western 47, Florida St. 20 | 1969 Auburn 34, Arizona 10 |
| 1942 Tulsa 6, Texas Tech 0 | 1956 Wyoming 21, Texas Tech 14 | 1969 (Dec.) Nebraska 45, Georgia 6 |
| 1943 Air Force 13, Hardin-Simmons 7 | 1957 Geo. Washington 13, Tex. Western 0 | 1970 Georgia Tech. 17, Texas Tech. 9 |
| 1944 Southwestern (Tex.) 7, New Mexico 0 | 1958 Louisville 34, Drake 20 | 1971 LSU 33, Iowa State 15 |
| 1945 Southwestern (Tex.) 35, U. of Mex. 0 | 1959 Wyoming 14, Hardin-Simmons 6 | 1972 North Carolina 32, Texas Tech 28 |
| 1946 New Mexico 34, Denver 24 | 1960 New Mexico St. 28, No. Texas St. 8 | 1973 Missouri 34, Auburn 17 |
| 1947 Cincinnati 38, Virginia Tech 6 | 1961 New Mexico St. 20, Utah State 13 | 1974 Mississippi St. 26, North Carolina 24 |
| 1948 Miami (O.) 13, Texas Tech 12 | 1962 Villanova 17, Wichita 9 | 1975 Pittsburgh 33, Kansas 19 |
| 1949 West Virginia 21, Texas Mines 12 | 1963 West Texas St. 15, Ohio U. 14 | 1977 (Jan.) Texas A&M 37, Florida 14 |
| | | 1977 Stanford 24, Louisiana St. 14 |

## Gator Bowl, Jacksonville

| | | |
|---|---|---|
| 1946 Wake Forest 26, So. Carolina 14 | 1957 Georgia Tech 21, Pittsburgh 14 | 1968 Penn State 17, Florida St. 17 |
| 1947 Oklahoma 34, N.C. State 13 | 1958 Tennessee 3, Texas A&M 0 | 1969 Missouri 35, Alabama 10 |
| 1948 Maryland 20, Georgia 20 | 1959 Mississippi 7, Florida 3 | 1969 (Dec.) Florida 14, Tenn. 13 |
| 1949 Clemson 24, Missouri 23 | 1960 Arkansas 14, Georgia Tech 7 | 1971 Auburn 35, Mississippi 28 |
| 1950 Maryland 20, Missouri 7 | 1961 Florida 13, Baylor 12 | 1972 Georgia 7, N. Carolina 3 |
| 1951 Wyoming 20, Wash. & Lee 7 | 1962 Penn State 30, Georgia Tech 15 | 1973 Auburn 24, Colorado 3 |
| 1952 Miami (Fla.) 14, Clemson 0 | 1963 Florida 17, Penn State 7 | 1973 (Dec.) Tex. Tech. 28, Tenn. 19 |
| 1953 Florida 14, Tulsa 13 | 1964 No. Carolina 35, Air Force 0 | 1974 Auburn 27, Texas 3 |
| 1954 Texas Tech 35, Auburn 13 | 1965 Florida St. 36, Oklahoma 19 | 1975 Maryland 13, Florida 0 |
| 1955 Auburn 33, Baylor 13 | 1966 Georgia Tech 31, Texas Tech 21 | 1976 Notre Dame 20, Penn State 9 |
| 1956 Vanderbilt 25, Auburn 13 | 1967 Tennessee 18, Syracuse 12 | 1977 Pittsburgh 34, Clemson 3 |

## Bluebonnet Bowl, Houston

| | | |
|---|---|---|
| 1959 Clemson 23, TCU 7 | 1966 Texas 19, Mississippi 0 | 1972 Tennessee 24, Louisiana St. 17 |
| 1960 Texas 3, Alabama 3 | 1967 Colorado 31, Miami (Fla.) 21 | 1973 Houston 47, Tulane 7 |
| 1961 Kansas 33, Rice 7 | 1968 SMU 28, Oklahoma 27 | 1974 N. Carolina St. 31, Houston 31 |
| 1962 Missouri 14, Georgia Tech 10 | 1969 Houston 36, Auburn 7 | 1975 Texas 38, Colorado 21 |
| 1963 Baylor 14, LSU 7 | 1970 Oklahoma 24, Alabama 24 | 1976 Nebraska 27, Texas Tech 24 |
| 1964 Tulsa 14, Mississippi 7 | 1971 Colorado 29, Houston 17 | 1977 USC 47, Texas A&M 28 |
| 1965 Tennessee 27, Tulsa 6 | | |

## Peach Bowl, Atlanta

| | | |
|---|---|---|
| 1968 LSU 31, Florida St. 27 | 1972 N. Carolina St. 49, W. Va. 13 | 1975 W. Virginia 13, No. Carolina St. 10 |
| 1969 West Virginia 14, S. Carolina 3 | 1973 Georgia 17, Maryland 16 | 1976 Kentucky 21, North Carolina 0 |
| 1970 Arizona St. 48, N. Carolina 26 | 1974 Vanderbilt 6, Texas Tech. 6 | 1977 N. Carolina St. 24, Iowa St. 14 |
| 1971 Mississippi 41, Georgia Tech. 18 | | |

## Tangerine Bowl, Orlando

| | | |
|---|---|---|
| 1968 Richmond 49, Ohio 42 | 1972 Tampa 21, Kent State 18 | 1976 Oklahoma St. 49, Brigham Young 21 |
| 1969 Toledo 56, Davidson 33 | 1973 Miami, Ohio 16, Florida 7 | |
| 1970 Toledo 40, William & Mary 12 | 1974 Miami, Ohio 21, Georgia 10 | 1977 Florida St. 40, Texas Tech 17 |
| 1971 Toledo 28, Richmond 3 | 1975 Miami, Ohio 20, South Carolina 7 | |

## Heisman Trophy Winners

Awarded annually to the nation's outstanding college football player

| | | |
|---|---|---|
| 1935 Jay Berwanger, Chicago, HB | 1950 Vic Janowicz, Ohio State, HB | 1964 John Huarte, Notre Dame, QB |
| 1936 Larry Kelley, Yale, E | 1951 Richard Kazmaier, Princeton, HB | 1965 Mike Garrett, USC, HB |
| 1937 Clinton Frank, Yale, QB | 1952 Billy Vessels, Oklahoma, HB | 1966 Steve Spurrier, Florida, QB |
| 1938 David O'Brien, Tex. Christian, QB | 1953 John Lattner, Notre Dame, HB | 1967 Gary Beban, UCLA, QB |
| 1939 Nile Kinnick, Iowa, QB | 1954 Alan Ameche, Wisconsin, FB | 1968 O. J. Simpson, USC, RB |
| 1940 Tom Harmon, Michigan, HB | 1955 Howard Cassady, Ohio St., HB | 1969 Steve Owens, Oklahoma, RB |
| 1941 Bruce Smith, Minnesota, HB | 1956 Paul Hornung, Notre Dame, QB | 1970 Jim Plunkett, Stanford, QB |
| 1942 Frank Sinkwich, Georgia, HB | 1957 John Crow, Texas A & M, HB | 1971 Pat Sullivan, Auburn, QB |
| 1943 Angelo Bertelli, Notre Dame, QB | 1958 Pete Dawkins, Army, HB | 1972 Johnny Rodgers, Nebraska, RB-R |
| 1944 Leslie Horvath, Ohio State, QB | 1959 Billy Cannon, La. State, HB | 1973 John Cappelletti, Penn State, RB |
| 1945 Felix Blanchard, Army, FB | 1960 Joe Bellino, Navy, HB | 1974 Archie Griffin, Ohio State, RB |
| 1946 Glenn Davis, Army, HB | 1961 Ernest Davis, Syracuse, HB | 1975 Archie Griffin, Ohio State, RB |
| 1947 John Lujack, Notre Dame, QB | 1962 Terry Baker, Oregon State, QB | 1976 Tony Dorsett, Pittsburgh, RB |
| 1948 Doak Walker, SMU, HB | 1963 Roger Staubach, Navy, QB | 1977 Earl Campbell, Texas, RB |
| 1949 Leon Hart, Notre Dame, E | | |

# College Football Teams

## Division I Teams

| Team | Nickname | Team colors | Conference | Coach | 1977 record (W-L-T) |
|---|---|---|---|---|---|
| Air Force | Falcons | Blue & silver | Independent | Bill Parcells | 2-8-1 |
| Alabama | Crimson Tide | Crimson & white | Southeastern | Paul Bryant | 11-1-0 |
| Alcom State | Braves | Purple & gold | Southwestern | Marino Casem | 3-8-0 |
| Appalachian State | Mountaineers | Black & gold | Southern | Jim Brakefield | 2-9-0 |
| Arizona | Wildcats | Red & blue | Pacific Ten | Tony Mason | 5-7-0 |
| Arizona State | Sun Devils | Maroon & gold | Pacific Ten | Frank Kush | 9-3-0 |
| Arkansas | Razorbacks | Cardinal & white | Southwest | Lou Holtz | 11-1-0 |
| Arkansas State | Indians | Scarlet & black | Southland | Bill Davidson | 7-4-0 |
| Army | Cadets | Black, gold, gray | Independent | Homer Smith | 7-4-0 |
| Auburn | Tigers | Orange & blue | Southeastern | Doug Barfield | 6-5-0 |
| Austin Peay State | Governors | Scarlet & white | Ohio Valley | James Donnelly | 8-3-0 |
| Ball State | Cardinals | Cardinal & white | Mid-American | Dwight Wallace | 9-2-0 |
| Baylor | Bears | Green & gold | Southwest | Grant Teaff | 5-6-0 |
| Boston College | Eagles | Maroon & gold | Independent | Ed Chiebek | 6-5-0 |
| Boston Univ. | Terriers | Scarlet & white | Yankee | Rick Taylor | 3-7-0 |
| Bowling Green St. | Falcons | Orange & brown | Mid-American | Denny Stolz | 5-7-0 |
| Brigham Young | Cougars | Royal blue & white | Western Athletic | LaVell Edwards | 9-2-0 |
| Brown | Bruins, Bears | Brown, cardinal, white | Ivy | John Anderson | 7-2-0 |
| Bucknell | Bisons | Orange & blue | Independent | Bob Curtis | 4-5-0 |
| California | Golden Bears | Blue & gold | Pacific-Ten | Roger Theder | 7-4-0 |
| Central Michigan | Chippewas | Maroon & gold | Mid-American | Roy Kramer | 10-1-0 |
| Cincinnati | Bearcats | Red & black | Indpendent | Ralph Staub | 5-4-2 |
| Citadel | Bulldogs | Blue & white | Southern | Art Baker | 5-6-0 |
| Clemson | Tigers | Purple & orange | Atlantic Coast | Charley Pell | 8-3-1 |
| Colgate | Red Raiders | Maroon | Independent | Fred Dunlap | 10-1-0 |
| Colorado State | Rams | Green & gold | Western Athletic | Sarkis Arslanian | 9-2-1 |
| Colorado | Buffaloes | Silver & gold | Big Eight | Bill Mallory | 7-3-1 |
| Columbia | Lions | Blue & white | Ivy | Bill Campbell | 2-7-0 |
| Connecticut | Huskies | Blue & white | Yankee | Walt Nadzak | 1-10-0 |
| Cornell | Big Red | Carnelian & white | Ivy | Bob Blackman | 1-8-0 |
| Dartmouth | Big Green | Dartmouth green | Ivy | Joe Yukica | 6-3-0 |
| Davidson | Wildcats | Red & black | Southern | Ed Farrell | 4-6-0 |
| Delaware State | Hornets | Red & blue | Mid-Eastern | Ed Wyche | 7-4-0 |
| Drake | Bulldogs | Blue & white | Missouri Valley | Chuck Shelton | 2-9-0 |
| Duke | Blue Devils | Royal blue & white | Atlantic Coast | Mike McGee | 5-6-0 |
| East Carolina | Pirates | Purple & gold | Independent | Pat Dye | 8-3-0 |
| East Tennessee St. | Buccaneers | Blue & gold | Southern | Jack Carlisle | 3-8-0 |
| Eastern Michigan | Hurons | Green & white | Mid-American | Mike Stock | 8-3-0 |
| Eastern Kentucky | Colonels | Maroon & white | Ohio Valley | Roy Kidd | 5-5-0 |
| Florida | Gators | Orange & blue | Southeastern | Doug Dickey | 6-4-1 |
| Florida State | Seminoles | Garnet & gold | Independent | Bobby Bowden | 10-2-0 |
| Fresno State | Bulldogs | Cardinal & blue | Pacific Coast | Bob Padilla | 9-2-0 |
| Fullerton, Cal. State | Titans | Blue, orange, white | Pacific Coast | Jim Colletto | 4-7-0 |
| Furman | Paladins | Purple & white | Southern | Dick Sheridan | 4-5-2 |
| Georgia | Bulldogs | Red & black | Southeastern | Vince Dooley | 5-6-0 |
| Georgia Tech | Yellow Jackets | Old gold & white | Independent | Pepper Rodgers | 6-5-0 |
| Grambling State | Tigers | Black & gold | Southwestern | Eddie Robinson | 10-1-0 |
| Harvard | Crimson | Crimson | Ivy | Joe Restic | 4-5-0 |
| Hawaii | Rainbow Warriors | Green & white | Western Athletic | Dick Tomey | 5-6-0 |
| Holy Cross | Crusaders | Royal purple | Independent | Neil Wheelwright | 2-9-0 |
| Houston | Cougars | Scarlet & white | Southwest | Bill Yeoman | 6-5-0 |
| Howard | Bison | Blue & white | Mid-Eastern | Douglas Porter | 5-5-0 |
| Idaho | Vandals | Silver & gold | Big Sky | Jerry Davitch | 3-8-0 |
| Idaho State | Bengals | Orange & black | Big Sky | Bud Hake | 3-8-0 |
| Illinois | Fighting Illini | Orange & blue | Big Ten | Gary Moeller | 3-8-0 |
| Illinois State | Redbirds | Red & white | Independent | Charley Cowdrey | 3-7-1 |
| Indiana | Fightin' Hoosiers | Cream & crimson | Big Ten | Lee Corso | 5-5-1 |
| Indiana State | Sycamores | Blue & white | Missouri Valley | Dick Jamieson | 3-7-0 |
| Iowa | Hawkeyes | Old gold & black | Big Ten | Bob Commings | 4-7-0 |
| Iowa State | Cyclones | Cardinal & gold | Big Eight | Earle Bruce | 8-4-0 |
| Jackson State | Tigers | Blue & white | Southwestern | W.C. Gorden | 8-3-0 |
| Kansas | Jayhawks | Crimson & blue | Big Eight | Bud Moore | 3-7-1 |
| Kansas State | Wildcats | Purple & white | Big Eight | Jim Dickey | 2-9-0 |
| Kent State | Golden Flashes | Blue & gold | Mid-American | Ron Blackledge | 6-5-0 |
| Kentucky | Wildcats | Blue & white | Southeastern | Fran Curci | 10-1-0 |
| Lafayette | Leopards | Maroon & white | Independent | Neil Putnam | 5-6-0 |
| Lamar | Cardinals | Red & white | Southland | Bob Frederick | 2-9-0 |
| Lehigh | Engineers | Brown & white | Independent | John Whitehead | 12-2-0 |
| Long Beach, Cal. State | Forty Niners | Brown & gold | Pacific Coast | Dave Currey | 4-6-0 |
| Louisiana State | Fighting Tigers | Purple & gold | Southeastern | Charles McClendon | 8-4-0 |
| Louisiana Tech | Bulldogs | Red & blue | Southland | Maxie Lambright | 9-1-2 |
| Louisville | Cardinals | Red, black, white | Independent | Vince Gibson | 7-4-1 |
| Maine | Black Bears | Blue & white | Yankee | Jack Bicknell | 3-7-0 |
| Marshall | Thundering Herd | Green & white | Southern | Frank Ellwood | 2-9-0 |
| Maryland | Terps | Red & white | Atlantic Coast | Jerry Claiborne | 8-4-0 |
| Massachusetts | Minutemen | Maroon & white | Yankee | Robert Pickett | 8-3-0 |
| McNeese State | Cowboys | Blue & gold | Southland | Jack Doland | 5-5-1 |
| Memphis State | Tigers | Blue & gray | Independent | Richard Williamson | 6-5-0 |
| Miami (Fla.) | Hurricanes | Orange, green, white | Independent | Lou Saban | 3-8-0 |
| Miami (Ohio) | Redskins | Red & white | Mid-American | Tom Reed | 10-1-0 |
| Michigan | Wolverines | Maize & blue | Big Ten | Bo Schembechler | 10-2-0 |

| Team | Nickname | Team colors | Conference | Coach | 1977 record (W-L-T) |
|---|---|---|---|---|---|
| Michigan State | Spartans | Green & white | Big Ten | Darryl Rogers | 7-3 |
| Middle Tennessee St. | Blue Raiders | Blue & white | Ohio Valley | Ben Hurt | 3-8 |
| Minnesota | Gophers | Maroon & gold | Big Ten | Cal Stoll | 7-5 |
| Mississippi | Rebels | Red & blue | Southeastern | Steve Sloan | 6-5 |
| Mississippi State | Bulldogs | Maroon & white | Southeastern | Bob Tyler | 0-11 |
| Missouri | Tigers | Old gold & black | Big Eight | Warren Powers | 4-7 |
| Montana | Grizzlies | Copper, silver, gold | Big Sky | Gene Carlson | 4-6 |
| Montana State | Bobcats | Blue & gold | Big Sky | Sonny Lubick | 6-4 |
| Morehead State | Eagles | Blue & gold | Ohio Valley | Wayne Chapman | 2-6 |
| Murray State | Racers | Blue & gold | Ohio Valley | Mike Gottfried | 6-5 |
| Navy | Midshipmen | Navy blue & gold | Independent | George Welsh | 5-6 |
| Nebraska | Cornhuskers | Scarlet & cream | Big Eight | Tom Osborne | 9-3 |
| Nevada-Las Vegas | Rebels | Scarlet & gray | Western Athletic | Tony Knap | 9-2 |
| Nevada-Reno | Wolf Pack | Silver & blue | Big Sky | Chris Ault | 8-3 |
| New Hampshire | Wildcats | Blue & white | Yankee | Bill Bowes | 8-2 |
| New Mexico | Lobos | Cherry & silver | Western Athletic | Bill Mondt | 5-7 |
| New Mexico State | Aggies | Crimson & white | Missouri Valley | Gil Krueger | 4-7 |
| North Carolina | Tar Heels | Blue & white | Atlantic Coast | Dick Crum | 8-3 |
| North Carolina A & T | Aggies | Blue & gold | Mid-Eastern | Jim McKinley | 7-4 |
| North Carolina State | Wolfpack | Red & white | Atlantic Coast | Bo Rein | 8-4 |
| North Texas State | Mean Green, Eagles | Green & white | Independent | Hayden Fry | 10-1 |
| Northeast Louisiana | Indians | Maroon & gold | Independent | John David Crow | 2-9 |
| Northeastern | Huskies | Red & black | Independent | Robert Lyons | 3-6 |
| Northern Arizona | Lumberjacks | Blue & gold | Big Sky | Joe Salem | 9-3 |
| Northern Illinois | Huskies | Cardinal & black | Mid-American | Pat Culpepper | 3-8 |
| Northwestern | Wildcats | Purple & white | Big Ten | Rick Venturi | 1-10 |
| Northwestern State | Demons | Burnt orange, purple, white | Independent | A.L. Williams | 6-5 |
| Notre Dame | Fighting Irish | Gold & blue | Independent | Dan Devine | 11-1 |
| Ohio State | Buckeyes | Scarlet & gray | Big Ten | Woody Hayes | 9-3 |
| Ohio Univ | Bobcats | Green & white | Mid-American | Bob Kappes | 1-10 |
| Oklahoma | Sooners | Crimson & cream | Big Eight | Barry Switzer | 10-2 |
| Oklahoma State | Cowboys | Orange & black | Big Eight | Jim Stanley | 4-7 |
| Oregon | Ducks | Green & yellow | Pacific Ten | Rich Brooks | 2-9 |
| Oregon State | Beavers | Orange & black | Pacific Ten | Craig Fertig | 2-9 |
| Pacific | Tigers | Orange & black | Pacific Coast | Chester Caddas | 6-5 |
| Penn State | Nittany Lions | Blue & white | Independent | Joe Paterno | 11-1 |
| Pennsylvania | Red & Blue, Quakers | Red & blue | Ivy | Harry Gamble | 5-4 |
| Pittsburgh | Panthers | Gold & blue | Independent | Jackie Sherrill | 9-2 |
| Portland State | Vikings | Green & white | Independent | Darrel Davis | 7-4 |
| Princeton | Tigers | Orange & black | Ivy | Frank Navarro | 3-6 |
| Purdue | Boilermakers | Old gold & black | Big Ten | Jim Young | 5-6 |
| Rhode Island | Rams | Blue & white | Yankee | Bob Griffin | 6-5 |
| Rice | Owls | Blue & gray | Southwest | Ray Alborn | 1-10 |
| Richmond | Spiders | Red & blue | Independent | Jim Tait | 3-8 |
| Rutgers | Scarlet Knights | Scarlet | Independent | Frank Burns | 8-3 |
| San Diego State | Aztecs | Scarlet & black | Western Athletic | Claude Gilbert | 10-1 |
| San Jose State | Spartans | Blue, gold & white | Pacific Coast | Lynn Stiles | 4-7 |
| South Carolina | Fighting Gamecocks | Garnet & black | Independent | Jim Carlen | 5-7 |
| South Carolina State | Bulldogs | Garnet & blue | Mid-Eastern | Willie Jeffries | 9-1 |
| Southern | Jaguars | Blue & gold | Southwestern | Cass Jackson | 3-7 |
| Southern California | Trojans | Cardinal & gold | Pacific Ten | John Robinson | 8-4 |
| Southern Illinois | Salukis | Maroon & white | Missouri Valley | Rey Dempsey | 3-8 |
| Southern Methodist | Mustangs | Red & blue | Southwest | Ron Meyer | 4-7 |
| Southern Mississippi | Golden Eagles | Black & gold | Independent | Bobby Collins | 6-6 |
| Southwestern La. | Ragin' Cajuns | Vermillion & white | Southland | Augie Tammariello | 6-4 |
| Stanford | Cardinals | Cardinal & white | Pacific Ten | Bill Walsh | 9-3 |
| Syracuse | Orangemen | Orange | Independent | Frank Maloney | 6-5 |
| Temple | Owls | Cherry & white | Independent | Wayne Hardin | 5-5 |
| Tennessee | Volunteers | Orange & white | Southeastern | John Majors | 4-7 |
| Tenn.-Chattanooga | Moccasins | Navy blue & gold | Southern | Joe Morrison | 9-1 |
| Tennessee State | Tigers | Blue & white | Independent | John A. Merritt | 8-1 |
| Tennessee Tech | Golden Eagles | Purple & gold | Ohio Valley | Don Wade | 9-2 |
| Texas | Longhorns | Orange & white | Southwest | Fred Akers | 11-1 |
| Texas-Arlington | Mavericks | Royal blue & white | Southland | Bud Elliott | 5-6 |
| Texas-El Paso | Miners | Orange & white | Western Athletic | Bill Michael | 1-10 |
| Texas A & M | Aggies | Maroon & white | Southwest | Emory Bellard | 8-4 |
| Texas Christian | Horned Frogs | Purple & white | Southwest | F.A. Dry | 2-9 |
| Texas Southern | Tigers | Maroon & gray | Southwestern | Wendell Mosley | 6-4 |
| Texas Tech | Red Raiders | Scarlet & black | Southwest | Rex Dockery | 7-5 |
| Toledo | Rockets | Blue & gold | Mid-American | Chuck Stobart | 2-9 |
| Tulane | Green Wave | Olive green & sky blue | Independent | Larry Smith | 3-8 |
| Tulsa | Golden Hurricane | Blue, red, gold | Missouri Valley | John Cooper | 3-8 |
| UCLA | Bruins | Navy blue & gold | Pacific Ten | Terry Donahue | 7-4 |
| Utah State | Aggies | Navy blue & white | Pacific Coast | Bruce Snyder | 4-7 |
| Utah | Utes | Crimson & white | Western Athletic | Wayne Howard | 3-8 |
| Vanderbilt | Commodores | Black & gold | Southeastern | Fred Pancoast | 2-9 |
| Villanova | Wildcats | Blue & white | Independent | Dick Bedesem | 4-7 |
| Virginia | Cavaliers | Orange & blue | Atlantic Coast | Dick Bestwick | 1-9 |
| Virginia Polytech Inst | Gobblers | Orange & maroon | Independent | Bill Dooley | 3-7 |
| VMI | Keydets | Red, white, yellow | Southern | Bob Thalman | 7-4 |
| Wake Forest | Demon Deacons | Old gold & black | Atlantic Coast | John Mackovic | 1-10 |
| Washington | Huskies | Purple & gold | Pacific Ten | Don James | 9-3 |
| Washington State | Cougars | Crimson & gray | Pacific Ten | Jim Walden | 6-5 |
| Weber State | Wildcats | Purple & white | Big Sky | Pete Riehlman | 4-6 |
| West Texas State | Buffaloes | Maroon & white | Missouri Valley | Bill Yung | 6-4 |

| Team | Nickname | Team colors | Conference | Coach | 1977 record (W-L-T) |
|---|---|---|---|---|---|
| West Virginia | Mountaineers | Old gold & blue | Independent | Frank Cignetti | 5-6-0 |
| Western Carolina | Catamounts | Purple & gold | Southern | Bob Waters | 6-4-1 |
| Western Kentucky | Hilltoppers | Red & white | Ohio Valley | Jimmy Feix | 1-8-1 |
| Western Michigan | Broncos | Brown & gold | Mid-American | Elliot Uzelac | 4-7-0 |
| Wichita State | Shockers | Gold & black | Missouri Valley | Jim Wright | 5-6-0 |
| William & Mary | Indians | Green, gold, silver | Independent | Jim Root | 6-5-0 |
| Wisconsin | Badgers | Cardinal & white | Big Ten | Dave McClain | 5-6-0 |
| Wyoming | Cowboys | Brown & yellow | Western Athletic | Bill Lewis | 4-6-1 |
| Yale | Bulldogs, Elis | Yale blue | Ivy | Carmen Cozza | 7-2-0 |

## Selected Division 2 and 3 Teams

| Team | Nickname | Team colors | Conference | Coach | Record |
|---|---|---|---|---|---|
| Akron | Zips | Blue & gold | Independent | Jim Dennison | 6-4-1 |
| Alma | Scots | Maroon & cream | Michigan | Phil Brooks | 6-3-0 |
| Amherst | Lord Jeffs | Purple & white | Little Three | James Ostendarp | 5-2-1 |
| Baldwin-Wallace | Yellow Jackets | Brown & gold | Ohio | Lee J. Tressel | 8-1-0 |
| Beloit | Buccaneers | Gold & blue | Midwest | Ed DeGeorge | 0-8-0 |
| Butler | Bulldogs | Blue & white | Indiana | Bill Sylvester | 5-5-0 |
| Carleton | Knights | Maize & blue | Midwest | Dale Quist | 1-7-0 |
| Case Reserve | Spartans | Blue & gray | Presidents Athletic | Bob DelRosa | 5-4-0 |
| Chico, Cal. St. | Wildcats | Cardinal & white | Far Western | Dick Trimmer | 6-2-1 |
| Coast Guard | Cadets, Bears | Blue & white | Independent | Bill Hickey | 5-4-0 |
| Coe | Kohawks | Crimson & gold | Midwest | Wayne Phillips | 5-3-0 |
| Dayton | Flyers | Red & blue | Independent | Rick Carter | 8-3-0 |
| Delaware | Fightin' Blue Hens | Blue & gold | Independent | Harold Raymond | 6-3-1 |
| Denison | Big Red | Red & white | Ohio | Keith Piper | 0-8-1 |
| Doane | Tigers | Orange & black | Nebraska Inter. | Joe Glenn | 5-5-0 |
| Emory & Henry | Wasps | Blue & gold | Old Dominion | Fred Selfe | 3-7-0 |
| Evansville | Purple Aces | Purple & white | Indiana | John Moses | 1-9-0 |
| Florida A & M | Rattlers | Orange & green | Southern IAC | Rudy Hubbard | 10-0-0 |
| John Carroll | Blue Streaks | Blue & gold | Presidents | Don Stupica | 2-7-0 |
| Kalamazoo | Hornets | Orange & black | Michigan | Ed Baker | 3-5-0 |
| Kenyon | Lords | Purple & white | Ohio | Tom McHugh | 4-5-0 |
| Knox | Siwash | Purple & gold | Midwest | Joe Campanelli | 2-5-1 |
| Lawrence | Vikings | Navy & white | Midwest | Ron Roberts | 7-1-0 |
| Michigan Tech. | Huskies | Silver & gold | Northern | Jim Kapp | 3-7-0 |
| Middlebury | Panthers | Blue & white | Independent | Mickey Heinecken | 7-1-0 |
| Morgan State | Bears | Blue & orange | Mid-Eastern | Clarence Thomas | 4-6-1 |
| Mt. Union | Purple Raiders | Purple & white | Ohio | Ken Wable | 4-5-0 |
| Muhlenberg | Mules | Cardinal & gray | Middle Atlantic | Frank Marino | 6-3-0 |
| Norfolk State | Spartans | Green & gold | Central | Dick Price | 4-6-1 |
| North Dakota State | Bison | Yellow & green | North Central | Jim Wacker | 8-1-1 |
| North Dakota | Sioux | Green & white | North Central | Gene Murphy | 4-6-1 |
| Northern Iowa | Panthers | Purple & old gold | North Central | Stan Sheriff | 6-5-0 |
| Northern Michigan | Wildcats | Old Gold & green | Independent | Bill Rademacher | 7-2-0 |
| Ohio Northern | Polar Bears | Orange & black | Ohio | A. Wallace Hood | 2-7-0 |
| Ohio Wesleyan | Battling Bishops | Red & black | Ohio | Jack Fouts | 2-6-1 |
| Olivet | Comets | Cardinal & white | Michigan | Chuck Cilibraise | 0-8-1 |
| Puget Sound | Loggers | Green & gold | Independent | Paul Wallrof | 6-4-0 |
| Redlands | Bulldogs | Maroon & gray | So. Cal. | Frank Serrao | 8-1-0 |
| Ripon | Redmen | Crimson & white | Midwest | Bob Giesey | 7-1-0 |
| Rochester | Yellow Jackets | Yellow & blue | Independent | Pat Stark | 6-3-0 |
| St. Cloud State | Huskies | Red & black | Northern | Mike Simpson | 5-6-0 |
| St. Lawrence | Saints | Scarlet & brown | ICAC | Ted Stratford | 7-2-0 |
| St. Norbert | Green Knights | Green & gold | Independent | Howie Kolstad | 0-10-0 |
| St. Olaf | Oles | Black & gold | Minn. IAC | Tom Porter | 5-4-1 |
| Santa Clara | Broncos | Cardinal & white | Independent | Pat Malley | 2-7-1 |
| Slippery Rock | Rockets, The Rock | Green & white | Pennsylvania | Bob DeSpirito | 4-6-1 |
| So. Dakota State | Jackrabbits | Yellow & blue | North Central | John Gregory | 8-1-1 |
| South Dakota | Coyotes | Vermilion & white | North Central | Bernard Cooper | 4-7-0 |
| Southern Oregon | Red Raiders | Red & black | Evergreen | Scott Johnson | 3-6-0 |
| Swarthmore | Little Quakers | Garnet | Middle Atlantic | Tom Lapinski | 4-4-1 |
| Thiel | Tomcats | Blue & gold | President's Athletic | James McCullough | 2-5-1 |
| Trenton State | Lions | Blue & gold | New Jersey State | Eric Hamilton | 4-5-0 |
| Tufts | Jumbos | Blue & brown | Independent | Paul Pawlak | 3-5-0 |
| Upsala | Vikings | Blue & gray | Middle Atlantic | John Hooper | 7-2-0 |
| Valparaiso | Crusaders | Brown & gold | Indiana | Bill Koch | 3-6-1 |
| Wash. & Jeff. | Presidents | Red & black | Presidents Athletic | Pat Mondock | 4-4-1 |
| Wash. & Lee | Generals | Royal blue, white | Old Dominion | Gary Fallon | 3-8-0 |
| Wayne State | Tartars | Green & gold | Great Lakes | Dick Lowry | 7-4-0 |
| Wesleyan | Cardinals | Red & black | Little Three | Bill MacDermott | 6-2-0 |
| Western Illinois | Leathernecks | Purple & gold | Independent | Bill Shanahan | 3-7-0 |
| Wilkes | Colonels | Navy & gold | Middle Atlantic | Roland Schmidt | 4-5-0 |
| Williams | Ephmen | Purple | Little Three | Robert Odell | 5-3-0 |
| Wittenberg | Tigers | Red & white | Ohio | Dave Maurer | 9-0-0 |
| Wooster | Fighting Scots | Black & gold | Ohio | Tom Hollman | 6-3-0 |
| Youngstown State | Penguins | Red & white | Independent | Bill Narduzzi | 7-3-0 |

## Women's Curling

The U.S. Women's Curling Association championship was won by the team from Wausau, Wis. The team was comprised of Sandy Robarge, Elaine Collins, Jo Shannon, and Virginia Morrison.

# College Football Conference Champions

## Atlantic Coast
| | |
|---|---|
| 1964 | No. Carolina St. |
| 1965 | Duke |
| 1966 | Clemson |
| 1967 | Clemson |
| 1968 | No. Carolina St. |
| 1969 | So. Carolina |
| 1970 | Wake Forest |
| 1971 | North Carolina |
| 1972 | North Carolina |
| 1973 | No. Carolina St. |
| 1974 | Maryland |
| 1975 | Maryland |
| 1976 | Maryland |
| 1977 | North Carolina |

## Ivy League
| | |
|---|---|
| 1964 | Princeton |
| 1965 | Dartmouth |
| 1966 | Dartmouth, Harvard, Princeton |
| 1967 | Yale |
| 1968 | Yale, Harvard |
| 1969 | Princeton, Dartmouth, Yale |
| 1970 | Dartmouth |
| 1971 | Dartmouth, Cornell |
| 1972 | Dartmouth |
| 1973 | Dartmouth |
| 1974 | Yale, Harvard |
| 1975 | Harvard |
| 1976 | Yale, Brown |
| 1977 | Yale |

## Big Eight
| | |
|---|---|
| 1964 | Nebraska |
| 1965 | Nebraska |
| 1966 | Nebraska |
| 1967 | Oklahoma |
| 1968 | Kansas, Oklahoma |
| 1969 | Missouri, Nebraska |
| 1970 | Nebraska |
| 1971 | Nebraska |
| 1972 | Nebraska |
| 1973 | Oklahoma |
| 1974 | Oklahoma |
| 1975 | Oklahoma, Nebraska |
| 1976 | Oklahoma, Colorado, Oklahoma State |
| 1977 | Oklahoma |

## Big Ten
| | |
|---|---|
| 1964 | Michigan |
| 1965 | Michigan State |
| 1966 | Michigan State |
| 1967 | Indiana, Purdue, Minn. |
| 1968 | Ohio State |
| 1969 | Michigan, Ohio State |
| 1970 | Ohio State |
| 1971 | Michigan |
| 1972 | Ohio State, Michigan |
| 1973 | Ohio State, Michigan |
| 1974 | Ohio State, Michigan |
| 1975 | Ohio State |
| 1976 | Michigan, Ohio State |
| 1977 | Michigan, Ohio State |

## Mid-America
| | |
|---|---|
| 1964 | Bowling Green |
| 1965 | Bowling Green, Miami |
| 1966 | Miami, Western Mich. |
| 1967 | Toledo, Ohio Univ. |
| 1968 | Ohio Univ. |
| 1969 | Toledo |
| 1970 | Toledo |
| 1971 | Toledo |
| 1972 | Kent State |
| 1973 | Miami |
| 1974 | Miami |
| 1975 | Miami |
| 1976 | Ball State |
| 1977 | Miami |

## Missouri Valley
| | |
|---|---|
| 1964 | Cincinnati |
| 1965 | Tulsa |
| 1966 | No. Texas, Tulsa |
| 1967 | North Texas |
| 1968 | Memphis State |
| 1969 | Memphis State |
| 1970 | Louisville |
| 1971 | Memphis State |
| 1972 | Louisville, W. Texas, Drake |
| 1973 | No. Texas St., Tulsa |
| 1974 | Tulsa |
| 1975 | Tulsa |
| 1976 | Tulsa, N. Mexico St. |
| 1977 | W. Texas St. |

## Southeastern
| | |
|---|---|
| 1964 | Alabama |
| 1965 | Alabama |
| 1966 | Alabama, Georgia |
| 1967 | Tennessee |
| 1968 | Georgia |
| 1969 | Tennessee |
| 1970 | Louisiana State |
| 1971 | Alabama |
| 1972 | Alabama |
| 1973 | Alabama |
| 1974 | Alabama |
| 1975 | Alabama |
| 1976 | Georgia |
| 1977 | Alabama |

## Southwest
| | |
|---|---|
| 1964 | Arkansas |
| 1965 | Arkansas |
| 1966 | Southern Methodist |
| 1967 | Texas A & M |
| 1968 | Texas, Arkansas |
| 1969 | Texas |
| 1970 | Texas |
| 1971 | Texas |
| 1972 | Texas |
| 1973 | Texas |
| 1974 | Baylor |
| 1975 | Texas A&M, Texas, Arkansas |
| 1976 | Houston |
| 1977 | Texas |

## Pacific Eight
| | |
|---|---|
| 1964 | Oregon St., USC |
| 1965 | UCLA |
| 1966 | USC |
| 1967 | USC |
| 1968 | USC |
| 1969 | USC |
| 1970 | Stanford |
| 1971 | Stanford |
| 1972 | USC |
| 1973 | USC |
| 1974 | USC |
| 1975 | UCLA, Cal. |
| 1976 | USC |
| 1977 | Washington |

## Southern
| | |
|---|---|
| 1964 | West Virginia |
| 1965 | West Virginia |
| 1966 | East Carolina, William & Mary |
| 1967 | West Virginia |
| 1968 | Richmond |
| 1969 | Richmond, Davidson |
| 1970 | William & Mary |
| 1971 | Richmond |
| 1972 | East Carolina |
| 1973 | East Carolina |
| 1974 | VMI |
| 1975 | Richmond |
| 1976 | East Carolina |
| 1977 | Tenn.-Chattanooga |

## Western Athletic
| | |
|---|---|
| 1964 | New Mexico, Arizona, Utah |
| 1965 | Brigham Young |
| 1966 | Wyoming |
| 1967 | Wyoming |
| 1968 | Wyoming |
| 1969 | Arizona State |
| 1970 | Arizona State |
| 1971 | Arizona State |
| 1972 | Arizona State |
| 1973 | Arizona State, Arizona |
| 1974 | Brigham Young |
| 1975 | Arizona State |
| 1976 | Wyoming, Brigham Young |
| 1977 | Brigham Young, Arizona St. |

## Pacific Coast
| | |
|---|---|
| 1969 | San Diego State |
| 1970 | Long Beach State |
| 1971 | Long Beach State |
| 1972 | San Diego State |
| 1973 | San Diego State |
| 1974 | San Diego State |
| 1975 | San Jose State |
| 1976 | San Diego State |
| 1977 | Fresno State |

# National College Football Champions

The NCAA recognizes as unofficial national champion the team selected each year by the AP (poll of writers) and the UPI (poll of coaches). When the polls disagree both teams are listed. The AP poll originated in 1936 and the UPI poll in 1950.

| | | | | | |
|---|---|---|---|---|---|
| 1936 | Minnesota | 1947 | Notre Dame | 1958 | Louisiana State |
| 1937 | Pittsburgh | 1948 | Michigan | 1959 | Syracuse |
| 1938 | Texas Christian | 1949 | Notre Dame | 1960 | Minnesota |
| 1939 | Texas A&M | 1950 | Oklahoma | 1961 | Alabama |
| 1940 | Minnesota | 1951 | Tennessee | 1962 | Southern Cal. |
| 1941 | Minnesota | 1952 | Michigan State | 1963 | Texas |
| 1942 | Ohio State | 1953 | Maryland | 1964 | Alabama |
| 1943 | Notre Dame | 1954 | Ohio State, UCLA | 1965 | Alabama, Mich. State |
| 1944 | Army | 1955 | Oklahoma | 1966 | Notre Dame |
| 1945 | Army | 1956 | Oklahoma | 1967 | Southern Cal. |
| 1946 | Notre Dame | 1957 | Auburn, Ohio State | | |

| | |
|---|---|
| 1968 | Ohio State |
| 1969 | Texas |
| 1970 | Nebraska, Texas |
| 1971 | Nebraska |
| 1972 | Southern Cal. |
| 1973 | Notre Dame, Alabama |
| 1974 | Oklahoma, So. Cal. |
| 1975 | Oklahoma |
| 1976 | Pittsburgh |
| 1977 | Notre Dame |

# Outland Awards

Honoring the outstanding interior lineman selected by the Football Writers' Association of America.

| | |
|---|---|
| 1946 | George Connor, Notre Dame, T |
| 1947 | Joe Steffy, Army, G |
| 1948 | Bill Fischer, Notre Dame, G |
| 1949 | Ed Bagdon, Michigan St., G |
| 1950 | Bob Gain, Kentucky, T |
| 1951 | Jim Weatherall, Oklahoma, T |
| 1952 | Dick Modzelewski, Maryland, T |
| 1953 | J. D. Roberts, Oklahoma, G |
| 1954 | Bill Brooks, Arkansas, G |
| 1955 | Calvin Jones, Iowa, G |
| 1956 | Jim Parker, Ohio State, G |

| | |
|---|---|
| 1957 | Alex Karras, Iowa, T |
| 1958 | Zeke Smith, Auburn, G |
| 1959 | Mike McGee, Duke, T |
| 1960 | Tom Brown, Minnesota, G |
| 1961 | Merlin Olsen, Utah State, T |
| 1962 | Bobby Bell, Minnesota, T |
| 1963 | Scott Appleton, Texas, T |
| 1964 | Steve Delong, Tennessee, T |
| 1965 | Tommy Nobis, Texas, G |
| 1966 | Loyd Phillips, Arkansas, T |
| 1967 | Ron Yary, Southern Cal, T |

| | |
|---|---|
| 1968 | Bill Stanfill, Georgia, T |
| 1969 | Mike Reid, Penn State, DT |
| 1970 | Jim Stillwagon, Ohio State, LB |
| 1971 | Larry Jacobson, Nebraska, DT |
| 1972 | Rich Glover, Nebraska, MG |
| 1973 | John Hicks, Ohio State, G |
| 1974 | Randy White, Maryland, DE |
| 1975 | Leroy Selmon, Oklahoma, DT |
| 1976 | Ross Browner, Notre Dame, DE |
| 1977 | Brad Shearer, Texas, DT |

# College Football Stadiums

| School | Capacity | School | Capacity |
|---|---|---|---|
| Alabama Univ. of (Denny Stad.), University, Ala. | 59,000 | North Carolina, Univ. of (Kenan Stad.) | 47,000 |
| Arizona State Univ. (Sun Devil), Tempe | 56,000 | North Texas St. Univ. (Fouts Field), Denton | 20,000 |
| Arizona, Univ. of (Arizona Stad.), Tucson | 57,000 | Northern Illinois Univ. (Huskie Stad.) DeKalb. | 20,257 |
| Arkansas, Univ. of (Razorback Stad.) Fayetteville | 43,500 | Northwestern Univ. (Dyche Stad.), Evanston, Ill. | 48,500 |
| Auburn Univ. (Jordan Hare Stad.), Auburn, Ala. | 61,291 | Notre Dame Stad., South Bend, Ind. | 59,075 |
| Baylor Univ. Stad., Waco, Texas | 48,000 | Ohio State Univ. (Ohio Stad.), Columbus | 83,112 |
| Boston Coll. (Alumni Stad.) Boston, Mass. | 32,000 | Oklahoma State (Lewis Stad.), Stillwater | 50,588 |
| Bowling Green State Univ. (Doyt Perry Field) | 23,272 | Oklahoma, Univ. of (Owen Field), Norman | 70,286 |
| Brigham Young Univ. Stad., Provo, Ut. | 30,000 | Old Dominion Univ. (Foreman Field), Norfolk | 32,000 |
| Cal., Univ. of (Memorial Stad.), Berkeley | 76,780 | Oregon St. Univ. (Parker Stad.), Corvallis | 41,000 |
| Central Mich. Univ. (Shorts Stad.), Mt. Pleasant | 20,000 | Oregon, Univ. of (Autzen Stad.), Eugene | 41,097 |
| Cincinnati, Univ. of (Nippert), Oh. | 25,692 | Pacific, Univ. of the (Pacific Memorial), Cal. | 33,345 |
| Citadel (Johnson Hagood Stad.), Charleston, S.C. | 22,500 | Penn. State Univ. (Beaver Stad.) | 60,203 |
| Clemson Univ. (Memorial Stad.), S.C. | 43,451 | Penn., Univ. of (Franklin Field), Phila. | 60,546 |
| Colorado St. Univ. (Hughes Stad.), Ft. Collins | 30,000 | Pittsburgh, Univ. of (Pitt. Stad.), Pa. | 56,500 |
| Colorado, Univ. of (Folsom Field), Boulder | 52,005 | Princeton (Palmer Stad.), Princeton, N.J. | 45,725 |
| Columbia Univ. (Baker Field), N.Y., N.Y. | 32,000 | Purdue, (Ross-Ade Stad.), Lafayette, Ind. | 69,250 |
| Cornell (Schoellkopf Crescent), Ithaca, N.Y. | 27,000 | Rice Stad., Houston, Texas | 70,000 |
| Dartmouth Coll. (Memorial Field), Hanover, N.H. | 20,416 | Rutgers Stad., New Brunswick, N.J. | 23,000 |
| Delaware, Univ. of (Delaware Stad.), Newark | 21,919 | So. Carolina, Univ. of (Williams-Brice), Columbia | 54,406 |
| Duke Univ., (Wade Stad.), Durham, N.C. | 44,000 | So. Illinois Univ. (McAndrew Stad.), Carbondale | 20,100 |
| N. Carolina Univ. (Ficklen Stad.), Greenville, N.C. | 20,000 | So. Miss., Univ. of (Roberts Stad.), Hattiesburg | 33,000 |
| Eastern Kentucky (Hanger Stad.), Richmond | 20,000 | Southwestern La., (Cajun Field), Lafayette | 24,610 |
| Florida State, (Campbell Stad.), Tallahassee | 40,500 | Stanford Stad., Stanford, Cal. | 86,307 |
| Florida, Univ. of (Florida Field), Gainesville | 62,000 | Syracuse Univ. (Archbold Stad.), N.Y. | 26,388 |
| Georgia Inst. of Tech. (Grant Field), Atlanta | 58,121 | Tampa, Univ. of (Tampa Stad.), Fla. | 47,000 |
| Georgia, Univ. of (Sanford Stad.), Athens | 59,200 | Tenn., Univ. of (Neyland Stad.), Knoxville | 80,250 |
| Harvard Stad., Boston, Mass. | 37,289 | Texas A. & M. Univ. (Kyle Field), College Station | 48,000 |
| Hawaii, Univ. of (Aloha Stad.), Honolulu | 50,000 | Texas Christian Univ. (TCU-Amon Carter Stad.) | 46,000 |
| Holy Cross (Fitton Field) Worcester, Mass. | 25,000 | Texas-El Paso (Sun Bowl) | 30,000 |
| Illinois, Univ. of (Memorial Stad.), Urbana | 71,229 | Texas Tech. Univ. (Jones Stad.), Lubbock | 47,000 |
| Indiana St. (Memorial Stad.), Terre Haute | 20,500 | Texas, Univ. of (Memorial Stad.), Austin | 80,000 |
| Indiana Univ. (Memorial Stad.), Bloomington | 52,354 | Trinity Univ. (Alamo Stad.), San Antonio, Tex. | 22,500 |
| Iowa State Univ. (Cyclone Stad.), Ames | 50,000 | Tulsa, Univ. of (Skelly Stad.), Okla. | 40,235 |
| Iowa, Univ. of (Kinnick Stad.), Iowa City | 60,200 | U.S. Air Force Acad. (Falcon Stad.), Col. | 49,668 |
| Kansas State Univ. Stad., Manhattan | 42,000 | U.S. Military Academy (Michie Stad.), West Point, N.Y. | 41,684 |
| Kansas, Univ. of (Memorial Stad.), Lawrence | 51,500 | U.S. Naval Academy (Navy-Marine Corps Mem. Stad.) | |
| Kent State Univ. (Dix Stad.), Kent, Oh. | 28,748 | Annapolis, Md. | 28,000 |
| Kentucky, Univ. of (Commonwealth), Lexington | 58,000 | Utah State Univ. (Romney Stad.), Logan | 20,000 |
| La. State Univ. (Tiger Stad.), Baton Rouge | 67,720 | Utah, Univ. of (Robert Rice Stad.), Salt Lake City | 30,000 |
| Louisiana Tech. Univ. (Joe Aillet Stad.), Ruston | 23,318 | Vanderbilt, (Dudley Stad.), Nashville | 34,000 |
| Maryland, Univ. of (Byrd), College Park | 45,000 | Va. Poly Inst. (Lane Stad.), Blacksburg | 40,000 |
| McNeese St. Univ. (Cowboy Stad.), | | Virginia, Univ. of (Scott Stad.), Charlottesville | 25,000 |
| Lake Charles, La. | 20,000 | Wake Forest (Groves Stad.), Winston-Salem, N.C. | 31,000 |
| Memphis State (Liberty Bowl) | 50,164 | Washington State Univ. (Clarence D. Martin) | 27,500 |
| Michigan State Univ. (Spartan Stad.), E. Lansing | 76,000 | Washington, Univ. of (Husky Stad.), Seattle | 58,946 |
| Michigan, Univ. of (Mich. Stad.), Ann Arbor | 101,701 | West Texas State Univ. (Kimbrough Stad.), Canyon | 20,000 |
| Minnesota, Univ. of (Memorial Stad.), Minneapolis | 56,725 | West Virginia Univ. (Mountaineer Field) | 34,000 |
| Mississippi St. Univ. (Scott Field) | 35,000 | Western Illinois Univ. (Hanson Field), Macomb | 18,000 |
| Mississippi, Univ. of (Hemingway Stad.) | 37,500 | Western Mich. Univ. (Waldo Stad.), Kalamazoo | 24,500 |
| Missouri, Univ. of (Faurot Field), Columbia | 55,000 | Wichita State Univ. (Cessna Stad.) | 30,500 |
| Nebraska, Univ. of (Memorial Stad.), Lincoln | 76,400 | Wisconsin, Univ. of (Camp Randall), Madison | 77,280 |
| New Mexico, Univ. Stad., Albuquerque | 31,500 | Wyoming, Univ. of (Memorial), Laramie | 27,000 |
| North Carolina St. U. (Carter Stad.), Raleigh | 44,000 | Yale Bowl, New Haven, Conn. | 70,874 |

# 33d Annual Field Archery Championships in 1978

Aurora, Ill., July 24 - 29, 1978

### Freestyle

**Professional Men**—Jack Cramer, Gettysburg, Pa.
**Professional Women**—Faye Binney, Moab, Ut.
**Open Men**—Paul Nazelrod, Cumberland, Md.
**Open Women**—Beverley Stout, Clinton, Ind.
**Amateur Men**—Barry Velarde, Ft. Knox, Ky.
**Amateur Women**—Judy Cockerham, Winston-Salem, N.C.

### Barebow

**Professional Men**—Eddie McCrary, Wylie, Tex.
**Open Men**—David Hughes, Mesquite, Tex.
**Open Women**—Gloria Shelley, Waterbury, Conn.
**Amateur Men**—Tyrus Baker, Centralia, Ill.

**Amateur Women**—Patti Lamb, Loves Park, Ill.

### Bowhunter

**Professional Men**—Ben Rogers, San Jose, Cal.
**Open Men**—James Brown, Marlow Heights, Md.
**Open Women**—June Hardy, Houston, Tex.
**Amateur Men**—John C. Saporiti, Rockford, Ill.
**Amateur Women**—Linda Carlson, Wildwood, Ill.

### Bowhunter Freestyle

**Professional Men**—Art Kurgin, Troy, Mich.
**Open Men**—Glenn Hummel, West Monroe, La.
**Open Women**—Sue Herbert, Prattville, Ala.
**Amateur Men**—Dennis Skinner, Chillicothe, Mo.

# National AAU Karate Championships in 1978

Hackensack, N.J., July 22-23, 1978

### Men

**Novice kata**—Thomas Cupo, Hawthorne, N.J.
**Intermediate kata**—Domingo Olivo, Haverstraw, N.Y.
**Advanced kata**—Domingo Llanos, Haverstraw, N.Y.
**Novice kumite**—Grant Frazer, Cleveland, Oh.
**Intermediate kumite**—Humberto Fontana, Miami, Fla.
**Advanced kumite**—Tokey Hill, Chillicothe, Oh.
**Weapons kata**—Yao Li, Revere, Mass.

### Women

**Novice kata**—Irene Crevani, Mahwah, N.J.
**Intermediate kata**—Barbara Merkley, Woodcliff Lake, N.J.
**Advanced kata**—Ellen Beal, Barrington, N.H.
**Novice kumite**—Gwen Hoffman, Freehold, N.J.
**Intermediate kumite**—Debbie Mazzochetti, Rochester, N.Y.
**Advanced kumite**—Rosine Hatem, Methuen, Mass.
**Weapons kata**—Roxanne Marcum, Tallmadge, Oh.

# Sports on Television

Source: Sports 1977, A.C. Nielsen Co.

| | Average Ratings and Viewer Composition | | | Ages of Men Viewers | | |
|---|---|---|---|---|---|---|
| | Household rating % | Percent men | Percent women | 18-34 | 35-49 | 50+ |
| **Football** | | | | | | |
| NFL Superbowl | 47.2 | 57 | 43 | 39% | 25% | 36% |
| ABC-NFL | 21.2 | 67 | 33 | 36 | 29 | 35 |
| CBS-NFL | 16.1 | 67 | 33 | 39 | 25 | 36 |
| NBC-NFL | 13.5 | 68 | 32 | 37 | 26 | 37 |
| College bowl games College All-Star games | 12.3 | 60 | 40 | 34 | 26 | 40 |
| NCAA regular season | 13.2 | 68 | 32 | 34 | 26 | 40 |
| **Baseball** | | | | | | |
| World Series | 29.8 | 58 | 42 | 30 | 26 | 44 |
| All-Star game | 24.5 | 60 | 40 | 34 | 19 | 47 |
| Regular season | 9.0 | 66 | 34 | 28 | 15 | 57 |
| **Horse racing** | | | | | | |
| Kentucky Derby | 14.9 | 51 | 49 | 36 | 21 | 43 |
| Preakness | 11.9 | 52 | 48 | 27 | 23 | 50 |
| **Basketball** | | | | | | |
| NBA regular season | 7.2 | 67 | 33 | 44 | 21 | 35 |
| NBA playoffs | 7.9 | 67 | 33 | 43 | 23 | 34 |
| NBA All-Star game | 8.6 | 60 | 40 | 49 | 21 | 30 |
| NBA championships | 12.7 | 67 | 33 | 49 | 17 | 34 |
| **Bowling** | | | | | | |
| Pro tour | 7.1 | 52 | 48 | 28 | 26 | 46 |
| Grand Prix | 6.0 | 54 | 46 | 27 | 23 | 50 |
| **Auto racing** | 8.3 | 59 | 41 | 41 | 23 | 36 |
| **Golf** | | | | | | |
| Tournaments | 5.8 | 60 | 40 | 28 | 20 | 52 |
| **Tennis** | | | | | | |
| World championship | 3.0 | 50 | 50 | 27 | 33 | 40 |
| World Invitational | 3.2 | 58 | 42 | 44 | 24 | 32 |
| **Multi-sports series** | | | | | | |
| American Sportsman | 7.5 | 53 | 47 | 35 | 30 | 35 |
| ABC WW Sports | | | | | | |
| Sat | 8.8 | 59 | 41 | 40 | 25 | 35 |
| Sun | 12.4 | 56 | 44 | 41 | 25 | 34 |
| CBS Sports Spectacular | 6.4 | 56 | 44 | 38 | 23 | 39 |

# Water Ski Champions in 1978

## 36th Annual National Water Ski Championships

Tivoli Gardens, Brighton, Mich., Aug. 23-27, 1978

Source: American Water Ski Association

**Men's Open Overall**—Ricky McCormick, Winter Haven, Fla., 2,663 points.

**Men's Open Slalom**—Bob LaPoint, Castro Valley, Cal., 55 buoys.

**Men's Open Tricks**—Cory Pickos, Eagle Lake, Fla., 6,080 points.

**Men's Open Jumping**—Robert Kempton, Tampa, Fla., 162 feet.

**Women's Open Overall**—Deena Brush, W. Sacramento, Cal., 3,021 points.

**Women's Open Slalom**—Deena Brush, 56 buoys.

**Women's Open Tricks**—Cyndi Matranga Benzel, Prior Lake, Minn., 3,750 points.

**Women's Open Jumping**—Deena Brush, 118 feet.

**Senior Men's Overall**—Ken White, Bynum, Tex. 2,746 points.

**Senior Men's Slalom**—Dr. J. D. Morgan, Pensacola, Fla., 51 buoys.

**Senior Men's Tricks**—Robert Hurm, St. Marys, Oh. 4,640 points.

**Senior Men's Jumping**—Dr. J. D. Morgan, 127 feet.

**Senior Women's Overall**—Vicki Johndrow, Odessa, Fla., 3,445 points.

**Senior Women's Slalom**—Vicki Johndrow, 44 1/2 buoys.

**Senior Women's Tricks**—Thelma Salmas, Canyon Lake, Cal 3,410 points.

**Senior Women's Jumping**—Vicki Johndrow, 111 feet.

**Boy's Overall**—Sammy Duvall, Greenville, S.C., 3,253 points.

**Boy's Slalom**—Mark Scharosch, Imola, Cal., 49 buoys.

**Boy's Tricks**—Craig Pickos, Eagle Lake, Fla., 5,170 points.

**Boy's Jumping**—Sammy Duvall, 142 feet.

**Girl's Overall**—Karin Roberge, San Diego, Cal., 2,733 points.

**Girl's Slalom**—Karin Roberge, 51 buoys.

**Girl's Tricks**—Kris Golden, Milford, Ind., 3,060 points.

**Girl's Jumping**—Karin Roberge, 109 feet.

**Junior Boy's Overall**—Billy Allen, San Mateo, Cal., 2,45 points.

**Junior Boy's Slalom**—Patrick Hill, Shawnee Mission, Kan., 4 1/4 buoys.

**Junior Boy's Tricks**—Billy Allen, 2,880 Points.

**Junior Boy's Jumping**—Ricky Meredith, Reddick, Ill., 96 feet.

**Junior Girl's Overall**—Nathalie Roberge, San Diego, Cal 3,516 points.

**Junior Girl's Slalom**—Nathalie Roberge, 51 buoys.

**Junior Girl's Tricks**—Sally Monnier, Rock Falls, Ill., 3,93 points.

**Junior Girl's Jumping**—Nathalie Roberge, 78 feet.

## 19th Annual Masters Tournament

Callaway Gardens, Ga., July 8-9, 1978

**Men's Overall**—Mike Hazelwood, London, England, 3,038 points.

**Men's Slalom**—Mike Hazelwood, 55 1/4 buoys.

**Men's Tricks**—Patrice Martin, Graslin, France, 6,090 points.

**Men's Jumping**—Lucky Lowe, Birmingham, Ala., 178 feet.

**Women's Overall**—Cindy Todd, Pierson, Fla., 2,447 points.

**Women's Slalom**—Patsy Messner, Ottawa, Canada, 50 buoys.

**Women's Tricks**—Pam Folsom, Boynton Beach, Fla., 4,36 points.

**Women's Jumping**—Deena Brush, W. Sacramento, Cal., 11 feet.

# North American Soccer League in 1978

### Final Standings

## National Conference

### Eastern Division

| | W | L | GF | GA | Bonus points | Total points |
|---|---|---|---|---|---|---|
| New York | 24 | 6 | 88 | 39 | 68 | 212 |
| Washington | 16 | 14 | 55 | 47 | 49 | 145 |
| Toronto | 16 | 14 | 58 | 47 | 48 | 144 |
| Rochester | 14 | 16 | 47 | 52 | 47 | 131 |

### Central Division

| | W | L | GF | GA | Bonus points | Total points |
|---|---|---|---|---|---|---|
| Minnesota | 17 | 13 | 58 | 43 | 54 | 156 |
| Tulsa | 15 | 15 | 49 | 46 | 42 | 132 |
| Dallas | 14 | 16 | 51 | 53 | 47 | 131 |
| Colorado | 8 | 22 | 34 | 66 | 33 | 81 |

### Western Division

| | W | L | GF | GA | Bonus points | Total points |
|---|---|---|---|---|---|---|
| Vancouver | 24 | 6 | 68 | 29 | 55 | 199 |
| Portland | 20 | 10 | 50 | 36 | 47 | 167 |
| Seattle | 15 | 15 | 50 | 45 | 48 | 138 |
| Los Angeles | 9 | 21 | 36 | 69 | 34 | 88 |

## American Conference

### Eastern Division

| | W | L | GF | GA | Bonus points | Total points |
|---|---|---|---|---|---|---|
| New England | 19 | 11 | 62 | 39 | 51 | 165 |
| Tampa Bay | 18 | 12 | 63 | 48 | 57 | 165 |
| Ft. Lauderdale | 16 | 14 | 50 | 59 | 47 | 143 |
| Philadelphia | 12 | 18 | 40 | 58 | 39 | 111 |

### Central Divison

| | W | L | GF | GA | Bonus points | Total points |
|---|---|---|---|---|---|---|
| Detroit | 20 | 10 | 68 | 36 | 56 | 176 |
| Chicago | 12 | 18 | 57 | 64 | 51 | 123 |
| Memphis | 10 | 20 | 43 | 58 | 41 | 101 |
| Houston | 10 | 20 | 37 | 61 | 36 | 96 |

### Western Division

| | W | L | GF | GA | Bonus points | Total points |
|---|---|---|---|---|---|---|
| San Diego | 18 | 12 | 63 | 56 | 56 | 164 |
| California | 13 | 17 | 43 | 49 | 37 | 115 |
| Oakland | 12 | 18 | 34 | 59 | 31 | 103 |
| San Jose | 8 | 22 | 36 | 81 | 35 | 83 |

**Playoff winner — New York Cosmos.**

Total points: Win - 6 pts., Loss - 0 pts. Bonus points: one point is awarded for each goal scored up to a maximum of 3 per team per game.

## Leading Scorers

| Player team | Goals | Assists | Points | Player, team | Goals | Assists | Points |
|---|---|---|---|---|---|---|---|
| Giorgio Chinaglia, New York | 34 | 11 | 79 | Karl-Heinz Granitza, Chicago | 19 | 9 | 47 |
| Mike Flanagan, New England | 30 | 8 | 68 | Alan Willey, Minnesota | 21 | 3 | 45 |
| Trevor Francis, Detroit | 22 | 10 | 54 | Ivan Lukacevic, Toronto | 16 | 5 | 37 |
| Kevin Hector, Vancouver | 21 | 10 | 52 | David Irving, Ft. Lauderdale | 16 | 5 | 37 |
| Rodney Marsh, Tampa Bay | 18 | 16 | 52 | Bob Lenarduzzi, Vancouver | 10 | 17 | 37 |
| Jeff Bourne, Dallas | 21 | 8 | 50 | Vladislav Bogicevic, New York | 10 | 17 | 37 |

## Leading Goalkeepers

| Player, team | *Minutes | Goals against | Average | Player, team | *Minutes | Goals against | Average |
|---|---|---|---|---|---|---|---|
| Phil Parkes, Vancouver | 2,650 | 28 | 0.95 | Zeljko Bilecki, Toronto | 1,550 | 23 | 1.34 |
| Erol Yasin, New York | 1,916 | 24 | 1.13 | Dave Jokerst, California | 1,574 | 24 | 1.37 |
| Mick Poole, Portland | 2,783 | 36 | 1.16 | Colin Boulton, Tulsa | 2,531 | 39 | 1.39 |
| Steve Hardwick, Detroit | 2,734 | 36 | 1.19 | Tony Chursky, Seattle | 2,617 | 41 | 1.41 |
| Kevin Keelan, New England | 2,609 | 36 | 1.24 | Bill Irwin, Washington | 2,362 | 39 | 1.49 |
| Winston Dubose, Tampa Bay | 1,352 | 19 | 1.26 | Keith Van Eron, Houston | 1,737 | 31 | 1.60 |

*At least 1,350 minutes needed to qualify.

# The World Cup

The World Cup, emblematic of International soccer supremacy, was won by Argentina on June 25, 1978, with a 3-1 over-time victory over the Netherlands. By winning the championship, Argentina became the fifth host country to emerge as champion since the competition began in 1930. Winners and sites of previous World Cup play follow:

| Year | Winner | Site | Year | Winner | Site |
|---|---|---|---|---|---|
| 1930 | Uruguay | Uruguay | 1962 | Brazil | Chile |
| 1934 | Italy | Italy | 1966 | England | England |
| 1938 | Italy | France | 1970 | Brazil | Mexico City |
| 1950 | Uruguay | Brazil | 1974 | W. Germany | W. Germany |
| 1954 | W. Germany | Switzerland | 1978 | Argentina | Argentina |
| 1958 | Brazil | Sweden | | | |

# Curling Champions

## World Champions

| Year | Country, skip | Year | Country, skip | Year | Country, skip |
|---|---|---|---|---|---|
| 1966 | Canada, Ron Northcott | 1971 | Canada, Don Duguid | 1975 | Switzerland, Otto Danieli |
| 1967 | Scotland, Chuck Hay | 1972 | Canada, Crest Melesnuk | 1976 | United States, Bruce Roberts |
| 1968 | Canada, Ron Northcott | 1973 | Sweden, Kjell Oscarius | 1977 | Sweden, Ragnar Kamp |
| 1969 | Canada, Ron Northcott | 1974 | United States, Bud Somerville | 1978 | United States, Bob Nichols |
| 1970 | Canada, Don Duguid | | | | |

## U.S. National Champions

| Year | State, skip | Year | State, skip | Year | State, skip |
|---|---|---|---|---|---|
| 1966 | North Dakota, Joe Zbacnik | 1971 | North Dakota, Dale Dalziel | 1975 | Washington, Ed Risling |
| 1967 | Washington, Bruce Roberts | 1972 | North Dakota, Bob LaBonte | 1976 | Minnesota, Bruce Roberts |
| 1968 | Wisconsin, Bud Somerville | 1973 | Massachusetts, Barry Blanchard | 1977 | Minnesota, Bruce Roberts |
| 1969 | Wisconsin, Bud Somerville | 1974 | Wisconsin, Bud Somerville | 1978 | Wisconsin, Bob Nichols |
| 1970 | North Dakota, Art Tallackson | | | | |

# Golf Records

## United States Open

| Year | Winner | Year | Winner | Year | Winner | Year | Winner |
|---|---|---|---|---|---|---|---|
| 1896 | James Foulis | 1916 | Chick Evans* | 1937 | Ralph Guldahl | 1960 | Arnold Palmer |
| 1897 | Joe Lloyd | 1917-18 | (Not played) | 1938 | Ralph Guldahl | 1961 | Gene Littler |
| 1898 | Fred Herd | 1919 | Walter Hagen | 1939 | Byron Nelson | 1962 | Jack Nicklaus |
| 1899 | Willie Smith | 1920 | Edward Ray | 1940 | Lawson Little | 1963 | Julius Boros |
| 1900 | Harry Vardon | 1921 | Jim Barnes | 1941 | Craig Wood | 1964 | Ken Venturi |
| 1901 | Willie Anderson | 1922 | Gene Sarazen | 1942-45 | (Not played) | 1965 | Gary Player |
| 1902 | L. Auchterlonie | 1923 | Bob Jones* | 1946 | Lloyd Mangrum | 1966 | Billy Casper |
| 1903 | Willie Anderson | 1924 | Cyril Walker | 1947 | L. Worsham | 1967 | Jack Nicklaus |
| 1904 | Willie Anderson | 1925 | Willie MacFarlane | 1948 | Ben Hogan | 1968 | Lee Trevino |
| 1905 | Willie Anderson | 1926 | Bob Jones* | 1949 | Cary Middlecoff | 1969 | Orville Moody |
| 1906 | Alex Smith | 1927 | Tommy Armour | 1950 | Ben Hogan | 1970 | Tony Jacklin |
| 1907 | Alex Ross | 1928 | John Farrell | 1951 | Ben Hogan | 1971 | Lee Trevino |
| 1908 | Fred McLeod | 1929 | Bob Jones* | 1952 | Julius Boros | 1972 | Jack Nicklaus |
| 1909 | George Sargent | 1930 | Bob Jones* | 1953 | Ben Hogan | 1973 | Johnny Miller |
| 1910 | Alex Smith | 1931 | Wm. Burke | 1954 | Ed Furgol | 1974 | Hale Irwin |
| 1911 | John McDermott | 1932 | Gene Sarazen | 1955 | Jack Fleck | 1975 | Lou Graham |
| 1912 | John McDermott | 1933 | John Goodman* | 1956 | Cary Middlecoff | 1976 | Jerry Pate |
| 1913 | Francis Ouimet* | 1934 | Olin Dutra | 1957 | Dick Mayer | 1977 | Hubert Green |
| 1914 | Walter Hagen | 1935 | Sam Parks Jr. | 1958 | Tommy Bolt | 1978 | Andy North |
| 1915 | Jerome Travers* | 1936 | Tony Manero | 1959 | Billy Casper | | |

*Amateur

## U.S. Women's Open Golf Champions

| Year | Winner | Year | Winner | Year | Winner | Year | Winner |
|---|---|---|---|---|---|---|---|
| 1948 | "Babe" Zaharias | 1956 | Mrs. K. Cornelius | 1964 | Mickey Wright | 1972 | Susie Maxwell Berning |
| 1949 | Louise Suggs | 1957 | Betsy Rawls | 1965 | Carol Mann | 1973 | Susie Maxwell Berning |
| 1950 | "Babe" Zaharias | 1958 | Mickey Wright | 1966 | Sandra Spuzich | 1974 | Sandra Haynie |
| 1951 | Betsy Rawls | 1959 | Mickey Wright | 1967 | Catherine Lacoste* | 1975 | Sandra Palmer |
| 1952 | Louise Suggs | 1960 | Betsy Rawls | 1968 | Susie Maxwell Berning | 1976 | JoAnne Carner |
| 1953 | Betsy Rawls | 1961 | Mickey Wright | 1969 | Donna Caponi | 1977 | Hollis Stacy |
| 1954 | "Babe" Zaharias | 1962 | Marie Lindstrom | 1970 | Donna Caponi | 1978 | Hollis Stacy |
| 1955 | Fay Crocker | 1963 | Mary Mills | 1971 | JoAnne Carner | | |

*Amateur

## Masters Golf Tournament Champions

| Year | Winner | Year | Winner | Year | Winner | Year | Winner |
|---|---|---|---|---|---|---|---|
| 1934 | Horton Smith | 1947 | Jimmy Demaret | 1958 | Arnold Palmer | 1969 | George Archer |
| 1935 | Gene Sarazen | 1948 | Claude Harmon | 1959 | Art Wall Jr. | 1970 | Billy Casper |
| 1936 | Horton Smith | 1949 | Sam Snead | 1960 | Arnold Palmer | 1971 | Charles Coody |
| 1937 | Byron Nelson | 1950 | Jimmy Demaret | 1961 | Gary Player | 1972 | Jack Nicklaus |
| 1938 | Henry Picard | 1951 | Ben Hogan | 1962 | Arnold Palmer | 1973 | Tommy Aaron |
| 1939 | Ralph Guldahl | 1952 | Sam Snead | 1963 | Jack Nicklaus | 1974 | Gary Player |
| 1940 | Jimmy Demaret | 1953 | Ben Hogan | 1964 | Arnold Palmer | 1975 | Jack Nicklaus |
| 1941 | Craig Wood | 1954 | Sam Snead | 1965 | Jack Nicklaus | 1976 | Ray Floyd |
| 1942 | Byron Nelson | 1955 | Cary Middlecoff | 1966 | Jack Nicklaus | 1977 | Tom Watson |
| 1943-1945 | (Not played) | 1956 | Jack Burke | 1967 | Gay Brewer Jr. | 1978 | Gary Player |
| 1946 | Herman Keiser | 1957 | Doug Ford | 1968 | Bob Goalby | | |

## Professional Golfer's Association Championships

| Year | Winner | Year | Winner | Year | Winner | Year | Winner |
|---|---|---|---|---|---|---|---|
| 1919 | Jim Barnes | 1934 | Paul Runyan | 1950 | Chandler Harper | 1965 | Dave Marr |
| 1920 | Jock Hutchison | 1935 | Johnny Revolta | 1951 | Sam Snead | 1966 | Al Geiberger |
| 1921 | Walter Hagen | 1936 | Denny Shute | 1952 | James Turnesa | 1967 | Don January |
| 1922 | Gene Sarazen | 1937 | Denny Shute | 1953 | Walter Burkemo | 1968 | Julius Boros |
| 1923 | Gene Sarazen | 1938 | Paul Runyan | 1954 | Melvin Harbert | 1969 | Ray Floyd |
| 1924 | Walter Hagen | 1939 | Henry Picard | 1955 | Doug Ford | 1970 | Dave Stockton |
| 1925 | Walter Hagen | 1940 | Byron Nelson | 1956 | Jack Burke | 1971 | Jack Nicklaus |
| 1926 | Walter Hagen | 1941 | Victor Ghezzi | 1957 | Lionel Hebert | 1972 | Gary Player |
| 1927 | Walter Hagen | 1942 | Sam Snead | 1958 | Dow Finsterwald | 1973 | Jack Nicklaus |
| 1928 | Leo Diegel | 1944 | Bob Hamilton | 1959 | Bob Rosburg | 1974 | Lee Trevino |
| 1929 | Leo Diegel | 1945 | Byron Nelson | 1960 | Jay Hebert | 1975 | Jack Nicklaus |
| 1930 | Tommy Armour | 1946 | Ben Hogan | 1961 | Jerry Barber | 1976 | Dave Stockton |
| 1931 | Tom Creavy | 1947 | Jim Ferrier | 1962 | Gary Player | 1977 | Lanny Wadkins |
| 1932 | Olin Dutra | 1948 | Ben Hogan | 1963 | Jack Nicklaus | 1978 | John Mahaffey |
| 1933 | Gene Sarazen | 1949 | Sam Snead | 1964 | Bob Nichols | | |

## Canadian Open Golf Champions

| Year | Winner | Year | Winner | Year | Winner | Year | Winner |
|---|---|---|---|---|---|---|---|
| 1942 | Craig Wood | 1952 | John Palmer | 1961 | Jacky Cupit | 1970 | Kermit Zarley |
| 1943-44 | (Not played) | 1953 | Dave Douglas | 1962 | Ted Kroll | 1971 | Lee Trevino |
| 1945 | Byron Nelson | 1954 | Pat Fletcher | 1963 | Doug Ford | 1972 | Gay Brewer |
| 1946 | George Fazio | 1955 | Arnold Palmer | 1964 | Kel Nagle | 1973 | Tom Weiskopf |
| 1947 | Bobby Locke | 1956 | Doug Sanders | 1965 | Gene Littler | 1974 | Bobby Nichols |
| 1948 | C.W. Congdon | 1957 | George Bayer | 1966 | Don Massengale | 1975 | Tom Weiskopf |
| 1949 | E. J. Harrison | 1958 | Wes Ellis Jr. | 1967 | Billy Casper | 1976 | Jerry Pate |
| 1950 | Jim Ferrier | 1959 | Doug Ford | 1968 | Bob Charles | 1977 | Lee Trevino |
| 1951 | Jim Ferrier | 1960 | Art Wall, Jr. | 1969 | Tommy Aaron | 1978 | Bruce Lietzke |

## Professional Golf Tournaments in 1978

| Date | Event | Winner | Score | Prize |
|------|-------|--------|-------|-------|
| Jan. 8 | Tucson Open | Tom Watson | 276 | $40,000 |
| Jan. 16 | Phoenix Open | Miller Barber | 272 | 40,000 |
| Jan. 23 | Bing Crosby National Pro-Am, Pebble Beach, Cal. | Tom Watson | *281 | 45,000 |
| Jan. 29 | Andy Williams-San Diego Open | Jay Haas | 278 | 40,000 |
| Feb. 4 | Hawaiian Open, Honolulu | Hubert Green | 274 | 50,000 |
| Feb. 13 | Bob Hope Desert Classic, Palm Springs, Cal. | Bill Rogers | 339 | 45,000 |
| Feb. 20 | Los Angeles Open | Gil Morgan | 278 | 40,000 |
| Feb. 26 | Jackie Gleason — Inverrary Classic, Ft. Lauderdale, Fla. | Jack Nicklaus | 276 | 50,000 |
| Mar. 5 | Florida Citrus Open, Orlando | Mac McLendon | 271 | 40,000 |
| Mar. 12 | Doral-Eastern Open, Miami, Fla. | Tom Weiskopf | 272 | 40,000 |
| Mar. 19 | Tournament Players Championship, Ponte Vedra Beach, Fla. | Jack Nicklaus | 289 | 60,000 |
| Mar. 26 | Heritage Classic, Hilton Head, S.C. | Hubert Green | 277 | 45,000 |
| Apr. 2 | Greater Greensboro Open, N.C. | Severiano Ballesteros | 282 | 49,000 |
| Apr. 9 | Masters Tournament, Augusta, Ga. | Gary Player | 277 | 45,000 |
| Apr. 16 | Tournament of Champions, Carlsbad, Cal. | Gary Player | 281 | 45,000 |
| Apr. 23 | Houston Open | Gary Player | 270 | 40,000 |
| Apr. 30 | New Orleans Open | Lon Hinkle | 271 | 40,000 |
| May 7 | Byron Nelson Classic, Dallas, Tex. | Tom Watson | 272 | 40,000 |
| May 14 | Colonial National Tournament, Ft. Worth, Tex. | Lee Trevino | 268 | 40,000 |
| May 21 | Memorial Tournament, Dublin, Oh. | Jim Simons | 284 | 50,000 |
| May 28 | Atlanta Classic | Jerry Heard | 269 | 40,000 |
| June 4 | Kemper Open, Charlotte, N.C. | Andy Bean | 273 | 60,000 |
| June 11 | Danny Thomas, Memphis Classic | Andy Bean | *277 | 50,000 |
| June 18 | U.S. Open, Denver | Andy North | 285 | 45,000 |
| June 25 | Canadian Open, Oakville, Ont. | Bruce Lietzke | 283 | 50,000 |
| July 3 | Western Open, Oak Brook, Ill. | Andy Bean | *282 | 50,000 |
| July 9 | Greater Milwaukee Open | Lee Elder | *275 | 30,000 |
| July 23 | Philadelphia Classic | Jack Nicklaus | 270 | 50,000 |
| July 30 | Hartford Open | Ron Funseth | 264 | 42,000 |
| Aug. 6 | PGA Championship, Oakmont, Pa. | John Mahaffey | *276 | 50,000 |
| Aug. 13 | Pleasant Valley Classic, Mass. | John Mahaffey | 270 | 45,000 |
| Aug. 20 | Westchester Classic, Harrison, N.Y. | Lee Elder | 274 | 60,000 |
| Aug. 27 | Hall of Fame Classic, Pinehurst, N.C. | Tom Watson | 277 | 50,000 |
| Sept. 3 | B.C. Open, Endicott, N.Y. | Tom Kite | 267 | 45,000 |
| Sept. 11 | Southern Open, Columbus, Ga. | Jerry Pate | 269 | 19,950 |
| Sept. 17 | Texas Open, San Antonio, Tex. | Ron Streck | 265 | 40,000 |
| Oct. 1 | World Series of Golf, Akron, Oh. | Gil Morgan | *278 | 100,000 |

### Women

| Date | Event | Winner | Score | Prize |
|------|-------|--------|-------|-------|
| Jan. 29 | Colgate Triple Crown, Palm Springs, Cal. | JoAnne Carner | 143 | $21,000 |
| Feb. 20 | Orange Blossom Classic, St. Petersburg, Fla. | Jane Blalock | 212 | 9,000 |
| Feb. 26 | Bent Tree Classic, Sarasota, Fla. | Nancy Lopez | 289 | 15,000 |
| Mar. 12 | Sunstar Classic, Los Angeles, Cal. | Nancy Lopez | 285 | 15,000 |
| Mar. 19 | Kathryn Crosby/Honda Civic Classic, San Diego, Cal. | Sally Little | 282 | 22,500 |
| Apr. 2 | Colgate-Dinah Shore Winners Circle Tournament | Sandra Post | 283 | 36,000 |
| Apr. 16 | Birmingham Classic, Ala. | Hollis Stacy | 207 | 9,000 |
| Apr. 23 | American Defender Classic, Raleigh, N.C. | Amy Alcott | *206 | 8,250 |
| Apr. 30 | Lady Tara Classic, Atlanta, Ga. | Janet Coles | *211 | 11,250 |
| May 8 | Women's International, Hilton Head, S.C. | Jan Stephenson | 283 | 12,000 |
| May 14 | Greater Baltimore Classic | Nancy Lopez | 212 | 9,750 |
| May 22 | LPGA Classic, Jamesburg, N.J. | Nancy Lopez | *210 | 15,000 |
| May 29 | LPGA Tournament, New Rochelle, N.Y. | Nancy Lopez | 277 | 15,000 |
| June 11 | LPGA Championship, Mason, Oh. | Nancy Lopez | 275 | 22,500 |
| June 18 | LPGA Tournament, Rochester, N.Y. | Nancy Lopez | 214 | 11,250 |
| June 25 | Lady Keystone Open, Hershey, Pa. | Pat Bradley | 206 | 7,500 |
| July 9 | Wheeling Classic, W. Va. | Jane Blalock | 207 | 10,000 |
| July 16 | Bordon Classic, Dublin, Oh. | JoAnne Carner | 209 | 12,750 |
| July 23 | U.S. Women's Open, Indianapolis | Hollis Stacy | 289 | 15,000 |
| July 30 | Hoosier Classic, Plymouth, Ind. | Pat Bradley | 206 | 9,000 |
| Aug. 6 | European LPGA Championship, Sunningdale, England | Nancy Lopez | 289 | 15,000 |
| Aug. 13 | Long Island Classic, Manhasset, N.Y. | Judy Rankin | 283 | 15,000 |
| Aug. 20 | LPGA Tournament, Dearborn, Mich. | Sandra Post | *286 | 22,500 |
| Aug. 27 | Patty Berg Classic, St. Paul, Minn. | Shelley Hamlin | 208 | 11,000 |
| Sept. 11 | National Jewish Hospital Open, Denver, Col. | Kathy Whitworth | 211 | 9,000 |
| Sept. 17 | LPGA Tournament, Alamo, Cal. | Donna Caponi Young | 282 | 15,000 |

*Won playoff

## PGA Hall of Fame

Established in 1940 to honor those who have made outstanding contributions to the game by their lifetime playing ability.

| | | | |
|---|---|---|---|
| Anderson, Willie | Dudley, Edward | Hutchison Sr., Jock | Runyan, Paul |
| Armour, Tommy | Dutra, Olin | Jones, Bob | Sarazen, Gene |
| Barnes, Jim | Evans, Chick | Little, W. Lawson | Shute, Denny |
| Berg, Patty | Farrell, Johnny | Mangrum, Lloyd | Smith, Alex |
| Boros, Julius | Ford, Doug | McDermott, John | Smith, Horton |
| Brady, Mike | Ghezzi, Vic | McLeod, Fred | Smith, MacDonald |
| Burke, Billy | Guldahl, Ralph | Middlecoff, Cary | Snead, Sam |
| Burke Jr., Jack | Hagen, Walter | Nelson, Byron | Travers, Jerry |
| Cooper, Harry | Harbert, M. R. (Chick) | Ouimet, Francis | Travis, Walter |
| Cruickshank, Bobby | Harper, Chandler | Picard, Henry | Wood, Craig |
| Demaret, Jimmy | Harrison, E. J. | Revolta, Johnny | Zaharias, Mildred (Babe) |
| Diegel, Leo | Hogan, Ben | | |

## British Open Golf Champions

| Year | Winner | Year | Winner | Year | Winner | Year | Winner |
|------|--------|------|--------|------|--------|------|--------|
| 1908 | James Braid | 1928 | Walter Hagen | 1949 | Bobby Locke | 1964 | Tony Lema |
| 1909 | J.H. Taylor | 1929 | Walter Hagen | 1950 | Bobby Locke | 1965 | Peter Thomson |
| 1910 | James Braid | 1930 | Bob Jones | 1951 | Max Faulkner | 1966 | Jack Nicklaus |
| 1911 | Harry Vardon | 1931 | Tommy Armour | 1952 | Bobby Locke | 1967 | Roberto de Vicenz |
| 1912 | Ted Ray | 1932 | Gene Sarazen | 1953 | Ben Hogan | 1968 | Gary Player |
| 1913 | J.H. Taylor | 1933 | Denny Shute | 1954 | Peter Thomson | 1969 | Tony Jacklin |
| 1914 | Harry Vardon | 1934 | Henry Cotton | 1955 | Peter Thomson | 1970 | Jack Nicklaus |
| 1915-19 | (Not played) | 1935 | Alf Perry | 1956 | Peter Thomson | 1971 | Lee Trevino |
| 1920 | George Duncan | 1936 | Alf Padgham | 1957 | Bobby Locke | 1972 | Lee Trevino |
| 1921 | Jock Hutchison | 1937 | T.H. Cotton | 1958 | Peter Thomson | 1973 | Tom Weiskopf |
| 1922 | Walter Hagen | 1938 | R.A. Whitcombe | 1959 | Gary Player | 1974 | Gary Player |
| 1923 | Arthur Havers | 1939 | Richard Burton | 1960 | Ken Nagle | 1975 | Tom Watson |
| 1924 | Walter Hagen | 1940-45 | (Not played) | 1961 | Arnold Palmer | 1976 | Johnny Miller |
| 1925 | Jim Barnes | 1946 | Sam Snead | 1962 | Arnold Palmer | 1977 | Tom Watson |
| 1926 | Bob Jones | 1947 | Fred Daly | 1963 | Bob Charles | 1978 | Jack Nicklaus |
| 1927 | Bob Jones | 1948 | Henry Cotton | | | | |

## U.S. Amateur

| Year | Winner | Year | Winner | Year | Winner | Year | Winner |
|------|--------|------|--------|------|--------|------|--------|
| 1903 | Walter Travis | 1922 | Jess Sweetser | 1940 | Dick Chapman | 1961 | Jack Nicklaus |
| 1904 | Chandler Egan | 1923 | Max Marston | 1941 | Bud Ward | 1962 | Labron Harris Jr. |
| 1905 | Chandler Egan | 1924 | Bob Jones | 1942-45 | (not played) | 1963 | Deane Beman |
| 1906 | Eben Byers | 1925 | Bob Jones | 1946 | Ted Bishop | 1964 | Bill Campbell |
| 1907 | Jerome Travers | 1926 | George Von Elm | 1947 | Skee Riegel | 1965 | Robert Murphy Jr. |
| 1908 | Jerome Travers | 1927 | Bob Jones | 1948 | Willie Turnesa | 1966 | Gary Cowan |
| 1909 | Robert Gardner | 1928 | Bob Jones | 1949 | Charles Coe | 1967 | Bob Dickson |
| 1910 | William Fownes Jr. | 1929 | Harrison Johnston | 1950 | Sam Urzetta | 1968 | Bruce Fleisher |
| 1911 | Harold Hilton | 1930 | Bob Jones | 1951 | Billy Maxwell | 1969 | Steve Melnyk |
| 1912 | Jerome Travers | 1931 | Francis Ouimet | 1952 | Jack Westland | 1970 | Lanny Wadkins |
| 1913 | Jerome Travers | 1932 | Ross Somerville | 1953 | Gene Littler | 1971 | Gary Cowan |
| 1914 | Francis Ouimet | 1933 | George Dunlap Jr. | 1954 | Arnold Palmer | 1972 | Vinnie Giles |
| 1915 | Robert Gardner | 1934 | Lawson Little | 1955 | Harvie Ward | 1973 | Craig Stadler |
| 1916 | Chick Evans Jr. | 1935 | Lawson Little | 1956 | Harvie Ward | 1974 | Jerry Pate |
| 1917-18 | (not played) | 1936 | John Fischer | 1957 | Hillman Robbins | 1975 | Fred Ridley |
| 1919 | Davidson Herron | 1937 | John Goodman | 1958 | Charles Coe | 1976 | Bill Sander |
| 1920 | Chick Evans Jr. | 1938 | Willie Turnesa | 1959 | Jack Nicklaus | 1977 | John Fought |
| 1921 | Jesse Guilford | 1939 | Bud Ward | 1960 | Deane Beman | 1978 | John Cook |

## Women's U.S. Amateur

| Year | Winner | Year | Winner | Year | Winner | Year | Winner |
|------|--------|------|--------|------|--------|------|--------|
| 1907 | Margaret Curtis | 1925 | Glenna Collett | 1942-45 | (not played) | 1962 | JoAnne Gunderson |
| 1908 | Kate Harley | 1926 | Mrs. G. Stetson | 1946 | "Babe" Zaharias | 1963 | Anne Q. Welts |
| 1909 | Dorothy Campbell | 1927 | Mrs. M. Horn | 1947 | Louise Suggs | 1964 | Barbara McIntire |
| 1910 | Dorothy Campbell | 1928 | Glenna Collett | 1948 | Grace Lenczyk | 1965 | Jean Ashley |
| 1911 | Margaret Curtis | 1929 | Glenna Collett | 1949 | Dorothy Porter | 1966 | JoAnne Carner |
| 1912 | Margaret Curtis | 1930 | Glenna Collett | 1950 | Beverly Hanson | 1967 | Lou Dill |
| 1913 | Gladys Raven Scroft | 1931 | Helen Hicks | 1951 | Dorothy Kirby | 1968 | JoAnn Carner |
| 1914 | Mrs. H. A. Jackson | 1932 | Virginia Van Wie | 1952 | Jackie Pung | 1969 | Catherine Lacoste |
| 1915 | Mrs. C. H. Vanderbeck | 1933 | Virginia Van Wie | 1953 | Mary Faulk | 1970 | Martha Wilkinson |
| 1916 | Alexa Stirling | 1934 | Virginia Van Wie | 1954 | Barbara Romack | 1971 | Laura Baugh |
| 1917-18 | (not played) | 1935 | Glenna C. Vare | 1955 | Pat Lesser | 1972 | Mary Budke |
| 1919 | Alexa Stirling | 1936 | Pamela Barton | 1956 | Marlene Stewart | 1973 | Carol Semple |
| 1920 | Alexa Stirling | 1937 | Mrs. J. A. Page | 1957 | JoAnne Gunderson | 1974 | Cynthia Hill |
| 1921 | Marion Hollins | 1938 | Patty Berg | 1958 | Anne Quast | 1975 | Beth Daniel |
| 1922 | Glenna Collett | 1939 | Betty Jameson | 1959 | Barbara McIntire | 1976 | Donna Horton |
| 1923 | Edith Cummings | 1940 | Betty Jameson | 1960 | JoAnne Gunderson | 1977 | Beth Daniel |
| 1924 | Mrs. D.C. Hurd | 1941 | Mrs. Frank New | 1961 | Anne Q. Decker | 1978 | Cathy Sherk |

## LPGA Leading Money Winners

| Year | Winner | Dollars | Year | Winner | Dollars | Year | Winner | Dolla |
|------|--------|---------|------|--------|---------|------|--------|-------|
| 1952 | Betsy Rawls | 14,505 | 1961 | Mickey Wright | 22,236 | 1970 | Kathy Whitworth | 30,23 |
| 1953 | Louise Suggs | 19,816 | 1962 | Mickey Wright | 21,641 | 1971 | Kathy Whitworth | 41,18 |
| 1954 | Patty Berg | 16,011 | 1963 | Mickey Wright | 31,269 | 1972 | Kathy Whitworth | 65,06 |
| 1955 | Patty Berg | 16,492 | 1964 | Mickey Wright | 29,800 | 1973 | Kathy Whitworth | 82,85 |
| 1956 | Marlene Hagge | 20,235 | 1965 | Kathy Whitworth | 28,658 | 1974 | JoAnne Carner | 87,09 |
| 1957 | Patty Berg | 16,272 | 1966 | Kathy Whitworth | 33,517 | 1975 | Sandra Palmer | 94,80 |
| 1958 | Beverly Hanson | 12,629 | 1967 | Kathy Whitworth | 32,937 | 1976 | Judy Rankin | 150,73 |
| 1959 | Betsy Rawls | 26,774 | 1968 | Kathy Whitworth | 48,379 | 1977 | Judy Rankin | 122,89 |
| 1960 | Louise Suggs | 16,892 | 1969 | Carol Mann | 49,152 | | | |

## LPGA Career Money Winners

(as of January 1, 1978)

| Player | Dollars | Player | Dollars | Player | Dolla |
|--------|---------|--------|---------|--------|-------|
| Kathy Whitworth | 745,359 | Donna Caponi Young | 381,422 | Sandra Post | 254,20 |
| Judy Rankin | 600,789 | Mickey Wright | 349,638 | Debbie Austin | 241,09 |
| Sandra Palmer | 500,631 | Marlene Hagge | 329,602 | Clifford Ann Creed | 233,39 |
| Sandra Haynie | 490,337 | Jo Ann Prentice | 315,295 | Betty Burfeindt | 213,34 |
| Carol Mann | 481,970 | Betsy Rawls | 302,664 | Sandra Spuzich | 202,39 |
| Jane Blalock | 475,942 | Marilynn Smith | 293,102 | Pat Bradley | 202,13 |
| JoAnne Carner | 443,668 | Mary Mills | 277,374 | Kathy Cornelius | 200,17 |

## PGA Leading Money Winners

| Year | Player | Dollars | Year | Player | Dollars | Year | Player | Dollars |
|---|---|---|---|---|---|---|---|---|
| 45 | Byron Nelson | 52,511 | 1956 | Ted Kroll | 72,835 | 1967 | Jack Nicklaus | 188,988 |
| 46 | Ben Hogan | 42,556 | 1957 | Dick Mayer | 65,835 | 1968 | Billy Casper | 205,168 |
| 47 | Jimmy Demaret | 27,936 | 1958 | Arnold Palmer | 42,407 | 1969 | Frank Beard | 175,223 |
| 48 | Ben Hogan | 36,812 | 1959 | Art Wall Jr. | 53,167 | 1970 | Lee Trevino | 157,037 |
| 49 | Sam Snead | 31,593 | 1960 | Arnold Palmer | 75,262 | 1971 | Jack Nicklaus | 244,490 |
| 50 | Sam Snead | 35,758 | 1961 | Gary Player | 64,540 | 1972 | Jack Nicklaus | 320,542 |
| 51 | Lloyd Mangrum | 26,088 | 1962 | Arnold Palmer | 81,448 | 1973 | Jack Nicklaus | 308,362 |
| 52 | Julius Boros | 37,032 | 1963 | Arnold Palmer | 128,230 | 1974 | Johnny Miller | 353,201 |
| 53 | Lew Worsham | 34,002 | 1964 | Jack Nicklaus | 113,284 | 1975 | Jack Nicklaus | 323,149 |
| 54 | Bob Toski | 65,819 | 1965 | Jack Nicklaus | 140,752 | 1976 | Jack Nicklaus | 266,438 |
| 55 | Julius Boros | 65,121 | 1966 | Billy Casper | 121,944 | 1977 | Tom Watson | 310,653 |

## PGA Career Money Winners

(as of January 1, 1978)

| Player | Dollars | Player | Dollars | Player | Dollars |
|---|---|---|---|---|---|
| Jack Nicklaus | 3,092,721 | Hale Irwin | 1,234,230 | George Archer | 967,449 |
| Arnold Palmer | 1,762,082 | Johnny Miller | 1,144,065 | Bobby Nichols | 925,353 |
| Billy Casper | 1,658,468 | Al Geiberger | 1,077,972 | Hubert Green | 895,696 |
| Lee Trevino | 1,620,723 | Dave Hill | 1,055,898 | Don January | 892,528 |
| Tom Weiskopf | 1,553,826 | Ray Floyd | 1,039,168 | Lou Graham | 853,528 |
| Gene Littler | 1,383,772 | Julius Boros | 1,000,642 | Tom Watson | 838,962 |
| Bruce Crampton | 1,374,294 | Frank Beard | 983,317 | J. C. Snead | 824,771 |
| Gary Player | 1,329,307 | Dave Stockton | 967,785 | Charles Coody | 822,878 |
| Miller Barber | 1,249,864 | | | | |

## Ryder Cup Matches

United States vs. Great Britain Professional (biennial)
Series Standing — United States 18, Great Britain 3, 1 tie

| Series record | | Series record | |
|---|---|---|---|
| 1955 | United States 8; Great Britain 4 | 1967 | United States 23½; Great Britain 8½ |
| 1957 | Great Britain 7; United States 4 | 1969 | United States 16; Great Britain 16 |
| 1959 | United States 8½; Great Britain 3½ | 1971 | United States 18½; Great Britain 13½ |
| 1961 | United States 14½; Great Britain 9½ | 1973 | Great Britain 13; United States 10 |
| 1963 | United States 23; Great Britain 9 | 1975 | United States 21; Great Britain 11 |
| 1965 | United States 19½; Great Britain 12½ | 1977 | United States 12½; Great Britain 7½ |

## International Walker Cup Golf Match

United States vs. Great Britain — Men's Amateur (biennial)
Series Standing — United States, 23, Great Britain 2, 1 tie

| Series record | | Series record | |
|---|---|---|---|
| 1955 | United States 10; Great Britain 2 | 1967 | United States 13; Great Britain 7 |
| 1957 | United States 10; Great Britain 2 | 1969 | United States 10; Great Britain 8 |
| 1959 | United States 9; Great Britain 3 | 1971 | Great Britain 13; United States 11 |
| 1961 | United States 11; Great Britain 1 | 1973 | United States 14; Great Britain 10 |
| 1963 | United States 9; Great Britain 3 | 1975 | United States 15½; Great Britain 8½ |
| 1965 | United States 11; Great Britain 11 | 1977 | United States 16; Great Britain 8 |

## International Curtis Cup Golf Match

United States vs. Great Britain (plus Ireland) — Women's Amateur (biennial)
Series standing — United States 16, Great Britain 2, 2 ties

| Series record | | Series record | |
|---|---|---|---|
| 1954 | United States 6; Great Britain 3 | 1968 | United States 10½; Great Britain 7½ |
| 1957 | Great Britain 5; United States 4 | 1970 | United States 11½; Great Britain 6½ |
| 1959 | Great Britain 4½; United States 4½ | 1972 | United States 10; Great Britain 8 |
| 1960 | United States 6½; Great Britain 2½ | 1974 | United States 13; Great Britain 5 |
| 1962 | United States 8; Great Britain 1 | 1976 | United States 11½; Great Britain 6½ |
| 1964 | United States 10½; Great Britain 7½ | 1978 | United States 12; Great Britain 6 |
| 1966 | United States 13; Great Britain 5 | | |

## Quarter Horse Racing

The richest horse race in the world, the All American Futurity is run each Labor Day at Ruidoso Downs, New Mexico. It is open to 2-year-old Quarter Horses. The distance of the event was 400 yards through 1972; 440 yards starting in 1973.

| Year | Winner | Time | Value to winner | Jockey | Year | Winner | Time | Value to winner | Jockey |
|---|---|---|---|---|---|---|---|---|---|
| 1963 | Goetta | 20.40 | $127,500 | C. Smith | 1971 | Mr. Kid Charge | 19.65 | $200,841 | J. Cox |
| 1964 | Decketta | 20.30 | 134,030 | B. Morris | 1972 | Possumjet | 20.04 | 336,629 | P. Herrera |
| 1965 | Savannah Jr. | 20.30 | 192,730 | J. Wallace | 1973 | Time To Thinkrich | 21.58 | 330,000 | J. Watson |
| 1966 | Go Dick Go | 20.27 | 198,300 | B. Nesmith | 1974 | Easy Date | 21.60 | 330,000 | D. Knight |
| 1967 | Laico Bird | 20.11 | 228,300 | B. Harmon | 1975 | Bugs Alive in 75 | 21.98 | 330,000 | J. Burgess |
| 1968 | Three Oh's | 20.06 | 160,372 | J. Nicodemus | 1976 | Real Wind | 21.70 | 330,000 | G. Sumpter |
| 1969 | Easy Jet | 20.46 | 159,840 | W. Lovell | 1977 | Hot Idea | 21.75 | 330,000 | T. Lipman |
| 1970 | Rocket Wrangler | 20.09 | 178,488 | J. Nicodemus | 1978 | Moon Lark | 21.84 | 437,500 | J. Martin |

# Professional Sports Directory

## Baseball

Commissioner's Office
75 Rockefeller Plaza
New York, NY 10019

**National League**

National League Office
1 Rockefeller Plaza
New York, NY 10019

Atlanta Braves
PO Box 4064
Atlanta, GA 30302

Chicago Cubs
Wrigley Field
Chicago, IL 60613

Cincinnati Reds
100 Riverfront Stadium
Cincinnati, OH 45202

Houston Astros
Astrodome
Houston, TX 77001

Los Angeles Dodgers
Dodger Stadium
1000 Elysian Park Ave.
Los Angeles, CA 90012

Montreal Expos
PO BOX 500, Station R
Montreal, Quebec H1V 3P2

New York Mets
William A. Shea Stadium
Roosevelt Ave. & 126th St.
Flushing, NY 11368

Philadelphia Phillies
Philadelphia Veterans Stadium
Broad St. & Pattison Ave.
Philadelphia, PA 19148

Pittsburgh Pirates
600 Stadium Circle
Pittsburgh, PA 15212

St. Louis Cardinals
Busch Memorial Stadium
250 Stadium Plaza
St. Louis, MO 63102

San Diego Padres
PO Box 2000
San Diego, CA 92120

San Francisco Giants
Candlestick Park
San Francisco, CA 94124

**American League**

American League Office
280 Park Ave.
New York, NY 10017

Baltimore Orioles
Memorial Stadium
Baltimore, MD 21218

Boston Red Sox
24 Jersey St.
Boston, MA 02215

California Angels
Anaheim Stadium
2000 State College Blvd.
Anaheim, CA 92806

Chicago White Sox
Comiskey Park
Dan Ryan & 35th St.
Chicago, IL 60616

Cleveland Indians
Cleveland Stadium
Cleveland, OH 44114

Detroit Tigers
Tiger Stadium
Detroit, MI 48216

Kansas City Royals
Harry S. Truman Sports Compl
PO Box 1969
Kansas City, MO 64141

Milwaukee Brewers
Milwaukee County Stadium
Milwaukee, WI 53214

Minnesota Twins
Metropolitan Stadium
8001 Cedar Ave.
Bloomington, MN 55420

New York Yankees
Yankee Stadium
Bronx, NY 10451

Oakland A's
Oakland-Alameda County
   Coliseum
Oakland, CA 94621

Seattle Mariners
PO Box 4100
Seattle, WA 98104

Texas Rangers
Arlington Stadium
PO Box 1111
Arlington, TX 76010

Toronto Blue Jays
Exhibition Stadium
Toronto, Ont.

## National Basketball Association

League Office
Olympic Tower
645 5th Ave.
New York, NY 10022

Atlanta Hawks
100 Techwood Drive NW
Atlanta, GA 30303

Boston Celtics
North Station
Boston, MA 02114

Chicago Bulls
333 North Michigan Ave.
Chicago, IL 60601

Cleveland Cavaliers
The Coliseum
2923 Streetsboro Rd.
Richfield, OH 44286

Denver Nuggets
PO Box 4286
Denver, CO 80204

Detroit Pistons
Cobo Hall
Detroit, MI 48226

Golden State Warriors
Oakland Coliseum Arena
Oakland, CA 94621

Houston Rockets
The Summit
Houston, TX 77046

Indiana Pacers
Market Square Center
151 N. Delaware
Indianapolis, IN 46204

Kansas City Kings
1800 Genessee
Kansas City, MO 64102

Los Angeles Lakers
The Forum
3900 W. Manchester Blvd.
   or PO Box 10
Inglewood, CA 90306

Milwaukee Bucks
901 North 4th St.
Milwaukee, WI 53203

New Jersey Nets
30 Park Avenue
Rutherford, NJ 07070

New Orleans Jazz
Louisiana Superdome
Box 53213
New Orleans, LA 70153

New York Knickerbockers
Madison Square Garden
Center
4 Pennsylvania Plaza
New York, NY 10001

Philadelphia 76ers
The Spectrum
Philadelphia, PA 19148

Phoenix Suns
PO Box 1369
Phoenix, AZ 85001

Portland Trail Blazers
Lloyd Bldg.
700 NE Multnomah St.
Portland, OR 97232

San Antonio Spurs
HemisFair Arena
P.O. Box 530
San Antonio, TX 78292

San Diego Clippers
San Diego Sports Arena
3500 Sports Arena Blvd.
San Diego, CA 92110

Seattle SuperSonics
221 West Harrison St.
Seattle, WA 98119

Washington Bullets
Capital Centre
Landover, MD 20786

## Hockey

**National Hockey League**

League Headquarters
920 Sun Life Bldg.
Montreal, Quebec H3B 2W2

League Services
2 Pennsylvania Plaza
New York, NY 10001

Atlanta Flames
100 Techwood Dr. NW
Atlanta, GA 30303

Boston Bruins
150 Causeway St.
Boston, MA 02114

Buffalo Sabres
Memorial Auditorium
Buffalo, NY 14202

Chicago Black Hawks
1800 W. Madison St.
Chicago, IL 60612

Colorado Rockies
McNichols Sports Arena
Denver, CO 80204

Detroit Red Wings
5920 Grand River
Detroit, MI 48208

Los Angeles Kings
PO Box 10
Inglewood, CA 90306

Minnesota North Stars
7901 Cedar Ave. S.
Bloomington, MN 55420

Montreal Canadiens
2313 St. Catherine St., West
Montreal, Quebec H3H 1N2

New York Islanders
1155 Conklin St.
Farmingdale, NY 11735

New York Rangers
Madison Square Garden
Pennsylvania Plaza
New York, NY 10001

Philadelphia Flyers
The Spectrum
Pattison Place
Philadelphia, PA 19148

Pittsburgh Penguins
Civic Arena
Pittsburgh, PA 15219

St. Louis Blues
5700 Oakland Ave.
St. Louis, MO 63110

Toronto Maple Leafs
60 Carlton St.
Toronto, Ont. M5B 1L1

Vancouver Canucks
100 North Renfrew St.
Vancouver, B.C. V5K 3N7

Washington Capitals
Capital Centre
Landover, MD 20786

**World Hockey Assn.**

League Office
One Financial Plaza
Hartford, CT 06103

Birmingham Bulls
1 Civic Center Plaza
Birmingham, AL 35203

Cincinnati Stingers
Riverfront Coliseum
Cincinnati, OH 45202

Edmonton Oilers
Edmonton Coliseum
Edmonton, Alta. T5B 4M9

Indianapolis Racers
Market Square Center
Indianapolis, IN 46204

New England Whalers
1 Civic-Center Plaza
Hartford, CT 06103

Quebec Nordiques
2025 Ave. Du Colisee
Quebec, Quebec G1L 4W7

Winnipeg Jets
15-1430 Maroons Rd.
Winnipeg, Man. R3G 0L5

## National Football League

League Office
410 Park Avenue
New York, NY 10022

Atlanta Falcons
521 Capitol Ave. SW
Atlanta, GA 30312

Baltimore Colts
Executive Plaza
Hunt Valley, MD 21031

Buffalo Bills
1 Bills Drive
Orchard Park, NY 14127

Chicago Bears
55 E. Jackson
Chicago, IL 60604

Cincinnati Bengals
200 Riverfront Stadium
Cincinnati, OH 45202

Cleveland Browns
Cleveland Stadium
Cleveland, OH 44114

Dallas Cowboys
6116 North Central Expressway
Dallas, TX 75206

Denver Broncos
5700 Logan St.
Denver, CO 80216

Detroit Lions
1200 Featherstone Rd.
Box 4200
Pontiac, MI 48057

Green Bay Packers
1265 Lombardi Ave.
Green Bay, WI 54303

Houston Oilers
P.O. Box 1516
Houston, TX 77001

Kansas City Chiefs
1 Arrowhead Drive
Kansas City, MO 64129

Los Angeles Rams
10271 W. Pico Blvd.
Los Angeles, CA 90064

Miami Dolphins
330 Biscayne Blvd. Bldg.
Miami, FL 33132

Minnesota Vikings
7110 France Ave. So.
Edina, MN 55435

New England Patriots
Schaefer Stadium
Foxboro, MA 02035

New Orleans Saints
944 St. Charles
New Orleans, LA 70130

New York Giants
Giants Stadium
E. Rutherford, NJ 07073

New York Jets
598 Madison Ave.
New York, NY 10022

Oakland Raiders
7811 Oakport St.
Oakland, CA 94621

Philadelphia Eagles
Veterans Stadium
Philadelphia, PA 19148

Pittsburgh Steelers
Three Rivers Stadium
Pittsburgh, PA 15212

St. Louis Cardinals
200 Stadium Plaza
St. Louis, MO 63102

San Diego Chargers
San Diego Stadium
P.O. Box 20666
San Diego, CA 92120

San Francisco 49ers
711 Nevada St.
Redwood City, CA 94061

Seattle Seahawks
5305 Lake Washington Blvd.
Kirkland, WA 98033

Tampa Bay Buccaneers
1 Buccaneer Place
Tampa, FL 33607

Washington Redskins
PO Box 17247
Dulles Intl. Airport
Washington, DC 20041

## North American Soccer League

League Office
1133 Ave. of the Americas
Suite 3500
New York, NY 10036

California Surf
PO Box 4449
Anaheim, CA 92803

Chicago Sting
Suite 1525
333 N. Michigan Ave.
Chicago, IL 60601

Caribous of Colorado
Diamond Hill
Suite 170, Bldg. C
2460 W. 26th Ave.
Denver, CO 80211

Dallas Tornado
6116 N. Central Expwy.
Dallas, TX 75206

Detroit Express
Pontiac Silverdome
1200 Featherstone Road
Pontiac, MI 48057

Ft. Lauderdale Strikers
1350 North East 56th St.
Ft. Lauderdale, FL 33348

Houston Hurricane
PO Box 42999
Suite 569
Houston, TX 77042

Los Angeles Aztecs
9171 Wilshire Blvd.
Suite A
Beverly Hills, CA 90210

Memphis Rogues
2200 Union Ave.
Memphis, TN 38104

Minnesota Kicks
7200 France Ave. So.
Minneapolis, MN 55435

New England Tea Men
34 Mechanic St.
Foxboro, MA 02543

New York Cosmos
75 Rockefeller Plaza
New York, NY 10019

Oakland Stompers
7901 Oakport Blvd.
Oakland, CA 94621

Philadelphia Fury
Veterans Stadium
Broad St. & Pattison Ave.
Philadelphia, PA 19148

Portland Timbers
Suite 101 D
10151 S.W. Barbur Blvd.
Portland, OR 97219

Rochester Lancers
812 Wilder Bldg.
Rochester, NY 14614

San Diego Sockers
San Diego Stadium
9449 Friars Road
San Diego, CA 92108

San Jose Earthquakes
Suite 272
2025 Gateway Place
San Jose, CA 95110

Seattle Sounders
300 Metropole Bldg.
Seattle, WA 98104

Tampa Bay Rowdies
Suite 109
1311 N. West Shore Blvd.
Tampa, FL 33607

Toronto Metros
Pro Soccer Ltd.
1678 Bloor St., West
Toronto, Ontario M6P 1A8

Tulsa Roughnecks
PO Box 35190
Tulsa, OK 75135

Vancouver Whitecaps
Suite 110
885 Dunsmuir St.
Vancouver, B.C. V6C 1N5

Washington Diplomats
RFK Stadium
E. Capitol Sts. & 22nd NE
Washington, DC 20003

## Little League World Series in 1978

Taiwan won the 1978 Little League World Series by defeating Danville (Cal.) 11-1 at Williamsport, Pa. on Aug. 26. The victory was Taiwan's 7th world title in the past 10 years.

# Baseball

## Major League Pennant Winners, 1901–1978

### National League        American League

| Year | Winner | Won | Lost | Pct | Manager | Year | Winner | Won | Lost | Pct | Manager |
|------|--------|-----|------|-----|---------|------|--------|-----|------|-----|---------|
| 1901 | Pittsburgh | 90 | 49 | .647 | Clarke | 1901 | Chicago | 83 | 53 | .610 | Griffith |
| 1902 | Pittsburgh | 103 | 36 | .741 | Clarke | 1902 | Philadelphia | 83 | 53 | .610 | Mack |
| 1903 | Pittsburgh | 91 | 49 | .650 | Clarke | 1903 | Boston | 91 | 47 | .659 | Collins |
| 1904 | New York | 106 | 47 | .693 | McGraw | 1904 | Boston | 95 | 59 | .617 | Collins |
| 1905 | New York | 105 | 48 | .686 | McGraw | 1905 | Philadelphia | 92 | 56 | .622 | Mack |
| 1906 | Chicago | 116 | 36 | .763 | Chance | 1906 | Chicago | 93 | 58 | .616 | Jones |
| 1907 | Chicago | 107 | 45 | .704 | Chance | 1907 | Detroit | 92 | 58 | .613 | Jennings |
| 1908 | Chicago | 99 | 55 | .643 | Chance | 1908 | Detroit | 90 | 63 | .588 | Jennings |
| 1909 | Pittsburgh | 110 | 42 | .724 | Clarke | 1909 | Detroit | 98 | 54 | .645 | Jennings |
| 1910 | Chicago | 104 | 50 | .675 | Chance | 1910 | Philadelphia | 102 | 48 | .680 | Mack |
| 1911 | New York | 99 | 54 | .647 | McGraw | 1911 | Philadelphia | 101 | 50 | .669 | Mack |
| 1912 | New York | 103 | 48 | .682 | McGraw | 1912 | Boston | 105 | 47 | .691 | Stahl |
| 1913 | New York | 101 | 51 | .664 | McGraw | 1913 | Philadelphia | 96 | 57 | .627 | Mack |
| 1914 | Boston | 94 | 59 | .614 | Stallings | 1914 | Philadelphia | 99 | 53 | .651 | Mack |
| 1915 | Philadelphia | 90 | 62 | .592 | Moran | 1915 | Boston | 101 | 50 | .669 | Carrigan |
| 1916 | Brooklyn | 94 | 60 | .610 | Robinson | 1916 | Boston | 91 | 63 | .591 | Carrigan |
| 1917 | New York | 98 | 56 | .636 | McGraw | 1917 | Chicago | 100 | 54 | .649 | Rowland |
| 1918 | Chicago | 84 | 45 | .651 | Mitchell | 1918 | Boston | 75 | 51 | .595 | Barrow |
| 1919 | Cincinnati | 96 | 44 | .686 | Moran | 1919 | Chicago | 88 | 52 | .629 | Gleason |
| 1920 | Brooklyn | 93 | 60 | .604 | Robinson | 1920 | Cleveland | 98 | 56 | .636 | Speaker |
| 1921 | New York | 94 | 59 | .614 | McGraw | 1921 | New York | 98 | 55 | .641 | Huggins |
| 1922 | New York | 93 | 61 | .604 | McGraw | 1922 | New York | 94 | 60 | .610 | Huggins |
| 1923 | New York | 95 | 58 | .621 | McGraw | 1923 | New York | 98 | 54 | .645 | Huggins |
| 1924 | New York | 93 | 60 | .608 | McGraw | 1924 | Washington | 92 | 62 | .597 | Harris |
| 1925 | Pittsburgh | 95 | 58 | .621 | McKechnie | 1925 | Washington | 96 | 55 | .636 | Harris |
| 1926 | St. Louis | 89 | 65 | .578 | Hornsby | 1926 | New York | 91 | 63 | .591 | Huggins |
| 1927 | Pittsburgh | 94 | 60 | .610 | Bush | 1927 | New York | 110 | 44 | .714 | Huggins |
| 1928 | St. Louis | 95 | 59 | .617 | McKechnie | 1928 | New York | 101 | 53 | .656 | Huggins |
| 1929 | Chicago | 98 | 54 | .645 | McCarthy | 1929 | Philadelphia | 104 | 46 | .693 | Mack |
| 1930 | St. Louis | 92 | 62 | .597 | Street | 1930 | Philadelphia | 102 | 52 | .622 | Mack |
| 1931 | St. Louis | 101 | 53 | .656 | Street | 1931 | Philadelphia | 107 | 45 | .704 | Mack |
| 1932 | Chicago | 90 | 64 | .584 | Grimm | 1932 | New York | 107 | 47 | .695 | McCarthy |
| 1933 | New York | 91 | 61 | .599 | Terry | 1933 | Washington | 99 | 53 | .651 | Cronin |
| 1934 | St. Louis | 95 | 58 | .621 | Frisch | 1934 | Detroit | 101 | 53 | .656 | Cochrane |
| 1935 | Chicago | 100 | 54 | .649 | Grimm | 1935 | Detroit | 93 | 58 | .616 | Cochrane |
| 1936 | New York | 91 | 62 | .597 | Terry | 1936 | New York | 102 | 51 | .667 | McCarthy |
| 1937 | New York | 95 | 57 | .625 | Terry | 1937 | New York | 102 | 52 | .662 | McCarthy |
| 1938 | Chicago | 89 | 63 | .586 | Hartnett | 1938 | New York | 99 | 53 | .651 | McCarthy |
| 1939 | Cincinnati | 97 | 57 | .630 | McKechnie | 1939 | New York | 106 | 45 | .702 | McCarthy |
| 1940 | Cincinnati | 100 | 53 | .654 | McKechnie | 1940 | Detroit | 90 | 64 | .584 | Baker |
| 1941 | Brooklyn | 100 | 54 | .649 | Durocher | 1941 | New York | 101 | 53 | .656 | McCarthy |
| 1942 | St. Louis | 106 | 48 | .688 | Southworth | 1942 | New York | 103 | 51 | .669 | McCarthy |
| 1943 | St. Louis | 105 | 49 | .682 | Southworth | 1943 | New York | 98 | 56 | .636 | McCarthy |
| 1944 | St. Louis | 105 | 49 | .682 | Southworth | 1944 | St. Louis | 89 | 65 | .578 | Sewell |
| 1945 | Chicago | 98 | 56 | .636 | Grimm | 1945 | Detroit | 88 | 65 | .575 | O'Neill |
| 1946 | St. Louis | 98 | 58 | .628 | Dyer | 1946 | Boston | 104 | 50 | .675 | Cronin |
| 1947 | Brooklyn | 94 | 60 | .610 | Shotton | 1947 | New York | 97 | 57 | .630 | Harris |
| 1948 | Boston | 91 | 62 | .595 | Southworth | 1948 | Cleveland | 97 | 58 | .626 | Boudreau |
| 1949 | Brooklyn | 97 | 57 | .630 | Shotton | 1949 | New York | 97 | 57 | .630 | Stengel |
| 1950 | Philadelphia | 91 | 63 | .591 | Sawyer | 1950 | New York | 98 | 56 | .636 | Stengel |
| 1951 | New York | 98 | 59 | .624 | Durocher | 1951 | New York | 98 | 56 | .636 | Stengel |
| 1952 | Brooklyn | 96 | 57 | .627 | Dressen | 1952 | New York | 95 | 59 | .617 | Stengel |
| 1953 | Brooklyn | 105 | 49 | .682 | Dressen | 1953 | New York | 99 | 52 | .656 | Stengel |
| 1954 | New York | 97 | 57 | .630 | Durocher | 1954 | Cleveland | 111 | 43 | .721 | Lopez |
| 1955 | Brooklyn | 98 | 55 | .641 | Alston | 1955 | New York | 96 | 58 | .623 | Stengel |
| 1956 | Brooklyn | 93 | 61 | .604 | Alston | 1956 | New York | 97 | 57 | .630 | Stengel |
| 1957 | Milwaukee | 95 | 59 | .617 | Haney | 1957 | New York | 98 | 56 | .636 | Stengel |
| 1958 | Milwaukee | 92 | 62 | .597 | Haney | 1958 | New York | 92 | 62 | .597 | Stengel |
| 1959 | Los Angeles | 88 | 68 | .564 | Alston | 1959 | Chicago | 94 | 60 | .610 | Lopez |
| 1960 | Pittsburgh | 95 | 59 | .617 | Murtaugh | 1960 | New York | 97 | 57 | .630 | Stengel |
| 1961 | Cincinnati | 93 | 61 | .604 | Hutchinson | 1961 | New York | 109 | 53 | .673 | Houk |
| 1962 | San Francisco | 103 | 62 | .624 | Dark | 1962 | New York | 96 | 66 | .593 | Houk |
| 1963 | Los Angeles | 99 | 63 | .611 | Alston | 1963 | New York | 104 | 57 | .646 | Houk |
| 1964 | St. Louis | 93 | 69 | .574 | Keane | 1964 | New York | 99 | 63 | .611 | Berra |
| 1965 | Los Angeles | 97 | 65 | .599 | Alston | 1965 | Minnesota | 102 | 60 | .630 | Mele |
| 1966 | Los Angeles | 95 | 67 | .586 | Alston | 1966 | Baltimore | 97 | 63 | .606 | Bauer |
| 1967 | St. Louis | 101 | 60 | .627 | Schoendienst | 1967 | Boston | 92 | 70 | .568 | Williams |
| 1968 | St. Louis | 97 | 65 | .599 | Schoendienst | 1968 | Detroit | 103 | 59 | .636 | Smith |

## National League

| Year | Winner | East | | | Manager | Winner | West | | | Manager | Playoff winner |
|------|--------|------|------|------|---------|--------|------|------|------|---------|----------------|
| | | W | L | Pct | | | W | L | Pct | | |
| 1969 | N.Y. Mets | 100 | 62 | .617 | Hodges | Atlanta | 93 | 69 | .574 | Harris | New York |
| 1970 | Pittsburgh | 89 | 73 | .549 | Murtaugh | Cincinnati | 102 | 60 | .630 | Anderson | Cincinnati |
| 1971 | Pittsburgh | 97 | 65 | .599 | Murtaugh | San Francisco | 90 | 72 | .556 | Fox | Pittsburgh |
| 1972 | Pittsburgh | 96 | 59 | .619 | Virdon | Cincinnati | 95 | 59 | .617 | Anderson | Cincinnati |
| 1973 | N.Y. Mets | 82 | 79 | .509 | Berra | Cincinnati | 99 | 63 | .611 | Anderson | New York |
| 1974 | Pittsburgh | 88 | 82 | .543 | Murtaugh | Los Angeles | 102 | 60 | .630 | Alston | Los Angeles |
| 1975 | Pittsburgh | 92 | 69 | .571 | Murtaugh | Cincinnati | 108 | 54 | .667 | Anderson | Cincinnati |

| Year | Winner | East W | L | Pct | Manager | Winner | West W | L | Pct | Manager | Playoff winner |
|---|---|---|---|---|---|---|---|---|---|---|---|
| 976 | Philadelphia | 101 | 61 | .623 | Ozark | Cincinnati | 102 | 60 | .630 | Anderson | Cincinnati |
| 977 | Philadelphia | 100 | 61 | .621 | Ozark | Los Angeles | 98 | 64 | .605 | Lasorda | Los Angeles |
| 978 | Philadelphia | 90 | 72 | .556 | Ozark | Los Angeles | 95 | 67 | .586 | Lasorda | Los Angeles |

## American League

| Year | Winner | East W | L | Pct | Manager | Winner | West W | L | Pct | Manager | Playoff winner |
|---|---|---|---|---|---|---|---|---|---|---|---|
| 969 | Baltimore | 109 | 53 | .673 | Weaver | Minnesota | 97 | 65 | .599 | Martin | Baltimore |
| 970 | Baltimore | 108 | 54 | .677 | Weaver | Minnesota | 98 | 64 | .605 | Rigney | Baltimore |
| 971 | Baltimore | 101 | 57 | .639 | Weaver | Oakland | 101 | 60 | .627 | Williams | Baltimore |
| 972 | Detroit | 86 | 70 | .551 | Martin | Oakland | 93 | 72 | .600 | Williams | Oakland |
| 973 | Baltimore | 97 | 65 | .599 | Weaver | Oakland | 94 | 68 | .580 | Williams | Oakland |
| 974 | Baltimore | 91 | 71 | .562 | Weaver | Oakland | 90 | 72 | .556 | Dark | Oakland |
| 975 | Boston | 95 | 65 | .594 | Johnson | Oakland | 98 | 64 | .605 | Dark | Boston |
| 976 | New York | 97 | 62 | .610 | Martin | Kansas City | 90 | 72 | .556 | Herzog | New York |
| 977 | New York | 100 | 62 | .617 | Martin | Kansas City | 102 | 60 | .630 | Herzog | New York |
| 978 | New York | 100 | 63 | .613 | Martin, Lemon | Kansas City | 92 | 70 | .568 | Herzog | New York |

## All-Star Baseball Games, 1933-1978

| Year | Winner | Score | Location | Year | Winner | Score | Location |
|---|---|---|---|---|---|---|---|
| 933 | American | 4-2 | Chicago | 1958 | American | 4-3 | Baltimore |
| 934 | American | 9-7 | New York | 1959 | National | 5-4 | Pittsburgh |
| 935 | American | 4-1 | Cleveland | 1959 | American | 5-3 | Los Angeles |
| 936 | National | 4-3 | Boston | 1960 | National | 5-3 | Kansas City |
| 937 | American | 8-3 | Washington | 1960 | National | 6-0 | New York |
| 938 | National | 4-1 | Cincinnati | 1961 | National (3) | 5-4 | San Francisco |
| 939 | American | 3-1 | New York | 1961 | Called-Rain | 1-1 | Boston |
| 940 | National | 4-0 | St. Louis | 1962 | National (3) | 3-1 | Washington |
| 941 | American | 7-5 | Detroit | 1962 | American | 9-4 | Chicago |
| 942 | American | 3-1 | New York | 1963 | National | 5-3 | Cleveland |
| 943* | American | 5-3 | Philadelphia | 1964 | National | 7-4 | New York |
| 944* | National | 7-1 | Pittsburgh | 1965 | National | 6-5 | Minnesota |
| 945 | (not played) | | | 1966 | National (3) | 2-1 | St. Louis |
| 946 | American | 12-0 | Boston | 1967 | National (4) | 2-1 | Anaheim |
| 947 | American | 2-1 | Chicago | 1968* | National | 1-0 | Houston |
| 948 | American | 5-2 | St. Louis | 1969 | National | 9-3 | Washington |
| 949 | American | 11-7 | New York | 1970* | National (2) | 5-4 | Cincinnati |
| 950 | National (1) | 4-3 | Chicago | 1971* | American | 6-4 | Detroit |
| 951 | National | 8-3 | Detroit | 1972* | National | 4-3 | Atlanta |
| 952 | National | 3-2 | Philadelphia | 1973* | National | 7-1 | Kansas City |
| 953 | National | 5-1 | Cincinnati | 1974* | National | 7-2 | Pittsburgh |
| 954 | American | 11-9 | Cleveland | 1975* | National | 6-3 | Milwaukee |
| 955 | National (2) | 6-5 | Milwaukee | 1976* | National | 7-1 | Philadelphia |
| 956 | National | 7-3 | Washington | 1977* | National | 7-5 | New York |
| 957 | American | 6-5 | St. Louis | 1978* | National | 7-3 | San Diego |

1) 14 innings, (2) 12 innings, (3) 10 innings, (4) 15 innings *Night game.

## Baseball Stadiums

### National League

| Team | | Home run distances (ft.) LF | Center | RF | Seating capacity |
|---|---|---|---|---|---|
| Atlanta Braves | Atlanta-Fulton County Stadium | 330 | 402 | 330 | 51,556 |
| Chicago Cubs | Wrigley Field | 355 | 400 | 353 | 37,741 |
| Cincinnati Reds | Riverfront Stadium | 330 | 404 | 330 | 51,963 |
| Houston Astros | Astrodome | 340 | 406 | 340 | 45,000 |
| Los Angeles Dodgers | Dodger Stadium | 330 | 395 | 330 | 56,000 |
| Montreal Expos | Olympic Stadium | 330 | 400 | 330 | 60,000 |
| New York Mets | Shea Stadium | 341 | 410 | 341 | 55,300 |
| Philadelphia Phillies | Veterans Stadium | 330 | 408 | 330 | 58,651 |
| Pittsburgh Pirates | Three Rivers Stadium | 335 | 400 | 335 | 50,235 |
| St. Louis Cardinals | Busch Memorial Stadium | 330 | 414 | 330 | 50,100 |
| San Diego Padres | San Diego Stadium | 330 | 410 | 330 | 48,460 |
| San Francisco Giants | Candlestick Park | 335 | 410 | 335 | 58,000 |

### American League

| Team | | Home run distances (ft.) LF | Center | RF | Seating capacity |
|---|---|---|---|---|---|
| Baltimore Orioles | Memorial Stadium | 309 | 405 | 309 | 52,137 |
| Boston Red Sox | Fenway Park | 315 | 420 | 302 | 33,513 |
| California Angels | Anaheim Stadium | 333 | 404 | 333 | 43,250 |
| Chicago White Sox | Comiskey Park | 352 | 440 | 352 | 44,492 |
| Cleveland Indians | Cleveland Stadium | 320 | 400 | 320 | 76,713 |
| Detroit Tigers | Tiger Stadium | 340 | 440 | 325 | 54,226 |
| Kansas City Royals | Royals Stadium | 330 | 410 | 330 | 40,762 |
| Milwaukee Brewers | Milwaukee County Stadium | 320 | 402 | 315 | 54,187 |
| Minnesota Twins | Metropolitan Stadium | 343 | 402 | 330 | 45,919 |
| New York Yankees | Yankee Stadium | 312 | 417 | 310 | 57,145 |
| Oakland A's | Oakland-Alameda County Coliseum | 330 | 400 | 330 | 49,649 |
| Seattle Mariners | Kingdome | 316 | 405 | 316 | 59,059 |
| Texas Rangers | Arlington Stadium | 330 | 400 | 330 | 35,698 |
| Toronto Blue Jays | Exhibition Stadium | 330 | 400 | 330 | 40,000 |

# Home Run Leaders

| National League | | American League | |
|---|---|---|---|
| **Year** | **HR** | **Year** | **HR** |
| 1921 George Kelly, New York | 23 | 1921 Babe Ruth, New York | 59 |
| 1922 Rogers Hornsby, St. Louis | 42 | 1922 Ken Williams, St. Louis | 39 |
| 1923 Cy Williams, Philadelphia | 41 | 1923 Babe Ruth, New York | 41 |
| 1924 Jacques Fournier, Brooklyn | 27 | 1924 Babe Ruth, New York | 46 |
| 1925 Rogers Hornsby, St. Louis | 39 | 1925 Bob Meusel, New York | 33 |
| 1926 Hack Wilson, Chicago | 21 | 1926 Babe Ruth, New York | 47 |
| 1927 Hack Wilson, Chicago; Cy Williams, Philadelphia | 30 | 1927 Babe Ruth, New York | 60 |
| 1928 Hack Wilson, Chicago; Jim Bottomley, St. Louis | 31 | 1928 Babe Ruth, New York | 54 |
| 1929 Charles Klein, Philadelphia | 43 | 1929 Babe Ruth, New York | 46 |
| 1930 Hack Wilson, Chicago | 56 | 1930 Babe Ruth, New York | 49 |
| 1931 Charles Klein, Philadelphia | 31 | 1931 Babe Ruth, Lou Gehrig, New York | 46 |
| 1932 Charles Klein, Philadelphia, Mel Ott, New York | 38 | 1932 Jimmy Foxx, Philadelphia | 58 |
| 1933 Charles Klein, Philadelphia | 28 | 1933 Jimmy Foxx, Philadelphia | 48 |
| 1934 Collins, St. Louis; Mel Ott, New York | 35 | 1934 Lou Gehrig, New York | 49 |
| 1935 Walter Berger, Boston | 34 | 1935 Jimmy Foxx, Philadelphia, Hank Greenberg, Detroit | 36 |
| 1936 Mel Ott, New York | 33 | 1936 Lou Gehrig, New York | 49 |
| 1937 Mel Ott, New York; Joe Medwick, St. Louis | 31 | 1937 Joe DiMaggio, New York | 46 |
| 1938 Mel Ott, New York | 36 | 1938 Hank Greenberg, Detroit | 58 |
| 1939 John Mize, St. Louis | 28 | 1939 Jimmy Foxx, Boston | 35 |
| 1940 John Mize, St. Louis | 43 | 1940 Hank Greenberg, Detroit | 41 |
| 1941 Dolph Camilli, Brooklyn | 34 | 1941 Ted Williams, Boston | 37 |
| 1942 Mel Ott, New York | 30 | 1942 Ted Williams, Boston | 36 |
| 1943 Bill Nicholson, Chicago | 29 | 1943 Rudy York, Detroit | 34 |
| 1944 Bill Nicholson, Chicago | 33 | 1944 Nick Etten, New York | 22 |
| 1945 Tommy Holmes, Boston | 28 | 1945 Vern Stephens, St. Louis | 24 |
| 1946 Ralph Kiner, Pittsburgh | 23 | 1946 Hank Greenberg, Detroit | 44 |
| 1947 Ralph Kiner, Pittsburgh; John Mize, New York | 51 | 1947 Ted Williams, Boston | 32 |
| 1948 Ralph Kiner, Pittsburgh; John Mize, New York | 40 | 1948 Joe DiMaggio, New York | 39 |
| 1949 Ralph Kiner, Pittsburgh | 54 | 1949 Ted Williams, Boston | 43 |
| 1950 Ralph Kiner, Pittsburgh | 47 | 1950 Al Rosen, Cleveland | 37 |
| 1951 Ralph Kiner, Pittsburgh | 42 | 1951 Gus Zernial, Chicago-Philadelphia | 33 |
| 1952 Ralph Kiner, Pittsburgh; Hank Sauer, Chicago | 37 | 1952 Larry Doby, Cleveland | 32 |
| 1953 Ed Mathews, Milwaukee | 47 | 1953 Al Rosen, Cleveland | 43 |
| 1954 Ted Kluszewski, Cincinnati | 49 | 1954 Larry Doby, Cleveland | 32 |
| 1955 Willie Mays, New York | 51 | 1955 Mickey Mantle, New York | 37 |
| 1956 Duke Snider, Brooklyn | 43 | 1956 Mickey Mantle, New York | 52 |
| 1957 Hank Aaron, Milwaukee | 44 | 1957 Roy Sievers, Washington | 42 |
| 1958 Ernie Banks, Chicago | 47 | 1958 Mickey Mantle, New York | 42 |
| 1959 Ed Mathews, Milwaukee | 46 | 1959 Rocky Colavito, Cleveland, Harmon Killebrew, Washington | 42 |
| 1960 Ernie Banks, Chicago | 41 | 1960 Mickey Mantle, New York | 40 |
| 1961 Orlando Cepeda, San Francisco | 46 | 1961 Roger Maris, New York | 61 |
| 1962 Willie Mays, San Francisco | 49 | 1962 Harmon Killebrew, Minnesota | 48 |
| 1963 Hank Aaron, Milwaukee; Willie McCovey, San Francisco | 44 | 1963 Harmon Killebrew, Minnesota | 45 |
| 1964 Willie Mays, San Francisco | 47 | 1964 Harmon Killebrew, Minnesota | 49 |
| 1965 Willie Mays, San Francisco | 52 | 1965 Tony Conigliaro, Boston | 32 |
| 1966 Hank Aaron, Atlanta; Willie McCovey, San Francisco | 44 | 1966 Frank Robinson, Baltimore | 49 |
| 1967 Hank Aaron, Atlanta | 39 | 1967 Carl Yastrzemski, Boston, Harmon Killebrew, Minnesota | 44 |
| 1968 Willie McCovey, San Francisco | 36 | 1968 Frank Howard, Washington | 44 |
| 1969 Willie McCovey, San Francisco | 45 | 1969 Harmon Killebrew, Minnesota | 49 |
| 1970 Johnny Bench, Cincinnati | 45 | 1970 Frank Howard, Washington | 44 |
| 1971 Willie Stargell, Pittsburgh | 48 | 1971 Bill Melton, Chicago | 33 |
| 1972 Johnny Bench, Cincinnati | 40 | 1972 Dick Allen, Chicago | 37 |
| 1973 Willie Stargell, Pittsburgh | 44 | 1973 Reggie Jackson, Oakland | 32 |
| 1974 Mike Schmidt, Philadelphia | 36 | 1974 Dick Allen, Chicago | 32 |
| 1975 Mike Schmidt, Philadelphia | 38 | 1975 George Scott, Milwaukee; Reggie Jackson, Oakland | 36 |
| 1976 Mike Schmidt, Philadelphia | 38 | 1976 Graig Nettles, New York | 32 |
| 1977 George Foster, Cincinnati | 52 | 1977 Jim Rice, Boston | 39 |
| 1978 George Foster, Cincinnati | 40 | 1978 Jim Rice, Boston | 46 |

**All-time Major League Record (154-game Season)—60**—Babe Ruth, New York Yankees (A), 1927. **(162-game Season)—61**—Roger Maris, New York Yankees, 1961. Prior to the 1931 season a batted ball that bounced into the stands was a home run (now a ground-rule double). None of Babe Ruth's record 60 homers bounced into the stands.

# Runs Batted In Leaders

| National League | | American League | |
|---|---|---|---|
| **Year** | **RBI** | **Year** | **RBI** |
| 1941 Dolph Camilli, Brooklyn | 120 | 1941 Joe DiMaggio, New York | 125 |
| 1942 John Mize, New York | 137 | 1942 Ted Williams, Boston | 137 |
| 1943 Bill Nicholson, Chicago | 128 | 1943 Rudy York, Detroit | 118 |
| 1944 Bill Nicholson, Chicago | 122 | 1944 Vern Stephens, St. Louis | 109 |
| 1945 Dixie Walker, Brooklyn | 124 | 1945 Nick Etten, New York | 111 |
| 1946 Enos Slaughter, St. Louis | 130 | 1946 Hank Greenberg, Detroit | 127 |
| 1947 John Mize, New York | 138 | 1947 Ted Williams, Boston | 114 |
| 1948 Stan Musial, St. Louis | 131 | 1948 Joe DiMaggio, New York | 155 |
| 1949 Ralph Kiner, Pittsburgh | 127 | 1949 Ted Williams, Vern Stephens, Boston | 159 |
| 1950 Del Ennis, Philadelphia | 126 | 1950 Walt Dropo, Vern Stephens, Boston | 144 |
| 1951 Monte Irvin, New York | 121 | 1951 Gus Zernial, Chicago-Philadelphia | 129 |
| 1952 Hank Sauer, Chicago | 121 | 1952 Al Rosen, Cleveland | 105 |
| 1953 Roy Campanella, Brooklyn | 142 | 1953 Al Rosen, Cleveland | 145 |
| 1954 Ted Kluszewski, Cincinnati | 141 | 1954 Larry Doby, Cleveland | 126 |
| 1955 Duke Snider, Brooklyn | 136 | 1955 Ray Boone, Detroit, Jack Jensen, Boston | 116 |
| 1956 Stan Musial, St. Louis | 109 | 1956 Mickey Mantle, New York | 130 |
| 1957 Hank Aaron, Milwaukee | 132 | 1957 Roy Sievers, Washington | 114 |
| 1958 Ernie Banks, Chicago | 129 | 1958 Jack Jensen, Boston | 122 |

| Year | | RBI | Year | | RBI |
|---|---|---|---|---|---|
| 59 | Ernie Banks, Chicago | 143 | 1959 | Jack Jensen, Boston | 112 |
| 60 | Hank Aaron, Milwaukee | 126 | 1960 | Roger Maris, New York | 112 |
| 61 | Orlando Cepeda, San Francisco | 142 | 1961 | Roger Maris, New York | 142 |
| 62 | Tommy Davis, Los Angeles | 153 | 1962 | Harmon Killebrew, Minnesota | 126 |
| 63 | Hank Aaron, Milwaukee | 130 | 1963 | Dick Stuart, Boston | 118 |
| 64 | Ken Boyer, St. Louis | 119 | 1964 | Brooks Robinson, Baltimore | 118 |
| 65 | Deron Johnson, Cincinnati | 130 | 1965 | Rocky Colavito, Cleveland | 108 |
| 66 | Hank Aaron, Atlanta | 127 | 1966 | Frank Robinson, Baltimore | 122 |
| 67 | Orlando Cepeda, St. Louis | 111 | 1967 | Carl Yastrzemski, Boston | 121 |
| 68 | Willie McCovey, San Francisco | 105 | 1968 | Ken Harrelson, Boston | 109 |
| 69 | Willie McCovey, San Francisco | 126 | 1969 | Harmon Killebrew, Minnesota | 140 |
| 70 | Johnny Bench, Cincinnati | 148 | 1970 | Frank Howard, Washington | 126 |
| 71 | Joe Torre, St. Louis | 137 | 1971 | Harmon Killebrew, Minnesota | 119 |
| 72 | Johnny Bench, Cincinnati | 125 | 1972 | Dick Allen, Chicago | 113 |
| 73 | Willie Stargell, Pittsburgh | 119 | 1973 | Reggie Jackson, Oakland | 117 |
| 74 | Johnny Bench, Cincinnati | 129 | 1974 | Jeff Burroughs, Texas | 118 |
| 75 | Greg Luzinski, Philadelphia | 120 | 1975 | George Scott, Milwaukee | 109 |
| 76 | George Foster, Cincinnati | 121 | 1976 | Lee May, Baltimore | 109 |
| 77 | George Foster, Cincinnati | 149 | 1977 | Larry Hisle, Minnesota | 119 |
| 78 | George Foster, Cincinnati | 120 | 1978 | Jim Rice, Boston | 139 |

## Batting Champions

| | **National League** | | | | **American League** | | |
|---|---|---|---|---|---|---|---|
| Year | Player | Club | Pct. | Year | Player | Club | Pct. |
| 15 | Larry Doyle | New York | .320 | 1915 | Ty Cobb | Detroit | .369 |
| 16 | Hal Chase | Cincinnati | .339 | 1916 | Tris Speaker | Cleveland | .386 |
| 17 | Edd Rousch | Cincinnati | .341 | 1917 | Ty Cobb | Detroit | .383 |
| 18 | Zack Wheat | Brooklyn | .335 | 1918 | Ty Cobb | Detroit | .382 |
| 19 | Edd Roush | Cincinnati | .321 | 1919 | Ty Cobb | Detroit | .384 |
| 20 | Rogers Hornsby | St. Louis | .370 | 1920 | George Sisler | St. Louis | .407 |
| 21 | Rogers Hornsby | St. Louis | .397 | 1921 | Harry Heilmann | Detroit | .394 |
| 22 | Rogers Hornsby | St. Louis | .401 | 1922 | George Sisler | St. Louis | .420 |
| 23 | Rogers Hornsby | St. Louis | .384 | 1923 | Harry Heilmann | Detroit | .403 |
| 24 | Rogers Hornsby | St. Louis | .424 | 1924 | Babe Ruth | New York | .378 |
| 25 | Rogers Hornsby | St. Louis | .403 | 1925 | Harry Heilmann | Detroit | .393 |
| 26 | Eugene Hargrave | Cincinnati | .353 | 1926 | Henry Manush | Detroit | .378 |
| 27 | Paul Waner | Pittsburgh | .380 | 1927 | Harry Heilmann | Detroit | .398 |
| 28 | Rogers Hornsby | Boston | .387 | 1928 | Goose Goslin | Washington | .379 |
| 29 | Lefty O'Doul | Philadelphia | .398 | 1929 | Lew Fonseca | Cleveland | .369 |
| 30 | Bill Terry | New York | .401 | 1930 | Al Simmons | Philadelphia | .381 |
| 31 | Chick Hafey | St. Louis | .349 | 1931 | Al Simmons | Philadelphia | .390 |
| 32 | Lefty O'Doul | Brooklyn | .368 | 1932 | Dale Alexander | Detroit-Boston | .367 |
| 33 | Charles Klein | Philadelphia | .368 | 1933 | Jimmy Foxx | Philadelphia | .356 |
| 34 | Paul Waner | Pittsburgh | .362 | 1934 | Lou Gehrig | New York | .363 |
| 35 | Arky Vaughan | Pittsburgh | .385 | 1935 | Buddy Myer | Washington | .349 |
| 36 | Paul Waner | Pittsburgh | .373 | 1936 | Luke Appling | Chicago | .388 |
| 37 | Joe Medwick | St. Louis | .374 | 1937 | Charlie Gehringer | Detroit | .371 |
| 38 | Ernie Lombardi | Cincinnati | .342 | 1938 | Jimmy Foxx | Boston | .349 |
| 39 | John Mize | St. Louis | .349 | 1939 | Joe DiMaggio | New York | .381 |
| 40 | Debs Garms | Pittsburgh | .355 | 1940 | Joe DiMaggio | New York | .352 |
| 41 | Pete Reiser | Brooklyn | .343 | 1941 | Ted Williams | Boston | .406 |
| 42 | Ernie Lombardi | Boston | .330 | 1942 | Ted Williams | Boston | .356 |
| 43 | Stan Musial | St. Louis | .357 | 1943 | Luke Appling | Chicago | .328 |
| 44 | Dixie Walker | Brooklyn | .357 | 1944 | Lou Boudreau | Cleveland | .327 |
| 45 | Phil Cavarretta | Chicago | .355 | 1945 | George Stirnweiss | New York | .309 |
| 46 | Stan Musial | St. Louis | .365 | 1946 | Mickey Vernon | Washington | .353 |
| 47 | Harry Walker | Philadelphia | .363 | 1947 | Ted Williams | Boston | .343 |
| 48 | Stan Musial | St. Louis | .376 | 1948 | Ted Williams | Boston | .369 |
| 49 | Jackie Robinson | Brooklyn | .342 | 1949 | George Kell | Detroit | .343 |
| 50 | Stan Musial | St. Louis | .346 | 1950 | Billy Goodman | Boston | .354 |
| 51 | Stan Musial | St. Louis | .355 | 1951 | Ferris Fain | Philadelphia | .344 |
| 52 | Stan Musial | St. Louis | .336 | 1952 | Ferris Fain | Philadelphia | .327 |
| 53 | Carl Furillo | Brooklyn | .344 | 1953 | Mickey Vernon | Washington | .337 |
| 54 | Willie Mays | New York | .345 | 1954 | Roberto Avila | Cleveland | .341 |
| 55 | Richie Ashburn | Philadelphia | .338 | 1955 | Al Kaline | Detroit | .340 |
| 56 | Hank Aaron | Milwaukee | .328 | 1956 | Mickey Mantle | New York | .353 |
| 57 | Stan Musial | St. Louis | .351 | 1957 | Ted Williams | Boston | .388 |
| 58 | Richie Ashburn | Philadelphia | .350 | 1958 | Ted Williams | Boston | .328 |
| 59 | Hank Aaron | Milwaukee | .355 | 1959 | Harvey Kuenn | Detroit | .353 |
| 60 | Dick Groat | Pittsburgh | .325 | 1960 | Pete Runnels | Boston | .320 |
| 61 | Roberto Clemente | Pittsburgh | .351 | 1961 | Norm Cash | Detroit | .361 |
| 62 | Tommy Davis | Los Angeles | .346 | 1962 | Pete Runnels | Boston | .326 |
| 63 | Tommy Davis | Los Angeles | .326 | 1963 | Carl Yastrzemski | Boston | .321 |
| 64 | Roberto Clemente | Pittsburgh | .339 | 1964 | Tony Oliva | Minnesota | .323 |
| 65 | Roberto Clemente | Pittsburgh | .329 | 1965 | Tony Oliva | Minnesota | .321 |
| 66 | Matty Alou | Pittsburgh | .342 | 1966 | Frank Robinson | Baltimore | .316 |
| 67 | Roberto Clemente | Pittsburgh | .357 | 1967 | Carl Yastrzemski | Boston | .326 |
| 68 | Pete Rose | Cincinnati | .335 | 1968 | Carl Yastrzemski | Boston | .301 |
| 69 | Pete Rose | Cincinnati | .348 | 1969 | Rod Carew | Minnesota | .332 |
| 70 | Rico Carty | Atlanta | .366 | 1970 | Alex Johnson | California | .328 |
| 71 | Joe Torre | St. Louis | .363 | 1971 | Tony Oliva | Minnesota | .337 |
| 72 | Billy Williams | Chicago | .333 | 1972 | Rod Carew | Minnesota | .318 |
| 73 | Pete Rose | Cincinnati | .338 | 1973 | Rod Carew | Minnesota | .350 |
| 74 | Ralph Garr | Atlanta | .353 | 1974 | Rod Carew | Minnesota | .364 |
| 75 | Bill Madlock | Chicago | .354 | 1975 | Rod Carew | Minnesota | .359 |
| 76 | Bill Madlock | Chicago | .339 | 1976 | George Brett | Kansas City | .333 |
| 77 | Dave Parker | Pittsburgh | .338 | 1977 | Rod Carew | Minnesota | .388 |
| 78 | Dave Parker | Pittsburgh | .334 | 1978 | Rod Carew | Minnesota | .333 |

# National League Records in 1978

## Final Standings

### East Division

| Club | W | L | Pct | GB |
|---|---|---|---|---|
| Philadelphia | 90 | 72 | .556 | ... |
| Pittsburgh | 88 | 73 | .547 | 1½ |
| Chicago | 78 | 83 | .488 | 11 |
| Montreal | 76 | 86 | .469 | 14 |
| St. Louis | 69 | 93 | .426 | 21 |
| New York | 66 | 96 | .407 | 24 |

### West Division

| Club | W | L | Pct | GB |
|---|---|---|---|---|
| Los Angeles | 95 | 67 | .586 | ... |
| Cincinnati | 92 | 69 | .571 | 2½ |
| San Francisco | 89 | 73 | .549 | 6 |
| San Diego | 84 | 78 | .519 | 11 |
| Houston | 74 | 88 | .457 | 21 |
| Atlanta | 69 | 93 | .426 | 26 |

## National League Playoffs

Oct. 4 — Los Angeles 9, Philadelphia 5.      Oct. 6 — Philadelphia 9, Los Angeles 4.
Oct. 5 — Los Angeles 4, Philadelphia 0.      Oct. 7 — Los Angeles 4, Philadelphia 3.

## Club Batting

| Club | Pct. | AB | R | H | HR | SB |
|---|---|---|---|---|---|---|
| Chicago | .264 | 5532 | 664 | 1461 | 72 | 110 |
| Los Angeles | .264 | 5437 | 727 | 1435 | 149 | 137 |
| Houston | .258 | 5458 | 605 | 1408 | 70 | 178 |
| Philadelphia | .258 | 5448 | 708 | 1404 | 133 | 152 |
| Pittsburgh | .257 | 5406 | 684 | 1390 | 115 | 213 |
| Cincinnati | .256 | 5392 | 710 | 1378 | 136 | 137 |
| Montreal | .254 | 5530 | 633 | 1404 | 121 | 80 |
| San Diego | .252 | 5360 | 591 | 1349 | 75 | 152 |
| St. Louis | .249 | 5415 | 600 | 1351 | 79 | 97 |
| San Francisco | .248 | 5364 | 613 | 1331 | 117 | 87 |
| New York | .245 | 5433 | 607 | 1332 | 86 | 100 |
| Atlanta | .244 | 5381 | 600 | 1312 | 123 | 90 |

## Club Pitching

| Club | ERA | CG | IP | H | BB | S |
|---|---|---|---|---|---|---|
| Los Angeles | 3.12 | 46 | 1440 | 1362 | 573 | 440 | 8 |
| San Diego | 3.28 | 21 | 1434 | 1385 | 598 | 483 | 7 |
| San Francisco | 3.30 | 42 | 1455 | 1377 | 594 | 453 | 8 |
| Philadelphia | 3.33 | 38 | 1436 | 1343 | 586 | 393 | 8 |
| Pittsburgh | 3.41 | 30 | 1445 | 1366 | 637 | 499 | 8 |
| Montreal | 3.42 | 42 | 1448 | 1332 | 611 | 572 | 7 |
| St. Louis | 3.58 | 32 | 1438 | 1300 | 657 | 600 | 8 |
| Houston | 3.63 | 48 | 1440 | 1327 | 634 | 578 | 9 |
| Cincinnati | 3.81 | 16 | 1448 | 1437 | 688 | 567 | 9 |
| New York | 3.87 | 21 | 1455 | 1447 | 690 | 531 | 7 |
| Chicago | 4.05 | 24 | 1455 | 1475 | 724 | 539 | 7 |
| Atlanta | 4.08 | 29 | 1440 | 1404 | 750 | 624 | 8 |

## Individual Batting

Leaders—440 or More at Bats

| Player, club | Pct. | AB | R | H | HR | RBI | SB |
|---|---|---|---|---|---|---|---|
| Parker, Pittsburgh† | .334 | 581 | 102 | 194 | 30 | 117 | 20 |
| Buckner, Chicago† | .323 | 446 | 47 | 144 | 5 | 74 | 7 |
| Garvey, Los Angeles | .316 | 639 | 89 | 202 | 21 | 113 | 10 |
| Cruz, Houston† | .315 | 565 | 79 | 178 | 10 | 83 | 37 |
| Madlock, San Francisco | .309 | 447 | 76 | 138 | 15 | 44 | 16 |
| Winfield, San Diego | .308 | 587 | 88 | 181 | 24 | 97 | 21 |
| Richards, San Diego† | .308 | 555 | 90 | 171 | 4 | 45 | 37 |
| Clark, San Francisco | .306 | 592 | 90 | 181 | 25 | 98 | 15 |
| Rose, Cincinnati | .302 | 655 | 103 | 198 | 7 | 52 | 13 |
| Burroughs, Atlanta | .301 | 488 | 72 | 147 | 23 | 77 | 1 |
| Concepcion, Cincinnati | .301 | 565 | 75 | 170 | 6 | 67 | 23 |

## Individual Pitching

Leaders—162 or More Innings

| Pitcher, club | W | L | ERA | G | IP | H | BB | S |
|---|---|---|---|---|---|---|---|---|
| Swan, New York | 9 | 6 | 2.43 | 29 | 207 | 164 | 58 | 1 |
| Rogers, Montreal | 13 | 10 | 2.47 | 30 | 219 | 186 | 64 | 1 |
| Vuckovich, St. Louis | 12 | 12 | 2.55 | 45 | 198 | 187 | 59 | 1 |
| Knepper, San Francisco† | 17 | 11 | 2.63 | 36 | 260 | 218 | 85 | 1 |
| Hooton, Los Angeles | 19 | 10 | 2.71 | 32 | 236 | 196 | 61 | 1 |
| Perry, San Diego | 21 | 6 | 2.72 | 37 | 261 | 241 | 66 | 1 |
| Blue, San Francisco† | 18 | 10 | 2.79 | 35 | 258 | 233 | 70 | 1 |
| Carlton, Philadelphia† | 16 | 13 | 2.84 | 34 | 247 | 228 | 63 | 1 |
| Halicki, San Francisco | 9 | 10 | 2.85 | 29 | 199 | 166 | 45 | 1 |
| Seaver, Cincinnati | 16 | 14 | 2.87 | 36 | 260 | 218 | 89 | 2 |

*Rookie †Bats or pitches lefthanded ‡Switch hitter

## Individual Batting (over 100 at-bats); Individual Pitching (over 50 innings)

### Atlanta Braves

| Batting | Pct. | G | AB | R | H | HR | RBI | SB |
|---|---|---|---|---|---|---|---|---|
| Burroughs | .301 | 153 | 488 | 72 | 147 | 23 | 77 | 1 |
| Matthews | .283 | 129 | 474 | 75 | 134 | 18 | 62 | 8 |
| Asselstine† | .272 | 39 | 103 | 11 | 28 | 2 | 13 | 2 |
| *Horner | .266 | 89 | 323 | 50 | 86 | 23 | 63 | 0 |
| Royster | .259 | 140 | 529 | 67 | 137 | 2 | 35 | 27 |
| *Hubbard | .258 | 44 | 163 | 15 | 42 | 2 | 13 | 2 |
| Office† | .250 | 146 | 404 | 40 | 101 | 9 | 40 | 8 |
| Gilbreath | .245 | 116 | 326 | 22 | 80 | 3 | 31 | 7 |
| Beall‡ | .243 | 108 | 185 | 29 | 45 | 1 | 16 | 4 |
| Pocoroba‡ | .242 | 92 | 289 | 21 | 70 | 6 | 34 | 0 |
| Bonnell | .240 | 117 | 304 | 36 | 73 | 1 | 16 | 12 |
| Nolan† | .230 | 95 | 213 | 22 | 49 | 4 | 22 | 3 |
| Murphy | .226 | 151 | 530 | 66 | 120 | 23 | 79 | 11 |

| Pitching | W | L | ERA | G | IP | H | BB | SO |
|---|---|---|---|---|---|---|---|---|
| Garber | 6 | 5 | 2.15 | 65 | 117 | 84 | 24 | 84 |
| *McWilliams† | 9 | 3 | 2.82 | 15 | 99 | 84 | 35 | 42 |
| Niekro | 19 | 18 | 2.88 | 44 | 334 | 295 | 102 | 248 |
| Camp | 2 | 4 | 3.77 | 42 | 74 | 99 | 32 | 23 |
| Solomon | 4 | 6 | 4.08 | 37 | 106 | 98 | 50 | 64 |
| Skok† | 3 | 2 | 4.35 | 43 | 62 | 64 | 27 | 28 |
| *Mahler† | 4 | 11 | 4.67 | 34 | 135 | 130 | 66 | 92 |
| Campbell | 4 | 4 | 4.83 | 53 | 69 | 67 | 49 | 45 |
| Hanna | 7 | 13 | 5.14 | 29 | 140 | 132 | 93 | 90 |
| Easterly† | 3 | 6 | 5.65 | 37 | 78 | 91 | 45 | 42 |
| Devine | 5 | 4 | 5.95 | 31 | 65 | 84 | 25 | 26 |
| Boggs | 2 | 8 | 6.71 | 16 | 59 | 80 | 26 | 21 |

### Chicago Cubs

| Batting | Pct. | G | AB | R | H | HR | RBI | S |
|---|---|---|---|---|---|---|---|---|
| Vail | .333 | 74 | 180 | 15 | 60 | 4 | 33 | |
| Buckner† | .323 | 117 | 446 | 47 | 144 | 5 | 74 | |
| Scott† | .282 | 78 | 227 | 41 | 64 | 0 | 15 | 2 |
| Cox | .281 | 59 | 121 | 10 | 34 | 2 | 18 | |
| Murcer† | .281 | 146 | 499 | 66 | 140 | 9 | 64 | |
| DeJesus | .278 | 160 | 619 | 104 | 172 | 3 | 35 | 4 |
| White‡ | .267 | 77 | 146 | 24 | 39 | 1 | 10 | |
| Kingman | .266 | 119 | 395 | 65 | 105 | 28 | 79 | |
| Gross† | .265 | 124 | 347 | 34 | 92 | 1 | 39 | |
| Trillo | .261 | 152 | 552 | 53 | 144 | 4 | 55 | |
| Clines | .258 | 109 | 229 | 31 | 59 | 0 | 17 | |
| Biittner† | .257 | 120 | 343 | 32 | 88 | 4 | 50 | |
| Ontiveros‡ | .243 | 82 | 276 | 34 | 67 | 1 | 22 | |
| Johnson | .232 | 68 | 138 | 19 | 32 | 4 | 20 | |
| Blackwell‡ | .223 | 49 | 103 | 8 | 23 | 0 | 7 | |
| Rader† | .203 | 116 | 305 | 29 | 62 | 3 | 36 | |

| Pitching | W | L | ERA | G | IP | H | BB | S |
|---|---|---|---|---|---|---|---|---|
| Sutter | 8 | 10 | 3.18 | 64 | 99 | 82 | 34 | 10 |
| McGlothen | 5 | 3 | 3.29 | 54 | 93 | 92 | 43 | 6 |
| *Lamp | 7 | 15 | 3.29 | 37 | 224 | 221 | 56 | 7 |
| R. Reuschel | 14 | 15 | 3.41 | 35 | 243 | 235 | 54 | 11 |
| Hernandez | 8 | 2 | 3.75 | 54 | 60 | 57 | 35 | 3 |
| Krukow | 9 | 3 | 3.91 | 27 | 138 | 125 | 53 | 8 |
| Moore | 9 | 7 | 4.11 | 71 | 103 | 117 | 31 | 5 |
| Burris | 7 | 13 | 4.75 | 40 | 199 | 210 | 79 | 9 |
| Roberts† | 6 | 8 | 5.26 | 35 | 142 | 159 | 56 | 5 |
| Holtzman† | 0 | 3 | 6.11 | 23 | 53 | 61 | 35 | 3 |

## Cincinnati Reds

| Batting | Pct. | G | AB | R | H | HR | RBI | SB |
|---|---|---|---|---|---|---|---|---|
| Rose‡ | .302 | 159 | 655 | 103 | 198 | 7 | 52 | 13 |
| Concepcion | .301 | 153 | 565 | 75 | 170 | 6 | 67 | 23 |
| Griffey† | .288 | 158 | 614 | 90 | 177 | 10 | 63 | 23 |
| Foster | .281 | 158 | 604 | 97 | 170 | 40 | 120 | 4 |
| Lum† | .269 | 86 | 145 | 15 | 39 | 6 | 23 | 0 |
| Bench | .260 | 120 | 393 | 52 | 102 | 23 | 73 | 4 |
| Kennedy | .255 | 89 | 157 | 22 | 40 | 0 | 11 | 4 |
| Driessen† | .250 | 153 | 524 | 68 | 131 | 16 | 70 | 28 |
| Correll | .238 | 52 | 105 | 9 | 25 | 1 | 6 | 0 |
| Morgan‡ | .236 | 132 | 441 | 68 | 104 | 13 | 75 | 19 |
| Geronimo† | .226 | 122 | 296 | 28 | 67 | 5 | 27 | 8 |
| Collins‡ | .216 | 102 | 102 | 13 | 22 | 0 | 7 | 7 |

| Pitching | W | L | ERA | G | IP | H | BB | SO |
|---|---|---|---|---|---|---|---|---|
| Bair | 7 | 6 | 1.98 | 70 | 100 | 87 | 38 | 91 |
| Seaver | 16 | 14 | 2.87 | 36 | 260 | 218 | 89 | 226 |
| Bonham | 11 | 5 | 3.54 | 23 | 140 | 151 | 50 | 83 |
| Norman† | 11 | 9 | 3.71 | 36 | 177 | 173 | 82 | 111 |
| Moskau | 6 | 4 | 3.97 | 26 | 145 | 139 | 57 | 88 |
| Hume | 8 | 11 | 4.14 | 42 | 174 | 198 | 50 | 90 |
| Sarmiento | 9 | 7 | 4.39 | 63 | 127 | 109 | 54 | 72 |
| *LaCross | 4 | 8 | 4.50 | 16 | 96 | 104 | 46 | 31 |
| Morbon | 8 | 2 | 5.00 | 62 | 99 | 102 | 27 | 35 |
| Tomlin† | 9 | 1 | 5.81 | 57 | 62 | 88 | 30 | 32 |

## Houston Astros

| Batting | Pct. | G | AB | R | H | HR | RBI | SB |
|---|---|---|---|---|---|---|---|---|
| Alou | .324 | 77 | 139 | 7 | 45 | 2 | 19 | 0 |
| Cruz‡ | .315 | 153 | 565 | 79 | 178 | 10 | 83 | 37 |
| Cabell | .295 | 162 | 660 | 92 | 195 | 7 | 71 | 33 |
| Howe | .293 | 119 | 420 | 46 | 123 | 7 | 55 | 2 |
| Puhl | .289 | 149 | 585 | 87 | 169 | 3 | 35 | 32 |
| Watson | .289 | 139 | 461 | 51 | 133 | 14 | 79 | 3 |
| Cedeno | .281 | 50 | 192 | 31 | 54 | 7 | 23 | 23 |
| *Bochy | .266 | 54 | 154 | 8 | 41 | 3 | 15 | 0 |
| *Landestoy‡ | .266 | 59 | 218 | 18 | 58 | 0 | 9 | 7 |
| *Walling† | .251 | 120 | 247 | 30 | 62 | 3 | 36 | 9 |
| Gonzalez | .233 | 78 | 223 | 24 | 52 | 1 | 16 | 6 |
| *Bergman† | .231 | 104 | 186 | 15 | 43 | 0 | 12 | 2 |

| Pitching | W | L | ERA | G | IP | H | BB | SO |
|---|---|---|---|---|---|---|---|---|
| Ruhle | 3 | 3 | 2.12 | 13 | 68 | 57 | 20 | 27 |
| Forsch | 10 | 6 | 2.71 | 52 | 133 | 136 | 37 | 71 |
| Sambito† | 4 | 9 | 3.07 | 62 | 88 | 85 | 32 | 96 |
| Richard | 18 | 11 | 3.11 | 36 | 275 | 192 | 141 | 303 |
| Andujar | 5 | 7 | 3.32 | 35 | 111 | 87 | 58 | 55 |
| Niekro | 14 | 14 | 3.86 | 35 | 203 | 190 | 73 | 97 |
| Lemongello | 9 | 14 | 3.94 | 33 | 210 | 204 | 66 | 77 |
| *Dixon | 7 | 11 | 3.99 | 30 | 140 | 140 | 40 | 66 |
| Bannister† | 3 | 9 | 4.83 | 28 | 110 | 120 | 63 | 94 |

## Los Angeles Dodgers

| Batting | Pct. | G | AB | R | H | HR | RBI | SB |
|---|---|---|---|---|---|---|---|---|
| Garvey | .316 | 162 | 639 | 89 | 202 | 21 | 113 | 10 |
| Smith‡ | .295 | 128 | 447 | 82 | 132 | 29 | 93 | 12 |
| Russell | .286 | 155 | 625 | 72 | 179 | 3 | 46 | 10 |
| Lopes | .278 | 151 | 587 | 93 | 163 | 17 | 58 | 45 |
| Cey | .270 | 159 | 555 | 84 | 150 | 23 | 84 | 2 |
| Baker | .262 | 149 | 522 | 62 | 137 | 11 | 66 | 12 |
| Lacy | .261 | 103 | 245 | 29 | 64 | 13 | 40 | 7 |
| Monday† | .254 | 119 | 342 | 54 | 87 | 19 | 57 | 2 |
| North† | .234 | 110 | 304 | 54 | 71 | 0 | 10 | 27 |
| Ferguson | .224 | 118 | 348 | 40 | 78 | 14 | 50 | 1 |
| Yeager | .193 | 94 | 228 | 19 | 44 | 4 | 23 | 0 |

| Pitching | W | L | ERA | G | IP | H | BB | SO |
|---|---|---|---|---|---|---|---|---|
| *Forster† | 5 | 4 | 1.94 | 47 | 65 | 56 | 23 | 46 |
| *Welch | 7 | 4 | 2.03 | 23 | 111 | 92 | 26 | 66 |
| Hooton | 19 | 10 | 2.71 | 32 | 236 | 196 | 61 | 104 |
| *Rautzhan† | 2 | 1 | 2.95 | 43 | 61 | 61 | 19 | 25 |
| Rau† | 15 | 9 | 3.26 | 30 | 199 | 219 | 68 | 95 |
| *Hough | 5 | 5 | 3.29 | 55 | 93 | 69 | 48 | 66 |
| John† | 17 | 10 | 3.30 | 33 | 213 | 230 | 53 | 124 |
| Sutton | 15 | 11 | 3.55 | 34 | 238 | 228 | 54 | 154 |
| Rhoden | 10 | 8 | 3.65 | 30 | 165 | 160 | 51 | 79 |

## Montreal Expos

| Batting | Pct. | G | AB | R | H | HR | RBI | SB |
|---|---|---|---|---|---|---|---|---|
| Cromartie† | .297 | 159 | 607 | 77 | 180 | 10 | 56 | 8 |
| Perez | .290 | 148 | 544 | 63 | 158 | 14 | 78 | 2 |
| Valentine | .289 | 151 | 570 | 75 | 165 | 25 | 76 | 13 |
| Parrish | .277 | 144 | 520 | 68 | 144 | 15 | 70 | 2 |
| Carter | .255 | 157 | 533 | 76 | 136 | 20 | 72 | 10 |
| Dawson | .253 | 157 | 609 | 84 | 154 | 25 | 72 | 28 |

---

| Batting | Pct. | G | AB | R | H | HR | RBI | SB |
|---|---|---|---|---|---|---|---|---|
| Cash | .252 | 159 | 658 | 66 | 166 | 3 | 43 | 12 |
| Speier | .251 | 150 | 501 | 47 | 126 | 5 | 51 | 1 |
| *Papi | .230 | 67 | 152 | 15 | 35 | 0 | 11 | 0 |
| Unser† | .196 | 130 | 179 | 16 | 35 | 2 | 15 | 2 |

| Pitching | W | L | ERA | G | IP | H | BB | SO |
|---|---|---|---|---|---|---|---|---|
| *Dues | 5 | 6 | 2.36 | 25 | 99 | 85 | 42 | 36 |
| Knowles† | 3 | 3 | 2.38 | 60 | 72 | 63 | 30 | 34 |
| Rogers | 13 | 10 | 2.47 | 30 | 219 | 186 | 64 | 126 |
| *Sanderson | 4 | 2 | 2.51 | 10 | 61 | 52 | 21 | 50 |
| Grimsley‡ | 20 | 11 | 3.05 | 36 | 263 | 237 | 67 | 84 |
| *Schatzeder† | 7 | 7 | 3.06 | 29 | 144 | 108 | 68 | 69 |
| Bahnsen | 1 | 5 | 3.84 | 44 | 75 | 74 | 31 | 44 |
| May† | 8 | 10 | 3.88 | 27 | 144 | 141 | 42 | 87 |
| Fryman† | 7 | 11 | 4.20 | 32 | 150 | 157 | 74 | 81 |
| Garman | 4 | 7 | 4.38 | 57 | 78 | 69 | 34 | 28 |
| Twitchell | 4 | 12 | 5.38 | 33 | 112 | 121 | 71 | 69 |

## New York Mets

| Batting | Pct. | G | AB | R | H | HR | RBI | SB |
|---|---|---|---|---|---|---|---|---|
| Mazzilli‡ | .273 | 148 | 542 | 78 | 148 | 16 | 61 | 20 |
| Valentine | .269 | 69 | 160 | 17 | 43 | 1 | 18 | 1 |
| S. Henderson | .266 | 157 | 587 | 83 | 156 | 10 | 65 | 3 |
| Stearns | .264 | 143 | 477 | 65 | 126 | 15 | 73 | 25 |
| Maddox | .257 | 119 | 389 | 43 | 100 | 2 | 39 | 2 |
| Foli | .257 | 143 | 413 | 37 | 106 | 1 | 27 | 2 |
| Montanez† | .256 | 159 | 609 | 66 | 156 | 17 | 96 | 9 |
| Hodges† | .255 | 47 | 102 | 4 | 26 | 0 | 7 | 1 |
| Youngblood | .252 | 113 | 266 | 40 | 67 | 7 | 30 | 4 |
| Flynn | .237 | 156 | 532 | 37 | 126 | 0 | 36 | 3 |
| Randle‡ | .233 | 132 | 437 | 53 | 102 | 2 | 35 | 14 |
| Boisclair† | .224 | 107 | 214 | 24 | 48 | 4 | 15 | 3 |
| Grieve | .208 | 54 | 101 | 5 | 21 | 2 | 8 | 0 |

| Pitching | W | L | ERA | G | IP | H | BB | SO |
|---|---|---|---|---|---|---|---|---|
| Swan | 9 | 6 | 2.43 | 29 | 207 | 164 | 58 | 125 |
| Kobel† | 5 | 6 | 2.92 | 32 | 108 | 95 | 30 | 51 |
| Zachry | 10 | 6 | 3.33 | 21 | 138 | 120 | 60 | 78 |
| Lockwood | 7 | 13 | 3.56 | 57 | 91 | 78 | 31 | 73 |
| Koosman† | 3 | 15 | 3.75 | 38 | 235 | 221 | 84 | 160 |
| Murray | 9 | 6 | 3.78 | 68 | 119 | 119 | 53 | 62 |
| Hausman | 3 | 4 | 4.67 | 10 | 52 | 58 | 9 | 16 |
| Espinosa | 11 | 15 | 4.72 | 32 | 204 | 230 | 75 | 76 |
| *Bruhert | 4 | 11 | 4.77 | 27 | 134 | 171 | 34 | 56 |

## Philadelphia Phillies

| Batting | Pct. | G | AB | R | H | HR | RBI | SB |
|---|---|---|---|---|---|---|---|---|
| Bowa‡ | .294 | 156 | 654 | 78 | 192 | 3 | 43 | 27 |
| Maddox | .288 | 155 | 598 | 62 | 172 | 11 | 68 | 33 |
| Boone | .283 | 132 | 435 | 48 | 123 | 12 | 62 | 2 |
| Hebner† | .283 | 137 | 435 | 61 | 123 | 17 | 71 | 4 |
| Martin | .271 | 128 | 266 | 40 | 72 | 9 | 36 | 9 |
| McBride† | .269 | 122 | 472 | 68 | 127 | 10 | 49 | 28 |
| Luzinski | .265 | 155 | 540 | 85 | 143 | 35 | 101 | 8 |
| Schmidt | .251 | 145 | 513 | 93 | 129 | 21 | 78 | 19 |
| Cardenal | .249 | 87 | 201 | 27 | 50 | 4 | 33 | 2 |
| McCarver† | .247 | 90 | 146 | 18 | 36 | 1 | 14 | 2 |
| Sizemore | .219 | 108 | 351 | 38 | 77 | 0 | 25 | 8 |
| Harrelson‡ | .214 | 71 | 103 | 16 | 22 | 0 | 9 | 5 |
| *Morrison | .157 | 53 | 108 | 12 | 17 | 3 | 10 | 1 |

| Pitching | W | L | ERA | G | IP | H | BB | SO |
|---|---|---|---|---|---|---|---|---|
| Reed | 3 | 4 | 2.23 | 66 | 109 | 87 | 23 | 85 |
| Brusstar | 6 | 3 | 2.33 | 58 | 89 | 74 | 30 | 60 |
| Carlton† | 16 | 13 | 2.84 | 34 | 247 | 228 | 63 | 161 |
| McGraw† | 8 | 7 | 3.20 | 55 | 90 | 82 | 23 | 63 |
| Christenson | 13 | 14 | 3.24 | 33 | 228 | 209 | 47 | 131 |
| Ruthven | 15 | 11 | 3.38 | 33 | 232 | 214 | 56 | 120 |
| Lerch† | 11 | 8 | 3.96 | 33 | 184 | 183 | 70 | 96 |
| Kaat† | 8 | 5 | 4.11 | 26 | 140 | 150 | 32 | 48 |
| Lonborg | 8 | 10 | 5.21 | 22 | 114 | 132 | 45 | 48 |

## Pittsburgh Pirates

| Batting | Pct. | G | AB | R | H | HR | RBI | SB |
|---|---|---|---|---|---|---|---|---|
| Parker† | .334 | 148 | 581 | 102 | 194 | 30 | 117 | 20 |
| Stargell† | .295 | 122 | 390 | 60 | 115 | 28 | 97 | 3 |
| Taveras | .278 | 157 | 654 | 81 | 182 | 0 | 38 | 46 |
| Milner† | .271 | 108 | 295 | 39 | 80 | 6 | 38 | 5 |
| Ott‡ | .269 | 112 | 379 | 49 | 102 | 9 | 38 | 4 |
| Sanguillen | .264 | 85 | 220 | 15 | 58 | 3 | 16 | 2 |
| Garner | .261 | 154 | 528 | 66 | 138 | 10 | 66 | 27 |
| B. Robinson | .246 | 136 | 499 | 70 | 123 | 14 | 80 | 14 |
| Stennett | .243 | 106 | 333 | 30 | 81 | 3 | 35 | 2 |
| Moreno† | .235 | 155 | 515 | 95 | 121 | 2 | 33 | 71 |
| Brye | .235 | 66 | 115 | 16 | 27 | 1 | 9 | 2 |
| Gaston | .233 | 62 | 120 | 6 | 28 | 1 | 9 | 0 |
| Dyer | .211 | 58 | 175 | 7 | 37 | 0 | 13 | 2 |
| *Berra | .207 | 56 | 135 | 16 | 28 | 6 | 14 | 3 |

| Pitching | W | L | ERA | G | IP | H | BB | SO |
|---|---|---|---|---|---|---|---|---|
| Tekulve . . . . . . . . . | 8 | 7 | 2.33 | 91 | 135 | 115 | 55 | 77 |
| Blyleven . . . . . . . . | 14 | 10 | 3.02 | 34 | 244 | 217 | 66 | 182 |
| Kison . . . . . . . . . . | 6 | 6 | 3.19 | 28 | 96 | 81 | 39 | 62 |
| Candelaria† . . . . . | 12 | 11 | 3.24 | 30 | 189 | 191 | 49 | 94 |
| Jackson† . . . . . . . . | 7 | 5 | 3.27 | 60 | 77 | 89 | 32 | 45 |
| *Whitson . . . . . . . . | 5 | 6 | 3.28 | 43 | 74 | 66 | 37 | 64 |
| *D. Robinson . . . . | 14 | 6 | 3.47 | 35 | 228 | 203 | 57 | 135 |
| Bibby . . . . . . . . . . | 8 | 7 | 3.53 | 34 | 107 | 100 | 39 | 72 |
| Rooker† . . . . . . . . | 9 | 11 | 4.25 | 28 | 163 | 160 | 81 | 76 |
| Reuss† . . . . . . . . . | 3 | 2 | 4.88 | 23 | 83 | 97 | 23 | 42 |

## St. Louis Cardinals

| Batting | Pct. | G | AB | R | H | HR | RBI | SB |
|---|---|---|---|---|---|---|---|---|
| Simmons‡ . . . . . . | .287 | 152 | 516 | 71 | 148 | 22 | 80 | 1 |
| Templeton‡ . . . . . | .280 | 155 | 647 | 82 | 181 | 2 | 47 | 34 |
| Swisher . . . . . . . . | .278 | 45 | 115 | 11 | 32 | 1 | 10 | 1 |
| Hendrick . . . . . . . | .278 | 138 | 493 | 64 | 137 | 20 | 75 | 2 |
| Phillips‡ . . . . . . . | .268 | 76 | 164 | 14 | 44 | 1 | 28 | 0 |
| Mumphrey‡ . . . . . | .262 | 125 | 367 | 41 | 96 | 2 | 37 | 14 |
| Hernandez† . . . . . | .255 | 159 | 542 | 90 | 138 | 11 | 64 | 13 |
| Garrett† . . . . . . . . | .250 | 82 | 132 | 17 | 33 | 2 | 12 | 1 |
| Reitz . . . . . . . . . . | .246 | 150 | 540 | 41 | 133 | 10 | 75 | 1 |
| Morales . . . . . . . . | .239 | 130 | 457 | 44 | 109 | 4 | 46 | 4 |
| Tyson . . . . . . . . . . | .233 | 125 | 377 | 26 | 88 | 3 | 26 | 2 |
| Scott‡ . . . . . . . . . | .228 | 96 | 219 | 28 | 50 | 1 | 14 | 5 |
| Brock† . . . . . . . . . | .221 | 92 | 298 | 31 | 66 | 0 | 12 | 17 |

| Pitching | W | L | ERA | G | IP | H | BB | SO |
|---|---|---|---|---|---|---|---|---|
| Bruno . . . . . . . . . . | 4 | 3 | 1.98 | 18 | 50 | 38 | 17 | 33 |
| Vuckovich . . . . . . | 12 | 12 | 2.55 | 45 | 198 | 187 | 59 | 149 |
| Littell . . . . . . . . . | 4 | 8 | 2.80 | 72 | 106 | 80 | 59 | 130 |
| Denny . . . . . . . . . | 14 | 11 | 2.96 | 33 | 234 | 200 | 74 | 103 |
| *Martinez . . . . . . | 9 | 8 | 3.65 | 22 | 138 | 114 | 71 | 45 |
| Forsch . . . . . . . . . | 11 | 17 | 3.69 | 34 | 234 | 205 | 97 | 114 |
| Schultz† . . . . . . . | 2 | 4 | 3.80 | 62 | 83 | 68 | 36 | 70 |
| *Lopez . . . . . . . . . | 4 | 2 | 4.29 | 25 | 65 | 52 | 32 | 46 |
| Urrea . . . . . . . . . . | 4 | 9 | 5.36 | 27 | 99 | 108 | 47 | 61 |
| Falcone† . . . . . . . | 2 | 7 | 5.76 | 19 | 75 | 94 | 28 | 28 |

## San Diego Padres

| Batting | Pct. | G | AB | R | H | HR | RBI | SB |
|---|---|---|---|---|---|---|---|---|
| Winfield . . . . . . . . | .308 | 158 | 587 | 88 | 181 | 24 | 97 | 21 |
| Richards† . . . . . . . | .308 | 154 | 555 | 90 | 171 | 4 | 45 | 37 |
| Turner† . . . . . . . . | .280 | 106 | 225 | 28 | 63 | 8 | 37 | 6 |
| Gamble† . . . . . . . . | .275 | 126 | 375 | 46 | 103 | 7 | 47 | 1 |

| Batting | Pct. | G | AB | R | H | HR | RBI | SB |
|---|---|---|---|---|---|---|---|---|
| *Smith‡ . . . . . . . . | .258 | 159 | 590 | 69 | 152 | 1 | 46 | 46 |
| Almon . . . . . . . . . | .252 | 138 | 405 | 39 | 102 | 0 | 21 | 17 |
| Gonzales . . . . . . . | .246 | 110 | 341 | 29 | 84 | 2 | 29 | 4 |
| Ashford . . . . . . . . | .245 | 75 | 155 | 11 | 38 | 3 | 26 | 1 |
| *Perkins‡ . . . . . . | .240 | 62 | 217 | 14 | 52 | 2 | 33 | 4 |
| Thomas‡ . . . . . . . | .227 | 128 | 352 | 36 | 80 | 3 | 26 | 11 |
| Tenace . . . . . . . . . | .224 | 142 | 401 | 60 | 90 | 16 | 61 | 6 |
| *Sweet‡ . . . . . . . . | .221 | 88 | 226 | 15 | 50 | 1 | 11 | 1 |

| Pitching | W | L | ERA | G | IP | H | BB | SO |
|---|---|---|---|---|---|---|---|---|
| D'Acquisto . . . . . | 4 | 3 | 2.13 | 45 | 93 | 60 | 56 | 104 |
| Fingers . . . . . . . . | 6 | 13 | 2.52 | 67 | 107 | 84 | 29 | 72 |
| Perry . . . . . . . . . . | 21 | 6 | 2.72 | 37 | 261 | 241 | 66 | 154 |
| Jones‡ . . . . . . . . . | 13 | 14 | 2.88 | 37 | 253 | 263 | 64 | 71 |
| *Lee . . . . . . . . . . . | 5 | 1 | 3.28 | 56 | 85 | 74 | 36 | 31 |
| Owchinko† . . . . . | 10 | 13 | 3.56 | 36 | 202 | 198 | 78 | 94 |
| Shirley† . . . . . . . . | 8 | 11 | 3.69 | 50 | 166 | 164 | 61 | 102 |
| Rasmussen . . . . . . | 14 | 15 | 4.09 | 37 | 207 | 215 | 63 | 91 |

## San Francisco Giants

| Batting | Pct. | G | AB | R | H | HR | RBI | SB |
|---|---|---|---|---|---|---|---|---|
| Madlock . . . . . . . . | .309 | 122 | 447 | 76 | 138 | 15 | 44 | 16 |
| Ivie . . . . . . . . . . . | .308 | 117 | 318 | 34 | 98 | 11 | 55 | 3 |
| Clark . . . . . . . . . . | .306 | 156 | 592 | 90 | 181 | 25 | 98 | 15 |
| Whitfield† . . . . . . | .289 | 149 | 488 | 70 | 141 | 10 | 32 | 5 |
| Herndon . . . . . . . . | .259 | 151 | 471 | 52 | 122 | 1 | 32 | 13 |
| Metzger‡ . . . . . . . | .246 | 120 | 358 | 28 | 88 | 0 | 23 | 8 |
| Evans† . . . . . . . . . | .243 | 159 | 547 | 82 | 133 | 20 | 78 | 4 |
| Hill . . . . . . . . . . . | .243 | 117 | 358 | 20 | 87 | 3 | 36 | 1 |
| Sadek . . . . . . . . . . | .239 | 40 | 109 | 15 | 26 | 2 | 9 | 1 |
| LeMaster . . . . . . . | .235 | 101 | 272 | 23 | 64 | 1 | 14 | 6 |
| McCovey† . . . . . . | .228 | 108 | 351 | 32 | 80 | 12 | 64 | 1 |
| Cruz . . . . . . . . . . . | .227 | 109 | 273 | 27 | 62 | 8 | 33 | 0 |
| Dwyer† . . . . . . . . | .223 | 107 | 238 | 30 | 53 | 6 | 26 | 7 |
| Andrews . . . . . . . . | .220 | 79 | 177 | 21 | 39 | 1 | 11 | 5 |
| Harris‡ . . . . . . . . | .150 | 53 | 100 | 8 | 15 | 1 | 11 | 0 |

| Pitching | W | L | ERA | G | IP | H | BB | SO |
|---|---|---|---|---|---|---|---|---|
| Knepper† . . . . . . . | 17 | 11 | 2.63 | 36 | 260 | 218 | 85 | 147 |
| Blue† . . . . . . . . . . | 18 | 10 | 2.79 | 35 | 258 | 233 | 70 | 171 |
| Halicki . . . . . . . . | 9 | 10 | 2.85 | 29 | 199 | 166 | 45 | 105 |
| Moffitt . . . . . . . . . | 8 | 4 | 3.29 | 70 | 82 | 79 | 33 | 52 |
| Lavelle† . . . . . . . . | 13 | 10 | 3.31 | 67 | 98 | 96 | 44 | 63 |
| Barr . . . . . . . . . . . | 8 | 11 | 3.53 | 32 | 163 | 180 | 35 | 44 |
| Curtis† . . . . . . . . . | 4 | 3 | 3.71 | 46 | 63 | 60 | 29 | 38 |
| Montefusco . . . . . | 11 | 9 | 3.80 | 36 | 239 | 233 | 68 | 177 |

## Leading Pitchers, Earned-Run Average

| | National League | | | | | | American League | | | |
|---|---|---|---|---|---|---|---|---|---|---|
| Year | Player, club | G | IP | ERA | | Year | Player, club | G | IP | ERA |
| 1961 | Warren Spahn, Milwaukee . . . | 38 | 263 | 3.01 | | 1961 | Dick Donovan, Washington . . . . | 23 | 169 | 2.40 |
| 1962 | Sandy Koufax, Los Angeles . . | 28 | 184 | 2.54 | | 1962 | Hank Aguirre, Detroit . . . . . . . | 42 | 216 | 2.21 |
| 1963 | Sandy Koufax, Los Angeles . . | 40 | 311 | 1.88 | | 1963 | Gary Peters, Chicago . . . . . . . | 41 | 243 | 2.33 |
| 1964 | Sandy Koufax, Los Angeles . . | 29 | 223 | 1.74 | | 1964 | Dean Chance, Los Angeles . . . . | 46 | 278 | 1.56 |
| 1965 | Sandy Koufax, Los Angeles . . | 43 | 336 | 2.04 | | 1965 | Sam McDowell, Cleveland . . . . | 42 | 274 | 2.18 |
| 1966 | Sandy Koufax, Los Angeles . . | 41 | 323 | 1.73 | | 1966 | Gary Peters, Chicago . . . . . . . | 29 | 204 | 2.03 |
| 1967 | Phil Niekro, Atlanta . . . . . . . | 46 | 207 | 1.87 | | 1967 | Joe Horlen, Chicago . . . . . . . . | 35 | 258 | 2.06 |
| 1968 | Bob Gibson, St. Louis . . . . . | 34 | 305 | 1.12 | | 1968 | Luis Tiant, Cleveland . . . . . . . | 34 | 258 | 1.60 |
| 1969 | Juan Marichal, San Francisco . | 37 | 300 | 2.10 | | 1969 | Dick Bosman, Washington . . . . | 31 | 193 | 2.19 |
| 1970 | Tom Seaver, New York . . . . . . | 37 | 291 | 2.81 | | 1970 | Diego Segui, Oakland . . . . . . . | 47 | 162 | 2.56 |
| 1971 | Tom Seaver, New York . . . . . . | 36 | 286 | 1.76 | | 1971 | Vida Blue, Oakland . . . . . . . . | 39 | 312 | 1.82 |
| 1972 | Steve Carlton, Philadelphia . . . | 41 | 346 | 1.98 | | 1972 | Luis Tiant, Boston . . . . . . . . . | 43 | 179 | 1.91 |
| 1973 | Tom Seaver, New York . . . . . . | 36 | 290 | 2.07 | | 1973 | Jim Palmer, Baltimore . . . . . . | 38 | 296 | 2.40 |
| 1974 | Buzz Capra, Atlanta . . . . . . . | 39 | 217 | 2.28 | | 1974 | Catfish Hunter, Oakland . . . . . | 41 | 318 | 2.49 |
| 1975 | Randy Jones, San Diego . . . . . | 37 | 285 | 2.24 | | 1975 | Jim Palmer, Baltimore . . . . . . | 39 | 323 | 2.09 |
| 1976 | John Denny, St. Louis . . . . . . | 30 | 207 | 2.52 | | 1976 | Mark Fidrych, Detroit . . . . . . | 31 | 250 | 2.34 |
| 1977 | John Candelaria, Pittsburgh . . . | 33 | 231 | 2.34 | | 1977 | Frank Tanana, California . . . . . | 31 | 241 | 2.54 |
| 1978 | Craig Swan, New York . . . . . . | 29 | 207 | 2.43 | | 1978 | Ron Guidry, New York . . . . . . | 35 | 274 | 1.74 |

ERA is computed by multiplying earned runs allowed by 9, then dividing by innings pitched.

## Major League Perfect Games Since 1900

| Year | Player | Clubs | Score | | Year | Player | Clubs | Score |
|---|---|---|---|---|---|---|---|---|
| 1904 | Cy Young . . . . . | Boston vs. Phil. (AL) . . . . . | 3-0 | | 1956 | Don Larson (b) | . . N.Y. Yankees vs. Brooklyn . | 2-0 |
| 1908 | Addie Joss . . . . . | Cleveland vs. Chicago (AL) . . | 1-0 | | 1964 | Jim Bunning . . . . . | Phil. vs. N.Y. Mets (NL) . . . | 6-0 |
| 1971 | Ernie Shore (a) . . | Boston vs. Wash. (AL) . . . . | 4-0 | | 1965 | Sandy Koufax . . . | Los Angeles vs. Chic. (NL) . . | 1-0 |
| 1922 | Charles Robertson | Chicago vs. Detroit (AL) . . . | 2-0 | | 1968 | Jim Hunter . . . . . | Oakland vs. Minn. (AL) . . . . | 4-0 |

(a) Babe Ruth, the starting pitcher, was ejected from the game after walking the first batter. Shore replaced him and the base-runner was out stealing. Shore retired the next 26 batters. (b) World Series.

## Most Valuable Player
Baseball Writers' Association

### National League

| Year | Player, team | Year | Player, team | Year | Player, team |
|---|---|---|---|---|---|
| 931 | Frank Frisch, St. Louis | 1947 | Bob Elliott, Boston | 1963 | Sandy Koufax, Los Angeles |
| 932 | Charles Klein, Philadelpha | 1948 | Stan Musial, St. Louis | 1964 | Ken Boyer, St. Louis |
| 933 | Carl Hubbell, New York | 1949 | Jackie Robinson, Brooklyn | 1965 | Willie Mays, San Francisco |
| 934 | Dizzy Dean, St. Louis | 1950 | Jim Konstanty, Philadelphia | 1966 | Roberto Clemente, Pittsburgh |
| 935 | Gabby Hartnett, Chicago | 1951 | Roy Campanella, Brooklyn | 1967 | Orlando Cepeda, St. Louis |
| 936 | Carl Hubbell, New York | 1952 | Hank Sauer, Chicago | 1968 | Bob Gibson, St. Louis |
| 937 | Joe Medwick, St. Louis | 1953 | Roy Campanella, Brooklyn | 1969 | Willie McCovey, San Francisco |
| 938 | Ernie Lombardi, Cincinnati | 1954 | Willie Mays, New York | 1970 | Johnny Bench, Cincinnati |
| 939 | Bucky Walters, Cincinnati | 1955 | Roy Campanella, Brooklyn | 1971 | Joe Torre, St. Louis |
| 940 | Frank McCormick, Cincinnati | 1956 | Don Newcombe, Brooklyn | 1972 | Johnny Bench, Cincinnati |
| 941 | Dolph Camilli, Brooklyn | 1957 | Henry Aaron, Milwaukee | 1973 | Pete Rose, Cincinnati |
| 942 | Mort Cooper, St. Louis | 1958 | Ernie Banks, Chicago | 1974 | Steve Garvey, Los Angeles |
| 943 | Stan Musial, St. Louis | 1959 | Ernie Banks, Chicago | 1975 | Joe Morgan, Cincinnati |
| 944 | Martin Marion, St. Louis | 1960 | Dick Groat, Pittsburgh | 1976 | Joe Morgan, Cincinnati |
| 945 | Phil Cavarretta, Chicago | 1961 | Frank Robinson, Cincinnati | 1977 | George Foster, Cincinnati |
| 946 | Stan Musial, St. Louis | 1962 | Maury Wills, Los Angeles | | |

### American League

| Year | Player, team | Year | Player, team | Year | Player, team |
|---|---|---|---|---|---|
| 931 | Lefty Grove, Philadelphia | 1947 | Joe DiMaggio, New York | 1963 | Elston Howard, New York |
| 932 | Jimmy Foxx, Philadelphia | 1948 | Lou Boudreau, Cleveland | 1964 | Brooks Robinson, Baltimore |
| 933 | Jimmy Foxx, Philadelphia | 1949 | Ted Williams, Boston | 1965 | Zoilo Versailles, Minnesota |
| 934 | Mickey Cochrane, Detroit | 1950 | Phil Rizzuto, New York | 1966 | Frank Robinson, Baltimore |
| 935 | Henry Greenberg, Detroit | 1951 | Yogi Berra, New York | 1967 | Carl Yastrzemski, Boston |
| 936 | Lou Gehrig, New York | 1952 | Bobby Shantz, Philadelphia | 1968 | Denny McLain, Detroit |
| 937 | Charley Gehringer, Detroit | 1953 | Al Rosen, Cleveland | 1969 | Harmon Killebrew, Minnesota |
| 938 | Jimmy Foxx, Boston | 1954 | Yogi Berra, New York | 1970 | John (Boog) Powell, Baltimore |
| 939 | Joe DiMaggio, New York | 1955 | Yogi Berra, New York | 1971 | Vida Blue, Oakland |
| 940 | Hank Greenberg, Detroit | 1956 | Mickey Mantle, New York | 1972 | Dick Allen, Chicago |
| 941 | Joe DiMaggio, New York | 1957 | Mickey Mantle, New York | 1973 | Reggie Jackson, Oakland |
| 942 | Joe Gordon, New York | 1958 | Jackie Jensen, Boston | 1974 | Jeff Burroughs, Texas |
| 943 | Spurgeon Chandler, New York | 1959 | Nellie Fox, Chicago | 1975 | Fred Lynn, Boston |
| 944 | Hal Newhouser, Detroit | 1960 | Roger Maris, New York | 1976 | Thurman Munson, New York |
| 945 | Hal Newhouser, Detroit | 1961 | Roger Maris, New York | 1977 | Rod Carew, Minnesota |
| 946 | Ted Williams, Boston | 1962 | Mickey Mantle, New York | | |

## Rookie of the Year
Baseball Writers' Association

1947—Combined selection—Jackie Robinson, Brooklyn, 1b
1948—Combined selection—Alvin Dark, Boston, N.L. ss

### National League

| Year | Player, team | Year | Player, team | Year | Player, team |
|---|---|---|---|---|---|
| 1949 | Don Newcombe, Brooklyn, p | 1959 | Willie McCovey, S.F., 1b | 1969 | Ted Sizemore, Los Angeles, 2b |
| 1950 | Sam Jethroe, Boston, of | 1960 | Frank Howard, Los Angeles, of | 1970 | Carl Morton, Montreal, p |
| 1951 | Willie Mays, New York, of | 1961 | Billy Williams, Chicago, of | 1971 | Earl Williams, Atlanta, c |
| 1952 | Joe Black, Brooklyn, p | 1962 | Ken Hubbs, Chicago, 2b | 1972 | Jon Matlack, New York, p |
| 1953 | Jim Gilliam, Brooklyn, 2b | 1963 | Pete Rose, Cincinnati, 2b | 1973 | Gary Matthews, S.F., of |
| 1954 | Wally Moon, St. Louis, of | 1964 | Richie Allen, Philadelphia, 3b | 1974 | Bake McBride, St. Louis, of |
| 1955 | Bill Virdon, St. Louis, of | 1965 | Jim Lefebvre, Los Angeles, 2b | 1975 | John Montefusco, S.F., p |
| 1956 | Frank Robinson, Cincinnati, of | 1966 | Tommy Helms, Cincinnati, 2b | 1976 | (tie) Butch Metzger, San Diego, p |
| 1957 | Jack Sanford, Philadelphia, p | 1967 | Tom Seaver, New York, p | | Pat Zachry, Cincinnati, p |
| 1958 | Orlando Cepeda, S.F., 1b | 1968 | Johnny Bench, Cincinnati c | 1977 | Andre Dawson, Montreal, of |

### American League

| Year | Player, team | Year | Player, team | Year | Player, team |
|---|---|---|---|---|---|
| 1949 | Roy Sievers, St. Louis, of | 1959 | Bob Allison, Washington, of | 1969 | Lou Piniella, Kansas City, of |
| 1950 | Walt Dropo, Boston, 1b | 1960 | Ron Hansen, Baltimore, ss | 1970 | Thurman Munson, New York, c |
| 1951 | Gil McDougald, New York, 3b | 1961 | Don Schwall, Boston, p | 1971 | Chris Chambliss, Cleveland, 1b |
| 1952 | Harry Byrd, Philadelphia, p | 1962 | Tom Tresh, New York, if-of | 1972 | Carlton Fisk, Boston, c |
| 1954 | Harvey Kuenn, Detroit, ss | 1963 | Gary Peters, Chicago, p | 1973 | Al Bumbry, Baltimore, of |
| 1954 | Bob Grim, New York, p | 1964 | Tony Oliva, Minnesota, of | 1974 | Mike Hargrove, Texas, 1b |
| 1955 | Herb Score, Cleveland, p | 1965 | Curt Blefary, Baltimore, of | 1975 | Fred Lynn, Boston, of |
| 1956 | Luis Aparicio, Chicago, ss | 1966 | Tommie Agee, Chicago, of | 1976 | Mark Fidrych, Detroit, p |
| 1957 | Tony Kubek, New York, if-of | 1967 | Rod Carew, Minnesota, 2b | 1977 | Eddie Murray, Baltimore, dh |
| 1958 | Albie Pearson, Washington, of | 1968 | Stan Bahnsen, New York, p | | |

## Triple Crown Winners
Players leading league in batting, runs batted in, and homers in a single season

| Year | Player, team | Year | Player, team |
|---|---|---|---|
| 1909 | Ty Cobb, Detroit Tigers | 1937 | Joe Medwick, St. Louis Cardinals |
| 1922 | Rogers Hornsby, St. Louis Cardinals | 1942 | Ted Williams, Boston Red Sox |
| 1925 | Rogers Hornsby, St. Louis Cardinals | 1947 | Ted Williams, Boston Red Sox |
| 1933 | Jimmy Foxx, Philadelphia Athletics | 1956 | Mickey Mantle, New York Yankees |
| 1933 | Chuck Klein, Philadelphia Phillies | 1966 | Frank Robinson, Baltimore Orioles |
| 1934 | Lou Gehrig, New York Yankees | 1967 | Carl Yastrzemski, Boston Red Sox |

A recent review of baseball statistics indicates that Heinie Zimmerman, formerly credited with winning the triple crown in 1912, did not lead the NL in RBIs that year.

# American League Records in 1978

### Final Standings

## East Division

| Club | W | L | Pct. | GB |
|---|---|---|---|---|
| New York | 100 | 63 | .613 | ... |
| Boston | 99 | 64 | .607 | 1 |
| Milwaukee | 93 | 69 | .574 | 6½ |
| Baltimore | 90 | 71 | .559 | 9 |
| Detroit | 86 | 76 | .531 | 13½ |
| Cleveland | 69 | 90 | .434 | 29 |
| Toronto | 59 | 102 | .366 | 40 |

## West Division

| Club | W | L | Pct. | GB |
|---|---|---|---|---|
| Kansas City | 92 | 70 | .568 | ... |
| California | 87 | 75 | .537 | 5 |
| Texas | 87 | 75 | .537 | 5 |
| Minnesota | 73 | 89 | .451 | 19 |
| Chicago | 71 | 90 | .441 | 20½ |
| Oakland | 69 | 93 | .426 | 23 |
| Seattle | 56 | 104 | .350 | 35 |

### American League Playoffs

Oct. 3 — New York 7, Kansas City 1.
Oct. 4 — Kansas City 10, New York 4.

Oct. 6 — New York 6, Kansas City 5.
Oct. 7 — New York 2, Kansas City 1.

### Club Batting

| Club | Pct. | AB | R | H | HR | SB |
|---|---|---|---|---|---|---|
| Milwaukee | .276 | 5536 | 804 | 1530 | 173 | 95 |
| Detroit | .271 | 5601 | 714 | 1520 | 129 | 90 |
| Kansas City | .268 | 5474 | 743 | 1469 | 98 | 216 |
| Boston | .267 | 5587 | 796 | 1493 | 172 | 74 |
| New York | .267 | 5583 | 735 | 1489 | 125 | 98 |
| Minnesota | .267 | 5522 | 666 | 1472 | 82 | 99 |
| Chicago | .264 | 5393 | 634 | 1423 | 106 | 83 |
| Cleveland | .261 | 5365 | 639 | 1400 | 106 | 64 |
| California | .259 | 5472 | 691 | 1417 | 108 | 86 |
| Baltimore | .258 | 5422 | 659 | 1397 | 154 | 75 |
| Texas | .253 | 5347 | 692 | 1353 | 132 | 196 |
| Toronto | .250 | 5430 | 590 | 1358 | 98 | 28 |
| Seattle | .248 | 5358 | 614 | 1327 | 97 | 123 |
| Oakland | .245 | 5321 | 532 | 1304 | 100 | 144 |

### Club Pitching

| Club | ERA | CG | IP | H | R | BB | SO |
|---|---|---|---|---|---|---|---|
| New York | 3.18 | 39 | 1461 | 1321 | 582 | 478 | 817 |
| Texas | 3.36 | 54 | 1456 | 1431 | 632 | 421 | 771 |
| Kansas City | 3.44 | 53 | 1439 | 1350 | 634 | 478 | 657 |
| Boston | 3.54 | 57 | 1473 | 1530 | 657 | 464 | 700 |
| Baltimore | 3.57 | 65 | 1429 | 1340 | 633 | 509 | 754 |
| Oakland | 3.62 | 26 | 1433 | 1401 | 690 | 582 | 755 |
| Detroit | 3.64 | 60 | 1456 | 1441 | 653 | 503 | 684 |
| California | 3.65 | 44 | 1456 | 1382 | 666 | 599 | 892 |
| Milwaukee | 3.67 | 62 | 1436 | 1442 | 650 | 398 | 572 |
| Minnesota | 3.69 | 48 | 1460 | 1468 | 678 | 520 | 701 |
| Cleveland | 3.97 | 36 | 1407 | 1397 | 694 | 568 | 739 |
| Chicago | 4.22 | 38 | 1409 | 1380 | 731 | 586 | 712 |
| Toronto | 4.55 | 35 | 1429 | 1529 | 775 | 614 | 758 |
| Seattle | 4.70 | 28 | 1419 | 1540 | 834 | 567 | 630 |

### Individual Batting

Leaders—440 or more at bats

| Player, Club | Pct. | AB | R | H | HR | RBI | SB |
|---|---|---|---|---|---|---|---|
| Carew, Minnesota† | .333 | 564 | 85 | 188 | 5 | 70 | 27 |
| Oliver, Texas† | .324 | 525 | 65 | 170 | 14 | 89 | 8 |
| Rice, Boston | .315 | 677 | 121 | 213 | 46 | 139 | 7 |
| Piniella, New York | .314 | 472 | 67 | 148 | 6 | 69 | 3 |
| Oglivie, Milwaukee† | .303 | 469 | 71 | 142 | 18 | 72 | 11 |
| Roberts, Seattle | .301 | 472 | 78 | 142 | 22 | 92 | 6 |
| Otis, Kansas City | .298 | 486 | 74 | 145 | 22 | 96 | 32 |
| Lynn, Boston† | .298 | 541 | 75 | 161 | 22 | 82 | 3 |
| LeFlore, Detroit | .297 | 666 | 126 | 198 | 12 | 62 | 68 |
| Munson, New York | .297 | 617 | 73 | 183 | 6 | 71 | 2 |

### Individual Pitching

Leaders—162 or more innings

| Pitcher, Club | W | L | ERA | G | IP | H | BB | SO |
|---|---|---|---|---|---|---|---|---|
| Guidry, New York† | 25 | 3 | 1.74 | 35 | 274 | 187 | 72 | 248 |
| Matlack, Texas† | 15 | 13 | 2.30 | 35 | 270 | 252 | 51 | 157 |
| Caldwell, Milwaukee† | 22 | 9 | 2.37 | 37 | 293 | 258 | 54 | 131 |
| Palmer, Baltimore | 21 | 12 | 2.46 | 38 | 296 | 246 | 97 | 138 |
| Goltz, Minnesota | 15 | 10 | 2.50 | 29 | 220 | 209 | 67 | 111 |
| Gura, Kansas City† | 16 | 4 | 2.72 | 35 | 222 | 183 | 60 | 81 |
| Figueroa, New York | 20 | 9 | 2.99 | 35 | 253 | 233 | 77 | 92 |
| Eckersley, Boston | 20 | 8 | 2.99 | 35 | 268 | 258 | 71 | 162 |
| Zahn, Minnesota† | 14 | 14 | 3.04 | 35 | 252 | 260 | 81 | 106 |
| Jenkins, Texas | 18 | 8 | 3.04 | 34 | 249 | 228 | 41 | 157 |

*Rookie †Bats or pitches lefthanded ‡Switch hitter

## Individual Batting (over 100 at-bats); Individual Pitching (over 50 innings)

### Baltimore Orioles

| Batting | Pct. | G | AB | R | H | HR | RBI | SB |
|---|---|---|---|---|---|---|---|---|
| Singleton† | .293 | 149 | 502 | 67 | 147 | 20 | 81 | 0 |
| DeCinces | .286 | 142 | 511 | 72 | 146 | 28 | 80 | 7 |
| Murray‡ | .285 | 161 | 610 | 85 | 174 | 27 | 95 | 6 |
| Kelly† | .274 | 100 | 274 | 38 | 75 | 11 | 40 | 10 |
| Dauer | .264 | 133 | 459 | 57 | 121 | 6 | 46 | 0 |
| Garcia | .263 | 79 | 186 | 17 | 49 | 0 | 13 | 7 |
| Smith‡ | .260 | 85 | 250 | 29 | 65 | 5 | 30 | 3 |
| Dempsey | .259 | 136 | 441 | 41 | 114 | 6 | 32 | 7 |
| May | .246 | 148 | 556 | 56 | 137 | 25 | 80 | 5 |
| Harlow† | .243 | 147 | 460 | 67 | 112 | 8 | 26 | 14 |
| Lopez | .238 | 129 | 193 | 21 | 46 | 4 | 20 | 5 |
| Bumbry† | .237 | 33 | 114 | 21 | 27 | 2 | 6 | 5 |
| Mora | .214 | 76 | 229 | 21 | 49 | 8 | 14 | 0 |
| Belanger | .213 | 135 | 348 | 39 | 74 | 0 | 16 | 6 |

| Pitching | W | L | ERA | G | IP | H | BB | SO |
|---|---|---|---|---|---|---|---|---|
| Palmer | 21 | 12 | 2.46 | 38 | 296 | 246 | 97 | 138 |
| Stanhouse | 6 | 9 | 2.88 | 56 | 75 | 60 | 52 | 42 |
| McGregor† | 15 | 13 | 3.32 | 35 | 233 | 217 | 47 | 94 |
| D. Martinez | 16 | 11 | 3.55 | 40 | 276 | 257 | 93 | 142 |
| Flanagan† | 19 | 15 | 4.04 | 40 | 281 | 271 | 87 | 167 |
| Briles | 4 | 4 | 4.67 | 16 | 54 | 58 | 21 | 30 |
| Kerrigan | 3 | 1 | 4.75 | 26 | 72 | 75 | 36 | 41 |
| T. Martinez† | 3 | 3 | 4.83 | 42 | 69 | 77 | 40 | 57 |

### Boston Red Sox

| Batting | Pct. | G | AB | R | H | HR | RBI | SB |
|---|---|---|---|---|---|---|---|---|
| Rice | .315 | 163 | 677 | 121 | 213 | 46 | 139 | 7 |
| Lynn† | .298 | 150 | 541 | 75 | 161 | 22 | 82 | 3 |
| Fisk | .284 | 157 | 571 | 94 | 162 | 20 | 88 | 7 |
| Remy† | .278 | 148 | 583 | 87 | 162 | 2 | 44 | 30 |
| Yastrzemski† | .277 | 144 | 523 | 70 | 145 | 17 | 81 | 4 |
| Duffy | .260 | 64 | 104 | 12 | 27 | 0 | 4 | 1 |
| Hobson | .250 | 147 | 512 | 65 | 128 | 17 | 80 | 1 |
| Burleson | .248 | 145 | 626 | 75 | 155 | 5 | 49 | 8 |
| Evans | .247 | 147 | 497 | 75 | 123 | 24 | 63 | 8 |
| Brohamer† | .234 | 81 | 244 | 34 | 57 | 1 | 25 | 1 |
| Scott | .233 | 120 | 412 | 51 | 96 | 12 | 54 | 1 |

| Pitching | W | L | ERA | G | IP | H | BB | SO |
|---|---|---|---|---|---|---|---|---|
| Stanley | 15 | 2 | 2.60 | 52 | 142 | 142 | 34 | 38 |
| Eckersley | 20 | 8 | 2.99 | 35 | 268 | 258 | 71 | 162 |
| Drago | 4 | 4 | 3.04 | 37 | 77 | 71 | 32 | 42 |
| Tiant | 13 | 8 | 3.31 | 32 | 212 | 185 | 57 | 114 |
| Lee† | 10 | 10 | 3.46 | 28 | 177 | 198 | 59 | 44 |
| *Wright | 8 | 4 | 3.57 | 24 | 116 | 122 | 24 | 56 |
| Campbell | 7 | 5 | 3.88 | 29 | 51 | 62 | 17 | 47 |
| Hassler† | 3 | 5 | 3.89 | 24 | 88 | 114 | 37 | 49 |
| Torrez | 16 | 13 | 3.96 | 36 | 250 | 272 | 99 | 120 |
| Burgmeier† | 2 | 1 | 4.43 | 35 | 61 | 74 | 23 | 24 |
| *Ripley | 2 | 5 | 5.55 | 15 | 73 | 92 | 22 | 26 |

## California Angels

### Batting

| Batting | Pct. | G | AB | R | H | HR | RBI | SB |
|---|---|---|---|---|---|---|---|---|
| Jackson | .297 | 105 | 387 | 49 | 115 | 6 | 57 | 2 |
| Bostock† | .296 | 147 | 568 | 74 | 168 | 5 | 71 | 15 |
| Lansford | .294 | 121 | 453 | 62 | 133 | 8 | 52 | 20 |
| Rettenmund | .269 | 50 | 108 | 16 | 29 | 1 | 14 | 0 |
| R. Miller† | .263 | 132 | 475 | 66 | 125 | 1 | 37 | 3 |
| Rudi | .256 | 133 | 497 | 58 | 127 | 17 | 79 | 2 |
| Baylor | .255 | 158 | 591 | 103 | 151 | 34 | 99 | 22 |
| Downing | .255 | 133 | 412 | 42 | 105 | 7 | 46 | 3 |
| Chalk | .253 | 135 | 470 | 42 | 119 | 1 | 34 | 5 |
| Grich | .251 | 144 | 487 | 68 | 122 | 6 | 42 | 4 |
| *Landreaux† | .223 | 93 | 260 | 38 | 58 | 5 | 23 | 7 |
| Humphrey | .219 | 53 | 114 | 11 | 25 | 1 | 9 | 0 |
| Fairly† | .217 | 91 | 235 | 23 | 51 | 10 | 40 | 0 |
| *Anderson | .194 | 48 | 108 | 6 | 21 | 0 | 7 | 0 |
| Mulliniks† | .185 | 50 | 119 | 6 | 22 | 1 | 6 | 2 |

### Pitching

| Pitching | W | L | ERA | G | IP | H | BB | SO |
|---|---|---|---|---|---|---|---|---|
| *Frost | 5 | 4 | 2.59 | 11 | 80 | 71 | 24 | 30 |
| D. Miller | 6 | 2 | 2.65 | 41 | 85 | 85 | 41 | 34 |
| LaRoche | 10 | 9 | 2.81 | 59 | 96 | 73 | 48 | 70 |
| Hartzell | 6 | 10 | 3.44 | 54 | 157 | 168 | 41 | 55 |
| Tanana† | 18 | 12 | 3.65 | 33 | 239 | 239 | 60 | 137 |
| Ryan† | 10 | 13 | 3.71 | 31 | 235 | 183 | 148 | 260 |
| Griffin | 3 | 4 | 4.02 | 24 | 56 | 63 | 31 | 35 |
| Aase | 11 | 8 | 4.02 | 29 | 179 | 185 | 80 | 93 |
| Knapp | 14 | 8 | 4.21 | 30 | 188 | 178 | 67 | 126 |
| Brett† | 3 | 5 | 4.95 | 31 | 100 | 100 | 42 | 43 |

## Chicago White Sox

### Batting

| Batting | Pct. | G | AB | R | H | HR | RBI | SB |
|---|---|---|---|---|---|---|---|---|
| Nordhagen | .301 | 68 | 206 | 28 | 62 | 5 | 35 | 0 |
| Lemon | .300 | 105 | 357 | 51 | 107 | 13 | 55 | 5 |
| *Squires† | .280 | 46 | 150 | 25 | 42 | 0 | 19 | 4 |
| Garr† | .275 | 118 | 443 | 67 | 122 | 3 | 29 | 7 |
| Orta† | .274 | 117 | 420 | 45 | 115 | 13 | 53 | 1 |
| L. Johnson | .273 | 148 | 498 | 52 | 136 | 8 | 72 | 6 |
| *Colbern | .270 | 48 | 141 | 11 | 38 | 2 | 20 | 0 |
| Bosley† | .269 | 66 | 219 | 25 | 59 | 2 | 13 | 12 |
| *Molinaro† | .262 | 105 | 286 | 39 | 75 | 6 | 27 | 22 |
| *Pryor | .261 | 82 | 222 | 27 | 58 | 2 | 15 | 3 |
| Soderholm | .258 | 143 | 457 | 57 | 118 | 20 | 67 | 2 |
| Kessinger† | .255 | 131 | 431 | 35 | 110 | 1 | 31 | 2 |
| Washington† | .253 | 98 | 356 | 34 | 90 | 6 | 33 | 5 |
| *Nahorodny | .236 | 107 | 347 | 29 | 82 | 8 | 35 | 1 |
| Blomberg† | .231 | 61 | 156 | 16 | 36 | 5 | 22 | 0 |
| Bannister | .224 | 49 | 107 | 16 | 24 | 0 | 8 | 3 |

### Pitching

| Pitching | W | L | ERA | G | IP | H | BB | SO |
|---|---|---|---|---|---|---|---|---|
| *Proly | 5 | 2 | 2.73 | 14 | 66 | 63 | 12 | 19 |
| *Wortham† | 3 | 2 | 3.05 | 8 | 59 | 59 | 23 | 25 |
| Kucek | 2 | 3 | 3.29 | 10 | 52 | 42 | 27 | 30 |
| Willoughby | 1 | 6 | 3.87 | 59 | 93 | 95 | 19 | 36 |
| Hinton† | 2 | 6 | 4.00 | 29 | 81 | 78 | 28 | 48 |
| Barrios | 9 | 15 | 4.04 | 33 | 196 | 180 | 85 | 79 |
| Kravec† | 11 | 16 | 4.08 | 30 | 203 | 188 | 95 | 154 |
| Scheuler | 3 | 5 | 4.28 | 30 | 82 | 76 | 39 | 40 |
| Stone | 12 | 12 | 4.37 | 30 | 212 | 196 | 84 | 118 |
| LaGrow | 6 | 5 | 4.40 | 52 | 88 | 85 | 38 | 42 |
| Torrealba† | 4 | 4 | 4.73 | 25 | 57 | 69 | 39 | 23 |
| Wood† | 10 | 10 | 5.20 | 28 | 168 | 187 | 74 | 69 |

## Cleveland Indians

### Batting

| Batting | Pct. | G | AB | R | H | HR | RBI | SB |
|---|---|---|---|---|---|---|---|---|
| Kuiper† | .283 | 149 | 547 | 52 | 155 | 0 | 43 | 4 |
| Norris† | .283 | 113 | 315 | 41 | 89 | 2 | 27 | 12 |
| Bell | .282 | 142 | 556 | 71 | 157 | 6 | 62 | 1 |
| Carbo† | .282 | 77 | 220 | 28 | 62 | 5 | 22 | 2 |
| Veryzer | .271 | 130 | 421 | 48 | 114 | 1 | 32 | 1 |
| Manning† | .263 | 148 | 566 | 65 | 149 | 3 | 50 | 12 |
| Thornton | .262 | 145 | 508 | 97 | 133 | 33 | 105 | 4 |
| Dade | .254 | 93 | 307 | 37 | 78 | 3 | 20 | 0 |
| Blanks | .254 | 70 | 193 | 19 | 49 | 2 | 20 | 0 |
| *Diaz | .236 | 44 | 127 | 12 | 30 | 2 | 11 | 0 |
| Pruitt | .235 | 71 | 187 | 17 | 44 | 6 | 17 | 2 |
| *Cox | .233 | 82 | 227 | 14 | 53 | 1 | 19 | 0 |
| *Speed | .226 | 70 | 106 | 13 | 24 | 0 | 4 | 2 |
| Alexander | .225 | 148 | 498 | 57 | 112 | 27 | 84 | 0 |

### Pitching

| Pitching | W | L | ERA | G | IP | H | BB | SO |
|---|---|---|---|---|---|---|---|---|
| Monget | 4 | 3 | 2.75 | 48 | 85 | 71 | 51 | 54 |
| Kern | 10 | 10 | 3.09 | 58 | 99 | 77 | 58 | 95 |
| Reuschel | 2 | 4 | 3.10 | 18 | 90 | 95 | 22 | 24 |
| Waits† | 13 | 15 | 3.21 | 34 | 230 | 206 | 86 | 97 |
| Spillner | 3 | 1 | 3.70 | 16 | 56 | 54 | 21 | 48 |
| Paxton | 12 | 11 | 3.86 | 33 | 191 | 179 | 63 | 96 |
| Clyde† | 8 | 11 | 4.29 | 28 | 153 | 166 | 60 | 83 |

---

### Pitching (Detroit Tigers — continued top right)

| Pitching | W | L | ERA | G | IP | H | BB | SO |
|---|---|---|---|---|---|---|---|---|
| Wise | 9 | 19 | 4.33 | 33 | 212 | 226 | 59 | 106 |
| Hood† | 5 | 6 | 4.47 | 36 | 155 | 166 | 77 | 73 |

## Detroit Tigers

### Batting

| Batting | Pct. | G | AB | R | H | HR | RBI | SB |
|---|---|---|---|---|---|---|---|---|
| LeFlore | .297 | 155 | 666 | 126 | 198 | 12 | 62 | 68 |
| Thompson† | .287 | 153 | 589 | 79 | 169 | 26 | 96 | 0 |
| *Whitaker† | .285 | 139 | 484 | 71 | 138 | 3 | 58 | 7 |
| Wockenfuss | .283 | 71 | 187 | 23 | 53 | 7 | 22 | 0 |
| Kemp† | .277 | 159 | 582 | 75 | 161 | 15 | 79 | 2 |
| Mankowski† | .275 | 88 | 222 | 28 | 61 | 4 | 24 | 2 |
| Staub† | .273 | 162 | 642 | 75 | 175 | 24 | 121 | 3 |
| *Trammell | .268 | 139 | 448 | 49 | 120 | 2 | 34 | 3 |
| Corcoran† | .265 | 116 | 324 | 37 | 86 | 1 | 27 | 3 |
| Rodriguez | .265 | 134 | 385 | 40 | 102 | 7 | 43 | 0 |
| Stanley | .265 | 53 | 151 | 15 | 40 | 3 | 8 | 0 |
| May† | .250 | 105 | 352 | 24 | 88 | 10 | 37 | 0 |
| Wagner | .239 | 39 | 109 | 10 | 26 | 0 | 6 | 1 |
| Dillard | .223 | 56 | 130 | 21 | 29 | 0 | 7 | 1 |
| *Parrish | .219 | 85 | 288 | 37 | 63 | 14 | 41 | 0 |

### Pitching

| Pitching | W | L | ERA | G | IP | H | BB | SO |
|---|---|---|---|---|---|---|---|---|
| Hiller† | 9 | 4 | 2.35 | 51 | 92 | 64 | 35 | 74 |
| *Young | 6 | 7 | 2.80 | 14 | 106 | 94 | 30 | 49 |
| Rozema | 9 | 12 | 3.14 | 28 | 209 | 205 | 41 | 57 |
| Wilcox | 13 | 12 | 3.77 | 29 | 215 | 208 | 68 | 132 |
| Billingham | 15 | 8 | 3.88 | 30 | 202 | 218 | 65 | 59 |
| Sykes† | 6 | 6 | 3.93 | 22 | 94 | 99 | 34 | 58 |
| Slaton | 17 | 11 | 4.12 | 35 | 234 | 235 | 85 | 92 |
| Morris | 3 | 5 | 4.33 | 28 | 106 | 107 | 49 | 48 |
| *Baker | 2 | 4 | 4.57 | 15 | 63 | 66 | 42 | 39 |

## Kansas City Royals

### Batting

| Batting | Pct. | G | AB | R | H | HR | RBI | SB |
|---|---|---|---|---|---|---|---|---|
| Wathan | .300 | 68 | 190 | 19 | 57 | 2 | 28 | 2 |
| Otis | .298 | 141 | 486 | 74 | 145 | 22 | 96 | 32 |
| LaCock† | .295 | 118 | 322 | 44 | 95 | 5 | 48 | 1 |
| Brett† | .294 | 128 | 510 | 79 | 150 | 9 | 62 | 23 |
| White | .275 | 143 | 461 | 66 | 127 | 7 | 50 | 13 |
| Cowens | .274 | 132 | 485 | 63 | 133 | 5 | 63 | 14 |
| McRae | .273 | 156 | 623 | 90 | 170 | 16 | 72 | 17 |
| Porter† | .265 | 150 | 520 | 77 | 138 | 18 | 78 | 0 |
| *Hurdle† | .264 | 133 | 417 | 48 | 110 | 7 | 56 | 1 |
| *Washington‡ | .264 | 69 | 129 | 10 | 34 | 0 | 9 | 12 |
| Zdeb | .252 | 60 | 127 | 18 | 32 | 0 | 11 | 3 |
| Braun† | .251 | 96 | 211 | 27 | 53 | 3 | 29 | 4 |
| Patek | .248 | 138 | 440 | 54 | 109 | 2 | 46 | 38 |
| *Wilson‡ | .217 | 127 | 198 | 43 | 43 | 0 | 16 | 46 |
| Poquette† | .216 | 80 | 204 | 16 | 44 | 4 | 30 | 2 |
| Terrell | .203 | 73 | 133 | 14 | 27 | 0 | 8 | 8 |

### Pitching

| Pitching | W | L | ERA | G | IP | H | BB | SO |
|---|---|---|---|---|---|---|---|---|
| Gura† | 16 | 4 | 2.72 | 35 | 222 | 183 | 60 | 81 |
| Mingori† | 1 | 4 | 2.74 | 45 | 69 | 64 | 16 | 28 |
| Hrabosky† | 8 | 7 | 2.88 | 58 | 75 | 52 | 35 | 60 |
| *Gale | 14 | 8 | 3.09 | 31 | 192 | 171 | 100 | 88 |
| Pattin | 3 | 3 | 3.30 | 32 | 79 | 72 | 25 | 30 |
| Leonard | 21 | 17 | 3.33 | 40 | 295 | 283 | 78 | 183 |
| Splittorff† | 19 | 13 | 3.40 | 39 | 262 | 244 | 60 | 76 |
| Bird | 6 | 5 | 5.27 | 40 | 99 | 110 | 31 | 48 |

## Milwaukee Brewers

### Batting

| Batting | Pct. | G | AB | R | H | HR | RBI | SB |
|---|---|---|---|---|---|---|---|---|
| Cooper† | .312 | 107 | 407 | 60 | 127 | 13 | 54 | 3 |
| Oglivie† | .303 | 128 | 469 | 71 | 142 | 18 | 72 | 11 |
| Wohlford | .297 | 46 | 118 | 16 | 35 | 1 | 19 | 3 |
| Money | .293 | 137 | 518 | 88 | 152 | 14 | 54 | 3 |
| Yount | .293 | 127 | 502 | 66 | 147 | 9 | 71 | 16 |
| Lezcano | .292 | 132 | 442 | 62 | 129 | 15 | 61 | 3 |
| Hisle | .290 | 142 | 520 | 96 | 151 | 34 | 115 | 10 |
| Bando | .285 | 152 | 540 | 85 | 154 | 17 | 78 | 3 |
| *Molitor | .273 | 125 | 521 | 73 | 142 | 6 | 45 | 30 |
| Moore | .269 | 96 | 268 | 30 | 72 | 5 | 31 | 4 |
| *Davis | .248 | 69 | 218 | 28 | 54 | 5 | 24 | 1 |
| Thomas | .246 | 137 | 452 | 70 | 111 | 32 | 86 | 3 |
| Martinez | .219 | 89 | 256 | 26 | 56 | 1 | 20 | 1 |

### Pitching

| Pitching | W | L | ERA | G | IP | H | BB | SO |
|---|---|---|---|---|---|---|---|---|
| Castro | 5 | 4 | 1.80 | 42 | 50 | 43 | 14 | 17 |
| Caldwell† | 22 | 9 | 2.37 | 37 | 293 | 258 | 54 | 131 |
| Sorensen | 18 | 12 | 3.20 | 37 | 281 | 277 | 50 | 78 |
| McClure† | 2 | 6 | 3.74 | 44 | 65 | 53 | 30 | 47 |
| Rodriguez | 5 | 5 | 3.94 | 32 | 105 | 107 | 26 | 51 |
| *Replogle | 9 | 5 | 3.99 | 32 | 149 | 177 | 47 | 41 |
| Travers† | 12 | 11 | 4.45 | 28 | 176 | 184 | 58 | 66 |
| Augustine† | 13 | 12 | 4.55 | 35 | 188 | 204 | 61 | 59 |
| *Stein | 3 | 2 | 5.30 | 31 | 73 | 78 | 39 | 42 |

## Minnesota Twins

| Batting | Pct. | G | AB | R | H | HR | RBI | SB |
|---|---|---|---|---|---|---|---|---|
| Carew† | .333 | 152 | 564 | 85 | 188 | 5 | 70 | 27 |
| Morales | .314 | 101 | 242 | 22 | 76 | 2 | 38 | 0 |
| Cubbage† | .282 | 125 | 394 | 40 | 111 | 7 | 57 | 3 |
| Ford | .274 | 151 | 592 | 78 | 162 | 11 | 82 | 7 |
| Smalley‡ | .273 | 158 | 586 | 80 | 160 | 19 | 77 | 2 |
| Rivera | .271 | 101 | 251 | 35 | 68 | 3 | 23 | 5 |
| Randall | .270 | 119 | 330 | 36 | 89 | 0 | 21 | 5 |
| Chiles† | .268 | 87 | 198 | 22 | 53 | 1 | 22 | 1 |
| Wilfong† | .266 | 92 | 199 | 23 | 53 | 1 | 11 | 8 |
| Adams† | .258 | 116 | 310 | 27 | 80 | 7 | 35 | 0 |
| Norwood | .255 | 125 | 428 | 56 | 109 | 8 | 46 | 25 |
| *Powell† | .247 | 121 | 381 | 55 | 94 | 3 | 31 | 11 |
| *Wolfe | .234 | 88 | 235 | 25 | 55 | 3 | 25 | 0 |
| Wynegar‡ | .229 | 135 | 454 | 36 | 104 | 4 | 45 | 1 |
| Borgmann | .211 | 48 | 123 | 16 | 26 | 3 | 15 | 0 |
| Kusick | .173 | 97 | 191 | 23 | 33 | 4 | 20 | 3 |

| Pitching | W | L | ERA | G | IP | H | BB | SO |
|---|---|---|---|---|---|---|---|---|
| Marshall | 10 | 12 | 2.45 | 54 | 99 | 80 | 37 | 56 |
| Goltz | 15 | 10 | 2.50 | 29 | 220 | 209 | 67 | 116 |
| Zahn† | 14 | 14 | 3.04 | 35 | 252 | 260 | 81 | 106 |
| *Erickson | 14 | 13 | 3.96 | 37 | 266 | 268 | 79 | 121 |
| Serum | 9 | 9 | 4.11 | 34 | 184 | 188 | 44 | 80 |
| *Jackson† | 4 | 6 | 4.50 | 19 | 92 | 89 | 48 | 54 |
| Thormodsgard | 1 | 6 | 5.05 | 12 | 66 | 81 | 17 | 23 |
| Perzanowski | 2 | 7 | 5.21 | 13 | 57 | 59 | 26 | 31 |

## New York Yankees

| Batting | Pct. | G | AB | R | H | HR | RBI | SB |
|---|---|---|---|---|---|---|---|---|
| Piniella | .314 | 130 | 472 | 67 | 148 | 6 | 69 | 3 |
| Munson | .297 | 154 | 617 | 73 | 183 | 6 | 71 | 2 |
| Randolph | .279 | 134 | 499 | 87 | 139 | 3 | 42 | 36 |
| Nettles† | .276 | 159 | 587 | 81 | 162 | 27 | 93 | 1 |
| Jackson† | .274 | 139 | 511 | 82 | 140 | 27 | 97 | 14 |
| Chambliss† | .274 | 162 | 625 | 81 | 171 | 12 | 90 | 2 |
| White‡ | .269 | 103 | 346 | 44 | 93 | 8 | 43 | 10 |
| Rivers† | .265 | 141 | 559 | 78 | 148 | 11 | 48 | 25 |
| Dent | .243 | 123 | 379 | 40 | 92 | 5 | 40 | 3 |
| Thomasson† | .233 | 101 | 270 | 37 | 63 | 8 | 36 | 4 |
| Spencer† | .227 | 71 | 150 | 12 | 34 | 7 | 24 | 0 |
| Stanley | .219 | 81 | 160 | 14 | 35 | 1 | 9 | 0 |
| Johnson | .184 | 76 | 174 | 20 | 32 | 6 | 19 | 0 |
| Blair | .176 | 75 | 125 | 10 | 22 | 2 | 13 | 1 |

| Pitching | W | L | ERA | G | IP | H | BB | SO |
|---|---|---|---|---|---|---|---|---|
| Guidry† | 25 | 3 | 1.74 | 35 | 274 | 187 | 72 | 248 |
| Gossage | 10 | 11 | 2.01 | 63 | 134 | 87 | 59 | 122 |
| Figueroa | 20 | 9 | 2.99 | 35 | 253 | 233 | 77 | 92 |
| Lyle† | 9 | 3 | 3.46 | 59 | 112 | 116 | 33 | 33 |
| Hunter | 12 | 6 | 3.58 | 21 | 118 | 98 | 35 | 56 |
| *Beattie | 6 | 9 | 3.73 | 25 | 128 | 123 | 51 | 65 |
| Tidrow | 7 | 11 | 3.84 | 31 | 185 | 191 | 53 | 73 |
| Lindblad† | 1 | 1 | 3.88 | 25 | 58 | 62 | 23 | 34 |
| Clay | 3 | 4 | 4.26 | 28 | 76 | 89 | 21 | 32 |

## Oakland A's

| Batting | Pct. | G | AB | R | H | HR | RBI | SB |
|---|---|---|---|---|---|---|---|---|
| Page† | .285 | 147 | 516 | 62 | 147 | 17 | 70 | 23 |
| Carty | .283 | 145 | 527 | 70 | 149 | 31 | 99 | 1 |
| Guerrero | .275 | 143 | 505 | 28 | 139 | 3 | 38 | 0 |
| *Edwards | .274 | 142 | 413 | 48 | 113 | 1 | 23 | 27 |
| *Revering† | .271 | 152 | 521 | 48 | 141 | 16 | 46 | 0 |
| *Duncan | .257 | 104 | 319 | 25 | 82 | 2 | 37 | 1 |
| Newman | .239 | 105 | 268 | 25 | 64 | 9 | 32 | 0 |
| Wallis‡ | .237 | 85 | 279 | 28 | 66 | 6 | 26 | 1 |
| Burke | .235 | 78 | 200 | 19 | 47 | 1 | 14 | 15 |
| Dilone† | .228 | 135 | 259 | 34 | 59 | 1 | 14 | 50 |
| Essian | .223 | 126 | 278 | 21 | 62 | 3 | 26 | 2 |
| Armas | .213 | 91 | 239 | 17 | 51 | 2 | 13 | 1 |
| Alston† | .205 | 61 | 176 | 17 | 36 | 1 | 10 | 11 |
| Gross† | .199 | 118 | 286 | 18 | 57 | 7 | 23 | 0 |

| Pitching | W | L | ERA | G | IP | H | BB | SO |
|---|---|---|---|---|---|---|---|---|
| Sosa | 8 | 2 | 2.64 | 68 | 109 | 106 | 44 | 61 |
| Lacey† | 8 | 9 | 3.00 | 74 | 120 | 126 | 35 | 60 |
| *Keough | 8 | 15 | 3.24 | 32 | 197 | 178 | 85 | 108 |
| Heaverlo | 3 | 6 | 3.25 | 69 | 130 | 141 | 41 | 71 |
| *Johnson† | 11 | 10 | 3.39 | 33 | 186 | 164 | 82 | 91 |
| Langford | 7 | 13 | 3.43 | 37 | 176 | 169 | 56 | 92 |
| *Wirth | 5 | 6 | 3.44 | 16 | 81 | 72 | 34 | 31 |
| Renko | 6 | 12 | 4.29 | 27 | 151 | 152 | 67 | 89 |
| Broberg | 10 | 12 | 4.61 | 35 | 166 | 174 | 65 | 94 |

## Seattle Mariners

| Batting | Pct. | G | AB | R | H | HR | RBI | SB |
|---|---|---|---|---|---|---|---|---|
| Roberts | .301 | 134 | 472 | 78 | 142 | 22 | 92 | |
| Paciorek | .299 | 70 | 251 | 32 | 75 | 4 | 30 | 2 |
| Reynolds† | .292 | 148 | 548 | 57 | 160 | 5 | 44 | 9 |
| Bochte† | .263 | 140 | 486 | 58 | 128 | 11 | 51 | 5 |
| Stein | .261 | 114 | 403 | 41 | 105 | 4 | 37 | |
| Stinson‡ | .258 | 124 | 364 | 46 | 94 | 11 | 55 | |
| Ru. Jones† | .235 | 129 | 472 | 48 | 111 | 6 | 46 | 22 |
| Cruz‡ | .235 | 147 | 550 | 77 | 129 | 1 | 25 | 59 |
| Bernhardt | .230 | 54 | 165 | 13 | 38 | 2 | 12 | |
| Robertson | .230 | 64 | 174 | 17 | 40 | 8 | 28 | 0 |
| Meyer† | .227 | 123 | 444 | 38 | 101 | 8 | 56 | |
| Milbourne‡ | .226 | 93 | 234 | 31 | 53 | 2 | 20 | 5 |
| Stanton | .182 | 93 | 302 | 24 | 55 | 3 | 24 | |
| Hale† | .171 | 107 | 211 | 24 | 36 | 4 | 22 | 3 |

| Pitching | W | L | ERA | G | IP | H | BB | SO |
|---|---|---|---|---|---|---|---|---|
| Romo | 11 | 7 | 3.70 | 56 | 107 | 88 | 39 | 62 |
| Todd | 3 | 4 | 3.87 | 49 | 107 | 113 | 61 | 37 |
| *Rawley† | 4 | 9 | 4.14 | 52 | 111 | 114 | 51 | 66 |
| Mitchell | 4 | 8 | 4.23 | 29 | 168 | 173 | 79 | 75 |
| *McLaughlin | 4 | 8 | 4.37 | 20 | 107 | 97 | 39 | 87 |
| Houser | 5 | 4 | 4.73 | 34 | 116 | 130 | 35 | 25 |
| *Honeycutt† | 5 | 11 | 4.90 | 26 | 134 | 150 | 49 | 50 |
| *Parrott | 1 | 5 | 5.16 | 27 | 82 | 108 | 32 | 41 |
| Colborn | 4 | 12 | 5.22 | 28 | 143 | 156 | 50 | 34 |
| Abbott | 7 | 15 | 5.28 | 29 | 155 | 191 | 44 | 67 |
| Pole | 4 | 11 | 6.45 | 21 | 99 | 122 | 41 | 41 |

## Texas Rangers

| Batting | Pct. | G | AB | R | H | HR | RBI | SB |
|---|---|---|---|---|---|---|---|---|
| Oliver† | .324 | 133 | 525 | 65 | 170 | 14 | 89 | 8 |
| Sundberg | .278 | 149 | 518 | 54 | 144 | 6 | 58 | 2 |
| Grubb† | .276 | 133 | 410 | 62 | 113 | 15 | 67 | 6 |
| Bonds | .267 | 156 | 565 | 93 | 151 | 31 | 90 | 43 |
| Zisk | .262 | 140 | 511 | 68 | 134 | 22 | 85 | 3 |
| Beniquez | .260 | 127 | 473 | 61 | 123 | 11 | 50 | 10 |
| Hargrove† | .251 | 146 | 494 | 63 | 124 | 7 | 40 | 2 |
| Wills‡ | .250 | 157 | 539 | 78 | 135 | 9 | 57 | 52 |
| Harrah | .229 | 139 | 450 | 56 | 103 | 12 | 59 | 31 |
| *Thompson‡ | .225 | 64 | 120 | 23 | 27 | 2 | 12 | 7 |
| Lowenstein† | .222 | 77 | 176 | 28 | 39 | 5 | 21 | 16 |
| Bevacqua | .221 | 90 | 249 | 21 | 55 | 6 | 30 | 1 |
| Mason† | .190 | 55 | 105 | 10 | 20 | 0 | 3 | 0 |
| Campaneris | .186 | 98 | 269 | 30 | 50 | 1 | 17 | 22 |

| Pitching | W | L | ERA | G | IP | H | BB | SO |
|---|---|---|---|---|---|---|---|---|
| Matlack† | 15 | 13 | 2.30 | 35 | 270 | 252 | 51 | 157 |
| *Comer | 11 | 5 | 2.31 | 30 | 117 | 107 | 37 | 65 |
| Jenkins | 18 | 8 | 3.04 | 34 | 249 | 228 | 41 | 157 |
| Cleveland | 5 | 8 | 3.08 | 54 | 76 | 66 | 23 | 46 |
| Medich | 9 | 8 | 3.68 | 28 | 171 | 166 | 52 | 71 |
| Alexander | 9 | 10 | 3.86 | 31 | 198 | 198 | 71 | 81 |
| D. Ellis | 9 | 7 | 4.21 | 22 | 141 | 131 | 46 | 45 |
| Umbarger† | 5 | 8 | 4.51 | 32 | 98 | 116 | 36 | 60 |
| Barker | 1 | 5 | 4.85 | 29 | 52 | 63 | 29 | 33 |

## Toronto Jays

| Batting | Pct. | G | AB | R | H | HR | RBI | SB |
|---|---|---|---|---|---|---|---|---|
| Howell† | .270 | 140 | 551 | 67 | 149 | 8 | 61 | 0 |
| Velez | .266 | 91 | 248 | 29 | 66 | 9 | 38 | 1 |
| Bailor | .264 | 154 | 621 | 74 | 164 | 1 | 52 | 5 |
| Ashby‡ | .261 | 81 | 264 | 27 | 69 | 9 | 29 | 1 |
| *Bosetti | .259 | 136 | 568 | 61 | 147 | 5 | 42 | 6 |
| Hutton† | .254 | 64 | 173 | 19 | 44 | 2 | 9 | 1 |
| Horton | .252 | 115 | 393 | 38 | 99 | 11 | 60 | 3 |
| Mayberry† | .250 | 152 | 515 | 51 | 129 | 22 | 70 | 1 |
| A. Woods† | .241 | 62 | 220 | 19 | 53 | 3 | 25 | 1 |
| Ault | .240 | 54 | 104 | 10 | 25 | 3 | 7 | 0 |
| McKay‡ | .238 | 145 | 504 | 59 | 120 | 7 | 45 | 4 |
| *Upshaw† | .237 | 95 | 224 | 26 | 53 | 1 | 17 | 4 |
| Cerone | .223 | 88 | 282 | 25 | 63 | 3 | 20 | 0 |
| Gomez | .223 | 153 | 413 | 39 | 92 | 0 | 32 | 2 |

| Pitching | W | L | ERA | G | IP | H | BB | SO |
|---|---|---|---|---|---|---|---|---|
| Coleman | 5 | 0 | 3.83 | 41 | 80 | 79 | 35 | 32 |
| Murphy | 6 | 9 | 3.93 | 50 | 94 | 87 | 37 | 35 |
| Clancy | 10 | 12 | 4.08 | 31 | 194 | 199 | 91 | 106 |
| Underwood† | 6 | 14 | 4.09 | 31 | 198 | 201 | 87 | 140 |
| Kirkwood | 4 | 5 | 4.24 | 16 | 68 | 76 | 25 | 29 |
| Jefferson | 7 | 16 | 4.37 | 31 | 212 | 214 | 86 | 97 |
| Willis† | 3 | 7 | 4.54 | 44 | 101 | 104 | 39 | 52 |
| Moore† | 6 | 9 | 4.94 | 37 | 144 | 165 | 54 | 75 |
| Garvin† | 4 | 12 | 5.65 | 26 | 145 | 189 | 48 | 67 |
| Lemanczyk | 4 | 14 | 6.24 | 29 | 137 | 170 | 65 | 62 |

## Members of National Baseball Hall of Fame and Museum

The shrine of organized baseball, dedicated June 12, 1939, is located in Cooperstown, N. Y.

Alexander, Grover Cleveland
Anson, Cap
Appling, Luke
Averill, Earl
Baker, Home Run
Bancroft, Dave
Banks, Ernie
Barrow, Edward G.
Beckley, Jake
Bell, Cool Papa
Bender, Chief
Berra, Yogi
Bottomley, Jim
Boudreau, Lou
Bresnahan, Roger
Brouthers, Dan
Brown (Three Finger), Mordecai
Bulkeley, Morgan C.
Burkett, Jesse C.
Campanella, Roy
Carey, Max
Cartwright, Alexander
Chadwick, Henry
Chance, Frank
Charleston, Oscar
Chesbro, John
Clarke, Fred
Clarkson, John
Clemente, Roberto
Cobb, Ty
Cochrane, Mickey
Collins, Eddie
Collins, James
Combs, Earle

Comiskey, Charles A.
Conlan, Jocko
Connolly, Thomas H.
Connor, Roger
Coveleski, Stan
Crawford, Sam
Cronin, Joe
Cummings, Candy
Cuyler, Kiki
Dean, Dizzy
Delahanty, Ed
Dickey, Bill
DiHigo, Martin
DiMaggio, Joe
Duffy, Hugh
Evans, Billy
Evers, John
Ewing, Buck
Faber, Urban
Feller, Bob
Flick, Elmer H.
Ford, Whitey
Foxx, Jimmy
Frick, Ford
Frisch, Frank
Galvin, Pud
Gehrig, Lou
Gehringer, Charles
Gibson, Josh
Gomez, Lefty
Goslin, Goose
Greenberg, Hank
Griffith, Clark

Grimes, Burleigh
Grove, Lefty
Hafey, Chick
Haines, Jesse
Hamilton, Bill
Harridge, Will
Harris, Bucky
Hartnett, Gabby
Heilmann, Harry
Herman, Billy
Hooper, Harry
Hornsby, Rogers
Hoyt, Waite
Hubbard, Cal
Hubbell, Carl
Huggins, Miller
Irvin, Monte
Jennings, Hugh
Johnson, Byron
Johnson, William (Rudy)
Johnson, Walter
Joss, Addie
Keefe, Timothy
Keeler, William
Kelley, Joe
Kelly, George
Kelly, King
Kiner, Ralph
Klem, Bill
Koufax, Sandy
Lajoie, Napoleon
Landis, Kenesaw M.
Lemon, Bob

Leonard, Buck
Lindstrom, Fred
Lloyd, Pop
Lopez, Al
Lyons, Ted
Mack, Connie
MacPhail, Larry
Mantle, Mickey
Manush, Henry
Maranville, Rabbit
Marquard, Rube
Mathews, Eddie
Mathewson, Christy
McCarthy, Joe
McCarthy, Thomas
McGinnity, Joe
McGraw, John
McKechnie, Bill
Medwick, Joe
Musial, Stan
Nichols, Kid
O'Rourke, James
Ott, Mel
Paige, Satchel
Pennock, Herb
Plank, Ed
Radbourne, Charlie
Rice, Sam
Rickey, Branch
Rixey, Eppa
Roberts, Robin
Robinson, Jackie
Robinson, Wilbert

Roush, Edd
Ruffing, Red
Rusie, Amos
Ruth, Babe
Schalk, Ray
Sewell, Joe
Simmons, Al
Sisler, George
Spahn, Warren
Spalding, Albert
Speaker, Tris
Stengel, Casey
Terry, Bill
Thompson, Sam
Tinker, Joe
Traynor, Pie
Vance, Dazzy
Waddell, Rube
Wagner, Honus
Wallace, Roderick
Walsh, Ed.
Waner, Lloyd
Waner, Paul
Ward, John
Weiss, George
Welch, Mickey
Wheat, Zach
Williams, Ted
Wright, George
Wright, Harry
Wynn, Early
Young, Cy
Youngs, Ross

## Major League Baseball Attendance

| | National League | | | | American League | | |
| Club | 1978 | 1977 | Change | Club | 1978 | 1977 | Change |
|---|---|---|---|---|---|---|---|
| Atlanta | 905,178 | 872,464 | + 32,714 | Baltimore | 1,051,316 | 1,195,769 | − 144,453 |
| Chicago | 1,525,311 | 1,439,834 | + 85,477 | Boston | 2,322,578 | 2,074,549 | + 248,029 |
| Cincinnati | 2,532,497 | 2,519,670 | + 12,827 | California | 1,754,986 | 1,432,633 | + 322,353 |
| Houston | 1,126,754 | 1,109,560 | + 17,194 | Chicago | 1,671,009 | 1,657,135 | + 13,874 |
| Los Angeles | 3,347,776 | 2,955,087 | + 392,689 | Cleveland | 806,081 | 900,365 | − 94,284 |
| Montreal | 1,426,907 | 1,433,757 | − 6,850 | Detroit | 1,746,422 | 1,359,856 | + 386,566 |
| New York | 1,007,328 | 1,006,825 | − 59,497 | Kansas City | 2,255,566 | 1,852,603 | + 402,963 |
| Philadelphia | 2,570,738 | 2,700,070 | − 129,332 | Milwaukee | 1,601,306 | 1,114,938 | + 486,368 |
| Pittsburgh | 964,196 | 1,237,349 | − 273,153 | Minnesota | 787,603 | 1,162,727 | − 375,124 |
| St. Louis | 1,278,175 | 1,659,287 | − 381,112 | New York | 2,320,572 | 2,103,092 | + 217,480 |
| San Diego | 1,669,299 | 1,376,269 | + 293,030 | Oakland | 527,007 | 495,599 | + 31,408 |
| San Francisco | 1,739,349 | 700,056 | + 1,039,293 | Seattle | 872,672 | 1,338,511 | − 465,839 |
| | | | | Texas | 1,446,963 | 1,250,722 | + 196,241 |
| | | | | Toronto | 1,562,585 | 1,701,052 | − 138,467 |
| **Totals** | **20,093,508** | **19,070,228** | **+ 1,023,280** | **Totals** | **20,726,666** | **19,639,551** | **+ 1,087,115** |

## Major League Attendance Records

**Season, both leagues**—40,820,174 in 1978.
**Season, one club**—3,347,776—Los Angeles Dodgers,1978.
**World Series**—420,784—1959 Series between Los Angeles Dodgers and Chicago White Sox.
**World Series game**—92,706—fifth game, 1959, Los Angeles, Oct. 6.
**Regular season game**—84,587—Municipal Stadium, Cleveland, Sept. 12, 1954, in doubleheader between the Indians and Yankees. (Not including pass list of 1,976).
**Regular season single game**—78,672—Los Angeles Memorial Coliseum, April 18, 1958, in opening game between Los Angeles Dodgers and San Francisco Giants.

## All-Time Home Run Leaders

| Player | HR | Player | HR | Player | HR | Player | HR | Player | HR |
|---|---|---|---|---|---|---|---|---|---|
| Hank Aaron | 755 | Willie McCovey | 505 | Rocky Colavito | 374 | Hank Greenberg | 331 | Hank Sauer | 288 |
| Babe Ruth | 714 | Lou Gehrig | 493 | Gil Hodges | 370 | Lee May | 325 | Del Ennis | 288 |
| Willie Mays | 660 | Stan Musial | 475 | Ralph Kiner | 369 | Roy Sievers | 318 | Willie Horton | 287 |
| Frank Robinson | 586 | Willie Stargell | 429 | Joe DiMaggio | 361 | Tony Perez | 310 | Frank Thomas | 286 |
| Harmon Killebrew | 573 | Billy Williams | 426 | John Mize | 359 | Johnny Bench | 310 | Ken Boyer | 282 |
| Mickey Mantle | 536 | Duke Snyder | 407 | Yogi Berra | 358 | Al Simmons | 307 | Ted Kluszewski | 279 |
| Jimmy Foxx | 534 | Al Kaline | 399 | Dick Allen | 351 | Rogers Hornsby | 302 | Rudy York | 277 |
| Ted Williams | 521 | Carl Yastrzemski | 383 | Ron Santo | 342 | Chuck Klein | 300 | Roger Maris | 275 |
| Ed Mathews | 512 | Frank Howard | 382 | Reggie Jackson | 340 | Bobby Bonds | 296 | Reggie Smith | 270 |
| Ernie Banks | 512 | Orlando Cepeda | 379 | John (Boog) Powell | 339 | Jim Wynn | 291 | Brooks Robinson | 268 |
| Mel Ott | 511 | Norm Cash | 377 | Joe Adcock | 336 | Robert Johnson | 288 | Vic Wertz | 266 |

# World Series, 1978

## Composite Box Score

### New York Yankees

| | g | ab | r | h | 2b | 3b | hr | rbi | bb | so | ba | po | a | e | fa |
|---|---|---|---|---|---|---|---|---|---|---|---|---|---|---|---|
| Brian Doyle, 2b | 6 | 16 | 4 | 7 | 1 | 0 | 0 | 2 | 0 | 0 | .438 | 17 | 7 | 0 | 1.000 |
| Bucky Dent, ss | 6 | 24 | 3 | 10 | 1 | 0 | 0 | 7 | 1 | 2 | .417 | 8 | 16 | 2 | .923 |
| Reggie Jackson, dh | 6 | 23 | 2 | 9 | 1 | 0 | 2 | 8 | 3 | 7 | .391 | 0 | 0 | 0 | .000 |
| Paul Blair, cf-ph-pr | 6 | 8 | 2 | 3 | 1 | 0 | 0 | 0 | 1 | 4 | .375 | 5 | 0 | 0 | 1.000 |
| Roy White, lf | 6 | 24 | 9 | 8 | 0 | 0 | 1 | 4 | 4 | 5 | .333 | 15 | 0 | 0 | 1.000 |
| Mickey Rivers, cf-ph | 5 | 18 | 2 | 6 | 0 | 0 | 0 | 1 | 0 | 2 | .333 | 7 | 0 | 0 | 1.000 |
| Thurman Munson, c | 6 | 25 | 5 | 8 | 3 | 0 | 0 | 7 | 3 | 7 | .320 | 33 | 5 | 0 | 1.000 |
| Lou Piniella, rf | 6 | 25 | 3 | 7 | 0 | 0 | 0 | 0 | 3 | 0 | .280 | 14 | 1 | 0 | 1.000 |
| Gary Thomasson, cf-lf | 3 | 4 | 0 | 1 | 0 | 0 | 0 | 0 | 0 | 1 | .250 | 3 | 0 | 0 | 1.000 |
| Fred Stanley, 2b | 3 | 5 | 0 | 1 | 1 | 0 | 0 | 0 | 0 | 1 | .200 | 5 | 2 | 0 | 1.000 |
| Chris Chambliss, 1b | 3 | 11 | 1 | 2 | 0 | 0 | 0 | 0 | 1 | 0 | .182 | 17 | 1 | 0 | 1.000 |
| Jim Spencer, 1b-ph | 4 | 12 | 3 | 2 | 0 | 0 | 0 | 0 | 2 | 4 | .167 | 23 | 2 | 0 | 1.000 |
| Craig Nettles, 3b | 6 | 25 | 2 | 4 | 0 | 0 | 0 | 1 | 0 | 6 | .160 | 8 | 18 | 0 | 1.000 |
| Cliff Johnson, ph | 2 | 2 | 0 | 0 | 0 | 0 | 0 | 0 | 0 | 0 | .000 | 0 | 0 | 0 | .000 |
| Jim Beattie, p | 1 | 0 | 0 | 0 | 0 | 0 | 0 | 0 | 0 | 0 | .000 | 0 | 1 | 0 | 1.000 |
| Ken Clay, p | 1 | 0 | 0 | 0 | 0 | 0 | 0 | 0 | 0 | 0 | .000 | 0 | 0 | 0 | .000 |
| Ed Figueroa, p | 2 | 0 | 0 | 0 | 0 | 0 | 0 | 0 | 0 | 0 | .000 | 0 | 0 | 0 | .000 |
| Rich Gossage, p | 3 | 0 | 0 | 0 | 0 | 0 | 0 | 0 | 0 | 0 | .000 | 0 | 0 | 0 | .000 |
| Ron Guidry, p | 1 | 0 | 0 | 0 | 0 | 0 | 0 | 0 | 0 | 0 | .000 | 0 | 0 | 0 | .000 |
| Mike Heath, c | 1 | 0 | 0 | 0 | 0 | 0 | 0 | 0 | 0 | 0 | .000 | 1 | 1 | 0 | 1.000 |
| Catfish Hunter, p | 2 | 0 | 0 | 0 | 0 | 0 | 0 | 0 | 0 | 0 | .000 | 2 | 0 | 0 | 1.000 |
| Jay Johnstone, rf | 2 | 0 | 0 | 0 | 0 | 0 | 0 | 0 | 0 | 0 | .000 | 1 | 0 | 0 | 1.000 |
| Paul Lindblad, p | 1 | 0 | 0 | 0 | 0 | 0 | 0 | 0 | 0 | 0 | .000 | 0 | 0 | 0 | .000 |
| Dick Tidrow, p | 2 | 0 | 0 | 0 | 0 | 0 | 0 | 0 | 0 | 0 | .000 | 0 | 0 | 0 | .000 |
| Totals | 6 | 222 | 36 | 68 | 8 | 0 | 3 | 34 | 16 | 40 | .306 | 159 | 54 | 2 | .991 |

### Los Angeles Dodgers

| | g | ab | r | h | 2b | 3b | hr | rbi | bb | so | ba | po | a | e | fa |
|---|---|---|---|---|---|---|---|---|---|---|---|---|---|---|---|
| Johnny Oates, ph-c | 1 | 1 | 0 | 1 | 0 | 0 | 0 | 0 | 1 | 0 | 1.000 | 3 | 1 | 0 | 1.000 |
| Joe Ferguson, c | 2 | 4 | 1 | 2 | 0 | 0 | 0 | 0 | 0 | 1 | .500 | 11 | 0 | 1 | .917 |
| Bill Russell, ss | 6 | 26 | 1 | 11 | 2 | 0 | 0 | 2 | 2 | 2 | .423 | 11 | 20 | 3 | .912 |
| Vic Davalillo, ph-dh | 2 | 3 | 0 | 1 | 0 | 0 | 0 | 0 | 0 | 0 | .333 | 0 | 0 | 0 | .000 |
| Dave Lopes, 2b | 6 | 26 | 7 | 8 | 0 | 0 | 3 | 7 | 2 | 1 | .308 | 10 | 19 | 1 | .967 |
| Ron Cey, 3b | 6 | 21 | 2 | 6 | 0 | 0 | 1 | 4 | 3 | 3 | .286 | 2 | 12 | 0 | 1.000 |
| Dusty Baker, lf | 6 | 21 | 2 | 5 | 0 | 0 | 1 | 1 | 1 | 3 | .238 | 12 | 0 | 0 | 1.000 |
| Steve Yeager, c | 5 | 13 | 2 | 3 | 1 | 0 | 0 | 1 | 1 | 2 | .231 | 23 | 2 | 0 | 1.000 |
| Steve Garvey, 1b | 6 | 24 | 1 | 5 | 1 | 0 | 0 | 0 | 1 | 7 | .208 | 58 | 3 | 1 | .984 |
| Reggie Smith, rf | 6 | 25 | 3 | 5 | 0 | 0 | 1 | 5 | 2 | 6 | .200 | 11 | 1 | 1 | .923 |
| Rick Monday, cf-dh | 5 | 13 | 2 | 2 | 1 | 0 | 0 | 1 | 4 | 3 | .154 | 5 | 0 | 0 | 1.000 |
| Lee Lacy, dh | 4 | 14 | 0 | 2 | 0 | 0 | 0 | 1 | 1 | 0 | .143 | 0 | 0 | 0 | .000 |
| Bill North, ph-cf | 4 | 8 | 2 | 1 | 1 | 0 | 0 | 2 | 1 | 0 | .125 | 7 | 0 | 0 | 1.000 |
| Terry Forster, p | 3 | 0 | 0 | 0 | 0 | 0 | 0 | 0 | 0 | 0 | .000 | 0 | 0 | 0 | .000 |
| Jerry Grote, c | 2 | 0 | 0 | 0 | 0 | 0 | 0 | 0 | 0 | 0 | .000 | 0 | 1 | 0 | 1.000 |
| Burt Hooton, p | 2 | 0 | 0 | 0 | 0 | 0 | 0 | 0 | 0 | 0 | .000 | 3 | 0 | 0 | 1.000 |
| Charlie Hough, p | 2 | 0 | 0 | 0 | 0 | 0 | 0 | 0 | 0 | 0 | .000 | 1 | 0 | 0 | 1.000 |
| Tommy John, p | 2 | 0 | 0 | 0 | 0 | 0 | 0 | 0 | 0 | 0 | .000 | 1 | 0 | 0 | 1.000 |
| Manny Mota, ph | 1 | 0 | 0 | 0 | 0 | 0 | 0 | 0 | 0 | 0 | .000 | 0 | 4 | 0 | 1.000 |
| Doug Rau, p | 1 | 0 | 0 | 0 | 0 | 0 | 0 | 0 | 0 | 0 | .000 | 0 | 1 | 0 | 1.000 |
| Lance Rautzhan, p | 2 | 0 | 0 | 0 | 0 | 0 | 0 | 0 | 0 | 0 | .000 | 0 | 0 | 0 | .000 |
| Don Sutton, p | 2 | 0 | 0 | 0 | 0 | 0 | 0 | 0 | 0 | 0 | .000 | 0 | 2 | 0 | 1.000 |
| Bob Welch, p | 3 | 0 | 0 | 0 | 0 | 0 | 0 | 0 | 0 | 0 | .000 | 0 | 0 | 0 | .000 |
| Totals | 6 | 199 | 23 | 52 | 8 | 0 | 6 | 22 | 20 | 31 | .261 | 158 | 64 | 7 | .969 |

## Pitching Summary

### New York

| | g | gs | cg | ip | h | r | er | bb | so | hb | wp | w | l | pct | era |
|---|---|---|---|---|---|---|---|---|---|---|---|---|---|---|---|
| Rich Gossage | 3 | 0 | 0 | 6 | 1 | 0 | 0 | 4 | 0 | 0 | 1 | 0 | 0 | .000 | 0.00 |
| Ron Guidry | 1 | 1 | 1 | 9 | 8 | 1 | 1 | 7 | 4 | 0 | 0 | 1 | 0 | 1.000 | 1.00 |
| Dick Tidrow | 2 | 0 | 0 | 4²/₃ | 4 | 1 | 1 | 0 | 5 | 0 | 0 | 0 | 0 | .000 | 1.93 |
| Jim Beattie | 1 | 1 | 1 | 9 | 9 | 2 | 2 | 4 | 8 | 0 | 0 | 1 | 0 | 1.000 | 2.00 |
| Catfish Hunter | 2 | 2 | 0 | 13 | 13 | 6 | 6 | 1 | 5 | 0 | 0 | 1 | 1 | .500 | 4.15 |
| Ed Figueroa | 2 | 2 | 0 | 6²/₃ | 9 | 6 | 6 | 2 | 2 | 0 | 0 | 0 | 1 | .000 | 8.10 |
| Ken Clay | 1 | 0 | 0 | 2¹/₃ | 4 | 3 | 3 | 2 | 2 | 0 | 1 | 0 | 0 | .000 | 11.57 |
| Paul Lindblad | 1 | 0 | 0 | 2¹/₃ | 4 | 4 | 3 | 0 | 1 | 0 | 0 | 0 | 0 | .000 | 11.57 |
| Totals | 6 | 6 | 2 | 53 | 52 | 23 | 22 | 20 | 31 | 0 | 1 | 4 | 2 | .667 | 3.74 |

Saves—none; shutouts—none.

### Los Angeles

| | g | gs | cg | ip | h | r | er | bb | so | hb | wp | w | l | pct | era |
|---|---|---|---|---|---|---|---|---|---|---|---|---|---|---|---|
| Terry Forster | 3 | 0 | 0 | 4 | 5 | 0 | 0 | 1 | 6 | 1 | 0 | 0 | 0 | .000 | 0.00 |
| Doug Rau | 1 | 0 | 0 | 2 | 1 | 0 | 0 | 3 | 0 | 0 | 0 | 0 | 0 | .000 | 0.00 |
| Tommy John | 2 | 2 | 0 | 14²/₃ | 14 | 8 | 5 | 4 | 6 | 0 | 0 | 1 | 0 | 1.000 | 3.07 |
| Bob Welch | 3 | 0 | 0 | 4¹/₃ | 3 | 3 | 2 | 6 | 0 | 0 | 1 | 0 | 0 | .000 | 6.23 |
| Burt Hooton | 2 | 2 | 0 | 8¹/₃ | 13 | 7 | 6 | 3 | 6 | 1 | 1 | 1 | 1 | .500 | 6.48 |
| Don Sutton | 2 | 2 | 0 | 12 | 17 | 10 | 10 | 4 | 8 | 0 | 1 | 0 | 2 | .000 | 7.50 |
| Charlie Hough | 2 | 0 | 0 | 5¹/₃ | 10 | 5 | 5 | 2 | 6 | 0 | 0 | 0 | 0 | .000 | 8.44 |
| Lance Rautzhan | 2 | 0 | 0 | 2 | 4 | 3 | 3 | 0 | 0 | 0 | 0 | 0 | 0 | .000 | 13.50 |
| Totals | 6 | 6 | 0 | 52²/₃ | 68 | 36 | 32 | 16 | 40 | 2 | 4 | 2 | 4 | .333 | 5.46 |

Save—Welch; shutouts—none.

# 1978 World Series Box Scores

## First Game

Dodger Stadium, Los Angeles, Oct. 10

| Yankees | ab | r | h | bi | Dodgers | ab | r | h | bi |
|---|---|---|---|---|---|---|---|---|---|
| Rivers cf | 4 | 0 | 0 | 0 | Lopes 2b | 5 | 2 | 2 | 5 |
| Blair cf | 1 | 0 | 0 | 0 | Russell ss | 5 | 1 | 3 | 0 |
| White lf | 4 | 0 | 1 | 0 | Smith rf | 5 | 0 | 1 | 1 |
| Munson c | 4 | 1 | 0 | 0 | Garvey 1b | 5 | 1 | 2 | 0 |
| Jackson dh | 4 | 1 | 3 | 0 | Cey 3b | 4 | 1 | 1 | 0 |
| Piniella rf | 4 | 2 | 1 | 0 | Baker lf | 4 | 2 | 3 | 1 |
| Nettles 3b | 4 | 0 | 1 | 1 | Monday cf | 2 | 2 | 1 | 0 |
| Chambliss 1b | 4 | 1 | 1 | 0 | North cf | 1 | 1 | 1 | 2 |
| Stanley 2b | 2 | 0 | 1 | 0 | Lacy dh | 3 | 0 | 1 | 1 |
| Johnson ph | 1 | 0 | 0 | 0 | Yeager c | 4 | 1 | 0 | 0 |
| Doyle 2b | 0 | 0 | 0 | 0 | | | | | |
| Dent ss | 4 | 0 | 1 | 2 | | | | | |
| Totals | 36 | 5 | 9 | 5 | Totals | 38 | 11 | 15 | 10 |

New York . . . . . 0 0 0   0 0 0   3 2 0—5
Los Angeles . . . . 0 3 0   3 1 0   3 1 x—11

E-Dent, Lopes, Russell, DP-New York 2, Los Angeles 1 LOB-New York 6, Los Angeles 6. 2B-Monday, Stanley, North, Russell, HR-Lopes (2), Baker (1), Jackson (1).

| | ip | h | r | er | bb | so |
|---|---|---|---|---|---|---|
| Figueroa (L,0-1) | 1 2-3 | 5 | 3 | 3 | 1 | 0 |
| Clay | 2 1-3 | 4 | 4 | 3 | 2 | 2 |
| Lindblad | 2 1-3 | 4 | 3 | 3 | 0 | 1 |
| Tidrow | 1 2-3 | 2 | 1 | 1 | 0 | 1 |
| John (W, 1-0) | 7 2-3 | 8 | 5 | 3 | 2 | 4 |
| Forster | 1 1-3 | 1 | 0 | 0 | 0 | 3 |

WP-Clay. T—2:48. A—55,997.

**How runs were scored**—Three in Dodgers third: Baker hit a home run. Monday doubled. Lopes hit a home run.

Three in Dodgers sixth: Monday walked. Yeager reached first on an error. Lopes hit a home run.

One in Dodgers fifth: two singles and a wild pitch.

Three in Yankees seventh: Jackson hit a home run. Dent singled in two runs.

Three in Dodgers seventh: Garvey and Baker singled. North doubled scoring Garvey and Baker. Lacy singled scoring North.

Two in Yankees eighth; One in Dodgers eighth.

## Second Game

Dodger Stadium, Los Angeles, Oct. 11

| Yankees | ab | r | h | bi | Dodgers | ab | r | h | bi |
|---|---|---|---|---|---|---|---|---|---|
| White lf | 5 | 2 | 2 | 0 | Lopes 2b | 4 | 1 | 1 | 0 |
| Thomsn cf | 3 | 0 | 1 | 0 | Russell ss | 4 | 0 | 1 | 0 |
| Blair cf | 1 | 0 | 0 | 0 | Smith rf | 4 | 2 | 1 | 0 |
| Munson c | 4 | 1 | 1 | 0 | Garvey 1b | 3 | 0 | 1 | 0 |
| Jacksn dh | 4 | 0 | 1 | 0 | Cey 3b | 3 | 1 | 2 | 4 |
| Nettles 3b | 4 | 0 | 0 | 0 | Baker lf | 3 | 0 | 0 | 0 |
| Piniella rf | 4 | 0 | 2 | 0 | Monday cf | 3 | 0 | 0 | 0 |
| Spencer 1b | 4 | 0 | 1 | 0 | North cf | 0 | 0 | 0 | 0 |
| Doyle 2b | 3 | 0 | 1 | 0 | Lacy dh | 3 | 0 | 0 | 0 |
| Johnsn ph | 1 | 0 | 0 | 0 | Yeager c | 3 | 0 | 1 | 0 |
| Stanley 2b | 0 | 0 | 0 | 0 | | | | | |
| Dent ss | 4 | 0 | 1 | 0 | | | | | |
| Totals | 37 | 3 | 11 | 3 | Totals | 30 | 4 | 7 | 4 |

New York . . . 0 0 2   0 0 0   1 0 0—3
Los Angeles . . . 0 0 0   1 0 3   0 0 x—4

DP—New York 1, Los Angeles 1. LOB—New York 10, Los Angeles 2. 2B—Munson, Jackson, Blair. HR—Cey (1). SB—White.

| | ip | h | r | er | bb | so |
|---|---|---|---|---|---|---|
| Hunter (L, 0-1) | 6 | 7 | 4 | 4 | 0 | 2 |
| Gossage | 2 | 0 | 0 | 0 | 0 | 0 |
| Hooton (W, 1-0) | 6 | 8 | 3 | 3 | 1 | 5 |
| Forster | 2 1-3 | 3 | 0 | 0 | 1 | 3 |
| Welch | 2-3 | 0 | 0 | 0 | 0 | 1 |

Save—Welch (1). HBP—Jackson (by Hooton). WP—Hooton. T—2:37. A—55,982.

**How runs were scored**—Two in Yankees third: White singled. Munson walked. Jackson doubled scoring White and Munson.

One in Dodgers fourth: Smith and Garvey singled. Cey singled scoring Smith.

Three in Dodgers sixth: Lopes and Smith singled. Cey hit a home run.

One in Yankees seventh: White singled. Blair doubled. Jackson grounded out scoring White.

## Third Game

Yankee Stadium, New York, Oct. 13

| Dodgers | ab | r | h | bi | Yankees | ab | r | h | bi |
|---|---|---|---|---|---|---|---|---|---|
| Lopes 2b | 5 | 0 | 1 | 0 | Rivers cf | 4 | 0 | 3 | 0 |
| Russell ss | 4 | 0 | 2 | 1 | Blair cf | 0 | 0 | 0 | 0 |
| Smith rf | 4 | 0 | 0 | 0 | White lf | 3 | 2 | 1 | 1 |
| Garvey 1b | 4 | 0 | 1 | 0 | Munson c | 4 | 1 | 1 | 1 |
| Cey 3b | 3 | 0 | 0 | 0 | Jackson dh | 3 | 0 | 1 | 1 |
| Baker lf | 3 | 0 | 2 | 0 | Piniella rf | 4 | 0 | 1 | 1 |
| Lacy dh | 4 | 0 | 1 | 0 | Nettles 3b | 4 | 1 | 0 | 0 |
| North cf | 3 | 1 | 0 | 0 | Chambliss 1b | 3 | 0 | 1 | 0 |
| Yeager c | 1 | 0 | 0 | 0 | Doyle 2b | 4 | 0 | 0 | 0 |
| Mota ph | 0 | 0 | 0 | 0 | Dent ss | 4 | 1 | 1 | 0 |
| Grote c | 0 | 0 | 0 | 0 | Guidry p | 0 | 0 | 0 | 0 |
| Ferguson c | 1 | 0 | 0 | 0 | | | | | |
| Sutton p | 0 | 0 | 0 | 0 | | | | | |
| Rautzhan p | 0 | 0 | 0 | 0 | | | | | |
| Hough p | 0 | 0 | 0 | 0 | | | | | |
| Totals | 32 | 1 | 8 | 1 | Totals | 33 | 5 | 10 | 5 |

Dodgers . . . . . . 0 0 1   0 0 0   0 0 0—1 8 1
Yankees . . . . . . 1 1 0   0 0 0   3 x—5 10 1

E—Dent. DP—Yankees 2. LOB—Dodgers 11, Yankees 7. 2b—Garvey. HR—White (1). SB—North, Piniella.

| | ip | h | r | er | bb | so |
|---|---|---|---|---|---|---|
| Sutton (L, 0-1) | 6 1-3 | 9 | 5 | 5 | 3 | 2 |
| Rautzhan | 2-3 | 1 | 0 | 0 | 0 | 0 |
| Hough | 1 | 0 | 0 | 0 | 0 | 0 |
| Guidry (W, 1-0) | 9 | 8 | 1 | 1 | 7 | 4 |

T—2:27. A—56,447.

**How runs were scored**—One in Yankees first: White hit a home run.

One in Yankees second: Nettles singled. Chambliss walked. Nettles scored on an infield out.

One in Dodgers third: Russell singled scoring North.

Three in Yankees seventh: Dent and Rivers singled. White forced Rivers at second. Munson singled scoring Dent. Jackson singled scoring White. Piniella grounded out scoring Munson.

## Fourth Game

Yankee Stadium, New York, Oct. 14

| Dodgers | ab | r | h | bi | Yankees | ab | r | h | bi |
|---|---|---|---|---|---|---|---|---|---|
| Lopes 2b | 4 | 1 | 0 | 0 | Blair cf | 4 | 1 | 2 | 0 |
| Russell ss | 5 | 0 | 2 | 0 | Rivers ph | 1 | 0 | 0 | 2 |
| Smith rf | 4 | 1 | 1 | 3 | White lf | 3 | 2 | 1 | 0 |
| Garvey 1b | 4 | 0 | 0 | 0 | Munson c | 3 | 1 | 2 | 1 |
| Cey 3b | 4 | 0 | 1 | 0 | Jackson dh | 4 | 0 | 2 | 1 |
| Baker lf | 4 | 0 | 1 | 0 | Piniella rf | 5 | 0 | 1 | 1 |
| Monday dh | 2 | 0 | 1 | 0 | Nettles 3b | 4 | 0 | 0 | 0 |
| North cf | 4 | 0 | 0 | 0 | Chambliss 1b | 4 | 0 | 0 | 0 |
| Yeager c | 3 | 1 | 1 | 0 | Stanley 2b | 3 | 0 | 0 | 0 |
| Davalillo ph | 1 | 0 | 0 | 0 | Spencer ph | 1 | 0 | 0 | 2 |
| | | | | | Doyle 2b | 0 | 0 | 0 | 0 |
| | | | | | Dent ss | 4 | 0 | 1 | 0 |
| Totals | 35 | 3 | 6 | 3 | Totals | 36 | 4 | 9 | 3 |

Los Angeles . . . . 0 0 0   0 3 0   0 0 0—3
New York . . . . . . 0 0 0   0 0 2   0 1 0   1—4

Two out when winning run scored.

E—Russell. DP—New York 1. LOB—Los Angeles 7, New York 8. 2B—Yeager, Munson. HR—Smith (1). SB—Garvey, Munson. S—White.

| | ip | h | r | er | bb | so |
|---|---|---|---|---|---|---|
| John | 7 | 6 | 3 | 2 | 2 | 2 |
| Forster | 1-3 | 1 | 0 | 0 | 0 | 0 |
| Welch (L,0-1) | 2 1-3 | 2 | 1 | 1 | 1 | 3 |
| Figueroa | 5 | 4 | 3 | 3 | 4 | 2 |
| Tidrow | 3 | 2 | 0 | 0 | 0 | 4 |
| Gossage (W, 1-0) | 2 | 0 | 0 | 0 | 0 | 2 |

HBP—Jackson (by Forster). T—3:17. A—56,445.

**How runs were scored**—Three in Dodgers fifth: Yeager doubled. Lopes walked. Smith hit a home run.

Two in Yankees sixth: White singled. Munson walked. Jackson singled scoring White. Munson scored on a throwing error.

One in Yankees eighth: Blair singled. Munson doubled scoring Blair.

One in Yankees tenth: White walked. Jackson singled. Piniella singled scoring White.

## Fifth Game

Yankee Stadium, New York, Oct. 15

| Dodgers | ab | r | h | bi | | Yankees | ab | r | h | bi |
|---|---|---|---|---|---|---|---|---|---|---|
| Lopes 2b . . . | 4 | 2 | 2 | 0 | | Rivers cf . . . | 5 | 2 | 3 | 1 |
| Russell ss . . . | 5 | 0 | 2 | 1 | | Blair cf . . . . | 1 | 1 | 0 | 0 |
| Smith rf. . . . | 4 | 0 | 1 | 1 | | White lf . . . . | 5 | 2 | 2 | 3 |
| Garvey 1b . . | 4 | 0 | 1 | 0 | | Johnston rf. . . | 0 | 0 | 0 | 0 |
| Cey 3b . . . . | 3 | 0 | 1 | 0 | | Munson c . . . | 5 | 1 | 3 | 5 |
| Baker lf . . . . | 4 | 0 | 0 | 0 | | Heath c. . . . | 0 | 0 | 0 | 0 |
| Monday cf . . | 3 | 0 | 0 | 0 | | Jackson dh . . | 3 | 0 | 1 | 0 |
| Lacy dh . . . . | 4 | 0 | 0 | 0 | | Piniella lf . . . | 4 | 0 | 1 | 1 |
| Yeager c . . . | 2 | 0 | 1 | 0 | | Thomasson lf . | 1 | 0 | 0 | 0 |
| Oates c. . . . | 1 | 0 | 1 | 0 | | Nettles 3b . . . | 5 | 0 | 1 | 0 |
| | | | | | | Spencer 1b . . | 4 | 2 | 1 | 0 |
| | | | | | | Doyle 2b . . . | 5 | 2 | 3 | 0 |
| | | | | | | Dent ss . . . . | 4 | 2 | 3 | 1 |
| Totals . . . . | 34 | 2 | 9 | 2 | | Totals . . . . | 42 | 12 | 18 | 11 |

Los Angeles . . . . . . 1 0 1 0 0 0 0 0 0—2
New York . . . . . . . 0 0 4 3 0 0 4 1 x—12

E—Russell, Smith, Garvey. DP—Los Angeles 2, New York 1. LOB—Los Angeles 9, New York 10. 2B—Russell, Munson, Dent. SB—Lopes, Rivers, White, Russell.

| | ip | h | r | er | bb | so |
|---|---|---|---|---|---|---|
| Hooton (L,1-1) . . | 2 1-3 | 5 | 4 | 3 | 2 | 1 |
| Rautzhan . . . . | 1 1-3 | 3 | 3 | 3 | 0 | 0 |
| Hough . . . . . . | 4 1-3 | 10 | 5 | 5 | 2 | 5 |
| Beattie (W,1-0) . | 9 | 9 | 2 | 2 | 4 | 8 |

WP—Hough. PB—Yeager, Oates. T—2:56. A—56,448.

**How runs were scored**—One in Dodgers first: Lopes singled and stole second. Smith singled scoring Lopes.

One in Dodgers third: Lopes singled. Russell doubled scoring Lopes.

Four in Yankees third: Dent walked. Rivers singled. White singled scoring Dent. Munson singled scoring Rivers and White. Piniella singled scoring Munson.

Three in Yankees fourth: Doyle singled. Dent singled. Rivers singled scoring Doyle. Dent scored on an infield out. Munson singled scoring Rivers.

Four in Yankees seventh: Spencer and Doyle singled. Spencer scored on a wild pitch. White singled scoring Doyle. Munson hit a home run.

One in Yankees eighth.

## Sixth Game

Dodger Stadium, Los Angeles, Oct. 17

| Yankees | ab | r | h | bi | | Dodgers | ab | r | h | b |
|---|---|---|---|---|---|---|---|---|---|---|
| Rivers cf . . . | 4 | 0 | 0 | 0 | | Lopes 2b . . . | 4 | 1 | 2 | 2 |
| Blair cf . . . . | 1 | 0 | 0 | 0 | | Russell ss . . . | 3 | 0 | 1 | 0 |
| White lf . . . . | 4 | 1 | 1 | 0 | | Smith rf. . . . | 4 | 0 | 0 | 0 |
| Thomasson lf . | 0 | 0 | 0 | 0 | | Garvey 1b . . | 4 | 0 | 0 | 0 |
| Munson c . . . | 5 | 0 | 0 | 0 | | Cey 3b . . . . | 4 | 0 | 1 | 0 |
| Jackson dh . . | 5 | 1 | 1 | 2 | | Baker lf . . . . | 3 | 0 | 0 | 0 |
| Piniella rf . . . | 4 | 1 | 1 | 0 | | Monday cf . . | 3 | 0 | 0 | 0 |
| Johnston rf . . | 0 | 0 | 0 | 0 | | Ferguson c . . | 3 | 1 | 2 | 0 |
| Nettles 3b . . . | 4 | 1 | 1 | 0 | | Davalillo dh . . | 2 | 0 | 1 | 0 |
| Spencer 1b . . | 3 | 1 | 0 | 0 | | | | | | |
| Doyle 2b . . . | 4 | 2 | 3 | 2 | | | | | | |
| Dent ss . . . . | 4 | 0 | 3 | 3 | | | | | | |
| Totals . . . . | 38 | 7 | 11 | 7 | | Totals . . . . | 30 | 2 | 7 | 2 |

New York . . . . . . . 0 3 0 0 0 2 2 0 0—7
Los Angeles . . . . . . 1 0 1 0 0 0 0 0 0—2

E—Ferguson. DP—New York 2. LOB—New York 6, Los Angeles 3. 2B—Ferguson 2, Doyle, Dent. HR—Lopes (3), Jackson (2). SB—Lopes. S—Davalillo.

| | ip | h | r | er | bb | so |
|---|---|---|---|---|---|---|
| Hunter (W, 1-1) . . | 7 | 6 | 2 | 2 | 1 | 3 |
| Gossage . . . . . | 2 | 1 | 0 | 0 | 0 | 2 |
| Sutton (L, 0-2) . . . | 5 2-3 | 8 | 5 | 5 | 1 | 6 |
| Welch . . . . . . . | 1 1-3 | 2 | 2 | 2 | 1 | 2 |
| Rau . . . . . . . . | 2 | 1 | 0 | 0 | 0 | 3 |

WP—Sutton. T—2:34. A—55,985.

**How runs were scored**—One in Dodgers first: Lopes hit a home run.

Three in Yankees second: Nettles singled. Spencer walked. Doyle doubled scoring Nettles. Dent singled scoring Spencer and Doyle.

One in Dodgers third: Ferguson doubled. Lopes singled scoring Ferguson.

Two in Yankees sixth: Piniella singled and went to second on a wild pitch. Doyle singled scoring Piniella. Dent singled scoring Doyle.

Two in Yankees seventh: White walked. Jackson hit a home run.

## World Series Results, 1903-1978

1903 Boston AL 5, Pittsburgh NL 3
1904 No Series
1905 New York NL 4, Philadelphia AL 1
1906 Chicago AL 4, Chicago NL 2
1907 Chicago NL 4, Detroit AL 0, 1 tie
1908 Chicago NL 4, Detroit AL 1
1909 Pittsburgh NL 4, Detroit AL 3
1910 Philadelphia AL 4, Chicago NL 1
1911 Philadelphia AL 4, New York NL 2
1912 Boston AL 4, New York NL 3, 1 tie
1913 Philadelphia AL 4, New York NL 1
1914 Boston NL 4, Philadelphia AL 0
1915 Boston AL 4, Philadelphia NL 1
1916 Boston AL 4, Brooklyn NL 1
1917 Chicago AL 4, New York NL 2
1918 Boston AL 4, Chicago NL 2
1919 Cincinnati NL 5, Chicago AL 3
1920 Cleveland AL 5, Brooklyn NL 2
1921 New York NL 5, New York AL 3
1922 New York NL 4, New York AL 0, 1 tie
1923 New York AL 4, New York NL 2
1924 Washington AL 4, New York NL 3
1925 Pittsburgh NL 4, Washington AL 3
1926 St. Louis NL 4, New York AL 3
1927 New York AL 4, Pittsburgh NL 0
1928 New York AL 4, St. Louis NL 0

1929 Philadelphia AL 4, Chicago NL 1
1930 Philadelphia AL 4, St. Louis NL 2
1931 St. Louis NL 4, Philadelphia AL 3
1932 New York AL 4, Chicago NL 0
1933 New York NL 4, Washington AL 1
1934 St. Louis NL 4, Detroit AL 3
1935 Detroit AL 4, Chicago NL 2
1936 New York AL 4, New York NL 2
1937 New York AL 4, New York NL 1
1938 New York AL 4, Chicago NL 0
1939 New York AL 4, Cincinnati NL 0
1940 Cincinnati NL 4, Detroit AL 3
1941 New York AL 4, Brooklyn NL 1
1942 St. Louis NL 4, New York AL 1
1943 New York AL 4, St. Louis NL 1
1944 St. Louis NL 4, St. Louis AL 2
1945 Detroit AL 4, Chicago NL 3
1946 St. Louis NL 4, Boston AL 3
1947 New York AL 4, Brooklyn NL 3
1948 Cleveland AL 4, Boston NL 2
1949 New York AL 4, Brooklyn NL 1
1950 New York AL 4, Philadelphia NL 0
1951 New York AL 4, New York NL 2
1952 New York AL 4, Brooklyn NL 3
1953 New York AL 4, Brooklyn NL 2

1954 New York NL 4, Cleveland AL 0
1955 Brooklyn NL 4, New York AL 3
1956 New York AL 4, Brooklyn NL 3
1957 Milwaukee NL 4, New York AL 3
1958 New York AL 4, Milwaukee NL 3
1959 Los Angeles NL 4, Chicago AL 2
1960 Pittsburgh NL 4, New York AL 3
1961 New York AL 4, Cincinnati NL 1
1962 New York AL 4, San Francisco NL 3
1963 Los Angeles NL 4, New York AL 0
1964 St. Louis NL 4, New York AL 3
1965 Los Angeles NL 4, Minnesota AL 3
1966 Baltimore AL 4, Los Angeles NL 0
1967 St. Louis NL 4, Boston AL 3
1968 Detroit AL 4, St. Louis NL 3
1969 New York NL 4, Baltimore AL 1
1970 Baltimore AL 4, Cincinnati NL 1
1971 Pittsburgh NL 4, Baltimore AL 3
1972 Oakland AL 4, Cincinnati NL 3
1973 Oakland AL 4, New York NL 3
1974 Oakland AL 4, Los Angeles NL 1
1975 Cincinnati NL 4, Boston AL 3
1976 Cincinnati NL 4, New York AL 0
1977 New York AL 4, Los Angeles NL 2
1978 New York AL 4, Los Angeles NL 2

## Amateur Softball Association Champions in 1978

**Men's major fast pitch**—Billard Barbell, Reading, Pa.
**Women's major fast pitch**—Raybestos Brakettes, Stratford, Conn.
**Men's major slow pitch**—Campbell's Carpet, Concord, Cal.
**Women's major slow pitch**—Bob Hoffman Dots, Miami, Fla.
**Industrial major slow pitch**—G.E.-Waco, Louisville, Ky.
**Men's class A fast pitch**—S & K Rigging, Arcola, Ill.
**Women's class A fast pitch**—Hank's Painting, Binghamton, N.Y.

**Men's class A slow pitch**—Port City Ford, Houston, Tex.
**Women's class A slow pitch**—Stillwater A's, Stillwater, Okla.
**Modified fast pitch**—Marianao's, Miami, Fla.
**Church slow pitch**—Grace Methodist Blacks, Oklahoma City, Okla.
**Industrial class A slow pitch**—Peabody Coal Co., Rockport, Ky.

## Cy Young Award Winners

| Year | Player, club | Year | Player, club | Year | Player, club |
|---|---|---|---|---|---|
| 1956 | Don Newcombe, Dodgers | 1968 | (NL) Bob Gibson, Cardinals | 1974 | (NL) Mike Marshall, Dodgers |
| 1957 | Warren Spahn, Braves | | (AL) Dennis McLain, Tigers | | (AL) Jim (Catfish) Hunter, A's |
| 1958 | Bob Turley, Yankees | 1969 | (NL) Tom Seaver, Mets | 1975 | (NL) Tom Seaver, Mets |
| 1959 | Early Wynn, White Sox | | (AL) (tie) Dennis McLain, Tigers | | (AL) Jim Palmer, Orioles |
| 1960 | Vernon Law, Pirates | | Mike Cuellar, Orioles | 1976 | (NL) Randy Jones, Padres |
| 1961 | Whitey Ford, Yankees | 1970 | (NL) Bob Gibson, Cardinals | | (AL) Jim Palmer, Orioles |
| 1962 | Don Drysdale, Dodgers | | (AL) Jim Perry, Twins | 1977 | (NL) Steve Carlton, Phillies |
| 1963 | Sandy Koufax, Dodgers | 1971 | (NL) Ferguson Jenkins, Cubs | | (AL) Sparky Lyle, Yankees |
| 1964 | Dean Chance, Angels | | (AL) Vida Blue, A's | 1978 | (NL) Gaylord Perry, Padres |
| 1965 | Sandy Koufax, Dodgers | 1972 | (NL) Steve Carlton, Phillies | | (AL) Ron Guidry, Yankees |
| 1966 | Sandy Koufax, Dodgers | | (AL) Gaylord Perry, Indians | | |
| 1967 | (NL) Mike McCormick, Giants | 1973 | (NL) Tom Seaver, Mets | | |
| | (AL) Jim Lonborg, Red Sox | | (AL) Jim Palmer, Orioles | | |

## Selected Major League Records

### Batting

**Highest batting average lifetime**—.367, Ty Cobb.
**Highest batting average, season**—.424, Rogers Hornsby, St. Louis, 1924.
**Most years led league in batting**—Ty Cobb, AL.
**Most years batting .300 or more**—Ty Cobb.
**Most hits, lifetime**—4,191, Ty Cobb.
**Most hits, season**—257, George Sisler, St. Louis, (AL), 1920.
**Most consecutive games batted safely**—56, Joe DiMaggio, New York (AL), 1941.
**Most runs, lifetime**—2,244, Ty Cobb.
**Most runs, season**—177, Babe Ruth, New York (AL), 1921.
**Most runs batted in, lifetime**—2,297, Henry Aaron.
**Most runs batted in, season**—190, Hack Wilson, Chicago (NL), 1930.
**Highest slugging percentage, lifetime**—.690, Babe Ruth.
**Most home runs, lifetime**—755, Henry Aaron.
**Most home runs, season**—61, Roger Maris, New York (AL), 1961.
**Most years home run leader**—12, Babe Ruth.
**Most grand slam home runs, lifetime**—23, Lou Gehrig.
**Most walks, season**—170, Babe Ruth, New York (AL), 1923.
**Most pinch hits, lifetime**—145, Smokey Burgess.

**Most stolen bases, lifetime**—Lou Brock.
**Most stolen bases, season**—118, Lou Brock, St. Louis (NL), 1974.

### Pitching

**Most games won, lifetime**—511, Cy Young.
**Most games won, season**—41, Jack Chesbro, New York (AL), 1904.
**Most consecutive games won, season**—19, Rube Marquard, New York (NL), 1912.
**Most shutouts, lifetime**—113, Walter Johnson.
**Most shutouts, season**—16, Grover Cleveland Alexander, Philadelphia (NL), 1916.
**Most consecutive shutout innings, seasons**—58, Don Drysdale, Los Angeles (NL), 1968.
**Lowest earned run average, season**—1.01, Hubert Leonard, Boston (AL), 1914.
**Most consecutive years lowest earned run average**—5, Sandy Koufax.
**Most strikeouts, lifetime**—3,508, Walter Johnson.
**Most strikeouts, season**—383, Nolan Ryan, California (AL), 1973.
**Most strikeouts in 9-inning game**—9, Steve Carlton, St. Louis (NL), 1969; Tom Seaver, New York (NL), 1970; Nolan Ryan, California (AL), 1977.

## College World Series

The University of Southern California won the 1978 College World Series by defeating Arizona State 10-3 at Omaha, Neb.

## New York City Marathon in 1978

Bill Rodgers of Newington, Conn. won the New York City Marathon for the third consecutive year by running the 26-mile, 385-yard course in 2 hours 12 minutes 12 seconds on Oct. 22, 1978. Grete Waitz of Norway set a women's record of 2 hours 32 minutes 29.8 seconds.

## Ten Most Dramatic Sports Events, Nov. 1977—Oct. 1978

### Selected by The World Almanac sports staff

—Pete Rose of the Cincinnati Reds hitting safely in 44 consecutive games to tie the National League record set by Willie Keeler in 1897.

—Affirmed winning a dramatic stretch run by a head against his arch rival, Alydar, in the Belmont Stakes. He was the 11th horse to win racing's triple crown.

—Leon Spinks winning the heavyweight title by upsetting Muhammad Ali. Ali later defeated Spinks to regain the title.

—Argentina defeating the Netherlands 3-1 in overtime to win the World Cup, emblematic of world soccer supremacy.

—Notre Dame defeating No. 1 ranked Texas 38-10 in the Cotton Bowl. The victory made the Fighting Irish the top ranked team in the final polls.

—Bucky Dent of the N.Y. Yankees hitting a 3-run home run in the 7th inning to wipe out a 2-0 Red Sox lead in the one-game playoff for the American League East championship. The Yankees won the game 5-4.

—Gordie Howe of the New England Whalers scoring the 1,000th goal of his pro hockey career. The 50-year-old former National Hockey League great had 2 of his sons as teammates.

—Walter Payton of the Chicago Bears rushing for 275 yards in a game against the Minnesota Vikings to break the NFL record held by O.J. Simpson.

—Pete Rose becoming the 13th player in history to get 3,000 major league hits.

—Nancy Lopez winning 5 consecutive golf tournaments, a feat unprecedented in the LPGA's 28-year history.

# College Basketball

## NCAA Division I Champions

| Year | Champion | Year | Champion | Year | Champion | Year | Champion |
|------|----------|------|----------|------|----------|------|----------|
| 1939 | Oregon | 1949 | Kentucky | 1959 | California | 1969 | UCLA |
| 1940 | Indiana | 1950 | CCNY | 1960 | Ohio State | 1970 | UCLA |
| 1941 | Wisconsin | 1951 | Kentucky | 1961 | Cincinnati | 1971 | UCLA |
| 1942 | Stanford | 1952 | Kansas | 1962 | Cincinnati | 1972 | UCLA |
| 1943 | Wyoming | 1953 | Indiana | 1963 | Loyola (Chi.) | 1973 | UCLA |
| 1944 | Utah | 1954 | La Salle | 1964 | UCLA | 1974 | No. Carolina State |
| 1945 | Oklahoma A&M | 1955 | San Francisco | 1965 | UCLA | 1975 | UCLA |
| 1946 | Oklahoma A&M | 1956 | San Francisco | 1966 | Texas Western | 1976 | Indiana |
| 1947 | Holy Cross | 1957 | North Carolina | 1967 | UCLA | 1977 | Marquette |
| 1948 | Kentucky | 1958 | Kentucky | 1968 | UCLA | 1978 | Kentucky |

## National Invitation Tournament Champions

| Year | Champion | Year | Champion | Year | Champion | Year | Champion |
|------|----------|------|----------|------|----------|------|----------|
| 1938 | Temple | 1949 | San Francisco | 1959 | St. John's | 1969 | Temple |
| 1939 | Long Island Univ. | 1950 | CCNY | 1960 | Bradley | 1970 | Marquette |
| 1940 | Colorado | 1951 | Brigham Young | 1961 | Providence | 1971 | North Carolina |
| 1941 | Long Island Univ. | 1952 | LaSalle | 1962 | Dayton | 1972 | Maryland |
| 1942 | West Virginia | 1953 | Seton Hall | 1963 | Providence | 1973 | Virginia Tech |
| 1943 | St. John's | 1954 | Holy Cross | 1964 | Bradley | 1974 | Purdue |
| 1944 | St. John's | 1955 | Duquesne | 1965 | St. John's | 1975 | Princeton |
| 1945 | De Paul | 1956 | Louisville | 1966 | Brigham Young | 1976 | Kentucky |
| 1946 | Kentucky | 1957 | Bradley | 1967 | Southern Illinois | 1977 | St. Bonaventure |
| 1947 | Utah | 1958 | Xavier (Ohio) | 1968 | Dayton | 1978 | Texas |
| 1948 | St. Louis | | | | | | |

## NCAA Division II Champions

| Year | Champion | Year | Champion | Year | Champion | Year | Champion |
|------|----------|------|----------|------|----------|------|----------|
| 1959 | Evansville | 1964 | Evansville | 1969 | Kentucky Wesleyan | 1974 | Morgan State |
| 1960 | Evansville | 1965 | Evansville | 1970 | Philadelphia Textile | 1975 | Old Dominion |
| 1961 | Wittenberg | 1966 | Kentucky Wesleyan | 1971 | Evansville | 1976 | Puget Sound |
| 1962 | Mt. St. Mary's | 1967 | Winston-Salem | 1972 | Roanoke | 1977 | Tennessee-Chattanooga |
| 1963 | South Dakota St. | 1968 | Kentucky Wesleyan | 1973 | Kentucky Wesleyan | 1978 | Cheyney State |

## Division 1 Records

(Restricted to games between 4-year colleges.)

### Season Scoring Averages

| Player, team | Year | Games | FG | FT | Pts | Avg |
|--------------|------|-------|----|----|-----|-----|
| Pete Maravich, LSU | 1970 | 31 | 522 | 337 | 1,381 | 44.5 |
| Pete Maravich, LSU | 1969 | 26 | 433 | 282 | 1,148 | 44.2 |
| Pete Maravich, LSU | 1968 | 26 | 432 | 274 | 1,138 | 43.8 |
| Frank Selvy, Furman | 1954 | 29 | 427 | 355 | 1,209 | 41.7 |
| Johnny Neumann, Mississippi | 1971 | 23 | 366 | 191 | 923 | 40.1 |
| Billy McGill, Utah | 1962 | 26 | 394 | 221 | 1,009 | 38.8 |
| Freeman Williams, Portland State | 1977 | 26 | 417 | 176 | 1,010 | 38.8 |
| Calvin Murphy, Niagara | 1968 | 24 | 337 | 242 | 916 | 38.2 |
| Austin Carr, Notre Dame | 1970 | 29 | 444 | 218 | 1,106 | 38.1 |
| Austin Carr, Notre Dame | 1971 | 29 | 430 | 241 | 1,101 | 38.0 |
| Rick Barry, Miami (Fla.) | 1965 | 26 | 340 | 293 | 973 | 37.4 |

# National AAU Wrestling Championships in 1978

| Freestyle | Greco Roman |
|-----------|-------------|
| **105.5 lbs.**—Bob Weaver, New York AC. | **105.5 lbs.**—Wilfredo Leiva, U.S. Marines. |
| **114.5 lbs.**—Jim Haines, Wisconsin WC. | **114.5 lbs.**—James Howard, U.S. Marines. |
| **125.5 lbs.**—Tomiyama Hideaki, Japan. | **125.5 lbs.**—Bruce Thompson, Minnesota WC. |
| **136.5 lbs.**—Tim Cysewski, Hawkeye WC. | **136.5 lbs.**—Abdurrahim Kuzu, Nebraska Olympic Club. |
| **149.5 lbs.**—Jim Humphrey, Oklahoma Underdogs. | **149.5 lbs.**—Abdul Raheem-Ali, Minnesota WC. |
| **163 lbs.**—Chuck Yagla, Hawkeye WC. | **163 lbs.**—John Matthews, Michigan WC. |
| **180.5 lbs.**—John Peterson, Athletes-In-Action. | **180.5 lbs.**—Dan Chandler, Minnesota WC. |
| **198 lbs.**—Ben Peterson, Wisconsin WC. | **198 lbs.**—Frank Anderson, Sweden. |
| **220 lbs.**—Larry Bielenberg, Sunkist Kids. | **220 lbs.**—Brad Rheingans, Minnesota WC. |
| **Heavyweight**—Greg Wojciechowski, Toledo WC. | **Unlimited**—Greg Wojciechowski, Toledo WC. |
| **Team champion**—New York Athletic Club. | **Team champion**—Minnesota Wrestling Club. |

## NCAA Wrestling Champions

| Year | Champion | Year | Champion | Year | Champion | Year | Champion | Year | Champion |
|------|----------|------|----------|------|----------|------|----------|------|----------|
| 1960 | Oklahoma | 1964 | Oklahoma State | 1968 | Oklahoma State | 1972 | Iowa State | 1976 | Iowa |
| 1961 | Oklahoma State | 1965 | Iowa State | 1969 | Iowa State | 1973 | Iowa State | 1977 | Iowa State |
| 1962 | Oklahoma State | 1966 | Oklahoma State | 1970 | Iowa State | 1974 | Iowa State | 1978 | Iowa |
| 1963 | Oklahoma | 1967 | Michigan State | 1971 | Oklahoma State | 1975 | Iowa | | |

# Speed Skating in 1978

Eric Heiden, a student at the Univ. of Wisconsin won his sixth consecutive world title at the world speed skating championships at Gothenburg, Sweden on Feb. 26, 1978.

# Tennis
## USTA National Champions
### Men's Singles

| Year | Champion | Final opponent | Year | Champion | Final opponent |
|------|----------|----------------|------|----------|----------------|
| 1920 | Bill Tilden | William Johnston | 1950 | Arthur Larsen | Herbert Flam |
| 1921 | Bill Tilden | Wallace Johnston | 1951 | Frank Sedgman | E. Victor Seixas Jr. |
| 1922 | Bill Tilden | William Johnston | 1952 | Frank Sedgman | Gardnar Mulloy |
| 1923 | Bill Tilden | William Johnston | 1953 | Tony Trabert | E. Victor Seixas Jr. |
| 1924 | Bill Tilden | William Johnston | 1954 | E. Victor Seixas Jr. | Rex Hartwig |
| 1925 | Bill Tilden | William Johnston | 1955 | Tony Trabert | Ken Rosewall |
| 1926 | Rene Lacoste | Jean Borotra | 1956 | Ken Rosewall | Lewis Hoad |
| 1927 | Rene Lacoste | Bill Tilden | 1957 | Malcolm Anderson | Ashley Cooper |
| 1928 | Henri Cochet | Francis Hunter | 1958 | Ashley Cooper | Malcolm Anderson |
| 1929 | Bill Tilden | Francis Hunter | 1959 | Neale A. Fraser | Alejandro Olmedo |
| 1930 | John Doeg | Francis Shields | 1960 | Neale A. Fraser | Rod Laver |
| 1931 | H. Ellsworth Vines | George Lott | 1961 | Roy Emerson | Rod Laver |
| 1932 | H. Ellsworth Vines | Henri Cochet | 1962 | Rod Laver | Roy Emerson |
| 1933 | Fred Perry | John Crawford | 1963 | Rafael Osuna | F. A. Froehling 3d |
| 1934 | Fred Perry | Wilmer Allison | 1964 | Roy Emerson | Fred Stolle |
| 1935 | Wilmer Allison | Sidney Wood | 1965 | Manuel Santana | Cliff Drysdale |
| 1936 | Fred Perry | Don Budge | 1966 | Fred Stolle | John Newcombe |
| 1937 | Don Budge | Baron G. von Cramm | 1967 | John Newcombe | Clark Graebner |
| 1938 | Don Budge | C. Gene Mako | 1968 | Arthur Ashe | Tom Okker |
| 1939 | Robert Riggs | S. Welby Van Horn | 1969 | Rod Laver | Tony Roche |
| 1940 | Don McNeill | Robert Riggs | 1970 | Ken Rosewall | Tony Roche |
| 1941 | Robert Riggs | F. L. Kovacs | 1971 | Stan Smith | Jan Kodes |
| 1942 | F. R. Schroeder Jr. | Frank Parker | 1972 | Ilie Nastase | Arthur Ashe |
| 1943 | Joseph Hunt | Jack Kramer | 1973 | John Newcombe | Jan Kodes |
| 1944 | Frank Parker | William Talbert | 1974 | Jimmy Connors | Ken Rosewall |
| 1945 | Frank Parker | William Talbert | 1975 | Manuel Orantes | Jimmy Connors |
| 1946 | Jack Kramer | Thomas Brown Jr. | 1976 | Jimmy Connors | Bjorn Borg |
| 1947 | Jack Kramer | Frank Parker | 1977 | Guillermo Vilas | Jimmy Connors |
| 1948 | Pancho Gonzales | Eric Sturgess | 1978 | Jimmy Connors | Bjorn Borg |
| 1949 | Pancho Gonzales | F. R. Schroeder Jr. | | | |

### Men's Doubles

| Year | Champions | Year | Champions |
|------|-----------|------|-----------|
| 1921 | Bill Tilden—Vincent Richards | 1950 | John Bromwich—Frank Sedgman |
| 1922 | Bill Tilden—Vincent Richards | 1951 | Frank Sedgman—Kenneth McGregor |
| 1923 | Bill Tilden—Brian Norton | 1952 | Mervyn Rose—E. Victor Seixas Jr. |
| 1924 | Howard Kinsey—Robert Kinsey | 1953 | Rex Hartwig—Mervyn Rose |
| 1925 | R. Norris Williams—Vincent Richards | 1954 | E. Victor Seixas Jr.—Tony Trabert |
| 1926 | R. Norris Williams—Vincent Richards | 1955 | Kosei Kamo—Atsushi Miyagi |
| 1927 | Bill Tilden—Francis Hunter | 1956 | Lewis Hoad—Ken Rosewall |
| 1928 | George Lott—John Hennessey | 1957 | Ashley Cooper—Neale Fraser |
| 1929 | George Lott—John Doeg | 1958 | Hamilton Richardson—Alejandro Olmedo |
| 1930 | George Lott—John Doeg | 1959 | Neale A. Fraser—Roy Emerson |
| 1931 | Wilmer Allison—John Van Ryn | 1960 | Neale A. Fraser—Roy Emerson |
| 1932 | H. Ellsworth Vines—Keith Gledhill | 1961 | Dennis Ralston—Chuck McKinley |
| 1933 | George Lott—Lester Stoefen | 1962 | Rafael Osuna—Antonio Palafox |
| 1934 | George Lott—Lester Stoefen | 1963 | Dennis Ralston—Chuck McKinley |
| 1935 | Wilmer Allison—John Van Ryn | 1964 | Dennis Ralston—Chuck McKinley |
| 1936 | Don Budge—C. Gene Mako | 1965 | Roy Emerson—Fred Stolle |
| 1937 | Baron G. von Cramm—Henner Henkel | 1966 | Roy Emerson—Fred Stolle |
| 1938 | Don Budge—C. Gene Mako | 1967 | John Newcombe—Tony Roche |
| 1939 | Adrian Quist—John Bromwich | 1968 | Robert Lutz—Stan Smith |
| 1940 | Jack Kramer—Frederick Schroeder Jr. | 1969 | Fred Stolle—Ken Rosewall |
| 1941 | Jack Kramer—Frederick Schroeder Jr. | 1970 | Pierre Barthes—Nicki Pilic |
| 1942 | Gardnar Mulloy—William Talbert | 1971 | John Newcombe—Roger Taylor |
| 1943 | Jack Kramer—Frank Parker | 1972 | Cliff Drysdale—Roger Taylor |
| 1944 | Don McNeill—Robert Falkenburg | 1973 | John Newcombe—Owen Davidson |
| 1945 | Gardnar Mulloy—William Talbert | 1974 | Bob Lutz—Stan Smith |
| 1946 | Gardnar Mulloy—William Talbert | 1975 | Jimmy Connors—Ilie Nastase |
| 1947 | Jack Kramer—Frederick Schroeder Jr. | 1976 | Marty Riessen—Tom Okker |
| 1948 | Gardnar Mulloy—William Talbert | 1977 | Bob Hewitt—Frew McMillan |
| 1949 | John Bromwich—William Sidwell | 1978 | Stan Smith—Bob Lutz |

### Mixed Doubles

| Year | Champions | Year | Champions |
|------|-----------|------|-----------|
| 1945 | Margaret Osborne—William Talbert | 1962 | Margaret Smith—Fred Stolle |
| 1946 | Margaret Osborne—William Talbert | 1963 | Margaret Smith—Kenneth Fletcher |
| 1947 | A. Louise Brough—John Bromwich | 1964 | Margaret Smith—John Newcombe |
| 1948 | A. Louise Brough—Thomas Brown Jr. | 1965 | Margaret Smith—Fred Stolle |
| 1949 | A. Louise Brough—Eric Sturgess | 1966 | Donna Floyd Fales—Owen Davidson |
| 1950 | Mrs. M. O. duPont—Kenneth MacGregor | 1967 | Billie Jean King—Owen Davidson |
| 1951 | Doris Hart—Frank Sedgman | 1968 | Mary Ann Eisel—Peter Curtis |
| 1952 | Doris Hart—Frank Sedgman | 1969 | Margaret S. Court—Marty Riessen |
| 1953 | Doris Hart—E. Victor Seixas Jr. | 1970 | Margaret S. Court—Marty Riessen |
| 1954 | Doris Hart—E. Victor Seixas Jr. | 1971 | Billie Jean King—Owen Davidson |
| 1955 | Doris Hart—E. Victor Seixas Jr. | 1972 | Margaret S. Court—Marty Riessen |
| 1956 | Mrs. M. O. duPont—Ken Rosewall | 1973 | Billie Jean King—Owen Davidson |
| 1957 | Althea Gibson—Kurt Nielsen | 1974 | Pam Teeguarden—Geoff Masters |
| 1958 | Mrs. M. O. duPont—Neale Fraser | 1975 | Rosemary Casals—Dick Stockton |
| 1959 | Mrs. M. O. duPont—Neale Fraser | 1976 | Billie Jean King—Phil Dent |
| 1960 | Mrs. M. O. duPont—Neale Fraser | 1977 | Betty Stove—Frew McMillan |
| 1961 | Margaret Smith—Robert Mark | 1978 | Betty Stove—Frew McMillan |

## Womens Singles

| Year | Champion | Year | Champion | Year | Champion | Year | Champion |
|------|----------|------|----------|------|----------|------|----------|
| 1935 | Helen Jacobs | 1946 | Pauline Betz | 1957 | Althea Gibson | 1968 | Virginia Wade |
| 1936 | Alice Marble | 1947 | A. Louise Brough | 1958 | Althea Gibson | 1969 | Margaret Smith Court |
| 1937 | Anita Lizana | 1948 | Mrs. Margaret O. du Pont | 1959 | Maria Bueno | 1970 | Margaret Smith Court |
| 1938 | Alice Marble | 1949 | Mrs. Margaret O. du Pont | 1960 | Darlene Hard | 1971 | Billie Jean King |
| 1939 | Alice Marble | 1950 | Mrs. Margaret O. du Pont | 1961 | Darlene Hard | 1972 | Billie Jean King |
| 1940 | Alice Marble | 1951 | Maureen Connolly | 1962 | Margaret Smith | 1973 | Margaret Smith Court |
| 1941 | Mrs. Sarah P. Cooke | 1952 | Maureen Connolly | 1963 | Maria Bueno | 1974 | Billie Jean King |
| 1942 | Pauline Betz | 1953 | Maureen Connolly | 1964 | Maria Bueno | 1975 | Chris Evert |
| 1943 | Pauline Betz | 1954 | Doris Hart | 1965 | Margaret Smith | 1976 | Chris Evert |
| 1944 | Pauline Betz | 1955 | Doris Hart | 1966 | Maria Bueno | 1977 | Chris Evert |
| 1945 | Sarah P. Cooke | 1956 | Shirley J. Fry | 1967 | Billie Jean King | 1978 | Chris Evert |

## Women's Doubles

| Year | Champions | Year | Champions |
|------|-----------|------|-----------|
| 1935 | Helen Jacobs—Mrs. Sarah P. Fabyan | 1957 | A. Louise Brough—Mrs. M. O. du Pont |
| 1936 | Mrs. M. G. Van Ryn—Carolin Babcock | 1958 | Darlene Hard—Jeanne Arth |
| 1937 | Mrs. Sarah P. Fabyan—Alice Marble | 1959 | Darlene Hard—Jeanne Arth |
| 1938 | Alice Marble—Mrs. Sarah P. Fabyan | 1960 | Darlene Hard—Maria Bueno |
| 1939 | Alice Marble—Mrs. Sarah P. Fabyan | 1961 | Darlene Hard—Lesley Turner |
| 1940 | Alice Marble—Mrs. Sarah P. Fabyan | 1962 | Maria Bueno—Darlene Hard |
| 1941 | Mrs. S. P. Cooke—Margaret Osborne | 1963 | Margaret Smith—Robyn Ebbern |
| 1942 | A. Louise Brough—Margaret Osborne | 1964 | Billie Jean Moffit—Karen Susman |
| 1943 | A. Louise Brough—Margaret Osborne | 1965 | Carole C. Graebner—Nancy Richey |
| 1944 | A. Louise Brough—Margaret Osborne | 1966 | Maria Bueno—Nancy Richey |
| 1945 | A. Louise Brough—Margaret Osborne | 1967 | Rosemary Casals—Billie Jean King |
| 1946 | A. Louise Brough—Margaret Osborne | 1968 | Maria Bueno—Margaret S. Court |
| 1947 | A. Louise Brough—Margaret Osborne | 1969 | Francoise Durr—Darlene Hard |
| 1948 | A. Louise Brough—Mrs. M. O. du Pont | 1970 | M. S. Court—Judy Tegart Dalton |
| 1949 | A. Louise Brough—Mrs. M. O. du Pont | 1971 | Rosemary Casals—Judy Tegart Dalton |
| 1950 | A. Louise Brough—Mrs. M. O. du Pont | 1972 | Francoise Durr—Betty Stove |
| 1951 | Doris Hart—Shirley Fry | 1973 | Margaret S. Court—Virginia Wade |
| 1952 | Doris Hart—Shirley Fry | 1974 | Billie Jean King—Rosemary Casals |
| 1953 | Doris Hart—Shirley Fry | 1975 | Margaret Court—Virginia Wade |
| 1954 | Doris Hart—Shirley Fry | 1976 | Linky Boshoff—Ilana Kloss |
| 1955 | A. Louise Brough—Mrs. M. O. du Pont | 1977 | Betty Stove—Martina Navratilova |
| 1956 | A. Louise Brough—Mrs. M. O. du Pont | 1978 | Martina Navratilova—Billie Jean King |

## British Champions, Wimbledon

### Inaugurated 1877

| Year | Men's singles | Women's singles | Year | Men's singles | Women's singles |
|------|---------------|-----------------|------|---------------|-----------------|
| 1947 | Jack Kramer | Margaret Osborne | 1963 | Chuck McKinley | Margaret Smith |
| 1948 | Bob Falkenburg | A. Louise Brough | 1964 | Roy Emerson | Maria Bueno |
| 1949 | Fred R. Schroeder | A. Louise Brough | 1965 | Roy Emerson | Margaret Smith |
| 1950 | Budge Patty | A. Louise Brough | 1966 | Manuel Santana | Billie Jean King |
| 1951 | Dick Savitt | Doris Hart | 1967 | John Newcombe | Billie Jean King |
| 1952 | Frank Sedgman | Maureen Connolly | 1968 | Rod Laver | Billie Jean King |
| 1953 | Victor Seixas | Maureen Connolly | 1969 | Rod Laver | Ann Jones |
| 1954 | Jaroslav Drobny | Maureen Connolly | 1970 | John Newcombe | Margaret S. Court |
| 1955 | Tony Trabert | A. Louise Brough | 1971 | John Newcombe | Evonne Goolagong |
| 1956 | Lewis Hoad | Shirley Fry | 1972 | Stan Smith | Billie Jean King |
| 1957 | Lewis Hoad | Althea Gibson | 1973 | Jan Kodes | Billie Jean King |
| 1958 | Ashley Cooper | Althea Gibson | 1974 | Jimmy Connors | Chris Evert |
| 1959 | Alex Olmedo | Maria Bueno | 1975 | Arthur Ashe | Billie Jean King |
| 1960 | Neale Fraser | Maria Bueno | 1976 | Bjorn Borg | Chris Evert |
| 1961 | Rod Laver | Angela Mortimer | 1977 | Bjorn Borg | Virginia Wade |
| 1962 | Rod Laver | Karen Hantze Susman | 1978 | Bjorn Borg | Martina Navratilova |

## Men's Indoor Champions

| Year | Singles | Doubles | Year | Singles | Doubles |
|------|---------|---------|------|---------|---------|
| 1967 | Charles Pasarell | Arthur Ashe—Charles Pasarell | 1973 | Jimmy Connors | Juan Gisbert—Jurgen Fassbender |
| 1968 | Cliff Richey | Thomas Koch—Tom Okker | 1974 | Jimmy Connors | Jimmy Connors—Frew McMillan |
| 1969 | Stan Smith | Stan Smith—Robert Lutz | 1975 | Jimmy Connors | Jimmy Connors—Ilie Nastase |
| 1970 | Stan Smith | Stan Smith—Arthur Ashe | 1976 | Ilie Nastase | Sherwood Stewart—Fred McNair |
| 1971 | Clark Graebner | Juan Gisbert—Manuel Orantes | 1977 | Bjorn Borg | Sherwood Stewart—Fred McNair |
| 1972 | Stan Smith | Andres Gimano—Manuel Orantes | 1978 | Jimmy Connors | Brian Gottfried—Raul Ramirez |

## Women's Indoor Champions

| Year | Singles | Doubles | Year | Singles | Doubles |
|------|---------|---------|------|---------|---------|
| 1963 | Carol Hanks | Carol Hanks—Mary Ann Eisel | 1970 | Mary Ann E. Curtis | Peaches Bartkowicz—Nancy Richey |
| 1964 | Mary Ann Eisel | Mary Ann Eisel—Katherine Hubbell | | | |
| 1965 | Nancy Richey | Carol Hanks Aucamp—Mary Ann Eisel | 1971 | Billie Jean King | Billie Jean King—Rosemary Casals |
| | | | 1972 | Virginia Wade | Rosemary Casals—Virginia Wade |
| 1966 | Billie Jean King | Billie Jean King—Rosemary Casals | 1973 | Evonne Goolagong | Olga Morozova—Marina Kroskina |
| 1967 | Billie Jean King | Carol Hanks Aucamp—Mary Ann Eisel | 1974 | Billie Jean King | none |
| | | | 1975 | Martina Navratilova | Billie Jean King—Rosemary Casals |
| 1968 | Billie Jean King | Billie Jean King—Rosemary Casals | 1976 | Virginia Wade | Francoise Durr—Rosemary Casals |
| 1969 | Mary Ann E. Curtis | Mary Ann Eisel—Valerie Ziegenfuss | 1977 | Chris Evert | Martina Navratilova—Betty Stove |
| | | | 1978 | Chris Evert | Kerry Reid—Wendy Turnbull |

## WCT-World Series of Tennis in 1978

| Dates | Event - city | Singles winner | Doubles winners |
|---|---|---|---|
| Jan. 9-15 | Birmingham International Indoor Tennis Tournament, Birmingham, Ala. | Bjorn Borg | Vitas Gerulaitis-Sandy Mayer |
| Jan. 23-29 | INA-U.S. Pro Indoor Championships, Philadelphia, Pa. | Jimmy Connors | Bob Hewitt-Frew McMillan |
| Jan. 30-Feb. 5 | United Virginia Bank Tennis Classic, Richmond, Va. | Vitas Gerulaitis | Bob Hewitt-Frew McMillan |
| Feb. 6-12 | St. Louis Tennis Classic, St. Louis, Mo. | Sandy Mayer | Bob Hewitt-Frew McMillan |
| Mar. 27-Apr. 2 | The Ramazzotti Tennis Cup, Milan, Italy | Bjorn Borg | Jose Higueras-Victor Pecci |
| Apr. 3-9 | ABN Wereldtennis Toernooi, Rotterdam, Netherlands | Jimmy Connors | Fred McNair-Raul Ramirez |
| Apr. 10-16 | Internationaux de Tennis de Monte Carlo, Monte Carlo, Monaco | Raul Ramirez | Peter Fleming-Tomas Smid |
| Apr. 17-23 | River Oaks/Houston National Bank Tennis Tournament, Houston, Tex. | Brian Gottfried | Wojtek Fibak-Tom Okker |

### WCT-Final Championship Summaries

**Singles Quarterfinals**
Borg def. Stockton 4-6, 6-2, 6-1, 6-0.
Gerulaitis def. Ramirez 6-1, 2-6, 6-2, 6-1.
Dibbs def. Nastase 6-3, 6-3, 6-0.
Barazzutti def. Gottfried 6-4, 2-6, 1-6, 6-1, 6-3.
**Semifinals**
Gerulaitis def. Borg (by default).
Dibbs def. Barazzutti 6-2, 7-6, 6-4.
**Third Place**
Barazzutti over Borg (by default).
**WCT Final**
Gerulaitis def. Dibbs 6-3, 6-2, 6-1.
**Group 1—Doubles**
Higueras-Pecci def. Barazzutti-Zugarelli 5-7, 6-1, 6-3.

Fibak-Okker def. Higueras-Pecci 6-1, 6-1.
Nastase-Fillol def. Barazzutti-Zugarelli 6-3, 6-3.
Fibak-Okker def. Nastase-Fillol 6-3, 6-4.
Nastase-Fillol def. Higueras-Pecci 6-3, 6-2.
Fibak-Okker def. Barazzutti-Zugarelli 6-2, 3-6, 6-3.
**Group 2—Doubles**
Smith-Lutz def. Leonard-Machette 7-6, 7-6.
Stewart-McNair def. Cahill-Moor 7-5, 4-6, 7-6.
Stewart-McNair def. Leonard-Machette 6-2, 6-2.
Smith-Lutz def. Cahill-Moor 6-2, 6-4.
Cahill-Moor def. Leonard-Machette 6-2, 6-4.
Smith-Lutz def. Stewart-McNair 7-5, 3-6, 7-6.
**WCT Final**
Fibak-Okker def. Smith-Lutz 6-7, 6-4, 6-0, 6-3.

## Shakey's Tournament of Champions

Las Vegas, Nev., Mar. 20-26, 1978

**Quarterfinals**
Solomon def. Borowiak 6-4, 6-2.
Gerulaitis def. Mayer 6-4, 5-6, 6-3.
Dibbs def. Rosewall 6-3, 6-4.
Drysdale def. Gullikson 6-1, 6-2.
Roche def. Stockton 5-6, 6-4, 6-5.
Borg def. Laver 6-4, 6-2.

**Semifinals**
Drysdale def. Dibbs 6-3, 6-2.
Borg def. Roche 6-4, 6-2.
Gerulaitis def. Solomon 6-4, 6-1.
**Finals**
Borg def. Gerulaitis 6-5, 5-6, 6-4, 6-5.
Borg def. Drysdale 6-4, 6-5.

## Forest Hills Invitational

New York, N.Y., July 10-16, 1978

**Round-robin singles**
Gerulaitis def. Dent 6-1, 7-6.
Pecci def. Rosewall 6-3, 6-1.
McEnroe def. Newcombe 1-6, 6-4, 7-5.
Fibak def. Martin 6-2, 6-4.
Dent def. Rosewall 7-5, 6-1.
Nastase def. Fleming 5-7, 7-6, 6-4.
Fibak def. Newcombe 6-1, 6-2.
Nastase def. Alexander 6-2, 6-2.
Stockton def. Fleming 7-6, 3-6, 6-3.
Gerulaitis def. Rosewall 6-3, 6-2.
McEnroe def. Martin 7-5, 4-6, 7-5.
Alexander def. Fleming 6-2, 2-6, 6-3.
Nastase def. Stockton 5-7, 7-5, 6-3.
Gerulaitis def. Pecci 6-4, 1-6, 7-5.
Dent def. Pecci 6-4, 0-6, 6-2.
McEnroe def. Fibak 6-2, 6-3

Martin def. Newcombe 6-3, 7-6.
Stockton def. Alexander 3-6, 6-2, 6-1.
**Semifinals**
Nastase def. McEnroe 6-3, 7-6.
Gerulaitis def. Fibak 6-2, 6-3.
**Final**
Gerulaitis def. Nastase 6-2, 6-0.
**Round-robin doubles:**
McNair-Stewart def. Alexander-Dent 6-0, 5-7, 6-1.
McEnroe-Fibak def. McNair-Stewart 7-6, 7-6.
McNair-Stewart def. Rosewall-Newcombe 6-4, 4-6, 6-4.
Alexander-Dent def. Rosewall-Newcombe 6-4, 7-5.
Alexander-Dent def. McEnroe-Fibak 6-4, 6-2.
Rosewall-Newcombe def. McEnroe-Fibak 6-4, 6-3.
**Final**
Alexander-Dent def. McNair-Stewart 7-6, 7-6.

## NCAA Tennis Champions

| Year | Singles | College | Doubles | College |
|---|---|---|---|---|
| 1968 | Stan Smith | USC | Stan Smith—Bob Lutz | USC |
| 1969 | Joaquin Loyo Mayo | USC | Joaquin Loyo Mayo—Marcelo Lara | USC |
| 1970 | Jeff Borowiak | UCLA | Pat Cramer—Luis Garcia | Miami (Fla.) |
| 1971 | Jimmy Connors | UCLA | Jeff Borowiak—Haroon Rahim | UCLA |
| 1972 | Dick Stockton | Trinity (Tex.) | Sandy Mayer—Roscoe Tanner | Stanford |
| 1973 | Sandy Mayer | Stanford | Sandy Mayer—Jim Delaney | Stanford |
| 1974 | John Whitlinger | Stanford | John Whitlinger—Jim Delaney | Stanford |
| 1975 | Billy Martin | UCLA | Butch Walts—Bruce Manson | USC |
| 1976 | Bill Scanlon | Trinity | Peter Fleming—Ferdi Taygan | UCLA |
| 1977 | Matt Mitchell | Stanford | Bruce Manson—Chris Lewis | USC |
| 1978 | John McEnroe | Stanford | Bruce Nichols—John Austin | UCLA |

## Clay Court Champions

| Year | Champion | Year | Champion | Year | Champion | Year | Champion |
|---|---|---|---|---|---|---|---|
| 1955 | Tony Trabert | 1961 | Bernard Bartzen | 1967 | Arthur Ashe | 1973 | Manuel Orantes |
| 1956 | Herbert Flam | 1962 | Chuck McKinley | 1968 | Clark Graebner | 1974 | Jimmy Connors |
| 1957 | E. Victor Seixas, Jr. | 1963 | Chuck McKinley | 1969 | Zeljko Franulovic | 1975 | Manuel Orantes |
| 1958 | Bernard Bartzen | 1964 | Dennis Ralston | 1970 | Cliff Richey | 1976 | Jimmy Connors |
| 1959 | Bernard Bartzen | 1965 | Dennis Ralston | 1971 | Zeljko Franulovic | 1977 | Manuel Orantes |
| 1960 | Barry MacKay | 1966 | Cliff Rickey | 1972 | Bob Hewitt | 1978 | Jimmy Connors |

## Davis Cup Challenge Round

| Year | Result | Year | Result | Year | Result |
|------|--------|------|--------|------|--------|
| 1900 | United States, 5 British Isles 0 | 1927 | France 3, United States 2 | 1955 | Australia 5, United States 0 |
| 1901 | (not played) | 1928 | France 4, United States 1 | 1956 | Australia 5, United States 0 |
| 1902 | United States 3, British Isles 2 | 1929 | France 3, United States 2 | 1957 | Australia 3, United States 2 |
| 1903 | British Isles 4, United States 1 | 1930 | France 4, United States 1 | 1958 | United States 3, Australia 2 |
| 1904 | British Isles 5, Belgium 0 | 1931 | France 3, Great Britain 1 | 1959 | Australia 3, United States 2 |
| 1905 | British Isles 5, United States 0 | 1932 | France 3, United States 2 | 1960 | Australia 4, Italy 1 |
| 1906 | British Isles 5, United States 0 | 1933 | Great Britain 3, France 2 | 1961 | Australia 4, Italy 0 |
| 1907 | Australia 3, British Isles 2 | 1934 | Great Britain 4, United States 1 | 1962 | Australia 5, Mexico 0 |
| 1908 | Australasia 3, United States 2 | 1935 | Great Britain 5, United States 0 | 1963 | United States 3, Australia 2 |
| 1909 | Australasia 5, United States 0 | 1936 | Great Britain 3, Australia 2 | 1964 | Australia 3, United States 2 |
| 1910 | (not played) | 1937 | United States 4, Great Britain 1 | 1965 | Australia 4, Spain 1 |
| 1911 | Australasia 5, United States 0 | 1938 | United States 3, Australia 2 | 1966 | Australia 4, India 1 |
| 1912 | British Isles 3, Australasia 2 | 1939 | Australia 3, United States 2 | 1967 | Australia 4, Spain 1 |
| 1913 | United States 3, British Isles 2 | 1940-45 | (not played) | 1968 | United States 4, Australia 1 |
| 1914 | Australasia 3, United States 2 | 1946 | United States 5, Australia 0 | 1969 | United States 5, Romania 0 |
| 1915-18 | (not played) | 1947 | United States 4, Australia 1 | 1970 | United States 5, W. Germany 0 |
| 1919 | Australasia 4, British Isles 1 | 1948 | United States 5, Australia 0 | 1971 | United States 3, Romania 2 |
| 1920 | United States 5, Australasia 0 | 1949 | United States 4, Australia 1 | 1972 | United States 3, Romania 2 |
| 1921 | United States 5, Japan 0 | 1950 | Australia 4, United States 1 | 1973 | Australia 5, United States 0 |
| 1922 | United States 4, Australasia 1 | 1951 | Australia 3, United States 2 | 1974 | South Africa (default by India) |
| 1923 | United States 4, Australasia 1 | 1952 | Australia 4, United States 1 | 1975 | Sweden 3, Czech. 2 |
| 1924 | United States 5, Australasia 0 | 1953 | Australia 3, United States 2 | 1976 | Italy 4, Chile 1 |
| 1925 | United States 5, France 0 | 1954 | United States 3, Australia 2 | 1977 | Australia 3, Italy 1 |
| 1926 | United States 4, France 1 | | | | |

## National Junior Tennis Champions

### Boys' 18 singles
1972 Patrick DuPre
1973 Billy Martin
1974 Ferd Taygan
1975 Howard Schoenfield
1976 Larry Gottfried
1977 Van Winitsky
1978 David Dowlen

### Girls' 18 singles
1972 Ann Kiyomura
1973 Carrie Fleming
1974 Rayni Fox
1975 Beth Norton
1976 Lynn Epstein
1977 Tracy Austin
1978 Tracy Austin

### Boys' 18 doubles
1972 Steve Mott and Brian Teachar
1973 Billy Martin and Trey Waitke
1974 Francisco Gonzalez and Rocky Maguire
1975 Larry Gottfried and John McEnroe
1976 Larry Gottfried and John McEnroe
1977 Robert Van'tHov and Van Winitsky
1978 Scott Bondurant and Blaine Willenborg

### Girls' 18 doubles
1972 Marita Redondo and Laurie Tenney
1973 Susan Boyle and Kathy May
1974 Anne Bruning and Barbara Halliquist
1975 Lea Antonoplis and Berta McCallum
1976 Sherry Acker and Anne Smith
1977 Lea Antonoplis and Kathy Jordan
1978 Tracy Austin and Maria Fernandez

### Boys' 16 singles
1972 Bill Maze
1973 Ben McKnown
1974 Walter Redondo
1975 Larry Gottfried
1976 Tim Wilkison
1977 Ramesh Krishnan
1978 Ben Testerman

### Girls' 16 singles
1972 Marita Redondo
1973 Betsy Nagelson
1974 Zenda Leiss
1975 Lea Antonoplis
1976 Peanut Louie
1977 Linda Siegel
1978 Tracy Austin

### Boys' 16 doubles
1972 Bruce Manson and Perry Wright
1973 Nial Brash and Matt Mitchell
1974 Jeff Robbins and Van Winitsky
1975 Tony Giammalua and Billy Scanlon
1976 Murray Robinson and Tim Wilkison
1977 Sean Brawley and David Siegler
1978 Scott Davis and Ben Testerman

### Girls' 16 doubles
1972 Jeanne Evert and Kathy Kendall
1973 Susan Mehmedbasich and Robin Tenney
1974 Sherry Acker and Anne Smith
1975 Lea Antonoplis and Berta McCallum
1976 Lucia Fernandez and Trey Lewis
1977 Tracy Austin and Maria Fernandez
1978 Pam Shriver and Barbara Potter

## Tennis Championships in 1978

**Australian Open (Melbourne)** — Men's Singles: Vitas Gerulaitis def. John Lloyd 6-3, 7-6, 5-7, 3-6, 6-2; Men's Doubles: Ruffels-Stone def. Alexander-Dent 7-6, 7-6; Women's Singles: Evonne Goolagong def. Helen Cawley 6-3, 6-0; Women's Doubles: Goolagong-Cawley vs. Matison-Whytcross (cancelled by rain).

**Italian Open (Rome)** — Men's Singles: Bjorn Borg def. Adriano Panatta 1-6, 6-3, 6-1, 4-6, 6-3; Men's Doubles: Pecci-Prajoux def. Kodes-Smid 6-7, 7-6, 6-1; Women's Singles: Regina Marsikova def. Virginia Ruzici 7-5, 7-5; Women's Doubles: Jausovec-Ruzici def. Mihai-Nagelsen 6-2, 2-6, 7-5.

**French Open (Paris)** — Men's Singles: Bjorn Borg def. Guillermo Vilas 6-1, 6-1, 6-3; Men's Doubles: Mayer-Pfister def. Orantes-Higueras 6-3, 6-2, 6-2; Women's Singles: Virginia Ruzici def. Mima Jausovec 6-2, 6-2; Women's Doubles: Jausovec-Ruzici def. Bowrey-Lovera 6-4, 6-3.

**Women's Collegiates** — Singles: Stacy Margolin, USC; Doubles: Sherry Acker-Judy Acker, Univ. of Fla.

## World Team Tennis in 1978

The Los Angeles Strings won its first WTT championship by defeating the Boston Lobsters 3-1 in the best-of-five championship series. Chris Evert of Los Angeles was named the outstanding player in the series.

## Leading Tennis Money Winners in 1977

| Men | | Women | |
|---|---|---|---|
| 1. Jimmy Connors, Belleville, Ill. | $922,657 | 1. Chris Evert, Fort Lauderdale, Fla. | $503,134 |
| 2. Guillermo Vilas, Argentina | 800,642 | 2. Martina Navratilova, Dallas, Tex. | 300,317 |
| 3. Bjorn Borg, Sweden | 480,661 | 3. Virginia Wade, Great Britain | 258,746 |
| 4. Brian Gottfried, Lauderhill, Fla. | 478,988 | 4. Betty Stove, The Netherlands | 229,162 |
| 5. Dick Stockton, Carrolton, Tex. | 311,856 | 5. Billie Jean King, New York, N.Y. | 193,194 |
| 6. Ilie Nastase, Romania | 306,956 | 6. Sue Barker, Great Britain | 190,498 |
| 7. Vitas Gerulaitis, Kings Point, N.Y. | 294,324 | 7. Kerry Reid, Australia | 156,234 |
| 8. Eddie Dibbs, North Miami Beach, Fla. | 283,691 | 8. Rosemary Casals, Sausalito, Cal. | 126,193 |
| 9. Roscoe Tanner, Lookout Mountain, Tenn. | 281,131 | 9. Dianne Fromholtz, Australia | 106,410 |
| 10. Raul Ramirez, Mexico | 245,007 | 10. Wendy Turnbull, Australia | 98,568 |

# National Skeet Shooting Assn. Championship in 1978

San Antonio, Tex., July 31 - August 6, 1978

### High Overall Championship - 550 targets

**Champion** — Walt Badorek, Klamath Falls, Ore., 550.
**Women** — Ila Hill, Birmingham, Mich., 543.
**Industry** — Jimmy Prall, Tulsa, Okla., 546.
**Veteran** — Tom Sanfilipo, Fairfield, Cal., 532.
**Sub-senior** — Larry Drennan Jr., Ada, Okla., 546.
**Senior** — Tom Hanzel, San Antonio, Tex., 535.
**Junior** — John Dail, Anderson, S.C., 546.
**Collegiate** — Chip Youngblood, Ft. Lauderdale, Fla., 546.

**Veteran** — George Vicknair, Baton Rouge, La., 97.
**Sub-senior** — Larry Drennan Jr., Ada, Okla., 100.
**Senior** — Tom Hanzel, San Antonio, Tex., 99.
**Junior** — John Dail, Anderson, S.C., 100.
**Collegiate** — Todd Bender, Fountain Valley, Cal., 99.

### 12 Gauge 250 Targets

**Champion** — Chip Youngblood, Ft. Lauderdale, Fla., 250.
**Women** — Gena Clark, Delmar, Cal., 250.
**Industry** — Jimmy Prall, Tulsa, Okla., 249.
**Veteran** — George Vicknair, Baton Rouge, La., 245.
**Sub-senior** — Russell Dorris, Franklin, Tenn., 250.
**Senior** — D.L. Cool, Louisville, Ky., 248.
**Junior** — Eric McClendon, Amite, La., 249.
**Collegiate** — Chip Youngblood, 250.

### 28 Gauge 100 Targets

**Champion** — John Dail, Anderson, S.C., 100.
**Women** — Virginia Schmidt, Prior Lake, Minn., 100.
**Industry** — Earl Larson, Bridgeport, Conn., 100.
**Veteran** — George Vicknair, Baton Rouge, La., 98.
**Sub-senior** — Jim Dozier, Crowville, La., 100.
**Senior** — Tom Hanzel, San Antonio, Tex., 98.
**Junior** — John Dail, 100.
**Collegiate** — Chip Youngblood, Ft. Lauderdale, Fla., 100.

### 20 Gauge 100 Targets

**Champion** — John Dail, Anderson, S.C., 100.
**Women** — Ila Hill, Birmingham, Mich., 99.
**Industry** — Tony Rosetti, Jr., Hagerstown, Md., 98.

### .410 Gauge 100 Targets

**Champion** — Walt Badorek, Klamath Falls, Ore., 100.
**Women** — Susan Pockmire, Pinehurst, N.C., 98.
**Industry** — Jimmy Prall, Tulsa, Okla., 100.
**Veteran** — Tom Sanfillipo, Fairfield, Cal., 97.
**Sub-senior** — Decatur Holcombe, Houston, Tex., 99.
**Senior** — Gen. Ken Pletcher, Bellevue, Neb., 94.
**Junior** — David Stone, Corpus Christi, Tex., 98.
**Collegiate** — Sheri Confer, San Antonio, Tex., 98.

# World Pocket Billiards Champions

| | | | | | |
|---|---|---|---|---|---|
| 1931 | Ralph Greenleaf | 1945 | Willie Mosconi | 1965 | Joe Balsis |
| 1932 | Ralph Greenleaf | 1946 | Irving Crane | 1966 | Luther Lassiter |
| 1933 | Erwin Rudolph | 1947 | Willie Mosconi | 1967 | Luther Lassiter |
| 1934 | Erwin Rudolph | 1948 | Willie Mosconi | 1968 | Irving Crane |
| 1935 | Andrew Ponzi | 1949 | James Caras | 1969 | Ed Kelly |
| 1936 | James Caras | 1950 | Willie Mosconi | 1970 | Irving Crane |
| 1937 | Ralph Greenleaf | 1951 | Willie Mosconi | 1971 | Ray Martin |
| 1938 | James Caras | 1952 | Willie Mosconi | 1972 | Irving Crane |
| 1939 | James Caras | 1953 | Willie Mosconi | 1973 | Lou Butera |
| 1940 | Andrew Ponzi | 1954 | none | 1974 | Ray Martin |
| 1941 | Willie Mosconi, Erwin Rudolph | 1955 | Irving Crane, Willie Mosconi | 1975 | none |
| 1942 | Irving Crane | 1956-62 | none | 1976 | Larry Lisciotti |
| 1943 | Andrew Ponzi | 1963 | Luther Lassiter | 1977 | Allen Hopkins |
| 1944 | Willie Mosconi | 1964 | Luther Lassiter, Arthur Cranfield | 1978 | Ray Martin |

## U.S. Open Pocket Billiards Champions

| | | | | | | | |
|---|---|---|---|---|---|---|---|
| 1967 | James Caras | 1970 | Steve Mizerak | 1973 | Steve Mizerak | 1976 | Tom Jennings |
| 1968 | Joe Balsis | 1971 | Steve Mizerak | 1974 | Joe Balsis | 1977 | Tom Jennings |
| 1969 | Luther Lassiter | 1972 | Steve Mizerak | 1975 | Dallas West | 1978 | none |

# Intercollegiate Rowing Association Championship

Onondaga Lake, Syracuse, N.Y. (3 miles)

| Year | Winner | Time | Year | Winner | Time | Year | Winner | Time |
|---|---|---|---|---|---|---|---|---|
| 1958 | Cornell | 17:12.1 | 1965 | Navy | 16:51.3 | 1972 | Penn (a) | 6:22.6 |
| 1959 | Wisconsin | 18:01.7 | 1966 | Wisconsin | 16:03.4 | 1973 | Wisconsin (a) | 6:21.0 |
| 1960 | California | 15:57.0 | 1967 | Penn | 16:15.9 | 1974 | Wisconsin (a) | 6:33.0 |
| 1961 | California | 16:49.2 | 1968 | Penn (a) | 6:15.6 | 1975 | Wisconsin (a) | 6:08.2 |
| 1962 | Cornell | 17:02.9 | 1969 | Penn (a) | 6:30.4 | 1976 | California (a) | 6:31.0 |
| 1963 | Cornell | 17:24.0 | 1970 | Washington (a) | | 1977 | Cornell (a) | 6:32.4 |
| 1964 | California (a) | 6:31.1 | 1971 | Cornell (a) | 6:06.0 | 1978 | Syracuse (a) | 6:39.5 |

(a) race at 2,000 meters

# Auto Racing

## Indianapolis 500 Winners

| Year | Winner | Chassis | Engine | MPH | Purse | Runner up |
|------|--------|---------|--------|-----|-------|-----------|
| 1948 | Mauri Rose | Deidt | Offenhauser | 119.814 | $171,075 | Bill Holland |
| 1949 | Bill Holland | Deidt | Offenhauser | 121.327 | 179,050 | Johnnie Parsons |
| 1950 | Johnnie Parsons | Kurtis Kraft | Offenhauser | 124.002(a) | 201,135 | Bill Holland |
| 1951 | Lee Wallard | Kurtis Kraft | Offenhauser | 126.244 | 207,650 | Mike Nazaruk |
| 1952 | Troy Ruttman | Kuzma | Offenhauser | 128.922 | 230,100 | Jim Rathmann |
| 1953 | Bill Vukovich | Kurtis Kraft 500A | Offenhauser | 128.740 | 246,300 | Art Cross |
| 1954 | Bill Vukovich | Kurtis Kraft 500A | Offenhauser | 130.840 | 269,375 | Jim Bryan |
| 1955 | Bob Sweikert | Kurtis Kraft 500C | Offenhauser | 128.209 | 270,400 | Tony Bettenhausen |
| 1956 | Pat Flaherty | Watson | Offenhauser | 128.490 | 282,052 | Sam Hanks |
| 1957 | Sam Hanks | Epperly | Offenhauser | 135.601 | 300,252 | Jim Rathmann |
| 1958 | Jimmy Bryan | Epperly | Offenhauser | 133.791 | 305,217 | George Amick |
| 1959 | Rodger Ward | Watson | Offenhauser | 135.857 | 338,100 | Jim Rathmann |
| 1960 | Jim Rathmann | Watson | Offenhauser | 138.767 | 369,150 | Rodger Ward |
| 1961 | A.J. Foyt | Watson | Offenhauser | 139.130 | 400,000 | Eddie Sachs |
| 1962 | Rodger Ward | Watson | Offenhauser | 140.293 | 426,152 | Len Sutton |
| 1963 | Parnelli Jones | Watson | Offenhauser | 143.137 | 494,031 | Jim Clark |
| 1964 | A.J. Foyt | Watson | Offenhauser | 147.350 | 506,625 | Rodger Ward |
| 1965 | Jim Clark | Lotus | Ford | 151.388 | 628,399 | Parnelli Jones |
| 1966 | Graham Hill | Lola | Ford | 144.317 | 691,809 | Jim Clark |
| 1967 | A.J. Foyt | Coyote | Ford | 151.207 | 737,109 | Al Unser |
| 1968 | Bobby Unser | Eagle | Offenhauser | 152.882 | 809,627 | Dan Gurney |
| 1969 | Mario Andretti | Hawk | Ford | 156.867 | 805,127 | Dan Gurney |
| 1970 | Al Unser | P.J. Colt | Ford | 155.749 | 1,000,002 | Mark Donohue |
| 1971 | Al Unser | P.J. Colt | Ford | 157.735 | 1,001,604 | Peter Revson |
| 1972 | Mark Donohue | McLaren | Offenhauser | 163.465 | 1,011,846 | Al Unser |
| 1973 | Gordon Johncock | Eagle | Offenhauser | 159.014(b) | 1,011,846 | Billy Vukovich |
| 1974 | Johnny Rutherford | McLaren | Offenhauser | 158.589 | 1,015,686 | Bobby Unser |
| 1975 | Bobby Unser | Eagle | Offenhauser | 149.213(c) | 1,101,322 | Johnny Rutherford |
| 1976 | Johnny Rutherford | McLaren | Offenhauser | 148.725(d) | 1,037,775 | A.J. Foyt |
| 1977 | A.J. Foyt | Coyote | Ford | 161.331 | 1,116,807 | Tom Sneva |
| 1978 | Al Unser | Lola | Cosworth | 161.363 | 1,145,225 | Tom Sneva |

(a) 345 miles. (b) 332.5 miles. (c) 435 miles. (d) 255 miles. Race record—163.465 MPH, Mark Donohue, 1972.

## 1978 Indianapolis 500 Final Standings

1—Al Unser, Albuquerque, N.M., Lola-Cosworth; 200 laps; 161.363 miles per hour.

2—Tom Sneva, Spokane, Wash., Penske-Cosworth; 200 laps; 161.244.

3—Gordon Johncock, Phoenix, Ariz., Wildcat-SGD; 200 laps; 159.861.

4—Steve Krisiloff, Dana Point, Cal., Wildcat-SGD; 198 laps; 159.242.

5—Wally Dallenbach, Basalt, Col., McLaren-Cosworth; 195 laps; 158.926.

6—Bobby Unser, Albuquerque, N.M., Eagle-Cosworth; 195 laps; 157.279.

7—A.J. Foyt, Houston, Tex., Coyote-Foyt; 191 laps; 153.874.

8—George Snider, Bakersfield, Cal., Coyote-Foyt; 191 laps; 152.928.

## World's Land Speed Records—Evolution of the Mile Record

| Date | Driver | Car | MPH | Date | Driver | Car | MPH |
|------|--------|-----|-----|------|--------|-----|-----|
| 12/18/98 | Chasseloup-Laubat | Jeantaud | 39.24 | 4/22/28 | Keech | White Triplex | 207.552 |
| 4/29/99 | Jenatzy | Jamais Contente | | 3/11/29 | Seagrave | Irving-Napier | 231.446 |
| | Jenatzy | | 65.79 | 2/ 5/31 | Campbell | Napier-Campbell | 246.086 |
| 11/17/02 | Augieres | Mars | 77.13 | 2/24/32 | Campbell | Napier-Campbell | 253.96 |
| 11/ 5/03 | Duray | Gabron-Brillie | 84.73 | 2/22/33 | Campbell | Napier-Campbell | 272.109 |
| 12/30/04 | Barras | Darracq | 109.65 | 9/ 3/35 | Campbell | Bluebird Special | 301.13 |
| 1/25/05 | Bowden | Mercedes | 109.75 | 11/19/37 | Eyston | Thunderbolt 1 | 311.42 |
| 1/26/06 | Marriott | Stanley (Steam) | 127.659 | 9/16/38 | Eyston | Thunderbolt 1 | 357.5 |
| 3/16/10 | Oldfield | Benz | 131.724 | 8/23/39 | Cobb | Railton | 368.9 |
| 4/23/11 | Burman | Benz | 141.732 | 9/16/47 | Cobb | Railton-Mobil | 394.2 |
| 2/12/19 | DePalma | Packard | 149.875 | 8/ 5/63 | Breedlove | Spirit of America | 407.45 |
| 4/27/20 | Milton | Dusenberg | 155.046 | 10/27/64 | Arfons | Green Monster | 536.71 |
| 4/28/26 | Parry-Thomas | Thomas Spl. | 170.624 | 11/15/65 | Breedlove | Spirit of America | 600.601 |
| 3/29/27 | Seagrave | Sunbeam | 203.790 | 10/23/70 | Gabelich | Blue Flame | 622.407 |

## World Grand Prix Champions

| Year | Driver | Year | Driver | Year | Driver |
|------|--------|------|--------|------|--------|
| 1950 | Nino Farina, Italy | 1960 | Jack Brabham, Australia | 1969 | Jackie Stewart, Scotland |
| 1951 | Juan Fangio, Argentina | 1961 | Phil Hill, United States | 1970 | Jochen Rindt, Austria |
| 1952 | Alberto Ascari, Italy | 1962 | Graham Hill, England | 1971 | Jackie Stewart, Scotland |
| 1953 | Alberto Ascari, Italy | 1963 | Jim Clark, Scotland | 1972 | Emerson Fittipaldi, Brazil |
| 1954 | Juan Fangio, Argentina | 1964 | John Surtees, England | 1973 | Jackie Stewart, Scotland |
| 1955 | Juan Fangio, Argentina | 1965 | Jim Clark, Scotland | 1974 | Emerson Fittipaldi, Brazil |
| 1956 | Juan Fangio, Argentina | 1966 | Jack Brabham, Australia | 1975 | Nicki Lauda, Austria |
| 1957 | Juan Fangio, Argentina | 1967 | Denis Hulme, New Zealand | 1976 | James Hunt, England |
| 1958 | Mike Hawthorne, England | 1968 | Graham Hill, England | 1977 | Nicki Lauda, Austria |
| 1959 | Jack Brabham, Australia | | | | |

## American Automobile Assn. National Champions

| Year | Driver | Year | Driver | Year | Driver | Year | Driver |
|------|--------|------|--------|------|--------|------|--------|
| 1954 | Jimmy Bryan | 1960 | A. J. Foyt | 1966 | Mario Andretti | 1972 | Joe Leonard |
| 1955 | Bob Sweikert | 1961 | A. J. Foyt | 1967 | A. J. Foyt | 1973 | Roger McCluskey |
| 1956 | Jimmy Bryan | 1962 | Rodger Ward | 1968 | Bobby Unser | 1974 | Bobby Unser |
| 1957 | Jimmy Bryan | 1963 | A. J. Foyt | 1969 | Mario Andretti | 1975 | A. J. Foyt |
| 1958 | Tony Bettenhausen | 1964 | A. J. Foyt | 1970 | Al Unser | 1976 | Gordon Johncock |
| 1959 | Rodger Ward | 1965 | Mario Andretti | 1971 | Joe Leonard | 1977 | Tom Sneva |

## Grand Prix for Formula 1 Cars in 1978

| Grand Prix | Winner, car | Grand Prix | Winner, car |
|---|---|---|---|
| Argentine | Mario Andretti, Lotus | German | Mario Andretti, Lotus 79 |
| Austrian | Ronnie Peterson, Lotus 79 | Italian | Niki Lauda, Brabham |
| Belgian | Mario Andretti, Lotus 79 | Long Beach | Carlos Reutemann, Ferrari |
| British | Carlos Reutemann, Ferrari | Monaco | Patrick DePailler, Tyrrell |
| Brazilian | Carlos Reutemann, Ferrari | South African | Ronnie Peterson, Lotus |
| Canadian | Gilles Villeneuve, Ferrari | Spanish | Mario Andretti, Lotus 79 |
| Dutch | Mario Andretti, Lotus 79 | Swedish | Niki Lauda, Brabham |
| French | Mario Andretti, Lotus | United States | Carlos Reutemann, Ferrari |

# NASCAR Racing in 1978

## Winston Cup Grand National Races

| Date | Race, site | Winner | Car | Winnings |
|---|---|---|---|---|
| Jan. 22 | Winston Western 500, Riverside, Cal. | Cale Yarborough | Oldsmobile | $16,200 |
| Feb. 19 | Daytona 500, Daytona Beach, Fla. | Bobby Allison | Ford | 44,300 |
| Feb. 26 | Richmond 400, Richmond, Va. | Benny Parsons | Chevrolet | 11,225 |
| Mar. 5 | Carolina 500, Rockingham, N.C. | David Pearson | Mercury | 10,605 |
| Mar. 19 | Atlanta 500, Atlanta, Ga. | Bobby Allison | Ford | 26,900 |
| Apr. 2 | Southeastern 500, Bristol, Tenn. | Darrell Waltrip | Chevrolet | 17,050 |
| Apr. 9 | Rebel 500, Darlington, S.C. | Benny Parsons | Chevrolet | 14,450 |
| Apr. 16 | Staley 400, No. Wilkesboro, N.C. | Darrell Waltrip | Chevrolet | 11,200 |
| Apr. 23 | Virginia 500, Martinsville, Va. | Darrell Waltrip | Chevrolet | 20,300 |
| May 14 | Winston 500, Talladega, Ala. | Cale Yarborough | Oldsmobile | 27,100 |
| May 21 | Mason-Dixon 500, Dover, Del. | David Pearson | Mercury | 11,700 |
| May 28 | World 600, Charlotte, N.C. | Darrell Waltrip | Chevrolet | 36,075 |
| June 3 | Music City USA 420, Nashville, Tenn. | Cale Yarborough | Oldsmobile | 9,065 |
| June 11 | Napa Riverside 400, Riverside, Cal. | Benny Parsons | Chevrolet | 14,500 |
| June 18 | Gabriel 400, Brooklyn, Mich. | Cale Yarborough | Oldsmobile | 16,055 |
| July 4 | Firecracker 500, Daytona Beach, Fla. | David Pearson | Mercury | 13,525 |
| July 15 | Nashville 420, Nashville, Tenn. | Cale Yarborough | Oldsmobile | 9,090 |
| July 30 | Coca-Cola 500, Pocono, Pa. | Darrell Waltrip | Chevrolet | 14,515 |
| Aug. 6 | Talladega 500, Talledaga, Ala. | Lennie Pond | Oldsmobile | 19,600 |
| Aug. 20 | Champion Spark Plug 400, Brooklyn, Mich. | David Pearson | Mercury | 12,000 |
| Aug. 26 | Volunteer 500, Bristol, Tenn. | Cale Yarborough | Oldsmobile | 13,760 |
| Sept. 4 | Southern 500, Darlington, S.C. | Cale Yarborough | Oldsmobile | 26,200 |
| Sept. 10 | Capital City 400, Richmond, Va. | Darrell Waltrip | Chevrolet | 11,700 |
| Sept. 17 | Delaware 500, Dover, Del. | Bobby Allison | Ford | 14,600 |
| Sept. 24 | Old Dominion 500, Martinsville, Va. | Cale Yarborough | Oldsmobile | 22,550 |

## Daytona 500 Winners

| Year | Driver, car | Avg. MPH | Year | Driver, car | Avg. MPH |
|---|---|---|---|---|---|
| 1961 | Marvin Panch, Pontiac | 149.601 | 1970 | Pete Hamilton, Plymouth | 149.601 |
| 1962 | Fireball Roberts, Pontiac | 152.529 | 1971 | Richard Petty, Plymouth | 144.456 |
| 1963 | Tiny Lund, Ford | 151.566 | 1972 | A. J. Foyt, Mercury | 161.550 |
| 1964 | Richard Petty, Plymouth | 154.334 | 1973 | Richard Petty, Dodge | 157.205 |
| 1965 | Fred Lorenzen, Ford (a) | 141.539 | 1974 | Richard Petty, Dodge (c) | 140.894 |
| 1966 | Richard Petty, Plymouth (b) | 160.627 | 1975 | Benny Parsons, Chevrolet | 153.649 |
| 1967 | Mario Andretti, Ford | 146.926 | 1976 | David Pearson, Mercury | 152.181 |
| 1968 | Cale Yarborough, Mercury | 143.251 | 1977 | Cale Yarborough, Chevrolet | 153.218 |
| 1969 | Lee Roy Yarborough, Ford | 160.875 | 1978 | Bobby Allison, Ford | 159.730 |

(a) 322.5 miles because of rain. (b) 495 miles because of rain. (c) 450 miles.

## Leading Daytona 500 Finishers in 1978

| | Driver, car | Laps | Winnings | | Driver, car | Laps | Winnings |
|---|---|---|---|---|---|---|---|
| 1 | Bobby Allison, Ford | 200 | $44,300 | 6 | Dave Marcis, Chevrolet | 198 | $14,450 |
| 2 | Cale Yarborough, Oldsmobile | 200 | 39,550 | 7 | Buddy Baker, Oldsmobile | 196 | 16,395 |
| 3 | Benny Parsons, Oldsmobile | 199 | 26,550 | 8 | Bill Eliott, Mercury | 195 | 11,935 |
| 4 | Ron Hutcherson, Buick | 199 | 19,950 | 9 | Ferrel Harris, Dodge | 195 | 11,025 |
| 5 | Richard Brooks, Mercury | 198 | 18,275 | 10 | Lennie Pond, Oldsmobile | 195 | 10,035 |

## Grand National Champions (NASCAR)

| Year | Driver | Year | Driver | Year | Driver | Year | Driver |
|---|---|---|---|---|---|---|---|
| 1951 | Herb Thomas | 1958 | Lee Petty | 1965 | Ned Jarrett | 1972 | Richard Petty |
| 1952 | Tim Flock | 1959 | Lee Petty | 1966 | David Pearson | 1973 | Benny Parson |
| 1953 | Herb Thomas | 1960 | Rex White | 1967 | Richard Petty | 1974 | Richard Petty |
| 1954 | Lee Petty | 1961 | Ned Jarrett | 1968 | David Pearson | 1975 | Richard Petty |
| 1955 | Tim Flock | 1962 | Joe Weatherly | 1969 | David Pearson | 1976 | Cale Yarborough |
| 1956 | Buck Baker | 1963 | Joe Weatherly | 1970 | Bobby Isaac | 1977 | Cale Yarborough |
| 1957 | Buck Baker | 1964 | Richard Petty | 1971 | Richard Petty | | |

# Motorcycle Racing

## Grand National Champion

| Year | Champion | Year | Champion | Year | Champion | Year | Champion |
|---|---|---|---|---|---|---|---|
| 1954 | Joe Leonard | 1960 | Carroll Resweber | 1966 | Bart Markel | 1972 | Mark Brelsford |
| 1955 | Brad Andres | 1961 | Carroll Resweber | 1967 | Gary Nixon | 1973 | Ken Roberts |
| 1956 | Joe Leonard | 1962 | Bart Markel | 1968 | Gary Nixon | 1974 | Ken Roberts |
| 1957 | Joe Leonard | 1963 | Dick Mann | 1969 | Mert Lawwill | 1975 | Gary Scott |
| 1958 | Carroll Resweber | 1964 | Roger Reiman | 1970 | Gene Romero | 1976 | Jay Springsteen |
| 1959 | Carroll Resweber | 1965 | Bart Markel | 1971 | Dick Mann | 1977 | Jay Springsteen |

## U.S. Amateur Roller Skating Championship in 1978

**American Senior Dance**—John LaBriola-Debra Coyne, Fountain Valley, Cal.
**American Esquire Dance**—Joseph Tarvis-Virginia Johnson, Norwood, Mass.
**American Free Dance**—Robert Sutherland-Theresa Schiavoni, Waltham, Mass.
**International Senior Dance**—Dan Littel-Fleurette Arseneault, East Meadow, N.Y.
**International Junior Dance**—David Golub-Wendy Galante, East Meadow, N.Y.
**American Senior Men's Figures**—Curt Craton, Fountain Valley, Cal.
**American Senior Ladies Figures**—Patti Marshalewski, Concord Ville, Pa.
**American Junior Men's Figures**—Mike Ricigliane, Hayward, Cal.
**American Junior Ladies Figures**—Beverly Perfect, Cincinnati, Oh.
**American Senior Men's Singles**—Paul Jones, Flint, Mich.
**American Senior Ladies Singles**—Robbie Coleman, Memphis, Tenn.

**International Senior Men's Singles**—Lex Kane, Toledo, Oh.
**International Senior Ladies Singles**—Natalie Dunn, Bakersfield, Cal.
**American Junior Men's Singles**—Kevin Kerwin, Bakersfield, Cal.
**American Junior Ladies Singles**—Amy Fosgate, Monroe, Mich.
**American Senior Pairs**—Paul Price-Tina Kneisley, Brighton, Mich.
**American Junior Pairs**—Kimberley Campbell-Kurt Anselmi, Pontiac, Mich.

### Speed
**Senior Men's**—Tom Peterson, Tacoma, Wash.
**Senior Ladies**—Linda Dorso, Cincinnati, Oh.
**Junior Men's**—Kenneth Sutton, Waukesha, Wis.
**Junior Ladies**—Lin Peterson, Tacoma, Wash.
**Senior Four Man Relay**—Tom Peterson, Stewart Roy, Jim Flaherty, Steve Clemons, Tacoma, Wash.
**Senior Four Lady Relay**—Linda Dorso, Lisa Bantin, Lisa Ashby, Mary Hohl, Cincinnati, Oh.

# Chess

Chess dates back to antiquity. Its exact origin is unknown. The strongest players of their time, and therefore regarded by later generations as world champions, were Francois Philidor, France; Alexandre Deschappelles, France; Louis de la Bourdonnais, France; Howard Staunton, England; Adolph Anderssen, Germany and Paul Morphy, United States. In 1866 Wilhelm Steinitz of Czechoslovakia defeated Adolph Anderssen and claimed the title of world champion. The official world champions, since the title was first used follow:

| | | |
|---|---|---|
| **1866-1894** Wilhelm Steinitz, Czech. | **1937-1946** Dr. Alexander A. Alekhine, USSR | **1961-1963** Mikhail Botvinnik, USSR |
| **1894-1921** Dr. Emanuel Lasker, Germany | | **1963-1969** Tigran Petrosian, USSR |
| **1921-1927** Jose R. Capablanca, Cuba | **1948-1957** Mikhail Botvinnik, USSR | **1969-1972** Boris Spassky, USSR |
| **1927-1935** Dr. Alexander A. Alekhine, USSR | **1957-1958** Vassily Smyslov, USSR | **1972-1975** Bobby Fischer, U.S. (a) |
| | **1958-1959** Mikhail Botvinnik, USSR | **1975**          Anatoly Karpov, USSR |
| **1935-1937** Dr. Max Euwe, Netherlands | **1960-1961** Mikhail Tal, USSR | |

(a) Defaulted championship after refusal to accept International Chess Federation rules for a championship match, April 1975.

## United States Champions

| Unofficial champions | Official champions | | |
|---|---|---|---|
| **1857-1871** Paul Morphy | **1891-1892** Jackson Showalter | **1944-1946** Arnold Denker | **1968-1969** Larry Evans |
| **1871-1876** George Mackenzie | **1892-1894** S. Lipschutz | **1946-1948** Samuel Reshevsky | **1969-1972** Samuel Reshevsky |
| **1876-1880** James Mason | **1894**          Jackson Showalter | **1948-1951** Herman Steiner | **1972-1973** Robert Byrne |
| **1880-1889** George Mackenzie | **1894-1895** Albert Hodges | **1951-1954** Larry Evans | **1973-1974** Lubomir Kavalek, John Grefe |
| **1889-1890** S. Lipschutz | **1895-1897** Jackson Showalter | **1954-1957** Arthur Bisguier | |
| **1890**          Jackson Showalter | **1897-1909** Harry Pillsbury | **1957-1961** Bobby Fischer | **1974-1977** Walter Browne |
| **1890-1891** Max Judd | **1909-1936** Frank Marshall | **1961-1962** Larry Evans | **1978**          Lubomir Kavalek |
| | **1936-1944** Samuel Reshevsky | **1962-1968** Bobby Fisher | |

# Polo Records

| | U.S. Open |
|---|---|
| 1969 | Tulsa Green Hill 11, Milwaukee 10. |
| 1970 | Tulsa Green Hill 9, Oak Brook 5. |
| 1971 | Oak Brook 8, Green Hill Farm 7. |
| 1972 | Milwaukee 9, Tulsa 5. |
| 1973 | Oak Brook 9, Willow Bend 4. |
| 1974 | Milwaukee 7, Houston 6. |
| 1975 | Milwaukee 14, Tulsa-Dallas 6. |
| 1976 | Willow Bend 10, Tulsa 5. |
| 1977 | Retama 11, Wilson Ranch 7. |

| | Silver Cup |
|---|---|
| 1969 | Oak Brook 7, Milwaukee 6. |
| 1970 | Oak Brook 9, Tulsa Green Hill 7. |
| 1971 | Green Hill Farm 8, Milwaukee 6. |
| 1972 | Red Doors Farm 10, Sun Ranch 6. |
| 1973 | Houston 6, Willow Bend 4. |
| 1974 | Houston 7, Willow Bend 6. |
| 1975 | Lone Oak-Bunntyco 8, Tulsa 5. |
| 1976 | Wilson Ranch 10, Tulsa 8. |
| 1977 | Boca Raton 6, Houston 5. |
| 1978 | Abercrombie & Kent 7, Tulsa 6. |

| | Intercollegiate Championship |
|---|---|
| 1969 | Yale 17, Cornell 16 |
| 1970 | Yale 22, Cornell 10 |
| 1971 | Yale 12, Virginia 11 |
| 1972 | Univ. of Conn. 17, Univ. of Virginia 15 |
| 1973 | Univ. of Conn. 19, Univ. of Virginia 10 |
| 1974 | Univ. of Conn. 18, Cornell 16 |
| 1975 | Univ. of Cal.-Davis 15, Yale 12 |
| 1976 | Xavier Univ. 25, Cornell 12. |
| 1977 | Xavier Univ. 13, Univ. of Cal.-Davis 9. |
| 1978 | Univ. Cal.-Davis 13, Xavier Univ. 7. |

### Other tournaments in 1978
**Delegate's Cup**—Boca Raton 8, Chukker Hill 6.
**America Cup**—Boca Raton 8, Chattanooga.
**Butler Handicap**—Smallwood 9, Jet Mix 5.
**Continental Cup**—Dahlwood 9, Narco 4.
**Gold Cup**—Abercrombie & Kent 8, Wilson Ranch 5.
**National President's Cup**—Fairlane 7, Longwood 5.
**Copper Cup**—Village Farms 8, Gone Away 7.

# Commonwealth Games in 1978

Canada won 109 medals-45 of them gold-to top the 47 nations that competed in the Commonwealth Games at Edmonton, Alta. Graham Smith of Canada won 6 gold medals.

# Trotting and Pacing Records

Source: Martin J. Evans, U.S. Trotting Assn.; records to Sept., 1978

## Trotting Records

Asterisk (*) denotes record was made against the clock. Times—seconds in fifths.

### One mile records (mile track)

**All-age — *1:54.4** — Nevele Pride, Indianapolis, Ind., Aug. 31, 1969.
**Two-year-old — 1:57** — Brisco Hanover, Du Quoin, Ill., Sept. 2, 1977.
**Three-year-old — 1:55** — Speedy Somolli and Florida Pro, Du Quoin, Ill., Sept. 2, 1978.

### (Half-mile track)

**All-age — 1:56.4** — Nevele Pride, Saratoga Springs, N.Y., Sept. 6, 1969.
**Two-year-old — 2:00.1** — Ayres, Delaware, Oh., 1963.
**Three-year-old — 1:58.3** — Songcan, Delaware, Oh., 1972.

### (Five Eighth-mile track)

**All-Age — 1:57.3** — Dream of Glory, Chicago, Ill., Aug. 21, 1976; Green Speed, Chicago, Ill., Aug. 25, 1978.
**Two-year-old — 2:01** — Starlark Hanover, Wilkes-Barre, Pa., Aug. 30, 1973; Green Speed, Philadelphia, Pa., Oct. 19, 1976.
**Three-year old — 1:58.1** — Speedy Somolli, Meadow Lands, Pa., Aug. 4, 1978.

### Odd distances

**1-1/16 Miles — 2:05.3** — Senator Frost, Inglewood, Cal., Oct. 17, 1959.
**1-1/8 — 2:12.3** — Keystone Pioneer, Inglewood, Cal., Nov. 12, 1976.
**1¼ Miles — 2:30.3** — Pronto Don, Inglewood, Cal., Nov. 24, 1951.
**1¼ Miles, half-mile track — 2:31.2** — Speedy Scot, Westbury, N.Y., Aug. 15, 1964; Noble Victory, Westbury, N.Y., July 2, 1966.
**1½ Miles — *3:02.1** — Greyhound, Indianapolis, Ind., Sept. 14, 1937.
**1½ Miles, half-mile track — 3:01.3** — Kash Minbar, Westbury, N.Y., July 30, 1977.
**2 Miles — *4:06** — Greyhound, Indianapolis, Ind., Sept. 19, 1939.

### Heat racing

**All-age — 1:55.3, 1:55.3** — Green Speed, Du Quoin, Sept. 3, 1977.
**Two-year-old — 1:59.1, 1:58.2** — Nevele Pride, Lexington, Ky., Oct. 4, 1967.
**Three-year-old — 1:55.3, 1:55.3** — Green Speed, Du Quoin, Ill., Sept. 3, 1977.

## Pacing Records

### One mile records (mile track)

**All-age — *1:52** — Steady Star, Lexington, Ky., Oct. 1, 1971.
**Two-year-old — 1:54.1** — Jade Prince, Lexington, Ky., Oct. 5, 1976.
**Three-year-old — *1:53.1** — Windshield Wiper, Lexington, Ky., Oct. 3, 1976.

### (Half-mile track)

**All-age — 1:55.3** — Adios Butler, Delaware, Oh., Sept. 21, 1961; Albatross, Delaware, Oh., 1972.
**Two-year-old — 1:58.4** — Columbia George, Yonkers, N.Y., Nov. 8, 1969; J. R. Skipper, Delaware, Oh., 1972; Armbro Ranger, Delaware, Oh., 1975.
**Three-year-old — 1:56** — Sundance Skipper, Saratoga Springs, N.Y., July 22, 1978.

### (Five Eighth-mile track)

**All-Age — 1:54.3** — Albatross, Chicago, Ill., 1972; Rambling Willie, Wilmington, Del., Sept. 4, 1977; Governor Skipper, Montreal, Que., Aug. 28, 1977.
**Two-year-old — 1:57** — Wellwood Hanover, Philadelphia, Pa., Oct. 11, 1977.
**Three-year-old — 1:54.3** — Governor Skipper, Montreal, Que., Aug. 28, 1977.

### Odd distances

**1-1/16 Miles — 2:03.1** — Adios Vic, Inglewood, Cal., Oct. 23, 1965.
**1⅛ Miles — 2:09.1** — True Duane, Inglewood, Cal., Nov. 5, 1966.
**1¼ Miles, half-mile track — 2:28.3** — Armbro Ranger, Yonkers, N.Y., June 18, 1977.
**1½ Miles, half-mile track — 3:01.4** — Handle With Care, Yonkers, N.Y., Aug. 21, 1976.

### Heat racing

**All-age — 1:54.4, 1:54.3** — Taurus Bomber, Springfield, Ill., Aug. 20, 1976; 1:55.1, 1:54.1 — Jade Prince, Lexington, Ky., Oct. 5, 1976.
**Two-year-old — 1:55.1, 1:54.1** — Jade Prince, Lexington, Ky., Oct. 5, 1976.
**Three-year-old — 1:54.4, 1:54.4** — Albatross, Lexington, Ky., Oct. 2, 1971.

## The Hambletonian (3-year-old trotters)

Du Quoin, Ill.

| Year | Winner | Driver | Purse | Year | Winner | Driver | Purse |
|---|---|---|---|---|---|---|---|
| 1947 | Hoot Mon | S.F. Palin | $46,267 | 1963 | Speedy Scot | Ralph Baldwin | $115,549 |
| 1948 | Demon Hanover | Harrison Hoyt | 59,941 | 1964 | Ayres | John Simpson Sr. | 115,281 |
| 1949 | Miss Tilly | Fred Egan | 69,791 | 1965 | Egyptian Candor | Del Cameron | 122,245 |
| 1950 | Lusty Song | Del Miller | 75,209 | 1966 | Kerry Way | Frank Ervin | 122,540 |
| 1951 | Mainliner | Guy Crippen | 95,263 | 1967 | Speedy Streak | Del Cameron | 122,650 |
| 1952 | Sharp Note | Bion Shively | 87,637 | 1968 | Nevele Pride | Stanley Dancer | 116,190 |
| 1953 | Helicopter | Harry Harvey | 117,118 | 1969 | Lindy's Pride | Howard Beissinger | 124,910 |
| 1954 | Newport Dream | Del Cameron | 106,830 | 1970 | Timothy T | John Simpson Sr. | 143,630 |
| 1955 | Scott Frost | Joe O'Brien | 86,863 | 1971 | Speedy Crown | Howard Beissinger | 128,770 |
| 1956 | The Intruder | Ned Bower | 98,591 | 1972 | Super Bowl | Stanley Dancer | 119,090 |
| 1957 | Hickory Smoke | John Simpson Sr. | 111,126 | 1973 | Flirth | Ralph Baldwin | 144,710 |
| 1958 | Emily's Pride | Flave Nipe | 106,719 | 1974 | Christopher T | Bill Haughton | 160,150 |
| 1959 | Diller Hanover | Frank Ervin | 125,284 | 1975 | Bonefish | Stanley Dancer | 232,192 |
| 1960 | Blaze Hanover | Joe O'Brien | 144,590 | 1976 | Steve Lobell | Bill Haughton | 263,524 |
| 1961 | Harlan Dean | James Arthur | 131,573 | 1977 | Green Speed | Bill Haughton | 284,131 |
| 1962 | A.C. Os Viking | Sanders Russell | 116,312 | 1978 | Speedy Somolli | Howard Beissinger | 241,280 |

## Harness Horse of the Year

(Chosen by the U.S. Trotting Assn. and the U.S. Harness Writers Assn.)

| | | | | | |
|---|---|---|---|---|---|
| 1948 | Rodney | 1956 | Scott Frost | 1964 | Bret Hanover | 1971 | Albatross |
| 1949 | Good Time | 1957 | Torpid | 1965 | Bret Hanover | 1972 | Albatross |
| 1950 | Proximity | 1958 | Emily's Pride | 1966 | Bret Hanover | 1973 | Sir Dalrae |
| 1951 | Pronto Don | 1959 | Bye Bye Byrd | 1967 | Nevele Pride | 1974 | Delmonica Hanover |
| 1952 | Good Time | 1960 | Adios Butler | 1968 | Nevele Pride | 1975 | Savior |
| 1953 | Hi Lo's Forbes | 1961 | Adios Butler | 1969 | Nevele Pride | 1976 | Keystone Ore |
| 1954 | Stenographer | 1962 | Su Mac Lad | 1970 | Fresh Yankee | 1977 | Green Speed |
| 1955 | Scott Frost | 1963 | Speedy Scot | | | | |

## Little Brown Jug (3-year-old pacers)

Delaware, Oh.

| Year | Winner | Driver | Purse | Year | Winner | Driver | Purse |
|---|---|---|---|---|---|---|---|
| 1955 | Quick Chief | Billy Haughton | $66,608 | 1967 | Best of All | James Hackett | $84,778 |
| 1956 | Noble Adios | John Simpson Sr. | 52,666 | 1968 | Rum Customer | Billy Haughton | 104,226 |
| 1957 | Torpid | John Simpson Sr. | 73,528 | 1969 | Laverne Hanover | Billy Haughton | 109,731 |
| 1958 | Shadow Wave | Joe O'Brien | 65,252 | 1970 | Most Happy Fella | Stanley Dancer | 100,110 |
| 1959 | Adios Butler | Clint Hodgins | 76,582 | 1971 | Nansemond | Herve Filion | 102,944 |
| 1960 | Bullet Hanover | John Simpson Sr. | 66,510 | 1972 | Strike Out | Keith Waples | 104,916 |
| 1961 | Henry T. Adios | Stanley Dancer | 70,069 | 1973 | Melvin's Woe | Joe O'Brien | 120,000 |
| 1962 | Lehigh Hanover | Stanley Dancer | 75,038 | 1974 | Ambro Omaha | Billy Haughton | 132,630 |
| 1963 | Overtrick | John Patterson Sr. | 68,294 | 1975 | Seatrain | Ben Webster | 147,813 |
| 1964 | Vicar Hanover | Billy Haughton | 66,590 | 1976 | Keystone Ore | Stanley Dancer | 153,799 |
| 1965 | Bret Hanover | Frank Ervin | 71,447 | 1977 | Gov. Skipper | John Chapman | 150,000 |
| 1966 | Romeo Hanover | George Sholty | 74,616 | 1978 | Happy Escort | Bill Popfinger | 186,760 |

## Leading Drivers

### Races Won

| Year | Driver | | Year | Driver | | Year | Driver | | Year | Driver | |
|---|---|---|---|---|---|---|---|---|---|---|---|
| 1958 | Bill Haughton | 176 | 1963 | Donald Busse | 201 | 1968 | Herve Filion | 407 | 1973 | Herve Filion | 445 |
| 1959 | William Gilmour | 165 | 1964 | Bob Farrington | 312 | 1969 | Herve Filion | 394 | 1974 | Herve Filion | 637 |
| 1960 | Del Insko | 156 | 1965 | Bob Farrington | 310 | 1970 | Herve Filion | 486 | 1975 | Daryl Buse | 360 |
| 1961 | Bob Farrington | 201 | 1966 | Bob Farrington | 283 | 1971 | Herve Filion | 543 | 1976 | Herve Filion | 445 |
| 1962 | Bob Farrington | 203 | 1967 | Bob Farrington | 277 | 1972 | Herve Filion | 605 | 1977 | Herve Filion | 441 |

### Money Won

| Year | Driver | Dollars | Year | Driver | Dollars | Year | Driver | Dollars |
|---|---|---|---|---|---|---|---|---|
| 1957 | Bill Haughton | 586,950 | 1964 | Stanley Dancer | 1,051,538 | 1971 | Herve Filion | 1,915,945 |
| 1958 | Bill Haughton | 816,659 | 1965 | Bill Haughton | 889,943 | 1972 | Herve Filion | 2,473,265 |
| 1959 | Bill Haughton | 711,435 | 1966 | Stanley Dancer | 1,218,403 | 1973 | Herve Filion | 2,233,302 |
| 1960 | Del Miller | 567,282 | 1967 | Bill Haughton | 1,305,773 | 1974 | Herve Filion | 3,474,315 |
| 1961 | Stanley Dancer | 674,723 | 1968 | Bill Haughton | 1,654,172 | 1975 | Carmine Abbatiello | 2,275,093 |
| 1962 | Stanley Dancer | 760,343 | 1969 | Del Insko | 1,635,463 | 1976 | Herve Filion | 2,241,045 |
| 1963 | Bill Haughton | 790,086 | 1970 | Herve Filion | 1,647,837 | 1977 | Herve Filion | 2,551,058 |

## Annual Leading Money-Winning Horses

### Trotters

| Year | Horse | Dollars | Year | Horse | Dollars | Year | Horse | Dollars |
|---|---|---|---|---|---|---|---|---|
| 1952 | Sharp Note | 101,625 | 1961 | Su Mac Lad | 245,750 | 1970 | Fresh Yankee | 359,002 |
| 1953 | Newport Dream | 94,933 | 1962 | Duke Rodney | 206,113 | 1971 | Fresh Yankee | 293,950 |
| 1954 | Katie Key | 84,867 | 1963 | Speedy Scot | 144,403 | 1972 | Super Bowl | 437,108 |
| 1955 | Scott Frost | 186,101 | 1964 | Speedy Scot | 235,710 | 1973 | Spartan Hanover | 262,023 |
| 1956 | Scott Frost | 85,851 | 1965 | Dartmouth | 252,348 | 1974 | Delmonica Hanover | 252,165 |
| 1957 | Hoot Song | 114,877 | 1966 | Noble Victory | 210,696 | 1975 | Savoir | 351,385 |
| 1958 | Emily's Pride | 118,830 | 1967 | Carlisle | 231,243 | 1976 | Steve Lobell | 338,770 |
| 1959 | Diller Hanover | 149,897 | 1968 | Nevele Pride | 427,440 | 1977 | Green Speed | 584,405 |
| 1960 | Su Mac Lad | 159,662 | 1969 | Lindy's Pride | 323,997 | | | |

### Pacers

| Year | Horse | Dollars | Year | Horse | Dollars | Year | Horse | Dollars |
|---|---|---|---|---|---|---|---|---|
| 1952 | Good Time | 110,299 | 1961 | Adios Butler | 180,250 | 1970 | Most Happy Fella | 387,239 |
| 1953 | Keystoner | 59,131 | 1962 | Henry T. Adios | 220,302 | 1971 | Albatross | 558,009 |
| 1954 | Red Sails | 66,615 | 1963 | Overtrick | 208,833 | 1972 | Albatross | 459,921 |
| 1955 | Adios Harry | 98,900 | 1964 | Race Time | 199,292 | 1973 | Sir Dalrae | 307,354 |
| 1956 | Adios Harry | 129,912 | 1965 | Bret Hanover | 341,784 | 1974 | Armbro Omaha | 345,146 |
| 1957 | Torpid | 113,982 | 1966 | Bret Hanover | 407,534 | 1975 | Silk Stockings | 336,312 |
| 1958 | Belle Action | 167,887 | 1967 | Romulus Hanover | 277,636 | 1976 | Keystone Ore | 539,762 |
| 1959 | Bye Bye Byrd | 199,933 | 1968 | Rum Customer | 355,618 | 1977 | Governor Skipper | 522,148 |
| 1960 | Bye Bye Byrd | 187,612 | 1969 | Overcall | 373,150 | | | |

## Leading Money-Winning Horses

(As of Jan. 1, 1978)

| Trotters | | | | Pacers | | | |
|---|---|---|---|---|---|---|---|
| Bellino II | $1,960,945 | Timothy T. | $894,237 | Albatross | $1,201,470 | Laverne Hanover | $868,557 |
| Une de Mai | 1,660,627 | Su Mac Lad | 885,095 | Rambling Willie | 1,066,437 | Handle With Care | 809,689 |
| Savoir | 1,307,595 | Nevele Pride | 873,238 | Rum Customer | 1,001,548 | Overcall | 783,948 |
| Fresh Yankee | 1,294,252 | Delmonica Hanover | 832,925 | Cardigan Bay | 1,000,837 | Henry T. Adios | 706,833 |
| Roquepine | 956,161 | Tidalium Pelo | 758,603 | Bret Hanover | 922,616 | Silk Stockings | 694,894 |

## Tour de France in 1978

Bernard Hinault of France won the Tour de France, the world's most prestigious bicycle endurance race, on July 23, 1978. The event covered 2,500 miles from Leiden, in the Netherlands, to Paris.

## NCAA Volleyball in 1978

Pepperdine won its first NCAA Volleyball by defeating UCLA 15-12, 11-15, 15-8, 5-15, and 15-12 at Columbus, Oh.

# CHRONOLOGY OF THE YEAR'S EVENTS

## Reported Month by Month in 3 Categories: National, International, and General — Nov. 1, 1977, to Nov. 1, 1978

## NOVEMBER

### National

**Prices, Unemployment, Trade Deficit Up**—The labor department, Nov. 3, reported that wholesale prices had risen by 0.8% during October, the largest gain in 6 months. On Nov. 4, it reported further that the nation's jobless rate had risen by 0.1% to 7% during the month of October. The White House described the news as a "disappointment" and as an indication that "economic growth has not picked up as fast as we expected." On Nov. 28, the commerce department indicated that the U.S. had registered a $3.1 billion trade deficit during October. It was the first time in the nation's history that the excess in imports over exports had topped $3 billion. The large deficit was laid chiefly to the East and Gulf coast dockers' strike which had begun Oct. 1.

**Helms Fined**—Federal District Judge Barrington D. Parker, in Washington, D.C., Nov. 4, fined former CIA Director Richard Helms $2,000, and gave him a 2-year suspended prison sentence and a stern rebuke for falsely testifying to a Senate committee in 1973 on covert operations in Chile. Barrington told Helms, "You dishonored your oath and you now stand before this court in disgrace and shame." After the sentencing, Helms replied that he had felt bound by his oath as an intelligence official "to protect intelligence sources and methods" when he had testified falsely before the Senate.

**Carter Vetoes Tennessee Reactor**—Wielding his first presidential veto, Pres. Jimmy Carter, Nov. 5, rejected legislation authorizing $80 million for a controversial nuclear breeder reactor on the Clinch River in Tennessee. Carter maintained that the project would be "technically and economically unnecessary" and that the plutonium-fueled reactor would "imperil the administration's policy to curb proliferation of nuclear weapons technology."

**Dock Strike Settled**—Ending a 60-day strike that had paralyzed container shipping from Maine to Texas, dockworkers, Nov. 29, accepted a new 3-year master contract by a 5-to-1 margin. The contract, negotiated between the International Longshoremen's Association and North Atlantic shipping employers Nov. 13, provided for a job security program and for wage and benefit increases of 30% over the term of the contract. ILA Pres. Thomas W. Gleason called the contract "a real breakthrough" in providing job security and a guaranteed annual income for longshoremen.

**Korean CIA Plan Disclosed**—The House Subcommittee on International Organizations, Nov. 29, disclosed the details of a plan created in 1976 by the South Korean CIA to manipulate the Ford administration, Congress, American news organizations, and the clergy to Seoul's advantage. The plan was more sophisticated and wider in scope than any yet revealed in the ongoing investigation of Korean influence buying in the U.S. The plan included actions to implant "an intelligence network in the White House" during the final year of the Ford administration, to win over the Democratic party's policy research committee in Congress, to create U.S. policy favorable to South Korea through various lures, including invitations to influential U.S. journalists to visit South Korea.

### International

**U.S. Withdraws From ILO**—U.S. Pres. Jimmy Carter, Nov. 1, withdrew the U.S. from the International Labor Organization effective Nov. 5. The action elicited generally harsh criticism from UN members; Secretary-General Kurt Waldheim called the move a "retrogressive step." The U.S. decision meant an end to its annual contribution of $20 million, a quarter of the annual ILO budget. U.S. Labor Secretary Ray Marshall stated that some U.S. contribution would continue indirectly through the UN Development Program. The decision stemmed from 1974 when an Arab-Communist coalition in the ILO secured majority support for a resolution condemning Israel for "racism" and occupying Arab lands. U.S. Secretary of State Henry A. Kissinger had threatened U.S. withdrawal within 2 years unless the ILO ceased such political activity. According to Marshall, the Carter administration had evaluated Kissinger's threat and decided to follow his policy.

**Giscard d'Estaing Supports Lévesque**—At a luncheon in honor of Quebec Premier Rene Lévesque, French Pres. Valery Giscard d'Estaing, Nov. 3, in Paris, expressed support for Quebec's right to self-determination. The statement, coming shortly after Giscard d'Estaing had taken the unusual step of making Lévesque a grand officer of the Legion of Honor, angered the Canadian government. Canadian Prime Minister Pierre Elliott Trudeau, at a press conference in Ottawa, took exception to references by French officials to the problem of French Canadian separatism. The Canadian government, Nov. 4, expressing irritation over the award of the Legion of Honor, reminded France that Canadians were not allowed to accept foreign honors without the express approval of their government.

**UN Votes South African Arms Embargo**—The UN Security Council, Nov. 4, unanimously voted a mandatory embargo on arms and military material to South Africa. The action, the first such punitive measure against one of its members in the UN's 32-year history, was directed against South Africa's repressive racial policies. South African Foreign Minister Roelof F. Botha called the embargo an incitement to violence and claimed it would stiffen the resolve of South Africans to defend their country. Specifically, the resolution obliged the UN's 149 members to "cease forthwith" the provision of arms, ammunition, military vehicles, equipment, and spare parts to South Africa, as well as new licenses for manufacturing such materials.

**Israel Bombs Southern Lebanon**—Israeli fighter-bombers, Nov. 9, conducted heavy bombing raids over southern Lebanon, ostensibly in reprisal for a recent attack on Nahariya in northern Israel. The Lebanese government reported that more than 100 persons, most of them civilians, were killed. The targets, according to Israeli officials, had been Palestinian guerrilla enclaves near Tyre held responsible for the attack on Nahariya. On Nov. 7, Israel had warned that its forces would "act intensively and quickly to restore quiet" in the Lebanese border area if Palestinian guerrillas continued to shell northern Israeli communities. On Nov. 11, Israeli fighter-bombers again raided southern Lebanon, wounding 14 persons.

**Somalia Expels Soviets, Cubans**—In a dramatic diplomatic turn, Somalia, Nov. 13, expelled all Soviet advisers, ordering them to leave within 7 days, and broke diplomatic relations with Cuba. In expelling the Soviets, Somalia, which for 8 years was Moscow's prime ally in East Africa, ended Soviet use of strategic naval facilities on the Indian Ocean. The Cubans were given 48 hours to leave the country. The sudden move was spurred by Somalia's anger over Soviet support for Ethiopia in the 4-month-old war in Ethiopia's Ogaden district and by the presence there of Cuban advisers. In a statement over Mogadishu radio, Minister of Information Abdulkassim Salad Hassan attacked "governments that have brazenly interfered in the struggle of the peoples fighting for their liberation from the Ethiopian government" and charged that their "intention is to launch a joint attack on Somalia."

**Rhodesian Leader Accepts Majority Rule**—Following the breakdown of the latest British-American peace effort, Rhodesian Prime Minister Ian D. Smith, Nov. 24, stated that he was prepared to accept majority rule based on universal suffrage as a starting point for negotiations with black nationalist leaders living in Rhodesia. Smith indicated that he had abandoned his long-held opposition to majority rule because the black nationalists had agreed to seek to safeguard the confidence of white Rhodesians in a black government. Such

915

safeguards, Smith said, would include an independent judicial system and special representation for minorities. On Nov. 25, the African National Council and the Zimbabwe United People's Organization stated that they were prepared to begin negotiations. On Nov. 26, Bishop Muzorewa, considered the major black nationalist spokesman in Rhodesia, said he would also negotiate if he were certain that Smith's offer was genuine.

### General

**Two Convicted in Bolles Death**—A Phoenix, Ariz., jury, Nov. 6, convicted Max Dunlap, a contractor, and James Robison, a plumber, of murder and conspiracy in the 1976 death of Don Bolles, an *Arizona Republic* reporter who had been investigating land fraud, organized crime, and the Arizona Racing Commission. The 2 men were also convicted of plotting to kill Bruce Babbitt, the Arizona attorney general, and Al (King Alfonso) Lizanetz, a former advertising man. Bolles died 11 days after he had been maimed in a bomb blast in his car. The prosecution based its case on the testimony of John Harvey Adamson, who had confessed to the killing and implicated Dunlap and Robison. Both Dunlap and Robison, **Jan. 10**, were sentenced to death in the gas chamber for the murder charge. Both were also sentenced to 29 to 30 years in prison on the conspiracy charge.

**KKK Figure Convicted**—Fourteen years after the fact, a Birmingham, Ala., jury, Nov. 18, convicted former Ku Klux Klansman Robert E. Chambliss of first-degree murder in the 1963 bombing of a Baptist church that resulted in the deaths of 4 young black girls. The 73-year-old former klansman was sentenced to life imprisonment. Chambliss, whose attorneys said he would appeal, claimed innocence: "God knows I have never killed anybody. . . . God knows I have never bombed anything in my life and wasn't down at that church." The prosecution announced jubilantly that they would seek further indictments in the case.

**Women's Conference Approves Rights Agenda**—The National Women's Conference, Nov. 21, in Houston, Tex., ended a 3-day convention by approving a 25-point plan for national action on women's equality. Only one point of the original agenda, a cabinet-level women's department, was rejected by the 1,442 voting delegates. Three points — re-productive freedom (abortion), homosexual rights, and passage of the Equal Rights Amendment — drew the most debate and controversy. In the closing moments of the conference, some 300 "pro-life" and "pro-family" delegates who opposed these points, as well as most of the agenda, marched off the convention floor singing "God Bless America." The group had complained that selective exercise of parliamentary procedure had prevented minority delegates from speaking or amending resolutions. The 25-point agenda also included recommendations for expanded child-care centers, federal programs for battered wives and abused children, affirmation of rights of older and disabled women, and the elimination of discrimination in employment, insurance, credit, and other institutional policies.

**Disasters**—Torrential rains, Nov. 6, collapsed an earthen dam on the outskirts of Toccoa, Ga., releasing a 35-foot-wall of water that swept through a trailer park on the Toccoa Falls Bible College campus, killing some 37 persons and injuring 45 others . . . . A typhoon swept the northern Philippines, Nov. 14, leaving some 80 persons dead and 50,000 persons homeless; of the 80 dead, 47 expired in a wind-swept fire at the Filipinas Hotel in Manila . . . . A TAP Portuguese airliner, Nov. 19, crashed in a rainstorm at the Funchal, Madeira, airport, killing 130 persons . . . . Some 20,000 persons were dead and more than 2 million homeless after a cyclone, Nov. 19, swept the coast of Andhra Pradesh in southern India . . . . Some 70 persons were left dead, 254 injured, and 10,000 homeless when an earthquake struck western Argentina, Nov. 23.

## DECEMBER

### National

**FBI Releases JFK Assassination Files** — Responding to several requests under the Freedom of Information Act, the FBI, Dec. 7, released 40,000 pages of files from its investigation of the 1963 assassination of Pres. John F. Kennedy. Though little new or dramatic information was contained in the 200 volumes of material, it represented the first time the FBI had released secret documents in the Kennedy case. Among the memoranda, reports, and other papers was a

---

### Sadat Goes to Israel to Promote Middle East Peace; Sadat and Begin Confer and Pledge "No More War"

For the first time since the creation of the Israeli state in 1948, an Egyptian leader, Nov. 19, met with an Israeli leader on Israeli soil. Upon his arrival in Jerusalem, Pres. Anwar Sadat received all the honors of a visiting head of state and was greeted by Israeli Prime Minister Menahem Begin and Pres. Ehpraim Katzir. Also on hand to greet Sadat were a host of prominent throughout the years of Egyptian-Israeli hostility: Golda Meir, Moshe Dyan, Yitzak Rabin, and Gen. Ariel Sharon.

The genesis of the historic meeting which captivated both the Israeli and Egyptian people came Nov. 9 in Cairo when Sadat told the Egyptian parliament, "I am ready to go to the Israeli parliament itself" to discuss procedural difficulties in reconvening a Geneva conference on Middle East peace. Following overwhelming approval by the Israeli parliament, Begin, Nov. 14, formally invited the Egyptian leader to address the Knesset. Despite harsh criticism in the Arab world and following an unsuccessful trip, Nov. 16, to persuade Syrian Pres. Hafez al-Assad to support him, Sadat, Nov. 17, accepted Begin's invitation. Within hours of the decision Egyptian Foreign Minister Ismail Fahmy had resigned in protests and bombs were set off near the Egyptian embassy in Damascus. Waves of protest, Nov. 18, continued to sweep Middle East capitals as Arab unity, based primarily on a common stand against Israel, seemed to founder.

On Nov. 20, Sadat met with a warm, enthusiastic reception as he delivered an eloquent plea for peace to the Knesset. While he made it clear that Egypt accepted the existence of Israel, Sadat underlined that a lasting Middle East peace depended on Israeli withdrawal from occupied Arab lands, including East Jerusalem, and recognition of the rights of the Palestinians. Sadat welcomed Israelis to live "among us with all security and safety," but warned that "you have to give up once and for all the dreams of conquest and to give up the belief that force is the best method in dealing with the Arabs."

Begin, in response, praised Sadat personally for his courage in coming to Jerusalem and stated that Israel did "not believe in might" and had never put its "trust in might in dealing with an Arab country." Begin also said that henceforth all Egyptians would be free to come to Israel and urged the leaders of other Arab "confrontation" states to come to Israel for talks.

On Nov. 21, Sadat and Begin made repeated pledges of "no more war" and issued a communique pledging to continue the dialogue they had begun both in public and private meetings.

Arab reaction to the Begin-Sadat meetings crystallized Nov. 22. Syria denounced the visit in the UN General Assembly as a "visit of shame" and a "stab in the back of the Arab people." On Nov. 25, Syria ruled out participation in a Geneva peace conference under the present circumstances, saying that the visit had split the Arab world and encouraged Israel to be intransigent. But Syria indicated it might make a negotiated settlement with Israel and was not yet ready to join a group of rejectionist states consisting of Libya, Iraq, Algeria, and South Yemen.

Continuing his peace effort, Sadat, Nov. 26, invited all parties involved, including Israel, the U.S., the USSR, and UN Secretary General Kurt Waldheim, to send representatives to Cairo to hold talks aimed at removing obstacles to a Geneva conference. Israel promptly accepted the invitation. Syrian Foreign Minister Abdel Halim Khaddam rejected the proposal as did the Palestine Liberation Organization. U.S. administration officials, Nov. 28, indicated that Pres. Jimmy Carter had decided to accept the Sadat invitation. The USSR, Nov. 29, rejected the invitation.

memo dated Dec. 12, 1963, from then-Director J. Edgar Hoover stating his belief Lee Harvey Oswald was the assassin, but possibly not the only one. Another release of materials from the files was set for Jan. 1978.

**Wholesale and Consumer Prices Up; Employment Rises Sharply** — The government announced, Dec. 8, that the November wholesale price index rose 0.7% over the previous month, an increase that was less than expected. Farm prices rose 3% during November. The Consumer Price Index for November was up 0.5%. Government economists, Dec. 21, blamed food price inflation and mark-ups for Toyota cars imported from Japan for the increase, which was the highest in 5 months. Even though 950,000 more people were employed in November than October, it was reported, Dec. 2, unemployment rate was still 6.9% nationwide, only an 0.1% drop from October. A record 63% of all working age Americans were employed in November.

**Congress Raises Social Security Tax** — After months of negotiation, what had been described by opponents as the "biggest peacetime tax increase in history" was passed Dec. 15 by Congress, mandating a series of increases starting in 1979 that will raise an estimated $227.3 billion for the nation's faltering Social Security system. The bill, which passed 56-21 in the Senate and 189-163 in the House, was designed to end deficits that drained cash from the Social Security trust funds and that threatened to force an end to disability payments in 1979 and old age pensions in 1982. Under the new legislation, which Pres. Carter signed Dec. 20, the maximum amount of social security tax paid by an employee would raise from $965 per year in 1977 to $3,046 per year by 1987. Also included in the compromise bill was a provision liberalizing benefits for Social Security recipients who work, raising the amount pensioners could earn without penalty to $6,000 per year by 1982.

**Farmers Strike for Higher Prices** — Many of the nation's farmers, angered at the high cost of farming and the low prices received from what they produce, began a strike, Dec. 14, to seek the Carter Administration's approval for higher floor prices for crops and 100% parity. A group calling itself the American Agriculture Movement and claiming support of 800,000 of the nation's 2.5 million farmers, said they would refuse to buy equipment and supplies for spring planting unless the government came to the farmer's aid. In a demonstration of anger by farmers, 4,000 tractors had crammed the streets of Plains, Ga., on Nov. 24, Thanksgiving Day, and 1,500 appeared again, Dec. 24. Pres. Carter met with the farmers, Dec. 24, and urged them to plant crops, but said he was unable to support 100% parity. Farmers' picket lines prevented grain ships from unloading in Portland and Seattle, Dec. 21. Commodity brokers, however, said the strike had little impact on either the market or farm prices.

**61 Americans Released from Mexican Prisons** — In a festive scene of banners, balloons, and cheers from onlookers at the San Diego Airport, Dec. 9, 61 Americans (and an 18-month-old child of one of them) who had been jailed in Mexico, returned to the U.S. in the first phase of a prisoner exchange. Jailed in the early 1970s at the peak of a drug trafficking crackdown by the Mexican government, the 35 men and 26 women were the first of as many as 300 Americans expected to be released. Another 66 Americans arrived Dec. 10. Earlier in the day, Dec. 9, the same chartered DC-9 jet had picked up 11 Mexican nationals held as prisoners in Houston, and 25 held in San Diego, and flew them back to Mexico City. The American group included 2 women in their 60s arrested for cocaine smuggling. Many of the Americans faced a continuation of their prison terms in U. S. jails, though some were to be released.

**Lance Sells Bank Stock; Carter Names His Successor** — Former budget director Bert Lance agreed, Dec. 21, to sell 60% of his stock in the National Bank of Georgia to Ghaith R. Pharaon, a Saudi Arabian businessman, for $20 per share, approximately $3 more per share than Lance originally paid for the 120,000 shares. An "agreement in principle" had been reached to sell the stock to Pharaon, who also owns interests in banks in Houston and Detroit. In a related development, Pres. Carter, Dec. 28, appointed Lance's former deputy, James T. McIntyre to Lance's old job as head of the Office of Management and Budget. McIntyre, a former Georgia budget director, had been acting director of

OMB since Lance's Sept. 21 resignation.

**U. S. Steel Raises Prices 5.5%** — The nation's largest steel company, U. S. Steel, announced, Dec. 11, an average 5.5% price increase, beginning Feb. 1, 1978. Bethlehem Steel and National Steel Corp., the nation's 2d and 3d largest producers, had previously announced similar prices hikes, Dec. 19 and 22. The price increases were sought to aid the industry, which had lost 60,000 jobs in 1977 and suffered from foreign imports which sold at $40-50 less per ton than U. S.-made steel. Government economists, while not pleased with the price hike, felt they "weren't out of line with the general inflation rate."

**Carter Approves 1979 Military Budget** — Pres. Carter, Dec. 22, approved a $126 billion budget for the Department of Defense for fiscal 1979. The budget was $4 billion less than requested by Defense Secretary Harold Brown, and was approved after what an Administration source characterized as "internal debate and horse trading" between the White House and Pentagon. Hardest hit by the cut was the U. S. Navy, whose excess costs of $6 billion in the last 8 years were reported to be one major source of contention between the military and the White House. A senior Pentagon official warned the cuts were "bound to have some impact on our readiness." The defense budget increased 2% over the fiscal 1978 budget.

**Burns Out as Federal Reserve Chairman** — In a surprise move, Pres. Carter, Dec. 28, announced he would replace Federal Reserve Board Chairman Dr. Arthur F. Burns with G. William Miller, chairman of Textron, Inc., a Rhode Island-based manufacturer. Burns' term as head of the board was to expire Jan. 31, 1978, though his term as one of 7 governors to the Fed expires in 1984. Burns, a fiscal conservative and vocal critic of the Administration's economic policies, had clashed most recently with the White House over the board's policies of tightening interest rates. Vice President Mondale, Treasury Secy. W. Michael Blumenthal and other liberal counselors had lobbied to replace Burns, and Carter's decision ended months of speculation about the Fed's direction both here and abroad. "The President has chosen wisely and well," Burns said of his successor. The financial community generally praised the choice, though it expressed some uncertainty about Miller's views on monetary policy and a concern over the future independence of the Fed.

## International

**Police Absolved in Biko Death** — After a 3-week inquest, South African security police and others involved in the arrest and interrogation of black leader Stephen Biko were absolved, Dec. 2, of any responsibility in his death from brain injuries, Sept. 12. A few hours before Magistrate Marthinus J. Prins announced the verdict, police arrested some 13 members of Biko's "Black Consciousness" group, including his brother, Kaya, and a cousin, Solomon. The inquest verdict found that Biko's injuries had resulted from a scuffle with police on Sept. 7, not from beatings by his interrogators, as lawyers for Biko's family charged. The inquest was marked by admissions from police that Biko had been kept naked in his cell for most of the 19 days prior to his death, that he had been shackled and handcuffed up to 50 hours at a time, and that police had prevented doctors from hospitalizing him after he was injured. The inquest verdict came on the heels of a Dec. 1 election, when the National Party of Prime Minister John Vorster won 134 seats in the 165-member Assembly.

**$5 Million Property Damages in Bermuda Riots** — After 250 British soldiers were flown to the island, Bermuda police were able to restore order, Dec. 4, after 3 nights of rioting in protest over the hanging of 2 criminals on Dec. 2. Even a dawn-to-dusk curfew announced by the government did not deter mobs of angry blacks from rioting in Hamilton. Arsonists set fire to a liquor warehouse, supermarkets, and other buildings, as police used tear gas against the rioters. Three persons, including two Americans, died when the luxury Southampton Princess Hotel burned, Dec. 2, a fire police suspected may have been set. The 2 hanged criminals, Erskine Burrows and Larry Tacklyn, had been convicted of several murders, including the murder of Bermuda's Governor Sir Richard Sharples in 1972.

**Egypt Severs Ties with Arab States** — President Anwar

Sadat, Dec. 5, announced Egypt was breaking diplomatic relations with Syria, Iraq, Libya, Algeria, and S. Yemen. On Dec. 7, he ordered closing of some Soviet-bloc cultural centers and consulates in Egypt, in retaliation for what he saw as Soviet interference with Mideast peace efforts. The 5 Arab states, and the PLO, were all participants in a conference held at Tripoli, Libya, Dec. 2-4, to discuss their response to the Sadat peace initiative. A declaration at the end of the conference strongly criticized Sadat's actions and announced a "freeze" on diplomatic relations with Egypt and a boycott of Egyptian companies that do business with Israel. Sadat said Egypt would carry negotiations "through to the end," alone if necessary.

Soviets Arrest 20 on Human Rights Day — In an unusual celebration of UN Human Rights Day, Dec. 10, the Soviet government placed some 20 prominent dissidents under house arrest, cutting off telephones, and threatening to break up a planned silent demonstration in Pushkin Square. While Pravda and other Soviet papers decried human rights violations elsewhere in the world, plainclothes secret police stationed themselves outside the residences of the dissidents. The demonstration, to mark the 1948 adoption of the Universal Declaration of Human Rights by the United Nations, was held anyway, when 25 people gathered silently at the statue of Pushkin for several minutes, without interference.

Egypt, Israel Meet on Mideast Peace Plans — Representatives of Egypt, Israel, the U. S. and the UN met in Cairo, Dec. 14, to begin procedural negotiations for a future conference on Mideast peace. Syria, Jordan, Lebanon, the USSR, and the PLO were all invited, but did not attend. All sides in attendance reported progress after a closed-door meeting, Dec. 15. U. S. Secy. of State Cyrus Vance had visited 6 Mideast countries, Dec. 9-14, to show U. S. backing for the conference. As the Cairo meeting got underway, Israeli Prime Minister Menahem Begin flew to the United States, Dec. 14, and met with Pres. Carter, Dec. 16, to unveil Israel's latest peace proposal, which included restoration to Egypt of complete sovereignty over the Sinai Peninsula and to give Palestinians control over the internal affairs in the West Bank of the Jordan River and the Gaza Strip, Israel to maintain a military presence in all three areas.

Kidnapers Release Cyprus President's Son — Achilleas Kyprianou, the son of Cyprus' President Spyros Kyprianou, was released unharmed, Dec. 18, after members of the right-wing group EOKA-B had kidnaped him Dec. 14. Achilleas, a second lieutenant in the island nation's National Guard, was siezed at the gate of a military camp in the Troodas Mountains. EOKA-B, which wants political union with Greece, demanded the release of 25 imprisoned members in exchange for Kyprianou's life. The Cypriot president declined to release the prisoners, but promised no action would be taken against the kidnapers if his son was released.

Sadat, Begin Meet on Mideast Peace — A summit meeting between Egyptian President Anwar Sadat and Israeli Prime Minister Menahem Begin, Dec. 25-26, in Ismalia, Egypt, produced no joint declaration of principles for establishing peace in the Middle East, but both men said in separate statements they felt progress had been made. The traditional stumbling blocks, Israeli troop withdrawal from occupied lands and the establishment of a Palestinian state (which Sadat called the "crux of the problem") were not resolved, but both sides pledged to continue discussions. Sadat also announced upgrading of the procedural conference in Cairo to foreign minister status, and said that 2 joint committees would begin work in Jan. 1978 on substantive military and political issues. Begin, who called the summit "successful," presented a 26-point peace plan to Sadat, which was, Dec. 28, passed by Israel's Knesset (parliament).

Cambodia, Vietnam Break Relations — Accusing Vietnam of "ferocious and barbarous aggression," the Cambodian government, Dec. 31, broke diplomatic ties with its ally. Vietnamese diplomats were given until Jan. 7, 1978, to leave Phnom Penh, the Cambodian capital. The action stemmed from fierce border fighting earlier in December, when Vietnamese forces occupied the "Parrot's Beak" area of Cambodia, after a Cambodian raid into Tay Ninh province that killed or injured 2,000 persons.

S. African Editor Flees — Donald Woods, banned from all forms of public expression for his criticism of the government's racial policies, Dec. 31, fled to the neighboring black state of Lesotho, on the first leg of a journey to freedom in Great Britain. Woods, the editor of S. Africa's East London Daily Dispatch, hitchhiked 185 miles to the border in disguise, hiked 12 miles in mountainous terrain and swam across a river to reach his wife, Wendy, and their 5 children in Maseru, Lesotho's capital. Woods was a close friend and supporter of slain black leader Stephen Biko.

### General

Major Drug Figure Convicted — Leroy (Nicky) Barnes, 45, described as one of New York City's principal drug dealers, was found guilty, Dec. 2, in Manhattan, on charges of heading an operation that sold 40 pounds of heroin per month from a Harlem garage. Barnes, reputed to be the head of a narcotics ring that sold millions of dollars of heroin and cocaine nationwide, was known as "Mr. Untouchable" because he had successfully avoided prosecution or won acquittals on a variety of charges in the past. Barnes faced life in prison as the result of his U. S. District Court conviction.

Escapee Joan Little Recaptured — Joan Little, whose 1975 trial for the murder of the prison guard she alleged had raped her attracted worldwide attention from women's and civil rights groups, was arrested with a companion, Dec. 7, in Brooklyn, N. Y., after a car chase. Little had escaped Oct. 15 from a North Carolina minimum security women's prison where she was serving 7-10 years for breaking and entering. Charged with being a fugitive and assault, Little was held pending extradition hearings. Attorney William Kunstler vowed to fight Little's extradition, saying "she doesn't have a chance in Carolina." Police were led to Little by an informant, who claimed she was pregnant with his child.

VA Poisoning Nurses Win New Trial — Filipina B. Narciso, 32, and Leonora M. Perez, 33, 2 Ann Arbor, Mich., VA hospital nurses, won a new trial, Dec. 19, on charges they poisoned 5 patients. Federal Dist. Judge Philip Pratt, in ordering the new trial, accused government prosecutors of "persistent misconduct" in the trial of the case which ended, July 13, in the conviction of Narciso and Perez. It was considered unusual that Pratt, the judge who sat on the first trial, had ordered a new trial after letting the first proceed full course. The two Filipino women had been accused of injecting a muscle-paralyzing drug into patients' intravenous medication tubes.

Calif. Bus Kidnapers Found Guilty — Retired Calif. Superior Court Judge Lee Duga, Dec. 15, found Richard A. Schoenfeld, 26, his brother James L. Schoenfeld, 23, and Frederick Newhall Woods, 26, guilty[6] of "causing bodily harm" to 3 of 26 children they admitted kipnaping aboard a Chowchilla, Calif. school bus, July 15, 1976. The ruling, after a 16-day, non-jury trial in Oakland, required the 3 men be sentenced to life in prison without possibility of parole.

Chemical Firm Indicted for Hiding Test Data — The Chicago-based Velsicol Chemical Corporation, and 6 present and former employees, were indicted, Dec. 12, on charges of conspiring to hide test data that allegedly showed 2 of its pesticides could produce cancer in humans. The 11-count Federal indictment charged there was a conspiracy to "defraud . . . and conceal material facts" from the U.S. Environmental Protection Agency. Velsicol had not submitted data that tended to show heptachlor and chlordane induced cancer in laboratory animals. It was the first time the EPA had sought action over the alleged failure of a company to report adverse product information. Company president Bruce Hoffman called the indictment an "outrage," and claimed it was based on the use of disputed test data. Sales of the two pesticides accounted for $44.7 million of Velsicol's revenues.

Disasters: At least 56 persons were killed, Dec. 2, when a chartered Bulgarian airliner carrying Moslem pilgrims home from Mecca, crashed while attempting an emergency landing near the Egypt-Libya border . . . All 100 persons aboard a hijacked Malaysian jetliner died Dec. 4, when the plane exploded and crashed near Johore Bharu in S. Malaysia, enroute to Singapore . . . The University of Evansville (Ind.) basketball team was among the 28 persons killed Dec. 13, when a chartered DC-3 crashed and burned soon after take-off from Evansville; 3 persons survived the fiery crash in rain and heavy fog. . . . An earthquake devastated 16 villages in southeastern Iran, Dec. 20, killing 589, injuring 700, and leaving thousands homeless.

## JANUARY

### National

**U.S. to Act to Prop Up Dollar** — The Treasury and the Federal Reserve Board announced, Jan. 4, a plan to end the decline of the dollar. In response, the dollar jumped 6% in trading in New York. On Jan. 5, however, the dollar fell again in trading, as bankers remained skeptical of the U.S. ability to defend the dollar unless the nation's trade deficit were corrected. The Federal Reserve Board, Jan. 6, raised the discount rate from 6 to 6½% because of "the recent disorder in foreign exchange markets." According to Pres. Carter, Jan. 12, the failure of Congress to approve his energy program and the continued high level of American oil imports were responsible for the instability of the dollar.

**Unemployment Down** — The national unemployment rate dropped to a 1977 year-end figure of 6.4%, down from 6.7% in November, the Labor Department reported, Jan. 11. Employment climbed a record 4.1 million for the year; Courtney M. Slater, a Commerce Department economist, testified before the Joint Economic Committee of Congress that she expected the unemployment rate to be "slightly over 6%" by the end of 1978. Unemployment declined among all groups but remained high among minorities and the young.

**Humphrey Dead at 66** — Sen. Hubert H. Humphrey, Democrat of Minnesota, died, Jan. 13, of cancer. Humphrey had been in public service 32 years, serving as mayor of Minneapolis, senator from Minnesota and 38th vice president of the United States. In 1968, he failed, by 500,000 votes, to be elected to the White House. Humphrey's body lay in state in the Capitol, while the nation's leaders, including Pres. Carter, Vice Pres. Mondale and ex-Presidents Nixon and Ford, eulogized him in a memorial service as "the conscience of his country" and "the most beloved of all Americans." On Jan. 25, Muriel Humphrey, the senator's widow, was appointed to fill her late husband's U.S. Senate seat.

**Webster Named FBI Head** — Attorney General Griffin B. Bell, Jan. 19, announced the nomination of William H. Webster, U. S. appellate judge in St. Louis, to be director of the Federal Bureau of Investigation. Judge Webster, a 53-year-old Republican, had served as federal prosecutor, U. S. attorney in St. Louis and, since 1971, on the U. S. Court of Appeals for the Eighth Circuit. The attorney general specified that Judge Webster would be directly accountable to him and not to the president. "I do not want the head of the F. B. I. involved in White House operations," Bell said. "We've been down that road before."

**Carter Delivers First State of the Union** — In his first State of the Union message to Congress, Pres. Jimmy Carter, Jan. 19, called for a $25-billion tax cut, Senate ratification of the Panama Canal treaties, a new federal department of education and a strong energy bill. The state of the union was good, Carter said, "militarily, politically, economically and in spirit." Carter stressed economic and domestic needs, calling on Congress and the nation to "come to grips with some of the hardest questions facing our society." Turning to foreign affairs, he emphasized the nation's need to remain militarily strong but also stressed its commitment to arms negotiations with the Soviet Union, peace talks in the Middle East and human rights. The speech was accompanied by a special written message in which the president promised also to cut the taxes paid by 96% of Americans and urged a modest expansion of federal job programs. He failed to recommend an increase in federally funded jobs in municipal governments under the Comprehensive Employment and Training Act. Carter also announced a proposal for a comprehensive reform of the federal civil service system.

**Federal Prosecutor Fired** — U. S. Attorney in Philadelphia David W. Marston was fired, Jan. 20, by Attorney General Griffin B. Bell. Marston, a Republican who had been investigating Democratic politicans charged with corruption, called the ouster "purely political." Bill Brock, the Republican national chairman, Jan. 13, had referred to the pending removal of Marston as having "overtones of political cover-up." Marston, who had been investigating charges against Pennsylvania Representatives Daniel J. Flood and Joshua Eilberg, said that the F. B. I. should investigate the question of whether obstruction of justice was involved in his firing but the Justice Department said, Jan. 24, that both

Pres. Carter and Attorney General Bell had been cleared of such allegations. The president, in a Jan. 30 news conference, said that he asked Bell on Nov. 6 or 7 to "expedite" the replacement of Marston by a Democrat as a "routine matter" and that neither of them had known of the Flood-Eilberg investigation at the time.

**Carter Sends First Budget to Congress** — Pres. Carter, Jan. 23, presented Congress with a $500-billion budget plan for fiscal year 1979. It allowed for a deficit of $60.6 billion, $1.2 billion less than that estimated for fiscal 1978. The main points of the budget included a $25-billion tax cut to keep the economy growing, emphasis on energy conservation and the development of alternative sources of energy, a $5.4 billion increase in health care funds, no increase in public service employment, a $117.8 billion outlay for defense, an increase in spending on mass transit to $2.3 billion, and a drop from the record $7.9 billion for farm supports for 1978 to an estimated $4.2 billion. On Jan. 20, Carter had announced a program of voluntary wage and price ceilings and on Jan. 21 had proposed tax reforms which would make the tax system "fairer and simpler." The proposals included significant tax reductions for individuals and couples with annual incomes of $30,000 or less and proposals to reduce tax deductions for business entertainment.

**Congressmen Linked to Tongsun Park Gifts** — Tongsun Park, South Korean rice dealer, reportedly gave Justice Department investigators in Seoul, Jan. 26, evidence that 15 to 18 current members of Congress may have received cash gifts in violation of ethical standards. Acting Deputy Attorney General Benjamin R. Civiletti said that about $1 million had been given to American officials. Park told investigators, Jan. 24, that he had made financial contributions to at least 5 U. S. senators, including Hubert H. Humphrey.

**Record Trade Deficit** — The Commerce Department announced, Jan. 30, a record trade deficit of $26.7 billion, more than 4 times the 1976 deficit and the largest in U. S history. U. S. imports of oil, amounting to $44.3 billion (up from $34 billion in 1976), as well as higher imports of machinery, cars, coffee and sugar, accounted for a total increase of 22%, while U. S. exports increased by only 4.6%.

**Committee OKs Canal Treaties** — The Senate Foreign Relations Committee approved, Jan. 30, by a vote of 14 to 1, treaties which will hand over the Panama Canal to Panama by the year 2000. Secretary of State Cyrus R. Vance had begun, Jan. 11, a nationwide speaking tour to rally support for the treaties. Opponents, led by Ronald Reagan and other conservative Republicans, came to Denver, Jan. 19, to organize pressure on senators who are still undecided on the treaties. The Senate committee agreed, Jan. 27, to recommend to the Senate that it adopt an amendment to the neutrality treaty which would allow the U. S. to defend the canal even after the year 2000.

### International

**Vietnam Occupies Cambodian Territory** — U. S. officials announced, Jan. 3, that Vietnamese troops were occupying some 400 square miles of Cambodian territory in the border region of the 2 nations. Zbigniew Brzezinski, Pres. Jimmy Carter's national security adviser, said, Jan. 8, that the Vietnamese-Cambodian fighting represented a "proxy war" between China and the Soviet Union. Vietnamese Deputy Foreign Minister Vo Dong Giang said, Jan. 12, that Vietnam would not withdraw its troops unless Cambodia agreed to negotiations.

**Carter Returns from World Tour** — Pres. Jimmy Carter returned to Washington, Jan. 6, from a 9-day, 16,000-mile journey. Carter visited Poland, Iran, India, Saudi Arabia, Egypt, France, and Belgium. The president's visit to Poland was marked by an embarrassing incident in which a State Department interpreter mistranslated, Dec. 29, the president's remarks into Polish so that the president seemed to have "abandoned" (left) Washington and spoke of the "lusts" (desires) of the Polish people. In India, Jan. 2, Carter and Prime Minister Morarji R. Desai disagreed sharply over American shipments of nuclear fuel to India. The president inadvertently made the disagreement public when he mentioned it to Secretary of State Cyrus R. Vance, not knowing that his voice was being picked up by nearby television microphones. A visit with Egyptian Pres. Anwar Sadat was arranged mid-tour and at Aswan, Jan. 4, Carter read a prepared statement in which he referred to the participation of the Palestinians "in the determination of their own future." Israeli Prime Minister Menahem Begin, in Jerusalem, expressed satisfaction that the words "Palestinian state" were not mentioned in the statement. Back in Washington, **Jan. 6,** Carter explained that the U.S. favored a referendum for the Palestinians but that an independent state was not one of the options. Earlier on **Jan. 6,** Carter, in France, met with French Socialist leader Francois Mitterand and expressed to him his concern about the possibility of a renewed Socialist-Communist alliance.

**Hungarian Crown Returned** — The Crown of St. Stephen, the symbol of the Hungarian nation since the year 1000 and held in American custody since the end of World War II, was returned, **Jan. 6,** by Secretary of State Cyrus R. Vance at a formal ceremony in Budapest. Anti-Communist Hungarian Americans had protested the return and Representative Mary Rose Oaker, Democrat of Ohio, whose Cleveland constituency includes the largest Hungarian population in the U. S., had tried to block the return of the crown. The Roman Catholic Primate of Hungary, Laszlo Cardinal Lekai, and leaders of the Protestant and Jewish communities attended the Budapest ceremony. Antal Apro, president of the Hungarian National Assembly, formally accepted the crown, claiming that the return of the "invaluable national relics" had demonstrated an improvement in U. S.-Hungarian relations.

**Nicaraguan Editor Shot** — Pedro Joaquín Chamorro Cardenal, the 53-year-old editor and publisher of *La Prensa,* the only opposition newspaper in Nicaragua, was shot to death, **Jan. 10.** Rioting broke out in Managua, **Jan. 12,** after some 40,000 people attended his funeral and on **Jan. 28** Pres. Anastasio Somoza Debayle imposed emergency rule, hoping to end the nationwide strike aimed at forcing him to resign.

**U.S.-Japan Accord** — Robert S. Strauss, American special representative for trade negotiations, and Nobuhiko Ushiba, Japanese minister of state for external economic affairs, announced, **Jan. 13,** in Tokyo, agreement on economic measures aimed at easing the trade relationship of the 2 nations. Japan agreed to reduce some protectionist import duties, liberalize some agricultural import quotas, and commit itself to achieving "basic equity" in its trade relations. Strauss claimed that the agreement was necessary because of the "rising tide of protectionism" in the U. S. Congress.

**Italian Government Resigns** — Christian Democrat Giulio Andreotti resigned, **Jan. 16,** as prime minister, ending Italy's 18-month-old minority government. Communists, Socialists, and Republicans had demanded a role for the Communists in the government, which the Christian Democrats rejected, and refused to promise continued tacit support of the Christian Democrats by abstaining in votes on government-sponsored legislation.

**Sadat Suspends Peace Talks** — Pres. Anwar Sadat recalled the Egyptian delegation, **Jan. 18,** from peace talks in Jerusalem, because, he reportedly explained to Pres. Jimmy Carter, Israel was seeking "land and not peace." American Secretary of State Cyrus R. Vance had participated in talks, **Jan. 17,** with the foreign ministers of Israel and Egypt aimed at establishing "principles which would govern the negotiation of a comprehensive peace settlement in the Middle East." Military talks had been held in Cairo **Jan. 11** and **12** between Israel Defense Minister Ezer Weizman and Egyptian War Minister Mohammed el-Gamasy to negotiate "military and security issues between Egypt and Israel, including the Israeli settlements in the Sinai."

**Soviet Nuclear Satellite Disintegrates over Canada** — A Soviet spy satellite powered by a nuclear reactor broke up over northwestern Canada **Jan. 24.** A U.S.-Canadian search team detected strong radiation, **Jan. 26,** in the area where the satellite was thought to have re-entered the earth's atmosphere and 2 U. S. wildlife and weather observers found, **Jan. 30,** a "moderately radioactive" piece of the satellite near Warden's Grove, a weather station in Canada's Northwest Territories. Canadian and American scientists had retrieved additional satellite fragments, some radioactive, at 6 sites along a 200-mile track, by **Feb. 4.** Canadian Defense Minister Barney Danson, **Feb. 4,** estimated the cost of the search at $1 million. Pres. Jimmy Carter called on the Soviet Union, **Jan. 31,** to sign a pact banning the use of nuclear

reactors in earth satellites.

### General

**India's Worst Aviation Disaster** — An Air India 747 jumbo jet, with 213 people aboard, exploded and crashed into the sea, **Jan. 1,** shortly after take-off from Bombay. There were no survivors in the 3rd worst aviation disaster in history.

**Hartford Civic Center Roof Collapses** — The $1.4 million roof of the Hartford Civic Center's coliseum caved in, **Jan. 18,** under 4.8 inches of wet snow. There were no injuries, as the coliseum was empty at the time, although 5,000 people had been watching a basketball game there just 6 hours earlier. According to the final report issued **June 15,** the collapse resulted from design deficiencies.

**Storms Batter Northeast, Mid-West** — Blizzards struck, **Jan. 20,** from Washington to New England, burying the New York region under 13 inches of snow and up to 20 inches in some suburbs. Businesses were forced to close and hundreds of motorists were stranded on the highways. At least 13 people died from heart attacks as a result of the storm. The National Weather Service had predicted a 3-inch snowfall. On **Jan. 26,** a storm swept the Middle West, with 15-inch snows in Michigan and Indiana, killing more than 70 people and stranding thousands of motorists. In Ohio, about 150,000 homes were without heat or electricity when the storm knocked out power lines, and in West Virginia, rivers overflowed their banks and forced at least 3,000 people to flee.

**Belgian Industrialist Kidnapped** — Baron Edouard-Jean Empain, a 40-year-old Belgian industrialist, was kidnapped **Jan. 23** in Paris. His abductors, apparently not political, demanded $8.6 million in ransom. On **Mar. 24,** French police prevented the Baron's family from paying the ransom but on **Mar. 27** he was released by the kidnappers outside of Paris. The Baron told police that he had been kept in chains for the two months.

### FEBRUARY
### National

**U.S. Sues Teamsters' Trustees** — The Department of Labor brought suit, **Feb. 1,** in Federal District Court in Chicago, against Frank E. Fitzsimmons, president of the International Brotherhood of Teamsters, and 18 other former trustees and employees of the union's principal pension fund. The suit charged them with having made imprudent loans and sought to force them to repay losses resulting from those loans. Secretary of Labor Ray Marshall, in Washington, said he did not know yet how much money the government would eventually seek to recover, because many of the loans would not come due for years. Loans itemized in the suit came to more than $130 million.

**Pentagon Seeks $56 Billion Budget Increase** — Secretary of Defense Harold Brown told the House Armed Services Committee, **Feb. 2,** that the Pentagon needed to increase its budgets from $116.8 billion for fiscal 1978 to $172.7 billion by fiscal 1983, in order to maintain the present nuclear balance with the Soviet Union. Gen. George S. Brown, chairman of the Joint Chiefs of Staff, told the committee that the B-1 bomber program should be kept alive. The Soviet Union, **Feb. 11,** blamed Congress and the Pentagon for lack of progress in arms negotiations. In an editorial in Pravda, the Carter administration was warned, also, not to try to obtain concessions from the Soviets with threats of a Senate rejection of a treaty to limit strategic nuclear weapons.

**Unemployment Down Again, Consumer Prices Up** — The Bureau of Labor Statistics reported, **Feb. 3,** that the unemployment rate for January was 6.3%, down from 6.4% for December and 6.7% for November. Unemployment dropped to 6.1% for women but remained unchanged for adult men and teen-agers. Unemployment among black workers remained unchanged at 12.7%. The Bureau reported, **Feb. 27,** that consumer prices rose 0.8% in January, led by food, housing, and medical-care costs. The January rise was about double the average monthly increase since July.

**Committee Investigates Congressmen** — The House Committee on Standards of Official Conduct opened investigations, **Feb. 8,** into charges against Rep. Daniel J. Flood nd Rep. Joshua Eilberg, Democrats of Pennsylvania. Flood has been charged with unethical activities in connection with J.S. aid to Haiti and the Bahamas. Flood and Eilberg were already under investigation by the U.S. Attorney in Philadelphia, in connection with the financing of a hospital building project there.

**Intelligence Proposals Offered** — The Senate Select Committee on Intelligence proposed, **Feb. 9**, legislation to curb U.S. intelligence agents and protect American civil liberties. The bill prohibits political assassinations, covert operations "likely to result in. . .the overthrow of democratic governments, or the support of actions by foreign police, intelligence, or internal security forces of countries which violate human rights." The American Civil Liberties Union praised the proposals for better civil liberties safeguards than those in Pres. Jimmy Carter's executive order on intelligence reorganization, **Jan. 24**, but expressed reservations that "important principles" were still being overlooked.

**Carter Urges More Funds for Education** — Pres. Jimmy Carter asked Congress, **Feb. 28**, to approve a 24% increase in federal spending on education. On **Feb. 8**, Carter and HEW Secretary Joseph Califano presented a $1.2 billion aid program for college students from middle-income families. Carter said that his program of scholarships, work-study subsidies, and guaranteed loans was "far more beneficial" than Congressional proposals to grant tax credits for tuition payments and that he would not accept both. The House voted, **June 1**, however, to give tax credits to parents of college students and private elementary and secondary school pupils. On **June 8**, Carter threatened to veto the tuition-credits bill, partly because provisions regarding parochial schools would be held unconstitutional. The president also threatened to veto his own education aid proposals, since Senate and House committees had added more than $200 million to his plan and, said Carter, "Some one has to hold the line on the budget."

## International

**Sadat Visits Washington** — Egyptian Pres. Anwar Sadat visited Washington, **Feb. 3**, to confer with Pres. Jimmy Carter on the Mideast situation. Israeli Foreign Minister Moshe Dayan visited New York City, **Feb. 9**, to meet with Assistant Secretary of State Alfred L. Atherton Jr., in an attempt to offset Sadat's visit. After leaving Washington, **Feb. 8**, Sadat met in London with Prime Minister James Callaghan and in Hamburg with Chancellor Helmut Schmidt, **Feb. 9**. Chancellor Bruno Kreisky of Austria arranged a meeting between Sadat and Shimon Peres, the leader of Israel's opposition Labor Party, in Salzburg, **Feb. 11**.

**Vietnam Envoy Expelled** — The U.S., **Feb. 3**, ordered Dinh Ba Thi, Vietnam's chief delegate to the U.N., to leave the country, because of charges implicating him in an espionage case. Thi at first defied the U.S. order but, on **Feb. 5**, received instructions from Hanoi to return home. Thi had been named as a co-conspirator in an indictment against Ronald L. Humphrey, U.S. Information Agency official, and Truong Dinh Hung, a Vietnamese national, whose father had been the "peace candidate" in South Vietnam's 1967 presidential election. Humphrey and Truong were arrested Jan. 31 in Washington, on charges of spying for Vietnam, and were convicted by a federal jury in Arlington, Va., **May 19**.

**Guerillas Join Anti-Somoza Forces** — Leftist guerrillas attacked National Guard barracks in 2 Nicaraguan cities, **Feb. 3**, joining the forces trying to oust Pres. Anastasio Somoza Debayle. Somoza replied that he would not give up his office before his term ends in 1981. On **Feb. 8**, Venezuela asked the Organization of American States to investigate charges of human rights violations in Nicaragua. Guerrillas clashed again with government troops, **Feb. 27**, and 10 persons were killed. The crisis in Nicaragua began, **Jan. 10**, with the murder of Pedro Joaquin Chamorro Cardenal, the editor of Nicaragua's only opposition newspaper.

**Syrians, Lebanese Clash** — Syrian-dominated Arab peacekeeping forces in Lebanon clashed, **Feb. 7-10**, with Lebanese army regulars and Christian militiamen, in Beirut. Unofficial estimates put the death toll at 100 Syrians and 50 Lebanese. Fighting began again in southern Lebanon, **Feb. 13**, between Christian militiamen and Palestinians. The Pal-

estinians claimed that Israeli forces had aided the Christians but Israel denied the charge.

**U.S., Israel Feud on Settlements** — The U.S. re-iterated, **Feb. 7**, **Feb. 10**, and **Feb. 13**, its opposition to Israeli settlements in occupied Arab territories but the Israeli cabinet decided, **Feb. 26**, not to change its limited policy of establishing settlements in Sinai and the West Bank. Prime Minister Menahem Begin denied, **Feb. 3**, the Carter administration's charge that Israel had promised the U.S. "there would not be more settlements." The Israeli opposition Labor Party criticized, **Feb. 2**, Begin's policy on the settlements, charging, specifically, that the archeological excavations at Shiloh were being used to disguise a new settlement and that Israel would be perceived, especially in American public opinion, as "deceptive."

**Israel, Arab Jet Sales** — The U.S. government announced, **Feb. 14**, that it would sell $4.8 billion worth of jet warplanes to Egypt, Israel, and Saudi Arabia. The decision, which would require Congressional approval, included selling Saudi Arabia 60 F-15 jets for $2.5 billion and Israel 15 F-15's for $400 million and 75 F-16 fighter-bombers for $1.5 billion. Egypt would get 50 F-5 fighters for $400 million. The McDonnell Douglas F-15 is described as the most advanced plane in the U.S. Air Force. The Northrop Corp. F-5's, which would be sold to Egypt, are less sophisticated than the F-15 or the F-16 and are not used by the U.S. Air Force at all. Israeli Prime Minister Begin deplored the decision, **Feb. 15**, fearing that Saudi Arabia would give its planes to Egypt to use against Israel. Sen. Daniel P. Moynihan, Democrat of N.Y., said, **Feb. 14**, that the sale to Saudi Arabia "could in time pose a threat to Israel's security." Secretary of State Cyrus R. Vance told a House Appropriations subcommittee on foreign operations, **Feb. 24**, that the sale to the 3 countries was "a package" and that if Congress rejected the sales to the Arabs, the Carter administration would veto the sale to Israel. On **Feb. 21**, Vance had told the House International Relations Committee that the administration had made it clear to Saudi Arabia that they could not transfer these planes to Egypt without American approval. On **Mar. 10**, a majority of the members of the committee informed Pres. Jimmy Carter, hours before he was to see Israel Defense Minister Ezer Weizman, that they opposed his decision to make the sale of advanced planes to Israel contingent upon their sale to Saudi Arabia and Egypt. The Senate, **May 15**, voted 54-44 to support the sales, after intense lobbying by the president. Since both chambers of Congress would have to veto the deal to block it, the Senate vote meant that the sales would go through. The need of Saudi Arabia to defend its oil fields and the U.S. need of Saudi influence in resisting OPEC price increases were cited in the debate. Israel complained, **May 16**, that the "package" deal was a violation of the 1975 agreement under which Israel withdrew forces from Sinai in exchange for American warplanes. The administration sought to mollify the American Jewish community, which had strongly opposed the sale to the Arabs, in a speech delivered by Vice President Walter F. Mondale, **May 18**, to the annual meeting of the American Jewish Congress, in New York City. Mondale conceded that arguments over the sale had produced "painful divisions" but contended that the "special relationship" between Israel and the U.S. would remain unaffected.

**Japan, China Sign $20 Billion Pact** — Japan and China signed, **Feb. 16**, in Peking, an 8-year, $20-billion trade agreement. The pact, under negotiation for a year, represents the most important single link between the 2 nations since the establishment of diplomatic relations in 1972. Provisions of the agreement include $7-8 billion worth of Japanese plants and technology to be purchased by China and 47.1 million tons of oil, up to 5.3 million tons of coking coal, and up to 3.9 million tons of other coal to be sold by China to Japan. The pact provided an opening for Japanese industry into the vast Chinese market and promised China advanced industrial technology. The Soviet Union had long opposed such links between the 2 nations.

**Ulster Bombing** — At least 12 people were killed in the bombing of a crowded restaurant, **Feb. 17**, in a Protestant district of Belfast, Northern Ireland. The Provisional Irish Republican Army claimed, **Feb. 19**, responsibility for the bombing. Catholic, Protestant, Irish, and British leaders condemned the bombing, as did the Provisional Sinn Fein, an IRA-affiliated group, **Feb. 21.** On **Feb. 28,** IRA forces ambushed and killed a British soldier in Belfast, apparently having decided to attack soldiers rather than civilians, following the reaction to the civilian deaths in the restaurant bombing.

**Egyptians, Cypriots Battle at Airport** — Cypriot soldiers opened fire on Egyptian commandos, **Feb. 19,** as the commandos attempted to storm a Cyprus Airways DC-8 at Larnaca Airport in Cyprus. The commandos were attempting to rescue 15 hostages held by 2 Palestinians who had killed the editor of the leading Egyptian newspaper, *Al Ahram,* **Feb. 18,** in Nicosia. Immediately after the assassination, the Palestinians took 30 hostages to the airport where they traded 15 hostages for a jet. After they were refused permission to land in Kuwait, Libya, Greece, and South Yemen, they landed in the East African country of Djibouti, **Feb. 19,** where they refueled and then returned to Cyprus. Of the 70 Egyptian commandos, 15 were killed and 17 wounded. On **Feb. 22,** Egypt broke diplomatic relations with Cyprus, even though Pres. Anwar Sadat conceded that the Cypriots had not been told in advance of the attack. On **Feb. 27,** Egypt withdrew the special privileges held since 1956 by Palestinians living in Egypt. The 2 terrorists were sentenced to death, **Apr. 4,** by a court in Nicosia. The U.S. State Department applauded the decision, welcoming "anything which serves to curb or penalize terrorism." The Palestine Liberation Organization charged, **Feb. 20,** that the terrorists had been acting under orders from Iraq.

### General

**Nurses Poisoning Charges Dropped** — U.S. Attorney James K. Robinson announced, **Feb. 1,** in Detroit, that the government was dropping all charges against Filipina Narciso and Leonora Perez, the Filipino nurses who had been granted a new trial after having been convicted of poisoning patients at a Veterans Administration hospital in Michigan. Robinson agreed with the judge who granted the new trial that "no clear evidence of motive is available" and said it was unlikely that a conviction could be obtained in a 2d trial.

**Calvin Klein's Daughter Kidnapped** — The 11-year-old daughter of designer Calvin Klein was kidnapped, **Feb. 3,** and was released, hours later, when her father paid $100,000 in ransom. Police arrested a former baby-sitter of the girl, **Feb. 4,** and all but $100 of the ransom money was recovered.

**Storms Batter Northeast, California** — A 40-hour snowstorm almost paralyzed the New York metropolitan region, **Feb. 6-7,** dropping 17.7 inches on New York City, the heaviest snowfall in the city since 1947. The storm crippled New England and buried Boston under 27 inches of snow, the worst in its history. About 50 deaths were attributed to the storm in N.Y., N.J., New England and Pennsylvania. The worst storm since 1969 hit drought-stricken southern California, **Feb. 10,** killing nearly 20 people and leaving 700 homeless. Heavy rains, 90 mph winds, floods, and mudslides did an estimated $23-million damage. Pres. Jimmy Carter, **Feb. 16,** declared a major disaster area in the counties hardest hit by the storm. National Weather Service officials said, **Feb. 14,** that cloud seeding hours before the rainstorm had possibly intensified the storm but did not start it. Further flooding and mud-slides, resulting in at least 8 deaths and damage to more than 600 homes, followed another torrential storm, **Mar. 6,** in the same area.

**Abzug Defeated Again** — Republican S. William Green defeated ex-Congresswoman Bella S. Abzug, **Feb. 14,** in a special election to fill New York City Mayor Edward I. Koch's vacant House seat. Abzug had had the State Supreme Court reverse, **Jan. 18,** the Democratic Party's nomination of former city-councilman Carter Burden. Abzug had served 3 terms in the House before running unsuccessfully, in 1976, for the Senate. In 1977, she lost the mayoral primary to Koch.

**Chowchilla Kidnappers Get Life** — The 3 men convicted of the 1976 kidnapping of 26 Chowchilla, Calif. school children and their bus driver were sentenced, **Feb. 17,** to life terms. Richard Schoenfeld, 23, could be considered for parole in 6 months as a youthful offender. James Schoenfeld, Richard's 26-year-old brother, and Frederick Newhall

Woods, also 26, were given no chance of parole, because 3 of the children had suffered "bodily harm."

**Disasters** — Avalanches killed at least 21 people in the Alps, **Feb. 4-5.** . . .A Pacific Western Airways Boeing 737 crashed, **Feb. 11,** while landing in heavy snow in Cranbrook British Columbia, killing 40 people. There were 7 survivors. . .A passenger train crashed into a trailer truck and derailed **Feb. 24,** in northern Argentina. At least 53 passengers were killed and about 100 injured. . . .A derailed railroad tanker car, loaded with liquid propane, exploded, **Feb. 24,** killing 21 and injuring 145 in Waverly, Tenn.

## MARCH

### National

**Carter Seeks Civil Service Reform** — Pres. Jimmy Carter asked Congress, **Mar. 2,** to approve his plan to revise the federal civil service system to allow more flexibility in rewarding merit and penalizing incompetence. Carter proposed replacing the Civil Service Commission, which controls personnel decisions regarding 2.1 million federal employees, with an office of personnel management and a merit system protection board. The president also submitted a new civil service law that would provide for incentive bonuses to replace automatic pay increases and would allow incompetent workers to be fired.

**Senate Confirms Miller to Head Federal Reserve** — G. William Miller was confirmed, **Mar. 3,** by the Senate, to succeed Arthur F. Burns, as chairman of the Federal Reserve Board. Sen. William Proxmire, Democrat of Wisconsin and chairman of the Senate Banking Committee, cast the only dissenting vote. The committee had spent 5 weeks investigating charges that Miller, as chairman of Textron, Inc., had been involved in a $2.9 million payment to an Iranian firm. Miller had argued that the payment was a legitimate sales commission, not a bribe. Miller was sworn in as head of the Federal Reserve at a White House ceremony, **Mar. 8.** Burns resigned from the board, **Jan. 31.** His term as a board member would not have expired until 1984, although his term as chairman ended Jan. 31, but he said, in a letter to the president, that his presence would be a "complicating distraction" for Miller.

**Carter Invokes Taft-Hartley to End Mine Strike** — Pres. Jimmy Carter invoked the mandatory back-to-work provisions of the Taft-Hartley Act, **Mar. 6,** in an effort to end the 91-day coal mine strike by the United Mine Workers, saying, "The law will be enforced." The 160,000 soft-coal miners had rejected, **Mar. 5,** by more than 2 to 1, a settlement urged on them by Carter and Arnold R. Miller, the union president. After a 55-minute hearing, **Mar. 9,** Federal District Court Judge Aubrey Robinson signed an order requiring the miners to go back to work and not to interfere with other miners returning to work. The miners, however, ignored the order and instead, on **Mar. 25,** ratified a new settlement, ending, in its 110th day, the longest strike in the industry's history. The main issues in the strike had concerned pensions, productivity, and health care. Increases had been demanded by the miners to bring the pensions of older retired miners up to the level of those who had retired in the last 3 years. Stiff measures to curb wildcat strikes and incentives to spur greater productivity were sought by the coal companies. Also, the companies wanted the miners to begin paying part of their own medical care costs. The 3-year contract, signed **Mar. 25,** reportedly increased the pensions of miners who had retired before 1976 from $250 to $275 a month, dropped a provision in the rejected settlement to discipline wildcat strike leaders, and reduced the "deductibles" on medical benefits from $700 a year to $200 for working miners and $150 for retirees. The return to work was completed, **Apr. 5,** when the U.M.W.'s 10,000 mine-construction members also ratified a new 3-year contract. The strike, together with 1978's severe winter weather, was blamed for subsequent increases in the price of steel and in the nation's trade deficit, the lag in business activity, first quarter declines in the GNP and in corporate profits, record losses for the nation's railroads, and the persistence of the worst inflation in American history.

**Unemployment at 3-Year Low; Prices, Deficit Up** — The unemployment rate for February fell to 6.1%, the Labor Department reported, **Mar. 10**, the lowest since October, 1974. Black unemployment fell from 12.7% to 11.8%. The rate for women declined from 6.1% to 5.7% and for adult men, from 4.7% to 4.5%. Treasury Secretary W. Michael Blumenthal and Charles L. Schultze, chairman of the Council of Economic Advisers, warned Pres. Jimmy Carter, **Mar. 17**, that inflation had replaced unemployment as the nation's worst economic problem. The House of Representatives, however, had voted **Mar. 16**, 257 to 152, to approve the Humphrey-Hawkins bill, which would attempt to reduce unemployment to 4% and guarantee all Americans the opportunity of employment. The Consumer Price Index rose 0.6% for February, the Labor Department reported **Mar. 28**, led by a 1.2% increase in food prices. The severe winter was blamed for much of the increase, but this rise and the January rise of 0.8% were even higher than the government had anticipated. The U.S. trade deficit for February was the largest in history, the Commerce Department announced **Mar. 31**. Imports exceeded exports by $4.52 billion, putting U.S. trade in the red for the 21st consecutive month.

**Congressman Indicted on Kickbacks** — Rep. Charles C. Diggs Jr., Democrat of Michigan, was indicted, **Mar. 23**, by a federal grand jury on charges of taking kickbacks from 3 Congressional employees and keeping on his Congressional payroll 3 other employees who did no work for Congress. The indictment charged that kickbacks and illegal payments amounted to more than $101,000 between 1973 and 1977. Diggs was charged with 14 counts of mail fraud and 21 counts of making false statements to the government. Diggs, the senior black member of the House, was on a tour of Africa as chairman of the Subcommittee of the House International Relations Committee when the charges were announced. He complained that the charges, which he denied, showed "an unfortunate insensitivity" to his "mission to Africa" and could undermine a meeting in which he was to join Pres. Jimmy Carter for talks in Nigeria.

**Carter Proposes Urban Aid Program** — Pres. Jimmy Carter proposed, **Mar. 27**, a broad program designed to aid the recovery of the nation's cities. The long-awaited program contained about 30 separate items, most of which would have to be approved by Congress. The plan would include a "national development bank" to provide up to $11 billion over a 3-year period in low-interest loans, to encourage industrial development in depressed areas. Other features of the plan included "urban impact analysis" of every new federal program, "supplementary fiscal assistance" to aid local governments in cities with unusually high unemployment, incentives to business to hire the chronically unemployed, and provisions for $350 million in loans for housing and mass-transit rehabilitation and another $150 million to improve social service programs such as day-care and "meals on wheels" in poverty areas. Carter asked Congress to increase his 1979 budget request by $4.4 billion to pay for the program. Vernon E. Jordan Jr., executive director of the National Urban League, called the plan a "significant step" but "disheartening" and a "missed opportunity" and renewed his call for an "urban Marshall Plan." New York City Mayor Edward I. Koch called the plan "encouraging" but said that the housing program was "very inadequate."

## International

**Internal Rhodesian Accord Signed** — Prime Minister Ian D. Smith and 3 black nationalist leaders signed an agreement, **Mar. 3**, to transfer power to Rhodesia's black majority by the end of the year. A transitional government would supervise the election of a new parliament and the enactment of a new constitution for the nation, to be renamed Zimbabwe. The UN Security Council, **Mar. 14**, by a vote of 10 to 0 with Canada, France, Great Britain, the U.S., and West Germany abstaining, declared the settlement "illegal and unacceptable." Leaders of the Patriotic Front guerrilla forces had denounced the agreement, **Mar. 9**, before the UN Security Council, as a "sellout," designed to allow the white minority government to retain control. Bishop Abel Muzowera, one of the leaders who had signed the accord, decided to abandon efforts to defend it before the Security Council when it became obvious that 3rd world and Communist members would vote against his appearance. On **Mar. 14**, the Patriotic Front rejected British appeals to join the nationalists who had signed the accord, declaring, "The war

still goes on." Bishop Muzowera, returning to Salisbury, **Mar. 19**, was welcomed by some 150,000 black Rhodesians, apparently representing substantial support in the black community for the bishop and the internal settlement. The Patriotic Front asserted, **Mar. 20**, however, that the guerrillas controlled areas in which 700,000 of the 3 million black Rhodesians lived and that Bishop Muzowera's support in Salisbury did not reflect the feelings of the rest of the black community. On **Mar. 21**, Bishop Muzowera, and the other signers of the accord, Rev. Ndabaningi Sithole, and Sen. Jeremiah Chirau, were sworn in as co-leaders of the provisional government with Prime Minister Smith. On **Mar. 26**, Angola, Botswana, Mozambique, Tanzania, and Zambia called on the U.S. and Great Britain to covene a meeting with the guerrillas and to support the Anglo-American plan for majority rule in Rhodesia. On a tour of southern Africa **Mar. 21-26**, U.S. Ambassador to the U.N. Andrew Young said that the U.S. would not support the internal settlement because it was "something less than majority rule" and would not end the fighting with the guerrillas. On **Mar. 27**, the U.S. State Department denounced the internal settlement as illegal, because the Smith government was illegal, and inadequate, because it would not end the fighting.

**China Adopts New Constitution** — China's nominal legislature, meeting in Peking, adopted **Mar. 5**, a new charter, stressing economic development over revolutionary ideology. The new constitution restored the office of prosecutor, which had been abolished during the Cultural Revolution of the late 1960s, and called for the modernization of the army, which had been weakened as a result of the political factionalism of those years. The new charter merely enshrined "the great banner of Chairman Mao," a subtle reversal of the old, 1975 constitution, which had called Maoist thought "the doctrine of the state." The National People's Congress, meeting **Feb. 26-Mar. 5**, also reappointed Hua Kuo-feng, 59-year-old chairman of the Chinese Communist party, as prime minister, and 80-year-old Marshal Yeh Chien-ying was named chairman of the Congress' Standing Committee, making him honorary chief of state. Teng Hsiao-ping, the man generally considered to hold the real power in China, remained First Deputy Prime Minister and the 3d ranking member in the party hierarchy. His predominance in the government could be seen, however, in the Congress' choice of a slate of 13 deputy prime ministers and a cabinet heavily weighted toward Teng's associates and programs. The Congress also adopted a new 10-year economic plan, aimed at turning China into a modern state by the year 2000. Wage increases and other material incentives, long barred by Mao, would be given to factory workers and managers whose production plans are fulfilled. The Chinese People's Political and Consultative Conference, which had not met since 1964, was convened in Peking, **Feb. 24-Mar. 8**, and approved the new constitution. In addition to Communist Party members, the conference was attended by representatives of China's 40 million minority group members, including the Tibetan Panchen Lama. The women's federation, religious groups and unions, scientists, artists, writers, and overseas Chinese were also represented. The convening of the conference was thought to indicate a desire for unity by the Peking government and an attempt to return to the relative tranquillity of the pre-Cultural Revolution period. The same purpose seemed to be behind the decision, announced **Feb. 26** by Prime Minister Hua, in convening the Congress, to abolish the provincial revolutionary committees formed by Mao in the late 1960's to run schools, factories, and farm brigades.

**Somalia to Pull Out of Ethiopia** — Pres. Jimmy Carter announced, **Mar. 9**, that Somalia had agreed to withdraw its troops from Ethiopia's Ogaden region. The Somali government requested the withdrawal of all foreign powers from the Horn of Africa, an apparent reference to Soviet and Cuban forces aiding the Ethiopians. Somalia also called for the right of the people of Ogaden to self-determination. The Somali withdrawal followed a swift Ethiopian advance through Ogaden which included the recapture of the town of Jijiga, **Mar. 5**, the most vital point the Somalis had been able to take in earlier fighting. Richard Moose, U.S. assistant secretary of state for African affairs, and several other high ranking American officials, visited Somalia, **Mar. 18-23**, in an effort to improve relations following Somalia's defeat in its attempt to take Ogaden. The U.S. refused, however, to consider sales of arms to rebuild Somalia's shattered army unless that country renounced its claims fo Ethiopian, Kenyan, and Djibouti territories populated by Somali-speaking people. Somalia reported, **Mar. 24**, that its regular forces had completed their withdrawal from Ogaden. Ethiopia, **Mar. 24**, said that it was in complete control of the Ogaden region, having wiped out remaining pockets of guerrilla resistance, but, on **May 12**, Ethiopian leader Lt. Col. Mengistu Haile Mariam warned that Ethiopia would go to war unless Somalia ceased supporting guerrillas in Ogaden. Somalia, refused arms by the U.S., signed a cooperation agreement, **Apr. 13-18**, with China, but there was no indication that the Chinese would actually sell them arms.

**Grigorenko, Rostropoviches Citizenships Revoked** —The Soviet Union announced, **Mar. 10**, that it had revoked the citizenship of former Gen. Pyotr G. Grigorenko and, on **Mar. 15**, that of cellist and conductor Mstislav Rostropovich and his wife former Bolshoi Opera soprano Galina Vishnevskaya. Grigorenko, a prominent dissident stripped of his military rank in 1961, was on a 6-month personal visit in the U.S. when the announcement was made. Grigorenko was granted asylum by the U.S. **Apr. 19**. When Soviet Pres. Leonid I. Brezhnev was in West Germany, **May 4-7**, to confer with German leaders, Grigorenko led a parade there to protest human rights violations in the U.S.S.R. Rostropovich and Vishnevskaya, friends of dissident Aleksandr Solzhenitsyn, had been living abroad since 1974, not intending to return to the Soviet Union until full artistic freedom was achieved there. A U.S. State Department spokesman said, **Mar. 16**, that the revocation of the Rostropoviches' citizenship was in conflict with internationally accepted standards of human rights.

**Germany, Japan Try to Help Dollar** — The U.S. and Germany announced, **Mar. 13**, a series of joint actions to stabilize the dollar, which had been declining in value against other currencies since late February. Foreign exchange dealers were disappointed with the limited scope of the plan, however, and the dollar continued to lose ground. On **Mar. 28**, when the dollar was under unprecedented selling pressure in Tokyo, the Bank of Japan purchased more than $1 billion, but was unable to prevent the dollar from reaching new postwar lows against the yen. News of the record U.S. trade deficit for February also depressed the value of the dollar in Frankfurt, Paris, London, and Zurich. Arthur F. Burns, former chairman of the Federal Reserve Board, called on the U.S., **Mar. 31**, to sell part of the nation's $50 billion gold reserves to "stop the deterioration" of the dollar. G. William Miller, the new head of the Federal Reserve, told the Senate Banking Committee, **Mar. 15**, that the dollar's weakness could be cured only by reducing oil imports and by a "very aggressive" anti-inflation program.

**Dutch Marines Rescue Hostages** — An anti-terrorist team of 60 Dutch marines stormed a government building in Assen, the Netherlands, **Mar. 14**, and freed all 70 hostages held by 3 South Moluccan terrorists. The South Asian nationalists had seized the building and hostages, **Mar. 13**, demanding the release of other South Moluccans imprisoned in the Netherlands. Previous terrorist acts had aimed at dramatizing their demands for Dutch help in winning independence for their home islands from Indonesia. One man was killed when the terrorists' seized the building. The 3 terrorists, aged 19, 20, and 22, were captured by the marines. Their fathers and other South Moluccans who had served in the Dutch colonial army fled to the Netherlands in 1949 when Indonesia became independent.

**Bhutto Condemned** — Former Prime Minister Zulfikar Ali Bhutto of Pakistan was condemned to death, **Mar. 18**, on charges of having ordered the murder of a political opponent in 1974. Bhutto, who was overthrown by a military coup in July, 1977, filed an appeal with the Pakistan Supreme Court, **Mar. 25**. According to reports from Teheran, **May 19**, the Shah of Iran warned Pakistan that it would lose its $300 million in annual aid from Iran if it executed Bhutto.

**Leftists Lose in French Elections** — The government center-right coalition defeated the Socialists and Communists, **Mar. 19**, in legislative elections in France. The government emerged with a 90-seat majority in the 491-seat Chamber of Deputies. Polls had predicted that the left would win the election. Socialist leader Francois Mitterand blamed the Communists, **Mar. 20**, for the defeat. The Communists had repeatedly attacked the Socialists during the election campaign. Pres. Valery Giscard d'Estaing reappointed Premier Raymond Barre, **Mar. 31**, to head the government. Barre named a cabinet, **Apr. 5**, that included most of the members of his previous cabinet; he promised to continue the conservative economic policies that were said to have won him the election. Giscard met, **Mar. 26-31**, with Socialist and Communist leaders, the first time in 20 years that a French head of state met with opposition leaders, and appealed to them

## Israel Invades, Occupies Southern Lebanon

Israeli ground forces, estimated between 10,000 and 22,000 men, supported by air and naval forces, invaded southern Lebanon, **Mar. 14**, to "root out terrorist bases" used by Palestinian guerrillas for attacks within Israel. The invasion went beyond reprisal for an Al Fatah assault **Mar. 11** on the Haifa-Tel Aviv road, in which more than 30 Israeli civilians were killed. Israel announced, **Mar. 15**, that its troops would occupy a 4- to 6-mile-wide "security belt," on the Lebanese side of the border from the Mediterranean to the foothills of Mt. Hermon. Among the targets struck were PLO strongholds in the area and the port of Tyre, which had been an entry point for Palestinian arms shipments. Israeli planes also bombed Damur, about 20 miles south of Beirut, which had been the staging ground for the **Mar. 11** raid, an Israeli spokesman explained.

Civilian casualties in the Israeli invasion were said to be heavy and more than 100,000 Palestinian and Lebanese civilians fled to Beirut, **Mar. 15**, to escape the bombing in the south. Virtually all the refugees were Moslems. Lebanese Christians, who had sided with Israel in the 1976 Lebanese civil war, welcomed the Israelis. Israel reported, **Mar. 16**, that its losses totaled 11 killed and 57 wounded and that about 100 Palestinians had been killed. Syrian anti-aircraft guns fired on Israeli planes bombing Damur but otherwise the 30,000-man Syrian-dominated peacekeeping force in Lebanon stayed out of the fighting.

The U.S. reacted sympathetically to the Israeli invasion but Secretary of State Cyrus R. Vance conceded, **Mar. 15**, that the invasion and the Palestinian raid that had inspired it had raised "impediments to the peace process." Egyptian Pres. Anwar Sadat had broken with the rest of the Arab world, **Mar. 14**, in denouncing the Palestinian raid as "irresponsible" and "sad and tragic" but on **Mar. 15**, Egyptian Foreign Minister Mohammed Ibrahim Kamel called the Israeli invasion an act of "organized genocide" and said that it threatened hopes for peace in the Middle East. The Egyptian government declared, **Mar. 25**, however, that it was prepared to go ahead with its efforts for peace despite the invasion.

On **Mar. 19**, the UN Security Council voted 12 to 0 to adopt a U.S.-sponsored resolution calling on Israel to withdraw from Lebanon and establishing a 4,000-man U.N. force to enforce a ceasefire in the area. On **Mar. 21** Israel Defense Minister Ezer Weizman issued a unilateral ceasefire after Israeli forces had completed the takeover of most of southern Lebanon up to the Litani River, except for the port city of Tyre.

A vanguard of the UN force, about 100 men, arrived in Lebanon **Mar. 22** and Israel announced it would withdraw "in a matter of days." Sporadic firing continued between Israelis and Palestinians during the week Mar. 22-29. More Unifil (UN Interim Forces in Lebanon) troops moved into Lebanon, **Mar. 23**, including 200 French paratroopers. The French had previously avoided participation in such activities but Pres. Valery Giscard d'Estaing explained, **Mar. 22**, that France had decided to be part of the force because of its traditional links with the Lebanese people.

A Swedish Unifil soldier was killed and another wounded, **Mar. 29**, in a mine explosion. On **Mar. 28**, PLO leader Yasir Arafat promised Maj. Gen. Emmanuel Erskine of Ghana, head of Unifil, that the PLO would help the UN force "carry out its mission." More radical PLO factions vowed, **Mar. 28**, to keep fighting until the Israelis were defeated.

to promote "reasonable co-existence" between the right and left.

**Protesters Close New Tokyo Airport** — About 7,000 rioters destroyed, **Mar. 26,** the control tower of the new international airport at Narita, 44 miles east of Tokyo. The site had been the scene, since construction began in 1971, of frequent demonstrations by farmers whose land had been appropriated and by environmentalists concerned about noise and air pollution. Radicals, intending to damage the government politically, led the latest protest. Police stormed a handmade concrete fortress, **Mar. 27,** and arrested 165 protesters. The airport, originally scheduled to open **Mar. 30,** finally began operations **May 21.**

**Namibian Leader Killed** — Chief Clemens Kapuo, leader of the Namibian (South-West African) Herero tribe, was murdered, **Mar. 27,** by gunmen in Windhoek, the territory's capital. Kapuo was president of the Democratic Turnhalle Alliance, a multiracial party favoring cooperation with South Africa in working toward Namibian independence. Five persons were killed, **Apr. 8,** when fighting broke out at Kapuo's funeral, between members of the Herero and Ovambo tribes. Most Ovambos support SWAPO (the South-West African People's Organization), the guerrilla group fighting against South Africa. A SWAPO spokesman in Zambia, **Mar. 28,** denied any connection with the Kapuo murder. The murderers were not captured.

### General

**Chaplin Body Stolen** — The body of Charlie Chaplin was stolen, **Mar. 2,** from a Swiss cemetery. It was recovered, **May 17,** in a cornfield 10 miles away and police arrested 2 men, a Pole and a Bulgarian, after tracing telephone calls demanding ransom. In recent years attempts have been made to steal the remains also of Maria Callas, Elvis Presley, Marshal Phillipe Pétain, and former UN Secretary General U Thant.

**Hustler Owner Shot** — Larry Flynt, 35-year-old owner of the sexually-explicit magazine *Hustler*, was shot, **Mar. 6,** in Lawrenceville, Ga. Flynt, who was left paralyzed from the waist down, had been in Georgia to testify in his own defense on charges of distributing obscene material. After the shooting, the judge declared a mistrial. Flynt's assailant got away. Pres. Jimmy Carter's evangelist sister, Ruth Carter Stapleton, whom Flynt had credited with his conversion to a "born-again Christian," flew to Flynt's bedside to pray for his recovery.

**Worst Oil Spill Pollutes French Coast** — The supertanker *Amoco Cadiz* broke in two, **Mar. 17,** after running aground in heavy seas off the Brittany coast, in France. More than 1.3 million of its 1.6 million barrels of crude oil were dumped in the sea. Hope of salvaging any of the oil was abandoned, **Mar. 27.** The oil slick from the spill covered 110 miles of coastline by **Mar 29,** destroying, at least temporarily, the area's fishing industry and threatening the tourist season. French Premier Raymond Barre blamed the wreck, **Mar. 23,** on the "grave negligence" of the captains of the *Amoco Cadiz* and the tug that tried to rescue it. During Pres. Jimmy Carter's visit to Liberia, **Apr. 3,** as part of his tour of Africa, Secretary of State Cyrus R. Vance expressed his concern over the loose safety standards of oil tankers, such as the *Amoco Cadiz,* that fly the Liberian flag.

**Davis Cup Protests** — Thousands of demonstrators marched through Nashville, Tenn. **Mar. 17-19,** protesting the participation of South Africa in the Davis Cup tennis matches at Vanderbilt University. South Africa had named an 18-year-old player of mixed race, Peter Lamb, to its team, **Feb. 12,** but the NAACP called the action "tokenism." The U.S. team defeated South Africa in the competition.

**Berkey Awarded Record Damages from Kodak** — Berkey Photo Inc. was awarded a record $112.8 million, **Mar. 22,** in its civil anti-trust suit against the Eastman Kodak Company. A jury had decided, **Jan. 21,** after a 6-month trial and a full week of deliberation, that Kodak had used its technological dominance to monopolize most of the amateur photographic business in the U.S. A Federal District Court judge in Manhattan reduced the award, **June 18,** to a little more than $81 million and rejected Berkey's request that Kodak be stripped of some of its major facilities to assure increased competition. Kodak said it would appeal the

jury's verdict. The key issues had to do with the way Kodak introduced its new pocket instamatic cameras in 1972.

**Olin Indicted** — The Olin Corporation and 3 former officials were indicted, **Mar. 23,** on charges of concealing the dumping of 38 tons of mercury into the Niagara River at Niagara Falls, N.Y., from 1970 to 1977. Environmental officials said that the mercury represented a serious hazard to anyone eating the fish caught in the river. In an unrelated case, a U.S. federal judge ordered Olin, **Mar. 30,** to set up a $510,000 charity fund as a penalty for illegal firearms sales to South Africa. In both cases the company claimed that it had discovered the illegal acts itself and had cooperated with government investigations.

**Begelman Charged** — David Begelman, former head of Columbia Pictures, was charged, **Mar. 31,** with embezzling $40,000 from the company. Begelman resigned, **Feb. 9,** amid controversy over financial practises in the film industry. If convicted, Begelman could face up to 10 years in prison on a charge of grand larceny and up to 14 years on each of 3 counts of forgery. He was said to have accomplished the theft by illegally endorsing checks made out to director Martin Ritt, actor Cliff Robertson, and Los Angeles restaurant owner Pierre Groleau.

**Disasters** — A Continental Air Lines DC-10, taking off in a rainstorm, **Mar. 1,** at Los Angeles International Airport, blew out 2 tires and ran off the runway. The plane burst into flames, killing 2 persons and injuring 50. . . .A Bulgarian airliner crashed, **Mar. 16,** shortly after takeoff from Sofia, killing all 73 persons aboard. . . .A Burmese 2-engine turboprop crashed, **Mar. 25,** shortly after takeoff from Rangoon, killing all 48 persons aboard.

### APRIL

#### National

**Steel Price Hike Reduced** — U.S. Steel Corp. rolled back, **Apr. 3,** a steel price increase that had been denounced, **Mar. 30,** by Pres. Jimmy Carter as "excessive" and "inflationary." U.S. Steel had announced, **Mar. 29,** that it was increasing the price of steel 2.2% or $10.50 a ton, to "cover the cost of the new coal labor contract." The president's Council on Wage and Price Stability had argued that the coal miners' settlement would add no more than $4 a ton to the cost of steel. The company reduced the increase to $5.50 a ton. The steel industry had been given, **Jan. 3,** special protection against low-priced foreign steel imports. The director of the Council on Wage and Price Stability was quoted, **June 19,** in *Fortune,* as saying, "If some industry comes in and asks for protection from foreign competition, the government at the same time has a right to ask them to exercise restraint in their pricing."

**Retirement Age Raised to 70** — Pres. Jimmy Carter signed into law, **Apr. 6,** a bill to raise the legal mandatory retirement age from 65 to 70 for most workers, effective Jan. 1, 1979. Private businesses with fewer than 20 employees would not be affected nor would the law affect early voluntary retirement. The law also abolished entirely the mandatory retirement age of 70 for most federal employees.

**Unemployment Up Slightly, Economy Declines** — Unemployment rose in March to 6.2%, the Labor Department announced **Apr. 7,** up from 6.1% in February. Economic growth declined 0.6% for the first quarter of 1978, the Commerce Department announced **Apr. 19.** The severe winter weather and the coal miners' strike were blamed.

**Neutron Bomb Deferred** — Pres. Jimmy Carter announced, **Apr. 7,** that he had "decided to defer production" of the controversial neutron bomb. This decision could be reversed, the president said, if the Soviet Union failed to show restraint in future arms deployments. The bomb uses enhanced radiation to kill enemy soldiers while doing relatively less damage to property. Tass, the Soviet news agency, responded that the Soviet Union was willing to consider mutual renunciation of the neutron bomb but not the kind of trade-off suggested by Carter. In his **Apr. 25** press conference, the president replied that such mutual renunciation had "no significance at all," since the Soviets had no need for a neutron bomb. The weapon was designed to offset superior Soviet tank forces in Europe. NATO defense ministers, meeting **Apr. 18-19** in Denmark, approved the U.S. decision to delay production of the bomb, but also kept open the option of introducing it in Europe in the future. Gen. Alexander Haig, NATO's supreme allied commander, denied, **Apr. 25,** a *New York Times* story that he would resign because of the decision. Maj. Gen. John K. Singlaub, who was relieved as chief of staff of U.S. troops in Korea last year for criticizing the president's planned troop withdrawal, "agreed to retire" from the army, **Apr. 28,** after calling Carter's neutron bomb decision "ridiculous" and "militarily unsound." Demonstrators broke into the French Consulate in Melbourne, Australia, **Apr. 21,** to protest France's testing of a neutron bomb in the South Pacific. The French government, **Apr. 24,** denied reports of the test.

**Former FBI Head Indicted** — L. Patrick Gray 3d, former acting head of the FBI, and 2 other ex-FBI officials were indicted, **Apr. 10,** on charges of conspiring to deprive U.S. citizens of their civil rights. Gray, W. Mark Felt, and Edward S. Miller were charged with having used illegal entries and searches in locating members of the radical Weatherman anti-war group in 1972 and 1973. Felt had been acting associate director of the FBI and Miller, chief of the bureau's counterintelligence section. Attorney General Griffin B. Bell, in announcing the indictments, also mentioned that charges against John J. Kearney were being dismissed. Evidence showed that Kearney, a lower-level FBI official formerly in New York City and involved in the same case, had been acting under orders from his superiors.

**Carter Announces Anti-Inflation Plan** — Pres. Jimmy Carter announced, **Apr. 11,** new steps to fight inflation, including a 5.5% limit on federal employees' salary increases and a freeze on White House staff pay. The president ruled out mandatory wage and price controls but appealed to industry and labor to show restraint. Industrial leaders praised Carter's decision not to impose mandatory controls but the financial community was disappointed with his failure to deal with what they consider the chief causes of inflation, the federal budget deficit, and the rapid growth of the U.S. money supply. George Meany, president of the AFL-CIO, meeting with Carter **May 10,** refused to support the president's call for a "deceleration" of wage increases. Inflation worsened in the first quarter of 1978, the Commerce Department reported **Apr. 19.** Prices increased at an adjusted annual rate of 7.1%, compared with 5.9% for the 4th quarter of 1977. According to a special report in *Business Week,* **May 22,** the U.S. "is caught in the grip of the worst, most prolonged and most pernicious inflation in its history." *Fortune,* **June 19,** blamed the recent worsening of the inflation on the federal budget deficit, the government's approval of the new coal miners' contract, higher farm price supports, increased Social Security taxes, and an increase in the minimum wage.

**Record Trading in 10-Day Stock Market Rally** — During a 10-day trading period **Apr. 13-26,** the New York Stock Exchange saw an unprecedented 431.88 million shares traded and a rise of 62 points in the Dow Jones industrial average. On **Apr. 17,** a volume of 63.5 million shares was traded, the heaviest in the exchange's history. The nation's major economic problems, inflation, energy, and the trade deficit, had not improved but institutional investors, who accounted for 75% of the volume, had accumulated huge cash reserves and were ready to pour them into the market, according to a story in *Newsweek,* **May 1.** The dollar recovered from its decline when the Treasury announced, **Apr. 19,** its plan to sell some of the U.S. gold reserve. This small recovery may have been responsible for part of the rally. When foreign investors began to join the rally, they bought dollars to pay for their purchases, further pushing up the value of the dollar.

**Carter Tax Plan in Trouble** — The House Ways and Means Committee rejected, **Apr. 17-19,** a series of Pres. Jimmy Carter's proposed tax reforms. The reforms would have eliminated or reduced certain tax deductions, both to make the tax system fairer and to generate more tax revenue to offset part of the president's proposed tax cut of about $25 billion. On **Apr. 20,** 3 members of the committee met with Carter at the White House and warned him that he would not be able to get his plan through Congress. On **Apr. 25,** G. William Miller, chairman of the Federal Reserve Board, recommended that the tax cut be put off until 1979. Carter, in a press conference later that day, rejected either delaying or paring down his proposed tax reduction, saying that it was "about the right figure" and that "the best time

to make it effective is the first of October." Carter agreed, **May 12,** to reduce his tax-cut package to $19.4 billion and to make it effective Jan. 1, 1979. The reversal was based or worsening inflation, reduced unemployment, and pressure from Congress and the Federal Reserve.

**Supreme Court Withholds Nixon Tapes** — The Supreme Court ruled, **Apr. 18,** by a 7-to-2 vote, that broadcasters and recording companies would not have automatic access to former Pres. Richard M. Nixon's White House tapes. In a majority opinion, Justice Lewis F. Powell Jr. argued that the press had no "special benefits" beyond "the right to attend the trial and report what they have observed." The court ruled, **Apr. 3,** by a vote of 7 to 0 that federal judges cannot block the construction of nuclear power plants by imposing extreme safety standards. On **Apr. 25,** the court banned, 6 to 2, pension plans with higher costs for women than men and declared unconstitutional, 5 to 4, a Massachusetts law prohibiting corporations from financing campaigns relating to ballot issues not directly affecting their interests.

**U.S. to Give Up Panama Canal** — The Senate voted, **Apr. 18,** to turn over the Panama Canal to Panama on Dec. 31, 1999. The 68-32 vote, one more than the two-thirds majority needed to ratify the treaty, was the same as the vote **Mar. 16** approving the treaty that guarantees the neutrality of the canal after the year 2000. Reservations added to the treaty would allow the U.S. to use its troops to re-open the canal if necessary but not to interfere with Panamanian sovereignty. Pres. Jimmy Carter, who had lobbied intensively for the treaties, and Panama's chief of state, Brig. Gen. Omar Torrijos, hailed the ratification. Torrijos added that, if the treaties had been rejected, Panama would have seized the canal by force. On **Apr. 17,** the U.S. Supreme Court had refused to issue an injunction sought by members of Congress to bar the treaties until the court could consider claims that the House as well as the Senate had to ratify them. On **May 15,** the court declined to review that decision.

**Natural Gas Accord** — Senior members of a House-Senate conference committee reached a compromise, **Apr. 21,** in closed session, on natural gas pricing, a crucial element in Pres. Jimmy Carter's energy plan. The agreement to deregulate the price of natural gas by 1985 still had to be approved by the full conference committee, as well as the House and Senate. The conferees had met, **Apr. 12,** in the White House, with the president and Energy Secretary James Schlesinger present. The House voted, **Apr. 13,** 371-6, against such closed sessions but one of the conferees said that the meetings would not be affected by the vote. **Apr. 20,** the anniversary of Carter's presentation of the energy plan, was marked by critical members of Congress with a cake in the shape of a turkey and a large doughnut with a single candle in the hole. It was estimated that the Apr. 21 compromise agreement would cost consumers $25 billion to $31 billion more than the 1977 House bill maintaining price controls and about $30 billion less than the 1977 Senate bill which called for quicker deregulation. The full conference committee finally approved the plan, **June 13.**

**Carter Slows Korea Troop Withdrawal** — Pres. Jimmy Carter announced, **Apr. 21,** that only 800 U.S. troops and 2,600 support personnel would be withdrawn from South Korea in 1978. Carter had announced in 1977 that about 32,000 troops would leave over a 4- to 5-year period. The reason for the withdrawal slowdown was Congressional inaction on Carter's proposed transfer of $800 million in military equipment and $275 million in arms credits to the Korean government. South Korea, **Apr. 22,** welcomed the president's decision. The Soviet Union, **Apr. 22,** and China and North Korea, **May 7,** criticized it, demanding the total withdrawal of American forces from Korea. The U.S. House of Representatives, **May 24,** rejected an attempt to require the U.S. to keep at least 26,000 troops in South Korea until South Korea and North Korea had signed a peace treaty.

**Carter Rating Drops** — Pres. Jimmy Carter's popularity dropped to 39%, according to a Gallup poll released **Apr. 24,** 9 points down from the March Gallup poll. Carter's loss in popularity was generally attributed to his handling of the economy.

**Ex-Rep. Hanna Sentenced** — Former Rep. Richard T. Hanna (D, Cal.), was sentenced, **Apr. 24,** to serve 6 to 30 months in prison for conspiring to defraud the U.S. in the Korean influence-buying scandal. Hanna, 63, was the first person to be sent to prison in the case. Former Rep. Otto E.

assman, Democrat of Louisiana, was indicted, **Mar. 31**, on imilar charges, and on **Apr. 28**, on a charge of tax evasion. assman, 77, had been in the Touro Infirmary in New Orleans since the end of March, suffering from "significant depression" and senility, according to his lawyer. A U.S. district judge said, **Apr. 19**, he would appoint doctors to determine whether Passman was competent to stand trial. Hanna was convicted and Passman indicted on charges of accepting bribes from Tongsun Park, the Korean businessman accused of buying influence in Congress. Hancho C. Kim, a Korean-born naturalized American citizen, was sentenced, **May 19**, to serve 6 months in prison for having conspired with the Korean Civil Intelligence Agency to bribe American Congressmen.

**SEC Accuses Lance of Fraud** — Former Budget Director Bert Lance was charged by the SEC, **Apr. 26**, with civil fraud and "unsafe and unsound banking practices and financial irregularities." Also charged were the Calhoun First National Bank and the National Bank of Georgia, the 2 Georgia banks Lance, still a friend of Pres. Jimmy Carter, headed before joining the administration. Lance and the banks settled the complaint as soon as it was filed, by promising not to violate, in the future, the laws cited in the complaint, but neither denied nor admitted guilt. Lance had settled, similarly, **Mar. 19**, SEC charges that he and 9 others, including 4 wealthy Arabs, had violated federal law in failing to disclose their attempted takeover of Financial Bankshares Inc., Washington's 2d largest bank-holding company.

## International

**Carter Tours South America, Africa** — Pres. Jimmy Carter returned to Washington, **Apr. 3**, from a 7-day, 14,000-mile South American and African journey. Carter visited Venezuela, Brazil, Nigeria, and Liberia. In Venezuela, **Mar. 28**, Carter endeared himself to his hosts by delivering 2 short speeches in Spanish. Carter and Venezuelan Pres. Carlos Andres Perez issued a statement noting strong agreement on the importance of the Panama Canal treaties, the seriousness of the abuses of human rights in Nicaragua, and the problem of Cuban involvement in Africa. Carter arrived in Brazil, **Mar. 29**, and immediately raised the 2 issues that had brought U.S.-Brazilian relations to a "30-year low," human rights and nuclear proliferation. Brazil had abrogated the U.S.-Brazilian military assistance treaty last year after Carter criticized the military government of Pres. Ernesto Geisel for its abuses of human rights. The U.S. had also opposed a Brazilian plan to import a West German uranium-reprocessing plant that could be used in the production of nuclear weapons. The Brazilian government gave Carter a cool welcome. On **Mar. 31**, Carter met with 6 prominent Brazilians, some of whom had publicly opposed the Geisel regime. Nevertheless, Carter publicly stressed the U.S. need for strong ties between Brazil and the U.S. and seemed to have reduced tensions somewhat. Later on **Mar. 31**, Carter flew to Nigeria, where he was joined by U.N. Ambassador Andrew Young. The president called for the withdrawal of the 16,000 to 17,000 Cuban troops in Ethiopia and for majority-rule governments in Rhodesia and Namibia (South-West Africa). Carter announced, **Apr. 2**, that the U.S. and Great Britain were trying to convene a meeting of all parties involved in the Rhodesian situation, including both the Patriotic Front guerrillas and the Ian Smith government. The plan was rejected, **Apr. 3**, by 2 of the 3 black nationalist groups participating in the transitional government with Smith. Carter stopped in Liberia, **Apr. 3**, on his way back to Washington, as a gesture to the Liberian people, some of whom are descended from freed American slaves.

**More French Troops to Chad** — French government sources, **Apr. 6**, confirmed that at least 150 additional advisers had been sent to Chad to help the government fight Moslem guerrillas. Chad, **Feb. 6**, had broken diplomatic relations with Libya because of Libyan aid to Frolinat, the Chad national liberation front, which began the civil war in 1965. Libya, Chad, Sudan, and Niger, **Feb. 24**, signed an agreement to end the war, whereby Frolinat leaders were to meet with Chad Pres. Félix Malloum in Libya in March. Fighting broke out again, however, and on **Apr. 19**, according to Reuters, another 200 French Foreign Legion troops were flown to Chad to counter the new rebel drive. Reports, **May 10**, indicated that as many as 1,700 French troops were

protecting the Malloum regime from the guerrillas, who had gotten to within 250 miles of Ndjamena, the capital. The *Wall Street Journal*, **May 24**, reported that there were 12,000 French troops in Africa helping the governments of Zaire, Chad, and Mauritania against guerrillas, as well as French bases in Gabon, Senegal, and the Ivory Coast, and 4,500 French troops in Djibouti, guarding the Horn of Africa and the approaches to the Red Sea. French forces in Africa, bolstering economic and cultural ties between France and the former colonies, were second only, among foreigners, to the Cubans.

**Fraud Charges in Philippine Elections** — Pres. Ferdinand E. Marcos' government won Philippine legislative elections, **Apr. 7**, amid opposition charges of electoral fraud. The antigovernment People's Force party charged, **Apr. 8**, that hundreds of its poll watchers had been forced away from the polling places. Police arrested, **Apr. 9**, about 600 marchers who were protesting the election. The marchers were released, **Apr. 11**, but the 8 organizers of the demonstration, including 6 People's Front leaders, were detained. On **May 26**, the Philippine government postponed municipal and provincial elections scheduled to be held later in 1978, because of the "disruptions" in the April balloting. On **June 3**, Marcos ordered the release of 5 of the imprisoned People's Force leaders.

**Europeans to Devise Independent Economic Recovery** — The European Community's heads of state, at their annual meeting **Apr. 7-8** in Copenhagen, decided to formulate an economic recovery plan independently of the U.S. The plan called for closer coordination of the members currencies to protect them from the dollar's weakness. The West German mark, already linked with the Belgian, Dutch, Danish, and Norwegian currencies, would be linked also with the British pound and the French franc. The Europeans also rejected the U.S. demand for a new nuclear fuel supply treaty.

**Soviet U.N. Aide Defects** — U.N. and State Department spokesmen announced, **Apr. 10**, that Arkady N. Shevchenko, top-ranking Soviet official in the U.N. Secretariat, had defected from the Soviet Union. Shevchenko, 47, applied for asylum in the U.S., **Apr. 26**, and announced he was resigning from the UN. He had originally tried to retain his post even after his defection but the Soviet Union insisted on his replacement. According to the *New York Times*, **Apr. 17**, Shevchenko had met with FBI and CIA agents for several years. Shevchenko's wife Leongina, 48, committed suicide in Moscow, **May 8**, apparently as a result of her husband's defection.

**Initial Israeli Withdrawals from Lebanon** — Israeli forces began to withdraw, **Apr. 11**, from southern Lebanon. A contingent of 150 Norwegian Unifil (U.N. Interim Force in Lebanon) troops occupied 6 villages in the area near the Syrian border evacuated by Israel. The Israelis had occupied most of southern Lebanon in March, forcing out Palestinian guerrillas who had killed 36 Israeli civilians in a raid, **Mar. 11**, inside Israel. As the Israelis pulled back, Lebanese and Palestinians who had fled to Beirut during the Israeli invasion began returning to their villages in the south. Israeli troops withdrew from an additional area, **Apr. 14**, and were replaced by Nepalese Unifil troops. On **April 30**, the Israelis turned over more positions to Unifil, remaining in control of only the 6-mile buffer zone which had been the original objective of their invasion. Unifil troops were fired on by Palestinian guerrillas, **Apr. 7**, and one Norwegian was killed. PLO leader Yasir Arafat was reported, **Apr. 17**, to have promised UN Secretary General Kurt Waldheim that the PLO would not interfere with Unifil troops. Arafat, also the leader of Al Fatah, the guerrilla group responsible for the Mar. 11 raid, was reported **Apr. 24**, to have ordered the arrest of 123 guerrillas who had entered Lebanon from Iraq to fight Israeli and Unifil soldiers. The arrest order led to fighting within Al Fatah and 3 men were killed. Fighting broke out in Beirut again, **Apr. 9**, between Lebanese Moslems and Christians. Syrian-dominated Arab peacekeeping forces in Lebanon intervened and by the time a ceasefire was announced **Apr. 13**, 102 persons were reported killed, including at least 5 Syrians, and 294 wounded.

**Gandhi Party Official Opposition** — Former Prime Minister Indira Gandhi's new party was recognized, **Apr. 12**, by the Indian parliament as the official opposition. The Congress Party-I (I for Indira) had won elections **Feb. 25** in the states of Andhra Pradesh and Karnataka and made a better showing in Maharashtra and Assam than had been expected. In elections in Haryana state, **Apr. 2**, her party was defeated by the ruling Janata party. On **Apr. 5**, Gandhi charged electoral fraud there, saying that untouchables had been intimidated against voting. Congress-I was declared the official opposition when it came to hold 71 seats in the lower house of parliament compared to the regular Congress party's 68. Congress-I also won a by-election, **May 9**, in the important state of Uttar Pradesh and 2 seats in the Uttar Pradesh state legislature. These victories were considered important in Gandhi's drive to regain power.

**U.S., Britain Fail to Arrange Rhodesia Talks** — U.S. Secretary of State Cyrus R. Vance and British Foreign Minister David Owen met, **Apr. 13-17**, with all sides in the Rhodesian conflict but were unable to arrange a conference. Vance and Owen met in Tanzania, **Apr. 14**, with Rhodesian Patriotic Front guerrilla leaders and with British and U.N. officials who would administer Rhodesia during a transition period under the Anglo-American plan. They also met there with leaders of Tanzania, Angola, Botswana, Zambia, and Nigeria. Patriotic Front leaders Joshua Nkomo and Robert Mugabe accepted the Anglo-American invitation to an all-party conference but only on the condition that they be given the dominant role in the transitional government. Mugabe, **Apr. 15**, said that the new Rhodesian state should have a one-party Marxist government. In South Africa, **Apr. 16**, Vance and Owen met with South African Foreign Minister Roelof Botha, who gave strong backing to the Anglo-American plan. On **Apr. 17**, Vance and Owen completed their trip with talks in Salisbury, Rhodesia, with the government of Ian Smith and the 3 black nationalist leaders who were participating in the transitional government not recognized by most nations. The Salisbury leaders rejected the guerrillas' participation in an accord, despite Anglo-American warnings that the internal settlement, by excluding the Patriotic Front, could eventually lead to a full-fledged war with Soviet and Cuban support for the guerrillas. The Rhodesian government began, **Apr. 13**, to release black nationalist political prisoners, including supports of both the Patriotic Front and the 3 groups in the government. An 18-member Council of Ministers was sworn in, **Apr. 14**, in Salisbury, composed of 9 ministries, each headed jointly by one black minister and one white. On **Apr. 28**, Byron Hove, the black justice minister, was fired after criticizing the Rhodesian courts.

**Vance in Moscow Arms Talks** — U.S. Secretary of State Cyrus R. Vance met, **Apr. 20-22**, with Soviet leaders in Moscow. After meeting with Soviet Pres. Leonid I. Brezhnev and Foreign Minister Andrei A. Gromyko, Vance reported "some progress" in talks aimed at strategic arms limitations (SALT), which had seen little progress in more than 3 years. Vance returned to Washington, **Apr. 24**, after a 13-day 25,000-mile trip to Africa, the Soviet Union, and England. Vance briefed the British, German, French, and Canadian foreign ministers, **Apr. 23**, in London, on the Moscow talks. He was reported to have told them that a clause had been added to the draft treaty on strategic arms limitations barring U.S. or Soviet circumvention of the treaty, but that disagreement remained on 2 other issues. The U.S. had not been successful in getting specific written limitations on the Soviet Backfire bomber nor a clause limiting the modernization of existing missiles. Vance refused publicly to reveal the content of the Moscow talks, saying Soviet officials insisted on secrecy in the negotiations.

**South Africa OKs Namibian Independence** — South African Prime Minister John Vorster announced, **Apr. 25**, that his government would accept a Western plan for the independence of Namibia (South-West Africa). South Africa would withdraw its troops as soon as the UN approved the plan but not until there was a "complete cessation" of SWAPO (South-West African People's Organization) guerrilla activities. The future of Walvis Bay, the only deepwater port in the territory, was left up to the future Namibian government and South Africa.

**American Charged in Letelier Murder** — The U.S., **Apr. 26**, charged Michael Townley, a 35-year-old American, with conspiracy in the 1976 murder of Orlando Letelier, former Chilean ambassador to the U.S., in Washington. Townley had been extradited, **Apr. 8**, to the U.S. from Chile. FBI agents testified, **June 2**, at a court hearing related to the case, that Townley was a former agent of DINA, the Chil-

ean secret police. The agents said that he had revealed them the details of the assassination. He had come to the U.S. Sept. 9, 1976, on a DINA assignment to arrange the murder of Letelier. He and 4 anti-Castro Cubans placed a bomb under Letelier's car, which was detonated Sept. 2 killing Letelier and Ronni K. Moffitt, his colleague at Wash ington's Institute for Policy Studies. The U.S. recalled ambassador from Chile, **June 23**, charging that Chile's mil tary government was not cooperating with the investigatic of the murder.

**Military Coup in Afghanistan** — A military junta ove threw, **Apr. 27**, the government of Pres. Mohammad Dau Khan of Afghanistan. Daud, who was killed resisting t coup, had come to power himself in a coup in 1973. A ne government was proclaimed **Apr. 30**, headed by N Mohammad Taraki, leader of an Afghan communist par known as Khalq. Taraki, **May 6**, denied as "imperialist pr paganda" claims that large numbers of people had died the takeover. Reports from Teheran and Islamabad, M 19, indicated that Iran and Pakistan were concerned abo information they had had that Taraki was meeting daily with t Soviet ambassador in Kabul and receiving advice from hi about what policies to follow. They feared, specifically, th the Soviets might encourage Afghanistan to revive its aid the separatist movement in the Pakistani province of Bal chistan (known also as Pushtunistan). A Pakistani press port, **June 5**, said that about 250 Afghan army officers ha fled to Pakistan.

**Moslems Flee Burma** — The Bangladesh governmer **Apr. 30**, reported that about 70,000 Moslems had fled Bangladesh to escape anti-Moslem terror in neighborin Burma during the previous 3 weeks. The Burmese gover ment denied charges of persecutions, saying that Burme Moslems had lived happily with the Buddhist majority f centuries. The refugees, they claimed, were in fact Benga who were fleeing to avoid an investigation of illegal imm gration. More Moslems fled in the following weeks. On Ju 9, an agreement was signed by Burma and Bangladesh repatriate the 200,000 refugees to Burma.

### General

**Music Hall Rescued** — Radio City Music Hall, the lar est theater in the U.S., was saved from closing, for at least year, by a plan announced **Apr. 13**. Rockefeller Center Inc the theater's owner, and New York state officials agreed share the costs of maintaining the midtown Manhattan m sic hall, famous for its art deco design and Rockettes dan ers, which had been scheduled to close because of mounti financial losses. The state also agreed to provide $200,000 study the feasability of subsidizing the music hall with ren from a 20-story office tower to be built over it.

**Air-Fare Cuts Proposed** — The Civil Aeronautics Boar proposed, **Apr. 14**, that airlines be allowed to reduce dome tic fares up to 50% without prior approval, while fare i creases would still require CAB permission. The propos was part of the Carter administration policy aimed at dere ulating the airline industry. It would open the way to fa competition among airlines flying the same route. On Ap 6, the airlines had been granted a 3% increase on domesl fares. On **May 8**, the CAB gave them permission to redu first-class fares between 13% and 20%, bringing them dow to about 30% higher than coach. The Apr. 14 deregulatio proposal, which was still under consideration, had include a provision eliminating the CAB rule that first-class fares at least 50% higher than coach.

**Soviets Force Down Korean Plane** — A Korean A Lines Boeing 707 passenger plane was forced down, **Apr. 2** when it strayed over Soviet territory near the Arctic Circ on a flight from Paris to Seoul. The jet, carrying 113 peopl was forced to crash-land on a frozen lake, killing 2 and i juring 13, when a Soviet jet-fighter began firing on t plane. The passengers were flown to Helsinki, **Apr. 23**, by Pan American Airways rescue plane, and, on **Apr. 24**, in a other Korean plane, to Seoul and Tokyo. The pilot and na igator, who had been detained by Soviet authorities, we released **Apr. 29**.

**Rubens Stolen, Recovered** — Thieves stole the Rube masterpiece "The Three Graces" and 9 other Flemish work **Apr. 21**, from the Pitti Palace in Florence, Italy. The pain ings, estimated at more than $1 million in value, were reco ered undamaged by police, **Apr. 23.**

**Sun Life to Leave Quebec** — Shareholders of Sun Life Assurance Co. of Canada, the country's largest life insurance company, voted, **Apr. 25,** to move company headquarters from Montreal to Toronto. Quebec legislation making French the official language of the province and the Quebec separatist movement were factors in the decision. The Quebec National Assembly, **Apr. 26,** passed a resolution deploring the vote. According to the Canadian government, **Apr. 25,** more than 23,000 people emigrated from Quebec, mostly to neighboring Ontario, in the year ending May 31, 1977, compared to fewer than 13,000 the previous year.

**Scaffold Collapses, 51 Dead** — Scaffolding inside a cooling tower being built for a utility company in West Virginia collapsed, **Apr. 27,** throwing 51 workers 170 feet to their death. The Occupational Safety and Health Administration announced **June 8,** that the company that was building the tower, the general engineering contractor, and a subcontractor for testing the concrete had been charged with willful and serious violations and that punitive damages were being sought. The survivors of the victims had also filed separate civil suits.

**J. P. Stevens, NLRB Suit Settled** — The J. P. Stevens Company and the National Labor Relations Board, **Apr. 28,** announced an agreement to settle a suit involving charges by the AFL-CIO Amalgamated Clothing and Textile Workers Union. The NLRB had, **Jan. 24,** asked U.S. district court to enjoin the nation's 2d largest textile company from alleged illegal anti-union activity. Under the agreement, the request for the injunction was withdrawn and the company agreed to re-hire 13 of 15 employees the union had contended were fired because of union organizing. A boycott of Stevens, a symbol of union-resistance in the South, had been maintained by organized labor for a year.

**Nixon Memoirs Published** — Excerpts from former Pres. Richard M. Nixon's memoirs were published, starting **Apr. 30,** in installments, by many U.S. newspapers. Nixon was quoted as saying in regard to the Watergate affair, the cause of his resignation from the presidency, "I told myself that I had not been involved in the things that gave [H. R. Haldeman, Nixon's chief of staff, and John Ehrlichman, his domestic adviser] potential criminal vulnerability. But there were things that I had known. I had talked with [presidential adviser Charles] Colson about clemency [for the Watergate burglers] . . . and I had been aware that attorneys' fees and family support funds were going to [them.] The difference between us was that Haldeman and Ehrlichman had become trapped . . . ; so far, I was not. I was faced with having to fire my friends for things I myself was part of."

**Disasters** — A passenger boat carrying 200 people capsized, **Apr. 8,** in a storm in the Bay of Bengal off Burma. More than 100 were presumed drowned. . . . About 1,000 people were reported drowned, **Apr. 9,** when the same storm sank 100 cargo boats in the Bay of Bengal off Bangladesh. . . At least 43 people were killed and over 100 hurt when 2 trains collided, **Apr. 15,** in the mountains between Bologna and Florence, Italy. . . . Tornadoes in eastern India killed 600 people, **Apr. 17.**

## MAY

### National

**Farm Prices Raised** — Congress, **May 4,** authorized the administration to raise grain and cotton price supports for the next 4 years. The House, **Apr. 12,** had defeated a bill which had provided even higher subsidies and which Pres. Jimmy Carter had threatened to veto as inflationary.

**Unemployment at 3½-Year Low, Prices Up** — Unemployment fell to 6% in April, the Labor Department reported **May 5,** the lowest rate in 3½ years. Consumer prices rose 0.6%, led by a record 6.6% increase in the price of beef, for the same period, the Bureau of Labor Statistics announced, **May 31.** Inflation was thus at a double-digit annual rate, again. Robert S. Strauss, Pres. Jimmy Carter's chief inflation adviser, said, **May 10,** that the president was deeply disappointed with organized labor's rejection of his request for voluntary wage-price guidelines to fight inflation. The AFL-CIO said that the emphasis should be on price controls rather than on wages.

**FBI Arrests 2 as Soviet Spies** — FBI agents, **May 20,**

arrested 2 Soviet citizens in New Jersey as spies. A 3d Soviet citizen was picked up and released because, as a member of the Soviet UN delegation, he was covered by diplomatic immunity. The 3 were caught in the act of picking up classified documents relating to U.S. Navy underwater warfare projects. An FBI agent said that all 3 were KGB (Soviet intelligence) agents. The State Department asked, **May 20,** that the UN delegate leave the U.S.

**Supreme Court Allows Newsroom Searches** — The Supreme Court, **May 31,** ruled, 5 to 3, that police could obtain warrants to search the property of newspapers without prior warning and that the papers had no right to contest such searches in court before they were conducted. The decision was condemned by reporters as an attack on First Amendment freedom of the press. The court also ruled, **May 23,** by a vote of 8 to 1, that judges and juries should not consider the possible reactions of children when deciding whether material was obscene in terms of "contemporary community standards." On **May 30,** the court ruled, in 2 separate cases, that lawyers could not solicit cases for personal gain but that they could do so when they represented nonprofit organizations or when they volunteered their services.

### International

**UN, Palestinians Clash in Lebanon** — French and Senegalese Unifil (UN Interim Force in Lebanon) troops, **May 1,** clashed with Palestinian guerrillas in Lebanon, hours after the 3d partial withdrawal of Israeli troops occupying southern Lebanon. In 2 separate incidents, 2 guerrillas and 3 UN soldiers were killed. On **May 2,** 3 French UN soldiers were killed and 7 wounded when gunmen attacked Unifil troops near Tyre, the port city controlled by Palestinians, and on **May 3,** the French commander called off patrols in the Tyre area. In view of the clashes, the UN voted to increase the Unifil force from 4,000 to 6,000 men. On **May 8,** the UN force moved its headquarters from a site north of Tyre to a village in the Israeli-held strip along the Lebanese-Israeli border. On **May 13,** Unifil discovered an 80-man guerrilla unit, and on **May 15,** one of about 20 men, in the UN controlled zone. The UN negotiated to have the guerrillas leave, in order to fulfill its mandate to obtain complete Israeli withdrawal from Lebanon. After yet another French-Palestinian clash, **May 17,** PLO leader Yasir Arafat, **May 24,** agreed to keep guerrillas out of southern Lebanon. PLO militants, however, challenged Arafat's rule. On **May 20,** 3 terrorists were killed in an attack on El Al passengers at Orly Airport in Paris. The Organization of the Sons of Southern Lebanon claimed responsibility for the attack, which they said was merely the first reply to the Israeli invasion.

**Prisoners Exchanged** — The U.S., East Germany, and Mozambique completed, **May 1,** a 3-way exchange of prisoners. A Soviet spy, convicted in the U.S., was released in West Berlin in exchange for an American arrested by East Germany for trying to help 3 East Germans leave the country. On **Apr. 23,** an Israeli businessman had been released by Mozambique as part of the deal.

**Chinese Flee Vietnam** — Hundreds of ethnic Chinese were reported, **May 1,** to be fleeing Vietnam after the nationalization of their businesses there. The Peking government, **May 24,** accused Vietnam of abusing and expelling 70,000 Chinese residents and announced, **May 27,** it would send ships to evacuate them. Vietnam, **May 28,** denied that the Chinese there had been mistreated. On **June 22,** the Vietnamese Foreign Ministry refused to allow the 2 Chinese ships sent to evacuate the ethnic Chinese to land, because of procedural disagreements. Nationalist China announced, **June 20,** that it would evacuate the 1,500 Chinese remaining in Ho Chi Minh City (Saigon).

**Rhodesian Guerrilla Parties Legalized** — Rhodesia, **May 2,** legalized ZAPU and ZANU, the Patriotic Front parties led by, respectively, Joshua Nkomo and Robert Mugabe. The interim government of Ian Smith and 3 black nationalist leaders removed the bans imposed on the Zimbabwe African People's Union in 1962 and the Zimbabwe African National Union in 1964 and promised to release all the political prisoners in Rhodesia. Zimbabwe is the nationalist name for Rhodesia. The moves were immediately dismissed by the guerrillas, who said their armed opposition to the government would continue. On **May 27,** at the first legal

ZAPU rally in Rhodesia in 15 years, a crowd of 50,000 roared its opposition to the biracial interim government.

**South Africa Attacks Guerrillas in Angola** — Between 300 and 700 South African troops, **May 4,** raided SWAPO (South-West African People's Organization) bases in Angola. The raid was in response to recent guerrilla attacks in Namibia (South-West Africa). SWAPO headquarters and 2 smaller bases were destroyed. Angola claimed, **May 6,** that 504 Namibian refugees and 16 Angolan soldiers had been killed in the attack. The UN Security Council, **May 6,** condemned the raid as a violation of Angolan sovereignty. On **May 12,** South Africa denounced the U.S. for condemning the raid while ignoring SWAPO attacks.

**Sanjay Gandhi Jailed** — Sanjay Gandhi, son of former Indian Prime Minister Indira Gandhi, was jailed for a month, **May 5,** on charges of tampering with witnesses in a case in which he was involved. A commission of inquiry, **May 15,** denounced him and his mother for illegal and repressive acts during her emergency rule government in 1975. Sanjay Gandhi was ordered, **May 25,** to face trial for refusing to testify before the commission.

**West Germany, USSR Sign 25-Year Economic Pact** — Soviet Pres. Leonid I. Brezhnev and West German Chancellor Helmut Schmidt, **May 6,** signed a 25-year economic cooperation agreement. Brezhnev visited Bonn, West Germany, **May 4-7.** The agreement called for doubling German-Soviet trade by 1980. Schmidt said, **May 17,** on the basis of his talks with Brezhnev, that he expected progress soon at the deadlocked talks on reducing troops in Central Europe.

**Rioting in Iran** — Moslem anti-government riots swept Iran, **May 8-11,** with dozens of people reported killed. Rioting had first begun **Feb. 23** and broke out again **Mar. 26-Apr. 2,** as religious leaders opposed government modernization plans and demanded the return of mosque lands confiscated under the shah's land reform program. The government, **May 10,** condemned the rioters as an "unholy alliance" of Moslem extremists and Communists. The shah, who appeared unworried by the rioting, warned, **May 31,** that pro-Soviet communists would take over if his government were to fall.

**USSR, China Border Raid** — China, **May 11,** accused the Soviet Union of a boat and helicopter raid at the Manchurian border and of attacking Chinese citizens. The Soviets, **May 12,** apologized for the incident, claiming that border guards, pursuing criminals, had thought they were on an island in the Ussuri river, when in fact they had crossed to the Chinese bank. Peking rejected the Soviet explanation. The Chinese Communist party, **May 14,** warned that war with the Soviet Union was inevitable.

**Coup in Comoro Islands** — A coup, **May 13,** deposed the government of Comoro Islands Pres. Ali Solih. The coup was carried out by members of the government deposed by Solih in a coup in 1975. Most of the 230,000 Moslem inhabitants of the Indian Ocean republic had resisted Solih's attempts to impose a Chinese-style revolutionary system, and the new regime announced that it would restore freedom of religion and property rights, which Solih had tried to suppress. Solih was killed, **May 29,** in an attempt to escape house arrest. The Comoro Islands delegation, **July 8,** was expelled from the annual summit meeting of the Organization of African Unity. The OAU foreign ministers charged that white mercenaries had helped overthrow Solih. The Comoro government, **July 23,** announced that Bob Denard, the Belgian who had led a group of about 50 white mercenaries in the coup, would remain in charge of the island nation's armed forces.

**Rioting, Martial Law in Peru** — Riots and a general strike began, **May 15,** in Peru, after the government announced a series of price increases from 30% to 120% for food, gasoline, and transportation. Peru had been subsidizing low-income consumers but was forced to institute austerity economic measures in order to obtain refinancing of the nation's large short-term debt from the International Monetary Fund. The riots began as clashes between police and university students in Lima and spread to other cities the next day. The government decided, **May 19,** to postpone legislative elections scheduled for June 4. Twelve left-wing politicians, who were to run in those elections, called for a general strike for **May 22-23** to protest the price increases. They were arrested. A state of emergency was proclaimed **May 20,** but the 2-day strike went off as planned. Clashes between police and demonstrators, **May 22-23,** in 28 cities were said to have resulted in the deaths of 20 people. The 12 leftists were expelled to Argentina, **May 25,** and other leftist leaders went underground to avoid arrest.

**Ethiopian Offensive in Eritrea** — Ethiopian forces, reportedly supported by Cuban troops, began, **May 16,** a major offensive against secessionist guerrillas in the coastal province of Eritrea. An Ethiopian force of 10,000 to 20,000 men, besieged in Asmara, the provincial capital, for 2 years, broke through rebel lines but after 3 days of heavy fighting

---

### Aldo Moro Found Dead; Kidnaped, "Tried" by Red Brigades Terrorists

The bullet-ridden body of former Italian Prime Minister Aldo Moro was found, **May 9,** abandoned in a parked car in Rome. Moro, who probably would have become Italy's next president, had been kidnaped in Rome, **Mar. 16,** by Red Brigades urban guerrillas. All 5 of his bodyguards were killed. The Red Brigades, Italy's largest terrorist organization, announced that Moro would be killed unless 15 guerrilla leaders on trial in Turin were freed. The Italian government deployed up to 50,000 policemen and troops to search for Moro and decided, **Mar. 19,** to continue the trial of the terrorists.

The kidnapers, **Mar. 25,** announced that they had begun a "people's trial" of Moro, accusing him of being the leading representative of a repressive regime for 30 years. On **Mar. 29,** a letter in Moro's handwriting was delivered to the government. Moro appealed to the interior minister to negotiate with the terrorists, and said he feared he might otherwise be forced to reveal state secrets. The government and Moro's ruling Christian Democratic party refused to negotiate.

On **Apr. 15,** the kidnapers announced that Moro's "trial" had been completed and that he had been sentenced to death. A message was found, **Apr. 18,** saying that Moro had been killed and his body thrown into a mountain lake near Rome. Italian troops on skis and in helicopters searched the area for 3 days, in vain. On **Apr. 20** a photograph was released showing that Moro was still alive. Moro's wife Eleonora appealed, in vain, to his party to negotiate his release and Pope Paul VI, **Apr. 22 and 23,** in dramatic messages, begged the terrorists to release Moro.

The Red Brigades announced, **May 5,** that they were carrying out the "death sentence" against Moro. Mrs. Moro, **May 7,** received a farewell letter in which the former prime minister wrote, "They have told me that they will kill me shortly. I kiss you for the last time; give a kiss to the children."

Moro was buried, **May 10,** in a simple ceremony. Party and government leaders, who had refused to negotiate Moro's release, were barred from the funeral at the family's request. On **May 13,** a memorial service for Moro was held at the Basilica of St. John Lateran, in Rome, attended by the Pope, Italian Pres. Giovanni Leone, and many other top Italian and foreign leaders.

During and after the period Moro was being held, Red Brigades members continued terrorist bombings and shootings in many Italian cities, including, **May 11,** the wounding of the manager of the Chemical Bank branch in Milan. On **May 15,** the Christian Democrats made substantial gains in local elections, apparently out of a sympathetic reaction against the Moro slaying and anger at the terrorists. The Communists suffered losses, even though they had totally dissociated themselves from the Red Brigades and had been denounced by the terrorists as spies for the government.

On **May 18-19** police discovered 3 Red Brigades hideouts and arrested 10 persons, 6 of whom were charged, **June 5,** with complicity in the Moro kidnaping. On **June 23** the trial of the terrorists in Turin was completed and 29 Red Brigades members were sentenced to up to 15 years in prison.

vere forced to retreat. The 2 main guerrilla groups, the Eritrean Liberation Front and the Eritrean People's Liberation Front, Apr. 27, had agreed to merge forces but the *New York Times*, May 26, reported that Ethiopia was aiming to eliminate the weaker ELF and then open negotiations with the ELPF, to which the Ethiopian regime was closer in ideology. Iraq was reported, May 25, to have threatened to break diplomatic relations with the Soviet Union if the Soviets helped the Ethiopians against the Eritreans, who were being supported by Iraq. It was also reported that Cuban Pres. Fidel Castro, who met with Ethiopian leader Lt. Col. Mengistu Haile Mariam Apr. 21-27, was reluctant to commit Cuban troops to fight in Eritrea.

**Opposition Wins Dominican Elections** — Dominican Republic Pres. Joaquín Balaguer was defeated, May 16, by Dominican Revolutionary party (PRD) candidate Antonio Guzmán. The PRD also won control of both houses of the Dominican congress but Balaguer's Reformist party (PR) won 40 mayoral elections to the PRD's 34. Army troops interrupted the vote count May 17-18, but when the elections board declared the results May 26, Balaguer and the army, under U.S. pressure, promised to respect them. The elections board ruled on July 8, however, that the PR had actually won a 16-11 majority in the upper house of the congress. The Dominican supreme court, July 20, rejected an appeal by the PRD against the ruling, which had awarded 4 contested seats to the PR. The outgoing congress, July 19, had limited Guzmán further, taking certain powers away from the government and giving them to the armed forces.

**Cambodian-Vietnamese Fighting Stepped Up** — Heavy fighting again broke out it was reported May 17 from Thailand, on the Cambodian-Vietnamese border, after a 2-month lull. Cambodian prisoners-of-war seemed to have been indoctrinated by the Vietnamese to be infiltrated back into Cambodia to help replace the Pol Pot regime there with a pro-Vietnamese one. Chinese tanks and arms were said to have been sent to Cambodia for use against Vietnam.

**Dissident Orlov Sentenced** — Soviet physicist Yuri Orlov, May 18, was sentenced to 7 years' imprisonment and 5 years' internal exile for "anti-Soviet agitation." He had been in the forefront of a group monitoring Soviet compliance with the 1975 Helsinki agreement on human rights. The U.S. State Department, the U.S. scientific community, the British Labor party, the French government, and the Italian Communist party newspaper strongly condemned the trial and the sentence. Orlov had not been allowed to call defense witnesses.

**French, Belgian Paratroopers to Zaire** — French and Belgian paratroopers were dropped, May 19-20, into the copper-mining town of Kolwezi in Zaire's Shaba (formerly Katanga) province. The paratroopers were sent in to rescue more than 2,500 Europeans trapped there in fighting between Zairian troops and secessionist rebels. The U.S. Air Force provided 18 transport planes for the operation. Guerillas had invaded Shaba, May 11, occupying Kolwezi and the town of Mutshatsha. The Zairian government of Pres. Mobutu Sese Seko accused Cuban forces of aiding the rebels. Cuban Pres. Fidel Castro, May 17, denied the charge but the French Foreign Ministry, May 19, reported that Cuban and Soviet advisers had been spotted with the rebels. The Western rescue was condemned by the Soviet Union, May 22, and endorsed by most of the African leaders, including Mobutu, attending the Franco-African annual summit in Paris, May 22-23. French paratroopers began to withdraw from Kolwezi May 25, leaving only a token force in place. The Zairian Red Cross, May 30, said that 720 people had been killed in Kolwezi, including 132 foreigners.

**Sadat Restricts Opposition** — A nationwide referendum in Egypt, May 21, overwhelmingly endorsed Pres. Anwar Sadat's plan to curb political opposition from both left and right. Sadat promised, however, that the restrictions would not lead to a return to the sometimes repressive measures of former Egyptian Pres. Gamal Abdel Nasser. On May 26 it was disclosed that Sadat had called home 30 Egyptian journalists living abroad to face charges that they had been working "against the national objectives of the Egyptian people." The conservative New Wafd party, June 2, disbanded in protest over the curbs. The leftist Progressive Union party, June 5, suspended activities, leaving Egypt with only the ruling Arab Socialist Union and the small Liberal party, which usually supported the government.

**UN Disarmament Session** — A special 5-week UN General Assembly session on disarmament opened, May 23. U.S. Vice Pres. Walter F. Mondale addressed the session, May 24, criticizing the Soviet Union for its deployments in Europe and the Indian Ocean. Many diplomats felt that Pres. Jimmy Carter's absence showed that the U.S. gave priority to direct arms talks with the Soviet Union over diarmament talks in a UN context. Soviet Foreign Minister Andrei Gromyko responded to Mondale, May 26, saying that the Soviet Union was prepared to discuss "substantial" nuclear arms reductions when the SALT treaty was concluded. French Pres. Valéry Giscard d'Estaing, May 25, and Chinese Foreign Minister Huang Hua, May 29, hinted to the General Assembly that they might join the Geneva disarmament talks if those talks were not controlled by the U.S. and the USSR. Huang also called the Soviet Union the "most dangerous source of a new world war" and warned the U.S. against a policy of appeasement. The Soviet delegate walked out during Huang's speech.

**Brzezinski Completes Trip** — National Security Adviser Zbigniew Brzezinski returned, May 25, to Washington from a 5-day tour of China, Japan, and South Korea. In China, May 20-22, Brzezinski briefed Chinese officials on U.S.-Soviet arms talks, in an effort to "underline the long-term strategic nature of the United States' relationship to China." He said also that the U.S. had "made up its mind" to move toward full diplomatic relations with China. In Japan, May 23-24, Brzezinski briefed Japanese officials on his talks in Peking and told Japanese Premier Takeo Fukuda that China was interested in resuming peace-treaty talks, suspended since 1975, with Japan. Brzezinski's visit, May 25, to South Korea did not calm Korean fears of U.S. troop withdrawals, despite his assurances of continued U.S. support.

**Yugoslavia, Bulgaria Arrest West German Terrorists** — The West German government, May 29, disclosed that Yugoslavia had arrested 4 of West Germany's most-wanted terrorists. Their extradition to West Germany was held up while Yugoslavia tried to extradite Croatian nationalists held in West Germany. Bulgaria, June 21, arrested 4 more suspected terrorists and turned them over to West Germany in a matter of hours.

**Carter Attacks Cuban, Soviet Role in Africa** — Pres. Jimmy Carter, May 30, attacked Cuban and Soviet actions in Africa, in his address to the 2-day meeting of NATO heads of state in Washington, D.C. There are an estimated 40,000 Cuban soldiers and advisers in Africa, mainly in Angola and Ethiopia. According to the *Washington Post*, May 14, Cubans had arrived in Zambia to train Rhodesian guerrillas. NATO leaders cautioned Moscow, May 31, that Soviet actions in Africa endangered détente. Cuba, May 30, continued to deny charges that Cuban forces had been involved in the recent rebel invasion of the Zairian province of Shaba. The Soviet Union, May 31, said that the Western rescue of Europeans in Shaba was a pretext for intervention in the internal affairs of African countries and was harmful to détente. Carter, May 19, had criticized the "very tight constraints" Congress had placed on aid to friendly African nations. As a result, the president said, the U.S. role in the Zaire airlift had been "very limited." On May 23, Carter reiterated his complaints to a group of senators, explaining that, because of the limits, the U.S. was not able to assist pro-Western guerrillas fighting the 20,000 Cubans stationed in Angola. Carter, at a press conference May 25, added that U.S. ability "to help countries whose security is threatened" had been limited by the restrictions. Zbigniew Brezezinski, the president's national security adviser, May 28, agreed that the president faced too many such restrictions.

## General

**Harvard Stiffens Requirements** — The faculty of Harvard University voted, May 2, to replace the current "general education" program with a stiffer "core curriculum." The new program, which would be introduced gradually and apply in full to the class of 1986, would require students to choose about one-quarter of their courses from a list of 80 to 100 "core" courses. The change reflects a new attitude in favor of stricter curriculum requirements at American colleges and universities, in contrast to the situation in the 1960s when, under pressure from students, many curriculum requirements were dropped.

**Patricia Hearst Back in Prison** — Patricia Hearst, **May 15,** returned to the medium-security federal prison at Pleasanton, Calif. She had been free on $1.5 million bail since November 19, 1976. On **Apr. 24,** the Supreme Court had declined to review her 7-year sentence for bank robbery. She had spent 14 months at Pleasanton before her release and would have to serve an additional 14 months before becoming eligible for parole.

**Courts, Voters Decide Homosexuals' Rights** — The U.S. Supreme Court, **May 15,** declined to review and so let stand a decision affirming the constitutionality of a North Carolina law which made homosexual relations between consenting adults a criminal offense. Justice William Rehnquist, **Feb. 21,** had objected to a similar decision, saying that the court should not "flee to escape from controversial or sensitive cases." The Florida State Supreme Court, **Mar. 20,** had ruled that acknowledgement of homosexual preference was not in itself grounds to deny a qualified applicant the right to practise law in the state. City ordinances prohibiting discrimination in housing, employment, and public accommodations on the basis of sexual or affectional preference were repealed in referenda in St. Paul, Minnesota, **Apr. 25;** Wichita, Kansas, **May 9,** and Eugene, Oregon, **May 23.** The United Presbyterian Church, **May 22,** voted against the ordination of "practicing" homosexuals, in spite of the recommendation in favor of ordination by a 19-member church task force that had spent 15 months studying the question.

**Indian Activists Acquitted** — A Los Angeles jury, **May 24,** acquitted 2 Indian activists charged with the murder and robbery of a cab driver in 1974. The trial and pre-trial hearings had lasted 3½ years and cost $1.25 million. Leaders of the American Indian Movement had claimed that Paul Skyhorse and Richard Mohawk were being prosecuted because of their political activities.

**Princess Margaret Divorced** — Princess Margaret of Britain and her husband of 18 years, the Earl of Snowden, were divorced, **May 24,** in London. The uncontested divorce was granted on grounds that "the marriage was irretrievably broken down."

**Atlantic City Casino Opened** — Legalized casino gambling began, **May 26,** in Atlantic City, N.J., the nation's first legal casino outside of Nevada. The Resorts International Hotel Casino reported, **June 5,** that it had taken in over $2.6 million in the first 6 days of operation.

**Disasters** — A tornado killed 2 and injured 96, **May 4,** at an elementary school in Clearwater, Florida. . . .Heavy rains left 4 dead and an estimated $60 million in damage, **May 4,** in New Orleans. . . .A landslide struck a passenger train in Iran, **May 24,** killing at least 17 people. . . .At least 3 persons were killed, **May 27,** when 2 days of heavy rains sent a 12-foot wall of water surging through a canyon in the Texas panhandle. . . .A series of explosions at an oil refinery, **May 30,** at Texas City, Texas, killed 4 people, injured 11 others,

and blew up two 55,000-gallon gasoline tanks.

## JUNE

### National

**Prices, Unemployment Up Slightly** — The Bureau of Labor Statistics, **June 2,** reported that May wholesale prices and unemployment increased slightly, indicating that inflation might be slowing down. The Consumer Price Index rose 0.9% for May, however, the Labor Department reported **June 30.** The White House admitted this was "not good news." Consumers' purchasing power declined 1.3%. The trade deficit for May, $2.24 billion, was the smallest since Sept. 1977, the Commerce Department reported, **June 27,** was, however, the 24th consecutive monthly deficit.

**Supreme Court Ends Cities' Immunity** — The Supreme Court, **June 6,** voted 7 to 2 to overturn a 1961 ruling and end the immunity of municipalities from civil rights suits. Cities, counties, and other local governments would become liable for acts depriving residents of their civil rights. The liabilities would apply only when municipal employees were acting in their official capacities. On **June 5,** the court had declined to review and so let stand a decision that a New Hampshire statutory rape law was unconstitutional. The law, since replaced, had made it a crime for an adult to have sexual relations with an under-age consenting female but ignored relations with under-age males. The court in June also handed down 2 decisions affecting the press. On **June 12** the court ruled that newspapers could not acquire radio or television stations in their own communities. All but 7 of the more than 140 existing media combinations were allowed to continue. The 16 required to dissolve were in communities where the only newspaper owned the only radio or television station. On **June 26** the court ruled that the press had no "constitutional right of access" to prisons beyond the rights of all citizens. The 4-to-3 decision was not considered unequivocal, however, as Justice Potter Stewart, who cast the deciding vote, did not join in the majority opinion. In a separate opinion he recognized that the press had the right of "effective access" to prisons, meaning that even if the general public were barred from bringing cameras into prisons, the press might still have the right to do so, or if the prison was opened to the public at all.

**California Taxes Cut by Voters** — California voters, **June 6,** approved, by a 65% majority, Proposition 13, a ballot initiative to cut property taxes 57%. Budget cutbacks and hiring freezes were imposed at the state and local levels immediately. Gov. Edmund G. Brown Jr. of California, **June 9,** urged the state legislature to use the state's almost $5 billion surplus to help schools and municipalities offset their $7 billion in losses resulting from the initiative. Brown, **July 6,** cut $388.5 million from the state budget, vetoing an $80.8 million salary increase for state employees. The cuts, the governor

---

## Supreme Court Upholds Some Affirmative Action Plans; Orders Alan Bakke Admitted to Medical School

The Supreme Court, **June 28,** voted 5 to 4 to allow some affirmative action plans by colleges but ordered Alan Bakke admitted to the University of California at Davis Medical College. Bakke, a 38-year-old white engineer, had argued that he had been denied admission while less qualified minority students had been accepted.

The court supported Bakke's claim of "reverse discrimination" while also upholding the legality of flexible race-based affirmative action plans. The Davis plan was considered extreme in setting aside a firm quota of 16 out of 100 places for minority group members.

Justice Lewis F. Powell, Jr., voting with the majority, said in the main opinion that while attaining a diverse student body was constitutionally permissible, that goal was improper if racial or ethnic quotas were used. Justice Powell cited a Harvard special-admissions plan to include students from all types of backgrounds.

Justice Thurgood Marshall wrote in a separate opinion that "during most of the past 200 years, the Constitution as interpreted by this court did not prohibit the most ingenious and pervasive forms of discrimination against the Negro.

Now, when a state acts to remedy the effects of that legacy of discrimination, I cannot believe that this same Constitution acts as a barrier."

Attorney General Griffin Bell told reporters that he and Pres. Jimmy Carter considered the decision a "great gain for affirmative action." The executive director of the NAACP called it a "clear-cut victory for voluntary affirmative action."

The general counsel of the Anti-Defamation League of B'nai Brith said that his organization was "comforted" that the court had held that "racial quotas are flatly illegal." Robert Bork, Yale law professor and solicitor general in the Ford administration, commented on the decision, "We're told that we can count race somewhat, but not too much. That's going to be difficult to apply."

The Defense Department, **July 17,** tentatively concluded that the Bakke decision would have only a minor impact on equal opportunity efforts in defense contracting. The Justice Department, **July 26,** in its first official interpretation of the decision, urged approval of quotas for promoting black policemen in Detroit.

nor explained, were made necessary by the passage of Proposition 13. The California vote was one of a series of nation-wide tax revolts. On the same day, in Ohio, voters defeated nearly 60% of proposed school tax measures. In the New Jersey Republican senatorial primary, Jeffrey Bell, who had called for a 30% federal income tax cut in a one-issue campaign, upset 4-term incumbent Sen. Clifford Case.

**Supreme Court Saves Rare Species** — The Supreme Court, **June 15**, ruled that the Tennessee Valley Authority could not complete construction of a dam that threatened the survival of a rare species of fish. The T.V.A. agreed, **June 16**, to redesign the nearly completed $116-million Tellico dam in order to protect the habitat of the 3-inch-long snail darter, under the 1973 Endangered Species Act. The Senate, **July 19**, voted 94-3 to amend the act. A high-level committee would be empowered to exempt projects from the act if their benefits would "clearly outweigh" the value of an endangered species. The T.V.A. and the Interior Department announced, **Aug. 10**, that snail darters, transplanted by federal experts, were flourishing at a site 18 miles from the dam. It had not yet been decided whether to complete the dam, due to costs and other factors unrelated to the fish.

**Labor Law Filibustered Back to Committee** — The Senate, **June 22**, after a 19-day filibuster, returned to committee a bill to revise the national labor law. Senate majority leader Robert C. Byrd called the bill "still very much alive." Sen. Richard G. Lugar (R., Ind.), one of the leaders of the filibuster, said "the bill will never reappear on the floor of the Senate." The bitterly contested amendments to the labor law would block employers' efforts to resist union organizing. It would, among other provisions, withhold federal contracts from employers who violated the law. The House had already passed the bill and it had Carter administration approval.

**House Votes Korea Aid Cutoff** — The House of Representatives, **June 22**, voted, 273 to 125, to cut off $56 million in aid to South Korea. The House had warned, **May 31**, in a resolution adopted by a 321-46 vote, that aid would be cut off unless the Koreans cooperated fully with the House investigation into Korean influence-buying in the U.S. Congress. Korea responded, **May 31**, that a House demand that former Ambassador to the U.S. Kim Dong Jo testify before the ethics committee was "unacceptable." The aid cutoff involved only the Food for Peace program; military assistance, which represented much more money, was not affected.

**Carter Committee Fined** — Pres. Jimmy Carter's campaign committee, **June 26**, agreed to pay a $1,200 fine for the illegal use of a National Bank of Georgia airplane. The bank, headed at the time by Carter friend Bert Lance, agreed to pay a $5,000 fine. Neither the committee nor the bank admitted nor denied guilt. The plane had been used during the president's 1976 campaign. Federal election law barred candidates from receiving gifts from corporations.

## International

**Evidence Presented on Cubans in Africa** — Pres. Jimmy Carter, **June 2**, briefed Congressional leaders on CIA information that Cuba had trained and equipped the rebels who invaded Zaire's Shaba province in May. CIA Director Adm. Stansfield Turner testified before the House International Relations Committee, **June 8**, and the Senate Foreign Relations Committee, **June 9**, presenting evidence concerning Cuban involvement gained from prisoners, diplomatic sources, and from sources in countries bordering on Zaire. Those Senators and Representatives who had previously doubted the truth of Cuban involvement were still not convinced. Cuban Pres. Fidel Castro, **June 13**, told 2 U.S. Congressman that he had tried to block the invasion in February. Castro strongly reiterated his denial of Cuban complicity in the invasion. Carter, **June 14**, once again rejected the denial, saying "Castro could have done much more had he genuinely wanted to stop the invasion."

**U.S., Canada in Fishing Dispute** — The U.S. and Canada, **June 5**, began excluding one another's commercial fishing vessels from their respective waters. The U.S. also banned Canadian recreational fishing in U.S. waters. The 2 nations were careful to avoid arrests or other confrontations. The bans resulted from a failure to negotiate a fishing treaty. Recreational fishing by American tourists in Canada was not banned; it earns Canada about $230 million a year. Canadian commercial fishing in U.S. waters was worth many times the amount of U.S. fishing in Canadian waters. Further negotiations for a treaty were to be scheduled.

**Carter Warns Moscow** — Pres. Jimmy Carter, **June 7**, in a commencement address at the U.S. Naval Academy at Annapolis, Md., warned the Soviet Union to end confrontation with the U.S., saying that "competition without restraint and without shared rules will escalate into graver tensions." In his toughest speech to date on Soviet-U.S. relations, the president attacked the Soviet definition of détente, which, he said, "seems to mean a continuing aggressive struggle for political advantage and increased influence." Carter called on the Soviet Union to conclude a new strategic arms limitation agreement and to work together with the U.S. in bringing about black rule in Rhodesia and South-West Africa. He accused the Soviets of military build-up, of exploiting internal African conflicts, of human rights abuses, and of attempting "to export a totalitarian and repressive form of government." Carter pointed out the weaknesses of the Soviet economic system and added that the weakness of Soviet agriculture forced the government to import food from the U.S. and other nations. Pravda, the Soviet Communist party newspaper, **June 11**, accused Carter of "working up anti-Soviet hysteria." Zbigniew Brzezinski, the president's national security adviser, was blamed for the aggressive tone of Carter's speech.

**Somalis Reported in Ogaden** — Western diplomats in Nairobi, Kenya reported Somali soldiers fighting in Ethiopia's Ogaden region, again, according to the *N.Y. Times*, **June 7**. Regular Somali forces had withdrawn from Ogaden in March after an Ethiopian offensive aided by the Soviet Union and Cuba. The new reports indicated that some of the same Somali soldiers had begun guerrilla warfare against the Ethiopians, calling themselves the Western Somali Liberation Front. The guerrillas claimed, **July 3**, to have killed about 2,500 Ethiopian soldiers and a number of Cubans since early June. The claims were believed to be exaggerated. According to the Somali government, Ethiopian jets bombed Somali border towns **June 22-25** and **July 13**, killing at least 11 persons. Somalia claims the Somali-speaking people of Ogaden want to join their territory to Somalia.

**Rhodesia Death Toll Mounts** — An estimated 1,850 persons were reported, **June 12**, to have been killed in guerrilla warfare in Rhodesia since January, 1978. In a clash, **June 10**, between government forces and guerrillas, 22 black civilians were killed. Military censors, **June 12**, prohibited a broadcast criticizing the government's version of the incident. The criticism came from both ZANU (the Zimbabwe African National Union), the guerrilla group based in Mozambique, and Bishop Abel Muzorewa, one of the black leaders participating in the bi-racial interim government with Prime Minister Ian D. Smith. A terrorist attack, **June 23**, resulted in the deaths of 8 white missionaries and 4 of their young children. British Prime Minister James Callaghan resisted Conservative pressure, provoked by the attack, to endorse the internal Rhodesian settlement and abandon the Patriotic Front, the loose alliance of ZANU and ZAPU (the Zimbabwe African People's Union). On **June 27**, guerrillas shot to death 2 German missionaries, the 14th and 15th missionaries killed in Rhodesia in June. Joshua Nkomo, the leader of ZAPU, the guerrilla group based in Zambia, admitted for the first time publicly, **June 6**, that Cuban soldiers were training his 6,000-man army.

**Soviets Arrest U.S. Businessman** — An American businessman was arrested, **June 12**, by Soviet police and imprisoned on charges of violating currency regulations. F. Jay Crawford, an Internatioal Harvester representative, was dragged from his car when he stopped at a traffic light in Moscow. He was detained for 16 days on charges of having exchanged 20,000 rubles ($29,000 at the official rate of exchange) for dollars on the black market. Foreigners had long suspected that the black market which flourishes outside the Intourist Hotel, where Crawford lived, was maintained by Soviet police in order to entrap Westerners. Crawford, who denied the charges, was released, **June 28**, in the custody of U.S. Ambassador Malcolm Toon, apparently in exchange for 2 accused Soviet spies, who were released, **June 26**, on $2 million bail each, in the custody of Soviet Ambassador Anatoly F. Dobrynin, in Washington. Soviet Foreign Minister Andrei A. Gromyko had been reported, **June 14**, to have warned Secretary of State Cyrus R. Vance, early in June, that the Soviet Union would retaliate against the U.S.

if the accused spies were not released.

**Withdrawal Completed, Fighting Continues in Lebanon** — Israel, **June 13**, completed the withdrawal of its invasion forces from Lebanon. Most of the 6-mile-wide border strip still occupied by Israeli troops was handed over to Christian militiamen headed by Maj. Saad Haddad of the Lebanese Army. A few places, where there were no militiamen, were turned over to UN troops. Israel had announced, **June 11**, that it would hand over major strongpoints to the Christians rather than to Unifil (the UN Interim Force in Lebanon). The Israelis, who feared that Unifil was not stopping Palestinian guerrillas from moving back into southern Lebanon, argued that Haddad was listed as a member of the Lebanese Army and that the Security Council had called, in the resolution authorizing Unifil, for the eventual return of the territory to Lebanon. Haddad accepted a Lebanese government order to allow Unifil to take control in the area and was placed under house arrest, it was reported **June 16**, by militia forces who refused to obey the order. A unit of Irish Unifil troops, **June 23**, occupied a village near the Israeli-Lebanese border. The UN had announced, earlier that week, that Unifil had taken control in 14 "potentially key positions" since the Israeli pullout. Israeli commandos, **June 9**, had attacked an Al Fatah Palestinian guerrilla base north of the UN zone. Israel said that intelligence reports had indicated that the base was to have been used to stage a guerrilla attack against Israel in a matter of days. On **June 18** Israel seized a gunboat destined for the guerrillas, according to Lebanese reports. Israel admitted only that the vessel had been searched and released. In clashes between 2 Christian groups north of Beirut, **June 13**, at least 45 persons were killed, including Parliament member Tony Franjieh, son of former Pres. Suleiman Franjieh, and the younger Franjieh's wife and their 2-year-old daughter. Earlier in June, pro-Franjieh Christians had killed 5 members of the Phalangist party. Suleiman Franjieh, **June 14**, pledged "revenge in our style and at the proper time" against the Phalangists for the slaying of his son. As Tony Franjieh's funeral began, Syrian troops occupying Lebanon seized 15 Phalangists suspected of participation in the June 13 attack. A Lebanese soldier was killed and 5 militiamen wounded when villagers refused to surrender the Phalangists to the Syrians.

**Italian President Resigns** — Italian Pres. Giovanni Leone, **June 15**, resigned from office, hours after the Communist party called for his resignation, because of charges involving him in the Lockheed bribery scandal. The charges had been known for some time; the working relationship between the Communists and the governing Christian Democrats meant that Leone had no choice but to resign when the Communists applied pressure. Sandro Pertini, an 81-year-old Socialist was elected, **July 8**, as the new president by the Electoral Assembly. The Christian Democrats had at first resisted the election of Pertini but finally acquiesced in order to avoid a confrontation with the Communists.

**Panama-U.S. Treaty Ceremony** — Pres. Jimmy Carter and Brig. Gen. Omar Torrijos of Panama, **June 16**, exchanged the instruments of ratification of the new Panama Canal treaties at a ceremony in Panama City.

**Soviet Sentences Jewish Activists** — Vladimir Slepak, a 50-year-old engineer, and Ida Nudel, a 47-year-old economist, were sentenced, **June 21**, to exile in Siberia for "malicious hooliganism." The charges referred to their having hung banners from their apartments, **June 1**, pleading for permission to emigrate to Israel. Slepak was a member of the dissident group publicizing Soviet violations of the Helsinki human-rights agreement. He had been trying to emigrate since 1970 and had not been allowed to work since then. Nudel had been trying to emigrate since 1971. The U.S., **June 21**, condemned the sentences as unduly harsh and incompatible with the terms of the Helsinki accord.

**Yemen, South Yemen Presidents Slain** — Ahmed Hussein Ghashmi, president of Yemen, was assassinated, **June 24**, when a bomb exploded in the briefcase of a South Yemeni envoy. The South Yemeni was also killed. South Yemen, **June 25**, denied involvement in the assassination. Arab diplomats in Beirut believed that Yemeni exiles in South Yemen were responsible. On **July 17**, Col. Ali Abdullah Saleh succeeded Ghashmi as president of Yemen. Saleh had taken part in the 1974 coup that brought Ibrahim Mohammed Hamidi to power. Hamidi was assassinated in 1977 and was

succeeded by Ghashmi. On **June 26**, Salem Robaye Ali, president of South Yemen, was deposed and executed. It was reported **June 27** that a pro-Soviet group, including Abdel Fattah Ismail, secretary-general of the National Liberation Front, had taken over in South Yemen. Robaye had favored improved relations with the U.S. and Saudi Arabia. Ismail had preferred maintaining close relations with the Soviet Union, including continued Soviet and South Yemeni assistance to Ethiopia. The Arab League, **July 2**, voted to impose a blockade on South Yemen for its complicity in the assassination of Ghashmi. The League appeared to have accepted reports in the Cairo press that the pro-Soviet faction in South Yemen had plotted the assassination, blamed it on Robaye, and then killed him, too. The Arab League conference was boycotted by Djibouti, apparently because of its sensitive position in the Horn of Africa across the Red Sea from Yemen. Syria, Libya, Algeria, Iraq, South Yemen, and the PLO, also stayed away; they had been boycotting League functions since December, in protest against Egyptian Pres. Anwar Sadat's peace initiative.

**Versailles Bombed** — A bomb exploded, **June 26**, at the 17th-century palace at Versailles, France, wrecking 3 of the 14 ground-floor rooms and destroying precious works of art. It was estimated that repairs to the masonry alone would cost $1 million. The Breton Republican Army, a branch of the Breton Liberation Front, claimed responsibility for the bombing. The Front, responsible for 206 bombings since 1966, had been seeking autonomy for Brittany. Police arrested 2 members of the Breton Republican Army, **June 30**, who were said to have confessed to the Versailles bombing. Charges were brought against them and 6 other Breton nationalists, **July 4**, for numerous bombings and police claimed to have broken up the Breton Republican Army. According to the *Times* of London, **July 5**, none of the accused spoke Breton.

**Bomb in Jerusalem Kills 2** — A bomb exploded, **June 2**, in a Jerusalem market, killing 2 Israelis and wounding 35. A PLO-unit named after Ali Yasin claimed responsibility for the bombing. Yasin was a PLO leader in Kuwait who had been killed **June 15** in factional Palestinian fighting. The U.S. State Department, **June 30**, condemned Al Fatah, the largest group in the PLO, and Yasir Arafat, leader of both Al Fatah and the PLO, for the bombing. The U.S. statement was careful to avoid condemning the PLO itself. Al Fatah guerrillas, **June 12**, raided an Israeli settlement in the West Bank. Defenders of the settlement killed one terrorist in 15-minute skirmish. The remaining 3 raiders fled back to Jordan before Israeli troops arrived on the scene. It was the first PLO raid from Jordan since August, 1977.

**U.S.-China Ties Strengthened** — The Carter administration, **June 30**, in a gesture to the Chinese Communist government in Peking, announced that it had decided not to sell 60 F-4 fighter-bombers to Nationalist China. The $500 million sale was considered by the White House and the State Department to be inconsistent with the policy of "strong and secure" mainland China. The Nationalist government, **July 6**, rejected an administration proposal to substitute 50 to 60 Israeli Kfir jet fighters for the F-4s. The U.S. had feared that the F-4s would enable the Taiwan government to bomb deep within China while the Kfirs could be used only defensively. The administration was reported by the *New York Times*, **June 24**, to have decided that China and the U.S. shared major strategic concerns and that "strong and secure China" - in the words of national security adviser Zbigniew Brzezinski - served American interests. Brzezinski was reported to have told Chinese leaders during his trip to Peking in May that the U.S. favored China's purchase of military equipment and modern technology from the U.S., Western Europe, and Japan. On **June 9**, it had been decided to sell airborne geological survey equipment to China. The U.S. would not sell such equipment to the Soviet Union because of its potential for military use. The White House, **June 27**, announced that a top government science mission was being sent to China July 6-10. The mission had been proposed by Brzezinski in Peking. The president's science adviser, Frank Press, **July 14**, briefed reporters on the mission. He expressed hope that more scientific cooperation between the U.S. and China might lead to expanded trade. A similar mission by Press to the Soviet Union was canceled by Carter to protest trials of dissidents there. Soviet Pres.

Leonid I. Brezhnev, **June 25**, attacked the U.S. for trying 'to play the 'Chinese card' " against the Soviet Union.

## General

**NYC, Unions Agree on Contract** — New York City agreed, **June 5**, after 98 days of bargaining, to a $757-million 2-year contract with unions representing 200,000 municipal workers. The agreement did not include transit workers, police, or firemen. The Transit Authority and the Transport Workers Union, **Apr. 2**, had agreed to a 2-year contract with a 6% raise, averting a transit strike, but workers had not yet ratified it by the time the municipal workers' agreement was reached. Dissident bus and subway workers, **July 7**, obtained a court order blocking ratification of the transit agreement. Tentative agreements between the city and the Policemen's Benevolent Association were rejected **July 1** and **July 13** by the union's delegate assembly. A 3d agreement was accepted, **July 20**, which called for a 2-year contract, in which the average pay for the 2d year, including overtime and holiday pay, would come to $22,358, according to the union's calculations. The labor agreements were crucial in getting Congressional approval for federally guaranteed loans to keep the city out of bankruptcy.

**22 Indicted in Port Corruption** — A federal grand jury in Miami, **June 7**, indicted 22 union officials and shipping company executives on 70 counts of racketeering, kickbacks, embezzlement, and other illegal activities. Arrests were made in Miami, Jacksonville, Atlanta, Charleston, Mobile, and New York. International Longshoremen's Association officials were charged with attempting to control business activity on the docks through payoffs, kickbacks, extortion, and intimidation. The union officials were charged with obtaining hundreds of thousands of dollars over a 10-year period by threatening to cause labor problems. The investigation, which had been underway for 3 years, was still continuing in New York and more indictments were expected to follow.

**Skylab Save Attempted** — The National Aeronautics and Space Administration, **June 8-11**, attempted to re-orient, by radio commands, the 84-ton orbiting Skylab space station. Skylab's orbit had been deteriorating due to the interference of the upper atmosphere and sunspot-related ultraviolet radiation. NASA officials had feared that, even though most of the space station would probably disintegrate upon re-entry, large sections of it might land in populated areas if the deterioration of the orbit were not checked. They hoped to modify the orbit to give Skylab an additional 6 to 12 months. By that time, a space shuttle mission might be ready to lift Skylab to a higher, more stable orbit or to direct its descent so that it crashed into an uninhabited area of the South Pacific. The radio commands were successful, but a power failure, **July 9**, caused the satellite to start wobbling again. Additional maneuvers, **July 25**, were successful in putting Skylab into a position to minimize drag, but NASA engineers would not predict whether it would be able to hold that position until the space shuttle was ready.

**Mormons to Allow Black Priests** — The Church of Jesus Christ of Latter-Day Saints (Mormons) revoked, **June 9**, its 148-year-old policy of excluding black men from the priesthood, which is usually entered by all white Mormon males at age 12. Spencer W. Kimball, president of the 4.2 million member church, announced in Salt Lake City that the decision had been based on a revelation that had come to church leaders. Kimball said, "The long-promised day has come when every faithful, worthy man in the Church may receive the holy priesthood." The ban against black priests had become a source of tension between the church and minority groups. The change was expected to facilitate the church's active missionary program. Women were still not considered eligible for the priesthood.

**Joan Little Extradited to North Carolina** — Joan Little was extradited, **June 9**, from New York to North Carolina to complete her prison sentence there. The U.S. Supreme Court, **June 5**, had refused, without comment, to block her extradition. Little pleaded guilty, **July 12**, to the charge of having escaped from a North Carolina prison in October, 1977. She was sentenced to 6-months to 2-years additional imprisonment. Little, who had been convicted in 1974 of breaking and entering, stabbed to death, shortly afterwards, a jailer she said was sexually assaulting her. She was acquit-

ted, in 1975, of the slaying.

**"Son of Sam" Sentenced** — David Berkowitz, the convicted "Son of Sam" murderer, was sentenced, **June 13**, in New York City, to maximum prison terms for each of the 6 murders he had confessed committing in 1976 and 1977. Berkowitz would be eligible for parole in the year 2007, when he would be 54 years old. If he were released then, he would still be liable for prosecution for 2,000 fires he confessed having set. Judges from Brooklyn, Queens, and the Bronx, the 3 New York City boroughs where Berkowitz's nighttime slayings were carried out, took part in the sentencing. Berkowitz had been found mentally competent to stand trial before he was allowed to plead guilty to the charges, **May 8**. Another psychological examination was ordered before sentencing, after Berkowitz, **May 22**, disrupted the trial with a wild outburst against his victims and their families.

**Provenzano Convicted of Murder** — Teamster union leader Anthony Provenzano, 60, and Harold Konigsberg, 49, an alleged enforcer for organized crime, were convicted, **June 14**, of murdering Anthony Castellito, Provenzano's union rival, in 1961. Both were sentenced, **June 21**, to life in prison. Provenzano had been charged with paying Konigsberg $15,000 to kill Castellito. Provenzano also had been linked with the disappearance of former Teamsters Pres. James R. Hoffa. Neither Castellito's nor Hoffa's body was ever found. On **July 11**, Provenzano was sentenced to 4 years in prison on charges that he split a $230,000 kickback on a $2.3-million Teamsters pension fund loan. Provenzano had resigned, after the murder conviction, from his Secaucus, N.J. union post. His daughter, Josephine Provenzano, 20, was installed in the position June 23.

**Hussein Marries American** — King Hussein of Jordan, 42, married Elizabeth Halaby, a 26-year-old American, **June 15**, in a brief Moslem ceremony in Amman, Jordan. The bride, who had converted to Islam, was proclaimed Queen Noor al-Hussein, Arabic for "Light of Hussein." The bride's father, Najeeb Halaby, was a former president of Pan American World Airways. The marriage was Hussein's fourth.

**Nazis Call Off Skokie March** — The National Socialist Party of America, **June 22**, called off plans for a march through Skokie, Illinois, a predominantly Jewish suburb of Chicago. The U.S. Supreme Court, **June 12**, had denied the town's request for a stay against the march. The American Civil Liberties Union had been split over its decision to defend the Nazis' right to march. On **July 9**, the Nazis held a rally in Chicago, at which 72 persons were arrested.

**Disasters** — The strongest earthquake to hit Japan in 14 years struck, **June 12**, at Sendai, Japan, killing at least 21 people and injuring 350. The earthquake, which registered 7.5 on the Richter scale, set skyscrapers swaying in Tokyo, 180 miles away. . . . A powerful earthquake hit Thessalonika, Greece, **June 20-21**, killing at least 14 people and injuring 150. The tremors, which reached 6.5 on the Richter scale, were felt also in Yugoslavia and Bulgaria. A state of emergency was declared in the Thessalonika region.

## JULY

### National

**Attorney General Held in Contempt** — Attorney General Griffin B. Bell was held in contempt of court, **July 6**, for refusing to turn over files on 18 informants who had spied on the Socialist Workers Party for the FBI. Bell, **July 7**, in federal appeals court, won a stay of the contempt order, pending appeal. The appeal could take several weeks, eventually reaching the U.S. Supreme Court. The Socialist Workers had long been seeking the files in its $40-million suit against the FBI. Evidence had already been introduced that the FBI had used about 1,300 informants in its investigation of the small Trotskyite party.

**FBI Informer Linked to Klan Terrorism** — The Justice Department, **July 12**, began an investigation into the activities of the FBI's chief paid informant in the Ku Klux Klan in Alabama in the 1960s. Gary Thomas Rowe Jr. had told Alabama authorities that he had been directly involved in several incidents of racial violence then, including the murder of a black man in Birmingham, following a riot in 1963. Rowe claimed that the FBI agent he told of the murder had instructed him to say nothing about it. The agent called

Rowe's claims "an absolute falsehood." Rowe received over $12,000 from the FBI from 1960 to 1965. He claimed also to have received an additional $10,000 to relocate after testifying, in 1965, that he had been with the Klansmen who killed civil-rights marcher Viola Liuzzo. The Justice Department investigation would seek to determine whether Rowe had, as an agent provocateur, helped initiate Klan violence he was paid to inform on.

**O'Neill Cleared of Charges** — Speaker of the House Thomas P. O'Neill Jr. (D., Mass.) was cleared, **July 13**, of all but one charge in the House ethics committee investigation of the Korean influence-buying scandal. O'Neill was criticized in the committee's report for having accepted 2 parties in his honor from Korean businessman Tong Sun Park. The committee concluded that this did not warrant disciplinary proceedings. The report criticized 4 other Congressmen for having accepted gifts from Park.

**Mexican-Americans Protest in Texas** — Hundreds of Mexican-Americans, **July 15**, demonstrated in 104-degree weather in Plainview, Texas, to protest alleged Carter administration reluctance to prosecute police officers charged in the deaths of Hispanic Americans. The Justice Department had announced that it would not bring federal charges against a Dallas policeman who was serving a 5-year sentence for having killed a 12-year-old Mexican-American boy there in 1973. The Justice Department, in Oct., 1977, had obtained a federal indictment against 4 Houston policemen on charges of violating the civil rights of a 23-year-old Mexican American they had allegedly killed earlier that year. An all-white Texas jury had previously given the officers suspended sentences. In a similar case in 1975, a Texas town marshal had been sentenced to 2-10 years in prison for the death of a 26-year-old Mexican-American. The Justice Department brought federal civil rights charges against the marshal and in 1977 he was sentenced to life imprisonment.

**Indians Demonstrate Against "Backlash"** — Nearly 1,000 American Indians and their supporters marched to the steps of the U.S. Capitol in Washington, **July 17**, completing a 2,700-mile walk. The "longest walk" had begun **Feb. 11** on Alcatraz Island, Calif. Only Sen. Alan Cranston (D., Calif.), the Senate majority whip and long-time supporter of Indian causes, attended the rally at the Capitol steps. It was intended to publicize Indian fears of a "Red backlash" in legislation pending in Congress which they felt was anti-Indian. On **July 18**, about 25 Indian elders and religious leaders met with Vice Pres. Walter F. Mondale and Interior Secretary Cecil Andrus. Andrus conveyed to Pres. Carter an Indian request to meet with him. Carter did not meet with them. Vernon Bellecourt, a walk coordinator and American Indian Movement (AIM) leader, admitted at the end of the walk, **July 23**, that the demonstrations had had little impact on Congress. But, he added, they had focused "attention on the plight of Indians in the United States when Pres. Carter was protesting human rights violations abroad."

**Carter Civil Service Plan Amended** — The House Post Office and Civil Service Committee, **July 19**, approved a bill to reform the U.S. civil service. Pres. Carter, in a news conference **July 20**, said he hoped the House would remove some "very adverse" amendments the committee had attached to his proposals. Carter's original version of the bill would have simplified hiring and firing procedures for most of the 2.8-million U.S. employees. It would also have substituted performance bonuses for automatic advancement for senior executives. Hiring and firing would be simplified only slightly in the amended bill. Rep. Morris K. Udall (D., Ariz.), the vice-chairman of the committee, admitted that the major accomplishment of the committee was that it had gotten a bill onto the House floor and that the final form of the bill would have to be worked out there.

**Carter's Drug Adviser Resigns** — Dr. Peter G. Bourne resigned, **July 20**, from his post as Pres. Jimmy Carter's top adviser on drug abuse. Bourne had admitted, **July 19**, that he had written a prescription for Quaalude, a powerful sedative, for one of his aides, using a fictitious name. A friend of the aide had been arrested while trying to fill the prescription. Bourne said that he had used the false name to protect the confidentiality of his aide, who, he said, had a real medical need for the drug. Bourne's incidental reference in his resignation announcement to a "high incidence" of marijuana use among the White House staff unleashed a storm of criticism from government officials. The president, **July 24**, warned his staff to obey the drug laws or to "seek employment elsewhere." In his campaign, Carter had advocated decriminalizing the possession of marijuana. Virginia and U.S. prosecutors announced, **Aug. 21**, that they would not bring charges against Bourne.

**Postal Workers Agreement Reached** — The U.S. Postal Service and the postal unions reached an agreement, **July 21**, on a 3-year contract, averting the danger of a postal strike. The new contract would provide a 19.5% increase in wages and benefits over the 3 years and would preserve the no-layoff clause of the old contract. Wildcat strikes began at postal facilities in Jersey City, N.J., as soon as the agreement was announced, and at Richmond, Calif., **July 22**. A union convention in Chicago, **July 31**, voted to recommend that the union's 175,000 members reject the contract. J. Joseph Vacca, president of the National Association of Letter Carriers, vowed, **Aug. 1**, to continue working for union ratification of the contract, despite the convention's recommendation.

**Double-Digit Inflation in Second Quarter** — Consumer prices rose 0.9% during June, the Bureau of Labor Statistics reported **July 28**. The price rise sent the annual rate of inflation to 11.4% for the 2d quarter of 1978. Treasury Secretary W. Michael Blumenthal called the development "worrisome." Food prices were up 1.4% for the month, led by a 5.6% increase in the cost of beef. Beef prices had risen 30.7% since Oct., 1977. Unemployment was down to a 4-year low of 5.7%, the Labor Department reported **July 7**. Courtenay M. Slater, chief Commerce Department economist, warned that the decline in unemployment was the result of temporary factors and that a new rise would begin if the nation's economic growth slowed. The Council of Economic Advisers, **July 6**, had predicted a slower rate of economic growth than had previously been anticipated, because worsening inflation was expected to reduce consumer spending. The price of gold soared above $200 an ounce, **July 28**, reflecting the weakness of the U.S. dollar and the apparent difficulty in holding down inflation.

**Carter Announces Health Plan** — Pres. Jimmy Carter, **July 29**, outlined a national health plan in a directive to H.E.W. Secretary Joseph A. Califano Jr. Califano was instructed to formulate, on the basis of the president's outline, a more detailed program for submission to Congress in 1979. If enacted, the plan might be ready for implementation by 1983. The outline placed great emphasis on curbing medical costs. The House Commerce Committee, **July 18**, had defeated an administration anti-inflation proposal designed to impose mandatory curbs on hospital cost rises. The American Medical Association praised the committee's endorsement of its voluntary cost control program.

## International

**Syrians Shell Beirut Christians** — Syrian peacekeeping troops in Lebanon attacked, **July 1-6**, Christian militiamen in the Beirut area, killing, according to militia leaders, 450 persons and injuring 1,400. Camille Chamoun, leader of the Christian National Liberal Party, denounced the Syrians, **July 4**, as "protectors turned aggressors." Lebanese Pres. Elias Sarkis, **July 6** and again **July 9**, threatened to resign but both times was persuaded to stay on by Lebanese leaders and the U.S., Saudi Arabian, and British ambassadors. Israeli planes buzzed Beirut, **July 6**, warning Syria to cease shelling Christian neighborhoods. Israeli officials re-affirmed their committment "not to let the Christian population be annihilated in Lebanon." Christian sources said the Syrian attack was provoked by Christian factional strife, in June. A truce between Syria and the militiamen was reached **July 6** and the fighting slowed down. The Syrian Information Minister, **July 9**, said that Chamoun's party and the Phalangists had to submit to the Sarkis government "or be destroyed." Fighting ceased completely in Beirut **July 16**, for the first time in 2 weeks, apparently in response to Sarkis' own withdrawal, **July 15**, of his resignation. New fighting broke out, **July 22-29**, in a Christian suburb of Beirut. Heavy Syrian shelling there was reported to have killed 30 civilians and injured more than 50. The fighting had been provoked by the wounding of 2 Syrian soldiers by sniper fire, **July 21**, and the discovery, reported **July 23**, of the bodies of 2 other Syrians near Christian National Liberal Party headquarters in the town. The U.S., **July 27**, advised Americans to leave Lebanon and reduced the staff of its embassy in Beirut.

**China Ends Vietnam Aid** — The Chinese news agency Hsinhua, **July 3,** announced the end of all Chinese aid to Vietnam, citing Vietnam's reported mistreatment of its ethnic Chinese. Since 1958 China had given Vietnam $10 billion in aid. A Vietnamese deputy minister for foreign affairs, **July 4,** said the aid cutoff would "not affect us much." Diplomatic sources in Peking explained the cutoff as a result of the admission of Vietnam into the Soviet-bloc economic association, Comecon, **June 29,** and Vietnam's preference for closer relations with the Soviet Union. According to a Hanoi broadcast **July 11,** Chinese fighter planes had penetrated up to 19 miles into Vietnamese airspace **July 9.** China, **July 12,** called the charges "mere fabrication." Hsinhua reported, **July 11,** that talks to permit 2 Chinese ships to evacuate ethnic Chinese from Vietnam were deadlocked, because of Vietnam's "unreasonable attitude." On **July 13,** Peking announced restrictions on ethnic Chinese wishing to cross from Vietnam to China, fearing that "spies" might be included. Vietnam, **July 14,** denied that spies were being sent into China and claimed that the Chinese had engineered the exodus of 150,000 ethnic Chinese from Vietnam since May for propaganda purposes.

**Mondale Returns from Middle East** — Vice Pres. Walter F. Mondale returned to Washington, **July 4,** from a 4-day visit to Israel and Egypt. In Israel, **June 30-July 3,** for Israel's 30th anniversary celebrations, and in Egypt, **July 3,** Mondale presented letters from Pres. Jimmy Carter to Israeli and Egyptian leaders, urging them to resume peace talks soon. Mondale, **June 30,** visited the Western Wall, the last remnant of the Second Temple in Jerusalem. Mondale said it was merely a "personal visit." Jerusalem Mayor Teddy Kollek insisted that it constituted tacit U.S. recognition of the Israeli unification of Jerusalem.

**Ghana Leader Replaced** — Gen. Ignatius Acheampong resigned, **July 5,** as Ghana's head of state and was succeeded by Gen. Fred Akuffo, his deputy on the military council ruling Ghana. Akuffo, who was sworn in **July 6,** ordered the release of about 40 politicians who had been held since April because of their opposition to Acheampong's plan to restore civilian rule. Akuffo, **July 10,** announced an amnesty for all exiled Ghanaians and promised to hand over power to an elected civilian government by 1979.

**China to Expand Trade** — Communist Party Chairman Hua Kuo-feng, in a speech in Peking **July 7,** acknowledged that China needed to "learn from the advanced experience of other countries" to expand its economy and to increase its volume of international trade. Pragmatic policies, including the elimination of revolutionary committees managing factories and an end to the requirement that students interrupt their education with a 2-year period in factories or on farms, reflected a move away from Maoist ideology.

**Solomons, Others, Gain Independence** — The Solomon Islands, famous as a World War II battleground, became independent, **July 7,** after 85 years of British rule. The 900-mile chain of islands in the Coral Sea with a population of 200,000 had had interim self-government since 1976. It was announced, **June 30,** that Brunei, a territory of 163,000 inhabitants in northern Borneo, would become independent of Britain in 1983 and that Malaysia and Indonesia, her neighbors, would respect Brunei's independence. It was also announced, **July 21,** that the Caribbean island of Dominica would become independent. A British royal commission set up to investigate race riots in Bermuda in 1977, reported **Aug. 2,** that Bermuda ought to be given independence.

**Basques Riot in Spain** — Riots, demonstrations, and strikes broke out, **July 8,** in the Basque provinces of Spain, after police fired on secessionist demonstrators in the bullring at Pamplona. Rioting spread to San Sebastian, **July 11,** and 2 people were reported slain, **July 12,** in clashes between Spanish police and Basque nationalists. An estimated 15,000 demonstrators in San Sebastian, **July 16,** called on the Spanish government to withdraw the Civil Guard from the Basque region.

**Egyptian, Israeli Proposals Rejected** — The Israeli cabinet, **July 9,** rejected Egyptian Pres. Anwar Sadat's proposal for Israel's withdrawal from the West Bank and the Gaza Strip. Egypt, **July 25,** dismissed Israel's proposal to discuss the sovereignty of the 2 areas in 1983, if the Arabs accepted an Israeli plan to grant partial autonomy to the inhabitants. Sadat, **July 26,** ordered the expulsion of the Israeli military mission in Egypt. The Egyptian president explained to Alfred L. Atherton Jr., special U.S. envoy for the Middle East, on **July 30,** that he opposed a U.S.-sponsored meeting of the Israeli and Egyptian foreign ministers unless there was a prior agreement that territorial issues were not negotiable. The U.S., **July 31,** publicly rebuked Sadat for his rejection of the meeting. Israeli Foreign Minister Moshe Dayan, Egyptian Foreign Minister Mohammed Ibrahim Kamel, and U.S. Secretary of State Cyrus R. Vance had met, **July 18-19,** in England, to discuss their conflicting proposals regarding the West Bank and Gaza. The meeting, originally scheduled to be held in London, was moved to Leeds Castle in Kent, after British Prime Minister James Callaghan, **July 15,** received reports that Palestinian terrorists were planning to disrupt the meeting. The Israeli cabinet, **June 18,** had decided to support Prime Minister Menahem Begin's Dec., 1977, peace plan, calling for a 5-year period of autonomy for the Arab inhabitants of the 2 areas while Israel retained security forces there. The Egyptian plan rejected by Israel had also called for a 5-year transition period, but would have required immediate Israeli withdrawal from the territories. After 5 years of Egyptian-Jordanian rule, the inhabitants would be free to decide their own future. An Israeli foreign ministry legal adviser, **July 11,** criticized the Sadat plan point by point, including its references to Palestinian refugees but not to Jewish refugees from Arab lands as well as the fact that the plan contained "nothing contrary to the philosophy of the PLO." Israel had long opposed any plan that would allow the creation of a PLO state on its borders until, at least, the PLO renounced the clause in its covenant calling for the destruction of Israel.

**Military Coup in Mauritania** — Mauritanian Pres. Moktar Ould Daddah was overthrown, **July 10,** by a coup led by army chief of staff Col. Mustapha Ould Salek. The Algerian-backed Polisario Front guerrillas, **July 12,** declared a cease fire in their war against Mauritania for the independence of the former Spanish Sahara. The group said the cease-fire was intended to give the new Mauritanian government "a chance to review the criminal policy" of the previous government, which had refused to give up the portion of the Sahara it had received in 1975. Salek, **July 14,** said his government was determined to find a peaceful solution to the dispute.

**SWAPO Accepts Namibia Plan** — The South-West African People's Organization (SWAPO), the guerrilla group fighting South Africa for 11 years, agreed, **July 12,** to accept a Western plan for the independence of Namibia (South-West Africa). Negotiators from the U.S., Britain, France, Canada, and West Germany announced the agreement in Luanda, Angola, where they had been meeting with SWAPO leader Sam Nujoma. The plan had been accepted in April by South Africa, which held a League of Nations mandate over the territory. The UN Security Council, **July 27,** endorsed the plan by a vote of 13 to 0, with the Soviet Union and Czechoslovakia abstaining. South Africa, in a dispute with the UN over the future of Walvis Bay, the territory's only deep-water port, **July 31,** decided, to delay final approval of the plan. South Africa claimed that since it had had sovereignty over the port prior to the mandate, the 2 issues were separate. The South Africans insisted on negotiating the future of Walvis Bay with the Namibian government to be elected in 1979. A UN resolution adopted **July 27** had supported early "reintegration" of Walvis Bay into Namibia.

**China Ends Aid to Albania** — China and Albania announced, **July 13,** that all Chinese technical and economic aid to Albania was being terminated. Albanian students had already begun leaving Peking and Chinese technicians were to leave Albania in a matter of days. Chinese aid to Albania, once its closest ally, amounted to $5 billion since 1954. Chinese-Albanian relations, which had been strained for years, broke over Albanian support for Vietnam in its dispute with China and Chinese-supported Cambodia. The ultimate source of the strain, according to a 56-page letter from the central committee of the Albanian Communist party to its Chinese counterpart, made public **July 30,** was periodic Chinese attempts to improve relations with the Soviet Union and, at other times, with the U.S.

**Palestinians Clash in Southern Lebanon** — At least 12 persons were killed or wounded, **July 13-14,** when Al Fatah and pro-Iraqi Palestine Liberation Front (PLF) guerrillas fought with one another around the Lebanese port cities of Tyre and Saida. The fighting broke out over an incident, **July 12,** in which a 3-man French Unifil (UN Interim Forces in Lebanon) patrol had attempted to disarm PLF guerrillas behind UN lines. The UN soldiers were detained by the PLF and released the same day, following Palestine Liberation Organization (PLO) and UN intervention. A PLO representative, **July 30,** called the incident a "misunderstanding," saying that it was generally understood that Unifil troops were to bar guerrillas from entering the UN zone but not to interfere with them there. Israel had said, **July 4,** that more than 400 PLO guerrillas had infiltrated into southern Lebanon, with the tacit permission of French Unifil commanders. A UN spokesman denied there was an "agreement with anyone." Christian militiamen, **July 31,** prevented the newly reorganized Lebanese army from entering the south, charging that the government soldiers were under the control of Syria and the Palestinians. The Lebanese army had fallen apart during the civil war of 1975-76. The Christian commanders in the south, Maj. Saad Haddad and Maj. Sami Shidiak, who had been accused of collaborating with Israel, were ordered, **July 31,** to return to Beirut. Haddad refused to go, saying the order had been "issued under external pressure." Syrian Foreign Minister Abdel Halim Khaddam, **Aug. 3,** said that Syria would support the Lebanese army's attempt to deploy along the Israeli border.

**Economic Summit Meeting in Bonn** — Leaders of the U.S. and its 6 largest allies met **July 16-17,** at an economic summit meeting in Bonn, West Germany, and agreed on a package of moves to spur economic growth "without rekindling inflation." Pres. Jimmy Carter and the heads of government of Britain, West Germany, Japan, Italy, France, and Canada, as well as Roy Jenkins, president of the Common Market's executive commission, took part. Carter committed the U.S. to strengthen the U.S. dollar by reducing oil imports and fighting inflation, Japan promised to increase imports and reduce exports, and West Germany agreed to spur its own economic growth. The Germans had been resisting U.S. pressures to do so for fear of increasing the rate of inflation. Carter, **July 15,** conducted a "town meeting" in West Berlin, where he answered questions for almost an hour and pledged U.S. support for the city. The East Germans, earlier that day, had slowed down traffic on the highways connecting the city to West Germany, apparently to protest the presence of West German Chancellor Helmut Schmidt, who had accompanied Carter.

---

## Soviet Trials, Inconclusive Arms Talks Mark Low Point in U.S.-Soviet Relations

Harsh sentences given to Soviet dissidents, **July 13 and 14,** provoking sharp U.S. reactions, and inconclusive U.S.-Soviet arms talks, **July 12-13,** brought relations between the superpowers to a low point, raising serious questions about the future of detente.

Anatoly B. Shcharansky, a leader of the Jewish emigration movement in the Soviet Union, was sentenced, **July 14,** to 13 years in prison and labor camps for treason, espionage, and "anti-Soviet agitation." Aleksandr Ginzburg, a Soviet dissident who had managed a fund for families of political prisoners, had been sentenced, **July 13,** to 8 years in a forced-labor camp, for "anti-Soviet agitation and propaganda." It was the 3d prison sentence for Ginzburg in 20 years and his wife, Arina, doubted he could survive the harsh conditions in the camps. Shcharansky had been convicted of giving secrets to the CIA, despite Pres. Carter's assurances to Soviet leaders that Shcharansky had had no connections at all with the CIA.

Carter, **July 12,** in an interview with French and West German television correspondents, had called the trials "an attack on every human being who lives in the world who believes in basic human freedom and is willing to speak for these freedoms or fight for them." British Foreign Minister David Owen, **July 10,** had warned the Soviet Union that Britain would consider improving its ties with China as a result of the trials. The Italian Communist party newspaper, **July 11,** condemned the Soviet actions in a front-page editorial. New York University, **July 15,** canceled all its exchange programs with the Soviet Union until the Soviets released Shcharansky, Ginzburg, and Vladimir Slepak, who had been sentenced in June for waving a banner from his apartment appealing for the right to emigrate to Israel. Pres. Carter, **July 18,** decided to cancel the sale of a Sperry Univac computer to the Soviet Union and to place oil-technology exports under government control, in an attempt to give the U.S. leverage in influencing Soviet human rights treatment.

Carter, in a news conference **July 20,** seemed to imply that the U.S. was secretly negotiating the release of Shcharansky and Ginzburg. When asked if this were so, the president hesitated for a moment and said, "No, not specifically. We would like to see the prisoners released, but I can't go into that now." The U.S. and Britain announced, **July 22,** that they had withdrawn their military teams from the world helicopter championships in the Soviet Union to protest the trials.

U.S. Secretary of State Cyrus R. Vance met, **July 12-13** in Geneva, with Soviet Foreign Minister Andrei A. Gromyko, but 2 major issues blocking a new treaty on strategic arms limitations remained unresolved. Vance's decision to go ahead with the talks, despite the Shcharansky and Ginzburg trials, had been strongly criticized by Senators Henry M. Jackson (D., Wash.) and Daniel P. Moynihan (D., N.Y.). Vance had long rejected linking arms talks and human rights. Because the talks involved the possibility of "mutual annihilation," he explained, they had to receive "the highest priority." The issues blocking agreement were the U.S. desire to be able to develop mobile missiles during the life of the treaty, which would run until 1985, and U.S. concern that the Soviet Backfire bomber might become a threat to the U.S.

U.S. Ambassador to the UN Andrew Young, **July 12,** compared Soviet dissidents to U.S. civil rights protestors, saying there were "political prisoners" in both countries. Young, **July 13,** denied that he had meant to equate "the status of political freedom in the United States with that of the Soviet Union." A move to impeach Young for his remarks was defeated in the House of Representatives. The Soviet news agency Tass had reported that "a senior member" of the Carter administration had "admitted" that the U.S. had political prisoners, just as Pres. Carter was criticizing the trials of Soviet dissidents. Jody Powell, the president's press secretary, told reporters, **July 15,** that Young had agreed that his statement was "a mistake, and an unfortunate one, and he apologized for the problems he caused."

A Soviet court, **July 18,** convicted 2 American reporters of libeling Soviet television employees and ordered them to publish retractions and pay $1,647 each in court costs. Craig R. Whitney, of the *New York Times,* and Harold D. Piper, of the *Baltimore Sun,* had reported, **May 25,** from Moscow, that friends and relatives of a convicted Georgian dissident had called his television confession a fabrication. Whitney and Piper had refused to recognize the jurisdiction of the Soviet court, since the *Times* and the *Sun* were not available for sale in the Soviet Union. Their newspapers paid the fines for them, **Aug. 4,** plus additional fines of $72.50 each, for the failure to publish retractions. The reporters insisted they had not libeled anyone and that the fines were being paid under protest.

The U.S., **July 5,** had summoned 4 Soviet journalists to the White House to review their credentials, the first such review in 16 years. A senior official linked the review to the trial of Whitney and Piper. The administration had warned the Soviet Union, according to a *Washington Post* report **Aug. 19,** that escalation of the case could lead the U.S. to close the Soviet news bureau in San Francisco and expel several Soviet journalists from Washington.

The court, **Aug. 18,** closed the case, dropping its demand that retractions be printed. Whitney commented on the decision, "The important thing to me about this case is that a Soviet court has failed to dictate to newspapers in the United States what they may print." The Soviet Foreign Ministry, **Aug. 24,** warned Whitney and Piper that they "deserve to be deprived of accreditation" but, "guided by the interests of Soviet-American relations," they would receive only a warning.

**Anti-Somoza Strike in Nicaragua** — A 24-hour strike by business and labor was called, **July 19**, by the anti-Somoza Broad Opposition Front (FAO) in Nicaragua. At least 23 persons had been killed in political violence there in July as political, economic, and student groups formed the FAO to force the resignation of Pres. Anastasio Somoza Debayle. Pres. Jimmy Carter sent Somoza a letter in mid-July, congratulating him on promises he had made regarding human rights in Nicaragua. The *Washington Post* reported, **Aug. 1**, that the letter caused serious concern in the State Department because, at the time the letter was delivered, the U.S. was receiving additional reports of rights abuses by the Somoza government.

**Coup Follows Bolivian Elections** — Gen. Juan Pereda Asbún, **July 21**, seized control of the Bolivian government of Pres. Hugo Banzer Suárez. Pereda's election as president, **July 9**, had been annulled by a Bolivian court, **July 19**, on charges of electoral fraud. Banzer had planned to turn over power, **Aug. 6**, to an elected president and end 12 years of military rule in Bolivia. Pereda, **July 24**, argued that Bolivia could not "have the same kind of democracy as that experienced by industrialized countries." On **July 26**, he said that new elections could be held in 1980, if the electoral law could be reformed by then. The *Washington Post*, the same day, reported that the U.S. would re-direct $70 million earmarked for aid to Bolivia if the Carter administration were not persuaded, by the end of August, of the new regime's commitment to prompt elections and human rights. Pereda announced, **Aug. 6**, that elections would be held in 1980 and that he would not run for president.

**Mrs. Gandhi Charged with Conspiracy** — Former Prime Minister Indira Gandhi was formally charged by an Indian court, **July 22**, with conspiracy and criminal misconduct during her 1977 election campaign. She and 5 of her aides were accused of forcing businesses into providing 139 vehicles, without payment, for the campaign. On **July 11**, the former prime minister and her son, Sanjay Gandhi, were charged with abuses committed during her period of "emergency" rule in 1975. Home Minister Charan Singh and Health Minister Raj Narain had been forced to resign from Indian Prime Minister Morarji R. Desai's cabinet, **June 30**, after criticizing the government for its delay in prosecuting the Gandhis. On **July 2**, Rabi Ray resigned as general secretary of the ruling Janata Party because of the forced resignation of the 2 ministers.

**Tito, Others Warn against Cubans in Africa** — Yugoslav Pres. Tito, at the opening session of the conference of nonaligned nations in Belgrade, **July 25**, warned against Soviet-backed Cuban intervention in Africa. Tito called on the nonaligned nations to settle their own disputes through negotiation, warning that otherwise, "new forms of colonial presence, of bloc dependence, foreign influence, and domination" could result. A North Korean message to the conference also rejected the Soviet-Cuban presence. Lt. Gen. Olusegun Obasanjo, the leader of Nigeria's military government, speaking at a meeting of the Organization of African Unity in Khartoum, **July 19**, warned Cuba and the Soviet Union "not to overstay their welcome" in Africa. "Africa is not about to throw off one colonial yoke for another," he said. Pres. Samora M. Machel of Mozambique gave the meeting the opposite point of view, in a speech in which he called the Soviet Union and Cuba supporters of liberation in Africa. The radical African nations, such as Algeria, Libya, Ethiopia, and Angola, with about 40,000 Cuban troops within their borders, gave Machel's speech a storm of applause.

**Soares Government Falls in Portugal** — The 6-month-old government of Portuguese Premier Mario Soares fell, **July 27**, when the conservative Center Democrats (CDS) left the coalition led by Soares' Socialists. The CDS had accused Soares of delaying the return to private owners of farms seized by farm workers after the 1974 revolution. Pres. Antonio Ramalho Eanes warned, **Aug. 1**, in a national television speech, that he would appoint a government himself, under a constitutional provision, if the nation's leaders could not agree upon one. The CDS had also opposed the Socialists over bills to nationalize health care and prohibit fascist and regional separatist movements.

**Ethiopian Victories in Eritrea** — The Ethiopian government announced, **July 28**, that its forces had broken the siege of Asmara, the capital of the providence of Eritrea. Diplomatic sources believed that the Eritrean secessionists still controlled the area to the north of Asmara and that government forces had merely opened up the highway linking Asmara to Addis Ababa, the Ethiopian capital, in the south. The government had reported, **July 26**, the recapture of Tennesei, an important rebel supply town near the Sudanese border; Massawa, a strategic Red Sea port; and the town of Mendefra. The Eritreans denied, **July 27**, that the government had taken the 3 towns. The Ethiopians announced, **July 31**, and the rebels denied, the same day, that government forces had recaptured Decamere, a town 20 miles south of Asmara. The *New York Times* reported, **July 27**, that Cuban troops had not participated militarily in the Ethiopian offensive but had provided backup help in logistics, communications, and strategy.

**Rhodesians Raid Guerrillas in Mozambique** — Rhodesia, **July 30-31**, raided 10 Patriotic Front guerrilla bases in Mozambique, in what was described as a pre-emptive strike to prevent the overthrow of Rhodesia's transitional bi-racial government. A guerrilla spokesman reported, **July 31**, that 12 people had been killed and 110 wounded in the raids. None of the 3 black nationalist leaders participating in the transitional government condemned the raids and 2 of them issued strong statements, **Aug. 2**, in favor of them. The morale of white Rhodesians had been badly shaken, according to a *New York Times* report **July 23**, by charges that officials had diverted more than $1 million, and possibly as much as $15 million, from a secret arms-purchasing fund to private bank accounts in Switzerland. The U.S. Senate, **July 26**, voted to lift economic sanctions against Rhodesia if free elections were held and if the elected government would negotiate with the guerrillas. The House, **Aug. 2**, passed a less qualified version of the bill, omitting the requirement of negotiations. State Department officials commented that unless a House-Senate conference committee could produce a bill more like the Senate version, the U.S. would lose much of its power to influence Rhodesia to negotiate with the guerrillas. Rev. Ndabaningi Sithole, one of the leaders of the transitional government who had defended the Mozambique raids, added, **Aug. 2**, that the one-man, one-vote elections scheduled for December would proceed according to plan.

## General

**Municipal Workers Strike in Many Cities** — More than 400 fires broke out in Memphis, **July 1-4**, during a strike by the city's 1,400 firemen. The union, which had been demanding more pay for night duty, returned to work, **July 4**, when the city obtained a court order against the strike. On **July 1**, police charged 2 of the strikers with arson. Police in Cleveland went on strike, **July 13**, because of the city's dismissal of 13 policemen who refused to patrol what they considered to be dangerous housing projects alone during the daytime. Mayor Dennis J. Kucinich, facing a recall election in August, obtained an injunction against the striking policemen the same day. The city's 15,000 policemen returned to work **July 14**, when a judge ordered temporary reinstatement of the 13 dismissed policemen. Louisville, Kentucky's 600 firemen struck, **July 14**, ignoring a court order. They returned to work **July 18**, after accepting a 14% salary increase. More than 19,000 city workers, not including police or firemen, went on strike **July 14-21** in Philadelphia. The strike brought most government services to a halt. Strikers had demanded a contract commensurate with the one signed with police several weeks earlier, which provided for a 9% salary increase. The city had offered the municipal workers a 7% increase for 1978 and a 5% increase for 1979. The strike was provoked by Mayor Frank Rizzo's announcement that 3,000 municipal workers would have to be furloughed to pay the policemen's increases. A wildcat transit workers strike stranded Washington, D.C. commuters, **July 19-25** and a one-day transit strike in Boston, **July 6**, stranded a half million commuters.

**CIA Book Profits Forfeited** — A federal judge ruled, **July 7**, that ex-CIA agent Frank W. Snepp Jr. had to forfeit profits on an unauthorized book he had written about the agency. The judge ruled that even though the book contained no classified information, Snepp had violated a contractual agreement not to publish unauthorized material relating to CIA activity. The judge argued that *Decent Interval*, which dealt with the CIA's evacuation of Saigon at the end of the Vietnam War, had "caused the United States irreparable harm and loss." Snepp said he would appeal the ruling. The president of Random House, Snepp's publisher, commented that the "supreme irony" of the case was that Richard Helms, formerly head of the CIA, had been fined recently $2,000 "for lying to a Congressional committee and that Frank Snepp has suffered the impoundment of at least $60,000 for telling the truth."

**John D. Rockefeller 3d Dies** — John D. Rockefeller 3d, 72-year-old philanthropist and eldest of the 5 grandsons of the founder of the Standard Oil Co., whose name he bore, died, **July 10,** in an automobile accident near the family estate at Pocantico Hills, N.Y. A funeral service, **July 13,** filled the 2500-seat Riverside Church in N.Y.C., which his grandfather had helped build, to capacity. Leaders in politics, the arts, and philanthropy attended, as well as the entire Rockefeller family and large numbers of friends and employees.

**Laetrile Legal for the Terminally Ill** — A U.S. court of appeals, in Denver, **July 10,** ruled that terminally-ill cancer patients were legally entitled to use the controversial drug Laetrile. The court ruled that "safety" and "effectiveness" in the federal law banning the drug had no meaning when applied to the terminally ill. Laetrile had been legalized in 14 states but the Food and Drug Administration had been fighting to retain the ban on its use.

**Congress Approves NYC Aid** — The Senate and the House of Representatives reached a compromise on aid to New York City, **July 13,** agreeing to federal guarantees on $1.65 billion in loans to help the city avoid bankruptcy. Sen. William Proxmire (D., Wisc.), who, as chairman of the Senate Banking Committee, had long acted as the financially troubled city's main adversary, finally was instrumental in arranging a compromise between House and Senate versions of the bill. In his own words, he "caved in." Pres. Carter signed the bill, **Aug. 8,** at a gala celebration at New York City Hall. Carter commented, "Those who thought the United States was going to stand by while its greatest city went under were wrong."

**United Orders Boeing 767s** — United Airlines announced, **July 14,** that it had ordered $1.6-billion worth of jet airliners from the Boeing Co., including 30 Boeing 767s, for $1.2 billion, and 30 Boeing 727-200s, for $400 million. The 767 is a medium-size airliner being developed by Boeing to compete with the European Airbus. The United order was the largest, in dollar amount, in aviation history.

**3 Guards Slain in Illinois Prison Riot** — Rioting broke out in an Illinois prison, **July 22,** and 3 guards were stabbed to death. The riot was put down by hundreds of officers using tear gas. No reason for the riot could be determined.

**2 of Wilmington 10 Paroled** — James McKoy and Willie Earl Vereen, 2 of Wilmington 10 defendents, were paroled **July 25,** after 2½ years in prison. The Wilmington 10 are 9 black men and a white woman who had been convicted of firebombing a white-owned grocery store during racial violence in Wilmington, N.C. in 1971. Two other defendents had already been paroled and a 5th was scheduled to be paroled **July 28.** McKoy and Vereen reaffirmed their claims of innocence and pledged to work for the release of the members still in prison.

**"Test-Tube Baby" Born in England** — An Englishwoman gave birth, **July 25,** to a baby who had been conceived outside her body, the first authenticated instance of a "test-tube baby" in history. Lesley Brown, 31 had been unable to conceive in more than 10 years of marriage because of a defect in her Fallopian tubes. English doctors surgically removed an egg cell from Mrs. Brown's ovaries, **Nov. 10,** and fertilized it in a petri dish with sperm from her husband, John Brown, a 38-year-old truck driver from Bristol. The fertilized egg was implanted several days later in Mrs. Brown's uterus. The successful birth gave hope to the 20%-45% of women who are infertile because of blocked Fallopian tubes.

**Disasters** — A fire in Rio de Janeiro's Museum of Modern Art, **July 8,** destroyed more than 1,000 works of art. . . . Floods killed at least 122 people in Afghanistan and northwest Pakistan, it was reported **July 10.** . . . A tank truck exploded at a Spanish beach, **July 14,** killing at least 170 people and critically burning about 150 more. The truck, carrying liquid industrial gas, had overturned and exploded at a tourist campsite, engulfing whole families in flames. . . .

An 18-day heat wave had taken the lives of 21, mostly elderly, persons, by **July 19,** in the Dallas-Fort Worth area. . . . Floods in northwest India were reported **July 24** to have killed 100 and affected 2 million people, washing away 10 villages in the state of Uttar Pradesh. . . . More than 200 Vietnamese refugees drowned, it was reported **July 26,** when their boat capsized in the South China Sea.

## AUGUST

### National

**Brooke Not to be Charged** — The Suffolk County, Mass., District Attorney decided, **Aug. 1,** not to file perjury charges against Sen. Edward R. Brooke (R., Mass.) Brooke had admitted, **May 27,** to making a false statement under oath, concerning the source of a $49,000 loan, during his divorce proceedings in 1977. The decision not to prosecute was based on the fact that the "misstatements" were not sufficient to be covered by the state's perjury law.

**Jaworski Quits Korea Probe** — Leon Jaworski withdrew, **Aug. 2,** as special counsel to the House ethics committee investigating the Korean influence-buying scandal. Jaworski explained that the committee could accomplish "nothing else" without the testimony of Kim Dong Jo, former Korean ambassador to the U.S. The committee announced, **Aug. 3,** that it had accepted a Korean offer of Kim's written testimony. Jaworski had opposed written testimony as inadequate. The U.S. Parole Board announced, **Aug. 18,** that former Rep. Richard T. Hanna (D., Calif.), serving a 6- to 30-month sentence on a bribery conspiracy charge related to the scandal, would be paroled on Sept. 6, 1979. Hancho C. Kim, a Korean-born businessman involved in the scandal, pleaded guilty, **Aug. 24,** to a tax-evasion charge stemming from the investigations. Kim denied guilt and said he had entered the guilty plea only to protect his family. Kim was fined $10,000 and given a suspended sentence in exchange for the government's promise to drop tax charges against his wife.

**Crane Enters GOP Race for Presidency** — Rep. Philip M. Crane (R., Ill.) entered, **Aug. 2,** the race for the Republican nomination for the 1980 presidential election. Crane, the first of what was expected to be a crowded field, pledged to lead a "free people liberated from excessive government." Crane became known nationally through his travels in support of conservative causes, including the campaign against the Panama Canal treaties that featured him on television.

**New Stock Market Record Volume** — The N.Y. Stock Exchange, **Aug. 3,** recorded a volume of 65.4 million shares traded, breaking the former record of 63.49 million shares traded **Apr. 17.** The ticker tape ran as much as 22 minutes late during the record trading and the Dow Jones industrial average closed at 886.87, up 3.38 for the day. Volume for the week ending **Aug. 4** hit a record 220.58-million shares, compared to 152.8 million the previous week. The Dow Jones industrial average, **Aug. 27,** was off 10.6 points, its worst loss in 2 months, closing at 884.88. The loss was attributed to actions by the Federal Reserve to tighten credit in order to aid the dollar and fight inflation.

**O'Neill Protegé Given White House Job** — Robert T. Griffin, protegé of House Speaker Thomas P. O'Neill Jr., was appointed, **Aug. 3,** to a newly created federal job. Griffin had been dismissed, **July 28,** from his post as deputy director of the General Services Administration (GSA), a move which had severely strained relations between O'Neill and the White House. The dismissal resulted from a dispute between Griffin and GSA Administrator Jay Solomon over control of the agency. Griffin's new post as "senior assistant" to Robert S. Strauss, the Carter administration's chief inflation adviser, paid $50,000 a year, the same as his GSA position.

**Unemployment, Prices, Wages Up** — Unemployment rose to 6.2% for July, the Bureau of Labor Statistics reported **Aug. 4.** The drop in the jobless rate to 5.7% in June was explained as a "statistical aberration." Wages rose a record 2.1% for the 2d quarter of 1978, the Bureau of Labor Statistics reported **Aug. 30,** while the consumer price index rose even faster, 2.9%, during the same period. A governor of the Federal Reserve warned, **Aug. 30,** that inflation might amount to at least 8% through 1979. The Carter administraon had been predicting a 7.2% rate of inflation for 1978 nd 6.5% for 1979.

**House Passes Tax Cut** — The House of Representatives, ug. 10, by a 362-to-49 vote, passed a $16.3-billion tax cut. he bill gave tax reduction primarily to persons in the $15,000 to $100,000 tax brackets, rather than to those earn ng less than $15,000 a year, as in previous Democratic tax ats. Rep. Richard Bolling (D., Mo.) called it a "Republican ill with a Democratic label." The Senate Finance Commit e began hearings on the bill **Aug. 21.**

**House Rejects Aid Cut** — The House of Representatives efeated an attempt to cut $584 million from the Carter ad inistration's foreign aid bill, **Aug. 14.** Rep. Clarence Long D., Md.) had offered the cut, arguing that the money, hich was appropriated for 2 international development anks, would not go to the poor but to those with "political out" and those offering the "highest bribes."

**House Investigates King Assassination** — The House As ssinations Committee held public hearings on the assassi ation of the Rev. Martin Luther King Jr., **Aug. 14-18.** mes Earl Ray, the convicted assassin of King, testified be re the committee **Aug. 16-18,** denying his guilt and claim g that he had been framed by a man named "Roual." The ommittee hearings were run in the manner of a trial, which ay, who had pleaded guilty, had been demanding for ears. Cross examination of Ray by Rep. Louis Stokes (D., hio) exposed numerous contradictions in Ray's defense. he committee also called on Coy Dean Cowden, a man ho had told Ray's lawyer Mark Lane that he had seen Ray ½ blocks from the assassination site at the time of the ooting, to testify. Cowden retracted the alibi, saying he ad in fact been in Beaumont, Tex., at the time.

**House Votes to Extend ERA Deadline** — The House of epresentatives passed, **Aug. 15,** by a vote of 233 to 189, a 9-month extension of the deadline for states to ratify the qual Rights Amendment. The extension, which faced reats of filibuster in the Senate, would move the deadline om March 22, 1979 to June 30, 1982. The amendment had een ratified by 35 states and still required ratification by 3 ore in order to become law. The House defeated, 227 to 96, an amendment to the extension offered by Rep. Tom ailsback (R., Ill.) which would have allowed states to re ind their ratification. Courts had not ruled on the legality f votes by 4 state legislatures to rescind their earlier ratifi ations.

**Carter Vetoes Defense Bill** — Pres. Jimmy Carter vetoed $36-billion weapons bill, **Aug. 17,** because it included a 2-billion nuclear-powered aircraft carrier he opposed. A easure to override the veto fell 74 votes short of the re uired two-thirds majority, **Sept. 7,** constituting a major olitical victory for the president. Sen. John C. Stennis (D., iss.), chairman of the Senate Armed Services Committee, mmediately introduced an arms appropriations bill identical o the vetoed one but deleting the carrier. In explaining the eto, Carter argued in favor of spending the $2 billion on ilitary improvements that could be made in less time than e 8 to 10 years it would take to build a nuclear-powered arrier.

**Carter Compromises on Reactor Research** — Sen. James . McClure (R., Idaho) released, **Aug. 23,** details of his ompromise with Pres. Jimmy Carter on atomic breeder re ctor research. The president agreed to spend $1.55 billion ver a 3-year period on the research, which he had previ usly opposed as dangerous, in return for McClure's crucial ote for the natural gas pricing bill in the House-Senate con rence committee. The bill, stuck in Congress for 16 onths, still faced opposition in Congress and the business ommunity. Carter told reporters **Aug. 25** he had "always vored a research and development program" for breeder actors and that "Sen. McClure wanted to make it look as he had won a great victory."

**Talmadge Repays Improper Claims** — Sen. Herman E. almadge (D., Ga.) turned over to the Senate, **Aug. 18,** a ersonal check for $37,125.90 for improper claims made by s office from 1972 to 1977. Talmadge blamed "errors in dgment" by aides who had claimed more than $24,000 for penses never incurred and more than $11,000 for expenses ot allowable under Senate regulations. The Senate Ethics ommittee voted, **Aug. 17,** to accept Talmadge's payment at continued to investigate the senator's finances.

**Senate Passes DC Voting Amendment** — The Senate, **Aug. 22,** by a vote of 67 to 32, sent to the states for ratifica tion a constitutional amendment giving District of Columbia residents full congressional representation. The proposed amendment would give the district 2 senators and one or 2 representatives, depending on population figures. Referring to the 75% black population of the district, some supporters of the amendment called it the "Civil Rights Act of 1978." It was noted that the district outranked 11 states in taxes paid to the federal government and that of the 115 countries with elected legislatures, only the U.S. and Brazil denied representation to residents of their capital cities. New Jersey, on **Sept. 11,** became the first state to ratify the amendment. A total of 38 states would have to ratify by 1984 for the amendment to become part of the U.S. Constitution.

**Postal Strike Averted** — A nationwide mail strike was averted, **Aug. 28,** when the Postal Service and union leaders agreed, only hours before a midnight strike deadline, to re sume bargaining, to be followed by binding arbitration if a settlement could not be reached in 15 days. Director Wayne Horvitz of the Federal Mediation and Conciliation Service announced, **Aug. 29,** that he had appointed James J. Healy, a Harvard University labor-relations expert to oversee the 15-day bargaining and arbitration process. AFL-CIO Pres. George Meany had fought publicly with the White House, **Aug. 8-11,** criticizing as inadequate the government's offer to the postal workers as well as Pres. Jimmy Carter's failure to get Congress to pass the labor law reform legislation Meany favored.

**Trade Deficit Sends Dollar Plunging** — The dollar fell sharply in value, **Aug. 29,** after a $3-billion trade deficit was reported for July. The deficit was far worse than had been expected; the dollar's position had improved in anticipation of a favorable report. The dollar continued to slide, **Aug. 30,** on all markets except London. The Treasury had an nounced, **Aug. 22,** that it would more than double its gold sales to help prop up the dollar.

**Prime Rate Hits 9¼%** — Major banks lifted the prime rate to 9¼%, **Aug. 30.** Chase Manhattan Bank, which led off the prime rate increase, explained it had raised the rate its most credit-worthy customers had to pay because of Federal Reserve actions intended to fight inflation and prop up the dollar. The Federal Reserve had raised the interest rate on federal funds 3 times in the previous 2 weeks.

**Midge Costanza Replaced** — Pres. Jimmy Carter, **Aug. 31,** appointed Agriculture Department counsel Sarah Wed dington, a Texas lawyer and abortion rights advocate, to a $51,000-a-year women's issues position in the White House. Weddington replaced Margaret (Midge) Costanza, the con troversial aide who resigned **July 31,** after her responsibili ties were sharply reduced and her office moved from the main floor of the White House to a basement cubicle. A tele vision appearance scheduled for **July 25** for Costanza had been abruptly canceled by the White House in order to al low more time on the show for Carter adviser Stuart Eizen stat. The U.S. Catholic Conference, **Sept. 1,** in a letter from its general secretary to the president, attacked Weddington for her support of federal funding for abortions.

### International

**Letelier Assassination Conspirators Indicted** — A federal grand jury in Washington, D.C., indicted, **Aug. 1,** the for mer head of Chile's secret police and 6 others for the assas sination of Orlando Letelier in 1976 in the district. Gen. Juan Manuel Contreras Sepúlveda, former head of DINA, Chile's intelligence agency, 2 other Chileans, and 4 anti-Communist Cubans living in New Jersey were charged with murder and conspiracy to murder Letelier and his American colleague Ronni K. Moffit. Letelier, a former Chilean foreign minister, had become a strong critic of the Pinochet regime. Michael Townley, an American who had worked for DINA, admit ted to a Washington court, **Aug. 11,** that he had carried out the assassination under orders from DINA. In exchange for his testimony, Townley was sentenced to 3½ to 10 years in prison, with an agreement from the Justice Department that he be recommended for parole after he completed the mini mum sentence. The Chilean government announced, **Aug. 1,** that the 3 Chileans indicted had been arrested, at the request of the U.S., and the Justice Department announced that it would seek to extradite them.

**Turkish Arms Embargo Ended** — The U.S. House of Representatives voted, **Aug. 1,** to allow Pres. Jimmy Carter to end the embargo on sales of arms to Turkey. The Senate, **July 25,** had also voted to end the embargo. Carter had requested the embargo repeal in order to facilitate a settlement in the Cyprus situation and to strengthen NATO. The Greek government, **Aug. 2,** expressed "sorrow" at the decision, warning that it would make it more difficult to reach a solution in Cyprus. Cypriote Pres. Spyros Kyprianou described the embargo repeal as "tantamount to indirect legalization of the Turkish invasion [of Cyprus] using American weapons." Turkish Prime Minister Bulent Ecevit called the measure "positive," but said it also had "unrealistic" aspects, apparently referring to Senate amendments providing for close congressional oversight of negotiations over Cyprus and for strict parity in military aid to Greece and Turkey.

**Palestinians Attack, Israel Responds** — Palestinian terrorists set off a bomb, **Aug. 3,** in a crowded market in Tel Aviv killing one Israeli and wounding 50. Israeli jets struck, 5 hours later, at Palestinian bases in Lebanon, wounding 5 Lebanese civilians, according to the PLO. Israeli planes attacked 2 PLO bases in Lebanon, **Aug. 21,** a day after an El Al crew in London was attacked by Palestinian gunmen who killed a stewardess and wounded 9 persons, including 7 British bystanders. El Al, the Israeli airline, criticized the British government for forbidding El Al's security guards to carry weapons in Britain.

**Beirut Fighting Renewed** — Fighting broke out in Beirut, **Aug. 5,** between Lebanese Christians and Syrian troops, after a week's lull. A truce was announced **Aug. 9** but fighting erupted again on **Aug. 11.** Israeli Foreign Minister Moshe Dayan warned his senior staff, **Aug. 31,** of the "creeping occupation" of Lebanon by the Syrian army and said that the urgency of the situation of the Lebanese Christians would be conveyed to the "highest levels" of the U.S. government at the Camp David summit meetings to be held in September. Lebanese Army troops that had attempted to deploy along the Israeli border **July 31** began withdrawing from the region **Aug. 11,** as Christian militiamen refused to turn over control of the territory.

**Pope Paul VI Dies at 80** — Pope Paul VI died, **Aug. 6,** at the age of 80, of a heart attack, at the papal summer residence at Castel Gondolfo. The pope's body was returned to the Vatican, **Aug. 9,** and lay in state in St. Peter's Basilica, **Aug. 10-11,** in a simple wood coffin. An estimated 100,000 mourners attended a requiem mass, **Aug. 12,** in St. Peter's Square, which was televised live by satellite to tens of millions of viewers. During the mourning period, ½ million pilgrims were estimated to have filed past the pope's coffin. The pope's body was laid to rest in a simple grave in the crypt inside the basilica.

**Camp David Summit Arranged** — The White House announced, **Aug. 8,** that Israeli Prime Minister Menahem Begin and Egyptian Pres. Anwar Sadat had accepted invitations to meet with Pres. Carter **Sept. 5** at Camp David to discuss ways of resolving the Middle East deadlock. Sadat said, **Aug. 8,** that he had accepted the invitation because the U.S. would be participating as a "full partner" at the summit. Israel announced, **Aug. 14,** plans to establish 5 new Jewish settlements in the West Bank. The following day, criticized by Egypt, the U.S., and Israel's Deputy Prime Minister Yigael Yadin, the Israeli cabinet voted to shelve the plans for the settlements until after the Camp David talks. Israel, **Aug. 30,** responded coolly to Carter's reported offer to deploy U.S. forces on the West Bank and in the Gaza Strip, saying the Israel Defense Force had to be the "center pillar" of security there.

**Sino-Japanese Treaty Signed** — China and Japan signed a 10-year peace and friendship treaty, **Aug. 12,** in Peking. The Soviet news agency, Tass, denounced the treaty, because of "an article which is of an openly anti-Soviet character and serves the selfish interests" of China's leaders. The Chinese had proposed a clause specifically against Soviet hegemony; but the final treaty contained a Japanese compromise formula which opposed efforts by any nation or bloc to establish hegemony in the Far East. According to Japanese Foreign Minister Sunao Sonoda, China dropped its claim to the Senkaku Islands in the East China Sea, claimed also by Japan and Taiwan. Sonoda revealed also that China would terminate the 1950 Sino-Soviet friendship treaty in April,

1979. The *New York Times* reported, **July 23,** that Chines Japanese trade had been developing even more rapidly tha had been expected.

**Palestinians, Iraq in Factional Strife** — A Palestini building in Beirut was blown up, **Aug. 13,** killing 150 to 20 people, including members of both the PLO and its pr Iraqi rival, the Palestine Liberation Front (PLF). The hea of the PLF blamed the bombing on the pro-Syrian Popul Front for the Liberation of Palestine (PFLP). Iraq and t PLF had been opposing "moderate" PLO members w were reportedly willing to consider a negotiated settleme with Israel that would allow the survival of the Jewish sta and the creation of a Palestinian state on the West Bank an Gaza. The PLO, **July 13,** had accused Iraq of murdering PLO representative in Kuwait, **June 15,** another in Londc **Jan. 4,** and an Egyptian editor in Cyprus, **Feb. 18.** PL gunmen had attacked the Iraqi embassy in Paris, **July** and the Iraqi consulate in Karachi, Pakistan, **Aug. 2.** Pr Iraqi guerrillas retaliated, killing PLO representatives Paris, **Aug. 3,** and Islamabad, Pakistan, **Aug. 5.**

**Terrorists Burn Theater in Iran** — Terrorists set fire to crowded movie theater in Abadan, Iran, **Aug. 20,** killing 4 people. The Iranian government blamed the arson on Mo lem extremists who had been leading riots throughout t country for several months in protest against the Shah modernization policies. Iranian students demonstrated, Au **21,** in Washington, claiming the fire had in fact been set the Iranian government itself. The Shah, **Aug. 27,** appointe Jaffar Sharif Emami, a man of religious background wi links to the Moslem clergy, as premier, to head a reconcil ation government.

**Jomo Kenyatta Dies** — Jomo Kenyatta, president Kenya and a leader among Africa's fighters for indepe dence, died in his sleep, **Aug. 22,** in Mombasa, Keny Kenyatta, whose age was estimated at least 80, w interred in a mausoleum in Nairobi, **Sept. 1.** Daniel Ara Moi, Kenya's vice president, was sworn in, **Aug. 22,** as i terim president, to serve until elections, to be held in ' days, could determine who would succeed Kenyatta.

**Nicaraguan Guerrillas Seize National Palace** — The Ni araguan National Palace was seized, **Aug. 22,** by 23 San dinista National Liberation Front guerrillas, who threatene to kill their 1,500 hostages and demanded a cash ranso and the release of 59 political prisoners. The guerrillas r leased their hostages, **Aug. 24,** after Pres. Anastasio Somo Debayle paid the $500,000 ransom and released the priso ers. The guerrillas and the released prisoners flew to Pa ama. Nicaraguan businessmen voted, **Aug. 27,** to support nationwide strike aimed at forcing Somoza to resig Somoza, at a news conference, **Aug. 29,** vowed to remain office until the end of his term. The Nicaraguan Nation Guard launched an offensive, **Aug. 31,** against teenage rebe who had taken over about half the city of Matagalpa.

**China, Vietnam in Border Clash** — Chinese and Vietnam ese forces clashed, **Aug. 25,** in the Friendship Pass area the 2 nations' border. China claimed, **Aug. 28,** that at lea 400 Vietnamese soldiers had occupied a hill within Chine territory during the clash. Vietnam, **Aug. 31,** denied t charge.

**Pope John Paul I Elected** — Albino Cardinal Lucia was elected to succeed Pope Paul VI, **Aug. 26,** and chose th name John Paul I, a symbolic declaration of his intention follow in the spirit of both the previous pope and his pred cessor, John XXIII. The new pope, formerly patriarch Venice, was consecrated, **Sept. 3,** at a mass in St. Peter Square, without the pomp of the usual coronation or e thronement. The mass was attended by 200,000 worshippe and was telecast live, by satellite, worldwide.

**Independent Named Portuguese Premier** — Alfred Nobre da Costa, a politically independent technocrat, wa sworn in, **Aug. 28,** as premier of Portugal, after the nation political parties had been unable to agree on a coalition go ernment. Da Costa's government would have to face a vc of confidence in the National Assembly within 10 days.

**Hua Visits Romania, Yugoslavia** — Chinese Communi Party Chairman Hua Kuo-feng, **Aug. 29,** completed a vis to Eastern Europe, symbolizing an historic break with Ch na's traditional isolation. Hua visited Romania, **Aug. 17-2** and Yugoslavia, **Aug. 21-29,** delivering sharp attacks on th Soviet Union in both countries.

### General

**Christina Onassis Marries Russian** — Christina Onassis, heiress of a Greek shipping fortune, married Sergei Kauzov, a Soviet citizen, in Moscow, **Aug. 1.** Kauzov was a former official in the Soviet merchant marine, the largest in the world.

**Health Emergency Result of Pollution** — New York State's Health Commissioner declared a health emergency, **Aug. 2,** in the Love Canal area of Niagara Falls, N.Y. Chemical wastes dumped into canal landfill by Hooker Chemicals and Plastics Corporation between 1947 and 1952 had leaked into backyards and basements, endangering the health of residents. Pres. Jimmy Carter, **Aug. 7,** approved emergency federal aid for the area, to "save lives, protect property, public health and safety, or avert the threat of a disaster." New York Gov. Hugh Carey said that the state would contribute $4 million to relocate families and correct the pollution and that he expected federal aid to be the same amount. Hooker announced that it would contribute $280,000 to help drain the contaminated site but maintained its position "that it is not liable for any claims of damage or harm."

**Seabrook Power Plant Approved** — The Environmental Protection Agency approved, **Aug. 4,** an open-ocean cooling system for the Seabrook, N.H., nuclear power plant. The Nuclear Regulatory Commission had ordered a suspension of work on the $2.3-billion plant, **June 30,** to allow the agency to review the system. A coalition of anti-nuclear groups that had organized 2 mass protests at Seabrook called the ruling "a serious, even tragic, violation of the responsibilities given the EPA by the American people" and vowed a series of "nonviolent, civil disobedience" protests.

**Times Reporter Jailed in N.J.** — *New York Times* reporter M.A. Farber was jailed, **Aug. 4,** for contempt of court in refusing to turn over his files on his investigation of the suspicious deaths of 13 patients in a New Jersey hospital in 1965 and 1966. The files were subpoenaed by the defense in the trial of Dr. Mario Jascalevich, who was charged with murder as an outgrowth of Farber's interest in the case. Also on **Aug. 4,** the *New York Times* began to pay a fine of $5,000 a day for refusing to turn over its files on the case, as well as an additional $1,000-a-day fine leveled against Farber. The New Jersey Supreme Court, **Aug. 30,** ordered Farber released and the fines stayed, pending hearings, on Farber's claims that the First Amendment and New Jersey's shield law protected reporters' rights to keep sources confidential.

**Strike Closes NYC Newspapers** — New York City's 3 major newspapers, the *Daily News,* the *Times,* and the *Post,* were closed by a strike, beginning **Aug. 9.** The pressmen's union struck over work rules designed to reduce pressroom personnel over a period of years. By **Aug. 22,** interim newspapers, the *Daily Metro, Daily Press,* and *City News* were appearing daily.

**Major Advance in Nuclear Fusion** — The Energy Department announced, **Aug. 12,** that a major advance in controlled nuclear fusion had been made by Princeton University scientists. The director of energy research of the department warned, **Aug. 14,** that "the first fusion reactor won't be seen before the first decade of the next century and it could be another 20 years before fusion goes commercial." The process, using "heavy" hydrogen, available from sea water, as fuel, had the added advantage of leaving relatively little atomic waste. The fusion was produced in a magnetic "bottle", a donut-shaped device call Torus Tokamak, originally developed in the Soviet Union.

**Kucinich Narrowly Survives Recall** — Cleveland Mayor Dennis J. Kucinich was continued in office, **Aug. 13,** by a 36-vote margin in a recall election in which more than 20,000 votes were cast. The 31-year-old Kucinich, youngest mayor of a major U.S. city, had feuded with the Cleveland City Council, 20 of whose 33 members had supported the movement to recall him. Cleveland's financial agent warned the city council, **Aug. 23,** that the city was in danger of defaulting on $15.5 million in notes due in December.

**Natural Gas Found off N.J.** — Texaco Inc. announced, **Aug. 14,** it had struck natural gas in an offshore test well 90 miles east of Atlantic City, N.J. The find was the first discovery of oil or gas since drilling began in the offshore Baltimore Canyon area in April. Texaco said the find was "very encouraging" but that it would take 8 to 12 months to determine whether the discovery was commercially exploitable.

**Scientology Conspiracy Charged** — A Washington, D.C. federal grand jury filed a 42-page indictment, **Aug. 15,** against 11 high ranking officials of the Church of Scientology. The indictment charged the church leaders with a widespread conspiracy to spy on, bug, and steal documents from government agencies. The spies were alleged to have been seeking information concerning IRS and Justice Department actions on the church's application for tax-exempt status as well as "information about any potential legal action against L. Ron Hubbard," the church's founder. The church leaders pleaded innocent, **Aug. 29,** and asked for a new judge, arguing that the government had "shopped around" for a judge favorable to its side.

**Atlantic Crossed by Balloon** — The first successful transatlantic balloon flight was completed, **Aug. 17,** when 3 Americans landed their craft in a wheat field outside Paris. They had begun their 3,200-mile journey 6 days earlier at Presque Isle, Maine. At least 17 unsuccessful attempts at the Atlantic crossing had been made since 1873, taking at least 7 lives. The balloon, the *Double Eagle II,* had cost $150,000 to build and was filled with about $15,000 worth of helium.

**Memphis Police, Firemen End Strike** — Memphis policemen ended a 9-day wildcat strike, **Aug. 18,** when they accepted a new contract. Firemen, who had joined the strike **Aug. 14,** also approved a new contract and went back to work. National Guard troops numbering 1,500 had policed the city during the strike. A 2½-hour blackout, **Aug. 16,** set off by a drunken power company guard, brought out looters and resulted in more than 30 arrests.

**Homosexuals' Discharges Upgraded** — The Pentagon acknowledged, **Aug. 20,** that veterans who had received less-than-honorable discharges because they were homosexual could usually get them upgraded. It was estimated that 20,000 to 30,000 veterans had received less-than-honorable discharges because of homosexuality and, as a result, had been denied veteran's benefits. The change in Defense Department policy had not been announced publicly and was discovered by lawyers with the National Military Discharge Review Project using the Freedom of Information Act.

**Guilty Plea in Hearst Kidnaping** — William and Emily Harris pleaded guilty, **Aug. 31,** to kidnaping Patricia Hearst in 1974. The Symbionese Liberation Army members faced jail sentences up to life imprisonment. The other 6 members involved in the kidnaping died in a shootout with L.A. police in 1974.

**Disasters** — At least 26 people died in floods as 30 inches of rain, caused by tropical storm Amelia, ravaged central Texas, **Aug. 2-4.** . . . A bus carrying physically and mentally handicapped people crashed into a lake in Quebec, **Aug. 5,** drowning 41 persons. . . . A bus plunged into a river in Uganda, **Aug. 12,** killing 40 persons, mostly school children. . . . Tropical storm Carmen lashed South Korea, **Aug. 20,** killing 20 and causing an estimated $20 million in property losses. . . . Tropical storm Elaine turned into a typhoon, **Aug. 26,** killing 14 people in the Philippines and leaving 30 towns there under water.

### SEPTEMBER

### National

**Unemployment Drops Slightly**—Unemployment fell 0.3% in August to 5.9%, the Labor Department announced **Sept. 1.** The House of Representatives voted, **Sept. 22,** to eliminate 100,000 jobs from Pres. Jimmy Carter's request for public service employment for 1979 but would allow an increase if unemployment rose unexpectedly. Rep. John Conyers Jr. (D., Mich.) stalked out of a White House meeting, **Sept. 26,** when Carter rejected his call for a "Camp David summit conference" on unemployment.

**Rep. Flood Indicted**—Rep. Daniel J. Flood (D., Pa.) was indicted, **Sept. 5,** by a federal grand jury in Los Angeles on 3 counts of perjury. The 75-year-old, 15-term Congressman was charged with lying to a grand jury and to a trial jury about payoffs allegedly made to him and to Stephen Elko, a former aide. Elko was convicted in 1977 of soliciting a bribe, perjury, and obstruction of justice. Flood pleaded innocent, Oct. 19, in a Washington, D.C., court to bribery and conspiracy charges consolidated with the Los Angeles indictment. Robert Hudock, running against Flood for his seat in the House of Representatives, stood outside the courtroom and called on Flood to resign.

**Assassinations Committee Opens Hearings**—The House Assassinations Committee opened hearings, **Sept. 6,** on the 1963 assassination of Pres. John F. Kennedy. A panel of medical experts, testifying before the committee **Sept. 7,** backed the Warren Commission's conclusion that a single bullet killed Kennedy and wounded Texas Gov. John B. Connally, who was riding in the same car at the time of the assassination. Cuban Pres. Fidel Castro, in a tape recording played before the committee **Sept. 19,** denied any involvement in the assassination.

**Eilberg Charged by Ethics Committee**—A House of Representatives ethics committee charged Rep. Joshua Eilberg (D., Pa.), **Sept. 13,** with breaking House rules and federal law in connection with fees of over $100,000 paid to him for his help in getting a $14.5-million grant for a Philadelphia hospital in 1975. The charges could lead to Eilberg's censure or expulsion from the House. Eilberg was indicted, **Oct. 24,** by a federal grand jury in Philadelphia on charges that he violated a conflict of interests law. If convicted, Eilberg would be prohibited from holding public office again.

**Postal Contract Imposed**—Federal mediator James Healy imposed a contract settlement, **Sept. 15,** awarding Postal Service employes higher wages and lifetime job guarantees. The settlement also included a clause allowing the Postal Service to lay off workers hired in the future. Postmaster General William F. Bolger warned that the pay increase could lead to a postage rate increase.

**Discount Rate Boosted to Fight Inflation**—The Federal Reserve Board raised the discount rate to 8%, **Sept. 22,** continuing its attempts to hold down inflation and protect the dollar. Pres. Jimmy Carter told the joint annual meeting of the International Monetary Fund and the World Bank, **Sept. 25,** that he would keep the promises he made in July at the economic summit in Bonn to "fight inflation, reduce oil imports, and expand (American) exports." Consumer prices rose 0.6% in August, the Labor Department reported **Sept. 26.** Secretary of the Treasury W. Michael Blumenthal admitted that the August rate was still too high but predicted that "we can expect a considerable moderation" for the rest of 1978. The director of the president's Council on Wage and Price Stability, however, said in a speech in New York City that inflation was "worsening" and that the August increase, though lower than the 0.8% average monthly increase for the first half of 1978, was not "very encouraging."

**Labor Leaders Back Kennedy on Health Insurance**—Labor leaders approved, **Sept. 26,** a national health insurance plan proposed by Sen. Edward M. Kennedy (D., Mass.). Pres. Jimmy Carter had proposed a health insurance plan in July that would be adopted piece by piece as the nation's economy allowed. The Kennedy plan would go into effect 2 years after it was adopted by Congress and would attempt to hold health care cost increases down to the rate of inflation.

**Weapons Bill Approved Without Nuclear Carrier**—The Senate, **Sept. 26,** approved a $35.2-billion weapons procurement bill, omitting the nuclear aircraft carrier that had provoked Pres. Jimmy Carter's veto of the original bill. The new bill contained none of the $2.2 billion worth of weapons proposed by Carter to replace the carrier. The House subsequently passed the bill, allowing Congressional approval of the $126-billion overall Pentagon appropriation.

**Railroad Strike Ended**—A 4-day nationwide railroad strike came to an end, **Sept. 29,** when the railway clerks union accepted a federal court order to go back to work. Nearly 70% of the nation's rail lines were shut down and the automotive industry had begun layoffs. Pres. Jimmy Carter invoked the Railway Labor Act, **Sept. 27,** leading to the court order.

**First GSA Fraud Indictments**—A federal grand jury in Baltimore, **Sept. 30,** indicted 12 General Services Administration (GSA) store managers, 4 other federal employes, and the chairman and vice president of an office supply firm. The 18 were charged with conspiracy to defraud the government by arranging for payment for office supplies never de-

livered. More indictments were expected in the months [to] come as a result of the GSA's internal investigation. GS[A] Administrator Jay Solomon had indicated **Aug. 30** that [as] many as 50 GSA employes and suppliers might eventual[ly] be indicted. By **Oct. 17,** 15 of those named in the first i[n]dictment had entered guilty pleas and one a plea of n[o] guilty. A consultant hired to study GSA corruption [re]ported **Sept. 5** that more than $1 million worth of suppli[es] was being stolen by GSA employees annually. Solomon to[ld] a Senate subcommittee **Sept. 19** that GSA fraud uncover[ed] by the investigation was "only the beginning." Charges we[re] filed in federal court in Washington, D.C., **Oct. 18,** against [a] building maintenance contractors for receiving $580,0[00] from the GSA for repairs never made on federal buildin[gs] there. The same day, the FBI arrested a painting contracto[r] charging they had observed him in the act of offering [a] $5,000 bribe to a GSA inspector in the courtyard of a fe[d]eral building in Washington.

## International

**Guerrilla Missile Downs Rhodesian Plane**—An Air Rh[o]desia commercial jet liner was shot down, **Sept. 3,** by a su[r]face-to-air missile launched by ZAPU (Zimbabwe Africa[n] People's Union) guerrillas, killing 38 passengers in the cras[h]. ZAPU denied Rhodesian claims that guerrillas massacre[d] 10 of the 18 survivors at the site. Rhodesia announced, **Sep[t.] 27,** that 725 people had already been killed in Septembe[r,] making it the bloodiest month of the 6-year-old guerri[lla] war. The figure did not include the hundreds of guerrill[as] the government had reported it killed during air attac[ks] against guerrilla bases in Mozambique, **Sept. 20-22.**

**Crawford Given Suspended Sentence**—Francis J. Craw[w]ford, the American businessman convicted by a Soviet cou[rt] for currency violations, was given a 5-year suspended se[n]tence, **Sept. 7,** by a Moscow city court. Crawford's Russia[n] co-defendants received 4- to 5-year sentences. Crawford le[ft] the Soviet Union **Sept. 8** and his employers, the Interna[a]tional Harvester Co., resumed its sales to the USSR Sep[t.] 11.

**Martial Law Declared in Iran**—Martial law was declar[ed] in Iran, **Sept. 8,** and at least 95 people were killed whe[n] troops fired on demonstrators in Teheran who were protes[t]ing the declaration. Martial law had been imposed in rea[c]tion to a demonstration there **Sept. 7** by 100,000 protesto[rs] demanding the return of Ayatollah Ruhola Khomeini, [a] Moslem leader in exile in Iraq, and the establishment of a[n] "Islamic government" in Iran to replace the Shah's mona[r]chy.

**Bulgarian Defectors Poisoned**—Georgi Marcov, a 4[9-]year-old Bulgarian defector who worked as a broadcaster [in] England for anti-Communist Radio Free Europe, died, Sep[t.] 11, after he was stabbed in a London street with a poisone[d] umbrella. Vladimir Simeonov, 30, a Bulgarian defecto[r] working for the BBC, was found dead, **Oct. 2,** in his Lo[n]don home. Police were treating the death as suspicious. Vl[a]dimir Kostov, 46, an exiled Bulgarian journalist living [in] Paris, was stabbed in the back by a sharp object in the Par[is] subway, **Aug. 26,** and was reported, **Sept. 14,** to have su[f]fered a high fever and swelling afterwards. French docto[rs] removed a metal particle from Kostov's back and Frenc[h] and British police present at the operation sent the partic[le] to London for comparison with the one removed from Ma[r]cov.

**Portugal's Government Falls**—After 17 days in powe[r,] the government of Portuguese Prime Minister Alfred[o] Nobre da Costa was defeated, **Sept. 14,** by an _ad hoc_ coal[i]tion of Socialists and Center Democrats. Pres. Anton[io] Ramalho Eanes, **Sept. 22,** offered the nation's politic[al] parties a last chance to come up with a government befo[re] he dissolved the parliament and called new elections.

**Nicaraguan Troops Shell Rebels**—Nicaraguan troops b[e]gan rocket attacks, **Sept. 15,** in Leon, the country's 2d larg[g]est city, against Sandinista Liberation Front guerril[la] strongholds. The National Guard announced, **Sept. 16,** th[at] it had retaken the city from the guerrillas. National Gua[rd] attacks, **Sept. 22,** in the northern city of Esteli wiped out t[he] last guerrilla strongholds in Nicaragua. The guerrillas ha[d] launched an offensive, **Sept. 9,** designed to force the resign[a]tion of Pres. Anastasio Somoza Debayle. A general strik[e,] including the nation's farmers and businesses as well as l[a]bor, aimed also at forcing Somoza's resignation, continue[d] through September's fighting and, it was reported **Sept. 19** by the *Washington Post*, the nation was on "the brink of total economic collapse." About 1,500 people were estimated to have died in the fighting. Eyewitness accounts from Leon and other Nicaraguan cities reported National Guard atrocities, including indiscriminate close-range shooting of women and children and summary executions of 18- to 25-year-old men suspected of being rebels. The Nicaraguan government charged, **Sept. 17**, that Venezuelan warplanes had supported a guerrilla invasion force entering Nicaragua from Costa Rica. Costa Rica and the guerrillas denied the charge. Venezuela had sent planes the previous week to Costa Rica, which had no armed forces of its own, to protect that country from Nicaraguan troops who had crossed the border in pursuit of guerrillas. The U.S. Senate **Sept. 22**, voted to cut off most aid to the Somoza regime.

**South Africa Abandons UN Namibia Plan**—South Africa rejected, **Sept. 20**, the UN plan for the independence of Namibia (South-West Africa) and announced it would hold its own elections for a Namibian constituent assembly **Nov. 20-24** in preparation for Namibian independence **Dec. 31**. UN Secretary General Kurt Waldheim had recommended to the Security Council **Aug. 30** that a 7,500-man peacekeeping force be sent to Namibia and that elections not be held until 7 months after the council approved his report. The South-West African People's Organization (SWAPO), the guerrillas fighting for control of Namibia, vowed, **Sept. 22**, to step up their struggle and called on "socialist countries" to supply them with weapons. South African Prime Minister John Vorster justified abandoning the UN plan, saying, "The impartiality of the UN is rendered suspect by its continued and sustained assistance to SWAPO to the exclusion of all other parties in South-West Africa."

**Vorster Resigns**—South African Prime Minister John Vorster announced his resignation, **Sept. 20**. No reason was given but it was known that Vorster was ill. The South African parliament elected Vorster, **Sept. 29**, to the ceremonial post of president. Vorster was succeeded as prime minister, **Sept. 28**, by Pieter Willem Botha, the South African defense minister.

**Bombings in Corsica**—Opponents of the Corsican separatist movement exploded 5 bombs, **Sept. 23**, on the Mediterranean island, in protest against the separatist Corsican Liberation Front. The Front had claimed responsibility for over 200 bombings during 1978 in an attempt to gain Corsica's independence from France. Public anger against the small separatist movement had been particularly aroused by a 1977 bombing that destroyed the island's main television receiver, depriving Corsicans of television viewing.

**Pope John Paul I Dead**—Pope John Paul I died, **Sept. 29**, at age 65, apparently of a heart attack in his sleep, after a reign of 34 days. The pope was buried, **Oct. 4**, in a Vatican crypt near his predecessors John XXIII and Paul VI.

**Syrians, Christians Escalate Fighting in Lebanon**—Syrian troops exchange artillery fire with Lebanese Christian militiamen, **Sept. 30**, in and around Beirut. Unlike the previous rounds of fighting, the two sides also engaged in ground fighting. Scores of people, mostly civilians, were believed to have been killed or wounded. A Christian spokesman said the Syrian attacks were aimed against U.S. Pres. Jimmy Carter's **Sept. 28** proposal for an international conference to resolve the 3½-year-old Lebanese crisis. The Christians had staged a one-day strike, **Sept. 13**, to protest Syrian shelling and to demand that Syria withdraw its troops when the peacekeeping force's mandate expired in October.

## Camp David Summit Concluded;
## Carter, Sadat, Begin Sign Framework for Peace

The Middle East summit at Camp David was concluded, **Sept. 17**, with the signing of a framework for peace by Egyptian Pres. Anwar Sadat and Israeli Prime Minister Menahem Begin, with U.S. Pres. Jimmy Carter signing as a witness. The summit, opened by Carter **Sept. 6**, was conducted under a news blackout but Sadat, **Sept. 18**, confirmed reports that he had threatened to walk out of the meetings the previous week.

Under the accord, Egypt and Israel would sign a peace treaty within 3 months, Israel would begin to withdraw its troops from Sinai during the next 3 to 9 months after that, and then normal diplomatic relations would be established between the 2 nations. All Israeli troops would be withdrawn from the Sinai peninsula within 2 to 3 years after the signing of the peace treaty and the area would be demilitarized.

The agreement dealt also with the West Bank and Gaza Strip, providing for Israel, Egypt, Jordan, and the Palestinian Arabs to negotiate the future of those territories, after a 5-year transition period during which Israel would keep troops in specific areas. The Palestinians would elect representatives and determine their own local government.

Egyptian Foreign Minister Ibrahim Kamel and Ambassador to the U.S. Ashraf Ghorbal resigned, **Sept. 18**, to protest the agreements. The Egyptian cabinet, however, on **Sept. 19**, unanimously approved the accord. Sadat, on his return to Cairo **Sept. 23**, received a jubilant welcome as "hero of the peace."

PLO leader Yasir Arafat denounced the accord, **Sept. 18**, as "a dirty deal which the Egyptian people will reject and which does not decide our destiny." Arafat added that Carter would "pay" for the agreements and that "American interests in the Middle East" could come under guerrilla attack. A Soviet broadcast accused Sadat of "complete surrender before the expansionist ambitions of the Israeli aggressor."

Reaction in Israel was largely favorable to the accord and the Knesset (parliament) approved, **Sept. 28**, both the agreements and the removal of Jewish settlements in Sinai. Members of Gush Emunim, the Israeli nationalist group favoring unlimited Jewish settlement in the West Bank, were forcibly evicted by Israeli soldiers, **Sept. 21**, from illegal settlements they had established there in defiance of the accord.

U.S. Secretary of State Cyrus R. Vance flew to Jordan, Saudi Arabia, and Syria, **Sept. 20-21**, to brief the leaders of those Arab states on the Camp David summit. A State Department statement released on his return to Washington said that King Hussein of Jordan and Crown Prince Fahd of Saudi Arabia had been "vitally concerned" about peace negotiations. Syrian Pres. Hafez Assad, however, criticized the accord as giving "Israel everything it wanted" and going "against the basic Arab rights."

The White House, **Sept. 22**, released 9 letters exchanged by Carter with Sadat and Begin dealing with controversial issues in the accord, including the future status of Jerusalem. Begin and Sadat agreed the city should be "undivided." Sadat, however, insisted that East Jerusalem "be under Arab sovereignty" while Begin reiterated the Israeli position that "Jerusalem is one city indivisible, the capital of the state of Israel."

Carter challenged Begin, **Sept. 27**, on the Israeli Prime Minister's contention that they had agreed to a freeze on new settlements in the West Bank only for the negotiation period leading up to the signing of a peace treaty within 3 months. Carter said that Begin had in fact agreed to a 5-year freeze on new settlements in return for dropping Carter's demand that existing settlements not be expanded. Carter told a news conference, **Sept. 28**, that Begin and Sadat had agreed to defer the question of the settlements in the West Bank until after the peace treaty was signed.

The leaders of Syria, Algeria, South Yemen, Libya, and the PLO, meeting in Damascus **Sept. 21-24**, announced that they had severed all relations with Egypt because of the accord. The group, known as the "Steadfastness and Confrontation Front," pledged to work for the "fall" of Sadat's peace policies.

Carter's role in the summit led to a dramatic rise in the president's popularity in the U.S. A *Washington Post* poll indicated, **Sept. 24**, that his popularity had gone from 45% to 56% in 2 weeks.

The Carter administration released a letter to Israel, **Sept. 29**, in which it committed the U.S. to direct involvement, conceivably including Army engineers, in building 2 air bases in the Negev Desert to replace those that Israel agreed to give up in Sinai.

## General

**Legionnaires' Disease in New York**—Health inspectors checked air conditioners and water supplies in New York City's garment district, **Sept. 7**, looking for the source of an outbreak of Legionnaires' Disease that had taken 2 lives. All of the persons suspected of having the disease worked in the garment district.

**FBI Agent Indicted in Mafia Case**—FBI agent Joseph Stabile was indicted, **Sept. 15**, in New York for lying to a Brooklyn grand jury about a bribe he allegedly received from a member of the Mafia. Stabile was charged with having lied about $10,000 he received from John Caputo, reputedly a member of the Luchese family of the Mafia, to have gambling charges against him dismissed.

**Up to 15,000 Dead in Iran Earthquake**—The most powerful earthquake in recent Iranian history killed possibly as many as 15,000 people, **Sept. 16**, and destroyed entire villages and towns. The quake measured 7.7 on the Richter scale. A quake in the same region in 1968 which killed 12,000 people measured 6.5. Almost all the buildings in the town of Tabas, southeast of Teheran, crumbled to rubble in 90 seconds, burying alive 70% of the town's 12,000 inhabitants. Another 40 villages in the region were destroyed or damaged.

**KKK Informer Indicted**—Gary Thomas Rowe Jr. was indicted, **Sept. 20**, by an Alabama grand jury for the murder of civil rights worker Viola Liuzzo in 1965. Rowe had been an FBI informer in the Ku Klux Klan at the time.

**Planes Collide over San Diego**—A total of 150 people were killed, **Sept. 25**, when a Pacific Southwest Airlines Boeing 727 jetliner crashed in midair with a private Cessna 172 over San Diego. All 137 persons aboard the 2 planes were killed, as well as 13 people struck on the ground by debris from the crash, making it the worst air disaster in U.S. history. The jetliner was banking for a landing turn into San Diego's Lindbergh Field when it was struck in the wing by a smaller plane, which was apparently practicing landing approaches.

**Disasters**—A "Soviet expert" and 14 Guineans were killed when a Soviet-made Guinean passenger plane crashed in bad weather on a flight from Moscow to Conakry, Guinea, it was reported **Sept. 5**. . .Nearly 1,000 people were killed in monsoon floods in northern India by **Sept. 8** and officials predicted the situation would get worse.

## OCTOBER

### National

**Public Works Veto Sustained** — The House of Representatives voted, **Oct. 5**, to sustain Pres. Jimmy Carter's veto of the $10.1-billion public works appropriation bill. Carter had attacked the bill, **Oct. 3**, as "inflationary and wasteful" and "absolutely unacceptable," a classic example of "pork-barrel" legislation. The Senate Appropriations Committee passed, **Oct. 11**, a scaled-down substitute for the vetoed bill, omitting the 17 water projects the president opposed and leaving in 42 others.

**ERA Extension Voted** — Congress extended the deadline for ratification of the Equal Rights Amendment, **Oct. 6**, from March 22, 1979 to June 30, 1982. The Senate rejected, **Oct. 5-6**, proposals to allow states to rescind their ratifications of the ERA.

**House Reprimands Members** — The House of Representatives voted, **Oct. 13**, to reprimand 3 of its members for their involvements in the South Korean influence-buying scandal. A House ethics committee had recommended, **Sept. 27**, censure of Rep. Edward R. Roybal (D., Cal.) and reprimand of Representatives Charles H. Wilson (D., Cal.) and John J. McFall (D., Cal.). Committee chairman John J. Flynt Jr. (D., Ga.) criticized the House for reducing the censure of Roybal to a reprimand, saying that the committee had settled for a recommendation of censure but had been prepared to recommend Roybal's expulsion from the House. Roybal was charged with taking $1,000 for his own use from Korean businessman Tongsun Park in 1974 and lying repeatedly about it to the committee.

**Federal Civil Service Reform Adopted** — Pres. Jimmy Carter signed into law, **Oct. 13**, a bill to reform the federal civil service system. The bill, which had been passed by Congress the previous week, would make it easier to reward good workers and fire incompetent ones. The final version of the bill included most of Carter's original proposals, except for his plan to limit veterans' preference rights, which was successfully resisted by veterans' groups.

**Energy Package Passed** — Congress approved, **Oct. 15**, package of energy legislation which Pres. Carter had considered his top domestic priority. Although the package had been changed radically during a 1½-year congressional battle, Carter called it an "important beginning" in the effort to make the U.S. self-sufficient in its energy use. The package included price increases for natural gas, leading to deregulation of newly discovered natural gas in 1985; a tax on gas guzzling cars, starting in 1980; and measures to promote energy conservation.

**$18.7-Billion Tax Cut Passed** — Congress passed a $18.7-billion tax cut bill for 1979, **Oct. 15**, giving 79% of its benefits to individuals making $15,000 a year or more. Sen. Edward M. Kennedy (D., Mass.), **Oct. 18**, urged Pres. Carter to veto the bill, charging that Congress had yielded to "crass and selfish lobbying demands of the business and investment community" and "unfairly ignored the needs of the average taxpayer for tax relief." The bill included an increase in the personal exemption from $750 to $1,000 and $2.1-billion cut in capital gains taxes, more than 75% of which would benefit those making over $50,000 a year. Congress rejected most of Carter's tax-reform proposals, including his plan to end deductions for the "3-martini lunch". In his televised address to the nation on inflation, **Oct. 24**, Carter said he would oppose "any further reduction in federal income taxes until we have convincing prospects that inflation will be controlled." Carter, addressing a political rally in Miami Beach **Oct. 26**, said he would sign the tax cut bill when it reached his desk.

**Tuition Tax Credits Rejected** — The House and Senate failed to compromise on tuition tax credits and passed, instead, on **Oct. 15**, Pres. Jimmy Carter's plan to increase the income level eligible for federal aid for college from $15,000 to $26,000 a year. The House had passed, on **June 1**, a bill granting tax credits for tuition paid to private and religious elementary schools as well as colleges. The Senate subsequently passed a version limited to college tuition. A compromise, including secondary but not elementary schools, agreed to by a House-Senate conference committee **Sept. 28**, was not accepted by the Senate. Pres. Carter had threatened to veto the bill if Congress passed it.

**Humphrey-Hawkins Bill Passed** — Congress passed the Humphrey-Hawkins "full-employment" bill, **Oct. 15**. The bill set national goals of reducing unemployment from the 1978 level of 6% to 4% by 1983. The bill also set the goal of reducing inflation to 3% by 1983 and to zero by 1988, but not in such a way as to "impede" reducing unemployment. The bill, which was backed strongly by black leaders, initiated no programs and left it up to the president and Congress to determine means to achieve its goals. Pres. Carter signed the bill **Oct. 27**.

**Airline Deregulation Passed** — Congress voted, **Oct. 15**, to deregulate the airline industry, phasing out federal regulation of airline routes and fares, in an effort to fight inflation and make the industry more competitive. The new law, which Pres. Carter signed **Oct. 24**, will abolish the Civil Aeronautics Board (CAB) by 1984. CAB authority over routes will be eliminated by 1981 and over fares and mergers by 1982. Before then airlines would be allowed to lower their fares by up to 50% without CAB approval. Representatives of 20 airlines lined up outside the CAB **Oct. 19-25** to be among the first to apply for routes not being served by airlines which previously had been awarded them.

**Veterans' Benefits Increased** — Congress passed, **Oct. 15**, a bill providing a 7.3% cost-of-living increase in veterans benefits, a measure affecting more than 2.5 million Americans. The bill also raised the maximum federal home loan guarantee for veterans from $17,500 to $25,000 and from $25,000 to $30,000 for special housing for the severely disabled. Pres. Jimmy Carter signed the bill **Oct. 18**.

**Worst Week in Wall St. History** — The stock market, **Oct. 20**, closed the worst week in its history with a 59.08 loss in the Dow Jones industrial average, down to 838.01. Market analysts attributed the selling pressure to fears that interest rates, already high, might go even higher, possibly setting off a recession. The market resumed its slide, **Oct. 31**, with the Dow Jones industrials falling to 792.45, their lowest close since **April 13**.

**Carter Reveals Anti-Inflation Plan** — Pres. Jimmy Carter announced, **Oct. 24**, in a televised address, his voluntary anti-inflation wage-price guidelines, including a proposed tax rebate to complying workers if inflation exceeded 7% in 1978-79. The guidelines set a 7% limit on wage increases and a limit on price increases of $1/2$% below the average increase during 1976-77. Carter promised to reduce government spending and threatened to deny federal contracts to companies that did not comply with his guidelines. Republican National Committee chairman Bill Brock attacked the plan as "blatantly political" and "too little, too late." Carter appointed, **Oct. 25**, Alfred E. Kahn, chairman of the Civil Aeronautics Board, to head the anti-inflation program. The AFL-CIO, **Oct. 31**, rejected Carter's anti-inflation program, calling for mandatory wage-price controls. Carter responded, **Nov. 1**, that mandatory controls were "a very bad thing to do and which I do not intend to do."

**Dollar Hits Record Lows** — The U.S. dollar plunged to record lows against the Japanese yen and the West German mark, **Oct. 25-30**. Dollar purchases of over $2 billion by central banks in Tokyo, Europe, and New York succeeded only in keeping the dollar from slipping any further. Foreign exchange dealers explained that the markets were disappointed with Pres. Jimmy Carter's anti-inflation plan announced **Oct. 24**. The Justice Department confirmed, **Oct. 31**, that it was "in the early stages of a civil investigation" into charges that U.S. banks had illegally manipulated trading in the dollar.

**Interest Rates Hit Record Highs** — The Federal Reserve raised the discount rate, **Oct. 31**, to a record high of $9^{1/2}$%. The same day the Federal Reserve raised the interest rate on federal funds to $9^{3/8}$% and Chase Manhattan Bank raised its prime rate to $10^{1/2}$%.

### International

**U.S. Installations Reopen in Turkey** — The U.S. reopened 4 key installations in Turkey, **Oct. 9**. The installations, which had been closed down in 1975 in retaliation against the U.S. embargo on arms sales to Turkey, were of strategic importance for monitoring Soviet military activity. Turkish permission to reopen the facilities followed congressional repeal, **Sept. 26**, of the arms embargo.

**Polish Cardinal Elected Pope** — Polish Cardinal Karol Wojtyla was elected pope, **Oct. 16**, the first non-Italian to be elevated to the papacy in 456 years. Choosing the name John Paul II, the 58-year-old Wojtyla, who had been archbishop of Crakow, honored his predecessor, John Paul I, who had reigned for 34 days. According to church sources, Wojtyla was elected when the Italian cardinals became too sharply split to agree on a candidate. The new pope was installed in an open-air ceremony in St. Peter's Square, **Oct. 22**, eliminating the use of the papal throne and tiara, as had John Paul I. The installation was attended by top officials of Poland's Communist government as well as by thousands of Poles who had been issued special passports in order to be able to make the pilgrimage to Rome. In an address **Oct. 23** to representatives of 125 nations who had come to Rome for the installation, the pope endorsed dialogue with Communist nations as "the only way to ease" problems.

**China's Trade Up 44%** — China's foreign trade increased 44% during the first 6 months of 1978 compared to the first 6 months of 1977, a Japanese trade organization reported **Oct. 20**. French officials confirmed, **Oct. 21**, that France would sell China $700 million worth of missiles. Chinese Vice Premier Teng Hsiao-ping arrived in Japan, **Oct. 22**, for an historic 8-day visit, marking what Japanese businessmen saw as "totally a new age" in Sino-Japanese trade and cooperation. The Soviet Union warned of retaliation against nations selling arms to China, the *Washington Post* reported **Oct. 27**, but, according to a Western official, "In the end it will be all bluster."

**Saudis Replace Some Syrians in Lebanon** — Syrian troops were replaced by Saudi soldiers, **Oct. 20**, at 2 key positions in Christian East Beirut. Syria retained, through control of gun emplacements on hills surrounding Beirut, the ability to shell Christian neighborhoods if new fighting were to erupt. The replacement had been arranged by the foreign ministers of the 6 Arab nations that provided men and money for the peacekeeping force in Lebanon, at a meeting in Beirut **Oct. 14-19**. A ceasefire had been in effect since **Oct. 8**, ending the savage fighting between Syrians and Christians that had brought heavy casualties in Beirut's Armenian and Maronite Christian neighborhoods during the early part of October. The Arab League agreed, **Oct. 26**, to extend the mandate of the peacekeeping force for another 6 months.

**Castro Releases Political Prisoners** — Cuban Pres. Fidel Castro, in a conciliatory gesture to the U.S., allowed 46 former political prisoners and 33 of their relatives to fly to Miami, **Oct. 21**. The U.S. State Department had announced, **Oct. 13**, that it had approved the released prisoners and their relatives for immigration, following a 6-week screening to make certain there were no spies or terrorists among them. At a **Sept. 6** news conference, Castro had said that 2,000 to 3,000 political prisoners might eventually be allowed to leave Cuba.

**Assad Visits Iraq** — Syrian Pres. Hafez Assad visited Iraq, **Oct. 24-26**, to smooth over the 12-year feud between the 2 Arab nations and form a united "eastern front" against Israel. A joint communique issued **Oct. 26** said that Assad and Iraqi Pres. Ahmed Hassan Bakr had agreed to work together toward a "full military union" against Israel. Diplomatic sources in Beirut indicated, however, that Iraq would not send more than a token military force into Syria for fear of provoking Israel. Moderates, led by Saudi Arabia and Jordan, rejected a Syrian proposal at a meeting of Arab foreign ministers in Baghdad, **Nov. 1**, refusing to impose sanctions on Egypt for making peace with Israel.

**Nobel Peace Prize to Begin, Sadat** — The Nobel Peace Prize for 1978 was awarded, **Oct. 27**, to Egyptian Pres. Anwar Sadat and Israeli Prime Minister Menahem Begin. Egypt had recalled its negotiators from peace talks in Washington, that day, in reaction to an Israeli announcement, **Oct. 25**, that Israel would "thicken" its settlements in the West Bank. Following an angry letter from Pres. Jimmy Carter to Begin, **Oct. 27**, protesting the settlements policy, and a personal appeal by Carter to Sadat, **Oct. 28**, the Egyptian president reversed his decision and announced that the negotiators would remain. Begin said, **Oct. 31**, that he hoped that the Israeli-Egyptian peace treaty could be signed **Dec. 9**, the day before he and Sadat were to receive the Peace Prize in Oslo.

**Soviet Spies Sentenced** — Valdik Enger and Rudolf Chernayev, former Soviet UN employees convicted of espionage in trying to buy U.S. military secrets, were sentenced, **Oct. 30**, by a U.S. court in Newark, N.J., to 50 years each in prison. The Soviet Union had retaliated, when the 2 spies were arrested in May, by arresting U.S. businessman Francis J. Crawford in Moscow on currency charges.

**Oil Workers Strike in Iran** — Oil workers went on strike in Iran, **Oct. 31**, cutting oil production from 5.3 million barrels a day to 2 million barrels. The workers demanded higher wages and an end to martial law. Major demonstrations continued, **Oct. 29-30**, throughout Iran, as Moslem leaders protested the Shah's modernization programs. An estimated 1,000 persons had been killed in rioting during the first 10 months of 1978.

### General

**Harrises Sentenced to 10 Years to Life** — William and Emily Harris were sentenced, **Oct. 3**, to 10 years to life in prison for the kidnaping of Patricia Hearst. With time off for good behavior and credit for time served, the couple could be released in 1983. They were already serving an 11-year-to-life sentence for a Los Angeles shootout. In the Hearst case, a clemency petition, asking for her release from a 7-year sentence for armed robbery following her kidnaping, was delivered to the Justice Department, **Sept. 25**, by Rep. Leo Ryan (D., Calif.) and Sen. S. I. Hayakawa (R., Calif.).

**Canary Island Plane Crash Report** — The Spanish government released, **Oct. 18**, a report on the 1977 crash of 2 jumbo jets in the Canary Islands, in which 583 people were killed. According to the report, the accident, which was the worst air disaster in history, was caused when "the KLM captain took off without clearance." A possible contributing factor was that "2 important radio transmissions — one from the tower and the other from the Pan Am plane — took place at the same time." More than $50 million had been paid in out-of-court settlements by the airlines and the Spanish government to survivors of the victims and 89 out of 644 cases filed remained to be settled.

**Lung Cancer Rises, Heart Deaths Fall** — Lung cancer in women rose 30% between 1973 and 1976, the National Cancer Institute reported **Oct. 19.** Increases in the numbers of women smoking and working in formerly male occupations were given as likely causes for the increase. Deaths from heart disease dropped to a 14-year low in the U.S. in 1977, according to figures released **Oct. 24** by the National Heart, Lung and Blood Institute, although heart disease remained the nation's No. 1 killer. It was not clear whether the decline could be attributed to improved care, reduction of risk factors such as smoking, diet, and lack of exercise, or other, unrecognized, factors.

**Firestone to Recall 10 Million Tires** — The Firestone Tire & Rubber Co. agreed, **Oct. 20,** to replace 10 million of

its "500" steel-belted radial tires. It was estimated that the recall would cost the company between $100 million and $200 million.

**Jascalevich Acquitted, Farber Freed** — Dr. Mario Jascalevich was acquitted, **Oct. 24,** of murdering 3 patients with curare in a N.J. hospital in 1965-1966. The same day that the 8-month-long trial came to an end, *New York Times* reporter M.A. Farber was released from jail, where he had been held for 40 days on a contempt charge for refusing to hand over his investigative notes on the case. Jascalevich had been indicted in May, 1976, following Farber's *New York Times* stories about mysterious deaths at the hospital. Farber and the *Times* had argued that the First Amendment and N.J.'s shield law guaranteed reporters' rights to protect their sources.

**Disasters** — Heavy floods ravaged southeast Asia, it was reported **Oct. 4,** driving millions of families from their homes and causing outbreaks of cholera. . . . Fires in Texas, California, and New Jersey, **Oct. 24,** took at least 7 lives and caused millions of dollars worth of damage.

## 100 Years Ago

On the last day of 1879, Thomas Alva Edison transported some 3,000 spectators by train to his laboratory at Menlo Park, N. J., to see a demonstration of hundreds of burning incandescent lamps. On Oct. 21, following thousands of experiments, he had successfully demonstrated for the first time a carbon-filament incandescent lamp. The lamp, supplied with current from his special high-voltage dynamos, maintained incandescence for more than 40 hours. Edison had filed for a patent for his incandescent lamp on Nov. 4.

Edison, despite popular belief, did not invent the incandescent lamp. But his improvement of the lamp and development of a system making electricity suitable for home lighting and competitive with gas had a great impact. Even before his patent was granted the following month, gas company shares fell dramatically. Only 3 years later, the completion of the Pearl Street central power station in New York City initiated the eventual electric illumination of all the cities of the world.

### "5-and-10-cent" Stores Born

1879 was also a revolutionary year in merchandising. Frank W. Woolworth opened his first "5-and-10-cent" store in Lancaster, Pa., the beginning of a chain that included more than 1,000 stores by the time of his death in 1919. However, the great success story almost didn't get off the ground. His first attempt, a "5-cent" store with a more limited variety of goods, established in Utica, N.Y. earlier in the year, had failed. Woolworth's premise of a store purveying inexpensive merchandise was based on the success of a 5-cent counter he had set up in W.H. Moore's Utica store.

In another marketing first, the year witnessed the introduction of the first milk bottle. Made by Louis Porter Whiteman, owner of the Warren Glass Works in Cumberland, Md., the "Warren Glass Works Glass Air Tight Milk Jars" were used by the Echo Farms Dairy Company in New York City.

Also in New York City, at Madison Square Garden, Thomas L. Rankin built the country's first indoor ice skating rink. The rink covered 6,000 square feet, and was inaugurated with a gala carnival on Feb. 12.

### Gold for Paper

On Jan. 1, the U.S. resumed specie payment, the payment of coin or bullion for paper money, a policy authorized by the Act of 1875. The policy was successful largely because of the unusual demand abroad for American agricultural products, bringing large quantities of gold into the country for the first time. Greenbacks were now worth their face value in gold. And fortunately, because the public knew that gold was plentiful, there was no rush to redeem the greenbacks.

The first session of the 46th Congress convened on Mar. 18. For the first time in the nation's history, the Democrats controlled both houses of Congress.

On Sept. 3, the Apaches led by Victorio launched a war in New Mexico with a raid at Ojo Caliente. On Sept. 11, the

Apaches attacked a ranch near Hillsboro, N. Mex.

### Women Make Headline News

On Mar. 3, Belva Ann Bennett Lockwood became the first woman to practice before the U.S. Supreme Court. This notable first was made possible by a Congressional "act to relieve certain legal disabilities of women."

Mary Cassatt, the American impressionist painter who worked in Europe, became the first American invited to exhibit with the French impressionists.

Also in 1879, Mary Baker Eddy, the founder of the Christian Science religion, became the pastor of the Church of Christ, Scientist, Boston, the year the church was formally chartered. The first public Christian Science service had been held in 1875, also the year in which Eddy published the first edition of *Science and Health.*

### War in South Africa and South America

In South Africa, the British waged the Zulu War against the Zulu King Cetywayo who had built up the military power of the Zulus. The Zulus massacred the British at Isandhlwana on Jan. 22. The British sent reinforcements to the front and, on July 4, won a decisive victory at Ulundi, captured Cetywayo on Aug. 28, and made peace with the Zulu chiefs on Sept. 1.

In South America, Chile, Apr. 5, declared war on Bolivia and Peru, beginning the War of the Pacific, also called the "saltpeter war." Chile, in need of improving its balance of payments situation, wanted saltpeter mines in Bolivia and Peru. Alleged ill treatment of Chilean minorities in the areas of the mines and vague borders served as Chile's pretext for invasion. The Chilean invasion was successful in occupying the entire Bolivian littoral in 1879. The war lasted until 1884.

### Conditioned Reflex Discovered

In Russia, Ivan Petrovich Pavlov discovered the "conditioned reflex" and succeeded in inducing "experimental neurosis" in dogs. Pavlov made the discovery by showing that production of gastric juices in dogs could be achieved without introducing food into the stomach.

At Johns Hopkins University in Baltimore, Md., Constantine Fahlberg, working under the direction of Prof. Ira Remsen, discovered saccharin.

On the literary scene, Henrik Ibsen introduced *A Doll's House,* Henry James published *Daisy Miller,* and George Meredith finished *The Egoist.* Peter Illich Tchaikovsky composed "Eugene Onegin," Pierre-Auguste Renoir painted "Mme. Charpentier and Her Children," and Auguste Rodin sculpted his "John the Baptist Preaching."

Two Russian revolutionaries-to-be, Joseph Stalin and Leon Trotsky, were born in 1879, as was British author E.M. Forster, Swiss painter Paul Klee, British-Canadian newspaper magnate Lord Beaverbrook, and Albert Einstein.

The year's necrology listed Honore Daumier, the French artist, and William Lloyd Garrison, the abolitionist.

# Deaths, Nov. 1, 1977-Nov. 1, 1978

## A

**Acker, Jean,** 85; silent screen actress; first wife of Rudolph Valentino; Los Angeles, Aug. 16.

**Addinsell, Richard,** 73; British composer of film, television, and theater scores; London, Nov. 15.

**Ahn, Philip,** Oriental character actor in films and TV; Los Angeles, Feb. 28.

**Allen, Rep. Clifford,** 66; Tennessee Democrat elected to House in 1975; Nashville, June 18.

**Allen, Sen. James B.,** 65; Alabama Democrat who led the fight against the Panama Canal treaties; Foley, Ala., June 1.

**Anderson, Heartley (Hunk),** 79; football coach whose career spanned more than 40 years; W. Palm Beach, Fla., Apr. 24.

**Artime Buesa, Manuel,** 45; Cuban physician led Bay of Pigs invasion of Cuba in 1961; Miami, Nov. 18.

**Ascoli, Max,** 79; publisher-editor of The Reporter magazine; New York, Jan. 1.

**Astor, Gertrude,** 90; actress appeared in silent films and talkies in a career spanning 50 years; Hollywood, Cal., Nov. 9.

## B

**Baldwin, Faith,** 84; author of over 85 books, including 60 novels; Norwalk, Conn., Mar. 19.

**Balopoulos, Michael,** 57; Greek colonel led the 1967 military coup that overthrew that country's democratic government; Athens, Mar. 3.

**Barlow, Perry,** 85; cartoonist for The New Yorker magazine since 1925; Westport, Conn., Dec. 26.

**Barrie, Wendy,** 65; film actress and television personality; Englewood, N.J., Feb. 2.

**Begle, Edward G.,** 65; foremost proponent of the "new math;" Palo Alto, Cal., Mar. 2.

**Bergen, Edgar,** 75; ventriloquist whose career spanned 56 years in vaudeville, radio, television, and films; Las Vegas, Sept. 30.

**Best, Dr. Charles,** 79; physician and co-discoverer of insulin treatment for diabetes; Toronto, Mar. 31.

**Betz, Carl,** 56; actor starred in TV's "Judd for the Defense" and "The Donna Reed Show;" Los Angeles, Jan. 18.

**Biddle, Katherine,** 87; widow of former U.S. Attorney General Francis Biddle; poet and literary critic; Devon, Pa., Dec. 30.

**Bleibtrey, Ethelda,** 76; swimmer won 3 Olympic gold medals in 1920; W. Palm Beach, Fla., May 6.

**Bond, Johnny,** 63; country singer and songwriter; Burbank, Cal., June 12.

**Borland, Hal,** 77; writer and naturalist; Sharon, Conn., Feb. 22.

**Bostock, Lyman,** 27; outfielder for the California Angels; one of the highest paid players in baseball; Gary, Ind., Sept. 24.

**Boucher, Frank,** 76; hockey hall of famer won Lady Byng trophy 7 times; Ottawa, Dec. 12.

**Bowles, Heloise,** 58; author of the "Hints From Heloise" column which appeared in 600 newspapers; San Antonio, Dec. 28.

**Boyer, Charles,** 78; French actor famed as one of the screen's great lovers in the 30s and 40s; Phoenix, Aug. 26.

**Breech, Ernest Robert,** 81; executive headed Ford, Bendix, and TWA; Royal Oak, Mich., July 3.

**Brel, Jacques,** 49; Belgian composer and singer; Paris, Oct. 9.

**Bruce, David K. E.,** 79; diplomat headed U.S. embassies in London, Paris, and Bonn; headed delegation at the Paris Vietnam peace talks; Washington, D.C., Dec. 4.

**Brugnon, Jacques,** 82; one of the "four musketeers" of French tennis who dominated the sport between 1922-31; Paris, Mar. 20.

**Burch, Preston M.,** 93; thoroughbred horse trainer; Middleburg, Va., Apr. 4.

## C

**Carlson, Richard,** 65; actor appeared in over 40 films; starred in TV's "I Led Three Lives;" Encino, Cal., Nov. 25.

**Carter, Maybelle,** 69; singer and composer headed country music's Carter Family; Madison, Tenn., Oct. 23.

**Catton, Bruce,** 78; author and historian wrote 13 volumes on the Civil War; won Pulitzer prize for "A Stillness at Appomattox" in 1954; Frankfort, Mich., Aug. 28.

**Cazale, John,** 42; stage and film actor; New York, Mar. 12.

**Chaplin, Charlie,** 88; actor starred in over 80 films mostly as the Little Tramp; "The Gold Rush," "The Kid," "Modern Times;" Switzerland, Dec. 25.

**Chase, Ilka,** 72; actress of stage and screen; authored over a dozen books; Mexico City, Feb. 15.

**Chavez, Carlos,** 79; Mexican composer and conductor; Mexico City, Aug. 2.

**Clapper, Aubrey (Dit),** 70; hockey hall of famer played 20 seasons with the Boston Bruins; Peterborough, Ont., Jan. 20.

**Clark, Earl (Dutch),** 71; quarterback in NFL hall of fame; Canon City, Col., Aug. 5.

**Clay, Gen. Lucius D.,** 80; commander of U.S. forces in Europe after WW2; led Berlin airlift; Cape Cod, Mass., Apr. 16.

**Cole, Charles W.,** 71; president of Amherst College, 1946-60; U.S. ambassador to Chile; at sea, Feb. 6.

**Colombo Sr., Joseph,** 54; founder of the Italian-American Civil Rights League; Newburgh, N.Y., May 22.

**Combs, George Hamilton Jr.,** 78; radio commentator; W. Palm Beach, Fla., Nov. 29.

**Conant, James B.,** 84; scientist, diplomat, and educator; Hanover, N.H., Feb. 11.

**Cox, Billy,** 58; Brooklyn Dodgers 3d baseman in the 50s; Harrisburg, Pa., Mar. 31.

**Cozzens, James Gould,** 74; author wrote 16 books and countless short stories; won Pulitzer prize for novel "Guard of Honor" in 1948; Stuart, Fla., Aug. 9.

**Craig, Cleo F.,** 85; former head of American Telephone and Telegraph Co.; Ridgewood, N.J., Apr. 21.

**Crane, Bob,** 49; actor starred in TV's "Hogan's Heroes;" Scottsdale, Ariz., June 29.

**Crawford, Ralston,** 71; abstract painter and lithographer; Houston, Apr. 27.

**Cully, Zara,** 86; actress played Mother Jefferson on TV's "The Jeffersons;" Los Angeles, Feb. 28.

## D

**Dailey, Dan,** 62; actor and dancer starred in numerous musicals in the 40s and 50s; Hollywood, Cal., Oct. 17.

**Daly, James,** 59; character actor had over 600 television credits; Nyack, N.Y., July 3.

**Davis, F.W.,** 91; inventor of power steering unit; Cambridge, Mass., Apr. 16.

**Davis, Hal,** 63; president of the American Federation of Musicians since 1970;

New York, Jan. 11.

**Denny, Sandy,** 30; singer and composer twice voted Britain's top pop singer; London, Apr. 21.

**Diederichs, Nicholaas,** 74; president of South Africa since 1975; Cape Town, Aug. 21.

**Dill, Clarence C.,** 93; U.S. Senator from Washington, 1922-36; helped draft the Federal Communications Act; Spokane, Jan. 14.

**Dodd, Mrs. John,** 96; whose suggestion for a "Father's Day" was adopted in 1910; Spokane, Mar. 22.

**Doeg, John Hope,** 69; tennis star in the 30s; Redding, Cal., May 25.

**Downs, Joseph H.,** 72; White House policeman wounded in the 1950 attempted assassination of President Truman; Baltimore, July 13.

## E

**Eames, Charles,** 71; industrial designer best known for a molded plywood chair designed in 1940; St. Louis, Aug. 21.

**Eccles, Marriner S.,** 87; headed Federal Reserve Board, 1936-48; helped shape New Deal economic policy; Salt Lake City, Dec. 18.

**Eglevsky, Andre,** 60; ballet dancer; Elmira, N.Y., Dec. 4.

**Eilers, Sally,** 68; actress appeared in over 40 films mostly in the 30s; Beverly Hills, Cal., Jan. 5.

**Estabrook, Howard,** 94; Hollywood screenwriter won an Academy Award for "Cimarron" in 1931; Woodland Hills, Cal., July 16.

**Evans, Bergen,** 72; author and authority on the English language; TV host; Highland Park, Ill., Feb. 4.

## F

**Fabian, Robert,** 77; famed Scotland Yard detective; Surrey, Eng., June 14.

**Fields, Totie,** 48; comedienne starred on television and in nightclubs; Las Vegas, Aug. 2.

**Finney, Thomas D.,** 52; Washington attorney, political strategist, and advisor to Presidents Kennedy and Johnson; Ayer, Mass., Jan. 31.

**Fitch, Adm. Aubrey,** 94; commanded U.S. task force planes in the Battle of the Coral Sea in WW2; Newcastle, Me., May 22.

**Fontaine, Frank,** 58; veteran comedian best known for his character "Crazy Guggenheim;" Spokane, Wash., Aug. 4.

**Freeman, Don,** 69; illustrator, author of books for children; New York, Feb. 1.

**Frick, Ford,** 83; commissioner of baseball, 1951-65; Bronxville, N.Y., Apr. 8.

## G

**Gainza Paz, Alberto,** 78; Argentine newspaper publisher; Buenos Aires, Dec. 26.

**Gaud, William S.,** 70; administrator of the Agency for International Development, 1966-69; coined the term "the green revolution;" Washington, D.C., Dec. 5.

**Geer, Will,** 76; character actor whose career spanned 6 decades; best known as the grandfather on TV's "The Waltons;" Los Angeles, Apr. 22.

**Geller, Bruce,** 47; writer and producer originated the "Mission Impossible" and "Mannix" TV programs; Santa Barbara, Cal., May 21.

**Genn, Leo,** 72; British stage and screen actor; London, Jan. 26.

**Gilliam, Jim,** 49; baseball player and coach for the Dodgers since 1953; Inglewood, Cal., Oct. 8.

**Gilson, Etienne,** 86; French philosopher, historian; Cravant, Yonne, France, Sept. 19.

**Godel, Kurt,** 71; mathematical logician; colleague of Einstein; Princeton, N.J., Jan. 14.

**Goff, Norris,** 72; actor played Abner on the "Lum and Abner" radio comedy series; Palm Desert, Cal., June 7.

**Goldmark, Dr. Peter,** 71; scientist invented the LP phonograph record; Westchester Co., N.Y., Dec. 7.

**Gordon, Joe,** 63; baseball player was the American League's MVP in 1942; Sacramento, Cal., Apr. 15.

**Gordon, John F.,** 77; president of General Motors, 1958-65; Royal Oak, Mich., Jan. 6.

**Gordon, Robert Aaron,** 69; economist, an authority on business cycles and manpower policy; Berkeley, Cal., Apr. 7.

**Greenwood, Charlotte,** 87; stage and film comedian; Los Angeles, Jan. 18.

**Gronchi, Giovanni,** 91; president of Italy, 1955-1962; Rome, Oct. 17.

**Guenther, Rennert,** 67; German opera director who staged operas in Europe and the U.S.; Salzburg, July 29.

**H**

**Haddad, Dr. Wadi,** 49; guerrilla leader; a founder of the Popular Front for the Liberation of Palestine; Algiers, Mar. 28.

**Haines, Jesse,** 85; baseball hall of fame pitcher won 210 games for the St. Louis Cardinals; Columbus, Oh., Aug. 5.

**Haney, Fred,** 79; baseball manager and executive; Beverly Hills, Cal., Nov. 9.

**Harrah, William F.,** 67; Nevada casino pioneer; Rochester, Minn., June 30.

**Harris, Bucky,** 81; baseball hall of famer managed 5 major league teams; Bethesda, Md., Nov. 8.

**Hasselblad, Victor,** 72; Swedish industrialist and inventor of the cameras that took the first close-up pictures of the moon; Gothenburg, Sweden, Aug. 6.

**Hawks, Howard,** 81; film director, "Sgt. York," "Scarface," "Red River;" Palm Springs, Cal., Dec. 26.

**Homolka, Oscar,** 79; character actor in films, television, and the theater; Sussex, Eng., Jan. 27.

**Humphrey, Sen. Hubert H.,** 66; Minnesota Democrat spent 32 years in public service; vice president during the Johnson administration; candidate for president, 1968; Waverly, Minn., Jan. 13.

**Hyams, Leila,** 72; actress starred in films in the 20s and 30s; Bel-Air, Cal., Dec. 4.

**J**

**James, Charles,** 72; innovative dress designer; New York, Sept. 23.

**Jennewein, Carl Paul,** 87; neo-classical sculptor; Larchmont, N.Y., Feb. 22.

**John Paul I, Pope (Albino Luciani),** 65; spiritual leader whose papacy lasted but 34 days; Vatican City, Sept. 28.

**Johnston, Neil,** 49; basketball star led the NBA in scoring 3 times during his career; Bedford, Tex., Sept. 28.

**Josephson, Matthew,** 79; biographer whose writings ranged from French literary figures to American capitalists; Santa Cruz, Cal., Mar. 13.

**K**

**Karasavina, Tamara,** 93; Russian-born ballerina; London, May 26.

**Keller, Greta,** 70s; cabaret singer; Vienna, Nov. 4.

**Kelly, Stephen E.,** 58; publisher headed Saturday Evening Post, Holiday, and McCall's magazines; New York, Apr. 6.

**Kelso, James L.,** 85; archeologist credited with discovering ancient city of Bethel in Jordan; Pittsburgh, June 28.

**Kenny, Bill,** 55; tenor led Ink Spots vocal group in the 30s and 40s; Vancouver, B.C., Mar. 23.

**Kenyatta, Jomo,** 80s; President of Kenya and symbol of African nationalism during that continent's struggle for independence; Mombasa, Kenya, Aug. 22.

**Ketchum, Rep. William M.,** 56; California Republican entered the House in 1973; Bakersfield, Cal., June 24.

**Khachaturian, Aram,** 74; Soviet composer best known for his "Sabre Dance;" Moscow, May 1.

**Kiernan, Walter,** 75; newspaper columnist and radio and TV commentator, "One Man's Opinion;" Daytona Beach, Fla., Jan. 8.

**King, Carleton,** 73; New York Republican served 7 terms in congress, 1960-74; Bradenton, Fla., Nov. 19.

**King, Cyril E.,** 56; governor of the Virgin Islands; Charlotte Amalie, Jan. 2.

**King, Teddi,** 48; jazz singer; New York, Nov. 18.

**Kipnis, Alexander,** 87; Russian-born bass starred at the Metropolitan and Chicago Civic operas; Westport, Conn., May 14.

**Kompfner, Dr. Rudolf,** 68; physicist invented the traveling wave tube; Stanford, Conn., Dec. 3.

**Krag, Jens Otto,** 63; former Danish prime minister who led his nation into the Common Market; Denmark, June 22.

**Kulakov, Fyodor D.,** 60; Soviet Politburo member viewed as possible successor to Brezhnev; Moscow, July 16.

**L**

**Lear, William Powell,** 75; industrialist pioneered small jet aircraft; invented car radio, automatic pilot, 8-track stereo cartridge; Reno, Nev., May 14.

**Leavis, F.R.,** 82; British literary critic; Cambridge, Apr. 14.

**Leibowitz, Samuel S.,** 84; jurist, Scottsboro Case lawyer; Brooklyn, N.Y., Jan. 11.

**Lenham, Gen. Charles T.,** 76; leader of the first American military unit to reach Paris in WW2; Chevy Chase, Md., July 20.

**Lewis, Albert,** 93; Broadway producer whose hits included "Cabin in the Sky" and "Rain;" Beverly Hills, Cal., Apr. 6.

**Light, Enoch,** 71; bandleader and stereo recording innovator; New York, July 31.

**Lindner, Richard,** 76; figure painter; New York, Apr. 16.

**Lombardo, Guy,** 75; bandleader whose mellow music remained popular for a half century; famed for New Year's Eve celebrations; Houston, Nov. 5.

**Lubin, Isador,** 82; economist supervised and made famous the consumer price index; a leading member of the New Deal "brain trust;" Annapolis, Md., July 6.

**M**

**MacArthur, John D.,** 80; insurance magnate and real estate billionaire reputed to be one of the richest men in U.S.; W. Palm Beach, Fla., Jan. 6.

**Mallowan, Max,** 74; British archeologist best known for excavations in the Middle East; widower of Agatha Christie; Oxfordshire, Eng., Aug. 19.

**von Manteuffel, Hasso,** 81; German tank commander who drove a 50-mile wedge into the Allied lines during the Battle of the Bulge in 1944; Austria, Sept. 23.

**Marais, Josef,** 72; folk singer, writer, and composer; Los Angeles, Apr. 27.

**Marshall, Gen. S.L.A.,** 77; military historian; El Paso, Tex., Dec. 17.

**Martinson, Harry,** 73; Swedish poet and novelist won Nobel prize in 1974; Stockholm, Feb. 11.

**Mason, F. van Wyck,** 74; writer of 58 historical novels, mysteries, and spy stories; Bermuda, Aug. 28.

**McCarthy, Joe,** 90; baseball manager led the N.Y. Yankees to 8 AL pennants and 7 world series titles; Buffalo, N.Y., Jan. 14.

**McClellan, Sen. John L.,** 81; Arkansas Democrat served 35 years in the Senate; chairman of the Appropriation Committee; Little Rock, Nov. 27.

**McCoy, Tim,** 86; cowboy movie star appeared in some 80 films; Nogales, Ariz., Jan. 29.

**McGinley, Phyllis,** 72; poet won Pulitzer prize in 1961; New York, Feb. 22.

**McGrath, Paul,** 74; actor best known as the grim voiced host of the Inner Sanctum radio mysteries; London, Apr. 13.

**McNamara, Maggie,** 48; actress starred on stage and screen in "The Moon is Blue;" New York, Feb. 18.

**Meadows, Algur H.,** 79; oilman and philanthropist; Dallas, June 10.

**Menzies, Sir Robert G.,** 83; Australian political leader served 2 terms as prime minister; Melbourne, May 14.

**Mercader, Ramon,** 65; convicted assassin of exiled Communist leader Leon Trotsky in 1940; Havana, Oct.

**Messel, Oliver,** 74; British theatrical designer for opera, ballet, movies, and the theater; Barbados, July 13.

**Messerschmitt, Willy,** 80; German aircraft designer whose Me-109 ruled the skies early in WW2; Munich, Sept. 15.

**Metcalf, Sen. Lee,** 66; Montana Democrat served 18 years in the Senate; Helena, Mont., Jan. 12.

**Metcalfe, Rep. Ralph H.,** 68; represented Chicago's South Side in the House since 1970; former Olympic athlete; Chicago, Oct. 10.

**Meusel, Bob,** 81; N.Y. Yankee outfielder who was a member of the famed "murderers row;" Downey, Cal., Nov. 28.

**Mikoyan, Anastas,** 82; former president of the Soviet Union and a prominent figure in the Communist Party and Soviet government for half a century; USSR, Oct. 21.

**Montoya, Sen. Joseph M.,** 62; New Mexico Democrat served in the Senate 1964-76; Washington, D.C., June 5.

**Moon, Keith,** 31; drummer for the British rock group The Who; London, Sept. 7.

**Moore, Sir Henry,** 91; British admiral directed air-sea strikes against German units off Norway in 1944; Kent, Eng. Mar. 12.

**Moreell, Adm. Ben,** 85; organized the U.S. Navy's Seabee construction battalions during WW2; Pittsburgh, July 30.

**Moro, Aldo,** 61; former prime minister of Italy; Rome, May 9.

**Morris** 17; the finicky cat who starred on television for 10 years in a cat food commercial; Chicago, July 7.

**Morrison, Bret,** 66; actor played "The Shadow" on radio in the 30s and 40s; Hollywood, Cal., Sept. 25.

**Murphy, Robert D.,** 83; career diplomat; credited with planning the Allied invasion of North Africa in WW2; New York, Jan. 9.

**Murphy, William,** 78; Democrat served Illinois in the House, 1959-71; Oak Park, Ill., Jan. 29.

**N**

**Nabokov, Nicolas,** 75; Russian-born composer and writer; New York, Apr. 6.

**Nebel, Long John,** 66; hosted all-night radio talk show for 20 years; New York, Apr. 10.

**Nikodim, Archbishop Boris,** 48; metropolitan of Leningrad and a leader of the World Council of Churches; Vatican City, Sept. 5.

**Nilsson, Gunnar,** 29; Swedish Grand Prix racing driver; London, Oct. 20.

**Nobile, Gen. Umberto,** 93; Italian aviator and polar explorer; Rome, July 29.

**Noble, Ray,** 71; British orchestra leader and composer; London, Apr. 3.

**Norrish, Ronald,** 80; British chemist awarded Nobel prize in 1967; England, June 7.

**O**

**Oakie, Jack,** 74; comic actor appeared in over 100 movies; Northridge, Cal., Jan. 23.

**Obolensky, Serge,** 87; Russian-born society leader; kin to Tsars; Grosse Pointe, Mich., Sept. 29.

**O'Brien, Davey,** 60; Texas Christian quarterback won the Heisman trophy in 1938; Ft. Worth, Tex., Nov. 18.

**O'Neill, C. William,** 62; chief justice of the Ohio supreme court; former governor of that state; Columbus, Oh., Aug. 20.

**P**

**Paul, Dr. William D.,** 77; inventor of buffered aspirin; Iowa City, Ia., Dec. 19.

**Paul VI, Pope (Giovanni Battista Montini),** 80; spiritual leader of the Roman Catholic Church since 1963; Castel Gandolfo, Aug. 6.

**Payne, Frederick G.,** 73; former U.S. Senator and governor of Maine; Waldoboro, Me., June 15.

**Peckinpaugh, Roger,** 86; baseball player, manager, and front-office executive; New York, Nov. 17.

**Pei, Mario Andrew,** 77; linguist and author, "The Story of Language"; Glen Ridge, N.J., Mar. 2.

**Peterson, Ronnie,** 34; Swedish racing driver won 10 Grand Prix races; Milan, Italy, Sept. 12.

**Poulter, Thomas C.,** 81; scientist and inventor; 2d in command on Byrd's Arctic expedition, 1933-35; Menlo Park, Cal., June 14.

**Prabhupada, Swami (A.C. Bhaktivedanta),** 81; founder of Hare Krishna movement in the U.S.; Vrindaban, India; Nov. 14.

**Prima, Louis,** 66; bandleader famed for his jazz trumpet and raspy baritone; New Orleans, Aug. 24.

**R**

**Rattigan, Terence,** 66; British playwright, "Separate Tables;" Bermuda, Nov. 30.

**Rattner, Abraham,** 82; colorist painter, printmaker, and tapestry designer; New York, Feb. 14.

**Ray, Joie,** 84; distance runner amassed over 950 medals in his career; Benton Harbor, Mich., May 13.

**Rich, Lorimer,** 86; architect designed the Tomb of the Unknown Soldier at Arlington; Rome, N.Y., June 2.

**Ritchard, Cyril,** 79; Australian-born actor, singer, and director; Chicago, Dec. 18.

**Ritter, Willis W.,** 79; controversial chief judge of U.S. District Court in Utah; Salt Lake City, Mar. 4.

**Roberts, Gilbert,** 78; structural engineer designed Scotland's Firth of Forth bridge; England, Jan. 1.

**Robson, Mark,** 64; film director whose works include "Champion," "Earthquake," and "Peyton Place;" London, June 20.

**Rockefeller John D., 3d,** 72; philanthropist, eldest member of one of the nation's wealthiest families; Westchester Co., N.Y., July 10.

**Rockwell, George (Doc),** 88; comedian, writer, and cartoonist; Brunswick, Me., Mar. 3.

**Rockwell, William F.,** 90; founder of Rockwell International; Pittsburgh, Oct. 16.

**Rosenberg, Harold,** 72; art critic; The Springs, N.Y., July 11.

**Ross, Nellie Tayloe,** 101; first woman governor in the U.S., Wyoming, 1924; Washington, D.C., Dec. 19.

**Ross, Rev. Roy G.,** 79; religious leader helped found the National Council of Churches; Pompano Beach, Fla., Jan. 8.

**Rubicam, Raymond,** 85; co-founder of major U.S. advertising agency; Scottsdale, Ariz., May 8.

**Rueff, Jacques Leon,** 81; French economist advocated a return to the gold standard; Paris, Apr. 23.

**Rupp, Adolph F.,** 76; basketball coach at Univ. of Kentucky won record 879 games and 4 national championships; Lexington, Ky., Dec. 10.

**S**

**Schippers, Thomas,** 47; conductor of opera, symphony; New York, Dec. 16.

**Schoeffler, Paul,** 70; German-born opera baritone noted for Wagner roles; Amersham, Eng., Nov. 21.

**Schoyer, B. Preston,** 66; novelist and author of articles on China; Stamford, Conn., Mar. 13.

**Schuschnigg, Kurt,** 79; Austrian chancellor who was unsuccessful in stopping Germany's annexation of his country, 1938; Innsbruck, Nov. 18.

**Scott, Paul,** 57; British novelist "The Raj Quartet;" London, Mar. 1.

**Selwyn-Lloyd, Lord,** 73; British foreign secretary, 1956-60; speaker of the House of Commons, 1971-76; Oxfordshire, Eng., May 17.

**Serly, Tibor,** 78; Hungarian-born composer, conductor, and music theorist; London, Oct. 8.

**Shaw, Robert,** 51; British actor, novelist, and playwright; County Mayo, Ire., Aŭg. 28.

**Shay, Dorothy,** 57; singer billed as the "Park Avenue Hillbilly;" Santa Monica, Cal., Oct. 22.

**Sheekman, Arthur,** 76; Hollywood writer collaborated with Groucho Marx on comedy films; a founder of the Screen Writers Guild; Santa Monica, Cal., Jan. 12.

**Siegbahn, Manne,** 91; Swedish physicist won the Nobel prize in 1924; Stockholm, Sept. 30.

**Smith, Mayo,** 62; managed the Detroit Tigers to the world championship in 1968; Boynton Beach, Fla., Nov. 24.

**Sobukwe, Robert,** 53; black South African nationalist leader founded Pan-African Congress; Kimberley, So. Africa, Feb. 27.

**Solomon, Samuel J.,** 78; aviation industry pioneer; Bethesda, Md., Dec. 8.

**Spencer-Churchill, Lady Clementine;** 92; widow of Sir Winston Churchill; London, Dec. 12.

**Steinberg, William,** 78; German-born conductor headed the Pittsburgh and Boston symphonies; New York, May 16.

**Stone, Edward Durell,** 76; architect who designed buildings throughout the world including the U.S. Embassy in New Delhi and the Kennedy Center in Washington; New York, Aug. 6.

**Street, Mel,** 43; country music singer; Nashville, Oct. 21.

**Student, Gen. Kurt,** 88; German commander planned air rescue mission that freed Mussolini from detention in 1943; West Germany, July 1.

**Stulberg, Louis,** 76; president of the International Ladies Garment Worker's Union, 1966-75; New York, Dec. 14.

**Swenson, Karl,** 70; veteran character actor appeared on the stage, radio, television, and in films; Torrington, Conn., Oct. 8.

**T**

**Thomas, Alma,** 86; abstract painter; Washington, D.C., Feb. 24.

**Tourneur, Jacques,** 73; director known chiefly for horror films; Bergerac, France, Dec. 19.

**Traglia, Luigi Cardinal,** 82; dean of the Roman Catholic Sacred College of Cardinals since 1974; Rome, Nov. 22.

**Truesdell, Gen. Karl,** 70; leader of first Air Force daylight bombing of Berlin in WW2; Phoenix, Aug. 22.

**Turner, Thomas Wyatt,** 101; civil rights pioneer and educator; Washington, D.C., Apr. 21.

**U**

**Untermeyer, Louis,** 92; poet, critic, and producer of 90 anthologies; Newtown, Conn., Dec. 18.

**V**

**Vasilevsky, Marshall Aleksandr M.,** 82; Soviet army chief of staff during WW2; Moscow, Dec. 5.

**Venuti, Joe,** 80s; jazz violinist; Seattle, Aug. 14.

**Vidor, Florence,** 82; silent screen actress; Pacific Palisades, Cal., Nov. 3.

**W**

**Wallenda, Karl,** 73; patriarch of the famed troupe of high-wire performers; San Juan, P.R., Mar. 22.

**Warner, Jack L.,** 86; last of Warner Bros. film pioneers, led studio for 40 years; Los Angeles, Sept. 9.

**Warner, Sylvia Townsend,** 85; novelist, poet, and short-story writer; Dorset, Eng., May 1.

**Wengenroth, Stow,** 71; lithographer best known for scenes of New England; Gloucester, Mass., Jan. 22.

**Wheatley, Dennis,** 80; British author of mystery novels and historical romances; London, Nov. 11.

**Whitehead, Cmdr. Edward,** 69; businessman led Schweppes tonic water advertising campaign; Petersfield, Eng., Apr. 16.

**Widdemer, Margaret,** 93; prize-winning poet, author of 32 novels; Gloversville, N.Y., July 14.

**Williams, Jay,** 64; author wrote numerous historical novels and science fiction stories for children; England, July 12.

**Willkie, Edith Wilk,** 87; widow of Wendell Willkie, the 1940 Republican presidential nominee; Indianapolis, Apr. 16.

**Wilson, Michael,** 63; Hollywood screenwriter, "A Place in the Sun," "The Bridge on the River Kwai;" Beverly Hills, Cal., Apr. 9.

**Wolf, Steve,** 34; rock music promoter; Los Angeles, Nov. 21.

**Wolff, Robert J.,** 72; abstract painter; New Preston, Conn., Dec. 29.

**Wood, Peggy,** 86; actress appeared in over 70 Broadway plays; starred in TV's "I Remember Mama;" Stamford, Conn., Mar. 18.

**Woodworth, Laurance,** 59; chief draftsman of President Carter's tax proposals; Newport News, Va., Dec. 7.

**Wragge, Sydney,** 70; women's fashion designer; Boca Raton, Fla., Mar. 23.

**Wrathall, John James,** 65; British-born president of Rhodesia since 1976; Salisbury, Aug. 31.

**Wright, Lloyd,** 88; architect best known for his Wayfarer's Chapel in Los Angeles; son of Frank Lloyd Wright; Santa Monica, Cal., May 31.

**Y**

**Young, Gig,** 60; actor appeared in 55 Hollywood films, mostly as the second lead; New York, Oct. 19.

**Youngdahl, Luther,** 82; former federal judge and 3-term governor of Minnesota; Washington, D.C., June 21.

**Yu Pin, Paul,** 77; archbishop of Nanking, the Roman Catholic Church's only Chinese cardinal; Rome, Aug. 16.

**Z**

**Zukofsky, Louis,** 74; poet; Port Jefferson, N.Y., May 12.

# VITAL STATISTICS

Source: National Center for Health Statistics, U.S. Department of Health, Education, and Welfare

## January-June 1978

### Births

Birth statistics for the first half of 1978, 1,595,000 live births, were lower than comparable data for 1977, 1,610,000. The decline in the number of births amounted to about 1%. The birth rate for this period, 14.8 per 1,000 population, was also 1% lower than the rate for the corresponding period in 1977. The fertility rate was 3% lower, 64.5 per 1,000 women, compared with 66.4.

### Marriages

In the first half of 1978 a total of 1,049,000 marriages was reported, yielding an increase of 16,000 over the total for the first half of 1977. The marriage rate for this 6-month period, 9.7 per 1,000 population, was slightly higher than the rate for the corresponding period in 1977, 9.6.

### Divorces

Divorces totaled 552,000 for the first half of 1978. This represented an increase of 16,000, or 3%, over the number estimated for the period from January to June 1977. The divorce rate increased from 5.0 per 1,000 population for the first half of 1977 to 5.1 for the corresponding period of 1978.

### Deaths

For June 1978 the provisional count of deaths furnished by the 50 states and the District of Columbia totaled 153,000, which amounts to a rate of 8.5 deaths per 1,000 population. Among these 153,000 were 3,800 deaths at ages under 1 year, yielding an infant mortality rate of 14.2 deaths per 1,000 live births.

The provisional death rate for the 12 months ending with May 1978, 889.5 per 100,000 population, was 1% higher than the corresponding rate for the 12 months ending with May 1977, 874.1 per 100,000.

#### Provisional Statistics
12 months ending with June

|  | Number | | Rate* | |
|---|---|---|---|---|
|  | 1978 | 1977 | 1978 | 1977 |
| Live births . . . . | 3,298,000 | 3,265,000 | 15.2 | 15.2 |
| Deaths . . . . . . | 1,934,000 | 1,886,000 | 8.9 | 8.7 |
| Natural increase. | 1,364,000 | 1,379,000 | 6.3 | 6.5 |
| Marriages . . . . | 2,193,000 | 2,179,000 | 10.1 | 10.1 |
| Divorces . . . . . | 1,105,000 | 1,076,000 | 5.1 | 5.0 |
| Infant deaths . . . | 46,000 | 47,400 | 13.9 | 14.5 |
| Population base (in millions) . . . . . . . . . . . . . . . | | | 217.3 | 215.5 |

*Per 1,000 population

## Annual Report for the Year 1977 (Provisional Statistics)

### Births

The number of births in the United States rose during 1977. There were an estimated 3,313,000 live births, about 4% more than the final number for 1976.

The birth rate rose from 14.8 births per 1,000 population in 1976 to 15.3 in 1977. The fertility rate of 67.4 births per 1,000 women 15-44 years of age was 2% higher than the final rate for 1976.

The increase in the number of births is a result of the increase in the number of women in the child-bearing ages (15-44 years).

During 1977 the growth of the population due to natural increase (the excess of births over deaths) amounted to 1,415,000 persons. The rate of natural increase was 6.5 persons per 1,000 population compared with a final rate of 5.9 for 1976.

### Deaths

An estimated 1,898,000 deaths occurred in the United States during 1977. The provisional death rate was 8.8 per 1,000 population, a decline from the final rate for 1976.

In 1977 there were approximately 46,500 infant deaths resulting in the estimated infant mortality rate of 14.0 per 1,000 live births.

### Marriages and Divorces

Provisional reports indicate that 2,176,000 marriages were performed in 1977, about 21,000 greater than the 1976 final total of 2,154,807. The number of marriages in 1977 fell approximately 100,000 short of the record 2,277,000 marriages performed in 1973. In 1977 the provisional marriage rate rose. It was 10.1 per 1,000 population, 1% higher than the final rate for 1976, and 10% lower than the 22-year high reached in 1972.

According to provisional estimates, 1,090,000 divorces were granted in 1977, representing an increase of 7,000 or 0.6% over the final count in 1976. The number of divorces in the United States increased every year after 1962 and more than doubled between 1966 (499,000 divorces) and 1976 (1,083,000 divorces). In recent years the increase has slowed, and the additional number of divorces has been smaller each year since 1971.

While the increase in divorces has been diminishing, it still outpaced population growth, resulting in a higher divorce rate. Estimated from provisional reports, the 1977 divorce rate was 5.0 per 1,000 population, nearly double the 1967 divorce rate of 2.6. The divorce rate has increased every year since 1967, however, the rate of increase has declined in more recent years to remain the same, 5.0 per 1,000 population, as the 1976 final rate.

## Births and Deaths in the U.S.

Refers only to events occurring within the U.S., including Alaska and Hawaii beginning in 1960. Excludes fetal deaths. Rates per 1,000 population enumerated as of April 1 for 1955, and 1960; estimated as of July 1 for all other years. (p) provisional. (NA) not available.

| Year | Births | | | | Deaths | | | |
|---|---|---|---|---|---|---|---|---|
|  | Males | Females | Total number | Rate | Males | Females | Total number | Rate |
| 1955 . . . . . | 2,073,719 | 1,973,576 | 4,047,295 | 24.6 | 872,638 | 656,079 | 1,528,717 | 9.3 |
| 1960 . . . . . | 2,179,708 | 2,078,142 | 4,257,850 | 23.7 | 975,648 | 736,334 | 1,711,982 | 9.5 |
| 1965 . . . . . | 1,927,054 | 1,833,304 | 3,760,358 | 19.4 | 1,035,200 | 792,936 | 1,828,136 | 9.4 |
| 1970 . . . . . | 1,915,378 | 1,816,008 | 3,731,386 | 18.4 | 1,078,478 | 842,553 | 1,921,031 | 9.5 |
| 1973 . . . . . | 1,608,326 | 1,528,639 | 3,136,965 | 14.9 | 1,096,795 | 876,208 | 1,973,003 | 9.4 |
| 1975 . . . . . | 1,613,135 | 1,531,063 | 3,144,198 | 14.8 | 1,050,819 | 842,060 | 1,892,879 | 8.9 |
| 1976 . . . . . | 1,624,436 | 1,543,352 | 3,167,788 | 14.8 | 1,051,983 | 857,457 | 1,909,440 | 8.9 |
| 1977(p) . . . . . . . . | NA | NA | 3,313,000 | 15.3 | NA | NA | 1,898,000 | 8.8 |

## Births and Deaths by States

Source: National Center for Health Statistics, U.S. Department of Health, Education, and Welfare

| State | Births 1977p | Births 1976 | Deaths 1977p | Deaths 1976 | State | Births 1977p | Births 1976 | Deaths 1977p | Deaths 1976 |
|---|---|---|---|---|---|---|---|---|---|
| Alabama | 60,917 | 57,283 | 34,366 | 34,058 | Nebraska | 25,140 | 24,019 | 14,390 | 14,690 |
| Alaska | 8,379 | 7,816 | 1,688 | 1,649 | Nevada | 10,152 | 9,530 | 5,331 | 4,921 |
| Arizona | 41,591 | 40,044 | 18,459 | 17,881 | New Hampshire | 12,064 | 11,087 | 7,139 | 7,327 |
| Arkansas | 34,502 | 33,294 | 20,986 | 21,129 | New Jersey | 90,981 | 87,778 | 64,339 | 63,742 |
| California | 338,716 | 332,238 | 169,657 | 171,454 | New Mexico | 22,433 | 21,666 | 8,193 | 8,118 |
| Colorado | 43,424 | 41,345 | 18,494 | 18,668 | New York | 237,894 | 237,040 | 165,923 | 171,952 |
| Connecticut | 36,065 | 35,422 | 25,775 | 26,181 | North Carolina | 84,772 | 80,583 | 46,701 | 46,115 |
| Delaware | 8,771 | 8,300 | 4,884 | 4,970 | North Dakota | 12,228 | 11,398 | 5,492 | 5,751 |
| Dist. of Col. | 20,648 | 19,908 | 7,460 | 9,180 | Ohio | 162,353 | 155,546 | 96,238 | 95,814 |
| Florida | 111,414 | 104,005 | 93,559 | 91,257 | Oklahoma | 43,805 | 42,269 | 26,006 | 26,412 |
| Georgia | 85,138 | 80,880 | 43,431 | 42,196 | Oregon | 38,398 | 35,613 | 20,710 | 20,493 |
| Hawaii | 17,024 | 16,402 | 4,723 | 4,719 | Pennsylvania | 153,654 | 149,318 | 119,689 | 120,816 |
| Idaho | 18,242 | 16,884 | 6,146 | 6,323 | Rhode Island | 11,932 | 11,102 | 9,208 | 9,315 |
| Illinois | 173,945 | 167,679 | 100,998 | 101,221 | South Carolina | 48,419 | 46,082 | 23,916 | 23,027 |
| Indiana | 85,425 | 80,620 | 46,852 | 46,781 | South Dakota | 11,917 | 11,488 | 6,220 | 6,575 |
| Iowa | 45,270 | 42,131 | 26,355 | 27,572 | Tennessee | 70,032 | 65,653 | 41,128 | 41,324 |
| Kansas | 34,820 | 33,538 | 20,661 | 21,194 | Texas | 235,791 | 227,409 | 102,182 | 102,414 |
| Kentucky | 60,532 | 56,964 | 34,035 | 32,165 | Utah | 38,237 | 36,220 | 7,976 | 7,808 |
| Louisiana | 76,155 | 70,002 | 34,837 | 34,782 | Vermont | 6,413 | 6,444 | 4,345 | 4,373 |
| Maine | 15,695 | 14,519 | 10,178 | 10,401 | Virginia | 71,298 | 67,247 | 39,444 | 39,590 |
| Maryland | 47,909 | 45,514 | 31,338 | 31,706 | Washington | 55,038 | 52,804 | 30,074 | 30,565 |
| Massachusetts | 71,049 | 67,668 | 52,623 | 54,387 | West Virginia | 30,118 | 28,583 | 19,349 | 19,731 |
| Michigan | 137,565 | 130,259 | 73,124 | 74,959 | Wisconsin | 68,561 | 64,696 | 39,301 | 40,121 |
| Minnesota | 60,145 | 56,939 | 32,216 | 33,458 | Wyoming | 7,530 | 6,890 | 2,953 | 3,109 |
| Mississippi | 45,419 | 42,678 | 22,895 | 22,805 | | | | | |
| Missouri | 72,361 | 71,319 | 49,270 | 50,076 | **Total** | **3,313,000** | **3,167,788** | **1,898,000** | **1,909,440** |
| Montana | 13,004 | 12,360 | 6,304 | 6,632 | (p) provisional | | | | |

## Marriages and Divorces by States

Source: National Center for Health Statistics, U.S. Department of Health, Education, and Welfare

1977 provisional figures; divorces include reported annulments.

| State | Marriages | Divorces | State | Marriages | Divorces | State | Marriages | Divorces |
|---|---|---|---|---|---|---|---|---|
| Alabama | 45,394 | 23,505 | Louisiana | 38,343 | NA | Oklahoma | 41,440 | 21,450 |
| Alaska | 5,092 | 3,805 | Maine | 11,526 | 5,751 | Oregon | 20,850 | 16,623 |
| Arizona | 28,270 | NA | Maryland | 44,973 | 15,701 | Pennsylvania | 91,382 | 37,675 |
| Arkansas | 24,038 | 18,366 | Massachusetts | 39,728 | 16,040 | Rhode Island | 7,096 | 3,414 |
| California | 151,346 | 132,888 | Michigan | 86,221 | 42,081 | South Carolina | 51,157 | 11,428 |
| Colorado | 29,435 | 20,250 | Minnesota | 31,593 | 13,896 | South Dakota | 10,300 | NA |
| Connecticut | 22,851 | 11,859 | Mississippi | 26,481 | 12,828 | Tennessee | 55,327 | 28,227 |
| Delaware | 3,999 | 3,044 | Missouri | 52,138 | 25,621 | Texas | 161,331 | 83,215 |
| Dist. of Col. | 4,601 | 2,935 | Montana | 7,532 | 4,841 | Utah | 15,188 | 6,901 |
| Florida | 89,142 | 63,326 | Nebraska | 12,978 | 6,258 | Vermont | 4,825 | 1,938 |
| Georgia | 67,192 | 30,096 | Nevada | 108,013 | 10,301 | Virginia | 57,832 | 21,577 |
| Hawaii | 10,274 | 4,653 | New Hampshire | 8,792 | 4,256 | Washington | 41,308 | 25,646 |
| Idaho | 13,439 | 5,841 | New Jersey | 50,016 | 20,027 | West Virginia | 17,522 | 9,552 |
| Illinois | 108,051 | 50,553 | New Mexico | 12,445 | 6,880 | Wisconsin | 37,283 | 14,932 |
| Indiana | 56,290 | NA | New York | 131,611 | 50,171 | Wyoming | 5,789 | 3,085 |
| Iowa | 26,422 | 10,938 | North Carolina | 43,400 | 25,065 | | | |
| Kansas | 23,556 | 12,652 | North Dakota | 5,672 | 1,982 | **Total** | **2,176,000** | **1,090,000** |
| Kentucky | 34,030 | 16,156 | Ohio | 97,358 | 55,552 | (NA) not available. | | |

## Marriages, Divorces, and Rates in the U.S.

Source: National Center for Health Statistics, Public Health Service

Data refer only to events occurring within the United States, including Alaska and Hawaii beginning with 1960. Rates per 1,000 population.

| Year | Marriages[1] No. | Marriages[1] Rate | Divorces[2] No. | Divorces[2] Rate | Year | Marriages[1] No. | Marriages[1] Rate | Divorces[2] No. | Divorces[2] Rate |
|---|---|---|---|---|---|---|---|---|---|
| 1890 | 570,000 | 9.0 | 33,461 | 0.5 | 1940 | 1,595,879 | 12.1 | 264,000 | 2.0 |
| 1895 | 620,000 | 8.9 | 40,387 | 0.6 | 1945 | 1,612,992 | 12.2 | 485,000 | [3]3.5 |
| 1900 | 709,000 | 9.3 | 55,751 | 0.7 | 1950 | 1,667,231 | 11.1 | 385,144 | 2.6 |
| 1905 | 842,000 | 10.0 | 67,976 | 0.8 | 1955 | 1,531,000 | 9.3 | 377,000 | 2.3 |
| 1910 | 948,166 | 10.3 | 83,045 | 0.9 | 1960 | 1,523,000 | 8.5 | 393,000 | 2.2 |
| 1915 | 1,007,595 | 10.0 | 104,298 | 1.0 | 1965 | 1,800,000 | 9.3 | 479,000 | 2.5 |
| 1920 | 1,274,476 | 12.0 | 170,505 | 1.6 | 1970 | 2,158,802 | 10.6 | 708,000 | 3.5 |
| 1925 | 1,188,334 | 10.3 | 175,449 | 1.5 | 1975 | 2,152,662 | 10.1 | 1,036,000 | 4.9 |
| 1930 | 1,126,856 | 9.2 | 195,961 | 1.6 | 1976 | 2,154,807 | 10.0 | 1,083,000 | 5.0 |
| 1935 | 1,327,000 | 10.4 | 218,000 | 1.7 | 1977(p). | 2,176,000 | 10.1 | 1,090,000 | 5.0 |

(1) Includes estimates and marriage licenses for some states for all years. (2) Includes reported annulments. (3) Divorce rates for 1945 based on population including armed forces overseas. (p) provisional.

## Wedding Anniversaries

The traditional names for wedding anniversaries go back many years in social usage. As such names as wooden, crystal, silver, and golden were applied it was considered proper to present the married pair with gifts made of these products or or something related. While the list of permissible gifts is extensive, gifts are most appropriate when retaining a suggestion of the originals. Thus the wooden anniversary may call for anything of wood, including furniture, but as the years mount the gifts become more valuable until the 60th or diamond anniversary, calls for diamonds. The traditional list follows, with a few allowable revisions in parentheses.

| | | | |
|---|---|---|---|
| 1st—Paper | 6th—Iron | 11th—Steel | 20th—China | 45th—Sapphire |
| 2d—Cotton | 7th—Wool (copper) | 12th—Silk | 25th—Silver | 50th—Gold |
| 3d—Leather | 8th—Bronze | 13th—Lace | 30th—Pearl | 55th—Emerald |
| 4th—Linen (silk) | 9th—Pottery (china) | 14th—Ivory | 35th—Coral (jade) | 60th—Diamond |
| 5th—Wood | 10th—Tin (aluminum) | 15th—Crystal | 40th—Ruby | 75th—Diamond |

## Deaths and Death Rates for Selected Causes

Source: National Center for Health Statistics, U.S. Department of Health, Education, and Welfare

Rates per 100,000 population

| 1977* Cause of death | Number | Rate | 1977* Cause of death | Number | Rate |
|---|---|---|---|---|---|
| All causes . . . . . . . . . . . . . . . | 1,898,000 | 877.4 | Acute bronchitis and bronchiolitis . . . . . . | 680 | 0.3 |
| Enteritis and other diarrheal diseases . . . . | 1,510 | 0.7 | Influenza and pneumonia . . . . . . . . . . . | 49,960 | 23.1 |
| Tuberculosis, all forms . . . . . . . . . . | 2,960 | 1.4 | influenza . . . . . . . . . . . . . . . . | 1,060 | 0.5 |
| Syphilis and its sequelae . . . . . . . . . | 130 | 0.1 | Pneumonia . . . . . . . . . . . . . . . | 48,900 | 22.6 |
| Other infective and parasitic diseases. . . . | 3,840 | 1.8 | Bronchitis, emphysema, and asthma . . . . | 22,220 | 10.3 |
| Malignant neoplasms, including | | | Chronic and unqualified bronchitis . . . . | 4,310 | 2.0 |
| neoplasms of lymphatic and | | | Emphysema . . . . . . . . . . . . . . . | 16,320 | 7.5 |
| hematopoietic tissues . . . . . . . . . . | 387,430 | 179.1 | Asthma . . . . . . . . . . . . . . . . | 1,590 | 0.7 |
| Diabetes mellitus . . . . . . . . . . . . | 33,570 | 15.5 | Peptic ulcer. . . . . . . . . . . . . . . | 6,320 | 2.9 |
| Meningitis . . . . . . . . . . . . . . . | 1,620 | 0.7 | Hernia and intestinal obstruction. . . . . . . | 5,660 | 2.6 |
| Major cardiovascular diseases. . . . . . . | 960,090 | 443.8 | Cirrhosis of liver . . . . . . . . . . . . . | 31,260 | 14.5 |
| Diseases of heart . . . . . . . . . . | 717,320 | 331.6 | Cholelithiasis, cholecystitis, and cholangitis. | 2,770 | 1.3 |
| Active rheumatic fever and chronic | | | Nephritis and nephrosis. . . . . . . . . . | 8,130 | 3.8 |
| rheumatic heart disease . . . . . . . | 12,560 | 5.8 | Infections of kidney . . . . . . . . . . . | 3,650 | 1.7 |
| Hypertensive heart disease and | | | Hyperplasia of prostate . . . . . . . . . . | 910 | 0.4 |
| renal disease . . . . . . . . . . . | 3,700 | 1.7 | Congenital anomalies . . . . . . . . . . | 12,540 | 5.8 |
| Ischemic heart disease . . . . . . . . | 637,670 | 294.8 | Certain causes of mortality in early infancy. | 23,310 | 10.8 |
| Chronic disease of endocardium and | | | Symptoms and ill-defined conditions . . . . | 32,150 | 14.9 |
| other myocardial insufficiency . . . | 3,930 | 1.8 | All other diseases . . . . . . . . . . . . | 128,620 | 59.5 |
| All other forms of heart disease . . . . | 52,800 | 24.4 | Accidents . . . . . . . . . . . . . . . . | 105,020 | 48.5 |
| Hypertension . . . . . . . . . . . . . | 5,310 | 2.5 | Motor vehicle accidents . . . . . . . . . | 50,380 | 23.3 |
| Cerebrovascular diseases . . . . . . . | 182,840 | 84.5 | All other accidents . . . . . . . . . . | 54,640 | 25.3 |
| Arteriosclerosis. . . . . . . . . . . . | 29,040 | 13.4 | Suicide . . . . . . . . . . . . . . . . | 28,390 | 13.1 |
| Other diseases of arteries, | | | Homicide . . . . . . . . . . . . . . . | 21,090 | 9.7 |
| arterioles, and capillaries . . . . . | 25,580 | 11.8 | All other external causes . . . . . . . . . | 4,230 | 2.0 |

*Provisional. Due to rounding estimates of death, figures may not add to total. Data based on a 10% sampling of all death certificates for a 12-month (Jan.-Dec.) period.

## Principal Types of Accidental Deaths

Source: National Center for Health Statistics, U.S. Department of Health, Education, and Welfare

| Year | All types | Motor vehicle | Falls | Burns | Drowning | Firearms | Machinery | Poison gases | Other poisons |
|---|---|---|---|---|---|---|---|---|---|
| 1960 . . | 93,806 | 38,137 | 19,023 | 7,645 | 6,529 | 2,334 | 1,951 | 1,253 | 1,679 |
| 1965 . . | 108,004 | 49,163 | 19,984 | 7,347 | 6,799 | 2,344 | 2,054 | 1,526 | 2,110 |
| 1970 . . | 114,638 | 54,633 | 16,926 | 6,718 | 6,391 | 2,406 | . . . | 1,620 | 3,679 |
| 1975 . . | 103,030 | 45,853 | 14,896 | 6,071 | 6,640 | 2,380 | . . . | 1,577 | 4,694 |
| 1976 . . | 100,761 | 47,038 | 14,136 | 6,338 | 5,645 | 2,059 | . . . | 1,569 | 4,161 |
| | | | Death rates per 100,000 population | | | | | | |
| 1960 . . | 52.1 | 21.2 | 10.6 | 4.2 | 3.6 | 1.3 | 1.1 | 0.7 | 0.9 |
| 1965 . . | 55.7 | 25.4 | 10.3 | 3.8 | 3.5 | 1.2 | 1.1 | 0.8 | 0.1 |
| 1970 . . | 56.4 | 26.9 | 8.3 | 3.3 | 3.1 | 1.2 | . . . | 0.8 | 1.8 |
| 1975 . . | 48.4 | 21.5 | 7.0 | 2.8 | 3.1 | 1.1 | . . . | 0.7 | 2.2 |
| 1976 . . | 46.9 | 21.9 | 6.6 | 3.0 | 2.6 | 1.0 | . . . | 0.7 | 1.9 |

## Deaths in Civil Aviation Accidents

Source: National Safety Council

(includes only U.S. carriers)

| Year | Total deaths[1] | Passenger deaths in scheduled flights Domestic No. | Rate[2] | International No. | Rate[2] | General aviation deaths No. | Rate[2] |
|---|---|---|---|---|---|---|---|
| 1960. . . . . . . . . . . . | 1,286 | 297 | 0.93 | 10 | 0.12 | 787 | 24 |
| 1965. . . . . . . . . . . . | 1,279 | 205 | 0.38 | 21 | 0.12 | 1,029 | 21 |
| 1970. . . . . . . . . . . . | 1,454 | 0 | 0.00 | 2 | 0.01 | 1,310 | 20* |
| 1975. . . . . . . . . . . . | 1,448 | 113 | 0.09 | 0 | 0.00 | 1,345 | 16 |
| 1977p. . . . . . . . . . . | 1,843 | 64 | 0.04 | 0 | 0.00 | 1,437 | 16 |

(1) Includes some deaths not shown separately—crew members in scheduled operations and persons not in planes killed in airplane accidents. Excludes deaths in military plane accidents. (2) Rates are the number of deaths per 100,000,000 passenger miles. General aviation rates (NSC estimate) include deaths of general aviation passengers, pilots, and other crew members. *Rates for this year and subsequent years not comparable with prior years.—less than 0.005. (p) preliminary.

## Accidental Injuries by Severity of Injury

Source: National Safety Council

| 1977 Severity of injury | Total* | Motor vehicle | Work | Home | Public non-motor vehicle |
|---|---|---|---|---|---|
| Deaths* . . . . . . . . . . . . . . . . | 104,000 | 49,500 | 13,000 | 24,000 | 22,000 |
| Disabling injuries* . . . . . . . . . . . | 10,400,000 | 1,900,000 | 2,300,000 | 3,600,000 | 2,800,000 |
| Permanent impairments. . . . . | 380,000 | 150,000 | 80,000 | 100,000 | 70,000 |
| Temporary total disabilities . . . | 10,000,000 | 1,750,000 | 2,200,000 | 3,500,000 | 2,700,000 |
| | Certain Costs of Accidental Injuries, 1977 ($ billions) | | | | |
| Total* . . . . . . . . . . . . . . . | $62.0 | $30.5 | $20.7 | $6.6 | $5.4 |
| Wage loss . . . . . . . . . . . | 18.3 | 8.8 | 4.1 | 3.2 | 3.2 |
| Medical expense . . . . . . . . | 7.5 | 2.5 | 2.2 | 1.7 | 1.3 |
| Insurance administration . . . . | 12.3 | 9.1 | 3.0 | 0.1 | 0.1 |

*Duplication between motor vehicle, work, and home are eliminated in the total column.

## Physical Growth Range for Children from 1 to 17 Years

Source: Division of Health Examination Statistics, U.S. Department of Health, Education, and Welfare

### Boys

| Age | Shortest 5% | Median height | Tallest 5% | Lightest 5% | Median weight | Heaviest 5% |
|---|---|---|---|---|---|---|
| 1 | 30.1 | 32.6 | 35.5 | 21.3 | 25.5 | 32.2 |
| 2 | 33.4 | 35.7 | 38.7 | 24.4 | 29.8 | 36.0 |
| 3 | 36.2 | 38.7 | 41.6 | 28.4 | 34.3 | 40.7 |
| 4 | 38.4 | 41.7 | 44.9 | 31.0 | 38.8 | 47.0 |
| 5 | 41.2 | 44.5 | 47.4 | 35.5 | 44.0 | 56.8 |
| 6 | 42.9 | 46.5 | 50.2 | 37.6 | 47.5 | 61.9 |
| 7 | 45.4 | 49.2 | 52.7 | 41.5 | 54.3 | 70.9 |
| 8 | 47.4 | 50.7 | 54.1 | 45.1 | 56.5 | 71.4 |
| 9 | 48.3 | 53.2 | 57.0 | 50.5 | 67.5 | 93.0 |
| 10 | 51.4 | 55.0 | 59.4 | 56.2 | 73.1 | 110.5 |
| 11 | 53.4 | 57.4 | 61.3 | 62.7 | 81.6 | 116.3 |
| 12 | 55.0 | 60.1 | 65.4 | 69.4 | 93.3 | 134.3 |
| 13 | 57.2 | 62.4 | 68.7 | 77.1 | 107.8 | 147.1 |
| 14 | 59.9 | 65.6 | 70.4 | 91.5 | 119.8 | 164.1 |
| 15 | 61.6 | 67.5 | 72.7 | 93.4 | 127.8 | 171.6 |
| 16 | 64.1 | 69.0 | 74.0 | 112.9 | 144.9 | 197.4 |
| 17 | 64.8 | 69.5 | 73.7 | 113.6 | 144.8 | 202.8 |

### Girls

| Age | Shortest 5% | Median height | Tallest 5% | Lightest 5% | Median weight | Heaviest 5% |
|---|---|---|---|---|---|---|
| 1 | 28.1 | 31.9 | 34.5 | 18.8 | 23.8 | 29.5 |
| 2 | 32.6 | 35.4 | 38.4 | 23.7 | 28.2 | 34.1 |
| 3 | 36.0 | 38.3 | 41.4 | 27.3 | 32.8 | 40.3 |
| 4 | 37.8 | 41.0 | 44.8 | 29.8 | 36.5 | 46.6 |
| 5 | 40.7 | 44.0 | 47.6 | 33.4 | 41.7 | 58.6 |
| 6 | 43.3 | 46.5 | 50.0 | 37.5 | 46.9 | 60.7 |
| 7 | 45.9 | 48.7 | 53.0 | 42.5 | 51.6 | 70.0 |
| 8 | 46.9 | 50.9 | 54.4 | 45.8 | 57.6 | 86.0 |
| 9 | 49.6 | 53.3 | 58.0 | 52.3 | 69.3 | 98.0 |
| 10 | 50.8 | 55.4 | 61.2 | 56.4 | 71.8 | 104.0 |
| 11 | 53.1 | 58.4 | 63.8 | 63.1 | 87.2 | 131.4 |
| 12 | 56.2 | 60.8 | 65.0 | 72.0 | 99.0 | 143.8 |
| 13 | 59.0 | 62.6 | 65.6 | 83.9 | 108.9 | 166.0 |
| 14 | 59.4 | 63.4 | 67.4 | 88.5 | 112.5 | 166.8 |
| 15 | 60.0 | 64.3 | 69.3 | 95.6 | 119.9 | 170.4 |
| 16 | 59.6 | 63.5 | 68.0 | 95.4 | 120.0 | 171.8 |
| 17 | 59.3 | 63.5 | 68.1 | 94.1 | 125.3 | 186.9 |

This table simply gives a general picture for American children. When used as a standard, the individual variation in children's growth should not be overlooked. In most cases the height-weight relationship is probably a more valid index of weight status than a weight-for-age assessment.

## Average Weight of Americans by Height and Age

Source: Society of Actuaries; based on a 4-year study of 5,000,000 persons
The figures represent weights in ordinary indoor clothing and shoes, and heights with shoes.

| Height | Men 20-24 | 25-29 | 30-39 | 40-49 | 50-59 | Height | Women 20-24 | 25-29 | 30-39 | 40-49 | 50-59 |
|---|---|---|---|---|---|---|---|---|---|---|---|
| 5'0" | 122 | 128 | 131 | 134 | 136 | 4'10" | 102 | 107 | 115 | 122 | 125 |
| 5'1" | 125 | 131 | 134 | 137 | 139 | 4'11" | 105 | 110 | 117 | 124 | 127 |
| 5'2" | 128 | 134 | 137 | 140 | 142 | 5'0" | 108 | 113 | 120 | 127 | 130 |
| 5'3" | 132 | 138 | 141 | 144 | 145 | 5'1" | 112 | 116 | 123 | 130 | 133 |
| 5'4" | 136 | 141 | 145 | 148 | 149 | 5'2" | 115 | 119 | 126 | 133 | 136 |
| 5'5" | 139 | 144 | 149 | 152 | 153 | 5'3" | 118 | 122 | 129 | 136 | 140 |
| 5'6" | 142 | 148 | 153 | 156 | 157 | 5'4" | 121 | 125 | 132 | 140 | 141 |
| 5'7" | 145 | 151 | 157 | 161 | 162 | 5'5" | 125 | 129 | 135 | 143 | 148 |
| 5'8" | 149 | 155 | 161 | 165 | 166 | 5'6" | 129 | 133 | 139 | 147 | 152 |
| 5'9" | 153 | 159 | 165 | 169 | 170 | 5'7" | 132 | 136 | 142 | 151 | 156 |
| 5'10" | 157 | 163 | 170 | 174 | 175 | 5'8" | 136 | 140 | 146 | 155 | 160 |
| 5'11" | 161 | 167 | 174 | 178 | 180 | 5'9" | 140 | 144 | 150 | 159 | 164 |
| 6'0" | 166 | 172 | 179 | 183 | 185 | 5'10" | 144 | 148 | 154 | 164 | 169 |
| 6'1" | 170 | 177 | 183 | 187 | 189 | 5'11" | 149 | 153 | 159 | 169 | 174 |
| 6'2" | 174 | 182 | 188 | 192 | 194 | 6'0" | 154 | 158 | 164 | 174 | 180 |
| 6'3" | 178 | 186 | 193 | 197 | 199 | | | | | | |
| 6'4" | 181 | 190 | 199 | 203 | 205 | | | | | | |

## How to Obtain Birth, Marriage, Death Records

The United States government has published a series of inexpensive booklets entitled: Where to Write for Birth & Death Records; Where to Write for Marriage Records; Where to Write for Divorce Records; Where to Write for Birth and Death Records of U. S. Citizens Who were Born or Died Outside of the U. S.; Birth Certifications for Alien Children Adopted by U. S. Citizens; You May Save Time Proving Your Age and Other Birth Facts. They tell where to write to get a certified copy of an original vital record. Supt. of Documents, Government Printing Office, Washington, DC 20402.

# The Nation's Hospitals

Source: American Hospital Association

In 1977, there were 7,099 hospitals in the United States registered by the American Hospital Association. These institutions had about 1.41 million beds and reported admitting some 37.1 million inpatients. About $63.6 billion was spent to provide services for both inpatients and outpatients, or a cost of $294 per resident of the nation.

| State | Hospitals Fed. | Hospitals Non-fed. | Beds Fed. | Beds Non-fed. | Average daily census Fed. | Average daily census Non-fed. | Admissions Fed. | Admissions Non-fed. | Expenses ($1,000) Fed. | Expenses ($1,000) Non-fed. |
|---|---|---|---|---|---|---|---|---|---|---|
| Alabama . . . . | 8 | 141 | 2,734 | 22,464 | 2,268 | 16,979 | 38,639 | 690,601 | 113,823 | 821,691 |
| Alaska . . . . | 9 | 17 | 577 | 1,120 | 359 | 699 | 18,233 | 39,689 | 40,389 | 77,257 |
| Arizona . . . . | 17 | 63 | 1,756 | 9,384 | 1,287 | 6,818 | 56,770 | 310,967 | 117,471 | 522,096 |
| Arkansas . . . | 4 | 93 | 1,932 | 11,657 | 1,631 | 8,110 | 24,628 | 396,594 | 71,159 | 382,104 |
| California . . . | 32 | 593 | 10,323 | 105,055 | 7,484 | 73,198 | 221,186 | 3,123,862 | 671,078 | 6,276,628 |
| Colorado . . . | 7 | 96 | 1,851 | 13,224 | 1,511 | 9,186 | 41,547 | 430,876 | 122,042 | 635,214 |
| Connecticut . . | 5 | 59 | 1,014 | 18,065 | 724 | 14,385 | 17,898 | 437,052 | 60,599 | 902,191 |
| Delaware . . . | 2 | 14 | 367 | 4,321 | 281 | 3,741 | 6,216 | 76,632 | 17,358 | 161,072 |
| Dist. of Columbia | 4 | 16 | 4,097 | 5,753 | 3,804 | 4,527 | 38,967 | 173,500 | 253,355 | 416,680 |
| Florida . . . . | 14 | 233 | 4,080 | 50,774 | 3,322 | 36,469 | 98,430 | 1,472,130 | 270,267 | 2,221,293 |
| Georgia . . . | 10 | 178 | 3,032 | 28,141 | 2,331 | 20,083 | 56,658 | 874,925 | 161,459 | 1,064,718 |
| Hawaii . . . . | 1 | 27 | 530 | 3,338 | 442 | 2,529 | 20,075 | 98,731 | 40,255 | 169,372 |
| Idaho . . . . | 2 | 49 | 192 | 3,505 | 139 | 2,370 | 5,406 | 128,645 | 12,388 | 137,628 |
| Illinois . . . . | 10 | 276 | 6,187 | 69,948 | 4,842 | 54,198 | 78,349 | 1,955,925 | 261,369 | 3,562,738 |
| Indiana . . . . | 5 | 131 | 2,106 | 32,352 | 1,662 | 24,918 | 20,649 | 851,723 | 69,904 | 255,495 |
| Iowa . . . . . | 3 | 138 | 1,619 | 19,930 | 1,324 | 13,574 | 17,307 | 550,012 | 63,361 | 673,088 |
| Kansas . . . | 7 | 155 | 1,986 | 16,130 | 1,513 | 11,310 | 25,853 | 438,884 | 82,622 | 577,131 |
| Kentucky . . . | 5 | 117 | 1,851 | 16,898 | 1,601 | 13,060 | 44,339 | 601,005 | 101,633 | 642,454 |
| Louisiana . . . | 9 | 151 | 2,464 | 22,552 | 1,789 | 15,882 | 44,288 | 715,329 | 114,303 | 857,502 |
| Maine . . . . | 2 | 52 | 736 | 6,590 | 631 | 4,700 | 6,492 | 174,583 | 26,030 | 262,890 |
| Maryland . . . | 11 | 72 | 3,257 | 21,608 | 2,536 | 17,970 | 51,162 | 499,416 | 204,930 | 1,053,435 |
| Massachusetts | 7 | 186 | 3,802 | 43,833 | 3,211 | 34,878 | 30,251 | 919,677 | 142,519 | 2,387,727 |
| Michigan . . . | 8 | 244 | 2,699 | 49,724 | 1,971 | 38,969 | 34,822 | 1,452,128 | 112,065 | 2,678,758 |
| Minnesota . . | 5 | 184 | 1,791 | 29,350 | 1,542 | 21,068 | 22,584 | 703,966 | 78,135 | 1,077,246 |
| Mississippi . . | 5 | 109 | 1,716 | 15,214 | 1,432 | 10,901 | 30,724 | 432,178 | 75,131 | 434,093 |
| Missouri . . . | 7 | 162 | 3,183 | 32,484 | 2,538 | 24,033 | 56,592 | 908,652 | 198,218 | 1,359,874 |
| Montana . . . | 6 | 59 | 388 | 4,731 | 277 | 2,962 | 9,544 | 134,600 | 20,539 | 145,488 |
| Nebraska . . . | 5 | 103 | 954 | 10,519 | 705 | 6,860 | 20,398 | 282,187 | 46,772 | 365,846 |
| Nevada . . . . | 4 | 21 | 297 | 2,946 | 197 | 1,933 | 7,166 | 98,764 | 16,500 | 159,597 |
| New Hampshire | 2 | 31 | 263 | 4,734 | 229 | 3,420 | 5,742 | 130,716 | 19,273 | 171,614 |
| New Jersey . . | 4 | 136 | 2,918 | 42,281 | 2,267 | 33,665 | 31,985 | 1,056,039 | 109,767 | 1,852,351 |
| New Mexico . . | 11 | 43 | 1,015 | 5,537 | 725 | 3,771 | 32,598 | 153,437 | 57,635 | 209,710 |
| New York . . . | 16 | 367 | 10,052 | 130,727 | 8,455 | 110,432 | 98,560 | 2,687,226 | 411,621 | 6,698,322 |
| North Carolina . | 9 | 151 | 2,995 | 31,225 | 2,504 | 24,074 | 54,280 | 860,612 | 141,311 | 1,070,690 |
| North Dakota . | 5 | 56 | 392 | 5,607 | 260 | 3,900 | 11,985 | 135,111 | 21,255 | 170,406 |
| Ohio . . . . . | 6 | 242 | 4,358 | 63,411 | 3,468 | 50,417 | 43,825 | 1,815,944 | 171,828 | 2,917,189 |
| Oklahoma . . . | 12 | 130 | 1,135 | 16,151 | 844 | 11,052 | 39,250 | 469,802 | 81,452 | 593,764 |
| Oregon . . . . | 2 | 86 | 992 | 11,039 | 817 | 7,546 | 16,377 | 358,657 | 45,970 | 506,942 |
| Pennsylvania . . | 11 | 307 | 6,281 | 83,087 | 4,938 | 65,279 | 51,450 | 1,915,319 | 227,900 | 3,516,979 |
| Rhode Island . | 2 | 19 | 445 | 6,396 | 329 | 5,528 | 10,757 | 135,596 | 30,738 | 300,481 |
| South Carolina . | 7 | 82 | 1,601 | 15,736 | 1,273 | 11,804 | 47,751 | 428,652 | 96,854 | 504,935 |
| South Dakota . | 10 | 60 | 1,246 | 4,732 | 977 | 3,114 | 21,331 | 123,960 | 46,131 | 122,748 |
| Tennessee . . . | 5 | 159 | 2,882 | 28,353 | 2,445 | 21,660 | 41,951 | 872,901 | 110,457 | 1,042,651 |
| Texas . . . . . | 24 | 544 | 8,895 | 69,056 | 7,249 | 47,571 | 183,754 | 2,203,060 | 471,245 | 2,730,444 |
| Utah . . . . . | 2 | 38 | 541 | 4,495 | 382 | 3,191 | 12,455 | 189,761 | 29,435 | 224,539 |
| Vermont . . . . | 1 | 18 | 224 | 2,851 | 196 | 2,144 | 4,054 | 74,759 | 13,513 | 110,392 |
| Virginia . . . . | 11 | 124 | 3,285 | 28,927 | 2,671 | 21,976 | 67,380 | 719,772 | 200,414 | 1,037,955 |
| Washington . . | 11 | 117 | 2,544 | 13,706 | 1,781 | 9,250 | 49,481 | 537,870 | 141,049 | 703,377 |
| West Virginia . . | 6 | 77 | 1,272 | 14,238 | 1,032 | 10,897 | 18,725 | 376,544 | 57,008 | 468,913 |
| Wisconsin . . . | 3 | 169 | 2,182 | 27,575 | 1,760 | 19,383 | 23,338 | 759,621 | 93,964 | 1,170,547 |
| Wyoming . . . | 3 | 27 | 551 | 2,033 | 444 | 1,162 | 5,315 | 63,673 | 18,123 | 61,220 |
| Total U.S. . . . . | 377 | 6,722 | 123,590 | 1,283,507 | 98,400 | 967,546 | 2,017,517 | 35,042,265 | 6,162,623 | 57,467,475 |

---

# Selected Statistics on State and County Mental Hospitals

Source: National Institute of Mental Health

| Year | Total admitted | Net releases | Deaths in hospital | Residents end of year | Expense per patient |
|---|---|---|---|---|---|
| 1955 . . . . . . . . . . . . | 178,003 | NA | 44,384 | 558,922 | $1,116.59 |
| 1960 . . . . . . . . . . . . | 234,791 | NA | 49,748 | 535,540 | 1,702.41 |
| 1970 . . . . . . . . . . . . | 393,174 | 394,627 | 30,804 | 338,592 | 5,435.38 |
| 1973 . . . . . . . . . . . . | 377,020* | 386,962 | 19,899 | 248,562 | 9,207.92 |
| 1975 . . . . . . . . . . . . | 376,156 | 391,345 | 13,401 | 193,436 | 13,634.53 |
| 1976 . . . . . . . . . . . . | NA | NA | 10,922 | 170,619 | NA |

*Includes estimates. NA-not available. (1) Per average daily resident patient population.

---

# Patients in State and County Mental Hospitals

Source: National Institute of Mental Health

Average daily census 1976. The following data was based on reports of the 300 state and county hospitals.

| State | Number | State | Number | State | Number | State | Number |
|---|---|---|---|---|---|---|---|
| United States . . . | 177,760 | Arizona . . . . . . . | 642 | Colorado . . . . . . | 1,012 | District of Columbia | 2,484 |
| Alabama . . . . . . | 2,556 | Arkansas . . . . . . | 358 | Connecticut . . . . . | 4,483 | Florida . . . . . . . . | 5,922 |
| Alaska . . . . . . . | 129 | California . . . . . . | 7,989 | Delaware . . . . . . | 739 | Georgia . . . . . . . | 5,641 |

## Suicide Rates

Source: National Center for Health Statistics, U.S. Department of Health, Education, and Welfare

(Rates per 100,000 population) (1976)

| Age group | Total | Male | Female | White Total | White Male | White Female | All other Total | All other Male | All other Female |
|---|---|---|---|---|---|---|---|---|---|
| Total. . . . . . . | 12.5 | 18.7 | 6.7 | 13.3 | 19.8 | 7.2 | 7.0 | 11.0 | 3.2 |
| 10-14 years . . . | 0.8 | 1.2 | 0.4 | 0.8 | 1.3 | 0.3 | 0.6 | 0.5 | 0.7 |
| 15-19 years . . . | 7.4 | 11.4 | 3.2 | 7.7 | 11.9 | 3.3 | 5.4 | 8.4 | 2.5 |
| 20-24 years . . . | 16.4 | 26.4 | 6.4 | 16.8 | 27.0 | 6.6 | 13.8 | 22.6 | 5.7 |
| 25-29 years . . . | 15.8 | 24.1 | 7.6 | 16.0 | 24.1 | 7.8 | 14.7 | 24.4 | 6.4 |
| 30-34 years . . . | 16.0 | 22.9 | 9.3 | 16.4 | 23.1 | 9.7 | 13.2 | 20.8 | 6.7 |
| 35-39 years . . . | 15.9 | 22.6 | 9.6 | 16.7 | 23.2 | 10.5 | 10.5 | 18.5 | 4.0 |
| 40-44 years . . . | 16.8 | 23.0 | 10.8 | 17.8 | 24.0 | 11.6 | 9.8 | 15.1 | 5.5 |
| 45-49 years . . . | 19.1 | 25.9 | 12.7 | 20.4 | 27.3 | 13.7 | 9.4 | 14.6 | 5.0 |
| 50-54 years . . . | 19.3 | 26.5 | 12.7 | 20.7 | 28.1 | 13.9 | 7.7 | 12.3 | 3.7 |
| 55-59 years . . . | 20.4 | 29.4 | 12.3 | 21.9 | 31.3 | 13.3 | 6.9 | 11.2 | 3.2 |
| 60-64 years . . . | 19.4 | 30.3 | 9.9 | 20.7 | 32.0 | 10.7 | 7.5 | 13.7 | 2.3 |
| 65-69 years . . . | 19.1 | 32.3 | 8.6 | 20.4 | 34.5 | 9.2 | 7.7 | 13.1 | 3.5 |
| 70-74 years . . . | 20.2 | 36.4 | 8.2 | 21.2 | 38.6 | 8.5 | 9.1 | 14.0 | 4.9 |
| 75-79 years . . . | 20.9 | 41.6 | 7.6 | 22.1 | 44.3 | 8.1 | 7.3 | 13.9 | 2.1 |
| 80-84 years . . . | 20.5 | 44.5 | 7.0 | 21.8 | 47.8 | 7.4 | 6.2 | 12.2 | 2.2 |
| 85+ years . . . | 18.9 | 47.5 | 5.4 | 19.8 | 49.9 | 5.8 | 10.6 | 27.9 | 0.8 |

## U.S. Fires

Source: National Fire Protection Assn.

(1977 estimates)

### By Type of Fire

| | No. of fires | Property loss |
|---|---|---|
| Fires in structures . . . . . | 1,179,000 | $5,227,000,000 |
| Fires outside structures[1] . . | 161,000 | 196,000,000 |
| Fires in vehicles[2]. . . . . . . | 529,000 | 415,000,000 |
| Fires in brush, grass, wildland[3]. . . . . . . . . . | 845,000 | * |
| Fires in rubbish[4] . . . . . . . | 375,000 | * |
| All other fires. . . . . . . . . | 424,000 | 226,000,000 |
| Total[6]. . . . . . . . . . . . | 3,513,000 | $6,064,000,000 |

### By Property Use

| | No. of fires | Property loss |
|---|---|---|
| Public assembly . . . . . . . | 33,000 | $271,000,000 |
| Educational. . . . . . . . . . | 18,000 | 120,000,000 |
| Institutional. . . . . . . . . . | 23,000 | 16,000,000 |
| Residential . . . . . . . . . . | 797,000 | 2,849,000,000 |
| One-/2-family dwellings[5] | 678,000 | 2,345,000,000 |
| Apartments . . . . . . . | 92,000 | 381,000,000 |
| Hotels, motels . . . . . . | 14,000 | 96,000,000 |
| Other residential . . . . | 13,000 | 27,000,000 |
| Stores and offices. . . . . . | 68,000 | 486,000,000 |
| Industry, utility, defense[6] . . | 61,000 | 669,000,000 |
| Storage in structures[6] . . . . | 96,000 | 736,000,000 |
| Special structures. . . . . . | 83,000 | 80,000,000 |
| Total[6]. . . . . . . . . . . . | 1,179,000 | $5,227,000,000 |

*No value involved. (1) Includes outside storage, crops, timber, etc. (2) Includes highway vehicles, trains, boats and ships, aircraft, farm vehicles, and construction vehicles. (3) Excludes crops and timber. (4) Includes dumpsters. (5) Includes mobile homes. (6) Since some fires were not reported to the NFPA, the results presented represent only a portion of the total U.S. fires.

### Annual Fire Losses in the U.S.

Source: Insurance Services Office

| Year | Loss | Year | Loss | Year | Loss | Year | Loss |
|---|---|---|---|---|---|---|---|
| 1940 . . . . . . | $285,878,697 | 1955. . . . . . | $885,218,000 | 1970 . . . . | $2,264,000,000 | 1976 . . . . . | $3,558,000,000 |
| 1945 . . . . . . | 484,274,000 | 1960 . . . . . | 1,107,824,000 | 1973 . . . . . | 2,639,000,000 | 1977 . . . . . | 3,751,000,000 |
| 1950 . . . . . . | 648,909,000 | 1965 . . . . . | 1,455,631,000 | 1975 . . . . . | 3,560,000,000 | 1978 . . . . . | 2,110,000,000 |

### Fire Fighters: Deaths and Injuries

Source: International Association of Fire Fighters

U.S. and Canadian professional fire fighters

| Year | In line of duty Deaths | In line of duty Injuries | Occupational diseases[1] Deaths | Occupational diseases[1] Retirement | Year | In line of duty Deaths | In line of duty Injuries | Occupational diseases[1] Deaths | Occupational diseases[1] Retirement |
|---|---|---|---|---|---|---|---|---|---|
| 1970 | 115 | 38,583 | 233 | 465 | 1974 | 100 | 56,296 | 107 | 604 |
| 1971 | 106 | 50,976 | N/A | 511 | 1975 | 108 | 51,312 | 88 | 721 |
| 1972 | 100 | 62,682 | 133 | 695 | 1976 | 79 | 49,819 | 79 | 673 |
| 1973 | 90 | 62,619 | 111 | 702 | | | | | |

(1) Includes: heart and cardiovascular diseases; lung and respiratory diseases; and other occupational diseases. N/A: not available.

# Heart Disease

## Warning Signs

**Source:** American Heart Association

**Of Heart Attack**
• Prolonged, oppressive pain or unusual discomfort in the center of the chest
• Pain may radiate to the shoulder, arm, neck or jaw
• Sweating may accompany pain or discomfort
• Nausea and vomiting may also occur
• Shortness of breath may accompany other signs

The American Heart Association advises immediate action at the onset of these symptoms. The Association points out that over half of heart attack victims die before they reach the hospital and that the average victim waits 3 hours before seeking help.

**Of Stroke**
• Sudden temporary weakness or numbness of face or limbs
• Temporary loss of speech, or trouble speaking or understanding speech
• Temporary dimness or loss of vision, particularly in one eye
• An episode of double vision
• Unexplained dizziness or unsteadiness
• Change in personality, mental ability
• New or unusual pattern of headaches

## Major Risk Factors

Blood pressure— systolic pressure under 120 is normal; systolic pressure over 150
= 2 times the risk of heart attack
= 4 times the risk of stroke

Cholesterol— level under 194 is normal;
level of 250 or over
= 3 times the risk of heart attack or stroke

Cigarettes— with non-smoking considered normal;
smoking one pack a day
= 2 times the risk of heart attack
= 4 times the risk of stroke

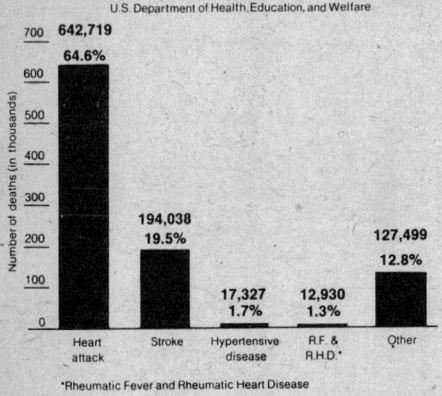

**U.S. Deaths Due to Cardiovascular Diseases by Major Type of Disorder,** 1975
**Source:** National Center for Health Statistics, U.S. Department of Health, Education, and Welfare

642,719
64.6%
Heart attack

194,038
19.5%
Stroke

17,327
1.7%
Hypertensive disease

12,930
1.3%
R.F. & R.H.D.*

127,499
12.8%
Other

Number of deaths (in thousands)

*Rheumatic Fever and Rheumatic Heart Disease

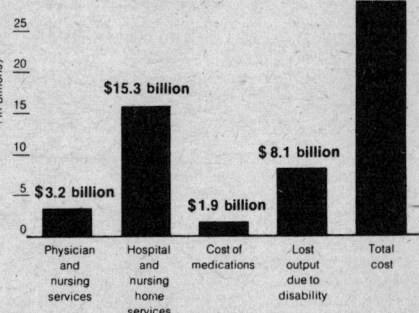

**Estimated Economic Costs of Cardiovascular Diseases by Type of Expenditure,** 1978
**Source:** American Heart Association

( in billions )

$3.2 billion — Physician and nursing services

$15.3 billion — Hospital and nursing home services

$1.9 billion — Cost of medications

$8.1 billion — Lost output due to disability

$28.5 billion — Total cost

## Cardiovascular Disease Statistical Summary

**Cost** — $28.5 billion (AHA est.) in 1978.

**Prevalence** — 29,780,000 Americans have some form of heart and blood vessel disease.
• hypertension — 24,080,000 (one in 6 adults).
• coronary heart disease — 4,120,000.
• rheumatic heart disease — 1,800,000.
• stroke — 1,840,000.

**Mortality** — 994,513 in 1975 (53% of all deaths). 1978 (AHA est.): 1,003,300 (52%).
• one-fourth of all persons killed by CVD are under age 65.

**Congenital or inborn heart defects** — 35 recognizable types of defects.
• more than 25,000 babies are born every year with heart defects.
• post-natal mortality from heart defects had been reduced to 6,440 in 1975.

**Heart attack** — caused 642,719 deaths in 1975.
• 4,120,000 alive today have history of heart attack and/or angina pectoris.
• 350,000 a year die of heart attack before they reach hospital.
• About 1,000,000 Americans will have a heart attack this year and about 650,000 of them will die.

**Stroke** — killed 194,038 in 1975; afflicts 1,840,000.

**CCU** — most of the 7,000 general hospitals in U.S. have coronary care capability.
• 1,800 have separate CCUs; 3,000 have combined intensive care and coronary care facilities.

**Hypertension (high blood pressure)** — 24,080,000 adults.
• easily detected and usually controllable, but only a minority have it under adequate control.

**Rheumatic heart disease** — 100,000 children; 1,700,000 adults.
• killed 12,930 in 1975. Modern antibiotic therapy has sharply reduced mortality in 5-24 age group.

# Marriage Information

Source: Compiled by William E. Mariano, Council on Marriage Relations, Inc.,
110 E. 42d St., New York, NY 10017 (as of Oct. 1, 1978)

Marriageable age, by states, for both males and females with and without consent of parents or guardians. But in most states, the court has authority, in an emergency, to marry young couples below the ordinary age of consent, where due regard for their morals and welfare so requires. In many states, under special circumstances, blood test and waiting period may be waived.

| State | With consent | | Without consent | | Blood test | | Wait for license | Wait after license |
|---|---|---|---|---|---|---|---|---|
| | Men | Women | Men | Women | Required | Other state accepted* | | |
| Alabama(b) | 17 | 14 | 21 | 18 | Yes | Yes | None | None |
| Alaska | 18 | 16 | 19 | 18 | Yes | No | 3 days | None |
| Arizona | 16(i) | 16 | 18 | 18 | Yes | Yes | None | None |
| Arkansas | 17 | 16(j) | 18 | 18 | Yes | No | 3 days | None |
| California | —(i) | —(i) | 18 | 18 | Yes | Yes | None | None |
| Colorado | 16 | 16 | 18 | 18 | Yes | ... | None | None |
| Connecticut | 16 | 16(m) | 18 | 18 | Yes | Yes | 4 days | None |
| Delaware | 18 | 16(j) | 18 | 18 | Yes | Yes | None | 24 hrs. (c) |
| District of Columbia | 18 | 16 | 21 | 18 | Yes | Yes | 3 days | None |
| Florida | 18 | 16 | 21 | 21 | Yes | Yes | 3 days | None |
| Georgia | 18 | 16 | 18 | 18 | Yes | Yes | None (b) | None (k) |
| Hawaii | 16 | 16 | 18 | 18 | Yes | Yes | None | None |
| Idaho | 16 | 16 | 18 | 18 | Yes (p) | Yes | None (l) | None |
| Illinois (a) | —(e) | 15(e) | 18 | 18 | Yes | Yes | None | None |
| Indiana | 17 | 17 | 18 | 18 | Yes | No | 3 days | None |
| Iowa | 16(e) | 16(e) | 18 | 18 | Yes | Yes | 3 days | None |
| Kansas | (i) | —(i) | 18 | 18 | Yes | Yes | 3 days | None |
| Kentucky | 18 | 16 | 18 | 18 | Yes | No | 3 days | None |
| Louisiana (a) | 18 | 16 | 18 | 18 | Yes | No | None | 72 hours |
| Maine | 16 | 16 | 18 | 18 | No | No | 5 days | None |
| Maryland | 18 | 16 | 21 | 18 | None | None | 48 hours | None |
| Massachusetts | —(i) | —(i) | 18 | 18 | Yes | Yes | 3 days | None |
| Michigan (a) | — | 16 | 18 | 18 | Yes | No | 3 days | None |
| Minnesota | — | 16(e) | 18 | 18 | None | ... | 5 days | None |
| Mississippi (b) | 17 | 15 | 17 | 15 | Yes | ... | 3 days | None |
| Missouri | 15 | 15 | 18 | 18 | Yes | Yes | 3 days | None |
| Montana | 16 | 16 | 18 | 18 | Yes | Yes | 3 days | None |
| Nebraska | 16 | 16 | 17 | 17 | Yes (p) | Yes | 5 days | None |
| Nevada | 18 | 16 | 21 | 18 | None | None | None | None |
| New Hampshire (a) | 14(e) | 13(e) | 18 | 18 | Yes | Yes | 5 days | None |
| New Jersey (a) | — | 16 | 18 | 18 | Yes | Yes | 72 hours | None |
| New Mexico | 16 | 16 | 21 | 21 | Yes | Yes | None | None |
| New York | 16 | 14 | 18 | 18 | Yes | No | None | 24 hrs.(g) |
| North Carolina (a) | 16 | 16 | 18 | 18 | Yes | Yes | None | None |
| North Dakota (a) | —(i) | 15 | 18 | 18 | Yes | ... | None | None |
| Ohio (a) | 18 | 16 | 18 | 18 | Yes | Yes | 5 days | None |
| Oklahoma | 16 | 16 | 18 | 18 | Yes | No | None (f)(h) | ... |
| Oregon | 18 (e) | 15 (e) | 18 | 18 | Yes | No | 7 days | None |
| Pennsylvania | 16 | 16 | 18 | 18 | Yes | Yes | 3 days | None |
| Rhode Island (a) (b) | 18 | 16 | 18 | 18 | Yes | No | None | None |
| South Carolina | 16 | 14 | 18 | 18 | None | None | 24 hrs. | None |
| South Dakota | 18 | 16 | 18 | 18 | Yes | Yes | None | None |
| Tennessee (b) | 16 | 16 | 21 | 21 | Yes | Yes | 3 days | None |
| Texas | 16 | 16 | 18 | 18 | Yes | Yes | None | None |
| Utah (a) | —(o) | —(o) | —(o) | —(o) | Yes | Yes | None | None |
| Vermont (a) | 18 | 16 | 18 | 18 | Yes | ... | None | 5 days |
| Virginia (a) | 16 | 16 | 18 | 18 | Yes | Yes (n) | None | None |
| Washington | 17 | 17 | 18 | 18 | (d) | ... | 3 days | None |
| West Virginia | (i) | 16 | 18 | 18 | Yes | No | 3 days | None |
| Wisconsin | 18 | 16 | 18 | 18 | Yes | Yes | 5 days | None |
| Wyoming | 18 | 16 | 21 | 21 | Yes | Yes | None | None |
| Puerto Rico | 16 | 16 | 21 | 21 | (f) | None | None | None |
| Virgin Island | 16 | 14 | 21 | 18 | None | None | 8 days | None |

**\*Many states have additional special requirements; contact individual state.** (a) Special laws applicable to non-residents. (b) Special laws applicable to those under 21 years; Ala., bond required if male is under 21, female under 18. (c) 24 hours if one or both parties resident of state; 96 hours if both parties are non-residents. (d) None, but male must file affidavit. (e) Parental consent plus court's consent required. (f) None, but a medical certificate is required. (g) Marriage may not be solemnized within 10 days from date of blood test. (h) If either under 21, 72 hrs. (i) Statute provides for obtaining license with parental or court consent with no state minimum age. (j) Under 16, with parental and court consent. (k) All those between 19-21 cannot waive 3 day waiting period. (l) if either under 18, wait 3 full days. (m) If under stated age, court consent required. (n) Va. blood test form must be used. (o) Ut. has recently amended its laws to eliminate distinctions of age based on sex. Current ages not available. (p) Applicant must also supply a certificate of immunity against German measles (rubella).

# Grounds for Divorce

**Source:** Compiled by William E. Mariano, Council on Marriage Relations, Inc.,
110 E. 42d St., New York, NY 10017 (as of Oct. 1, 1978)

Persons contemplating divorce should study latest decisions or secure legal advice before initiating proceedings since different interpretations or exceptions in each case can change the conclusion reached.

| State | Breakdown of marriage/incompatibility | Cruelty | Desertion | Non-support | Alcohol &/or drug addiction | Felony | Impotency | Insanity | Living separate and apart | Other grounds | Residence time | Time between interlocut'y and final decrees |
|---|---|---|---|---|---|---|---|---|---|---|---|---|
| Alabama | X | X | X | X | X | X | X | X | | A-E-K | 1 yr. | none-M |
| Alaska | X | X | X | | X | X | X | X | | C | 1 yr. | none |
| Arizona | X | | | | | | | | | | 90 days | none |
| Arkansas | | X | X | X | X | X | X | X | 3 yrs. | C | 3 mos. | none |
| California² | X | | | | | | | X | | | 6 mos. | 6 mos. |
| Colorado | X | | | | | | | | | | 90 days | none |
| Connecticut | X | X | X | X | X | X | | X | 18 mos. | B-K | 1 yr. | none |
| Delaware | X⁴ | | X | | | | | | 18 mos. | B-K | 3 mos. | 3 mos. |
| Dist. of Columbia | | | X | | | | X | X | 6 mos.-1 yr. | | 6 mos. | none |
| Florida | X | | | | | | | X | | | 6 mos. | none |
| Georgia | X | X | X | | X | X | X | X | | A-B-D | 6 mos. | L |
| Hawaii | X | | | | | | | | 2 yrs. | K | 6 mos. | L-N |
| Idaho | X | X | X | X | X | X | | X | 5 yrs. | | 6 wks. | none |
| Illinois | | X | X | | X | X | X | | | | 3 mos. | none |
| Indiana | X | | | | | | X | X | | | 6 mos. | none |
| Iowa | X | | | | | | | | | | 1 yr. | none-N |
| Kansas | X | X | X | X | X | X | X | X | | A-B-H-I | 60 days | none-M |
| Kentucky | X | | | | | | | | | | 180 days | none |
| Louisiana | | X | | | | X | | | 2 yrs. | K | 1 yr. | none-N |
| Maine | X | X | X | X | X | X | | X | 3 yrs. | K | 6 mos. | none |
| Maryland | | | X | | | X | X | X | 1-3 yrs. | | 1 yr. | none |
| Massachusetts | X⁴ | X | X | X | X | X | X | X | 6 mos.-1 yr. | | 2 yrs. | 6 mos. |
| Michigan | X⁴ | | | | | | | | | | 6 mos. | none |
| Minnesota | X⁴ | | | | | | | | 6 mos. | K | 6 mos. | none-O |
| Mississippi | X⁴ | X | X | | X | X | X | X | | A-D-I | 3 mos. | none-P |
| Missouri | X⁴ | | | | | | | | 1-2 yrs. | | 3 mos. | none |
| Montana | X | | | | | | | | | | 1 yr. | 6 mos. |
| Nebraska | X | | | | | | | | | | 6 wks. | none |
| Nevada | X | | | | | | | X | 1 yr. | | 6 wks. | none |
| New Hampshire³ | X | X | X | X | X | X | | | 6 mos. | K | 1 yr. | none |
| New Jersey | | X | X | | X | X | | X | 6 mos. | E-K | 1 yr. | none |
| New Mexico | X | X | X | | | | | | | | 6 mos. | none |
| New York | | X | X | | | X | | | 1 yr. | K | 1 yr. | none |
| North Carolina | | | | | | | X | X | 1 yr. | A-E | 6 mos. | none |
| North Dakota | X | X | X | X | X | X | X | X | | K | 1 yr. | none |
| Ohio | X | X | X | X | X | X | X | X | 2 yrs. | B-G-H-I | 6 mos. | none |
| Oklahoma | X | X | X | X | X | X | X | X | | A-B-G-H | 6 mos. | none |
| Oregon | X | | | | | | | | | | 6 mos. | 90 days |
| Pennsylvania | | X | X | | | X | X | X | 3 yrs. | B-C-D-I | 1 yr. | none |
| Rhode Island | | X | X | X | X | X | X | X | 3 yrs. | | 1 yr. | 6 mos. |
| South Carolina | | X | X | | X | | | | 3 yrs. | | 1 yr. | none |
| South Dakota | | X | X | X | X | X | | X | | | actual | none |
| Tennessee | X | X | X | X | X | X | X | X | | A-I-J-K | 6 mos. | none |
| Texas | X | X | X | | X | X | | X | 3 yrs. | K | 1 yr. | none-O |
| Utah | | X | X | X | X | X | X | X | 6 mos. | | actual | 3 mos. |
| Vermont | | X | X | | X | X | | | 6 mos. | | 6 mos. | 3 mos.-Q |
| Virginia | | X | X | | | X | | | 1 yr. | A-C | 6 mos. | none-P |
| Washington | X | | | | | | | | 2 yrs. | | actual | none-R |
| West Virginia | | X | X | | X | | X | X | 2 yrs. | | 2 yrs.-S | none |
| Wisconsin | X⁴ | | | | | | | | 1 yr. | K | 6 mos. | none-O |
| Wyoming | X | | | | | | | X | 2 yrs. | | 60 days | none |

Adultery is either grounds for divorce or evidence of irreconcilable differences and a breakdown of the marriage in all states. The plaintiff can invariably remarry in the same state where he or she procured a decree of divorce or annulment. Not so the defendant, who is barred in certain states for some offenses. After a period of time has elapsed even the offender can apply for permission.

(1) Generally 5 yrs. insanity but: permanent insanity in Ut.; incurable insanity in Col.; 1 yr. Wis.; 18 mos. Alas.; 2 yrs. Ga., Ha., Ind., Nev., N.J., Ore., Wash., Wy.; 3 yrs. Ark., Cal., Fla., Kan., Md., Minn., Miss., N.C., Tex., W. Va.; 6 yrs. Ida. (2) Cal. has a procedure whereby if the couple has been married less than 2 years, have no children, no real estate, little personal property, and few debts they can get a divorce without an attorney and without appearing in court. (3) Other grounds existing only in N.H. are: Joining a religious order disbelieving in marriage, treatment which injures health or endangers reason, wife without the state for 10 years, and wife in state 2 yrs. husband never in state and intends to become a citizen of a foreign country. (4) Provable only fault grounds, separation for some period, generally a year, proof of marital discord or commitment for mental illness. (A) Pregnancy at marriage. (B) Fraudulent contract. (C) Indignities. (D) Consanguinity. (E) Crime against nature. (F) Mental incapacity at time of marriage. (G) Procurement of out-of-state divorce. (H) Gross neglect of duty. (I) Bigamy. (J) Attempted homicide. (K) Separation by decree in Conn.; after decree: one yr. in La., N.Y., Wis.; 18 mos. in N.H.; 2 yrs. in Ala., Ha., Minn., N.C. Tenn.; 3 yrs. in Ut.; 4 yrs. in N.J., N.D.; 5 yrs. in Md. (L) Determined by court order. (M) 60 days to remarry. (N) One yr. to remarry except Ha. one yr. with minor child; La. 90 days. (O) 6 mos. to remarry. (P) Adultery cases, remarriage in court's discretion. (Q) Plaintiff, 6 mos.; defendant 2 yrs. to remarry. (R) No remarriage if an appeal is pending. (S) Actual domicile in adultery cases. **Enoch Arden Laws:** disappearance and unknown to be alive - Conn., 7 yrs. absence, N.H., 2 yrs., N.Y. 5 yrs. (called dissolution). Vt. 7 yrs.

N.B. Grounds not recognized for divorce may be recognized for separation or annulment. Local laws should be consulted.

# Canadian Marriage Information

**Source:** Compiled from information provided by the various provincial government departments and agencies concerned.

Marriageable age, by provinces, for both males and females with and without consent of parents or guardians. In some provinces, the court has authority, given special circumstances, to marry young couples below the minimum age. Most provinces waive the blood test requirement and the waiting period varies across the provinces.

| Province | With consent Men | With consent Women | Without consent Men | Without consent Women | Blood test other province Required | Blood test other province Accepted | Wait for license | Wait after license |
|---|---|---|---|---|---|---|---|---|
| Newfoundland | — | — | 19 | 19 | | | | |
| Prince Edward Island | 16 | 16 | 18 | 18 | Yes | Yes | 5 days | None |
| Nova Scotia | (1) | (1) | 19 | 19 | None | None | 5 days | None |
| New Brunswick | 14 | 14 | 18 | 18 | None | None | 5 days | None |
| Quebec | 14 | 12 | 18 | 18 | None | — | — | None[2] |
| Ontario | 16 | 16 | 18 | 18 | None | — | None[2] | 3 days |
| Manitoba | 16 | 16 | 18 | 18 | Yes | Yes | None | 24 hours |
| Saskatchewan | 15 | 15 | 18 | 18 | Yes | Yes | 5 days | None |
| Alberta | 18— | 18— | 18 | 18 | Yes[3] | Yes[4] | None[5] | None |
| British Columbia | 16[6] | 16[6] | 19 | 19 | None | None | 2 days[7] | None |
| Yukon Territory | 15 | 15 | 19 | 19 | None | None | None | 24 hours |
| Northwest Territories | 15 | 15 | 19 | 19 | None | Yes | None | None |

(1) There is no statutory minimum age in the province. Anyone under the age of 19 years must have consent for marriage and no person under the age of 16 may be married without authorization of a Family Court judge and in addition must have the necessary consent of the parent or guardian. (2) Special requirements applicable to nonresidents. (3) Applies only to applicants under 60 years of age. (4) This is upon filing of negative lab report indicating blood test was taken within 14 days preceding date of application for license. (5) Exception where consent is required by mail; depending receipt of divorce documents, etc. (6) Persons under 16 years of age (no minimum age specified) may also be married if they have obtained, in addition to the usual consent from parents or guardian, an order from a judge of the Supreme or County Court in this province. (7) Including day of application, e.g., a license applied for on a Monday cannot be issued until Wednesday.

# Grounds for Divorce in Canada

**Source:** Government of Canada Divorce Act

The grounds for divorce in Canada are the same for all the provinces and its territories. There are two categories of offense:

A. Marital Offense:
- Adultery
- Sodomy
- Bestiality
- Rape
- Homosexual act
- Subsequent marriage
- Physical cruelty
- Mental cruelty

B. Marriage breakdown by reason of:
- Imprisonment for aggregate period of not less than 3 years
- Imprisonment for not less than 2 years on sentence of death or sentence of 10 years or more
- Addiction to alcohol
- Addiction to narcotics
- Whereabouts of spouse unknown
- Non-consummation
- Separation for not less than 3 years
- Desertion by petitioner for not less than 5 years

Residence time: Domicile in Canada. Time between interlocutory and final decree: normally 3 months before final can be applied for.

# Canadian Motor Vehicle Traffic Deaths

**Source:** Statistics Canada

| Province | Number 1975 | Number 1974 | Province | Number 1975 | Number 1974 |
|---|---|---|---|---|---|
| Newfoundland | 104 | 117 | Saskatchewan | 286 | 306 |
| Prince Edward Island | 44 | 42 | Alberta | 527 | 573 |
| Nova Scotia | 242 | 268 | British Columbia | 717 | 844 |
| New Brunswick | 230 | 287 | Yukon | 8 | 8 |
| Quebec | 1,893 | 1,882 | Northwest Territories | 7 | 14 |
| Ontario | 1,800 | 1,748 | Total | 6,061 | 6,290 |
| Manitoba | 203 | 201 | | | |

# Birthstones

**Source:** Jewelry Industry Council

| Month | Ancient | Modern |
|---|---|---|
| January | Garnet | Garnet |
| February | Amethyst | Amethyst |
| March | Jasper | Bloodstone or Aquamarine |
| April | Sapphire | Diamond |
| May | Agate | Emerald |
| June | Emerald | Pearl, Moonstone, or Alexandrite |

| Month | Ancient | Modern |
|---|---|---|
| July | Onyx | Ruby |
| August | Carnelian | Sardonyx or Peridot |
| September | Chrysolite | Sapphire |
| October | Aquamarine | Opal or Tourmaline |
| November | Topaz | Topaz |
| December | Ruby | Turquoise or Zircon |

# Federal Bureau of Investigation

The Federal Bureau of Investigation (FBI) is the investigative arm of the Department of Justice, and is located at 9th St. and Pennsylvania Ave., Washington, DC 20535. It investigates all violations of federal laws except those specifically assigned to some other agency by legislative action, such violations including counterfeiting, and internal revenue, postal, and customs violations. It also investigates espionage, sabotage, treason, and other matters affecting internal security, as well as kidnaping, transportation of stolen goods across state lines, and violations of the federal bank and atomic energy laws.

The Identification Division has about 195 million fingerprint cards on file. While this division is of great usefulness in detecting criminals, it serves a wider purpose in recording the fingerprints of many other citizens who voluntarily make this record.

The FBI has 59 field divisions in the principal cities of the country. *Consult telephone directories for location and phone numbers.*

An applicant for the position of Special Agent of the FBI must be a citizen of the U.S. at least 23 and under 35 years old and graduate of a state-accredited resident law school or from a resident 4-year college with a major in accounting

with at least one year of practical accounting and/or auditing experience. In addition, applicants with a 4-year residential college degree with a major in certain areas or 3 years specialized experience of a professional, executive, or complex investigative nature are presently being considered on a limited basis. An agent gets 15 weeks of training.

William H. Webster, a federal appeals court judge from St. Louis, was confirmed as FBI Director for a 10-year term on Feb. 9, 1978. He replaced Clarence Kelley.

## U.S. Crime Reports

Source: Federal Bureau of Investigation

| Offense | Number 1977 est. | % change over[1] 1976 | 1973 |
|---|---|---|---|
| Murder | 19,120 | + 1.8 | − 2.6 |
| Rape | 63,020 | +11.1 | +22.6 |
| Robbery | 404,850 | − 3.7 | + 5.4 |
| Aggravated assault | 522,510 | + 6.4 | +24.2 |
| Burglary | 3,052,200 | − 1.2 | +19.0 |
| Larceny-theft | 5,905,700 | − 5.8 | +35.8 |
| Auto theft | 968,400 | + 1.1 | + 4.3 |

[1]Percent by which the rate of crime per 100,000 population changed in 1977 as compared with 1976 and 1973.

## U.S. Crime Rate Drops 4% in 1977

The rate of crime per 100,000 population decreased by 4% in 1977 as compared to 1976, according to the Crime Index offenses measured by the FBI. Violent crime rates were up 1.5%, with a 10.2% increase in the rate of reported rape and a 5.6% increase in the aggravated assault rate. The robbery rate declined 4.4% and the murder rate remained unchanged. Property crime rates fell 4.5%, with the larceny rate down 6.6% and burglary off by 2%. Auto theft increased by 0.3%.

## Reported Crime, 1976-77, by Size of Place
Source: 1977 Uniform Crime Reports, Federal Bureau of Investigation

| Population group (1977 estimates) | Crime index total | Violent crime | Property crime | Murder and non-negligent man-slaughter | Forcible rape | Robbery | Aggra-vated assault | Burglary-breaking or entering | Larceny-theft |
|---|---|---|---|---|---|---|---|---|---|
| **Total all agencies:** 10,513 agencies; total population 201,756,000: | | | | | | | | | |
| 1976 | 10,689,093 | 943,927 | 9,745,166 | 17,803 | 53,990 | 410,515 | 461,619 | 2,903,176 | 5,929,649 |
| 1977 | 10,284,575 | 956,218 | 9,328,357 | 18,240 | 59,800 | 393,275 | 484,903 | 2,852,212 | 5,554,355 |
| Percent change | −3.8 | +1.3 | −4.3 | +2.5 | +10.8 | −4.2 | +5.0 | −1.8 | −6.3 |
| **Total cities:** 7,926 cities; total population 141,634,000: | | | | | | | | | |
| 1976 | 8,734,621 | 796,341 | 7,938,280 | 13,653 | 42,237 | 377,690 | 362,761 | 2,265,239 | 4,887,626 |
| 1977 | 8,377,092 | 800,746 | 7,576,346 | 13,992 | 46,890 | 359,202 | 380,662 | 2,214,847 | 4,574,546 |
| Percent change | −4.1 | +.6 | −4.6 | +2.5 | +11.0 | −4.9 | +4.9 | −2.2 | −6.4 |
| **57 cities** over 250,000; population 41,774,000: | | | | | | | | | |
| 1976 | 3,455,940 | 460,311 | 2,995,629 | 8,158 | 22,729 | 262,781 | 166,643 | 956,192 | 1,623,321 |
| 1977 | 3,259,643 | 448,800 | 2,810,843 | 8,224 | 25,033 | 244,760 | 170,783 | 913,320 | 1,492,551 |
| Percent change | −5.7 | −2.5 | −6.2 | +.8 | +10.1 | −6.9 | +2.5 | −4.5 | −8.1 |
| **116 cities,** 100,000 to 250,000; population 16,557,000: | | | | | | | | | |
| 1976 | 1,214,594 | 93,247 | 1,121,347 | 1,641 | 5,716 | 39,628 | 46,262 | 319,945 | 702,185 |
| 1977 | 1,164,759 | 97,282 | 1,067,477 | 1,852 | 6,696 | 39,451 | 49,283 | 315,963 | 651,831 |
| Percent change | −4.1 | +4.3 | −4.8 | +12.9 | +17.1 | −.4 | +6.5 | −1.2 | −7.2 |
| **263 cities,** 50,000 to 100,000; population 18,067,000: | | | | | | | | | |
| 1976 | 1,101,061 | 72,953 | 1,028,108 | 1,107 | 4,574 | 27,938 | 39,334 | 282,787 | 658,044 |
| 1977 | 1,066,025 | 78,026 | 987,999 | 1,146 | 5,147 | 28,234 | 43,499 | 282,723 | 616,095 |
| Percent change | −3.2 | +7.0 | −3.9 | +3.5 | +12.5 | +1.1 | +10.6 | 0.0 | −6.4 |
| **640 cities,** 25,000 to 50,000; population 22,140,000: | | | | | | | | | |
| 1976 | 1,193,209 | 72,610 | 1,120,599 | 1,146 | 4,044 | 24,695 | 42,725 | 286,939 | 749,961 |
| 1977 | 1,151,266 | 74,640 | 1,076,626 | 1,097 | 4,524 | 24,129 | 44,890 | 285,808 | 703,360 |
| Percent change | −3.5 | +2.8 | −3.9 | −4.3 | +11.9 | −2.3 | +5.1 | −.4 | −6.2 |
| **1,504 cities,** 10,000 to 25,000; population 23,416,000: | | | | | | | | | |
| 1976 | 1,034,499 | 56,421 | 978,078 | 907 | 3,112 | 15,148 | 37,254 | 246,803 | 669,336 |
| 1977 | 1,008,566 | 59,244 | 949,322 | 980 | 3,282 | 15,068 | 39,934 | 243,418 | 640,319 |
| Percent change | −2.5 | +5.0 | −2.9 | +8.0 | +4.8 | −.5 | +7.2 | −1.4 | −4.3 |
| **5,346 cities** under 10,000; population 19,670,000: | | | | | | | | | |
| 1976 | 735,318 | 40,799 | 604,519 | 694 | 2,062 | 7,500 | 30,543 | 172,573 | 484,779 |
| 1977 | 726,833 | 42,754 | 684,079 | 693 | 2,228 | 7,560 | 32,273 | 173,615 | 470,390 |
| Percent change | −1.2 | +4.8 | −1.5 | −.1 | +8.1 | +.8 | +5.7 | +.6 | −3.0 |
| **Suburban area:** 4,465 agencies; population 73,154,000: | | | | | | | | | |
| 1976 | 3,256,317 | 204,374 | 3,051,943 | 3,626 | 14,045 | 59,612 | 127,091 | 882,537 | 1,940,786 |
| 1977 | 3,148,614 | 216,230 | 2,932,384 | 3,672 | 15,400 | 60,874 | 136,284 | 875,133 | 1,818,326 |
| Percent change | −3.3 | +5.8 | −3.9 | +1.3 | +9.6 | +2.1 | +7.2 | −.8 | −6.3 |
| **Rural area:** 1,900 agencies; population 26,778,000: | | | | | | | | | |
| 1976 | 536,088 | 43,902 | 492,186 | 1,955 | 3,309 | 5,221 | 33,417 | 198,397 | 266,759 |
| 1977 | 531,031 | 44,751 | 486,280 | 1,994 | 3,612 | 5,258 | 33,887 | 198,950 | 256,846 |
| Percent change | −.9 | +1.9 | −1.2 | +2.0 | +9.2 | +.7 | +1.4 | +.3 | −3.7 |

# Reported Crime in Metropolitan Areas, 1977

Source: 1977 Uniform Crime Reports, Federal Bureau of Investigation

The 28 Standard Metropolitan Statistical Areas listed below are those which appear most frequently among the top 30 cities in per capita reported crime rate for each of 7 kinds of major crime: the 5 listed below plus aggravated assault and auto theft.

The rates are for reported crimes only; they are not an accurate index of crimes actually committed. In many metropolitan areas an unknown number of crimes go unreported by victims. This is especially true of the crimes of rape, burglary, and larceny. Additionally, figures are often distorted for political reasons.

The number in parentheses following the city name indicates the number of categories (including auto theft and aggravated assault) in which the city appears among the top 30.

The numbers in parentheses following crime rate figures give that city's rank in that category of crime. If no number appears, the city is not among the top 30 in that category. The cities are listed in order of the diversity and violence of criminal activity.

| Metropolitan areas | Total[1] | Violent[2] | Property[3] | Murder[4] | Rape | Robbery | Burglary | Larceny |
|---|---|---|---|---|---|---|---|---|
| Las Vegas, Nev. (7) | 9,453.4 (3) | 961.1 (5) | 8,492.3 (3) | 20.5 (4) | 64.5 (6) | 452.4 (3) | 3,113.0 (2) | 4,699.6 (6) |
| Los Angeles-Long Beach, Cal. (6) | 7,013.1(29) | 1,004.1 (3) | 6,009.0 | 16.0(20) | 64.9 (5) | 429.0 (4) | 2,199.9(16) | 2,899.8 |
| New York, N.Y. (5) | 7,442.7(16) | 1,339.3 (1) | 6,103.4 | 17.1(15) | 42.8 | 810.2 (1) | 2,112.7(21) | 2,897.7 |
| Miami, Fla. (5) | 8,169.8 (6) | 1,084.8 (2) | 7,085.0(12) | 15.6(21) | 37.8 | 390.5 (6) | 2,124.6(20) | 4,393.9(12) |
| San Francisco-Oakland, Cal. (5) | 7,939.0 (8) | 768.8(17) | 7,170.2(11) | 11.9 | 51.9(15) | 378.6 (7) | 2,255.1(13) | 4,170.0(23) |
| Daytona Beach, Fla. (5) | 9,578.2 (2) | 755.8(19) | 8,822.4 (2) | 8.9 | 53.2(13) | 240.9(27) | 2,854.1 (3) | 5,505.8 (1) |
| Sacramento, Cal. (5) | 7,879.3(10) | 661.8 | 7,217.5(10) | 9.4 | 51.0(17) | 256.7(22) | 2,243.1(14) | 4,331.5(15) |
| Denver-Boulder, Col. (5) | 7,892.0 (9) | 650.2 | 7,241.8 (8) | 7.0 | 49.8(21) | 248.8(25) | 2,358.3 (9) | 4,264.0(18) |
| Orlando, Fla. (4) | 7,570.8(15) | 831.3 (9) | 6,739.5(17) | 7.5 | 65.8 (4) | 142.8 | 2,175.0(17) | 4,214.5(19) |
| Fresno, Cal. (4) | 8,118.6 (7) | 731.0(21) | 7,387.6 (6) | 21.9 (2) | 35.5 | 306.9(14) | 2,783.3 (4) | 3,932.3 |
| Stockton, Cal. (4) | 8,373.8 (4) | 654.2 | 7,719.6 (5) | 15.6(21) | 35.8 | 233.8 | 2,350.9(11) | 4,676.0 (7) |
| Gary-Hammond-E. Chicago, Ind. (4) | 5,417.8 | 598.5 | 4,819.3 | 16.7(17) | 49.8(21) | 256.6(23) | 1,296.7 | 2,645.8 |
| Lubbock, Tex. (4) | 7,613.8(14) | 558.7 | 7,055.1(14) | 19.1 (7) | 47.9(27) | 150.9 | 2,504.3 | 4,167.1(24) |
| Charleston-No. Charleston, S.C. (3) | 6,582.7 | 908.6 (6) | 5,674.1 | 9.2 | 47.6(28) | 200.5 | 2,060.3(28) | 3,235.1 |
| Fayetteville, N.C. (3) | 6,851.1 | 888.5 (7) | 5,962.6 | 16.4(19) | 47.0 | 215.2 | 2,305.4(12) | 3,217.2 |
| Columbia, S.C. (3) | 7,055.2(28) | 826.8(10) | 6,228.5 | 13.1 | 54.2(10) | 207.4 | 2,488.9 (7) | 3,351.7 |
| Detroit, Mich. (3) | 6,673.8 | 825.6(11) | 5,848.1 | 14.1 | 47.5(30) | 454.3 (2) | 1,661.3 | 3,296.7 |
| Savannah, Ga. (3) | 6,797.4 | 791.7(12) | 6,005.6 | 15.6(21) | 50.9(18) | 196.2 | 1,971.5 | 3,690.3 |
| Gainesville, Fla. (3) | 7,364.5(18) | 782.3(14) | 6,582.2(21) | 13.9 | 50.9(18) | 139.5 | 1,901.4 | 4,426.4(10) |
| Little Rock-N. Lit. Rock, Ark. (3) | 7,083.7(26) | 769.5(16) | 6,314.2(28) | 11.7 | 81.9 (1) | 301.2(16) | 2,053.1(29) | 3,800.4 |
| New Orleans, La. (3) | 6,003.2 | 752.7(20) | 5,250.6 | 19.2 (5) | 44.5 | 346.4(10) | 1,468.9 | 3,082.5 |
| Baton Rouge, La. (3) | 7,270.8(21) | 719.7 (24) | 6,551.1(22) | 13.6 | 48.6(25) | 122.9 | 1,941.1 | 4,204.0 |
| Riverside-San Bernadino-Ontario, Cal. (3) | 7,772.8(13) | 703.4(27) | 7,069.3(13) | 13.9 | 49.6(23) | 209.7 | 2,717.8 (5) | 3,844.9 |
| Memphis, Tenn.-Ark.-Miss. (3) | 5,841.1 | 695.0(29) | 5,146.2 | 13.2 | 73.4 (2) | 326.3(11) | 2,101.7(23) | 2,542.8 |
| Albany, Ga. (3) | 5,079.6 | 676.7 | 4,402.9 | 18.1(10) | 47.6(28) | 148.5 | 1,619.0 | 2,614.5 |
| Albuquerque, N.M. (2) | 7,125.1(24) | 722.4(23) | 6,402.8(26) | 9.4 | 67.3 (3) | 213.2 | 2,034.3 | 4,017.7 |
| Tallahassee, Fla. (2) | 6,737.4 | 710.5(25) | 6,026.9 | 5.7 | 62.2 (7) | 132.2 | 1,806.9 | 3,961.3 |
| Jacksonville, Fla. (2) | 6,247.9 | 707.4(26) | 5,540.4 | 13.2 | 49.5(24) | 234.0 | 1,724.3 | 3,514.4 |

(1) Other metro areas among the top 30 in total reported crime (predominantly property crime): Tucson, Ariz. (1); Phoenix, Ariz. (5); Bakersfield, Cal. (11); Ft. Lauderdale-Hollywood, Fla. (12); West Palm Beach-Boca Raton, Fla. (17); Reno, Nev. (19); Dallas-Ft. Worth, Tex. (20); Great Falls, Mont. (22); Pensacola, Fla. (23); Modesto, Cal. (25); Lakeland-Winter Haven, Fla. (27); Columbia, S.C. (28); Yakima, Wash. (30).

(2) Violent crime includes murder and non-negligent manslaughter, forcible rape, robbery, and aggravated assault. Other metro areas in the top 30 in violent crime are: Baltimore, Md. (4); West Palm Beach-Boca Raton, Fla. (13); Lafayette, La. (15); Flint, Mich. (18); Waco, Tex. (22); Kansas City, Mo.-Kans. (28); Saginaw, Mich. (30).

(3) Property crime includes burglary, larceny and auto theft. Other metro areas in the top 30 are: Tucson, Ariz. (1); Phoenix, Ariz. (4); Ft. Lauderdale, Fla. (7); Bakersfield, Cal. (9); Reno, Nev. (15); Great Falls, Mont. (16); Dallas, Tex. (18); Modesto, Cal. (19); West Palm Beach-Boca Raton, Fla. (20); Pensacola, Fla. (23); Yakima, Wash. (24); Lawrence, Kans. (25); Santa Cruz, Cal. (27); Springfield, Mo. (29); San Diego, Cal. (30).

(4) Of the top 30 cities in murder, all but 6 are in the South (18) or in Texas (6).

# Crime Rates by State

Source: 1977 Uniform Crime Reports, Federal Bureau of Investigation

(Rates per 100,000 population)

| State | Total | Violent | Property | Murder | Rape | Robbery | Assault | Burglary | Larceny | Auto theft |
|---|---|---|---|---|---|---|---|---|---|---|
| Alabama | 3,712.6 | 414.4 | 3,298.2 | 14.2 | 25.2 | 96.8 | 278.3 | 1,135.5 | 1,881.9 | 280.7 |
| Alaska | 5,898.0 | 443.2 | 5,454.8 | 10.8 | 51.6 | 96.8 | 284.0 | 1,331.7 | 3,369.4 | 753.3 |
| Arizona | 7,747.2 | 494.2 | 7,253.0 | 9.5 | 34.2 | 138.2 | 312.3 | 2,346.1 | 4,467.4 | 439.5 |
| Arkansas | 3,341.1 | 322.9 | 3,018.1 | 8.8 | 27.6 | 83.2 | 203.4 | 972.6 | 1,862.1 | 183.4 |
| California | 7,008.7 | 706.0 | 6,302.7 | 11.5 | 49.4 | 287.0 | 358.0 | 2,139.4 | 3,499.8 | 663.5 |
| Colorado | 6,827.5 | 511.9 | 6,315.6 | 6.3 | 42.0 | 170.7 | 292.9 | 1,935.2 | 3,903.2 | 477.1 |
| Connecticut | 4,842.1 | 282.3 | 4,559.8 | 4.2 | 16.8 | 129.5 | 131.8 | 1,346.0 | 2,620.7 | 593.2 |
| Delaware | 6,210.1 | 382.1 | 5,828.0 | 6.0 | 24.9 | 157.0 | 194.2 | 1,682.6 | 3,678.4 | 467.0 |
| Florida | 6,738.6 | 686.8 | 6,051.8 | 10.2 | 39.6 | 187.9 | 449.1 | 1,859.9 | 3,840.5 | 351.4 |
| Georgia | 4,259.1 | 439.8 | 3,819.2 | 11.7 | 31.1 | 140.5 | 256.5 | 1,351.1 | 2,170.2 | 297.9 |
| Hawaii | 6,546.1 | 224.8 | 6,321.3 | 7.2 | 25.5 | 128.0 | 64.1 | 1,911.5 | 3,920.4 | 489.4 |
| Idaho | 4,124.9 | 236.9 | 3,888.0 | 5.5 | 19.4 | 39.6 | 172.5 | 1,050.8 | 2,599.6 | 237.6 |
| Illinois | 4,894.1 | 452.0 | 4,442.1 | 9.9 | 21.8 | 211.3 | 209.0 | 1,085.0 | 2,828.5 | 528.6 |
| Indiana | 4,272.9 | 310.6 | 3,962.3 | 7.4 | 26.5 | 123.2 | 153.5 | 1,086.2 | 2,498.7 | 377.4 |
| Iowa | 3,861.5 | 144.0 | 3,717.5 | 2.3 | 10.6 | 41.2 | 89.8 | 812.5 | 2,685.1 | 219.9 |
| Kansas | 4,563.8 | 309.8 | 4,254.0 | 6.6 | 22.0 | 100.7 | 180.5 | 1,270.4 | 2,739.3 | 244.3 |
| Kentucky | 3,013.3 | 233.6 | 2,779.8 | 10.1 | 19.1 | 81.1 | 123.3 | 872.2 | 1,662.1 | 245.4 |
| Louisiana | 4,497.9 | 524.8 | 3,973.1 | 15.5 | 30.9 | 142.9 | 335.5 | 1,165.5 | 2,469.9 | 337.7 |

| State | Total | Violent | Property | Murder | Rape | Robbery | Assault | Burglary | Larceny | Auto theft |
|---|---|---|---|---|---|---|---|---|---|---|
| Maine | 4,075.4 | 224.7 | 3,850.7 | 2.4 | 13.5 | 38.7 | 170.0 | 1,253.1 | 2,350.7 | 246.9 |
| Maryland | 5,700.0 | 693.8 | 5,006.2 | 8.0 | 34.8 | 292.1 | 358.9 | 1,400.0 | 3,177.7 | 428.5 |
| Massachusetts | 5,409.0 | 425.3 | 4,983.7 | 3.1 | 20.8 | 169.1 | 231.6 | 1,532.2 | 2,311.3 | 1,140.1 |
| Michigan | 5,812.0 | 584.7 | 5,227.3 | 9.3 | 38.9 | 261.9 | 274.6 | 1,522.7 | 3,159.0 | 545.5 |
| Minnesota | 4,230.8 | 193.8 | 4,037.0 | 2.7 | 19.5 | 85.9 | 85.8 | 1,134.7 | 2,559.3 | 343.1 |
| Mississippi | 2,588.6 | 288.7 | 2,299.9 | 14.3 | 19.6 | 65.7 | 189.1 | 915.6 | 1,239.9 | 144.4 |
| Missouri | 4,581.3 | 460.4 | 4,120.8 | 9.6 | 28.3 | 189.0 | 233.5 | 1,318.3 | 2,424.2 | 378.4 |
| Montana | 4,105.3 | 218.0 | 3,887.3 | 5.4 | 16.7 | 39.2 | 156.8 | 804.9 | 2,773.2 | 309.2 |
| Nebraska | 3,524.6 | 199.4 | 3,325.2 | 3.9 | 18.1 | 64.7 | 112.7 | 760.0 | 2,316.1 | 249.1 |
| Nevada | 7,967.9 | 743.0 | 7,225.0 | 15.8 | 49.1 | 323.1 | 355.0 | 2,453.1 | 4,212.6 | 559.2 |
| New Hampshire | 3,792.1 | 113.1 | 3,679.0 | 3.2 | 10.7 | 23.2 | 76.0 | 1,041.7 | 2,343.9 | 293.4 |
| New Jersey | 5,113.9 | 392.0 | 4,721.8 | 5.6 | 21.0 | 180.4 | 185.1 | 1,435.8 | 2,774.5 | 511.5 |
| New Mexico | 5,187.6 | 500.9 | 4,686.7 | 8.8 | 39.1 | 109.6 | 343.4 | 1,418.7 | 3,008.6 | 259.5 |
| New York | 6,087.6 | 831.8 | 5,255.8 | 10.7 | 29.4 | 472.6 | 319.1 | 1,728.0 | 2,782.0 | 745.8 |
| North Carolina | 3,791.1 | 407.1 | 3,384.0 | 10.6 | 17.0 | 61.3 | 318.3 | 1,154.1 | 2,037.8 | 192.1 |
| North Dakota | 2,500.9 | 67.1 | 2,433.8 | 0.9 | 9.0 | 13.3 | 43.8 | 446.1 | 1,843.0 | 144.7 |
| Ohio | 4,719.9 | 406.7 | 4,313.2 | 7.8 | 27.3 | 190.5 | 181.1 | 1,216.0 | 2,696.8 | 400.4 |
| Oklahoma | 4,159.6 | 316.6 | 3,843.0 | 8.6 | 29.2 | 73.8 | 205.0 | 1,288.2 | 2,228.1 | 326.8 |
| Oregon | 5,987.2 | 455.8 | 5,531.4 | 4.9 | 39.9 | 124.1 | 286.9 | 1,636.4 | 3,506.1 | 388.9 |
| Pennsylvania | 3,117.5 | 282.8 | 2,834.7 | 5.6 | 19.0 | 130.3 | 128.0 | 877.5 | 1,624.1 | 333.2 |
| Rhode Island | 5,426.6 | 301.6 | 5,125.0 | 3.6 | 10.5 | 86.5 | 201.0 | 1,489.5 | 2,844.1 | 791.4 |
| South Carolina | 4,837.3 | 636.2 | 4,201.1 | 11.9 | 33.0 | 105.9 | 485.3 | 1,613.6 | 2,342.4 | 245.1 |
| South Dakota | 2,611.5 | 189.1 | 2,422.4 | 2.0 | 13.5 | 17.9 | 155.7 | 570.5 | 1,704.4 | 147.5 |
| Tennessee | 3,739.7 | 389.5 | 3,350.2 | 10.1 | 29.7 | 145.8 | 203.9 | 1,259.7 | 1,776.5 | 314.0 |
| Texas | 5,397.1 | 407.7 | 4,989.4 | 13.3 | 33.8 | 152.4 | 208.2 | 1,603.1 | 2,988.7 | 397.6 |
| Utah | 4,750.6 | 240.0 | 4,510.6 | 3.5 | 20.3 | 68.8 | 147.3 | 1,171.6 | 3,004.6 | 334.5 |
| Vermont | 3,964.0 | 149.5 | 3,814.5 | 1.4 | 15.9 | 30.8 | 101.2 | 1,348.2 | 2,201.0 | 265.2 |
| Virginia | 4,024.1 | 290.0 | 3,734.0 | 9.0 | 23.3 | 92.1 | 165.7 | 986.2 | 2,521.2 | 226.7 |
| Washington | 5,727.7 | 374.9 | 5,352.8 | 4.3 | 39.6 | 106.2 | 224.8 | 1,605.6 | 3,386.9 | 360.3 |
| West Virginia | 2,254.7 | 152.3 | 2,102.4 | 6.0 | 13.2 | 42.2 | 90.9 | 597.4 | 1,341.7 | 163.3 |
| Wisconsin | 3,813.4 | 131.5 | 3,681.9 | 2.8 | 12.9 | 52.2 | 63.7 | 846.9 | 2,614.2 | 220.7 |
| Wyoming | 4,106.7 | 240.9 | 3,865.8 | 5.4 | 21.9 | 39.7 | 173.9 | 811.6 | 2,772.2 | 282.0 |

## Total Arrest Trends by Sex, 1977

Source: 1977 Uniform Crime Reports, Federal Bureau of Investigation

| | Males | | | | Females | | | |
|---|---|---|---|---|---|---|---|---|
| | Total | | Under 18 | | Total | | Under 18 | |
| | 1977 | Per-cent change 1976-77 | 1977 | Per-cent change 1976-77 | 1977 | Per-cent change 1976-77 | 1977 | Per-cent change 1976-77 |
| Total[1] | 7,180,561 | − .5 | 1,621,764 | − 2.3 | 1,374,963 | + 2.5 | 443,605 | + .1 |
| Murder and non-negligent manslaughter | 14,032 | − 3.6 | 1,493 | + 1.9 | 2,384 | − 1.6 | 136 | − 23.6 |
| Manslaughter by negligence | 2,432 | − 6.3 | 261 | − 5.4 | 305 | + 7.0 | 47 | + 34.3 |
| Forcible rape | 24,324 | + 4.3 | 3,991 | + .7 | 260 | +21.5 | 101 | + 57.8 |
| Robbery | 110,489 | − 3.5 | 35,764 | − 1.7 | 8,851 | − .7 | 2,757 | − 1.5 |
| Aggravated assault | 184,293 | + 2.5 | 29,815 | − 2.6 | 27,238 | + 1.4 | 5,206 | − 7.0 |
| Burglary—breaking or entering | 404,638 | − 2.4 | 209,156 | − 1.9 | 25,860 | + 4.1 | 13,117 | + 6.9 |
| Larceny—theft | 656,619 | − 2.7 | 297,074 | − 2.0 | 306,898 | + .1 | 117,155 | − 1.3 |
| Motor vehicle theft | 119,071 | + 2.4 | 62,534 | + 4.1 | 10,492 | +16.5 | 6,198 | + 18.9 |
| Other assaults | 324,080 | − .2 | 57,899 | − 6.9 | 52,192 | − 1.2 | 15,099 | − 5.8 |
| Arson | 13,784 | + 2.6 | 7,054 | − 3.0 | 1,782 | + 5.4 | 731 | + .4 |
| Forgery and counterfeiting | 44,403 | +10.3 | 5,878 | + 26.5 | 18,529 | + 8.5 | 2,324 | + 9.5 |
| Fraud | 127,725 | +21.9 | 17,465 | +298.4 | 69,552 | +17.8 | 4,583 | +216.7 |
| Embezzlement | 4,761 | −20.4 | 581 | + 10.5 | 1,419 | −45.8 | 162 | + 57.3 |
| Stolen property; buying, receiving, possessing | 88,622 | − 2.9 | 29,961 | + 1.2 | 10,671 | − .4 | 2,832 | + 6.7 |
| Vandalism | 170,542 | + 1.3 | 104,331 | − 2.9 | 15,721 | + 4.9 | 8,495 | − 1.1 |
| Weapons; carrying, possessing, etc. | 120,235 | − 2.5 | 19,654 | − 4.2 | 10,558 | − 4.1 | 1,329 | + .2 |
| Prostitution and commercialized vice | 22,070 | +13.6 | 1,021 | + 59.5 | 53,212 | + 7.8 | 2,209 | + .3 |
| Sex offenses (except forcible rape and prostitution) | 53,100 | + 4.2 | 9,647 | − 3.9 | 5,265 | + 5.4 | 1,065 | − 5.3 |
| Drug abuse offenses | 462,154 | − 3.0 | 105,086 | − 4.1 | 74,415 | − 3.0 | 20,504 | − 3.2 |
| Gambling | 46,738 | −26.3 | 2,061 | − 25.4 | 4,593 | −31.4 | 113 | − 58.1 |
| Offenses against family, children | 42,446 | −20.0 | 1,880 | − 34.7 | 5,211 | −17.8 | 1,129 | − 16.7 |
| Driving under the influence | 954,261 | + 4.8 | 20,693 | + 12.6 | 86,735 | + 7.8 | 2,112 | + 27.3 |
| Liquor laws | 258,988 | − .2 | 89,031 | + 2.4 | 45,128 | + 6.3 | 24,457 | + 8.3 |
| Drunkenness | 1,074,243 | + .1 | 40,533 | − .3 | 82,864 | + .2 | 6,482 | + 5.1 |
| Disorderly conduct | 495,788 | −10.1 | 94,271 | − 9.0 | 103,655 | − 3.8 | 21,792 | − 1.4 |
| Vagrancy | 28,088 | − .3 | 4,364 | − 24.1 | 15,158 | +96.9 | 1,014 | − .3 |
| All other offenses (except traffic) | 1,193,112 | + 2.4 | 230,743 | − 3.1 | 216,571 | + 6.8 | 63,012 | + 2.4 |

(1) Totals will not add due to deletion of several minor arrest categories.

## Police Roster
**Source: Uniform Crime Reports**

Police officers and civilian employees in large cities as of Oct. 31, 1977

| City | Officer | Civilian | City | Officer | Civilian | City | Officer | Civilian |
|---|---|---|---|---|---|---|---|---|
| Anchorage, Alas. . . | 163 | 58 | Indianapolis, Ind. . . . | 1,069 | 299 | Phoenix, Ariz. . . . . | 1,532 | 469 |
| Atlanta, Ga. . . . . . | 1,225 | 328 | Jacksonville, Fla. . . . | 979 | 578 | Pittsburgh, Pa. . . . . | 1,416 | 34 |
| Baltimore, Md. . . . . | 3,410 | 601 | Kansas City, Mo. . . . | 1,226 | 500 | Portland, Ore. . . . . | 693 | 185 |
| Birmingham, Ala. . . | 679 | 155 | Little Rock, Ark. . . . . | 262 | 66 | Rochester, N.Y. . . . . | 645 | 138 |
| Boston, Mass. . . . . | 2,166 | 324 | Los Angeles, Cal. . . . | 7,299 | 2,719 | Sacramento, Cal. . . . | 492 | 168 |
| Bridgeport, Conn. . . | 365 | 23 | Louisville, Ky. . . . . | 727 | 211 | St. Louis, Mo. . . . . | 2,091 | 566 |
| Buffalo, N.Y. . . . . . | 1,092 | 129 | Memphis, Tenn. . . . . | 1,241 | 348 | St. Petersburg, Fla. . | 438 | 194 |
| Chicago, Ill. . . . . . | 13,214 | 1,654 | Miami, Fla. . . . . . . | 733 | 300 | San Antonio, Tex. . . | 1,102 | 239 |
| Cincinnati, Oh. . . . | 977 | 163 | Milwaukee, Wis. . . . . | 2,083 | 240 | San Diego, Cal. . . . | 1,092 | 309 |
| Cleveland, Oh. . . . . | 2,095 | 172 | Minneapolis, Minn. . . | 795 | 120 | San Francisco, Cal. . | 1,659 | 517 |
| Columbus, Oh. . . . | 1,087 | 170 | Newark, N.J. . . . . . | 1,463 | 278 | San Jose, Cal. . . . . | 787 | 172 |
| Dallas, Tex. . . . . . | 2,004 | 595 | New Orleans, La. . . . | 1,600 | 439 | Santa Ana, Cal. . . . | 322 | 123 |
| Denver, Col. . . . . . | 1,384 | 271 | New York, N.Y. . . . . | 24,895 | 4,702 | Seattle, Wash. . . . . | 1,013 | 302 |
| Detroit, Mich. . . . . | 5,703 | 610 | Norfolk, Va. . . . . . | 604 | 130 | Stockton, Cal. . . . . | 220 | 112 |
| Ft. Worth, Tex. . . . . | 671 | 205 | Oakland, Cal. . . . . . | 656 | 375 | Tampa, Fla. . . . . . | 612 | 176 |
| Fresno, Cal. . . . . . | 333 | 116 | Oklahoma City, Okl. . | 672 | 190 | Toledo, Oh. . . . . . | 733 | 102 |
| Hartford, Conn. , . . . | 427 | 93 | Omaha, Neb. . . . . . | 534 | 127 | Tucson, Ariz. . . . . . | 515 | 179 |
| Honolulu, Ha. . . . . | 1,471 | 349 | Pasadena, Cal. . . . . | 181 | 132 | Washington, D.C. . . . | 4,166 | 585 |
| Houston, Tex. . . . . | 2,817 | 770 | Philadelphia, Pa. . . . | 8,188 | 1,064 | Wichita, Kan. . . . . . | 391 | 134 |

### 1,094 Law Enforcement Officers Killed 1968-1977

| | | | |
|---|---|---|---|
| Responding to disturbance calls. . . . . . . . . . . . . . | 175 | Handling, transporting, custody of prisoners . . . . . . . | 53 |
| Burglaries in progress or pursuing suspect. . . . . . . . | 75 | Investigating suspicious persons and circumstances . . . | 81 |
| Robberies in progress or pursuing suspect. . . . . . . . | 212 | Ambush . . . . . . . . . . . . . . . . . . . . . . . . | 99 |
| Attempting other arrests . . . . . . . . . . . . . . . . | 241 | Mentally deranged . . . . . . . . . . . . . . . . . . . | 30 |
| Civil disorders . . . . . . . . . . . . . . . . . . . . . | 7 | Traffic stops . . . . . . . . . . . . . . . . . . . . . . | 121 |

Geographically for the period of 1968-1977 the 1,094 officers who were slain in the line of duty were divided in this fashion: Northeast 157; North Central 269; South 463; and West 177. Another 28 officers were killed in outlying territories.

### Crime Index Trends by Geographic Region 1977 over 1976
(rates per 100,000 population)

| Region[1] | Total | Violent | Property | Murder | Rape | Robbery | Assault | Burglary | Larceny | Auto theft |
|---|---|---|---|---|---|---|---|---|---|---|
| Northeast . . . . . . . . | -3.9 | -2.5 | -4.0 | -1.4 | +11.3 | -9.3 | +5.5 | -3.0 | -4.9 | -3.0 |
| North Central . . . . . . | -5.8 | -2.1 | -6.1 | -2.7 | +5.6 | -7.5 | +2.1 | -3.5 | -8.0 | -0.3 |
| South . . . . . . . . . | -3.5 | +5.2 | -4.3 | 0.0 | +11.8 | +0.3 | +7.6 | -0.8 | -7.1 | +4.9 |
| West . . . . . . . . . . | -3.1 | +5.0 | -3.8 | +9.4 | +11.1 | +3.3 | +5.3 | -1.5 | -5.9 | +2.4 |

(1) Northeast includes New England, New Jersey, New York, and Pennsylvania; North Central extends west through Nebraska and includes Missouri; South extends from Delaware, Maryland, and West Virginia to Oklahoma and Texas.

### Canada: Criminal Offenses and Crime Rate
**Source: Statistics Canada**

| | 1976 | | 1977[1] | | Percent change in rate |
|---|---|---|---|---|---|
| | Actual offenses | Rate[2] | Actual offenses | Rate[2] | |
| **Total criminal code** . . . . . . . . . . . . . . . . | 1,637,704 | 7086.9 | 1,650,382 | 7,085.9 | — |
| **Total homicide** . . . . . . . . . . . . . . . . . . | 1,360 | 5.9 | 1,389 | 6.0 | +0.1 |
| Murder, 1st degree . . . . . . . . . . . . . . . . | 12 | 0.05 | 199 | 0.9 | [3] |
| Murder, 2d degree . . . . . . . . . . . . . . . . | 603 | 2.61 | 425 | 1.8 | [3] |
| Manslaughter . . . . . . . . . . . . . . . . . . . | 48 | 0.2 | 78 | 0.3 | +50 |
| Infanticide . . . . . . . . . . . . . . . . . . . . | 5 | 0.02 | 5 | 0.02 | — |
| Attempted murder . . . . . . . . . . . . . . . . . | 692 | 3.0 | 682 | 2.9 | -3.3 |
| **Total sexual offenses** . . . . . . . . . . . . . . . | 10,611 | 45.9 | 10,919 | 46.9 | +2.2 |
| Rape . . . . . . . . . . . . . . . . . . . . . . | 1,828 | 7.9 | 1,892 | 8.1 | +2.5 |
| Indecent assault on female . . . . . . . . . . . . | 5,273 | 22.8 | 5,259 | 22.6 | -0.9 |
| Indecent assault on male. . . . . . . . . . . . . | 1,116 | 4.8 | 1,344 | 5.8 | +20.8 |
| Other sexual offenses . . . . . . . . . . . . . . | 2,394 | 10.4 | 2,424 | 10.4 | — |
| **Total crimes of violence** . . . . . . . . . . . . . | 136,935 | 592.6 | 135,479 | 581.7 | -1.8 |
| Assaults (not indecent) . . . . . . . . . . . . . | 104,914 | 445.4 | 103,708 | 445.3 | — |
| Robbery . . . . . . . . . . . . . . . . . . . . . | 20,050 | 86.8 | 19,463 | 83.6 | -3.7 |
| **Total property crimes** . . . . . . . . . . . . . . | 1,062,952 | 4,599.5 | 1,056,894 | 4,537.9 | -1.3 |
| Breaking and entering . . . . . . . . . . . . . . | 268,332 | 1,161.1 | 270,065 | 1,159.5 | -0.1 |
| Theft, motor vehicle. . . . . . . . . . . . . . . | 87,627 | 379.2 | 83,899 | 360.2 | -5.0 |
| Theft over $200 . . . . . . . . . . . . . . . . . | 105,381 | 456.0 | 113,660 | 488.0 | +10.7 |
| Theft $200 and under. . . . . . . . . . . . . . | 497,662 | 2,153.4 | 485,753 | 2,085 | -3.1 |
| Having stolen goods . . . . . . . . . . . . . . | 17,686 | 76.5 | 18,297 | 78.6 | +2.7 |
| Fraud . . . . . . . . . . . . . . . . . . . . . | 86,264 | 373.3 | 85,220 | 365.9 | -2.0 |
| **Total other crimes** . . . . . . . . . . . . . . . | 437,817 | 1,894.6 | 458,009 | 1,966.5 | +3.8 |
| Prostitution. . . . . . . . . . . . . . . . . . . | 2,841 | 12.3 | 2,840 | 12.2 | -0.8 |
| Gaming and betting . . . . . . . . . . . . . . . | 3,753 | 16.2 | 3,487 | 15.0 | -7.4 |
| Offensive weapons . . . . . . . . . . . . . . . | 13,512 | 58.5 | 13,424 | 57.6 | -1.5 |
| Other criminal code. . . . . . . . . . . . . . . | 417,711 | 1,807.5 | 438,258 | 1,881.7 | +4.1 |
| Federal statutes-drugs . . . . . . . . . . . . . | 62,916 | 272.3 | 63,843 | 274.1 | +.7 |
| Federal statutes-other[4] . . . . . . . . . . . . . | 50,497 | 218.5 | 65,779 | 282.4 | 29.2 |
| Provincial statutes[4] . . . . . . . . . . . . . . | 367,482 | 1,590.1 | 379,219 | 1,628.2 | +2.4 |
| Municipal bylaws[4] . . . . . . . . . . . . . . . | 64,178 | 277.7 | 61,282 | 263.1 | -5.3 |
| **Total - all offenses** . . . . . . . . . . . . . . | 2,182,777 | 9,445.6 | 2,220,505 | 9,533.7 | +0.9 |

(1) Preliminary. (2) Rate per 100,000 population. (3) Data within these categories reflect a 1976 Criminal Code murder reclassification. The rate for 1st and 2d degree murder (formerly capital and non-capital murder) combined is 2.7 for both years. (4) Excluding traffic offenses.

# POSTAL INFORMATION

## U.S. Postal Service

The Postal Reorganization Act, creating a government-owned postal service under the executive branch and replacing the old Post Office Department, was signed into law by President Nixon on Aug. 12, 1970. The service officially came into being on July 1, 1971.

The new U.S. Postal Service is governed by an 11-man Board of Governors. Nine members are appointed to 9-year terms by the president with Senate approval. These 9, in turn, choose a postmaster general, who is no longer a member of the president's cabinet. The board and the new post-master general choose the 11th member, who serves as deputy postmaster general. A new Postal Rate Commission of 5 members, appointed by the president, recommends postal rates to the governors for their approval.

The first postmaster general under the new system was Winton M. Blount. He resigned Oct. 29, 1971, and was replaced by his deputy, E. T. Klassen, Dec. 7, 1971. Benjamin F. Bailar succeeded him Feb. 16, 1975, and was succeeded by William F. Bolger on March 15, 1978.

As of June 30, 1977, there was a total of 30,521 post offices throughout the U.S. and possessions.

## U.S. Domestic Rates (in effect May 29, 1978)

Domestic includes the U.S., territories and possessions, APO and FPO.

### First Class

Letters written, and matter sealed against inspection, 15¢ for 1st ounce or fraction, 13¢ for each additional ounce or fraction.

U.S. Postal cards; single 10¢; double 20¢; private postcards, same.

First class includes written matter, namely letters, postal cards, postcards (private mailing cards) and all other matter wholly or partly in writing, whether sealed or unsealed, except manuscripts for books, periodical articles and music, manuscript copy accompanying proofsheets or corrected proofsheets of the same and the writing authorized by law on matter of other classes. Also matter sealed or closed against inspection, bills and statements of accounts.

### Greeting Cards

May be sent first class or single piece third class.

### Second Class

Single copy mailings by general public 10¢ for first 2 ounces and 6¢ for each additional ounce or the 4th class rate, whichever is lower. There are special rates for publications, newspapers, and bulk mailing, consult local postmasters for rates and permit.

### Third Class

Third class (limit up to but not including 16 ounces): Mailable matter not in 1st and 2d classes.

Single mailing: Greeting cards (sealed or unsealed), small parcels, printed matter, booklets and catalogs. 20¢ the first 2 ounces plus 20¢ for the next 2 ounces, plus 13¢ for each additional 2 ounces through 15.9 ounces.

Bulk material: books, catalogs of 24 pages or more, seeds, cuttings, bulbs, roots, scions, and plants. 36¢ per pound, 8.4¢ minimum per price.

Other matter: newsletters, shoppers' guides, advertising circulars. 41¢ per pound, 8.4¢ minimum per piece. Separate rates for some nonprofit organizations. Bulk mailing fee, $40 per calendar year. Apply to postmaster for permit. One-time fee for permit imprint, $30.

### Parcel Post—Fourth Class

Fourth class or parcel post (16 ounces and over): merchandise, printed matter, etc., may be sealed, subject to inspection.

On parcels weighing less than 15 lbs. and measuring more than 84 inches, but not more than 100 inches in length and girth combined, the minimum postal charge shall be the zone charge applicable to a 15-pound parcel.

### Priority Mail

First class mail of more than 12 ounces can be sent "Priority Mail (Heavy Pieces)" service. The most expeditious handling and transportation available will be used for fastest delivery.

### Forwarding Addresses

The mailer, in order to obtain a forwarding address, must endorse the envelope or cover "Address Correction Requested." The destination post office then will determine whether a forwarding address has been left on file and provide if for a fee of 25¢.

### Special Handling

Third and fourth class parcels will be handled and delivered as expeditiously as practicable (but not special delivery) upon payment, in addition to the regular postage: up to 2 lbs., 50¢; over 2 lbs. and up to 10 lbs., 70¢; over 10 lbs., $1.25. Such parcels must be endorsed, Special Handling.

### Special Delivery

First class mail up to 2 lbs. $2.00, over 2 lbs. and up to 10 lbs., $2.25; over 10 lbs. $2.85. All other classes up to 2 lbs. $2.25, over 2 and up to 10 lbs., $2.85, over 10 lbs. $3.25.

### Priority Mail

Packages weighing up to 70 pounds and exceeding 100 inches in length and girth combined, including written and other material of the first class, whether sealed or unsealed, fractions of a pound being charged as a full pound, except in the 1 to 5 pound weight category where half-pound weight increments apply.

Rates according to zone apply between the U.S. and Puerto Rico and Virgin Islands.

Parcels weighing less than 15 pounds, measuring over 84 inches but not exceeding 100 inches in length and girth combined are chargeable with a minimum rate equal to that for a 15 pound parcel for the zone to which addressed.

| Zones | To 1 lb. | 1½ | 2 | 2½ | 3 | 3½ | 4 | 4½ | 5 |
|---|---|---|---|---|---|---|---|---|---|
| 1, 2, 3 | $1.71 | $1.86 | $1.99 | $2.11 | $2.23 | $2.35 | $2.47 | $2.59 | $2.72 |
| 4 | 1.81 | 1.96 | 2.12 | 2.27 | 2.42 | 2.58 | 2.73 | 2.89 | 3.04 |
| 5 | 1.88 | 2.07 | 2.27 | 2.46 | 2.65 | 2.84 | 3.03 | 3.22 | 3.42 |
| 6 | 1.97 | 2.21 | 2.44 | 2.68 | 2.91 | 3.15 | 3.38 | 3.62 | 3.85 |
| 7 | 2.06 | 2.34 | 2.61 | 2.89 | 3.17 | 3.45 | 3.73 | 4.01 | 4.29 |
| 8 | 2.25 | 2.50 | 2.83 | 3.16 | 3.50 | 3.83 | 4.16 | 4.50 | 4.83 |

## Individual Piece Mailings
### (Fourth class catalogs)

| Weight lbs. | Local | 1&2 | 3 | 4 | 5 | 6 | 7 | 8 |
|---|---|---|---|---|---|---|---|---|
| | | | | Zones | | | | |
| 1.5 | .69 | .92 | .94 | .97 | 1.02 | 1.08 | 1.16 | 1.19 |
| 2 | .69 | .93 | .95 | .99 | 1.06 | 1.14 | 1.25 | 1.28 |
| 2.5 | .69 | .93 | .96 | 1.01 | 1.10 | 1.20 | 1.33 | 1.38 |
| 3 | .69 | .94 | .97 | 1.03 | 1.14 | 1.25 | 1.41 | 1.47 |
| 3.5 | .69 | .94 | .98 | 1.05 | 1.17 | 1.31 | 1.50 | 1.56 |
| 4 | .69 | .95 | .99 | 1.07 | 1.21 | 1.37 | 1.58 | 1.66 |
| 4.5 | .69 | .95 | 1.00 | 1.09 | 1.25 | 1.42 | 1.67 | 1.75 |
| 5 | .70 | .96 | 1.02 | 1.12 | 1.29 | 1.48 | 1.75 | 1.85 |
| 6 | .70 | .96 | 1.04 | 1.16 | 1.36 | 1.59 | 1.92 | 2.03 |
| 7 | .70 | .97 | 1.06 | 1.20 | 1.44 | 1.71 | 2.09 | 2.22 |
| 8 | .70 | .98 | 1.08 | 1.24 | 1.51 | 1.82 | 2.25 | 2.41 |
| 9 | .70 | .99 | 1.10 | 1.28 | 1.59 | 1.94 | 2.42 | 2.59 |
| 10 | .70 | 1.00 | 1.12 | 1.32 | 1.66 | 2.05 | 2.59 | 2.78 |
| Per piece (dollars) | .69 | .91 | .91 | .91 | .91 | .91 | .91 | .91 |
| Per pound (cents) | .1 | .9 | 2.1 | 4.1 | 7.5 | 11.4 | 16.8 | 18.7 |

### Zone Mileage

| | | | | | |
|---|---|---|---|---|---|
| 1 . . Up to 50 | 3 . . 150-300 | 5 . . 600-1,000 | 7 . 1,400-1,800 |
| 2 . . 50-150 | 4 . . 300-600 | 6 . . 1,000-1,400 | 8 . over, 1,800 |

## Domestic Mail Special Services

**Registry** — all mailable matter prepaid with postage at the first-class or airmail rate may be registered. The mailer is required to declare the value of mail presented for registration.

**Insurance** — is applicable to 3d and 4th class matter. Matter for sale addressed to prospective purchasers who have not ordered it or authorized its sending will not be insured.

**C.O.D.: Unregistered** — is applicable to 3d and 4th class matter and sealed domestic mail of any class bearing postage at the 1st class rate. Such mail must be based on bona fide orders or be in conformity with agreements between senders and addressees. **Registered** — for details consult postmaster.

**Certified mail** — service is available for any matter having no intrinsic value on which 1st class or air mail postage is paid. Receipt is furnished at time of mailing and evidence of delivery obtained. The fee is 80¢ in addition to postage. Return receipt, restricted delivery, and special delivery are available upon payment of additional fees. No indemnity.

### Registered Mail

| | |
|---|---|
| Indemnity to $100 . . . . . . . . . . . . . . . . . . . . . . | $3.00 |
| 100.01 to 200. . . . . . . . . . . . . . . . . . . . . . . | 3.30 |
| 200.01 to 400. . . . . . . . . . . . . . . . . . . . . . . | 3.70 |
| 400.01 to 600. . . . . . . . . . . . . . . . . . . . . . . | 4.10 |
| 600.01 to 800. . . . . . . . . . . . . . . . . . . . . . . | 4.50 |
| 800.01 to 1,000. . . . . . . . . . . . . . . . . . . . . | 4.90 |
| 1,000.01 to 2,000. . . . . . . . . . . . . . . . . . . | 5.30 |
| 2,000.01 to 3,000. . . . . . . . . . . . . . . . . . . | 5.70 |
| 3,000.01 to 4,000. . . . . . . . . . . . . . . . . . . | 6.10 |
| 4,000.01 to 5,000. . . . . . . . . . . . . . . . . . . | 6.50 |
| 5,000.01 to 6,000. . . . . . . . . . . . . . . . . . . | 6.90 |
| 6,000.01 to 7,000. . . . . . . . . . . . . . . . . . . | 7.30 |
| 7,000.01 to 8,000. . . . . . . . . . . . . . . . . . . | 7.70 |
| 8,000.01 to 9,000. . . . . . . . . . . . . . . . . . . | 8.10 |
| 9,000.01 to 10,000. . . . . . . . . . . . . . . . . | 8.50 |

Consult postmaster for registry rates above $10,000.

## Insured Mail

| | |
|---|---|
| $0.01 to $15. . . . . . . . . . . . . . . . . . . . . . . . . | $0.50 |
| 15.01 to 50. . . . . . . . . . . . . . . . . . . . . . . . | 0.85 |
| 50.01 to 100. . . . . . . . . . . . . . . . . . . . . . . | 1.10 |
| 100.01 to 150. . . . . . . . . . . . . . . . . . . . . . | 1.40 |
| 150.01 to 200. . . . . . . . . . . . . . . . . . . . . . | 1.75 |
| 200.01 to 300. . . . . . . . . . . . . . . . . . . . . . | 2.25 |
| 300.01 to 400. . . . . . . . . . . . . . . . . . . . . . | 2.75 |

Liability for insured mail is limited to $400.

## C.O.D. Mail

Consult postmaster for fees and conditions of mailing.

### Special Fourth Class Rate
(limit 70 lbs.)

First pound or fraction, 59¢ (52¢ if special rate matter is presorted to 5 digit ZIP code or 55¢ if presorted to 3 digits); each additional pound or fraction through 7 pounds, 22¢; each additional pound, 13¢. Only following specific articles: books 24 pages or more, at least 22 of which are printed consisting wholly of reading matter or scholarly bibliography containing no advertisement other than incidental announcements of books; 16 millimeter films in final form (except when mailed to or from commercial theaters); printed music in bound or sheet form; printed objective test materials; sound recordings, playscripts, and manuscripts for books, periodicals, and music; printed educational reference charts; loose-leaf pages and binders therefor consisting of medical information for distribution to doctors, hospitals, medical schools, and medical students. Package must be marked "Special 4th Class Rate" stating item contained.

### Library Rate (limit 70 lbs.)

First pound 38¢, each additional pound through 7 pounds, 13¢; each additional pound, 7¢. Books when loaned or exchanged between schools, colleges, public libraries, and certain non-profit organizations; books, printed music, bound academic theses, periodicals, sound recordings, other library materials, museum materials (specimens, collections), scientific or mathematical kits, instruments or other devices; also catalogs, guides or scripts for some of these materials. Must be marked "Library Rate".

### Postal Union Mail Special Services

**Registration** — available to practically all countries. Fee $3.00. The maximum indemnity payable — generally only in case of complete loss (of both contents and wrapper) — is $15.76. To Canada only the fees are $3.00 and $3.30, providing indemnity for loss up to $100 to $200, respectively.

**Return receipt** —fee is 45¢.

**Special delivery** — Available to most countries. Consult post office. Fees: for post cards, letter mail, and airmail "other articles," $2.00 up to 2 pounds; over 2 to 10 pounds, $2.25; over 10 pounds, $2.85. For surface "other articles," $2.25, $2.85, and $3.25, respectively.

**Marking** — an article intended for special delivery service must have affixed to the cover near the name of the country of destination "EXPRESS" (special delivery) label, obtainable at the post office, or it may be marked on the cover

## Parcel Post Rate Schedule

| 1 lb., not exceeding | Local | 1 & 2 | 3 | 4 | 5 | 6 | 7 | 8 |
|---|---|---|---|---|---|---|---|---|
| | | | | Zones | | | | |
| 2 | 1.15 | 1.35 | 1.39 | 1.56 | 1.72 | 1.84 | 1.98 | 2.22 |
| 3 | 1.23 | 1.45 | 1.53 | 1.73 | 1.86 | 2.04 | 2.24 | 2.61 |
| 4 | 1.29 | 1.50 | 1.65 | 1.82 | 2.00 | 2.23 | 2.50 | 3.00 |
| 5 | 1.36 | 1.66 | 1.77 | 1.92 | 2.14 | 2.43 | 2.77 | 3.39 |
| 6 | 1.42 | 1.71 | 1.84 | 2.01 | 2.28 | 2.62 | 3.03 | 3.78 |
| 7 | 1.47 | 1.76 | 1.90 | 2.11 | 2.41 | 2.82 | 3.29 | 4.17 |
| 8 | 1.51 | 1.80 | 1.97 | 2.20 | 2.55 | 3.02 | 3.56 | 4.55 |
| 9 | 1.54 | 1.85 | 2.03 | 2.29 | 2.69 | 3.21 | 3.82 | 4.95 |
| 10 | 1.57 | 1.89 | 2.10 | 2.39 | 2.83 | 3.41 | 4.08 | 5.34 |
| 11 | 1.60 | 1.94 | 2.17 | 2.50 | 3.00 | 3.65 | 4.42 | 5.73 |
| 12 | 1.64 | 1.98 | 2.22 | 2.56 | 3.09 | 3.77 | 4.57 | 6.12 |
| 13 | 1.67 | 2.02 | 2.27 | 2.63 | 3.17 | 3.89 | 4.72 | 6.41 |
| 14 | 1.70 | 2.05 | 2.32 | 2.69 | 3.25 | 3.99 | 4.86 | 6.62 |
| 15 | 1.73 | 2.09 | 2.36 | 2.74 | 3.33 | 4.09 | 4.99 | 6.30 |
| 16 | 1.76 | 2.13 | 2.41 | 2.80 | 3.40 | 4.19 | 5.11 | 6.98 |
| 17 | 1.79 | 2.16 | 2.45 | 2.85 | 3.47 | 4.28 | 5.23 | 7.15 |
| 18 | 1.82 | 2.20 | 2.49 | 2.91 | 3.54 | 4.37 | 5.34 | 7.31 |
| 19 | 1.86 | 2.23 | 2.53 | 2.96 | 3.61 | 4.46 | 5.45 | 7.47 |
| 20 | 1.89 | 2.27 | 2.58 | 3.01 | 3.67 | 4.54 | 5.55 | 7.52 |

Consult postmaster for parcels over 20 pounds or measuring more than 72 inches, length and girth.

boldly in red "EXPRESS" (special delivery).

**Special handling** — entitles AO surface packages to priority handling between mailing point and U.S. point of dispatch. Fees: 70¢ for packages to 10 pounds, and $1.25 for packages over 10 pounds.

**Airmail** — there is daily air service to practically all countries.

**Prepayment of replies from other countries** — a mailer who wishes to prepay a reply by letter from another country may do so by sending his correspondent one or more international reply coupons, which may be purchased at United States post offices. One coupon should be accepted in any country in exchange for stamps to prepay a surface letter of the first unit of weight to the U.S.

## Post Office-Authorized 2-Letter State Abbreviations

Gradually replacing the traditional abbreviations for the states of the United States are the two-letter ones approved by the Post Office Department when it introduced the ZIP Code in 1963. The official list follows, including the District of Columbia, Guam, Puerto Rico, the Canal Zone, and the Virgin Islands (all capital letters are used):

| | | | | | | | |
|---|---|---|---|---|---|---|---|
| Alabama | AL | Idaho | ID | Montana | MT | Rhode Island | RI |
| Alaska | AK | Illinois | IL | Nebraska | NE | South Carolina | SC |
| Arizona | AZ | Indiana | IN | Nevada | NV | South Dakota | SD |
| Arkansas | AR | Iowa | IA | New Hampshire | NH | Tennessee | TN |
| California | CA | Kansas | KS | New Jersey | NJ | Texas | TX |
| Canal Zone | CZ | Kentucky | KY | New Mexico | NM | Utah | UT |
| Colorado | CO | Louisiana | LA | New York | NY | Vermont | VT |
| Connecticut | CT | Maine | ME | North Carolina | NC | Virginia | VA |
| Delaware | DE | Maryland | MD | North Dakota | ND | Virgin Islands | VI |
| Dist. of Col. | DC | Massachusetts | MA | Ohio | OH | Washington | WA |
| Florida | FL | Michigan | MI | Oklahoma | OK | West Virginia | WV |
| Georgia | GA | Minnesota | MN | Oregon | OR | Wisconsin | WI |
| Guam | GU | Mississippi | MS | Pennsylvania | PA | Wyoming | WY |
| Hawaii | HI | Missouri | MO | Puerto Rico | PR | | |

Also approved for use in addressing mail are the following abbreviations:

| | | | | | | | |
|---|---|---|---|---|---|---|---|
| Alley | Aly | Courts | Cts | Heights | Hts | Rural | R |
| Arcade | Arc | Crescent | Cres | Highway | Hwy | Square | Sq |
| Boulevard | Blvd | Drive | Dr | Lane | Ln | Street | St |
| Branch | Br | Expressway | Expy | Manor | Mnr | Terrace | Ter |
| Bypass | Byp | Extended | Ext | Place | Pl | Trail | Trl |
| Causeway | Cswy | Extension | Ext | Plaza | Plz | Turnpike | Tpke |
| Center | Ctr | Freeway | Fwy | Point | Pt | Viaduct | Via |
| Circle | Cir | Gardens | Gdns | Road | Rd | Vista | Vis |
| Court | Ct | Grove | Grv | | | | |

## Commemorative Stamps and Regular Postal Issues 1978

| Date | Commemorative stamp | Value | From |
|---|---|---|---|
| Jan. 6 | Carl Sandburg | 13¢ | Galesburg, IL |
| Jan. 11 | Indian Head Penny test stamp | 13¢ | Kansas City, MO |
| Jan. 20 | Captain James Cook (pair) | 13¢ | Honolulu, HI |
| Feb. 1 | Harriet Tubman | 13¢ | Washington, DC |
| Mar. 8 | American Quilts (4 stamps) | 13¢ | Charleston, WV |
| Mar. 31 | Statue of Liberty (Americana Series) | 16¢ | New York, NY |
| Apr. 14 | Lighthouse (Americana Series) | 29¢ | Atlantic City, NJ |
| Apr. 26 | American Dance (4 stamps) | 13¢ | New York, NY |
| May 4 | French Alliance | 13¢ | York, PA |
| May 18 | Dr. George Papanicolaou | 13¢ | Washington, DC |
| May 24 | Jimmie Rodgers | 13¢ | Meridian, MS |
| June 26 | Photography | 15¢ | Las Vegas, NV |
| July 3 | George M. Cohan | 15¢ | Providence, RI |
| July 20 | Viking Missions | 15¢ | Hampton, VA |
| Aug. 26 | Owls (4 stamps) | 15¢ | Fairbanks, AK |
| Sept. 23 | Wright Brothers International Airmail (pair) | 31¢ | Dayton, OH |
| Oct. 9 | American Trees (four stamps) | 15¢ | Hot Springs Natl Park, AR |
| Oct. 18 | Della Robbia Art Masterpiece (Christmas) | 15¢ | Washington, DC |
| Oct. 18 | Hobby Horse-Contemporary (Christmas) | 15¢ | Holly, MI |

## Postal Receipts at Large Cities

| Fiscal year | Boston | Chicago | Detroit | L.A. | New York | Phila. | St. Louis | Wash., D.C. |
|---|---|---|---|---|---|---|---|---|
| 1972 | $109,178,539 | $332,951,729 | $85,997,396 | $172,644,940 | $395,523,484 | $120,059,844 | $73,246,822 | $99,980,611 |
| 1973 | 114,159,472 | 339,770,450 | 84,358,518 | 172,365,582 | 392,348,195 | 120,173,378 | 75,342,257 | 103,152,177 |
| 1974 | 123,164,661 | 347,561,637 | 87,784,811 | 176,847,940 | 409,392,651 | 130,655,216 | 79,412,843 | 133,458,807 |
| 1975 | 136,453,079 | 365,378,795 | 84,338,282 | 193,229,077 | 453,905,277 | 134,571,376 | 85,591,774 | 115,489,343 |
| 1976 | 151,642,227 | 384,380,826 | 95,527,250 | 203,413,409 | 484,180,727 | 147,650,431 | 96,844,188 | 125,997,649 |
| 1977 | 173,933,702 | 424,045,237 | 102,018,571 | 232,293,590 | 528,545,213 | 168,521,442 | 107,379,762 | 138,050,517 |

Other cities for fiscal year 1976: Atlanta, $126,323,319; Baltimore, $80,200,675; Cincinnati, $59,555,300; Cleveland, $92,027,408; Columbus, $71,531,507; Dallas, $125,101,004; Denver, $70,421,633; Houston, $108,229,165; Indianapolis, $73,346,326; Kansas City, $71,980,330; Minneapolis, $97,046,273; Pittsburgh, $78,346,484; San Francisco, $109,333,101; Seattle, $62,928,291.

# Air Mail, Parcel Post International Rates

**Aerogrammes** — 22¢ each to all countries.
**Air mail postcards** (single) - 21¢ to all countries except Canada and Mexico (14¢)

| Country | Misc. rates (see below) | Air parcel post rates — First 4 oz. | Each add'l. 4 oz. or fraction |
|---|---|---|---|
| Afghanistan | G | 3.14 | 1.20 |
| Albania | E | 3.33 | .79 |
| Algeria | F | 2.71 | .80 |
| Andorra | F | 2.79 | .70 |
| Angola | G | 2.93 | 1.01 |
| Anguilla | A | 1.78 | .36 |
| Antigua | A | 1.78 | .36 |
| Argentina | F | 2.46 | 1.07 |
| Aruba | C | 2.08 | .45 |
| Ascension Is. | E | (4) | — |
| Australia[3] | I | 2.62 | 1.21 |
| Austria | F | 2.70 | .74 |
| Azores | F | 1.95 | .56 |
| Bahamas | C | 2.19 | .27 |
| Bahrain | G | 2.42 | 1.03 |
| Bangladesh | G | 3.46 | 1.22 |
| Barbados | A | 1.90 | .51 |
| Barbuda | A | 1.78 | .36 |
| Belgium | F | 2.41 | .66 |
| Belize | C | 1.89 | .48 |
| Benin | I | 2.36 | .85 |
| Bermuda | B | 1.77 | .35 |
| Bhutan | * | (4) | — |
| Bolivia[3] | F | 2.47 | .69 |
| Bonaire | C | 2.08 | .45 |
| Botswana | G | 2.66 | 1.27 |
| Brazil | F | 2.94 | .79 |
| Br. Virgin Is. | A | 1.78 | .36 |
| Brunei | G | 3.01 | 1.47 |
| Bulgaria | E | 2.15 | .75 |
| Burma[3] | G | 3.30 | 1.43 |
| Burundi | G | 2.76 | 1.07 |
| Cameroon | G | 2.79 | .92 |
| Canada[3] | * | (6) | — |
| Canary, Balearic Is.[1] | F | 2.79 | .70 |
| Cape Verde | G | 2.72 | .81 |
| Cayman | A | 2.36 | .33 |
| Cen. African Emp. | I | 2.76 | 1.07 |
| Chad | I | 2.76 | 1.07 |
| Chile[3] | E | 2.92 | .89 |
| China, People's Rep.[7] | E | 3.08 | 1.37 |
| China. Rep. of | E | 2.46 | 1.05 |
| Colombia[3] | D | 2.86 | .50 |
| Comoro | I | 3.13 | 1.43 |
| Congo | I | 2.76 | 1.07 |
| Corsica | F | 2.98 | .66 |
| Costa Rica | F | 2.06 | .43 |
| Crete | * | 2.62 | .84 |
| Cuba | * | (4) | — |
| Curacao | C | 2.08 | .45 |
| Cyprus | F | 2.88 | .85 |
| Czechoslovakia | F | 2.17 | .76 |
| Denmark | F | 2.14 | .72 |
| Djibouti | I | 2.89 | 1.03 |
| Dominica | A | 2.39 | .48 |
| Dominican Rep. | C | 2.24 | .36 |
| East Timor | G | 3.64 | 1.72 |
| Ecuador | F | 2.78 | .48 |
| Egypt | C | 2.32 | .92 |
| El Salvador | C | 2.21 | .44 |
| Equatorial Guinea | I | 2.82 | 1.22 |
| Estonia[2] | I | 2.84 | .95 |
| Ethiopia | E | 2.83 | 1.10 |
| Falkland Is. | E | 2.99 | .85 |
| Fiji | F | 2.79 | .90 |
| Finland | F | 2.17 | .79 |
| France | F | 2.98 | .66 |
| French Guiana | F | 2.19 | .56 |
| Fr. Polynesia | I | 2.70 | .76 |
| Gabon. | F | 2.76 | 1.07 |
| Gambia | G | 2.39 | .76 |
| Germany, Fed. Rep. (West) | F | 2.10 | .70 |
| Germany (East) | E | 2.10 | .70 |
| Ghana. | G | 2.92 | .92 |
| Gilbraltar | E | 2.16 | .75 |
| Gilbert Is. | I | 2.66 | 1.00 |
| Great Britain | F | 2.08 | .66 |
| Greece | F | 2.62 | .84 |
| Greenland | F | 2.35 | .93 |
| Grenada | A | 2.39 | .48 |
| Guadeloupe | C | 2.00 | .36 |
| Guatemala | C | 2.51 | .46 |
| Guinea, Rep. of | I | 2.46 | .96 |
| Guinea-Bissau | G | 2.93 | 1.01 |
| Guyana | E | 2.42 | .50 |
| Haiti | C | 2.25 | .35 |
| Honduras[1] | C | 2.14 | .46 |
| Hong Kong | G | 2.65 | 1.24 |
| Hungary | F | 2.16 | .76 |
| Iceland | F | 2.66 | .56 |
| India[1] | I | 2.67 | 1.27 |
| Indonesia | G | 3.48 | 1.52 |
| Iran | I | 2.67 | .96 |
| Iraq | I | 2.98 | .95 |
| Ireland | E | 2.06 | .66 |
| Israel | H | 2.93 | .91 |
| Italy | F | 2.63 | .79 |
| Ivory Coast | I | 2.46 | .95 |
| Jamaica | A | 2.36 | .33 |
| Japan | G | 2.19 | .80 |
| Jordan | G | 2.72 | .90 |
| Kampuchea (Cambodia) | * | (4) | — |
| Kenya | I | 2.93 | 1.10 |
| Korea (Rep. of) | G | 2.25 | .85 |
| No. Korea[1] | * | (4) | — |
| Kuwait | I | 2.39 | 1.00 |
| Laos. | G | 3.35 | 1.37 |
| Latvia[2] | I | 2.84 | .95 |
| Lebanon[1] | I | 2.72 | .90 |
| Leeward Is. | A | 1.78 | .36 |
| Lesotho | G | 2.66 | 1.27 |
| Liberia | G | 2.24 | .84 |
| Libya | F | 2.70 | .85 |
| Liechtenstein | F | 2.39 | .67 |
| Lithuania[2] | I | 2.84 | .95 |
| Luxembourg | F | 2.47 | .65 |
| Macao | G | 3.20 | 1.24 |
| Madagascar | I | 3.09 | 1.22 |
| Madeira Is. | E | 2.10 | .72 |
| Malawi | G | 2.66 | 1.24 |
| Malaysia | G | 3.23 | 1.42 |
| Maldives | G | 3.59 | 1.29 |
| Mali | I | 3.46 | .82 |
| Malta | E | 2.61 | .79 |
| Martinique | C | 2.00 | .36 |
| Mauritania | I | 2.36 | .79 |
| Mauritius | G | 3.01 | 1.29 |
| Mexico | * | 1.77 | .35 |
| Monaco | F | 2.98 | .66 |
| Mongolia | * | (4) | — |
| Montserrat | C | 1.78 | .36 |
| Morocco | F | 2.63 | .79 |
| Mozambique | G | 3.43 | 1.28 |
| Namibia (SW Africa) | G | 2.66 | 1.27 |
| Nauru | G | 2.62 | 1.21 |
| Nepal | G | 2.66 | 1.27 |
| Netherlands | F | 2.36 | .66 |
| Neth. Antilles | C | 2.08 | .45 |
| Nevis | A | 1.78 | .36 |
| New Caledonia | I | 2.81 | .93 |
| New Hebrides | I | 2.65 | .93 |
| New Zealand | G | 2.98 | 1.07 |
| Nicaragua | C | 2.08 | .43 |
| Niger | I | 3.45 | .80 |
| Nigeria | G | 3.14 | .93 |
| Norway | F | 2.14 | .72 |
| Oman | I | 2.42 | 1.03 |
| Pakistan | G | 3.46 | 1.22 |
| Panama. | * | 2.50 | .45 |
| Papua New Guinea | I | 2.72 | 1.32 |
| Paraguay | F | 2.47 | .67 |
| Peru | F | 2.88 | .60 |
| Philippines[1] | I | 3.03 | 1.17 |
| Pitcairn | I | 2.89 | 1.03 |
| Poland | F | 2.61 | .75 |
| Portugal. | F | 2.05 | .64 |
| Qatar | G | 2.42 | 1.03 |
| Reunion | I | 2.89 | 1.27 |
| Rhodesia | G | 2.66 | 1.24 |
| Romania | E | 2.42 | .79 |

| Country | Misc. rates (see below) | Air parcel post rates First 4 oz. | Each add'l. 4 oz. or fraction | Country | Misc. rates (see below) | Air parcel post rates First 4 oz. | Each add'l. 4 oz. or fraction |
|---|---|---|---|---|---|---|---|
| Rwanda | G | 2.76 | 1.07 | Switzerland | F | 2.39 | .67 |
| Saba | C | 2.08 | .45 | Syria[1] | I | 2.47 | .92 |
| St. Christopher | A | 2.39 | .48 | Tanzania | G | 2.99 | 1.15 |
| St. Eustatius | C | 2.08 | .45 | Thailand | G | 3.28 | 1.17 |
| St. Helena | G | 3.01 | 1.22 | Togo | I | 2.57 | .95 |
| St. Lucia | A | 2.39 | .48 | Tonga | G | 2.34 | .93 |
| St. Pierre, Miquelon | C | 1.72 | .35 | Trinidad & Tobago | A | 2.37 | .45 |
| St. Vincent | A | 2.39 | .48 | Tristan da Cunha | G | 2.83 | 1.21 |
| Samoa | G | 2.71 | .80 | Tunisia | F | 2.62 | .75 |
| San Marino | F | 2.63 | .79 | Turkey | F | 2.26 | .85 |
| Santa Cruz Is. | G | 3.10 | 1.39 | Turks & Caicos | A | 2.25 | .33 |
| Sao Tome & Principe | G | 2.93 | 1.01 | Tuvalu (Ellice) | G | 2.66 | 1.00 |
| Saudi Arabia | G | 3.10 | 1.00 | Uganda | G | 2.93 | 1.10 |
| Senegal | I | 2.34 | .75 | USSR[2] | I | 2.84 | .95 |
| Seychelles | G | 2.53 | 1.12 | United Arab Emir | G | 2.42 | 1.03 |
| Sierra Leone | G | 3.09 | .81 | Upper Volta | I | 2.72 | .89 |
| Singapore | G | 3.23 | 1.42 | Uruguay | F | 2.93 | .90 |
| Solomon Is. | G | 3.12 | 1.39 | Vatican City | F | 2.42 | .74 |
| Somalia | G | 3.23 | 1.13 | Venezuela | D | 2.71 | .43 |
| South Africa | G | 2.66 | 1.27 | Vietnam[1] | * | (4) | — |
| Spain | F | 2.79 | .70 | Windward Is. | A | 2.39 | .4t |
| Sri Lanka (Ceylon) | G | 3.33 | 1.28 | Yemen (Aden) | I | 2.81 | 1.1t |
| Sudan | G | 3.13 | 1.01 | Yemen (Sanaa) | I | 3.04 | 1.55 |
| Surinam | F | 2.24 | .53 | Yugoslavia | F | 2.17 | .79 |
| Swaziland | G | 2.66 | 1.27 | Zaire | I | 2.76 | 1.07 |
| Sweden | F | 2.14 | .72 | Zambia | G | 2.66 | 1.24 |

## Miscellaneous Rates

| Group or country | Air service Letters and letter pkgs. per 1/2 oz. thru 2 oz. | per 1/2 oz. over 2 oz. | Other articles First 2 oz. | Each add'l. 2 oz. or fraction | Surface parcel post First 2 lbs. | Each add'l. pound or fraction | Max. wt. for parcel post (surface or air) lbs. |
|---|---|---|---|---|---|---|---|
| A | .25 | .21 | .60 | .16 | 2.19 | .52 | 22 |
| B | .25 | .21 | .60 | .16 | 2.19 | .52 | 33 |
| C | .25 | .21 | .60 | .16 | 2.19 | .52 | 44 |
| D | .25 | .21 | .60 | .16 | 2.34 | .59 | 44 |
| E | .31 | .26 | .73 | .29 | 2.34 | .59 | 22 |
| F | .31 | .26 | .73 | .29 | 2.34 | .59 | 44 |
| G | .31 | .26 | .86 | .42 | 2.34 | .59 | 22 |
| H | .31 | .26 | .86 | .42 | 2.34 | .59 | 33 |
| I | .31 | .26 | .86 | .42 | 2.34 | .59 | 44 |
| * Exceptions: | | | | | | | |
| Bhutan | .31 | .26 | .86 | .42 | ... | ... | (5) |
| Canada[3] | (oz.) .15 | (addl. oz.) .13 | (6) | ... | 2.19 | .52 | 35 |
| Cuba | .25 | .21 | .60 | .16 | ... | ... | (5) |
| Kampuchea (Cambodia) | .31 | .26 | (1) | ... | ... | ... | (5) |
| Korea, No. | .31 | .26 | .86 | .42 | ... | ... | (5) |
| Mexico | (oz.) .15 | (addl. oz.) .13 | .60 | .16 | 2.19 | .52 | 44 |
| Mongolia | .31 | .26 | .86 | .42 | ... | ... | (5) |
| Panama | .25 | .21 | .60 | .16 | 2.19 | .52 | 70 |
| Vietnam[1] | .31 | .26 | .86 | .42 | ... | ... | (5) |

(1) Restrictions apply; consult post office. (2) To facilitate distribution and delivery, include "Union of Soviet Socialist Republics" or "USSR" as part of the address. (3) Small packets weight limit one pound. (4) No air parcel post service. (5) No surface parcel post service. (6) No airmail AO or parcel post to Canada; prepare and prepay all airmail packages as letter mail. (7) The continental China postal authorities will not deliver articles unless addressed to show name of the country as "People's Republic of China"; also, only acceptable spelling of capital is "Peking."

---

## International Mails

### Weight and Dimensional Limits and Surface Rates

For air rates and parcel post see pages 973-974

**Letters and letter packages:** all written matter or correspondence recordings, must be sent as letter mail. Weight limit: 4 lbs. to all countries except Canada, which is 60 lbs. **Surface rates:** Canada and Mexico, 15¢ first ounce; 13¢ each additional ounce or fraction through 12 ounces; eighth-zone priority rates for heavier weights. Countries other than Canada and Mexico, 1 ounce, 20¢; over 1 to 2 ounces, 36¢; over 2 to 4 ounces, 42¢; over 4 to 8 ounces, 96¢; over 8 ounces to 1 pound, $1.84; over 1 to 2 pounds, $3.20; and over 2 to 4 pounds, $5.20. **Air rates:** Canada and Mexico, 15¢ first ounce; 13¢ each additional ounce or fraction. Central America, Colombia, Venezuela, the Caribbean Islands, Bahamas, Bermuda, and St. Pierre and Miquelon, 25¢ per half ounce up to and including 2 ounces; 21¢ each additional half ounce or fraction. All other countries, 31¢ per half ounce up to and including 2 ounces; 26¢ each additional half ounce or fraction. Aerogrammes, which can be folded into the form of an envelope and sent by air to all countries, are available at post offices for 22¢ each.

**Note.** Mail to Canada and Mexico bearing postage paid at the surface letter rate will receive first class service in the U.S. and airmail service in Canada and Mexico during the Postal Service First Class Mail Service Improvement Program.

**Postcards.** Surface rates to Canada and Mexico, 9¢; to all other countries, 14¢. By air, Canada and Mexico, 10¢; to all other countries, 21¢. Maximum size permitted, 6 x 4¼ in.; minimum, 5½ x 3½.

**Printed matter.** To Canada and Mexico, 20¢ the first 2 ounces, 20¢ for the next two ounces, plus 13¢ each add'l. 2 ounces or fraction through 1 pound; $1.26 for 1 to 2 pounds, $1.68 for 2 to 4 pounds. To other countries, 20¢ the first 2 ounces, 40¢ 2 to 4 ounces, 66¢ 4 to 8 ounces, $1.05 8 to 16 ounces, $1.26 1 to 2 pounds, $1.68 2 to 4 pounds. To countries admitting regular prints over 4 lbs. 84¢ for each additional 2 lbs. or fraction. (Consult post office for rates and conditions applying to certain publications mailed by the publishers or by registered news agents.) Book weight limit for most countries is 11 lbs; for exceptions see below. Consult post office for book rates.

**Exceptional weight limits for printed matter.** Printed matter may weigh up to 22 lbs. to Argentina, Bolivia, Brazil, Chile, Colombia, Costa Rica, Cuba, Dominican Republic, Ecuador, El Salvador, Guatemala, Haiti, Honduras, Mexico, Nicaragua, Panama, Paraguay, Peru, Spain (including Balearic Islands and Canary Islands) Surinam, Uruguay, and Venezuela. For other countries, limit for books is 11 lbs., all other prints, 4 lbs.

**Matter for the blind.** Surface rate free; air service to Canada for matter prepared as letters/letter packages is at the letter rate. (For all other countries, consult postmaster.) Weight limit 15 lbs.

**Small packets.** Postage rates for small items of merchandise and samples are lower than for letter packages or parcel post; consult post office for weight limits and requirements for customs declarations. Surface rates: Canada and Mexico,

20¢ the first 2 oz.; 40¢ for the next 2 oz.; plus 13¢ for each add'l 2 oz. or fraction. All other countries, 20¢ the first 2 oz.; 40¢ for the next 2 oz.; 4 to 8 oz. 66¢; 8oz. to 1 lb. $1.05; 1 to 2 lbs. $1.26. For other rates, see schedule "Air Service Other Articles" under heading of International Rates for Air Mail and Surface Parcel Post, pages 973-974.

## International Parcel Post
For rates see pages 973-974

**General dimensional limits** — greatest length, 3½ feet; greatest length and girth combined, 6 feet.

**Prohibited articles.** Before sending goods abroad the mailer should consult the post office that they will not be confiscated or returned because their importation is prohibited or restricted by the country of address.

**Packing.** Parcels for transmission overseas should be even more carefully packed than those intended for delivery within the continental U.S. Containers should be used which will be strong enough to protect the contents from the weight of other mail, from pressure and friction, climatic changes, and repeated handlings.

**Sealing.** Registered or insured parcels must be sealed. To some countries the sealing of ordinary (unregistered and uninsured) parcels is optional, and to others compulsory. Consult post office.

**Customs declarations and other forms.** At least one customs declaration is required for parcel post packages (surface or air) mailed to another country. In addition, to some countries, a dispatch note is required. The forms may be obtained at post offices.

## United Nations Postage Stamps Issued in 1978

UN stamps in United States denominations, valid for postage only on mail deposited at UN Headquarters, New York, and UN stamps in Swiss denominations, valid for postage only on mail deposited at the United Nations Office, Geneva, are available at face value from the UN Postal Administration in New York and Geneva and through sales agencies around the world. They may be obtained by mail or automatically through the Customer Deposit Account service, both in New York and Geneva. Revenue from the sale of UN stamps for postage purposes goes to the U.S. Postal Service and the Swiss PTT, respectively; from philatelic sales, revenue goes to the UN.

| Date | Stamp | Value | | |
|------|-------|-------|---|---|
| 27 Jan. | Definitives | 1¢, | 25¢, | $1.00 |
| 31 Mar. | Global Eradication of Smallpox | 13¢, | 31¢ | |
| 5 May | Namibia : Liberation, Justice, Co-operation | 13¢, | 18¢ | |
| 12 June | ICAO: Safety in the Air | 13¢, | 25¢ | |
| 15 Sept. | General Assembly | 13¢, | 18¢ | |
| 17 Nov. | Technical Co-operation Among Developing Countries | 13¢, | 31¢ | |

## Canadian Postal Rates
(in effect April 1, 1978)

**Letter mail and postcards.** Up to 1 oz. 14¢, over 1 and up to 2 oz. 22¢, over 2 and up to 4 oz. 34¢, over 4 and up to 6 oz. 50¢, over 6 and up to 8 oz. 66¢, plus 16¢ for each additional 2 oz. up to 16 oz.

**Parcels** (over 1 lb.) **First class** (maximum 66 lb.) parcels receive priority air service. **Fourth class** (maximum 35 lb.) parcels receive surface transmission.

The charges given below are for local (short haul) deliveries. A chart showing the cost for deliveries to all other postal zones may be obtained from your local postmaster.

| over/up to | 1 lb./2 | 2/3 | 3/4 | 4/5 | 5/6 | 6/7 | 7/8 | 8/9 | 9/10 | 10/15 |
|------------|---------|-----|-----|-----|-----|-----|-----|-----|------|-------|
| 1st class | $1.50 | 1.70 | 1.90 | 2.10 | 2.25 | 2.45 | 2.65 | 2.85 | 3.00 | 3.35 |
| 4th class | .80 | .90 | 1.05 | 1.15 | 1.30 | 1.40 | 1.50 | 1.65 | 1.75 | 1.95 |

| over/up to | 15 lb./20 | 20/25 | 25/30 | 30/35 | 35/40 | 40/45 | 45/50 | 50/55 | 55/60 | 60/65 |
|------------|-----------|-------|-------|-------|-------|-------|-------|-------|-------|-------|
| 1st class | 3.70 | 4.05 | 4.40 | 4.75 | 5.10 | 5.45 | 5.80 | 6.15 | 6.50 | 6.85 |
| 4th class | 2.15 | 2.35 | 2.55 | 2.75 | | | | | | |

**Third class.** Standard addressed rates (includes greeting cards). Up to 2 oz. 12¢ plus 7¢ for each additional 2 oz. up to a maximum of 1 lb.

**Premium Services.** Certified mail (proof of delivery service) 75¢ plus postage. Special Delivery first class postage plus 80¢ per item. Money order fee (maximum $200) - 35¢

## To U.S.A., Territories and Possessions

**Airmail letters and postcards,** up to and including 1 oz. 14¢ plus 12¢ for each additional oz. up to 1 lb. Over 1 lb. up to and including 2 lbs. $3.15 plus 80¢ for each additional lb. up to a maximum of 66 lbs.

**Surface parcel post.** Up to and including 2 lbs. $1.85 plus 50¢ for each additional lb. up to a maximum of 35 lbs.

# QUICK REFERENCE INDEX

## First Class Postal Rates in Brief

### U.S. Domestic (in effect May. 1978)

**Letters**—15¢ first ounce, 13¢ each additional ounce.
**Postal cards**—10¢ each (up to 4½ × 6 in.). Double cards, 20¢. Private cards, 10¢; double 20¢.

### U.S. International (in effect June, 1978)

**Letters**—(1) Canada (max. weight 60 lbs.) and Mexico (max. weight 4 lbs.), 15¢ first ounce, 13¢ each addl. ounce to 12 ounces; over 12 ounces to 1 pound, $2.25; over 1 pound to 1½ pounds, $2.50; over 1½ to 2 pounds, $2.83; over 2 to 2½ pounds, $3.16; over 2½ to 3 pounds, $3.50; over 3 to 3½ pounds, $3.83; over 3½ to 4 pounds, $4.16; over 4 to 4½ pounds, $4.50; over 4½ to 5 pounds, $4.83; over 5 pounds, $1.33 each additional 2 pounds. (2) Countries other than Canada and Mexico, 1 ounce, 20¢; over 1 to 2 ounces, 36¢; over 2 to 4 ounces, 48¢; over 4 to 8 ounces, 96¢; over 8 ounces to 1 pound, $1.84; over 1 to 2 pounds, $3.20; and over 2 to 4 pounds, $5.20.
**Air mail letters**—(1) Canada, and Mexico, same as domestic surface rates. (2) Cen. America, Colombia, Venezuela, the Caribbean Is., Bahamas, Bermuda, and St. Pierre and Miquelon, 25¢ per half ounce through 2 ounces; 21¢ each addl. ½ oz. (3) All other countries, 31¢ per half ounce through 2 ounces; 26¢ each addl. ½ oz.

**Aerogrammes**—to all countries, 22¢ each.
**Postal cards**—to Canada and Mexico 10¢ each. To all other countries, 14¢ each.
**Air mail postcards**—to Canada and Mexico 10¢ each, to other countries 21¢ each.

### Canada (in effect Apr., 1978)

**Letter mail and postcards**—1 oz. 14¢; 1-2 oz. 22¢; 2-4 oz. 34¢; 4-6 oz. 50¢; 6-8 oz. 66¢; 16¢ each additional 2 oz.
**To U.S.A. territories and possesions**—(1) Airmail letters and postcards, up to and including 1 oz. 14¢ plus 12¢ for each additional oz. up to 1 lb. Over 1 lb. up to and including 2 lbs. $3.15 plus 80¢ for each additional lb. up to a maximum of 66 lbs. (2) Surface parcel post. Up to and including 2 lbs. $1.85 plus 50¢ for each additional lb. up to a maximum of 35 lbs.